The Lutheran Annual 2026

of The Lutheran Church—Missouri Synod

Compiled by

The LCMS Office of the Secretary
Rosters, Statistics, and Research Services

Published by

1333 S. Kirkwood Road
St. Louis, MO 63122-7295

1-800-325-3040
cph.org

On the Cover:

The most enduring symbol of the Lutheran Reformation is the seal that Luther himself designed to represent his theology. By the early 1520s, this seal begins to appear on the title page of Luther's works.

Here is how Luther himself explained its meaning:

First, there is a black cross in a heart that remains its natural color. This is to remind me that it is faith in the Crucified One that saves us. Anyone who believes from the heart will be justified (Romans 10:10). It is a black cross, which mortifies and causes pain, but it leaves the heart its natural color. It doesn't destroy nature, that is to say, it does not kill us but keeps us alive, for the just shall live by faith in the Crucified One (Romans 1:17). The heart should stand in the middle of a white rose. This is to show that faith gives joy, comfort, and peace—it puts the believer into a white, joyous rose. Faith does not give peace and joy like the world gives (John 14:27). This is why the rose must be white, not red. White is the color of the spirits and angels (cf. Matthew 28:3; John 20:12). This rose should stand in a sky-blue field, symbolizing that a joyful spirit and faith is a beginning of heavenly, future joy, which begins now, but is grasped in hope, not yet fully revealed. Around the field of blue is a golden ring to symbolize that blessedness in heaven lasts forever and has no end. Heavenly blessedness is exquisite, beyond all joy and better than any possessions, just as gold is the most valuable and precious metal.

(From: Letter from Martin Luther to Lazarus Spengler, July 8, 1530 [WA Br 5:445]; tr. P. T. McCain)

Produced with the assistance of Livingstone (www.LivingstoneCorp.com).

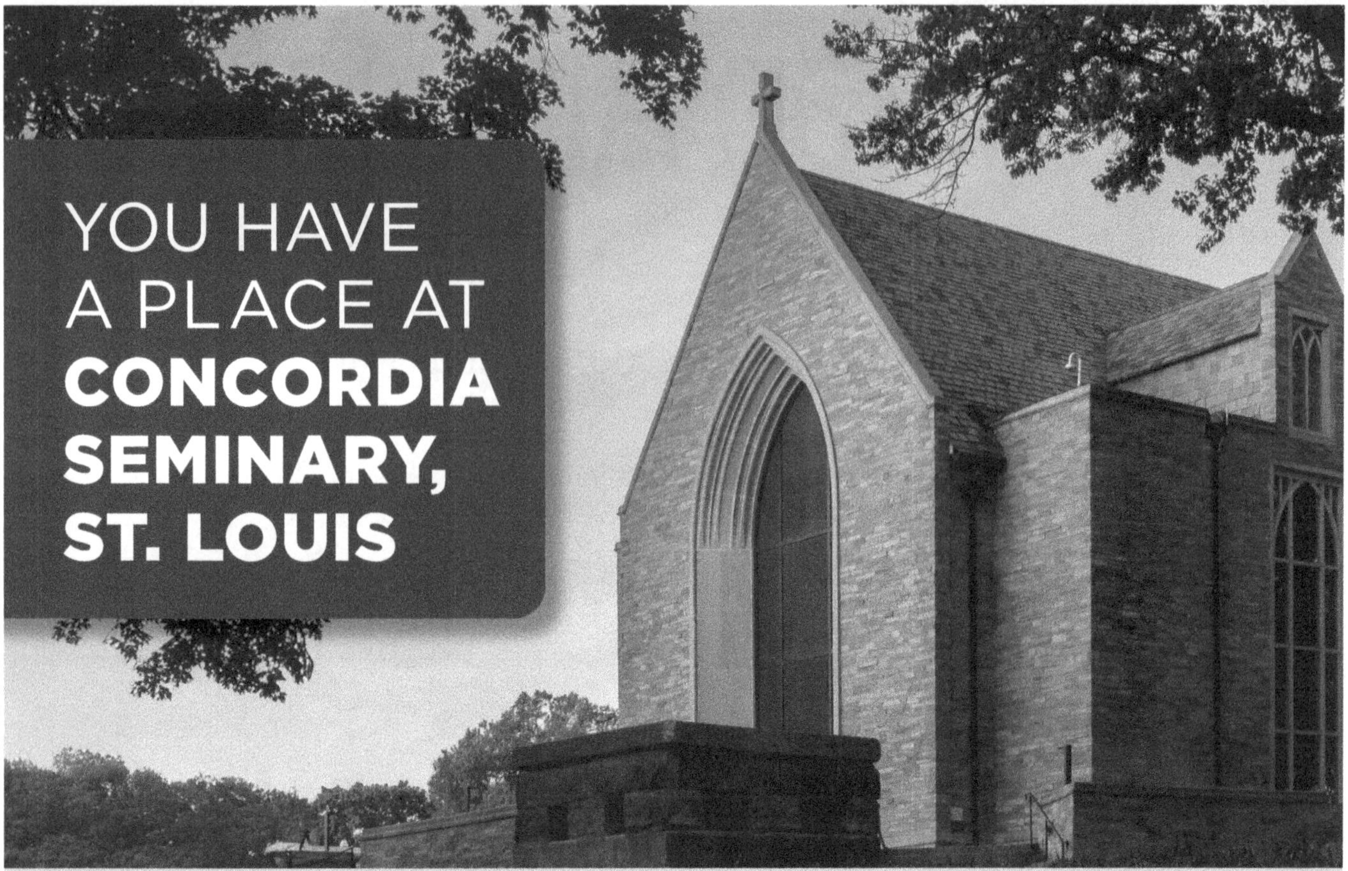

From the Editor and the Publisher

Welcome to *The Lutheran Annual 2026*, containing up-to-date information on LCMS ministries and 2024 statistical data as collected in 2025. This resource, a synodwide directory and statistical abstract, relies on the contributions of congregations' pastors and staffs (as enjoined by Bylaw 1.3.4.3); district presidents, their staffs, and circuit visitors (as enjoined by Bylaw 4.4.8); the Department of Rosters, Statistics, and Research Services (RSRS); and the publishing staff of Concordia Publishing House. For the contribution of all these labors, in view of the good ends of planning "current and future ministry efforts" and of lending "accuracy and integrity to Synod's delegate representation and voting processes," we are sincerely grateful.

This year, 78.5 percent of congregations and new church starts (up from 73.4 percent last year, as expected in a year of electoral circuit alignment) responded with fresh data. Where appropriate, and as indicated, cumulative data are reflected in the statistical tables of the LCMS General Information section. At present, 89.4 percent of congregational data (reflecting 95.3 percent of confirmed membership) is less than three years old. This year, we celebrate four districts, Atlantic, Iowa East, Iowa West, and Nebraska, having achieved the bylaw-expected "unanimous participation," with Kansas, Michigan, Missouri, Wyoming, and Mid-South notable as having achieved 90 percent reporting or better. And we did it in record time, just nineteen weeks. Thanks be to God! (Staleness of records does remain a challenge in the West-Southwest Region and non-geographical districts.)

These fresh data served as the basis for alignment of the Synod's 601 visitation circuits into 497 electoral circuits for representation at the 2026 Synod convention, a decrease from 532 in 2023 and a peak of 628 in 2007. Only 6.8 percent of the 2026 electoral circuits were granted exceptions by the President, the lowest rate since 1998. The 2023 Res. 9-06A task force is now concluding its work to propose any necessary change to circuit parameters and aiming to achieve equitable representation and an effective convention size, and to improve, if possible, the work of visitation and mutual encouragement that goes on in our Synod's visitation circuits. Its ability to do so thoughtfully has depended in great part on reliable data, so we are grateful for timely reporting.

Attendance across the Synod's five regions has, by 2024, generally recovered in the aggregate to the pre-COVID-19 trendline, though the stories of individual congregations surely vary. Roughly 25 percent of congregations report the same level of attendance they had five years ago; the top 10 percent have experienced more than 13 percent growth; and 55 percent have declined by at least 13 percent, which is approximately the general trend.

Our convention looks forward to the theme Christ Is Risen Indeed, drawing on 1 Cor. 15:20–22. Our collective statistics, to some extent, make clear that we do not yet *see* the consequence of the Resurrection of the Head: that the members of the Body, too, will be raised up. Of course, "time, like an ever-rolling stream, soon bears us all away" (*LSB* 733:5). But also, our parish life does not in every place resound with the irrepressible joy and hope of an Easter Dawn, suffering instead a dark night of Passover waiting. But where the Word is proclaimed, the Lord is bringing His own through death to life—for, in fact, "Christ has been raised from the dead" (1 Cor. 15:20). And we have in Him all the hope that there is in this world. And in it, we are here for one another.

We pray this book reminds you of the fellowship of the saints joined in our Synod in the confession of the Scriptures as the Word of God and the Lutheran Confessions as "true and unadulterated exposition" thereof, and for common mission, for and on behalf of all our member congregations (Constitution Articles II and III). The good Lord continue to make our Synod an instrument of His will that "the diversities of gifts should be for the common profit" (Const. Preface; 1 Cor 12:4–31), that His Church in all its fullness should be blessed. I+N+J

Dr. John W. Sias
Secretary
The Lutheran Church—
Missouri Synod
Editor, *The Lutheran Annual*

Jonathan D. Schultz
President and CEO
Concordia Publishing House
Publisher, *The Lutheran Annual*

CONTENTS

For your convenience, a table of abbreviations is now available on page 53.

2026 Church Festivals and Civil Holidays

New Year's Day	January 1
Epiphany	January 6
Martin Luther King Jr. Day	January 19
National Sanctity of Human Life Day	January 22
Washington's Birthday	February 22; obs. 16
Ash Wednesday	February 18
Palm Sunday	March 29
Good Friday	April 3
Easter	April 5
Easter Monday (Canada)	April 6
National Day of Prayer	May 7
Mother's Day	May 10
Ascension Day	May 14
Armed Forces Day	May 16
Victoria Day (Canada)	May 18
Pentecost (Whitsunday)	May 24
Memorial Day	May 25
Trinity Sunday	May 31
Flag Day	June 14
Father's Day	June 21
Canada Day	July 1
US Independence Day	July 4
Labor Day	September 7
Patriot Day	September 11
Columbus Day	October 12
Thanksgiving Day (Canada)	October 12
United Nations Day	October 24
Reformation Day	October 31
Veterans Day	November 11
Remembrance Day (Canada)	November 11
Thanksgiving Day (US)	November 26
Advent Sunday	November 29
Christmas Day	December 25

Certain other days are fixed by proclamation. Only Church days are noted in the daily calendar.

• CALENDAR FOR 2026 •

JANUARY

S	M	T	W	T	F	S
				1	2	3
4	5	6	7	8	9	10
11	12	13	14	15	16	17
18	19	20	21	22	23	24
25	26	27	28	29	30	31

FEBRUARY

S	M	T	W	T	F	S
1	2	3	4	5	6	7
8	9	10	11	12	13	14
15	16	17	18	19	20	21
22	23	24	25	26	27	28

MARCH

S	M	T	W	T	F	S
1	2	3	4	5	6	7
8	9	10	11	12	13	14
15	16	17	18	19	20	21
22	23	24	25	26	27	28
29	30	31				

APRIL

S	M	T	W	T	F	S
			1	2	3	4
5	6	7	8	9	10	11
12	13	14	15	16	17	18
19	20	21	22	23	24	25
26	27	28	29	30		

MAY

S	M	T	W	T	F	S
					1	2
3	4	5	6	7	8	9
10	11	12	13	14	15	16
17	18	19	20	21	22	23
24	25	26	27	28	29	30
31						

JUNE

S	M	T	W	T	F	S
	1	2	3	4	5	6
7	8	9	10	11	12	13
14	15	16	17	18	19	20
21	22	23	24	25	26	27
28	29	30				

JULY

S	M	T	W	T	F	S
			1	2	3	4
5	6	7	8	9	10	11
12	13	14	15	16	17	18
19	20	21	22	23	24	25
26	27	28	29	30	31	

AUGUST

S	M	T	W	T	F	S
						1
2	3	4	5	6	7	8
9	10	11	12	13	14	15
16	17	18	19	20	21	22
23	24	25	26	27	28	29
30	31					

SEPTEMBER

S	M	T	W	T	F	S
		1	2	3	4	5
6	7	8	9	10	11	12
13	14	15	16	17	18	19
20	21	22	23	24	25	26
27	28	29	30			

OCTOBER

S	M	T	W	T	F	S
				1	2	3
4	5	6	7	8	9	10
11	12	13	14	15	16	17
18	19	20	21	22	23	24
25	26	27	28	29	30	31

NOVEMBER

S	M	T	W	T	F	S
1	2	3	4	5	6	7
8	9	10	11	12	13	14
15	16	17	18	19	20	21
22	23	24	25	26	27	28
29	30					

DECEMBER

S	M	T	W	T	F	S
		1	2	3	4	5
6	7	8	9	10	11	12
13	14	15	16	17	18	19
20	21	22	23	24	25	26
27	28	29	30	31		

• CALENDAR FOR 2027 •

JANUARY

S	M	T	W	T	F	S
					1	2
3	4	5	6	7	8	9
10	11	12	13	14	15	16
17	18	19	20	21	22	23
24	25	26	27	28	29	30
31						

FEBRUARY

S	M	T	W	T	F	S
	1	2	3	4	5	6
7	8	9	10	11	12	13
14	15	16	17	18	19	20
21	22	23	24	25	26	27
28						

MARCH

S	M	T	W	T	F	S
	1	2	3	4	5	6
7	8	9	10	11	12	13
14	15	16	17	18	19	20
21	22	23	24	25	26	27
28	29	30	31			

APRIL

S	M	T	W	T	F	S
				1	2	3
4	5	6	7	8	9	10
11	12	13	14	15	16	17
18	19	20	21	22	23	24
25	26	27	28	29	30	

MAY

S	M	T	W	T	F	S
						1
2	3	4	5	6	7	8
9	10	11	12	13	14	15
16	17	18	19	20	21	22
23	24	25	26	27	28	29
30	31					

JUNE

S	M	T	W	T	F	S
		1	2	3	4	5
6	7	8	9	10	11	12
13	14	15	16	17	18	19
20	21	22	23	24	25	26
27	28	29	30			

JULY

S	M	T	W	T	F	S
				1	2	3
4	5	6	7	8	9	10
11	12	13	14	15	16	17
18	19	20	21	22	23	24
25	26	27	28	29	30	31

AUGUST

S	M	T	W	T	F	S
1	2	3	4	5	6	7
8	9	10	11	12	13	14
15	16	17	18	19	20	21
22	23	24	25	26	27	28
29	30	31				

SEPTEMBER

S	M	T	W	T	F	S
			1	2	3	4
5	6	7	8	9	10	11
12	13	14	15	16	17	18
19	20	21	22	23	24	25
26	27	28	29	30		

OCTOBER

S	M	T	W	T	F	S
					1	2
3	4	5	6	7	8	9
10	11	12	13	14	15	16
17	18	19	20	21	22	23
24	25	26	27	28	29	30
31						

NOVEMBER

S	M	T	W	T	F	S
	1	2	3	4	5	6
7	8	9	10	11	12	13
14	15	16	17	18	19	20
21	22	23	24	25	26	27
28	29	30				

DECEMBER

S	M	T	W	T	F	S
			1	2	3	4
5	6	7	8	9	10	11
12	13	14	15	16	17	18
19	20	21	22	23	24	25
26	27	28	29	30	31	

• CALENDAR FOR 2028 •

JANUARY

S	M	T	W	T	F	S
						1
2	3	4	5	6	7	8
9	10	11	12	13	14	15
16	17	18	19	20	21	22
23	24	25	26	27	28	29
30	31					

FEBRUARY

S	M	T	W	T	F	S
		1	2	3	4	5
6	7	8	9	10	11	12
13	14	15	16	17	18	19
20	21	22	23	24	25	26
27	28	29				

MARCH

S	M	T	W	T	F	S
			1	2	3	4
5	6	7	8	9	10	11
12	13	14	15	16	17	18
19	20	21	22	23	24	25
26	27	28	29	30	31	

APRIL

S	M	T	W	T	F	S
						1
2	3	4	5	6	7	8
9	10	11	12	13	14	15
16	17	18	19	20	21	22
23	24	25	26	27	28	29
30						

MAY

S	M	T	W	T	F	S
	1	2	3	4	5	6
7	8	9	10	11	12	13
14	15	16	17	18	19	20
21	22	23	24	25	26	27
28	29	30	31			

JUNE

S	M	T	W	T	F	S
				1	2	3
4	5	6	7	8	9	10
11	12	13	14	15	16	17
18	19	20	21	22	23	24
25	26	27	28	29	30	

JULY

S	M	T	W	T	F	S
						1
2	3	4	5	6	7	8
9	10	11	12	13	14	15
16	17	18	19	20	21	22
23	24	25	26	27	28	29
30	31					

AUGUST

S	M	T	W	T	F	S
		1	2	3	4	5
6	7	8	9	10	11	12
13	14	15	16	17	18	19
20	21	22	23	24	25	26
27	28	29	30	31		

SEPTEMBER

S	M	T	W	T	F	S
					1	2
3	4	5	6	7	8	9
10	11	12	13	14	15	16
17	18	19	20	21	22	23
24	25	26	27	28	29	30

OCTOBER

S	M	T	W	T	F	S
1	2	3	4	5	6	7
8	9	10	11	12	13	14
15	16	17	18	19	20	21
22	23	24	25	26	27	28
29	30	31				

NOVEMBER

S	M	T	W	T	F	S
			1	2	3	4
5	6	7	8	9	10	11
12	13	14	15	16	17	18
19	20	21	22	23	24	25
26	27	28	29	30		

DECEMBER

S	M	T	W	T	F	S
					1	2
3	4	5	6	7	8	9
10	11	12	13	14	15	16
17	18	19	20	21	22	23
24	25	26	27	28	29	30
31						

The Movable Festivals of the Church Year

The date of Easter determines the dates of all the movable festivals and days of the Church Year except those in Advent. *Advent 1* is always the Sunday nearest November 30, whether before or after. When the date of Easter has been determined, the Church Year will be arranged as follows:

Ash Wednesday, the beginning of Lent, is the Wednesday before the sixth Sunday before Easter (the fortieth weekday before Easter). *Ascension* is on the Thursday after the sixth Sunday of Easter. *Pentecost* is seven weeks after Easter.

Movable Dates in the Church Year, 2016–2036

Year	Sundays after Epiphany	Ash Wednesday	Easter	Ascension	Pentecost	Sundays after Pentecost	First Advent Sunday
2016	5	Feb. 10	March 27	May 5	May 15	27	Nov. 27
2017	8	March 1	April 16	May 25	June 4	25	Dec. 3
2018	6	Feb. 14	April 1	May 10	May 20	27	Dec. 2
2019	8	March 6	April 21	May 30	June 9	24	Dec. 1
2020	7	Feb. 26	April 12	May 21	May 31	25	Nov. 29
2021	6	Feb. 17	April 4	May 13	May 23	26	Nov. 28
2022	8	March 2	April 17	May 26	June 5	24	Nov. 27
2023	7	Feb. 22	April 9	May 18	May 28	26	Dec. 3
2024	6	Feb. 14	March 31	May 9	May 19	27	Dec. 1
2025	8	March 5	April 20	May 29	June 8	24	Nov. 30
2026	6	Feb. 18	April 5	May 14	May 24	26	Nov. 29
2027	5	Feb. 10	March 28	May 6	May 16	27	Nov. 28
2028	8	March 1	April 16	May 25	June 4	25	Dec. 3
2029	6	Feb. 14	April 1	May 10	May 20	27	Dec. 2
2030	8	March 6	April 21	May 30	June 9	24	Dec. 1
2031	7	Feb. 26	April 13	May 22	June 1	25	Nov. 30
2032	5	Feb. 11	March 28	May 6	May 16	27	Nov. 28
2033	8	March 2	April 17	May 26	June 5	24	Nov. 27
2034	7	Feb. 22	April 9	May 18	May 28	26	Dec. 3
2035	5	Feb. 7	March 25	May 3	May 13	28	Dec. 2
2036	7	Feb. 27	April 13	May 22	June 1	25	Nov. 30

JANUARY 2026

		Daily Lectionary	Dates of Historical Significance	Readings and Hymn of the Day	Liturgical Color
1	Thu	Isaiah 61:1–11 & Luke 1:57–80	**New Year's Day, Circumcision and Name of Jesus**		White
2	Fri	Isaiah 62:1–12 & Luke 2:1–20	J. K. Wilhelm Loehe, Pastor, d. 1872		
3	Sat	Isaiah 63:1–14 & Luke 2:21–40			
4		**SECOND SUNDAY AFTER CHRISTMAS**		***R:*** 1 Kings 3:4–15 ***E:*** Eph. 1:3–14 ***G:*** Luke 2:40–52 ***H:*** *LSB* 410—Within the Father's House	White
4	Sun	Isaiah 63:15–65:7 & Luke 2:41–52	Concordia Theological Seminary, Springfield, Ill., dedicated, 1874		
5	Mon	Isaiah 65:8–25 & Luke 3:1–20	C. F. W. Walther arrived at New Orleans, 1839		
6		**THE EPIPHANY OF OUR LORD**		***R:*** Isaiah 60:1–6 ***E:*** Eph. 3:1–12 ***G:*** Matt. 2:1–12 ***H:*** *LSB* 395—O Morning Star, How Fair and Bright	White
6	Tue	Isaiah 66:1–20 & Luke 3:21–38			
7	Wed	Ezek. 1:1–14, 22–28 & Rom. 1:1–17			
8	Thu	Ezek. 2:1–3:11 & Rom. 1:18–32	J. A. O. Preus, 9th LCMS pres., b. 1920		
9	Fri	Ezek. 3:12–27 & Rom. 2:1–16			
10	Sat	Ezek. 18:1–4, 19–32 & Rom. 2:17–29	Basil the Great of Caesarea, Gregory of Nazianzus, and Gregory of Nyssa, Pastors and Confessors		
11		**THE BAPTISM OF OUR LORD First Sunday after the Epiphany**		***R:*** Isaiah 42:1–9 ***E:*** Rom. 6:1–11 ***G:*** Matt. 3:13–17 ***H:*** *LSB* 406/407—To Jordan Came the Christ, Our Lord	White
11	Sun	Ezek. 33:1–20 & Rom. 3:1–18	Walter A. Maier, Lutheran Hour speaker, d. 1950		
12	Mon	Ezek. 34:1–24 & Rom. 3:19–31			
13	Tue	Ezek. 36:13–28 & Rom. 4:1–25			
14	Wed	Ezek. 36:33–37:14 & Rom. 5:1–21			
15	Thu	Ezek. 37:15–28 & Rom. 6:1–23			
16	Fri	Ezek. 38:1–23 & Rom. 7:1–20			
17	Sat	Ezek. 39:1–10, 17–29 & Rom. 7:21–8:17			
18		**SECOND SUNDAY AFTER THE EPIPHANY**		***R:*** Isaiah 49:1–7 ***E:*** 1 Cor. 1:1–9 ***G:*** John 1:29–42a ***H:*** *LSB* 402—The Only Son from Heaven	Green
18	Sun	Ezek. 40:1–4; 43:1–12 & Rom. 8:18–39	**The Confession of St. Peter**		White
19	Mon	Ezek. 44:1–16, 23–29 & Rom. 9:1–18			
20	Tue	Ezek. 47:1–14, 21–23 & Rom. 9:19–33	Sarah		
21	Wed	Joel 1:1–20 & Rom. 10:1–21			
22	Thu	Joel 2:1–17 & Rom. 11:1–24	National Sanctity of Human Life Day		
23	Fri	Joel 2:18–32 & Rom. 11:25–12:13			
24	Sat	Joel 3:1–21 & Rom. 12:14–13:14	**St. Timothy, Pastor and Confessor**		White
25		**THIRD SUNDAY AFTER THE EPIPHANY**		***R:*** Isaiah 9:1–4 ***E:*** 1 Cor. 1:10–18 ***G:*** Matt. 4:12–25 ***H:*** *LSB* 839—O Christ, Our True and Only Light	Green
25	Sun	Zech. 1:1–21 & Rom. 14:1–23	**The Conversion of St. Paul**		White
26	Mon	Zech. 2:1–3:10 & Rom. 15:1–13	**St. Titus, Pastor and Confessor**		White
27	Tue	Zech. 4:1–5:11 & Rom. 15:14–33	John Chrysostom, Preacher		
28	Wed	Zech. 6:1–7:14 & Rom. 16:17–27			
29	Thu	Zech. 8:1–23 & 2 Tim. 1:1–18	Gerald Kieschnick, 13th LCMS pres., b. 1943		
30	Fri	Zech. 9:1–17 & 2 Tim. 2:1–26			
31	Sat	Zech. 10:1–11:3 & 2 Tim. 3:1–17			

FEBRUARY 2026

		Daily Lectionary	Dates of Historical Significance	Readings and Hymn of the Day	Liturgical Color
1		**FOURTH SUNDAY AFTER THE EPIPHANY**		***R:*** Micah 6:1–8 ***E:*** 1 Cor. 1:18–31 ***G:*** Matt. 5:1–12 ***H:*** *LSB* 842—Son of God, Eternal Savior	Green
1	Sun	Zech. 11:4–17 & 2 Tim. 4:1–18			
2	Mon	Zech. 12:1–13:9 & Titus 1:1–2:6	**The Purification of Mary and the Presentation of Our Lord**		White
3	Tue	Zech. 14:1–21 & Titus 2:7–3:15			
4	Wed	Job 1:1–22 & John 1:1–18			
5	Thu	Job 2:1–3:10 & John 1:19–34	Jacob (Israel), Patriarch		
6	Fri	Job 3:11–26 & John 1:35–51			
7	Sat	Job 4:1–21 & John 2:1–12			
8		**FIFTH SUNDAY AFTER THE EPIPHANY**		***R:*** Isaiah 58:3–9a ***E:*** 1 Cor. 2:1–12 (13–16) ***G:*** Matt. 5:13–20 ***H:*** *LSB* 578—Thy Strong Word	Green
8	Sun	Job 5:1–27 & John 2:13–25			
9	Mon	Job 6:1–13 & John 3:1–21			
10	Tue	Job 6:14–30 & John 3:22–4:6	Silas, Fellow Worker of St. Peter and St. Paul		
11	Wed	Job 7:1–21 & John 4:7–26			
12	Thu	Job 8:1–22 & John 4:27–45			
13	Fri	Job 9:1–35 & John 4:46–54	Aquila, Priscilla, Apollos		
14	Sat	Job 10:1–22 & John 5:1–18	Valentine, Martyr		
15		**THE TRANSFIGURATION OF OUR LORD Last Sunday after the Epiphany**		***R:*** Ex. 24:8–18 ***E:*** 2 Peter 1:16–21 ***G:*** Matt. 17:1–9 ***H:*** *LSB* 413—O Wondrous Type! O Vision Fair	White
15	Sun	Job 11:1–20 & John 5:19–29	Philemon and Onesimus		
16	Mon	Job 12:1–6, 12–25 & John 5:30–47	Philipp Melanchthon, Confessor, b. 1497		
17	Tue	Job 13:1–12 & John 6:1–21			
18		**ASH WEDNESDAY**		***R:*** Joel 2:12–19 ***E:*** 2 Cor. 5:20b–6:10 ***G:*** Matt. 6:1–6, 16–21 ***H:*** *LSB* 607—From Depths of Woe I Cry to Thee	Black/Violet
18	Wed	Gen. 1:1–19 & Mark 1:1–13	Martin Luther, Doctor and Confessor, d. 1546		
19	Thu	Gen. 1:20–2:3 & Mark 1:14–28			
20	Fri	Gen. 2:4–25 & Mark 1:29–45	Ralph A. Bohlmann, 10th LCMS pres., b. 1932		
21	Sat	Gen. 3:1–24 & Mark 2:1–17	J. K. Wilhelm Loehe, Pastor, b. 1808		

22 **FIRST SUNDAY IN LENT**	*R:* Gen. 3:1–21	*E:* Rom. 5:12–19	*G:* Matt. 4:1–11	Violet
	H: LSB 656/657—A Mighty Fortress Is Our God			

22	Sun	Gen. 4:1–26 & Mark 2:18–28		
23	Mon	Gen. 6:1–7:5 & Mark 3:1–19	Polycarp of Smyrna, Pastor and Martyr, d. ca. 156 John W. Behnken, 7th LCMS pres., d. 1968	
24	Tue	Gen. 7:11–8:12 & Mark 3:20–35	**St. Matthias, Apostle**	Red
25	Wed	Gen. 8:13–9:17 & Mark 4:1–20		
26	Thu	Gen. 11:27–12:20 & Mark 4:21–41		
27	Fri	Gen. 13:1–18 & Mark 5:1–20		
28	Sat	Gen. 15:1–21 & Mark 5:21–43	Concordia Publishing House dedicated, 1870	

MARCH 2026

1 **SECOND SUNDAY IN LENT**	*R:* Gen. 12:1–9	*E:* Rom. 4:1–8, 13–17	*G:* John 3:1–17	Violet
	H: LSB 708—Lord, Thee I Love with All My Heart			

1	Sun	Gen. 16:1–9, 15–17:22 & Mark 6:1–13	Robert Kuhn, 12th LCMS pres., d. 2025
2	Mon	Gen. 18:1–15 & Mark 6:14–34	
3	Tue	Gen. 21:1–21 & Mark 6:35–56	
4	Wed	Gen. 22:1–19 & Mark 7:1–23	
5	Thu	Gen. 24:1–31 & Mark 7:24–37	
6	Fri	Gen. 24:32–52, 61–67 & Mark 8:1–21	
7	Sat	Gen. 27:1–29 & Mark 8:22–38	Perpetua and Felicitas, Martyrs, d. 203

8 **THIRD SUNDAY IN LENT**	*R:* Ex. 17:1–7	*E:* Rom. 5:1–8	*G:* John 4:5–26 (27–30, 39–42)	Violet
	H: LSB 823/824—May God Bestow on Us His Grace			

8	Sun	Gen. 27:30–45; 28:10–22 & Mark 9:1–13	
9	Mon	Gen. 29:1–30 & Mark 9:14–32	
10	Tue	Gen. 35:1–29 & Mark 9:33–50	
11	Wed	Gen. 37:1–36 & Mark 10:1–12	
12	Thu	Gen. 39:1–23 & Mark 10:13–31	
13	Fri	Gen. 40:1–23 & Mark 10:32–52	
14	Sat	Gen. 41:1–27 & Mark 11:1–19	Matthew C. Harrison, 14th LCMS pres., b. 1962

15 **FOURTH SUNDAY IN LENT**	*R:* Isaiah 42:14–21	*E:* Eph. 5:8–14	*G:* John 9:1–41 or John 9:1–7, 13–17, 34–39	Violet
	H: LSB 571—God Loved the World So That He Gave			

15	Sun	Gen. 41:28–57 & Mark 11:20–33		
16	Mon	Gen. 42:1–34, 38 & Mark 12:1–12		
17	Tue	Gen. 43:1–28 & Mark 12:13–27	Patrick, Missionary to Ireland, d. ca. 466	
18	Wed	Gen. 44:1–18, 32–34 & Mark 12:28–44		
19	Thu	Gen. 45:1–20, 24–28 & Mark 13:1–23	**St. Joseph, Guardian of Jesus** John W. Behnken, 7th LCMS pres., b. 1884	White
20	Fri	Gen. 47:1–31 & Mark 13:24–37		
21	Sat	Gen. 49:29–50:7, 14–26 & Mark 14:1–11	Johann Sebastian Bach, Kantor, b. 1685	

22 **FIFTH SUNDAY IN LENT**	*R:* Ezek. 37:1–14	*E:* Rom. 8:1–11	*G:* John 11:1–45 (46–53) or John 11:17–27, 38–53	Violet
	H: LSB 430—My Song Is Love Unknown			

22	Sun	Ex. 1:1–22 & Mark 14:12–31		
23	Mon	Ex. 2:1–22 & Mark 14:32–52	A. L. Barry, 11th LCMS pres., d. 2001	
24	Tue	Ex. 2:23–3:22 & Mark 14:53–72		
25	Wed	Ex. 4:1–18 & Mark 15:1–15	**The Annunciation of Our Lord**	White
26	Thu	Ex. 4:19–31 & Mark 15:16–32		
27	Fri	Ex. 5:1–6:1 & Mark 15:33–47		
28	Sat	Ex. 7:1–25 & Mark 16:1–20		

29 **SUNDAY OF THE PASSION** **Palm Sunday**	*R:* Isaiah 50:4–9a	*E:* Phil. 2:5–11	*G:* Matt. 26:1–27:66 or Matt. 27:11–66 or John 12:20–43	Scarlet/Violet
	H: LSB 438—A Lamb Goes Uncomplaining Forth			

29	Sun	Ex. 8:1–32 & Heb. 1:1–14	
30	Mon	Ex. 9:1–28 & Heb. 2:1–18	
31	Tue	Ex. 9:29–10:20 & Heb. 3:1–19	Joseph, Patriarch Concordia Historical Institute incorporated, 1927

APRIL 2026

1	Wed	Ex. 10:21–11:10 & Heb. 4:1–16

2 **HOLY (MAUNDY) THURSDAY**	*R:* Ex. 24:3–11	*E:* Heb. 9:11–22	*G:* Matt. 26:17–30	White/Scarlet/Violet
	H: LSB 617—O Lord, We Praise Thee			

2	Thu	Ex. 12:1–28 & Heb. 5:1–14

3 **GOOD FRIDAY**	*R:* Isaiah 52:13–53:12	*E:* Heb. 4:14–16; 5:7–9	*G:* John 18:1–19:42 or John 19:17–30	Black
	H: LSB 454—Sing, My Tongue, the Glorious Battle			

3	Fri	Ex. 12:29–32; 13:1–16 & Heb. 6:1–20
4	Sat	Ex. 13:17–14:9 & Heb. 7:1–22

5 **THE RESURRECTION OF OUR LORD** **Easter Day**	*R:* Acts 10:34–43 or Jer. 31:1–6	*E:* Col. 3:1–4	*G:* Matt. 28:1–10	White/Gold
	H: LSB 458—Christ Jesus Lay in Death's Strong Bands			

5	Sun	Ex. 14:10–31 & Heb. 7:23–8:13	H. C. Schwan, 4th LCMS pres., b. 1819 Robert Kuhn, 12th LCMS pres., b. 1937
6	Mon	Ex. 15:1–18 & Heb. 9:1–28	Lucas Cranach and Albrecht Dürer, Artists
7	Tue	Ex. 15:19–16:12 & Heb. 10:1–18	
8	Wed	Ex. 16:13–35 & Heb. 10:19–39	Martin Chemnitz, Pastor and Confessor, d. 1586
9	Thu	Ex. 17:1–16 & Heb. 11:1–29	

10 Fri	Ex. 18:5–27 & Heb. 12:1–24					
11 Sat	Ex. 19:1–25 & Heb. 13:1–21					
12	**SECOND SUNDAY OF EASTER**	***R:*** Acts 5:29–42 ***H:*** *LSB* 470/471—O Sons and Daughters of the King	***E:*** 1 Peter 1:3–9	***G:*** John 20:19–31	White	
12 Sun	Ex. 20:1–24 & Luke 4:1–15					
13 Mon	Ex. 22:20–23:13 & Luke 4:16–30					
14 Tue	Ex. 23:14–33 & Luke 4:31–44					
15 Wed	Ex. 24:1–18 & Luke 5:1–16	Walther-Marbach Debate, Altenburg, Mo., 1841				
16 Thu	Ex. 25:1–22 & Luke 5:17–39					
17 Fri	Ex. 31:1–18 & Luke 6:1–19					
18 Sat	Ex. 32:1–14 & Luke 6:20–38					
19	**THIRD SUNDAY OF EASTER**	***R:*** Acts 2:14a, 36–41 ***H:*** *LSB* 483—With High Delight Let Us Unite	***E:*** 1 Peter 1:17–25	***G:*** Luke 24:13–35	White	
19 Sun	Ex. 32:15–35 & Luke 6:39–49	Philipp Melanchthon, Confessor, d. 1560				
20 Mon	Ex. 33:1–23 & Luke 7:1–17	Johannes Bugenhagen, Pastor, d. 1558				
21 Tue	Ex. 34:1–28 & Luke 7:18–35	Anselm of Canterbury, Theologian, d. 1109				
22 Wed	Ex. 34:29–35:21 & Luke 7:36–50	Friedrich Pfotenhauer, 6th LCMS pres., b. 1859				
23 Thu	Ex. 38:21–39:8, 22–23, 27–31 & Luke 8:1–21					
24 Fri	Ex. 39:32–40:16 & Luke 8:22–39	Johann Walter, Kantor, d. 1570				
25 Sat	Ex. 40:17–38 & Luke 8:40–56	**St. Mark, Evangelist**			Red	
26	**FOURTH SUNDAY OF EASTER**	***R:*** Acts 2:42–47 ***H:*** *LSB* 709—The King of Love My Shepherd Is	***E:*** 1 Peter 2:19–25	***G:*** John 10:1–10	White	
26 Sun	Lev. 8:1–13, 30–36 & Luke 9:1–17	Missouri Synod organized, Chicago, 1847				
27 Mon	Lev. 9:1–24 & Luke 9:18–36					
28 Tue	Lev. 10:1–20 & Luke 9:37–62					
29 Wed	Lev. 16:1–24 & Luke 10:1–22					
30 Thu	Lev. 17:1–16 & Luke 10:23–42					

MAY 2026

1 Fri	Lev. 18:1–7, 20–19:8 & Luke 11:1–13	**St. Phillip and St. James, Apostles**			Red
2 Sat	Lev. 19:9–18, 26–37 & Luke 11:14–36	Athanasius of Alexandria, Pastor and Confessor, d. 373			
3	**FIFTH SUNDAY OF EASTER**	***R:*** Acts 6:1–9; 7:2a, 51–60 ***H:*** *LSB* 633—At the Lamb's High Feast We Sing	***E:*** 1 Peter 2:2–10	***G:*** John 14:1–14	White
3 Sun	Lev. 20:1–16, 22–27 & Luke 11:37–54				
4 Mon	Lev. 21:1–24 & Luke 12:1–12	Friedrich Wyneken, Pastor and Missionary, 2nd LCMS pres., d. 1876 F. W. Husmann, 1st sec. of LCMS, d. 1881			
5 Tue	Lev. 23:1–22 & Luke 12:13–34	Frederick the Wise, Christian Ruler, d. 1525			
6 Wed	Lev. 23:23–44 & Luke 12:35–53				
7 Thu	Lev. 24:1–23 & Luke 12:54–13:17	C. F. W. Walther, Theologian, 1st & 3rd LCMS pres., d. 1887			
8 Fri	Lev. 26:1–20 & Luke 13:18–35				
9 Sat	Lev. 26:21–33, 39–44 & Luke 14:1–24	Job			
10	**SIXTH SUNDAY OF EASTER**	***R:*** Acts 17:16–31 ***H:*** *LSB* 556—Dear Christians, One and All, Rejoice	***E:*** 1 Peter 3:13–22	***G:*** John 14:15–21	White
10 Sun	Num. 3:1–16, 39–48 & Luke 14:25–15:10				
11 Mon	Num. 8:5–26 & Luke 15:11–32	Cyril and Methodius, Missionaries to the Slavs			
12 Tue	Num. 9:1–23 & Luke 16:1–18				
13 Wed	Num. 10:11–36 & Luke 16:19–31	Friedrich Wyneken, Pastor and Missionary, 2nd LCMS pres., b. 1810			
14	**THE ASCENSION OF OUR LORD**	***R:*** Acts 1:1–11 ***H:*** *LSB* 491—Up through Endless Ranks of Angels	***E:*** Eph. 1:15–23	***G:*** Luke 24:44–53	White
14 Thu	Num. 11:1–23, 31–35 & Luke 17:1–19	Rosa Young, Pioneer Alabama African American Teacher, b. 1890			
15 Fri	Num. 11:24–29; 12:1–16 & Luke 17:20–37	English Synod joined LCMS, 1911			
16 Sat	Num. 13:1–3, 17–33 & Luke 18:1–17				
17	**SEVENTH SUNDAY OF EASTER**	***R:*** Acts 1:12–26 ***H:*** *LSB* 539—Christ Is the World's Redeemer	***E:*** 1 Peter 4:12–19; 5:6–11	***G:*** John 17:1–11	White
17 Sun	Num. 14:1–25 & Luke 18:18–34				
18 Mon	Num. 14:26–45 & Luke 18:35–19:10				
19 Tue	Num. 16:1–22 & Luke 19:11–28				
20 Wed	Num. 16:23–40 & Luke 19:29–48				
21 Thu	Num. 16:41–17:13 & Luke 20:1–18	Emperor Constantine, Christian Ruler, and Helena, Mother of Constantine			
22 Fri	Num. 20:1–21 & Luke 20:19–44				
23 Sat	Num. 20:22–21:9 & Luke 20:45–21:19				
24	**PENTECOST**	***R:*** Num. 11:24–30 ***H:*** *LSB* 497—Come, Holy Ghost, God and Lord	***E:*** Acts 2:1–21	***G:*** John 7:37–39	Red
24 Sun	Num. 21:10–35 & Luke 21:20–38	Esther			
25 Mon	Num. 22:1–20 & Luke 22:1–23	Bede the Venerable, Theologian, d. 735			
26 Tue	Num. 22:21–23:3 & Luke 22:24–46				
27 Wed	Num. 23:4–28 & Luke 22:47–71				
28 Thu	Num. 24:1–25 & Luke 23:1–25				
29 Fri	Num. 27:12–23 & Luke 23:26–56	H. C. Schwan, 4th LCMS pres., d. 1905 LCMS International Center dedicated, 1983			
30 Sat	Num. 32:1–6, 16–27 & Luke 24:1–27				
31	**THE HOLY TRINITY** **First Sunday after Pentecost**	***R:*** Gen. 1:1–2:4a ***H:*** *LSB* 498/499—Come, Holy Ghost, Creator Blest	***E:*** Acts 2:14a, 22–36	***G:*** Matt. 28:16–20	White
31 Sun	Num. 35:9–30 & Luke 24:28–53	**The Visitation** (three-year lectionary)			White

JUNE 2026

Date	Day	Readings	Commemoration	Color
1	Mon	Eccl. 9:1–17 & John 9:24–41	Justin, Martyr	
2	Tue	Eccl. 10:1–20 & John 10:1–21		
3	Wed	Eccl. 11:1–10 & John 10:22–42	Franz A. O. Pieper, 5th LCMS pres., d. 1931 Oliver Harms, 8th LCMS pres., d. 1980	
4	Thu	Eccl. 12:1–14 & John 11:1–16		
5	Fri	Prov. 1:8–33; John 11:17–37	Boniface of Mainz, Missionary to the Germans, d. 755	
6	Sat	Prov. 3:5–24; John 11:38–57		
7		**SECOND SUNDAY AFTER PENTECOST (Proper 5)**	***R:*** Hos. 5:15–6:6 ***E:*** Rom. 4:13–25 ***G:*** Matt. 9:9–13 ***H:*** *LSB* 689—Let Me Be Thine Forever	Green
7	Sun	Prov. 4:1–27 & John 12:1–19		
8	Mon	Prov. 5:1–23 & John 12:20–36a		
9	Tue	Prov. 8:1–21 & John 12:36b–50		
10	Wed	Prov. 8:22–36 & John 13:1–20		
11	Thu	Prov. 9:1–18 & John 13:21–38	**St. Barnabas, Apostle** First Building of Concordia Seminary, St. Louis, dedicated, 1850	Red
12	Fri	Prov. 10:1–23 & John 14:1–17	The Ecumenical Council of Nicaea, 325 Walther Mausoleum, St. Louis, dedicated, 1892	
13	Sat	Prov. 13:1–25 & John 14:18–31		
14		**THIRD SUNDAY AFTER PENTECOST (Proper 6)**	***R:*** Ex. 19:2–8 ***E:*** Rom. 5:6–15 ***G:*** Matt. 9:35–10:8 (9–20) ***H:*** *LSB* 571—God Loved the World So That He Gave	Green
14	Sun	Prov. 14:1–27 & John 15:1–11	Elisha	
15	Mon	Prov. 15:1–29 & John 15:12–27		
16	Tue	Prov. 16: 1–24 & John 16:1–16		
17	Wed	Prov. 17:1–28 & John 16:17–33		
18	Thu	Prov. 20:5–25 & John 17:1–26		
19	Fri	Prov. 22:1–21 & John 18:1–14		
20	Sat	Prov. 22:22–23:12 & John 18:15–40		
21		**FOURTH SUNDAY AFTER PENTECOST (Proper 7)**	***R:*** Jer. 20:7–13 ***E:*** Rom. 6:12–23 ***G:*** Matt.10:5a, 21–33 ***H:*** *LSB* 659—Lord of Our Life	Green
21	Sun	Prov. 24:1–22 & John 19:1–22		
22	Mon	Prov. 25:1–22 & John 19:23–42	Lutheran Laymen's League organized, 1917	
23	Tue	Prov. 27:1–24 & John 20:1–18		
24	Wed	Prov. 30:1–9, 18–33 & John 20:19–31	**The Nativity of St. John the Baptist**	White
25	Thu	Prov. 31:10–31 & John 21:1–25	Presentation of the Augsburg Confession, 1530	
26	Fri	Joshua 1:1–18 & Acts 8:1–25	Jeremiah	
27	Sat	Joshua 2:1–24 & Acts 8:26–40	Cyril of Alexandria, Pastor and Confessor, d. 444 Franz A. O. Pieper, 5th LCMS pres., b. 1852	
28		**FIFTH SUNDAY AFTER PENTECOST (Proper 8)**	***R:*** Jer. 28:5–9 ***E:*** Rom. 7:1–13 ***G:*** Matt. 10:34–42 ***H:*** *LSB* 685—Let Us Ever Walk with Jesus	Green
28	Sun	Joshua 3:1–17 & Acts 9:1–22	Irenaeus of Lyons, Pastor	
29	Mon	Joshua 4:1–24 & Acts 9:23–43	**St. Peter and St. Paul, Apostles**	Red
30	Tue	Joshua 5:1–6:5 & Acts 10:1–17	Rosa Young, Pioneer Alabama African American Teacher, d. 1971	

JULY 2026

Date	Day	Readings	Commemoration	Color
1	Wed	Joshua 6:6–27 & Acts 10:18–33		
2	Thu	Joshua 7:1–26 & Acts 10:34–48	**The Visitation** (one-year lectionary)	White
3	Fri	Joshua 8:1–28 & Acts 11:1–18		
4	Sat	Joshua 10:1–25 & Acts 11:19–30		
5		**SIXTH SUNDAY AFTER PENTECOST (Proper 9)**	***R:*** Zech. 9:9–12 ***E:*** Rom. 7:14–25a ***G:*** Matt. 11:25–30 ***H:*** *LSB* 699—I Heard the Voice of Jesus Say	Green
5	Sun	Joshua 23:1–16 & Acts 12:1–25		
6	Mon	Joshua 24:1–31 & Acts 13:1–12	Isaiah	
7	Tue	Judges 2:6–23 & Acts 13:13–41		
8	Wed	Judges 3:7–31 & Acts 13:42–52	Lutheran Women's Missionary League organized, 1942	
9	Thu	Judges 4:1–24 & Acts 14:1–18		
10	Fri	Judges 6:1–24 & Acts 14:19–15:5	Synodical Conference organized, 1872	
11	Sat	Judges 6:25–40 & Acts 15:6–21		
12		**SEVENTH SUNDAY AFTER PENTECOST (Proper 10)**	***R:*** Isaiah 55:10–13 ***E:*** Rom. 8:12–17 ***G:*** Matt. 13:1–9, 18–23 ***H:*** *LSB* 577—Almighty God, Your Word Is Cast	Green
12	Sun	Judges 7:1–23 & Gal. 1:1–24		
13	Mon	Judges 13:1–25 & Gal. 2:1–21		
14	Tue	Judges 14:1–20 & Gal. 3:1–22		
15	Wed	Judges 15:1–16:3 & Gal. 3:23–4:11		
16	Thu	Judges 16:4–30 & Gal. 4:12–31	Ruth	
17	Fri	1 Sam. 1:1–20 & Gal. 5:1–26		
18	Sat	1 Sam. 1:21–2:17 & Gal. 6:1–18		
19		**EIGHTH SUNDAY AFTER PENTECOST (Proper 11)**	***R:*** Isaiah 44:6–8 ***E:*** Rom. 8:18–27 ***G:*** Matt. 13:24–30, 36–43 ***H:*** *LSB* 772—In Holy Conversation	Green
19	Sun	1 Sam. 2:18–36 & Acts 15:22–41		
20	Mon	1 Sam. 3:1–21 & Acts 16:1–22	Elijah	
21	Tue	1 Sam. 4:1–22 & Acts 16:23–40	Ezekiel	
22	Wed	1 Sam. 5:1–6:3, 10–16 & Acts 18:1–11, 23–28	**St. Mary Magdalene**	White
23	Thu	1 Sam. 6:19–7:17 & Acts 19:1–22		
24	Fri	1 Sam. 8:1–22 & Acts 21:15–36	Ralph A. Bohlmann, 10th LCMS pres., d. 2016	
25	Sat	1 Sam. 9:1–27 & Acts 21:37–22:16	**St. James the Elder, Apostle**	Red
26		**NINTH SUNDAY AFTER PENTECOST (Proper 12)**	***R:*** Deut. 7:6–9 ***E:*** Rom. 8:28–39 ***G:*** Matt. 13:44–52 ***H:*** *LSB* 713—From God Can Nothing Move Me	Green
26	Sun	1 Sam. 10:1–27 & Acts 22:17–29		

Date	Day	Readings	Commemoration / Propers	Color
27	Mon	1 Sam. 12:1–25 & Acts 22:30–23:11		
28	Tue	1 Sam. 13:1–18 & Acts 23:12–35	Johann Sebastian Bach, Kantor, d. 1750	
29	Wed	1 Sam. 14:47–15:9 & Acts 24:1–23	Mary, Martha, and Lazarus of Bethany	
30	Thu	1 Sam. 15:10–35 & Acts 24:24–25:12	Robert Barnes, Confessor and Martyr, d. 1540	
31	Fri	1 Sam. 16:1–23 & Acts 25:13–27	Joseph of Arimathea	

AUGUST 2026

Date	Day	Readings	Commemoration / Propers	Color
1	Sat	1 Sam. 17:1–19 & Acts 26:1–23		
2	**TENTH SUNDAY AFTER PENTECOST (Proper 13)**		***R:*** Isaiah 55:1–5; ***E:*** Rom. 9:1–5 (6–13); ***G:*** Matt. 14:13–21; ***H:*** *LSB* 642—O Living Bread from Heaven	Green
2	Sun	1 Sam. 17:20–47 & Acts 26:24–27:8		
3	Mon	1 Sam. 17:48–18:9 & Acts 27:9–26	Joanna, Mary, and Salome, Myrrhbearers	
4	Tue	1 Sam. 18:10–30 & Acts 27:27–44	A. L. Barry, 11th LCMS pres., b. 1931	
5	Wed	1 Sam. 19:1–24 & Acts 28:1–15	Third Lutheran Free Conference, Cleveland, 1858	
6	Thu	1 Sam. 20:1–23 & Acts 28:16–31		
7	Fri	1 Sam. 20:24–42 & 1 Cor. 1:1–25		
8	Sat	1 Sam. 24:1–22 & 1 Cor. 1:26–2:16		
9	**ELEVENTH SUNDAY AFTER PENTECOST (Proper 14)**		***R:*** Job 38:4–18; ***E:*** Rom. 10:5–17; ***G:*** Matt. 14:22–33; ***H:*** *LSB* 717—Eternal Father, Strong to Save	Green
9	Sun	1 Sam. 25:1–22 & 1 Cor. 3:1–23		
10	Mon	1 Sam. 25:23–44 & 1 Cor. 4:1–21	Lawrence, Deacon and Martyr, d. 285	
11	Tue	1 Sam. 26:1–25 1 Cor. 5:1–13		
12	Wed	1 Sam. 28:3–25 & 1 Cor. 6:1–20		
13	Thu	1 Sam. 31:1–13 & 1 Cor. 7:1–24	J. A. O. Preus, 9th LCMS pres., d. 1994	
14	Fri	2 Sam. 1:1–27 & 1 Cor. 7:25–40		
15	Sat	2 Sam. 5:1–25 & 1 Cor. 8:1–13	**St. Mary, Mother of Our Lord**	White
16	**TWELFTH SUNDAY AFTER PENTECOST (Proper 15)**		***R:*** Isaiah 56:1, 6–8; ***E:*** Rom. 11:1–2a, 13–15, 28–32; ***G:*** Matt. 15:21–28; ***H:*** *LSB* 653—In Christ There Is No East or West	Green
16	Sun	2 Sam. 6:1–19 & 1 Cor. 9:1–23	Isaac	
17	Mon	2 Sam. 7:1–17 & 1 Cor. 9:24–10:22	Johann Gerhard, Theologian, d. 1637	
18	Tue	2 Sam. 7:18–29 & 1 Cor. 10:23–11:16		
19	Wed	2 Sam. 11:1–27 & 1 Cor. 11:17–34	Bernard of Clairvaux, Hymn Writer and Theologian, d. 1153 Gotthold Heinrich Löber, Pastor, d. 1849	
20	Thu	2 Sam. 12:1–25 & 1 Cor. 12:1–13	Samuel	
21	Fri	1 Kings 1:1–4, 15–35 & 1 Cor. 12:14–31	Formula of Concord signed at Gotha, 1577	
22	Sat	1 Kings 2:1–27 & 1 Cor. 13:1–13		
23	**THIRTEENTH SUNDAY AFTER PENTECOST (Proper 16)**		***R:*** Isaiah 51:1–6; ***E:*** Rom. 11:33–12:8; ***G:*** Matt. 16:13–20; ***H:*** *LSB* 645—Built on the Rock	Green
23	Sun	1 Kings 3:1–15 & 2 Cor. 1:1–22		
24	Mon	1 Kings 5:1–18 & 2 Cor. 1:23–2:17	**St. Bartholomew, Apostle**	Red
25	Tue	1 Kings 7:51–8:21 & 2 Cor. 3:1–18		
26	Wed	1 Kings 8:22–30, 46–63 & 2 Cor. 4:1–18		
27	Thu	1 Kings 9:1–9; 10:1–13 & 2 Cor. 5:1–21	Monica, Mother of Augustine	
28	Fri	1 Kings 11:1–26 & 2 Cor. 6:1–18	Augustine of Hippo, Pastor and Theologian, d. 430	
29	Sat	1 Kings 11:42–12:19 & 2 Cor. 7:1–16	**The Martyrdom of St. John the Baptist**	Red
30	**FOURTEENTH SUNDAY AFTER PENTECOST (Proper 17)**		***R:*** Jer. 15:15–21; ***E:*** Rom. 12:9–21; ***G:*** Matt. 16:21–28; ***H:*** *LSB* 531—Hail, Thou Once Despised Jesus	Green
30	Sun	1 Kings 12:20–13:5, 33–34 & 2 Cor. 8:1–24		
31	Mon	1 Kings 16:29–17:24 & 2 Cor. 9:1–15		

SEPTEMBER 2026

Date	Day	Readings	Commemoration / Propers	Color
1	Tue	1 Kings 18:1–19 & Eph. 1:1–23	Joshua	
2	Wed	1 Kings 18:20–40 & Eph. 2:1–22	Hannah	
3	Thu	1 Kings 19:1–21 & Eph. 3:1–21	Gregory the Great, Pastor	
4	Fri	2 Kings 2:1–18 & Eph. 4:1–24	Moses	
5	Sat	2 Kings 2:19–25; 4:1–7 & Eph. 4:25–5:14	Zacharias and Elizabeth	
6	**FIFTEENTH SUNDAY AFTER PENTECOST (Proper 18)**		***R:*** Ezek. 33:7–9; ***E:*** Rom. 13:1–10; ***G:*** Matt. 18:1–20; ***H:*** *LSB* 820—My Soul, Now Praise Your Maker	Green
6	Sun	2 Kings 4:8–22, 32–37 & Eph. 5:15–33		
7	Mon	2 Kings 4:38–5:8 & Eph. 6:1–24	First Issue of *Der Lutheraner*, 1844	
8	Tue	2 Kings 5:9–27 & Phil. 1:1–20		
9	Wed	2 Kings 6:1–23 & Phil. 1:21–2:11	Second Building of Concordia Seminary, St. Louis, dedicated, 1883	
10	Thu	2 Kings 9:1–13; 10:18–29 & Phil. 2:12–30		
11	Fri	2 Chron. 29:1–24 & Phil. 3:1–21	Concordia Publishing House founded, 1869	
12	Sat	2 Chron. 31:1–21 & Phil. 4:1–23		
13	**SIXTEENTH SUNDAY AFTER PENTECOST (Proper 19)**		***R:*** Gen. 50:15–21; ***E:*** Rom. 14:1–12; ***G:*** Matt. 18:21–35; ***H:*** *LSB* 501—Come Down, O Love Divine	Green
13	Sun	2 Chron. 32:1–22 & Col. 1:1–23		
14	Mon	2 Chron. 33:1–25 & Col. 1:24–2:7	**Holy Cross Day**	Red
15	Tue	2 Chron. 34:1–4, 8–11, 14–33 & Col. 2:8–23		
16	Wed	2 Chron. 35:1–7, 16–25 & Col. 3:1–25	Cyprian of Carthage, Pastor and Martyr, d. 258	
17	Thu	2 Chron. 36:1–23 & Col. 4:1–18		
18	Fri	Neh. 1:1–2:10 & 1 Tim. 1:1–20		
19	Sat	Neh. 2:11–20; 4:1–6 & 1 Tim. 2:1–15		
20	**SEVENTEENTH SUNDAY AFTER PENTECOST (Proper 20)**		***R:*** Isaiah 55:6–9; ***E:*** Phil. 1:12–14, 19–30; ***G:*** Matt. 20:1–16; ***H:*** *LSB* 555—Salvation unto Us Has Come	Green
20	Sun	Neh. 4:7–23 & 1 Tim. 3:1–16		
21	Mon	Neh. 5:1–16; 6:1–9, 15–16 & 1 Tim. 4:1–16	**St. Matthew, Apostle and Evangelist**	Red

22	Tue	Neh. 7:1–4; 8:1–18 & 1 Tim. 5:1–16	Jonah	
23	Wed	Neh. 9:1–21 & 1 Tim. 5:17–6:2		
24	Thu	Neh. 9:22–38 & 1 Tim. 6:3–21		
25	Fri	Mal. 1:1–14 & Matt. 3:1–17		
26	Sat	Mal. 2:1–3:5 & Matt. 4:1–11		

27 EIGHTEENTH SUNDAY AFTER PENTECOST (Proper 21) — ***R:*** Ezek. 18:1–4, 25–32 ***E:*** Phil. 2:1–4 (5–13) 14–18 ***G:*** Matt. 21:23–27 (28–32) — Green
H: *LSB* 655—Lord, Keep Us Steadfast in Your Word

27	Sun	Mal. 3:6–4:6 & Matt. 4:12–25		
28	Mon	Deut. 1:1–18 & Matt. 5:1–20		
29	Tue	Deut. 1:19–36 & Matt. 5:21–48	**St. Michael and All Angels**	White
30	Wed	Deut. 1:37–2:15 & Matt. 6:1–15	Jerome, Translator of Holy Scripture, d. 420	

OCTOBER 2026

1	Thu	Deut. 2:16–37 & Matt. 6:16–34		
2	Fri	Deut. 3:1–29 & Matt. 7:1–12	Lutheran Hour started by LLL, 1930	
3	Sat	Deut. 4:1–20 & Matt. 7:13–29		

4 NINETEENTH SUNDAY AFTER PENTECOST (Proper 22) — ***R:*** Isaiah 5:1–7 ***E:*** Phil. 3:4b–14 ***G:*** Matt. 21:33–46 — Green
H: *LSB* 544—O Love, How Deep

4	Sun	Deut. 4:21–40 & Matt. 8:1–17		
5	Mon	Deut. 5:1–21 & Matt. 8:18–34		
6	Tue	Deut. 5:22–6:9 & Matt. 9:1–17		
7	Wed	Deut. 6:10–25 & Matt. 9:18–38	Henry Melchior Muhlenberg, Pastor, d. 1787	
8	Thu	Deut. 7:1–19 & Matt. 10:1–23		
9	Fri	Deut. 8:1–20 & Matt. 10:24–42	Abraham Friedrich Pfotenhauer, 6th LCMS pres., d. 1939	
10	Sat	Deut. 9:1–22 & Matt. 11:1–19		

11 TWENTIETH SUNDAY AFTER PENTECOST (Proper 23) — ***R:*** Isaiah 25:6–9 ***E:*** Phil. 4:4–13 ***G:*** Matt. 22:1–14 — Green
H: *LSB* 510—A Multitude Comes from the East and the West

11	Sun	Deut. 9:23–10:22 & Matt. 11:20–30	Philip the Deacon	
12	Mon	Deut. 11:1–25 & Matt. 12:1–21		
13	Tue	Deut. 11:26–12:12 & Matt. 12:22–37		
14	Wed	Deut. 12:13–32 & Matt. 12:38–50		
15	Thu	Deut. 13:1–18 & Matt. 13:1–23		
16	Fri	Deut. 14:1–2, 22–23, 14:28–15:15 & Matt. 13:24–43		
17	Sat	Deut. 15:19–16:22 & Matt. 13:44–58	Ignatius of Antioch, Pastor and Martyr	

18 TWENTY-FIRST SUNDAY AFTER PENTECOST (Proper 24) — ***R:*** Isaiah 45:1–7 ***E:*** 1 Thess. 1:1–10 ***G:*** Matt. 22:15–22 — Green
H: *LSB* 940—Holy God, We Praise Thy Name

18	Sun	Deut. 17:1–20 & Matt. 14:1–21	**St. Luke, Evangelist**	Red
19	Mon	Deut. 18:1–22 & Matt. 14:22–36		
20	Tue	Deut. 19:1–20 & Matt. 15:1–20		
21	Wed	Deut. 20:1–20 & Matt. 15:21–39		
22	Thu	Deut. 21:1–23 & Matt. 16:1–12		
23	Fri	Deut. 24:10–25:10 & Matt. 16:13–28	**St. James of Jerusalem, Brother of Jesus and Martyr**	Red
24	Sat	Deut. 25:17–26:19 & Matt. 17:1–13		

25 TWENTY-SECOND SUNDAY AFTER PENTECOST (Proper 25) — ***R:*** Lev. 19:1–2, 15–18 ***E:*** 1 Thess. 2:1–13 ***G:*** Matt. 22:34–46 — Green
H: *LSB* 411—I Want to Walk as a Child of the Light

25	Sun	Deut. 27:1–26 & Matt. 17:14–27	Dorcas (Tabitha), Lydia, and Phoebe, Faithful Women C. F. W. Walther, Theologian, 1st & 3rd LCMS pres., b. 1811	
26	Mon	Deut. 28:1–22 & Matt. 18:1–20	Philipp Nicolai, Johann Heerman, and Paul Gerhardt, Hymn Writers	
27	Tue	Deut. 29:1–29 & Matt. 18:21–35		
28	Wed	Deut. 30:1–20 & Matt. 19:1–15	**St. Simon and St. Jude, Apostles**	Red
29	Thu	Deut. 31:1–29 & Matt. 19:16–30		
30	Fri	Deut. 31:30–32:27 & Matt. 20:1–16		

31 REFORMATION DAY — ***R:*** Rev. 14:6–7 ***E:*** Rom. 3:19–28 ***G:*** John 8:31–36 or Matt. 11:12–19 — Red
H: *LSB* 656/657 A Mighty Fortress Is Our God

31	Sat	Deut. 32:28–52 & Matt. 20:17–34	**Reformation Day**	Red

NOVEMBER 2026

1 ALL SAINTS' DAY Twenty-Third Sunday after Pentecost — ***R:*** Rev. 7:(2–8) 9–17 ***E:*** 1 John 3:1–3 ***G:*** Matt. 5:1–12 — White
H: *LSB* 677—For All the Saints

1	Sun	Deut. 34:1–12 & Matt. 21:1–22	**All Saints' Day**	White
2	Mon	Jer. 1:1–19 & Matt. 21:23–46		
3	Tue	Jer. 3:6–4:2 & Matt. 22:1–22		
4	Wed	Jer. 5:1–19 & Matt. 22:23–46		
5	Thu	Jer. 7:1–29 & Matt. 23:1–12		
6	Fri	Jer. 8:18–9:12 & Matt. 23:13–39		
7	Sat	Jer. 11:1–23 & Matt. 24:1–28	Synodical Conference Black Mission began, 1877	

8 TWENTY-FOURTH SUNDAY AFTER PENTECOST (Proper 27) — ***R:*** Amos 5:18–24 ***E:*** 1 Thess. 4:13–18 ***G:*** Matt. 25:1–13 — Green
H: *LSB* 516—Wake, Awake, for Night Is Flying

8	Sun	Jer. 20:1–18 & Matt. 24:29–51	Johannes von Staupitz, Luther's Father Confessor	
9	Mon	Jer. 22:1–23 & Matt. 25:1–13	Martin Chemnitz, Pastor and Confessor, b. 1522	
10	Tue	Jer. 23:1–20 & Matt. 25:14–30	Martin Luther, Doctor and Confessor, b. 1483	
11	Wed	Jer. 23:21–40 & Matt. 25:31–46	Martin of Tours, Pastor	
12	Thu	Jer. 25:1–18 & Matt. 26:1–19		
13	Fri	Jer. 26:1–19 & Matt. 26:20–35		
14	Sat	Jer. 29:1–19 & Matt. 26:36–56	Emperor Justinian, Christian Ruler and Confessor of Christ, d. 565	

15	**TWENTY-FIFTH SUNDAY AFTER PENTECOST (Proper 28)**	***R:*** Zeph. 1:7–16 ***H:*** *LSB* 508—The Day Is Surely Drawing Near	***E:*** 1 Thess. 5:1–11	***G:*** Matt. 25:14–30	Green

15 Sun Jer. 30:1–24 & Matt. 26:57–75
16 Mon Jer. 31:1–17, 23–34 & Matt. 27:1–10
17 Tue Jer. 33:1–22 & Matt. 27:11–32
18 Wed Jer. 37:1–21 & Matt. 27:33–56
19 Thu Jer. 38:1–28 & Matt. 27:57–66 — Elizabeth of Hungary, d. 1231
20 Fri Dan. 1:1–21 & Matt. 28:1–20
21 Sat Dan. 2:1–23 & Rev. 18:1–24

22 LAST SUNDAY OF THE CHURCH YEAR (Proper 29) — ***R:*** Ezek. 34:11–16, 20–24 ***E:*** 1 Cor. 15:20–28 ***G:*** Matt. 25:31–46 — Green
H: *LSB* 532—The Head That Once Was Crowned with Thorns

22 Sun Dan. 2:24–49 & Rev. 19:1–21
23 Mon Dan. 3:1–30 & Rev. 20:1–15 — Clement of Rome, Pastor
24 Tue Dan. 4:1–37 & Rev. 21:1–8
25 Wed Dan. 5:1–30 & Rev. 21:9–27

26 THANKSGIVING DAY (U.S.) — ***R:*** Deut. 8:1–10 ***E:*** Phil. 4:6–20 or 1 Tim. 2:1–4 ***G:*** Luke 17:11–19 — White
H: *LSB* 785—We Praise You, O God

26 Thu Dan. 6:1–28 & Rev. 22:1–21
27 Fri Isaiah 1:1–28 & 1 Peter 1:1–12
28 Sat Isaiah 2:1–22 & 1 Peter 1:13–25

29 FIRST SUNDAY IN ADVENT — ***R:*** Isaiah 64:1–9 ***E:*** 1 Cor. 1:3–9 ***G:*** Mark 11:1–10 or Mark 13:24–37 — Blue/Violet
H: *LSB* 332—Savior of the Nations, Come

29 Sun Isaiah 5:1–25 & 1 Peter 2:1–12 — Noah
30 Mon Isaiah 6:1–7:9 & 1 Peter 2:13–25 — **St. Andrew, Apostle** — Red

DECEMBER 2026

1 Tue Isaiah 7:10–8:8 & 1 Peter 3:1–22
2 Wed Isaiah 8:9–9:7 & 1 Peter 4:1–19
3 Thu Isaiah 9:8–10:11 & 1 Peter 5:1–14
4 Fri Isaiah 10:12–27a, 33–34 & 2 Peter 1:1–21 — John of Damascus, Theologian and Hymn Writer, d. 749
5 Sat Isaiah 11:1–12:6 & 2 Peter 2:1–22

6 SECOND SUNDAY IN ADVENT — ***R:*** Isaiah 40:1–11 ***E:*** 2 Peter 3:8–14 ***G:*** Mark 1:1–8 — Blue/Violet
H: *LSB* 344—On Jordan's Bank the Baptist's Cry

6 Sun Isaiah 14:1–23 & 2 Peter 3:1–18 — Nicholas of Myra, Pastor, d. 345 or 352
7 Mon Isaiah 24:1–13 & 1 John 1:1–2:14 — Ambrose of Milan, Pastor and Hymn Writer
8 Tue Isaiah 24:14–25:12 & 1 John 2:15–29
9 Wed Isaiah 26:1–19 & 1 John 3:1–24 — Log Cabin College, Perry Co., Mo., dedicated, 1839
10 Thu Isaiah 26:20–27:13 & 1 John 4:1–21
11 Fri Isaiah 28:14–29 & 1 John 5:1–21 — Oliver Harms, 8th LCMS pres., b. 1901
12 Sat Isaiah 29:1–14 & Jude 1–25

13 THIRD SUNDAY IN ADVENT — ***R:*** Isaiah 61:1–4, 8–11 ***E:*** 1 Thess. 5:16–24 ***G:*** John 1:6–8, 19–28 — Blue/Violet
H: *LSB* 345—Hark! A Thrilling Voice Is Sounding

13 Sun Isaiah 29:15–30:14 & Rev. 1:1–20 — Lucia, Martyr
14 Mon Isaiah 30:15–26 & Rev. 2:1–29
15 Tue Isaiah 30:27–31:9 & Rev. 3:1–22
16 Wed Isaiah 32:1–20 & Rev. 4:1–11
17 Thu Isaiah 33:1–24 & Rev. 5:1–14 — Daniel the Prophet and the Three Young Men
18 Fri Isaiah 34:1–2, 8–35:10 & Rev. 6:1–17
19 Sat Isaiah 40:1–17 & Rev. 7:1–17 — Adam and Eve

20 FOURTH SUNDAY IN ADVENT — ***R:*** 2 Sam. 7:1–11, 16 ***E:*** Rom. 16:25–27 ***G:*** Luke 1:26–38 — Blue/Violet
H: *LSB* 357—O Come, O Come, Emmanuel

20 Sun Isaiah 40:18–41:10 & Rev. 8:1–13 — Katharina von Bora Luther, d. 1555
21 Mon Isaiah 42:1–25 & Rev. 9:1–12 — **St. Thomas, Apostle** — Red
22 Tue Isaiah 43:1–24 & Rev. 9:13–10:11
23 Wed Isaiah 43:25–44:20 & Rev. 11:1–19

24 THE NATIVITY OF OUR LORD Christmas Eve — ***R:*** Isaiah 7:10–14 ***E:*** 1 John 4:7–16 ***G:*** Matt. 1:18–25 — White
H: *LSB* 359—Lo, How a Rose E'er Blooming

24 Thu Isaiah 44:21–45:13, 20–25 & Rev. 12:1–17

25 THE NATIVITY OF OUR LORD Christmas Day — ***R:*** Isaiah 52:7–10 ***E:*** Heb. 1:1–6 (7–12) ***G:*** John 1:1–14 (15–18) — White
H: *LSB* 382—We Praise You, Jesus, at Your Birth

25 Fri Isaiah 49:1–18 & Matt. 1:1–17
26 Sat Isaiah 49:22–26; 50:4–51:8, 12–16 & Matt. 1:18–25 — **St. Stephen, Martyr** — Red

27 FIRST SUNDAY AFTER CHRISTMAS — ***R:*** Isaiah 61:10–62:3 ***E:*** Gal. 4:4–7 ***G:*** Luke 2:22–40 — White
H: *LSB* 389—Let All Together Praise Our God

27 Sun Isaiah 51:17–52:12 & Matt. 2:1–12 — **St. John, Apostle and Evangelist** — White
28 Mon Isaiah 52:13–54:10 & Matt. 2:13–23 — **The Holy Innocents, Martyrs** — Red
29 Tue Isaiah 55:1–13 & Luke 1:1–25 — David
30 Wed Isaiah 58:1–59:3, 14–21 & Luke 1:26–38
31 Thu Isaiah 60:1–22 & Luke 1:39–56 — **New Year's Eve, Eve of the Circumcision and Name of Jesus** — White

THE LUTHERAN CHURCH—MISSOURI SYNOD

International Center
1333 S. Kirkwood Rd.
Saint Louis, MO 63122-7295
Phone: (314) 965-9000
Fax: (314) 996-1016
Website: lcms.org
Office Hours: Monday–Friday, 7:45 a.m.–4:15 p.m. (Central Time)

The year following each name indicates when the present term expires.

Officers of the Synod

PRESIDENT:	Matthew C. Harrison	(2026)
FIRST VICE PRESIDENT:	Peter K. Lange	(2026)
SECOND VICE PRESIDENT:	Benjamin T. Ball	(2026)
THIRD VICE PRESIDENT:	Scott R. Murray	(2026)
FOURTH VICE PRESIDENT:	Nabil S. Nour	(2026)
FIFTH VICE PRESIDENT:	Christopher S. Esget	(2026)
SIXTH VICE PRESIDENT:	John C. Wohlrabe Jr.	(2026)
SECRETARY:	John W. Sias	(2026)
CHIEF ADMINISTRATIVE OFFICER:	Felix L. Loc	(Appointed)
CHIEF FINANCIAL OFFICER:	Nathan M. Haak	(Appointed)
CHIEF MISSION OFFICER:	Dan Galchutt	(Appointed, Interim)

PRESIDENTS EMERITI:
Gerald B. Kieschnick

Board of Directors

OFFICERS:
Chairman: Christian A. Preus (2026)
Vice-Chairman: Andrew N. Grams (2026)
Secretary: John W. Sias (2026)

ORDAINED MEMBERS:
Roger B. Gallup (2029)
Matthew C. Harrison (2026)
Josemon T. Hoem (2029)
Peter K. Lange (2026)
John W. Sias (2026)

COMMISSIONED MEMBER:
Jan W. Lohmeyer (2026)

LAY MEMBERS:
Andrew N. Grams (2026)
Larry Harrington (2029)
Leo S. Mackay Jr. (2029)
Christian A. Preus (2026)
Rick H. Stathakis (2029)
K. Allan Voss (2029)
Jesse Yow, Jr. (2026)

NON-VOTING MEMBERS:
Peter K. Lange (2026)

ADVISORY:
Nathan M. Haak, Chief Financial Officer
Felix L. Loc, Chief Administrative Officer
Dan Galchutt, Interim Chief Mission Officer

LEGAL COUNSEL:
UB Greensfelder LLP, 10 South Broadway, St. Louis, MO 63102-1747

Standing Committee on Nominations

CHAIRMAN:
Christian A. Preus (2026)
VICE-CHAIRMAN:
Samuel M. Powell (2026)
SECRETARY:
Mark O. Stern (2026)

OFFICERS/STRUCTURE

COMMISSIONS

The year following each name indicates when the present term expires.

Theology & Church Relations (CTCR)

Phone: (314) 996-1433
1333 S. Kirkwood Rd.
St. Louis, MO 63122
Phone: (314) 996-1433
Email: ctcr@lcms.org
Website: lcms.org/ctcr

Commission Members:

Chairman:	Brian Saunders	(2026)
	Paul G. Alms	(2026)
	Joel Biermann	(2026)
	Gerhard Bode	(2026)
	Robert Dargatz	(2026)
	Bill Frerking	(2026)
	Joseph Gerth	(2029)
	Frederick Guengerich	(2026)
	Jack Kilcrease	(2029)
	Naomich Masaki	(2026)
	Mark Paterson	(2026)
	David Petersen	(2029)
	Andrea Pitkus	(2026)
	John Pless	(2026)
	Ely Prieto	(2026)
	Roland Ziegler	(2026)

Advisory Members:
Jon Bruss
Thomas Egger
Matthew C. Harrison
Peter Lange

Executive Director: Joel Lehenbauer
Associate Executive Director: Richard Serina
Assistant to the Executive Director: Larry Vogel

Doctrinal Review (CDR)

Phone: (314) 996-1406
1333 S. Kirkwood Rd.
St. Louis, MO 63122-7295

Commission Members:

Chairman:	Andrew E. Steinmann	(2026)
	Carl L. Beckwith	(2026)
	Jason D. Lane	(2026)
	Eric T. Lange	(2026)
	David I. Lewis	(2026)

Constitutional Matters (CCM)

Phone: (314) 996-1415
1333 S. Kirkwood Rd.
St. Louis, MO 63122-7295
Fax: (314) 996-1119
Website: lcms.org/ccm

Commission Members:

Chairman:	Larry A. Peters	(2026)
	Thomas Deadrick	(2026)
	Kevin A. Karner	(2029)
	Scott A. Killian	(2029)
	John W. Sias	(2026)
	David D. Vandercook Sr.	(2029)

Handbook (COH)

Phone: (314) 996-1415
1333 S. Kirkwood Rd.
St. Louis, MO 63122-7295
Fax: (314) 996-1119

Commission Members:

Chairman:	Ken R. Schurb	(2029)
	Heidi K. Abegg	(2029)
	Roger Carlisle	(2026)
	David K. Hawk	(2026)
	David W. Totsky	(2029)

Advisory Members:
Felix L. Loc
John W. Sias

MISSION BOARDS

The year following each name indicates when the present term expires.

Board for National Mission

Central Region:
- Michael Schuermann, Ordained (2026)
- Stephen Weller, Lay (2029)

East-Southeast Region:
- Tim Droegemueller, Ordained (2029)
- Janis McDaniels, Lay (2026)

Great Lakes Region:
- Peter Bender, Ordained (2026)
- Crysten Sanchez, Lay (2029)

Great Plains Region:
- Craig Niemeier, Ordained (2029)
- Carla Claussen, Lay (2026)

West-Southwest Region:
- Alfonso Espinosa, Ordained (2026)
- Carol Hack Broome, Lay (2029)

President's Representative:
- Dien Taylor, Ordained (2026)

Chairman:
- Alfonso Espinosa, Ordained

Board for International Mission

Central Region:
- James Gier, Ordained (2029)
- Michael Hawk, Lay (2029)

East-Southeast Region:
- James Douthwaite, Ordained (2026)
- James Wolf, Lay (2029)

Great Lakes Region:
- Vacant, Ordained/Commissioned ( )
- John Powers, Lay (2026)

Great Plains Region:
- Daniel Preus, Ordained (2029)
- John Edson, Lay (2029)

West-Southwest Region:
- Terrence Chan, Ordained (2029)
- Terence Lung, Lay (2026)

President's Representative:
- Elstner Lewis, Ordained (2026)

Chairman:
- John Edson, Lay

INTERNATIONAL CENTER MINISTRY UNITS

Chief Mission Officer, Interim: Dan Galchutt

Office of National Mission

OFFICE OF NATIONAL MISSION
Phone: (888) 843-5267
Fax: (314) 996-1124
Email: nationalmission@lcms.org
Website: lcms.org

Executive Director:
Dan Galchutt
All Nations Ministry Manager:
Stephen Heimer
Church Planting Director:
Quintin Cundiff
Congregations & Districts Managing Director & Disaster Training Director:
Michael Meyer
Disaster Response Director:
Ross Johnson
Discipleship Ministry Director:
Heath Trampe
Family Ministry Manager:
Andy Becker
Grantmaking Manager:
Maryann Hayter
Health Ministry Manager:
Stephanie Neugebauer
Human Care & Ministerial Support Managing Director & Life Ministry Director:
Tiffany Manor
Recognized Service Organization Director:
Dorothy Krans
School Ministry Director:
Alan Freeman
Specialized Spiritual Care Ministry Manager:
Brian Heller
Stewardship Ministry Manager:
(Vacant)
Worship Director:
Sean Daenzer
Youth Ministry Director:
Mark Kiessling

Office of International Mission

OFFICE OF INTERNATIONAL MISSION
Phone: (888) 843-5267
Website: international.lcms.org

Executive Director:
Cory J. Rajek
Managing Director – Global Business Operations:
Blake Warren
Managing Director – Global Mission Operations:
Brian Gauthier
Africa Regional Director:
Shauen Trump
Asia Regional Director:
Charles Ferry
Business Operations:
John Tape
Disaster Response Director (Int'l):
Ross Johnson
Eurasia Regional Director:
David Preus
Latin America /Caribbean Regional Director:
Theodore Krey
Ministry to the Armed Forces Director:
Craig Muehler
Missionary Recruitment:
Mark Rabe
Missionary Services Director:
Mark Wolfram
Short Term Mission Teams:
Erin Alter

Other Ministry Units

COMMUNICATIONS
Phone: (314) 996-1202
Fax: (314) 996-1126
Email: bonnie.parker@lcms.org
Website: lcms.org

Interim Executive Director:
Roy Askins
Managing Director, Production:
Jennifer Duffy
Managing Director, Editorial & Theological Content:
Roy Askins
Director, Video Services:
Drew Davidson
Director, Web Services:
Rudy Blank
Director, Design Services:
Erica Schwan

PASTORAL EDUCATION
Phone: (314) 996-1254
Website: lcms.org/pastoral

Executive Director:
James Baneck
Director, PALS & Continuing Education:
Jonathan Manor

KFUO RADIO
Phone: (314) 996-1518
Email: info@kfuo.org
Website: kfuo.org

Executive Director:
Gary Duncan
Associate Executive Director:
Andy Bates

MISSION ADVANCEMENT
Phone: (888) 930-4438
Email: Mission.Advancement@lcms.org
Website: lcms.org/about/directories/mission-advancement-staff

Interim Executive Director:
Shane Smithson
Director, Campaigns & Sp. Initiatives:
Martha Dahlke
Director, Member Engagement:
Shane Smithson
Director, Missionary Network Care:
Chandra Thurman
Director, Transformative Giving:
(Vacant)
Director, Managed Giving:
Brianne Gerzevske
Mission Central, Mapleton, Iowa:
Gary Thies

INTERNATIONAL CENTER SERVICE UNITS

Administrative Operations

Chief Administrative Officer: Felix Loc
Phone: (314) 996-1350
Email: felix.loc@lcms.org

HUMAN RESOURCES
Phone: (314) 996-1368
Fax: (314) 996-1121

Executive Director: Nathan Thomas
Email: nathan.thomas@lcms.org

EVENT PLANNING & PROCUREMENT
Phone: (314) 996-1355
Mobile: (314) 956-0452
Senior Director: Lynne C. Marvin
Email: lynne.marvin@lcms.org

OPERATIONS SUPPORT SERVICES
Phone: (314) 996-1875
Fax: (314) 996-1122

Executive Director: Joel A. Rivers
Email: joel.rivers@lcms.org

Technology Applications Group
Director: Mike Metcalf

Operations Service Coordination
Manager: Gina Grosz

Mail & Print Services
Manager: Chad Ray

Reception & Meeting Services
Reception Service Manager: Murel Warren
Meeting Service Manager: Meredith Gamache

FACILITIES MANAGEMENT SERVICES
Managed by Cushman & Wakefield

INFORMATION TECHNOLOGY DESKTOP & INFRASTRUCTURE SUPPORT SERVICES
Managed by Concordia Plans Services, Dalechek Technology Group, & Oakwood

Financial Operations

Chief Financial Officer: Nathan M. Haak
Phone: (314) 996-1425
Email: nathan.haak@lcms.org

ACCOUNTING
Phone: (314) 996-1425
Fax: (314) 996-1089

Interim Executive Director: Nathan Haak
Email: nathan.haak@lcms.org

Director, Synod Accounting:
Jim Ehlers

Director, Tax Reporting:
Pam Palmer

INTERNAL AUDIT
Phone: (314) 996-1108
Fax: (314) 996-1560

Executive Director: Christopher Wood
Email: chris.wood@lcms.org

International Center Chaplain

Chaplain/Director of Worship: Sean Daenzer
Phone: (314) 996-1740
Email: sean.daenzer@lcms.org

Rosters, Statistics & Research Services

LCMS Secretary: John W. Sias
Phone: (314) 996-1415
Email: john.sias@lcms.org

Director: Scott Kostencki
Phone: (314) 996-1369
Email: scott.kostencki@lcms.org

Research Services
Senior Research Analyst: Ryan Curnutt
Phone: (314) 996-1439
Email: ryan.curnutt@lcms.org

International Schools

Name	Address City State Zip	Phone Fax	Website
Concordia International School Hanoi Director: Doug Grove	Van Tri Golf Compound Kim No, Dong Anh Hanoi, Vietnam	84-24 3795 8878 84-24 3795 8879	www.concordiahanoi.org
Concordia International School Shanghai Director: Eric Semler	999 Mingyue Rd. Jinqiao, Pudong Shanghai, China 201206	(8621) 5899-0380 (8621) 5899-1685	www.concordiashanghai.org
Hong Kong International School Interim Director: Ron Roukema	1 Red Hill Rd. Tai Tam, Hong Kong	(852) 3149 7000 (852) 2813 8470	www.hkis.edu.hk

MILITARY CHAPLAINS

Phone: (800) 248-1930 ext. 1337 or (314) 996-1337
1333 S. Kirkwood Rd.
St. Louis, MO 63122-7295
Email: lcmschaps@lcms.org
Website: lcms.org/armedforces

Director, Ministry to the Armed Forces: Craig G. Muehler, CAPT, CHC, USN (Ret)
Assistant Director: Steven C. Hokana, LTC, USA (Ret)
Ministry to the Armed Forces Committee
Chairman: Chase Welton Jr., BG, USA (Ret)

U.S. Air Force Active Duty

Bueltmann, Kurtis
Edwards, David
Gandy, Amadeus
Genke, Quentin
Henry, Travis
Nelson, Robert
Potts, Chad
Riley, Benjamin
Schnake, Ryan
Shaw, Vincent
Smithley, Jon

U.S. Army Active Duty

Bain, Vincent
Boyer, Brad
Evans, Timothy
Giese, Joel
Gronewold, Geoffrey
Kearney, Michael
Kraft, Robert
Lorenz, Jonathan
Mietzner, Kyle
Mills, Ryan
Mortenson, Matthew
Niemtschk, Bobby
Norton, Cody
Schiff, Joshua
Wurdeman, David

U.S. Navy Active Duty

Ancira, Mario
Bell, Aaron
Bomberger, Kenneth
Chanthaphon, Pon
Engel, Ross
Engle, Tristan
Flynn, Patrick
Gibbs, Karl
Gledhill, Eric
Hamer, Brian
Mallie, Charles
Muehler, Carl
Nava, Jaime
Neider, Erik
Prince, Matthew
Rockrohr, Paul
Schleusener, David
Seifert, Joseph
Sluder, Jason
Sneath, Michael
Stephan, Merlin
Todd, Gregory
Varsogea, Charles

U.S. Air National Guard

Bahr, Benjamin
Banke, Brian
Boggs, Chad
Buckman, James
Frese, Michael
Grosskopf, Sol
Wismar, Eric
Wollberg, Trenton

U.S. Army National Guard

Cullen, Justin
Czischke, Chad
Grieser, Winston
Gustafson, Scott
Heinecke, Gerald
Meadows, Bryan
Price, Nicholas
Schneider, Joshua
Scott, Jacob
Witte, David

U.S. Navy Reserve

Bartok, James
Bombaro, John
Dart, Jason
DeMik, Stephen
Gorline, Jeremy
Hazel, Shawn
Maske, Daniel
Moreno, Mark
Schroeder, Benjamin
Sharp, Kevin

U.S. Air Force Reserve

Bredeson, Jason
Ferguson, Travis
Harbaugh, Darren
Jenson, Jens
Poock, Patrick
Schultz, Jonathan
Steele, Timothy
Witte, Keith

U.S. Army Reserve

Ayers, Raymond
Burfeind, Peter
Callahan, Phillip
Chisamore, Brian
Frandle, Andre
Geraci, Coleman
GeRue, Keith
Glover, Graham
Hoham, Theodore
Johnson, Ross
Knepper, Christopher
Krupsky, Justin
McCarthy, David
Radkey, Timothy
Sauer, Paul
Schultz, Richard
Yang, Lang
Yee, Travis

Coast Guard Auxiliary

Daub, James
Rudnik, Richard
Schmidt, William
Wurst, Robert

Civil Air Patrol

Beane, Larry
Bier, Louis
Doellinger, David
Gowen, Mitchell
Martin, Ronald
Williams, Guillaume
Williams, Jeffrey
Wismar, Eric
Yang, Lang

U.S. Army Directors of Religious Educ.

Roberts, James
Strong, Martha

Canadian Force Active Duty

Lutz, Gregory

NATIONAL MISSION MINISTRIES

Specialized Pastoral Ministries

Phone: (800) 248-1930, ext. 1388 or (314) 996-1388
1333 S. Kirkwood Rd.
St. Louis, MO 63122-7295
Fax: (314) 996-1124
Website: lcms.org/spm

INSTITUTIONAL CHAPLAINS

(List includes all who serve in specialized pastoral ministries [Bylaw 2.11.1(h)] and who may be designated as chaplain by the institution that they serve.)

Alabama
Birmingham—Margaret Anderson (EM) (SO)

Arizona
Green Valley—John Stieve (EN)

Arkansas
Bella Vista—John Lindner (MDS)

California
Lancaster—Wayne Anderson (PSW)
Mission Viejo—Mark Reschke (PSW)
Orange—Timothy Detviler (PSW)
San Diego—Charles Varsogea (EN)

Colorado
Lafayette—Brian Earl (RM)
Loveland—Bruce Rippe (RM)

Florida
Brooksville—Paul Meseke (FG)
Ft. Meyers—David Erbel (FG)
Homestead—Wilfredo Rivera Sr. (FG)
Miami—Jessie Perez (FG)
Erwin Perez-Arche (FG)
Benito Perez-Lopez (FG)

Georgia
Marietta—David Kruger (FG)

Illinois
Beason—Charles Olander (CI)
Carterville—Carl Miller (SI)
Crystal Lake—Thomas Tews (NI)
Lake Zurich—Jonathan Vierkant (NI)
Latham—Joel Cluver (CI)
Maeystown—Royal Boeder (SI)
Oak Lawn—Nora Ausra (NI)
Valdas Ausra (NI)
Park Ridge—Richard Heller (NI)
Philo—Jeffrey McPike (CI)
Rushville—Joseph Eckman (CI)
Springfield—Jeffrey Harter (CI)
Streamwood—Mark Frusti (NI)
Valley Park—Chris Nilges ((MO)
Wheaton—Donald Kretzschmar (NI)
Chad Leonard (NI)

Indiana
Columbus—Janice Kiel (IN)
Michael Malinsky (IN)
Crown Point—Cory Wielert (IN)
Ft. Wayne—Mary Barney (IN)
James Cotter (IN)
Karl Frincke (IN)
David Griebel (IN)
Roger Olson (IN)
Indianapolis—John Kolb (IN)
Udhayanesan Raji (IN)
La Porte—Richard Ungrodt (IN)
Seymour—Sara Lemon (EN)
Valparaiso—Michael Porter (IN)
Woodburn—Ralph Wetzel (IN)

Iowa
Cedar Rapids—Lawrence Schmidt (IE)
Dennison—William Wrede (IW)
Perry—Max Phillips (IW)

Kansas
Kincaid—Ervin Daugherty Jr. (KS)
McConnell AFB—Quentin Genke (SE)

Kentucky
Ashland—Mark Kloha (OH)
Burlington—Ronald Ewell (MDS)
Goshen—Margy Whitsett (IN)
Mark Whitsett (IN)

Maryland
Baltimore—Stephen Funck (SE)
Robert Kretzschmar (SE)

Massachusetts
Cohasset—Robert Schipul (NE)
N. Falmouth—Charles Mueller (NE)

Michigan
Frankenmuth—Joel Kaiser (MI)
Lansing—Steven Sutterer (EN)
Macomb—Gerald Grimm (MI)
Temperance—John Schinkel (MI)

Minnesota
Apple Valley—Roger Holland (MNS)
Centerville—Joel Lintner (MNS)
Fergus Falls—Craig Palach (MNN)
Minneapolis—Paul Emmel (MNS)
Northfield—David Habermas (MNS)
Waconia—Robert Alsleben (EN)

Mississippi
Picayune—Martin Gilliland (SO)

Missouri
Columbia—Jerry Riggert (MO)
Farmington—James King (MO)
Jefferson City—Alvin Lange (MO)
James Mueller (MO)
Liberty—Stephen Streufert (MO)
Macon—Ronald Hoehne (MO)
Manchester—Gayle Truesdell (MO)
St. Charles—Raymond Scholle (MO)
David Stratmann (MO)
Washington—Tim Weiser

Nebraska
Grand Island—John Nelson Sr. (NEB)
Norfolk—Adrian Hanft II (NEB)
James Wonnacott (NEB)
Omaha—Ken Hessel (NEB)
Seward—Ryan Matthias (NEB)

Nevada
Reno—Michael Benke (CNH)

New Jersey
W. Caldwell—Michael Dunne (NJ)

New Mexico
Rio Rancho—Raymond Fontaine (NI)

New York
Amherst—Robert Spilman (EA)
Brooklyn—Hugo Berger (AT)
Highland Falls—Rob Carter Jr. (AT)
Rochester—Maggie Harris (EA)
Troy—Joel Janzow (AT)

North Carolina
Charlotte—Richard Runge (SE)

North Dakota
W. Fargo—Michael Giddings (ND)

Ohio
Avon—Wayne Decker (OH)
Cleveland—James Jasper (EN)
N. Olmsted—Walther Marcis (OH)
Uniontown—Mark Luecke (OH)

Oklahoma
Oklahoma City—Kathleen Brown (OK)

Oregon
Hillsboro—Kasimir Kachmarek (NOW)
Medford—Dennis Wenholz (NOW)

Pennsylvania
Butler—Jack Hartman (EA)
Joel Dieterichs (EA)
Swissvale—Patrick Runk (EA)

South Carolina
Greer—James Balke (SE)

South Dakota
Sioux Falls—Matthew Nix (SD)

Tennessee
Rogersville—John Freitag (MDS)

Texas
Austin—William Knippa (TX)
Brownsville—Lori Bachmann (TX)
Lamarque—Robert Wedergren (TX)
Lubbock—Ronald Rodeck (TX)
New Braunfels—Sharon Teague (TX)
Pflugerville—Edward Banarsi (TX)
Rockwall—Jon Sciclune (TX)
San Antonio—Mark Steege (TX)
Spring—Walter Dube (TX)
Alvin Franzmeier (TX)

Vermont
Northfield—Calvin Kemp (NE)

Virginia
Fredericksburg—William Hughes III (SE)
Portsmouth—Richard Hill (S)
Williamsburg—Charles Froehlich (AT)

Washington
Buckley—Ronald Gocken (NOW)
Dorothy Prybylski (NOW)
Everett—Barry Stueve (NOW)
Kennewick—Arthur Rasch (NOW)
Lacey—David Hinz (NOW)
Renton—Arthur Werzner (NOW)
Snohomish—Phillip Streufert (NOW)
Spokane—Edwin Schultze (NOW)
Tacoma—Daniel Gerken (NOW)
Kirk Van Natta (NOW)
Tukwila—Ruth Shimoi (NOW)
Vancouver—Robert Kunz (NOW)

Wisconsin
Allis—Thomas Hinz (SW)
Beloit—Mark Yates (SW)
Cedarburg—Randolph Raasch (SW)
Wilmer Reichmann (SW)
Chippewa Falls—Charles Yunghans (NW)
Cottage Grove—Stephen Wenk (SW)
E. Troy—Maurice Lind (SW)
Eleva—Timothy Moe (NW)
Fond Du Lac—John Fuchs (SW)
Franklin—David Sorensen (SW)
Milwaukee—Ronald Albers (SW)
Paul Koester (EN)
Oconomowoc—Paul Borgman (SW)
Jon Pickelmann (SW)
Suring—David Behling (NW)
Tomahawk—Gary Uttech (NW)
Watertown—Michael Schempf (SW)
Victor Tegtmeier (SW)
Waupaca—Wayne Schwanke (NW)
Wauwatosa—Leroy Hass (SW)
Wild Rose—Eugene Trieglaff (NI)

British Columbia, Canada
Abbotsford—David Hilderman

Ontario, Canada
Windsor—Gregory Lutz (EN)

Japan
Saitama—Michael Piescer (CNH)

PASTORAL COUNSELORS

(Qualified by various professional organizations such as the American Association of Pastoral Counselors)

Alaska
Anchorage—Mark Wegner (NOW)

Arizona
Tucson—Luke Stephan (MI)

California
Rancho Cordova—Carlos Hernandez (MO)
Van Nuys—Ronald Rehrer (PSW)

Colorado
Littleton—Werner Boos (RM)

Florida
Orlando—R. Richard Armstrong (FG)
Palm City—David A. Mueller (EM) (FG)
Pensacola—Neil Pape (EM) (SO)

Indiana
Carmel—Randall Schroeder (IN)
Seymour—Edgar Keinath (IN)

Iowa
Sioux City—Gerald Bruhn (IW)
Cherryll Hoffman (IW)
W. Des Moines—Eric Schillo (EM) (IW)

Kansas
Topeka—Neil Buono (KS)

Michigan
Ann Arbor—John Rathje (MI)

Minnesota
Sartell—Donald Wilke (EM) (MNN)

Missouri
Richmond Heights—Bruce Hartung (MO)
St. Charles—Edward Arle (MO)
St. Louis—Dale Kuhn (MO)
Allen Schenk (MO)

New York
Flushing—Ronald Lehenbauer (AT)
Hawthorne—David Elseroad (AT)
Niagara Falls—Erwin Brese (EM) (EA)
Orchard Park—David F. C. Wurster (EA)

Ohio
Tiffin—Jan Kucera (OH)

Oregon
Albany—Terry Merrill (NOW)

South Carolina
Aiken—William Scar (PSW)
Hilton Head Island—Walt Warneck (FG)

Tennessee
Rogersville—John Freitag (MDS)

Virginia
Orchard Park—Philip Wurster (EM) EA)

VETERANS AFFAIRS CHAPLAINS

Full-Time
Elser, John—Amarillo, TX (TX)
Mueller, Robert—Albuquerque, NM (RM)
Wenholz, Dennis—White City, OR (NOW)

Part-Time
Earl, Brian—Albuquerque, NM (RM)

BUREAU OF PRISONS CHAPLAINS

Alms, Maurice—Troy, IL (SI)
Cook, Kevin—Staunton, IL (SI)
Kirchoff, Scott—Waycross, GA (FG)
Nehrt, Jeffery—Smithboro, IL (SI)
Schefelker, Perry—Centralia, IL (SI)
Stanley, Vince—St. Louis, MO (MO)
Voightmann, James—Pana, IL (SI)
Weber, Paul—E. Moline, IL (CI)
Wilbert, Lori—Crest Hill, IL (NI)
Willis, Ryan—Endeavor, WI (SW)

EMERGENCY SERVICES CHAPLAINS

Arizona
Peoria—Daryl Robarge (Police) (PSW)
Yuma—Joshua Keinath (Police/Sheriff) (PSW)

California
Anaheim—Kerry Duerr (Police) (PSW)
Chico—Donald Jordan (Fire) (CNH)
Encinitas—H. W. Mike Mitschke (Police) (EM) (PSW)
Grover Beach—George Lepper (Fire) (NOW)
Nipomo—George Lepper (Fire) (CNH)
Oceanside—Ralph Buchhorn (Police/Fire) (PSW)
Redwood City—Harold Draeger (Police) (CNH)
San Francisco—Curtis Binz (Police) (EN)
Santa Cruz—Richard Rice (Sheriff) (FG)
Sonora—David Shoemaker (Police) (EM) (CNH)
Temecula—Steve Leinhos (Police) (PSW)

Colorado
Colorado Springs—Dennis Lucero (Police) (PSW)
Englewood—Donald Hinchey (Police) (FG)

Connecticut
Greenwich—Ronald Erbe (Pastor/Police) (NE)
Lebanon—Scott Schuett (Fire) (NE)
Norwalk—Robert Beinke (Police) (NE)
W. Hartford—Dana Hallenbeck (Police) (NE)

Florida
Davie—George Poulos Jr. (State Police) (FG)
Darrell Stuehrendberg (Police) (FG)
Ft. Myers—Jon Zehnder (FG)
David Erbel (Police) (FG)
Lake Placid—Richard Norris (Fire/Police/Veterans) (FG)
Leesburg—Donald Roberts (FG)
North Palm Beach—Daniel McPherson (Police) (FG)
Oviedo—Brian Roberts (SELC)
Plantation—Walter Volz (Fire) (EM) (FG)
Rockledge—Douglas Fountain (Police) (EM) (CNH)
Sanford—Ed DeWitt (Police) (MO)
Venice—Randy Winkel (FG)

Georgia
Eatonton—Ronald Schornhorst (Co Dive Team/CISM Team) (FG)
Rome—John Karch (Police) (FG)

Hawaii
Kahilui—Milton Fricke (Police) (MO)

Idaho
Jerome—Baldwin Camin (NOW)

Illinois
Altamont—James Wright (CI)
Belleville—Daniel Berteau (Coast Guard) (NI)
Burbank—Steve Lee (Police) (NI)
Carbondale—Robert Gray (Fire) (EM) (SI)
Collinsville—William Engfehr III (Police) (SI)
Effingham—Jason Rensner (Police) (CI)
Groveland—Vernon Bettermann (Police) (CI)
Pleasant Plains—Donald Pritchard (CI)
Roanoke—Bruce Scarbeary (Fire) (CI)
Skokie—Matt Conrad (Police/Fire) (NI)
St. Joseph—Scott Weiler (Police) (EM) (CI)
Wheeler—Stephen Gillet (Fire/Hospital) (CI)

Indiana
Greenwood—Daniel Coffey (Police/Fire) (IN)
Seymour—Matthew Prince (Coast Guard) (IN)

Kentucky
Bowling Green—Andrew Toopes (Police/AFT/DEA) (MDS)

Michigan
Allen Park—Joel Holls (Police) (EN)
Ann Arbor—Michael Wentzel (Sheriff) (FG)
Beverly Hills—Daniel Grams (Police/Fire) (SW)
Grand Rapids—Michael Wentzel (MI)
Huntington Woods—Peter Nickel (MI)
Mt. Pleasant—Jonathon Bakker (Police) (MI)
Niles—Carl Bassett (VA) (IC) (FBI) (MI)
Penwater—Thomas Bye (Police) (MI)
Redford—Victor Halboth (Police) (EM) (EN)
Sanford—W. Roger Stauffer (Police/Fire) (MI)

Minnesota
Chisholm—Steven Breitbarth (Police/Fire) (MNN)
Mahtomedi—J. Nevin Crowther (Police) (MNS)
Mora—Greggory Coop (Sheriff Dept) (EM) (MNS)

Missouri
Cape Girardeau—David V. Dissen (MO)
Neosho—William Doubek III (Police) (MO)
St. James—Paul Goddard (Police) (MO)
St. Louis—Martin Liebman III (MO)
John Perling (Police) (SELC)
James Rhiver (Police) (PSW)
William Simmons (Police) (MO)

Nebraska
Norfolk—James Wonnacott (NEB)
Omaha—Kenneth Hessel (Police/Fire) (NEB)
Seward—Scott Bruick (Police/Fire) (NEB)

Nevada
Pahrump—Ronald Mayer (Police) (PSW)

New Jersey
Union—Donald Brand (Police/Fire) (MNN)

New York
Brockport—William Kay (Police) (EA)
Center Moriches—John Fleischmann (AT)

North Carolina
Gibsonville—David Tessmann (SE)
Hickory—Anton Lagoutine (Police/Fire) (SE)

North Dakota
Bismarck—Lester Wolfgram (Fire) (CI)
Wahpeton—Alan Werth (Police) (EA)

Ohio
Parma—Dean Kavouras (Police) (OH)

Oklahoma
Edmond—Mark Erler (Police) (OK)
Fairmont—Timothy Dorsch (Police/Fire) (CNH)

Oregon
Salem—Mark Lieske (Police) (EN)
Silverton—Joseph Hughes III (Fire) (NW)

Tennessee
Rogersville—John Freitag (Police) (MDS)

Texas
Granbury—Burt Benson (TX)
Groves—Richard Turner (Police/Fire) (EM) (TX)
La Grange—Bill Qualman (Police) (TX)
Waco—Matthew Canion (Police) (TX)

Washington
Bolling AFB—Gregory Todd (Fire) (EM) (SI)
Gig Harbor—Ron Norris (NOW)

West Virginia
Charleston—Frank Ruffatto (Police/Sheriff) (OH)

Wisconsin
Appleton—Marvin Ahlborn (Police) (SW)
Beloit—Bill Wagner (Police/Fire) (SW)
Janesville—Jack Fish (Police) (SW)
Paul Speerbrecker (Police) (NE)
Mauston—Steve Thomas (Fire) (SW)
Oconomowoc—Gary Tillmann (FBI/Police) (SW)
Platteville—Thomas Reeder Jr. (Police) (SW)
Pleasant Prairie—Donald Hackbarth (Police/Fire) (EM) (SW)
Plover—David Ficken (Police) (NW)

Wyoming
Ft. Washakie—James Judson Jr. (WY)
Rock Springs—Scott Shields (Police) (WY)

Ontario, Canada
Sarnia—Roger Ellis (Police) (SI)

SYNODWIDE TRUST ENTITIES

THE CONCORDIA PLANS

Concordia Retirement Plan
Concordia Disability & Survivor Plan
Concordia Health Plan
Concordia Retirement Savings Plan

Managing Agency

The year following each name indicates when the present term expires.

CONCORDIA PLAN SERVICES
Phone: (314) 965-7580 or (888) 927-7526
1333 S. Kirkwood Rd.
St. Louis, MO 63122-7226
Fax: (314) 996-1127
Email: info@ConcordiaPlans.org
Website: ConcordiaPlans.org

President & CEO: James F. Sanft
Vice President & Chief Administrative Officer/Chief Financial Officer:
Robert A. Bouche
Vice President & Chief Operating Officer: Kevin M. Herweck
Vice President & Chief Investment Officer: Brian K. Gardner
Vice President & General Counsel: Ann T. Stillman

Board of Directors—Concordia Plan Services
Board of Trustees—Concordia Plans

Chairman:	Scott A. Seefeld	(2027)
	Amber D. Bahr	(2026)
	Jon D. Boeche	(2027)
	Jason Burk	(2027)
	Daryl R. Dagit	(2026)
	Henry C. Eickelberg	(2027)
	David K. Hawk	(2028)
	Jesse P. Huber	(2028)
	Ronald L. Kuehn	(2028)
	Mark A. Miller	(2028)
	Roger Offermann	(2026)
	M. Douglas Peters	(2027)
	Judy Stromback	(2027)
	Mark O. Swenson	(2026)
	Renee C. Varga	(2026)

President's Representative to the Board:
Dr. Roger C. Paavola

SYNODWIDE CORPORATE ENTITIES

The year following each name indicates when the present term expires.

CONCORDIA HISTORICAL INSTITUTE
Phone: (314) 505-7900
804 Seminary Place
St. Louis, MO 63105-3014
Fax: (314) 505-7901
Email: info@concordiahistoricalinstitute.org
Website: concordiahistoricalinstitute.org

Executive Director: Daniel N. Harmelink

Board Members

Chairman:	John C. Wohlrabe Jr.	(2025)
	Rodney A. Benkendorf	(2026)
	Tim Good	(2025)
	Kathleen Graumann	(2026)
	David Millar	(2025)
	Paul Robinson	(2026)
	Robert V. Roethemeyer	(2026)
	Ross Stroh	(2029)

Advisory Members:
Daniel N. Harmelink
Lawrence R. Rast Jr.

President's Representative: John C. Wohlrabe Jr.
Ex-officio: John W. Sias

CONCORDIA PUBLISHING HOUSE
Phone: (314) 268-1000
3558 S. Jefferson Ave.
St. Louis, MO 63118-3968
Fax: (314) 268-1329
Email: cph@cph.org
Website: cph.org

President & Chief Executive Officer:
Jonathan D. Schultz
Vice President of Publishing:
Jacob Corzine
Chief Customer Impact & Growth Officer:
Rick Johnson
Chief Financial Officer:
Collin Bivens

Board Members:

Chairman:	Joe Olson	(2026)
	Heidi Abegg	(2026)
	Kurt Battles	(2029)
	Mark Birkholz	(2029)
	Stephanie Egger	(2026)
	Elaine Graff	(2029)
	Tom Halvorson	(2026)
	Jill Johnson	(2029)
	Pam Nielsen	(2029)

President's Representative to the Board: Dr. Jon Vieker
LCMS Board of Directors Representative (Non-Voting): Nathan Haak

CONCORDIA UNIVERSITY SYSTEM

Phone (314) 996-1252
1333 S. Kirkwood Rd.
St. Louis, MO 63122
Email: info@cus.edu
Website: cus.edu

President:
Jamison J. Hardy
Vice President:
Douglas H. Spittel

Board Members:

Chairman:	Mark Braden	(2029)
Vice Chairman:	Mark Nuckols	(2026)
	Dennis Eickhoff	(2026)
	Mark Franke	(2026)
	Stevin Gehrke	(2026)
	Jon Giordano	(2029)
	Mark Kalthoff	(2026)
	Ellen Lange	(2029)
	Gary Thompson	(2029)

Advisory Members/Ex-officio:
Brady Finnern
Felix Loc
Dennis Meyer
Michael Thomas
(Vacant)
(Vacant)

President's Representative: M. Alan Taylor (2026)

Institutional Advisory Council: Comprised of the presidents of the Concordia Colleges/Universities

Concordia University Education Network (CUEnet):
Website: cuenet.edu
Executive Director: Paul A. Philp

LUTHERAN CHURCH EXTENSION FUND

Phone: (800) 843-5233
10733 Sunset Office Dr., Suite 300
St. Louis, MO 63127-1020
Fax: (314) 996-1131
Website: lcef.org

President/CEO:
Bart Day

Finance:
Chief Financial Officer: Kevin Bremer
Growth Solutions:
Chief Growth Officer: Joseph Russo
Human Capital & Organizational Effectiveness:
Senior Vice President: Yvonne Schone
Legal/Risk Management:
Chief Legal Officer: Timothy Ramberger
Operations:
Chief Operating Officer: James O'Brien

Board of Directors:

Chairman:	Max Phillips	(2025)
	Linda Barnes	(2025)
	Jason Braaten	(2026)
	Gary Hemmer	(2027)
	Julie Johnson	(2026)
	Jonathan Kramer	(2026)
	Jaime Peters	(2027)
	Mark Pieper	(2026)
	Christopher Soyke	(2027)
	Dale Wagner	(2026)
	Bruce Winter	(2026)

Non-Voting Member:
Daniel Galchutt
Nathan Haak

THE LUTHERAN CHURCH—MISSOURI SYNOD FOUNDATION

Phone (800) 325-7912
1333 S. Kirkwood Rd.
St. Louis, MO 63122-7295
Fax: (314) 996-1132
Website: lcmsfoundation.org

President:
David Fiedler

Finance/Administration:
Senior Vice President: Mark Cannon
Gift Planning Services:
Senior Vice President: Philip Krupski
Marketing/Communications:
Senior Vice President: David O'Brien
Client Services:
Sr. Vice President Growth-Constituent Experience: Jeff Craig-Meyer
Sr. Vice President Legal & Data Management: Tina Clasquin

Board of Trustees:

Chairman:	Ralph Blomenberg	(2025)
	Carol Hack Broome	(2026)
	Melvin Faulkner	(2025)
	Dennis Fliehman	(2026)
	Brian Fricke	(2027)
	Russell Harms	(2026)
	Kay Kreklau	(2027)
	Kirk Mattes	(2027)
	Gregory Miller	(2026)
	Todd Riordan	(2026)
	Tim Sheldon	(2026)

Non-Voting Member: Nathan Haak

SPECIAL COMMITTEES

COLLOQUY COMMITTEE FOR THE PASTORAL MINISTRY

Peter Lange, Chair
Jon Bruss
Thomas Egger
(Vacant)

COLLOQUY COMMITTEE FOR COMMISSIONED MINISTERS

Peter Lange, Chair
Bernard Bull
Cari Chittick
Russell Dawn
Paul Philp
James Pingel
Lorinda Sankey

SEMINARIES

The year following each name indicates when the present term expires.

Concordia Seminary—St. Louis, MO

Phone: (314) 505-7000
801 Seminary Place
St. Louis, MO 63105-3199
Website: csl.edu
Year Founded: 1839

President: Thomas J. Egger

Board of Regents

Chairman:	W. Max Mons	(2028)
	Joel Brondos	(2026)
	Paul Edmon	(2029)
	Matthew Kenitzer	(2029)
	Bruce Keseman	(2026)
	Adam Koontz	(2029)
	W. Max Mons	(2028)
	Michael Staub	(2026)
	Mark Stern	(2026)
	Timothy Wood	(2031)

Advisory Member:
R. Lee Hagan
COP Representative:
Michael W. Mohr
President's Representative:
Peter K. Lange

Concordia Theological Seminary—Fort Wayne, IN

Phone: (260) 452-2100
6600 N. Clinton St.
Fort Wayne, IN 46825-4996
Email: info@ctsfw.edu
Website: ctsfw.edu
Year Founded: 1846

President: Jon S. Bruss

Board of Regents

Chairman:	Scott R. Murray	(2026)
	William M. Cwirla	(2026)
	David L. Daniels	(2026)
	Kaibo Feng	(2029)
	Marcheta Leighton-Beasley	(2028)
	Korey D. Maas	(2026)
	Mark W. Meehl	(2026)
	John L. Powers	(2029)
	Jeffrey J. Reuer	(2029)
	Matthew W. Rueger	(2029)
	Tim Sheldon	(2028)
	Beverly K. Yahnke	(2029)

COP Representative:
Roger C. Paavola (2025)
President's Representative:
Scott R. Murray (2026)

COLLEGES AND UNIVERSITIES

The year following each name indicates when the present term expires.

Concordia University Irvine

Phone: (949) 854-8002 or (800) 229-1200
Website: cui.edu
Year Founded: 1976

Turtle Rock Campus
1530 Concordia West
Irvine, CA 92612-3299

Spectrum Campus™
16355 Laguna Canyon Road
Irvine, CA 92618

President: Michael A. Thomas

Board of Regents

Chairman:	Ryan P. Ermeling	(2024)
	Jon Baermann	(2027)
	Jeffrey S. Beavers	(2026)
	Jason J. Bredeson	(2026)
	Matthew Flandermeyer	(2025)
	Timothy Gast	(2028)
	Michael E. Gibson	( )
	Anthony Harnack	(2024)
	David J. Hemker	(2026)
	Laura G. Hemminger	(2026)
	Scott Klemsz	(2026)
	Glenn Lucas	(2025)
	Michael McThrow	(2026)
	Craig Olson	(2026)
	Mary Scott	(2026)
	Veronica Steele	(2028)

Advisory Members:
Michael R. Lange
James Maxwell
Christopher Pond
Xavria Schwarz
Michael Von Behren

Concordia University Wisconsin & Ann Arbor

at Mequon, WI
Phone: (262) 243-5700
12800 N. Lake Shore Dr.
Mequon, WI 53097-2402
Fax: (262) 243-4351
Website: cuw.edu
Year Founded: 1881

at Ann Arbor, MI
Phone: (734) 995-7300 or (877) 995-7520
4090 Geddes Rd.
Ann Arbor, MI 48105-2797
Fax: (734) 995-4610
Website: cuaa.edu
Year Founded: 1963

President: Erik P. Ankerberg

Board of Regents

Chairman:	David Piehler	(2026)
Vice Chairman:	Jonah Burakowski	(2026)
	David Bliese	(2028)
	Terry Donovan	(2027)
	David Fleming	(2026)
	Paula Harris	(2026)
	Michael Henrichs	(2028)
	Jeff Jurss	(2028)
	Jennifer Knox	(2026)
	David Lambert	(2026)
	Joe Olson	(2028)
	Brian Peteson	(2028)
	Stephen Saunders	(2026)
	Jon Schumacher	(2026)
	Lisa Senkbeil	(2026)
	Terrance Wright	(2028)

District President: Nathan Meador

Concordia University Chicago

Phone: (708) 209-3011
7400 Augusta St.
River Forest, IL 60305-1499
Fax: (708) 209-3176
Email: admission@cuchicago.edu
Website: cuchicago.edu
Year Founded: 1864

President: Russell P. Dawn

Board of Regents

Chairman:	Michelle M. Kazmierczak	(2026)	Larry Richardson	(2027)
Vice Chairman:	Matthew Zickler	(2028)	Jeff Schwarz	(2027)
	Allan R. Buss	( )	Frank Simek	(2027)
	Seth Clemmer	(2028)	Jennifer Siukola	(2026)
	Kyle Knoepfel	(2028)	Virginia Terrell	(2028)
	John Krause	(2027)	John Thoelke	(2026)
	Gerhard Mundinger	(2028)	Alison Witte	(2026)
	Lawrence Rast	(2026)		

Concordia University at St. Paul, MN

Phone: (651) 641-8230
1282 Concordia Ave.
St. Paul, MN 55104
Fax: (651) 641-8782
Website: csp.edu
Year Founded: 1893

President: Brian L. Friedrich

Board of Regents

Chairman:	Mark L'Heureux	(2026)		
	Karl Abbott	(2026)	Roger Lindahl	(2028)
	Andrew Braun	(2027)	Jim Linnett	(2027)
	Esther Dale	(2028)	Carrie Meyer	(2026)
	Donald Fondow	(2026)	Marilyn Reineck	(2028)
	Keith Grimm	(2028)	Naomi Teske	(2026)
	Andrew Herzberg	(2026)	Lori Utech	(2025)
	Paul Hinz	(2026)	Pangjua Xiong	(2027)
	Paul Kieffer	(2027)	Daniel Zismer	(2026)

Ex-officio: Lucas Woodford (2028)

Concordia University Nebraska at Seward, NE

Phone: (402) 643-3651 or (800) 535-5494
800 N. Columbia Ave.
Seward, NE 68434
Fax: (402) 643-4073
Email: info@cune.edu
Website: cune.edu
Year Founded: 1894

President: Bernard Bull

Board of Regents

Chairman:	Dennis Meyer	(2026)	Timothy Hu	(2026)
Vice Chairperson:	Gail Hawkins	(2027)	Samuel Huebner	(2028)
	Scott Adle	(2026)	Trudy Meyer	(2027)
	Stuart Bartruff	(2027)	Timothy Moll	(2026)
	Craig Ernstmeyer	(2026)	Richard Snow	(2028)
	John Fraser	(2026)	Melanie Standiford	(2028)
	Douglas Gaunt	(2028)	Preston Sunderman	(2028)
	Dick Helms	(2028)	Douglas Tewes	(2026)
			Erik Vieselmeyer	(2027)

President's Representative: Benjamin Ball (2026)

DISTRICTS OF THE SYNOD

NORTHWEST	Washington, Oregon, Idaho, and Alaska
MONTANA	the State
NORTH DAKOTA	the State
SOUTH DAKOTA	the State
WYOMING	the State and western "Panhandle" of Nebraska
NEBRASKA	the State except western "Panhandle"
CALIFORNIA-NEVADA-HAWAII	California (except southern counties), Nevada (except southern tip), and Hawaii
KANSAS	the State
PACIFIC SOUTHWEST	Arizona, southern counties of California, and southern tip of Nevada
OKLAHOMA	the State
TEXAS	the State (except El Paso County)
ROCKY MOUNTAIN	Colorado, Utah, New Mexico, El Paso County, Texas
S.E.L.C.	represented in the following twelve states: Connecticut, Florida, Illinois, Indiana, Minnesota, Missouri, New Jersey, New York, Ohio, Pennsylvania, Virginia, Wisconsin, and in the provinces of Ontario and Quebec, Canada
MINNESOTA NORTH	Northern counties and Douglas County, Wisconsin
MINNESOTA SOUTH	Southern counties
NORTH WISCONSIN	including western part of Upper Peninsula of Michigan
SOUTH WISCONSIN	southern half
MICHIGAN	Lower Peninsula and eastern part of Upper Peninsula
EASTERN	western half of New York State, Pennsylvania (except York County), and Garrett County, Maryland
ATLANTIC	eastern half of New York State
NEW ENGLAND	Maine, Vermont, New Hampshire, Massachusetts, Connecticut, and Rhode Island
NEW JERSEY	the State
IOWA WEST	
IOWA EAST	vertical division approximately in the center
NORTHERN ILLINOIS	
CENTRAL ILLINOIS	Illinois
SOUTHERN ILLINOIS	
INDIANA	the State and north-central counties of Kentucky
OHIO	the State, West Virginia, and northeastern counties of Kentucky
SOUTHEASTERN	Maryland (except Garrett County), District of Columbia, Delaware, Virginia, North Carolina, South Carolina, and York County, Pennsylvania
MISSOURI	the State
MID-SOUTH	Arkansas, Tennessee, and southern counties of Kentucky
SOUTHERN	Louisiana, Mississippi, Alabama, and western tip of Florida
FLORIDA-GEORGIA	Florida (except western tip), Georgia, and Bahamas
ENGLISH	represented in the following fifteen states: Arizona, California, Florida, Georgia, Illinois, Indiana, Michigan, Minnesota, Missouri, Nebraska, New Jersey, New York, Ohio, Pennsylvania, Wisconsin, and in the provinces of Ontario and Quebec, Canada

DISTRICTS

Council of Presidents

Chairman: Brady L. Finnern		(2028)
Vice-Chairman: Allan R. Buss		(2028)
Secretary: Justin A. Panzer		(2028)
PROGRAM COMMITTEE:		
	Allan R. Buss	(2028)
	Brady L. Finnern	(2028)
	Michael E. Gibson	(2028)
	John E. Hill	(2028)
	Justin A. Panzer	(2028)
Ex-officio:	Matthew C. Harrison	(2026)
	Peter K. Lange	(2026)
Staff:	John W. Sias	(2026)

Atlantic

Phone: (914) 337-5700
7 Farragut Ave.
Hastings-on-Hudson, NY 10706-2304
Fax: (914) 337-7471
Website: www.ad-lcms.org
Office Hours: 9:00 a.m.–5:00 p.m. (Eastern Time)

Officers:
Dien Ashley Taylor, President
Matthew O. Staneck, First Vice President
David Wackenhuth, Second Vice President
Victor Nelson Jr., Third Vice President
Edward Alexander Marque, Fourth Vice President
Robert Hartwell, Secretary
Brian Martin, Treasurer

Circuit Visitor:
P. Wagner (1)
D. Cohn (2)
S. Gramenz (3)
R. Boehler (4)
J. Hollmann (5)
C. Dorsey (6)
J. Allstaedt (7)
B. Noack (8)
P. Deberny (9)

Staff:

Henry Albrechtsen, III	Atlantic District Lay Deacon Coordinator
George Carstensen	Director of Gospel Communications
Daniel Cohn	Finance Associate
Joshua Hollmann	Education Executive
Carol Mittelstaedt	Mission Society Coordinator
Johnson Rethinasamy	Mission Executive
(Vacant)	Administrative Assistant to the District President

Legal Counsel: Capell, Barnett, Matalon & Schoenfeld, 14 Pennsylvania Plaza, Suite #814, New York, NY 10122
Archivist: Dien Ashley Taylor (District Office)
Church Extension Chairman: AJ Sinisgalli (District Office)
Communications/PR Chairman: George Carstensen (District Office)
Congregation Constitutions Chairman: Robert Hartwell (District Office)
Continuing Education: Joshua Hollmann (District Office)
Evangelism: Johnson Rethinasamy (District Office)
Family Ministry: Carol Mittelstaedt (District Office)
Lutheran Witness Editor: Dien Ashley Taylor (District Office)
Ministerial Growth Chairman: Matthew O. Staneck (District Office)
Missions Chairman: Johnson Rethinasamy (District Office)
Parish Education Chairman: Joshua Hollmann (District Office)
Stewardship: Brian Martin (District Office)
Student Recruitment/Aid Chairman: Brian Martin (District Office)
Youth Ministry Chairperson: Carol Mittelstaedt (District Office)

California-Nevada-Hawaii

Phone: (925) 245-4000
2772 Constitution Dr.
Livermore, CA 94551-7566
Fax: (925) 245-1107
Website: www.cnh-lcms.org
Office Hours: 8:00 a.m.–4:30 p.m. (Pacific Time)

Officers:
Michael R. Lange, President
Mitchell W. Gowen, First Vice President
William Abbott, Regional Vice President
John Standley, Regional Vice President
Dan Truesdell, Regional Vice President
Eric Van Scharrel, Regional Vice President
Robert Weller, Regional Vice President
Jared Eggebraaten, Secretary
Donald Busse, Treasurer
Robert D. Newton, President Emeritus
Walter C. Tietjen, President Emeritus

Circuit Visitor:
L. Szeto (1)
M. Behrens (2)
K. Waetzig (3)
D. Hardin (4)
D. Schlensker (5)
A. Mundinger (7)
P. Schult (8)
A. Steinbeck (9)
M. Benke (10)
D. Truesdell (11)
B. Merrick (12)
J. Beyer (14)
D. Jung (15)
R. Rice (16)
J. Bestul (18)
A. Sommer (19)
M. Benke (20)

Staff:

L. Paul Ferguson, Jr.	Assistant to the President, Strategic Mission Leadership
Denise C. Lo	Assistant to the President, Operations Executive
Matthew Molinari	District Vice President, LCEF
Glenna Sanlis	Administrative Assistant to the District President
Joel D. Wahlers	Assistant to the President, Schools & Congregational Support

Legal Counsel: Steven Herum
Archivist: (Vacant)
Communications/PR Chairman: Douglas Benton (District Office)
Congregation Constitutions Chairman: Richard Rice
Disability Ministry Committee Chairperson: Dianne Flynn
Human Care Chairman: Phil Zabell
Ministerial Growth Chairman: (Vacant)
Missions Chairman: Mitchell Gowen
Student Recruitment/Aid Chairman: Eric Van Scharrel
Youth Ministry Chairperson: Jennifer de la Motte

Central Illinois

Phone: (217) 793-1802
1850 N. Grand Ave. W.
Springfield, IL 62702-1626
Fax: (217) 793-1822
Website: www.cidlcms.org
Office Hours: 8:00 a.m.–4:00 p.m. (or by appointment) (Central Time)

Officers:
Michael Mohr, President
Michael Burdick, First Vice President
Mark Eddy, Second Vice President
Justin Cullen, Secretary
Marcus Manley, Assistant Secretary
Robert Dalton, Financial Secretary
Joel Oschwald, Treasurer

Circuit Visitor:
R. Meyer (1)
J. Boehne (2)
A. Smith (3)
M. Stoerger (4)
B. Hinrichs (5)
S. Becker (6)
H. Minton (7)
B. Lesemann (8)
M. Berndt (9)
D. Ulrich (10)
K. Eckhoff (11)
M. Riley (12)
T. Nerud (13)
N. Woolery (14)
M. Schneider (15)
M. Kaufman (16)
G. Moyer (17)

Staff:

Christine Anderson	Executive Director, CID-CEF
Patrick Gumz	Administrative Assistant to the District President for Missions and Administration
William Jensen	Administrative Assistant to the District President for Stewardship
Charles Olander	Gift Planning Counselor
Trip Rodgers	Administrative Assistant to the District President for Education & Congregational Life
Ken Schurb	Administrative Assistant to the District President for Evangelism

Legal Counsel: David Rolf, 1 N. Old State Capitol Plaza, Springfield, IL 62701
Archivist: Mark Miller (District Office)
Church Extension Chairman: Darin Gehrke, 1604 W. Morton Ave., Jacksonville, IL 62650
Communications/PR Chairman: Trip Rodgers (District Office)
Congregation Constitutions Chairman: Daniel Bishop, 301 Beloit Rd., Marquette Heights, IL 61554
Congregational Life Chairman: Martin Kaufmann, 4630 Timberview Dr., Auburn, IL 62615
Education Chairman: Jonathan Buescher, 219 E. Cooke St., Mt. Pulaski, IL 62548
Evangelism Chairman: Kevin Wendorf, 1225 N. Main St., P.O. Box 377, Chatham, IL 62629
Human Care Chairman: Michael Koschmann, 705 E. Menard St., P.O. Box 380, Riverton, IL 62561
Ministerial Growth Chairman: Thomas Radtke, 7 Wildwood Rd., Springfield, IL 62704
Missions Chairman: Bruce Scarbeary, 202 W. Lincoln, P.O. Box 268, Roanoke, IL 61561
Stewardship Chairman: James Frazee, 17 Oak Grove Ln., Beardstown, IL 62618
Student Recruitment/Aid Chairman: Michael Mohr (District Office)
The GatePost Editor: Trip Rodgers (District Office)
Youth Ministry Chairman: Jonathan Guse, 85 Forestview Rd., Morton, IL 61550

Eastern

Phone: (716) 634-5111
5111 Main St.
Williamsville, NY 14221-5295
Website: www.lcmsed.org
Office Hours: 8:30 a.m.—4:30 p.m. Monday—Thursday (Eastern Time)

Officers:
John Pingel, President
Jeffrey Nickel, First Vice President
Edward Grimenstein, Second Vice President
John Zimmerman, Third Vice President
William Dorow, Fourth Vice President
Dennis Krueger, Secretary
Gary Krull, Treasurer
John G. Brunner, Honorary President Emeritus
Chris Wicher, Honorary President Emeritus

Circuit Visitor:
P. Schultz (1)
J. Duke, Jr. (2)
M. Schettler (3)
K. Schultz (4)
B. Bahr (5)
R. Pape (6)
C. Prostka (7)
M. Ball (8)
S. Kuntz (9)
D. Hahn (10)
S. Kerns (11)

Staff:

Kevin Gundell	Assistant to the President, Education Executive
John Fretthold	Accountant
Peter Johnson	Communications & Network Specialist
Stephanie Johnson	Communications & Network Specialist
Ruth Marzano	Administrative Assistant to the District President
Bruce Sutherland	Assistant to the President, Director of Discipleship Development

Legal Counsel: Dan Joyce, Fiegel, Carr & Joyce
Archivist: Bruce Sutherland
Church Extension Chairman: AJ Sinisgalli
Communications/PR Chairperson: Stephanie Johnson
Congregation Constitutions Chairman: Gordon Tresch
Stewardship: Bruce Sutherland

English

Phone: (248) 476-0039
33100 Freedom Rd.
Farmington, MI 48336-4030
Fax: (248) 476-0188
Website: www.englishdistrict.org
Office Hours: 8:30 a.m.— 5:00 p.m. Monday—Thursday; 8:30 a.m.— 12:00 p.m. Friday (Eastern Time)

Officers:
Jeffrey G. Miskus, President
Michael A. Morehouse, First Vice President (Western Region)
Robert J. Kieselowsky, Second Vice President (Eastern Region)
Zachary W. Marklevitz, Third Vice President (Lake Erie Region)
Anthony J. Oliphant, Fourth Vice President (Midwest Region)
Justin D. Laughridge, Secretary
Jamison J. Hardy, President Emeritus
David H. Ritt, President Emeritus
David P. Stechholz, President Emeritus

Circuit Visitor:
C. Stephens (1)
C. Seifferlein (2)
E. Linthicum (3)
A. Sterling (4)
D. Walsh (5)
J. Schmidt (6)
G. Luck (7)
J. Leistico (8)
R. Weldon, Sr. (9)
B. Scott (10)
T. Holzerland (11)
A. Sabol (12)
S. Barnett (13)
D. Hoag (14)
P. Bacon (15)
F. Reaman (16)

J. Gruen (17)
S. Lacey (18)
B. Crane (19)
B. von Hindenburg (20)
J. Huenink (21)
T. Utecht (22)
K. Belter (23)

Staff:

Albert Amling	School Ministry Executive
Natalya Hrecznyj	Accounting Assistant
J. Derek Mathers	Assistant to the President & Mission Executive
Sally L. Naglich	Executive Assistant to the President-Business, Finance-Treasurer
Peggy Oke	Administrative Assistant to the Business, Finance-Treasurer
Kathy Stanis	Administrative Assistant to the District President
John Hoover	District Vice President, LCEF

Legal Counsel: Douglas Abraham, 342 E. Main St., Suite 1, Northville, MI 48167, (734) 591-3737
Archivist: David Stechholz, 14374 Pere St., Livonia, MI 48154-4761
Auxiliary Services Committee Chairman: Gregory R. Lutz, padre.lutz@gmail.com
Campus Ministry Chairman: David A. Dressel, 444 Abbott Rd., E. Lansing, MI 48823
Communications Director: Linda Linthicum (District Office)
Congregation Constitutions Chairman: Luke Zimmerman, Interim
Endowment Fund Chairman: Fred Gerlach, 2501 E. Chandler Blvd., Phoenix, AZ 85048-5801
Evangelism: Brian Pratt, 10305 E. 550 S., Hudson, IN 46747
Gift Planning Counselor: Ron Grimm (District Office)
Human Care & Disaster Relief Chairman: James Robinson, 2214 Burcham Dr., E. Lansing, MI 48823-7243
Lifeline Ministry Chairman: Roni Grad, Tucson, AZ
Ministerial Health Commission Co-Chairmen: Timothy Holzerland, 4363 Kensington Ave., Detroit, MI 48224-2736 & J. Derek Mathers (District Office)
Mission Action Team Co-Chairmen: Justin D. Laughridge, 3200 Bayview, N. York, ON, Canada M2M 3R7 & J. Derek Mathers (District Office)
Parish Education Chairman: Albert Amling (District Office)
Stewardship: Michael Scheer, 8144 Loon Ln., Grand Blanc, MI 48439-7255
Student Recruitment/Aid Chairman: Albert Amling (District Office)
Youth Ministry Chairman: Rod Lane, 9541 S. 71st St., Lincoln, NE 68516-9512

Florida-Georgia

Phone: (407) 857-5556 or (877) 457-5556
5850 T. G. Lee Blvd., Ste. 500
Orlando, FL 32822-4410
Fax: (407) 857-5665
Website: www.flgadistrict.org
Office Hours: 8:00 a.m.–4:00 p.m. (Eastern Time)

Officers:
James H. Rockey, President
Jay Winters, First Vice President
David Brockhoff, Second Vice President
Charles Reich, Third Vice President
R. Scott Henze, Fourth Vice President
Jeffrey Jordan, Fifth Vice President
Gregory C. Michael, Secretary
Tracy Cripe, Treasurer
Gerhard C. Michael Jr., President Emeritus
Gregory S. Walton, President Emeritus
Thomas R. Zehnder, President Emeritus

Circuit Visitor:
D. Wesche (1)
D. Brammeier (2)
W. Heyliger (3)
A. Howe (4)
A. Matlock (5)
P. McKenzie (6)
J. Shanks (7)
G. Le Sieur (8)
J. Hohe (9)
M. Kappel (10)
R. Pennekamp (11)
S. McLean (12)
J. Zang (13)
P. O'Brien (14)
K. Yoakum (15)
R. Stolarczyk (16)
K. Lingsch (17)
S. Jensen (18)
J. Roedsens (19)
J. Wilhelm (20)
A. Mandile (21)

Staff:

Eric Sahlberg	Executive Director of Missions & Outreach
Jennifer Tanner	Executive Director of School & Youth Ministries
Jay Wendland	District Vice President, LCEF
Laura Zirbel	Executive Director Finance & Administration

Legal Counsel: William R. Huseman, P.A., 9310 Old Kings Rd. S., #702, Jacksonville, FL 32257
Archivist: (Vacant)
Communications/PR Chairman: Marketing Quorum, LLC, 971 Pepper Ridge Ter., Boca Raton, FL 33486
Congregation Constitutions Chairmen: Jay Winters, 925 W. Jefferson St., Tallahassee, FL 32304-8019
Continuing Education: (Vacant) (District Office)
District Youth Ministry Council Chairman: Nick Moss
Lutheran Witness Editor: Marketing Quorum, LLC, 971 Pepper Ridge Ter., Boca Raton, FL 33486
Stewardship: Jay Wendland (District Office)
Student Aid Chairperson: Lois Ford, 118 E. Wilt Ave., Eustis, FL 32726
Worker Care Chairman: Rick Armstrong, Lutheran Counseling Services, 1505 Orchid Ave., Winter Park, FL 32789

Indiana

Phone: (260) 423-1511
1145 S. Barr St.
Fort Wayne, IN 46802-3180
Fax: (260) 423-1514
Website: www.in.lcms.org
Office Hours: 8:00 a.m.–4:30 p.m. (Eastern Time)

Officers:
D. Richard Stuckwisch, President
Peter J. Brock, First Vice President
David Mueller, Second Vice President
Douglas Baumann, Third Vice President
Erich Fickel, Fourth Vice President
Keaton Christiansen, Secretary
Beth Maxwell, Treasurer

Circuit Visitor:
A. Krebs (1)
D. Solum (2)
D. Speckhard (3)
W. Carney (4)
A. Appel (5)
D. Griebel (6)
M. Trombley (7)
M. Blodgett (8)
S. Wirgau (9)
A. Keller (10)
F. Hearn (11)
S. Giger (12)
S. Mierow (13)
C. Truelsen (14)
E. Edwards (15)
J. Rodriguez (16)
J. McKinley (17)
J. Tucher (18)
J. Bowlds (19)
N. Rusert (20)
C. Eckels (21)
D. Becker (22)
A. Guagenti (23)

Staff:

J. Cody Dodson	Business Manager
T. J. Mattick	District Development, LCEF
Mark Muehl	Gift Planning
Diane Ottinger	District Accountant
Geoffrey Robinson	Outreach & Human Care
Lisa Slack	Exec. Administrative Assistant
Nathan Wingfield	Lutheran Education

Legal Counsel: Michael Hawk, 116 E. Berry St., Ste. 302, Ft. Wayne, IN 46802
Archivist: Nathan Bienz
Church Extension Chairman: T. J. Mattick (District Office)
Congregation Constitutions Chairman: Leonard Tanksley
Lutheran Witness Editor: Sara Pierce (District Office)

Iowa East

Phone: (319) 373-2112
1100 Blairs Ferry Rd.
Marion, IA 52302-3093
Website: www.lcmside.org
Office Hours: 8:15 a.m.–4:30 p.m. (Central Time)

Officers:
Brian S. Saunders, President
William Maximillian Mons, First Vice President
Stephen Preus, Second Vice President
Peter D. Hoft, Secretary
Zachary Rowley, Treasurer

Circuit Visitor:
D. Lingard (1)
S. Hansen (2A)
B. Hartwig (2B)
D. Redhage (3)
B. Ferch (4)
K. Kincaid (5)
A. Hambleton (6)
J. Koepp (7)
M. Scudder (8)
J. Burns (9)
D. Menet (10)
J. Ellingworth (11)
W. Karstens (12)

Staff:

Jan Doellinger	Assistant to the President for Schools
Ryan Johnson	Business Manager/Office Manager
Pam Krog	Administrative Assistant to the District President
Daniel Sanchez	District Services Coordinator

Legal Counselor: Shuttleworth & Ingersoll PLC of Cedar Rapids, IA 52406-2107
Archivist: Allen Konrad, P.O. Box 157, Rowley, IA 52329
Congregation Constitutions Chairman: Gary Sears
District Life Coordinator: Alex Post, 1603 S. 2nd Ave., Marshalltown, IA 50158-4016
District Vice President, LCEF: Josh Remington, IDW, 409 Kenyon Rd. Suite B, Fort Dodge, IA 50501
Missions Committee: David Menet
Operation Barnabas Representative: Michael Scudder
School Committee Chairman: Cody Collier
*Student Aid Chairm*an: David Lingard, P.O. Box 294, Van Horne, IA 52346-0294
Worship Chairman: Tom Van Hemert, 287 Roberts Ave., Marengo, IA
Youth Ministry Chairman: (Vacant)

OFFICERS/STRUCTURE

Iowa West

Phone: (515) 576-7666
409 Kenyon Rd., Ste. B
Fort Dodge, IA 50501
Website: www.iowadistrictwest.org
Office Hours: 8:00 a.m.–4:30 p.m. (Central Time)

Officers:
Paul Egger, President
Jonathan Riggert, First Vice President
Benjamin Dose, Second Vice President
Richard Merrill, Secretary
Scott Ernst, Treasurer

Circuit Visitor:
K. McBee (1)
P. Schulz (2)
D. Martens (3)
J. Conner (4)
D. Meyer (5)
N. Sherrill (6)
C. Trunkhill (7)
K. Johnson (8)
J. Stogdill (9)
J. Pierson (10)
M. Boothby (11)
N. Wehmas (12)
C. Nitzel (13)
D. Lyons (14)
J. Travis (15)
B. Ketcham (16)

Staff:

Roger Curtis	Business Manager
Jill Davis	Administrative Assistant to the District President
B. Keith Haney	Assistant to the President for Missions, Stewardship & Human Care
Pedro Lopez	Assistant to the President Missionary at Large
Julie Mann	Disaster Response Coordinator
Rhonda Mohr	Assistant to the President for Education, Youth & Family Life
Josh Remington	District Vice President, LCEF
Leon Schoenfeld	Gift Planning Counselor
Steve Schulz	Assistant Director-Mission Central
Gary Thies	Mission Development Counselor

Legal Counsel: Zachary J. Parle of BrownWinick Law Firm, 666 Grand Ave. #2000, Des Moines, IA 50309
Archivist: Aaron Zimmerman
Church Extension Chairman: Josh Remington
Congregation Constitutions Chairman: Richard Merrill
Human Care Chairman: Chadric Dietrich
Missions Chairman: Joshua Lowe
Parish Education Chairman: Paul Dare
Stewardship Chairman: Russell Senstad
Student Recruitment/Aid Chairman: Joseph Pierson
Youth Ministry Chairman: Ryan Roehrig

Kansas

Phone: (785) 357-4441
1000 S.W. 10th Ave.
Topeka, KS 66604
Fax: (785) 357-5071
Website: www.kslcms.org
Office Hours: 8:00 a.m.–4:30 p.m. (Central Time)

Officers:
Justin Panzer, President
Alan Stahlecker, First Vice President
Michael Schotte, Second Vice President
Andrew Wehling, Third Vice President
Philip Hoppe, Fourth Vice President
Joshua Woelmer, Secretary
Brad Brunkow, Treasurer

Circuit Visitor:
I. Kinney (1)
J. Boetcher (2)
J. Schultz (3N)
J. Keltner (3S)
T. Booth (4)
M. Jennings (5)
S. Kilgo (6)
W. Wingfield (7)
J. Woemler (8)
K. Letcher (9)
M. Bingenheimer (10)
M. Brockman (11)
T. Slater (12)
C. Craig (13)
M. Schmidt (15)
J. Toombs (16)

Staff:

Dan Grams	Assistant to the President for Congregations & School Services
Jeff Maltz	District Vice President, LCEF
Heather Williams	Business Manager

Legal Counsel: Eric Turner (District Office)
Archivist: Michael Grau (District Office)
Church Extension Chairman: Jeff Maltz (District Office)
Communications/PR Chairperson: Jackie Schaefer (District Office)
Congregation Constitutions Chairman: Joshua Woelmer (District Office)
Family Ministry: Philip Hoppe (District Office)
Human Care Chairman: Curt Engelbrecht (District Office)
Lutheran Witness Editor: Jackie Schaefer (District Office)
Ministerial Growth Chairman: Lee Hovel (District Office)
Missions Chairman: Marvin Schulteis (District Office)
Parish Education Chairman: Bruce Schultz
Stewardship: Dave Bruns
Student Recruitment/Aid Chairman: Sean Kilgo
Youth Ministry Chairman: (Vacant)

Michigan

Phone: (734) 665-3791 or (888) 225-2111
3773 Geddes Rd.
Ann Arbor, MI 48105-3098
Fax: (734) 665-0255
Website: www.michigandistrict.org
Instagram.com/milcms
Twitter.com/milcms
www.facebook.com/milcms
Office Hours: 8:45 a.m.–4:00 p.m. (Eastern Time)

Officers:
David Davis, President
Darryl Andrzejewski, First Vice President
Erik Cloeter, Second Vice President
Craig Bickel, Third Vice President
Andrew Gruenhagen, Fourth Vice President
Derek Riddle, Secretary
Bonnie Mann, Treasurer

Circuit Visitor:
C. Burhop (1)
J. Mandley (2)
F. Cordts (3)
T. Sheridan (4)
D. Kempin (5)
D. Jung (6)
M. Durance (7)
M. Boyer (8)
C. Steele (9)
C. Buckhahn (10)
T. Zucker (11)
M. Hein (12)
T. Frusti (13)
G. Doroh (14)
N. Gibbons (15)
N. Koy (16)
P. Undlin (17)
E. Gaertner (18)
M. Hetzner (19)
H. Avers (20)
R. Robinson (21)
J. Cashmer (23)
K. Jones (24)
J. Bellinghausen (26)
S. Newton (27)
D. Pezzica (28)
B. Schindel (29)
Z. Holdorf (30)
M. Peters (31)
M. Goers (32)
B. Woell (33)
P. Tonn (34)
W. Wangelin (35)
E. Filter (36)
W. Lahrman (38)
C. Boehnke (39)
G. Schaeffer (40)
B. West (41)
K. Strenge (42)
M. Roth (43)
K. Kuhlmann (44)

Staff:

Laurie Brown	Executive Assistant to the President
Debby Fall	Director of Communications
Travis Grulke	Superintendent of Schools
Randy Johnson	Director of District Facilitators
Scott Yakimow	Director of Mission Development
Robert Kasper	Director of Leadership Development
Laura Thomas	Director of Development
Martha Wohlfeil	Administrative Assistant, President's Office
Chad Woltemath	Vice President of Finance
John Bates	President, CEF
James Saalfeld	Chief Executive Officer, CEF
Andrew Sohn	Vice President of Strategy & Marketing, CEF

Archivist: Barbara Adler (District Office)
Church Extension Chairman: Timothy Haberling
Communications/PR Chairperson: Debby Fall (District Office)
Congregation Constitutions Chairman: Brad Hubbard
Family Ministry: Travis Grulke (District Office)
Foundation Gift Planning Counselor: Julie Burgess
Human Care Chairperson/Continuing Education: Debby Fall (District Office)
Lutheran Witness Editor: Debby Fall (District Office)
Ministerial Growth Chairman: Daniel Ramthun
Missions Chairman: Scott Yakimow (District Office)
Stewardship: Richard Wolfram (District Office)
Student/Aid Chairman: Chad Woltemath (District Office)
Youth Ministry Chairman: Travis Grulke (District Office)

Mid-South

Phone: (901) 373-1343 or (866) 373-1343
1675 Wynne Rd.
Cordova, TN 38016-4905
Fax: (901) 373-4826
Website: mid-southlcms.org
Office Hours: 8:15 a.m.–4:30 p.m. (Central Time)

Officers:
Roger Paavola, President
Joshua Willadsen, First Vice President (Region 1)
Kevin Conger, Second Vice President (Region 2)
Philip Young, Third Vice President (Region 3)
David Graves, Fourth Vice President (Region 4)
Larry Peters, Secretary
John Hofman, Treasurer
David C. Callies, President Emeritus
Kenneth Lampe, President Emeritus

Circuit Visitor:
D. Welmer (1)
B. Martin (2)
T. Bartzsch (3)
R. Herring (4)
C. LeFort (5)
K. Janneke (6)
E. Woerner (7)
C. Sellers (8)
K. Shaw (9)
T. McMinn (10)
D. Appold (11)
S. Marshall (12)
C. Shemwell (13)

Staff:
Michelle Fischer — Executive for Education-Youth & Family
Angela Fowler — Executive Director for Business & Finance
Scott Roberts — District Vice President, LCEF
Missy Washburn — Executive Administrative Assistant to the District President

Legal Counsel: Kevin Washburn, 80 Monroe Ave., #650, Memphis, TN 38103
Archivists: Nancy Lee, 2800 Elise, Hernando, MS 38632
Communication/PR Chairperson: Rhonda Anderson, 419 Nubia Rd., Westmoreland, TN 37186
Congregation Constitution Chairman: Ken Haydon, 8 Thomas Dr., Eureka Springs, AR 72632
Evangelism: Roger Paavola (District Office)
Human Care Co-Chairmen: Trae Fistler, 405 Shelia Dr., Hopkinsville, KY 42240; Kurt Ludwig, 2023 Hidden Meadow Dr., Adams, TN 37010
Lutheran Witness Editor: Judy Otto, 150 N. Maury, Holly Springs, MS 38635
Parish Education Chairperson: Michelle Fischer
Stewardship: Jack Ficken
Student Aid Chairperson: Angela Fowler (District Office)
Webmaster: Rhonda Anderson, 419 Nubia Rd., Westmoreland, TN 37186
World Missions Chairman: Bob Allen, 208 Peach Tree, White House, TN 39188
Youth Ministry Chairman: (Vacant)

Minnesota North

Phone: (218) 829-1781
7264 Fairview Rd.
Baxter, MN 56425
Email: mnndist@mnnlcms.org
Website: www.mnnlcms.org
Office Hours: 8:00 a.m.–4:30 p.m. Monday–Thursday (Central Time)

Officers:
Brady L. Finnern, President
Karl A. Weber, First Vice President
Bruce Timm, Second Vice President
Jeffrey Ross, Third Vice President
Martin Mably, Secretary
Mike Uran, Treasurer

Circuit Visitor:
D. Thompson (1)
R. Wentzel (2)
M. Vrudny (3)
J. Whitmore (4)
B. Rickbeil (5)
G. Coop (6)
J. Anthony (7)
T. Peperkorn (8)
B. Vogt (9)
T. Rehwaldt (10)
J. Gillard (11)
J. Reber (12)
R. Pumphrey (13)
R. Fritz (14)
D. Mommens (15)
W. Aufdenkamp (16)
(Vacant) (17)
D. Tilney (18)

Staff:
Albert Boldt — Business Manager
Vicent Grochow — District Vice President, LCEF
Sean Paul Martens — District Education Executive
Diana Ruopp — Executive Assistant to the District President
Mike Uran — Treasurer

Archivist: Mark Maunula, Isle, MN
Congregation Constitutions Chairman: John Beck, Sauk Rapids, MN
Crisis Consultation & Support: Steve Breitbarth, 3535 7th Ave. E., Hibbing, MN 55746
Lutheran Witness Editor: Travis Lauterbach, Backus, MN

Minnesota South

Phone: (952) 435-2550
14301 Grand Ave.
Burnsville, MN 55306
Fax: (952) 435-2581
Website: mnsdistrict.org
Office Hours: 8:00 a.m.–4:00 p.m. Monday–Friday (Central Time)

Officers:
Lucas V. Woodford, President
Mark S. Loder, First Vice President
Brent Parrish, Second Vice President
Joshua Miller, Third Vice President
Jonathan Vollrath, Fourth Vice President
Brian Thorson, Secretary
Jolene Peterman, Treasurer

Circuit Visitor:
P. Strawn (1)
S. Bielenberg (2)
T. Heinecke (3)
J. Vano (4)
S. Jones (5)
W. Hugo (6)
M. Engelhardt (7)
R. Neal (8)
D. Hormann (9)
T. Schmidt (10)
L. Sorenson (11)
T. Volker (12)
J. Kumfer (13)
J. Krusemark (14)
W. Odom (15)
B. Klein (16)
M. Trask (17)
R. Reed (18)
K. Grant (19)
A. Finney (20)
A. Bertram (21)
R. Bremseth (22)
A. Jacobsen (23)
S. Ethridge (24)

Staff:

Deborah Borchardt (FT)	Administrative Assistant to the District President, (952) 223-2158
Vincent Grochow	District Vice President, LCEF
Fredric Hinz (PT)	Public Policy Advocate, (507) 317-9634
Phillip Johnson (FT)	Assistant to the President for Mission Formation & Commissioned Ministers, (952) 223-2161
Christina Krentz	Administrative Assistant for Commissioned Ministers, (952) 223-2162
Vue Lee	Assistant to the President for Missions, (952) 223-2151
Sean Martens (FT)	Assistant to the President for Education and Commissioned Ministers/Teachers, (952) 223-2152
Nadine Meyer	Communications Director, (952) 223-2156
Scot Missling (PT)	Public Policy Advocate (612)845-1966
Jolene Peterman	Treasurer
Stefan Wismar (FT)	Executive Assistant to the President, (952) 223-2154

Archivist: (Vacant)
Communications: Nadine Meyer (District Office)
Congregation Constitutions Chairman: Matthew Moss, St. John Lutheran Church, 9141 County Rd. 101, Corcoran, MN 55340
Ministerial Health Chairman: Stefan Wismar (District Office)
Student Recruitment/Aid Chairman: Sean Martens (District Office)
Stewardship: Phillip Johnson (District Office)

Missouri

Phone: (314) 590-6200
660 Mason Ridge Center Dr., Ste. 100
St. Louis, MO 63141
Fax: (314) 590-6202
Website: mo.lcms.org
Office Hours: 8:00 a.m.–4:30 p.m. (Central Time)

Officers:
R. Lee Hagan, President
Craig Otto, First Vice President
Randy Asburry, Second Vice President
Samuel Powell, Third Vice President
Richard Cody, Fourth Vice President
Nicolas Hagerman, Secretary
Robert Uthoff, Treasurer
James Kalthoff, President Emeritus
Ray Mirly, President Emeritus

Circuit Visitor:
P. Winningham (1)
J. Wagner (2)
W. Wildauer (3)
E. Kohn (4)
A. Alter (5)
M. Junkin (6)
J. Kurz (7)
K. Castens (8)
J. May (9)
B. Whittle (10)
G. Stolle (11)
G. Reiser (12)
S. Andrews Jr. (13)
J. Dock (14)
J. Perling (15)
R. Taylor (16)
D. Moore (17)
D. Gruenwald (18)
T. Freudenburg (19)
S. Jonas (20)
N. Ruback (21)
M. Femmel (22)
M. Clark (23)
W. Smith (24)
A. Kennell (25)
J. Krueger (26)
D. Roth (27)
D. Stock (28)

Staff:

(Vacant)	Director of Mission Services
Marty Hasz	Director of Church Worker Support
Sarah Irwin	Administrative Assistant to the District President

Peter Kirby	Executive Director of Congregational Services
Peter Krege	Chief Financial Officer
Daniel Kreienkamp	Director of Youth Ministry
Pamela Nummela	Family Discipleship Coaching Facilitator
Leah Sieveking	Director of Mission Advancement
Joshua Swartz	Director of Schools
Mike Wadley	District Vice President, LCEF

Legal Counsel: David Castleman, 1 N. Brentwood Blvd., St. Louis, MO 63105
Archivist: (Vacant)
Church Extension Chairman: Mike Wadley (District Office)
Communications/PR Chair: Christie Hampton
Congregation Constitutions Chairman: Terry Weinhold
Continuing Education: Joshua Swartz (District Office)
Disaster Response: Marty Hasz (District Office)
Evangelism: (Vacant)
Family Ministry: Pamela Nummela (District Office)
Life Coordinator: Jason Wagner, 2308 Gravois Rd., High Ridge, MO 63049
Ministerial Growth Chairman: Marty Hasz (District Office)
Missions Chairman: (Vacant)
Stewardship: Peter Kirby (District Office)
Student Recruitment/Aid Chairman: Joshua Swartz (District Office)
Youth Ministry Chairman: Daniel Kreienkamp (District Office)

Montana

Phone: (406) 259-2908
759 Newman Ln., Ste. 2
Billings, MT 59101
Website: www.mtdistlcms.org
Office Hours: 9:00 a.m.–5:00 p.m. (Mountain Time)

Officers:
Ryan Wendt, President
Arlo Pullmann, First Vice President
Samuel Grayl, Second Vice President
David Behm, Secretary

Circuit Visitor:
R. Dewell (1)
A. Eckert (2)
M. Christensen (3)
J. Schultz (4)
G. Pullmann (5)
S. Thomas (6)

Staff:

Ruth Kosche	Administrative Assistant to the District President
Susan Loomans	Treasurer

Archivist: Jason Menagh, 2221 Willow Dr. Unit 107G, Livingston, MT 59047
Communication/PR Chairperson: Ruth Kosche (District Office)
Congregation Constitutions Chairman: Ryan Wendt (District Office)
Evangelism & Missions Chairman: (Vacant)
Human Care Chairperson: Lorraine Roach, 418 Foxtail Ln., Stevensville, MT 59870
Parish Education Chairperson: Sarah Elliott, 77 Konley Dr., Kalispell, MT 59901
Stewardship: Lorraine Roach, 418 Foxtail Ln., Stevensville, MT 59870
Youth Ministry Chairman: Sarah Elliott, 77 Konley Dr., Kalispell, MT 59901

Nebraska

Phone: (402) 643-2961
152 S. Columbia Ave.
Mail: P.O. Box 407
Seward, NE 68434
Website: ndlcms.org
Office Hours: 8:00 a.m.–5:00 p.m. (Central Time)

Officers:
Richard Snow, President
Michael Awe, First Vice President
James Moshier, Second Vice President
Scott Bruick, Third Vice President
Cory Burma, Fourth Vice President
Caleb Kruse, Secretary

Circuit Visitor:
L. Christensen (1)
W. Voelker (2)
B. Rick (3)
B. Francik (4)
P. Warneke (5)
A. Gerber (6)
B. Wright (7)
D. Olson (8)
R. Kuefner (9)
J. Scheich (10)
A. Moline (11)
B. Williams (12)
E. Jay (13)
R. Janke (14)
K. Hessel (15)
S. Kitzing (16)
J. Warner (17)
N. Henschen (18)
J. Dickmander (19)
M. Neidow (20)

Staff:

Justin Hannemann	Assistant to the President for Church Worker Care
Kim Hofer	Administrative Assistant to the District President
Lonnie Jacobsen	Assistant to the President for Mission & Revitalization
Elijah Luebbe	Treasurer
Nathan Meier	District Vice President, LCEF
Kimberly Myers	Communications Director
Vanessa Seifert	Assistant to the President for Lifelong Pastoral Formation
Craig Stirtz	Gift Planning Counselor, LCMS Foundation
Gary Thies	Mission Development Counselor
Robert Ziegler	Assistant to the President for Education and Youth

Legal Counsel: Tim Moll, Rembolt Ludtke Law Firm, 125 6th St., Seward, NE 68434
Archivist: David Palomaki, Redeemer Lutheran Church, P.O. Box 244, David City, NE 68632
Church Extension Chairman: Nathan Meier (District Office)
Communications: Kimberly Myers (District Office)
Congregation Constitutions Chairman: Caleb Kruse, Lord of Life Lutheran Church, 20844 Bonanza Blvd., Elkhorn, NE 68022
Family Ministry: Deb Jurchen, Concordia University, 800 N. Columbia Ave., Seward, NE 68434
Missions Chairman: Lonnie Jacobsen (District Office)
Parish Education Chair: Dr. Mark Blanke, 189 Wildwood Rd., Seward, NE 68434
Stewardship Chairman: Nathan Meier (District Office)
Student Recruitment/Aid Chairman: Robert Ziegler (District Office)

New England

Phone: (413) 783-0131
400 Wilbraham Rd.
Springfield, MA 01109
Fax: (413) 783-0909
Website: www.ned-lcms.org
Business Office Hours: 8:00 a.m.–4:30 p.m. Monday–Friday (Eastern Time)

Officers:
Robert Beinke, President
Peter Gregory, First Vice President
Randall Pekari, Second Vice President
Scott MacDonald, Third Vice President
Dwight Riley, Secretary
Kevin McCarthy, Treasurer

Circuit Visitor:
B. Akers (1)
J. Hopkins (2)
C. Chandler (3)
M. Clow (4)
R. Morris (5)

Staff:

Brenda Bacon	Business Manager & District Vice President, LCEF
(Vacant)	Administrative Assistant to the District President & Business Manager

Legal Counsel: (Vacant)
Archivist: Kevin McCarthy, 7 Brooke Meadow Rd., Kensington, CT 06037
Communications/PR Chairperson: Brenda Bacon (District Office)
Congregation Constitutions Chairman: (Vacant)
Evangelism: (Vacant)
Human Care: (Vacant)
Life Coordinator: Marla Zeneski, 78 Merriam District, N. Oxford, MA 01537
Lutheran Church Extension Vice President & NED News Editor: Brenda Bacon (District Office)
Parish Education Chairperson: Josephine Schiebel, 802 Lakeview Dr., China, ME 04358
Stewardship: (Vacant)
Student Recruitment/Aid Chairman: David Jacoby, 750 Ridge Rd., Fitchburg, MA 01420
Worship Chairman: Robert Morris, 85 Mt. Pleasant Rd., Newtown, CT 06470
Youth Ministry Chairman: (Vacant)

New Jersey

Phone: (908) 233-8111
1168 Springfield Ave.
Mountainside, NJ 07092
Fax: (908) 233-3883
Website: www.njdistrict.org
Office Hours: 8:30 a.m.–4:30 p.m. Monday–Thursday (Eastern Time)

Officers:
Stephen A. Gewecke, President
Deric Taylor, First Vice President
Jon Dunbar, Second Vice President
Jonathan Hodges, Third Vice President
Jonathan Iovine, Secretary
Christian Koerner, Treasurer

Circuit Visitor:
R. Holsten (1)
A. Giordano (2)
S. Vera (3)
G. Jans (4)
D. Small (5)
A. Wolfgram (6)

Staff:

(Vacant)	Education Executive
George Mikula	Communications
Roy Minnix, Jr.	Church Worker Wellness
Elaine Schleifer	Administrative Assistant to the President, Business & Office Manager
William Schmidt	Director, Ministry to Armed Forces & Veteran/Operation Barnabas
Christian Schonberg	Ministry Facilitator
AJ Sinisgalli	LCEF VP & Congregation Res. Counselor

Legal Counsel: Charles Karcher, 30 Linden Pl., Red Bank, NJ 07701
Archivist: Anthony Iovine (District Office)
Campus Ministry: Gregory Jans
Church Extension Chairman: AJ Sinisgalli
Communications/PR Chairman: George Mikula (District Office)
Congregation Constitutions Chairman: Anthony Iovine (District Office)
Congregation Revitalization: Larry Schumann (District Office)
Disaster Relief: Christian Schonberg (District Office)
Evangelism: Matthew Hass (District Office)
Family Ministry: (Vacant)
Ministerial Growth Chairman: (Vacant)
Missions Chairman: (Vacant)
Parish Education Chairman: (Vacant)
Parish Nurse: Colleen Bottcher (District Office)
Stewardship: David Small (District Office)
Youth Ministry Chairman: (Vacant) (District Office)

North Dakota

Phone: (701) 293-9001
P.O. Box 9029
Fargo, ND 58106
Website: nodaklcms.org
Office Hours: 9:00 a.m.–5:00 p.m. Monday– Friday (Central Time)

Officers:
Mark Chepulis, President
Paul Preus, First Vice President
Jonathan Walla, Second Vice President
Daniel Voth, Secretary
Kay Kreklau, Treasurer

Circuit Visitor:
B. Woodruff (1)
C. Waldvogel (2)
D. Provost (3)
T. Stout (4)
M. Grieve (5)
Z. Heide (6)

Staff:

Tana McKenna	Executive Administrator
Tamara Ulland	Business Manager
Adam Filipek	Board Vice Chairman
Tom Langer	Board Chairman

Legal Counsel: Niles Hanson & Davies Ltd, 201 5th St. N., Fargo, ND 58102
Archivist: Vicki Peihl, 2601 23rd Ave. S., Fargo, ND 58103
Communications/PR Chairperson: Dana Otto, 601 N. 32nd St, Bismarck, ND 58501
Congregation Constitutions Chairman: Daniel Voth, 2229 Fallcreek Ct., Grand Forks, ND 58201
Continuing Education: Clark Jahnke, 325 Cherry Ct., W. Fargo, ND 58078
District Vice President, LCEF: Kurt Primuth, Sioux Falls, SD
Evangelism: (Vacant)
Family Ministry: Brock Schmeling, 316 Iowa St., Barney, ND 58008
Human Care Chairman: Lester Wolfgram, 4601 Rolling Ridge Rd., Bismarck, ND 58053
Lutheran Witness Editor: Dana Otto, 601 N. 32nd St., Bismarck, ND 58501
Ministerial Growth Chairman: Clark Jahnke, 325 Cherry Ct., W. Fargo, ND 58078
Missions Chairman: Richard Jones, 5801 19th Ave. N.W., Minot, ND 58701
Parish Education Chairman: (Vacant)
Stewardship: Dennis Voss, 4703 Nova Ave., Mandan, ND 58554
Student Recruitment/Aid Chairperson: Tamara Ulland, 2601 23rd Ave. S., Fargo, ND 58103
Youth Ministry: *(Vacant)*

North Wisconsin

Phone: (715) 845-8241
3103 Seymour Ln.
Wausau, WI 54401
Website: www.nwdlcms.org
Office Hours: 8:00 a.m.–4:00 p.m. (Central Time)

Officers:
Timothy J. Shoup, President
Donald V. Engebretson, First Vice President
Preston A. Paul, Second Vice President
Ryan J. Fehrmann, Third Vice President
Travis R. Kleinschmidt, Secretary
Dwayne Maroszek, Treasurer

Circuit Visitor:

A. vonSeggern (1)	D. Sutton (6)	J. Mayland (11)	R. Anderson (16)
A. Gehrke (2)	P. Radke (7)	T. Jerabek (12)	T. Ritter (17)
J. Miels (3)	E. Clemens (8)	A. Zobel (13)	J. Smiles (18)
C. Zandi (4)	B. Thomas (9)	C. Nehring (14)	L. Yaw (19)
P. Kufahl (5)	R. Shorey (10)	D. Knefelkamp (15)	

Staff:

Lori Kavajecz	Executive Assistant to the President	DJ Schult	Assistant to the President
Sandie Pagel	Administrative Assistant		

Legal Counsel: David Piehler, Wausau, WI
Archivist: (Vacant)
Church Extension District Vice President, LCEF: Bill Jordan (District Office)
Communication/PR Chairman: DJ Schult (District Office)
Congregation Constitutions Chairman: Travis Kleinschmidt, Shawano, WI
Lutheran Witness Editor: Karol Selle, Stevens Point, WI
PALS: Joshua Errer, Green Bay, WI
Student Recruitment/Aid Chairman: Andrew Heren, Eau Claire, WI

Northern Illinois

Phone: (708) 449-3020
1107 Monroe Ave.
River Forest, IL 60305
Website: www.nidlcms.org
Office Hours: 8:00 a.m.–4:00 p.m. Monday–Thursday; 8:00 a.m.–3:00 p.m. Friday (Central Time)

Officers:
Allan R. Buss, President
Cory Estby, First Vice President
Caleb Schauer, Second Vice President
Michael Brown, Third Vice President
Steven Anderson, Fourth Vice President
David Totsky, Secretary
LeeAnn Acosta, Treasurer
William H. Ameiss, President Emeritus
Dan P. Gilbert, President Emeritus

Circuit Visitor:

E. Blonski (1)	C. James (6)	P. Robarge (11)	D. Balla (15)
K. Fay (2)	R. Krueger (7)	R. Tausz (12)	R. Schauer (16)
S. Maske (3)	P. Pinion (8)	V. Ausra (13A)	W. Ryden (17)
L. Tieman (4)	R. Rub Jr. (9)	M. Duer (13B)	E. Brown (18)
J. Hays (5)	D. Andermann (10)	E. Lewis (14)	J. LaMie (19)

Staff:

LeeAnn Acosta	Business Manager & Treasurer	Lois Stewart	Mission Facilitator Schools
Sue Green	District Services Coordinator	Kris Whitby	Assistant to the President-Mission & Ministry
Michelle La Velle	Administrative Assistant to the District President	Joe Willmann	District Vice President, LCEF
John Prohl	Assistant to the President (PT)		

Archivist: John Hallman, 6151 Lippicott Ln., Rockford, IL 61107
Congregational Constitutions Chairman: Davis Totsky, St. Peter's Ev. Lutheran Church, 310 N. Broadway, Joliet, IL 60435
Director of Communications: Ann Ciaccio
Human Care Chairman: Christopher Singer, President, Lutheran Church Charities, 3020 Milwaukee Ave., Northbrook, IL 60062
Missions Chairman: Kris Whitby (District Office)

Northwest

Phone: (503) 288-8383
1700 N.E. Knott
Portland, OR 97212
Fax: (503) 284-2785
Website: www.nowlcms.org
Office Hours: 8:00 a.m.–4:30 p.m. (Pacific Time)

Officers:
Michael Von Behren, President
Eric Lange, First Vice President
Jonathan Dinger, Second Vice President
Michael Warmbier, Third Vice President
Brian Bowes, Fourth Vice President
Tim Bayer, Fifth Vice President
(Vacant), Sixth Vice President
Steve Heinsen, District Secretary
Erhart L. Bauer, Honorary President Emeritus
Paul Linnemann, Honorary President Emeritus
Warren Schumacher, Honorary President Emeritus

Circuit Visitor:

J. Heimbuck (1)
J. Markus (2)
K. Hess (3)
N. Brandt (4)
J. Hughes III (5)
J. Sprengle (6)
D. Richard (7)
P. Brandt (8)
K. Oster (9)
R. Benscoter (10)
S. Barckholtz (11)
G. Pay (12)
P. Knutson (13)
M. Bertermann (14)
A. Bayless (15)
M. Gulseth (16)
S. Neider (17)
W. Berger (18)
D. Carnahan (19)
S. Berry (20)
K. Hulvey (21)
P. Mueller (22)
D. Freeman (23)
D. Gerken (24)
A. Schultz (25)
J. Davis (26)

Staff:

Marilyn Allen	Business Manager
Dustin Kunkel	Director of Ministry Leadership
Michael Madison	District Vice President, LCEF
Jenny McIvor	Administrative Assistant to the District President
James Scrivens	Director of Education Services

Archivist: (Vacant)
Church Extension Chairman: (Vacant)
Communications/PR Chairperson: Elena Scott (District Office)
Congregation Constitutions Chairman: Mark Hoelter (District Office)
Evangelism: Dustin Kunkel (District Office)
Family Ministry: Dustin Kunkel (District Office)
Missions Chairman: Dustin Kunkel (District Office)
Parish Education Chairman: James Scrivens (District Office)
Stewardship: Marilyn Allen (District Office)
Student Recruitment/Aid Chairperson: Marilyn Allen (District Office)
Youth Ministry Chairman: Dustin Kunkel (District Office)

Ohio

Phone: (440) 235-2297
Mail: 25000 Country Club Blvd., Ste. 220
North Olmsted, OH 44070
Fax: (440) 235-1970
Website: www.oh.lcms.org
Office Hours: 8:30 a.m.–4:30 p.m. (Eastern Time)

Officers:

Kevin A. Wilson, President
Paul R. Schlueter, First Vice President
Mark W. Love, Second Vice President
Everette E. Greene, Third Vice President
Michael S. Wallace, Fourth Vice President
Anders M. Davidson, Fifth Vice President
Philip Zielinski, Secretary

Circuit Visitor:

H. Folks (1)
L. Scheiwe (2)
M. Mapus (3)
A. Alberts (4)
D. Woolsey (5)
J. Schroeder (6)
W. Marcis (7)
P. Pirn (8)
S. Hackmann (9)
D. Luecke (10)
A. Stuckwisch (11)
T. Beck (12)
K. Witte (13)
M. Hartsough (14)
W. Hromowyk (15)
D. Golden (16)

Staff:

Karen Dutton	Youth Ministry Coordinator (PT)
Lisa Hall	District Vice President, LCEF
Cheryl Ohradzansky	Administrative Assistant to the District President
Lisa Rachul	Chief Financial Officer
Nicole Levy	Director of Education Services
John E. Greig	Director of Ministry Resources

Legal Counsel: Wegman Hessler, 6055 Rockside Woods Blvd., Ste. 200, Cleveland, OH 44131
Archivist: Paul Hoffman, 7900 Hollenbeck Cir., Parma, OH 44129
Communications/PR Chairperson: Sara Krek (District Office)
Congregation Constitutions Chairman: Paul Hoffman, 7900 Hollenbeck Cir., Parma, OH 44129
Continuing Education: (Vacant)
Human Care Chairman: (Vacant)
Ministerial Health Commission Chairman: Chris Eldridge, 530 McNaughten Rd., Columbus, OH 43213
Missions Chairman: (Vacant)
New Ministry Task Force: Mark Carlson, 4865 Wilmington Pike, Kettering, OH 45440
Stewardship: (Vacant)
Student Coordinator/Aid Chairman: Mark Matzke, 11900 Chillicothe Rd., Chesterland, OH 44026
Youth Ministry Coordinator: Karen Dutton (District Office)

Oklahoma

Phone: (405) 321-3443
603 Classen Blvd.
Norman, OK 73071
Website: www.oklahomalutherans.org
Office Hours: 9:00 a.m.—4:00 p.m. Tuesday—Friday (Central Time)

Officers:
David Nehrenz, President
Christopher Hall, First Vice President
Mark Muenchow, Second Vice President
Timothy McCarty, Third Vice President
Wayne Rostek, Secretary
Yvonne Moore, Treasurer

Circuit Visitor:
G. McClellan (1)
D. Schroeder (2)
R. Smith Jr. (3)
E. Schneider (4)
J. Wackler (5)
J. Hobson (6)
S. Burmeister (7)
R. Simpson (8)
C. Griffith (9)

Staff:

Sara Cage	Education Executive
Jeffrey Maltz	LCEF Vice President
Glenn Meyer	Mission Executive
Daniel Ross	Evangelism Executive
Lois Rostek	District President Administrative Assistant
Cyndi Smith	Communications Director
Rick Tabisz	Stewardship Executive
Suzanne Watt	Youth Executive

Legal Counsel: (Vacant)
Communications/PR Chairman: Mark Muenchow, 3600 N.W. Expressway, Oklahoma City, OK 73112-4410
Congregation Review Chairman: Ahren Reiter, 1545 NW 31st St., Lawton, OK 73505
Continuing Education: Jay Hobson, 320 Deer Creek Ln., Skiatook, OK 74070
Human Care Chairman: Ron Simpson, 700 N. Air Depot Blvd., Midwest City, OK 73110
Lutheran Witness Editor: Cyndi Smith, 12302 E. 79th Ct. N., Owasso, OK 74055
Ministerial Growth Chairman: (Vacant)
Ministerial Health/Worker Wellness: Clifton Loman, 25043 E. 727 Rd., Tahlequah, OK 74464
PALS Coordinator: (Vacant)
Student Recruitment/Aid Chairman: David Nehrenz, 603 Classen Blvd., Norman, OK 73071

Pacific Southwest

Phone: (949) 854-3232
16355 Laguna Canyon Rd. Suite 300
Irvine, CA 92618
Website: www.psd-lcms.org
Office Hours: 8:00 a.m.—4:00 p.m. Monday—Friday (Pacific Time)

Officers:
Michael Gibson, President
Vince Harman, First Vice President
Mark Manning, Second Vice President
Dustin Parker, Third Vice President
John Palka, Fourth Vice President
Jonathan Burkee, Secretary
Justin Stewart, Treasurer

Circuit Visitor:
P. Wenz (1)
P. Koch (2)
T. Jenks (3)
M. Harnack (4)
E. Killian (5)
M. Wait (6)
E. Eichinger (7)
S. Pica (8)
P. Terhune (9)
R. Paul (10)
J. Elmore (11)
D. Sheek (12)
G. Lucas (13)
W. Maggard (14)
P. Curley (15)
L. Bogardus (16)
L. Kastner (17)
J. Harris (18)
M. Hansen (19)
M. Knauss-Behal (20)
T. Gerdes (21)
R. Ross (22)
M. Kessler (23)
N. Schaus (24)
S. Seidler (25)
A. Burke (26)
M. Hoffman (27N)
G. Rachuy (27S)
P. Frank (28)
B. Wellik (29)
A. Stetson (30)

Staff:

Tyler Fewins	District Vice President, LCEF
Maddie Gong	Executive Assistant to the President
Jim Henkell	Ministry Executive
Eun Chu Kim	Superintendent of School Innovation
Xavria Schwarz	Executive Director of School Administration
Cathy Korp	Chief Financial Officer
Aaron Lucas	Director, Communication and IT
Jon Niederbrach	Chief Operating Officer

OFFICERS/STRUCTURE

Archivist: Bruce Benne (District Office)
Church Extension Chairman: James Clark
Congregation Constitutions Chairman: Paul Wenz
Disaster Response: Jason Johnson, Lutheran Church Charities (deployed)
Mission Training Center Director: Jonathan Priest (deployed)
Parish Nursing Representative: Sherri Spicer (deployed)
Prison Ministry: Art Stevens (deployed)

Rocky Mountain

Phone: (303) 695-8001
88 Inverness Cir. E.
Unit A-210
Englewood, CO 80112
Website: www.rm.lcms.org
Office Hours: 8:00 a.m.–4:30 p.m. (Mountain Time)

Officers:
James B. Maxwell, President
Jared Melius, First Vice President
Jason Rust, Second Vice President
Mark Nierman, Third Vice President
Michael Redeker, Fourth Vice President
Eli Lietzau, Secretary

Circuit Visitor:
B. Flamme (1)
G. Roberts (2)
J. Larson (3)
D. Magruder (4)
D. Escue (5)
N. Shults (6)
R. von Steinman (7)
J. Clarke (8)
K. VanFossan (9)
A. Cave (10)
W. Viergutz (11)
T. Norton (12)
J. Kern (13)
R. Wohletz (14)
J. Jacoby (15)
R. Langness (16)
D. Kear (17)

Staff:
Paul Albers — Executive, Congregational Services
Monique Hjalmquist — Administrative Assistant to the District President

Legal Counsel: Kim Seter: 7400 E. Orchard Rd., Ste. 3300, Greenwood Village, CO 80111
Archivist: (Vacant)
District Life Coordinator: (Vacant)

SELC (Non-Geographical District)

Phone: (610) 965-3265 (Church Office) & (484) 951-9441 (Cell)
C/O Concordia Lutheran Church
2623 Brookside Rd.
Macungie, PA 18062
Phone: (610) 392-4927 (Administrative Assistant)
Website: www.selc.lcms.org
Office Hours: 9:00 a.m.–5:00 p.m. (Eastern Time)

Officers:
Waldemar R. Vinovskis, President
Wally Arp, First Vice President
Christopher Cahill, Second Vice President
Jonathan Palmer, Third Vice President
John Telloni, Secretary
Robert Lange, Treasurer
Andrew Dzurovcik, President Emeritus
Carl H. Krueger, President Emeritus

Circuit Visitor:
R. Malec (1)
G. Hansell (2)
(Vacant) (3)
J. Fernandez (4)

Staff:
Irene Bray — Financial Secretary
Rod Jackson — District Education Executive
Patti Gates-Smith — Administrative Assistant to the District President

Legal Counsel: George S. Peek, 411 E. Wisconsin Ave. Suite 1000, Milwaukee, WI 53202
Church Extension Chairman: (Vacant)
Constitutional Review: Larry Schultz, 1566 Bushkill Center Rd., Bath, PA 18014
Continuing Education: Chris Cahill, 656 Wooster St., Lodi, OH 44254
Educational Executive: Rod Jackson, 2025 W. State Rd. 426, Oviedo, FL 32765
Evangelism: Mark C. Larson, 7100 Morganford Rd., St. Louis, MO 63116
LCMS Life Ministries: Ziggy Rein, 13030 Madison Ave., Lakewood, OH 44107
Ministerial Health: Chris Cahill, 656 Wooster St., Lodi, OH 44254
Mission Executive Secretary: Mark C. Larson, 7100 Morganford Rd., St. Louis, MO 63116

Pastoral Representative/Mission Focus: Tige Culbertson, St. Luke's Lutheran Church, 2021 W. State Rd. 426, Oviedo, FL 32765
Stewardship: Mark C. Larson, 7100 Morganford Rd., St. Louis, MO 63116
Student Aid: John Glanzer, 2025 W. State Rd. 426, Oviedo, FL 32765
Youth Group Advisor: Rachel Bublitz, 5127 Romaine Spring Dr., St. Louis, MO 63026

South Dakota

Phone: (605) 361-1514
3501 S. Gateway Blvd.
Sioux Falls, SD 57106-1557
Website: sddlcms.org
Office Hours: 8:30 a.m.–4:30 p.m. (Central Time)

Officers:
Randy Sturzenbecher, President
Matthew Wurm, First Vice President
Corey Aker, Second Vice President
Thomas Brown, Secretary
Kent Harnisch, Treasurer

Circuit Visitor:
J. Smith (1)
T. Rynearson (2)
D. Otten (3)
D. Warner (4)
R. Loeslie (5)
T. Christopher (6)
C. Ascher (7)
S. Weispfennig (8)

Staff:

Lori Hoffman	District President Administrative Assistant
Paul Winckler	Assistant to the President
Chad Zinnel	Business Manager
Kurt Primuth	Vice President, LCEF
Dawn Wombold	Education Executive

Legal Counsel: Matthew Naasz, P.O. Box 8045, Rapid City, SD 57709
Archivist: Bob & Kim Heckmann (District Office)
Congregations Constitutions Chairman: David Otten, 601 E. Logan Ave., Gettysburg, SD 57442
Continuing Education: (Vacant)
Disaster Response: Jeff Summers, 4564 Lahinch St., Rapid City, SD 57702
Lutheran Witness Editor: Kate Meadows, 420 East Liberty, Rapid City, SD 57701

South Wisconsin

Phone: (414) 464-8100
8100 W. Capitol Dr.
Milwaukee, WI 53222-1920
Fax: (414) 464-0602
Website: www.swd.lcms.org
Office Hours: 8:00 a.m.–4:30 p.m. (Central Time)

Officers:
Nathan Meador, President
Eric Skovgaard, First Vice President
John Berg, Second Vice President
Jonah Burakowski, Third Vice President
Daniel Torkelson, Fourth Vice President
Christian Gugel, Secretary
David Begalke, Treasurer

Circuit Visitor:
A. Koch (1)
B. Akers (2)
M. Schleider (3)
S. Voigt (4)
D. Paape (5)
M. Larson (6)
C. Lehenbauer (7)
D. Knuth (8)
M. Eckert (9)
D. Johnson (10)
A. Kretschmar (11)
K. Backhaus (12)
A. Cigelske (13)
R. Schroeder (14)
B. Fritsch (15)
L. Sheppard (16)
N. Rogness (17)
R. Poppe (18)
D. Juhl (19)
A. Strawn (20)
L. O'Donnell (21)
D. Bergelin (22)
C. Seeger (23)
A. Harris (24)
D. Ramirez (25)
J. Gilbert (26)

Staff:

(Vacant)	Superintendent of Schools, Youth & Family
(Vacant)	Mission & Mercy Ministry
Robin Mueller	Administrative Assistant to Schools, Youth, & Family
Karen Rayner	Administrative Assistant to the District President
Paul Reske	Business Manager
Christopher Rowan	District Vice President, LCEF

Legal Counsel: Attorney Thomas Balgeman, 1011 N. Mayfair Rd. Suite 200, Wauwatosa, WI 53226
Congregation Constitutions Chairman: Christian Gugel, 1614 S. 23rd St., Sheboygan, WI 53081

Southeastern

Phone: (703) 971-9371
2305 North Parham Rd., Ste. 200
Henrico, VA 23229
Website: www.se.lcms.org
Office Hours: 8:00 a.m.–4:30 p.m. (Eastern Time)

Officers:
William A. Harmon, President
Lloyd D. Gaines, First Vice President
David Ziehr, Second Vice President
Timothy Bohlmann, Third Vice President
Wayne Fredericksen, Secretary
Ronald L. Adolphi, Treasurer

Circuit Visitor:
M. Thress (1)
B. Sedney (2)
E. Bednash (3)
M. Hilpert (4)
A. Okai (5)
W. Stottlemyer (6)
P. Schiebel (7)
J. Kent (8)
A. Jagow (9A)
M. Shaltanis (9B)
R. Minnix (10)
E. Malmstrom (11)
L. Martin (12)
J. Daub (13E)
M. Merker (13W)
J. Scheuermann (14)
S. Newberg (15)
A. Lagoutine (16)
S. Pennington (17)
J. Engwall (18)
J. Christensen (19)

Staff:

John Denninger	District Gift Planning Counselor
Hannah Gillrup	Director of Communications
Travis Guse	Executive Director of Wellness & Coaching
Esseye Haile	Front Office Manager & Bookkeeper
Yared Halche	Executive Director of Witness
Sidney Heetland	Director of Business & Finance
Sally Hiller	District Disaster Response Coordinator
Kirk Hymes	Director for Stewardship and District Vice President, LCEF
Gina Jordan	Executive Assistant
Allison Klettke	Administrative Assistant to the District President
Thomas W. Kolb	Executive Director of Schools & Youth Ministry
Martin Schultheis	Chief Ministry Officer

Legal Counsel: Timothy Patterson
Archivist: Sally Hiller
Church Extension Chairman: Kirk Hymes (District Office)
Communications/PR Chairperson: Hannah Gillrup (District Office)
Congregation Constitutions Chairman: Robert Coyle
Continuing Education: Lannon Martin
Evangelism: Yared Halche
Family Ministry: Thomas W. Kolb (District Office)
Human Care Chairperson: Sally Hiller (District Office)
Lutheran Witness Editor: Martin Schultheis (District Office)
Ministerial Growth Chairman: Travis Guse (District Office)
Missions Chairman: Yared Halche
Parish Education Chairman: Thomas W. Kolb (District Office)
Stewardship: Kirk Hymes (District Office)
Student Recruitment/Aid Chairman: Sid Heetland (District Office)
Youth Ministry Chairman: Thomas W. Kolb (District Office)

Southern

Phone: (504) 282-2632
100 Mission Dr.
Slidell, LA 70460
Fax: (985) 871-9696
Website: www.southernlcms.org
Office Hours: 8:00 a.m.–5:00 p.m. Monday–Thursday (Central Time)

Officers:
Eric C. Johnson, President
John Bussman, First Vice President
Jerome Terry, Second Vice President
Randal Ehrichs, Third Vice President
Louis Boldt, Fourth Vice President
James Endrihs, Secretary
Patti Young, Treasurer

Circuit Visitor:
P. Sukstorf (1)
R. Rudnik (2)
J. Drosendahl (4)
R. Portier (5)
C. Miller (6)
S. Mazzaferro (7)
D. Waffel (8)
G. Murdaugh (9)
N. Ragazinskas (10)
W. Miller (11)
S. Washington (12)
M. Kocsis (13)
E. Gretarsson (14)
R. Parent (15)

Staff:

David M. Buss	Executive Assistant to District President
Michelle Fischer	Education Executive
Daisy Olmstead	Administrative Assistant to the District President

Legal Counsel: Gerald Cooper
Church Extension Chairman: Allan Parauka
Communications/PR Chairperson: Lisa Miller, l.miller@southernlcms.org
Congregation Constitutions Chairman: Charles Lehman
Lutheran Witness Editor: Ronnie Giaise
Missions Chairman: Jason Scheler (District Office)
Stewardship: (Vacant)
Student Recruitment/Aid Chairman: (Vacant)
Youth Ministry Chairman: Kyle Arnold

Southern Illinois

Phone: (618) 234-4767
2408 Lebanon Ave.
Belleville, IL 62221-2529
Website: sidlcms.org
Office Hours: 8:00 a.m.–4:00 p.m. (Central Time)

Officers:
Heath Curtis, President
Stephen Krenz, First Vice President
Mark Surburg, Second Vice President
Lyle Buettner, Secretary
Gary Hemmer, Treasurer

Circuit Visitor:
C. Prumm (1)
T. Appel (2)
S. Busacker (3)
A. Gray (4)
C. Spelbring (5)
R. Laufer (6)
J. Hennig (7)
E. Wood (8)
D. Kollmeyer (9)
S. Hojnacki (10)
J. Holden (11)

Staff:
Jeff Fick — Schools & General Executive
Elsa Mort — Administrative Assistant to the District President
Scott Radden — Gift Planning Counselor, The LCMS Foundation
Scott Roberts — District Vice President, LCEF
Anna Rowden — Bookkeeper

Congregation Constitutions Chairman: Peter Ill

Missions Chairman: David Schultz

Texas

Phone: (512) 926-4272 or (800) 951-3478
1221 Satellite View
Round Rock, TX 78665
Fax: (512) 926-1006
Website: www.txlcms.org
Office Hours: 8:00 a.m.–4:30 p.m. (Central Time)

Officers:
Jon Braunersreuther, President
John Davis Jr., First Vice President
Larry Krueger, Second Vice President
Nathan Wendorf, Third Vice President
Eric Hiner, Fourth Vice President
Brian Hesse, Secretary
Linda Hagge, Treasurer

Circuit Visitor:
J. Andrajack (1)
S. Misch (2)
E. Stadler (3)
R. Mittelstadt (4)
T. Chandler (5)
S. Brummett (6)
S. Sandfort (7)
P. Terral (8)
G. Beutel (9)
A. Whaley (10)
A. Douthwaite (11)
M. Huston (12)
S. Sundbye (13)
J. Mashburn (14)
H. Smith (15)
J. Thomas (16)
T. Ochsner (17)
M. Nemec (18)
S. Schaller (19)
J. Bontke (20)
R. Mittwede (21)
C. Roth (22)
N. Hill (23)
B. Kachelmeier (24)
E. Giese (25)
T. Winter (26)
M. Carnahan (27)
G. Lorenz (28)
C. Brynestad (29)
M. Dorn (30)
S. Heitshusen (31)
R. Lamb (32)
D. Theimer (33)
J. Knippa (34)
J. Salminen (35)
M. Brackman (36)
J. Moreno (37)
B. Jurischk (38)
G. Johnson (39)
T. Engel (40)

Staff:
David Bahn — Congregation Support Specialist (Area D)
Lisa Candido — External Relations Director
Ben Gonzales — Mission Strategist (B)
Lincon Guerra — Mission & Ministry Facilitator (Area A)
Noemi Guerra — Districtwide Evangelist Development Leader
Cindy Hilewitz — Administrative Assistant to the District President
William V. Hinz — Director of School Ministry
Christina Hobbs — Youth Ministry & Commissioned Minister Specialist
Becca Jones — Church Extension Fund Executive Director
Peter Mueller — Mission Strategist (Area C)
Larry Rietz — Congregation Support Specialist (Area C)
Martin Schardt — Congregation Support Specialist (Area B)
Stephen Sohns — Mission Strategist (Area D)
Andrew Walker — Administrative Assistant to the District President

Archivists: Karen Lacy, Holy Cross, College Station, TX
Church Extension Chairman: Dennis Huffman, Trinity Lutheran Church, Waco, TX
Communications/PR Chair: Lisa Candido (District Office)
Congregation Constitutions Chairman: Christopher Kennedy, Shepherd of the Hills Lutheran Church, San Antonio, TX
Disaster Response: Julie Tucker, Concordia Lutheran Church, San Antonio, TX
Evangelism: Noemi Guerra (District Office)

OFFICERS/STRUCTURE

Lutheran Witness Editor: Lisa Candido (District Office)
Missions Chairperson: Stephanie Knea, Gloria Dei Lutheran Church, Houston, TX
Student Recruitment/Aid Chairperson: Cindy Hilewitz (District Office)
Youth Ministry Chairperson: Christiane Hobbs (District Office)

Wyoming

2400 Hickory St.
Casper, WY 82604
Website: wylcms.org
Office Hours: 8:00 a.m.–5:00 p.m. (Mountain Time)

Officers:
John E. Hill, President
Paul Cain, First Vice President
Jonathan Lange, Second Vice President
Jeffrey Grams, Third Vice President
Zachary Viggers, Secretary
John Schmall, Treasurer

Circuit Visitor:
R. Neugebauer (1)
S. Firminhac (2)
J. Olson (3)
J. Korb (4)
T. Berg (5)
M. Mumme (6)

Staff:

Tiffany Hoff	Office Manager & Administrative Assistant to the President
Andrew Richard	District Education Executive
Jeffrey Snyder	District Vice President, LCEF & Business Manager

Legal Counsel: (Vacant)
Archivist: Tera Rice, 80 Running Dutchman, Glenrock, WY 82037
Church Extension Chairman: Jeffrey Snyder (District Office)
Communications/PR Chairman: (Vacant)
Congregation Constitutions Chairman: Jonathan Lange, 49 Straight & Narrow Dr., Evanston, WY 82930
Congregation Services Chairman: David Bott, P.O. Box 1624, Jackson, WY 83001
Continuing Education: (Vacant)
Education Chairman: Andrew Richard, 2300 Hickory St., Casper, WY 82604
Evangelism: Jon C. Olson, 1240 Missouri, Casper, WY 82609
Marriage, Life & Family Facilitator: Jonathan Lange, 49 Straight & Narrow Dr., Evanston, WY 82930
Missions Chairman: Patrick Baldwin, 1305 Ritter, Rawlins, WY 82301
Stewardship: (Vacant)
Student Recruitment/Aid Chairman: Richard Mueller, P.O. Box 715, Alliance, NE 69301
Youth Ministry Chairman: Zachary Viggers, 4102 Silver Spur Ave., Gillette, WY 82718

TABLE OF ABBREVIATIONS
(Key to Abbreviations)

Missouri Synod Districts

AT = Atlantic
CNH = Calif-Nev-Hawaii
CI = Central Illinois
EA = Eastern
EN = English
FG = Florida-Georgia
IN = Indiana
IE = Iowa East
IW = Iowa West
KS = Kansas
MI = Michigan
MDS = Mid-South
MNN = Minnesota North
MNS = Minnesota South
MO = Missouri
MT = Montana
NEB = Nebraska
NE = New England
NJ = New Jersey
ND = North Dakota
NW = North Wisconsin
NI = Northern Illinois
NOW = Northwest
OH = Ohio
OK = Oklahoma
PSW = Pacific Southwest
RM = Rocky Mountain
S = SELC (Slovak)
SD = South Dakota
SW = South Wisconsin
SE = Southeastern
SO = Southern
SI = Southern Illinois
TX = Texas
WY = Wyoming

Classifications

Commissioned Minister Section

DCE=Commissioned Director of Christian Education
DCO=Commissioned Director of Christian Outreach
DCE/DCO=Commissioned DCE/DCO
DCM=Commissioned Director of Church Ministries
Deaconess=Commissioned Deaconess
Deac/DCM=Commissioned Deaconess/DCM
Deac/Tch=Commissioned Deaconess/Teacher
DFLM= Commissioned Director of Family Life Ministry
DPM=Commissioned Director of Parish Music
Parish Assist=Commissioned Parish Assistant
Parish Assist/DFLM=Commissioned Parish Assistant/DFLM
PC=Partner Church Pastor
Teacher=Commissioned Teacher
Tch/DCE=Commissioned Teacher/DCE
Tch/DCE/DCO=Commissioned Teacher/DCE/DCO
Tch/DPM=Commissioned Teacher/DPM

Position Titles

Assoc=Associate Pastor
Asst=Assistant Pastor
Aux=Auxiliary Ministry
CCRA=Cooperative Church-Related Agency
Cmp P=Campus Pastor
D Ex/S=District Executive or Staff
Df Min=Missionary to the Deaf
D Miss=District Missionary
DP=District President
END=Endorsed by Synod
ExecDir= Executive Director
IndC P=Independent Congregation Pastor
Inst C=Institutional Chaplain
M Chap=Military Chaplain/Dir of Rel Ed
Mem C=Serving a Member Congregation
NILE=National Inter-Lutheran Entity
NMem C=Serving a Non-Member Congregation
O-Miss=Other Missionary
O-Sp Min=Other Special Ministry
P Df=Pastor to Deaf
Prin= Principal Only
Pro Stf=Professional Staff
P/Tchr=Principal and Teacher
RSO=Recognized Service Organization
S Adm=Synodical Administrator
S Ex/S=Synod Executive or Staff
S HS/C=Synod High School/ College/ University/Seminary
S Miss=Synodical Missionary
SMP=Pastor-Specific Ministry
Sn/Adm=Senior or Administrative Pastor
SP= Sole Pastor
Tchr=Teacher

Colleges/Universities/Seminaries/Programs

AA=Concordia, Ann Arbor, MI
AU=Concordia, Austin, TX
BR=Concordia, Bronxville, NY
CH=Concordia University Chicago, River Forest, IL (formerly Concordia River Forest, IL)
CQ=Colloquized
DITSL=Deaf Institute of Theology, St. Louis, MO
ED=Concordia College & Seminary, Edmonton, AB CANADA
EIITSL=Ethnic Immigrant Institute of Theology, St. Louis, MO
FW=Concordia Theological Seminary, Ft. Wayne, IN (formerly Springfield, IL)
FW-D=Concordia Theo Sem DELTO Program, Ft. Wayne, IN
FW-DEAC=Concordia Theo Sem Deaconess Program, Ft. Wayne, IN
FW-SMP=Concordia Theo Sem Specialized Ministry Program, Ft. Wayne, IN
HIT=Hispanic Institute of Theology, River Forest, IL
HITSL=Center for Hispanic Studies, St. Louis, MO
HK=Concordia Seminary, Hong Kong
IV=Concordia, Irvine, CA (formerly Christ College)
KO=Lutheran Seminary, South Korea
MQ=Concordia, Mequon, WI (formerly Milwaukee, WI)
MW=Concordia, Milwaukee, WI
NESC=Concordia Lutheran Theological Seminary, St. Catharines, ON CANADA
Other=Non-Synodical School
PO=Concordia, Portland, OR
RF=Concordia, River Forest, IL
S=Concordia, Seward, NE
SEL=Concordia, Selma, AL
SL=Concordia Seminary, St. Louis, MO
SL-D=Concordia Sem DELTO Program, St. Louis, MO
SL-DEAC=Concordia Sem Deaconess Program, St. Louis, MO
SL-SMP=Concordia Sem Specialized Ministry Program, St. Louis, MO
SP=Concordia, St. Paul, MN
SPR=Concordia Theological Seminary, Springfield, IL
TW=Lutheran Seminary, Taiwan
VB=Concordia Seminary, Villa Ballester, Argentina
WN=St. John College, Winfield, KS

LCMS ROSTER OF CONGREGATIONS

Corrected to September 18, 2025

The following list includes all congregations of The Lutheran Church—Missouri Synod. The legal or corporate name of the congregation is not listed. Only a form of the name is used that briefly identifies a congregation in a locality (example: St John, not Saint John's Lutheran Church). Congregation membership statistics are shown only for congregations that reported in the most recent data collection cycle. Congregations may have more services than are listed. Also included in this list are congregations' satellite worship sites with worship services. Contact the individual congregations for further detailed information or visit the LCMS Website at http://www.lcms.org and select Directories

CITY	CONGREGATION EMAIL WEBSITE	YEAR EST	LOCATION MAILING ADDRESS	ZIP CODE(S)	DIST.	PASTOR(S)	PHONE FAX	WS SS BC	SCHOOLS/ MINISTRIES	STATISTIC Bapt	Conf	Avg Attend
ALABAMA												
ALBERTVILLE	*CHRIST* secchristlutheran@clc35950.org christlutheranal.org	1982	9363 US HIGHWAY 431	35950	SO	Warren J Ruland	(256)891-0608	WS 1030 SS 915	ED/MD	45	43	35
ARLINGTON	*EPIPHANY*	1965	9975 Hwy 5 PO BOX 309	36722	SO	Anthony I Robinson Sr	(334)385-2435	WS 10 1120	ED			
ATMORE	*EBENEZER*	1925	109 Harris St PO BOX 947	36502 36504	SO	Perry L McCullam	(251)368-4719	SS 10	ED/HC	30	30	20
AUBURN	*TRINITY* mail@tlcauburn.org www.tlcauburn.org	1929	446 S GAY ST	36830	SO	Corey J Grunklee	(334)887-3901 (334)887-5937	WS 8 1030 SS 915	ED/HC/ MD/SN	153	101	137
BESSEMER	*ZION*	1951	1201 24th St N PO BOX 589	35020 35021	SO		(205)425-2091 (205)428-1774	WS 8 SS 930	HC	14	14	7
BIRMINGHAM	*FIRST* secretary@firstlutheranbham.org firstlutheranbham.org	1887	2507 HIGHLAND AVE S	35205	SO	Thomas T Presley Kurtis D Schultz	(205)933-0380	WS 1015 SS 9 BC 9	ED/HC/MD	95	90	41
	ST PAUL www.stpaullutheranbham.org	1940	132 6TH AVE S	35205	SO	Dr Piotr J Malysz	(205)324-2063 (205)326-2140	WS 1105 SS 920 BC 920	ED/HC/MD			
	TRINITY jmwyss@uab.edu	1948	1730 SAINT CHARLES AVE SW	35211	SO	Dr James M Wyss	(205)923-6494	WS 1030 SS 930 BC 930	ED/HC/SN	47	44	24
	UNITY unitylutheran@earthlink.net		447 1ST ST N	35204	SO		(205)251-3451	WS 11 SS 1130				
	VESTAVIA HILLS		See Vestavia Hills AL									
CAMDEN	*HOLY CROSS* holycrosscamden1@gmail.com	1925	1883 T L Threadgill Rd Ste 870655 PO BOX 314	36726	SO	Meredith B Jackson	(334)682-9552	WS 1115 SS 10	ED/HC/ MD/SN			
CHICKASAW	*GRACE*		See Mobile AL									
COOSADA	*MESSIAH*		See Prattville AL									
CULLMAN	*ST PAUL* revbussman@stpaulscullman.com stpaulscullman.com/	1885	513 4TH AVE SE	35055	SO	John M Bussman Christopher R Clark	(256)734-3575 (256)734-3540	WS 8 1030 SS 915 BC 915	EL/ED/HC/ MD	558	432	187
DAPHNE	*ASCENSION* ascensionlcms@bellsouth.net ourdaphne.church	1980	8888 COUNTY ROAD 64	36526	SO	Ralph C Hough	(251)626-7500	WS 8 1030 SS 915 BC 915	EC/ED/HC/ MD	111	95	64
	GRACE		See Mobile AL									
DEATSVILLE	*MESSIAH*		See Prattville AL									
DECATUR	*ST PAUL'S* churchoffice@stpaulsdec.com www.stpaulsdec.com	1898	1700 CARRIDALE ST SW	35601	SO	Dr Aaron C Kretzschmar	(256)353-8759	WS 815 1045 SS 930	EC/ED/HC/ MD/SN	409	360	141
DOTHAN	*CHRIST THE KING*		See Enterprise AL									
	TRINITY TrinityDothan@outlook.com www.TrinityLutheranDothan.org	1951	105 LUTHER WAY	36301	SO	Mark D Kocsis	(334)792-9745	WS 945 SS 830	ED/HC/ MD/SN	88	86	48
ELBERTA	*ST MARK* stmarks@gulftel.com www.stmarkslc.com	1908	13220 Main St 13220 N. MAIN STREET	36530	SO	Keith J Ringers	(251)986-8133 (251)986-8134	WS 730 945 SS 845 BC 845	EC/ED/HC/ MD	263	206	96
ENTERPRISE	*CHRIST THE KING* church.office@enterpriselutheran.org www.enterpriselutheran.org	1956	208 E WATTS ST	36330	SO	James E Endrihs	(334)347-6716	WS 1030 SS 9	ED/HC	141	119	59
FAIRHOPE	*ASCENSION*		See Daphne AL									
	CONCORDIA CLCLCMS@ATT.NET	1931	23986-A US HIGHWAY 98	36532	SO	Benjamin F Stallworth Sr	(251)929-2810	WS 12 BC 130	HC	85	74	25
	GRACE		See Mobile AL									
	REDEEMER redeemerfairhope@bellsouth.net redeemerfairhope.org	1949	200 S SECTION ST	36532	SO	William A Parsons III	(251)928-8397 (251)928-8397	WS 730 10 SS 845	ED/HC/ MD/SN	201	185	100
FLORALA	*FIRST* firstlutheranchurchflorala@gmail.com	1955	24512 5TH AVE	36442	SO	Sean R Ballard	(334)858-3515	WS 10 SS 1130	ED/HC/SN	30	30	20
FLORENCE	*OUR REDEEMER* info@our-redeemer-lutheran-church.com www.our-redeemer-lutheran-church.com	1935	630 N POPLAR ST	35630	SO	James L Garnett	(256)764-3902	WS 1030 SS 915 BC 915	HC	82	63	54
FOLEY	*ST PAUL* stpauls.lcms.foley@gmail.com www.stpaulslcms.com	1912	400 N Alston St PO BOX 1603	36535 36536	SO	Ryan A Cramer	(251)943-6931 (251)955-6931	WS 10 SS 830 BC 830	ED/MD/SN	198	169	120
FORT PAYNE	*PRINCE OF PEACE* sites.google.com/site/ princepeacelcms	1993	1519 SMITH GAP RD NW	35968	SO		(256)273-6311	WS 10	ED/HC/SN			
FORT RUCKER	*CHRIST THE KING*		See Enterprise AL									
GADSDEN	*ST PETER*	1962	104 GORDON ST	35903	SO				ED/MD			
	TRINITY tlcgadsden@gmail.com www.tlcgadsden.com	1908	1885 RAINBOW DR	35901	SO	Dr John D Reynolds	(256)546-1712	WS 1040 SS 930	ED/HC/MD	120	106	64
GARDENDALE	*GOOD SHEPHERD* www.gardendalegoodshepherd.org	1979	2456 DECATUR HWY	35071	SO	David C Moerbe Forrest E Brashier Jr	(205)631-6590	WS 9 11 SS 1015	ED/HC/ MD/SN			

*Indicates a new church start. A new church start is an intentionally organized gathering which comes together on a regular basis for the purpose of worship and/or Bible study and is intended to grow into a member LCMS congregation. WS =Worship Service; SS = Sunday School; BC =Bible Class; EC = Early Childhood; EL = Elementary School; HS = High School; ED =Education Ministry; HC =Human Care Ministry; SN = Special Needs Ministry; MD = Media Ministry (PC)=Partner Church Pastor. See Page 53 for the Table of Abbreviations for key to additional abbreviations

CITY	CONGREGATION EMAIL WEBSITE	YEAR EST	LOCATION MAILING ADDRESS	ZIP CODE(S)	DIST.	PASTOR(S)	PHONE FAX	WS SS BC	SCHOOLS/ MINISTRIES	STATISTIC Bapt	Conf	Avg Attend
GRANT	*TRINITY*		See Scottsboro AL									
GULF SHORES	*ST JUDE BY SEA* st.judeslutheranchurch@yahoo.com www.stjudesbythesea.org	1980	312 E 16th St PO BOX 1263	36547	SO	Deral E Rollings	(251)968-JUDE	WS 9 BC 1015	ED/HC/ MD/SN	30	27	52
GUNTERSVILLE	*TRINITY*		See Scottsboro AL									
HANCEVILLE	*TRINITY* trinityhanceville@gmail.com www.trinityhanceville.com	1885	505 COMMERCIAL ST SE	35077	SO	John D Jankens	(256)352-6442	WS 10 SS 845 BC 845	ED/HC/ MD/SN	164	141	74
HARTSELLE	*CHRIST OUR REDEEMER* corhartselle.org	2000	721 Pickens St 721 PICKENS ST SW	35640	SO		(256)773-2121	WS 1030 SS 915 BC 915	HC			
HUNTSVILLE	*ASCENSION* office@ascensionhsv.org www.ascensionhsv.org	1965	3801 OAKWOOD AVE NW	35810	SO	Derek C Waffel	(256)536-9987	WS 8 1045 SS 930 BC 930	EC/ED/MD	316	246	110
	GRACE secretary@gracelutheran-hsv.org www.gracelutheran-hsv.org	1958	3321 S Memorial Pkwy 3321 MEMORIAL PKWY SW	35801	SO	Russ W Gipson Andrew P Frerichs	(256)881-0552 (256)881-0563	WS 8 1045 SS 930 BC 930	EC/EL/ED/ HC/MD/SN	587	434	327
KINGS LANDING	*HOPE*	1924	104 County Road 128 PO BOX 44 SARDIS	36775	SO				ED/HC			
LILLIAN	*RESURRECTION*		See Pensacola FL									
	SHEP OF BAY shepherdofthebay@gmail.com shepherdofthebaylutheranchurch.com	1984	12851 PERDIDO ST	36549	SO		(251)962-7682	WS 9 SS 1030	HC/SN	77	77	45
LOXLEY	*ASCENSION*		See Daphne AL									
MADISON	*FAITH* church.office@faithmadison.org faithmadison.org	1990	660 GILLESPIE RD	35758	SO	Mark A Moldenhauer	(256)830-5600 (256)830-5660	WS 8 1030 BC 915	HC	186	132	132
MARBURY	*MESSIAH*		See Prattville AL									
MILLBROOK	*MESSIAH*		See Prattville AL									
MOBILE	*GRACE* grace@gracelutheranmobile.com gracelutheranmobile.com	1867	1356 GOVERNMENT ST	36604	SO	Wayne J Miller Dennis M Jacobson	(251)433-2749	WS 10 SS 915 BC 1145	ED/HC/MD	210	175	88
	HOLY CROSS church@holycrosslcms.org www.holycrosslcms.org	1959	3900 AIRPORT BLVD	36608	SO		(251)342-8755 (251)342-6934	WS 830 1030 SS 930 BC 930	ED/HC/MD	191	157	106
	MOUNT CALVARY mtcalvary6@att.net	1946	1660 Dominick St PO BOX 6010	36605 36660	SO	Jimmy Mc Cants Jr	(251)471-4200	WS 11 SS 1045 BC 6	ED/HC			
	OUR SAVIOR oslcmobile@gmail.com www.oursavior-mobile.org	1964	5101 GOVERNMENT BLVD	36693	SO		(251)305-3510	WS 930	HC	39	35	23
	REDEEMER		See Fairhope AL									
	TRINITY church@trinitylutheranmobile.org	1951	2668 BERKLEY AVE	36617	SO	Dr Ulmer Marshall Jr	(251)456-7929 (251)456-7909	WS 10 SS 9	EL/ED/HC/ MD	348	212	169
MONTGOMERY	*MESSIAH*		See Prattville AL									
	ST PAUL www.stpaulmontgomery.org	1965	4475 ATLANTA HWY	36109	SO	Carey P Elam James S Richardson	(334)272-6214	WS 8 1030 SS 915	ED/HC/ MD/SN	125	80	83
	UNITED lw0009@bellsouth.net www.ueluth.org	2003	1104 ROSA PARKS AVE	36108	SO	La Vaughn Wiggins	(334)262-4326 (334)263-3183	WS 1030 SS 930	ED/MD			
MUSCLE SHOALS	*CHRIST KING*		See Tuscumbia AL									
NEW BROCKTON	*CHRIST THE KING*		See Enterprise AL									
OAK HILL	*ST PAUL*	1922	4950 Highway 21 PO BOX 73	36766	SO			WS 11 SS 1030				
OZARK	*CHRIST THE KING*		See Enterprise AL									
	PRINCE PEACE www.princeofpeaceozark.org	1957	2454 ANDREWS AVE	36360	SO	Chad M Ingle	(334)774-6758	WS 1030 SS 9	ED/HC/ MD/SN	65	63	40
PINE LEVEL	*MESSIAH*		See Prattville AL									
POINT CLEAR	*BETHEL* bethellutheranch@aol.com bethelutheranchurch.org	1951	6725 County Road 32 PO BOX 337	36564	SO	Dr Ulmer Marshall Jr	(251)928-8327	WS 1	MD	134	69	35
PRATTVILLE	*BETHLEHEM* bethlehemlutheran1922@gmail.com	1922	2738 HIGHWAY 82 W	36067	SO	Jeffrey A Hesterman	(205)365-2088	WS 10 SS 9		51	38	35
	MESSIAH pastor@mymessiahchurch.org www.mymessiahchurch.org	2010	334 OLD FARM LANE S.	36066	SO	Tommy R Lee Sr	(334)290-5215	WS 1030 SS 915 BC 915	ED/HC/MD	65	45	36
PRICHARD	*FAITH* mthrash@swapte.org	1920	P.O. BOX 10369	36610	SO		(251)471-1629 (251)471-1629	WS 11 SS 10	HC/MD/SN			
RAINSVILLE	*TRINITY*		See Scottsboro AL									
ROBERTSDALE	*ASCENSION*		See Daphne AL									
SARALAND	*GRACE*		See Mobile AL									
	HOLY CROSS		See Mobile AL									
SATSUMA	*GRACE*		See Mobile AL									
SCOTTSBORO	*TRINITY* trinitylutheranscottsboro@gmail.com trinitylutheranscottsboro.com	1966	3512 S BROAD ST	35769	SO	Ival L Toepke	(256)574-4927	WS 930 SS 1045 BC 1045	ED/HC/MD	14	13	13
SELMA	*TRINITY* trinitylutheran1900@gmail.com	1924	1900 MARIE FOSTER ST	36703	SO	Steven Washington	(334)526-4455	WS 11 SS 945	ED/HC/ MD/SN	73	62	48
SEMMES	*GRACE*		See Mobile AL									
	HOLY CROSS		See Mobile AL									
SPANISH FORT	*ASCENSION*		See Daphne AL									
	GRACE		See Mobile AL									

*Indicates a new church start. A new church start is an intentionally organized gathering which comes together on a regular basis for the purpose of worship and/or Bible study and is intended to grow into a member LCMS congregation. WS =Worship Service; SS = Sunday School; BC =Bible Class; EC = Early Childhood; EL = Elementary School; HS = High School; ED =Education Ministry; HC =Human Care Ministry; SN = Special Needs Ministry; MD = Media Ministry (PC)=Partner Church Pastor. See Page 53 for the Table of Abbreviations for key to additional abbreviations

CITY	CONGREGATION EMAIL WEBSITE	YEAR EST	LOCATION MAILING ADDRESS	ZIP CODE(S)	DIST.	PASTOR(S)	PHONE FAX	WS SS BC	SCHOOLS/ MINISTRIES	STATISTIC Bapt	Conf	Avg Attend
SPANISH FORT	*HOLY CROSS*		See Mobile AL									
STEVENSON	*TRINITY*		See Scottsboro AL									
THEODORE	*GRACE*		See Mobile AL									
	HOLY CROSS		See Mobile AL									
TUSCALOOSA	*CHRIST*	1948	2901 18TH ST	35401	SO	Anthony I Robinson Sr	(205)752-0108	WS 1030 SS 930	MD	41	39	20
	HOLY CROSS tuscaholycross@aol.com holycrosstuscaloosa.weebly.com	1939	1401 UNIVERSITY BLVD E	35404	SO		(205)553-8004 (205)553-5408	WS 1030 SS 1030 BC 915	ED/HC/MD			
	UNIVERSITY uniluchap@bellsouth.net	1961	911 5TH AVE	35401	SO		(205)752-8784	WS 10 SS 9 BC 9	ED/HC/ MD/SN	28	28	37
TUSCUMBIA	*CHRIST KING* ctklutheran@comcast.net	1959	4801 HIGHWAY 43 S	35674	SO	Charles P Schaum	(256)381-3560 (256)381-3560	WS 1030 SS 915	MD	30	24	16
VESTAVIA HILLS	*VESTAVIA HILLS* lwalter@vestavialutheran.org www.vestavialutheran.org	1959	201 Montgomery Hwy S 201 MONTGOMERY HWY VESTAVIA	35216	SO	Michael D Ahlemeyer	(205)823-1883 (205)823-4549	WS 8 1030 SS 9 BC 9	EC/ED/HC/ MD/SN	560	445	305
VREDENBURGH	*IMMANUEL*	1917	PO BOX 195	36481	SO	Steven Washington	(251)789-2388	WS 1015 SS 1015	ED/HC/MD			
WETUMPKA	*MESSIAH*		See Prattville AL									

ALASKA

CITY	CONGREGATION EMAIL WEBSITE	YEAR EST	LOCATION MAILING ADDRESS	ZIP CODE(S)	DIST.	PASTOR(S)	PHONE FAX	WS SS BC	SCHOOLS/ MINISTRIES	STATISTIC Bapt	Conf	Avg Attend
ANCHORAGE	*ANCHORAGE* office@anchoragelutheran.org www.anchoragelutheran.org	1938	1420 N ST	99501	NOW	David Keddington Albino Y Kong	(907)272-5323	WS 830 11 SS 945 BC 945	EL/HS/ED/ HC/MD/SN	311	245	95
	BEAUTIFUL SAVIOR office@bslc.org www.bslc.org	1984	8100 ARCTIC BLVD	99518	NOW	Erik M Christensen	(907)522-3899 (907)522-3359	WS 830 1030 SS 915 BC 915	EL/HS/ED/ HC/MD			
	OUR REDEEMER		See Chugiak AK									
	ZION zion.anchorage@gmail.com www.zionanchorage.org	1963	2100 BONIFACE PKWY	99504	NOW		(907)338-3838 (907)333-4014	WS 930 BC 11	EL/HS	50	39	23
BIG LAKE	*LAMB OF GOD*		See Wasilla AK									
CHUGIAK	*OUR REDEEMER* office@orlc-ak.org www.orlc-ak.org	1962	18444 Old Glenn Hwy PO BOX 670150	99567	NOW		(907)688-2157	WS 10 SS 9 BC 9	EL/HS/ED/ HC/MD	206	190	107
COLLEGE	*ZION*		See Fairbanks AK									
COOPER LANDING	*COOPER LANDING COMMUNITY CHURCH* Satellite Site of Sterling Sterling AK	1998	37785 Snug Harbor Rd	99752								
COPPER CENTER	*MOUNT DRUM* mdlc907@gmail.com		Silver Springs Loop Rd PO BOX 421	99573	NOW		(907)822-5115 (907)822-5115	WS 11 SS 10	ED/HC	8	8	14
	PRINCESS HOTEL Satellite Site of Mount Drum Copper Center AK	2008	Princess Hotel	99573								
COPPER VALLEY	*MOUNT DRUM*		See Copper Center AK									
EAGLE RIVER	*OUR REDEEMER*		See Chugiak AK									
EIELSON AIR FORCE BASE	*ZION*		See Fairbanks AK									
ESTER	*ZION*		See Fairbanks AK									
FAIRBANKS	*ZION* admin@zionfairbanks.org www.zionfairbanks.org	1959	2982 DAVIS RD	99709	NOW	Andrew J Carlson Sr Scott A Barkdull	(907)456-7660	WS 9 6 SS 1015 BC 1030	EC/ED/HC/ MD/SN	350	300	124
FORT WAINWRIGHT	*ZION*		See Fairbanks AK									
FUNNY RIVER	*FUNNY RIVER*		See Soldotna AK									
GLENNALLEN	*MOUNT DRUM*		See Copper Center AK									
HOMER	*FAITH* office@faithhomer.org faithhomer.org	1970	1000 SOUNDVIEW AVE	99603	NOW		(907)235-7600 (907)235-7660	WS 1030 SS 915	EC/ED/HC/ MD/SN			
	PRINCE OF PEACE SELDOVIA AK Satellite Site of Faith Homer AK	1985	C/O Faith Lutheran Church 1000 Soundview Ave	99603								
HOUSTON	*LAMB OF GOD*		See Wasilla AK									
JUNEAU	*FAITH* faithlutheranjno@gci.net www.faithlutheranjuneau.org	1954	2500 SUNSET DR	99801	NOW	Aaron D Spratt	(907)789-7568	WS 10 SS 845	ED	66	56	34
KASILOF	*STAR OF THE NORTH*		See Kenai AK									
KENAI	*STAR OF THE NORTH* starofthenorthlc@gmail.com www.sotnlc.org	1960	216 N FOREST DR	99611	NOW	Scott L Shields	(907)283-4153	WS 11 SS 930	ED/SN	101	76	56
MEADOW LAKES	*LAMB OF GOD*		See Wasilla AK									
NIKISKI	*STAR OF THE NORTH*		See Kenai AK									
NORTH POLE	*ZION*		See Fairbanks AK									
PALMER	*ST JOHN* admin@stjohnpalmer.org stjohnpalmer.org	1935	440 E Elmwood Ave PO BOX 774	99645	NOW	Jeremy A Davis	(907)745-3338 (907)746-6117	WS 815 11 SS 945	ED/HC/MD	693	445	193
SALCHA	*ZION*		See Fairbanks AK									
SELDOVIA	*FAITH*		See Homer AK									
SOLDOTNA	*FUNNY RIVER* revacarlson@funnyriverlutheran.org funnyriverlutheran.org		35575 RABBIT RUN RD	99669	NOW		(907)262-7434	WS 11 SS 930 BC 930	ED/HC/MD			

*Indicates a new church start. A new church start is an intentionally organized gathering which comes together on a regular basis for the purpose of worship and/or Bible study and is intended to grow into a member LCMS congregation. WS =Worship Service; SS = Sunday School; BC =Bible Class; EC = Early Childhood; EL = Elementary School; HS = High School; ED =Education Ministry; HC =Human Care Ministry; SN = Special Needs Ministry; MD = Media Ministry (PC)=Partner Church Pastor. See Page 53 for the Table of Abbreviations for key to additional abbreviations

CONGREGATIONS

CITY	CONGREGATION EMAIL WEBSITE	YEAR EST	LOCATION MAILING ADDRESS	ZIP CODE(S)	DIST.	PASTOR(S)	PHONE FAX	WS SS BC	SCHOOLS/ MINISTRIES	STATISTIC Bapt	Conf	Avg Attend
SOLDOTNA	*STAR OF THE NORTH*		See Kenai AK									
STERLING	*STAR OF THE NORTH*		See Kenai AK									
	STERLING gpbowen@gci.net	1994	35100 McCall Rd PO BOX 187	99672	NOW		(907)262-9259	WS 11 BC 10	ED/HC/MD	20	19	14
WASILLA	*LAMB OF GOD* loglcms@mtaonline.net loglcms.org	1996	1221 N CHURCH RD	99654	NOW	Eugene A Larmi	(907)357-8077	WS 1030 BC 9	ED/HC/MD	55	46	23
WILLOW	*LAMB OF GOD*		See Wasilla AK									
ARIZONA												
AMADO	*CHRISTUS REX*		See Rio Rico AZ									
ANTHEM	*CROSS OF CHRIST* cathy@anthemcross.org www.anthemcross.org	2003	39808 N GAVILAN PEAK PKWY	85086	PSW	Kevin C Kosberg Martin D Strohschein	(623)551-9851	WS 8 10 SS 10	HS/ED/HC/ MD	566	503	345
APACHE JUNCTION	*FAITH IN ACTION* thoughland@faithinactionaz.org www.faithinactionaz.org	2018	1352 W 15TH LN	85120	PSW		(480)292-0794		ED/HC/MD			
	MOUNTAIN VIEW office@mountainviewlutheran.org www.mountainviewlutheran.org	1979	2122 S GOLDFIELD RD	85119	PSW	Mark D Friedrich	(480)982-8266	WS 8 1030 SS 915 BC 915	ED/HC/ MD/SN	279	233	291
	SHEPHERD OF CANYON		See Gold Canyon AZ									
ASHFORK	*SAVING GRACE*		See Chino Valley AZ									
BEAVER DAM	*MESQUITE*		See Mesquite NV									
BENSON	*PEACE VALLEY* pitv.office@gmail.com www.pitvbenson.org	1981	551 J Six Ranch Rd PO BOX 2467	85602	PSW	Ronald K York	(520)586-3171	WS 930 BC 11	ED/HC/ MD/SN	53	25	42
BUCKEYE	*LIVING WATER* office@livingwateraz.org www.LivingWaterAZ.org	2009	1495 S Verrado Way 1131 S 225TH LN	85326	PSW		(623)266-1835	WS 10 SS 10 BC 830	ED/HC/MD			
	SUMMIT COMMUNITY Office@summitcc.org www.summitcc.org	2003	20555 W ROOSEVELT ST	85326	PSW	Nathan E Schaus	(623)535-0251 (623)535-6605	WS 9 1045 SS 9 1045	ED/HC/MD	968	812	863
BULLHEAD CITY	*ST JOHN* office@stjohnbullhead.church stjohnbullhead.church	1974	1664 CENTRAL AVE	86442	PSW	Daniel J Chrismer Sr	(928)758-2301	WS 8 11 SS 930 BC 915	ED/HC/ MD/SN	323	273	131
CAREFREE	*DESERT FOOTHILLS*		See Scottsdale AZ									
CASA GRANDE	*TRINITY* churchoffice@tlcscg.org www.tlcscg.org	1964	1515 N TREKELL RD	85122	PSW	Jonathan R Burkee	(520)836-2451	WS 845 11	EC/ED/HC/ MD	218	218	210
CATALINA	*CATALINA*		See Tucson AZ									
CAVE CREEK	*DESERT FOOTHILLS*		See Scottsdale AZ									
CHANDLER	*EPIPHANY* info@epiphanychandler.org www.epiphanychandler.org	1964	800 W RAY RD	85225	PSW	Mark W Rossington	(480)963-6105 (480)963-6170	WS 830 11 SS 945 BC 945	ED/HC/ MD/SN	256	223	156
	RISEN SAVIOR info@risensavioraz.org www.risensavioraz.org	1992	23914 S ALMA SCHOOL RD	85248	PSW	Ronald D Burcham Dr Kevin W Austin	(480)895-6782 (480)718-8252	WS 8 9 930 1030 11 1130 SS 1030 BC 915	EC/ED/HC/ MD/SN	1607	1317	946
CHINO VALLEY	*SAVING GRACE* sglcvaz@gmail.com savinggracelutherancvaz.org	2006	440 W Palomino Rd PO BOX 721	86323	PSW	Michael J Dueppen	(928)636-9533	WS 10 BC 1130	ED/HC/ MD/SN	39	39	22
	SHEPHERD HILLS		See Prescott AZ									
CLARKDALE	*ROCK OF AGES*		See Sedona AZ									
COOLIDGE	*CHRIST* pastorclc@hotmail.com christlutherancoolidge.com	1958	615 W Vah Ki Inn Rd PO BOX 632	85128	PSW	Mark J Hoffmann	(520)723-7428	WS 9	ED/HC/ MD/SN	129	99	72
CORDES LAKES	*MOUNTAIN OF FAITH* mtnoffaithcdl@outlook.com	1990	20135 E STAGECOACH TRL	86333	PSW		(928)821-3703	WS 9 BC 1030	ED/HC/MD	18	18	15
COTTONWOOD	*FAITH* cottonwoodlutheran@netzero.com cottonwoodfaithlutheran.org	1970	2021 E Fir St PO BOX 3732	86326	PSW	Karl E Schloeman	(928)634-7876	WS 9 SS 1045 BC 1045	EC/ED/ HC/SN	155	146	65
	ROCK OF AGES		See Sedona AZ									
DESERT FOOTHILLS	*DESERT FOOTHILLS*		See Scottsdale AZ									
DEWEY	*SHEPHERD HILLS*		See Prescott AZ									
FLAGSTAFF	*PEACE* plcflagstaff@gmail.com www.peacelutheranflagstaff.org	1965	3430 N 4th St 3430 NORTH FOURTH ST	86004	PSW	William M Weiss Jr	(928)526-9578	WS 10 BC 1130	ED/HC/ MD/SN	55	52	50
FOUNTAIN HILLS	*TRINITY* www.tlcfhaz.org	1992	13770 N Fountain Hills Blvd PO BOX 17270 FOUNTAIN HLS	85268 85269	PSW	John R Koczman	(480)837-0130 (480)837-7453	WS 930 BC 1045	ED/HC/ MD/SN	180	180	102
GILBERT	*CHRIST GREENFIELD* jgerhauser@cglchurch.org christgreenfield.church	1980	425 N GREENFIELD RD	85234	PSW	Timothy P Ahlman Jeffrey W Sutherlin Michael L Heiden	(480)892-8521 (480)503-0437	WS 730 9 1045 SS 9 BC 9	EC/EL/HS/ ED/HC/ MD/SN	2341	1969	827
	SAVING GRACE		See Queen Creek AZ									
GLENDALE	*ATONEMENT* church@atonementlc.org www.atonementlc.org	1979	4001 W BEARDSLEY RD	85308	PSW	Daniel J Larson Jais H Tinglund	(623)582-8785 (623)587-8512	WS 8 1030 SS 915 BC 915	EL/HS/ED/ HC/MD/SN	427	367	191
	MOUNT ZION		See Peoria AZ									
GOLD CANYON	*MOUNTAIN VIEW*		See Apache Junction AZ									

*Indicates a new church start. A new church start is an intentionally organized gathering which comes together on a regular basis for the purpose of worship and/or Bible study and is intended to grow into a member LCMS congregation. WS =Worship Service; SS = Sunday School; BC =Bible Class; EC = Early Childhood; EL = Elementary School; HS = High School; ED =Education Ministry; HC =Human Care Ministry; SN = Special Needs Ministry; MD = Media Ministry (PC)=Partner Church Pastor. See Page 53 for the Table of Abbreviations for key to additional abbreviations

CITY	CONGREGATION EMAIL WEBSITE	YEAR EST	LOCATION MAILING ADDRESS	ZIP CODE(S)	DIST.	PASTOR(S)	PHONE FAX	WS SS BC	SCHOOLS/ MINISTRIES	STATISTIC Bapt	Conf	Avg Attend
GOLD CANYON	*SHEPHERD OF CANYON* office@shepherdofthecanyon.org shepherdofthecanyon.org		6499 S KINGS RANCH RD SUITE 13	85118	EN	Dr Mark A Wood	(623)396-5262	WS 1045 BC 945				
GRAYHAWK	*DESERT FOOTHILLS*		See Scottsdale AZ									
GREEN VALLEY	*RISEN SAVIOR* www.risen-savior.com	1964	555 S LA CANADA DR	85614	EN	Todd W Arnold Nicholas D Wirtz	(520)625-2612 (520)625-2635	WS 9 BC 1030	ED/HC/ MD/SN	242	233	140
GREER	*SHEP MOUNTAINS*		See Pinetop AZ									
KINGMAN	*GOOD SHEPHERD* gslc1955@gmail.com www.goodshepherdlckingman.org	1986	3958 N BANK ST	86409	PSW	Timothy A Barkett	(928)757-3525	WS 10	ED/HC/MD	75	71	54
LAKE HAVASU CITY	*LAMB OF GOD* office.loglhcaz@gmail.com lambofgodlhcaz.org	1998	2791 INCA DR LK HAVASU CTY	86406	PSW	Leonard R Nizinski	(928)854-7170 (928)854-7172	WS 9 BC 1030	ED/HC/ MD/SN	128	98	128
LAKESIDE	*SHEP MOUNTAINS*		See Pinetop AZ									
LITCHFIELD PARK	*TRINITY* rbolte@trinitylc.org www.trinitylcs.org	1980	830 E PLAZA CIR LITCHFIELD PK	85340	PSW	David J Bolte	(623)935-4665 (623)935-5540	WS 730 9 1015 1130 6 SS 1015 BC 845 1015	EL/HS/ED/ HC/MD/SN			
MARANA	*ALIVE IN CHRIST* aliveinchristmarana@gmail.com www.aliveinchristmarana.org	2016	Dove Mountain CSTEM K-8 5650 W. Moore Road PO BOX 90685 TUCSON	85658 85752	PSW	Justin W Wixon	(520)401-3989	WS 9 SS 1015 BC 1015	ED/HC/ MD/SN	69	65	34
	ASCENSION		See Tucson AZ									
	CATALINA		See Tucson AZ									
MARICOPA	*RISEN SAVIOR*		See Chandler AZ									
MAYER	*MOUNTAIN OF FAITH*		See Cordes Lakes AZ									
MESA	*CHRIST GREENFIELD*		See Gilbert AZ									
	CHRIST GREENFIELD | EAST MESA Satellite Site of Christ Greenfield Gilbert AZ	2020	9737 East Toledo Avenue	85212				WS 9 SS 9				
	ETERNAL LIFE office@eternallifelutheran.org www.eternallifelutheran.org	1964	50 S JEFFERSON AVE	85208	EN	Brian T Crane Robert M Doughty III	(480)985-0224 (480)985-2393	WS 9 SS 1045 BC 1045	ED/HC/ MD/SN	135	113	95
	HOSANNA info@hosanna-lcms.com www.hosanna-lcms.com	1988	9601 E BROWN RD	85207	PSW	Paul J Frank	(480)984-1414 (480)984-7839	WS 8 1030 SS 930 BC 930	EC/ED/HC/ MD	391	311	175
	LA MESA Satellite Site of Christ Greenfield Gilbert AZ	2014	805 N Country Club	85201								
	MOUNTAIN VIEW		See Apache Junction AZ									
	SAVING GRACE		See Queen Creek AZ									
	ST LUKE office@stlukemesa.com www.stlukemesa.com	1961	807 N STAPLEY DR	85203	PSW	Luke N Hennings	(480)969-4414 (480)969-4801	WS 8 1030 SS 930 BC 930	ED/HC/ MD/SN	422	348	338
NOGALES	*CHRISTUS REX*		See Rio Rico AZ									
ORO VALLEY	*ASCENSION*		See Tucson AZ									
	CATALINA		See Tucson AZ									
OVERGAARD	*FAITH* church@faithlutheranovergaard.org faithlutheranovergaard.org	1993	2750 Mogollon Dr PO BOX 683	85933	EN	Rodney L Schmeltz	(928)535-9575	WS 1030 BC 9	ED/MD	37	29	24
PAGE	*SHEPHERD OF DESERT* pageazlcms@gmail.com www.pageazlutherans.com	1957	331 S Lake Powell Blvd PO BOX 343	86040	RM	Thomas P Henkes	(928)645-0078	WS 10	EC/ED/HC/ MD			
PARADISE VALLEY	*ST MARK*		See Phoenix AZ									
PARKER	*MESSIAH* messiahchurch@earthlink.net www.azmessiahlutheran.org	1959	800 S Mohave Ave PO BOX 1576	85344	EN		(928)669-8964 (928)669-8964	WS 10 BC 9				
PAULDEN	*SAVING GRACE*		See Chino Valley AZ									
PAYSON	*SHEP OF THE PINES* sotppayson@gmail.com www.shepherdofthepineslutheran.com	1985	507 W WADE LN	85541	EN		(928)474-5440 (928)472-1125	WS 10 SS 830 BC 9	ED/HC			
PEORIA	*APOSTLES* secretary.apostles@phxcoxmail.com www.apostles-az.org	1979	7020 W CACTUS RD	85381	PSW	Andrew K Byars Ramon Cabrales	(623)979-3497 (623)979-5778	WS 8 11 SS 11 BC 930	ED/HC/MD	174	115	92
	LIFE IN CHRIST officeadmin@licl.org www.licl.org	2004	14802 N 75TH AVE	85381	PSW	Christopher D Crume	(623)773-1234 (623)776-2944	WS 8 11 BC 930	HS/ED/HC/ MD/SN	358	254	215
	MOUNT ZION office@mtzionaz.com www.mtzionaz.com	1996	8902 W DEER VALLEY RD	85382	PSW	Mark P Brown	(623)825-9221 (623)825-6021	WS 9 SS 1030 BC 1030	ED/HC/ MD/SN	129	122	85
PHOENIX	*ATONEMENT*		See Glendale AZ									
	CHRIST christchurch@cclphoenix.org www.cclphoenix.org	1953	3901 E INDIAN SCHOOL RD	85018	PSW	Dr Jeffery T Schrank David R Schmidt Andrew J Wilson	(602)955-4830 (602)955-8073	WS 8 830 1030 1045 SS 940 BC 940	EL/HS/ED/ HC/MD			
	CHRIST REDEEMER ctrlutheran@ctr.phxcoxmail.com www.ctrlutheran.org	1969	8801 N 43RD AVE	85051	PSW		(623)934-3286 (623)934-3298	WS 9 SS 1030 BC 1030	HS/ED/HC			
	DESERT FOOTHILLS		See Scottsdale AZ									
	FAMILY OF CHRIST church@familyofchristlutheranaz.org FamilyofChristLutheranAZ.org	1989	3501 E CHANDLER BLVD	85048	EN	Fred H Gerlach	(480)759-4047 (480)759-9004	WS 930	EC/ED/HC			

*Indicates a new church start. A new church start is an intentionally organized gathering which comes together on a regular basis for the purpose of worship and/or Bible study and is intended to grow into a member LCMS congregation. WS =Worship Service; SS = Sunday School; BC =Bible Class; EC = Early Childhood; EL = Elementary School; HS = High School; ED =Education Ministry; HC =Human Care Ministry; SN = Special Needs Ministry; MD = Media Ministry (PC)=Partner Church Pastor. See Page 53 for the Table of Abbreviations for key to additional abbreviations

CONGREGATIONS

CITY	CONGREGATION EMAIL WEBSITE	YEAR EST	LOCATION MAILING ADDRESS	ZIP CODE(S)	DIST.	PASTOR(S)	PHONE FAX	WS SS BC	SCHOOLS/ MINISTRIES	STATISTIC Bapt	Conf	Avg Attend
PHOENIX	*MOUNT CALVARY* khellwig@vlhs.org www.mclcphx.org	1950	5105 N 7TH AVE	85013	PSW	Kurt W Hellwig	(602)230-1600 (602)263-0403	WS 10 BC 9	HS/ED/HC/ MD	73	64	60
	MOUNTAIN VIEW		See Apache Junction AZ									
	OROMO dserba07@gmail.com		3901 E Indian School Rd 8801 N 43RD AVE	85018 85051	PSW		(480)742-8954		ED/HC/MD	86	47	45
	ST MARK church@hopephx.com www.stmarkphx.org	1967	3030 E THUNDERBIRD RD	85032	PSW	Michael B Sheldon Timothy S Duerr	(602)992-1980 (602)992-7125	WS 8 930 11 SS 1030	EC/ED/HC/ MD/SN	576	497	317
	ST PAUL info@stpaullutheran-az.com www.stpaullutheran-az.com	1959	6301 W INDIAN SCHOOL RD	85033	PSW		(623)846-2228 (623)846-1851	WS 930 SS 11 BC 11	MD	104	84	38
	THE MASTER lcomaz@yahoo.com www.lcomaz.org	1962	2340 W CACTUS RD	85029	PSW	Jacob D Wampfler	(602)997-7439 (602)674-0232	WS 9 SS 1030 BC 1030	ED/HC/MD	50	48	26
	TRINITY		See Litchfield Park AZ									
	WORD OF LIFE		See Surprise AZ									
PINETOP	*SHEP MOUNTAINS* shepherdpinetop@gmail.com www.shepherdofthemountains.com	1979	2035 S PENROD LN	85935	EN	Michael W Mathews	(928)367-1183	WS 1030 SS 915 BC 915	ED	66	63	58
PRESCOTT	*SAVING GRACE*		See Chino Valley AZ									
	SHEPHERD HILLS office@prescottshepherd.org www.prescottshepherd.org	1978	1202 GREEN LN STE A	86305	PSW	Adam M Burke	(928)778-9122 (928)778-6952	WS 930 BC 11	ED/HC/ MD/SN	114	98	78
PRESCOTT VALLEY	*SAVING GRACE*		See Chino Valley AZ									
	SHEPHERD HILLS		See Prescott AZ									
	TRINITY tlcofpv@gmail.com www.tlcpv.360unite.com/home	1972	3950 N VALORIE DR PRESCOTT VLY	86314	PSW		(928)772-8845 (928)772-2455	WS 8 11 SS 930 BC 930	EC/ED/HC/ MD/SN	126	126	68
QUEEN CREEK	*SAVING GRACE* info@savinggracelc.org www.savinggracelc.org	2002	24414 S ELLSWORTH RD	85142	PSW	Timothy A Lawson Ryan N Golden	(480)888-9673	WS 830 10 SS 945	EC/HC/SN	348	348	305
QUEEN VALLEY	*SHEPHERD OF CANYON*		See Gold Canyon AZ									
RIMROCK	*GRACE COMMUNITY*	1996	5100 N Stevenson Dr PO BOX 1078	86335	PSW			WS 1030 BC 10	ED/HC/SN	33	31	19
RIO RICO	*CHRISTUS REX* Pastor@ChristusRexLutheran.org www.ChristusRexLutheran.org	1970	282 Rio Rico Dr PO BOX 4070	85648	EN		(520)243-0284	WS 9 BC 1015	ED			
RIO VERDE	*DESERT FOOTHILLS*		See Scottsdale AZ									
SADDLEBROOKE	*CATALINA*		See Tucson AZ									
SAFFORD	*OUR SAVIOR* www.oursaviorchurch.net	2008	1124 Thatcher Blvd Suite 200 860 W MOHAWK DR	85546	PSW		(928)428-7262	WS 10	ED/HC/MD			
SAHUARITA	*CROSSPOINT* admin@crosspointlutheranchurch.org www.crosspointlutheranchurch.org	2011	2285 E SAHUARITA RD	85629	EN	Jason J Hong	(520)977-2638	WS 9 SS 1015 BC 1015	ED/HC	75	60	43
SAN TAN VALLEY	*MOUNTAIN VIEW*		See Apache Junction AZ									
	SAVING GRACE		See Queen Creek AZ									
SCOTTSDALE	*DESERT FOOTHILLS* officeadmin@dflc.org www.dflc.org	1995	29305 N SCOTTSDALE RD	85266	PSW	Dr Mark K McCrory Jeremy J DaPena	(480)585-8007	WS 830 1030	EC/ED/HC/ MD/SN	524	487	254
	HOLY CROSS churchoffice@scottsdaleholycross.org www.scottsdaleholycross.org	1960	3110 N HAYDEN RD	85251	PSW	Jon A Bjorgaard	(480)994-4848 (480)994-5004	WS 9 1045 BC 1030	ED/HC/ MD/SN	137	127	265
	SCOTTSDALE VILLAGE SQUARE Satellite Site of Holy Cross Scottsdale AZ	2024	2620 N. 68th Street	85257								
	SHEPHERD DESERT info@sotdaz.org www.shepherdaz.church	1978	9590 E SHEA BLVD	85260	PSW	Dr Scott K Seidler John D Karolus Alan P Rosnau	(480)860-1188 (480)860-4152	WS 8 930 BC 930	EC/HS/ED/ HC/MD/SN	1055	887	433
	SHEPHERD OF THE DESERT LUTHERAN CHURCH Satellite Site of Shepherd Desert Scottsdale AZ	2010	9400 E Mountain View Rd	85258				WS 930 SS 930				
	THE SPRINGS Satellite Site of Holy Cross Scottsdale AZ	2023	3212 N Miller Rd	85251								
	WESTMINSTER VILLAGE Satellite Site of Holy Cross Scottsdale AZ	2023	12000 N 90th St	85260								
SEDONA	*ROCK OF AGES* info@sedonalcms.org www.sedonalcms.org	1989	390 DRY CREEK RD	86336	PSW		(928)282-4091 (928)282-5660	WS 9	EC/ED/HC/ MD/SN			
SELIGMAN	*SAVING GRACE*		See Chino Valley AZ									
SHOW LOW	*SHEP MOUNTAINS*		See Pinetop AZ									
SIERRA VISTA	*IMMANUEL* sec@grace2u.org www.grace2u.org	1984	2145 S CORONADO DR	85635	PSW	Gary M Brown	(520)458-3883 (520)458-3883	WS 930 SS 11 BC 11	ED/HC/ MD/SN	227	188	130
SNOWFLAKE	*SHEP MOUNTAINS*		See Pinetop AZ									
SUN CITY	*FOUNTAIN OF LIFE* execsecretary@suncitylutheran.org www.suncitylutheran.org	1966	15630 N DEL WEBB BLVD	85351	PSW		(623)933-8246 (623)876-0190	WS 10	HC/MD/SN	170	170	141
	MOUNT ZION		See Peoria AZ									

*Indicates a new church start. A new church start is an intentionally organized gathering which comes together on a regular basis for the purpose of worship and/or Bible study and is intended to grow into a member LCMS congregation. WS =Worship Service; SS = Sunday School; BC =Bible Class; EC = Early Childhood; EL = Elementary School; HS = High School; ED =Education Ministry; HC =Human Care Ministry; SN = Special Needs Ministry; MD = Media Ministry (PC)=Partner Church Pastor. See Page 53 for the Table of Abbreviations for key to additional abbreviations

CITY	CONGREGATION EMAIL WEBSITE	YEAR EST	LOCATION MAILING ADDRESS	ZIP CODE(S)	DIST.	PASTOR(S)	PHONE FAX	WS SS BC	SCHOOLS/ MINISTRIES	STATISTIC Bapt	Conf	Avg Attend
SUN CITY WEST	*CROWN OF LIFE* office@colchurch.com www.colchurch.com	1986	13131 W SPANISH GARDEN DR	85375	PSW		(623)546-6228 (623)975-2329	WS 9 BC 1015	ED/HC/MD	679	673	415
SUN LAKES	*RISEN SAVIOR*		See Chandler AZ									
SURPRISE	*WORD OF LIFE* finance@wordoflifeaz.org www.wordoflifeaz.org	2002	17525 W BELL RD	85374	PSW	Dr David W Martin	(623)544-3000	WS 8 945 SS 945	EC/ED/MD	284	250	148
TATUM RANCH	*DESERT FOOTHILLS*		See Scottsdale AZ									
TEMPE	*BEAUTIFUL SAVIOR* office@beautifulsaviortempe.org www.beautifulsaviortempe.org	1960	1337 W 11TH ST	85281	PSW	Timothy W Anderson	(480)967-2660	WS 10 SS 10 BC 830	ED/HC/ MD/SN	56	56	44
	CONNECTING INTERNATIONAL COMMUNITIES Satellite Site of Beautiful Savior Tempe AZ	2011	1034 S Mill Ave	85281				BC 6				
	GETHSEMANE info@gctempe.org gctempe.org	1973	1035 E GUADALUPE RD	85283	PSW		(480)839-0906 (480)839-8876	WS 8 10 SS 10 BC 915	EC/ED/HC/ MD	575	347	273
	TEMPE TABLE Satellite Site of Christ Greenfield Gilbert AZ	2022	1337 W 11th Street	85281								
TERRAVITA	*DESERT FOOTHILLS*		See Scottsdale AZ									
TUBAC	*CHRISTUS REX*		See Rio Rico AZ									
TUCSON	*AFRIA COMPANNA DEL RIO INDEPENDENT* Satellite Site of Ascension Tucson AZ	2017	1550 E River Rd	85718				WS 5				
	AMBER LIGHTS ASSISTED Satellite Site of Ascension Tucson AZ	2017	6231 N Montebella Rd	85704				WS 3				
	ASCENSION receptionist@alcs-az.org www.ascensiontucson.org	1961	1220 W MAGEE RD	85704	EN	Thomas P Braun Samuel M St John Stephen W Martin	(520)297-3095 (520)742-4781	WS 830 1031 SS 935 BC 935	EC/ED/HC/ MD/SN	512	418	263
	ASSISTED FOUNTAIN AT LA CHOLLA Satellite Site of Ascension Tucson AZ	2017	2001 W Rudasill Rd	85704				WS 130				
	CATALINA office@catalinalutheran.org www.catalinalutheran.org	1982	15855 N TWIN LAKES DR	85739	EN	Dr Michael A Morehouse Bruce J von Hindenburg	(520)825-9255	WS 9 5 SS 1030 BC 1030	ED/HC/ MD/SN	200	156	112
	COPPER CAYON SPECIAL CARE CENTER Satellite Site of Ascension Tucson AZ	2013	5901 N Lacholla Blvd	85741								
	CROSS AND CROWN crossandcrowntucson@gmail.com crossandcrowntucson.org	2019	2435 E 17TH ST	85719	PSW	Joshua S Palmer Colter A Knippa	(520)222-7453	WS 1030 SS 12		162	117	121
	FAITH churchoffice@faith-lutheran.org www.faithlutherantucson.org	1949	3925 E 5TH ST	85711	EN	M T Zill	(520)326-2262 (520)325-5625	WS 9 BC 1015	EL/ED/HC/ MD/SN			
	FOUNTAIN OF LIFE receptionist@follutheran.org FOLLutheran.org	1958	710 S KOLB RD	85710	PSW	William R Hartley	(520)747-1213 (520)747-9444	WS 8 1015 SS 1030 BC 1030	ED/HC/ MD/SN	371	322	177
	HOLY TRINITY holytrinitytucson@gmail.com holytrinitytucson.org	1961	5975 W WESTERN WAY CIR SUITES 117-118	85713	EN		(520)294-8851	WS 9 BC 1015	HC/MD/SN			
	IGLESIA LUTERANA SANTA TRINIDAD Satellite Site of Faith Tucson AZ	2021	3925 E. 5th St.	85711				WS 1030				
	KATALING VILLAGE ASSISTED Satellite Site of Ascension Tucson AZ	2017	5324 E 1st St	85711								
	LA ROSA SENIOR RETIREMENT ASSISTED LIVING COMMUNITY Satellite Site of Ascension Tucson AZ	2012	7500 N Calle San Envidia	85704								
	MESSIAH lpesala@msn.com	1990	1220 W Magee Rd PO BOX 262 CORTARO	85704 85652	EN	Luther P Esala	(520)401-7849 (520)579-7140	WS 915 SS 930 BC 1030				
	MOUNT OLIVE ChurchMTO@gmail.com www.mountolivetucson.com	1972	2005 S HOUGHTON RD	85748	EN	Isaac H Wirtz	(520)298-0996	WS 10 SS 9 BC 9	ED/HC/ MD/SN	96	80	72
	MOUNTAIN VIEW CARE CENTER Satellite Site of Ascension Tucson AZ	2012	1313 W Magee Rd	85704								
	MT VIEW RETIREMENT VILLAGE Satellite Site of Ascension Tucson AZ	2017	7900 N LaCanada	85704								
	SPLENDIDO AT RANCHO VISTOSO Satellite Site of Ascension Tucson AZ	2011	13500 N Rancho vistoso	85755				WS 930				
	SUNRISE SENIOR LIVING MEMORY Satellite Site of Ascension Tucson AZ	2017	4971 N 1st Ave	85718								

*Indicates a new church start. A new church start is an intentionally organized gathering which comes together on a regular basis for the purpose of worship and/or Bible study and is intended to grow into a member LCMS congregation. WS =Worship Service; SS = Sunday School; BC =Bible Class; EC = Early Childhood; EL = Elementary School; HS = High School; ED =Education Ministry; HC =Human Care Ministry; SN = Special Needs Ministry; MD = Media Ministry (PC)=Partner Church Pastor. See Page 53 for the Table of Abbreviations for key to additional abbreviations

CITY	CONGREGATION EMAIL WEBSITE	YEAR EST	LOCATION MAILING ADDRESS	ZIP CODE(S)	DIST.	PASTOR(S)	PHONE FAX	WS SS BC	SCHOOLS/ MINISTRIES	STATISTIC Bapt	Conf	Avg Attend
VAIL	*CHRIST* info@christlutheranvail.org www.christlutheranvail.org	2006	14600 E COLOSSAL CAVE RD	85641	PSW	David J Hook	(520)468-7075 (520)254-6021	WS 9 SS 9 BC 10	EL/ED/HC/ MD	218	194	137
VILLAGE OF OAK CREEK	*ROCK OF AGES*		See Sedona AZ									
WICKENBURG	*REDEEMER* wickenburgredeemer@gmail.com wickenburgredeemer.org	1962	450 ROSE LN	85390	PSW	Vincent W Barringer	(928)684-2729	WS 10 BC 830	ED/HC/ MD/SN	102	83	76
WILLIAMS	*SAVING GRACE*		See Chino Valley AZ									
YUMA	*CALVARY* calvarylutheranyuma@gmail.com www.calvary-lutheran.com	1931	711 S 7TH AVE	85364	PSW	Michael E Kessler	(928)783-3024 (772)325-0310	WS 9 BC 1030	ED/MD			
	CHRIST churchoffice@christyuma.org www.ChristYuma.org	1965	2555 S ENGLER AVE	85365	PSW	Vincent R Harman	(928)726-0773 (928)726-6674	WS 8 10 SS 10 BC 930	EL/ED/HC/ MD/SN	805	554	210
	SHEP OF THE HILLS sothyuma@gmail.com www.sothyuma.org	2002	11201 E 38TH PL	85367	PSW	Jonathan R Stites	(928)345-9694	WS 930 BC 815	ED/HC/MD	79	79	88
				ARKANSAS								
ALEXANDER	*IMMANUEL*	1880	15224 S Alexander Rd PO BOX 119	72002	MDS	Steven W Teske		WS 9 BC 1015		35	19	10
ASH FLAT	*SHEPHERD HILLS*		See Horseshoe Bend AR									
AVILLA	*ZION* zionlutheranavilla.org	1882	300 AVILLA E ALEXANDER	72002	MDS	Willie T Grills	(501)408-4630	WS 9 SS 1030 BC 1030	ED/HC/ MD/SN	320	290	109
AVOCA	*HOLY TRINITY*		See Rogers AR									
BATESVILLE	*HOPE* batesvillehopelutheran@gmail.com www.hopelutheranbatesville.org	1972	2415 E MAIN ST	72501	MDS	Gerald D Heinecke	(870)793-3078	WS 1045 SS 945	ED/HC/SN	79	62	45
BELLA VISTA	*BELLA VISTA* office@bvlutheran.com www.bvlutheran.com	1989	1990 FOREST HILLS BLVD	72715	MDS	Dr Paul E Hass Christopher L Gorshe	(479)855-0272 (479)876-6097	WS 830 1045 SS 945 BC 945	ED/HC/MD	613	562	344
BENTON	*FIRST* jburns7165@sbcglobal.net www.flcbenton.com	1960	18181 Hwy I-30 18181 INTERSTATE 30 S	72015	MDS	James D Burns	(501)231-8329	WS 10 SS 9	ED/MD	98	89	64
BENTONVILLE	*FAITH* office@faithbentonville.com www.faithbentonville.com	1976	1602 NW 12TH ST	72712	MDS	David P Schmidt	(479)273-9419 (479)271-7532	WS 1015 SS 9 BC 9	ED/HC/MD	158	109	89
	HOLY TRINITY		See Rogers AR									
	LIVING SAVIOR		See Springdale AR									
BLYTHEVILLE	*FIRST* bp_hanson@bellsouth.net	1929	108 N 6th St PO BOX 573	72315 72316	MDS		(251)454-1169	WS 1030	HC/MD/SN			
	FIRST LUTHERAN CHURCH Satellite Site of All Saints Jonesboro AR	2025	108 N 6th St	72315								
BRINKLEY	*OUR SAVIOR*	1951	11935 Hwy 49 S 11935 HIGHWAY 49	72021	MDS	Jeremy T McDonald		WS 1 SS 2		17	17	12
BROOKLAND	*ALL SAINTS*		See Jonesboro AR									
BRYANT	*FOX RIDGE* Satellite Site of Friends In Christ BRYANT AR	2007	4216 Fox Ridge Dr	72022				WS 230				
	FRIENDS IN CHRIST emilwoerner63@gmail.com	1999	4305 HIGHWAY 5 N	72022	MDS	Emil L Woerner	(501)749-4574	WS 1030 SS 930	ED/HC/MD	124	118	47
CABOT	*OUR SAVIOR* oursaviorcabot@gmail.com www.oslcabot.org		301 S PINE ST	72023	MDS	Addison V Pope	(501)605-8082	WS 830 11 SS 945	ED/HC/MD	150	150	96
CAVE SPRINGS	*HOLY TRINITY*		See Rogers AR									
CENTERTON	*HOLY TRINITY*		See Rogers AR									
CHEROKEE VILLAGE	*PEACE* peace_cv@hotmail.com peacecv.net	1967	4 IROQUOIS DR CHEROKEE VLG	72529	MDS	Brian L Pummill	(870)257-3957 (870)257-3957	WS 9 1115 SS 1015 BC 1015	ED/HC/MD	146	138	76
CLARKSVILLE	*RIVER VALLEY GRACE*		See Lamar AR									
CONWAY	*PEACE* plc@conwaycorp.net www.peaceconway.org	1964	800 S DONAGHEY AVE	72034	MDS	Thomas R Boeck	(501)329-3854 (501)327-7980	WS 9 SS 1030 BC 1030	ED/HC/MD	147	123	82
	ST MATTHEW stmatthewlcmsconway@gmail.com www.stmatthewconway.com	1998	900 FARRIS RD	72034	MDS	Kory A Janneke	(501)358-6252	WS 10 BC 9	ED/HC/ MD/SN	108	94	69
CORNING	*ST MATTHEW* lwfarm@usa.net	1893	501 N Missouri Ave PO BOX 399	72422	MDS	Jon C Bischof	(870)323-0338	WS 830	ED	79	44	22
DE WITT	*ST LUKE*	1945	903 E 2ND ST	72042	MDS	Jonathan E Holmes				65	45	20
EL DORADO	*OUR SAVIOR* OurSaviorLutheranChurch_ELDO@ outlook.com www.eldoradolutherans.com	1931	900 W FAULKNER ST	71730	MDS		(870)862-1443	WS 1030 SS 930				
EUREKA SPRINGS	*GRACE*		See Holiday Island AR									
FAIRFIELD BAY	*FAITH* faithfairfieldbay@gmail.com	1972	310 SNEAD DR	72088	MDS	Donald R Hefta	(501)884-3375	WS 930 BC 830	ED/HC	42	42	30
FAYETTEVILLE	*LIVING SAVIOR*		See Springdale AR									
	RESTORATION jd.zischke@gmail.com restorationlutheran.com		2730 E TOWNSHIP ST.	72703	MDS	John David K Zischke	(210)601-0682	WS 9 SS 1030 BC 1030	ED	85	73	81

*Indicates a new church start. A new church start is an intentionally organized gathering which comes together on a regular basis for the purpose of worship and/or Bible study and is intended to grow into a member LCMS congregation. WS =Worship Service; SS = Sunday School; BC =Bible Class; EC = Early Childhood; EL = Elementary School; HS = High School; ED =Education Ministry; HC =Human Care Ministry; SN = Special Needs Ministry; MD = Media Ministry (PC)=Partner Church Pastor. See Page 53 for the Table of Abbreviations for key to additional abbreviations

CITY	CONGREGATION EMAIL WEBSITE	YEAR EST	LOCATION MAILING ADDRESS	ZIP CODE(S)	DIST.	PASTOR(S)	PHONE FAX	WS SS BC	SCHOOLS/ MINISTRIES	STATISTIC Bapt	Conf	Avg Attend
FAYETTEVILLE	*ST JOHN* stjohnslcmsfay@gmail.com sites.google.com/site/ stjohnslutheranchurchlcsm/	1944	2730 E TOWNSHIP ST	72703	MDS		(479)443-3609	WS 9 SS 10 BC 10	EC/ED/HC/ MD/SN	85	73	81
FORREST CITY	*FAITH*	1968	4525 N WASHINGTON ST	72335	MDS		(870)633-8312	WS 1045 SS 930 BC 930	HC	43	31	6
FORT SMITH	*BETHEL* office@bethelfortsmith.org www.bethelfortsmith.org	1939	5400 EUPER LN	72903	MDS	Joshua J Willadsen	(479)452-1521 (479)452-1521	WS 1015 SS 9 BC 9	ED/HC/MD	61	58	43
	FIRST 1stlutheran.com	1868	1115 North D St 1115 N D ST	72901	MDS	John F Merrill	(479)785-2886 (479)785-2902	WS 1015 SS 9 BC 9	EL/ED/HC/ MD/SN	328	292	127
	FIRST LUTHERAN SCHOOL Satellite Site of First Fort Smith AR	1976	2407 Massard Rd	72901								
	OUR REDEEMER office@ORLC.arcoxmail.com OurRedeemerFortSmith.360unite.com	1964	2100 CAVANAUGH RD	72908	MDS	Dr Richard A Davenport	(479)646-7611	WS 1015 SS 9 BC 9		79	72	35
GARFIELD	*HOLY TRINITY*		See Rogers AR									
GENTRY	*CHRIST*		See Siloam Springs AR									
GILLETT	*ST PAUL* splcg@centurytel.net	1893	206 Rose Ave PO BOX 419	72055	MDS	Jonathan E Holmes	(870)548-2554	SS 10		125	108	35
GRAVETTE	*HOLY TRINITY*		See Rogers AR									
GREENBRIER	*PEACE*		See Conway AR									
GREENWOOD	*GRACE* gracegreenwoodlcms@gmail.com gracegreenwood.com	1991	18218 US Hwy 71 S 18218 HIGHWAY 71 S	72936	MDS	Jason P Zirbel	(479)996-7747	WS 8 1015 SS 9 BC 9	HC/MD/SN	89	83	65
HARDY	*PEACE*		See Cherokee Village AR									
HARRISBURG	*ALL SAINTS*		See Jonesboro AR									
HARRISON	*FIRST* office@flchar.com www.flchar.com	1960	515 S LOCUST	72601	MDS		(870)741-9777	WS 1030 SS 9	ED/HC/ MD/SN			
HOLIDAY ISLAND	*GRACE* gracelutheranHI@cox.net www.gracelutheranhi.org	1972	179 HOLIDAY ISLAND DR HOLIDAY ISLE	72631	MDS	Myles R Schultz	(479)253-9040	WS 930 BC 11	ED/HC/ MD/SN			
HORSESHOE BEND	*SHEPHERD HILLS* batesvillehopelutheran@gmail.com	1974	508 PROFESSION DR HORSE- SHOE BND	72512	MDS	Gerald D Heinecke	(870)793-3078	WS 9 SS 915 BC 915	ED/HC/ MD/SN	21	21	18
HOT SPRINGS	*FIRST* flchs@flchs.com www.flchs.com	1915	105 VILLAGE RD	71913	MDS	Jonathan M Beyer Anthony M Johnson	(501)525-0322 (501)525-0142	WS 830 11 SS 950 BC 950	ED/HC/ MD/SN	403	328	196
HOT SPRINGS VILLAGE	*FAITH* faithluth@sbcglobal.net www.faithhsv.com	1986	1196 De Soto Blvd 1196 DESOTO BLVD HOT SPRINGS	71909	MDS	Robert J Benke	(501)922-5700 (501)922-9780	WS 10 BC 845	ED/HC/ MD/SN	159	152	84
JACKSONVILLE	*HOPE* hopelutheranchurch@ymail.com www.hopelutheranjacksonville.org	1970	1904 Mc Arthur Dr 1904 MCARTHUR DR	72076	MDS	Kevin R Conger	(501)982-1333	WS 10 SS 9 BC 9	ED/MD/SN	209	173	87
JONESBORO	*ALL SAINTS* pastor@allsaintsjonesboro.org allsaintsjonesboro.org	1958	1812 RAINS ST	72401	MDS	Joshua P Leigeber Jerome P Leckband Andrew S Lehman Daniel P Suelzle	(870)935-2001	WS 9 SS 1030 BC 1030	EL/HS/ED	145	131	85
LAFE	*ST JOHN* saintjohnslafe@gmail.com www.stjohnslafe.org	1886	11530 Hwy 135N 11530 HIGHWAY 135 N	72436	MDS	Aaron J Neugebauer	(870)586-0319 (870)586-9291	WS 830 1030 SS 915	ED/HC/MD	398	309	200
LAMAR	*RIVER VALLEY GRACE*	1961	922 W MAIN	72846	MDS	Thomas W Bartzsch	(479)754-2769	WS 1015 SS 9 BC 9	HC	44	39	27
LITTLE FLOCK	*HOLY TRINITY*		See Rogers AR									
LITTLE ROCK	*CHRIST* www.christlittlerock.com	1980	315 S HUGHES ST	72205	MDS	Matthew L Albright	(501)663-5232 (501)663-9542	WS 8 1030 SS 915 BC 915	EL/ED/HC/ MD	375	325	135
	CHRIST LITTLE ROCK WEST Satellite Site of Christ Little Rock AR	2020	16025 Taylor Loop Road	72205				WS 530				
	COMMUNITY OF FAITH rosielew@comcast.net	1997	9300 S Chicot Rd PO BOX 190042	72209 72219	MDS	Randall C Lewis	(501)562-7704 (501)379-9334	WS 11 SS 10	ED/HC/MD	8	8	15
	FIRST firstlutheranlr@gmail.com www.firstlutheranlr.com	1868	314 E 8TH ST	72202	MDS	Ronald J Bacic	(501)372-1023	WS 1030 SS 9	ED/HC/ MD/SN	146	122	35
	GRACE office@glclr.org www.gracelutheranlr.org	1941	5124 HILLCREST AVE	72205	MDS	David M Buchs David R Witte	(501)663-3631	WS 10 SS 9 BC 9	EC/ED/HC	338	270	110
	ZION		See Avilla AR									
LONDON	*ZION* rev.jralston@gmail.com zionaugsburg.org	1883	93 Augsburg Rd PO BOX 327 DOVER	72847 72837	MDS	Joshua A Ralston	(479)331-3277	WS 10 SS 9 BC 9	ED/HC	154	133	69
LOWELL	*HOLY TRINITY*		See Rogers AR									
MAGNOLIA	*FAITH*	1960	1700 N Jackson St 1700 N JACKSON	71753	MDS		(870)234-2040 (870)234-3839	WS 10 BC 1115	ED	4	4	3
MALVERN	*ST LUKE*	1965	820 SULPHUR SPRINGS RD	72104	MDS			WS 9		15	15	7
MAUMELLE	*SHEPHERD OF PEACE* sopmaumelle@gmail.com shepeace.com	1991	449 MILLWOOD CIR	72113	MDS		(501)851-4546	WS 9 SS 8 BC 8	ED/HC	70	58	38

*Indicates a new church start. A new church start is an intentionally organized gathering which comes together on a regular basis for the purpose of worship and/or Bible study and is intended to grow into a member LCMS congregation. WS =Worship Service; SS = Sunday School; BC =Bible Class; EC = Early Childhood; EL = Elementary School; HS = High School; ED =Education Ministry; HC =Human Care Ministry; SN = Special Needs Ministry; MD = Media Ministry (PC)=Partner Church Pastor. See Page 53 for the Table of Abbreviations for key to additional abbreviations

CITY	CONGREGATION EMAIL WEBSITE	YEAR EST	LOCATION MAILING ADDRESS	ZIP CODE(S)	DIST.	PASTOR(S)	PHONE FAX	WS SS BC	SCHOOLS/ MINISTRIES	STATISTIC Bapt	Conf	Avg Attend
MAYFLOWER	*PEACE*		See Conway AR									
MELBOURNE	*SHEPHERD HILLS*		See Horseshoe Bend AR									
MENA	*TRINITY* tlcmenaar@gmail.com www.trinitylutheranmena.com	1900	1010 De Queen PO BOX 1305	71953	MDS	Timothy J Henning	(479)394-1290	WS 10 SS 9 BC 9	ED/HC/ MD/SN	28	25	19
MORRILTON	*PEACE*		See Conway AR									
MOUNTAIN HOME	*REDEEMER* rlcmhoffice@gmail.com redeemermtnhome.org	1959	312 W NORTH ST	72653	MDS	Kevin S McReynolds	(870)425-6071 (870)425-2844	WS 830 11 SS 945 BC 945	ED/HC/ MD/SN	345	335	248
NORTH LITTLE ROCK	*TRINITY* trinitynlr@gmail.com trinitynlr.com	1943	3802 N OLIVE ST	72116	MDS		(501)753-6824	WS 11 SS 10 BC 10	SN	47	46	22
OAK GROVE	*SHEPHERD HILLS*		See Kimberling City MO									
PARAGOULD	*ALL SAINTS*		See Jonesboro AR									
	REDEEMER pastorkirkneugebauer@gmail.com	1958	829 W KINGSHIGHWAY	72450	MDS	Kirk C Neugebauer	(870)236-2162	WS 10 SS 9 BC 9	MD	165	137	104
PEA RIDGE	*MESSIAH* office@nwamessiah.org		15315 N Hwy 94 15315 N HIGHWAY 94	72751	MDS	Richard H Mayer	(479)451-0021	WS 1030 SS 930	ED/HC	167	152	65
PINE BLUFF	*TRINITY* trinityowr@gmail.com www.trinitylutheranpb.org	1894	4200 OLD WARREN RD	71603	MDS	Stewart A Marshall	(870)534-4316 (870)534-5494	WS 1045 SS 930	ED/HC/ MD/SN	133	104	40
PRAIRIE CREEK	*HOLY TRINITY*		See Rogers AR									
ROGERS	*HOLY TRINITY* tabby@holytrin.org www.holytrin.org	1962	1101 W HUDSON RD	72756	MDS	Eric A Longman Michael J Meyer	(479)636-1135	WS 8 1045 SS 930 BC 930	EC/ED/HC/ MD/SN	492	408	176
	LIVING SAVIOR		See Springdale AR									
RUSSELLVILLE	*ST JOHN* stjohnschurch@suddenlinkmail.com www.stjohns-lutheranchurch.org	1923	500 N CUMBERLAND AVE	72801	MDS	Joshua K Schooping	(479)968-1309 (479)968-1309	WS 1015 SS 915 BC 915	ED/HC/MD	219	219	61
	ZION		See London AR									
SEARCY	*OUR SHEPHERD* office@ourshepherdlutheran.com www.ourshepherdlutheran.com	1981	2610 S MAIN ST	72143	MDS	Jeffrey W King	(501)268-1613 (501)268-1613	WS 10 SS 845 BC 845	ED/HC/ MD/SN	90	81	36
SILOAM SPRINGS	*CHRIST* christsiloamlcms@gmail.com sites.google.com/view/ christlutheran/home	2008	920 S CARL ST BLDG 1 SUITE #3	72761	MDS	Russell L Shewmaker	(870)897-4443	WS 1030		55	50	21
SPRINGDALE	*LIVING SAVIOR* livingsaviorlutheran@gmail.com www.livingsavior.us	1996	1600 BUTTERFIELD COACH RD.	72764	MDS	Roger D Sterle	(479)770-2124	WS 10	ED/HC/ MD/SN	20	20	15
	SALEM ddiercouff@aol.com salemspringdale.org	1876	1800 W EMMA AVE	72762	MDS	Adam C Gless Brandon L Martin	(479)751-9500 (479)750-2028	WS 8 1015 SS 915 BC 915	EC/ED/HC/ MD/SN	392	283	244
STUTTGART	*SAINT JOHNS* secretary@stjohnsluth.com www.stjohnsstuttgartar.org	1882	205 E 5TH ST	72160	MDS		(870)673-2858 (870)673-2936	WS 9 SS 1015 BC 8 1015	EL/ED/HC/ MD/SN	348	322	100
ULM	*ZION* zionlutheran@hotmail.com	1881	252 E 2nd St PO BOX 158	72170	MDS	Jeremy T McDonald	(870)241-1040	WS 11 SS 10	ED	64	55	41
VILONIA	*PEACE*		See Conway AR									
WALDENBURG	*ZION*	1881	5612 Highway 14 East PO BOX 40	72475	MDS		(870)579-2276	WS 8	ED/HC/SN	56	46	16
	ZION LUTHERAN CHURCH Satellite Site of All Saints Jonesboro AR	2025	5612 AR-14	72475				WS 745				

CALIFORNIA

CITY	CONGREGATION EMAIL WEBSITE	YEAR EST	LOCATION MAILING ADDRESS	ZIP CODE(S)	DIST.	PASTOR(S)	PHONE FAX	WS SS BC	SCHOOLS/ MINISTRIES	Bapt	Conf	Avg Attend
AGOURA HILLS	*ST PAUL* www.stpaulagoura.com	1965	30600 THOUSAND OAKS BLVD	91301	PSW	Matthew T Nolte	(818)889-1620 (818)889-1649	WS 1030 SS 1145 BC 1145	ED/HC			
ALHAMBRA	*EMMAUS* jameshoiyue@rocketmail.com www.emmausalhambra.org	1923	840 S ALMANSOR ST	91801	PSW	James H Yue	(626)289-3664 (626)576-0476	WS 9 SS 1010 BC 1020	EL/ED/HC/ MD/SN	61	61	140
ALMADEN	*SHEP OF VALLEY*		See San Jose CA									
ALTA LOMA	*SHEPHERD HILLS*		See Rancho Cucamonga CA									
ANAHEIM	*EMERALD COURT* Satellite Site of Prince Peace Anaheim CA	2018	1731 W Medical Center Dr	92801								
	HEPHATHA HephathaChurch@Hephatha.net www.hephatha.net	1974	5900 E SANTA ANA CANYON RD	92807	PSW	Arthur F Andrews	(714)637-0887 (714)637-6088	WS 8 930 11 SS 1015 BC 935	EL/HS/ED/ MD	244	196	180
	PRINCE PEACE Church@princeofpeaceanaheim.org princeofpeaceanaheim.org	1955	1421 W BALL RD	92802	PSW	Darrin D Sheek	(714)774-0993	WS 8 1030 SS 9	EC/EL/HS/ ED/HC/ MD/SN	110	85	60
	SALEM		See Orange CA									
	TRINITY office@tlcanaheim.com www.tlcanaheim.com	1966	4101 E NOHL RANCH RD	92807	PSW	James A Elmore	(714)637-8370	WS 1030 SS 915 BC 915	ED/SN	101	91	80
	ZION church@zionanaheim.org www.zionanaheim.org	1903	222 N EAST ST	92805	PSW	Timothy E Eaton	(714)535-1169 (657)232-9188	WS 830 1010	EC/EL/HS/ ED/HC/ MD/SN	175	135	142

*Indicates a new church start. A new church start is an intentionally organized gathering which comes together on a regular basis for the purpose of worship and/or Bible study and is intended to grow into a member LCMS congregation. WS =Worship Service; SS = Sunday School; BC =Bible Class; EC = Early Childhood; EL = Elementary School; HS = High School; ED =Education Ministry; HC =Human Care Ministry; SN = Special Needs Ministry; MD = Media Ministry (PC)=Partner Church Pastor. See Page 53 for the Table of Abbreviations for key to additional abbreviations

CITY	CONGREGATION EMAIL WEBSITE	YEAR EST	LOCATION MAILING ADDRESS	ZIP CODE(S)	DIST.	PASTOR(S)	PHONE FAX	WS SS BC	SCHOOLS/ MINISTRIES	STATISTIC Bapt	Conf	Avg Attend
ANAHEIM HILLS	*SALEM*		See Orange CA									
ANTELOPE	*HOLY CROSS*		See Rocklin CA									
ANTIOCH	*ST ANDREW* standrewsluth@gmail.com	1957	2507 SAN JOSE DR	94509	CNH	Roger R Kuehn Herman A Sealey	(925)757-1672 (925)757-5709	WS 10	ED/HC/MD	40	40	25
ANZA	*SHEP OF VALLEY* anzas.church@gmail.com shepherdofthevalleyanza.org	1980	56095 Pena Rd PO BOX 390668	92539	PSW		(951)708-8415	WS 9 BC 1030	ED/HC/ MD/SN	16	14	15
APPLE VALLEY	*ASCENSION* office@ascensionav.org ascensionav.org	1959	22130 Ottawa Rd PO BOX 1645	92308 92307	PSW	James C Harris	(760)247-7392 (760)247-9014	WS 9 BC 1030	ED/HC/MD	151	142	49
APTOS	*MOUNT CALVARY*		See Soquel CA									
ARCADIA	*OUR SAVIOR* oslcarcadia@aol.com www.oslcarcadia.com	1954	512 W DUARTE RD	91007	PSW	Eric T Eichinger	(626)447-7690 (626)447-9301	WS 8 1015 SS	ED/HC/ MD/SN	420	365	180
ARROYO GRANDE	*COMMUNITY BIBLE STUDY* Satellite Site of Peace Arroyo Grande CA	2023	1142 Branch St	93420								
	PEACE info@peacearroyogrande.com www.peacearroyogrande.com	1954	244 OAK PARK BLVD	93420	CNH	John A Huss	(805)489-2708 (805)474-1823	WS 10	EC/ED/HC/ MD/SN	90	83	60
ARVIN	*ST JOHNS VALLEY OF FAITH* Satellite Site of St John Bakersfield CA	2015	500 Campus Dr	93203								
ATASCADERO	*OF THE REDEEMER* office.redeemeratascadero@gmail.com www.redeemeratascadero.org	1954	4500 EL CAMINO REAL	93422	CNH		(805)466-9350 (805)461-9649	WS 1015 BC 915	ED/HC/SN	67	61	31
	TRINITY		See Paso Robles CA									
ATWATER	*HOLY CROSS* holycrossatwater.wordpress.com	1957	1495 UNDERWOOD AVE	95301	CNH		(209)358-3471	WS 1015 BC 9	ED			
AUBURN	*GRACE*		See Grass Valley CA									
	ST PAUL stpaulaubca@gmail.com stpaulauburn.org	1947	275 NATION DR	95603	CNH	David F Poganski	(530)885-5378	WS 9 SS 1030	HC/MD/SN	89	84	35
BAKERSFIELD	*BETHANY* blc@bak.rr.com	1962	900 DAY AVE	93308	CNH	Stephen E Asche	(661)399-3532	WS 11 SS 930	HC/SN	32	18	15
	GRACE gracelutheranbakersfield@gmail.com	1949	2530 DRAKE ST	93301	CNH		(661)324-4315 (661)324-4315	WS 1030 SS 915 BC 930				
	PRAYER office@lcop.org www.lcop.org	1957	8001 PANORAMA DR	93306	CNH	Dwayne R Hendricks	(661)871-1289 (661)872-6302	WS 9 SS 1030 BC 1030	EC/ED/HC/ MD/SN			
	ST JOHN office@sjlchurch.org www.sjlchurch.org	1904	4500 BUENA VISTA RD	93311	CNH	Eric J Van Scharrel Marvin F St Pierre Benjamin J Schrank	(661)665-7815 (661)665-7821	WS 9 1030 SS 9 1030 BC 10	EL/ED/HC/ MD/SN	1277	957	751
BANNING	*GRACE* office@glcbanning.org www.glcbanning.org	1926	1000 W WILSON ST	92220	PSW	Brian F Barlow	(951)849-3232	WS 9 SS 1015 BC 1015	ED/MD	105	95	70
BARSTOW	*CONCORDIA* concordialutheranbarstow@gmail.com www.concordialutheranbarstow.org	1944	420 AVENUE E	92311	PSW	Timothy M Kohlmeier	(760)256-2036 (760)256-2036	WS 9 SS 1030 BC 1030	EC/ED			
BAY AREA	*FIRST IMMANUEL*		See San Jose CA									
BEAUMONT	*GRACE*		See Banning CA									
BELL GARDENS	*SS PEDRO/PABLO*	1947	6430 COLMAR AVE	90201	PSW		(323)773-3056	WS 930	ED/HC	20	10	15
BENICIA	*BENICIA* blcoffice@sbcglobal.net benicialutheranchurch.com	1976	201 RAYMOND DR	94510	CNH		(707)746-0201	WS 930 SS 10	EC/ED/HC/ MD	72	61	42
BERKELEY	*BETHLEHEM*	1899	3100 TELEGRAPH AVE	94705	CNH		(510)848-8821			5	5	3
	BETHLEHEM ETHIOPIAN	2009	3100 Telegraph Ave 17238 VIA DEL REY SAN LORENZO	94705 94580	CNH	Dr Dereje Fantaye	(510)551-7450					
BEVERLY HILLS	*MOUNT CALVARY* clausengang@yahoo.com www.beverlyhillslutheran.com	1940	436 S BEVERLY DR	90212	PSW	John W Berg	(310)277-1164 (310)277-8024	WS 1030 BC 1145	ED/HC/ MD/SN	50	30	25
	OROMO wowwla2003@gmail.com oromoevangelicallutheranchurch inlosangeles.com	2009	C/O MT CALVARY LUTHERAN CHURCH 436 S BEVERLY DR	90212	PSW		(661)317-1505			87	57	40
BIG BEAR CITY	*SHEPHERD INTHE PINES*		See Big Bear Lake CA									
BIG BEAR LAKE	*SHEPHERD INTHE PINES* shepherditp@gmail.com SITPbigbear.org	1977	42450 N Shore PO BOX 1606	92315	PSW		(909)866-8718 (909)866-8718	WS 10	ED			
BIG RIVER	*MESSIAH*		See Parker AZ									
BIG SUR	*BETHLEHEM*		See Monterey CA									
BISHOP	*GRACE* glcbishopca@schat.net	1945	711 N FOWLER ST	93514	PSW	Timothy M Homan	(760)872-9791	WS 1045 BC 930	ED/HC/ MD/SN	125	113	40
BLUE JAY	*MOUNT CALVARY*		See Lake Arrowhead CA									
BLYTHE	*ZION* zionlutheranblythe@outlook.com zionlutheranblythe.org	1950	721 E Chanslor Way 701 E CHANSLOR WAY	92225	PSW	Jonathan M Manthei	(760)922-7321 (760)922-7456	WS 9 SS 9	ED/HC/MD			
BONITA	*VICTORY*		See Chula Vista CA									
BORREGO SPRINGS	*BORREGO* borregolutheranchurch.com	1986	601 Diamond Bar Rd PO BOX 1122 BORREGO SPGS	92004	EN	Michael A Matthews		WS 10	ED/HC/MD			

*Indicates a new church start. A new church start is an intentionally organized gathering which comes together on a regular basis for the purpose of worship and/or Bible study and is intended to grow into a member LCMS congregation. WS =Worship Service; SS = Sunday School; BC =Bible Class; EC = Early Childhood; EL = Elementary School; HS = High School; ED =Education Ministry; HC =Human Care Ministry; SN = Special Needs Ministry; MD = Media Ministry (PC)=Partner Church Pastor. See Page 53 for the Table of Abbreviations for key to additional abbreviations

CITY	CONGREGATION EMAIL WEBSITE	YEAR EST	LOCATION MAILING ADDRESS	ZIP CODE(S)	DIST.	PASTOR(S)	PHONE FAX	WS SS BC	SCHOOLS/ MINISTRIES	STATISTIC Bapt	 Conf	 Avg Attend
BRAWLEY	*TRINITY* trinitylutheranbrawley@yahoo.com	1938	275 N First St 275 N 1ST ST	92227	PSW		(760)344-1635 (760)344-8778	WS 9 SS 1030 BC 1030				
BREA	*CHRIST* pmartinez@christbrea.org www.christbrea.org	1962	820 W IMPERIAL HWY	92821	PSW	Eric K Clausen	(714)529-2984	WS 8 1030 SS 930 BC 930	EL/HS/ED/ HC/MD/SN	798	733	260
BRENTWOOD	*RESURRECTION* rezministry@outlook.com rezministry.org	1992	1275 FAIRVIEW AVE	94513	CNH		(925)634-5180	WS 930 SS 1045 BC 830 1045	EC/ED/HC/ MD/SN	121	52	101
BUENA PARK	*BETHEL* bpbethellutheran@gmail.com bethellutheranbp.com	1957	6441 LINCOLN AVE	90620	PSW	Timothy C Potthoff	(714)527-4776 (714)527-4788	WS 9	HS/ED/HC/ MD/SN	149	144	57
	GOOD NEWS KOREAN kimbg1212@gmail.com	1992	6625 DALE ST.	90621	PSW	Byung G Kim Soon S Jang	(714)681-6770		HC/MD	20	20	18
	MESSIAH MessiahLuBP@gmail.com www.MessiahBP.com	1947	6625 DALE ST	90621	PSW	Mark H Baumbach	(714)752-6040	WS 10 SS 9 BC 9	ED/HC	62	55	33
BURBANK	*CHRIST* jhirsch@alumni.nmu.edu	1941	2400 W BURBANK BLVD	91506	PSW		(818)846-4415	WS 10 SS 930				
	FIRST church@firstlutheranburbank.org www.firstlutheranburbank.org	1921	1001 S GLENOAKS BLVD	91502	PSW	Michael E Harnack	(818)848-7432 (818)848-3801	WS 10 SS 9	ED/HC/ MD/SN	45	40	20
BURLINGAME	*TRINITY* office@trinityburlingame.org trinityburlingame.org	1951	1245 EL CAMINO REAL	94010	CNH	Jeffrey L Schufreider	(650)347-4100 (650)347-6681	WS 1045 SS 930	EC/ED	54	54	29
BURNEY	*FAITH*	1968	20400 TIMBER DR	96013	CNH		(530)335-3723	WS 930 BC 1030	ED			
CABAZON	*GRACE*		See Banning CA									
CALEXICO	*GRACE*		See El Centro CA									
CALIMESA	*GRACE*		See Banning CA									
CAMARILLO	*PEACE* office@peacecamarillo.com www.peacecamarillo.com	1976	71 LOMA DR	93010	PSW	Michael A Schultze	(805)482-3313 (805)482-6044	WS 9 11 SS 920 BC 1015	EC/ED/HC/ MD/SN	308	250	98
CAMERON PARK	*LIGHT OF THE HILLS* loth@loth.org www.loth.org	1990	3100 RODEO RD	95682	CNH	Alan J Sommer	(530)677-9536 (530)677-4376	WS 8 1045 SS 930 BC 930	ED/HC/ MD/SN	300	272	180
CAMPBELL	*HOLY CROSS*		See Los Gatos CA									
	OUR SAVIOR		See Cupertino CA									
CANOGA PARK	*CANOGA PARK* lauriec@cplchurch.org www.cplchurch.org	1945	7357 JORDAN AVE	91303	PSW	Timothy A Jenks	(818)348-5714 (818)348-1516	WS 930 SS 1045 BC 1045	MD	173	149	64
	OUR REDEEMER		See Winnetka CA									
CANYON COUNTRY	*BETHLEHEM*		See Santa Clarita CA									
CAPISTRANO BEACH	*FAITH* office@faithcapo.com www.faithcapo.com	1965	34381 CALLE PORTOLA CAPO BEACH	92624	PSW	Jeremy D Rhode	(949)496-1901 (949)496-1992	WS 8 1030 1230 SS 920 BC 920	ED/HC/ MD/SN	255	227	176
CAPITOLA	*MOUNT CALVARY*		See Soquel CA									
CARLSBAD	*REDEEMER BY THE SEA* kay@redeemerbythesea.org www.redeemerbythesea.org	1990	6600 BLACK RAIL RD	92011	PSW		(760)431-8990	WS 830 1015 SS 1045	EC/ED/ MD/SN	245	230	146
CARMEL	*FAITH*		See Seaside CA									
CARMEL VALLEY	*FAITH*		See Seaside CA									
CARMEL-BY-THE-SEA	*THE COTTAGES OF CARMEL* Satellite Site of Bethlehem Monterey CA	2023	26245 Carmel Rancho Blvd	93923								
CARPINTERIA	*FAITH* paul@islandbrewingcompany.com www.faithcarpinteria.org	1959	1335 VALLECITO PL	93013	PSW		(805)684-4707 (805)566-0073	WS 9	ED/HC/ MD/SN			
CARUTHERS	*OUR SAVIOUR* oscaruthers@gmail.com	1923	13441 S Quince St PO BOX 215	93609	CNH	Scott A Jacobsen	(559)864-3008	WS 1030 BC 915	HC			
CASTROVILLE	*FAITH*		See Seaside CA									
CEDAR GLEN	*MOUNT CALVARY*		See Lake Arrowhead CA									
CERRITOS	*CONCORDIA* church@concordia.org www.concordia.org	1970	13633 183RD ST	90703	PSW	Dr Dustin T Parker	(562)926-7416 (562)407-0610	WS 9 SS 1045	EC/ED/HC/ MD/SN	322	302	82
CHERRY VALLEY	*GRACE*		See Banning CA									
CHESTER	*OUR SAVIOR*	1950	161 Aspen St PO BOX 706	96020	CNH		(530)258-2347	WS 9	ED/HC/SN			
CHICAGO PARK	*GRACE*		See Grass Valley CA									
CHICO	*REDEEMER* redeemerchicooffice@gmail.com redeemerchico.org	1910	750 MOSS AVE	95926	CNH	Brennan T DeForest	(530)342-6085	WS 10 SS 845 BC 845	ED	131	117	70
CHINO	*EDGEWATER*		See Eastvale CA									
	IMMANUEL Office.ImmanuelChino@gmail.com www.immanuelchino.org	1950	5648 JEFFERSON AVE	91710	PSW	Patrick W Curley	(909)628-2823	WS 10 BC 9	ED/HC/ MD/SN	90	75	50
CHINO HILLS	*LOVING SAVIOR* church@lovingsavior.org www.lovingsavior.org	1983	14816 PEYTON DR	91709	PSW	Andy Wu	(909)597-4668 (909)597-5739	WS 930 5	EL	260	230	180
CHOWCHILLA	*TRINITY* trinitylutheranchowchilla@gmail.com trinitylutheranchowchilla.com	1953	821 TRINITY AVE	93610	CNH		(209)665-4601	WS 930				

*Indicates a new church start. A new church start is an intentionally organized gathering which comes together on a regular basis for the purpose of worship and/or Bible study and is intended to grow into a member LCMS congregation. WS =Worship Service; SS = Sunday School; BC =Bible Class; EC = Early Childhood; EL = Elementary School; HS = High School; ED =Education Ministry; HC =Human Care Ministry; SN = Special Needs Ministry; MD = Media Ministry (PC)=Partner Church Pastor. See Page 53 for the Table of Abbreviations for key to additional abbreviations

CITY	CONGREGATION EMAIL WEBSITE	YEAR EST	LOCATION MAILING ADDRESS	ZIP CODE(S)	DIST.	PASTOR(S)	PHONE FAX	WS SS BC	SCHOOLS/ MINISTRIES	STATISTIC Bapt	Conf	Avg Attend
CHULA VISTA	*CONCORDIA* office@concordiachurch.com www.concordiachurch.com	1964	1695 DISCOVERY FALLS DR	91915	PSW	Richard W Schmidt Jr	(619)656-8100 (619)422-6620	WS 830 1030	EC/EL/HS/ ED/HC/MD			
	VICTORY church.office@victorysouthbay.org victorysouthbay.org		810 BUENA VISTA WAY	91910	PSW	Timothy A Gerdes	(619)262-4444	WS 8 11 SS 1115	EL/HS/ED/ HC/MD	409	206	125
CITRUS HEIGHTS	*HOLY CROSS*		See Rocklin CA									
	MESSIAH www.mlcch.org	1956	7801 ROSSWOOD DR CITRUS HTS	95621	CNH	Morris W Stephens Jr	(916)725-4550	WS 9 SS 1030 BC 1030	ED/HC/ MD/SN			
CLAREMONT	*ST LUKE* stlukelutheran.lcms@aol.com www.st-luke.info	1965	2050 N INDIAN HILL BLVD	91711	PSW	Timothy L Seals	(909)624-8898 (909)621-4299	WS 10 BC 9	ED/HC/MD	85	80	60
CLEARLAKE	*SAINT JOHNS* office@stjohnslutheranclearlake.org stjohnslutheranclearlake.org	1960	14310 Memory Ln PO BOX 338	95422	CNH		(707)994-2829	WS 10				
CLOVERDALE	*GRACE* GraceLutheranChurch@sonic.net GraceCloverdale.org	1952	890 N Cloverdale Blvd PO BOX 455	95425	CNH	Fred W Karlen	(707)894-2330	WS 10 SS 930	ED/HC/ MD/SN	86	76	43
CLOVIS	*EMMANUEL* office@emmanuelclovis.org www.emmanuelclovis.com	1890	785 N FOWLER AVE	93611	CNH	Daniel J Hues	(559)298-0725 (559)298-0727	WS 9 SS 1015 BC 1030	ED/HC/SN			
COARSEGOLD	*SHEP OF THE SIERRRA* shepherdofthesierra.tripod.com/ index.html		28420 Yosemite Springs Pkwy Suite E 45707 THREE BROTHER RD AHWAHNEE	93614 93601	CNH		(559)683-8873	WS 930 SS 11 BC 630	ED/HC/MD			
COLUSA	*BETHLEHEM* waltschedler@yahoo.com	1954	720 Ware Ave PO BOX 976	95932	CNH		(530)458-4943	WS 9	ED/HC/ MD/SN			
COMPTON	*ST PHILIP* saintphilip110@yahoo.com www.stphiliplutheran.org	1960	1110 N DWIGHT AVE	90222	PSW		(310)635-8600	WS 10	HC/MD	29	29	10
CONCORD	*FAITH*		See Pleasant Hill CA									
	FIRST office@flcconcord.org www.flcconcord.org	1940	4000 CONCORD BLVD	94519	CNH	Andrew R Jones	(925)671-9942 (925)671-9943	WS 930 SS 1045 BC 1045	EC/ED/HC/ MD/SN	167	136	98
	HOLY CROSS office@holycrossconcord.org www.holycrossconcord.org	1959	1092 ALBERTA WAY	94521	CNH	Andrew P Mundinger	(925)686-2000 (925)686-6894	WS 930 SS 11 BC 1115	ED/HC/MD	115	80	67
CORNING	*MOUNT OLIVE* mtocorning@gmail.com www.mtocorning.org	1959	341 Solano St 341 E SOLANO ST	96021	CNH	Sylvan N Finger	(530)824-5530	WS 1030	ED/HC/MD	26	24	14
CORONA	*AMAZING GRACE* amazinggracecorona@gmail.com www.amazinggracecorona.org	2017	2550 S Main St PO BOX 78413	92882 92877	PSW	Jason P Kilian	(951)433-0151	WS 10 SS 1015		125	92	57
	EDGEWATER		See Eastvale CA									
COSTA MESA	*CHRIST* mrs.culp@christcm.org christcm.org	1953	760 VICTORIA ST	92627	PSW	Andrew B Ross Jack Brouwer	(949)631-1611 (949)631-6224	WS 8 1030 SS 920 BC 920	EC/EL/HS/ ED/HC/ MD/SN	584	403	274
COTATI	*ST JOHN'S*		See Petaluma CA									
COVINA	*ST JOHN* office@stjohncovina.org www.stjohncovina.org	1911	304 E COVINA BLVD	91722	PSW	Justin S Wood	(626)332-3142	WS 9 SS 1015	ED/HC/ MD/SN	151	139	81
COWAN HEIGHTS	*SALEM*		See Orange CA									
CRESCENT CITY	*GRACE* secglc@YAHOO.COM gracelutheranevangelical.com	1951	188 E COOPER AVE	95531	CNH	Marty L Tyler	(707)464-4712 (707)464-4070	WS 1015 SS 9 BC 9	ED/HC/MD			
CREST PARK	*MOUNT CALVARY*		See Lake Arrowhead CA									
CRESTLINE	*MOUNT CALVARY*		See Lake Arrowhead CA									
CROWS LANDING	*SAINT JAMES*		See Newman CA									
CULVER CITY	*THE GOOD SHEPHERD*		See Inglewood CA									
CUPERTINO	*OUR SAVIOR* office@lcos.org www.lcos.org	1954	5825 BOLLINGER RD	95014	CNH	John C Bestul Dennis E Bestul Adam M Debner	(408)252-0345	WS 10 SS 830 BC 830	EL/ED/ MD/SN	358	257	103
CYPRESS	*HOLY CROSS LUTHERAN CHURCH* Satellite Site of Bethany Long Beach CA	2024	4321 Cerritos Ave.	90630				WS 11				
DALY CITY	*HOPE* info@hopedalycity.org www.hopedalycity.org	1949	55 SAN FERNANDO WAY	94015	CNH	Daniel K Woo Corey J Chang	(650)991-4673 (650)991-9723	WS 9 SS 1030 BC 1030	EC/ED	280	240	200
DANA POINT	*FAITH*		See Capistrano Beach CA									
DANVILLE	*MESSIAH* mlclcms@pacbell.net www.messiahlutherandanville.com	1979	2305 CAMINO TASSAJARA	94526	EN	Kevin P Belter	(925)736-2270 (925)736-0435	WS 10 SS 845 BC 845 7	ED/HC/SN	228	191	73
DAVS	*ST PAUL*		See Woodland CA									
DEL REY OAKS	*FAITH*		See Seaside CA									
DELANO	*OUR SAVIOUR*	1921	1522 11th Ave PO BOX 399	93215 93216	CNH		(661)725-2225	WS 1015 BC 9	ED			
DESERT HOT SPRINGS	*TRINITY*		See Indio CA									
DIAMOND BAR	*MT CALVARY* Rita.morena@mcldb.org www.mcldb.org	1968	23300 GOLDEN SPRINGS DR	91765	PSW	Luke S Huang	(909)861-2740 (909)861-5481	WS 9 SS 8	EL/ED/HC/ MD			

*Indicates a new church start. A new church start is an intentionally organized gathering which comes together on a regular basis for the purpose of worship and/or Bible study and is intended to grow into a member LCMS congregation. WS =Worship Service; SS = Sunday School; BC =Bible Class; EC = Early Childhood; EL = Elementary School; HS = High School; ED =Education Ministry; HC =Human Care Ministry; SN = Special Needs Ministry; MD = Media Ministry (PC)=Partner Church Pastor. See Page 53 for the Table of Abbreviations for key to additional abbreviations

CITY	CONGREGATION EMAIL WEBSITE	YEAR EST	LOCATION MAILING ADDRESS	ZIP CODE(S)	DIST.	PASTOR(S)	PHONE FAX	WS SS BC	SCHOOLS/ MINISTRIES	STATISTIC Bapt	Conf	Avg Attend
DINUBA	*FIRST* dinubalutheran@yahoo.com www.dinubalutheran.net	1907	961 E ELIZABETH WAY	93618	CNH		(559)591-0375	WS 1030				
DOWNEY	*GOOD SHEPHERD* goodshepherddowney@yahoo.com www.downeygoodshepherd.org	1954	13200 COLUMBIA WAY	90242	PSW	Sean G Pica Kbrab Issak John H Kim	(562)803-4459 (562)803-4450	WS 9 SS 1030 BC 1030	ED/HC/ MD/SN	81	79	65
	MESSIAH messiahdowney@gmail.com www.messiahlutherandowney.com	1943	10711 PARAMOUNT BLVD	90241	PSW		(562)923-1215 (562)923-9211	WS 9 SS 1030 BC 1030	ED/HC/ MD/SN	116	111	45
	PEACE		See Pico Rivera CA									
DOWNTOWN SAN JOSE	*FIRST IMMANUEL*		See San Jose CA									
DUBLIN	*ST PHILIP* admin@stphilipchurch.com www.stphilipchurch.com	1963	8850 DAVONA DR	94568	CNH	David E Ficken	(925)828-2117	WS 10	EC/ED/HC/ MD			
DUCOR	*ZION*		See Terra Bella CA									
EARP	*MESSIAH*		See Parker AZ									
EAST LOS ANGELES	*FAITH*		See Whittier CA									
EAST PALO ALTO	*HOPE*		See Fremont CA									
EAST WHITTIER	*FAITH*		See Whittier CA									
EASTON	*OUR SAVIOUR*		See Caruthers CA									
EASTVALE	*EDGEWATER* pastorjosh@edgewaterlutheran.org www.edgewaterlutheran.org	2010	14977 Walters St Multipurpose Room 12672 LIMONITE AVE STE 3E #231	92880	PSW	Joel J Held	(478)919-6187	WS 10 SS 10	ED/MD	108	88	61
EL CAJON	*FIRST* admin@youhaveaplace.com www.youhaveaplace.com	1946	867 S LINCOLN AVE	92020	EN	James E Huenink	(619)444-7444 (619)444-9892	WS 9 11 BC 945	EC/EL/HS/ ED/HC/MD	180	180	110
	MORNING STAR		See Lakeside CA									
EL CENTRO	*GRACE* glcelcentro@gmail.com gracelutheranelcentro.org	1935	768 W Holt Ave PO BOX 1530	92243 92244	PSW		(760)352-5715	WS 11 BC 9	ED/MD	99	74	20
	ST PAUL		See Holtville CA									
EL CERRITO	*GRACE* www.graceelcerrito.org	1935	15 SANTA FE AVE	94530	CNH	Temesgen M Dabsu	(510)525-9004 (510)525-9087	WS 10 SS 10 BC 1145	ED/HC/ MD/SN	32	21	8
EL MONTE	*FIRST*	1937	4900 KINGS ROW	91731	PSW		(626)863-8397		ED/HC	26	26	11
EL SEGUNDO	*ST JOHN* karinaw@stjohnspreschooles.org stjohnses.com	1954	1611 E SYCAMORE AVE	90245	PSW	Dr Scott F Geminn	(310)615-1072 (310)615-0640	WS 10 SS 10	EC/ED	29	29	16
EL TORO	*ABIDING SAVIOR*		See Lake Forest CA									
ELK GROVE	*LIGHT OF THE VALLEY* pastor@lightofthevalley.net LightoftheValley.net	1952	9270 BRUCEVILLE RD	95758	CNH	James W Reed	(916)691-3568 (916)686-9682	WS 845 1030 11 SS 845 1030	HC/MD/SN	167	153	115
ENCINITAS	*ST MARK* stmark@stmarkchurch.net www.stmarkchurch.net	1945	552 S EL CAMINO REAL	92024	PSW		(760)753-4776 (760)753-4857	WS 930 SS 1045	EC/ED/HC/ MD/SN	150	127	100
ESCONDIDO	*COMMUNITY* churchoffice@clcfamily.org www.clcfamily.org	1989	3575 E Valley Parkway 3575 E VALLEY PKWY	92027	PSW	Robert M Hiller Matthew A Knauss-Behal	(760)739-1650 (760)739-8655	WS 8 1030 BC 915	EC/ED/MD	529	505	230
	GLORIA DEI office@gdlutheran.org gdlutheran.org	1978	1087 W COUNTRY CLUB LN	92026	PSW	Jeffrey P Horn	(760)743-2478	WS 9 SS 1030 BC 1030	ED/HC/ MD/SN	118	104	70
	GRACE asmith@gracelcms.net www.gracelutheranescondido.org/contact	1919	643 W 13TH AVE	92025	PSW	Aaron R Smith	(760)745-0831 (760)888-9240	WS 9 SS 1030 BC 1030	EL/ED/MD	312	229	140
EUREKA	*ST MARK*		See Ferndale CA									
EXETER	*TRINITY* tlcexeter@verizon.net tlcexeter.com	1955	420 SEQUOIA DR	93221	CNH		(559)592-4070	WS 9 SS 1030 BC 1030	EC/ED/HC/ MD	70	50	35
FAIR OAKS	*FAITH* faithfairoaks.com	1940	4000 SAN JUAN AVE	95628	CNH	Jared A Eggebraaten	(916)961-4252 (916)961-2604	WS 930 SS 1045 BC 1045	EC/ED/HC/ MD/SN	203	168	128
FAIRFIELD	*TRINITY* pastordanmolyneux@yahoo.com www.tlcfairfield.org	1910	2075 Dover Ave PO BOX 182	94533	CNH		(707)425-2944 (707)435-1122	WS 10 BC 845	ED/HC/ MD/SN			
FALLBROOK	*ZION* zionchurch@zlcs.org www.zionfallbrook.org	1954	1405 E FALLBROOK ST	92028	PSW	Aaron A Pingel	(760)728-8288	WS 9 SS 1030 BC 1030	EC/EL/HS/ ED/MD			
FERNDALE	*ST MARK* stmarksferndaleoffice@gmail.com www.stmarksferndale.com	1905	795 Berding St PO BOX 1016	95536	EN	Tyrel E Bramwell	(707)786-9353	WS 1030 BC 9	ED/HC/ MD/SN	58	46	34
FOLSOM	*MOUNT OLIVE* office.molc@gmail.com www.mountolivefolsom.com	1963	320 MONTROSE DR	95630	CNH	Daniel X Vang	(916)985-2984	WS 10 BC 9	ED/HC			
	MOUNT OLIVE BIBLE STUDY Satellite Site of Mount Olive Folsom CA	2018	110 Dyrell Way	95630								
FONATANA	*IGLESIA LUTERANA LA SANTISIMA TRINIDAD-FONTANA* Satellite Site of Iglesia La Santisima San Bernardino CA	2022	9315 Citrus Ave	92335				WS 1230				

*Indicates a new church start. A new church start is an intentionally organized gathering which comes together on a regular basis for the purpose of worship and/or Bible study and is intended to grow into a member LCMS congregation. WS =Worship Service; SS = Sunday School; BC =Bible Class; EC = Early Childhood; EL = Elementary School; HS = High School; ED =Education Ministry; HC =Human Care Ministry; SN = Special Needs Ministry; MD = Media Ministry (PC)=Partner Church Pastor. See Page 53 for the Table of Abbreviations for key to additional abbreviations

CONGREGATIONS

CITY	CONGREGATION EMAIL WEBSITE	YEAR EST	LOCATION MAILING ADDRESS	ZIP CODE(S)	DIST.	PASTOR(S)	PHONE FAX	WS SS BC	SCHOOLS/ MINISTRIES	STATISTIC Bapt	 Conf	 Avg Attend
FONTANA	*FIRST* 1stlutheranfontana@sbcglobal.net www.firstfontana.com	1925	9315 CITRUS AVE	92335	PSW	Jose S Villalobos	(909)823-3457 (866)591-3222	WS 9 BC 1030	ED/HC/MD	51	49	28
FORTUNA	*ST MARK*		See Ferndale CA									
FREMONT	*FREMONT OAK GARDENS* Satellite Site of Memorial-Deaf FREMONT CA	2000	2681 Driscoll Rd	94539								
	HOPE hopelutheranfmt@gmail.com www.hopelutheranfremont.org		3800 BEARD RD	94555	EN	Raymond A Hulett	(510)793-8691	WS 10 BC 9	HC/MD/SN	57	49	25
	MEMORIAL-DEAF gomez.andylorena@sbcglobal.net	1937	C/O PRINCE OF PEACE CHURCH AND SCHOOL 38451 FREMONT BLVD	94536	CNH	Andrew D Gomez Jr	(510)499-8473	WS 12 BC 930	ED/HC/ MD/SN	24	24	12
	PRINCE OF PEACE sabraham@popfremont.org www.popfremont.org	1953	38451 FREMONT BLVD	94536	CNH	Dr Thomas J Zelt David M Sauer	(510)793-3366 (510)793-6993	WS 830 11 SS 945 11 BC 945	EL/ED/HC/ MD/SN			
	PRINCE OF PEACE-MISSION HILLS Satellite Site of Prince of Peace Fremont CA	2019	858 Washington Blvd	94536								
FRESNO	*EMMANUEL*		See Clovis CA									
	PEACE peace@pacbell.net www.peacelutheranfresno.org	1958	4672 N CEDAR AVE	93726	CNH	Clinton S Hoff Khai N Lee	(559)222-2320 (559)222-2750	WS 9 SS 9 1030 BC 1030	ED/HC/ MD/SN	396	230	184
	REDEEMER office@redeemerfresno.com www.redeemerfresno.com	1954	1084 W BULLARD AVE	93711	CNH	Clarence H Eisberg James B Fennacy	(559)439-8500 (559)439-8585	WS 8 1030 SS 915 BC 915	ED/HC/ MD/SN	238	218	88
FULLERTON	*SEARCHLIGHT* office@searchlightministries.com www.SearchlightMinistries.com	2015	2311 E CHAPMAN AVE	92831	PSW	Mark L Manning	(714)871-1711		EC	70	65	90
	TRUE LOVE mankang1957@gmail.com	1991	1521 W ORANGETHORPE AVE	92833	PSW	Man S Kang Seung W Kim	(714)992-5008 (714)827-9424	WS 930 11	EC			
GALT	*SHEPHERD OF VALLEY* office.svlc@gmail.com	1948	604 E ST	95632	CNH	Michael S Dube	(209)745-1825 (209)745-6781	WS 10	ED/HC/ MD/SN	79	72	36
GARDEN GROVE	*ST LUKE*		See Westminster CA									
	ST PAUL vukinh@yahoo.com	1951	13082 BOWEN ST	92843	PSW	Kinh T Vu Van M Pinkerton	(714)537-4245 (714)741-8353	WS 8 930 11 SS 930 BC 930 11	HS/ED	54	50	30
GEORGETOWN	*TRINITY* tlc3office@gmail.com	1983	6417 Main St PO BOX 115	95634	CNH	Richard E Toms	(530)333-0798 (530)333-0798	WS 9 SS 1030	ED/HC	34	32	27
GLENDALE	*ZION* leighghart@yahoo.com classicedlearning.org	1923	301 N ISABEL ST	91206	PSW	Leigh G Hart	(818)243-3119 (818)243-9640	WS 8	ED/HC/ MD/SN			
GLENDORA	*HOPE* adminoffice@hopeglendora.org www.hopeglendora.org	1955	1041 E FOOTHILL BLVD	91741	PSW	Dr Steven R Parks	(626)335-5315 (626)852-0836	WS 9 SS 930 BC 1035	EL/ED/ HC/SN	281	202	114
GOLETA	*GOOD SHEPHERD* gslc2@yahoo.com www.gslcms.org	1959	380 N FAIRVIEW AVE	93117	PSW	Keith R Jones	(805)967-1416 (805)692-5236	WS 930 BC 11	EC/ED/HC/ MD	196	174	77
GRANADA HILLS	*OUR SAVIOR FIRST* cadmin@osflcs.com www.osflcs.com	1954	16603 SAN FERNANDO MISSION BLV	91344	PSW		(818)363-9505 (818)831-9222	WS 10 BC 9 1130	EL/ED/HC/ MD/SN	60	43	49
GRANITE BAY	*HOLY CROSS*		See Rocklin CA									
GRASS VALLEY	*GRACE* admin@gracelutherangv.org gracelutherangv.org	1945	1979 RIDGE RD	95945	CNH		(530)273-7043 (530)273-4206	WS 9 SS 1030 BC 1030	ED/HC/ MD/SN			
GREENVILLE	*FIRST*	1951	120 Bush St PO BOX 598	95947	CNH		(530)258-2347	WS 11	HC/SN			
GRIDLEY	*GRACE* gracelutherangridley@gmail.com	1950	150 FORD AVE	95948	CNH	Jeffrey W Tuft	(530)846-4736 (530)846-4736	WS 10 BC 9	ED/HC/MD	23	23	16
GROVER BEACH	*PEACE*		See Arroyo Grande CA									
GUSTINE	*SAINT JAMES*		See Newman CA									
HACIENDA HEIGHTS	*HOLY TRINITY* matthew.morrison@htlcms.org www.htlcms.org	1962	15710 NEWTON ST HACIENDA HTS	91745	PSW	Dr Clinton J Armstrong	(626)333-9017 (626)333-6468	WS 9 SS 1030 BC 1030	ED/HC	125	80	80
HANFORD	*FIRST* pastorhalakhe@flchanford.org www.flchanford.org	1947	9075 12TH AVE.	93230	CNH	John H Halakhe	(559)582-2463	WS 10 SS 9 BC 9	ED/HC/ MD/SN	70	65	35
HAWTHORNE	*THE GOOD SHEPHERD*		See Inglewood CA									
HAYWARD	*GOOD SHEPHERD* office@gslchayward.org www.gslchayward.org	1953	166 W HARDER RD	94544	CNH	Dawit A Bokre Joshua M Woodrow	(510)782-0872 (510)781-0317	WS 930 10 SS 11 1145 BC 830 9 1145	ED/HC/ MD/SN	257	190	210
	GRACE grace_lutheran@att.net www.gracehayward.org	1931	1836 B St 166 W HARDER RD	94541 94544	CNH		(510)581-6620 (510)881-8045	WS 9	ED/SN			
	HOPE		See Fremont CA									
	*OROMO** teme_meng@yahoo.com		166 WEST HARDER RD	94544	CNH		(510)754-1494					
HEALDSBURG	*GOOD SHEPHERD* goodshepherd@mygslc.com www.mygslc.com	1954	1402 UNIVERSITY ST	95448	CNH	Philip J Beyer	(707)433-3835 (707)433-4863	WS 930	EC/ED/HC/ MD	68	64	36
HEMET	*FUENTE DE VIDA*	2000	26410 Columbia St 186 W 5TH ST SAN JACINTO	92544 92583	PSW	Dr Juan D Herrera	(951)654-8691	WS 5 SS 6				

*Indicates a new church start. A new church start is an intentionally organized gathering which comes together on a regular basis for the purpose of worship and/or Bible study and is intended to grow into a member LCMS congregation. WS =Worship Service; SS = Sunday School; BC =Bible Class; EC = Early Childhood; EL = Elementary School; HS = High School; ED =Education Ministry; HC =Human Care Ministry; SN = Special Needs Ministry; MD = Media Ministry (PC)=Partner Church Pastor. See Page 53 for the Table of Abbreviations for key to additional abbreviations

CITY	CONGREGATION EMAIL WEBSITE	YEAR EST	LOCATION MAILING ADDRESS	ZIP CODE(S)	DIST.	PASTOR(S)	PHONE FAX	WS SS BC	SCHOOLS/ MINISTRIES	STATISTIC Bapt	Conf	Avg Attend
HEMET	*PRINCE OF PEACE* jen@princeofpeacehemet.org www.princeofpeacehemet.org	1979	701 N SANDERSON AVE	92545	PSW	Luis E Barreto Lugo	(951)925-6121 (951)766-6779	WS 830 1030 SS 945 BC 930	EC/ED/HC/ MD/SN	95	85	68
	ST JOHN nbellamy@stjohnshemet.org www.stjohnshemet.org	1928	26410 COLUMBIA ST	92544	PSW	Luke W Kastner	(951)925-7756 (951)925-6136	WS 815 1015 BC 930	EL/ED/HC/ MD	294	275	95
HERALD	*SHEPHERD OF VALLEY*		See Galt CA									
HERMOSA BEACH	*IMMANUEL*		See Redondo Beach CA									
HESPERIA	*ASCENSION*		See Apple Valley CA									
	FAITH faithhesperia@verizon.net	1963	9600 7TH AVE	92345	PSW	Dr Elroi Reimnitz	(760)244-5943 (760)956-7636	WS 1030 BC 9	ED/HC/ MD/SN	75	67	55
HIGHLAND	*MESSIAH* messiah7@empirenet.com www.empirenet.com/~messiah7	1960	7070 Palm Ave PO BOX 372	92346	PSW	John P Juedes	(909)862-2923	WS 1015 SS 9		22	20	16
HOLTVILLE	*ST PAUL* 548stpaul@gmail.com www.stpaulsholtville.com	1929	562 Chestnut Ave 548 CHESTNUT AVE	92250	PSW	Davin J Alberson	(760)356-4315	WS 9 SS 1015 BC 1030	ED/HC/MD	236	194	83
HUNTINGTON BEACH	*CHRIST*		See Costa Mesa CA									
	CHRIST LUTHERAN Satellite Site of Christ Costa Mesa CA	2023	8200 Ellis Ave	92646				WS 930				
	MEDHANE ALEM wasfawz5@gmail.com	2009	8200 ELLIS AVE	93646	PSW		(714)995-7324	WS 10		78	55	50
	REDEEMER churchoffice@redeemer-lutheran.net www.redeemer-lutheran.net	1963	16351 SPRINGDALE ST HUN-TINGTN BCH	92649	PSW	Ernest C Jeong Thomas R Miller	(714)846-6330 (714)840-2679	WS 8 11 SS 930 BC 930	EC/HS/ED/ HC/MD/SN	201	194	113
	ST LUKE		See Westminster CA									
IMPERIAL	*GRACE*		See El Centro CA									
	ST PAUL		See Holtville CA									
IMPERIAL BEACH	*SAINT JAMES* office@stjamesib.org stjamesib.org	1954	866 IMPERIAL BEACH BLVD IMPERIAL BCH	91932	PSW	Ramon Contreras	(619)424-6166	WS 9 SS 1030 BC 1030	EL/HS/ED	99	88	63
INDIAN WELLS	*TRINITY*		See Indio CA									
INDIO	*TRINITY* trinity81500@verizon.net www.trinityindio.org	1949	81500 Miles Ave P.O. BOX 1586	92201 92202	PSW	Robert E Smith	(760)347-3971	WS 830 11 SS 10 1115 BC 10	ED/HC/MD			
INGLEWOOD	*FAITH* anthony_foster@sbcglobal.net www.faithing.org	1966	3320 W 85th St 8517 S 11TH AVE	90305	PSW	Anthony K Foster	(323)750-3552 (323)750-4136	WS 9 BC 11	HC/MD	175	175	35
	THE GOOD SHEPHERD GoodShepherdLC@sbcglobal.net tgslcms.org	1935	902 S MAPLE ST	90301	PSW	Edward J Killian	(310)671-7644 (310)673-7488	WS 10 BC 830	EL/HS/ED/ HC/MD/SN			
IRVINE	*ETHIOPIAN*	2009	18182 Culver Dr	91612	PSW		(562)437-8532			20	20	15
	FAITH	1925	PO BOX 4970	92616	PSW		(213)700-3504					
	JESUS LOVE lutheran1031@gmail.com	2015	18182 CULVER DR	92612	PSW	Chimin Jun Theodore S Kim	(949)878-1970					
	LIGHT OF CHRIST churchoffice@locirvine.com www.lightofchristirvine.com	1980	18182 CULVER DR	92612	PSW	Jim B Gwaltney III Jonathan B Ruehs	(949)786-3326	WS 8 1030 SS 915 BC 915	EC/ED/HC	180	169	180
	ST PAUL office@saintpaulsirvine.com www.saintpaulsirvine.org	1945	SAINT PAUL'S LUTHERAN CHURCH OF IRVINE 16355 LAGUNA CANYON RD	92618	PSW	Dr Alfonso O Espinosa Dr Steven P Mueller	(949)599-4760	WS 930 BC 11	HS/ED/HC/ MD	225	175	80
LA CRESCENTA	*GETHSEMANE* glcmslc@gmail.com www.glcmslc.org	1955	2723 ORANGE AVE	91214	PSW	Dr James P Edwards	(818)248-3738 (818)248-3487	WS 10 BC 9	ED	21	21	16
LA JOLLA	*UNIVERSITY* ucsdlutheran.net	1963	9595 LA JOLLA SHORES DR	92037	PSW	Peter C Alexander	(858)453-0561 (858)453-9932	WS 1015	ED	20	20	30
LA MESA	*CHRIST* info@christlamesa.org www.christlamesa.org	1942	7929 LA MESA BLVD	91942	PSW	Travis W Ferguson	(619)462-5211 (619)462-5275	WS 8 1030 SS 915 BC 915	EL/HS/ED/ HC/MD/SN	552	450	420
	MORNING STAR		See Lakeside CA									
	ST LUKES office-sllc@att.net www.st-lukes-la-mesa.org	1944	5150 WILSON ST	91942	EN	Mark D Menacher	(619)463-6633	WS 9 SS 1030		179	132	68
	TRINITY		See San Diego CA									
LA QUINTA	*TRINITY*		See Indio CA									
LA VERNE	*ST PAULS*		See Pomona CA									
LADERA HEIGHTS	*THE GOOD SHEPHERD*		See Inglewood CA									
LAGUNA HILLS	*ABIDING SAVIOR*		See Lake Forest CA									
LAKE ARROWHEAD	*MOUNT CALVARY* info@mclutheran.com www.mclutheran.com	1957	27415 School Rd PO BOX 250 LK ARROWHEAD	92352	PSW		(909)337-1412	WS 8 930 11 SS 930 BC 930	EL/ED/HC/ MD	441	372	157
LAKE ELSINORE	*FIRST* pastor@firstluth.com www.firstluth.com	1946	600 W Sumner 600 W SUMNER AVE	92530	PSW	Kevin L Kolander	(951)674-2757	WS 1030 SS 9	ED/HC/ MD/SN			
LAKE FOREST	*ABIDING SAVIOR* abidingsavior.com	1965	23262 EL TORO RD	92630	PSW	Glenn A Lucas	(949)830-1460 (949)830-6783	WS 8 1015 SS 1015 BC 915	EL/HS/ED/ HC/MD/SN	2081	1148	326
LAKE ISABELLA	*SHEPHERD HILLS* sothlica@yahoo.com www.shepherdothills.org	1969	377 Highway 155 PO BOX S	93240	CNH	Daniel A Schlenske	(760)379-2343 (760)379-2343	WS 11 SS 930 BC 930	ED/HC/ MD/SN	51	50	22

*Indicates a new church start. A new church start is an intentionally organized gathering which comes together on a regular basis for the purpose of worship and/or Bible study and is intended to grow into a member LCMS congregation. WS =Worship Service; SS = Sunday School; BC =Bible Class; EC = Early Childhood; EL = Elementary School; HS = High School; ED =Education Ministry; HC =Human Care Ministry; SN = Special Needs Ministry; MD = Media Ministry (PC)=Partner Church Pastor. See Page 53 for the Table of Abbreviations for key to additional abbreviations

CITY	CONGREGATION EMAIL WEBSITE	YEAR EST	LOCATION MAILING ADDRESS	ZIP CODE(S)	DIST.	PASTOR(S)	PHONE FAX	WS SS BC	SCHOOLS/ MINISTRIES	STATISTIC Bapt	Conf	Avg Attend
LAKE VIEW TERRACE	*PEACE* peacelutheran2023lvt.ca@gmail.com www.peacelutheran-ca.org	1962	11690 FENTON AVE LAKE VIEW TER	91342	PSW		(818)899-3950		ED/HC/MD	55	55	53
LAKESIDE	*CELEBRATION** hjmajewski@cox.net	1992	Morning Starr Luth Church 12821 Ha Hana Rd 8828 PEBBLE BEACH CT SANTEE	92040 92071	PSW		(619)916-8310	WS 1030 SS 1030	EL/HS	40	40	20
	MORNING STAR mstarpastor@gmail.com www.morningstarlcms.org	1972	12821 HA HANA RD	92040	PSW	Richard Ross	(619)443-6032	WS 845 SS 10 BC 10	EL/HS/ED/MD	32	32	20
LANCASTER	*GRACE* church@gracelancaster.org www.gracelancaster.org	1921	856 W NEWGROVE ST	93534	PSW	Michael D Hall	(661)948-1018 (661)948-2731	WS 10 BC 11	EL/ED	211	180	105
	RESURRECTION		See Quartz Hill CA									
LEMON GROVE	*TRINITY*		See San Diego CA									
LINCOLN	*HOLY CROSS*		See Rocklin CA									
LINDSAY	*MOUNT OLIVE* scottscheeremt@aol.com	1949	1044 PARKSIDE AVE	93247	CNH	Scott C Scheer	(559)359-2022	WS 10 SS 1130				
LIVERMORE	*OUR SAVIOR* oslm@oslm.net oslm.net	1954	1385 S LIVERMORE AVE	94550	CNH	Joseph E Robb	(925)447-1246 (925)447-0201	WS 9 1115 SS 1030 BC 1030	EL/ED/HC/MD/SN	314	310	222
LIVINGSTON	*SAINT JAMES*		See Newman CA									
LODI	*REDEEMER* redeemerlutheranlodi@gmail.com	1982	1845 S HAM LN	95242	CNH	Bruce E Berndt	(209)368-2288 (209)334-5431	WS 9 BC 1020				
	ST PETER church@stpeterlodi.org splodichurch.org/	1898	2400 OXFORD WAY	95242	CNH	Timothy A Blau	(209)333-2223 (209)297-4349	WS 830 1045 SS 9 1115 BC 930	EL/ED/HC/MD	367	308	261
	ZION office@zlclodi.org www.zlclodi.org		105 S HAM LN	95242	CNH	Jason M Weber	(209)369-1919 (877)335-2264	WS 10 BC 845 630	EC/ED/MD/SN	86	78	50
LOMPOC	*BETHANY* bethanylompoc@gmail.com bethanylompoc.org	1951	135 S E ST	93436	CNH	Joseph A Byrd	(805)736-8615 (805)735-6178	WS 10 BC 1115	ED/HC/MD/SN			
	CLEAR PROMISE jpuscheck@clearpromise.com www.clearpromise.com		1305 North H St Ste A 1305 N H ST STE A PMB 256	93436	CNH	John E Puscheck	(805)698-9846			13	9	10
LONG BEACH	*BETHANY* www.bethanylutheran.org	1944	4644 CLARK AVE	90808	PSW	Kevin L Kritzer John M Alwood	(562)421-4711 (562)429-1693	WS 8 930 SS 930	EC/EL/ED/HC/MD/SN	1817	1448	450
	ST PAUL info@stpaulslb.org www.stpaulslb.org	1955	2283 PALO VERDE AVE	90815	EN	Mark A Pierson	(562)596-4409 (562)598-5629	WS 930 SS 1130 BC 1130	EC/ED/MD			
LOOMIS	*HOLY CROSS*		See Rocklin CA									
LOS ANGELES	*ARK OF NOAH* arkofnoahchurch@gmail.com www.arkofnoahchurch.org	1988	3735 HUGHES AVE	90034	PSW	Yeong K Kim Ung W Cho	(310)836-8342		ED/HC/MD	40	40	37
	CHRIST info@christlutheranla.com	1905	1966 CONCORDIA WALK	90062	PSW		(323)815-4344	WS 10	MD	30	30	20
	FIRST info@firstlutherancc.org	1927	3735 HUGHES AVE	90034	PSW	Matthew Wait	(310)838-6076	WS 10		30	24	18
	GRACE jeanenockberus@gmail.com	1906	936 W VERNON AVE	90037	PSW	Arthur J Stevens	(213)359-5740	WS 9	ED/HC/MD/SN	39	39	36
	HIGHLAND PARK revnwirtz@yahoo.com hplutheran.tripod.com	1922	6310 ALDAMA ST	90042	EN		(323)255-0309 (323)255-0309	WS 9 SS 1015 BC 1015	ED/HC			
	HOPE MEMORIAL	1951	3401 SOMERSET DR	90016	PSW		(213)731-1721 (323)731-1761	WS 10 SS 11				
	JOBBER MISSION OF USA Satellite Site of Ark Of Noah Los Angeles CA	2003	1015 S Crocker St #S-27	90021								
	LA SANTA CRUZ	1957	753 CAMULOS ST	90023	PSW	Marcello Gomez	(626)298-0193					
	LIGHT OF LIGHT dongjoon815@hotmail.com	1997	1308 S New Hampshire Ave #403 1644 4TH AVE	90006 90019	PSW	Dong J Kim	(213)598-1196					
	OUR SAVIOR oursav@sbcglobal.net www.childrenofoursaviorwestchester.org	1952	6705 W 77TH ST WEST-CHESTER	90045	PSW		(310)670-7272 (310)649-5440	WS 10 SS 9 BC 9	EC/EL/HS/ED/HC/MD	34	27	22
	PALISADES		See Pacific Palisades CA									
	*REFORMATION ETHIOPIA** chariotchurch@yahoo.com		3401 S Somerset Dr	90016	PSW		(626)298-9788		ED/HC/MD			
	ST PAUL jeanenockberus@gmail.com stpaullutheranla.org	1925	3901 W ADAMS BLVD	90018	PSW	Jean-Enock Berus	(323)731-8384 (310)887-4856	WS 830 11 SS 1115 BC 930	ED/HC/MD/SN	85	52	30
	THE GOOD SHEPHERD		See Inglewood CA									
	TRINITY CENTRAL tclc1882@gmail.com	1882	987 S GRAMERCY PL	90019	PSW	Michael P Pavich	(323)737-2790	WS 10				
LOS GATOS	*HOLY CROSS* secretary@holycrosslosgatos.com www.holycrosslosgatos.com	1958	15885 LOS GATOS ALMADEN RD	95032	CNH	Andrew M Koschmann	(408)356-3525 (408)358-4982	WS 930 BC 1045	EL/ED/HC/MD	154	137	61
LUCERNE	*FIRST* nanoom212003@yahoo.com firstlutheran-lucerne.org	1953	3863 Country Club Dr PO BOX 458	95458	CNH		(707)274-5572	WS 11 SS 11 BC 10	ED/HC/SN	22	18	15
LUCERNE VALLEY	*ASCENSION*		See Apple Valley CA									
MADERA	*EMMANUEL*		See Clovis CA									

*Indicates a new church start. A new church start is an intentionally organized gathering which comes together on a regular basis for the purpose of worship and/or Bible study and is intended to grow into a member LCMS congregation. WS =Worship Service; SS = Sunday School; BC =Bible Class; EC = Early Childhood; EL = Elementary School; HS = High School; ED =Education Ministry; HC =Human Care Ministry; SN = Special Needs Ministry; MD = Media Ministry (PC)=Partner Church Pastor. See Page 53 for the Table of Abbreviations for key to additional abbreviations

CITY	CONGREGATION EMAIL WEBSITE	YEAR EST	LOCATION MAILING ADDRESS	ZIP CODE(S)	DIST.	PASTOR(S)	PHONE FAX	WS SS BC	SCHOOLS/ MINISTRIES	STATISTIC Bapt	Conf	Avg Attend
MAMMOTH LAKES	*MAMMOTH LAKES* revkpuls@gmail.com www.mammothlakeslutheranchurch.com	1976	379 Old Mammoth Rd PO BOX 7218	93546	PSW	Timothy M Homan	(760)934-4051	WS 845	ED/HC/MD			
MANHATTAN BEACH	*FIRST* flcoffice@first-lutheran.com www.flcol.org	1948	1100 N POINSETTIA AVE MANHATTAN BCH	90266	PSW	Bartholomew C Loos	(310)545-5653 (310)545-5654	WS 10 BC 845	EC/EL/HS/ ED/HC/MD	86	80	65
MARINA	*BETHLEHEM*		See Monterey CA									
	FAITH		See Seaside CA									
MARTINEZ	*FAITH*		See Pleasant Hill CA									
MAYWOOD	*PALABRA DE DIOS* palabradediosmaywood@gmail.com	1997	4421 E 61ST ST	90270	PSW	Dr Antonio J Lopez	(323)404-8583		ED/HC/ MD/SN	48	47	21
MENLO PARK	*BETHANY* revjon@bethany-mp.org www.bethany-mp.org	1950	1095 CLOUD AVE	94025	CNH	Thomas G Norris Jr	(650)854-5897 (650)854-5910	WS 930 SS 945	EC/ED/HC/ MD			
MERCED	*ST PAUL* churchoffice@stpaulmerced.com stpaulmerced.com	1940	2916 N Mc Kee Rd 2916 MCKEE RD	95340	CNH	Doua Xiong	(209)383-3301 (209)383-3642	WS 10 SS 1115 BC 9 1115	EL/ED/HC/ MD	248	120	67
MILL VALLEY	*PEACE* pastor@plcmarin.org www.plcmarin.org	1949	205 TENNESSEE VALLEY RD	94941	CNH		(415)388-2065 (415)381-7290	WS 930 SS 11	ED/HC/ MD/SN			
MILPITAS	*MOUNT OLIVE* office@mt-olive.org www.mt-olive.org	1962	1989 E CALAVERAS BLVD	95035	CNH		(408)262-0506 (408)262-9359	WS 9 SS 1015 BC 1030	ED/HC/MD			
MISSION HILLS	*THE CROSS*	1955	10000 SEPULVEDA BLVD	91345	EN	William G Naumann Victor M de la Rosa	(818)892-8490	WS 10 BC 9	ED/HC			
MISSION VIEJO	*ABIDING SAVIOR*		See Lake Forest CA									
MODESTO	*GRACE* gracemodesto@gmail.com www.gracemodesto.org	1920	617 W ORANGEBURG AVE	95350	CNH	Grant A Knepper	(209)522-8890 (209)529-7721	WS 9 BC 9	EC/ED	297	267	115
MONROVIA	*FIRST* firstlutheranchurch@outlook.com church.lutheranmonrovia.org	1926	1323 S MAGNOLIA AVE	91016	PSW	Michael E Powers	(626)357-3543 (626)357-8296	WS 9	EC/ED/HC/ MD/SN	78	76	70
MONTCLAIR	*TRINITY* pastor.lirey@gmail.com www.tlcmontclair.org	1957	5080 KINGSLEY ST	91763	PSW	Lance A Irey	(909)626-6552	WS 10 BC 1115	ED/HC/MD	30	30	22
MONTE SERENO	*HOLY CROSS*		See Los Gatos CA									
MONTEBELLO	*ST JOHN*	1906	433 N 18TH ST	90640	PSW		(323)477-1275	WS 1030	EC/ED/HC/ MD/SN			
MONTEREY	*BETHLEHEM* blcmonterey@gmail.com letsgotobethlehem.org	1925	800 CASS ST	93940	CNH	Joshua A Schmidt	(831)373-1523	WS 10 BC 9	ED/HC/ MD/SN	81	75	52
	FAITH		See Seaside CA									
	MERRILL GARDENS Satellite Site of Bethlehem Monterey CA	2023	200 Iris Canyon Rd.	93940								
MONTEREY PARK	*EMMAUS*		See Alhambra CA									
MOORPARK	*FAITH* faith@faithmoorpark.com www.faithmoorpark.com	1985	123 PARK LN	93021	PSW	Sean K Deming	(805)532-1049 (805)532-1049	WS 915 SS 1045 BC 1045	ED/HC/ MD/SN	161	148	65
MORENO VALLEY	*SHEP OF THE VALLEY* office@svlcmoval.net www.svlcmoval.net	1978	11650 PERRIS BLVD	92557	PSW	Anthony P Yearyean	(951)924-4688 (951)243-1834	WS 930 BC 1045	EC/ED/HC/ MD/SN	93	93	48
MOUNTAIN VIEW	*ST PAUL* andrewc@st-paul.org www.st-paul.org	1951	1075 EL MONTE AVE	94040	CNH		(650)967-0666	WS 9 SS 1030 BC 1030	EC/ED			
MURRIETA	*PROMISE* office@promise.family www.promise.family	2003	25664 Madison Ave 39590 SUNROSE DR	92562	PSW		(951)600-8201 (877)698-4593	WS 8 915 11 SS 915 11	ED/HC/ MD/SN	237	237	141
	TRINITY		See Temecula CA									
NAPA	*ST JOHN'S* churchoffice@stjohnsnapa.org www.stjohnslutheran.net	1904	3521 LINDA VISTA AVE	94558	CNH	Michael A Schmid	(707)255-0119 (707)255-3041	WS 930 SS 950 BC 11	EL/ED/HC/ MD/SN	515	437	178
NATIONAL CITY	*VICTORY*		See Chula Vista CA									
NEEDLES	*GRACE* gracelutheran.us	1937	1605 WASHINGTON ST	92363	PSW		(706)326-3128	WS 10	ED/HC/MD			
NEVADA CITY	*GRACE*		See Grass Valley CA									
NEWARK	*HOPE*		See Fremont CA									
NEWBURY PARK	*CHRIST KING* admin@ctknp.com www.ctknp.com	1964	3947 KIMBER DR	91320	PSW	Benjamin J Mai	(805)498-2217	WS 830 1030 SS 1130 BC 9	EC/ED/HC/ MD	78	75	55
NEWMAN	*SAINT JAMES* SJLC-Newman@outlook.com	1893	1102 P St PO BOX 816	95360	CNH	Daniel E Junkin	(209)862-3438	WS 10 BC 1115		32	29	13
NEWPORT BEACH	*CHRIST*		See Costa Mesa CA									
NORCO	*EDGEWATER*		See Eastvale CA									
NORTH HIGHLANDS	*ZION* zionnhsec@gmail.com www.ZionLutheranNH.org	1954	3644 BOLIVAR AVE N HIGHLANDS	95660	CNH		(916)332-4001 (916)332-4030	WS 8 1045 SS 11 BC 11	ED/HC/ MD/SN	156	145	43
NORTH TUSTIN	*SALEM*		See Orange CA									
NORWALK	*PEACE*		See Pico Rivera CA									
	TRINITY www.trinitywhittier.org	1909	11909 Rosecrans Ave 11716 FLORAL DR WHITTIER	90650 90601	PSW		(562)699-7431	WS 9 SS 1030	MD/SN			

*Indicates a new church start. A new church start is an intentionally organized gathering which comes together on a regular basis for the purpose of worship and/or Bible study and is intended to grow into a member LCMS congregation. WS =Worship Service; SS = Sunday School; BC =Bible Class; EC = Early Childhood; EL = Elementary School; HS = High School; ED =Education Ministry; HC =Human Care Ministry; SN = Special Needs Ministry; MD = Media Ministry (PC)=Partner Church Pastor. See Page 53 for the Table of Abbreviations for key to additional abbreviations

CITY	CONGREGATION EMAIL WEBSITE	YEAR EST	LOCATION MAILING ADDRESS	ZIP CODE(S)	DIST.	PASTOR(S)	PHONE FAX	WS SS BC	SCHOOLS/ MINISTRIES	STATISTIC Bapt	Conf	Avg Attend
NORWALK	*TRINITY* tlc.norwalk@yahoo.com www.tlc-norwalk.org	2008	11507 STUDEBAKER RD	90650	PSW	Eduardo Cuen	(562)864-3713 (562)864-1761	WS 10 SS 845	EC/EL/ ED/HC	76	75	44
OAKLAND	*ZION*		See Piedmont CA									
OCEANO	*PEACE*		See Arroyo Grande CA									
OCEANSIDE	*IMMANUEL* office@immanueloceanside.com www.ilcoceanside.org	1947	1900 S NEVADA ST	92054	PSW	Michael A Hansen	(760)458-6570	WS 930 BC 11	EL/HS/ MD/SN	87	74	74
	SHEP OF VALLEY SVLCOceanside@gmail.com www.svlchurch.org	1973	4510 N River Rd PO BOX 406 SAN LUIS REY	92057 92068	PSW	Joel A Luckemeyer	(760)433-9250 (760)433-9757	WS 10 SS 9 BC 9	ED/MD	133	114	40
ONTARIO	*REDEEMER* secretary@redeemer4me.com www.redeemer4me.com	1943	920 W 6TH ST	91762	PSW	Daniel M Grabowski	(909)986-2615	WS 9 SS 1030 BC 1030	EC/ED/HC/ MD/SN	227	209	117
ORANGE	*IMMANUEL* church@immanuelorange.org www.immanuelorange.com	1922	802 E CHAPMAN AVE	92866	EN	Dr Robb C Ring	(714)538-2373 (714)538-7952	WS 8 1045 BC 930	EC/EL/HS/ ED/MD/SN			
	SAINT JOHNS www.stjohnsorange.org	1882	154 S SHAFFER ST	92866	PSW	Timothy M Klinkenberg Trevor E Van Blarcom	(714)288-4400 (714)288-4411	WS 830 1030 SS 1030 BC 945 630	EL/HS/ED/ HC/MD/SN	5494	4249	1164
	SALEM church@salemorange.com www.salemorange.com	1965	6500 E SANTIAGO CANYON RD	92869	PSW	Roger P Frick	(714)633-2366 (714)633-6937	WS 830 10 SS 830 1030 BC 930	EL/HS/ED/ HC/MD	234	198	245
	ST PAUL churchoffice@splsorange.org www.stpaulsorange.org	1907	1250 E HEIM AVE	92865	PSW	Dr Larry A Stoterau Carlos V Velazquez	(714)637-2640 (714)637-1963	WS 9 1030	EC/EL/HS/ ED/HC/ MD/SN	953	745	436
	TRINITY		See Anaheim CA									
ORANGE PARK ACRES	*SALEM*		See Orange CA									
ORANGEVALE	*HOLY CROSS*		See Rocklin CA									
ORCUTT	*GRACE*		See Santa Maria CA									
OROVILLE	*CALVARY* calvary.lutheran2@gmail.com www.calvarylutheranoroville.org	1939	10 CONCORDIA LN	95966	CNH	Jeffrey W Tuft	(530)533-5017 (530)533-5203	WS 845 BC 1015	ED/HC/ MD/SN	45	43	32
OXNARD	*CENTRO CRISTIANO* velascom72@gmail.com www.centrocristianohispano.com	1985	1500 North C St 1500 N C ST	93030	PSW		(805)727-0127		ED/HC	55	45	45
	ST JOHN'S vmoore@stjohnsoxnard.com www.stjohnsoxnard.com	1897	1500 N C ST	93030	PSW	Todd M Niebling	(805)983-0330 (805)983-2171	WS 930 SS 11	ED/HC	230	190	60
PACIFIC GROVE	*BETHLEHEM*		See Monterey CA									
	FAITH		See Seaside CA									
PACIFIC PALISADES	*PALISADES* LCMS@plc.cc plc.cc	1948	15905 W SUNSET BLVD	90272	PSW	Dr Martin E Lee	(310)459-2358	WS 9 BC 1115	ED/HC/ MD/SN	35	35	35
PACIFICA	*OUR SAVIOR'S* oursaviorslutheranpacifica.com/	1955	4400 CABRILLO HWY	94044	CNH	Kevin D Hempe	(650)359-1550	WS 10 SS 845 BC 845	MD			
PALM DESERT	*PEACE/DESERT* peacelutheranpd@gmail.com www.peacechurchlcms.org	1994	74200 Country Club Dr 74200 COUNTRY CLUB DR STE 4	92260	EN	James F Bowes	(760)776-7100	WS 10	ED/HC/ MD/SN	58	58	54
	TRINITY		See Indio CA									
PALM SPRINGS	*OUR SAVIOR'S* oscadmin@oursaviors.org www.oursaviors.org	1953	1020 E RAMON RD	92264	PSW		(760)327-5611	WS 10 SS 10	ED/HC/ MD/SN	50	45	65
	TRINITY		See Indio CA									
PALMDALE	*FIRST*	1954	38343 15TH ST E	93550	PSW		(661)947-6230 (661)947-6230	WS 1015 SS 9 BC 9				
	RESURRECTION		See Quartz Hill CA									
PALO ALTO	*TRINITY* trinitylutheranpa@gmail.com www.trinitylutheranpaloalto.com	1925	1295 MIDDLEFIELD RD	94301	CNH	Stewart D Crown	(650)853-1295	WS 930 SS 11 BC 11	ED/HC	120	110	39
PANORAMA CITY	*EL REDENTOR*	1957	14445 TERRA BELLA ST	91402	PSW		(818)891-1038	WS 11 SS 10				
PARADISE	*OUR SAVIOR* oslcinparadise@gmail.com www.oslcparadise.org	1964	6404 PENTZ RD	95969	CNH	Brandon P Merrick	(530)877-7321	WS 10 BC 9	ED/HC	87	80	45
PASADENA	*ETHIOPIAN CHARIOT** chariotchurch@yahoo.com www.ethiochurch.org		393 Lake Ave Ortlund Hall #201	91101	PSW		(626)298-9788					
	FAITH	1952	835 HASTINGS RANCH DR	91107	PSW		(626)351-5413 (626)351-5414	WS 1030 SS 915 BC 915	ED/HC/ MD/SN			
	FIRST www.historicfirstlutheran.org	1892	808 N LOS ROBLES AVE	91104	PSW	Christopher G Schaar	(626)793-1139 (626)793-6642	WS 10 SS 9 BC 9	ED/HC/ MD/SN	91	78	57
	MOUNT OLIVE mountolivepasadena@gmail.com www.mountolivelc.org	1925	1118 N ALLEN AVE	91104	PSW	Mark C Jasa	(626)794-2294	WS 1030 SS 930 BC 9	ED/MD			
PASO ROBLES	*TRINITY* church@trinitypaso.org www.trinitypaso.org	1921	940 CRESTON RD	93446	CNH	Christopher M Simmons	(805)238-3702 (805)238-7501	WS 930 SS 930 BC 1045	EL			
PATTERSON	*SAINT JAMES*		See Newman CA									
PEBBLE BEACH	*BETHLEHEM*		See Monterey CA									

*Indicates a new church start. A new church start is an intentionally organized gathering which comes together on a regular basis for the purpose of worship and/or Bible study and is intended to grow into a member LCMS congregation. WS =Worship Service; SS = Sunday School; BC =Bible Class; EC = Early Childhood; EL = Elementary School; HS = High School; ED =Education Ministry; HC =Human Care Ministry; SN = Special Needs Ministry; MD = Media Ministry (PC)=Partner Church Pastor. See Page 53 for the Table of Abbreviations for key to additional abbreviations

CITY	CONGREGATION EMAIL WEBSITE	YEAR EST	LOCATION MAILING ADDRESS	ZIP CODE(S)	DIST.	PASTOR(S)	PHONE FAX	WS SS BC	SCHOOLS/ MINISTRIES	STATISTIC Bapt	 Conf	 Avg Attend
PEBBLE BEACH	*FAITH*		See Seaside CA									
PENN VALLEY	*GRACE*		See Grass Valley CA									
PENNGROVE	*ST JOHN'S*		See Petaluma CA									
PENRYN	*HOLY CROSS*		See Rocklin CA									
PETALUMA	*ST JOHN'S* stjohn@lcmsj.org www.lcmsj.org	1910	455 MCNEAR AVE	94952	CNH		(707)762-4466 (707)766-6043	WS 2	ED	52	50	16
	ST MARK		See Santa Rosa CA									
PICO RIVERA	*PEACE* peaceluthch@gmail.com www.peacepicorivera.org	1952	9412 SHADE LN	90660	PSW	Alex Zavala	(562)949-5203	WS 9 SS 1030 BC 1030	ED/HC/ MD/SN	37	37	29
PIEDMONT	*ZION* churchoffice@zionlutheran.net zionlutheran.net	1882	5201 PARK BLVD	94611	CNH	Peter B Dorn	(510)530-4213 (510)530-2635	WS 9 SS 8 BC 8	ED/HC/ MD/SN	215	210	52
PINOLE	*OUR SAVIOR* osl@att.net www.facebook.com/oslcofpinole	1952	3110 AVIS WAY	94564	CNH	Nickolas E Teller	(510)275-3494	WS 1030 SS 915	HC/MD	60	60	45
PISMO BEACH	*PEACE*		See Arroyo Grande CA									
PITTSBURG	*GRACE* graceluthchurch@sbcglobal.net	1931	195 Alvarado Ave 1092 ALBERTA WAY CONCORD	94565 94521	CNH		(925)439-5857 (925)439-0563	WS 930 BC 11	HC/MD/SN			
PLACERVILLE	*FIRST* firstlutheran@sbcglobal.net www.first4others.org	1952	1200 PINECREST CT	95667	CNH	Mark A Oatman	(530)622-3022	WS 10 BC 9	ED/HC/ MD/SN	101	101	80
PLEASANT HILL	*FAITH* info@welcome2faith.com www.welcome2faith.com	1950	50 WOODSWORTH LN	94523	CNH	David A Floyd	(925)685-7353	WS 9 SS 1030 BC 1030	EC/ED/HC/ MD/SN			
POMONA	*ST PAULS* pomonalutheran@yahoo.com www.pomonalutheran.org	1920	610 N San Antonio Ave 101 W MISSION BLVD # 110-123	91767 91766	PSW	Neal R Blanke	(909)623-6368	WS 9 SS 1030 BC 1030	ED/MD/SN			
PORTERVILLE	*MOUNT OLIVE*		See Lindsay CA									
	ZION		See Terra Bella CA									
PORTOLA	*ST LUKE*	1952	496 W SIERRA ST	96122	CNH			WS 10	HC/SN	7	7	10
POWAY	*MOUNT OLIVE* mountolivepoway@gmail.com mountolivepoway.com	1960	14280 POWAY RD	92064	PSW	Quincy D Koll	(858)748-3871 (858)748-0693	WS 830 SS 830 BC 10	EC/EL/HS/ ED/MD/SN	110	95	60
PRATHER	*EMMANUEL*		See Clovis CA									
PRUNEDALE	*FAITH*		See Seaside CA									
QUARTZ HILL	*RESURRECTION* relcqh@gmail.com www.relcqh.org	1988	42217 55th St W 2010 W AVE K BOX 630 LANCASTER	93536	PSW		(661)943-8433	WS 9 BC 930	ED/MD	66	50	50
RAISIN CITY	*OUR SAVIOUR*		See Caruthers CA									
RAMONA	*RAMONA* church.office@ramonalutheran.org	1958	520 16TH ST	92065	PSW	Terry L Meyer	(760)789-1367	WS 9 SS 1045 BC 1045	EL/HS/ ED/HC			
RANCHO CORDOVA	*CORDOVA* cordovalutheran@gmail.com www.corluth.org	1957	10400 COLOMA RD	95670	CNH	Matthew D Peters	(916)363-5687 (253)669-6489	WS 10 BC 9	ED/HC	37	35	21
RANCHO CUCAMONGA	*SHEPHERD HILLS* www.soth.org	1977	6080 HAVEN AVE RCH CUCAMONGA	91737	PSW	Scott E Christenson Harry H Wang	(909)989-6500 (909)989-4905	WS 830 1030 SS 930 BC 930	ED/HC/MD	711	711	150
RANCHO MIRAGE	*TRINITY*		See Indio CA									
RANCHO PALOS VERDES	*CHRIST* office@clschool.org www.christrpv.com	1925	28850 S WESTERN AVE RCH PALOS VRD	90275	PSW	Dr Jonathan L Bran- denburg	(310)831-0848 (310)831-0090	WS 1030 SS 9 BC 9	EL/HS/ED/ MD	150	120	82
	MOUNT OLIVE admin@mtoliverpv.com www.mtoliverpv.com	1963	5975 ARMAGA SPRING RD RCH PALOS VRD	90275	PSW		(310)377-8541 (310)377-9903	WS 10 SS 10 BC 9	EC/ED/HC/ MD/SN	75	58	55
RED BLUFF	*ST PAUL* lutheranchurchredbluff@gmail.com lutheranchurch-redbluff.org	1947	455 Jefferson St PO BOX 726	96080	CNH	Dallas D Dubke	(530)527-3414	WS 10 BC 9	HC/MD	101	95	50
REDDING	*TRINITY* office@reddingtlc.org www.reddingtlc.org	1939	2440 HILLTOP DR	96002	CNH	Brian K Cummins	(530)221-6686 (530)232-2397	WS 9 SS 9 BC 9	EC/ED/HC/ MD/SN	262	218	75
REDLANDS	*CHRIST KING* ctklutheranpax@verizon.net www.ctkredlands.org	1967	1505 FORD ST	92373	PSW	Wiley J Smith	(909)793-5703	WS 9 SS 1030 BC 1030	EC/ED/HC/ MD	250	210	150
REDONDO BEACH	*IMMANUEL* immanuelrb706@gmail.com immanuelrb.com	1925	706 KNOB HILL AVE	90277	PSW	George W Lowrey Jr	(310)540-4435	WS 10 BC 830	EL/HS/ED/ MD/SN			
REDWOOD CITY	*BRIDGE CITY* hello@bridgecity.cc www.bridgecitychurch.online/	1926	468 GRAND ST	94062	CNH	Corey R Garrity Paul T Schult	(650)366-5892 (650)366-5898	WS 930 11 SS 930 BC 930	EL/ED/HC/ MD/SN	250	62	140
RIALTO	*GRACE* gracelutheranrialto@gmail.com www.gracelutheranrialto.com	1954	539 N ACACIA AVE	92376	PSW	William R Maggard Jr Daniel A Holm	(909)875-3163 (909)875-5232	WS 9 SS 1030 BC 1030	ED/HC/SN	41	34	28
RICHMOND	*MOUNT ZION* johnz@mahays.com	1955	5714 SOLANO AVE	94805	CNH	Timothy W Schepman Moises Morales	(510)685-9662 (510)233-2299	WS 10 SS 9 BC 9	SN	28	24	12
RIDGECREST	*OUR SAVIOR* secretary@oslc-rc.org www.oslc-rc.org	1947	735 N Fairview St 725 N FAIRVIEW ST	93555	PSW		(760)375-7921 (760)375-7921	WS 1015 SS 9 BC 9	EL/HS/ED/ HC/MD/SN	48	39	40
RIMFOREST	*MOUNT CALVARY*		See Lake Arrowhead CA									
RIVERDALE	*OUR SAVIOUR*		See Caruthers CA									

*Indicates a new church start. A new church start is an intentionally organized gathering which comes together on a regular basis for the purpose of worship and/or Bible study and is intended to grow into a member LCMS congregation. WS =Worship Service; SS = Sunday School; BC =Bible Class; EC = Early Childhood; EL = Elementary School; HS = High School; ED =Education Ministry; HC =Human Care Ministry; SN = Special Needs Ministry; MD = Media Ministry (PC)=Partner Church Pastor. See Page 53 for the Table of Abbreviations for key to additional abbreviations

CITY	CONGREGATION EMAIL WEBSITE	YEAR EST	LOCATION MAILING ADDRESS	ZIP CODE(S)	DIST.	PASTOR(S)	PHONE FAX	WS SS BC	SCHOOLS/ MINISTRIES	STATISTIC Bapt	Conf	Avg Attend
RIVERSIDE	*FAITH* faithriverside@att.net flcriv.org	1937	4785 JACKSON ST	92503	PSW	Eugene N Smith	(951)689-2626 (909)689-3829	WS 9	HC/MD	190	151	58
	IMMANUEL info@immanuelriverside.com www.immanuelriverside.com	1909	5455 ALESSANDRO BLVD	92506	PSW	Steven B Borst John W McCombs Robert M Jones	(951)682-7613 (951)682-9403	WS 930 SS 930 1030	EL/ED/SN	819	600	212
RIVERSIDE COUNTY	*PROMISE*		See Murrieta CA									
ROCKLIN	*HOLY CROSS* staff@holycrossrocklin.org www.holycrossrocklin.org	1986	4701 GROVE ST	95677	CNH	William M Shamburger III	(916)624-8185 (916)624-0813	WS 8 1045 SS 930 BC 930	EC/ED/HC/ MD/SN	270	208	185
	ST MATTHEW office@stmatthewrocklin.com www.stmatthewrocklin.com	1966	3785 PLACER CORPORATE DRIVE SUITE 600	95765	CNH	Bradley G Cusson	(916)435-0330	WS 830 10 SS 830 10 BC 10	ED/HC/MD			
ROHNERT PARK	*ST JOHN'S*		See Petaluma CA									
	ST MARK		See Santa Rosa CA									
ROSEMEAD	*ZION* iscahw@gmail.com	1938	3366 GLADYS AVE	91770	PSW		(626)589-8875	WS 10 SS 12 BC 1130	HC			
ROSEVILLE	*HOLY CROSS*		See Rocklin CA									
RUNNING SPRINGS	*MOUNT CALVARY*		See Lake Arrowhead CA									
SACRAMENTO	*CORDOVA*		See Rancho Cordova CA									
	FAITH		See Fair Oaks CA									
	GREENHAVEN office@greenhavenlutheran.org www.greenhavenlutheran.org	1968	475 FLORIN RD	95831	CNH	Derek M Evans	(916)428-8449 (916)428-3213	WS 1015 SS 1015 BC 845	EC/ED/ MD/SN	246	196	75
	PEACE peacelutherannatomas@yahoo.com www.peacelutherannatomas.org	1965	924 San Juan Rd 1520 W EL CAMINO AVE #206	95834 95833	CNH	James A Pevy	(916)927-5934 (916)927-5418	WS 9 SS 10 BC 1045	HC/MD/SN	94	61	34
	TOWN AND COUNTRY tclc@tclutheranchurch.org www.tclutheranchurch.org	1949	4049 MARCONI AVE	95821	CNH	Trevor A Mankin	(916)481-2542 (916)514-5057	WS 930 SS 11 BC 11	ED/HC/ MD/SN	118	95	73
	TRINITY tlcchurchsecretary@gmail.com www.tlc-sacramento.org	1915	1500 27TH ST	95816	CNH	Jason J Bredeson	(916)456-8701 (916)736-2369	WS 1015 SS 9 BC 9	ED/HC/ MD/SN	343	245	70
	ZION		See North Highlands CA									
SALINAS	*BETHLEHEM*		See Monterey CA									
	OUR SAVIOR office@SalinasLutheran.com www.salinaslutheran.com	1942	1230 LUTHER WAY	93901	CNH	Scott C Klemsz	(831)422-6352 (831)422-5320	WS 930 SS 830 BC 830	EC/ED			
SAN BERNARDINO	*IGLESIA LA SANTISIMA* stpmark@aol.com	1995	2900 N E ST	92405	PSW	Mark L McKenzie	(909)999-8311			96	12	31
	MESSIAH		See Highland CA									
	TRINITY www.trinitylutheransb.org	1910	2900 North E St 2900 N E ST SN BERNRDNO	92405	PSW	Jeffrey J Johnson	(909)882-2989	WS 1030 BC 9	ED/HC/ MD/SN	209	102	22
SAN CLEMENTE	*FAITH*		See Capistrano Beach CA									
SAN DIEGO	*BETHANY* admin@bethanylutheranob.org bethanylutheranob.org	1937	2051 SUNSET CLIFFS BLVD	92107	PSW	Wallace J Kimari	(619)222-7295	WS 11	ED/HC	26	25	20
	CHRIST		See La Mesa CA									
	CHRIST CORNERSTONE info@ctc-academy.org www.ctc-academy.org	1971	9028 WESTMORE RD	92126	PSW	Quincy D Koll	(858)566-1741 (858)566-1965	WS 1030 SS 1030 BC 9	EL/ED/MD	100	84	48
	FAITH flcms_1@att.net	1931	4335 Van Dyke Ave Parish House 4050 OLYMPIC ST	92105 92115	PSW	Dr Assefa Z Gugsa	(619)582-1068	WS 10	EL/HS/ED/ HC/MD/SN	26	26	20
	FIRST		See El Cajon CA									
	GLORIA DEI		See Escondido CA									
	GOOD SHEPHERD	1927	4335 VAN DYKE AVE	92105	PSW	William P Smith	(619)284-7228	WS 11	ED/HC/ MD/SN	21	11	18
	GRACE gjordan@gracesandiego.com www.gracesandiego.com	1912	3967 PARK BLVD	92103	PSW	Brian W Thomas	(619)299-2890 (619)295-4472	WS 8 1030 SS 1015	EL/HS/ED/ HC/MD/SN	148	122	104
	HOPE LINDA VISTA churchoffice@hope4sandiego.org hope4sandiego.org	1945	6749 TAIT ST	92111	PSW	Kevin G Sharp Gabriel S Ochoa Dr Laerte Tardelli H Voss	(858)268-4688	WS 930 BC 1045	EL/HS/ED/ HC/MD/SN	63	57	41
	LIVING WATER LivingWaterSD7@gmail.com livingwatersd.org	1990	Hampton Inn 11920 El Camino Real PMB 254 3525 DEL MAR HEIGHTS RD	92130	EN		(858)792-7691	WS 845 BC 10				
	MEDHANIALEM ETHIOPIA flcms_1@att.net	2008	4335 Van Dyke Ave	92105	PSW		(619)582-1068	WS 12 SS 10 BC 1030	MD			
	MORNING STAR		See Lakeside CA									
	MOUNT OLIVE		See Poway CA									
	OROMO nadhiilove@gmail.com		1370 EUCLID AVE	92105	PSW		(701)200-7796			15	8	8
	OUR REDEEMER ourredeemer@orlcsd.org www.ourredeemersandiego.com	1951	1370 EUCLID AVE	92105	PSW	David A Weber	(619)262-0757 (619)262-0403	WS 830 11 SS 10 BC 10	EL/HS/ED/ HC/MD/SN	123	108	75
	PRINCE PEACE churchoffice@princeofpeacesd.net www.princeofpeacesd.net	1955	6801 EASTON CT	92120	PSW	Paul L Willweber	(619)583-1436 (619)501-8710	WS 9 SS 1030 BC 1030	EL/HS	46	45	35

*Indicates a new church start. A new church start is an intentionally organized gathering which comes together on a regular basis for the purpose of worship and/or Bible study and is intended to grow into a member LCMS congregation. WS =Worship Service; SS = Sunday School; BC =Bible Class; EC = Early Childhood; EL = Elementary School; HS = High School; ED =Education Ministry; HC =Human Care Ministry; SN = Special Needs Ministry; MD = Media Ministry (PC)=Partner Church Pastor. See Page 53 for the Table of Abbreviations for key to additional abbreviations

CONGREGATIONS

CITY	CONGREGATION EMAIL WEBSITE	YEAR EST	LOCATION MAILING ADDRESS	ZIP CODE(S)	DIST.	PASTOR(S)	PHONE FAX	WS SS BC	SCHOOLS/ MINISTRIES	STATISTIC Bapt	 Conf	 Avg Attend
SAN DIEGO	*ST JAMES SHIELD MEN'S MINISTRY* Satellite Site of Saint James Imperial Beach CA	2020	615 Saturn Blvd	92154								
	ST PAULS rhartford@stpaulspb.com www.stpaulspb.com	1943	1376 FELSPAR ST	92109	PSW	Nathan A Hausch Isaac J Davis	(858)272-6363 (858)272-4822	WS 830 10 SS 10 BC 10	EL/HS/ED/ HC/MD/SN	363	326	150
	TRINITY sdtrinityluth@aol.com www.tlcsd.org	1897	7210 LISBON ST	92114	PSW	Richard P Stark	(619)262-1089	WS 1030 SS 9 BC 9	EL/HS/ED/ HC/MD	100	80	30
	UNIVERSITY		See La Jolla CA									
	VICTORY		See Chula Vista CA									
SAN DIMAS	*ST PAULS*		See Pomona CA									
SAN FRAN BAY AREA	*FIRST IMMANUEL*		See San Jose CA									
SAN FRANCISCO	*ADDIS KIDAN*		745 Buchanan St 2525 ALEMANY BLVD	94102 94112	CNH		(408)728-5900					
	BETHEL	1925	2525 ALEMANY BLVD	94112	CNH	Dr Terrence C Chan	(415)587-2525 (415)585-7320	WS 1030 SS 9 BC 9	HC/SN			
	BIBLE STUDY Satellite Site of Shepherd Hills San Francisco CA	2023	395 Addison Street	94131								
	CANAAN	1996	498 Funston St 498 FUNSTON AVE	94118	CNH		(415)221-0250	WS 930 BC 11	ED/HC			
	CHRIST ALL NATIONS		465 WOOLSEY ST	94134	CNH	Dr Terrence C Chan	(415)468-2937	WS 1030 SS 9 BC 9	HC			
	GRACE	1908	465 WOOLSEY ST	94134	CNH	Dr Terrence C Chan	(415)468-2937 (415)468-7320	WS 1030 SS 9 BC 9	ED/HC	26	25	12
	HOLY SPIRIT adminoffice@lcholyspirit.org www.lcholyspirit.org	1964	2400 NORIEGA ST	94122	CNH	Dr Shiu M Lau Christopher H Ng	(415)661-1120	WS 930 SS 11 BC 11	EC/ED/HC/ MD	338	323	272
	LAGUNA HONDA HOSPITAL & REHABILITATION CENTER Satellite Site of New Life Chinese San Francisco CA	2004	375 Laguna Honda Boulevard	94116								
	NEW LIFE CHINESE newlifechineselutheranchurch@ gmail.com www.newlifechinesesf.com	1994	395 ADDISON ST	94131	EN	Charles A Fox	(415)508-9552 (415)586-6526	WS 1145 SS 1030 BC 1030	ED/HC/MD	89	79	46
	SHEPHERD HILLS shepherdofthehillssf@gmail.com	1967	395 ADDISON ST	94131	CNH	Charles A Fox Otis L Byrd	(415)859-9603	WS 1030 BC 9	ED/HC/ MD/SN	20	20	15
	WEST PORTAL admin.church@wplsf.com www.westportallutheran.org	1943	200 SLOAT BLVD	94132	EN	Curtis A Binz Jacob D Swenson	(415)661-0242 (415)661-8402	WS 10 SS 9 BC 9	EL/ED	621	439	138
	ZION www.zionsf.org	1905	495 9TH AVE	94118	CNH	Lenny Szeto	(415)221-7500	WS 10 BC 830	EL/ED/HC	204	144	63
SAN GABRIEL	*EMMAUS*		See Alhambra CA									
SAN JOSE	*CHRIST THE LIFE* christthelifelutheran@gmail.com www.christthelife.org	1978	3412 SIERRA RD	95132	CNH		(408)259-1670 (408)259-0574	WS 10 SS 9 BC 9	ED/MD/SN			
	FIRST IMMANUEL office@firstimmanuel.org www.firstimmanuel.org	1882	374 S 3RD ST	95112	CNH		(408)292-5404 (408)297-8748	WS 9 SS 1030 BC 1015	ED/HC/ MD/SN			
	HOLY CROSS		See Los Gatos CA									
	OUR SAVIOR		See Cupertino CA									
	SHEP OF VALLEY www.sanjoselutheran.org	1969	1281 REDMOND AVE	95120	CNH	Robert D Weller	(408)997-4848 (408)997-4842	WS 830 11 SS 945 BC 945	EC/ED			
	TRINITY trinity1500@att.net	1932	1500 LEIGH AVE	95125	CNH	Eloy S Gonzalez Jose L Cervantes	(408)377-4411 (408)377-4414	WS 9 SS 1030 BC 1030	ED/HC/ MD/SN	45	38	25
SAN JUAN BAUTISTA	*BETHLEHEM*		See Monterey CA									
SAN JUAN CAPISTRANO	*FAITH*		See Capistrano Beach CA									
SAN LEANDRO	*HOPE*	1953	1801 MANOR BLVD	94579	CNH		(510)351-7410	WS 11	ED/HC	22	22	12
	ST PETER'S splcsl@att.net	1933	1801 MANOR BLVD C/O HOPE LUTHERAN CHURCH	94579	CNH		(510)638-7017	WS 930 BC 1045	ED/HC/ MD/SN			
SAN LORENZO	*CALVARY* churchsecretary@calvarysanlorenzo. com www.calvarysanlorenzo.com	1948	17200 VIA MAGDALENA	94580	CNH	Matthew J Behrens	(510)278-2555 (510)278-2557	WS 9	ED/MD/SN	88	76	55
SAN LUIS OBISPO	*ZION* zion@zionslo.com www.zionslo.com	1908	1010 Foothill Blvd 1010 EAST FOOTHILL BLVD SN LUIS OBISP	93405	CNH	Aleksandr A Von Schmidt	(805)543-8327 (805)543-8331	WS 8 1030 SS 930 BC 930	ED/HC/ MD/SN			
SAN MARCOS	*COMMUNITY*		See Escondido CA									
	COMMUNITY LUTHERAN CHURCH SAN MARCOS Satellite Site of Community Escondido CA	2012	340 Rancheros Dr Suite 160	92069				WS 930 BC 1045				
	GLORIA DEI		See Escondido CA									
SAN MARINO	*EMMAUS*		See Alhambra CA									
SAN MATEO	*GRACE* office@glcssm.org www.gracelutheransanmateo.org	1925	2825 ALAMEDA DE LAS PULGAS	94403	CNH	Dr Martin R Noland Frank J Balgeman	(650)345-9068	WS 9 SS 1015 BC 1030	ED/MD/SN	147	138	35

*Indicates a new church start. A new church start is an intentionally organized gathering which comes together on a regular basis for the purpose of worship and/or Bible study and is intended to grow into a member LCMS congregation. WS =Worship Service; SS = Sunday School; BC =Bible Class; EC = Early Childhood; EL = Elementary School; HS = High School; ED =Education Ministry; HC =Human Care Ministry; SN = Special Needs Ministry; MD = Media Ministry (PC)=Partner Church Pastor. See Page 53 for the Table of Abbreviations for key to additional abbreviations

CITY	CONGREGATION EMAIL WEBSITE	YEAR EST	LOCATION MAILING ADDRESS	ZIP CODE(S)	DIST.	PASTOR(S)	PHONE FAX	WS SS BC	SCHOOLS/ MINISTRIES	STATISTIC Bapt	Conf	Avg Attend
SAN PABLO	*ROLLINGWOOD* www.rollingwoodlutheran.org	1944	2393 GREENWOOD DR	94806	CNH	Timothy W Schepman	(510)223-1932	WS 11 BC 1230	ED			
SAN PEDRO	*CHRIST*		See Rancho Palos Verdes CA									
SAN RAFAEL	*RESURRECTION* lcrsanrafael672@gmail.com www.lcrsr.com	1953	1100 LAS GALLINAS AVE	94903	CNH	Thomas R Hurley	(415)479-1334 (415)479-1334	WS 930 SS 930 BC 1030	ED/HC/ MD/SN			
	TRINITY secretary@trinitysanrafael.org trinitysanrafael.org	1938	333 WOODLAND AVE	94901	CNH		(415)454-4135 (415)454-6230	WS 10 SS 1020 BC 9	EC/ED/HC/ MD/SN	78	52	45
SAND CITY	*BETHLEHEM*		See Monterey CA									
SANGER	*EMMANUEL*		See Clovis CA									
SANTA ANA	*PEACE* office@peacetustin.org peacetustin.org	1956	18542 VANDERLIP AVE	92705	PSW	Thomas N Huse	(714)731-2226	WS 930	ED/HC/SN	134	115	125
	SALEM		See Orange CA									
	TRINITY CRISTO REY	1909	902 S Broadway PO BOX 2241	92701 92707	PSW		(714)542-0784 (714)543-0388	WS 9 SS 1030 BC 10	HS			
SANTA BARBARA	*EMANUEL* emanuelluthsb@gmail.com emanuellutheransb.org	1915	3721 MODOC RD	93105	PSW	Dr Paul G Wenz	(805)687-3734	WS 930 SS 11 BC 11	ED/HC/SN	95	79	66
	GRACE		See Ventura CA									
SANTA CLARA	*REDEEMING GRACE* steveroma88@gmail.com		2495 CABRILLO AVE	95051	CNH	Stephan A Roma Muluneh Taye	(408)736-6605					
SANTA CLARITA	*BETHLEHEM* office@bethlehemscv.com www.bethlehemscv.com	1964	27265 LUTHER DR	91351	PSW		(661)252-0622 (661)252-5043	WS 8 10 BC 915	EC	207	201	159
SANTA CRUZ	*MESSIAH* pastor@messiah-lutheran.us www.messiah-lutheran.us	1930	801 HIGH ST	95060	CNH	Richard R Rice	(831)423-8330 (831)423-6677	WS 10	EC/ED/HC/ MD	119	85	28
SANTA MARIA	*GOOD SAMARITAN SHELTER* Satellite Site of Grace Santa Maria CA	2006	519 W Morrison Ave	93454								
	GRACE glc.sm@hotmail.com gracelutheransm.org	1938	423 E FESLER ST	93454	CNH		(805)925-3818 (805)347-7713	WS 930 SS 930 BC 815	EC/ED/HC/ MD/SN			
	OUR SAVIOR lcosoffice22@gmail.com www.lcos.net	1961	4725 S BRADLEY RD	93455	CNH	Brenden M Harrell	(805)937-1116 (805)937-2107	WS 10 SS 10 BC 9	EC/ED/HC/ MD	181	137	109
SANTA MONICA	*PILGRIM* amenmail@aol.com www.pilgrimsm.org	1913	1730 WILSHIRE BLVD	90403	PSW		(310)829-4113 (310)829-4970	WS 10 BC 9	ED/HC/ MD/SN	65	65	45
SANTA PAULA	*CENTRO CRISTIANO* pastordennis@centrocristianohispano. com www.centrocristianohispano.com	2009	505 W Harvard Blvd PO BOX 952	93060 93061	PSW	Marcelino Velasco	(805)525-5911		ED	80	75	55
SANTA ROSA	*ST LUKE* marie@stluke-lcms.org www.stluke-lcms.org	1888	905 MENDOCINO AVE	95401	CNH		(707)545-6772 (707)544-2112	WS 10 BC 1030	EC/ED/HC/ MD/SN	86	73	49
	ST MARK gary@stmarklc.org www.stmarklc.org	1962	4325 MAYETTE AVE	95405	CNH	Gary M Gerloff	(707)545-1230	WS 9 1110 SS 1010 BC 1010	ED/HC/ MD/SN	270	91	152
SANTA YNEZ	*SHEP OF VALLEY* sotvlco@outlook.com www.sotvsy.org	1978	3550 BASELINE AVE	93460	PSW	Jess M Knauft	(805)688-8938	WS 10 SS 10 BC 845	MD/SN	110	95	60
SANTEE	*MORNING STAR*		See Lakeside CA									
SARATOGA	*HOLY CROSS*		See Los Gatos CA									
	OUR SAVIOR		See Cupertino CA									
SEASIDE	*BETHLEHEM*		See Monterey CA									
	FAITH office@faithseaside.org www.faithseaside.org	1964	1460 HILBY AVE	93955	CNH	Darren M Harbaugh	(831)394-1312 (831)394-1312	WS 10 SS 9	ED/HC/ MD/SN			
SEBASTOPOL	*MOUNT OLIVE* www.mtolivelutheran.info	1954	460 MURPHY AVE	95472	CNH		(707)823-6316	WS 10 BC 9	ED/HC/MD			
	ST MARK		See Santa Rosa CA									
SELMA	*ST PAUL*	1907	2131 Stillman St PO BOX 409	93662	CNH			WS 9 SS 1015	ED/HC/MD	36	32	16
SHERMAN OAKS	*SHERMAN OAKS* shermanoakslutheran@yahoo.com www.shermanoakslutheran.org	1946	14847 DICKENS ST	91403	EN	Titus A Utecht	(818)789-0215 (818)789-0373	WS 10 SS 1015 BC 9	EC/ED/HC/ MD	127	112	75
SILLICON VALLEY	*FIRST IMMANUEL*		See San Jose CA									
SIMI VALLEY	*TRINITY* trinity@tlcsimi.com www.trinitylutheranchurchsimi.com	1959	2949 ALAMO ST	93063	PSW	Robert L Barker III	(805)526-2429 (805)526-4857	WS 9 1030 SS 930	EC/EL/ED/ HC/MD/SN	625	510	275
SKYFOREST	*MOUNT CALVARY*		See Lake Arrowhead CA									
SONOMA	*FAITH* faithlutheransv@att.net www.flcsv.org	1943	19355 ARNOLD DR	95476	CNH		(707)996-7365 (707)996-4231	WS 11	ED/HC/ MD/SN	67	67	33
SONORA	*ST MATTHEW* stmattsonora@gmail.com www.stmatthewchurchsonora.org	1941	13880 Joshua Wy 13880 JOSHUA WAY	95370	CNH	Thomas M Sharpe	(209)532-4639	WS 8 1030 SS 915 BC 915	ED/HC/ MD/SN			
SOQUEL	*MOUNT CALVARY* mtcal@cruzio.com www.mtcalvarysoquel.org	1965	2402 CABRILLO COLLEGE DR	95073	CNH	Stanley R Abraham	(831)475-6962	WS 9 BC 1030	HC	40	38	23

*Indicates a new church start. A new church start is an intentionally organized gathering which comes together on a regular basis for the purpose of worship and/or Bible study and is intended to grow into a member LCMS congregation. WS =Worship Service; SS = Sunday School; BC =Bible Class; EC = Early Childhood; EL = Elementary School; HS = High School; ED =Education Ministry; HC =Human Care Ministry; SN = Special Needs Ministry; MD = Media Ministry (PC)=Partner Church Pastor. See Page 53 for the Table of Abbreviations for key to additional abbreviations

CITY	CONGREGATION EMAIL WEBSITE	YEAR EST	LOCATION MAILING ADDRESS	ZIP CODE(S)	DIST.	PASTOR(S)	PHONE FAX	WS SS BC	SCHOOLS/ MINISTRIES	STATISTIC Bapt	Conf	Avg Attend
SOUTH GATE	*REDEEMER* www.redeemersouthgate.org	1924	2626 LIBERTY BLVD	90280	PSW	Blaise E Marin	(323)588-0934 (323)588-0701	WS 9 1115	ED/HC/MD	30	30	25
SOUTH PASADENA	*EMMAUS*		See Alhambra CA									
SOUTH SAN FRANCISCO	*FIRST* schufreider@gmail.com firstlutheranssf.org	1954	350 DOLORES WAY S SAN FRAN	94080	CNH	Jeffrey L Schufreider	(650)583-5131	WS 915		50	50	37
SPRING VALLEY	*ATONEMENT* atonement.sv@gmail.com www.atonementspringvalley.org	1961	10245 LOMA RANCHO DR	91978	PSW	Wallace J Kimari	(619)670-7174	WS 9	EL/HS/ED/ HC/MD	100	90	42
SPRINGVILLE	*ZION*		See Terra Bella CA									
STOCKTON	*ST ANDREW* office@stalc.org www.stalc.org	1943	4910 CLAREMONT AVE	95207	CNH	Brian C Muldowney	(209)957-8750 (209)957-1887	WS 830 1045 SS 945 BC 945	EC/ED/HC/ MD/SN			
	TRINITY jeffmorey@sbcglobal.net www.trinitylutheranstockton.org	1882	444 N AMERICAN ST	95202	CNH	Jeffrey D Morey	(209)464-1936 (209)464-0965	WS 9 BC 1030	ED/HC/ MD/SN			
SUN CITY	*GOOD SHEPHERD* gslcmenifee@gmail.com	1986	27010 Encanto Dr 26876 CHERRY HILLS RD	92586	PSW	Larry D Bogardus	(951)672-6675 (951)672-6680	WS 10 SS 10 BC 830	ED/HC/ MD/SN	45	45	32
SUNLAND	*FAITH*		See Tujunga CA									
SUNNYVALE	*OUR SAVIOR*		See Cupertino CA									
SUSANVILLE	*ST PAUL* stpaulssus@frontiernet.net	1896	105 ASH ST	96130	CNH		(530)257-2223	WS 10	ED/HC/ MD/SN			
TAFT	*PEACE* www.peacelutherantaft.org	1910	26 Emmons Park Dr 26 COUGAR CT	93268	CNH		(661)765-2488 (661)765-2822		MD/SN			
TEHACHAPI	*GOOD SHEPHERD* secretarygslc@att.net goodshepherdtehachapi.org/	1960	329 S MILL ST	93561	PSW	Kenneth W Burton III	(661)822-6817 (661)823-1554	WS 830 11 SS 1030 BC 1030	EC/ED/HC/ MD/SN	331	247	78
TEMECULA	*TRINITY* contact@trinitytemecula.info www.trinitytemecula.info	1989	30470 PAUBA RD	92592	PSW	James L Kirkman Jr	(951)676-1492 (951)695-1520	WS 8 930 11 BC 1045	EC/ED/HC/ MD/SN	685	613	399
TEMECULA VALLEY	*PROMISE*		See Murrieta CA									
TEMPLE CITY	*FIRST* admin@firstlutherantc.org firstlutherantc.org	1945	9123 BROADWAY	91780	PSW		(626)287-0968 (626)285-8648	WS 830 SS 945 BC 945	ED	26	26	20
TERRA BELLA	*ZION* zionlutheran@ocsnet.net www.zionterrabella.org	1909	10341 ROAD 256	93270	CNH		(559)535-4952 (559)535-2719	WS 1030 SS 915 BC 915	EL/ED/HC/ MD/SN	252	174	70
THORNTON	*SHEPHERD OF VALLEY*		See Galt CA									
THOUSAND OAKS	*REDEEMER*	1962	667 Camino Dos Rios PO BOX 1563	91360 91358	PSW	Matthew T Nolte	(805)498-4813 (805)498-7847	WS 9 SS 9 BC 1030				
TOLLHOURSE	*EMMANUEL*		See Clovis CA									
TORRANCE	*ASCENSION* churchoffice@ascensiontorrance.org www.ascensiontorrance.org	1954	17910 PRAIRIE AVE	90504	PSW	Michael R Abram	(310)793-0071	WS 830 1030	EC/EL/HS/ ED/HC/ MD/SN	385	379	112
	IMMANUEL		See Redondo Beach CA									
TRACY	*ST PAUL* www.stpaulstracy.org	1892	1635 CHESTER DR	95376	CNH	Kalvin L Waetzig Joel D Rockemann	(209)835-7438 (209)835-7951	WS 830 10 SS 10 BC 1115	EL/ED/HC			
TUJUNGA	*FAITH* faithtujunga@hotmail.com www.faithlutherantujunga.org	1946	7749 Apperson St PO BOX 577	91042 91043	PSW		(818)352-4444	WS 10 SS 9 BC 9				
TURLOCK	*GOOD SHEPHERD* office@gslct.org www.gslct.org	1942	640 Minaret Ave 640 N MINARET AVE	95380	CNH	Dr Mark A Koch	(209)667-7712 (209)667-9532	WS 9 1020 11	ED/HC/ MD/SN	558	489	175
TUSTIN	*PEACE*		See Santa Ana CA									
	SALEM		See Orange CA									
UKIAH	*FAITH* faithlc560@gmail.com flcukiah.org	1942	560 PARK BLVD	95482	CNH	Stuart A Sultze	(707)462-2618 (707)462-5546	WS 9 BC 1030	ED/HC/MD	30	30	22
UNION CITY	*HOPE*		See Fremont CA									
VACAVILLE	*BETHANY* mychurch@gobethany.com www.gobethany.com	1953	1011 ULATIS DRIVE	95687	CNH		(707)451-6675 (707)451-1740	WS 11 BC 10	EL/ED/HC/ MD/SN	132	116	71
VALLEY CENTER	*COMMUNITY*		See Escondido CA									
	LIGHT VALLEY lovlutheran@gmail.com	1978	28330 LILAC RD	92082	PSW		(760)749-9733 (760)749-8370	WS 9 SS 9 BC 1030	ED/HC/MD	77	74	44
VALLEY HOME	*SAINTS JOHN AND LUKE*	1906	4606 Michigan Ave PO BOX 2151 OAKDALE	95361	CNH	Bruce E Berndt	(209)847-0607					
VALLEY SPRINGS	*FOOTHILL LUTHERAN CHURCH* Satellite Site of Zion Lodi CA	2024	225 Hwy 12	95252				WS 10				
VAN NUYS	*FIRST* firstlutheran6952@sbcglobal.net www.flvn.org	1920	6952 VAN NUYS BLVD	91405	PSW	Erik J Loza	(818)989-5844 (818)989-0337	WS 830 BC 1030	ED/HC/MD	16	15	22
	SHERMAN OAKS		See Sherman Oaks CA									
VENICE	*FIRST* info@flvenice.org flvenice.org	1945	815 VENICE BLVD	90291	PSW	John M Palka	(310)821-2740	WS 830 11 5 SS 1230 BC 945	ED/HC	118	88	76
VENTURA	*GRACE* churchoffice@gracelutheranventura.com www.gracelutheranventura.com	1963	6190 TELEPHONE RD	93003	PSW	Paul E Koch	(805)642-2267	WS 9 SS 1045 BC 1045	HC/MD	175	160	100

*Indicates a new church start. A new church start is an intentionally organized gathering which comes together on a regular basis for the purpose of worship and/or Bible study and is intended to grow into a member LCMS congregation. WS =Worship Service; SS = Sunday School; BC =Bible Class; EC = Early Childhood; EL = Elementary School; HS = High School; ED =Education Ministry; HC =Human Care Ministry; SN = Special Needs Ministry; MD = Media Ministry (PC)=Partner Church Pastor. See Page 53 for the Table of Abbreviations for key to additional abbreviations

CITY	CONGREGATION EMAIL WEBSITE	YEAR EST	LOCATION MAILING ADDRESS	ZIP CODE(S)	DIST.	PASTOR(S)	PHONE FAX	WS SS BC	SCHOOLS/ MINISTRIES	STATISTIC Bapt	Conf	Avg Attend
VICTORVILLE	*ASCENSION*		See Apple Valley CA									
	ZION secretary@zionvv.org www.zionvv.org	1948	15342 JERALDO DR	92394	PSW	Lewis M Busch	(760)245-9725 (760)245-5945	WS 9 SS 1030 BC 1030	EL/ED/HC	315	208	95
VILLA PARK	*SALEM*		See Orange CA									
VISALIA	*GRACE* business@gracevisalia.org gracevisalia.org	1907	1111 S CONYER ST	93277	CNH	David S Jung Soun See	(559)734-7694 (559)734-0146	WS 8 1030 1 SS 930	EL/ED/ MD/SN	123	110	105
VISTA	*FAITH* churchoffice@faithvista.org www.faithvista.org	1960	700 E BOBIER DR	92084	PSW	David L Keane Paul A Martin	(760)724-7700 (760)724-6151	WS 8 1030 SS 915 BC 915	ED/HC/ MD/SN	212	198	127
WALNUT	*CHRIST THE KING* geopam24@verizon.net www.christthekingwalnut.org	1964	555 Gartel Dr PO BOX 462	91789 91788	PSW		(909)595-3819	WS 9	HC	12	12	11
WALNUT CREEK	*FAITH*		See Pleasant Hill CA									
WATSONVILLE	*TRINITY*	1931	175 LAWRENCE AVE	95076	CNH	Juan G Vallejo	(831)724-0176 (831)724-0176	WS 9	HC			
WEST COVINA	*IMMANUEL FIRST* info@immanuelfirst.org www.immanuelfirst.org	1953	512 S VALINDA AVE	91790	PSW	Dr Mason K Okubo	(626)919-1530 (626)919-5979	WS 9 SS 930 BC 1030	ED/HC/ MD/SN	187	122	57
WEST LOS ANGELES	*FIRST*		See Los Angeles CA									
WESTMINSTER	*BETHANY KOREAN* bdnchurch@protonmail.com		13552 GOLDENWEST	92683	PSW		(714)403-6803		MD			
	ST LUKE www.lukeslutheran.org	1957	13552 GOLDENWEST ST	92683	PSW		(800)972-1605	WS 930 BC 11	ED/HC	28	20	20
WHITTIER	*FAITH* dawnlangemeier@yahoo.com www.flcwhittier.org	1953	9920 MILLS AVE	90604	PSW		(562)941-0245 (562)941-4451	WS 9 SS 1030 BC 1030	HC/MD			
	PEACE		See Pico Rivera CA									
WILLITS	*ST JOHN* vicki_ham@yahoo.com	1953	24 MILL CREEK DR	95490	CNH		(707)459-2988	WS 11 SS 930	ED/HC/SN	26	26	32
WILLOWS	*FIRST* flcwillows@gmail.com flcwillows.org	1950	333 VINE ST	95988	CNH	Sylvan N Finger	(530)934-2140	WS 830	ED/HC/MD	41	33	17
WILTON	*SHEPHERD OF VALLEY*		See Galt CA									
WINNETKA	*OUR REDEEMER* church@our-redeemer.org www.our-redeemer.org	1957	8520 WINNETKA AVE	91306	PSW	Gregory J Barth	(818)341-3460 (818)772-2788	WS 830 11 BC 930	EC/ED/HC/ MD	168	143	89
WOODLAND	*ST PAUL* office@stpaulswoodland.org stpaulswoodland.org	1912	625 W GIBSON RD	95695	CNH	David S Hardin Berhanu K Didanu	(530)662-1935 (530)662-1999	WS 1030	EC/ED/HC/ MD			
YORBA LINDA	*HEPHATHA*		See Anaheim CA									
	TRINITY		See Anaheim CA									
YUBA CITY	*FIRST* www.flcyc.org	1932	850 COOPER AVE	95991	CNH	Nathan D Linehan	(530)673-8894 (530)673-3454	WS 830 1051 SS 10	ED/HC/MD			
YUCAIPA	*GOOD SHEPHERD* prayer@goodshepherdyucaipa.com www.goodshepherdyucaipa.com	1956	34215 AVENUE E	92399	PSW	Aaron G Kangas	(909)790-1863	WS 9 SS 1030 BC 1030	ED/HC/MD	45	40	30
YUCCA VALLEY	*GOOD SHEPHERD* goodshepherdyv@gmail.com goodshepherdlutheranchurch. shutterfly.com	1961	59077 YUCCA TRL	92284	PSW		(760)365-2548	WS 10 BC 9	ED/HC/ MD/SN	214	159	30

COLORADO

CITY	CONGREGATION EMAIL WEBSITE	YEAR EST	LOCATION MAILING ADDRESS	ZIP CODE(S)	DIST.	PASTOR(S)	PHONE FAX	WS SS BC	SCHOOLS/ MINISTRIES	Bapt	Conf	Avg Attend
ADAMS COUNTY	*MOUNT ZION*		See Denver CO									
AKRON	*TRINITY* trinityakron.weebly.com	1916	202 Birch PO BOX 575	80720	RM		(970)345-2303	WS 8 BC 915	ED/HC/SN	20	16	10
ALAMOSA	*TRINITY* tlcoffice52@gmail.com	1919	52 El Rio Dr PO BOX 1323	81101	RM	Jason K Cody	(719)589-4611	WS 10 SS 845 BC 845	EL/ED/HC/ MD	87	84	54
AMHERST	*ST PAUL* stpaulcone@pctelcom.coop	1909	300 Monmouth Ave PO BOX 7	80721	RM	Kurt T Hatteberg	(970)854-4310	WS 1015	ED/HC/ MD/SN	80	73	26
	ST PAUL		See Venango NE									
ARRIBA	*IMMANUEL*	1907	204 Colorado Ave P.O. BOX 75 FLAGLER	80804 80815	RM		(719)768-3429	WS 3		18	15	16
ARRIOLA	*TRINITY*		See Cortez CO									
ARVADA	*KING OF KINGS* Kok8300pomona@outlook.com kingofkingsarvada.org	1973	8300 Pomona Dr 8300 W POMONA DR	80005	RM		(303)425-7096 (303)425-5608	WS 8 1045 SS 930 BC 930	HS/ED/HC/ MD/SN	59	56	40
	PEACE peace@peacelutheran.net www.peacelutheran.net	1955	5675 FIELD ST	80002	RM	Guy W Roberts Timothy J Lindeman	(303)424-4454 (303)940-7683	WS 8 1030 SS 915 BC 915	EC/HS/ED/ HC/MD/SN	894	785	426
	RISEN CHRIST President@RisenChristLutheran.org www.risenchristlutheran.org	1994	14850 W 72nd Ave 14850 WEST 72ND AVENUE	80007	RM	Dr Robert D Macina	(303)421-5872	WS 8 1030 SS 930 BC 930	ED/MD	133	115	70
AURORA	*HOPE* office@hopeaurora.org www.hopeaurora.org	1953	1345 MACON ST	80010	RM	Jonathan T Olson	(303)364-7416	WS 915 SS 1045 BC 1045	ED/HC/ MD/SN	329	273	69
	INDIA PAKISTAN		11453 Wesley Ave C/O MT OLIVE LUTHERAN CHURCH 11453 WESLEY AVE	80014	RM							
	MOUNT OLIVE finance@mtolc.org www.mtoliveluth.org	1964	11453 E WESLEY AVE	80014	RM	Robert D Harmon	(303)755-9123	WS 8 1045 SS 10 BC 10	EC/HS/ED/ HC/MD/SN	188	181	160

CONGREGATIONS

*Indicates a new church start. A new church start is an intentionally organized gathering which comes together on a regular basis for the purpose of worship and/or Bible study and is intended to grow into a member LCMS congregation. WS =Worship Service; SS = Sunday School; BC =Bible Class; EC = Early Childhood; EL = Elementary School; HS = High School; ED =Education Ministry; HC =Human Care Ministry; SN = Special Needs Ministry; MD = Media Ministry (PC)=Partner Church Pastor. See Page 53 for the Table of Abbreviations for key to additional abbreviations

CITY	CONGREGATION EMAIL WEBSITE	YEAR EST	LOCATION MAILING ADDRESS	ZIP CODE(S)	DIST.	PASTOR(S)	PHONE FAX	WS SS BC	SCHOOLS/ MINISTRIES	STATISTIC Bapt	Conf	Avg Attend
AURORA	*PEACE W CHRIST* pwcoffice@pwclc.org www.pwclc.org	1982	3290 S TOWER RD	80013	RM	Joshua R Krepel Dr Michael E Paulison	(303)693-5618 (303)699-2777	WS 8 1015 SS 915 BC 915	EC/EL/HS/ ED/HC/ MD/SN	456	394	272
BAILEY	*SHEP ROCKIES* shepherdofrockies@gmail.com www.shepherdoftherockies.org	1980	106 ROSALIE RD	80421	RM	John H Graham	(303)838-2161 (303)838-2161	WS 9 SS 1045 BC 1045	ED/MD			
BENNETT	*CHRIST REDEEMER* www.christourredeemerlcms.org	1985	275 S Ash St PO BOX 537	80102	RM	Dr George N Guirguis	(303)644-3044	WS 930 SS 1045 BC 1045	ED	96	75	45
BERTHOUD	*FAITH*		See Johnstown CO									
BOULDER	*MOUNT HOPE* mthopelutheran@gmail.com www.mthopeboulder.org	1966	1345 S BROADWAY ST	80305	RM	David J Ahlman	(303)499-9800	WS 930 SS 1045 BC 1045	ED/HC/ MD/SN	65	65	62
	MOUNT ZION mtzionboulder.org	1956	1680 BALSAM AVE	80304	RM	Allen D Anderson	(303)443-4151 (303)448-9547	WS 9 SS 10 BC 10	EC/ED/HC/ MD/SN			
	UNIVERSITY pastor@universitylutheranchapel.com universitylutheranchapel.org	1958	1202 FOLSOM ST	80302	RM	Robert W Jarvis	(303)443-8720 (303)443-4847	WS 10	ED			
BRECKENRIDGE	*CHRIST* info@christlutheranbreck.org www.christlutheranbreck.org	1994	16072 Hwy 9 PO BOX 3314	80424	RM		(970)453-8019	WS 930 SS 10	ED/HC/MD	50	37	46
BRIGHTON	*SUMMIT PEACE*		See Thornton CO									
	ZION church@zionbrighton.org www.zionbrighton.org	1900	1400 SKEEL ST	80601	RM	Andrew D Roettjer	(303)659-2339 (303)659-2342	WS 815 1045 SS 930 BC 930	EL/ED/HC/ MD/SN	1007	727	282
BROOMFIELD	*BEAUTIFUL SAVIOR* bslcsec@yahoo.com bslcms.com	1958	6995 W 120th Ave PO BOX 8	80020 80038	RM	Richard D Langness	(303)469-1785	WS 9 SS 1030 BC 1030	EL/HS/ ED/HC	137	91	65
	RISEN SAVIOR office@rslc.org www.rslc.org	1987	3031 W 144TH AVE	80023	RM		(303)469-3521 (303)635-0201	WS 8 1030 SS 915 BC 915	HS/ED/HC/ MD	537	471	150
BUENA VISTA	*FAITH* faithlutheranbv.org	1978	15440 Main St PO BOX 1448	81211	RM	James T Sorensen	(719)395-2039	WS 1030 SS 9 BC 9	ED/HC/MD			
BURLINGTON	*TRINITY* trinitylutheranburlington@gmail.com	1923	338 7TH ST	80807	RM	William H Viergutz	(719)346-7401	WS 10 BC 9	ED/HC/ MD/SN	180	160	58
CAMPION	*FAITH*		See Johnstown CO									
CANON CITY	*ST JOHN* pastor@stjohncanoncity.org www.stjohncanoncity.org	1986	790 GREYDENE AVE	81212	RM	Daniel B Kletke	(719)275-0111	WS 9 SS 1030 BC 1030	ED/HC/MD	137	116	85
CARBONDALE	*FAITH* pastor@faithcarbondale.org faithcarbondale.org		1340 Hwy 133 1340 HIGHWAY 133	81623	RM		(970)510-5046	WS 9 SS 1015 BC 1015	EC/ED/HC/ MD/SN	25	25	20
CASTLE PINES	*GRACE*		See Parker CO									
CASTLE ROCK	*EPIPHANY* office@epiphanylc.org www.epiphanylc.org	1999	550 E WOLFENSBERGER RD	80109	RM	Christopher S Matthis Michael J Huntley	(303)688-4435 (303)688-8655	WS 8 11 SS 930 BC 930	HS/ED/HC/ MD	357	289	151
	MOUNT ZION mtzionpastor@hotmail.com mountzionlutheran.org	1959	750 CANTRIL ST	80104	RM	Carlton K Hein	(303)688-9550	WS 9 SS 1030 BC 1030	MD			
	TRINITY		See Franktown CO									
CENTENNIAL	*GRACE*		See Parker CO									
	OUR FATHER info@oflc.net www.ourfatherlutheran.net	1974	6335 S HOLLY ST	80121	RM	Scott F Abel Micah P Steiner Nathan F Peregoy	(303)779-1332 (303)779-1668	WS 8 1045 SS 930	EC/HS/ED/ HC/MD/SN	1314	889	698
	SHEPHERD HILLS info@sothfamily.org www.shepherdhills-church.org	1963	7691 S UNIVERSITY BLVD	80122	RM	Dr Bradley R Stoltenow Benjamin T Oesch	(303)798-0711 (303)707-4399	WS 8 1045 SS 930 BC 930	EC/HS/ED/ HC/MD	726	643	249
CHEYENNE WELLS	*GRACE*	1920	825 North First West PO BOX 728 CHEYENNE WLS	80810	RM	Steven C Zandstra	(719)767-5913	WS 9 SS 1015		38	30	17
COLORADO SPRINGS	*FAMILY OF CHRIST* office@foccs.net www.foccs.net	1994	675 W BAPTIST RD COLORADO SPGS	80921	RM	Dr Mark C Moreno Aidan M Moon	(719)481-2255 (719)481-1366	WS 8 945 11 SS 11	EC/ED/HC/ MD/SN	900	830	467
	FAMILY OF FAITH		See Falcon CO									
	HOLY CROSS christineb@holycrosscs.org holycrosscs.org	1965	4125 CONSTITUTION AVE COLORADO SPGS	80909	RM	Gregory A Zillinger	(719)596-0661 (719)596-0699	WS 9 SS 930 BC 930	EC/ED/HC/ MD/SN	1255	953	357
	IMMANUEL church_office@ilc-cos.org www.ilc-cos.org	1900	846 E PIKES PEAK AVE COLO-RADO SPGS	80903	RM	Jonathan M Kern	(719)636-5011 (719)636-5292	WS 9 SS 1045 BC 1045	HC/MD	245	199	125
	REDEEMER redeemercos@gmail.com www.redeemerlutheran-cs.org	1950	2226 N Corona St 2221 N WAHSATCH AVE COLO-RADO SPGS	80907	RM	Donal C Widger	(719)633-7661	WS 9 SS 1015 BC 1015	ED/HC/MD	146	117	62
	RESURRECTION office@resurrectionlcms.com www.resurrectionlcms.com	1979	4444 MOONBEAM DR COLO-RADO SPGS	80916	RM	Dr Dennis F Lucero	(719)392-7045	WS 10 SS 830 BC 830	ED/HC/MD	93	64	43
	ROCK OF AGES roachurchoffice@gmail.com roalcms.org	1957	120 N 31st St PO BOX 6941 COLORADO SPGS	80904 80934	RM	James B Maxwell Daniel M Warner William V Beck	(719)632-9394 (719)632-0772	WS 9 SS 1030 BC 1030	EC/ED/HC/ MD	215	169	127
	SHEP SPRINGS sslc.cos@gmail.com www.sslc-cos.org	1981	6755 Earl St Suite 100 6755 EARL DR STE 100 COLO-RADO SPGS	80918	RM	Jeffery L Patterson	(719)396-4710	WS 9 SS 1030 BC 1030	ED/MD	65	58	40
COMMERCE CITY	*OUR SAVIOUR* secretary@oursaviourlcms.com www.oursaviourlcms.com	1953	6770 MONACO ST	80022	RM	David W Baker	(303)288-9577	WS 845	HS/ED/HC	53	53	28

*Indicates a new church start. A new church start is an intentionally organized gathering which comes together on a regular basis for the purpose of worship and/or Bible study and is intended to grow into a member LCMS congregation. WS =Worship Service; SS = Sunday School; BC =Bible Class; EC = Early Childhood; EL = Elementary School; HS = High School; ED =Education Ministry; HC =Human Care Ministry; SN = Special Needs Ministry; MD = Media Ministry (PC)=Partner Church Pastor. See Page 53 for the Table of Abbreviations for key to additional abbreviations

CITY	CONGREGATION EMAIL WEBSITE	YEAR EST	LOCATION MAILING ADDRESS	ZIP CODE(S)	DIST.	PASTOR(S)	PHONE FAX	WS SS BC	SCHOOLS/ MINISTRIES	STATISTIC Bapt	Conf	Avg Attend
COMMERCE CITY	*ZION*		See Brighton CO									
CORTEZ	*TRINITY* TrinityLCCortez@gmail.com www.TrinityLutheranChurchCortez.com	1952	208 N DOLORES RD	81321	RM	Luke P Scheele	(970)565-9346	WS 9 SS 1045 BC 1045	EC/ED/HC/ MD	182	156	70
CRAIG	*FAITH* faith_lutheranchurch@yahoo.com	1960	580 Green St PO BOX 428	81625 81626	RM	John S Turner	(970)824-3043	WS 9 SS 1030 BC 1030				
CREEDE	*LCMS PREACHING STATION* Satellite Site of St Peter Monte Vista CO	1983	502 South Main St	81130								
DELTA	*REDEEMER* rlclcms@deltalutheran.org deltalutheran.org	1946	1000 PIONEER RD	81416	RM	Jordan E Schaller	(970)874-3052 (970)874-7495	WS 9 SS 1030 BC 1030	EL/ED/HC/ MD/SN	157	122	96
DENVER	*BETHLEHEM*		See Lakewood CO									
	CHRIST christlutheransecretary2695@ gmail.com	1944	2695 S FRANKLIN ST	80210	RM	Roger C Wohletz	(303)722-1424	WS 9 BC 8 1030	EC/HS/ED/ MD/SN	181	146	50
	CORDERO DE DIOS corderodedioslcms@gmail.com	1989	5200 TEJON ST	80221	RM	Juan L Hormachea	(303)579-6564	WS 10 SS 915	ED/HC/MD	97	69	53
	FAITH faithdenver@eoni.com www.faith-lutheran-lcms.org	1944	4785 ELM CT	80211	RM	Terry L Neustel II	(303)455-5878	WS 930 SS 830 BC 830	HS/ED/HC/ MD/SN	47	47	25
	HOPE		See Aurora CO									
	IMMANUEL		See Englewood CO									
	MOUNT ZION office@mtzionlcms.org www.mtzionlcms.org	1955	500 DRAKE ST	80221	RM	Jared K Melius Gregory N Thompson	(303)429-0165	WS 930 SS 11 BC 11	HS/ED/HC/ MD	255	175	112
	PEACE		See Arvada CO									
	RENEWAL CHURCH Satellite Site of St Johns Denver CO	2017	3120 Irving St	80211								
	RESURRECTION CITY mtcalvarydenver@yahoo.com resurrectioninthecity.com/	1938	3560 York St 3560 N YORK ST	80205	RM	Duane P Meissner	(346)616-8090	WS 10	HS/ED/HC/ MD	36	27	30
	ST JOHNS church@sjdenver.org www.sjdenver.org	1879	700 S FRANKLIN ST	80209	RM	Andrew W Farhat Paul J Aarsvold	(303)733-3777 (303)778-6070	WS 8 945	EL/HS/ED/ HC/MD/SN	463	371	331
	ST LUKE		See Golden CO									
	SUMMIT PEACE		See Thornton CO									
	TRINITY trinitylutheran@gototrinity.com www.trinitylutherandenver.com	1956	4225 W YALE AVE	80219	RM	Adrian N Sherrill James D Bauer North P Sherrill Jr Thomas E Lock Dr Charles W Westby	(303)406-3143	WS 9 SS 1030 BC 1030	HS/ED/HC/ MD/SN	245	157	201
	UNIVERSITY HILLS churchsecretary@uhillslutheran.org www.uhillslutheran.org	1952	4949 E EASTMAN AVE	80222	RM	David R Vanderhyde Jr	(303)759-0161	WS 12 SS 1030 BC 1030	ED/HC	63	48	25
DILLON	*CHRIST*		See Breckenridge CO									
DOLORES	*TRINITY*		See Cortez CO									
DOVE CREEK	*TRINITY*		See Cortez CO									
DURANGO	*ST PAUL'S* STPAULSDURANGO@GMAIL.COM www.stpaulsdurango.org	1881	2611 JUNCTION ST	81301	RM	Benjamin J Delin	(970)247-0357	WS 930 SS 11 BC 11	ED/HC/ MD/SN			
EAGLE	*GRACE FELLOWSHIP*		See Gypsum CO									
EDGEWATER	*BETHLEHEM*		See Lakewood CO									
EDWARDS	*GRACIOUS SAVIOR* graciousssaviorchurch@gmail.com www.gracioussavior.org	1984	33520 Hwy 6 PO BOX 250	81632	RM	Jason M Haynes	(970)926-3550	WS 930 SS 930 BC 11	ED/HC/ MD/SN	151	129	73
ELIZABETH	*CHRIST OUR SAVIOR* office@cos-lutheran.org www.cos-lutheran.org	1981	4022 PARK LN	80107	RM	Geoffrey A Wagner	(303)646-1378	WS 10 SS 9 BC 9		52	44	27
ENGLEWOOD	*IMMANUEL* godwithus@englewoodlutheran.org immanuellutheran.net	1925	3695 S ACOMA ST	80110	RM	James A Tuell	(303)781-5887	WS 10 SS 845 BC 845	HS/ED/ MD/SN	40	36	32
ERIE	*ETERNAL SAVIOR*		See Lafayette CO									
	RISEN SAVIOR		See Broomfield CO									
	SUMMIT PEACE		See Thornton CO									
ESTES PARK	*MOUNT CALVARY* secretary@mtcalvaryep.org www.mtcalvaryep.360unite.com	1944	950 N SAINT VRAIN AVE	80517	RM	Paul G Rhode	(970)586-4646	WS 9 SS 1030 BC 1030	ED/HC	71	68	48
EVERGREEN	*MOUNT HOPE* mounthopeluth@aol.com	1980	30571 CHESTNUT DR	80439	RM	Carl R Frank	(303)670-1387	WS 9 SS 1030 BC 1030	HS/ED/MD			
FALCON	*FAMILY OF FAITH* Family_of_FaithPeyton@yahoo.com falconfamilyoffaith.com		6355 E BLANEY RD PEYTON	80831	RM		(719)367-5303	WS 10 SS 9 BC 9	ED/MD	86	70	65
FEDERAL HEIGHTS	*MOUNT ZION*		See Denver CO									
FIRESTONE	*FAITH*		See Johnstown CO									
FLAGLER	*ZION*	1911	722 Main Ave PO BOX 267	80815	RM			WS 9 SS 1030 BC 1030		46	34	24
FORT COLLINS	*PEACE W CHRIST* pwcfcoffice@gmail.com pwchrist.360unite.com	1972	1412 W SWALLOW RD	80526	RM	David B Magruder	(970)226-4721 (970)204-1570	WS 8 1045 SS 930	ED/HC/ MD/SN	295	255	150

*Indicates a new church start. A new church start is an intentionally organized gathering which comes together on a regular basis for the purpose of worship and/or Bible study and is intended to grow into a member LCMS congregation. WS =Worship Service; SS = Sunday School; BC =Bible Class; EC = Early Childhood; EL = Elementary School; HS = High School; ED =Education Ministry; HC =Human Care Ministry; SN = Special Needs Ministry; MD = Media Ministry (PC)=Partner Church Pastor. See Page 53 for the Table of Abbreviations for key to additional abbreviations

CITY	CONGREGATION EMAIL WEBSITE	YEAR EST	LOCATION MAILING ADDRESS	ZIP CODE(S)	DIST.	PASTOR(S)	PHONE FAX	WS SS BC	SCHOOLS/ MINISTRIES	STATISTIC Bapt	 Conf	 Avg Attend
FORT COLLINS	*REDEEMER* redeemer@redeemerconnect.com www.redeemerconnect.com	1988	7755 Greenstone Trail 7755 GREENSTONE TRL	80525	RM	Timothy D Runtsch Caleb C Cox Michael S Curtis	(970)225-9020 (970)225-9870	WS 8 930 11 SS 930	EC/ED/HC/ MD/SN	2994	2462	956
	SAINT JOHN'S church@stjohnsfc.org www.stjohnsfc.org	1908	305 E ELIZABETH ST	80524	RM	Shawn P Nettleton	(970)482-5316	WS 9 SS 1030 BC 1030	EC/ED/HC/ MD/SN	277	277	99
FORT LUPTON	*MOUNT CALVARY* secretary@mtcalvaryluth.org www.mtcalvaryluth.org	1937	650 S PARK AVE	80621	RM	Keith L Besel	(303)857-6827 (303)312-1656	WS 9 SS 1045 BC 1045	ED/HC/MD	122	106	60
FORT MORGAN	*TRINITY* church.secretary@trinitylutheran fortmorgan.com www.trinitylutheranfortmorgan.com	1906	1215 W 7TH AVE	80701	RM	Bror M Erickson	(970)867-5721 (970)867-5139	WS 9 SS 1015 BC 1015	EL/ED/HC/ MD	496	369	94
FRANKTOWN	*TRINITY* trinitychurch@tlcas.org www.tlcas.org	1982	4740 N State Hwy 83 4740 N STATE HIGHWAY 83	80116	RM	Robert W Walston	(303)841-4660 (303)841-2761	WS 8 1030 SS 930 BC 930	EL/HS/ED/ HC/MD	441	374	271
FREDERICK	*FAITH*		See Johnstown CO									
FRISCO	*CHRIST*		See Breckenridge CO									
GENOA	*TRINITY*	1902	214 2nd St 31320 COUNTY ROAD 3K	80818	RM		(719)763-2289	WS 9	ED	20	20	13
GOLDEN	*NEW HOPE*	1986	16600 W 50TH AVE	80403	RM		(303)279-2070	WS 9 BC 1030	HS			
	ST LUKE office@stlukes-golden.org stlukes-golden.org	1980	13119 W 20TH AVE	80401	RM	Edward H Schmidt	(303)233-5658	WS 9 SS 1030 BC 1030	HS/ED/HC/ MD/SN	103	85	43
GRAND JUNCTION	*MESSIAH* Admin@mlgj.org lutheranchurchandschoolofmessiah. org/	1933	840 N 11TH ST GRAND JCT	81501	RM	Michael J Redeker	(970)245-2838 (970)245-8145	WS 9 SS 1030 BC 1030	EL/ED/HC/ MD/SN	769	608	200
GREELEY	*FAITH*		See Johnstown CO									
	GLORIA CHRISTI gloriachristioffice@gmail.com www.gloriachristi.org	1963	1322 31ST AVE	80634	RM	Stephen T Weiss	(970)353-2554 (970)353-6555	WS 9 SS 1030 BC 1030	ED/HC/ MD/SN	127	118	71
	TRINITY office@tlgreeley.com www.tlgreeley.org	1904	3000 35TH AVE	80634	RM	Joshua S Vanderhyde	(970)330-2485	WS 8 1030 SS 920 BC 920	EL/ED/HC/ MD/SN	322	262	135
GROVER	*ZION*	1916	52701 County Rd 124 PO BOX 670 PINE BLUFFS	80729 82082	WY	Lincoln C Winter	(307)245-3390	WS 4		15	15	12
GUNNISON	*MOUNT CALVARY* pastor@mountcalvarygunnison.com www.mountcalvarygunnison.com	1961	711 N Main St PO BOX 662	81230	RM	Jacob A With	(970)641-1860	WS 10 SS 9	ED/HC/MD			
GYPSUM	*GRACE FELLOWSHIP* austin@gracegypsum.com www.gracefellowshipgypsum.com		525 McGregor Dr F PO BOX 4280	81637	RM	Austin D Kraft	(970)445-3101 (970)328-1240	WS 9 11 SS 915 1115 BC 1015	ED/HC/MD	255	96	165
HAXTUN	*IMMANUEL* churchladytana@gmail.com www.haxtunimmanuellutheran.org/	1919	400 N Colorado Ave PO BOX 116	80731	RM	Timothy R Hahn	(970)774-6236	WS 930 BC 830	ED	105	99	40
HENDERSON	*ZION*		See Brighton CO									
HIGHLANDS RANCH	*HOLY CROSS* office@hclchr.org www.hclchr.org	1994	9770 FOOTHILLS CANYON BLVD HGHLNDS RANCH	80129	RM	Bruce A Skelton	(303)683-1300 (303)470-0165	WS 9 SS 1030 BC 1030	HS/ED/HC/ MD			
HOLYOKE	*ZION* zion@pctelcom.coop zionholyoke.com	1906	240 S HIGH SCHOOL AVE	80734	RM	Gary A Rahe	(970)854-2615 (970)854-2314	WS 915 SS 815 BC 815	ED/HC/ MD/SN			
HUDSON	*GRACE* www.gracehudsonlcms.org	1937	400 Cherry St PO BOX 409	80642	RM	David W Baker	(303)536-4734	WS 1045 SS 915 BC 915	ED			
JOHNSTOWN	*FAITH* faithjohnstown@yahoo.com www.faithjohnstown.org	1958	3999 West South 1st St PO BOX 70	80534	RM	Brandon W Ross Victor P Young	(970)587-6460	WS 9 SS 1030 BC 1030	ED/HC/MD			
JULESBURG	*ST PAUL* stpauljules@gmail.com www.stpaulsjulesburg.org	1921	621 Maple St PO BOX 72	80737	RM	Trenton D Christensen	(970)474-2592	WS 9 SS 8 BC 8	ED/HC/MD	115	113	38
KEYSTONE	*CHRIST*		See Breckenridge CO									
KIT CARSON	*TRINITY*	1914	PO BOX 306	80825	RM	Thomas M Barton		WS 11 SS 10		25	20	15
LA JUNTA	*TRINITY* admin@trinitylajunta.com	1924	1601 Raton Ave PO BOX 1069	81050	RM	Rick L Miller	(719)384-6555	WS 1030 SS 9 BC 9	ED/HC	72	60	35
LAFAYETTE	*ETERNAL SAVIOR* secretary@eternalsavior-lutheran.org www.eternalsavior-lutheran.org	1971	2688 North Park Dr 2688 NORTHPARK DR	80026	RM	Clint O Thorson	(303)665-6105	WS 9 SS 1030	ED/HC/ MD/SN	170	136	72
LAKEWOOD	*BETHLEHEM* bethlehem@bethlehemdenver.com www.bethlehemdenver.com	1930	2100 WADSWORTH BLVD	80214	RM	David J Langewisch Timothy J Wendelin David L Dyer	(303)238-7676 (303)237-4011	WS 745 830 9 10 1030 SS 9 1030 BC 830 10	EL/HS/ED/ HC/MD/SN	1690	1218	465
	CONCORDIA concordia@clcgrace.org www.clcgrace.org	1964	13371 W ALAMEDA PKWY	80228	RM		(303)989-5260	WS 815 1015 SS 1015 BC 1015	EC/HS/ED/ HC/MD/SN	354	332	123
	IMMANUEL		See Englewood CO									
	TRINITY		See Denver CO									
LAMAR	*GRACE* nrhavenstein@netscape.net gracelutheranlamar.org	1959	1 MEMORIAL DR	81052	RM	Thomas M Barton	(719)336-5500	WS 9	ED/HC/MD	50	35	30
LEADVILLE	*GOOD SHEPHERD* www.goodshepherdleadville.org	1960	530 W 8TH ST	80461	RM		(719)486-0280	WS 9 BC 1015	ED/HC/ MD/SN	20	15	10

*Indicates a new church start. A new church start is an intentionally organized gathering which comes together on a regular basis for the purpose of worship and/or Bible study and is intended to grow into a member LCMS congregation. WS =Worship Service; SS = Sunday School; BC =Bible Class; EC = Early Childhood; EL = Elementary School; HS = High School; ED =Education Ministry; HC =Human Care Ministry; SN = Special Needs Ministry; MD = Media Ministry (PC)=Partner Church Pastor. See Page 53 for the Table of Abbreviations for key to additional abbreviations

CITY	CONGREGATION EMAIL WEBSITE	YEAR EST	LOCATION MAILING ADDRESS	ZIP CODE(S)	DIST.	PASTOR(S)	PHONE FAX	WS SS BC	SCHOOLS/ MINISTRIES	STATISTIC Bapt	Conf	Avg Attend
LEWIS	*TRINITY*		See Cortez CO									
LIMON	*TRINITY*		See Genoa CO									
LITTLETON	*ASCENSION* office@alutheran.org www.alutheran.org	1955	1701 W CALEY AVE	80120	RM	John R Larson	(303)794-4636	WS 8 1030 SS 915 BC 1015	EC/HS/ED/ HC/MD/SN	504	444	213
	HOLY CROSS		See Highlands Ranch CO									
	HOSANNA hosanna.lutheran@att.net www.myhosanna.org	1974	10304 W BELLEVIEW AVE	80127	RM	Gregory G Peters	(303)973-1706 (303)973-1422	WS 8 1030 SS 915 BC 915	HS/ED/HC/ MD			
	IMMANUEL		See Englewood CO									
	OUR FATHER		See Centennial CO									
	SHEPHERD HILLS		See Centennial CO									
LOCHBUIE	*ZION*		See Brighton CO									
LONE TREE	*GRACE*		See Parker CO									
LONGMONT	*CHRIST OUR SAVIOR* church.office@coslongmont.org www.coslongmont.org	1976	640 ALPINE ST	80504	RM	John A Thieme	(303)776-1789	WS 830 1030 BC 930	ED/HC/ MD/SN			
	FAITH		See Johnstown CO									
	MESSIAH mlcs_office@mlcslongmont.org www.messiahlongmont.org	1926	1335 FRANCIS ST	80501	RM	Ronald S Rieger	(303)776-2573 (303)776-2599	WS 10 SS 10 BC 845	ED/HC/SN	100	91	55
LOUISVILLE	*ETERNAL SAVIOR*		See Lafayette CO									
LOVELAND	*FAITH*		See Johnstown CO									
	IMMANUEL churchoffice@immanuelloveland.org www.immanuelloveland.org	1931	4650 SUNVIEW DR	80538	RM	Dr Glen A Schlecht Dr Robin J Dugall	(970)667-4506 (970)624-3422	WS 8 1030 SS 930 BC 930	EL/HS/ED/ HC/MD/SN	540	433	256
	MOUNT OLIVE mountoliveloveland@yahoo.com www.mountolivelutheranchurch. 360unite.com	1975	3411 S TAFT AVE	80537	RM	Mark J Nierman	(970)669-7350 (970)669-4715	WS 9 SS 1030 BC 1030	ED/MD	196	161	89
MANCOS	*TRINITY*		See Cortez CO									
MEAD	*FAITH*		See Johnstown CO									
MILLIKEN	*FAITH*		See Johnstown CO									
MONTE VISTA	*ST PETER* stpeters1907@yahoo.com www.splcmv.wordpress.com	1907	1811 Grande Ave 1821 GRANDE AVE	81144	RM		(719)852-3424	WS 1015 SS 9 BC 9	MD	153	118	35
MONTROSE	*CHRIST* montroselutheran@gmail.com www.montroselutheranchurch.org	2019	1980 N Townsend Ave PO BOX 871	81401	RM	Timothy G Onnen	(970)633-0226	WS 9 920 SS 1030	ED	25	23	18
	HOPE hopelutheranmontrose.com	1984	600 N 2ND ST	81401	RM	Darryl S Hannenberg	(970)249-8811	WS 9 SS 1030 BC 1030				
MONUMENT	*FAMILY OF CHRIST*		See Colorado Springs CO									
NORTHGLENN	*GETHSEMANE* church@glutheran.com glutheran.com	1961	10675 N Washington St 10675 WASHINGTON ST	80233	RM		(303)451-6895	WS 8 1030 BC 1020	HS/ED/HC/ MD	259	218	66
	MOUNT ZION		See Denver CO									
PAGOSA SPRINGS	*OUR SAVIOR* oslcpagosa@gmail.com www.oslcpagosa.org	1968	56 MEADOWS DR PAGOSA SPGS	81147	RM	Dustin C Atkinson John G Widmer	(970)731-4668 (970)731-4668	WS 9 SS 1030 BC 1030	EL/ED/MD	123	99	70
PAONIA	*IMMANUEL* uskav34@protonmail.com	1952	602 5TH ST	81428	RM	Kurt A Van Fossan	(970)238-6551	WS 8 SS 1030 BC 1030		28	27	18
PARKER	*GRACE* officeSecretary@glcparker.org www.glcparker.org	2002	11135 NEWLIN GULCH BLVD	80134	RM	Joseph G Murphy	(303)840-5493	WS 8 1030 SS 915 BC 915	HS/ED/ MD/SN	332	248	184
	TRINITY		See Franktown CO									
PEYTON	*FAMILY OF FAITH*		See Falcon CO									
PLATTEVILE	*FAITH*		See Johnstown CO									
PLEASANT VIEW	*TRINITY*		See Cortez CO									
PUEBLO	*BETHANY* pastor@bethanypueblo.org bethanypueblo.org	1957	1802 SHERIDAN RD	81001	RM	Nicholas R Shults	(719)544-5269	WS 1045 BC 930	ED/HC/ MD/SN			
	OUR SAVIOR'S		See Pueblo West CO									
	TRINITY trinitychurchoffice24@gmail.com www.trinitylutheranpueblo.org	1888	701 W EVANS AVE	81004	RM	Robert W Hauter	(719)544-3016	WS 9 SS 1015 BC 1015	EC/EL/ ED/HC	387	286	50
PUEBLO WEST	*OUR SAVIOR'S* pastor@oursaviorspueblowest.com oursaviorspueblowest.com	1982	275 W JOHN POWELL BLVD	81007	RM	Nicholas R Shults	(719)547-2300	WS 9 SS 8 BC 8	ED/HC/ MD/SN			
RIFLE	*EMMANUEL* elcrifle@gmail.com www.elcrifle.com	1950	652 E 5TH ST	81650	RM	Dallas C Dubke	(970)625-2369 (970)625-2157	WS 9 SS 1030 BC 1030	EL/ED/ MD/SN			
ROCKY FORD	*ST PETER*	1906	952 Washington Ave 18410 COUNTY ROAD EE	81067	RM		(719)254-6064	WS 1030 SS 9 BC 9				
SALIDA	*FIRST* flcsalida@flc-salida.org www.flc-salida.org	1956	1237 F ST	81201	RM	James T Sorensen	(719)539-4311 (719)539-9373	WS 830 SS 930 BC 930	ED/HC			
SILVERTHORNE	*CHRIST*		See Breckenridge CO									
STEAMBOAT SPRINGS	*CONCORDIA* concordia@steamboatlutheran.com www.steamboatlutheran.com	1936	755 CONCORDIA LN STEAM- BOAT SPR	80487	RM	Jonathan T Muhly	(970)879-0175	WS 9 BC 1030	ED/HC/MD	168	147	80

*Indicates a new church start. A new church start is an intentionally organized gathering which comes together on a regular basis for the purpose of worship and/or Bible study and is intended to grow into a member LCMS congregation. WS =Worship Service; SS = Sunday School; BC =Bible Class; EC = Early Childhood; EL = Elementary School; HS = High School; ED =Education Ministry; HC =Human Care Ministry; SN = Special Needs Ministry; MD = Media Ministry (PC)=Partner Church Pastor. See Page 53 for the Table of Abbreviations for key to additional abbreviations

CITY	CONGREGATION EMAIL WEBSITE	YEAR EST	LOCATION MAILING ADDRESS	ZIP CODE(S)	DIST.	PASTOR(S)	PHONE FAX	WS SS BC	SCHOOLS/ MINISTRIES	STATISTIC Bapt	Conf	Avg Attend
STERLING	*FIRST ENGLISH* firstenglish701@gmail.com www.firstenglish701.org/main	1927	701 FAIRHURST ST	80751	RM	Richard von Steinman	(970)522-5142	WS 1030 SS 9 BC 9	ED/HC/ MD/SN			
	TRINITY tlchurch732@yahoo.com trinitylutheransterling.org	1912	732 CLARK ST	80751	RM	Pedro G Jofre	(970)522-5942 (970)521-7763	WS 8 1045 SS 930 BC 930 6	EC/ED/HC/ MD/SN	470	376	150
THORNTON	*SUMMIT PEACE* office@summitofpeace.org www.summitofpeace.org	1986	4661 E 136TH AVE	80602	RM	Jeremy M Jacoby	(303)452-0448	WS 930 BC 930	ED/HC/MD	566	345	157
VAIL	*GRACE FELLOWSHIP*		See Gypsum CO									
	GRACIOUS SAVIOR		See Edwards CO									
WESTCLIFFE	*HOPE* www.hopelutheranwestcliffe.org	1872	312 S 3rd St 312 3RD ST	81252	RM		(719)783-9773	WS 2 BC 315	HC	29	29	16
WESTMINISTER	*MOUNT ZION*		See Denver CO									
WESTMINSTER	*WITHOUT WALLS* pastorcraighenningfield@gmail.com	2007			RM		(303)725-6760		ED/HC/SN			
WHEAT RIDGE	*BETHLEHEM*		See Lakewood CO									
	WHEAT RIDGE office@wrlutheran.org www.wrlutheran.org	1954	8600 W 38TH AVE	80033	RM	Eli J Lietzau	(303)424-3161 (303)424-4378	WS 10 SS 845 BC 845	HS/ED/HC/ MD			
WOODLAND PARK	*FAITH* office@faithteller.org www.faithteller.org	1955	1310 EVERGREEN HEIGHTS DR	80863	RM	Gary S Schuschke	(719)687-2303 (719)687-4576	WS 9 SS 1030 BC 1030	EC/ED/HC/ MD	207	151	51
WRAY	*CALVARY* pastor@calvarywray.org www.calvarywray.org	1928	518 DEXTER ST	80758	RM	Benjamin D Vanderhyde	(970)630-5636 (970)332-4023	WS 11 SS 930 BC 930	ED/HC/ MD/SN	175	159	60
YELLOW JACKET	*TRINITY*		See Cortez CO									
YUMA	*ST JOHN* stjohnslutheran@centurylink.net	1916	405 S Albany St PO BOX 436	80759	RM	Dennis G Fitzpatrick Jr	(970)848-2210 (970)848-2210	WS 930 SS 1045 BC 1045	ED/MD/SN			

CONNECTICUT

CITY	CONGREGATION EMAIL WEBSITE	YEAR EST	LOCATION MAILING ADDRESS	ZIP CODE(S)	DIST.	PASTOR(S)	PHONE FAX	WS SS BC	SCHOOLS/ MINISTRIES	Bapt	Conf	Avg Attend
AMSTON	*CHRIST* www.clchebron.org	1985	330 CHURCH ST	06231	NE	Matthew D Hardaway	(860)228-1152 (860)228-1062	WS 9 SS 930 BC 1030	EC/ED/HC/ MD	72	56	33
ANSONIA	*ZION*		See Orange CT									
BEACON FALLS	*ST PAUL*		See Naugatuck CT									
BETHEL	*CHRIST KING*		See Newtown CT									
BRIDGEPORT	*ZION* zionbpt@gmail.com	1892	612 GRAND ST	06604	NE		(203)367-4521	WS 9				
BRISTOL	*IMMANUEL* lroaas@ilcs.org www.ilcs.org	1892	154 MEADOW ST	06010	NE	Kevin A Karner Robert D Beinke	(860)583-5649 (860)585-4785	WS 8 1045 SS 930 BC 930	EL/ED/HC/ MD	914	664	110
BROOKFIELD	*CHRIST KING*		See Newtown CT									
CHESHIRE	*CHESHIRE* office@cheshirelutheran.org www.cheshirelutheran.org	1956	660 W Main St PO BOX 157	06410	NE	Dr David P Rowold	(203)272-5106 (203)272-3523	WS 8 1030 SS 910 BC 910	EC/ED/HC/ MD/SN	511	432	103
COVENTRY	*PRINCE OF PEACE* www.princeofpeace-lcms.org	1961	10 N RIVER RD	06238	NE		(860)742-7548	WS 12	ED/HC/ MD/SN			
DANBURY	*IMMANUEL DANBURY* churchoffice@immanueldanbury.org www.immanueldanbury.org	1881	18 CLAPBOARD RIDGE RD	06811	NE	Ryan J Oakes	(203)748-3320 (203)748-5022	WS 9 SS 1030 BC 1030	EL/ED/HC/ MD	370	282	112
DARIEN	*ST PETER*		See Norwalk CT									
DERBY	*ZION*		See Orange CT									
EAST GANBY	*GOOD SHEPHERD*		See Suffield CT									
EAST HAVEN	*ZION*		See Orange CT									
EAST WINDSOR	*OUR REDEEMER*		See Enfield CT									
ENFIELD	*OUR REDEEMER* lcorct@gmail.com lcorenfieldct.org	1958	20 NORTH ST	06082	NE	Michael J Coons	(860)749-3167	WS 8 1030 SS 920 BC 920	ED/HC/MD	165	142	42
GREENWICH	*ST PAUL* stpaulgreenwich@gmail.com	1902	286 DELAVAN AVE	06830	NE	Evan P Scamman	(203)531-8466	WS 9 BC 1030	ED/HC/SN	128	110	50
GROTON	*FAITH* president@faithgroton.org www.faithgroton.org	1955	625 POQUONNOCK RD	06340	NE	Christopher L Chandler	(860)445-0483	WS 11 BC 1215	ED/MD/SN	55	51	30
	OUR REDEEMER		See New London CT									
HAMDEN	*ZION*		See Orange CT									
HEBRON	*CHRIST*		See Amston CT									
LEBANON	*REDEEMER* secretary@RLC-Lebanon-CT.org	1916	321 VILLAGE HILL RD	06249	NE	Michael A Skarda	(860)423-4320 (860)450-1064	WS 9 SS 1030 BC 1030	ED/HC/ MD/SN	151	118	50
LITCHFIELD	*SHEPHERD/HILLS*		See Morris CT									
MADISON	*MADISON* lcofmadison@aol.com www.lutheranchurchofmadison.com	1949	9 BRITTON LN	06443	NE	Volker S Heide	(203)245-4145	WS 10	ED/HC/ MD/SN	230	222	74
MANCHESTER	*ZION* zionlutheranct@outlook.com	1890	112 Cooper St 120 COOPER ST	06040	NE	Gregory Dwyer	(860)649-4243	WS 930 BC 1045	ED/HC	25	20	15
MANSFIELD	*HOPE*		See Storrs CT									
MERIDEN	*ST JOHN* office@saintjohnmeriden.org www.saintjohnmeriden.org	1865	520 PADDOCK AVE	06450	NE	Scott M MacDonald	(203)238-2331	WS 10 SS 9 BC 9	EC/ED/HC/ MD/SN	160	141	58
	ZION		See Wallingford CT									

*Indicates a new church start. A new church start is an intentionally organized gathering which comes together on a regular basis for the purpose of worship and/or Bible study and is intended to grow into a member LCMS congregation. WS =Worship Service; SS = Sunday School; BC =Bible Class; EC = Early Childhood; EL = Elementary School; HS = High School; ED =Education Ministry; HC =Human Care Ministry; SN = Special Needs Ministry; MD = Media Ministry (PC)=Partner Church Pastor. See Page 53 for the Table of Abbreviations for key to additional abbreviations

CITY	CONGREGATION EMAIL WEBSITE	YEAR EST	LOCATION MAILING ADDRESS	ZIP CODE(S)	DIST.	PASTOR(S)	PHONE FAX	WS SS BC	SCHOOLS/ MINISTRIES	STATISTIC Bapt	Conf	Avg Attend
MIDDLETOWN	*GRACE* grace.evan.lutheran@snet.net www.gracemiddletown.org	1901	1055 RANDOLPH RD	06457	NE	Mark R Clow	(860)346-2641 (860)344-0611	WS 930 SS 1045 BC 1045	EC/ED/HC/ MD/SN	431	310	43
MILFORD	*ZION*		See Orange CT									
MORRIS	*SHEPHERD/HILLS* shepherdofthehills.morris@gmail.com	1995	Morris Congregational 9 East St PO BOX 47 BANTAM	06763 06750	NE		(860)480-5357			25	22	15
MYSTIC	*FAITH*		See Groton CT									
NAUGATUCK	*ST PAUL* mjbatta@comcast.net	1903	350 MILLVILLE AVE	06770	NE		(203)729-8610	WS 915				
NEW BRITAIN	*ST MATTHEW* www.stmatthewslc.org	1887	99 FRANKLIN SQ	06051	NE	Mark S Valigorsky	(860)223-3503 (860)223-3503	WS 9	ED	145	145	20
NEW CANAAN	*ST PETER*		See Norwalk CT									
NEW FAIRFIELD	*GOOD SHEPHERD* office@goodshepherdnewfairfield.org goodshepherdnewfairfield.org	1969	2 COLONIAL RD	06812	NE	Philip D Bartelt	(203)746-9022 (203)746-9022	WS 1030 SS 9 BC 915	ED/HC	124	124	37
NEW HARTFORD	*SAINT PAULS* slutheranchurch@snet.net www.stpaulsnewhartford.org	1895	39 PROSPECT ST NEW HARFORD	06057	NE	Kevin A Mongeau	(860)379-3172	WS 9 SS 1030 BC 1030	ED/HC/MD	106	96	58
NEW HAVEN	*ZION*		See Orange CT									
NEW LONDON	*FAITH*		See Groton CT									
	OUR REDEEMER ornl1930@gmail.com WWW.ourredeemernl.org	1916	35 Cedar Grove Ave 31 CEDAR GROVE AVE	06320	NE			WS 6	ED/MD			
NEW MILFORD	*TRINITY* cathy_f_mcgrath@yahoo.com www.Trinitylutherannewmilford.org	1958	107 Kent Rd PO BOX 388	06776	NE	F Christian J Bunzel	(860)354-3450	WS 1030 SS 9 BC 9		102	90	40
NEWTOWN	*CHRIST KING* ctknewtown@gmail.com www.ctklutherannewtown.org	1960	85 MOUNT PLEASANT RD	06470	NE	Robert H Morris II	(203)426-6300 (203)270-8178	WS 930 5 SS 1045 BC 1045	ED/HC	379	327	134
NIANTIC	*CHRIST* office@clcniantic.org www.clcniantic.org	1962	24 SOCIETY RD	06357	NE	Paul L Scheyder	(860)739-6849 (860)739-6849	WS 830 11 SS 945 BC 945	ED	298	215	105
NORTH HAVEN	*ZION*		See Orange CT									
	ZION		See Wallingford CT									
NORWALK	*ST PETER* office@stpeternorwalk.org www.stpeternorwalk.org	1911	208 NEWTOWN AVE	06851	NE	Gem Gabriel	(203)847-1252 (203)846-4415	WS 10 SS 845 BC 845	ED/MD	135	120	45
NORWICH	*FAITH*		See Groton CT									
ORANGE	*ZION* pastor@zion-orange.com www.zion-orange.com	1883	780 GRASSY HILL RD	06477	NE	Kevin McGladdery	(203)795-3916	WS 1030 SS 930 BC 930	ED/HC/MD	90	70	26
RIDGEFIELD	*ST PETER*		See Norwalk CT									
ROWAYTON	*ST PETER*		See Norwalk CT									
SOMERS	*OUR REDEEMER*		See Enfield CT									
SOUTH WINDSOR	*OUR SAVIOR* churchoffice@oursaviorct.org www.oursaviorct.org	1958	239 GRAHAM RD	06074	NE	Randall L Pekari	(860)644-3350 (860)644-9068	WS 815 1030 SS 915 BC 915	EC/ED/HC/ MD	393	312	175
SOUTHBURY	*CHRIST KING*		See Newtown CT									
STAMFORD	*ST PAUL*		See Greenwich CT									
	ST PETER		See Norwalk CT									
STORRS	*HOPE* hopechurchstorrs@gmail.com www.hope-lcms.org	1962	62 DOG LN STORRS MANFLD	06269 06268	NE		(860)429-5409	WS 1030	ED/HC/MD			
SUFFIELD	*GOOD SHEPHERD* gslcsuffieldct@gmail.com GSLCSuffield.org	1957	585 South St PO BOX 155	06078	NE	Adam P Moore	(860)668-2790	WS 9		36	36	27
TERRYVILLE	*HOLY TRINITY* htlc08@sbcglobal.net www.holytrinityterryville.org	1896	8 MAPLE ST	06786	NE	Joel D Kotila	(860)582-0723 (860)583-1981	WS 9 SS 1045	SN	113	113	30
TRUMBULL	*HOLY CROSS* office@holycrosstrumbull.com www.holycrosstrumbull.org	1958	5995 MAIN ST	06611	NE		(203)268-7555 (203)268-5499	WS 10 BC 1045	EC/ED/HC/ MD	270	227	86
WALLINGFORD	*ZION* zion-aa@sbcglobal.net www.zionlutheranwlfd.org	1891	235 POND HILL RD	06492	NE	Robert C Hass	(203)269-6847	WS 1030 SS 915 BC 915	EC/ED/HC/ MD/SN	248	219	65
WATERFORD	*OUR REDEEMER*		See New London CT									
WEST HARTFORD	*BETHANY* elizabeth@blcwh.org www.blcwh.org	1945	1655 BOULEVARD	06107	NE	Jason E Reitz	(860)521-5076	WS 1030 SS 915	EC/ED/HC			
WEST HAVEN	*ZION*		See Orange CT									
WESTPORT	*ST PAUL* acct@stpaulwestport.org www.stpaulwestport.org	1921	41 EASTON RD	06880	S		(203)227-7441 (203)222-9205	WS 10 BC 9	EC/ED/HC/ MD/SN	150	150	95
WILTON	*ST PETER*		See Norwalk CT									
WINDSOR LOCKS	*GOOD SHEPHERD*		See Suffield CT									
WOODBRIDGE	*ZION*		See Orange CT									

DELAWARE

CITY	CONGREGATION EMAIL WEBSITE	YEAR EST	LOCATION MAILING ADDRESS	ZIP CODE(S)	DIST.	PASTOR(S)	PHONE FAX	WS SS BC	SCHOOLS/ MINISTRIES	STATISTIC Bapt	Conf	Avg Attend
BEAR	*FAITH* info@faith-lutheran.church www.faith-lutheran.church	1954	2265 RED LION RD	19701	SE	Michael P Thress	(302)834-1214 (302)834-3417	WS 815 1030 SS 1030 BC 930	EC/ED/HC/ MD	213	184	72
	OUR REDEEMER		See Newark DE									

*Indicates a new church start. A new church start is an intentionally organized gathering which comes together on a regular basis for the purpose of worship and/or Bible study and is intended to grow into a member LCMS congregation. WS =Worship Service; SS = Sunday School; BC =Bible Class; EC = Early Childhood; EL = Elementary School; HS = High School; ED =Education Ministry; HC =Human Care Ministry; SN = Special Needs Ministry; MD = Media Ministry (PC)=Partner Church Pastor. See Page 53 for the Table of Abbreviations for key to additional abbreviations

CITY	CONGREGATION EMAIL WEBSITE	YEAR EST	LOCATION MAILING ADDRESS	ZIP CODE(S)	DIST.	PASTOR(S)	PHONE FAX	WS SS BC	SCHOOLS/ MINISTRIES	STATISTIC Bapt	Conf	Avg Attend
CHRISTIANA	*OUR REDEEMER*		See Newark DE									
DOVER	*ST JOHN* secretary@sjldover.com www.sjldover.com	1923	113 LOTUS ST	19901	SE	Dr Charles E Ransdell Jr	(302)734-7078	WS 915 SS 11 BC 11	ED/HC/MD			
EASTERN SUSSEX COUNTY	*OUR SAVIOR*		See Rehoboth Beach DE									
LEWES	*OUR SAVIOR*		See Rehoboth Beach DE									
NEW CASTLE	*FAITH*		See Bear DE									
	OUR REDEEMER		See Newark DE									
NEWARK	*OUR REDEEMER* secretary.orlcde@outlook.com www.ourredeemernewark.org	1957	10 JOHNSON RD	19713	SE	Jeremy D Loesch	(302)737-6176	WS 10 SS 1015 BC 845	HC/MD	60	60	28
REHOBOTH BEACH	*OUR SAVIOR* lcosoffice@yahoo.com www.lcosrehoboth.org	1961	20276 BAY VISTA RD REHO-BOTH BCH	19971	SE		(302)227-3066	WS 8 1030 SS 930 BC 930	ED/HC/ MD/SN	268	195	180
SEAFORD	*CHRIST* christlutheranseaford.com	1955	315 N SHIPLEY ST	19973	SE		(302)629-9755	WS 830 11 SS 945	ED/HC/ MD/SN			
SMYRNA	*PEACE*	1975	5048 WHEATLEYS POND RD	19977	SE		(302)653-4312	WS 1030	ED/HC/MD			
WILMINGTON	*CONCORDIA* info@concordiade.com concordiade.com	1931	3003 SILVERSIDE RD	19810	SE	David J Kummer	(302)478-3004	WS 1030 SS 915 BC 915	EC/ED/HC/ MD	193	93	75
	OUR REDEEMER		See Newark DE									
	TRINITY		See Carneys Point NJ									

DISTRICT OF COLUMBIA

CITY	CONGREGATION EMAIL WEBSITE	YEAR EST	LOCATION MAILING ADDRESS	ZIP CODE(S)	DIST.	PASTOR(S)	PHONE FAX	WS SS BC	SCHOOLS/ MINISTRIES	Bapt	Conf	Avg Attend
WASHINGTON	*CHRIST DEAF*		See Silver Spring MD									
	DMV MEKANE YESUS dmvmekaneyesus@gmail.com		1725 MICHIGAN AVE NE	20017	SE		(202)403-9493	WS 10				
	*ELSHADDAI** gemechisfeyisa747@gmail.com		7005 PINE BRANCH RD	20012	SE		(240)701-4196					
	IMMANUEL		See Alexandria VA									
	MESSIAH		See Germantown MD									
	MOUNT OLIVE mtolivetdc@gmail.com mountolivetdc.org	1933	1306 Vermont Ave NW 1308 VERMONT AVE NW	20005	SE	Dr John F Johnson	(202)667-5357 (202)234-6631	WS 10 SS 920 BC 920	ED/HC/ MD/SN	113	84	32
	PEACE peacedc@msn.com peacelutherandc.org	1960	15 49th Pl NE 4929 AMES ST NE	20019	SE	Dr Lloyd D Gaines Sr	(202)398-5503 (202)388-4667	WS 830 1030 SS 930	ED/HC/MD	332	230	68
WASHINGTON DC	*CONCORDIA*		See Upper Marlboro MD									

FLORIDA

CITY	CONGREGATION EMAIL WEBSITE	YEAR EST	LOCATION MAILING ADDRESS	ZIP CODE(S)	DIST.	PASTOR(S)	PHONE FAX	WS SS BC	SCHOOLS/ MINISTRIES	Bapt	Conf	Avg Attend
ALACHUA	*FIRST*		See Gainesville FL									
ALTOONA	*FAITH*		See Eustis FL									
APOLLO BEACH	*CHRIST THE KING*		See Riverview FL									
APOPKA	*ST PAUL* stpaullcms@embarqmail.com StPaulLCMS.org	1964	261 S Mc Gee Ave 261 S MCGEE AVE	32703	FG	Donald A Moore Jr	(407)889-2634	WS 10 SS 9 BC 9	ED/HC/MD			
	WOODLANDS		See Montverde FL									
ARCADIA	*GRACE*	1979	1004 W OAK ST	34266	FG	Anthony A Arias	(863)494-7008 (863)494-7008	WS 11	ED/HC/ MD/SN	45	42	14
	OF THE CROSS		See Port Charlotte FL									
ARIPEKA	*HOPE*		See Hudson FL									
ASTATULA	*THE CROSS*		See Mount Dora FL									
AVENTURA	*HOLY CROSS*		See North Miami FL									
AVON PARK	*CHRIST* sjmclean@embarqmail.com christlutheranavonpark.org	1998	1320 County Road 64 E PO BOX 819	33825 33826	FG	Scott J McLean	(863)471-2663	WS 10 BC 830	HC/MD	40	37	23
BABCOCK RANCH	*FAITH*		See Punta Gorda FL									
BARTOW	*REDEEMER*	1957	390 E Parker St PO BOX 1380	33830 33831	FG	Jonathan R Horsman	(863)512-3652	WS 1015 BC 9	ED/HC/ MD/SN			
BELLE GLADE	*ST PETER* jordine@aol.com	1938	125 E CANAL ST N	33430	FG			WS 10		11	10	8
BELLEAIR BEACH	*CHRIST THE KING*		See Largo FL									
BELLEAIR BLUFFS	*CHRIST THE KING*		See Largo FL									
BELLEVIEW	*AMAZING GRACE*		See Oxford FL									
	TRINITY		See Summerfield FL									
BEULAH	*TRINITY*		See Cantonment FL									
BITHLO	*ST LUKE*		See Oviedo FL									
BOCA GRANDE	*TRINITY SW FL*		See Port Charlotte FL									
BOCA RATON	*ST PAUL* contactus@stpaulboca.com www.stpaulboca.com	1957	701 W PALMETTO PARK RD	33486	FG	Stephen P Carretto Jacob R Scheler	(561)395-0433 (561)395-5348	WS 9 1045 SS 945	EL/ED/HC/ MD	2136	1618	385
	TRINITY		See Delray Beach FL									
BONIFAY	*GRACE*	1979	3309 Hwy 90 East PO BOX 972	32425	SO	Richard T Wright	(850)547-9898	WS 815	ED/HC/MD	5	5	9
BONITA SPRINGS	*AMIGOS EN CRISTO** bobselle@amigoscenter.org www.amigoscenter.org		25999 OLD 41 RD BONITA SPGS	34135	FG		(239)437-6727 (239)466-7927		HC/MD			
	HOPE info@hopebonita.org	1986	25999 OLD 41 RD BONITA SPGS	34135	FG	Richard L Browning	(239)992-6952 (239)992-3254	WS 9 1030	ED/HC/ MD/SN	350	320	275

*Indicates a new church start. A new church start is an intentionally organized gathering which comes together on a regular basis for the purpose of worship and/or Bible study and is intended to grow into a member LCMS congregation. WS =Worship Service; SS = Sunday School; BC =Bible Class; EC = Early Childhood; EL = Elementary School; HS = High School; ED =Education Ministry; HC =Human Care Ministry; SN = Special Needs Ministry; MD = Media Ministry (PC)=Partner Church Pastor. See Page 53 for the Table of Abbreviations for key to additional abbreviations

CITY	CONGREGATION EMAIL WEBSITE	YEAR EST	LOCATION MAILING ADDRESS	ZIP CODE(S)	DIST.	PASTOR(S)	PHONE FAX	WS SS BC	SCHOOLS/ MINISTRIES	STATISTIC Bapt	 Conf	 Avg Attend
BONITA SPRINGS	*THRIVE COMMUNITY*		See Estero FL									
BOWLING GREEN	*PEACE VALLEY*		See Wauchula FL									
BOYNTON BEACH	*SON LIFE* sonlifelutheran@bellsouth.net www.sonlifelutheran.org	1984	9301 Jog Rd 9301 S JOG RD	33437	FG		(561)738-5433 (561)364-7884	WS 10 SS 9 BC 9	ED/HC			
	TRINITY		See Delray Beach FL									
BRADENTON	*HOPE* office@hopelutheranfl.org www.hopelutheranfl.org	1959	4635 26TH ST W	34207	FG	James M Krach	(941)755-3256	WS 830 1030 SS 945 1045 BC 945 1045	ED/HC/ MD/SN	129	125	130
BRANDON	*IMMANUEL* info@immanuelbrandon.com www.immanuelbrandon.com	1970	2913 JOHN MOORE RD	33511	FG	Philip W Ressler Miguel A Sanabria Jr	(813)689-1787	WS 8 1015 SS 915 BC 915	EL/ED/ HC/SN	360	307	215
BROOKSVILLE	*CHRIST* office@clcfla.org clcfla.org	1962	475 NORTH AVE W	34601	FG	Paul R Meseke	(352)796-8331 (352)754-4380	WS 10 SS 845 BC 845	ED/HC/ MD/SN	117	114	95
	HOLY TRINITY		See Masaryktown FL									
CALLAHAN	*OUR REDEEMER*		See Jacksonville FL									
CALLAWAY	*GOOD SHEPHERD* rev.ehrichs@gmail.com www.gslcpc.org	1967	929 S TYNDALL PKWY PANAMA CITY	32404	SO	Randal G Ehrichs	(850)871-6311	WS 9 SS 1045 BC 1045	ED/HC/SN	161	161	92
CANTONMENT	*RESURRECTION*		See Pensacola FL									
	TRINITY OfficeAdmin@trinity-lutheranchurch.org www.trinity-lutheranchurch.org	1974	2385 HIGHWAY 297A	32533	SO	Sanford D Stanton Jackson D Onkka	(850)607-9524	WS 10 SS 830	ED/HC/ MD/SN	85	56	47
CAPE CANAVERAL	*CHRIST* clccc@cfl.rr.com www.christlutheranchurchcape canaveral.org	1959	7511 N ATLANTIC AVE CPE CANAVERAL	32920	FG	Gregory M Le Sieur	(321)783-3303 (321)783-1089	WS 10	ED/HC/MD	96	96	75
CAPE CORAL	*FAITH*		See Punta Gorda FL									
	THRIVE COMMUNITY		See Estero FL									
	TRINITY church@trinitycapecoral.org www.trinitycapecoral.org	1984	706 SW 6TH AVE	33991	FG	Gary E Koltz	(239)772-0172 (239)772-4691	WS 10	ED/HC/ MD/SN	202	123	73
CARRABELLE	*TRINITY*		See Crawfordville FL									
CARROLLWOOD	*MESSIAH* tnunes@messiahtampa.com messiahtampa.com	1982	14920 HUTCHISON RD TAMPA	33625	FG	Mark J Adrian Jr John F Cobos	(813)961-2182 (813)961-0592	WS 830 11 SS 945 BC 945	EC/ED/HC/ MD/SN	700	641	214
CASSELBERRY	*ASCENSION* mmueller@ascensionlcms.org www.ascensionlcms.org	1960	351 ASCENSION DR	32707	FG	Mark A Mueller Raleigh N Sims	(407)831-7788	WS 830 11 SS 10 BC 10	ED/MD/SN	201	181	101
	ST LUKE		See Oviedo FL									
CELEBRATION	*GRACE*		See Saint Cloud FL									
CHIEFLAND	*GOOD SHEPHERD* gslutheran@bellsouth.net lutheranchurchchiefland.org	1982	14303 NW HWY 19	32626	FG	Dr Larry J Griffin	(352)493-4597	WS 1030	ED/HC/ MD/SN	52	50	40
CHULUOTA	*ST LUKE*		See Oviedo FL									
CLEARWATER	*BETHEL* blutheranchurch@tampabay.rr.com bethellutheranclearwater.org	1975	3166 Mc Mullen Booth Rd 3166 N MCMULLEN BOOTH RD	33761	FG	Aaron D Schnelle	(727)799-3010 (727)796-4889	WS 8 1030 SS 915 BC 915	ED/MD/SN	579	438	191
	CHRIST THE KING		See Largo FL									
	FAITH		See Dunedin FL									
	FIRST info@flcclearwater.org flcclearwater.org	1941	1644 NURSERY RD	33756	FG	Andrew D Apple	(727)462-8000 (727)442-7473	WS 930 SS 945 BC 1045	EL/ED/HC/ MD	241	197	152
CLEARWATER BEACH	*CHRIST THE KING*		See Largo FL									
CLERMONT	*WOODLANDS*		See Montverde FL									
CLEWISTON	*FAITH* www.faithclewistonfl.org	1989	810 CEDAR ST	33440	FG	Seth T DeBartolo	(863)983-7302	WS 11	ED/HC/MD	32	31	21
COCOA	*TRINITY*		See Rockledge FL									
CRAWFORDVILLE	*TRINITY* bert.matlock@gmail.com www.trinitylutheranofwakulla.com	1981	3254 Coastal Hwy PO BOX 940	32327 32326	FG	Albert H Matlock	(850)926-7808	WS 1017		73	55	35
CRESTVIEW	*GOOD SHEPHERD*		See Shalimar FL									
	OUR SAVIOR oselc@oselc.gccoxmail.com www.oselc.net	1952	178 W NORTH AVE	32536	SO	Raymond D Parent II	(850)682-3154 (850)682-6008	WS 10 BC 9	ED/HC/MD	66	66	39
CRYSTAL RIVER	*FAITH*		See Lecanto FL									
DAVIE	*GLORIA DEI* office@gloria-dei.org www.gloria-dei.org	1973	7601 SW 39TH ST	33328	FG	George E Poulos Jr	(954)475-0683 (954)474-2313	WS 10 SS 1130 BC 1130	EC/ED/HC/ MD	396	268	55
DAYTONA BEACH	*HOLY CROSS*		See South Daytona FL									
	TRINITY		See Holly Hill FL									
DE FUNIAK SPRINGS	*HOPE ON THE BEACH*		See Santa Rosa Beach FL									
DEER ISLAND	*THE CROSS*		See Mount Dora FL									
DELAND	*REDEEMER*		See Sanford FL									
	WELLSPRING CHURCH Satellite Site of Holy Cross Lake Mary FL	2016	111 S Alabama Ave	32724				WS 10 SS 10				
DELRAY BEACH	*EMMANUEL HAITIAN*	1990	1699 SW 6th St PO BOX 7142	33482	FG	Daniel A Bartley	(561)889-4835			79	69	78

*Indicates a new church start. A new church start is an intentionally organized gathering which comes together on a regular basis for the purpose of worship and/or Bible study and is intended to grow into a member LCMS congregation. WS =Worship Service; SS = Sunday School; BC =Bible Class; EC = Early Childhood; EL = Elementary School; HS = High School; ED =Education Ministry; HC =Human Care Ministry; SN = Special Needs Ministry; MD = Media Ministry (PC)=Partner Church Pastor. See Page 53 for the Table of Abbreviations for key to additional abbreviations

CITY	CONGREGATION EMAIL WEBSITE	YEAR EST	LOCATION MAILING ADDRESS	ZIP CODE(S)	DIST.	PASTOR(S)	PHONE FAX	WS SS BC	SCHOOLS/ MINISTRIES	STATISTIC Bapt	Conf	Avg Attend
DELRAY BEACH	*TRINITY* info@trinitydelray.org www.trinitydelray.org	1904	400 N SWINTON AVE	33444	FG	Gary P Boye Jacob J Roedsens	(561)278-1737 (561)272-3215	WS 830 1030	EL/ED/HC/ MD	160	160	141
DELTONA	*PROVIDENCE* lutheranchurchofprovidence@gmail.com lutheranprovidence.org	1966	1696 PROVIDENCE BLVD	32725	FG		(386)789-3300 (386)789-0132	WS 1030 SS 11 BC 915	SN	127	94	80
DESTIN	*GOOD SHEPHERD*		See Shalimar FL									
	GRACE pastorkevin@gracedestin.com www.gracedestin.org	1982	125 MAIN STREET	32541	SO	Dr Kevin M Wendt	(850)353-2996	WS 930 SS 1115 BC 1115	ED/HC/ MD/SN	101	88	61
	HOPE ON THE BEACH		See Santa Rosa Beach FL									
DUKE FIELD	*GOOD SHEPHERD*		See Shalimar FL									
DUNEDIN	*BETHEL*		See Clearwater FL									
	FAITH office@faithdunedin.org www.faithdunedin.org	1958	1620 PINEHURST RD	34698	FG	Andrew J Sorenson	(727)733-2657	WS 1015 SS 915 BC 915	ED/HC/MD	121	109	79
DUNNELLON	*PEACE* peacelutheran.dunnellon@gmail.com peacelutheranonline.com	1962	7201 S Hwy 41 7201 S US HIGHWAY 41	34432	FG	Terry L McKee	(352)489-5881	WS 10 SS 9 BC 9	HC/MD	69	68	49
EGLIN AFB	*GOOD SHEPHERD*		See Shalimar FL									
ELLENTON	*FAITH*		See Parrish FL									
ENGLEWOOD	*FAITH*		See Punta Gorda FL									
	LAKESIDE		See Venice FL									
	REDEEMER church.office@redeemerfl.com www.redeemerfl.com	1978	6465 Mayport St 6970 MINEOLA RD	34224	FG	Craig A Mathews	(941)475-2410 (941)475-9726	WS 915 SS 1045 BC 1045	EL/ED/HC/ MD/SN	158	106	41
	TRINITY SW FL		See Port Charlotte FL									
ENSLEY	*TRINITY*		See Cantonment FL									
ESTERO	*AMIGOS EN CRISTO** bobselle@amigoscenter.org www.amigoscenter.org		20041 S Tamiami Trl Suite 1 20041 S TAMIAMI TRL SUITE 1	33928	FG		(239)657-3822		HC			
	HOPE		See Bonita Springs FL									
	THRIVE COMMUNITY info@thrive-fl.org www.thrive-fl.org		20041 S Tamiami Trail Suite 1 20041 S TAMIAMI TRL STE 1	33978 33928	FG	Dr John D Roth	(239)687-3430	WS 10	ED/HC/MD			
EUSTIS	*FAITH* dheilman@flcse.org www.faitheustis.org	1953	2727 S GROVE ST	32726	FG	Marc A Kappel	(352)589-5433 (352)589-1886	WS 10 SS 845 BC 845	EL/ED/HC/ MD/SN	419	330	136
	THE CROSS		See Mount Dora FL									
	WOODLANDS		See Montverde FL									
FERN PARK	*ST LUKE*		See Oviedo FL									
FERNANDING BEACH	*HOLY TRINITY*		See Kingsland GA									
FERRY PASS	*TRINITY*		See Cantonment FL									
FLEMING ISLAND	*ST PETER*		See Middleburg FL									
FORT LAUDERDALE	*GLORIA DEI*		See Davie FL									
	GOOD SHEPHERD jannicesmith17@gmail.com	1954	1201 NW 27TH AVE FT LAUDERDALE	33311	FG			WS 1030	ED/HC/MD	25	25	17
	GRACE TABERNACLE pastoroslet@hotmail.com		1161 SW 30TH AVE FT LAUDERDALE	33312	FG	Bernard Julmiste				5	5	230
	MONT GARIZIM	2008	1161 SW 30th Ave	33312	FG	Oslet Maccenat						
	SHEP OF THE COAST rmurphy@shepherdofthecoast.org www.shepherdofthecoast.org		1901 E COMMERCIAL BLVD FT LAUDERDALE	33308	FG	Chad T Czischke	(954)772-8010 (954)772-2232	WS 830 1030 SS 930 BC 930	EL/ED/HC/ MD/SN	170	134	85
	ST PAUL		See Weston FL									
	TRINITY trinityftlauderdale@gmail.com www.trinityftl.org	1927	11 SW 11TH ST FT LAUDERDALE	33315	FG	Jeffrey M Wilhelm	(954)463-2450 (954)767-4776	WS 10	ED/HC/ MD/SN	40	40	28
	*TRINITY HAITIAN**		11 SW 11TH ST FT LAUDERDALE	33315	FG							
FORT MYERS	*BETHLEHEM* bethlehemlc@gmail.com www.blcefm.org	1982	14531 OLD OLGA RD	33905	FG	Karl P Glander	(239)694-3878 (239)694-9868	WS 1030 SS 1130 BC 1130	ED/HC/ MD/SN	84	81	65
	FAITH		See Punta Gorda FL									
	HOPE		See Bonita Springs FL									
	ST MICHAEL saintmichaellutheran@gmail.com www.smlcftmyers.com	1941	3595 BROADWAY	33901	FG	David J Bass Dr Roy R Peterson	(239)939-1218 (239)939-1839	WS 8 1045 SS 930 BC 930	EL/ED/HC/ MD/SN	945	709	352
	THRIVE COMMUNITY		See Estero FL									
	TRINITY		See Cape Coral FL									
	ZION info@zionfm.org www.zionfm.org	1971	7401 WINKLER RD	33919	FG	Dr Curtis L Deterding	(239)481-4040 (239)481-4102	WS 9 1030 SS 9	EC/ED/HC/ MD/SN	379	324	300
FORT PIERCE	*TRINITY* trinitychurch4u@gmail.com TrinityChurch4U.com	1952	2011 S 13TH ST	34950	FG		(772)461-7272 (772)461-5999	WS 10 SS 9 BC 9	EL/ED/HC/ MD/SN			
FORT WALTON BEACH	*GOOD SHEPHERD*		See Shalimar FL									
	GRACE		See Destin FL									
FREEPORT	*HOPE ON THE BEACH*		See Santa Rosa Beach FL									
FRUIT COVE	*CELEBRATION*		See Saint Johns FL									

*Indicates a new church start. A new church start is an intentionally organized gathering which comes together on a regular basis for the purpose of worship and/or Bible study and is intended to grow into a member LCMS congregation. WS =Worship Service; SS = Sunday School; BC =Bible Class; EC = Early Childhood; EL = Elementary School; HS = High School; ED =Education Ministry; HC =Human Care Ministry; SN = Special Needs Ministry; MD = Media Ministry (PC)=Partner Church Pastor. See Page 53 for the Table of Abbreviations for key to additional abbreviations

CITY	CONGREGATION EMAIL WEBSITE	YEAR EST	LOCATION MAILING ADDRESS	ZIP CODE(S)	DIST.	PASTOR(S)	PHONE FAX	WS SS BC	SCHOOLS/ MINISTRIES	STATISTIC Bapt	Conf	Avg Attend
FRUITLAND PARK	*TRINITY*		See Summerfield FL									
GAINESVILLE	*ABIDING SAVIOR* office@abidingsavior.info www.abidingsavior.info	1991	9700 W NEWBERRY RD	32606	FG	Graham B Glover	(352)331-4409 (352)331-7777	WS 8 1045 SS 945 BC 945	EC/ED/HC/ MD	239	193	136
	FIRST office@flcgainesville.org www.flcgainesville.org	1931	1801 NW 5TH AVE	32603	FG	Christopher J Kollmann	(352)376-2062 (352)376-3822	WS 10 BC 845	EC/ED/HC/ MD/SN	204	199	112
GOLDENROD	*ST LUKE*		See Oviedo FL									
GONZALEZ	*TRINITY*		See Cantonment FL									
GRAND ISLAND	*FAITH*		See Eustis FL									
	THE CROSS		See Mount Dora FL									
GREEN COVE SPRINGS	*ST PETER*		See Middleburg FL									
GROVELAND	*WOODLANDS*		See Montverde FL									
GULF BREEZE	*GOOD SHEPHERD* goodshepherdgb@outlook.com goodshepherdgb.com	1964	4237 GULF BREEZE PKWY	32563	SO		(850)932-3263	WS 8 1030	EL/ED/MD			
GULF COVE	*TRINITY SW FL*		See Port Charlotte FL									
HARMONY	*GRACE*		See Saint Cloud FL									
HIALEAH	*FAITH* flcs@faithlutheranhialeah.org www.faithlutheranhialeah.org	1948	293 HIALEAH DR	33010	FG	Dr James C Tino	(305)888-6706 (305)885-2845	WS 930 SS 11 BC 11	EL/ED/HC/ MD	37	37	15
	ST ANDREW	1958	575 W 68th St	33014	FG	Enrique A Orozco	(305)821-3622	WS 9 SS 1015 BC 1015	HC			
HIGH SPRINGS	*FIRST*		See Gainesville FL									
HOBE SOUND	*BETHEL* bethellutheran.hobesound@gmail.com bethel-lutheranhobesound.org	1982	7905 SE FEDERAL HWY	33455	FG	Scott A Jensen	(772)546-5399 (772)546-9847	WS 10 BC 9	EC/ED	40	38	35
HOLIDAY	*HOPE*		See Hudson FL									
HOLLY HILL	*TRINITY* tlchurch@cfl.rr.com www.trinityhollyhill.org	1949	1205 RIDGEWOOD AVE	32117	FG	Russell A Anderson	(386)255-7580	WS 1015 BC 9	ED/HC/ MD/SN	150	150	104
HOLLYWOOD	*PRINCE PEACE* juanmartin87800@yahoo.com	1956	3000 N 75TH AVE	33024	FG	Eliexer Ramirez	(954)495-0712	WS 1230 SS 130	ED/HC/ MD/SN			
HOMESTEAD	*HOSPITAL DEL ALMA*		See Leisure City FL									
HOMOSASSA SPRINGS	*FAITH*		See Lecanto FL									
HOWEY IN THE HILLS	*THE CROSS*		See Mount Dora FL									
HUDSON	*HOPE* hopelutheranhudson@gmail.com www.hopelchudson.com	1975	12321 CANTON AVE	34669	FG	James T Zang III	(727)863-6446 (727)861-1820	WS 10 SS 10 BC 830	ED/HC/ MD/SN	226	176	141
HURLBURT FIELD	*GOOD SHEPHERD*		See Shalimar FL									
IMMOKALEE	*BETHLEHEM HAITIAN*		106 S 2ND ST	34142	FG	Andre F Mezilus	(239)657-3822		ED/HC/ MD/SN			
	IMMOKALEE LUTHERAN MISSION Satellite Site of Amigos En Cristo Bonita Springs FL	2008	106 S 2nd St	34142								
INDIAN ROCKS BEACH	*CHRIST THE KING*		See Largo FL									
INVERNESS	*FIRST* 1stlutheransecretary@gmail.com www.1stlutheraninverness.org	1963	1900 HIGHWAY 44 W	34453	FG	Thomas R Beaverson	(352)726-1637 (352)344-0628	WS 9 BC 1030	ED/HC/ MD/SN	327	206	89
	TREE OF LIFE info@treeoflifelc.org www.treeoflifelc.org		2991 E THOMAS ST	34453	EN	Eric R Linthicum	(352)419-4100	BC 9		29	29	15
JACKSONVILLE	*GRACE* church_office@gracelutheraneagles.org www.gracelcms.com	1989	12200 MCCORMICK RD	32225	FG	Michael S Popp	(904)928-9136 (904)928-0181	WS 830 11 SS 945 BC 945	EL/ED/HC/ MD/SN	364	224	186
	HOLY CROSS pfeiferk36@bellsouth.net www.facebook.com/holycrossjax/	1955	6620 ARLINGTON EXPY	32211	FG	Dr Leon M Roberts	(904)477-0800	WS 9 SS 10	ED/MD	30	30	10
	HOPE hopelutheranjax@gmail.com hopelutheranjax.com		8570 Philips Hwy Philips Plaza No 104 8570 PHILIPS HWY STE 104	32256	FG	Patrick C McKenzie	(904)677-4506	WS 915 SS 1030 BC 1030	ED/HC/MD	59	49	42
	OUR REDEEMER revbillreister@aol.com www.ourredeemerjax.org	1960	5401 DUNN AVE	32218	FG	William P Reister	(904)766-4728	WS 10 SS 845 BC 845	ED/HC/ MD/SN	101	76	65
	ST PAUL splcjax@gmail.com www.splcjax.org	1956	2730 EDGEWOOD AVE W	32209	FG	Stephen A Wiggins Sr	(904)765-4219 (904)765-7737	WS 10	ED/HC/ MD/SN	110	93	45
	ST PETER		See Middleburg FL									
JACKSONVILLE BEACH	*BETHLEHEM* officeadmin@bethlehemlutheranjaxbeach.org www.blcjaxbeach.org	1949	1423 8TH AVE N JAX BCH	32250	FG	Dana A Brones David K Horn Nathan A McCarty	(904)249-5418 (904)249-7572	WS 8 930 11 SS 930 BC 930	EC/ED/HC/ MD/SN	477	417	252
JENSEN BEACH	*REDEEMER*		See Stuart FL									
KENANSVILLE	*GRACE*		See Saint Cloud FL									
KEY WEST	*GRACE* gracelutherankw@att.net www.gracelutherankw.360unite.com	1942	2713 FLAGLER AVE	33040	FG	Nathan P LeGreco	(305)296-5161 (305)296-0622	WS 9 SS 1030 BC 1030	EL/ED/HC/ MD			

*Indicates a new church start. A new church start is an intentionally organized gathering which comes together on a regular basis for the purpose of worship and/or Bible study and is intended to grow into a member LCMS congregation. WS =Worship Service; SS = Sunday School; BC =Bible Class; EC = Early Childhood; EL = Elementary School; HS = High School; ED =Education Ministry; HC =Human Care Ministry; SN = Special Needs Ministry; MD = Media Ministry (PC)=Partner Church Pastor. See Page 53 for the Table of Abbreviations for key to additional abbreviations

CITY	CONGREGATION EMAIL WEBSITE	YEAR EST	LOCATION MAILING ADDRESS	ZIP CODE(S)	DIST.	PASTOR(S)	PHONE FAX	WS SS BC	SCHOOLS/ MINISTRIES	STATISTIC Bapt	 Conf	 Avg Attend
KISSIMMEE	*GRACE*		See Saint Cloud FL									
LABELLE	*CHRIST KING* PastorSeth@CTKLaBelle.com	1983	350 CR 78 PO BOX 2925	33935 33975	FG	Seth T DeBartolo	(863)323-2734	WS 915 SS 930	ED/HC/ MD/SN	66	57	49
LADY LAKE	*TRINITY*		See Summerfield FL									
LAKE BUENA VISTA	*GRACE*		See Saint Cloud FL									
LAKE CITY	*OUR REDEEMER* lcmsourredeemerlakecity@gmail.com lakecitylutheran.com	1964	5056 SW STATE ROAD 47	32024	FG	Stephen T Fair	(386)755-4299	WS 10 SS 12	ED/HC/MD	86	65	40
LAKE MARY	*HOLY CROSS* dennis@hclm.org www.hclm.org	1984	960 PAUL HOYER WAY	32746	S	Russell A Peterson Benjamin Hoyer	(407)333-0797 (407)333-9977	WS 8 10 SS 10 BC 9	EL/HS/ED/ HC/MD	1093	722	312
	REDEEMER		See Sanford FL									
LAKE PLACID	*TRINITY* trinitylpfl@gmail.com www.trinitylutheranlp.com	1974	25 LAKEVIEW ST	33852	FG	Richard A Norris Marthinus J Olckers	(863)465-5253 (863)465-1074	WS 10 SS 830 BC 830	EC/ED/HC/ MD/SN	138	125	101
LAKE SUZY	*OF THE CROSS*		See Port Charlotte FL									
LAKE WALES	*LAKE WALES* lakewaleslutheran@gmail.com www.facebook.com/LakeWales LutheranChurch	1953	640 S SCENIC HWY	33853	FG	William K Whitehead	(863)676-4715 (863)676-8484	WS 915 BC 1030	ED/HC/ MD/SN	57	57	54
LAKE WORTH	*EPIPHANY* admin@epiphanylakeworth.org Epiphanylakeworth.com	1976	4460 LYONS RD	33467	FG		(561)968-3627 (561)968-8142	WS 830 11 SS 945	EC/ED/ MD/SN			
	OUR SAVIOR osl@osl-lw.org osl-lw.org	1927	1615 LAKE AVE LAKE WORTH BEACH	33460	FG		(561)582-4430	WS 10 SS 9 BC 9	ED/HC/ MD/SN	215	118	80
	SALEM HAITIAN	1990	1020 S DIXIE HWY	33460	FG		(561)586-5691 (561)582-4319					
	TRINITY		See Delray Beach FL									
LAKELAND	*CHRIST* clcsecretary@gmail.com www.clclakeland.org	1963	2715 LAKELAND HILLS BLVD	33805	FG	Christopher A Hazzard	(863)682-7802	WS 10 SS 9 BC 830	ED/HC/ MD/SN	201	184	107
	ST PAUL churchinfo@stpaullakeland.org www.stpaullakeland.org	1912	4450 HARDEN BLVD	33813	FG	Andrew J Ritchie Kenneth Sherman	(863)644-7710 (863)644-7491	WS 830 1047 SS 945 BC 945	EL/ED/HC/ MD/SN	1416	1105	363
LAND O LAKES	*HOLY TRINITY*		See Lutz FL									
	HOPE		See Hudson FL									
LARGO	*CHRIST THE KING* office@ctklc.org www.ctklc.org	1958	11220 OAKHURST RD	33774	FG	Michael W Mast	(727)595-2117 (727)593-3477	WS 9 11 SS 930 BC 930	EL/ED/HC/ MD	243	209	70
LECANTO	*FAITH* connect@faithlecanto.org www.faithlecanto.com	1990	935 S CRYSTAL GLEN DR	34461	FG	Patrick J Galligar	(352)527-3325 (352)527-7043	WS 930 SS 11 BC 11	ED/HC/ MD/SN	184	176	129
LEESBURG	*BETHANY* BLCLeesburg@gmail.com bethanylutheranleesburg.com	1962	1334 GRIFFIN RD	34748	FG	Michael H Hanel	(352)787-7275	WS 1030 SS 915 BC 915	ED/HC/ MD/SN	202	193	160
	FAITH		See Eustis FL									
	THE CROSS		See Mount Dora FL									
	TRINITY		See Summerfield FL									
	WOODLANDS		See Montverde FL									
LEHIGH ACRES	*BEAUTIFUL SAVIOR* treasury@beautifulsaviorswfl.org www.beautifulsaviorswfl.org	1992	215 RICHMOND AVE N	33936	FG		(239)368-7897	WS 10 SS 9 BC 9	ED	4	4	8
LEISURE CITY	*HOSPITAL DEL ALMA* BPerez6950@aol.com	1997	29501 SW 152 Ave 29501 SW 152ND AVE HOMESTEAD	33033	FG		(305)247-0459 (305)247-1117	WS 1030 SS 930 BC 930				
LITHIA	*IMMANUEL*		See Brandon FL									
LITTLE RIVER	*OUR SAVIOUR* semaj44@aol.com www.oursaviourmiami.org	1950	2362 NW 95th St C/O MR. ANDRE KIRBY 1301 EAST BROWARD BLVD SUITE 300 FORT LAUDERDALE	33147 33301	FG		(305)691-1672	WS 10 SS 9 BC 9				
LONGWOOD	*HOLY CROSS*		See Lake Mary FL									
	REDEEMER		See Sanford FL									
LUTZ	*FAITH*		See Wesley Chapel FL									
	FAMILY OF CHRIST		See Tampa FL									
	HOLY TRINITY htlutzoffice@verizon.net www.holytrinitylutz.com	1973	20735 LEONARD RD	33558	FG	Justin R Pahl	(813)949-7173 (813)949-7173	WS 9 SS 1015 BC 1030	EL/ED/HC/ MD/SN	145	133	72
MADEIRA BEACH	*CHRIST THE KING*		See Largo FL									
MAITLAND	*ST LUKE*		See Oviedo FL									
MARATHON	*MARTIN LUTHER* mlcmarathon@gmail.com martinlutherchapel.com	1956	325 122nd St Gulf 325 122ND STREET GULF	33050	FG	Anthony B Mandile III	(305)289-0700 (305)289-0700	WS 10 BC 1130	ED/MD	73	72	32
MARCO ISLAND	*MARCO* office@marcolutheran.org www.marcolutheran.org	1974	525 N COLLIER BLVD	34145	FG	James E Thelen	(239)394-0332 (239)394-9073	WS 930 BC 930	ED/HC/ MD/SN	444	444	297
MARIANNA	*ASCENSION* MariannaAscensionLutheran.org	1958	3975 Hwy 90 3975 HIGHWAY 90	32446	SO	Richard T Wright	(850)482-4691	WS 11	ED/HC/SN	23	23	16
	GRACE		See Bonifay FL									
MARY ESTHER	*GOOD SHEPHERD*		See Shalimar FL									

*Indicates a new church start. A new church start is an intentionally organized gathering which comes together on a regular basis for the purpose of worship and/or Bible study and is intended to grow into a member LCMS congregation. WS =Worship Service; SS = Sunday School; BC =Bible Class; EC = Early Childhood; EL = Elementary School; HS = High School; ED =Education Ministry; HC =Human Care Ministry; SN = Special Needs Ministry; MD = Media Ministry (PC)=Partner Church Pastor. See Page 53 for the Table of Abbreviations for key to additional abbreviations

CITY	CONGREGATION EMAIL WEBSITE	YEAR EST	LOCATION MAILING ADDRESS	ZIP CODE(S)	DIST.	PASTOR(S)	PHONE FAX	WS SS BC	SCHOOLS/ MINISTRIES	STATISTIC Bapt	Conf	Avg Attend
MASARYKTOWN	*HOLY TRINITY* htlc@tampabay.rr.com www.htlc.us	1943	1214 BROAD ST BROOKSVILLE	34604	FG	Dr David D Brockhoff	(352)796-4066 (352)593-6812	WS 8 1030 SS 915 BC 915	ED/HC/ MD/SN	201	179	123
MASCOTTE	*WOODLANDS*		See Montverde FL									
MELBOURNE	*HOPE VIERA* admin@hope-brevard.org hopebrevard.org		4541 N WICKHAM RD	32935	S	James F Fernandez	(321)622-6126	WS 830 1030 SS 940 BC 940	ED/HC/MD	123	113	88
MERRITT ISLAND	*FAITH* office@faithlutheranmi.org www.faithlutheranmi.org	1964	280 E MERRITT AVE MERRITT IS	32953	FG	Andrew D Schermbeck	(321)452-4080 (321)452-9147	WS 8 1030 SS 915 BC 915	EC/ED/HC/ MD/SN	477	399	189
	TRINITY		See Rockledge FL									
MIAMI	*BAY SHORE* epereza@aol.com	1944	5051 BISCAYNE BLVD	33137	FG	Erwin Perez-Arche	(305)758-1344	WS 11 SS 10 BC 10				
	CONCORDIA concordiakendall@bellsouth.net www.concordiakendall.org	1957	8701 SW 124TH ST	33176	FG		(305)235-6123 (305)235-6525	WS 930 BC 11	EC/ED/MD	70	45	35
	HOLY CROSS		See North Miami FL									
	HOSPITAL DEL ALMA		See Leisure City FL									
	SAN PABLO APOSTOL stpaulmia@bellsouth.net	1985	10700 SW 56TH ST	33165	FG	William A Sielk	(305)271-3171		ED/HC/MD			
	ST MATTHEW	1924	621 BEACOM BLVD	33135	FG	Luis M Santana	(305)642-2860 (305)642-3477	WS 9 11 SS 1015 BC 10	ED/HC/ MD/SN			
	ST PAUL stpaulmia@bellsouth.net www.StPaulLutheranMiami.org	1959	10700 SW 56TH ST	33165	FG	William A Sielk	(305)271-3171	WS 9 SS 1045 BC 1045	ED/HC/MD			
MIAMI SHORES	*HOLY CROSS*		See North Miami FL									
MICANOPY	*FIRST*		See Gainesville FL									
MIDDLEBURG	*ST PETER* www.stplutheran.com	1983	1614 S Blanding Blvd 1614 BLANDING BLVD	32068	FG	Logan P Landes	(904)282-8876	WS 8 1030 SS 915 BC 915	ED/HC/ MD/SN	231	209	140
	SUPPORT ARMED FORCES MINISTRY Satellite Site of St Peter Middleburg FL	2009	1614 Blanding Blvd	32068								
MILTON	*ETERNAL TRINITY* pastor@eternaltrinitylutheran.com eternaltrinitylutheran.com/	1960	6076 OLD BAGDAD HWY	32583	SO	Dr Daniel E Thies	(850)623-5780 (850)626-3335	WS 915 SS 1030				
	RESURRECTION		See Pensacola FL									
MINNEOLA	*WOODLANDS*		See Montverde FL									
MIRAMAR	*MIRAMAR* pastor@miramarlutheran.org	1960	7790 LASALLE BLVD	33023	FG		(954)987-1234 (954)987-2532		HC			
MIRAMAR BEACH	*GRACE*		See Destin FL									
MOLINO	*TRINITY*		See Cantonment FL									
MONTVERDE	*WOODLANDS* office@woodlandschurch.com www.woodlandschurch.com	1988	15333 COUNTY ROAD 455	34756	FG	Joshua M Pettit Dr Robert M Roegner	(407)469-2525 (407)469-3199	WS 830 11 SS 945 BC 945	EC/ED/HC/ MD/SN	594	439	313
MOUNT DORA	*FAITH*		See Eustis FL									
	THE CROSS jacob@thecross.family thecross.family	2017	4425 CO RD 19A	32757	S	Jacob T Baumann Mark Crossman	(352)602-4635	WS 9 11 SS 9 11 BC 745	ED/HC/ MD/SN	650	550	800
	WOODLANDS		See Montverde FL									
MOUNT PLYMOUTH	*THE CROSS*		See Mount Dora FL									
NAPLES	*ALL SAINTS** mbonnough@srdentbill.com		5100 POST OAK LN	34105	S		(419)261-8307					
	CONEXION orlandoapa@gmail.com		4472 25TH AVE SW	34116	FG	Orlando Ramirez	(239)821-0660			43	34	35
	FAITH faith@flcnaples.com www.flcnaples.com	1985	4150 GOODLETTE RD N	34103	EN	Donald E Treglown Bradford W Hildebrandt Owen D Duncan	(239)434-5811	WS 8 915 11 SS 1015 BC 1015	EC/ED/HC/ MD/SN	738	642	337
	GRACE office@graceofnaples.com www.graceofnaples.com	1955	860 BANYAN BLVD	34102	FG	Keith A Lingsch	(239)261-7421 (239)261-9337	WS 8 1030 SS 915	EC/ED/HC/ MD	490	475	213
	HOPE		See Bonita Springs FL									
	PEACE info@peacelutherannaples.org www.peacenaples.org		9850 IMMOKALEE RD	34120	FG	Dr Richard M Mokry Rochenel Jean Jacques	(239)354-9144	WS 930 SS 10	EC/ED/HC/ MD	151	113	73
	THE PELICAN pastormarknaples@hotmail.com		5800 GOLDEN GATE PKWY	34116	FG	Mark T Eisold	(239)307-7336					
	THRIVE COMMUNITY		See Estero FL									
NAVARRE	*GOOD SHEPHERD*		See Gulf Breeze FL									
NAVARRE BEACH	*GOOD SHEPHERD*		See Gulf Breeze FL									
NEW PORT RICHEY	*FAITH* frontoffice@faithnpr.org www.faithnpr.org	1957	5443 SUNSET RD NEW PRT RCHY	34652	FG	Dr Thomas K Fuqua	(727)849-4418	WS 10 SS 9 BC 9	ED/HC/ MD/SN	110	100	75
	HOPE		See Hudson FL									
NEWBERRY	*FIRST*		See Gainesville FL									
NICEVILLE	*GOOD SHEPHERD*		See Shalimar FL									
	GRACE		See Destin FL									

*Indicates a new church start. A new church start is an intentionally organized gathering which comes together on a regular basis for the purpose of worship and/or Bible study and is intended to grow into a member LCMS congregation. WS =Worship Service; SS = Sunday School; BC =Bible Class; EC = Early Childhood; EL = Elementary School; HS = High School; ED =Education Ministry; HC =Human Care Ministry; SN = Special Needs Ministry; MD = Media Ministry (PC)=Partner Church Pastor. See Page 53 for the Table of Abbreviations for key to additional abbreviations

CITY	CONGREGATION EMAIL WEBSITE	YEAR EST	LOCATION MAILING ADDRESS	ZIP CODE(S)	DIST.	PASTOR(S)	PHONE FAX	WS SS BC	SCHOOLS/ MINISTRIES	Bapt	Conf	Avg Attend
NOKOMIS	*LAKESIDE*		See Venice FL									
NORTH FORT MEYERS	*FAITH*		See Punta Gorda FL									
NORTH FORT MYERS	*GOOD SHEPHERD* pastordavis@goodshepofnfm.com www.goodshepofnfm.com	1965	4770 ORANGE GROVE BLVD N FT MYERS	33903	FG	Robert S Davis	(239)995-7711 (239)217-7445	WS 10 1130 SS 9	EL/HS/ED/ HC/MD	76	50	76
NORTH MIAMI	*HOLY CROSS* dbartels@holycross-nm.org www.holycrossnm.com	1949	650 NE 135TH ST	33161	FG		(305)893-0371 (305)893-1845	WS 1030 SS 915 BC 915	EL/ED/HC/ MD/SN	296	175	120
NORTH MIAMI BEACH	*HOLY CROSS*		See North Miami FL									
NORTH PALM BEACH	*FAITH* church@faithnpb.com faithlutheran-npb.com	1958	555 US HIGHWAY 1 N PALM BEACH	33408	FG	Mark G Stillman	(561)848-4737 (561)881-1613	WS 845 1045	EC/ED/HC/ MD/SN			
NORTH PORT	*LAKESIDE*		See Venice FL									
	OF THE CROSS		See Port Charlotte FL									
	TRINITY SW FL		See Port Charlotte FL									
OCALA	*OUR REDEEMER* churchoffice@ourredeemerocala.org www.ourredeemerocala.org	1984	5200 SW COLLEGE RD	34474	FG	Joseph D Signore III	(352)237-2233	WS 10 SS 845 BC 845 11	ED/HC/ MD/SN	292	269	126
	ST JOHN Tracy.williams@stjohnocala.org www.stjohnocalachurch.org	1945	1915 SE LAKE WEIR AVE	34471	FG	Jeffrey P Shanks Timothy L Mehl	(352)629-1794 (352)622-5564	WS 830 1045 BC 945	EL/HS/ED/ HC/MD/SN	540	459	249
	TRINITY trinitylutheranocala@gmail.com trinitylutheranocala.org	1989	4001 NE 25TH AVE	34479	EN	Danlias F Howe	(352)840-0711 (352)840)-5978	WS 10	ED	52	50	37
	TRINITY		See Summerfield FL									
OCKLAWAHA	*TRINITY*		See Summerfield FL									
OCOEE	*WOODLANDS*		See Montverde FL									
OKAHUMPKA	*THE CROSS*		See Mount Dora FL									
OKEECHOBEE	*PEACE* www.peaceokee.org	1969	750 NW 23RD LN	34972	FG	Deon L Hull	(863)763-5042 (863)763-0143	WS 1030 BC 915	EC/ED/HC/ MD	362	285	71
OLDSMAR	*BETHEL*		See Clearwater FL									
ORANGE PARK	*ST PETER*		See Middleburg FL									
ORLANDO	*ASCENSION*		See Casselberry FL									
	CHRIST KING ctklc407@gmail.com www.ctkorlando.com	1984	4962 S APOPKA VINELAND RD	32819	FG	Timothy C Brown	(407)876-2771	WS 8 1030 SS 915 BC 915	EC/ED/SN			
	ESPERANZA VIVA eduardo.martinez@trinitydowntown.com		123 E. LIVINGSTON STREET	32801	FG	Eduardo M Martinez	(321)278-4612		ED/MD	8	8	6
	GRACE		See Saint Cloud FL									
	HOPE office@hopeoforlando.org hopeoforlando.org	1971	2600 N DEAN RD	32817	FG	Paul W vonWerder	(407)657-4556 (407)657-8806	WS 9 BC 1045	EC/ED/HC/ MD			
	NEW CITY adam@newcitynow.com newcitynow.com	2010	4071 L B MCLEOD RD SUITE H	32811	S	Matthew W Fitzpatrick	(407)595-2299	SS 930		49	27	40
	OUR SAVIOR oursaviororlando@gmail.com OurSaviorOrlando.com	1957	1750 BRUTON BLVD	32805	FG	Leo P Luke	(407)295-0261 (407)295-9044	WS 10	ED/HC/MD			
	PRINCE OF PEACE staff@poporlando.com www.poporlando.com	1957	1515 S SEMORAN BLVD	32807	FG	Kenneth D Green II Adolfo Borges	(407)277-3945 (407)380-1802	WS 9 11 SS 10 BC 10	EC/ED/HC/ MD/SN	622	470	259
	ST LUKE		See Oviedo FL									
	THE CROSS ORLANDO Satellite Site of Holy Cross Lake Mary FL	2016	1010 W Church St	32803				WS 10 SS 10				
	TRINITY tlc@trinitydowntown.com www.trinitydowntown.com	1919	123 East Livingston St 123 E LIVINGSTON ST	32801	FG	Douglas L Kallesen Eduardo M Martinez Jean C Picard	(407)488-1919 (407)488-1230	WS 9 1115 SS 1015 BC 1015	EC/ED/HC/ MD/SN	496	391	156
	WOODLANDS		See Montverde FL									
	ZION		See Winter Garden FL									
OVIEDO	*ST LUKE* email@sllcs.org sllcs.org	1912	2021 W STATE ROAD 426	32765	S	Dr Tige A Culbertson Scott M Coerber John M Elliott Samuel A Shick	(407)365-3408 (407)366-9346	WS 8 930 935 11 1105 SS 930 BC 930 11	EL/ED/HC/ MD/SN	4383	3501	1237
OXFORD	*AMAZING GRACE* office@aglc.org www.amazinggracelc.org		4886 COUNTY ROAD 472	34484	FG	Dr Paul S Burtzlaff	(352)748-1201	WS 8 1015 SS 915 BC 915	EC/ED/HC/ MD/SN	282	277	205
	TRINITY		See Summerfield FL									
PACE	*ETERNAL TRINITY*		See Milton FL									
	RESURRECTION		See Pensacola FL									
	TRINITY		See Cantonment FL									
PALM BAY	*RISEN SAVIOR* jkfaithful@gmail.com risensaviorpalmbay.org	1961	2220 PORT MALABAR BLVD NE	32905	FG		(321)984-8987 (321)984-2108	WS 930 BC 830	ED/MD	38	33	45
	ZION HAITIAN jeanparent19@aol.com		2220 PORT MALABAR BLVD NE	32905	FG	Jean A Parent	(321)984-8987					
PALM CITY	*REDEEMER*		See Stuart FL									
PALM COAST	*SHEPHERD COAST* sotcms@gmail.com www.sotcpc.com	1989	101 PINE LAKES PKWY S	32164	EN	Gregory S Michel	(386)446-2481	WS 815 11 BC 940	ED/HC/ MD/SN	267	245	147

*Indicates a new church start. A new church start is an intentionally organized gathering which comes together on a regular basis for the purpose of worship and/or Bible study and is intended to grow into a member LCMS congregation. WS =Worship Service; SS = Sunday School; BC =Bible Class; EC = Early Childhood; EL = Elementary School; HS = High School; ED =Education Ministry; HC =Human Care Ministry; SN = Special Needs Ministry; MD = Media Ministry (PC)=Partner Church Pastor. See Page 53 for the Table of Abbreviations for key to additional abbreviations

CITY	CONGREGATION EMAIL WEBSITE	YEAR EST	LOCATION MAILING ADDRESS	ZIP CODE(S)	DIST.	PASTOR(S)	PHONE FAX	WS SS BC	SCHOOLS/ MINISTRIES	STATISTIC Bapt	Conf	Avg Attend
PALM HARBOR	*BETHEL*		See Clearwater FL									
PALMETTO	*FAITH*		See Parrish FL									
PANAMA CITY	*GOOD SHEPHERD*		See Callaway FL									
	TRINITY TLCPCOffice@gmail.com www.trinitylutheranpanamacity.org	1952	1001 W 11th S 1001 W 11TH ST	32401	SO	Paul M Mc Comack Paul E Zeigler	(850)763-2412	WS 830 11 SS 10	ED/HC/ MD/SN	165	149	84
PANAMA CITY BEACH	*CHRIST OUR SAV* church@christoursaviorpcb.com www.christoursaviorpcb.com	1988	300 CLARA AVE P C BEACH	32407	SO	Paul M Mc Comack Paul E Zeigler	(850)233-6249 (850)233-9900		ED	53	52	49
	HOPE ON THE BEACH		See Santa Rosa Beach FL									
PARRISH	*FAITH* office@faithlutheranfl.com	1978	9608 US HIGHWAY 301 N	34219	FG	Patrick W Poock	(941)776-1395	WS 8 1030 BC 915	ED/HC/ MD/SN	236	198	146
PENNEY FARMS	*ST PETER*		See Middleburg FL									
PENSACOLA	*GOOD SHEPHERD*		See Gulf Breeze FL									
	GRACE grace@gracepensacola.org www.gracepensacola.org	1958	6601 N 9TH AVE	32504	SO	Bernhard J Huesmann	(850)476-5667	WS 8 1030 SS 915 BC 915	EC/ED/HC/ MD	247	206	120
	IMMANUEL office@immlu.com immlu.com	1885	24 W Wright St PO BOX 12912	32501 32591	SO	Randy M Blankschaen	(850)438-8138	WS 9 SS 1030 BC 1030	ED/HC/ MD/SN			
	JEHOVAH jehovahlcms@aol.com	1924	2801 N 9TH AVE	32503	SO	Ferry L Nye Sr	(850)433-2091 (850)433-9767		ED/HC/SN			
	REDEEMER redeemerpensacola@yahoo.com www.redeemerlutheranpensacola.com	1953	333 COMMERCE ST	32507	SO		(850)455-0330 (850)455-3083	WS 930 SS 815 BC 815	EL/ED/HC/ MD/SN	257	193	71
	RESURRECTION resurrection.lcotr@outlook.com resluthpns.com	1959	6305 N Blue Angel Parkway 6305 N BLUE ANGEL PKWY	32526	SO	Nathan P Ragazinskas	(850)944-3777 (850)332-5509	WS 9 SS 1015	ED/HC/MD	360	273	107
	ST MATTHEW smlcpensacola@gmail.com	1947	7049 PENSACOLA BLVD	32505	SO	Reholma Mc Cants	(850)477-0567 (850)477-1000	WS 11 SS 945	ED/HC/ MD/SN	75	75	50
	TRINITY		See Cantonment FL									
PENSACOLA BEACH	*GOOD SHEPHERD*		See Gulf Breeze FL									
PERDIDO KEY	*RESURRECTION*		See Pensacola FL									
PINELLAS PARK	*CHRIST THE KING*		See Largo FL									
PLANT CITY	*HOPE* hopelutheranpc@gmail.com www.hopeplantcity.com	1957	2001 N PARK RD	33563	FG	Dean R Pfeffer	(813)752-4622 (813)707-1244	WS 915 SS 1030 BC 1030	ED/HC/ MD/SN	373	328	151
	*HOPE HISPANIC** jfcobos26@gmail.com		2001 N Park Rd 14920 HUTCHISON RD TAMPA	33563 33625	FG		(347)693-6766	WS 4 SS 330	ED/HC	31	31	29
	IMMANUEL		See Brandon FL									
PLANTATION	*OUR SAVIOR* church@oursaviorplantation.org www.oslplantation.church	1961	8001 NW 5TH ST	33324	FG	Kenneth A Durante	(954)473-6888	WS 8 1030 SS 1030 BC 915	EL/ED	287	287	138
PLANTATION KEY	*IMMANUEL* stierdon@aol.com www.keyslutheran.org	1952	108 OCEAN DR TAVERNIER	33070	FG	Donald L Stier	(305)852-8711 (305)852-8711	WS 10	HC	40	37	45
PORT CHARLOTTE	*FAITH*		See Punta Gorda FL									
	OF THE CROSS secretary@lccross.org www.lccross.org	1982	2300 LUTHER RD PUNTA GORDA	33983	FG	Dr Raymond B Stolarczyk	(941)627-6060 (941)627-5467	WS 730 1030 SS 9 BC 9	ED/HC/ MD/SN	265	240	160
	TRINITY SW FL TLCswfl3@gmail.com trinitylutheranchurchswfl.org	2015	1379 McCall Rd 1379 S MCCALL RD PT CHARLOTTE	33981	FG	Brian A Albrecht	(941)828-1910	WS 830 1030 SS 945 BC 945	ED/HC/MD	214	138	119
PORT RICHEY	*HOPE*		See Hudson FL									
PORT SAINT LUCIE	*GRACE* office@gracelutheranpsl.org www.GraceLutheranPSL.com	1990	555 SW CASHMERE BLVD PORT ST LUCIE	34986	FG	Christopher W Escher	(772)871-6599	WS 830 1015	ED/HC/ MD/SN	171	153	106
	TRINITY		See Fort Pierce FL									
PUNTA GORDA	*FAITH* faithadmin88@embarqmail.com www.faithlutheranpg.com	1972	4005 PALM DR	33950	FG	Dana A Narring	(941)639-6309	WS 930 SS 930	ED/HC/ MD/SN	220	219	179
	OF THE CROSS		See Port Charlotte FL									
REDINGTON	*CHRIST THE KING*		See Largo FL									
REDINGTON BEACH	*CHRIST THE KING*		See Largo FL									
RIVERVIEW	*CHRIST THE KING* revkev@ctklcms.org www.ctklcms.org	1990	11421 BIG BEND RD	33579	FG	Kevin L Yoakum	(813)677-1332	WS 10 SS 9 BC 9	ED/HC	124	43	83
	IMMANUEL		See Brandon FL									
ROCKLEDGE	*FAITH VIERA* info@faithviera.org www.faithviera.org	1996	5550 FAITH DR	32955	S	Troy A Countryman Jonathan J Moyer	(321)636-5504 (321)636-2030	WS 8 930 11 SS 930 BC 915	EC/ED/HC/ MD/SN	874	805	451
	TRINITY church@trinity-rockledge.org www.trinity-rockledge.org	1952	1330 S FISKE BLVD	32955	FG		(321)636-5431 (321)638-4498	WS 1030 SS 910 BC 9	EL/ED/HC/ MD/SN			
ROTONDA WEST	*TRINITY SW FL*		See Port Charlotte FL									
SAINT AUGUSTINE	*CHRIST OUR SAVIOR* coslecsa@gmail.com coselc.org	1994	21 MILTON ST ST AUGUSTINE	32084	FG	Mark B Stirdivant	(904)829-6823	WS 1030 BC 9	HC/SN	75	75	51
SAINT CLOUD	*GRACE* pastor@graceofstcloud.org www.graceofstcloud.org	1955	1123 LOUISIANA AVE	34769	FG	John W Hohe	(407)892-4653 (888)254-4559	WS 845 11 SS 11 BC 10	EC/ED/HC/ MD	138	125	83

*Indicates a new church start. A new church start is an intentionally organized gathering which comes together on a regular basis for the purpose of worship and/or Bible study and is intended to grow into a member LCMS congregation. WS =Worship Service; SS = Sunday School; BC =Bible Class; EC = Early Childhood; EL = Elementary School; HS = High School; ED =Education Ministry; HC =Human Care Ministry; SN = Special Needs Ministry; MD = Media Ministry (PC)=Partner Church Pastor. See Page 53 for the Table of Abbreviations for key to additional abbreviations

CITY	CONGREGATION EMAIL WEBSITE	YEAR EST	LOCATION MAILING ADDRESS	ZIP CODE(S)	DIST.	PASTOR(S)	PHONE FAX	WS SS BC	SCHOOLS/ MINISTRIES	STATISTIC Bapt	Conf	Avg Attend
SAINT JOHNS	*CELEBRATION* contact@celebrationlutheran.org	1994	810 ROBERTS RD	32259	EN		(904)230-2496	WS 9 SS 1130 BC 9	ED/HC/SN			
SAINT PETERSBURG	*CHRIST THE KING*		See Largo FL									
	GRACE churchoffice@grace-lutheran.com www.grace-lutheran.com	1928	4301 16TH ST N ST PETERS-BURG	33703	FG	Kevin R Loughran Steven M Massey	(727)527-6213 (727)522-4535	WS 830 11 SS 945 BC 945	EL/ED/HC/ MD	775	491	231
	OUR SAVIOR info@oursaviorfl.org oursaviorfl.org/	1954	301 58TH ST S ST PETERSBURG	33707	FG	Daniel R Ritter Christopher Y Futch	(727)344-2684	WS 8 10 SS 10 BC 9	EL/ED/HC/ MD/SN	1415	938	475
SAN ANTONIO	*FAITH*		See Wesley Chapel FL									
SANFORD	*HOLY CROSS*		See Lake Mary FL									
	REDEEMER office@redeemersanford.org www.redeemersanford.org	1953	2525 S OAK AVE	32773	FG	Edward J DeWitt	(407)322-3552 (407)302-5625	WS 1030 BC 9	ED/HC/SN	95	70	35
	RESURRECTION CHURCH Satellite Site of Holy Cross Lake Mary FL	2023	100 Aero Lane	32771				WS 11 SS 11				
SANIBEL	*THRIVE COMMUNITY*		See Estero FL									
SANTA ROSA BEACH	*GRACE*		See Destin FL									
	HOPE ON THE BEACH kristie@hopeonthebeach.com hopeonthebeach.com	2001	3834 US Hwy 98 W 3834 US HIGHWAY 98 W STE 7 SANTA RSA BCH	32459	SO	Jason J Scheler	(850)267-0322	WS 11 SS 11	ED/HC/ MD/SN	120	109	250
	HOPE ON THE BEACH CHURCH Satellite Site of Hope on the Beach Santa Rosa Beach FL	2018	1875 S. Co Hwy 393	32459				WS 920				
	HOPE ON THE BEACH CHURCH Satellite Site of Hope on the Beach Santa Rosa Beach FL	2004	4447 W County Hwy 30A	32459				WS 8				
SARASOTA	*BEAUTIFUL SAVIOR* office@beautifulsaviorlcms.com beautifulsaviorlcms.com	1987	7461 PROSPECT RD	34243	FG	Rossetter T Leavitt Todd A Kuehn	(941)355-2798	WS 8 1030 SS 915 BC 915	ED/HC/SN	331	319	200
	CONCORDIA concordia5@juno.com ConcordiaSarasota.org	1948	2185 WOOD ST	34237	FG		(941)365-0844	WS 9 1015 1045 SS 10 BC 9 10	ED/HC/ MD/SN	247	216	146
	GOOD SHEPHERD parishcoord@goodshepherdsarasota.org goodshepherdsarasota.org/	1981	5659 HONORE AVE	34233	FG	Steven P Anderson	(941)921-3673 (941)923-3659	WS 915 BC 1030	EC/ED/HC/ MD/SN	198	198	103
SEBASTIAN	*REDEEMER*		See Vero Beach FL									
SEBRING	*FAITH* faithlutheransebring@comcast.net	1951	2740 LAKEVIEW DR	33870	FG	Robert J Maulella	(863)385-7848 (863)385-2740	WS 9 SS 1015	EC/ED/HC/ MD/SN	173	153	100
SEFFNER	*IMMANUEL*		See Brandon FL									
SEMINOLE	*CHRIST THE KING*		See Largo FL									
SHALIMAR	*GOOD SHEPHERD* churchsecretary@gslcshalimar.org www.shalimar.church	1956	1 MEIGS DR	32579	SO	Melvin R Angerman Eric E Klemme	(850)651-1022	WS 8 1045 SS 930	ED/HC/ MD/SN	249	196	111
SILVER SPRINGS	*FOREST* joanb654@hughes.net www.forestlutheran.org	1987	1663 SE 183 Ave Rd 1663 SE 183RD AVENUE RD SILVER SPGS	34488	FG		(352)625-8700	WS 1030 SS 915 BC 915	ED/HC	23	21	17
SORRENTO	*THE CROSS*		See Mount Dora FL									
SOUTH DAYTONA	*HOLY CROSS* sdhc1960@aol.com holycrossdaytona.com	1960	724 BIG TREE RD	32119	FG	David R Schillinger Sr Brett N Snider	(386)767-6542	WS 830 1015	HC/MD/SN			
SPRING HILL	*CHRIST*		See Brooksville FL									
	FOREST OAKS folcoffice2@tampabay.rr.com www.forestoakslutheran.com	1984	8555 FOREST OAKS BLVD	34606	FG	Glenn E Fischer	(352)683-9731 (352)683-1641	WS 930 SS 1045 BC 11	ED/HC/ MD/SN	217	201	117
	HOPE		See Hudson FL									
STARKE	*GOOD SHEPHERD* gslcstarke@gmail.com Goodshepherdlcmsstarke.org		4900 NW 182nd Way PO BOX 217	32091	FG		(904)386-6987	WS 10	ED/HC/SN	18	18	15
STUART	*REDEEMER* church@redeemerstuart.com www.redeemerstuart.com	1958	2450 SE OCEAN BLVD	34996	FG	Stanley E Allen Jr	(772)286-0911 (772)286-5645	WS 830 11 SS 945 BC 945	EL/ED/HC/ MD/SN	467	434	273
SUMMERFIELD	*AMAZING GRACE*		See Oxford FL									
	TRINITY office@trinitysummerfield.org www.trinitysummerfield.com	1996	17330 S Hwy 441 17330 S US HIGHWAY 441	34491	FG		(352)307-4500 (352)307-4502	WS 8 1030 BC 915	ED/HC/ MD/SN	526	524	275
SUN CITY CENTER	*CHRIST THE KING*		See Riverview FL									
TALLAHASSEE	*EPIPHANY* chafner@epiphanystar.org	1950	8300 Deerlake Rd West 8300 DEERLAKE RD W	32312	FG	Timothy D Barber	(850)385-7373	WS 815 1030 SS 930	EC/ED/HC/ MD/SN	275	262	94
	TRINITY		See Crawfordville FL									
	UNIVERSITY pastor@universitylutheranchurch.org www.universitylutheranchurch.org	1999	925 W JEFFERSON ST	32304	FG	Jay A Winters	(850)778-5854	WS 11 BC 930	ED/MD	90	83	51
TAMPA	*FAITH*		See Wesley Chapel FL									
	FAMILY OF CHRIST info@familyofchrist.org www.familyofchrist.org	1999	16190 BRUCE B DOWNS BLVD	33647	S	Landon M Ledlow David M Haara	(813)558-9343 (813)558-8576	WS 9 11 SS 9 11	EL/ED/HC/ MD	712	415	265
	HOLY TRINITY office@holytrinitytampa.org www.holytrinitytampa.org	1955	3712 W EL PRADO BLVD	33629	FG	Dr Daniel R Prugh	(813)839-6847 (813)839-2706	WS 9 1030 SS 9 BC 9	EL/ED/HC/ MD/SN	335	228	163
	IMMANUEL		See Brandon FL									

*Indicates a new church start. A new church start is an intentionally organized gathering which comes together on a regular basis for the purpose of worship and/or Bible study and is intended to grow into a member LCMS congregation. WS =Worship Service; SS = Sunday School; BC =Bible Class; EC = Early Childhood; EL = Elementary School; HS = High School; ED =Education Ministry; HC =Human Care Ministry; SN = Special Needs Ministry; MD = Media Ministry (PC)=Partner Church Pastor. See Page 53 for the Table of Abbreviations for key to additional abbreviations

CITY	CONGREGATION EMAIL WEBSITE	YEAR EST	LOCATION MAILING ADDRESS	ZIP CODE(S)	DIST.	PASTOR(S)	PHONE FAX	WS SS BC	SCHOOLS/ MINISTRIES	STATISTIC Bapt	Conf	Avg Attend
TAMPA	*MESSIAH*		See Carrollwood FL									
	*MESSIAH HISPANIC** jfcobos26@gmail.com		14920 HUTCHISON RD	33625	FG		(347)693-6766	WS 1 SS 1 BC 12	ED/HC	215	170	65
	OUR SAVIOR		See Zephyrhills FL									
	ZION ZionLutheranTampa.com	1893	2901 N HIGHLAND AVE	33602	FG		(727)228-8272 (727)228-9532	WS 815	ED/HC	15	15	12
TARPON SPRINGS	*BETHEL*		See Clearwater FL									
TAVARES	*BETHANY*		See Leesburg FL									
	FAITH		See Eustis FL									
	THE CROSS		See Mount Dora FL									
	WOODLANDS		See Montverde FL									
TEMPLE TERRACE	*FAMILY OF CHRIST*		See Tampa FL									
THE VILLAGES	*AMAZING GRACE*		See Oxford FL									
	BETHANY		See Leesburg FL									
	TRINITY		See Summerfield FL									
TITUSVILLE	*GOOD SHEPHERD* office@titusvillelutherans.org www.titusvillelutherans.org	1957	2073 Garden Street BLDG A 2073 GARDEN ST BLDG A	32796	FG		(321)267-4323 (321)267-1702	WS 930 SS 11 BC 11	EC/ED/HC/ MD	160	160	73
TREASURE ISLAND	*CHRIST THE KING*		See Largo FL									
TRINITY	*TRINITY* www.tlctrinity.org		3100 Starkey Rd 3100 STARKEY BLVD	34655	FG	Marc E Nauman	(727)364-4667	WS 830 10	ED/HC/MD	271	189	140
UMATILLA	*FAITH*		See Eustis FL									
	THE CROSS		See Mount Dora FL									
UNION PARK	*ST LUKE*		See Oviedo FL									
VALPARAISO	*GOOD SHEPHERD*		See Shalimar FL									
VALRICO	*IMMANUEL*		See Brandon FL									
VENICE	*LAKESIDE* llc@lakesidelutheran.net www.lakesidelutheran.net	1954	2401 TAMIAMI TRL S	34293	FG	David J Dahlke	(941)493-5102	WS 9 1030	ED/HC/ MD/SN	197	163	261
VERO BEACH	*REDEEMER* office@redeemerverobeach.com www.redeemerverobeach.com	1971	900 27TH AVE	32960	FG	Joseph M Adams II	(772)567-8193	WS 8 1030 BC 915	ED/MD	170	169	93
VIERA	*FAITH VIERA*		See Rockledge FL									
WAUCHULA	*PEACE VALLEY* pvlc1962@gmail.com www.peacevalleylutheran.org	1962	1643 STENSTROM RD	33873	FG	Anthony A Arias	(863)773-2858	WS 9		17	17	29
WEIRSDALE	*TRINITY*		See Summerfield FL									
WESLEY CHAPEL	*FAITH* church@faithwesleychapel.com www.faithwesleychapel.com	2018	27221 Foamflower Blvd 4414 CRYSTAL DOWNS CT	33544 33543	S	Kurt R Steinbrueck	(813)602-1104	WS 11	ED/HC/MD	29	24	32
	FAMILY OF CHRIST		See Tampa FL									
WEST PALM BEACH	*NEW ALLIANCE HAITIAN* revmichelovil@gmail.com newlifealliance.org		2300 S DIXIE HWY WEST PALM BCH	33401	FG	Michel J Ovil		WS 1115 730 SS 10	HC/MD	16	16	16
	REDEEMER info@redeemerwpb.org redeemerwpb.org	1925	2300 S DIXIE HWY WEST PALM BCH	33401	FG	Daniel P Mc Pherson	(561)832-8705 (561)832-3237	WS 10 SS 845 BC 845	ED/SN	45	40	30
WESTON	*ST PAUL* office@stpaulweston.org www.stpaulweston.org	1989	580 Indian Trace 580 INDIAN TRCE	33326	FG	Richard S Henze	(954)384-9096 (954)384-1037	WS 830 11 SS 945 BC 10	EC/ED/HC/ MD	739	686	275
WILDWOOD	*AMAZING GRACE*		See Oxford FL									
	TRINITY		See Summerfield FL									
	TRINITY SOUTH Satellite Site of Trinity Summerfield FL	2018	1477 Huey St	34785								
WILLIAMSBURG	*GRACE*		See Saint Cloud FL									
WIMAUMA	*CHRIST THE KING*		See Riverview FL									
WINTER GARDEN	*ZION* churchadmin@zionwg.org www.zionwg.org	1886	16173 MARSH ROAD	34787	FG	Roberto E Rojas Jr Frank G Frye Bradley D Heinecke James T Kress Sr	(407)743-5533	WS 9 SS 1045 BC 1045	MD	187	144	127
	WOODLANDS		See Montverde FL									
WINTER HAVEN	*GRACE* swilson@glwh.org www.glwh.org	1948	327 AVENUE C SE	33880	FG	Charles T Reich	(863)293-8447 (863)291-0935	WS 830 1045 SS 950 BC 950	EL/ED/HC/ MD/SN	1300	1038	391
WINTER PARK	*ST LUKE*		See Oviedo FL									
WINTER SPRINGS	*ST LUKE*		See Oviedo FL									
YALAHA	*THE CROSS*		See Mount Dora FL									
YULEE	*HOLY TRINITY*		See Kingsland GA									
ZELLWOOD	*THE CROSS*		See Mount Dora FL									
ZEPHYRHILLS	*FAITH*		See Wesley Chapel FL									
	OUR SAVIOR ochurch@tampabay.rr.com www.oursaviorlutheranzephyrhills.org	1951	5626 20TH ST	33542	FG		(813)782-1369	WS 10 BC 9	MD	154	143	97
ZOLFO SPRINGS	*PEACE VALLEY*		See Wauchula FL									

GEORGIA

CITY	CONGREGATION	YEAR EST	LOCATION	ZIP	DIST.	PASTOR(S)	PHONE	WS	SCHOOLS/MINISTRIES	Bapt	Conf	Avg Attend
ACWORTH	*FAITH*		See Marietta GA									
	LIVING HOPE		See Kennesaw GA									

*Indicates a new church start. A new church start is an intentionally organized gathering which comes together on a regular basis for the purpose of worship and/or Bible study and is intended to grow into a member LCMS congregation. WS =Worship Service; SS = Sunday School; BC =Bible Class; EC = Early Childhood; EL = Elementary School; HS = High School; ED =Education Ministry; HC =Human Care Ministry; SN = Special Needs Ministry; MD = Media Ministry (PC)=Partner Church Pastor. See Page 53 for the Table of Abbreviations for key to additional abbreviations

CONGREGATIONS

CITY	CONGREGATION EMAIL WEBSITE	YEAR EST	LOCATION MAILING ADDRESS	ZIP CODE(S)	DIST	PASTOR(S)	PHONE FAX	WS SS BC	SCHOOLS/ MINISTRIES	STATISTIC Bapt	Conf	Avg Attend
ALBANY	*PEACE*		See Tifton GA									
	TRINITY tlcalbany@gmail.com www.tlcalbany.org	1962	1508 WHISPERING PINES RD	31707	FG	Gary V Bowman	(229)436-5272 (229)436-5272	WS 11 SS 930 BC 930	ED/HC/ MD/SN	51	49	31
ALPHARETTA	*CHRIST SHEPHERD* pastor@cts.org www.cts.org	1990	4655 WEBB BRIDGE RD	30005	EN	Kevin P Elseroad Aaron D Sterling	(770)475-0640 (770)442-1043	WS 830 1045 BC 940	EL/ED/HC/ MD/SN	506	414	220
	LIVING FAITH		See Cumming GA									
ATHENS	*CHRISTUS VICTOR* pastor.christusvictor@gmail.com www.christusvictor.net	1999	1010 S LUMPKIN ST	30605	FG	Dr Gregory C Michael	(706)543-3801	WS 1030 SS 9 BC 9	ED	70	64	41
	TRINITY nburger@trinity-athens.org trinity-athens.org	1939	2535 JEFFERSON RD	30607	FG	Timothy P Davis	(706)546-0670 (706)546-0150	WS 8 10 SS 9	EC/ED/HC/ MD	170	147	72
ATLANTA	*ASCENSION* office@ascension-lcms.com www.ascension-lcms.com	1955	4000 ROSWELL RD NE	30342	EN	David V Miller	(404)255-0224 (404)256-0037	WS 10 SS 9 BC 9	EC/ED/ HC/SN	95	55	50
	CHRIST		See East Point GA									
	FAITH		See Marietta GA									
	GRACE pastor@gracemidtown.com www.gracemidtown.com	1922	1155 N HIGHLAND AVE NE	30306	FG	Adam G Ellsworth	(404)875-5411 (404)875-5411	WS 10 SS 9 BC 9		91	76	37
	INCARNATE WORD		See Stone Mountain GA									
	PEACE		See Decatur GA									
	PRINCE PEACE		See Douglasville GA									
AUGUSTA	*BETHLEHEM*		See Aiken SC									
	OUR REDEEMER info@orlcaugusta.com orlcaugusta.com	1937	402 AUMOND RD	30909	FG	Roger A Schwartz	(706)733-6076 (706)733-3324	WS 815 11 SS 940 BC 940	ED/HC/ MD/SN	511	385	197
BALL GROUND	*KING OF KINGS*		See Jasper GA									
BARNESVILLE	*CHRIST OUR SAVIOR*		See Griffin GA									
BLAIRSVILLE	*ALL SAINTS* aslconnecting@gmail.com www.allsaintslcms.org	1990	83 EARL SHELTON RD	30512	FG	Timothy P Handrick	(706)745-7777 (706)745-7757	WS 10 SS 830	ED/HC/ MD/SN	121	121	83
BLUE RIDGE	*ALL SAINTS*		See Blairsville GA									
BRUNSWICK	*MESSIAH** MessiahBrunswick@att.net messiahlcmsbrunswick.360unite. com/home		5661 New Jesup Hwy Building D 5661 NEW JESUP HWY BLDG D	31523	FG		(912)264-6116	WS 1030		16	15	12
CANTON	*FAITH*		See Marietta GA									
	KING OF KINGS		See Jasper GA									
CARTERSVILLE	*SAVIOR OF ALL* pastor@saviorofall.org www.saviorofall.org	1989	35 Indian Trail 35 INDIAN TRL SE	30120	FG	Bruce A Alberts Dr David F Kruger	(770)387-0379	WS 8 1030 SS 915 BC 915		190	155	92
CLARKSVILLE	*GRACE LUTHERAN CHURCH* Satellite Site of Trinity Eastanollee GA	2010	1121 Hwy 441 North	30523				WS 945 SS 11				
CLAYTON	*RESURRECTION*		See Franklin NC									
COLUMBUS	*BETHLEHEM* bethlehemlutherangeorgia@gmail.com	1963	621 17TH AVE	31906	FG	Bradley P Arnholt	(706)327-8756	WS 11 SS 10		71	65	30
	REDEEMER rls31904@hotmail.com www.redeemercolumbusga.org	1940	4700 ARMOUR RD	31904	FG	John C Bumgardner	(706)322-5026	WS 1030 SS 915 BC 915	ED/MD/SN	168	141	72
COMMERCE	*CHRIST THE KING* ctkcommercega@gmail.com www.ctkcommerce.org	2014	3100 Ila Rd PO BOX 314	30530 30529	FG		(706)423-9813	WS 1030 SS 915	ED/HC/MD	28	28	19
CORDELE	*CHRIST*		See Perry GA									
	PEACE		See Tifton GA									
CUMMING	*LIVING FAITH* lflcoffice@gmail.com www.livingfaithlutheran.com	2001	1171 Atlanta Hwy PO BOX 992	30040 30028	FG	Timothy J Droegemueller	(770)887-0184	WS 1015 SS 9 BC 9	ED/HC/MD	345	264	166
	VILLAS AT CANTERFIELD Satellite Site of Living Faith Cumming GA	2017	815 Atlanta Highway	30040				WS 10 BC 10				
DAHLONEGA	*ST PETER* church@stpeter-lutheran.org www.stpeter-lutheran.org	2018	3460 S CHESTATEE	30533	FG	Charles J Kanefke	(706)864-6001	WS 1030 SS 915 BC 915	ED/HC/MD	71	61	37
DALLAS	*FAITH*		See Marietta GA									
DAWSONVILLE	*LIVING FAITH*		See Cumming GA									
	ST PETER		See Dahlonega GA									
DECATUR	*PEACE* peacedecatur@gmail.com peacelutherandecaturga.com	1955	1679 COLUMBIA DR	30032	FG	Terrell L Davis Sr	(404)289-1474 (404)289-1494	WS 1030 SS 9	HC/MD/SN	72	72	39
DOUGLASVILLE	*FAITH*		See Marietta GA									
	PRINCE PEACE princeofpeace30135@gmail.com poplcga.org/	1970	3988 HIGHWAY 5	30135	FG	Timothy M Faile	(770)942-4681 (770)942-4632	WS 10 SS 9	EC/MD			
EAST POINT	*CHRIST* revsaw4@aol.com www.AliveAtChrist.com	1952	2719 Delowe Dr PO BOX 162165 ATLANTA	30344 30321	FG		(678)900-6315	WS 10	ED/HC/MD			

*Indicates a new church start. A new church start is an intentionally organized gathering which comes together on a regular basis for the purpose of worship and/or Bible study and is intended to grow into a member LCMS congregation. WS =Worship Service; SS = Sunday School; BC =Bible Class; EC = Early Childhood; EL = Elementary School; HS = High School; ED =Education Ministry; HC =Human Care Ministry; SN = Special Needs Ministry; MD = Media Ministry (PC)=Partner Church Pastor. See Page 53 for the Table of Abbreviations for key to additional abbreviations

CITY	CONGREGATION EMAIL WEBSITE	YEAR EST	LOCATION MAILING ADDRESS	ZIP CODE(S)	DIST.	PASTOR(S)	PHONE FAX	WS SS BC	SCHOOLS/ MINISTRIES	Bapt	Conf	Avg Attend
EASTANOLLEE	*TRINITY* trinitytoccoa@windstream.net www.trinitytoccoa.com	1970	4041 Highway 17 PO BOX 1154 TOCCOA	30538 30577	FG	Roland D Vega	(706)886-6723	WS 1045 SS 930 BC 930	ED/HC/ MD/SN	53	51	37
EATONTON	*LAKE OCONEE* officelolc@gmail.com www.lakeoconeelutheran.org	1999	1089 Lake Oconee Parkway 1089 GREENSBORO RD	31024	FG	Steven J Hayden	(706)485-4600	WS 1030 SS 9	ED/HC/ MD/SN	131	121	81
ELLIJAY	*KING OF KINGS*		See Jasper GA									
EVANS	*OUR REDEEMER*		See Augusta GA									
FORT OGLETHORPE	*GOOD SHEPHERD*		See Chattanooga TN									
FORT VALLEY	*CHRIST*		See Perry GA									
GAINESVILLE	*GOOD SHEPHERD* gslcsecretary@gmail.com www.goodshepherd.info	1960	600 S ENOTA DR NE	30501	FG	Daniel P Sparling	(770)532-2428 (770)532-2428	WS 830 1045 SS 945 BC 945	ED/HC/ MD/SN	216	202	113
GREENSBORO	*LAKE OCONEE*		See Eatonton GA									
GRIFFIN	*CHRIST OUR SAVIOR* ChristOurSaviorGriffin@gmail.com christoursaviorlutheran.org	2005	3235 TEAMON RD	30223	FG	Joseph M Warnke	(770)227-4082	WS 930 SS 11 BC 11	ED/HC/MD	85	78	50
HAMPTON	*CHRIST OUR SAVIOR*		See Griffin GA									
HAWKINSVILLE	*CHRIST*		See Perry GA									
HIAWASSEE	*ALL SAINTS*		See Blairsville GA									
HIRAM	*PRINCE PEACE*		See Douglasville GA									
HOSCHTON	*ST JOHN THE APOSTLE* stjohntheapostlelutheranchurch@ gmail.com www.stjohntheapostlelutheran.com	2012	5609 Grand Reunion Dr PO BOX 106 BUFORD	30548 30515	FG	Brian C Wachter	(678)858-4961	WS 1030 SS 935 BC 10	HC/MD	26	23	21
JACKSON	*CHRIST OUR SAVIOR*		See Griffin GA									
JASPER	*KING OF KINGS* kingofkingslcmsga@gmail.com kingofkingsga.org		744 NOAH DRIVE STE 113-132	30143	FG	Jefrey S Jensen	(706)301-9191 (706)301-9191	WS 1030 BC 9	ED/HC/ MD/SN	100	98	75
KATHLEEN	*CHRIST*		See Perry GA									
KENNESAW	*FAITH*		See Marietta GA									
	LIVING HOPE office@livinghopega.com www.livinghopega.com	1993	3450 STILESBORO RD NW	30152	FG	John R Schubert	(770)425-6726 (770)425-1142	WS 930 11 BC 1045	ED/HC/ MD/SN	308	257	197
KINGSLAND	*HOLY TRINITY* holytrinity@tds.net holytrinitykingsland.com	1983	165 Camden Woods Pkwy 165 CAMDEN WOODS PKWY E	31548	FG	Dr Joel P Meyer Adam H Gray	(912)729-6085	WS 1030 SS 915 BC 915	ED/HC	165	149	70
LAWRENCEVILLE	*ST JOHN THE APOSTLE*		See Hoschton GA									
LEESBURG	*TRINITY*		See Albany GA									
LILBURN	*MEKANE YESUS ATLANTA** atlecmy@gmail.com		1004 OAK RD SW	30047	FG		(470)223-2522					
	OAK ROAD oakroadlutheran@gmail.com oakroadlutheranchurch.org	1984	1004 OAK RD SW	30047	FG		(770)979-6391 (770)979-9619	WS 8 1045 SS 930 BC 930	ED/HC	215	210	91
LOCUST GROVE	*CHRIST OUR SAVIOR*		See Griffin GA									
MABLETON	*FAITH*		See Marietta GA									
MACON	*HOLY TRINITY* lchtmacon@gmail.com www.holytrinitymacon.org	1951	1899 TUCKER RD	31220	FG	Laird W Van Gorder		WS 11 BC 10	ED/HC	26	21	15
MARIETTA	*FAITH* faithlc@faithmarietta.org faithmarietta.com	1955	2111 LOWER ROSWELL RD	30068	FG	Shaun M Daugherty	(770)973-8877 (770)971-7796	WS 815 11 SS 945 BC 945	EL/ED/HC/ MD	309	233	135
	LIVING HOPE		See Kennesaw GA									
MC DONOUGH	*CHRIST OUR SAVIOR*		See Griffin GA									
MONTEZUMA	*CHRIST*		See Perry GA									
NORCROSS	*EMMANUEL** lflcpastor@gmail.com emmanuellutheran.net		Emmanuel Lutheran Church at Norcross Community Center 10 College St PO BOX 206	30071 30091	FG		(470)302-4815					
	*TRINITY** samil2110@gmail.com		150 Hunt St 355 OAK SPRINGS DR LAW-RENCEVILLE	30071 30043	FG		(678)622-2717	WS 2				
PEACHTREE CITY	*ST PAUL* www.church.stpaulptc.org	1995	700 ARDENLEE PKWY PEACHTREE CTY	30269	FG	Mark D Dahn Dr Joel M Dietrich	(770)487-0339 (770)692-6389	WS 830 1045 SS 930 BC 930	EL/ED/HC/ MD	271	209	155
PERRY	*CHRIST* christlutheranperry@gmail.com www.christlutheranperry.org		208 LANGSTON RD	31069	FG	Alan I Mueller	(478)987-6016	WS 1030 SS 930	EL/ED/HC/ MD	173	155	88
POWDER SPRINGS	*FAITH*		See Marietta GA									
RINGGOLD	*FIRST*		See Chattanooga TN									
	GOOD SHEPHERD		See Chattanooga TN									
ROME	*HOLY TRINITY* www.romehtlc.org	1955	3000 Garden Lakes Blvd 3000 GARDEN LAKES BLVD NW	30165	FG		(706)232-7257	WS 1030 SS 930 BC 930	HC	92	82	30
	RENAISSANCE MARQUIS Satellite Site of Holy Trinity Rome GA	2000	3126 Cedartown Hwy SW	30161								
ROSSVILLE	*FIRST*		See Chattanooga TN									
	GOOD SHEPHERD		See Chattanooga TN									
ROSWELL	*FAITH*		See Marietta GA									
	RIVERCLIFF		See Sandy Springs GA									
SAINT MARYS	*HOLY TRINITY*		See Kingsland GA									

*Indicates a new church start. A new church start is an intentionally organized gathering which comes together on a regular basis for the purpose of worship and/or Bible study and is intended to grow into a member LCMS congregation. WS =Worship Service; SS = Sunday School; BC =Bible Class; EC = Early Childhood; EL = Elementary School; HS = High School; ED =Education Ministry; HC =Human Care Ministry; SN = Special Needs Ministry; MD = Media Ministry (PC)=Partner Church Pastor. See Page 53 for the Table of Abbreviations for key to additional abbreviations

CITY	CONGREGATION EMAIL WEBSITE	YEAR EST	LOCATION MAILING ADDRESS	ZIP CODE(S)	DIST.	PASTOR(S)	PHONE FAX	WS SS BC	SCHOOLS/ MINISTRIES	STATISTIC Bapt	Conf	Avg Attend
SANDY SPRINGS	*RIVERCLIFF* member-care@rivercliff.org www.rivercliff lutheran.org	1968	8750 ROSWELL RD SANDY SPGS	30350	FG	Jeffrey W Jordan Jacob M Berlinski	(770)993-4316	WS 830 11 SS 945 BC 945	ED/HC/MD	326	244	167
SAVANNAH	*TRINITY* trinityoffice@bellsouth.net www.trinitylutheransavannah.com	1946	12391 MERCY BLVD	31419	FG	Jeffrey N Webb	(912)925-4839 (912)925-4056	WS 830 11 SS 945 BC 945	HC/MD	271	185	117
SMYRNA	*FAITH*		See Marietta GA									
STATESBORO	*ST PAUL* www.stpaulstatesboro.org	1969	1608 FAIR RD	30458	FG	Samuel P Clay	(912)681-2481 (912)681-2481					
STOCKBRIDGE	*HOLY CROSS* holycrossga@att.net	1964	3250 MOUNT ZION RD	30281	FG		(770)507-5910	SS 930	ED/HC/ MD/SN			
	LORD OF LIFE earhartgeorge@yahoo.com www.lordoflifevision.com	1979	3250 MOUNT ZION RD	30281	FG	Carl R Morten	(470)278-5837	WS 830 1045 SS 945 BC 530	ED/HC/MD			
STONE MOUNTAIN	*INCARNATE WORD* wiltonheyliger@gmail.com		4950 Hugh Howell Rd 50 HARMONY GROVE RD LILBURN	30087 30047	FG	Dr Wilton E Heyliger	(404)936-0628	WS 845		41	28	16
SUGAR HILL	*ST JOHN THE APOSTLE*		See Hoschton GA									
SUWANNEE	*LIVING FAITH*		See Cumming GA									
	ST JOHN THE APOSTLE		See Hoschton GA									
SYLVESTR	*TRINITY*		See Albany GA									
TATE	*KING OF KINGS*		See Jasper GA									
TIFTON	*PEACE* peace.tifton@gmail.com PeaceLutheranTifton.org	1962	604 Tennessee Dr 604 TENNESSEE AVE	31794	FG		(229)382-7344	WS 5 BC 1030	ED/HC/ MD/SN	26	26	18
TOCCOA	*TRINITY*		See Eastanollee GA									
TUCKER	*ST MARK* saintmarktucker@yahoo.com www.saintmarklutheranchurch.org	1966	2110 BROCKETT RD	30084	FG	Hiruy B Gebremichael	(770)938-4546 (770)938-4546	WS 930 SS 11 BC 11	ED/HC/MD			
VALDOSTA	*MESSIAH* messiahluth500@gmail.com www.MessiahLutheranVLD.com	1955	500 BAYTREE RD	31602	FG	Stephen D Wareham	(229)244-0143	WS 1030 SS 915 BC 915	ED/HC/SN	108	106	78
	PEACE		See Tifton GA									
VILLA RICA	*PRINCE PEACE*		See Douglasville GA									
WARNER ROBINS	*CHRIST*		See Perry GA									
	MOUNT CALVARY office@mountcalvaryga.org www.mountcalvaryga.org	1980	336 CARL VINSON PKWY	31088	FG	Andrew J Howe Peter J LeBorious	(478)922-1418 (478)922-7215	SS 930 BC 930	ED/HC	574	475	226
WINSTON	*PRINCE PEACE*		See Douglasville GA									
WOODBINE	*HOLY TRINITY*		See Kingsland GA									
WOODSTOCK	*FAITH*		See Marietta GA									
	TIMOTHY timothylutheran@tlcwoodstock.org www.tlcwoodstock.org	1979	556 ARNOLD MILL RD	30188	FG	Daniel G Brammeier	(770)928-2812 (678)445-7151	WS 830 11 SS 945 BC 945	EC/ED/HC/ MD	432	338	144
ZEBULON	*CHRIST OUR SAVIOR*		See Griffin GA									
					HAWAII							
AIEA	*OUR SAVIOR* office@oursaviorhawaii.com www.oursaviorhawaii.com	1961	98-1098 Moanalua Rd 98-325 KOAUKA ST	96701	CNH	Mitchell W Gowen	(808)488-3654	WS 815 1045	EL/ED/ MD/SN	277	195	1
EWA BEACH	*OUR SAVIOR*		See Aiea HI									
EWA BEACH-OAHU	*MESSIAH* info@messiahlutheranhawaii.org messiahlutheranhawaii.org/	1960	91-679 FORT WEAVER RD EWA BEACH	96706	CNH	Kanagasabai Uma-Shankar	(808)321-3941	WS 10 SS 9 BC 9	ED/HC/SN			
HAIKU	*EMMANUEL*		See Kahului-maui HI									
HALEIWA	*TRINITY*		See Wahiawa HI									
HILO	*CHRIST* christlchilo@gmail.com ChristHilo.org	1954	595 KAPIOLANI ST	96720	CNH		(808)935-8612	WS 8 1030 SS 915	ED/HC/ MD/SN	134	120	97
HONOLULU	*GOOD SHEPHERD* goodshepherdhnl@gmail.com www.jesus4hawaii.com	1955	638 N KUAKINI ST	96817	CNH	Robert R Mabry Uchel R Naito	(808)523-2927 (808)536-1923	WS 9 BC 9	EC/ED/HC	60	60	40
	OUR REDEEMER office@ourredeemerlutheran.us ourredeemerlutheran.us	1945	1404 UNIVERSITY AVE	96822	CNH		(808)946-4223 (808)943-1027	WS 9 BC 1015	ED/HC/ MD/SN			
	OUR SAVIOR		See Aiea HI									
	TRINITY		See Wahiawa HI									
KAHULUI-MAUI	*EMMANUEL* pastor@elcs-maui.org www.elc-maui.org	1967	520 W One St 520 ONE ST KAHULUI	96732	CNH	Edward Hosch III	(808)877-3037	WS 8 1045 SS 915 BC 915	EL/ED/HC/ MD	135	116	70
KAILUA	*ST MARK*		See Kaneohe HI									
KANEOHE	*ST MARK* PastorDan@StMarkHawaii.Org www.stmarkhawaii.org	1952	45-725 Kamehameha Highway 45-725 KAMEHAMEHA HWY	96744	CNH	Daniel B Truesdell	(808)227-3930	WS 9 SS 1030 BC 1030	EL/ED/HC	110	110	100
KIHEI	*EMMANUEL*		See Kahului-maui HI									
KOLOA	*ST MATTHEW* williampierce@stmatthewsofkauai.org		3540 Koloa Rd 5750 KUAMOO RD KAPAA KAUAI	96756 96746	CNH	William J Pierce	(808)639-9166	WS 5 SS 4 BC 4	ED/HC/MD			
LAHAINA	*EMMANUEL*		See Kahului-maui HI									
MILILANI	*TRINITY*		See Wahiawa HI									
PAIA	*EMMANUEL*		See Kahului-maui HI									
PEARL CITY	*OUR SAVIOR*		See Aiea HI									

*Indicates a new church start. A new church start is an intentionally organized gathering which comes together on a regular basis for the purpose of worship and/or Bible study and is intended to grow into a member LCMS congregation. WS =Worship Service; SS = Sunday School; BC =Bible Class; EC = Early Childhood; EL = Elementary School; HS = High School; ED =Education Ministry; HC =Human Care Ministry; SN = Special Needs Ministry; MD = Media Ministry (PC)=Partner Church Pastor. See Page 53 for the Table of Abbreviations for key to additional abbreviations

CITY	CONGREGATION EMAIL WEBSITE	YEAR EST	LOCATION MAILING ADDRESS	ZIP CODE(S)	DIST.	PASTOR(S)	PHONE FAX	WS SS BC	SCHOOLS/ MINISTRIES	Bapt	Conf	Avg Attend
SCHOFIELD BARRACKS	*TRINITY*		See Wahiawa HI									
WAHIAWA	*TRINITY* churchoffice@tls-hawaii.org www.trinity-hawaii.org	1950	1611 CALIFORNIA AVE	96786	CNH	Dr Stephen H Becker	(808)621-6033	WS 10 BC 9	EL/ED/ MD/SN	81	69	52
WAIKOLOA	*WAIKOLOA* pastorjmueller@gmail.com www.waikoloalutheranchurch.com	1989	Waikoloa Vlg Golfcourse 68_1792 Melia St PO BOX 383046	96738	CNH	Jeffrey E Mueller	(808)883-9255	WS 10 SS 9 BC 9	ED/MD	38	29	32
WAILUKU	*EMMANUEL*		See Kahului-maui HI									
WAIPAHU	*OUR SAVIOR*		See Aiea HI									

IDAHO

CITY	CONGREGATION EMAIL WEBSITE	YEAR EST	LOCATION MAILING ADDRESS	ZIP CODE(S)	DIST.	PASTOR(S)	PHONE FAX	WS SS BC	SCHOOLS/ MINISTRIES	Bapt	Conf	Avg Attend
ABERDEEN	*FAITH*		See Pocatello ID									
ASHTON	*ZION* zionashton@myidahomail.com	1906	9 Main St PO BOX 387	83420	NOW		(208)652-7438 (208)652-7438	WS 1030 SS 915	ED/HC/ MD/SN			
ATHOL	*BLESSED SACRAMENT*		See Hayden ID									
	FIRST		See Spirit Lake ID									
BAYVIEW	*BLESSED SACRAMENT*		See Hayden ID									
	FIRST		See Spirit Lake ID									
BELMONT	*BLESSED SACRAMENT*		See Hayden ID									
BLANCHARD	*FIRST*		See Spirit Lake ID									
BOISE	*BEAUTIFUL SAVIOR* bslcboise@gmail.com bslcboise.org	1980	2981 E BOISE AVE	83706	NOW	Dennis J Durham	(208)336-3616	WS 930 SS 1045 BC 1045	EC/ED/SN	246	180	96
	FRIENDSHIP		See Meridian ID									
	GOOD SHEPHERD info@gslcboise.org www.gslcboise.org	1954	5009 Cassia St 5009 W CASSIA ST	83705	NOW	Timothy J Pauls	(208)343-7212	WS 8 1045 SS 930 BC 930	ED/HC/MD			
BUHL	*CLOVER TRINITY* clovertlchurch@gmail.com www.clovertrinity.org	1915	3552 N 1825 E	83316	NOW	Steven A Barckholtz	(208)326-4950 (208)326-5105	WS 1030 SS 11 BC 1145	EL/ED/ MD/SN			
	ST JOHN stjohnsbuhl@cableone.net	1943	1128 POPLAR ST	83316	NOW		(208)543-4282	WS 1030 SS 9 BC 9				
BURLEY	*TRINITY*		See Rupert ID									
	ZION	1948	2410 MILLER AVE	83318	NOW	Alexander G Lissow	(208)678-4167	WS 10 SS 845 BC 845	ED/HC/MD	22	22	18
CALDWELL	*GRACE* graceonkimball@gmail.com www.gracelutherancaldwell.org	1941	2700 S KIMBALL AVE	83605	NOW	Jason E Gullidge	(208)459-4191	WS 1030 SS 915 BC 915 6	EC/ED/HC/ MD	217	183	147
CASCADE	*SHEP OF THE MOUNTAIN*	1987	212 N Hwy 55 PO BOX 37	83611	NOW		(208)382-4422	WS 830 BC 945	ED/HC			
CHALLIS	*CHRIST OUR SAVIOR* coschallis@gmail.com		695 Challis Creek Rd PO BOX 1163	83226	MT	Michael A Musegades	(208)756-4429	SS	ED	11	8	20
	SHEP OF THE VALLEY		See Salmon ID									
CHILCO	*BLESSED SACRAMENT*		See Hayden ID									
CHUBBUCK	*FAITH*		See Pocatello ID									
CLARK FORK	*LIVING WATER* livingwater.clarkfork@gmail.com livingwaterclarkfork.org		317 E 2nd Ave PO BOX 406	83811	NOW	Nicholas L Larsen	(208)266-1282	WS 9 1030	ED/HC/MD			
COEUR D'ALENE	*BLESSED SACRAMENT*		See Hayden ID									
	CHRIST KING info@ctkcda.com www.ctkcda.com	1955	1700 E PENNSYLVANIA AVE	83814	NOW	Daniel D Deuel Larry E Comer	(208)664-9231 (208)664-9233	WS 830 11 SS 10 BC 10	EC/ED/HC/ MD/SN	586	522	280
DALTON GARDENS	*BLESSED SACRAMENT*		See Hayden ID									
DECLO	*TRINITY*		See Rupert ID									
EAGLE	*FRIENDSHIP*		See Meridian ID									
EDEN	*TRINITY* trinityeden@trinitylutheraneden.org www.trinitylutheraneden.org	1916	1602 E 1100 S	83325	NOW	Mark E Schulze	(208)825-5277 (208)825-5277	WS 9 SS 1015 BC 1015	EC/ED/HC/ MD/SN			
EMMETT	*OUR REDEEMER* facebook.com/ourredeemer.emmett	1921	407 S Hayes 407 S HAYES AVE	83617	NOW	David K Reeder	(208)365-5231	WS 1030 SS 9 BC 9		61	43	45
FERNAN LAKE VILLAGE	*BLESSED SACRAMENT*		See Hayden ID									
FILER	*CLOVER TRINITY*		See Buhl ID									
	PEACE peace@filertel.com peacelutheranfiler.org	1963	600 Stevens Ave PO BOX 33	83328	NOW		(208)326-5450	WS 9 SS 1030 BC 1030	ED/HC/ MD/SN			
FORT HALL	*FAITH*		See Pocatello ID									
GARWOOD	*BLESSED SACRAMENT*		See Hayden ID									
	SHEPHERD HILLS		See Rathdrum ID									
GOODING	*CALVARY LUTHERAN CHURCH SATELLITE LOCATION* Satellite Site of St Paul Jerome ID	2020	633 Pine St	83330								
GRANGEVILLE	*TRINITY* info@grangevilletrinitylutheran.org	1892	210 N MILL ST	83530	NOW	Steven A Naylor	(208)983-0562	WS 930 SS 11 BC 11	ED/HC/ MD/SN	50	50	40
HAILEY	*VALLEY OF PEACE* richardandjenniferstahl@verizon.net www.haileyvop.org/	1974	740 Wintergreen PO BOX 218	83333	NOW	Gerald R Reinke	(814)251-2852	WS 10	ED/HC/MD			

*Indicates a new church start. A new church start is an intentionally organized gathering which comes together on a regular basis for the purpose of worship and/or Bible study and is intended to grow into a member LCMS congregation. WS =Worship Service; SS = Sunday School; BC =Bible Class; EC = Early Childhood; EL = Elementary School; HS = High School; ED =Education Ministry; HC =Human Care Ministry; SN = Special Needs Ministry; MD = Media Ministry (PC)=Partner Church Pastor. See Page 53 for the Table of Abbreviations for key to additional abbreviations

CITY	CONGREGATION EMAIL WEBSITE	YEAR EST	LOCATION MAILING ADDRESS	ZIP CODE(S)	DIST.	PASTOR(S)	PHONE FAX	WS SS BC	SCHOOLS/ MINISTRIES	STATISTIC Bapt	Conf	Avg Attend
HARRISON	*BLESSED SACRAMENT*		See Hayden ID									
HAUSER	*BLESSED SACRAMENT*		See Hayden ID									
	SHEPHERD HILLS		See Rathdrum ID									
HAYDEN	*BLESSED SACRAMENT* info@blessedsacramentlutheran church.com www.blessedsacramentlutheran church.com	2020	9140 N Reed Rd 8989 N HUETTER RD RATH-DRUM	82835 83858	EN	Marcus A Williams Marc G DiConti	(406)262-3298	BC 2	ED	58	41	48
	SHEPHERD HILLS		See Rathdrum ID									
HAYDEN LAKE	*BLESSED SACRAMENT*		See Hayden ID									
HAZELTON	*TRINITY*		See Eden ID									
HEYBURN	*TRINITY*		See Rupert ID									
HOMEDALE	*MOUNT CALVARY*	1939	621 W IDAHO AVE	83628	NOW	Sean L Rippy	(208)337-4248	WS 10 SS 9	ED			
IDAHO FALLS	*HOPE* hlcs@allabouthope.org www.allabouthope.org	1957	2071 12TH ST	83404	NOW	Garen R Pay Robert A Carabotta	(208)529-8080 (208)529-8880	WS 930 SS 830 BC 830	EL/ED/MD	164	138	93
	ST JOHN office@stjohnministries.net www.stjohnministries.net	1913	290 7TH ST	83401	NOW	Stephen B Weems	(208)522-5650 (208)522-6652	WS 930 SS 1045 BC 1045	HC			
INKOM	*FAITH*		See Pocatello ID									
JEROME	*ST PAUL* www.stpaulsjerome.org	1937	1301 N Davis St PO BOX 502	83338	NOW		(208)324-2842 (208)324-2842	WS 10 SS 845 BC 845	ED/HC/SN			
KELLOGG	*EMMANUEL*		See Mullan ID									
KETCHUM	*VALLEY OF PEACE*		See Hailey ID									
KIMBERLY	*KIMBERLY CAMPUS* Satellite Site of XrossWay TWIN FALLS ID	2023	400 Irene St	83341								
KUNA	*KUNA* kunalutheranchurch@gmail.com www.flmkuna.org/		128 E. PORTER ST	83634	NOW	Joel A Beyer	(208)860-1274	WS 530				
LEWISTON	*CONCORDIA*		See Pullman WA									
MCCALL	*OUR SAVIOR* officemanager@oslcmccall.com www.oslcmccall.com	1954	100 N Mission St PO BOX 912	83638	NOW	Dr Kirk A Hille	(208)634-5905	WS 11 BC 10	ED/HC/ MD/SN	64	63	62
MERIDIAN	*BEAUTIFUL SAVIOR*		See Boise ID									
	CHRIST office@clcmeridian.org www.clcmeridian.org	1972	1406 W CHERRY LN	83642	NOW	Daniel G Jones	(208)888-1622	WS 10 SS 1130	EC/ED/HC/ MD/SN			
	FRIENDSHIP office@friendshipcelebration.org www.friendshipcelebration.org	1998	765 E Chinden 765 E CHINDEN BLVD	83646	NOW	Dr Matthew R Henry	(208)288-2404 (208)288-2402	WS 815 11 SS 945 BC 945	EC/ED/HC/ MD/SN	511	405	285
MOSCOW	*AUGUSTANA* jkrenz98@hotmail.com moscowlutheran.org		217 E. 6th Street PO BOX 9625	83843 83848	NOW	Jonathon T Krenz Douglas J Taylor	(208)892-9224	WS 2 SS 330	ED/MD	86	69	65
	CONCORDIA		See Pullman WA									
MOUNTAIN HOME	*FAITH* faith.mtnhome@gmail.com faithlutheranchurchidaho.org/	1956	1190 N 6TH E	83647	NOW	Dr Richard J Davis	(208)587-4127 (208)587-4127	WS 1030 SS 915	ED/HC	70	58	34
MULLAN	*EMMANUEL* www.mullanelc.org	1945	124 Terrell Loop PO BOX 434	83846	NOW		(208)744-1324	WS 930				
MURTAUGH	*TRINITY*		See Eden ID									
NAMPA	*ZION* office@zionlutherannampa.com www.zionlutherannampa.com	1917	404 NECTARINE ST	83686	NOW	Jason A Swan	(208)466-6746	WS 1030 SS 9	EC/EL/HS/ ED/HC/ MD/SN			
NEW PLYMOUTH	*IMMANUEL* fayedykema@gmail.com	1904	320 W Elm St PO BOX 553	83655	NOW		(208)278-3080	WS 11 SS 12 BC 10	ED/HC/MD	26	22	19
OSBURN	*EMMANUEL*		See Mullan ID									
PAUL	*TRINITY*		See Rupert ID									
PLUMMER	*BLESSED SACRAMENT*		See Hayden ID									
POCATELLO	*FAITH* www.faithpocatello.org	1955	856 W ELDREDGE RD	83201	NOW		(208)237-2391	WS 10 SS 9	ED/HC/MD			
	GRACE churchoffice01@gracepocatello.org www.gracepocatello.org	1926	1350 BALDY AVE	83201	NOW	Jonathan M Dinger	(208)237-0467 (208)237-0931	WS 830 11 5 SS 10 BC 10	EL/HS/ED/ HC/MD/SN	856	620	411
POST FALLS	*BLESSED SACRAMENT*		See Hayden ID									
	SHEPHERD HILLS		See Rathdrum ID									
RATHDRUM	*BLESSED SACRAMENT*		See Hayden ID									
	FIRST		See Spirit Lake ID									
	SHEPHERD HILLS SOTHSecretary@outlook.com www.shepherdofthehills-rathdrum.org	1980	13541 W Hwy 53 13541 W HIGHWAY 53	83858	NOW	Benjamin J Ulledalen Sr	(208)687-1809	WS 1015 SS 9	EC/ED/HC/ MD/SN	240	240	170
RIGBY	*CROWN OF LIFE* collcms.org	1989	3856 E 300 N	83442	NOW		(208)419-9532	WS 11 SS 945 BC 10	ED/HC/MD			
RUPERT	*TLC OUTREACH CENTER AND PRESCHOOL* Satellite Site of Trinity Rupert ID	2023	923 8th	83350								
	TRINITY tlcrupert@gmail.com www.tlcrupert.com	1914	909 8TH ST	83350	NOW	Dr James A Von Busch	(208)436-3413	WS 1030 SS 915 BC 915	EC/ED/HC/ MD/SN	180	143	100

*Indicates a new church start. A new church start is an intentionally organized gathering which comes together on a regular basis for the purpose of worship and/or Bible study and is intended to grow into a member LCMS congregation. WS =Worship Service; SS = Sunday School; BC =Bible Class; EC = Early Childhood; EL = Elementary School; HS = High School; ED =Education Ministry; HC =Human Care Ministry; SN = Special Needs Ministry; MD = Media Ministry (PC)=Partner Church Pastor. See Page 53 for the Table of Abbreviations for key to additional abbreviations

CITY	CONGREGATION EMAIL WEBSITE	YEAR EST	LOCATION MAILING ADDRESS	ZIP CODE(S)	DIST.	PASTOR(S)	PHONE FAX	WS SS BC	SCHOOLS/ MINISTRIES	STATISTIC Bapt	Conf	Avg Attend
SAINT ANTHONY	*TRINITY* trinitysaintanthony@gmail.com		48 E 1 N C/O JOHN SCAFE PO BOX 772 ASHTON	83445 83420	NOW	Alan L Nedrow	(208)624-0357	WS 1030 SS 915 BC 915	ED/HC/MD	31	26	14
SALMON	*SHEP OF THE VALLEY* office@sotvlutheran.org sotvlutheran.org	1978	178 HIGHWAY 28	83467	MT	Michael A Musegades	(208)756-4429 (208)756-4429	WS 930 SS 1045 BC 1045	ED/HC	80	74	39
SANDPOINT	*CHRIST OUR REDEEMER* corlc@corsandpoint.org www.corsandpoint.org	1987	1900 W Pine St 1900 PINE ST	83864	NOW	Mark W Airey	(208)263-7516 (877)295-0294	WS 10 BC 9	EC/ED/HC/ MD/SN			
SILVERTON	*EMMANUEL*		See Mullan ID									
SODA SPRINGS	*HOPE* rdierks208@gmail.com	1974	25 S Hooper Ave PO BOX 85	83276	NOW		(208)821-0125	WS 11 BC 10				
SPIRIT LAKE	*BLESSED SACRAMENT*		See Hayden ID									
	FIRST chelleyeend3@gmail.com	1909	32529 N 6th St PO BOX 100	83869	NOW	Daniel A Wurster	(208)623-2275	WS 10 SS 9 BC 9	ED/HC/SN	35	35	35
STATE LINE	*BLESSED SACRAMENT*		See Hayden ID									
SUN VALLEY	*VALLEY OF PEACE*		See Hailey ID									
SWAN VALLEY	*CHRIST OUR SAVIOR*		See Nordic Ranches WY									
TWIN FALLS	*IMMANUEL* church@immanueltf.org immanueltf.org	1909	2055 FILER AVE E	83301	NOW	Roger M Sedlmayr	(208)733-7820 (208)735-9770	WS 815 1045 SS 930 BC 930	EC/EL/ED/ HC/MD/SN	456	358	250
	XROSSWAY info@xrossway.org www.xrossway.org		1385 Park View Dr #103 400 IRENE ST KIMBERLY	83301 83341	NOW	Clinton J Lutz	(208)423-5139	WS 1030 SS 930 BC 930	EC/ED/HC/ MD/SN			
TWIN LAKES	*BLESSED SACRAMENT*		See Hayden ID									
WALLACE	*EMMANUEL*		See Mullan ID									
WEISER	*CONCORDIA*	1943	402 E COURT ST	83672	NOW		(208)608-1061	WS 10 BC 11	ED/HC/MD			
WORLEY	*BLESSED SACRAMENT*		See Hayden ID									

ILLINOIS

CITY	CONGREGATION EMAIL WEBSITE	YEAR EST	LOCATION MAILING ADDRESS	ZIP CODE(S)	DIST.	PASTOR(S)	PHONE FAX	WS SS BC	SCHOOLS/ MINISTRIES	STATISTIC Bapt	Conf	Avg Attend
ADDISON	*ST PAUL* stpauladdison@gmail.com stpauladdison.com	1906	37 W ARMY TRAIL BLVD	60101	NI	Kevin P Peterson	(630)543-6909 (630)543-5768	WS 9 BC 1045	EL/HS/ED/ HC/MD/SN	245	208	71
ALEDO	*ZION*		See Taylor Ridge IL									
	ZION AT BROOKSTONE OF ALEDO Satellite Site of Zion Taylor Ridge IL	2007	Brookstone of Aledo 405 SE 13th Ave	61231				WS 3				
ALGONQUIN	*CROSSPOINT LAKEWOOD*		See Lakewood IL									
	ST JOHN churchoffice@stjohnsalgonquin.org www.stjohnsalgonquin.org	1876	300 JEFFERSON ST	60102	NI	Jeremy A Latzke	(847)658-9300 (847)658-5766	WS 9 SS 1015 BC 1015	ED/HC/MD	467	387	157
ALSIP	*HOLY CROSS* secretary@hc-lc.org www.hc-lc.org	1939	4041 W 120TH ST	60803	S		(708)597-5209 (708)597-5209	WS 11	ED/HC/MD	36	32	20
ALTAMONT	*BETHLEHEM* bethlehemaltamont@gmail.com www.bethlehemaltamont.org	1861	6351 N 200th St 6409 N. 200TH ST.	62411	CI	Marcus G Manley	(618)483-6756	WS 930 SS 1045 BC 1045	EL/ED/HC/ MD	214	142	118
	IMMANUEL immalt22@gmail.com immanuelaltamont.org	1874	203 E DIVISION ST	62411	CI	Scott A Niermann	(618)483-6395	WS 830 11 SS 945 BC 945	EL/ED/HC/ MD/SN	745	615	405
	ST PAUL stpaulbluepoint.org	1869	14026 N 500TH ST	62411	CI	David R Speers	(618)483-6993 (618)483-6993	WS 930 SS 830 BC 830	EL			
	ZION zion.altamont@gmail.com zionaltamont.org	1893	5534 E 600TH AVE	62411	CI	Marcus G Manley		WS 8 SS 915	EL	53	45	38
ALTON	*HOPE*		See Jerseyville IL									
	MESSIAH messiahalton@gmail.com www.messiahalton.com	1943	920 MILTON RD	62002	SI		(618)465-5343	WS 9 SS 1015 BC 1015	ED/MD			
ANDREW	*GOOD SHEPHERD*		See Sherman IL									
ANNA	*TRINITY*	1930	205 W Jefferson 205 W JEFFERSON ST	62906	SI		(618)833-2475	WS 11	ED	60	56	17
ANTIOCH	*BEAUTIFUL SAVIOR* Pastor@BSLCAntioch.com BSLCAntioch.com	1996	1501 Deep Lake Road 1501 DEEP LAKE RD	60002	NI	Jonathan D Petzold	(847)395-9400	WS 9 SS 1030 BC 1030	ED/HC/MD	155	123	71
ARCOLA	*IMMANUEL*		See Tuscola IL									
ARENZVILLE	*TRINITY* secretary@trinityarenzville.org trinityarenzville.org	1872	Frederick St PO BOX 49	62611	CI	Andrew P Dierks	(217)997-5534	WS 10 SS 9 BC 9	EL/ED/MD	420	285	103
ARLINGTON HEIGHTS	*FAITH* office@faithlutheran-ah.org faithlutheran-ah.org	1947	431 S ARLINGTON HEIGHTS RD ARLINGTON HTS	60005	EN		(847)253-4839 (847)398-5010	WS 10 BC 945	EC/ED/HC/ MD			
	LIVING CHRIST lclcoffice@aol.com www.livingchristlutheran.org	1965	625 E DUNDEE RD ARLINGTON HTS	60004	NI	William L Harder	(847)577-7133	WS 10	ED/HC/MD	140	108	33
	ST PETER agill@fulllifeinchrist.org fulllifeinchrist.org	1860	111 W OLIVE ST ARLINGTON HTS	60004	NI	Micah D Greiner Dr Randall L Rozelle David W Ficken Charles W Kittel	(847)259-4114 (847)259-4185	WS 845 915 11 SS 10 BC 10	EL/ED/HC/ MD/SN	2608	1940	411
AROMA PARK	*ST PAUL*		See Bourbonnais IL									
ARTHUR	*IMMANUEL*		See Tuscola IL									

*Indicates a new church start. A new church start is an intentionally organized gathering which comes together on a regular basis for the purpose of worship and/or Bible study and is intended to grow into a member LCMS congregation. WS =Worship Service; SS = Sunday School; BC =Bible Class; EC = Early Childhood; EL = Elementary School; HS = High School; ED =Education Ministry; HC =Human Care Ministry; SN = Special Needs Ministry; MD = Media Ministry (PC)=Partner Church Pastor. See Page 53 for the Table of Abbreviations for key to additional abbreviations

CITY	CONGREGATION EMAIL WEBSITE	YEAR EST	LOCATION MAILING ADDRESS	ZIP CODE(S)	DIST.	PASTOR(S)	PHONE FAX	WS SS BC	SCHOOLS/ MINISTRIES	STATISTIC Bapt	Conf	Avg Attend
ATHENS	*IMMANUEL*	1907	306 W WASHINGTON ST	62613	CI	Richard A Becker		WS 10 BC 915		16	15	9
ATWOOD	*IMMANUEL*		See Tuscola IL									
AUBURN	*TRINITY* www.trinityauburn.org	1953	1201 W JACKSON ST	62615	CI	Martin J Kaufmann	(217)438-6820	WS 9 SS 8 BC 8	EC/ED/ HC/SN	366	314	99
AURORA	*BETHANY*		See Naperville IL									
	EMMANUEL emmanuel.staff@yahoo.com emmanuelaurora.org	1901	550 4TH AVE	60505	NI	Jacob A Stoltzman	(630)851-2200 (630)851-7269	WS 9 SS 1030 BC 1030	ED/HC/MD	104	89	28
	HOPE hope4aurora@sbcglobal.net www.Hope4Aurora.com	1950	1575 RECKINGER RD	60505	NI	John A Fritz	(630)898-6754	WS 9	SN	45	33	19
	NEW SONG hello@newsongaurora.com www.newsongaurora.com/	2000	2858 HAFENRICHTER RD	60503	NI	Angel G Morales	(630)499-0542	WS 930	ED/HC/MD			
	SAN PABLO IGLESIALUTERANASP@GMAIL.COM	2005	555 E BENTON ST	60505	NI	Alex L Merlo Jorge Mazariegos	(630)820-3450 (630)820-3451	WS 1030 SS 915	ED/HC			
	ST LUKE		See Montgomery IL									
	ST PAUL info@stpaulaurora.org www.stpaulaurora.org	1857	85 S CONSTITUTION DR	60506	NI	Gary H Schultz	(630)896-3250	WS 8 1030 BC 930	ED/MD			
	ZION		See Naperville IL									
BALDWIN	*ST JOHN* stjohnch@egyptian.net stjohnbaldwin.ctsmemberconnect.net	1883	312 S 5th St P.O. BOX 162	62217	SI	Brian L Nowak	(618)785-2344	WS 9 BC 1015	ED/HC	229	207	45
BARRINGTON	*ST MATTHEW* office@stmatthewbarrington.org www.stmatthewbarrington.org	1932	720 DUNDEE AVE	60010	NI	Michael A Brown	(847)382-7002 (847)382-7017	WS 10 SS 9 BC 830	ED/HC	255	234	105
BARTLETT	*IMMANUEL* immanuelbartlett@sbcglobal.net immanuellutheranbartlett.com	1871	1116 E DEVON AVE	60103	NI	James G Bauman	(630)837-1166 (630)837-1193	WS 930 BC 1045	ED/HC/ MD/SN			
BATAVIA	*IMMANUEL* church@immanuelbatavia.org www.immanuelbatavia.org	1882	950 HART RD	60510	NI	Noah A Kegley Micah R Brown	(630)879-7163 (630)879-7614	WS 8 930 1045 SS 930 BC 930	EL/ED/HC/ MD/SN	1760	1725	380
	LORD OF LIFE		See Elburn IL									
BATH	*ST JOHN* banblesemann@juno.com stjohnsbath.weebly.com	1849	10844 N CR 1400 E 13961 E CR 1100N	62617	CI	Brian A Lesemann	(309)546-2434			250	186	40
BEARDSTOWN	*EVERGREEN PLACE* Satellite Site of St John Beardstown IL	2006	8570 St. Lukes Dr	62618								
	HERITAGE HEATH Satellite Site of St John Beardstown IL	2006	8306 St. Lukes dr	62618								
	ST JOHN stjohnslutheranbt@gmail.com	1848	601 Jefferson St 214 E 6TH ST	62618	CI	Keith A Kettner	(217)323-1288 (217)323-1288	WS 10 SS 9 BC 9	ED/HC/MD	225	167	73
BEECHER	*PEACE* secretary@ourpeacelutheran.org www.ourpeacelutheran.org/		540 Oak Park Ave 540 OAK PARK AVE P.O. BOX 369	60401	NI	Julian A LaMie	(708)946-2271	WS 1030		496	449	191
	PEACE LUTHERAN CHURCH Satellite Site of Peace Beecher IL	2023	28054 S Yates Ave	60401				WS 8				
BELLEVILLE	*BELLEVILLE HEALTHCARE CENTER* Satellite Site of Christ Our Savior Freeburg IL	2013	727 North 17th Street	62226								
	SIGNAL HILL welcome@signalhillchurch.org www.signalhillchurch.org	1931	8100 W MAIN ST	62223	SI	Mark D Wiesner	(618)397-1407 (618)397-9220	WS 8 920 1040 BC 1030	ED/HC/ MD/SN	123	119	52
	ZION churchoffice@zionbelleville.org www.zionbelleville.org	1861	1810 MCCLINTOCK AVE	62221	SI	Christopher A Spelbring Joshua A Kintz	(618)233-2299 (618)233-2324	WS 8 1045 SS 930 BC 930	EL/ED/HC/ MD/SN	1475	1138	402
BELVIDERE	*IMMANUEL* info@immanuelbelvidere.org www.immanuelbelvidere.org	1869	1045 Belvidere Rd 1225 E 2ND ST	61008	NI	Braun C Campbell Keith R Richard Carl M Gnewuch	(815)544-8058 (815)544-8059	WS 8 915 11 SS 915 BC 915	EL/HS/ED/ HC/MD/SN	1961	1606	371
BENSENVILLE	*ZION* pastor@zionconcord.org www.zionconcord.org	1837	865 S CHURCH RD	60106	NI	Stephen M Heuser	(630)766-1039 (630)766-2205	WS 9 SS 915 BC 920	EL/HS/ED/ HC/MD	279	259	117
BERWYN	*CONCORDIA* www.concordiaberwyn.org	1923	3144 HOME AVE	60402	EN	Christopher J Kolupa	(708)484-9784 (708)484-9832	WS 9 SS 1030 BC 1030	EC/EL/HS/ ED/HC/ MD/SN			
	GOOD SHEP/REDEEMER gsor.berwyn@gmail.com		6717 W 19th St 6717 19TH ST	60402	NI		(708)788-9054 (708)484-0525	WS 1230	ED/HC			
BETHALTO	*ZION* churchoffice@zionbethalto.org www.zionbethalto.org	1859	625 CHURCH DR	62010	SI	Kale W Hanson Brandon W Metcalf	(618)377-8314 (618)377-8740	WS 815 1045 SS 930	EL/ED/HC/ MD/SN	1534	1260	372
BEVERLY	*ST JOHN DIVINE*		See Chicago IL									
BIG ROCK	*IMMANUEL*		See Hinckley IL									
BLOOMINGTON	*GOOD SHEPHERD* office@goodshepherdblm.org www.goodshepherdblm.org	1993	3516 WHITE EAGLE DR	61704	CI	Chad D Lueck	(309)662-8905	WS 9 SS 1015 BC 1015	ED/HC/MD	121	115	78

*Indicates a new church start. A new church start is an intentionally organized gathering which comes together on a regular basis for the purpose of worship and/or Bible study and is intended to grow into a member LCMS congregation. WS =Worship Service; SS = Sunday School; BC =Bible Class; EC = Early Childhood; EL = Elementary School; HS = High School; ED =Education Ministry; HC =Human Care Ministry; SN = Special Needs Ministry; MD = Media Ministry (PC)=Partner Church Pastor. See Page 53 for the Table of Abbreviations for key to additional abbreviations

CITY	CONGREGATION EMAIL WEBSITE	YEAR EST	LOCATION MAILING ADDRESS	ZIP CODE(S)	DIST.	PASTOR(S)	PHONE FAX	WS SS BC	SCHOOLS/ MINISTRIES	STATISTIC Bapt	Conf	Avg Attend
BLOOMINGTON	*OUR REDEEMER* office@ourredeemerlcms.net www.ourredeemerlcms.net	1958	1822 E LINCOLN ST	61701	CI	Andrew D Smith	(309)662-3935 (309)662-5338	WS 9 SS 1015 BC 1015	ED/HC/MD	248	221	86
	TRINITY info@trinluth.org trinluth.org	1858	801 S MADISON ST	61701	CI	Charles A Bahn David L McBurney	(309)828-6265 (309)828-0831	WS 815 1030 SS 930 BC 930	EL/ED/HC/ MD/SN	2863	2180	467
BLUE ISLAND	*SALEM* salemchurch@comcast.net	1909	12951 S Maple Ave 12951 MAPLE AVE	60406	NI	Steven D Warren	(708)388-1830 (708)388-5176	WS 9	HC/MD	41	37	25
	ST JOHN DIVINE		See Chicago IL									
BLUFFS	*TRINITY*	1870	1585 Trinity Rd PO BOX 78	62621	CI		(217)754-3517	WS 9 SS 10	MD			
BOLINGBROOK	*DIVINE SHEPHERD* office@ds-lcms.org ds-lcms.org	1977	985 LILY CACHE LN	60440	NI	David C Zimmer	(630)759-5300	WS 830 SS 10 BC 10	ED/HC/ MD/SN	99	81	40
	ZION		See Naperville IL									
BONFIELD	*ZION* zionon17@outlook.com zionbonfield.org	1859	11478 W STATE ROUTE 17	60913	NI	Dwight D Wyeth	(815)426-2650	WS 10 SS 9 BC 9	ED/HC/MD			
BOURBONNAIS	*ST PAUL* kkoeppen@stpaulslutheran.net www.stpaulslutheran.net	1859	1780 CAREER CENTER RD	60914	NI	Karl J Koeppen Roger A Drinnon	(815)932-0312 (815)932-7588	WS 830 1105 SS 950 BC 950	EL/ED/HC/ MD/SN			
BOWEN	*ST PAUL'S* brosenda@adams.net	1932	202 W 5th St	62316	CI	Marcus R Jauss	(217)430-9372	WS 1030		60	47	25
BRADLEY	*ST PAUL*		See Bourbonnais IL									
BRIMFIELD	*ST PAUL*	1879	204 W Clay St PO BOX 297	61517	CI	Michael G Wagnitz	(309)446-3233	WS 10 SS		99	96	33
BROADLANDS	*IMMANUEL* crystal@immanuelbroadlands.com immanuelbroadlands.com	1876	390 COUNTY ROAD 2400 E	61816	CI		(217)834-3289	WS 9 SS 1015 BC 1015	HS/ED/MD	412	341	133
BROOKFIELD	*ST PAUL* stpaulbrookfield@comcast.net www.stpaulsbrookfield.org	1902	9035 GRANT AVE	60513	NI	Dr Edward A Naumann	(708)485-6987	WS 9 SS 1030 BC 1030	EL/ED/HC/ MD	238	198	152
BROWNSVILLE	*OUR SAVIOR*		See Carmi IL									
BRUSSELS	*ST MATTHEW*	1861	Prosker Ln PO BOX 14	62013	SI		(618)883-2351	WS 1030	ED/MD/SN			
BUCKLEY	*ST JOHNS* churchoffice@stjohnsbuckley.com www.stjohnsbuckley.com/Church.htm	1870	109 N Oak PO BOX 6	60918	CI	Jon K Wyckoff	(217)394-2444 (217)394-2444	WS 9 SS 10 BC 10	EL/HS/ED/ HC/MD	729	543	130
BUFFALO	*RISEN SAVIOR* pastordave@bueltmann.org		110 West Mc Manus PO BOX 212	62515	CI		(217)364-4513	SS 9 BC 9	ED/HC/MD	20	12	3
BUFFALO GROVE	*LIVING CHRIST*		See Arlington Heights IL									
BUNKER HILL	*ZION* zionbunkerhill@gmail.com	1892	609 E WARREN ST	62014	SI		(618)585-3606 (618)585-3606	WS 10 SS 845 BC 845	ED/HC/MD	340	232	86
BURBANK	*HOLY TRINITY* holytrinitynewlife@gmail.com www.holytrinitynewlife.org	1941	8659 S Sayre 8659 SAYRE AVE	60459	NI		(708)598-8070 (708)598-7305	WS 9 BC 1010	ED/HC			
BURNT PRAIRIE	*OUR SAVIOR*		See Carmi IL									
BURR RIDGE	*TRINITY* csecretary@tlbr.org www.tlbr.org	1865	11500 German Church Rd 11503 GERMAN CHURCH RD	60527	NI	Robert E Geaschel Christian B Dollar Luther G Albrecht	(708)839-1200 (708)839-8503	WS 830 11 SS 945 BC 945	EL/HS/ED/ HC/MD/SN	782	618	242
CALEDONIA	*IMMANUEL NORTH* Satellite Site of Immanuel Belvidere IL	2011	2940 Charleston Ct.	61011				WS 930 BC 1030				
CALUMET PARK	*MOUNT CALVARY* klaserrl@yahoo.com	1954	1301 W VERMONT AVE	60827	NI		(708)389-1010	WS 1045 SS 1210	HC	43	40	17
CALVIN	*OUR SAVIOR*		See Carmi IL									
CAMARGO	*IMMANUEL*		See Tuscola IL									
CAMPBELL HILL	*IMMANUEL* secretary@imstp.org www.imstp.org	1876	1699 Westpoint Rd 11854 WINE HILL RD STEELE- VILLE	62916 62288	SI	John M Sedwick	(618)426-3154	WS 8	ED/HC/ MD/SN			
	ST PETER spchlcms@gmail.com	1890	601 W Church St PO BOX 69	62916	SI		(618)426-9091	WS 9 SS 845	ED/HC/ MD/SN	282	244	49
CAMPTON HILLS	*LORD OF LIFE*		See Elburn IL									
CANTRALL	*GOOD SHEPHERD*		See Sherman IL									
CARBONDALE	*OUR SAVIOR* lutheran@siu.edu www.oslcdale.org	1930	700 S UNIVERSITY AVE	62901	SI	Jason S Holden Peter J Weeks	(618)549-1694	WS 10 SS 9 BC 11	ED/HC/ MD/SN	298	267	120
CARLINVILLE	*ZION* zioncarl2@frontier.com www.zion-carlinville.org	1856	501 S BROAD ST	62626	SI		(217)854-8514 (217)854-8514	WS 11 SS 945 BC 945	ED/HC/ MD/SN	531	317	35
CARLYLE	*BETHLEHEM*		See Ferrin IL									
	MESSIAH carlylemlc@sbcglobal.net	1934	1091 13TH ST	62231	SI	Timothy J Scharr	(618)594-3912 (618)594-3959		EC/HS/ ED/HC			
CARMI	*OUR SAVIOR* OurSaviorLutheran@protonmail.com facebook.com/OSLCarmi	1948	1102 JILL ST	62821	SI	Dean H Spooner	(618)384-5291	WS 930 SS 1045 BC 1045	ED/HC/SN			
CAROL STREAM	*OUR SAVIOR* office@oursavior.com www.oursavior.com	1981	1244 W ARMY TRAIL RD	60188	NI	Kenneth A Estes	(630)830-4833 (630)483-3148	WS 930 BC 1045	ED/HC/MD	265	231	98
CARPENTER	*ZION*	1902	6409 QUERCUS GROVE RD EDWARDSVILLE	62025	SI	Dustin J Krystowiak	(618)656-4492	WS 8 SS 730 BC 730				
CARPENTERSVILLE	*CROSSPOINT LAKEWOOD*		See Lakewood IL									

*Indicates a new church start. A new church start is an intentionally organized gathering which comes together on a regular basis for the purpose of worship and/or Bible study and is intended to grow into a member LCMS congregation. WS =Worship Service; SS = Sunday School; BC =Bible Class; EC = Early Childhood; EL = Elementary School; HS = High School; ED =Education Ministry; HC =Human Care Ministry; SN = Special Needs Ministry; MD = Media Ministry (PC)=Partner Church Pastor. See Page 53 for the Table of Abbreviations for key to additional abbreviations

CITY	CONGREGATION EMAIL WEBSITE	YEAR EST	LOCATION MAILING ADDRESS	ZIP CODE(S)	DIST.	PASTOR(S)	PHONE FAX	WS SS BC	SCHOOLS/ MINISTRIES	STATISTIC Bapt	Conf	Avg Attend
CARPENTERSVILLE	*FAITH* faithlc61@att.net www.faithlccville.com	1960	2505 Helm Rd PO BOX 366 CARPENTERSVLE	60110	NI	Mark A Frusti Carlos Catalan	(847)428-2079 (847)428-2079	WS 10 BC 9	ED/HC			
CARROLLTON	*OUR REDEEMER* ourredeemercarrollton@gmail.com www.our-redeemer-lutheran-church.org	1933	208 7TH ST	62016	SI	Steven J Jacobsen	(217)942-3168	WS 9 SS 1015 BC 1015	ED/HC/ MD/SN	244	173	36
CARTHAGE	*ST PAUL'S*		See Bowen IL									
CARY	*CROSSPOINT LAKEWOOD*		See Lakewood IL									
	HOLY CROSS hclchurch@holycrosscary.org www.holycrosscary.org	1911	2107 Three Oaks Rd 2107 3 OAKS RD	60013	NI	Zachary J Patterson	(847)639-1702 (847)639-6702	WS 830 1045 SS 1030	EL/ED/HC/ MD/SN	324	324	103
CASEY	*TRINITY* TrinityLutheranCasey@hotmail.com	1947	201 E Colorado Ave PO BOX 295	62420	CI	Adrian L Piazza	(217)932-2645	WS 830 SS 745	ED/HC/ MD/SN	91	86	25
CASEYVILLE	*HOLY CROSS*		See Collinsville IL									
CENTRALIA	*TRINITY* tlcsecretary@trinitycentralia.org www.trinitycentralia.org	1892	201 S PLEASANT AVE	62801	SI	James L Hennig	(618)532-2614	WS 830 SS 10 BC 10	EL/HS/ED/ HC/MD/SN	425	356	85
CHAMPAIGN	*FRIENDSHIP/JOY* officemanager@friendshiplutheran.com www.friendshiplutheran.com	1991	3601 S DUNCAN RD	61822	CI	Glen M Triplett	(217)355-0454	WS 9 SS 1015 BC 1015	ED/HC/MD	92	88	44
	ST JOHN churchoffice@stjohn-lcms.church www.stjohn-lcms.org	1855	509 S MATTIS AVE	61821	CI	Jeffrey E Caithamer	(217)359-1123	WS 8 1045 SS 930 BC 930	EL/ED/HC/ MD	984	712	286
	UNIVERSITY churchoffice@uniluchampaign.org uniluchampaign.org	1941	604 E Chalmers 604 E CHALMERS ST	61820	CI	Michael P Schuermann	(217)344-1558	WS 1030 BC 930	ED/MD			
CHANDLERVILLE	*SALEM* banblesemann@juno.com salemchandlerville.weebly.com	1871	Mechanics St PO BOX 221	62627	CI	Brian A Lesemann	(309)546-2434	SS 830		70	57	15
CHANNAHON	*RIVER OF LIFE* www.rolchannahon.org	1997	24901 S SAGE ST	60410	NI	Jackson R Scofield	(815)467-0641	WS 9 SS 1015 BC 1015				
CHAPIN	*ST PAUL*	1850	1931 St Pauls Church Rd 1931 SAINT PAULS CHURCH RD	62628	CI	Andrew P Dierks	(217)472-7891	WS 10 SS 9 BC 9				
CHARLESTON	*IMMANUEL* office@immanuelcharleston.com immanuelcharleston.com	1925	902 CLEVELAND AVE	61920	CI	Samuel S Smith	(217)345-3008	WS 9 SS 915	EC/ED/HC/ MD/SN	190	132	56
CHATHAM	*ST JOHN* stjohnsoffice@comcast.net www.stjohnschathamil.org	1877	1225 N MAIN ST	62629	CI	Kevin C Wendorf	(217)483-2612	WS 9 SS 1030 BC 1030	EC/HS/ED/ HC/MD/SN	358	283	109
CHEBANSE	*ZION* zionoffice@comcast.net zionchebanse.net	1895	190 CONCORDIA DR	60922	NI	Benjamin M Hayter	(815)697-2212 (815)697-3302	WS 930 BC 1045	HS/ED/ MD/SN	587	433	64
CHENOA	*ST PAUL* stpaullutheranchenoa@gmail.com www.stpaulchenoa.org	1864	800 S Division St 405 EMMA ST	61726	CI	Kyle C Ronchetto	(815)945-5331	WS 1030 SS 930 BC 930	ED/HC/ MD/SN	296	228	66
CHESTER	*ST JOHN* sjschurchsecretary@gmail.com www.sjshornets.com	1849	302 W HOLMES ST	62233	SI	Timothy A Sims	(618)826-3545	WS 745 10 SS 9 BC 9	EL/ED/HC/ MD/SN	976	784	217
CHESTNUT	*ZION* zionlutheranchestnut@frontier.com christandzionlutheran.org	1892	401 N Logan St PO BOX 107	62518	CI	David M Dunlop	(217)796-3386	WS 1030 SS 9 BC 9	ED/HC/MD	124	84	65
CHICAGO	*BETHANY* stevebaldauf73@gmail.com	1905	Graceland Cemetary Chapel 4001 N Clark	60639	EN		(331)356-2084	WS 945	ED			
	BETHESDA	1920	6803 N CAMPBELL AVE	60645	EN	Dr Paul E Bacon Jean A Bingue Dr Shadrach Katari	(773)743-6460 (773)743-4415	WS 1030	EL/ED/HC			
	CHATHAM FIELDS chathamfields@yahoo.com chathamfields.org	1939	8050 S SAINT LAWRENCE AVE	60619	EN	Keith Kinslow	(773)723-3661 (773)723-3672	WS 1030 SS 9				
	CHRIST ENGLISH christenglish1@aol.com www.christenglcms.org	1891	1511 N LONG AVE	60651	EN	Clarence J Wright Sr	(773)637-4800 (708)889-9921	WS 12	ED/HC/MD			
	CHRIST KING geribrazeal@gmail.com	1951	3715-3719 S Lake Park Ave 3701 S LAKE PARK AVE	60653	NI	John Brazeal	(773)536-1984	WS 11 12 SS 10	EL/ED/HC/ MD/SN			
	CONCORDIA info@concordiabelmont.org concordiabelmont.org	1891	2645 W BELMONT AVE	60618	NI		(773)207-5811	WS 9				
	DR MARTIN LUTHER dadchilos@gmail.com	1913	5344 S FRANCISCO AVE	60632	S	Richard L Ramirez	(440)360-0390	WS 10 BC 1115	ED/HC	32	22	23
	EPHPHATHA-DEAF ephphathalutheran@gmail.com elcofthedeaf.weebly.com/	1920	7956 S M L King Dr 7956 S KING DR	60619	EN	Prentice D Marsh	(773)723-3232					
	FAITH	1911	8300 S SANGAMON ST	60620	EN		(773)488-8286 (773)488-0468	WS 11 SS 930	ED/HC			
	FIRST BETHLEHEM office@fblcchicago.org www.fblcchicago.org	1871	1649 W LE MOYNE ST	60622	NI		(773)276-2338	WS 1045 BC 930	ED/HC/ MD/SN			
	FIRST ST PAUL office@fspauls.org www.fspauls.org	1846	1301 N LA SALLE DR	60610	NI	Dr Jeffrey W Leininger	(312)642-7172 (312)642-1608	WS 930 SS 1045 BC 1045	ED/HC	195	179	96
	GLORIA DEI secretary@mygloriadei.com www.mygloriadei.com	1940	5259 S MAJOR AVE	60638	NI	Steven J Anderson	(773)767-2771 (773)767-4670	WS 9 BC 8	ED/MD/SN			

*Indicates a new church start. A new church start is an intentionally organized gathering which comes together on a regular basis for the purpose of worship and/or Bible study and is intended to grow into a member LCMS congregation. WS =Worship Service; SS = Sunday School; BC =Bible Class; EC = Early Childhood; EL = Elementary School; HS = High School; ED =Education Ministry; HC =Human Care Ministry; SN = Special Needs Ministry; MD = Media Ministry (PC)=Partner Church Pastor. See Page 53 for the Table of Abbreviations for key to additional abbreviations

CITY	CONGREGATION EMAIL WEBSITE	YEAR EST	LOCATION MAILING ADDRESS	ZIP CODE(S)	DIST.	PASTOR(S)	PHONE FAX	WS SS BC	SCHOOLS/ MINISTRIES	STATISTIC Bapt	Conf	Avg Attend
CHICAGO	*GRACE ENGLISH* graceenglish@comcast.net www.graceenglish.org	1920	2725 N LARAMIE AVE	60639	EN		(773)637-1177 (773)637-1188	WS 9	ED			
	HOLY CROSS holycross1886@gmail.com www.holycrosschicago.net	1886	3116 S RACINE AVE	60608	NI	Dr Carlos A Ortiz-Lugo	(773)523-3838	WS 1030 SS 1030	ED/MD/SN	99	71	20
	HOLY CROSS		See Alsip IL									
	JEHOVAH-EL BUEN PAST rsalgado@gscachicago.org	1904	3740 W BELDEN AVE	60647	NI	Fernando Gomez	(773)342-5854 (773)342-6048	WS 1030	EL/ED/HC/ MD/SN	38	38	40
	MESSIAH messiahchgo@sbcglobal.net www.messiahchicago.org	1924	6201 W PATTERSON AVE	60634	NI		(773)725-8903 (773)202-7671	WS 930	ED/HC/SN	106	73	30
	MOUNT GREENWOOD mtgrnwdluthchurch@gmail.com	1943	10901 S TRUMBULL AVE	60655	NI		(773)445-6080 (773)445-6080	WS 930	ED/MD	43	40	10
	OUR SAVIOUR pastor@oursaviourls.org www.oursaviourls.org	1933	3457 N NEVA AVE	60634	NI		(773)736-1120 (773)736-4851	WS 930	ED/SN	50	45	18
	RESURRECTION rlc9349@gmail.com www.resurrectionchicago.com/	1952	9349 S WENTWORTH AVE	60620	NI		(773)928-6311	WS 1045	ED/HC			
	SAINT JAMES church@stjames-lutheran.org stjameschicago.com	1869	2050 N Fremont St 2101 N FREMONT ST	60614	NI	Joel A Hess Ethan M Boester	(773)549-1615 (773)326-3645	WS 830 11 SS 945 BC 10	EL/ED/HC/ MD/SN	1057	753	396
	SALEM		See Homewood IL									
	ST JOHN office@stjohnschicago.org www.stjohnschicago.org	1875	4939 W MONTROSE AVE	60641	NI	Jacob W Ehrhard	(773)736-1112 (773)736-3614	WS 9 6 SS 1015 BC 1015	EL/ED/HC	597	511	81
	ST JOHN DIVINE sjdchicago@outlook.com ChicagoLutheran.com	1928	10511 S OAKLEY AVE	60643	EN		(773)238-2320	WS 1030 BC 12	ED/HC/MD	40	30	36
	ST MATTHEW ceelly1973@gmail.com stmatthewchicago.org	1871	2108 W 21ST ST	60608	NI	Cesar G Sifuentes	(312)636-6496 (773)847-6471			62	62	40
	ST PAUL stpauloffice2@yahoo.com www.stpaulaustin.com	1886	857 N Menard Ave 846 N MENARD AVE	60651	NI		(773)378-6644 (773)378-7442	WS 10 BC 9	EL/HS/ED/ HC/SN			
	ST PAUL stpauldorchester76@att.net www.stpauldorchester.com	1888	7621 S Dorchester 7621 S DORCHESTER AVE	60619	NI	Jeffrey P Howell	(773)721-2350 (773)721-1749	WS 10 SS 915	EL/ED/HC			
	ST PAUL		See Melrose Park IL									
	ST PAUL		See Norwood Park Twp IL									
	ST PETER	1871	8550 S KEDVALE AVE	60652	NI		(773)582-0470	WS 9	HC			
	ST PHILIP	1926	6232 S EBERHART AVE	60637	NI	Elstner C Lewis Jr	(773)493-3865 (773)493-8680	WS 11 BC 930	ED/HC			
	ST PHILIP NORTH www.stphiliplutheran.com	1893	2500 W BRYN MAWR AVE	60659	NI	Thomas E Engel	(773)561-9830 (773)561-9831	WS 10 SS 9 BC 9	EL			
	ST STEPHEN	1886	910 W 65th St 6455 S PEORIA ST	60621	NI		(773)783-0416	WS 11 SS 9	ED/HC/MD			
	TABOR info@taborchicago.org taborchicago.org	1906	3542 W SUNNYSIDE AVE	60625	NI	Philip D Robarge Walter J Ramirez	(773)588-4040	WS 10 SS 10	ED/HC/MD	95	76	55
	TRINITY	1887	13200 S BURLEY AVE	60633	NI		(773)646-3811	WS 9				
	TRINITY		See Lisle IL									
	TRINITY GALEWOOD Satellite Site of Trinity Lisle IL	2015	1701 N Narragansett Ave	60639				WS 1030 SS 1030				
CHICAGO HEIGHTS	*ST PAUL* spchurchoffice@yahoo.com stpaulsch.com	1882	330 W HIGHLAND DR CHICAGO HTS	60411	NI	Dr Vernon E Wendt Jr	(708)754-4493	WS 1015 SS 930 BC 930	ED/HC/ MD/SN			
CICERO	*FAITH*	1945	6011 W 36th St 3615 S 61ST AVE	60804	NI	Guillermo Jerez	(708)439-8839	WS 8 SS 1130	EL/HS			
CISSNA PARK	*IMMANUEL*	1882	996 N State Route 49 PO BOX 95	60924	CI							
	ST JOHN'S		See Onarga IL									
	TRINITY trinitycissna@yahoo.com www.facebook.com/profile. php?id=61550058556343	1928	302 S 4TH ST	60924	CI	Dale A Fjordbotten	(815)457-2739	WS 830 SS 930 BC 930	ED/MD	325	257	54
CLAYTON	*GOOD SHEPHERD*	1934	103 E Morgan 103 E MORGAN ST	62324	CI	Kirk R Cunningham	(217)894-7717	WS 9 SS 10 1011 BC 10	ED/HC	50	50	34
CLINTON	*CHRIST* pastordunlop@gmail.com christandzionlutheran.org	1957	701 S MULBERRY ST	61727	CI	David M Dunlop	(217)935-5808	WS 815	EC/ED/HC	104	80	42
COAL CITY	*FRIENDS IN CHRIST*		See Morris IL									
COAL VALLEY	*TRINITY* trinityCV1@gmail.com trinitylutherancv.org	1916	2815 W 3rd St PO BOX 160	61240	CI	David C Anderson	(309)799-5650 (309)799-5603	WS 9 SS 1015 BC 1015	ED/HC/ MD/SN	131	116	62
COLLINSVILLE	*GOOD SHEPHERD* www.goodshepherdcollinsville.org	1959	1300 BELT LINE RD	62234	SI	Andrew L Packer Michael P Walther Andrew W Gray	(618)344-3151 (618)344-3378	WS 8 1030 SS 915 BC 915	EL/HS/ED/ HC/MD/SN	1326	1122	440

*Indicates a new church start. A new church start is an intentionally organized gathering which comes together on a regular basis for the purpose of worship and/or Bible study and is intended to grow into a member LCMS congregation. WS =Worship Service; SS = Sunday School; BC =Bible Class; EC = Early Childhood; EL = Elementary School; HS = High School; ED =Education Ministry; HC =Human Care Ministry; SN = Special Needs Ministry; MD = Media Ministry (PC)=Partner Church Pastor. See Page 53 for the Table of Abbreviations for key to additional abbreviations

CITY	CONGREGATION EMAIL WEBSITE	YEAR EST	LOCATION MAILING ADDRESS	ZIP CODE(S)	DIST.	PASTOR(S)	PHONE FAX	WS SS BC	SCHOOLS/ MINISTRIES	STATISTIC Bapt	Conf	Avg Attend
COLLINSVILLE	*HOLY CROSS* office@holycross-collinsville.org www.holycross-collinsville.org	1848	304 SOUTH ST	62234	SI	Dale A Skeesick	(618)344-3145 (618)344-1222	WS 8 1030 SS 915 BC 915	EL/HS/ED/ HC/MD	1005	778	250
	JERUSALEM dougnicely81@gmail.com	1903	305 Collinsville Ave 514 W SOUTH ST MASCOUTAH	62234 62258	SI	Dr Douglas A Nicely	(618)346-1925	WS 10 SS 9 BC 9	HC			
COLUMBIA	*ST PAUL'S* secretary@stpauls-lcms.org www.stpauls-lcms.org	1841	227 N Goodhaven St 227 GOODHAVEN ST	62236	SI	Dr Stephen N Krenz	(618)281-4600 (618)281-4600	WS 8 1030 SS 915 BC 915	EC/ED/HC/ MD/SN	636	501	135
	THE WAY info@theway618.church theway618.church	2022	600 COLUMBIA CENTER DR	62236	S	Jonathan R Palmer	(618)504-8585	WS 9 1030 1045	ED/HC/MD	237	234	191
CONANT	*TRINITY*		See Pinckneyville IL									
CORTLAND	*LORD OF LIFE*		See Elburn IL									
COUNTRY CLUB HILLS	*ST JOHN'S* secretary@sjcch.com www.sjcch.org	1849	4247 W. 183RD ST	60478	NI		(708)798-4131	WS 9 BC 945	ED/HC/MD			
COUNTRYSIDE	*HOPE* hopelcl@comcast.net www.hopecountrysideil.org	1957	6455 JOLIET RD LAGRANGE HLDS	60525	NI	Steven J Anderson	(708)354-6176 (708)588-9723	WS 1045 SS 930 BC 930	ED/HC/MD	30	30	18
COVINGTON	*ST LUKE*		See Okawville IL									
CRESTWOOD	*HOLY CROSS*		See Alsip IL									
CROSSVILLE	*OUR SAVIOR*		See Carmi IL									
CRYSTAL LAKE	*CROSSPOINT LAKEWOOD*		See Lakewood IL									
	IMMANUEL www.immanuelcl.org	1870	300 S PATHWAY CT	60014	NI	Dr Larry W Tieman James A Kirk	(815)459-1441 (815)459-1462	WS 8 930 11 SS 930 BC 930	EL/ED/HC/ MD/SN	2006	1253	582
	PRINCE PEACE info@prince-of-peace.org www.prince-of-peace.org	1974	932 McHenry Ave 932 S MCHENRY AVE	60014	NI	Larry D Rubeck	(815)455-3200 (815)455-6323	WS 830 1030 SS 1030 BC 940	EC/ED/MD	283	239	74
	THE POINTE Satellite Site of Immanuel Crystal Lake IL	2003	5650 Northwest Hwy	60014								
DALTON CITY	*MOUNT CALVARY*		See Decatur IL									
DANVERS	*ZION* Fwz@frontiernet.net ziondanvers.com	1872	204 W North St PO BOX 545	61732	CI	Frank W Zimmerman	(309)963-4825	WS 1030	HC/MD			
DANVILLE	*HAWTHORNE INN* Satellite Site of Trinity Danville IL	2014	3222 Independence Dr	61832								
	IMMANUEL ilcd.churchsec@gmail.com www.ilcdanville.com	1896	1930 N Bowman Ave 1930 N BOWMAN AVENUE RD	61832	CI	James E Yonkers	(217)442-5675	WS 930 SS 830 BC 830	EC/ED/HC/ MD	589	428	111
	TRINITY trinitylutheranchurch824@gmail.com trinitylutherandanvilleil.com	1863	824 E MAIN ST	61832	CI	Kent A Tibben	(217)446-4300	WS 930 SS 830 BC 830	EL/ED/HC/ MD	499	393	111
DARIEN	*ST JOHN* office@stjohndarienil.org www.stjohndarienil.org	1859	7214 S CASS AVE	60561	NI	Eli B Voigt	(630)969-7987 (630)969-8204	WS 9 SS 1015 BC 1030	ED/HC/MD			
DARMSTADT	*TRINITY* stpaultrinity@gmail.com	1865	900 BELSHA ST NEW ATHENS	62264	SI	Lyle E Buettner	(618)696-2649	WS 9 SS 10	MD/SN			
DECATUR	*CONCORDIA* concordiadecatur@comcast.net www.concordialutherandecatur.com	1964	3303 E MARYLAND ST	62521	CI	Dr David J Bueltmann	(217)428-6421 (217)428-6421	WS 9 SS 1015 BC 1015	EL/HS/SN	94	75	24
	MOUNT CALVARY office@mtcalvarydecatur.org mtcalvarydecatur.org	1954	2055 S Franklin St Rd 2055 S FRANKLIN STREET RD	62521	CI	Brett M Hinrichs	(217)428-0641	WS 9 SS 1030 BC 1030	EC/EL/HS/ ED/HC/MD	325	261	115
	ST JOHN office@stjohnsdecatur.com www.stjohnsdecatur.com	1891	2727 N UNION BLVD	62526	CI	Adam M Ray Aaron T Bird	(217)875-3656 (217)875-7242	WS 830 11 SS 930 BC 930	EL/HS/ED/ HC/MD	1300	1108	185
	ST PAUL'S info@spldecatur.org spldecatur.org	1860	1 BACHRACH CT	62526	CI	Robert L Goodwin Mark A Gearig William D Grueninger	(217)423-6955	WS 8 1030 SS 915 BC 915	EL/HS/ED/ HC/MD/SN	2802	1874	559
	TRINITY office@trinitydecatur.com www.trinitydecatur.com	1927	1960 E JOHNS AVE	62521	CI	Matthew O Versemann	(217)422-3630 (217)422-8901	WS 9 SS 1015 BC 1015	EL/HS/ED/ HC/MD	218	170	70
DEKALB	*IMMANUEL* office@godwithusilc.org www.immanuelDeKalb.com	1909	511 RUSSELL RD	60115	NI	Martin L Marks	(815)756-6669 (815)756-9585	WS 8 1030 SS 915 BC 915	EC/ED/HC/ MD			
	IMMANUEL		See Hinckley IL									
	LORD OF LIFE		See Elburn IL									
DELAVAN	*CHRIST* pr.jsiegel@gmail.com	1957	306 N Locust St PO BOX 477	61734	CI		(309)244-7200 (309)244-7200	WS 830 BC 915	ED/MD			
DES PLAINES	*IMMANUEL* immanueldp@immanueldp.org www.immanueldp.org	1871	855 LEE ST	60016	NI	Christopher J LaBoube Dr Tony Davison	(847)824-3652 (847)824-3687	WS 9 SS 1015 BC 1015	ED/HC/ MD/SN	145	136	50
DIETERICH	*GRACE*	1915	206 Fayette St PO BOX 1	62424	CI		(217)925-5349		ED/HC/ MD/SN	111	84	12
	ST JOHN dualparish@mmtcnet.com www.stjohndieterich.com	1860	22775 E 700th Ave PO BOX 18	62424	CI	Dean Z Herberts	(217)739-2252	WS 830 SS 930 BC 930	ED/HC/SN	208	150	77
DIXON	*CHRIST OUR SAVIOR* coslcdixon@gmail.com coslcdixon.org	1984	2035 IL ROUTE 26	61021	NI	David J Andermann	(815)284-4554 (815)284-4556	WS 9 SS 1020 BC 1020	EL/ED/HC/ MD/SN	78	76	33

*Indicates a new church start. A new church start is an intentionally organized gathering which comes together on a regular basis for the purpose of worship and/or Bible study and is intended to grow into a member LCMS congregation. WS =Worship Service; SS = Sunday School; BC =Bible Class; EC = Early Childhood; EL = Elementary School; HS = High School; ED =Education Ministry; HC =Human Care Ministry; SN = Special Needs Ministry; MD = Media Ministry (PC)=Partner Church Pastor. See Page 53 for the Table of Abbreviations for key to additional abbreviations

CITY	CONGREGATION EMAIL WEBSITE	YEAR EST	LOCATION MAILING ADDRESS	ZIP CODE(S)	DIST.	PASTOR(S)	PHONE FAX	WS SS BC	SCHOOLS/ MINISTRIES	STATISTIC Bapt	Conf	Avg Attend
DORSEY	*EMMAUS* www.emmauslcmsdorsey.org/home.html	1859	5215 LOOP RD	62021	SI		(618)377-6221	WS 10 SS 9 BC 9	HC			
DOWNERS GROVE	*IMMANUEL* ilcdg@ilcdg.org www.ilcdg.org	1909	5211 CARPENTER ST	60515	NI	Dr Christopher N James	(630)968-3112	WS 8 10	EC/ED/HC/ MD/SN	874	630	210
DU QUOIN	*BETHEL* bethelduquoin@gmail.com www.bethelduquoin.org	1928	699 W MAIN ST	62832	SI		(618)542-3418	WS 1045				
DUNDEE	*BETHLEHEM*		See West Dundee IL									
	IMMANUEL		See East Dundee IL									
	ST PETER stpeterlutheran@stpeterlutheran.org stpeterlutheran.org	1887	18N377 GALLIGAN RD	60118	NI	Bruce P Milash	(847)428-4054 (847)428-1640	WS 9 1030 SS 1030 BC 6	ED/HC/MD			
DWIGHT	*EMMANUEL* emmanueldwight@gmail.com www.emmanueldwight.org	1867	325 E MAZON AVE	60420	NI	Dr John F Mueller	(815)584-3433 (815)584-1291	WS 10 SS 9 BC 830	ED/HC/ MD/SN	198	162	55
	TRINITY	1854	515 E Stonewall Rd PO BOX 27	60420	NI	William T Mitschke		WS 930	ED	54	35	26
EAST DUBUQUE	*ST PAUL*		See Dubuque IA									
EAST DUNDEE	*IMMANUEL* immanuel@immanuel-ed.org www.immanuel-ed.org	1854	310 E MAIN ST	60118	NI	William P Yonker Adam L Tanney Bruce W Meissner	(847)428-4477 (847)428-4580	WS 8 1030 BC 915	EL/ED/HC/ MD/SN			
EAST MOLINE	*CHRIST THE KING* cristorey-em@sbcglobal.net		1301 19th Street 1301 19TH ST	61244	CI	Pablo G Dominguez	(309)738-6124		ED/HC/MD	28	18	18
	HOPE CREEK CARE NURSING HOME Satellite Site of Trinity Coal Valley IL	1971	4343 Kennedy Dr	61244								
	ST JOHN office@stjohnsem.org www.stjohnsem.org	1918	1450 30TH AVE	61244	CI		(309)792-0755 (309)792-0776	WS 9 SS 1015 BC 1015	ED/HC/ MD/SN	494	424	123
	ZION zlchamptonbluff@gmail.com www.ZionEM.com	1852	17628 HUBBARD RD	61244	CI	Gary A Wright	(309)496-2186 (309)469-9076	WS 9 SS 1015	HC/MD/SN			
EAST PEORIA	*ST PETERS* secretary@stpeters-epil.org www.stpeters-epil.com	1895	200 E Cole St 200 COLE ST	61611	CI	Brian N Pape	(309)699-5411 (309)699-9776	WS 8 1045 SS 925 BC 930		187	187	75
EAST SAINT LOUIS	*UNITY*	1901	4200 CASEYVILLE AVE	62204	SI	Dr Willie P Stallworth Sr	(618)874-6600 (618)874-7546	WS 12 SS 11	EL/ED/HC/ MD/SN			
EDINBURG	*TRINITY* tlcedinburg@gmail.com www.trinitylutheranedinburg.com	1894	205 N Campbell PO BOX 259	62531	CI	Gaylord J Spilker	(618)267-5673	WS 10 SS 9 BC 9	ED/HC/MD	194	132	25
EDWARDSVILLE	*TRINITY* church@trinitylutheranministries.org trinitylutheranministries.org	1901	600 WATER ST	62025	SI	John C Shank Jess R Biermann	(618)656-2918 (618)656-5941	WS 8 1030 SS 915 BC 915	EL/HS/ED/ HC/MD/SN	1739	1395	420
	ZION		See Carpenter IL									
EFFINGHAM	*ST JOHN* office@stjohnslcms.net www.stjohnslcms.net	1866	901 W JEFFERSON AVE	62401	CI	Michael H Burdick Trey R Dille	(217)342-4334	WS 8 1030 SS 915 BC 915	EC/ED/HC/ MD/SN	986	785	399
EL PASO	*TRINITY* trinitylutheranelpaso@gmail.com www.trinitylutheranchurchelpaso.com	1947	533 W 3RD ST	61738	CI	Jonathan P Boehne	(309)527-4333	WS 10 SS 9 BC 9	EC/ED/HC/ MD	222	199	110
ELBURN	*LORD OF LIFE* lol@lolchurch.net lolchurch.net	1990	40W605 Rt 38 40W605 IL RTE 38	60119	NI	Matthew D Blackford	(630)513-5325	WS 830 10 SS 10	EC/ED/HC/ MD			
ELDORADO	*FAITH SALINE COUNTY** otter59@hotmail.com		901 STATE ST STE C	62930	SI		(618)273-9792	WS 9 SS 8	HC/MD			
ELGIN	*CALVARY* office@clce.org clce.org	1956	535 N Mc Lean Blvd 535 N MCLEAN BLVD.	60123	NI	Mark C Bestul	(847)741-5433	WS 8 1045 SS 925 BC 915	ED/HC	295	250	186
	GOOD SHEPHERD choffice@gselgin.org www.gselgin.org	1939	195 NESLER RD	60124	NI	Steven R Maske	(847)741-7788 (847)697-4916	WS 830 10 SS 10	EC/ED/HC/ MD/SN	432	349	175
	KING OF GLORY kogelgin@gmail.com www.kogelgin.org	1989	36W720 HOPPS RD	60123	NI	Matthew S Kusch	(847)931-1520	WS 815 1045 SS 9 BC 930	ED	125	120	75
	LORD OF LIFE		See Elburn IL									
	SAINT JOHN'S churchoffice@stjohnselgin.org www.stjohnselgin.org	1859	115 N. Spring Street 101 N. SPRING STREET	60120	NI	Aaron R Levenhagen	(847)741-0814 (847)741-0859	WS 1030 SS 930 BC 1015	EL/ED/HC/ MD/SN	420	308	130
ELIZABETH	*ST PAUL* stpaulelizabethil@gmail.com www.stpaulelizabeth.org	1895	411 W Catlin St 411 W CATLIN ST P O BOX 506	61028	NI	Michael A Nesbit	(815)858-3334	WS 9 BC 10	ED/HC/MD	171	147	85
ELK GROVE VILLAGE	*HOLY SPIRIT* secretary@holyspiritegv.org www.holyspiritegv.org	1957	150 LIONS DR ELK GROVE VLG	60007	EN		(847)437-5897 (847)437-5899	WS 9 SS 1030 BC 1030	ED/HC/MD			
ELMHURST	*IMMANUEL* office@immanuelelmhurst.org www.immanuelelmhurst.org	1892	142 E 3RD ST	60126	NI	David W Seabaugh Jeremy A Steinke	(630)832-1649	WS 830 11 SS 945 BC 945	EL/HS/ED/ HC/MD/SN	932	786	270
	MESSIAH mlcelmhurst@gmail.com www.messiahelmhurstlcms.org	1961	130 W BUTTERFIELD RD	60126	EN	Bradford C Maxon	(630)279-4775	WS 1030 SS 915	ED/HC/ MD/SN			

*Indicates a new church start. A new church start is an intentionally organized gathering which comes together on a regular basis for the purpose of worship and/or Bible study and is intended to grow into a member LCMS congregation. WS =Worship Service; SS = Sunday School; BC =Bible Class; EC = Early Childhood; EL = Elementary School; HS = High School; ED =Education Ministry; HC =Human Care Ministry; SN = Special Needs Ministry; MD = Media Ministry (PC)=Partner Church Pastor. See Page 53 for the Table of Abbreviations for key to additional abbreviations

CONGREGATIONS

CITY	CONGREGATION EMAIL WEBSITE	YEAR EST	LOCATION MAILING ADDRESS	ZIP CODE(S)	DIST.	PASTOR(S)	PHONE FAX	WS SS BC	SCHOOLS/ MINISTRIES	STATISTIC Bapt	Conf	Avg Attend
ELMHURST	*REDEEMER* office345@redeemerlcms.com www.redeemerlcms.com	1928	123 E. ST. CHARLES ROAD	60126	EN	Anthony J Oliphant	(630)834-1411	WS 10 SS 9 BC 9	ED/MD/SN	212	178	68
EMMA	*OUR SAVIOR*		See Carmi IL									
ENFIELD	*OUR SAVIOR*		See Carmi IL									
EPWORTH	*OUR SAVIOR*		See Carmi IL									
EUREKA	*OUR REDEEMER* orlceureka@gmail.com	1923	698 Reagan Dr PO BOX 273	61530	CI	Joseph G Burns	(309)467-5477	WS 930 SS 945 BC 945	ED/HC/ MD/SN	147	115	55
EVANSTON	*BETHLEHEM* pastorbroecker@aol.com www.bethlehemevanston.com	1872	1334 WESLEY AVE	60201	NI	Mark F Broecker	(847)328-9454 (847)328-9467	WS 10 SS 9 BC 9	ED/HC/SN			
EVANSVILLE	*ST JOHN* stjohnlutheranruma@gmail.com www.stjohnlutheranruma.com	1848	8446 1ST RD	62242	SI		(618)282-6060	WS 830 SS 930	ED/HC	125	49	15
	ST JOHN		See Baldwin IL									
	ST PETER	1871	900 Church St PO BOX 27	62242	SI		(618)853-2322	WS 830 10 SS 9	ED/HC/SN			
FAIRVIEW HEIGHTS	*BETHANY* www.bethanylcms.org	1977	5600 OLD COLLINSVILLE RD FAIRVIEW HTS	62208	SI	Jeffrey B Hemmer	(618)632-6906	WS 930 SS 1045 BC 1045	ED/HC	65	53	33
	HOLY CROSS		See Collinsville IL									
FARMERSVILLE	*ZION* zionevanlc@gmail.com	1889	501 Nobbe St PO BOX 19	62533	SI	Dr Micheal M Strong	(217)725-1717	WS 10 SS 9 BC 9	ED/HC/ MD/SN	65	52	15
FERRIN	*BETHLEHEM* bethlehemferrinchurch@gmail.com www.bethlehemlutheranferrin.org	1905	12903 CLARA ST CARLYLE	62231	SI	Jonathan P Jennings	(618)545-9543	WS 930 SS 830 BC 830	EC/HS/ED/ MD	248	210	84
FLORA	*FAITH*	1929	600 W 12TH ST	62839	SI	Paul M Pater	(618)662-9500	WS 10	ED/HC/ MD/SN	39	32	15
FOREST PARK	*ST JOHN* stjohnchurch@stjohnforestpark.org stjohnforestpark.org	1867	305 CIRCLE AVE	60130	NI	Dr Leonard R Payton Roney C Riley	(708)366-3226	WS 930 SS 830	ED/SN	214	189	81
FORSYTH	*ST PAUL'S*		See Decatur IL									
FOX LAKE	*BEAUTIFUL SAVIOR*		See Antioch IL									
FRANKFORT	*GOOD SHEPHERD* office@goodshepherdfrankfort.org www.goodshepherdfrankfort.org	1956	177 LUTHER LN	60423	NI	Kevin E Hahn	(815)469-2549 (815)469-1028	WS 8 1046 SS 930 BC 930	ED/HC/SN			
FRANKLIN PARK	*MOUNT CALVARY* mtcalvary32@yahoo.com mtcalvarysecretary.googlepages.com	1950	3222 ROSE ST	60131	NI	Mark D Post	(847)678-5565	WS 830	EL/HS			
FREEBURG	*CHRIST OUR SAVIOR* coslc@att.net coslc-online.org	1991	612 N STATE ST	62243	SI	Adam R Hiles	(618)539-5664	WS 9 SS 1030 BC 1030	ED/HC/MD	237	196	70
	FREEBURG BIBLE STUDY AT CEDAR TRAILS Satellite Site of Christ Our Savior Freeburg IL	2016	490 Urbanna Dr	62243								
FREEPORT	*IMMANUEL* church@ourgodwithus.com www.ourgodwithus.com	1877	1993 W. CHURCH ST.	61032	NI	Zachary A Klatt	(815)235-1993 (815)233-9158	WS 9	EL/HS/ED/ HC/MD/SN			
	OUR REDEEMER ourredeemerfreeport@gmail.com ourredeemerfreeport.org	1910	1320 S BLACKHAWK AVE	61032	NI	Dr Willis R Schwicht-enberg	(815)232-6934 (815)232-0036	WS 9 SS 9 BC 1030	ED/HC/ MD/SN			
GALESBURG	*MOUNT CALVARY* office@mclcgalesburg.org mclcgalesburg.org	1937	1372 W FREMONT ST	61401	CI	Steven L Sommerer	(309)342-7083	WS 10 SS 845 BC 845	EC/ED/MD	192	164	108
GARRETT	*IMMANUEL*		See Tuscola IL									
GENESEO	*CONCORDIA* concordia@geneseolutheranchurch.com www.geneseolutheranchurch.com	1864	316 S OAKWOOD AVE	61254	CI	Stephen M Mueller	(309)944-3993 (309)945-1060	WS 8 1030 SS 930 BC 930	EC/ED/HC/ MD	401	308	121
	ST JOHN churchoffice@stjohnsgeneseo.org www.stjohnsgeneseo.org	1869	8948 N 1900TH AVE	61254	CI	Timothy L Nerud	(815)989-2025	WS 10 SS 845 BC 845	ED/HC/ MD/SN	193	167	47
GENEVA	*FAITH* faithoffice@flcgeneva.net www.flcgeneva.net	1961	1745 Kaneville Rd 1745 KANEVILLE RD STE 1	60134	NI	Dr Dennis A Aubey	(630)232-8420	WS 9 BC 1030	ED/HC/MD	23	23	28
	LORD OF LIFE		See Elburn IL									
GENOA	*TRINITY* trinity@tlcgenoa.org www.tlcgenoa.org	1878	33930 N STATE RD	60135	NI	Derek S Paetow	(815)784-2522 (815)784-5208	WS 8 1030 SS 915 BC 915	EC/ED/HC/ MD/SN			
GIRARD	*TRINITY* jjane2515@gmail.com www.tlcgirard.org	1903	32946 ROUTE 4	62640	SI	Kelly G Mitteis	(217)697-0072	BC 8	ED/HC/ MD/SN	295	225	45
GLEN CARBON	*SAINT JAMES* cheryl@stjamesglencarbon.org stjamesglencarbon.org	1982	146 N Main St P.O. BOX 644	62034	SI		(618)288-6120	WS 9 BC 1030	HS/HC	268	224	147
GLENDALE HEIGHTS	*FAMILY IN FAITH* fifcc@fifcc.org www.fifcc.org	1996	1480 BLOOMINGDALE RD GLENDALE HTS	60139	NI	Stephen R Kass	(630)653-5030 (630)653-5249	WS 8 1030 BC 915	ED/HC/ MD/SN	120	120	60
GLENVIEW	*IMMANUEL* info@immanuelglenview.org www.immanuelglenview.org	1876	1850 CHESTNUT AVENUE	60025	NI	Matthew G Douglas	(847)724-1034 (847)724-1038	WS 10 SS 845	EC/ED/HC	136	114	60

*Indicates a new church start. A new church start is an intentionally organized gathering which comes together on a regular basis for the purpose of worship and/or Bible study and is intended to grow into a member LCMS congregation. WS =Worship Service; SS = Sunday School; BC =Bible Class; EC = Early Childhood; EL = Elementary School; HS = High School; ED =Education Ministry; HC =Human Care Ministry; SN = Special Needs Ministry; MD = Media Ministry (PC)=Partner Church Pastor. See Page 53 for the Table of Abbreviations for key to additional abbreviations

CITY	CONGREGATION EMAIL WEBSITE	YEAR EST	LOCATION MAILING ADDRESS	ZIP CODE(S)	DIST.	PASTOR(S)	PHONE FAX	WS SS BC	SCHOOLS/ MINISTRIES	STATISTIC Bapt	Conf	Avg Attend
GODFREY	*FAITH* church@flcgodfrey.org www.flcgodfrey.org	1953	6809 GODFREY RD	62035	SI	Timothy A Appel	(618)466-3833 (618)466-3839	WS 9 SS 1030 BC 1030	HS/HC/MD	382	308	122
GOLCONDA	*OUR REDEEMER* orlg@shawneelink.net www.orlcgolconda.org	1865	405 S Franklin St PO BOX 580	62938	SI		(618)683-8621	WS 11 SS 10	ED/HC/ MD/SN			
GOLDEN	*HOLY CROSS* hcsecretary@adams.net	1852	205 W 3rd St PO BOX 116	62339	CI		(605)519-3488	WS 830 SS 5	ED/HC/MD	119	79	50
GRANITE CITY	*CONCORDIA*	1922	2305 GRAND AVE	62040	SI	Brian J Feicho	(618)451-9925	WS 1015 SS 9				
	HOPE hopelutherangc@gmail.com www.hopelutherangc.org	1948	3715 WABASH AVE	62040	SI	Alan R Beuster	(618)876-7568	WS 930 SS 830 BC 830	ED/HC/MD	215	177	48
	ST JOHN stjohnlutherangc@gmail.com www.stjohngranitecity.org	1923	2001 SAINT CLAIR AVE	62040	S	William E Hale	(618)451-7788 (618)451-5855	WS 1030 SS 1040 BC 9		103	86	37
GRANT PARK	*ZION* ziongrantpark@yahoo.com	1872	11456 N 11000E RD	60940	NI	Cory A Estby	(815)361-0056	WS 10 SS 845 BC 845	ED/HC/SN	419	351	107
GRAYSLAKE	*LORD OF GLORY* cindy@lordofglory.org www.lordofglory.org	1995	607 W BELVIDERE RD	60030	NI	Brian K Davies	(847)548-5673 (847)548-6796	WS 8 1030 SS 915 BC 915	EC/ED/HC/ MD	842	667	280
GRAYVILLE	*OUR SAVIOR*		See Carmi IL									
GREEN VALLEY	*ST JOHN* secretary@stjsp.org www.stjsp.org	1876	13443 TOWNLINE RD	61534	CI	James C Sansom	(309)348-3180	WS 8 1045 SS 930	EL/ED/HC/ MD	1277	915	113
GREENVILLE	*OUR REDEEMER* ourredeemergreenville@gmail.com www.ourredeemergreenville.org	1932	1540 E St Route 140 1540 E STATE ROUTE 140	62246	SI	Dr Jeffery D Nehrt	(618)664-0223	WS 1015 SS 9	ED/HC/ MD/SN			
GURNEE	*BETHEL* office@bethelgurnee.org www.bethelgurnee.org	1966	5110 GRAND AVE	60031	NI	Dr Benjamin C Squires	(847)244-9647	WS 9 SS 1030 BC 1030	EC/ED/MD	321	297	115
HAMPSHIRE	*LORD OF LIFE*		See Elburn IL									
	ST JOHN stjohnlutheran@foxvalley.net www.stjohnburlington.com	1888	13N535 French Rd PO BOX 85 BURLINGTON	60140 60109	NI	Patrick D Pinion	(847)683-2338 (847)683-2521	WS 8 1030 SS 915 BC 915	ED/HC/ MD/SN			
	ST PETER'S office@stpetersnorthplato.org www.stpetersnorthplato.org	1884	43W301 PLANK RD	60140	NI	Thomas E Eaves	(847)464-5721	WS 9 SS 10 BC 1030	EC/ED/HC/ MD	167	143	68
	TRINITY trinityhampshire@sbcglobal.net	1883	135 TERWILLIGER AVE	60140	NI		(847)683-2238 (847)683-2238	WS 9 SS 1015 BC 1015	HC	74	47	25
HAMPTON	*ZION*		See East Moline IL									
HANOVER PARK	*ST JOHN*		See Schaumburg IL									
HARDIN	*ST MATTHEW*		See Brussels IL									
HARRISTOWN	*ST PAUL'S*		See Decatur IL									
HARVARD	*ST PAUL* stpaullutheran@risebroadband.net	1905	1601 N Garfield Rd 1601 GARFIELD RD	60033	NI		(815)943-5330	WS 10	MD	250	250	30
HARVEL	*TRINITY* trinitylutheranharvel@gmail.com tlcharvel.org	1894	402 N Monroe PO BOX 207	62538	SI		(217)229-3143	WS 11	ED/HC/MD			
HARWOOD HEIGHTS	*OUR SAVIOUR*		See Chicago IL									
HAVANA	*ST JOHN*		See Bath IL									
	ST PAUL www.stpaulslutheranhavana.com	1850	121 N Pearl St PO BOX 534	62644	CI	Ian M Heinze	(309)543-4850 (309)543-1245	WS 9 SS 1015	ED/HC/MD	200	169	133
HAWTHORN WOODS	*ST MATTHEW* smlcs@stmattsonline.com stmatts.net	1863	24500 N Old Mc Henry Rd 24500 N OLD MCHENRY RD HAWTHORN WDS	60047	NI	Edward A Blonski Sr Ryan M Ferguson	(847)438-7709	WS 8 1045 SS 930 BC 930	EC/ED/HC/ MD	1056	832	230
HAZEL CREST	*WATERFORD ESTATES RETIREMENT COMMUNITY* Satellite Site of Salem Homewood IL	1997	17400 Kedzie Ave	60429								
HERSCHER	*TRINITY* trinityher1@comcast.net trinitylutheranherscher.org	1909	255 E Third St PO BOX 414	60941	NI	Eric J Brown	(815)426-2262	WS 830 SS 930 BC 945	EC/ED/HC/ MD/SN	572	399	123
HIGHLAND	*HOPE* hopelutheranchurchlcms@gmail.com www.hopelutheranhighland.church	1941	2745 BROADWAY	62249	SI	Dr Scott M Busacker	(618)654-7891	WS 9 SS 1015 BC 1015		344	281	150
HIGHLAND PARK	*FAITH*		See Lake Forest IL									
HILLSBORO	*OUR SAVIOR*	1946	510 E TREMONT ST	62049	SI		(217)532-3463	WS 915	ED/HC/ MD/SN	70	70	20
HILLSIDE	*HOPE* hopehillside@gmail.com	2000	5159 Madison 5159 MADISON ST	60162	NI	Ralph G Tausz	(708)449-8688 (708)449-8688	WS 1015 SS 1130 BC 1130	EL/HS			
	IMMANUEL general@immanuel-hillside.org www.immanuel-hillside.org	1858	2317 S WOLF RD	60162	NI	Steve C Deombeleg	(708)562-5590 (708)562-6085	WS 930 BC 11	EL/ED/HC/ MD	220	184	52
HINCKLEY	*IMMANUEL* office@immanuel-hinckley.org www.immanuel-hinckley.org	1865	12760 LEE RD	60520	NI	James A Barbey	(815)286-3885 (815)286-3885	WS 1015 SS 9 BC 9	ED/MD/SN	231	186	48
HINDSBORO	*IMMANUEL*		See Tuscola IL									

*Indicates a new church start. A new church start is an intentionally organized gathering which comes together on a regular basis for the purpose of worship and/or Bible study and is intended to grow into a member LCMS congregation. WS =Worship Service; SS = Sunday School; BC =Bible Class; EC = Early Childhood; EL = Elementary School; HS = High School; ED =Education Ministry; HC =Human Care Ministry; SN = Special Needs Ministry; MD = Media Ministry (PC)=Partner Church Pastor. See Page 53 for the Table of Abbreviations for key to additional abbreviations

CITY	CONGREGATION EMAIL WEBSITE	YEAR EST	LOCATION MAILING ADDRESS	ZIP CODE(S)	DIST.	PASTOR(S)	PHONE FAX	WS SS BC	SCHOOLS/ MINISTRIES	STATISTIC Bapt	Conf	Avg Attend
HINSDALE	*ZION* info@zionhinsdale.org www.zionhinsdale.org	1888	204 S GRANT ST	60521	NI	David S Nieman	(630)323-0384 (630)323-0694	WS 930	EC/EL/HS/ ED/HC/ MD/SN	216	151	64
HODGKINS	*IMMANUEL* www.immanuelhodgkins.org	1911	6605 S Kane Ave 6605 KANE AVE	60525	NI	Eric N Andersen	(708)354-0692 (708)478-8429	WS 11 SS 1215				
HOFFMAN	*TRINITY* churchoffice@trinityhoffman.org www.trinityhoffman.org	1874	8700 Huey Rd PO BOX 200	62250	SI	Brett A Jones	(618)495-2545 (618)495-2692	WS 830 SS 945 BC 945	EL/HS/ED/ HC/MD	623	488	142
HOFFMAN ESTATES	*ST JOHN*		See Schaumburg IL									
HOMER	*IMMANUEL*		See Broadlands IL									
HOMEWOOD	*SALEM* salemlutheranhomewood@gmail.com salemhomewood.org	1919	18324 ASHLAND AVE	60430	NI	Brian P Mayo Sr	(708)798-1820	WS 930 SS 9 BC 1045	EC/ED/HC/ MD/SN			
HOOPESTON	*GOOD SHEPHERD* goodshepherdhoopeston@gmail.com www.goodshepherdhoopeston.org	1946	302 N MARKET ST	60942	CI		(217)283-7966	WS 1045	ED/HC	33	26	15
HOUSTON	*ST JOHN*		See Baldwin IL									
HOYLETON	*TRINITY* www.trinityhoyleton.org	1867	205 N Main St PO BOX 176	62803	SI	Nathan T Wollenberg	(618)493-6226 (618)493-7754	WS 930 SS 830 BC 830	EL/HS/ED/ HC/MD/SN			
HUNTLEY	*CROSSPOINT LAKEWOOD*		See Lakewood IL									
	TRINITY office@trinityhuntley.org www.trinityhuntley.org	1871	11008 N CHURCH ST	60142	NI	Andrew B Hatesohl	(847)669-5780 (847)669-5978	WS 8 1030 SS 915 BC 915	ED/HC/MD	332	268	153
INGLESIDE	*ZION*		See McHenry IL									
ISLAND LAKE	*ST JOHN* gospel4all@yahoo.com www.stjohnislandlake.com	1942	405 W State Road # 176 PO BOX 370	60042	NI	Michael H Tanney	(847)526-7614 (847)526-7672	WS 9 SS 1030 BC 1030	ED/HC/MD			
ITASCA	*ST LUKE* www.saintlukeitasca.org	1907	410 S RUSH ST	60143	NI	Terry A McReynolds	(630)773-0396 (630)773-0786	WS 8 1030 SS 915 BC 915	EL/HS/ED/ HC/MD/SN	530	384	120
IUKA	*TRINITY* revkangas@yahoo.com	1873	8250 TRINITY LN	62849	SI	Paul M Pater	(618)323-6586	WS 9 SS 815 BC 815	ED/HC/MD	156	127	55
JACKSONVILLE	*CHRIST DEAF* cid_deaf@hotmail.com www.illinoisdeaflutheran.org	1948	104 FINLEY ST	62650	CI		(217)245-0180	WS 10 BC 830	ED/HC/ MD/SN			
	OUR REDEEMER sec1975orlc@yahoo.com orlcjaxil.org	1975	405 MASSEY LN	62650	CI		(217)243-3939	WS 9	ED/MD/SN	176	147	74
	SALEM businessmanager@salemjaxschool.net www.salemjax.net	1858	222 E BEECHER AVE	62650	CI	Jonah J Schultz	(217)243-3419 (217)245-0289	WS 9 SS 1030 BC 1030	EL/ED/HC/ MD/SN	828	663	132
JACOB	*CHRIST*	1876	184 W JACOB RD	62950	SI	Gunnar G Campbell	(618)763-4663	WS 9 SS 1015 BC 1015				
JERSEYVILLE	*HOPE* hopelutheran@gtec.com www.hopejerseyville.com	1953	1009 N STATE ST	62052	SI	David L Otten	(618)498-3423	WS 930 SS 830 BC 830	HC	146	109	46
JOHNSBURG	*BEAUTIFUL SAVIOR*		See Antioch IL									
JOLIET	*OUR SAVIOR* oursaviorjoliet@gmail.com www.oursaviorjoliet.org	1956	1910 BLACK RD	60435	NI	Matthew G Carlson	(815)725-1606 (815)725-1689	WS 9 SS 1015 BC 1015	EC/ED/HC/ MD/SN	484	417	120
	ST PETER stpeterjoliet@aol.com stpeterjoliet.org	1857	310 N BROADWAY ST	60435	NI	David W Totsky	(815)722-3567	WS 9 SS 1030 BC 1030	MD	335	273	50
KAMPSVILLE	*ST JOHN* ourredeemercarrollton@gmail.com	1859	316 S St Louis Ave 453 S SAINT LOUIS AVE	62053	SI	Steven J Jacobsen				77	70	11
	ST MATTHEW		See Brussels IL									
KANKAKEE	*ST PAUL*		See Bourbonnais IL									
	ST PAULS LUTHERAN Satellite Site of St Paul Bourbonnais IL	2010	348 E Merchant	60901								
KEWANEE	*FAITH* hahn.gary@comcast.net www.faithkewanee.org	2000	620 Hepner Dr 620 HEPNER ST	61443	CI	Paul M Weber	(309)852-2787	WS 9 BC 1030	ED/HC/ MD/SN	150	109	21
	ST PAUL stpaulskewanee@gmail.com www.stpaulskewanee.org	1862	109 S ELM ST	61443	CI	Winston P Grieser	(309)852-2461	WS 9 SS 1030	ED/HC/ MD/SN	42	36	35
LA GRANGE	*HOPE*		See Countryside IL									
	SAINT JOHNS churchoffice@stjohnslagrange.org sjlagrange.com/church/	1886	505 S PARK RD	60525	NI	Mark R Stapleton	(708)354-1690 (708)354-4910	WS 8 1045 SS 925 BC 925	EL/ED/HC/ MD/SN			
LAKE FOREST	*FAITH* office@faithlakeforest.org www.faithlakeforest.org	2002	680 W DEERPATH	60045	NI	James D Buckman	(847)234-1868 (847)234-1929	WS 8 1030 SS 915 BC 915	ED/HC/ MD/SN	445	376	105
LAKE IN THE HILLS	*CROSSPOINT LAKEWOOD*		See Lakewood IL									
LAKE VILLA	*BEAUTIFUL SAVIOR*		See Antioch IL									
	GOOD SHEPHERD lindagallu@juno.com www.goodshepherd-lakevilla.org	1962	25100 W Grand Ave 215 VILLA AVE	60046	NI		(847)356-5158	WS 10	ED/MD/SN	41	32	8
LAKE ZURICH	*ST MATTHEW*		See Hawthorn Woods IL									
LAKEMOOR	*ZION*		See McHenry IL									

*Indicates a new church start. A new church start is an intentionally organized gathering which comes together on a regular basis for the purpose of worship and/or Bible study and is intended to grow into a member LCMS congregation. WS =Worship Service; SS = Sunday School; BC =Bible Class; EC = Early Childhood; EL = Elementary School; HS = High School; ED =Education Ministry; HC =Human Care Ministry; SN = Special Needs Ministry; MD = Media Ministry (PC)=Partner Church Pastor. See Page 53 for the Table of Abbreviations for key to additional abbreviations

CITY	CONGREGATION EMAIL WEBSITE	YEAR EST	LOCATION MAILING ADDRESS	ZIP CODE(S)	DIST.	PASTOR(S)	PHONE FAX	WS SS BC	SCHOOLS/ MINISTRIES	STATISTIC Bapt	Conf	Avg Attend
LAKEWOOD	*CROSSPOINT LAKEWOOD* info@crosspointlakewood.org cplakewood.info	2010	8505 REDTAIL DR VLG OF LAKEWD	60014	NI	Tyler R Coyne	(815)893-0888	WS 10 SS 10		220	177	63
LANSING	*STJOHNS* stjohnslansing@comcast.net www.stjohnschurchlansing.org	1883	18100 WENTWORTH AVE	60438	NI	Dr John M Richy	(708)895-9240	WS 930 BC 815	ED/HC/MD	236	204	58
	TRINITY church@tlclansing.org www.tlclansing.org	1864	2501 INDIANA AVE	60438	NI	Ryan D Reese	(708)474-7997 (708)474-0820	WS 930 BC 815	ED/HC/ MD/SN	691	533	76
LAWRENCEVILLE	*OUR SAVIOR*	1932	1411 15th St PO BOX 643	62439	CI		(618)943-6680	WS 8 SS 915 BC 915	HC	49	42	19
LEBANON	*MESSIAH* messiahlutheranlcms@gmail.com www.messiahlebanon.org	1988	801 N MADISON ST	62254	SI	Karl W Gregory	(618)537-2300	WS 9 SS 1015 BC 1015		31	25	23
LEMONT	*ST MATTHEW* office.stmatthewlemont@gmail.com www.stmatthewlemont.org	1874	305 LEMONT ST	60439	NI	Michael R Gudgel	(630)257-5000	WS 9 SS 1015 BC 1015	ED/HC/ MD/SN	450	351	95
LENA	*ST JOHN* office@stjohnslena.org www.stjohnslena.org	1890	625 Country Lane Dr 625 COUNTRY LANE DR P.O. BOX 216	61048	NI	Jason A Shaw	(815)369-4035 (815)369-2535	WS 8 1030 SS 915 BC 915	ED/HC/ MD/SN	667	553	238
LENZBERG	*ST JOHN*		See Baldwin IL									
LEXINGTON	*ST PAUL* stpaul@stpaul-lex.org www.stpaul-lex.org	1956	107 E CHATHAM ST	61753	CI	Kyle C Ronchetto	(309)365-5000	WS 9 SS 1005 BC 8	EC/ED/MD	259	208	54
LINCOLN	*FAITH* faithlincolnil@gmail.com	1968	2320 N Kickapoo 2320 N KICKAPOO ST	62656	CI	Noah R Kerstein	(217)732-4901	WS 10 SS 9 BC 9	ED/HC/ MD/SN	404	326	70
	ZION zlcsecretary@comcast.net www.zlclinc.org	1871	205 PULASKI ST	62656	CI	Mark A Thompson	(217)732-3946 (217)732-5876	WS 8 1030 SS 920 BC 920	EL/ED/ MD/SN	375	303	174
LINDENHURST	*BEAUTIFUL SAVIOR*		See Antioch IL									
LINDENWOOD	*IMMANUEL* office@immanuel-lindenwood.org www.immanuel-lindenwood.org	1882	16060 E LINDENWOOD RD	61049	NI	Dr Matthew D Rosebrock	(815)393-4500 (815)393-4500	WS 9 SS 1030 BC 1030	ED/HC/ MD/SN	57	45	41
LISLE	*TRINITY* office@tlc4u.org www.tlc4u.org	1960	1101 KIMBERLY WAY	60532	NI	Nicholas M Price Paul A Horstmeyer	(630)964-1272 (630)964-1468	WS 830 10 SS 10 BC 10	EC/ED/HC/ MD/SN			
	TRINITY GREEN TRAILS Satellite Site of Trinity Lisle IL	2010	2701 Maple Ave	60532				WS 9 11 SS 9 11				
LITCHFIELD	*ZION* www.zionlutheranlitchfield.com	1886	1301 N STATE ST	62056	SI	Fred H Kraemer	(217)324-2033 (217)324-3166	WS 8 1030 SS 915	EL/ED/MD			
LIVINGSTON	*HOLY CROSS* hclc@madisontelco.com	1937	460 Church St PO BOX 397	62058	SI		(618)637-2146	WS 10 SS 9 BC 915	ED/HC/ MD/SN			
LOCKPORT	*ST PAUL* spchoff@gmail.com www.stpaulslockport.org	1871	1500 S BRIGGS ST	60441	NI	Christopher O Antonetti	(815)838-1832 (815)838-4732	WS 9 SS 1040 BC 1040		169	144	61
LODA	*IMMANUEL* immanuel.loda@gmail.com	1949	215 N Poplar St PO BOX 338	60948	CI		(217)781-1264	WS 8 BC 930	HS	78	75	24
LOMBARD	*PEACE* office@peacehome.org www.peacehome.org	1969	21W500 BUTTERFIELD RD	60148	NI	Steven M Hufford Hesham A Shehab	(630)627-1101 (630)627-1103	WS 815 1045 SS 815 1045 BC 930	EC/ED/HC/ MD/SN			
	ST JOHN church@stjohnslombard.org www.stjohnslombard.org	1893	215 S LINCOLN ST	60148	NI	Dr Daniel J Wegrzyn Peter R Imlah	(630)629-2515 (630)282-0436	WS 8 1030 SS 915 BC 915	EL/HS/ED/ HC/MD/SN	1200	934	507
	TRINITY secretary@trinitylombard.org trinitylombard.org	1868	1165 S WESTMORE-MEYERS RD	60148	NI	Steven E Wagner	(630)629-8765	WS 9 SS 1015 BC 1030	EL/HS/ED/ HC/MD/SN	297	248	80
LOUISVILLE	*ST JOHN* stjohnlutheran@wabash.net stjohnlouisville.org	1867	17684 E 1st Ave 17684 1ST AVE	62858	CI	Emmett A Bartens	(618)686-2971	WS 10 SS 9 BC 9	ED/HC/MD	336	243	132
LOVES PARK	*ST ANDREW*		See Rockton IL									
LYONS	*ZION* zionevlutheranoffice@yahoo.com www.zionlyons.org	1884	7930 OGDEN AVE	60534	NI	Mark W Duer	(708)447-4499 (708)447-1565	WS 11 SS 945	ED/HC/MD			
MACHESNEY PARK	*CONCORDIA* contactus.concordia@gmail.com www.ConcordiaMP.com	1952	7424 N 2ND ST MACHESNEY PK	61115	NI	Steven A Benson	(815)633-4983 (815)633-1345	WS 930 BC 1030	EL/HS/ED/ MD/SN	167	150	53
	ST ANDREW		See Rockton IL									
MACOMB	*IMMANUEL* immanuellutheranmacomb@gmail.com www.immanuelmacomb.com	1956	906 E Grant St 303 N. CLAY ST.	61455	CI	Christopher J Hull	(309)833-5483	WS 830 SS 945 BC 945	ED/MD	212	163	72
	IMMANUEL LUTHERAN STUDENT CENTER Satellite Site of Immanuel Macomb IL	2014	303 N Clay St	61455				WS 11				
MACON	*MOUNT CALVARY*		See Decatur IL									
MANITO	*ST PAUL*	1868	21819 County Road N 3300 E 21819 N COUNTY ROAD 3300 E	61546	CI	Matthew C Berndt	(309)968-2872	WS 1015 SS 9 BC 9	ED/HC/MD	171	138	50
	TRINITY trinitymanito@gmail.com	1959	110 S PARK AVE	61546	CI	Matthew C Berndt	(309)968-6984	WS 830 SS 945 BC 945	ED	121	107	35

*Indicates a new church start. A new church start is an intentionally organized gathering which comes together on a regular basis for the purpose of worship and/or Bible study and is intended to grow into a member LCMS congregation. WS =Worship Service; SS = Sunday School; BC =Bible Class; EC = Early Childhood; EL = Elementary School; HS = High School; ED =Education Ministry; HC =Human Care Ministry; SN = Special Needs Ministry; MD = Media Ministry (PC)=Partner Church Pastor. See Page 53 for the Table of Abbreviations for key to additional abbreviations

CITY	CONGREGATION EMAIL WEBSITE	YEAR EST	LOCATION MAILING ADDRESS	ZIP CODE(S)	DIST.	PASTOR(S)	PHONE FAX	WS SS BC	SCHOOLS/ MINISTRIES	STATISTIC Bapt	Conf	Avg Attend
MANTENO	*RISEN SAVIOR* risensavior.manteno@gmail.com www.risensaviormanteno.org	1990	1881 W DIVISION ST	60950	NI	Kevin L Werner	(815)468-2011	WS 9 SS 1015 BC 1015	ED/HC/ MD/SN	125	101	60
	ST PAUL		See Bourbonnais IL									
MARENGO	*FLORENCE NURSING HOME* Satellite Site of Zion Marengo IL	1990	546 E Grant Hwy	60152								
	ZION www.zionmarengo.net	1880	412 JACKSON ST	60152	NI	Jonathan M Ripke Jonathon H Rusche	(815)568-6564 (815)568-0547	WS 8 1030 SS 915 BC 930	EL/HS/ED/ HC/MD/SN	1864	1470	313
MARION	*GOOD SHEPHERD* gshepherdmarion@frontier.com gslcmarion.com	1984	1801 WESTMINSTER DR	62959	SI	Mark P Surburg	(618)993-3649	WS 9 SS 1015 BC 1015	ED/MD	146	113	72
MARIONETTE PARK	*HOLY CROSS*		See Alsip IL									
MARISSA	*ST JOHN*		See Baldwin IL									
MARKHAM	*MARKHAM* MLCoffice@markhamlutheranchurch.org markhamlutheranchurch.org	1940	3518 W 160 St 3518 W 160TH ST	60428	EN	Dr Larry G Schneekloth	(708)331-4885	WS 1015 SS 9 BC 9	ED/HC/MD	124	97	21
MARSEILLES	*TRINITY* trinitymarseilles@outlook.com	1866	621 UNION ST	61341	NI		(815)795-2031	WS 1030 SS 915 BC 915	ED			
MASCOUTAH	*ZION* churchoffice@zionmascoutah.org www.zionmascoutah.org	1868	101 S Railway 101 S RAILWAY ST	62258	SI	Joel A Dietrich	(618)566-7345 (618)566-9519	WS 10 SS 845 BC 845	EC/ED/HC/ MD/SN			
MASON CITY	*CHRIST* christlumc@casscomm.com	1946	114 E WALNUT ST	62664	CI	Brandon M Sullivan	(217)482-5168	WS 10 SS 11 BC 11	EC/ED/HC/ MD	194	194	67
MATTESON	*IMMANUEL*		See Richton Park IL									
	ST PAUL churchsec@stpaulsonline.org www.stpaulsonline.org	1868	6201 VOLLMER RD	60443	NI	Matthew D Troester Lawrence M Ruger	(708)720-0880	WS 9 SS 1030 BC 1030	ED/HC/ MD/SN	580	535	119
MATTOON	*ST JOHNS* churchoffice@stjohns-mattoon.org www.stjohns-mattoon.org	1893	200 CHARLESTON AVE	61938	CI	Andrew E Herzberg	(217)234-4923 (217)234-4925	WS 9 SS 1020 BC 1020	EL/HS/ED/ MD/SN	945	713	213
	ST PAULS stpaulsmattoon@gmail.com	1880	8975 E COUNTY ROAD 1200N	61938	CI	Daniel M Ulrich	(217)234-9880	WS 10 SS 930 BC 930	ED/HC/ MD/SN	143	109	68
MAUNIE	*OUR SAVIOR*		See Carmi IL									
MAYWOOD	*ST PAUL*		See Melrose Park IL									
MAZON	*FRIENDS IN CHRIST*		See Morris IL									
MCHENRY	*FELLOWSHIP OF FAITH* ministry@fellowshipoffaith.org www.fellowshipoffaith.org	1999	6120 MASON HILL RD	60050	NI	David C Gaddini Thaddeus S Wielgos	(815)759-0739 (815)759-0792	WS 10 SS 945 5 BC 945	ED/HC/ MD/SN	279	225	287
	ZION office@zionmchenry.org zionmchenry.org	1876	4206 W ELM ST	60050	NI	Mark T Buetow	(815)385-0859 (815)385-0878	WS 9 SS 1015 BC 8	EL/ED/HC/ MD/SN			
MCLEANSBORO	*OUR SAVIOR*		See Carmi IL									
MEDINAH	*ST JOHN*		See Schaumburg IL									
MELROSE PARK	*APOSTLES* church@apostlesmelrosepark.org www.apostlesmelrosepark.org	1939	10429 W FULLERTON AVE	60164	NI	Ralph G Tausz	(847)455-0903 (847)455-0915	WS 930 SS 1030 BC 1030	ED/HC/MD			
	ST PAUL stpaulmp@yahoo.com www.stpaulmp.org	1892	1025 Lake St 1025 W LAKE ST	60160	NI	Michael F Duffy Martin M Zarate	(708)343-1000 (708)343-8635	WS 9 BC 1030	EL/HS/ED/ HC/MD/SN			
MILAN	*ST MATTHEW* stmatthewmilan@gmail.com www.stmatthewmilan.org	1960	115 12TH AVE W	61264	CI	Kurt R Larson	(309)787-4295 (309)787-4291	WS 10 SS 845 BC 845	ED/HC/ MD/SN	735	583	162
MILFORD	*OUR SAVIOR* secretary@oursaviormilford.com www.oursaviormilford.com	1932	209 W Jones St PO BOX 188	60953	CI	Harold D Minton Jr	(815)889-4121	WS 9 SS 1030 BC 1030	MD	211	176	77
	ST PAUL stpaulswoodworth@yahoo.com www.stpaulswoodworth.org	1872	113 W WOODWORTH RD	60953	CI	Michael J Ruhlig	(815)889-4209 (815)889-4364	WS 9 SS 1030 BC 1030	EL/HS/ED/ MD	419	330	120
MILLBROOK	*LORD OF LIFE* cms21749@sbcglobal.net	2013	8360 Fox River Dr PO BOX 251 SERENA	60536 60549	NI	Charles M Sampson Jr	(815)496-2284	WS 1130	ED/MD	44	27	28
MILLSTADT	*TRINITY* secretary@trinitymillstadt.org trinitymillstadt.org	1849	503 E WASHINGTON ST	62260	SI	Peter W Ill Todd A Wilken	(618)476-3101	WS 9 SS 1015 BC 1015	ED/HC/ MD/SN	226	196	66
MINIER	*GOOD SHEPHERD* fwz@frontiernet.net goodshepherdminier.com	1977	101 E Garfield PO BOX 858	61759	CI	Frank W Zimmerman	(309)963-4825	WS 830 SS 945	ED/HC/MD			
MINOOKA	*FRIENDS IN CHRIST*		See Morris IL									
MOKENA	*IMMANUEL* office@immanuelmokena.org www.immanuelmokena.org	1850	10731 W LA PORTE RD	60448	NI	Aaron M Schellhas	(708)479-5600 (708)479-2248	WS 9 SS 1015 BC 1015	EC/ED/ MD/SN	397	322	128
MOLINE	*HOLY CROSS* holycrosslutheran@mchsi.com www.holycrossmoline-lcms.org	1950	4107 21ST AVE	61265	CI		(309)764-9720 (309)764-0505	WS 815 1045 SS 930 BC 930	ED/HC/ MD/SN	258	185	80
	ST JOHN		See East Moline IL									
MOMENCE	*OUR SAVIOR* revgreg88030@yahoo.com	1891	118 N PINE ST	60954	NI	Gregory W Brown	(580)571-4288	WS 10 BC 845		43	42	25
	ST PAUL		See Bourbonnais IL									
MONTGOMERY	*NEW SONG*		See Aurora IL									

*Indicates a new church start. A new church start is an intentionally organized gathering which comes together on a regular basis for the purpose of worship and/or Bible study and is intended to grow into a member LCMS congregation. WS =Worship Service; SS = Sunday School; BC =Bible Class; EC = Early Childhood; EL = Elementary School; HS = High School; ED =Education Ministry; HC =Human Care Ministry; SN = Special Needs Ministry; MD = Media Ministry (PC)=Partner Church Pastor. See Page 53 for the Table of Abbreviations for key to additional abbreviations

CITY	CONGREGATION EMAIL WEBSITE	YEAR EST	LOCATION MAILING ADDRESS	ZIP CODE(S)	DIST.	PASTOR(S)	PHONE FAX	WS SS BC	SCHOOLS/ MINISTRIES	STATISTIC Bapt	Conf	Avg Attend
MONTGOMERY	*ST LUKE* churchoffice@stlcfamily.org www.stlcfamily.org	1959	63 FERNWOOD RD	60538	NI	Aaron J Mol	(630)892-9309	WS 9 BC 1030	ED/HC/ MD/SN	404	317	63
MONTICELLO	*FAITH* Faithmonticello@gmail.com www.faithmonticello.org/		1201 Bear Lane 1201 BEAR LN	61856	CI	David E Daniel	(217)762-9235	WS 10 SS 9 BC 9		105	57	60
MORRIS	*FRIENDS IN CHRIST* office@ficlc.org www.ficlc.org		1338 CLAY ST	60450	NI	Jackson R Scofield	(815)941-1255 (815)941-1255	WS 930 BC 1030	ED/HC/ MD/SN			
MORRISON	*ST PETER* stpeterslutheranchurch01@gmail.com stpetersmorrison.com	1885	601 N JACKSON ST	61270	NI		(815)772-3386	WS 930 SS 1045 BC 930 1045	EL/HC	369	292	63
MORRISONVILLE	*TRINITY*		See Harvel IL									
MORTON	*BETHEL* church@bethelmorton.org blcmorton.org	1945	325 E QUEENWOOD RD	61550	CI	Jeffrey M Anderson Gregory S Moyer	(309)263-2417 (309)263-7902	WS 8 1045 SS 930 BC 930	EL/HS/ED/ HC/MD	1815	1498	683
MOUNT CARMEL	*HOPE* hopelutheranmc@frontier.com www.facebook.com/mchopelutheran	1946	1512 N CHERRY ST	62863	SI	Thomas F Kramer	(618)240-3220	WS 10 SS 10	ED/HC/SN			
MOUNT GREENWOOD	*ST JOHN DIVINE*		See Chicago IL									
MOUNT OLIVE	*IMMANUEL* immanuelmtolive@frontiernet.net	1881	111 E MAIN ST	62069	SI	James F Ritter	(217)999-7442	WS 1030 SS 915 BC 915	HC	336	292	42
MOUNT PROSPECT	*ST JOHN* jeffgavin@sbcglobal.net www.stjohn-mpil.org	1848	1100 S Linneman Rd 1100 LINNEMAN RD	60056	NI	Jeff G Gavin	(847)593-7670 (847)593-2601	WS 8 1030 SS 915				
	ST PAUL church@saint-paul.org www.saint-paul.org	1912	100 S SCHOOL ST	60056	NI	Bo G Graham Peter W Berauer Erwin A Valencia	(847)255-0332 (847)255-0948	WS 8 10 SS 905	EL/ED/HC/ MD/SN	2751	1751	420
MOUNT PULASKI	*ZION* office@zionmp.org www.zionmp.org	1851	203 S VINE ST	62548	CI	Jonathan W Buescher	(217)792-5965 (217)792-5915	WS 10 SS 9 BC 9	EL/ED/HC/ MD/SN	357	289	69
MOUNT STERLING	*FIRST*	1957	111 W SOUTH ST	62353	CI		(217)322-4237	WS 1030 SS 930 BC 10				
MOUNT VERNON	*FAITH* faluth41@hotmail.com faithmvil.org	1913	1104 N 42ND ST	62864	SI	Joseph M Nehring	(618)242-4330 (618)316-9289	WS 930 SS 11	HC/SN			
MOUNT ZION	*MOUNT CALVARY*		See Decatur IL									
	MOUNT ZION www.mtzion-lutheran.org/	1977	1475 W MAIN ST	62549	CI	Robert L Bruer	(217)864-4958	WS 1030 SS 930 BC 930	ED/HC/MD			
	ST PAUL'S		See Decatur IL									
MURPHYSBORO	*IMMANUEL* secretary@immanuelmurphy.com immanuelmurphy.com	1897	1915 PINE ST	62966	SI	Matthew J Christian	(618)684-3012 (618)684-5115	WS 9 SS 1015 BC 1015	EL/ED/HC/ MD	374	308	83
NAPERVILLE	*BETHANY* sclemmer@bethanylcs.org www.bethanylcs.org	1928	1550 MODAFF RD	60565	NI	Seth M Clemmer Stephen O Schumacher	(630)355-2198 (630)355-2216	WS 830 11 SS 10 BC 10	EL/ED/HC/ MD	734	604	320
	TRINITY		See Lisle IL									
	WORD OF LIFE pastor@wordoflife.net www.wordoflife.net	1987	879 TUDOR DR	60563	NI	Joshua A Schoon	(630)355-9655 (630)355-2220	WS 830 1045 SS 940 BC 945	EC/ED/HC			
	ZION office@zionnaperville.org www.zionnaperville.org	1864	11007 S Book Rd 11007 BOOK RD	60564	NI	Dr Mark W Birkholz	(630)904-1124 (630)904-4149	WS 8 1045 SS 930 BC 930	ED	270	231	143
NASHVILLE	*ST LUKE*		See Okawville IL									
	TRINITY trinitystjohn@gmail.com www.trinity-nashville.org	1886	680 W WALNUT ST	62263	SI	David E Benning	(618)327-3311 (618)327-4540	WS 930 SS 830 BC 830	EL/HS/ED/ HC/MD			
NEUNERT	*CHRIST*		See Jacob IL									
NEW ATHENS	*ST PAUL* stpaultrinity@gmail.com	1948	513 Church St 900 BELSHA ST	62264	SI	Lyle E Buettner	(618)696-2649	WS 1030 SS 930	MD/SN			
NEW BERLIN	*ST JOHN* info@stjnb.org stjnb.org	1870	308 E Gibson 308 E GIBSON ST	62670	CI	Jacob M Moore	(217)488-3190	WS 10 SS 9 BC 9		181	144	66
NEW HAVEN	*OUR SAVIOR*		See Carmi IL									
NEW HOLLAND	*ZION* zlcnewholland@gmail.com	1902	105 N Logan St PO BOX 199	62671	CI	Brandon M Sullivan	(217)445-2264	WS 9 SS 10 BC 10	ED/HC/ MD/SN	84	73	30
NEW LENOX	*TRINITY* tlcsecretary508@gmail.com www.trinitynewlenox.org	1940	508 N CEDAR RD	60451	EN	Douglas E Hoag	(815)485-6973	WS 8 9 1030 SS 9	EC/ED/HC/ MD			
NEW MEMPHIS	*ST PETER* pastorstsalvator@aol.com	1863	153 E Church St PO BOX 261	62266	SI		(618)824-6366	WS 830	HC			
NEW MINDEN	*ST JOHN* tpm@frontiernet.net stjohnnewminden.360unite.com	1846	15538 STATE ROUTE 127 NASHVILLE	62263	SI	Timothy P Mueller	(618)478-5544	WS 10 SS 9 BC 9	EL/HS/ED/ HC/MD	358	289	93
NEWARK	*LORD OF LIFE*		See Millbrook IL									
NEWMAN	*IMMANUEL*		See Tuscola IL									
	IMMANUEL		See Broadlands IL									
NEWTON	*GOOD SHEPHERD*	1980	110 E Edwards St 110 EDWARDS ST	62448	CI		(618)707-8607	WS 1015 BC 1115		42	36	12

CONGREGATIONS

*Indicates a new church start. A new church start is an intentionally organized gathering which comes together on a regular basis for the purpose of worship and/or Bible study and is intended to grow into a member LCMS congregation. WS =Worship Service; SS = Sunday School; BC =Bible Class; EC = Early Childhood; EL = Elementary School; HS = High School; ED =Education Ministry; HC =Human Care Ministry; SN = Special Needs Ministry; MD = Media Ministry (PC)=Partner Church Pastor. See Page 53 for the Table of Abbreviations for key to additional abbreviations

CITY	CONGREGATION EMAIL WEBSITE	YEAR EST	LOCATION MAILING ADDRESS	ZIP CODE(S)	DIST.	PASTOR(S)	PHONE FAX	WS SS BC	SCHOOLS/ MINISTRIES	STATISTIC Bapt	Conf	Avg Attend
NILES	*ASCENSION* office@ascensionniles.com www.ascensionniles.com	2015	7429 N MILWAUKEE AVE	60714	NI	Matthew J Uttenreither	(847)647-9867	WS 930 SS 1045 BC 11	ED/SN			
NOKOMIS	*ST PAUL'S* stpaulnokomis@gmail.com	1870	22009 E 19TH RD	62075	SI	Christen E Prumm	(217)563-2487 (217)563-2487	WS 930 SS 830 BC 830	ED/HC/SN	197	154	107
	TRINITY trinitynokomis@consolidated.net www.trinitylutherannokomis.com	1893	204 N PINE ST	62075	SI	Justin D Massey Josef L Muench	(217)563-2718 (217)563-7371	WS 10 SS 845 BC 9	ED/HC/MD			
NORMAL	*CHRIST* CLCMS@ChristLutheranNormal.org www.christlutherannormal.org	1947	311 HERSHEY RD	61761	CI	Dr Timothy J Fitzner	(309)452-5609 (309)888-9085	WS 8 1045 SS 925 BC 925	ED/HC/ MD/SN	656	534	195
	GOOD SHEPHERD		See Bloomington IL									
	TRINITY		See Bloomington IL									
	*WITTENBERG** wittenberglcms@gmail.com www.wittenberg-lcms.org		201 S Main 201 S MAIN ST	61761	CI		(309)452-5971 (309)454-2483	WS 1030 BC 930	ED			
NORRIDGE	*OUR SAVIOUR*		See Chicago IL									
	ZION zion.lutheran1963@gmail.com www.zionnorridgeil.org	1909	8600 W LAWRENCE AVE	60706	S	Michael A Croon Sr	(773)747-0160	WS 930 SS 1035 BC 1045		57	54	20
NORRIS CITY	*OUR SAVIOR*		See Carmi IL									
NORTHBROOK	*GRACE* churchoffice@gracenorthbrook.org www.gracenorthbrook.org	1950	2245 WALTERS AVE	60062	NI		(847)498-3060 (847)498-3061	WS 930 BC 11	EC/ED/HC/ MD/SN	109	97	40
	IMMANUEL		See Glenview IL									
NORWOOD PARK TOWNSHIP	*ST PAUL* ministry@stpaulcanfield.org www.stpaulcanfield.org	1903	5650 N CANFIELD AVE CHICAGO	60631	NI	Todd W Roberts	(708)867-5044 (708)867-0083	WS 930 BC 11	ED/HC/SN	213	169	52
OAK LAWN	*FAITH* faith_oaklawn@sbcglobal.net www.faithoaklawn.org	1940	9701 MELVINA AVE	60453	NI	Dr Dean D Pittelko	(708)424-1059 (708)424-1059	WS 9 SS 1015 BC 1030	ED/HC/MD			
	ST PAUL prjohn99@stpauloaklawn.org stpauloaklawn.org	1948	4660 W 94TH ST	60453	NI		(708)423-1040 (708)423-1588	WS 9 SS 1015 BC 1015	ED/HC/ MD/SN	364	284	81
	ZION zionlithlutheran@aol.com	1910	9000 MENARD AVE	60453	NI	Dr Valdas Ausra	(708)422-1433 (708)422-1485	WS 930 SS 10	ED/HC/ MD/SN			
OAK PARK	*CHRIST ENGLISH*		See Chicago IL									
O'FALLON	*BLESSED SAVIOR* pastor@mybslc.org www.mybslc.org	1992	1205 N LINCOLN AVE	62269	SI		(618)632-0126 (618)632-0927	SS 1045 BC 1045	ED/HC/ MD/SN			
OKAWVILLE	*IMMANUEL* principal@immanuelokawville.org www.immanuelokawville.org	1908	206 E SCHUMACHER ST	62271	SI	Eric R Wood	(618)243-6216 (618)243-6562	WS 10 SS 9 BC 9	EL/ED/ HC/SN	431	348	99
	OLIVE BRANCH olivebranchlutheranchurch@yahoo.com olivebranchlcms.org	1865	11265 State Route 177 11235 STATE ROUTE 177	62271	SI		(618)243-5498	SS 9 BC 9	EL			
	ST LUKE tpm@frontiernet.net	1885	16365 Covington Rd 15538 STATE ROUTE 127 NASHVILLE	62271 62263	SI	Timothy P Mueller	(618)478-5544	WS 830	MD	36	32	18
OLMSTED	*ST LUKE*	1906	680 E Cedar St PO BOX 87	62970	SI		(618)742-6238	WS 10		46	28	8
OMAHA	*OUR SAVIOR*		See Carmi IL									
ONARGA	*ST JOHN'S* stjohnsashgrove@outlook.com www.facebook.com/profile. php?id=100064643891286	1887	1180 E 1000 N Rd 1180 E 1000 NORTH ROAD	60955	CI	Dale A Fjordbotten	(815)457-2909	WS 1015 SS 930 BC 930		253	188	62
ORLAND PARK	*CHRIST* info@christlutheranorland.com www.christlutheranorland.com	1888	14700 S 94TH AVE	60462	NI	Charles D Johnson	(708)349-0431 (708)349-0668	WS 8 10 SS 10 BC 10	EC/ED/HC/ MD			
	LIVING WORD intouchlwlc@yahoo.com www.livingwordorland.org	1990	16301 WOLF RD	60467	NI		(708)403-9673	WS 10 BC 915	EC/ED/HC/ MD/SN			
OSMAN	*IMMANUEL* info@osmanlutheran.org www.osmanlutheran.org	1895	100 N Mc Clean County Road 942 GRAPE AVE FISHER	61843	CI	Jeffrey D Mc Pike	(217)897-6170	WS 930 SS 830 BC 830	ED/HC/ MD/SN	100	100	43
OSWEGO	*ST LUKE*		See Montgomery IL									
	ZION		See Naperville IL									
OTTAWA	*ZION*	1860	622 W JEFFERSON ST	61350	NI		(815)433-1408 (815)433-1597	WS 9 SS 1030 BC 1030	ED/MD			
PALATINE	*IMMANUEL* Immanuel@ilcp.org immanuelpalatine.org	1869	200 N PLUM GROVE RD	60067	NI	Warren K Schilf Dr Donald M Antor	(847)359-1549 (847)359-1583	SS 1045 BC 915	EL/ED/HC/ MD/SN	1794	1291	260
	PRINCE PEACE office@pop.church www.pop.church	1970	1190 N HICKS RD	60067	NI	Karl R Fay Matthew L Koenig	(847)359-3451 (847)359-3471	WS 9 1030 SS 9 BC 9	ED/HC/ MD/SN	705	587	298
	THE GATHERING PLACE Satellite Site of Immanuel Palatine IL	2018	Facebook	60067								
PALOS HEIGHTS	*HOLY CROSS*		See Alsip IL									
PANA	*ST PAUL* stpaulpana@gmail.com	1924	208 E 4TH ST	62557	CI	Keith A Bueltmann	(217)562-4731 (217)562-3689	WS 1015	ED/HC			

*Indicates a new church start. A new church start is an intentionally organized gathering which comes together on a regular basis for the purpose of worship and/or Bible study and is intended to grow into a member LCMS congregation. WS =Worship Service; SS = Sunday School; BC =Bible Class; EC = Early Childhood; EL = Elementary School; HS = High School; ED =Education Ministry; HC =Human Care Ministry; SN = Special Needs Ministry; MD = Media Ministry (PC)=Partner Church Pastor. See Page 53 for the Table of Abbreviations for key to additional abbreviations

CITY	CONGREGATION EMAIL WEBSITE	YEAR EST	LOCATION MAILING ADDRESS	ZIP CODE(S)	DIST.	PASTOR(S)	PHONE FAX	WS SS BC	SCHOOLS/ MINISTRIES	STATISTIC Bapt	Conf	Avg Attend
PARIS	*GRACE* graceparisoffice@gmail.com graceparis.org	1939	711 S Main St PO BOX 493	61944	CI	Daniel M Smith	(217)466-1215	WS 8 1030 SS 915	EC/ED/HC/ MD/SN	245	215	105
PARK RIDGE	*ST ANDREWS* www.standrewsparkridge.org	1909	260 N NORTHWEST HWY	60068	NI	Matthew J Hoffmann Ethan W Luft	(847)823-6656 (847)823-1846	WS 830 11 SS 945 BC 945	EL/ED/HC/ MD			
PAXTON	*IMMANUEL*		See Loda IL									
PECATONICA	*ST JOHN* stjohn.office.61063@gmail.com	1875	1301 N Jackson St 1301 JACKSON ST	61063	NI	Phillip J Allman	(815)239-2400	WS 9 SS 1015 BC 1015	ED/MD	213	175	83
PEKIN	*ST JOHN* stjohnsec@grics.net www.stjohnpekin.com	1852	711 COURT ST	61554	CI	Daniel J Bishop	(309)347-2136	WS 8 1030 7 SS 915 BC 915	EL/ED/HC/ MD	1015	527	110
	TRINITY trinity.lutheran.pekin@gmail.com www.trinitypekin.com	1941	700 S 4TH ST	61554	CI	Mark R Drews	(309)346-1391	WS 9 BC 1015	EL/ED/HC/ MD	335	261	66
PEORIA	*CHRIST* info@christlutheranpeo.org www.christlutheranpeo.org	1894	2020 W MALONE ST	61605	CI	Karl F Eckhoff	(309)637-5309 (309)637-6033	WS 9 SS 1030 BC 1030	EL/ED/HC/ MD/SN	557	438	126
	MOUNT CALVARY mtcalvary@mtcalvarypeoria.org MtCalvaryPeoria.org	1932	908 W HANSSLER PL	61604	CI	Barry A Long	(309)688-4321 (309)688-3062	WS 9 1145 SS 1030 BC 1030	EL/ED/HC/ MD	401	308	84
	REDEEMER www.redeemerlutheran.com	1949	6801 N ALLEN RD	61614	CI	Frank E Winter III	(309)691-2333 (309)691-4388	WS 815 1045 SS 930 BC 930	EC/EL/ED/ HC/MD/SN	1149	901	410
	TRINITY tlc@trinitypeoria.com www.trinitypeoria.com	1857	135 NE RANDOLPH AVE	61606	CI	Mark J Nelson Matthew B Synnott	(309)676-4609 (309)676-4689	WS 8 1045 SS 930 BC 940	EL/ED/HC/ MD/SN	590	509	326
PERCY	*EMMANUEL* emmanuellutheranpercy@gmail.com www.emmanuelpercy.org	2015	110 E Pine St PO BOX 400	62272	SI	Dr Alan W Janneke	(618)317-4416		HC			
PETERSBURG	*BETHLEHEM* blcpburgil@gmail.com www.bethlehempetersburg.org	1881	120 W MONROE ST	62675	CI	Jeffrey A Gross	(217)632-2453	WS 10 SS 9 BC 9	ED/HC/ MD/SN	439	399	60
PHILLIPSTOWN	*OUR SAVIOR*		See Carmi IL									
PINCKNEYVILLE	*TRINITY* contact@ziontrinity.org ziontrinity.org	1897	2338 Mountain Lion Rd 508 S MILL ST	62274	SI	David L Kollmeyer	(618)357-2818	WS 830 SS 830 930	ED/HC/ MD/SN			
	ZION www.zionpinckneyville.org	1886	508 S MILL ST	62274	SI	David L Kollmeyer	(618)357-2818	WS 10 SS 9	ED/HC/MD			
PITTSFIELD	*ST PAUL* stpaullutheranpittsfield@gmail.com	1949	1234 W Washington 1234 W WASHINGTON ST	62363	CI		(217)491-2548	WS 10 SS 9				
PLAINFIELD	*DIVINE SHEPHERD*		See Bolingbrook IL									
	PEACE plc@peaceplainfield.org www.peaceplainfield.org	1956	24024 W Main 24024 W MAIN ST	60544	NI	Dr David P Balla	(815)436-9847	WS 830 11 SS 945 BC 945	ED/HC/ MD/SN	208	177	87
	ZION		See Naperville IL									
PLANO	*LORD OF LIFE*		See Millbrook IL									
PLEASANT PLAINS	*ZION* zionpp@casscomm.com www.zionpp.net	1965	525 N Cartwright PO BOX 167	62677	CI	Donald F Pritchard	(217)626-1282	WS 830 SS 930 BC 930	HS/ED/HC/ MD/SN	193	152	36
PRAIRIE	*ST JOHN*		See Baldwin IL									
PRAIRIETOWN	*ST PETER* splcasop@gomadison.com www.saintpeterslutheran.org	1855	7183 RENKEN RD DORSEY	62021	SI	Oliver Q LaMie	(618)888-2250 (618)888-2353	WS 10 SS 9 BC 9	EL/ED/HC/ MD	301	257	95
PROSPECT HEIGHTS	*OUR REDEEMER* ourredeemerluth@sbcglobal.net www.ourredeemerprospectheights.org	1957	304 W PALATINE RD PROSPECT HTS	60070	NI	Jeffery H Leichman	(847)537-4430	WS 9	EC/ED/HC/ MD/SN	60	60	34
QUINCY	*OUR REDEEMER* Secretary@OurRedeemerQuincy.org www.OurRedeemerQuincy.org	1940	2701 COLLEGE AVE	62301	CI	Martin R Eden	(217)223-1769 (217)223-2392	WS 9 SS 1010 BC 1010	ED/HC/ MD/SN	546	430	134
	SAINT JAMES churchoffice@stjamesquincy.org www.stjamesquincy.org	1851	900 South 17th St 900 S 17TH ST	62301	CI	Matthew E Riley Marlin R Rempfer	(217)222-8447 (217)222-3415	WS 8 1030 SS 915 BC 915	EL/ED/HC/ MD/SN	605	444	160
	ST JOHN secretary@lcosj.org www.lcosj.org	1837	3340 STATE ST	62301	CI	Steven L Hayden	(217)222-8579 (217)222-1182	WS 8 1030 SS 915	ED/HC/MD	780	547	197
RAYMOND	*TRINITY*		See Harvel IL									
RED BUD	*ST JOHN* office@stjohnsredbud.org www.stjohnsredbud.org/church	1855	508 Bloom St 808 S MAIN ST	62278	SI	Mark P Winkelman Brian L Nowak	(618)282-3873 (618)282-4087	WS 8 1030 SS 930 BC 930	EL/ED/HC/ MD/SN			
	ST JOHN		See Baldwin IL									
	TRINITY trinitypastor@htc.net www.trinityredbud.com	1842	10235 S PRAIRIE RD	62278	SI	Scott E Hojnacki	(618)282-2883 (618)282-4045	WS 10 SS 9 BC 9	EL/ED/MD			
RENAULT	*HOLY CROSS* holycros@htc.net holycrossrenault.org	1853	2033 Kaskaskia Rd PO BOX 7	62279	SI	Terry L Grebing	(618)458-6680	WS 10 SS 9 BC 9	ED/HC/ MD/SN			
RICHTON PARK	*IMMANUEL* immanuelrichtonpark@gmail.com www.immanuelrp.com	1852	4800 SAUK TRL	60471	NI	Bryan A Reeves	(708)748-0558 (708)748-6593	WS 9	ED/HC/MD	82	68	50
RISING SUN	*OUR SAVIOR*		See Carmi IL									
RIVER GROVE	*BETHLEHEM* gallup57@juno.com www.bethlehemrivergrove.org	1898	2624 OAK ST	60171	NI	Roger B Gallup	(708)453-1113	WS 945 SS 945 BC 845				

*Indicates a new church start. A new church start is an intentionally organized gathering which comes together on a regular basis for the purpose of worship and/or Bible study and is intended to grow into a member LCMS congregation. WS =Worship Service; SS = Sunday School; BC =Bible Class; EC = Early Childhood; EL = Elementary School; HS = High School; ED =Education Ministry; HC =Human Care Ministry; SN = Special Needs Ministry; MD = Media Ministry (PC)=Partner Church Pastor. See Page 53 for the Table of Abbreviations for key to additional abbreviations

CONGREGATIONS

CITY	CONGREGATION EMAIL WEBSITE	YEAR EST	LOCATION MAILING ADDRESS	ZIP CODE(S)	DIST.	PASTOR(S)	PHONE FAX	WS SS BC	SCHOOLS/ MINISTRIES	STATISTIC Bapt	Conf	Avg Attend
RIVERTON	*IMMANUEL*	1893	705 E Menard St PO BOX 380	62561	CI	Michael A Koschmann	(217)629-8415	WS 830 SS 930 BC 930				
ROANOKE	*TRINITY* trinity_roanoke@frontier.com trinityroanokeil.com/#/	1871	202 W Lincoln PO BOX 268	61561	CI	Bruce W Scarbeary	(309)923-5251	WS 10 SS 915 BC 915	EC/ED/SN	73	68	42
ROBBINS	*HOLY CROSS*		See Alsip IL									
ROBINSON	*OUR REDEEMER*	1982	801 W Emmons St PO BOX 42	62454	CI	Adrian L Piazza	(618)546-5210	WS 11 SS 1015	ED/HC	39	36	22
ROCHELLE	*ST PAUL* stpaul2@rochelle.net www.stpaulev.org	1897	1415 10TH AVE	61068	NI		(815)562-2744 (815)561-8074	WS 9 SS 1015 BC 1015	EL/ED/HC/ MD/SN	518	432	112
ROCHESTER	*GOOD SHEPHERD* goodshepherdroch@sbcglobal.net	1962	1 Camelot Dr PO BOX 587	62563	CI	Samuel J Janssen	(217)498-7991	WS 10 SS 9 BC 9	ED			
ROCK FALLS	*GOOD SHEPHERD* goodshepherdlutheran@live.com www.gslcrf.org	1962	435 MARTIN RD	61071	NI	John W Sharp	(815)625-3376	WS 1015 SS 915 BC 915	EL/ED/HC/ MD	203	157	50
ROCK ISLAND	*IMMANUEL* officeimmanuelri@gmail.com www.immanuelri.org	1856	3300 24TH ST	61201	CI	Leonard A Astrowski Jr	(309)786-3391	WS 9 SS 1015 BC 1015	ED/HC/MD	306	228	60
ROCKFORD	*CHRIST THE ROCK* office@ctrockford.org www.CTRockford.org	1991	8330 NEWBURG RD	61108	NI	James W Mc Coid	(815)332-7191 (815)986-2104	WS 8 1030 SS 915 BC 915	EC/EL/HS/ ED/HC/ MD/SN	255	204	186
	CONCORDIA		See Machesney Park IL									
	MOUNT OLIVE secretary@mtolivelutheran.com www.mtolivelutheran.com	1956	2001 N ALPINE RD	61107	NI	Steven A Benson	(815)399-3171 (815)399-3174	WS 8 11 SS 915 BC 915	EL/HS/ED/ HC/MD/SN	333	309	140
	REDEEMER pharrison.redeemerlcms@gmail.com www.redeemerlcms.org/	1930	827 16TH ST	61104	NI	Kevin R Olson	(815)397-2227 (815)397-3191	WS 8 1030 SS 915 BC 915	EL/HS/ED/ HC/MD/SN			
	RESURRECTION roloegg2@yahoo.com rlcrockford.org		600 N HORSMAN ST	61101	NI		(815)965-3335	WS 920 BC 1030	EL/HS	36	36	21
	ROCKFORD DEAF	1960	827 16TH ST	61104	NI		(815)397-2227					
	ST ANDREW		See Rockton IL									
	ST PAUL church.office@sp815.org www.stpaulrockford.org	1888	4881 Kilburn Avenue 4881 KILBURN AVE	61101	NI	Jonathan M Fisk	(815)963-5435	WS 8 10	EL/HS/ED/ HC/MD	217	200	91
ROCKTON	*ST ANDREW* office@standrewrockton.com standrewrockton.com	1963	511 W ROCKTON RD	61072	NI	Donald C Stein	(815)624-6051	WS 8 1045 SS 915 BC 915	EL/HS/ED/ HC/MD/SN	300	250	176
ROMEOVILLE	*DIVINE SHEPHERD*		See Bolingbrook IL									
ROSCOE	*CHRIST OUR SAVIOR* www.cosroscoe.org	1976	5506 REIMER DR	61073	NI	Eugene C Dassow	(608)481-1162	WS 930 SS 930 BC 1030	EL/HS/ED/ HC/MD	65	65	55
	ST ANDREW		See Rockton IL									
ROSECRANS	*BEAUTIFUL SAVIOR*		See Antioch IL									
ROSELLE	*ST JOHN*		See Schaumburg IL									
	TRINITY pastorkeith@trinityroselle.com www.trinityroselle.com	1910	405 RUSH ST	60172	NI	Keith A Speaks Dr James F Bach Douglas R Warmann	(630)894-3263 (630)894-1430	WS 830 11 6 SS 10 BC 945	EL/ED/HC/ MD/SN			
ROUND LAKE	*BEAUTIFUL SAVIOR*		See Antioch IL									
ROUND LAKE BEACH	*BEAUTIFUL SAVIOR*		See Antioch IL									
RUSHVILLE	*ST JOHN*	1957	424 W WASHINGTON ST	62681	CI		(217)322-4237	WS 830 SS 930 BC 745	ED/HC/ MD/SN			
SADORUS	*ST PAUL* stpaulsadorus@gmail.com www.stpaulsadorus.com	1875	101 E Church St PO BOX 230	61872	CI		(217)598-2259	WS 10 SS 9 BC 9	EC/HC			
SAINT ANNE	*ST PAUL*		See Bourbonnais IL									
SAINT CHARLES	*LORD OF LIFE*		See Elburn IL									
	ST MARK info@stmarkslife.org www.stmarkslife.org	1907	101 S 6TH AVE	60174	NI	James A Holt Ray A Krueger	(630)584-8638 (630)584-8646	WS 830 11 SS 945 BC 945	EC/ED/HC/ MD	992	746	228
SAINT PETER	*ST PETER* bharpster.spls@gmail.com	1869	605 E 3RD ST	62880	CI	Ryan W Meyer	(618)349-8321 (618)349-8321	WS 9 SS 1030 BC 1030	EL/ED/HC/ MD/SN	614	489	152
SALEM	*SALEM* pastormike@salemlc.org salemlc.org	1928	1401 HAWTHORN RD	62881	CI	Michael W Feldmann Ethan D Hart	(618)548-3190 (618)548-3206	WS 8 1015 SS 9 BC 9	EC/HS/ED/ HC/MD/SN	498	399	212
SAN JOSE	*ST LUKE* 4johnsons2009@live.com www.stluke-sanjose.org	1908	15757 N CR 3600E PO BOX 407	62682	CI		(217)482-5822	WS 1030 SS 930	ED/MD	133	115	30
SANDWICH	*IMMANUEL*		See Hinckley IL									
	LORD OF LIFE		See Millbrook IL									
SAVOY	*UNIVERSITY*		See Champaign IL									
SCHAUMBURG	*HISTORIC CHAPEL* Satellite Site of St Peter Schaumburg IL	2007	218 E Schaumburg Rd	60194				WS 10				
	ST JOHN secretary@stjohnschaumburg.org www.stjohnschaumburg.org	1851	1800 S RODENBURG RD	60193	NI	Robert D Etheridge	(847)524-9746 (847)524-6376	WS 9 SS 1015 BC 1015	EC/ED/HC/ MD/SN	123	106	26
	ST PETER churchinfo@stpeterlcms.org stpeterlcms.org	1847	202 E SCHAUMBURG RD	60194	NI	Jerry D Hays Matthew R Dubensky	(847)885-3350 (847)885-1106	WS 745 9 11 SS 10 BC 1010	EL/ED/HC/ MD/SN	1532	1272	385

*Indicates a new church start. A new church start is an intentionally organized gathering which comes together on a regular basis for the purpose of worship and/or Bible study and is intended to grow into a member LCMS congregation. WS =Worship Service; SS = Sunday School; BC =Bible Class; EC = Early Childhood; EL = Elementary School; HS = High School; ED =Education Ministry; HC =Human Care Ministry; SN = Special Needs Ministry; MD = Media Ministry (PC)=Partner Church Pastor. See Page 53 for the Table of Abbreviations for key to additional abbreviations

CITY	CONGREGATION EMAIL WEBSITE	YEAR EST	LOCATION MAILING ADDRESS	ZIP CODE(S)	DIST.	PASTOR(S)	PHONE FAX	WS SS BC	SCHOOLS/ MINISTRIES	STATISTIC Bapt	Conf	Avg Attend
SECOR	*ST JOHN* stjohn-secor.org	1865	212 N 2nd PO BOX 229	61771	CI	Michael J Peters	(309)744-2255	WS 10 SS 9 BC 9	ED/SN	232	232	21
SENECA	*FRIENDS IN CHRIST*		See Morris IL									
SHABBONA	*IMMANUEL*		See Hinckley IL									
SHELBYVILLE	*HOLY CROSS* holycrosslutheranshelbyvilleil@gmail.com www.holycrosslutherans.com	1883	1201 N CHESTNUT ST	62565	CI	Nathan P Woolery	(217)774-2952 (217)774-3675	WS 9 SS 10 BC 10	ED/HC/ MD/SN	330	289	100
SHERMAN	*GOOD SHEPHERD* churchoffice@gsslcms.org gsslcms.org	1981	500 South Sherman Boulevard PO BOX 237	62684	CI	Matthew L Schneider Joshua W Theilen	(217)496-3149	WS 9 SS 1030 BC 1030	EC/HS/ED/ HC/MD/SN	586	451	97
SHOBONIER	*IMMANUEL* augsburg@augsburgchurch.com www.augsburgchurch.com	1876	1297 E 900 AVE	62885	CI	Timothy J Landskroener	(618)846-8383	WS 10 SS 9 BC 9	ED	299	222	54
	ST PAUL	1864	1608 E 800 AVE	62885	CI		(618)349-6291	WS 9 SS 1015 BC 1015				
SHOREWOOD	*HOPE* office@shorewoodhopelutheran.org www.shorewoodhope.org	1980	305 E BLACK RD	60404	NI	William C Ryden	(815)741-2428	WS 8 1030 SS 915	ED/HC/ MD/SN			
	TIMBERS RETIREMENT COMMUNITY Satellite Site of Hope Shorewood IL	2009	1100 N River Rd	60404								
SHUMWAY	*FAITH* Rev.j.peiser@gmail.com faithlutheranchurchshumway.org	1986	7707 East State Highway 33 7707 E STATE HIGHWAY 33	62461	CI	Jordan R Peiser	(217)868-5484	WS 10 SS 9 BC 9	ED/HC/MD	246	180	60
SIDNEY	*IMMANUEL*		See Broadlands IL									
SIGEL	*ST PAUL*	1865	201 E Washington PO BOX 182	62462	CI		(217)844-2019	WS 8	HC	142	112	23
SILVIS	*ST JOHN*		See East Moline IL									
SKOKIE	*ST PAUL* office@stpaulskokie.org www.stpaulskokie.org	1881	7870 Niles Center Rd 5201 GALITZ ST	60077	NI	Henry H Biar II	(847)673-5030	WS 9 SS 1015 BC 1015	ED/HC/ MD/SN	254	218	57
SOUTH BELOIT	*ST ANDREW*		See Rockton IL									
SOUTH ELGIN	*KING OF GLORY*		See Elgin IL									
	LORD OF LIFE		See Elburn IL									
SPARTA	*ST JOHN*	1910	1110 N MARKET ST	62286	SI	Carl H Miller	(618)443-3634	WS 830 1045 SS 945 BC 945	EC/ED/HC			
	ST JOHN		See Baldwin IL									
SPRING GROVE	*BEAUTIFUL SAVIOR*		See Antioch IL									
	COMMUNITY FAITH communityoffaith@hotmail.com	1995	3010 E SOLON RD	60081	NI		(815)675-1074	WS 9 SS 930	ED/HC/MD			
	ZION		See McHenry IL									
SPRINGERTON	*OUR SAVIOR*		See Carmi IL									
SPRINGFIELD	*CHRIST DEAF*		See Jacksonville IL									
	CONCORDIA clc.ps.concordia@gmail.com www.concordiacares.org	1930	2300 E WILSHIRE RD	62703	CI		(217)529-3307	WS 10 BC 9	EL/HS/ ED/HC	171	151	50
	GOOD SHEPHERD		See Sherman IL									
	HOLY TRINITY www.holytrinitylutheranspringfield.org	1888	119 N 15TH ST	62703	CI		(217)528-9894					
	IMMANUEL immanuellutheranspi@gmail.com	1929	2750 E SANGAMON AVE	62702	CI	Adam L Rouse	(217)528-5232 (217)523-5453	WS 9 BC 1015	HS/HC/ MD/SN	149	133	76
	IMMANUEL LUTHERAN CHAPEL Satellite Site of Immanuel Springfield IL	2021	1800 N. Grand Avenue West	62702				WS 2				
	OUR SAVIOR'S info@oursaviors-church.org www.oursaviors-church.org	1960	2645 OLD JACKSONVILLE RD	62704	CI	Joshua T Traxel Joel W Springer	(217)546-4531 (217)546-0293	WS 8 10 SS 915 BC 9	EL/HS/ED/ HC/MD	1572	1283	386
	TRINITY church@trinity-lutheran.com www.trinity-lutheran.com	1841	220 S 2nd St 515 S MACARTHUR BLVD	62701 62704	CI	Aaron J Mueller Jonathan M Sharp	(217)787-2323 (217)522-7059	WS 8 1030	EL/HS/ED/ HC/MD	1088	827	398
	TRINITY LUTHERAN SCHOOL Satellite Site of Trinity Springfield IL	2012	515 S Mac Arthur Blvd	62704				BC 940 SS 940				
STAUNTON	*ZION* zionlutheranstaunton@gmail.com www.zion-luth.org	1846	311 S ELM ST	62088	SI		(618)635-2880 (618)635-3994	WS 8 1030 SS 930	EL/ED/MD	991	728	175
STEELEVILLE	*IMMANUEL*		See Campbell Hill IL									
	ST MARK STMARKS.STEELEVILLE@GMAIL.COM	1872	105 N GARFIELD ST	62288	SI	Mark E Harriss	(618)965-3192	WS 9 SS 1015 BC 1015	EL/ED/ MD/SN			
	ST PAUL'S secretary@imstp.org www.imstp.org	1859	11854 WINE HILL RD	62288	SI	John M Sedwick	(618)965-3831	WS 10 SS 845	ED/HC/ MD/SN	223	185	70
STEGER	*IMMANUEL* ilcsteger.secretary@gmail.com www.ilcsteger.org	1899	24 W 34th Place 24 W 34TH PL	60475	NI	Dr Vernon E Wendt Jr	(708)754-2345	WS 8 BC 930	ED/HC/ MD/SN			
STERLING	*MESSIAH* melcoffice@comcast.net mlcsterling.org	1875	1601 Ave F 1601 AVENUE F	61081	NI	Chad R Bolosan	(815)625-2284 (815)625-1804	WS 9 SS 1015 BC 1015	EL/ED/MD	273	217	90

*Indicates a new church start. A new church start is an intentionally organized gathering which comes together on a regular basis for the purpose of worship and/or Bible study and is intended to grow into a member LCMS congregation. WS =Worship Service; SS = Sunday School; BC =Bible Class; EC = Early Childhood; EL = Elementary School; HS = High School; ED =Education Ministry; HC =Human Care Ministry; SN = Special Needs Ministry; MD = Media Ministry (PC)=Partner Church Pastor. See Page 53 for the Table of Abbreviations for key to additional abbreviations

CITY	CONGREGATION EMAIL WEBSITE	YEAR EST	LOCATION MAILING ADDRESS	ZIP CODE(S)	DIST.	PASTOR(S)	PHONE FAX	WS SS BC	SCHOOLS/ MINISTRIES	STATISTIC Bapt	Conf	Avg Attend
STERLING	*OUR SAVIOR*	1875	21496 HAZEL RD	61081	NI	Philip M Heuser	(815)772-4345	WS 9 SS 10 BC 10	EL/ED/HC/ MD/SN			
STEWARDSON	*TRINITY* trinitylutheranchurchandschool@ hotmail.com www.trinitystewardsonil.org	1868	113 S Walnut St PO BOX 307	62463	CI	David J Weaver	(217)682-5722 (217)682-3881	WS 10 SS 9 BC 9	EL/ED	506	401	136
STRASBURG	*GRACE* gracestrasburg@gmail.com	1897	109 N Locust St PO BOX 336	62465	CI	Kene A Whybrew	(217)644-2452	WS 1030 SS 930 BC 930	ED/MD/SN	150	96	54
	ST PAUL'S stpaulsstrasburg@gmail.com www.stpaul-strasburg.com	1866	511 S Walnut 511 S WALNUT ST	62465	CI	Kene A Whybrew	(217)644-2661	WS 830 1015 SS 9 BC 930	ED/HC/MD			
STREAMWOOD	*GRACE* pastorpaulcutler@yahoo.com www.graceistheplace.net	1959	780 S BARTLETT RD	60107	NI	Paul J Cutler	(630)289-3996 (630)289-7104	WS 815 1045 SS 930 BC 930				
STREATOR	*HOLY TRINITY* htlc.streator@gmail.com www.holytrinitystreator.org	1884	101 TRINITY DR	61364	S	John E Gutz	(815)672-2393	WS 9 SS 1015 BC 1015	EC/ED/HC/ MD/SN	328	253	103
SUGAR LOAF TOWNSHIP	*HOLY CROSS* hcsugarloaf@gmail.com	1841	7640 TRIPLE LAKES RD E CARONDELET	62240	SI	Ralph E Laufer	(618)538-5600	WS 1030 SS 915 BC 915		70	50	25
SULLIVAN	*FAITH* church@faithsullivan.org www.faithsullivan.org	1969	1185 State Hwy 32 PO BOX 109	61951	CI	Justin W Cullen	(217)728-7711	WS 10 SS 9 BC 9 530	ED/HC/ MD/SN	185	169	74
SUMMIT	*ZION* zionevlcms@gmail.com www.zionlutheransummit.org	1871	5865 S ARCHER RD SUMMIT ARGO	60501	NI	Eric N Andersen	(708)563-0777	WS 9 BC 8	ED/HC/ MD/SN			
SYCAMORE	*IMMANUEL*		See Hinckley IL									
	ST JOHN office@stjohnsycamore.org www.stjohnsycamore.org	1876	26555 BRICKVILLE RD	60178	NI	Paul G Mumme	(815)895-4477	WS 9 SS 1030 BC 1030	ED/HC/MD	477	441	222
TAYLOR RIDGE	*ZION* zionlcms@juno.com zionlutherantaylorridge.org/	1854	18121 134TH AVE W	61284	CI	Mark R Eddy	(309)795-1063	WS 8 1030 SS 920 BC 920	ED/HC/MD	366	212	67
TAYLORVILLE	*TRINITY* trinitychurch@tlctaylorville.com trinitylutherantaylorville.org	1896	1010 N WEBSTER ST	62568	CI	Brian C Johnston	(217)824-8148	WS 915 SS 1030	EC/ED/HC/ MD	641	414	70
THAWVILLE	*ST PETER*	1886	114 N Mc Neil St PO BOX 157	60968	CI		(217)387-2381	WS 930 SS 1030				
THOMASBORO	*PEACE* peacelutheran@gmail.com peace-thomasboro.org	1880	200 W Arnold Ave PO BOX 428	61878	CI	Michael W Stoerger	(217)643-3265	WS 930 SS 830	HS/ED/HC/ MD/SN			
THORNTON	*ST PAUL* office@splcms.org www.splcms.org	1859	508 CHICAGO RD	60476	NI		(708)877-6564 (708)877-6564	WS 930 SS 1030				
TINLEY PARK	*TRINITY* church@tlcs.org tlcs.org	1859	6850 W 159th St 6850 159TH ST	60477	NI	Paul O Strand Richard V Schauer	(708)532-9395 (708)532-0750	WS 8 930 11 SS 930 BC 930	EL/ED/HC/ MD/SN	1429	894	626
TROY	*ST PAUL* church@saintpaulstroy.org www.saintpaulstroy.org	1867	106 N BORDER ST	62294	SI	Dr Albert B Collver III	(618)667-6681	WS 9 SS 1030 BC 1030	EC/ED/HC	563	464	136
TUSCOLA	*IMMANUEL* immanuel.tuscola@gmail.com www.immanueltuscola.org	1897	600 E NORTHLINE RD	61953	CI	Jason M Braaten	(217)253-4341	WS 9 SS 1030 BC 1030	ED/MD	186	158	106
UNION	*ST JOHN* contact@stjohnsluth.org www.stjohnsluth.org	1887	6821 MAIN ST	60180	NI	Caleb J Schauer Mark D Novacek	(815)923-2733 (815)923-2734	WS 745 1030 SS 9 BC 915	EL/HS/ED/ HC/MD/SN	922	749	195
URBANA	*TRINITY* office@trinity-urbana.org www.trinity-urbana.org	1953	701 E FLORIDA AVE	61801	CI		(217)367-8923 (217)367-8928	WS 830 1045 SS 945 BC 945	EC/ED/HC/ MD/SN	131	131	81
	UNIVERSITY		See Champaign IL									
VANDALIA	*HOLY CROSS* hclchurch@att.net www.holycrossvandalia.org	1934	726 W FILLMORE ST	62471	CI	Brett E Cornelius Michael W Mohr	(618)283-1133 (618)283-1133	WS 9 SS 1030 BC 1030	ED/HC/MD	180	139	69
VARNA	*ST PAUL* stpaulsvarna@gmail.com	1871	80 CHESTNUT ST	61375	CI	Mark E Gruden		WS 830 SS 945 BC 945	ED	135	117	35
VENEDY	*ST SALVATOR* Pastor.JimdEntremont@gmail.com www.stsalvator.ctshost.org	1842	179 W CHURCH ST	62214	SI		(618)824-6366	WS 10 SS 9	EL/ED/ MD/SN	245	171	77
VILLA GROVE	*IMMANUEL*		See Tuscola IL									
VILLA PARK	*TRINITY* margaret@trinityvp.com www.trinitylutheranvp.com	1913	300 S ARDMORE AVE	60181	EN	Robert A Rogers	(630)834-3440 (630)834-5232	WS 8 1030 SS 915 BC 915	ED/HC/ MD/SN	450	394	104
WADSWORTH	*BEAUTIFUL SAVIOR*		See Antioch IL									
WAGGONER	*TRINITY*		See Harvel IL									
WALNUT	*HOLY TRINITY* www.htlcwalnut.org	1966	404 E North St PO BOX 550	61376	NI	Phillip J Fischaber	(815)379-2839	WS 830 BC 10	EL/ED/HC			
WALSH	*ST JOHN*		See Baldwin IL									
WARRENSBURG	*ST PAUL'S*		See Decatur IL									
WARSAW	*CONCORDIA*	1845	801 Lafayette 801 LAFAYETTE ST	62379	CI	Marcus R Jauss	(217)256-3215	WS 830 BC 945	ED/SN			
WASCO	*LORD OF LIFE*		See Elburn IL									
WASHBURN	*ST JOHN* tlh262@gmail.com	1875	400 North Jefferson PO BOX 437	61570	CI	Mark E Gruden	(309)431-1704	WS 10	HC	67	50	19

*Indicates a new church start. A new church start is an intentionally organized gathering which comes together on a regular basis for the purpose of worship and/or Bible study and is intended to grow into a member LCMS congregation. WS =Worship Service; SS = Sunday School; BC =Bible Class; EC = Early Childhood; EL = Elementary School; HS = High School; ED =Education Ministry; HC =Human Care Ministry; SN = Special Needs Ministry; MD = Media Ministry (PC)=Partner Church Pastor. See Page 53 for the Table of Abbreviations for key to additional abbreviations

CITY	CONGREGATION EMAIL WEBSITE	YEAR EST	LOCATION MAILING ADDRESS	ZIP CODE(S)	DIST.	PASTOR(S)	PHONE FAX	WS SS BC	SCHOOLS/ MINISTRIES	STATISTIC Bapt	Conf	Avg Attend
WASHINGTON	*OUR SAVIOR* secretary@oslwashington.org www.oslwashington.org	1965	1209 KINGSBURY RD	61571	CI	Frank M Gallagher	(309)444-4030 (309)444-8817	WS 815 11 SS 945	EC/ED/HC/ MD/SN	325	280	120
WATERLOO	*HOLY CROSS* hcwartb@htc.net www.holycrosswartburg.com	1841	5765 MAEYSTOWN RD	62298	SI	Daniel A Ostlund	(618)939-7094 (618)939-7094	WS 9 SS 1015 BC 1015	ED/HC			
	IMMANUEL immanuelwaterloo@gmail.com www.immanuelwaterloo.org	1901	522 S CHURCH ST	62298	SI	Dr Antonin C Troup	(618)939-6480 (618)939-7010	WS 745 1015 SS 9 BC 9	EC/ED/ HC/SN	775	607	187
WATERMAN	*IMMANUEL*		See Hinckley IL									
WATSEKA	*CALVARY* calvarywatseka@gmail.com calvarywatseka.com	1930	120 E HICKORY ST	60970	CI	Aaron D Uphoff	(815)432-4136 (815)432-3535	WS 9 SS 1015 BC 1015	EC/ED/HC/ MD	441	338	100
WAUKEGAN	*REDEEMER* lcmsredeemer@aol.com	1927	620 Grove Ave 620 W GROVE AVE	60085	NI	Wayne P Jahn	(847)336-4891	WS 9 BC 1015				
WAVERLY	*CHRIST* katco@speednet.com	1939	185 E TREMONT ST	62692	CI	Keith R Pereira	(217)435-9685	WS 10 SS 9 BC 9	ED/HC/ MD/SN			
WAYNE	*LORD OF LIFE*		See Elburn IL									
WENONA	*ZION* zionlutheranwenona@gmail.com www.zionlutheranwenona.org	1883	117 WALNUT PO BOX 245	61377	CI	Mark E Gruden	(815)853-4479		ED/HC/ MD/SN	61	44	20
WEST CHICAGO	*TRINITY* secretary@trinitywc.org www.trinitywc.org	1884	328 GEORGE ST	60185	NI	Dr Eric J Moeller Fred A Gaede	(630)231-1175 (630)231-6926	SS 1030 BC 1030	ED			
WEST DUNDEE	*BETHLEHEM* bethchurchdun@aol.com www.bethlehemdundee.org	1909	401 W MAIN ST	60118	NI	Joseph S Glombicki	(847)426-7311	WS 8 1030	ED/HC			
	VIDA Y FE/LIFE FAITH vidayfe.elgin@gmail.com vidayfechurch.org		417 W MAIN ST	60118	NI		(224)802-2949	WS 11	ED/MD			
WEST FRANKFORT	*ST PAULS* stpaulwestfrankfort@gmail.com stpaulwflcms.org	1926	1 West Frankfort Plaza 1 WEST FRANKFORT PLZ W FRANKFORT	62896	SI	Dr Alan W Janneke	(618)932-3450	WS 1030 SS 9 BC 9	HC/MD/SN			
WEST POINT	*IMMANUEL*		See Campbell Hill IL									
WESTCHESTER	*FAITH* pastor.prentice@comcast.net faith-lutheran-church.com	1949	1124 Westchester Blvd 1118 WESTCHESTER BLVD	60154	NI	David L Prentice Jr	(708)885-0001	WS 9 11 SS 1015 BC 1015	ED/HC	44	40	25
WESTERN SPRINGS	*GRACE* gracelutheran.ws@gmail.com www.grace-lutheranws.org	1925	4101 WOLF RD WESTERN SPRGS	60558	NI	Matthew L Zickler	(708)246-0536 (708)246-1005	WS 9 SS 1015 BC 1015	EL/HS	157	131	70
WESTMONT	*BETHEL* www.bethelwestmont.org	1921	36 N GRANT ST	60559	NI	David K Szeto	(630)968-3232 (630)968-2030	WS 1015 SS 9 BC 9	EC/ED/HC/ MD	261	229	71
WHEATON	*ST JOHN* mnelson@stjohnwheaton.org www.stjohnwheaton.org	1867	410 N CROSS ST	60187	NI	Marcus J Nelson Dr Scott A Bruzek Eamonn M Ferguson Alvaro J Witt Duarte Nathan S LeMahieu	(630)668-0701 (630)682-1504	WS 830 11 SS 10 BC 10	EC/ED/HC/ MD/SN	809	631	675
WHEELER	*ST PAUL* dualparish@mmtcnet.com	1871	13204 N 2300TH ST	62479	CI	Dean Z Herberts	(217)924-4498	WS 10 SS 9 BC 9	ED/HC/ MD/SN	162	134	60
WILLIAMSVILLE	*GOOD SHEPHERD*		See Sherman IL									
WILLOW SPRINGS	*GRACE* gracewillowsprings@gmail.com gracewillowsprings.org	1928	212 S NOLTON AVE WILLOW SPGS	60480	NI	Mark W Duer	(708)839-5255	WS 9 SS 1030	ED/HC/ MD/SN	95	90	45
WINCHESTER	*CHRIST* christwinchester@gmail.com	1966	125 W JEFFERSON ST	62694	CI		(217)742-3919	WS 1030	ED	57	42	19
WINDSOR	*WINDSOR LUTHERAN CENTER* Satellite Site of Faith Sullivan IL	2023	1102 Maine Street	61957								
WINE HILL	*ST PAUL'S*		See Steeleville IL									
WINFIELD	*CHRIST OUR SAVIOR*	1963	O S 501 SUMMIT DR	60190	NI	Jesus G Morales	(630)665-5110 (630)665-5262	WS 9 SS 10 1015 BC 10 1015				
WONDER LAKE	*ZION*		See McHenry IL									
WOOD DALE	*ZION*		See Bensenville IL									
WOOD RIVER	*ST PAUL* churchoffice@stpaulwoodriver.com www.stpaulwoodriver.com	1916	1327 VAUGHN RD	62095	SI	Dr David M Schultz	(618)259-0257 (618)259-0055	WS 8 1030 SS 915 BC 915	EC/HS/ED/ HC/MD/SN	836	672	303
WOODRIDGE	*BETHANY*		See Naperville IL									
	DIVINE SHEPHERD		See Bolingbrook IL									
	IMMANUEL LUTHERAN CHURCH SATELLITE Satellite Site of Immanuel Downers Grove IL	2003	Hollywood Blvd Theater 1001 W 75th ST at Lemont Rd	60517				WS 1010 BC 9				
WOODSTOCK	*CROSSPOINT LAKEWOOD*		See Lakewood IL									
	ST JOHNS office@stjohnswoodstock.com www.stjohnswoodstock.com	1875	401 St Johns Rd 401 SAINT JOHNS RD	60098	NI		(815)338-5159	WS 9 SS 1015 BC 1015	ED/HC/ MD/SN			
WORDEN	*ST PAUL* jmertz@stpaulhamel.org www.stpaulhamel.org	1856	6969 W Frontage Rd PO BOX 247 HAMEL	62097 62046	SI	Benjamin T Ball Rene G Castillero William C Weedon	(618)633-2209	WS 745 10 SS 9 BC 9	EC/EL/HS/ ED/HC/ MD/SN	738	582	325
	TRINITY tlc@madisontelco.com www.trinityworden.org	1877	512 Main St PO BOX 296	62097	SI	Dustin J Krystowiak	(618)459-3991	WS 9 SS 10 BC 10	HS/ED			
YORKVILLE	*CROSS* churchinfo@hiscross.org www.hiscross.org	1881	8609 STATE ROUTE 47	60560	NI	Erik A Gauss Matthew J Conrad	(630)553-7335 (630)553-2580	WS 8 930 11 BC 930	EL/ED/HC/ MD/SN	910	579	316

*Indicates a new church start. A new church start is an intentionally organized gathering which comes together on a regular basis for the purpose of worship and/or Bible study and is intended to grow into a member LCMS congregation. WS =Worship Service; SS = Sunday School; BC =Bible Class; EC = Early Childhood; EL = Elementary School; HS = High School; ED =Education Ministry; HC =Human Care Ministry; SN = Special Needs Ministry; MD = Media Ministry (PC)=Partner Church Pastor. See Page 53 for the Table of Abbreviations for key to additional abbreviations

INDIANA

CITY	CONGREGATION EMAIL WEBSITE	YEAR EST	LOCATION MAILING ADDRESS	ZIP CODE(S)	DIST.	PASTOR(S)	PHONE FAX	WS SS BC	SCHOOLS/ MINISTRIES	STATISTIC Bapt	Conf	Avg Attend
ANDERSON	*CHRIST* christlutheranchurchanderson@ gmail.com www.christlutherananderson.com	1903	716 Rainbow Blvd 2751 N SCATTERFIELD RD	46012	IN	John A Jameson	(765)642-2154	WS 1015 SS 9 BC 9	ED/HC/ MD/SN	280	202	79
ANGOLA	*PEACE*		See Fremont IN									
ARCADIA	*EMANUEL*	1852	355 SHAFFER ST	46030	IN	Dr Jerrell S Simmerman	(317)418-5509	WS 9 BC 1030	ED/SN			
AUBURN	*TRINITY* pastor@trinitylutheran-auburn.org www.trinitylutheran-auburn.org	1871	1801 N MAIN ST	46706	IN	Jonathan C Nack	(260)925-2440	WS 9 SS 1015 BC 1015	EC/ED/HC/ MD/SN	167	148	80
AURORA	*ST JOHN* office@sjlsaurora.com stjohnaurora.org	1860	220 MECHANIC ST	47001	IN	Mark W Hesse	(812)926-3337 (812)926-7603	WS 10 BC 9	EL/ED/HC/ MD			
AVILLA	*IMMANUEL* imavilla@embarqmail.com immanuellutheran-avilla.com	1844	111 W Albion St PO BOX 188	46710	IN	Patrick J Kuhlman	(260)897-2071	WS 930 SS 830 BC 830	ED/HC/ MD/SN	547	401	66
AVON	*LIVING CHRIST*		See Plainfield IN									
	OUR SHEPHERD office@ourshepherd.org www.ourshepherd.org	1971	9201 E County Rd 100 N 9201 E COUNTY ROAD 100 N	46123	IN	Andrew G Berg Daniel K Coffey	(317)271-9103 (317)271-3084	WS 9 1115 SS 1015	EL/HS/ ED/HC/ MD/SN	847	627	347
BARGERSVILLE	*CHRIST THE KING*		See Mooresville IN									
BEAN BLOSSOM	*SHEPHERD HILLS* shepherd.of.the.hills.5802@gmail.com sothbrowncounty.org	1966	5802 N OLD SETTLERS RD MORGANTOWN	46160	IN	Scott P Roberts	(812)988-8057	WS 1015 BC 9	ED/MD/SN	34	26	25
BEDFORD	*CALVARY* bedfordcalvary@gmail.com www.calvarylutheranbedford.com	1931	3705 AUSTIN DR	47421	IN	Grant A Sorenson	(812)275-5488	WS 1030 SS 930	EC/ED/ HC/MD	146	122	73
	EMMANUEL emmanuellutheranleesville@frontier.com	1947	4340 LEESVILLE RD	47421	IN	Kenneth G Keily	(812)797-3693	WS 9	ED			
BEECH GROVE	*ASCENSION* bascension@aol.com hometown.aol.com/markewagnr/ myhomepage/business.html	1972	602 S 9TH AVE	46107	IN	Mark E Wagner	(317)788-1118 (317)780-7063	WS 10	HS/ED			
BERNE	*PEACE* peaceberne@gmail.com	1966	201 FULTON ST	46711	IN	Russell D Fuhrmann	(260)589-3848 (219)589-3848	WS 1030 SS 915 BC 915	ED/HC	44	36	15
BLOOMINGTON	*FAITH* office@faithbtown.org faithbtown.org	1963	2200 S HIGH ST	47401	IN	Eric J Edwards Liwei Sui	(812)332-1668 (812)332-2206	WS 8 1030 5 SS 915 BC 915	EC/ED/HC/ MD/SN			
	PRINCE OF PEACE		See Martinsville IN									
	TRINITY		See Ellettsville IN									
	UNIVERSITY indianalutheran@gmail.com www.indianalutheran.com	1929	607 E 7TH ST	47408	IN	Timothy J Winterstein	(812)336-5387	WS 1030 SS 915 BC 915	ED/HC/MD			
BLUFFTON	*NEW HOPE*		See Ossian IN									
BREMEN	*ST PAUL* church@stpaulsbremen.org www.stpaulsbremen.org	1846	605 S CENTER ST	46506	IN	Neil K Wonnacott	(574)546-2332	WS 930 SS 830 BC 830	EL/ED/HC/ MD	407	324	129
BRISTOL	*PRINCE PEACE*		See Goshen IN									
	TRINITY		See Elkhart IN									
BROWNSBURG	*ADVENT*		See Zionsville IN									
	CHRIST celc701@gmail.com www.christlutheran-indy.org	1976	701 E TILDEN DR	46112	IN	Christopher D Truelsen	(317)852-3343	WS 10 SS 1115	EC/ED/HC/ MD/SN	138	127	73
	CORNERSTONE		See Carmel IN									
	OUR SHEPHERD		See Avon IN									
BROWNSTOWN	*ST PAUL*	1856	1165 E COUNTY ROAD 400 S	47220	IN	Joel W Meyer	(812)358-2334	WS 10 SS 915 BC 915	EL/HS/ED	384	310	147
	ST PETER office@stpetersbrownstown.org www.facebook.com/people/ Stpetersbrownstown/ 100083201228897/#	1900	403 W BRIDGE ST	47220	IN	Ryan B Schneider	(812)358-2539	WS 8 1030 SS 915	EL/ED/HC/ MD/SN	703	551	268
CARMEL	*ADVENT*		See Zionsville IN									
	CORNERSTONE info@cornerstonelutheran.church www.cornerstonelutheran.church	1976	4850 E MAIN ST	46033	IN	Scott W Giger Shawn R Hecksel Dale B Ward Max J Murphy Kevin C Thomson	(317)814-4252	WS 830 1045 SS 945 BC 945	EC/HS/ ED/HC/ MD/SN			
CEDAR LAKE	*TRINITY*		See Lowell IN									
CHESTERTON	*ST PAUL* www.saintpaul-chesterton.org	1887	106 E County Road 1100 N 106 E COUNTY RD 1100 N	46304	IN	Erich R Fickel	(219)926-1556 (219)926-2638	WS 9 SS 1030				
CHURUBUSCO	*FAITH* flcbusco@yahoo.com www.flcbusco.org	1961	9251 E STATE ROAD 205	46723	IN	Adam L Sorenson	(260)693-6254	WS 8 10 SS 9 BC 9	ED	373	311	154
CLEAR LAKE	*CLEAR LAKE*		See Fremont IN									
COLUMBIA	*FAITH*		See Thompsons Station TN									
COLUMBIA CITY	*ST JOHN* dmommens@icloud.com stjohnlutheranchurch.webs.com	1847	2465 W KEISER RD	46725	IN	Gino C Marchetti II	(260)244-3712 (260)244-5870	WS 9 SS 1030 BC 1030	ED/HC/ MD/SN	313	227	76
	ZION zionccdq@gmail.com www.zionlutherancc.com	1861	101 E NORTH ST	46725	IN	David J Whan	(260)244-5513	WS 1015 SS 9 BC 9	ED/HC/ MD/SN	168	120	47

*Indicates a new church start. A new church start is an intentionally organized gathering which comes together on a regular basis for the purpose of worship and/or Bible study and is intended to grow into a member LCMS congregation. WS =Worship Service; SS = Sunday School; BC =Bible Class; EC = Early Childhood; EL = Elementary School; HS = High School; ED =Education Ministry; HC =Human Care Ministry; SN = Special Needs Ministry; MD = Media Ministry (PC)=Partner Church Pastor. See Page 53 for the Table of Abbreviations for key to additional abbreviations

CITY	CONGREGATION EMAIL WEBSITE	YEAR EST	LOCATION MAILING ADDRESS	ZIP CODE(S)	DIST.	PASTOR(S)	PHONE FAX	WS SS BC	SCHOOLS/ MINISTRIES	STATISTIC Bapt	Conf	Avg Attend
COLUMBUS	*FAITH* office@faithontheweb.org www.faithontheweb.org	1962	6000 W State Road 46 PO BOX 1164	47201 47202	IN	Josiah J Fitch	(812)342-3587 (812)342-7267	WS 9 SS 1030 BC 1030	EC/HS/ ED/HC/ MD/SN	305	248	64
	GRACE office@gracecolumbus.org www.gracecolumbus.org	1955	3201 CENTRAL AVE	47203	IN	Todd C Riordan	(812)372-4859	WS 8 1030 SS 930 BC 930	HS/ED/ HC/MD/ SN	416	289	135
	ST JOHN www.whitecreek.org	1840	16270 S 300 W	47201	IN	James A Haugen Jr	(812)342-6832	WS 9 SS 1015	EL/HS/ED/ MD			
	ST PAUL pastorbauman@stpaulcolumbus.org www.stpaulcolumbus.org	1848	6045 East State St 6045 E STATE ST	47201	IN	Douglas D Bauman Daniel P Fickenscher Jeffrey D Patterson	(812)376-6504	WS 8 1045 SS 930 BC 930	EC/HS/ED/ HC/MD	629	515	364
	ST PETER info@stpeters-columbus.org www.stpeterscolumbus.org	1858	719 5TH ST	47201	IN	John Cordrey Timothy R Carter James A Rodriguez	(812)372-1571 (844)718-0102	WS 8 1045 SS 930 BC 930	EL/HS/ED/ HC/MD	3454	2600	727
	ST PETER		See Waymansville IN									
CONNERSVILLE	*BETHANY* snretreat@hotmail.com	1944	2907 VIRGINIA AVE	47331	IN	Gene A Ott	(765)338-6527	WS 1030 BC 930				
CORUNNA	*ZION* ZionLutheranCorunna@gmail.com www.zionlutherancorunna.org	1846	389 COUNTY ROAD 12	46730	IN	Brian T Stark	(260)668-0250	WS 10 SS 9	ED/HC/ MD/SN	170	145	70
CRAWFORDSVILLE	*HOLY CROSS* wshelton@mfgqsinc.com www.holycross-crawfordsville.org	1954	1414 E WABASH AVE CRAW-FORDSVLLE	47933	IN	David L Putz	(765)362-5599	WS 1015 SS 9 BC 9	ED/HC/MD	55	54	30
CROSS PLAINS	*ST PAUL'S* stpaullutheran@seidata.com www.stpaulsdewberry.com	1851	5588 E COUNTY ROAD 900 S	47017	IN	Jared C Tucher	(812)667-5700	WS 9 SS 1015		192	146	30
CROWN POINT	*RESURRECTION* relc1992@yahoo.com www.reson30.org/	1992	8061 E US Highway 30 8061 E LINCOLN HWY	46307	S		(219)942-6604 (219)942-6604	WS 9 SS 9 BC 1030	ED/HC/MD			
	TRINITY info@trinitycp.org www.trinitycp.org	1868	250 S INDIANA AVE	46307	IN	Alan M Toenjes Cory A Wielert	(219)663-1578 (219)663-9606	WS 8 1030 BC 930	EL/ED/HC/ MD/SN	1128	763	432
CULVER	*TRINITY*	1958	430 ACADEMY RD	46511	IN	Timothy P Anderson	(574)842-3175	WS 9 BC 10	SN	27	23	20
DANVILLE	*LIVING CHRIST*		See Plainfield IN									
	OUR SHEPHERD		See Avon IN									
DARMSTADT	*TRINITY* trinitydarmstadt.org	1847	1401 W Boonville New Harmony 1401 W BOONVILLE NEW HARMONY R EVANSVILLE	47725	IN	James D Glowinski	(812)867-5279 (812)867-5333	WS 930 SS 11 BC 11	EC/ED/ MD/SN	174	153	70
DECATUR	*IMMANUEL*	1849	8538 N 500 E	46733	IN		(260)724-7680	WS 9 SS 1030 BC 1030	EL/ED/HC/ MD/SN	492	390	149
	ST JOHN churchoffice@stjohnbingen.com www.stjohnbingen.com	1845	11555 N US Hwy 27 11555 N US HIGHWAY 27	46733	IN	Peter J Brock Berett J Steffen	(260)639-6178	WS 8 1030 SS 915 BC 915	EL/ED/HC/ MD/SN	947	701	400
	ST PAUL andrewtyeager@gmail.com www.stpaulpreble.org	1873	4510 W 750 N	46733	IN	Andrew T Yeager I Dr Daniel J Brege	(260)547-4176	WS 8 1015 SS 915 BC 915	EL	533	426	187
	ST PETER leonard.tanksley@gmail.com www.stpeterdecatur.org	1845	1033 E 1100 N	46733	IN	Leonard E Tanksley	(260)724-7533	WS 9 SS 1015 BC 1015	EL/ED	464	292	115
	ZION pastor@zionfriedheim.org www.zionfriedheim.org	1838	10653 N 550 W	46733	IN	Matthew T Ulmer	(260)547-4248	WS 9 SS 9 1015 BC 9 1015	EL/ED/HC/ MD/SN	637	471	176
	ZION church@ziondecaturchurch.com www.ziondecatur.com	1901	1010 W MONROE ST	46733	IN	Zachary R Oedewaldt	(260)724-7177	WS 8 1030 SS 915 BC 915	EL/ED/HC/ MD			
DELPHI	*ST MATTHEWS* st.matthewsdelphi@gmail.com stmatthewsdelphi.org		1301 S WASHINGTON ST	46923	IN	Paul D Norris	(765)564-3200	WS 1030 SS 930 BC 930	ED/HC/MD	91	75	40
DEMOTTE	*FAITH* faithsecretary987@gmail.com www.faithdemotte.org	1958	1700 S HALLECK ST	46310	IN	Brett A Satkowiak	(219)987-3730	WS 9 SS 1030 BC 1030	EC/ED/ HC/MD	260	226	106
DENHAM	*ST PAUL* stpauldenham@gmail.com stpauldenham.org	1873	6692 N 575 W WINAMAC	46996	IN	Mark I Fakih	(574)896-5090	WS 10 SS 10 BC 9	HC/MD	74	56	38
DILLSBORO	*TRINITY* dillstrinity@yahoo.com	1903	9901 Central Ave PO BOX 578	47018	IN	Richard K Kolaskey	(812)432-5406	WS 10 SS 9 BC 915	ED/HC/MD	232	193	48
DUDLEYTOWN	*EMANUEL* pastor@emanueldudleytown.com	1857	2174 S COUNTY ROAD 750 E SEYMOUR	47274	IN	Kenneth J Davidson	(812)523-8234	WS 830 SS 945 BC 945	EL/HS/ED/ HC/MD			
DYER	*GRACE* gracelutheran.dyer@gmail.com gracedyer.org	1960	8303 SHEFFIELD AVE	46311	IN	Dale L Hetherington	(219)865-1137 (219)865-1137	WS 9 BC 1030	ED/HC/ MD/SN	86	72	54
EAGLE CREEK	*CORNERSTONE*		See Carmel IN									
EDWARDSVILLE	*SHEPHERD HILLS*		See Georgetown IN									
ELKHART	*PRINCE PEACE*		See Goshen IN									
	ST PETER		See Mishawaka IN									
	TRINITY www.trinityL.org	1874	30888 CR 6 30888 COUNTY ROAD 6	46514	IN	Spencer A Mielke Mason W Vieth	(574)674-8800 (574)674-6410	WS 830 11 BC 10	EL/ED/HC/ MD/SN	886	713	501
ELLETTSVILLE	*TRINITY* pastor@trinitylutheranellettsville.org www.trinitylutheranellettsville.org		501 E TEMPERANCE ST	47429	IN		(812)876-0996	WS 9 SS 1030 BC 1030	HC	39	38	16
EMMINENCE	*CHRIST THE KING*		See Mooresville IN									

*Indicates a new church start. A new church start is an intentionally organized gathering which comes together on a regular basis for the purpose of worship and/or Bible study and is intended to grow into a member LCMS congregation. WS =Worship Service; SS = Sunday School; BC =Bible Class; EC = Early Childhood; EL = Elementary School; HS = High School; ED =Education Ministry; HC =Human Care Ministry; SN = Special Needs Ministry; MD = Media Ministry (PC)=Partner Church Pastor. See Page 53 for the Table of Abbreviations for key to additional abbreviations

CITY	CONGREGATION EMAIL WEBSITE	YEAR EST	LOCATION MAILING ADDRESS	ZIP CODE(S)	DIST.	PASTOR(S)	PHONE FAX	WS SS BC	SCHOOLS/ MINISTRIES	STATISTIC Bapt	Conf	Avg Attend
EVANSTON	*ST JOHN* stjohnlutheranchurch07@gmail.com	1842	12308 E CR 1160 N 12308 E COUNTY ROAD 1160 N	47531	IN	Steven A Shank	(812)547-2007 (812)547-9620	WS 930 SS 830 BC 830	EC/ED/HC/ MD/SN	175	147	64
EVANSVILLE	*CONCORDIA* concordiaevansville@gmail.com concordiaevansville.org	1938	2451 STRINGTOWN RD	47711	IN	David E Wiist	(812)422-0384	WS 1030 SS 9 BC 9	ED/HC/ MD/SN			
	IMMANUEL immanuel-lutheranchurch.org	1854	1925 VOLKMAN RD	47725	IN	Kirk P Horstmeyer	(812)867-5088 (812)867-5088	WS 8 1015 SS 910 BC 910				
	OUR REDEEMER front.desk@redeemerchurch.org www.redeemerchurch.org	1928	1811 LINCOLN AVE	47714	IN	Dr Thomas D Wenig Jeremy B Seger Jason P Yunker	(812)476-9991 (812)476-4561	WS 8 1030 SS 930 BC 930	EC/EL/ ED/HC/ MD/SN			
	ST PAUL stpaulslcms@stpaulslcms.org stpaulslcms.org	1887	100 E MICHIGAN ST	47711	IN	Chad M Eckels Case A Farney Futao Liu	(812)422-5414 (812)422-5363	WS 8 1030 SS 915 BC 915	EL/ED/HC/ MD	1183	894	236
	TRINITY		See Darmstadt IN									
FAIR OAKS	*FAITH*		See Demotte IN									
FARMERS RETREAT	*ST JOHN* stjohnsfr@seidata.com Stjohnsfr.com	1843	7291 STATE ROAD 62 DILL-SBORO	47018	IN	Jared C Tucher	(812)667-5281	WS 1030 SS 930	ED/HC/MD	295	223	50
FISHERS	*CHRIST*		See Noblesville IN									
	CORNERSTONE		See Carmel IN									
	CORNERSTONE LUTHERAN CHURCH FISHERS Satellite Site of Cornerstone Carmel IN	2016	13450 E 116th St	46037				WS 845 11 SS 10				
	HOLY CROSS		See Indianapolis IN									
	JOURNEY pastor@journeylutheranministries.org www.journeylutheranministries.org		10401 E 116TH ST	46037	IN	Jonathan van Sliedrecht	(407)489-7727	WS 9				
FORT WAYNE	*ABOITE* info@aboitelutheran.org www.aboitelutheran.org	1987	10312 ABOITE CENTER RD	46804	IN	Richard Pagan	(260)436-5673 (260)436-9990	WS 830 11 SS 830 11 BC 945	HS/HC			
	ASCENSION office@alcsfw.org www.alcsfw.org	1977	8811 SAINT JOE RD	46835	IN	James D Gier Jr Dr Gary W Zieroth	(260)486-2226 (260)486-5793	WS 8 1045 SS 930 BC 930	EL/HS/ED	402	333	226
	BETHANY study@bethanylc.org www.bethanylc.org	1952	2435 ENGLE RD	46809	EN	Chad D Trouten	(260)747-0713 (260)747-8011	WS 930 SS 1045	ED			
	BETHLEHEM bethfw@yahoo.com www.bethlehemlcms.org	1926	3705 S ANTHONY BLVD	46806	IN	Benjamin T Ahlersmeyer	(260)744-3228 (260)744-3229	WS 9 BC 1030	EL/HS/ HC/SN	622	444	100
	CONCORDIA www.concordiachurch.org	1899	4245 LAKE AVE	46815	IN	Douglas E Croucher Joseph D Reineke Steven M Ahlersmeyer	(260)422-2429 (260)422-3415	WS 830 9 11 SS 10 BC 945	EL/HS/ ED/HC	1735	1427	583
	EMMANUEL becki@emmanuellutheran.org www.emmanuellutheran.org	1867	917 W JEFFERSON BLVD	46802	IN	Thomas A Eggold Daniel M Sheafer	(260)423-1369 (260)426-6147	WS 8 1030 SS 915 BC 915	EL/ED/HC/ MD/SN	2599	2029	592
	EMMANUEL churchofficeemmanuelsoest@gmail.com emmanuelsoest.ctshost.org	1845	9909 WAYNE TRCE	46816	IN	Josef J Henning	(260)447-3005 (260)447-3840	WS 8 10 SS 915 BC 915	EC/EL/HS/ ED/HC/ MD/SN	628	509	220
	EMMAUS eberg@emmausfortwayne.org emmausfortwayne.org	1900	8626 COVINGTON RD	46804	IN	Roy C Olsen III	(260)459-7722 (260)459-7766	WS 9 SS 1030 BC 1030	EL/HS/ ED/HC/ MD/SN	208	178	111
	FAITH		See Churubusco IN									
	GLORIA DEI	1937	6222 Parrott Rd 32 W 200 N BLUFFTON	46803 46714	IN		(260)307-1047	WS 7				
	HOLY CROSS hgraf@holycrossfw.org www.holycrossfw.org	1945	3425 CRESCENT AVE	46805	IN	Dr Thomas R Ahlersmeyer Daniel A Kinley Chad M Van Meter	(260)483-3173 (260)471-6141	WS 815 1030	EL/HS/ ED/HC/ MD/SN	1717	1379	588
	JACOBS WELL team@jacobswell.us jacobswell.us		10707 COLDWATER RD	46845	EN	David C Adams	(260)312-6294	WS 1030	EC			
	MOUNT CALVARY church@mtcfw.org www.mtcfw.org	1929	6721 Old Trail Rd Suite 300 PO BOX 9590	46809 46899	IN		(260)747-4121	WS 930 BC 1045	EL/HS/ ED/HC/ MD/SN	73	73	30
	NEW LIFE nl4u@hotmail.com www.NL4U.org	1992	2424 S COLISEUM BLVD	46803	IN	James N Keller	(260)420-3024	WS 11 SS 12 BC 12 6	HS/HC	175	88	130
	PEACE secretary@peacelutheranfw.org www.peacelutheranfw.org	1946	4900 FAIRFIELD AVE	46807	IN	Kevin D Mann	(260)744-3869	WS 9 SS 1030 BC 1030	EC/EL/HS/ ED/HC/ MD/SN	277	235	79
	PRAISE office@praiselutheran.org praiselutheran.org	1994	1115 W DUPONT RD	46825	IN		(260)490-7729 (260)490-0364	WS 1030 BC 930	EC/ED/HC/ MD/SN	118	92	51
	PROMISE office@promisefw.com www.promisefw.com	1996	7323 SCHWARTZ RD	46835	IN	Scott R Hedtke Sean W Sheppard	(260)493-9953 (260)749-8119	WS 9 1030 SS 9	HC/MD	652	490	361
	REDEEMER secretary.redeemer@gmail.com redeemer-fortwayne.org	1892	202 W RUDISILL BLVD	46807	EN	Dr David H Petersen Shawn T Barnett	(260)744-2585	WS 8 1030 SS 915 BC 915	HS/ED	328	221	300
	SAINT AUGUSTINE dhenry@holycrossfw.org		3425 CRESCENT AVE	46805	IN		(260)739-6517	WS 1030 SS 1030 BC 10	ED/HC/MD			
	SHEPHERD OF THE CITY shepherdfw1@gmail.com shepherdofthecitylutheran.org	1970	1301 S ANTHONY BLVD	46803	IN		(260)422-3790	WS 930 SS 11 BC 11	ED/HC	108	63	36

*Indicates a new church start. A new church start is an intentionally organized gathering which comes together on a regular basis for the purpose of worship and/or Bible study and is intended to grow into a member LCMS congregation. WS =Worship Service; SS = Sunday School; BC =Bible Class; EC = Early Childhood; EL = Elementary School; HS = High School; ED =Education Ministry; HC =Human Care Ministry; SN = Special Needs Ministry; MD = Media Ministry (PC)=Partner Church Pastor. See Page 53 for the Table of Abbreviations for key to additional abbreviations

CITY	CONGREGATION EMAIL WEBSITE	YEAR EST	LOCATION MAILING ADDRESS	ZIP CODE(S)	DIST.	PASTOR(S)	PHONE FAX	WS SS BC	SCHOOLS/ MINISTRIES	STATISTIC Bapt	Conf	Avg Attend
FORT WAYNE	*SOUTHWEST* swlc@southwestlutheran.org www.southwestlutheran.org	2002	5120 HOMESTEAD RD	46814	IN	Joseph W Ferry Soe Moe	(260)436-4474	WS 915 SS 1045 BC 1045	ED/HC/MD	150	126	64
	ST MICHAEL jenny@stmfw.org stmfw.org	1953	2131 GETZ RD	46804	IN	Dr Dennison J Goff Shawn P Davis	(260)432-2033 (260)432-8363	WS 8 1045 SS 930 BC 930	EL/HS/ ED/HC/ MD/SN	1148	1053	519
	ST PAUL		See New Haven IN									
	ST PAULS churchoffice@stpaulsfw.org www.stpaulsfw.org	1837	1145 BARR ST	46802	IN	Josemon T Hoem Peter C Cage	(260)423-2496 (260)423-2497	WS 930 BC 1045	EL/HS/ ED/HC/ MD/SN	916	793	299
	ST PETER'S churchoffice@stpetersfw.org www.stpetersfw.org	1855	7710 E STATE BLVD	46815	IN	Daniel A Eggold Adam M McDowell Nathan C Widener	(260)749-5816 (260)749-0472	WS 8 1030 SS 915 BC 915	EL/HS/ED/ HC/MD	1631	1273	525
	SUB BETHLEHEM sbl@deeplyrootedtogrow.org www.deeplyrootedtogrow.org	1898	6318 W CALIFORNIA RD	46818	IN	William E Mueller Alexander L Duff	(260)484-7873 (260)483-9016	WS 8 1030 SS 930 BC 930	EL/HS/ ED/HC/ MD/SN	952	707	402
	TRINITY trinityfortwayne@gmail.com www.trinityfortwayne.com	1853	7819 DECATUR RD	46816	IN	Michael W Trombley	(260)447-2411	WS 9 SS 1030 BC 1030		141	105	70
	TRINITY secretary@trinitylutheranfw.com trinitylutheranfw.com	1895	1636 SAINT MARYS AVE	46808	IN	David W Griebel	(260)422-7931 (260)969-4005	WS 930 SS 1045 BC 1045	ED/HC/ MD/SN	192	123	94
	URBAN MISSION LEWIS KING Satellite Site of Holy Cross Fort Wayne IN	2015	502 E Pontiac	46806				BC 2				
	WORSHIP IN THE PARK Satellite Site of Trinity Fort Wayne IN	1979	3411 Sherman Blvd	46808								
	ZION office@zionfw.org www.zionfw.org	1883	2313 Hanna St 2313 S HANNA ST	46803	IN	Douglas D Punke	(260)744-1389 (260)744-2421	WS 9 SS 1045 BC 1045	EL/HS/ ED/HC/ MD/SN	337	239	85
FORTVILLE	*CORNERSTONE*		See Carmel IN									
FRANKLIN	*CHRIST THE KING*		See Mooresville IN									
	CONCORDIA		See Greenwood IN									
	GOOD SHEPHERD gslcfranklin@gmail.com www.gslcfranklin.org	1969	1300 S Morton PO BOX 265	46131	IN	Roger W Daene	(317)736-7849	WS 10 SS 9 BC 9	ED/HC/ MD/SN			
FREMONT	*CLEAR LAKE* clearlakelutheran@gmail.com www.clearlakelutheran.org	1968	270 Outer Dr Clear Lk 270 OUTER DR	46737	IN	Jeffrey J Corder	(260)495-9219	WS 9 BC 10	ED/HC/MD	122	102	49
	LAKE GEORGE lakegeorgelutheranchapel@gmail. com lakegeorgelutheran.org	1967	1540 W 800 N	46737	IN	Paul E Shoemaker	(260)615-9580	WS 9	ED/MD	42	42	57
	PEACE admin@plcms.org www.plcms.org	1985	355 E STATE ROAD 120	46737	EN	Jeffrey S Teeple Jared E Rudolph	(260)495-4306 (260)495-5076	WS 8 1030 SS 915 BC 915	EC/ED/HC/ MD/SN	503	481	211
GARRETT	*ZION* zelcgarrett@gmail.com ziongarrett.org	1887	1349 S RANDOLPH ST	46738	IN	Keaton G Christiansen	(260)553-4202	WS 9 SS 1030	EC/ED/ HC/SN	299	203	80
GARY	*GOOD SHEPHERD* Goodshepherdluther@sbcglobal.net	1943	719 W 25TH AVE	46407	IN		(219)885-2109 (219)885-2109	WS 11 SS 930 BC 930				
	ST JOHN secretary@historicstjohngary.net	1870	2271 W 10th Ave 1139 NOBLE ST	46404	IN		(219)944-0654 (219)944-3577	WS 9 SS 1015	HC/MD	25	22	20
GEORGETOWN	*SHEPHERD HILLS* pastor@sothluth.org sothluth.org	1969	5231 STATE ROAD 62	47122	IN	Dale A Becker	(812)945-2101	WS 9 SS 1015 BC 1015	EC/ED/MD	161	143	80
GOODLAND	*TRINITY* davidmueller66@yahoo.com	1873	217 W JASPER ST	47948	IN	David R Mueller	(219)297-3556	WS 8 SS 930	ED			
GOSHEN	*PRINCE PEACE* popgoshen@gmail.com www.popgoshen.org	1981	18548 COUNTY ROAD 18	46528	IN	Andrew J Wollman	(574)533-7705	WS 9 SS 1015 BC 1015	ED/HC/MD	88	73	45
	TRINITY		See Elkhart IN									
GRABILL	*PRINCE OF PEACE* www.princeofpeacegrabill.com	1966	12640 St Joe Rd 12640 SAINT JOE RD	46765 46741	IN	Robert E Eickmann Jr	(260)627-5621	WS 9 SS 1030 BC 1030	ED/MD/SN			
GRANGER	*ST PETER*		See Mishawaka IN									
	TRINITY		See Elkhart IN									
GREENCASTLE	*PEACE* peacegreencastlein@gmail.com www.peacelutherangreencastle.org	1954	1421 S Bloomington St PO BOX 778	46135	IN	William J Winter	(765)653-6995 (765)653-6995	WS 1015 BC 9	ED/HC/ MD/SN	66	62	45
GREENFIELD	*FAITH* secretary@faithgreenfield.org www.faithgreenfield.org	1957	200 W Mc Kenzie Rd 200 W MCKENZIE RD	46140	IN	William D O'Connor	(317)462-4609 (317)468-0721	WS 915 SS 11 BC 11	EC/HS/ ED/HC/ MD/SN	135	120	89
GREENSBURG	*HOLY TRINITY* mail2holytrinity@gmail.com www.htlcg.org	1935	1219 S MICHIGAN AVE	47240	IN	Aaron M West	(812)663-8192	WS 10 SS 9 BC 9	ED/HC	140	108	35
GREENWOOD	*CALVARY*		See Indianapolis IN									
	CHRIST THE KING		See Mooresville IN									
	CONCORDIA concordia@concordia-lcms.com www.concordia-lcms.com	1956	305 N Howard Rd 305 HOWARD RD	46142	IN	Henry S Scheltens	(317)881-4477 (317)881-4498	WS 930 SS 1045	EC/HS/ED/ HC/MD	313	238	94
HAMLET	*ST MATTHEW*	1885	6 W INDIANA AVE	46532	IN		(574)867-8704	WS 9 SS 10 BC 1015	ED/MD/SN	57	50	30

*Indicates a new church start. A new church start is an intentionally organized gathering which comes together on a regular basis for the purpose of worship and/or Bible study and is intended to grow into a member LCMS congregation. WS =Worship Service; SS = Sunday School; BC =Bible Class; EC = Early Childhood; EL = Elementary School; HS = High School; ED =Education Ministry; HC =Human Care Ministry; SN = Special Needs Ministry; MD = Media Ministry (PC)=Partner Church Pastor. See Page 53 for the Table of Abbreviations for key to additional abbreviations

CITY	CONGREGATION EMAIL WEBSITE	YEAR EST	LOCATION MAILING ADDRESS	ZIP CODE(S)	DIST.	PASTOR(S)	PHONE FAX	WS SS BC	SCHOOLS/ MINISTRIES	STATISTIC Bapt	Conf	Avg Attend
HAMLET-TRACY	*IMMANUEL* davidmalbertin@gmail.com www.tracylutheran.org	1875	8705 S 100 E HAMLET	46532	IN	Dr David M Albertin	(219)921-9378	WS 9 SS 10	ED/HC/ MD/SN	45	40	25
HAMMOND	*TRINITY* trinityluthham@yahoo.com www.trinityhammond.com	1918	7227 HOHMAN AVE	46324	IN		(219)932-4660	WS 9 SS 1030 BC 1030	ED/HC/MD	125	113	52
HANNA	*FIRST* firstlutheran46340@gmail.com	1884	15 E Wheeler PO BOX 26	46340	IN	Michael J Osbun Kendall L Schaeffer	(219)797-4855	WS 9	ED/HC/SN	68	61	25
HARTFORD CITY	*PRINCE OF PEACE* princeofpeacehc@gmail.com	1994	Mill And Van Cleve Sts PO BOX 86	47348	IN		(317)410-4799	WS 9 SS 1015		22	22	10
HEBRON	*FAITH*		See Demotte IN									
HIGHLAND	*REDEEMER* info@redeemerhighland.org www.redeemerhighland.org	1954	9009 KENNEDY AVE	46322	IN	Eric A Kleinschmidt	(219)838-4898 (219)838-3197	WS 8 1045 SS 915 BC 915	ED/MD/SN	450	360	134
HOBART	*TRINITY* tlc900churchsec@comcast.net www.trinityhobart.org	1873	900 LUTHER DR	46342	IN	Nathan G Kramer	(219)942-2589 (219)942-7459	WS 9 SS 1030 BC 1030	EL/ED/HC/ MD/SN	630	550	145
HOWE	*MESSIAH*		See Wolcottville IN									
HUDSON	*PRINCE PEACE* office.pop.stroh@gmail.com princeofpeacestroh.org	1977	10275 E 550 S PO BOX 358 STROH	46747 46789	EN	Brian V Pratt	(260)351-2144	WS 9 BC 1030	ED/HC/MD	99	89	61
HUNTERTOWN	*OUR HOPE* ourhopeinfo@gmail.com www.ourhopelutheran.com	1963	1826 Trinity Dr PO BOX 36	46748	IN	Roger B James	(260)637-3625 (260)637-4673	WS 830 11 SS 10 BC 10	EC/ED/HC	369	192	85
HUNTINGTON	*ST PETER* spelcsecretary@gmail.com stpeterhuntington.org	1849	648 N La Fontaine St 605 POLK ST	46750	IN	Timothy J Lorenz	(260)356-6528 (260)356-6528	WS 1015 SS 9 BC 9	ED/HC/ MD/SN	316	239	85
INDIANAPOLIS	*ADVENT*		See Zionsville IN									
	CALVARY churchsecretary@clcs.org www.clcs.org	1931	6111 SHELBY ST	46227	IN	Kurt A Ebert Samuel R Troemel Udhayanesan Raji Dr Mark E Schumm	(317)783-2000 (317)783-7096	WS 8 1045 SS 925 BC 925	EL/HS/ED/ HC/MD	1195	996	381
	CHRIST		See Noblesville IN									
	CHRIST THE KING		See Mooresville IN									
	CONCORDIA		See Greenwood IN									
	CORNERSTONE		See Carmel IN									
	CORNERSTONE LUTHERAN CHURCH EAGLE CREEK Satellite Site of Cornerstone Carmel IN	2022	6100 N Raceway Rd	46234				WS 930 SS 1045				
	CORNERSTONE LUTHERAN INDIANAPOLIS Satellite Site of Cornerstone Carmel IN	2016	2837 E New York St	46201				WS 9 11 BC 10				
	EMMAUS emmauschurchindy@gmail.com www.elcindy.org	1903	1224 LAUREL ST	46203	IN		(317)632-1486 (317)632-2620	WS 10 SS 845 BC 845	HS/HC/MD	130	114	66
	FIRST TIMOTHY church@firsttimothylcms.org www.firsttimothylcms.org	1989	2190 Lafayette Rd PO BOX 88465	46222 46208	IN	Cleveland A Lewis	(317)257-6383	WS 1015 SS 930	ED/HC/MD	51	32	16
	HOLY CROSS hclc@hclc.info www.hclcindy.org	1989	8115 OAKLANDON RD	46236	IN	Daniel L Hauser David R McClean	(317)823-5801 (317)762-7904	WS 8 9 10 11	EL/HS/ ED/HC/ MD/SN	1520	1103	494
	JOURNEY		See Fishers IN									
	OUR SAVIOR	1942	261 W 25TH ST	46208	IN		(317)925-3737 (317)925-3744	WS 11 BC 930	HS			
	OUR SHEPHERD		See Avon IN									
	PRINCE OF PEACE		See Martinsville IN									
	SAINT PETERS prmierow@gmail.com www.stpetersindy.org	1896	2525 E 11TH ST	46201	IN	Seth A Mierow	(317)638-7245	WS 1015 SS 1035 BC 1035	HS/ED/ HC/MD/ SN	267	197	89
	ST JOHN info@stjohnindy.org www.stjohnindy.org	1852	6630 SOUTHEASTERN AVE	46203	IN	Collin P Duling	(317)352-9196 (317)352-9740	WS 8 1045 SS 945 BC 945	EC/EL/HS/ ED/HC/ MD/SN	1077	670	261
	ST PAULS stpaulsindy@gmail.com www.stpaulsindy.com	1842	3932 MICASA AVE	46237	IN	David A Shadday Anthony Nwokeneme	(317)787-4464 (317)787-0838	WS 930 SS 1045	HS/ED/ HC/MD/ SN	255	205	97
	TRINITY www.Trinityindy.org	1875	8540 E 16TH ST	46219	IN		(317)897-0243	WS 830 11 SS 9 BC 9	EL/HS/ED/ HC/MD	226	185	101
	TRINITY LUTHERAN CHURCH LATINO WORSHIP Satellite Site of Trinity Indianapolis IN	2019	8540 East 16th Street	46219				WS 330				
	ZION		See New Palestine IN									
JONESVILLE	*ST PAUL* stpaulsjonesville@gmail.com	1877	609 MILL ST	47247	IN	Matthew P Jung	(812)523-9994	WS 1015 SS 9 BC 9	HS			
KENDALLVILLE	*MESSIAH*		See Wolcottville IN									
	ST JOHN sjlc.net	1859	301 S OAK ST	46755	IN	Dr Philip J Rigdon	(260)347-2158 (260)349-2854	WS 8 1030 SS 920 BC 920	EL/ED/HC/ MD/SN	511	464	175
KNOX	*BASS LAKE MINISTRY* Satellite Site of St Paul Denham IN	1997	7055 S U S 35	46534								

*Indicates a new church start. A new church start is an intentionally organized gathering which comes together on a regular basis for the purpose of worship and/or Bible study and is intended to grow into a member LCMS congregation. WS =Worship Service; SS = Sunday School; BC =Bible Class; EC = Early Childhood; EL = Elementary School; HS = High School; ED =Education Ministry; HC =Human Care Ministry; SN = Special Needs Ministry; MD = Media Ministry (PC)=Partner Church Pastor. See Page 53 for the Table of Abbreviations for key to additional abbreviations

CITY	CONGREGATION EMAIL WEBSITE	YEAR EST	LOCATION MAILING ADDRESS	ZIP CODE(S)	DIST.	PASTOR(S)	PHONE FAX	WS SS BC	SCHOOLS/ MINISTRIES	STATISTIC Bapt	Conf	Avg Attend
KNOX	*MELODY DRIVE IN THEATER* Satellite Site of St Peter North Judson IN	2014	7055 S US 35	46534								
	MELODY DRIVE-IN Satellite Site of Our Redeemer Knox IN	1995	7055 S US Hwy 35	46534								
	OUR REDEEMER office@ourredeemerknox.com	1940	1600 S HEATON ST	46534	IN		(574)772-4186	WS 9 SS 1015 BC 1015	EC/ED/HC/ MD/SN			
KOKOMO	*GOOD SHEPHERD* www.goodshepherdkokomo.org	1977	121 SANTA FE BLVD	46901	IN	John C Kolb	(765)457-4968 (765)457-8526	WS 1015 SS 9 BC 9	ED/HC/SN	65	62	18
	OUR REDEEMER LCOR@RedeemerKokomo.org www.RedeemerKokomo.org	1918	705 E SOUTHWAY BLVD	46902	IN	John M Dreyer Carl D Hingst	(765)453-0969 (765)864-6470	WS 830 11 BC 945 345	EL/ED/HC/ MD/SN	775	659	230
KOUTS	*ST PAUL* stpaullutheranchurch@frontier.com www.facebook.com/koutslutheran	1873	507 South Rose St PO BOX 547	46347	IN	Brian P Westgate	(219)766-2395 (219)766-2395	WS 9	ED/HC/ MD/SN	193	171	47
LA PORTE	*TRINITY* trinitylaporte@gmail.com	1925	907 MICHIGAN AVE	46350	EN		(219)362-4932 (219)362-4932	WS 9 SS 1015 BC 1015	ED/HC/MD	69	63	20
LACROSSE	*ST JOHN*	1906	301 N Washington St PO BOX 359 LA CROSSE	46348	IN	Joel S Zipay	(219)754-2296		HC			
LAFAYETTE	*GRACE* office@gracelaf.org www.gracelaf.org	1976	102 BUCKINGHAM DR	47909	IN		(765)474-1887	WS 8 1030 SS 915 BC 915	ED/HC/MD	397	332	214
	SAINT JAMES churchoffice@stjameslaf.org www.stjameslaf.org	1850	800 CINCINNATI STREET	47901	IN	Dr John J Bombaro Adam L Barcott	(765)423-1616 (765)742-4642	WS 930 SS 930 BC 930	EL/ED/ MD/SN	664	513	251
LAGRANGE	*MESSIAH*		See Wolcottville IN									
LANESVILLE	*SAINT JOHN* info@stjohnslanesville.com www.stjohnslanesville.com	1846	1505 SAINT JOHNS CHURCH RD NE	47136	IN	Michael D Terkula	(812)952-3711	WS 9 SS 1015 BC 1015	EL/ED	441	345	125
LAPORTE	*IMMANUEL*		See Hamlet-tracy IN									
	SAINT JOHNS churchoffice@stjohnslaporte.org www.stjohnslaporte.org	1857	111 KINGSBURY AVE LA PORTE	46350	IN	John M Albers	(219)362-3726	WS 8 930	EL/ED/HC/ MD/SN			
	TRINITY		See La Porte IN									
LAWRENCE	*HOLY CROSS*		See Indianapolis IN									
LEBANON	*ADVENT*		See Zionsville IN									
LOGANSPORT	*SAINT JAMES* Pastor.Dehning@gmail.com stjameslogansport.org	1848	430 9TH ST	46947	IN	Scott A Woodhouse	(574)753-4227	WS 1030 SS 9 BC 9	ED/HC/SN			
LOWELL	*TRINITY* office@trinitylowell.com www.trinitylowell.com	1926	631 W Commercial Ave PO BOX 236	46356	IN	Richard A Heinz	(219)696-9338	WS 8 1030 SS 925 BC 930	ED/HC/MD	451	371	168
MADISON	*FAITH* faithinfo.lcms@gmail.com www.faithlutheran-madison.org	1961	3024 MICHIGAN RD	47250	IN	Jeffery D Pflug	(812)273-1371 (440)325-8942	WS 10 SS 9 BC 9	HC/MD	121	96	39
MARION	*SAINT JAMES* church@stjamesmarion.org www.stjamesmarion.org	1950	1206 N MILLER AVE	46952	IN	Fredrick C Hearn	(765)662-3092 (765)662-9197	WS 830 1045 SS 945	SN	215	198	117
MARTINSVILLE	*CHRIST THE KING*		See Mooresville IN									
	PRINCE OF PEACE popchurchlcms@hotmail.com www.popmartinsville.org	1961	3496 E MORGAN ST	46151	IN	Nathan L Janssen	(765)342-2004 (765)813-0036	WS 9 SS 1030 BC 1030	EC/ED/HC/ MD/SN	369	261	138
MCCORDSVILLE	*CORNERSTONE*		See Carmel IN									
	HOLY CROSS		See Indianapolis IN									
MEDARYVILLE	*ST MARK*	1876	US 421 5950 E 700 N	47957	IN		(574)205-2274	WS 11 SS 10	HC/MD			
MEDORA	*EMMANUEL*		See Bedford IN									
	GOOD SHEPHERD	1940	186 W Main St PO BOX 310	47260	IN	Janis C Mikits		WS 11				
MERRILLVILLE	*RESURRECTION*		See Crown Point IN									
	TRINITY MEMORIAL office@tmlchurch.com www.tmlchurch.com	1940	7950 MARSHALL STREET	46410	IN	Brian J Nygaard	(219)769-5376 (219)769-1265	WS 9 SS 1020 BC 1030	ED/HC/ MD/SN	326	267	90
MICHIGAN CITY	*IMMANUEL* immanuellutheran1237@gmail.com www.immanuelmc.com	1904	1237 E COOLSPRING AVE	46360	IN	David R Solum	(219)872-4419 (219)872-4870	WS 10 SS 845 BC 845	MD	337	263	116
MIDDLEBURY	*PRINCE PEACE*		See Goshen IN									
	TRINITY		See Elkhart IN									
MISHAWAKA	*ST PETER* office@splcm.org www.splcm.org	1847	437 E DRAGOON TRL	46544	IN	Dr Adam C Clark Bryan G Borger	(574)255-5585 (574)259-1726	WS 1015 SS 9 BC 9	EL/ED/HC/ MD/SN	192	163	128
	TRINITY		See Elkhart IN									
MONROEVILLE	*ST JOHN* churchoffice@saintjohnflatrock.org saintjohnflatrock.org	1847	12912 FRANKE RD	46773	IN	Douglas M Christian	(260)639-6404 (260)639-6404	WS 815 1030 7 SS 1015 BC 1015	EL/ED	460	404	147
MONROVIA	*CHRIST THE KING*		See Mooresville IN									
MONTICELLO	*OUR SAVIOUR* lutheranchurchofoursaviour.0catch. com	1957	122 CONDO ST	47960	IN	Jeffrey S Zell	(574)583-5005	WS 10	ED/MD/SN			
MOORESVILLE	*CHRIST THE KING* eric.ebb@hotmail.com www.christthekingmooresville.com	2013	6845 E OLD STATE ROAD 144	46158	IN	Jefferson M Arnold	(260)750-8198	WS 10 SS 9 BC 9	ED/MD/SN			
	LIVING CHRIST		See Plainfield IN									

*Indicates a new church start. A new church start is an intentionally organized gathering which comes together on a regular basis for the purpose of worship and/or Bible study and is intended to grow into a member LCMS congregation. WS =Worship Service; SS = Sunday School; BC =Bible Class; EC = Early Childhood; EL = Elementary School; HS = High School; ED =Education Ministry; HC =Human Care Ministry; SN = Special Needs Ministry; MD = Media Ministry (PC)=Partner Church Pastor. See Page 53 for the Table of Abbreviations for key to additional abbreviations

CITY	CONGREGATION EMAIL WEBSITE	YEAR EST	LOCATION MAILING ADDRESS	ZIP CODE(S)	DIST.	PASTOR(S)	PHONE FAX	WS SS BC	SCHOOLS/ MINISTRIES	STATISTIC Bapt	Conf	Avg Attend
MOORESVILLE	*PRINCE OF PEACE*		See Martinsville IN									
MOUNT VERNON	*OUR SAVIOR*		See Carmi IL									
MUNCIE	*GRACE* graceutheran2@sbcglobal.net www.gracemuncielcms.com	1938	610 N RESERVE ST	47303	IN	Daniel P Mackey	(765)282-2537	WS 8 1030 SS 920 BC 920	ED/HC	230	191	85
MUNSTER	*ST PAUL* StPaul@STPLmunster.com www.stplmunster.com	1882	8601 HARRISON AVE	46321	IN	Peter A Speckhard Adrian J Krebs	(219)836-6270 (219)836-3724	WS 8 1015 SS 915 BC 915	EL/ED/ MD/SN	1109	937	307
NASHVILLE	*SHEPHERD HILLS*		See Bean Blossom IN									
NEW ALBANY	*GRACE* karen.meredith@glcna.com www.glcna.com	1927	1787 KLERNER LN	47150	IN	Matthew B Woods	(812)944-1267 (812)941-8519	WS 8 1030 SS 915	EC/ED/HC/ MD/SN			
NEW HARMONY	*OUR SAVIOR*		See Carmi IL									
NEW HAVEN	*EMANUEL* churchoffice@emanuelnh.org www.emanuelnh.org	1858	800 GREEN ST	46774	IN	Scott A Zeckzer David O Stecker	(260)749-2163 (260)493-3425	WS 8 1030 SS 915 BC 915	EL/ED/HC/ MD	1287	1002	436
	MARTINI martinichurchoffice@gmail.com MartiniNH.com	1853	333 MOELLER RD	46774	IN	Kyle E Brown	(260)749-0014	WS 9 SS 1030 BC 1030	EC/EL/ ED/HC/ MD/SN	255	186	78
	ST PAUL garcreekoffice@gmail.com stpaulgarcreek.org	1880	1910 N BERTHAUD RD	46774	IN	Michael S Blodgett	(260)749-5444	WS 8 1030 SS 915 BC 915	EL/ED/HC/ MD/SN	330	273	150
	ST PETER'S		See Fort Wayne IN									
NEW PALESTINE	*ZION* zionchurch@zionnewpal.org www.zionnewpal.org	1853	6513 W 300 S	46163	IN	Jason W Taylor Brady D Gurganious	(317)861-5544 (317)861-8153	WS 8 1030 SS 915 BC 915	EL/HS/ ED/HC/ MD/SN	746	576	300
NEW SALISBURY	*EPIPHANY* revmbboyd@gmail.com	1985	8600 HIGHWAY 135 NE	47161	IN		(812)725-6955	WS 10 SS 9 BC 9	ED/HC			
NEWBURGH	*OUR REDEEMER LUTHERAN NEWBURGH CAMPUS* Satellite Site of Our Redeemer Evansville IN	2016	7811 Oak Grove Rd	47630								
NOBLESVILLE	*ADVENT*		See Zionsville IN									
	CHRIST office@clc-in.org www.clc-in.org	1937	10055 E 186TH ST	46060	IN	Jacob R Hercamp	(317)773-3669	WS 9 SS 1030 BC 1030	ED/HC/ MD/SN	171	158	88
	CORNERSTONE		See Carmel IN									
	LORD OF LIFE		See Westfield IN									
NORTH JUDSON	*ST PETER* church@stpeternorthjudson.org www.stpeternorthjudson.org	1872	810 W TALMER AVE	46366	IN	Daniel A Speckhard	(574)896-2025 (574)896-2082	WS 9 SS 1030 BC 1030	EL/ED/HC/ MD	540	417	214
NORTH MANCHESTER	*NORTH MANCHESTER** lcmsnorthmanchester@gmail.com		Manchester University 604 E College Ave C/O ST JOHNS LUTHERAN 2465 W KEISER RD COLUMBIA CITY	46962 46725	IN		(260)244-3712					
NORTH VERNON	*LORD OF LIFE* lordoflifenv.com	1981	3300 N State Hwy 3 PO BOX 910	47265	IN		(812)346-6400	WS 9 SS 1015 BC 8	HS/ED/ HC/MD/ SN			
OAKLANDON	*HOLY CROSS*		See Indianapolis IN									
OSCEOLA	*ST PETER*		See Mishawaka IN									
OSSIAN	*BETHLEHEM* bethlehemossiansec@gmail.com www.bethlehemossian.org	1897	6514 E 750 N	46777	IN	Samuel S Wirgau Anthony C Dodgers	(260)597-7121 (260)597-7366	WS 9 SS 1015 BC 1015	EL/ED/HC/ MD/SN	505	391	212
	NEW HOPE newhopelutheranossian@gmail.com newhopelutheranossian.org	1977	8824 N STATE ROAD 1	46777	IN	Raymond T Doubrava II	(260)622-7954 (260)622-7956	WS 10 SS 845 BC 845	EC/ED/MD			
PERU	*ST JOHN* stjohnsperu@yahoo.com stjohnsperu.org	1858	181 W MAIN ST	46970	IN	Joshua P Dub	(765)473-6659 (765)473-6659	WS 930 SS 1045	EC/ED/ HC/MD	479	349	59
PLAINFIELD	*CHRIST THE KING*		See Mooresville IN									
	LIVING CHRIST admin.assistant@livingchristplainfield.com livingchristplainfield.com	1997	726 MOON RD	46168	IN	Steven D Latzke	(317)839-4800 (317)839-8825	WS 1030	EC/ED	73	70	27
	OUR SHEPHERD		See Avon IN									
PLYMOUTH	*CALVARY* church@calvarylutheranplymouth.org www.calvarylutheranplymouth.org	1933	1314 N MICHIGAN ST	46563	IN	Eric M Ahlemeyer Roger E Rohde	(574)936-2903	WS 815 1045 SS 930 BC 930	EC/ED/HC	448	321	128
PORTAGE	*ST PETER* office@stpeterportage.com www.stpeterportage.com	1882	6540 CENTRAL AVE	46368	IN	Brian C Doel	(219)762-2673 (219)764-1072	WS 10	ED/HC/MD	144	135	56
RENSSELAER	*ST JOHN*	1894	2723 N County Road 700 W 2723 N 700 W	47978	IN	David R Mueller	(219)208-2469	WS 1015	ED	36	32	17
	ST LUKE stlukerensselaer@gmail.com www.saintlukeev.weebly.com	1947	704 E GRACE ST	47978	IN	Jeffrey S Zell	(219)866-7681	WS 8 SS 915	EC/ED/SN	328	246	36
REYNOLDS	*SAINT JAMES* stjamesreynolds@yahoo.com www.st-james-lutheran.org	1861	110 N Kenton St PO BOX 327	47980	IN	Andrew P Keller	(219)984-5421 (219)984-5421	WS 9 SS 1015	EC	506	341	74
RICHMOND	*BETHANY*		See Connersville IN									
ROANOKE	*FAITH* faithlcms@gmail.com faithlcmsroanoke.com	1996	3416 E 900 N PO BOX 219	46783	IN	Shayne M Jonker	(260)672-1140	WS 9 SS 1015 BC 1015	ED/HC	219	180	103

*Indicates a new church start. A new church start is an intentionally organized gathering which comes together on a regular basis for the purpose of worship and/or Bible study and is intended to grow into a member LCMS congregation. WS =Worship Service; SS = Sunday School; BC =Bible Class; EC = Early Childhood; EL = Elementary School; HS = High School; ED =Education Ministry; HC =Human Care Ministry; SN = Special Needs Ministry; MD = Media Ministry (PC)=Partner Church Pastor. See Page 53 for the Table of Abbreviations for key to additional abbreviations

CITY	CONGREGATION EMAIL WEBSITE	YEAR EST	LOCATION MAILING ADDRESS	ZIP CODE(S)	DIST.	PASTOR(S)	PHONE FAX	WS SS BC	SCHOOLS/ MINISTRIES	STATISTIC Bapt	Conf	Avg Attend
ROCHESTER	*ST JOHNS* stjohnlutheran@rtcol.com www.stjohns-churchlcms.org	1928	404 JEFFERSON ST	46975	IN	Curtis A May	(574)223-6898	WS 930 SS 1030 BC 1030	ED/HC/MD	111	90	35
ROME CITY	*MESSIAH*		See Wolcottville IN									
ROSELAWN	*FAITH*		See Demotte IN									
SAINT JOHN	*TRINITY*		See Lowell IN									
SALEM	*FAITH*	1966	1200 S Lake Salinda Rd 1200 LAKE SALINDA RD	47167	IN	Janis C Mikits	(314)931-6003	WS 9 SS 830 BC 815		60	50	43
SAVAH	*OUR SAVIOR*		See Carmi IL									
SCOTTSBURG	*HOLY CROSS* holycrosslutheran.scott.co@gmail.com	2013	200 N Washington St PO BOX 572	47170	IN		(812)530-1974	WS 8 930 11 BC 12	ED/MD	7	7	13
SEYMOUR	*IMMANUEL* info@immanuelseymour.com www.immanuelseymour.com	1870	605 S WALNUT ST	47274	IN	Dr Ralph Blomenberg Philip E Bloch William G Fredstrom James A Rodriguez Jr	(812)522-3118 (812)522-6675	WS 9 1115 SS 1015 BC 1015	EC/EL/HS/ ED/HC/ MD/SN	3762	2823	841
	PEACE churchoffice@peaceseymour.org www.seymourpeacelutheran.com	2005	330 W TIPTON ST	47274	IN	Alarik D Morris	(812)523-3838	WS 930 SS 830 BC 830	HS/ED/HC	114	99	48
	REDEEMER redeemerseymour@gmail.com www.rlcseymour.org	1946	504 N WALNUT ST	47274	IN	Andrew J Currao Zachary R Huffman	(812)522-1837	WS 8 1030 SS 915	EL/HS/ ED/HC/ MD/SN	1148	894	219
	ST JOHN pastor@sjsauerslutheran.org stjohnsauers.org	1838	1108 S COUNTY ROAD 460 E	47274	IN	Craig A Muhlbach	(812)523-3131	WS 930 SS 830	EL/HS/ED/ HC/MD	683	532	225
	ST PETER		See Waymansville IN									
	ST PETER		See Brownstown IN									
	ZION zlc@zionseymour.org zionseymour.org	1959	1501 GAISER DR	47274	IN	Jeffrey L Stuckwisch	(812)522-1089 (812)523-7526	WS 8 1030 SS 915 BC 915	EL/HS/ ED/SN	679	538	217
SHELBYVILLE	*ST MARK*	1957	1560 N MICHIGAN RD	46176	IN		(317)398-7990	WS 1030 SS 915 BC 915	HC			
SOLITUDE	*OUR SAVIOR*		See Carmi IL									
SOUTH BEND	*EMMAUS* emmaus24@emmaus24.org www.emmaus24.org	1923	929 MILTON ST	46613	IN	Ronald A Stephens Dr Don R Stuckwisch Jr	(574)287-4151	WS 9 SS 1045 BC 1045	ED/HC/MD	145	118	105
	OUR REDEEMER ourredeemersb@aol.com www.ourredeemersb.360unite.com	1928	805 S 29TH ST	46615	IN		(574)288-8288 (574)288-0517	WS 10 SS 9 BC 9	EL/ED/HC/ MD			
	ST PAUL stpaulsboffice@gmail.com www.stpaulsb.org	1878	51490 LAUREL RD	46637	IN	Matthew P Schiemann	(574)271-1050	WS 1015 SS 9 BC 9	EL	157	130	92
	ST PETER		See Mishawaka IN									
	TRINITY		See Elkhart IN									
SOUTHPORT	*CALVARY*		See Indianapolis IN									
SPEEDWAY	*CORNERSTONE*		See Carmel IN									
SPENCER	*TRINITY*		See Ellettsville IN									
SPRING HILL	*FAITH*		See Thompsons Station TN									
STROH	*PRINCE PEACE*		See Hudson IN									
SYRACUSE	*SHEP BY LAKES* office@sbtl-lcms.com www.sbtl-lcms.com	1994	7449 E 1000 N	46567	IN	Dr Jerry D Winegarden	(574)528-6137 (574)528-6127	WS 930 SS 1045	ED/HC/MD	103	84	50
TELL CITY	*EMMANUEL* emmanuel@psci.net www.tellcitylutheran.org	1951	1105 Pestalozzi St PO BOX 116	47586	IN	Nathan J Rusert	(812)547-4215	WS 10 SS 845 BC 845	ED/HC/MD	283	205	74
TERRE HAUTE	*IMMANUEL* stacy.gibbens@ielcth.org ielcth.org	1858	645 POPLAR ST	47807	IN	Kurt R Cockran	(812)232-4972 (812)234-3935	WS 1030 SS 9 BC 9	ED/HC/ MD/SN	360	279	100
TIPTON	*EMANUEL* emanueltiptonin@gmail.com www.emanueltipton.org	1896	1385 S Main St PO BOX F	46072	IN	Dr Robb W Roloff David L Stout	(765)675-4090 (765)675-4200	WS 815 1045 SS 930 BC 930	ED/HC/ MD/SN	374	334	128
TOPEKA	*MESSIAH*		See Wolcottville IN									
VALLONIA	*TRINITY* tlcvallonia@gmail.com www.trinityvallonia.com	1874	4413 S STATE ROAD 135	47281	IN	Jordan J McKinley	(812)358-3225	WS 930 SS 830 BC 830	EL/ED	272	220	106
VALPARAISO	*FAITH MEMORIAL* www.faithvalpo.org	1956	753 N CALUMET AVE	46383	IN	Eric W Schoech James A Wetzstein	(219)462-7684 (219)477-5304	WS 9 SS 1030 BC 1030	ED/HC/MD			
	HERITAGE heritagelc@heritagelutheran.comcastbiz.net www.heritagelcmsvalpo.org	1976	308 WASHINGTON ST	46383	IN	Dr Stanton J Temme	(219)464-2810 (219)477-2677	WS 9 SS 1030 BC 1030	ED/MD	325	280	94
	IMMANUEL churchoffice@immanuelvalpo.org www.immanuelvalpo.org	1864	1700 MONTICELLO PARK DR	46383	IN	Andrew T Fields Casey T Kegley Jose Tomas Angon	(219)462-8207 (219)531-2238	WS 8 1045 SS 930 BC 930	EL	1051	774	458
	PRINCE PEACE princeofpeacelutheranchurch@gmail.com www.princeofpeacevalparaiso.com	1986	234 W DIVISION RD	46385	IN	William E Foy	(219)464-4911	WS 9 SS 1030 BC 1030	ED/HC/ MD/SN			
VINCENNES	*ST JOHN* stjohnlcmsvin@gmail.com	1859	707 N 8TH ST	47591	IN	Ronnie D Maxwell	(812)882-4662 (812)882-0213	WS 9 SS 1015 BC 1015	EC/ED	295	214	58
	ST PETER stpeter.lcms.vin@gmail.com www.stpeterlcmsvincennes.weebly.com	1869	7000 S DECKER RD	47591	IN	Nathan P Rastl	(812)882-8229 (812)882-0018	WS 10 SS 9 BC 9	ED/HC/MD	349	260	58

*Indicates a new church start. A new church start is an intentionally organized gathering which comes together on a regular basis for the purpose of worship and/or Bible study and is intended to grow into a member LCMS congregation. WS =Worship Service; SS = Sunday School; BC =Bible Class; EC = Early Childhood; EL = Elementary School; HS = High School; ED =Education Ministry; HC =Human Care Ministry; SN = Special Needs Ministry; MD = Media Ministry (PC)=Partner Church Pastor. See Page 53 for the Table of Abbreviations for key to additional abbreviations

CITY	CONGREGATION EMAIL WEBSITE	YEAR EST	LOCATION MAILING ADDRESS	ZIP CODE(S)	DIST.	PASTOR(S)	PHONE FAX	WS SS BC	SCHOOLS/ MINISTRIES	STATISTIC Bapt	 Conf	 Avg Attend
WABASH	*ZION* Secretary@zionwabash.org www.zionwabash.org	1946	173 HALE DR	46992	IN	Nathan D Schieber	(260)563-1886 (260)569-1919	WS 1030 SS 915 BC 915	ED/HC/MD	125	113	34
WANATAH	*ST JOHN*	1876	15496 S 900 W	46390	IN	Joel S Zipay	(219)733-9475		ED/HC			
WARSAW	*REDEEMER* churchoffice@redeemerwarsaw.org www.redeemerwarsaw.org	1937	1720 E CENTER ST	46580	IN	William M Carney	(574)267-5656 (574)267-6289	WS 9 1130 SS 1015	EC/ED/ MD/SN			
WAYMANSVILLE	*ST PETER* stpeterwaymansville.com	1871	11750 W 930 S COLUMBUS	47201	IN	Erik J Sorenson	(812)343-1688	WS 9 SS 10 BC 10	HS	120	102	89
WEST LAFAYETTE	*REDEEMER* revjet54@frontier.com www.redeemerwl.org	1953	510 LINDBERG AVE W LAFAYETTE	47906	IN	Joseph E Townsend	(765)463-5851	WS 930 SS 1045 BC 1045	ED/HC/ MD/SN	150	125	63
	UNIVERSITY ulutheranchurch@gmail.com www.ulupurdue.org	1945	460 NORTHWESTERN AVE W LAFAYETTE	47906	IN	Jared S DeBlieck	(765)743-2472	WS 1030 5 SS 915	ED/HC/MD	167	133	115
WESTFIELD	*ADVENT*		See Zionsville IN									
	CORNERSTONE		See Carmel IN									
	EPIPHANY adminasst@epiphanylcms.org www.epiphanylcms.org	2008	15605 DITCH RD	46074	IN	Jeremy H Mills	(317)815-3884	WS 830 1030 SS 1030 BC 1030	ED/MD	356	282	168
	LORD OF LIFE info@lollutheran.org www.lordoflife.family	1999	4283 E 191st St PO BOX 1075	46062 46074	IN	Ethan P Spira	(317)867-5673 (317)867-3973	WS 8 1045 SS 930 BC 930	ED/HC/MD			
WHEATFIELD	*EMMANUEL* rev.markifakih@gmail.com	1985	Hwy 10 PO BOX 142	46392	IN		(219)956-4513	WS 1030 SS 1030		29	23	18
	FAITH		See Demotte IN									
WHITELAND	*CONCORDIA*		See Greenwood IN									
WHITING	*ST PAUL* www.stpaulwhiting.org	1904	1801 ATCHISON AVE	46394	S		(219)659-0303	WS 930 6 SS 1045 BC 1045	ED			
WINAMAC	*ST LUKE* stluke3501@live.com www.stlukewinamac.org/	1944	721 S MARKET ST	46996	IN		(574)946-3501	WS 9 SS 10 BC 8	ED			
	ST PAUL		See Denham IN									
WOLCOTTVILLE	*MESSIAH* messiahwolcottville@gmail.com	1960	2955 E 700 S	46795	IN	Anthony E Appel	(260)854-3129	WS 930 SS 1030 BC 1030		126	101	53
WOLF LAKE	*LIVING WATER* livingwaterwolflakeon33@gmail.com livingwaterwolflake.com	2002	1197 S US Highway 33 PO BOX 297 1197 S. US HIGHWAY 33 WOLFLAKE	46796	IN	Lynn A Hanson	(260)635-2336	WS 915 SS 1015 BC 1015	ED/HC	84	74	25
WOODBURN	*CHRIST* christlutheransecretary@frontier.com www.christlutheranchurchwoodburn.360unite.com	1898	4412 Park St PO BOX 127	46797	IN	Timothy L Edwards	(260)632-4821	WS 8 1030	EL/ED/HC/ MD	311	261	115
	ZION secretary@zionwoodburn.org www.zionwoodburn.org	1888	7616 BULL RAPIDS RD	46797	IN	Mark J Peters	(260)632-4679 (260)632-4679	WS 830 BC 930	EL/ED/HC/ MD/SN	205	160	80
WOODLAND	*ST PAUL* rundershepherd@gmail.com stpaulwoodland.org	1851	15697 NEW RD MISHAWAKA	46544	IN	Raymond J Salemink	(574)633-4888	WS 10	MD/SN	106	80	40
ZIONSVILLE	*ADVENT* info@adventlutheran.org www.adventlutheran.org	1993	11250 N MICHIGAN RD	46077	EN	Marcus J Mackay Aaron A Schultz	(317)873-6318 (317)873-6369	WS 815 1045 SS 930 BC 930	EL/ED/HC/ MD/SN	688	532	338

IOWA

CITY	CONGREGATION EMAIL WEBSITE	YEAR EST	LOCATION MAILING ADDRESS	ZIP CODE(S)	DIST.	PASTOR(S)	PHONE FAX	WS SS BC	SCHOOLS/ MINISTRIES	Bapt	Conf	Avg Attend
ADEL	*FAITH* office@faithadel.com www.faithadel.com	1971	602 S 14TH ST	50003	IW	Matthew M Krause	(515)993-3848 (515)993-4756	WS 8 1030 SS 915 BC 915	EC/ED/ HC/MD	425	302	140
	TRINITY		See Van Meter IA									
ALBERT CITY	*ZION*		See Storm Lake IA									
ALDEN	*ST PAUL'S* stpaulsalden806@gmail.com	1913	806 Mill St PO BOX 27	50006	IE	Jay A Jaeger	(515)859-3901	WS 1015	ED/HC	66	63	26
ALGONA	*TRINITY* office@trinityalgona.org www.trinityalgona.org	1903	520 N GARFIELD ST	50511	IW	Benjamin J Dose Briton J Nelson	(515)295-3518 (515)295-3519	WS 8 1045 SS 915 BC 915	ED/HC/ MD/SN	1316	1061	215
ALTA	*ST JOHN* stjohnlutheranhanover@gmail.com www.stjohnhanover.org	1880	169 630TH ST	51002	IW	Merritt M Demski	(712)284-1450	WS 10 SS 9 BC 9	ED/HC/SN	263	193	114
	ST PAUL stpaulalta@gmail.com www.stpaulalta.org	1936	Fourth and Division 405 DIVISION ST	51002	IW	Alan J Miller	(712)200-1133	WS 10 SS 845 BC 845	ED/MD/SN	326	243	75
ALTOONA	*CHRIST KING* christthekingaltoona@gmail.com www.christthekingaltoona.com	1974	600 1ST AVE N	50009	IW	John R Schonkaes	(515)967-3349 (515)967-3254	WS 9 SS 1015 BC 8 1030	EC/ED/HC	136	119	79
AMES	*MEMORIAL* mlcsecretary1940@gmail.com www.memoriallutheranchurch.org	1940	2228 W Lincoln Way 2228 LINCOLN WAY	50014	IW	Mark T Heilman David R Beagley	(515)292-5005	WS 830 11 SS 940 BC 10	ED/HC/ MD/SN	974	688	260
	ST PAUL office@saintpaulames.org www.saintpaulames.org	1953	610 15TH ST	50010	IW	Dr Todd A Jenks	(515)232-5838 (515)232-2168	WS 830 11 SS 9 BC 9	EC/ED/ HC/MD	408	343	161
	TRINITY		See State Center IA									
ANITA	*HOLY CROSS*	1939	401 Maple St 704 MAPLE ST	50020	IW	Theodore F Weishaupt Jr	(712)249-0240	WS 9 SS 10	MD	135	117	25
ANKENY	*BEAUTIFUL SAVIOR*		See Polk City IA									

*Indicates a new church start. A new church start is an intentionally organized gathering which comes together on a regular basis for the purpose of worship and/or Bible study and is intended to grow into a member LCMS congregation. WS =Worship Service; SS = Sunday School; BC =Bible Class; EC = Early Childhood; EL = Elementary School; HS = High School; ED =Education Ministry; HC =Human Care Ministry; SN = Special Needs Ministry; MD = Media Ministry (PC)=Partner Church Pastor. See Page 53 for the Table of Abbreviations for key to additional abbreviations

CITY	CONGREGATION EMAIL WEBSITE	YEAR EST	LOCATION MAILING ADDRESS	ZIP CODE(S)	DIST.	PASTOR(S)	PHONE FAX	WS SS BC	SCHOOLS/ MINISTRIES	STATISTIC Bapt	Conf	Avg Attend
ANKENY	*CHRIST* pastor@christankeny.org www.christankeny.org	2017	2325 SW STATE ST SUITE C	50023	IW	Paul L Rieger	(515)261-2131	WS 930 SS 11 BC 11		154	114	50
	OUR SAVIOUR		See Des Moines IA									
	ST PAUL info@stpaulankeny.org stpaulankeny.org	1966	1100 SE SHARON DR	50021	IW	Joel L Newton David P Kottlowski	(515)964-1250	WS 8 1045 SS 930 BC 930	ED/HC/ MD/SN	710	598	310
	SUDANESE syiech@yahoo.com		1100 SE SHARON DR	50021	IW		(515)279-3609 (515)274-6806	WS 1130	HC	50	50	10
ANTHON	*TRINITY* trinity51004@gmail.com	1946	106 ARNOLD ST	51004	IW	Martin W Davis		WS 9	ED/HC	114	99	33
ARCADIA	*ZION* zionluth@westianet.net www.zionarcadia.com	1879	118 W Tracy St PO BOX 59	51430	IW	Andrew C Noble	(712)689-2441	WS 10 SS 9 BC 9	ED/HC	587	396	88
ARNOLD PARK	*IMMANUEL*		See Terril IA									
ARTESIAN	*ST PAUL*		See Waverly IA									
ASBURY	*ST PAUL*		See Dubuque IA									
ATKINS	*SAINT STEPHENS* office@sslchurch.org sslchurch.org	1869	303 3rd Ave PO BOX 203	52206	IE	Douglas M Woltemath	(319)446-7675 (319)446-7679	WS 9 SS 1015 BC 1015	EL/ED/MD	594	461	140
ATLANTIC	*ZION* zionatlantic@hotmail.com www.zionatlantic.com/	1877	811 OAK ST	50022	IW	Kyle A McBee	(712)243-2927	WS 915 SS 1030 BC 1030	ED/HC/ MD/SN	326	285	60
AUBURN	*ZION* cboljbet@netins.net	1873	212 Ash St PO BOX 246	51433	IW	Charles R Bettin			SN	43	31	18
AUDUBON	*ST JOHN* bodkinsm@gmail.com	1945	815 E Division St PO BOX 123	50025	IW	Michael D Bodkins	(712)563-3333	WS 8	EC/ED	74	62	27
AURELIA	*ST PAUL* spaurelia@newulmtel.net	1925	501 LOCUST ST BOX 278	51005	IW	Joseph M Eggerman	(712)434-2331	WS 930 SS 1030 BC 1030	ED/HC/ MD/SN	313	258	92
AYRSHIRE	*ZION* p.schulz571@gmail.com	1892	1008 Burns St 311 N HIGHWAY 4 MALLARD	50515 50562	IW	Paul A Schulz	(712)425-3328	WS 8		35	25	18
BATTLE CREEK	*ST JOHN* stjohns_bc@yahoo.com	1883	608 Fifth St PO BOX 286	51006	IW	Randall D Cormeny	(712)365-4477	WS 930 SS 830 BC 830	ED/HC/ MD/SN	139	122	57
	ST PAUL stpaulsmonica@yahoo.com	1892	2326 STORY AVE	51006	IW	Martin W Davis	(712)365-4328	WS 1030	ED/HC/SN	108	88	34
BEDFORD	*ST TIMOTHY*	1966	1308 MADISON ST	50833	IW		(712)523-2874			8	8	6
BELLE PLAINE	*FIRST* firstlutheranbp1925@gmail.com	1925	1523 SUNSET DR	52208	IE	Dean H Duncan	(319)444-2849 (319)444-2849	WS 1015 SS 9 BC 7	EC/ED/ HC/MD	235	203	49
BENNETT	*ST PAUL*	1935	260 E 4th St PO BOX J	52721	IE	Dr Andrew C Watkins	(563)890-6619	WS 9	ED	33	30	21
BETTENDORF	*OUR SAVIOR* oursaviorbett@gmail.com oursaviorbett.org	1948	3775 MIDDLE RD	52722	IE	Keith A Piotter Gary M Timm	(563)332-5141 (563)332-2117	WS 8 1045 SS 930	EC/ED/ HC/SN	1371	1012	533
BLAIRSTOWN	*GRACE* gracebtown@gmail.com www.gracelutheranbtown.org	1912	100 Locust NE PO BOX 156	52209	IE	Jeffrey A Schanbacher	(319)454-6941	WS 10 SS 9 BC 9	ED	470	381	87
BOONE	*ST PAUL* stpaulboone.org	1868	281 SPRUCE LN	50036	IW	Michael R Standfest	(515)432-4470 (515)432-4470	WS 1030 SS 915 BC 915	ED	190	152	68
	TRINITY trinitylutheranchurch01@gmail.com trinitylutheranboone.com	1866	712 12TH ST	50036	IW	Jessten P Heimer Michael R Standfest	(515)432-5140 (515)432-1059	WS 8 1030 SS 1015 BC 1015	EL/ED/MD	681	540	237
BUCKEYE	*ST PAUL*	1890	408 Berlin St PO BOX 8 ALDEN	50043 50006	IE	Jay A Jaeger	(515)855-4240	WS 830	HC	106	77	33
BURLINGTON	*CONCORDIA* concordiabrl@yahoo.com concordiabrl.com	1934	2901 CLIFF RD	52601	IE	Christopher A Roepke	(319)754-4246	WS 10 SS 9	ED/MD	77	67	25
	WORD OF GOD - BURLINGTON Satellite Site of Word Of God Of Cedar Rapids IA	2014	2901 Cliff Rd	52601								
BURT	*ST JOHN* churchoffice@stjohnsburt.org www.stjohnsburt.org	1913	109 Maple St PO BOX 98	50522	IW	Benjamin J Dose Briton J Nelson	(515)924-3344	WS 930 SS 830 BC 815	ED/HC/ MD/SN	221	186	50
CALAMUS	*IMMANUEL*		See Grand Mound IA									
CARLISLE	*HOLY CROSS* www.holycrosscarlisle.org	1963	1100 MARKET ST	50047	IW	Kevin L Johnson	(515)989-3841	WS 9 SS 1045 BC 1045	ED/HC/MD	171	132	105
CARROLL	*ST PAUL* stpaul@stpaul-ia.com www.stpaul-ia.com	1886	1844 HIGHLAND DR	51401	IW	Ryan K Roehrig	(712)792-4354	WS 9 SS 1015 BC 1015	EC/ED/HC/ MD/SN	398	327	148
CASEY	*ST JOHN* stjohnslutheran@netins.net	1882	104 E 1st St PO BOX 73	50048	IW	Jeffrey M Keuning	(641)746-2734	WS 1030 SS 915	ED/HC/SN	133	118	31
CEDAR FALLS	*COLLEGE HILL* www.college-hill.org	1942	2322 OLIVE ST	50613	IE	John H Wegener	(319)266-1274	WS 10 SS 9 BC 9	ED/HC/ MD/SN	201	166	78
	IMMANUEL office@immanuelcf.com www.ilcv.org	1878	4820 OSTER PKWY	50613	IE	Dr Gerald C Kapanka Kevin C Richter	(319)260-2000	WS 8 1030 SS 915 BC 930	EC/EL/HS/ ED/HC/ MD	681	518	233
	OUR REDEEMER orlc@cfu.net www.theforgivenessplace.org	1962	904 BLUFF ST	50613	IE	Matthew J Baker Michael R Knox Dr Brian S Saunders	(319)266-2509	WS 9 SS 1030	ED/HC/ MD/SN	167	153	105
	WORD OF GOD - WATERLOO Satellite Site of Word Of God Of Cedar Rapids IA	2014	4820 Oster Parkway	50613								

*Indicates a new church start. A new church start is an intentionally organized gathering which comes together on a regular basis for the purpose of worship and/or Bible study and is intended to grow into a member LCMS congregation. WS =Worship Service; SS = Sunday School; BC =Bible Class; EC = Early Childhood; EL = Elementary School; HS = High School; ED =Education Ministry; HC =Human Care Ministry; SN = Special Needs Ministry; MD = Media Ministry (PC)=Partner Church Pastor. See Page 53 for the Table of Abbreviations for key to additional abbreviations

CITY	CONGREGATION EMAIL WEBSITE	YEAR EST	LOCATION MAILING ADDRESS	ZIP CODE(S)	DIST.	PASTOR(S)	PHONE FAX	WS SS BC	SCHOOLS/ MINISTRIES	STATISTIC Bapt	Conf	Avg Attend
CEDAR RAPIDS	*BETHANY* office.bethanycr@gmail.com www.bethanycr.org	1932	2202 FOREST DR SE	52403	IE	Michael W Erickson	(319)364-6026 (319)366-4891	WS 830 11 SS 945	ED/HC/ MD/SN	662	472	186
	CONCORDIA concordia@imonmail.com www.concordia-cr.org	1957	4210 JOHNSON AVE NW	52405	IE	Brad A Brown	(319)396-9035 (319)261-0559	WS 830 BC 10	EC/ED/ MD/SN	298	286	64
	KING OF KINGS office@kingofkingscr.org www.kingofkingscr.org	1981	3275 N CENTER POINT RD	52411	IE	Christopher A Navurskis Noah A Russell	(319)393-2438	WS 8 1045 SS 930 BC 930	ED/HC/MD	879	648	275
	ST PAUL		See Williamsburg IA									
	ST SILAS		See North Liberty IA									
	TRINITY churchoffice@trinitycr.org www.trinitycr.org	1884	1363 1ST AVE SW	52405	IE	Theodore W Groth Daryn A Bahn	(319)366-1569 (877)687-7670	WS 9 SS 1030 BC 1030	EL/ED/HC/ MD/SN	684	540	191
	WORD OF GOD DF iowaeastdeaf@yahoo.com www.iowaeastdeaf.org	1969	1515 29TH ST NE	52402	IE	Timothy C Eckert	(319)450-7699	WS 11 BC 10	MD/SN	33	32	15
CENTER POINT	*ST JOHN* prtcvanhemert@gmail.com www.stjohnlutherancp.org	1947	316 Vine Street PO BOX 244	52213	IE		(319)849-1251	WS 9 SS 1015 BC 1015	ED/HC	160	144	70
CHARITON	*TRINITY* pastorknaus@gmail.com www.trinity-chariton.org	1989	825 N 7TH ST	50049	IE	Nathan K Knaus	(641)774-8335	WS 9 SS 1015 BC 1030	ED/MD	65	62	29
CHARLES CITY	*NEW HOPE* isaacrwj@gmail.com newhopecharlescity.weebly.com/	2011	607 N MAIN ST	50616	IE	Isaac R Johnson	(641)552-4831	WS 9 BC 1015		44	31	28
CHARLOTTE	*IMMANUEL*	1873	Hwy 136 235 First St PO BOX 239	52731	IE	Lloyd W Redhage	(563)677-2756	WS 10 SS 9 BC 9		300	229	65
CHARTER OAK	*IMMANUEL*	1889	1512 130TH ST	51439	IW	Richard C Merrill	(712)678-3630		ED/HC/ MD/SN	57	47	37
	ST JOHN stjohnco@frontiernet.net stjohncharteroak.blogspot.com	1881	104 Birch Ave PO BOX 73	51439	IW	Richard C Merrill	(712)678-3630	WS 10 SS 845 BC 9	ED/HC/ MD/SN	503	400	97
	ST PAUL	1877	1743 G Ave PO BOX 74 SCHLESWIG	51439 51461	IW	Richard C Merrill	(712)679-2425		ED/HC	95	79	37
CHEROKEE	*TRINITY* nancy@trinitycherokee.org www.trinitycherokee.org	1890	230 N ROOSEVELT AVE	51012	IW	Jonathan R Riggert	(712)225-4332	WS 9 SS 10 BC 10	EC/ED/ HC/MD	534	384	291
CLARINDA	*IMMANUEL* immanuellutheran.clarinda@gmail.com www.immanuelclarinda.org	1869	1614 P AVE	51632	IW	Wade M Brandt	(712)542-3283 (712)586-4537	WS 9 BC 1015	ED/HC/MD	381	244	53
	ST JOHN stjohnlcms@mediacombb.net www.stjohnclarinda.org	1906	301 N 13TH ST	51632	IW	Mitchel E Schuessler	(712)542-3708	WS 1030 SS 9 BC 9	EC/ED/ HC/MD	564	439	130
	ST PAUL stpaul@myfmtc.com www.stpaulslutheranchurch.net	1895	2463 State Hwy 2 2463 STATE HIGHWAY 2	51632	IW	David D Herald	(712)542-1505	WS 10 SS 11 BC 11	EL	228	173	80
CLARION	*IMMANUEL* mcjems6@gmail.com mountcalvary-immanuel.org	1976	2153 Hwy 69 PO BOX 52 ROWAN	50525 50470	IW	Mark P Eichler	(641)580-1209	WS 1030	ED/HC/SN	32	30	16
CLEAR LAKE	*REDEEMER*		See Ventura IA									
CLIMBING HILL	*ST JOHN*	1940	157 DEER RUN TRL	51015	IW	David A Schoop	(712)239-3655	WS 930 SS 1045 BC 1045	ED/HC	56	50	25
CLINTON	*ST JOHN* cdell@stjohn-clinton-ia.org stjohn-clinton-ia.org/	1855	416 MAIN AVE	52732	IE	Dr Daniel P Pool	(563)242-5588	WS 745 1015 SS 9 BC 9	EC/ED/ HC/MD	646	537	158
	TRINITY trinitylutheranclinton.org	1932	656 5TH AVE S	52732	IE	Nathan J Wille	(563)242-5328	WS 9 SS 1030 BC 1030	ED/HC/ MD/SN	92	82	56
CLIVE	*LIVING FAITH* emile@livingfaithclive.com www.LivingFaithClive.com		2180 NW 142ND ST	50325	IW	Luke R Timm Daniel G Petrak	(515)987-4030	WS 930 SS 10	EC/ED/HC	352	297	175
	TRINITY		See Van Meter IA									
COLUMBUS JUNCTION	*ST PAUL*		See Wapello IA									
CONROY	*TRINITY* glsears@iowatelecom.net	1905	626 8th Ave PO BOX 66	52220	IE	Gary L Sears	(319)662-4075	WS 930 SS 830 BC 830	EL	189	155	52
COON RAPIDS	*TRINITY*	1886	2174 B AVE	50058	IW		(712)684-5118	WS 1030 SS 930	ED/HC/MD	96	74	37
CORALVILLE	*PRINCE OF PEACE* popcoralville@msn.com popcoralville.com	1980	1701 8TH ST	52241	IE	Dr Mitchell E Otto Michael D Musick	(319)338-1842	WS 8 1015 SS 9 BC 9	EC/ED/HC/ MD/SN	173	150	65
	ST SILAS		See North Liberty IA									
CORNING	*REDEEMER* redeemerlutherancorning@gmail.com	1953	800 17TH ST	50841	IW		(641)322-3498	WS 830	ED/HC	60	55	21
CORRECTIONVILLE	*GRACE*	1948	828 Driftwood 828 DRIFTWOOD ST CORRECTIONVLE	51016	IW		(712)539-8801	WS 1	ED/HC	44	40	10
COUNCIL BLUFFS	*FAITH* faithlutherancboffice@gmail.com www.faithlutherancouncilbluffs.org/	1948	2100 S 11th St 2100 S. 11TH STREET	51501	IW	Robert R Rosenkaimer II	(712)323-6445	WS 9 BC 1015	MD/SN	165	148	60
	HARMONY COURT RETIREMENT COMMUNITY Satellite Site of Timothy Council Bluffs IA	2012	173 Bennett Ave	51503				WS 3				

*Indicates a new church start. A new church start is an intentionally organized gathering which comes together on a regular basis for the purpose of worship and/or Bible study and is intended to grow into a member LCMS congregation. WS =Worship Service; SS = Sunday School; BC =Bible Class; EC = Early Childhood; EL = Elementary School; HS = High School; ED =Education Ministry; HC =Human Care Ministry; SN = Special Needs Ministry; MD = Media Ministry (PC)=Partner Church Pastor. See Page 53 for the Table of Abbreviations for key to additional abbreviations

CITY	CONGREGATION EMAIL WEBSITE	YEAR EST	LOCATION MAILING ADDRESS	ZIP CODE(S)	DIST.	PASTOR(S)	PHONE FAX	WS SS BC	SCHOOLS/ MINISTRIES	STATISTIC Bapt	Conf	Avg Attend
COUNCIL BLUFFS	*ST PAULS* splccboffice@gmail.com www.stpaulscouncilbluffs.org	1881	239 FRANK ST COUNCIL BLFS	51503	IW	Nathan A Sherrill Timothy A Frank	(712)322-4729 (712)322-8832	WS 8 1045 SS 930 BC 930	EC/ED/HC/ MD/SN	552	552	295
	TIMOTHY secretary@timothylutheran.net www.timothylutheran.net	1945	3112 W BROADWAY COUNCIL BLFS	51501	IW	William R Clark	(712)323-0693 (712)323-7582	WS 8 1030 SS 915 BC 915	ED/HC/MD	437	335	105
CRESCENT	*ST JOHN*		See Honey Creek IA									
CRESTON	*TRINITY* pastor@trinitycreston.org www.trinitycreston.org	1926	800 N SUMNER AVE	50801	IW	John B Rutz	(641)782-5095	WS 9 SS 1030 BC 8	EC/ED/HC/ MD/SN	281	229	86
CUMMING	*TRINITY*		See Van Meter IA									
CYLINDER	*ST LUKE*	1895	5652 340TH ST	50528	IW		(515)889-2769	WS 1030 SS 930	ED/HC	144	86	37
DALLAS CENTER	*TRINITY*		See Van Meter IA									
DAVENPORT	*HOLY CROSS* office@holycrossdav.org www.holycrossdav.org	1902	1705 E LOCUST ST	52803	IE	Terry L Quick	(563)322-2654	WS 9 BC 1030	ED/HC/ MD/SN	135	120	36
	IMMANUEL IMMANUEL.LCMS.DAVENPORT@ GMAIL.COM www.immanueldavenport.org	1924	3834 ROCKINGHAM RD	52802	IE	Bradley E Ferch	(563)324-6431	WS 9 SS 1020 BC 1020	ED/HC/ MD/SN	240	219	72
	RISEN CHRIST info@rclcqc.org www.rclcqc.org	1985	6021 NORTHWEST BLVD	52806	IE	Brian C Licht	(563)386-2342 (563)386-8969	WS 9 SS 1030 BC 1030	EC/ED/HC/ MD/SN	337	177	95
	TRINITY janet.levetzow@trinitydavenport.org trinitydavenport.org	1870	1122 W CENTRAL PARK AVE	52804	IE	Randall L Golter Matthew B Schilling	(563)323-8001 (563)324-9153	WS 8 1045 SS 930 BC 930	EL/ED/HC/ MD/SN	2187	1340	276
	WORD OF GOD - DAVENPORT Satellite Site of Word Of God Of Cedar Rapids IA	2014	1705 E Locust St	52803								
DE SOTA	*TRINITY*		See Van Meter IA									
DEEP RIVER	*CALVARY*	1942	401 Church St PO BOX 273	52222	IE	Michael J Kolesar		WS 10 SS 930	ED/HC/SN	123	86	17
DELAWARE	*ST PAUL* vesey99@gmail.com www.stpaulsdelaware.ctshost.org	1880	200 4TH ST	52036	IE	Matthew W Vesey	(563)922-2364	WS 9 BC 1030	ED/HC	210	164	38
DELOIT	*FAITH* sjlcmski@schallertel.net	1953	211 WALL ST	51441	IW		(712)675-4881	WS 9	ED/MD	53	41	15
DENISON	*AMIGOS EN CRISTO* pastorgrills@gmail.com		1004 1ST AVE S	51442	IW		(712)263-2235		ED/HC/MD	17	17	15
	CHRIST christlutherandenison@gmail.com		Boulders Conference Center 2507 Boulders Dr PO BOX 122 18 SOUTH MAIN ST	51442	IW	Theodore D Torreson				82	65	103
	OUR SAVIOR office@oursaviordenison.com www.oursaviordenison.com	1970	500 N 24TH ST	51442	IW	Chad A Trunkhill	(712)263-3282	WS 9 SS 10 BC 10	ED/HC/ MD/SN	1026	824	206
	ZION info@ziondenison.org ziondenison.org	1872	1004 1ST AVE S	51442	IW	Jeffrey E Wade	(712)263-2235	WS 9 SS 1015 BC 1015	ED/MD	1466	1124	140
DENVER	*ST JOHN* secretary@stjohndenver.com stjohndenver.360unite.com	1921	641 LINCOLN ST	50622	IE	Jesse S Schlie	(319)984-5351	WS 9 SS 1015 BC 1030	EL/HS/ED/ MD	346	273	99
DES MOINES	*ASIAN*		3223 UNIVERSITY AVE	50311	IW		(515)729-3987 (515)274-6806	SS 915 BC 9		13	13	15
	CALVARY DEAF	1947	3909 E 42ND ST	50317	IW		(515)518-6934	WS 10	ED/HC/SN	11	11	11
	CHRIST		See Ankeny IA									
	HOPE churchoffice@hopelutheran-dsm.org www.hopelutheran-dsm.org	1959	3857 E 42ND ST	50317	IW	Timothy P Braun Shane D Acers	(515)265-2057	WS 9 SS 1015 BC 1015	EC/ED/HC/ MD/SN	376	316	191
	MOUNT OLIVE school.office@molcs.org www.molcs.org	1953	5625 FRANKLIN AVE	50310	IW	Garret A Kasper	(515)277-8349	WS 9 SS 930 BC 945	EL/ED/HC/ MD	185	165	90
	OUR SAVIOUR oursavioursecretary@gmail.com www.oursaviour-lutheran.org	1946	4003 2ND AVE	50313	IW	David P Kuhfal	(515)244-9347	WS 9 SS 1030 BC 1030	ED/HC/ MD/SN	127	102	67
	PEACE peace@peacedsm.com www.peacedsm.com	1958	5615 SW 14TH ST	50315	IW		(515)285-3769	WS 10 SS 1115		251	199	44
	SHEP OF THE VALLEY		See West Des Moines IA									
	ST PAUL		See Williamsburg IA									
	TRINITY trinityofficeDSM@gmail.com Trinitydesmoines.org	1901	3223 UNIVERSITY AVE	50311	IW	Carl E Wendorff	(515)279-3609 (515)274-6806	WS 10 SS 845 BC 845	ED/HC/ MD/SN	126	108	70
DEWITT	*GRACE* kgood@gracedewitt.org www.gracedewitt.org	1925	415 10th St PO BOX 156	52742	IE		(563)659-9153 (563)659-9154	WS 8 1030 SS 915 BC 915	EC/ED/HC/ MD/SN	515	425	130
	GRACE CAMP Satellite Site of Grace DeWitt IA	2016	2675 242nd St	52742								
DEXTER	*ZION* Zion.Dexter.Office@gmail.com	1871	309 Marshall St PO BOX 127	50070	IW	Jeffrey M Keuning	(515)729-2977	WS 830 SS 945	ED	202	162	73
DIXON	*IMMANUEL*		See Grand Mound IA									
DONAHUE	*IMMANUEL*		See Grand Mound IA									
DOW CITY	*BETHLEHEM*	1939	110 Logan St PO BOX 167	51528	IW	Chad A Trunkhill	(712)674-3323	WS 1030 SS 915 BC 915		340	208	38

*Indicates a new church start. A new church start is an intentionally organized gathering which comes together on a regular basis for the purpose of worship and/or Bible study and is intended to grow into a member LCMS congregation. WS =Worship Service; SS = Sunday School; BC =Bible Class; EC = Early Childhood; EL = Elementary School; HS = High School; ED =Education Ministry; HC =Human Care Ministry; SN = Special Needs Ministry; MD = Media Ministry (PC)=Partner Church Pastor. See Page 53 for the Table of Abbreviations for key to additional abbreviations

CITY	CONGREGATION EMAIL WEBSITE	YEAR EST	LOCATION MAILING ADDRESS	ZIP CODE(S)	DIST.	PASTOR(S)	PHONE FAX	WS SS BC	SCHOOLS/ MINISTRIES	STATISTIC Bapt	Conf	Avg Attend
DUBUQUE	*OUR REDEEMER* orlcdbq@gmail.com ourredeemerdubuque.360unite.com	1961	2145 JOHN F KENNEDY RD	52002	IE	Jesse K Cearlock Mark G Zieroth	(563)588-1247	WS 8 1030 SS 915 BC 915	EC/ED/ HC/MD	1004	693	185
	ST PAUL stpsecretary@msn.com stpauldbq.com	1865	2025 JACKSON ST	52001	IE	Jonathan T Crawford	(563)556-7636	WS 9 SS 1030 BC 1030	ED/HC/MD	320	251	88
	WORD OF GOD - DUBUQUE Satellite Site of Word Of God Of Cedar Rapids IA	2005	2145 John F Kennedy Rd	52002								
EAGLE GROVE	*MOUNT CALVARY* emporiahusker@gmail.com mountcalvary-immanuel.org	1947	400 W Broadway St 400 W BROADWAY ST PO BOX 194	50533	IW	Mark P Eichler	(515)448-4668	WS 830	ED/HC/MD	60	58	14
EARLHAM	*TRINITY*		See Van Meter IA									
EARLY	*FAITH* cboljbet@netins.net	1959	202 E 6th St PO BOX 24	50535	IW	Charles R Bettin	(712)660-0193	WS 10	SN	48	43	26
ELDORA	*ST PAUL* godshous1@heartofiowa.net stpauleldora.com	1882	1105 Washington St 1109 WASHINGTON ST	50627	IE	Aaron M Hambleton	(641)858-2464 (641)858-2464	WS 930 SS 830 BC 830	EC/ED/ HC/MD	441	352	119
ELDRIDGE	*PARK VIEW* secretary.pvlcms@outlook.com www.pvlcms.org	1970	14 GROVE RD	52748	IE	Peter D Hoft	(563)285-9035 (563)285-8054	WS 8 1030 SS 915 BC 915	EC/ED/ HC/MD	516	418	160
ELMA	*ST PETER* bhmklm1@aol.com stpeterelma.blogspot.com	1889	107 Wood St PO BOX 346	50628	IE	Bruce H Miller	(641)393-2558	WS 9 BC 1015	ED	50	47	32
ELY	*KING OF GLORY*		See Swisher IA									
EMMETSBURG	*ST PAUL* stpaulemmetsburg@gmail.com www.stpaulemmetsburg.org	1911	805 HARRISON ST	50536	IW	Keith P Christiansen	(712)852-2367	WS 830	ED/HC/MD	203	173	43
ESTHERVILLE	*IMMANUEL* Immanuel1331@msn.com	1892	409 N 6TH ST	51334	IW	Thomas J Marth	(712)362-3237 (712)362-5807	WS 9 SS 1030 BC 1045	ED/HC/ MD/SN	275	235	49
EVANSDALE	*ST PAUL*	1942	735 CENTRAL AVE	50707	IE	Dr David S Hasselbrook	(319)232-7657	WS 10 BC 1115	ED/SN	28	26	15
FAIRBANK	*ST JOHN'S* stjohnsandgracelp@gmail.com stjohnsandgracelp.com	1868	208 N 4th St PO BOX 465	50629	IE	Grant P Tapken	(319)635-2181	WS 10 SS 945	ED/HC/SN	146	133	29
FAIRFAX	*KING OF GLORY*		See Swisher IA									
FAIRFIELD	*IMMANUEL* ilcmsfairfield@gmail.com www.ilcms.com	1964	1601 S MAIN ST	52556	IE		(641)472-5333	WS 9 SS 1030 BC 1030	EC/ED	223	164	58
FARNHAMVILLE	*HOLY TRINITY* htlcsec@wccta.net www.holytrinityfarnhamville.com/	1961	805 Garfield Ave PO BOX 125	50538	IW	Aaron A Zimmerman	(515)544-3264	WS 1030 SS 930 BC 930	ED/HC/MD	250	194	83
FAYETTE	*GRACE*	1942	201 King St PO BOX 446	52142	IE	Kent A Peck	(563)425-3544	WS 8 SS 9 BC 9		105	98	30
FENTON	*ST JOHN*	1902	600 ASH	50539	IW		(515)889-2812	WS 1015 SS 9	ED/HC/MD	120	120	50
FORT DODGE	*GOOD SHEPHERD* office@goodshepfortdodge.org www.goodshepfortdodge.org	1947	1436 21ST AVE N	50501	IW	Nicholas J Thackery	(515)573-3174	WS 8 1030 SS 1030 BC 1030	EC/ED/MD	562	532	134
	PRINCE PEACE poplcfd@gmail.com www.princeofpeacefd.com	1924	1023 S 27TH ST	50501	IW	Kendall L Meyer	(515)573-8618 (515)573-8629	WS 915 SS 1015	HC/MD/SN	206	156	42
	ST PAUL stpaulfd@stpaulfd.org www.stpaulfd.org	1863	400 S 13TH ST	50501	IW	Kendall L Meyer	(515)955-7285 (515)955-2263	WS 8 1030 SS 915 BC 915	EL/ED/HC/ MD/SN	953	758	200
	TRINITY	1890	1446 JOHNSON AVE	50501	IW		(515)546-6331	WS 845 SS 945	ED/SN	62	58	25
FORT MADISON	*OUR SAVIOR* oslcftmadison@gmail.com	1960	2121 AVENUE A	52627	IE	Christopher A Roepke	(319)372-7952	WS 815		24	24	10
FREDERICKSBURG	*ST PAUL* stpaulfburg@gmail.com www.stpaulfburg.blogspot.com	1890	222 S Washington Ave PO BOX 336 FREDERICKSBRG	50630	IE	Ronnie L Koch	(319)269-2220	WS 830 SS 10 BC 10	EC/ED	211	183	59
GALVA	*ST JOHN*	1896	406 Monona 406 MONONA ST	51020	IW		(712)282-4700	WS 10 SS 9 BC 9	ED/MD	324	324	131
GARNER	*ST JOHN* stjohnparsonage@cltel.net www.st-john.church	1887	2404 260th St 2405 260TH ST	50438	IW	Mark P Lund	(641)829-4493	WS 10 SS 9 BC 9		246	165	70
	ST PAUL stpauloffice@comm1net.net stpaulgarner.org	1894	810 STATE ST	50438	IW	Scott A Kozisek	(641)923-2261 (641)923-2190	WS 9 SS 1015 BC 1015	EC/ED/HC/ MD/SN	444	342	112
GARRISON	*ST MARK*	1951	101 N WALNUT AVE	52229	IE	Zachary S Johnson	(319)477-5141	WS 8 SS 9		149	147	30
GERMANTOWN	*ST JOHN* stjohnlutheran@tcaexpress.net stjohngermantown.org	1878	5092 480TH ST PAULLINA	51046	IW	Carl B Stenzel	(712)448-2630	WS 10 SS 9 BC 9	EL/ED/HC/ MD	240	208	82
GLADBROOK	*CHRIST*	1951	PO BOX 43	50635	IE	Fred L Berry Jr	(641)473-2527		ED/MD	61	45	22
GLENWOOD	*FIRST*		See Plattsmouth NE									
	TRINITY trinitylutheran@q.com tlcglenwood.org	1945	512 2ND ST	51534	IW	Michael J Metzler	(712)527-4667	WS 10 SS 845 BC 845	ED/HC/MD	489	352	92
GLIDDEN	*PEACE* peacegli@iowatelecom.net	1898	226 W 7th St PO BOX 448	51443	IW		(712)659-3875	WS 9 SS 1015 BC 8	ED/HC/MD	100	99	38
GRAETTINGER	*IMMANUEL*		See Terril IA									

*Indicates a new church start. A new church start is an intentionally organized gathering which comes together on a regular basis for the purpose of worship and/or Bible study and is intended to grow into a member LCMS congregation. WS =Worship Service; SS = Sunday School; BC =Bible Class; EC = Early Childhood; EL = Elementary School; HS = High School; ED =Education Ministry; HC =Human Care Ministry; SN = Special Needs Ministry; MD = Media Ministry (PC)=Partner Church Pastor. See Page 53 for the Table of Abbreviations for key to additional abbreviations

CITY	CONGREGATION EMAIL WEBSITE	YEAR EST	LOCATION MAILING ADDRESS	ZIP CODE(S)	DIST.	PASTOR(S)	PHONE FAX	WS SS BC	SCHOOLS/ MINISTRIES	STATISTIC Bapt	Conf	Avg Attend
GRAND MOUND	*IMMANUEL* churchesbulletin@gmail.com www.immanuelgrandmound.com	1871	706 Smith St PO BOX 166	52751	IE	John M Dolde	(563)847-2631	WS 10 SS 9 BC 9	ED	204	204	63
GREENFIELD	*IMMANUEL* keithlcms@gmail.com www.immanuelgreenfield.org	1874	505 NE Dodge St PO BOX 359	50849	IW	Dr Keith W Schweitzer	(641)745-5143	WS 845 SS 1015 BC 1015	EC/ED/HC/ MD/SN	145	129	50
GRIMES	*BEAUTIFUL SAVIOR*		See Polk City IA									
	TRINITY		See Van Meter IA									
GRINNELL	*IMMANUEL* lcms.immanuelgrinnell@gmail.com www.immanuelgrinnell.org	1978	229 11TH AVE W	50112	IE	Dr Joel G Koepp	(641)236-6691	WS 9 SS 1030	ED/HC/ MD/SN	128	100	60
GUTHRIE CENTER	*IMMANUEL* churchinfoilc@gmail.com immanuelgc.org	1954	713 N 12TH ST GUTHRIE CTR	50115	IW	Steven D Wichtendahl	(641)332-2918	WS 9 SS 1015	ED/HC	186	141	75
GUTTENBERG	*TRINITY* www.listentojesus.info	1930	106 S RIVER PARK DR	52052	IE	Michael B Keller	(563)252-1476	WS 830 SS 930	ED/HC/ MD/SN	92	70	28
HAMPTON	*TRINITY* trinityhamptonoffice@gmail.com www.trinityhampton.com	1916	16 12TH AVE NE	50441	IE	Karl C Bollhagen	(641)456-4816	WS 830 SS 945 BC 945	ED/MD	368	350	95
HARTLEY	*ST PAUL* splhart@tcaexpress.net stpaullutheranhartley.com	1909	60 N Central Ave PO BOX 88	51346	IW	Christopher A Nitzel	(712)728-2711	WS 9 SS 1030 BC 1030	ED/HC/MD	378	305	100
HASTINGS	*ST JOHN* sjspdualparish@gmail.com	1873	56020 340TH ST	51540	IW	Christopher A Maronde		WS 830	ED/HC/SN	66	62	28
HAWARDEN	*TRINITY* trinityhawarden@gmail.com trinityhawarden.com	1900	1103 CENTRAL AVE	51023	IW	Dr Joshua T Lowe	(712)551-2743	WS 1030 SS 915	ED/HC/ MD/SN	373	262	114
HIAWATHA	*ZION* www.zionhiawatha.org	1954	201 1ST AVE	52233	IE	Kevin C Zellers Jr	(319)393-2013 (319)393-2012	WS 9 SS 1015 BC 1015	EC/ED/HC/ MD/SN	328	285	83
HINTON	*TRINITY* tlchinton@mtcnet.net	1885	29014 LAKE AVE	51024	IW	Alex J Kaldahl	(712)947-4435	WS 930	ED/HC/ MD/SN	265	222	44
HOMESTEAD	*ST JOHN* sjlchomestead@gmail.com	1864	1928 V AVE	52236	IE	Gary L Sears	(319)662-4286	WS 745 SS 915	EL/ED/HC/ MD	136	118	44
HONEY CREEK	*ST JOHN* stjohnshcsecretary@gmail.com www.stjohnshoneycreek.org	1894	30907 COLDWATER AVE	51542	IW		(712)545-3022	WS 10	ED	294	245	89
HORNICK	*ST JOHN*		See Climbing Hill IA									
HUBBARD	*ST JOHN* stjohnhubbard@hotmail.com www.stjohnhubbard.com	1879	124 S Iowa St PO BOX 267	50122	IE	Dr Matthew W Rueger	(641)864-2672 (641)864-2672	WS 10 SS 9 BC 9	ED/HC/MD	358	280	150
HUMBOLDT	*ZION* zion@goldfieldaccess.net zioninhumboldt.org	1884	1005 11TH AVE N	50548	IW	Aaron G Flatau Mark A Hansen	(515)332-3279 (515)332-3295	WS 10 SS 845 BC 845	ED/HC/ MD/SN	1233	902	190
IDA GROVE	*ST PAUL* stpaulidagrove@gmail.com www.stpaulig.org	1888	100 7TH ST	51445	IW	Neil E Wehmas	(712)364-2918	WS 9 SS 1015 BC 1030	ED/HC/ MD/SN	870	702	165
INDEPENDENCE	*OUR REDEEMER*	1989	120 17TH AVE NE	50644	IE	Jay R Weideman	(319)334-2745	WS 1030 SS 1130 BC 1130	ED/HC/MD	69	63	33
INDIANOLA	*MOUNT CALVARY* office@mt-calvary.com www.mt-calvary.com	1954	2214 East Second Ave PO BOX 174	50125	IW	Thomas W Vanderbilt	(515)961-4321 (515)961-2986	WS 8 1030 SS 915 BC 915	ED/MD	554	442	131
IOWA CITY	*OUR REDEEMER* redeemer@ourredeemer.org www.ourredeemer.org	1957	2301 E COURT ST	52245	IE	Brent M Hartwig	(319)338-5626 (319)338-9171	WS 8 1030 SS 920 BC 920	EC/ED/ HC/MD	1222	956	272
	ST PAUL stpaulschapel.iowacity@gmail.com www.stpaulic.com	1942	404 E JEFFERSON ST	52245	IE	William M Mons	(319)337-3652 (319)337-4102	WS 9 SS 1015 BC 1015	ED/HC/MD	30	24	40
	ST PAUL		See Williamsburg IA									
	ST SILAS		See North Liberty IA									
IOWA FALLS	*IMMANUEL* immanuellutheranchurchif@outlook.com www.immanuellutheraniowafalls.org	1932	313 LEE LN	50126	IE	Paul L Beisel	(641)648-3756	WS 10 SS 845 BC 845	ED/MD	239	204	110
IRETON	*ST JOHN*	1875	4755 FIR AVE	51027	IW	Michael J Boothby		WS 815	HC	32	24	17
	ST PAUL secretarystpauls2324@gmail.com stpaulsireton.weebly.com	1886	602 Main St PO BOX 66	51027	IW	Michael J Boothby	(712)278-2324	WS 9 SS 1015 BC 1015		303	271	95
JEFFERSON	*TRINITY* tlcjeffia.360unite.com	1939	801 W LINCOLN WAY	50129	IW	Dennis L Martens	(515)386-3517 (515)386-5262	WS 930 SS 1045	ED/HC/ MD/SN	487	391	85
JESUP	*GRACE* stjohnsandgracelp@gmail.com stjohnsandgracelp.com	1934	633 Purdy St PO BOX 523	50648	IE	Grant P Tapken	(319)827-1257	WS 830 SS 930	ED/HC/ MD/SN	55	55	25
JOHNSTON	*BEAUTIFUL SAVIOR*		See Polk City IA									
	MESSIAH pastor@messiahjohnston.com www.messiahjohnston.com	2008	6270 MERLE HAY RD	50131	IW	James A Stogdill	(515)270-6268 (515)270-8611	WS 930 SS 1045 BC 1045	EC/ED/HC/ MD/SN	113	96	46
KEYSTONE	*ST JOHN* stjnluth@netins.net www.stjohnkeystone.org	1895	201 4th Ave PO BOX 176	52249	IE	Josiah J Schultz	(319)442-3514	WS 10 SS 1015 BC 1015	EL/ED/HC/ MD/SN	420	347	71
KINGSLEY	*FIRST* firstluth.kingsley@gmail.com	1935	406 Main St PO BOX 306	51028	IW	Jason M Letsche	(712)378-2129	WS 9 SS 10 BC 10	ED/HC/ MD/SN	257	164	111
KIRON	*ST JOHN* sjlcmski@schallertel.net	1891	17 S Orchard PO BOX 216	51448	IW		(712)675-4881	WS 1030	ED/MD	129	95	25

*Indicates a new church start. A new church start is an intentionally organized gathering which comes together on a regular basis for the purpose of worship and/or Bible study and is intended to grow into a member LCMS congregation. WS =Worship Service; SS = Sunday School; BC =Bible Class; EC = Early Childhood; EL = Elementary School; HS = High School; ED =Education Ministry; HC =Human Care Ministry; SN = Special Needs Ministry; MD = Media Ministry (PC)=Partner Church Pastor. See Page 53 for the Table of Abbreviations for key to additional abbreviations

CITY	CONGREGATION EMAIL WEBSITE	YEAR EST	LOCATION MAILING ADDRESS	ZIP CODE(S)	DIST.	PASTOR(S)	PHONE FAX	WS SS BC	SCHOOLS/ MINISTRIES	STATISTIC Bapt	Conf	Avg Attend
KNOXVILLE	*TRINITY* office@trinityknoxville.org trinityknoxville.org	1946	814 W PLEASANT ST	50138	IE	Joel T Picard	(641)842-4724	WS 1030 SS 915 BC 915	ED/HC/MD	448	326	96
LACONA	*ST PAUL*	1854	2002 20TH PL	50139	IE			WS 1030 SS 930	ED	114	86	38
LAKE CITY	*PILGRIM* pastorpaulferderer82@gmail.com www.pilgrimlakecity.com	1928	720 E MAIN ST	51449	IW	Paul A Ferderer	(712)464-3130	WS 9 BC 8	ED/HC/ MD/SN	196	166	55
LAKE PARK	*CONCORDIA* tlcsv@hotmail.com www.concordialp.com	1942	306 E 4th St PO BOX 597	51347	IW	Adam E Jacobsen	(712)832-3503	WS 1045 SS 945	ED/SN	171	140	45
	TRINITY		See Sioux Valley Twp MN									
LAKE VIEW	*EMMANUEL* lakeviewemmanuel@outlook.com www.lakeviewemmanuel.com	1912	115 2nd St PO BOX 260	51450	IW	Donald E Peterson III	(712)657-3324	WS 10 SS 9 BC 9	ED/HC/MD	324	297	80
LARCHWOOD	*ENGLISH*	1941	603 Fell St 1690 130TH ST	51241	IW	John A Sloter	(712)477-2387	WS 8	HC/MD	20	20	17
LATIMER	*ST PAUL* jcollier@stpaulslatimer.org	1895	304 West Main St PO BOX 697	50452	IE	Joel P Wagner	(641)579-6281	WS 9 SS 1015 BC 1015	EL/HS/HC/ MD	149	121	70
LAWTON	*BETHEL* bethel@wiatel.net www.bethellawton.org	1934	322 Pine St PO BOX 218	51030	IW	Robert J Zellmer	(712)944-5580	WS 1015 SS 9 BC 9	ED/HC/ MD/SN	124	106	39
LE MARS	*GRACE* gracelutheranchurch@ymail.com www.gracelemars.org	1942	1430 7TH AVE SE	51031	IW	Timothy P Geitz Daniel D Mapur	(712)546-5516 (712)546-5527	WS 9 SS 1015 BC 1015	MD/SN	402	300	130
LEEDS	*CALVARY*		See Sioux City IA									
LEON	*OUR SAVIOR'S* pr.awendorff@gmail.com	1970	709 W 1st St PO BOX 418	50144	IW	Aaron N Wendorff	(507)766-2165	WS 11 SS 1015		71	46	32
LIDDERDALE	*IMMANUEL*	1872	103 4th St PO BOX 100	51452	IW		(712)822-5512			47	37	27
LIVERMORE	*IMMANUEL*	1932	301 K Rd PO BOX 29	50558	IW	Steven M Struecker	(515)379-1287	WS 815	ED/HC/MD	80	73	25
LOGAN	*IMMANUEL* immanuelluth@iowatelecom.net www.ilclogan.org	1931	311 E 6TH ST	51546	IW	Daniel P Steeb	(712)644-2384	WS 9 SS 1015 BC 1015		107	97	49
LONE ROCK	*IMMANUEL* lottscreekilc@gmail.com	1875	2706 50TH AVE	50559	IW		(515)925-3597	WS 9 SS 945	ED/HC/ MD/SN	137	116	41
LOST NATION	*IMMANUEL*		See Grand Mound IA									
LOWDEN	*TRINITY* tlclowden@fbcom.net www.trinitylowden.org	1870	801 Washington Ave 474 PO BOX 399	52255	IE	Daniel T Redhage	(563)941-5853	WS 10 SS 845 BC 845 11	ED/HC/MD	284	245	85
LU VERNE	*ZION* skafarms@ncn.net	1880	1002 HAYES ST	50560	IW	Steven M Struecker	(515)882-3347	WS 10 SS 845	ED/HC/ MD/SN	125	99	21
LUZERNE	*ST PAUL* stpauls1859@gmail.com	1859	107 MAPLE ST	52257	IE	Dean H Duncan	(319)444-2378	WS 830 SS 945 BC 945	ED/HC	66	54	21
LYTTON	*ST PAUL'S*		See Sac City IA									
MALLARD	*TRINITY* p.schulz571@gmail.com	1893	311 North Highway 4 311 N HIGHWAY 4	50562	IW	Paul A Schulz	(712)425-3328	WS 945 SS 11 BC 11	ED/HC/ MD/SN	126	100	70
MANCHESTER	*OUR SAVIOR* oursav@iowatelecom.net www.oursaviormanchester.com	1964	116 Guetzko Ct PO BOX 247	52057	IE	Isaiah A Armbrecht	(563)927-4860 (563)927-4860	WS 9 SS 1015 BC 1015	ED/HC/ MD/SN	349	285	87
MANILLA	*TRINITY* trinitymanilla@gmail.com trinitylutheranmanilla.com	1886	641 3rd Ave PO BOX 340	51454	IW	Zachary A Staehr	(712)654-3031		ED/HC/MD	207	166	60
MANNING	*ZION* zionmanninglcms@gmail.com zionmanning.com	1900	1204 CENTER ST	51455	IW	Jonathan E Conner	(712)655-2352 (712)655-2237	WS 9 SS 1030 BC 1030	EC/ED/ HC/MD	765	571	186
MANSON	*TRINITY* www.churchesinthecountry.org	1875	3335 220TH ST	50563	IW	Chadric A Dietrich	(515)463-2244	WS 1045		125	113	23
MAPLETON	*ST MATTHEW* office@stmatthewmapleton.org stmatthewmapleton.org	1902	504 WALNUT ST	51034	IW		(712)881-2243 (712)881-1163	WS 8 SS 945 BC 945	ED/MD	372	296	47
MAQUOKETA	*IMMANUEL*		See Grand Mound IA									
MARCUS	*PEACE* marcusplcsec@midlands.net	1944	300 E Spruce St PO BOX 428	51035	IW	Larry K Roop	(712)376-4818	WS 930 SS 1030 BC 1030	ED/HC/ MD/SN	265	248	58
	TRINITY trinitysecretary.marcus@gmail.com	1879	5289 C AVE	51035	IW	Alex J Kaldahl	(712)376-2666	WS 10 SS 11 BC 11	ED/HC/ MD/SN	100	84	50
MARENGO	*ST JOHNS* stjohns2@netins.net www.stjohnsmarengo.org	1885	780 COURT AVE	52301	IE	Thomas C Van Hemert	(319)642-5452	WS 845 SS 10 BC 10	ED/HC	597	478	114
MARION	*ST PAUL* office@stpaulsmarioniowa.org www.mystpauls.org	1923	915 27TH ST	52302	IE	Alan R Kornacki Jr	(319)377-4687	WS 8 1030 SS 915 BC 915	ED/HC/ MD/SN	446	368	185
MARSHALLTOWN	*REDEEMER* www.redeemerlutheranmarshalltown.org	1926	1600 S CENTER ST	50158	IE	Alexander C Post	(641)753-9565	WS 9 SS 1015 BC 1015	ED/HC/ MD/SN	312	239	110
	TRINITY		See State Center IA									
	TRINITY DILLON	1870	2702 DILLON RD	50158	IE	Fred L Berry Jr	(641)479-2170	WS 1015 SS 915 BC 915		278	199	62
MASON CITY	*BETHLEHEM* bethinfo@bethlcms.org bethlcms.org	1919	419 N DELAWARE AVE	50401	IE	Karl C Bollhagen	(641)423-0438 (641)423-0459	WS 1045 SS 930 BC 930	EC/ED/HC/ MD/SN	325	242	87

*Indicates a new church start. A new church start is an intentionally organized gathering which comes together on a regular basis for the purpose of worship and/or Bible study and is intended to grow into a member LCMS congregation. WS =Worship Service; SS = Sunday School; BC =Bible Class; EC = Early Childhood; EL = Elementary School; HS = High School; ED =Education Ministry; HC =Human Care Ministry; SN = Special Needs Ministry; MD = Media Ministry (PC)=Partner Church Pastor. See Page 53 for the Table of Abbreviations for key to additional abbreviations

CITY	CONGREGATION EMAIL WEBSITE	YEAR EST	LOCATION MAILING ADDRESS	ZIP CODE(S)	DIST.	PASTOR(S)	PHONE FAX	WS SS BC	SCHOOLS/ MINISTRIES	STATISTIC Bapt	Conf	Avg Attend
MASON CITY	*MESSIAH* pottedplantproduction@yahoo.com www.messiahlutheranmc.com	1992	2620 4TH ST SE	50401	IE	Dr Byron Northwick	(641)423-2970	WS 9 SS 1015 BC 1030	ED/MD	113	89	55
MCGREGOR	*ST PAUL* trinitylcms@gmail.com www.listentojesus.info	1932	630 Main St PO BOX 368	52157	IE	Michael B Keller	(563)873-3341	WS 1030 SS 915	ED/HC	109	91	39
MEDIAPOLIS	*ST PAUL*		See Wapello IA									
MELCHER - DALLAS	*ST JOHN* stjohnchurchmd@gmail.com	1921	709 SW MAIN ST	50062	IE		(641)947-6904	WS 9 SS 1015	ED/MD/SN	86	68	35
MILFORD	*IMMANUEL*		See Terril IA									
MINBURN	*CHRIST*		See Perry IA									
MISSOURI VALLEY	*FIRST* flcmovalley@msn.com www.facebook.com/FLCMoValley	1928	724 N 8TH ST MISSOURI VLY	51555	IW	Joseph D Hanson	(712)642-2483	WS 930 SS 830 BC 830	ED/HC	170	127	45
MONTICELLO	*ST JOHN* stjohnsjd@hotmail.com stjohnslutheranmonticello.com/	1864	18927 Hwy 38 18927 HIGHWAY 38	52310	IE	Caleb W Schewe	(319)465-4842	WS 955 SS 845 BC 845	ED	349	255	57
MOUNT PLEASANT	*FAITH* faithlc39@gmail.com www.faithsonshine.com	1941	910 E MAPLELEAF DR	52641	IE	Michael R Scudder	(319)385-8427	WS 930 SS 815 BC 815	EC/ED/ HC/MD	325	250	86
MOUNT VERNON	*ST PAUL* info@splcmv.org www.splcmv.org	1957	600 5TH AVE SW	52314	IE	Sean D Hansen	(319)895-8772 (319)895-4089	WS 930 SS 815	ED	347	252	91
MUSCATINE	*OUR SAVIOR* oslcp@machlink.com www.oursaviormuscatine.org	1962	2611 LUCAS ST	52761	IE	Jeffrey W Pautz	(563)263-0347	WS 9 SS 1030 BC 1030	ED	86	73	52
NEWELL	*ST PETER* stpeter_newell@iowatelecom.net stpeterlutheran-newell-iowa.weebly.com	1905	314 S Clark St PO BOX 393	50568	IW		(712)272-3739	WS 10	ED/MD	126	118	24
	ZION		See Storm Lake IA									
NEWHALL	*ST JOHN* stjohnnewhall@southslope.net www.stjohnofnewhall.org	1871	310 2nd St E PO BOX 390	52315	IE	Nickalaus W Palmer	(319)223-5593	WS 8 1030 SS 915 BC 915	EL/ED/HC/ MD/SN	921	734	230
NEWTON	*OUR SAVIOR* oursavr@windstream.net www.oursavlutheran.com	1961	1900 N 4TH AVE E	50208	IE	Michael J Manz	(641)792-1084	WS 9 SS 1030	ED/HC/ MD/SN	291	229	57
NORTH LIBERTY	*ST SILAS* smayderm@gmail.com www.stsilaslutheran.org	2013	70 CIRCLE DR STE C	52317	IE		(319)626-3961	WS 10 SS 9 BC 9	ED	37	30	26
OAKLAND	*ST PAUL* sjspdualparish@gmail.com	1878	735 N HIGHWAY ST	51560	IW	Christopher A Maronde	(712)482-3028	WS 1030 SS 930	ED/HC	72	62	22
OCHEYEDAN	*ST JOHN* beahappy40@yahoo.com	1888	6665 FREDERICK AVE MAY CITY	51354	IW	Richard W Milbrandt	(712)735-4401	WS 1015 SS 10 BC 915	ED/HC/MD	96	84	21
	ST PETER www.osceolacolutherans.org	1901	1077 Pine St PO BOX 56	51354	IW	Richard W Milbrandt	(712)758-3425	WS 1015	ED/HC/MD	133	123	35
	ZION www.osceolacolutherans.org	1887	1303 TANAGER AVE	51354	IW	Richard W Milbrandt	(712)758-3483	WS 1015	ED/MD/SN	70	68	34
ODEBOLT	*TRINITY* odebolttrinity@netins.net	1946	612 S Dewey St PO BOX 470	51458	IW	David E Clark	(712)668-4201	WS 1015 BC 9	ED/HC	263	217	104
OELWEIN	*PEACE* peaceoelwein@gmail.com	1961	1308 E CHARLES ST	50662	IE	Jay R Weideman	(319)283-5778	WS 830	ED/HC/MD	102	83	35
OGDEN	*ZION* zionogdenoffice@netins.net	1872	319 W Elm St PO BOX L	50212	IW	Max A Phillips Christopher M Walters Stephen C Ude	(515)275-2234	WS 915 SS 1015	EC/ED/ HC/MD	269	219	70
OKOBOJI	*IMMANUEL*		See Terril IA									
ORANGE CITY	*FAITH* faithlutheran@premieronline.net www.faithlutheranorangecity.com/	1970	710 8TH ST SE	51041	IW	Thomas C Batchelder	(712)737-2112	WS 9 SS 1015 BC 1015	ED/HC/MD	229	193	86
OSAGE	*ST JOHN*	1874	1921 317th St PO BOX 153	50461	IE	Dr Byron Northwick	(641)395-2914		HC	33	31	20
	TRINITY secretary@trinityosage.org trinityosage.org	1932	402 STATE ST	50461	IE	James L Rockhill	(641)732-4771	WS 10 SS 9 BC 9		332	279	82
OSCEOLA	*IMMANUEL* pr.awendorff@gmail.com www.immanuelosceola.org	1946	101 E VIEW PL	50213	IW	Aaron N Wendorff	(507)766-2165	WS 830 SS 945 BC 945	EC/ED	134	103	75
OSKALOOSA	*ST JOHN* pastor@stjohnosky.org www.stjohnosky.org	1892	2370 MERINO AVE	52577	IE	Samuel G Beltz	(641)673-6546	WS 9 SS 10 BC 10	ED	292	246	80
OTTUMWA	*TRINITY* jamespreus@gmail.com www.trinitylutheranottumwa.com	1934	295 SHAUL AVE	52501	IE	James A Preus	(641)684-7279	WS 9 SS 1030 BC 1030	MD	161	136	74
OXFORD	*ST SILAS*		See North Liberty IA									
PANORA	*ST THOMAS* stthomas@netins.net www.panoralutheran.com	1973	2106 Hwy 4 PO BOX 509	50216	IW	Steven D Wichtendahl	(641)755-2051	WS 1030 SS 9 BC 915	ED/MD	156	156	23
PANORE	*PANORATELECO* Satellite Site of St Thomas Panora IA	2004	114 E Main	50216								
PAULLINA	*BETHEL*		See Sutherland IA									
	ST JOHN		See Germantown IA									
	ZION zionsec@tcaexpress.net zlcpaullina.360unite.com	1892	101 E Bertha PO BOX 509	51046	IW	Donald J Meyer David H Matthews Jr	(712)949-3910	WS 930 SS 1030 BC 1045	EL/ED/HC/ MD	447	360	120

*Indicates a new church start. A new church start is an intentionally organized gathering which comes together on a regular basis for the purpose of worship and/or Bible study and is intended to grow into a member LCMS congregation. WS =Worship Service; SS = Sunday School; BC =Bible Class; EC = Early Childhood; EL = Elementary School; HS = High School; ED =Education Ministry; HC =Human Care Ministry; SN = Special Needs Ministry; MD = Media Ministry (PC)=Partner Church Pastor. See Page 53 for the Table of Abbreviations for key to additional abbreviations

CITY	CONGREGATION EMAIL WEBSITE	YEAR EST	LOCATION MAILING ADDRESS	ZIP CODE(S)	DIST.	PASTOR(S)	PHONE FAX	WS SS BC	SCHOOLS/ MINISTRIES	STATISTIC Bapt	Conf	Avg Attend
PEOSTA	*ST PAUL*		See Dubuque IA									
PERRY	*CHRIST* rev.max.phillips@gmail.com www.facebook.com/CLCBouton/	1892	1300 28th PO BOX 100 BOUTON	50220 50039	IW	Max A Phillips Christopher M Walters Stephen C Ude	(515)676-2289	WS 1030 SS 930 BC 930	ED/HC/ MD/SN	198	176	82
	PERRY LUTHERAN HOME Satellite Site of Christ Perry IA	2015	2323 E Willis Ave	50220				WS 830				
	TRINITY officetlcp@gmail.com	1938	2715 IOWA ST	50220	IW	Kenneth A Bose	(515)465-3272	WS 5	ED/HC/ MD/SN	54	54	11
PERSIA	*TRINITY*	1898	301 1st Ave PO BOX 86	51563	IW	Merlene D Ostebee	(712)488-2023	WS 830 SS 945 BC 945		34	33	14
POLK CITY	*BEAUTIFUL SAVIOR* secretary@polkcity.church polkcity.church	1992	1701 W JESTER PARK DR	50226	IW		(515)984-6146	WS 815 1030 SS 920 BC 920	EC/ED/HC/ MD/SN	543	335	135
POMEROY	*IMMANUEL* pastorzimmerman2019@gmail.com immanuel-pomeroy.weebly.com/	1879	302 S Seneca St PO BOX 211	50575	IW		(712)468-2211	WS 8	ED/SN	43	41	20
QUIMBY	*PILGRIM* plcquimby@midlands.net	1941	301 N Main PO BOX 146	51049	IW	Alex J Kaldahl	(712)445-2549	WS 8 SS 9	ED/HC	128	71	21
READLYN	*IMMANUEL* immanuelstpaul@gmail.com	1873	2683 QUAIL AVE	50668	IE	Miguel A Gonzalez-Feliciano	(319)279-3977	WS 10 SS 9 BC 9	EL/ED/HC/ MD	203	151	71
	ST PAUL	1909	120 W 4th PO BOX 57	50668	IE	Miguel A Gonzalez-Feliciano	(319)279-3961	WS 830 BC 3	EL/ED/HC/ MD/SN	223	180	57
REINBECK	*ST JOHN'S* sjluth@reinbeck.net stjohnreinbeck.360unite.com/home	1896	207 RANDALL ST	50669	IE	Kevin C Richter	(319)345-2766 (319)345-2766	WS 9 SS 1015 BC 1015	EL/HS/ED/ MD	110	90	52
REMSEN	*CHRIST* christlutheran51050@gmail.com www.clcremsen.com/	1887	503 S Washington St PO BOX 570	51050	IW	Matthew A Martin	(712)786-2225	WS 9 SS 1015 BC 1030	ED/HC/ MD/SN	237	187	64
RICEVILLE	*ST PETER* Matthias.wollberg@ctsfw.edu saintpetersriceville.com	1870	105 W 6th St PO BOX 255	50466	IE	Matthias C Wollberg	(641)985-2421	WS 930 SS 830 BC 830	ED/HC/ MD/SN	216	199	50
ROCK RAPIDS	*PEACE* plc@premieronline.net www.peacelutheranrr.com	1901	902 S CARROLL ST	51246	IW	John A Sloter	(712)472-3226	WS 1015 SS 9 BC 9	ED/HC/ MD/SN	303	272	101
ROCKWELL CITY	*IMMANUEL* immanueltrinity03@gmail.com www.churchesinthecountry.org	1878	3010 270TH ST	50579	IW	Chadric A Dietrich	(712)297-7708	WS 845 SS 10		263	209	89
	TRINITY		See Manson IA									
SAC CITY	*ST PAUL*		See Schaller IA									
	ST PAUL'S saintpaulsac@gmail.com stpaulssac.org	1938	1112 BAILEY ST	50583	IW	Cory J Kroonblawd	(712)662-7029	WS 9 SS 1015 BC 8	ED/HC/ MD/SN	378	318	91
	ST PETER'S dianegottol@gmail.com	1879	3541 300TH ST	50583	IW		(712)466-2488	WS 830	HC	48	36	30
SAINT ANSGAR	*IMMANUEL* ilstaworks@gmail.com www.immanuelsta.org	1872	308 W 5th St PO BOX 339	50472	IE	Mark R Squire	(641)713-4782	WS 9 SS 10 BC 10	ED/HC/SN	461	348	92
SANBORN	*ST JOHN* stjohnschurch86@gmail.com www.stjohnsia.org/	1886	305 ANGIE ST	51248	IW	Nicholas J Sinatra	(712)729-3800	WS 9	ED/HC/MD	147	109	47
SCHALLER	*ST PAUL* schallerlutheranchurch@gmail.com	1920	402 E 3rd PO BOX 368	51053	IW	David W Lyons	(712)275-4299	WS 10 SS 9 BC 9	ED/HC	285	225	100
SCHLESWIG	*IMMANUEL* immansch@iowatelecom.net	1912	501 GLAD ST	51461	IW	Merle F Mahnken	(712)676-2235	WS 9 SS 1015 BC 1015	EC/ED	615	513	148
SERGEANT BLUFF	*SHEPHERD OF PEACE* sopoffice@longlines.com www.shepherdofpeacechurch.com	1975	203 Port Neal Rd PO BOX 36 SERGEANT BLF	51054	IW	Benjamin D Perkins	(712)943-4502 (712)943-4506	WS 9 SS 1030 BC 1030	ED/HC/ MD/SN	138	91	65
SHELDON	*OUR SAVIOR* oursaviorsheldonlcms@gmail.com www.oursaviorsheldon.org		1225 S 2nd Ave 1225 2ND AVE	51201	IW	George H Clausen	(712)324-9725	WS 9 SS 1015 BC 1015	ED/HC/MD	22	22	13
SHELL ROCK	*PEACE* pastorknox@theforgivenessplace.org	1943	121 E Washington St PO BOX 625	50670	IE	Michael R Knox	(319)885-4440		ED	20	20	15
SHELLSBURG	*ZION*	1939	209 Grand Ave Sw PO BOX 268	52332	IE	Zachary S Johnson	(319)436-2524	WS 10 SS 845		227	184	35
SHENANDOAH	*TRINITY* pastorimmanuelclartrinityshen@ gmail.com www.trinityShenandoah.org	1928	713 CHURCH ST	51601	IW	Wade M Brandt	(712)246-1131	WS 1045 SS 930 BC 930	ED/HC/ MD/SN	106	90	30
SHERRILL	*ST MATTHEW*	1855	5350 SHERRILL RD	52073	IE	Mark G Zieroth Jesse K Cearlock		WS 1130	ED	34	30	20
SIGOURNEY	*HOPE*	1975	315 Kelley St PO BOX 246	52591	IE	Richard A Meyer	(319)668-2999			54	22	19
SIOUX CITY	*BETHANY*	1949	1201 DUBUQUE ST	51105	IW		(712)255-4900	WS 1030 SS 1030	ED/HC/ MD/SN	82	51	22
	CALVARY calvarysecretary@aol.com www.calvarylutheransiouxcityia.org	1935	4410 Central St 4400 CENTRAL ST	51108	IW	James W Travis Alexander L Smith	(712)239-1575	WS 8 1030 SS 915 BC 915	ED/HC/ MD/SN	764	619	167
	FAITH faithsc3101@gmail.com faithlutheranchurch.net	1959	3101 HAMILTON BLVD	51104	IW	Ezra G Grabau	(712)258-4820	WS 915 SS 1030 BC 1030	HC/SN	294	208	68
	REDEEMER redeemerchurchsc@gmail.com www.redeemersiouxcity.com	1926	3204 S LAKEPORT ST	51106	IW	Russell C Senstad David N Zirpel	(712)276-1125 (712)276-1146	WS 815 1045 SS 930 BC 930	EC/ED/HC/ MD/SN	1216	948	298

*Indicates a new church start. A new church start is an intentionally organized gathering which comes together on a regular basis for the purpose of worship and/or Bible study and is intended to grow into a member LCMS congregation. WS =Worship Service; SS = Sunday School; BC =Bible Class; EC = Early Childhood; EL = Elementary School; HS = High School; ED =Education Ministry; HC =Human Care Ministry; SN = Special Needs Ministry; MD = Media Ministry (PC)=Partner Church Pastor. See Page 53 for the Table of Abbreviations for key to additional abbreviations

CITY	CONGREGATION EMAIL WEBSITE	YEAR EST	LOCATION MAILING ADDRESS	ZIP CODE(S)	DIST.	PASTOR(S)	PHONE FAX	WS SS BC	SCHOOLS/ MINISTRIES	STATISTIC Bapt	Conf	Avg Attend
SIOUX CITY	*ST PAULS* siouxcitystpauls@gmail.com www.siouxcitystpauls.org	1877	612 JENNINGS ST	51101	IW		(712)252-0338 (712)252-1141	WS 815 1045 SS 930 BC 930	EL/ED/HC/ MD/SN	811	680	138
SOLON	*KING OF GLORY*		See Swisher IA									
	ST SILAS		See North Liberty IA									
SPENCER	*CHRIST KING* www.ctkspencer.com	1982	500 4TH AVE SW	51301	IW	Michael J McGinley	(712)262-2244	WS 9 SS 1030 BC 1030	ED/MD	120	97	67
	FIRST ENGLISH felc5598@gmail.com spencer-church.com	1892	1311 E 18TH ST	51301	IW	Paul E Kaldahl Jr	(712)262-5598 (712)262-8396	WS 8 1045 SS 930 BC 930	EC/ED/HC/ MD/SN	818	632	191
SPIRIT LAKE	*IMMANUEL* lcmslakes@gmail.com www.lcmslakes.org	1871	2300 27th St PO BOX 422	51360	IW	Paul W Dare	(712)336-1010 (712)336-5734	WS 9 SS 1005 BC 1015	EC/ED/HC/ MD/SN	860	732	232
SPRING FOUNTAIN	*ST JOHN*		See Sumner IA									
STANWOOD	*ST PAUL*	1875	313 S Ash St PO BOX 236	52337	IE	Dr Andrew C Watkins	(563)942-3924	WS 9	ED	21	18	21
STATE CENTER	*TRINITY* sectrinitysc@gmail.com tlcscia.com/	1945	206 1st Ave S PO BOX 632	50247	IE	Robert W Ricard	(641)483-2682	WS 10 SS 9 BC 9	ED/HC/ MD/SN	235	190	61
STORM LAKE	*GRACE* lutherangrace1951@gmail.com gracestormlake.org	1951	1407 W 5TH ST	50588	IW	Bradley W Ketcham	(712)732-5005 (712)732-3791	WS 9 SS 1015 BC 1015	EC/ED/HC/ MD/SN	265	218	64
	ST JOHN stjohnstormlake@gmail.com www.stjohnstormlake.org	1885	402 LAKE AVE	50588	IW	Bruce H Lesemann	(712)732-2400 (712)732-2401	WS 9 SS 1015 BC 1015	ED/HC/ MD/SN	323	262	86
	ST PAUL		See Schaller IA									
	ZION ZionStormLake@gmail.com	1871	1725 555TH ST	50588	IW	Lucas W Booher	(712)732-5223	WS 10 SS 845	MD	326	242	98
SUMNER	*ST JOHN* piehldmap@gmail.com www.stpaulstjohnsumner.org	1875	1490 Tahoe Ave 612 W 3RD ST	50674	IE	Tanner B Post	(563)578-3315	WS 8	ED	81	68	24
	ST PAUL piehldmap@gmail.com www.stpaulstjohnsumner.org	1915	612 W 3RD ST	50674	IE	Tanner B Post	(563)578-3315	WS 10 SS 11	ED	159	123	44
SUTHERLAND	*BETHEL* bethel@midlands.net blcsuth.360unite.com/home	1934	502 Ash St PO BOX 20	51058	IW	Donald J Meyer David H Matthews Jr	(712)446-3630	WS 1030 SS 915 BC 915	ED/MD/SN	277	275	57
SWEA CITY	*OUR SAVIOR* nina.harbaugh67@gmail.com	1959	710 5th St N PO BOX 297	50590	IW	David P Schultz	(515)538-0620	WS 9 BC 930	EC/ED/MD	27	25	17
SWISHER	*KING OF GLORY* kingofgloryswisher@gmail.com Kingofgloryswisher.org	1988	2720 120TH ST NE	52338	IE	Brad A Brown	(319)431-5431	WS 1130	ED	24	20	16
	ST SILAS		See North Liberty IA									
TERRIL	*IMMANUEL*	1890	206 Terril Ave PO BOX 98	51364	IW		(712)853-6192	WS 1030 BC 1130		147	125	20
TIFFIN	*ST SILAS*		See North Liberty IA									
URBANDALE	*GLORIA DEI* office@gdlc.church www.gdlc.church	1965	8301 AURORA AVE	50322	IW	Benjamin C Johnson Dr Joseph M Meyer Timothy J Phillips Christian L Pieper	(515)276-1700 (515)276-5939	WS 730 9 1030 SS 915 1045	EC/ED/HC/ MD/SN	3276	2436	866
	TRINITY		See Van Meter IA									
UTE	*ST PAUL* stpaulute@gmail.com stpaulsute.org	1898	303 E 4th St PO BOX 139	51060	IW	Nathan A Peitsch	(712)885-2221 (712)885-2020	WS 10 SS 930	ED/HC/ MD/SN	369	272	66
VAN HORNE	*ST ANDREW*	1895	307 3rd Ave PO BOX 294	52346	IE	David C Lingard	(319)228-8325	WS 10 BC 8	HC/MD/SN	200	168	40
VAN METER	*TRINITY* trinity.lcms@yahoo.com www.trinity-vm.org/index.html	1885	1195 Prairieview Ave 1193 PRAIRIEVIEW AVE	50261	IW	Edward E Durand III	(515)996-2093	WS 9 SS 1015 BC 1015	ED/HC	165	137	41
VENTURA	*REDEEMER* rlc1946@cltel.net	1946	301 S Main St PO BOX 138	50482	IE	Jesse A Burns	(641)829-3650 (641)829-3612	WS 9	EL/ED/MD	296	247	82
	ST JOHN		See Garner IA									
VICTOR	*SAINT JAMES* stjlcv@netins.net	1910	502 Washington St PO BOX 127	52347	IE	Michael J Kolesar	(319)647-3375	WS 9 SS 1030 BC 1030	ED	180	138	77
	SAINT JOHNS st.johnslchurch@gmail.com	1868	2656 CC Ave 2653 CC AVE	52347	IE	Stuart A Rethwisch	(319)685-4400	WS 830 SS 930 BC 930	ED/SN	287	225	93
VILLISCA	*MOUNT CALVARY*	1938	107 S 5th Ave PO BOX 204	50864	IW	Jerome Wagoner	(712)826-7202	WS 9 SS 10		107	75	30
VINTON	*TRINITY* trinityvinton@gmail.com trinitylcmsvinton.org	1923	1002 E 13TH ST	52349	IE	Stephen K Preus	(319)472-5571	WS 9 SS 1020 BC 1020	EC/ED/HC/ MD/SN	438	350	129
WALL LAKE	*PEACE* peacewalllake@gmail.com	1882	406 Stuart St PO BOX 189	51466	IW	David L Wenndt	(712)664-2961	WS 10 SS 830 BC 830	ED/HC/MD	490	413	84
WALNUT	*OUR SAVIOR*	1982	903 Antique City Dr PO BOX 344	51577	IW	Merlene D Ostebee	(712)784-3644	WS 1030 BC 1030		41	40	16
WAPELLO	*ST PAUL* stpaulwapello.org	1949	226 WASHINGTON ST	52653	IE	Mark T Kluzek	(712)265-1286	WS 9 BC 1015	ED/HC	54	49	15
WASHINGTON	*ST PAUL*		See Wapello IA									
WATERLOO	*FAITH* faithluth@aol.com www.faithupontherock.com	1979	1555 W RIDGEWAY AVE	50701	IE	David M Menet	(319)236-1771	WS 9 SS 1015 BC 1015	EL/HS	144	107	92

*Indicates a new church start. A new church start is an intentionally organized gathering which comes together on a regular basis for the purpose of worship and/or Bible study and is intended to grow into a member LCMS congregation. WS =Worship Service; SS = Sunday School; BC =Bible Class; EC = Early Childhood; EL = Elementary School; HS = High School; ED =Education Ministry; HC =Human Care Ministry; SN = Special Needs Ministry; MD = Media Ministry (PC)=Partner Church Pastor. See Page 53 for the Table of Abbreviations for key to additional abbreviations

CITY	CONGREGATION EMAIL WEBSITE	YEAR EST	LOCATION MAILING ADDRESS	ZIP CODE(S)	DIST.	PASTOR(S)	PHONE FAX	WS SS BC	SCHOOLS/ MINISTRIES	STATISTIC Bapt	Conf	Avg Attend
WATERLOO	*GRACE* officeadmin@gracewaterloo.org www.gracewaterloo.org	1938	1024 W 8TH ST	50702	IE	Justin D Kane	(319)235-6705 (319)235-6735	WS 9 SS 1020 BC 1020	EL/HS/ED/ HC/MD	541	413	68
WAUKEE	*LIVING FAITH*		See Clive IA									
WAVERLY	*ST JOHN* stjohnlcmswaverly@gmail.com www.stjohnlutheranwaverly.org	1913	415 4TH ST SW	50677	IE	Jon M Ellingworth	(319)352-2314	WS 9 SS 1030 BC 1030	ED/HC/ MD/SN	375	315	97
	ST PAUL revfeldt@stjohndenver.com	1871	2022 LARRABEE AVE	50677	IE		(319)984-5351	WS 1030 BC 1130	EL/HS	40	35	15
WEBSTER CITY	*ST PAUL'S* stpaulwebstercity@gmail.com stpaulwebstercity.org	1874	1005 BEACH ST	50595	IW	Joseph B Pierson	(515)832-3043 (515)832-3069	WS 10 SS 9 BC 9	EC/ED/HC/ MD/SN	451	293	90
WELLMAN	*GOOD SHEPHERD*	1860	401 5th St PO BOX 116	52356	IE	Gary L Sears	(319)646-2702	WS 11		6	6	6
WELLSBURG	*ST JOHN*	1942	600 6th St PO BOX Q	50680	IE	Bruce L Zimmermann	(641)869-3838	WS 9 SS 945 BC 945	ED/HC/MD	67	59	34
WELTON	*IMMANUEL*		See Grand Mound IA									
WEST BEND	*PEACE* peacewb@ncn.net	1907	703 2nd Ave SE PO BOX 100	50597	IW	Keith P Christiansen	(515)887-3261	WS 1030	ED/HC/ MD/SN	139	114	27
WEST DES MOINES	*LIVING FAITH*		See Clive IA									
	SHEP OF THE VALLEY angie@sotv-wdm.org www.shepherd-valley.org	1967	3900 Ashworth Rd 3900 ASHWORTH RD.	50265	IW	John D Mull Eugene R Krueger	(515)225-1623 (515)225-0871	WS 8 1030 SS 915 BC 915	EC/ED/HC/ MD/SN	771	518	257
	TRINITY		See Van Meter IA									
WESTGATE	*ST PETER*	1885	280 MAIN ST	50681	IE	Kent A Peck	(563)578-8664	WS 1030 SS 9	ED/HC	343	249	80
WHITTEMORE	*ST PAUL* angelaresner85@gmail.com	1885	513 Clay St PO BOX 248	50598	IW	Mark A Resner	(515)884-2629	WS 9	ED/HC/SN	90	80	20
WILLIAMSBURG	*IMMANUEL*	1898	2978 225TH ST	52361	IE	Richard A Meyer	(319)668-2999		EL/ED/MD	465	370	205
	ST PAUL stpaullcmswburg@gmail.com www.stpaullcmswburg.com	1904	500 Clark St PO BOX 42	52361	IE	Jason B Zoske	(319)668-1266 (319)668-9436	WS 9 SS 1030 BC 1030	EL/ED/HC/ MD/SN	638	525	135
WILTON	*ZION* zionchurch@netwtc.net www.zionwilton.org	1856	1000 MAURER ST	52778	IE	Daniel F Ognoskie	(563)732-3651 (563)732-2106	WS 9 SS 1015 BC 1015	EC/ED/HC/ MD/SN	483	408	100
WINTERSET	*FAITH* keithlcms@gmail.com www.faithwinterset.org	2003	815 S 2nd Ave PO BOX 532	50273	IW	Dr Keith W Schweitzer	(641)745-5143	WS 1030 SS 930 BC 930	ED/HC/ MD/SN	40	38	30
	FAITH LUTHERAN Satellite Site of Immanuel Greenfield IA	2004	2223 204th Ct	50273				WS 11 SS 1015 BC 1015				
	TRINITY		See Van Meter IA									
WIOTA	*FIRST* pastormike@q.com	1882	70139 Memphis 70139 MEMPHIS RD	50274	IW	Michael D Bodkins	(712)774-5787	WS 1030 SS 930 BC 930	MD/SN	112	92	42
WOODWARD	*CHRIST*		See Perry IA									

KANSAS

CITY	CONGREGATION EMAIL WEBSITE	YEAR EST	LOCATION MAILING ADDRESS	ZIP CODE(S)	DIST.	PASTOR(S)	PHONE FAX	WS SS BC	SCHOOLS/ MINISTRIES	Bapt	Conf	Avg Attend
ABILENE	*FAITH* faithabilene@gmail.com www.faithabilene.org	1948	1600 N BUCKEYE AVE	67410	KS	Nathan A Harkins	(785)263-1842	WS 9 SS 1015 BC 1015	ED/HC/ MD/SN	291	223	93
ALICEVILLE	*ST JOHN* www.stjohnlutheranalicevilleks.org	1883	114 2nd 114 2ND ST WESTPHALIA	66093	KS	Timothy D Booth		WS 10 SS 9 BC 9	ED/HC/ MD/SN	179	153	78
ALMA	*ST JOHN* STJOHNALMA@GMAIL.COM www.stjohnalma.org	1861	218 W Second St PO BOX 365	66401	KS	Robert W Grimm	(785)765-3632	WS 930 SS 830 BC 830	EL/ED/HC/ MD/SN	542	413	130
ALTA VISTA	*ST PAUL* stpaulav@hotmail.com	1907	303 Main St PO BOX 235	66834	KS	John J Fries	(785)499-6623	WS 930		96	95	40
ANDOVER	*PEACE* office@peacelutheranandover.com www.peacelutheranandover.com	1984	405 W 21ST ST	67002	KS	Stephen K Wipperman	(316)733-2633	WS 8 1030 SS 915 BC 915	ED/HC/MD	227	195	54
ARGONIA	*ZION* davidpersland@gmail.com www.forministry.com/67004ZL	1885	101 E Cherry PO BOX 205	67004	KS	David P Ersland	(620)435-6524	WS 1045		30	27	11
ARKANSAS CITY	*REDEEMER* secretaryrlc320@gmail.com www.rlcarkcity.com	1925	320 W CENTRAL AVE	67005	KS	Christopher W Warneke	(620)442-5240	WS 1015 SS 9	ED/HC/ MD/SN	214	168	58
ATCHISON	*TRINITY* churchoffice@trinityatchison.org www.trinityatchison.org	1866	603 N 8TH ST	66002	KS	Jacob W Dandy Michael R Carney Marty E Reed	(913)367-2837	WS 8 1030 630 SS 915 BC 915	EL/ED/HC/ MD	1060	811	262
ATWOOD	*REDEEMER* redluth03@gmail.com www.rlcatwood.com	1993	808 S 1ST ST	67730	KS	Richard J Schneider Jr	(785)626-3178	WS 9 SS 1015 BC 1015	EC/ED/ HC/MD	316	316	100
AUGUSTA	*CHRIST* christaugusta@gmail.com www.christlutheranaugusta.com	1934	1500 CRON ST	67010	KS		(316)775-7301	WS 11 SS 940 BC 940	ED/HC	164	146	40
BALDWIN CITY	*IMMANUEL*		See Lawrence KS									
BARNES	*ST PETER* stpetersbarnes@gmail.com	1883	2647 3rd Rd PO BOX 64	66933	KS	Randall L Jahnke		WS 8	HC	127	89	42
BASEHOR	*RISEN SAVIOR* weinkauf@rslcms.church risensaviorlcms.org	1908	14700 LEAVENWORTH RD	66007	KS	Robert C Weinkauf Zachariah E Burgdorf	(913)724-2900	WS 8 1030 SS 915 BC 915	EL/HS/ED/ HC/MD	565	460	294

*Indicates a new church start. A new church start is an intentionally organized gathering which comes together on a regular basis for the purpose of worship and/or Bible study and is intended to grow into a member LCMS congregation. WS =Worship Service; SS = Sunday School; BC =Bible Class; EC = Early Childhood; EL = Elementary School; HS = High School; ED =Education Ministry; HC =Human Care Ministry; SN = Special Needs Ministry; MD = Media Ministry (PC)=Partner Church Pastor. See Page 53 for the Table of Abbreviations for key to additional abbreviations

CITY	CONGREGATION EMAIL WEBSITE	YEAR EST	LOCATION MAILING ADDRESS	ZIP CODE(S)	DIST.	PASTOR(S)	PHONE FAX	WS SS BC	SCHOOLS/ MINISTRIES	STATISTIC Bapt	Conf	Avg Attend
BASEHOR	*TRINITY FAMILY FAITH* adminassistant@gatheringinchrist.org gatheringinchrist.org		16928 EVANS RD	66007	KS	Jason D Boetcher	(913)724-4441	WS 8 1030 SS 915	EC/ED/MD	227	165	91
BONNER SPRINGS	*RISEN SAVIOR*		See Basehor KS									
	TRINITY FAMILY FAITH		See Basehor KS									
BREMEN	*BETHLEHEM*	1901	401 ARROWHEAD RD	66412	KS			WS 1015	EL/ED/MD	124	94	68
	IMMANUEL info@immanuelbremen.org www.immanuelbremen.org	1869	570 3RD RD	66412	KS		(785)337-2472	WS 1015	EL/ED/HC	280	227	96
BURLINGTON	*TRINITY* secretarytlcburlington@gmail.com www.tlcburlingtonks.org	1951	902 KENNEDY ST	66839	KS	Timothy J Wilcoxen	(620)364-2283	WS 9 SS 1030 BC 1030	EC/ED/ HC/MD	112	84	53
CANEY	*TRINITY* klmcintosh48@gmail.com www.trinitycaney.net	1960	108 N BRADLEY AVE	67333	KS			WS 10 SS 9 BC 9	MD/SN	83	71	50
CANTON	*IMMANUEL* immanuellcms@hometelco.net www.immanuellutherancanton.com	1878	703 26TH AVE	67428	KS	Troy L Slater	(620)628-4801	WS 1030 SS 930 BC 930	ED/HC/MD	195	169	90
CHANUTE	*ZION* zionchanute@sbcglobal.net	1943	1202 W MAIN ST	66720	KS		(620)431-1341	WS 930 SS 1030 BC 1030	EC/ED/ HC/MD	120	105	49
CHENEY	*ST PAUL* office@stpaulscheney.com stpaulscheney.com	1884	639 Lincoln St PO BOX 397	67025	KS	Anthony D Masinelli	(316)540-0115 (316)542-0115	WS 8 1030 SS 915 BC 915	EL/ED/HC/ MD	454	359	134
CLAFLIN	*ZION*	1884	121 Fifth St PO BOX 415	67525	KS	Daniel E Harders	(620)587-3698	WS 1030 SS 915 BC 915	ED/HC	58	55	12
CLAY CENTER	*ST PAUL* spluther@sbcglobal.net www.claycenterlutheran.com	1888	816 9TH ST	67432	KS	Paul D Tessaro Matthew E Vatthauer	(785)632-5301	WS 9 SS 1030 BC 1030	EC/ED/HC/ MD/SN	749	578	150
COFFEYVILLE	*ST PAUL* pastor.splccoffeyville@gmail.com splccoffeyville.org	1892	506 W 9TH ST	67337	KS	Jon T Franson	(620)251-2927	WS 1030 SS 9 BC 9	ED/MD/SN	83	71	55
COLBY	*TRINITY* lutheran@st-tel.net www.trinitycolby.org	1935	855 E 5TH ST	67701	KS	Philip C Hoppe	(785)462-3497	WS 1030 SS 915 BC 915	ED/HC/ MD/SN	159	137	98
CONCORDIA	*ZION LUTHERAN CHURCH-CON-CORDIA OUTREACH* Satellite Site of Zion Downs KS	2017	117 W 8th St	66901				WS 3				
COUNCIL GROVE	*CALVARY* www.facebook.com/calvary.lutheran.5015	1945	715 E MAIN ST	66846	KS	Adam W Reichart	(620)767-6772	WS 11 SS 10 BC 10	ED/HC/MD	123	98	38
DE SOTO	*LIGHT OF WORLD LUTHERAN CHURCH* Satellite Site of Beautiful Savior Olathe KS	2023	33391 Lexington Avenue Suite B	66018				WS 9 BC 10:15				
DEERFIELD	*IMMANUEL*		See Lakin KS									
DELIA	*CALVARY*		See Topeka KS									
DENISON	*CALVARY*		See Topeka KS									
DERBY	*FAITH* office@faithderby.com www.flcderby.com	1954	214 S DERBY AVE	67037	KS	Thomas R Johnson	(316)788-1715 (316)789-0043	WS 815 1045 SS 930	ED/HC	301	249	87
DODGE CITY	*HOLY CROSS* office@hclc.kscoxmail.com hclcdodgecity.org	1911	2200 3RD AVE	67801	KS	Robert F Allmann	(620)227-6204	WS 8 1030 SS 915 BC 915	ED/HC/MD	400	330	67
DOWNS	*ZION* zlcdowns@ruraltel.net	1892	1019 Blunt St PO BOX 163	67437	KS	Sherman D Stenson	(785)454-3733	WS 8 SS 10 BC 10	MD/SN	150	121	43
DULUTH	*ST PAULS* ricktwenhafel@gmail.com	1875	21185 DULUTH RD	66521	KS	Ricky J Twenhafel	(785)456-4606	WS 1030 SS 1045	HC/MD	103	83	46
EASTON	*ST JOHN*	1880	34771 243RD ST	66020	KS		(913)773-8591	WS 8	HC/MD/SN			
EDWARDSVILLE	*TRINITY FAMILY FAITH*		See Basehor KS									
EL DORADO	*GRACE* glcldks@gmail.com sites.google.com/site/graceeldorado	1929	1124 W CENTRAL AVE	67042	KS		(316)321-2423	WS 9 BC 10	ED/HC/ MD/SN	131	111	42
ELKHART	*CHRIST* christlutheranelkhart@gmail.com	1960	813 South Baca PO BOX 39	67950	OK	Mark A Schlamann	(620)697-2284	WS 1030 BC 930	ED/HC/MD	25	24	15
ELLINWOOD	*ST JOHN* info@stjohnellinwood.org www.stjohnellinwood.org	1877	512 N WILHELM AVE	67526	KS	Kenton L Abbott	(620)564-2044 (620)564-3024	WS 8 1045 SS 915 BC 930	EC/ED/HC/ MD/SN	406	310	125
ELLSWORTH	*HOEGER CHAPEL* Satellite Site of Immanuel Ellsworth KS	2014	204 Bickerdyke Blvd	67439								
	IMMANUEL immanuelellsworth@gmail.com	1916	905 Stanberry St PO BOX 133	67439	KS	Luther C Brown	(785)472-4045	WS 10 SS 9	ED/HC/ MD/SN	211	165	63
	ST PAUL christopher.craig@ctsfw.edu www.facebook.com/stpaulsellsworth/	1878	449 13TH RD	67439	KS		(785)472-8912	WS 930 SS 930 BC 930	ED/HC/ MD/SN	316	250	90
EMPORIA	*FAITH* faithemporia@gmail.com www.faithemporia.org	1982	1348 TRAILRIDGE RD	66801	KS	Adam W Reichart	(620)342-3590	WS 830 SS 930 BC 930	EC/ED	150	137	20
	MESSIAH cvantuyl@messiahlutheran.org www.messiahlutheran.org	1923	1101 NEOSHO ST	66801	KS		(620)342-8181 (620)342-6090	WS 830 11 SS 945	ED/HC/MD	1006	723	167

*Indicates a new church start. A new church start is an intentionally organized gathering which comes together on a regular basis for the purpose of worship and/or Bible study and is intended to grow into a member LCMS congregation. WS =Worship Service; SS = Sunday School; BC =Bible Class; EC = Early Childhood; EL = Elementary School; HS = High School; ED =Education Ministry; HC =Human Care Ministry; SN = Special Needs Ministry; MD = Media Ministry (PC)=Partner Church Pastor. See Page 53 for the Table of Abbreviations for key to additional abbreviations

CITY	CONGREGATION EMAIL WEBSITE	YEAR EST	LOCATION MAILING ADDRESS	ZIP CODE(S)	DIST.	PASTOR(S)	PHONE FAX	WS SS BC	SCHOOLS/ MINISTRIES	STATISTIC Bapt	 Conf	 Avg Attend
ERIE	*GOOD SHEPHERD* pastor.gslcerie@gmail.com goodshepherderie.wordpress.com/	1980	603 N MILDFELT ST	66733	KS	Caleb D Stoever	(620)244-5555	WS 830	ED/HC	67	37	24
ESKRIDGE	*ST PAUL*		See Alta Vista KS									
EUDORA	*IMMANUEL*		See Lawrence KS									
FAIRVIEW	*ST PAUL* office@nekpartnership.org	1882	112 E Maple St C/O ST. PAUL-ZION DUAL PAR-ISH 613 S 1ST HIAWATHA	66425 66434	KS	Brian G Holle	(785)742-3995	WS 830 SS 930 BC 930	EC/ED/HC	83	73	44
FORT LEAVENWORTH	*TRINITY*		See Leavenworth KS									
FORT SCOTT	*TRINITY* office-tlc@trinity-fs.us	1947	2824 S Horton 2824 S HORTON ST	66701	KS	Michael A Apfel	(620)223-3596	WS 9 SS 1030 BC 1030	EC/ED/HC	87	76	35
GALVA	*IMMANUEL*		See Canton KS									
GARDEN CITY	*TRINITY* trinitygcks@gmail.com www.tlcgck.org	1922	1010 FLEMING ST	67846	KS	Michael S Hageman Magdiel U Fajardo	(620)276-3110 (620)276-3169	WS 9 SS 1030 BC 1030	EC/ED/HC/ MD/SN	492	362	115
GARDNER	*KING OF KINGS* info@kingofkingsks.org www.kingofkingsks.org	1986	306 E Madison St PO BOX 364	66030	KS	Daniel L Wehmeier	(913)856-2500 (913)856-4260	WS 8 1030 SS 920 BC 920	EL/ED/HC/ MD/SN	598	380	124
	REDEEMER		See Olathe KS									
GIRARD	*TRINITY* trinitylutherangirard@gmail.com www.trinitygirard.org	1947	109 W SAINT JOHN ST	66743	KS	Michael L Hofmann	(620)724-8895	WS 1030 SS 915 BC 915	ED/MD	425	322	145
GOESSEL	*IMMANUEL*		See Canton KS									
GRANTVILLE	*CALVARY*		See Topeka KS									
GREAT BEND	*OUR SAVIOUR* oursaviourgb@gmail.com	1976	5860 EISENHOWER AVE	67530	KS		(620)617-2441	WS 230		35	30	18
GREENLEAF	*BETHLEHEM* bethlehemgreenleaf@hotmail.com	1917	2054 10TH RD	66943	KS	Randall L Jahnke	(785)747-2407	WS 8 SS 1045 BC 1045	ED/HC/ MD/SN	195	153	62
GREENSBURG	*PEACE* Info@peacekansas.org	1954	321 S WALNUT ST	67054	KS	David A McCloskey	(620)966-8845	WS 1030 SS 915 BC 915	ED	19	19	15
GRIDLEY	*TRINITY*		See Burlington KS									
HANOVER	*TRINITY* trinityhanover@gmail.com www.trinitylutheranhanoverks.org	1880	2942 27TH RD	66945	KS	Travis N Orr	(785)713-2764	WS 10 SS 9 BC 9	ED/HC/MD	201	169	84
HARTFORD	*TRINITY*		See Burlington KS									
HAVEN	*ST PAUL'S* info@stpaulshaven.com www.stpaulshaven.com	1880	8513 E ARLINGTON RD	67543	KS	Nathan S Dudley	(620)465-3427	WS 1030 SS 9	ED/HC/MD	308	246	66
HAYS	*MESSIAH* messiahsec@ruraltel.net www.messiahlutheranhays.com	1950	2000 MAIN ST	67601	KS		(785)625-2057	WS 830 11 SS 945 BC 945	ED/HC/MD	237	186	130
HEPLER	*IMMANUEL* pastor.ilchepler@gmail.com immanuelhepler.wordpress.com	1879	673 W 680TH AVE	66746	KS	Caleb D Stoever	(620)395-2692	WS 11 SS 10 BC 10	HC	138	111	35
HERINGTON	*IMMANUEL* jaronpmelin@protonmail.com heringtonlcms.wordpress.com/	1887	2201 1000th Ave 2201 1000 AVE	67449	KS	Jaron P Melin	(785)258-3003			80	60	25
	OUR REDEEMER orlcherington@gmail.com heringtonlcms.wordpress.com/	1927	802 E TRAPP ST	67449	KS	Jaron P Melin	(785)258-3122	WS 1030 BC 7	EC/ED/MD	256	180	60
	ST JOHN jaronpmelin@protonmail.com heringtonlcms.wordpress.com/	1861	2124 Hwy 4 2124 HIGHWAY 4	67449	KS	Jaron P Melin	(785)366-0270		HC	58	58	25
	THE LEGACY OF HERINGTON Satellite Site of Our Redeemer Herington KS	1995	2 E Ash Street	67449								
HESSTON	*IMMANUEL*		See Canton KS									
HIAWATHA	*ZION* zionhiawatha@rainbowtel.net	1895	613 S 1ST ST	66434	KS	Brian G Holle	(785)742-3995	WS 1030 SS 915 BC 915	ED	123	105	46
HILL CITY	*GRACE*	1961	519 N 11th Ave PO BOX 40	67642	KS		(785)421-2481	WS 6 SS 3 BC 3	ED/HC	45	35	10
HILLSBORO	*ZION* zionlutheranhillsboro@gmail.com www.facebook.com/profile. php?id=61552100987299	1883	106 N LINCOLN ST	67063	KS	Frank E Johnson	(620)947-3522	WS 1030 SS 915 BC 915	ED/MD/SN	88	76	46
HOISINGTON	*CONCORDIA* gapswolf@sbcglobal.net www.concordia-hoisington.org	1955	460 W 9th 460 W 9TH ST	67544	KS	Gary C Wolf	(620)653-4644	WS 10 SS 9 BC 9	ED/HC/ MD/SN	124	98	55
HOLTON	*CALVARY*		See Topeka KS									
	TRINITY trinitylutheranholton@gmail.com	1926	401 CHEYENNE DR	66436	KS	Dr Jerome A Brownlee Sr	(785)364-2206	WS 10 SS 9 BC 9	ED/HC/ MD/SN	233	166	56
HOLYROOD	*ST PETER*	1883	209 S County Road PO BOX 46	67450	KS	Daniel E Harders	(785)252-3275	WS 9 SS 1015 BC 1015	ED/HC/ MD/SN	166	124	22
HOPE	*ST JOHN*		See Herington KS									
HOXIE	*IMMANUEL* immanuel.lutheran.hoxie@gmail.com	1888	1400 Locust PO BOX 672	67740	KS		(785)675-3608	WS 8 BC 930	ED/HC/ MD/SN	119	90	20
HOYT	*CALVARY*		See Topeka KS									
HUMBOLDT	*ST PETER* office@stpetershumboldt.org www.stpetershumboldt.org	1863	910 AMOS ST	66748	KS	Matthew H Jennings Donald Copley	(620)473-2343	WS 930 SS 830 BC 830	ED/HC/ MD/SN	240	189	88

*Indicates a new church start. A new church start is an intentionally organized gathering which comes together on a regular basis for the purpose of worship and/or Bible study and is intended to grow into a member LCMS congregation. WS =Worship Service; SS = Sunday School; BC =Bible Class; EC = Early Childhood; EL = Elementary School; HS = High School; ED =Education Ministry; HC =Human Care Ministry; SN = Special Needs Ministry; MD = Media Ministry (PC)=Partner Church Pastor. See Page 53 for the Table of Abbreviations for key to additional abbreviations

CITY	CONGREGATION EMAIL WEBSITE	YEAR EST	LOCATION MAILING ADDRESS	ZIP CODE(S)	DIST.	PASTOR(S)	PHONE FAX	WS SS BC	SCHOOLS/ MINISTRIES	STATISTIC Bapt	Conf	Avg Attend
HUNTER	*TRINITY*	1886	101 Wagoner St PO BOX 128	67452	KS	Matthew M Schneider	(785)529-2715	WS 10 SS 9	ED/HC/MD	208	135	46
HUTCHINSON	*OUR REDEEMER* orlbusinessmgr@gmail.com orlhutch.org	1922	407 E 12th St 407 E 12TH AVE	67501	KS	Quentin T Nuttmann Henry A Blickhahn III	(620)662-5642 (620)662-4074	WS 830 11 SS 945 BC 945	ED/HC/ MD/SN	614	517	160
INDEPENDENCE	*ZION* zionofficeindy@gmail.com church.zionindy.com	1872	219 S 10th St 215 S 10TH ST	67301	KS	Kevin M Peterson	(620)332-3300	WS 8 1030 SS 1015 BC 1015	EL/ED/HC/ MD/SN	245	224	99
IOLA	*GRACE* gracelcmsiolaks@gmail.com gracelcmsiolaks.org	1949	117 E MILLER RD	66749	KS	Joseph R Goodroad	(620)365-6468	WS 1030 SS 9 BC 9	ED	125	102	47
JETMORE	*ST PAUL*	1962	S Bowles St PO BOX 97	67854	KS				ED	15	12	10
JUNCTION CITY	*IMMANUEL* ilcoffice@yahoo.com www.immanueljc.org	1926	630 S EISENHOWER DR	66441	KS	George T Mc Call	(785)238-6007	WS 9 SS 1030 BC 930	EC/ED/ HC/SN	250	100	55
	ST PAUL	1861	9719 CLARKS CREEK RD	66441	KS	John J Fries		WS 11 SS 10 BC 10	ED	70	63	20
KANSAS CITY	*BETHEL* revken1@msn.com www.bethellutherankansascity.com	1955	2801 N 83RD ST	66109	KS		(913)299-6478	WS 10 SS 9 BC 9		14	14	4
	FAITH	1948	530 QUINDARO BLVD	66101	KS	Kenneth J Nettling	(913)321-1326			14	14	7
	GRACE revken1@msn.com	1927	3333 WOOD AVE	66102	KS		(913)281-1621	WS 745 SS 930 BC 9		14	14	8
	IMMANUEL revken1@msn.com	1884	3232 METROPOLITAN AVE	66106	KS		(913)831-4542	WS 945 SS 9 BC 9	HC	16	16	7
	OUR SAVIOUR www.oskc.org	1926	4153 RAINBOW BLVD	66103	KS	James W Bender	(913)236-6228 (913)236-8522	WS 9 BC 1015	EC/ED/HC/ MD/SN	261	261	70
	RISEN SAVIOR		See Basehor KS									
KANSAS CITY/PIPER	*TRINITY FAMILY FAITH*		See Basehor KS									
KENSINGTON	*FIRST ST JOHN* 1stjohn@ruraltel.net www.1stjohnlutheran.com	1874	332 N Adams Ave PO BOX 57	66951	KS	David L Hutson	(785)476-2246 (785)476-2283	WS 10 SS 9 BC 9	EC/ED/HC/ MD/SN	200	134	65
KINSLEY	*OUR REDEEMER* orlckinsley@gmail.com	1947	201 MASSACHUSETTS AVE	67547	KS	Stanley E Palmer	(620)659-2262	WS 9 SS 1015 BC 1015	ED/MD	104	104	37
LAKE WABAUNSEE	*ST PAUL*		See Alta Vista KS									
LAKIN	*IMMANUEL* www.immanuellakin.org	1906	1304 Mattie PO BOX 46	67860	KS	Michael S Hageman Magdiel U Fajardo	(620)355-7161	WS 11 BC 1215	ED/HC/ MD/SN	34	33	22
LANSING	*RISEN SAVIOR*		See Basehor KS									
	TRINITY		See Leavenworth KS									
	TRINITY FAMILY FAITH		See Basehor KS									
LARNED	*GRACE* gracelarned@gmail.com	1949	524 Carroll Ave PO BOX 424	67550	KS		(620)285-2013		ED/HC/SN	12	10	5
LAWRENCE	*IMMANUEL* officemanager@immanuellawrence.org immanuellawrence.org	1928	2104 BOB BILLINGS PKWY	66049	KS	Andrew A Wehling	(785)843-0620	WS 9 SS 1030 BC 1030	ED/HC/ MD/SN	320	249	126
	REDEEMER redeemer.lutheran@att.net www.Redeemer-Lawrence.org	1976	2700 LAWRENCE AVE	66047	KS	Sean R Kilgo	(785)843-8181 (785)331-2926	WS 10 SS 9	ED/HC/MD	202	152	87
LEAVENWORTH	*ST PAUL* office@splcs.org stpaul-lcms.org	1862	311 N 7TH ST	66048	KS	Dale G Skurla	(913)682-0387 (913)682-1139	WS 10 SS 845 BC 845	EL/ED/HC/ MD/SN	372	336	60
	TRINITY officetlc@tlcleavenworth.org www.tlcleavenworth.org	1955	2101 10TH AVE	66048	KS	Dr Damian M Snyder Nathan R Nelson	(913)682-7474 (913)297-0777	WS 8 930 1045 SS 930 BC 930	ED/HC/ MD/SN	456	376	171
LEAWOOD	*LORD OF LIFE* office.lordlife@gmail.com www.lordoflifekc.com	1988	3105 W 135TH ST	66224	KS	Dr Scott Holder	(913)681-5167	WS 8 1030 SS 915 BC 915	EC/ED/HC/ MD/SN	368	265	229
LEBO	*TRINITY*		See Burlington KS									
LECOMPTON	*IMMANUEL*		See Lawrence KS									
LENEXA	*REDEEMER*		See Olathe KS									
LEROY	*TRINITY*		See Burlington KS									
LIBERAL	*GRACE* gelcks@hotmail.com www.gracelutheran-ks.org	1945	1200 W 11th 1200 W 11TH ST	67901	KS	Jason W Toombs	(620)624-5900	WS 1030 SS 9 BC 9	ED/HC/MD	263	204	60
LINCOLN	*ST JOHN* www.lutheranlincolnks.com	1881	966 N Hwy 14 966 N HIGHWAY 14	67455	KS	Don M Haselhuhn	(785)524-4039 (785)524-4039	WS 1030 SS 930 BC 930	ED/HC/MD	359	278	59
	ST PAUL stpauls.1911@gmail.com www.stpaulslincoln.org	1911	2282 E FOX DR	67455	KS	Don M Haselhuhn	(785)524-4046	WS 9		101	81	24
LINCOLNVILLE	*ST JOHN*	1877	220 Sixth St PO BOX 187	66858	KS	Alan R Stahlecker	(620)924-5236	WS 1045 SS 945 BC 945	ED/HC/SN	197	157	34
LINN	*IMMANUEL*	1882	712 HERITAGE RD	66953	KS	Mark Gaschler	(785)348-5892	WS 930 SS 1030 BC 1030	ED/HC/ MD/SN	197	152	78
	ZION zionoffice@bluevalley.net www.zionlinn.org	1887	210 CHURCH ST	66953	KS	Timothy A Koch	(785)348-5332	WS 930 SS 1030 BC 1030	EL/ED	360	270	153
LINWOOD	*TRINITY FAMILY FAITH*		See Basehor KS									
LOGAN	*FIRST*		See Phillipsburg KS									

*Indicates a new church start. A new church start is an intentionally organized gathering which comes together on a regular basis for the purpose of worship and/or Bible study and is intended to grow into a member LCMS congregation. WS =Worship Service; SS = Sunday School; BC =Bible Class; EC = Early Childhood; EL = Elementary School; HS = High School; ED =Education Ministry; HC =Human Care Ministry; SN = Special Needs Ministry; MD = Media Ministry (PC)=Partner Church Pastor. See Page 53 for the Table of Abbreviations for key to additional abbreviations

CITY	CONGREGATION EMAIL WEBSITE	YEAR EST	LOCATION MAILING ADDRESS	ZIP CODE(S)	DIST.	PASTOR(S)	PHONE FAX	WS SS BC	SCHOOLS/ MINISTRIES	STATISTIC Bapt	Conf	Avg Attend
LOUISBURG	*CHRIST OUR SAVIOR* pastorandy4@yahoo.com christoursaviorlouisburg.com		5 South 8th 5 S 8TH ST	66053	KS	James A Keltner	(913)837-4502	WS 8 1030 7 SS 915	ED/HC/ MD/SN	245	196	110
LUCAS	*BETHLEHEM*		See Sylvan Grove KS									
LURAY	*BETHLEHEM*		See Sylvan Grove KS									
LYONS	*GRACE* graceinlyonsks@gmail.com	1942	1111 W LINCOLN ST	67554	KS		(620)257-2204	WS 1015 SS 9	ED/SN	51	50	30
MANHATTAN	*CHRIST* christlutheran.mhk@gmail.com www.christlutheranmanhattan.org/	1996	4592 GREEN VALLEY RD	66502	KS	James D Woelmer	(785)776-2227	WS 1030 SS 930 BC 930	ED/HC	83	62	38
	ST LUKES office@stlukesmanhattan.org www.stlukesmanhattan.org	1911	4801 ANDERSON AVENUE	66503	KS	Michael J Schmidt	(785)539-2604	WS 830 11 SS 945 BC 945	EC/ED/HC/ MD/SN	523	388	211
MARION	*OUR SAVIOR*	1940	320 S CEDAR ST	66861	KS	Frank E Johnson	(620)382-2432	WS 9 SS 10 BC 8	ED/HC/ MD/SN	88	65	26
MARYSVILLE	*MOUNT CALVARY* mtcsecretary@bluevalley.net www.mtcsecretary.wixsite.com/ mtcalvarymville	1928	1710 JENKINS ST	66508	KS	Philip T Miller Jay D Williamson	(785)562-2046	WS 8 1030 SS 1015 BC 1015	EL/ED/HC/ MD/SN	355	291	132
	SPECIAL SAINTS SERVICE Satellite Site of Mount Calvary Marysville KS	2016	Fellowship Hall 1710 Jenkins St	66508								
MAYETTA	*CALVARY*		See Topeka KS									
MC FARLAND	*TRINITY* www.tlcmcfarland.com	1893	322 Main Street PO BOX 67	66501	KS		(785)765-3755	WS 10 SS 9 BC 9	EL	161	140	39
MCPHERSON	*GRACE* PrDumperth@att.net macgracelcms.360unite.com/home	1945	800 E 1ST ST	67460	KS	Dale A Dumperth	(620)241-1627	WS 1030 SS 9	ED/HC/MD	123	102	57
	IMMANUEL		See Canton KS									
MEADE	*ST JOHN* stjohnmeade@gmail.com	1887	208 E Grant St PO BOX 772	67864	KS	Mark A Mozeik	(620)873-2966	WS 1030 SS 930 BC 930	ED/HC	432	307	35
MEDICINE LODGE	*TRINITY* trinitymlks@sctelcom.net	1954	908 N Guffey St PO BOX 161 MEDICINE LDG	67104	KS		(620)886-3397 (620)886-3397	WS 830 SS 915 BC 915	ED/HC/ MD/SN	38	32	21
MERIDEN	*CALVARY*		See Topeka KS									
MISSION	*TRINITY* tlcinfo@tlcms.org www.tlcms.org	1940	5601 W 62ND ST	66202	KS	Luke A Jacob Daniel J Martinez Mark C Wood	(913)432-5441	WS 830 945 11 SS 945 BC 945	EC/ED/ HC/MD	1535	1283	429
MOUNDRIDGE	*IMMANUEL*		See Canton KS									
NASHVILLE	*ST JOHN* stjohns@havilandtelco.com	1893	516 S Main St PO BOX 105	67112	KS		(620)246-5220	WS 1030 SS 945 BC 945	ED/MD/SN	62	50	30
NATOMA	*PEACE* peacenatoma@yahoo.com	1962	705 5th St PO BOX 292	67651	KS	Michael J Schmidt	(785)885-4718	WS 1030 SS 930 BC 930	ED/HC/ MD/SN	200	160	38
NEOSHO RAPIDS	*TRINITY*		See Burlington KS									
NETAWAKA	*IMMANUEL* ilcnetawaka@gmail.com	1893	302 KANSAS ST	66516	KS			WS 9 SS 10 BC 930	ED	134	125	20
NEW STRAWN	*TRINITY*		See Burlington KS									
NEWTON	*ZION* secretary@zionnewton.com www.zionnewton.com	1886	225 S Poplar 225 S POPLAR ST	67114	KS	Kurt R Letcher	(316)283-1441 (316)283-0950	WS 10 SS 845	EC/ED/HC/ MD/SN	268	239	94
NORTON	*IMMANUEL* ilcnorton@ruraltel.net immanuelstar.substack.com	1908	14715 W Washington St 14715 WASHINGTON RD	67654	KS	Matthew D Goehring	(785)877-2430	WS 1030 SS 9 BC 9 7	ED/HC/MD	208	160	63
NORTONVILLE	*ST MATTHEW* office@stmatthewlcms.org www.stmatthewslcms.org	1897	312 Elm St PO BOX 297	66060	KS	Richard A Lally Jr	(913)886-6331	WS 915 SS 8 BC 8	HC	260	165	85
OAKLEY	*IMMANUEL* immoak77@gmail.com	1949	206 E 7TH ST	67748	KS		(785)672-3833	WS 11 SS 10	ED/SN	54	50	17
OBERLIN	*ST JOHN'S* stjohns@kitusa.com stjohnsoberlin.com	1886	510 N WILSON AVE	67749	KS	Paul B Rick	(785)475-2333	WS 9 SS 1015 BC 1015	ED/HC/MD	173	157	45
OFFERLE	*ZION* orlckinsley@gmail.com	1878	13307 JEWELL RD	67563	KS	Stanley E Palmer	(620)659-2078	WS 1045 SS 945		95	95	22
OLATHE	*BEAUTIFUL SAVIOR* office@bslcks.org www.bslcks.org	1992	13145 S BLACKBOB RD	66062	KS	Joel S Schultz Michael Ada	(913)780-6023 (913)780-0602	WS 8 1045 SS 930 BC 930	EC/HS/ ED/HC/ MD/SN	757	603	397
	CEDAR LAKE VILLAGE LUTHER-AN WORSHIP Satellite Site of Redeemer Olathe KS	2016	15325 S Lone Elm Rd	66061								
	LORD OF LIFE		See Leawood KS									
	REDEEMER office@redeemerolathe.org www.redeemerolathe.org	1962	920 S ALTA LN	66061	KS	David A Kahle	(913)764-2359	WS 830 11 SS 10 BC 10	EC/ED/HC/ MD/SN	333	284	197
ONAGA	*ST PAULS*		See Duluth KS									
OSWEGO	*ST PAUL* stpaulslutheran.oswegoks@gmail.com www.facebook.com/stpauls. churchoswego	1918	522 5TH ST	67356	KS		(620)795-4887	WS 1045 SS 9 BC 9	ED/HC/ MD/SN	45	33	10
OTTAWA	*FAITH* office@faithottawa.org www.faithottawa.org	1943	1320 W 15TH ST	66067	KS	Timothy L Roth	(785)242-1906	WS 8 9 1030	EC/ED/HC/ MD/SN	344	260	129

*Indicates a new church start. A new church start is an intentionally organized gathering which comes together on a regular basis for the purpose of worship and/or Bible study and is intended to grow into a member LCMS congregation. WS =Worship Service; SS = Sunday School; BC =Bible Class; EC = Early Childhood; EL = Elementary School; HS = High School; ED =Education Ministry; HC =Human Care Ministry; SN = Special Needs Ministry; MD = Media Ministry (PC)=Partner Church Pastor. See Page 53 for the Table of Abbreviations for key to additional abbreviations

CITY	CONGREGATION EMAIL WEBSITE	YEAR EST	LOCATION MAILING ADDRESS	ZIP CODE(S)	DIST.	PASTOR(S)	PHONE FAX	WS SS BC	SCHOOLS/ MINISTRIES	STATISTIC Bapt	Conf	Avg Attend
OVERLAND PARK	*BETHANY* cstelmachowicz@bethany-joco.org www.bethany-joco.org	1961	9101 LAMAR AVE	66207	KS	Sean M Baker Robert E Choate	(913)648-2228 (913)648-2283	WS 830 11 SS 945 BC 945	EC/EL/HS/ ED/HC/ MD/SN	957	777	308
	CHRIST info@clcop.org www.clcop.org	1980	11720 NIEMAN RD	66210	KS	Rocky W Mease Jeffrey T Meyers	(913)345-9700 (913)345-9707	WS 815 1045 SS 930 BC 930	EC/EL/HS/ ED/HC/ MD/SN	1547	1251	488
	LORD OF LIFE		See Leawood KS									
	REDEEMER		See Olathe KS									
OZAWKIE	*CALVARY*		See Topeka KS									
PALMER	*ST JOHN* www.stjohnpalmer.net	1878	304 National Rd 312 NATIONAL RD	66962	KS	John T Werner	(785)692-4228	WS 930 SS 1045 BC 1045	EL/ED/MD	322	229	155
PAOLA	*FIRST* flcpaolaks@gmail.com www.firstlutheranpaola.org	1921	401 E PIANKISHAW ST	66071	KS		(913)294-3476	WS 9 SS 1030 BC 1030	EC/ED/HC/ MD/SN	283	213	79
	TRINITY trinitylutheranblock@gmail.com www.trinitylcms.org	1868	34868 BLOCK RD	66071	KS	Joshua J Woelmer	(913)849-3344	WS 10 SS 9 BC 9	ED/MD	595	431	98
PARSONS	*TRINITY* trinitylc021@gmail.com	1936	2911 CRAWFORD AVE	67357	KS	Theodore E Cook Sr		WS 1130 SS 9 BC 9	ED/HC/ MD/SN	75	51	20
PERRY	*CALVARY*		See Topeka KS									
PHILLIPSBURG	*FIRST* firstlutheranchurch@hotmail.com firstlutheranpburg.360unite.com/home	1945	1035 1ST ST	67661	KS		(785)543-5046	WS 1130 SS 3 BC 3	ED/HC/SN	142	120	30
PITTSBURG	*ZION* zionpitt@ckt.net www.zionpittsburg.org	1876	102 W JACKSON ST	66762	KS	Theodore E Cook Sr	(620)231-4267 (620)231-4267	WS 8		172	128	22
PLAINVILLE	*FIRST*	1954	705 S JEFFERSON ST	67663	KS	Michael J Schmidt	(785)434-2874	WS 9 SS 1015	ED/HC/MD	80	60	28
POWHATTAN	*ZION*	1900	202 W Main 641 130TH ST	66527	KS		(402)245-2162	WS 8	ED/HC/MD	6	6	6
PRATT	*ASCENSION* office@ascensionpratt.org www.ascensionpratt.org		502 E Second St PO BOX 846	67124	KS	Matthew C Schultz		WS 10 SS 9	ED	115	95	95
PRESTON	*ST PAUL* splcms@sctelcom.net www.stpaulpreston.org	1900	40291 NE 40TH AVE	67583	KS	Michael L Schotte	(620)672-5354	WS 10 SS 9 BC 9	ED/MD	218	182	67
RAMONA	*TRINITY* revclark@tctelco.net	1906	401 E Street PO BOX 8	67475	KS	Clark M Davis	(785)965-2234	WS 1045	ED/HC/MD	36	36	14
SABETHA	*FIRST* firstlutheranoffice225@gmail.com neklutherans.org	1946	311 Cedar St FIRST LUTHERAN CHURCH 311 CEDAR	66534	KS	Ian P Kinney	(785)284-3566	WS 1030 SS 915 BC 915	EC/ED/ HC/MD	214	157	104
SAINT GEORGE	*CHRIST*		See Manhattan KS									
SALINA	*CHRIST KING* ctklcsecretary@gmail.com www.ctksalina.org	1963	111 W MAGNOLIA RD	67401	KS	Aaron D Wagner Timothy P Wangerin	(785)827-7492	WS 8 1030 SS 915 BC 915	ED/HC/ MD/SN	561	387	138
	TRINITY trinitysalina@gmail.com www.trinitysalina.org	1934	702 S 9TH ST	67401	KS	Mark D Boxman Dennis L Kootz	(785)823-7151 (785)823-3898	WS 830 11 SS 945 BC 945	ED/HC/ MD/SN	642	515	252
SCOTT CITY	*HOLY CROSS* hclcscottcityks@gmail.com www.hclcscottcity.org	1925	1102 Court St PO BOX 283	67871	KS	Matthew C Koterba	(620)872-2294	WS 1015 SS 9 BC 9	ED/HC/MD	120	107	35
SHAWNEE	*AUGSBURG* paterjww@sbcglobal.net augsburglutheranchurch.org		13902 W 67TH ST	66216	KS	Jay W Watson	(913)403-6194	WS 9 SS 1015 BC 1015	HS/ED	48	43	30
	HOPE church@hopelutheran.org www.hopelutheran.org	1954	6308 QUIVIRA RD	66216	KS	Jacob T Mueller	(913)631-6940 (913)268-9525	WS 8 1030 SS 920 BC 920	EL/HS/ ED/HC/ MD/SN	759	636	233
	TRINITY LUTHERAN CHURCH SHAWNEE CAMPUS Satellite Site of Trinity Mission KS	2006	21320 Midland Dr	66218				WS 830 11 SS 945 BC 945				
SHAWNEE MISSION	*BETHANY*		See Overland Park KS									
SILVER LAKE	*CALVARY*		See Topeka KS									
STOCKTON	*FIRST*		See Phillipsburg KS									
STRONG CITY	*GRACE*	1884	501 Central Ave PO BOX 366	66869	KS			WS 9 SS 1030 BC 1030	ED	53	43	25
SUMMERFIELD	*FIRST*	1947	305 Front St PO BOX 70	66541	NEB	Gregory L Stuckwisch	(785)244-6529	WS 730	ED	65	62	12
SYLVAN GROVE	*BETHLEHEM* bethlehem@wtciweb.com bethlehemsylvangrove.org	1881	308 N INDIANA AVE	67481	KS	Christopher M Craig	(785)526-7152	WS 10 BC 1130	ED/MD/SN	244	171	57
TAMPA	*ST JOHN* norsk58@hotmail.com	1893	425 Main St 102 W 5TH	67483	KS	Clark M Davis	(785)965-2234	WS 915	ED/HC/MD	49	46	35
TONGANOXIE	*TRINITY FAMILY FAITH*		See Basehor KS									
TOPEKA	*CALVARY* calvarylcms@calvarytopeka.org www.calvarytopeka.org	1965	4211 NW TOPEKA BLVD	66617	KS	Benjamin R Ockree	(785)286-1431 (785)286-1516	WS 9 SS 1015 BC 1015	EC/ED/HC/ MD/SN	405	346	132
	CHRIST office@christlcms.org www.christlcms.org		3509 SW BURLINGAME RD	66611	KS	Avery E Hjulberg	(785)266-6263	WS 8 1030 SS 915 BC 915	ED/MD/SN	499	389	140
	FAITH office@faithlutherantopeka.com www.faithlutherantopeka.com	1948	1716 SW GAGE BLVD	66604	KS	Jacob P Heine Martin K Albrecht William J Lane	(785)272-4214	WS 8 930 11 SS 930 BC 930	ED/HC/ MD/SN	912	815	377

*Indicates a new church start. A new church start is an intentionally organized gathering which comes together on a regular basis for the purpose of worship and/or Bible study and is intended to grow into a member LCMS congregation. WS =Worship Service; SS = Sunday School; BC =Bible Class; EC = Early Childhood; EL = Elementary School; HS = High School; ED =Education Ministry; HC =Human Care Ministry; SN = Special Needs Ministry; MD = Media Ministry (PC)=Partner Church Pastor. See Page 53 for the Table of Abbreviations for key to additional abbreviations

CONGREGATIONS

CITY	CONGREGATION EMAIL WEBSITE	YEAR EST	LOCATION MAILING ADDRESS	ZIP CODE(S)	DIST.	PASTOR(S)	PHONE FAX	WS SS BC	SCHOOLS/ MINISTRIES	STATISTIC Bapt	Conf	Avg Attend
TOPEKA	*PRINCE OF PEACE* office@princeofpeacetopeka.org www.princeofpeacetopeka.org	1988	3625 SW WANAMAKER RD	66614	KS	Kevin G DeHope	(785)271-0808 (785)271-5324	WS 10 SS 9 BC 9	EC/ED/HC/ MD/SN	205	177	82
	SAINT JOHNS secretary@stjlcms.org www.stjohnlcmstopeka.org	1874	901 SW FILLMORE ST	66606	KS	Boyd A Wright	(785)354-7132	WS 8 11 SS 945 BC 945	EL/ED/ MD/SN	490	416	251
ULYSSES	*GRACE* grace4u@pld.com graceulysses.org	1953	205 E Patterson 205 E PATTERSON AVE	67880	KS	Michael S Hageman Magdiel U Fajardo	(620)356-3161	WS 9 BC 8	ED/HC/ MD/SN	49	45	21
VASSAR	*ZION* office@zionvassar.org www.zionvassar.org	1893	23167 TOPEKA	66543	KS	James E Kirschenmann	(785)828-4482	WS 9 SS 1030 BC 1030	ED/HC/MD	156	124	65
WAMEGO	*MOUNT CALVARY* mclc.wamego@gmail.com www.mtcalvarylutheranchurch.org	1948	17535 SAY RD	66547	KS	James M Price	(785)456-2444	WS 8 1030 SS 915 BC 915	ED/HC/ MD/SN	487	407	217
WATERVILLE	*TRINITY* revtimkoch@gmail.com	1886	196 Navajo Rd 165 HARVEST ROAD BREMEN	66548 66412	KS		(785)348-5550	WS 9	ED/HC/SN	11	11	10
WATHENA	*CHRIST*	1884	2108 Hwy 36 2108 HIGHWAY 36	66090	KS	Philip B Wolf	(785)989-3348	WS 1015 SS 9 BC 9	HC/MD	165	100	43
WAVERLY	*TRINITY*		See Burlington KS									
WELLINGTON	*CALVARY* calvarylcms@yahoo.com www.calvarywellington.org	1954	1300 North C St 1300 N C ST	67152	KS		(620)326-7715	WS 1030 SS 915 BC 915	ED/HC	101	87	18
WESTPHALIA	*ST JOHN*		See Aliceville KS									
WHEATON	*ST LUKE* vicardegiovanni@yahoo.com www.stlukewheaton.com	1897	129 RAILROAD ST	66521	KS	Terry L De Giovanni	(785)396-4411	WS 10 SS 845 BC 9	ED/MD	316	271	47
WICHITA	*ASCENSION* cbressler@ascension-lcms.org www.ascension-lcms.org	1960	842 N TYLER RD	67212	KS	Dr Michael R Bingen-heimer Scott L Goltl Brendon T Moore	(316)722-4694 (316)729-7027	WS 830 11 SS 945 BC 945	EC/ED/ HC/MD	1622	1124	460
	BETHANY office@bethanylutheranwichita.org www.bethanylutheranwichita.org	1957	1000 W 26TH ST S	67217	KS	Nicholas R Cordt	(316)265-7415 (316)265-0887	WS 9 SS 1030	EC/ED/HC	340	333	81
	HOLY CROSS office@hcwichita.net www.holycrosslutheran.net	1942	600 N GREENWICH RD	67206	KS	Shawn D Fenske Ryan J Ankersen Scott A Snow	(316)684-5201 (316)684-2847	WS 8 1037 11 SS 930 BC 930	EL/ED/HC	1794	1338	634
	IMMANUEL secretary@ilchurch.org www.ilchurch.org/team-3	1909	909 S MARKET ST	67211	KS	Mark D Lovett	(316)264-0639	WS 930 SS 11	ED/MD/SN	193	148	88
	MAPLE CAMPUS Satellite Site of Ascension Wichita KS	2001	12885 W Maple	67235				WS 10 SS 9 BC 9				
	RISEN SAVIOR www.RisenSavior.net	1993	6770 E 34TH ST N	67226	KS	Calvin W Luttinen Matthew B Goltl	(316)683-5538 (316)683-5536	WS 8 1030 SS 915 BC 915	ED/HC/ MD/SN	574	485	276
	SAINT ANDREWS office@standrewswichita.org www.standrewswichita.org	1971	2555 Hyacinth Ln 2555 N HYACINTH LN	67204	KS		(316)838-0944 (316)838-0948	WS 1030 SS 9 BC 9	ED/HC/MD	86	73	43
	TRINITY office@tlc.kscoxmail.com www.tlcwichita.org	1934	611 S ERIE ST	67211	KS	Aaron M Filipek Daniel J Metzger	(316)685-1571	WS 9 SS 1030 BC 1030	ED/HC/ MD/SN	251	213	110
WILSON	*BETHLEHEM*		See Sylvan Grove KS									
WINFIELD	*TRINITY* trinitywinfield@hotmail.com trinitylutheranwinfield.com	1883	910 MOUND ST	67156	KS	Seth A Meyer Christopher W Warneke	(620)221-9460 (620)221-3779	WS 9 SS 1020 BC 1020	EL/ED/HC/ MD	381	261	170
YATES CENTER	*TRINITY*		See Burlington KS									

KENTUCKY

CITY	CONGREGATION EMAIL WEBSITE	YEAR EST	LOCATION MAILING ADDRESS	ZIP CODE(S)	DIST.	PASTOR(S)	PHONE FAX	WS SS BC	SCHOOLS/ MINISTRIES	Bapt	Conf	Avg Attend
ASHLAND	*ST PAUL*	1866	1320 BATH AVE	41101	OH	Mark A Kloha	(606)324-3515	WS 1045 SS 930 BC 930	EC/ED/ HC/MD	149	122	48
BARDSTOWN	*GOOD SHEPHERD* goodshepherdluthchc2000@gmail.com www.bardstownlutheran.org	2000	1126 BLOOMFIELD RD	40004	IN		(502)349-3130	WS 1030 SS 930 BC 930	ED/HC/MD	64	60	30
BENTON	*IMMANUEL*		See Murray KY									
BOWLING GREEN	*HOLY TRINITY* church.admin@htlc-bg.org www.htlc-bgky.com	1961	553 ASHMOOR AVE	42101	MDS	Dr Mark G Press	(270)843-9595 (270)843-7466	WS 8 1030 SS 915 BC 915	EL/ED/HC/ MD/SN	477	385	211
BRANDENBURG	*GRACE*		See Vine Grove KY									
BROOKS	*DIVINE SAVIOR*		See Shepherdsville KY									
COVINGTON	*BETHANY*		See Erlanger KY									
CYNTHIANA	*BREAD OF LIFE*		See Georgetown KY									
DANVILLE	*OUR SAVIOR* pastoroslutheran@gmail.com	1967	285 Hill N Dale 285 HILL N DALE ST	40422	IN	Justin M Mason	(330)432-2678	WS 930 SS 1045 BC 1045	ED/HC/SN	55	53	35
EDGEWOOD	*BETHANY*		See Erlanger KY									
ELIZABETHTOWN	*GLORIA DEI* pastor.gdlchtlc@gmail.com www.gloriadeietown.org	1969	1701 Ring Rd E 1701 RING RD	42701	IN	Monty D Gleitz	(270)769-5910 (270)769-5703	WS 9 SS 1015 BC 1015	EC/ED/HC/ MD/SN	164	119	92
	GRACE		See Vine Grove KY									
ERLANGER	*BETHANY* BethanyLutheranChurchky@gmail.com www.bethanylutheran.net	1934	3501 TURKEYFOOT RD	41018	OH	Brett A Matz	(859)331-3501	WS 845 11 SS 1015 BC 1015		88	78	57

*Indicates a new church start. A new church start is an intentionally organized gathering which comes together on a regular basis for the purpose of worship and/or Bible study and is intended to grow into a member LCMS congregation. WS =Worship Service; SS = Sunday School; BC =Bible Class; EC = Early Childhood; EL = Elementary School; HS = High School; ED =Education Ministry; HC =Human Care Ministry; SN = Special Needs Ministry; MD = Media Ministry (PC)=Partner Church Pastor. See Page 53 for the Table of Abbreviations for key to additional abbreviations

CITY	CONGREGATION EMAIL WEBSITE	YEAR EST	LOCATION MAILING ADDRESS	ZIP CODE(S)	DIST.	PASTOR(S)	PHONE FAX	WS SS BC	SCHOOLS/ MINISTRIES	STATISTIC Bapt	 Conf	 Avg Attend
FLORENCE	*GOOD SHEPHERD* secretary@gslcky.org gslcky.org/	1995	9066 GUNPOWDER RD	41042	OH	Michael J Poynter	(859)746-9066	WS 10 SS 845 BC 845	ED/HC/ MD/SN	130	117	75
FORT KNOX	*GLORIA DEI*		See Elizabethtown KY									
	GRACE		See Vine Grove KY									
FRANKFORT	*BREAD OF LIFE*		See Georgetown KY									
GEORGETOWN	*BREAD OF LIFE* georgetown.breadoflife@email.com www.breadoflifeky.com		700 CLAYTON AVE	40324	IN	Lohn M Johnson		WS 10 SS 9 BC 9	ED/HC			
HARRODSBURG	*OUR SAVIOR*		See Danville KY									
HENDERSON	*TRINITY* trinity125henderson@gmail.com www.trinityhenderson.org	1896	501 N ELM ST	42420	IN	Michael D Liese	(270)826-4337	WS 10 SS 845 BC 845	ED/HC/MD	165	123	45
HILLVIEW	*DIVINE SAVIOR*		See Shepherdsville KY									
HOPKINSVILLE	*FAITH* pastor@faithhopkinsville.com www.faithhopkinsville.com	1962	405 SHEILA DR	42240	MDS	Trae L Fistler	(270)885-3969 (270)885-3969	WS 10 SS 11 BC 9	HC/MD/SN	60	60	40
INDEPENDENCE	*BETHANY*		See Erlanger KY									
LA GRANGE	*HOLY TRINITY* pastor@htlc-lagrange.org www.htlc-lagrange.org	1980	2416 S HIGHWAY 53	40031	IN	Jason A Reed	(502)222-5827	WS 930 SS 11 BC 11	ED/HC/MD			
LAWRENCEBURG	*OUR SAVIOR*		See Danville KY									
LEBANON JUNCTION	*DIVINE SAVIOR*		See Shepherdsville KY									
LEITCHFIELD	*HOLY TRINITY* pastor.gdlchtlc@gmail.com	1983	889 LILAC RD	42754	IN	Monty D Gleitz	(270)259-9241	WS 1030		22	20	16
LEXINGTON	*BREAD OF LIFE*		See Georgetown KY									
	GOOD SHEPHERD church@gslclexington.org www.gslclexington.org	1983	425 PATCHEN DR	40517	IN		(859)269-6517	WS 1030	EC/ED/MD			
	OUR REDEEMER office@orlutheran.com www.orlutheran.com	1964	2255 EASTLAND PKWY	40505	IN	Michael W Huebner	(859)299-9615 (859)299-9615	WS 1015 SS 9 BC 9	EC/ED/MD			
	ST JOHN office@stjohnslexington.org www.stjohnslexington.org	1892	516 PASADENA DR	40503	IN	Micah D Schmidt	(859)277-6391	WS 8 1030 SS 915 BC 915	EC/ED/ HC/MD	551	406	210
LOUISVILLE	*CONCORDIA* mail@concordia-lutheran.com www.concordia-lutheran.com	1878	1127 E BROADWAY	40204	IN	Eric M Estes	(502)585-4459	WS 745 10 SS 850 BC 9	ED/HC/ MD/SN	291	248	137
	DIVINE SAVIOR		See Shepherdsville KY									
	FAITH faithlcmslou@aol.com faithlutheranlouisville.org	1954	7635 Old 3rd St Rd 7635 3RD STREET RD	40214	IN	John T Stebbins	(502)367-8513 (502)368-2463	WS 10 SS 1145	MD			
	OUR SAVIOR www.oursaviorlouisville.com	1942	8305 NOTTINGHAM PKWY	40222	IN		(502)426-1130 (502)394-0648	WS 830 11 SS 945 BC 945	EL/ED/HC/ MD/SN	404	326	210
	REDEEMER office@redeemerlouky.com www.redeemerlouky.com	1888	3640 RIVER PARK DR	40211	IN		(502)776-5945	WS 10	ED/HC/MD	198	150	51
	RESURRECTION kydobe@hotmail.com www.mylouisvillechurch.org/		4205 GARDINER VIEW AVE	40213	IN		(502)883-0032	WS 1030 SS 930 BC 930	ED/HC/ MD/SN			
MAYFIELD	*IMMANUEL*		See Murray KY									
MAYSVILLE	*TRINITY* maysvilletlc@maysvilleky.net www.trinitylutheranmaysville.org	1925	621 PARKER RD	41056	OH		(606)564-3566	WS 915	ED/HC/MD			
MIDDLESBORO	*CHRIST CUMBERLANDS*		See Harrogate TN									
MOUNT WASHINGTON	*DIVINE SAVIOR*		See Shepherdsville KY									
MURRAY	*IMMANUEL* info@immanuel.am www.immanuel.faith	1966	100 S 15TH ST	42071	MDS	Joshua P Reifsteck	(270)753-6712	WS 1030 SS 915 BC 915	ED/HC/ MD/SN	160	128	89
OWENSBORO	*PEACE* peacelutheranowensboro@gmail.com www.peaceelc.org	1955	2200 CARTER RD	42301	IN	Adam A Sternquist	(270)685-0249	WS 10 SS 9 BC 9	ED/MD/SN			
PADUCAH	*ST PAUL* stpauls@stpaulpaducah.org www.stpaulpaducah.org	1868	211 S 21ST ST	42003	MDS	David R Appold	(270)442-8343 (270)441-7571	WS 8 1045 SS 930 BC 930	ED/HC/MD	391	317	150
PARIS	*BREAD OF LIFE*		See Georgetown KY									
RADCLIFF	*GLORIA DEI*		See Elizabethtown KY									
	GRACE		See Vine Grove KY									
SHELBYVILLE	*HOLY CROSS* secretary@holycrosslutheran-ky.org holycross.360unite.com	1989	181 OLD SEVEN MILE PIKE	40065	IN	Andrew D Guagenti	(502)647-3696 (502)647-4994	WS 11 SS 945 BC 945	ED/HC/ MD/SN	200	147	49
SHEPHERDSVILLE	*DIVINE SAVIOR* divinesaviorshepherdsville@gmail.com divinesaviorshepherdsville.org	1985	1025 N BUCKMAN ST	40165	IN	Thomas J Elbert Jr	(502)543-2905	WS 1030 SS 9	ED/HC/MD			
SMITHS GROVE	*HOLY TRINITY* Satellite Site of Holy Trinity Bowling Green KY	2019	First Christian Church	42171								
STANFORD	*OUR SAVIOR*		See Danville KY									
TAYLORSVILLE	*RISEN LORD* office@risenlordchurch.com www.risenlordchurch.com	2007	5138 TAYLORSVILLE RD	40071	IN	Jonathan R Mueller	(502)477-6557	WS 11	MD			
VINE GROVE	*GRACE*	2010	398 KNOX AVE	40175	EN	Jonathan S Lackey	(270)877-2855	WS 1030 SS 930 BC 930	MD			

*Indicates a new church start. A new church start is an intentionally organized gathering which comes together on a regular basis for the purpose of worship and/or Bible study and is intended to grow into a member LCMS congregation. WS =Worship Service; SS = Sunday School; BC =Bible Class; EC = Early Childhood; EL = Elementary School; HS = High School; ED =Education Ministry; HC =Human Care Ministry; SN = Special Needs Ministry; MD = Media Ministry (PC)=Partner Church Pastor. See Page 53 for the Table of Abbreviations for key to additional abbreviations

CITY	CONGREGATION EMAIL WEBSITE	YEAR EST	LOCATION MAILING ADDRESS	ZIP CODE(S)	DIST.	PASTOR(S)	PHONE FAX	WS SS BC	SCHOOLS/ MINISTRIES	STATISTIC Bapt	Conf	Avg Attend
						LOUISIANA						
ALEXANDRIA	*AUGUSTANA* phyllis_culbert@yahoo.com	1915	2732 3rd St PO BOX 7912	71302 71306	SO		(318)613-8351	WS 5	HC			
	REDEEMER	1918	4809 MASONIC DR	71301	SO	Donald F Thompson Jr	(318)442-4325	WS 1030 SS 930 BC 930	MD	131	128	21
BATON ROUGE	*CROSS OF CALVARY* chapelcrossluthbr@yahoo.com		3235 DALRYMPLE DR	70802	SO	Gary I Peterson	(225)383-2962	WS 2				
	GOOD SHEPHERD	1999	5990 PERKINS RD	70808	SO	Paul N Anderson	(225)766-4610					
	TRINITY www.tlcbr.org	1957	15160 S HARRELLS FERRY RD	70816	SO	William L Crowe	(225)272-3110 (225)272-9517	WS 830 11 SS 945 BC 945	EC/ED/ HC/MD	651	573	276
	TRINITY LUTHERAN SCHOOL Satellite Site of Trinity Baton Rouge LA	2018	15160 S. Harrell's Ferry Rd.	70816								
BOGALUSA	*ZION*	1911	135 RIO GRANDE ST	70427	SO		(985)732-4701	WS 1030 SS 9	ED/HC			
BOSSIER CITY	*IMMANUEL* ilcbossier.net@gmail.com www.ilcbossier.net	1963	2565 AIRLINE DR	71111	SO	Robert M Portier Christopher J Yeager	(318)746-2215 (318)746-8374	WS 9 SS 1030 BC 1030	ED/HC/ MD/SN	342	298	117
CHALMETTE	*CHRIST* christlutheranchalmette@yahoo.com www.facebook.com/ groups/1559044474351682	1903	3300 JUPITER DR	70043	SO			WS 10 BC 6	ED/MD	62	51	16
CLINTON	*ZION*	1892	11007 Plank Rd PO BOX 281	70722	SO	David R Mc Intyre	(225)683-5592	WS 1030 SS 915 BC 915	ED/HC/MD			
COVINGTON	*HOLY TRINITY* office@htlministries.org www.htlministries.org	1960	1 N MARIGOLD DR	70433	SO	Daniel M Koyn	(985)892-6146 (985)892-3012	WS 8 1030 SS 915 BC 915	EC/ED/ HC/MD	274	239	150
CROWLEY	*FIRST*	1894	121 W 8th St PO BOX 1446	70526 70527	SO		(337)783-8713	WS 11 SS 1015 BC 1015	HC/MD			
DE RIDDER	*REDEEMER* www.facebook.com/profile. php?id=61555379111443	1932	811 SHIRLEY ST DERIDDER	70634	SO	Kermit C Bostelman	(337)463-8427	WS 1045 SS 930 BC 930	HC/MD	54	42	18
DENHAM SPRINGS	*ABSOLUTION* Pastor@absolutionchurch.com		30851 LA HIGHWAY 16	70726	SO	Michael F Gibney	(225)347-8721			52	52	50
FOLSOM	*NEW LIFE* newlifelutheran.folsom@gmail.com		82392 Hwy 25 PO BOX 1617	70437	SO		(504)300-9380	WS 10	HC			
FORT POLK	*TRINITY*		See Leesville LA									
GONZALES	*SAINT JAMES* stjamesgonzales@gmail.com www.stjameslutheran.net	1972	1415 E HIGHWAY 30	70737	SO	Karl D Hollibaugh	(225)644-2432	WS 930 SS 1045 BC 1045	ED/HC/ MD/SN			
GRETNA	*SALEM* pastorbeane@gmail.com salemlutherangretna.org	1871	418 4TH ST	70053	SO	Larry L Beane II	(504)367-5126	WS 10 SS 9 BC 9				
HAMMOND	*ST PAUL* office@stpaulhammond.org www.stpaulhammond.org	1893	707 W DAKOTA ST	70401	SO	Louis A Boldt	(985)345-6008 (985)345-6027	WS 1015 SS 9 BC 9	ED/MD	162	138	64
HARAHAN	*FAITH*	1954	300 COLONIAL CLUB DR	70123	SO	David J Lofthus	(504)737-0448 (504)739-9470	WS 745 1030 SS 915 BC 915	EL/HS			
HARVEY	*CHRIST OUR SAVIOR* www.coslcms.com	1985	3150 DESTREHAN AVE	70058	SO	Brandon J Simoneaux	(504)348-1212 (504)348-1212	WS 9 SS 1015 BC 1015	HC			
HOUMA	*GRACE* secretary@gracehouma.org www.gracehouma.org	1956	422 VALHI BLVD	70360	SO	Richard D Rudnik	(985)879-1865	WS 9 SS 1045	ED/HC/MD	170	118	35
IOTA	*ST JOHN*	1901	222 N 3rd St PO BOX 125	70543	SO			WS 8 SS 9 BC 9	ED/HC/MD			
JENNINGS	*IMMANUEL*	1895	114 N Cutting Ave PO BOX 530	70546	SO		(337)824-3546	WS 930	ED			
LACOMBE	*THE VILLAGE* village@villagelutheran.org www.villagelutheran.org		29180 Highway 190 PO BOX 1219	70445	SO	Paul M Ernewein	(985)882-5727	WS 9 SS 1015	ED/HC/MD	228	193	95
LAFAYETTE	*FAITH* faithlutheranlafayette@gmail.com facebook.com/faithlutheranlft/	2002	104 RUE FONTAINE	70508	SO	Brandon M Carlone	(337)216-9658	WS 1030 SS 915 BC 915	SN	125	98	68
LAKE CHARLES	*ST JOHN* stjohnlcla@gmail.com saintjohnlutheranchurch.com	1888	600 UNIVERSITY DR	70605	SO	Charles R Lehmann Charles R Miller	(337)478-5666 (337)478-8196	WS 1030 SS 915 BC 915	EC/ED/MD	209	133	75
LEESVILLE	*TRINITY* trinityleesville@gmail.org trinityleesville.org	1953	120 Alexandria Highway 120 ALEXANDRIA HWY	71446	SO	Kermit C Bostelman	(337)239-2457	WS 9 SS 1015 BC 1015	ED/HC/ MD/SN	59	51	25
MANDEVILLE	*REDEEMER* redeemermandeville@gmail.com www.redeemerla.net		22531 HIGHWAY 1088	70448	SO	John C Drosendahl	(985)674-0377	WS 1030 SS 9 BC 9	ED			
	THE VILLAGE		See Lacombe LA									
MANY	*GRACE* info@gracetoledobend.org www.gracetoledobend.org	2003	12951 Texas Hwy 265 PINTO DR N HEMPHILL	71449 75948	SO		(816)244-7342	WS 1030 SS 9 BC 9	ED/HC/MD	17	17	14
METAIRIE	*ATONEMENT* churchoffice@alcs.org www.alcs.org	1958	6500 RIVERSIDE DR	70003	SO		(504)887-0225 (504)887-0225	WS 10 SS 9 BC 9	EL/HS/ED/ HC/MD			

*Indicates a new church start. A new church start is an intentionally organized gathering which comes together on a regular basis for the purpose of worship and/or Bible study and is intended to grow into a member LCMS congregation. WS =Worship Service; SS = Sunday School; BC =Bible Class; EC = Early Childhood; EL = Elementary School; HS = High School; ED =Education Ministry; HC =Human Care Ministry; SN = Special Needs Ministry; MD = Media Ministry (PC)=Partner Church Pastor. See Page 53 for the Table of Abbreviations for key to additional abbreviations

CITY	CONGREGATION EMAIL WEBSITE	YEAR EST	LOCATION MAILING ADDRESS	ZIP CODE(S)	DIST.	PASTOR(S)	PHONE FAX	WS SS BC	SCHOOLS/ MINISTRIES	STATISTIC Bapt	Conf	Avg Attend
METAIRIE	*FIRST ENGLISH* church@firstenglishmetairie.com www.firstenglishmetairie.com	1888	3701 CLEARY AVE	70002	SO	John C Ramsey II	(504)455-5562 (504)455-5537	WS 9 SS 10 BC 10	HS/ED/ HC/MD/ SN	171	168	75
	MONTE DE OLIVE godmonte@hotmail.com	1980	4105 DAVID DR	70003	SO	Jesus M Gonzales	(504)451-9172		ED/HC/MD			
	MOUNT OLIVE mtolivelutheranmetairie@gmail.com www.mountolivelutheran.net	1945	315 RIDGELAKE DR	70001	SO	Bradley A Drew	(504)833-4963 (504)833-0154	WS 8 1030 SS 915 BC 915	HS/ED	247	212	91
	ST JOHN		See New Orleans LA									
MONROE	*TRINITY* tlcmonroesecretary@gmail.com tlcinmonroe.org	1925	1301 OLIVER RD	71201	SO		(318)322-3507 (318)325-4619	WS 1030 SS 915	ED/HC/ MD/SN	137	120	56
MORGAN CITY	*GRACE*		See Houma LA									
NATCHITOCHES	*CHRIST KING* ChristTheKingNatchitoches.com	1964	305 ROYAL ST	71457	SO		(318)352-8708	WS 1015 SS 9	ED/HC/MD			
NEW ORLEANS	*BETHEL* bethelnola@att.net	1963	4127 FRANKLIN AVE	70122	SO	Jerome N Terry	(504)941-5888	WS 9	ED/HC/MD	32	24	28
	CHRIST		See Chalmette LA									
	CHRIST OUR SAVIOR		See Harvey LA									
	EPIPHANY epiphanylutheran@att.net	2000	9004 HICKORY ST	70118	SO	Collis Parham Sr	(504)861-7093 (504)431-3417	WS 745 SS 930	ED/HC/ MD/SN			
	FIRST ENGLISH		See Metairie LA									
	GLORIA DEI www.gloriadeinola.com	1935	2021 S DUPRE ST	70125	SO	Gregory T Manning	(504)822-7229 (504)822-7229	WS 1030 SS 915 BC 915	HS/ED			
	HOLY CROSS hc@61.nocoxmail.com holycrosslcno.com	1961	6154 PRESS DR	70126	SO	Aubrey J Watson Jr	(504)288-3437	WS 10 SS 9	ED/HC/ MD/SN	150	119	65
	MOUNT ZION vbsmzlc1401@gmail.com www.Mzlcnola.org	1878	1401 SIMON BOLIVAR AVE	70113	SO	Limakatso Nare	(504)522-9951 (504)522-9951	WS 9 SS 930	HS/ED/ HC/MD	80	68	98
	SALEM		See Gretna LA									
	ST JOHN admin@stjohnlutherannola.com www.stjohnlutherannola.com	1852	3937 CANAL ST	70119	SO	Perry T Sukstorf	(504)482-2118 (504)482-2101	WS 915 SS 1045 BC 1045	EL/HS/ED/ MD/SN	158	130	69
	ST PAUL president@stpaulmarigny.org stpaulmarigny.org	1840	2624 BURGUNDY ST	70117	SO	Christian J Rasmussen	(504)945-3741 (504)945-3743	WS 1030 SS 1030 BC 915	HS/ED/ HC/SN	170	149	65
	ST PAUL NE splc1@att.net www.splcnola.org	1881	1625 ANNETTE ST	70116	SO		(504)944-5401 (504)948-1864	WS 1030	ED/HC	346	257	48
	ST STEPHEN st2secretary@att.net	1954	6336 BERKLEY DR	70131	SO	Kenneth J DeSoto	(504)394-4956 (504)394-4970	WS 9 SS 9 BC 1030	MD	161	122	23
	TRINITY	1875	620 ELIZA ST	70114	SO	Kenneth J DeSoto	(504)368-0411 (504)368-0425	WS 10	ED/HC/ MD/SN			
	ZION rbobbelknap@gmail.com www.ZionLA.com	1847	1924 Saint Charles Ave 1539 SAINT ANDREW ST	70130	SO	Dr Robert H Belknap	(504)524-1025 (504)524-1025	WS 1030 SS 9 BC 9	HS/ED/ HC/MD			
PINEVILLE	*PRINCE PEACE* DKCepc03@msn.com pinevillelutheran.com	1986	2063 JOHN H KING SERVICE RD	71360	SO		(318)473-0812 (318)473-0812	WS 3 BC 9	MD/SN	69	60	23
RUSTON	*ST PAUL*	1962	504 Tech Dr PO BOX 752	71270 71273	SO			WS 5 BC 4		7	7	8
SHREVEPORT	*CHRIST* christlutheranlcms.org		290 IDEMA ST	71106	SO	Perry A Culver	(318)671-1363	WS 1030 SS 9 BC 9	ED/HC/MD			
	FAITH FaithLutheranChurchLA@gmail.com faithlutheranchurchla.org	1984	4175 LAKESHORE DR	71109	SO	Michael K Shannon	(318)635-8084 (318)635-1339	WS 1030 SS 915	ED/HC/MD	120	90	75
	IMMANUEL		See Bossier City LA									
SLIDELL	*BETHANY* office@openarmsslidell.org www.openarmsslidell.org	1928	1340 8TH ST	70458	SO	Emil Y Gretarsson	(985)643-3043 (985)643-1698	WS 9	EC/HS/ED/ MD	239	166	80
	GOOD SHEPHERD gsslidell@att.net goodshepherdslidellchurch.com		35300 HOME ESTATE DR	70460	SO	Carl L Noble I	(985)641-2109 (985)641-2110	WS 1030 SS 9 BC 9	ED/HC/ MD/SN			
	LAMB OF GOD lambofgodslidell@gmail.com www.lambofgodslidell.com	1997	57210 ALLEN RD	70461	SO		(985)847-1877	WS 8 1030	ED/HC/ MD/SN	165	162	75
	THE VILLAGE		See Lacombe LA									
SULPHUR	*TRINITY*	1949	766 S Post Oak Road 766 S POST OAK RD	70663	SO	Joseph L Arthur IV	(337)625-3276	WS 830 1030 SS 930 BC 930	ED			
THIBODAUX	*GRACE*		See Houma LA									
VIDALIA	*FIRST*		See Natchez MS									
WEST MONROE	*TRINITY*		See Monroe LA									

MAINE

CITY	CONGREGATION EMAIL WEBSITE	YEAR EST	LOCATION MAILING ADDRESS	ZIP CODE(S)	DIST.	PASTOR(S)	PHONE FAX	WS SS BC	SCHOOLS/ MINISTRIES	STATISTIC Bapt	Conf	Avg Attend
GORHAM	*REDEEMER* redeemermaine@gmail.com www.redeemermaine.org	1962	410 Main St PO BOX 427	04038	NE	Gabriel Strawn	(207)839-7100	WS 1015 SS 9 BC 9	ED/HC/MD	139	110	60
HAMPDEN	*HOPE* HopeLutheran1517@gmail.com hopebangor.org	2001	41 Canoe Club Road Hampden VFW PO BOX 2282 BANGOR	04444 04402	NE	Benjamin M Akers		WS 230	ED/HC/ MD/SN	19	18	15

*Indicates a new church start. A new church start is an intentionally organized gathering which comes together on a regular basis for the purpose of worship and/or Bible study and is intended to grow into a member LCMS congregation. WS =Worship Service; SS = Sunday School; BC =Bible Class; EC = Early Childhood; EL = Elementary School; HS = High School; ED =Education Ministry; HC =Human Care Ministry; SN = Special Needs Ministry; MD = Media Ministry (PC)=Partner Church Pastor. See Page 53 for the Table of Abbreviations for key to additional abbreviations

CONGREGATIONS

CITY	CONGREGATION EMAIL WEBSITE	YEAR EST	LOCATION MAILING ADDRESS	ZIP CODE(S)	DIST.	PASTOR(S)	PHONE FAX	WS SS BC	SCHOOLS/ MINISTRIES	STATISTIC Bapt	 Conf	 Avg Attend
PORTLAND	*REDEEMER*		See Gorham ME									
SANFORD	*REDEEMER LUTHERAN CHURCH* Satellite Site of Redeemer Gorham ME	2019	1725 Main St #9	04073								
SCARBOROUGH	*REDEEMER*		See Gorham ME									
WATERVILLE	*RESURRECTION* info@lcrwaterville.org lcrwaterville.org	1964	36 Cool St PO BOX 2884	04901 04903	NE	Benjamin M Akers	(207)872-5208	WS 10 SS 845		139	122	75
WINDHAM	*REDEEMER*		See Gorham ME									

MARYLAND

CITY	CONGREGATION EMAIL WEBSITE	YEAR EST	LOCATION MAILING ADDRESS	ZIP CODE(S)	DIST.	PASTOR(S)	PHONE FAX	WS SS BC	SCHOOLS/ MINISTRIES	Bapt	Conf	Avg Attend
ACCIDENT	*ST JOHN* stjohncove@gmail.com www.stjohncove.org	1860	1065 COVE RD	21520	EA	Benjamin D Hertel	(301)746-8466 (301)746-8466	WS 9				
	ZION office@zionaccident.com www.zionaccident.com	1854	209 N Main St PO BOX 171	21520	EA	Benjamin D Hertel	(301)746-8170	WS 1030 SS 930 BC 930	ED/HC/ MD/SN			
ANNAPOLIS	*ST PAUL* stpaulannapolis@gmail.com www.stpaullutheranchurchannapolis. org	1952	31 Roscoe Rowe Blvd 31 ROWE BLVD	21401	SE	John M Holyer	(410)268-2400 (410)268-2884	WS 930 SS 1115 BC 1115	ED/HC/ MD/SN	134	114	60
ARBUTUS	*HOLY NATIVITY* secretary@holy-nativity.com www.holy-nativity.com	1927	1200 LINDEN AVE BALTIMORE	21227	SE	Dr Andrew T Okai	(410)242-9441 (410)242-0295	WS 830 1030 SS 1030	ED/HC/MD	200	100	75
BALTIMORE	*BEREA* berealutheran2999@gmail.com bereabaltimore.org	1963	2999 BELAIR RD	21213	SE		(410)732-5160	WS 1130 SS 1015	HC/MD	82	18	18
	BETHLEHEM church@bethleheminbaltimore.org www.bethleheminbaltimore.org	1887	4815 HAMILTON AVE	21206	SE		(410)488-4445 (410)488-2599	WS 10 SS 9 BC 9	EL/HS/ ED/HC/ MD/SN	453	274	38
	CALVARY www.calvarylutherancs.org	1915	2625 E NORTHERN PKWY	21214	SE	Kevin D Barron	(410)426-4301 (410)426-7590	WS 10 BC 845	EL/HS/ED/ HC/MD	186	150	59
	EMMANUEL		See Catonsville MD									
	HOLY NATIVITY		See Arbutus MD									
	IMMANUEL ilcadmin@immanuellutheran.org www.immanuellutheran.org	1864	5701 Loch Raven Blvd P. O. BOX 66475	21239	SE	Charles C Minetree III	(410)435-6861	WS 10 SS 9 BC 9	EL/HS/ED/ HC/MD	156	114	50
	LIVING WATER		See Rosedale MD									
	MARTINI secretary@martinilutheran.org martinilutheran.org	1867	100 W HENRIETTA ST	21230	SE	Philip J Jaseph	(410)752-7817 (410)752-7817	WS 11 SS 945 BC 945	EL/HS/ ED/HC/ MD/SN	405	189	44
	NAZARETH nazarethlutheran@msn.com www.nazarethonline.org	1905	3401 Bank St PO BOX 12179	21224 21281	SE		(410)732-3125 (410)732-3125		EL/HS/ ED/HC			
	OROMO		929 INGLESIDE AVE	21228	SE		(240)713-8154					
	OUR SAVIOUR oursaviourbaltimore.org	1892	3301 THE ALAMEDA	21218	SE	Charles L Mc Clean	(410)235-9553 (410)235-1913	WS 11 SS 945	EL/HS	71	67	23
	PILGRIM pilgrimlc05@yahoo.com www.bcpl.net/~pcds/pcds_ pilgrimlutheranchurch.html	1924	7200 LIBERTY RD	21207	SE		(410)484-6692 (410)484-6692	WS 9 SS 1030 BC 1030	EL/HS/ED/ HC/MD			
	REDEEMER church@redeemerlutheranbaltimore.org redeemerlutheranbaltimore.org	1898	4211 VERMONT AVE	21229	SE	Roy A Coats	(410)644-0544 (410)644-6781	WS 1030	EL/HS/ ED/HC/ MD/SN	62	41	30
	REDEEMER		See Parkton MD									
	RESURRECTION		See Brooklyn Park MD									
	SAINT PAUL		See Catonsville MD									
	ST JAMES OF OVERLEA		See Overlea MD									
	ST THOMAS st.thomaslutheran@yahoo.com www.stthomaslutheran.weebly.com	1889	339 S PULASKI ST	21223	SE			WS 10	EL/HS	80	65	11
BEL AIR	*ADVENT*		See Forest Hill MD									
	ST MATTHEW office@smlc.org www.smlc.org	1955	1200 E CHURCHVILLE RD	21014	SE	Garet M Ellis David A Rodgers Paul R Schmidt Jr	(410)838-3178	WS 8 1015 SS 1015 BC 915	EC/EL/HS/ ED/HC/ MD/SN	859	510	291
BELTSVILLE	*OUR SAVIOR*		See Laurel MD									
BETHESDA	*PILGRIM* office@pilgrimbethesda.org www.pilgrimbethesda.org	1946	5500 MASSACHUSETTS AVE	20816	SE	Joshua D Rusert	(301)229-2800 (301)320-7085	WS 815 10 SS 9 BC 9	ED/HC	86	72	54
BOWIE	*TRINITY* churchoffice@tlcbowie.org www.tlcbowie.org	1967	6600 LAUREL BOWIE RD	20715	SE	David H Daumer	(301)262-5475 (301)352-9067	WS 830 11 SS 945 BC 945	ED/HC/ MD/SN	150	115	60
	ZION PRAISE jakeharris_2002@yahoo.com		6600 LAUREL BOWIE RD	20715	SE	Jacob T Harris Henry G Greenfield II	(301)442-6726					
BROOKLYN PARK	*RESURRECTION*	1936	601 HAMMONDS LN BALTI- MORE	21225	SE		(410)789-0415	WS 1030 SS 930 BC 930	SN			
BRYANS ROAD	*OUR SAVIOR* office@lcoos.org www.lcoos.org	1911	7365 INDIAN HEAD HWY	20616	SE	Christopher M Ogne	(301)375-7507 (301)375-8077	WS 830 11 SS 945	ED/HC/ MD/SN	324	194	192
BURTONSVILLE	*OUR SAVIOR*		See Laurel MD									
CATONSVILLE	*EMMANUEL* churchoffice@emmanuelbaltimore.org www.emmanuelbaltimore.org	1888	929 INGLESIDE AVE BALTI- MORE	21228	SE	Falak Robson	(410)744-0016 (410)744-1199	WS 10 SS 9 BC 9	EL/HS/ED/ HC/MD			

*Indicates a new church start. A new church start is an intentionally organized gathering which comes together on a regular basis for the purpose of worship and/or Bible study and is intended to grow into a member LCMS congregation. WS =Worship Service; SS = Sunday School; BC =Bible Class; EC = Early Childhood; EL = Elementary School; HS = High School; ED =Education Ministry; HC =Human Care Ministry; SN = Special Needs Ministry; MD = Media Ministry (PC)=Partner Church Pastor. See Page 53 for the Table of Abbreviations for key to additional abbreviations

CITY	CONGREGATION EMAIL WEBSITE	YEAR EST	LOCATION MAILING ADDRESS	ZIP CODE(S)	DIST.	PASTOR(S)	PHONE FAX	WS SS BC	SCHOOLS/ MINISTRIES	STATISTIC Bapt	Conf	Avg Attend
CATONSVILLE	*SAINT PAUL* secretary@stpaulcatonsville.org stpaulcatonsville.org	1866	2001 OLD FREDERICK RD	21228	SE	Paul G Alms	(410)747-1897 (410)747-7248	WS 10 SS 845	EL/HS/ED/ HC/MD	260	235	118
CHESTER	*GALILEE* galileelcms@gmail.com galileelutheranki.org	1961	1934 HARBOR DR	21619	SE	Belete D Belay	(410)643-6545	WS 9 BC 1030	ED/MD	24	10	18
CHESTERTOWN	*TRINITY* trinitylutheran2@verizon.net www.tlcctown.org/	1929	101 Greenwood Ave PO BOX 597	21620	SE	Keffie A Deen II	(410)778-2744	WS 10 SS 10	ED/HC/ MD/SN	143	135	39
COLUMBIA	*CROSSWALK* info@crosswalkmd.com www.crosswalkmd.com	1969	8940 C-D Route 108 8940 STATE ROUTE 108 STE C	21045	SE	Suah S Deddeh	(410)730-8765	WS 930 SS 11 BC 11	EL/HS/HC	151	104	68
	OUR SAVIOR		See Laurel MD									
CROFTON	*ST PAUL*		See Gambrills MD									
CUMBERLAND	*TRINITY* trinitylcms@atlanticbbn.net	1853	326 N CENTRE ST	21502	SE		(301)777-1800	WS 10 BC 850		84	77	27
EASTON	*IMMANUEL* immanuel@goeaston.net www.ImmanuelEaston.org	1928	7215 OCEAN GTWY	21601	SE	Mark D Tooley	(410)822-5665 (410)763-7372	WS 830 11 SS 945	ED/HC/ MD/SN	125	108	77
ELDERSBURG	*FAITH* office@faithmd.org www.faithlutheraneldersburg.com	1977	1700 SAINT ANDREWS WAY	21784	SE	Christopher N Sperb	(410)795-8082	WS 8 1045 SS 930	ED/HC/ MD/SN	322	253	169
ELKTON	*OUR REDEEMER*		See Newark DE									
FOREST HILL	*ADVENT* adventluth21050@gmail.com www.adventluthch.org	1993	2230 ROCK SPRING RD	21050	SE		(443)655-3962	WS 930 BC 11	EL/HS/ ED/HC/ MD/SN	47	46	27
FREDERICK	*PEACE IN CHRIST*		See Walkersville MD									
FREELAND	*REDEEMER*		See Parkton MD									
FRIENDSVILLE	*ZION*		See Accident MD									
FROSTBURG	*TRINITY*		See Cumberland MD									
FUNKSTOWN	*CONCORDIA*		See Hagerstown MD									
GAMBRILLS	*ST PAUL* info@stpaulscrofton.com www.stpaulscrofton.com	1947	1370 DEFENSE HWY	21054	SE	Iromar Schreiber	(410)721-2332	WS 930 1030 SS 930	ED/HC/ MD/SN	138	115	50
GERMANTOWN	*MESSIAH* PastorandTrustees@Messiah LutheranGermantown.org messiahlutherangermantown.org	1976	13901 CLOPPER RD	20874	SE	David M Seeger	(301)972-2130	WS 930 SS 1045 BC 1045	EC/ED/MD	134	114	83
GLEN ARM	*ST JOHN BLENHEIM* office@stjohnslcms.org www.stjohnslcms.org	1849	13300 MANOR RD	21057	SE	Frederick H Hoffman	(410)592-8018	WS 915 1045	EC/EL/HS/ ED/HC/ MD	171	134	83
GLEN BURNIE	*GALILEE*		See Pasadena MD									
	GALILEE AT GLEN SQUARE Satellite Site of Galilee Pasadena MD	2003	102 North Crain Highway	21061								
	ST PAUL'S churchoffice@stpaulsgb.org www.stpaulsgb.org	1908	308 OAK MANOR DR	21061	SE	Kevin M Scott Ryan E Barnett	(410)766-2283 (410)766-2281	WS 8 1030 SS 915 BC 915	EL/HS/ ED/HC/ MD/SN	488	360	223
GRANTSVILLE	*ST JOHN*		See Accident MD									
	TRINITY		See Cumberland MD									
	ZION		See Accident MD									
GREENBELT	*EL-SHADDAI* gemechisfeyisa747@gmail.com		6905 GREENBELT RD	20770	SE	Wasihun Gutema	(240)701-4196	WS 10				
	HOLY CROSS myholycrosslcms@gmail.com www.myholycross.com	1951	6905 GREENBELT RD	20770	SE	James H Helms Jr	(301)345-5111	WS 930 BC 11	ED/HC/MD			
HAGERSTOWN	*CONCORDIA* concordia.hagerstown@gmail.com www.concordiahagerstown.org	1960	17906 GARDEN LN	21740	SE	Mark D Moretz	(301)797-5955	WS 8 11 SS 930 BC 930	EC/ED/ HC/MD	225	209	200
HANCOCK	*ST PAUL* saintpaulslutheranhancockmd@ gmail.com www.stpaulhancockmd.org	1909	3738 RESLEY RD	21750	SE	William K Stottlemyer	(301)678-7180	WS 10 SS 845		97	65	57
HUNTINGTOWN	*FIRST* flc@firstlutheranchurch.org www.firstlutheranchurch.org	1976	6300 SOUTHERN MARYLAND BLVD	20639	SE	James E Kent	(410)257-3030	WS 8 1045 SS 930	EC/ED/HC/ MD/SN	212	211	100
HYATTSVILLE	*CHRISTOS SENOR/VIDA**	1994	3799 E West Hwy 3041 DUBARRY LN BROOKEV-ILLE	20782 20833	SE		(301)277-4729					
	*MEDHANIALEM ETHIOPIA** mountzionem@yahoo.com		3799 EAST WEST HWY	20782	SE		(619)397-8893					
	REDEEMER office@redeemer-lutheran.us www.redeemer-lutheran.us	1956	3799 East-West Hwy 3799 EAST WEST HWY	20782	SE		(301)277-2302 (301)277-2303	WS 10 BC 9	ED/HC/MD	205	128	60
INDIAN HEAD	*INDIAN HEAD SENIOR CENTER* Satellite Site of Our Savior Bryans Road MD	2004	100 Cornwallis Square	20640								
KENSINGTON	*OROMO RESURRECTION* teka.obsa@gmail.com		3101 UNIVERSITY BLVD W	20895	SE	Teka O Fogi	(301)942-7759			480	241	160
KENT ISLAND	*GALILEE*		See Chester MD									
KINGSVILLE	*ST PAULS* abrintnall@stpaulskingsville.org www.stpaulskingsville.org	1850	12022 JERUSALEM RD	21087	SE	Timothy R Seban	(410)592-8100 (410)592-3282	SS 830	EL/HS/ED/ HC/MD	370	350	130
LA PLATA	*CHARLES COUNTY DETENTION CENTER* Satellite Site of Our Savior Bryans Road MD	2006	6905 Crain Highway	20646								

*Indicates a new church start. A new church start is an intentionally organized gathering which comes together on a regular basis for the purpose of worship and/or Bible study and is intended to grow into a member LCMS congregation. WS =Worship Service; SS = Sunday School; BC =Bible Class; EC = Early Childhood; EL = Elementary School; HS = High School; ED =Education Ministry; HC =Human Care Ministry; SN = Special Needs Ministry; MD = Media Ministry (PC)=Partner Church Pastor. See Page 53 for the Table of Abbreviations for key to additional abbreviations

CITY	CONGREGATION EMAIL WEBSITE	YEAR EST	LOCATION MAILING ADDRESS	ZIP CODE(S)	DIST.	PASTOR(S)	PHONE FAX	WS SS BC	SCHOOLS/ MINISTRIES	STATISTIC Bapt	Conf	Avg Attend
LA PLATA	*GRACE* church@growingwithgrace.org www.growingwithgrace.org	1961	1200 CHARLES ST	20646	SE	Jeffrey D Marquardt Edward R Huber	(301)932-0963 (301)934-1459	WS 830 11 SS 945 BC 945	EL/ED/HC	332	293	125
LANDOVER HILLS	*ASCENSION* ascenluth@aol.com www.alutheranchurch.com	1950	7415 BUCHANAN ST LANDOVER HLS	20784	SE	Paul C Agne	(301)577-0500 (301)577-9558	WS 9 SS 1030	ED/HC	203	181	43
	LAMB OF GOD		7415 BUCHANAN ST LANDOVER HLS	20784	SE	Robert W Sawah	(202)394-0356	WS 1	ED/HC			
LAUREL	*FIRST* firstlutherbowie@aol.com	1910	12710 Duckettown Rd PO BOX 120 BOWIE	20708 20719	SE		(301)464-2599	WS 9	HC/MD/SN	12	11	17
	OUR SAVIOR office@oslclaurel.org www.oslclaurel.org	1969	13611 LAUREL BOWIE RD	20708	SE	John O Flahn	(301)776-7670	WS 815 1045 BC 930	EC/ED/HC/ MD/SN	580	433	158
LEXINGTON PARK	*TRINITY* office@trinitylutheranlp.org www.trinitylutheranlp.org	1954	46707 Shangri La Dr 46707 S SHANGRI LA DR LEXINGTON PK	20653	SE	Dr Matthew E Borrasso	(301)863-9512 (301)863-8185	WS 10 SS 9 BC 9	EC/ED/ HC/SN	202	146	95
MCHENRY	*ST JOHN*		See Accident MD									
	ZION		See Accident MD									
MECHANICSVILLE	*SAINT PAULS* info@stpaulssomd.com www.stpaulssomd.com	1909	37707 New Market-Turner Rd 37707 NEW MARKET TURNER RD MECHANICSVLLE	20659	SE		(301)884-5184 (301)884-2063	WS 10 SS 845 BC 845	ED/HC/ MD/SN	180	120	60
MIDDLE RIVER	*FAITH*	1956	2200 OLD EASTERN AVE BALTIMORE	21220	SE	Raymond H Rohrs	(410)687-7500	WS 1030				
MOUNT RAINIER	*TRINITY* trinity-elc-office@verizon.net www.tlcmr.org	1931	4000 30TH ST	20712	SE	Peter A Schiebel Gugssa Biru	(301)864-4340 (301)779-5629	WS 930 SS 830	HC/MD	162	111	21
OAKLAND	*ST JOHN*		See Accident MD									
	ZION		See Accident MD									
ODENTON	*FIRST* churchoffice@felcodenton.org www.felcodenton.org	1940	8397 Piney Orchard Parkway 8397 PINEY ORCHARD PKWY	21113	SE	Corey S Brooks	(410)672-3352	WS 1030 SS 9	ED/HC/MD			
	OUR SAVIOR		See Laurel MD									
OLNEY	*GOOD SHEPHERD* office@olneygoodshepherd.org LCGS.church	1963	4200 Olney Laytonsville Rd PO BOX 280	20832 20830	SE	Timothy M Boerger	(301)774-9125 (301)774-9649	WS 11 SS 930 BC 930	EC/ED/ HC/MD	217	165	77
OVERLEA	*ST JAMES OF OVERLEA* saintjamesbaltimore@gmail.com www.saintjamesbaltimore.com	1906	8 W OVERLEA AVE BALTIMORE	21206	SE	Eric Z Bednash	(410)668-0158	WS 10 SS 9 BC 9	EL/HS/ED/ HC/MD	70	66	45
OWINGS MILLS	*CHRIST KING* ctklclcms@yahoo.com ctklchurch.org	1964	515 ACADEMY AVE	21117	SE	Harry M Krolus	(410)356-3400 (410)356-3400	WS 1030 SS 9 BC 9	EL/HS/ED/ HC/MD	138	110	47
PARKTON	*REDEEMER* info@redeemerparkton.org redeemerparkton.org	1981	20440 DOWNES RD	21120	SE		(410)343-1665	WS 10 SS 9 BC 9	ED/MD	116	104	48
PASADENA	*FOREST OF FAITH* Satellite Site of Galilee Pasadena MD	2023	4652 Mountain Road	21122								
	GALILEE office@glcpasadena.org www.glcpasadena.org	1966	4652 MOUNTAIN RD	21122	SE	Matthew R Hilpert	(410)255-8236	WS 8 1045 SS 9 BC 915 5	EC/ED/HC/ MD/SN	555	463	230
	GALILEE YOUTH GROUP Satellite Site of Galilee Pasadena MD	2019	19 Milburn Circle	21122								
PRESTON	*IMMANUEL* immanuellutheranpreston@verizon.net ilcpreston.org	1896	242 Main St PO BOX 39	21655	SE	David D Casey-Motley	(410)673-7107 (410)673-1426	WS 1030 SS 915 BC 915	EC/ED/HC/ MD/SN	340	226	59
REISTERSTOWN	*CHRIST KING*		See Owings Mills MD									
ROCKVILLE	*OF THE CROSS* office@lccrockville.org www.lccrockville.org	1960	12801 FALLS RD	20854	SE	Aurelio Magarino	(301)762-7565 (301)762-7551	WS 1030 SS 915 BC 915	ED/HC	90	70	26
ROSEDALE	*LIVING WATER* livingwater.lutheran@outlook.com		8912 PHILADELPHIA RD BALTIMORE	21237	SE	Richard K Parron	(410)391-0755	WS 10	EL/HS/ ED/HC			
ROSSVILLE	*LIVING WATER*		See Rosedale MD									
SALISBURY	*BETHANY* office.bethanylutheran@gmail.com	1931	817 CAMDEN AVE	21801	SE	Dr Alemu E Katiso	(410)742-1737 (410)742-3506	WS 8 11 SS 930 BC 945	HC/MD			
SEVERNA PARK	*GALILEE*		See Pasadena MD									
SILVER SPRING	*CALVARY* pastor.alex@calvarysilverspring.org calvarysilverspring.org	1941	9545 GEORGIA AVE	20910	SE	Alexander Q Harris	(301)589-4001 (301)589-0931	WS 930	HC/MD/SN			
	CHRIST DEAF christdeaf@verizon.net www.christdeaf.org	1974	9545 GEORGIA AVE	20910	SE	Andrew D Petajan	(301)251-5953 (301)251-8986	WS 930 BC 11	ED/HC/ MD/SN	33	33	12
	*HOPE OF GLORY** simretmulgeta24@gmail.com		8120 FENTON ST	20910	SE		(240)529-4372					
	*MEKANE-YESUS** gugwengiel@aol.com		9545 GEORGIA AVE	20910	SE		(410)730-3440					
	ST ANDREW office@mystandrew.org www.mystandrew.org	1953	15300 NEW HAMPSHIRE AVE	20905	SE	Mark A Hricko Nicholas O Gonzalez	(301)384-4394 (301)384-4450	WS 8 930 11 SS 930 BC 930	EC/ED/HC/ MD/SN	2184	1588	751
SMITHSBURG	*CONCORDIA*		See Hagerstown MD									
SOUTHERN MARYLAND	*CONCORDIA*		See Upper Marlboro MD									
TOWSON	*HOLY CROSS* office@holycrosstowson.org www.holycrosstowson.org	1952	8516 LOCH RAVEN BLVD	21286	SE		(410)825-7905 (410)825-7905	WS 10 BC 1130	EC/ED/HC	85	71	25

*Indicates a new church start. A new church start is an intentionally organized gathering which comes together on a regular basis for the purpose of worship and/or Bible study and is intended to grow into a member LCMS congregation. WS =Worship Service; SS = Sunday School; BC =Bible Class; EC = Early Childhood; EL = Elementary School; HS = High School; ED =Education Ministry; HC =Human Care Ministry; SN = Special Needs Ministry; MD = Media Ministry (PC)=Partner Church Pastor. See Page 53 for the Table of Abbreviations for key to additional abbreviations

CITY	CONGREGATION EMAIL WEBSITE	YEAR EST	LOCATION MAILING ADDRESS	ZIP CODE(S)	DIST.	PASTOR(S)	PHONE FAX	WS SS BC	SCHOOLS/ MINISTRIES	STATISTIC Bapt	Conf	Avg Attend
TOWSON	*NEW THING* ministryassistant@newthing.live newthing.live	2022	1145 CONCORDIA DRIVE	21286	SE	Peter T Couser	(410)825-8770	WS 10	EL/HS/ ED/HC/ MD/SN	68	62	51
UPPER MARLBORO	*CONCORDIA* info@concordialutheranum.org www.concordialutheranum.org	1974	8677 Crain Highway 8677 CRAIN HWY UPPR MARLBORO	20772	SE		(301)952-0009 (301)856-4636	WS 11 SS 10	ED/MD/SN	30	30	17
WALDORF	*CHARLESTON SENIOR CENTER* Satellite Site of Our Savior Bryans Road MD	2022	45 St Patrick Drive	20603								
WALKERSVILLE	*PEACE IN CHRIST* office@peaceinchrist.org www.peaceinchrist.org	1975	8798 ADVENTURE AVE	21793	SE	Bradley J Singer Richard L Benjamin John P Jakupciak	(301)845-6300	WS 1030 BC 9	ED/HC/SN			
WESTMINSTER	*CHRIST KING*		See Owings Mills MD									
WILLIAMSPORT	*CONCORDIA*		See Hagerstown MD									
MASSACHUSETTS												
ACTON	*BETHEL OROMO*		472 MASSACHUSETTS AVE	01720	NE	Adam K Teferi						
	MOUNT CALVARY info@mtcalvaryacton.org mtcalvaryacton.org	1909	472 Massachusetts Ave PO BOX 986	01720	NE	Eric S Sahlberg Jr	(978)263-5156 (978)264-0167	WS 1030 SS 9	EC/ED/ HC/MD	506	248	157
AGAWAM	*OUR REDEEMER*		See Enfield CT									
	ST JOHN'S		See Westfield MA									
BEDFORD	*OF THE SAVIOR* church@lcsavior.org www.lcsavior.org	1957	426 DAVIS RD	01730	NE	Nils P Niemeier	(781)275-6013 (781)275-9308	WS 8 1045 SS 930 BC 930	EC/ED/HC/ MD/SN	167	145	64
BOSTON	*FIRST* admin@flc-boston.org www.flc-boston.org	1839	299 BERKELEY ST	02116	NE	James P Hopkins Miguel A Barcelos Jacob W Rhodes	(617)536-8851 (617)247-9827	WS 8 11 SS 930 BC 930	ED/HC/ MD/SN	508	421	143
CANTON	*SAINT JAMES* www.stjamescanton.org	1959	214 YORK ST	02021	NE		(781)828-0620 (781)821-4752	WS 10	ED/HC/ MD/SN			
CLINTON	*TRINITY* pastorgramit@yahoo.com www.trinitylutheranclintonma.org	1915	117 CHACE ST	01510	NE	Paul E Gramit	(978)365-6888	WS 10 SS 9 BC 9	ED/MD			
DEDHAM	*ST LUKES* office@stlukesdedham.org www.stlukesdedham.org	1892	950 EAST ST	02026	NE	James E Butler	(781)326-1346	WS 930 SS 845 BC 830	EC/ED/HC/ MD/SN	153	126	58
EASTHAMPTON	*TRINITY* tlceasthampton@gmail.com www.tlceasthampton.org	1893	2 CLARK ST	01027	NE	James W Rice	(413)527-3311	WS 9 SS 9	ED/HC/MD	29	24	30
FEEDING HILLS	*ST JOHN'S*		See Westfield MA									
FITCHBURG	*MESSIAH* messiah.fitchburg@gmail.com www.messiahfitchburg.com	1893	750 RINDGE RD	01420	NE	David S Jacoby	(978)343-7397 (978)345-5954	WS 10 SS 9 BC 9	EC/ED	210	184	56
HANOVER	*OF THE CROSS* admin@crosshanover.org www.crosshanover.org	1961	77 ROCKLAND ST	02339	NE	Paul L Lantz	(781)826-5121 (781)826-5122	WS 9 SS 915	EC/ED/HC/ MD/SN	172	172	74
HOLYOKE	*FIRST* secretaryflc@comcast.net www.lutheranholyoke.org	1867	1810 NORTHAMPTON ST	01040	NE	Randall T Bessette Sr	(413)534-7071 (413)534-7071	WS 9 SS 1015 BC 1015	ED	72	72	40
LEOMINSTER	*TRINITY*		See Clinton MA									
LONGMEADOW	*OUR REDEEMER*		See Enfield CT									
LYNNFIELD	*MESSIAH* jeremy.pekari@gmail.com www.messiahspirit.org	1959	708 LOWELL ST	01940	NE	Dr Jeremy R Pekari David E Brezina	(781)334-4111	WS 1030 SS 9 BC 9	ED/HC/MD	106	86	43
MARLBOROUGH	*TRINITY*		See Clinton MA									
MIDDLETON	*MESSIAH*		See Lynnfield MA									
NORTH READING	*MESSIAH*		See Lynnfield MA									
PEABODY	*MESSIAH*		See Lynnfield MA									
PLYMOUTH	*OF THE WAY*		See Raynham MA									
QUINCY	*WOLLASTON* steve@wlchurch.org www.wlchurch.org	1931	550 HANCOCK ST	02170	NE	Steve T Law	(617)773-5482 (617)471-0235	WS 845 SS 10	ED/HC/SN	174	133	80
RAYNHAM	*OF THE WAY* admin@familiesinchrist.org www.familiesinchrist.org	1965	110 ROBINSON ST	02767	NE	Jacob S Dickerhoff	(508)822-5900 (508)822-5900	WS 9 SS 1030 BC 1030	ED/HC/MD			
READING	*MESSIAH*		See Lynnfield MA									
ROSLINDALE	*TRINITY*		See West Roxbury MA									
SAUGUS	*MESSIAH*		See Lynnfield MA									
SHREWSBURY	*TRINITY*		See Clinton MA									
SOUTHWICK	*GOOD SHEPHERD*		See Suffield CT									
	ST JOHN'S		See Westfield MA									
SPRINGFIELD	*TRINITY* tlcspringfieldma@gmail.com www.tlcspringfield.360unite.com	1889	400 WILBRAHAM RD	01109	NE		(413)783-9112	WS 1115 SS 10	ED/HC			
TAUNTON	*OF THE WAY*		See Raynham MA									
TOPSFIELD	*OUR SAVIOR* office@oslcma.com www.oslcma.com	1962	478 BOSTON ST	01983	NE	Joseph R Nollet	(978)887-5701 (978)887-9548	WS 815 1030 SS 930 BC 930	ED/HC/ MD/SN	156	132	120
WAKEFIELD	*MESSIAH*		See Lynnfield MA									
WEST ROXBURY	*TRINITY*	1871	1195 Centre St PO BOX C ROSLINDALE	02132 02131	NE	Stephen A Vekasy	(617)327-5155	WS 930 SS 1030 BC 1030	ED/HC	44	44	22
WEST SPRINGFIELD	*ST JOHN'S*		See Westfield MA									

*Indicates a new church start. A new church start is an intentionally organized gathering which comes together on a regular basis for the purpose of worship and/or Bible study and is intended to grow into a member LCMS congregation. WS =Worship Service; SS = Sunday School; BC =Bible Class; EC = Early Childhood; EL = Elementary School; HS = High School; ED =Education Ministry; HC =Human Care Ministry; SN = Special Needs Ministry; MD = Media Ministry (PC)=Partner Church Pastor. See Page 53 for the Table of Abbreviations for key to additional abbreviations

CONGREGATIONS

CITY	CONGREGATION EMAIL WEBSITE	YEAR EST	LOCATION MAILING ADDRESS	ZIP CODE(S)	DIST.	PASTOR(S)	PHONE FAX	WS SS BC	SCHOOLS/ MINISTRIES	STATISTIC Bapt	Conf	Avg Attend
WESTFIELD	*ST JOHN'S* info@stjohnswestfield.org stjohnswestfield.org	1901	60 BROAD ST	01085	NE	Dwight D Riley Jeffrey M Windoloski	(413)568-1417	WS 10 SS 830 BC 830	ED/HC/ MD/SN			
WESTMINSTER	*CAMP PINESHORE* Satellite Site of Messiah Fitchburg MA	2014	Pineshore Rd	01473								
	OUR SAVIOR office@oursaviorlcms.com www.oursaviorlcms.com	1961	1 Hagar Park Rd PO BOX 459	01473	NE	Peter F Gregory Edward C Schneeflock	(978)874-2504 (978)874-2479	WS 10 6 SS 1130 BC 1130	ED/HC/ MD/SN	280	214	145
WORCESTER	*TRINITY*		See Clinton MA									
			MICHIGAN									
ADA TOWNSHIP	*ST MATTHEW*		See Grand Rapids MI									
ADDISON	*OF THE LAKES* lcoloffice@gmail.com www.lcol.org	1990	8800 N ROLLIN HWY	49220	MI	James D Weist	(517)547-4261	WS 815 1030 SS 945 BC 945	ED/HC/ MD/SN	182	161	82
ADRIAN	*HOPE* hopelcms@tc3net.com www.hopeadrian.org	1972	5625 W US Highway 223 PO BOX 232	49221	MI	Paul W Herter	(517)263-4317 (517)265-5432	WS 9 SS 1030 BC 1030	ED/HC/MD	204	170	65
	ST JOHN pastor@stjohnsadrian.org stjohnsadrian.org	1847	3448 N ADRIAN HWY	49221	MI	Joel H Sarrault	(517)265-6998 (517)264-2512	WS 830 11 SS 945 BC 945	EC/ED/HC/ MD/SN	564	469	213
ALBION	*ST PAUL* office@stpaulalbion.org stpaulalbion.org	1868	100 LUTHER BLVD	49224	MI	Paul R Koehn	(517)629-8379 (517)629-8342	WS 815 1030 BC 9	EC/ED/HC/ MD/SN	248	196	100
ALGER	*FAITH*		See Prescott MI									
ALGOMA TOWNSHIP	*ST PETER*		See Rockford MI									
ALGONAC	*FIRST* firstofalgonac@sbcglobal.net	1944	510 Green St 1623 WASHINGTON ST	48001	MI		(810)794-4642	WS 1115	ED/HC/MD	52	46	35
ALLEN PARK	*ANGELICA* angelicalutheranoffice@gmail.com www.angelicalutheranchurch.org/	1947	8400 PARK AVE	48101	EN		(313)381-2080	WS 930 BC 1115	ED/MD	252	75	36
	CHRIST OUR REDEEMER joholls@aol.com www.christourredeemerlutheran.com		14722 MORRIS AVE	48101	EN	Joel M Holls	(313)429-3085	BC 1130		39	36	22
	MOUNT HOPE mthopeluthchurch@yahoo.com mthopelutheranchurch.com	1930	5323 SOUTHFIELD RD	48101	MI	Paul A Pollatz	(313)565-9445 (313)565-2426	WS 930 BC 1045	EC/ED/SN	90	90	35
ALLENDALE	*ST JOHN*		See Jenison MI									
ALMA	*PEACE* www.peacealma.org	1962	325 E WARWICK DR	48801	MI	Thomas C Messer	(989)463-5754	WS 930 SS 11 BC 11				
ALPENA	*BESSER SENIOR LIVING* Satellite Site of Immanuel Alpena MI	2021	325 Johnson Street	49707								
	FOWLER Satellite Site of Immanuel Alpena MI	2014	525 River St	49707								
	IMMANUEL jenniferheinze111@gmail.com www.immanuelalpena.org	1874	351 WILSON ST	49707	MI	James D Erickson Joshua M Schultz	(989)354-3443 (989)354-0122	WS 8 1030 SS 915 BC 915	EL/ED/HC/ MD/SN	1507	1051	303
	ST PAUL		See Hubbard Lake MI									
	TURNING BROOK OF ALPENA Satellite Site of Immanuel Alpena MI	2007	300 Oxbow Dr.	49707								
AMASA	*SION*	1905	413 W Pine St PO BOX 241	49903	NW		(906)822-7810		HC			
ANN ARBOR	*EMMAUS ** info@emmausannarbor.org emmausannarbor.org/		420 W LIBERTY ST	48103	MI		(810)990-7572			41	24	43
	FAITH		See Ypsilanti MI									
	LIVING WATER		See Whitmore Lake MI									
	PEACE peacelutheran@peaceaa.net www.peaceaa.net	1994	8260 JACKSON RD	48103	MI	Kurt E Lambart	(734)424-0899	WS 830 11 6 SS 945 11 BC 945	ED/HC/ MD/SN	499	394	135
	ST LUKE office@stlukeaa.org stlukeaa.org	1957	4205 WASHTENAW AVE	48108	MI	Kyle T Weeks	(734)971-0550	WS 830 11 SS 945 BC 945	ED/HC/ MD/SN	330	283	176
	ST PAUL priehs6@yahoo.com www.stpaulannarbor.org	1908	420 W LIBERTY ST	48103	MI	Dr Theodore J Hopkins Aaron W Roggow	(734)665-9117	WS 830 SS 945 BC 945	EL/HS/ ED/HC/ MD/SN	949	738	332
	ST THOMAS stthomaslutheranaa@gmail.com www.stthomaslcms.org	1842	10001 W ELLSWORTH RD	48103	MI	Coleman K Geraci	(734)663-7511	WS 9		40	35	24
	ST. PAUL LUTHERAN CHURCH-SCHOOL MAIN CAMPUS Satellite Site of St Paul Ann Arbor MI	2005	495 Earhart Rd	48105				WS 1045 SS 945 BC 945				
	UNIVERSITY CHAPEL info@ulcannarbor.org ulcannarbor.org		1511 WASHTENAW AVE	48104	MI	Robert G Kasper Randall S Duncan Marcus J Lane	(734)663-5560	WS 8 945 1130 SS 9	ED	365	301	271
ARCADIA	*TRINITY* trinityarcadiami@gmail.com www.trinityarcadiami.org/	1881	17191 Third St PO BOX 139	49613	MI	Dr Justin P Rossow	(231)889-3620	WS 930 10 SS 11 BC 11	ED/HC/MD	359	325	135
ARMADA	*OUR SAVIOUR* oslchurch@teleweb.net www.oslc-armada.org	1947	22511 West Main St 22511 W MAIN ST	48005	MI	Alexander A Schrader	(586)784-9088	WS 8 1045 BC 930	HS/ED/ HC/MD/ SN	210	183	56

*Indicates a new church start. A new church start is an intentionally organized gathering which comes together on a regular basis for the purpose of worship and/or Bible study and is intended to grow into a member LCMS congregation. WS =Worship Service; SS = Sunday School; BC =Bible Class; EC = Early Childhood; EL = Elementary School; HS = High School; ED =Education Ministry; HC =Human Care Ministry; SN = Special Needs Ministry; MD = Media Ministry (PC)=Partner Church Pastor. See Page 53 for the Table of Abbreviations for key to additional abbreviations

CITY	CONGREGATION EMAIL WEBSITE	YEAR EST	LOCATION MAILING ADDRESS	ZIP CODE(S)	DIST.	PASTOR(S)	PHONE FAX	WS SS BC	SCHOOLS/ MINISTRIES	STATISTIC Bapt	Conf	Avg Attend
ARMADA	*ST JOHN*		See Ray MI									
AU GRES	*ST JOHN* office@stjohnaugres.com www.stjohnaugres.org	1911	206 N Court St PO BOX 763	48703	MI	Sean R McNeil	(989)876-8910	WS 9 BC 1015	ED/HC	348	246	49
AUBURN	*GRACE* office.graceauburn@gmail.com graceauburn.org	1959	303 RUTH ST	48611	MI	Aaron T Schian	(989)662-6161	WS 9 SS 1030 BC 1030 12	ED/HC/ MD/SN	461	362	178
	ZION office@zionauburn.com www.zionauburn.com	1887	1557 W Seidlers Rd 1557 SEIDLERS RD	48611	MI	Andrew P Menz Seth R Hemme	(989)662-4264 (989)662-7052	WS 9 SS 1015 BC 1015	EL/HS/ ED/HC/ MD/SN	1049	802	214
AUBURN HILLS	*CROWN OF LIFE*		See Rochester Hills MI									
	GOOD SHEPHERD		See Lake Orion MI									
	ST PAUL		See Pontiac MI									
BAD AXE	*OUR SAVIOR* oslcbadaxe@gmail.com www.badaxelutheran.org	1946	123 W IRWIN ST	48413	MI	Andrew M Simpson	(989)269-7642 (989)269-7131	WS 8 11 SS 930 BC 930	EC/ED/HC/ MD/SN	536	415	165
BALDWIN	*GRACE* graceluthbaldwin@att.net graceluthbaldwin.org	1978	8636 S M 37	49304	MI	Daniel H Fienen	(231)745-7521	WS 1030 BC 930	ED/HC/MD	65	60	27
BATTLE CREEK	*REDEMPTION* redemption@outlook.com www.redemptionlutheranchurchbc.org.	1954	2450 MICHIGAN AVE W	49037	MI	Karl N Strenge	(269)964-2321 (269)964-6691	WS 1030 SS 9 BC 9	ED/HC/MD	253	234	62
	ST MARK office@stmark.net stmark.net	1957	114 E MINGES RD.	49015	MI	Christopher K Paavola	(269)964-0401 (269)964-4766	WS 8 930 11 SS 930 11	EC/ED/HC/ MD/SN	667	482	350
	ST PAUL saintpaul1916@gmail.com www.facebook.com/share/ g/1E1jo5C9US/	1916	349 CAPITAL AVE NE	49017	MI	Larry R Gorlitz	(269)968-3055	WS 1030 SS 9 BC 9	ED/HC/MD	105	105	37
BAY CITY	*FAITH* office@faithbaycity.org www.faithbaycity.org	1960	3033 WILDER RD	48706	MI	James D Chinery	(989)684-3430 (989)684-3545	WS 8 1030 SS 1030 BC 915	EL/HS/ ED/HC/ MD/SN	600	539	207
	GRACE		See Auburn MI									
	IMMANUEL ilc@immanuelbaycity.com immanuelbaycity.com	1861	300 N SHERIDAN ST	48708	MI	Adan C Garcia	(989)893-4088	WS 10 SS 845 BC 845	EL/ED/HC/ MD/SN	1850	1047	254
	ST JOHN office@amelith.org www.amelith.org	1852	1664 AMELITH RD	48706	MI	Gerald A Gauthier II	(989)686-0176	WS 930 BC 1030	EL/HS/ ED/HC/ MD/SN	644	499	122
	ST PAUL office@stpaulbaycity.org www.stpaulbaycity.org	1848	6100 Westside Saginaw Rd 6094 WESTSIDE SAGINAW RD	48706	MI	Dr Dennis W Matyas David M Schultz	(989)684-4450 (989)684-0882	WS 8 1030 SS 930 BC 930	EL/HS/ ED/HC/ MD/SN	935	759	420
	TRINITY churchsecretary@trinitymonitor.org www.trinitymonitor.org	1880	20 E SALZBURG RD	48706	MI	Seth C Kaiser	(989)662-6093 (989)662-6173	WS 830 1030 SS 940 BC 940	EL/HS/ ED/HC/ MD/SN	743	608	197
	ZION secretary@zionbaycity.org www.zionbaycity.org	1901	510 W IVY ST	48706	MI	Phillip A Baerwolf	(989)894-2611	WS 930 BC 830	EL/ED/HC/ MD/SN	825	697	138
	ZION		See Auburn MI									
BELDING	*HOLY CROSS* crossh667@gmail.com www.holycrossbelding.org	1939	422 W HIGH ST	48809	MI	Robert V Wagner	(616)794-1310 (616)794-1170	WS 1030	HC/MD	71	71	27
BELLAIRE	*HOPE* hopeinbellaire@gmail.com	1973	2680 S M-88 Hwy PO BOX 160	49615	EN	Wade M Seaver	(231)533-8129	WS 9 SS 1030 BC 1030		38	36	30
BELLEVILLE	*FAITH*		See Ypsilanti MI									
	OPEN ARMS dreszke@openarmscenter.com www.openarmscenter.com		7865 BELLEVILLE RD	48111	MI		(734)699-5000 (734)697-0947	WS 10	EC/HS/ED/ HC/MD	136	82	87
BELMONT	*ST PETER*		See Rockford MI									
BENTLEY	*BETHLEHEM*		See Standish MI									
BENZONIA	*OUR SAVIOR* oursaviormi@gmail.com oursaviormich.com	1946	6790 FRANKFORT HWY	49616	MI		(231)882-4326	WS 1030	ED/HC/MD	83	53	22
BERGLAND	*TRINITY*	1923	404 Birch St PO BOX 367	49910	NW	Bryan L Hopfensperger		WS 9				
BERRIEN SPRINGS	*TRINITY* churchoffice@trinityberrien.org www.trinityberrien.org	1912	9123 GEORGE AVE BERRIEN SPRGS	49103	MI	Dr James F Wright	(269)473-1811 (269)471-7013	WS 915 BC 1030	EL/ED/ HC/SN	293	284	80
BESSEMER	*OUR REDEEMER*		See Ramsay MI									
BEVERLY HILLS	*ASCENSION/CHRIST* info@ascensionofchrist.org www.ascensionofchrist.org	1950	16935 W 14 MILE RD	48025	EN	Larry K Loree Jr	(248)644-8890 (248)644-1181	WS 1015 SS 9 BC 9	EC/EL/ED/ HC/MD			
	OUR SAVIOR DF tyler.walworth@gmail.com www.oslcd.org	1910	16935 W 14 MILE RD	48025	MI	Tyler A Walworth	(816)590-1692	WS 1	HS/ED/ MD/SN	38	36	15
	OUR SHEPHERD		See Birmingham MI									
BIG RAPIDS	*ST PETER'S* office@stpetersbr.org www.stpetersbr.org	1870	408 W BELLEVUE ST	49307	MI	Tyson V Bentz Tyler D Carter	(231)796-6684 (231)796-1186	WS 10	EL/HS/ED/ HC/MD	647	207	148
BIRCH RUN	*ST MARTIN* secretary@stmartinbirchrun.org www.stmartinbirchrun.org	1988	10995 CANADA RD	48415	MI		(989)624-9204 (989)624-0298	WS 830 1115 SS 10 BC 10	EC/ED/HC/ MD/SN	439	314	163
BIRMINGHAM	*ASCENSION/CHRIST*		See Beverly Hills MI									

*Indicates a new church start. A new church start is an intentionally organized gathering which comes together on a regular basis for the purpose of worship and/or Bible study and is intended to grow into a member LCMS congregation. WS =Worship Service; SS = Sunday School; BC =Bible Class; EC = Early Childhood; EL = Elementary School; HS = High School; ED =Education Ministry; HC =Human Care Ministry; SN = Special Needs Ministry; MD = Media Ministry (PC)=Partner Church Pastor. See Page 53 for the Table of Abbreviations for key to additional abbreviations

CITY	CONGREGATION EMAIL WEBSITE	YEAR EST	LOCATION MAILING ADDRESS	ZIP CODE(S)	DIST.	PASTOR(S)	PHONE FAX	WS SS BC	SCHOOLS/ MINISTRIES	STATISTIC Bapt	Conf	Avg Attend
BIRMINGHAM	*OUR SHEPHERD* churchoffice@ourshepherd.net www.ourshepherd.net	1949	2225 E 14 MILE RD	48009	MI	Dr Evan P Gaertner Michael S Vieregge Stephen W Woodfin	(248)646-6100 (248)646-6176	WS 830 11 SS 945 BC 945	EL/HS/ ED/HC/ MD/SN	1318	1006	413
	REDEEMER redeemer@redeemerbirmingham.org redeemerbirmingham.org	1924	1800 W MAPLE RD	48009	MI	Randall J Schlak James H Greenwalt II	(248)644-4010	WS 8 9 1030 SS 1030	EC/EL/ ED/HC/ MD/SN	1760	1488	397
BLENDON TOWNSHIP	*ST JOHN*		See Jenison MI									
BLISSFIELD	*BLESSED SAVIOR*	1993	8995 Thompson Hwy PO BOX 65	49228	MI		(517)486-2990	WS 8 SS 915	ED/HC/SN	14	10	11
BLOOMFIELD HILLS	*CROSS CHRIST* office@bloomfieldcross.org www.bloomfieldcross.org	1960	1100 Lone Pine Rd 1100 LONE PINE RD BLDG 1 BLOOMFIELD	48302	MI		(248)646-5886 (248)646-5968	WS 1030 SS 915 BC 915	EL/ED/HC/ MD/SN	416	352	92
BLOOMFIELD TOWNSHIP	*OUR SHEPHERD*		See Birmingham MI									
BOYNE CITY	*CHRIST* christlutheranboyne@gmail.com www.clcboyne.org	1903	1250 BOYNE AVE	49712	MI	Charles R Hoffman	(231)582-9301	WS 8 1030 SS 915 BC 915	ED/HC/MD	284	238	117
BRANT	*ST JOHN MARION SPR* richelewis@gmail.com		12140 S MERRILL RD	48614	MI	Richard E Lewis	(989)715-4555	WS 10	ED/HC/SN	107	97	31
BRIDGEPORT	*FAITH* faithluthchurch@yahoo.com www.faithlutheranbridgeport.org	1948	4241 Williamson Rd PO BOX 242	48722	MI	Timothy J Behnke	(989)777-2600 (989)777-5069	WS 9 SS 1015 BC 1015	EC/HS/ ED/HC/ MD/SN	258	213	113
BRIDGMAN	*BREAKFAST WITH JESUS* Satellite Site of Immanuel Bridgman MI	2016	9673 Red Arrow Highway	49106								
	IMMANUEL ilc@immanuelbridgman.org www.immanuelbridgman.org	1896	9650 Church St PO BOX 26	49106	MI	Dr Douglas A Krengel	(269)465-6031 (269)465-6409	WS 9 1030 SS 1045	EC/ED/HC/ MD/SN	590	536	161
BRIGHTON	*LIVING WATER*		See Whitmore Lake MI									
	SHEP LAKES info@sotlchurch.com www.sotlchurch.com	1973	2101 S HACKER RD	48114	MI	Dr Scott G Sommerfeld Keith E Dwyer	(810)227-5099 (810)227-3566	WS 815 1030 SS 930	EL/HS/ ED/HC/ MD/SN	1026	871	335
BRITTON	*EMMANUEL* office@emmanuelontheridge.com www.emmanuelontheridge.com	1859	9950 RIDGE HWY	49229	MI	Peter J Burch	(517)451-8148	WS 1030 SS 9 BC 9	ED/HC/ MD/SN	157	135	55
BRONSON	*ST PAUL*		See Coldwater MI									
BROOKLYN	*ST MARK* info@stmarksih.org www.stmarksirishhills.org	1952	11151 US HIGHWAY 12	49230	MI	Bryan K Schindel Bryan S Varblow	(517)467-7565	WS 10 SS 9	ED/HC/MD	116	104	49
	TABLE TALK MEN'S GROUP Satellite Site of St Mark Brooklyn MI	2023	211 Chicago St.	49230								
BUCHANAN	*ST PAUL* buchsmp@gmail.com www.stpaulbuch.org	1933	212 W FRONT ST	49107	MI	Daniel S Barz	(269)695-9061	WS 930 BC 8	ED/HC/MD	76	63	26
BURR OAK	*ST JOHN* st.johnsburroak@juno.com www.stjohnsburroak.charterinternet.com	1863	218 W Main St PO BOX 72	49030	MI	Kurt P Kuhlmann	(269)489-5539	WS 8 1045 SS 915 BC 915	ED/HC/MD	137	120	49
BURTON	*PILGRIM* office@pilgrimburton.com pilgrimburton.com	1968	3222 S GENESEE RD	48519	MI	Mark T Matheny	(810)744-1188	WS 1030 SS BC 915	HC	138	121	50
BYRON CENTER	*EPIPHANY*		See Dorr MI									
CADILLAC	*EMMANUEL* office@emmanuelcadillac.org www.emmanuelcadillac.org	1884	11198 E M-55 11198 E M 55	49601	MI	Brennan A Woell	(231)775-3261 (231)775-2754	WS 830 11 SS 945 BC 945	EC/ED/HC/ MD/SN	332	260	154
CALEDONIA	*ST PAUL* officestaff@stpaulcaledonia.org www.stpaulcaledonia.org	1869	8436 KRAFT AVE SE	49316	MI	David L Miller III	(616)891-8688 (616)891-0598	WS 830 11 BC 945	EC/ED/HC/ MD/SN	408	408	138
CANADIAN LAKES	*CHAPEL LAKES*		See Mecosta MI									
CANNONSBURG	*ST PETER*		See Rockford MI									
CANNONSBURG TOWNSHIP	*ST PETER*		See Rockford MI									
CANTON	*FAITH*		See Ypsilanti MI									
	GRACE stevenewt10@gmail.com	2004	46001 WARREN RD	48187	MI	Steven M Newton	(734)414-7422 (734)414-7422	WS 845 BC 8	HC	30	30	22
	OPEN ARMS		See Belleville MI									
	RISEN CHRIST		See Plymouth MI									
CAPAC	*FAMILY OF CHRIST*		See Imlay City MI									
CARO	*ST PAUL* church@stpaulcaro.org stpaulcaro.org	1915	503 S STATE ST	48723	MI	Richard L Boshoven	(989)673-4214 (989)673-5518	WS 830 11 SS 945 BC 945	ED/HC/ MD/SN	604	499	154
CARROLLTON	*MESSIAH*		See Saginaw MI									
CARSON CITY	*CALVARY* calvarylutheran.mi@gmail.com www.calvarylutheranmi.org	1952	509 W Elm St PO BOX 703	48811	MI	Thomas C Messer	(989)584-6068	WS 9	ED/HC			
CASCADE TOWNSHIP	*ST MATTHEW*		See Grand Rapids MI									
CASEVILLE	*GOOD SHEPHERD*		See Pigeon MI									
CASS CITY	*GOOD SHEPHERD* goodshepherdcasscity1@gmail.com goodshepherdcasscity.com	1945	6820 Main St PO BOX 164	48726	MI	George S Bagnall	(989)872-2770	WS 930 SS 11 BC 11	ED/HC/ MD/SN	355	281	88
CASSOPOLIS	*CASS CO MEDICAL CARE FACILITY* Satellite Site of St Paul Cassopolis MI	2011	23770 Hospital St	49031								

*Indicates a new church start. A new church start is an intentionally organized gathering which comes together on a regular basis for the purpose of worship and/or Bible study and is intended to grow into a member LCMS congregation. WS =Worship Service; SS = Sunday School; BC =Bible Class; EC = Early Childhood; EL = Elementary School; HS = High School; ED =Education Ministry; HC =Human Care Ministry; SN = Special Needs Ministry; MD = Media Ministry (PC)=Partner Church Pastor. See Page 53 for the Table of Abbreviations for key to additional abbreviations

CITY	CONGREGATION EMAIL WEBSITE	YEAR EST	LOCATION MAILING ADDRESS	ZIP CODE(S)	DIST.	PASTOR(S)	PHONE FAX	WS SS BC	SCHOOLS/ MINISTRIES	STATISTIC Bapt	Conf	Avg Attend
CASSOPOLIS	*ST PAUL* office@stpaulcass.org stpaulcass.org	1951	305 W State St PO BOX 382	49031	MI	Paul M Doellinger	(269)445-3950	WS 9 10 SS 1030 BC 1030	EC/ED/HC/ MD/SN	131	100	74
CEDAR	*ST PAUL*		See Good Harbor MI									
CEDAR SPRINGS	*ST PETER*		See Rockford MI									
CENTREVILLE	*ST PAUL* churchsp@outlook.com	1878	585 W BURR OAK ST	49032	MI	Philip R Rittner II	(269)467-4355	WS 10	ED/HC/MD	62	62	38
CHARLEVOIX	*BETHANY* bethanycharlevoix@sbcglobal.net www.bethanycharlevoix.com	1947	11906 US-31 North 11906 US HIGHWAY 31 N	49720	MI		(231)547-9446	WS 4	ED/HC/ MD/SN	33	33	13
CHARLOTTE	*FIRST* flcchurchoffice@gmail.com firstlutherancharlotte.org	1942	550 E SHEPHERD ST	48813	MI	Sean M Esterline Mark A Gawura Daniel R Longden	(517)543-4360 (517)543-9836	WS 830 1115 SS 10 BC 10	EC/ED/HC/ MD/SN	327	252	112
CHATHAM	*SION* sionlutheran@tds.net	1901	N5177 Rock River St Hwy M94 PO BOX 131	49816	NW		(906)439-5222	WS 1030 SS 915 BC 915	ED/HC/SN	435	412	85
CHEBOYGAN	*ST JOHN* SJLC49721@gmail.com stjohncheboygan.org	1898	8757 N STRAITS HWY	49721	MI	Michael W Schaedig	(231)627-5149	WS 830 11 SS 1045 BC 1045	ED/SN	167	157	85
CHELSEA	*OUR SAVIOR* pastor.pezzica@oursaviorchelsea.com www.oursaviorchelsea.com	1969	1515 S MAIN ST	48118	MI	Daniel W Pezzica	(734)475-1404	WS 815 1030 SS 915 BC 915	ED/HC/MD	198	168	98
	ST THOMAS		See Ann Arbor MI									
CHESANING	*CHESANING LUTHERAN MISSION* Satellite Site of Nativity Saint Charles MI	2018	9381 Volkmer Rd	48616								
CHESTERFIELD	*GOOD SHEPHERD* revgoodshepherd@yahoo.com	1968	31100 23 MILE RD	48047	MI	Timothy D Storck	(586)949-9440	WS 915 BC 1030	HS/ED/ HC/MD	71	61	35
CHESTERFIELD TOWNSHIP	*ST JOHN*		See Ray MI									
CHINA	*IMMANUEL*		See Saint Clair MI									
CLARE	*PRINCE PEACE* claremipeace@gmail.com	1965	10333 S CLARE AVE	48617	MI		(989)386-2687	WS 10 BC 845	ED/HC/SN	78	48	25
CLARKSTON	*GOOD SHEPHERD*		See Lake Orion MI									
	ST TRINITY office@sainttrinitylutheran.com www.sainttrinitylutheran.com	1885	7925 SASHABAW RD	48348	MI	Paul J Undlin Michael D DeVries	(248)625-4644	WS 930 SS 1045	EC/ED/HC/ MD/SN	331	296	128
CLAY TOWNSHIP	*LIVING FAITH*		See Marine City MI									
CLINTON	*ST MARK*		See Brooklyn MI									
CLINTON COUNTY	*ST JOHN'S*		See Saint Johns MI									
CLINTON TOWNSHIP	*ALL NATIONS* church_allnations@yahoo.com www.allnationslutheranchurch.org/	1996	17345 15 MILE ROAD	48035	MI	Khurram M Khan Farrukh M Khan	(586)636-5688	WS 12 SS 12 BC 10 12	ED/HC	94	89	55
	CROSS POINT khurram@pablo.org crosspointchurchmi.com	2021	17345 FIFTEEN MILE RD	48035	MI		(586)477-0234			20	20	14
	ST LUKE church@stlukemi.org www.stlukemi.org	1953	21400 S NUNNELEY RD CLINTON TWP	48035	MI	Roderick D Schultz	(586)791-1150 (586)791-1880	WS 930 BC 1045	HS/ED/MD	481	391	75
	TRINITY church@trinityct.org www.trinityct.org	1885	38900 HARPER AVE CLINTON TWP	48036	MI	Benjamin R Burge Jeremy R Ashley	(586)463-2921 (586)463-2389	WS 9 11	EC/EL/HS/ ED/HC/ MD/SN	1904	1542	565
	TRINITY		See Clinton Township MI									
CLIO	*MESSIAH* office@messiahclio.org www.messiahclio.org	1961	520 Butler St PO BOX 10	48420	MI	Erik K Cloeter	(810)686-0740 (810)686-4299	WS 8 930 11 SS 930	HS/ED/ HC/MD/ SN	1813	1485	302
COLDWATER	*ST PAUL* churchoffice@stpaulcoldwater.com www.stpaulcoldwater.com	1860	95 W STATE ST	49036	MI	Aaron B Chittick	(517)278-8061	WS 9 1130 SS 1030 BC 1030	EC/ED/HC/ MD/SN	234	183	75
COLOMA	*SALEM* salem_lcms@comcast.net salemcoloma.org	1919	275 MARVIN ST	49038	MI	Alex W Hoffmeyer	(269)468-6567	WS 9 SS 1015 BC 1015	EC/ED/HC/ MD/SN	245	224	78
COLON	*ST PAUL* www.stpaulscolon.com	1892	484 S BURR OAK RD	49040	MI		(269)432-3807	WS 9 BC 8	ED/HC/ MD/SN	37	37	19
COMMERCE TOWNSHIP	*OUR SAVIOR DF*		See Beverly Hills MI									
COMSTOCK PARK	*ST PETER*		See Rockford MI									
CONKLIN	*TRINITY* office@tlc-conklin.org www.tlc-conklin.org	1865	1379 HARDING ST	49403	MI	Timothy J Brand	(616)899-2167	WS 930 SS 1045 BC 1045	EL/ED/HC/ MD/SN	532	431	125
CONSTANTINE	*ST PAUL*		See Centreville MI									
COOPERSVILLE	*GRACE* secretary@gracecoopersville.org www.gracecoopersville.org	1991	300 CLEVELAND ST E	49404	MI	Joel F Hoyer	(616)837-7831	WS 9 SS 1030	ED/HC/MD	267	249	104
	LAKESHORE		See Spring Lake MI									
	TRINITY		See Conklin MI									
COTTRELLVILLE	*LIVING FAITH*		See Marine City MI									
COURTLAND TOWNSHIP	*ST PETER*		See Rockford MI									
COVINGTON	*TRINITY* tlc1919@outlook.com	1910	12677 Hwy M-28 PO BOX 140	49919	NW	Corey J Harman	(906)355-2534	WS 9 SS 10	ED/HC/SN	226	212	31
CURTIS	*BETHLEHEM*		See Engadine MI									
	GRACE		See Germfask MI									

*Indicates a new church start. A new church start is an intentionally organized gathering which comes together on a regular basis for the purpose of worship and/or Bible study and is intended to grow into a member LCMS congregation. WS =Worship Service; SS = Sunday School; BC =Bible Class; EC = Early Childhood; EL = Elementary School; HS = High School; ED =Education Ministry; HC =Human Care Ministry; SN = Special Needs Ministry; MD = Media Ministry (PC)=Partner Church Pastor. See Page 53 for the Table of Abbreviations for key to additional abbreviations

CONGREGATIONS

CITY	CONGREGATION EMAIL WEBSITE	YEAR EST	LOCATION MAILING ADDRESS	ZIP CODE(S)	DIST.	PASTOR(S)	PHONE FAX	WS SS BC	SCHOOLS/ MINISTRIES	STATISTIC Bapt	Conf	Avg Attend
DAVISON	*TRINITY* office@trinitydavison.org www.trinitydavison.org	1941	706 W FLINT ST	48423	MI	Todd I Frusti Robert G Geisler	(810)658-3000 (810)653-4155	WS 10 SS 11 BC 9		514	401	101
DE TOUR VILLAGE	*REDEEMER*	1988	210 Superior St PO BOX 62 DE TOUR VLG	49725	MI			WS 830	ED	14	14	9
DEARBORN	*EMMANUEL* emmanuelchurchoffice@gmail.com www.emmanueldearborn.org	1895	800 S MILITARY ST	48124	MI	Tyler A Walworth Joel R Baseley Paul A Wolff	(313)565-4002	WS 915 SS 11 BC 11	EL/HS/ ED/SN	302	246	140
	GUARDIAN church@guardianlutheran.org www.guardianlutheranchurch.org	1947	24544 CHERRY HILL ST	48124	MI	Daniel W Ramthun	(313)274-1414 (313)274-2076	WS 8 11 SS 930 BC 930	EL/HS/ED/ HC/MD	951	744	315
	SALEM NATIONAL		See Westland MI									
DEARBORN HEIGHTS	*EMMANUEL*		See Dearborn MI									
	IMMANUEL info@immanuellutheranchurch.org www.immanuellutheranchurch.org	1865	27035 ANN ARBOR TRL DEAR- BORN HTS	48127	MI	Daniel P Murray	(313)278-5755	WS 11	ED	28	27	20
DECKERVILLE	*ST JOHN*		See Palms MI									
DETROIT	*BETHANY* bethanydetroitlcms@bethanydetroit.org bethanydetroit.org	1889	11475 E OUTER DR	48224	MI		(313)885-7721 (313)885-7722	WS 930 SS 1045	ED/HC/ MD/SN	98	82	34
	EAST BETHLEHEM asaphjames@yahoo.com www.ebethlehem.org	1873	3510 E OUTER DR	48234	MI	Asaph A James	(313)892-2670 (313)892-2670	WS 10 SS 230	ED/HC/MD	75	47	39
	EMMANUEL		See Dearborn MI									
	EVERGREEN william20418@yahoo.com	1945	8680 EVERGREEN AVE	48228	MI	William F Danowski	(313)584-0450 (313)584-2029	WS 10 SS 10 BC 9	EL			
	FAMILY OF GOD jim@fogdetroit.com www.fogdetroit.com		8941 West Vernor 7354 WHITTAKER ST	48209	MI	James M Hill Timothy J LeClair Nicholas C Gapski Alexander R Ogden	(586)722-3996	WS 3	ED/HC/MD	100	54	40
	GRACE		See Redford Township MI									
	HIST TRINITY church@historictrinity.org www.historictrinity.org	1850	1345 GRATIOT AVE	48207	MI	Darryl L Andrzejewski	(313)567-3100	WS 9 1030 SS 9 BC 9	EL/HS/ED/ HC/MD	1960	1024	370
	MOUNT CALVARY mtcalvarylutheranoffice@gmail.com www.mtcalvarydetroit.org	1922	17100 CHALMERS ST	48205	MI		(313)527-3366	WS 9	ED/HC/ MD/SN	143	116	24
	NAZARETH	1913	4321 VICKSBURG ST	48204	MI		(313)897-8622	WS 1230	ED/HC			
	OUTER DR FAITH odflc1@yahoo.com	1936	17500 JAMES COUZENS HWY	48235	MI	Eddie Morales	(313)341-4095 (313)341-2926	WS 830 11 BC 9	ED/HC/MD	105	105	60
	PAN DE VIDA pandevidadetroit.org	1887	7354 Whittaker St 17500 JAMES COUZENS FWY	48209 48235	MI		(313)841-2377 (313)887-4164		ED/HC	68	54	60
	PEACE peacedetroit@gmail.com	1927	15700 E WARREN AVE	48224	MI		(313)882-0254 (313)882-4570	WS 10 SS 1030 BC 930	ED/HC/MD	124	100	20
	ST JOHN eric7935@gmail.com	1879	4950 OAKMAN BLVD	48204	MI	Richard E Robinson	(313)933-9360 (313)933-5842	WS 11 SS 10 BC 10	ED/HC/MD	65	65	65
	ST MATTHEW		See Westland MI									
	ST PHILIP splc84233@yahoo.com	1933	2884 E GRAND BLVD	48202	MI		(313)872-1010 (313)872-2010	WS 11 SS 945	ED/HC/ MD/SN	146	140	60
	ST STEPHEN	1890	8736 Chamberlain St 1235 LAWNDALE ST	48209	MI	James M Hill Nicholas C Gapski	(313)841-7940 (313)841-7963	WS 1030 BC 915	ED/HC/MD			
	ZION Church@ZionDetroit.org www.ZionDetroit.org	1882	4305 MILITARY	48210	EN	Mark P Braden	(313)894-7450 (313)894-7871	WS 10 SS 1130 BC 1130	HS	83	72	32
DEWITT	*HOPE* dewitthopelutheran@yahoo.com www.hopelutherandewitt.com/	1968	1180 W HERBISON RD	48820	MI	Dr Edward A Sikora Sr	(517)669-3930 (517)669-1580	WS 815 1045 SS 930 BC 11	EL/ED/HC/ MD/SN	236	205	100
DEXTER	*PEACE*		See Ann Arbor MI									
	ST THOMAS		See Ann Arbor MI									
DORR	*EPIPHANY* office@epiphanydorr.org www.epiphanydorr.org	1994	4219 Park Ln PO BOX 245	49323	EN	Ryan D Beffrey	(616)681-0791	WS 915 SS 11 BC 11	ED/HC/ MD/SN	132	113	54
DRUMMOND ISLAND	*DRUMMOND ISLAND*	1986	29515 E Channel Rd PO BOX 269 DRUMMOND IS	49726	MI	Dennis L Dufon	(906)493-5982 (906)493-5982	WS 1030	ED/HC/MD	95	67	35
DRYDEN	*HOLY REDEEMER* holyredlc@yahoo.com holyred.org	1971	4538 DRYDEN RD	48428	MI	Evan C Veen	(810)796-3951 (810)796-4157	WS 930 BC 8 11	EC/ED/ HC/MD	228	157	89
EAGLE	*ST ANDREW*		See Portland MI									
EAST CHINA	*IMMANUEL*		See Saint Clair MI									
EAST CHINA TOWNSHIP	*LIVING FAITH*		See Marine City MI									
EAST LANSING	*ASCENSION* office@ascensioneastlansing.org www.ascensioneastlansing.org	1956	2780 HASLETT RD	48823	MI	Sean Q McCoy	(517)337-9703 (517)337-4840	WS 10 SS 845	EL/ED/MD	150	119	85
	MARTIN LUTHER CHAPEL mlc@martinlutherchapel.org www.martinlutherchapel.org	1952	444 ABBOT RD	48823	EN	Curtis E Dwyer James B Robinson	(517)332-0778	WS 1030 7 BC 930	ED/HC/MD	322	274	85
EASTPOINTE	*BETHANY*		See Detroit MI									
	SAINT PETERS www.stpeterslutheranchurch.net	1845	23000 GRATIOT AVE	48021	MI	Douglas M Adams	(586)777-6300 (586)771-2524	WS 8 1030 SS 930 BC 915	EL/HS/ ED/HC/ MD/SN	955	725	226
	ST THOMAS churchoffice@stl-eastpointe.org www.stl-eastpointe.org	1876	23801 KELLY RD	48021	MI	Dietrick A Gladden Richard A VanBriggle	(586)772-3370 (586)772-6265	WS 930 SS 1045 BC 1045	HS/ED/ HC/MD	415	331	95

*Indicates a new church start. A new church start is an intentionally organized gathering which comes together on a regular basis for the purpose of worship and/or Bible study and is intended to grow into a member LCMS congregation. WS =Worship Service; SS = Sunday School; BC =Bible Class; EC = Early Childhood; EL = Elementary School; HS = High School; ED =Education Ministry; HC =Human Care Ministry; SN = Special Needs Ministry; MD = Media Ministry (PC)=Partner Church Pastor. See Page 53 for the Table of Abbreviations for key to additional abbreviations

CITY	CONGREGATION EMAIL WEBSITE	YEAR EST	LOCATION MAILING ADDRESS	ZIP CODE(S)	DIST.	PASTOR(S)	PHONE FAX	WS SS BC	SCHOOLS/ MINISTRIES	STATISTIC Bapt	 Conf	 Avg Attend
EATON RAPIDS	*ST MATTHEW*		See Holt MI									
EDWARDSBURG	*TRINITY*		See Elkhart IN									
ELK RAPIDS	*GRACE* info@ergracelcms.org ergracelcms.org	1949	16194 WANIGAN DR	49629	MI	James C Redmann	(231)264-5312 (231)264-5312	WS 10	ED/HC/ MD/SN	99	78	26
ENGADINE	*BETHLEHEM* bethlehemlcmsengadine@gmail.com www.facebook.com/ bethlehemengadine	1903	N8696 M-117	49827	MI	Kyle I Kuehl		WS 1145	ED/HC/SN	79	76	25
ESCANABA	*OUR SAVIOR* oursavior87@gmail.com oursavioresky.org	1987	2401 N LINCOLN RD	49829	NW	Benjamin H Ramthun	(906)789-9350	WS 8 1030 SS 915 BC 915	ED/HC/ MD/SN	192	142	97
	SION		See Chatham MI									
ESSEXVILLE	*PILGRIM* pilgrimessexville@gmail.com	1942	1705 NEBOBISH AVE	48732	MI	Erwin M Hutter	(989)893-7224 (989)893-7263	WS 1030 BC 9	ED/HC/ MD/SN	150	132	55
FAIR HAVEN	*ST PETER* secretary@stpeterfairhaven.org www.stpeterfairhaven.org	1880	6745 PALMS RD	48023	MI	Steven R Hoerr	(810)765-8161	WS 930 SS 930 BC 830	ED/HC/ MD/SN	125	105	70
FAIRGROVE	*GRACE* gracefairgrove@airadvantage.net www.gracefairgrove.org	1945	1809 S MAIN ST	48733	MI	Joshua T Haller	(989)693-6322	WS 915 SS 1045 BC 1045	MD	93	64	79
FARMINGTON HILLS	*OUR SAVIOR DF*		See Beverly Hills MI									
	PRINCE PEACE office@princeofpeacefhills.org www.princeofpeacefhills.org	1958	28000 NEW MARKET RD FARM- INGTN HLS	48334	MI	Alexander J Hinojosa	(248)553-3380	WS 930 SS 815 BC 815	ED/HC/ MD/SN	101	87	44
	SHADOW OF THE CROSS sotclutheran.officemanager@gmail.com shadowofthecrosslc.org	2019	20805 MIDDLEBELT RD	48336	MI	Brian C Dupre	(248)474-0675	WS 945 145 SS 10 BC 11	ED/HC/ MD/SN	317	242	80
FENTON	*TRINITY FENTON* office@tlcfenton.org www.trinityfenton.com	1932	1025 MAIN ST	48430	MI	Peter C Ahlersmeyer	(810)629-7861	WS 830 11 SS 945 BC 945	HC	462	345	247
FERRYSBURG	*LAKESHORE*		See Spring Lake MI									
FLAT ROCK	*COMMUNITY* office@clcflatrock.com www.clcflatrock.com	1979	23984 GIBRALTAR RD	48134	MI		(734)782-0563 (734)782-1541	WS 9 SS 1015 BC 1015	EC/ED/ HC/MD	261	115	125
FLINT	*CHRIST KING*	1959	402 S Ballenger Hwy 402 S. BALLENGER HWY.	48532	MI	Brant A Engel Dean G Dumbrille Thomas W Dunseth	(810)239-6200	WS 10	SN	36	34	14
	*FRANKLIN AVENUE** shannon@franklinavemission.org www.franklinavemission.org		2210 N FRANKLIN AVE	48506	MI		(810)285-9598		ED/HC/MD	9	7	9
	LAMB OF GOD lambofgodflint@gmail.com www.lambofgodlutheranflint.com		2051 W MAPLE AVE	48507	MI	Mark E Pretznow	(810)234-2423 (810)234-5699	WS 10 SS 9 BC 9	ED/HC/ MD/SN	194	167	103
	NEWLIFE COMMUNITY		See Swartz Creek MI									
	OUR SAVIOR oslflint@gmail.com www.oslflint.org	1926	6901 N SAGINAW ST	48505	MI		(810)789-1361	WS 1030 SS 1130 BC 1130	ED/HC/SN	143	112	28
	ST MARK office@stmarkflint.org www.stmarkflint.com	1957	5073 DALY BLVD	48506	MI	Jeffrey D Frechette Sr Morgan J Garrett	(810)736-6680	WS 8 1045 SS 1045 BC 1045	ED/HC/MD	637	506	113
	ST PAUL www.stpaulflint.com	1910	402 S BALLENGER HWY	48532	MI	Brant A Engel Dean G Dumbrille Thomas W Dunseth	(810)239-6200 (810)239-5466	WS 10 SS 9	EL/ED/HC/ MD/SN	373	366	107
	UNITED IN CHRIST churchoffice@uiclutheran.org www.uiclutheran.org	1931	6330 Corunna Rd G-6330 CORUNNA RD	48532	MI		(810)732-3730	WS 1030 SS 9 BC 9	ED/MD/SN	125	105	27
FLUSHING	*HOLY CROSS* secretary@holycrosslutheran.com www.holycrosslutheran.com	1956	1209 COUTANT ST	48433	MI	Tyge C Zucker	(810)659-5926 (810)496-2768	WS 9 1030 1115 SS 10	ED/HC/ MD/SN	326	270	110
FORESTVILLE	*ST JOHN*		See Palms MI									
	TRINITY hchales@hotmail.com	1882	5034 Bay City Forestville Rd 5034 E BAY CITY FORESTVILLE RD MINDEN CITY	48434 48456	MI	Henry J Hales	(989)864-3745	WS 1030		59	46	38
	TRINITY LUTHERAN CHURCH Satellite Site of St John Palms MI	2021	5034 E. Bay City Forestville Rd.	48456				WS 9				
FOWLER	*ST PAUL* revpmclark@gmail.com	1878	329 N SORRELL ST	48835	MI	Paul M Clark Lance D Klamer	(517)420-4826	WS 9 SS 1030 BC 1030	ED/HC/ MD/SN	116	91	70
FRANKENLUST TOWNSHIP	*ST PAUL*		See Bay City MI									
FRANKENMUTH	*IMMANUEL*		See Saginaw MI									
	ST LORENZ www.stlorenz.org	1845	1030 W Tuscola St 850 W GENESEE	48734	MI	Bradley B Hubbard Joel S Eden Joel C Kaiser	(989)652-6141 (989)652-9071	WS 8 930 1045 SS 930 BC 930	EL/ED/HC/ MD/SN	5264	4181	1205
FRASER	*ST JOHN* churchinfo@stjohnfraser.org www.stjohnfraser.org	1864	16339-14 MILE RD	48026	MI	Bradley A Smith Joel D Haak	(586)293-0333 (586)293-5442	WS 8 11 SS 930 BC 930	EL/HS/ ED/HC/ MD/SN	1329	1037	653
FREELAND	*GRACE*		See Auburn MI									
	ST JOHN		See Bay City MI									
	ST MARK		See Saginaw MI									
FREMONT	*REDEEMER* redeemerfremont@comcast.net	1954	680 E MAIN ST	49412	MI	Dr Mark A Bowditch Dr K F Graves	(231)924-2707	WS 9 SS 1015 BC 1015		89	72	42
FRUITPORT	*LAKESHORE*		See Spring Lake MI									

*Indicates a new church start. A new church start is an intentionally organized gathering which comes together on a regular basis for the purpose of worship and/or Bible study and is intended to grow into a member LCMS congregation. WS =Worship Service; SS = Sunday School; BC =Bible Class; EC = Early Childhood; EL = Elementary School; HS = High School; ED =Education Ministry; HC =Human Care Ministry; SN = Special Needs Ministry; MD = Media Ministry (PC)=Partner Church Pastor. See Page 53 for the Table of Abbreviations for key to additional abbreviations

CONGREGATIONS

CITY	CONGREGATION EMAIL WEBSITE	YEAR EST	LOCATION MAILING ADDRESS	ZIP CODE(S)	DIST.	PASTOR(S)	PHONE FAX	WS SS BC	SCHOOLS/ MINISTRIES	STATISTIC Bapt	 Conf	 Avg Attend
GAYLORD	*TRINITY* trinitygaylord-secretary@outlook.com trinitymthope.360unite.com/home	1946	1354 S OTSEGO AVE	49735	MI	Kurt C Klingbeil	(989)732-4816 (989)732-2346	WS 9 SS 1015 BC 1030	ED/HC/MD	174	152	88
GERMFASK	*GRACE* gracegermfasklcms@gmail.com www.facebook.com/gracegermfask	1930	7920 Pine St PO BOX 69 CURTIS	49836 49820	MI	Kyle I Kuehl	(906)586-6900	WS 8 BC 945	ED/HC/MD	81	71	26
GIRARD	*ST PAUL*		See Coldwater MI									
GLADWIN	*OUR SAVIOR* oursaviorgladwin@gmail.com www.oursaviorgladwin.com	1902	331 Clendening Road 331 CLENDENING RD P.O. BOX 527	48624	MI	Adam R Flanick	(989)426-9689	WS 10	ED/HC/ MD/SN	240	216	160
GLEN ARBOR	*BETHLEHEM* secretary@bethlehemglenarbor.com www.bethlehemglenarbor.com	1932	6012 S Lake St PO BOX 353	49636	MI	James L Nihiser	(231)334-4180 (231)334-4180	WS 930 SS 1045 BC 1045	ED/HC/ MD/SN	79	79	28
GLENDORA	*TRINITY* telcglendora@gmail.com www.tlcglendora.org	1919	1733 W GLENDORA RD BUCHANAN	49107	MI	Jonathan A Liebich	(269)422-2554 (269)422-2009	WS 10 SS 845 BC 845	ED/HC/MD	506	393	136
GLENNIE	*OUR SAVIOR*	1955	3639 S M-65 3639 STATE RD	48737	MI	Glen W Bromm	(989)735-2710	WS 9	ED/HC	28	24	15
GOBLES	*TRINITY*		See Paw Paw MI									
GOOD HARBOR	*ST PAUL* stpaulsgoodharbor.com	1877	2943 SW Manitou Trl 2943 S MANITOU TRL CEDAR	49621	MI	Mark C Reinsch	(231)228-6888	WS 10 SS 1130 BC 1130		52	49	34
GOODELLS	*HOPE* hope@hopegoodells-lcms.org www.hopegoodells-lcms.org	1965	2792 Goodells Rd PO BOX 158	48027	MI		(810)325-1169	WS 1030	MD			
GOODRICH	*CHRIST* christ@christluth.org www.christluth.org	1958	5245 HADLEY RD	48438	MI	Kelly D Todd	(810)255-1185	WS 10 BC 9	ED/MD	36	32	31
GOULD CITY	*BETHLEHEM*		See Engadine MI									
GRAND BLANC	*FAITH* churchoffice@faithgb.org www.faithgb.org	1956	12534 HOLLY RD	48439	MI	Jeffrey E Heimsoth Robert G Scott	(810)694-9351 (810)694-3949	WS 815 1045 SS 930 BC 930	EC/EL/ED/ HC/MD	1815	1176	375
	TRINITY FENTON		See Fenton MI									
GRAND HAVEN	*ST JOHN* office@stjohnsgrandhaven.com www.stjohnsgrandhaven.com	1865	527 TAYLOR AVE	49417	MI	Aaron H Vergin	(616)842-4510	WS 815 1030 SS 930 BC 930	EL/ED/HC/ MD/SN	675	525	240
	LAKESHORE		See Spring Lake MI									
GRAND MARAIS	*GRACE*		See Germfask MI									
GRAND RAPIDS	*EPIPHANY*		See Dorr MI									
	HOPE cnuttelman@hopegrandrapids.org www.hopegrandrapids.org	1914	100 PACKARD AVE SE	49503	EN	Christopher K Nuttelman	(616)459-2941	WS 10 SS 1215 BC 1215	ED	155	90	29
	IMMANUEL office@immanuelgr.org www.immanuelgr.org	1856	2 MICHIGAN ST NE	49503	MI	Craig L Bickel Thomas M Gustafson	(616)454-3655 (616)454-3427	WS 830 11 SS 950 BC 950	EL/HS/ ED/HC/ MD/SN	646	498	270
	MESSIAH messiahgr@messiahgr.org www.messiahgr.org	1964	2727 5 MILE RD NE	49525	MI	Eric S Black	(616)363-2553 (616)363-7843	WS 10 SS 9 BC 9	EC/ED/HC/ MD/SN	311	248	93
	OUR SAVIOR churchsecretary@oursavior-gr.org www.oursavior-gr.org	1961	2900 BURTON ST SE	49546	MI	Jeremy M Swem David C Fleming	(616)949-0710 (616)975-7840	WS 8 11 SS 940 BC 940	EL/HS/ED	627	281	252
	SAINT JAMES office@stjamesgr.com stjamesgr.com	1929	2040 OAKWOOD AVE NE	49505	MI	Dr Glenn E Schaeffer	(616)363-7718	WS 930 BC 11	EL/ED/HC/ MD/SN	152	133	75
	ST MARK		See Kentwood MI									
	ST MATTHEW info@stmatthewgr.com www.stmatthewgr.com	1970	5125 CASCADE RD SE	49546	MI	Jonathan C Meyer Maxx J Fisher	(616)942-9091	WS 830 1045 SS 945 BC 945	ED/HC/ MD/SN	814	611	362
	THE VINE pastorjim@onthevinechurch.com onthevinechurch.com		3950 LEONARD ST NW	49534	MI	James F Richter	(616)202-1540	WS 10	ED/MD	71	34	61
	TRINITY		See Conklin MI									
GRANDVILLE	*BETHEL* officebethel@att.net www.bethelingrandville.com	1954	3655 WILSON AVE SW	49418	MI	Robert A Gerke	(616)534-3364	WS 10 BC 9	ED/MD	53	53	41
GRATTAN	*ST PETER*		See Rockford MI									
GRAWN	*REDEEMER INTERLOCHEN* redeemer@redeemerofinterlochen.com www.redeemerofinterlochen.com	1973	1896 Rogers Rd PO BOX 184 INTERLOCHEN	49637 49643	MI	Jason C Bauer	(231)276-6372 (231)276-5141	WS 8 1030 SS 930 BC 930	ED/HC/MD	275	205	120
GRAYLING	*MOUNT HOPE* mthopelcms@gmail.com	1950	905 N I 75 BUSINESS LOOP	49738	MI	Kurt C Klingbeil	(989)348-5921 (989)348-0166	WS 11 BC 10 12	ED/HC/MD	114	102	56
GREENVILLE	*MOUNT CALVARY* mclc908@sbcglobal.net www.mclc908.org	1951	908 W OAK ST	48838	MI	Daniel J Lepley Robert B Appold	(616)754-4886 (616)754-4886	WS 930 SS 11 BC 11	EC/ED/ HC/MD	167	149	89
GROSSE POINTE	*BETHANY*		See Detroit MI									
GROSSE POINTE WOODS	*CHRIST KING* admin@christthekinggp.org www.christthekinggp.org	1940	20338 MACK AVE GROSSE PT WDS	48236	EN	Solomon K Spangler	(313)884-5090	WS 815 1045 SS 930 BC 830	EC/ED/MD	227	195	86
GULLIVER	*GRACE*		See Germfask MI									
HALE	*SAINT PAUL* stphalesecretary@gmail.com stplutheranhale.com	1935	407 S Washington St PO BOX 307	48739	MI	Dean R Muhle	(989)728-4082	WS 1015 SS 9 BC 9	ED/HC/ MD/SN	418	291	50
HAMBURG	*ST PAUL HAMBURG*		See Whitmore Lake MI									
HAMILTON	*CHRIST OUR SAVIOR*		See Holland MI									

*Indicates a new church start. A new church start is an intentionally organized gathering which comes together on a regular basis for the purpose of worship and/or Bible study and is intended to grow into a member LCMS congregation. WS =Worship Service; SS = Sunday School; BC =Bible Class; EC = Early Childhood; EL = Elementary School; HS = High School; ED =Education Ministry; HC =Human Care Ministry; SN = Special Needs Ministry; MD = Media Ministry (PC)=Partner Church Pastor. See Page 53 for the Table of Abbreviations for key to additional abbreviations

CONGREGATIONS

CITY	CONGREGATION EMAIL WEBSITE	YEAR EST	LOCATION MAILING ADDRESS	ZIP CODE(S)	DIST.	PASTOR(S)	PHONE FAX	WS SS BC	SCHOOLS/ MINISTRIES	STATISTIC Bapt	Conf	Avg Attend
HANCOCK	*SS PETER AND PAUL*		See Houghton MI									
HARBOR BEACH	*ZION* pastor@zionlcs.com www.zionlcs.com	1881	299 GARDEN ST	48441	MI	Dr Matthew H Durance	(989)479-3615 (989)479-6551	WS 9 BC 1015	EL/ED/HC/ MD/SN	535	375	150
HARPER WOODS	*BETHANY*		See Detroit MI									
HARRISON	*ST LUKE* stlukeharrison@yahoo.com www.stlukeharrison.com	1973	616 S 4th St PO BOX 623	48625	MI	Timothy J Sheridan	(989)539-6312 (989)539-1457	WS 1030 SS 915	ED/HC/SN	144	136	62
HARTFORD	*SALEM*		See Coloma MI									
HARTLAND	*OUR SAVIOR* gshelton@oursaviorhartland.org www.oursaviorhartland.org	1955	13667 W Highland Rd 13667 HIGHLAND RD	48353	EN	Dr Christopher I Thoma Dr Jamison J Hardy	(248)887-4300 (248)887-3596	WS 930 SS 11 BC 11	EL/ED/ MD/SN	711	527	280
	TRINITY FENTON		See Fenton MI									
	WHALEN LAKE SERVICE Satellite Site of Salem National Westland MI	2010	12601 Hibner Rd	48353								
HASLETT	*ASCENSION*		See East Lansing MI									
	ST LUKE pastortsutton@knowingjesus.org www.knowingjesus.org	1986	5589 VAN ATTA RD	48840	MI	Dr August T Sutton Michael S Stainbrook Zerehaimanot Z Yohannes Elamin M Baggor	(517)339-9119 (517)339-5430	WS 830 11 SS 945 BC 945	EC/EL/ ED/HC/ MD/SN	897	733	489
HAWKS	*FAITH*	1873	8201 County Road 451 PO BOX 131	49743	MI	Dr Jack D Ferguson		WS 9 BC 1015	ED/HC			
HEMLOCK	*ST MARK*		See Saginaw MI									
	ST PETER church@stpeterhemlock.org www.stpeterhemlock.org	1880	2461 N RAUCHOLZ RD	48626	MI	Dr William L Morris Michael P Speckhard	(989)642-8188	WS 930 SS 915 BC 915	EL/HS/ ED/HC/ MD/SN	1330	1044	268
	ZION admin@zionhemlock.org www.zionhemlock.org	1895	17927 DICE RD	48626	MI	Larry A Warsinski	(989)642-5909 (989)642-4416	WS 930	HS/ED/ HC/MD/ SN	380	311	63
HERRON	*ST PAUL*		See Hubbard Lake MI									
HIGHLAND	*FAITH* office@faithhighland.com faithhighland.com	1962	3501 E HIGHLAND RD	48356	MI		(248)887-5550 (248)889-8115	WS 830 11 SS 945 BC 945	ED/HC/MD	463	374	95
HILLMAN	*ST JOHN*	1888	22000 COUNTY ROAD 452	49746	MI	Jason L Mandley	(989)742-4400	WS 10 SS 9 BC 9	EC	398	335	86
HILLSDALE	*ST PAUL* officestaff.stpauls@gmail.com www.stpauls-hillsdale.org	1860	2551 W BACON RD	49242	MI	Sean A Willman Andrew R Twietmeyer Dr Korey D Maas	(517)437-2762 (517)439-1328	WS 8 1030 SS 915 BC 915	ED/MD/SN	468	359	289
HOLLAND	*CHRIST OUR SAVIOR* coshlld@sbcglobal.net www.cosholland.net	1992	3151 N 120TH AVE	49424	MI	Russell D Johnson	(616)738-0100	WS 1015 SS 915 BC 915	ED/HC/ MD/SN	111	73	60
	ZION office@zionholland.org www.zionholland.com	1893	77 W 32ND ST	49423	MI	Ryan A Winningham	(616)392-7151 (616)392-7180	WS 830 1030 SS 945	ED/HC/MD	363	313	176
HOLLY	*TRINITY FENTON*		See Fenton MI									
HOLT	*MESSIAH* office@messiahlutheranholt.org www.messiahlutheranholt.org	1978	5740 West Holt Rd 5740 HOLT RD	48842	MI	Mark A Werner	(517)694-1280 (517)694-1492	WS 830 11 SS 9 BC 9	EC/EL/ ED/HC/ MD/SN	289	265	95
	ST MATTHEW smlchurchoffice@gmail.com www.smlministries.net	1964	2418 AURELIUS RD	48842	MI	Dean R Poellet	(517)694-0978 (517)694-6371	WS 1030 SS 9 BC 915	EL/ED/HC/ MD/SN	153	122	65
HOPKINS	*EPIPHANY*		See Dorr MI									
HOUGHTON	*SS PETER AND PAUL* secretary@copperluth.org www.copperluth.org	1867	1010 MADELEINE ST	49931	NW	Aaron R Gehrke Kevin J Bender	(906)482-4750 (906)482-7425	WS 830 11 SS 10 BC 10	EC/ED/HC/ MD/SN	692	484	248
HOUGHTON LAKE	*ST JOHN* office@stjohnhl.com www.stjohnhl.com	1940	2888 W HOUGHTON LAKE DR	48629	MI	Paul G Kruse	(989)366-5164 (989)366-4420	WS 9 SS 10	ED/HC/ MD/SN	297	260	129
HOWARD CITY	*BETHEL* bethellutheranhc@outlook.com www.bethellutheranhc.com/	1961	18645 W Howard City Edmore Rd 18645 HOWARD CITY EDMORE RD	49329	MI	Richard A Townes Jr	(231)937-4921 (231)937-4921	WS 930 SS 11 BC 11	ED/HC	132	120	80
HOWELL	*HEART OF THE SHEP* office@heartoftheshepherd.church heartoftheshepherd.church		228 North Burkhart Rd 228 N BURKHART RD	48843	MI	Samuel V Fink	(517)552-7218 (517)552-5210	WS 1030 BC 9	EC/ED/HC	206	173	122
	IMMANUEL immanuel_lutheran_howell@juno.com	1982	1944 Oak Grove Rd PO BOX 656	48855 48844	EN	Eric C Forss	(517)548-2066	WS 1015 SS 9 BC 9	ED/HC/ MD/SN			
HUBBARD LAKE	*ST PAUL* office.stpaulhl@gmail.com stpaulhubbardlake.org	1894	6891 NICHOLSON HILL RD	49747	MI	Joseph J Llewellyn	(989)727-2496	WS 930 SS 930 BC 11	EC/ED/HC/ MD/SN	330	271	143
HUBBELL	*ST JOHN* stpaulstjohnlcms.org	1893	26847 W 13th PO BOX 6	49934	NW	Bryan G Lundquist	(906)934-8470	WS 830				
HUDSON	*OUR SAVIOUR* www.oslhudson.org	1950	751 N Maple Grove Ave PO BOX 3	49247	MI		(517)448-6271	WS 1015 SS 9 BC 9		84	66	25
HUDSONVILLE	*NEW HOPE* busadmin@nhlchurch.org www.nhlchurch.org	1992	3232 PORT SHELDON ST	49426	MI	Adam P Kosberg	(616)669-2790	WS 1015 SS 9 BC 9	ED/HC/ MD/SN	145	117	81
	ST JOHN		See Jenison MI									
HULBERT	*TRINITY*		See Newberry MI									
HUNTINGTON WOODS	*HUNTINGTON WOODS* office@hwlc.org www.hwlc.org	1945	12935 W 11 MILE RD HUNTINGTN WDS	48070	MI	Mark R Doede	(248)542-3007 (248)542-0709	WS 8 10 BC 9	EC/ED/ HC/SN	282	246	78

*Indicates a new church start. A new church start is an intentionally organized gathering which comes together on a regular basis for the purpose of worship and/or Bible study and is intended to grow into a member LCMS congregation. WS =Worship Service; SS = Sunday School; BC =Bible Class; EC = Early Childhood; EL = Elementary School; HS = High School; ED =Education Ministry; HC =Human Care Ministry; SN = Special Needs Ministry; MD = Media Ministry (PC)=Partner Church Pastor. See Page 53 for the Table of Abbreviations for key to additional abbreviations

CITY	CONGREGATION EMAIL WEBSITE	YEAR EST	LOCATION MAILING ADDRESS	ZIP CODE(S)	DIST.	PASTOR(S)	PHONE FAX	WS SS BC	SCHOOLS/ MINISTRIES	STATISTIC Bapt	Conf	Avg Attend
IMLAY CITY	*FAMILY OF CHRIST* church@lutheranfamilyofchrist.org lutheranfamilyofchrist.org		7191 E IMLAY CITY RD	48444	MI		(810)724-2620 (810)724-2640	WS 1030 SS 1030	ED/HC/ MD/SN	54	54	32
	SERENITY GARDENS Satellite Site of Family of Christ Imlay City MI	2020	600 Maple Vista	48444								
INTERLOCHEN	*REDEEMER INTERLOCHEN*		See Grawn MI									
IONIA	*ST JOHN* office@stjohnionia.org www.stjohnionia.org	1870	617 N JEFFERSON ST	48846	MI		(616)527-1250	WS 830 SS 945 BC 945	ED/HC/ MD/SN	69	69	30
IRON RIVER	*ST PAULS* stpaullcmsironriver@yahoo.com	1904	4221 W US Highway 2 P.O. BOX 499	49935	NW	Charles Sheffler	(906)265-4750	WS 10 SS 9 BC 11	ED/HC/ MD/SN	43	35	29
IRONWOOD	*IMMANUEL*	1946	Little Girls Point 1898 BRACE RD	49938	NW			SS 1030	ED/HC	63	44	18
	TRINITY trinityironwood@yahoo.com	1954	E5104 Margaret St E5104 E MARGARET ST	49938	NW	Dr David K Jacob	(906)932-3022 (906)932-5583	WS 9 BC 1015	EC/ED/HC/ MD/SN	209	187	55
ISHPEMING	*CHRIST KING* ctkishpeming@gmail.com www.ctkishpeming.org	1977	440 STONEVILLE RD	49849	NW	Michael P Fox	(906)485-4432 (906)485-4496	WS 1045 6 SS 10	EC/ED/ HC/SN			
JACKSON	*GRACE*		See Leslie MI									
	REDEEMER office@redeemerjackson.org www.redeemerjackson.org/	1961	3637 SPRING ARBOR RD	49201	MI	Zachary J Holdorf	(517)750-3100 (517)750-4590	WS 8 1030 SS 930 BC 930	HC	348	287	175
	TRINITY holesoa.tlm@gmail.com www.tlmjackson.com	1868	122 W WESLEY ST	49201	MI	J D Riddle	(517)784-3135 (517)784-4344	WS 9 BC 1030	EL/ED/HC/ MD	330	285	120
JENISON	*HOLY CROSS* office@holycrossjenison.org www.holycrossjenison.org	1965	1481 BALDWIN ST	49428	MI	Brian D West Adam J Peck	(616)457-2420	WS 830 11 SS 945 BC 945	ED/HC	1583	1319	355
	ST JOHN stjohnlutheran@outlook.com www.stjohnlutherans.org	1871	9628 48TH AVE	49428	MI		(616)895-4826	WS 10 BC 9	ED/HC	31	14	19
JONESVILLE	*ST PAUL*		See Coldwater MI									
KALAMAZOO	*CAMPUS MINISTRY* Satellite Site of Zion Kalamazoo MI	2002	c/o Western MI Univ Solid Grounds Stud Min	49008				WS 12				
	IMMANUEL ilckalamazoo@gmail.com www.ilckalamazoo.org	1953	3000 W MAIN ST	49006	MI	Joshua Grotelueschen	(269)345-8090 (269)345-4825	WS 10 SS 9	ED/HC/ MD/SN	145	126	75
	TRINITY		See Paw Paw MI									
	ZION zionkazoo.org	1868	2122 BRONSON BLVD	49008	MI	Michael W Saylor Mark T Couch Timothy W Seeber	(269)382-2360	WS 8 1030 SS 915 BC 915	EC/ED/ HC/MD	507	415	208
KALKASKA	*ST PAUL* stpaulkalkaska2470@gmail.com www.stpaulkalkaska.org	1962	2470 BEEBE RD	49646	MI	Thomas P Phillips	(231)258-9258	WS 10 BC 1130	ED	378	299	35
KENTWOOD	*ST MARK* office@saintmarkgr.org www.saintmarkgr.org	1966	1934 52ND ST SE	49508	MI	Andrew P Bartholomew	(616)455-5320 (616)455-8487	WS 10 BC 9	EC/EL/HS/ ED/HC/ MD/SN	274	234	132
KILMANAGH	*ST JOHN* stjohnssec.office@airadv.net	1876	9476 KILMANAGH RD SEBEWAING	48759	MI	Thomas B Garrison	(989)883-3807	WS 10 SS 10	ED/HC/MD	221	157	61
KINCHELOE	*ST PAUL* cbburhop@att.net	1991	16811 S Water Tower Dr PO BOX 5003	49788	MI	Charles B Burhop	(906)635-2940	WS 830	ED/HC/MD	6	6	6
KINDE	*ST PETER*	1873	5098 Dwight St PO BOX 177	48445	MI		(989)553-6357	WS 930	HC	83	69	36
KINDERHOOK	*ST PAUL*		See Coldwater MI									
KINGSFORD	*OUR REDEEMER* secretary@ourredeemerkingsford.org www.ourredeemerkingsford.org	1924	420 W BREITUNG AVE	49802	NW	Matthew D Ruesch	(906)774-1844 (906)774-2967	WS 10 SS 845 BC 845	ED/HC/MD	470	367	99
LACHINE	*ST PAUL*		See Hubbard Lake MI									
LAKE ORION	*CROWN OF LIFE*		See Rochester Hills MI									
	GOOD SHEPHERD church@gsls.org www.goodshepherdlakeorion.com	1971	1950 S BALDWIN RD	48360	MI	Benjamin G Oelschlaeger	(248)391-1170 (248)391-1680	WS 830 11 SS 9 BC 9	EC/ED/ HC/MD	199	151	99
	JOURNEY		See Oxford MI									
LAKEVIEW	*HOLY TRINITY* htlclakeview@gmail.com www.htlclakeview.com	1947	8890 TAMARACK RD	48850	EN	Alexander W Sabol	(989)352-6374	WS 1030 BC 12	ED/HC	120	108	49
LAMBERTVILLE	*CHRIST KING* ctkl@bex.net www.ctkbedford.org	1962	2843 STERNS RD	48144	MI	Timothy J Loewe	(734)856-1461 (734)856-1461	WS 930 SS 945 BC 1045	ED/MD	137	137	30
LANSING	*GOOD SHEPHERD* office@gslansing.org www.gslansing.org	1964	7000 W SAGINAW HWY	48917	MI	Delwyn X Campbell Sr	(517)321-6100 (517)321-1161	WS 1045	EL/ED/ HC/SN			
	LIVING WORD africanlivingwordlansing@gmail.com		C/O Trinity Lutheran Church 501 West Saginaw St TRINITY LUTHERAN CHURCH 501 W SAGINAW ST	48933	MI	Moses G Dangba	(517)490-5135	WS 4	ED/HC	48	10	44
	OUR SAVIOR ssundstrom@oursaviorlansing.org www.oursaviorlansing.org	1956	7910 E ST JOE HWY	48917	MI	William R Wangelin Christopher M Deneen	(517)882-8665	WS 830 1030	EL/ED/HC/ MD	1232	933	404
	SAINT LUKE- CHRIST CAMPUS Satellite Site of St Luke Haslett MI	2016	122 S Pennsylvania Ave	48912				WS 11 2 6 SS 945 BC 945				

*Indicates a new church start. A new church start is an intentionally organized gathering which comes together on a regular basis for the purpose of worship and/or Bible study and is intended to grow into a member LCMS congregation. WS =Worship Service; SS = Sunday School; BC =Bible Class; EC = Early Childhood; EL = Elementary School; HS = High School; ED =Education Ministry; HC =Human Care Ministry; SN = Special Needs Ministry; MD = Media Ministry (PC)=Partner Church Pastor. See Page 53 for the Table of Abbreviations for key to additional abbreviations

CITY	CONGREGATION EMAIL WEBSITE	YEAR EST	LOCATION MAILING ADDRESS	ZIP CODE(S)	DIST.	PASTOR(S)	PHONE FAX	WS SS BC	SCHOOLS/ MINISTRIES	STATISTIC Bapt	Conf	Avg Attend
LANSING	*ST MATTHEW*		See Holt MI									
	TRINITY telclansingmi@gmail.com www.trinitylutheranlansing.org	1871	501 W SAGINAW ST	48933	MI	Delwyn X Campbell Sr	(517)372-1631 (517)372-5026	WS 845 BC 10	EC/EL/ ED/HC/ MD/SN	132	89	31
LAPEER	*ST PAUL* office@stpaul-lapeer.org www.stpaul-lapeer.org	1873	90 MILLVILLE RD	48446	MI	Jared R Nies	(810)664-6653 (810)245-4082	WS 830 11 SS 915 BC 915	EL/ED/HC/ MD/SN	1122	730	189
LAURIUM	*SAINT PAUL* stpaulstjohnlcms.org	1879	146 TAMARACK ST	49913	NW	Bryan G Lundquist	(906)337-3810	WS 1030 SS 9	ED/HC/ MD/SN	110	100	50
LAWTON	*TRINITY*		See Paw Paw MI									
LELAND	*IMMANUEL* immanuelleland@gmail.com www.immanuelleland.com	1869	303 E Pearl St PO BOX 436	49654	MI		(231)256-9464 (231)256-2052	WS 930 SS 1040 BC 1040	ED/HC/ MD/SN	138	135	75
LEONIDAS	*CREATORS PRAISE**		See Mendon MI									
LESLIE	*GRACE* Gracelutheranchurchleslie@gmail.com www.gracelutheranleslie.org	1989	212 S SHERMAN ST	49251	MI		(517)589-0250	WS 10 SS 9	ED/HC/ MD/SN	48	43	19
LEWISTON	*BETHLEHEM* bethlehemlewiston@gmail.com www.bethlehemlewiston.360unite.com	1940	3805 COUNTY ROAD 612	49756	MI		(989)786-3713 (989)786-3713	WS 1030 SS 1030 BC 9	ED/HC/ MD/SN	159	134	53
LEXINGTON	*ST MATTHEW* smlclex@gmail.com	1949	7155 Huron PO BOX 160	48450	MI	Christopher D Jung	(810)359-8411	WS 930 SS 1045	ED/HC/ MD/SN	306	306	90
LINCOLN PARK	*CALVARY* calvarylutheran11@yahoo.com calvarylplcms.org	1924	3320 ELECTRIC AVE	48146	MI		(313)381-6715 (313)381-3584	WS 1030	ED/HC/MD	131	120	40
LINDEN	*HOPE* hopelclm@gmail.com www.hopelinden.org	1974	7355 SILVER LAKE RD PO Box 188 PO BOX 188 LINDEN	48451	MI	Paul K Kollek	(810)735-4807 (810)735-4807	WS 930 SS 1030 BC 1030	ED/MD	184	164	47
	TRINITY FENTON		See Fenton MI									
LINKVILLE	*ST PAUL* lvlspaul40@gmail.com stpaullinkville.org	1894	7292 KILMANAGH RD PIGEON	48755	MI	Christopher S Suggitt	(989)453-2271	WS 830 SS 945		414	365	72
LIVONIA	*CHRIST OUR SAVIOR* admin@christoursavior.org www.christoursavior.org	1977	14175 FARMINGTON RD	48154	MI	Dean M Davenport Joel A Werner	(734)522-6830 (734)522-5949	WS 830 11 SS 945 BC 945	EC/HS/ ED/HC/ MD/SN	1572	1242	523
	SALEM NATIONAL		See Westland MI									
LOWELL	*GOOD SHEPHERD* mailbox@gslc.church gslc.church	1973	10305 BLUEWATER HWY	49331	MI		(616)897-8307	WS 1030		63	57	30
LUDINGTON	*ST JOHN* stjohns@stjohnslutheranludington.com www.stjohnsludington.org	1872	209 N Rowe St PO BOX 209	49431	MI	David P Goehmann	(231)843-9188	WS 10	ED/HC/ MD/SN	282	237	64
LUPTON	*FAITH*		See Prescott MI									
MACOMB	*IMMANUEL* sgrunewald@immlutheran.org www.immlutheran.org/	1853	47120 Romeo Plank 21Mile Rd 47120 ROMEO PLANK RD	48044	MI	Dr Charles Y Foster Douglas J Bender Nikolai J Gibbons	(586)286-4231 (586)286-8645	WS 8 930 11 SS 930 BC 930	EL/HS/ ED/HC/ MD/SN	3701	2289	1657
	ST JOHN		See Ray MI									
	ST PETER kwenzelburger@splcs.net www.stpetermacomb.com	1882	17051 24 MILE RD	48042	MI	Kurt R Wenzelburger Dante B Pronsati	(586)781-3434 (586)781-6564	WS 8 930 11 SS 930 BC 930	EL/HS/ ED/HC/ MD/SN	4539	3414	932
MANCELONA	*ST MATTHEW* stmatthewmancelona@gmail.com stmatthewmancelona.com	1891	211 E Hinman PO BOX 469	49659	MI	Thomas P Phillips	(231)916-2555	WS 1030 SS 1030	ED/HC/ MD/SN	99	97	11
MANCHESTER	*ST THOMAS*		See Ann Arbor MI									
MANISITQUE	*GRACE*		See Germfask MI									
MANISTEE	*BEAUTIFUL SAVIOR*		See Wellston MI									
	NORWALK jbmatt46@yahoo.com	1980	5614 Chippewa Highway 5614 CHIPPEWA HWY.	49660	MI		(231)889-3550	WS 9	ED/HC/MD	87	60	28
	TRINITY trinluthman@trinitymanistee.com www.trinitymanistee.com	1869	420 OAK ST	49660	MI	Dennis D Rahn	(231)723-5149 (231)723-9755	WS 10 SS 845 1020 BC 845	EL/ED/HC/ MD/SN	813	533	92
MARENISCO	*TRINITY*		See Boulder Junction WI									
MARINE CITY	*LIVING FAITH* livingfaithlutheranmc@gmail.com www.livingfaithlc.org	2007	310 South Parker 310 S PARKER ST	48039	MI	Paul E Yanke	(810)765-8440	WS 930 SS 1045 BC 1045	ED	50	46	30
MARLETTE	*OUR SAVIOR* churchoffice@oslmarlette.com www.oslmarlette.com	1974	6770 MARLETTE ST	48453	MI	Timothy D Kern	(989)635-7994 (989)635-8306	WS 9 SS 1030 BC 1030	ED/MD	192	157	59
MARQUETTE	*REDEEMER* redeemer@redeemermqt.org redeemermqt.org	1873	1700 W FAIR AVE	49855	NW	Chad M Ott Daniel P Ondov	(906)228-9883 (906)228-8912	WS 906 11 SS 1010	EC/ED/ HC/MD	1224	985	334
	SION		See Chatham MI									
MARSHALL	*AGNUS DEI* cyril9@aol.com agnusdeimarshall.com	2018	719 E MANSION ST	49068	EN	Peter M Burfeind	(419)324-5535	WS 11 BC 1215				
	CHRIST clcsecretary1@att.net www.christlutheranmarshall.com/	1970	440 WEST DR N	49068	MI	David R Moran	(269)781-5842 (269)727-0078	WS 10 SS 9 BC 9	EC/ED/ HC/MD	170	100	35
MARYSVILLE	*LIGHT OF CHRIST* office@locm.us www.LightofChristMarysville.org		4053 Ravenswood 4053 RAVENSWOOD RD	48040	MI	Scott S Magneson	(810)334-6756	WS 10 SS 11	ED/HC/MD	97	74	75
MASON	*GRACE*		See Leslie MI									
	ST MATTHEW		See Holt MI									
MATTAWAN	*TRINITY*		See Paw Paw MI									

*Indicates a new church start. A new church start is an intentionally organized gathering which comes together on a regular basis for the purpose of worship and/or Bible study and is intended to grow into a member LCMS congregation. WS =Worship Service; SS = Sunday School; BC =Bible Class; EC = Early Childhood; EL = Elementary School; HS = High School; ED =Education Ministry; HC =Human Care Ministry; SN = Special Needs Ministry; MD = Media Ministry (PC)=Partner Church Pastor. See Page 53 for the Table of Abbreviations for key to additional abbreviations

CITY	CONGREGATION EMAIL WEBSITE	YEAR EST	LOCATION MAILING ADDRESS	ZIP CODE(S)	DIST.	PASTOR(S)	PHONE FAX	WS SS BC	SCHOOLS/ MINISTRIES	STATISTIC Bapt	Conf	Avg Attend
MCMILLAN	*TRINITY*		See Newberry MI									
MECOSTA	*CHAPEL LAKES* cllcmsweb@gmail.com chapelofthelakesmecosta.com	1980	9407 90TH AVE	49332	MI	Mark E Gilson	(231)972-7891 (231)972-2929	WS 930 BC 1050	ED/HC/ MD/SN	95	95	56
MEMPHIS	*ST ANDREW* www.memphislutheran.com	1994	775 Kinney Rd PO BOX 52	48041	MI	Ronald B Roland	(810)392-2392	WS 9 SS 1030 BC 1030	ED/HC			
MENDON	*CREATORS PRAISE** pastor@creatorspraiseministries.org www.creatorspraiseministries.org	2020	163 West Main Street PO BOX 204 163 WEST MAIN STREET	49072	MI		(269)689-7482	WS 10				
	ST PAUL		See Centreville MI									
MESICK	*FAITH* faithmesick.org	1979	320 N Clark St PO BOX 603	49668	MI	Timothy C Selim	(231)885-1072	WS 10 BC 9	ED/HC	23	19	15
MIDDLEVILLE	*GOOD SHEPHERD* goodshepherdlcms@gmail.com goodshepherdlcms.googlepages.com/home	1987	908 W MAIN ST	49333	MI	Robert W Wurst Jr	(269)795-2391	WS 930 BC 1045	ED	39	38	25
MIDLAND	*GRACE*		See Auburn MI									
	LORD/NEW LIFE lordofnewlife@outlook.com lordofnewlife.org	1996	3021 E HUBBARD RD	48642	MI	Carl F Trosien	(989)837-2856	WS 930 SS 10 BC 11				
	MESSIAH messiah@messiahbc.org	1971	1550 S POSEYVILLE RD	48640	MI	Edward F Doerner Dennis J Kreil Stephen A Lampi Matthew S Lytikainen	(989)631-5200 (989)835-5325	WS 930 11 SS 930	ED/HC	1873	1291	480
	OUR SAVIOR oursaviormidland@sbcglobal.net www.oursaviormidland.com	1955	1501 N SAGINAW RD	48640	MI	Gary D Lyvere	(989)832-3667	WS 930 BC 1045	ED/HC/ MD/SN	92	78	37
	ST JOHN'S office@sjlmidland.org www.sjlmidland.org	1884	505 E CARPENTER ST	48640	MI	Daniel A Kempin Joshua J Parsons	(989)835-5861 (989)835-2443	WS 8 1045 SS 930 BC 930	EL/ED/HC/ MD/SN	1259	1020	304
	ZION		See Auburn MI									
MILAN	*ST PAUL* secretary.stpausmilan@gmail.com www.stpaulslutheranmilan.com	1939	106 DEXTER ST	48160	MI	Coleman K Geraci	(734)439-2806	WS 11 SS 945 BC 945	ED/HC	119	102	59
MILFORD	*CHRIST* office@christlutheranmilford.org www.christlutheranmilford.org	1947	620 GENERAL MOTORS RD	48381	MI	Dr Andrew M Johnson	(248)684-0895 (248)685-7703	WS 830 11 SS 945 BC 945	EC/ED/ HC/MD	373	265	141
MILLINGTON	*ST PAUL* church.office@spmill.org www.stpaul-millington.org	1897	4941 CENTER ST	48746	MI	James R Bruner Timothy D Martinal	(989)871-4581 (989)871-5573	WS 830 11 SS 10 BC 10	EL/ED/HC/ MD/SN	1330	1164	241
MINDEN CITY	*ST JOHN*		See Palms MI									
MIO	*LIVING WATER* livingwatermio@gmail.com	1999	207 E 4th St PO BOX 247	48647	MI	Glen W Bromm	(989)826-1688 (989)826-6398	WS 11		45	43	20
MONROE	*GRACE* church@gracelutheranmonroe.org www.gracelutheranmonroe.org	1930	630 N MONROE ST	48162	MI	Mark K Witte	(734)242-1401 (734)243-2629	WS 8 1030 SS 915 BC 915	ED/HC/ MD/SN	266	242	121
	HOLY GHOST holyghostmonroe@gmail.com www.holyghostmonroe.org	1844	3589 HEISS RD	48162	MI	D L Cullen Jr	(734)242-0509	WS 9 SS 1030 BC 1030	EL/ED/HC/ MD	618	491	125
	IMMANUEL eastidaimmanuellutheran@gmail.com www.eastidaimmanuel.com	1847	6272 W ALBAIN RD	48161	MI	Curtis D Garland	(734)269-2961	WS 9 SS 1015 BC 1030	ED/MD	456	336	91
	TRINITY info@trinitylutheranmonroe.org www.tlcmonroe.org	1844	323 SCOTT ST	48161	MI	Greyson D Grenz Mark A Duerr	(734)242-2308 (734)242-2762	WS 830 1030 BC 930	EL/ED/HC/ MD/SN	1271	1016	291
MONTAGUE	*SAINT JAMES* stjamestz@frontier.com stjamesmontague.com	1871	8945 STEBBINS ST	49437	MI	Eric M Nelson	(231)894-8471 (231)893-0198	WS 815 1045 SS 930 BC 930	EC/ED/HC/ MD/SN	576	493	170
MOUNT CLEMENS	*IMMANUEL*		See Macomb MI									
	ST LUKE		See Clinton Township MI									
MOUNT PLEASANT	*CHRIST THE KING LUTHERAN CHAPEL* Satellite Site of Zion Mount Pleasant MI	1968	1401 S Washington	48858				WS 11				
	ZION zion@zionmpmi.org www.zionchristtheking.org	1889	3401 E RIVER RD MT PLEASANT	48858	MI	Jesse R Greenhagen	(989)772-1516 (989)772-7640	WS 830 SS 945 BC 945	EC/ED/HC/ MD/SN	560	433	140
MULLIKEN	*ST ANDREW*		See Portland MI									
MUNGER	*TRINITY-ST JAMES* tsjloffice@gmail.com tsjmunger.com	1980	119 E Munger Rd PO BOX 156	48747	MI	Jimmy K Riley	(989)659-2506 (989)659-2506	WS 9 SS 1015	EL/ED/HC	511	350	72
MUNISING	*GOOD SHEPHERD* goodshepherd@jamadots.com goodshepherdmunising.org	1987	E 9035 State Hwy 28 E 9035 STATE HWY M 28	49862	NW		(906)387-3579	WS 10 SS 9 BC 9	EC/ED/HC/ MD/SN	88	74	40
	SION		See Chatham MI									
MUSKEGON	*LAKESHORE*		See Spring Lake MI									
	ST MARK sml.muskegon@yahoo.com stmarkmuskegon.com	1953	4475 HENRY ST	49441	MI	Scott M Faith	(231)798-2197	WS 930 5 SS 930	ED/HC/ MD/SN	400	305	138
	TRINITY business@tlcmuskegon.org tlcmuskegon.360unite.com/	1885	3225 ROOSEVELT RD	49441	MI	Paul C Appold	(231)755-1292	WS 8 1030 SS 1045 BC 915	EL/ED/HC/ MD/SN	475	359	133
NAUBINWAY	*BETHLEHEM*		See Engadine MI									

*Indicates a new church start. A new church start is an intentionally organized gathering which comes together on a regular basis for the purpose of worship and/or Bible study and is intended to grow into a member LCMS congregation. WS =Worship Service; SS = Sunday School; BC =Bible Class; EC = Early Childhood; EL = Elementary School; HS = High School; ED =Education Ministry; HC =Human Care Ministry; SN = Special Needs Ministry; MD = Media Ministry (PC)=Partner Church Pastor. See Page 53 for the Table of Abbreviations for key to additional abbreviations

CITY	CONGREGATION EMAIL WEBSITE	YEAR EST	LOCATION MAILING ADDRESS	ZIP CODE(S)	DIST.	PASTOR(S)	PHONE FAX	WS SS BC	SCHOOLS/ MINISTRIES	STATISTIC Bapt	Conf	Avg Attend
NEW BALTIMORE	*CHRIST* CLCnewbaltimore@gmail.com www.christlutherannewbaltimore.com	1947	50750 WALPOLE ST	48047	MI	Daniel H Harrison	(586)725-1431	WS 9 SS 1030 BC 1030	ED/HC/ MD/SN	90	77	49
NEW BOSTON	*ST PAUL* churchoffice@stpaulsnewboston.org www.stpaulsnewboston.org	1878	19109 Craig St 19109 CRAIG ST PO BOX 274	48164	MI	Scott L Blevins	(734)753-9048 (734)753-9710	WS 10 SS 11 BC 9	ED/HC	148	125	68
NEW HAVEN	*ST JOHN*		See Ray MI									
NEWBERRY	*TRINITY* trinitynewberrylcms@gmail.com www.facebook.com/tlcnewberry	1935	711 NEWBERRY AVE	49868	MI	Kyle I Kuehl	(906)293-9340	WS 10 SS 915	ED/HC/MD	123	95	36
NILES	*ST PAUL* office@stpaulsniles.org www.stpaulsniles.org	1919	1340 SYCAMORE ST	49120	MI		(269)683-0771	WS 10	EL/ED/HC/ MD/SN	275	200	65
NORTH BRANCH	*NEW LIFE IN CHRIST*	1985	6007 FISH LAKE RD	48461	MI	Joseph S Schierlinger	(810)688-2747	WS 1030 SS 9 BC 9	ED/HC	108	108	28
NORTH MUSKEGON	*LAKESHORE*		See Spring Lake MI									
NORTHVILLE	*RISEN CHRIST*		See Plymouth MI									
	ST PAUL stpaulnorthville@ameritech.net www.stpaulnorthville.org	1896	201 ELM ST	48167	MI	Christopher D Fairbairn James M Frusti	(248)349-3140 (248)349-7493	WS 830 11 SS 945 BC 945	EL/ED/HC/ MD	466	382	161
NOTTAWA	*CREATORS PRAISE**		See Mendon MI									
NUNICA	*ST LUKE* stlukenunica@gmail.com stlukenunica.org	1902	17122 2nd Street 17122 2ND ST	49448	MI	Micah J Brooks	(616)837-6059	WS 9 SS 1030 BC 1030	ED/HC/ MD/SN	223	179	96
OKEMOS	*ASCENSION*		See East Lansing MI									
OMER	*BETHLEHEM*		See Standish MI									
ONAWAY	*HOLY CROSS* holycrossonaway@gmail.com holycrossonaway.com	1933	3786 GLASIER RD	49765	MI	Trenton N Wollberg	(989)733-8412 (989)733-8412	WS 10	EC/ED/HC/ MD/SN	84	76	45
ONEKAMA	*TRINITY* trinityonekama@sbcglobal.net trinityonekama.org	1887	5471 Fairview St PO BOX 119	49675	MI	Jacob T Sherry	(231)889-4429 (231)889-4429	WS 1030 SS 930 BC 930	SN	153	141	58
ONSTED	*ST MARK*		See Brooklyn MI									
ONTONAGON	*ST PAUL* stpaul@jamadots.com	1931	107 E River St PO BOX 85	49953	NW		(906)884-4788	WS 9	ED/HC/ MD/SN			
ORTONVILLE	*PRINCE OF PEACE* poportonville@gmail.com www.princeofpeacelcms.org	1979	180 Grange Hall Rd PO BOX 156	48462	MI		(248)627-6222	WS 1030	ED/HC/MD	54	48	19
OSCODA	*TRINITY* churchoffice@trinityoscoda.org trinityoscoda.org	1960	5625 N US HIGHWAY 23	48750	MI	Stephen E Schilke	(989)739-9292 (989)739-9295	SS 930 BC 1045	HC/MD/SN	160	131	68
OSSINEKE	*GOOD SHEPHERD*	1988	12365 US Hwy 23 S PO BOX 175	49766	MI		(989)471-5428	WS 1030 BC 9	ED/HC	30	30	22
	ST PAUL		See Hubbard Lake MI									
OTISVILLE	*ST TIMOTHY* pastor@sttimothyotisville.org sttimothyotisville.org	1972	450 E Wilson Rd 450 WILSON RD	48463	MI	E E Nevis	(810)631-4730	WS 830 11 SS 945 BC 945	ED/HC/MD	228	169	69
OTSEGO	*EPIPHANY*		See Dorr MI									
OWOSSO	*ST PHILIP* www.stphilipowosso.org	1986	219 W Oliver St PO BOX 155	48867	MI	Brian F Heidt	(989)723-6238	WS 10 SS 9 BC 9	HC/MD	95	85	42
OXFORD	*CROWN OF LIFE*		See Rochester Hills MI									
	GOOD SHEPHERD		See Lake Orion MI									
	JOURNEY info@journeylutheran.church www.journeylutheran.church	2021	136 S WASHINGTON ST	48371	MI	Benjamin A Spaulding	(248)628-2011	WS 845 11	EC	356	277	142
PALMS	*ST JOHN* hchales@hotmail.com	1916	6600 N Ruth Rd 6600 RUTH RD N	48465	MI	Henry J Hales	(989)864-3663 (989)864-3663	WS 9	ED/SN	77	69	30
	ST. JOHN LUTHERAN CHURCH Satellite Site of Trinity Forestville MI	2021	6600 Ruth Rd. N.	48465				WS 1030				
PARADISE	*TRINITY*		See Newberry MI									
PAW PAW	*TRINITY* churchoffice@trinitylutheran.com www.trinitylutheran.com	1932	721 PINE ST	49079	MI		(269)657-4840	WS 11 SS 1015 BC 1015	EL/ED/HC/ MD/SN	598	492	170
PENTWATER	*LIGHTHOUSE* revjohn.hansen@gmail.com		8786 US 31 PO BOX 235	49449	MI	John G Hansen	(231)869-2527	WS 11	ED/HC	58	58	32
PETERSBURG	*ST PETER* secretary@stpeterslutheranchurch.com stpeterslutheranchurch.com/	1876	343 E CENTER ST	49270	MI	Peter D Candreva	(734)279-1949	WS 1030 SS 9 BC 9		141	128	42
PETOSKEY	*ZION* office@zionlutheranpetoskey.org www.zionlutheranpetoskey.org	1879	500 W MITCHELL ST	49770	MI	Matthew A Peters	(231)347-3438 (231)348-7606	WS 8 1030 SS 915 BC 915	EC/ED/ HC/MD	254	251	112
PIGEON	*GOOD SHEPHERD* goodsheplc@gmail.com goodshepherdcaseville.org	1971	7899 CRESCENT BEACH RD	48755	MI	Christopher S Suggitt	(989)856-4850	WS 1030 BC 1130		102	91	35
PINCKNEY	*TRINITY* trinitylutheranpinckney@yahoo.com www.trinitypinckney.org	1977	5758 W M 36	48169	MI	Kenneth A Huner	(734)878-5977 (734)878-6261	WS 10 SS 9 BC 9	ED/HC/MD	155	120	57
PINCONNING	*ST JOHN* churchoffice@mysjp.org www.mysjp.org	1888	1633 E Pinconning Rd PO BOX 56	48650	MI	Gregory D Hyatt	(989)879-2377 (989)879-6343	WS 9 SS 1015 BC 1030	ED/HC/ MD/SN	247	200	80
PLAINFIELD TOWNSHIP	*MESSIAH*		See Grand Rapids MI									

*Indicates a new church start. A new church start is an intentionally organized gathering which comes together on a regular basis for the purpose of worship and/or Bible study and is intended to grow into a member LCMS congregation. WS =Worship Service; SS = Sunday School; BC =Bible Class; EC = Early Childhood; EL = Elementary School; HS = High School; ED =Education Ministry; HC =Human Care Ministry; SN = Special Needs Ministry; MD = Media Ministry (PC)=Partner Church Pastor. See Page 53 for the Table of Abbreviations for key to additional abbreviations

CITY	CONGREGATION EMAIL WEBSITE	YEAR EST	LOCATION MAILING ADDRESS	ZIP CODE(S)	DIST.	PASTOR(S)	PHONE FAX	WS SS BC	SCHOOLS/ MINISTRIES	STATISTIC Bapt	Conf	Avg Attend
PLAINFIELD TOWNSHIP	*ST PETER*		See Rockford MI									
PLAINWELL	*EPIPHANY*		See Dorr MI									
PLYMOUTH	*FAITH*		See Ypsilanti MI									
	GRACE		See Canton MI									
	RISEN CHRIST www.risenchrist.info	1964	46250 ANN ARBOR RD W	48170	EN	Reinald W Kaufmann	(734)453-5252 (734)453-0224	WS 930 BC 9	ED/HC/ MD/SN	92	68	60
PONTIAC	*ST PAUL* stpauloffice1133@gmail.com stpaulpontiac.com	2008	1133 JOSLYN AVE	48340	MI	Gerald H Corbett Jr	(248)758-9019	WS 11 SS 1215	ED/HC	45	10	25
PORT HOPE	*SAINT JOHN* stjohnsec@stjohnporthope.org www.stjohnporthope.org	1868	4527 Second St PO BOX 206	48468	MI	David A Dodge	(989)428-4140 (989)428-4811	WS 8 10 SS 9	ED/HC/ MD/SN	595	447	94
PORT HURON	*FAITH* faithlutheran3455@comcast.net www.faithporthuron.org	1956	3455 STONE ST	48060	MI	Mark L Huff	(810)985-5733 (810)985-3841	WS 815 11 SS 945 BC 945	ED/HC/ MD/SN	527	359	173
	LIGHT OF CHRIST		See Marysville MI									
	TRINITY office.secretary@tlc1517.org www.tlc1517.org	1871	1517 10TH ST	48060	MI	Dr Mark J Madson	(810)984-2993 (810)982-3906	WS 930 SS 1030 BC 815	ED/HC/MD	1230	759	94
PORT SANILAC	*ST JOHN*	1857	246 N RIDGE RD	48469	MI	Randy D Lett	(810)425-3085	WS 1130 BC 10	HC	69	61	25
PORTAGE	*ST MICHAEL* tsonger@mightymessengers.org www.mightymessengers.org	1960	7211 OAKLAND DR	49024	MI	Dr Paul R Naumann Daniel S Maske	(269)327-7832	WS 830 11 SS 945 BC 945	EL/ED/HC/ MD/SN	758	555	328
PORTLAND	*ST ANDREW* portlandstandrew@gmail.com www.portlandstandrew.com	1983	8867 KENT ST	48875	MI	Roger K Straub	(517)647-4473	WS 10 SS 9 BC 1130	EC/ED/ HC/SN	70	57	33
PRESCOTT	*FAITH* faithfamily303@gmail.com	1969	5315 HENDERSON LAKE RD	48756	MI	Edward A Meyer	(989)873-4506	WS 10 SS 9 BC 9	ED/HC/ MD/SN	207	162	67
QUINCY	*ST PAUL*		See Coldwater MI									
RAMSAY	*OUR REDEEMER* staff@ourredeemerlutheran.net	1924	E8223 SANDERS RD BESSEMER	49959 49911	NW	Bryan L Hopfensperger	(906)663-4318	WS 1030		125	117	53
RAVENNA	*TRINITY*		See Conklin MI									
RAY	*ST JOHN* pastor@stjohnray.comcastbiz.net	1884	62657 NORTH AVE	48096	MI	Joshua T Ball	(586)749-5286 (586)749-7778	WS 9 SS 1030 BC 1030	HS/ED/ HC/MD/ SN			
REDFORD TOWNSHIP	*GRACE* glcms41@gmail.com www.gracelutheranredford.org	1941	25630 GRAND RIVER AVE REDFORD	48240	EN	Timothy P Halboth	(313)532-2266 (313)532-0643	WS 915 11 SS 915 11	ED/HC/ MD/SN			
REED CITY	*TRINITY* office@trinitylutheran-rc.org www.trinitylutheran-rc.org	1867	19778 US Hwy 10 19778 US HIGHWAY 10	49677	MI	Paul A Tonn	(231)832-5186 (231)832-0107	WS 9 615 SS 1020 BC 1020	EL/ED/MD	504	444	106
REESE	*TRINITY* trinityreeseoffice@gmail.com www.trinityreese.org	1903	9858 NORTH ST	48757	MI	Daniel G Burhop	(989)868-9901 (989)868-3702	WS 815 1045 SS 930 BC 930	EC/EL/HS/ ED/HC/ MD	965	780	262
RICHMOND	*ST PETER* officemanager@splschoolrichmond.org www.stpetersrichmond.org	1872	67055 GRATIOT AVE	48062	MI	Mark J Haller	(586)727-9693 (586)727-3370	WS 8 1045 SS 930 BC 930	EL/HS/ ED/HC/ MD/SN	1419	1113	424
RICHVILLE	*ST MICHAEL* church@stmichaelsrichville.org stmichaelsrichville.org	1851	3455 S Van Buren Rd 3455 S. VAN BUREN ROAD REESE	48758	MI	Keith E Knea Wesley S Gillaspie	(989)868-4791	WS 745 1030 SS 915 BC 915	EL/ED/HC/ MD/SN	1302	1062	446
ROCHESTER	*GOODLIFE* glclutheran@gmail.com	1944	1892 E AUBURN RD ROCHES-TER HLS	48307	MI	Dr David L Prout	(248)852-5510 (888)893-7594	WS 930 BC 1045	ED/MD	32	32	18
	GOODLIFE CHURCH-CEDARBROOK Satellite Site of GoodLife Rochester MI	2019	790 Letica Dr	48307								
	ST JOHN church@stjohnrochester.org www.stjohnrochester.org	1920	1011 W UNIVERSITY DR	48307	MI	Marc N Schwichtenberg Tyler R Cronkright Stephen D Grafe	(248)402-8000	WS 8 930 1045 11 SS 930 BC 930	EL/HS/ ED/HC/ MD/SN	2462	1837	939
ROCHESTER HILLS	*CROWN OF LIFE* office@crownoflifechurch.org www.crownoflifechurch.org	1978	2975 DUTTON RD ROCHESTER HLS	48306	MI	Terry A Baughman	(248)652-7720 (248)652-1387	WS 9 1030	EC/ED/ HC/MD	84	65	60
	EPIC		See Shelby Township MI									
	GOODLIFE CHURCH-AMERICAN HOUSE VILLAGE Satellite Site of GoodLife Rochester MI	2015	3617 S Adams Rd Manor #5	48309								
	GOODLIFE CHURCH-ANTHOLOGY Satellite Site of GoodLife Rochester MI	2019	1775 S Rochester Rd	48307								
	GOODLIFE CHURCH-BELLBROOK Satellite Site of GoodLife Rochester MI	2014	873 W Avon Rd	48307				WS 330				
	GOODLIFE CHURCH-ELMWOOD Satellite Site of GoodLife Rochester MI	2017	2251 W Auburn Rd	48309								
	GOODLIFE CHURCH-POMEROY Satellite Site of GoodLife Rochester MI	2018	3434 W South Blvd	48309								
ROCKFORD	*BISHOP HILLS* Satellite Site of St Peter Rockford MI	2012	4951 11 Mile Rd NE	49341				WS 3				

*Indicates a new church start. A new church start is an intentionally organized gathering which comes together on a regular basis for the purpose of worship and/or Bible study and is intended to grow into a member LCMS congregation. WS =Worship Service; SS = Sunday School; BC =Bible Class; EC = Early Childhood; EL = Elementary School; HS = High School; ED =Education Ministry; HC =Human Care Ministry; SN = Special Needs Ministry; MD = Media Ministry (PC)=Partner Church Pastor. See Page 53 for the Table of Abbreviations for key to additional abbreviations

CONGREGATIONS

CITY	CONGREGATION EMAIL WEBSITE	YEAR EST	LOCATION MAILING ADDRESS	ZIP CODE(S)	DIST.	PASTOR(S)	PHONE FAX	WS SS BC	SCHOOLS/ MINISTRIES	STATISTIC Bapt	Conf	Avg Attend
ROCKFORD	*ST PETER* secretary@stpetersrockford.org www.stpetersrockford.org	1963	310 E DIVISION ST	49341	MI	Jason P Peterson	(616)866-1818	WS 930 SS 1030 BC 1030	EC/ED/HC/ MD/SN	257	224	34
ROGERS CITY	*HILLTOP MANOR* Satellite Site of St John Rogers City MI	2013	643 W Erie St	49779								
	IMMANUEL immanuelofmoltke@outlook.com www.immanuelmoltke.org	1873	7134 CHURCH HWY	49779	MI	Joseph L Bangert	(989)474-4032	WS 830	MD	179	158	47
	PEACE office@peacelcms.org www.peacelcms.org	1993	1401 M-68 Hwy 1401 M 68	49779	MI	Jonathan A Dueker	(989)734-7621	WS 930 1115 SS 10	EL/ED/HC/ MD	403	323	89
	ST JOHN sjlcrogerscity@gmail.com stjohnlutheranchurchrcmi.org	1873	460 W Erie Ave 460 W ERIE AVENUE	49779	MI	Joseph L Bangert	(989)590-2643	WS 1030 SS 10	EL/ED/ MD/SN	325	256	90
	ST MICHAEL stmichaelbelknaplcms.org	1871	5918 COUNTY ROAD 451	49779	MI	Paul M Boerger	(989)734-3007	WS 10 SS 845 BC 845		323	248	60
ROMEO	*GRACE FELLOWSHIP* pastormajeski@graceromeo.com www.graceromeo.com	1989	7525 32 MILE RD BRUCE TWP	48065	MI	Eric W Majeski Michael G Phillips	(586)752-9800 (586)752-8996	WS 830 11 SS 945 BC 945	EC/HS/ED/ HC/MD	743	562	269
ROSE CITY	*ST JOHN*		See West Branch MI									
ROSEVILLE	*BETHLEHEM*	1924	29675 GRATIOT AVE	48066	MI		(586)777-9128 (586)777-1788	WS 10 BC 845	EC/HS/ED	125	89	30
ROYAL OAK	*OUR SHEPHERD*		See Birmingham MI									
	ST PAUL prodway@stpaulroyaloak.org www.stpaulroyaloak.org	1873	202 E 5TH ST	48067	MI	Jakob A Andrzejewski	(248)541-0613 (248)541-6965	WS 815 11 SS 945 BC 945	EL/ED/HC/ MD/SN	925	653	228
RUTH	*ST JOHN*		See Palms MI									
SAGINAW	*BETHLEHEM* churchoffice@bethlehemsaginaw.org www.bethlehemsaginaw.org	1914	808 WEISS ST	48602	MI	Gary L Bender	(989)755-1144 (989)755-3969	WS 9 1030 SS 915 BC 915	EL/HS/ ED/HC/ MD/SN	1110	650	215
	FAITH		See Bridgeport MI									
	GOOD SHEPHERD office@goodshepherdsaginaw.com goodshepherdsaginaw.com	1955	5335 BROCKWAY RD	48638	MI	Dr Paul R Biber	(989)793-8201 (989)793-9525	WS 8 1030 SS 915 BC 915	EC/HS/ ED/HC/ MD/SN	808	669	186
	GRACE		See Auburn MI									
	HOLY CROSS church@hclc.org www.fb.me/hclc.sag.org	1849	600 COURT ST	48602	MI	Kurt A Brandon	(989)793-9723 (989)793-7441	WS 915 BC 1020	EL/HS/ED/ MD	349	303	130
	IMMANUEL churchoffice@frankentrost.org www.frankentrost.org	1847	8220 E HOLLAND RD	48601	MI	Mark A Loest Daniel A Wojtowicz	(989)754-0929 (989)754-0454	WS 8 1030 SS 915 BC 915	EL/HS/ED	557	456	180
	MESSIAH office@messiahcarrollton.org messiahsaginaw.360unite.com/home	1964	4640 N MICHIGAN AVE	48604	MI	Christian Q Mundorf	(989)753-7281	WS 930 SS 1045 BC 1045	HS/ED/ HC/MD/ SN	100	90	51
	PEACE lhall@peacesaginaw.org www.peacesaginaw.org	1941	3427 ADAMS AVE	48602	MI	Erik R Schmidt Matthew J Hauser	(989)793-9025 (989)921-1201	WS 9 11 SS 9 BC 9	EL/HS/ ED/HC/ MD/SN	2426	1841	611
	ST JOHN		See Bay City MI									
	ST MARK stmark@stmarksaginaw.org www.stmarksaginaw.com	1979	2565 N MILLER RD	48609	MI	Kirk W Abatelli	(989)781-3205	WS 8 1030 SS 915 BC 915	EC/HS/ED/ MD/SN	264	234	116
SAINT CHARLES	*NATIVITY* nativitylutheran625@gmail.com	1985	625 W CLINTON ST	48655	MI	Kevin C Jones	(989)865-9964 (989)865-9906	WS 10	ED/HC/MD	109	98	44
SAINT CLAIR	*IMMANUEL* nancy@immanuelsc.org immanuelsc.org	1898	415 N 9TH ST	48079	MI	James O Murr Jr David W DuBois	(810)329-7174 (810)329-4104	WS 8 1030 SS 9 915 BC 9 915	EC/HS/ED/ HC/MD	738	508	276
SAINT CLAIR SHORES	*REDEEMER*	1921	30003 JEFFERSON AVE	48082	EN		(586)294-0640	WS 8 1045 SS 915 BC 915	EC			
	ST PAUL st.pauls.scs@gmail.com www.stpaulsmi.com	1926	22915 GREATER MACK AVE ST CLAIR SHORES	48080	EN	Simeon J Cornwell	(586)777-0215 (586)777-0216	WS 930 SS 1045 BC 1045	ED/HC/SN	161	134	50
SAINT CLAIR TOWNSHIP	*IMMANUEL*		See Saint Clair MI									
SAINT HELEN	*HOPE* hopesthelen@charter.net www.hopesthelen.org	1976	635 N Saint Helen Rd PO BOX 297	48656	MI	Carl R Petzold	(989)389-7715	WS 10 SS 930 BC 845	ED/HC/ MD/SN	102	102	30
SAINT JOHNS	*ST JOHN'S* churchoffice@stjohns1869.org www.stjohns1869.org	1869	511 E STURGIS ST	48879	MI	James M Pearl	(989)224-6796	WS 8 1030 SS 915 BC 915	ED/HC/MD	327	266	144
	ST PETER church@stpeterriley.org www.stpeterriley.org	1869	8990 CHURCH RD	48879	MI	Timothy A Bayer	(989)224-3178 (989)224-8962	WS 930 SS 11 BC 11	EL/ED/HC/ MD/SN	234	180	90
SAINT JOSEPH	*SALEM*		See Coloma MI									
	TRINITY betty.perrone@discovertrinity.org www.trinitystjoe.org	1867	609 Court St 619 MAIN ST	49085	MI	Michael J Roth Joseph T Liss Benjamin P Micheel David A Rutter	(269)983-5000 (269)983-8933	WS 8 930 11 SS 930 BC 930	EL/ED/HC/ MD/SN	1052	926	331
SALINE	*CHRIST OUR KING* office@c-o-k.org www.christ-our-king.org	1979	3255 SALINE WATERWORKS RD	48176	MI	Joseph W Polzin	(734)429-9200 (734)944-5432	WS 815 11 SS 945	ED/HC/ MD/SN	545	487	198
	ST THOMAS		See Ann Arbor MI									
SAND LAKE	*RESURRECTION* churchresurrection@yahoo.com	1979	180 Northland Dr PO BOX 172	49343	MI	Phillip W Chaffee	(616)636-5502	WS 930 BC 1050	ED/HC/MD	167	135	70

*Indicates a new church start. A new church start is an intentionally organized gathering which comes together on a regular basis for the purpose of worship and/or Bible study and is intended to grow into a member LCMS congregation. WS =Worship Service; SS = Sunday School; BC =Bible Class; EC = Early Childhood; EL = Elementary School; HS = High School; ED =Education Ministry; HC =Human Care Ministry; SN = Special Needs Ministry; MD = Media Ministry (PC)=Partner Church Pastor. See Page 53 for the Table of Abbreviations for key to additional abbreviations

CITY	CONGREGATION EMAIL WEBSITE	YEAR EST	LOCATION MAILING ADDRESS	ZIP CODE(S)	DIST.	PASTOR(S)	PHONE FAX	WS SS BC	SCHOOLS/ MINISTRIES	STATISTIC Bapt	Conf	Avg Attend
SANDUSKY	*HOLY REDEEMER*	1987	85 E Miller Rd PO BOX 64	48471	EN		(810)648-3190	WS 10 SS 9 BC 9	HC/MD/SN			
	PEACE secretary@peacelutheransandusky.com www.peacelutheransandusky.com	1950	92 N FLYNN ST	48471	MI		(810)648-3241 (810)648-3336	WS 9 SS 1030 BC 1030	EC/ED/MD	352	288	114
SANFORD	*ST PAUL* stpaullutheran@tds.net www.stpaulsanford.org	1948	2045 LYNN ST	48657	MI	Christopher P Vossler	(989)687-2824	WS 930 SS 1030 BC 11	ED/HC	321	274	92
SARANAC	*GOOD SHEPHERD*		See Lowell MI									
SAULT SAINTE MARIE	*SAINT BARNABAS* saintbarnabas@sblcms.org saintbarnabas-saultsaintemarie.org	1994	701 E Easterday Ave PO BOX 308 SAULT STE MARIE	49783	MI	Charles B Burhop	(906)632-7796	WS 1030	ED/HC/MD	106	64	25
SAWYER	*TRINITY* trinity_lutheran@yahoo.com trinitylutheransawyer.com	1911	5791 Sawyer Rd PO BOX 247	49125	MI	Brandon M Wittig	(269)426-3937 (269)426-3151	WS 930 BC 1045	EC/ED/HC/MD/SN	252	197	59
SCOTTS	*CREATORS PRAISE**		See Mendon MI									
SCOTTVILLE	*OUR SAVIOR* oursaviorlutheranscottville@gmail.com www.scottvillelutheran.com	1958	765 W US Highway 10 31 PO BOX 66	49454	MI	Kenneth L Williamson	(231)757-2271 (231)757-4320	WS 1030 SS 1030 BC 930	ED/HC/MD/SN	359	305	143
SEBEWAING	*IMMANUEL* church@ilcmi.org www.ilcmi.org	1845	800 E BAY ST	48759	MI	Michael D Boyer	(989)883-3050	WS 9 SS 1015 BC 1015	EL/ED/HC/MD/SN	888	757	210
	ST PETER thomgarrison@aol.com	1912	9653 Bach Rd 9456 KILMANAGH RD	48759	MI	Thomas B Garrison	(989)977-1044	WS 830	ED/HC/MD	69	63	30
SENEY	*GRACE*		See Germfask MI									
SHELBY	*ST STEPHEN* StStephensShelby@gmail.com pomegranate-flounder-4by6.squarespace.com	1870	7400 W JOHNSON RD	49455	MI	Kurt R Overway	(231)861-2952	WS 930 SS 11 BC 11	ED/MD/SN	32	30	30
SHELBY TOWNSHIP	*EPIC* office@epicchurch.com www.epicchurch.com	2004	47488 DEQUINDRE RD SHELBY TWP	48317	EN	John A Hile	(248)606-4348	WS 10 SS 10	HC			
	PEACE info@peaceshelby.org www.peaceshelby.org	1959	6580 24 MILE RD	48316	MI	David R Klemm	(586)731-4120 (586)731-8935	WS 830 1030 SS 1030	EL/HS/ED/HC/MD/SN	737	525	260
	SHEPHERD'S GATE office@sgatechurch.org www.sgatechurch.org	1980	12400 23 MILE RD	48315	MI	Timothy R Bollinger Benjamin D Marsh Eric J Shanburn	(586)731-4544 (586)731-8658	WS 830 1030 SS 9 11	HS/ED/HC	972	786	722
SHIELDS	*ST MARK*		See Saginaw MI									
SOUTH HAVEN	*SALEM*		See Coloma MI									
SOUTH LYON	*CROSS CHRIST* cofcsouthlyon@gmail.com www.cofcsl.org/	1973	24155 GRISWOLD RD	48178	MI	Jake B Bellinghausen	(248)437-8810	WS 10 SS 10 BC 9	EC/ED/HC/MD	441	292	58
	LIVING WATER		See Whitmore Lake MI									
SOUTHGATE	*CHRIST THE KING* staff@ctk.me www.ctk.me	1951	15600 TRENTON RD	48195	MI	Jason D Cashmer Patrick J Brooks	(734)285-9695 (734)285-4188	WS 9 11 SS 10 BC 10	EL/HS/ED/HC/MD	1689	1339	527
	CHRIST THE KING LUTHERAN CHURCH Satellite Site of Christ The King Southgate MI	2007	16700 Pennsylvania Rd	48195				WS 9 11 BC 10				
SPARTA	*ST PETER*		See Rockford MI									
	TRINITY		See Conklin MI									
SPRING LAKE	*LAKESHORE* info@lakeshorefellowship.com www.lakeshorefellowship.com	1987	16790 VAN WAGONER RD	49456	MI	Christopher M Boehnke	(616)846-8556	WS 10 SS 1015	ED/HC/MD	275	251	124
	ST MATTHEW office@smslm.org www.smslm.org	1969	15395 RANNES ST	49456	MI	Michael W Hughes	(616)846-2490 (616)846-7670	WS 930 SS 11 BC 11	EC/ED/MD/SN	97	91	62
SPRUCE	*ST PAUL*		See Hubbard Lake MI									
STANDISH	*BETHLEHEM* bethlehem1903@yahoo.com blcstandish.org	1903	5622 JOHNSFIELD RD	48658	MI	Matthew T Dent	(989)846-4972	WS 1030 SS 9 BC 9	ED/HC/MD/SN	244	174	52
STANTON	*HOPE*	1881	4741 W STANTON RD	48888	MI	Alexander W Sabol	(989)831-5594	WS 830	ED/HC	29	29	17
STANWOOD	*CHAPEL LAKES*		See Mecosta MI									
STERLING	*BETHLEHEM*		See Standish MI									
	FAITH		See Prescott MI									
STERLING HEIGHTS	*ST PAUL* stpaullutheransh@yahoo.com www.saintpaullutheran.com	1875	42681 HAYES RD STERLING HTS	48313	MI	Michael G Duchene	(586)247-4645 (586)247-1476	WS 8 1030 SS 915 BC 915	HS/ED/MD	162	162	90
STEVENSVILLE	*CHRIST* clcoffice@christstevensville.com www.Christ-luth.org	1955	4333 CLEVELAND AVE	49127	MI	Martin P Measel	(269)429-7222 (269)429-3788	WS 8 1045 SS 930 BC 930	EL/ED/HC/MD	802	661	143
STURGIS	*CREATORS PRAISE**		See Mendon MI									
	SALEM millerjjm@yahoo.com	1870	23269 Banker St Rd 23269 BANKER ST	49091	MI		(269)651-2846	WS 9 SS 1015		30	30	25
	ST PAUL		See Centreville MI									
	TRINITY church@trinitysturgis.com www.trinitylutheransturgis.com	1864	406 S Lakeview St 406 S LAKEVIEW AVE	49091	MI	Kaleb J Yaeger	(269)651-6511 (269)659-2909	WS 10 BC 845	EL/ED/HC/MD/SN	490	397	157
SUMPTER TOWNSHIP	*OPEN ARMS*		See Belleville MI									

*Indicates a new church start. A new church start is an intentionally organized gathering which comes together on a regular basis for the purpose of worship and/or Bible study and is intended to grow into a member LCMS congregation. WS =Worship Service; SS = Sunday School; BC =Bible Class; EC = Early Childhood; EL = Elementary School; HS = High School; ED =Education Ministry; HC =Human Care Ministry; SN = Special Needs Ministry; MD = Media Ministry (PC)=Partner Church Pastor. See Page 53 for the Table of Abbreviations for key to additional abbreviations

CITY	CONGREGATION EMAIL WEBSITE	YEAR EST	LOCATION MAILING ADDRESS	ZIP CODE(S)	DIST.	PASTOR(S)	PHONE FAX	WS SS BC	SCHOOLS/ MINISTRIES	STATISTIC Bapt	Conf	Avg Attend
SUNFIELD	ST ANDREW		See Portland MI									
SWARTZ CREEK	NEWLIFE COMMUNITY Info@newlifelutheran.net www.newlifelutheran.net	1995	7235 TORREY RD	48473	MI	Matthew C Hein	(810)655-3336	WS 9 1030 SS 1030	ED/HC	237	195	156
TAWAS CITY	ZION tawaszion@gmail.com ziontawas.com	1870	720 2nd St PO BOX 307	48763 48764	MI	Gabriel J Martin	(989)362-5712	WS 930 BC 1045	ED/MD	291	239	74
TAYLOR	EMMANUEL		See Dearborn MI									
	ST JOHNS stephanie@stjohnstaylor.org stjohnstaylor.org	1887	13115 TELEGRAPH RD	48180	MI	Mark C Whittaker	(734)287-2080 (734)287-0532	WS 9 SS 11 BC 11	ED/HC/ MD/SN	155	148	60
TECUMSEH	ST MARK		See Brooklyn MI									
TEKONSHA	ST PAUL		See Coldwater MI									
THREE RIVERS	CREATORS PRAISE*		See Mendon MI									
	ST PAUL		See Centreville MI									
	ST PETER stpeterstr@frontier.com www.stpeterstr.org	1896	PO BOX 327	49093	MI		(269)278-8415	WS 915 SS 1030 BC 1030	ED/HC/ MD/SN	125	125	40
TIPTON	ST MARK		See Brooklyn MI									
TRAVERSE CITY	ST MICHAEL stmichaelstcmi@gmail.com stmichaelstc.org	1955	912 S Garfield Ave PO BOX 5945	49686 49696	MI	Mark E Latham	(231)947-5293	WS 10	ED/HC	89	86	59
	TRINITY info@tctrinity.org www.tctrinity.org	1883	1003 S MAPLE ST	49684	MI	Michael M Goers Bruce K Lucas	(231)946-2720 (231)946-4796	WS 830 11 SS 945 BC 945	EL/ED/HC/ MD/SN	1343	997	382
TRENTON	ST PAUL staff@splconline.com splconline.com	1941	2550 EDSEL DR	48183	MI	John S Carrier Christopher P Harding Benjamin A Roberts	(734)676-1565 (734)676-1573	WS 930 11 SS 11 BC 830	EC/ED/HC/ MD/SN	1016	800	462
TROUT LAKE	BETHLEHEM		See Engadine MI									
TROY	FAITH hello@faithtroy.org www.faithtroy.org	1965	37635 DEQUINDRE RD	48083	MI	Joseph A Casiglia Richard J Grunewald Matthew G Schuler	(248)689-4664 (248)689-1554	WS 915 11 SS 915 11 BC 915 11	EC/HS/ ED/HC/ MD/SN	2398	2398	700
	FAITH TAMIL		37635 DEQUINDRE RD	48083	MI	Arul J Alexander	(248)689-4664 (248)689-1554	WS 915 SS 915	ED/HC/MD			
	GOODLIFE		See Rochester MI									
	OUR SHEPHERD		See Birmingham MI									
	SAINT AUGUSTINE churchoffice@saltchurch.net saltchurch.net	1961	5475 LIVERNOIS RD	48098	MI	Paul C Monson Franklin J Dohanyos	(248)879-6400 (248)879-1578	WS 830 11 SS 945 BC 945	EC/HS/ ED/HC	170	164	101
UNION CITY	OUR SAVIOR	1953	405 SAINT JOSEPH ST	49094	MI	Peter M Burfeind	(517)741-7643 (517)741-7643	WS 9 SS 10 BC 8	ED/HC/MD			
UNIONVILLE	ST PAUL stpaulunionville@gmail.com	1876	6356 Center St PO BOX 178	48767	MI	Steven M Stolarczyk	(989)674-8681	WS 9 SS 1015 BC 1015	EL/ED/HC/ MD	269	217	95
UTICA	GOODLIFE		See Rochester MI									
	PEACE		See Shelby Township MI									
	SHEPHERD'S GATE		See Shelby Township MI									
	TRINITY churchoffice@trinityutica.com www.trinityutica.com	1882	45160 VAN DYKE AVE	48317	MI	Justin A Krupsky Joshua D Britton Nicholas T Duerr Christian M Jones Chad E Wright	(586)731-4490 (586)731-1071	WS 8 930 945 1115 SS 930	EL/HS/ ED/HC/ MD/SN	3932	2826	938
VICKSBURG	CREATORS PRAISE*		See Mendon MI									
	ST PAUL		See Centreville MI									
WAKEFIELD	OUR REDEEMER		See Ramsay MI									
WALKER	THE VINE		See Grand Rapids MI									
WALLED LAKE	ST MATTHEW churchoffice@st-matthew.org www.st-matthew.org	1948	2040 S COMMERCE RD	48390	MI	Paul M Moldenhauer	(248)624-7676 (248)624-0685	WS 845 11 SS 10 BC 10	EC/EL/HS/ ED/HC/ MD/SN	1634	1196	423
WALTZ	ST JOHNS churchoffice@stjohnswaltz.org www.stjohnswaltzchurch.org	1857	28320 WALTZ RD NEW BOSTON	48164	MI	Kyle E Jones	(734)654-6366 (734)654-3675	WS 8 11	EL/HS/ ED/HC/ MD/SN	649	542	304
WARREN	EAST BETHLEHEM		See Detroit MI									
	HOLY CROSS office@holycrosswarren.com holycrosswarren.com	1960	30003 RYAN RD	48092	MI	Eric J Shanburn	(586)751-2550	WS 10 SS 9 BC 9	EL/HS/ ED/HC/ MD/SN	238	211	97
	HOPE office@hopewarren.com www.hopewarren.com	1966	32400 HOOVER RD	48093	MI	Daniel C Howard	(586)979-9055 (586)979-5570	WS 930 BC 11	HS/ED/ HC/MD	372	356	153
WASHINGTON	OUR REDEEMER Secretary@ourredeemer-lcms.org www.ourredeemer-lcms.org	1947	8600 27 MILE RD	48094	MI	Keith H Lemley	(586)781-5567 (586)781-0672	WS 8 1030 SS 915 BC 915	EC/HS/ ED/HC/ MD/SN	368	315	162
WATERFORD	PEACE peacewaterford@gmail.com www.peacewaterford.org	1963	7390 Elizabeth Lake Road 7390 ELIZABETH LAKE RD	48327	MI	Russell S Tkac	(248)681-9360 (248)681-9361	WS 1030 BC 915	ED/HC/ MD/SN	194	163	55
	ST PAUL		See Pontiac MI									
	ST STEPHEN office@ststephenwaterford.org www.ststephenwaterford.org	1956	3795 SASHABAW RD	48329	MI	Robert A Hoffman	(248)673-6621 (248)673-6683	WS 830 1045 SS 945 BC 945	ED/MD	281	220	120
WATERSMEET	HOPE hopelutheranlol@gmail.com www.hopelutheranlol.org	1951	N1764 Highway 45 PO BOX 477 LAND O LAKES	49969 54540	NW	Jeffrey G Mueller	(906)544-2259	WS 930 BC 815	ED/HC	114	104	62
WATERVLIET	SALEM		See Coloma MI									
WAYLAND	EPIPHANY		See Dorr MI									

*Indicates a new church start. A new church start is an intentionally organized gathering which comes together on a regular basis for the purpose of worship and/or Bible study and is intended to grow into a member LCMS congregation. WS =Worship Service; SS = Sunday School; BC =Bible Class; EC = Early Childhood; EL = Elementary School; HS = High School; ED =Education Ministry; HC =Human Care Ministry; SN = Special Needs Ministry; MD = Media Ministry (PC)=Partner Church Pastor. See Page 53 for the Table of Abbreviations for key to additional abbreviations

CITY	CONGREGATION EMAIL WEBSITE	YEAR EST	LOCATION MAILING ADDRESS	ZIP CODE(S)	DIST.	PASTOR(S)	PHONE FAX	WS SS BC	SCHOOLS/ MINISTRIES	STATISTIC Bapt	Conf	Avg Attend
WAYNE	*ST MICHAEL* churchoffice@stmichaellutheran.org stmichaellutheran.org	1962	3003 HANNAN RD	48184	MI	Andrew D Gruenhagen Martin C Banks	(734)728-1950 (734)728-9569	WS 830 11 SS 10 BC 10	EL/HS/ED/ HC/MD	493	426	240
WELLSTON	*BEAUTIFUL SAVIOR* AQUATICPLANTLADY@GMAIL.COM	2000	16486 STEINBERG RD	49689	MI		(231)848-4838	WS 11 BC 10	ED/HC/ MD/SN	11	11	10
WEST BLOOMFIELD	*SHEPHERD KING* office@shepherdkinglcms.org shepherdkinglcms.org	1956	5300 W MAPLE RD W BLOOMFIELD	48322	EN	Timothy A Holzerland	(248)626-2121 (248)626-0324	WS 10 SS 845 BC 845	EC/ED/ HC/MD	109	82	45
WEST BRANCH	*FAITH*		See Prescott MI									
	NEW BEGINNINGS sdan.08@gmail.com		960 S M 33 PO BOX 337	48661	EN	Daniel L Jansen	(989)836-3042	WS 9 SS 915 BC 10	ED/HC/MD	53	53	25
	ST JOHN stjohnwb@gmail.com www.stjohnwb.org	1900	155 N FAIRVIEW ST	48661	MI	Carl R Petzold	(989)345-0120	WS 9 SS 1030	HC/MD	127	110	75
WEST OLIVE	*CHRIST* christevangelicallutheran.org		15424 LAKE MICHIGAN DR	49460	EN		(616)534-0805					
	UNITED gwenulc@gmail.com	1996	15424 LAKE MICHIGAN DR	49460	MI		(616)846-4790	WS 10	HC	49	31	18
WESTLAND	*RISEN CHRIST*		See Plymouth MI									
	SALEM NATIONAL salemwestland@att.net www.salemwestland.com	1921	32430 ANN ARBOR TRL	48185	MI	Steven M Newton	(734)422-5550	WS 1045 SS 930 BC 930		96	85	55
	ST MATTHEW church@stmatthew.info www.stmatthew.info	1935	5885 N VENOY RD	48185	MI	Bryce S Rosche Samuel P Watters	(734)425-0260 (734)425-7932	WS 9 1115 SS 1020 BC 1020	EL/HS/ED/ HC/MD	465	376	157
WESTPHALIA	*ST ANDREW*		See Portland MI									
WHEELER	*IMMANUEL* Immanuel.Wheeler@gmail.com wheelerimanuellutheran.org/	1900	10020 E MONROE RD	48662	MI	Michael A Podeszwa	(989)842-3459 (989)842-3359	WS 930 SS 1045	MD	128	118	39
WHITE CLOUD	*CHRIST* christlutheranwc@att.net clcwhitecloud.org	1925	701 S Evergreen Dr PO BOX 625	49349	MI	Dr Mark A Bowditch	(231)689-1704	WS 930 SS 1045 BC 1045	ED/HC/SN	125	100	40
WHITE PIGEON	*ST PAUL*		See Centreville MI									
WHITEHALL	*FAITH* info@faithwhitehall.org www.faithwhitehall.org	1954	711 ALICE ST	49461	MI	Matthew J Gunia	(231)893-7722 (231)894-6636	WS 1030 SS 915 BC 915	ED/HC/ MD/SN	176	129	65
WHITMORE LAKE	*LIVING WATER* lbowen@livingwatermi.org livingwatermi.org		200 BARKER RD	48189	MI	Matthew J Canion	(734)426-4006	WS 1015 SS 9 BC 9	ED/HC/MD	69	55	45
	ST PAUL HAMBURG stpaul@stpaulhamburg.com www.stpaulhamburg.com	1952	7701 East M-36 7701 E MICHIGAN STATE RD 36	48189	MI	Jeffrey S Burgess	(810)231-1033 (810)231-1016	WS 815 11 SS 945 BC 945	ED/HC/MD	828	571	262
WHITTEMORE	*FAITH*		See Prescott MI									
	GOOD NEWS goodnewslutheran@centurytel.net	1987	3107 S M 65 PO BOX 64	48770	MI		(989)756-2159	WS 830 SS 945 BC 945	ED/HC	63	31	18
WILLIAMSTON	*ST MATTHEW*		See Holt MI									
WIXOM	*ST MATTHEW*		See Walled Lake MI									
	ST MATTHEW LUTH CHURCH WIXOM CAMPUS Satellite Site of St Matthew Walled Lake MI	2000	Wixom Campus 48380 Pontiac Trl	48393				WS 9 1020 SS 1020 BC 1020				
WYANDOTTE	*TRINITY* tlm@wyan.org www.trinitywyandotte.org	1861	505 Oak St 465 OAK ST	48192	MI		(734)282-5877 (734)282-2707	WS 11 SS 10 BC 10	ED/HC	352	269	60
WYOMING	*GRACE* gracelc.office@gmail.com www.gracelc.net	1949	150 50TH ST SW	49548	EN	Zachary W Marklevitz	(616)534-0805 (616)534-2308	WS 9 SS 1045 BC 1045	EL/HS/ ED/HC/ MD/SN	155	109	94
YPSILANTI	*CROSS RESURRECTION* contactus@crossandres.org www.crossandres.org		812 ANN ST	48197	MI	Bryan K Schindel	(734)829-0148 (734)487-1404	WS 1039 SS 930 BC 930	ED/HC/ MD/SN	74	47	61
	FAITH faithypsi11@comcast.net www.faithypsilanti.com	1941	1255 E FOREST AVE	48198	MI	Dr James A Waddell	(734)482-9412	WS 1015 SS 9 BC 9				
	OPEN ARMS		See Belleville MI									
	ST PAUL		See Ann Arbor MI									
ZEELAND	*CHRIST OUR SAVIOR*		See Holland MI									
MINNESOTA												
ADA	*ST JOHN* www.stjohnsada.com	1882	2948 240TH AVE	56510	MNN	Caleb J Worral	(218)784-4644	WS 1030 SS 930	ED/HC/MD			
	ZION zion.ada@loretel.net www.zionada.com	1919	410 3rd Ave W PO BOX 147	56510	MNN	Caleb J Worral	(218)784-7103	WS 9 SS 1015 BC 8	ED/MD/SN			
AFTON	*AFTON LAND* Satellite Site of Woodbury Woodbury MN	2008	Manning and Bailey Rd	55001								
	ST PETER stpeter@stpeterafton.org stpeterafton.org	1863	880 NEAL AVE S	55001	MNS	David A Domanski	(651)436-3357	WS 9 SS 1015 BC 1015	ED/HC/ MD/SN	260	190	91
	WOODBURY		See Woodbury MN									
AITKIN	*IMML IRON HUB* ilcih.lcms@gmail.com	1888	26535 IRON HUB RD	56431	MNN	Donald M Klatt	(218)546-6910	WS 1030 SS 9	ED/MD			

*Indicates a new church start. A new church start is an intentionally organized gathering which comes together on a regular basis for the purpose of worship and/or Bible study and is intended to grow into a member LCMS congregation. WS =Worship Service; SS = Sunday School; BC =Bible Class; EC = Early Childhood; EL = Elementary School; HS = High School; ED =Education Ministry; HC =Human Care Ministry; SN = Special Needs Ministry; MD = Media Ministry (PC)=Partner Church Pastor. See Page 53 for the Table of Abbreviations for key to additional abbreviations

CITY	CONGREGATION EMAIL WEBSITE	YEAR EST	LOCATION MAILING ADDRESS	ZIP CODE(S)	DIST.	PASTOR(S)	PHONE FAX	WS SS BC	SCHOOLS/ MINISTRIES	STATISTIC Bapt	Conf	Avg Attend
AITKIN	*ST JOHN* stjohnaitkin@gmail.com www.stjohnaitkin.org	1926	324 3RD ST NW	56431	MNN		(218)927-3170	WS 9 SS 1015	ED/HC/SN	452	329	97
AKELEY	*ST JOHN* stjohnsakeley.org	1917	PO BOX 160	56433	MNN	Karl J Yahr	(218)652-3779	WS 9 SS 1015 BC 1015	ED/HC/ MD/SN	53	45	35
ALBANY	*IMMANUEL* immanuellutheranchurchms@gmail.com www.ilcms.org	1873	23845 County Road 40 PO BOX 340	56307	MNN	David L Steege	(320)845-2620	WS 930	ED/MD	147	131	43
	POND VEIW ESTATES Satellite Site of Immanuel Albany MN	2022	334 Golf View Drive	56307								
	SONRISE		See Avon MN									
ALBERT LEA	*ALBERT LEA MN* Satellite Site of Sudanese Mankato MN	2009	924 Bridge Ave	56007				WS 12				
	ZION zion@zion4jesus.org	1945	924 BRIDGE AVE	56007	MNS	Matthew L Lehman	(507)373-8609 (507)373-7114	WS 9 SS 1015 BC 1015	ED/HC/ MD/SN			
ALBERTVILLE	*LIFE IN CHRIST* lic_admin@embarqmail.com lifeinchristonline.org	1977	5015 MAIN AVE NE	55301	MNS	Michael A Trask	(763)497-3799	WS 9 SS 1015 BC 1015	EC/ED/ HC/MD	482	353	151
	SAMARITANS HILL kharste@samaritanshill.com www.samaritanshill.com	2014	6826 LAKETOWNE PLACE NE	55301	MNS	Kenneth K Harste Kyle L Johnson	(763)595-1199	WS 10 SS 10	HS	63	47	49
ALEXANDRIA	*EBENEZER*	1874	13070 COUNTY ROAD 6 NW	56308	MNN	Scott D Brown	(309)231-4878	WS 1030 SS 1015	ED	200	169	66
	GOOD SHEPHERD goodshepherdalexsec@gmail.com www.goodshepherdalex.com	1982	2702 STATE HIGHWAY 29 N	56308	MNN	Jonathan C Jahnke	(320)762-5152	WS 9 SS 1015 BC 1015	ED/HC/ MD/SN	545	425	163
	SAINT JAMES		See Parkers Prairie MN									
	ZION zionchurch@zionalex.org www.zionalex.org	1880	300 LAKE ST	56308	MNN	Matthew S Lorenz Hayden A Brown	(320)763-4842 (320)763-3676	WS 8 1030 SS 920 BC 920	EL/ED/HC/ MD/SN	1000	754	268
ALPHA	*TRINITY*	1906	225 S Main St PO BOX 71	56111	MNS	Richard L Bremseth	(507)639-5645					
AMBOY	*ST PAUL*	1887	241 South St E PO BOX 245	56010	MNS		(507)674-3916	WS 8 SS 9	ED/HC			
ANDOVER	*FAMILY CHRIST*		See Ham Lake MN									
ANNANDALE	*BETHLEHEM* info@bethlehemlutheranchurchmn.org www.bethlehemlutheranchurchmn.org	1878	7809 County Road 35W 7809 COUNTY ROAD 35 W	55302	MNS	Brian J Thorson	(320)963-3592	WS 9 SS 1015 BC 1015		173	147	79
	ZION info@zionannandale.org zionannandale.org	1887	360 CHESTNUT ST E	55302	MNS		(320)274-5226	WS 9 SS 1015 BC 1015	ED/HC/ MD/SN	324	280	103
ANOKA	*MOUNT OLIVE* mtolive@mtolive-anoka.org www.mtolive-anoka.org	1936	700 WESTERN ST	55303	MNS		(763)421-3223 (763)576-9626	WS 8 1030 SS 915 BC 915	EC/ED/HC/ MD/SN	1145	953	295
APPLE VALLEY	*ASCENSION*		See Burnsville MN									
	MESSIAH		See Lakeville MN									
APPLETON	*TRINITY* trinityappletonmn@outlook.com trinitychurchappleton.com	1918	27 E THIELKE AVE	56208	MNN	John A Ramsbacher	(320)289-1342	WS 9 BC 10	MD	172	156	60
ARDEN HILLS	*THE GATHERING PLACE* office@gplacelm.com		3245 NEW BRIGHTON RD	55112	MNS	Yia S Lor Johnny Vang	(651)633-2402		ED	247	151	45
ARLINGTON	*PEACE* office@peacearlington.org www.peacearlington.org	1983	514 Freedom Dr PO BOX 333	55307	MNS	Craig T McCourt	(507)964-2959	WS 930 SS 815 BC 1045	ED/HC/MD	367	282	138
	ST JOHN	1859	38597 State Hwy 19 38597 STATE HIGHWAY 19	55307	MNS	Gary L Ruckman	(507)964-2400	WS 10 SS 9 BC 9				
ATWATER	*ST JOHN* stjohnlchurch@gmail.com www.stjohnatwater.com	1871	19903 56TH AVE NE	56209	MNS	John C Strickland	(320)974-8984 (320)974-8982	WS 10 SS 9 BC 9	ED/HC/ MD/SN	277	209	94
AURORA	*REDEEMER* redeemeraurora@gmail.com www.gdrlutheran.com	1955	500 CENTRAL AVE W	55705	MNN	Zachary T Klumpp	(218)229-3208	WS 11	ED/HC/ MD/SN	46	41	35
AUSTIN	*HOLY CROSS* holycrossaustin@hotmail.com	1945	300 16th St NE 300 16TH ST NE STE 2	55912	MNS	Gemechu Olana	(507)437-2107 (507)437-2107	WS 1015 BC 9	MD	48	48	14
	ST JOHN stjohns@stjohnsaustinlcms.org www.stjohnsaustinlcms.org	1908	1200 13TH AVE NW	55912	MNS		(507)433-2642	WS 9 SS 1015 BC 1015	ED/HC/MD	230	182	56
	TRINITY pastorkrusemark@yahoo.com www.facebook.com/trinitywaltham	1877	29972 570th Ave 57043 300TH ST WALTHAM	55912 55982	MNS	Jesse E Krusemark	(507)567-2272	WS 1030 SS 1030 BC 1030	ED			
AVON	*SONRISE* jmanthe24@gmail.com www.sonriseavon.org		501 Cty Rd 9 PO BOX 448	56310	MNN	Jeffrey D Manthe	(320)761-0715	WS 9 SS 1010 BC 1010	ED/HC/MD			
BABBITT	*GOOD SHEPHERD* goodshepherd1@frontiernet.net www.goodshepherdbabbitt.org	1956	10 CENTRAL BLVD	55706	MNN		(218)827-2301	WS 830 SS 930 10 BC 930	ED/MD/SN			
BACKUS	*EMMANUEL* backusoffice@tds.net www.emmanuelbackus.org	1948	603 State 371 NW PO BOX 12	56435	MNN	Travis E Lauterbach	(218)947-4182	WS 10 SS 11	ED	167	129	42
BAGLEY	*REDEEMER* www.redeemerbagley.org	1947	11 Red Lake Ave SW PO BOX E	56621	MNN		(218)694-6258	WS 930 SS 1045 BC 1045	ED/HC/ MD/SN			

*Indicates a new church start. A new church start is an intentionally organized gathering which comes together on a regular basis for the purpose of worship and/or Bible study and is intended to grow into a member LCMS congregation. WS =Worship Service; SS = Sunday School; BC =Bible Class; EC = Early Childhood; EL = Elementary School; HS = High School; ED =Education Ministry; HC =Human Care Ministry; SN = Special Needs Ministry; MD = Media Ministry (PC)=Partner Church Pastor. See Page 53 for the Table of Abbreviations for key to additional abbreviations

CITY	CONGREGATION EMAIL WEBSITE	YEAR EST	LOCATION MAILING ADDRESS	ZIP CODE(S)	DIST.	PASTOR(S)	PHONE FAX	WS SS BC	SCHOOLS/ MINISTRIES	STATISTIC Bapt	Conf	Avg Attend
BARNESVILLE	*SAINT JOHNS* secretary@stjohnsbarnesville.org www.stjohnsbarnesville.org	1947	1103 4TH AVE NE	56514	MNN	Gregory A DeMuth	(218)354-7158 (218)354-7003	WS 9 SS 1030 BC 1030	ED/MD	245	186	59
BARNUM	*EMMANUEL* pastorbradvogt@hotmail.com	1889	3756 FAIR ST	55707	MNN	Bradley A Vogt Walter Lehenbauer	(218)389-6849	WS 9 SS 8 BC 8	ED/HC/MD			
BAUDETTE	*BETHLEHEM* www.lcmsbaudette.org	1930	310 W Main PO BOX 694	56623	MNN	William F Moeller Jr	(218)634-1532	WS 9 SS 8 BC 8				
BAXTER	*PRINCE OF PEACE* info@princeofpeacelutheran.church www.princeofpeacelutheran.church	1979	6311 MILDRED RD	56425	MNN	Greggory S Coop	(218)829-7092	WS 9 SS 1030 BC 1030	ED/HC/ MD/SN	216	171	80
BECKER	*GRACE* gracelutheran@sherbtel.net www.gracebecker.org	1997	11185 27th Ave SE PO BOX 252	55308	MNN	David M Johnson	(763)262-7782 (763)262-2871	WS 9 SS 1030 BC 1030	ED/HC/ MD/SN			
BELLINGHAM	*TRINITY* revnathanielbrown@protonmail.com	1882	3197 141ST AVE	56212	MNN	Nathaniel W Brown	(320)568-2551	WS 1030 BC 1130	ED/HC/MD			
BEMIDJI	*TRINITY* trinity3@paulbunyan.net www.trinitybemidji.org	1921	123 29TH ST NE	56601	MNN		(218)444-4441 (218)444-4443	WS 9 SS 1030 BC 1030	EC/ED/MD	475	386	115
	TRINITY		See Lake George MN									
BENSON	*ST MARK* stmarksbenson@gmail.com www.stmarksbenson.org	1939	414 15TH ST N	56215	MNN	David H Baumgarn	(320)843-4131	WS 8 1030 SS 915 BC 915	ED/HC/MD	525	428	87
BERTHA	*ST PAUL* stpaulsbertha@gmail.com www.stpaulsbertha.ctshost.org	1915	203 1st Ave SE PO BOX 296 203 1 AVE SE	56437	MNN	Blake A Rickbeil	(218)924-4051	WS 9 SS 1015 BC 1015	ED/HC/ MD/SN	92	79	31
BIG LAKE	*LORD OF GLORY*		See Elk River MN									
BIWABIK	*REDEEMER*		See Aurora MN									
BLACKDUCK	*HOLY TRINITY* ruds1974@gmail.com	1921	125 1st St NW PO BOX 219	56630	MNN		(218)835-4423	WS 6				
BLAINE	*KING OF GLORY* secretary@kingofglory.org www.kingofglory.org	1969	10103 UNIVERSITY AVE NE	55434	MNS		(763)784-4229	WS 1030 SS 930 BC 930	ED/HC/MD			
BLOOMINGTON	*ASCENSION*		See Burnsville MN									
	HOLY EMMANUEL pastork@holyemmanuel.org holyemmanuel.org	1888	201 E 104TH ST	55420	MNS	Paul D Krentz	(952)888-2345 (952)888-2349	WS 930 SS 1045 BC 830 1045	EC/ED/MD	178	124	38
	MOUNT HOPE church@mthopelutheran.org www.mthopelutheran.org	1956	3601 W OLD SHAKOPEE RD	55431	MNS	Francis T Green	(952)888-5059 (952)888-7538	WS 930 SS 1045 BC 1045	ED/HC/MD	150	123	50
	REDEMPTION info@redemptionmn.org www.redemptionmn.org	1955	927 E OLD SHAKOPEE RD	55420	MNS	Joshua L Parrish	(952)881-0035	WS 9 SS 1030 BC 1030	ED/HC/ MD/SN	274	244	110
	ST MICHAELS office@smlcb.org www.smlcb.org	1964	9201 NORMANDALE BLVD	55437	MNS	Patrick S Simmons Ryan C Alvey Hunde G Takele	(952)831-5276	WS 830 10 SS 10 BC 830	EC/ED/HC/ MD/SN	868	762	285
BLUE EARTH	*IMMANUEL*	1868	43103 120th St PO BOX 392	56013	MNS		(507)526-2072	WS 8	ED/HC/ MD/SN	104	88	26
	ST PAUL stpauloffice@bevcomm.net stpaulblueearth.weebly.com	1887	305 E 5th St PO BOX 423	56013	MNS		(507)526-7318	WS 930 SS 1045 BC 1045	ED/MD/SN	572	487	87
BOCK	*ST PAUL'S*		See Milaca MN									
BOVEY	*MOUNT OLIVE* mount_olive_lutheran_church@q.com	1923	620 4th St PO BOX 508	55709	MNN	Richard G Kelm	(218)245-3983	WS 9 SS 1130	ED			
BOYD	*ZION* zionlutheran@outlook.com	1889	3472 260 Ave 3472 260TH AVE	56218	MNN	Dean G Rager	(320)855-2554	WS 830 SS 915	ED/HC/SN			
BRAHAM	*ST STEPHENS* ststephens1913@msn.com www.ststephensbraham.org	1913	400 8TH ST SE	55006	MNN	Grant T Bode	(320)396-3103 (320)396-3103	WS 1030 SS 915 BC 915	ED/MD	256	184	55
BRAINERD	*ZION* zionspt@brainerd.net www.zionbrainerd.com	1889	220 N 8TH ST	56401	MNN		(218)829-4317 (218)829-1282	WS 9 SS 1015 BC 1015	ED/MD/SN	624	490	140
BRANDON	*TRINITY*		See Evansville MN									
BRECKENRIDGE	*GRACE* gracelutheranbreck@gmail.com www.facebook.com/profile. php?id=100068121644421	1952	1100 MAIN ST	56520	MNN	Ross M Fritz	(218)643-5286	WS 9 SS 1030 BC 1030	ED/HC/ MD/SN	139	129	38
BREEZY POINT	*BREEZY POINT CHAPEL* Satellite Site of Gloria Dei Pequot Lakes MN	2011	9252 Breezy Point Dr	56472								
BREWSTER	*TRINITY*	1886	1025 4th Ave PO BOX 308	56119	MNS	David P Mc Donald	(507)842-5982					
BROOKLYN CENTER	*TRIUNE GOD* info@triunegod.net www.triunegod.net	1954	5827 HUMBOLDT AVE N BROOKLYN CTR	55430	MNS	David J Farley	(763)561-6470	WS 9 SS 1015 BC 1015	MD/SN	139	113	29
BROOKLYN PARK	*ETERNAL HOPE* office@eternalhopelutheran.com www.eternalhopelutheran.com	1972	10508 DOUGLAS DR N	55443	MNS	William J Hillyer	(763)424-8245	WS 8 1030 SS 915 BC 915	ED/HC/SN	258	205	57
	GRACE grace@gracelcms.org www.gracelcms.org	1961	6810 WINNETKA AVE N	55428	MNS		(763)533-4411 (763)533-4434	WS 8 1045 SS 930 BC 930	ED/HC/MD	319	235	53
	ST PAUL		See Osseo MN									
BROWNS VALLEY	*ZION*	1899	106 1st St S PO BOX 318	56219	MNN	Jonathan J Varns	(320)695-2354	WS 9	ED/HC/MD			

*Indicates a new church start. A new church start is an intentionally organized gathering which comes together on a regular basis for the purpose of worship and/or Bible study and is intended to grow into a member LCMS congregation. WS =Worship Service; SS = Sunday School; BC =Bible Class; EC = Early Childhood; EL = Elementary School; HS = High School; ED =Education Ministry; HC =Human Care Ministry; SN = Special Needs Ministry; MD = Media Ministry (PC)=Partner Church Pastor. See Page 53 for the Table of Abbreviations for key to additional abbreviations

CITY	CONGREGATION EMAIL WEBSITE	YEAR EST	LOCATION MAILING ADDRESS	ZIP CODE(S)	DIST.	PASTOR(S)	PHONE FAX	WS SS BC	SCHOOLS/ MINISTRIES	STATISTIC Bapt	Conf	Avg Attend
BROWNSDALE	*OUR SAVIOR* oursavior1@frontiernet.net oursaviorbrownsdale.com/default/	1937	411 W MAIN ST	55918	MNS	Gemechu Olana	(507)567-2329	WS 830 SS 945	ED/HC/MD	93	85	19
BROWNTON	*IMMANUEL* immanuellutheranbrownton.org	1895	700 Division St PO BOX 147	55312	MNS	Russell A Reed	(320)328-5522	WS 9	EC/ED/MD	578	479	119
	OUR SAVIOR		See Hutchinson MN									
BRUNO	*ST PAUL* peacelutheranmn@outlook.com	1916	7572 Pine St PO BOX 60 FINLAYSON	55712 55735	MNN	Nathaniel W Konkel	(320)233-6138	WS 1045 SS 10	ED/MD			
BUFFALO	*ST JOHN* info@stjohnsbuffalo.org stjohnsbuffalo.org	1887	302 2ND ST NE	55313	MNS	Ryan M Clark Christopher M Ryan	(763)682-1883 (763)682-1936	WS 8 1030 SS 910 BC 910	EC/ED/HC/ MD/SN	1179	761	492
BURNSVILLE	*ASCENSION* office@ascensionburnsville.org www.ascensionburnsville.org	1964	1801 E Cliff Rd 1801 CLIFF RD E	55337	MNS	Joel M Vano	(952)890-3412	WS 830 11 SS 1015 BC 945	ED/HC/ MD/SN	114	91	78
BYRON	*MOUNT MORIAH* secretary@mtmoriahluth.org mtmoriahluth.org	1977	923 2ND AVE NW	55920	MNS		(507)775-2460 (507)775-2479	WS 1045 SS 915 BC 915	ED/MD/SN	55	55	22
CALLAWAY	*BEAUTIFUL SAVIOR* beautifulsavior@arvig.net www.beautifulsaviorcallaway.com		23115 County Highway 14 PO BOX 98	56521	MNN	Matthew J Meyer	(218)375-2786	WS 930 SS 1030 BC 1030	ED/HC			
CAMBRIDGE	*JOY* ptl4joy@yahoo.com www.joylutheran.net	1970	1155 Joy Circle 1155 JOY CIR SW	55008	MNN	James P Ritter	(763)689-4355	WS 8 1030 SS 945 BC 945	ED/HC/MD	249	206	90
	ZION		See Princeton MN									
CAMPBELL	*ST PAUL* www.runestone.net/~ggroth/ churches.htm	1900	324 Connecticut Ave PO BOX 38	56522	MNN	Craig M Palach	(218)630-5377	WS 10 SS 9				
CANBY	*NICOLAI* nicolailutheranchurch@frontier.com	1884	103 HUMPHREY DR	56220	MNN	Dean G Rager	(507)223-5223	WS 830 1030 SS 945	ED/HC/ MD/SN			
CARLOS	*GOOD SHEPHERD*		See Alexandria MN									
	TRINITY TrinityLutheranCarlos@gmail.com		16 N Douglas Ave PO BOX 26	56319	MNN		(320)852-7530 (320)852-7853	WS 1045		98	90	27
CARVER	*LIVING CHRIST*		See Chanhassen MN									
	NEW CREATION		See Shakopee MN									
	SAINT JOHNS		See Chaska MN									
	TRINITY office@trinitycarver.com www.trinitycarver.com	1866	417 Oak St N PO BOX 124	55315	MNS		(952)448-3628	WS 10 SS 845 BC 845	ED/HC/MD	186	149	36
CEYLON	*OUR SAVIOR* russellreimers@frontiernet.net	1900	306 W Main St PO BOX 247	56121	MNS		(507)236-6659					
	ST PAUL pastor@sjlsherburn.com www.sjlsherburn.com/ st-pauls-wilbert-page	1890	1669 40TH ST	56121	MNS		(507)764-5312	WS 930	EL/HS/MD	155	141	60
CHANHASSEN	*LIVING CHRIST* office@livingchrist.org www.livingchrist.org	1969	820 LAKE DR	55317	MNS	Todd D Stocker	(952)934-5110 (952)934-8155	WS 8 930 SS 930	ED/HC/MD	407	349	146
	TRINITY		See Carver MN									
CHASKA	*CHRIST VICTORIOUS* mail@christvictorious.org www.christvictorious.org	1992	9860 SHADY OAK DR	55318	MNS	Aaron J Kuehn Tobias P Schmidt	(952)443-2993	WS 815 1045 SS 930	ED/HC/ MD/SN	784	613	292
	LIVING CHRIST		See Chanhassen MN									
	NEW CREATION		See Shakopee MN									
	SAINT JOHNS churchoffice@stjohns-chaska.org stjohnschaska.org	1884	300 4th St E 300 E 4TH ST	55318	MNS	Gregory J Snow Matthew A Barry	(952)448-2433 (952)448-9500	WS 8 930 1045 SS 930 BC 930	EL/HS/ ED/HC/ MD/SN	1061	835	452
	TRINITY		See Carver MN									
CHATFIELD	*CHOSEN VALLEY CARE CENTER* Satellite Site of St Paul Chatfield MN	2017	1102 Liberty St SE	55923								
	ST PAUL pastorhaugen@stpaulchatfield.org www.stpaulchatfield.org	1909	128 FILLMORE ST SE	55923	MNS	Peter J Haugen	(507)867-4604	WS 10 BC 1045	ED/HC/ MD/SN	247	172	67
CHISAGO CITY	*LORD OF LAKES*		See Forest Lake MN									
CHISHOLM	*GRACE* glcchisholm@gmail.com	1927	508 9TH ST NW	55719	MNN	Bradley N Felix	(218)254-3466	WS 1045 SS 9 1015 BC 9 1015	ED/HC/ MD/SN			
CIRCLE PINES	*GOOD SHEPHERD* office@goodshepherdlink.org www.goodshepherdlink.org	1955	1 SHEPHERD CT	55014	MNS	Theodore J Diedrick	(763)784-8417 (763)783-0977	WS 815 1045 SS 930 BC 945	ED/HC/ MD/SN	477	345	146
CLAREMONT	*ST JOHN* sjlcofcloffice@gmail.com	1865	4532 SE 84TH AVE	55924	MNS	Alan L Broadwell	(507)528-2404	WS 1030 SS 915	ED/HC/ MD/SN	239	187	25
	TRINITY		See Medford MN									
CLARISSA	*ST MATTHEW* immanuelstmatthewlcms@gmail.com	1896	101 Howe St N PO BOX 425	56440	MNN		(218)756-2395	WS 9 SS 9		100	80	8
CLEAR LAKE	*TRINITY* trinityclearlake@gmail.com trinityclearlake.org	1912	8690 1st Ave E PO BOX 152	55319	MNN	Joshua S Reber	(320)743-2919	WS 845	ED/HC/ MD/SN			
CLEMENTS	*TRINITY*		See Sanborn MN									
CLOQUET	*HOPE* hopelutheranmunger.org/	1912	4093 MUNGER SHAW RD	55720	MNN	Stafford L Thompson	(218)729-6380	WS 9 SS 1030 BC 1030	ED/HC	112	81	51

*Indicates a new church start. A new church start is an intentionally organized gathering which comes together on a regular basis for the purpose of worship and/or Bible study and is intended to grow into a member LCMS congregation. WS =Worship Service; SS = Sunday School; BC =Bible Class; EC = Early Childhood; EL = Elementary School; HS = High School; ED =Education Ministry; HC =Human Care Ministry; SN = Special Needs Ministry; MD = Media Ministry (PC)=Partner Church Pastor. See Page 53 for the Table of Abbreviations for key to additional abbreviations

CONGREGATIONS

CITY	CONGREGATION EMAIL WEBSITE	YEAR EST	LOCATION MAILING ADDRESS	ZIP CODE(S)	DIST.	PASTOR(S)	PHONE FAX	WS SS BC	SCHOOLS/ MINISTRIES	STATISTIC Bapt	Conf	Avg Attend
CLOQUET	*OUR REDEEMER* ourredeemer@orlcp.com www.orlcp.com	1901	515 SKYLINE BLVD	55720	MNN	Matthew P Kohl	(218)879-3380 (218)879-0258	WS 9 1030 SS 1030	EC/ED/ HC/SN			
COHASSET	*OUR REDEEMER* www.ourredeemercohasset.org	1971	35568 Foxtail Ln 35568 FOXTAIL LN PO BOX 8	55721	MNN		(218)328-5165	WS 10 SS 9 BC 9	EC/ED/HC/ MD/SN			
COLD SPRING	*ST PAUL*		See Eden Valley MN									
COLOGNE	*LIVING CHRIST*		See Chanhassen MN									
	ZION office@zion-cologne.org www.zion-cologne.org	1854	14745 COUNTY ROAD 153	55322	MNS	Eric L Zacharias	(952)466-3379 (952)466-2703	WS 930 SS 10	EL/HS/ED/ HC/MD	483	400	120
COLUMBIA HEIGHTS	*ST MATTHEW* www.stmatthew-ch.org	1932	4101 WASHINGTON ST NE COLUMBIA HTS	55421	MNS	William D Hugo	(763)788-9427 (763)788-5772	WS 8 1045 SS 845 BC 830	EC/ED/HC/ MD/SN	655	385	66
CORCORAN	*ST JOHN'S* secretary@stjlutheran.org www.stjlutheran.org	1856	9141 COUNTY ROAD 101	55340	MNS	Matthew V Moss Matthew P Johnson Dr Steven C Briel	(763)420-2426 (763)420-7198	WS 8 1030 SS 930 BC 930	EL/ED/MD	727	580	280
CORRELL	*GRACE* revnathanielbrown@protonmail.com	1927	309 Highway 7 N 309 STATE HIGHWAY 7	56227	MNN	Nathaniel W Brown	(320)568-2551	WS 1030 BC 1130	ED/HC			
COTTAGE GROVE	*ROSE OF SHARON* pastor@roseofsharonlutheran.org www.roseofsharonlutheran.org	1960	6875 JAMAICA AVE S	55016	MNS	Martin T Schoenfeld	(651)459-3551 (651)459-6245	WS 9 SS 1030 BC 1030	EC/ED/ HC/MD	296	281	68
	THEALLEY info@thealley.church www.theAlley.church		8944 Indahl Ave S PO BOX 489	55016	MNS	Martin D Cornes Bennego G Kangar	(651)459-2063	WS 10 SS 1030	ED/HC/MD	75	57	45
	WOODBURY		See Woodbury MN									
COTTONWOOD	*ST LUKE*		See Wood Lake MN									
COURTLAND	*IMMANUEL* church@immanuelcourtland.com www.immanuelcourtland.com	1859	County Road 25 50490 - 478TH ST	56021	MNS		(507)359-2505	WS 930	EL/ED/HC/ MD/SN	469	393	101
CROMWELL	*VILLA VISTA/CARDINAL COURT NURING AND ASSISTED LIVING* Satellite Site of St John WRIGHT MN	1974	1220 Villa Ct Dr	55726								
CROOKSTON	*OUR SAVIOR* bookkeeper.oslds@midconetwork.com www.oursaviorslutheranchurch crookston.org	1890	217 S BROADWAY	56716	MNN	Steven W Bohler	(218)281-1239	WS 8 11 SS 930 BC 930	EL/ED/HC/ MD/SN	488	372	119
CROSBY	*ZION* zip.lcms@gmail.com www.zionatcrosby.com	1924	225 4TH ST NW	56441	MNN	Donald M Klatt	(218)546-6910 (218)546-6905	WS 830 SS 10	ED/HC/ MD/SN	45	43	42
CROSSLAKE	*MISSION OF THE CROSS* motc@crosslake.net missionofthecross.org	1989	13716 COUNTY ROAD 103 PO BOX 718	56442	MNN	William J Traphagan	(218)692-4228	WS 930 SS 1045 BC 1045	ED/HC/MD	71	71	39
CROWN	*ZION*		See Saint Francis MN									
DALBO	*ZION*		See Princeton MN									
DASSEL	*OUR SAVIOR*		See Hutchinson MN									
DAYTON	*SAMARITANS HILL*		See Albertville MN									
DEEPHAVEN	*LIVING CHRIST*		See Chanhassen MN									
DEER CREEK	*TRINITY* pastortdc@arvig.net www.trinitydeercreek.org	1915	221 Clark St N PO BOX 237	56527	MNN	Donald R Wagner	(218)462-2465	WS 930 SS 10		320	250	58
DEER RIVER	*REDEEMER* janthony@paulbunyan.net	1923	41 5TH AVE NE	56636	MNN	James W Anthony	(218)259-0115	WS 1030 SS 945				
DENT	*IMMANUEL*	1911	PO BOX 127	56528	MNN	Dan C Abrahams	(218)841-8130	WS 9	ED/HC/ MD/SN			
	ST JOHN	1899	40989 355th Ave 40989 330TH AVE	56528	MNN		(218)758-2679	WS 11 SS 10	ED/HC			
DETROIT LAKES	*BEAUTIFUL SAVIOR*		See Callaway MN									
	ZION zionlcms@arvig.net www.zionlutherandl.org	1885	1100 LAKE AVE	56501	MNN	Andrew C Mussell Bruce E Noennig	(218)847-7630	WS 8 1030 SS 915 BC 915	ED/HC/MD	556	556	278
DODGE CENTER	*GRACE* info@gracedc.church gracedc.church	1892	404 CENTRAL AVE N	55927	MNS	Elliott R Malm	(507)633-2253	WS 9 SS 1030 BC 1030	EL/ED/ MD/SN	156	128	59
DORSET	*FIRST ENGLISH* information@dorsetlutheran.org	1884	20252 STATE 226 PARK RAPIDS	56470	MNN	Jordan L DeBoer	(218)732-9466	WS 9 SS 1030 BC 1030		366	228	57
DULUTH	*CHRIST*		See Superior WI									
	MOUNT OLIVE mtoliveduluth@msn.com mtoliveduluth.org	1919	2012 E SUPERIOR ST	55812	MNN	Robert C Franck	(218)724-2500 (218)728-0801	WS 930 SS 825 BC 825 630	ED/HC/ MD/SN	224	202	63
	PEACE CHRIST		See Hermantown MN									
	PERKINS FAMILY RESTERANT Satellite Site of Mount Olive Duluth MN	1994	2502 London Rd	55812								
	REDEEMER RLChurchDuluth@gmail.com	1927	9503 GRAND AVE	55808	MNN		(218)626-1630	WS 1045				
EAGAN	*ASCENSION*		See Burnsville MN									
	CHRIST christlutheraneagan@outlook.com www.christlutheraneagan.org	1910	1930 DIFFLEY RD	55122	MNS	Jared A Cooksey	(651)454-4091 (651)405-6881	WS 9 BC 1030	ED/HC/ MD/SN	613	568	75
	TRINITY LONE OAK office@trinityloneoak.org www.trinityloneoak.org	1880	2950 HIGHWAY 55	55121	MNS	James L Kroonblawd	(651)454-7235 (651)454-0109	WS 8 1030 SS 915 BC 915	EL/HS/ ED/HC/ MD/SN	524	398	120

*Indicates a new church start. A new church start is an intentionally organized gathering which comes together on a regular basis for the purpose of worship and/or Bible study and is intended to grow into a member LCMS congregation. WS =Worship Service; SS = Sunday School; BC =Bible Class; EC = Early Childhood; EL = Elementary School; HS = High School; ED =Education Ministry; HC =Human Care Ministry; SN = Special Needs Ministry; MD = Media Ministry (PC)=Partner Church Pastor. See Page 53 for the Table of Abbreviations for key to additional abbreviations

CITY	CONGREGATION EMAIL WEBSITE	YEAR EST	LOCATION MAILING ADDRESS	ZIP CODE(S)	DIST.	PASTOR(S)	PHONE FAX	WS SS BC	SCHOOLS/ MINISTRIES	STATISTIC Bapt	Conf	Avg Attend
EAGLE BEND	*IMMANUEL* immanuelstmatthewlcms@gmail.com	1916	308 South St W PO BOX 35	56446	MNN		(218)738-3912	WS 9 SS 9	ED/SN			
EAST GRAND FORKS	*FIRST* firstlutheranegf@gmail.com	1945	203 5TH ST NW E GRAND FORKS	56721	MNN	David E Laue	(218)773-0181	WS 1030 SS 915		42	39	32
ECHO	*ST LUKE*		See Wood Lake MN									
EDEN PRAIRIE	*BETHLEHEM*		See Minnetonka MN									
	LIVING CHRIST		See Chanhassen MN									
	VICTORY admin@victorylcms.org www.victorylcms.org	1991	16200 BERGER DR	55347	MNS	Brendan S Prigge	(952)934-0956	WS 9 SS 1015 BC 1015	ED/MD	156	96	110
EDEN VALLEY	*ST PAUL* stpaulsevlc@outlook.com	1911	852 Stearns Ave W PO BOX 59	55329	MNN	Benjamin A Hollingsead	(320)453-2472	WS 930 SS 815 BC 815	ED	150	120	80
EDINA	*CROSS VIEW* FrontDesk@crossview.net www.crossview.net	1969	6645 Mc Cauley Trl 6645 MCCAULEY TRL W	55439	MNS	Steven J Wheeler Dr Robert R Lessing	(952)941-1094	WS 815 1045 SS 930 BC 930	EC/ED/HC/ MD/SN	741	621	326
	ST PETERS info@stpetersedina.org www.stpetersedina.org	1929	5421 FRANCE AVE S	55410	MNS	Mark W Shockey	(952)927-8400 (952)977-9909	WS 930 SS 945 BC 1045	EC/ED/HC/ MD/SN	130	97	65
ELBOW LAKE	*CHRIST* christ@runestone.net www.christ-zion.org	1900	20 3rd Ave NE PO BOX 479	56531	MNN	William M Aufdenkamp	(218)685-5213	WS 830 SS 945 BC 945	ED/HC/ MD/SN			
ELDRED	*FIRST ENGLISH*	1928	33276 339th Ave SW PO BOX 477 CROOKSTON	56523 56716	MNN	Steven W Bohler	(218)281-1239	WS 930	ED/HC	23	18	8
ELGIN	*IMMANUEL*	1873	7134 HIGHWAY 247 NE	55932	MNS	Dean D Zemple	(507)876-2585	WS 930 SS 1030 BC 830	ED/HC/ MD/SN	119	108	35
	TRINITY trinitylutheranelgin@gmail.com www.trinitylutheranelgin.org	1894	305 1ST ST NW	55932	MNS	Joshua P Moldenhauer	(507)876-2671	WS 830 SS 830 BC 10	ED/HC/ MD/SN	538	393	80
ELIZABETH	*ST JOHN*	1873	102 Broadway W PO BOX 385 FERGUS FALLS	56533 56538	MNN		(218)736-3413			84	84	10
ELK RIVER	*EMMANUEL* emmanlutherer@gmail.com www.emmanuel-elkriver.org	1918	1506 MAIN ST NW	55330	MNN	Terry L Grzybowski	(763)441-2555	WS 8 1030 SS 1015 BC 845	EC/HS/ ED/HC/ MD/SN	163	162	63
	FAITH COMMUNITY		See Zimmerman MN									
	LORD OF GLORY office@lordofglorylutheran.org www.lordofglorylutheran.org	1977	15550 190TH AVE NW	55330	MNN	Carl J Seim	(763)263-3090	WS 8 1030 SS 915	HS/ED/ HC/SN	452	349	118
ELKO NEW MARKET	*ST JOHN*		See Webster MN									
ELLENDALE	*TRINITY*		See Medford MN									
ELMORE	*ST JOHN* mvklatt@gmail.com	1884	3893 420TH AVE	56027	MNS	Michael V Klatt	(507)943-3390	WS 10 BC 9	HC	107	105	37
ELY	*FIRST* secretary@firstlutheranely.org www.firstlutheranely.org	1890	915 E CAMP ST	55731	MNN		(218)365-3348	WS 1030	HC/MD/SN	87	63	33
ELYSIAN	*BETHLEHEM*	1921	200 Park Ave NW PO BOX 282	56028	MNS	John A Pasche	(507)362-8381	WS 830				
EMBARRASS	*REDEEMER*		See Aurora MN									
ESKO	*ST MATTHEWS* stmattsesko@aol.com stmatthewsesko.org	1902	4 ELIZABETH AVE	55733	MNN	Martin W Mably	(218)879-3510	WS 8 1030 SS 915 BC 915	EC/ED/HC/ MD/SN	612	439	169
EUCLID	*ST PAUL*	1891	13219 275th Ave SW 26395 140TH ST SW	56722	MNN	Douglas S Thompson		WS 8 SS 915	ED/HC			
EVANSVILLE	*TRINITY*	1892	19237 County Road 53 17001 COUNTY ROAD 5 NW	56326	MNN	James S Walburg	(320)876-4021	WS 9 SS 1015 BC 1015	ED/HC/ MD/SN	66	51	45
EXCELSIOR	*LIVING CHRIST*		See Chanhassen MN									
	OUR SAVIOR oursavior@oslcs.org www.oslcs.org	1924	23290 HIGHWAY 7	55331	MNS	Adam M Hengst Frederick B Limmel	(952)474-5181 (952)470-1985	WS 815 1045 BC 930	EC/EL/HS/ ED/HC/ MD/SN	532	396	184
EYOTA	*OUR SAVIOR* pastorjonvollrath@yahoo.com oursaviorseyota.org	1949	770 Robert Ave SW PO BOX 417	55934	MNS	Jonathan H Vollrath	(507)545-2067	WS 8 1030 SS 915 BC 915	ED/HC/ MD/SN	320	285	100
FAIR HAVEN	*CONCORDIA* david.buchs@gmail.com www.concordialcms.com	1887	13455 BLUFFTON RD SOUTH HAVEN	55382	MNN		(320)236-7550	WS 9 SS 1030 BC 1030	ED/HC/ MD/SN	203	151	84
FAIRFAX	*ST PETER'S*		See Gibbon MN									
FAIRMONT	*IMMANUEL* immanuel_fairmont@yahoo.com www.immanuel-fairmont.org	1897	1200 N NORTH AVE	56031	MNS	Wade A Daul Alexander A Goodwin	(507)238-1387 (507)238-2544	WS 8 1030 SS 915 BC 915	EL/HS/ED/ HC/MD	477	454	165
	ST PAUL splcoffice@splfairmont.org splfairmont.org	1883	211 BUDD ST	56031	MNS	Anthony T Bertram Michael G Holmen	(507)238-9491 (507)235-6226	WS 9 SS 1015 BC 1015	EL/HS/ ED/HC/ MD/SN	901	757	306
	ZION sjlnorthrop@gmail.com zionfraser.com	1890	1623 170TH ST	56031	MNS	John C Henry III	(507)436-5289	WS 10 SS 845 BC 845	EL/HS/ED/ HC/SN	282	218	100
FARIBAULT	*PEACE* peacelutheranlcms@gmail.com www.peace-lcms.org	1947	213 6TH AVE SW	55021	MNS		(507)334-9610	WS 8 1030 SS 920 BC 920	EC/EL/ED/ HC/MD	476	362	128
	ST JOHN		See Webster MN									
	TRINITY jenniek@trinityfaribo.org www.trinityfaribault.org	1870	530 4TH ST NW	55021	MNS	Peter L Gueldner	(507)331-6579 (507)331-0986	WS 8 1030 SS 915 BC 915	EL/ED/HC/ MD/SN	1028	785	212
	TRINITY		See Medford MN									

*Indicates a new church start. A new church start is an intentionally organized gathering which comes together on a regular basis for the purpose of worship and/or Bible study and is intended to grow into a member LCMS congregation. WS =Worship Service; SS = Sunday School; BC =Bible Class; EC = Early Childhood; EL = Elementary School; HS = High School; ED =Education Ministry; HC =Human Care Ministry; SN = Special Needs Ministry; MD = Media Ministry (PC)=Partner Church Pastor. See Page 53 for the Table of Abbreviations for key to additional abbreviations

CITY	CONGREGATION EMAIL WEBSITE	YEAR EST	LOCATION MAILING ADDRESS	ZIP CODE(S)	DIST.	PASTOR(S)	PHONE FAX	WS SS BC	SCHOOLS/ MINISTRIES	STATISTIC Bapt	Conf	Avg Attend
FARMINGTON	*TRINITY* secretary@trinityfarmington.org www.trinityfarmington.org	1937	600 WALNUT ST	55024	MNS	Dr Christian J Einertson Dr Lucas V Woodford	(651)463-7225 (651)463-7225	WS 9 SS 1030 BC 1030	ED/HC/SN	250	209	86
FERGUS FALLS	*FAITH* faithlutheran.secretary@prtel.com	1960	333 E CEDAR AVE	56537	MNN		(218)736-5352	WS 9 SS 1030 BC 1030	HC/MD	103	87	23
	IMMANUEL immanuellutheranfergusfalls@gmail.com immanuelfergusfalls.360unite.com	1872	22083 Co Hwy 10 22083 COUNTY HIGHWAY 10	56537	MNN	Keith B Ratcliffe	(218)736-6228	WS 10 SS 9 BC 9	ED/HC/MD	67	65	30
	LADIES AID / LWML Satellite Site of Immanuel Fergus Falls MN	2019	808 Sharidan St. So.	56537								
	LAKE REGION HOSP Satellite Site of Faith Fergus Falls MN	2005	712 S Cascade	56537								
	TRINITY info@trinityff.org www.trinityff.org	1873	1150 Cavour Ave W 1150 W CAVOUR AVE	56537	MNN	Christopher A Lieske	(218)736-4869 (218)739-3667	WS 9 SS 1030 BC 1030	EC/ED/HC/ MD/SN	273	234	109
FINLAYSON	*PEACE* peacelutheranmn@outlook.com www.plcms.com	1905	2177 Hwy 18 PO BOX 60	55735	MNN	Nathaniel W Konkel	(320)233-6138	WS 9 SS 1015	ED/HC/ MD/SN	280	179	79
	ST PAUL		See Bruno MN									
FISHER	*ST PAUL*		See Euclid MN									
	TRINITY	1886	305 3rd St S PO BOX 175	56723	MNN	Douglas S Thompson	(218)891-4581	WS 11 SS 10 BC 10	ED/HC/MD			
FOLEY	*ST PAUL* stpaulparishministry@gmail.com	1910	724 11th Ave 724 11TH AVE N	56329	MNN		(320)968-6400	WS 9 SS 1015	ED/HC/ MD/SN			
FOREST LAKE	*LORD OF LAKES* lotloffice@gmail.com www.lordofthelakes.org	1977	25402 ITASCA AVE	55025	MNN	Craig C Bertram	(651)462-3535	WS 8 1030 SS 930 BC 930	ED/HC/MD	332	281	129
	MESSIAH www.messiahlutheranmn.com	1972	807 Hwy 97 SE 807 HIGHWAY 97 SE	55025	EN	Gregory S Musolf	(651)464-6842	WS 9 SS 1030 BC 1030	HS			
FORESTON	*ST PAUL'S*		See Milaca MN									
FRAZEE	*BETHLEHEM* bethlech@loretel.net www.bethlehemfrazee.org	1901	210 E Maple Ave PO BOX 335	56544	MNN		(218)334-2866	WS 9 SS 10	ED/HC/MD	646	594	125
	ST JOHN	1890	37425 County Hwy 56 37425 COUNTY HIGHWAY 56	56544	MNN		(218)252-0199	WS 9 SS 1030	HC/SN			
	ST PAUL stpaulev@loretel.net	1899	13130 COUNTY HIGHWAY 39	56544	MNN		(218)334-8125	WS 9 SS 10 BC 10	ED/MD			
FULDA	*ST PAUL* stpaulsfulda@yahoo.com www.stpaulsfulda.org	1886	400 N Maryland Ave PO BOX 384	56131	MNS	Shawn P Ethridge	(507)425-2258	WS 9 SS 1015 BC 1015	ED/HC/ MD/SN	417	334	89
GARFIELD	*GOOD SHEPHERD*		See Alexandria MN									
	ST JOHN sjlgarfield.com	1910	101 Park St PO BOX 18	56332	MNN	Jeffrey C Ross	(320)834-2248	WS 9 SS 10 BC 1030	ED/HC/MD	178	144	74
	TRINITY		See Evansville MN									
GARRISON	*SHEP OF THE LAKE* sotl1982@gmail.com www.shepherdofthelake.org	1979	10583 US Highway 169 PO BOX 155	56450	MNN		(320)692-4581 (320)692-4581	WS 10 BC 830	ED/HC/ MD/SN	100	82	38
GAYLORD	*IMMANUEL* immluth55334@aol.com immanuelgaylord.org	1882	312 5th PO BOX 448	55334	MNS	Bradley D Akey	(507)237-2380 (507)237-2899	WS 930 SS 1015 BC 1015	EL/ED/HC/ MD/SN	515	431	168
	ST JOHN stjohnmtv@gmail.com	1855	23677 491 Ave 23677 491ST AVE	55334	MNS	Michael D Harman	(507)237-2782	WS 8 SS 905 BC 905	ED/HC/ MD/SN			
GIBBON	*ST PETER'S* splcgibbon@gmail.com www.splcgibbon.org	1879	63924 240TH ST	55335	MNS	Karl M Grant	(507)834-6676	WS 10 SS 830 BC 845	ED/HC/MD	246	208	96
GIESE	*IMMANUEL* pastorlanghorst@yahoo.com		12987 State Hwy 18 12987 STATE HIGHWAY 18	55735	MNN	Richard E Langhorst	(218)273-6248	WS 9				
GLEN LAKE	*BETHLEHEM*		See Minnetonka MN									
GLENCOE	*FIRST* office@1stglencoe.org firstglencoe.org	1876	925 13TH ST E	55336	MNS	Daniel J Welch Michael W Ewert	(320)864-5522 (320)864-6813	WS 8 1030 SS 915 BC 915	EL/ED/HC/ MD	1750	1493	313
	GOOD SHEPHERD office@gslcglencoe.org gslcglencoe.org	1960	1407 CEDAR AVE N	55336	MNS	Jon E Niebuhr	(320)864-6157 (320)864-8519	WS 9 SS 10 BC 10	ED/HC/ MD/SN	741	595	250
	OUR SAVIOR		See Hutchinson MN									
GOLDEN VALLEY	*GOLDEN VALLEY* mail@gvlc.net www.gvlc.net	1946	5501 GLENWOOD AVE	55422	MNS		(763)544-2810 (763)542-7824	WS 10 SS 815 BC 915	EC/ED/HC/ MD/SN	327	253	120
GOOD THUNDER	*ST JOHN* ministry@hickorytech.net www.stjohngoodthunder.org	1870	137 S Hoak St PO BOX 37	56037	MNS		(507)278-3635 (507)278-3966	WS 930 SS 1030 BC 1030	EC/EL/HS/ ED/HC/ MD/SN	420	304	59
GOODHUE	*IMMANUEL*		See Hay Creek MN									
	ST PETER tarakehren@hotmail.com	1873	28961 365TH ST	55027	MNS	Steven N Frentz	(651)923-4438	WS 1030 SS 930	ED/HC/MD	246	213	51
GRAND MARAIS	*LIFE IN CHRIST* pastor@licgm.org licgm.org	2000	2017 West Highway 61 PO BOX 765	55604	MNN	Jonathan C Watt	(515)462-0566	WS 9 BC 1030	ED/HC/MD			

*Indicates a new church start. A new church start is an intentionally organized gathering which comes together on a regular basis for the purpose of worship and/or Bible study and is intended to grow into a member LCMS congregation. WS =Worship Service; SS = Sunday School; BC =Bible Class; EC = Early Childhood; EL = Elementary School; HS = High School; ED =Education Ministry; HC =Human Care Ministry; SN = Special Needs Ministry; MD = Media Ministry (PC)=Partner Church Pastor. See Page 53 for the Table of Abbreviations for key to additional abbreviations

CITY	CONGREGATION EMAIL WEBSITE	YEAR EST	LOCATION MAILING ADDRESS	ZIP CODE(S)	DIST.	PASTOR(S)	PHONE FAX	WS SS BC	SCHOOLS/ MINISTRIES	STATISTIC Bapt	Conf	Avg Attend
GRAND MARAIS	*LIFE IN CHRIST ON GUNFLINT LAKE* Satellite Site of Life In Christ Grand Marais MN	2013	Hestons Lodge 579 S Gunflint Lake Rd	55604								
GRAND RAPIDS	*FIRST* firstev@paulbunyan.net www.flcgr.org	1917	735 NE 1ST AVE	55744	MNN	Dr Patrick S Lovejoy	(218)326-5453 (218)326-9729	WS 8 1030 SS 915 BC 915	ED/HC/ MD/SN			
	OUR REDEEMER		See Cohasset MN									
GRANITE FALLS	*ST PAUL* stpaulgf@embarqmail.com stpaulgf.org	1899	1050 10TH AVE	56241	MNN		(320)564-2221	WS 930 BC 830	ED/HC/ MD/SN	403	319	57
	WOMEN'S BIBLE STUDY Satellite Site of St Paul Granite Falls MN	2019	500 Skyview Drive	56241								
GREEN ISLE	*ST PAUL* lutheranchurchesofgi@gmail.com stpaulsgreenisle.org	1924	240 Cleveland Ave PO BOX 25	55338	MNS	Eric W Rapp	(507)326-3451	WS 9 BC 8	ED/HC/MD	234	147	46
	ZION lutheranchurchesofgi@gmail.com ziongreenisle.org	1871	20199 385th Ave PO BOX 25	55338	MNS	Eric W Rapp	(507)326-3451 (507)326-5123	WS 1030	HC/MD	121	75	27
GREY EAGLE	*ST JOHN*	1920	219 Cedar St S PO BOX 127	56336	MNN	Micheal J Bitz	(320)285-2902	WS 9 SS 10 BC 10				
GROVE LAKE	*TRINITY* ryan.j.pumphrey@gmail.com Facebook.com/LCMSinPopeCountyMN	1912	20129 County Road 29 PO BOX 36 VILLARD	56334 56385	MNN	Ryan J Pumphrey	(320)554-2161	WS 9 SS 1015 BC 6	ED/HC/SN	90	72	35
HAM LAKE	*FAMILY CHRIST* office@foclutheran.org www.foclutheran.org	1978	16345 POLK ST NE	55304	MNS	Keith H Grimm Craig A Quiring	(763)434-7337	WS 9 1030 SS 9 BC 9	EC/HS/ ED/HC/ MD/SN	1280	938	522
	SPIRIT CHRIST secretary@soclc.org www.spiritofchristhamlake.org	1982	2749 BUNKER LAKE BLVD NE	55304	MNS	Jason D Neel	(763)755-7234	WS 9 SS 1015 BC 8	ED/HC/MD			
HAMBURG	*EMANUEL* sunday.bulletinnote@gmail.com www.elchamburg.org	1857	18175 COUNTY ROAD 50	55339	MNS	Todd A Bentz	(952)467-2788 (952)467-2907	WS 9	EL/HS/ ED/HC/ MD/SN	527	452	160
HAMEL	*ST JOHN'S*		See Corcoran MN									
HAMMOND	*ST JOHN*	1895	80 3RD AVE S	55991	MNS	Dean D Zemple	(507)753-2388	WS 11 SS 12 BC 12	ED/HC/ MD/SN	56	50	18
HANLEY FALLS	*ST LUKE*		See Wood Lake MN									
HARDWICK	*ZION* zionoffice@alliancecom.net zionlutheranhardwick.com	1892	305 E 2nd St PO BOX 36	56134	MNS	Edwin J Borchardt	(507)669-2855	WS 9 SS 1030 BC 1030	ED/HC/ MD/SN	189	143	76
HASTINGS	*HOPE* office@hopeofhastings.com www.hopeofhastings.com	2002	16898 MICHAEL AVE	55033	EN	Kenneth J Boudreau	(651)480-2273	WS 9 SS 1030 BC 1030	EC/ED/MD			
	SHEP VALLEY chad@ReDOfitness.org	1985	1450 4TH ST W	55033	MNS	Chad A Kirchoff	(651)437-7010	WS 10	ED/HC/ MD/SN	64	50	60
HAY CREEK	*IMMANUEL* immanuellcms@yahoo.com www.immanuel-lcms.org	1858	24686 OLD CHURCH RD RED WING	55066	MNS	Dr Lowell S Sorenson	(651)388-4577	WS 10 SS 9 BC 9	ED/HC/ MD/SN			
HEIGHT OF LAND TOWNSHIP	*ST JOHN*		See Frazee MN									
HENDERSON	*CENTENNIAL* centenniallc@gmail.com	1939	701 Locust St PO BOX 487	56044	MNS		(507)248-3888	WS 9 SS 1015 BC 1015	HC/MD			
HENNING	*ST PAUL* stpaulsec@arvig.net stpaulhenning.net	1906	700 Douglas Ave PO BOX 332	56551	MNN	Daniel C Larsen	(218)583-2707	WS 930 SS 1040				
HERMAN	*BETHLEHEM*	1919	206 Fourth St E PO BOX 192	56248	MNN	Craig M Palach	(320)219-2154	WS 8		36	34	18
HERMANTOWN	*PEACE CHRIST* picoffice@piclutheran.org www.piclutheran.org	1990	5007 MAPLE GROVE RD	55811	MNN	Timothy J Ludwig Caleb P Weight	(218)729-9473	WS 8 1045 SS 930 BC 930	EC/ED/HC			
HERON LAKE	*OUR REDEEMER*		See Okabena MN									
HEWITT	*TRINITY*	1899	524 Front St PO BOX 116	56453	MNN			WS 11		146	97	8
HIBBING	*GRACE* office@gracehibbing.com www.gracehibbing.com	1917	4010 W 9th Ave 4010 9TH AVE W	55746	MNN	Timothy N Yearyean	(218)263-3955 (218)262-1455	WS 9 SS 1030 BC 1030	EC/ED/HC/ MD/SN	289	218	96
HILL CITY	*TRINITY* www.trinityluthhc.com	1928	113 Ione Ave PO BOX 299	55748	MNN	Michael L Eckert	(218)398-0859	WS 9	ED/HC	30	30	10
HINCKLEY	*ST JOHN*	1902	3289 VELVET ST	55037	MNN		(320)384-6884	WS 9 SS 10	ED/HC/SN			
	ST PAUL st.paulhinckley@yahoo.com stpaulhinckleymn.org	1897	405 2nd St NW PO BOX 99	55037	MNN		(320)384-6267 (320)384-6267	WS 9 SS 10 BC 1030	EC/ED/HC/ MD/SN	200	185	60
HOFFMAN	*ZION* christ@runestone.net www.christ-zion.org	1919	106 6th St S PO BOX 367	56339	MNN	William M Aufdenkamp	(320)986-2897	WS 11 SS 945	ED/HC/SN			
HOKAH	*MESSIAH*		See La Crescent MN									
HOLLAND	*SAINT JAMES* stjames@woodstocktel.net stjamesholland.com	1891	300 CARTER AVE	56139	MNS	David J Petrich	(507)347-3357 (507)347-3357	WS 10 SS 9 BC 9	ED/HC	165	145	44
HOLLANDALE	*ST PAUL'S* pastorkrusemark@yahoo.com www.facebook.com/stpaulshollandale	1926	202 Park Ave E PO BOX 219	56045	MNS	Jesse E Krusemark	(507)567-2272	WS 830				

*Indicates a new church start. A new church start is an intentionally organized gathering which comes together on a regular basis for the purpose of worship and/or Bible study and is intended to grow into a member LCMS congregation. WS =Worship Service; SS = Sunday School; BC =Bible Class; EC = Early Childhood; EL = Elementary School; HS = High School; ED =Education Ministry; HC =Human Care Ministry; SN = Special Needs Ministry; MD = Media Ministry (PC)=Partner Church Pastor. See Page 53 for the Table of Abbreviations for key to additional abbreviations

CITY	CONGREGATION EMAIL WEBSITE	YEAR EST	LOCATION MAILING ADDRESS	ZIP CODE(S)	DIST.	PASTOR(S)	PHONE FAX	WS SS BC	SCHOOLS/ MINISTRIES	STATISTIC Bapt	Conf	Avg Attend
HOLLOWAY	*IMMANUEL*	1909	510 Olivia St 1750 30TH ST NW	56249	MNN		(320)394-2308	SS 930	ED/MD/SN			
	TRINITY	1876	1746 30th St Nw 1750 30TH ST NW	56249	MNN		(320)394-2308	WS 10 SS 845	ED/HC/ MD/SN	93	93	40
HOPKINS	*BETHLEHEM*		See Minnetonka MN									
	ZION zionlutheran@zionhopkins.org www.zionhopkins.org	1915	241 5TH AVE N	55343	MNS	Randall A Neal Daniel E Schultz Howard A Krienke	(952)938-7661 (952)938-7662	WS 830 11 SS 940 BC 940	EC/ED/HC/ MD/SN			
HOVLAND	*LIFE IN CHRIST*		See Grand Marais MN									
HOWARD LAKE	*SAINT JAMES* church@stjameshl.org www.stjameshl.org	1875	1000 7th Ave PO BOX 680	55349	MNS	Mark S Loder	(320)543-2766 (320)543-3063	WS 8 1030 SS 915 BC 915	EL/HS/ ED/HC/ MD/SN	949	798	230
HOYT LAKES	*REDEEMER*		See Aurora MN									
HUGO	*NEW LIFE* newlifehugo@gmail.com newlifehugo.org	1973	6000 N 148th St 6000 148TH ST N	55038	MNS	Timothy N Heinecke	(651)429-1975 (651)429-1975	WS 9 SS 1030 BC 1030	ED/HC/ MD/SN	209	171	85
HUTCHINSON	*OUR SAVIOR* oslsecretary@oslhutch.com www.oslhutch.com	1957	800 BLUFF ST NE	55350	MNS	Daniel J Gadbaw	(320)587-3318 (320)234-7861	WS 9 SS 1015 BC 1015	EC/ED/ HC/MD	403	341	113
	PEACE office@plchutch.org www.plchutch.org	1891	400 FRANKLIN ST SW	55350	MNS	Kurt A Weber	(320)587-3031 (320)587-1162	WS 8 915 1030	EC/ED/ HC/MD	1655	1313	289
	ST JOHN sjlchrch@hutchtel.net sjlcms.org	1892	60929 110TH ST	55350	MNS	David J Markworth	(320)587-4853	WS 9 SS 1015 BC 1015	ED/HC/MD	373	314	123
INTERNATIONAL FALLS	*ST PAUL* stpaulslutheranchurch@frontier.com www.stpaulifalls.com	1913	1324 9TH ST INTL FALLS	56649	MNN		(218)283-8642 (218)283-9123	WS 11 SS 10	ED/HC/MD	247	204	35
INVER GROVE HEIGHTS	*EMANUEL* info@emanuellutheranchurch.org www.emanuellutheranchurch.org	1856	2075 70TH ST E INVER GROVE	55077	MNS	Thomas L Evans Michael R Mulso	(651)457-3929	WS 8 1030	HS/ED/ HC/MD/ SN	364	350	211
	WOODBURY		See Woodbury MN									
ISLE	*TRINITY* trinitylutheranchurchislemn@gmail.com www.trinitylutheranisle.com	1920	880 Island Ave PO BOX 51	56342	MNN	Mark L Maunula	(320)676-8774	WS 9 SS 1030 BC 1030	ED/HC/ MD/SN			
JACKSON	*OUR REDEEMER* orlc@msn.com ourredeemerjackson.org	1949	101 KIMBALL AVE	56143	MNS	John A Schuetz	(507)847-3693	WS 9 SS 1015 BC 1015	ED/MD	449	366	70
JANESVILLE	*IMMANUEL* revsipe@gmail.com www.facebook.com/profile. php?id=100057300696283	1874	30266 35TH ST	56048	MNS	Larry R Sipe Jr	(507)835-2621	WS 9 SS 10				
	TRINITY Donita@TrinityJanesville.com www.trinityjanesville.com	1880	412 N MAIN ST	56048	MNS	Jason M Wolter Timothy D Contreras	(507)231-5189	WS 8 1015 BC 915	EL/ED/HC/ MD/SN	1786	1356	311
JASPER	*TRINITY* pastormoeller@threestrandsparish.com www.threestrandsparish.com	1894	401 Wall St E PO BOX 326	56144	MNS		(507)348-4186	WS 1015	ED/MD			
JORDAN	*LIVING CHRIST*		See Chanhassen MN									
	TRINITY		See Carver MN									
KANDIYOHI	*LIVING WORD*		See New London MN									
KASOTA	*RIVER OF LIFE*		See Saint Peter MN									
KENYON	*TRINITY*		See Medford MN									
KIMBALL	*ST JOHN* stjohnskimball@gmail.com stjohnslutherankimball.org	1901	8871 135th St PO BOX 307	55353	MNN	James R Gimbel	(320)398-7151	WS 9 SS 1015 BC 1015	ED/HC/MD	526	260	92
LA CRESCENT	*MESSIAH* LCMessiahLutheran@outlook.com www.messiahlacrescent.org	1993	825 JONATHAN LN	55947	MNS	Mark R Meier Sr	(507)895-5673	WS 10 SS 9 BC 9	HS/ED/HC	93	82	25
LAKE CITY	*BETHANY* bethanylc4@hotmail.com www.bethanylutheranlakecity.com	1948	525 S 6TH ST	55041	MNS	Steven N Frentz	(651)345-2424	WS 9 SS 9	ED/HC/MD	320	284	60
LAKE CRYSTAL	*TRINITY* www.trinitylakecrystal.com	1945	342 S Main St PO BOX 873	56055	MNS	Paul A Lauer		WS 9 SS 815	EL/HS			
LAKE ELMO	*WOODBURY*		See Woodbury MN									
LAKE GEORGE	*TRINITY* trinitylakegeorge.org	1948	37115 US 71 PO BOX 1644	56458	MNN	Philip G Houser	(218)699-3693	WS 9 SS 1030 BC 1030	HC	125	110	48
LAKE SHORE	*LIVING SAVIOR* livingsavior@gmail.com www.livingsaviorchurch.org	1997	8327 INTERLACHEN RD	56468	MNN	Dr Richard J Hans	(218)963-9733 (218)961-9734	WS 9 SS 10 BC 1030	ED/HC/ MD/SN	142	110	68
LAKEFIELD	*HOLY TRINITY*	1896	76084 460th Ave PO BOX 1010	56150	MNS	Dale R Hedstrom	(308)991-7074	WS 10 SS 9 BC 9		195	158	75
	IMMANUEL immanuel@immanuellakefield.com www.immanuellakefield.com	1890	604 BUSH ST	56150	MNS	Eric P Obermann	(507)662-5718 (507)662-5820	WS 1045 SS 1015 BC 1015	EL/ED/MD	590	433	131
	ST PAUL stpaullutheranlakefield@gmail.com www.stpaulrost.com	1884	38886 800TH ST	56150	MNS	Jeffery J Sage	(507)853-4512	WS 830 SS 930	ED/MD	167	129	74
	ST PETER	1878	87977 State Hwy 86 PO BOX 1010	56150	MNS	Dale R Hedstrom	(308)991-7074	WS 830 SS 945 BC 945		174	148	62
LAKEVILLE	*MESSIAH* www.messiahonline.org	1986	16725 HIGHVIEW AVE	55044	MNS	Kurt R Klaus	(952)431-5959 (952)431-5980	WS 8 1030 SS 915 BC 915	ED/HC	1024	1024	460

*Indicates a new church start. A new church start is an intentionally organized gathering which comes together on a regular basis for the purpose of worship and/or Bible study and is intended to grow into a member LCMS congregation. WS =Worship Service; SS = Sunday School; BC =Bible Class; EC = Early Childhood; EL = Elementary School; HS = High School; ED =Education Ministry; HC =Human Care Ministry; SN = Special Needs Ministry; MD = Media Ministry (PC)=Partner Church Pastor. See Page 53 for the Table of Abbreviations for key to additional abbreviations

CITY	CONGREGATION EMAIL WEBSITE	YEAR EST	LOCATION MAILING ADDRESS	ZIP CODE(S)	DIST.	PASTOR(S)	PHONE FAX	WS SS BC	SCHOOLS/ MINISTRIES	STATISTIC Bapt	Conf	Avg Attend
LAKEVILLE	*ST JOHN*		See Webster MN									
LAMBERTON	*TRINITY*		See Sanborn MN									
LEAF VALLEY	*EBENEZER*		See Alexandria MN									
	SAINT JAMES		See Parkers Prairie MN									
LESTER PRAIRIE	*SAINT PAUL* stpaulslp@embarqmail.com www.stpaullp.org	1905	124 Maple St N PO BOX 38 LESTER PR	55354	MNS	Joseph J Barlau	(320)395-2573 (320)395-2037	WS 8 1030 SS 915 BC 915	ED/HC/MD	820	665	159
	ST PETER stpeterslp@gmail.com	1871	77 S Second Ave 77 2ND AVE S LESTER PR	55354	MNS	Joshua B Arndt	(320)395-2811	WS 9 SS 1015 BC 1015	ED/HC	169	136	58
LESUEUR	*RIVER OF LIFE*		See Saint Peter MN									
LEWISTON	*IMMANUEL* secretary@immanuelsilo.org www.immanuelsilo.org	1862	22577 COUNTY ROAD 25	55952	MNS	Herbert C Mueller III	(507)523-2228	WS 815 1030 SS 930 BC 930	EL/HS/ED/ HC/MD	676	429	233
LEWISVILLE	*TRINITY* pastorvolbrecht@gmail.com www.trinityfieldon.org	1890	47334 132nd St 109 3RD ST SE MADELIA	56060 56062	MNS	Gregory H Volbrecht	(507)642-8414	WS 730	EL/HS/ED/ MD	48	39	26
LITCHFIELD	*IMMANUEL* ilc.litch@gmail.com www.immanuellutheranlitchfield.net	1962	175 W 11TH ST	55355	MNS		(320)693-6155	WS 9 SS 1015 BC 1015	ED/MD/SN	72	68	20
	OUR SAVIOR		See Hutchinson MN									
LITTLE FALLS	*ZION* zionlf@yahoo.com www.zionlf.com	1902	411 3RD AVE NE	56345	MNN	Brandon R Johnson	(320)632-5792	WS 9 SS 1015 BC 1030	ED/HC/ MD/SN	149	141	78
LONG PRAIRIE	*TRINITY* office@trinitylp.com www.trinitylp.com	1881	610 2ND AVE SE	56347	MNN	Noah J Wehrspann	(320)732-2238 (320)732-3435	WS 9 SS 945	EC/ED/HC/ MD/SN			
LONSDALE	*ST JOHN*		See Webster MN									
LOON LAKE	*ST PAUL*		See Vergas MN									
LUTSEN	*LIFE IN CHRIST*		See Grand Marais MN									
LUVERNE	*ST JOHN* office@stjohnluverne.org stjohnluverne.org	1892	803 N CEDAR ST	56156	MNS	Dr Phillip E Booe	(507)283-2316	WS 9 SS 1015 BC 1015	EC/ED/ HC/MD	478	398	156
MADELIA	*SALEM* salemlutheran1@comcast.net	1943	109 3RD ST SE	56062	MNS	Gregory H Volbrecht	(507)642-8414	WS 9 BC 10	EL/HS/ED/ MD	123	86	45
MADISON	*MADISON HEALTHCARE SERVICES* Satellite Site of St John Madison MN	2023	900 2nd Ave	56256								
	ST JOHN stjohnslutheran@farmerstel.net	1903	822 W 6TH ST	56256	MNN	Thomas L Puffe	(320)598-7550	WS 9 BC 1015	ED/MD	264	231	38
MAHNOMEN	*BETHLEHEM*	1911	524 W Monroe Ave PO BOX 328	56557	MNN							
MAHTOMEDI	*WOODBURY*		See Woodbury MN									
MANKATO	*GOOD SHEPHERD*		See North Mankato MN									
	HOSANNA hosanna@hosanna.church hosanna.church	1972	105 HOSANNA DR	56001	MNS	Mark A Biebighauser Michael J Omtvedt Darren K Scruggs Austin M Wellhousen	(507)388-1766	WS 8 930 11 SS 930 11	ED/HC/ MD/SN			
	HOSANNA HIGHLAND CAMPUS Satellite Site of Hosanna Mankato MN	2013	329 Ellis St	56001				WS 10 SS 9				
	OUR SAVIOR contact@oslcmankato.org www.oslcmankato.org	1950	1103 N BROAD ST	56001	MNS	Adam M Matheny John H Koopman	(507)385-2180 (507)345-5113	WS 8 1030 SS 925 BC 925	ED/MD	985	791	191
	RIVER OF LIFE		See Saint Peter MN									
	SUDANESE slcmankato.org		220 E Main St Suite 2 105 HOSANNA DR	56001	MNS	James N Ruey Gatluk L Reat	(507)385-2186					
MAPLE GROVE	*BEAUTIFUL SAVIOR*		See Plymouth MN									
	SHEPHERD GROVE office@sotg.org	1974	11875 W EAGLE LAKE DR	55369	MNS	Chou Vang	(763)425-5941 (763)425-0622	WS 8 1030 BC 915	EC/ED/HC/ MD/SN	145	145	81
	ST JOHN'S		See Corcoran MN									
	ST PAUL		See Osseo MN									
MAPLETON	*ECUMEN/ THE BEACON* Satellite Site of St John Good Thunder MN	2011	206 3rd Ave NE	56065								
	MAPLETON COMMUNITY HOME Satellite Site of St John Good Thunder MN	2011	301 Trondel St SW	56065								
MAPLEWOOD	*CORNERSTONE*		See White Bear MN									
	WOODBURY		See Woodbury MN									
MARBLE	*GRACE* gracemarble@mchsi.com	1928	200 Ethel St PO BOX 430	55764	MNN	Richard G Kelm	(218)247-7451		HC			
MARSHALL	*GOOD SHEPHERD* office@gslcmarshall.org www.gslcmarshall.org	1964	1600 E COLLEGE DR	56258	MNS	James J Stefanic	(507)532-4857	WS 9 SS 1030 BC 1030	ED/HC/ MD/SN	410	240	90
MAYER	*ZION* church.office@zionmayer.org www.zionmayer.org	1883	121 Bluejay Ave 209 BLUEJAY AVENUE	55360	MNS		(952)657-2339 (952)657-7868	WS 8 1030 SS 915 BC 915	EL/HS/ED/ HC/MD	665	539	257
MC GREGOR	*OUR SAVIOR* oslutheranmcg@gmail.com oursaviorslutheranchurch.weebly.com/	1943	135 S 1ST ST MCGREGOR	55760	MNN	John M Thomson	(218)768-3198 (218)768-3198	WS 9 SS 10	ED/HC/ MD/SN			

*Indicates a new church start. A new church start is an intentionally organized gathering which comes together on a regular basis for the purpose of worship and/or Bible study and is intended to grow into a member LCMS congregation. WS =Worship Service; SS = Sunday School; BC =Bible Class; EC = Early Childhood; EL = Elementary School; HS = High School; ED =Education Ministry; HC =Human Care Ministry; SN = Special Needs Ministry; MD = Media Ministry (PC)=Partner Church Pastor. See Page 53 for the Table of Abbreviations for key to additional abbreviations

CITY	CONGREGATION EMAIL WEBSITE	YEAR EST	LOCATION MAILING ADDRESS	ZIP CODE(S)	DIST.	PASTOR(S)	PHONE FAX	WS SS BC	SCHOOLS/ MINISTRIES	STATISTIC Bapt	 Conf	 Avg Attend
MC INTOSH	*IMMANUEL* jstark@gvtel.com	1918	305 Jackson Ave Nw PO BOX 128 MCINTOSH	56566 56556	MNN	Bruce L Blocker	(218)563-2121	WS 9 SS 1015				
MCGRATH	*GRACE*	1922	Hwy 65 21995 230TH LN MC GRATH	56350	MNN		(320)592-3682	WS 11 SS 10				
MEDFORD	*TRINITY* tlcmedfordoffice@gmail.com www.tlcmedford.org	1935	102 3rd St SW PO BOX 209	55049	MNS	Ian O Thormodson	(507)451-0447	WS 9 SS 9 BC 9	ED/HC/ MD/SN	397	292	76
MELROSE	*SAINT PAULS* stpauls@meltel.net www.stpaulsmelrose.org	1884	207 5TH ST NE	56352	MNN	David R Mommens	(320)256-3847	WS 9 SS 1020 BC 1020	ED/HC			
MENAHGA	*REDEEMER*	1890	15 12th St SE PO BOX 306	56464	MNN	Terry L Yahr	(218)564-4931	WS 9	ED/HC/MD	80	80	21
MILACA	*ST PAUL'S* church@stpaulsmilaca.org www.stpaulsmilaca.org	1920	12662 Hwy 23 12662 STATE HIGHWAY 23	56353	MNN	Daniel R Carlson	(320)982-6703	WS 9 SS 1030 BC 1030	ED/MD/SN	123	104	50
	ZION		See Princeton MN									
MILLERVILLE	*TRINITY*		See Evansville MN									
MILTONA	*MOUNT CALVARY* mtcalvarystpauls@arvig.net	1942	149 4th Ave PO BOX 52	56354	MNN		(218)943-5251	WS 845	ED/HC			
	ST PAUL		See Parkers Prairie MN									
MINNEAPOLIS	*BEREA*		See Richfield MN									
	FAITH felc@q.com faithlutheranmpls.org	1926	3430 E 51ST ST	55417	MNS	Dr Jared D Yogerst	(612)729-5463 (612)729-1856	WS 9 SS 1030 BC 1030	ED/SN	89	67	18
	GLORIA DEI info@gloriadeilcms.org www.gloriadeilcms.org	1951	3014 MCKINLEY ST NE	55418	MNS	Matthew A Cephus	(612)781-1989 (612)789-9727	WS 10	ED/HC/ MD/SN	47	47	28
	JAPANESE FELLOWSHIP genhashim1@gmail.com	1981	4217 BLOOMINGTON AVE S	55407	MNS		(612)722-8234					
	MOUNT HOPE		See Bloomington MN									
	ROYAL FAMILY mattcephus7@yahoo.com		C/O GLORIA DEI LUTHERAN CHURCH 3014 MCKINLEY ST NE	55418	MNS		(612)781-1989			80	80	40
	SAINT JAMES		See West Saint Paul MN									
	ST MATTHEW		See Columbia Heights MN									
	ST PETERS		See Edina MN									
	TRINITY FIRST info@trinityfirst.org www.trinityfirst.org	1856	1115 E 19TH ST	55404	MNS	Jonathan D Kuehne	(612)870-9487 (612)871-6550	WS 930	EL/ED/HC			
	UNIV CHAPEL revkind@gmail.com ulcmn.com	1925	316 10TH AVE SE	55414	MNS	David A Kind	(612)331-2747	WS 10 SS 845 BC 845	ED/HC/MD	159	138	126
MINNESOTA LAKE	*ST JOHN* revsipe@gmail.com www.facebook.com/profile.php?id=61550721968292	1873	11593 626 Ave 62747 121ST ST MINNESOTA LK	56068	MNS	Larry R Sipe Jr				75	74	18
MINNETONKA	*BETHLEHEM* office@blcmtka.org blcmtka.org	1948	5701 EDEN PRAIRIE RD	55345	MNS		(952)934-9633 (952)934-9633	WS 930 SS 1045 BC 1045	ED/HC/ MD/SN			
	LIVING CHRIST		See Chanhassen MN									
MINNETRISTA	*LIVING CHRIST*		See Chanhassen MN									
MONTEVIDEO	*ST JOHN'S* SJTLutheran@gmail.com www.sj-lutheran.org	1885	3090 40th Ave SW 4005 40TH ST SW	56265	MNN	Kent A Borglum	(605)999-5591	WS 1030 SS 930	ED/HC/ MD/SN	116	101	35
	ST PAUL office@stpaulmonte.org	1916	321 N 5TH ST	56265	MNN	Keith A Brustuen	(320)269-7145	WS 9 SS 1015 BC 1015	ED/HC/ MD/SN	285	224	59
	TRINITY SJTLutheran@gmail.com	1894	1055 20th St NE 4005 40TH ST SW	56265	MNN	Kent A Borglum	(605)999-5591	WS 9	ED/MD	53	48	18
MONTGOMERY	*ST JOHN*		See Webster MN									
MONTICELLO	*SAMARITANS HILL*		See Albertville MN									
MOORHEAD	*OUR REDEEMER* orlcmoorhead@outlook.com www.ourredeemermoorhead.org	1941	1000 14TH ST S	56560	MNN	David S Pitsch	(218)233-7569	WS 8 1030 SS 915 BC 915	EL/ED/HC/ MD/SN	672	491	201
MOOSE LAKE	*ST PETER* pastorbradvogt@hotmail.com	1895	1030 Folz Blvd 4600 FOLZ BLVD	55767	MNN	Bradley A Vogt Walter Lehenbauer	(218)485-4902	WS 1030 BC 1130	ED/HC/MD			
MORA	*ZION*	1902	401 HIGHWAY 65 S	55051	MNN	Anthony C Cloose	(320)679-1094 (320)679-1096	WS 930 SS 1045 BC 1045	EC/ED/HC/ MD/SN			
MORRIS	*WEST CENTRAL HOMES* Satellite Site of Zion Morris MN	2012	6 Thomas Ave	56267								
	ZION zion@hometownsolutions.net zion-morris.360unite.com	1960	315 S COLUMBIA AVE	56267	MNN	Reed J Stockman	(320)589-2744	WS 9 BC 1030	EC/ED/ MD/SN	161	133	57
MORRISTOWN	*BETHLEHEM* blcmorristown@gmail.com Bethlehem-morristown.org	1910	404 W Franklin St PO BOX 346	55052	MNS	Weslie T Odom	(507)685-4338	WS 9 SS 1030 BC 1030	ED/HC/ MD/SN	338	240	117
	TRINITY www.schm12.wix.com/morristowntlccom	1868	10500 215TH ST W	55052	MNS	Juan D Palm	(507)685-2307	WS 930 SS 1045 BC 830	EL/ED	300	232	65
MOTLEY	*ST JOHN* stjohnsmotley@brainerd.net	1926	497 3RD AVE S	56466	MNN	Paul E Koehler	(218)352-6399 (218)352-8322	WS 930	ED/HC/MD	150	122	27
MOUND	*LIVING CHRIST*		See Chanhassen MN									

*Indicates a new church start. A new church start is an intentionally organized gathering which comes together on a regular basis for the purpose of worship and/or Bible study and is intended to grow into a member LCMS congregation. WS =Worship Service; SS = Sunday School; BC =Bible Class; EC = Early Childhood; EL = Elementary School; HS = High School; ED =Education Ministry; HC =Human Care Ministry; SN = Special Needs Ministry; MD = Media Ministry (PC)=Partner Church Pastor. See Page 53 for the Table of Abbreviations for key to additional abbreviations

CONGREGATIONS

CITY	CONGREGATION EMAIL WEBSITE	YEAR EST	LOCATION MAILING ADDRESS	ZIP CODE(S)	DIST.	PASTOR(S)	PHONE FAX	WS SS BC	SCHOOLS/ MINISTRIES	STATISTIC Bapt	Conf	Avg Attend
MOUND	*MOUNT OLIVE* admin@mountolivelcms.org www.mountolivelcms.org	1927	5218 BARTLETT BLVD	55364	MNS	Michael E Michalk	(952)472-2756	WS 9 SS 950	ED/HC/ MD/SN	147	116	52
MOUNDS VIEW	*MESSIAH* messiah@messiah-lutheran.org messiah-lutheran.org	1941	2848 COUNTY ROAD H2	55112	MNS	Paul J Pfotenhauer	(763)784-1786 (763)784-1927	WS 8 1030 SS 915 BC 915	EC/ED/HC/ MD/SN	882	691	210
MOUNTAIN LAKE	*TRINITY* trinitylutheransec@gmail.com trinitymtnlake.360unite.com	1898	1418 2ND AVE	56159	MNS	Richard L Bremseth	(507)427-2451 (507)427-2611	WS 830 SS 945	HC/MD	496	382	73
MUNGER	*HOPE*		See Cloquet MN									
NEW GERMANY	*ST JOHN* djmahlum@embarqmail.com www.stjohnlutheranhollywood.org	1865	17725 53RD ST	55367	MNS		(952)353-2406 (952)353-1619	WS 930 SS 1030 BC 1030	EL/HS/ ED/HC/ MD/SN			
	ST MARK stmarknewgermany@gmail.com	1914	510 E Broadway PO BOX 69	55367	MNS	Aaron J Beckman	(952)353-2464	WS 9 SS 1015 BC 1015	EL/HS/ ED/HC/ MD/SN	315	276	120
NEW LONDON	*LIVING WORD* www.livingwordlutheran.net	2005	16245 County Road 9 NE PO BOX 242	56273	MNN	David A Dauk	(320)354-4637	WS 10 SS 9 BC 9	ED/HC/MD			
NEW PRAGUE	*ST JOHN*		See Webster MN									
NEW ULM	*REDEEMER* redeemer@newulmtel.net www.redeemernewulm.net	1947	700 S BROADWAY ST	56073	MNS	Brian R Scoles	(507)233-3470 (507)359-7789	WS 9 SS 1015 BC 1030	EC/ED/MD	443	358	102
NEW YORK MILLS	*TRINITY* trinity1892@nymtrinity.org nymtrinity.org	1892	424 E Gilman St PO BOX J NEW YORK MLS	56567	MNN	Kirk D Douglas	(218)385-2450 (218)385-4533	WS 8 1030 SS 915 BC 915	EC/ED/HC/ MD/SN	950	629	229
NEWPORT	*WOODBURY*		See Woodbury MN									
NICOLLET	*GOOD SHEPHERD*		See North Mankato MN									
NIMROD	*NIMROD* gracesebeka@wcta.net www.facebook.com/gracesebeka/	1946	28134 County Road 26 500 WELLS AVE N SEBEKA	56478 56477	MNN		(218)472-3306		ED			
NORTH BRANCH	*LIVING BRANCH* pastorglenkleppe@livingbranch.org www.LivingBranch.org	1997	6486 Elm St PO BOX 335	55056	MNN	Glen A Kleppe	(651)674-5576	WS 8 SS 9 BC 9	ED/HC	73	60	33
	ST JOHN stjohnlutheranweber@gmail.com	1870	28168 JODRELL ST NE	55056	MNN	Paul D Anderson	(763)444-5988	WS 9 SS 1030 BC 1030	ED/HC			
NORTH MANKATO	*GOOD SHEPHERD* goodshepmankato@gmail.com www.goodshepherdmankato.org	1957	2101 LOR RAY DR	56003	MNS	LeRoy J LaPlant	(507)388-4336 (507)388-2160	WS 9 SS 1015 BC 1015	EL/ED/ MD/SN	218	109	78
	RIVER OF LIFE		See Saint Peter MN									
NORTH SAINT PAUL	*WOODBURY*		See Woodbury MN									
NORTHFIELD	*ST JOHN*		See Webster MN									
	TRINITY inquiries@trinitynorthfield.org www.trinitynorthfield.org	1932	803 WINONA ST	55057	MNS	Dr Brent A Klein Dr Armand J Boehme	(507)645-4438 (507)645-0658	WS 9 SS 1030 BC 1030	ED/HC/MD	515	384	87
NORTHROP	*SAINT JAMES* sjlnorthrop@gmail.com www.sjlnorthrop.com	1889	108 S James St PO BOX 315	56075	MNS	John C Henry III	(507)436-5289	WS 830 SS 945 BC 945	EL/HS/ ED/HC	393	298	101
NORWOOD YOUNG AMERICA	*ST JOHN* churchoffice@stjohnsnya.org www.stjohnsnya.org	1865	101 SE 2nd Ave 101 2ND AVE SE NYA	55397	MNS	Joshua P Bernau Joshua W Hoffman	(952)467-2740 (952)467-2846	WS 830 1030 SS 945 BC 945	EL/HS/ ED/HC/ MD/SN	1080	857	432
NOWTHEN	*ST JOHN* michelle.gueldner@sjlcas.com	1876	9231 VIKING BLVD NW ELK RIVER	55330	MNS	Eric W Voigt	(763)441-3646	WS 8 1030 SS 915 BC 915	EL/HS/ ED/HC/ MD/SN			
OAKDALE	*PEACEFUL LODGE SENIOR LIVING APARTMENTS* Satellite Site of Eastern Hghts Saint Paul MN	2017	6630 Hudson Blvd	55128								
	WOODBURY		See Woodbury MN									
ODESSA	*TRINITY* revnathanielbrown@protonmail.com	1892	204 Cedar Ave S PO BOX 38	56276	MNN	Nathaniel W Brown	(320)568-2551	WS 830 BC 1130	MD	28	28	21
OGILVIE	*ST PAUL* splcogilvie@gmail.com www.luther95.com/SPLC-OMN	1912	301 Church Ave PO BOX 67	56358	MNN		(320)272-4352 (320)272-4352	WS 9	ED/MD/SN	122	101	31
OKABENA	*OUR REDEEMER* sporchurch@yahoo.com	1949	120 NORTH FRONT ST	56161	MNS	Jeffery J Sage	(507)853-4512	WS 8	ED/MD	126	114	24
ONAMIA	*ST PAUL'S*		See Milaca MN									
ORMSBY	*IMMANUEL* trinitytrimont@gmail.com	1885	2325 120TH AVE	56162	MNS	Logan S Smith	(507)639-4111	WS 1045	EL/HS/HC/ MD	82	75	23
ORROCK	*FAITH COMMUNITY*		See Zimmerman MN									
ORTONVILLE	*TRINITY* ofc.tlcort@midconetwork.com www.trinitylutheranortonville.org	1896	341 PARK ST	56278	MNN		(320)839-3422 (320)839-2672	WS 9 SS 10 BC 10	ED/HC/ MD/SN	523	375	140
OSAKIS	*GOOD SHEPHERD*		See Alexandria MN									
	REDEEMER redeemerisalive@outlook.com	1948	418 3RD AVE W	56360	MNN		(320)859-2769		ED/HC/SN			
OSSEO	*ST JOHN'S*		See Corcoran MN									
	ST PAUL office@stpaulsosseo.org www.stpaulsosseo.org	1867	710 BROADWAY ST E	55369	MNS	Daniel R Burns	(763)425-2238	WS 830 SS 915 BC 915	HC/MD	367	290	78
OTSEGO	*SAMARITANS HILL*		See Albertville MN									
OTTERTAIL	*ST JOHN* stjohnot@arvig.net www.stjohnottertail.org	1885	31963 County Hwy 61 PO BOX 125	56571	MNN	Karl A Weber	(218)367-2470	WS 930 SS 1045 BC 1045	ED/HC/MD	377	344	101

*Indicates a new church start. A new church start is an intentionally organized gathering which comes together on a regular basis for the purpose of worship and/or Bible study and is intended to grow into a member LCMS congregation. WS =Worship Service; SS = Sunday School; BC =Bible Class; EC = Early Childhood; EL = Elementary School; HS = High School; ED =Education Ministry; HC =Human Care Ministry; SN = Special Needs Ministry; MD = Media Ministry (PC)=Partner Church Pastor. See Page 53 for the Table of Abbreviations for key to additional abbreviations

CITY	CONGREGATION EMAIL WEBSITE	YEAR EST	LOCATION MAILING ADDRESS	ZIP CODE(S)	DIST.	PASTOR(S)	PHONE FAX	WS SS BC	SCHOOLS/ MINISTRIES	STATISTIC Bapt	 Conf	 Avg Attend
OTTERTAIL	*ST PAUL*		See Richville MN									
OWATONNA	*GOOD SHEPHERD* info@gsowatonna.com www.goodshepherdowatonna.com	1984	2500 7TH AVE NE	55060	MNS	Gregory A Schlicker Daniel G Borkenhagen Harold A Storm	(507)451-4125	WS 830 10 SS 10	EC/ED/HC/ MD/SN	1329	989	364
	TRINITY		See Medford MN									
PARK RAPIDS	*ST JOHN* stjohnslutheranpr@gmail.com www.stjohnspr.org	1908	Hwy 34 W 803 1ST ST W	56470	MNN	James H Neubauer Chad S Berg	(218)732-9783 (218)237-9785	WS 8 1030 SS 915 BC 915	EC/ED/ MD/SN	829	652	178
	TRINITY		See Lake George MN									
PARKERS PRAIRIE	*IMMANUEL* immanuel@midwestinfo.net www.immanuelparkersprairie.com	1905	709 S Douglas Ave PO BOX 66 PARKERS PR	56361	MNN	Kirk E Lee	(218)338-2511 (218)338-5106	WS 9 SS 1030 BC 1030	ED/HC/MD	849	648	115
	MOUNT CALVARY		See Miltona MN									
	SAINT JAMES	1874	10159 County Hwy 63 10159 COUNTY RD 63 PARKERS PRARE	56361	MNN	Scott D Brown	(320)760-5328	WS 1030 SS 9	ED/HC	86	76	40
	ST PAUL	1890	19020 W Miltona Rd NE 123 COUNTY ROAD 63 NW PARKERS PR	56361	MNN		(218)943-4774	WS 1030 SS 10				
	ZION dwangland@gmail.com	1884	14570 500TH AVE PARKERS PR	56361	MNN	Dennis W Angland	(320)760-5328	WS 930				
PAYNESVILLE	*LIVING WORD*		See New London MN									
	ST PAUL		See Eden Valley MN									
PEASE	*ST PAUL'S*		See Milaca MN									
PEQUOT LAKES	*GLORIA DEI* info@gloriadeipl.org	1959	30701 Patriot Avenue PO BOX 126	56472	MNN	Monte L Meyer	(218)568-5668	WS 9 SS 10 BC 1015	ED/HC/ MD/SN			
PERHAM	*ST JOHN* www.stjohnsperham.org	1891	49658 County Hwy 53 49658 COUNTY HIGHWAY 53	56573	MNN	Justin D Whitmore	(218)346-4302 (218)346-4302	WS 930 SS 830 BC 830	ED/HC/ MD/SN			
	ST PAUL churchoffice@stpaulsperham.org www.stpaulsperham.org	1875	500 6TH AVE SW	56573	MNN	Andrew B Ratcliffe	(218)346-7725	WS 9 SS 1015 BC 1015	EL/ED/HC/ MD/SN	927	657	235
PINE CITY	*ZION* zionpinecity@gmail.com www.zionpinecity.org	1884	410 MAIN ST S	55063	MNN		(320)629-3683	WS 8 SS 930 BC 930	EC/ED/HC/ MD/SN			
PINE RIVER	*GOOD SAMARITAN INDEPENDENT LIVING* Satellite Site of Emmanuel Backus MN	2016	2175 White Pine Point Rd SW	56474								
	GOOD SAMARITAN SOCIETY Satellite Site of Mission Of The Cross CROSSLAKE MN	2011	2175 White Pine Rd SW	56474								
PIPESTONE	*OUR SAVIOUR* secretaryoslc@gmail.com www.threestrandsparish.com	1955	1102 7TH AVE SW	56164	MNS		(507)825-4124	WS 1015 SS 1115 BC 1115	ED/HC/ MD/SN	125	104	28
	SAINT JAMES		See Holland MN									
	ST PAUL stpaulpipestone@gmail.com www.stpaulpipestone.com	1892	621 W MAIN ST	56164	MNS	Christopher M Amen	(507)825-5271 (507)825-2499	WS 9 SS 10 BC 10	EC/ED/HC/ MD/SN			
PLAINVIEW	*IMMANUEL* office@immanuelplainview.org immanuelplainview.org	1875	45 W BROADWAY	55964	MNS	John P Augustine	(507)534-3700	WS 8 1015 SS 915 BC 915	EL/HS/ ED/HC/ MD/SN	740	588	156
PLATO	*ST JOHN* secretary@christ-4-u.org www.christ-4-u.org	1879	216 Mc Leod Ave N 216 MCLEOD AVE N	55370	MNS	Tyson F Mastin	(320)238-2338	WS 9 SS 1010 BC 1010	ED/MD	286	276	45
PLUMMER	*REDEEMER*	1919	170 Pleth Ave W 19288 190TH ST SE	56748	MNN	Jeffrey S Lytle				30	30	13
PLYMOUTH	*BEAUTIFUL SAVIOR* info@beautifulsaviorlc.org www.beautifulsaviorlc.org	1923	5005 NORTHWEST BLVD	55442	MNS	Joseph C Behnke	(763)550-1000	WS 830 1045 SS 945 1045	EC/ED/HC/ MD/SN	1752	1367	605
	GLORY OF CHRIST secretary@gloryofchrist.org www.gloryofchrist.org	1985	4040 Highway 101 N 4040 COUNTY ROAD 101 N	55446	MNS	Jeremiah D Johnson Kyle D Krueger John R Fehrmann	(763)478-6031	WS 8 1045 SS 930 BC 930	ED/HC/MD	557	444	297
POSEN TOWNSHIP	*ST LUKE*		See Wood Lake MN									
PRINCETON	*FAITH COMMUNITY*		See Zimmerman MN									
	ST PAUL'S		See Milaca MN									
	ZION zlc1@live.com www.zionprinceton.com	1876	5972 70th Ave PO BOX 310	55371	MNN	Steven L Tischer	(763)389-1286	WS 10 SS 9 BC 9		125	125	85
PRIOR LAKE	*HOLY CROSS* holycross@holycross-pl.org www.holycross-pl.org	1989	14085 PIKE LAKE TRL NE	55372	MNS	Marc T Engelhardt	(952)445-1779 (952)445-6997	WS 815 11 SS 945 BC 945	ED/HC	71	59	51
	IMMANUEL office@immanuel-fishlake.org www.immanuel-fishlake.org	1871	20200 FAIRLAWN AVE	55372	MNS	Dr Brent L Parrish	(952)492-6010 (952)492-2810	WS 8 1030 SS 915 BC 915	ED/HC/ MD/SN			
	ST JOHN		See Webster MN									
	ST PAUL church_admin@stpaulspriorlake.org www.stpaulspriorlake.org	1924	5634 LUTHER RD SE	55372	MNS		(952)447-2117 (952)447-2119	WS 8 1030 BC 915	EL/ED/HC/ MD/SN	382	204	127
RACINE	*IMMANUEL* marc.freiberg.sr@gmail.com	1874	73297 310 St 73278 310TH ST	55967	MNS	Marc L Freiberg Sr	(507)754-5782	WS 830 SS 930	ED/HC/MD			
RADIUM	*IMMANUEL*		See Warren MN									
RAMEY	*BETHANY*	1922	34238 NATURE RD FOLEY	56329	MNN		(320)355-2604	WS 10				

*Indicates a new church start. A new church start is an intentionally organized gathering which comes together on a regular basis for the purpose of worship and/or Bible study and is intended to grow into a member LCMS congregation. WS =Worship Service; SS = Sunday School; BC =Bible Class; EC = Early Childhood; EL = Elementary School; HS = High School; ED =Education Ministry; HC =Human Care Ministry; SN = Special Needs Ministry; MD = Media Ministry (PC)=Partner Church Pastor. See Page 53 for the Table of Abbreviations for key to additional abbreviations

CITY	CONGREGATION EMAIL WEBSITE	YEAR EST	LOCATION MAILING ADDRESS	ZIP CODE(S)	DIST.	PASTOR(S)	PHONE FAX	WS SS BC	SCHOOLS/ MINISTRIES	STATISTIC Bapt	Conf	Avg Attend
RANDALL	*ST PETER* stpeterrandalllcms@brainerd.net	1895	413 Parkview Dr PO BOX 32	56475	MNN	Joseph E Crosswhite III	(320)749-2477	WS 1015 SS 9		77	72	18
RED LAKE FALLS	*ST JOHN* stjohnrlf@gvtel.com www.stjohnrlf.org	1888	702 Main Ave S PO BOX 387 RL FALLS	56750	MNN	Jeffrey S Lytle	(218)253-2987	WS 1030 SS 9 BC 920	ED/MD	160	104	72
RED WING	*CONCORDIA* concordiarw@outlook.com	1947	1805 BUSH ST	55066	MNS		(651)388-5447 (651)388-3839	WS 930 SS 830 BC 830	EC/ED/ HC/MD	160	160	50
REDWOOD FALLS	*TRINITY*		See Sanborn MN									
RICE	*SHEPHERD PINES* office@sotpministries.com www.sotpministries.com	1989	1950 125TH ST NW	56367	MNN	Timothy D Schiller	(320)393-4295 (320)393-4885	WS 9 SS 1020 BC 1030	ED/HC/MD	418	338	134
RICHFIELD	*BEREA* info@berealutheran.org www.berealutheran.org	1945	7538 EMERSON AVE S	55423	MNS	Kevin N Tiaden	(612)861-7121 (612)869-5141	WS 9 SS 1015 BC 1015	ED/HC/ MD/SN	317	270	68
	MOUNT CALVARY info@mtcalvaryrichfield.org www.mtcalvaryrichfield.org	1933	6544 16TH AVE S	55423	MNS	Jason D Krause	(612)866-5405 (612)866-6005	WS 9 SS 1030 BC 1030	EC/ED/MD	175	154	57
	ST PETERS		See Edina MN									
RICHMOND	*ST PAUL*		See Eden Valley MN									
RICHVILLE	*ST PAUL* www.stpaulslcms.net	1926	750 W 1ST ST	56576	MNN	Karl A Weber		WS 8				
ROBBINSDALE	*GRACE INTERNATIONAL* isaacnbrenda@aol.com		C/O PEACE LUTHERAN CHURCH 4512 FRANCE AVE N	55422	MNS	Isaac T Williams	(651)890-6708	WS 1145 SS 11				
	PEACE office@peacelutheranmn.org www.peacelutheranmn.org	1945	4512 FRANCE AVE N	55422	MNS	Steven M Jones	(763)533-0570	WS 915 SS 1030	ED/HC/ MD/SN	182	160	57
	REDEEMER redeemer.ev@q.com www.redeemer-lutheran-robbinsdale.org	1924	4201 REGENT AVE N	55422	MNS		(763)533-2564 (763)533-1075	WS 9 SS 1030 BC 1030	ED/HC/ MD/SN	85	85	14
ROCHESTER	*GRACE* office@gracebythelake.org www.gracebythelake.org	1944	800 E Silver Lake Dr 800 E SILVER LAKE DR NE	55906	MNS	Dr William L Keller II	(507)289-7833 (507)289-2888	WS 9 SS 1030 BC 1030	EL/ED/ HC/SN			
	HOLY CROSS office@holycross-church.org www.holycross-church.org	1962	2703 9TH AVE NW	55901	MNS	Jeffrey W Niederstadt	(507)289-1354 (507)289-4815	WS 930 SS 1045 BC 1045	EL/ED/HC/ MD/SN	377	227	143
	REDEEMER office@redeemer-rochester.com www.redeemer-rochester.com	1932	869 7TH AVE SE	55904	MNS	Adam B Koglin Andrew M Pronsati	(507)289-5147 (507)289-7887	WS 8 1040 SS 920 BC 920	ED/HC/ MD/SN	1169	973	449
	ROCHESTER WORSHIP SVC & BIBLE ST. Satellite Site of Japanese Fellowship Minneapolis MN	2019	869 7th ave SE	55904				WS 11				
	TRINITY office@trinitylutheranchurch.org www.trinitylutheranchurch.org	1867	222 6TH AVE SW	55902	MNS	Nathaniel R Schwartz Timothy D Smith	(507)289-1531 (507)287-9882	WS 8 1030 SS 915 BC 915	EL/ED/HC/ MD/SN	1065	876	401
ROGERS	*SAMARITANS HILL*		See Albertville MN									
	ST JOHN'S		See Corcoran MN									
ROSEMOUNT	*OUR SAVIOR* kghhsu@yahoo.com www.osfamily.org	1965	14980 DIAMOND PATH W	55068	MNS	Kenneth G Hsu	(651)423-2580 (651)423-2581	WS 830 10 SS 10	EC/ED/ HC/MD			
	SAINT JOHN sjrv.office@frontier.com stjohnsrichvalley.com	1911	14385 Blaine Ave E 14385 BLAINE AVE	55068	MNS	Christopher P Horton	(651)423-2149	WS 930 SS 1045 BC 1045	ED/SN	182	137	46
ROSEVILLE	*KING OF KINGS* churchoffice@kingofkingsroseville.org kingofkingsroseville.org	1963	2330 DALE ST N	55113	MNS	Steven M Bielenberg Matthew D Lane	(651)484-5142 (612)540-0739	WS 830 11 SS 945 BC 945	EL/HS/ ED/HC/ MD/SN	956	667	254
ROUND LAKE	*BETHEL*	1931	501 MAIN ST	56167	MNS		(507)945-8102	WS 9	ED/HC/ MD/SN			
ROYALTON	*BETHANY*		See Ramey MN									
	ST JOHN	1886	26733 63rd St 27066 93RD ST PIERZ	56373 56364	MNN		(320)420-2276	WS 930 SS 1030	ED/HC/ MD/SN			
	ST PAUL	1947	13 S Driftwood St PO BOX 216	56373	MNN	Joseph E Crosswhite III	(320)584-8367	WS 830 SS 945	ED/HC/MD			
RUSH CITY	*ST JOHNS* stjohns@midco.net www.stjohnsrushcity.org	1873	980 W 4th St PO BOX 368	55069	MNN	Grant T Bode	(320)358-3623	WS 845 SS 955 BC 730	HC/MD			
RUSHFORD	*ST JOHN* stjohnshart@acegroup.cc	1862	31497 Highway 43 31497 STATE HIGHWAY 43	55971	MNS	Thomas G Volker	(507)864-2585	WS 1015 SS 9	HS/ED/MD			
	ST MARK stmarks@acegroup.cc	1951	104 E NORTH ST	55971	MNS	Thomas G Volker	(507)864-7111 (507)864-4017	WS 8 830 SS 930	HS/ED/ HC/MD			
RUSHMORE	*ST JOHN*	1894	420 4th St PO BOX 128	56168	MNS	David P Mc Donald	(507)478-4922	WS 1030	ED/SN	50	50	12
RUTHTON	*SAINT JAMES*		See Holland MN									
SABIN	*TRINITY* tlcsabin@gmail.com www.tlcsabin.360unite.com	1890	100 2nd Ave W PO BOX 198	56580	MNN	Brett D Hartwig	(218)789-7259	WS 9 SS 1015 BC 1015	EL/ED/HC/ MD			
SAINT CHARLES	*ST MATTHEW* stm55972@gmail.com www.stm55972.org	1889	555 E 12TH ST	55972	MNS	Thomas E Fast	(507)932-4246	WS 9 SS 1015 BC 1015	EC/HS/ED/ HC/MD	432	320	85
SAINT CLOUD	*FAITH* faithlutheransc@msn.com www.faithsc.com	1957	3000 COUNTY ROAD 8 SE	56304	MNN	Joshua S Reber	(320)252-3315 (320)252-3315	WS 1015 SS 9 BC 9				
	GOOD SHEPHERD		See Sauk Rapids MN									

*Indicates a new church start. A new church start is an intentionally organized gathering which comes together on a regular basis for the purpose of worship and/or Bible study and is intended to grow into a member LCMS congregation. WS =Worship Service; SS = Sunday School; BC =Bible Class; EC = Early Childhood; EL = Elementary School; HS = High School; ED =Education Ministry; HC =Human Care Ministry; SN = Special Needs Ministry; MD = Media Ministry (PC)=Partner Church Pastor. See Page 53 for the Table of Abbreviations for key to additional abbreviations

CONGREGATIONS

CITY	CONGREGATION EMAIL WEBSITE	YEAR EST	LOCATION MAILING ADDRESS	ZIP CODE(S)	DIST.	PASTOR(S)	PHONE FAX	WS SS BC	SCHOOLS/ MINISTRIES	STATISTIC Bapt	Conf	Avg Attend
SAINT CLOUD	*HOLY CROSS* holy-cross@hclutheranchurch.org hclutheranchurch.org	1890	2555 CLEARWATER RD	56301	MNN	Zachary E Hoffman	(320)251-8416	WS 8 1030 SS 915 BC 915	EL/ED/HC/ MD/SN			
	LOVE OF CHRIST office@loveofchrist.org www.loveofchrist.org	1993	1971 Pinecone Rd 1971 PINE CONE RD	56303	MNN	Joel D Kosberg	(320)253-7453 (320)251-5396	WS 930 SS 930	EL/ED/HC/ MD	868	619	236
	REDEEMER office@redeemerstcloud.org www.redeemerstcloud.org	1945	2719 3RD ST N	56303	MNN	Bruce A Timm	(320)252-8171 (320)240-9353	WS 9 SS 1030 BC 1030	EL/ED/HC/ MD/SN	251	234	137
SAINT FRANCIS	*FAITH COMMUNITY*		See Zimmerman MN									
	TRINITY office@trinitysf.org www.trinitysf.org	1963	3812 229TH AVE NW	55070	MNS	Timothy B Vaughan	(763)753-1234 (763)753-1774	WS 9 SS 1030 BC 1030	EL/HS/ED/ HC/MD	879	684	112
	ZION zioncrown@connections-etc.net zionlutherancrown.com	1877	7515 269TH AVE NW	55070	MNN	Timothy H Lamkin Sr	(763)856-2099 (844)273-4576	WS 9 SS 1015 BC 1015	EL/HS/ED			
SAINT JAMES	*ST JOHN* sbranch@sjsbant.org www.sjsbant.org	1887	South Branch 41486 760TH AVE	56081	MNS	Matthew L Rusert	(507)375-4228	WS 10 SS 9	EL/HS/ED			
	ST JOHN		See Truman MN									
SAINT LOUIS PARK	*ST PETERS*		See Edina MN									
SAINT MICHAEL	*SAMARITANS HILL*		See Albertville MN									
SAINT PAUL	*BETHEL* blc@bethelstpaul.com www.bethelstpaul.com	1930	670 WHEELOCK PKWY W	55117	MNS	Lusienie Fofana	(651)300-2642	WS 930 SS 11 BC 11	HS/ED/ HC/MD			
	BETHLEHEM bethstpaullcms@Gmail.com www.bethlehem-eaststpaul.org	1887	655 FOREST ST	55106	MNS	Scot D Missling	(651)776-4737	WS 9 SS 1015 BC 1015	HS/ED/ HC/MD			
	CORNERSTONE		See White Bear MN									
	CRISTO EL REDENTOR www.cristoelredentor.org	1979	784 Jackson St 674 JOHNSON PKWY	55117 55106	MNS		(651)291-2757		ED			
	EASTERN HGHTS office@ehlc.org www.EHLC.org	1947	616 RUTH ST N	55119	MNS	Steven M Benson Bradley C Asmus Charles S Fenton	(651)735-4202 (651)714-4684	WS 830 10 11 BC 10	EC/HS/ ED/HC/ MD/SN	680	409	110
	EMMAUS emmaus.lutheran.office@gmail.com emmaus-lutheran-church.org	1948	1074 IDAHO AVE W	55117	MNS	Nickolas M Kooi	(651)489-9426	WS 930 BC 1030	HS/MD	244	199	76
	*EMMAUS OROMO**		1074 W Idaho Ave 1074 IDAHO AVE W	55117	MNS							
	HMONG hmonglutheranchurch@gmail.com	1986	784 JACKSON ST	55117	MNS	Richard X Her			ED/HC/MD	385	263	79
	JEHOVAH office@jehovahlutheran.org www.jehovahlutheran.org	1923	1566 THOMAS AVE	55104	MNS	Dr Joshua C Miller	(651)644-1421	WS 930 SS 11 BC 11	HS	255	215	70
	KING OF KINGS		See Roseville MN									
	MEKANE YESUS		1566 W Thomas Ave 1566 THOMAS AVE	55104	MNS	Hailu H Gorobo	(651)644-1421		MD	120	92	72
	MESSIAH		See Mounds View MN									
	SERENITY MARIAN CENTER SENIOR LIVING APARTMENTS Satellite Site of Eastern Hghts Saint Paul MN	2017	200 Earl Street	55106								
	ST PETER stpetersstpaul@gmail.com www.saintpeterslutheranchurch.com	1886	530 VICTORIA ST S	55102	MNS	Christopher J Weber	(651)228-1482	WS 830 SS 945 BC 945	HS/ED/ HC/MD/ SN	95	84	38
	ST STEPHANUS saintstephanus@comcast.net www.saintstephanus.org	1890	739 LAFOND AVE	55104	MNS	Andrew P Thompson Yohannes Ghebru	(651)228-1486 (651)335-0921	WS 930 SS 1045 BC 11	HS/ED/ HC/MD/ SN	181	166	73
	SUMMIT HILL SENIOR LIVING APARTMENTS Satellite Site of Eastern Hghts Saint Paul MN	2012	1824 Old Hudson Rd	55119								
	UNIV CHAPEL		See Minneapolis MN									
SAINT PAUL PARK	*WOODBURY*		See Woodbury MN									
SAINT PETER	*GOOD SHEPHERD*		See North Mankato MN									
	RIVER OF LIFE office@riveroflifelutheran.com riveroflifelutheran.com	2016	830 SUNRISE DR	56082	MNS	Brian S Mc Quiggin	(507)934-0063	WS 9 SS 845 BC 845 6	ED/HC/ MD/SN	306	205	142
SANBORN	*TRINITY* pastor@trinitysanborn.org www.trinitysanborn.org	1888	20476 LASER AVE	56083	MNS	Benjamin K Rucker	(507)342-5544	WS 9 10	ED/HC/ MD/SN			
SANDSTONE	*TRINITY* pastorlanghorst@yahoo.com		200 3rd St PO BOX 656	55072	MNN	Richard E Langhorst	(320)245-2700	WS 1030				
SARGEANT	*ST JOHNS* marc.freiberg.sr@gmail.com	1897	28959 630 Ave 28959 630TH AVE	55973	MNS	Marc L Freiberg Sr	(507)754-5782	WS 1015 SS 9 BC 915	ED/HC/MD	149	122	24
SARTELL	*GOOD SHEPHERD*		See Sauk Rapids MN									
	MESSIAH messiahlc@charter.net www.messiahsartell.com	1980	320 4TH AVE N	56377	MNN	Justin T Hesterman	(320)252-5883 (320)252-2814	WS 9 SS 1020 BC 1020	ED/HC			
SAUK CENTRE	*ZION* zionpastor@arvig.net	1898	316 MAPLE ST	56378	MNN	Marty L Porter	(320)352-3447	WS 10	ED/HC			

*Indicates a new church start. A new church start is an intentionally organized gathering which comes together on a regular basis for the purpose of worship and/or Bible study and is intended to grow into a member LCMS congregation. WS =Worship Service; SS = Sunday School; BC =Bible Class; EC = Early Childhood; EL = Elementary School; HS = High School; ED =Education Ministry; HC =Human Care Ministry; SN = Special Needs Ministry; MD = Media Ministry (PC)=Partner Church Pastor. See Page 53 for the Table of Abbreviations for key to additional abbreviations

CITY	CONGREGATION EMAIL WEBSITE	YEAR EST	LOCATION MAILING ADDRESS	ZIP CODE(S)	DIST.	PASTOR(S)	PHONE FAX	WS SS BC	SCHOOLS/ MINISTRIES	STATISTIC Bapt	 Conf	 Avg Attend
SAUK RAPIDS	*GOOD SHEPHERD* keithweise@gsc-mn.org www.goodshepherdcampus.org/ spiritual-services-chapel	2003	325 11TH ST N	56379	MNN	Gregory J Tomhave	(320)259-3474	WS 10	ED/MD/SN			
	ST JOHN	1890	6855 GOLDEN SPIKE RD NE	56379	MNN	Dr Timothy J Rehwaldt	(320)968-7047	WS 1030 SS 930	ED/HC/SN			
	TRINITY office@trinitysr.org www.trinitysr.org	1887	2163 MAYHEW LAKE RD NE	56379	MNN	David W Hinz Levi R Willms	(320)252-3670 (320)202-1095	WS 9 SS 1015 BC 1015	EL/ED/HC/ MD			
SAVAGE	*ASCENSION*		See Burnsville MN									
	LIVING CHRIST		See Chanhassen MN									
	ST PAUL		See Prior Lake MN									
SCHRODER	*LIFE IN CHRIST*		See Grand Marais MN									
SEBEKA	*GRACE* gracesebeka@wcta.net www.facebook.com/gracesebeka/	1898	500 Wells Ave NW 500 WELLS AVE N	56477	MNN		(218)837-5565		ED/HC/SN			
	ZION gracesebeka@wcta.net www.facebook.com/gracesebeka/	1893	26985 COUNTY ROAD 23	56477	MNN			BC 330	ED/HC/ MD/SN	52	39	26
SHAKOPEE	*LIVING CHRIST*		See Chanhassen MN									
	NEW CREATION ncshakopee.org/	2009	1053 JEFFERSON ST S	55379	MNS	Jorge Gomez		WS 10 BC 9	ED/HC/MD			
	SAINT JOHNS		See Chaska MN									
	TRINITY		See Carver MN									
SHERBURN	*ST JOHN* church@sjlsherburn.com www.stjohnlutheransherburn.org	1890	317 S Main St PO BOX 760	56171	MNS	Steven D Wilson Jeffrey D Hagen	(507)764-5312	WS 8 1030 SS 915 BC 915	ED/HC/MD	595	472	197
SHOREWOOD	*LIVING CHRIST*		See Chanhassen MN									
SILVER BAY	*FAITH* www.faithlutheransilverbay.com	1958	105 OUTER DR	55614	MNN	Troy W Peperkorn	(218)226-3908	WS 930 SS 11 BC 11	ED/HC/SN			
SILVER CREEK	*IMMANUEL*	1928	11390 ELLIOT AVE NW MAPLE LAKE	55380 55358	MNS	Kenneth L Tatkenhorst	(763)878-2820	WS 9 SS 10 BC 10	ED/HC/ MD/SN	26	24	12
SILVER LAKE	*OUR SAVIOR*		See Hutchinson MN									
SIOUX VALLEY TOWNSHIP	*TRINITY* tlcsv@hotmail.com www.trinitysv.com	1921	38523 730TH ST LAKEFIELD	56150	MNS	Adam E Jacobsen	(507)839-3086	WS 9 SS 1015	ED/MD	201	174	47
SLAYTON	*TRINITY* sec@trinityslayton.info www.trinityslayton.info	1890	2105 KING AVE	56172	MNS	Dr Jeffrey B Williams	(507)836-8129	WS 9 SS 1015 BC 1015	EC/ED/ MD/SN	173	170	45
SNELLMAN	*GETHSEMANE*	1911	46913 St Hwy 34 46913 STATE HWY 34 OSAGE	56570	MNN		(218)573-3574	WS 1030 SS 930				
SOUTH HAVEN	*CONCORDIA*		See Fair Haven MN									
SOUTH SAINT PAUL	*WAKOTA RIDGE CAMPUS* Satellite Site of Woodbury Woodbury MN	2021	255 W Douglas St.	55075				WS 9 SS 915				
	WOODBURY		See Woodbury MN									
SPICER	*LIVING WORD*		See New London MN									
SPRING LAKE PARK	*PRINCE OF PEACE* office@ppslp.org ppslp.org	1959	7700 MONROE ST NE SPRING LK PK	55432	MNS	Paul M Strawn	(763)786-1706	WS 930 SS 1040 BC 815 1040	HS/ED/ HC/SN	410	369	75
	PRINCE PEACE DF dgehlbach@aol.com	1908	7700 Monroe St NE PO BOX 32961 FRIDLEY	55432	MNS	Daryl D Gehlbach	(763)786-1706		SN			
SPRING VALLEY	*FIRST ENGLISH* fel@mediacombb.net	1938	217 W GRANT ST	55975	MNS	Loel A Wessel	(507)346-2793	WS 830 10	ED/HC/ MD/SN	157	147	41
SPRINGFIELD	*ZION* church@zionspringfieldmn.org www.zionspringfieldmn.org/	1897	122 W CENTRAL ST	56087	MNS	Benjamin K Rucker	(507)723-5609	WS 9	ED/MD			
SQUAW LAKE	*CENTENNIAL*	1937	Highway 46 PO BOX 395	56681	MNN	James W Anthony	(218)259-0115		ED/HC			
STAPLES	*TRINITY* trnty3n1@gmail.com www.trinitylutheranstaples.com	1933	1000 4TH ST NE	56479	MNN	Paul E Koehler	(218)894-2372	WS 9 SS 1030 BC 1030	ED/HC/ MD/SN			
STEWART	*ST PETER'S*		See Gibbon MN									
STEWARTVILLE	*ST JOHNS* pastorjustin@stjohnsandweecare.org www.stjohnsandweecare.org	1892	111 2ND AVE NE	55976	MNS	Justin A Kumfer Nicholas M Wagenknecht	(507)533-4420	WS 8 1030 SS 915 BC 915	ED/HC	634	490	175
STILLWATER	*FAMILY OF CHRIST*		See Houlton WI									
	OAK HILL CAMPUS Satellite Site of Woodbury Woodbury MN	2012	9050 60th St N	55082				WS 9 1030 SS 915 BC 915				
	WOODBURY		See Woodbury MN									
SWANVILLE	*ST PETER* stpeters@swanvillelutheran.org swanvillelutheran.org	1890	503 Berkey Ave PO BOX 126	56382	MNN	Timothy D Schmeisser	(320)547-2928	WS 9 SS 1015 BC 1015	ED			
THIEF RIVER FALLS	*ST JOHNS*	1895	101 PINE AVE S THIEF RVR FLS	56701	MNN		(218)681-4488	WS 1045 SS 930 BC 930	EL/HS/ED	71	66	35
TOFTE	*LIFE IN CHRIST*		See Grand Marais MN									
TOWER	*GREENWOOD TOWN HALL* Satellite Site of Gloria Dei Virginia MN	1981	3000 County Rd 77	55790				WS 730				

*Indicates a new church start. A new church start is an intentionally organized gathering which comes together on a regular basis for the purpose of worship and/or Bible study and is intended to grow into a member LCMS congregation. WS =Worship Service; SS = Sunday School; BC =Bible Class; EC = Early Childhood; EL = Elementary School; HS = High School; ED =Education Ministry; HC =Human Care Ministry; SN = Special Needs Ministry; MD = Media Ministry (PC)=Partner Church Pastor. See Page 53 for the Table of Abbreviations for key to additional abbreviations

CITY	CONGREGATION EMAIL WEBSITE	YEAR EST	LOCATION MAILING ADDRESS	ZIP CODE(S)	DIST.	PASTOR(S)	PHONE FAX	WS SS BC	SCHOOLS/ MINISTRIES	STATISTIC Bapt	Conf	Avg Attend
TRIMONT	*TRINITY* trinitytrimont@gmail.com	1903	31 Main St W PO BOX 321	56176	MNS	Logan S Smith	(507)639-4111	WS 830 SS 945 BC 945	EL/HS/ ED/HC/ MD/SN	157	148	43
TROSKY	*ST JOHN* pastormoeller@threestrandsparish.com threestrandsparish.com	1911	210 Ridge St PO BOX 323 PIPESTONE	56144 56164	MNS		(605)321-1641	WS 845 SS 945 BC 8	HC			
TRUMAN	*ST JOHN* sbranch@sjsbant.org	1870	41486 760TH AVE SAINT JAMES	56088 56081	MNS	Matthew L Rusert	(507)776-6487	WS 830 SS 930	EL/HS			
	ST PAUL stpaul98@frontiernet.net stpaulstruman.weebly.com	1900	110 E 4TH ST N	56088	MNS		(507)776-2801 (507)776-3060	WS 9 SS 1015 BC 1015	EL/HS/ ED/HC/ MD/SN	541	433	112
TWIN VALLEY	*TRINITY* trinity.tv248@gmail.com	1947	106 Stenseth Ave. SW PO BOX 248	56584	MNN		(218)584-8440	WS 9 SS 1030		205	172	69
TWO HARBORS	*SHEP OF THE LAKE* loghome42jb@gmail.com www.shepherdofthelake.com/		2014 7TH AVE	55616	MNN	John C Bonk	(218)834-5345 (218)834-5395	WS 930 BC 1045	ED/HC/MD	42	42	22
TYLER	*SAINT JAMES*		See Holland MN									
VERGAS	*ST JOHN* stjohnvergas@arvig.net	1915	410 E SCHARF AVE	56587	MNN	Steven J Frank	(218)342-2791	WS 845 SS 9	EC/ED/HC/ MD/SN	229	210	64
	ST PAUL parishsecretary@eot.com vergaslutheran.org	1885	31385 Co Hwy 4 31385 COUNTY HIGHWAY 4	56587	MNN	Steven J Frank	(218)342-2379	WS 10 SS 915 BC 9	EC/ED/HC/ MD/SN			
VERNDALE	*IMMANUEL* robin.fish@hotmail.com	1898	17097 - 460th Street PO BOX 37	56481	MNN	Robin D Fish Sr	(573)286-1009	WS 9 BC 1030	ED/MD	73	62	37
VERNON CENTER	*ST JOHN* stjohnswillowcreek@gmail.com stjohnswillowcreek.org	1869	13148 499 Ave 13148 499TH AVE	56090	MNS	John C Bennett	(507)549-3760	WS 9 SS 10 BC 1015	EL/HS/ ED/HC/ MD/SN			
	ST PETER stplcms@hickorytech.net stpetersvc.org	1910	202 EAST KENDALL ST PO BOX 415	56090	MNS	Adam C Finney	(507)549-3166	WS 930 SS 1030	ED/HC/MD	268	195	130
VICTORIA	*CHRIST VICTORIOUS*		See Chaska MN									
	LIVING CHRIST		See Chanhassen MN									
	SAINT JOHNS		See Chaska MN									
	TRINITY		See Carver MN									
VILLARD	*SAINT JOHNS* ryan.j.pumphrey@gmail.com Facebook.com/LCMSinPopeCountyMN	1885	341 Commercial Ave PO BOX 36	56385	MNN	Ryan J Pumphrey	(320)554-2161	WS 1030	ED/HC/SN			
	TRINITY		See Grove Lake MN									
VIRGINIA	*GLORIA DEI* gloriadeisecretary@gmail.com www.gdrlutheran.com	1957	6959 HIGHWAY 169	55792	MNN	Zachary T Klumpp	(218)741-1977	WS 9 SS 10	ED/SN	142	129	62
	REDEEMER		See Aurora MN									
	TRINITY carpfishermen@msn.com tlcvirginiamn.com	1921	900 13TH ST S	55792	MNN	Bradley N Felix	(218)741-1911	WS 9 SS 1015	HC/MD/SN	483	163	67
WACONIA	*LIVING CHRIST*		See Chanhassen MN									
	TRINITY www.trinitywaconia.org	1865	601 E 2nd St 601 E 2ND ST STE A	55387	MNS	Duncan B McLellan Bryan D Stecker	(952)442-4165 (952)442-4644	WS 815 1045 SS 930 BC 930	EL/HS/ ED/HC/ MD/SN			
WADENA	*ST JOHN* stjohnwadena1@yahoo.com www.stjohnwadena.org	1914	710 FRANKLIN AVE SW	56482	MNN	Stephen N Meltzer	(218)631-3000	WS 9 SS 1015 BC 1015	ED/HC/MD	804	608	116
WAITE PARK	*GOOD SHEPHERD*		See Sauk Rapids MN									
WALDORF	*FIRST* flcwaldorf@gmail.com flcwaldorf.wixsite.com/flcwaldorf	1910	120 3rd Ave PO BOX 216	56091	MNS	Larry R Sipe Jr	(507)239-2431	WS 8 SS 915 BC 915	ED	166	151	36
WALKER	*IMMANUEL* immanuellutheran@arvig.net www.immanuellutheranwalker.org	1915	4656 STATE 200 NW	56484	MNN	Matthew J Vrudny	(218)547-3156 (218)547-4139	WS 9 SS 1015 BC 1030	EL/ED/HC/ MD/SN	185	157	67
WANDA	*TRINITY*		See Sanborn MN									
WARREN	*IMMANUEL*	1897	23511 260TH AVE NW	56762	MNN		(701)361-9414	WS 1 SS 2 BC 2	ED/HC			
	ZION	1911	Highway 1 E PO BOX 102	56762	MNN		(218)745-4766	WS 845				
WARROAD	*BETHLEHEM* www.bethlehemwarroad.org	1987	32442 580TH AVE	56763	MNN	William F Moeller Jr	(218)386-3555	WS 1115 SS 1030	ED/HC/MD			
WASECA	*ST PAUL* stpaulwa@hickorytech.net www.stpaulwaseca.org	1909	314 4TH AVE NE	56093	MNS	Michael J Grannis	(507)835-2647	WS 9 SS 1015 BC 1030	ED/MD	410	326	120
	TRINITY revsipe@gmail.com www.facebook.com/ TrinityLutheranChurchWilton/	1872			MNS	Larry R Sipe Jr	(507)676-7956	WS 1045	ED/HC/MD			
	TRINITY		See Medford MN									
WATERTOWN	*ST PAULS* office.stpaulswatertown@gmail.com www.stpaulswatertown.org	1949	505 Westminster Ave SW PO BOX 697	55388	MNS	George W Morris II Gerald A Schwanke	(952)955-1498	WS 8 1030 SS 915 BC 915	EL/HS/ ED/HC/ MD/SN			
	ST PETER stpeterlc.org	1867	3030 Navajo Ave PO BOX 508	55388	MNS	William H Kirmsse	(952)955-1679 (952)955-1679	WS 9 SS 1015 BC 1015	EL/HS/ED/ HC/MD	125	100	45
WATERVILLE	*ST PETER*	1867	21377 TETONKA LAKE RD	56096	MNS	John A Pasche	(507)362-8381	WS 10 SS 845	ED/HC/ MD/SN			
	TRINITY tlchurch@frontiernet.net	1909	415 LAKE ST W	56096	MNS	David C Mumme	(507)362-4454	WS 9 BC 10	ED/HC/MD	576	476	143
WATKINS	*ST PAUL*		See Eden Valley MN									

*Indicates a new church start. A new church start is an intentionally organized gathering which comes together on a regular basis for the purpose of worship and/or Bible study and is intended to grow into a member LCMS congregation. WS =Worship Service; SS = Sunday School; BC =Bible Class; EC = Early Childhood; EL = Elementary School; HS = High School; ED =Education Ministry; HC =Human Care Ministry; SN = Special Needs Ministry; MD = Media Ministry (PC)=Partner Church Pastor. See Page 53 for the Table of Abbreviations for key to additional abbreviations

CITY	CONGREGATION EMAIL WEBSITE	YEAR EST	LOCATION MAILING ADDRESS	ZIP CODE(S)	DIST.	PASTOR(S)	PHONE FAX	WS SS BC	SCHOOLS/ MINISTRIES	STATISTIC Bapt	Conf	Avg Attend
WAYZATA	*BEAUTIFUL SAVIOR*		See Plymouth MN									
	REDEEMER khanson@redeemerwayzata.org www.redeemerwayzata.org	1924	115 WAYZATA BLVD W	55391	MNS	Steven E Ferber	(952)473-1281 (952)473-3186	WS 8 1030 SS 1045 BC 915	EL/ED/ HC/SN			
WEBSTER	*ST JOHN* www.stjwebster.com	1865	4376 41ST ST W	55088	MNS	Donavon L Riley	(952)652-2844	WS 10 SS 845 BC 845	MD			
WEST CONCORD	*TRINITY*		See Medford MN									
WEST SAINT PAUL	*SAINT JAMES* stjlc@saintjameslutheran.com	2022	460 W ANAPOLIS ST	55118	MNS	Jordan R Voges	(651)457-9232	WS 9		1079	730	123
	THE SANCTUARY SENIOR LIVING APARTMENTS Satellite Site of Eastern Hghts Saint Paul MN	2017	1746 Oakdale Ave	55118								
	WOODBURY		See Woodbury MN									
WHEATON	*IMMANUEL*	1885	7006 - Cty Rd 16 7006 COUNTY ROAD 16	56296	MNN	Daniel G Gifford		WS 1030 SS 930	ED/HC/SN			
	ST JOHN stjohn96@runestone.net stjohnwheatonmn.org	1896	1603 BROADWAY	56296	MNN	Daniel G Gifford	(320)563-4143 (320)563-4143	WS 9 SS 915	ED/HC/MD	397	364	78
WHITE BEAR	*CORNERSTONE* cornerstone@cllc.church www.cllc.church		1830 Stillwater St 674 JOHNSON PARKWAY SAINT PAUL	55110 55106	MNS	Daniel Thao Joel V Her	(952)239-9136	WS 1030 BC 1030	ED/HC/MD	136	136	82
WHITE BEAR LAKE	*BELLAIRE BEACH* Satellite Site of South Shore Trinity White Bear Lake MN	1980	Bellaire Ave & S Shore Blvd Lakeside	55110								
	SOUTH SHORE TRINITY info@sstwbl.org www.sstwbl.org	1943	2480 S SHORE BLVD WHITE BEAR LK	55110	MNS		(651)429-4293 (651)653-3634	WS 8 1045 SS 930	EC/HS/ ED/HC/ MD/SN	526	430	167
	WOODBURY		See Woodbury MN									
WILLMAR	*LIVING WORD*		See New London MN									
	REDEEMER redeemer@redeemerwillmar.org www.redeemerwillmar.org	1927	1401 6TH ST SW	56201	MNN	Craig J Donofrio	(320)235-4685 (320)235-1879	WS 8 1030 SS 915 BC 915	EC/ED/HC/ MD/SN	674	620	173
WINDOM	*OUR SAVIOR* lcoos@windomnet.com oursaviorslutheran.net	1884	1157 3RD AVE	56101	MNS	Paul M Sajban	(507)831-3522 (507)831-1781	WS 9 SS 1030 BC 1030	ED/HC/ MD/SN	509	433	93
WINNEBAGO	*OUR SAVIOR* jeremiah@oslwinnebago.org oslwinnebago.org	1933	121 1st Ave SE PO BOX 455	56098	MNS		(507)893-3320	WS 10 SS 1015	EL/HS/ ED/HC/ MD/SN	327	247	118
WINONA	*CAMPUS BIBLE STUDY* Satellite Site of St Martin Winona MN	2011	Huff and Howard Sts	55987								
	GRACE graceevanluth.org	1891	8110 W MAIN ST	55987	MNS	Mark R Meier Sr	(507)689-2777	WS 8	HS			
	REDEEMER pastor@rlcwinona.com www.rlcwinona.com/	1957	1664 KRAEMER DR	55987	MNS	Ryan L Eden	(507)452-3828	WS 9 SS 1015 BC 1015	HS/ED/ HC/MD/ SN	49	46	20
	ST MARTIN church@stmartinswinona.org www.stmartinswinona.com	1856	328 E BROADWAY ST	55987	MNS	Richard A Moore Kyle A Lewis	(507)452-6928 (507)457-0884	WS 8 1030 SS 915 BC 915	EL/HS/ ED/HC/ MD/SN			
WINSTED	*ST JOHN* revdaveh@gmail.com stjohnswinsted.com	1872	414 Westgate Drive PO BOX 67	55395	MNS	David L Hormann	(320)485-2522	WS 830 1015	HC/MD	382	248	138
WINTHROP	*ST PETER'S*		See Gibbon MN									
WOLF LAKE	*CHRIST* mariepie29@yahoo.com	1900	233 N Manninen Ave PO BOX 305	56593	MNN	Terry L Yahr	(218)538-6694	WS 1030 SS 930	ED/HC/MD			
WOOD LAKE	*ST LUKE* dmtilney@hotmail.com www.yourstlukes.com	1875	5597 130TH AVE	56297	MNN	David M Tilney	(507)485-3527	WS 930 SS 1030 BC 1030	ED/HC/MD	203	157	58
WOODBURY	*ST JOHN* stjohn@stjohnwoodbury.org www.stjohnwoodbury.org	1868	1975 SAINT JOHNS DR	55129	MNS	David N Larson	(651)436-6621	WS 8 1030 SS 915 BC 915	ED/HC/ MD/SN	407	285	178
	VALLEY CREEK CAMPUS Satellite Site of Woodbury Woodbury MN	1968	7380 Afton Road	55125				WS 9 1030 SS 9				
	WOODBURY wlc@woodburylutheran.org wlc.church	1968	7380 Afton Road 7380 AFTON RD	55125	MNS	Thomas J Pfotenhauer Dean A Dunavan Joel E Symmank Daniel J Langewisch Timothy J Marshall	(651)739-5144 (651)739-3536	WS 9 1030 SS 9	EC/HS/ ED/HC/ MD/SN	3059	2233	1239
WORTHINGTON	*ST MATTHEW* stmattchurchoffice@gmail.com stmatthewworthington.com	1891	1505 DOVER ST	56187	MNS	David G Hahn	(507)376-6168 (507)376-6915	WS 8 1015 SS 915 BC 915	ED/HC/ MD/SN	957	756	183
WRIGHT	*ST JOHN* sjlutheranwri@gmail.com oursaviorslutheranchurch.weebly.com/	1906	1417 2ND ST	55798	MNN	John M Thomson	(218)768-3198	WS 1030 SS 930 BC 930	ED/HC/ MD/SN			
WYKOFF	*ST JOHNS* CHURCH@STJOHNS-WYKOFF.COM www.stjohns-wykoff.org	1874	241 Line St S PO BOX 128	55990	MNS		(507)352-2296	WS 8 SS 1030 BC 1030	EL/ED/HC/ MD/SN	339	306	76
ZIMMERMAN	*FAITH COMMUNITY* faith_clc@yahoo.com www.faithclc.com	1993	12266 255th Ave PO BOX 156	55398	MNN	Jacob S Gillard	(763)856-3600	WS 10 BC 845	HS/ED/ HC/MD/ SN	126	111	85
ZUMBROTA	*IMMANUEL*		See Hay Creek MN									

*Indicates a new church start. A new church start is an intentionally organized gathering which comes together on a regular basis for the purpose of worship and/or Bible study and is intended to grow into a member LCMS congregation. WS =Worship Service; SS = Sunday School; BC =Bible Class; EC = Early Childhood; EL = Elementary School; HS = High School; ED =Education Ministry; HC =Human Care Ministry; SN = Special Needs Ministry; MD = Media Ministry (PC)=Partner Church Pastor. See Page 53 for the Table of Abbreviations for key to additional abbreviations

MISSISSIPPI

CITY	CONGREGATION EMAIL WEBSITE	YEAR EST	LOCATION MAILING ADDRESS	ZIP CODE(S)	DIST.	PASTOR(S)	PHONE FAX	WS SS BC	SCHOOLS/ MINISTRIES	STATISTIC Bapt	Conf	Avg Attend
BILOXI	*GOOD SHEPHERD* goodshepherdbiloxi@gmail.com www.goodshepherdbiloxi.com	1953	2004 PASS RD	39531	SO	Raymond B Cox	(228)388-5767	WS 1030 SS 9 BC 9		126	104	48
BYRAM	*OUR REDEEMER*		See Clinton MS									
CLINTON	*OUR REDEEMER* secretary@orlcms.org www.orlcms.org	1930	1799 Clinton-Raymond Rd 1799 CLINTON RAYMOND RD	39056	SO	Alfred W Schubert III	(601)924-9999	WS 8 1030 SS 915 BC 915	ED/HC/ MD/SN	343	268	99
COLUMBIA	*ST JOHN*		See Hattiesburg MS									
COLUMBUS	*OUR SAVIOR* www.oursaviorlutheranms.org	1952	1211 18TH AVE N	39701	SO	David M Hartung	(662)323-3050	WS 2 BC 1130	ED/HC/ MD/SN	35	35	18
CORINTH	*PRINCE OF PEACE*	1963	4203 SHILOH RD	38834	SO	Michael W Dixon		WS 2 BC 3	ED/HC	20	18	12
FLOWOOD	*GOOD SHEPHERD* seelsorge@aol.com www.gslc-gsls.com	1987	6035 Hwy 25 PO BOX 5013 BRANDON	39232 39047	SO	James R Sawyer Jr	(601)992-4752	WS 9 SS 1030 BC 1030	EL/ED/HC/ MD			
GAUTIER	*CHRIST*		See Pascagoula MS									
GULFPORT	*ST MATTHEW* m1919@bellsouth.net stmatthewgulfport.tripod.com	1919	11213 HIGHWAY 49	39503	SO		(228)864-6264	WS 10 SS 9 BC 9	ED/HC/ MD/SN	120	105	60
HATTIESBURG	*HOLY CROSS* holycrosslutheranhattiesburg@gmail.com holycrosslutheranhattiesburg.org		5296 OLD HIGHWAY 11 STE 5A	39402	SO	James R Sawyer Jr	(601)402-8147	WS 11 BC 10	ED	13	13	8
	ST JOHN stjohnlutheranchurch@gmail.com saintjohnhattiesburg.com	1946	2001 HARDY ST	39401	SO	Chet L Scherbarth	(601)583-4898 (601)583-4886	WS 1030 SS 915 BC 915	ED/HC/ MD/SN	163	124	58
HOLLY SPRINGS	*ZION* sarahjliddy@hotmail.com	1961	945 Highway 311 310 CEDAR HILLS RD	38635	SO	Wallace L Bostelmann	(662)252-4513	WS 1030 BC 7				
JACKSON	*CHRIST* sistersara@christlutheranjacksonms.org www.ChristLutheranJacksonMS.org	1956	4423 I-55 N 4423 I 55 N	39206	SO	George N Fields	(601)366-2055	WS 1030 SS 9 BC 9	SN			
	EPIPHANY epiphanylutheranchurch156@gmail.com		1230 Isaiah Montgomery PO BOX 20027	39203 39289	SO	Raymond W Gage	(601)353-0504 (601)353-0714		HC	43	43	15
	OUR REDEEMER		See Clinton MS									
JACKSON RESERVOIR	*GOOD SHEPHERD*		See Flowood MS									
MAGNOLIA	*TRINITY*		See McComb MS									
MCCOMB	*TRINITY* office@trinitylutheranchurchmccomb.org trinitylutheranchurchmccomb.org	1962	1622 Virginia Ave P O BOX 656 SUMMIT	39648 39666	SO	Warren J Schulingkamp II	(769)276-1897	WS 3	ED	4	4	4
MERIDIAN	*TRINITY* trinity3460@bellsouth.net www.tlcms.com	1996	4805 HIGHWAY 39 N	39301	SO	Steven D Mazzaferro	(601)483-5457	WS 10 SS 845 BC 845	ED/HC/MD	52	45	29
MOSS POINT	*CHRIST*		See Pascagoula MS									
NATCHEZ	*FIRST*	1957	70 Sgt S Prentiss Dr 70 SGT PRENTISS DR	39120	SO	Warren J Schulingkamp II	(601)442-1397	WS 1030	ED/MD	12	11	9
OLIVE BRANCH	*BEAUTIFUL SAVIOR* churchbslc@gmail.com www.beautifulsaviorlutheran.org	1971	7630 DAVIDSON RD	38654	MDS	Sawyer A Meyers	(662)890-7272	WS 1015	ED/HC/ MD/SN	105	82	60
OXFORD	*PEACE* peaceoxfordms@gmail.com www.peaceoxford.org	1930	407 JACKSON AVE W	38655	SO		(662)234-6568	WS 3 SS 415 BC 415	ED/HC/ MD/SN	70	61	33
PASCAGOULA	*CHRIST* clc1888@outlook.com www.christlutheranchurchms.org	1888	3042 Pascagoula St PO BOX 877	39567 39568	SO		(228)762-1754	WS 10 SS 9 BC 9	ED/SN	134	109	45
PETAL	*ST JOHN*		See Hattiesburg MS									
PICAYUNE	*ST PAUL* www.stpaullutheranpicayune.org	1954	1309 HIGHWAY 11 S	39466	SO	Bradley S Aumann	(601)798-4586	WS 1030 SS 9 BC 9	ED/HC/ MD/SN	83	71	56
RAYMOND	*OUR REDEEMER*		See Clinton MS									
SOUTHAVEN	*PRINCE OF PEACE* wrpellom@aol.com www.peaceinsouthaven.org	1962	8089 US Highway 51 N 8089 HIGHWAY 51 N	38671	SO	Warren R Pellom	(662)393-3432	WS 930 SS 1045 BC 1045	MD	258	238	63
STARKVILLE	*ST LUKE* office@saintlukestarkville.org www.saintlukestarkville.org	1965	1104 LOUISVILLE ST	39759	SO	David M Hartung	(662)323-3050 (662)323-3050	WS 1030 BC 930	ED/HC/ MD/SN			
TUPELO	*HOLY TRINITY* www.holytrinitylcms.net	1956	1305 LAWHON DR	38804	SO	David E Mac Kain	(662)350-3679	WS 10 SS 9 BC 9	ED/MD	139	106	67
VICKSBURG	*MESSIAH* www.lutheranchurchmessiahvicksburg.org	1950	301 CAIN RIDGE RD	39180	SO	James R Sawyer Jr	(601)636-1894	WS 3 SS 415				
WAVELAND	*OF THE PINES* office@lutheranchurchofthepines.org lutheranchurchofthepines.org	1962	309 HIGHWAY 90	39576	SO	Brock A Cain	(228)467-6771 (228)467-6771	WS 10 SS 9	ED/HC/MD	138	122	79

*Indicates a new church start. A new church start is an intentionally organized gathering which comes together on a regular basis for the purpose of worship and/or Bible study and is intended to grow into a member LCMS congregation. WS =Worship Service; SS = Sunday School; BC =Bible Class; EC = Early Childhood; EL = Elementary School; HS = High School; ED =Education Ministry; HC =Human Care Ministry; SN = Special Needs Ministry; MD = Media Ministry (PC)=Partner Church Pastor. See Page 53 for the Table of Abbreviations for key to additional abbreviations

MISSOURI

CITY	CONGREGATION EMAIL WEBSITE	YEAR EST	LOCATION MAILING ADDRESS	ZIP CODE(S)	DIST.	PASTOR(S)	PHONE FAX	WS SS BC	SCHOOLS/ MINISTRIES	STATISTIC Bapt	Conf	Avg Attend
AFFTON	*REFORMATION* office@reformationstl.org www.reformationstl.org	1954	7910 MACKENZIE RD SAINT LOUIS	63123	MO	Robert O Riebau	(314)352-1355	WS 9 SS 1030 BC 1030	HS/ED/ HC/SN	193	164	71
	RESURRECTION		See Sunset Hills MO									
ALMA	*TRINITY* secretary@trinitylutheranalma.com www.trinitylutheranalma.com	1875	310 WAVERLY	64001	MO	Bernard M Ross III	(660)674-2376 (660)674-2747	WS 930 SS 830 BC 830	EL/ED/HC/ MD	598	429	156
ALTENBURG	*IMMANUEL*	1857	8234 Main St PO BOX 26	63732	MO	Frank E Lucas	(573)824-5636	WS 9 SS 8 BC 8	HS/ED/HC			
	TRINITY trinity.altenburg1@att.net trinityaltenburg.com/	1839	57 Church St PO BOX 66	63732	MO		(573)824-5847	WS 9 SS 8 BC 8	EL/HS/ED/ HC/MD/SN			
APPLETON CITY	*TRINITY* trinitylutheran.appleton@gmail.com	1870	300 E 1ST ST	64724	MO	William G Smith Jr	(660)476-5438	WS 10 SS 9	ED/HC/ MD/SN	134	114	52
ARCADIA	*ST PAUL*		See Ironton MO									
ARNOLD	*GOOD SHEPHERD* goodsheparnold@sbcglobal.net www.goodshepherdarnold.org	1969	2211 TENBROOK RD	63010	MO	Warren R Woerth	(636)296-1292	WS 9 SS 1030 BC 1030	ED/MD/SN	204	132	50
	RESURRECTION		See Sunset Hills MO									
	ST JOHNS jschultz@sjlarnold.org www.sjlarnold.org	1848	3517 JEFFCO BLVD	63010	MO	Jeremy J Schultz Benjamin C Berteau	(636)464-0096	WS 8 930 1050 SS 930 BC 930	EL/HS/ED/ HC/MD/SN	2210	1553	700
ASHLAND	*FAMILY OF CHRIST*		408 S Main St PO BOX 475	65010	MO		(573)657-1463	WS 9 SS 1015 BC 1015	HC	103	94	32
AUGUSTA	*CHRIST* clcaugustamo.org	1858	123 CHURCH RD	63332	MO	Randall D Bell	(636)228-4642	WS 10 SS 9 BC 9	ED/HC/MD	113	95	47
AURORA	*GRACE* klampe@mid-southlcms.com www.gracelutheranaurora.com	1948	1120 S PARK AVE	65605	MO	Daniel W Heitshusen	(417)678-3603 (417)678-3603	WS 10 SS 9 BC 9	ED/HC/MD	89	86	41
BABBTOWN	*ST JOHN*		See Meta MO									
BARNHART	*IMMANUEL* immanuellutheranchurchbarnhart@ yahoo.com	1870	6500 METROPOLITAN BLVD	63012	MO	Bruce H Elliott	(636)464-4114 (636)464-4114	WS 9 SS 1015 BC 1015	HS/ED/HC/ MD	115	93	52
BEAUFORT	*ST JOHNS* segelhorst@yhti.net stjohns-beaufortmo.com/	1852	2149 LUTHERAN CHURCH RD	63013	MO	John F Schoedel	(573)484-3575	WS 10 SS 9 BC 9		323	241	75
BELLE	*MOUNT CALVARY* Pr.David.Roth@gmail.com	1949	508 Taylor Ave PO BOX 833	65013	MO	David J Roth Jr	(573)207-4148	WS 1045		57	48	29
BELLEFONTAINE NGHBRS	*GRACE CHAPEL* churchoffice@gracechapelstl.org www.gracechapelstl.org	1953	10015 LANCE DR SAINT LOUIS	63137	MO	Nathan A Ruback Eric T Stacy	(314)868-3232 (314)868-2485	WS 8 1030 SS 915 BC 915	EL/HS/ED/ HC/MD/SN	423	377	125
BELTON	*BETHLEHEM*		See Raymore MO									
	HOLY TRINITY		See Grandview MO									
BETHANY	*HOPE*	1963	1205 S 25TH ST	64424	MO		(660)425-3627	WS 9 SS 1015 BC 1015		34	26	17
BISMARCK	*ST JOHN*	1870	1146 Cedar St PO BOX 537	63624	MO	Lawrence L Eatherton	(573)779-3820			21	17	16
BLACK JACK	*SALEM* salemchurch@salembjmo.org www.salembjmo.org	1849	5180 PARKER RD	63033	MO	Dr Martin B Dressler	(314)741-6781 (314)741-1797	WS 10 SS 845 BC 845	EL/HS/ED/ HC/MD/SN	279	260	119
BLACKBURN	*ZION*	1897	207 Churchill PO BOX 196	65321	MO	Timothy C Miille	(660)538-4688	WS 10 SS 11 BC 11		124	90	37
BLUE EYE	*SHEPHERD HILLS*		See Kimberling City MO									
BLUE SPRINGS	*POINTE OF HOPE* connect@pointeofhope.org www.pointeofhopechurch.com	2000	1215-A N 7 Highway 1215-A NW STATE ROUTE 7	64014	MO	Brian J Hetzel	(816)220-2609 (816)220-2608	WS 10	HC/MD	312	149	82
	TIMOTHY www.timothylutheran.com	1961	301 EAST WYATT RD	64014	MO	Ryan W Hochgrebe	(816)228-5300 (816)228-5323	WS 9 1030	EL/HS/ED/ HC/MD	1943	1528	398
BOLIVAR	*ZION* zionbolivar@windstream.net www.zionlutheranbolivar.org	1976	600 E Aldrich Rd PO BOX 5	65613	MO	Jeffrey E Sippy	(417)326-5506	WS 11 BC 945	ED/HC/ MD/SN	99	81	44
BONNE TERRE	*ST MATTHEW* StMatthewBT@gmail.com stmatthewbt.org	1900	340 SUMMIT ST	63628	MO		(314)518-7511	WS 9	ED/HC/ MD/SN	25	25	15
BOONVILLE	*IMMANUEL* immanuel.boonville@gmail.com immanuelboonvillemo.church	1915	1001 IMMANUEL DR	65233	MO	Joshua C Ketelsen	(660)882-2208	WS 9 SS 1015 BC 1015	EC/ED/HC/ MD	322	257	70
	TRINITY		See Clarks Fork MO									
BOURBON	*CONCORDIA* concordiabourbon@gmail.com concordiabourbon.com	1902	642 E Pine St PO BOX 359	65441	MO		(573)732-4477	WS 845 SS 945 BC 945	ED/HC/MD	177	128	34
BOWLING GREEN	*GOOD SHEPHERD* www.goodshepherdbg.org	1980	1806 W MAIN ST	63334	MO	Jeffrey M Dock	(573)754-6120	WS 845 SS 10 BC 10	ED/MD/SN	117	98	59

*Indicates a new church start. A new church start is an intentionally organized gathering which comes together on a regular basis for the purpose of worship and/or Bible study and is intended to grow into a member LCMS congregation. WS =Worship Service; SS = Sunday School; BC =Bible Class; EC = Early Childhood; EL = Elementary School; HS = High School; ED =Education Ministry; HC =Human Care Ministry; SN = Special Needs Ministry; MD = Media Ministry (PC)=Partner Church Pastor. See Page 53 for the Table of Abbreviations for key to additional abbreviations

CITY	CONGREGATION EMAIL WEBSITE	YEAR EST	LOCATION MAILING ADDRESS	ZIP CODE(S)	DIST.	PASTOR(S)	PHONE FAX	WS SS BC	SCHOOLS/ MINISTRIES	STATISTIC Bapt	Conf	Avg Attend
BRANSON	*FAITH* faithbranson@gmail.com faithbranson.org	1999	221 Malone PO BOX 1807	65616 65615	MO	Joel A Krueger Joseph R Bluege	(417)334-2469	WS 1030 SS 915 BC 915	EL/ED/HC/ MD/SN	533	470	210
	PRAISE AND WORSHIP		See Branson West MO									
BRANSON WEST	*PRAISE AND WORSHIP* email@branson.church www.branson.church		9138 E. STATE HIGHWAY 76	65737	MO	Matthew W Canaday	(417)386-2422	WS 10 BC 9		125	117	75
	SHEPHERD HILLS		See Kimberling City MO									
BRENTWOOD	*MOUNT CALVARY* office@mtcalvarylcms.org www.mtcalvarylcms.org	1930	9321 LITZSINGER RD	63144	MO	Karl W Hanke IV	(314)968-2360 (314)968-4943	WS 9 SS 945	EC/HS/ED	163	120	80
BRIDGETON	*BEAUTIFUL SAVIOR* beautifulsavior1@sbcglobal.net www.bslcms.org	1965	12397 NATURAL BRIDGE RD	63044	MO	Timothy J Ostermeyer	(314)291-2395 (314)291-0202	WS 9 SS 1030 BC 1030	EL/HS/ED/ HC/MD/SN	134	114	50
	TRINITY kdanielbrock@gmail.com www.trinity-lutheran.org	1964	3765 Mc Kelvey Rd 3765 MCKELVEY RD	63044	MO	Keith D Ellerbrock	(314)739-0022	WS 1015 SS 9 BC 9	ED/SN	112	83	52
BROOKFIELD	*ST PAUL* lddorrell@sbcglobal.net	1975	806 S BRUNSWICK ST	64628	MO			WS 10 BC 915	ED	10	9	6
BRUNSWICK	*ST JOHN* blutheran@outlook.com	1871	319 E BROADWAY ST	65236	MO	Benjamin J Theiss	(660)548-3642	WS 10 SS 9 BC 9	ED	257	174	54
BUCKHORN	*FAITH*		See Saint Robert MO									
BUFFALO	*OUR SAVIOR* oursaviorlutheranbuffalo@gmail.com sites.google.com/view/oslc	1952	107 S ELDER ST	65622	MO	Jeffrey E Sippy	(417)986-3048	WS 9 BC 8	HC	29	29	23
BUNCETON	*ZION*	1896	9195 B HWY	65237	MO	Paul C Weisenborn	(660)838-6428	WS 10 SS 9 BC 9	EL/ED/HC/ MD	319	249	64
CABOOL	*HOLY CROSS*		See Houston MO									
CALIFORNIA	*ST PAUL'S* office@stpaulslutheran1860.com www.stpaulslutheran1860.com	1860	207 N OWEN ST	65018	MO	Evandro Kopper Sr	(573)796-2735 (573)796-2735	WS 9 SS 1030 BC 1030	EC/ED/HC/ MD/SN	438	337	114
CAMDENTON	*PEACE* plccamdenton@gmail.com www.plccamdenton.org	1989	9307 N State Hwy 5 9307 N STATE HIGHWAY 5	65020	MO		(573)836-8141	WS 9 SS 1030 BC 1030		69	69	40
CAMERON	*PRINCE PEACE* princeofpeacelutherancameron@ gmail.com cameronlutheran.360unite.com	1969	209 LITTLE BRICK ST	64429	MO	Mark A Goucher	(816)632-7904		EC/ED/HC/ MD	131	92	25
CAPE GIRARDEAU	*CHRIST*		See Gordonville MO									
	GOOD SHEPHERD secretary@gslccape.org www.gslccape.org	1967	1904 W CAPE ROCK DR CPE GIRARDEAU	63701	MO	Weston J Wildauer	(573)335-3974	WS 8 1030 SS 915	HS/ED/ HC/SN	203	168	93
	HANOVER office@hanoverlutheran.com www.hanoverlutheran.com	1846	2949 PERRYVILLE RD CPE GIRARDEAU	63701	MO	Rodney A Benkendorf	(573)335-8583 (573)335-4741	WS 745 1015 SS 9 BC 9	HS/ED/HC/ MD/SN	385	320	200
	ONLINE Satellite Site of St Andrew Cape Girardeau MO	2021	804 N Cape Rock Drive	63701				WS 8 930 11				
	ST ANDREW office@lglomd.org www.lglomd.org	1957	804 N CAPE ROCK DR	63701	MO	John A Dehne Timothy J Koehler Jared L Tanz	(573)334-3200 (573)335-8589	WS 8 1030 SS 915 BC 915	HS/ED/HC/ MD/SN	387	341	349
	THE EXCHANGE		See Jackson MO									
	TRINITY office@t-lutheran.org www.t-lutheran.org	1854	100 N FREDERICK ST CPE GIRARDEAU	63701	MO	Douglas C Breite	(573)335-8224 (573)335-1146	WS 8 1030 SS 915 BC 915	EL/HS/ED/ HC/MD	1280	1028	400
	TRINITY trinity.egyptmills@gmail.com tlcem.org	1867	5665 COUNTY ROAD 635 CPE GIRARDEAU	63701	MO	Eric S Ronsick	(573)334-4549 (573)334-4549	WS 745 10 SS 9 BC 9		164	142	58
CARROLLTON	*IMMANUEL* ImmanuelCarrolltonMO@gmail.com www.immanuelcarrollton.com	1882	402 S FOLGER ST	64633	MO	Samuel J Aizenberg	(660)542-2064	WS 10 SS 9 BC 9	ED/MD	250	189	110
CARTHAGE	*GOOD SHEPHERD* goodshepherd@ecarthage.com www.gslc-carthage.com	1986	8975 County Ln 170 PO BOX 257	64836	MO	Silas C Mehl	(417)358-1325	WS 9 SS 1030 BC 1030	ED/HC/ MD/SN	461	375	86
CASCADE	*ZION*		See Gravelton MO									
CEDAR HILL	*CEDAR HILL* chlutheran@gmail.com chlutheran.org	1983	8600 SILVER LN	63016	MO	Dr Darrell W Zimmerman	(636)274-4802 (636)274-9080	WS 730 9 1030 SS 1030 BC 915	ED/HC/ MD/SN	182	155	99
CENTER	*TRINITY*	1978	22227 HWY EE 22227 HIGHWAY EE	63436	MO	William O Blankenship		WS 10	ED/MD	47	31	20
CENTRALIA	*GOOD SHEPHERD* office@goodshepherdcentralia.org goodshepherdcentralia.org	1958	120 W GANO CHANCE DR	65240	MO	James R Lanning	(573)682-3941	WS 10 SS 9 BC 9	ED/HC/MD	88	70	49
CHAFFEE	*ST PAUL*	1917	201 GRAY ST	63740	MO	Daniel E Warner	(573)204-1944	WS 8 SS 9 BC 9	HS	41	41	16
CHAMOIS	*PILGRIM* pilgrimlutheranfreedom.com	1868	310 State Hwy N PO BOX 585 LINN	65024 65051	MO	Paul D Landgraf	(314)791-6401	WS 1030 BC 930		91	65	18

*Indicates a new church start. A new church start is an intentionally organized gathering which comes together on a regular basis for the purpose of worship and/or Bible study and is intended to grow into a member LCMS congregation. WS =Worship Service; SS = Sunday School; BC =Bible Class; EC = Early Childhood; EL = Elementary School; HS = High School; ED =Education Ministry; HC =Human Care Ministry; SN = Special Needs Ministry; MD = Media Ministry (PC)=Partner Church Pastor. See Page 53 for the Table of Abbreviations for key to additional abbreviations

CITY	CONGREGATION EMAIL WEBSITE	YEAR EST	LOCATION MAILING ADDRESS	ZIP CODE(S)	DIST.	PASTOR(S)	PHONE FAX	WS SS BC	SCHOOLS/ MINISTRIES	STATISTIC Bapt	Conf	Avg Attend
CHESTERFIELD	*KING OF KINGS* officeadmin@kokstl.org www.kokstl.org	1969	13765 OLIVE BLVD	63017	MO	Douglas W Chinberg Alexander S Pitsch	(314)469-2224 (314)469-0601	WS 8 930 11 SS 930 BC 930 1045	EC/EL/HS/ ED/HC/ MD/SN	834	661	237
	LORD OF LIFE secretary@lordoflifelcms.org www.lordoflifelcms.org	1976	15750 BAXTER RD	63017	MO	Trevor A Freudenburg	(636)532-0400 (636)536-2322	WS 8 1030 SS 915 BC 915	EC/ED/HC/ MD/SN	212	194	117
CHILLICOTHE	*ST JOHN* halljo55@yahoo.com stjohnchillicothe.org	1929	1001 Calhoun St PO BOX 426	64601	MO	Lloyd A Hubbard	(660)646-5944	WS 10 SS 1115 BC 1115	ED/HC/MD	38	32	17
CLARKS FORK	*TRINITY* pastorpete067@gmail.com	1860	20209 ELLIS DAVIS RD BOONVILLE	65233	MO	Dr Peter M Kurowski	(605)471-0293	WS 830	ED/HC/SN	155	130	43
CLINTON	*TRINITY* trinityclinton@outlook.com www.trinityclintonmo.com	1932	1267 E HIGHWAY 7	64735	MO	James B Stockland	(660)885-4728	WS 1 SS 12 BC 12	ED/HC	217	165	51
COLE CAMP	*HOLY CROSS* colecamplutheran@gmail.com holycrosslutheranchurchcolecamp. weebly.com	1842	11357 Lake Creek Ave 210 N PINE ST	65325	MO	Tyler P Poppen	(660)668-0117	WS 1030 SS 930 BC 930	EL/HS/ED/ HC/MD	246	193	95
	MOUNT HULDA mthuldalutheranchurch@gmail.com www.facebook.com/MtHulda LutheranChurch/	1853	22303 Mount Hulda Ave 22303 MT HULDA AVE	65325	MO	Allen L Braun	(660)668-9981	WS 10	ED	89	78	25
	ST JOHN colecamplutheran@gmail.com holycrosslutheranchurchcolecamp. weebly.com	1842	24295 Cheese Creek Rd 210 N PINE ST	65325	MO	Tyler P Poppen	(660)668-0117	WS 8 SS 9 BC 9	EL/HS/ED/ HC/MD	74	58	30
	TRINITY info@trinitycolecamp.org www.trinitycolecamp.org	1896	104 E BUTTERFIELD TRAIL	65325	MO	Dr Gregory R Truwe	(660)668-2364	WS 9 SS 1030 BC 1030	EC/EL/HS/ ED/HC/ MD/SN	505	406	197
COLUMBIA	*ALIVE IN CHRIST* aicoffice@aic.org www.aic.org	1992	201 SOUTHAMPTON DR	65203	MO	Timothy E Morris David J Prill	(573)499-0443 (573)499-0452	WS 830 11 SS 10 BC 10	ED/HC/MD	574	472	309
	CAMPUS office@campuslutheran.org www.campuslutheran.org	1959	304 S COLLEGE AVE	65201	MO	Dr Kent D Pierce	(573)442-5942 (573)442-6930	WS 830 11 SS 945 BC 945	ED/HC/ MD/SN	348	267	151
	TRINITY church@trinity-lcms.org trinity-lcms.org	1922	2201 W Rollins Rd 2201 ROLLINS RD	65203	MO	Brian K Thieme Joseph M McCalley	(573)445-2112 (573)445-4078	WS 8 1030 SS 915 BC 915	EC/ED/HC/ MD/SN	632	528	236
CONCORDIA	*LUTHERAN GOOD SHEPHERD HOME* Satellite Site of St Paul Concordia MO	2007	202 S West St	64020				WS 930				
	ST PAUL office@stpaulsconcordia.org stpaulsconcordia.org	1840	401 S Main St PO BOX 60	64020	MO	Michael T Pottschmidt Andrew A Lehenbauer	(660)463-2291 (660)463-7173	WS 8 1030 SS 915 BC 915	EL/ED/HC/ MD/SN	1610	1315	552
CONWAY	*IMMANUEL*	1885	97 ORCHID RD	65632	MO		(417)589-2402	WS 10 SS 9	ED	107	82	40
CORDER	*ZION*	1889	500 N Elizabeth PO BOX 224	64021	MO	Mark R Junkin	(660)394-2322	WS 1030 SS 930 BC 930	EL/ED/HC	239	200	60
COTTLEVILLE	*HOLY CROSS*		See O'fallon MO									
CREIGHTON	*TRINITY*	1904	206 A St PO BOX 123	64739	MO	C R Malone Sr	(660)499-2205	WS 11 SS 930 940 BC 930	ED/HC/MD	49	47	24
CRESTWOOD	*CHRIST MEMORIAL*		See Saint Louis MO									
	PRINCE OF PEACE www.princeofpeacecrestwood.com	1963	8646 NEW SAPPINGTON RD SAINT LOUIS	63126	MO	Hans W Fiene	(314)843-8448 (314)843-5653	WS 9 SS 1030 BC 1030	EL/HS/ ED/HC	234	197	105
	RESURRECTION		See Sunset Hills MO									
CROCKER	*FAITH*		See Saint Robert MO									
CROSSTOWN	*ZION* salemlutheran@hotmail.com salemlutheran8.wixsite.com/ SalemandZion	1901	21202 Hwy C 21202 HIGHWAY C PERRYVILLE	63775	MO	John P Hellwege Jr	(573)824-5728	WS 730 SS 830	HS/ED	170	129	57
CRYSTAL CITY	*IMMANUEL* secretary@ilcfestus.org ilcfestus.org	1892	220 BRIERTON LN 221 BRIERTON LN FESTUS	63019 63028	MO	Kyle D Castens	(636)937-5525 (636)937-9332	WS 8 1030 SS 915 BC 915	EC/ED/HC/ MD	460	347	160
CUBA	*ST PAUL* stpauls@centurytel.net	1915	730 FLEENOR RD	65453	MO		(573)885-7234 (573)885-7234	WS 1030 SS 915	ED	161	129	31
DARDENNE PRAIRIE	*HOLY CROSS*		See O'fallon MO									
	PEACE		See Weldon Spring MO									
DE SOTO	*GRACE* gracelutheranchurchdesoto@gmail.com glcdesoto.org	1984	121 W KELLEY ST	63020	MO		(636)535-7252	WS 1045 BC 930	ED/HC/ MD/SN	68	62	32
DES PERES	*LIVING STONE SERVICE* Satellite Site of St Paul Des Peres MO	2015	1300 N Ballas Rd	63131				WS 1045				
	ST PAUL church@stpaulsdp.org www.stpaulsdesperes.org	1849	12345 MANCHESTER RD SAINT LOUIS	63131	MO	Lawton D Thompson Tanner S Wade	(314)822-0447 (314)822-3555	WS 8 930 1045 SS 930 BC 930	EC/EL/HS/ ED/HC/ MD/SN	2462	1988	956
DEVILS ELBOW	*FAITH*		See Saint Robert MO									

*Indicates a new church start. A new church start is an intentionally organized gathering which comes together on a regular basis for the purpose of worship and/or Bible study and is intended to grow into a member LCMS congregation. WS =Worship Service; SS = Sunday School; BC =Bible Class; EC = Early Childhood; EL = Elementary School; HS = High School; ED =Education Ministry; HC =Human Care Ministry; SN = Special Needs Ministry; MD = Media Ministry (PC)=Partner Church Pastor. See Page 53 for the Table of Abbreviations for key to additional abbreviations

CONGREGATIONS

CITY	CONGREGATION EMAIL WEBSITE	YEAR EST	LOCATION MAILING ADDRESS	ZIP CODE(S)	DIST.	PASTOR(S)	PHONE FAX	WS SS BC	SCHOOLS/ MINISTRIES	STATISTIC Bapt	Conf	Avg Attend
DEXTER	*FAITH* flcdexter@gmail.com	1959	1002 SADDLE SPUR RD	63841	MO	Justin C Sponaugle	(573)624-4921	WS 930	ED	48	48	25
DIGGINS	*ZION* rcpeckman77@att.net	1896	492 South Diggins Main St PO BOX 68	65636	MO			WS 1030 BC 930	ED	60	53	26
DIXON	*FAITH*		See Saint Robert MO									
DONIPHAN	*TRINITY*	1973	801 RIPLEY 160 E-2	63935	MO		(573)996-3061	WS 11		30	25	10
DRAKE	*ST JOHN* stjohnlutheran-drake.com	1871	2840 CHARLOTTE CHURCH RD OWENSVILLE	65066	MO	Paul D Landgraf	(314)791-6401	WS 830 SS 930	ED/MD	93	67	26
EGYPT MILLS	*TRINITY*		See Cape Girardeau MO									
ELDON	*BETHANY* www.bethanyeldon.com	1947	1000 N Grand 1000 N GRAND AVE	65026	MO	Peter A Lange	(573)392-4603	WS 9 SS 1015 BC 1015	ED/HC/MD			
ELK PRAIRIE	*PEACE*	1884	PO BOX 1573 ROLLA	65401 65402	MO		(573)341-3482	WS 10 BC 930				
ELLISVILLE	*PATHFINDER* churchinfo@pathfinderstl.org pathfinderstl.org	1851	15800 MANCHESTER RD	63011	MO	Dion T Garrett Andrew J Mastic Douglas E Mauss	(636)394-4100 (636)394-9853	WS 9 11 SS 9 11	EL/ED/HC/ MD/SN	3381	2757	856
EMMA	*HOLY CROSS* office@holycrossemma.org www.holycrossemma.org	1865	504 N Elm PO BOX 121	65327	MO		(660)463-7869	WS 9 SS 1015 BC 1015	EL/ED/HC/ MD/SN	463	351	160
ERNESTVILLE	*ST MATTHEW* pastor@saintmatthewlcms.org www.saintmatthewlcms.org	1899	2095 Hwy KK 2095 HIGHWAY KK CON- CORDIA	64020	MO	William P Copus Jr	(660)463-2717	WS 10 SS 9 BC 9	EL/ED/HC/ MD/SN	152	124	58
EUREKA	*ST MARK* sstuart@stmarkseureka.org www.stmarkseureka.org	1948	500 MERAMEC BLVD	63025	MO	Robert O Liebmann Joshua W Rusnak	(636)938-4432	WS 930 SS 11 BC 11	EL/ED/HC/ MD/SN	577	466	240
EXCELSIOR SPRINGS	*MOUNT CALVARY* mtcalvarylutheranes@yahoo.com www.mtcalvarylutheran.org	1932	1215 Baldwin St 1215 BALDWIN LN EXCELSIOR SPG	64024	MO	Mark J Kranz	(816)637-9800	WS 9 SS 1030 BC 1030	ED/HC/ MD/SN	115	94	73
FARLEY	*ST JOHN* info@stjohnsfarley.com www.stjohnsfarley.com	1872	98 Main St PO BOX 117	64028	MO	Gregg A Reiser	(816)330-3314	WS 1030 SS 930 BC 930	EL/ED/HC/ MD	122	108	54
FARMINGTON	*ST PAUL* jmestp@yahoo.com stpaulfarmington.com	1873	609 E Columbia St 608 E COLUMBIA ST	63640	MO		(573)756-7872 (573)756-0934	WS 9 SS 1015	EL/HS/ED/ HC/MD/SN	848	672	250
FARRAR	*SALEM* salemlutheran@hotmail.com salemlutheran8.wixsite.com/ SalemandZion	1859	299 PCR 328	63746	MO	John P Hellwege Jr	(573)824-5728	WS 9 SS 815 BC 815	EL/HS/ED/ MD	332	261	127
FAYETTE	*SHEP OF THE HILLS* pastor@shlcfayettemo.com shlcfayettemo.com	1979	402 PARK RD	65248	MO	Andrew R Etzler	(660)248-3486	WS 10 SS 9		107	90	21
FENTON	*OUR SAVIOR* gkeeve@oursaviorlcs.org www.oursaviorlcs.org	1961	1500 SAN SIMEON WAY	63026	MO	Mark E Sell Dr Ryan R Rupe	(636)343-2192 (636)343-9936	WS 8 1030 SS 915 BC 915	EL/HS/ED/ MD	1196	845	138
	RESURRECTION		See Sunset Hills MO									
FESTUS	*IMMANUEL*		See Crystal City MO									
FLAT RIVER	*TRINITY*		See Park Hills MO									
FLORISSANT	*BLESSED SAVIOR* office@blessedsavior-lcms.org www.BlessedSavior-LCMS.org	1980	2615 SHACKELFORD RD	63031	MO	Matthew D Roeglin	(314)831-1300	WS 8 1030 SS 915 BC 915	EL/HS/MD	120	107	48
	SALEM		See Black Jack MO									
FOREST GREEN	*SALEM*		See Salisbury MO									
FORSYTH	*SHEP OF THE LAKES* shepherd13904@gmail.com www.sheplakeslcms.com	1993	13904 US Highway 160 PO BOX 235	65653	MO	David M Oddi	(417)546-2246 (417)546-4966	WS 9 SS 1030 BC 1030	HC	74	63	27
FORT LEONARD WOOD	*FAITH*		See Saint Robert MO									
FREDERICKTOWN	*TRINITY* sthilary@trinityfredericktown.net	1922	601 Kingsbury 601 KINGSBURY BLVD	63645	MO		(573)783-2405	WS 1045 SS 945 BC 945		79	76	57
FREISTATT	*TRINITY* trinityfreistatt@gmail.com www.trinity1874.com	1874	207 North Main 207 N MAIN ST	65654	MO	Jacob E Sletten	(417)235-7300 (417)235-6336	WS 10 SS 845 BC 845	EL/ED/HC/ MD/SN	582	438	174
FRIEDHEIM	*TRINITY* trinitylutheranfriedheim@yahoo.com 65.websitex5.me/Trinity	1848	3700 COUNTY ROAD 415	63747	MO	Michael T Winckler	(573)788-2536	WS 8 SS 930 BC 930	HS	277	216	102
FROHNA	*CONCORDIA* concordiafrohna@att.net www.concordiafrohna.org	1839	10172 HIGHWAY C	63748	MO		(573)824-5435	WS 9	EL/HS/ED/ MD/SN	339	280	126
FULTON	*ST PAULS* stpaulslutheranfultonlcms@gmail.com stpaulsfulton.org	1954	1703 PLAZA DR	65251	MO	William C Heaton	(573)642-2856 (573)642-2856	WS 1030 SS 930 BC 930	ED	93	81	61
GLENDALE	*GLENDALE* glendalelutheranchurch@gmail.com glendalelutheranchurch.org	1943	1365 N SAPPINGTON RD SAINT LOUIS	63122	MO	Scott E Jonas	(314)966-3220 (314)966-3243	WS 915 SS 1045 BC 1045	EL/HS/ED/ HC/MD/SN	345	293	88
GORDONVILLE	*CHRIST* admin@christgordonville.org www.christgordonville.org	1899	248 Albert St PO BOX 72	63752	MO	Jacob T May	(573)243-5639	WS 10 SS 9 BC 9	HS/ED/HC	200	175	95
	ST PAUL		See Chaffee MO									

*Indicates a new church start. A new church start is an intentionally organized gathering which comes together on a regular basis for the purpose of worship and/or Bible study and is intended to grow into a member LCMS congregation. WS =Worship Service; SS = Sunday School; BC =Bible Class; EC = Early Childhood; EL = Elementary School; HS = High School; ED =Education Ministry; HC =Human Care Ministry; SN = Special Needs Ministry; MD = Media Ministry (PC)=Partner Church Pastor. See Page 53 for the Table of Abbreviations for key to additional abbreviations

CITY	CONGREGATION EMAIL WEBSITE	YEAR EST	LOCATION MAILING ADDRESS	ZIP CODE(S)	DIST.	PASTOR(S)	PHONE FAX	WS SS BC	SCHOOLS/ MINISTRIES	STATISTIC Bapt	Conf	Avg Attend
GORDONVILLE	*ZION* zlcgordonville@gmail.com www.zlcgordonville.org/	1865	176 Country Rd 226 176 COUNTY ROAD 226 CPE GIRARDEAU	63752 63701	MO	Daniel E Warner	(573)204-1944	WS 1015 SS 915 BC 915	HS	253	203	66
GRANDVIEW	*HOLY TRINITY* churchofficeholytrinity@gmail.com www.holytrinitylcms.org	1957	5901 E 135TH ST	64030	MO	Keith E Emshoff	(816)763-3211	WS 8 1030 SS 915 BC 915	EC/HS/ED/ HC/MD/SN	421	352	83
GRAVELTON	*ZION* sthilary@trinityfredericktown.net	1857	601 KINGSBURY BLVD FREDERICKTOWN	63645	MO		(573)783-2405	WS 8		44	36	38
GREENVIEW	*PEACE*		See Camdenton MO									
HANNIBAL	*IMMANUEL* immanuellutheranchurch@live.com	1869	6508 COUNTY ROAD 263	63401	MO	Scott A Salo	(573)221-7051 (573)248-8210	WS 1030 SS 930 BC 930	ED/HC/ MD/SN	190	138	80
	ST JOHNS church@stjohnshannibal.org www.stjohnshannibal.org	1860	1201 Lyon St 1317 LYON ST	63401	EN	Eric S Carlson	(573)221-0615 (573)221-8384	WS 10 SS 830 BC 830	EL/ED/HC/ MD/SN	689	519	145
HARRISONVILLE	*BETHLEHEM*		See Raymore MO									
HERMANN	*SHEPHERD HILLS* shepherdofthehillsluth@gmail.com sothhermann.com	1982	1952 W Hwy 100 1952 HIGHWAY 100	65041	MO		(573)486-3335	WS 930 SS 815 BC 815	ED/HC	67	63	30
HERMITAGE	*HOPE* marthabreedlove40@gmail.com	1990	23055 W 54 Hwy PO BOX 346	65668	MO		(417)253-2619	WS 1030	HC	11	11	10
HIGGINSVILLE	*IMMANUEL* immanuellutheran@ctcis.net www.immanuellutheranhigginsville.com/	1891	1501 LIPPER AVE	64037	MO		(660)584-3541 (660)584-5914	WS 1015 SS 9 BC 9	EL/ED/ MD/SN	647	474	121
HIGH RIDGE	*HOPE* hopehighridge@sbcglobal.net www.hopehighridge.org	1937	2308 GRAVOIS RD	63049	MO	Dr Jason M Wagner	(636)677-8788	WS 8 1045 SS 930 BC 930	EC/HS/ED/ HC/MD	428	411	177
HIGHLANDVILLE	*MY CHURCH*		See Ozark MO									
HILLSBORO	*ZION* office@zionhb.org www.zionhb.org	1853	9700 ZION LUTHERAN CHURCH RD	63050	MO		(636)797-4211	WS 9 SS 1030 BC 1030	ED/HC/ MD/SN	237	188	98
HOLTS SUMMIT	*GRACE* graceholtssummitmo@gmail.com www.GraceLutheranHS.com	1990	618 HALIFAX RD	65043	MO	Michael J Diener	(573)896-8824 (573)896-5836	WS 10 SS 9 BC 9	EC/HS/ED/ HC/MD/SN	236	187	92
HOUSTON	*HOLY CROSS* salemlchpas@gmail.com	1969	1419 S SAM HOUSTON BLVD	65483	MO	David L Kettner	(417)967-2204	WS 8 SS 930	MD	113	87	46
IMPERIAL	*RESURRECTION*		See Sunset Hills MO									
	ST PAUL'S saintpaulsoffice@att.net www.saintpaulslcms.org	1856	6550 State Rt 21 6550 OLD STATE ROUTE 21	63052	MO		(636)942-4250	WS 10 SS 845 BC 845	ED/HC/MD	149	124	37
INDEPENDENCE	*ASCENSION*		See Kansas City MO									
	MESSIAH mlc@messiahlcms.net www.messiahlcms.net	1936	613 S MAIN ST	64050	MO		(816)254-9405	WS 9 SS 1015 BC 1015	HS/HC/ MD/SN	410	406	67
	ST PAULS secretary172stpl@comcast.net www.stpaulsindependencemo.com	1908	17200 E 39TH ST S	64055	MO		(816)373-5290	WS 9 BC 1015	HS/ED/MD	146	142	35
IRONTON	*IMMANUEL*		See Pilot Knob MO									
	ST PAUL	1917	101 E DENT ST	63650	MO		(573)880-0175	WS 9 SS 10 BC 10		43	40	28
ISABELLA	*FAITH*	1974	Hwy 160 8615 US HIGHWAY 160	65676	MO				HC	17	17	8
JACKSON	*CHRIST*		See Gordonville MO									
	IMMANUEL	1866	496 STATE HIGHWAY F	63755	MO	Mark A Boettcher	(573)204-4700	WS 845 SS 10 BC 10	HS			
	ST PAUL office@stpauljackson.com www.stpauljackson.com	1893	223 W ADAMS ST	63755	MO	Joshua W Schmidt	(573)243-2236 (573)243-6238	WS 745 915 1045 SS 915 BC 915	HS/ED/HC/ MD/SN	2185	1727	567
	THE EXCHANGE TheExchangeSemo@gmail.com theexchangecommunity.org		5195 OLD CAPE RD E	63755	MO	Cory S Stallings		WS 830 1030	HS	89	68	50
	ZION		See Pocahontas MO									
JAMESTOWN	*IMMANUEL* pastorpete067@gmail.com	1989	148 CEDAR ST	65046	MO	Dr Peter M Kurowski	(605)471-0293	SS 9		34	29	35
JEFFERSON CITY	*FAITH* office@faithinjeffcity.org faithinjeffcity.org	1950	2027 INDUSTRIAL DR JEFFERSON CTY	65109	MO	Richard D Steensma Jr	(573)636-4602 (573)632-7739	WS 745 10 1130 SS 9	HS/ED/HC/ MD/SN	684	494	334
	IMMANUEL ilhcchurch@midmoimmanuel.com www.midmoimmanuel.com	1870	8231 TANNER BRIDGE RD JEFFERSON CTY	65101	MO	Steven A Resner	(573)496-3451	WS 930 SS 815 BC 815	EL/HS/ED/ HC/MD	490	404	249
	ST JOHN stjohnslutheranjcmo@gmail.com www.stjohnslutheranjc.com	1869	Us Highway 50 4409 SAINT JOHNS RD JEFFERSON CTY	65101	MO	Ryan M Groh	(573)395-4591 (573)395-9954	WS 10 SS 915 BC 930	HS/ED/ MD/SN	258	203	100
	ST JOHN		See Lohman MO									
	TRINITY churchoffice@trinityjc.org www.trinityjc.org	1870	803 SWIFTS HWY JEFFERSON CTY	65109	MO	Samuel M Powell	(573)636-6750	WS 8 1030 SS 915	EL/HS/ED/ HC/MD/SN	1648	1250	401

*Indicates a new church start. A new church start is an intentionally organized gathering which comes together on a regular basis for the purpose of worship and/or Bible study and is intended to grow into a member LCMS congregation. WS =Worship Service; SS = Sunday School; BC =Bible Class; EC = Early Childhood; EL = Elementary School; HS = High School; ED =Education Ministry; HC =Human Care Ministry; SN = Special Needs Ministry; MD = Media Ministry (PC)=Partner Church Pastor. See Page 53 for the Table of Abbreviations for key to additional abbreviations

CITY	CONGREGATION EMAIL WEBSITE	YEAR EST	LOCATION MAILING ADDRESS	ZIP CODE(S)	DIST.	PASTOR(S)	PHONE FAX	WS SS BC	SCHOOLS/ MINISTRIES	STATISTIC Bapt	Conf	Avg Attend
JONESBURG	*ST PAUL* church_office@stpaulsjonesburg.com stpaulsjonesburg.com	1884	204 Jones St PO BOX 328	63351	MO	Dr Kevin J Kohnke	(636)488-5235 (636)488-5205	WS 9 SS 1030	ED/HC/ MD/SN	190	152	55
JOPLIN	*IMMANUEL* churchoffice@immanueljoplin.com www.immanueljoplin.com	1897	2616 CONNECTICUT AVE	64804	MO	Christopher M Ramstad	(417)624-0333 (417)624-2774	WS 8 1030 SS 920 BC 920	EL/ED/HC/ MD/SN	783	625	170
KANSAS CITY	*ASCENSION* secretary@ascensionlckc.org www.ascensionlutherankc.org	1964	4900 BLUE RIDGE BLVD	64133	MO		(816)358-1919	WS 930 SS 830 BC 815	HS/ED/HC/ MD/SN	168	114	62
	BETHLEHEM		See Raymore MO									
	CALVARY churchoffice@calvarykc.com www.calvarykc.com	1925	7500 OAK ST	64114	MO	Bryce A Bereuter	(816)444-6908 (816)444-5696	WS 8 940 11 430 SS 930 BC 930 545	EL/HS/ED/ HC/MD/SN	785	537	150
	CHRIST		See Platte Woods MO									
	HOLY CROSS church@holycrosskc.org www.holycrosskc.org	1951	2003 NE ENGLEWOOD RD	64118	MO	Dr Craig A Meissner	(816)452-9113 (816)452-8263	WS 10 SS 845 BC 845	EC/ED/HC	323	278	85
	HOLY TRINITY		See Grandview MO									
	IMMANUEL Immanuelkc42@gmail.com www.immanuellcmskcmo.org	1885	4203 Tracy Ave 4205 TRACY AVE	64110	MO		(816)561-0561 (816)561-0612	WS 1030	HS/ED/HC/ MD	27	21	20
	JESUS EL BUEN PASTOR pastorfee@gmail.com	1983	3007 Mercier 3007 MERCIER ST	64108	MO		(913)707-3518 (913)948-6650		ED/HC/MD	78	62	56
	KING OF KINGS koklc@kokkc.org kingofkingsKC.org	1967	1701 NE 96TH ST	64155	MO	Frank N Greene III Daniel J Clemens	(816)436-7680 (816)436-2876	WS 8 1030 SS 930 BC 930	EC/EL/ED/ MD	1123	896	290
	MESSIAH		See Independence MO									
	OUR REDEEMER Office@OurRedeemerKC.com www.OurRedeemerKC.com	1922	711 BENTON BLVD	64124	MO	Vicente Sanchez-Zapata	(816)241-2334	WS 915	HS/ED/HC	50	50	45
	PEACE peacelutheranlcms@att.net www.peacelutheranlcms.org	1954	8240 BLUE RIDGE BLVD	64138	MO	David M Rolf	(816)353-3813	WS 830 11 SS 945 BC 945	EC/HS/ED/ HC/MD	337	290	90
	ST MATTHEW		See Lees Summit MO									
	TRINITY		See Mission KS									
KEARNEY	*TRINITY* gnuguy1946@gmail.com www.trinitykearney.org	1978	1715 S Jefferson St PO BOX 440	64060	MO		(816)628-6644	WS 9 SS 1030 BC 1030	ED	265	207	92
KENNETT	*REDEEMER*	1963	1004 FALCON DR	63857	MO		(573)888-4638					
KIMBERLING CITY	*SHEPHERD HILLS* sheplutheran@live.com www.kimberlinglutheran.com	1973	71 Kimberling Blvd PO BOX 484 KIMBERLING CY	65686	MO	Richard K Futrell	(417)739-2512	WS 930 SS 815 BC 815	ED/HC/ MD/SN	104	101	58
KIRKSVILLE	*FAITH* secretaryatfaith@hotmail.com www.faithlutherankv.org	1938	1820 S BALTIMORE ST	63501	MO		(660)665-6122 (660)627-0101	WS 1015 SS 9 BC 9	EL/ED/ HC/SN	139	111	73
KIRKWOOD	*CONCORDIA* lwatson@ckhome.org www.ckhome.org	1874	505 S KIRKWOOD RD SAINT LOUIS	63122	MO	Stephen H Bongard David L Meggers Charles B Kieschnick	(314)822-7772	WS 815 930 1045 SS 930 BC 930	EL/HS/ED/ HC/SN	2379	1868	640
KNOB NOSTER	*FAITH* faithknobnoster@gmail.com www.youtube.com/@faith lutheranknobnostermo3305	1983	507 S Washington Ave PO BOX 42	65336	MO	Jon-Michael Schweigert	(660)563-5973	WS 930 SS 1045	ED	86	60	45
LA GRANGE	*ST PETER* stpeterslg@gmail.com	1855	300 S 7TH ST	63448	MO		(573)655-4416	WS 930 BC 9	EC/ED/HC/ MD	253	250	58
LADUE	*VILLAGE* www.villagelutheranchurch.org	1946	9237 CLAYTON RD SAINT LOUIS	63124	MO	Dr Matthew C Harrison	(314)993-1834 (314)993-8920	WS 815 1045 SS 945	EC/EL/HS/ ED/MD/SN	484	391	244
LAKE OZARK	*CHRIST KING* ctk@ctklo.org www.ctklo.com	1996	1700 BAGNELL DAM BLVD	65049	MO	Ronald P Lehenbauer	(573)365-5212 (573)365-5356	WS 8 1045	EL/ED/HC/ MD/SN	696	532	330
LAKE SAINT LOUIS	*HOLY CROSS*		See O'fallon MO									
	PEACE		See Weldon Spring MO									
LAMAR	*GRACE* www.lamarGLC.com	1947	208 POPLAR ST	64759	MO	Galen M Friedrichs	(417)682-2257	WS 1030 SS 915 BC 915	ED/HC/ MD/SN	120	110	55
LAMPE	*SHEPHERD HILLS*		See Kimberling City MO									
LAQUEY	*FAITH*		See Saint Robert MO									
LEBANON	*TRINITY* secretary@trinitylebanon.com www.trinitylebanon.com	1934	1300 KENT DR	65536	MO	David L Oberdieck	(417)532-2717 (417)532-2677	WS 9 SS 1030 BC 915	ED/HC/ MD/SN	150	148	73
LEES SUMMIT	*BEAUTIFUL SAVIOR* office@beautifulsavior-lsmo.org www.beautifulsavior-lsmo.org	1978	615 SE TODD GEORGE PKWY	64063	EN	Jonathan P Gruen Devin J Burmeister	(816)524-7288 (816)897-0311	WS 8 930 11 SS 930 BC 930	EC/ED/HC/ MD/SN	902	714	281
	HOLY TRINITY		See Grandview MO									
	ST MATTHEW secretary@gracefaithlove.org www.GraceFaithLove.org	1960	700 NE CHIPMAN RD	64063	MO	Craig D Otto Steven P Andrews Jr	(816)524-7068 (816)524-9012	WS 8 1045 SS 930 BC 930	EC/ED/HC/ MD/SN	737	571	293
LEMAY	*GETHSEMANE* gethsemane765@gmail.com www.glcl.church	1905	765 LEMAY FERRY RD SAINT LOUIS	63125	MO		(314)631-7331 (314)631-0265	WS 10 BC 9	EL/HS/ED/ HC/MD/SN	181	177	80

*Indicates a new church start. A new church start is an intentionally organized gathering which comes together on a regular basis for the purpose of worship and/or Bible study and is intended to grow into a member LCMS congregation. WS =Worship Service; SS = Sunday School; BC =Bible Class; EC = Early Childhood; EL = Elementary School; HS = High School; ED =Education Ministry; HC =Human Care Ministry; SN = Special Needs Ministry; MD = Media Ministry (PC)=Partner Church Pastor. See Page 53 for the Table of Abbreviations for key to additional abbreviations

CITY	CONGREGATION EMAIL WEBSITE	YEAR EST	LOCATION MAILING ADDRESS	ZIP CODE(S)	DIST.	PASTOR(S)	PHONE FAX	WS SS BC	SCHOOLS/ MINISTRIES	Bapt	Conf	Avg Attend
LEMAY	*RESURRECTION*		See Sunset Hills MO									
LESLIE	*EBENEZER* info@ebenezerporthudson.com ebenezerporthudson.com	1846	9100 Hwy YY 9100 HIGHWAY YY	63056	MO	James M Wilshusen	(573)459-6432 (573)459-2203	WS 1030 SS 930 BC 930	MD/SN			
LEXINGTON	*GRACE* office@gracelutheranlexington.org www.gracelutheranlexington.org	1920	806 S Business Hwy 13 806 S BUSINESS HIGHWAY 13	64067	MO	Jeffrey M Kuddes	(660)259-2932	WS 10 SS 10 BC 10	EC/ED/HC/ MD/SN	192	148	48
LIBERTY	*ST STEPHEN* office@teamjesusliberty.org www.teamjesusliberty.org	1960	205 N FOREST AVE	64068	MO	Jose J Rodriguez Jr	(816)781-3377 (816)866-9216	WS 8 1030 SS 915 BC 915	EC/EL/HS/ ED/HC/ MD/SN	530	410	239
LINCOLN	*IMMANUEL* zionandimmanuel@gmail.com www.zionimmanuel.org	1898	17430 N Lincoln Rd PO BOX 278	65338	MO	Stephen W Rutherford	(660)547-3399	WS 1015 SS 9		103	76	30
	ZION zionandimmanuel@gmail.com www.zionimmanuel.org	1859	21011 Rotermund Ave PO BOX 278	65338	MO	Stephen W Rutherford	(660)547-3399	WS 830 SS 930 BC 7		258	230	66
LINDBERG	*RESURRECTION*		See Sunset Hills MO									
LOCKWOOD	*GOOD SHEPHERD NURSING HOME* Satellite Site of Immanuel Lockwood MO	1993	200 W 12th Street	65682								
	IMMANUEL churchoffice@immanuellcms.net www.immanuellcms.net	1882	212 W 4th St PO BOX H	65682	MO	Kyle J Fittje	(417)232-4642 (417)232-4476	WS 8 1030 SS 915 BC 915	EL/ED/HC/ MD/SN	448	349	199
LOHMAN	*ST JOHN* stjohnstringtown@gmail.com www.stjohnstringtown.org	1867	4420 STRINGTOWN RD	65053	MO	Brian C Whittle	(573)782-3191	WS 10 SS 9 BC 9	HS			
LONGTOWN	*ZION*		See Perryville MO									
LOUISIANA	*TRINITY* www.trinitylouisiana.org	1949	3405 GEORGIA ST	63353	MO	Jeffrey M Dock	(573)754-6120	WS 11 SS 945 BC 945	ED/MD	83	58	15
MACON	*ZION* zionmacon@cvalley.net www.zionmacon.org	1866	32405 Business Hwy 36E 32405 BUSINESS ROUTE 36 E	63552	MO	Elden D Kohn	(660)385-4433 (660)395-7021	WS 10 SS 845 BC 845	ED/HC/ MD/SN	403	320	121
MAPLEWOOD	*CONCORDIA* office@concordiamaplewood.org www.concordiamaplewood.org	1892	7291 SARAH AVE.	63143	MO	Erik L Johnson	(314)647-1215 (314)646-1255	WS 930 SS 11 BC 11	HS/ED/ MD/SN	61	53	35
MARSHALL	*OUR REDEEMER* office@orlutheran.org www.orlutheran.org	1914	361 W SUMMIT ST	65340	MO	Brett A Arrasmith	(660)886-2270 (660)886-9717	WS 9 SS 1015 BC 1015	EC/ED/HC/ MD/SN	534	385	110
MARSHFIELD	*ST PAULS* office@stpaulslutheranmarshfield.org www.stpaulslutheranmarshfield.org	1875	609 N LOCUST ST	65706	MO		(417)468-2577 (417)468-5005	WS 10 SS 9 BC 9	ED/HC/MD	486	344	53
MARYLAND HEIGHTS	*ZION* church@zionmh.org www.zionmh.org	1869	12075 DORSETT ROAD	63043	MO	Dr Mark D Femmel	(314)739-6121	WS 8 1030 SS 930 BC 930	EC/ED/HC/ MD	200	175	118
MARYVILLE	*HOPE* hopelutheranlcms@gmail.com www.maryvillehopelcc.org	1948	931 S MAIN ST	64468	MO		(660)582-3262 (660)582-3262	WS 10 SS 9 BC 9	ED/MD/SN	104	84	63
MEHLVILLE	*RESURRECTION*		See Sunset Hills MO									
MEMPHIS	*ST PAUL*	1963	North Hwy 15 14970 STATE ROUTE T BARING	63555 63531	MO		(660)883-5516	WS 1015 SS 9 BC 9	ED/HC/MD	11	9	6
META	*ST JOHN*	1871	7075 Hwy P 7075 HIGHWAY P WESTPHALIA	65085	MO	Ryan M Groh	(314)395-4591	WS 8 SS 910 BC 910		27	26	18
MEXICO	*ST JOHN* office@stjohnsmexico.com www.stjohnsmexico.com	1884	1000 Dorcas St PO BOX 320	65265	MO	Donaldo Sonntag	(573)581-5655 (573)581-1173	WS 9 1115 SS 1015 BC 1015	ED/HC/ MD/SN	299	263	86
MILAN	*PEACE*	1978	Route E C/O FAITH LUTHERAN CHURCH 1820 S BALTIMORE ST KIRKSVILLE	63556 63501	MO		(660)265-4104 (660)265-4908	WS 815 SS 915	ED/HC	33	28	23
MOBERLY	*ZION* secretary@zionlutheranmoberly.com www.zionlutheranchurchlcmsmoberly.com	1887	1075 E URBANDALE DR	65270	MO	Matthew T Resner	(660)263-3256	WS 10 SS 9 BC 9	ED/MD	153	108	51
MONETT	*ST JOHNS* stjohnmonett@gmail.com www.stjohnsmonett.com	1919	23237 HIGHWAY H	65708	MO	Andrew C Kennell	(417)235-3416	WS 10 SS 9 BC 9	ED/HC/ MD/SN	95	90	60
MONROE CITY	*OUR SAVIOR* immanuellutheranchurch@live.com www.oursaviormonroecity.wordpress.com	1985	317 S MAIN ST	63456	MO	Scott A Salo	(573)221-7051 (573)248-8210	WS 845	ED/HC/MD	81	59	20
MOUND CITY	*HOLY TRINITY* office@holytrinitymcmo.org www.holytrinitymcmo.org		1413 NEBRASKA ST	64470	MO	Daniel S Broaddus	(660)442-1029	WS 1030 SS 915 BC 915	HC/MD	236	200	110
NEOSHO	*FIRST* 1stlutheran.neosho@gmail.com	1945	431 CEMETERY RD	64850	MO	Steven R Gillmore	(417)451-2464	WS 1030 SS 915	ED/HC/ MD/SN	83	61	49
NEVADA	*TRINITY* trinity1630@gmail.com	1947	1630 N Ash St PO BOX 583	64772	MO	Johannes W Brann	(417)667-5676	WS 830	ED/SN	33	33	17
NEW HAVEN	*BETHLEHEM* www.bethlehemlutheran newhavenmo.wordpress.com	1852	3825 BOEUF LUTHERAN RD	63068	MO	James M Wilshusen	(573)237-2602 (573)237-2602	WS 8 SS 9 BC 9	ED/HC/SN	176	150	49

*Indicates a new church start. A new church start is an intentionally organized gathering which comes together on a regular basis for the purpose of worship and/or Bible study and is intended to grow into a member LCMS congregation. WS =Worship Service; SS = Sunday School; BC =Bible Class; EC = Early Childhood; EL = Elementary School; HS = High School; ED =Education Ministry; HC =Human Care Ministry; SN = Special Needs Ministry; MD = Media Ministry (PC)=Partner Church Pastor. See Page 53 for the Table of Abbreviations for key to additional abbreviations

CITY	CONGREGATION EMAIL WEBSITE	YEAR EST	LOCATION MAILING ADDRESS	ZIP CODE(S)	DIST.	PASTOR(S)	PHONE FAX	WS SS BC	SCHOOLS/ MINISTRIES	STATISTIC Bapt	Conf	Avg Attend
NEW HAVEN	*TRINITY* www.trinitynewhaven.com		9521 Hwy 100 9521 HIGHWAY 100	63068	MO	Andrew J Preus	(573)237-3026	WS 10 SS 9 BC 9		151	118	85
NEW WELLS	*IMMANUEL* ielcnw@gmail.com	1853	304 County Rd 516 304 COUNTY ROAD 516	63732	MO		(573)833-6933	WS 9 SS 815 BC 815	HS/ED/MD	166	148	61
NIANGUA	*IMMANUEL*		See Conway MO									
NIXA	*REDEEMER - NIXA* Satellite Site of Redeemer Springfield MO	2006	911 W Mt Vernon	65714				WS 8 1045 SS 930 BC 930				
NORBORNE	*TRINITY*	1869	204 N PINE ST	64668	MO	Tysen L Bibb	(660)593-3721	WS 9 SS 1015 BC 1015		279	214	97
OAK GROVE	*SHEPHERD OF VALLEY* shepherdofthevalley@comcast.net	1974	600 SE 12TH ST	64075	MO		(816)690-4020	WS 10 BC 9		34	29	25
OAKVILLE	*FAITH* info@faithoakville.org faithoakville.org	1945	6101 TELEGRAPH RD SAINT LOUIS	63129	MO	Matthew J Peeples Brandon J Boos Cyril D Loum Samuel O Maconachy	(314)846-8612 (314)846-7157	WS 9 1045 SS 9 1030	EC/HS/ED/ HC/SN	1536	1228	710
O'FALLON	*HOLY CROSS* secretary@hcross.com www.hcross.com	1960	8945 VETERANS MEMORIAL PKWY	63366	MO	Andrew J Gimbel Jason P Kohm	(636)272-4505 (636)980-9581	WS 8 1045 SS 930 BC 930	EC/HS/ED/ HC/MD	886	687	261
	MESSIAH		See Weldon Spring MO									
OLIVETTE	*IMMANUEL* rkarg@immanuelolivette.org www.immanuelolivette.org	1844	9733 OLIVE BLVD	63132	MO	Rory C Karg	(314)993-2394 (314)993-0311	WS 8 1030 SS 915 BC 930	EL/HS/ED/ HC/MD	767	610	249
	OUR REDEEMER		See Overland MO									
OSAGE BEACH	*HOPE* office@hopelutheranchapel.org www.hopelutheranchapel.org	1965	1027 Industrial Dr 5709 OSAGE BEACH PKWY	65065	MO	Guillaume J Williams Sr	(573)348-2108	WS 10 SS 1120 BC 1120	ED/HC/ MD/SN	63	56	33
OTTO	*ST PAUL'S*		See Imperial MO									
OVERLAND	*OUR REDEEMER* elcoroffice@ourredeemerstl.org www.ourredeemerstl.org	1912	9135 SHELLEY AVE	63114	MO	David R Boisclair Scott R Schilbe	(314)427-3444	WS 8 1045 BC 930	EL/HS/ED/ MD/SN	570	553	85
OWENSVILLE	*ZION* zionowensville@gmail.com facebook.com/zionowensville	1906	211 E Madison PO BOX 137	65066	MO	David J Roth Jr	(573)207-4148	WS 845 SS 10		54	40	27
OZARK	*MY CHURCH* info@mychurchozark.org www.mychurchozark.org	2019	727 N 9th Street 2610 S LILAC	65721	MO	James L Bartok	(734)624-3422	WS 10	EC	52	11	65
PACIFIC	*NEW BEGINNINGS* staff@nblc.net www.nblc.net		791 NEW BEGINNINGS DR	63069	MO	Joseph D Sullivan	(636)257-4455	WS 9 1030 SS 1030	ED/MD	567	442	367
PALMYRA	*ZION* zionpalmyra@gmail.com www.zionpalmyra.org	1847	120 S SPRING ST	63461	MO	Wesley A Gehrke	(573)769-2739 (573)769-4014	WS 8 1030 SS 915	EC/ED	616	449	135
PARK HILLS	*TRINITY* tlcparkhills@gmail.com www.trinitylutheranchurchparkhills.com	1898	309 TAYLOR AVE	63601	MO	Jeremy D May David E Schmitt	(573)431-3442	WS 1030 SS 9 BC 9	HS/ED/HC/ MD	141	125	50
PARKVILLE	*CHRIST*		See Platte Woods MO									
PECULIAR	*BETHLEHEM*		See Raymore MO									
PERRYVILLE	*IMMANUEL* Churchoffice@ilsperryville.org www.ilsperryville.org	1866	453 N WEST ST	63775	MO	Matthew T Marks Joseph E Schlie	(573)547-8317 (573)547-7254	WS 730 10 SS 850 BC 850	EL/HS/ED/ HC/MD	1447	1131	534
	ZION gracezionchurch@gmail.com	1897	6483 S HIGHWAY 61	63775	MO	Edward B Andrada	(573)788-2432	WS 10 SS 915 BC 915	HS/ED/MD	102	86	42
	ZION		See Crosstown MO									
PEVELY	*ZION* bryanroberts@email.com www.zionpevely.com	1918	310 CENTRAL ST	63070	MO	Bryan L Roberts	(636)475-4486	WS 915 SS 1030 BC 1030	ED/HC/MD	190	165	125
PILOT KNOB	*IMMANUEL* in_man_pam@yahoo.com	1861	701 N Ziegler St PO BOX 326	63663	MO	Lawrence L Eatherton	(573)546-2373	WS 1 BC 10	ED	22	15	11
	ST PAUL		See Ironton MO									
PLATTE CITY	*OUR SAVIOR* oursaviorpc@gmail.com www.oursaviorchurch.net	1991	14155 N Hwy 14155 N HIGHWAY	64079	MO	Timothy R Swanson Larry H Block	(816)335-4049	WS 9 1030 SS 930 BC 8 930	EL/HS/ED/ HC/MD/SN	296	238	87
PLATTE WOODS	*CHRIST* christlc@christlc.com www.christlc.net	1957	6700 NW 72ND ST	64151	MO	Brandon J Froiland Thomas J Cowell Abdi M Selbana	(816)741-0483	WS 8 1045 SS 930 BC 930	EC/EL/HS/ ED/HC/ MD/SN	853	566	214
	OROMO oromo.evangelical.lutheran.church@gmail.com		6700 NW 72ND ST	64151	MO		(816)672-9902			113	76	55
PLEASANT HILL	*AMAZING GRACE* amazinggraceph@embarqmail.com amazinggraceph.com	1998	313 Cedar 313 CEDAR ST	64080	MO	C R Malone Sr	(816)540-5150	WS 830	ED/HC	40	40	15
POCAHONTAS	*TRINITY*		See Shawneetown MO									
	ZION zionlutheran@cablerocket.com	1889	264 Pocahontas Main St PO BOX 60	63779	MO	Virgil M Kelm	(573)833-6055 (573)833-6055	WS 1015 SS 930 BC 930	HS/ED/SN	89	71	24

*Indicates a new church start. A new church start is an intentionally organized gathering which comes together on a regular basis for the purpose of worship and/or Bible study and is intended to grow into a member LCMS congregation. WS =Worship Service; SS = Sunday School; BC =Bible Class; EC = Early Childhood; EL = Elementary School; HS = High School; ED =Education Ministry; HC =Human Care Ministry; SN = Special Needs Ministry; MD = Media Ministry (PC)=Partner Church Pastor. See Page 53 for the Table of Abbreviations for key to additional abbreviations

CITY	CONGREGATION EMAIL WEBSITE	YEAR EST	LOCATION MAILING ADDRESS	ZIP CODE(S)	DIST.	PASTOR(S)	PHONE FAX	WS SS BC	SCHOOLS/ MINISTRIES	STATISTIC Bapt	Conf	Avg Attend
POPLAR BLUFF	*ZION* zionlutheranchurchpoplarbluff@bigrivertel.net www.zionlutheranpb.org	1897	450 N MAIN ST PO BOX 3955	63901 63902	MO	Justin C Sponaugle	(573)785-3936 (573)785-7273	WS 8 SS 930 BC 930	ED	102	97	38
POTOSI	*REDEEMER*	1966	312 E HIGH ST	63664	MO		(573)438-7161	WS 1030 BC 1130	ED/MD	21	19	17
PRAIRIE HOME	*IMMANUEL* pastorpete067@gmail.com	1844	13002 CAMPBELL BRIDGE DR	65068	MO	Dr Peter M Kurowski	(605)471-0293		HC/SN	25	18	31
PURDY	*ST JOHN* stjohnslcmspurdy@gmail.com sites.google.com/site/lcmsstjohnslutheran	1884	5732 Farm Rd 1057 5732 FARM ROAD 1057	65734	MO	James F Schnackenberg	(417)442-3836	WS 1030 SS 930 BC 930	ED/HC/MD/SN	183	161	80
RAYMORE	*BETHLEHEM* info@bethlehem-raymore.org www.bethlehem-raymore.org	1987	310 JOHNSTON PKWY	64083	MO	Dr Matthew D Priem	(816)322-3606 (816)322-9673	WS 8 1045 SS 930 BC 930	EC/ED/MD	627	517	188
	HOLY TRINITY		See Grandview MO									
REEDS SPRING	*SHEPHERD HILLS*		See Kimberling City MO									
REPUBLIC	*HOPE* secretary@hopelc.com www.hopelc.com	1985	218 E STATE ROUTE 174	65738	MO		(417)647-2183	WS 1030 SS 915 BC 915	EC/ED/HC/MD/SN	160	110	76
RICHLAND	*FAITH*		See Saint Robert MO									
RICHMOND	*FAITH* faithrichmond@gmail.com www.faithlutheranrichmond.org	1972	805 E LEXINGTON ST	64085	MO		(816)776-5550	WS 930 BC 11	ED/HC/MD	90	84	30
RICHMOND HEIGHTS	*CONCORDIA*		See Maplewood MO									
ROBY	*FAITH*		See Saint Robert MO									
ROCK PORT	*TRINITY*		See Auburn NE									
ROCKVILLE	*ZION* zionlutheranprairiecitymo@gmail.com zionrockville.org	1868	10135 SE COUNTY ROAD 9526	64780	MO	Jeffrey B Kyler	(660)598-6215	WS 10 SS 9 BC 9	EL/ED/HC	262	235	102
ROLLA	*IMMANUEL* ilc@ilcrolla.org www.ilcrolla.org/	1925	801 W 11TH ST	65401	MO	Eric D Swyres	(573)364-4525	WS 9 SS 1030 BC 1030	ED/HC/MD/SN	486	401	140
	REDEEMER info@RedeemerRolla.org www.redeemerrolla.org	1975	1701 HWY 72 E	65401	MO	Dr Nathan A Kuhlman	(573)364-7071	WS 830 11 SS 845 BC 845	ED/HC	140	114	51
ROSEBUD	*IMMANUEL* immanuel@fidnet.com	1905	229 Hwy 50 300 1ST ST N	63091	MO		(573)764-2564	WS 10 SS 9 BC 9	EL/ED/HC/MD	339	249	85
SAINT ANN	*HOPE* school@hopelutheranstann.org hopelutheranstann.org	1945	10701 SAINT COSMAS LN	63074	MO	William J Orr	(314)429-3808 (314)429-3809	WS 9 SS 1030 BC 1030	ED/HC/MD/SN	160	137	55
	OUR REDEEMER		See Overland MO									
SAINT CHARLES	*IMMANUEL* www.immanuelstcharles.org	1847	115 S 6TH ST	63301	MO	Scott A Schmieding Ryan S Taylor Matthew H Bohlmann	(636)946-2656 (636)946-0166	WS 8 930 1045 SS 930 BC 930	EL/HS/ED/HC/MD/SN	3415	2588	1000
	MESSIAH		See Weldon Spring MO									
	OUR SAVIOR cari.oslc@yahoo.com www.oslcecc.org	1959	2800 W Elm St 2800 ELM ST	63301	MO	Dr Mike A Iannelli Jr	(636)947-8010 (636)947-1925	WS 815 11 SS 945 BC 945	EC/EL/HS/ED/HC/MD/SN	567	453	200
	PEACE		See Weldon Spring MO									
	TRINITY jthomas@trinityof.org www.trinityorchardfarm.com	1875	4795 N Hwy 94 4795 N HIGHWAY 94	63301	MO	James M Thomas	(636)250-3350 (636)250-3351	WS 8 1030 SS 915 BC 915	EL/ED/HC/MD/SN	706	502	125
	ZION vadams@zionharvester.org www.zionharvester.org	1884	3866 S Old Hwy 94 3866 S OLD HIGHWAY 94	63304	MO	Mark A Rouland Dr Michael T Fieberkorn	(636)441-7425 (636)447-3008	WS 8 1030 SS 930 BC 930	EL/HS/ED/HC/MD/SN	3471	2596	827
SAINT CLAIR	*HOLY TRINITY* htlcclerk@yahoo.com htlcstc.org	1963	1500 S OUTER RD	63077	MO		(636)629-3355	WS 9 BC 1045	EC/ED/HC/MD/SN	118	65	27
SAINT JAMES	*ST JOHN* www.stjlutheranchurch.com/	1880	229 W James Blvd PO BOX 57	65559	MO		(573)265-3226	WS 1030 SS 930 BC 915	ED/HC/MD	82	80	42
SAINT JOSEPH	*ST PAUL* church@splcc.org www.splcc.org	1881	4715 FREDERICK AVE	64506	MO	David W Moore Barrett R Buchmueller	(816)279-1110 (816)279-1114	WS 815 1045 SS 930 BC 930	EL/ED/HC	872	708	239
	ST PETER stpeterlutheran1891@gmail.com www.stpeter-stjomo.com	1891	3524 SAINT JOSEPH AVE	64505	MO	Richard S Cody	(816)279-8190 (816)279-8190	WS 9 SS 1030	ED/HC/MD/SN	173	140	84
SAINT LOUIS	*ABIDING SAVIOR* info@abidingsaviorlutheran.org www.knowthesavior.org	1983	4355 BUTLER HILL RD	63128	MO	Adam D Parvey David S Andrus	(314)894-9200	WS 8 1030 SS 915 BC 915	EL/HS/ED/HC/MD	604	559	337
	ASCENSION office@ascensionstl.com www.ascensionstl.com	1936	5347 DONOVAN AVE	63109	MO	Dr Matthew J Clark Matthew C Kobs	(314)832-5600 (314)832-5601	WS 830 11 SS 945 BC 945	EL/HS/ED/HC/MD/SN	659	551	222
	BETHLEHEM Bethlehem.lutheran@bethlehemstlouis.org bethlehemstlouis.org	1849	2153 SALISBURY ST	63107	MO	Dr Gerard I Bolling Christopher D Knepper	(314)231-4702	WS 950	EC/EL/HS/ED/HC/MD/SN	214	117	189

*Indicates a new church start. A new church start is an intentionally organized gathering which comes together on a regular basis for the purpose of worship and/or Bible study and is intended to grow into a member LCMS congregation. WS =Worship Service; SS = Sunday School; BC =Bible Class; EC = Early Childhood; EL = Elementary School; HS = High School; ED =Education Ministry; HC =Human Care Ministry; SN = Special Needs Ministry; MD = Media Ministry (PC)=Partner Church Pastor. See Page 53 for the Table of Abbreviations for key to additional abbreviations

CITY	CONGREGATION EMAIL WEBSITE	YEAR EST	LOCATION MAILING ADDRESS	ZIP CODE(S)	DIST.	PASTOR(S)	PHONE FAX	WS SS BC	SCHOOLS/ MINISTRIES	STATISTIC Bapt	Conf	Avg Attend
SAINT LOUIS	*BETHLEHEM LUTHERAN CHILDCARE* Satellite Site of Bethlehem Saint Louis MO	2025	11645 Benham Road	63136								
	CHRIST MEMORIAL churchoffice@cmstl.org cmstl.org	1948	5252 S Lindbergh 5252 S LINDBERGH BLVD	63126	MO	Jeffrey P Cloeter Paul N Dickerson Benjamin D Haupt	(314)631-0304 (314)631-8583	WS 745 9 1045 SS 10 BC 9 10	EC/EL/HS/ ED/HC/ MD/SN	1794	1496	610
	CONCORDIA		See Maplewood MO									
	CONG CHAI V SHALOM www.chaivshalom.com	1998	6327 CLAYTON AVE	63139	MO	Kevin D Parviz	(314)645-4456		ED/HC/MD	37	28	30
	EBENEZER ebenluth@att.net www.facebook.com/ebenezer lutheranchurchlcms	1869	1011 THEOBALD ST	63147	MO		(314)388-2777 (314)388-4903	WS 10 SS 9 BC 9	EL/HS/ED/ HC/SN	40	37	25
	EMMAUS pastor@jamstl.org	1894	2241 S JEFFERSON AVE	63104	MO	George A Denholm	(314)782-7678	WS 5	HS/ED/HC/ MD	15	10	20
	EPIPHANY church@elcstl.org www.elcstl.org	1941	4045 HOLLY HILLS BLVD	63116	MO	Timothy W Staffeld	(314)752-7065 (314)752-7066	WS 930 SS 1045 BC 1045	HS/ED/HC/ MD	181	143	79
	GLENDALE		See Glendale MO									
	GRACE CHAPEL		See Bellefontaine Nghbrs MO									
	GREAT COMMISSION greatcommissionlc1@gmail.com		4364 DR MARTIN LUTHER KING DR	63113	MO	Dwight E Dickinson Sr	(314)773-9182	WS 11 SS 945	EL/HS/ED/ HC/MD			
	HOLY CROSS hclcstl@gmail.com www.holycrossstl.org	1858	2650 Miami St 3636 TEXAS AVE	63118	MO	Robert K Bernhardt Paul R Gaschler	(314)772-8633 (314)772-0071	WS 1030 SS 915 BC 915	HS/ED/HC/ MD	159	145	82
	HOLY CROSS DF danthemech56@gmail.com HolyCrossDeaf.org	1930	Concordia Lutheran Church 505 S Kirkwood Rd	63122	MO			WS 10 SS 10 BC 10	MD/SN	31	26	22
	HOPE hopestl@hopelutheranstl.org www.hopelutheranstl.org	1916	5218 NEOSHO ST	63109	MO	Randy K Asburry	(314)352-0014 (314)352-1944	WS 9 SS 1030 BC 1030	EL/HS/ED/ HC/MD	396	323	80
	IMMANUEL		See Olivette MO									
	JACOBS WELL jacobswellstl@yahoo.com		1916 BOOKBINDER DR	63146	S	David B Corson	(314)603-4821					
	MESSIAH office@messiahstl.org messiahstl.org	1908	2846 S GRAND BLVD	63118	MO	Stephen W Miller Michael Okine	(314)772-4474	WS 10 SS 9 BC 9	ED/HC/MD	195	144	92
	MOUNT CALVARY		See Brentwood MO									
	MOUNT OLIVE lcmspadre@gmail.com	1926	4246 Shaw Blvd 4052 DE TONTY ST	63110	MO		(314)307-9021	WS 1045 SS 9 BC 930	ED/HC/ MD/SN	15	15	8
	PEACE		See Saint Louis County MO									
	PRINCE OF PEACE		See Crestwood MO									
	RELIANT Satellite Site of Christ Memorial Saint Louis MO	2010	3500 Caroline St	63104				WS 1115				
	SAINT LUKES st.lukeslutheran@yahoo.com	1896	3415 TAFT AVE	63111	MO	David L Dittmar	(314)352-1224 (314)352-1224	WS 930 SS 1045 BC 1045	HS/ED/HC	42	28	12
	SALEM churchoffice@slcas.org www.slcas.org	1909	8343 GRAVOIS RD AFFTON	63123	MO	Wayne K Huebner Christopher T Hill	(314)352-4454 (314)353-9328	WS 8 1030 SS 920 BC 920	EL/HS/ED/ HC/MD/SN	937	749	244
	ST JOHNS stjohnslcstl@gmail.com stjohnslutheranstlouis.org	1865	3738 MORGANFORD RD	63116	MO	Benjamin M Wescoatt Ratna B Mangar Nabin Samal	(314)773-0126	WS 9 BC 1030	HS/ED/HC/ MD	89	73	45
	ST LUCAS office@stlucaslcms.org stlucaslcms.org	1905	7100 MORGANFORD RD	63116	S	Dr Mark C Larson	(314)351-2628 (314)351-1174	WS 8 1030 SS 915 BC 915	EC/EL/HS/ ED/HC/ MD/SN	340	287	103
	ST MATTHEW stmatthewsecretary1@gmail.com stmatthewstl.org	1901	5402 WREN AVE	63120	MO	Johnathan C Lewis	(314)261-7765 (314)261-7707	WS 11 SS 10 BC 10	EL/HS/ED/ HC/MD	73	59	30
	ST PAUL stpaulcollegehill@gmail.com stpaulscollegehill.org	1872	2137 E John Ave 2141 E JOHN AVE	63107	MO		(314)534-0372	WS 9 BC 1015	EL/HS/HC	47	43	17
	ST PETER		See Spanish Lake MO									
	ST TRINITY office@sainttrinity.org www.sainttrinity.org	1859	7404 Vermont Ave 517 KOELN AVE	63111	MO	David A Lewis Lewi J Jermiya Idonis M King	(314)353-3276 (314)353-3276	WS 10 SS 9 BC 9	HS/ED/HC	157	118	48
	THE WAY		See Columbia IL									
	TIMOTHY office@timothystl.org www.timothystl.org	1927	6704 FYLER AVE	63139	MO	Andrew D Dinger Matthew N Gerzevske Minh Chau N Vo	(314)781-8673	WS 8 1045 SS 930 BC 930	EL/HS/ED/ HC/MD/SN	310	234	165
	TRANSFIGURATION tlccongregation@att.net	1904	1807 BIDDLE ST	63106	MO		(314)621-7845 (314)621-9390	WS 11 SS 945 BC 10	EL/HS/HC	39	36	30
	TRINITY office@trinitystlouis.com trinitystlouis.com	1839	1805 S 8th St 812 SOULARD ST	63104	MO	Dr Joshua M Hatcher Steven H Albers	(314)231-4092	WS 815 1015 SS 915 BC 915	EL/HS/ED/ HC/MD/SN	901	694	245
	WEBSTER GARDENS		See Webster Groves MO									

*Indicates a new church start. A new church start is an intentionally organized gathering which comes together on a regular basis for the purpose of worship and/or Bible study and is intended to grow into a member LCMS congregation. WS =Worship Service; SS = Sunday School; BC =Bible Class; EC = Early Childhood; EL = Elementary School; HS = High School; ED =Education Ministry; HC =Human Care Ministry; SN = Special Needs Ministry; MD = Media Ministry (PC)=Partner Church Pastor. See Page 53 for the Table of Abbreviations for key to additional abbreviations

CITY	CONGREGATION EMAIL WEBSITE	YEAR EST	LOCATION MAILING ADDRESS	ZIP CODE(S)	DIST.	PASTOR(S)	PHONE FAX	WS SS BC	SCHOOLS/ MINISTRIES	STATISTIC Bapt	Conf	Avg Attend
SAINT LOUIS	*ZION*		See Maryland Heights MO									
SAINT LOUIS COUNTY	*CHAPEL CROSS* chapelofthecross@sbcglobal.net www.chapelofthecross.org	1965	11645 BENHAM RD SAINT LOUIS	63136	EN	Theodore L Laesch Jr Ellory W Glenn	(314)741-3737 (314)741-3746	WS 830 11 SS 945 BC 945	EL/HS/ED/ HC/MD/SN	1066	861	225
	PEACE office@peacelutheranstl.org www.PeaceLutheranSTL.org	1945	737 BARRACKSVIEW RD SAINT LOUIS	63125	MO	Dr Jon C Furgeson Robert M Brown	(314)892-5610 (314)892-7345	WS 8 920 1030 SS 915 BC 915	EC/EL/HS/ ED/HC/ MD/SN	1529	1289	630
	PRINCE OF PEACE		See Crestwood MO									
SAINT PAUL	*HOLY CROSS*		See O'fallon MO									
SAINT PETERS	*CHAPEL OF THE CROSS* office@chapelofthecrosslutheran.org chapelofthecrosslutheran.org	1982	907 JUNGERMANN RD	63376	MO	Dr Mark R Hoehner James R Uglum James M Prince	(636)928-5885	WS 8 1015 SS 915 BC 915	EC/ED/HC/ MD/SN	1115	933	425
	CHILD OF GOD churchoffice@coglcs.com coglcs.com	2003	650 SALT LICK RD	63376	MO	Jeremy D Gorline	(636)970-7080 (636)970-7083	WS 930 SS 1030 BC 1030	EL/HS/ED/ HC/MD/SN	195	179	100
SAINT ROBERT	*FAITH* office@felclcms.org www.felclcms.org	1962	981 HIGHWAY Z	65584	MO	John F Perling	(573)336-4464	WS 1030 SS 9	ED/HC/ MD/SN	168	168	70
SAINTE GENEVIEVE	*HOLY CROSS* holycrossstegen@gmail.com www.holycrossstegen.org	1867	200 MARKET ST STE GEN-EVIEVE	63670	MO		(573)883-5361	WS 9 BC 10	ED/HC/ MD/SN	96	94	47
SALEM	*SALEM* salemlchpas@gmail.com	1949	403 E SCENIC RIVERS BLVD	65560	MO	David L Kettner Dennis D Roedemeier	(573)729-5512	WS 1045 SS 930 BC 930	MD	154	98	62
SALISBURY	*IMMANUEL*	1890	124 W 3RD ST	65281	MO	Glen E Gutz	(660)388-5192 (660)388-5192	WS 1015 SS 9 BC 9	EC/ED/HC/ MD	242	188	81
	SALEM	1861	36157 SALEM AVE	65281	MO	Noah E Burgdorf	(660)481-2249	WS 10 SS 9 BC 9	ED/HC	161	150	60
SAPPINGTON	*RESURRECTION*		See Sunset Hills MO									
SARCOXIE	*TRINITY*	1883	300 S 9th St PO BOX 612	64862	MO	Gary W Griffin		WS 1030 SS 930	ED/HC/MD	35	30	35
SCHUBERT	*ST JOHN*		See Jefferson City MO									
SCOTT CITY	*EISLEBEN* eislebenlutheranchurch@gmail.com www.lutheranchurchscottcity.org	1851	432 LUTHERAN LN	63780	MO		(573)264-2762 (573)264-2762	WS 10 SS 9 BC 9	HS/ED/HC/ MD/SN	186	147	81
SEDALIA	*AMIGOS DE CRISTO* amigosdecristo1@gmail.com	1998	3003 W 11th 3003 W 11TH ST	65301	MO		(660)826-2788 (660)826-1925		ED/HC/MD	59	48	35
	OUR SAVIOR oslsecretary123@gmail.com sedaliaoursavior.org	1959	US 50 Highway 3700 W BROADWAY BLVD	65301	MO	Andrew T Tessone	(660)827-0226 (660)829-1834	WS 9 SS 1015 BC 1015	ED/HC/ MD/SN	383	260	95
	ST PAUL sedaliasaintpauls@gmail.com sedaliasaintpauls.org	1882	701 S MASSACHUSETTS AVE	65301	MO	Jeremy M Freeman	(660)826-1164 (660)826-1925	WS 9 SS 1015 BC 1015	EL/ED/ MD/SN	495	413	131
SEYMOUR	*ZION*		See Diggins MO									
SHAWNEETOWN	*TRINITY* pastorvkelm@sbcglobal.net	1909	175 SHAWNEETOWN RD JACKSON	63755	MO	Virgil M Kelm	(573)833-6055	WS 1015 SS 930	HS/ED/SN	80	72	30
SHELL KNOB	*PEACE*	1982	Hwy 39 N PO BOX 407	65747	MO	Steven J Okpisz	(417)858-3900	WS 10 SS 1015 BC 11		25	25	14
SHREWSBURY	*CONCORDIA*		See Maplewood MO									
SIKESTON	*CONCORDIA* concordialutheranchurch@gmail.com Concordiasikeston.org	1911	836 PARK AVE	63801	MO	Matthew C Berry	(573)471-5842 (573)471-5842	WS 1030 SS 915 BC 915	HS/ED/MD	144	104	57
SLATER	*PEACE*	1954	408 N Porter 37507 E HIGHWAY P	65349	MO	Walter P Snyder	(660)529-2248	WS 9 SS 10	ED/HC			
	ST PAUL	1880	37507 E Hwy P 37507 E HIGHWAY P	65349	MO	Walter P Snyder		WS 1030 SS 930	ED/HC			
SMITHVILLE	*OUR SAVIOR*		See Platte City MO									
	OUR SAVIOR LUTHERAN CHURCH - SMITHVILLE Satellite Site of Our Savior Platte City MO	2014	1103 SOUTH COMMERCIAL	64089				WS 10 BC 9				
SPANISH LAKE	*ST PETER*	1863	1120 TRAMPE AVE SAINT LOUIS	63138	MO	Johnny L Greer	(314)741-2485	WS 10	EL/HS	10	10	6
SPARTA	*MY CHURCH*		See Ozark MO									
SPRINGFIELD	*FAITH* faithlutheransec@gmail.com www.flc-s.org	1974	1517 E VALLEY WATER MILL RD	65803	MO	Timothy J Steckling	(417)833-3749	WS 830 11 SS 945 BC 945	ED/HC/ MD/SN	173	159	104
	REDEEMER rlc@rlcmail.org growsharecare.org	1961	2852 S DAYTON AVE	65807	MO	Jarod P Koenig Stephen C Moser	(417)881-5470 (417)889-6218	WS 8 1045 SS 930 BC 930	EC/EL/ED/ HC/MD	1582	1271	514
	TRINITY tlcoffice@trinitylutheranspfd.org www.trinity-springfield.org	1910	1415 S HOLLAND AVE	65807	MO	Dr Nicholas L Hagerman	(417)866-5878 (417)866-5629	WS 815 11 SS 945 BC 945	ED/HC/MD	648	536	397
STOCKTON	*ST ANDREW* standrewstocktonmo@yahoo.com www.standrewlutheranstocktonmo.weebly.com	1987	15080 S Hwy 39 PO BOX 516	65785	MO		(417)276-3511	WS 930 BC 1030	ED/HC/ MD/SN	184	154	74
STOVER	*ST PAUL*	1857	407 W 3RD ST	65078	MO	Kevin M Koester	(573)377-2690 (573)377-2690	WS 10 SS 845 BC 845	EL/ED/HC	184	177	73

*Indicates a new church start. A new church start is an intentionally organized gathering which comes together on a regular basis for the purpose of worship and/or Bible study and is intended to grow into a member LCMS congregation. WS =Worship Service; SS = Sunday School; BC =Bible Class; EC = Early Childhood; EL = Elementary School; HS = High School; ED =Education Ministry; HC =Human Care Ministry; SN = Special Needs Ministry; MD = Media Ministry (PC)=Partner Church Pastor. See Page 53 for the Table of Abbreviations for key to additional abbreviations

CITY	CONGREGATION EMAIL WEBSITE	YEAR EST	LOCATION MAILING ADDRESS	ZIP CODE(S)	DIST.	PASTOR(S)	PHONE FAX	WS SS BC	SCHOOLS/ MINISTRIES	STATISTIC Bapt	Conf	Avg Attend
SULLIVAN	*ST MATTHEW* stmatt@fidnet.com www.stmatthewsullivan.com	1895	528 N CHURCH ST	63080	MO	Lewis S Ensor	(573)468-4245	WS 1030 SS 915 BC 915	ED/MD	134	126	35
SUNSET HILLS	*RESURRECTION* church@lcrstl.org www.lcrstl.org	1956	9907 SAPPINGTON RD SAINT LOUIS	63128	MO	David A Gruenwald Nicholas A Schram	(314)843-6633	WS 830 11 SS 945 BC 945	EC/EL/HS/ ED/HC/ MD/SN	809	636	349
SWEET SPRINGS	*CHRIST*	1899	Hwy EE 14178 HIGHWAY EE	65351	MO		(660)335-6807	WS 1015	HC/SN	16	14	14
	IMMANUEL ssimmanuellutheran@gmail.com www.ImmanuelSweetSprings.com	1878	110 MAIN ST	65351	MO		(660)335-4141 (660)335-4140	WS 9 SS 1015	ED/HC/MD	241	198	100
	ROYAL OAKS Satellite Site of Immanuel Sweet Springs MO	2024	507 E. Marshall	65351								
TAOS	*ST JOHN*		See Jefferson City MO									
TRENTON	*IMMANUEL*	1949	1711 HILLCREST DR	64683	MO		(660)359-3076	WS 2 SS 3 BC 3	MD	50	45	18
TROY	*TRINITY* trinitytroymo@gmail.com www.tlctroylcms.org	1963	1307 W Boone St 1307 BOONE ST	63379	MO	Garry A McCracken	(636)528-4999 (636)528-2970	WS 830 11 SS 945 BC 945		216	216	88
UNION	*ST PAUL* secretarystpaulhp@outlook.com www.inunionwithchrist.org	1921	208 W SPRINGFIELD AVE	63084	MO	Mathew A Hayter	(636)583-2209 (636)583-1155	WS 730 10 SS 845 BC 845	EC/ED/HC	579	423	128
UNIONTOWN	*GRACE* gracezionchurch@gmail.com	1840	53 GRACE LN	63783	MO	Edward B Andrada	(573)788-2342	WS 830 BC 8	HS/ED/HC/ MD	259	210	101
	ZION		See Perryville MO									
UNIVERSITY CITY	*ALL NATIONS* info@allnationschurch.net	1960	7860 OLIVE BLVD	63130	MO		(314)226-1999					
	BETHLEHEM LUTHERAN CHILDCARE Satellite Site of Bethlehem Saint Louis MO	2025	7860 Olive Blvd	63130								
	GRACE gracelutheran6@att.net	1872	7860 OLIVE BLVD	63130	MO		(314)727-3030	WS 9	EL/HS	12	12	11
	SAINT JAMES welawrence2002@yahoo.com	1932	1401 N HANLEY RD UNIVERSITY CY	63130	MO	Wayne E Lawrence	(314)727-3253 (314)727-3263	WS 10 SS 9 BC 9	EL/HS			
VALLEY PARK	*ZION* info@zionlutheranvp.org www.zionlutheranvp.org	1912	531 MERAMEC STATION RD	63088	MO	John S Weiler	(636)225-7780	WS 925 BC 1045	MD/SN	125	110	39
VANDALIA	*ST JOHN*	1874	414 S MAIN ST	63382	MO		(573)594-6640	WS 8	ED/HC	25	22	15
VERSAILLES	*GRACE*	1951	403 S BURKE ST	65084	MO	Erik J Rottmann	(573)378-5512	WS 1030 SS 930	ED	160	145	43
WARRENSBURG	*BETHLEHEM* csmith@blchurch.com www.blchurch.com	1939	607 N MAGUIRE ST	64093	MO	Joel R Kurz	(660)747-6742	WS 1030 SS 915 BC 915	ED/MD/SN	413	351	94
	LUTHERAN CAMPUS CENTER Satellite Site of Bethlehem Warrensburg MO	2007	215 S Holden St	64093								
WARRENTON	*ST JOHN* sjwarrlutheran@gmail.com www.stjohnswarrenton.com	1921	950 S State Hwy 47 950 S STATE HIGHWAY 47	63383	MO	Jeremy R Klaustermeier	(636)456-2888 (636)456-0882	WS 930 BC 830	EC/ED/HC/ MD	516	394	112
WARSAW	*FAITH* faithwarsawlcms@gmail.com www.faithwarsaw.com	1976	1201 Dogwood 1201 DOGWOOD ST	65355	MO		(660)438-6948	WS 10 BC 9	ED/HC/MD	125	79	57
WASHINGTON	*A BRIDGE TO FAITH* Church@Bridgetofaithchurch.church bridgetofaith.church	1986	1008 BIEKER RD	63090	MO	Andrew T Yount	(314)974-9833	WS 1030 SS 915 BC 915	ED/HC/ MD/SN	35	15	50
	IMMANUEL churchsecretary@imlutheran.org www.imlutheran.org	1862	214 W 5TH ST	63090	MO	Craig B Wehmeyer Jacob A Sipes	(636)239-4705 (636)239-0589	WS 8 1045 SS 930 BC 930	EL/ED/HC/ MD/SN	1965	1275	490
WAVERLY	*IMMANUEL*	1897	116 W Kelling Ave PO BOX 62	64096	MO	Mark R Junkin	(660)394-2322			89	52	21
WAYNESVILLE	*FAITH*		See Saint Robert MO									
WEBSTER GROVES	*WEBSTER GARDENS* office@webstergardens.org www.webstergardens.org	1949	8749 WATSON RD WEBSTER GRVS	63119	MO	David M McGinley Brian J King William M Murphy	(314)961-5275 (314)961-4764	WS 815 1030 SS 915 BC 930	EL/HS/ED/ HC/MD/SN	2261	1652	701
WELDON SPRING	*MESSIAH* churchoffice@messiahnetwork.org www.messiahstcharles.org	1987	5911 S Hwy 94 5911 S HIGHWAY 94	63304	MO	Dr James L Mueller Charles S Schlie	(636)926-9773 (636)926-9924	WS 9 1030 SS 9	EL/HS/ED/ HC/MD/SN	2381	1832	520
	PEACE michelle@peacewinghaven.org www.peacewinghaven.org		Breeze Park 600 Breeze Park Dr 907 JUNGERMANN RD SAINT PETERS	63304 63376	MO		(636)561-8282 (636)561-8282	WS 1015 SS 9 BC 9	HS/ED/HC/ MD/SN	120	83	31
WELLSVILLE	*GRACE* gracelcms@sbcglobal.net www.graceinwellsville.com	1947	528 W HUDSON ST	63384	MO	Luke B Wolters	(573)684-2106 (573)684-2106	WS 10 SS 9 BC 9	ED/HC	390	313	137
	TRINITY info@trinitylutheranonline.com www.trinitylutheranonline.com	1897	105 Trinity Church Rd 61 FREIE RD MIDDLETOWN	63384 63359	MO		(573)684-6232	WS 945 1030 SS 930 BC 930	ED/HC/ MD/SN	45	35	25
WENTZVILLE	*IMMANUEL* jauringer@ilcsw.net www.ilcsw.net	1874	632 E Hwy N 632 E HIGHWAY N	63385	MO	Jason P Auringer Thomas R Roma	(636)327-4416 (636)639-9944	WS 8 930 11 SS 930 BC 930	EL/HS/ED/ HC/MD	1990	1492	777

*Indicates a new church start. A new church start is an intentionally organized gathering which comes together on a regular basis for the purpose of worship and/or Bible study and is intended to grow into a member LCMS congregation. WS =Worship Service; SS = Sunday School; BC =Bible Class; EC = Early Childhood; EL = Elementary School; HS = High School; ED =Education Ministry; HC =Human Care Ministry; SN = Special Needs Ministry; MD = Media Ministry (PC)=Partner Church Pastor. See Page 53 for the Table of Abbreviations for key to additional abbreviations

CITY	CONGREGATION EMAIL WEBSITE	YEAR EST	LOCATION MAILING ADDRESS	ZIP CODE(S)	DIST.	PASTOR(S)	PHONE FAX	WS SS BC	SCHOOLS/ MINISTRIES	STATISTIC Bapt	Conf	Avg Attend
WENTZVILLE	*PEACE*		See Weldon Spring MO									
WEST PLAINS	*IMMANUEL* immanuellutheranwp@gmail.com	1978	1051 PREACHER ROE BLVD	65775	MO	Wade R Mattsfield	(417)256-3407	WS 9 SS 1030 BC 1030	ED/HC/ MD/SN	107	78	66
WESTON	*TRINITY*		See Leavenworth KS									
WILDWOOD	*ST PAULS* Pastor@stpaulswildwood.org stpaulswildwood.org	1883	955 HWY 109	63038	MO	Christopher L Biernacki	(636)273-6239	WS 9 SS 1030 BC 1030	ED/HC/ MD/SN	185	160	70

MONTANA

CITY	CONGREGATION EMAIL WEBSITE	YEAR EST	LOCATION MAILING ADDRESS	ZIP CODE(S)	DIST.	PASTOR(S)	PHONE FAX	WS SS BC	SCHOOLS/ MINISTRIES	Bapt	Conf	Avg Attend
ACTON	*MOUNT OLIVE*		See Billings MT									
ANACONDA	*REDEEMER* redeemeranaconda@gmail.com www.redeemer-anaconda.church	1896	1321 W 5TH ST	59711	MT		(406)797-7211	WS 1030 BC 1130	HC/MD/SN	12	11	10
BELFRY	*ST JOHN* shupepr@outlook.com	1916	103 Vaill PO BOX 201	59008	MT	Paul R Shupe	(406)662-3776	WS 9 SS 1030	ED/HC			
BELGRADE	*HOLY TRINITY* holytrinityandgrace@gmail.com www.holytrinitybelgrade.org	2002	102 N Weaver 102 N WEAVER ST	59714	MT		(406)388-0432 (406)388-0432	WS 830 SS 930 BC 930	ED/HC/MD			
BIG TIMBER	*EMMAUS MT*		See Livingston MT									
BIGFORK	*CHAPEL OF PINES* Satellite Site of Trinity Kalispell MT	1986	450 Pierce Ln	59911								
BILLINGS	*CHRIST THE KING* pastorwendt@ctkbillings.org www.ctkbillings.org	1966	759 NEWMAN LN	59101	MT	Ryan D Wendt John M Donnan	(406)252-9250	WS 10 SS 845 BC 845	ED/HC/ MD/SN	143	118	87
	HOPE	1972	1911 US Hwy 87 E 1911 US HIGHWAY 87 E	59101	MT	Robert A Lane	(406)245-4605 (406)245-4605	WS 845 SS 1015 BC 1015	HC			
	MOUNT OLIVE businessmanager@mountolive.com www.mountolive.com	1959	2336 SAINT JOHNS AVE	59102	MT	Willis J McCall	(406)656-6687 (406)656-1211	SS 1030 BC 1030	EC/EL/ED/ HC/MD/SN	382	314	122
	OUR REDEEMER		See Worden MT									
	OUR SAVIOR	1982	1603 Saint Andrews Dr 1603 ST ANDREWS DR	59105	MT	Kenneth H Zoeller	(406)252-5141	WS 930 SS 1045 BC 1045	ED/HC/MD	85	71	44
	TRINITY church@trinitybillings.org www.trinitybillings.org	1919	537 GRAND AVE	59101	MT	Daniel P Keinath David M Mews	(406)245-3984 (406)245-3923	WS 8 1030 SS 930 BC 930	EL/ED/HC/ MD/SN	1421	1104	321
BOULDER	*FAITH* gideonpullmann@gmail.com www.faithlutheranboulder.com	1953	317 S Main St PO BOX 586	59632	MT	Gideon J Pullmann	(402)243-3185	WS 10 SS 11 BC 11	ED/HC/SN	39	36	24
BOZEMAN	*EMMAUS MT*		See Livingston MT									
	FIRST office@firstlutheranbozeman.com www.firstlutheranbozeman.com	1929	225 S BLACK AVE	59715	MT	Samuel J Grayl	(406)586-5374 (406)586-1626	WS 9 SS 1030 BC 1030	ED/HC/ MD/SN			
BRIDGER	*ST PAUL* shupepr@outlook.com	1912	404 S 3rd St PO BOX 310	59014	MT	Paul R Shupe	(406)662-3776	WS 1030	ED/HC			
BUTTE	*ST MARK* stmarkbutte@outlook.com stmarkzion.com	1888	223 S MONTANA ST	59701	MT		(406)782-5935	WS 1030 SS 9 BC 9		187	147	39
CHINOOK	*ZION LUTHERAN* www.stpaul-zion.com	1913	803 Illinois Ave PO BOX 743	59523	MT		(406)357-2516	WS 9 SS 10	ED/HC/SN	62	57	28
COLSTRIP	*MOUNT CALVARY* blakemarshallrollf@gmail.com www.mtcalvary-colstrip.org	1973	430 Olive Dr PO BOX 218	59323	MT		(406)748-2516	WS 830 BC 730				
COLUMBIA FALLS	*OUR REDEEMER* www.ourredeemerlc.org	1956	640 7th St W PO BOX 2005 COLUMBIA FLS	59912	MT	Matthew E Nelson	(406)892-4074	WS 830 11 SS 945 BC 945	EC/ED/HC/ MD/SN			
CONDON	*FAITH*	1966	6853 Hwy 83 PO BOX 1039	59826	MT	Erik J Iverson	(406)677-2281	WS 11				
CROW AGENCY	*CROW*	1997	Crow Indian Reservation PO BOX 335	59022	MT		(406)638-2331	WS 930 SS 3	ED/HC/MD	70	39	1
DEER LODGE	*ST JOHN* stjohndeerlodge@yahoo.com	1915	410 MISSOURI AVE	59722	MT		(406)846-1755	WS 4	ED/HC/SN			
DENTON	*OUR SAVIOR* stpaul@midrivers.com	1951	1102 Lehman PO BOX 924	59430	MT	Mark R Wiegert	(406)535-8563	WS 8		19	19	12
DILLON	*LIVING WATER* lwlc@yahoo.com		33 N WASHINGTON ST	59725	MT	Kenneth O Stensrud	(406)684-5153	WS 12 SS 1 BC 1		18	18	16
ENNIS	*SHEPHERD HILLS* sothmt@gmail.com	1982	507 Madison PO BOX 785	59729	MT	Kenneth O Stensrud	(406)682-4910	WS 9	ED/HC	71	51	30
EUREKA	*HOLY CROSS* treasurerholycrosseureka@yahoo.com	1955	Highway 93 North PO BOX 332	59917	MT	David J McCarthy	(406)297-2116	WS 1030 SS 9 BC 9				
FAIRFIELD	*ST JOHN*	1955	PO BOX 241	59436	MT		(406)467-2847	WS 9 SS 1015				
FAIRVIEW	*ST JOHN* www.trinitystjohn.org	1930	310 Ellery and 2nd St PO BOX 2	59221	MT	John C Baseley	(406)742-5332	WS 8 BC 9	ED/HC/ MD/SN			
FALLON	*GRACE*	1931	421 Curry Ave PO BOX 234	59326	MT	Gregory J Lucido		WS 8	HC	16	16	9

*Indicates a new church start. A new church start is an intentionally organized gathering which comes together on a regular basis for the purpose of worship and/or Bible study and is intended to grow into a member LCMS congregation. WS =Worship Service; SS = Sunday School; BC =Bible Class; EC = Early Childhood; EL = Elementary School; HS = High School; ED =Education Ministry; HC =Human Care Ministry; SN = Special Needs Ministry; MD = Media Ministry (PC)=Partner Church Pastor. See Page 53 for the Table of Abbreviations for key to additional abbreviations

CITY	CONGREGATION EMAIL WEBSITE	YEAR EST	LOCATION MAILING ADDRESS	ZIP CODE(S)	DIST.	PASTOR(S)	PHONE FAX	WS SS BC	SCHOOLS/ MINISTRIES	STATISTIC Bapt	Conf	Avg Attend
FORSYTH	*CONCORDIA* concordialutheranforsyth@gmail.com www.facebook.com/profile. php?id=61576215204822	1929	310 8th Ave N PO BOX 1258	59327	MT	Dr Matthew C Christensen	(406)346-7614	WS 1030 SS 915 BC 915 1145	ED/HC/ MD/SN	156	109	40
FORT BENTON	*FIRST* pastor@peacelutherangreatfalls.org	1948	PO BOX 896	59442	MT	Joshua C Reinke		WS 3 SS 4 BC 4	SN			
GLASGOW	*FAITH*	1958	909 8TH AVE N	59230	MT		(406)228-8550	WS 1030 SS 915 BC 915	ED/MD	20	19	11
GLENDIVE	*OUR SAVIOR* oslc@midrivers.com	1938	322 N RIVER AVE	59330	MT	Gregory J Lucido	(406)377-3890 (406)377-8825	WS 10 5 SS 9 BC 9 11	EC/ED/HC/ MD/SN	279	231	88
GREAT FALLS	*CHRIST DEAF* www.peacelutherangreatfalls.org	1961	3340 11th Ave South 3340 11TH AVE S	59405	MT	Joshua C Reinke	(406)761-7343 (406)452-3884		ED/MD/SN			
	PEACE peacesecretary@bresnan.net www.peacelutherangreatfalls.org	1956	3340 11TH AVE S	59405	MT	Joshua C Reinke	(406)761-7343 (406)452-3884	WS 930 SS 1130 BC 1130	MD/SN	134	112	47
	TRINITY trinity@trinity-mt.org www.trinity-mt.org	1892	1226 1ST AVE N	59401	MT	Jonathan G Schultz	(406)452-2121 (406)453-0398	WS 10 SS 830 BC 830	EC/ED/ MD/SN	326	262	143
HAMILTON	*GRACE* gracelutheranhamilton@gmail.com www.gracelutheranhamilton.com	1905	275 HATTIE LN	59840	MT	Justin A Herman	(406)363-1924 (406)363-1925	WS 3 SS 1045 BC 1045	EC/ED/HC/ MD/SN	298	238	83
HARDIN	*REDEEMER* jameskoss54@gmail.com	1942	323 N CRAWFORD AVE	59034	MT	James M Koss	(406)679-0733	WS 1030 SS 9 BC 9	ED/HC	80	68	28
HARLOWTON	*TRINITY* ewegner@mtintouch.net	1911	2nd St SE and A Ave PO BOX 665	59036	MT	Terry R Forke	(406)632-4214	WS 11 BC 10	ED	31	28	18
HAVRE	*ST PAUL* dane.breitung@ctsfw.edu www.stpaul-zion.com	1919	1100 11TH AVE	59501	MT		(406)265-7637	WS 11 SS 945 BC 945	ED/HC/ MD/SN	122	98	55
HELENA	*FIRST* churchoffice@firstlutheranhelena.org www.firstlutheranhelena.org	1887	2231 E Broadway 2231 E BROADWAY ST	59601	MT	Larry A Miller	(406)442-5367 (406)442-5285	WS 815 11 SS 945 BC 945	EC/ED/HC/ MD/SN	596	465	201
HYSHAM	*TRINITY* concordiatrinity@gmail.com	1942	302 Summit PO BOX 466	59038	MT		(406)346-7614	WS 5	ED/MD			
KALISPELL	*CRESTON* thechurchatcrestonlcms@gmail.com www.thechurchatcreston.org	2004	5447 HWY 35	59901	MT	Kyle C Winter	(406)752-1205	WS 930 SS 1045 BC 1045	ED/HC/MD	151	58	153
	TRINITY trinity@trinitykalispell.org www.trinitykalispell.org	1895	400 W CALIFORNIA ST	59901	MT	Brian D Lee	(406)257-5683 (406)257-5684	WS 8 1045 SS 930 BC 930	EL/ED/HC/ MD/SN	795	630	350
LAME DEER	*CIRCLE OF LIFE* circleoflife@rangeweb.net	1997	PO BOX 458	59043	MT		(406)477-6797	WS 11 SS 10 BC 10	HC			
LAUREL	*ST JOHN* stjohnlaurelmt@juno.com stjohnlaurel.org	1913	417 W 9th St PO BOX 185	59044	MT	Arlo W Pullmann	(406)628-4775 (406)628-1591	WS 9 SS 1015 BC 1015	MD	482	382	100
LEWISTOWN	*ST PAUL* stpaul@midrivers.com	1917	125 C ST	59457	MT	Mark R Wiegert	(406)535-8563	WS 1030 SS 930 BC 930				
LIBBY	*ST JOHN* info@sjlc-libbymt.org www.sjlc-libbymt.org	1912	1017 MONTANA AVE	59923	MT	Steven C Thomas	(406)293-4024	WS 1030 SS 915 BC 915	ED/MD	145	106	57
LIVINGSTON	*EMMAUS MT* pastormerz@gmail.com emmauslutheranmt.org		801 E PARK ST	59047	MT	Jacob R Corrigan		WS 10 BC 9	ED	24	18	15
LODGE GRASS	*CROW*		See Crow Agency MT									
MILES CITY	*TRINITY* trinity@midrivers.com www.trinitylutheranchurch.360unite. com	1906	221 S CENTER AVE	59301	MT	Erik D Saunders	(406)234-4983 (406)234-8033	WS 8 1030 SS 1030 BC 1030	EL/ED/HC/ MD	421	298	98
MISSOULA	*FIRST* churchoffice@firstlutheranmissoula.com www.firstlutheranmissoula.com	1900	2808 SOUTH AVE W	59804	MT	David Johnson Steven C Carlson	(406)549-3311	WS 830 11 SS 945 BC 945	EC/EL/ED/ HC/MD/SN	565	483	158
	MESSIAH LutheranMessiah24@outlook.com www.messiahmissoulalcms.org/	1966	3718 RATTLESNAKE DR	59802	MT	Russell E Fitch	(406)549-9222 (406)543-4845	WS 1030 SS 915 BC 915	ED/SN	70	65	30
MOLT	*MOUNT OLIVE*		See Billings MT									
PARK CITY	*ST PAUL'S* StPaulParkCity@gmail.com	1913	301 1st St SW P.O. BOX 188 301 1ST ST SW	59063	MT	Russell L Dewell	(406)633-2356	WS 10	EC/ED/MD			
PLAINS	*SHEP OF THE VALLEY*		See Thompson Falls MT									
PLENTYWOOD	*TRINITY* hep_cab@nemont.net video.ibm.com/channel/tinymt	1912	212 N Maurice St PO BOX 306	59254	MT		(406)765-1365 (406)385-2544	WS 1030 BC 9	ED/HC/MD	65	53	15
POLSON	*MT CALVARY* mail@mtcalvary-polson.org mtcalvary-polson.org	1981	1609 2ND ST W	59860	MT	Kyle T Whaley	(406)883-4041	WS 11	EC/ED/HC/ MD/SN	32	29	19
	ST JOSEPH ASSISTED LIVING Satellite Site of MT Calvary Polson MT	2010	11 17th Ave E B	59860				WS 2				
POWER	*ZION*	1913	302 Teton Ave PO BOX 265	59468	MT		(406)463-2541	WS 11 SS 950 BC 950	ED/HC/MD			

*Indicates a new church start. A new church start is an intentionally organized gathering which comes together on a regular basis for the purpose of worship and/or Bible study and is intended to grow into a member LCMS congregation. WS =Worship Service; SS = Sunday School; BC =Bible Class; EC = Early Childhood; EL = Elementary School; HS = High School; ED =Education Ministry; HC =Human Care Ministry; SN = Special Needs Ministry; MD = Media Ministry (PC)=Partner Church Pastor. See Page 53 for the Table of Abbreviations for key to additional abbreviations

CITY	CONGREGATION EMAIL WEBSITE	YEAR EST	LOCATION MAILING ADDRESS	ZIP CODE(S)	DIST.	PASTOR(S)	PHONE FAX	WS SS BC	SCHOOLS/ MINISTRIES	STATISTIC Bapt	Conf	Avg Attend
RONAN	*ST PAUL* stpaullutheranchurch@ronan.net www.facebook.com/RonanLutheran	1915	35681 TERRACE LAKE RD	59864	MT		(406)676-8280	WS 1015 SS 9	EC/ED/HC/ MD	56	56	30
ROUNDUP	*ST PAUL* dom99@midrivers.com	1912	1009 1ST ST W	59072	MT	Terry R Forke	(406)947-2360		ED/HC/MD			
SAINT IGNATIUS	*ZION* mt_upsguy@msb.com lcmsmontana.org	1947	300 2nd Ave PO BOX 607 ST IGNATIUS	59865	MT	Kyle T Whaley	(406)745-4149	WS 9 SS 815	ED/HC/MD	27	21	18
SALTESE	*EMMANUEL*		See Mullan ID									
SEELEY LAKE	*FAITH*		See Condon MT									
	HOLY CROSS lutefisk777@yahoo.com	1966	1655 Airport Rd PO BOX 869	59868	MT	Erik J Iverson	(406)677-2281	WS 9 SS 9	ED/HC/MD	42	36	20
SIDNEY	*CRESTWOOD APARTMENT SERVICE* Satellite Site of Trinity Sidney MT	2009	410 3rd Ave SW	59270								
	TRINITY tlchurch@midrivers.com www.trinitystjohn.org	1928	214 LINCOLN AVE S	59270	MT	John C Baseley	(406)433-2050 (406)433-2051	WS 1015 SS 915 BC 915	ED/MD			
STANFORD	*TRINITY*	1954	520 3rd St S PO BOX 214	59479	MT	Mark R Wiegert	(406)566-2723	WS 8 SS 915 BC 915				
STEVENSVILLE	*OUR SAVIOR* oursaviorstevi@gmail.com www.oslcmt.weebly.com	1954	184 PINE HOLLOW RD	59870	MT	Andrew W Eckert	(406)777-5625 (406)777-5625	WS 9 SS 1030 BC 1030	EC/ED/HC	70	37	55
SUPERIOR	*TRINITY* tlclcms@blackfoot.net	1960	6th Ave and Pike St PO BOX 790	59872	MT	Russell E Fitch	(406)822-4547	WS 230 BC 330	SN	28	28	15
THOMPSON FALLS	*SHEP OF THE VALLEY* shepherd@blackfoot.net www.shepherdofthevalleylcms.org		1192 Mt Silcox Dr PO BOX 2508 THOMPSON FLS	59873	MT	Jakob D Berger	(406)827-9570	WS 930 SS 1130 BC 1130	ED/HC/MD	41	37	24
THREE FORKS	*GRACE* holytrinityandgrace@gmail.com www.gracethreeforks.org	1926	305 5th Ave E PO BOX 857	59752	MT		(406)285-6865 (406)285-6865	WS 1030 SS 1130 BC 1130	EC/ED/HC/ MD			
TROUT CREEK	*SHEP OF THE VALLEY*		See Thompson Falls MT									
WHITEFISH	*ST PETER* stpeterlcms16@gmail.com www.stpeterwhitefish.org	1959	201 Wisconsin Ave PO BOX 883	59937	MT	Edward W Wright Jr	(406)862-3008	WS 930 SS 1045 BC 1045	ED	40	40	30
	ST. PETER LCMS Satellite Site of St Peter Whitefish MT	2000	6570 US Highway 93 South	59937								
WHITEHALL	*ZION* zionwhitehall@gmail.com www.zionwhitehall.org/	1958	301 W 1st St PO BOX 84	59759	MT		(406)782-5935	WS 830 SS 945		85	76	31
WOLF POINT	*TRINITY*	1930	121 Benton St PO BOX 862	59201	MT		(406)653-2289	WS 1030 SS 945 BC 930				
WORDEN	*OUR REDEEMER*	1993	1495 Ash St PO BOX 116	59088	MT	Robert A Lane	(406)656-2860	WS 1030 SS 945 BC 945				

NEBRASKA

CITY	CONGREGATION EMAIL WEBSITE	YEAR EST	LOCATION MAILING ADDRESS	ZIP CODE(S)	DIST.	PASTOR(S)	PHONE FAX	WS SS BC	SCHOOLS/ MINISTRIES	Bapt	Conf	Avg Attend
ADAMS	*IMMANUEL*		See Sterling NE									
AINSWORTH	*ZION* zion.lutheran.ainsworth@gmail.com zionainsworth.com	1884	318 E 4TH ST	69210	NEB	Lynn W Christensen	(402)387-1512	WS 10 SS 9 BC 9	ED/HC/MD	225	175	81
ALEXANDRIA	*IMMANUEL*		See Daykin NE									
ALLIANCE	*IMMANUEL* immanuelevlcms@gmail.com immanuelevlutheran.org	1911	1024 Box Butte Ave PO BOX 715	69301	WY	Richard C Mueller	(308)762-4663 (308)762-8218	WS 1030 SS 9 BC 9	EL/HS/ED/ HC/MD	444	309	136
ALTONA	*FIRST TRINITY*		See Wayne NE									
AMHERST	*TRINITY* TrinityAmherst@outlook.com	1907	301 E Garfield PO BOX 157	68812	NEB	Nicholas K Whitney	(308)826-3421	WS 10 SS 9 BC 9	ED/HC/ MD/SN	340	283	108
ARAPAHOE	*TRINITY* trinity@trinityarapahoe.org www.trinityarapahoe.org	1879	1005 9TH ST	68922	NEB	James A Moshier	(308)962-7667	WS 10 SS 915 BC 915	ED/HC/MD	558	441	131
ARLINGTON	*ST PAUL* stpaul@stpaulsarlington.org www.stpaulsarlington.org	1869	8951 COUNTY ROAD 9	68002	NEB	Rick G Kanoy Jason A Duley	(402)478-4278 (402)478-5378	WS 815 1030 SS 930 BC 930	EL/HS/ED/ HC/MD	938	681	241
ASHLAND	*PEACE*		See Waverly NE									
ATKINSON	*IMMANUEL* IMMANUEL_ATK@YAHOO.COM	1899	903 N State Hwy 11 903 N STATE HIGHWAY 11	68713	NEB	Leif R Hasskarl	(402)925-2851	WS 1045 SS 930 BC 930	ED/HC/MD	280	228	64
AUBURN	*TRINITY* trinityaub@outlook.com www.trinityaubne.org	1940	634 ALDEN DR	68305	NEB	Brent W Berg	(402)274-4210 (402)274-4204	WS 9 BC 10	ED/MD	142	120	53
AURORA	*CROSS OF CHRIST* crossofchristaurora@gmail.com www.crossofchristaurora.org		209 S 16th PO BOX 14	68818	NEB	Timothy M Wells	(402)694-4209	WS 9 SS 1015 BC 1015	ED/HC/ MD/SN	105	95	46
BANCROFT	*ST PAUL* splc.bancroft@gmail.com	1905	501 Park St PO BOX 306	68004	NEB	Nathan P Henschen	(402)648-7689	WS 1030 SS 915	ED/HC/MD	416	347	42

*Indicates a new church start. A new church start is an intentionally organized gathering which comes together on a regular basis for the purpose of worship and/or Bible study and is intended to grow into a member LCMS congregation. WS =Worship Service; SS = Sunday School; BC =Bible Class; EC = Early Childhood; EL = Elementary School; HS = High School; ED =Education Ministry; HC =Human Care Ministry; SN = Special Needs Ministry; MD = Media Ministry (PC)=Partner Church Pastor. See Page 53 for the Table of Abbreviations for key to additional abbreviations

CITY	CONGREGATION EMAIL WEBSITE	YEAR EST	LOCATION MAILING ADDRESS	ZIP CODE(S)	DIST.	PASTOR(S)	PHONE FAX	WS SS BC	SCHOOLS/ MINISTRIES	STATISTIC Bapt	Conf	Avg Attend
BANCROFT	*ZION* pastormike01@gmail.com	1874	1710 20TH RD	68004	NEB	Michael G Belinsky Sr	(402)648-3314	WS 1030 SS 10		139	90	35
BATTLE CREEK	*ST JOHN* churchsecretary@stjohnbc.net www.stjohnbc.net	1872	308 S 2nd PO BOX 87	68715	NEB		(402)675-3155 (402)675-1400	WS 9 SS 1030 BC 1030	EL/HS/ED/ HC/MD/SN	1028	838	245
BAYARD	*MOUNT CALVARY* mtcalv69334@gmail.com	1954	1237 Ave A PO BOX 488	69334	WY	George E Naylor	(308)586-1300	WS 9 SS 1015 BC 1015		51	44	27
BAZILE MILLS	*CHRIST* christlutheranbazile@gmail.com	1882	101 BAZILE MAIN ST CREIGHTON	68729	NEB	Justin M Hildebrand	(402)358-5298	WS 9 SS 10 BC 8	ED/SN	227	180	80
BEATRICE	*FIRST TRINITY* www.firsttrinitylutheran.org	1875	11668 W State Hwy 4 11668 W STATE HIGHWAY 4	68310	NEB	Timothy W Wagner	(402)228-0216	WS 915 SS 1030 BC 1030	ED/HC/ MD/SN	152	131	61
	SAINT PAUL'S stpaulbeatrice@gmail.com www.stpaulbeatrice.org	1915	321 N 10TH ST	68310	NEB		(402)228-1540	WS 9 SS 1015 BC 1015	EL/ED/MD	691	548	107
BEAVER LAKE	*FIRST*		See Plattsmouth NE									
BEEMER	*IMMANUEL* imm.zsj@gmail.com www.facebook.com/ImmanuelBeemer	1868	1101 K RD	68716	NEB	Robert J Mayes	(402)528-7253		ED/MD	76	74	24
	ST JOHN pastormike01@gmail.com	1892	334 LAMBRECHT ST	68716	NEB	Michael G Belinsky Sr	(402)528-7278	WS 9 SS 10 BC 8	ED/HC/ MD/SN	145	118	45
	ZION-ST JOHN		See Wisner NE									
BELLEVUE	*FIRST*		See Plattsmouth NE									
	PILGRIM lburton.pilgrim@gmail.com www.pilgrimbellevue.org	1943	2311 FAIRVIEW RD	68123	NEB	Burt L Garwood	(402)291-2848	WS 1030 SS 1045 BC 915	EC/HS/ED/ HC/MD/SN	351	282	80
BELVIDERE	*IMMANUEL*		See Daykin NE									
BIG SPRINGS	*ST JOHN'S*		See Brule NE									
	ZION pcstpaul@hotmail.com	1910	100 W 4th St PO BOX 104	69122	RM	Trenton D Christensen	(970)474-4757	WS 11 SS 10	HC	55	51	14
BINGHAM	*BINGHAM* janajensen@nebcommfound.org	1998	1084 MCADOO AVE	69335	NEB		(308)458-9685	WS 1030	EC/ED/HC	39	33	18
BLAIR	*TRINITY* trinitylutheranblair@gmail.com www.TrinityLutheranBlair.com	1889	141 S 20TH ST	68008	NEB		(402)426-2851	WS 9 SS 1015 BC 1015	ED/SN	199	169	78
BLOOMFIELD	*FIRST TRINITY* ftlcsec@gpcom.net www.firsttrinitylutheranchurch.com	1895	402 E Main St PO BOX 540	68718	NEB		(402)373-4797	WS 5 SS 4	ED/HC/MD	313	244	62
	GOLGOTHA		See Wausa NE									
BLUE HILL	*TRINITY* tlchurchsecretary@gmail.com	1882	301 N Pine PO BOX 355	68930	NEB	Glen D Wurdeman	(402)756-2102	WS 1030 SS 930 BC 945	ED/HC/ MD/SN	296	257	75
BRIDGEPORT	*ST PAUL* www.stpaulsbridgeport.org	1943	506 Main PO BOX 40	69336	WY	Peter D Preus	(308)262-0424	WS 830 SS 1030 BC 1030	ED/HC/MD	170	134	55
BROWNVILLE	*TRINITY*		See Auburn NE									
BRULE	*ST JOHN'S* stjohnsbrulelcms@gmail.com www.stjohnsbrule.org	1927	411 W 6th St PO BOX 98	69127	NEB	Jon M Dickmander	(308)287-2394	WS 830 SS 945		72	64	45
	TRINITY		See Ogallala NE									
BRUNING	*IMMANUEL*		See Daykin NE									
BURTON	*GRACE* cindyandclint@hotmail.com	1947	HC 80 Box 44 44489 STATE HWY 12 SPRINGVIEW	68777 68778	NEB	William C Serr	(402)497-2507	SS 10		74	48	40
BURWELL	*ST JOHNS* stjohnslutheranburwell@gmail.com www.stjohnslutheranburwell.org	1926	350 N 8th Avenue PO BOX 595	68823	NEB	Timothy M Reicks	(308)346-5060	WS 1030 SS 1015	EC/ED	100	100	34
BUTTE	*IMMANUEL*	1891	241 Walnut St PO BOX 260	68722	NEB	Leif R Hasskarl	(402)775-2194	WS 830	ED	67	62	12
CAIRO	*CHRIST* christcairo@gmail.com www.christlutheranchurchcairo.com	1920	503 W Medina St PO BOX 9	68824	NEB	Brian L Wright	(308)485-4863	WS 1030 1130 SS 9 10 BC 9 10	ED/HC/MD	330	264	84
CAMBRIDGE	*ST PAUL* stpaulscambridge@yahoo.com www.stpaulscambridge.weebly.com	1931	719 PARK AVE	69022	NEB	Daniel T Wiese	(308)697-3725	WS 9 SS 1015 BC 1015	ED/HC/ MD/SN	179	179	60
CAMPBELL	*TRINITY* trinitylutherancampbell@ouylook.com FB.me/trinitylutherancampbell	1897	360 Stewart St PO BOX 146	68932	NEB	Gregory R Volzke	(402)756-8552	WS 9 SS 1030	ED/HC/MD	112	86	44
CARROLL	*ST PAUL*	1897	411 Nebraska St PO BOX 117	68723	NEB	Alexander J Blanken	(402)375-1291	WS 8 SS 9		25	23	15
CEDAR BLUFFS	*ST MATTHEW* stmatthewslutheran@windstream.net	1876	300 S 2nd St PO BOX 8	68015	NEB		(402)628-3015	WS 9 SS 10 BC 10	ED	262	203	75
CEDAR RAPIDS	*ST JOHN* rbketelsen@yahoo.com	1887	111 S 3rd PO BOX 361	68627	NEB	Brian L Ketelsen		WS 830		103	77	27
CENTRAL CITY	*ST PAULS* stpaullccc@gmail.com	1924	820 G AVE	68826	NEB	Erik J Hart	(308)946-2680	WS 930 1030 SS 930 BC 930	ED/HC/ MD/SN	310	268	70
CHADRON	*OUR SAVIOR* oursavior@bbc.net www.oursaviorschadron.com	1924	702 E 9TH ST	69337	WY	Travis W Sherman	(308)432-5698 (308)432-5698	WS 10 SS 10	ED	153	123	40

*Indicates a new church start. A new church start is an intentionally organized gathering which comes together on a regular basis for the purpose of worship and/or Bible study and is intended to grow into a member LCMS congregation. WS =Worship Service; SS = Sunday School; BC =Bible Class; EC = Early Childhood; EL = Elementary School; HS = High School; ED =Education Ministry; HC =Human Care Ministry; SN = Special Needs Ministry; MD = Media Ministry (PC)=Partner Church Pastor. See Page 53 for the Table of Abbreviations for key to additional abbreviations

CITY	CONGREGATION EMAIL WEBSITE	YEAR EST	LOCATION MAILING ADDRESS	ZIP CODE(S)	DIST.	PASTOR(S)	PHONE FAX	WS SS BC	SCHOOLS/ MINISTRIES	STATISTIC Bapt	Conf	Avg Attend
CHAMBERS	*ST PAUL*	1906	102 West Wry PO BOX 67	68725	NEB	Timothy M Reicks	(402)482-5835	WS 1030 11 SS 930 BC 930	EC/ED/HC/ MD	91	68	35
CHAPPELL	*ZION*	1917	650 5th St PO BOX 307	69129	WY	Neil L Carlson	(308)874-2533	WS 830 1030 SS 915 930 BC 915 930	ED/HC/ MD/SN	77	76	15
CHESTER	*ST JOHN* stjohnchester@hotmail.com	1898	805 Church St PO BOX 211	68327	NEB	Jacob T Garrison	(402)324-8075	WS 1030	ED/HC/ MD/SN	92	85	35
CLEARWATER	*CONCORDIA*	1944	601 IOWA ST	68726	NEB		(402)485-2596	WS 915 SS 10	ED/MD/SN	121	103	60
COLUMBUS	*1C THE SANCTUARY* office@1cchurch.com www.1cchurch.com		2200 28TH AVE	68601	NEB	Bradley D Knorr Randall D Longacre	(402)835-5511	WS 9 11	ED/HC/ MD/SN	768	547	500
	CHRIST christ1871@frontiernet.net www.christcolumbusschool.org	1871	32392 122ND AVE	68601	NEB	William J Voelker	(402)563-1314 (402)564-5680	WS 10 SS 9 BC 9	EL/ED	460	314	153
	IMMANUEL office@immanuelweb.org www.immanuelweb.org	1883	2406 14th St 1470 24TH AVE	68601	NEB	Patrick R Sparling	(402)564-0502 (402)564-8851	WS 8 1030 SS 1015 BC 1015	EL/ED/HC/ MD/SN	1334	929	282
	PEACE church@peacecolumbus.org www.peacecolumbus.org	1961	2720 28TH ST	68601	NEB	Cory W Burma Joel D Ripke	(402)564-8311 (402)564-8643	WS 8 1030 BC 1015	EC/EL/ED/ HC/MD/SN	1176	923	256
	ST JOHN sjlc@telebeep.com	1879	39452 205TH AVE	68601	NEB	Paul D Rempfer	(402)285-0335 (402)285-0335	WS 10 SS 9 BC 910	EL/ED/MD	655	449	314
CONCORD	*ST PAUL*	1892	58085 867th Rd 58085 867 RD	68728	NEB	William R Bertrand	(402)584-2557	WS 8 BC 9	ED/HC	55	50	17
CORDOVA	*SAINT JOHN* stjohnscordova@gmail.com stjohnscordova.com/	1887	200 Paris St PO BOX 167	68330	NEB	Brian D Tuma	(402)576-3211	WS 9 SS 1030	ED/HC/ MD/SN	269	217	87
CRAWFORD	*BETHLEHEM* belccrawford@gmail.com www.belccrawford.org/	1918	916 2ND ST	69339	WY		(308)665-2058	WS 4 SS 3	ED	59	52	49
CREIGHTON	*GOLGOTHA*		See Wausa NE									
CRESTON	*ST JOHN*		See Columbus NE									
CRETE	*BETHLEHEM* bethlehem.lutheran.crete@gmail.com www.bethlehemlutherancrete.org	1889	805 Hawthorne Ave PO BOX 249	68333	NEB		(402)826-4359	WS 9 SS 1015 BC 1015	EC/ED/HC/ MD/SN	718	545	165
	ST JOHN www.stjohnkramer.org	1874	11400 W PANAMA RD	68333	NEB	Maynard L Toensing Jr	(402)826-3883	WS 9 SS 1015 BC 1030	ED/HC/ MD/SN	456	317	90
CROFTON	*FIRST TRINITY*		See Bloomfield NE									
CULBERTSON	*ST JOHN*	1907	712 Colorado 712 COLORADO ST	69024	NEB	Paul B Rick	(308)278-2575	WS 9 SS 10 BC 10	ED/HC/ MD/SN	242	155	24
CURTIS	*ST JOHN* pastorpeterson8@gmail.com facebook.com/stjohncurtis	1948	504 Wallace Ave PO BOX 64	69025	NEB	James M Peterson	(308)367-4238	WS 9 SS 1030 BC 1030	ED/HC/ MD/SN	163	117	47
DAVENPORT	*ST PETERS* revgregschaffer@gmail.com	1912	208 W 10th St PO BOX 160	68335	NEB	Gregory A Schaffer	(402)364-2182	WS 830 SS 945 BC 945	ED/HC/ MD/SN	244	182	97
DAVID CITY	*REDEEMER* redeemerlc@windstream.net www.redeemerlcms-dc.com	1940	695 N 9th St PO BOX 244	68632	NEB	David W Palomaki	(402)367-3859	WS 1045 SS 930 BC 930	EC/ED/MD	346	274	74
DAYKIN	*IMMANUEL* ilcdaykin@gmail.com	1891	72430 567TH AVE	68338	NEB	Alexander D Bjoraker	(402)446-7357	WS 1030 SS 930	ED/HC/ MD/SN	121	103	35
DECATUR	*TRINITY* tolzie@abbnebraska.com	1954	603 N 4th Ave PO BOX 272	68020	NEB	Brion P Tolzman	(402)349-5541	WS 9 SS 10	ED/MD/SN	87	63	17
DESHLER	*ST PETER* stpeterdeshler@gmail.com www.stpeterdeshler.org	1888	400 E Hebron Ave PO BOX 69	68340	NEB	Brian D Francik	(402)365-4341	WS 945 SS 11 BC 11	EL/ED/HC/ MD/SN	300	249	104
DEWITT	*IMMANUEL*		See Daykin NE									
DONIPHAN	*ST PAUL* stpauldoniphan@gmail.com spdoniphan.360unite.com	1887	207 N 4th St PO BOX 185	68832	NEB	Tyler D Hauptmeier	(402)845-2340	WS 9 SS 1015 BC 8		142	117	50
DOUGLAS	*IMMANUEL*		See Sterling NE									
EAGLE	*IMMANUEL* immanueloffice@windstream.net www.immanueleagle.org	1900	1009 G ST	68347	NEB	Scott T Porath	(402)781-2190	WS 9 SS 1015 BC 1015		227	189	92
	PEACE		See Waverly NE									
ELGIN	*TRINITY* trinityelginne@gmail.com trinityelgin.blogspot.com/	1905	200 N 5th St PO BOX 378	68636	NEB		(402)887-4791	WS 8	ED	81	68	26
ELK CREEK	*ST PETER* stpeterselkcreek@gmail.com stpeterselkcreek.weebly.com	1871	71955 Hwy 50 71955 HIGHWAY 50	68348	NEB		(402)335-2686	WS 10 SS 930 BC 930	ED/HC/MD	330	277	101
ELKHORN	*GRACEHILL* info@gracehillomaha.com www.gracehillomaha.com	2016	18751 HARNEY STREET	68022	NEB	Justin A Bell Brady W Betten	(402)403-4941	WS 8 930 11	EL/HS	918	619	570
	LORD OF LIFE PastorDavid@LordofLifeElkhorn.org www.lordoflifeelkhorn.org	1981	20844 BONANZA BLVD	68022	NEB	David H Linkugel Caleb J Kruse	(402)289-3437	WS 8 930 1045 SS 930 BC 930	EC/EL/HS/ ED/HC/MD	465	351	200

*Indicates a new church start. A new church start is an intentionally organized gathering which comes together on a regular basis for the purpose of worship and/or Bible study and is intended to grow into a member LCMS congregation. WS =Worship Service; SS = Sunday School; BC =Bible Class; EC = Early Childhood; EL = Elementary School; HS = High School; ED =Education Ministry; HC =Human Care Ministry; SN = Special Needs Ministry; MD = Media Ministry (PC)=Partner Church Pastor. See Page 53 for the Table of Abbreviations for key to additional abbreviations

CITY	CONGREGATION EMAIL WEBSITE	YEAR EST	LOCATION MAILING ADDRESS	ZIP CODE(S)	DIST.	PASTOR(S)	PHONE FAX	WS SS BC	SCHOOLS/ MINISTRIES	STATISTIC Bapt	Conf	Avg Attend
ELWOOD	*OUR REDEEMER* rredeemer@q.com www.ourredeemerelwood.org	1948	704 Smith Ave PO BOX 42	68937	NEB	Aaron M Witt	(308)785-2875	WS 10 BC 9	EC/ED/HC/ MD/SN	356	305	66
FAIRBURY	*GRACE* gl92901@windstream.net gracelutheranfairbury.com	1923	1100 G ST	68352	NEB	Glen A Emery	(402)729-5163	WS 830 11 SS 945 BC 945	ED/HC/ MD/SN	780	667	168
FALLS CITY	*CHRIST* christlutheran@sentco.net fallscitylcms.blogspot.com	1883	2310 BARADA ST	68355	NEB	Kenneth L Humphrey	(402)245-3324	WS 9 SS 1015	ED/MD	180	122	45
	ST PAUL stpauls6n@sentco.net fallscitylcms.blogspot.com	1881	65103 712 RD	68355	NEB	Kenneth L Humphrey	(402)245-4643 (402)245-4643	WS 1030 SS 930 BC 930	ED/HC	177	151	48
FARNAM	*ST JOHN*		See Curtis NE									
FOSTER	*TRINITY* TLCFosterNE@gmail.com	1913	305 N PINE ST	68765	NEB	Terry J Makelin	(402)329-4262	WS 10 SS 11	EL	162	131	54
FRANKLIN	*GRACE*	1926	1206 N ST	68939	NEB			WS 430 SS 330		18	17	12
FREMONT	*KING OF KINGS LUTHERAN CHURCH FREMONT* Satellite Site of King Of Kings Omaha NE	2024	1440 E Military Ave	68137				WS 915 11				
	TRINITY church@trinityfremont.org www.trinityfremont.com	1884	1546 N LUTHER RD	68025	NEB	Anthony J Gerber Greg D Rathke	(402)721-5536 (402)721-5537	WS 8 1030 SS 915 BC 915	EL/HS/ED/ HC/MD/SN	1283	1030	292
FRIEND	*IMMANUEL*		See Daykin NE									
FULLERTON	*MOUNT CALVARY* mtcalvaryfullerton@gmail.com www.mtcalvarylutheran.net	1935	401 Irving St PO BOX 7	68638	NEB	Allen L Pingel	(308)536-2635	WS 9 SS 1015	ED/HC/MD	214	151	70
GARLAND	*IMMANUEL*		See Seward NE									
	ZION church2229@windstream.net	1886	370 4th St PO BOX 106	68360	NEB	David F Dobbertien	(402)588-2229	WS 9		143	126	40
GERING	*FAITH* secretary@keepfaithlutheran.org keepfaithlutheran.org	1963	2055 U St PO BOX 307	69341	WY	Richard H Neugebauer	(308)436-4307 (308)436-3232	WS 9 SS 1030	EC/ED/HC/ MD	319	259	113
GILEAD	*IMMANUEL*		See Daykin NE									
GLADSTONE	*IMMANUEL*		See Daykin NE									
GOEHNER	*HOLY CROSS* hclchurch@windstream.net	1933	1042 May St PO BOX 92	68364	NEB		(402)523-4705	WS 930 SS 1030 BC 1030	ED/HC	123	99	65
GORDON	*FAITH**	1974	33393 FAWN LAKE RD	69343	NEB		(308)458-2565	WS 3	EC	7	7	4
	GRACE office@gordongrace.org gordongrace.org	1921	801 N Elm St PO BOX 239	69343	WY	Travis W Sherman	(308)282-0584	WS 10 SS 930	EC/ED/ HC/SN	226	175	37
GRAND ISLAND	*CRISTO CORDERO/DIOS* panchitaportillo@hotmail.com	1998	512 E 2ND ST	68801	NEB		(308)391-0169	WS 11 BC 10		55	55	15
	GRACE graceofc@gracegi.net gracelcmsgi.org	1956	545 E Memorial Dr 545 MEMORIAL DR	68801	NEB	Daniel G Bremer	(308)382-1190	WS 9 SS 1030 BC 1030	EL/HS/MD	240	206	120
	PEACE office@peacegi.org www.peacegi.org	1976	1710 N NORTH RD	68803	NEB	Justin R Bangert Carl A Eliason	(308)384-5673	WS 815 830 1030 1045 SS 945 BC 945	EC/EL/HS/ ED/HC/ MD/SN	1703	1187	715
	TRINITY trinitylutherangi.org	1878	212 W 12TH ST	68801	NEB	Adam J Snoberger	(308)382-0753 (308)384-6722	WS 8 1030 BC 915	EL/HS/ED/ HC/MD/SN	956	691	262
GRANT	*ZION* grantzion@gpcom.net www.ziongrant.org/	1924	705 Central Ave PO BOX 740	69140	NEB	Michael A Heckmann	(308)352-4107	WS 930 SS 1030 BC 1045	ED/HC/ MD/SN	308	270	96
GREENWOOD	*PEACE*		See Waverly NE									
GRESHAM	*ST PETER*	1909	2320 Hwy 69 2320 HIGHWAY 69	68367	NEB	Lee D Seetin	(402)735-7333	WS 1030 SS 930		182	147	30
GRETNA	*GOOD SHEPHERD* jan.kounkel@gslcgretna.org www.gslcgretna.org	1979	11204 S 204th St PO BOX 39	68028	NEB	Eric G Larson	(402)332-3345 (402)332-4821	WS 8 930 1045 SS 915 BC 915	EC/EL/HS/ ED/HC/ MD/SN	1391	1055	400
GURLEY	*SALEM*	1910	506 Washington PO BOX 117	69141	WY			WS 1035 SS 1045 BC 1045	ED/HC/ MD/SN	116	101	37
HAMPTON	*ZION* notifications@mychurchwebsite.net www.zionhampton.com	1870	1511 N Y RD	68843	NEB		(402)725-3320 (402)725-3326	WS 10 SS 9 BC 9	ED/MD	398	337	102
HARBINE	*ZION*	1901	58115 718TH RD JANSEN	68377	NEB	Gregory L Stuckwisch	(402)754-4522	WS 1045		88	76	32
HARRISON	*REDEEMER* relcharrison@gmail.com relcharrison.org	1929	296 Rose St PO BOX 482	69346	WY		(308)665-2058	WS 8 SS 915		30	20	12
HARTINGTON	*FIRST TRINITY*		See Bloomfield NE									
HASTINGS	*FAITH* office@afamilyoffaith.com www.afamilyoffaith.com	1956	837 CHESTNUT AVE	68901	NEB	Paul T Dunbar Joshua P Davis	(402)462-5044 (402)462-5404	WS 8 1030 SS 915 BC 915	ED/HC/ MD/SN	1861	1389	376
	PEACE peacelutheranhastings@gmail.com www.peacelutheranhastings.org	1948	906 N CALIFORNIA AVE	68901	NEB	Micah R Gaunt	(402)462-9023 (402)463-3749	WS 9 BC 1030	EL/ED/HC/ MD/SN	312	272	94

*Indicates a new church start. A new church start is an intentionally organized gathering which comes together on a regular basis for the purpose of worship and/or Bible study and is intended to grow into a member LCMS congregation. WS =Worship Service; SS = Sunday School; BC =Bible Class; EC = Early Childhood; EL = Elementary School; HS = High School; ED =Education Ministry; HC =Human Care Ministry; SN = Special Needs Ministry; MD = Media Ministry (PC)=Partner Church Pastor. See Page 53 for the Table of Abbreviations for key to additional abbreviations

CITY	CONGREGATION EMAIL WEBSITE	YEAR EST	LOCATION MAILING ADDRESS	ZIP CODE(S)	DIST.	PASTOR(S)	PHONE FAX	WS SS BC	SCHOOLS/ MINISTRIES	STATISTIC Bapt	Conf	Avg Attend
HASTINGS	*SENIOR BIBLE STUDY AND LUNCH* Satellite Site of Peace Hastings NE	2022	1100 N 6th Ave	68901				WS 2				
	ZION office.ZionHastings@gmail.com www.zionhastings.org	1900	465 S MARIAN RD	68901	NEB	Benjamin R Siebert	(402)469-2133	WS 9 SS 1015 BC 1015	EL/ED/ MD/SN	241	206	78
HAY SPRINGS	*ZION*	1929	224 S Main St PO BOX 177	69347	WY	Allan D Wierschke	(308)638-7575	WS 1030 SS 915 BC 915	ED	110	95	33
HAZARD	*FAITH* lutheranfaith77@gmail.com gracefaithlutheran.com		308 MUNN ST	68844	NEB	Dean A Hanson		WS 9		158	150	65
HEBRON	*FAITH* faithlutheranhebron@gmail.com	1963	420 CHARLES RD	68370	NEB	Brian D Francik	(402)710-6679	WS 830 SS 930	ED/HC/ MD/SN	97	74	41
	TRINITY	1874	1364 ROAD 5600	68370	NEB	Jose Flores	(402)365-4317	WS 10 SS 1115 BC 1115	EL/ED/HC/ MD/SN	142	104	64
HENRY	*TRINITY*		See Morrill NE									
HERSHEY	*OUR REDEEMER*		See North Platte NE									
HOLDREGE	*MOUNT CALVARY* mtcalfinance@gmail.com mtcalvaryholdrege.org	1937	1419 EAST AVE	68949	NEB	Kenton J Birtell	(308)995-2208 (308)995-3834	WS 830 1045 SS 945 BC 945	ED/HC/ MD/SN	625	455	251
HOLSTEIN	*ST PAUL* prspnzn@gmail.com	1899	18260 W Sundown Rd PO BOX 88	68950	NEB	Lon E Landsmann	(402)200-0078	WS 1030	ED/SN	74	67	21
HOOPER	*IMMANUEL* immanuelhooperne@gmail.com www.immanuelhooper.com	1876	27052 Co Rd 12 27052 COUNTY ROAD 12	68031	NEB	Stuart W Freese	(402)654-3663	WS 10 SS 9 BC 9	EC/HS/ ED/HC	171	147	70
HOWELLS	*TRINITY* trinityluthhowells@outlook.com	1900	505 Ann St PO BOX 436	68641	NEB		(402)986-1254	WS 8 BC 915	ED	100	93	25
HUMBOLDT	*COLONIAL ACRES NURSING HOME* Satellite Site of Faith Humboldt NE	2014	1043 Tenth St	68376								
	FAITH faith.humboldt@windstream.net	1948	948 CENTRAL AVE	68376	NEB	Timothy J Llewellyn	(402)862-2437	WS 1030 SS 930	ED/HC/ MD/SN	211	171	22
HUMPHREY	*ST PETER*	1884	PO BOX 325	68642	NEB		(402)246-2730	WS 830		20	20	8
HYANNIS	*FAITH**		See Gordon NE									
	SHEPHERD OF HILLS susan@artcottage.com	1969	609 N Hwy 61 609 N HIGHWAY 61	69350	NEB	Jonathan W Oetting	(308)458-2831	WS 9	EC/ED/MD	103	85	32
IMPERIAL	*ZION* office@zionimperial.com zionimperial.com	1917	1305 Broadway PO BOX 1199	69033	NEB	Scott T Adle	(308)882-5655	WS 9 SS 1015 BC 1015	ED/HC/ MD/SN	576	483	170
JAMISON	*IMMANUEL*	1925	Main St 90897 W JAMISON RD NEWPORT	68759	NEB	William C Serr			ED/HC	64	50	25
JOHNSON	*TRINITY*		See Auburn NE									
JUNIATA	*CHRIST* welcome@christjuniata.org christjuniata.org	1882	13175 W 70TH ST	68955	NEB	Darren R Olson	(402)744-4991	WS 10 SS 9 BC 9	EL/ED/HC/ MD	446	404	110
	FAITH		See Hastings NE									
	ZION prspnzn@gmail.com	1878	4080 S WANDA AVE	68955	NEB	Lon E Landsmann		WS 8 BC 915	EL/ED	34	28	14
KEARNEY	*HOLY CROSS* office@hclk.org holycrosskearney.org	1965	3315 11TH AVE	68845	NEB	Dr John W Rasmussen Timothy J Barone	(308)237-2944 (308)237-2695	WS 8 930 11 5 SS 930 BC 930	EC/ED/HC/ MD/SN	1370	1031	610
	ZION james.deloach@zionkearney.com www.zionkearney.com	1913	2421 Ave C 2421 C AVE	68847	NEB	James H DeLoach Douglas A Gaunt	(308)234-3410 (308)236-8100	WS 9 5 SS 1030 BC 1030	EL/ED/MD	561	392	170
KENESAW	*ST PAUL* stpaulskenesaw@gmail.com stpaulskenesaw.org	1904	310 N 4th Ave PO BOX 36	68956	NEB	Paul S Duffy	(402)752-3421	WS 10 SS 9 BC 930	ED/HC/MD	442	380	95
	ST PAUL		See Lowell Township NE									
KIMBALL	*ST JOHNS* Pastor.Steffensen@protonmail.com wyobraskalcms.org	1916	601 LOCUST ST	69145	WY	Ellery J Steffensen	(308)235-2582	WS 10 SS 11 BC 11		107	87	44
LA PLATTE	*FIRST*		See Plattsmouth NE									
LAUREL	*IMMANUEL* secretary@immanuellutheran laurelne.com immanuellutheranlaurelne.com	1895	301 Alma St PO BOX 597	68745	NEB	Jeffery P Warner	(402)256-3314	WS 10 SS 9 BC 9	ED/HC/MD	292	235	79
LAVISTA	*BEAUTIFUL SAVIOR* info@bslcomaha.org www.bslcomaha.org	1962	7706 S 96TH ST	68128	NEB	Calvin R Kapels James R Haack	(402)331-7376 (402)331-1123	WS 8 930 11 SS 930	EC/EL/HS/ ED/HC/ MD/SN	1029	886	657
LEIGH	*ZION* zionlutheran68643@gmail.com zionleigh.org	1894	405 Main St PO BOX 215	68643	NEB		(402)487-2502	WS 1030 SS 930	EC/ED/MD	179	131	56
LEXINGTON	*FIRST* vicandrogene@gmail.com	1890	42956 BUFFALO RD	68850	NEB	Victor J Rasmussen	(308)627-6263	WS 1030 SS 1130 BC 1130	HC/MD	57	43	37

*Indicates a new church start. A new church start is an intentionally organized gathering which comes together on a regular basis for the purpose of worship and/or Bible study and is intended to grow into a member LCMS congregation. WS =Worship Service; SS = Sunday School; BC =Bible Class; EC = Early Childhood; EL = Elementary School; HS = High School; ED =Education Ministry; HC =Human Care Ministry; SN = Special Needs Ministry; MD = Media Ministry (PC)=Partner Church Pastor. See Page 53 for the Table of Abbreviations for key to additional abbreviations

CITY	CONGREGATION EMAIL WEBSITE	YEAR EST	LOCATION MAILING ADDRESS	ZIP CODE(S)	DIST.	PASTOR(S)	PHONE FAX	WS SS BC	SCHOOLS/ MINISTRIES	STATISTIC Bapt	Conf	Avg Attend
LEXINGTON	*TRINITY* mrodriguez@tlclex.org www.tlclex.org	1930	205 E 7th St PO BOX L	68850	NEB	Robert C Kuefner Jr	(308)324-4341	WS 10 SS 845 BC 845	ED/HC/ MD/SN	363	307	110
LINCOLN	*CALVARY* jenny@calvarylincoln.org www.calvarylutheranlincoln.org	1930	2788 Franklin St 2764 FRANKLIN ST	68502	NEB	Benjamin M Vineyard	(402)476-1567	WS 8 1030 SS 930 BC 930	EL/HS/ED/ HC/MD/SN	351	263	194
	CHRIST contact@christlincoln.org www.christlincoln.org	1949	6700 Chatsworth Lane 4325 SUMNER ST	68516 68506	NEB	Dr Michael A Eckelkamp Michael P Kasaty Joseph M Beran Aaron L Hutton Dr Daniel A Potts Jeffrey L Scheich Dr Luke R Schnake William J Steinbauer James C Riang	(402)483-7774 (402)483-7776	WS 8 930 11 SS 920 BC 930	EL/HS/ED/ HC/MD	3815	3032	2200
	CHRIST LINCOLN - YANKEE HILL CAMPUS Satellite Site of Christ Lincoln NE	2014	6700 Chatsworth Lane	68516				WS 9 1030 SS 9 BC 9				
	FAITH lhumlicek@faithlincoln.org www.faithlincoln.org	1952	8701 ADAMS ST	68507	NEB	Dr William D Miller Daniel M McMahan	(402)466-6861 (402)466-3857	WS 8 1030 530 SS 930 BC 930 7	EL/HS/ED/ HC/MD/SN	884	691	300
	FAITH OF OUR FATHERS		See Roca NE									
	GOOD SHEPHERD info@goodshepherdlincoln.org www.goodshepherdlincoln.org	1978	3825 WILDBRIAR LN	68516	NEB	Adam S Moline Thomas E Goodroad	(402)423-7639 (402)423-0984	WS 8 1030 SS 920 BC 920	ED/HC/ MD/SN	659	531	358
	GOOD SHEPHERD		See Milford NE									
	HOLY SAVIOR office.admin@holysavior.org www.holysavior.org	1992	4710 N 10TH ST	68521	NEB	James M Irwin	(402)434-3325	WS 1030 SS 915	EL/HS/ED/ HC/MD	417	324	155
	IMMANUEL immanuellc@hotmail.com www.immanuellincolnlcms.com	1909	2001 S 11TH ST	68502	NEB	Jeffrey L Bloom	(402)474-6275	WS 8 1045 SS 930 BC 930	ED/HC/ MD/SN	318	280	104
	IMMANUEL		See Sterling NE									
	LIFE cjmeyer333@gmail.com		2816 TENNYSON ST	68516	NEB		(402)450-5320			5	4	35
	MESSIAH info@messiah.us www.messiah.us	1988	1800 S 84TH ST	68506	NEB	John R Kunze Andrew T Greer Dustin P Lappe David P Loeschen	(402)489-3024	WS 8 930 11	EL/HS/ED/ HC/MD/SN	3324	2389	1205
	PEACE		See Waverly NE									
	REDEEMER valerie.coleman@redeemerlincoln.org redeemerlincoln.org	1917	510 S 33RD ST	68510	EN	Samuel L Bobby	(402)477-1710 (402)477-5240	WS 830 11 SS 945 BC 945	EL/HS/ED/ HC/MD/SN	815	709	263
	TRINITY churchoffice@trinityoflincoln.org trinityoflincoln.org/	1881	724 S 12TH ST	68508	NEB	Daniel S Wing	(402)474-0606	WS 8 1030 6 SS 915	EL/HS/ED/ HC/MD/SN	689	538	295
	TRINITY		See Walton NE									
	WORD OF LIFE WOLLincolnOffice@gmail.com www.wordoflifelincoln.org		200 Fletcher 200 FLETCHER AVE	68521	NEB		(402)742-9673	WS 1030 SS 915 BC 915	EL/HS/ED/ HC/MD/SN	172	125	95
LOUISVILLE	*FIRST*		See Plattsmouth NE									
	IMMANUEL immanuel.lutheran@windstream.net www.Immanuel-Louisville.org	1871	36712 CHURCH RD	68037	NEB	Jon J Sollberger	(402)234-5980	WS 10 SS 830 BC 830	ED	189	172	86
LOUP CITY	*IMMANUEL* immanuel.loupcity@aol.com	1882	205 N 1ST ST	68853	NEB		(308)745-0808	WS 9 SS 10 BC 8	ED/HC/SN	187	153	65
LOWELL TOWNSHIP	*ST PAUL*	1889	2294 X RD KENESAW	68956	NEB		(308)647-6776	WS 8		52	48	20
LYMAN	*TRINITY*		See Morrill NE									
LYNCH	*CHRIST* www.immanuelchristlutheran. blogspot.com	1950	518 W Hoffmann St PO BOX 113	68746	NEB	John E Nelson Jr	(402)589-1323	WS 5 SS 4		61	41	28
LYONS	*ST JOHN* rrsimonsen@yahoo.com	1874	1543 County Road 13 PO BOX 357	68038	NEB	Nathan P Henschen	(402)648-7689	WS 845 SS 10	ED/MD	108	95	26
MADISON	*ST JOHN* stjohngg@telebeep.com	1877	82664 547th Ave 82664 547 AVE	68748	NEB	Barry A Williams	(402)454-2823	WS 9 SS 8 BC 8	ED/HC/MD	122	101	45
	TRINITY trinitylutheranmadison@gmail.com trinitylutheranmadison.com	1885	508 S Jackson St PO BOX 367	68748	NEB	Todd E Kollbaum	(402)454-3532 (402)454-3476	WS 930 SS 830 BC 830	EL/HS/ED/ HC/MD	352	329	103
MALCOLM	*ST PAUL* pastor@parishmusic.org stpaulsmalcolm.org	1922	375 S LINCOLN ST	68402	NEB	Brent S Horne	(402)796-2396 (402)796-2406	WS 10 BC 845	ED/HC/MD	164	150	59
MARTINSBURG	*TRINITY* trinitylutheran@nntc.net trinitylutheranmartinsburg. godaddysites.com	1875	5106 DOUGLAS ST PONCA	68770	NEB	Martin R Hill	(402)945-2160	WS 9 SS 1030	ED/HC/SN	210	121	47
MAXWELL	*OUR REDEEMER*		See North Platte NE									
MAYWOOD	*ST JOHN*		See Curtis NE									
MCCOOK	*PEACE* office@plcmccook.org www.plcmccook.org	1908	411 E 6th St PO BOX 240	69001	NEB	Lonnie R Felcher	(308)345-2595 (308)345-2596	WS 8 1030 SS 915 BC 915	EC/ED/HC/ MD/SN	474	366	135

*Indicates a new church start. A new church start is an intentionally organized gathering which comes together on a regular basis for the purpose of worship and/or Bible study and is intended to grow into a member LCMS congregation. WS =Worship Service; SS = Sunday School; BC =Bible Class; EC = Early Childhood; EL = Elementary School; HS = High School; ED =Education Ministry; HC =Human Care Ministry; SN = Special Needs Ministry; MD = Media Ministry (PC)=Partner Church Pastor. See Page 53 for the Table of Abbreviations for key to additional abbreviations

CITY	CONGREGATION EMAIL WEBSITE	YEAR EST	LOCATION MAILING ADDRESS	ZIP CODE(S)	DIST.	PASTOR(S)	PHONE FAX	WS SS BC	SCHOOLS/ MINISTRIES	STATISTIC Bapt	 Conf	 Avg Attend
MCCOOK	*ST JOHN* kelley.brothers@plantpioneer.com www.stjohnsmccook.org	1884	39097 ROAD 712	69001	NEB		(308)364-2706	WS 1030 SS 930 BC 930	ED/MD	95	84	35
MEADOW GROVE	*ST MATTHEW* stmatthewmg@gmail.com	1910	216 1st St PO BOX 48	68752	NEB	Chad U Boggs	(402)368-5690	WS 8 BC 930	HS/ED/HC/ MD/SN	60	58	20
MERNA	*IMMANUEL* churchemanuel2@outlook.com	1938	328 E Brotherton Ave PO BOX 185	68856	NEB		(308)643-2302	WS 11	ED/MD/SN	80	60	29
MERRIMAN	*GRACE*	1978	2nd Ave And Main St PO BOX 116	69218	NEB		(402)425-3357	WS 4		16	12	4
MILFORD	*GOOD SHEPHERD* goodshepherdmilfordne@gmail.com www.goodshepherd-milford.org	1973	2668 PIONEERS RD	68405	NEB		(402)761-3146	WS 10 SS 9 BC 9	ED/HC/ MD/SN	151	126	68
MILLIGAN	*IMMANUEL*		See Daykin NE									
MINDEN	*ST PAUL* stpaulminden@gmail.com www.stpaulserving.com	1878	206 N COLORADO AVE	68959	NEB	William F Zwick	(308)832-1343	WS 1015 SS 9 BC 9		334	277	108
MITCHELL	*TRINITY*		See Morrill NE									
MOOREFIELD	*ST JOHN*		See Curtis NE									
MORRILL	*TRINITY* trinitymorrill@gmail.com trinitymorrill.blogspot.com	1946	405 JACKSON CT	69358	WY	Scott G Firminhac	(308)247-2432 (509)561-3437	WS 9 BC 215	ED/HC/ MD/SN	116	103	26
MURDOCK	*TRINITY* trinitymurdock.weebly.com	1892	31104 CHURCH RD	68407	NEB	Brent W Kuhlman	(402)867-2916	WS 1030 SS 915 BC 915	ED	437	373	175
MURRAY	*FIRST*		See Plattsmouth NE									
NEBRASKA CITY	*CHRIST* www.christlutherannebcity.org	1950	2201 2ND AVE	68410	NEB	Paul M Warneke	(402)873-6824	WS 1030 SS 915	ED/HC/SN	95	77	25
NELIGH	*GRACE* graceneligh@gmail.com www.facebook.com/profile. php?id=100064519337093	1929	508 K ST	68756	NEB		(402)887-4791	WS 1030 SS 930 BC 930	ED/HC/MD	406	321	75
NORFOLK	*CHRIST* info@clnorfolk.org www.clnorfolk.org	1871	605 S 5TH ST	68701	NEB	Michael P Moreno James P Carretto	(402)371-1210 (402)371-1228	WS 8 1030 SS 915 BC 915	EL/HS/ED/ HC/MD	2120	1641	503
	GRACE glnorfolk416@gmail.com www.gracelutherannorfolk.com	1919	416 Park Ave 416 W PARK AVE	68701	NEB	Christopher P Asbury Ray S Wilke	(402)371-1044	WS 10 SS 830 BC 845	EL/HS/ED/ HC/MD/SN	978	721	200
	MOUNT OLIVE mtolivechurchnorfolk@gmail.com www.mountolivenorfolk.com	1931	1212 S 2ND ST	68701	NEB	Robert D Wiest	(402)371-1238	WS 1030 BC 915	EL/HS/ED/ HC/MD/SN	145	128	38
	OUR SAVIOR oursavior@oursav.org www.oursav.org	1962	2420 W OMAHA AVE	68701	NEB	Kenneth L Weander Jr Eric T Gradberg Caleb J Wehling	(402)371-9005 (402)371-1378	WS 9 1030 SS 9 BC 9	EL/HS/ED/ HC/MD	2753	2516	1142
NORTH BEND	*ST PETER* st.peter@gpcom.net stpeternorthbend.org	1943	920 Linden Dr PO BOX 496	68649	NEB	Lawson K Short	(402)652-8215	WS 9 SS 930	EC/ED/HC	347	274	94
NORTH PLATTE	*BEAUTIFUL SAVIOR* bslc@bslcnp.com www.bslcnp.com	1980	402 S BAYTREE AVE	69101	NEB		(308)534-7004 (308)534-3177	WS 845 11 SS 10 BC 10	EC/ED/ MD/SN	444	418	125
	OUR REDEEMER orlcs.np.ne@gmail.com ourredeemer.life	1926	1400 East E St 1400 E E ST	69101	NEB	Daniel J Ramsey	(308)532-4753 (308)532-0295	WS 10 SS 845 BC 845 630	EL/ED/HC/ MD	515	386	112
OAKDALE	*GRACE*		See Neligh NE									
	TRINITY		See Elgin NE									
ODELL	*OUR SAVIOR* oursaviorodell@diodecom.net	1926	421 Maple St PO BOX A	68415	NEB	Gregory L Stuckwisch	(402)766-3688	WS 9 SS 10 BC 10		321	259	100
OGALLALA	*ST JOHN* sjlcogallala@gmail.com	1886	466 Rd E G S 466 ROAD EAST G S	69153	NEB	Albert J Bader	(308)284-6015	WS 1030 SS 930 BC 930	ED/HC	172	150	54
	ST JOHN'S		See Brule NE									
	ST PAUL contact@stpaulsogallala.org www.stpaulsogallala.org	1926	317 W 2nd St 312 W 3RD ST	69153	NEB	Timothy D Steele II	(308)284-2944 (308)284-2688	WS 830 SS 940 BC 940	EL/ED/HC/ MD/SN	242	218	77
	TRINITY trinityogallalalcms@gmail.com stjohnsbrule.org	1886	32695 ROAD 768	69153	NEB	Jon M Dickmander	(308)352-4079	WS 1030 SS 945 BC 7	ED/HC/MD	45	41	28
OHIOWA	*IMMANUEL*		See Daykin NE									
OMAHA	*DIVINE SHEPHERD* admin@dsomaha.org www.dsomaha.org	1973	15005 Q ST	68137	NEB	Dr Brent D Smith James D Rasmussen	(402)895-1500 (402)895-5377	WS 815 10 SS 915	EC/EL/HS/ ED/HC/MD	1208	1060	650
	FAITH		See Council Bluffs IA									
	GRACEHILL		See Elkhorn NE									
	HOPE	1946	2723 N 30TH ST	68111	NEB		(402)453-1583	WS 11 SS 1015	HC/MD	51	51	35
	KING OF KINGS gg@kingofkings.org www.kingofkings.org	1962	11615 I ST	68137	NEB	Greg S Griffith Seth T Flick Dr Roger P Theimer Zachary A Zehnder	(402)333-6464 (402)333-0644	WS 8 9 11 SS 9 11	EC/EL/HS/ ED/HC/MD	4464	1961	1277
	KING OF KINGS LUTHERAN CHURCH NORTHWEST Satellite Site of King Of Kings Omaha NE	2023	15656 Fort Street	68116				WS 915 11				

*Indicates a new church start. A new church start is an intentionally organized gathering which comes together on a regular basis for the purpose of worship and/or Bible study and is intended to grow into a member LCMS congregation. WS =Worship Service; SS = Sunday School; BC =Bible Class; EC = Early Childhood; EL = Elementary School; HS = High School; ED =Education Ministry; HC =Human Care Ministry; SN = Special Needs Ministry; MD = Media Ministry (PC)=Partner Church Pastor. See Page 53 for the Table of Abbreviations for key to additional abbreviations

CITY	CONGREGATION EMAIL WEBSITE	YEAR EST	LOCATION MAILING ADDRESS	ZIP CODE(S)	DIST.	PASTOR(S)	PHONE FAX	WS SS BC	SCHOOLS/ MINISTRIES	STATISTIC Bapt	Conf	Avg Attend
OMAHA	*LAMB OF GOD*		See Papillion NE									
	LIVING WATER info@livingwateromaha.org livingwateromaha.org/		4141 N 156th St 4141 N 156TH ST LL	68116	NEB	Joseph R Eisenbacher Mark A Anderson	(402)431-2593		EL/HS	303	213	290
	LORD OF LIFE		See Elkhorn NE									
	MOUNT CALVARY office@mountcalvary-lcms.org www.mountcalvary-lcms.org	1926	5529 LEAVENWORTH ST	68106	NEB	Andrew S Gerike	(402)551-0244	WS 10 SS 845 BC 845	EL/HS	192	141	105
	MOUNT OLIVE office@mountoliveomaha.org www.mountoliveomaha.com	1927	7301 N 28TH AVE	68112	NEB	Paul F Albers	(402)455-8700	WS 9 SS 1020 BC 1020	EL/HS/ ED/HC	260	184	92
	OUR REDEEMER		See Springfield NE									
	PACIFIC HILLS KimKielty@PacificHillsLutheran.org www.pacifichillslutheran.org	1955	1110 S 90TH ST	68124	NEB	Bryan E Drebes	(402)391-9625	WS 8 1030 SS 915 BC 915	EL/HS/ED/ HC/MD/SN	231	201	110
	RIVER OF LIFE office@riveroflifeomaha.org riveroflifelutheran.org	1939	5151 NW RADIAL HWY	68104	NEB	Kevin M Foley Joseph C Haggas	(402)558-6212 (402)561-6928	WS 930 5 SS 1045 BC 1045	EL/HS/ED/ HC/MD/SN	139	118	82
	ST JOHN secretary@stjohnomaha.com www.stjohnomaha.com	1902	11120 Calhoun Rd 9910 N 48TH ST STE 104	68152	NEB	Ronald E Holling	(402)451-2441	WS 9 SS 1015 BC 1015	EL/HS/HC/ MD	75	75	36
	ST MARK info@stmarkomaha.org www.stmarkomaha.org	1956	1821 N 90TH ST	68114	NEB	Eric L Jay	(402)391-6148 (402)399-1682	WS 1030 SS 930 BC 930	EL/HS/ED/ HC/MD/SN	445	321	275
	ST PAULS		See Council Bluffs IA									
	SUNDAY NIGHT ZOOM BIBLE STUDY Satellite Site of Pacific Hills Omaha NE	2020	16019 Lake Circle	68114								
	ZION zionjcohrs@gmail.com www.zionwest.org	1886	14205 IDA ST	68142	NEB	Lance D Berndt Philip W Hale	(402)493-1744 (402)965-8706	WS 8 1030 SS 915 BC 930	EL/HS/ED/ MD/SN	554	457	241
	ZOOM COMMUNION Satellite Site of Pacific Hills Omaha NE	2021	1110 S 90th Street	68124								
O'NEILL	*CHRIST* clcsecretary@hotmail.com christlutheranoneill.org/	1941	129 N 7th St PO BOX 736	68763	NEB	John E Nelson Jr Jordan B Schut	(402)336-1884	WS 9 SS 1010	EC/ED/HC/ MD	487	401	103
ORCHARD	*ST PAUL* virginia.vonseggern251@gmail.com	1914	51301 876 Rd 87127 512 AVE	68764	NEB	Ryan M Janke	(402)655-2246 (402)655-2213	WS 8	ED/HC	41	37	20
	ST PETER stpetersluthchurch@gmail.com	1909	230 N Cherry St PO BOX 217	68764	NEB	Ryan M Janke	(402)893-2390	WS 930 SS 1045 BC 1045	ED	148	113	60
ORD	*ST JOHN* stjohnsord@gmail.com	1889	725 S 14TH ST	68862	NEB	Adam K Archer	(308)728-5111	WS 9 SS 1030 BC 1030	ED/HC/MD	199	163	51
OSMOND	*GOLGOTHA*		See Wausa NE									
	IMMANUEL immanuelosmond@gmail.com www.immanuelosmond.com	1902	808 Fulton Street PO BOX 10	68765	NEB		(402)748-3301	WS 930 BC 9	EC/ED/HC/ MD	631	473	121
	TRINITY		See Foster NE									
OXFORD	*ST JOHN* sjlcoxford@gmail.com	1885	418 Globe St PO BOX 68	68967	NEB	Eric D Souer	(308)824-3269	WS 10 SS 930 BC 930	ED/HC/ MD/SN	165	118	42
PALMER	*ST JOHNS* inhishand23@yahoo.com www.facebook.com/StJohnsPalmer	1901	504 Utica Ave PO BOX 157	68864	NEB	John M Doolittle	(308)894-3545	WS 8 SS 915	ED/HC/MD	217	168	35
PAPILLION	*FIRST* 1st-lutheran.org	1876	332 N Washington St 420 N WASHINGTON ST	68046	NEB	Karl P Ziegler Ronald J Benson	(402)339-3668 (402)339-3693	WS 8 1030 SS 915 BC 915	EC/EL/HS/ ED/HC/ MD/SN	907	734	346
	LAMB OF GOD www.lambofgodlcms.org	2003	1414 S Washington 1414 S WASHINGTON ST	68046	NEB		(402)934-9045 (402)964-2292	WS 9 SS 1030	ED/HC/ MD/SN	60	51	30
PAWNEE CITY	*ZION* zionlcpc@gmail.com	1953	504 12th St NE 504 12TH ST	68420	NEB	Timothy J Llewellyn	(402)852-2671	WS 830	ED/HC/SN	97	82	27
PENDER	*ST JOHN* stjohnspender@gmail.com	1885	2175 15TH RD	68047	NEB	Robert G Schilling	(402)385-2447	WS 9 SS 1015 BC 8	ED/HC/ MD/SN	215	164	95
PERU	*TRINITY*		See Auburn NE									
PETERSBURG	*TRINITY*		See Elgin NE									
PIERCE	*ST JOHN'S* office@stjohnspierce.org www.stjohnspierce.org	1871	55203 854 Rd 55203 854TH RD	68767	NEB	Jacob B Tuma	(402)329-4298	WS 9 SS 1015 BC 1015	ED/HC/ MD/SN	234	183	64
	TRINITY		See Foster NE									
	ZION churchoffice@zionlutheranpierce.com zionlutheranpierce.com	1903	520 E MAIN ST	68767	NEB		(402)329-4313	WS 8 10	EL/HS/ED/ HC/MD/SN	1240	858	180
PILGER	*ST JOHN* stjohnspilger@gmail.com	1915	150 N Monroe 150 N MONROE ST	68768	NEB		(402)396-3478	WS 930	ED/HC/ MD/SN	109	87	21
PLAINVIEW	*TRINITY*		See Foster NE									
	ZION zionplvw@plvwtelco.net www.zionlutheranplainview.org	1889	102 N 6th PO BOX 159	68769	NEB		(402)582-3312 (402)582-3912	WS 8 SS 10 BC 10	EL/HS/ED/ HC/MD/SN	341	252	76

*Indicates a new church start. A new church start is an intentionally organized gathering which comes together on a regular basis for the purpose of worship and/or Bible study and is intended to grow into a member LCMS congregation. WS =Worship Service; SS = Sunday School; BC =Bible Class; EC = Early Childhood; EL = Elementary School; HS = High School; ED =Education Ministry; HC =Human Care Ministry; SN = Special Needs Ministry; MD = Media Ministry (PC)=Partner Church Pastor. See Page 53 for the Table of Abbreviations for key to additional abbreviations

CITY	CONGREGATION EMAIL WEBSITE	YEAR EST	LOCATION MAILING ADDRESS	ZIP CODE(S)	DIST.	PASTOR(S)	PHONE FAX	WS SS BC	SCHOOLS/ MINISTRIES	STATISTIC Bapt	 Conf	 Avg Attend
PLATTE CENTER	*GRACE*	1940	216 1st St PO BOX 259	68653	NEB		(402)246-2730	WS 10	ED/SN	8	8	6
	ST PETER		See Humphrey NE									
PLATTSMOUTH	*FIRST* flcplattsmouth@gmail.com flcplattsmouth.360unite.com	1940	1025 AVENUE D	68048	NEB	Ryan D Maser	(402)296-2832	WS 9 SS 9 BC 9	HS/ED/HC/ MD/SN	280	217	91
PLEASANT DALE	*BETHLEHEM*	1899	101 Maple St PO BOX 127	68423	NEB	Timothy A Gall	(402)795-3885	WS 9 SS 1015 BC 1025	ED/HC/MD	198	156	55
PLEASANTON	*GRACE* gracelutheran@frontiernet.net gracefaithlutheran.com	1955	29577 Highway 10 PO BOX 218	68866	NEB	Dean A Hanson	(308)627-6200	WS 1030 SS 1130 BC 7	ED/MD	313	275	75
PLYMOUTH	*IMMANUEL*		See Daykin NE									
POLK	*IMMANUEL*	1879	2406 E 26TH RD	68654	NEB	David D Ohlman	(402)765-7252	WS 930 SS 1045 BC 1045	EL/ED	194	146	71
PONCA	*TRINITY*		See Martinsburg NE									
POTTER	*ST PAUL* luther2@vistabeam.com	1918	4450 Rd 89 4450 ROAD 89	69156	WY		(308)879-4437 (308)879-4437	WS 8 SS 915	ED/HC/ MD/SN	80	72	27
RAVENNA	*BETHLEHEM* bethluthoffice@gmail.com www.bethlehemlutheranravenna.com	1918	324 Kufus Ave PO BOX 64	68869	NEB	Russell D Bonine	(308)452-3685 (308)452-3685	WS 9	ED/HC/ MD/SN	278	227	74
RED CLOUD	*ZION* zionrc@gpcom.net	1933	802 N FRANKLIN ST	68970	NEB	Glen D Wurdeman	(402)746-2859	WS 830 BC 930	HC	133	120	22
RISING CITY	*IMMANUEL* redeemerlc@windstream.net www.redeemerlcms-dc.com/	1883	2991 I Rd PO BOX 288 DAVID CITY	68658 68632	NEB	David W Palomaki	(402)367-4685	WS 830 SS 930 BC 930	ED	165	141	37
ROCA	*FAITH OF OUR FATHERS* foofchurch@yahoo.com www.foofchurch.org	1990	15580 E St PO BOX 57	68430	NEB	Keith H Burk	(402)421-2222	WS 9 SS 1030 BC 1030		57	49	30
ROSEMONT	*CALVARY*	1950	2013 Rosemont Rd PO BOX 397 BLUE HILL	68930	NEB		(402)756-2568	WS 10	MD	32	22	25
RUSHVILLE	*ST PAUL*	1889	419 Main St PO BOX 531	69360	WY	Allan D Wierschke	(308)327-2220	WS 9	ED/HC/ MD/SN	70	53	21
RUSKIN	*ST MARK*	1904	290 MAIN ST	68974	NEB	Jose Flores	(402)226-2391		ED/MD	41	35	16
SAINT EDWARD	*FAITH* rbketelsen@yahoo.com	1982	508 Water PO BOX 349	68660	NEB	Brian L Ketelsen	(402)678-3343	WS 830		115	92	22
SAINT LIBORY	*ZION* www.zionworms.org	1874	1653 WORMS RD	68872	NEB	Craig K Niemeier	(308)687-6314	WS 1015 SS 9 BC 9	ED/HC/MD	384	292	90
SAINT PAUL	*CHRIST* clchurch1946@outlook.com www.clcstpaulne.org	1946	1022 ELM ST	68873	NEB	John M Doolittle	(308)754-5135	WS 10 BC 9	EC/ED/HC	219	175	70
SCHUYLER	*TRINITY* trinity.schuyler@gmail.com	1933	1617 Colfax St PO BOX 126	68661	NEB	Aaron J Hannemann	(402)352-2307	WS 9	EL/HC/MD	122	112	43
SCOTIA	*ZION* contact@zionscotia.org www.zionscotia.org	1884	201 Scotia Ave PO BOX 334	68875	NEB	Mark G Middendorf	(308)245-4151	WS 1030 BC 9	ED/HC/SN	184	142	75
SCOTTSBLUFF	*SAINT JAMES*	1908	1117 E 14TH ST	69361	WY	George E Naylor	(308)632-8001	WS 11	ED/MD/SN	26	24	12
	ST JOHN stjohns.lcms@outlook.com ScottsbluffLutheran.org	1916	2220 BROADWAY	69361	WY	Jeffery W Grams	(308)635-1722	BC 1015	ED/HC/ MD/SN	226	185	86
SCRIBNER	*ST PETER* stpeter125@gpcom.net	1884	600 Baker St PO BOX 409	68057	NEB	Bruce L Schut	(402)664-3462	WS 10 SS 9 BC 9		430	345	52
SEWARD	*GOOD SHEPHERD*		See Milford NE									
	IMMANUEL	1870	1838 ALVO RD	68434	NEB	Louis E Griser	(402)795-3770	WS 9 SS 1030 BC 1045	ED/MD	74	72	30
	OUR REDEEMER		See Staplehurst NE									
	ST JOHN sjcstaff@stjohnseward.org www.stjohnseward.org	1877	919 N COLUMBIA AVE	68434	NEB	Scott D Bruick Nathan D Scheck David P Rempfer	(402)643-2983 (402)643-2985	WS 830 11 SS 10 BC 10	EL/ED/HC/ MD/SN	2823	2119	773
	THE ROCK pastor@therockseward.org www.therockseward.org		237 S 3rd St PO BOX 199	68434	NEB	Jonathan M Bartels	(402)643-6624	WS 10	EL/HS/ED/ HC/MD	323	218	163
SHELTON	*ST PAUL* revrcstephens@gmail.com	1946	705 A St PO BOX 326	68876	NEB	Don F Pobanz	(308)647-6733	WS 10 SS 1030	ED/MD	131	102	81
SHICKLEY	*ZION*	1884	402 W Murray PO BOX 135	68436	NEB	James P Moll	(402)366-5818	WS 830 BC 945	HC/SN	47	33	27
SIDNEY	*ST PAUL*	1915	1424 Maple St 1432 15TH AVE	69162	WY		(308)254-3144	WS 11 SS 1015	ED/MD/SN	221	180	47
	TRINITY	1886	12108 Rd 6 PO BOX 314	69162	WY	Neil L Carlson	(308)254-3062	WS 830 1030 SS 930	ED/HC/MD	141	109	42
SOUTH SIOUX CITY	*HOPE* angie@hopelutheranssc.com Hopelutheranssc.com	1947	218 W 18TH ST S SIOUX CITY	68776	NEB	Michael A Awe Henry F Witte	(402)494-1847 (402)494-8304	WS 930 SS 1030 BC 1030	ED/HC/ MD/SN	348	187	84
SPENCER	*CHRIST*		See Lynch NE									

*Indicates a new church start. A new church start is an intentionally organized gathering which comes together on a regular basis for the purpose of worship and/or Bible study and is intended to grow into a member LCMS congregation. WS =Worship Service; SS = Sunday School; BC =Bible Class; EC = Early Childhood; EL = Elementary School; HS = High School; ED =Education Ministry; HC =Human Care Ministry; SN = Special Needs Ministry; MD = Media Ministry (PC)=Partner Church Pastor. See Page 53 for the Table of Abbreviations for key to additional abbreviations

CITY	CONGREGATION EMAIL WEBSITE	YEAR EST	LOCATION MAILING ADDRESS	ZIP CODE(S)	DIST.	PASTOR(S)	PHONE FAX	WS SS BC	SCHOOLS/ MINISTRIES	STATISTIC Bapt	Conf	Avg Attend
SPENCER	*IMMANUEL*	1902	308 Hill Crest Blvd PO BOX 308	68777	NEB	John E Nelson Jr	(402)589-1323	WS 11 SS 10	ED/HC/ MD/SN	155	115	55
SPRINGFIELD	*OUR REDEEMER* ourredeemerspringfield@gmail.com orspfld.360unite.com	1964	305 N 3rd St PO BOX 529	68059	NEB	Kenneth N Hessel	(402)253-2893	WS 9 SS 1015 BC 1015	EL/HS/ED	31	21	21
SPRINGVIEW	*GRACE*		See Burton NE									
STANTON	*FAITH* faithlutheranstanton@gmail.com	1962	506 16th St PO BOX 685	68779	NEB		(402)439-2104	WS 8 11 SS 915 BC 915 930		242	209	28
STAPLEHURST	*OUR REDEEMER* redeemsec@clarks.net orlcne.org	1870	3743 MARYSVILLE RD	68439	NEB	Shawn L Kitzing	(402)535-2251	WS 9 SS 1030 BC 1030	EL/ED/HC/ MD	448	340	158
	OUR REDEEMER LUTHERAN SCHOOL Satellite Site of Our Redeemer Staplehurst NE	2020	425 South St	68439								
STERLING	*IMMANUEL* secretary_stjohnlutherantec@ outlook.com www.2gatherinchrist.org	1874	60798 Hwy 41 PO BOX 397	68443	NEB	Marcel L Kohlmeyer	(402)335-3816	WS 830 SS 930	ED/HC	94	74	51
SUMNER	*GRACE*	1929	407 Oak St PO BOX 112	68878	NEB	Victor J Rasmussen		WS 830 SS 930	ED/HC/MD	97	67	30
SUPERIOR	*CENTENNIAL* centennialsecretary@gmail.com	1938	855 N Dakota St PO BOX 231	68978	NEB	Jacob T Garrison	(402)879-3137	WS 1030 SS 915 BC 915	ED/MD	152	137	61
SUTHERLAND	*OUR REDEEMER*		See North Platte NE									
SWANTON	*IMMANUEL*		See Daykin NE									
TECUMSEH	*ST JOHN* secretary_stjohnlutherantec@ outlook.com www.2gatherinchrist.org	1885	1260 WEBSTER ST	68450	NEB	Marcel L Kohlmeyer	(402)335-3816	WS 10 BC 1115	ED/HC/ MD/SN	207	160	59
THEDFORD	*TRINITY*	1973	408 Locust St PO BOX 254	69166	NEB	Benjamin P Eickhoff	(308)645-2254	WS 7 SS 6	ED	20	20	10
TILDEN	*IMMANUEL* immanuel@ilctilden.com www.ilctilden.com/home	1887	500 S CENTER ST	68781	NEB	Chad U Boggs	(402)368-5690 (402)368-5690	WS 1030 SS 915 BC 930	EC/HS/ED/ HC/MD/SN	621	463	150
	ST PAUL splbuffalocreek@gmail.com www.splbuffalocreek.wix.com/saint-paul-lutheran	1892	53626 836TH RD	68781	NEB	Barry A Williams	(402)454-2823	WS 1045 SS 930 BC 930	HS/ED/HC	75	70	23
TOBIAS	*IMMANUEL*		See Daykin NE									
	ZION zionlutherantobias@gmail.com zionimmanuellutheran.org	1879	2247 Co Rd 400 2247 COUNTY ROAD 400	68453	NEB	Alexander D Bjoraker	(402)243-2353	WS 9 SS 10 BC 8	ED/HC	318	259	90
TRYON	*OUR REDEEMER*		See North Platte NE									
UTICA	*ST PAUL* church.secretary@stpaulutica.com stpaulutica.com	1899	1100 D ST	68456	NEB	Drew R Oswald Terence R Groth	(402)534-2200 (888)534-3015	WS 9 SS 1015 BC 1015	EL/ED/HC/ MD/SN	845	583	242
VALENTINE	*OUR SAVIOR* oursaviorvalentine@gmail.com www.oursaviorvalentine.org	1965	130 E 3RD ST	69201	NEB	Andrew E Utecht	(605)828-2695	WS 9 BC 1030	ED/HC/MD	225	175	80
VENANGO	*ST PAUL* stpaulcone@pctelcom.coop	1907	322 S Pennsylvania PO BOX 26	69168	RM	Kurt T Hatteberg	(970)854-4310	WS 830 BC 10	ED/HC/SN	44	36	19
	ST PAUL		See Amherst CO									
VENUS	*ST PAUL*		See Orchard NE									
VERDIGRE	*BETHLEHEM*	1947	310 Quimby Ave PO BOX 359	68783	NEB	Justin M Hildebrand	(402)668-2846	WS 7	ED/HC/ MD/SN	102	82	22
WACO	*PEACE*	1908	107 BLAINE ST	68460	NEB	Charles M Ramsey III	(402)728-5227	WS 9 SS 1030 BC 1030		31	26	22
	ST JOHN stjohnswaco@gmail.com	1872	1011 ROAD U	68460	NEB	Matthew L Mau	(402)728-5446	WS 9 SS 1030 BC 1030	EL/ED/ HC/SN	225	186	91
WAHOO	*OUR REDEEMER* ourredeemerwahoo@yahoo.com ourredeemerwahoo.org	1964	1245 N LOCUST ST	68066	NEB	Zachary A Courie	(402)443-4450	WS 1030 SS 9 BC 9	ED/HC/SN	181	142	39
WAKEFIELD	*IMMANUEL*	1882	57885 860 RD	68784	NEB	William R Bertrand	(402)375-3616	WS 930 SS 1030		80	75	20
	ST JOHN stjohnwakefieldne@gmail.com	1908	412 W 7TH ST	68784	NEB	William R Bertrand	(402)287-2385	WS 11 SS 10 BC 10	HS/ED/ MD/SN	135	127	35
WALTHILL	*TRINITY* tolzie@abbnebraska.com	1936	207 North Broughton PO BOX 252	68067	NEB	Brion P Tolzman	(402)846-5935	WS 1045 SS 945	ED/MD/SN	154	121	26
	TRINITY		See Decatur NE									
WALTON	*TRINITY* TrinityWaltonPastor@gmail.com www.trinitywalton.org	1880	5315 S 162ND ST	68461	NEB	Luke J Watt	(402)782-6515	WS 10 SS 9 BC 9	ED/HC/MD	236	133	80
WAUNETA	*REDEEMER*	1940	233 S Arapahoe PO BOX 278	69045	NEB	Keith B Wellman	(308)394-5522	WS 830	ED/HC/ MD/SN	90	90	36
	ST PAUL	1907	33851 ROAD 726	69045	NEB	Keith B Wellman	(308)394-5562	WS 10 SS 845 BC 845	HC/MD	92	86	42
WAUSA	*GOLGOTHA*	1896	87242 543rd Ave PO BOX 11	68786	NEB	Terry J Makelin	(402)586-2412	WS 8		115	99	35

*Indicates a new church start. A new church start is an intentionally organized gathering which comes together on a regular basis for the purpose of worship and/or Bible study and is intended to grow into a member LCMS congregation. WS =Worship Service; SS = Sunday School; BC =Bible Class; EC = Early Childhood; EL = Elementary School; HS = High School; ED =Education Ministry; HC =Human Care Ministry; SN = Special Needs Ministry; MD = Media Ministry (PC)=Partner Church Pastor. See Page 53 for the Table of Abbreviations for key to additional abbreviations

CITY	CONGREGATION EMAIL WEBSITE	YEAR EST	LOCATION MAILING ADDRESS	ZIP CODE(S)	DIST.	PASTOR(S)	PHONE FAX	WS SS BC	SCHOOLS/ MINISTRIES	STATISTIC Bapt	Conf	Avg Attend
WAVERLY	*PEACE* office@peacewaverly.org www.peacewaverly.org	1969	9831 N 145TH ST	68462	NEB	Neil D Wheeler	(402)786-2345 (402)786-2346	WS 8 1030 SS 915 BC 915	EC/EL/HS/ ED/HC/ MD/SN	414	301	177
WAYNE	*FIRST TRINITY* firsttrinityaltona@gmail.com	1881	57741 847TH RD	68787	NEB		(402)375-1291	WS 8 11	HS/ED/HC/ MD	91	67	15
	GRACE kwiser@gracewayne.com www.gracewayne.com	1925	904 LOGAN ST	68787	NEB	Paul S Hammes	(402)375-1905	WS 8 1030 SS 915 BC 915	EC/HS/ED/ HC/MD	765	629	164
	ST PAUL		See Carroll NE									
WEEPING WATER	*ST PAUL*	1950	607 S Randolph St PO BOX 427	68463	NEB	Paul M Warneke	(402)267-5206	WS 830	HC	72	70	15
WELLFLEET	*OUR REDEEMER*		See North Platte NE									
WEST POINT	*IMMANUEL*		See Beemer NE									
	ST PAUL stpauloffice@stpaulwp.org www.stpaulwp.org	1871	434 N LINCOLN ST	68788	NEB	John P Gierke	(402)372-2111 (402)372-2742	WS 9 SS 1015 BC 1015	EL/ED/MD	871	700	149
WESTERN	*IMMANUEL*		See Daykin NE									
WILBER	*IMMANUEL*		See Daykin NE									
WILCOX	*ST JOHN* stjohnslutheranwilcox.org	1881	104 South Stockton PO BOX 214	68982	NEB		(308)478-5466	WS 930 SS 1045 BC 1045	ED/HC/ MD/SN	206	162	90
WINSIDE	*ST PAUL* stpaulwinside@gmail.com www.stpaulwinside.com	1890	218 Miner St PO BOX 98	68790	NEB	Alexander J Blanken	(402)286-4929	WS 1030 SS 915 BC 915	HS/ED/HC/ MD/SN	276	242	53
WISNER	*ST PAUL* secretary@stpaulwisner.onmicrosoft.com stpaullutheranwisner.360unite.com	1903	509 13th St PO BOX 797	68791	NEB	Jared P Hartman	(402)529-6583	WS 1030 SS 915 BC 915	ED/HC/ MD/SN	390	320	154
	ZION-ST JOHN www.facebook.com/ZionSt JohnWisner	1969	999 6th Rd 1065 6TH RD	68791	NEB	Robert J Mayes	(402)528-7253		ED/HC/ MD/SN	147	142	32
WOOD RIVER	*GRACE* dpobanz@gmail.com	1940	1100 East St PO BOX 327	68883	NEB	Don F Pobanz	(308)583-2820	WS 830 SS 945 BC 945	ED/HC	135	109	27
WYMORE	*ST PETER* st.peterslutheranchurch@windstream.net	1936	304 S 10th St PO BOX 3	68466	NEB	Gregory L Stuckwisch	(402)645-8215	WS 1045 SS 945 BC 945	ED/MD/SN	125	89	18
YORK	*EMMANUEL* www.emmanuelyorkne.com	1903	806 Beaver 806 N BEAVER AVE	68467	NEB	Michael P Neidow Benjamin J Kaiser	(402)362-3655 (402)362-5485	WS 8 1030 SS 915 BC 915	EL/ED/HC/ MD/SN	1365	1064	298
	FAITH faithlutheranyork@gmail.com www.faithlutheranyork.com	1963	1214 N OHIO AVE	68467	NEB	Benjamin J Francisco	(402)362-3000	WS 9 SS 1030 BC 1030	EL/ED/HC/ MD/SN	335	308	185
			NEVADA									
BATTLE MOUNTAIN	*CHRIST* clc_lcms48@yahoo.com	1968	55 BASTIAN RD BATTLE MTN	89820	CNH	Jason L Iwen	(775)635-2290 (775)635-2263	WS 430 SS 330 BC 330	EC/ED			
BOULDER CITY	*CHRIST* clcinbc@gmail.com christlutheranbc.org	1951	1401 5TH ST	89005	PSW	Adam Stetson	(702)293-4332	WS 930 BC 8	EC/EL/HS/ ED/HC	83	65	50
CARSON CITY	*BETHLEHEM* lspiker@blcs.org www.blcs.org	1956	1837 MOUNTAIN ST	89703	CNH	Dr Jedidiah T Maschke	(775)882-5252 (775)882-9278	WS 915 SS 8 BC 8	EL/HS/ED/ HC/MD			
	SHEPHERD OF SIERRA office@sotsl.org sotsl.org/	1997	3680 Highway 395 South 3680 US HIGHWAY 395 SOUTH	89705	CNH	James S Cleland	(775)267-3680	WS 930	HS/ED/HC/ MD/SN			
DAYTON	*RIVER OF LIFE* waabbott@sbcglobal.net	2001	801 Overland Loop Suite 401 PO BOX 221	89403	CNH		(310)344-3439	WS 1030 BC 930	ED/HC/SN			
ELKO	*ST MARK* stmarkelko@gmail.com stmarkelko.com	1958	277 WILLOW ST	89801	CNH	Jacob W Eisinger	(775)738-5436	WS 9 SS 1030 BC 1030	EC/ED	134	106	65
FALLON	*ST JOHN* office@stjohnsfallon.org www.stjohnsfallon.org	1946	1170 S TAYLOR ST	89406	CNH	Chad A Biar	(775)423-4146 (775)423-6596	WS 10 BC 830	EC/ED/HC/ MD/SN	89	81	49
GARDNERVILLE	*TRINITY* communications@trinitygv.com trinitygv.com	1895	1480 DOUGLAS AVE	89410	CNH	Jonathan R Zoch	(775)782-8153 (775)782-8154	WS 8 1045 SS 930 BC 930	EC/HS/ED/ MD			
HAWTHORNE	*BETHANY* bethanylutheran89415@gmail.com	1944	204 C St PO BOX 1207	89415	CNH		(775)312-1953	WS 1030 SS 915		24	16	20
HENDERSON	*GRACE* gracelutheranchurchnv@gmail.com www.gracelutheranhenderson.org	2001	2657 W Horizon Ridge Pkwy 2657 W HORIZON RIDGE PKWY STE 120	89052	PSW	Anthony J DiLiberto	(702)492-4701	WS 8 1045 SS 930 BC 930	EL/HS/ ED/HC	419	322	181
	OUR SAVIOR	1952	59 Lynn Ln PO BOX 91449	89015 89009	PSW	Edward V Bruning Jr	(702)565-9154 (702)565-6246	WS 9 1030 1045 SS 9	EL/HS/ED/ HC/MD/SN			
LAS VEGAS	*FAITH COMMUNITY* churchoffice@faithlasvegas.org www.faithlasvegas.org	1998	3505 S TOWN CENTER DR	89135	PSW	Craig A Michaelson Brandon D Larson	(702)921-2700	WS 8 930 11 SS 9 1030	EC/EL/HS/ ED/HC/ MD/SN	1903	1803	814

*Indicates a new church start. A new church start is an intentionally organized gathering which comes together on a regular basis for the purpose of worship and/or Bible study and is intended to grow into a member LCMS congregation. WS =Worship Service; SS = Sunday School; BC =Bible Class; EC = Early Childhood; EL = Elementary School; HS = High School; ED =Education Ministry; HC =Human Care Ministry; SN = Special Needs Ministry; MD = Media Ministry (PC)=Partner Church Pastor. See Page 53 for the Table of Abbreviations for key to additional abbreviations

CITY	CONGREGATION EMAIL WEBSITE	YEAR EST	LOCATION MAILING ADDRESS	ZIP CODE(S)	DIST.	PASTOR(S)	PHONE FAX	WS SS BC	SCHOOLS/ MINISTRIES	STATISTIC Bapt	Conf	Avg Attend
LAS VEGAS	*FIRST GOOD SHEP* fgschurchoffice@fgslc.org www.fgslc.org	1940	301 S MARYLAND PKWY	89101	PSW	Bradley P Beckman	(702)384-6106	WS 1030 BC 9	EL/HS/ED/ HC/MD	167	167	115
	LAMB OF GOD churchinfo@lambofgodlv.com www.lambofgodlv.org	1992	6220 N JONES BLVD	89130	PSW	Jared C Townley	(702)645-4998 (702)645-7605	WS 8 1045 SS 930 BC 930	EL/HS/ED/ HC/MD/SN	378	280	200
	MOUNTAIN VIEW churchoffice@mvlcs.org www.mvlcs.org	1957	9550 W CHEYENNE AVE	89129	PSW	Derek S Klemm Bradley M Wellik	(702)360-8290 (702)360-2099	WS 8 1030 SS 930 BC 930	EL/HS/ED/ HC/MD	416	361	216
	OROMO churchoffice@faithlasvegas.org	2017	2700 S TOWN CENTER DR	89135	PSW		(702)921-2700		ED/HC			
	REDEEMER sue@redeemerlasvegas.com www.redeemerlasvegas.com	1962	1730 N PECOS RD	89115	PSW		(702)642-7744 (702)642-7744	WS 9 SS 1015 BC 1015	EC/EL/HS/ ED/HC	64	46	40
LAUGHLIN	*LIVING CHRIST LUTHERAN CHURCH* Satellite Site of St John Bullhead City AZ	2015	1650 Casino Dr	89028								
LOGANDALE	*MESQUITE*		See Mesquite NV									
MESQUITE	*MESQUITE* pastor@mesquitelutheran.org www.mesquitelutheran.org	1998	450 TURTLEBACK RD	89027	PSW	David P Constien	(702)346-5811 (702)346-4367	WS 10 BC 830	EC/ED	148	141	90
	PRINCE OF PEACE princeofpeace@rconnects.com princeofpeacelutheranchurch mesquitenv.org/		350 Falcon Ridge Pkwy Bldg 600 350 FALCON RIDGE PKWY STE 600	89027	EN	Robert Q Bruggeman	(702)345-2160	WS 1015 BC 9	ED/HC/ MD/SN	68	67	58
OVERTON	*MESQUITE*		See Mesquite NV									
PAHRUMP	*SHEP/VALLEY*	1984	650 South Blagg Rd PO BOX 2435	89048 89041	PSW	Andrew C Safarik	(775)727-4098	WS 745 930 SS 930 BC 1040	HC/MD/SN	89	83	85
RENO	*OUR SAVIOR*		See Sparks NV									
	ST LUKES admin@stlukesreno.org www.stlukesreno.org	1902	3835 Lakeside Dr		CNH		(775)825-0588	WS 830 1015 SS 845 BC 9 530	HS/ED/HC/ MD/SN			
ROUND MOUNTAIN	*GRACE**		95 A Hadley Cir PO BOX 1949	89045	CNH							
SPARKS	*OUR SAVIOR* office-oslc-sparks@att.net www.oslcsparks.org	1956	1900 1ST ST	89431	CNH		(775)358-0743 (775)358-8015	WS 10 SS 9 BC 9	ED/HC/MD			
SUMMERLIN	*FAITH COMMUNITY*		See Las Vegas NV									
WELLS	*ST MARK*		See Elko NV									
WINNEMUCCA	*ZION* churchoffice@zionwinnemucca.org www.zionwinnemucca.org	1960	3205 Highland Dr 3205 N HIGHLAND DR	89445	CNH	Jason L Iwen	(775)623-3796	WS 1030 SS 915	EC/ED/HC			
YERINGTON	*FAITH* faithlutheranyerington@gmail.com www.faithyerington.info	1962	12 N. WEST ST. 12 N WEST ST	89447	CNH	Steven B Tomac	(775)463-5675	WS 9	ED/HC/ MD/SN	55	36	40

NEW HAMPSHIRE

CITY	CONGREGATION EMAIL WEBSITE	YEAR EST	LOCATION MAILING ADDRESS	ZIP CODE(S)	DIST.	PASTOR(S)	PHONE FAX	WS SS BC	SCHOOLS/ MINISTRIES	Bapt	Conf	Avg Attend
KEENE	*CHRIST*		See Troy NH									
	TRINITY tlckeene.nh@gmail.com www.tlckeene.org	1952	100 MAPLE AVE	03431	NE	Edwin T Harkey	(603)352-4446 (603)358-3405	WS 1030 SS 9 BC 9	EL/ED/HC/ MD/SN	184	166	88
MANCHESTER	*IMMANUEL* secretary@immanuel-mnh.org www.immanuel-mnh.org	1895	673 WESTON RD	03103	NE	Donald L Colageo	(603)622-1514 (603)622-5203	WS 10 BC 9	ED/HC/ MD/SN	174	167	105
MOULTONBOROUGH	*LAKES REGION LUTHERAN CHURCH* Satellite Site of Grace Nashua NH	2023	1070 Whittier Hwy. (Rt. 25) Unit 1	03254				WS 930				
NASHUA	*GRACE* churchsecretary@grace lutherannashua.org www.gracelutherannashua.org	1961	130 SPIT BROOK RD	03062	NE	George A Ruwisch V Lesley W Chen	(603)888-7579	WS 815 1045 SS 930 BC 930	ED/HC/ MD/SN	419	331	229
NEW IPSWICH	*OUR REDEEMER* orlcnh@comcast.net ourredeemerNH.org	1960	200 ASHBY RD	03071	NE	Dagan W Siepert	(603)878-1837 (603)878-0891	WS 9 10 SS 9	EC/ED/HC	46	42	34
PETERBOROUGH	*GOOD SHEPHERD* goodshepherdnh@gmail.com goodshepherdnh.wordpress.com	1985	280 Dublin Rd 280 DUBLIN RD PO BOX 37	03458	NE	David L Mueller	(603)924-4019	WS 10 BC 9	MD	49	36	18
TROY	*CHRIST* office@clctroy.org www.clctroy.org	1912	4 Fitzwilliam Rd PO BOX 189	03465	NE		(603)242-7283	WS 10	MD	87	83	33

NEW JERSEY

CITY	CONGREGATION EMAIL WEBSITE	YEAR EST	LOCATION MAILING ADDRESS	ZIP CODE(S)	DIST.	PASTOR(S)	PHONE FAX	WS SS BC	SCHOOLS/ MINISTRIES	Bapt	Conf	Avg Attend
ABSECON	*PEACE*		See Galloway NJ									
BASKING RIDGE	*SOMERSET HILLS* shlc@shlc.net www.shlc.net	1958	350 LAKE RD	07920	NJ	Jose D Fenco	(908)766-2858 (908)766-6546	WS 930 SS 945 BC 1045	EC/ED/ HC/SN	163	122	57

*Indicates a new church start. A new church start is an intentionally organized gathering which comes together on a regular basis for the purpose of worship and/or Bible study and is intended to grow into a member LCMS congregation. WS =Worship Service; SS = Sunday School; BC =Bible Class; EC = Early Childhood; EL = Elementary School; HS = High School; ED =Education Ministry; HC =Human Care Ministry; SN = Special Needs Ministry; MD = Media Ministry (PC)=Partner Church Pastor. See Page 53 for the Table of Abbreviations for key to additional abbreviations

CITY	CONGREGATION EMAIL WEBSITE	YEAR EST	LOCATION MAILING ADDRESS	ZIP CODE(S)	DIST.	PASTOR(S)	PHONE FAX	WS SS BC	SCHOOLS/ MINISTRIES	STATISTIC Bapt	Conf	Avg Attend
BLACKWOOD	*LUTHER MEMORIAL* ebmallepalle@yahoo.com www.lmlchurch.net	1959	401 Erial Rd PO BOX 186	08012	NJ	Ebenezer C Mallepalle	(856)227-2209	WS 9 SS 1015 BC 1015	ED	124	73	51
BLAIRSTOWN	*GOOD SHEPHERD* lcgsoffice@gmail.com www.lcotgs.com	1977	168 STATE ROUTE 94	07825	NJ	Jason T Kiefer	(908)362-9405 (908)362-9405	WS 1030 SS 1030	EC/ED/MD	67	54	25
BLOOMFIELD	*ST JOHN* stjohnsecy@gmail.com www.saintjohnsbloomfield.org	1896	216 LIBERTY ST	07003	NJ		(973)429-8654	WS 830	ED/HC/MD	73	59	18
BORDENTOWN TOWNSHIP	*HOLY CROSS* info@hclconline.org www.hclc.life	1959	280 CROSSWICKS RD BOR-DENTOWN	08505	NJ		(609)298-2880 (609)298-1411	WS 10	EC/ED/HC/MD	379	298	32
BOUND BROOK	*ST JOHN* stjohnboundbrook@gmail.com www.sjlcbb.org	1916	108 W Union Ave 319 WINSOR ST	08805	S		(732)356-4850	WS 1115 SS 10 BC 10	MD	36	31	12
BRIDGETON	*ST JOHN* secretarystjohnluth@verizon.net www.stjohnsbridgeton.com	1858	61 Oak St 59 OAK ST	08302	NJ		(856)451-0141	WS 1015 BC 9	ED/HC/MD			
CARNEYS POINT	*TRINITY* trinitylutheranchurchcp@gmail.com	1939	320 GEORGETOWN RD	08069	NJ		(856)299-4304 (856)299-4304	WS 1030 SS 915 BC 915	ED	20	13	21
CLARK	*REDEEMER*		See Westfield NJ									
	ZION zionclarknj@gmail.com www.zionlutheranclark.org	1928	559 RARITAN RD	07066	S	Allen S Dass	(732)382-7320	WS 1030 SS 915 BC 915	EC/ED/HC/MD/SN	226	155	77
CLIFFSIDE PARK	*TRINITY* trinitycp@outlook.com	1900	238 Columbia Ave PO BOX 1936 CLIFFSIDE PK	07010	NJ	John H Schroter	(201)943-0088	WS 11	ED/SN			
CLIFTON	*ST JOHN'S* prayinghands810@gmail.com www.stjohnsclifton.org	1886	810 BROAD ST	07013	NJ		(973)778-1412	WS 9 BC 1015		40	40	30
CLINTON	*ST PAUL*		See Flemington NJ									
CLOSTER	*ST PAUL'S* stpaulscloster@gmail.com saintpaulsofcloster.com	1887	171 CLOSTER DOCK RD	07624	NJ		(201)768-6310 (201)768-6444	WS 830 10 BC 830	ED/HC/MD/SN	164	164	23
EAST BRUNSWICK	*CHRIST MEMORIAL* christmemorial@verizon.net www.cmlceb.org	1956	114 OLD STAGE RD E BRUNS-WICK	08816	NJ	Luke D Elowsky	(732)251-5454 (732)723-9026	WS 8 1030 SS 915 BC 915	EC/ED/HC/MD	144	100	81
EAST RUTHERFORD	*IMMANUEL* immanuellutheranchurch@yahoo.com www.immanuellutheranchurch eastrutherford.com	1908	78 WASHINGTON PL E RUTHERFORD	07073	NJ	Timothy A Casaday	(201)939-2386	WS 930	ED/MD/SN	8	8	8
EWING	*BETHANY* www.bethanyewing.org	1934	1125 PARKSIDE AVE	08618	EN		(609)883-2860 (609)883-8075	WS 9 SS 1030	ED/HC/MD/SN			
FAIR LAWN	*OUR SAVIOR* churchoffice@oursaviornj.org www.oursaviornj.org	1941	22-15 BROADWAY	07410	NJ	Deric A Taylor	(201)796-3007 (201)796-7949	WS 815 1045 SS 930 BC 930	EC/ED/HC/MD/SN	364	310	82
FLEMINGTON	*ST PAUL* info@stpaulnj.com www.stpaulnj.com	1955	201 STATE ROUTE 31	08822	NJ	Robert B Mueller	(908)782-5120 (908)782-1633	WS 8 10 SS 10 BC 10	EC/ED/HC/MD/SN	760	689	272
FORDS	*OUR REDEEMER* pastorsadlo@yahoo.com www.ourredeemer-fords.com	1921	28 S 4TH ST	08863	NJ	Christopher N Sadlo	(732)738-7470 (732)738-6547	WS 930 SS 930 BC 830	ED/MD	455	329	42
FRANKLIN	*PRINCE PEACE*		See Hamburg NJ									
FRANKLIN PARK	*HOLY TRINITY*		See Somerset NJ									
FRENCHTOWN	*ST PAUL*		See Flemington NJ									
GALLOWAY	*PEACE* PeaceChurchWeb@gmail.com	1992	328 E Great Creek Rd 328 GREAT CREEK RD	08205	S		(609)748-1777 (609)748-1005	WS 10 SS 930	EC/ED/HC/MD	65	53	20
GARFIELD	*HOLY TRINITY* htlcnj@gmail.com	1892	100 SPRING ST	07026	S		(973)478-7434	WS 1130 SS 1230	ED/HC/MD/SN	68	63	35
HACKETTSTOWN	*GETHSEMANE* gethsemanehtown@gmail.com www.glc.church	1957	409 E BALDWIN ST	07840	NJ	Timothy G Drawbaugh	(908)852-2156 (908)852-8556	WS 1030 SS 915 BC 915	EC/ED/HC/MD/SN	226	205	56
HAMBURG	*PRINCE PEACE* poplc.hamburg@gmail.com www.poplc-hamburg.org	1963	3320 STATE RT 94	07419	NJ	John J Babbitts	(973)827-5080 (973)827-5163	WS 930 SS 1030 BC 1030	ED/HC/MD	99	99	35
HARDYSTON	*PRINCE PEACE*		See Hamburg NJ									
HILLSBOROUGH	*HOLY TRINITY*		See Somerset NJ									
HOPEWELL	*ST PETER*		See Hopewell Township NJ									
HOPEWELL TOWNSHIP	*ST PETER* secretary@stpeternj.org stpeternj.org	1962	1608 HARBOURTON ROCK-TOWN RD LAMBERTVILLE	08530	NJ	Jon M Dunbar	(609)466-0939	SS 815 BC 815	EC/ED/HC/MD	221	202	57
HOWELL	*PRINCE PEACE* popchurch@optonline.net www.princeofpeacehowellnj.org	1960	434 ALDRICH RD	07731	NJ		(732)363-0732 (732)534-7744	WS 8 1015 SS 9	ED/HC/MD/SN	200	180	65
JERSEY CITY	*TUMANIN KRISTO*		68 Martin Luther King Dr C/O HARON ORUTWA 582 WESTSIDE AVE	07305 07304	NJ				ED/HC/SN			

*Indicates a new church start. A new church start is an intentionally organized gathering which comes together on a regular basis for the purpose of worship and/or Bible study and is intended to grow into a member LCMS congregation. WS =Worship Service; SS = Sunday School; BC =Bible Class; EC = Early Childhood; EL = Elementary School; HS = High School; ED =Education Ministry; HC =Human Care Ministry; SN = Special Needs Ministry; MD = Media Ministry (PC)=Partner Church Pastor. See Page 53 for the Table of Abbreviations for key to additional abbreviations

CITY	CONGREGATION EMAIL WEBSITE	YEAR EST	LOCATION MAILING ADDRESS	ZIP CODE(S)	DIST.	PASTOR(S)	PHONE FAX	WS SS BC	SCHOOLS/ MINISTRIES	STATISTIC Bapt	Conf	Avg Attend
LANOKA HARBOR	*VILLAGE* joelle@villagelutheranchurch.net www.villagelutheranchurch.net	1972	701 WESTERN BLVD	08734	NJ	Matthew C Hass	(609)693-1333 (609)693-6975	WS 9 11 SS 10 BC 1015	EC/ED/HC/ MD/SN	285	285	150
LAWRENCE	*HOLY TRINITY*		See Lawrenceville NJ									
LAWRENCEVILLE	*HOLY TRINITY* htlc_nj@comcast.net www.htlc-nj.org	1911	2730 PRINCETON PIKE	08648	NJ		(609)882-7891	WS 930 SS 1045 BC 1045		35	35	18
LITTLE FALLS	*ST JOHN'S*		See Clifton NJ									
LIVINGSTON	*GRACE* rvossler@minister.com GraceLutheranLivingstonNJ.org	1946	290 W HOBART GAP RD	07039	NJ	Dr Lawrence R Vossler Jr	(973)992-0145	WS 1015 SS 9 BC 9		56	50	25
LYNDHURST	*ST MATTHEW* www.stmatthewselc-lcms.org	1913	295 TRAVERS PL	09071	NJ		(201)939-2134	WS 11		23	23	15
MANALAPAN	*ST THOMAS* STLC.Manalapan@gmail.com	1967	203 Taylors Mill Rd 203 TAYLORS MILLS RD	07726	NJ	Peter Wee	(732)252-9550	WS 1030 SS 930 BC 1130	HC	26	26	12
MANCHESTER	*REDEEMER* redeemermanchester@gmail.com www.redeemermanchester.org	1986	2309 Highway 70 E 2309 ROUTE 70	08759	S	Daniel C Berteau	(732)657-2828	WS 1015 SS 9 BC 9	EC/ED/HC/ MD/SN	220	178	106
MANCHESTER TOWNSHIP	*REDEEMER*		See Manchester NJ									
MAYWOOD	*ZION* zionmaywood@verizon.net zionmaywood.com	1899	120 E PLEASANT AVE	07607	NJ		(201)843-5916 (201)843-4109	WS 930 SS 1045 BC 1045	ED/HC/SN	48	41	18
MEDFORD	*CALVARY* office@calvary-medford.org calvary-Medford.org	1958	3 EAYRESTOWN RD	08055	NJ	David C Small	(609)654-2489	WS 10 SS 9 BC 9	ED/HC/ MD/SN	63	60	48
MIDDLESEX	*HOLY TRINITY*		See Somerset NJ									
MILFORD	*ST PAUL*		See Flemington NJ									
MONTVILLE	*HOLY SPIRIT* pastormike.holyspirit@gmail.com holyspiritmontville.org	1962	70 RIVER RD	07045	NJ	Michael P Dunne	(973)263-1696	WS 11 SS 9 BC 10	SN	26	23	15
MORRIS PLAINS	*TRINITY* tlcmorrisplains@gmail.com www.tlcmp.com	1947	131 MOUNTAIN WAY	07950	NJ	David J Russert	(973)538-7606 (973)538-6763	WS 10 SS 9	ED/HC/MD			
MOUNTAIN LAKES	*KING OF KINGS* admin@kofkluther.com www.kingofkingslutheranchurchnnj.org	1955	145 Route 46 145 US HIGHWAY 46 MOUNTAIN LKS	07046	NJ	Steven R Vera	(973)334-8333 (973)334-6726	WS 9 SS 1015 BC 1015	EC/ED/HC/ MD/SN	173	158	82
MULLICA HILL	*TRINITY*		See Carneys Point NJ									
NEW BRUNSWICK	*HOLY TRINITY*		See Somerset NJ									
NEW MILFORD	*ST MATTHEW* stmatthewsnj@gmail.com www.smlcnewmilford.org	1895	225 Center St PO BOX 339	07646	NJ	Anthony J Iovine	(201)262-5092	SS 845	ED/HC/ MD/SN	75	65	20
NEWARK	*CHRIST ASSEMBLY*	1999	664 BROADWAY	07104	NJ	Borbor A Zolue	(973)485-7096 (973)485-4819	WS 9 1030				
NEWTON	*REDEEMER* redeemersec37@gmail.com redeemernewton.net	1954	37 NEWTON SPARTA RD	07860	NJ	Brian W Handrich	(973)383-3945 (973)383-3954	WS 9 11	EC/ED/HC/ MD	72	68	38
NORTH BRUNSWICK	*HOLY TRINITY*		See Somerset NJ									
NUTLEY	*ST JOHN'S*		See Clifton NJ									
OAK RIDGE	*HOLY FAITH* holyfaith@verizon.net www.holyfaith.org	1960	104 PARADISE RD	07438	NJ	Craig E Lutz	(973)697-6060 (973)697-4231	SS 10 BC 7	ED/HC/ MD/SN	388	287	77
OLD BRIDGE	*GOOD SHEPHERD* office@gs4nj.org gs4nj.org	1961	3139 County Road 516 3139 HIGHWAY 516	08857	NJ	Garrett L Knudson Jeffrey Campbell	(732)679-8883 (732)679-8996	WS 10 SS 9	EC/ED/ MD/SN	401	352	85
PALISADES PARK	*GRACE* graceevlutheran@yahoo.com www.graceevlutheran.blogspot.com	1919	9 E HOMESTEAD AVE PALI-SADES PK	07650	EN	Peter A Bauernfeind	(201)944-2107 (201)592-0254	WS 11	ED/HC/MD			
	KOREAN CHO WON njklchurch@gmail.com palparkchurch.org		9 E HOMESTEAD AVE PALI-SADES PK	07650	EN	Philip Sang S Rey	(201)852-3600 (844)777-0010					
PASSAIC	*ST JOHN'S*		See Clifton NJ									
PATERSON	*ST JOHN'S*		See Clifton NJ									
PENNINGTON	*ST PETER*		See Hopewell Township NJ									
PENNSAUKEN	*MARTIN LUTHER* mlcemail2019@gmail.com www.mlchapel.org	1932	4100 TERRACE AVE	08109	EN	Daniel L Gray	(856)665-0116 (856)665-5312	WS 10 BC 9	ED/HC/MD	211	173	80
PENNSGROVE	*TRINITY*		See Carneys Point NJ									
PENNSVILLE	*TRINITY*		See Carneys Point NJ									
PHILLIPSBURG	*ST PAUL*		See Flemington NJ									
PISCATAWAY	*HOLY TRINITY*		See Somerset NJ									
POINT PLEASANT	*GOOD SHEPHERD* gsppnj@gmail.com www.gsppnj.org	1951	708 Ocean Rd 708 ROUTE 88 PT PLEASANT	08742	NJ	Andrew C Wolfgram	(732)892-4492 (732)899-3605	WS 10 SS 930 BC 9	ED/HC/ MD/SN	125	87	36
POMPTON LAKES	*ST PAUL INCARNATION* pastormike.holyspirit@gmail.com	1948	220 HAMBURG TPKE	07442	NJ	Michael P Dunne	(973)835-5537	WS 930		44	37	17
PRINCETON	*MESSIAH* lcmprinceton@gmail.com www.princetonlutheranchurch.org	1947	407 Nassau St 407 NASSAU ST STE 1	08540	EN	Dr Martin K Erhardt	(609)924-3642	WS 1030 SS 9 BC 9	ED	55	48	40

*Indicates a new church start. A new church start is an intentionally organized gathering which comes together on a regular basis for the purpose of worship and/or Bible study and is intended to grow into a member LCMS congregation. WS =Worship Service; SS = Sunday School; BC =Bible Class; EC = Early Childhood; EL = Elementary School; HS = High School; ED =Education Ministry; HC =Human Care Ministry; SN = Special Needs Ministry; MD = Media Ministry (PC)=Partner Church Pastor. See Page 53 for the Table of Abbreviations for key to additional abbreviations

CITY	CONGREGATION EMAIL WEBSITE	YEAR EST	LOCATION MAILING ADDRESS	ZIP CODE(S)	DIST.	PASTOR(S)	PHONE FAX	WS SS BC	SCHOOLS/ MINISTRIES	STATISTIC Bapt	Conf	Avg Attend
RANDOLPH	*GOOD SHEPHERD* gsrandolphnj@gmail.com www.randolphlutheran.org	1914	319 QUAKER CHURCH RD	07869	NJ	Adam E Carnehl	(973)366-4267	WS 10 SS 9 BC 9	ED/HC/MD	90	65	50
RARITAN	*CAMINO DE FE*		See Somerville NJ									
	ST PAUL stpaulraritan@gmail.com www.stpaulraritan.org	1894	15 W SOMERSET ST	08869	S		(908)722-6111 (908)722-6114	WS 930				
RIDGEWOOD	*BETHLEHEM* office@blcmail.org www.bethlehemchurch.live/	1905	155 LINWOOD AVE	07450	NJ	Peter T De Mik	(201)444-3600 (201)444-2549	WS 9 SS 930	EC/ED/HC/ MD/SN	489	346	95
RINGOES	*ST PETER*		See Hopewell Township NJ									
RINGWOOD	*CHRIST KING* ctkringwood@optimum.net www.ctk-ringwood.org	1962	50 ERSKINE RD	07456	NJ	Jonathan E Hodges	(973)962-6384 (973)962-6581	WS 1030 SS 915 BC 915	EC/ED/HC/ MD/SN	143	117	55
SALEM	*TRINITY*		See Carneys Point NJ									
SMITHVILLE	*PEACE*		See Galloway NJ									
SOMERSET	*HOLY TRINITY* pastor@htlsomerset.org www.htlsomerset.org	1961	1640 AMWELL RD	08873	NJ	Gregory D Jans	(732)873-2888	WS 10 SS 1130 BC 1130	ED/HC/ MD/SN	95	77	38
SOMERVILLE	*CAMINO DE FE* pastordan@caminodefe.church caminodefe.church/		64 MERCER ST	08876	NJ	Jose D Fenco	(908)922-7491		HC			
STANHOPE	*OUR SAVIOR* oursavior.stanhope@gmail.com oursaviorstanhope.org	1959	143 BROOKLYN RD	07874	NJ		(973)347-1212 (973)347-5060	WS 1045 SS 9		83	79	48
SWEDESBORO	*TRINITY*		See Carneys Point NJ									
TINTON FALLS	*LUTHER MEMORIAL* officelmc818@gmail.com lmcnj.org	1960	818 TINTON AVE	07724	NJ		(732)542-2727 (732)542-6087	WS 9 11 SS 10 BC 10	EC/ED/HC/ MD/SN	200	155	74
TITUSVILLE	*ST PETER*		See Hopewell Township NJ									
TOTOWA	*ST JOHN'S*		See Clifton NJ									
TRENTON	*BETHANY*		See Ewing NJ									
UNION	*REDEEMER*		See Westfield NJ									
UPPER MONTCLAIR	*ST JOHN'S*		See Clifton NJ									
VERONA	*CALVARY* calvaryverona@verizon.net veronalutheran.com	1928	23 S PROSPECT ST	07044	NJ	Anthony J Giordano	(973)239-0577 (973)239-6719	WS 1030 SS 830	ED/HC/ MD/SN	78	78	35
WAYNE	*ST PAUL INCARNATION*		See Pompton Lakes NJ									
WESTFIELD	*REDEEMER* rlc@redeemerwestfield.com www.redeemerwestfield.com	1930	229 COWPERTHWAITE PL	07090	NJ		(908)232-1517	WS 10 SS 10 BC 9	HC/MD	268	210	58
WESTWOOD	*ZION* office@zionwestwoodnj.org zionwestwoodnj.org	1905	155 2ND AVE	07675	NJ	Thomas J Pranschke William H Schmidt Sr	(201)664-1325 (201)664-4393	WS 8 1015 SS 1015 BC 915	EC/ED/HC/ MD/SN	440	375	124
WOODLAND PARK	*ST JOHN'S*		See Clifton NJ									

NEW MEXICO

CITY	CONGREGATION EMAIL WEBSITE	YEAR EST	LOCATION MAILING ADDRESS	ZIP CODE(S)	DIST.	PASTOR(S)	PHONE FAX	WS SS BC	SCHOOLS/ MINISTRIES	STATISTIC Bapt	Conf	Avg Attend
ALAMOGORDO	*TRINITY* tlchurchlcms@yahoo.com trinityalamogordo.org	1952	1505 COLLEGE AVE	88310	RM		(575)437-1482 (575)437-1482	WS 1015 SS 9 BC 9	ED/HC/ MD/SN	125	106	69
ALBUQUERQUE	*CALVARY*		See Rio Rancho NM									
	CHRIST admin@christabq.org christabq.org	1960	7701 CANDELARIA RD NE	87110	RM	Eric W Robinson	(505)884-3876 (505)888-0655	WS 815 11 SS 945 BC 945	EL/ED/HC/ MD	293	189	145
	CHRIST OUR REDEEMER admin@rlchurch.org www.faithinchristlutheran.org	1978	1750 Faith Court NE 1750 FAITH CT NE	87112	RM	William B Wilder	(505)256-9881	WS 1015 SS 1030 BC 1045	ED/MD			
	GRACE officesecretary@comcast.net www.gracelutheran-nm.org	1985	7550 EUBANK BLVD NE	87122	RM	Aaron M Richert	(505)823-9100 (505)823-1681	WS 9 SS 1030	EC/ED/MD	277	237	105
	IMMANUEL churchoffice@ilcabq.org www.ilcabq.org	1914	300 GOLD AVE SE	87102	RM	Dustin K Kear	(505)242-0616	WS 815 1045 SS 930 BC 930	EL/ED/HC/ MD/SN			
	OUR SAVIOR oslcabq@gmail.com oslcnm.com	1961	4301 ATRISCO DR NW	87120	RM		(505)836-7007	WS 9 SS 915 BC 1015	ED/HC	32	32	30
	PRINCE OF PEACE		See Cedar Crest NM									
	SAINT ANDREW alanarnoldnm@gmail.com www.saintandrewlutheran.church/	2019	6230 Isleta Blvd SW PO BOX 19245	87105 87119	RM		(505)514-3736	WS 930 3		17	15	12
ANGEL FIRE	*CHRIST OUR SAVIOR* christoursavioraf@gmail.com www.angelfirelutheranchurch.org	1982	13 Elliott Barker Ln PO BOX 102	87710	RM	Benjamin R Davis	(575)377-2814	WS 11	ED/HC/MD	18	8	15
BELEN	*BELEN MEADOWS NURSING HOME* Satellite Site of Christ/King Los Lunas NM	1999	1831 Camino Del Llano	87002								
CARLSBAD	*IMMANUEL* immanuel.carlsbad@gmail.com immanueleddycolcms.com	1936	901 N HALAGUENO ST	88220	RM	Karl F Wright	(575)885-5780	WS 1030 SS 930 BC 930	ED/HC/ MD/SN			

*Indicates a new church start. A new church start is an intentionally organized gathering which comes together on a regular basis for the purpose of worship and/or Bible study and is intended to grow into a member LCMS congregation. WS =Worship Service; SS = Sunday School; BC =Bible Class; EC = Early Childhood; EL = Elementary School; HS = High School; ED =Education Ministry; HC =Human Care Ministry; SN = Special Needs Ministry; MD = Media Ministry (PC)=Partner Church Pastor. See Page 53 for the Table of Abbreviations for key to additional abbreviations

CITY	CONGREGATION EMAIL WEBSITE	YEAR EST	LOCATION MAILING ADDRESS	ZIP CODE(S)	DIST.	PASTOR(S)	PHONE FAX	WS SS BC	SCHOOLS/ MINISTRIES	STATISTIC Bapt	Conf	Avg Attend
CEDAR CREST	*PRINCE OF PEACE* poplcmsnm@gmail.com pop14.com	1984	12121 HWY N 14	87008	RM	Michael O Feuer Doyle W Boykin	(505)596-6142	WS 9 SS 1030	ED/HC/ MD/SN	60	51	43
CHAPARRAL	*ZION*		See El Paso TX									
CLOVIS	*IMMANUEL* ilcsecretaryclovis@gmail.com www.immanuellutheranclovisnm.org	1941	1021 N PRINCE ST	88101	RM	Thomas N Reeder Jr	(575)763-4526	WS 1030 SS 915 BC 915	EC/ED/HC/ MD/SN	52	51	34
CORRALES	*CALVARY*		See Rio Rancho NM									
DEMING	*REDEEMER* redeemerlutherandeming@hotmail.com	1960	600 W FLORIDA ST	88030	RM		(575)546-3348	WS 1030 BC 930	ED/MD/SN			
EAGLE NEST	*CHRIST OUR SAVIOR*		See Angel Fire NM									
EDGEWOOD	*GOOD SHEPHERD* office@gslcnm.org www.gslcnm.org	1988	#5 Entrada Del Norte PO BOX 1298	87015	RM		(505)281-2013 (505)281-2013	WS 9 SS 1030 BC 1030	HC/MD/SN	127	98	66
FARMINGTON	*ZION* zionfarmington@gmail.com zionfarmingtonlcms.org	1953	7455 FOOTHILLS DR	87402	RM	Nathanael R Biberdorf	(505)325-3420 (866)453-4474	WS 8 1015 BC 9	ED/HC/ MD/SN	75	70	52
GALLUP	*TRINITY* tlcgallup@gmail.com	1956	1100 E Mesa Ave PO BOX 2860	87301 87305	RM		(505)863-3375	WS 10 SS 845	ED/HC			
HOBBS	*GRACE* www.gracelutheranhobbs.org/	1948	100 E BERRY DR	88240	RM	Thaine L Kister	(575)393-4911	WS 1030 SS 930 BC 930	ED/HC	45	40	22
LAS CRUCES	*MISSION* secretary@missionlutheran.net missionlutheran.net	1988	2752 N ROADRUNNER PKWY	88011	RM	Andrew L Cave	(575)522-0465	WS 9 SS 1030 BC 1030	EL/ED/HC/ MD/SN	165	141	85
LAS VEGAS	*IMMANUEL* ken@krusemarks.com	1921	2100 7TH ST	87701	RM	Solomona J Rakotonirina	(505)652-2562	WS 10 BC 10		26	26	18
LOS ALAMOS	*REDEEMER* pastornieminen@gmail.com www.redeemerlosalamos.org	2008	2000 DIAMOND DR	87544	RM	Johannes Nieminen	(505)662-0782	WS 930 SS 11 BC 11	ED/MD	43	39	33
LOS LUNAS	*CHRIST/KING* www.christthekingnm.org	1978	700 Camelot Blvd SW PO BOX 907	87031	RM		(505)865-9226 (505)865-9226	WS 10 SS 10 BC 9	ED/HC/MD	33	33	22
	HOPE		See Socorro NM									
LOVINGTON	*OUR SAVIOR* www.oslclovington.org	1953	600 S 9TH ST	88260	RM	Thaine L Kister	(575)396-4549	WS 830 SS 745 BC 745	ED/HC			
NAVAJO	*SHEP OF THE VALLEY* sotvnavpastor@gmail.com www.navajolutheranoutreach.org	2002	PO BOX 444	87328	RM	Timothy P Norton	(505)567-4316		ED/HC	33	10	19
PORTALES	*FAITH IN CHRIST* ficlc@yucca.net	1997	1024 W 14TH LN	88130	RM		(575)356-2510	WS 9 SS 1020 BC 1020	ED			
RIO RANCHO	*CALVARY* calvarylutheranrr@gmail.com calvaryLCMS.com/	1980	305 UNSER BLVD NE	87124	RM	Adam J DeGroot	(505)892-9407 (505)891-2080	WS 9 SS 1030 BC 1030	ED/HC/ MD/SN	170	159	90
ROSWELL	*IMMANUEL* lcms_row_c@plateautel.net www.immanuelroswell.org	1933	1405 N Sycamore 1405 N SYCAMORE AVE	88201	RM	Anthony B Flamme	(575)622-2853	WS 9 SS 1030 BC 1030	EL/HS/ED/ MD/SN	267	182	83
RUIDOSO	*SHEPHERD HILLS* shlcruidoso@shlcruidoso.org www.shlcruidoso.org	1984	1120 HULL RD	88345	RM	Jason S Rust	(575)258-4191	WS 1030 SS 9 BC 9	HC/MD	95	92	53
SANTA FE	*IMMANUEL* Immanuellcms@hotmail.com ilc-sfnm.org	1938	209 E BARCELONA RD	87505	RM	Douglas K Escue	(505)983-7568	WS 930 SS 1045	EC/ED/HC/ MD			
SANTA TERESA	*ZION*		See El Paso TX									
SILVER CITY	*MESSIAH* messiahlutheransc.com	1954	2501 N SWAN ST	88061	RM	Joseph E Pellegrino	(505)538-9446	WS 9 SS 1015	HC	60	50	27
SOCORRO	*CHRIST/KING*		See Los Lunas NM									
	HOPE wmguske@gmail.com	1988	908 Leroy Pl PO BOX 1907	87801	RM		(309)945-7452	WS 4	ED	11	11	8
SPRINGER	*IMMANUEL*	1950	301 Summit Ave PO BOX 672	87747	RM		(575)707-0579	WS 2	ED/HC/MD	6	6	6
TAOS	*SANGRE DE CRISTO* taoslutheran.360unite.com	1993	116 DONA ANA DR	87571	RM	Benjamin R Davis	(575)758-5944	WS 9	HC/MD	18	18	16
WHITE ROCK	*REDEEMER*		See Los Alamos NM									

NEW YORK

CITY	CONGREGATION EMAIL WEBSITE	YEAR EST	LOCATION MAILING ADDRESS	ZIP CODE(S)	DIST.	PASTOR(S)	PHONE FAX	WS SS BC	SCHOOLS/ MINISTRIES	Bapt	Conf	Avg Attend
ADIRONDACK	*SONRISE*		See Pottersville NY									
AKRON	*HOLY CROSS*		See Clarence NY									
ALBANY	*ST MATTHEW* jimdorner@gmail.com www.unitylutheranalbany.org	1854	75 Whitehall Rd	12209	AT	James E Dorner II	(518)464-2648	WS 10 SS 11	ED/HC	47	47	30
	ST PAULS stpaulslc.pastor@gmail.com www.stpaulsalbanyny.com	1838	475 STATE ST		AT	James E Dorner II	(518)464-2648	SS 11 BC 11	ED/HC/MD	36	31	27
AMHERST	*CALVARY* kschmidt184@verizon.net	1891	575 AYER RD	14221	EN		(716)835-7567	WS 1030 SS 1030 BC 9	ED/HC/ MD/SN			
	HOLY CROSS		See Clarence NY									

*Indicates a new church start. A new church start is an intentionally organized gathering which comes together on a regular basis for the purpose of worship and/or Bible study and is intended to grow into a member LCMS congregation. WS =Worship Service; SS = Sunday School; BC =Bible Class; EC = Early Childhood; EL = Elementary School; HS = High School; ED =Education Ministry; HC =Human Care Ministry; SN = Special Needs Ministry; MD = Media Ministry (PC)=Partner Church Pastor. See Page 53 for the Table of Abbreviations for key to additional abbreviations

CITY	CONGREGATION EMAIL WEBSITE	YEAR EST	LOCATION MAILING ADDRESS	ZIP CODE(S)	DIST.	PASTOR(S)	PHONE FAX	WS SS BC	SCHOOLS/ MINISTRIES	STATISTIC Bapt	Conf	Avg Attend
AMITYVILLE	*SAINT PAUL'S* office@stpaulsamityville.org stpaulsamityville.org	1930	147 PARK AVE	11701	AT	Thomas W Cusanelli	(631)264-0763 (631)264-0372	WS 10 SS 10 BC 9	EL/HS	285	271	70
ANGELICA	*ST PAUL*	1865	COUNTY ROAD 15	14709	EA		(585)760-4689	WS 10 SS 11	ED/MD	20	20	18
ANGOLA	*ST JOHN* churchoffice@stjohnangola.org www.stjohnangola.org	1940	962 GOLD ST	14006	EA		(716)549-2144 (716)549-2144	WS 1030 SS 915 BC 9	ED/HC/ MD/SN	139	104	60
AQUEBOGUE	*OUR REDEEMER* ourredeemerli@gmail.com	1918	269 Main Rd P. O BOX 960	11931	AT	Charles R Byer	(631)722-4000	WS 9 BC 1015	ED/HC/ MD/SN	90	70	42
AUBURN	*REDEEMER* redeemerauburn@gmail.com	1948	10 PROSPECT ST	13021	EA		(315)252-7409 (315)252-4646	WS 1030 SS 915 BC 915	ED/HC/ MD/SN	26	26	17
AVON	*EPIPHANY* czuber1@rochester.rr.com	1963	6050 Avon Lima Rd 6050 E AVON LIMA RD	14414	EA	Clayton G Zuber	(585)226-2200	WS 1030 SS 1030 BC 930	ED/HC/ MD/SN			
BATAVIA	*ST PAUL* stpaulbatavia@gmail.com www.stpaulbatavia.org	1873	31 WASHINGTON AVE	14020	EA	Thompson Marin	(585)343-0488 (585)344-0470	WS 1015 SS 9 BC 9	EL/ED/HC/ MD	160	142	89
BAYSIDE	*GLORY KOREAN* kennethkko@gmail.com	1997	210-10 Horace Harding Expwy 61-48 212TH ST OAKLAND GDNS	11364	AT		(718)224-8423	WS 1230 SS 1230		6	6	6
	REDEEMER www.rlcb.org	1915	3601 BELL BLVD	11361	AT	John S Stohlmann	(718)229-5770 (718)229-5770	WS 1030 SS 930 BC 930	EL/HS/ED	38	36	26
BEACON	*OUR SAVIOR*		See Fishkill NY									
BERGHOLTZ	*HOLY GHOST* office@hgl.church holyghostlcms.org	1843	6630 LUTHER ST NIAGARA FALLS	14304	EA	Denton W White	(716)731-3030	WS 8 1030 SS 1015 BC 1015	EL/ED/HC/ MD	631	479	154
BETHPAGE	*ST PAUL* office@stpaulbethpage.com www.stpaulbethpage.com	1923	449 STEWART AVE	11714	AT		(516)931-8262 (516)827-0882	WS 1030	EC/EL/ HS/ED	40	38	33
BINGHAMTON	*HOLY TRINITY* admin@holytrinitylc.net HTLCB.ch	1965	216 KATTELVILLE RD	13901	EA	Martin A Seel Jr	(607)204-0704	WS 930 BC 11		50	50	19
BOSTON	*ST MARTIN*	1854	8304 Cole Rd PO BOX 26 COLDEN	14025 14033	EA	Domenick A Lettieri	(716)941-5419 (716)941-9124	WS 1115 SS 1030	ED/HC/MD			
BRANT LAKE	*SONRISE*		See Pottersville NY									
BROCKPORT	*HOPE CHURCH BROCKPORT CAMPUS* Satellite Site of Hope Rochester NY	2022	6601 Fourth Section Road	14420				WS 930 SS 930				
BRONX	*BRONX PSYCHIATRIC CENTER* Satellite Site of Immanuel Whitestone NY	2009	1500 Water Place	10461								
	OUR SAVIOUR mgonzalez@oursaviourbronx.org www.oursaviourbronx.org	1927	1734 WILLIAMSBRIDGE RD	10461	AT	Matthew R Gonzalez John R Hannah	(718)792-5665	WS 930	EL/HS/ED	90	81	100
	REDEEMER office@redeemerlutheranbronx.org www.redeemerlutheranbronx.org	1928	4360 BOYD AVE	10466	AT	Dr Dien A Taylor	(718)324-1288 (718)324-2056	WS 8 11 SS 945 BC 7	ED/HC/ MD/SN	672	464	194
	TRINITY trinitylutheranbronx@gmail.com www.trinitylutheranbronx.org	1913	2125 WATSON AVE	10472	AT	Matthew R Gonzalez Warren L Lattimore	(718)828-3532	WS 11 SS 10	ED/HC/MD	115	74	50
BRONXVILLE	*THE VILLAGE* vlcmail@vlc-ny.org www.vlc-ny.org	1916	172 WHITE PLAINS RD	10708	AT	Dr Robert E Hartwell Mark D Budenholzer	(914)337-0207 (914)771-9711	WS 9 1045 SS 9	EL/ED/HC/ MD/SN	1342	812	164
BROOKLYN	*GOOD SHEPHERD*	1908	2139 NEW YORK AVE	11210	AT	Hugo E Berger	(718)338-6424	WS 1015	ED/HC/MD	37	36	15
	RISEN CHRIST	1965	250 Blake Ave C/O PASTOR STEVEN HICKS 116-12 204TH STREET ST. ALBANS	11212 11412	AT		(646)339-9279	WS 11 SS 10 BC 10	ED/HC/SN	35	29	15
	ST JOHN office@sjebrooklyn.org www.sjebrooklyn.org	1844	195 MAUJER ST	11206	AT		(718)963-2100	WS 11 BC 930	EL/HS/ED/ HC/MD/SN	80	75	27
	ST MATTHEW church@smlbrooklyn.com www.smlbrooklyn.com/	1879	1187 E 92ND ST 1182 EAST 93RD STREET	11236	AT	Christoph M Schulze	(347)659-7562	WS 1130 SS 1	EL/HS/ED/ HC/MD	62	29	27
	ST PAUL tentinasia@aol.com	1887	592 KNICKERBOCKER AVE	11221	AT	Christoph M Schulze	(718)443-2220	WS 9	EL/HS	124	61	42
	ST PETERS dhbad@aol.com www.spbklyn.org	1897	105 HIGHLAND PL	11208	AT	Dr David H Benke Henry D Chanderdatt	(718)647-1014 (718)229-1262	WS 945 SS 1015 BC 1130	EC/EL/HS/ ED/HC/ MD/SN	152	85	81
	TRINITY www.trinitybayridge.org	1886	9020 3RD AVE	11209	AT		(718)745-0138	WS 1030	ED/MD/SN	5	2	4
BUFFALO	*FIRST TRINITY*		See Tonawanda NY									
	HANANIAH hlcbuffalo@gmail.com		900 Genesee 900 GENESEE ST	14211	EA		(716)240-9476 (716)725-6865	WS 1 SS 12				
	IMMANUEL	1892	1084 E LOVEJOY ST	14206	EA		(716)896-8035	WS 9 SS 9				
	OUR SAVIOR oursaviorbuffalo@gmail.com www.oursaviorbuffalo.org	1926	26 BRUNSWICK BLVD	14208	EA	Christopher C Browne	(716)885-1108 (716)883-5480	WS 11	ED	70	62	45

*Indicates a new church start. A new church start is an intentionally organized gathering which comes together on a regular basis for the purpose of worship and/or Bible study and is intended to grow into a member LCMS congregation. WS =Worship Service; SS = Sunday School; BC =Bible Class; EC = Early Childhood; EL = Elementary School; HS = High School; ED =Education Ministry; HC =Human Care Ministry; SN = Special Needs Ministry; MD = Media Ministry (PC)=Partner Church Pastor. See Page 53 for the Table of Abbreviations for key to additional abbreviations

CITY	CONGREGATION EMAIL WEBSITE	YEAR EST	LOCATION MAILING ADDRESS	ZIP CODE(S)	DIST.	PASTOR(S)	PHONE FAX	WS SS BC	SCHOOLS/ MINISTRIES	Bapt	Conf	Avg Attend
BUFFALO	*SALEM* salemoncircle@yahoo.com www.salembuffalo.com	1917	10 Mc Clellan Cir 10 MCCLELLAN CIR	14220	EA	John D Duke Jr	(716)824-2787 (716)824-3193	WS 815 1045 SS 930 BC 930	ED/HC/ MD/SN	344	294	95
	ST JOHNS		See Depew NY									
BURNT HILLS	*IMMANUEL*		See Niskayuna NY									
CAIRO	*RESURRECTION* rlc.office.lj@gmail.com www.rlc.life	1959	186 Main St PO BOX 563	12413	AT	Samuel J Sessa Victor H Nelson Jr	(518)622-3286 (518)622-2083	WS 815 1030 SS 915 BC 915	EC/ED/ HC/SN	463	440	127
CANANDAIGUA	*GOOD SHEPHERD* office@goodshepherdcdga.org goodshepherdcdga.org	1961	320 S Pearl St PO BOX 690	14424	EA	Steven R Geske	(585)394-2760 (585)394-2760	WS 8 11 SS 915 BC 930	EC/ED/HC/ MD/SN			
CANASTOTA	*GRACE* gracelc.canastota.ny@gmail.com www.grace-lcms-cny.org		3965 CARTER RD	13032	EA	James R Burch II	(315)697-2128	WS 10 SS 845 BC 845	ED/HC/ MD/SN	186	186	50
	REDEEMER	2003	400 S Peterboro St PO BOX 201 WAMPSVILLE	13032 13163	EA	Peter N Saie	(315)697-3332	WS 4 BC 3				
CATSKILL	*ST MARKS SECOND*		See Hudson NY									
CATTARAUGUS	*IMMANUEL* ottoimmanuel@gmail.com	1864	9037 OTTO EAST OTTO RD	14719	EA	Timothy D Klahn	(716)220-6748	WS 1115 SS 10 BC 10	ED/HC/ MD/SN			
CAYUGA LAKE	*CHRIST*		See Interlaken NY									
CENTER MORICHES	*CHRIST*		See East Moriches NY									
CENTEREACH	*OUR SAVIOR* rwstelzer@optonline.net www.oursaviorlongisland.org	1958	140 MARK TREE RD	11720	AT	Ronald W Stelzer	(631)588-2757 (631)588-2617	WS 8 1030 SS 915 BC 915	EL/HS/ED/ HC/MD/SN	396	309	170
CENTRAL ISLIP	*GRACE* yrudy@optoline.net	1943	75 CALEBS PATH	11722	AT		(631)234-8524	WS 930	EC/ED/HC	12	12	12
CHEEKTOWAGA	*ST JOHNS*		See Depew NY									
	ST LUKE secretary@stluke-buffalo.org stluke-buffalo.org	1945	900 MARYVALE DR	14225	EA	Phillip R Schultz	(716)633-6752 (716)635-0718	WS 830 11 SS 11 BC 945	ED/HC/MD			
CHESTERTOWN	*SONRISE*		See Pottersville NY									
CLARENCE	*HOLY CROSS* holycrossclarence@gmail.com www.holycrossclarence.com	1959	8900 SHERIDAN DR	14031	EA	Jeffrey D Nickel	(716)634-2332	WS 8 11 SS 930 BC 930	ED/HC/ MD/SN	275	213	91
CLARENCE CENTER	*HOLY CROSS*		See Clarence NY									
	ST PAUL www.jesusintheclarencecenter.org		7720 GOODRICH RD CLARENCE CTR	14032	EA	Rako D Zech	(716)741-2500	WS 930 SS 1030				
COHOCTON	*ST PAULS* cedrum1@gmail.com	1860	97 Maple Ave PO BOX 316	14826	EA	Robert C Crane	(585)384-5667	WS 9 SS 1015 BC 1015	ED/SN			
COLDEN	*REDEEMER* aredeemerluther1@roadrunner.com www.redeemerlutherancolden.org	1920	8740 SUPERVISOR AVE	14033	EA	Domenick A Lettieri	(716)941-5419	WS 10 SS 10	ED/HC/MD	172	171	55
COLLEGE POINT	*ST JOHNS* stjchofc@aol.com www.sjlcp.org	1857	2201 123RD ST	11356	AT	Desmond A Sukhdeo	(718)463-4790	WS 9 10 SS 1130	EL/HS/ED/ HC/MD	133	102	45
COLONIE	*OUR SAVIOR* information@oursaviors.com www.oslalbany.com	1929	63 MOUNTAIN VIEW AVE ALBANY	12205	AT		(518)459-2248 (518)459-1330	WS 830 11 SS 945 BC 945	EL/ED/HC/ MD/SN	145	130	95
CORNING	*FAITH* faithlutheran2@verizon.net www.faithlutherancorning.org	1977	71 W 1ST ST	14830	EA	Phillip J Callahan	(607)962-4970	WS 11 BC 930	HC			
CORONA	*CHRIST*		See Woodside NY									
	EMANUEL-CORONA QUEENS Satellite Site of Christ Woodside NY	2010	37 57 104th St	11368								
CORTLAND	*ST PAUL* StPaulCortlandNY@gmail.com WWW.splccortland.org	1926	45 HAMLIN ST	13045	EA	Cory J Eckstrom	(607)591-5919	WS 1030	EC/ED	21	19	10
CORTLANDT MANOR	*ST LUKE*		See Putnam Valley NY									
DELHI	*IMMANUEL* delawarepastor@gmail.com immanueldelhi.org	1941	565 Andes Rd PO BOX 68	13753	AT	Robert C Wilson	(607)746-2098	WS 11 SS 12	ED/HC/ MD/SN	214	169	32
DELMAR	*BETHLEHEM* office@blcdelmar.com www.blcdelmar.com	1954	85 ELM AVE	12054	AT	Jessy J Wilson David W Dietsche	(518)439-4328 (518)439-3022	WS 830 11 SS 945 BC 945	ED/HC/ MD/SN	622	482	207
DEPEW	*ST JOHNS* Secretary@sjlcdepew.com sjlcdepew.com	1895	67 LITCHFIELD AVE	14043	EA	Galen M Purpura Jr	(716)683-3947 (716)683-3295	WS 830 1115 SS 10 BC 10	ED/HC/ MD/SN	424	321	174
DIX HILLS	*ST LUKE* laura@stlukedixhills.org www.stlukedixhills.org	1962	20 CANDLEWOOD PATH	11746	AT	Dr Thomas R Johnson	(631)499-8656 (631)462-6496	WS 815 1045 SS 1045 BC 930	EC/EL/HS/ ED/HC/ MD/SN	859	634	130
DONAGAN HILLS	*ST MATTHEW*		See Staten Island NY									
DUNKIRK	*ST PAUL*		See Fredonia NY									
EAST AMHERST	*HOLY CROSS*		See Clarence NY									
EAST AURORA	*IMMANUEL*	1929	43 PINE ST	14052	EA	Dennis J Krueger	(716)652-4240 (716)652-4243	WS 1030	ED/HC/SN	39	39	20
EAST BLOOMFIELD	*ST MARK*		See Mendon NY									
EAST MEADOW	*CALVARY* office@calvarylc.org www.calvarylc.org	1950	36 TAYLOR AVE	11554	AT	Sean C Chapman	(516)735-1473 (516)735-1804	WS 10 SS 10	EC/EL/HS/ ED/HC/ MD/SN	150	150	70

*Indicates a new church start. A new church start is an intentionally organized gathering which comes together on a regular basis for the purpose of worship and/or Bible study and is intended to grow into a member LCMS congregation. WS =Worship Service; SS = Sunday School; BC =Bible Class; EC = Early Childhood; EL = Elementary School; HS = High School; ED =Education Ministry; HC =Human Care Ministry; SN = Special Needs Ministry; MD = Media Ministry (PC)=Partner Church Pastor. See Page 53 for the Table of Abbreviations for key to additional abbreviations

CITY	CONGREGATION EMAIL WEBSITE	YEAR EST	LOCATION MAILING ADDRESS	ZIP CODE(S)	DIST.	PASTOR(S)	PHONE FAX	WS SS BC	SCHOOLS/ MINISTRIES	STATISTIC Bapt	Conf	Avg Attend
EAST MORICHES	*CHRIST* clcem@optonline.net www.clcem.net	1961	177 Frowein Road PO BOX 580	11940	AT	Dr John G Fleischmann II	(631)878-2277 (631)878-8672	WS 8 11 SS 930 BC 9	ED/HC/ MD/SN	150	135	70
EAST SETAUKET	*MESSIAH* info@messiahny.org www.messiahny.org	1961	465 POND PATH	11733	AT		(631)751-1775	WS 830 11 SS 945	ED/HC/MD	564	399	80
EASTPORT	*CHRIST*		See East Moriches NY									
EDEN	*ST PAUL* splc@stpaulseden.com stpaulseden.com	1849	3487 N BOSTON RD	14057	EA	Thomas S Lutz	(716)992-9112 (716)992-3113	WS 830 1045 SS 930 BC 930	ED/HC/ MD/SN			
ELMA	*FAITH* faithelmaoffice@gmail.com www.faithlutheranelma.com	1929	1230 BOWEN RD	14059	EA	Dennis J Krueger	(716)652-2221 (716)652-2386	WS 930 SS 11 BC 11	ED/HC/ MD/SN			
FAIRPORT	*RISEN CHRIST* rclc.office@gmail.com risenchristfamily.com	1974	1000 MOSELEY RD	14450	EA		(585)223-5757	WS 930 SS 830 BC 830	EC/ED/HC/ MD/SN	145	92	60
FARMINGTON	*ST JOHN* stjohns@pumpkinhook.org pumpkinhook.org	1886	153 CHURCH AVE	14425	EA		(315)986-3045 (315)986-3045	WS 830 11 SS 945 BC 945	EC/ED/HC/ MD/SN			
FISHKILL	*OUR SAVIOR* office@oursaviorlutheran.org www.oursaviorlutheran.org	1957	1400 ROUTE 52	12524	AT	John M Young	(845)897-4423	WS 820 945 1110 SS 1015	EC/ED/HC	566	438	120
FLUSHING	*ASCENSION*		See Jamaica NY									
	GLORY KOREAN		See Bayside NY									
	IMMANUEL KOREAN lee.attorney77@gmail.com	1978	15514 35TH AVE	11354	EN	Ho J Lee	(718)460-5736 (718)961-6062	WS 11 SS 10 BC 10				
	RESURRECTION resurrection.lutheran@verizon.net www.homestead.com/rlcflushing	1936	44-16 192nd St 4410 192ND ST	11358	AT	James T Gajadhar	(718)463-4292 (718)463-4677	WS 915	EL/HS/ED/ HC/MD	15	15	12
	ST JOHN www.saintjohnsflushing.com	1893	14746 SANFORD AVE	11355	AT	James T Gajadhar	(718)463-2959	WS 1030 SS 1030 BC 915	EL/HS/ED/ HC/MD	40	38	13
FREDONIA	*ST PAUL* stpaullcfredonia@outlook.com www.stpaulfredonia.org	1887	334 TEMPLE ST	14063	EA	Matthew C Schettler	(716)672-6731	WS 1030 SS 915 BC 915	ED/HC/MD	172	123	51
FRESH MEADOWS	*GLORY KOREAN*		See Bayside NY									
GARDEN CITY	*RESURRECTION* office@resgc.org resgc.org/	1948	420 STEWART AVE	11530	AT	Jeffrey S Browning	(516)746-4426 (516)746-6638	WS 830 945 11 SS 945 BC 945	EC/EL/HS/ ED/HC/MD	1150	934	253
GARRISON	*ST LUKE*		See Putnam Valley NY									
GERMANTOWN	*ST MARKS SECOND*		See Hudson NY									
GETZVILLE	*HOLY CROSS*		See Clarence NY									
GLEN COVE	*TRINITY* trinitygcofficemanager@gmail.com trinitylutheranglencove.com	1920	74 FOREST AVE	11542	AT		(516)676-1340	WS 930 BC 830	EL/HS/ED/ HC/MD/SN	85	85	30
GLENDALE	*REDEEMER* dorsey.curtis@gmail.com www.redeemerglendale.org	1909	6907 COOPER AVE	11385	AT	Curtis R Dorsey	(718)456-5292 (718)456-5292	WS 1030 SS 9 BC 915	EL/HS/ED	50	45	25
	ST JOHN stjohnslutheranglendale@gmail.com www.saintjohnsglendale.org/	1844	8824 MYRTLE AVE	11385	AT	Matthew O Staneck	(718)847-3188	WS 9	EL/HS/ ED/HC	50	33	30
GLENS FALLS	*GOOD SHEPHERD* goodshepherd543@aol.com goodshepherdgf.360unite.com	1947	543 GLEN ST	12801	AT	Paul R Wagner	(518)792-7971	WS 9 SS 10 BC 10	ED/HC/ MD/SN	491	253	66
GOWANDA	*IMMANUEL*	1898	40 S CHAPEL ST	14070	EA		(716)532-4342 (716)532-4342	WS 845 SS 10	ED/HC/ MD/SN			
HAMLIN	*ST JOHN* stjohnhamlin@hotmail.com www.stjohnhamlin.org	1874	1107 Lake Rd West Fork 1107 LAKE ROAD WEST FRK	14464	EA	Christian D Bode	(585)964-2550 (585)964-8933	WS 830 11 SS 945 BC 945	HC/MD/SN			
HAMPTON BAYS	*CHRIST OUR SAVIOUR* ckenreich@aol.com www.lutheranchurchhamptonbays.com	1959	9 TERRACE DR	11946	AT	John A Kenreich	(631)728-3288 (631)728-6716	WS 9 1030 SS 9	ED/HC/MD	80	60	55
HAWTHORNE	*TRINITY* trinityhawthorne292@gmail.com trinityhawthorne.org	1894	292 ELWOOD AVE	10532	AT	Dr David A Elseroad	(914)769-2546 (914)769-5326	WS 1015 SS 9 BC 9	EC/ED/HC/ MD/SN	120	86	43
HENRIETTA	*PINNACLE*		See Rochester NY									
	ST MARK		See Mendon NY									
	ST MARK		See West Henrietta NY									
HICKSVILLE	*TRINITY* churchoffice@trinityhicksville.org www.trinityhicksville.org	1850	40 W NICHOLAI ST	11801	AT	Dr Johnson E Rethinasamy	(516)931-2225	WS 9 1045 SS 9	EL/HS/ED/ HC/MD	857	836	93
HILTON	*ST PAUL* churchoffice@stpaulhilton.org www.stpaulhilton.org	1898	158 EAST AVE	14468	EA	Mark D Ball	(585)392-4000 (585)392-4001	WS 830 11 SS 945 BC 945	EL/ED/HC/ MD/SN	568	469	239
HOLBROOK	*SAINT JOHN* stjholbrook@gmail.com www.stjohnsholbrook.com	1904	1675 COATES AVE	11741	AT		(631)588-6050 (631)588-6059	WS 9 11 SS 9	EC/ED/HC	970	516	90
HOLLIS HILLS	*THE REDEEMER*	1941	220-16 Union Turnpike 22016 UNION TPKE	11364	AT		(718)465-4236 (718)465-2808	WS 1030	EL/HS/ ED/HC	24	24	13
HONEOYE FALLS	*PINNACLE*		See Rochester NY									
	ST MARK		See Mendon NY									

*Indicates a new church start. A new church start is an intentionally organized gathering which comes together on a regular basis for the purpose of worship and/or Bible study and is intended to grow into a member LCMS congregation. WS =Worship Service; SS = Sunday School; BC =Bible Class; EC = Early Childhood; EL = Elementary School; HS = High School; ED =Education Ministry; HC =Human Care Ministry; SN = Special Needs Ministry; MD = Media Ministry (PC)=Partner Church Pastor. See Page 53 for the Table of Abbreviations for key to additional abbreviations

CITY	CONGREGATION EMAIL WEBSITE	YEAR EST	LOCATION MAILING ADDRESS	ZIP CODE(S)	DIST.	PASTOR(S)	PHONE FAX	WS SS BC	SCHOOLS/ MINISTRIES	STATISTIC Bapt	Conf	Avg Attend
HUDSON	*ST MARKS SECOND* st.marks.lutheran.hudson@gmail.com www.stmarkslutheranchurchhudson.org	1932	8 STORM AVE	12534	AT	Daniel F Cohn	(518)828-9514 (518)828-9514	WS 930 SS 930	ED/HC/ MD/SN	93	82	45
HURLEY	*GOOD SHEPHERD* gselc@usinternet.com www.gskingston.org	1977	470 HURLEY AVE	12443	AT		(845)338-5262	WS 11 SS 1015	HC/MD/SN	38	36	20
HYDE PARK	*ST TIMOTHY* pastor@sttimothyhp.org www.sttimothyhp.org	1959	1348 Rt 9G 1348 ROUTE 9G	12538	AT		(845)229-2758	WS 10 SS 9	ED/HC/ MD/SN	19	19	13
INTERLAKEN	*CHRIST*	1959	7966 CR 153 7966 COUNTY ROAD 153	14847	EA	Cory J Eckstrom		WS 9	ED/HC/MD	52	41	10
IONIA	*ST MARK*		See Mendon NY									
ISLIP	*TRINITY* trinityislip@optonline.net www.trinityislip.org	1927	111 NASSAU AVE	11751	AT	Michael C Staneck	(631)277-1555 (631)277-3134	WS 8 10 SS 10	EC/ED/HC/ MD	1144	951	160
ITHACA	*TRINITY* tlc@trinityithaca.org www.trinityithaca.org	1961	149 HONNESS LN	14850	EA	Robert M Foote	(607)273-9017 (607)273-9438	WS 1030 SS 9 BC 9	ED/HC/ MD/SN			
JACKSON HEIGHTS	*CHRIST*		See Woodside NY									
JAMAICA	*ASCENSION*	1942	8010 MAIN ST	11435	AT	Jimmy A Lalljie	(718)380-1892	WS 1115		12	12	9
	GRACE	1920	14412 89TH AVE	11435	AT	Charles L Persaud	(718)526-6290		ED/HC/ MD/SN	154	121	23
	REDEEMER		See Saint Albans NY									
	TRINITY	1954	172-61 Baisley Blvd 17261 BAISLEY BLVD	11434	AT	David E Haberer	(718)525-3689 (718)525-3354	WS 11	EL/HS	66	62	45
KENMORE	*LA SANTA CRUZ* lasantacruz716@gmail.com	1988	c/o Pilgrim Lutheran Church 22 Chapel Rd 240 ABBOTT RD BUFFALO	14217 14220	EA	Luis J Florez	(716)875-5485	WS 1	HC			
	PILGRIM beneder@aol.com www.pilgrimkenmorelcms.org	1922	44 CHAPEL RD	14217	EN	David J Walsh	(716)875-5485 (716)875-5485	WS 10 SS 9				
KINDERHOOK	*ST MARKS SECOND*		See Hudson NY									
KINGSTON	*GOOD SHEPHERD*		See Hurley NY									
LAGRANGEVILLE	*ALL SAINTS* allsaintsevangelical@gmail.com allsaints-lcms.org	1985	133 Cross Rd 133 N CROSS RD	12540	AT		(845)223-5288	WS 9 BC 10	ED/HC/ MD/SN	95	92	20
LAKE PEEKSKILL	*ST LUKE*		See Putnam Valley NY									
LANCASTER	*HOLY CROSS*		See Clarence NY									
	ST JOHNS		See Depew NY									
LATHAM	*IMMANUEL*		See Niskayuna NY									
	RESURRECTION ResurrectionLutheranLatham@ gmail.com	1958	645 WATERVLIET SHAKER RD	12110	AT		(518)785-8286 (518)785-8286	WS 930	ED/HC/MD	15	11	6
LAURELTON	*GOOD SHEPHERD* goodshepherd5@aol.com	1927	13452 228 St 134-52 228TH ST	11413	AT		(718)528-5068 (718)276-5444	WS 11 SS 930 BC 930	EL/HS/ED/ MD	45	45	35
LOCKPORT	*IMMANUEL*	1905	7147 RIDGE RD	14094	EA	Kenneth L Craig	(716)434-0521 (716)434-0521	WS 930 SS 10				
	MOUNT OLIVE Office@mtolivelockport.org www.mtolivelockport.org	1960	6965 CHESTNUT RIDGE RD	14094	EA		(716)434-8500 (716)434-8500	WS 1015 SS 9 BC 9	ED/HC/MD	159	158	45
	ST PETER offices@stpeternorthridge.org www.stpeternorthridge.org	1865	4169 CHURCH RD	14094	EA	William F Wrede	(716)433-9014	WS 930 BC 1045	SN	285	218	50
	TRINITY tlclockport@gmail.com www.tlclockport.org	1871	67 SAXTON ST	14094	EA		(716)434-3106	WS 1045	ED/HC/ MD/SN	373	253	32
MACEDON	*ST JOHN*		See Farmington NY									
MANHATTAN	*MOUNT ZION* Mtzion@yahoo.com mtzionlc.wordpress.com	1947	421 W 145TH ST NEW YORK	10031	AT	George R Ramsudh	(646)370-3940 (646)370-3940	WS 11 SS 930 BC 930		97	97	50
	TRUE LIGHT		See New York NY									
MANORVILLE	*CHRIST*		See East Moriches NY									
MASTIC	*CHRIST*		See East Moriches NY									
MASTIC BEACH	*CHRIST*		See East Moriches NY									
	GRACE church@graceinmb.org www.graceinmb.org	1955	240 MASTIC RD	11951	AT	Peter J Deberny	(631)281-8196 (631)281-7871	WS 745 915 SS 915	ED/HC/MD	217	217	147
MEDINA	*TRINITY*	1886	1212 WEST AVE	14103	EA		(585)798-0525 (585)798-0525	WS 930				
MENDON	*ST MARK* secretary@stmarkmendon.org www.stmarkmendon.org	1901	18 Victor Mendon Rd PO BOX 239	14506	EA	Bradley P Urlaub	(585)624-1766	WS 9 SS 1030 BC 1030	ED/HC/MD	122	107	40
MIDDLE ISLAND	*HOLY TRINITY* office@htlcny.org www.htlcny.org	1953	Yaphank-Middle Island Rd PO BOX 36	11953	AT	David Santos	(631)924-6991 (631)924-0415	WS 9 11 SS 9 11	ED/HC/MD	375	341	203
MIDDLEPORT	*HOLY CROSS* holycrossmid@gmail.com holycrossmiddleport.com	1954	133 Telegraph Rd PO BOX 128	14105	EA	Richard P Wolf	(716)735-7209	WS 10	ED/HC/ MD/SN	40	40	23

*Indicates a new church start. A new church start is an intentionally organized gathering which comes together on a regular basis for the purpose of worship and/or Bible study and is intended to grow into a member LCMS congregation. WS =Worship Service; SS = Sunday School; BC =Bible Class; EC = Early Childhood; EL = Elementary School; HS = High School; ED =Education Ministry; HC =Human Care Ministry; SN = Special Needs Ministry; MD = Media Ministry (PC)=Partner Church Pastor. See Page 53 for the Table of Abbreviations for key to additional abbreviations

CITY	CONGREGATION EMAIL WEBSITE	YEAR EST	LOCATION MAILING ADDRESS	ZIP CODE(S)	DIST.	PASTOR(S)	PHONE FAX	WS SS BC	SCHOOLS/ MINISTRIES	STATISTIC Bapt	Conf	Avg Attend
MIDDLETOWN	*FAMILY OF FAITH* familyoffaith@frontiernet.net FamilyofFaithMiddletown.org	1989	240 Midland Lakes Rd 240 MIDLAND LAKE RD	10941	AT	Dr Kenneth J Doka	(845)692-7075 (845)692-7075	WS 1015 SS 1045 BC 915	ED/HC/ MD/SN	50	30	25
MONROE	*ST PAUL* church@stpaulmonroe.org www.stpaulmonroe.org	1962	21 STILL RD	10950	AT		(845)782-5600 (845)782-3703	WS 9 SS 10 BC 9	EL/ED/HC/ MD	436	311	88
MOUNT VERNON	*IMMANUEL* immanuelmtv@aol.com	1897	15 E GRAND STREET	10552	AT		(212)567-5948	WS 1030	ED/HC	55	40	10
NEW HYDE PARK	*TRINITY* www.trinitynewhydepark.org	1942	5 DURHAM RD	11040	AT	Jimmy A Lalljie	(516)354-8883	WS 930 SS 930 BC 1115	ED/HC/MD	79	68	50
NEW YORK	*ST MATTHEW* stmatthewnyc@aol.com www.stmatthewnyc.org	1664	178 BENNETT AVE	10040	AT	Peter A Deebrah	(212)567-5948 (212)567-5948	WS 130 SS 245	ED/HC	108	68	20
	ST PAUL		See Brooklyn NY									
	ST PAUL		See Greenwich CT									
	TRINITY		See Scarsdale NY									
	TRUE LIGHT office@truelightlutheran.org truelightlutheran.org	1936	195 WORTH ST	10013	AT	Dr Joshua D Hollmann	(212)962-1482 (212)962-1483	WS 1030	ED/HC/MD	475	350	95
NEW YORK CITY	*EMMAUS*		See Ridgewood NY									
	IMMANUEL		See Whitestone NY									
NEWARK	*REDEEMER*	1925	102 HOPE AVE	14513	EA		(315)331-0662 (315)331-0662	WS 1030 SS 930 BC 930	MD			
NEWFANE	*CONCORDIA*	1876	3121 BEEBE RD	14108	EA		(716)751-6939	WS 1045		133	127	23
NIAGARA FALLS	*GRACE* office@gracenf.org www.gracenf.org	1907	736 CAYUGA DR	14304	EA	Benjamin G Bahr	(716)283-1843 (716)283-1843	WS 1030 SS 9 BC 9	ED/HC/ MD/SN	289	175	69
	HOLY GHOST		See Bergholtz NY									
	OUR SAVIOR thomasjamesharris2017@gmail.com	1991	2759 MILITARY RD	14304	EA	Kurt D Schultz	(716)297-3880 (716)297-6348	WS 1045				
NISKAYUNA	*IMMANUEL* office@immanuelniskayuna.org	1902	1850 UNION ST	12309	AT	George D Carstensen	(518)346-1958	WS 1015	ED/HC/MD	91	84	45
NORTH TONAWANDA	*REDEEMER* rlcntoffice@yahoo.com www.rlcnt.com	1897	365 Thompson St 265 FALCONER ST N TONAWANDA	14120	EN		(716)692-5734	WS 1030 SS 9				
	ST JOHN churchoffice@stjohnnt.com www.stjohnnt.com	1853	6950 WARD RD N TONAWANDA	14120	EA	Michael R Borgstede	(716)693-9677 (716)693-2686	WS 9 SS 1015 BC 1015	EL/ED/HC/ MD	439	349	99
	ST MARK NT office@stmarknt.org www.stmarknt.org	1891	1135 OLIVER ST N TONAWANDA	14120	EA	David T Keating	(716)693-3715 (716)693-3932	WS 1030	EC/ED/MD	378	332	102
	ST MATTHEW office@stmatthewlutheran.net www.stmatthewlutheran.net	1890	875 EGGERT DR N TONAWANDA	14120	EA	Robert B Jorg	(716)692-6862	WS 915 SS 1015	ED/HC/ MD/SN	151	147	100
	ST PAUL stpaulnt@gmail.com www.stpaulnt.com	1861	453 OLD FALLS BLVD N TONAWANDA	14120	EA	Ernest R Green III William J Novack	(716)692-3255 (716)692-3643	WS 8 1045 SS 930 BC 930	EC/ED/HC/ MD/SN	1621	1044	252
OAKLAND GARDENS	*IMMANUEL CHINESE* skmchung@yahoo.com	1977	21010 Horace Harding Expway 4410 192ND ST FLUSHING	11364 11358	AT		(718)873-6719			95	95	71
OLD WESTBURY	*THE LIFE* pastor@thelifeny.org www.thelifeny.org		1 OLD WESTBURY RD	11568	AT	Justin K Vetrano Brian M Crocitto Alessandro A Rubino Adam R Schoepflin	(516)333-3355 (516)333-7046	WS 9 1030	EC/EL/HS/ ED/HC/MD	583	583	304
ORCHARD PARK	*ST JOHN* www.stjohnsop.com	1908	4536 S Buffalo 4536 S BUFFALO ST	14127	EA	Nathan C Hartke	(716)662-4747 (716)667-1290	WS 8 930 11 SS 930 BC 930	ED/HC/ MD/SN	1627	1046	316
OWEGO	*ZION* zionowego@pm.me www.zionowego.org	1921	3917 WAVERLY RD	13827	EA		(607)687-1205 (607)687-6375	WS 1030 SS 930 BC 930	ED/HC/MD			
PATCHOGUE	*CHRIST*		See East Moriches NY									
	EMANUEL emanluthbm@gmail.com www.emanluthpatch.org	1912	179 E MAIN ST	11772	AT	Steven J Williamson-Link	(631)758-2240 (631)758-2418	WS 9 11 SS 9	EC/ED/HC/ MD	180	164	141
PAWLING	*CHRIST THE KING* info@pawlinglutheran.org pawlinglutheran.org	1963	14 PINE DR	12564	AT	Stefan M Gramenz	(845)855-3169 (845)855-3169	WS 930 SS 11 BC 11		120	85	49
PEEKSKILL	*OUR REDEEMER* prwpt@optonline.net www.ourredeemerlcms.org	1932	714 HUDSON AVE	10566	AT	William P Terjesen	(914)293-0081	WS 1030 SS 9 BC 915	ED/HC/MD	45	40	22
	ST LUKE		See Putnam Valley NY									
PEKIN	*ST ANDREW* standrewlutheranpekin@gmail.com www.standrewlutheranpekin.org/	1896	3229 UPPER MOUNTAIN RD SANBORN	14132	EA	Kurt D Schultz	(716)731-5863 (716)731-5863	WS 9		100	100	52
PENFIELD	*FAITH* www.faithpenfield.org	1956	2576 Browncroft Boulivard 2576 BROWNCROFT BLVD ROCHESTER	14526 14625	EA	Peter D Johnson	(585)381-3970 (585)381-6407	WS 830 1045 SS 945	EL/ED/HC/ MD/SN	1032	700	307
PHILMONT	*ST MARKS SECOND*		See Hudson NY									
PITTSFORD	*PINNACLE*		See Rochester NY									

*Indicates a new church start. A new church start is an intentionally organized gathering which comes together on a regular basis for the purpose of worship and/or Bible study and is intended to grow into a member LCMS congregation. WS =Worship Service; SS = Sunday School; BC =Bible Class; EC = Early Childhood; EL = Elementary School; HS = High School; ED =Education Ministry; HC =Human Care Ministry; SN = Special Needs Ministry; MD = Media Ministry (PC)=Partner Church Pastor. See Page 53 for the Table of Abbreviations for key to additional abbreviations

CITY	CONGREGATION EMAIL WEBSITE	YEAR EST	LOCATION MAILING ADDRESS	ZIP CODE(S)	DIST.	PASTOR(S)	PHONE FAX	WS SS BC	SCHOOLS/ MINISTRIES	STATISTIC Bapt	Conf	Avg Attend
PITTSFORD	*ST MARK*		See Mendon NY									
POTTERSVILLE	*SONRISE* www.sonriselc.org	2000	7996 Route 9 PO BOX 51	12860	AT	Bruce E Rudolf	(772)321-8692	WS 930	ED/HC	23	23	25
PUTNAM VALLEY	*ST LUKE* stlukepv@gmail.com www.stlukesputnamvalley.org	1942	65 Oscawana Lake Rd PO BOX 64	10579	AT	William M Vangor	(845)528-8858	WS 930	EC/ED/HC/ MD	51	38	24
QUEENS	*CHRIST*		See Woodside NY									
	EMMAUS		See Ridgewood NY									
	OUR SAVIOUR NEW YORK		See Rego Park NY									
	REDEEMER		See Saint Albans NY									
	RESURRECTION		See Flushing NY									
RED CREEK	*HOPE COMMUNITY* cohawkin@yahoo.com www.hopelutheranredcreek.org		6847 Main St PO BOX 54	13143	EA	Charles E Madison	(585)690-1648	WS 11 SS 1015	HC/MD	46	30	16
REGO PARK	*OUR SAVIOUR NEW YORK* aforgione@our-saviour.org www.oursaviournewyork.com	1926	9214 63RD DR	11374	AT	Anthony Forgione	(718)275-2825	WS 1030 SS 1030	EC/EL/HS/ ED/MD	65	27	85
RIDGEWOOD	*EMMAUS* www.emmausnyc.org	1904	6010 67TH AVE	11385	AT	John A Stoudt	(718)821-5253 (718)381-6719	WS 1030	EL/HS/ ED/HC	22	20	16
RIVERHEAD	*OUR REDEEMER*		See Aquebogue NY									
ROCHESTER	*ALPHA DEAF* revjohnrushton@gmail.com	1923	250 Pinnacle Rd PO BOX 24708	14623 14624	EA	John S Rushton	(585)286-2600	WS 11	ED/MD/SN	33	27	15
	HOPE connect@sharethehope.org www.sharethehope.org	1929	1301 VINTAGE LN	14626	EA	Kirk D Dueker Jeffrey A Reuter Larry S Stojkovic	(585)723-4673 (585)723-8549	WS 930 1115 SS 930	EC/ED/HC/ MD/SN	1398	1104	664
	PINNACLE office@pinnaclelutheran.org www.pinnaclelutheran.org	1957	250 PINNACLE RD	14623	EA		(585)334-1392 (585)334-6022	WS 10 SS 9 1015 BC 9	ED/HC/ MD/SN	160	155	74
	RISEN CHRIST		See Fairport NY									
	ST MARK		See West Henrietta NY									
ROME	*BREAD OF LIFE* allen@breadoflifelutheran.org BreadOfLifeLutheran.org	2018	700 WEST LIBERTY ST	13440	EA			WS 11	MD	7	7	14
	ROME RESCUE MISSION Satellite Site of Bread of Life Rome NY	2018	413 E Dominick St	13440								
	ST JOHN Office@StJohnsLutheranRome. onmicrosoft.com www.stjohnslutheranchurchromeny.com/	1848	502 W CHESTNUT ST	13440	EA	Robert Catherwood Jr	(315)336-8090	WS 10 SS 9 BC 9	ED/MD/SN	150	65	74
ROTTERDAM	*IMMANUEL*		See Niskayuna NY									
RUSH	*PINNACLE*		See Rochester NY									
	ST MARK		See Mendon NY									
SAINT ALBANS	*REDEEMER* www.englishredeemerchurch.com	1926	11601 204TH ST	11412	EN	Steven B Hicks	(718)525-3233	WS 1045 SS 915 BC 930	ED/HC/MD			
SAINT JAMES	*SAINT JAMES* office@stjlc.com www.stjameslutheranchurch.com	1923	230 2ND AVE	11780	AT	Neil A Mittelstaedt Conner E Forbes	(631)584-5212	WS 830 10 SS 10	EC/ED/HC/ MD	2674	1651	190
SARATOGA SPRINGS	*MEN'S BREAKFAST BIBLE STUDY* Satellite Site of St Paul Saratoga Springs NY	2008	120 West Avenue	12866								
	ST PAUL office@spalutheran.org www.spalutheran.org	1894	149 LAKE AVE SARATOGA SPGS	12866	AT	Adam C Wiegand	(518)584-0904 (518)584-2180	WS 10 SS 1130	EC/ED/HC/ MD/SN	574	574	129
SAYVILLE	*ST JOHN* stjohns11782@aol.com www.stjohnsayville.org	1897	48 GREENE AVE	11782	AT	Brian B Noack	(631)589-3202 (631)589-1419	WS 745 9 11 SS 9	ED/HC/ MD/SN	306	235	126
SCARSDALE	*TRINITY* lutheranchurchtrinity@gmail.com www.trinityscarsdale.org	1924	25 CRANE RD	10583	EN	Curtis D Stephens	(914)723-1998	WS 10 SS 9 BC 9	ED/HC/MD	49	42	26
SCHENECTADY	*IMMANUEL*		See Niskayuna NY									
	TRINITY www.trinitylutheranchurchschenectady.org	1905	35 FURMAN ST	12304	AT	Mohan P Singh	(518)346-5646 (518)346-4982	WS 9 1130 SS 1015 BC 1015	ED/HC/ MD/SN	98	90	80
	ZION zion@zionlcny.org www.zion.lc	1872	153 Nott Ter PO BOX 915	12308 12301	AT	Francis S Rigobert	(518)374-1811 (518)374-4438	WS 10 SS 910 BC 830	ED/HC/ MD/SN	429	425	90
SCHODACK	*LOVE* johnbuzz01@yahoo.com	1958	114 Birchwood 10 GREENWOOD DR PO BOX 118 E GREENBUSH	12033 12061	AT		(518)477-8685	WS 10 SS 9 BC 9	ED/HC/ MD/SN	42	34	16
SCHROON LAKE	*SONRISE*		See Pottersville NY									
SCOTIA	*IMMANUEL*		See Niskayuna NY									
SETAUKET	*MESSIAH*		See East Setauket NY									
SHIRLEY	*CHRIST*		See East Moriches NY									
SILVER CREEK	*TRINITY*	1833	15 PORTER AVE	14136	EA		(716)934-2002 (716)934-9549	WS 1045 SS 1015 BC 10	ED/HC/ MD/SN			

*Indicates a new church start. A new church start is an intentionally organized gathering which comes together on a regular basis for the purpose of worship and/or Bible study and is intended to grow into a member LCMS congregation. WS =Worship Service; SS = Sunday School; BC =Bible Class; EC = Early Childhood; EL = Elementary School; HS = High School; ED =Education Ministry; HC =Human Care Ministry; SN = Special Needs Ministry; MD = Media Ministry (PC)=Partner Church Pastor. See Page 53 for the Table of Abbreviations for key to additional abbreviations

CITY	CONGREGATION EMAIL WEBSITE	YEAR EST	LOCATION MAILING ADDRESS	ZIP CODE(S)	DIST.	PASTOR(S)	PHONE FAX	WS SS BC	SCHOOLS/ MINISTRIES	STATISTIC Bapt	Conf	Avg Attend
SMITHTOWN	*SAINT JAMES*		See Saint James NY									
SPENCERPORT	*TRINITY* trinitylutheran191@gmail.com www.trinityspencerport.org	1958	191 NICHOLS ST	14559	EA		(585)352-3143 (585)352-3172	WS 9 11 SS 10 BC 10	EC/ED/HC/ MD/SN	316	232	78
SPRINGVILLE	*SALEM* office@salemspringville.org www.salemspringville.org	1871	91 W MAIN ST	14141	EA	Eric A Goodwin	(716)592-4893 (716)592-1881	WS 1030 SS 9	EC/ED/HC/ MD/SN	410	319	102
	TRINITY		See West Valley NY									
STAMFORD	*TRINITY*	1966	126 Route 10 126 STATE ROUTE 10	12167	AT	Robert C Wilson	(607)652-2711	WS 9		34	34	14
STATEN ISLAND	*CHRIST ASSEMBLY* calclcms1@gmail.com	1996	27 HUDSON ST	10304	AT	Philip S Saywrayne Zaza L Kandakai	(718)556-2652 (718)420-9423	WS 11 SS 1030	ED/HC	440	405	160
	ST JOHN sjlcouncil663@gmail.com www.stjohnslutheransi.org	1852	216 Jewett Ave 663 MANOR RD	10302 10314	AT	Michael R Bagnall	(718)761-1600	WS 1030 BC 9	EL/ED/MD	120	107	60
	ST JOHNS LUTHERAN SCHOOL Satellite Site of St John Staten Island NY	1950	663 Manor Rd	10314								
	ST MATTHEW StMatthewsLCMS_10304@yahoo.com stmatthews-statenisland.com	1915	96 ALTER AVE	10304	AT	Philip S Saywrayne	(718)351-0866	WS 10 SS 9		28	24	9
STONY POINT	*ATONEMENT* atonementlutheranchurch.net	1959	71 CENTRAL HWY	10980	AT	Martin A Tyce	(845)942-0121	WS 1045 SS 930	ED/MD/SN	97	71	36
STUYVESANT	*ST JOHN* stjohnsstuyvesant@gmail.com www.stjohnsstuyvesant.org	1870	159 Route 26A 159 COUNTY ROUTE 26A	12173	AT		(518)758-1891	WS 1015 SS 9	ED/HC/MD	77	72	24
SYRACUSE	*HOPE COMMUNITY* johnsonabednego@yahoo.com		620 W GENESEE ST	13204	EN		(315)251-4141 (315)299-7148	WS 2 SS 130	HC/MD/SN			
THE BRONX	*OUR SAVIOUR*		See Bronx NY									
	REDEEMER		See Bronx NY									
	TRINITY		See Bronx NY									
TONAWANDA	*FIRST TRINITY* office@firsttrinity.com www.FirstTrinity.com	1839	1570 NIAGARA FALLS BLVD	14150	EA	Dr Charles E Whited Jr Jason A Christ	(716)835-2220 (716)833-6998	WS 845 1115 SS 10 BC 10	EC/ED/HC/ MD/SN	927	810	252
	IMMANUEL immanuel14150@gmail.com www.ilctny.org	1868	107 SCOTT ST	14150	EA	Michael R Dobler	(716)692-6200 (716)692-3435	WS 1030 SS 9 BC 9	ED/HC/MD	310	297	44
TROY	*IMMANUEL*		See Niskayuna NY									
UTICA	*TRINITY* trinity.utica@verizon.net www.trinitylutheranutica.com	1881	2620 GENESEE ST	13502	EA	Peter N Saie	(315)732-7869 (315)732-7869	WS 10 SS 9 BC 9	EC/ED/HC	128	109	38
VALLEY STREAM	*OUR SAVIOUR* Pastoralfy@gmail.com www.oursaviourvalleystream.com	1932	888 ROCKAWAY AVE	11581	EN	Alfred R Thiagarajan	(516)825-5453 (516)825-5453	WS 930 SS 930	ED/HC/ MD/SN	35	35	35
VESTAL	*GRACE* gracevestal709@gmail.com gracelutheranchurchvestal.com	1950	709 MAIN ST	13850	EA		(607)748-0840 (607)748-0840	WS 930 SS 1045 BC 1045	EC/ED/HC/ MD/SN			
VICTOR	*ST MARK*		See Mendon NY									
WARWICK	*GOOD SHEPHERD* gslc@warwick.net www.goodshepherdwarwick.org	1964	95 Kings Hwy PO BOX 218	10990	AT	Henry Albrechtsen III	(845)986-3040 (845)986-3050	WS 930 SS 1050 BC 1050		246	233	45
	ST PETER st.petercontact@gmail.com stpeterwarwick.org	1897	70 LITTLE YORK RD	10990	AT	Dr Kenneth J Doka	(845)258-4541	WS 11	HC	50	50	13
WATERLOO	*CALVARY* calluth@rochester.twcbc.com calvarylutheranwaterloo.com	1951	2414 Route 414 N 2414 STATE ROUTE 414	13165	EA	William R Dorow Jr	(315)539-8053 (315)539-6225	WS 930 SS 1045 BC 1045	ED/HC/ MD/SN	107	71	62
WELLSVILLE	*TRINITY* churchofficetrinity@gmail.com www.trinitylutheranwellsvilleny.org	1859	470 N MAIN ST	14895	EA		(585)593-3311 (585)593-1194	WS 1030 SS 9 BC 9	EC/ED/HC/ MD/SN	213	195	54
WEST BLOOMFIELD	*ST MARK*		See Mendon NY									
WEST HENRIETTA	*ST MARK* pastor@saintmarkslutheran.org www.saintmarkslutheran.org	1901	779 Erie Station Rd PO BOX 287 W HENRIETTA	14586	EA		(585)334-4795	WS 10 SS 1130	ED/HC/MD	75	60	29
WEST SENECA	*TRINITY* trinitylutheranchurch146@verizon.net trinitywestseneca.com	1849	146 RESERVE RD	14224	EA	Nycholas C Greig	(716)674-9188 (716)674-9188	WS 1030 SS 915 BC 915	EL/ED/HC/ MD/SN	474	372	146
WEST VALLEY	*TRINITY* ashfordtrinitylutheranchurch@ gmail.com	1866	10377 DUTCH HILL RD	14171	EA	Timothy D Klahn	(716)570-5953	WS 945 SS 1045	ED/HC/MD			
WHITESTONE	*IMMANUEL* immwhitestone@aol.com www.immanuelwhitestone.com	1895	149 40 11th Ave 1210 150TH ST	11357	AT	Travis J Yee	(718)767-5656 (718)747-1124	WS 10 SS 1020 11 BC 915	EL/HS/ED/ HC/MD/SN	380	250	100
	THE GRAND REHABILITATION CENTER Satellite Site of Immanuel Whitestone NY	2012	157-15 19th Ave	11357								

*Indicates a new church start. A new church start is an intentionally organized gathering which comes together on a regular basis for the purpose of worship and/or Bible study and is intended to grow into a member LCMS congregation. WS =Worship Service; SS = Sunday School; BC =Bible Class; EC = Early Childhood; EL = Elementary School; HS = High School; ED =Education Ministry; HC =Human Care Ministry; SN = Special Needs Ministry; MD = Media Ministry (PC)=Partner Church Pastor. See Page 53 for the Table of Abbreviations for key to additional abbreviations

CITY	CONGREGATION EMAIL WEBSITE	YEAR EST	LOCATION MAILING ADDRESS	ZIP CODE(S)	DIST.	PASTOR(S)	PHONE FAX	WS SS BC	SCHOOLS/ MINISTRIES	STATISTIC Bapt	Conf	Avg Attend
WILLIAMSVILLE	*AMBERLEIGH RETIREMENT COMMUNITY* Satellite Site of Calvary Amherst NY	1990	2330 Maple Rd	14221				WS 2				
	HOLY CROSS		See Clarence NY									
WILLISTON PARK	*SAINT JOHN'S* office@stjohns-wp.org www.stjohns-wp.org	1932	47 WINTHROP ST WILLISTON PK	11596	AT	Jacob C Allstaedt	(516)742-5858	WS 1015 BC 915	ED/HC/ MD/SN	327	312	50
WILSON	*CONCORDIA*		See Newfane NY									
WOLCOTTSVILLE	*ST MICHAEL* stmichaelsakron@gmail.com www.stmichaelsakron.org	1859	6379 WOLCOTTSVILLE RD AKRON	14001	EA		(716)542-2886	WS 9	EC/ED/ HC/SN	101	101	45
WOODSIDE	*CHRIST* clcny@aol.com www.christchurchwoodside.com	1896	3357 58TH ST	11377	AT	Edward A Marque	(718)639-3945 (718)205-1426	WS 11 SS 945 BC 945	EL/HS/ED/ HC/MD	128	74	45
	UNITED BENGALI roy_js52@yahoo.com	2001	3357 58TH ST	11377	AT	James S Roy	(718)639-3945 (718)740-2824	WS 5 SS 5 BC 4	ED/HC/MD	100	100	45
YONKERS	*HOLY TRINITY* pastor@htlcyonkers.org www.htlcyonkers.org	1895	60 Mulberry St 56-69 MULBERRY ST	10701	AT		(914)965-3884	WS 10 SS 1130	ED/HC	93	93	22
	ST MARK office@smlcyonkers.org www.smlcyonkers.org	1911	7 SAINT MARKS PL	10704	AT	Robert A Boehler	(914)237-8199 (914)237-1346	WS 10	EL/ED/HC	92	92	29
YOUNGSTOWN	*ST JOHN* stjohnyny@verizon.net sjlcy.org	1900	420 Lockport St PO BOX 365	14174	EA	William F Wrede	(716)745-3443 (716)745-3443	WS 1030	ED/HC/SN			

NORTH CAROLINA

CITY	CONGREGATION EMAIL WEBSITE	YEAR EST	LOCATION MAILING ADDRESS	ZIP CODE(S)	DIST.	PASTOR(S)	PHONE FAX	WS SS BC	SCHOOLS/ MINISTRIES	STATISTIC Bapt	Conf	Avg Attend
ABERDEEN	*ST PAUL*		See Whispering Pines NC									
APEX	*JORDAN* pastor@jordanapex.org www.jordanapex.org		309 Holleman Street 1031 PEMBERTON HILL RD STE 202	27502	SE	Michael S Merker	(919)303-1613	WS 10 SS 9 BC 9	ED/HC/MD	234	167	139
	OUR SAVIOR		See Raleigh NC									
	RESURRECTION		See Cary NC									
ASHEVILLE	*EMMANUEL* churchoffice@elcsmail.org www.emmanuellutheran.info	1904	51 WILBURN PL	28806	SE	Dr Jeffrey E Skopak	(828)252-1795 (828)285-0064	WS 830 11 SS 945 BC 945	EL/ED/HC/ MD/SN	272	260	150
	OUR SAVIOR		See Clyde NC									
	RESURRECTION		See Franklin NC									
BLOWING ROCK	*MOUNTAINSIDE*		See Linville NC									
BOONE	*MOUNTAINSIDE*		See Linville NC									
BURLINGTON	*REDEEMER* redeemerburlington@gmail.com www.redeemerlove.com/	1958	2306 LACY ST	27215	SE	Dr Charles W Spomer	(336)227-7092	WS 11 SS 10 BC 10	ED/HC/ MD/SN			
CAMERON	*ST PAUL*		See Whispering Pines NC									
CANTON	*OUR SAVIOR*		See Clyde NC									
CAROLINA BEACH	*MESSIAH*		See Wilmington NC									
CARY	*ETHIOPIAN MEKANE* endalk@aol.com		100 W LOCHMERE DR	27518	SE		(919)201-1637			93	0	61
	JORDAN		See Apex NC									
	OROMO NC dantene2012@gmail.com		110 SE Maynard Rd 100 W LOCHMERE DR	27511 27518	SE		(614)772-5579					
	OUR SAVIOR		See Raleigh NC									
	RESURRECTION office@rlcary.org www.rlcary.org	1978	100 W LOCHMERE DR	27518	SE	Dr Jonathan A Blanke Alan C Shaw Zachery R Sarrault	(919)851-7248 (919)851-6411	WS 8 930 11 SS 930	EC/EL/ED/ HC/MD/SN	1174	938	377
CATAWBA	*REDEEMER* pastor@redeemercatawba.com www.redeemercatawba.com	1916	200 S Main St PO BOX 187	28609	SE	David M Daniels	(828)241-2371 (828)241-2371	WS 10 SS 9	ED/HC/ MD/SN	335	280	90
	ST JOHN		See Conover NC									
CHAPEL HILL	*ADVENT* www.adventlutheranch.org	1988	230 ERWIN RD	27514	SE	Richard S Lohman	(919)968-7690	WS 1030 SS 905 BC 905				
	OUR SAVIOR		See Raleigh NC									
CHARLOTTE	*ABUNDANT LIFE* pastorstout@yahoo.com	2001	908 Kenilworth Ave C/O ASCENSION LUTHERAN CHURCH 1225 E MOREHEAD ST	28204	SE	Christopher T Stout	(704)750-1463 (704)531-9000	WS 11 SS 10 BC 10	ED/HC/ MD/SN	15	13	8
	ALL SAINTS allsaintscharlotte@outlook.com www.allsaintslutheran.org	1956	17030 LANCASTER HWY	28277	SE	Jeffrey W Ware	(704)752-4287 (704)752-4283	WS 1030 SS 9 BC 9	ED/MD	191	153	121
	ASCENSION www.AscensionCharlotte.org	1931	1225 E MOREHEAD ST	28204	SE	Steven E Newberg	(704)372-7317	WS 830 11 SS 945	ED/HC/ MD/SN	305	248	176
	CENTER GROVE		See Kannapolis NC									
	MESSIAH office@messiah-nc.org www.messiah-nc.org	1980	8300 PROVIDENCE RD	28277	SE	Steven B Patton Roger Penny	(704)541-1624 (704)541-1292	WS 815 1045 SS 945 BC 945	EC/ED/HC/ MD/SN	420	385	220

*Indicates a new church start. A new church start is an intentionally organized gathering which comes together on a regular basis for the purpose of worship and/or Bible study and is intended to grow into a member LCMS congregation. WS =Worship Service; SS = Sunday School; BC =Bible Class; EC = Early Childhood; EL = Elementary School; HS = High School; ED =Education Ministry; HC =Human Care Ministry; SN = Special Needs Ministry; MD = Media Ministry (PC)=Partner Church Pastor. See Page 53 for the Table of Abbreviations for key to additional abbreviations

CITY	CONGREGATION EMAIL WEBSITE	YEAR EST	LOCATION MAILING ADDRESS	ZIP CODE(S)	DIST.	PASTOR(S)	PHONE FAX	WS SS BC	SCHOOLS/ MINISTRIES	STATISTIC Bapt	Conf	Avg Attend
CHARLOTTE	*PRINCE OF PEACE* www.popnc.org	1964	3001 BEATTIES FORD RD	28216	SE		(704)392-6098 (704)392-4452	WS 10	ED/HC/MD	31	31	23
CLAREMONT	*BETHEL* churchoffice@bethelms.org bethelms.org	1870	5759 BOLICK RD	28610	SE	Eric C Hollar Morgan S Lane	(828)459-7378 (828)459-7841	WS 8 1030 SS 915	ED/HC/ MD/SN			
	CONCORDIA		See Conover NC									
	ST JOHN		See Conover NC									
CLAYTON	*HOLY CROSS* william.beyer@holycrossclayton.com www.holycrossclayton.com	2001	2920 VETERANS PARKWAY	27520	SE	William D Beyer	(919)553-4784 (919)553-6061	WS 830 11 SS 10	EC/ED/HC/ MD/SN	690	605	288
	OUR SAVIOR		See Raleigh NC									
CLYDE	*OUR SAVIOR* office@oslcnc.com www.oslcnc.com	1961	785 PARAGON PKWY	28721	SE	Jonathan Z Misch	(828)456-6493	WS 1030 SS 930	MD	78	60	63
COLUMBUS	*TRINITY*		See Tryon NC									
CONCORD	*CENTER GROVE*		See Kannapolis NC									
	GRACE lebuick@aol.com www.gracelutheran-concordnc.org	1891	58 Chestnut Dr SW PO BOX 891	28025 28026	SE	Donald E Anthony	(704)782-7620 (704)795-5475	WS 11 SS 930				
	ST PETER stpeterlutheran@windstream.net www.saintpeters-lutheran.org	1895	2400 WARD AVE	28025	SE		(704)786-2507	WS 11 SS 945	ED/HC/MD			
CONOVER	*CONCORDIA* sharman@concordianc.org concordianc.org/home.php	1878	216 5TH AVE SE	28613	SE	Michael A Geml	(828)464-3324 (828)464-3400	WS 9 11 SS 1010	EL/ED/HC/ MD/SN	1090	852	216
	CONOVER NURSING HOME Satellite Site of Immanuel Conover NC	2004	920 4th St SW	28613								
	IMMANUEL	1894	2448 EMMANUEL CHURCH RD	28613	SE	Robert J Stevens	(828)464-4050	WS 10 SS 9 BC 9	HC/MD/SN			
	SAINT PETER'S secretary@stpetersconover.org www.stpetersconover.org	1825	6175 Saint Peters Church Rd 6175 ST PETERS CHURCH RD	28613	SE	Peter A Frank Robert E Hauss	(828)256-2970	WS 815 1045 SS 930 BC 930	ED/HC/ MD/SN	465	426	225
	ST JOHN secretary@stjohnsconover.com www.stjohnsconover.com	1798	2126 SAINT JOHNS CHURCH RD NE	28613	SE	Anton G Lagoutine Luke W Self	(828)464-4071 (828)464-6590	WS 8 1030 SS 930	EC/ED/HC/ MD/SN	1124	828	300
DENVER	*LAKE NORMAN* officelnlc@gmail.com www.lakenormanlutheran.com	1978	1445 N Highway 16 1445 N. NC 16 BUSINESS HIGHWAY	28037	SE	Mark A Schild	(704)483-2130 (704)483-3427	WS 830 11 SS 9 BC 845	ED/HC/ MD/SN	118	105	73
DURHAM	*GRACE* office@gracedurham.org gracedurham.org	1942	824 N BUCHANAN BLVD	27701	SE	David H Brooks Richard R Kuehn	(919)682-6030	WS 830 11	ED/HC/SN	192	172	75
FAYETTEVILLE	*OUR REDEEMER* orlc_pastor@ncrrbiz.com www.faylcms.org	1961	1605 VAN BUREN AVE	28303	SE	Tod R Rappe	(910)488-6010 (910)823-9122	WS 1030 SS 9 BC 9	ED/HC/MD	170	120	89
FRANKLIN	*RESURRECTION* resurrectionlutheran22@gmail.com rlcfranklin.org/	1977	38 Wayah St PO BOX 2215	28734 28744	SE	Glenn A Roseman Sr	(828)524-5996	WS 1030 SS 915	EC/ED/HC/ MD/SN	126	56	59
GARNER	*JORDAN*		See Apex NC									
GOLDSBORO	*PEACE* peacelutherangoldsboro@gmail.com peacelutherangoldsboro.360unite. com/home	1968	1002 GARDNER MANOR DR	27534	SE		(919)778-2230	WS 11 BC 9				
GREENSBORO	*EBENEZER* office@ebenezerlutheranchurch.com www.ebenezerlutheranchurch.com	1907	310 S TREMONT DR	27403	SE	John H Scheuermann Jr	(336)272-5321 (336)272-5320	WS 830 11 SS 945 BC 945	HC/MD/SN			
	FOUNTAIN OF LIFE		See Kernersville NC									
	GRACE cgracelutheran13@att.net	1897	1315 E WASHINGTON ST	27401	SE		(336)272-1174 (336)272-1176	WS 11 SS 930 BC 930	ED/HC/SN			
HAMPSTEAD	*MESSIAH*		See Wilmington NC									
HAVELOCK	*ST PAUL* saintpaulpastor@gmail.com www.stpaulhavelock.com	1956	305 US Hwy 70 West 305 US HIGHWAY 70 W	28532	SE	James M Daub	(252)447-3826 (252)447-0714	WS 9 11	ED/HC/ MD/SN	118	109	70
HAYESVILLE	*ALL SAINTS*		See Blairsville GA									
	RESURRECTION		See Franklin NC									
HENDERSONVILLE	*MOUNT PISGAH* mtpisgahlcms@gmail.com www.mtpisgahlutheran.com	1956	2606 CHIMNEY ROCK RD HENDERSONVLLE	28792	SE	Jonathan K Christensen	(828)692-7027 (828)692-7667	WS 10 SS 830	EC/ED/HC/ MD/SN	136	119	75
HICKORY	*AUGUSTANA* church@augustanalcms.org www.AugustanaLutheranHickory.com	1905	1523 16TH ST SE	28602	SE	Devin M Kerns	(828)328-6706	WS 1030 BC 930	ED/HC/ MD/SN			
	CHRIST clcs@clchickory.com www.christlutheranchurhhickory.com	1900	324 2ND AVE SE	28602	SE	Alexander R Fisher Richard J Tucker Sr David J Ludwig	(828)328-1483 (828)328-9841	WS 9 1030 SS 915 BC 9 1030	ED/HC/SN	299	225	110
	CONCORDIA		See Conover NC									
	OUR SAVIOR osluthhickory@gmail.com www.oursaviorhickory.org	1960	2160 35TH AVENUE DR NE	28601	SE	Mark M Seaman	(828)256-5469 (828)256-2160	WS 10 SS 845	ED/HC	156	101	55

*Indicates a new church start. A new church start is an intentionally organized gathering which comes together on a regular basis for the purpose of worship and/or Bible study and is intended to grow into a member LCMS congregation. WS =Worship Service; SS = Sunday School; BC =Bible Class; EC = Early Childhood; EL = Elementary School; HS = High School; ED =Education Ministry; HC =Human Care Ministry; SN = Special Needs Ministry; MD = Media Ministry (PC)=Partner Church Pastor. See Page 53 for the Table of Abbreviations for key to additional abbreviations

CITY	CONGREGATION EMAIL WEBSITE	YEAR EST	LOCATION MAILING ADDRESS	ZIP CODE(S)	DIST.	PASTOR(S)	PHONE FAX	WS SS BC	SCHOOLS/ MINISTRIES	STATISTIC Bapt	Conf	Avg Attend
HICKORY	*ST JOHN*		See Conover NC									
	ST STEPHEN sslcms.org	1898	2304 SPRINGS RD NE	28601	SE	David W Ziehr Shea R Pennington	(828)256-9865 (828)256-7994	WS 8 1030 SS 930	EL/ED/HC/ MD/SN	1961	1567	533
HIGH POINT	*FOUNTAIN OF LIFE*		See Kernersville NC									
	ST LUKE	1908	1711 Stonetbrook Dr		SE	James A McDaniels						
HIGHLANDS	*RESURRECTION*		See Franklin NC									
HOLLY SPRINGS	*JORDAN*		See Apex NC									
HUNTERSVILLE	*POINT OF GRACE* qgirard@bellsouth.net www.pointofgracelutheranchurch.com	2003	16214 Statesville Road PO BOX 1505	28078 28070	SE		(704)248-2776	WS 1130 BC 10	ED/HC/MD	22	20	10
JACKSONVILLE	*CALVARY* office@clcms.org clcms.org	1963	206 PINE VALLEY RD	28546	SE	Jason S Dart	(910)353-4016	WS 8 1030 SS 920	EC/ED/HC/ MD/SN	206	128	147
KANNAPOLIS	*CENTER GROVE* secretary@centergrovelcms.org www.centergrovelutheran.org	1876	1601 S Cannon Blvd P. O. BOX 934	28083 28082	SE	Christopher T Stout	(704)750-1463	WS 1145 SS 1030	ED/HC/MD	72	68	48
	MOUNT CALVARY MtCalvary1898@outlook.com mountcalvarylutheran.net	1898	204 N Little Texas Rd PO BOX 250	28083 28082	SE	Christopher T Stout	(704)932-2864 (704)292-4859	WS 10 SS 9	ED/HC/ MD/SN	190	134	56
KERNERSVILLE	*FOUNTAIN OF LIFE* churchinfo@folcp.com www.cometothefountain.com	1965	323 HOPKINS RD	27284	SE	Elliott M Lutz	(336)993-4447 (336)993-0941	WS 830 11 SS 950 BC 950	EC/ED/HC/ MD/SN	530	439	252
KILL DEVIL HILLS	*GRACE BY SEA*		See Nags Head NC									
KINGSTON	*KINGSTON REHABILITATION CENTER* Satellite Site of Faith Kinston NC	1996	Kingston Rehabilitation Center	28501								
KINSTON	*FAITH* faithlutherankinston@gmail.com www.faithlutherankinston.org	1940	709 W VERNON AVE	28501	SE	Frank X Kinast Jr	(252)523-6033 (252)523-2032	WS 11 SS 945	ED/HC/MD	129	120	49
KITTY HAWK	*GRACE BY SEA*		See Nags Head NC									
LELAND	*MESSIAH*		See Wilmington NC									
LINCOLNTON	*ST LUKES* www.stlukeslcms.org		4051 KING WILKINSON RD	28092	SE		(704)735-2968	WS 11 SS 10	ED/HC/ MD/SN			
LINVILLE	*MOUNTAINSIDE* mountainsidelutheran@gmail.com www.mountainsidelutheran.org	2003	1308 Linville Falls Highway PO BOX 235	28646	SE	Bryan J Chestnutt	(828)733-4404	WS 930 10 BC 1045 1115	ED/HC/MD	116	96	73
MAGGIE VALLEY	*OUR SAVIOR*		See Clyde NC									
MAIDEN	*CONCORDIA*		See Conover NC									
	ST JOHN		See Conover NC									
MANTEO	*GRACE BY SEA*		See Nags Head NC									
MARION	*ST MATTHEW* smlcinmarionnc@frontier.com	1932	241 W COURT ST	28752	SE		(828)659-1060	WS 1030 SS 915	HC	15	15	15
MATTHEWS	*ALL SAINTS*		See Charlotte NC									
	MESSIAH		See Charlotte NC									
MONROE	*ALL SAINTS*		See Charlotte NC									
MOORESVILLE	*CENTER GROVE*		See Kannapolis NC									
	NEW HOPE newhopelcms@gmail.com www.newhopelcms.org	2016	296 Faith Rd PO BOX 4922	28115 28117	SE		(704)997-5360	WS 10 BC 915	HC	44	40	28
MOREHEAD CITY	*ST PAUL*		See Havelock NC									
MORRISVILLE	*JORDAN*		See Apex NC									
MURPHY	*ALL SAINTS*		See Blairsville GA									
NAGS HEAD	*GRACE BY SEA* gracelutheranobx@gmail.com www.gracelutheranobx.org	1981	4212 S Croatan Hwy PO BOX 1356	27959	SE	Peter D Grana	(252)441-1530	WS 9 SS 1030	ED/HC	86	79	71
NEW BERN	*ST PAUL*		See Havelock NC									
NEW HILL	*JORDAN*		See Apex NC									
NEWPORT	*ST PAUL*		See Havelock NC									
NEWTON	*CONCORDIA*		See Conover NC									
	MOUNT OLIVE mtolivelutheranchurchnewton@gmail.com www.mtolivenewton.org	1895	2103 MOUNT OLIVE CHURCH RD	28658	SE	Ralph A Abernethy III	(828)464-2407 (828)464-2419	WS 10 SS 9	ED/HC/ MD/SN	165	129	25
	ST JOHN		See Conover NC									
	TRINITY HMONG hmonglutheranmission@gmail.com		2110 MOUNT OLIVE CHURCH RD	28658	SE	Zang Yang	(336)325-5268		ED/HC			
PINEHURST	*ST PAUL*		See Whispering Pines NC									
PITTSBORO	*JORDAN*		See Apex NC									
PORTERS NECK	*MESSIAH*		See Wilmington NC									
PUMPKIN CENTER	*ST LUKES*		See Lincolnton NC									
RALEIGH	*HOPE*		See Wake Forest NC									
	JORDAN		See Apex NC									

*Indicates a new church start. A new church start is an intentionally organized gathering which comes together on a regular basis for the purpose of worship and/or Bible study and is intended to grow into a member LCMS congregation. WS =Worship Service; SS = Sunday School; BC =Bible Class; EC = Early Childhood; EL = Elementary School; HS = High School; ED =Education Ministry; HC =Human Care Ministry; SN = Special Needs Ministry; MD = Media Ministry (PC)=Partner Church Pastor. See Page 53 for the Table of Abbreviations for key to additional abbreviations

CITY	CONGREGATION EMAIL WEBSITE	YEAR EST	LOCATION MAILING ADDRESS	ZIP CODE(S)	DIST.	PASTOR(S)	PHONE FAX	WS SS BC	SCHOOLS/ MINISTRIES	Bapt	Conf	Avg Attend
RALEIGH	*OUR SAVIOR* secretary@oslcraleigh.org www.oslcraleigh.org	1941	1500 GLENWOOD AVE	27608	SE	Kevin W Martin	(919)832-8822 (866)906-9895	WS 830 11 SS 945 BC 945	ED/HC	291	261	150
	RESURRECTION		See Cary NC									
RIDGEWAY	*ST PAULS* splcridgeway@gmail.com www.splcridgeway.net	1898	438 Ridgeway-Drewry Rd 114 POPLAR MOUNT RD NORLINA	27570 27563	SE		(252)456-2747 (252)456-2747	WS 1030 SS 915 BC 915	HC/MD	263	213	73
SALISBURY	*CENTER GROVE*		See Kannapolis NC									
	CROWN IN GLORY	1899	517 E Bank St PO BOX 1384	28144 28145	SE		(704)633-0067 (704)633-0067	WS 9 SS 1030	ED/HC/MD			
SANFORD	*JORDAN*		See Apex NC									
SEVEN LAKES	*ST PAUL*		See Whispering Pines NC									
SHELBY	*MEN'S MATINS/BIBLE CLASSS* Satellite Site of Trinity Tryon NC	2023	232 S Lafayette St	28150								
SOUTHERN PINES	*SAINT JAMES* saintjamessouthernpines@gmail.com www.saintjamessouthernpines.com	1898	983 W NEW HAMPSHIRE AVE SOUTHERN PNES	28387	SE	David M Miedema		WS 11	HC	60	51	46
SOUTHPORT	*MESSIAH*		See Wilmington NC									
SPRING LAKE	*ST PAUL*		See Whispering Pines NC									
STATESVILLE	*HOLY TRINITY*	1929	465 HARTNESS RD	28677	SE		(704)873-3591 (704)873-8146	WS 830 11 SS 945 BC 945	ED/HC/MD			
TAYLORSVILLE	*SALEM* www.salemnc.org	1854	4005 NC Hwy 16 N 4046 NC HIGHWAY 16 N	28681	SE	Reed T Shoaff	(828)632-4863 (828)632-4863	WS 10 SS 9 BC 9	ED/HC/ MD/SN			
TRYON	*TRINITY* pto351@gmail.com www.trinitylutherantryon.com	1989	3353 US 176 HWY	28782	SE	Thomas L Olson	(828)859-0379	WS 1015 BC 9		108	84	53
VASS	*ST PAUL*		See Whispering Pines NC									
WAKE FOREST	*HOPE* bevans@hopelutheranwf.org www.hopelutheranwf.org	1996	3525 ROGERS RD	27587	SE	Devin K Murphy	(919)554-8109 (919)554-0412	WS 830 11 SS 945 BC 945	EC/ED/HC/ MD/SN	1863	1509	649
	OUR SAVIOR		See Raleigh NC									
WAXHAW	*ALL SAINTS*		See Charlotte NC									
	MESSIAH		See Charlotte NC									
WAYNESVILLE	*OUR SAVIOR*		See Clyde NC									
WEST JEFFERSON	*MOUNTAINSIDE*		See Linville NC									
WHISPERING PINES	*ST PAUL* parishpost1@gmail.com sites.google.com/view/ saintpaullutheranchurch	2001	3253 NIAGARA CARTHAGE RD	28327	SE	Dakota S Monday	(910)949-2345	WS 9 SS 1030	ED/HC	59	59	45
WILMINGTON	*MESSIAH* office@messiahwilmington.org www.messiahwilmington.org	1966	3302 S COLLEGE RD	28412	SE	Timothy C Steele	(910)791-7040	WS 930 SS 1045 BC 830	ED/HC/ MD/SN	151	133	97
WILSON	*OUR REDEEMER* kappelbeverly@yahoo.com	1938	612 NE Vance St 612 VANCE ST NE	27893	SE		(252)955-0522	WS 830 BC 10		55	55	23
WINSTON-SALEM	*FOUNTAIN OF LIFE*		See Kernersville NC									
	ST JOHN churchsecretary@stjohnsws.org stjohnsws.com	1924	2415 Silas Creek Parkway 2415 SILAS CREEK PKWY	27103	SE	Hans T Labuhn	(336)725-1651 (336)725-1603	WS 830 1030 SS 930 BC 930	EL/ED/HC/ MD	329	250	175
	ST MARK bmartinwatson@triad.rr.cm	1921	1151 E 14TH ST	27105	SE		(336)391-5701		ED/HC/ MD/SN			
WRIGHTSVILLE BEACH	*MESSIAH*		See Wilmington NC									

NORTH DAKOTA

CITY	CONGREGATION EMAIL WEBSITE	YEAR EST	LOCATION MAILING ADDRESS	ZIP CODE(S)	DIST.	PASTOR(S)	PHONE FAX	WS SS BC	SCHOOLS/ MINISTRIES	Bapt	Conf	Avg Attend
ADRIAN	*TRINITY*	1897	8895 56TH ST SE	58472	ND	Thomas R Eckstein	(701)778-5181	WS 11 SS 10		40	32	12
ANAMOOSE	*ST MARTIN*	1899	Ave E West & 1st St W #006 PO BOX 179	58710	ND	Timothy L Stout	(701)465-3585	WS 830 SS 930 BC 930	ED/HC/MD	101	85	23
BARNEY	*PEACE* www.peacetrinitylcms.org/	1899	300 MAIN ST	58008	ND	Brock W Schmeling	(701)439-2429	WS 1030 SS 915 BC 1130	ED/HC/ MD/SN	83	71	27
BEACH	*ST PAUL* stpaulbeach@midstate.net www.stpaulbeach.org	1909	387 S Central Ave PO BOX 549	58621	ND		(701)872-4700	WS 1015 SS 1115 BC 1115		119	101	44
	ST PETER		See Belfield ND									
BELFIELD	*ST PETER*	1902	12934 33RD ST SW	58622	ND		(701)872-4700	WS 8	ED	33	25	16
BEULAH	*CONCORDIA* www.concordiabeulah.org	1947	801 Beacon Ln PO BOX 189	58523	ND	Toby H Heller	(701)873-4388	WS 10 SS 11 BC 11	ED/HC/MD	345	285	74
BINFORD	*ZION* bnrahlf@ictc.com	1907	10369 4th St NE 271 GROVE ST SUTTON	58416 58484	ND				SN	25	21	16
BISMARCK	*BETHEL* secretary@bethelbismarck.com www.bethelbismarck.com	1967	615 E TURNPIKE AVE	58501	ND	Jonathan J Walla Justin E Woodside	(701)255-1433	WS 830 11 SS 945 BC 945	EL/ED/HC/ MD/SN	622	480	207

*Indicates a new church start. A new church start is an intentionally organized gathering which comes together on a regular basis for the purpose of worship and/or Bible study and is intended to grow into a member LCMS congregation. WS =Worship Service; SS = Sunday School; BC =Bible Class; EC = Early Childhood; EL = Elementary School; HS = High School; ED =Education Ministry; HC =Human Care Ministry; SN = Special Needs Ministry; MD = Media Ministry (PC)=Partner Church Pastor. See Page 53 for the Table of Abbreviations for key to additional abbreviations

CITY	CONGREGATION EMAIL WEBSITE	YEAR EST	LOCATION MAILING ADDRESS	ZIP CODE(S)	DIST.	PASTOR(S)	PHONE FAX	WS SS BC	SCHOOLS/ MINISTRIES	STATISTIC Bapt	Conf	Avg Attend
BISMARCK	*HOLY CROSS* mt@midco.net www.holycrossbismarck.org	2010	7111 WILLIAMSON DR.	58503	ND	Matthew R Thompson	(701)426-4877	WS 9 SS 1030 BC 8	EL/ED/HC/ MD/SN	129	105	65
	SHEP VALLEY pastor.wolfgram@gmail.com sotv-bis.org	1977	801 E DENVER AVE	58504	ND	Lester J Wolfgram Justin E Woodside	(701)258-4231	WS 9 SS 1030	EL/ED/HC/ MD/SN	185	159	81
	ZION zionlcmsbis@gmail.com www.zionbismarck.org	1924	413 E AVENUE D	58501	ND	Thomas R Marcis Jr Vincent J Otto	(701)223-8286 (701)258-2146	WS 830 1045 SS 930 BC 930	EL/ED/HC/ MD/SN	1089	875	250
BOTTINEAU	*OUR SAVIOR'S* oslcsecretary@utma.com www.oslcb.com	1941	709 11TH ST E	58318	ND	Christopher J Neuendorf	(701)228-3021 (701)228-3021	WS 11 SS 945	ED/HC/SN	363	300	70
CARRINGTON	*GRACE* gracesp@daktel.com	1941	95 1st St N PO BOX 436 95 1ST STREET N.	58421	ND		(701)652-2204	WS 830 BC 930	ED/HC/ MD/SN	155	138	35
CAVALIER	*OUR SAVIOR* oslccavalier@gmail.com	1948	508 Division Ave N PO BOX 88	58220	ND	Aaron Parkhurst	(701)265-4408	WS 945 SS 845	ED/HC/ MD/SN	194	159	46
COOPERSTOWN	*GRACE* ljwhite@mlgc.com www.cooperstownd.com	1948	1010 Burrel Ave SE PO BOX 674	58425	ND				ED/HC/ MD/SN	27	21	14
CRETE	*ST JOHNS*		See Oakes ND									
CRYSTAL	*ST JOHN*	1878	8294 Highway 18 8389 HIGHWAY 18	58222	ND		(701)657-2323	WS 8	HC	11	11	1
DEVILS LAKE	*ST PETER* stpeterslcms@gondtc.com	1893	623 7th Ave NE PO BOX 834	58301	ND		(701)662-2245	WS 11 SS 10	ED/MD	50	50	35
DICKINSON	*REDEEMER* rlc4him@ndsupernet.com redeemerdickinson.org	1928	711 10TH AVE W	58601	ND	Michael D Wolters	(701)483-4463	WS 9 SS 1030 BC 1030	ED/HC/ MD/SN	225	186	102
DRAYTON	*TRINITY*	1947	307 N Main St PO BOX 25	58225	ND	Daniel M Provost		WS 930 SS 1030	ED/HC/SN			
EDGELEY	*ZION* zionlcmspastor@drtel.net sites.google.com/view/edgeley-lcms/ home	1888	110 2nd Ave W PO BOX 96	58433	ND	Brandon D Woodruff	(701)493-2537	WS 1030 SS 9 BC 1145	ED/MD/SN	186	166	72
ELLENDALE	*ZION* zionlutheran@drtel.net zionlutheranellendale.com	1923	121 2nd St S PO BOX 793	58436	ND	Paul O Preus Dwaine D Doremus	(701)349-4147	WS 930 SS 1030 BC 1030	ED/HC/ MD/SN	232	172	80
FARGO	*BEAUTIFUL SAVIOR* office@bslcfargo.org www.beautifulsaviorfargo.com	1982	2601 23RD AVE S	58103	ND	Christopher C Waldvogel Daniel E Bodin Samuel G Majak	(701)293-1047 (701)293-9022	WS 815 1045 SS 930 BC 930	EL/ED/HC/ MD	522	374	203
	CROSSPOINTE office@crosspointelutheran.org www.crosspointelutheran.org		4550 South 37th Ave 4550 37TH AVE S	58104	ND				EL/ED/HC	152	110	55
	GRACE gracelutheran@gracefargo.org www.gracefargo.org	1898	821 5TH AVE S	58103	ND	Michael D Suelzle	(701)232-1516	WS 10 SS 1045 BC 1045	EL/ED/HC/ MD	419	345	96
	IMMANUEL immanuel.fargo@gmail.com www.immanuelfargo.org	1950	1258 Broadway 1258 BROADWAY N	58102	ND	Bernard M Worral Scott E Johnson	(701)293-7979 (701)293-5075	WS 815 11 SS 930 BC 930	EL/ED/HC/ MD/SN	740	578	245
	ST JOHN		See Hillsboro ND									
FORBES	*BETHLEHEM* zionlcmspastor@drtel.net sites.google.com/view/blcforbes-lcms/ home	1923	28 Lewis St PO BOX 95	58439	ND	Brandon D Woodruff	(701)357-7521 (605)358-8721	WS 830 SS 930	ED/SN	72	53	35
FULLERTON	*ST JOHNS*		See Oakes ND									
GARRISON	*PEACE* peace@restel.net	1972	505 2nd St NW PO BOX 756	58540	ND		(701)463-2073	WS 5 SS 4	ED	74	65	37
GLEN ULLIN	*ZION*	1924	111 S 2nd St PO BOX 129	58631	ND	Toby H Heller	(701)348-3172	WS 8 SS 9		45	34	24
GLOVER	*ST JOHNS*		See Oakes ND									
GRAFTON	*ZION ENGLISH* sites.google.com/view/zetlutheran/ home	1887	1100 Hill Ave PO BOX 457	58237	ND	Daniel M Provost	(701)352-2869	WS 11 BC 12	ED/HC/MD			
GRAND FORKS	*IMMANUEL* immanuel@immanuelgf.org www.immanuelgf.org	1900	1710 CHERRY ST	58201	ND	Daniel C Voth	(701)775-7125	WS 830 11 SS 945 BC 945	EC/ED/HC/ MD/SN	720	596	196
	REDEEMER redeemergf@gmail.com	1948	815 N 20TH ST	58203	ND	David E Laue	(701)772-0706	WS 1030 SS 915 BC 915		67	56	24
	ST JOHN		See Hillsboro ND									
GRASSY BUTTE	*REDEEMER*	1925	PO BOX 161	58634	ND		(701)863-6845	WS 5 BC 6				
GREAT BEND	*TRINITY* www.peacetrinitylcms.org/	1875	206 SCHOOL ST	58075	ND	Brock W Schmeling	(701)545-7422	WS 830 SS 930	MD			
GUELPH	*ST JOHNS*		See Oakes ND									
GWINNER	*ZION* secretary@ziongwinner.org www.ziongwinner.org	1908	420 1st St SE PO BOX 118	58040	ND	Michael S Grieve	(701)678-2401	WS 10 SS 845 BC 845	ED/HC/ MD/SN	216	111	53
HANKINSON	*IMMANUEL* immanuelhankinson.net	1902	205 2nd Ave NE PO BOX 440	58041	ND	Thomas J Clark	(701)242-7834	WS 945 SS 845 BC 11	ED/MD	375	276	73

*Indicates a new church start. A new church start is an intentionally organized gathering which comes together on a regular basis for the purpose of worship and/or Bible study and is intended to grow into a member LCMS congregation. WS =Worship Service; SS = Sunday School; BC =Bible Class; EC = Early Childhood; EL = Elementary School; HS = High School; ED =Education Ministry; HC =Human Care Ministry; SN = Special Needs Ministry; MD = Media Ministry (PC)=Partner Church Pastor. See Page 53 for the Table of Abbreviations for key to additional abbreviations

CITY	CONGREGATION EMAIL WEBSITE	YEAR EST	LOCATION MAILING ADDRESS	ZIP CODE(S)	DIST.	PASTOR(S)	PHONE FAX	WS SS BC	SCHOOLS/ MINISTRIES	STATISTIC Bapt	Conf	Avg Attend
HANKINSON	*ST JOHN* www.sendlcms.org/belford	1883	16656 88th St SE PO BOX 440	58041	ND	Thomas J Clark	(701)242-7741	WS 815 SS 915	ED/MD	145	111	34
HANNOVER	*ST PETER* stpeter@westriv.com stpeterzion.org	1889	2095 HIGHWAY 31	58563	ND	Zelwyn C Heide	(701)794-8705	WS 1030 SS 930 BC 6	ED/MD	229	182	42
HAZEN	*ST MATTHEW* stmatthazennd@westriv.com www.stmatthewhazen.org	1915	302 3rd St NW PO BOX 523	58545	ND		(701)748-2680	WS 9 SS 1015 BC 10	ED/HC/ MD/SN	271	206	57
	TRINITY stjohns@westriv.com	1926	Hwy 200 540 HIGHWAY 200 N	58545	ND		(701)442-3409	WS 11	ED			
HILLSBORO	*ST JOHN* trinitystjohn@outlook.com www.trinitystjohn.com	1875	204 2nd St NW PO BOX 99	58045	ND		(701)636-4692	WS 1030 SS 915	ED/HC/ MD/SN	192	144	39
HOPE	*TRINITY* clemley@ictc.com	1908	270 7th Street SE 518 5TH STREET NE	58046	ND		(701)361-9241	WS 830	ED/HC/ MD/SN	32	30	16
JAMESTOWN	*CONCORDIA* concordiajt@daktel.com www.concordiajt.org	1953	502 1ST AVE N	58401	ND	Thomas R Eckstein	(701)252-2819 (701)252-1165	WS 8 1030 SS 915 BC 915	ED/HC/ MD/SN	607	455	131
KENSAL	*ST PAUL* stpaulw@daktel.com www.stpaulw.org	1905	510 2nd Ave PO BOX 195 WIMBLEDON	58455 58492	ND	Robert T Hill	(701)435-2873	WS 830 11	ED/MD/SN	99	64	20
KONGSBERG	*ST JOHN*	1912	3037 10TH AVE N VOLTAIRE	58792	ND	Timothy L Stout	(701)626-7510	WS 1030 SS 930		25	25	18
KRAMER	*ZION*	1900	560 Rudolph St PO BOX 86	58748	ND	Jonathan R Bonine	(701)359-4461	WS 930	ED/HC	85	73	27
LAKOTA	*GRACE*	1949	415 West C PO BOX 645	58344	ND			WS 930		27	25	10
LANGDON	*REDEEMER*	1948	823 9th Ave PO BOX 526	58249	ND	Aaron Parkhurst	(701)265-4408	WS 8	ED/HC/ MD/SN	17	17	10
LARIMORE	*ST ANDREW*		See Niagara ND									
LIDGERWOOD	*HOLY CROSS* hcilcndlcms@gmail.com www.hcilc.com	1906	101 2nd Ave SE PO BOX I	58053	ND	Dr Adam T Filipek	(701)538-4688	WS 830 SS 940 BC 940		323	286	60
	IMMANUEL holycross@rrt.net www.hcilc.com	1884	9690 Hwy 18 9702 HIGHWAY 18	58053	ND	Dr Adam T Filipek	(701)538-4688	WS 11 SS 10				
	ZION		See Claire City SD									
LISBON	*REDEEMER* redeemer.lisbon@gmail.com www.facebook.com/redeemer.lisbon	1912	801 Forest St PO BOX 582	58054	ND	Christopher D Durham	(701)683-3462	WS 9 SS 1045 BC 1045	ED/HC/ MD/SN	82	66	37
LUDDEN	*ST JOHNS*		See Oakes ND									
MANDAN	*BETHEL*		See Bismarck ND									
	MESSIAH messiahsecretary@midconetwork.com www.messiahmandan.org	1956	1020 BOUNDARY ST NW	58554	ND	Kevin C Zellers	(701)663-8545	WS 9 SS 1045 BC 1045	EL/ED/HC/ MD	233	156	81
MAX	*ST MATTHEW*	1903	313 Main St PO BOX 274	58759	ND		(701)463-2073	WS 9 SS 10	ED/HC	65	59	35
MAYVILLE	*FIRST AMERICAN* yohound50@yahoo.com		213 3RD AVE NE	58257	ND	Adam D Harvala	(218)779-5620	WS 10	ED/HC/MD	22	22	18
MCCLUSKY	*ST JOHN* sjlcmc@live.com	1910	103 AVE F W PO BOX 635	58463	ND	Matthew R Thompson	(701)363-2636	WS 1130 SS 1030 BC 1030	ED/HC/ MD/SN	95	81	45
MINOT	*OUR SAVIOR* oslc@srt.com www.oslcminot.com	1985	3705 11TH ST SW	58701	ND		(701)852-6404	WS 815 930 11 SS 930 BC 930	ED/HC/ MD/SN	1377	963	268
	ST MARK stmarks@srt.com minotstmarks.com	1956	2209 4TH AVE NW	58703	ND	Philip J Beyersdorf	(701)839-4663	WS 930 SS 11 BC 11	ED/HC/MD	386	346	73
	ST PAUL stpaulsofc@outlook.com www.anchoredminot.com	1905	200 BURDICK EXPY E	58701	ND	Dr Matthew R Richard Carlyle L Roth	(701)852-2821	WS 8 1030 SS 915 BC 915	ED/HC/ MD/SN	477	386	189
MUNICH	*ZION*	1908	PO BOX 130	58352	ND	Scott A Ramey	(701)682-5126					
NAPOLEON	*ST MATTHEW* tmarcisjr@gmail.com	1907	402 Broadway PO BOX 205	58561	ND	Thomas R Marcis Jr		WS 2		16	15	5
	TRINITY LUTHERAN CHURCH Satellite Site of St Matthew Napoleon ND	2005	423 2 STE	58561								
NEW SALEM	*ZION*	1910	407 N 5th St PO BOX 376	58563	ND	Zelwyn C Heide	(701)843-7202	WS 1030	ED/HC	61	61	25
	ZION		See Glen Ullin ND									
NEWBURG	*BETHLEHEM/ST JOHN*		PO BOX 441	58762	ND	Jonathan R Bonine		WS 11 BC 945	ED/HC/MD			
NIAGARA	*ST ANDREW*	1894	407 Baker Ave PO BOX 70	58266	ND		(701)397-5713	WS 8 SS 920 BC 920	ED/HC/ MD/SN			
OAKES	*ST JOHNS* stjohnsoakes@gmail.com www.stjohnsoakes.org	1905	120 S 9TH ST	58474	ND	Christopher W Brade- meyer	(701)742-2595	WS 9 SS 1015 BC 1015	ED/HC/ MD/SN	288	252	115
PETTIBONE	*OUR SAVIOR* stpaulw@daktel.com www.stpaulw.org	1966	104 N Main St PO BOX 195 WIMBLEDON	58475 58492	ND		(701)435-2873	WS 830 11 SS 930	ED/MD/SN	125	90	23
ROCK LAKE	*ALL NATIONS* pastor_scott_ramey@hotmail.com	1898	22 S Sibley St PO BOX 213 ROCKLAKE	58365	ND	Scott A Ramey	(701)266-5361	WS 930	ED/MD			

*Indicates a new church start. A new church start is an intentionally organized gathering which comes together on a regular basis for the purpose of worship and/or Bible study and is intended to grow into a member LCMS congregation. WS =Worship Service; SS = Sunday School; BC =Bible Class; EC = Early Childhood; EL = Elementary School; HS = High School; ED =Education Ministry; HC =Human Care Ministry; SN = Special Needs Ministry; MD = Media Ministry (PC)=Partner Church Pastor. See Page 53 for the Table of Abbreviations for key to additional abbreviations

CITY	CONGREGATION EMAIL WEBSITE	YEAR EST	LOCATION MAILING ADDRESS	ZIP CODE(S)	DIST.	PASTOR(S)	PHONE FAX	WS SS BC	SCHOOLS/ MINISTRIES	STATISTIC Bapt	Conf	Avg Attend
ROLLA	*IMMANUEL*	1896	10 1st Ave SE PO BOX 37	58367	ND	Scott A Ramey	(701)477-5122	WS 11 SS 930	MD/SN			
RUGBY	*ST PAUL* saintpaulrugby@gmail.com www.stpaulrugby.org/	1942	320 8TH ST SW	58368	ND	Christopher J Neuendorf	(701)776-6739	WS 8 SS 9		214	182	37
SAINT THOMAS	*ST PAUL*	1882	8750 144TH AVE NE	58276	ND	Aaron Parkhurst	(701)257-6747	WS 1115	ED/HC	114	90	18
SAWYER	*ST PETER*	1927	210 Dakota Ave S PO BOX 196	58781	ND	Timothy L Stout	(701)624-5688	WS 5 SS 4				
STIRUM	*ST JOHNS*		See Oakes ND									
TOLLEY	*TRINITY* lorettabuch@yahoo.com	1916	202 Bertleson PO BOX 127	58787	ND	Joel L Brandvold	(701)386-2246	WS 10 BC 11	ED	56	54	16
TOWNER	*FAITH*	1987	405 1st St NW PO BOX 180	58788	ND	Jonathan R Bonine	(701)537-5815	WS 8 BC 730	ED	57	39	17
UNDERWOOD	*ST JOHN*	1903	213 Summit St PO BOX 757	58576	ND		(701)442-5467	WS 9		34	33	12
UPHAM	*BETHLEHEM/ST JOHN*		See Newburg ND									
VERONA	*ST JOHNS*		See Oakes ND									
VOLTAIRE	*ST JOHN*		See Kongsberg ND									
WAHPETON	*IMMANUEL* immanuel@702com.net www.immanuelwahp.com	1900	420 3RD AVE N	58075	ND		(701)642-6910 (701)642-1481	WS 9 SS 1015 BC 1015	ED/MD/SN	595	464	100
WEST FARGO	*ST ANDREW* office@standrewlcms.org www.standrewlcms.org	1960	1005 1st St E 1005 1ST ST	58078	ND	Clark H Jahnke Dylan K Meyer	(701)282-4195 (701)282-4204	WS 8 1045 SS 930 BC 930	EL/ED/HC/ MD/SN	599	478	151
WILLISTON	*CONCORDIA* concordia@nccray.net www.concordiawilliston.com	1933	1805 MAIN ST	58801	MT	David M Behm	(701)572-9021	WS 930 SS 11 BC 11	ED/MD/SN	93	78	47
WILLOW CITY	*IMMANUEL* oslcsecretary@utma.com www.immanuelwillowcreek.org	1889	8230 6th Ave NE C/O OUR SAVIOR'S LUTHERAN CHURCH 709 11TH ST E BOTTINEAU	58384 58318	ND	Christopher J Neuendorf		WS 930	ED/HC/MD	62	60	32
WIMBLEDON	*ST PAUL* stpaulw@daktel.com www.stpaulw.org	1908	307 Gibson St PO BOX 195	58492	ND	Robert T Hill	(701)435-2873	WS 830 11	ED/HC/ MD/SN	140	110	25
WOODWORTH	*REDEEMER* stpaulw@daktel.com www.stpaulw.org	1966	123 2nd Ave NE PO BOX 195 WIMBLEDON	58496 58492	ND		(701)435-2873	WS 830 11	ED/MD/SN	107	83	21
OHIO												
AKRON	*CONCORDIA* secretary@celc.org CELC.org	1904	724 SUMNER ST	44311	EN		(330)535-1330 (330)535-4577	WS 12 BC 1030	HC/MD	182	180	30
	FAIRLAWN		See Fairlawn OH									
	HOPE		See Coventry Township OH									
	REDEEMER		See Cuyahoga Falls OH									
	ROYAL REDEEMER		See North Royalton OH									
	ST JOHN stjohnlcms550@sbcglobal.net	1908	550 E WILBETH RD	44301	OH	John C Voelker II	(330)773-4128	WS 10 SS 9 BC 9	ED/HC	135	133	30
	ZION churchinfo@zionorthehill.org www.zionorthehill.org	1854	139 S HIGH ST	44308	OH	Keith J Johnson	(330)253-3136	WS 8 1015 BC 915	ED/HC/ MD/SN	240	221	50
AMHERST	*ST PAUL* churchoffice@stpaulamherst.com www.stpaulamherst.com	1875	115 CENTRAL DR	44001	OH	Paul G Werner	(440)988-4157 (440)988-5436	WS 830 10 SS 930 BC 1045	EC/ED/HC/ MD	619	454	73
ANDERSON TOWNSHIP	*ZION*		See Cincinnati OH									
ANTWERP	*MOUNT CALVARY* lutheranmountcalvary@gmail.com	1939	3495 Co Rd 424 PO BOX 1024	45813	OH	Mark J Peters	(419)258-6505	WS 1015 SS 9 BC 9		144	120	55
ARCHBOLD	*EMMAUS*		See Wauseon OH									
	SAINT JAMES bpbeers@williams-net.com	1846	22881 MONROE ST	43502	OH	James C Strawn	(419)445-4750	WS 930 SS 815	EC/ED/HC/ MD/SN	340	259	99
ASHTABULA	*LIGHTED CROSS* jackiepanich@yahoo.com		2310 W 9th St PO BOX 766	44004 44005	OH	Frederick E Davison	(440)466-6890	WS 1030				
	ST JOHN		See Geneva OH									
AUBURN TOWNSHIP	*HOPE*		See Aurora OH									
AURORA	*HOPE* hopelcaurora@gmail.com www.hlcaurora.org	1969	456 S CHILLICOTHE RD	44202	OH	Daniel D Esala	(330)562-9660 (330)562-9092	WS 10 BC 9	EC/ED/HC/ MD	93	84	44
AUSTINTOWN	*REDEEMER* redeemerlutheran@zoominternet.net www.redeemer-austintown.org	1949	2305 S CANFIELD NILES RD	44515	OH	Dale R Krienke	(330)799-7823	WS 1030 SS 9 BC 9	ED/HC/ MD/SN	180	154	72
AVON	*FAITH* www.faithavon.com	1961	2265 GARDEN DR	44011	OH	David C Woolsey	(440)934-4710 (440)934-1917	WS 8 1030 SS 915 BC 915	EC/EL/HS/ ED/HC/ MD/SN	458	346	182
BARNESBURG	*TRINITY*		See Cincinnati OH									
BATH	*FAIRLAWN*		See Fairlawn OH									
BEAVERCREEK	*EMMANUEL*		See Kettering OH									
BELLBROOK	*EMMANUEL*		See Kettering OH									

*Indicates a new church start. A new church start is an intentionally organized gathering which comes together on a regular basis for the purpose of worship and/or Bible study and is intended to grow into a member LCMS congregation. WS =Worship Service; SS = Sunday School; BC =Bible Class; EC = Early Childhood; EL = Elementary School; HS = High School; ED =Education Ministry; HC =Human Care Ministry; SN = Special Needs Ministry; MD = Media Ministry (PC)=Partner Church Pastor. See Page 53 for the Table of Abbreviations for key to additional abbreviations

CITY	CONGREGATION EMAIL WEBSITE	YEAR EST	LOCATION MAILING ADDRESS	ZIP CODE(S)	DIST.	PASTOR(S)	PHONE FAX	WS SS BC	SCHOOLS/ MINISTRIES	STATISTIC Bapt	Conf	Avg Attend
BEREA	*ST JOHN*		See Strongsville OH									
BEXLEY	*BETHANY*		See Columbus OH									
BLACKLICK	*BETHANY*		See Columbus OH									
BRISTOLVILLE	*TRINITY*		See Warren OH									
BROADVIEW HEIGHTS	*COMMUNITY HOPE* office@cohchurch.com cohchurch.com	1991	1435 West Royalton Rd 1435 W ROYALTON RD BROAD-VIEW HTS	44147	OH	Douglas S Seletzky	(440)457-2296	WS 9 1045 SS 9 1045 BC 9	EL/HS/ED/ MD	279	216	254
BROOK PARK	*CROSSROADS CLE* info@CrossroadsCLE.com www.crossroadsCLE.com	2014	16311 BROOKPARK RD	44142	OH	David L Walters	(216)816-1615	WS 1030	ED/HC/MD			
BROOKLYN	*UNITY*		See Cleveland OH									
BRUNSWICK	*FAITHWALK* office@Faithwb.org www.myhopestartshere.org	2006	1480 Pearl Rd Unit 5 13485 W. RIVER RD COLUMBIA STATION	44212 44028	OH	Philip D McClelland	(440)462-9021	WS 10 SS 9	ED/HC/MD	63	56	35
	ST MARK cgordon@stmarkbrunswick.org www.stmarkbrunswick.org	1956	1330 N CARPENTER RD	44212	OH	Steven D Girard	(330)225-3110 (330)225-4380	WS 815 11 SS 930 BC 930	ED/HC/MD	197	163	290
CANAL WINCHESTER	*BETHANY*		See Columbus OH									
CANTON	*HOLY CROSS*		See North Canton OH									
CENTERVILLE	*EMMANUEL*		See Kettering OH									
CHAGRIN FALLS	*HOPE*		See Aurora OH									
	VALLEY office@valleylutheran.org www.valleylutheran.org	1938	87 E ORANGE ST	44022	OH	Michael B Henn	(440)247-0390 (440)247-0125	WS 9 1030 SS 1030	EC	467	344	76
CHAMPION	*TRINITY*		See Warren OH									
CHARDON	*PEACE* plcchardon424@gmail.com peacelutheranmunson.org	1958	12686 BASS LAKE RD	44024	OH		(440)286-1266	WS 1030 SS 915 BC 915	EC/ED/HC	56	56	34
CHESTERLAND	*ST MARK* mail@stmarkchester.org www.stmarkchester.org	1961	11900 CHILLICOTHE RD	44026	OH	Mark G Matzke Christopher A Ryan	(440)729-1668	WS 8 1015 SS 915 BC 915	EC/ED/HC/ MD/SN	561	342	158
CHILLICOTHE	*OUR SAVIOR* oslc151@gmail.com oschillicothe.ctshost.org	1953	151 UNIVERSITY DR	45601	OH		(740)775-2470	WS 1030 SS 1145 BC 1145	ED/HC/ MD/SN	61	61	12
CINCINNATI	*CHRIST* om@christ-lcms.org www.christ-lcms.org/	1955	3301 COMPTON RD	45251	OH	Andrew S Norris Jason D von der Lage	(513)385-8342	WS 10 SS 9 BC 9	ED/HC/ MD/SN	200	156	110
	GRACE ministry@gracemin.org www.gracemin.org	1914	3628 BOUDINOT AVE	45211	OH	Gregory W Enterline	(513)661-5166 (513)661-3728	WS 9 1115 SS 1010 BC 1010	ED/HC/ MD/SN	195	155	67
	IMMANUEL egreene1@fuse.net www.immanuellutherancincy.org	1926	544 ROCKDALE AVE	45229	OH	Everette E Greene	(513)961-3407	WS 1145 SS 1230				
	KING OF KINGS		See Mason OH									
	PEACE peacechurchlink@hotmail.com PeaceChurchLink.com	1962	1451 EBENEZER RD	45233	OH		(513)941-5177	WS 1030 SS 915 BC 915	ED/HC/MD	179	139	64
	PRINCE OF PEACE info@poplcmscinci.org www.poplcmscinci.org	1968	1528 Race St PO BOX 881	45202 45201	OH	Joel C Morgan	(513)621-7265	WS 10 BC 1130	ED/HC	20	20	17
	ST PAUL stpaulcinci@yahoo.com www.stpaulcinci.org	1868	5433 MADISON RD	45227	OH	Timothy E Beck	(513)271-4147 (513)271-4152	WS 9 SS 1030 BC 1030	ED/HC/MD	93	93	70
	ST PAUL VILLAGE ASSISTED LIVING Satellite Site of St Paul Cincinnati OH	1978	5515 Madison Ave	45227								
	TRINITY cschneider9988@gmail.com www.facebook.com/ TrinityLutheranChurch1845	1845	5921 SPRINGDALE RD	45247	OH	Everette E Greene	(513)385-7024	WS 945	ED/HC/ MD/SN	20	20	15
	ZION office@zionlc.org www.zionlc.org	1951	1175 Birney Ln 1175 BIRNEY LANE	45230	OH	Jason A Hoerth	(513)231-2253 (513)231-5303	WS 830 11 SS 945 BC 945	ED/HC/SN	386	282	173
CLEVELAND	*CHRIST* pastordck@gmail.com www.christlutherancleveland.org	1889	13812 BELLAIRE RD	44135	OH	Dean Kavouras	(216)252-4711	WS 1030 BC 9	ED/MD	60	55	40
	CONCORDIA		See Independence OH									
	CRISTIANA HISPANA ICHRCC@aol.com	1988	2970 W 30TH ST	44113	EN		(216)785-9003	WS 1015 SS 1030 BC 7				
	CROSSROADS CLE		See Brook Park OH									
	EL BUEN PASTOR	1988	2059 W 28TH ST	44113	OH		(216)631-4634		EL			
	GRACE		See Lakewood OH									
	HOLY CROSS hclutheran@sbcglobal.net www.hclcas.org	1944	4260 ROCKY RIVER DR	44135	EN		(216)252-2348 (216)941-3035	WS 9 SS 1015 BC 1015	EL/HS/ED/ HC/MD			
	IMMANUEL immanluth1@sbcglobal.net immanuellutherantremont.org	1880	2928 SCRANTON RD	44113	OH	Jerry Witt-Jablonski	(216)781-9511	WS 9 1030 SS 1030	EL/HS/ED/ HC/MD/SN	181	150	48

*Indicates a new church start. A new church start is an intentionally organized gathering which comes together on a regular basis for the purpose of worship and/or Bible study and is intended to grow into a member LCMS congregation. WS =Worship Service; SS = Sunday School; BC =Bible Class; EC = Early Childhood; EL = Elementary School; HS = High School; ED =Education Ministry; HC =Human Care Ministry; SN = Special Needs Ministry; MD = Media Ministry (PC)=Partner Church Pastor. See Page 53 for the Table of Abbreviations for key to additional abbreviations

CITY	CONGREGATION EMAIL WEBSITE	YEAR EST	LOCATION MAILING ADDRESS	ZIP CODE(S)	DIST.	PASTOR(S)	PHONE FAX	WS SS BC	SCHOOLS/ MINISTRIES	STATISTIC Bapt	Conf	Avg Attend
CLEVELAND	*OUR SAVIOR*		See Mayfield Heights OH									
	OUR SAVIOR		See North Royalton OH									
	ROYAL REDEEMER		See North Royalton OH									
	SAINT JAMES stjamessecretary4771@gmail.com www.stjameslcms.com	1933	4771 BROADVIEW RD	44109	OH	Mark J Renner	(216)351-6499 (216)351-7815	WS 1015 BC 9	EL/HS/ED/ HC/MD/SN	172	138	80
	SHORE HAVEN		See Euclid OH									
	ST JOHN churchoffice@stjohnnottingham.org www.stjohnnottingham.org	1890	17403 NOTTINGHAM RD	44119	OH	Dr Walther P Marcis Ronald W Rollins	(216)531-1156	WS 945	EL/HS/ED/ HC/MD	190	170	61
	ST MARK smelccleveland@gmail.com	1897	4464 PEARL RD	44109	OH		(216)749-3545 (216)749-1503	WS 11 BC 10	ED/MD	58	46	20
	ST PHILIP speigk@yahoo.com www.stphilip.com	1928	11315 REGALIA AVE	44104	OH		(216)991-0655 (216)991-5900	WS 11	HS/ED/HC/ MD/SN	15	15	10
	TRINITY trinityohiocity@gmail.com trinityohiocity.org/home	1853	2031 W 30TH ST	44113	OH		(216)281-1700 (216)281-4406	WS 10 SS 10	EL/HS/HC			
	UNITY uelc@unity-lutheran.org www.unity-lutheran.org	1914	4542 PEARL RD	44109	OH	Peeter Pirn	(216)741-2085 (216)741-1505	WS 930 7 SS 11	EL/HS/ED/ MD	85	56	15
	ZION zionchurch@sbcglobal.net	1843	2062 E 30TH ST	44115	OH		(216)331-0156	WS 1015 BC 9	ED/HC			
COLERAIN HEIGHTS	*TRINITY*		See Cincinnati OH									
COLUMBIA STATION	*HOSANNA* hosannacolumbiastation@gmail.com www.hosannalutheranchurch.com	1974	13485 W RIVER RD COLUMBIA STA	44028	OH	Philip D McClelland	(440)328-7167	WS 12 BC 930	EC/ED/HC/ MD	13	13	9
COLUMBUS	*ATONEMENT* coa@atonementchurch.com atonementchurch.com	1965	1621 FRANCISCO RD	43220	OH	Eric R Gawura	(614)451-1880	WS 930 SS 11	EC/ED/HC/ MD/SN	230	203	89
	BETHANY bethanycolumbus@sbcglobal.net bethanylutherancolumbus.com	1958	1000 NOE BIXBY RD	43213	OH	Paul E Shaw	(614)866-7755	WS 9 SS 1030 BC 1030	ED/HC/ MD/SN	137	119	46
	CONCORDIA concordiacolumbus@gmail.com www.concordiacolumbus.org	1929	225 SCHOOLHOUSE LN	43228	OH		(614)878-7800 (614)853-1795	WS 10	ED/HC	59	50	24
	EBENEZER		See Whitehall OH									
	HOLY CROSS OF/DEAF predwinlot@gmail.com	1946	360 MORSE RD	43214	OH	Edwin L Bergstresser II	(614)429-1351	WS 1030	ED/HC/SN	36	35	22
	OROMO y.gemta@yahoo.com		1763 BAIRSFORD DR	43232	OH	Yoseph G Gemta	(614)322-1184					
	PRINCE OF PEACE info@poplutheran.net www.poplutheran.net	1977	530 Mc Naughten Rd 530 MCNAUGHTEN RD	43213	OH	Christopher R Eldridge	(614)863-3124	WS 8 1030 SS 930 BC 930	ED/HC/MD	240	212	80
	SAINT JAMES stjames@ohiostjames.com www.stjameslutherancolumbus.com	1847	5660 TRABUE RD	43228	OH	James D Jordan	(614)878-5158	WS 845 1115 SS 945 BC 945	ED/HC/ MD/SN	329	278	120
	ST JOHN		See Dublin OH									
	ZION office@zionlcms.org www.zionlcms.org	1882	766 S HIGH ST	43206	OH	Wesley T Hromowyk	(614)444-3456 (614)443-4818	WS 8 1030 SS 930 BC 930	ED/HC/ MD/SN	356	289	193
CONDIT	*HOPE* hopelutheransunbury@gmail.com www.hopelutheransunbury.org	1978	15370 Meredith State Rd PO BOX 255 SUNBURY	43074	OH	Benjamin C Meyer	(740)965-1685	WS 815 1030 SS 930 BC 930	ED/HC/MD	175	153	98
CONVOY	*REDEEMER* redeemerlutheran111@gmail.com www.redeemerconvoy.org	1961	6727 St Rt 49 PO BOX 10	45832	OH	Stephen O Shrum	(419)749-2167	WS 830 1045 SS 945	ED/HC/ MD/SN	358	220	175
COPLEY	*FAIRLAWN*		See Fairlawn OH									
CORTLAND	*TRINITY*		See Warren OH									
COVENTRY TOWNSHIP	*HOPE* churchoffice@hopelcmsakron.org www.hopelcmsakron.org	1951	999 PORTAGE LAKES DR.	44319	OH	Jack A Kozak	(330)644-3522 (330)644-8747	WS 1030 SS 915 BC 915	EC/ED/HC/ MD/SN	204	173	71
CUYAHOGA FALLS	*REDEEMER* churchoffice@redeemerlutheran.us www.redeemerlutheran.us	1918	2141 5TH ST CUYAHOGA FLS	44221	OH	Paul C Frerichs	(330)923-1445 (330)923-4517	WS 830 1115 BC 10	EL/ED/ HC/SN	325	283	156
DAYTON	*CONCORDIA* info@concordiaoakwood.com www.concordiaoakwood.com	1926	250 PEACH ORCHARD AVE OAKWOOD	45419	OH	Anthony D Sobocinski	(937)299-1912 (937)299-6618	WS 915 SS 1030 BC 1030	ED/HC/ MD/SN	98	88	44
	EMMANUEL		See Kettering OH									
	MOUNT CALVARY mtcalvarylutheran1@gmail.com mtcalvaryonline.net	1951	9100 N MAIN ST ENGLEWOOD	45415	OH	Stephen D Gettinger	(937)836-2238 (937)836-1518	WS 1030 SS 930 BC 930		127	105	58
	ST MATTHEW		See Huber Heights OH									
	ST TIMOTHY		See Huber Heights OH									

*Indicates a new church start. A new church start is an intentionally organized gathering which comes together on a regular basis for the purpose of worship and/or Bible study and is intended to grow into a member LCMS congregation. WS =Worship Service; SS = Sunday School; BC =Bible Class; EC = Early Childhood; EL = Elementary School; HS = High School; ED =Education Ministry; HC =Human Care Ministry; SN = Special Needs Ministry; MD = Media Ministry (PC)=Partner Church Pastor. See Page 53 for the Table of Abbreviations for key to additional abbreviations

CITY	CONGREGATION EMAIL WEBSITE	YEAR EST	LOCATION MAILING ADDRESS	ZIP CODE(S)	DIST.	PASTOR(S)	PHONE FAX	WS SS BC	SCHOOLS/ MINISTRIES	STATISTIC Bapt	Conf	Avg Attend
DEFIANCE	*CHRIST OUR SAVIOR* rldpkd65@att.net www.cosdefiance.com	1989	301 CARTER RD	43512	OH		(419)782-6688	WS 930 SS 830 BC 830		81	68	35
	ST JOHN business.admin@stjohntigers.com www.stjohndefiance.com	1851	655 WAYNE AVE	43512	OH	Kurt F Mews	(419)782-5766 (419)782-0954	WS 9 11 BC 10	EL/ED/HC/ MD/SN	820	736	244
	ST STEPHEN StStephenLutheran43512@gmail.com	1853	30304 New Bavaria Rd 30328 NEW BAVARIA RD	43512	OH	William J Stottlemyer	(419)395-1507	WS 10 SS 9 BC 9	MD	220	184	43
DELAWARE	*BEAUTIFUL SAVIOR*		See Powell OH									
DELHI HILLS	*PEACE*		See Cincinnati OH									
DELTA	*EMMAUS*		See Wauseon OH									
DENT	*TRINITY*		See Cincinnati OH									
DUBLIN	*ATONEMENT*		See Columbus OH									
	BEAUTIFUL SAVIOR		See Powell OH									
	ST JOHN office@stjohndublin.org www.stjohndublin.org	1855	6135 RINGS RD	43016	OH	Adam J Steinbrenner	(614)889-2284 (614)760-0412	WS 8 1045 SS 930 BC 930	EL/ED/HC/ MD/SN	451	368	257
	ST PAUL		See Milford Center OH									
EDGERTON	*ZION*	1846	1018 CICERO RD	43517	OH	Isaac M Spangler	(419)298-2594	WS 10 SS 9 BC 9	ED/HC	129	124	35
ELMORE	*TRINITY* tlcelmore1@gmail.com trinityelmore.360unite.com	1865	412 Fremont St PO BOX 22	43416	OH	Stephen H Lutz	(419)862-3461	WS 8 1045 SS 930	EC/ED/MD	407	344	129
ELYRIA	*GRACE* graceelyria@gmail.com www.gracelcelyria.org	1907	9685 E RIVER RD	44035	EN	Robert F Weldon Sr Glenn A Mertz	(440)322-5497 (440)322-5495	WS 8 1030 SS 920	EC/ED/HC/ MD/SN	418	331	83
	ST JOHN sjlc1@neohio.twcbc.com www.stjohnlutheranchurchelyria.org	1851	1140 W RIVER RD N	44035	OH		(440)324-4070	WS 9	ED/HC/MD	215	131	40
ENGLEWOOD	*MOUNT CALVARY*		See Dayton OH									
	ST TIMOTHY		See Huber Heights OH									
ETNA	*BETHANY*		See Columbus OH									
EUCLID	*SHORE HAVEN* office@shorehavenlutheran.org www.shorehavenlutheran.org	1921	280 E 222ND ST	44123	OH	Steven M Hackmann	(216)731-4100 (216)731-6821	WS 10 SS 1115 BC 9	EL/HS/ED/ HC/MD	276	206	49
FAIRBORN	*BETHLEHEM* bethlehem7@aol.com bethlehem7.org	1955	1240 S MAPLE AVE	45324	OH	Keith F Witte	(937)878-0651 (937)878-8794	WS 8 1045 SS 930 BC 930	EL/ED/ HC/SN	395	306	133
	ST TIMOTHY		See Huber Heights OH									
FAIRLAWN	*FAIRLAWN* admin.jessica@fairlawnlutheran.org www.fairlawnlutheran.org	1955	3415 W MARKET ST	44333	EN	James A Gau	(330)836-7286	WS 10 SS 9 BC 9	EC/ED/HC/ MD/SN	430	430	240
FARMINGTON	*TRINITY*		See Warren OH									
FINDLAY	*CONCORDIA* pastor@concordiafindlay.com www.concordiafindlay.com	1959	1431 6TH ST	45840	OH	David M DePaoli	(419)422-4209	WS 1015 SS 9 BC 9	ED/MD	154	115	36
	FINDLAY LIVING STONES Satellite Site of Good Shep Deaf Toledo OH	2013	109 E Lincoln	45840								
FLATROCK	*ST PAUL*		See Napoleon OH									
FREMONT	*TRINITY*		See Elmore OH									
GAHANNA	*BETHANY*		See Columbus OH									
	NEW HOPE		See Newark OH									
GALENA	*LIVING WORD* info@livingwordgalena.com www.livingwordgalena.com		7539 DUSTIN RD	43021	OH	Derrick N Hurst	(740)965-3335	WS 1030 SS 9 BC 9	MD			
GARFIELD HEIGHTS	*ST JOHN LUTHERAN* sjlutheran@att.net sjlutheran.net	1854	11333 GRANGER RD	44125	OH		(216)587-4222	WS 9	ED/HC/SN	332	187	40
GENEVA	*CHAPEL FOR SHUT-INS* Satellite Site of St John Geneva OH	2015	60 W Main St 60 W Main St	44041								
	ST JOHN Stjohnsgeneva20@gmail.com stjohnsgeneva.org	1915	811 S Broadway PO BOX 500	44041	OH	Jonathan C Schroeder	(440)466-2473 (440)415-0659	WS 1030 SS 915 BC 930	EC/EL/ED/ HC/MD/SN	248	242	82
GRANVILLE	*NEW HOPE*		See Newark OH									
	NEW HOPE GRANVILLE CAMPUS Satellite Site of New Hope Newark OH	2015	309 W Broadway	43023				WS 9 BC 8				
GREENHILLS	*MESSIAH* churchoffice@messiahgrh.org www.messiahgrh.org	1958	10416 BOSSI LN CINCINNATI	45218	OH	Allen D Stuckwisch	(513)825-4768	WS 830 1045 SS 930 BC 930	ED/HC/ MD/SN	215	215	90
GROSBECK	*TRINITY*		See Cincinnati OH									
GROVEPORT	*BETHANY*		See Columbus OH									

*Indicates a new church start. A new church start is an intentionally organized gathering which comes together on a regular basis for the purpose of worship and/or Bible study and is intended to grow into a member LCMS congregation. WS =Worship Service; SS = Sunday School; BC =Bible Class; EC = Early Childhood; EL = Elementary School; HS = High School; ED =Education Ministry; HC =Human Care Ministry; SN = Special Needs Ministry; MD = Media Ministry (PC)=Partner Church Pastor. See Page 53 for the Table of Abbreviations for key to additional abbreviations

CITY	CONGREGATION EMAIL WEBSITE	YEAR EST	LOCATION MAILING ADDRESS	ZIP CODE(S)	DIST.	PASTOR(S)	PHONE FAX	WS SS BC	SCHOOLS/ MINISTRIES	STATISTIC Bapt	Conf	Avg Attend
HAMILTON	*IMMANUEL* immanuelhamilton@gmail.com www.immanuelhamiltonchurch.com	1896	1285 MAIN ST	45013	OH	Kevin R Jud	(513)893-6792 (513)863-2502	WS 8 1045 SS 945 BC 945	EL/HS/ED/ HC/MD/SN	440	229	221
	ROYAL REDEEMER		See Liberty Township OH									
HAMLER	*IMMANUEL* lutheranchurchhamler@gmail.com www.ilcho.org	1896	G-983 SR 109 G983 STATE ROUTE 109 PO BOX 274	43524	OH	Dr Richard S Lofgren	(419)274-4811	WS 10 SS 9 BC 9	ED/HC/ MD/SN	353	280	81
HARRISON	*AMAZING GRACE* hugh69marie@gmail.com	1993	9961 NEW HAVEN RD	45030	OH	William R Ritchie	(513)367-5094	WS 1030 BC 915	ED/HC/MD			
HEATH	*NEW HOPE*		See Newark OH									
HEBRON	*NEW HOPE*		See Newark OH									
HOLGATE	*ST JOHN* christine.k.stober@gmail.com www.stjohnlutheranholgate.org/	1875	501 N WILHELM ST	43527	OH	James A Haugen III	(419)264-4641	WS 10 SS 9 BC 9	EC	185	134	58
HOWLAND	*TRINITY*		See Warren OH									
HUBBARD	*TRINITY*		See Warren OH									
HUBER HEIGHTS	*ST MATTHEW* st_matthew_ev_jesu@att.net www.stmatthewlutheran huberheights.com	1962	5566 CHAMBERSBURG RD	45424	OH	Kelly Reagan	(937)233-4632	WS 930 SS 11	ED/HC/MD	87	75	54
	ST TIMOTHY office@sttimothylutheran.net www.sttimothylutheran.net	1959	5040 RYE DR	45424	OH		(937)233-2443 (937)233-0028	WS 1030 SS 9	ED/SN	161	119	86
HUDSON	*GLORIA DEI* office@gloriadeihudson.org www.gloriadeihudson.org	1967	2113 RAVENNA ST	44236	OH	Dr Eric E Tritten	(330)650-6550 (330)650-6685	WS 815 1045 SS 930 BC 930	EC/ED/HC/ MD/SN	528	438	194
INDEPENDENCE	*CONCORDIA* office@myconcordia.org myconcordia.org	1965	6705 BRECKSVILLE RD	44131	OH	Matthew M Garred	(216)524-2188 (216)573-9005	WS 930 BC 1045	ED/HC/MD	62	60	17
JEFFERSON	*ST JOHN*		See Geneva OH									
JOHNSTOWN	*NEW HOPE*		See Newark OH									
KETTERING	*CONCORDIA*		See Dayton OH									
	EMMANUEL office@emmanuellc.org www.emmanuellc.org	1973	4865 WILMINGTON PIKE	45440	OH	Mark E Carlson	(937)434-1798 (937)434-2234	WS 9 SS 930 BC 930	ED/HC/MD	433	334	263
LAKE MILTON	*GETHSEMANE*		See North Jackson OH									
LAKEWOOD	*FEDOR MANOR* Satellite Site of Grace Lakewood OH	2008	12400 Madison Ave	44107								
	GETHSEMANE office.gethsemane@gmail.com gethsemanelakewood.org	1948	14560 MADISON AVE	44107	OH	Michael S Wallace	(216)521-0434 (216)226-4082	WS 930 SS 1030 BC 1030	EL/HS/ED/ HC/MD			
	GRACE graceluthlake1@att.net www.gracelutheranlakewood.org	2002	13030 MADISON AVE	44107	S	John W Milligan	(216)221-4959 (216)221-7286	WS 9 SS 945 BC 945	EC/EL/HS/ ED/HC			
LANCASTER	*EMANUEL* elclancaster@gmail.com elclancaster.wixsite.com/lcms	1847	231 E Mulberry St PO BOX 2270	43130	OH		(740)653-1847	WS 1015 SS 9 BC 9	ED/HC/ MD/SN	308	250	83
	REDEEMER 1400redeemeroffice@gmail.com www.redeemerlancaster.com	1958	1400 CONCORDIA DR	43130	OH	Dr John C Davidson	(740)653-4083 (740)653-0801	WS 1015 SS 9	EC/ED/MD	178	139	56
LEBANON	*KING OF KINGS*		See Mason OH									
LEWIS CENTER	*BEAUTIFUL SAVIOR*		See Powell OH									
LIBERTY CENTER	*ST PAUL* stpaullc@embarqmail.com www.saintpaullc.org	1931	8074 COUNTY ROAD T LIBERTY CTR	43532	OH	Charles E Kramer	(419)533-3041	WS 10 SS 9 BC 9	EC/ED/HC/ MD	259	257	50
LIBERTY TOWNSHIP	*ROYAL REDEEMER* churchoffice@royalredeemer.org www.royalredeemer.org	1988	7127 DUTCHLAND PKWY LIBERTY TWP	45044	OH	John V Benham III	(513)779-4740 (513)779-0597	WS 9 1030 SS 1030	EC/ED/HC/ MD	316	234	200
LIMA	*IMMANUEL* immanuel@wcoil.com ImmanuelLima.org	1901	2120 LAKEWOOD AVE	45805	OH	Michael A Phillips	(419)222-2541	WS 10 BC 9	ED/HC/MD	104	91	56
LINCOLN VILLAGE	*CONCORDIA*		See Columbus OH									
LITHOPOLIS	*BETHANY*		See Columbus OH									
LODI	*CHRIST KING* ctklutheranlodi@gmail.com www.christthekinglodi.org	1980	8080 Lafayette Rd PO BOX 183	44254	S	Dr Christopher T Cahill	(330)948-3000 (330)948-3000	WS 815 1045 BC 930	HC/MD	122	109	42
LOGAN	*TRINITY* trinityluthsecretary@gmail.com trinitylcmslogan.com/	1882	430 N Mulberry St PO BOX 586	43138	OH		(740)281-7593	WS 1045	ED/HC/ MD/SN	64	55	37
LORAIN	*SS PETER AND PAUL*	1905	1500 LINCOLN BLVD	44055	S	Edgar O Anthony	(440)233-5166	WS 10	ED/HC/ MD/SN	18	18	12
	ZION zionlorain@gmail.com	1900	5100 ASHLAND AVE	44053	OH	William F Mugnolo	(440)282-8418 (440)282-8418	WS 11	ED/HC/MD			
LORDSTOWN	*GETHSEMANE*		See North Jackson OH									
LOVELAND	*KING OF KINGS*		See Mason OH									
MADISON	*HOLY CROSS* sberndt@holycrossmadison.church holycrossmadison.church	1965	3050 MCMACKIN RD	44057	OH	Steve C Berndt	(440)812-1635	WS 930	EL			

*Indicates a new church start. A new church start is an intentionally organized gathering which comes together on a regular basis for the purpose of worship and/or Bible study and is intended to grow into a member LCMS congregation. WS =Worship Service; SS = Sunday School; BC =Bible Class; EC = Early Childhood; EL = Elementary School; HS = High School; ED =Education Ministry; HC =Human Care Ministry; SN = Special Needs Ministry; MD = Media Ministry (PC)=Partner Church Pastor. See Page 53 for the Table of Abbreviations for key to additional abbreviations

CITY	CONGREGATION EMAIL WEBSITE	YEAR EST	LOCATION MAILING ADDRESS	ZIP CODE(S)	DIST.	PASTOR(S)	PHONE FAX	WS SS BC	SCHOOLS/ MINISTRIES	STATISTIC Bapt	Conf	Avg Attend
MADISON	*ST JOHN*		See Geneva OH									
MAINEVILLE	*KING OF KINGS*		See Mason OH									
MALVERN	*RESURRECTION* resurrectionlutheranmalvern@yahoo.com www.resurrectionlutheranonline.com		105 S Reed Ave PO BOX 632	44644	S	Kevin A McLeod	(330)312-7039	WS 930 SS 1045 BC 1045		75	63	18
MANTUA	*CHRIST* clcmantua737@yahoo.com christlutheranmantua.org	1953	10827 N Main St PO BOX 737 10827 MAIN ST.	44255	OH	Blake J Martzowka	(330)274-2849	WS 11 SS 945	ED/HC/MD	115	86	56
	HOPE		See Aurora OH									
MARION	*GETHSEMANE* ttrpg@yahoo.com gethsemanelcms.org/	1998	219 E CHURCH ST	43302	OH	Cody A Schrepferman	(740)375-0599	WS 1030 SS 915	ED/HC/MD			
MARYSVILLE	*ST JOHN'S* stjohns@stjohnsmarysville.org stjohnsmarysville.360unite.com	1838	12809 STATE ROUTE 736	43040	OH	Jack D Heino Drake M Peterson	(937)644-5540 (937)644-1086	WS 9 11 SS 10 BC 10	EL/ED/HC/ MD/SN	1167	970	301
	ST PAUL		See Milford Center OH									
MASON	*KING OF KINGS* office@koklcms.org www.koklcms.org	1978	3621 SOCIALVILLE FOSTER RD	45040	OH	Douglas R Swanson	(513)398-6089 (513)459-9896	WS 815 11 SS 945 BC 945	EC/ED/HC/ MD	198	198	157
MASSILLON	*ST JOHN* stjohnmassillon@gmail.com www.stjohnlutheranmassillon.org/	1909	1900 WALES RD NE	44646	S	John L Telloni	(330)837-4645	WS 10 SS 845 BC 845	ED/HC/ MD/SN	503	334	64
MAUMEE	*CONCORDIA*		See Toledo OH									
MAYFIELD HEIGHTS	*OUR SAVIOR* mayfieldlutherans@gmail.com www.oursavior-church.org	1947	2154 SOM CENTER RD MAY- FIELD HTS	44124	OH		(440)442-4455 (440)442-4995	WS 9 1115 SS 1015 BC 1015	ED/HC	42	34	15
MECHANICSBURG	*ST PAUL*		See Milford Center OH									
MEDINA TOWNSHIP	*PRINCE PEACE* admin@princepeace.org www.princepeace.org	1963	3355 MEDINA RD MEDINA	44256	EN		(330)723-8293	WS 8 1030 SS 930 BC 930	HC/MD	383	338	186
MENTOR	*FAITH* faith.lutheran@att.net faithmentor.org	1953	8125 MENTOR AVE	44060	OH	Dr Kevin L Guynn	(440)255-2229	WS 930 SS 1030 BC 1030	EL/ED/HC/ MD/SN	219	195	83
MIAMISBURG	*EMMANUEL*		See Kettering OH									
MIDDLETOWN	*MESSIAH* pastor_herb@sbcglobal.net www.mlcm.org	1955	4715 HOLLY AVE	45044	OH	Daniel J Herb	(513)422-2441	WS 1030 SS 9 BC 9	ED/HC/MD	88	79	50
	ROYAL REDEEMER		See Liberty Township OH									
MILFORD	*ST MARK* stmarksmilford@hotmail.com www.stmarksmilford.org	1958	5849 BUCKWHEAT RD	45150	OH		(513)575-0292 (513)575-2472	WS 8 1030 6 SS 915 BC 915	EL/ED/HC/ MD			
MILFORD CENTER	*ST PAUL* www.stpaulchuckery.church	1893	7960 STATE ROUTE 38 MIL- FORD CTR	43045	OH	Dr Paul R Schlueter	(937)349-2405 (937)349-5939	WS 1015 SS 9 BC 9	EC/ED/ HC/SN	425	354	103
MONTROSE-GHENT	*FAIRLAWN*		See Fairlawn OH									
MORROW	*KING OF KINGS*		See Mason OH									
MOUNT HOPE	*ST JOHN*	1842	8084 State Route 241 PO BOX 11	44660	OH		(330)674-5191	WS 915	HC	35	35	18
MOUNT VERNON	*NEW HOPE*		See Newark OH									
NAPOLEON	*EMMAUS*		See Wauseon OH									
	ST JOHN www.sjl.org	1869	16035 COUNTY ROAD U	43545	OH		(419)598-8961 (419)598-8518	WS 9 SS 1020 BC 1020	EL/ED/HC/ MD/SN	764	540	190
	ST PAUL stpaulflatrock@gmail.com www.facebook.com/stpaulflatrockohio/	1851	12-868 County Road K K980 COUNTY ROAD 17D	43545	OH	Jacob A Stuenkel		WS 830 SS 945		182	159	55
	ST PAUL church@stpaulnapoleon.org www.stpaulnapoleon.org	1851	1075 GLENWOOD AVE	43545	OH	Peter C Marcis Brandon M Bettcher Logan B Scheiwe	(419)592-3535 (419)592-0652	WS 745 9 11 SS 1010 BC 1010	EL/ED/HC/ MD/SN	2884	2171	558
	ST PETER stpeterflorida@gmail.com www.stpeterfloridaohio.com	1875	K980 COUNTY ROAD 17D	43545	OH	Jacob A Stuenkel	(419)762-5075	WS 10 SS 9 BC 9	EC/ED/MD	171	143	40
NEW ALBANY	*NEW HOPE*		See Newark OH									
NEW CARLISLE	*ST TIMOTHY*		See Huber Heights OH									
NEWARK	*HOPES DOOR* Satellite Site of New Hope Newark OH	2017	27 N 4th Street	43055								
	NEW HOPE office@newhopelickingcounty.org www.newhopelickingcounty.org	2015	1137 SHARON VALLEY RD	43055	OH	Mark R Hartsough Terry J Worst	(740)366-6459 (740)366-6459	WS 1045 SS 930	ED/HC/ MD/SN	98	81	62
NILES	*TRINITY*		See Warren OH									
NORTH CANTON	*HOLY CROSS* holycross@holycrossnorthcanton.com www.holycrossnorthcanton.com	1965	7707 MARKET AVE N N CANTON	44721	OH	Anders M Davidson Alexander C Kauffman	(330)499-3307 (330)499-2319	WS 815 1030 SS 930 BC 930	EC/ED/HC/ MD/SN	698	564	270
NORTH JACKSON	*GETHSEMANE* revroll@ourglc.org	1971	1110 N SALEM WARREN RD	44451	OH	Zachary H Roll	(330)538-2630 (330)538-0569	WS 9 SS 1015 BC 1015	ED/HC	175	163	56
NORTH OLMSTED	*ASCENSION* ascnlutheran@gmail.com www.ascensionnortholmsted.org	1948	28081 LORAIN RD	44070	EN	Joshua R Ulm	(440)777-6365 (440)777-1609	WS 945 SS 1045 BC 830	EC/ED			
NORTH RIDGEVILLE	*HOPE*		See Sheffield Village OH									

*Indicates a new church start. A new church start is an intentionally organized gathering which comes together on a regular basis for the purpose of worship and/or Bible study and is intended to grow into a member LCMS congregation. WS =Worship Service; SS = Sunday School; BC =Bible Class; EC = Early Childhood; EL = Elementary School; HS = High School; ED =Education Ministry; HC =Human Care Ministry; SN = Special Needs Ministry; MD = Media Ministry (PC)=Partner Church Pastor. See Page 53 for the Table of Abbreviations for key to additional abbreviations

CITY	CONGREGATION EMAIL WEBSITE	YEAR EST	LOCATION MAILING ADDRESS	ZIP CODE(S)	DIST.	PASTOR(S)	PHONE FAX	WS SS BC	SCHOOLS/ MINISTRIES	STATISTIC Bapt	Conf	Avg Attend
NORTH RIDGEVILLE	*SHEPHERD RIDGE* churchofficesotr@gmail.com shepherdoftheridge.org	1965	34555 CENTER RIDGE RD N RIDGEVILLE	44039	OH		(440)327-7321	BC 930	ED/HC/ MD/SN			
NORTH ROYALTON	*OUR SAVIOR* info@oursaviornorthroyalton.org oursaviornorthroyalton.org	2021	4000 WALLINGS RD	44133	EN	Jonathan C McCall	(216)381-2873	WS 1030 330	MD	25	23	19
	ROYAL REDEEMER info@royred.org www.royred.org	1957	11680 ROYALTON RD	44133	OH	John C Zahrte Mark A Rein David S Luecke David H Timm	(440)237-7958 (440)237-6992	WS 830 930 10 11 SS 930	EL/HS/ED/ HC/SN	2016	1617	940
NORTON	*ST MATTHEW* stmatthewpastor1530@gmail.com www.saintmatthewnorton.com	1910	5451 Cleveland Massillon Rd 5451 S CLEVELAND MASSILLON RD	44203	S	Jon C Carpenter	(330)825-4100	WS 1030 SS 930 BC 930	ED/HC/ MD/SN			
OAKWOOD	*CONCORDIA*		See Dayton OH									
OBERLIN	*GRACE* www.grace-church-oberlin.org	1936	310 W LORAIN ST	44074	EN		(440)775-3271	WS 10 BC 1115	ED/HC	91	78	26
OHIO CITY	*ST THOMAS* StThomas1847@outlook.com stthomaslcms.com/	1847	6299 GERMAN CHURCH RD	45874	OH		(419)495-2408	WS 9 SS 1015 BC 1015	ED/HC	118	99	45
OREGON	*PRINCE OF PEACE* office@princeofpeaceoregon.com www.princeofpeaceoregon.com	1960	4155 PICKLE RD	43616	OH	John W Genszler	(419)691-9407 (419)691-8406	WS 8 1030 SS 915 BC 915	EC/ED/HC	373	360	119
PAINESVILLE	*ST PAUL* office@splcpainesville.org www.splcpainesville.org	1958	250 BOWHALL RD	44077	OH		(440)354-3000 (440)354-7085	WS 930 SS 930 BC 830 1045	EC/EL/ED/ MD/SN	132	111	61
	ZION office@zelc.com www.zionpainesville.com	1893	508 MENTOR AVE	44077	OH	Dr Kurt R Ziemann	(440)357-5174	WS 9 1130 SS 1015 BC 1015	EL/ED/HC/ MD/SN	723	620	247
PARMA	*BETHANY* www.bethanyparma.org	1929	6041 RIDGE RD	44129	OH	Benjamin W Vogel	(440)884-1230 (440)884-9813	WS 830 11 SS 945 BC 945	EL/HS/ED/ HC/MD	992	835	349
	BETHLEHEM secretary@blc7500.com www.blc7500.com	1904	7500 STATE RD	44134	OH	Robert L Green	(440)845-2230	WS 9 SS 1030 BC 1030	ED/HC/ MD/SN	205	164	117
	CALVARY churchoffice@calvaryparma.org www.calvaryparma.org	1954	6906 W PLEASANT VALLEY RD	44129	S		(440)845-0070	WS 10 SS 9 BC 9	ED/HC/ MD/SN	287	227	49
	HOLY TRINITY hlytrinity@aol.com www.holytrinity.ctsmemberconnect.net	1892	6220 BROADVIEW RD	44134	S	John W Milligan	(216)741-2602 (216)661-3111	WS 10	MD	36	36	15
	UNITY		See Cleveland OH									
PATASKALA	*NEW HOPE*		See Newark OH									
PEACH GROVE	*TRINITY*		See Cincinnati OH									
PERRYSBURG	*SHEP OF VALLEY* sovlcms@att.net www.sov-lcms.org	1967	13101 FIVE POINT RD	43551	OH	John M Rutz	(419)874-6939 (419)874-6939	WS 1015 SS 9 BC 9		106	96	43
PETTISVILLE	*EMMAUS*		See Wauseon OH									
PICKERINGTON	*BETHANY*		See Columbus OH									
PIGEON CREEK	*FAIRLAWN*		See Fairlawn OH									
PLAIN CITY	*ST PAUL*		See Milford Center OH									
PLEASANT CITY	*HOLY TRINITY*	1902	10252 Pine Street PO BOX 309	43772	S		(740)685-5991	WS 930 4		30	30	10
POWELL	*BEAUTIFUL SAVIOR* pastorchris@bslcoh.org www.bslcoh.org		3924 HOME RD	43065	OH	Christopher W Schneider	(740)938-4248	WS 830 1045 SS 945 BC 945	EC/ED/HC/ MD	259	224	98
REMINDERVILLE	*HOPE*		See Aurora OH									
REYNOLDSBURG	*BETHANY*		See Columbus OH									
RIDGEVILLE CORNERS	*ZION* zionrco@bright.net www.zionrco.org	1904	20141 County Road X PO BOX 37 RDGVILLE CORS	43555	OH		(419)267-3429	WS 10 SS 845 BC 845	ED/HC/ MD/SN	91	89	38
RIVERSIDE	*EMMANUEL*		See Kettering OH									
ROCKY RIVER	*ST THOMAS* office@stcr.org www.stcr.org	1945	21211 DETROIT RD	44116	OH	Jeremiah N Jording	(440)331-2680 (440)331-2681	WS 9 BC 1015	EC/EL/HS/ ED/HC/ MD/SN	186	158	60
SHAKER HEIGHTS	*ST PETER* church@stpeterslc.org www.stpeterslc.org	1883	18000 VAN AKEN BLVD SHAKER HTS	44122	OH	Dr Troy R Neujahr	(216)561-2511	WS 930 SS 1115 BC 1115	EL/HC	54	52	48
SHEFFIELD VILLAGE	*HOPE* hopelutheransheffield@gmail.com	1971	4792 OSTER RD SHEFFIELD VLG	44054	OH		(440)949-2620	WS 930 SS 830 BC 830	EC/ED/HC/ MD	165	114	26
SHERWOOD	*ST JOHN* stjohnlutheransherwood@gmail.com www.facebook.com/stjohnsherwood	1859	9088 OPENLANDER RD	43556	OH	Eric M Moquin	(419)899-2850	WS 1015 SS 9 BC 9	ED/HC/ MD/SN	595	457	144
SIDNEY	*REDEEMER* rlcsidney@embarqmail.com redeemersidney.ctshost.org	1961	300 W MASON RD	45365	OH		(937)492-2461	WS 9 SS 1030	HC/MD/SN	127	126	37
SOLON	*HOPE*		See Aurora OH									
	OUR REDEEMER orlc@sbcglobal.net www.orlcsolon.org	1958	7196 S O M Center Rd 7196 SOM CENTER RD	44139	OH	Jonathan A Torreson	(440)248-4066 (440)248-9413	WS 8 1030 SS 915 BC 915	EC/ED/HC	628	479	135
SOUTH EUCLID	*ST JOHN* SJSE2017@att.net	1853	4386 MAYFIELD RD	44121	OH		(216)381-9396 (216)381-1564	WS 11 BC 10	EL/HS/ED/ HC/SN	78	69	33

*Indicates a new church start. A new church start is an intentionally organized gathering which comes together on a regular basis for the purpose of worship and/or Bible study and is intended to grow into a member LCMS congregation. WS =Worship Service; SS = Sunday School; BC =Bible Class; EC = Early Childhood; EL = Elementary School; HS = High School; ED =Education Ministry; HC =Human Care Ministry; SN = Special Needs Ministry; MD = Media Ministry (PC)=Partner Church Pastor. See Page 53 for the Table of Abbreviations for key to additional abbreviations

CITY	CONGREGATION EMAIL WEBSITE	YEAR EST	LOCATION MAILING ADDRESS	ZIP CODE(S)	DIST.	PASTOR(S)	PHONE FAX	WS SS BC	SCHOOLS/ MINISTRIES	STATISTIC Bapt	Conf	Avg Attend
SPRINGBORO	*EMMANUEL*		See Kettering OH									
SPRINGFIELD	*RISEN CHRIST* churchofficemanager@risenchristlcms.org www.risenchristlcms.org	1988	41 E POSSUM RD	45502	OH	Bradley D Viken	(937)323-3688	WS 10 SS 9 BC 9	EL/HS/ED/ HC/MD	161	108	60
STEUBENVILLE	*ST MARK* saintmarklcms@gmail.com www.stmarkluth.org	1928	133 LOVERS LN	43953	S		(740)264-2561 (740)264-2561	WS 1 BC 9	ED/HC/ MD/SN	28	3	18
STREETSBORO	*ST THOMAS* st.telc@gmail.com stthomasstreetsboro.com/		9042 State Rt 43 PO BOX 2247	44241	EN	Blake J Martzowka	(330)626-4945	WS 9		51	51	30
	HOPE		See Aurora OH									
STRONGSVILLE	*ST JOHN* office@stjohnluth.org stjohnluth.org	1890	8888 PROSPECT RD	44149	OH	Anthony B Mandile IV	(440)234-5806 (440)234-5821	WS 930 BC 830 1045	ED/HC/ MD/SN	150	140	64
STRYKER	*SPENDWK* Satellite Site of Good Shep Deaf Toledo OH	1985	611 S Defiance St	43557								
	ST JOHN stjohn6and66@bright.net www.stjohnstryker.org	1859	T-079 STATE ROUTE 66	43557	OH	Aaron J Bueltmann	(419)267-5266	WS 8 1030 SS 915 BC 915	ED/HC/ MD/SN	415	327	218
SUGAR GROVE	*TRINITY* trinitylutheransec@gmail.com www.trinitysugargrove.com/	1839	7120 SPONAGLE RD	43155	OH	Richard Sovitzky IV	(740)281-7593	WS 815 SS 930 BC 9	ED/HC/SN	110	83	26
SUNBURY	*HOPE*		See Condit OH									
SYLVANIA	*KING OF GLORY* kingof.glory@bex.net www.kingofglorysylvania.org	1963	6517 BRINT RD	43560	EN	Paul R Schmidlin	(419)882-6488 (419)882-6488	WS 815 1030 SS 930	ED/HC/SN			
TALLMADGE	*TALLMADGE* secretary@tlcoh.org www.tlcoh.org	1959	759 EAST AVE	44278	OH	Andrew W Alberts	(330)633-4775 (330)633-4846	WS 8 1030 SS 915 BC 915	EC/ED/HC/ MD	246	226	183
THOMPSON	*GRACE* sberndt@gracethompson.church	1955	8091 PLANK RD	44086	OH	Steve C Berndt	(440)298-3822 (440)298-1842	WS 1030 SS 9 BC 9	EL/ED/ HC/SN			
	ST JOHN		See Geneva OH									
TIFFIN	*REDEEMER* redeemerlutherantiffin@gmail.com	1966	2467 S State Rt 231 2467 S STATE ROUTE 231	44883	OH	Dr Jan S Kucera	(419)447-7794		ED/HC/ MD/SN	119	100	67
TIPP CITY	*ST TIMOTHY*		See Huber Heights OH									
TOLEDO	*CONCORDIA* office@concordiatoledo.org concordiatoledo.org	1932	3636 S DETROIT AVE	43614	OH	Michael A Mapus II	(419)382-0410 (419)382-6383	WS 930 SS 11	EC/ED/HC/ MD	65	65	43
	GOOD SHEP DEAF goodshepherddeaf@bex.net	1906	5845 ELMER DR	43615	OH	Matthew W Bergstresser	(419)536-3370	WS 1030	ED/MD/SN	102	87	37
	GOOD SHEPHERD gslcms@bex.net www.goodshepherdtoledo.org	1955	3934 W LASKEY RD	43623	EN	Bradford E Scott	(419)474-0529 (419)474-0520	WS 1030 SS 9 BC 9	ED/MD			
	IMMANUEL csf_oregon@yahoo.com	1888	710 BUCKEYE ST	43611	OH	Matthew W Bergstresser	(419)726-3991 (419)727-9197	WS 9 SS 1015	ED/HC	68	63	24
	PRINCE OF PEACE		See Oregon OH									
	ST PHILIP stphiliplutheran@hotmail.com	1949	3002 UPTON AVE	43606	OH		(419)475-2835 (419)472-9032	WS 11 SS 930	ED/HC/ MD/SN	27	27	16
	TRINITY info@trinitylutheran.org www.trinitylutheran.org	1874	4560 GLENDALE AVE	43614	OH	Mark W Love Ryan D Kleimola	(419)385-2651 (419)385-2636	WS 8 930 11 SS 930 BC 930 11	EL/ED/HC/ MD/SN	920	752	354
TRUMBULL COUNTY	*TRINITY*		See Warren OH									
TWINSBURG	*HOPE*		See Aurora OH									
UPPER ARLINGTON	*ATONEMENT*		See Columbus OH									
UTICA	*NEW HOPE*		See Newark OH									
VALLEY CITY	*ST PAUL* secretary@spvc.org www.spvc.org	1846	1377 LESTER RD	44280	OH	Philip E Zielinski	(330)483-3883	WS 8 1030 SS 915 BC 930	HC/MD/SN	511	435	145
VAN WERT	*EMMANUEL* emluch@gmail.com www.stjohnsemmanuel.com	1870	705 S WASHINGTON ST	45891	OH	Thomas J Chamberlain	(419)238-4992	WS 830	ED/HC/ MD/SN	124	118	35
VANDALIA	*ST TIMOTHY*		See Huber Heights OH									
VERMILION	*ST MATTHEW* stmatthewvermilion@gmail.com	1978	15617 Mason Rd PO BOX 774	44089	OH		(440)967-9886	WS 1030 SS 1030	ED/HC/MD			
VERMINON	*KINGSTON OF VERMINON* Satellite Site of St Matthew Vermilion OH	2012	6010 W Lake Rd	44089								
WAPAKONETA	*ST JOHN* www.stjohnsemmanuel.com	1848	15321 PUSHETA RD	45895	OH	Thomas J Chamberlain	(419)738-6746	WS 1030 SS 930 BC 930	ED/HC/ MD/SN	104	50	45
WARREN	*TRINITY* trinitylutheranwarren@gmail.com www.trinitylutheranwarren.org	1943	2742 NORTH RD NE	44483	OH	Robert J Wacker	(330)647-6402	WS 1015 SS 9	HC			
WAUSEON	*EMMAUS* office@emmauslutheranchurch.com www.emmauslutheranchurch.com	1913	841 N SHOOP AVE	43567	OH		(419)335-7446 (419)335-7446	WS 10 BC 830	EC/ED/HC	254	202	40

*Indicates a new church start. A new church start is an intentionally organized gathering which comes together on a regular basis for the purpose of worship and/or Bible study and is intended to grow into a member LCMS congregation. WS =Worship Service; SS = Sunday School; BC =Bible Class; EC = Early Childhood; EL = Elementary School; HS = High School; ED =Education Ministry; HC =Human Care Ministry; SN = Special Needs Ministry; MD = Media Ministry (PC)=Partner Church Pastor. See Page 53 for the Table of Abbreviations for key to additional abbreviations

CITY	CONGREGATION EMAIL WEBSITE	YEAR EST	LOCATION MAILING ADDRESS	ZIP CODE(S)	DIST.	PASTOR(S)	PHONE FAX	WS SS BC	SCHOOLS/ MINISTRIES	STATISTIC Bapt	Conf	Avg Attend
WAUSEON	*ST LUKE* stlukelutheran@bright.net st-lukechurch.org	1910	1588 STATE ROUTE 108	43567	OH	Chris L Sigmon	(419)335-9170 (419)335-9170	WS 10 SS 9 BC 9	ED/MD	135	120	40
WAYNESVILLE	*EMMANUEL*		See Kettering OH									
WELLINGTON	*BETHANY* bethanylutheranwellington@gmail.com blcwellington.org	1962	231 E Hamilton St PO BOX 310	44090	OH	Garrett K Buvinghausen	(440)647-5300	WS 1015 SS 9 BC 1130		119	117	41
WEST CARROLLTON	*EMMANUEL*		See Kettering OH									
WEST CHESTER	*KING OF KINGS*		See Mason OH									
	ROYAL REDEEMER		See Liberty Township OH									
WEST FARMINGTON	*TRINITY*		See Warren OH									
WESTERVILLE	*BETHANY*		See Columbus OH									
	HOLY CROSS OF THE DEAF SATELLITE Satellite Site of Holy Cross Of/Deaf Columbus OH	1972	1150 Colony Dr	43081								
WESTLAKE	*ST PAUL* churchoffice@stpaulwestlake.org www.stpaulwestlake.org	1857	27993 DETROIT RD	44145	OH	Jeffery M Smith Joshua A Gremminger	(440)835-3050	WS 815 945 11 SS 945 BC 945	EL/HS/ED/ HC/MD/SN	1447	1174	414
	ST THOMAS		See Rocky River OH									
WHITE OAK	*TRINITY*		See Cincinnati OH									
WHITEHALL	*BETHANY*		See Columbus OH									
	EBENEZER arsseber@gmail.com		700 BERNHARD RD	43213	OH	Berhanu D Arsse	(614)377-8350					
WILLOUGHBY	*TRINITY* tlcoffice@trinitywilloughby.org www.trinitywilloughby.org	1926	37728 EUCLID AVE	44094	OH		(440)942-7766 (440)942-2021	WS 1045 SS 930 BC 930	ED/HC/ MD/SN	290	263	77
WILLOWICK	*BETHEL* office@bethelwillowick.org www.bethelwillowick.org	1949	32410 WILLOWICK DR	44095	OH	Donald P Beaumont	(440)943-5000	WS 10 BC 1115	ED/HC/ MD/SN	340	247	45
	SHORE HAVEN		See Euclid OH									
WILLSHIRE	*ZION* pastor@zionschumm.org www.zionschumm.org	1846	17434 SCHUMM RD	45898	OH	Hayden M Folks	(419)495-2398	WS 10 SS 9 BC 9	ED/HC/MD	488	336	115
WILMINGTON	*WILMINGTON* wlmc757@swohio.twcbc.com wilmingtonlutheran.com	2011	757 W Main St PO BOX 1028	45177	OH	Kenneth R Castor	(937)366-6108	WS 930 BC 11	ED/HC	35	27	13
WINTERSVILLE	*ST MARK*		See Steubenville OH									
WORTHINGTON	*ATONEMENT*		See Columbus OH									
	BEAUTIFUL SAVIOR		See Powell OH									
YOUNGSTOWN	*CONCORDIA*	1922	125 N BROCKWAY AVE	44509	S		(330)792-1805	WS 10		30	25	17
	REDEEMER		See Austintown OH									
	ST MARK	1927	280 MILL CREEK DR	44512	OH		(330)788-8995 (330)788-8995	WS 1045 SS 1015 BC 1015	EC			
ZANESVILLE	*TRINITY* telcz@sbcglobal.net www.trinityzanesville.org	1844	128 S 7TH ST	43701	OH		(740)453-0744 (740)453-2331	WS 8 1030 SS 915 BC 915	EC/ED/HC/ MD	506	344	155

OKLAHOMA

CITY	CONGREGATION EMAIL WEBSITE	YEAR EST	LOCATION MAILING ADDRESS	ZIP CODE(S)	DIST.	PASTOR(S)	PHONE FAX	WS SS BC	SCHOOLS/ MINISTRIES	Bapt	Conf	Avg Attend
ADA	*FIRST* Lutheranchurchlcmsada@gmail.com www.firstlutheranada.org	1949	1319 E 18TH ST	74820	OK		(580)332-3433 (580)332-3433	WS 1030 SS 915 BC 915	ED/MD	86	40	28
ADAIR	*BETHLEHEM* www.facebook.com/bethlehem lutheranchurchadairok/	1919	6911 W 380 RD	74330	OK	Dwight F Moeller	(918)785-2994	WS 9 SS 1015 BC 1015	ED/HC			
ALTUS	*FAITH* bj.armstrong@lutheranok.com lutheranok.org	1978	2401 N PARK LN	73521	OK	Brandon J Armstrong	(580)482-2222 (580)846-5672	WS 1030 SS 915	ED/HC/MD	26	18	23
ALVA	*ZION* zionalvapastor@gmail.com www.zionalva.org	1899	218 MAPLE ST	73717	OK	Timothy C Roggow	(580)327-0510 (580)327-0552	WS 1030 SS 915 BC 915	ED/HC/ MD/SN	272	198	81
ANADARKO	*FIRST*		See Chickasha OK									
ARDMORE	*TRINITY* pastor@trinitylutheranardmore.org www.trinitylutheranardmore.org	1934	1624 HARRIS ST NW	73401	OK		(580)223-3048 (580)223-0344	WS 10 SS 9 BC 9	ED/MD/SN	87	68	37
BARTLESVILLE	*REDEEMER* redeemer@redeemerbartlesville.org redeemerbartlesville.org	1931	3700 SE Woodland Rd 3700 WOODLAND RD	74006	OK	Dr William J Shupe	(918)333-6022 (918)333-2691	WS 815 1045 SS 1015 BC 1015	ED/HC/ MD/SN	190	162	100
BEAVER	*PEACE* 4x4starrs@gmail.com	1968	10th & G PO BOX 323	73932	KS	Jason W Toombs	(580)527-1816	WS 6 SS 5 BC 5		37	27	23
BETHANY	*OUR SAVIOR* secretary@oursaviorokc.org www.oursaviorokc.org	1962	6501 NW 23RD ST	73008	OK	Dr Gary E Rohwer	(405)495-1605 (405)495-8386	WS 10 SS 9	ED	130	112	52
BLACKWELL	*ST JOHN'S* StJohnsnkbklutheran@outlook.com www.nkbklutheran.com	1901	1998 North S St 1998 N S ST PONCA CITY	74631 74601	OK		(580)362-3750	WS 11 SS 10 BC 10	HC			

*Indicates a new church start. A new church start is an intentionally organized gathering which comes together on a regular basis for the purpose of worship and/or Bible study and is intended to grow into a member LCMS congregation. WS =Worship Service; SS = Sunday School; BC =Bible Class; EC = Early Childhood; EL = Elementary School; HS = High School; ED =Education Ministry; HC =Human Care Ministry; SN = Special Needs Ministry; MD = Media Ministry (PC)=Partner Church Pastor. See Page 53 for the Table of Abbreviations for key to additional abbreviations

CITY	CONGREGATION EMAIL WEBSITE	YEAR EST	LOCATION MAILING ADDRESS	ZIP CODE(S)	DIST.	PASTOR(S)	PHONE FAX	WS SS BC	SCHOOLS/ MINISTRIES	STATISTIC Bapt	Conf	Avg Attend
BLACKWELL	*TRINITY* church@trinityblackwell.org trinityblackwell.org	1925	125 Vinnedge Ave PO BOX 545	74631	OK	James S Bozarth	(580)363-4026	WS 1045 SS 915 BC 915	ED/HC/ MD/SN	153	148	36
BLANCHARD	*FIRST*		See Chickasha OK									
BOISE CITY	*HOPE*	1928	408 W Main St PO BOX 628	73933	OK	Mark A Schlamann	(580)544-2420	WS 9 SS 10	ED/HC/ MD/SN			
BRECKINRIDGE	*IMMANUEL* immanuel.breckinridge@juno.com www.facebook.com/Immanuel LutheranBreckinridge/	1899	4324 N 102ND ST ENID	73701	OK		(580)446-5521	WS 1030 SS 930 BC 930	ED/MD	103	87	40
BROKEN ARROW	*IMMANUEL* tseeman@immanuelba.org www.immanuelba.org	1912	400 N ASPEN AVE	74012	OK	Benjamin A Braun	(918)258-5506 (918)251-8365	WS 10 SS 9	EC/EL/HS/ ED/SN	531	404	333
	TRINITY office@tlcba.org www.tlcba.org	1983	5750 S ELM PL	74011	OK	John M Wilke	(918)455-5750 (918)455-7726	WS 9 SS 1030 BC 1030	ED/HC/ MD/SN	400	301	150
BUFFALO	*ZION* www.zionlutheranbuffalo.com	1903	19015 US Hwy 64 PO BOX 632	73834	OK		(580)735-2733	WS 4 SS 5	ED/HC/MD	66	60	18
CHICKASHA	*FIRST* pr.kpnelson@gmail.com firstchickasha.org	1913	828 Minnesota Ave PO BOX 387	73018 73023	OK	Kyle P Nelson	(405)224-1552	WS 1030 SS 930 BC 930	ED/HC/MD	86	62	43
CHOCTAW	*GOOD SHEPHERD*		See Midwest City OK									
CLAREMORE	*REDEEMER* rluther@sbcglobal.net www.rlccok.org	1949	220 N SEMINOLE AVE	74017	OK	Ryan L Honeycutt	(918)341-1429 (918)343-3724	WS 1030 SS 9	ED/HC/SN			
COVINGTON	*ST JOHNS* sjlchurchcovington@gmail.com www.facebook.com/StJohns LutheranChurchInCovington/	1897	205 E Jackson P.O. BOX 345	73730	OK		(580)864-7965	WS 10 BC 9	ED/HC	149	96	32
COYLE	*ZION*		See Guthrie OK									
CUSHING	*OUR REDEEMER* revrafferty@gmtel.net www.facebook.com/ Lutheran-Church-of-our-Rede emer-Cushing-112881827010521/	1923	730 E CHERRY ST	74023	OK	Charles R Rafferty	(918)225-4646	WS 1045 SS 930	ED/HC/SN			
DEL CITY	*GOOD SHEPHERD*		See Midwest City OK									
DUNCAN	*GOOD SHEPHERD* duncangoodshepherd@gmail.com www.duncangoodshepherd.org	1952	3965 COUNTRY CLUB RD	73533	OK		(580)255-3267 (580)255-3001	WS 10 SS 9 BC 9	ED/HC/ MD/SN	63	52	24
EDMOND	*HOLY TRINITY* info@holytrinityedmond.org www.holytrinityedmond.org	1986	308 NW 164TH ST	73013	OK	Paul C Hemenway Joshua Brakhage	(405)348-3292	WS 815 1030 1045 SS 930	EL/ED/HC/ MD/SN	906	763	450
	ST MARK office@stmarkedmond.org www.stmarkedmond.org	1980	1501 N BRYANT AVE	73034	OK	Mark R Erler	(405)340-0192 (405)340-0290	WS 815 1045 SS 930 BC 930	EC/ED/HC/ MD	350	247	90
EL RENO	*TRINITY* tlcelreno7116@gmail.com tlcelreno.org	1931	500 S COUNTRY CLUB RD	73036	OK	Aaron P Kotila	(405)262-7116	WS 1030 SS 915	EC/ED/MD	403	367	90
ELK CITY	*CHRIST* christlutheranelkcity@gmail.com www.clcelkcity.org/	1945	1023 W 2ND ST	73644	OK		(580)757-9696	WS 11 BC 945	HC/MD	26	26	17
ENID	*IMMANUEL*		See Breckinridge OK									
	REDEEMER pastor1rlc@gmail.com www.redeemerenid.com	1934	215 S CLEVELAND ST	73703	OK		(580)234-6622	WS 10 SS 845	ED/HC/ MD/SN	203	163	127
	SAINT PAUL'S office@stpaulsenid.com www.stpaulsenid.com	1909	1626 E BROADWAY AVE	73701	OK	Jonathan F Meyer	(580)234-6646 (580)234-6692	WS 9 SS 1015	EL/ED/HC/ MD	360	315	103
EUFAULA	*GOOD SHEPHERD* martymortensen@gmail.com	1982	Eunice Burns Rd PO BOX 687	74432	OK		(918)689-2169	WS 9 BC 1030				
FAIRLAND	*ST PAUL* stpaulluthch@aol.com	1910	513 W Washington Ave PO BOX 219	74343	OK		(918)676-3059 (918)676-3059	WS 1030 SS 915 BC 915	ED/HC/ MD/SN	18	18	13
FAIRMONT	*ZION* zlcfairmont@gmail.com www.facebook.com/ZLCFairmont/	1897	507 FAIRMONT RD	73736	OK	Mark J Blakeman	(580)358-2291	WS 1030 SS 915 BC 915	EC/ED/ MD/SN	313	213	37
GARBER	*IMMANUEL* immanuelgarber@gmail.com	1900	601 Arapaho St PO BOX 59	73738	OK	Clayton E Dodge	(580)863-2722	WS 1030 SS 930	ED/HC/MD	147	110	33
GLENPOOL	*KING OF KINGS* info@kingofkingsok.org www.kingofkingsok.org	2005	15251 S BROADWAY ST	74033	OK		(918)291-2005	WS 9 BC 1030	ED/HC/ MD/SN	50	42	26
GRANITE	*ST JOHN* bj.armstrong@lutheranok.com www.facebook.com/stjohnslutheran. granite	1909	507 Ada St PO BOX 56	73547	OK	Brandon J Armstrong	(580)535-4662	WS 845 SS 10		49	40	35
GROVE	*IMMANUEL* Immanuelgr706@gmail.com	2002	706 ROCKWOOD DR	74344	OK		(918)786-4585	WS 930 SS 9 BC 9	ED/HC/ MD/SN	36	35	28
GUTHRIE	*OUR SAVIOR* www.facebook.com/Our-Savior-Lut heran-Guthrie-101243928243847/	1994	735 S Santa Fe 735 S SANTA FE RD	73044	OK	John C Rumsey III	(405)282-5144	WS 1030 SS 915 BC 915	ED/HC/SN	39	31	27
	ZION zlcmsok@aol.com www.zlcguthrieok.org	1899	424 E WARNER AVE	73044	OK		(405)282-3914 (405)282-3918	WS 10 SS 9 BC 9		104	81	60

*Indicates a new church start. A new church start is an intentionally organized gathering which comes together on a regular basis for the purpose of worship and/or Bible study and is intended to grow into a member LCMS congregation. WS =Worship Service; SS = Sunday School; BC =Bible Class; EC = Early Childhood; EL = Elementary School; HS = High School; ED =Education Ministry; HC =Human Care Ministry; SN = Special Needs Ministry; MD = Media Ministry (PC)=Partner Church Pastor. See Page 53 for the Table of Abbreviations for key to additional abbreviations

CITY	CONGREGATION EMAIL WEBSITE	YEAR EST	LOCATION MAILING ADDRESS	ZIP CODE(S)	DIST.	PASTOR(S)	PHONE FAX	WS SS BC	SCHOOLS/ MINISTRIES	STATISTIC Bapt	Conf	Avg Attend
GUYMON	*TRINITY* wescoattmd@gmail.com www.facebook.com/TELCGuymon/	1908	1212 N CRUMLEY ST	73942	OK	Tyler R Arends	(580)338-3820	WS 1030 SS 915	EC/ED/ HC/SN			
HINTON	*ST JOHN* orval_peters@yahoo.com	1906	400 S Spencer St PO BOX 8	73047	OK	Orval F Peters	(405)542-6472	WS 11		25	20	12
HOOKER	*ST JOHN* stjohnslcms1@gmail.com	1917	301 N Jackson St PO BOX 65	73945	OK	Conrad W Oehlert	(580)652-2683	WS 1030 SS 930	ED/HC			
KINGFISHER	*EMMANUEL* revtimmcc@gmail.com elc1904.360unite.com/home	1904	124 W DOUGLAS AVE	73750	OK	Timothy L McCarty	(405)375-3431	WS 1030 SS 930 BC 930	ED/HC/ MD/SN	192	172	93
LAHOMA	*ZION* zionlahomasec@yahoo.com zionlahoma.com/	1902	518 OKLAHOMA ST	73754	OK	Randy C Foote	(580)796-2243	WS 1030 SS 930 BC 930	ED/HC/ MD/SN	87	75	43
LAWTON	*HOLY CROSS* holycrosslawton@gmail.com holycrosslawton.org	1965	2105 NW 38TH ST	73505	OK	Ahren L Reiter	(580)357-7684 (580)357-7684	WS 1030 SS 915	EC/ED/HC/ MD	131	84	75
	ST JOHN stjohnlcsec@gmail.com stjohnlutheranlawton.com/	1916	102 SW 7TH ST	73501	OK	Dr Eugene W Schneider III	(580)353-0556 (580)353-0646	WS 1030 SS 930 BC 930	EC/ED/ HC/SN	375	259	115
LONE WOLF	*ST JOHNS* bj.armstrong@lutheranok.com lutheranok.org	1903	214 Evans Ave PO BOX 368	73655	OK	Brandon J Armstrong	(580)471-9237	WS 9 SS 1015	ED/MD	55	45	35
MCALESTER	*TRINITY* trinity74501@sbcglobal.net trinitymcalester.com	1948	190 E STATE HIGHWAY 31	74501	OK	Glenn A Meyer	(918)426-4544 (918)426-4544	WS 1030 SS 915 BC 915	ED/HC/ MD/SN	125	97	18
MIAMI	*MOUNT OLIVE* mtolivechurchmiami@gmail.com	1944	2337 N MAIN ST	74354	OK		(918)542-4681 (918)542-4681	WS 1030 SS 9 BC 9	EL/HS/ED/ HC/MD/SN			
MIDWEST CITY	*GOOD SHEPHERD* secretary@gslok.org gslcmwc.com	1950	700 N AIR DEPOT BLVD	73110	OK	Ronald L Simpson	(405)732-2585 (405)732-7977	WS 8 1030 SS 915 BC 915	EL/ED/HC/ MD/SN	358	246	76
MOORE	*ST JOHN* office@stjohnsmoore.org www.stjohnsmoore.org	1963	1032 NW 12TH ST	73160	OK	Mark L Bersche	(405)794-5462	WS 8 1030 SS 915 BC 915	EL/ED/HC/ MD/SN	258	220	127
MUSKOGEE	*FIRST* pastor@firstlutherantahlequah.org	1913	428 E BROADWAY ST	74403	OK			WS 1	ED/MD			
MUSTANG	*CHRIST* christlutheranmustang@gmail.com www.christlutheranmustang.org	1974	501 N CLEAR SPRINGS RD	73064	OK	Daniel C Ross	(405)376-3116	WS 8 1030 SS 915	ED/HC/ MD/SN	201	168	140
NEWKIRK	*ST JOHNS* StJohnsnkbklutheran@outlook.com	1908	101 S Magnolia PO BOX 290	74647	OK		(580)362-3750	WS 9 SS 10				
NICOMA PARK	*GOOD SHEPHERD*		See Midwest City OK									
NINNEKAH	*FIRST*		See Chickasha OK									
NORMAN	*TRINITY* tlcnormanpastor@gmail.com www.tlcnorman.org	1901	603 CLASSEN BLVD	73071	OK	David R Nehrenz	(405)321-3443	WS 8 1030 SS 915 BC 915	EC/ED/HC/ MD	518	403	173
OKARCHE	*ST JOHNS* stjohns@pldi.net stjohnsokarche.com	1892	408 W Colorado PO BOX 66	73762	OK		(405)263-7311	WS 1015 SS 9 BC 9	EC/ED/ MD/SN	338	245	123
OKLAHOMA CITY	*CHRIST*		See Mustang OK									
	CRISTO REY abiutfajardo@gmail.com www.iglesialuteranacristorey.org/	2000	1140 SW 29TH ST	73109	OK	Abiut Fajardo-Ruiz	(405)636-1783		ED/HC/MD	275	261	45
	FAITH faithlcmsokc@gmail.com www.facebook.com/faith lutheranchurch2512/	1956	2512 S SHARTEL AVE	73109	OK	Adam W Ellison	(405)632-5744	WS 1015		27	27	12
	GOOD SHEPHERD		See Midwest City OK									
	HOLY TRINITY		See Edmond OK									
	IMMANUEL immanueloffice@yahoo.com www.ILC-OKC.com	1934	1800 NW 36TH ST	73118	OK		(405)525-5793	WS 1030 SS 930 BC 930	ED/HC/MD	285	140	44
	MESSIAH mmuenchow@messiahokc.org www.messiahokc.org	1956	3600 NW EXPRESSWAY	73112	OK	Mark R Muenchow Myron D Harms	(405)946-0681 (405)946-0682	WS 815 1045 SS 930 BC 930	EL/ED/HC/ MD/SN	476	428	161
	ZION zionluthokc@hotmail.com zionluthokc.360unite.com	1900	7701 W BRITTON RD	73132	OK	Ronald E Christie	(405)615-1292	WS 1030 SS 915	ED/HC	98	76	40
OKMULGEE	*TRINITY* tlcoksecretary@gmail.com trinityokmulgee.org	1930	1314 E 6TH ST	74447	OK	Richard M Dailey	(918)756-6046 (918)756-6046	WS 1045 SS 930	ED/HC/ MD/SN	84	66	40
OWASSO	*FAITH* lutheranowasso@sbcglobal.net www.faithlutheranowasso.org	1980	9222 N GARNETT RD	74055	OK	Mark A Neumann	(918)272-9858 (918)272-4629	WS 8 1030 SS 915	ED/HC/ MD/SN	263	210	124
PERRY	*CHRIST* lutheranperry@sbcglobal.net www.perrylutheran.com/	1901	1301 N 7TH ST	73077	OK	Aaron J Ferguson	(580)336-2347	WS 10 SS 845 BC 845	ED/HC/SN	461	309	54
PONCA CITY	*FIRST* flcsponcacity@flcspc.com flcspc.360unite.com/home	1925	1101 N 4TH ST	74601	OK	Joseph C Highley	(580)762-1111 (580)762-1111	WS 9 BC 1030	EL/ED/HC/ MD/SN	437	328	148
	ST JOHN'S		See Blackwell OK									

*Indicates a new church start. A new church start is an intentionally organized gathering which comes together on a regular basis for the purpose of worship and/or Bible study and is intended to grow into a member LCMS congregation. WS =Worship Service; SS = Sunday School; BC =Bible Class; EC = Early Childhood; EL = Elementary School; HS = High School; ED =Education Ministry; HC =Human Care Ministry; SN = Special Needs Ministry; MD = Media Ministry (PC)=Partner Church Pastor. See Page 53 for the Table of Abbreviations for key to additional abbreviations

CONGREGATIONS

CITY	CONGREGATION EMAIL WEBSITE	YEAR EST	LOCATION MAILING ADDRESS	ZIP CODE(S)	DIST.	PASTOR(S)	PHONE FAX	WS SS BC	SCHOOLS/ MINISTRIES	STATISTIC Bapt	Conf	Avg Attend
POND CREEK	*FIRST* bjkemna@yahoo.com	1987	221 5th St PO BOX 218	73766	OK		(580)532-6531					
PRYOR	*ST JOHN* stjohnpryor@yahoo.com www.stjohnpryor.org	1955	607 SE 9TH ST	74361	OK		(918)825-1926	WS 1030 BC 930	HC/MD/SN	34	28	20
SALLISAW	*TRINITY* www.tlcsallisaw.org/	1982	2000 S KERR BLVD	74955	MDS	Joshua J Willadsen	(918)775-6753	WS 1015		20	19	10
SHATTUCK	*CHRIST* www.facebook.com/ Christ-Lutheran-Church-Shat tuck-OK-1622641194656150/	1902	212 S Charles St PO BOX 456	73858	OK	Gary W Mc Clellan	(580)938-5208	WS 11 BC 10		34	32	24
SHAWNEE	*REDEEMER* redeemer.lutheranok@gmail.com redeemershawnee.org	1982	39307 Mac Arthur St 39307 MACARTHUR ST	74804	OK	Matthew W Tassey	(405)273-6286 (405)214-4476	WS 930 SS 1045 BC 1045	ED	200	140	63
SKIATOOK	*SHEPHERD OF THE HILL* office@sothlc.org www.sothlc.org		724 N 52nd W Ave PO BOX 871	74070	OK	Jay G Hobson	(918)895-2611	WS 930 SS 1045	ED/MD	121	94	80
STILLWATER	*ZION* zionluth2@sbcglobal.net www.zionlutheranstw.com	1926	504 S KNOBLOCK ST	74074	OK	John E Wackler	(405)372-3703 (405)372-0372	WS 8 1030 SS 915	ED/HC/SN	251	223	124
SULPHUR	*HOPE* wpwpayne@gmail.com	1967	208 E 3rd St 220 EAST 3 RD STREET	73086	OK		(580)332-3433	WS 745 SS 845				
TAHLEQUAH	*FIRST* pastor@firstlutherantahlequah.org www.firstlutherantahlequah.org	1970	2111 MAHANEY AVE	74464	OK	Clifton R Loman	(918)456-5070	WS 1030 SS 12	ED/MD			
TEXHOMA	*ST PAUL* StPaul.Texhoma.ok@gmail.com www.facebook.com/groups/StPaul LutheranChurchTexhoma/	1936	416 N 2nd PO BOX 465	73949	OK	Thomas W House	(580)423-7353	WS 1030 SS 930 BC 930	ED/HC			
TULSA	*ABLAZE CHURCH* Satellite Site of Our Savior Tulsa OK	2017	4901 S 177 E Ave	74134				WS 1030 SS 11				
	CHRIST THE REDEEMER christredeemer@ctrtulsa.org www.ctrtulsa.org	1953	2550 E 71ST ST	74136	OK	Scott E Burmeister	(918)492-6451	WS 815 1045 1215 SS 930 BC 930	ED/HC/ MD/SN			
	GOOD SHEPHERD gslcoffc@gslctulsa.org www.gslctulsa.org	1946	8730 E SKELLY DR	74129	OK	Bernardo Rangel Sr	(918)622-2905 (918)622-3805	WS 830 11 SS 945	ED/HC/MD			
	GRACE secretary@glctulsa.org www.glctulsa.org	1922	2331 E 5TH PL	74104	OK	Christopher D Hall	(918)592-2999	WS 8 1030 SS 915	ED/HC/ MD/SN	360	340	133
	IMMANUEL		See Broken Arrow OK									
	OUR SAVIOR pastor@osltulsa.org www.osltulsa.org	1949	4901 S 177 E AVE	74134	OK	Timothy P Dreier	(918)836-3752 (918)836-4538	WS 9 SS 1030 BC 1030	EC/ED/HC/ MD/SN	333	272	156
TUTTLE	*FIRST*		See Chickasha OK									
VINITA	*MESSIAH*	1989	460 N Wilson St PO BOX 392	74301	OK	Bruce C Cottrell	(918)256-3223	WS 10 SS 9 BC 9	ED/HC	14	9	9
WATONGA	*MOUNT CALVARY* orval_peters@yahoo.com	1933	621 N LEACH AVE	73772	OK	Orval F Peters	(580)623-5099	WS 9 SS 10 BC 10	ED	102	75	40
WELLSTON	*ST PAUL* www.facebook.com/stpaulswellstonok	1986	706 Birch PO BOX 333	74881	OK	Christopher C Griffith Michael S Monterastelli	(405)356-4203	WS 9 BC 1015	ED	80	56	45
WOODWARD	*TRINITY* revgreg88030@yahoo.com	1901	1518 14TH ST	73801	OK		(580)256-2524		ED/HC	67	54	8
YUKON	*TRINITY*		See El Reno OK									

OREGON

CITY	CONGREGATION EMAIL WEBSITE	YEAR EST	LOCATION MAILING ADDRESS	ZIP CODE(S)	DIST.	PASTOR(S)	PHONE FAX	WS SS BC	SCHOOLS/ MINISTRIES	STATISTIC Bapt	Conf	Avg Attend
ALBANY	*HOLY CROSS* holycrosslutheranalbany@gmail.com www.holycrosslutheranalbany.org	1982	2515 QUEEN AVE SE	97322	NOW	Alexander J Lange	(541)928-0214 (541)928-0200	WS 1030 SS 915 BC 915	ED/HC/MD	112	90	58
	IMMANUEL ilchurch2009@gmail.com Immanuelalbany.org	1891	154 MADISON ST SE	97321	NOW	Larry L Oliver	(541)926-3495	WS 1030 SS 1030 BC 9	HC/MD	55	55	42
	SHEPHERD OF VALLEY		See Corvallis OR									
	ZION		See Corvallis OR									
ALOHA	*BETHLEHEM* office@blcfamily.org www.blcfamily.org	1958	18865 SW JOHNSON ST	97003	NOW		(503)649-3380 (503)649-1530	WS 830 11 SS 945 BC 945	EC/EL/ED/ HC/MD/SN			
AMITY	*TRINITY*		See Sheridan OR									
ASHLAND	*GRACE* gracelutheranashland@gmail.com www.gracelutheranashland.org	1948	660 FRANCES LN	97520	NOW	Joshua J Heimbuck	(541)482-1661 (541)482-2860	WS 10 BC 9	ED/HC/ MD/SN	77	77	49
BEAVERTON	*PILGRIM* k.darby@pilgrimbeaverton.com www.pilgrimbeaverton.com	1942	5650 SW HALL BLVD	97005	NOW	Shawn F Hazel	(503)644-8697 (503)644-8182	WS 9 SS 1015	EL/ED			
	PRINCE OF PEACE		See Portland OR									

*Indicates a new church start. A new church start is an intentionally organized gathering which comes together on a regular basis for the purpose of worship and/or Bible study and is intended to grow into a member LCMS congregation. WS =Worship Service; SS = Sunday School; BC =Bible Class; EC = Early Childhood; EL = Elementary School; HS = High School; ED =Education Ministry; HC =Human Care Ministry; SN = Special Needs Ministry; MD = Media Ministry (PC)=Partner Church Pastor. See Page 53 for the Table of Abbreviations for key to additional abbreviations

CITY	CONGREGATION EMAIL WEBSITE	YEAR EST	LOCATION MAILING ADDRESS	ZIP CODE(S)	DIST.	PASTOR(S)	PHONE FAX	WS SS BC	SCHOOLS/ MINISTRIES	STATISTIC Bapt	Conf	Avg Attend
BEND	*TRINITY* church@saints.org www.saints.org	1926	2550 NE BUTLER MARKET RD	97701	NOW	Caleb M Adams Donald J Heien	(541)382-1832	WS 930 BC 1045	EL/HS/ED/ HC/MD			
BORING	*CHRIST THE VINE*		See Damascus OR									
BROOKINGS	*GRACE*		See Crescent City CA									
BURNS	*FIRST*	1929	349 S EGAN AVE	97720	NOW		(541)589-3153	WS 3				
CANBY	*CHRIST THE VINE*		See Damascus OR									
CENTRAL POINT	*GLORIA DEI* www.gloriadeicp.org	1964	745 N 10TH ST	97502	NOW	Herbert M Percy Jr	(541)664-3724 (541)664-3724	WS 9 SS 1045 BC 1045	ED/HC/ MD/SN			
CLACKAMAS	*BEAUTIFUL SAVIOR*		See Portland OR									
COOS BAY	*CHRIST* office@coosbaylutheran.org www.coosbaylutheran.org	1908	1835 N 15TH ST	97420	NOW		(541)267-3851 (541)267-3331	WS 1030 BC 1130	ED/HC/MD			
COQUILLE	*SAINT JAMES*		See Myrtle Point OR									
CORNELIUS	*ST PETER* office-stpeters-lcms@coho.net www.stpeterscornelius.org	1882	4265 SW GOLF COURSE RD	97113	NOW	Michael G Warmbier	(503)357-3863 (503)357-6418	WS 1030 SS 915 BC 915	EL/ED/HC/ MD/SN	373	256	85
CORVALLIS	*PEACE*		See Philomath OR									
	SHEPHERD OF VALLEY svlc.corvallis@gmail.com svlc-corvallis.org	1966	2650 NW HIGHLAND DR	97330	NOW	Eric C Bohlmann	(541)753-2816	WS 9 SS 1030 BC 1030	ED/HC/MD	58	58	45
	ZION zion@proaxis.com zioncorvallis.org	1905	2745 NW HARRISON BLVD	97330	NOW	Theodore P Schaefer	(541)757-0946	WS 9 11 BC 1010	EL/ED/HC/ MD/SN	202	190	100
COTTAGE GROVE	*TRINITY* tlc@tlccg.com www.tlccg.com	1947	675 S 7TH ST	97424	NOW		(541)942-2373 (541)942-5321	WS 1030 SS 915 BC 915	ED/HC/ MD/SN			
COVE	*FAITH*		See La Grande OR									
DALLAS	*FAITH*		See Monmouth OR									
DAMASCUS	*CHRIST THE VINE* kristina@christthevinelutheran.org christthevinelutheran.org	1978	18677 SE HIGHWAY 212	97089	NOW	Jesse L Brubaker	(503)658-5650	WS 930 SS 830	EL/ED/HC/ MD	279	228	112
EAGLE CREEK	*CHRIST THE VINE*		See Damascus OR									
EAGLE POINT	*ST JOHN* church@stjohnep.org www.stjohnep.org	1978	42 Alta Vista Rd PO BOX 1049	97524	NOW	Gary L Clark	(541)826-4334	WS 8 1030 SS 915	ED/HC/ MD/SN	50	40	38
ELGIN	*FAITH*		See La Grande OR									
ENTERPRISE	*FAITH*		See La Grande OR									
	WALLOWA COUNTY OUTREACH Satellite Site of Faith La Grande OR	2004	409 Main St	97828				WS 2				
ESTACADA	*CHRIST THE VINE*		See Damascus OR									
	PEACE	1971	29455 SE Eagle Creek Rd PO BOX 930	97023	NOW		(503)630-4049	WS 10 SS 9 BC 9	ED/HC/SN			
EUGENE	*GRACE* glc@glchurch.org www.graceeugene.org	1920	710 E 17TH AVE	97401	NOW	Joseph M Baumgarten	(541)342-4844 (541)342-2241	WS 10 BC 9	ED/HC/ MD/SN	322	238	99
	HOPE		See Springfield OR									
	MESSIAH office@messiaheugene.org	1957	3280 RIVER RD	97404	NOW	John W Schatz	(541)688-0735	WS 9 BC 1015	ED/HC/MD			
FLORENCE	*RESURRECTION* ResurrectionLutheranFlorence@ gmail.com puppro.wixsite.com/rlcflorence	2003	85294 Hwy 101 South PO BOX 1957	97439	NOW	Dr Steven M Waterman	(541)997-8038	WS 10 BC 9	ED/HC/ MD/SN	54	54	45
FOREST GROVE	*MOUNT OLIVE* info@MtOliveFG.org www.MtOliveFG.org	1932	2327 17TH AVE	97116	NOW	Nicholas W Koschmann	(503)357-2511	WS 10 SS 9 BC 9	EC/EL/ED/ HC/MD/SN			
GLADSTONE	*CHRIST THE VINE*		See Damascus OR									
GRANDE RONDE	*TRINITY*		See Sheridan OR									
GRANTS PASS	*ST PAUL* office@stpaulsgp.com stpaulsgp.com	1928	865 NW 5TH ST	97526	NOW	Eli T Davis	(541)476-2565	WS 10 SS 845 BC 845	ED/HC/SN	139	139	51
GRESHAM	*CHRIST THE VINE*		See Damascus OR									
	REDEEMER rdmr-lcms@juno.com wheretheliturgylives.org	1935	795 E POWELL BLVD	97030	NOW	Eric T Lange	(503)665-5414 (503)665-1297	WS 10 SS 845 BC 845	ED/HC/ MD/SN	103	103	61
HAPPY VALLEY	*CHRIST THE VINE*		See Damascus OR									
HERMISTON	*BETHLEHEM* pastor.bethlehemhermiston@gmail.com www.bethlehemhermiston.org	1953	515 SW 7TH ST	97838	NOW	Mark E Adams	(541)567-6811 (541)289-0114	WS 1030 BC 9	EC/ED/HC/ MD	159	113	41
HILLSBORO	*TRINITY* office@trinityhillsboro.com www.trinityhillsboro.org	1917	2194 SE MINTER BRIDGE RD	97123	NOW	Jason A Taber Joshua D Nix	(503)640-1693 (503)640-1342	WS 8 1030	EC/EL/ED/ HC/MD/SN	503	481	229
	ZION zionhillsb@aol.com www.zionhillsboro.org	1904	30900 NW Evergreen Rd 178 NE EVERGREEN RD	97124	NOW		(503)640-8914	WS 1030 SS 915 BC 915	EC/EL/ED/ HC/MD	73	60	45
HOOD RIVER	*IMMANUEL* Church@immanuelhr.org immanuelhr.org	1902	305 9TH ST	97031	NOW	Tyler C Moore	(541)386-3046	WS 10 SS 10	ED/HC/ MD/SN	150	120	70

*Indicates a new church start. A new church start is an intentionally organized gathering which comes together on a regular basis for the purpose of worship and/or Bible study and is intended to grow into a member LCMS congregation. WS =Worship Service; SS = Sunday School; BC =Bible Class; EC = Early Childhood; EL = Elementary School; HS = High School; ED =Education Ministry; HC =Human Care Ministry; SN = Special Needs Ministry; MD = Media Ministry (PC)=Partner Church Pastor. See Page 53 for the Table of Abbreviations for key to additional abbreviations

CITY	CONGREGATION EMAIL WEBSITE	YEAR EST	LOCATION MAILING ADDRESS	ZIP CODE(S)	DIST.	PASTOR(S)	PHONE FAX	WS SS BC	SCHOOLS/ MINISTRIES	STATISTIC Bapt	Conf	Avg Attend
IMBLER	*FAITH*		See La Grande OR									
INDEPENDENCE	*FAITH*		See Monmouth OR									
IONE	*CHRIST ALONE LUTHERAN CHURCH* Satellite Site of Bethlehem Hermiston OR	2011	Ione Market 245 W Main	97843				WS 8 BC 7				
JOHN DAY	*REDEEMER* redeemerlutheranjohnday@yahoo.com	1950	627 SE HILLCREST RD	97845	NOW		(541)575-2348	WS 10 SS 11	SN	15	14	12
JOSEPH	*FAITH*		See La Grande OR									
JUNCTION CITY	*SHEP OF VALLEY* secretarysotvlc@gmail.com www.shepherdofthevalleylutheran.org	1977	29357 Lingo Ln 29357 LINGO LN P.O. BOX 706	97448	NOW	John W Schatz	(541)998-6659		ED/HC/ MD/SN	25	24	12
KENO	*SAVING GRACE* henryjvester@gmail.com	1987	15681 HIGHWAY 66	97627	NOW		(541)882-4629	WS 830	ED	16	3	9
KLAMATH FALLS	*SAVING GRACE*		See Keno OR									
	ZION www.zionklamathfalls.org	1924	1025 HIGH ST	97601	NOW		(541)884-6793 (541)884-6868	WS 1015 SS 9 BC 9	ED/HC/ MD/SN			
LA GRANDE	*FAITH* flglcmspastor@gmail.com lgfaithlcms.org	1958	104 S 12TH ST	97850	NOW	Samuel C Wiseman	(541)963-2831	WS 10 SS 845 BC 845	EC/ED/HC/ MD/SN	103	79	42
	GRANDE RONDE RETIREMENT BIBLE STUDY Satellite Site of Faith La Grande OR	2004	1809 Gekeler Ln	97850								
LA PINE	*FAITH* faithlutheranlapine@gmail.com	1972	52315 S Huntington Rd PO BOX 1280	97739	NOW	Peter Pagel	(541)536-1198	WS 10 BC 9	MD	132	119	58
LAKE OSWEGO	*TRIUMPHANT KING* Office@tklc-lcms.org www.tklc-lcms.org	1960	4700 LAMONT WAY	97035	NOW	Philemon O Ngare	(503)636-3436	WS 11 SS 10	EC	34	33	19
LAKEVIEW	*FIRST*	1954	Highway 395 North PO BOX 69	97630	NOW		(541)417-1946	WS 1030				
LEBANON	*BETHLEHEM* office@blclebanon.org www.blclebanon.org	1911	434 E Grant St 900 CLEVELAND ST	97355	NOW	Michael A Miller	(541)258-6393	WS 1030 SS 9 BC 9	HC/MD/SN	96	53	41
LINCOLN CITY	*LAKEVIEW SENIOR LIVING* Satellite Site of St Peter Fisherman Lincoln City OR	2012	2690 NE Yacht	97367								
	ST PETER FISHERMAN stpeterlc@yahoo.com www.stpeterthefishermanlcms.org	1967	1226 SW 13th St PO BOX 169	97367	NOW	James M Kyes	(541)994-8793	WS 1030 SS 1030 BC 9	HC/MD/SN	108	79	49
MCMINNVILLE	*ST JOHN* churchoffice@stjohnmac.org www.stjohnmac.org	1939	2142 NE Mc Donald Ln 2142 NE MCDONALD LN	97128	NOW		(503)472-6677 (503)472-6677	WS 1030 SS 915	MD/SN	57	57	25
	TRINITY		See Sheridan OR									
MEDFORD	*ST PETER* luth1020@gmail.com stpeterlutheran-medford.org	1928	1020 E MAIN ST	97504	NOW	William H Lehmann III	(541)772-4395 (541)245-4242	WS 930 SS 11 BC 11	EC/ED/HC/ MD/SN			
MILWAUKIE	*BEAUTIFUL SAVIOR*		See Portland OR									
	CHRIST THE VINE		See Damascus OR									
MOLALLA	*GRACE* gracemolalla@yahoo.com www.gracemolalla.com	1947	510 May St PO BOX 329	97038	NOW		(503)829-2250	WS 10 SS 10 BC 845	ED/HC/ MD/SN			
MONMOUTH	*FAITH* faithlutheranmon@aol.com faithlutheranmonmouth.org	1964	200 Monmouth Independence Hwy PO BOX 327	97361	NOW		(503)838-3459	WS 10 SS 845 BC 845	ED/HC/ MD/SN	107	85	54
MOUNT ANGEL	*TRINITY* trinitymtangel@gmail.com www.trinitymtangel.org	1890	15534 E MARQUAM RD NE	97362	NOW	John S Karay	(503)634-2437	WS 1030 BC 9	ED/MD			
MYRTLE POINT	*SAINT JAMES*	1938	510 Railroad Ave PO BOX 157	97458	NOW	Gregory J Howald	(541)572-5665	WS 10 SS 9 BC 1130	HC			
NEWPORT	*ALL NATIONS* anlc_office@allnationslutheran.org www.allnationslutheran.org	1945	358 NE 12TH ST	97365	NOW	Nathan M Brandt	(541)265-2503	WS 11 BC 945	ED/HC/MD	30	30	34
NORTH POWDER	*FAITH*		See La Grande OR									
OAKRIDGE	*ST LUKE*	1953	47477 Teller Rd PO BOX 674	97463	NOW		(541)782-2030	WS 10 SS 845	ED/HC			
ONTARIO	*PILGRIM* pilgrimontario@yahoo.com www.pilgrimlutheran.net	1942	208 SW 1ST AVE	97914	NOW	LeRoy D Raynor	(541)889-5458	WS 1045 SS 930 BC 930	ED/HC	100	93	45
OREGON CITY	*CHRIST THE VINE*		See Damascus OR									
	TRINITY office@trinityoc.org trinityoc.org	1921	16000 S HENRICI RD	97045	NOW		(503)632-5554 (503)632-5546	WS 10 SS 11 BC 11	ED/HC/MD	191	188	73
PHILOMATH	*PEACE* pastorlucke@gmail.com www.peaceinphilomath.com	1950	2540 APPLEGATE ST	97370	NOW	Jeremy N Lucke	(541)929-5504	WS 10 SS 9 BC 9	ED/HC/MD			
	SHEPHERD OF VALLEY		See Corvallis OR									
	ZION		See Corvallis OR									

*Indicates a new church start. A new church start is an intentionally organized gathering which comes together on a regular basis for the purpose of worship and/or Bible study and is intended to grow into a member LCMS congregation. WS =Worship Service; SS = Sunday School; BC =Bible Class; EC = Early Childhood; EL = Elementary School; HS = High School; ED =Education Ministry; HC =Human Care Ministry; SN = Special Needs Ministry; MD = Media Ministry (PC)=Partner Church Pastor. See Page 53 for the Table of Abbreviations for key to additional abbreviations

CITY	CONGREGATION EMAIL WEBSITE	YEAR EST	LOCATION MAILING ADDRESS	ZIP CODE(S)	DIST.	PASTOR(S)	PHONE FAX	WS SS BC	SCHOOLS/ MINISTRIES	STATISTIC Bapt	Conf	Avg Attend
PLEASANT HILL	*PLEASANT HILL* churchongaupp@gmail.com www.phlutheran.org	1965	84421 GAUPP LN	97455	NOW		(541)747-8913	WS 1 BC 2	ED/HC/MD	60	60	30
PORTLAND	*ASCENSION* office@alcportland.org www.alcportland.org	1958	1440 SE 182ND AVE	97233	NOW	James J Sprengle	(503)665-8821	WS 830 11 SS 945 BC 945	ED/HC/ MD/SN	189	167	124
	BEAUTIFUL SAVIOR info@bslc.com www.bslc.com	1955	9800 SE 92ND AVE	97086	NOW	Kevin A Hohnstadt John M Durkin	(503)788-7000 (503)788-8468	WS 9 SS 1030 BC 1030	ED/HC/MD	281	246	164
	CHRIST THE VINE		See Damascus OR									
	EBENEZER	2003	6700 NE 29TH AVE	97211	NOW	Gemedo E Adema	(971)344-9437					
	HOLY CROSS office@hclcpdx.org hclcpdx.org	1947	8705 E BURNSIDE ST	97216	NOW	John C Eggert	(503)254-8705	WS 1030 BC 9	ED/HC/ MD/SN	88	75	37
	IMMANUEL ilcpdxoffice@gmail.com www.immanuelpdx.com	1908	7810 SE 15TH AVE	97202	NOW	Philemon O Ngare	(503)236-7823	WS 9	ED/HC	51	46	28
	IMMANUEL		See Hood River OR									
	LIVING SAVIOR		See Tualatin OR									
	PRINCE OF PEACE office@princeofpeacelc.org www.princeofpeacelc.org	1960	14175 NW CORNELL RD	97229	NOW		(503)645-1211 (503)531-2534	WS 10 SS 845 BC 845	EC/EL/ED/ HC/MD	180	150	90
	RUSSELLVILLE PARK WORSHIP Satellite Site of Holy Cross Portland OR	2010	20 Se 103rsd Ave	97216				WS 1				
	SAINT MICHAEL'S secretary@stmikeslutheran.org www.stmikeslutheran.org	1948	6700 NE 29TH AVE	97211	NOW	Phillip L Brandt	(503)493-6333	WS 10 BC 9	ED/HC			
	THE MASTER		2646 NE 102nd 2650 NE 102ND AVE	97220	NOW	Van C Phan	(503)257-9323					
	TRINITY office@trinityportland.org www.trinityportland.org	1890	5520 NE KILLINGSWORTH ST	97218	NOW	Ruberto Ek Yah	(503)288-6403	WS 830 11 SS 945 BC 945	EL/ED/MD	324	240	110
	ZION zion@zion-portland.org www.zion-portland.org	1889	1015 SW 18TH AVE	97205	NOW		(503)221-1343 (503)228-6484	WS 11 BC 945	ED/HC/ MD/SN	111	92	52
RAINIER	*GRACE*		See Longview WA									
REDMOND	*BROOKDALE NURSING HOME SERVICE* Satellite Site of Emmaus Redmond OR	2025	1942 SW Canyon Dr.	97756				WS 130				
	EMMAUS elder@emmauslcms.org www.emmauslcms.org	1981	2175 SW SALMON AVE	97756	NOW	Karl R Hess	(541)508-1927	WS 9 SS 1045 BC 1045	ED/HC	65	62	60
	JUNIPER SPRINGS SERVICE Satellite Site of Emmaus Redmond OR	2025	590 NW 23rd St.	97756				WS 3				
REEDSPORT	*BEAUTIFUL SAVIOR* beautifulsaviorreedsport.org	1957	2160 ELM AVE	97467	NOW	James H Cavener	(541)271-2633	WS 10 BC 9	ED	30	28	25
RILEY	*FIRST LUTHERAN CHURCH* Satellite Site of First Burns OR	2006	68178 Silver Creek Rd	97758								
ROGUE RIVER	*FAITH* www.faithrogueriver.org	1985	8582 Rogue River Highway PO BOX 428	97537	NOW	Jonah Q Laws Michael L Mc Coy		WS 10 SS 845 BC 845	ED/HC/ MD/SN	100	75	36
ROSEBURG	*ST PAUL* churchoffice@stpaulroseburg.org www.stpaulroseburg.org	1936	750 W KEADY CT	97471	NOW	David Weir	(541)673-7212	WS 1030 SS 915 BC 915	EC/ED/HC/ MD	158	149	95
SAINT HELENS	*CALVARY* calvarylcms1@gmail.com	1947	58251 S DIVISION RD	97051	NOW	Mark Dennis	(503)397-1739	WS 1030 SS 1045 BC 915	ED			
SALEM	*MESSIAH* messiahlcms97305@outlook.com www.messiahlcms.org	1977	4965 INDIANA AVE NE	97305	NOW		(503)362-4960	WS 10 SS 9	ED/MD/SN			
	PEACE office@peacelutheransalem.org peacelutheransalem.org	1957	1525 GLEN CREEK RD NW	97304	NOW		(503)362-8500	WS 915 BC 1045	ED/HC/ MD/SN			
	REDEEMER office@redeemer-lcms.org www.redeemer-lcms.org	1962	4663 LANCASTER DR NE	97305	NOW	John C Rallison	(503)393-7121 (503)463-8267	WS 10 SS 9 BC 9	EC/ED/HC/ MD/SN	146	111	67
	ST JOHN office@stjohnsalem.org www.stjohnsalem.org	1899	1350 COURT ST NE	97301	NOW	James R Fryckman Harry M Stratton	(503)588-0171 (503)585-2801	WS 10 BC 9	EC/ED/HC/ MD	154	130	58
	ZION		See Corvallis OR									
SANDY	*IMMANUEL* office@immanuelsandy.com www.immanuelsandy.com	1907	39901 Pleasant St PO BOX 686 39901 PLEASANT ST	97055	NOW		(503)668-6232 (503)668-6232	WS 10	ED/MD	81	81	27
SCAPPOOSE	*GRACE* church@gracescappoose.org www.gracescappoose.org	1943	51737 COLUMBIA RIVER HWY	97056	NOW	Joshua C Wiley	(503)543-6555	WS 1015 SS 1015 BC 9	EC/ED/HC/ MD/SN	98	69	46
SCIO	*ZION*		See Corvallis OR									

*Indicates a new church start. A new church start is an intentionally organized gathering which comes together on a regular basis for the purpose of worship and/or Bible study and is intended to grow into a member LCMS congregation. WS =Worship Service; SS = Sunday School; BC =Bible Class; EC = Early Childhood; EL = Elementary School; HS = High School; ED =Education Ministry; HC =Human Care Ministry; SN = Special Needs Ministry; MD = Media Ministry (PC)=Partner Church Pastor. See Page 53 for the Table of Abbreviations for key to additional abbreviations

CITY	CONGREGATION EMAIL WEBSITE	YEAR EST	LOCATION MAILING ADDRESS	ZIP CODE(S)	DIST.	PASTOR(S)	PHONE FAX	WS SS BC	SCHOOLS/ MINISTRIES	STATISTIC Bapt	Conf	Avg Attend
SHERIDAN	*TRINITY* stefaniem@sheridantlc.org www.SheridanTLC.org	1901	311 SE Schley St PO BOX 128	97378	NOW	William T Hering	(503)843-4747	WS 1030 BC 910	ED/HC/MD	84	59	58
SHERWOOD	*ST PAUL* office@stpaulsherwood.org www.stpaulsherwood.org	1878	17500 Cedarview Way 17500 SW CEDARVIEW WAY	97140	NOW	Donald F Richard	(503)625-6648 (503)625-8976	WS 830 1045 SS 940 BC 940	EC/ED/HC/ MD/SN	187	170	128
SPRINGFIELD	*HOPE* garyrt2@gmail.com	1946	1369 B St 1355 B ST	97477	NOW		(541)746-1255	WS 1 BC 12	ED/HC/ MD/SN	45	40	35
STAYTON	*CALVARY* calvary@calvarystayton.com www.calvarystayton.com	1946	198 Fern Ridge Rd SE 198 FERN RIDGE RD	97383	NOW	Dr Joseph W Hughes III	(503)769-6144 (503)767-6144	WS 930 SS 10	ED/HC/ MD/SN			
SUMMERVILLE	*FAITH*		See La Grande OR									
SUTHERLIN	*ST JOHNS* sjlc1950@gmail.com	1946	1101 W 6th Ave PO BOX 620	97479	NOW	Brandt E Hoffman Sr	(541)459-3701	WS 10	ED/HC/MD			
THE DALLES	*FAITH* faithlutherantd@gmail.com faithlutherantd.com	1954	2810 W 10TH ST	97058	NOW	Luke M Shirley	(541)296-3586	WS 10 BC 9	ED/HC/ MD/SN			
TIGARD	*OUR REDEEMER* office@orlc.net www.orlc.net	1989	13401 SW BENISH ST	97223	NOW	Patrick M Rooney	(503)524-6646 (503)213-5937	WS 10 SS 9	EC/ED/HC/ MD/SN	200	182	78
TILLAMOOK	*REDEEMER* redeemertillamook@gmail.com www.redeemertillamook.com	1926	302 GROVE AVE	97141	NOW	Kevin W Oster	(503)842-4823 (503)842-4823	WS 1030 SS 930 BC 930	HC/SN			
TROUTDALE	*CHRIST THE VINE*		See Damascus OR									
TUALATIN	*LIVING SAVIOR* lslc@living-savior.org www.living-savior.org	1978	8740 SW SAGERT ST	97062	NOW	Kevin W Fenster	(503)692-3490 (503)691-6508	WS 10 BC 845	EC/ED/HC/ MD/SN	400	290	169
UNION	*FAITH*		See La Grande OR									
VENETA	*CHRIST* christlutheranveneta@gmail.com	1957	25157 LUTHER LN	97487	NOW	John W Luther	(541)935-1335 (541)935-1335	WS 10	ED			
WALDPORT	*OUR SAVIOR* oslc@peak.org www.oursaviorlutheranwaldport.org	1996	38 N Bayview Rd PO BOX 2458	97394	NOW	John A Westhafer	(541)563-7729	WS 10 SS 10 BC 11	ED/HC/MD	45	35	22
WALDPORT HWY 101	*OUR SAVIOR*		See Waldport OR									
WEST LINN	*CHRIST THE VINE*		See Damascus OR									
WEST SALEM	*PEACE*		See Salem OR									
WILLAMINA	*TRINITY*		See Sheridan OR									
WOODBURN	*HOPE* info@hopewoodburn.org hopewoodburn.org	1967	211 Parr Rd PO BOX 355	97071	NOW	Zabdi Lopez	(503)981-0400 (503)981-0400	WS 930	ED/HC/MD	107	86	79
			PENNSYLVANIA									
ALBION	*HOLY TRINITY* htlcalbn@gmail.com mikeyytaylor.wixsite.com/ holytrinity-albion	1911	80 3RD AVE	16401	EN	Michael S Taylor	(814)756-3426 (814)756-3426	WS 10 SS 9 BC 9	EC/ED/HC			
ALLENTOWN	*CONCORDIA*		See Northampton PA									
	CONCORDIA		See Macungie PA									
ALTOONA	*TRINITY*		See Cumberland MD									
AMBRIDGE	*ST JOHN'S* office@stjohnsambridge.org	1907	1320 CHURCH ST	15003	EA	Joel N Lissy	(724)266-5618	WS 2	ED/HC/MD	48	32	35
ARNOLD	*JOHN HUSS*	1916	1539 KENNETH AVE	15068	S	Jerome E Panzigrau	(724)334-2272	WS 930 SS 830 BC 830		96	75	16
BATH	*CONCORDIA*		See Northampton PA									
BEAVER FALLS	*MOUNT OLIVE* secretary@mtolivechurch.net www.mtolivechurch.net	1952	1154 SHENANGO RD	15010	EA	Joel N Lissy	(724)650-5682 (724)843-1921	WS 930 SS 1045	ED/HC/MD			
BEDFORD	*TRINITY*		See Cumberland MD									
BETHEL PARK	*PEACE*		See McMurray PA									
BETHLEHEM	*CHRIST*		See Freemansburg PA									
	CONCORDIA		See Northampton PA									
BLUE BELL	*GLORIA DEI* office@gloriadeibluebell.org www.gloriadeibluebell.org	1955	6024 BUTLER PIKE	19422	EN	David M Young	(215)646-0848	WS 930 SS 11 BC 11	ED/HC			
BRACKENRIDGE	*JOHN HUSS*		See Arnold PA									
BRADFORD	*GRACE* glmoffice@agraceplace.org www.agraceplace.org	1928	79 MECHANIC ST	16701	EA		(814)362-3244 (814)362-6085	WS 10 SS 9	ED/SN			
BRENTWOOD	*CONCORDIA* concordia-brentwood@outlook.com	1924	3109 BROWNSVILLE RD PITTSBURGH	15227	EA	Ronald L Cox	(412)881-3005	WS 1030 SS 9 BC 9	ED/HC/ MD/SN			
BRIDGEVILLE	*ZION* secretary@zlcb.org www.zlcb.org	1898	3197 WASHINGTON PIKE	15017	EA	Dr Edward O Grimenstein	(412)221-4776 (412)221-4780	WS 8 1030 SS 915 BC 915	EC/ED/HC/ MD	271	228	143
BUTLER	*ST. LUKE BUTLER* Satellite Site of St Luke Cabot PA	2019	241 Freeport Road	16002								

*Indicates a new church start. A new church start is an intentionally organized gathering which comes together on a regular basis for the purpose of worship and/or Bible study and is intended to grow into a member LCMS congregation. WS =Worship Service; SS = Sunday School; BC =Bible Class; EC = Early Childhood; EL = Elementary School; HS = High School; ED =Education Ministry; HC =Human Care Ministry; SN = Special Needs Ministry; MD = Media Ministry (PC)=Partner Church Pastor. See Page 53 for the Table of Abbreviations for key to additional abbreviations

CITY	CONGREGATION EMAIL WEBSITE	YEAR EST	LOCATION MAILING ADDRESS	ZIP CODE(S)	DIST.	PASTOR(S)	PHONE FAX	WS SS BC	SCHOOLS/ MINISTRIES	STATISTIC Bapt	Conf	Avg Attend
CABOT	*ST LUKE* stluke@stlukecabot.org www.stlukecabot.org	1835	330 HANNAHSTOWN RD	16023	EA	Brian C Bocian	(724)352-2777 (724)352-2355	WS 8 1030 SS 915 BC 915	EL/ED/HC/ MD	1341	1066	331
CAMP HILL	*CALVARY*		See Mechanicsburg PA									
CANONSBURG	*PEACE*		See McMurray PA									
CARLISLE	*CALVARY*		See Mechanicsburg PA									
CECIL	*ZION*		See Bridgeville PA									
CENTRAL CITY	*SS PETER AND PAUL*	1918	881 MAIN ST	15926	EA	Brett P Witmer	(814)539-0123	WS 11	HC/SN	45	39	12
CHAMBERSBURG	*CONCORDIA*		See Hagerstown MD									
COLUMBIA	*ST PAUL* llhines229@gmail.com stpcolumbia.wix.com/stpaulslutheran	1862	555 LOCUST ST	17512	SE	Geoffrey S Abendschoen	(717)764-4746	WS 9 SS 915 BC 1015	HC	35	26	20
CRANBERRY	*PRINCE PEACE*		See Freedom PA									
CREIGHTON	*JOHN HUSS*		See Arnold PA									
CROYDON	*ST LUKE* pastor@stlukescroydon.org www.stlukescroydon.org	1930	1305 STATE RD	19021	EA	James A Eckert	(215)788-8951 (215)788-3838	WS 1030 SS 9 BC 915		28	26	20
DICKSON CITY	*ST STEPHEN* www.ststephensdicksoncity.com	1894	701 W Lackawanna Ave 25 HILLCREST DR	18447	S		(570)489-2462	WS 930 BC 1045	ED/HC			
EASTON	*FAITH* faithlcms@outlook.com www.faithlcms.com	1950	2012 SULLIVAN TRL	18040	EA	Douglas S Kerns II	(610)253-1625	WS 945 SS 830	EC/ED/HC/ MD/SN	167	129	75
EPHRATA	*MOUNT CALVARY*		See Lititz PA									
ERIE	*TRINITY* churchoffice@tlcerie.com www.tlcerie.com	1881	14 E 38TH ST	16504	EN	Travis J Schmidt	(814)452-4888 (814)456-1703	WS 9 6 SS 5 BC 10	ED/MD			
FAIRHOPE	*TRINITY* trinityofglensavage@gmail.com www.trinityofglensavage.org	1868	630 CHURCH RD	15538	EA	Kyle S Mullins	(814)267-4474	WS 1030 SS 930 BC 930	ED/HC/ MD/SN			
FAYETTEVILLE	*CONCORDIA*		See Hagerstown MD									
FOREST HILLS	*CHRIST* pastor@christlutheranfh.org www.christlutheranfh.org	1933	400 BARCLAY AVE PITTSBURGH	15221	EA	Ronald M Breight	(412)271-7173 (412)271-4921	WS 10 SS 845 BC 845	ED/HC/MD	147	131	56
FORKS TOWNSHIP	*FAITH*		See Easton PA									
FREEDOM	*PRINCE PEACE* popluthsecy@comcast.net www.princeofpeacefreedom.com	1849	60 ROCHESTER RD	15042	EA	Sean G Walters	(724)728-3881 (724)728-6708	WS 1015 SS 9 BC 9	EC/ED/HC	84	72	70
FREEMANSBURG	*CHRIST* christ302main@rcn.com		302 MAIN ST	18017	EA		(610)866-5578	WS 1030 SS 915 BC 915	ED/HC/MD			
GLENSHAW	*BETHEL* info@bethelglenshaw.org www.bethelglenshaw.org	1938	301 SCOTT AVE	15116	EA	Donn E Woolweber	(412)486-5777 (412)487-8328	WS 1015 SS 9 BC 9	HC/MD	190	101	35
GROVE CITY	*ALL SAINTS*		See Slippery Rock PA									
HARRISBURG	*CALVARY*		See Mechanicsburg PA									
HAZLETON	*ST JOHN* stjohnshazleton@gmail.com www.stjohnshazleton.org	1921	621 N VINE ST	18201	S	Gordon S Naumann	(570)459-6423 (570)455-5280	WS 9 SS 1015 BC 1015		117	85	27
HERNDON	*FAITH*	1980	2354 STATE ROUTE 225	17830	EA		(570)758-4970	WS 1030 SS 915	ED/HC/SN	65	61	12
HERSHEY	*CALVARY*		See Mechanicsburg PA									
HOP BOTTOM	*GRACE* hbgrace@epix.net www.grace-lutheran-church.net	1942	351 GREENWOOD ST	18824	EA		(570)289-4468 (570)289-4468	WS 10 SS 9 BC 845	EC/ED/HC/ MD/SN			
JOHNSTOWN	*HOLY CROSS* holycrossjohnstown@gmail.com holycrossjohnstown.org	1914	711 CHESTNUT ST	15906	S	Brett P Witmer	(814)539-0123	WS 10	HC/MD	52	52	15
LANCASTER	*MOUNT CALVARY*		See Lititz PA									
LANDENBERG	*OUR REDEEMER*		See Newark DE									
LEVITTOWN	*HOPE* info@hopelcs.org www.hopelcs.org	1952	2600 HAINES RD	19055	EA	Philip W Twietmeyer	(215)946-3467 (215)946-5926	WS 930 SS 1045 BC 1045	EL/ED/HC/ MD/SN			
LITITZ	*MOUNT CALVARY* office@lancasterlutheran.com www.lancasterlutheran.com	1904	308 PETERSBURG RD	17543	EN	Christopher M Seifferlein	(717)560-6751	WS 9 SS 1030 BC 1030	ED/HC/ MD/SN	272	239	164
LOWER BURRELL	*JOHN HUSS*		See Arnold PA									
MACUNGIE	*CONCORDIA* concordia.macungie@gmail.com www.concordia-macungie.com	1987	2623 BROOKSIDE RD	18062	S	Waldemar R Vinovskis	(610)965-3265	WS 8 1045 SS 930 BC 930	EC/ED/HC/ MD	257	183	100
	LEHIGH COMMONS SENIOR LIVING Satellite Site of Concordia Macungie PA	2006	1680 Spring Creek Rd	18062								
MALVERN	*CHRIST MEMORIAL* office@christmemorial.us www.christmemorial.us	1957	89 LINE RD	19355	EA	Frederick M Hoover Jr Carl D Emberger Sr Jon F Hofmeister	(610)644-4508 (610)644-4677	WS 830 11 SS 945 BC 945	EC/ED/HC/ MD	404	307	107
MCDONALD	*ZION*		See Bridgeville PA									
MCMURRAY	*PEACE* secretary@peacelutheranpgh.org www.peacelutheranpgh.org		107 CAROL DR	15317	EN	Justin R Schmidt	(724)941-9441 (724)941-9442	WS 1030 SS 9 BC 9	ED/HC/ MD/SN	183	150	80

*Indicates a new church start. A new church start is an intentionally organized gathering which comes together on a regular basis for the purpose of worship and/or Bible study and is intended to grow into a member LCMS congregation. WS =Worship Service; SS = Sunday School; BC =Bible Class; EC = Early Childhood; EL = Elementary School; HS = High School; ED =Education Ministry; HC =Human Care Ministry; SN = Special Needs Ministry; MD = Media Ministry (PC)=Partner Church Pastor. See Page 53 for the Table of Abbreviations for key to additional abbreviations

CITY	CONGREGATION EMAIL WEBSITE	YEAR EST	LOCATION MAILING ADDRESS	ZIP CODE(S)	DIST.	PASTOR(S)	PHONE FAX	WS SS BC	SCHOOLS/ MINISTRIES	STATISTIC Bapt	Conf	Avg Attend
MECHANICSBURG	*CALVARY* office@calvarymechanicsburg.org www.calvarymechanicsburg.org	1899	208 WOODS DR	17050	EN	Luke T Zimmerman	(717)697-9771	WS 1030 SS 9 BC 9	ED/HC/ MD/SN	277	216	99
MILLVALE	*SAINT JOHNS* stjohnsmill.office@gmail.com STJPittsburgh.org	1877	501 NORTH AVE PITTSBURGH	15209	EA	Daniel A Hahn Jr	(412)821-6266	WS 9 SS 1015 BC 1015	ED/HC/ MD/SN	234	210	65
MONROEVILLE	*HOLY CROSS*		See Johnstown PA									
MOUNT JOY	*MOUNT CALVARY*		See Lititz PA									
MOUNT LEBANON	*PEACE*		See McMurray PA									
MOUNT POCONO	*OUR SAVIOR* mtpoursavior@verizon.net	1963	675 BELMONT AVE	18344	EA	Peter A Richert	(570)839-9868 (570)839-9868	WS 10	ED/HC/MD	155	124	53
MUNSON	*ST JOHN* kzitsch@hotmail.com stjohnsforest.org	1893	3495 WINBURNE MUNSON RD MORRISDALE	16858	EA	Kenneth E Zitsch Jr	(814)345-5741 (814)345-5741	WS 1030 BC 915	ED/HC/ MD/SN			
MURRYSVILLE	*CALVARY* calvarylut@clcs.comcastbiz.net calvarylcms.org	1956	4725 OLD WILLIAM PENN HWY	15668	EA	Joshua P Obermann	(724)327-2898 (724)327-2878	WS 830 11 SS 945 BC 945	EC/ED/HC/ MD/SN	241	231	99
NATORNA HEIGHTS	*JOHN HUSS*		See Arnold PA									
NAZARETH	*CONCORDIA*		See Northampton PA									
NEW CASTLE	*CHRIST* clcmos@aol.com christlutheran-newcastle.org/	1925	1302 E WASHINGTON ST	16101	EA	James A Driskell	(724)658-8009	WS 1030 SS 9	ED/HC/ MD/SN			
NEW FREEDOM	*REDEEMER*		See Parkton MD									
NEW HOPE	*ST PETER*		See Hopewell Township NJ									
NEW KENSINGTON	*JOHN HUSS*		See Arnold PA									
	ST PAUL stpaulnk@comcast.net	1909	1001 KNOLLWOOD RD NEW KENSINGTN	15068	EA	Roger D Nuerge	(724)339-2829 (724)339-8905	WS 1045 SS 1015 BC 1015	ED/HC/ MD/SN			
NORTH EAST	*ST PAUL* splcnepa@gmail.com	1864	30 CLINTON ST	16428	EA	William N Ringer	(814)725-4395	WS 1030 SS 930 BC 930	ED/HC/SN	114	90	50
NORTHAMPTON	*CONCORDIA* office@concordialv.org www.concordialv.org	1911	3285 Pheasant Drive 3285 PHEASANT DR	18067	S	Raymond A Malec	(610)262-8500 (610)882-0561	WS 930	ED/HC/SN	119	104	48
OAKMONT	*REDEEMER* info@redeemer.oakmont.org www.redeemer-oakmont.org	1900	1261 PENNSYLVANIA AVE	15139	EN	Dr Adam C Koontz	(412)828-9323	WS 1045 SS 930 BC 930	EL/HS/ED/ HC/MD/SN	175	156	75
OIL CITY	*CHRIST* christluth@comcast.net christlutheranoilcitylcms.org	1898	1029 GRANDVIEW RD	16301	EA	David A Oester	(814)677-4484	WS 1030 SS 915 BC 915	HC/MD	76	64	40
PENN HILLS	*GRACE* revgreenway@verizon.net www.gracelutheranpgh.org	1931	2931 UNIVERSAL RD	15235	EA	Berton L Greenway	(412)793-1394 (412)793-0529	WS 1015 SS 9	HC	183	148	52
PETERS TOWNSHIP	*PEACE*		See McMurray PA									
PHILADELPHIA	*CHRIST ASSEMBLY*	1997	229 N 63RD ST	19139	EA	William Y Boymah	(610)241-6532					
	CONCORDIA		See Wilmington DE									
	HOLY CROSS	1954	500 E MOUNT PLEASANT AVE	19119	EA	Timothy S Green	(215)242-0530 (215)248-0584	WS 9 SS 1030	HC			
	LOGOS LUTHERAN CHURCH Satellite Site of St John Springfield PA	2015	628 N Broad St	19130				WS 3				
	SAINT PHILIPS	1917	Holy Cross Lutheran Church 500 E Mt Pleasant Ave	19119	EA			WS 9				
PITTSBURGH	*ASCENSION* secretary@ascensionpgh.com www.ascensionpgh.com	1952	8225 PEEBLES RD	15237	EA	Adam R Thompson	(412)364-4463 (412)369-0599	WS 930 SS 11 BC 11	ED/HC/ MD/SN	160	122	72
	CONCORDIA		See Brentwood PA									
	FAITH	1936	7060 Lemington Ave PO BOX 523 MONROEVILLE	15206 15146	EA	Stephen M Niermann	(412)363-8520 (412)363-8760	WS 10	ED/HC/MD			
	FIRST TRINITY info@firsttrinity.net www.firsttrinity.net	1837	531 N Neville St 535 N NEVILLE ST	15213	EN	Eric R Andrae Benjamin N Janssen	(412)683-4121	WS 11 SS 945 BC 945	ED/HC/SN	185	150	63
	GOOD SHEPHERD S HILL office@goodshepherdpittsburgh.org goodshepherdpittsburgh.org/	1960	418 MAXWELL DR	15236	EA		(412)884-3232 (412)884-3233	WS 1015 SS 915 BC 915	EC/ED/HC/ MD	181	181	65
	HOLY CROSS EVANGELICAL-LUTHERAN CHAPEL Satellite Site of First Trinity Pittsburgh PA	2019	5319 Second Ave	15207								
	MOUNT CALVARY		See West View PA									
	TRINITY DEAF	1922	409 SWISSVALE AVE	15221	EA	Ronald M Breight	(412)727-7632	WS 1030 SS 915 BC 915				
	ZION pastor.zelc@verizon.net www.zionevangelicallutheran.org	1868	237 37TH ST	15201	EA	Donn E Woolweber	(412)621-2720 (412)621-2720	WS 1130	HC			
	ZION		See Bridgeville PA									
PITTSTON	*ST JOHN* stjohnslutheranchurch@aol.com	1857	9 WOOD ST	18640	EA	John M Zimmerman	(570)655-2505	WS 8	ED/MD			

*Indicates a new church start. A new church start is an intentionally organized gathering which comes together on a regular basis for the purpose of worship and/or Bible study and is intended to grow into a member LCMS congregation. WS =Worship Service; SS = Sunday School; BC =Bible Class; EC = Early Childhood; EL = Elementary School; HS = High School; ED =Education Ministry; HC =Human Care Ministry; SN = Special Needs Ministry; MD = Media Ministry (PC)=Partner Church Pastor. See Page 53 for the Table of Abbreviations for key to additional abbreviations

CITY	CONGREGATION EMAIL WEBSITE	YEAR EST	LOCATION MAILING ADDRESS	ZIP CODE(S)	DIST.	PASTOR(S)	PHONE FAX	WS SS BC	SCHOOLS/ MINISTRIES	STATISTIC Bapt	Conf	Avg Attend
PUNXSUTAWNEY	*MARTIN LUTHER* mlcpunxsy@hotmail.com mlcpunxsy.webstarts.com	1853	230 N PENN ST	15767	EA		(814)938-9792	WS 3 SS 2 BC 2	ED/MD/SN	33	25	16
RIDLEY PARK	*REHOBOTH AFAAN OROMO* rehoboth.oromochurchphl@gmail. com		628 E CHESTER PIKE	19078	EN		(571)489-3594	WS 2				
ROCHESTER	*PRINCE PEACE*		See Freedom PA									
SCRANTON	*IMMANUEL* ILCScranton@gmail.com www.immanuelscranton.org	1895	238 REESE ST	18508	EA	John M Zimmerman	(570)342-3374	WS 1015 SS 1130 BC 1130	EC/ED/HC/ MD/SN	180	160	47
	PEACE pastor@yourpeace.org www.yourpeace.org	1917	2506 N Main Ave 60 E PARKER ST	18508 18509	EA		(570)703-0607	WS 815 1030 SS 915	EL/ED/HC/ MD			
SHARON	*SS PETER AND PAUL* church@saintspeterandpaul.net www.saintspeterandpaul.net	1917	699 STAMBAUGH AVE	16146	S	Jacob T Deal	(724)347-3620	WS 9	ED/HC/ MD/SN	99	93	39
SHREWSBURY	*REDEEMER*		See Parkton MD									
SLIPPERY ROCK	*ALL SAINTS* Church@Rocklutheran.org RockLutheran.Org	1977	351 S MAIN ST	16057	EN		(724)794-4334	WS 1130 BC 1015 7	ED	103	88	45
SOUTH FAYETTE	*PEACE*		See McMurray PA									
	ZION		See Bridgeville PA									
SPRINGFIELD	*ST JOHN* info@stjohnspringfieldpa.org www.stjohnspringfieldpa.org	1848	25 E Scenic Rd 25 SCENIC RD	19064	EN	Robert J Kieselowsky Jr	(610)543-3100	WS 1045 SS 930 BC 930		75	66	60
STATE COLLEGE	*GOOD SHEPHERD* goodshepherdsc@comcast.net www.goodshepherdsc.org	1985	851 N Science Park Rd 851 SCIENCE PARK RD	16803	EA	Bryan J Spang	(814)234-8177	WS 8 1030 SS 1030 BC 915	EC/ED/HC/ MD/SN	134	113	84
STEWARTSTOWN	*REDEEMER*		See Parkton MD									
TARENTUM	*JOHN HUSS*		See Arnold PA									
TUNKHANNOCK	*ST PAUL'S* pastorjosh@stpaulslutheranpa.org st-pauls-lutheran-pa.org	1971	5672 US 6	18657	EA	Joshua A Makey	(570)836-2301	WS 9 SS 915	ED/HC/MD	91	79	25
UNIVERSAL	*GRACE*		See Penn Hills PA									
UPPER SAINT CLAIR	*PEACE*		See McMurray PA									
VERONA	*REDEEMER*		See Oakmont PA									
	REDEEMER LUTHERAN SCHOOL Satellite Site of Redeemer OAKMONT PA	2011	700 Idaho Ave	15147								
WARMINSTER	*GRACE*	1960	1169 W Street Rd PO BOX 196	18974	EN	David M Young	(215)442-5500	WS 1130	ED/HC/MD	44	41	30
WASHINGTON	*PEACE*		See McMurray PA									
WAYNESBORO	*CONCORDIA*		See Hagerstown MD									
WELLSBORO	*TRINITY* trinitylutheran16901@yahoo.com www.trinitylutheranwellsboro.org	1942	53 WEST AVE	16901	EA	Joseph P Weatherell	(570)724-2316 (570)723-1053	WS 10 BC 9	EL/ED	98	86	30
WEST VIEW	*MOUNT CALVARY* revkuntz@wmconnect.com www.mtcalvarywv.com	1929	285 HIGHLAND AVE	15229	EA	Scott A Kuntz	(412)931-4500 (412)931-3414	WS 1015 BC 9	ED/HC			
WILKES-BARRE	*ST MATTHEW* www.stmatthewwb.org	1896	667 N Main St 663 N MAIN ST	18705	S	Peter J Haenftling	(570)822-8233	WS 930 SS 1040 BC 1110	ED/HC			
	ST PETER splcsec@gmail.com www.splcwb.org	1901	1000 S MAIN ST HANOVER TWP	18706	EA		(570)823-7332	WS 9 SS 1030 BC 1030	ED/HC/MD			
WILLIAMSPORT	*TRINITY*		See Wellsboro PA									
YORK	*FIRST ST JOHNS* firststjohns@verizon.net www.firststjohns.com	1874	140 W KING ST	17401	SE	Geoffrey S Abendschoen	(717)843-8597 (717)843-8597	WS 11 BC 9	ED/HC/MD	78	63	20
	GOOD SHEPHERD gs_york@verizon.net gsyork.wix.com/goodshepherdlutheran	1922	2121 ROOSEVELT AVE	17408	SE	Brian K Smith	(717)764-4746	WS 9 11 SS 10	ED/HC/ MD/SN	334	198	99
	REDEEMER		See Parkton MD									
	ST JOHN stjohn-yorkpa@comcast.net www.stjohnyorkpa.com	1874	2580 MOUNT ROSE AVE	17402	SE	Tab E Cosgrove	(717)840-0382 (717)840-1845	WS 830 11 SS 10	ED/HC/ MD/SN	310	274	148

RHODE ISLAND

CITY	CONGREGATION EMAIL WEBSITE	YEAR EST	LOCATION MAILING ADDRESS	ZIP CODE(S)	DIST.	PASTOR(S)	PHONE FAX	WS SS BC	SCHOOLS/ MINISTRIES	Bapt	Conf	Avg Attend
ASHAWAY	*TRINITY* trinitylutheranashaway@gmail.com www.trinityashaway.org	1922	110 HIGH ST	02804	NE	Christopher L Chandler	(401)377-4340	WS 9 SS 1015	EC/ED/ HC/SN	112	93	35
GREENVILLE	*OUR REDEEMER*		See Smithfield RI									
PROVIDENCE	*ST PAUL* stpaulschurch445@gmail.com stpaulsprov.org	1866	445 ELMWOOD AVE	02907	NE		(401)941-5100	WS 10 SS 10 BC 1130	ED/HC	250	225	125
SMITHFIELD	*OUR REDEEMER* office@orelc.org www.orelc.org	1989	54 CEDAR SWAMP RD	02917	NE	Aaron A Stinnett	(401)232-7575 (401)232-7575	WS 915 SS 1045 BC 1045	ED/HC/SN	227	196	100
WESTERLY	*TRINITY*		See Ashaway RI									

*Indicates a new church start. A new church start is an intentionally organized gathering which comes together on a regular basis for the purpose of worship and/or Bible study and is intended to grow into a member LCMS congregation. WS =Worship Service; SS = Sunday School; BC =Bible Class; EC = Early Childhood; EL = Elementary School; HS = High School; ED =Education Ministry; HC =Human Care Ministry; SN = Special Needs Ministry; MD = Media Ministry (PC)=Partner Church Pastor. See Page 53 for the Table of Abbreviations for key to additional abbreviations

SOUTH CAROLINA

CITY	CONGREGATION EMAIL WEBSITE	YEAR EST	LOCATION MAILING ADDRESS	ZIP CODE(S)	DIST.	PASTOR(S)	PHONE FAX	WS SS BC	SCHOOLS/ MINISTRIES	STATISTIC Bapt	Conf	Avg Attend
AIKEN	*BETHLEHEM* blcalkensc@gmail.com bethlehemlutheranaiken.org	1952	902 Hitchcock Dr 902 HITCHCOCK DR SW	29803	SE	John B Engwall	(803)649-6417	WS 1030 SS 9 BC 9	ED/HC/ MD/SN	96	93	39
ANDERSON	*ABIDING SAVIOR* pastor@abidingsavior.net www.abidingsavior.net	1981	1905 E GREENVILLE ST	29621	SE		(864)225-6438	WS 1030 SS 915 BC 915	HC	193	159	63
BEAUFORT	*FAITH* faithlutheranbeaufort@gmail.com www.faithlutheranbeaufort.org	2008	37 MARSHELLEN DR	29935	SE		(843)379-9772	WS 1030 BC 915	MD	33	30	30
CHARLESTON	*CALVARY* calvary.lutheran@calvarylutheranchas.com www.calvarycharleston.org	1943	Hwy 7 1400 MANOR BLVD	29407	SE	Marin Cerchez	(843)766-3113 (843)766-7919	WS 10 SS 845	ED/HC/SN	200	194	106
COLUMBIA	*HOLY TRINITY* holytrinitylcms.contactus@gmail.com www.holytrinitylutheranchurchlcms.org	1907	2200 Lee St PO BOX 5692	29205 29250	SE	Christopher A Burger Scott E Simpson	(803)799-7224	WS 1030 SS 9 BC 930	ED/HC/SN	55	43	43
	MOUNT OLIVE lcms@mtolivesc.org www.mtolivesc.org	1930	1541 LAKE MURRAY BLVD	29212	SE	Walter J Harper Colin E Ford	(803)781-5845	WS 8 1030 SS 915 BC 915	EC/ED/HC/ MD/SN	391	323	196
CONWAY	*HOLY LAMB*		See Myrtle Beach SC									
FLORENCE	*INCARNATE WORD* pastor.jeffords@yahoo.com www.facebook.com/IncarnateWordSC	1968	1900 2ND LOOP RD	29501	SE	Matthew K Jeffords	(843)662-9639	WS 1030 SS 9 BC 9		53	32	37
FORT MILL	*ALL SAINTS*		See Charlotte NC									
GILBERT	*BETHLEHEM*		See Aiken SC									
GRANITEVILLE	*BETHLEHEM*		See Aiken SC									
GREENVILLE	*GOOD SHEPHERD* Parish.secretary@lcgs.org www.lcgs.org	1953	1601 N PLEASANTBURG DR	29609	SE	Dr Jeffrey A Dukeman	(864)244-5825	WS 8 1030 SS 915 BC 915	ED/HC/MD	121	115	137
GREENWOOD	*GREENWOOD* greenwoodlutheran@wctel.net	1996	343 West Cambridge Ave. PO BOX 49369	29646 29649	SE		(864)223-9500	WS 1030 BC 930	ED/HC/ MD/SN	16	16	10
HILTON HEAD ISLAND	*ISLAND* office@islandlutheran.org www.islandlutheran.org	1985	4400 MAIN ST HILTON HEAD	29926	SE	Jeffrey D Dorth Kevin D Duff Andrew J Wrasman	(843)689-5200 (843)684-5201	WS 830 11 SS 940 BC 940	ED/HC/ MD/SN	425	385	202
INDIAN LAND	*ALL SAINTS*		See Charlotte NC									
LANCASTER	*ALL SAINTS*		See Charlotte NC									
MONETTA	*BETHLEHEM*		See Aiken SC									
MOUNT PLEASANT	*GOOD SHEPHERD* pastor@goodshepherdcharleston.org www.goodshepherdcharleston.org		937 Bowman Rd PO BOX 62135 N. CHARLESTON	29464 29419	SE	Allen C Bergstrazer	(843)814-7221	WS 10	ED/HC/ MD/SN	36	33	22
MURRELLS INLET	*HOLY LAMB*		See Myrtle Beach SC									
MYRTLE BEACH	*HOLY LAMB* holylamblcms@aol.com www.holylambmyrtlebeach.org	1985	2541 FORESTBROOK RD	29588	SE	Scott W Kirchoff	(843)236-1344	WS 8 1030 BC 915	ED/HC/ MD/SN	114	103	60
	RISEN CHRIST risenchristlutheran@gmail.com www.risenchristmb.org	1976	10595 N Kings Highway 10595 N KINGS HWY	29572	SE	Joshua A Keinath Timothy J Phanco	(843)272-5845 (843)272-4039	WS 830 1030 BC 930 12	EL/HS/ED/ HC/MD	295	251	240
NEW ELLENTON	*BETHLEHEM*		See Aiken SC									
NORTH AUGUSTA	*BETHLEHEM*		See Aiken SC									
	OUR REDEEMER		See Augusta GA									
NORTH MYRTLE BEACH	*RISEN CHRIST*		See Myrtle Beach SC									
OKATIE	*OKATIE PINES RETIREMENT COMMUNITY* Satellite Site of Faith Beaufort SC	2024	142 Okatie Center Blvd N	29909								
PORT ROYAL	*HELENA PLACE ASSISTED LIVING* Satellite Site of Faith Beaufort SC	2011	1624 Paris Ave	29935								
RIDGE SPRING	*BETHLEHEM*		See Aiken SC									
ROCK HILL	*ALL SAINTS*		See Charlotte NC									
	EMMANUEL emmanuelrh@comporium.net www.emmanuelrockhill.com	2005	636 Hollis Lakes Rd PO BOX 37892	29732	SE	Jeffrey L Coble	(803)324-2283	WS 1030 SS 915	ED	39	33	31
SENECA	*ETERNAL SHEPHERD* office@eternalshepherd.org www.eternalshepherd.org	1984	220 CARSON RD	29678	SE	David M Hammer	(864)882-3209 (864)882-5512	WS 830 11 SS 945	EC/ED/HC/ MD	344	311	180
SIMPSONVILLE	*IMMANUEL* office@immanuellutheranchurch.com www.immanuellutheranchurch.com	1988	2820 WOODRUFF RD	29681	SE	Jeffrey M VanOsdol	(864)297-5815 (864)297-1771	WS 8 1030 SS 930 BC 915	EC/ED/HC/ MD	371	300	216
SPARTANBURG	*IMMANUEL LUTHERAN HOUR* Satellite Site of Immanuel Albuquerque NM	1989	292 S Pine St	29302				WS 9				
SUMMERVILLE	*GRACE* office@gracesummerville.org www.gracesummerville.org	1978	1600 OLD TROLLEY RD	29485	SE	Wendell R Willsea III	(843)871-5444 (843)871-5763	WS 8 930 11 SS 930 BC 930	ED/HC/ MD/SN	247	194	137
WAGENER	*BETHLEHEM*		See Aiken SC									

*Indicates a new church start. A new church start is an intentionally organized gathering which comes together on a regular basis for the purpose of worship and/or Bible study and is intended to grow into a member LCMS congregation. WS =Worship Service; SS = Sunday School; BC =Bible Class; EC = Early Childhood; EL = Elementary School; HS = High School; ED =Education Ministry; HC =Human Care Ministry; SN = Special Needs Ministry; MD = Media Ministry (PC)=Partner Church Pastor. See Page 53 for the Table of Abbreviations for key to additional abbreviations

SOUTH DAKOTA

CITY	CONGREGATION EMAIL WEBSITE	YEAR EST	LOCATION MAILING ADDRESS	ZIP CODE(S)	DIST.	PASTOR(S)	PHONE FAX	WS SS BC	SCHOOLS/ MINISTRIES	STATISTIC Bapt	Conf	Avg Attend
ABERDEEN	*OUR SAVIOR* oursaviorlutheran@nvc.net www.oursaviorlutheranchurch aberdeen.com	1947	624 N JAY ST	57401	SD	Chad C Schopp Dr Alan G Ludwig	(605)225-7106	WS 1045 SS 930	ED/HC/MD	339	276	100
	PARKSIDE ASSISTED LIVING CENTER Satellite Site of Trinity MANSFIELD SD	2005	1324 12th Ave SE	57401								
	PRIMROSE PLACE (ASSISTED LIVING) Satellite Site of Trinity MANSFIELD SD	2017	1801 3rd Ave S.E	57460								
	ST JOHNS palssew@nrctv.com www.tri-parishlutheran.com	1888	37900 140TH ST	57401	SD	Bret R Bierman	(605)228-4032	WS 11 SS 945	ED/HC/ MD/SN	111	82	27
	ST PAUL www.stpaulsaberdeen.org	1888	214 7TH AVE SW	57401	SD	Ryan A Drevlow Ray N Anderson Jacob E Smith	(605)225-1847 (605)225-1848	WS 8 1045 SS 930 BC 930	EC/ED/ MD/SN	457	295	231
ALCESTER	*PEACE* peacealcester@gmail.com	1878	106 CHURCH ST	57001	SD	Donald E Erickson	(605)934-2365	WS 9 SS 1015 BC 1015	ED/HC/ MD/SN	106	89	42
ALEXANDRIA	*ST MARTIN*	1888	500 5th St PO BOX 126	57311	SD	Thomas D Christopher	(605)239-4421			109	88	40
ANDOVER	*ZION*	1902	301 Pew St PO BOX 16	57422	SD	Jeremy T Yeadon			ED			
ARMOUR	*REDEEMER* redeemarmour@unitelsd.com	1941	403 3rd St PO BOX 158	57313	SD	Jens B Jenson	(605)724-2489 (605)724-2489	WS 930 SS 1030 BC 1030	ED/HC/MD	270	193	82
AVON	*ZION* zion@gwtc.net	1893	314 Pine St PO BOX 243	57315	SD	Kenneth P Johnson	(605)286-3256	WS 10 SS 1115 BC 1130	ED/MD/SN	298	213	111
BLACK HAWK	*DIVINE SHEPHERD* dslcsecretary@divineshep.org www.divineshep.org	1987	7308 WEDGEWOOD DR	57718	SD	Dennis D Mercer	(605)787-6438	WS 8 1030 SS 915 BC 915	EC/ED/HC/ MD/SN	619	455	150
BLUNT	*TRINITY*	1965	108 W Fair St PO BOX 98	57522	SD	David F Strable	(605)962-6489		ED			
BRANDON	*BLESSED REDEEMER* brlc@alliancecom.net www.blessedredeemer.com	1990	705 S Sioux Blvd PO BOX 289	57005	SD		(605)582-2396 (605)582-6870	WS 9 SS 1015 BC 1015	EC/ED	348	267	130
BRITTON	*ST JOHN* pastor@stjohnbritton.com stjohnbritton.com	1892	401 N Main PO BOX J	57430	SD	Robert E Moeller Jr	(605)448-5235	SS 10	ED/HC/SN	157	138	29
BROOKINGS	*MOUNT CALVARY* mountcalvary@swiftel.net www.mountcalvary1.org	1928	629 9TH AVE	57006	SD	Matthew E Wurm	(605)692-2678	WS 8 1030 SS 920 BC 920	ED/MD	535	429	187
	PEACE peacelut@brookings.net www.peacebrookings.org	1996	1104 22ND AVE S	57006	SD	Timothy J Rynearson Samuel R Thole	(605)692-5272	WS 1030 SS 9	EL/ED/ MD/SN	444	314	180
BUFFALO GAP	*BETHESDA*		See Hot Springs SD									
CANISTOTA	*ZION* saint_johns_lutheran_church@ hotmail.com www.zionandstjohn.com	1885	350 W ELM ST	57012	SD	Timothy M Schleusener	(605)296-3166	WS 845	EC/ED/MD	301	233	44
CENTERVILLE	*FIRST ENGLISH* www.FirstEnglishCenterville.org	1934	351 Broadway St PO BOX 129	57014	SD	Kurt G Laskowsky	(605)563-2904	WS 1030	ED/MD/SN	80	63	25
CHAMBERLAIN	*ZION* zionlutheran@midstatesd.net www.zionchamberlain.com	1917	314 S MAIN ST	57325	SD		(605)234-9466	WS 9 SS 10 BC 1015	ED/MD			
CLAIRE CITY	*ZION*	1894	45697 101ST ST NEW EFFINGTON	57224 57255	MNN	Jonathan J Varns	(320)695-2354	WS 11 SS 10				
COLUMBIA	*ST JOHN*	1887	23 N JAMES ST	57433	SD	Chad C Schopp Dr Alan G Ludwig	(605)225-7106	WS 815	ED/MD	123	101	30
CORONA	*TRINITY*	1890	209 3rd St PO BOX 93	57227	SD	Arthur J Drehman		WS 9	ED/HC/MD	167	129	33
CREIGHTON	*EMMANUEL* walllutheran@gwtc.net	1910	21605 Creighton Rd PO BOX 327 WALL	57790	SD	Christopher R McCarthy	(605)457-3171	WS 11 SS 10 BC 1230	ED	73	55	26
CRESBARD	*CONCORDIA* www.concordiacresbard.org	1948	307 Swift Ave PO BOX 106	57435	SD		(605)324-3318	WS 9 BC 8				
	IMMANUEL		See Wecota SD									
CUSTER	*BETHESDA*		See Hot Springs SD									
	OUR REDEEMER orlc@gwtc.net	1932	744 Harney St PO BOX 907	57730	SD	David M Warner	(605)673-4361	WS 10 BC 1115	ED/HC/ MD/SN	243	196	64
	OUR SAVIOR		See Hill City SD									
DAKOTA DUNES	*HOLY CROSS* holycrossdakotadunes@gmail.com www.holycrossdakotadunes.org	1994	149 Bison Tr 149 BISON TRL	57049	SD	Jeremy D Richert Dr Michael L Kumm	(605)232-9117 (605)235-1688	WS 915 SS 1030 BC 1030	EC/ED/HC	272	225	107
DEADWOOD	*GRACE* glc.belc.secretary@gmail.com	1936	827 MAIN ST	57732	SD	Robert M Hinckley Jr	(605)578-2219	WS 830	ED/HC	80	66	38

*Indicates a new church start. A new church start is an intentionally organized gathering which comes together on a regular basis for the purpose of worship and/or Bible study and is intended to grow into a member LCMS congregation. WS =Worship Service; SS = Sunday School; BC =Bible Class; EC = Early Childhood; EL = Elementary School; HS = High School; ED =Education Ministry; HC =Human Care Ministry; SN = Special Needs Ministry; MD = Media Ministry (PC)=Partner Church Pastor. See Page 53 for the Table of Abbreviations for key to additional abbreviations

CONGREGATIONS

CITY	CONGREGATION EMAIL WEBSITE	YEAR EST	LOCATION MAILING ADDRESS	ZIP CODE(S)	DIST.	PASTOR(S)	PHONE FAX	WS SS BC	SCHOOLS/ MINISTRIES	STATISTIC Bapt	Conf	Avg Attend
DELMONT	*ZION* zionlutherandelmont@midstatesd.net	1896	101 SOUTH SEAMAN STREET PO BOX 204	57330	SD	Brian S Lemcke	(605)779-5181	WS 9 SS 1015	ED/MD/SN	117	95	70
DIMOCK	*IMMANUEL* www.immanueldimock.weebly.com	1882	40205 270TH ST	57331	SD	Ryan L Loeslie	(605)928-3117	WS 9 SS 1015 BC 1015	ED/MD/SN	153	126	77
DOLAND	*MESSIAH* messiahredeemerlcms@gmail.com www.messiahredeemerlcms.org	1946	402 SD-37 225 E 1ST ST REDFIELD	57436 57469	SD	Kevin D Moore	(605)472-0730	WS 9 SS 1015	SN	184	144	35
	REDEEMER messiahredeemerlcms@gmail.com www.messiahredeemerlcms.org	1932	402 SD-37 225 E 1ST ST REDFIELD	57436 57469	SD	Kevin D Moore	(605)472-0730	WS 11		30	29	12
DRAPER	*ST PAUL*	1906	200 N Main PO BOX 469 MURDO	57531 57559	SD	Ray A Greenseth	(605)669-2406	WS 11	ED/HC/MD			
EDGEMONT	*BETHESDA*		See Hot Springs SD									
EMERY	*ST PETER*	1886	42652 272nd St 42654 272ND ST	57332	SD	Joseph R Greenmyer	(605)825-4222	WS 1045 SS 10	ED	63	56	34
EUREKA	*ST PAUL'S*		See Leola SD									
FAIRFAX	*TRINITY* cckehn@gwtc.net	1892	307 5th St PO BOX 237	57335	SD			WS 1030 BC 930	ED/HC/MD	113	79	67
FERNEY	*ST PAUL*	1900	301 S 2nd Ave PO BOX 835	57439	SD	Robert E Moeller Jr	(605)395-6420 (605)395-6420	WS 9 SS 1015 BC 1015	ED/HC/MD			
FLANDREAU	*REDEEMER*	1921	508 W 1ST AVE	57028	SD	Timothy J Rynearson Samuel R Thole	(605)997-3848	WS 830	EC/ED/HC/ MD/SN	35	29	20
FREEMAN	*ST PAUL* stpaulfreeman@gmail.com www.stpaulfreeman.org	1882	615 E 7th St PO BOX 96	57029	SD		(605)925-7219	WS 930 SS 1030 BC 830	ED/HC/MD	293	228	64
GETTYSBURG	*EMMANUEL*	1925	601 E LOGAN AVE	57442	SD	David G Otten Thomas Penrod	(605)765-9201	WS 1030 SS 915	ED			
GREGORY	*ST JOHN* stjohn@gwtc.net	1905	211 CHURCH AVE	57533	SD	Marcus J Ring	(605)835-9214 (605)835-9214	WS 930 SS 1030 BC 830	ED			
GROTON	*ST JOHN* stjohnsgroton@gmail.com	1893	308 N 2nd PO BOX 348	57445	SD	Jeremy T Yeadon	(605)397-2386	WS 9 SS 10 BC 8	EC/ED/SN			
HAMILL	*ZION* christzionlutheran.wordpress.com	1913	B & Main St 730 E 6TH ST WINNER	57534 57580	SD	Wade M Harr	(605)842-0780	WS 11 SS 10	MD			
HARROLD	*IMMANUEL*	1910	201 EAST 2 ST	57536	SD	David F Strable		WS 11		28	20	6
HARTFORD	*TRINITY* pastor@hartfordtlc.com www.hartfordtlc.com	1881	46448 263RD ST	57033	SD	Zachary T Wessel Albert F Althoff Jr	(605)526-3571	WS 9 SS 1030 BC 1030	ED/HC/ MD/SN	150	103	68
HILL CITY	*OUR REDEEMER*		See Custer SD									
	OUR SAVIOR	1947	244 Elm St PO BOX 356 244 ELM ST.	57745	SD	David M Warner	(605)673-4361	WS 815		39	34	20
HOT SPRINGS	*BETHESDA* bethesda@gwtc.net www.bethesdahssd.org	1919	1537 BALTIMORE AVE	57747	SD	Peter M Utecht	(605)745-4834 (605)745-6676	WS 9 SS 1030 BC 8 1030	EL/ED/HC/ MD			
HOWARD	*ST JOHN*	1887	502 S Main St PO BOX 607	57349	SD	Joshua D Mork	(605)256-4483	WS 1030 SS 945	ED/HC/MD	174	135	65
HURLEY	*ZION*	1898	700 Oregon PO BOX 356	57036	SD	Kurt G Laskowsky	(605)563-2904	WS 830	ED	28	23	13
HURON	*MOUNT CALVARY* office.mclc@midconetwork.com www.mtcalvaryhuron.org	1927	688 DAKOTA AVE S	57350	SD		(605)352-7121 (605)353-6047	WS 8 1030 SS 915 BC 915	EC/ED/ MD/SN	957	767	160
IPSWICH	*ST PAUL'S*		See Leola SD									
LEBANON	*CHRIST*	1906	3rd St 601 E LOGAN AVE GETTYS-BURG	57455 57442	SD	David G Otten Thomas Penrod	(605)765-9201					
LEOLA	*ST PAUL'S*	1921	Sherman St PO BOX 317	57456	SD	Ryan A Drevlow Ray N Anderson	(605)439-3531	WS 1030 SS 930	ED			
LONG LAKE	*ST PAUL'S*		See Leola SD									
MADISON	*OUR SAVIOR* oursaviorlutheran17@gmail.com www.oslcmadison.com	1957	1010 N WASHINGTON AVE	57042	SD	Joshua D Mork	(605)256-4483	WS 830 SS 930	ED	234	205	71
MANSFIELD	*TRINITY* thatchurchguy@yahoo.com	1888	14908 377TH AVE	57460	SD	Bret R Bierman	(605)887-3696	WS 930 SS 1030	HC/MD/SN	366	266	53
MARION	*BETHESDA*	1912	200 E State St PO BOX 358	57043	SD	Brian M Mosemann	(605)387-5188		ED	50	46	20
MENNO	*IMMANUEL*	1889	255 W Juniper PO BOX 467	57045	SD	Brian M Mosemann	(605)387-5188			66	66	21
MIDLAND	*ST PETER*	1906	25185 CHURCH RD	57552	SD	Gregory S Hinners	(605)843-2274	WS 11 SS 12				
MILBANK	*BETHLEHEM*	1882	15048 484th Ave PO BOX 38 REVILLO	57252 57259	SD	Nathan T Neugebauer	(605)623-4280	WS 815 SS 915 BC 745	ED/MD			
	EMANUEL elc@itcmilbank.com www.elcmilbank.org	1889	701 S 1ST ST	57252	SD	Dr Christopher B Davis	(605)432-9555	WS 9 SS 1015 BC 1015	EC/ED/HC/ MD/SN	722	564	192
	TRINITY		See Corona SD									
MITCHELL	*ZION* office@zionmitchell.org www.zionmitchell.org	1892	620 E 3RD AVE	57301	SD	Daniel P Grimmer	(605)996-7530	WS 8 1030 SS 915 BC 915	ED/HC/ MD/SN	588	490	268
MONTROSE	*ST JOHN* zionandstjohn.com/	1939	201 E Clark St PO BOX 295	57048	SD	Timothy M Schleusener	(605)363-5023	WS 1030	ED/MD	146	119	26
MURDO	*MESSIAH*	1920	308 Cedar Ave PO BOX 469	57559	SD	Ray A Greenseth	(605)669-2406	WS 9 SS 10 BC 10	ED/HC/MD			

*Indicates a new church start. A new church start is an intentionally organized gathering which comes together on a regular basis for the purpose of worship and/or Bible study and is intended to grow into a member LCMS congregation. WS =Worship Service; SS = Sunday School; BC =Bible Class; EC = Early Childhood; EL = Elementary School; HS = High School; ED =Education Ministry; HC =Human Care Ministry; SN = Special Needs Ministry; MD = Media Ministry (PC)=Partner Church Pastor. See Page 53 for the Table of Abbreviations for key to additional abbreviations

CITY	CONGREGATION EMAIL WEBSITE	YEAR EST	LOCATION MAILING ADDRESS	ZIP CODE(S)	DIST.	PASTOR(S)	PHONE FAX	WS SS BC	SCHOOLS/ MINISTRIES	STATISTIC Bapt	 Conf	 Avg Attend
NORRIS	*ST JOHN*	1918	27281 251st Ave 25049 SD HIGHWAY 63	57560	SD	Gregory S Hinners	(605)462-6169	WS 8 SS 9 BC 910				
NORTH SIOUX CITY	*HOLY CROSS*		See Dakota Dunes SD									
OELRICHS	*BETHESDA*		See Hot Springs SD									
ONIDA	*HOLY CROSS* holycross@venturecomm.net	1951	408 S Main St PO BOX 49	57564	SD	David F Strable	(605)258-2207	WS 815 SS 930	ED	114	101	23
ORAL	*BETHESDA*		See Hot Springs SD									
PARKER	*FIRST ENGLISH*	1892	197 E 6th St PO BOX 117	57053	SD	Brian M Mosemann	(605)387-5188		ED/HC	37	31	9
PARKSTON	*FAITH*	1956	201 W Cherry 201 W CHERRY ST	57366	SD	Joseph R Greenmyer	(605)928-3876	WS 9 SS 10		249	196	96
PHILIP	*OUR REDEEMER*	1919	200 SW Ave PO BOX 964	57567	SD	Gregory S Hinners	(605)859-2721	WS 1				
PIERRE	*FAITH* faith@faithluth.com www.faithluth.com	1932	714 N GRAND AVE	57501	SD	Samuel P Handschke	(605)224-2216 (605)224-2226	WS 830 11 SS 945	EC/ED/HC/ MD	1886	1469	263
PLANKINTON	*ST PAUL'S* stpaulplankinton@gmail.com www.stpaulplankinton.com	1910	109 W STATE ST	57368	SD		(605)942-7364	WS 1030	ED	174	138	21
	ST PAUL'S LUTHERAN CHURCH Satellite Site of Trinity White Lake SD	2024	109 W State St	57368				WS 1030				
PRESHO	*ZION* zionlcms.presho@gmail.com zionandtrinity.ctshost.org	1920	200 Main Ave PO BOX 266	57568	SD	Ray A Greenseth	(605)895-2334	WS 9				
RAPID CITY	*BETHESDA*		See Hot Springs SD									
	BETHLEHEM bethlehem@rushmore.com www.bethlehemlcms.net	1950	1630 RUSHMORE ST	57702	SD	Dr Joshua H Jones	(605)343-2011	WS 9 SS 1015 BC 1015	ED/HC/ MD/SN	631	452	171
	OUR REDEEMER secretary_orlc@rushmore.com www.rapidcitylutheran.net	1999	910 WOOD AVE	57701	SD	Lucas W Edwards	(605)388-0032 (605)716-2894	WS 9 SS 1030 BC 1030	ED/MD	127	126	70
	PEACE office@peacelutheranrc.org www.peacelutheranrc.org	1970	219 E SAINT ANNE ST	57701	SD	David J Lindenberg	(605)721-6480 (605)721-6483	WS 930 SS 815 BC 815	ED/HC/ MD/SN	661	494	103
	ZION www.zionrc.org	1910	4550 S Highway 16 4550 MOUNT RUSHMORE RD	57701	SD	Bryan W Meadows Gary R Schulte	(605)342-5749 (605)342-4469	WS 8 1045 SS 930 BC 930	EL/ED/MD	654	514	297
REDFIELD	*REDEEMER LUTHERAN BIBLE STUDY* Satellite Site of Redeemer Doland SD	2022	602 N Main St	57469				BC 4				
	SUNDAY BIBLE STUDY Satellite Site of Messiah Doland SD	2022	602 N Main Street	57469								
RELIANCE	*TRINITY* christzionlutheran.wordpress.com	1917	PO BOX 943	57569	SD	Wade M Harr	(605)842-0780	WS 1				
REVILLO	*BETHLEHEM*		See Milbank SD									
	ST JOHN'S	1911	100 N Dillman Ave PO BOX 38	57259	SD	Nathan T Neugebauer	(605)623-4280	WS 1030 SS 930 BC 945	ED/HC/MD			
ROSEBUD	*ROSEBUD LUTHERAN CHURCH* Satellite Site of Our Savior VALENTINE NE	1997	sioux BLVD	57570				WS 11				
SCOTLAND	*ST PAUL*	1901	940 S 1st PO BOX 484	57059	SD	Brian M Mosemann	(605)387-5188		HC	26	26	12
SIOUX FALLS	*CHRIST* pastor@christsiouxfalls.org www.christsiouxfalls.org	1957	4801 E 6TH ST	57110	SD	Matthew W Nix	(605)338-3769 (605)330-0706	WS 930 SS 1045	ED/HC/ MD/SN			
	FAITH faithlutheransf@gmail.com www.faithlutheransiouxfalls.org	1929	601 N CLIFF AVE	57103	SD	Corey W Aker Jason E Rensner	(605)332-3401	WS 9 SS 1015 BC 1015	EL/HS/ED/ HC/MD	798	578	219
	LORD OF LIFE wmeyer@lordoflifelutheran.org www.lordoflifelutheran.org	1989	2600 S SYCAMORE AVE	57110	SD	William J Newell Chera H Nemera	(605)371-3501 (605)371-3592	SS 1015 BC 1030	EL/HS/ED/ HC/MD	209	163	130
	MEMORIAL info@memoriallutheran.net www.memoriallutheran.net	1944	5000 S WESTERN AVE	57108	SD	Douglas J Slavens	(605)334-7133 (605)334-7177	WS 8 930 11 SS 930 BC 930	EL/HS/ED/ HC/MD			
	OUR REDEEMER office@ourredeemersf.org www.ourredeemersf.org	1954	2200 S WESTERN AVE	57105	SD	Brett E Simek	(605)338-6957	WS 8 1030 SS 915 BC 915	EL/HS/ED/ HC/MD/SN	335	282	167
	RESURRECTION office@resurrectionsf.org resurrectionsf.org	1991	5500 W 26TH ST	57106	SD	Dr Christopher D Ascher Albert T Bakat	(605)361-6631 (605)361-6575	WS 9 SS 11 BC 11	EC/EL/HS/ ED/HC/SN	348	252	143
	RISEN SAVIOR		See Tea SD									
	TRINITY		See Hartford SD									
	TRINITY DEAF mw_nix@yahoo.com	1947	4801 E 6TH ST	57110	SD	Matthew W Nix	(605)330-0724	WS 830	ED/HC/ MD/SN			
	ZION zion@zionlutheransf.com www.zionlutheransf.com	1889	1400 S DULUTH AVE	57105	SD	Gregory A Lehr	(605)338-5226 (605)338-8936	WS 8 1030 SS 915 BC 930	ED/HC/MD	934	710	297
SISSETON	*EMANUEL* elc.lcms@gmail.com www.emanuelzion.com	1898	321 7TH AVE E	57262	SD	Thomas P Mueller	(605)698-7116	WS 9 SS 10 BC 8	ED/HC	111	98	39

*Indicates a new church start. A new church start is an intentionally organized gathering which comes together on a regular basis for the purpose of worship and/or Bible study and is intended to grow into a member LCMS congregation. WS =Worship Service; SS = Sunday School; BC =Bible Class; EC = Early Childhood; EL = Elementary School; HS = High School; ED =Education Ministry; HC =Human Care Ministry; SN = Special Needs Ministry; MD = Media Ministry (PC)=Partner Church Pastor. See Page 53 for the Table of Abbreviations for key to additional abbreviations

CITY	CONGREGATION EMAIL WEBSITE	YEAR EST	LOCATION MAILING ADDRESS	ZIP CODE(S)	DIST.	PASTOR(S)	PHONE FAX	WS SS BC	SCHOOLS/ MINISTRIES	STATISTIC Bapt	Conf	Avg Attend
SPEARFISH	*ST PAUL* stpspear@rushmore.com www.stpaul-spearfish.org	1940	846 N 7TH ST	57783	SD	Dr Thomas C Brown	(605)642-2929	WS 8 1030 SS 915 BC 915	ED/HC/ MD/SN	346	283	160
SPENCER	*TRINITY*	1892	416 Fuller PO BOX 39	57374	SD	Thomas D Christopher	(605)246-2760	WS 830 SS 930 BC 10		89	79	42
SPRINGFIELD	*OUR SAVIOR* oslc.springfield@gmail.com	1956	613 12th St PO BOX 426	57062	SD	Kenneth P Johnson	(605)369-2386	WS 830 SS 915	ED	40	26	20
STRATFORD	*ST PAUL* jmmilbrandt@gmail.com	1907	593 N 3RD ST	57474	SD	Bret R Bierman	(605)395-6549	WS 8	ED/HC/ MD/SN	62	38	12
STURGIS	*BLESSED EMMANUEL* blessedemmanuelsturgis@yahoo.com	1998	2942 Pine Tree Trail 2942 PINE TREE TRL	57785	SD	Robert M Hinckley Jr	(605)423-5870	WS 1030 SS 915 BC 915	ED/HC/ MD/SN			
TEA	*RISEN SAVIOR* risensaviortea@gmail.com www.risensaviortea.org	2003	1401 N MAIN AVE	57064	SD	Tanner T Sutcliffe	(605)498-5050	WS 9 SS 1030 BC 1030	EC/ED	135	114	63
TRIPP	*EMMAUS* zionlutherandelmont@midstatesd.net	1901	400 South Dobson PO BOX M	57376	SD	Brian S Lemcke	(605)935-6725	WS 1030 SS 930	ED	57	48	28
TYNDALL	*ST JOHN* pastorschroeder@hcinet.net www.stjohnstyndalllcms.org	1924	108 W 23RD AVE	57066	SD	Dean F Schroeder	(605)589-3195	WS 830 SS 10	ED	183	143	57
UTICA	*MARTINUS* pastorschroeder@hcinet.net martinuslutheran.org	1882	43804 300TH ST	57067	SD	Dean F Schroeder	(605)589-3195	WS 1030 SS 930	ED			
VERMILLION	*CONCORDIA* pastor@lcmsvermillion.org lcmsvermillion.org	1949	7 S UNIVERSITY ST	57069	SD	Matthew A Bless	(605)624-3459	WS 10 SS 9 BC 9	ED/HC/MD	90	73	41
WAGNER	*ST JOHN* stjohntrinityluth@gmail.com	1899	110 High Ave NW PO BOX 506	57380	SD		(605)384-3500	WS 830 SS 930	ED/MD			
	TRINITY		See Fairfax SD									
WALL	*FIRST* walllutheran@gwtc.net firstlutheranwall.wordpress.com	1946	504 Norris St PO BOX 327	57790	SD	Christopher R McCarthy	(605)279-2453	WS 9 BC 8	ED	291	226	69
WATERTOWN	*MOUNT OLIVE* mtolive@tnics.com www.mtolivewatertownsd.org	1956	715 2ND ST NE	57201	SD	Brad E Birtell	(605)886-5671	WS 9 SS 1015 BC 1030	ED/MD			
WAUBAY	*ZION*	1892	224 W 5th Ave 224 W 5TH AVE PO BOX 325	57273	SD	Thomas P Mueller	(605)520-9919	WS 11 SS 10	ED/HC/MD	100	94	30
WECOTA	*IMMANUEL* www.immanuelwecota.org	1888	35439 SD Hwy 20 PO BOX 106 CRESBARD	57438 57435	SD		(605)324-3318	WS 1030 SS 930				
WENTWORTH	*SAINT PETER'S* stpeter@itctel.com www.stpeterswentworth.com	1882	316 S Main Ave 316 S MAIN AVE PO BOX 125	57075	SD		(605)483-3129 (605)483-1302	WS 9 SS 1030 BC 1030	MD	248	187	118
WESSINGTON SPRINGS	*ZION*	1916	312 Barrett Ave PO BOX 308 WESSINGTN SPG	57382	SD	Leonard S Spiehs Richard D Weeman	(605)539-1297	WS 930				
WHITE	*ZION* zionluthwhite@gmail.com	1897	203 S Sherwood Ave PO BOX 601	57276	SD	Timothy J Rynearson Samuel R Thole	(605)629-2951	WS 945 SS 9	HC	82	63	23
WHITE LAKE	*ST PAUL'S*		See Plankinton SD									
	TRINITY trinitywhitelake@gmail.com www.trinitywhitelake.com	1884	304 S JOHNSTON ST	57383	SD		(605)249-2333	WS 830	ED	131	112	20
	TRINITY LUTHERAN CHURCH Satellite Site of St Paul's Plankinton SD	2024	304 S Johnston St	57383				WS 830				
WILMOT	*OUR SAVIOR*	1967	401 Main St PO BOX 7	57279	SD	Arthur J Drehman		WS 1030 SS 10	ED/HC/MD	201	160	33
	TRINITY		See Corona SD									
WINNER	*CHRIST* christzionlutheran.wordpress.com	1957	798 E 5th St 730 E 6TH ST	57580	SD	Wade M Harr	(605)842-0780	WS 9	ED/MD			
WOLSEY	*ST JOHN*	1884	241 Commercial Ave NW PO BOX 327	57384	SD	Leonard S Spiehs Richard D Weeman	(605)883-4972	WS 1030 SS 915 BC 915	ED/HC/MD			
WOONSOCKET	*MOUNT OLIVE*	1930	PO Box 264 PO BOX 327 WOLSEY	57385 57384	SD	Leonard S Spiehs Richard D Weeman	(605)796-4141 (605)796-4143	WS 8				
YANKTON	*ST JOHN* office@stjohnsyankton.com www.stjohnsyankton.com	1882	1009 JACKSON ST	57078	SD	Steven A Weispfennig Dr Jacob C Bobby	(605)665-7337 (605)665-7293	WS 8 1030 SS 915 BC 915	EC/ED/HC/ MD/SN			

TENNESSEE

CITY	CONGREGATION EMAIL WEBSITE	YEAR EST	LOCATION MAILING ADDRESS	ZIP CODE(S)	DIST.	PASTOR(S)	PHONE FAX	WS SS BC	SCHOOLS/ MINISTRIES	Bapt	Conf	Avg Attend
ALCOA	*PRAISE*		See Maryville TN									
ATHENS	*ATHENS* athenslutherantn@gmail.com athenslutheranchurch.org	1973	710 Forrest Ave PO BOX 841	37303 37371	MDS	Benjamin L Heinz	(423)745-9419	WS 8 1030 SS 915	ED/HC/SN	100	75	48
ATOKA	*GRACEPOINT* secretary@gpcmunford.org gpctiptonco.org		245 COMMERCIAL DRIVE	38004	MDS	Daniel D Hawkins	(901)840-2086	WS 10	ED/HC/MD	68	59	80
BARTLETT	*IMMANUEL*		See Memphis TN									
BRISTOL	*HOLY TRINITY* pastor@lutheranbristol.org www.holytrinitylutheran.us/	2002	1909 Volunteer Pkwy 1909 VOLUNTEER PARKWAY	37620 37602	SE	Timothy E Winslett		WS 11 SS 10	ED/HC/ MD/SN			
BURNS	*ST JOHN* stjohnburns@gmail.com www.blessedbythelord.org	1995	2300 HIGHWAY 96	37029	MDS	Nathan R Jansen	(615)446-2332 (615)446-0023	WS 830 11 SS 1005 BC 1005		337	258	95

*Indicates a new church start. A new church start is an intentionally organized gathering which comes together on a regular basis for the purpose of worship and/or Bible study and is intended to grow into a member LCMS congregation. WS =Worship Service; SS = Sunday School; BC =Bible Class; EC = Early Childhood; EL = Elementary School; HS = High School; ED =Education Ministry; HC =Human Care Ministry; SN = Special Needs Ministry; MD = Media Ministry (PC)=Partner Church Pastor. See Page 53 for the Table of Abbreviations for key to additional abbreviations

CITY	CONGREGATION EMAIL WEBSITE	YEAR EST	LOCATION MAILING ADDRESS	ZIP CODE(S)	DIST.	PASTOR(S)	PHONE FAX	WS SS BC	SCHOOLS/ MINISTRIES	STATISTIC Bapt	Conf	Avg Attend
CHATTANOOGA	*CROSS OF CHRIST* church@cocluth.com www.cocluth.com	1958	3204 HIXSON PIKE	37415	MDS	Patrick M Cox II	(423)877-7447 (423)870-2990	WS 9 SS 1015 BC 1015	ED/HC/ MD/SN	168	147	82
	FIRST office@first4u.org www.first4u.org	1887	2800 MCCALLIE AVE	37404	MDS	Donald N Welmer	(423)629-5990	WS 830 11 SS 945 BC 945	EL/ED/HC/ MD/SN	233	178	155
	GOOD SHEPHERD OFFICE@GSLCFLOCK.ORG www.gslcflock.org	1951	822 BELVOIR AVE	37412	MDS	Harry C Sheets Dr Edward K Rosser	(423)629-4661 (423)629-1431	WS 9 1115 SS 1010 BC 2	EL/ED/HC/ MD/SN	355	325	186
	SPIRIT OF JOY		8705 E BRAINERD RD	37421	MDS		(423)645-3583	WS 930	EL/ED/HC/ MD	5	5	6
	ST PHILIP	1947	51 W 25th St PO BOX 23304	37408	MDS	Joseph L Jacks	(423)267-1475 (423)267-1475	WS 11 SS 10	ED/HC			
CLARKSVILLE	*GRACE* office@glctn.org glctn.org	1958	2041 MADISON ST	37043	MDS	Sean R Smith James S Martin	(931)647-6750 (931)645-3374	WS 815 1045 SS 930 BC 945	EC/ED/HC/ MD/SN	649	498	290
CLEVELAND	*FIRST* firstluthcl@bellsouth.net firstlutheranclevelandtn.360unite.com	1950	195 MCINTIRE AVE NE	37312	MDS	Robert G Seaton	(423)472-6811	WS 815 1045 SS 930 BC 930	ED/HC/MD	321	291	138
	FIRST		See Chattanooga TN									
COLLIERVILLE	*FAITH* office@faithcollierville.com faithcollierville.com	1984	507 NEW BYHALIA RD	38017	MDS	Robert N Harbin Justin C Sellers	(901)853-4673 (901)853-5015	WS 815 11 SS 940 BC 940	EC/ED/HC/ MD	442	373	179
COLUMBIA	*OUR SAVIOR*		See Nashville TN									
	TRINITY ChurchOffice@trinitycolumbia.org www.trinitycolumbia.org	1963	5001 TROTWOOD AVE	38401	MDS	William B Wagner Jr	(931)388-0790 (931)388-0790	WS 830 11 SS 945 BC 945	EC/ED/HC/ MD	122	104	95
COOKEVILLE	*HEAVENLY HOST* office@heavenlyhostlcms.org heavenlyhostlcms.org	1965	777 S WILLOW AVE	38501	MDS	Todd A Bunge	(931)526-3423 (931)520-3766	WS 8 1030 SS 915 BC 915	EC/ED/HC/ MD/SN	219	205	126
CORDOVA	*BEAUTIFUL SAVIOR*		See Olive Branch MS									
	GRACE CELEBRATION admin@gracecelebration.org www.gracecelebration.org	1993	8601 TRINITY RD	38018	MDS	Dr Terry D Tieman James E Belles	(901)737-6010 (901)737-6084	WS 10 SS 845	ED/HC/ MD/SN	150	120	112
	IMMANUEL		See Memphis TN									
CROSSVILLE	*SHEP OF THE HILLS* finance@sothmail.org www.shepherdcrossville.com	1977	1461 SPARTA HWY	38572	MDS	John L Beabout	(931)484-3461 (931)707-0042	WS 8 1030 SS 915 BC 915	EC/ED/HC/ MD/SN	407	402	236
CUMBERLAND GAP	*CHRIST CUMBERLANDS*		See Harrogate TN									
DANDRIDGE	*ST PAUL*		See Sevierville TN									
DICKSON	*ST JOHN*		See Burns TN									
DYERSBURG	*CANTERBURY ASSISTED LIVING* Satellite Site of Trinity Dyersburg TN	2014	1900 Highway 51 Bypass N	38024				BC 1030				
	TRINITY	1978	1500 US HIGHWAY 51 BYP N	38024	MDS	Paul A Leigeber	(731)285-9691	WS 11 SS 9	ED/HC			
EAST RIDGE	*FIRST*		See Chattanooga TN									
	GOOD SHEPHERD		See Chattanooga TN									
ELIZABETHTON	*REDEEMER* redeemerlcmseliz@gmail.com redeemerlcmselizabethton. freechurchwebsites.com	1937	234 West F St 234 W F ST	37643	MDS	Mark A Kophamer	(423)543-1132	WS 1030 BC 915	ED/HC/MD	33	33	15
FRANKLIN	*FAITH*		See Thompsons Station TN									
	REDEEMER		See Nashville TN									
GALLATIN	*TRINITY* trinitygallatin@trinitygallatin.org www.trinitygallatin.org	1984	720 LOCK 4 RD	37066	MDS	Kenneth B Shaw	(615)452-3352	WS 930 SS 1045 BC 1045	ED/HC/MD	180	123	45
GATLINBURG	*ST PAUL*		See Sevierville TN									
GERMANTOWN	*FAITH*		See Collierville TN									
GOODLETTSVILLE	*ASCENSION*		See Madison TN									
GREENBACK	*PRAISE*		See Maryville TN									
HARRIMAN	*REDEEMER* redeemerharriman@att.net www.redeemerharriman.org	1952	1658 ROANE STATE HWY	37748	MDS	Michael M Miller	(865)376-7647	WS 1030 SS 915	ED/HC/ MD/SN	127	111	46
HARROGATE	*CHRIST CUMBERLANDS*	1987	190 Forge Ridge Rd PO BOX 4069	37752	MDS	Gordon L Smith	(423)869-4359 (423)869-4359	WS 9 SS 930 BC 815				
HENDERSONVILLE	*ASCENSION*		See Madison TN									
HERMITAGE	*EMMANUEL* office@emmanuelhermitage.org www.emmanuelhermitage.org	1961	1003 HICKORY HILL LN	37076	MDS	Andrew J Abraham Timothy R Hunze	(615)883-7533 (615)885-5815	WS 8 1030 SS 915 BC 915	ED/HC/ MD/SN	204	199	115
HIXSON	*FIRST*		See Chattanooga TN									
	GOOD SHEPHERD		See Chattanooga TN									
JACKSON	*CONCORDIA* lcmsconcordia@gmail.com concordiajacksontn.wixsite.com/ concordia-lutheran-c	1935	637 WALLACE RD	38305	MDS	Eric M Rudsenske	(731)668-0757 (731)668-7820	WS 1015 SS 9 BC 9	ED/MD/SN	112	95	69
JOHNSON CITY	*BETHLEHEM* bethlehemstar@embarqmail.com www.bethlehemjc.org	1924	201 E WATAUGA AVE	37601	MDS	Charles V Shemwell	(423)926-5261 (423)926-0102	WS 8 1045 SS 915 BC 915	ED/HC/SN	200	180	120

*Indicates a new church start. A new church start is an intentionally organized gathering which comes together on a regular basis for the purpose of worship and/or Bible study and is intended to grow into a member LCMS congregation. WS =Worship Service; SS = Sunday School; BC =Bible Class; EC = Early Childhood; EL = Elementary School; HS = High School; ED =Education Ministry; HC =Human Care Ministry; SN = Special Needs Ministry; MD = Media Ministry (PC)=Partner Church Pastor. See Page 53 for the Table of Abbreviations for key to additional abbreviations

CITY	CONGREGATION EMAIL WEBSITE	YEAR EST	LOCATION MAILING ADDRESS	ZIP CODE(S)	DIST.	PASTOR(S)	PHONE FAX	WS SS BC	SCHOOLS/ MINISTRIES	STATISTIC Bapt	Conf	Avg Attend
KINGSPORT	*CONCORDIA* pastor@concordiakingsport.org concordiakingsport.org	1959	725 TRUXTON DR	37660	MDS		(423)247-3582	WS 1030 SS 9	ED/HC/MD	118	100	74
KINGSTON SPRINGS	*REDEEMER*		See Nashville TN									
KNOXVILLE	*CHRISTUS VICTOR* wondracka@gmail.com www.cvlcknox.org	1967	4110 Central Ave Pike 4110 CENTRAL AVENUE PIKE	37912	MDS	William J Ondracka	(865)687-6622 (865)687-9206	WS 815 1045 SS 930 BC 930	ED/HC/ MD/SN	178	150	50
	FIRST office@firstknoxville.org firstknoxville.org	1869	1207 N BROADWAY ST	37917	MDS	Edward J Maanum	(865)524-0308 (865)524-5636	WS 930 SS 1045	EL/ED	439	343	129
	GRACE glc@visitgrace.org visitgrace.org	1957	9076 MIDDLEBROOK PIKE	37923	MDS	Robert D Anderson Jacob L Childers	(865)691-2823 (865)691-4895	WS 8 930 11 SS 930 BC 945	ED/HC/MD	1164	955	448
	PRAISE		See Maryville TN									
	THE POINT hello@thepointknox.com thepointknox.com/	2010	211 West Fifth Avenue P.O. BOX 10626	37917 37939	MDS	Adam T Woldt	(402)681-5708	WS 1030 SS 1030		208	165	128
KODAK	*ST PAUL*		See Sevierville TN									
LOUDON	*CHRIST OUR SAVIOR* christrs@bellsouth.net coslctn.org	1997	260 Wade Rd West 260 WADE RD W	37774	MDS	Mark R Rhoads	(865)458-9407 (865)458-8531	WS 830 11 SS 10 BC 10	ED/HC/ MD/SN	315	297	203
LOUISVILLE	*PRAISE*		See Maryville TN									
MADISON	*ASCENSION* office@ascensionmadison.com www.ascensionmadison.com	1955	610 W OLD HICKORY BLVD	37115	MDS	Gregory D Bauch	(615)868-2346 (615)868-7674	WS 1030 SS 9	ED/HC/MD	162	123	55
MARYVILLE	*PRAISE* pastor@praiselutheran.com www.praiselutheran.com	2000	315 Southdowne Drive 315 SOUTHDOWNE DR	37801	MDS	Derek A Roberts	(865)977-5810	WS 9 11 SS 945 BC 945	ED/HC/MD	304	249	176
MCMINNVILLE	*SHEPHERD HILLS* pastor@sothlutheran.org www.sothlutheran.org	1977	4083 YAGER RD	37110	MDS	Theodore D McMinn III	(931)815-7684	WS 9 BC 1030	ED/HC	65	57	49
MEMPHIS	*CHRIST THE KING* churchoffice@ctkmemphis.com ctkmemphis.com	1959	5296 PARK AVE	38119	MDS	Mark D Goble Matthew S Lynch	(901)682-8404 (901)682-7687	WS 830 11 SS 945	EL/ED/HC/ MD	1147	921	325
	CROSS OF CALVARY crossofcalvarylutheranchurch@gmail.com atthecrossmemphis.org	1993	4327 ELVIS PRESLEY BLVD	38116	MDS	Russell S Belisle	(901)396-5566	WS 10 SS 9	ED/HC/ MD/SN	127	126	35
	FAITH		See Collierville TN									
	IMMANUEL churchoffice@immanuelmemphis.org www.ilcmemphis.org	1924	6325 Raleigh La Grange Rd 6325 RALEIGH LAGRANGE RD	38134	MDS	Jonathan E Petering	(901)373-4486 (901)373-4487	WS 830 11 SS 950 BC 950	EL/ED/HC/ MD/SN	349	311	147
	MESSIAH messiahmemphis@aol.com Messiah-memphis.org	1961	3743 AUSTIN PEAY HWY	38128	MDS		(901)386-3401 (901)386-3401	WS 9 SS 1015 BC 1015	ED/HC/MD	52	46	24
	TRINITY office@trinitymemphis.org www.trinitymemphis.org	1855	210 WASHINGTON AVE	38103	MDS	Michael L Croom II	(901)525-1056	WS 10 SS 1130 BC 1130	ED/HC/ MD/SN	134	109	63
MORRISTOWN	*OUR SAVIOR* oslc@musfiber.com www.oursaviormorristown.org	1962	2717 BUFFALO TRL	37814	MDS	Gordon L Smith	(423)586-8818 (423)586-8818	WS 11 BC 930	ED/HC/ MD/SN	78	76	47
MURFREESBORO	*GRACE* contact@glc-lcms.org www.glc-lcms.org	1960	811 E CLARK BLVD	37130	MDS	Alan M Thoe	(615)893-0338 (615)225-8939	WS 8 1045 SS 930 BC 930	ED/HC/ MD/SN	303	249	135
	MIDDLE TENNESSEE STATE UNIVERSITY Satellite Site of Grace Murfreesboro TN	2025	1301 E Main St	37132								
NASHVILLE	*ASCENSION*		See Madison TN									
	CONCORDIA concordialutherannashville@gmail.com www.concordianashville.com	1930	3501 CENTRAL AVE	37205	MDS	Eric G Phillips	(615)292-0982	WS 1030 BC 915	ED/HC/MD			
	EMMANUEL		See Hermitage TN									
	HOPE		See Smyrna TN									
	OUR SAVIOR allison.lynch@oslcnashville.org www.oslcnashville.org	1967	5110 Franklin Rd 5110 FRANKLIN PIKE	37220	MDS	Lane B Reuter Mark R Bushuiakovish Tracy T Nelson	(615)833-1500 (615)331-1123	WS 8 1045 SS 930 BC 930	EC/ED/HC/ MD	1170	872	450
	REDEEMER rlcnashville@bellsouth.net www.redeemernashville.org	1982	800 BELLEVUE RD	37221	MDS	Philip H Young	(615)646-3150	WS 930 SS 1045 BC 1045	ED/HC	103	93	60
	TRINITY		See Gallatin TN									
OAK RIDGE	*FAITH* faith@faithlutheranoakridge.org www.faithlutheranoakridge.org	1944	1300 Oak Ridge Turnpike 1300 OAK RIDGE TPKE	37830	MDS	Chase K Lefort George E Smith	(865)483-5431	WS 1030 SS 930 BC 9	ED/HC/ MD/SN	116	103	87
OAKLAND	*HOLY SPIRIT* holyspiritoakland@outlook.com www.holyspiritoakland.com		14615 Hwy 194 PO BOX 571	38060	MDS	Gerald Stobaugh	(901)465-6103	WS 930		20	20	11
OOLTEWAH	*FIRST*		See Chattanooga TN									
	GOOD SHEPHERD		See Chattanooga TN									
PARIS	*CHRIST LUTHERAN* CLC@ChristLutheranParis.org christlutheranparis.org	1971	3235 Hwy 79 S 3235 HIGHWAY 79 S	38242	MDS	Koh M Yamamoto	(731)642-6620	WS 1030 SS 9 BC 9	ED/HC/MD	85	83	56

*Indicates a new church start. A new church start is an intentionally organized gathering which comes together on a regular basis for the purpose of worship and/or Bible study and is intended to grow into a member LCMS congregation. WS =Worship Service; SS = Sunday School; BC =Bible Class; EC = Early Childhood; EL = Elementary School; HS = High School; ED =Education Ministry; HC =Human Care Ministry; SN = Special Needs Ministry; MD = Media Ministry (PC)=Partner Church Pastor. See Page 53 for the Table of Abbreviations for key to additional abbreviations

CITY	CONGREGATION EMAIL WEBSITE	YEAR EST	LOCATION MAILING ADDRESS	ZIP CODE(S)	DIST.	PASTOR(S)	PHONE FAX	WS SS BC	SCHOOLS/ MINISTRIES	STATISTIC Bapt	Conf	Avg Attend
PARIS	*IMMANUEL*		See Murray KY									
PIGEON FORGE	*ST PAUL*		See Sevierville TN									
RALEIGH	*MESSIAH*		See Memphis TN									
RED BANK	*FIRST*		See Chattanooga TN									
	GOOD SHEPHERD		See Chattanooga TN									
ROCKFORD	*PRAISE*		See Maryville TN									
ROGERSVILLE	*HAWKINS COUNTY**	2006	355 LAUDERBACH GAP TRL	37857	MDS		(423)272-4834	WS 4 BC 5	ED/HC/MD			
SEVIERVILLE	*ST PAUL* splctn@gmail.com www.splctn.com	1994	1610 PULLEN RD	37862	MDS	Seth P Korte	(865)365-8551	WS 1015 BC 9	ED/HC/ MD/SN	139	136	109
SEYMOUR	*CELEBRATION* celebrationseymour@gmail.com www.celebrationseymour.com	1976	10330 Chapman Highway PO BOX 1550	37865	MDS	Raymond D Krieg	(865)579-2218	WS 9 BC 9	ED/HC/MD	21	21	19
SHARPS CHAPEL	*GOOD SHEPHERD* chapelofthegoodshepherd@outlook.com www.goodshepherdsharpschapel.com		681 Sharps Chapel Rd PO BOX 35	37866	MDS	Paul E Kritsch	(865)279-1279	WS 1030		38	35	35
SIGNAL MOUNTAIN	*GOOD SHEPHERD*		See Chattanooga TN									
SMYRNA	*HOPE* hopeinsmyrna@gmail.com		1450 Sam Davis Rd Suite 130 1450 SAM DAVIS RD STE 130	37167	MDS		(615)984-7664					
SODDY DAISY	*FIRST LUTHERAN CHURCH CAMP* Satellite Site of First Chattanooga TN	2014	1621 Lee Pike	37379								
	GOOD SHEPHERD		See Chattanooga TN									
SPRING HILL	*OUR SAVIOR*		See Nashville TN									
	OUR SAVIOR LUTHERAN CHURCH | SPRING HILL Satellite Site of Our Savior Nashville TN	2024	220 Town Center Parkway	37174				WS 1030				
TAZEWELL	*CHRIST CUMBERLANDS*		See Harrogate TN									
THOMPSONS STATION	*FAITH* pastorcurthoover@gmail.com www.faithlutheran-tn.org	1990	2640 BUCKNER RD THOMPSONS STN	37179	MDS	Curtis R Hoover Craig A Fiebiger Fasil G Alemayehu	(615)791-1880	WS 1030 SS 915 BC 915	ED/HC/ MD/SN	301	236	100
	OUR SAVIOR		See Nashville TN									
TOWNSEND	*PRAISE*		See Maryville TN									
TULLAHOMA	*FAITH* jesusisthelight@lighttube.net www.faithlutherantullahoma.com	1951	101 BRAGG CIR	37388	MDS	Martin S Nutter	(931)455-3510 (931)455-1862	WS 8 1030 SS 915 BC 915	EC/ED/HC/ MD/SN	271	249	108
UNION CITY	*FAITH*	1964	2012 E REELFOOT AVE	38261	MDS	Paul A Leigeber	(731)885-9562	WS 930 SS 1015	ED/HC/ MD/SN			
WARTBURG	*ST PAUL* stpaulluthrn@highland.net www.splcwartburg.org	1846	222 S Church St PO BOX 67	37887	MDS	David W Graves	(423)346-3554 (423)346-3554	WS 830 11 SS 10 BC 10	EC/ED/HC/ MD	308	252	135
WHITE HOUSE	*PRINCE OF PEACE* rmsak@comcast.net www.princeofpeacelutheran whitehouse.com		4095 Highway 31 W PO BOX 1528	37188	MDS	Randy K Sakach	(615)362-1902	WS 915 SS 1030 BC 1030	ED/HC/SN	103	87	58

TEXAS

CITY	CONGREGATION EMAIL WEBSITE	YEAR EST	LOCATION MAILING ADDRESS	ZIP CODE(S)	DIST.	PASTOR(S)	PHONE FAX	WS SS BC	SCHOOLS/ MINISTRIES	Bapt	Conf	Avg Attend
ABILENE	*OUR SAVIOR* oslcabilene@gmail.com oslcabilene.org	1953	4933 S 7TH ST	79605	TX	Robert J Pase	(325)692-6163 (325)692-6521	WS 1030 SS 915 BC 915		205	184	75
	ZION office@zion-abilene.org www.zion-abilene.org	1894	2801 ANTILLEY RD	79606	TX	Clyde J Kieschnick Randall C Sanders	(325)690-0121 (325)690-1069	WS 830 1045 SS 945 BC 945	EC/ED/HC/ MD	706	549	205
ADDISON	*LORD OF LIFE*		See Plano TX									
ALAMO	*ZION* churchoffice@zionalamo.org www.zionalamo.org	1927	226 S Alamo Rd PO BOX 805	78516	TX	Carlos R Sandoval	(956)787-1584	WS 9 SS 1015	ED/HC/ MD/SN	60	60	41
ALBANY	*TRINITY* trinitypastortom@gmail.com www.albanylutheran.com	1909	733 Hwy 180 E PO BOX 2255	76430	TX	Thomas B Chandler	(325)762-2557	WS 1030 SS 930 BC 930	ED/HC/ MD/SN	119	114	23
ALEDO	*REDEEMER*		See Fort Worth TX									
	ST PAUL		See Fort Worth TX									
	THE SUMMIT Satellite Site of St Paul Fort Worth TX	2009	111 Maverick St	76008				WS 915 1045				
ALLEN	*IMMANUEL*		See Fairview TX									
	LORD OF LIFE		See Plano TX									
	TANGIBLE GRACE Office@tangiblegrace.com Www.tangiblegrace.com	2016	605 S Greenville Ave 190 E STACY RD STE 306 BOX 313	75002	TX		(972)246-8411	WS 9 SS 930 BC 1030				

*Indicates a new church start. A new church start is an intentionally organized gathering which comes together on a regular basis for the purpose of worship and/or Bible study and is intended to grow into a member LCMS congregation. WS =Worship Service; SS = Sunday School; BC =Bible Class; EC = Early Childhood; EL = Elementary School; HS = High School; ED =Education Ministry; HC =Human Care Ministry; SN = Special Needs Ministry; MD = Media Ministry (PC)=Partner Church Pastor. See Page 53 for the Table of Abbreviations for key to additional abbreviations

CITY	CONGREGATION EMAIL WEBSITE	YEAR EST	LOCATION MAILING ADDRESS	ZIP CODE(S)	DIST.	PASTOR(S)	PHONE FAX	WS SS BC	SCHOOLS/ MINISTRIES	STATISTIC Bapt	Conf	Avg Attend
ALLEN	*VERITAS COMMUNITY**		See Wylie TX									
	WATERS EDGE		See Frisco TX									
ALPINE	*REDEEMER* atxredeemer@yahoo.com redeemeralpinetx.com	1940	1003 West Holland Avenue P.O. BOX 1287	79830 79831	TX		(432)279-0744	WS 5	ED/HC/MD	24	24	21
AMARILLO	*PRINCE PEACE* office@popamarillo.org www.popamarillo.org	1980	6900 HILLSIDE RD	79109	TX		(806)359-7700 (806)359-7719	WS 830 11 SS 945 BC 945	ED/MD	261	210	88
	TRINITY churchoffice@trinityama.org www.trinityama.org	1921	5005 I-40 W 5005 W INTERSTATE 40	79106	TX	Ricky C Black	(806)352-5629 (806)353-7785	WS 9 6 SS 915	EL/ED/HC/ MD/SN	311	280	165
ANDERSON	*ZION* revrlamb@gmail.com	1882	455 FM 149 W PO BOX 409	77830	TX	Richard E Lamb	(936)873-2175 (936)873-2175	WS 10 SS 9 BC 9	ED/HC			
ANGLETON	*GOOD SHEPHERD* TedFelder@centurylink.net www.goodshepherdangleton.org	1982	1601 E HENDERSON RD	77515	TX	Robert L Sweet	(979)849-2223	WS 930 SS 1045 BC 1045	HC	74	62	31
ARANSAS PASS	*FAITH* faithlcaptx@gmail.com	1953	938 W LOTT AVE	78336	TX	David H Bergquist	(361)758-3145 (361)758-3145	WS 9 SS 11 BC 10	ED/HC	25	21	23
ARGYLE	*THE GROVE* rosalie@grovechurchntx.org grovechurchntx.org	2018	825 Sam Davis Rd 2650 FM 407 E SUITE 145-110 BARTONVILLE	76226	TX	Benjamin I Scheck	(817)709-9401	WS 9	ED/HC/MD	154	117	92
ARLINGTON	*BEAUTIFUL SAVIOR* churchoffice@bslcarlington.org www.bslcarlington.org	1986	5851 NEW YORK AVE	76018	TX		(817)465-3164	WS 1030 SS 9	ED/HC/MD	72	67	36
	GRACE churchoffice@grace.lc grace.lc	1952	210 W PARK ROW DR	76010	TX	Douglas D Widger Steven M Roth	(817)274-1626 (817)861-0193	WS 930 SS 1045 BC 1045	EC/ED/HC/ MD/SN	371	346	178
	HOLY CROSS jaimeb@holycrossarlington.org www.holycrossarlington.org	1975	4400 W ARKANSAS LN	76016	TX	Luke C Madsen	(817)451-7561	WS 1030 SS 915 BC 915	ED/HC/ MD/SN	185	167	89
	*IGLESIA GRACIA** j.zamora77@yahoo.com		210 W PARK ROW DR	76010	TX		(817)751-0583					
	ST PAUL		See Fort Worth TX									
ATASCOCITA	*LAMB OF GOD*		See Humble TX									
ATASOCITA	*JOY*		See Houston TX									
ATHENS	*ST JOHN* lcmsathens@gmail.com stjohnathens.org	1982	451 LILA LN	75751	TX	Dr Seth T Davidson	(903)675-9598	WS 1030 SS 9	ED/HC/ MD/SN			
ATLANTA	*REDEEMER*	1980	Laws Chapel Rd FM 2328 PO BOX 882	75551	TX		(903)796-9030	WS 10 BC 9	HC/MD	34	33	25
AUBREY	*SAINT JOHN*		See The Colony TX									
AUSTIN	*ACTS* info@actschurchlakeway.com www.actschurchlakeway.com	2002	1304 R R 620 N 1304 RANCH ROAD 620 N LAKEWAY	78734	TX	Peter E Mueller	(512)263-8175	WS 10 SS 10	ED/HC/MD	180	149	55
	BEAUTIFUL SAVIOR bslcaustin@sbcglobal.net www.bslcaustin.com	1978	6830 S PLEASANT VALLEY RD	78744	TX	Jonathan C Bontke	(512)443-4947 (512)443-4947	WS 1045 SS 930 BC 930	ED/HC/MD	85	78	40
	BETHANY info@bethanyaustin.com www.bethanyaustin.com	1962	3701 W SLAUGHTER LN	78749	TX	Martin D Danner Bill R Woolsey	(512)292-8778	WS 745 9 11 SS 10 BC 10	EC/ED/HC/ MD/SN	1381	1071	648
	CHRIST office@christaustin.org www.christaustin.org	1946	300 E MONROE ST	78704	TX	John C Stennfeld	(512)442-5844 (512)707-8082	WS 930 BC 1045	HS/ED/HC/ MD	150	132	73
	GOOD SHEPHERD		See Cedar Park TX									
	HOPE officemanager@hopelutheranaustin.org www.hopelutheranaustin.org	1960	6414 N HAMPTON DR	78723	TX		(512)926-8574 (512)926-0708	WS 9 SS 1015 BC 1015	HS/ED/HC/ MD	130	99	45
	HOPE INTERNATIONAL nvicprov2918atx@hotmail.com		1811 Cameron Rd # 500 1500 W ANDERSON LANE	78753 78757	TX		(512)203-7140					
	JESUS OF THE DEAF jesusdeafchurch@gmail.com jesusdeafchurch.com	1960	1307 NEWTON ST	78704	TX	C B Wolfmueller	(512)442-1715	WS 3 BC 2	ED/HC/SN	20	19	15
	KING OF KINGS		See Round Rock TX									
	MOUNT OLIVE info@connectwithjesus.org www.mtoliveaustin.org	1978	10408 HIGHWAY 290 W	78736	TX	Jason D Wallingsford	(512)288-2370 (512)288-2375	WS 830 1030 BC 940	EC/ED/HC/ MD/SN	324	286	103
	OUR SAVIOR churchoffice@oslaustin.org www.oslaustin.org	1973	1513 E YAGER LN	78753	TX	Eric E Borchers	(512)836-9600 (512)836-4660	WS 9 SS 1030 BC 1030	HS/ED/HC/ MD/SN	263	198	88
	POINT OF GRACE		See Pflugerville TX									
	REDEEMER info@redeemer.net www.redeemer.net	1954	1500 W ANDERSON LN	78757	TX	Kevin T Westergren Michael S Knippa	(512)459-1500 (512)610-8809	WS 8 930 11 SS 930 BC 930	EL/HS/ED/ HC/MD/SN	1634	1321	607

*Indicates a new church start. A new church start is an intentionally organized gathering which comes together on a regular basis for the purpose of worship and/or Bible study and is intended to grow into a member LCMS congregation. WS =Worship Service; SS = Sunday School; BC =Bible Class; EC = Early Childhood; EL = Elementary School; HS = High School; ED =Education Ministry; HC =Human Care Ministry; SN = Special Needs Ministry; MD = Media Ministry (PC)=Partner Church Pastor. See Page 53 for the Table of Abbreviations for key to additional abbreviations

CITY	CONGREGATION EMAIL WEBSITE	YEAR EST	LOCATION MAILING ADDRESS	ZIP CODE(S)	DIST.	PASTOR(S)	PHONE FAX	WS SS BC	SCHOOLS/ MINISTRIES	STATISTIC Bapt	Conf	Avg Attend
AUSTIN	*REDEEMING GRACE* pastorfick@gmail.com www.rglcms.org		1010 W FM 1626	78748	TX	Steven J Fick	(512)695-2087	WS 1030 SS 9	ED/HC	91	84	45
	ST PAUL churchoffice@stpaulaustin.org www.stpaulaustin.org	1891	3501 RED RIVER ST	78705	TX	C B Wolfmueller William R Davis	(512)472-8301 (512)682-3404	WS 8 11 SS 930 BC 930	HS/ED/HC/ MD/SN	711	711	408
	UNIVERSITY Richard@ULCaustin.com ulcaustin.com	1953	2100 San Antonio 2100 SAN ANTONIO ST STE 110	78705	TX		(512)461-3425 (512)472-1199	WS 5	ED	1	1	15
AZLE	*ST PAUL*		See Fort Worth TX									
	THE EDGE edge.azle@gmail.com edge4all.com	1963	1313 Southeast Parkway 1313 SOUTHEAST PKWY	76020	TX	Stephen D Sandfort	(817)237-4822	WS 930 11	ED/HC/SN	174	133	127
BALLINGER	*BETHEL*	1950	1701 N BROADWAY ST	76821	TX	Thomas W Baden	(325)942-9275	WS 9 BC 8	ED			
BANDERA	*MESSIAH*		See Boerne TX									
BARTLETT	*FORTRESS*		See Harker Heights TX									
BASTROP	*EPIPHANY* church@epiphanybastrop.org epiphanybastrop.org	2021	SDA 3300 Highway 21 E 489 AGNES SUITE 112 BOX 117	78602	TX	Edward B Holschuh III	(512)907-0717	WS 1130 BC 10	HS/ED/HC/ MD	29	24	24
	HOLY CROSS		See Giddings TX									
BAYTOWN	*REDEEMER* redeemer.baytown@gmail.com www.redeemer-baytown.com	1927	1200 E LOBIT ST	77520	TX	Daniel M Schuetz	(281)422-2207	WS 10 SS 9 BC 9	EL/ED/MD	158	133	57
	*VERDAD Y VIDA** rev.antonio@yahoo.com		1200 E LOBIT ST	77520	TX		(281)422-2207					
BEAUMONT	*REDEEMER* bmiller328@gt.rr.com www.rlccc.com	1959	4330 CROW RD	77706	TX	Micah J Drengler	(409)892-3286	WS 10 SS 9 BC 9	EC	171	133	53
	ST JOHN secretary@stjohnbeaumont.org www.stjohnbeaumont.com	1903	2955 S MAJOR DR	77707	TX		(409)840-9915 (409)840-9140	WS 11 SS 10 BC 10	ED/HC/ MD/SN	266	189	77
BEDFORD	*CONCORDIA* mlasch@concordialutheran.org www.concordialutheran.org	1967	2503 BEDFORD RD	76021	TX	Dr Mark F Lasch	(817)283-3560 (817)283-2877	WS 9 11 SS 10 BC 10	ED/HC/ MD/SN	324	242	106
BELLMEAD	*ST PAUL* wecare@splcwaco.com www.splcwaco.com	1956	1301 HOGAN LN WACO	76705	TX	Dr Brian J Hesse	(254)799-3211 (254)412-0529	WS 8 1030 SS 915	ED/HC/ MD/SN	892	832	260
BELTON	*FORTRESS*		See Harker Heights TX									
	IMMANUEL LUTHERAN MINISTRIES Satellite Site of Immanuel Temple TX	2012	1215 S Wall ST	76513				WS 1030 SS 915				
BENBROOK	*CHRIST*		See Fort Worth TX									
	REDEEMER		See Fort Worth TX									
	ST PAUL		See Fort Worth TX									
BEXAR	*ST PAUL*		See San Antonio TX									
BIG SPRING	*ALIVE IN CHRIST* aliveinchristtx@gmail.com aicbigspring.org		2805 Lynn St 2805 LYNN DR	79720	TX	Robert C Roever	(432)264-7818 (432)264-7818	WS 1030 SS 930 BC 930	ED	30	25	25
	ST PAUL stpaullc@sbcglobal.net	1929	810 Scurry St PO BOX 3705	79720 79721	TX		(432)267-7163 (432)267-8876	WS 9 SS BC 915	ED/HC/MD	30	20	24
BISHOP	*ST PAUL* office@stpaulbishop.org www.stpaulbishop.org	1911	801 E MAIN ST	78343	TX	Thomas J Thierfelder	(361)584-2778	WS 1045 SS 930 BC 930		140	128	40
BOERNE	*MESSIAH* mmaloy@messiahboerne.org www.messiahboerne.org	1991	9401 DIETZ ELKHORN RD	78015	TX	Neil S Vanderbush	(830)755-4300 (830)981-8035	WS 1030 SS 915	EC/HS/ED/ HC/MD	212	192	83
BONHAM	*CLYDE COSPER TEXAS STATE VETERANS HOME* Satellite Site of Grace Paris TX	2008	1300 Seven Oak Rd	75418				WS 330				
BORGER	*GOOD SHEPHERD* gslcborgertx@gmail.com www.gslcborger.com	1998	100 Caprock PO BOX 656	79007 79008	TX		(806)274-2455	WS 9 SS 1015	ED/HC	28	23	13
	TRINITY tlc2737546@gmail.com	1939	212 W Jefferson St PO BOX 545	79007 79008	TX		(806)273-7546	WS 1030 BC 930	HC	43	37	12
BOWIE	*ST PETER* stpetertexscty@gmail.com www.stpetertex.com	1894	906 Hwy 59 N PO BOX 133	76230	TX	Mark K De Young	(940)872-1886 (940)872-8837	WS 1030 SS 930	ED/MD/SN	293	211	70
BRACKETVILLE	*CRISTO EL SALVADOR**		See Del Rio TX									
BRADY	*MOUNT CALVARY* mountcalvarybrady@gmail.com mclcbrady.wordpress.com	1923	814 SAN ANGELO HWY	76825	TX	Lewis L Lubke	(325)597-2498	WS 1030 SS 930 BC 930	ED/HC	36	31	22
BRENHAM	*BETHLEHEM* office@bethlehemwmpenn.org www.bethlehemwmpenn.org	1860	10202 FM 1935	77833	TX	Kelly D Krieg	(979)836-7303	WS 1015 SS 9 BC 9	ED/HC/ MD/SN	331	254	154
	GRACE grace@glcsbren.org www.gracebrenham.org	1935	1212 W JEFFERSON ST	77833	TX	Ryan J Ogrodowicz William H Holzer Isaac S Schuller	(979)836-3475 (979)836-0510	WS 9 SS 1030 BC 1030	EL/HS/ED/ HC/MD			
	HOLY CROSS		See Giddings TX									

*Indicates a new church start. A new church start is an intentionally organized gathering which comes together on a regular basis for the purpose of worship and/or Bible study and is intended to grow into a member LCMS congregation. WS =Worship Service; SS = Sunday School; BC =Bible Class; EC = Early Childhood; EL = Elementary School; HS = High School; ED =Education Ministry; HC =Human Care Ministry; SN = Special Needs Ministry; MD = Media Ministry (PC)=Partner Church Pastor. See Page 53 for the Table of Abbreviations for key to additional abbreviations

CITY	CONGREGATION EMAIL WEBSITE	YEAR EST	LOCATION MAILING ADDRESS	ZIP CODE(S)	DIST.	PASTOR(S)	PHONE FAX	WS SS BC	SCHOOLS/ MINISTRIES	STATISTIC Bapt	Conf	Avg Attend
BRIDGEPORT	*TRINITY* trinitylutheranbridgeport@yahoo.com www.trinitylutheranbridgeport.org	1893	1307 10th St PO BOX 247	76426	TX	Gerald N Epperson	(940)683-5604	WS 10 SS 845 BC 845	ED/HC	39	36	19
BRIGGS	*FORTRESS*		See Harker Heights TX									
BROOKSHIRE	*CHRIST* christlutheran@consolidated.net www.christlutheranchurchpattison.org	1890	35912 Royal Rd PO BOX 507 PATTISON	77423 77466	TX	Kory B Boster	(281)934-8218	WS 1030 SS 9 BC 9		55	45	28
	MEMORIAL LUTHERAN		See Katy TX									
BROWNSVILLE	*TRINITY* tlcbrownsville@att.net	1934	901 BOCA CHICA BLVD	78520	TX	Steven A Morfitt	(956)542-7024	WS 9	ED/HC/MD			
BROWNWOOD	*GRACE* glcpastor1@outlook.com glcbrownwood.com	1916	1401 1ST ST	76801	TX	Richard A Mittelstadt	(325)646-2045	WS 1015 SS 9 BC 9	ED/HC/ MD/SN	114	94	58
BRYAN	*BETHEL* office@blcbcs.org www.blcbcs.org	1940	4221 BOONVILLE RD	77802	TX	Randall C Bard Timothy P Eden	(979)822-2742 (979)822-4082	WS 830 1115 SS 10 BC 10	EC/ED	915	717	400
BUCHANAN DAM	*GENESIS* genesisoffice1225@gmail.com www.genesislutheranchurch.org	1994	15946 E State Highway 29 PO BOX 994	78609	TX		(512)793-6800	WS 10 SS 845 BC 845	ED/HC/MD	89	85	54
BUDA	*ST JOHN*		See Uhland TX									
BUFFALO	*OUR SAVIOR*		See Centerville TX									
BULVERDE	*MESSIAH*		See Boerne TX									
BURKBURNETT	*GRACE* graceburkburnett@sbcglobal.net	1945	410 E 3RD ST	76354	TX	William M Cody	(940)569-2706	WS 930 SS 830 BC 830		71	56	20
	TRINITY		See Iowa Park TX									
BURLESON	*CHRIST*		See Fort Worth TX									
	ST PAUL		See Fort Worth TX									
BURNET	*GENESIS*		See Buchanan Dam TX									
CANTON	*HOLY CROSS* holycrosscanton@yahoo.com www.holycrosscanton.com	1996	28171 W Hwy 64 PO BOX 851	75103	TX	Mark T Huston	(903)603-5071	WS 10 SS 9 BC 9		59	53	28
CANYON	*ST PAUL* lutheranchurchstpaul@hotmail.com www.stpaulcanyon.com	1952	2600 4TH AVE	79015	TX	Brian T Shane	(806)655-4086 (806)655-3870	WS 1030 SS 915 BC 915	ED	85	71	45
CARROLLTON	*LORD OF LIFE*		See Plano TX									
	*PRINCE OF PEACE** jaimegdesantiago@gmail.com		4000 MIDWAY RD	75007	TX		(469)653-7086					
	PRINCE PEACE sandy.ericksen@princeofpeace.org www.princeofpeace.org	1965	4000 MIDWAY RD	75007	TX	Micah D Miller Jeremiah A Bauer Sabir N Bashir	(972)447-9887 (972)447-0450	WS 8 1030 SS 915 BC 915	ED/HC/MD	958	773	441
	SOULTHIRST		See The Colony TX									
CASTROVILLE	*DIVINE SAVIOR*		See Devine TX									
	MOUNT OLIVE		See San Antonio TX									
CEDAR PARK	*GOOD SHEPHERD* pastoralcare@gstx.org www.gstx.org	1973	700 W WHITESTONE BLVD	78613	TX	Steven M Headley	(512)258-6227	WS 8 1030 SS 10 BC 10	EC/HS/ED/ HC/MD	580	525	350
	KING OF KINGS		See Round Rock TX									
CELINA	*SAINT JOHN*		See The Colony TX									
	*THE TABLE** kc@thetablecelina.org www.thetablecelina.org		229 Pecan St	75009	TX		(816)810-6940			35	23	25
CENTERVILLE	*OUR SAVIOR* pastor@oursaviortx.org www.oursaviortx.org	1976	171 Hwy 75 N PO BOX 505	75833	TX	Keith E Bowman Jr	(903)536-2019	WS 1030 SS 915 BC 915	ED/HC/MD	91	82	36
CHANNELVIEW	*JOY*		See Houston TX									
CIBOLO	*WORD OF LIFE* betterlife@wordoflife4u.com www.wordoflife4u.com		213 COY LN	78108	TX	Kenneth R Mitschke Philip S Doublestein	(210)566-2237	WS 830 945 11 SS 945 11	ED/HC	154	125	100
CINCO RANCH	*CHRIST*		See Brookshire TX									
CISCO	*REDEEMER* redeemerlutheranchurchcisco@ gmail.com www.redeemercisco.org	1965	1711 CONRAD HILTON BLVD	76437	TX	Keith A Reich	(254)442-2090	WS 1030 SS 915 BC 915	EC/ED/HC	153	129	59
CLARA	*TRINITY*		See Iowa Park TX									
CLARKSVILLE	*ST JOHN*	1918	Highway 82 W 2709 W MAIN ST	75426	TX	Mike L Kimmel		WS 8 SS 915				
CLEBURNE	*ASCENSION* church@ascensioncleburne.org www.ascensioncleburne.org	1962	205 S RIDGEWAY DR	76033	TX	Eddie R Scheler Jr	(817)645-9452	WS 8 1030 SS 9 BC 9	EC/ED/HC/ MD	262	211	116
CLEVELAND	*GOOD SHEPHERD* sec_gslc.lcms@yahoo.com	1967	901 PLUM GROVE RD	77327	TX		(281)592-6803	WS 1030 SS 915 BC 915		68	64	30
	*MI SALVADOR** nelsonhernandez@glocalmission.org		1680 Rd 3549 12510 DONNA DR HOUSTON	77067	TX		(713)351-9986					
CLIFTON	*IMMANUEL* immanuelclifton1@gmail.com	1886	911 W 3RD ST	76634	TX	James D Burke	(254)675-3281	WS 1030 SS 915 BC 915	ED/HC/MD	159	148	65

*Indicates a new church start. A new church start is an intentionally organized gathering which comes together on a regular basis for the purpose of worship and/or Bible study and is intended to grow into a member LCMS congregation. WS =Worship Service; SS = Sunday School; BC =Bible Class; EC = Early Childhood; EL = Elementary School; HS = High School; ED =Education Ministry; HC =Human Care Ministry; SN = Special Needs Ministry; MD = Media Ministry (PC)=Partner Church Pastor. See Page 53 for the Table of Abbreviations for key to additional abbreviations

CITY	CONGREGATION EMAIL WEBSITE	YEAR EST	LOCATION MAILING ADDRESS	ZIP CODE(S)	DIST.	PASTOR(S)	PHONE FAX	WS SS BC	SCHOOLS/ MINISTRIES	Bapt	Conf	Avg Attend
COAHOMA	*ALIVE IN CHRIST*		See Big Spring TX									
COLLEGE STATION	*BETHEL*		See Bryan TX									
	HOLY CROSS office@holycrossbcs.org www.holycrossbcs.org	1983	1200 FOXFIRE DR COLLEGE STA	77845	TX	Michael A Hafer	(979)764-3992 (979)693-2950	WS 815 1045 SS 930 BC 930	EC/ED/HC/ MD/SN	801	671	389
	*UNIV CHAPEL** UniveristyLutheranCS@gmail.com ulctamu.org	1965	500 College Main PO BOX 315	77840 77841	TX		(979)846-6687	WS 1030	ED/HC			
COLLEYVILLE	*CONCORDIA*		See Bedford TX									
	CROWN OF LIFE church@crownoflife.org www.crownoflife.church	1989	6605 PLEASANT RUN RD	76034	TX	James M Richardson Jr Travis M Hartjen	(817)421-5683 (817)421-9263	WS 815 1045 SS 930	EL/ED/HC/ MD/SN	668	536	300
COMFORT	*MESSIAH*		See Boerne TX									
COMMERCE	*TRINITY* trinitycommerce1502@gmail.com	1968	1502 MONROE ST	75428	TX	Arthur B Farrow	(903)583-5155	WS 9 BC 8	ED/HC/SN	30	30	26
CONROE	*LAZARUS*		See Spring TX									
	LIVING SAVIOR		See Montgomery TX									
	PROJECT 242 AT BRISTOL PARK Satellite Site of Joy Houston TX	2024	608 Conroe Medical Dr	77304								
	PROJECT 242 AT VILLAGE GREEN CONROE Satellite Site of Joy Houston TX	2024	404 S Loop 336 W	77304								
	ST MARK office@stmarkconroe.org stmarkconroe.org	1958	2100 TICKNER ST	77301	TX	Brian R Bestian	(936)756-6335	WS 9 SS 1030 BC 1030	HS/HC/SN	255	215	131
	ST THOMAS		See Magnolia TX									
CONVERSE	*WORD OF LIFE*		See Cibolo TX									
COPPERAS COVE	*FORTRESS*		See Harker Heights TX									
	IMMANUEL teamilc125@gmail.com	1894	922 LUTHERAN CHURCH RD	76522	TX	David D Reedy	(254)547-3498 (254)547-3498	WS 11 SS 10	ED/HC/SN	120	115	55
	TRINITY trinitylcms76522@gmail.com www.trinitycopperascove.com	1956	518 E Highway 190 518 E BUSINESS 190	76522	TX	David D Reedy	(254)547-2225 (254)547-2225	WS 930 SS 1030	ED/HC/SN	129	94	47
COPPERFIELD	*EPIPHANY*		See Houston TX									
COPPERSCOVE	*STONEY BROOK ASSISTED LIVING* Satellite Site of Trinity Copperas Cove TX	2017	1808 Martin Luther King Jr Dr	76523								
CORINTH	*HOPE* hlct.net		2550 POST OAK DR	76210	TX	Charles W Hamit	(940)497-4753	WS 1030 SS 9	ED/HC/SN			
CORPUS CHRISTI	*LORD OF LIFE* lordoflifecorpuschristi.org	1989	1317 FLOUR BLUFF DR CORP CHRISTI	78418	TX		(361)937-8158 (361)937-1796	WS 9 SS 1030 BC 1030	EC/ED	59	59	45
	MESSIAH mlc@stx.rr.com messiahlcms-cc.org	1982	4102 TRINITY RIVER DR	78410	TX	John S Cotner	(361)387-7748 (361)767-1768	WS 9 SS 10 BC 10	ED/HC/ MD/SN	156	130	31
	MOUNT OLIVE mtoliveluthcc@gmail.com www.mtoliveluthcc.org	1952	5101 SARATOGA BLVD CORP CHRISTI	78413	TX	Kevin M Jennings	(361)991-3416 (361)991-8851	WS 8 1030 SS 915 BC 915	MD	246	167	94
	TRINITY OUR SAVIOR info@trinityoursaviorlutheran.com		808 LOUISIANA AVE	78404	TX		(361)884-4041	WS 1045	HC/MD	193	173	73
CORSICANA	*FAITH* jqmash@gmail.com www.faithlutherancorsicana.org	1964	3824 W Highway 22 3824 W STATE HIGHWAY 22	75110	TX	Joe Q Mashburn	(903)874-8795	WS 1030 SS 9 BC 9	ED/HC/ MD/SN	59	53	30
CRANDALL	*WATER OF LIFE*		See Forney TX									
CRESSON	*ST PAUL*		See Fort Worth TX									
CROCKETT	*GRACE* glccrocketttx@ymail.com gracelutherancrockett.org	1979	925 W LOOP 304	75835	TX	Thomas R St Jean	(936)544-3508 (936)544-3508	WS 1030 SS 9 BC 9	ED/HC/SN			
CROWLEY	*CHRIST*		See Fort Worth TX									
	ST PAUL		See Fort Worth TX									
CUERO	*CHRIST THE KING*		See Victoria TX									
CYPRESS	*CYPRESS CHAPEL* jerry@mcnamaras.org		c/o Creekwood Grill 12710 Telge Rd 14207 IMPERIAL SPRINGS CT	77429	TX		(832)576-6716					
	EPIPHANY		See Houston TX									
	*IGLESIA CAMINO NUEVO** angel@iglesiacaminonuevo.net		C/O SAINT JOHN LUTHERAN 15235 SPRING CYPRESS RD C/O SAINT JOHN LUTHERAN CHURCH 15235 SPRING CYPRESS RD	77429	TX		(832)946-2108					

*Indicates a new church start. A new church start is an intentionally organized gathering which comes together on a regular basis for the purpose of worship and/or Bible study and is intended to grow into a member LCMS congregation. WS =Worship Service; SS = Sunday School; BC =Bible Class; EC = Early Childhood; EL = Elementary School; HS = High School; ED =Education Ministry; HC =Human Care Ministry; SN = Special Needs Ministry; MD = Media Ministry (PC)=Partner Church Pastor. See Page 53 for the Table of Abbreviations for key to additional abbreviations

CITY	CONGREGATION EMAIL WEBSITE	YEAR EST	LOCATION MAILING ADDRESS	ZIP CODE(S)	DIST.	PASTOR(S)	PHONE FAX	WS SS BC	SCHOOLS/ MINISTRIES	STATISTIC Bapt	Conf	Avg Attend
CYPRESS	*LIFEBRIDGE* pastormichael@lifebridgecypress.org www.lifebridgecypress.org		16614 MUESCHKE RD	77433	TX	Michael J Meissner	(832)628-0072	WS 10	ED/HC			
	MEMORIAL LUTHERAN		See Katy TX									
	ST JOHN trueriches@stjohn.tv stjohn.tv	1853	15235 SPRING CYPRESS RD	77429	TX	David V Schultz	(281)373-0503 (281)373-5102	WS 815 11 SS 945 BC 945	EC/ED/HC/ MD/SN	2080	2080	683
	ST TIMOTHY		See Houston TX									
	THE FAMILY/FAITH dbo@thefamilyoffaith.org www.thefamilyoffaith.org	1991	9230 Fry Road 16710 FM 529 RD HOUSTON	77095	TX		(281)855-2950 (281)855-8301	WS 930 BC 1045	EC/ED/HC/ MD/SN	210	177	50
	ZION		See Tomball TX									
DALHART	*GRACE* vermedahl@xit.net	1977	1311 E 16th St PO BOX 1025	79022	TX		(806)244-2606	WS 830 SS 930 BC 930	ED	88	67	13
DALLAS	*BETHEL* churchoffice@betheldallas.org www.betheldallas.org	1953	11211 E NORTHWEST HWY	75238	TX	Christopher S Holder	(214)348-0420 (214)348-7756	WS 830 1030 BC 10 12 530	EC/EL/HS/ ED/HC/ MD/SN	238	171	173
	*BETHEL KINYARWANDAN** pastor.jospehng@gmail.com		11211 E NORTHWEST HIGHWAY	75238	TX		(214)348-0420					
	*BETHEL** walkernery@hotmail.com		11211 E NORTHWEST HWY	75238	TX		(214)348-0420					
	*COMUNIDAD** oscararicianga@hotmail.com		6121 E LOVERS LN	75214	TX		(214)284-4240					
	EMMANUEL ETHIOPIAN mekru4@gmail.com www.eecdallas.org		11211 E NORTHWEST HWY	75238	TX	Mekru Bekele	(972)674-7914 (214)348-7756	WS 11 SS 10	ED/HC/ MD/SN			
	*ERITREAN** kbrab@linchouston.org		6121 E LOVERS LN	75214	TX		(281)235-7707					
	HOLY CROSS admin@hcdallas.org hcdallas.org	1956	11425 MARSH LN	75229	TX	Noah T Menke Edilberto M Alzate	(214)358-4396	WS 930 BC 1045	EL/HS/ED/ HC/MD/SN	110	100	65
	*IGLESIA SANTA CRUZ** balzate@hcdallas.org		11425 MARSH LN	75229	TX		(214)358-4396					
	LORD OF LIFE		See Plano TX									
	OUR REDEEMER thickman@orlcs.com www.orlcs.com	1941	7611 PARK LN	75225	TX	Geoffrey B McGuire Adam N Douthwaite	(214)368-1371 (214)368-1473	WS 8 1045 SS 930 BC 930	EL/HS/ ED/HC			
	OUR SAVIOR	1949	3621 W Clarendon Dr C/O DON DORWARD 3319 W JEFFERSON BLVD	75211	TX		(214)331-6105	WS 1030 SS 915 BC 915				
	PRINCE PEACE		See Carrollton TX									
	ST PAUL www.splcdallas.org	1956	5725 S MARSALIS AVE	75241	TX	Byron R Williams Sr	(214)371-9429 (214)371-1211	WS 1030 SS 915	ED/HC/MD	120	110	60
	TREE OF LIFE		See Garland TX									
	*UMOJA INTERNATIONAL ** umojachurch3@gmail.com		11425 MARSH LN	75229	TX		(469)651-9813					
	WATER OF LIFE		See Forney TX									
	ZION rgoodwin@ziondallas.org www.ziondallas.org	1874	6121 E LOVERS LN	75214	TX	James H Ebersole Benyam Weldtensai	(214)363-1639	WS 8 1030 SS 910	EL/HS/ED/ HC/MD/SN	1083	848	300
	*ZION MULTIETHNIC** benaflus@gmail.com		6121 E LOVERS LN	75214	TX		(619)841-8030	WS 9				
DEER PARK	*CHRIST REDEEMER*		See La Porte TX									
DEL RIO	*CRISTO EL SALVADOR** info@cristoelsalvador.org cristoelsalvador.org	1982	204 WERNETT ST	78840	TX		(830)775-9904		HC	61	45	35
	GRACE www.gracelutherandelrio.360unite.com	1942	201 WESTERN DR	78840	TX	David G Nielsen	(830)308-3311	WS 9 SS 1030 BC 1030 4	ED/HC	23	18	12
DENISON	*GRACE* office@glcdenison.org www.glcdenison.org	1942	2411 WOODLAKE RD	75021	TX	David A Edge	(903)465-1016	WS 8 1030 SS 920	ED/HC/ MD/SN	280	218	135
	SAINT JAMES		See Windom TX									
DENTON	*ST PAUL* office@splcdenton.org www.splcdenton.org	1921	703 N ELM ST	76201	TX		(940)387-1575 (940)566-0005	WS 815 1045	EC/ED/HC/ MD/SN	231	175	135
	*THE STATION**		Unt University Union 1155 Union Cr #310710 C/O LAMB OF GOD LUTHERAN 1401 CROSS TIMBERS RD FLOWER MOUND	76203 75028	TX				ED			

*Indicates a new church start. A new church start is an intentionally organized gathering which comes together on a regular basis for the purpose of worship and/or Bible study and is intended to grow into a member LCMS congregation. WS =Worship Service; SS = Sunday School; BC =Bible Class; EC = Early Childhood; EL = Elementary School; HS = High School; ED =Education Ministry; HC =Human Care Ministry; SN = Special Needs Ministry; MD = Media Ministry (PC)=Partner Church Pastor. See Page 53 for the Table of Abbreviations for key to additional abbreviations

CITY	CONGREGATION EMAIL WEBSITE	YEAR EST	LOCATION MAILING ADDRESS	ZIP CODE(S)	DIST.	PASTOR(S)	PHONE FAX	WS SS BC	SCHOOLS/ MINISTRIES	Bapt	Conf	Avg Attend
DESOTO	*CROSS CHRIST* crossofchrist.org	1984	512 N COCKRELL HILL RD	75115	TX	John E De Young	(972)223-9340 (972)223-8432	WS 9 SS 1030 BC 1030	ED/HC/ MD/SN	165	160	48
DEVINE	*DIVINE SAVIOR* www.divinesaviorlc.org	1990	405 Ingram 405 INGRAM RD	78016	TX	Randall C Wehmeyer	(830)663-3735	WS 1030 SS 9 BC 9	ED/HC/ MD/SN	84	70	68
DIME BOX	*TRINITY* trinitydimebox@gmail.com	1900	3887 E Hwy 21 3887 E HIGHWAY 21	77853	TX	Bernard J Schey	(979)884-1471 (979)884-0441	WS 9 BC 1015				
DONNA	*ZION*		See Alamo TX									
DRIPPING SPRINGS	*MOUNT OLIVE*		See Austin TX									
DUMAS	*ST JOHN*	1943	207 S MEREDITH AVE	79029	TX	Troy D Scroggins	(806)935-2974	WS 1030 SS 9 BC 9	HC/MD	91	69	25
EDEN	*TRINITY*	1921	701 W Broadway PO BOX 245	76837	TX	Thomas F Obersat Sr	(325)869-4031	WS 11 SS 10	ED/MD	50	40	12
EDINBURG	*ZION*		See Alamo TX									
EDNA	*ST PAUL* stpauldnatx@att.net www.stpaullutheranednatx.com	1912	108 E GAYLE ST	77957	TX	Paul M Kaiser	(361)782-3037 (361)782-3364	WS 1030 SS 915 BC 915	EC/ED/HC/ MD	76	69	28
EL PASO	*ASCENSION* alc6520@swbell.net www.alconnect.faith	1960	6520 LOMA DE CRISTO DR	79912	RM	Richard K Schlak	(915)833-1009 (915)581-3216	WS 1030 SS 9 BC 9	EC/ED/HC/ MD/SN			
	CROSSPOINT mike@crosspointelpaso.com www.crosspointelpaso.com	1994	11995 MONTWOOD DR	79936	RM	David K Boone	(915)857-7492 (915)857-2679	WS 9 11 SS 9 11	ED/HC/ MD/SN			
	GRACE elpgraceoffice@att.net www.elpgrace.org	1957	9301 DIANA DR	79924	RM		(915)755-1322	WS 1030 SS 915 BC 915	ED/HC/ MD/SN			
	SAN PABLO sanpablolutheranchurch@gmail.com	1982	301 S SCHUTZ DR	79907	RM		(915)858-2588 (915)858-2708	WS 11 SS 1130 BC 945	ED/HC/ MD/SN			
	ZION info@zionelpaso.org www.zionelpaso.org	1898	2800 PERSHING DR	79903	RM	Dr Kirk E Triplett	(915)566-4667 (915)566-6677	WS 1030 SS 915 BC 915	EC/ED/HC/ MD/SN	345	251	82
ELECTRA	*IMMANUEL*		See Harrold TX									
	TRINITY		See Iowa Park TX									
ELGIN	*GRACE* GraceElginLCMS@Gmail.com www.graceelgin.org	1943	801 W 11TH ST	78621	TX	Carl D Roth	(512)281-3367	WS 915 SS 845 BC 845		244	197	94
ELLINGER	*MOUNT CALVARY*		See La Grange TX									
ENNIS	*GRACE* olarmy02@gmail.com www.gracelutheranennis.com/	1994	2402 W ENNIS AVE	75119	TX		(972)875-7680	WS 1015 SS 915 BC 915	HC	36	25	40
EOLA	*MOUNT CALVARY*	1930	12358 County Road 5500 PO BOX 636	76937	TX	Thomas W Baden	(325)942-9275	WS 11 SS 10 BC 10				
EULESS	*CONCORDIA*		See Bedford TX									
	OUR REDEEMER		See Irving TX									
	ST PAUL		See Fort Worth TX									
EVERMAN	*ST PAUL*		See Fort Worth TX									
FAIRFIELD	*TRINITY* trinitylutheranfairfield@gmail.com www.trinityfairfield.com	1973	1100 E COMMERCE ST	75840	TX		(903)389-4005	WS 9 SS 1030	ED/HC	35	35	21
FAIRVIEW	*IMMANUEL* immanuelfairview@att.net www.immanuelfairview.org	1995	301 COUNTRY CLUB RD	75069	TX	Tab C Ottmers	(972)540-1036	WS 8 1045 SS 915 BC 915	ED/HC/MD	162	111	114
FARWELL	*ST JOHN*		See Lariat TX									
FAYETTEVILLE	*MOUNT CALVARY*		See La Grange TX									
FEDOR	*HOLY TRINITY*		See Lexington TX									
FLATONIA	*MOUNT CALVARY*		See La Grange TX									
FLORENCE	*FORTRESS*		See Harker Heights TX									
FLOWER MOUND	*LAMB OF GOD* info@log.org www.log.org	1969	1401 CROSS TIMBERS RD	75028	TX	Dr Rance A Settle Mark E Payne Jae H Park	(972)539-5200 (972)539-8194	WS 8 1030 SS 915 BC 915	EC/ED/HC/ MD	976	837	437
FORNEY	*WATER OF LIFE* terri@wateroflifelc.org www.wateroflifelc.org		12340 FM 1641	75126	TX	Shawn L Deterding	(972)552-9393	WS 8 1030 SS 845	ED/HC/MD	168	137	65
FORSAN	*ALIVE IN CHRIST*		See Big Spring TX									
FORT HOOD	*FORTRESS*		See Harker Heights TX									
FORT STOCKTON	*FAITH* faithfortstockton@gmail.com www.redeemeralpinetx.com/faith-ftstockton	1956	705 N Rio St PO BOX 1481	79735	TX			WS 10				
FORT WORTH	*CHRIST* office@christfortworth.com www.christfortworth.com	1952	4409 SYCAMORE SCHOOL RD	76133	TX	Dr Stacy D Rollefson	(817)370-6242 (817)370-8600	WS 930 SS 11	ED/HC/ MD/SN	203	175	81

*Indicates a new church start. A new church start is an intentionally organized gathering which comes together on a regular basis for the purpose of worship and/or Bible study and is intended to grow into a member LCMS congregation. WS =Worship Service; SS = Sunday School; BC =Bible Class; EC = Early Childhood; EL = Elementary School; HS = High School; ED =Education Ministry; HC =Human Care Ministry; SN = Special Needs Ministry; MD = Media Ministry (PC)=Partner Church Pastor. See Page 53 for the Table of Abbreviations for key to additional abbreviations

CONGREGATIONS

CITY	CONGREGATION EMAIL WEBSITE	YEAR EST	LOCATION MAILING ADDRESS	ZIP CODE(S)	DIST.	PASTOR(S)	PHONE FAX	WS SS BC	SCHOOLS/ MINISTRIES	STATISTIC Bapt	Conf	Avg Attend
FORT WORTH	*LIGHT OF THE WORLD* office@lotwchurch.org www.lotwchurch.org		8750 N RIVERSIDE DR	76244	TX	Dr Gregory D Beutel	(817)750-0444 (817)750-0447	WS 830 945 11 SS 945	EC/ED/MD	365	300	365
	MESSIAH		See Keller TX									
	REDEEMER www.redeemerfw.org	1954	4513 WILLIAMS RD BEN-BROOK	76116	TX	Richard C Stephens	(817)560-0030 (817)560-0031	WS 1030 SS 9	ED/HC/MD			
	ST PAUL daphne.fernstrom@sharingnewlife.com www.sharingnewlife.com	1893	1800 WEST FWY	76102	TX	Andrew A Audette Troy A Miklos Nathan A Abel Barrett H Grebing Isaac L Lujang	(817)332-2281 (817)332-2640	WS 8 1050 11 SS 930 BC 930	EL/ED/HC/ MD/SN	1875	1352	970
	THE EDGE		See Azle TX									
FRANKLIN	*SHEPHERD PRAIRIE* sotp@windstream.net		105 E Decherd St PO BOX 1296	77856	TX		(979)828-3807	WS 10 SS 9	ED/HC			
FREDERICKSBURG	*RESURRECTION* resurrectionfbgtx@gmail.com www.resurrectionfbg.org	1989	2215 N LLANO ST FREDER-ICKSBRG	78624	TX		(830)997-9408	WS 1030 SS 9 BC 9	HC	79	79	45
FRIENDSWOOD	*HOPE* kkohn@hope-lutheran.org www.hope-lutheran.org	1962	1804 S FRIENDSWOOD DR	77546	TX	Dr Joshua M LeBorious	(281)482-7943	WS 8 11 SS 1045 BC 1045	EC/ED/MD	616	537	298
	MOUNT OLIVE		See Houston TX									
FRISCO	*LORD OF LIFE*		See Plano TX									
	SAINT JOHN		See The Colony TX									
	SOUTHIRST		See The Colony TX									
	WATERS EDGE office@watersedgefrisco.com www.watersedgefrisco.com		5475 Coit Rd PO BOX 894	75035 75034	TX	Troy M Schmidt Karl A Ashcraft Oscar O Benavides William R Kemp Andrew D Whaley	(972)712-7377	WS 10 SS 10	ED/MD	607	485	360
FT. DAVIS	*REDEEMER*		See Alpine TX									
FULSHEAR	*CHRIST*		See Brookshire TX									
	MEMORIAL LUTHERAN		See Katy TX									
GAINESVILLE	*FAITH* faithgainesville@outlook.com www.faithgainesville.net	1975	1823 Luther Ln PO BOX 1199	76240 76241	TX	Paul Q Terral	(940)668-7147 (940)668-1412	WS 1015 SS 9	ED/HC	88	85	58
GALENA PARK	*PEACE*	1946	1810 11TH ST	77547	TX		(713)674-3111 (713)674-3111	WS 10 SS 11 BC 11				
GALVESTON	*ST JOHN* patmostx@gmail.com www.stjohngalveston.org	1921	1121 39TH ST	77550	TX	M A Taylor	(409)762-2702 (409)762-2702	WS 1015	ED/HC/MD	158	147	60
GARDEN RIDGE	*WORD OF LIFE*		See Cibolo TX									
GARLAND	*ALL NATIONS** irfanwilson@yahoo.com		2929 S 1ST ST	75041	TX							
	CONCORDIA concordia@concordiatx.org www.ConcordiaTX.org	1981	5702 N JUPITER RD	75044	TX	Kenneth C Knippa	(972)495-4714	WS 8 1045 SS 930 BC 930	EL/HS/ED/ HC/MD/SN	156	145	80
	*NEW LIFE COMMUNITY**	2009	2929 S First St 1419 RIO HONDO DR DALLAS	75041 75218	TX		(214)563-7463	WS 1130 SS 10	ED			
	TREE OF LIFE tolsec@treeoflifelcms.org www.treeoflifelcms.org	1986	6318 LYONS RD	75043	TX	Mark T Couser Mark A Hotopp	(972)226-6086 (972)226-1545	WS 1030 SS 9	ED/HC/ MD/SN	236	225	78
GATESVILLE	*ST PAUL*		See The Grove TX									
GEORGETOWN	*FAITH* secfaith@flcms.org flcms.org	1981	4010 WILLIAMS DR	78628	TX	Dr James F Marriott John F Selle	(512)863-7332 (512)819-0430	WS 815 11 SS 945 BC 945	EC/HS/ED/ HC/MD/SN	1069	949	484
	KING OF KINGS		See Round Rock TX									
	NARRATIVE		See Round Rock TX									
	ZION church@zionwalburg.org www.zionwalburg.org	1882	6001 FM 1105	78626	TX	Zachary McIntosh Kyle D Borcherding Kevin J Hintze	(512)863-3065 (512)869-5659	WS 8 1045 SS 930 BC 930	EL/HS/ED/ HC/MD	1165	745	411
GIDDINGS	*HOLY CROSS* holycross@cvctx.com www.holycrosswarda.com	1873	600 Farm to Market 1482 PO BOX 69 WARDA	78942 78960	TX	Dustin M Beck	(979)242-3333 (979)242-3416	WS 9 SS 1015 BC 1015	HS/ED/MD	347	275	142
	IMMANUEL church@ilgtx.com www.ilgtx.com	1883	300 N Grimes 300 N GRIMES ST	78942	TX	Robert J Tiner Joshua R Hahn	(979)542-2918	WS 8 1030 SS 930 BC 930	EL/HS/ED/ HC/MD/SN			
GODLEY	*ST PAUL*		See Fort Worth TX									
GONZALES	*ABIDING WORD* abidingword@gvtc.com www.abidingwordgonzales.com		1020 St Louis St 1020 SAINT LOUIS ST	78629	TX		(830)519-4058	WS 1030	ED/HC/MD	38	38	32
GRAHAM	*FAITH* faithlutheran.graham@gmail.com	1969	1618 HWY 380 BYP	76450	TX	Dr Douglas R Kabell	(940)549-5155	WS 1030 SS 915	ED/HC/MD	34	28	13
GRANBURY	*OUR SAVIOR* oursavior.tx@gmail.com www.oursaviorgranbury.com	1974	1400 N MEADOWS DR	76048	TX	David E Schatte	(817)573-5011 (817)579-9479	WS 10 SS 845 BC 845	EC/ED/HC/ MD/SN	179	169	119
	ST PAUL		See Fort Worth TX									

*Indicates a new church start. A new church start is an intentionally organized gathering which comes together on a regular basis for the purpose of worship and/or Bible study and is intended to grow into a member LCMS congregation. WS =Worship Service; SS = Sunday School; BC =Bible Class; EC = Early Childhood; EL = Elementary School; HS = High School; ED =Education Ministry; HC =Human Care Ministry; SN = Special Needs Ministry; MD = Media Ministry (PC)=Partner Church Pastor. See Page 53 for the Table of Abbreviations for key to additional abbreviations

CITY	CONGREGATION EMAIL WEBSITE	YEAR EST	LOCATION MAILING ADDRESS	ZIP CODE(S)	DIST.	PASTOR(S)	PHONE FAX	WS SS BC	SCHOOLS/ MINISTRIES	STATISTIC Bapt	Conf	Avg Attend
GRAND PRAIRIE	*BEAUTIFUL SAVIOR*		See Arlington TX									
	FAITH admin@flcgp.com www.flcgp.com	1946	2200 SW 3RD ST	75051	TX		(972)264-2511	WS 1045 BC 930	ED/HC/ MD/SN	119	90	45
	OUR REDEEMER		See Irving TX									
GRAPEVINE	*OUR REDEEMER*		See Irving TX									
GROVES	*LA TRINIDAD** mario@linchouston.org		5801 W JEFFERSON BLVD	77619	TX		(832)262-5355					
	PEACE peacelutheran.groves@gmail.com peacelutherangroves.org	2022	5801 W JEFFERSON	77619	TX	Phillip L Phifer	(409)962-1133	WS 9 SS 1030	ED/HC/ MD/SN	181	157	80
GUN BARREL CITY	*ST PETER* Stpetergbc.org	1974	130 LUTHER LN GUN BARREL CY	75156	TX		(903)887-0436 (903)887-3051	WS 10 BC 845	EC/ED/HC/ MD/SN			
HAMILTON	*SAINT PAULS*	1886	1446 FM3340 1446 FM 3340	76531	TX		(254)386-5976	WS 1030 SS 930 BC 930	ED			
	ST JOHN stjohnlutheranoffice@gmail.com www.stjohnhamilton.org	1936	122 CHEYENNE MESA	76531	TX	Aaron C Kalbas	(254)386-3158 (254)386-3159	WS 10 SS 9 BC 9	EC/ED/HC/ MD	581	464	165
HARKER HEIGHTS	*FORTRESS* ryan@fortress.today www.fortress.today	2018	13960 FM 2410 PO BOX 3678	76548	TX	Ryan W Pennington	(254)393-0669	WS 10 SS 9 BC 9	ED/HC/ MD/SN	84	56	54
HARLINGEN	*ST PAUL* church@splch.com www.stpaultexas.com	1923	602 MORGAN BLVD	78550	TX	Nathan M Wendorf Jose M Franco-Arango	(956)423-3924 (956)423-3942	WS 830 1030 SS 915 BC 915	EC/ED/HC/ MD/SN	663	459	226
HARROLD	*IMMANUEL*	1933	19113 COUNTY ROAD 132 E	76364	TX		(940)886-2342	WS 8 4 SS 9 BC 9		50	40	32
HASLET	*HOLY SHEPHERD* cb2890@att.net holy-shepherd.com/	1995	1500 FM 156 S	76052	TX	Christopher J Bramich	(817)439-2100 (817)439-2100	WS 1030 SS 915	EC/ED	191	165	94
HAWKINS	*TRINITY-HAWKINS* Satellite Site of Trinity Tyler TX	2004	3718 S FM 2869	75765				WS 1030 BC 9				
HELOTES	*MOUNT OLIVE*		See San Antonio TX									
HEMPSTEAD	*SALEM*		See Navasota TX									
	ST THOMAS		See Magnolia TX									
HEREFORD	*IMMANUEL*	1914	100 AVENUE B	79045	TX		(806)346-2740			13	11	8
HEWITT	*PEACE*		See Waco TX									
	TRINITY		See Woodway TX									
HILLSBORO	*CHRIST* clchillsboro@att.net	1947	915 CORSICANA HWY	76645	TX	Michael C Nemec	(254)582-5782 (254)582-5782	WS 1030 SS 9 BC 9	ED/HC/MD	215	177	71
HILLTOP LAKES	*OUR SAVIOR*		See Centerville TX									
HOCKLEY	*ST THOMAS*		See Magnolia TX									
HOLLAND	*FORTRESS*		See Harker Heights TX									
HONDO	*DIVINE SAVIOR*		See Devine TX									
HONEY GROVE	*SAINT JAMES*		See Windom TX									
HORIZON CITY	*ZION*		See El Paso TX									
HORSESHOE BAY	*GENESIS*		See Buchanan Dam TX									
HOUSTON	*CENTRO DE FEY**		1300 Hugh Rd	77067	TX		(713)673-7862 (713)673-4439	WS 1030 SS 12 BC 12				
	*CENTRO FAMILIAR** jesussantos70@hotmail.com		1353 WITTE RD	77055	TX		(713)826-6573					
	CHRIST MEMORIAL admin@cmlhouston.org www.CMLHouston.org	1966	14200 MEMORIAL DR	77079	TX	Jason A Moreno	(281)497-0250	WS 815 1045 SS 930	EC/ED/HC/ MD/SN	279	250	139
	CONCORDIA church@clc-h.org concordialutheranhouston.com	1958	4115 BLALOCK RD	77080	TX	Russell A Etzel	(713)462-4040	WS 9 SS 1015 BC 1015	ED/HC/ MD/SN	102	90	40
	*CRISTIAN EL BUEN** noenoe3481@gmail.com		5645 Hillcroft St #203 5645 HILLCROFT ST STE 203	77036	TX		(281)222-7938					
	*CRISTIANA EMANUEL** nelo1881@hotmail.com		1504 JOHNSON ST	77007	TX		(703)973-3996					
	EPIPHANY congillett@elcsh.org www.elcsh.org	1984	14423 WEST RD	77041	TX	Jeffrey A Muchow David A Leeland	(713)896-1773 (713)896-7568	WS 8 1045 SS 930	EL/HS/ED/ HC/MD/SN			
	ERITREAN		8601 Chimney Rock 8601 CHIMNEY ROCK RD	77096	TX		(713)666-3693		ED/HC/MD			
	FISHERS OF MEN		See Sugar Land TX									
	GETHSEMANE glchouston@sbcglobal.net www.gethsemanelutheran.org	1953	4040 WATONGA BLVD	77092	TX	James R Jennings	(713)688-5227 (713)688-5235	WS 9 SS 1015	EC/ED/MD	394	299	60
	GLORIA DEI gloriadei@gdlc.org www.gdlc.org	1966	18220 UPPER BAY RD	77058	TX	Daniel W Schepmann Steven A Garrabrant Randy J Miller Nelson Rodriguez	(281)333-4535	WS 830 11 SS 945 BC 945	EC/ED/HC/ MD	1861	1372	994
	HILLTOP seungwoong@gmail.com hilltophouston.org		St Andrew Lutheran Church 1353 Witte Rd 1353 WITTE RD	77055	TX	Seungwoong Ok	(713)463-5954 (713)463-8837	WS 1130 SS 1030	ED/HC/ MD/SN	75	73	40

*Indicates a new church start. A new church start is an intentionally organized gathering which comes together on a regular basis for the purpose of worship and/or Bible study and is intended to grow into a member LCMS congregation. WS =Worship Service; SS = Sunday School; BC =Bible Class; EC = Early Childhood; EL = Elementary School; HS = High School; ED =Education Ministry; HC =Human Care Ministry; SN = Special Needs Ministry; MD = Media Ministry (PC)=Partner Church Pastor. See Page 53 for the Table of Abbreviations for key to additional abbreviations

CITY	CONGREGATION EMAIL WEBSITE	YEAR EST	LOCATION MAILING ADDRESS	ZIP CODE(S)	DIST.	PASTOR(S)	PHONE FAX	WS SS BC	SCHOOLS/ MINISTRIES	STATISTIC Bapt	Conf	Avg Attend
HOUSTON	*HOLY CROSS* holycross_ht@att.net www.holycross-lcms-houston.org	1940	2702 Rosalie PO BOX 8099	77004 77288	TX		(713)524-0192 (713)524-0192	WS 11 SS 10	ED/HC/MD			
	HOLY THREE IN ONE MarkDYMT@aol.com	1960	8311 Waterbury St PO BOX 801917	77055 77280	TX		(713)468-1815 (713)468-6735	WS 11 BC 930				
	*IGLESIA GLOCAL** nelsonhernandez@glocalmission.org		12510 DONNA DR	77067	TX		(713)351-9986					
	IMMANUEL churchoffice@immanuelhouston.org immanuelhouston.org	1919	306 E 15TH ST	77008	TX	Ian S Pacey Claudio Perez Sr	(713)864-2651 (713)864-8163	WS 9 SS 1030 BC 1030	EC/ED	141	112	68
	*JESUS CHRIST**		8601 CHIMNEY ROCK RD	77096	TX				ED/HC/ MD/SN			
	JOY joylutheranoffice@gmail.com www.joysummerwood.com		14450 WOODSON PARK DRIVE	77044	TX	Vernon J Sansom III	(832)850-5070	WS 1030 SS 915	MD	96	80	118
	LAMB OF GOD		See Humble TX									
	LIVING WATER	1962	10635 HOMESTEAD RD	77016	TX		(713)633-7276	WS 9	ED/MD			
	*MANANTIALES** rodrigo@linchouston.org		14225 HARGRAVE RD	77070	TX		(281)857-1878					
	MEMORIAL nmoerbe@mlchouston.org www.mlchouston.org	1956	5800 WESTHEIMER RD	77057	TX	Ned A Moerbe Dr Christopher S Ahlman Preus A Hasselbrook Robert W Paul	(713)782-6079 (713)975-1684	WS 815 11 SS 945 BC 945	EL/HS/ED	1198	968	459
	MEMORIAL LUTHERAN		See Katy TX									
	MESSIAH messiahhouston@att.net mlhouston.org	1923	816 ROY ST	77007	TX	Timothy A Engel	(713)861-3072	WS 9 BC 1015	EC/ED/HC/ MD	101	81	30
	MOUNT OLIVE sharon@mountolivehouston.org www.mountolivehouston.org	1945	10310 SCARSDALE BLVD	77089	TX		(281)922-5673 (281)922-5914	WS 1015 SS 9	EC/ED/HC/ MD	327	184	45
	OIKOS www.oikoschurch.org	2013	522 LINDALE ST	77022	TX	Aaron L Lytle Robert J Donaldson	(832)236-0645	WS 10	ED/HC/MD	104	47	35
	OUR SAVIOR church@osl.cc www.osl.cc	1945	5000 West Tidwell Rd 5000 W TIDWELL RD	77091	TX	Laurence L White Steven T Cholak	(713)290-9087 (713)290-0224	WS 930 SS 1045 BC 815	EL/ED/ MD/SN	997	806	388
	PILGRIM churchoffice@plchouston.org www.plchouston.org	1947	8601 CHIMNEY ROCK RD	77096	TX	Joshua P Duffy	(713)432-7082 (713)666-6585	WS 11 BC 9	ED/HC/ MD/SN	210	180	95
	*REDEEMED CHRISTIAN** george.adegboye@att.net		10800 Gessner Rd C/O LINC HOUSTON 1504 JOHNSON ST	77071 77007	TX		(713)927-4967					
	SAINT PETER pastor.raymond@stpeterdowntown houston.org www.StPeterDowntownHouston.org	1937	1501 HOUSTON AVE	77007	TX	Raymond J Van Buskirk Jose R Argueta	(713)485-6889	WS 930 BC 1045	ED	57	52	35
	SAVIOR REDEEMER bgadd@alivewithchrist.org www.alivewithchrist.org		215 RITTENHOUSE	77076	TX	Russell M Strimple	(713)691-2203	WS 9 1		75	63	61
	ST ANDREW office@standrew-lcms.org www.standrew-lcms.org	1954	1353 WITTE RD	77055	TX	Wynn T Derong	(713)468-9565 (713)468-1064	WS 930 SS 11 BC 1045	EC/ED/MD	129	96	34
	ST LUKE www.saintlukelutheran.org	1950	11025 ALDINE WESTFIELD RD	77093	TX	Scott R Heise	(281)442-2180	WS 9 SS 1015 BC 1015	ED/HC/MD	80	80	13
	ST MARK info@stmarkhouston.org www.stmarkhouston.org	1948	1515 HILLENDAHL BLVD	77055	TX	Matthew L Popovits Thomas J Winters	(713)468-2623 (713)468-6735	WS 9 1030 SS 9 1030 BC 9 1030	EL/ED/HC/ MD/SN	909	658	455
	ST MATTHEW office@stmatthewhouston.org www.stmatthewhouston.org	1926	5315 MAIN ST	77004	TX	Mark R Wiesenborn	(713)526-5731 (713)524-1709	WS 8 1045 SS 930 BC 930				
	ST MATTHEW WESTFIELD office.smlcw@gmail.com www.stmatthewlcms.com	1900	21434 E HARDY RD	77073	TX	Dr Ronald A Bogs Arturo G Mendez	(281)443-2304 (281)443-8463	WS 10 SS 845 BC 845	ED/MD	186	115	85
	ST TIMOTHY contactus@stlhouston.org www.stlhouston.org	1973	14225 HARGRAVE RD	77070	TX	Bradley W Jurischk Alexander D Lahue	(281)469-2457 (281)469-2921	WS 8 1045 SS 930 BC 930	EC/HS/ED/ HC/MD/SN	850	697	365
	THE TEGULU-REDEEMER		8888 W Bellfort St C/O PILGRIM LUTHERAN CHURCH 8601 CHIMNEY ROCK RD	77031 77096	TX	Vijay Gurrala						
	TRINITY kdavis@trinitydt.org www.trinitydt.org	1879	800 HOUSTON AVE	77007	TX	Michael P Dorn Donald G Black Gregory A Finke Lonnie A Gonzales	(713)224-0684 (713)224-0685	WS 9 SS 1015 BC 1015	ED/HC/ MD/SN	1253	1002	260
	TRINITY LUTHERAN CHURCH SATELLITE SERVICE Satellite Site of Trinity Houston TX	2017	1316 Washington Ave	77002								
	*VIDA NUEVA** vidanuevapastoralfredo@gmail.com		16710 FM 529 15427 HAZEL THICKET TRL CYPRESS	77095 77429	TX		(832)618-5956					
	VIETNAMESE nguyendungandrew@yahoo.com vietnameselutheranchurch.net	1992	14200 MEMORIAL DR.	77079	TX	Dung C Nguyen	(503)516-4660 (503)516-4660		ED/HC/ MD/SN	12	5	20
	ZION		See Tomball TX									

*Indicates a new church start. A new church start is an intentionally organized gathering which comes together on a regular basis for the purpose of worship and/or Bible study and is intended to grow into a member LCMS congregation. WS =Worship Service; SS = Sunday School; BC =Bible Class; EC = Early Childhood; EL = Elementary School; HS = High School; ED =Education Ministry; HC =Human Care Ministry; SN = Special Needs Ministry; MD = Media Ministry (PC)=Partner Church Pastor. See Page 53 for the Table of Abbreviations for key to additional abbreviations

CITY	CONGREGATION EMAIL WEBSITE	YEAR EST	LOCATION MAILING ADDRESS	ZIP CODE(S)	DIST.	PASTOR(S)	PHONE FAX	WS SS BC	SCHOOLS/ MINISTRIES	Bapt	Conf	Avg Attend
HUDSON OAKS	*ST PAUL*		See Fort Worth TX									
HUFFMAN	*LAMB OF GOD*		See Humble TX									
	OUR SHEPHERD secretary@voicehandsfeet4him.org voicehandsfeet4him.org	1964	24915 FM 2100 PO BOX 1509	77336	TX	John M Moore		WS 9 SS 1015 BC 1015		207	146	68
HUMBLE	*JOY*		See Houston TX									
	LAMB OF GOD office@lambofgod.net www.lambofgod.net	1977	1400 BYPASS 1960 E	77338	TX	Anthony F Kobak	(281)446-8427 (281)446-0289	WS 8 1030 SS 915 BC 915	EC/ED/HC/ MD/SN	425	420	225
HUNTSVILLE	*FAITH* www.faithhuntsville.org	1957	111 SUMAC RD	77340	TX	Robert W Hemsath	(936)295-5298 (936)295-8266	WS 1030 SS 915	EL/ED/MD			
HURST	*GRACE DIVINE* minroberts1@yahoo.com		941 W BEDFORD EULESS RD	76053	TX	Sammy G Roberts	(817)404-7539					
	PEACE info@peacechurch.org www.peacechurch.org	1959	941 Bedford-Euless Rd 941 W BEDFORD EULESS RD	76053	TX	Brian S Weaver Jerome A De Beir Jr William D Rowland Wichieng T Wetnyangran	(817)284-1677 (817)284-3731	WS 830 11 BC 945	EC/ED/HC/ MD	778	742	393
	ST PAUL		See Fort Worth TX									
HUTTO	*POINT OF GRACE*		See Pflugerville TX									
IOWA PARK	*GOOD SHEPHERD* goodshepherdlcms.org	1972	801 N 1st St PO BOX 386	76367	TX	William M Cody	(940)631-5219	WS 11 SS 10		9	9	6
	TRINITY trinitylcmsatclara@gmail.com www.trinitylutheranchurchofclara.org	1900	11867 FM 1813	76367	TX		(940)636-7433	WS 3	MD	20	18	11
IRVING	*OUR REDEEMER* orlc@orlc.org www.orlc.org	1964	2505 W NORTHGATE DR	75062	TX	Harry R Smith Juan A Zamora Nelson S Ortega	(972)255-0595 (972)257-0033	WS 10 BC 1115	ED/HC/SN	204	156	97
	OUR REDEEMER LUTHERAN MEN'S BIBLE STUDY Satellite Site of Our Redeemer Irving TX	2014	8120 Esters Blvd	75063								
JARRELL	*FORTRESS*		See Harker Heights TX									
JASPER	*ST PAUL* stjasperjasper@gmail.com	1972	P. O. BOX 1080	75951	TX		(409)384-8317	WS 11 SS 10	ED/MD	15	15	11
JEWETT	*OUR SAVIOR*		See Centerville TX									
JOSHUA	*CHRIST*		See Fort Worth TX									
	ST PAUL		See Fort Worth TX									
JUSTIN	*RECLAIM** travis.hartjen@icloud.com		15824 CABALLERO DR	76247	TX		(972)740-6033					
	ST PETER		See Roanoke TX									
KATY	*CHRIST*		See Brookshire TX									
	CROSSROAD info@crossroadkaty.org www.crossroadkaty.org	2022	700 S WESTGREEN BLVD	77450	TX	Dr Michael J Weider George D Holleway IV	(281)398-6464	WS 10	EC/ED/HC	800	500	475
	LIFEBRIDGE		See Sealy TX									
	MEMORIAL LUTHERAN assistant@mlckaty.com www.mlckaty.com	1945	5810 THIRD ST	77493	TX	Dr John F Davis Jr Dimas Jimenez	(281)391-0171	WS 9 BC 1030	EC/MD	610	450	277
	NEWCHURCH NewChurchTX@gmail.com newchurchtexas.com		26100 Cinco Ranch Blvd 7710 CHERRY PARK SUITE T-362 HOUSTON	77494 77095	TX	Henry F Hart	(832)786-8212	WS 10 SS 9 BC 9		145	140	100
KELLER	*LIGHT OF THE WORLD*		See Fort Worth TX									
	MESSIAH churchoffice@messiahkeller.org www.messiahkeller.org	1980	1308 WHITLEY RD	76248	TX	Thomas E Chryst Brennick T Christiansen	(817)431-2345 (817)431-8536	WS 8 1045 SS 930 BC 930	EL/ED/HC/ MD			
	ST PETER		See Roanoke TX									
KENEDY	*EAGLE FORD**	2014	PO BOX 52	78119	TX		(210)897-4880					
KERMIT	*ZION* zionkermit@gmail.com www.redeemeralpinetx.com/ zion-kermit	1958	400 Ne Ave PO BOX 516	79745	TX		(432)279-0744	WS 9				
KERRVILLE	*HOSANNA* heidi@hosannakerrville.org www.hosannakerrville.org	1989	134 CAMP MEETING RD	78028	TX	Timothy M Radkey	(830)257-6767 (830)257-4283	WS 830 11 SS 945 BC 945	ED/HC/MD	327	242	165
KILGORE	*PILGRIM* secretary@pilgrimlc.org www.pilgrimlc.org	1949	713 FLOREY ST	75662	TX	Dr Jayson S Galler	(903)984-4333 (903)984-4333	WS 1045 SS 930 BC 930	HC/MD	64	54	34
KILLEEN	*FORTRESS*		See Harker Heights TX									
	GRACE church@gracelcs.com www.gracelcs.com	1954	1007 BACON RANCH RD	76542	TX	Andrew W Green	(254)392-0717	WS 830 1115 SS 830 BC 830	EC/ED/HC/ MD/SN	202	178	95
KINGSBURY	*EVANGELISTS* ydavetrue@gmail.com	1887	7745 KINGSBURY RD	78638	TX	David L Truenow	(830)639-4906	WS 1030 SS 915 BC 930		48	48	20
KINGSLAND	*GENESIS*		See Buchanan Dam TX									
KINGSVILLE	*ST PAUL* stpaulsec@gmail.com www.stpaulkingsville.com	1918	521 E Doddridge PO BOX 1581	78363 78364	TX	Thomas J Thierfelder	(361)592-6531 (361)592-4134	WS 845 SS 1020 BC 1020	HC	244	185	58

*Indicates a new church start. A new church start is an intentionally organized gathering which comes together on a regular basis for the purpose of worship and/or Bible study and is intended to grow into a member LCMS congregation. WS =Worship Service; SS = Sunday School; BC =Bible Class; EC = Early Childhood; EL = Elementary School; HS = High School; ED =Education Ministry; HC =Human Care Ministry; SN = Special Needs Ministry; MD = Media Ministry (PC)=Partner Church Pastor. See Page 53 for the Table of Abbreviations for key to additional abbreviations

CITY	CONGREGATION EMAIL WEBSITE	YEAR EST	LOCATION MAILING ADDRESS	ZIP CODE(S)	DIST.	PASTOR(S)	PHONE FAX	WS SS BC	SCHOOLS/ MINISTRIES	STATISTIC Bapt	Conf	Avg Attend
KINGWOOD	*CHRIST KING* www.christ4u.net	1989	3803 W LAKE HOUSTON PKWY	77339	TX	Allen F Doering Mark A Hunsaker	(281)360-7936 (281)360-2965	WS 8 1030 SS 910 BC 910	EC/ED/HC/ MD	725	598	378
	LAMB OF GOD		See Humble TX									
KLEIN	*TRINITY KLEIN* www.trinityklein.org	1874	5201 SPRING CYPRESS RD	77379	TX	Lee A Hopf James A Bretthauer II Gene E Johnson Luis G Martinez	(281)376-5773 (281)251-7021	WS 815 1045 SS 930	EL/HS/ED/ HC/MD/SN	2251	1650	888
KYLE	*ST JOHN*		See Uhland TX									
LA GRANGE	*HOLY CROSS*		See Giddings TX									
	MOUNT CALVARY secretary@mtcalvary-lcms.org www.mtcalvary-lcms.org	1962	800 N FRANKLIN ST	78945	TX	Jason M Kaspar	(979)968-3938 (979)968-2918	WS 9 SS 10 BC 1015	EC/HS/ED/ HC/MD/SN	308	265	116
	ST MICHAEL'S		See Winchester TX									
LA PORTE	*CHRIST REDEEMER*	1973	8909 SPENCER HWY	77571	TX	Jesus Santos	(281)479-2201	WS 1030 SS 915 BC 915	MD			
	IGLESIA CRISTIANA * jesus@glocalmission.org		8909 Spencer Hwy 12510 DONNA DR HOUSTON	77571 77067	TX		(713)826-6573					
LACKLAND AFB	*MOUNT OLIVE*		See San Antonio TX									
LACOSTE	*DIVINE SAVIOR*		See Devine TX									
LAGO VISTA	*CHRIST OUR SAVIOR* coslutheran@live.com coslvtx.org	1987	21900 FM 1431 PO BOX 4973	78645	TX	Andrew L Thompson	(512)267-7121	WS 1030 BC 915	HS/ED/HC	120	116	49
LAKE JACKSON	*ST MARK* stmarksec@stmarklj.org stmarklj.org	1956	501 WILLOW DR	77566	TX	Terrance S Adamson	(979)297-2667 (979)299-3291	WS 8 1030 SS 915 BC 915	ED/HC/ MD/SN	342	272	70
LAKE WORTH	*THE EDGE - LAKE WORTH* Satellite Site of The Edge Azle TX	2020	3980 Boat Club Rd Suite 117	76135				WS 1030				
LAKEWAY	*ACTS*		See Austin TX									
LAMESA	*GRACE* glclamesa@gmail.com	1949	202 N Avenue G 380 PO BOX 380	79331	TX		(806)872-2858	WS 9 SS 1030	MD/SN	38	35	17
LAMPASAS	*FAITH* revtim@sbcglobal.net faithlampasas.com	1958	182 CR 4006 PO BOX 884	76550	TX	Timothy L Ochsner	(512)556-3514 (512)556-3514	WS 1045 SS 930 BC 930		162	139	60
LAREDO	*FAITH* faithlutheranchurchlaredo@outlook.com faithlutheranlaredo.org/	1947	2419 N Seymour Ave PO BOX 451610	78040 78045	TX	Erik J Ommen	(956)602-0175	WS 11 SS 930 BC 930	ED	33	32	15
LARIAT	*ST JOHN* st.johnlariat@gmail.com stjohnlutheranlariat.com	1921	US Hwy 84 725 COUNTY ROAD DD FARWELL	79325	TX	William D Rose	(806)825-2409 (806)825-2409	WS 930 SS 1045 BC 1045	EC/ED/HC/ MD/SN	149	99	30
LEAGUE CITY	*SOUTH LAKE* RBailey@SouthLakeLC.org southlakelc.org/		Hometown Heroes Park 1001 E League City Pkwy 240 W GALVESTON ST 2844	77573 77574	TX	Robert A Bailey Jr	(346)708-1202	WS 9 1030		105	90	58
LEANDER	*ACTS* hello@actschurchleander.com www.actschurchleander.com		1195 Sonny Dr PO BOX 1596	78641 78646	TX	Joshua M Miller	(512)337-6524	WS 930 1115	ED/HC/MD			
	GOOD SHEPHERD		See Cedar Park TX									
LEONA	*OUR SAVIOR*		See Centerville TX									
LEVELLAND	*EMMANUEL*		See Littlefield TX									
LEWISVILLE	*LAMB OF GOD*		See Flower Mound TX									
LEXINGTON	*HOLY TRINITY* trinity-stjames.org	1870	1035 County Rd 309 PO BOX 247	78947	TX	Jonathan D Meyer	(979)773-2634	WS 830 BC 8		178	153	43
	SAINT JAMES trinity-stjames.org	1891	320 N Rockdale St PO BOX 247	78947	TX	Jonathan D Meyer	(979)773-2634	WS 1030 SS 945 BC 10		345	266	54
LIBERTY HILL	*LIBERTY HILL* office@missionlibertyhill.com www.missionlibertyhill.com		381 COUNTY ROAD 213	78642	TX	Michael D Cofer	(512)778-9310	WS 10 SS 9		114	111	58
LINCOLN	*CHRIST*		See Loebau TX									
	ST JOHN stjohnlincoln@yahoo.com	1886	Fm 1624 1012 PRIVATE ROAD 8012 GIDDINGS	78948 78942	TX	Dale E Bohm	(512)253-6350	WS 9 SS 8 BC 8		469	379	178
LITTLE ELM	*SAINT JOHN*		See The Colony TX									
	SOULTHIRST		See The Colony TX									
	WATERS EDGE		See Frisco TX									
LITTLE RIVER ACADEMY	*FORTRESS*		See Harker Heights TX									
LITTLEFIELD	*EMMANUEL*	1917	409 W 3RD ST	79339	TX	Travis A Pittock		WS 1030 SS 930 BC 930				
LIVE OAK	*WORD OF LIFE*		See Cibolo TX									
LIVINGSTON	*TRINITY* trinitylivingston@gmail.com trinitylivingston.org	1967	221 Pan American Dr PO BOX 1163	77351	TX	Alexander C Garber IV	(936)327-3239 (936)327-3239	WS 1030 SS 9 BC 9	ED/HC/ MD/SN	65	57	40

*Indicates a new church start. A new church start is an intentionally organized gathering which comes together on a regular basis for the purpose of worship and/or Bible study and is intended to grow into a member LCMS congregation. WS =Worship Service; SS = Sunday School; BC =Bible Class; EC = Early Childhood; EL = Elementary School; HS = High School; ED =Education Ministry; HC =Human Care Ministry; SN = Special Needs Ministry; MD = Media Ministry (PC)=Partner Church Pastor. See Page 53 for the Table of Abbreviations for key to additional abbreviations

CONGREGATIONS

CITY	CONGREGATION EMAIL WEBSITE	YEAR EST	LOCATION MAILING ADDRESS	ZIP CODE(S)	DIST.	PASTOR(S)	PHONE FAX	WS SS BC	SCHOOLS/ MINISTRIES	STATISTIC Bapt	Conf	Avg Attend
LLANO	*GENESIS*		See Buchanan Dam TX									
LOCKHART	*ST JOHN*		See Uhland TX									
LOEBAU	*CHRIST* christloebau@zochnet.com www.christloebau.com	1892	4654 CR 114 4654 COUNTY ROAD 114 LINCOLN	78948	TX	David P Mumm		WS 9 SS 1015 BC 1015	HS/MD	177	133	55
LONGVIEW	*OUR REDEEMER* orlclview@gmail.com orlctx.jimdo.com	1966	1300 JUDSON RD	75601	TX	Loucan E Saling	(903)758-2019 (903)757-0554	WS 11 SS 930 BC 930	ED/MD	105	92	53
LORENA	*TRINITY*		See Woodway TX									
LOS FRESNOS	*JESUS AND TACOS BIBLE STUDY* Satellite Site of Table of Los Fresnos Los Fresnos TX	2025	116 E Ocean Blvd	78566								
	TABLE OF LOS FRESNOS thetablelf@gmail.com www.thetableoflosfresnos.org	2021	Los Fresnos Community Center 204 North Brazil St 111 E 7TH ST	78566	TX	Chad R Bresson	(956)254-0294			52	38	32
LUBBOCK	*CHRIST* secretary@christlutheranlubbock.org www.christlutheranlubbock.org/	1954	7801 INDIANA AVE	79423	TX	Daniel A Hinton	(806)799-0162 (806)799-2273	WS 1015 SS 9 BC 9	ED/HC/MD	181	149	83
	HOPE ehiner@hopelubbock.com www.hopelubbock.com	1989	5700 98TH ST	79424	TX	Eric D Hiner Stephen R DeMik	(806)798-2747 (806)798-3019	WS 830 11 SS 945 BC 945	EC/ED/HC/ MD	474	363	276
	REDEEMER redeemerlcms@yahoo.com www.rlcms.org	1932	2221 AVENUE W	79411	TX	Charles E Nemec	(806)744-6178 (806)744-3889	WS 930 SS 1045 BC 1045	ED/HC/MD	69	55	71
	*STUDENT CENTER** lsclubbock@gmail.com www.lsftech.org	1964	2615 19th St P.O. BOX 6176	79410 79493	TX		(806)763-3644	BC 5	ED			
LUCAS	*IMMANUEL*		See Fairview TX									
LUFKIN	*FIRST* firstlutheranlufkin@gmail.com sites.google.com/view/ first-lutheran-church-lufkin/home	1940	1001 ATKINSON DR	75901	TX	Kenneth L Bunge	(936)634-7468 (936)634-7469	WS 1015 SS 9 BC 9	ED/HC/MD	185	132	31
LYTLE	*DIVINE SAVIOR*		See Devine TX									
	MOUNT OLIVE		See San Antonio TX									
MAGNOLIA	*ST PAUL* secretary@saintpaulmagnolia.org saintpaulmagnolia.org	1975	21088 FM 1488 PO BOX 553	77355 77353	TX	Kenneth M Burkhard	(281)259-7818	WS 1015 SS 9 BC 9		54	48	42
	ST THOMAS office@stthomastx.church stthomastx.church	2024	Klein Funeral Home 14711 FM 1488 18640 FM 1488 STE A BOX 133	77354	EN	Stanley J Lacey	(281)206-4043	WS 9 BC 1015		72	49	53
	ST TIMOTHY		See Houston TX									
	ZION		See Tomball TX									
MANCHACA	*REDEEMING GRACE*		See Austin TX									
MANHEIM	*EBENEZER* manheim@zochnet.com	1876	4146 W HIGHWAY 21 PAIGE	78659	TX		(512)253-6636 (512)253-6797	WS 8 SS 9 BC 9	ED/HC/ MD/SN	115	93	65
MANSFIELD	*BEAUTIFUL SAVIOR*		See Arlington TX									
	ST JOHN info@stjohnmansfield.org stjohnmansfield.org	1980	1218 E DEBBIE LN	76063	TX	Jonathan R Thomas Jarrett D Jones Timothy B Perkins	(817)473-4889	WS 8 930 11 SS 930 BC 930	EC/ED/HC/ MD/SN	653	556	426
	ST PAUL		See Fort Worth TX									
MARATHON	*REDEEMER*		See Alpine TX									
MARBLE FALLS	*GENESIS*		See Buchanan Dam TX									
	HOPE hopeluthmf@gmail.com www.hopelutheranmf.org		3411 US 281 N PO BOX 656	78654	TX		(830)220-3664	WS 1030 SS 9 BC 9		53	52	36
MARFA	*REDEEMER*		See Alpine TX									
MARION	*WORD OF LIFE*		See Cibolo TX									
MARLIN	*GRACE*	1924	432 HOUGHTON AVE	76661	TX	Kurt G Rutz	(254)803-2475 (254)803-2475	WS 1030				
MARQUEZ	*OUR SAVIOR*		See Centerville TX									
MART	*GRACE*	1935	814 E TEXAS AVE	76664	TX	Kurt G Rutz	(254)876-2314 (254)876-2314	WS 830 SS 930 BC 930	HC/SN			
MATHIS	*TRINITY*		See Odem TX									
MCALLEN	*EL BUEN PASTOR* buenpastoronpecan@yahoo.com	1954	1929 W Pecan Blvd 1929 PECAN BLVD	78501	TX		(956)322-3887		ED/HC/ MD/SN			
	ST PAUL churchsecretary@stpaulmcallen.org www.stpaulmcallen.org	1916	300 W PECAN BLVD	78501	TX	Gregory M Lorenz	(956)682-2345 (956)682-7148	WS 8 11 BC 930	EL/ED/HC/ MD/SN	477	296	180
	ZION		See Alamo TX									
MCGREGOR	*TRINITY*		See Woodway TX									
MCKINNEY	*IMMANUEL*		See Fairview TX									
	OUR SAVIOR www.oslmckinney.org	1977	2708 W Virginia Pkwy 2708 VIRGINIA PKWY	75071	TX	Mark C Bray David R Thompson	(972)562-9944 (972)548-9673	WS 830 11 SS 945 BC 945	EC/ED/HC/ MD	832	740	463
	SAINT JOHN		See The Colony TX									
	WATERS EDGE		See Frisco TX									
MENARD	*GRACE* gracelutheranmenard@gmail.com www.facebook.com/Grace-Luthe ran-Church-Menard-83523161653 7687/	1938	Callan St PO BOX 715	76859	TX	Timothy S Rosenthal	(325)456-1875	WS 9 SS 10	ED/HC/MD			

*Indicates a new church start. A new church start is an intentionally organized gathering which comes together on a regular basis for the purpose of worship and/or Bible study and is intended to grow into a member LCMS congregation. WS =Worship Service; SS = Sunday School; BC =Bible Class; EC = Early Childhood; EL = Elementary School; HS = High School; ED =Education Ministry; HC =Human Care Ministry; SN = Special Needs Ministry; MD = Media Ministry (PC)=Partner Church Pastor. See Page 53 for the Table of Abbreviations for key to additional abbreviations

CITY	CONGREGATION EMAIL WEBSITE	YEAR EST	LOCATION MAILING ADDRESS	ZIP CODE(S)	DIST.	PASTOR(S)	PHONE FAX	WS SS BC	SCHOOLS/ MINISTRIES	Bapt	Conf	Avg Attend
MERCEDES	*IMMANUEL* immanuelmercedes@sbcglobal.net www.immanuellutheranmercedes.com	1909	703 W 3RD ST	78570	TX	Edmund J Weber	(956)565-1518 (956)565-1518	SS 1030 BC 1030	EL/ED/HC/ MD/SN	114	95	65
	*MISSION EMANUEL**		257 S WASHINGTON AVE	78570	TX		(956)463-1305			292	92	24
MEXIA	*FAITH* faithlutheran2013@att.net	1989	401 S Highway 14 PO BOX 1456	76667	TX	Joel D Hall	(254)562-7756	WS 930 SS 1045	HC			
MEYERSVILLE	*CHRIST THE KING*		See Victoria TX									
MIDLAND	*GRACE* office@gracelutheranmidlandtx.org www.GraceLutheranMidland.org	1930	3000 W GOLF COURSE RD	79701	TX	Dr John M Ramey	(432)697-3221 (432)697-3536	WS 1030 SS 915 BC 915	EC/ED/HC/ MD/SN	377	279	125
	HOLY CROSS holycross@holycrossmidland.org holycrossmidland.org	1990	5110 N GARFIELD ST	79705	TX		(432)570-8149 (432)618-0607	WS 930 SS 1045				
MIDLOTHIAN	*BEAUTIFUL SAVIOR*		See Arlington TX									
MILLSAP	*ST PAUL*		See Fort Worth TX									
MINERAL WELLS	*ST MARK* stmk@sbcglobal.net	1964	1201 SE 25TH AVE	76067	TX		(940)325-4282 (940)325-4384	WS 1030 SS 930 BC 930	ED/HC/MD			
MOFFAT	*ST PAUL*		See The Grove TX									
MONAHANS	*ST PAUL* stpaulmonahans@gmail.com www.redeemeralpinetx.com/stpaul-monahans	1952	1500 SOUTH MAIN STREET	79756	TX		(432)279-0744	WS 11 BC 9				
MONTGOMERY	*LIVING SAVIOR* office@livingsaviortexas.org livingsaviortexas.org	2008	310 LOUISA ST	77356	TX	David R Bailes Timothy S Douglas Jr	(936)597-8013 (936)597-7544	WS 8 1045 SS 930 BC 930	ED/HC/ MD/SN	355	297	166
	ST THOMAS		See Magnolia TX									
MOODY	*FORTRESS*		See Harker Heights TX									
	ST PAUL		See The Grove TX									
MOUNT PLEASANT	*GOOD SHEPHERD* goodshepherdmtpleasant@gmail.com www.goodshepherdmtpleasant.com	1975	2820 W FERGUSON RD	75455	TX	Mike L Kimmel	(903)572-4470	WS 1030 SS 930 BC 930	ED/MD	83	74	43
MURPHY	*FAITH*		See Wylie TX									
NACOGDOCHES	*REDEEMER* rlcnac@yahoo.com www.redeemerlutherannac.com	1960	2306 APPLEBY SAND RD	75965	TX	John W Cain	(936)564-6729 (936)564-2171	WS 9 SS 1020	ED/HC/MD	130	117	71
NASSAU BAY	*GLORIA DEI*		See Houston TX									
NATALIA	*DIVINE SAVIOR*		See Devine TX									
NAVASOTA	*SALEM* salemlutheranchurchwh@gmail.com www.salemwhitehall.org/	1893	2373 FM 2988	77868	TX		(828)838-5745	WS 10 SS 9 BC 9		110	102	47
	TRINITY office@tlcnavasota.com www.tlcnavasota.com	1933	1530 E WASHINGTON AVE	77868	TX	Matthias J Dinger	(936)825-6851	WS 9 SS 1030 BC 1030	EC/ED/HC/ MD	333	286	106
NEDERLAND	*HOLY CROSS* secretary@holycrossnederland.net holycrossnederland.com	1957	2711 HELENA AVE	77627	TX	Joshua A Knippa	(409)722-1609 (409)722-1194	WS 1030 SS 930 BC 930	EC/ED/HC/ MD	623	508	77
NEW BRAUNFELS	*CROSS* church@crossnbtx.org crossnbtx.org	1928	2171 COMMON ST	78130	TX	Dale L Brynestad	(830)625-3969	WS 10 SS 9 BC 9	EL/ED/HC/ MD/SN			
NEWARK	*VICTORY IN CHRIST* churchoffice@viclutheranchurch.org www.viclutheranchurch.org		508 MAIN ST	76071	TX	Dr Philip J Schielke	(817)489-5400	WS 10 SS 11 BC 11	EL/HS/ED/ HC/MD	68	56	34
NOACK	*CHRIST*		See Taylor TX									
NOLANVILLE	*FORTRESS*		See Harker Heights TX									
NORMANGEE	*OUR SAVIOR*		See Centerville TX									
NORTH RICHLAND HILLS	*GRACE DIVINE ** minroberts1@yahoo.com		7801 BRANDI LN SUITE G	76182	TX		(817)479-4914					
	LIGHT OF THE WORLD		See Fort Worth TX									
NORTH ZULCH	*BETHLEHEM* bethlehemnz@windstream.net	1882	5084 CHURCH LN	77872	TX	Randall J Smith	(936)399-5563	WS 945 SS 830 BC 830		127	90	55
NORTHLAKE	*ST PETER*		See Roanoke TX									
	THE GROVE		See Argyle TX									
NURSERY	*CHRIST THE KING*		See Victoria TX									
OAKWOOD	*OUR SAVIOR*		See Centerville TX									
ODEM	*TRINITY* patrick.kieschnick@gmail.com	1937	7912 FM 796	78370	TX		(361)364-2367 (361)364-2367	WS 930 SS 1030 BC 1030	ED/HC/MD	47	46	24
ODESSA	*EMMANUEL* dspiva@emmausalhambra.org www.emmanuellutheranodessa.org	1990	6450 E HIGHWAY 191	79762	TX		(432)366-9311 (432)366-6731	WS 11 SS 930 BC 930				
	HOLY CROSS		See Midland TX									
	REDEEMER rlc_824@hotmail.com www.redeemerodessa.org	1946	824 E 18TH ST	79761	TX	Erik W Stadler	(806)416-0951	WS 10 SS 9	ED/HC/ MD/SN	145	130	41
OKLAUNION	*IMMANUEL*		See Harrold TX									

*Indicates a new church start. A new church start is an intentionally organized gathering which comes together on a regular basis for the purpose of worship and/or Bible study and is intended to grow into a member LCMS congregation. WS =Worship Service; SS = Sunday School; BC =Bible Class; EC = Early Childhood; EL = Elementary School; HS = High School; ED =Education Ministry; HC =Human Care Ministry; SN = Special Needs Ministry; MD = Media Ministry (PC)=Partner Church Pastor. See Page 53 for the Table of Abbreviations for key to additional abbreviations

CITY	CONGREGATION EMAIL WEBSITE	YEAR EST	LOCATION MAILING ADDRESS	ZIP CODE(S)	DIST.	PASTOR(S)	PHONE FAX	WS SS BC	SCHOOLS/ MINISTRIES	STATISTIC Bapt	Conf	Avg Attend
OLNEY	*ST LUKE* stluke@brazosnet.com	1897	1302 W Oak St PO BOX 626	76374	TX	Sean D Reeves	(940)564-5466 (940)564-5466	WS 1030 SS 930 BC 930		158	132	45
ORANGE	*GRACE* gracelutheranchurchorange@ gmail.com	1958	2300 EDDLEMAN RD	77632	TX		(409)883-5145 (409)882-0034	WS 1030 SS 930 BC 930	HC/MD			
ORANGE GROVE	*FIRST EV* firstog@msn.com	1913	600 S Dibrell St PO BOX 605	78372	TX		(361)384-2712			139	116	73
OZONA	*FAITH*	1965	801 1st St PO BOX 818	76943	TX	Thomas W Baden	(325)942-9275	WS 7 BC 6				
PALACIOS	*OUR REDEEMER* orlc11@yahoo.com	1911	1206 4th St PO BOX 943	77465	TX		(361)972-3852	WS 8 SS 915				
PALESTINE	*BETHLEHEM* belctx@outlook.com www.belctx.org	1945	1515 S LOOP 256	75801	TX		(903)729-6362 (903)729-6362	WS 1015 SS 9	ED/HC/ MD/SN	100	92	46
PAMPA	*ZION* www.pampalutheran.org/	1942	1200 DUNCAN ST	79065	TX	Michael K Erickson	(806)669-2774	WS 1030 SS 915 BC 915		108	84	52
PARIS	*GRACE* secretary@graceluthparistx.com www.graceluthparistx.com	1947	739 19th St SE PO BOX 603	75460 75461	TX		(903)784-3753	WS 9 SS 1030 BC 1030	ED/HC/ MD/SN			
	ST PAUL church@stpaul-paris.com www.stpaul-paris.com	2024	VIP INN & SUITES 3560 NE LOOP 286	75460	EN	Toby O Byrd		WS 9 930 SS 1030 BC 1030		27	22	20
	SAINT JAMES		See Windom TX									
PASADENA	*ZION* zlcpastorbrady@gmail.com www.zionpasadena.com	1943	5050 E SAM HOUSTON PKWY S	77505	TX	Brady W Blasdel	(281)991-8600	WS 8 11 SS 930 BC 930	ED/HC/ MD/SN	277	252	142
PATTISON	*CHRIST*		See Brookshire TX									
PEARLAND	*EPIPHANY* pastor_jon@epiphanypearland.org www.shiningthelight.org	1990	5515 BROADWAY ST	77581	TX	Jon D Salminen	(281)485-7833 (281)485-5040	WS 830 1045 SS 945 BC 945	EC/ED/MD	958	809	313
	MOUNT OLIVE		See Houston TX									
PEARSALL	*ST PETER* st.peter.pearsall@gmail.com www.stpeterpearsall.org	1929	819 E BRAZOS ST	78061	TX	Thomas W Winter	(830)334-2336	WS 1030 SS 915 BC 915	HC/MD	52	42	23
PERRYTON	*BETHLEHEM*	1924	611 S Grinnel PO BOX 672	79070	TX		(806)435-3522		ED	11	11	7
PFLUGERVILLE	*KING OF KINGS*		See Round Rock TX									
	POINT OF GRACE pog@pointofgracechurch.org www.pog.church	2003	19507 FM 685	78660	TX	Delton R Weiser	(512)251-9095 (512)251-9095	WS 930 11 SS 11	EC/HS/ ED/HC	229	194	206
PHARR	*ZION*		See Alamo TX									
PLAINVIEW	*ST PAUL* Pastor_nathan@stpaulplainview.com www.stpaulplainview.com	1930	901 Oakland St PO BOX 595	79072 79073	TX	Stephen N Misch	(806)293-1697 (806)293-8420	WS 9 SS 1015 BC 1015	ED/HC/ MD/SN	155	125	63
PLANO	*FAITH* church@faithplano.org www.faithplano.org	1964	1701 E PARK BLVD	75074	TX	Mark M Taylor Timmothy W Heath Jr	(972)423-7447 (972)423-9618	WS 8 1045 SS 930 BC 930	EL/HS/ED/ HC/MD/SN	640	553	310
	FAITH		See Wylie TX									
	*GRACE** graceccir@yahoo.com		1801 W Plano Parkway 7217 SATURN DR ROWLETT	75075 75089	TX		(214)603-2703					
	LORD OF LIFE cindy@planolutheran.com www.planolutheran.com	1990	3601 W 15TH ST	75075	TX	Joel A Shaltanis	(972)867-5588 (972)985-5588	WS 8 1045 SS 930	ED/HC/ MD/SN	237	217	140
	MESSIAH messiah@messiahlutheran.com www.messiahlutheran.com	1957	1801 West Plano Pkwy 1801 W PLANO PKWY	75075	TX	Dr Victor J Kollmann Matthew A Lee Jace C Detrie	(972)398-7500 (972)398-7597	WS 830 11 SS 945 BC 945	EC/EL/HS/ ED/HC/ MD/SN	2712	2144	891
	*OROMO DALLAS** syadessa@gmail.com		1701 E PARK BLVD	75074	TX		(214)326-5969		ED/HC			
	SAINT JOHN		See The Colony TX									
	ST PAUL office@stpaulplano.org www.stpaulplano.org	1981	6565 INDEPENDENCE PKWY	75023	TX		(972)618-4266	WS 830 11 BC 10	EC/ED/HC/ MD/SN	118	86	52
	WATERS EDGE		See Frisco TX									
PLANTERSVILLE	*ST THOMAS*		See Magnolia TX									
PORT ISABEL	*FISHERS OF MEN* fishersofmenportisabel@gmail.com www.fishersofmenlutheran.com/	1991	603 S TARNAVA ST	78578	TX		(956)943-2005	WS 830 BC 930	ED/HC/ MD/SN			
PORTER	*LAMB OF GOD*		See Humble TX									
	THE DWELLING thedwellingtx@gmail.com		24862 Highway 59 PO BOX 2006 NEW CANEY	77365 77357	TX	Seth L Kunze	(281)299-1909			158	138	144
POST	*ST PAUL*		See Wilson TX									
PROSPER	*SAINT JOHN*		See The Colony TX									
RAYMONDVILLE	*MOUNT CALVARY* mtcalvaryraymondville@gmail.com mtcalvaryraymondville.org	1940	181 E WOOD AVE	78580	TX	Steven A Morfitt	(956)689-2224	WS 11 SS 10 BC 10	ED/HC/SN			
RICHARDSON	*CONCORDIA*		See Garland TX									

*Indicates a new church start. A new church start is an intentionally organized gathering which comes together on a regular basis for the purpose of worship and/or Bible study and is intended to grow into a member LCMS congregation. WS =Worship Service; SS = Sunday School; BC =Bible Class; EC = Early Childhood; EL = Elementary School; HS = High School; ED =Education Ministry; HC =Human Care Ministry; SN = Special Needs Ministry; MD = Media Ministry (PC)=Partner Church Pastor. See Page 53 for the Table of Abbreviations for key to additional abbreviations

CITY	CONGREGATION EMAIL WEBSITE	YEAR EST	LOCATION MAILING ADDRESS	ZIP CODE(S)	DIST.	PASTOR(S)	PHONE FAX	WS SS BC	SCHOOLS/ MINISTRIES	STATISTIC Bapt	Conf	Avg Attend
RICHARDSON	*LORD OF LIFE*		See Plano TX									
	MESSIAH		See Plano TX									
RICHMOND	*MEMORIAL LUTHERAN*		See Katy TX									
	SPIRIT OF LIFE life4u@sbcglobal.net		2414 HORSESHOE LN	77406	TX	Chad M Miller	(281)238-5531					
RIESEL	*TRINITY* bookkeeping@tlcriesel.org www.tlcriesel.org	1883	264 CR 143 PO BOX 447	76682	TX	Larry N Knobloch	(254)896-6043	WS 10 SS 9 BC 9	EC/ED/HC/ MD/SN	147	139	65
RIVER OAKS	*REDEEMER*		See Fort Worth TX									
ROANOKE	*ST PETER* www.stpeterfw.org	2006	15701 CLEVELAND GIBBS RD NORTHLAKE	76262	TX	Robert A Balduc	(817)491-2010 (817)491-2022	WS 10	EC/ED/HC/ MD	214	162	144
ROBINSON	*GATHERING* pastor@gatheringwaco.org gatheringwaco.org		635 NORTH ROBINSON DRIVE	76706	TX		(254)300-1466			77	52	59
ROCKDALE	*GRACE*	1955	247 N Wilcox St PO BOX 1416	76567	TX		(512)446-2978	WS 10 SS 9 BC 9				
ROCKPORT	*PEACE* www.rockportpeace.com	1968	1302 W MARKET ST	78382	TX		(361)729-7264 (361)729-5852	WS 11 SS 1010 BC 1010	ED/HC/MD	60	49	30
ROCKWALL	*COMUNIDAD CRISTIANA* jaimedesantiago@gmail.com		Our Savior Lutheran 3003 Horizon Rd PO BOX 52	75032 75087	TX	Jaime Gonzalez	(214)395-6222					
	OUR SAVIOR office@oslcrockwall.org oslcrockwall.org	1974	3003 HORIZON RD	75032	TX		(972)771-8118 (972)771-8753	WS 9 1045 SS 1010 BC 1010	EL/HS/ED/ HC/MD/SN	450	227	233
	WATER OF LIFE		See Forney TX									
ROSEBUD	*FIRST*	1946	105 W Ave E PO BOX 503	76570	TX		(254)583-7505	WS 10 SS 9 BC 9	ED/HC/ MD/SN	30	0	15
ROSENBERG	*TRINITY* revwishbone@gmail.com trinitylutheran.cc	1906	1512 LOUISE ST	77471	TX	Steven L Wiechman	(281)341-1451 (281)232-3803	WS 1015 SS 9	HC/MD			
ROUND ROCK	*KING OF KINGS* office@kingofkingstx.org www.kingofkingstx.org	1980	17000 SMYERS LN	78681	TX	Christopher P Brynestad	(512)255-0829 (512)255-4582	WS 8 10 1045 SS 1030 BC 1030	EC/HS/ED/ HC/MD/SN	345	245	127
	NARRATIVE ted@narrative.church WWW.NARRATIVE.CHURCH	2015	1221 SATELLITE VIEW	78665	TX	Theodore A Doering		WS 10 SS 10		50	50	60
	POINT OF GRACE		See Pflugerville TX									
ROUND TOP	*MOUNT CALVARY*		See La Grange TX									
ROWLETT	*FAITH*		See Wylie TX									
SAGINAW	*HOLY SHEPHERD*		See Haslet TX									
	LIGHT OF THE WORLD		See Fort Worth TX									
	ST PAUL		See Fort Worth TX									
	THE EDGE		See Azle TX									
SALADO	*FORTRESS*		See Harker Heights TX									
SAN ANGELO	*TRINITY* trinity@tlcsanangelo.com www.tlcsanangelo.com	1927	3536 LUTHERAN WAY	76904	TX	Allan C Eckert	(325)944-8660 (325)223-9770	WS 8 1030 SS 915 BC 915	EL/HS/ED/ HC/MD/SN	379	311	165
SAN ANTONIO	*ABUNDANT GRACE*		5063 RIGSBY AVE	78222	TX	Arturo Pena	(210)648-5509					
	*BROOKS** philipd@lincsa.org		Greenline Park on Brooks Campus 5323 BLANCO RD	78217 78216	TX		(210)846-8505					
	CHRIST OUR SAVIOR admin@coslc.org www.coslc.org	2000	5323 BLANCO RD	78216	TX	Edward P Giese	(210)732-7223 (210)732-9288	WS 1030 SS 9 BC 9	EC/ED/HC			
	CONCORDIA www.concordia.cc	1951	16801 HUEBNER RD	78258	TX	William H Tucker Corey J Christians Jeffrey D Tucker	(210)479-1477 (210)479-9348	WS 8 930 11 SS 930 BC 930	EL/HS/ED/ HC/MD/SN			
	CROWN OF LIFE office@crownoflifesa.org www.crownoflifesa.org	1982	19291 STONE OAK PKWY	78258	TX	Dr Brian L Kachelmeier Chase M Greenhagen	(210)490-6886 (210)490-1552	WS 8 1045 SS 930 BC 930	EC/HS/ ED/SN	522	397	215
	HOLY CROSS	1945	3118 S NEW BRAUNFELS AVE	78210	TX	Elder McCants	(210)532-1300	WS 1015 SS 9 BC 9	ED/HC/ MD/SN			
	KING OF KINGS office@satx-kingofkings.church www.satx-kingofkings.church	1975	13888 DREAMWOOD DR	78233	TX	Neldo Schmidt	(210)656-6508 (210)564-0970	WS 8 1045 SS 930 BC 930	EL/ED/HC/ MD	326	286	135
	MESSIAH		See Boerne TX									
	MORNINGSIDE MANOR Satellite Site of Redeemer San Antonio TX	2024	137 West French Place	78212								
	MOUNT CALVARY mtcalvary@mtcsa.org www.mtcsa.org	1922	308 Mount Calvary Dr 308 MOUNT CALVARY	78209	TX	Craig D Meissler Michael S Middaugh	(210)824-8748 (210)804-0052	WS 930 SS 1045 BC 1045	HS/ED/HC/ MD/SN	267	240	149
	MOUNT OLIVE dbhouse47@att.net www.mtolivesa.org	1926	3200 W LOOP 1604 S	78245	TX	David A Brockhouse Derek W Easterling	(210)675-6394	WS 1030 SS 930 BC 915	ED/MD/SN	118	87	60

*Indicates a new church start. A new church start is an intentionally organized gathering which comes together on a regular basis for the purpose of worship and/or Bible study and is intended to grow into a member LCMS congregation. WS =Worship Service; SS = Sunday School; BC =Bible Class; EC = Early Childhood; EL = Elementary School; HS = High School; ED =Education Ministry; HC =Human Care Ministry; SN = Special Needs Ministry; MD = Media Ministry (PC)=Partner Church Pastor. See Page 53 for the Table of Abbreviations for key to additional abbreviations

CITY	CONGREGATION EMAIL WEBSITE	YEAR EST	LOCATION MAILING ADDRESS	ZIP CODE(S)	DIST.	PASTOR(S)	PHONE FAX	WS SS BC	SCHOOLS/ MINISTRIES	STATISTIC Bapt	Conf	Avg Attend
SAN ANTONIO	*REDEEMER* www.redeemersatx.com	1942	2507 FREDERICKSBURG RD	78201	TX	Michael P Bailey	(210)732-4112	WS 1015 SS 9 BC 9	HS/ED/ MD/SN	54	54	28
	SHEPHERD HILLS church@shlutheran.org shepherdlutheran.com	1969	6914 WURZBACH RD	78240	TX	Dr Christopher M Kennedy Andrew J Johnson	(210)614-3742 (210)692-7554	WS 9 1030 BC 8	EL/HS/ED/ HC/MD/SN	1016	790	422
	ST PAUL stpaullu@stpaulsa.org www.stpaulsa.org	1913	2302 S PRESA ST	78210	TX	David J Murillo	(210)532-7341 (210)534-2998	WS 9 SS 1030 BC 1030	EC/ED/HC			
SAN JUAN	*ZION*		See Alamo TX									
SAN MARCOS	*CROSS*		See New Braunfels TX									
	GRACE gracesanmarcossecretary@yahoo.com www.gracesanmarcos.com	1957	1250 BELVIN ST	78666	TX	Dr Craig A DuBois Jerrell P Hein	(512)392-4241	WS 1015 SS 9 BC 9	ED/HC	166	146	88
	ST JOHN		See Uhland TX									
SCHERTZ	*CROSS*		See New Braunfels TX									
	WORD OF LIFE		See Cibolo TX									
SCHULENBURG	*MOUNT CALVARY*		See La Grange TX									
	ZION secretary@zionschulenburg.org www.zionschulenburg.org	1944	103 KEUPER AVE	78956	TX		(979)743-3842 (979)743-3842	WS 10 SS 845 BC 845	HS/MD/SN	95	79	38
SEALY	*LIFEBRIDGE* pastor@lifebridgesealy.com www.lifebridgesealy.com	2012	2162 FM 2187 Rd PO BOX 934	77474	TX	Scott E Heitshusen	(979)885-7270	WS 10 BC 830	ED/HC	142	100	136
	TRINITY pastorken@tlcsealy.org www.tlcsealy.org	1883	402 ATCHISON ST	77474	TX	Kenneth J Bersche	(979)885-2211 (979)885-7003	WS 10 SS 9 BC 9	EC/ED/HC/ MD/SN	364	298	92
SEGUIN	*GRACE* secretaryofgrace@sbcglobal.net gracelutheranchurchseguin.com	1948	935 E MOUNTAIN ST	78155	TX	Roger A Hotopp	(830)379-1690 (830)379-2487	WS 10 SS 9 BC 9	EC/ED/ MD/SN			
SELMA	*WORD OF LIFE*		See Cibolo TX									
SERBIN	*ST PAUL* st.paulserbin@verizon.net www.stpaulserbin.org	1854	1572 CR 211 1572 COUNTY ROAD 211 GIDDINGS	78942	TX	John E Schmidt	(979)366-9650 (979)366-2200	WS 830 SS 930 BC 930	EL/HS/ED/ MD/SN	718	591	252
SEYMOUR	*TRINITY*	1953	500 S Main St PO BOX 53	76380	TX			WS 8				
SHALLOWATER	*EMMANUEL*		See Littlefield TX									
SHAMROCK	*TRINITY*	1917	900 S Main St PO BOX 44	79079	TX		(806)256-2355	WS 11 SS 945	ED/HC	20	16	7
SHENANDOAH	*PROJECT 242 AT AVANTI* Satellite Site of Joy Houston TX	2024	120 Vision Park Blvd	77384								
SHERMAN	*GRACE*		See Denison TX									
SINTON	*TRINITY*		See Odem TX									
SLATON	*ST PAUL*		See Wilson TX									
SMITHVILLE	*GRACE* gracelutheransmithville@gmail.com www.glcs.org	1927	308 BYRNE ST	78957	TX	David C Woelmer	(512)237-2108 (512)237-2832	WS 10 SS 845 BC 845	HS/ED	327	220	112
SNYDER	*GRACE*		5500 COLLEGE AVE	79549	TX	Dr Jimmie L Wright	(325)436-0414		ED/HC			
SOMERSET	*MOUNT OLIVE*		See San Antonio TX									
SONORA	*HOPE*	1958	419 E 2nd St 417 E 2ND ST	76950	TX	Thomas W Baden	(325)942-9275	WS 4 BC 3				
SPICEWOOD	*MOUNT OLIVE*		See Austin TX									
SPRING	*BEAUTIFUL SAVIOR OUR REDEEMER NORTH* Satellite Site of Savior Redeemer Houston TX	2018	1804 N Spring Dr	77373								
	COMMUNITY OF HOPE pj@hope68.com		9225 Crescent Clover Dr PO BOX 11963	77379 77391	TX	Jonathan A Goeke	(281)716-2929		HS			
	*IGNITE** paul.korabandi@gmail.com		1612 MEADOW EDGE LN	77388	TX		(346)386-7509	WS 1030				
	LAZARUS pulliammarkt@gmail.com www.LazarusChurch.com	2023	31150 BIRNHAM WOODS DR	77388	TX	Mark T Pulliam	(210)643-4319	WS 10	ED/HC/MD	100	60	72
	RESURRECTION brenda@churchthatcares.org churchthatcares.org	1971	1612 MEADOW EDGE LN	77388	TX	Thayer K Benson Daniel T Brummet Paul A Korabandi	(281)353-4413 (281)353-1642	WS 815 11 SS 945 BC 945	EC/HS/ED/ HC/MD	480	379	415
	ST THOMAS		See Magnolia TX									
	ST TIMOTHY		See Houston TX									
	ZION		See Tomball TX									
SPRINGTOWN	*THE EDGE*		See Azle TX									
STEPHENVILLE	*FAITH* church.office@ faithlutheranstephenville.com faithlutheranstephenville.com	1962	3000 NORTHWEST LOOP	76401	TX	Jeffrey A Lee	(254)968-2710 (254)968-2344	WS 8 1045 SS 945	EC/ED/HC/ MD	221	169	106

*Indicates a new church start. A new church start is an intentionally organized gathering which comes together on a regular basis for the purpose of worship and/or Bible study and is intended to grow into a member LCMS congregation. WS =Worship Service; SS = Sunday School; BC =Bible Class; EC = Early Childhood; EL = Elementary School; HS = High School; ED =Education Ministry; HC =Human Care Ministry; SN = Special Needs Ministry; MD = Media Ministry (PC)=Partner Church Pastor. See Page 53 for the Table of Abbreviations for key to additional abbreviations

CITY	CONGREGATION EMAIL WEBSITE	YEAR EST	LOCATION MAILING ADDRESS	ZIP CODE(S)	DIST.	PASTOR(S)	PHONE FAX	WS SS BC	SCHOOLS/ MINISTRIES	STATISTIC Bapt	Conf	Avg Attend
STONE OAK	*CROWN OF LIFE*		See San Antonio TX									
SUGAR LAND	*FAITH* information@faithsugarland.org www.faithsugarland.org	1972	800 BROOKS ST	77478	TX	Jeffrey G Wuertz	(281)242-7729 (281)242-8749	WS 930 BC 1115	ED/HC	158	141	97
	FISHERS OF MEN office@fishersofmen.org www.fishersofmen.org	1989	2011 AUSTIN PKWY	77479	TX	Charles E Ridley	(281)242-7711 (281)242-2164	WS 830 11 SS 945 BC 945	EC/ED/HC/ MD/SN	557	517	228
SULPHUR SPRINGS	*OUR SAVIOR* ourchurch@oursaviorsstx.org www.oursaviorsstx.org	1954	1000 TEXAS ST SULPHUR SPGS	75482	TX	Mark R Elliott	(903)885-5787 (903)885-3107	WS 1030 SS 9 BC 9	ED/HC/MD			
SWEENY	*ST LUKE* stlukesweeny@windstream.net	1961	1402 North Main PO BOX 97	77480	TX		(979)548-3535	WS 11 SS 945				
SWEETWATER	*FAITH* faithrus@suddenlinkmail.com	1967	1607 JOSEPHINE ST	79556	TX	Keith M Hills Jr	(325)235-2773	WS 1045	ED/HC	16	16	10
TAHOKA	*ST PAUL*		See Wilson TX									
TAYLOR	*CHRIST*	1891	6730 FM 112	76574	TX		(512)352-3644	WS 10 SS 9 BC 9				
	TRINITY www.trinity-taylor.org	1950	3505 N Main 3505 N MAIN ST	76574	TX	Scott A Schaller	(512)352-6958 (512)352-7350	WS 8 1015 SS 915 BC 915	EC/ED/HC/ MD			
TEMPLE	*FORTRESS*		See Harker Heights TX									
	IMMANUEL info@ilmtexas.org www.ilmtexas.org	1926	2109 W AVENUE H	76504	TX	Grayson E Albers	(254)773-3898 (254)791-5659	WS 8 1030 SS 915 BC 915	ED/HC/ MD/SN	515	444	340
	ST PAUL		See The Grove TX									
TERLINGUA	*REDEEMER*		See Alpine TX									
TERRELL	*WATER OF LIFE*		See Forney TX									
TEXARKANA	*FIRST* scottsundbye@gmail.com www.firstlutheranchurchtexarkana.org	1919	4600 TEXAS BLVD	75503	TX	Scott A Sundbye	(903)792-5253 (903)794-0999	WS 10 SS 9 BC 9	HC/MD	238	178	63
TEXAS CITY	*PEACE* peacelutherantc@yahoo.com	1947	9111 EMMETT F LOWRY EXPY	77591	TX	Matthew S Brackman	(409)938-1277 (409)938-7764	WS 1030 SS 915 BC 915		194	128	53
THE COLONY	*LORD OF LIFE*		See Plano TX									
	SAINT JOHN pastor@sjlcfrisco.com stjohnfrisco.org		4809 S. Colony Blvd. P.O. BOX 528 FRISCO	75056 75034	TX	Thomas C Stark	(469)573-0885	WS 930 BC 115		100	80	60
	SOULTHIRST soulthirstchurch@gmail.com www.soulthirstchurch.com	1983	4700 Nash Dr 4704 NASH DR	75056	TX	James P Miller William R Brimer Jason P Hamre	(469)353-8655	WS 10 SS 1030 BC 11	ED/HC/MD			
THE GROVE	*ST PAUL* pastor@stpaulthegrove.org www.stpaulthegrove.org	1883	220 THE GROVE RD GATES-VILLE	76528	TX	John M Heckmann	(254)986-2607	WS 1015 SS 9 BC 9	ED/HC/ MD/SN	405	324	194
THE WOODLANDS	*LAZARUS*		See Spring TX									
	LIVING WORD lisa@lwlc.org www.lwlc.org	1978	9500 N PANTHER CREEK DR	77381	TX	Douglas W Dommer Micah J Drengler	(281)363-4860 (281)363-3447	WS 10 SS 830 BC 830	EC/HS/ED/ HC/MD/SN	430	317	180
	ST THOMAS		See Magnolia TX									
THORNDALE	*ST PAUL* churchoffice@stpaulthorndale.com www.stpaulthorndale.com	1890	101 N 3rd St PO BOX 369	76577	TX	Jeffrey S Doria	(512)898-5455 (512)898-5298	WS 930 SS 830 BC 830	EL/ED/HC/ MD	779	602	209
TODD MISSION	*ST THOMAS*		See Magnolia TX									
TOMBALL	*SALEM* lstetler@salem4u.com www.salem4u.com	1851	22601 LUTHERAN CHURCH RD	77377	TX	Timothy R Niekerk Vincent S Parks III Jason P Schleicher	(281)351-8223	WS 9 1030 BC 9 1030	EL/HS/ED/ HC/SN	2148	1733	1142
	ST THOMAS		See Magnolia TX									
	ST TIMOTHY		See Houston TX									
	ZION zion@ziontomballtx.org www.ziontomballtx.org	1906	907 HICKS ST	77375	TX	Scott E Herbert	(281)351-5757 (281)255-8696	WS 930 SS 11 BC 11	EC/HS/ED/ MD/SN	574	448	85
TYLER	*TRINITY* office@tlctyler.org www.tlctyler.org	1933	2001 HUNTER ST	75701	TX	John L Scheusner Benjamin T Prohl	(903)593-1526 (903)593-7664	WS 830 11 SS 950 BC 950	EC/ED/HC/ MD	520	449	256
UHLAND	*ST JOHN* st_john_lcms.uhland@yahoo.com		20 North Camino Real 9865 CAMINO REAL	78640	TX	Ben Jore	(512)668-4542	WS 1030 SS 9 BC 9	HC/MD			
UNIVERSAL CITY	*WORD OF LIFE*		See Cibolo TX									
UVALDE	*TRINITY* trinityuvalde@gmail.com www.trinitylutheranuvalde.com	1946	762 N GETTY ST	78801	TX		(830)278-9474	WS 1030 SS 915 BC 915	ED	86	80	39
VERNON	*IMMANUEL*		See Harrold TX									
	ST PAUL stpaulv@yahoo.com stpaulvernon.net	1912	4405 HOSPITAL DR	76384	TX	Craig S Rendahl	(940)552-2495 (940)552-6616	WS 1030 SS 930 BC 930	EC/ED/MD	225	193	60
	ZION zionlockettpastor@gmail.com	1893	14570 FM 2074	76384	TX	Steven R Brummett	(940)552-7164	WS 1045 SS 945 BC 945	ED/HC/ MD/SN	160	145	70
VICTORIA	*CHRIST THE KING* lutheranctk@gmail.com christthekingmv.com	2013	563 FM 237	77905	TX		(361)433-5009	WS 10 SS 9 BC 630	ED	25	25	16

*Indicates a new church start. A new church start is an intentionally organized gathering which comes together on a regular basis for the purpose of worship and/or Bible study and is intended to grow into a member LCMS congregation. WS =Worship Service; SS = Sunday School; BC =Bible Class; EC = Early Childhood; EL = Elementary School; HS = High School; ED =Education Ministry; HC =Human Care Ministry; SN = Special Needs Ministry; MD = Media Ministry (PC)=Partner Church Pastor. See Page 53 for the Table of Abbreviations for key to additional abbreviations

CITY	CONGREGATION EMAIL WEBSITE	YEAR EST	LOCATION MAILING ADDRESS	ZIP CODE(S)	DIST.	PASTOR(S)	PHONE FAX	WS SS BC	SCHOOLS/ MINISTRIES	STATISTIC Bapt	 Conf	 Avg Attend
VICTORIA	*GRACE* office@gracelutheran-tx.org www.gracelutheran-tx.org	1952	9806 NE ZAC LENTZ PKWY	77904	TX	Dr Keith D Aschenbeck	(361)573-2232 (361)573-0867	WS 910 SS 1030 BC 1030	ED/HC/ MD/SN	273	226	106
	ZION zlmv@ccwip.net www.zionlutheranmv.org		12183 FM 236	77905	TX		(361)578-5447 (361)578-5659	WS 10 SS 9 BC 9	ED/HC/ MD/SN	288	222	94
WACO	*PEACE* pastor@peacehewitt.org www.peacehewitt.org	1978	9301 PANTHER WAY	76712	TX	Dr Robert W Holaday	(254)420-4729 (254)420-4729	WS 9 SS 1030 BC 1030	ED/HC/ MD/SN			
	ST MARK office@stmarkwaco.com stmarkwaco.com	1917	2000 CLAY AVE	76706	TX	Peter C Kolb	(254)754-0644	WS 9 SS 1030 BC 1030	ED/HC/ MD/SN			
	ST PAUL		See Bellmead TX									
	TRINITY		See Woodway TX									
WALBURG	*ZION*		See Georgetown TX									
WALLER	*CROSS OF CHRIST* crossofchrist.waller_tx@yahoo.com		19361 FM 362 S	77484	TX	David C Cecil	(979)702-0658	WS 10 SS 9 BC 9				
	ST THOMAS		See Magnolia TX									
WALLIS	*ST PAUL* office@stpaulwallis.org www.stpaulwallis.org	1900	515 Cedar PO BOX 427	77485	TX		(979)478-6741	WS 9 SS 1030 BC 1030	HC/MD	64	52	22
WATAUGA	*GRACE KOREAN* son3006@hotmail.com		6416 WATAUGA RD	76148	TX	DongSu Son	(817)427-2909					
	ST PAUL		See Fort Worth TX									
WAXAHACHIE	*CHRIST KING* ctkwax@gmail.com www.christthekingwax.org	1968	301 W HIGHWAY 287 BYP	75165	TX	Jared M Raebel	(972)938-1633 (972)938-1633	WS 8 1045 SS 930 BC 930	HC/MD	277	246	143
WEATHERFORD	*ST PAUL*		See Fort Worth TX									
	TRINITY churchoffice@trinityweatherford.org www.trinityweatherford.org	1958	1500 W BALL ST	76086	TX		(817)613-1939	WS 1015 SS 9 BC 9	HC	289	249	107
WEST POINT	*MOUNT CALVARY*		See La Grange TX									
WHARTON	*ST JOHN* stjohns-wharton.org	1898	614 PECAN ST	77488	TX	Robert W Lutjens	(979)532-4522	WS 10 SS 9 BC 9	MD/SN	178	144	54
WHITE SETTLEMENT	*REDEEMER*		See Fort Worth TX									
	ST PAUL		See Fort Worth TX									
WHITNEY	*OUR SAVIOR* www.oslcwhitney.org	1977	117 HCR 2129 East PO BOX 2172	76692	TX	Philip C Wottrich	(254)694-3234	WS 10 SS 845 BC 845		105	96	29
WICHITA FALLS	*OUR REDEEMER* orlcwf@yahoo.com www.orlcwf.org	1948	4605 CYPRESS AVE	76310	TX	Duane R Bamsch	(940)692-3690 (940)692-0382	WS 8 1030 SS 915	ED/HC/ MD/SN	364	306	198
	ST PAUL stpaulwf@att.net www.saintpaullutheran.org	1894	1417 11th St PO BOX 126	76301 76307	TX	Eric A Stinnette	(940)322-6112 (940)322-6135	WS 1015 BC 9	ED/HC/ MD/SN	192	120	52
WILLS POINT	*HOLY CROSS*		See Canton TX									
WILSON	*ST PAUL* splcwilson@gmail.com	1926	1611 16th St PO BOX 136	79381	TX		(806)800-1012	WS 1015 SS 915 BC 915		142	108	51
WINCHESTER	*ST MICHAEL'S* secretary@stmichaelswinchester.org www.stmichaelswinchester.org	1876	700 FRIO ST	78945	TX	Nathaniel W Hill	(979)242-3444 (979)242-3444	WS 9 SS 1030 BC 1030	HS/ED/HC/ MD/SN	254	213	93
WINDOM	*SAINT JAMES* saintjamesac@gmail.com www.stjameswindom.org/	1884	14394 E FM 1396	75492	TX	Arthur B Farrow	(903)583-5155	WS 11	HC	42	42	34
WINNIE	*HOPE* hopelutheranwinnie@gmail.com	1973	1322 9th St PO BOX 701	77665	TX		(409)296-2377	WS 930 SS 1045 BC 1045	ED/HC/SN	116	80	40
WOLFFORTH	*ST PAUL*		See Wilson TX									
WOODVILLE	*FAITH* Faithlutheran789@gmail.co	1981	704 W HOLLY ST	75979	TX		(409)283-7171	WS 9 SS 1015 BC 730	ED	36	34	18
WOODWAY	*TRINITY* nikki@fullerheaven.com www.fullerheaven.com	1945	2 RITCHIE RD	76712	TX	Kevin D Lentz	(254)772-4225	WS 830 1030 SS 930 BC 930	ED/HC/ MD/SN	426	349	200
WYLIE	*FAITH* faithlutheranwylie@gmail.com www.faithlutheranwylie.org	2020	615 PARKER RD	75098	TX	Kurt A Ulmer	(972)461-2777	WS 930 BC 1115		138	110	76
	*VERITAS COMMUNITY** mhotopp@veritaslife.org veritasacademics.org		3104 Savoy Ct 1345 E FM 544	75098	TX		(469)661-8002	WS 1030	EL/HS/ ED/HC			
YORKTOWN	*CHRIST THE KING*		See Victoria TX									
ZAPATA	*ABIDING SAVIOR* pastor.abidingsaviorzapata@gmail.com	1971	1314 14TH ST	78076	TX		(956)763-0468			20	20	26

*Indicates a new church start. A new church start is an intentionally organized gathering which comes together on a regular basis for the purpose of worship and/or Bible study and is intended to grow into a member LCMS congregation. WS =Worship Service; SS = Sunday School; BC =Bible Class; EC = Early Childhood; EL = Elementary School; HS = High School; ED =Education Ministry; HC =Human Care Ministry; SN = Special Needs Ministry; MD = Media Ministry (PC)=Partner Church Pastor. See Page 53 for the Table of Abbreviations for key to additional abbreviations

UTAH

CITY	CONGREGATION EMAIL WEBSITE	YEAR EST	LOCATION MAILING ADDRESS	ZIP CODE(S)	DIST.	PASTOR(S)	PHONE FAX	WS SS BC	SCHOOLS/ MINISTRIES	Bapt	Conf	Avg Attend
BOUNTIFUL	*CROSS CHRIST* church@crossofchristutah.com www.CrossofChristUtah.com	1958	1840 S 75 E	84010	RM		(801)295-7677	WS 8 SS 9	ED/HC/ MD/SN			
CEDAR CITY	*TRINITY* LD.hehn@gmail.com cedarlutheran.org	1976	410 E 1935 N	84720 84721	RM	Robert A Sharp	(435)586-7103	WS 10 SS 10 BC 845	ED/MD	47	47	50
LOGAN	*HOLY TRINITY* htlcloganut@msn.com www.holytrinitylutheranlogan.org	1962	581 N 700 E	84321	RM		(435)752-1453	WS 1030 SS 930 BC 930	ED/HC/MD	62	53	45
MOAB	*GRACE* widmerjg@gmail.com gracelutheranmoab.weebly.com	1946	360 W 400 N PO BOX 760	84532	RM		(970)946-4740	WS 10 SS 11	ED	21	21	13
MURRAY	*CHRIST* www.christlutheranmurray.com	1931	240 E 5600 S	84107	RM	Justin C Clarke	(801)266-8714	WS 9 SS 1030 BC 1030	ED/HC			
OGDEN	*ST PAUL* pastor@stpaulutah.org www.stpaulutah.org	1940	3329 HARRISON BLVD	84403	RM	Mark E Christ	(801)392-6368 (801)392-7562	WS 830 11 SS 945 BC 945	ED/HC/ MD/SN	208	194	128
RICHFIELD	*GOOD SHEPHERD*		1310 W 1800 S	84701	RM	Robert M Bennett		WS 3 BC 430				
RIVERTON	*HOLY TRINITY* pastor@holytrinityut.org www.holytrinityut.org		13249 S REDWOOD RD	84065	RM	Alan D Borcher	(801)860-6412	WS 9 SS 10 BC 10	EL/ED/HC/ MD	346	250	104
SAINT GEORGE	*MESQUITE*		See Mesquite NV									
	TRINITY trinityl@infowest.com www.trinitystgeorge.org	1978	2260 Red Cliff Dr 2260 RED CLIFFS DR	84790	RM	John Manweiler	(435)628-1850 (435)628-1850	WS 8 1030 SS 1030 BC 1030	EL/ED/HC/ MD/SN	195	167	96
SALT LAKE CITY	*CHRIST*		See Murray UT									
	REDEEMER jjohnson@rlcs-slc.org www.rlcs-slc.org	1950	1955 E STRATFORD AVE SALT LAKE CTY	84106	RM	Mark G Below	(801)467-4352 (801)463-7904	WS 930	EL/ED/HC/ MD	115	101	50
	ST JOHNS www.stjohnslutheranslc.org	1898	1030 S 500 E 475 E HERBERT AVE SALT LAKE CTY	84105 84111	RM	Henry B Malone	(801)364-2873	WS 10 SS 9	EC/ED/HC			
SANDY	*GRACE* church@gracesandy.org www.gracesandy.org	1981	1815 E 9800 S	84092	RM	Jeremy D Lamont	(801)572-6375 (801)553-2403	WS 930 SS 1130	EL/ED/HC/ MD	512	475	64
TOOELE	*FIRST* www.firstlutherantooele.org	1952	349 N 7th St PO BOX 738	84074	RM		(435)882-1172	WS 10 SS 11 BC 11				
VERNAL	*OUR SAVIOUR* oslvernal@gmail.com www.oursaviourvernal.org	1960	370 South 500 West PO BOX 342	84078	RM	Derrick C Brown	(435)789-1421	WS 1115 SS 10	ED/MD	97	74	40

VERMONT

CITY	CONGREGATION EMAIL WEBSITE	YEAR EST	LOCATION MAILING ADDRESS	ZIP CODE(S)	DIST.	PASTOR(S)	PHONE FAX	WS SS BC	SCHOOLS/ MINISTRIES	Bapt	Conf	Avg Attend
GRANITEVILLE	*WILLIAMSTOWN* WLCvermont@gmail.com WLCvermont.org	1991	2828 Graniteville Rd. 2828 GRANITEVILLE RD	05654	NE	Stephen C Sweyko	(802)479-1164	WS 1015 SS 9	ED/HC/SN	102	83	38
SOUTH BURLINGTON	*COMMUNITY* clcvt@comcast.net www.communitylutheranvt.org	1952	1560 WILLISTON RD S BURLINGTON	05403	NE	Matthew G Rasmussen	(802)864-5537 (802)864-5537	WS 930 SS 1030 BC 1030	ED/HC/SN	245	210	100
WILLIAMSTOWN	*WILLIAMSTOWN*		See Graniteville VT									

VIRGINIA

CITY	CONGREGATION EMAIL WEBSITE	YEAR EST	LOCATION MAILING ADDRESS	ZIP CODE(S)	DIST.	PASTOR(S)	PHONE FAX	WS SS BC	SCHOOLS/ MINISTRIES	Bapt	Conf	Avg Attend
ALDIE	*VINE AND BRANCHES* churchoffice@vablc.org vineandbranches.com	2015	25615 LENNOX HALE DR	20105	SE	Christopher M Conkling	(571)267-5900	WS 830 1030 SS 930	EC/ED/HC/ MD	257	180	95
ALEXANDRIA	*BETHANY* office@bethany-lcms.org www.bethany-lcms.org	1953	2501 BEACON HILL RD	22306	SE	Andrew W Jagow Joseph B Davis	(703)765-8255 (703)765-0307	WS 815 10 SS 9	EL/ED/HC/ MD	194	155	70
	IMMANUEL church@immanuelalexandria.org immanuelalexandria.org	1870	1801 RUSSELL RD	22301	EN	Christopher S Esget Theodore A Hoham	(703)549-0155	WS 10 SS 845 BC 845	EL/ED/ MD/SN			
	SAINT ATHANASIUS		See Vienna VA									
	SHALOM ETHIOPIAN mitikuzeleke22@gmail.com		5952 FRANCONIA RD	22310	SE	Dr Mitiku Zeleke	(571)422-7930	WS 11 SS 11	ED/HC			
	ST JOHNS office@sjlc.com www.sjlc.com	1956	5952 FRANCONIA RD	22310	SE	John S Meehan	(703)971-2210	WS 1030 BC 915	EC/ED/HC/ MD/SN	273	239	107
AMELIA	*ST PAUL* www.splc-amelia.com	1910	Eggleston St 4721 WEST CREEK RD AMELIA CT HSE	23002	SE			WS 11 SS 10	ED/HC/SN	34	32	21
ANNANDALE	*VA MEKANE YESUS* alabachew2005@yahoo.com		3901 Gallows Rd PO BOX 11129 ALEXANDRIA	22003 22312	SE	Eyob B Kassa	(202)215-7269					
APPOMATTOX	*OUR SAVIOR*		See Lynchburg VA									
ARLINGTON	*OUR SAVIOR* office@osva.org www.osva.org	1941	825 S TAYLOR ST	22204	SE	Wayne P Fredericksen David H Labuhn Dr Jeffrey J Kloha	(703)892-4846 (703)892-4847	WS 815 11 SS 940 BC 940	EL/ED/HC/ MD/SN	393	243	212
ASHBURN	*OUR SAVIOR'S WAY* churchoffice@oswlc.org www.oswlc.org	1994	43115 WAXPOOL RD BROADLANDS	20148	SE	John W Scott	(703)858-9254 (703)729-9149	WS 8 930 11 SS 930 BC 930	EC/ED/HC/ MD/SN			

*Indicates a new church start. A new church start is an intentionally organized gathering which comes together on a regular basis for the purpose of worship and/or Bible study and is intended to grow into a member LCMS congregation. WS =Worship Service; SS = Sunday School; BC =Bible Class; EC = Early Childhood; EL = Elementary School; HS = High School; ED =Education Ministry; HC =Human Care Ministry; SN = Special Needs Ministry; MD = Media Ministry (PC)=Partner Church Pastor. See Page 53 for the Table of Abbreviations for key to additional abbreviations

CITY	CONGREGATION EMAIL WEBSITE	YEAR EST	LOCATION MAILING ADDRESS	ZIP CODE(S)	DIST.	PASTOR(S)	PHONE FAX	WS SS BC	SCHOOLS/ MINISTRIES	STATISTIC Bapt	Conf	Avg Attend
ASHLAND	*TRINITY LUTHERAN CHURCH ASHLAND CAMPUS* Satellite Site of Trinity Richmond VA	2017	11515 Ashcake Rd	23005								
BEDFORD	*OUR SAVIOR*		See Lynchburg VA									
BLACKSBURG	*OUTREACH VA TECH** LOVT@gslcp.org		War Memorial Chapel 601 Drillfield Dr 1887 ELECTRIC RD ROANOKE	24061 24018	SE		(540)774-8746	WS 330				
BUENA VISTA	*CONCORDIA* concordialutheranmission3@gmail.com concordiaandkoinonia.wordpress.com/	2010	Ben Salem Presbyterian Church 34 Ben Salem Ln PO BOX 1012	24450 24416	SE		(540)784-5622	WS 1030 BC 930				
CALLAO	*GOOD SHEPHERD* www.goodshepherdcallao.org	1981	1717 Hampton Hall Rd PO BOX 576	22435	SE	Robert C Hull	(804)529-5948	WS 9 SS 1030	HC/MD/SN	57	54	31
CHANTILLY	*VINE AND BRANCHES*		See Aldie VA									
CHARLOTTESVILLE	*IMMANUEL* churchoffice@immanuel charlottesville.com www.immanuelcharlottesville.com	1869	2416 JEFFERSON PARK AVE CHARLOTTESVLE	22903	SE	Benjamin O Maton	(434)295-4038	WS 1015 SS 915 BC 915	ED/HC/ MD/SN	290	235	117
CHESAPEAKE	*COMMUNITY OF HOPE* office@ccohchurch.com www.ccohchurch.com		1009 Scenic Parkway Ste J 1009 SCENIC PKWY UNIT J	23323	SE	Nathan D Speerbrecker	(757)436-0079	WS 10 SS 1045 BC 1145	ED/HC/MD	115	93	95
CHESTER	*GRACE* churchoffice@gracelutheranva.org www.gracechester.com	1964	13028 HARROWGATE RD	23831	SE	Jaim E Gann	(804)748-6058 (804)748-8126	WS 815 1045 SS 930	ED/HC/MD	192	174	128
CHESTERFIELD	*GRACE*		See Chester VA									
	NEW HOPE www.thenewhope.com	1997	14851 Hull St Rd 14851 HULL STREET RD	23832	SE	Gary R Pomrenke			EC/ED/MD			
CHINCOTEAGUE	*SAINT LUKE'S EVANGELICAL LUTHERAN CHAPEL* Satellite Site of Immanuel Alexandria VA	2025	6202 Quillen Dr	23336				WS 10				
COLONIAL HEIGHTS	*GRACE*		See Chester VA									
CROZET	*BETHANY-TRINITY*		See Fishersville VA									
DANVILLE	*CHRIST KING* office@ctk-lc.org www.ctk-lc.org	1962	1172 FRANKLIN TPKE	24540	SE	Norbert Folwaczny	(434)836-6888	WS 11 BC 930	ED/HC/MD	46	45	26
EMPORIA	*ST JOHN* saintjohnthebaptistlutheran@gmail.com www.saintjohnlutheranemporiava.com	1909	1351 W ATLANTIC ST	23847	SE		(434)634-4515	WS 11 BC 930	ED/HC/ MD/SN	122	115	39
EWING	*CHRIST CUMBERLANDS*		See Harrogate TN									
FAIRFAX STATION	*LIVING SAVIOR* secretary@livingsaviorlutheran.org www.livingsaviorlutheran.org	1983	5500 OX RD FAIRFAX STA	22039	SE		(703)352-1421 (703)352-1421	WS 830 11 SS 945 BC 945	EC/ED/HC	613	402	120
FALLS CHURCH	*ST PAUL* Secretary@stpaulsfallschurch.org www.stpaulsfallschurch.org	1952	7426 IDYLWOOD RD	22043	SE	Mark A Shaltanis Chris X Yang	(703)573-0295 (703)573-3273	WS 8 1030 SS 915 BC 915	EC/ED/HC	685	485	110
FALMOUTH	*SUNDAY SERVICE AT CHARTER* Satellite Site of Redeemer Fredericksburg VA	2024	20 Heartfields Ln.	22405								
FARMVILLE	*ST JOHN* pastor@stjohnsfarmville.org www.stjohnsfarmville.org	1904	1301 MILNWOOD RD	23901	SE	Matthew D Sorenson	(434)392-1875	WS 8 1030 SS 915 BC 915	ED/HC/ MD/SN	89	80	66
FISHERSVILLE	*BETHANY-TRINITY* bethtrin@bethanylcw.org www.bethanylcw.org	1772	PO BOX 389	22939	SE	Timothy P Bohlmann	(540)942-4361 (877)480-8840	WS 830 11 SS 945 BC 945	EC/ED/HC/ MD/SN	461	413	140
FOREST	*OUR SAVIOR*		See Lynchburg VA									
FRANCONIA	*ST JOHNS*		See Alexandria VA									
FREDERICKSBURG	*LUTHERAN SERVICE OF THE SACRAMENT AT CHANCELLOR'S VILLAGE* Satellite Site of Redeemer Fredericksburg VA	2022	12100 Chancellors Village Ln	22407								
	REDEEMER info@redeemerfxbg.org www.redeemerfxbg.org	1978	5120 HARRISON RD FREDER-ICKSBRG	22408	SE	David B Miner	(540)898-4748 (540)891-9106	WS 8 11 SS 945 BC 945	EC/ED/HC/ MD/SN	435	316	248
	SUNDAY SERVICE AT HARMONY Satellite Site of Redeemer Fredericksburg VA	2015	60 Brimley Dr	22406								
HARRISONBURG	*BETHANY-TRINITY*		See Fishersville VA									
HERNDON	*GOOD SHEPHERD* gslc@gslcva.org www.gslcva.org	1970	1133 RESTON AVE	20170	SE	Jotham S Johann Gary B James	(703)437-5020	WS 8 11 SS 930 BC 930	EC/ED	470	367	200
	OUR SAVIOR'S WAY		See Ashburn VA									
HOPEWELL	*NAZARETH* nazluthchurch@gmail.com www.nazluthchurch.org	1928	1711 GRANT ST	23860	SE		(804)458-7994 (804)458-7994	WS 1030 SS 915 BC 915	ED/HC/SN			
KING GEORGE	*PEACE* www.peacekg.com	1963	5590 KINGS HWY	22485	SE	John M Duran Eugene Bostwick	(540)775-9131 (540)775-9131	WS 830 11 SS 945	EC/ED/HC/ MD/SN	153	140	95
KINGSTOWNE	*ST JOHNS*		See Alexandria VA									
LEESBURG	*CHRIST COMMUNITY* info@christcommunityleesburg.org christcommunityleesburg.org/		826 S King St 818 S KING ST	20175	SE		(571)223-6736	WS 10 SS 1020	EC/ED/HC/ MD	46	30	37

*Indicates a new church start. A new church start is an intentionally organized gathering which comes together on a regular basis for the purpose of worship and/or Bible study and is intended to grow into a member LCMS congregation. WS =Worship Service; SS = Sunday School; BC =Bible Class; EC = Early Childhood; EL = Elementary School; HS = High School; ED =Education Ministry; HC =Human Care Ministry; SN = Special Needs Ministry; MD = Media Ministry (PC)=Partner Church Pastor. See Page 53 for the Table of Abbreviations for key to additional abbreviations

CITY	CONGREGATION EMAIL WEBSITE	YEAR EST	LOCATION MAILING ADDRESS	ZIP CODE(S)	DIST.	PASTOR(S)	PHONE FAX	WS SS BC	SCHOOLS/ MINISTRIES	STATISTIC Bapt	Conf	Avg Attend
LEESBURG	*OUR SAVIOR'S WAY*		See Ashburn VA									
LEXINGTON	*BETHANY-TRINITY*		See Fishersville VA									
	CONCORDIA LUTHERAN MISSION Satellite Site of Concordia Buena Vista VA	2019	409 S Main St	24450				BC 930				
LYNCHBURG	*OUR SAVIOR* oslc.office@oursaviorlynchburg.org oursaviorlynchburg.org	1959	2940 LINK RD	24503	SE	Aaron E Yaeger Richard E Malmstrom	(434)384-6651 (434)384-6651	WS 1030 SS 915	ED/MD	89	64	66
MANASSAS	*HOPE* www.hopemanassas.org	1978	10391 SUDLEY MANOR DR	20109	SE	Joel D Wallschlaeger	(703)361-8732	WS 8 1030 SS 915 BC 915	ED/HC/ MD/SN	200	175	130
MECHANICSVILLE	*ST PAUL* www.saintpaul-lcms.com	1960	8100 SHADY GROVE RD MECHANICSVLLE	23111	SE	Rodney E Bitely	(804)427-7500 (804)427-7500	WS 1030 SS 915 BC 915		201	177	68
MEHERRIN	*ST MATTHEW*	1883	1364 Free State Rd PO BOX 91	23954	SE		(434)390-0714	WS 130	HC	29	18	16
	ST PAULS	1894	4472 Patrick Henry Hwy PO BOX 92	23954	SE		(804)379-4565	WS 130				
MIDLOTHIAN	*GOOD SHEPHERD* www.GoodShepherdMidlo.com		1401 OLD HUNDRED RD	23114	SE	George D Lippitt	(804)897-0262 (804)897-0266	WS 1030 SS 915	EL/ED			
NEWPORT NEWS	*RESURRECTION* news@rlcnn.org www.rlcnn.org	1956	765 J CLYDE MORRIS BLVD	23601	SE	Adam F Kuder	(757)596-5808 (757)596-5010	WS 9 SS 1045 BC 1045	EC/ED/HC/ MD/SN	255	132	99
NORFOLK	*CHRIST* office@christnorfolk.hrcoxmail.com www.christnorfolk.org	1953	6510 N MILITARY HWY	23518	SE	Sean M Tietze	(757)853-5655 (757)858-5094	WS 10 SS 10 BC 9	HC/MD	45	45	25
	TRINITY churchoffice@tlcnorfolk.com www.tlcnorfolk.com	1920	6001 GRANBY ST	23505	SE	James M Doebler	(757)489-2551 (757)489-8413	WS 10 SS 9	ED	143	124	93
	UNITY		2801 E PRINCESS ANNE RD	23504	SE		(757)627-3498 (757)627-3498	WS 11 BC 930	ED/MD			
PORTSMOUTH	*REDEEMER* redeemerlcms@gmail.com redeemerportsmouth.com	1944	1901 AIRLINE BLVD	23701	SE		(757)397-8362	WS 11 SS 10	HC	63	42	22
PRINCE GEORGE	*GRACE*		See Chester VA									
PROVIDENCE FORGE	*KING OF GLORY* larry.mcreynolds@kognk.org www.kognk.org		9120 Pocahontas Trail PO BOX 37	23140	SE	Lawrence J McReynolds	(804)966-5525	WS 8 10 6 SS 10	ED/HC/MD	174	144	64
PURCELLVILLE	*HOPE LUTHERAN MISSION* Satellite Site of Saint Athanasius Vienna VA	2019	37018 Glendale Street	20132								
	SAINT ATHANASIUS		See Vienna VA									
RICHMOND	*BETHLEHEM* golson9350@gmail.com	1852	1100 W GRACE ST	23220	SE	Jonathan A Scheck	(804)353-4413 (804)353-4860	WS 10 SS 845	ED/HC/ MD/SN			
	REDEEMER info@redeemerric.org www.redeemerric.org	1948	9400 REDBRIDGE RD N CHESTERFLD	23236	SE	Dr Matthew D Bean	(804)272-7973 (804)272-6310	WS 830 11 SS 945 BC 945	EC/ED/HC/ MD/SN	808	660	337
	RESURRECTION	1963	2500 SEMINARY AVE	23220	SE		(804)321-7291 (804)228-1025	WS 11 SS 945	HC			
	ST PAUL		See Mechanicsville VA									
	TRINITY admin@tlcrva.org www.tlcrva.org	1956	2315 N Parham Rd PO BOX 31354 HENRICO	23229 23294	SE	Dr Roy W Minnix III Zachary N Bultemeier Samuel R Hoag	(804)270-4626	WS 830 915 1030	EC/ED/HC/ MD/SN			
ROANOKE	*GOOD SHEPHERD* gslcp@gslcp.org gslcp.org	1962	1887 ELECTRIC RD	24018	SE	Derrick K Beasley	(540)774-8746 (540)774-4741	WS 1015 SS 9	EC/ED	137	108	83
RUSTBURG	*OUR SAVIOR*		See Lynchburg VA									
SOUTH CHESTERFIELD	*GRACE*		See Chester VA									
SOUTH RIDING	*OUR SAVIOR'S WAY*		See Ashburn VA									
SPRINGFIELD	*NUEVA VIDA*		See Woodbridge VA									
	PRINCE OF PEACE brad.womble@poplc.org www.poplc.org	1962	8304 OLD KEENE MILL RD	22152	SE	Dr Michael E Hayes Mark L Boriack Robert D Winston	(703)451-5855 (703)569-0978	WS 8 1030 SS 915	EC/ED/HC/ MD/SN	1181	752	460
STAFFORD	*LIVING HOPE* office@livinghopestafford.org www.livinghopestafford.org	2000	325 COURTHOUSE RD	22554	SE	Marcus A Breitbarth	(540)657-4105	WS 815 1045 SS 1030 BC 1030	EC/ED/HC/ MD/SN	150	120	55
	REDEEMER		See Fredericksburg VA									
STAUNTON	*BETHANY-TRINITY*		See Fishersville VA									
STERLING	*OUR SAVIOR'S WAY*		See Ashburn VA									
TRIANGLE	*CONCORDIA* office3637.clc@gmail.com www.concordialutheranva.org	1960	3637 Graham Park Rd PO BOX 336	22172	SE	Dr James R Knill John M McElvain	(703)221-3703	WS 1030 BC 9	ED/HC/ MD/SN	30	28	15
VIENNA	*SAINT ATHANASIUS* salchurch7@gmail.com www.saint-athanasius.org	1999	Vienna Spanish SDA Church 114 Kingsley Rd SW 3057 NUTLEY ST STE 822 FAIRFAX	22180 22031	S	James A Douthwaite	(703)455-4003	WS 1015 SS 9 BC 9	ED/HC/MD	99	72	60

*Indicates a new church start. A new church start is an intentionally organized gathering which comes together on a regular basis for the purpose of worship and/or Bible study and is intended to grow into a member LCMS congregation. WS =Worship Service; SS = Sunday School; BC =Bible Class; EC = Early Childhood; EL = Elementary School; HS = High School; ED =Education Ministry; HC =Human Care Ministry; SN = Special Needs Ministry; MD = Media Ministry (PC)=Partner Church Pastor. See Page 53 for the Table of Abbreviations for key to additional abbreviations

CITY	CONGREGATION EMAIL WEBSITE	YEAR EST	LOCATION MAILING ADDRESS	ZIP CODE(S)	DIST.	PASTOR(S)	PHONE FAX	WS SS BC	SCHOOLS/ MINISTRIES	STATISTIC Bapt	Conf	Avg Attend
VIRGINIA BEACH	*HOPE* connect@hopevabeach.org www.hopevabeach.org	1974	5350 PROVIDENCE RD VIRGINIA BCH	23464	SE	Dr Alexander Whitfield	(757)424-4848 (757)424-7626	WS 815 11 SS 945	EC/ED/HC/ MD/SN	454	326	208
	PRINCE OF PEACE office@princeofpeacevb.org princeofpeacevb.org	1960	424 KINGS GRANT RD VIR-GINIA BCH	23452	SE		(757)340-8420 (757)340-8421	WS 830 11 SS 945 BC 945	EC/ED/HC/ MD/SN	160	145	92
WAYNESBORO	*BETHANY-TRINITY*		See Fishersville VA									
WILLIAMSBURG	*KING OF GLORY* office@kogva.org www.kogva.org	1990	4897 LONGHILL RD	23188	SE	Dr Lannon R Martin Shawn C Linnell	(757)258-9701 (757)564-9810	WS 8 930 11 SS 930 BC 930	EC/ED/HC/ MD	914	744	569
WINCHESTER	*CONCORDIA*		See Hagerstown MD									
	OUR SAVIOR oslc.lcms.2800@gmail.com www.oursavior-lcms.org	1981	2800 MILLWOOD PIKE	22602	SE	Gregory J Cumbee II	(540)667-1459	WS 10 SS 9 BC 9	ED/HC/ MD/SN	114	97	94
WOODBRIDGE	*GRACE* grace@glcvirginia.org www.glcvirginia.org	1962	1601 PRINCE WILLIAM PKWY	22191	SE	Wayne D Puls Dr Young S Yun	(703)494-4600	WS 10 SS 845 BC 845	ED/HC/ MD/SN	239	193	147
	NUEVA VIDA robert.winston@poplc.org www.facebook.com/profile.php?id=100065023803126		Fred Lynn Middle School 1650 Prince William Pkwy C/O PRINCE OF PEACE LUTHERAN CHURCH 8304 OLD KEENE MILL RD SPRINGFIELD	22191 22152	SE		(703)789-3208		MD			

WASHINGTON

CITY	CONGREGATION EMAIL WEBSITE	YEAR EST	LOCATION MAILING ADDRESS	ZIP CODE(S)	DIST.	PASTOR(S)	PHONE FAX	WS SS BC	SCHOOLS/ MINISTRIES	STATISTIC Bapt	Conf	Avg Attend
ABERDEEN	*CALVARY* calvaryaberdeen@gmail.com	1920	2515 Sumner Ave PO BOX 1957	98520	NOW	Daniel D Vines	(360)532-3980 (360)637-8639	WS 10 SS 9 BC 9	EC/ED/HC/ MD	58	45	29
ALDERWOOD	*SAINT TIMOTHY*		See Edmonds WA									
ALGONA	*NEW HOPE*		See Pacific WA									
ANACORTES	*CONCORDIA*		See Oak Harbor WA									
ANDERSON ISLAND	*IN FAITH DEPENDENT*		11408 GUTHRIE RD ANDER-SON IS	98303	NOW	Steven T Cook	(253)884-4974	WS 11 BC 10	SN			
AUBURN	*NEW HOPE*		See Pacific WA									
	OF THE CROSS		See Kent WA									
	OUR SAVIOR		See Tacoma WA									
BASIN CITY	*MESSIAH*		See Mesa WA									
BATTLE GROUND	*PRINCE OF PEACE* office@princeofpeacebg.com www.princeofpeacebg.org	1979	14208 NE 249TH ST	98604	NOW	David M Zemke	(360)687-7455 (360)687-7862	WS 1030 SS 9	EC/ED/MD			
BELLEVUE	*ALL SAINTS* office@allsaints-lcms.com www.allsaints-lcms.com	1974	5501 148TH AVE NE	98007	NOW	Benjamin A Dolby	(425)881-2925	WS 8 1045 SS 915 BC 915	EC/ED/HC/ MD	186	152	91
	JOY staff@joylutheranwa.org www.joylutheranwa.org	2022	10420 SE 11TH ST	98004	NOW		(425)454-1162	WS 9 SS 1030 BC 1030	EC/ED	158	144	91
	REDEEMER		See Mercer Island WA									
BELLINGHAM	*REDEEMER* office@redeemerbellingham.com www.redeemerbellingham.com	1977	858 W SMITH RD	98226	NOW	Rex E Watt	(360)384-5923	WS 1030 SS 9 BC 915	EC/ED	78	76	55
	TRINITY church@trinitybellingham.org www.trinitybellingham.org	1906	119 TEXAS ST	98225	NOW	David S Wagner	(360)734-2770 (360)734-2795	WS 9 11 SS 10 BC 10	EC/ED/HC/ MD/SN	275	225	137
BENTON CITY	*MESSIAH*		See Prosser WA									
BINGEN	*OUR SAVIOR* garymhagen@comcast.net	1953	100 E Jefferson St PO BOX 237	98605	NOW		(509)493-2499	WS 9 SS 1015 BC 8	ED/MD			
BIRCH BAY	*GRACE*		See Blaine WA									
BLAINE	*GRACE* office@bglutheran.com www.blaine-grace-lutheran.org		702 G St PO BOX 1646	98230 98231	NOW	Aaron T Zuch	(360)332-6589 (360)332-6590	WS 1030 430 SS 9 BC 9	EC/ED/HC/ MD			
BONNEY LAKE	*OUR REDEEMER*		See Buckley WA									
	OUR SAVIOR		See Tacoma WA									
BOTHELL	*EPIPHANY*		See Kenmore WA									
	SAINT JAMES www.stjames-lcms.com	1978	19510 Bothell Everett Hwy PO BOX 12806 MILL CREEK	98012 98082	NOW	James B Jenson	(425)745-9859	WS 11 SS 945	EL/MD			
	SHEPHERD HILLS		See Snohomish WA									
BREMERTON	*EVERGREEN*		See Seabeck WA									
	PEACE churchoffice@peacebremerton.org www.peacebremerton.org	1965	1234 NE RIDDELL RD	98310	NOW		(360)377-6253 (360)377-0587	WS 930 SS 930 BC 1030	EL/ED/HC/ MD/SN	416	301	94
BREWSTER	*HOPE* hopeservingjesus@gmail.com	1980	1520 SUNSET DRIVE 1520 SUNSET DR PO BOX 1084	98812	NOW		(509)689-3106	WS 11	ED/HC/ MD/SN			
BRIDGEPORT	*HOPE*		See Brewster WA									
BUCKLEY	*OUR REDEEMER* ourredeemerlutheran@hotmail.com www.ourredeemerlutheran.org	1987	10411 234th Ave E PO BOX 7127 BONNEY LAKE	98321 98391	NOW		(253)862-0715	WS 11 SS 930 BC 930	ED/HC	43	39	27
BURIEN	*ATONEMENT*		See Seattle WA									
	RESURRECTION		See Des Moines WA									
CASTLE ROCK	*GRACE*		See Longview WA									

*Indicates a new church start. A new church start is an intentionally organized gathering which comes together on a regular basis for the purpose of worship and/or Bible study and is intended to grow into a member LCMS congregation. WS =Worship Service; SS = Sunday School; BC =Bible Class; EC = Early Childhood; EL = Elementary School; HS = High School; ED =Education Ministry; HC =Human Care Ministry; SN = Special Needs Ministry; MD = Media Ministry (PC)=Partner Church Pastor. See Page 53 for the Table of Abbreviations for key to additional abbreviations

CITY	CONGREGATION EMAIL WEBSITE	YEAR EST	LOCATION MAILING ADDRESS	ZIP CODE(S)	DIST.	PASTOR(S)	PHONE FAX	WS SS BC	SCHOOLS/ MINISTRIES	STATISTIC Bapt	 Conf	 Avg Attend
CHEHALIS	*PEACE* peacelc@yahoo.com www.chehalislutheran.org/	1914	2071 BISHOP RD	98532	NOW	Daniel L Freeman Larry W Bergman	(360)748-4108	WS 9 SS 1045	EC/ED/HC/ MD/SN	393	242	106
CHELAN	*HOPE*		See Brewster WA									
CLARKSTON	*CONCORDIA*		See Pullman WA									
CLINTON	*CONCORDIA*		See Oak Harbor WA									
COSMOPOLIS	*CALVARY*		See Aberdeen WA									
COULEE CITY	*BETHEL* www.ziongrandcoulee.org	1949	102 N 2nd St PO BOX 446	99115	NOW	Shawn F Neider	(509)633-2566	WS 9 BC 8	ED/HC/ MD/SN	16	11	9
COUPEVILLE	*CONCORDIA*		See Oak Harbor WA									
COVINGTON	*OF THE CROSS*		See Kent WA									
DAVENPORT	*ZION-EMMANUEL*		See Odessa WA									
DEER PARK	*FAITH*	1977	214 S WEBER RD	99006	NOW	Steven J Brehmer	(509)276-5268	WS 10	EC			
DES MOINES	*RESURRECTION* secretary@resurrection-lcms.org www.resurrection-lcms.org	1956	134 S 206TH ST	98198	NOW	Matthew R Mantey	(206)824-2978 (206)824-2979	WS 8 1030 SS 915 BC 930	ED/HC/MD			
DUVALL	*SHEPHERD HILLS*		See Snohomish WA									
EAST WENATCHEE	*FAITH* office@faithlutheranwen.com www.faithlutheranwen.com	1956	171 EASTMONT AVE E WENATCHEE	98802	NOW	Gary A Krumdieck	(509)884-7623 (509)888-6463	WS 930 SS 11 BC 11	EC/ED/HC/ MD/SN	142	130	70
EATONVILLE	*OUR SAVIOR*		See Tacoma WA									
EDMONDS	*SAINT TIMOTHY* stlc_office@frontier.com www.sainttimothylutheran.net	1964	16431 52ND AVE W	98026	NOW	Sean G Berry	(425)743-2323 (425)745-4744	WS 10 SS 1045 BC 1045		75	67	38
ENUMCLAW	*OUR REDEEMER*		See Buckley WA									
	OUR SAVIOR		See Tacoma WA									
EPHRATA	*OUR SAVIOR'S* oursaviorsstaff@hotmail.com	1955	471 NAT WASHINGTON WAY PO BOX 156	98823	NOW		(509)754-3468	WS 10 SS 845 BC 845	ED/HC/MD	97	79	40
EVERETT	*IMMANUEL* office@immanueleverett.org www.immanueleverett.org	1901	2531 Lombard Ave 2521 LOMBARD AVE	98201	NOW		(425)252-7038 (425)258-2729	WS 930 SS 11 BC 11	ED/MD/SN	231	204	115
FEDERAL WAY	*LIGHT OF CHRIST* info@thelight.org www.thelight.org	1987	2400 SW 344TH ST	98023	NOW	Dr Paul K Gossman	(253)874-2517	WS 10 SS 1030 BC 845	EC/ED/HC/ MD/SN			
	ST LUKES church@stlukes-church.com www.stlukes-church.com	1959	515 S 312TH ST	98003	NOW	Daniel J Weber	(253)941-3000 (253)941-8994	WS 815 1045 SS 930 BC 930	EC/EL/ED/ HC/MD/SN	477	422	346
FIFE	*OUR SAVIOR*		See Tacoma WA									
FREDRICKSON	*OUR SAVIOR*		See Tacoma WA									
GEORGE	*CHRIST SAVIOR* ctslcgeorge@gmail.com	1962	214 Deacon Ave PO BOX 5325	98848 98824	NOW			WS 930 SS 11 BC 11				
GIG HARBOR	*KING OF GLORY* office@kingofglorygh.org www.kingofglorygh.org	1973	6411 154TH ST NW	98332	NOW	Stephen K Willweber	(253)857-4574	WS 1015 BC 9	HC			
GRAHAM	*OUR SAVIOR*		See Tacoma WA									
	ST PAUL secretary@lcspgraham.org www.lcspgraham.org	1980	22419 108th Ave E PO BOX 1186	98338	NOW	Matthew G Warmbier	(253)847-3084	WS 9 SS 1015 BC 1015	ED/HC/ MD/SN			
GRAND COULEE	*ZION* ziongrandcoulee@gmail.com www.ziongrandcoulee.org	1934	348 Mead St PO BOX 4	99133	NOW	Shawn F Neider	(509)633-2566	WS 11	ED/HC/ MD/SN	77	45	25
GRANDVIEW	*MESSIAH*		See Prosser WA									
GRANITE FALLS	*CHAPEL ON HILL* www.lutheranchapelonthehill.com	1988	18212 Engebretsen Rd PO BOX 344	98252	NOW		(360)691-2467	WS 2 SS 3 BC 3	ED/MD			
GREENACRES	*REDEEMER*		See Spokane WA									
HARRINGTON	*ZION-EMMANUEL*		See Odessa WA									
HOQUIAM	*CALVARY*		See Aberdeen WA									
KALAMA	*GRACE*		See Longview WA									
KELSO	*GRACE*		See Longview WA									
KENMORE	*EPIPHANY* epiphany@epiphanyonline.org www.epiphanyonline.org	1962	16450 JUANITA DR NE	98028	NOW	Jacob S Mueller	(425)488-9606 (425)488-3212	WS 9 BC 1030	EC/EL	157	140	80
KENNEWICK	*BETHLEHEM* churchoffice@blcbls.org www.blcbls.org	1909	2505 W 27TH AVE	99337	NOW	Joshua M Hileman	(509)582-5858	WS 8 11 SS 930 BC 930	EL/ED/ HC/SN	455	403	228
	EMMAUS		See Pasco WA									
KENT	*KING OF KINGS*		See Renton WA									
	OF THE CROSS office@lutheranchurchofthecross.net www.lutheranchurchofthecross.net	1968	23810 112TH AVE SE	98031	NOW	Kirk S Hulvey	(253)854-3240 (253)854-2721	WS 930 SS 930 BC 930	EL/ED/HC/ MD/SN	282	201	104
	PEACE office@peacecovington.org www.peacecovington.org	1985	18615 SE 272ND ST	98042	NOW	Steven R Heinsen	(253)631-3454 (253)639-4686	WS 8 1045 SS 930	EC/ED/HC/ MD/SN	206	173	116
KINGSTON	*FAITH* Faithlutherankingston@gmail.com www.faithkingston.org	1972	26736 Miller Bay Rd NE PO BOX 1603	98346	NOW		(360)297-2736	WS 1030 SS 930	ED/HC/ MD/SN			
KLICKITAT	*GRACE* garymhagen@comcast.net	1924	84 Parsonage Rd PO BOX 66	98628	NOW		(509)369-4972	WS 11 SS 1215 BC 1215				

*Indicates a new church start. A new church start is an intentionally organized gathering which comes together on a regular basis for the purpose of worship and/or Bible study and is intended to grow into a member LCMS congregation. WS =Worship Service; SS = Sunday School; BC =Bible Class; EC = Early Childhood; EL = Elementary School; HS = High School; ED =Education Ministry; HC =Human Care Ministry; SN = Special Needs Ministry; MD = Media Ministry (PC)=Partner Church Pastor. See Page 53 for the Table of Abbreviations for key to additional abbreviations

CITY	CONGREGATION EMAIL WEBSITE	YEAR EST	LOCATION MAILING ADDRESS	ZIP CODE(S)	DIST.	PASTOR(S)	PHONE FAX	WS SS BC	SCHOOLS/ MINISTRIES	Bapt	Conf	Avg Attend
LACEY	*FAITH* churchoffice@faithcampus.org www.faithlutheranlacey.org	1963	7075 PACIFIC AVE SE	98503	NOW	Gregory A Strand	(360)491-3552 (360)459-3784	WS 830 1115 SS 10 BC 10	EL/ED/ HC/SN			
LAKE STEVENS	*LAMB OF GOD* secretary@lambofgod-lakestevens.org www.lambofgod-lakestevens.org	1994	3923 103RD AVE SE	98258	NOW	George M May	(425)377-2173	WS 1015 SS 9 BC 9	EL/ED/HC	240	198	60
LAKEWOOD	*GRACE* pastor@gracelutherantacoma.org gracelutherantacoma.org	1924	10333 Bridgeport Way SW PO BOX 9292 TACOMA	98499 98490	NOW	James A Matthews	(253)472-7105	WS 8 11 BC 930	ED/MD			
	OUR SAVIOR		See Tacoma WA									
	PRINCE OF PEACE office@poplakewood.org www.poplakewood.org	1959	10333 BRIDGEPORT WAY SW	98499	NOW		(253)584-2565	WS 8 11 BC 930	ED/HC/ MD/SN			
LANGLEY	*CONCORDIA*		See Oak Harbor WA									
LIBERTY LAKE	*BLESSED SACRAMENT*		See Hayden ID									
	REDEEMER		See Spokane WA									
LIND	*ZION-EMMANUEL*		See Odessa WA									
LONG BEACH	*ST JOHN*		See Seaview WA									
LONGVIEW	*GRACE* gracelutheranchurch2@gmail.com glclongview.org	1926	2725 DOVER ST	98632	NOW	Eli J Thomas	(360)423-2114	WS 1	ED/HC/ MD/SN	154	127	23
LYNNWOOD	*SAINT TIMOTHY*		See Edmonds WA									
MALTBY	*SHEPHERD HILLS*		See Snohomish WA									
MARLIN	*SALEM*	1903	375 W 1st P.O. BOX 32 WILSON CREEK	98832 98860	NOW		(509)345-2564	WS 8				
MARYSVILLE	*MESSIAH* secretary@messiah-lcms.org www.messiah-lcms.org	1956	9209 STATE AVE	98270	NOW	Kurt D Onken	(360)659-4112 (360)658-1814	WS 8 1045 SS 930 BC 930	EL/ED/HC/ MD/SN			
MELROSE	*MESSIAH*		See Lynnfield MA									
MERCER ISLAND	*REDEEMER* office@redeemerlutheranmi.org www.redeemerlutheranmi.org	1961	6001 ISLAND CREST WAY	98040	NOW	Eugene W Baade	(206)232-1711 (206)275-1424	WS 10 SS 10 BC 11	ED/HC/ MD/SN	57	56	20
MESA	*MESSIAH* goatfarmer@hotmail.com	1962	291 Loen Dr PO BOX 406	99343	NOW	James R Pierce	(509)492-7399	WS 9		35	33	28
MILL CREEK	*SAINT JAMES*		See Bothell WA									
	SHEPHERD HILLS		See Snohomish WA									
MILTON	*BEAUTIFUL SAVIOR* staff@mybslc.com www.mybslc.com	1963	2306 MILTON WAY	98354	NOW	Samuel P Schuldheisz	(253)922-6977 (253)922-7953	WS 930 SS 1045 BC 1045	EC/EL/HS/ ED/HC/MD	211	184	120
	OUR SAVIOR		See Tacoma WA									
MONROE	*PEACE* peacechurchmonroe@live.com www.peacemonroe.org	1949	202 DICKINSON RD	98272	NOW	Todd E Roeske	(360)794-2082	WS 10 SS 1015 BC 845	EC/EL/ED/ MD	153	123	54
MONTESANO	*CALVARY*		See Aberdeen WA									
MOSES LAKE	*THE APOSTOLIC* winstongrieser@gmail.com alcml.org		422 ROAD S NE GETZINGER FARMS	98837	EN		(509)760-4278	WS 930 SS 11	ED/HC	30	22	25
MOUNT VERNON	*TRINITY* office@tlcmv.com tlcmv.com	1927	301 S 18TH ST	98274	NOW	Kevin L Schubkegel	(360)428-0290	WS 1030 SS 930 BC 930	EC/ED/HC/ MD/SN	142	120	66
MOUNTLAKE TERRACE	*MEKANE YESUS*		21428 44TH AVE W	98043	NOW	Berhanu Seyoum	(206)371-2938					
	SAINT TIMOTHY		See Edmonds WA									
MUKILTEO	*SAINT TIMOTHY*		See Edmonds WA									
NEAH BAY	*MAKAH*	1974	1290 Back Track Rd PO BOX 600	98357	NOW		(360)645-2523	WS 11 SS 930	ED/HC/MD			
NEWMAN LAKE	*BLESSED SACRAMENT*		See Hayden ID									
NORMANDY PARK	*RESURRECTION*		See Des Moines WA									
NORTH BEND	*CHAPEL OF THE CROSS*	2002	49515 SE MIDDLE FORK RD	98045	NOW							
OAK HARBOR	*CONCORDIA* Clcwhidbey@gmail.com www.ConcordiaOakHarbor.org	1959	590 N OAK HARBOR ST	98277	NOW	Mark T Hanson	(360)675-2548	WS 930	ED/HC/MD	78	52	40
OCEAN SHORES	*CALVARY*		See Aberdeen WA									
ODESSA	*ZION-EMMANUEL* pastor@zionemmanuel.org www.zionemmanuel.org	1959	4279 STATE ROUTE 21 N	99159	NOW	Pierce H Chadburn	(509)982-2402	WS 1030 BC 930		54	50	20
OKANOGAN	*OUR SAVIOR* deacon@ncidata.com	1960	2262 BURTON AVE	98840	NOW	Brian Bowes	(509)429-1567	WS 9	ED/HC/MD	46	27	27
OLYMPIA	*FAITH*		See Lacey WA									
	TRINITY tlcolympiaoffice@trinityolympia.comcastbiz.net www.trinityolympia.org	1908	2020 FRANKLIN ST SE	98501	NOW	Michael D Wenzel	(360)357-6574	WS 830 11 SS 945 BC 945	ED/HC/MD			
OROVILLE	*FAITH* flc.oroville@gmail.com	1956	1019 Ironwood St PO BOX 338	98844	NOW		(509)476-2426	WS 9	ED/HC/MD	12	12	9

*Indicates a new church start. A new church start is an intentionally organized gathering which comes together on a regular basis for the purpose of worship and/or Bible study and is intended to grow into a member LCMS congregation. WS =Worship Service; SS = Sunday School; BC =Bible Class; EC = Early Childhood; EL = Elementary School; HS = High School; ED =Education Ministry; HC =Human Care Ministry; SN = Special Needs Ministry; MD = Media Ministry (PC)=Partner Church Pastor. See Page 53 for the Table of Abbreviations for key to additional abbreviations

CITY	CONGREGATION EMAIL WEBSITE	YEAR EST	LOCATION MAILING ADDRESS	ZIP CODE(S)	DIST.	PASTOR(S)	PHONE FAX	WS SS BC	SCHOOLS/ MINISTRIES	STATISTIC Bapt	Conf	Avg Attend
ORTING	*OUR SAVIOR*		See Tacoma WA									
OTIS ORCHARDS	*BLESSED SACRAMENT*		See Hayden ID									
PACIFIC	*NEW HOPE*	1989	603 3RD AVE SE	98047	NOW	Mark E Gause	(253)351-0450	WS 10 SS 11	ED/HC/SN			
PARKLAND	*OUR SAVIOR*		See Tacoma WA									
PASCO	*BETHLEHEM*		See Kennewick WA									
	EMMAUS pastor@emmauspasco.org www.emmauspasco.org	1954	Holiday Inn Express 4525 Convention Pl PO BOX 2960	99301 99302	NOW	James R Pierce	(509)547-3466	WS 11 SS 1015		41	41	36
PATEROS	*HOPE*		See Brewster WA									
PORT ANGELES	*ST MATTHEW* stmatthewpa@gmail.com stmatthewportangeles.org	1938	132 E 13TH ST	98362	NOW		(360)457-4122 (360)457-4122	WS 10 BC 845	EC/ED/HC/ MD	285	220	87
PROSSER	*MESSIAH* messiahprosser@gmail.com messiahprosser.org	1949	801 LUTHER LN	99350	NOW	Don M Petersen	(509)786-2011 (509)786-7820	WS 9	EC/ED/HC	85	71	35
	SUN TERRACE Satellite Site of Messiah Prosser WA	2005	2131 Wine Country Rd	99350								
PULLMAN	*CONCORDIA* info@concordiapullman.org www.concordiapullman.org	1955	1015 NE ORCHARD DR	99163	NOW	Matthew M Gulseth	(509)332-2830	WS 10 SS 9 BC 9	EC/ED/HC/ MD/SN	163	121	112
PUYALLUP	*OUR SAVIOR*		See Tacoma WA									
	OUR SAVIOR - IMMANUEL CAMPUS Satellite Site of Our Savior Tacoma WA	2025	720 W Main	98371								
QUINCY	*CHRIST SAVIOR*		See George WA									
REDMOND	*ALL SAINTS*		See Bellevue WA									
RENTON	*AMAZING GRACE* drzimmerman@rentonprep.org www.rentonprep.org	1952	C/O RENTON PREP CHRISTIAN SCHOOL 200 MILL AVE S SUITE 110	98057	NOW	Dr David P Zimmerman	(206)723-5526		EL/HS/ED	5	5	2
	KING OF KINGS office@king-of-kings.org www.king-of-kings.org	1960	18207 108TH AVE SE	98055	NOW	Paul D Birner	(425)226-1480 (425)276-5327	WS 830 11 SS 945 BC 945	ED/HC/ MD/SN	243	162	96
	OF THE CROSS		See Kent WA									
REPUBLIC	*TRINITY* iam4givn1944@yahoo.com	1961	118 E Delaware Ave PO BOX 615	99166	NOW	Kenneth E Schauer	(509)775-2617	WS 11 BC 930	ED/HC	35	33	15
RICHLAND	*BETHLEHEM*		See Kennewick WA									
	EMMAUS		See Pasco WA									
	REDEEMER office@richlandredeemer.org www.richlandredeemer.org	1945	520 THAYER DR	99352	NOW	Todd E Schroeder	(509)943-4967 (509)946-6817	WS 9 SS 1015 BC 1030	ED/MD/SN	262	241	93
RIDGEFIELD	*CHRIST COMMUNITY* office@ccridgefield.com ccridgefield.com		2724 S Hillhurst Rd 202 S 4TH AVE	98642	NOW	Eli J Thomas	(360)727-3578	WS 930 SS 930	ED/HC/ MD/SN	115	88	70
RITZVILLE	*ZION-EMMANUEL*		See Odessa WA									
SEABECK	*EVERGREEN* evergreenlutheran@wavecable.com www.seabecklutheran.com	1980	3200 Seabeck Holly Rd NW PO BOX 740	98380	NOW	David A Carnahan	(360)830-4180	WS 10 SS 830	EC/ED/HC/ MD/SN			
SEATTLE	*ATONEMENT* atone@atonement-lcms.org www.atonement-lcms.org	1946	740 S 128TH ST	98168	NOW		(206)244-3020	WS 930 SS 11 BC 11	ED/HC/SN	75	64	36
	BEAUTIFUL SAVIOR beautiful-savior-seatac@comcast.net www.beautifulsaviorseatac.org	1951	16919 33RD AVE S SEATAC	98188	NOW	Christopher N Howell	(206)246-9533	WS 9 SS 1030 BC 1030	EC/ED/ MD/SN	282	174	30
	CHAPEL ON THE AVE Satellite Site of Trinity Seattle WA	2005	4130 University Way NE	98105								
	CHRIST SON OF GOD	2015	1720 S FOREST ST	98144	NOW	Beniam B Habthemariam						
	ERITREAN		12509 27th Ave NE 4701 154TH PL SW LYNNWOOD	98125 98087	NOW							
	GOOD SHEPHERD lcgs22un@outlook.com	1951	2116 E UNION ST	98122	NOW	Nathan C Whittaker	(206)325-2733	WS 11 SS 10 BC 10	EL/ED/HC/ MD			
	HOPE church@hopeseattle.org www.hopeseattle.org	1919	4456 42ND AVE SW	98116	NOW	Peter C Mueller	(206)937-9330 (206)937-9332	WS 9 1045 SS 1030 BC 930	EL/ED/HC/ MD	383	321	117
	LAMB OF GOD www.lambofgodseattle.org	2008	12509 27TH AVE NE	98125	NOW	Paul E Winterstein	(206)363-0110	WS 1030 SS 9 BC 9	EL/ED/HC/ MD/SN			
	MESSIAH office@messiahseattle.org www.messiahseattle.org	1947	7050 35TH AVE NE	98115	NOW	Dr Peter W Elliott	(206)524-0024 (206)524-4119	WS 9 SS 1030 BC 1030	EL/ED/ MD/SN	235	190	159
	REDEEMER		See Mercer Island WA									
	REFORMATION EMMANUEL cgmpastor23@hotmail.com		2116 E UNION ST	98122	NOW							

*Indicates a new church start. A new church start is an intentionally organized gathering which comes together on a regular basis for the purpose of worship and/or Bible study and is intended to grow into a member LCMS congregation. WS =Worship Service; SS = Sunday School; BC =Bible Class; EC = Early Childhood; EL = Elementary School; HS = High School; ED =Education Ministry; HC =Human Care Ministry; SN = Special Needs Ministry; MD = Media Ministry (PC)=Partner Church Pastor. See Page 53 for the Table of Abbreviations for key to additional abbreviations

CITY	CONGREGATION EMAIL WEBSITE	YEAR EST	LOCATION MAILING ADDRESS	ZIP CODE(S)	DIST.	PASTOR(S)	PHONE FAX	WS SS BC	SCHOOLS/ MINISTRIES	STATISTIC Bapt	Conf	Avg Attend
SEATTLE	*RESURRECTION*		See Des Moines WA									
	TRINITY office@tlcseattle.org tlcseattle.org	1901	1200 10TH AVE E	98102	NOW	Dillon M Weber	(206)324-1066	WS 10 BC 9	EL/ED/HC/ MD	84	66	42
	W WASH DEAF	1921	766 John St C/O BEAUTIFUL SAVIOR LUTHERAN CHURCH 16919 33RD AVE S SEATAC	98109 98188	NOW		(206)246-9533	WS 11 BC 10	ED/SN			
SEAVIEW	*ST JOHN* stjohnseaview@gmail.com	1972	5000 N Place PO BOX 271	98644	NOW		(360)642-4930	WS 10				
	ST. JOHN LUTHERAN CHURCH Satellite Site of St John Seaview WA	2023	5000 N Place	98644				WS 10				
SELAH	*MEN'S BIBLE STUDY* Satellite Site of Peace Selah WA	2024	307 South First Street	98942								
	PEACE peacelutheranselah@gmail.com peacelutheranchurch.360unite.com/	1961	91 Wernex Loop 91 WERNEX LOOP RD	98942	NOW		(509)697-4353 (509)697-6471	WS 9 SS 915 BC 1030	ED/HC/ MD/SN	112	86	35
SEQUIM	*FAITH* faithlutheransequim@yahoo.com www.faithlutheransequim.org	1964	382 West Cedar PO BOX 925	98382	NOW	Roger E Stites Jr	(360)683-4803 (360)683-1206	WS 830 11 SS 945 BC 945	EC			
SHELTON	*ALPINE WAY* Satellite Site of Mount Olive Shelton WA	2022	900 Alpine Way	98584				WS 2				
	MOUNT OLIVE molcshelton@comcast.net www.mtoliveshelton.org	1926	206 E WYANDOTTE AVE	98584	NOW	William C Baker	(360)426-6353	WS 830 11 SS 10	EC/ED/HC/ MD/SN			
SHORELINE	*SAINT TIMOTHY*		See Edmonds WA									
SILVERDALE	*EVERGREEN*		See Seabeck WA									
SNOHOMISH	*LAMB OF GOD*		See Lake Stevens WA									
	SHEPHERD HILLS snohomishshepherd@gmail.com www.snohomishshepherd.org	1972	9225 212TH ST SE	98296	NOW	Warrens E Berger	(360)668-7881	WS 8 1045 SS 1045 BC 1045	EC/ED	376	314	132
	ZION snohomishsecretary@gmail.com zionsnohomish.360unite.com	1892	329 Ave A 331 UNION AVE	98290	NOW	Don A Stults	(360)568-2700 (360)568-2700	WS 9 SS 1030 BC 1030	EL/ED/HC/ MD	155	141	53
SOUTH HILL	*OUR SAVIOR*		See Tacoma WA									
SPANAWAY	*OUR SAVIOR*		See Tacoma WA									
SPOKANE	*BEAUTIFUL SAVIOR* office@beautifulsaviorspokane.org www.beautifulsaviorspokane.org	1956	4320 S CONKLIN ST	99203	NOW	Justin M Chester	(509)747-6806 (509)747-7342	WS 9 SS 1030 BC 1030	EC/ED/HC/ MD	209	209	102
	HOLY CROSS secretary@holycrosslcms.net www.holycrosslcms.net	1949	7307 N NEVADA ST	99208	NOW	Shaun P Adams	(509)483-4218 (509)483-4293	WS 830 1045 BC 830 1030	EC/ED/HC/ MD/SN	664	558	212
	HOPE		See Spokane Valley WA									
	NEW VISION dougwagley@outlook.com		3307 W Rowan 3307 W ROWAN AVE	99205	NOW	Douglas L Wagley	(509)499-0121	WS 945 SS 1115	ED/HC/SN	75	70	75
	PILGRIM pilgrimchurchspokane@gmail.com www.pilgrimchurchspokane.org	1927	2733 W NORTHWEST BLVD	99205	NOW		(509)325-5738	WS 9 SS 1015 BC 1015	EC/ED/HC/ MD/SN	160	159	81
	REDEEMER frontdesk@redeemeralive.org www.redeemeralive.org	1926	3606 S SCHAFER RD SPO-KANE VLY	99206	NOW	David C Noll Andrew C Bayless	(509)926-6363 (509)926-4573	WS 830 1030	EC/ED/HC/ MD/SN			
	ST JOHN'S frontdesk@sjlspokane.org sjlspokane.org	1900	5810 S MEADOWLANE RD	99224	NOW	David C LaFore	(509)747-0984 (509)443-5902	WS 10 SS 930 BC 930 630	ED	103	103	95
SPOKANE VALLEY	*BLESSED SACRAMENT*		See Hayden ID									
	HOPE pastorwulf@hlcms.org www.hlcms.org	1951	17909 E BROADWAY AVE SPOKANE VLY	99016	NOW	Craig M Wulf Kerry E Torske	(509)924-1630	WS 930 SS 1030 BC 8	ED/HC/MD	130	128	75
SUMNER	*OUR REDEEMER*		See Buckley WA									
SUNNYSIDE	*CALVARY* calvary_lc@hotmail.com	1939	804 S 11th St PO BOX 507	98944	NOW	Don M Petersen	(509)837-5662	WS 11 BC 10	EC/ED	63	43	20
TACOMA	*GOOD SHEPHERD* secretary@goodshepherdluth.com www.goodshepherdluth.com	1950	140 E 56TH ST	98404	NOW	Dr Joel M Schuldheisz	(253)473-4848 (253)473-4849	WS 9 BC 1030	EC/EL/HS/ ED/HC/MD	133	112	95
	GRACE		See Lakewood WA									
	OUR SAVIOR info@oslc.com oslc.com	1962	4519 112TH ST E	98446	NOW	Timothy R Bayer Matthew J Cario	(253)531-2112 (253)531-2997	WS 9 1030 SS 9 1030	EC/EL/HS/ ED/HC/ MD/SN	1073	926	766
	ZION ziontacoma@gmail.com zion-tacoma.org	1890	3410 6TH AVE	98406	NOW	Jeffrey E Ries	(253)752-1264	WS 8 1030 SS 915 BC 915	EL/HS/ED/ HC/MD/SN			
TONASKET	*HOPE*	1942	623 S Whitcomb PO BOX 607	98855	NOW	Brian Bowes	(509)486-2254	WS 1115	ED/HC/MD	23	19	18
	IMMANUEL immanuel@nvinet.com	1905	1608 HAVILLAH RD	98855	NOW		(509)485-3342 (509)485-3342	WS 9 SS 1030 BC 1030	ED/HC/SN	45	35	22
TWISP	*HOPE*		See Brewster WA									
VANCOUVER	*GOOD SHEPHERD* office@vanflock.org www.vanflock.org	1992	16001 NE 34TH ST	98682	NOW	Dr Theodore C Moeller III	(360)254-5158 (360)254-1679	WS 9 11 SS 1015 BC 1015	ED/HC/ MD/SN	267	251	116

*Indicates a new church start. A new church start is an intentionally organized gathering which comes together on a regular basis for the purpose of worship and/or Bible study and is intended to grow into a member LCMS congregation. WS =Worship Service; SS = Sunday School; BC =Bible Class; EC = Early Childhood; EL = Elementary School; HS = High School; ED =Education Ministry; HC =Human Care Ministry; SN = Special Needs Ministry; MD = Media Ministry (PC)=Partner Church Pastor. See Page 53 for the Table of Abbreviations for key to additional abbreviations

CITY	CONGREGATION EMAIL WEBSITE	YEAR EST	LOCATION MAILING ADDRESS	ZIP CODE(S)	DIST.	PASTOR(S)	PHONE FAX	WS SS BC	SCHOOLS/ MINISTRIES	STATISTIC Bapt	Conf	Avg Attend
VANCOUVER	*GRACE* office@gracevancouver.org www.gracevancouver.org	1958	9900 SE Mill Plain Blvd PO BOX 873129	98664 98657	NOW	Gary A Syth Jr	(360)892-7850	WS 10 SS 1115 BC 1115	EC/ED/MD	106	91	43
	MEMORIAL office@mlc.org www.mlc.org	1943	2700 E 28 St 2602 E 28TH ST	98661	NOW	Daniel J Adams	(360)695-7501	WS 815 1045 SS 930 BC 930	ED/HC/ MD/SN	165	140	150
	ST JOHN info@stjohnlc.com stjohnlc.com	1908	11005 NE HIGHWAY 99	98686	NOW	Brian T Larson	(360)573-1461 (360)574-8726	WS 815 11 SS 945 BC 945	EL/ED/HC	492	400	141
	VIETNAMESE GRACE andrew.d.nguyen@biola.edu www.vnglc.org	2020	16001 NE 34th St 11005 NE HIGHWAY 99	98682 98686	NOW		(503)516-4660					
WALLA WALLA	*TRINITY* tlcwallawalla@gmail.com tlcwallawalla.weebly.com	1908	109 S ROOSEVELT ST	99362	NOW	Dr Stephen P Juergensen	(509)525-2493 (509)525-2493	WS 10 SS 1115 BC 1115	ED/MD	130	101	43
WASHOUGAL	*ST MATTHEW* stmatthewlcms@comcast.net www.stmattlutheran.com	1941	716 WASHOUGAL RIVER RD	98671	NOW	Robert G Barber Jr	(360)835-5533 (360)835-7755	WS 1030 SS 9 BC 9	ED/HC/ MD/SN	71	71	70
WENATCHEE	*ST PAUL* office@stpaulwen.com www.stpaulwen.com	1913	312 PALOUSE ST	98801	NOW	Dr Donald E Ray	(509)662-8790	WS 1015 SS 9 BC 9	EL/HS/ED/ HC/MD	158	108	92
WEST RICHLAND	*EMMAUS*		See Pasco WA									
WILBUR	*ZION-EMMANUEL*		See Odessa WA									
WINTHROP	*HOPE*		See Brewster WA									
WOODINVILLE	*SHEPHERD HILLS*		See Snohomish WA									
YAKIMA	*BETHLEHEM* blcofyakima@gmail.com blcyakima.org	1902	801 TIETON DR	98902	NOW		(509)457-5822	WS 11 SS 930 BC 930	ED/HC/ MD/SN	101	86	55
	MOUNT OLIVE info4me@mountoliveyakima.org mountoliveyakima.org	1965	7809 TIETON DR	98908	NOW	Peter J Knutson	(509)966-2190 (509)972-4932	WS 9 SS 1015 BC 1015	EC/ED/HC/ MD	207	183	101

WEST VIRGINIA

CITY	CONGREGATION EMAIL WEBSITE	YEAR EST	LOCATION MAILING ADDRESS	ZIP CODE(S)	DIST.	PASTOR(S)	PHONE FAX	WS SS BC	SCHOOLS/ MINISTRIES	Bapt	Conf	Avg Attend
ALDERSON	*CHRIST OUR SAVIOR** edwarduncleshrek@aol.com		103 Railroad Ave PO BOX 292	24910	OH		(304)445-2286	WS 11 SS 10	ED/HC/MD	4	4	11
BRIDGEPORT	*ST JOHN'S* info@stjohnslutheranwv.org www.stjohnslutheranwv.org		721 HALL ST	26330	EN	Christopher D Harrison	(304)608-3597	WS 11 SS 10		68	45	31
CHARLESTON	*REDEEMER* church@redeemerwv.org www.redeemerwv.org	1953	#1 Deerwalk Ln 1 DEERWALK LN	25314	OH	Frank C Ruffatto	(304)345-6251	WS 1045 SS 930	ED/HC/ MD/SN	91	86	57
CLARKSBURG	*ST JOHN'S*		See Bridgeport WV									
FAIRMONT	*ST JOHN'S*		See Bridgeport WV									
FALLING WATERS	*CONCORDIA*		See Hagerstown MD									
FORT ASHBY	*TRINITY*		See Cumberland MD									
HUNTINGTON	*OUR REDEEMER* orelc.wv@gmail.com www.ourredeemerhuntington.org	1952	3047 WASHINGTON BLVD	25705	OH		(304)529-7365	WS 10 SS 1115	HC			
KEYSER	*TRINITY*		See Cumberland MD									
MARTINSBURG	*CONCORDIA*		See Hagerstown MD									
PARKERSBURG	*ST PAUL* office@stpaulwv.org www.stpaulwv.org	1887	3500 BROAD ST	26104	OH	Daniel S Golden	(304)428-5826	WS 1015 SS 9 BC 9	MD/SN	150	129	65
RIDEGELY	*TRINITY*		See Cumberland MD									
ROMNEY	*TRINITY*		See Cumberland MD									

WISCONSIN

CITY	CONGREGATION EMAIL WEBSITE	YEAR EST	LOCATION MAILING ADDRESS	ZIP CODE(S)	DIST.	PASTOR(S)	PHONE FAX	WS SS BC	SCHOOLS/ MINISTRIES	Bapt	Conf	Avg Attend
ABBOTSFORD	*CHRIST* clcabby@frontier.com www.christlutheranabby.org	1915	308 W LINDEN ST	54405	NW	Donald Bruce	(715)223-4315 (715)223-8183	WS 10 SS 11 BC 11	ED/MD	211	200	60
ADAMS	*IMMANUEL* ilcmsaf@hotmail.com www.adamsimmanuellutheran.com	1933	243 N LINDEN ST	53910	SW	John R Krebs	(608)339-6102	WS 9 SS 8	ED/MD	194	178	60
	ST JOHN janegrabarski@gmail.com	1875	2823 COUNTY ROAD Z	53910	SW	Brian M Beardsley	(608)339-7869	WS 9 SS 1015	ED	51	47	35
ADELL	*EMMANUEL* secretary@emmanueladell.org emmanueladell.org	1915	326 CENTER AVE	53001	SW	Paul W Marks	(920)994-9005	WS 9 SS 1015 BC 1015	ED/HC/MD	235	182	99
	ST PAULS		See Cascade WI									
	ST STEPHEN		See Batavia WI									
ALGOMA	*ST JOHN'S* mail@stjohnsalgoma.org stjohnsalgoma.org	1867	E5221 CHURCH RD	54201	NW	Dr Christopher Jackson	(920)487-2335 (920)487-2335	WS 830 SS 945 BC 945	ED/HC/ MD/SN	275	222	83
ALLENTON	*IMMANUEL*		See Mayville WI									
ALMA CENTER	*GRACE* gracelms@centurytel.net	1908	136 W Main PO BOX 156	54611	NW		(715)964-2203	WS 1030 SS 9 BC 9	ED/MD/SN	265	199	44
ALMENA	*ST MATTHEW* stmatthewchurch@chibardun.net	1896	315 CLINTON ST S P.O. BOX 28	54805	NW	Isaac W Nicholson	(715)357-3267	WS 1030 SS 9 BC 930	ED/HC/MD	309	153	61

*Indicates a new church start. A new church start is an intentionally organized gathering which comes together on a regular basis for the purpose of worship and/or Bible study and is intended to grow into a member LCMS congregation. WS =Worship Service; SS = Sunday School; BC =Bible Class; EC = Early Childhood; EL = Elementary School; HS = High School; ED =Education Ministry; HC =Human Care Ministry; SN = Special Needs Ministry; MD = Media Ministry (PC)=Partner Church Pastor. See Page 53 for the Table of Abbreviations for key to additional abbreviations

CITY	CONGREGATION EMAIL WEBSITE	YEAR EST	LOCATION MAILING ADDRESS	ZIP CODE(S)	DIST.	PASTOR(S)	PHONE FAX	WS SS BC	SCHOOLS/ MINISTRIES	STATISTIC Bapt	Conf	Avg Attend
ALMOND	*ST JOHN* stjohnsalmond@gmail.com www.stjohnsalmond.com	1870	1165 COUNTY ROAD D	54909	NW	Richard O Bartholomew	(715)366-2480	WS 10 SS 845	ED/HC	115	97	34
ALTOONA	*BETHLEHEM* pastortim@blcaltoona.org www.blcaltoona.org	1906	2245 HAYDEN AVE	54720	NW	Timothy A Stein	(715)832-9953	WS 830 1045 SS 945 BC 10	EC/ED/HC/ MD	307	254	167
AMERY	*REDEEMER* rlcpo@amerytel.net redeemerlutheranchurch-amery.com	1918	600 KELLER AVE S	54001	NW	Edward E Clemens	(715)268-7283	WS 930 SS 1045 BC 1045	ED/HC/ MD/SN			
AMHERST	*ST PAUL* stpaul@wi-net.com	1860	203 GRANT ST	54406	NW	Gerhard Wilch	(715)824-3314	WS 8 1030 SS 9 BC 9	ED/HC/ MD/SN			
ANIWA	*ZION*		See Wausau WI									
ANTIGO	*PEACE* peace.info@peaceantigo.org www.peaceantigo.org	1884	300 LINCOLN ST	54409	NW	David B Karolus Jarod M Fenske	(715)623-2200 (715)627-0845	WS 8 1030 BC 915	EL/ED/HC/ MD/SN	1040	802	348
	ST PETER	1886	N2891 COUNTY RD S	54409	NW	Donald V Engebretson	(715)623-6921	WS 9 SS 10 BC 10				
APPLETON	*FAITH* churchoffice@faithfv.org www.faithfoxvalley.org	1949	601 E GLENDALE AVE	54911	NW	Daniel P Thews Richard A Bridgman	(920)739-9191 (920)739-6030	WS 8 920 1040 SS 920 BC 920	EL/ED/HC/ MD/SN			
	FAITH LUTHERAN CHURCH - CELEBRATION MINISTRY CENTER Satellite Site of Faith Appleton WI	2009	3100 E Evergreen Dr	54913				WS 9 SS 1020 BC 1020				
	GOOD SHEPHERD goodshep@gslchurch.net www.goodsheplutheran.net	1962	2220 E COLLEGE AVE	54915	NW	Timothy M Seabaugh	(920)734-9643 (920)882-8978	WS 8 1030 SS 915	ED/HC/ MD/SN	1536	1164	248
	NEW HOPE		See Neenah WI									
ARBOR VITAE	*PEACE* office@peacearborvitae.org www.peacearborvitae.org	2000	10868 Old Hwy 51 N 10868 OLD 51 N	54568	NW	Jonathan C Rathjen	(715)358-8338 (715)358-3759	WS 9	ED/HC/MD	115	112	49
	TRINITY		See Boulder Junction WI									
ARKDALE	*IMMANUEL*		See Adams WI									
ARLINGTON	*ST PETER* stpeterluth@gmail.com www.stpetersarlington.org	1907	303 Park St PO BOX 45	53911	SW	David M Juhl	(608)635-4825 (608)635-2753	WS 8 1030 SS 915 BC 915	EL/ED/MD	625	470	114
ASHLAND	*ZION* secretary@zionlutheranashland.com zionashland.org	1884	1111 11TH AVE W	54806	NW	Richard F Williams	(715)682-6075	WS 9 SS 845 BC 1015	EC/ED/ HC/SN	658	459	70
ATHENS	*BETHLEHEM* secretary@stjbeth.org www.stjbeth.org	1907	233500 COUNTY ROAD E	54411	NW		(715)352-2888	WS 8 SS 915	ED/HC/SN			
	ST JOHN dlwglw1@gmail.com	1867	486 County Rd F 134058 COUNTY ROAD L	54411	NW	Donald G Love	(715)536-1810	WS 830 SS 930	EC/ED/HC/ MD			
	TRINITY trinitylutheranchurchandschool@gmail.com www.trinityathens.net	1882	301 Elm St PO BOX 100	54411	NW	Mark L Schwarz	(715)257-7526 (715)257-7559	WS 9 SS 10 BC 10	EL/ED/MD	774	595	170
AUBURNDALE	*ST JOHN*	1878	10571 George Ave PO BOX 96	54412	NW	Mark A Lundgren	(715)652-2213 (715)652-2213	WS 9 SS 10 BC 8	ED/HC/SN			
AUGUSTA	*GRACE* graceaugusta@plbb.us	1870	814 HUDSON ST	54722	NW	Jonathan A Wessel	(715)286-2116	WS 9 SS 1015 BC 1015	ED/HC/ MD/SN	458	366	93
AURORAVILLE	*IMMANUEL*	1887	N2506 STATE ROAD 49 BERLIN	54923	SW	Ryan S Willis Sr	(920)361-1812	WS 830	ED/HC	52	51	40
BARABOO	*OUR SAVIOR*	1973	1120 DRAPER ST	53913	SW	Matthew J Gehrke	(608)356-9792 (608)356-9792	WS 8 SS 930 BC 930	EC/ED	99	90	15
BARRON	*SALEM* salembarron@gmail.com salembarron.com	1893	1360 E LA SALLE AVE	54812	NW		(715)537-3011 (715)537-5949	WS 9 SS 1030 BC 1030	EC/ED/MD	228	165	61
BATAVIA	*ST STEPHEN* lutheransinbatavia.ctshost.org	1884	N1510 Highway 28 N1510 STATE ROAD 28 ADELL	53001	SW	Brian L Krueger	(920)994-9060	WS 1030	ED/HC/MD			
BEAR CREEK	*GRACE*	1924	409 W Willow St PO BOX 187	54922	NW		(715)752-4855	WS 830 SS 945	ED/SN	167	137	81
	TRINITY www.gracetrinitylcms.org	1875	E8010 STATE ROAD 22	54922	NW		(715)752-3601 (715)752-3601	WS 1015 SS 9	ED/HC/ MD/SN	246	222	92
BEAVER DAM	*PEACE* office@bdpeacelutheran.org www.beaverdampeace.360unite.com	1964	400 HILLCREST DR	53916	SW	Jesse R Gullion	(920)887-1272	WS 8 1030 SS 1030 BC 1030	ED/HC/ MD/SN	328	298	126
	ZION		See Burnett WI									
BELGIUM	*ST MARK* stmarkbelgium1@gmail.com www.stmarklutheranbelgium.org	1987	200 PARK ST	53004	SW	Lewis R Polzin	(262)285-3820	WS 9 SS 1015 BC 1015	ED/HC/ MD/SN	113	113	52
BELOIT	*MESSIAH* messiahlutheransecretary@gmail.com mlcbeloit.com	1959	1531 TOWNLINE AVE	53511	SW	Daniel C Eddy	(608)365-3794	WS 9 11 SS 10	ED/HC/ MD/SN	390	264	115

*Indicates a new church start. A new church start is an intentionally organized gathering which comes together on a regular basis for the purpose of worship and/or Bible study and is intended to grow into a member LCMS congregation. WS =Worship Service; SS = Sunday School; BC =Bible Class; EC = Early Childhood; EL = Elementary School; HS = High School; ED =Education Ministry; HC =Human Care Ministry; SN = Special Needs Ministry; MD = Media Ministry (PC)=Partner Church Pastor. See Page 53 for the Table of Abbreviations for key to additional abbreviations

CITY	CONGREGATION EMAIL WEBSITE	YEAR EST	LOCATION MAILING ADDRESS	ZIP CODE(S)	DIST.	PASTOR(S)	PHONE FAX	WS SS BC	SCHOOLS/ MINISTRIES	STATISTIC Bapt	Conf	Avg Attend
BELOIT	*SAINT JOHNS* officestjohnsbeloit@gmail.com www.stjohnsbeloit.com	1895	1000 BLUFF ST	53511	SW	Zachary A Kreitler	(608)362-8595 (608)361-0989	WS 9 SS 1030 BC 10	ED/HC/ MD/SN	114	86	50
	ST ANDREW		See Rockton IL									
	TRINITY trinity@trinitybeloit.org www.trinitybeloit.org	1939	1850 CRANSTON RD	53511	SW		(608)362-3607 (608)362-6753	WS 930 BC 830	EL/HS/ED/ MD	176	163	61
BERLIN	*IMMANUEL*		See Auroraville WI									
	ST JOHN church@stjohnberlin.org www.stjohnberlin.org	1852	168 MOUND ST	54923	SW	Robert M Schrader	(920)361-9935	WS 9 SS 1015 BC 1015	EL/ED/HC/ MD/SN	545	449	224
BIG FALLS	*ST LUKE*	1898	130 Harrison Street PO BOX 66 130 HARRISON STREET	54926	NW	Jeffrey A Smiles	(920)596-3241	WS 830 SS 930	HC	36	32	21
BIRCHWOOD	*FIRST*		See Rice Lake WI									
BIRNAMWOOD	*ST PAUL* stpaulbirnamwoodsecretary@gmail.com www.stpaulbirnamwood.jigsy.com	1898	N9035 US Highway 45 PO BOX 208	54414	NW	Matthew J Christians	(715)449-2101	WS 1030 SS 9 BC 9	ED/MD	288	232	62
BLACK RIVER FALLS	*MEN'S BIBLE BREAKFAST* Satellite Site of Grace Alma Center WI	2022	502 N Water Street	54615								
	ST JOHN stjohnbrf@gmail.com www.SJLchurchBRF.com	1909	351 W JEFFERSON ST BLK RIVER FLS	54615	NW	David F Shudy	(715)284-7003	WS 9 SS 10 BC 8	ED/HC/MD	133	108	43
BONDUEL	*ST PAUL* stpaultnwashington@gmail.com www.stpaulimmanuel.org	1868	W4496 County Road E W4496 COUNTY RD E	54107	NW	Craig J Nehring	(715)745-4096	WS 830	ED/SN	123	104	45
	ST PAUL t.anderson@stpaulbonduel.com www.stpaulbonduel.com	1863	240 E Green Bay St PO BOX 577	54107	NW	Ryan J Fehrmann Mark R Palmer	(715)758-8559 (715)758-6352	WS 8 1015	EL/HS/ED/ HC/MD/SN	1987	1546	463
	ZION zion.lcmszachow@gmail.com	1900	N4437 County F N4437 COUNTY ROAD F	54107	NW	Richard R Buhrke		WS 10 SS 915 BC 9	HS	79	74	23
BOSCOBEL	*HICKORY GROVE* mkufahl@cuw.edu hickorygrovelutheran.com	1872	15934 COUNTY ROAD T	53805	SW	Mark C Kufahl		WS 9 SS 8 BC 8	ED/HC/ MD/SN			
BOULDER JUNCTION	*TRINITY* trinityboulderjct@icloud.com www.trinityboulderjunction.net	1946	5434 Church St PO BOX 24 BOULDER JCT	54512	NW	Kevin J Hoogland	(715)385-2267	WS 10 SS 1130	ED/HC/ MD/SN	84	80	35
BOWLER	*ST PAUL*	1924	201 Wall St 201 E WALL ST	54416	NW	Walter K Gilkey	(715)793-4608	WS 9 BC 1115	HS/ED/HC	330	281	30
BOYCEVILLE	*GRACE*		See Connorsville WI									
	HOLY TRINITY	1917	N11550 COUNTY RD O	54725	S	Michael A Penikis		WS 1030 SS 930		46	40	23
BOYD	*ST PETER* sjlcoffice@centurytel.net	1874	212 E Murray St PO BOX 9 CADOTT	54726 54727	NW	Robert D Hopkins	(715)289-4521 (715)289-4521	WS 1030 SS 915		152	132	40
BREED	*EMMANUEL* breedemmanuelwi@gmail.com	1911	13346 COUNTY HWY AA SURING	54174	NW	Steven E Stoll	(920)842-4600	WS 10 SS 9	ED/HC/ MD/SN	183	119	30
BRILLION	*SAINT BARTHOLOMEW* sblcoffice105@gmail.com www.stbartbrillion.org	1858	105 HORN ST	54110	SW	Joshua J Brandmahl	(920)756-3031	WS 9 SS 830 BC 10	ED/MD/SN	281	230	92
BRISTOL	*BEAUTIFUL SAVIOR*		See Antioch IL									
	GRACE		See Racine WI									
BROCKWAY	*ST JOHN*		See Black River Falls WI									
BROOKFIELD	*BLESSED SAVIOR*		See New Berlin WI									
	BROOKFIELD contactus@goblc.org www.brookfieldlutheran.org	1950	18500 W BURLEIGH RD	53045	SW	Robert A Mrosko Richard E Schneider	(262)783-4270 (262)783-4616	WS 8 915 1045 SS 915 BC 915	HS/ED/HC/ MD/SN	1005	803	507
	IMMANUEL kgraf@immanuelbrookfield.org www.immanuelbrookfield.org	1912	13445 W Hampton Rd 13445 HAMPTON RD	53005	SW	Stephen P Henderson Colby C Howell	(262)781-7140	WS 8 1030 SS 930 BC 930	EL/HS/ED/ HC/MD/SN	1301	1000	508
	LAMB OF GOD		See Pewaukee WI									
BROWN DEER	*ST PAUL* officestpaulsbd@gmail.com www.stpaulsbrowndeer.org	1938	8080 N 47TH ST	53223	SW	Dennis M Roser	(414)355-5030 (414)354-7230	WS 9 SS 1015 BC 1015	ED/HC/ MD/SN	271	194	106
BROWNSVILLE	*IMMANUEL*		See Mayville WI									
BURLINGTON	*OUR SAVIOR* oursaviorburlingtonwi@gmail.com www.oursaviorburlington.com	1963	417 S KANE ST	53105	SW	Paul D Muther	(262)763-3281 (262)763-5716	WS 8 1045 SS 930 BC 930	EC/ED/HC	420	304	100
BURNETT	*IMMANUEL*	1873	N9520 STATE ROAD 26	53922	SW		(920)251-0170	WS 11	HC	13	12	9
	ZION timsallach@yahoo.com	1911	N8523 Front St PO BOX 185	53922	SW	Timothy L Sallach	(920)689-2280 (920)689-2280	WS 930 SS 845	HC/SN	138	130	37
BUTTERNUT	*ST PAUL* www.stpaulslutheranbutternut.com	1881	301 N Second St PO BOX 158	54514	NW	John A Deitz	(715)769-3731	WS 9 SS 1015 BC 1015	ED			

*Indicates a new church start. A new church start is an intentionally organized gathering which comes together on a regular basis for the purpose of worship and/or Bible study and is intended to grow into a member LCMS congregation. WS =Worship Service; SS = Sunday School; BC =Bible Class; EC = Early Childhood; EL = Elementary School; HS = High School; ED =Education Ministry; HC =Human Care Ministry; SN = Special Needs Ministry; MD = Media Ministry (PC)=Partner Church Pastor. See Page 53 for the Table of Abbreviations for key to additional abbreviations

CITY	CONGREGATION EMAIL WEBSITE	YEAR EST	LOCATION MAILING ADDRESS	ZIP CODE(S)	DIST.	PASTOR(S)	PHONE FAX	WS SS BC	SCHOOLS/ MINISTRIES	STATISTIC Bapt	Conf	Avg Attend
CABLE	*TRINITY* cabletlc@cheqnet.net	1914	13520 Spruce St PO BOX 145	54821	NW	Dr Arleigh F vonSeggern	(715)798-3417	WS 8	ED/HC	39	39	22
CADOTT	*ST JOHN* cadottlutheran@gmail.com www.cadottlutheran.org	1874	215 E Seminary St PO BOX 9	54727	NW	Robert D Hopkins	(715)289-4521	WS 9 SS 10	ED/HC/MD	347	299	80
	ST PETER		See Boyd WI									
CALEDONIA	*GRACE*		See Racine WI									
CAMERON	*FIRST*		See Rice Lake WI									
	ST JOHN r3babies@yahoo.com	1892	1115 W MAIN ST	54822	NW		(715)458-2602	WS 1045 SS 930	ED/HC/MD			
CAMPBELLSPORT	*ST JOHN*		See New Fane WI									
CAROLINE	*ST JOHN*		See Tigerton WI									
CASCADE	*ST PAULS* stpaulscascade@hotmail.com www.stpaulslcmscascade.com	1866	509 MILWAUKEE AVE	53011	SW	Richard M Bidinger	(920)528-8094	WS 730 10 SS 830 BC 845	ED/HC/MD			
CATARACT	*ST JOHN*		See Black River Falls WI									
CECIL	*IMMANUEL* imwclsec@gmail.com stpaulimmanuel.org	1880	W3110 WHITE CLAY LAKE DR	54111	NW	Craig J Nehring	(715)745-2364	WS 10 SS 845 BC 4	HS/ED/HC/ MD/SN	199	162	62
CEDAR GROVE	*ST PAULS*		See Cascade WI									
CEDARBURG	*FIRST IMMANUEL* connect@fils.org www.filministries.org	1853	W67N622 EVERGREEN BLVD	53012	SW	Vincent W Putnam Aaron T Hauser Daniel E Paavola	(262)377-6610 (262)377-9606	WS 730 9 1035 SS 9 1030 BC 845	EL/HS/ED/ HC/MD/SN	3520	2911	978
CENTER	*ZION* www.zionlutherantownofcenter.org	1884	2129 N CHURCH RD EVANS- VILLE	53536	SW	Donald G Fehlauer	(608)876-6667	WS 9 SS 1010 BC 1030	ED/SN	213	140	31
CHELSEA	*TRINITY* trinitylutheran.medford@gmail.com www.trinity-medford.org	1883	W5127 Elm St Chelsea W5334 DASSOW AVE MEDFORD	54451	NW	Ralph C Shorey III	(715)748-4181	WS 11 SS 10	MD	75	59	15
CHILI	*CHRIST*	1907	N5740 Maple St W1421 FREMONT RD GRANTON	54420 54436	NW	Daniel R Schoessow	(715)238-7422	WS 9 BC 8	ED/MD	166	156	27
CHILTON	*ST LUKE* stlukeluth@gmail.com	1912	W3102 KILLSNAKE RD	53014	SW	Mark E Peterson	(920)483-0956	WS 1030 SS 9	ED/SN	65	34	40
	ST MARTIN stmartinlcms@gmail.com www.stmartinlcms.org	1915	717 MEMORIAL DR	53014	SW	Thomas K Schmitt	(920)849-4421 (920)849-4421	WS 9 SS 1015 BC 1015	ED/HC/ MD/SN	373	314	88
CHIPPEWA FALLS	*FAITH* info@faithlutherancf.org www.faithlutherancf.org	1954	733 WOODWARD AVE CHIP- PEWA FLS	54729	NW	Dr Daniel A Wonderly	(715)723-7754	WS 8 1015 SS 9 BC 9	EC/ED/MD	339	281	137
	ZION secretaryzioncf@outlook.com www.zionlcmscf.org	1868	110 E GRAND AVE CHIPPEWA FLS	54729	NW	Brad Thomas Timothy A Jones	(715)723-6380 (715)723-8476	WS 9 SS 1015 BC 1015	MD	169	138	65
CLAYTON	*IMMANUEL* scott@berghammerbuilders.com facebook.com/Immanuel LutheranChurchLCMSClayton	1910	124 Church St PO BOX 174	54004	NW		(715)641-0054	WS 9	ED/MD	75	67	14
	SILVER CREEK lwmllaura@gmail.com	1897	483 7th Ave PO BOX 21	54004	NW		(715)243-9585	WS 9	ED/HC	63	58	25
CLEAR CREEK TOWNSHIP	*ST PETER*		See Osseo WI									
CLINTON	*CHRIST* office@christlutheranclinton.org christlutheranclinton.org	1882	300 High St PO BOX 308	53525	SW	Andrew M Harris	(608)676-4994	WS 9 SS 1030 BC 1030	ED/HC/MD	110	88	54
CLINTONVILLE	*ASTER RETIREMENT COMMUNITY* Satellite Site of Zion Embarrass WI	2001	38 N Main	54929								
	MEN'S BIBLE STUDY Satellite Site of Zion Embarrass WI	2018	70 Greentree Rd	54929								
	ST JOHN sjohnbp@gmail.com	1878	N3299 HUNTING RD	54929	NW	Todd R Jerabek	(715)851-5199	WS 1130 SS 1030				
	ST JOHN		See Tigerton WI									
	ST MARTIN contact@stmlc.org stmlc.org	1863	100 S CLINTON AVE	54929	NW	Jason W Zobel Hayden M Lukas	(715)823-6538	WS 8 1030 SS 910 BC 910	EL/HS/ED/ HC/MD/SN	1012	883	363
	ST PETER zionstpe@frontiernet.net	1878	N2730 Pella Opening Rd PO BOX 197 EMBARRASS	54929 54933	NW	Todd R Jerabek	(715)823-3889	WS 10 SS 845		125	105	30
	WOMEN'S BIBLE STUDY Satellite Site of Zion Embarrass WI	2024	76 W Greentree Rd	54929								
	WOMEN'S BIBLE STUDY Satellite Site of Zion Embarrass WI	2025	76 Greentree Rd	54929								
CLYMAN	*ZION* zionclyman@gmail.com www.zionclyman.org	1897	700 Main St 700 MAIN STREET PO BOX 220	53016	SW	Daniel L Bohn	(920)341-2025	WS 830 SS 945 BC 945				

*Indicates a new church start. A new church start is an intentionally organized gathering which comes together on a regular basis for the purpose of worship and/or Bible study and is intended to grow into a member LCMS congregation. WS =Worship Service; SS = Sunday School; BC =Bible Class; EC = Early Childhood; EL = Elementary School; HS = High School; ED =Education Ministry; HC =Human Care Ministry; SN = Special Needs Ministry; MD = Media Ministry (PC)=Partner Church Pastor. See Page 53 for the Table of Abbreviations for key to additional abbreviations

CITY	CONGREGATION EMAIL WEBSITE	YEAR EST	LOCATION MAILING ADDRESS	ZIP CODE(S)	DIST.	PASTOR(S)	PHONE FAX	WS SS BC	SCHOOLS/ MINISTRIES	STATISTIC Bapt	Conf	Avg Attend
COLBY	*ST PAUL* clcabby@frontier.com www.stpaulcolbywi.com	1879	N13520 County Road E PO BOX 206	54421	NW	Donald Bruce	(715)223-4315 (715)223-8183	WS 815 SS 915 BC 1230	ED/HC	64	51	30
	ZION admin@zionlutheranchurchcolbywi.com www.zionlutheranchurchcolbywi.com	1877	301 N 2nd St PO BOX 438	54421	NW	James H Groleau	(715)223-2166	WS 9 SS 1015	EC/ED/HC	336	266	100
COMSTOCK	*CHRIST*	1884	1994 20TH ST	54826	NW	Stephen C Miller	(715)931-0056	WS 1030 SS 930 BC 930	ED/HC/MD	171	156	29
CONNORSVILLE	*GRACE*	1922	E 1394 1260TH AVE BOY-CEVILLE	54725	NW		(715)269-5599	WS 1045 SS 930 BC 915	ED/HC	78	68	18
CONOVER	*TRINITY*		See Boulder Junction WI									
CORNELL	*ZION*		See Gilman WI									
COTTAGE GROVE	*MONONA*		See Monona WI									
CRANDON	*GOOD SHEPHERD* stjohngoodshepherd@gmail.com	1977	1507 N Lake Ave PO BOX 146	54520	NW	Jamie D Bauknecht	(715)478-3555	WS 1030		145	81	40
CUDAHY	*ST JOHN* office.stjohn@yahoo.com www.stjohncudahy.org	1906	4850 S LAKE DR	53110	S	Phillip M DeVries	(414)481-0520	WS 9 SS 1030 BC 1030	EC/ED/ HC/SN	308	297	96
CUMBERLAND	*BIBLE STUDY* Satellite Site of St Paul Cumberland WI	2021	1345 2nd Ave.	54829								
	CHRIST		See Comstock WI									
	ST PAUL churchoffice@stpaulcumberland.com www.stpaulcumberland.com	1900	743 22 1/2 AVE	54829	NW	John A Miels	(715)822-8690 (715)822-5018	WS 9 SS 1015 BC 1015	ED/HC/ MD/SN	303	237	135
DANCY	*ST JOHN* www.stjohnsdancy.org	1903	200950 SAINT JOHNS ROAD MOSINEE	54455	NW	Dr Timothy W Roser	(715)457-2405	WS 830 SS 10		170	146	41
DARIEN	*TRIUNE*		See Sharon WI									
DE FOREST	*BETHLEHEM*		See Sun Prairie WI									
DE PERE	*HOPE* office@hopedepere.org www.hopedepere.org	1951	700 S SUPERIOR ST	54115	NW	Matthew D Baye	(920)336-9843	WS 8 1027 SS 915 BC 930	EC/EL/HS/ ED/HC/MD	522	381	186
DEERBROOK	*ST MATTHEW* paul.radke@ctsfw.edu	1897	North 5674 County East N 5674 CTH E	54424	NW	Paul C Radke	(715)627-7989	WS 9 SS 1010				
DEFOREST	*CROSS*		See Westport WI									
DELAFIELD	*LAMB OF GOD*		See Pewaukee WI									
DELAVAN	*OUR REDEEMER* dmortlock@orlcs.org www.orlcs.org	1914	416 W GENEVA ST	53115	SW	Mark C Wilkens	(262)728-4266 (262)728-5581	WS 8 1030 SS 915 BC 915	EL/ED	2025	1342	230
DORCHESTER	*ST PETER* stpeterdorchester@gmail.com	1879	275 S 3RD ST	54425	NW	Shawn W Andersen	(715)654-5055	WS 9 SS 1015 BC 1030		129	102	94
DURAND	*ST JOHN* stjohnsdurand@gmail.com www.stjohnsdurand.org	1898	315 E Montgomery St PO BOX 34	54736	NW	Daniel M Pfaffe	(715)672-8787	WS 845 SS 10 BC 730 10	ED/HC/ MD/SN	140	113	36
EAGLE RIVER	*GRACE*		See Three Lakes WI									
	OUR SAVIOR oursavioreagleriver@gmail.com www.oursavioreagleriver.org	1955	223 SILVER LAKE RD	54521	NW	Peter J Kufahl	(715)479-6226 (715)479-7890	WS 730 10 SS 845 BC 845	ED/HC/ MD/SN	535	380	234
EAST TROY	*GOOD SHEPHERD* gslchurch@wi.rr.com www.gslet.org	1964	1936 EMERY ST	53120	SW	Dr Timothy A Prince	(262)642-3310	WS 9 SS 1030 BC 1030	EL/ED/SN	463	398	104
EAU CLAIRE	*BETHLEHEM*		See Altoona WI									
	OUR REDEEMER churchoffice@orlcms.net	1923	601 FALL ST	54703	NW	Jeffrey H Carlson	(715)835-5239 (715)835-9166	WS 830 1035 SS 930	EC/ED/HC/ MD/SN	448	368	126
	PEACE info@mypeacechurch.com www.mypeacechurch.com	1961	501 E FILLMORE AVE	54701	NW	Dr Mark W Schulz David L Forke Ethan M Luhman	(715)834-2486	WS 815 9 1015 SS 9	ED/HC/MD	1784	1495	388
	SAINT MATTHEW stmatthewinfo@gmail.com stmatthewec.org/	1934	1915 HOGEBOOM AVE	54701	NW		(715)834-4028	WS 815 1030 SS 920 BC 920	ED/HC/ MD/SN	292	245	112
	ZION		See Eleva WI									
EDGAR	*ST JOHN* secretary@stjbeth.org www.stjbeth.org	1869	119415 HUCKLEBERRY RD	54426	NW	Michael J Mathey	(715)352-2888	WS 1030 SS 915 BC 1145	ED/HC			
EDGERTON	*ST JOHN* stjohnevc@gmail.com stjohnevc.org	1872	207 E HIGH ST	53534	SW	Carl W Seeger	(608)884-3515	WS 9 SS 1030 BC 1030	ED/HC/ MD/SN	363	281	88
ELAND	*ZION*	1901	PO BOX 13	54427	NW	Walter K Gilkey	(715)253-3939	WS 1045		65	60	20
ELCHO	*ST LUKE* paul.radke@ctsfw.edu	1934	PO BOX 25	54428	NW	Paul C Radke	(715)275-3152	WS 1045				
ELEVA	*ZION* office@zioncleghorn.com www.zioncleghorn.com	1895	E3720 COUNTY ROAD HH	54738	NW	Preston A Paul	(715)878-4512 (715)878-4512	WS 930 SS 830 BC 830	ED/SN	359	285	117

*Indicates a new church start. A new church start is an intentionally organized gathering which comes together on a regular basis for the purpose of worship and/or Bible study and is intended to grow into a member LCMS congregation. WS =Worship Service; SS = Sunday School; BC =Bible Class; EC = Early Childhood; EL = Elementary School; HS = High School; ED =Education Ministry; HC =Human Care Ministry; SN = Special Needs Ministry; MD = Media Ministry (PC)=Partner Church Pastor. See Page 53 for the Table of Abbreviations for key to additional abbreviations

CITY	CONGREGATION EMAIL WEBSITE	YEAR EST	LOCATION MAILING ADDRESS	ZIP CODE(S)	DIST.	PASTOR(S)	PHONE FAX	WS SS BC	SCHOOLS/ MINISTRIES	STATISTIC Bapt	Conf	Avg Attend
ELKHART LAKE	*GRACE* lutheran_grace@yahoo.com www.graceserves.org	1961	210 N Lincoln Hwy 67 PO BOX 262	53020	SW	Peter M Peitsch	(920)781-5076	WS 8 1015 SS 915 BC 915	ED/HC/MD	313	267	93
ELM GROVE	*ELM GROVE* astroh@egl.org www.egl.org	1940	945 N Terrace Dr 945 TERRACE DR	53122	SW	Eric C Skovgaard Dr Samuel Lee Joshua D Teggatz	(262)797-2970 (262)797-2977	WS 9 SS 1030 BC 10	HS/ED/HC/ MD/SN	623	543	195
EMBARRASS	*ST PETER*		See Clintonville WI									
	ZION zionstpe@frontiernet.net	1888	118 Church St PO BOX 197	54933	NW	Todd R Jerabek	(715)823-3889	WS 8 SS 910	ED/HC/MD	256	256	53
EVANSVILLE	*ZION*		See Center WI									
FAIRCHILD	*ST PAUL* brentzimbauer@gmail.com	1884	324 Oak St PO BOX 163	54741	NW		(715)586-1203		ED/HC/MD			
FALL CREEK	*BETHLEHEM* countryc@centurylink.net www.zion-bethlehem.org	1896	E19675 STATE ROAD 27	54742	NW	James E Norton	(715)877-3249 (715)877-3249	WS 1030 SS 9	ED/HC/ MD/SN	295	235	48
	ST JOHN	1864	E11620 COUNTY ROAD JJ	54742	NW	Brendan G Harris	(715)877-3150	WS 10 SS 9	ED/HC/MD	118	101	42
	ST PAUL'S stpaulsecretaryfc@gmail.com www.stpaulstjohn.com/	1910	721 S STATE ST	54742	NW	Brendan G Harris	(715)877-2117 (715)877-3256	WS 815 SS 945	EC/ED/HC/ MD/SN	500	406	80
	ZION countryc@centurylink.net www.zion-bethlehem.org	1885	1286 150th Ave S 1286 S 150TH AVE	54742	NW	James E Norton	(715)877-3128 (715)877-3128	WS 9 SS 10	ED/HC/ MD/SN	217	176	40
FOND DU LAC	*HOPE* czoch@lifeathope.org www.lifeathope.org	1947	260 VINCENT ST	54935	SW	Phillip M Enderle	(920)922-5130 (920)922-9832	WS 8 1041 SS 915 BC 930	EC/ED/HC/ MD/SN	1311	1188	325
FORESTVILLE	*ST PETER* revcjackson@gmail.com www.saintpetersforestville.org	1875	316 W Main St PO BOX 85	54213	NW	Dr Christopher Jackson	(920)856-6420	WS 1030 SS 930	ED/HC/MD	232	162	60
FORT ATKINSON	*LIVING SAVIOR* livingsavior.360unite.com/home		1661 JANESVILLE AVE	53538	SW	David N Emmrich	(920)563-8050	WS 10 SS 9 BC 9	ED/HC/SN	43	37	41
FOXBORO	*CHRIST*		See Superior WI									
FRANKLIN	*RISEN SAVIOR* risensavior@sbcglobal.net www.risenlife.org	1983	9501 W DREXEL AVE	53132	SW	John H Schober II	(414)529-5647 (414)529-5673	WS 9 SS 1030 BC 1030	ED/HC/ MD/SN	421	334	90
FRANKSVILLE	*CHAPEL CROSS*		See Racine WI									
	GRACE		See Racine WI									
FREDERIC	*IMMANUEL* qabuech@gmail.com	1913	201 1ST AVE S	54837	NW		(715)307-4448		ED			
FREDONIA	*ST JOHN* www.stjohnfredonia.org	1861	824 FREDONIA AVE	53021	SW		(262)692-2734 (262)692-3297	WS 8 1030 SS 915 BC 915	EC/ED/HC/ MD/SN	457	341	211
FREISTADT	*TRINITY*		See Mequon WI									
FREMONT	*ST PAUL* kdelwiche@stpaulfremontwi.org stpaulfremontwi.org	1885	107 TUSTIN RD	54940	NW	Mark J Drengler	(920)446-3251 (920)446-2880	WS 745 1030 SS 8 BC 1030	EC/ED/ HC/SN	436	361	119
	ZION pastordoug@milwpc.com www.zionfremont.com	1861	E9016 MARSH RD	54940	NW	Douglas R Reinders	(920)667-4301	WS 9 SS 1015 BC 1015	ED/HC/MD	173	142	70
FRIENDSHIP	*IMMANUEL*		See Adams WI									
GERMANTOWN	*FAITH* faithlutheran@faithgtown.com www.faithgtown.com	1963	W172 N11187 DIVISION RD	53022	SW	Peter P Heckert	(262)251-8250	WS 9 SS 1015 BC 1015	ED/HC/ MD/SN	215	176	109
	LIVING WORD		See Jackson WI									
GILLETT	*CHRIST*	1892	6905 RED BANKS RD	54124	NW	Michael A Paholke		WS 830 SS 845	HS			
	FAITH UNITED faithunitedluth@gmail.com		11465 Old U Rd 11465 OLD U	54124	NW	John V Laatsch	(920)855-6464	WS 9 SS 10	HS/ED	202	202	90
	ST JOHN RIVERSIDE	1904	5686 State Hwy 32 S PO BOX 566	54124	NW		(920)855-2625	WS 830 SS 930	ED/HC	48	47	18
GILMAN	*ZION* trinity2011@centurylink.net ziontrinity-e.faithlifesites.com/?ssi=1	1919	205 N 5TH AVE	54433	NW		(715)447-8262	WS 830	ED	103	91	30
GILMANTON	*TRINITY*	1905	PO BOX 14	54743	NW			WS 10	ED/HC/SN	20	15	12
GLEASON	*LUTHER MEMORIAL* grlaska@yahoo.com	1964	N5302 Town Hall Rd PO BOX 39	54435	NW	Gregory R Laska	(715)873-4592	WS 1030 SS 930	ED/SN	550	481	81
	OUR SAVIOR www.oursaviorslcms.weebly.com	1937	W513 County Road D W516 COUNTY ROAD D	54435	NW		(715)362-2323	WS 830	ED/HC/MD			
GLENBEULAH	*WESTWARD HO CAMPGROUND* Satellite Site of St John Plymouth WI	1970	N5456 Division Rd	53023								
	ZION www.zionglen.org	1892	200 E Main St PO BOX 26	53023	SW		(920)526-3152	WS 10 BC 845	ED/HC/ MD/SN	100	80	25
GLENDALE	*ST JOHN* office@stjohnglendale.com www.stjohnglendale.com	1866	7877 N PORT WASHING-TON RD	53217	SW	Stephen J Klemp	(414)352-4150 (414)352-4221	WS 9 BC 1010	EL/ED/HC/ MD/SN	261	224	55
GLENWOOD CITY	*ST JOHN*	1898	2805 HWY 64	54013	NW			WS 9				
GLIDDEN	*TRINITY* tlcglidden@gmail.com	1885	76372 Lenz Rd PO BOX 161	54527	NW	Kenneth W Lahners	(715)264-3961	WS 9 SS 1015 BC 1015	ED/HC/MD	306	248	53

*Indicates a new church start. A new church start is an intentionally organized gathering which comes together on a regular basis for the purpose of worship and/or Bible study and is intended to grow into a member LCMS congregation. WS =Worship Service; SS = Sunday School; BC =Bible Class; EC = Early Childhood; EL = Elementary School; HS = High School; ED =Education Ministry; HC =Human Care Ministry; SN = Special Needs Ministry; MD = Media Ministry (PC)=Partner Church Pastor. See Page 53 for the Table of Abbreviations for key to additional abbreviations

CITY	CONGREGATION EMAIL WEBSITE	YEAR EST	LOCATION MAILING ADDRESS	ZIP CODE(S)	DIST.	PASTOR(S)	PHONE FAX	WS SS BC	SCHOOLS/ MINISTRIES	STATISTIC Bapt	Conf	Avg Attend
GORDON	*CHRIST*		See Superior WI									
GRAFTON	*ST PAUL* info@splgrafton.org splgrafton.org	1851	701 WASHINGTON ST	53024	SW	Luke J Anderson Dr Timothy H Maschke Jacob M Schultz	(262)377-4659 (262)377-7808	WS 8 930 11 SS 815 BC 930	EL/HS/ED/ HC/MD/SN	2431	1901	730
GRAND MARSH	*IMMANUEL*		See Adams WI									
GRANTON	*ZION* lutheranpastor@gmail.com	1863	W2894 Granton Rd W 2894 GRANTON RD	54436	NW	Daniel R Schoessow	(715)238-7422	WS 1030 SS 915	ED/HC/ MD/SN	308	240	63
GREEN BAY	*CHRIST OF BAY* secretary@cotbchurch.org cotbchurch.com	1976	450 LAVERNE DR	54311	NW		(920)468-4246	WS 9	EL/HS/HC	37	34	25
	FAITH office@flcgb.com www.flcgb.com	1945	2335 S WEBSTER AVE	54301	NW	Joshua S Errer	(920)435-5524 (920)435-6050	WS 8 1030 SS 915 BC 915	EC/EL/HS/ ED/HC/ MD/SN	742	603	268
	HMONG PILGRIM		1731 SAINT AGNES DR	54304	NW	Kue Ly	(920)965-2233 (920)965-2255		HC/MD	101	84	35
	OUR SAVIOUR info@oslc-gb.org www.oslc-gb.org	1942	120 S HENRY ST	54302	NW	David H Hatch	(920)468-4065 (920)468-5757	WS 745 915 SS 1030 BC 1030	EC/EL/HS/ ED/HC/ MD/SN	1038	853	282
	PILGRIM scottmalme@pilgrimluth.org www.pilgrimluth.org	1957	1731 SAINT AGNES DR	54304	NW	Dr Michael B Hanson Timothy D Fraker Scott C Malme	(920)965-2233 (920)965-2255	WS 745 9 1030 SS 9 10 BC 9 10	EL/HS/ED/ HC/MD/SN	2809	2257	708
	REDEEMER redeemergreenbay@gmail.com redeemerlutherangb.com	1937	210 S Oneida St 205 HUDSON ST	54303	NW	Paul K Pett	(920)499-1033 (920)496-0795	WS 915 SS 1025 BC 1025	EL/HS/ED/ HC/MD/SN	375	301	199
	ZION LUTHERAN CHURCH		See Oneida WI									
GREEN VALLEY	*ST JOHN*	1878	W1294 NAUMAN RD CECIL	54127 54111	NW		(715)745-4558	WS 1030				
GREENDALE	*OUR SHEPHERD* bethb@ourshepherdlutheran.org ourshepherdlutheran.org	1958	5901 Westway PO BOX 77	53129	SW	Douglas W Schroeder	(414)421-2060 (414)421-7927	WS 8 1030 SS 930 BC 915	HS/ED/HC/ MD	265	198	150
GREENFIELD	*MOUNT ZION* mountziongreenfield@gmail.com www.mountziongreenfield.org	1931	3820 W LAYTON AVE	53221	SW	Aaron A Koch	(414)282-4900	WS 9 SS 1020 BC 1020	SN	138	124	75
	OUR FATHER'S churchsecretary@ourfatherslutheran. org www.ofls.org	1946	6025 S 27TH ST	53221	SW	Aaron T Fenker Sr	(414)282-8220 (414)282-9737	WS 8 1045 SS 930 BC 930	EL/HS/ ED/HC	340	291	160
GREENLEAF	*ALLELUIA* alleluia.office@gmail.com www.alleluiawrightstown.org	2000	6725 ELMRO RD	54126	NW	Roger L Mackie	(920)532-3892	WS 9 BC 8	EC/ED/HC/ MD/SN	273	176	35
	ZION		See Wayside WI									
GREENVILLE	*SHEPHERD HILLS* office@shepherdhills.org www.shepherdhills.org	1970	N1615 MEADOWVIEW DR	54942	NW	Steven G Kline Chad J Starfeldt Grant E Thiel	(920)757-5722 (920)757-0461	WS 8 930 1045 SS 930 BC 930	EC/ED/HC/ MD/SN	1808	1485	560
GRESHAM	*IMMANUEL*		See Marion WI									
	IMMANUEL MOHICAN	1898	Cty Rd G N7691 JUNIPER RD	54128	NW		(715)787-3306	WS 1030				
	OUR SAVIOR	1932	N8035 Morgan Rd W11100 W TOWN HALL RD	54128	NW	Dr Roy W Rinehard	(715)526-5280	WS 10 SS 10	ED	59	49	17
HALES CORNERS	*HALES CORNERS* theise@hcl.org www.hcl.org/school-childcare	1928	12300 W JANESVILLE RD	53130	EN	Leon C Jameson Chad A Kogutkiewicz Aaron J Hickey Todd W Liefer Dr Christian R Wood	(414)529-6700 (414)529-6710	WS 745 915 1045 SS 915	EL/HS/ED/ HC/MD/SN	5721	4635	1441
HAMBURG	*ST JOHN*		See Athens WI									
	ST PAUL EVANGELICAL pastordanner@aol.com	1880	244526 GRASS CREEK LN	54411	NW	Joel S Danner	(715)536-7242	WS 830		99	78	42
HANCOCK	*GRACE* grceluth@gmail.com	1894	W10805 County Road C W10805 CTY RD C	54943	SW	Dale W Bahls	(715)249-3043	WS 1015				
HANOVER	*IMMANUEL*		See Orfordville WI									
HARSHAW	*FAITH* revsutton@outlook.com	1948	9160 Church Rd PO BOX 94	54529	NW	David J Sutton	(715)282-5550	WS 830 BC 1130				
HARTFORD	*DIVINE SAVIOR* chrissy.daniels@divinesaviorlutheran.com www.divinesaviorlutheran.com	1971	3200 Highway K South 3200 COUNTY ROAD K	53027	SW	Dr Douglas J Stowe	(262)673-5140	WS 8 930 11 SS 930 BC 930	ED/HC/MD	547	471	201
	LIVING WORD		See Jackson WI									
HARTLAND	*DIVINE REDEEMER* www.drlc.org	1972	N48 W31385 State Road 83 31385 W HILL RD	53029	SW	Graham J Jenkins Christopher J Sturges	(262)367-8400 (262)367-9410	WS 8 915 1030 SS 915 BC 915	EL/HS/ED/ HC/MD	1914	1530	567
	LAMB OF GOD		See Pewaukee WI									
HATFIELD	*ST JOHN*		See Black River Falls WI									
HAVEN	*GRACE* gracehavenw1264@gmail.com	1859	W1264 COUNTY ROAD FF	53083	SW	Adam P Barkley	(920)565-2186	WS 8	HS/ED/HC/ MD/SN	52	50	35
HAWTHORNE	*CHRIST*		See Superior WI									
HAYWARD	*TRINITY* office@trinitylutheranchurchhayward.org www.trinitylutheranchurchhayward.org	1904	10576 GRESYLON DR	54843	NW	Roy W Berquist	(715)634-2260 (715)934-2160	WS 930 SS 1030 BC 815	ED/MD/SN	115	105	49

*Indicates a new church start. A new church start is an intentionally organized gathering which comes together on a regular basis for the purpose of worship and/or Bible study and is intended to grow into a member LCMS congregation. WS =Worship Service; SS = Sunday School; BC =Bible Class; EC = Early Childhood; EL = Elementary School; HS = High School; ED =Education Ministry; HC =Human Care Ministry; SN = Special Needs Ministry; MD = Media Ministry (PC)=Partner Church Pastor. See Page 53 for the Table of Abbreviations for key to additional abbreviations

CITY	CONGREGATION EMAIL WEBSITE	YEAR EST	LOCATION MAILING ADDRESS	ZIP CODE(S)	DIST.	PASTOR(S)	PHONE FAX	WS SS BC	SCHOOLS/ MINISTRIES	STATISTIC Bapt	Conf	Avg Attend
HAZEL GREEN	*ST PAUL*		See Dubuque IA									
HAZELHURST	*PEACE*		See Arbor Vitae WI									
HERBSTER	*CHRIST*		See Superior WI									
HERMAN	*IMMANUEL*		See Mayville WI									
HEWITT	*IMMANUEL* secretary@immanuelhewitt.org immanuelhewitt.org	1892	7735 YELLOWSTONE DR	54441	NW	Dean T Pingel	(715)384-5153	WS 9 SS 1015 BC 1015	ED/HC/ MD/SN	688	481	217
HIGHLAND	*CHRIST* dwilkie595@aol.com	1895	303 Main St PO BOX 555 MUSCODA	53543 53573	SW	Dana M Wilkie	(608)739-4017	WS 830 SS 930	ED/MD	66	60	27
HILBERT	*ST LUKE*		See Chilton WI									
	ST PETER stpeterhilbert@gmail.com www.stpeterhilbert.org	1878	43 N 3RD ST	54129	SW	Mark E Peterson	(920)853-3217	WS 830	ED/HC/SN	187	158	61
HILES	*ST JOHN*		See Laona WI									
HILLPOINT	*ST PAUL* LoganPointLutheran@gmail.com	1870	E 4171 Village Rd PO BOX 9	53937	SW	Timothy A Anderson	(608)727-3841	WS 830 SS 930	ED/HC/MD	179	130	58
HIXTON	*ST JOHN*		See Black River Falls WI									
HOLCOMBE	*TRINITY*		See Sheldon WI									
HOLMEN	*GIFT OF GRACE* giftofgracelc@gmail.com www.giftofgracelc.org		642 Western Ave 642 WESTERN AVENUE PO BOX 642	54636	SW	Timothy A Duesenberg	(608)668-1587	WS 9		54	54	34
HORICON	*IMMANUEL*		See Mayville WI									
	ST JOHN saintjohnlc@aol.com www.stjohnshoricon.org	1866	N7074 Hwy V N7074 COUNTY ROAD V	53032	SW	Allen L Behnke	(920)387-3775	WS 9 SS 1030 BC 1030		111	106	64
	ST STEPHEN ststeph@ststephen-lcms.org www.ststephen-lcms.org	1858	505 N PALMATORY ST	53032	SW	Daniel J Seehafer	(920)485-6687 (920)485-2545	WS 9	EL/ED/HC/ MD/SN	835	741	227
	ZION		See Burnett WI									
HOULTON	*FAMILY OF CHRIST* fochoulton@gmail.com familyofchristhoulton.org	1991	285 County Road E 285 COUNTY RD E	54082	MNS	Jesse C Baker	(715)549-6140	WS 930 SS 1030 BC 1045	ED/HC/ MD/SN	252	223	63
HOWARDS GROVE	*GRACE*		See Elkhart Lake WI									
	TRINITY trinityhowardsgrove.org	1853	W 2776 STH 32	53083	SW	Noah A Fremer	(920)565-3669 (920)565-4592	WS 8 1030 SS 915 BC 915	EC/HS/ED/ HC/MD/SN			
HUDSON	*FAMILY OF CHRIST*		See Houlton WI									
	TRINITY trinity@trinityhudson.org www.trinityhudson.org	1909	1205 6TH ST	54016	MNS	Mark A Schreiber	(715)386-9313 (715)386-9707	WS 830 930 1030 SS 930 1030 BC 930	EL/HS/ED/ HC/MD/SN	1061	730	281
	TRINITY EAST CAMPUS Satellite Site of Trinity Hudson WI	2002	614 Badlands Rd	54016				WS 9 1030 SS 9 1030				
HURLEY	*TRINITY*		See Ironwood MI									
HUSTISFORD	*IMMANUEL*		See Mayville WI									
IRMA	*ST PAUL'S* revsutton@outlook.com	1924	N6537 OLD HIGHWAY 51 PO BOX 7	54442	NW	David J Sutton	(715)536-5069	WS 1030 SS 930 BC 930	ED			
JACKSON	*LIVING WORD* pastor.davis@mylivingword.com www.mylivingword.com	1997	2240 LIVING WORD LN	53037	SW	Christopher M Davis	(262)677-1685 (262)677-1695	WS 9 SS 1030 BC 1030	EC/HS/ED/ MD	222	183	148
JANESVILLE	*MOUNT CALVARY* secretary@mountcalvaryjanesville.org www.mountcalvaryjanesville.org	1942	2940 MINERAL POINT AVE	53548	SW	David A Bergelin	(608)754-4145	WS 9 BC 1030	ED/MD/SN	300	233	113
	OUR SAVIOR OurSavLuth@gmail.com www.oursaviorlcms.org/	1970	2015 KELLOGG AVE	53546	SW	Richard G Sears II	(608)563-2912	WS 930 SS 1030 BC 830 11		57	57	30
	ST MARK secretary@stmarkjvl.org www.stmarkjvl.org	1967	2921 MOUNT ZION AVE	53545	EN		(608)754-8115	WS 830 1030 SS 1040	ED/HC/ MD/SN	440	384	90
	ST PAUL'S churchoffice@stpaulsjanesville.com www.stpaulsjanesville.com	1863	1245 E Holmes St 210 S RINGOLD ST	53545	SW	Andrew J Nelson	(608)754-4471 (608)754-4050	WS 8 1030 BC 915	EL/ED	1656	1303	356
JUMP RIVER	*TRINITY*		See Sheldon WI									
	ZION		See Gilman WI									
JUNCTION CITY	*ST PAUL* twroser@yahoo.com www.stpaulsjunctioncity.org	1918	1225 MAIN ST	54443	NW	Dr Timothy W Roser	(715)457-2405	WS 1030 SS 9	HC/MD	153	127	39
JUNEAU	*CLEARVIEW* Satellite Site of Zion Burnett WI	1984	199 Home Rd	53039								
	ZION		See Burnett WI									
KANSASVILLE	*GRACE*		See Racine WI									
KAUKAUNA	*BETHANY* secretary@bethanykaukauna.org www.bethanykaukauna.org	1946	124 W 10TH ST	54130	NW	Rod M Krueger	(920)766-1452 (920)766-2697	WS 745 10 SS 855 BC 9	ED/HC/ MD/SN			
	ST LUKE		See Chilton WI									
KELLNER	*ST JOHN*		See Wisconsin Rapids WI									
KENNAN	*ZION* arndtshirley@hotmail.com	1897	W 10363 MAIN ST	54537	NW		(715)965-2469	WS 1030 SS 1030	HC/SN	89	69	10

*Indicates a new church start. A new church start is an intentionally organized gathering which comes together on a regular basis for the purpose of worship and/or Bible study and is intended to grow into a member LCMS congregation. WS =Worship Service; SS = Sunday School; BC =Bible Class; EC = Early Childhood; EL = Elementary School; HS = High School; ED =Education Ministry; HC =Human Care Ministry; SN = Special Needs Ministry; MD = Media Ministry (PC)=Partner Church Pastor. See Page 53 for the Table of Abbreviations for key to additional abbreviations

CITY	CONGREGATION EMAIL WEBSITE	YEAR EST	LOCATION MAILING ADDRESS	ZIP CODE(S)	DIST.	PASTOR(S)	PHONE FAX	WS SS BC	SCHOOLS/ MINISTRIES	STATISTIC Bapt	Conf	Avg Attend
KENOSHA	*GOOD SHEPHERD*		See Pleasant Prairie WI									
	GRACE		See Racine WI									
	MESSIAH secretary@messiahkenosha.org www.messiahkenosha.org	1961	2026 22ND AVE	53140	SW	James A Roemke	(262)551-8182 (262)597-5168	WS 9 SS 1045 BC 1045	MD	298	232	114
KEWASKUM	*ST ANDREW*		See West Bend WI									
	ST JOHN		See New Fane WI									
KIEL	*GRACE*		See Elkhart Lake WI									
KOHLER	*BETHANY* info@blckohler.com bethanylutherankohler.org	1909	222 CHURCH ST	53044	SW		(920)457-4681	WS 10	HS/ED	164	149	57
	IMMANUEL		See Sheboygan WI									
KOHLSVILLE	*IMMANUEL*		See Mayville WI									
LA CROSSE	*FAITH* pastor@faithonmain.com www.faithonmain.com	1956	1407 MAIN ST	54601	SW	Jacob J Eichers	(608)782-3696	WS 9 SS 1015 BC 1015	ED/HC/ MD/SN	193	169	83
	MESSIAH		See La Crescent MN									
	SHEPHERD HILLS		See Onalaska WI									
LA VALLE	*ST PAUL* jsjackson389@yahoo.com	1875	PO BOX 140	53941	SW		(608)985-7412	WS 1030	ED/HC	119	89	19
	ZION zionlutheranlavalle@gmail.com	1885	200 Union St PO BOX 140	53941	SW		(608)985-7412	WS 9 SS 10	ED/HC	139	105	28
LAC DU FLAMBEAU	*PEACE*		See Arbor Vitae WI									
	TRINITY		See Boulder Junction WI									
LADYSMITH	*SAINT JOHNS* stjohnladysmith@centurylink.net www.stjohnsladysmith.org	1916	515 COLLEGE AVE W	54848	NW	Craig S Zandi	(715)532-5780	WS 9 SS 1030 BC 1030	EC/ED/HC/ MD/SN	327	274	70
LAKE MILLS	*CHRIST* dukovandm@gmail.com christlutheranlakemills.org	1996	403 MULBERRY ST	53551	EN	David M Dukovan	(262)804-1087	WS 10 SS 9	ED/HC/ MD/SN			
LAKE TOMAHAWK	*PEACE*		See Arbor Vitae WI									
LAMPSON	*CHRIST* christlampson@centurytel.net	1925	W5523 County Hwy F W5523 COUNTY HIGHWAY F TREGO	54888	NW		(715)466-4516	WS 9 BC 1015	ED/HC/ MD/SN			
LAND O' LAKES	*TRINITY*		See Boulder Junction WI									
LAONA	*ST JOHN* stjohngoodshepherd@gmail.com	1915	5502 BEECH ST	54541	NW	Jamie D Bauknecht	(715)674-3836	WS 830		88	76	30
LEBANON	*ST PETER* congregation@stpetersoflebanonwi.org www.stpetersoflebanonwi.org	1881	W 4661 County Rd MM PO BOX 115	53047	SW	Douglas J Bergelin	(920)925-3547	WS 8 1030 SS 915 BC 915	EL/ED/HC/ MD/SN	452	332	137
LISBON	*LAMB OF GOD*		See Pewaukee WI									
LOGANVILLE	*ST JOHN* LoganPointLutheran@gmail.com	1854	380 E Walnut St PO BOX 94	53943	SW	Timothy A Anderson	(608)727-2000	WS 10 SS 9	ED/HC/MD	99	59	34
LOMIRA	*IMMANUEL*		See Mayville WI									
LUXEMBURG	*ST JOHN* secretary@stjohnlux.com www.stjohnlux.com	1874	700 HERITAGE RD	54217	NW	Carl A Brewer III Craig J VanPay	(920)845-5250 (920)845-9996	WS 8 1030 SS 915 BC 915	HS/ED/ HC/SN	777	607	340
	ST PAUL secretary@stpaullux.org www.stpaullux.org	1865	N4118 COUNTY ROAD AB	54217	NW	Dr Daniel A Olson	(920)845-2095 (920)845-9075	WS 930 SS 830 BC 830	EL/HS/ED/ MD	548	427	237
LYNDON STATION	*ST LUKE*	1897	377 ROGER ST LYNDON STA	53944	SW	Alan G Boeck	(608)666-4091	WS 9 SS 1015 BC 1015				
MADISON	*BETHLEHEM*		See Sun Prairie WI									
	CALVARY calvary@calvarymadison.org www.calvarymadison.org	1920	701 STATE ST	53703	SW	Allen K Strawn	(608)255-7214 (608)255-1857	WS 11	ED/HC/SN	25	25	20
	CHRIST MEMORIAL www.livelifetogether.com	1953	2833 RARITAN RD FITCH-BURG	53711	SW	Jeffrey S Meyer Matthew P Wipperman	(608)271-2811 (608)271-2849	WS 9 SS 915 BC 915 6	ED/HC/ MD/SN	244	196	121
	CROSS		See Westport WI									
	IMMANUEL office@Immanuelmadison.org www.immanuelmadison.org	1903	1021 SPAIGHT ST	53703	SW	Michael J Erdman	(608)257-5401 (608)257-8875	WS 9 BC 1015	ED/HC			
	LIVING CHRIST admin@living-christ.org www.living-christ.org	1980	110 N GAMMON RD	53717	SW	Daniel C Kowert	(608)829-2136 (608)829-3513	WS 8 915 SS 1030 BC 8 915 1030	EC/ED/ HC/SN	354	287	201
	MONONA		See Monona WI									
	MOUNT OLIVE office@molc.us www.molc.us	1941	110 N WHITNEY WAY	53705	SW	Daniel T Torkelson	(608)238-5656	WS 9 SS 1020 BC 1030	EC/ED/HC/ MD/SN	310	280	126
	ST PAUL office@stpaulmadison.org www.stpaulmadison.org	1939	2126 N SHERMAN AVE	53704	SW	Michael J Erdman	(608)244-8077	WS 930 BC 8	ED/HC/ MD/SN	116	87	43
MANAWA	*ST LUKE*		See Big Falls WI									
	ST MARK stmarksymco@yahoo.com	1880	N7534 CHURCH ST	54949	NW	Jeffrey A Smiles	(920)596-3241	WS 1015 SS 9	ED/HC/MD	397	348	82
	ST PAUL stpaulchurchmanawa2004@yahoo.com www.stpaulmanawa.org	1875	742 DEPOT ST	54949	NW	Nathan A Reichle	(920)596-2837 (920)596-2851	WS 815 1030 SS 920 BC 930	EL/ED/MD	1004	790	250
MANITOWISH WATERS	*TRINITY*		See Boulder Junction WI									

*Indicates a new church start. A new church start is an intentionally organized gathering which comes together on a regular basis for the purpose of worship and/or Bible study and is intended to grow into a member LCMS congregation. WS =Worship Service; SS = Sunday School; BC =Bible Class; EC = Early Childhood; EL = Elementary School; HS = High School; ED =Education Ministry; HC =Human Care Ministry; SN = Special Needs Ministry; MD = Media Ministry (PC)=Partner Church Pastor. See Page 53 for the Table of Abbreviations for key to additional abbreviations

CITY	CONGREGATION EMAIL WEBSITE	YEAR EST	LOCATION MAILING ADDRESS	ZIP CODE(S)	DIST.	PASTOR(S)	PHONE FAX	WS SS BC	SCHOOLS/ MINISTRIES	STATISTIC Bapt	Conf	Avg Attend
MANITOWOC	*REDEEMER* office@redeemermanty.com www.redeemermanty.com	1940	1712 MENASHA AVE	54220	SW	Jonathan P Huehn	(920)684-3989	WS 9 SS 1015 BC 1015	EC/ED/HC/ MD/SN	620	496	135
MAPLE	*FAITH* tvonhagel@yahoo.com	1897	4641 County Highway F PO BOX 187	54854	MNN		(715)363-2516 (715)363-2516	WS 10	ED			
MARENGO	*ST PAUL* www.stpaulmarengo.ctshost.org	1907	6391 Vista Rd 63491 VISTA RD	54855	NW	Dr Arleigh F vonSeggern	(715)278-3271	WS 1030 SS 915		110	99	30
MARINETTE	*FAITH* marinettefaithlutheran@gmail.com www.faithmarinette.org	1968	4009 IRVING ST	54143	NW	James F Krueger	(715)735-6506	WS 9 SS 1015 BC 1030	EC/ED/HC/ MD/SN	164	138	83
MARION	*IMMANUEL*	1864	W12136 County Rd M 1027 N MAIN ST	54950	NW	Dean M Suehring	(715)851-1151	WS 9 1030	ED/HC/ MD/SN			
	ST JOHN		See Tigerton WI									
MARSHALL	*BETHLEHEM*		See Sun Prairie WI									
MARSHFIELD	*CHRIST* christ.marshfield@gmail.com www.christmarshfield.org	1928	1208 W 14TH ST	54449	NW	Andrew D Belt	(715)384-3535	WS 9 SS 1030 BC 1030	ED/HC/ MD/SN	755	571	192
	IMMANUEL info@immanuelmarshfield.org www.immanuelmarshfield.org	1880	604 S CHESTNUT AVE	54449	NW	Chris A Schwanz Donn H Radde	(715)384-5121 (715)389-2963	WS 9 SS 10 BC 745	EL/ED/HC/ MD/SN	806	611	192
MATTOON	*ST JOHN* spockat53@yahoo.com	1885	304 Flint Ave PO BOX 260	54450	NW	Steven N Pockat Sr	(715)489-3471	WS 9 SS 10	ED/HC/SN	394	311	75
MAYVILLE	*IMMANUEL* pastorzahner@gmail.com www.immanuelmayville.com	1847	N 8092 County Hwy AY N8092 COUNTY ROAD AY	53050	SW	Douglas J Zahner	(920)387-5363 (920)387-2158	WS 930 SS 830 BC 830	EL/ED/HC/ MD/SN	184	134	91
	ST JOHN www.stjohnsmayville.com	1860	450 BRIDGE ST	53050	SW	Dr Mark G Cutler Joshua J Frazee	(920)387-3568 (920)387-2852	WS 9 SS 8 BC 8	EL/ED/HC/ MD/SN	823	708	199
MCFARLAND	*MONONA*		See Monona WI									
MEDFORD	*TRINITY*		See Chelsea WI									
	TRINITY trinitylutheran.medford@gmail.com www.trinity-medford.org	1883	W5334 DASSOW AVE	54451	NW	Ralph C Shorey III	(715)748-4181	WS 9 SS 10 BC 8	ED/HC/ MD/SN	572	448	76
MELLEN	*IMMANUEL* immanuelmellen@centurytel.net	1901	101 Thomas St PO BOX 18	54546	NW	Rod D Stewart Jr	(715)274-2751	WS 2 SS 10	ED/MD	277	231	45
MELROSE	*ST JOHN*		See Black River Falls WI									
MENASHA	*NEW HOPE*		See Neenah WI									
	ST LUKE		See Chilton WI									
	TRINITY kgerue@trinitymenasha.com www.trinitymenasha.com	1857	300 BROAD ST	54952	SW	Steven S Billings Keith E Ge Rue	(920)722-2662	WS 9 SS 1030 BC 1030	EL/ED/HC/ MD/SN	429	381	134
MENOMONEE FALLS	*GRACE* www.grace-connect.org	1933	W196N9525 CROSSVIEW WAY MENOMONEE FLS	53051	SW	Dr Joel R Howard Anthony C Sedotto	(262)251-0670 (262)251-8263	WS 8 10 SS 10	EL/HS/ED/ HC/MD			
	PRINCE PEACE office.popmf@gmail.com www.lcpopmf.com	1961	W156N7149 PILGRIM RD MENOMONEE FLS	53051	EN	Thomas E Engler	(262)251-3360	WS 9 BC 1015	ED/HC/SN			
	ZION www.zioninthefalls.org	1883	N48 W18700 Lisbon Rd N48W18700 LISBON RD	53051	SW	Dean A Dummer	(262)781-8133 (262)781-4656	WS 9 SS 930	EL/HS/ED/ MD	206	166	111
MENOMONIE	*FAITH*	1979	2220 21st St S 2220 21ST ST SE	54751	NW	Michael A Penikis	(715)235-1653	WS 845 SS 10				
MEQUON	*BEAUTIFUL SAVIOR* bslcmequon@gmail.com www.bslcmequon.com	1956	11313 N Riverland Rd #35W 11313 N RIVERLAND RD # 35W	53092	SW	Michael L Stein	(262)242-6650 (262)242-6650	WS 9 SS 1015 BC 1015	ED/HC/ MD/SN	334	271	80
	CONCORDIA UNIVERSITY Satellite Site of First Immanuel Cedarburg WI	2007	Outdoor Amphitheater 12800 N Lake Shore Dr	53097								
	TRINITY trinity@trinityfreistadt.com www.trinityfreistadt.com	1839	10729 West Freistadt Rd 10729 W FREISTADT RD	53097	SW	Carl W Lehenbauer Daniel Reh	(262)242-2045 (262)242-4407	WS 8 1045 BC 915	EL/HS/ED/ HC/MD/SN	787	627	309
MERCER	*FAITH* faithlutheranchurch@centurylink.net www.lcmsflm.org	1967	2701 W KICHAKS LANDING RD	54547	NW		(715)476-2626	WS 9	ED/HC/ MD/SN	49	43	18
MERRILL	*BELL TOWER SERVICE* Satellite Site of Trinity Merrill WI	2021	1500 ODay Street	54452								
	FAITH faithmerrillwi@gmail.com faithlutheranmerrill.com	1871	15425 County Road K S 15425 S COUNTY ROAD K	54452	NW	Donald G Love	(715)536-5443	WS 1015 SS 915 BC 1115		298	275	91
	IMMANUEL	1915	N1660 LEAFY GROVE RD	54452	NW	Joel S Danner	(715)536-7242	WS 10 SS 9 BC 9	ED/HC/MD	302	246	99
	JENNY TOWER SERVICES Satellite Site of Trinity Merrill WI	2021	711 E. First Street	54452								

*Indicates a new church start. A new church start is an intentionally organized gathering which comes together on a regular basis for the purpose of worship and/or Bible study and is intended to grow into a member LCMS congregation. WS =Worship Service; SS = Sunday School; BC =Bible Class; EC = Early Childhood; EL = Elementary School; HS = High School; ED =Education Ministry; HC =Human Care Ministry; SN = Special Needs Ministry; MD = Media Ministry (PC)=Partner Church Pastor. See Page 53 for the Table of Abbreviations for key to additional abbreviations

CITY	CONGREGATION EMAIL WEBSITE	YEAR EST	LOCATION MAILING ADDRESS	ZIP CODE(S)	DIST.	PASTOR(S)	PHONE FAX	WS SS BC	SCHOOLS/ MINISTRIES	STATISTIC Bapt	 Conf	 Avg Attend
MERRILL	*MEN'S BIBLE STUDY* Satellite Site of St John Merrill WI	2024	501 S Pine Ridge Avenue	54452								
	MEN'S BIBLE STUDY Satellite Site of St John Merrill WI	2024	Merrill	54452								
	PARK PLACE WORSHIP Satellite Site of Trinity Merrill WI	2021	215 Grand Ave.	54452								
	PINE CREST SERVICE Satellite Site of Trinity Merrill WI	2021	2100 E. 6th Street	54452								
	ST JOHN churchoffice@stjohnmerrill.org www.stjohnmerrill.org	1876	1104 E 3RD ST	54452	NW		(715)536-4722 (715)539-3381	WS 8 1030 SS 930 BC 930 7	EL/ED/HC/ MD/SN	1045	836	174
	ST PAUL	1892	W2604 COUNTY ROAD P	54452	NW	Gregory R Laska	(715)432-4954	WS 830 SS 930	ED/MD	215	154	56
	ST PAUL'S		See Irma WI									
	STONE BRIDGE SERVICE Satellite Site of Trinity Merrill WI	2021	307 W. Main Street	54452								
	TRINITY admin@trinitymerrill.com www.trinitymerrill.com	1885	107 N STATE ST	54452	NW	Scott A Gustafson Jonathan T Chapa	(715)536-5482 (715)539-2911	WS 8 1030 6 BC 915	EL/ED/HC/ MD/SN	1731	1468	379
	WOODLAND COURT SERVICE Satellite Site of Trinity Merrill WI	2021	1102 S. Center Ave.	54452								
MIDDLETON	*CROSS*		See Westport WI									
MILLSTON	*ST JOHN*		See Black River Falls WI									
	ST MATTHEW		See Warrens WI									
MILWAUKEE	*AGAPE HILL LUTHERAN CHURCH* Satellite Site of Berea Milwaukee WI	2013	4873 N 107th Street	53225				WS 1130				
	BEAUTIFUL SAVIOR admin@beautifulsaviorlc.com www.beautifulsaviorlc.com	1950	3205 N 85TH ST	53222	SW	Gregory A Mech	(414)871-6744 (414)871-6864	WS 930 BC 1045	EL/HS/ED/ HC/MD/SN	126	93	34
	BENEDICTION office@benediction-lcms.org www.benediction-lcms.org	1959	8475 W FOND DU LAC AVE	53225	SW	Donald T Hougard Moua Vang	(414)463-9158 (414)463-8338	WS 9 SS 1015 BC 1030	HS/ED/HC	397	264	77
	BEREA berealutheranchurch1957@gmail.com berealutheran.com	1956	4873 N 107TH ST	53225	SW		(414)466-9220	WS 9 1130 BC 1015	EL/HS/ED/ HC/MD/SN			
	BETHANY	1893	2031 N 38TH ST	53208	SW	Afam Afamefuna	(414)444-3131	WS 10 SS 9 BC 9	HS/HC	50	38	27
	BROOKFIELD		See Brookfield WI									
	CHAPEL OF THE CROSS luthchapel@gmail.com www.lutheranchapelofthecross.com	1948	3353 S WHITNALL AVE	53207	SW	David W Zeuschner	(414)481-1880 (414)481-1880	WS 9 SS 1015 BC 1015	ED/HC/MD	130	120	40
	COVENANT covenantlutheran@sbcglobal.net covenantlutheranmke.com	1948	8121 W HOPE AVE	53222	SW	Steven J Voigt	(414)464-2410	WS 930 SS 1045 BC 8 1045	EC/EL/HS/ ED/MD/SN	219	192	86
	DE SION		5740 N 86TH ST	53225	SW	Gui K Kasongo	(414)463-9158	WS 3		220	170	140
	DIVINE SHEPHERD Kristen@divineshepherdlc.org divineshepherdlc.org	1959	9741 W BELOIT RD	53227	SW	Barry A Akers	(414)321-0730 (414)321-5733	WS 930 SS 950 BC 1045	ED/MD/SN	122	112	67
	GOSPEL gospellutheran@gmail.com gospel.swdlcms.org	1918	1535 W CAPITOL DR	53206	SW	Gui K Kasongo	(414)562-1890 (414)562-6760	WS 1030 SS 915 BC 915	HS/ED/HC/ MD			
	GRACE info@grace-ok.org www.grace-ok.org	1895	3030 W OKLAHOMA AVE	53215	SW	Patrick W Randolph	(414)384-3520	WS 9 SS 9 BC 10	HS	145	140	76
	GREENFIELD PARK		See West Allis WI									
	HMONG HOPE Hmonghopemke@outlook.com	2000	4873 N 107TH ST	53225	SW	Faiv Neng B Her	(414)722-2024	WS 1130 SS 1030	HS/ED/HC/ MD			
	HOLY GHOST	1876	547 W Concordia Ave PO BOX 12045	53212	SW	Elijah A Ndon	(414)264-0372	WS 9 SS 1030 BC 1030	HS/ED/HC/ MD	76	54	45
	HOPE HopeLuthMKE@att.net www.hopeluthmke.com/	1924	1115 N 35TH ST	53208	SW	Dennis L Harmon	(414)342-0471	WS 1030 SS 915 BC 915	HS/HC/MD	104	104	50
	LUTHER MANOR Satellite Site of Berea Milwaukee WI	2020	4545 N. 92nd Street	53225								
	LUTHER MEMORIAL		See Shorewood WI									
	MISS OF CHRIST missionofchristlc@sbcglobal.net	1973	912 W Center St PO BOX 6499	53206	SW	Dennis L Harmon	(414)264-4050 (414)264-4237	WS 9 SS 8 BC 10	HS/HC	115	100	60
	MOUNT CALVARY pastorc@mtcalvary-mke.org www.mtcalvary-mke.org	1925	2862 N 53RD ST	53210	SW	Dr Daniel P Czaplewski · Howard L Thomas III	(414)873-3931 (414)873-0567	WS 9 SS 1015 BC 1015	EL/HS/ED/ HC/MD/SN	127	115	57

*Indicates a new church start. A new church start is an intentionally organized gathering which comes together on a regular basis for the purpose of worship and/or Bible study and is intended to grow into a member LCMS congregation. WS =Worship Service; SS = Sunday School; BC =Bible Class; EC = Early Childhood; EL = Elementary School; HS = High School; ED =Education Ministry; HC =Human Care Ministry; SN = Special Needs Ministry; MD = Media Ministry (PC)=Partner Church Pastor. See Page 53 for the Table of Abbreviations for key to additional abbreviations

CITY	CONGREGATION EMAIL WEBSITE	YEAR EST	LOCATION MAILING ADDRESS	ZIP CODE(S)	DIST.	PASTOR(S)	PHONE FAX	WS SS BC	SCHOOLS/ MINISTRIES	STATISTIC Bapt	Conf	Avg Attend
MILWAUKEE	*MOUNT OLIVE* info@mtolivemke.org www.mtolivemke.org	1894	5327 W WASHINGTON BLVD	53208	SW	Michael J Schleider Stephen M Rosebrock	(414)774-2200 (414)771-3855	WS 930 SS 11 BC 11	EL/HS/ED/ HC/MD/SN	350	320	168
	MOUNT ZION		See Greenfield WI									
	OKLAHOMA AVE secretary@oa-lc.org okavelutheran.org/	1934	5335 W OKLAHOMA AVE	53219	SW	Silas M Hasselbrook	(414)543-3580	WS 1030 BC 945	ED/HC/ MD/SN	86	74	42
	OUR SAVIOR		See Whitefish Bay WI									
	PILGRIM		See Wauwatosa WI									
	SHERMAN PARK	1923	2703 N SHERMAN BLVD	53210	SW	Benjamin T Schimm	(414)445-5185 (414)445-6556	WS 930 BC 1030	ED/HC/MD	34	34	23
	ST MARTINI	1884	1500 S Cesar E Chavez Dr 1512 S CESAR E CHAVEZ DR	53204	SW	Alfonso J Prada	(414)645-4094 (414)645-4094	WS 10	HS			
	ST PETER-IMMANUEL spi-mke.com	1973	7801 W ACACIA ST	53223	SW		(414)353-6800 (414)353-5510	WS 930	EL/HS/ ED/HC	52	49	28
	TRINITY UAC pastor@trinitymilwaukee.org www.trinitymilwaukee.org	1847	1046 N 9th St 1026 N 9TH ST	53233	SW	Matthew D Peters	(414)271-2219 (414)271-1530	WS 10 SS 1130 BC 830	ED/MD	166	142	75
MINOCQUA	*PEACE*		See Arbor Vitae WI									
	ROCK OF AGES rockofagesminocqua@gmail.com www.rockofages-minocqua.org	1979	10441 Hwy 70 W PO BOX 1131	54548	NW	Brian D Liermann	(715)356-3848 (715)356-4726	WS 9 BC 1015	ED/HC/ MD/SN	206	174	100
	TRINITY		See Boulder Junction WI									
MONDOVI	*ST PAUL*	1870	Steinke Vly Rd W1143 COUNTY ROAD A	54755	NW	Daniel M Pfaffe	(716)926-5973					
	ZION office@zionmondovi.com zionmondovi.com	1903	264 E MAIN ST	54755	NW		(715)926-3664	WS 9 SS 1030 BC 1030	ED/HC/MD	534	367	128
MONONA	*MONONA* mlc-ms@hotmail.com mononalutheran.org	1936	4411 MONONA DR	53716	SW	Thomas M Nowak	(608)222-7071 (608)222-0761	WS 9 SS 1015	ED/HC/ MD/SN	113	97	31
	OUR SAVIOR DEAF mlc-ms@hotmail.com osdlc.org	1949	MONONA EVANGELICAL LUTHERAN CHURCH 4411 MONONA DR	53716	SW		(608)222-7071	WS 1030	ED/SN	18	18	6
MONROE	*PEACE VALLEY** benish@swd.lcms.org peacevalleylcms.360unite.com/home	2024	113 W 8TH STREET	53566	SW		(608)377-3748	BC 1030		20	17	16
MONTELLO	*ST JOHN*		See Oxford WI									
	TRINITY	1865	W1164 Fern Rd W3008 COUNTY ROAD E NESHKORO	53949 54960	SW			WS 8	ED/HC	17	17	11
MONTICELLO	*PEACE VALLEY**		See Monroe WI									
MOSINEE	*ST JOHN*		See Dancy WI									
MOUNT HOREB	*CROSS*		See Westport WI									
MOUNT PLEASANT	*CHAPEL CROSS*		See Racine WI									
	GRACE		See Racine WI									
	HOLY CROSS		See Racine WI									
	PRIMROSE RETIREMENT COMMUNITIES Satellite Site of Living Hope Racine WI	2015	1775 N Newman Rd	53406				WS 8				
MOUNTAIN	*TABOR* taborlutheran@centurytel.net	1904	14153 Church Rd PO BOX 67	54149	NW	Steven E Stoll	(715)276-7707	WS 830	HS/ED/HC	151	144	35
MUSCODA	*ST PETERS* dwilkie595@aol.com	1870	210 W Beech St PO BOX 555	53573	SW	Dana M Wilkie	(608)739-4017	WS 1015 SS 930	ED/HC	109	88	30
NECEDAH	*SAINT JAMES* secretary@stjamesnecedah.com stjamesnecedah.com	1930	1106 S MAIN ST	54646	SW	Roger A Erdman	(608)565-7252 (608)565-2410	WS 1030 SS 9 BC 915	ED/HC/ MD/SN	95	90	32
NEENAH	*NEW HOPE* newhope@newhopeconnect.org www.newhopeconnect.org	1981	1850 AMERICAN DR	54956	SW	Gregory M Hintz	(920)725-4354 (920)725-4058	WS 9 SS 1015 BC 1015	EL/ED/HC/ MD/SN			
	PEACE pastor@peaceneenah.com www.peaceneenah.com	1960	1228 S PARK AVE	54956	SW	Marshal R Frisque	(920)725-0510	WS 9 SS 1030 BC 1030	ED/HC/ MD/SN	379	324	138
NEKOOSA	*BETHLEHEM* houseofbread@solarus.biz www.bethlehemnekoosa.org	1892	316 BUEHLER AVE	54457	NW	Dennis D Schwalenberg	(715)886-4081 (715)886-4094	WS 930 BC 11	ED/HC/ MD/SN	123	116	60
	LAKES AREA lakesarea@outlook.com lacfchurch.com		1167 ALPINE DR	54457	NW	Eric R Wenger	(715)325-5475	WS 930 BC 12		136	133	104

*Indicates a new church start. A new church start is an intentionally organized gathering which comes together on a regular basis for the purpose of worship and/or Bible study and is intended to grow into a member LCMS congregation. WS =Worship Service; SS = Sunday School; BC =Bible Class; EC = Early Childhood; EL = Elementary School; HS = High School; ED =Education Ministry; HC =Human Care Ministry; SN = Special Needs Ministry; MD = Media Ministry (PC)=Partner Church Pastor. See Page 53 for the Table of Abbreviations for key to additional abbreviations

CITY	CONGREGATION EMAIL WEBSITE	YEAR EST	LOCATION MAILING ADDRESS	ZIP CODE(S)	DIST.	PASTOR(S)	PHONE FAX	WS SS BC	SCHOOLS/ MINISTRIES	STATISTIC Bapt	Conf	Avg Attend
NEKOOSA	*LAKES AREA FELLOWSHP* Satellite Site of Bethlehem Nekoosa WI	2002	Rome Town Hall 1156 Alpine Dr	54457				WS 930 SS 1045 BC 1045				
NESHKORO	*ST PAUL*		See Westfield WI									
	TRINITY		See Montello WI									
	ZION zionlutheranneshkoro.com	1881	227 N State St 219 N STATE ST	54960	SW	Charles P Schultz	(920)293-4312	WS 10 SS 1115	ED/HC/MD	164	144	53
NEW BERLIN	*BLESSED SAVIOR* secretary.bslcnb@gmail.com blessedsaviorwi.org	1960	15250 W CLEVELAND AVE	53151	SW	Zachary M DeArmond	(262)786-6465 (262)786-6799	WS 8 1030 SS 915 BC 915	EC/HS/ED/ HC/MD/SN	463	410	150
	PEACE secretary@peacelutheran.org www.peacelutheran.org	1962	17651 W SMALL RD	53146	EN	Scott D Kruse	(262)679-1441 (262)679-0292	WS 8 1030 SS 920 BC 920	EC/ED/MD	360	332	146
NEW FANE	*ST JOHN* stjohnnewfane@outlook.com www.stjohnlutheran.yolasite.com	1859	N683 County Rd S N683 COUNTY ROAD S KEWASKUM	53040	SW	Mark W Eckert	(262)626-2309	WS 730 9 SS 1015 BC 830 1015	ED/HC/ MD/SN	609	458	191
NEW GLARUS	*PEACE VALLEY**		See Monroe WI									
NEW HOLSTEIN	*ZION* office@zionnewholstein.org	1915	1702 VAN BUREN ST	53061	SW	Brian A Cigelske	(920)898-5250	WS 745 1015 SS 9 BC 9	HC/MD/SN	355	291	141
NEW MINER	*ST PAUL*	1892	N15296 19th Ave 1106 S MAIN ST NECEDAH	54646	SW	Roger A Erdman	(608)565-7252 (608)565-2410	WS 8 BC 915	ED/HC/SN	59	52	15
NEW RICHMOND	*ST LUKE* jody@stlukesnr.org stlukesnr.org	1938	365 W RIVER DR	54017	NW	Dwain J Thomsen	(715)246-4861	WS 8 1030 SS 915 BC 930	ED/HC/MD	1073	758	250
NEWALD	*ST JOHN*		See Laona WI									
NORTH FOND DU LAC	*DIVINE SAVIOR* divinesaviorlcms@gmail.com www.divinesaviornfdl.org	1976	1081 PROSPECT AVE N FOND DU LAC	54937	SW	Allen H Bramstadt	(920)923-1532	WS 9 BC 1015	ED/MD			
NORTH PRAIRIE	*ST JOHNS* kathy@stjohnsnp.org stjohnsnp.org	1887	312 N MAIN ST	53153	SW	Dr Michael J Nielsen	(262)392-2170	WS 9 SS 1015 BC 8	EC/ED/HC/ MD	200	175	60
OAK CREEK	*GRACE* church@graceoakcreek.org www.graceoakcreek.org	1955	3381 E Puetz Rd 8537 S PENNSYLVANIA AVE	53154	SW	John M Taggatz	(414)762-8990 (414)762-8869	WS 8 1030 SS 915 BC 915	EC/EL/HS/ ED/HC/ MD/SN	451	335	94
	ST JOHN		See Cudahy WI									
OCONOMOWOC	*ST JOHN* pastor@stjohnashippun.com	1881	N1245 St Johns Way N1245 SAINT JOHNS WAY	53066	SW	Gary W Tillmann	(920)474-4749	WS 930 SS 8 BC 830	ED/HC/MD	319	285	80
	ST PAUL church@splco.org www.splco.org	1865	210 E PLEASANT ST	53066	SW	Lance A ODonnell Jason A Schockman	(262)567-5001 (262)567-1207	WS 8 1030 SS 915 BC 915	EL/HS/ED/ HC/MD/SN	1995	1204	370
OCONTO	*ZION* zionoconto@gmail.com www.zionoconto.org	1931	1700 Superior Ave PO BOX 259	54153	NW	Dustin E Ridings	(920)834-5037	WS 930 SS 9	ED/MD	52	41	28
OMRO	*GRACE* graceormo@att.net graceomro.com	1930	720 JACKSON AVE	54963	SW	Mark A Wenzel	(920)685-2621 (920)685-6549	WS 8 1030 SS 915 BC 915	EC/ED/HC/ MD	636	508	155
ONALASKA	*SHEPHERD HILLS* office@sothonalaska.com www.sothonalaska.org	1980	1215 REDWOOD ST	54650	SW		(608)783-0330	WS 9 1030 SS 1015 BC 1015	EC/HS/ED/ HC/MD/SN	306	261	152
ONEIDA	*ZION LUTHERAN CHURCH* pastor.ziononeida@gmail.com www.ziononeida.org	1923	453 ROSE HILL DR	54155	NW	Christian G Burg	(920)869-9466 (920)869-2777	WS 8 1030 SS 1015 BC 1015	ED/HC/MD	147	125	62
OOSTBURG	*ST PAULS*		See Cascade WI									
ORFORDVILLE	*IMMANUEL*	1883	8212 High St 8212 W HIGH ST	53576	SW		(608)751-4984	WS 9 SS 10 BC 10				
OSCEOLA	*SHEP OF VALLEY*		See Saint Croix Fls WI									
OSHKOSH	*GOOD SHEPHERD* church@oshkoshgoodshepherd.org www.goodshepherdinoshkosh.com	1968	2450 W 9TH AVE	54904	SW	Gregory A Koepsell	(920)231-0530 (920)651-8721	WS 8 1030 SS 915 BC 915	ED/HC/SN	547	435	270
	HMONG	1994	370 BOWEN ST	54901	SW	Blong Vang	(920)267-3305		ED/HC	26	24	17
	NEW HOPE		See Neenah WI									
	TRINITY church@trinityoshkosh.org www.trinityoshkosh.org	1856	370 BOWEN ST	54901	SW	James F Pemberton	(920)235-7440 (920)235-6940	WS 9 SS 1015 BC 1030	ED/HC/ MD/SN	597	455	69
OSSEO	*ST PAUL*		See Whitehall WI									
	ST PETER st.peter.54758@gmail.com	1884	E11770 COUNTY ROAD HH	54758	NW	David J Knefelkamp	(715)597-2431	WS 9 SS 1015	ED/HC/SN	182	149	34
OXFORD	*ST JOHN* StJohnsOxford0@gmail.com stjohn-trinity-lcms-marquette-co-wi.360unite.com	1895	330 E Vallette St PO BOX 127	53952	SW	Larry G Sheppard	(608)586-5877	WS 1030 SS 9	ED/HC/MD	250	172	34
PACKWAUKEE	*TRINITY*	1897	W5940 Chestnut PO BOX 628	53953	SW	Larry G Sheppard	(608)589-5138	WS 830 SS 945 BC 730	ED/HC/SN	74	55	27

*Indicates a new church start. A new church start is an intentionally organized gathering which comes together on a regular basis for the purpose of worship and/or Bible study and is intended to grow into a member LCMS congregation. WS =Worship Service; SS = Sunday School; BC =Bible Class; EC = Early Childhood; EL = Elementary School; HS = High School; ED =Education Ministry; HC =Human Care Ministry; SN = Special Needs Ministry; MD = Media Ministry (PC)=Partner Church Pastor. See Page 53 for the Table of Abbreviations for key to additional abbreviations

CITY	CONGREGATION EMAIL WEBSITE	YEAR EST	LOCATION MAILING ADDRESS	ZIP CODE(S)	DIST.	PASTOR(S)	PHONE FAX	WS SS BC	SCHOOLS/ MINISTRIES	Bapt	Conf	Avg Attend
PADDOCK LAKE	*BEAUTIFUL SAVIOR*		See Antioch IL									
PARK FALLS	*PEACE* peace2you@pctcnet.net peace2you.pctcnet.net	1903	600 2nd Ave N 598 2ND AVE N	54552	NW	Samuel L Morsching	(715)762-4541 (715)762-4009	WS 9 SS 1015 BC 1015	ED/HC/ MD/SN			
PEWAUKEE	*CHRIST THE LIFE*		See Waukesha WI									
	LAMB OF GOD lambofgod7@juno.com www.lambofgodlutheran.com	1979	N19 W25050 BLUEMOUND RD	53072	SW	Bruce W Harrmann	(262)691-3828	WS 10 SS 9 BC 9	HS/ED/HC/ MD/SN	122	97	77
	SHEPHERD/HILLS pastoraaron@sothpewaukee.org www.sothpewaukee.org	1990	N36W24130 Pewaukee Rd PO BOX 802	53072	SW	Aaron M Meyer Noah O Strand	(262)691-0700 (262)691-1627	WS 8 930 11 SS 930	HC	1207	969	404
PHILLIPS	*TRINITY* trinzion@pctcnet.net	1885	103 TRINITY DR	54555	NW	Samuel L Morsching	(715)339-3495	WS 830 SS 945 BC 945	ED/HC/ MD/SN	160	139	40
PICKEREL	*ST JOHN* bo.baumeister63@gmail.com	1902	N8934 State Hwy 55	54465	NW		(715)484-3382	WS 9 BC 730	ED/HC	237	129	36
PIPE LAKE	*CHRIST*		See Comstock WI									
PITTSVILLE	*ST JOHN* stjohnsecretary@tds.net	1888	8313 2nd St PO BOX 263	54466	NW	Gary L Markworth	(715)884-2211 (715)884-2211	WS 9 SS 930 BC 8	ED/HC/MD	330	287	69
	ST PAUL stjohnsecretary@tds.net	1925	Hwy 73 PO BOX 263	54466	NW	Gary L Markworth	(715)884-2211	WS 1030	MD	100	84	23
PLATTEVILLE	*ST PAUL*		See Dubuque IA									
PLEASANT PRAIRIE	*GOOD SHEPHERD* gslutheranoffice@gmail.com goodshepherdluth.org	1964	4311 104TH ST PLEASANT PR	53158	SW	Kyle T Verage	(262)694-4405 (262)694-0964	WS 9 SS 1015 BC 1015	ED/MD	262	203	126
	GRACE		See Racine WI									
PLOVER	*BEAUTIFUL SAVIOR* secretary@bsavior.onmicrosoft.com www.beautifulsaviorploverwi.com	1989	3210 MAPLE DR	54467	NW	Joseph L Leech	(715)341-2898 (715)342-5642	WS 930 SS 1045 BC 11	ED/HC/MD	187	159	67
PLUM CITY	*IMMANUEL*	1894	420 1ST ST	54761	NW	Daniel M Pfaffe	(715)647-2555	WS 1030 SS 930		93	84	34
PLYMOUTH	*GRACE*		See Elkhart Lake WI									
	ST JOHN office@sjlplymouth.com www.sjlplymouth.com	1855	222 N Stafford St 222 STAFFORD ST	53073	SW	John M Schultz Andrew S Thompson	(920)893-3071	WS 8 1030 SS 930 BC 930	EL/HS/ED/ HC/MD/SN	1873	1438	502
	ZION		See Glenbeulah WI									
POPLAR	*CHRIST*		See Superior WI									
PORT EDWARDS	*TRINITY* secretary@trinitylutheranpe.org www.trinitylutheranpe.org	1950	990 3RD ST	54469	NW		(715)887-3021	WS 9 BC 1015	ED	185	184	84
PORT WASHINGTON	*ST JOHNS* office@stjohns-port.com www.stjohns-port.com	1890	217 N FREEMAN DR PRT WASHINGTN	53074	SW	Dustin L Anderson Richard M Gaub	(262)284-2131 (262)268-6558	WS 9 SS 1015 BC 1015	ED/MD	372	297	64
PORT WING	*CHRIST*		See Superior WI									
PORTAGE	*ST JOHNS* churchoffice@stjohnsportage.com www.stjohnsportage.com	1859	850 ARMSTRONG ST	53901	SW	G G Hovland Rodney A Armon	(608)742-9000 (608)742-7154	WS 8 1030 BC 915	EL/ED/HC/ MD/SN	810	672	275
POTTER	*TRINITY* trinity.rantoulschool@gmail.com www.trinityrantoul.org	1858	N6080 West River Rd N6080 W RIVER RD HILBERT	54129	SW		(920)853-3134	WS 8 10 SS 9 BC 9	EL/ED/HC/ MD/SN	635	528	161
POY SIPPI	*EMMAUS* emmauspoysippi@gmail.com	1907	W2185 County H PO BOX 346	54967	SW	Brian G Weber	(920)987-5229	WS 8 SS 830	ED/HC/SN	186	158	42
PRAIRIE DU CHIEN	*ST PAUL*		See McGregor IA									
PRENTICE	*TRINITY* trinitylutheranprentice@gmail.com trinitylutheranprentice.weebly.com/	1967	W4594 US HIGHWAY 8	54556	NW		(715)428-2851		ED/HC/SN	38	37	17
PRESQUE ISLE	*TRINITY*		See Boulder Junction WI									
PRINCETON	*CALVARY* calvluthprinceton@gmail.com www.calvaryprinceton.org	1990	202 S Farmer St PO BOX 11	54968	SW	Charles P Schultz	(920)295-4747 (920)295-3421	WS 9 SS 9	ED/HC/ MD/SN	123	113	51
PULASKI	*ST JOHN* stjohn-lcms@netnet.net www.stjohnpulaskiwi.org	1956	910 S SAINT AUGUSTINE ST	54162	NW	Larry R Yaw	(920)822-3511	WS 9 SS 1030 BC 1030	ED/HC/ MD/SN			
RACINE	*CHAPEL CROSS* lutheranchapelofthecross@gmail.com lutheranchapelofthecross.org	1969	1426 N FANCHER RD MT PLEASANT	53406	SW	Paul D Ficken	(262)886-4755	WS 9 BC 1015	ED/SN	70	65	45
	CHRIST KING ctklutheranlcms@gmail.com www.christthekinglcms.wordpress.com	1954	3350 LaSalle St PO BOX 44288	53402 53404	SW	Luke H Otten	(262)639-5849	WS 8	HS/ED/HC	42	35	15
	GRACE gracelutheransecretary@yahoo.com gracelutheranracine.net	1918	3700 WASHINGTON AVE	53405	SW	John A Frahm III	(262)633-4831	WS 9 BC 1030	ED/HC/MD	218	192	65

*Indicates a new church start. A new church start is an intentionally organized gathering which comes together on a regular basis for the purpose of worship and/or Bible study and is intended to grow into a member LCMS congregation. WS =Worship Service; SS = Sunday School; BC =Bible Class; EC = Early Childhood; EL = Elementary School; HS = High School; ED =Education Ministry; HC =Human Care Ministry; SN = Special Needs Ministry; MD = Media Ministry (PC)=Partner Church Pastor. See Page 53 for the Table of Abbreviations for key to additional abbreviations

CITY	CONGREGATION EMAIL WEBSITE	YEAR EST	LOCATION MAILING ADDRESS	ZIP CODE(S)	DIST.	PASTOR(S)	PHONE FAX	WS SS BC	SCHOOLS/ MINISTRIES	STATISTIC Bapt	Conf	Avg Attend
RACINE	*HOLY CROSS* Office@HCLCRacine.com HCLCRacine.com	1960	3350 LATHROP AVE ELM-WOOD PARK	53405	SW	Luke H Otten	(262)554-7010	WS 10 BC 11	EL/HS/ ED/HC	58	55	26
	PENTECOST pentecostlutheran@gmail.com www.pentecost-racine.org	1908	2213 COOLIDGE AVE	53403	S	Brady N Retzlaff	(262)633-9674	WS 830 11 SS 945 BC 945	HS/ED	165	134	93
	PRINCE PEACE colleenoffice@wi.twcbc.com www.princeofpeaceracine.com	1978	4340 6 MILE RD	53402	SW	Christopher K Lockie	(262)639-1277 (262)898-2088	WS 9 SS 1015	EC/HS/ED			
	ST JOHN chapman@stjohnsracine.org www.stjohnsracine.org	1862	1501 Erie St 510 KEWAUNEE ST	53402	SW	Jacob A Gilbert Joshua K DeYoung	(262)637-7011 (262)637-7089	WS 745 1015 SS 9 BC 9	EL/HS/ED/ HC/MD/SN	665	514	227
	TRINITY aburke@trinityracine.com www.trinityracine.com	1905	2065 GENEVA ST	53402	SW	David F Gehne Stephen E Jennings	(262)632-2900 (262)632-3838	WS 8 1030 BC 915	EL/HS/ED/ HC/MD			
RANDOM LAKE	*IMMANUEL* lutheransinbeechwood.ctshost.org	1869	W8497 BRAZELTON DR	53075	SW	Brian L Krueger	(920)994-9060	WS 845 SS 945	ED/HC/ MD/SN	135	129	46
	ST JOHN church@stjohnrandomlake.org stjohnrandomlake.org	1855	W5406 COUNTY ROAD SS W5407 COUNTY ROAD SS	53075	SW	Christopher R Gillespie	(920)994-2228 (920)994-9721	WS 930 BC 815	EL/ED/HC/ MD/SN	399	313	86
REEDSBURG	*ST PETER* stpetersreedsburg@gmail.com www.stpetersreedsburg.com	1867	345 N PINE ST	53959	SW	Paul M Crolius	(608)524-4512 (608)524-8821	WS 9 SS 1015 BC 1015	EL/ED/HC/ MD/SN			
REESEVILLE	*IMMANUEL* immanuellc@tds.net	1895	210 Lincoln Ave 210 LINCOLN AVENUE P.O. BOX 272	53579	SW	Donald E Steinberg	(920)927-5734	WS 9 SS 1030 BC 1030	ED/MD	131	112	25
	TRINITY trinitylutheranchurchoffice@gmail.com	1858	N2296 COUNTY ROAD I	53579	SW		(920)927-5762	WS 10	ED	181	147	31
RHINELANDER	*GRACE*		See Three Lakes WI									
	ST MARK stmarkchurch@outlook.com www.stmarkrhinelander.org	1950	21 S BAIRD AVE	54501	NW	Richard C Miller	(715)362-2470 (715)362-2037	WS 9	ED/HC/ MD/SN	172	139	96
RIB MOUNTAIN	*RIB MOUNTAIN*		See Wausau WI									
	ST MARK		See Wausau WI									
RICE LAKE	*FIRST* talktous@firstlutheranricelake.com www.firstlutheranricelake.com	1889	15 E SAWYER ST	54868	NW	Jonathan D Cluppert	(715)234-7505 (715)434-6516	WS 830 1030 SS 930 BC 930	EC/ED/HC/ MD	346	311	130
	IMMANUEL revjse@gmail.com	1913	2476 27th St	54868	NW		(715)764-9362		ED/HC/MD	24	24	20
RICHLAND CENTER	*ST LUKE* mkufahl@cuw.edu www.stlukerichlandcenter.wordpress.com	1929	1096 North Main Street PO BOX 230 RICHLAND CTR	53581	SW	Mark C Kufahl	(608)334-2639	WS 11 BC 1215	ED/HC/MD			
RINGLE	*ZION*		See Wausau WI									
RIPON	*MESSIAH* contact@messiah.lc messiahlcripon.com/	1969	500 MAYPARTY DR	54971	SW	Bryan L Fritsch	(920)748-3882 (920)748-3882	WS 9 SS 1015 BC 1015	SN	295	240	88
RIVER FALLS	*LUTHER MEMORIAL* ministrycoordinator@lmcrf.org www.lmcrf.org	1950	420 S 4TH ST	54022	NW	Chad R Elfe	(715)425-2675	WS 8 1030 SS 915 BC 915 730	ED/HC/ MD/SN	353	329	160
SAINT CROIX FLS	*SHEP OF VALLEY* www.shepherdofthevalleyscf.org	1988	140 S MADISON ST SAINT CROIX FALLS	54024	NW	Mark K Schoen William A Boateng	(715)483-1186	WS 9 SS 1030 BC 1030	ED/HC/ MD/SN	254	212	143
SAINT FRANCIS	*ST JOHN*		See Cudahy WI									
SAINT GERMAIN	*PEACE*		See Arbor Vitae WI									
	TRINITY		See Boulder Junction WI									
SALEM	*BEAUTIFUL SAVIOR*		See Antioch IL									
	GRACE		See Racine WI									
SAUKVILLE	*RIVER OF LIFE* Satellite Site of First Immanuel Cedarburg WI	2005	598 W Hillcrest Rd	53080				WS 8 930 1045 SS 930 1045 BC 9				
SHARON	*TRIUNE* pastorblanchardlcms@gmail.com	1961	N1584 COUNTY ROAD K	53585	SW	Dale R Blanchard	(262)882-4000	WS 10 SS 845 BC 845	ED/HC	136	125	55
SHAWANO	*SAINT JAKOBI* church@stjakobi.org www.stjakobi.org	1883	N6386 E Hazel Rd W8089 COUNTY ROAD A	54166	NW	Travis R Kleinschmidt	(715)524-4347	WS 9 SS 1030 BC 1030	EL/HS/ED/ HC/MD/SN	704	552	191
	SAINT JAMES secretary@stjamesshawano.org stjames-shawano.org	1873	324 S ANDREWS ST	54166	NW	Andrew J Zobel	(715)524-4815 (715)524-4876	WS 8 930	HS/ED/HC/ MD	1616	1261	400
	SAINT PAUL stpaulstonyhill@gmail.com	1883	W9304 OAK AVE	54166	NW		(715)524-2350	WS 1030 SS 915	HS/ED/HC/ MD/SN	284	253	70
	ST JOHN		See Clintonville WI									
	ST JOHN		See Tigerton WI									
	ST JOHN HERMANSFORT pastor.conradt@yahoo.com	1876	N5633 COUNTY ROAD U	54166	NW		(715)526-5507	WS 9 SS 10	ED/HC/ MD/SN	192	168	61

*Indicates a new church start. A new church start is an intentionally organized gathering which comes together on a regular basis for the purpose of worship and/or Bible study and is intended to grow into a member LCMS congregation. WS =Worship Service; SS = Sunday School; BC =Bible Class; EC = Early Childhood; EL = Elementary School; HS = High School; ED =Education Ministry; HC =Human Care Ministry; SN = Special Needs Ministry; MD = Media Ministry (PC)=Partner Church Pastor. See Page 53 for the Table of Abbreviations for key to additional abbreviations

CITY	CONGREGATION EMAIL WEBSITE	YEAR EST	LOCATION MAILING ADDRESS	ZIP CODE(S)	DIST.	PASTOR(S)	PHONE FAX	WS SS BC	SCHOOLS/ MINISTRIES	STATISTIC Bapt	Conf	Avg Attend
SHEBOYGAN	*BETHLEHEM* infochurch@ourbethlehem.com www.ourbethlehem.com	1890	1121 GEORGIA AVE	53081	SW	John P Niles Jeremy C Hanson	(920)452-4331 (920)452-0209	WS 8 1030 SS 915 BC 915	EL/HS/ED/ HC/MD	923	601	475
	CHRIST christlutheransheboygan@gmail.com	1947	3816 S 12TH ST	53081	SW	Christian F Gugel	(920)457-9205	WS 8 SS 930	HS/ED	91	74	32
	GOOD SHEPHERD pastor@goodshepherdsheboygan.com www.goodshepherdsheboygan.com	1953	1614 S 23RD ST	53081	SW	Christian F Gugel David Blas	(920)452-8759	WS 930 SS 1030 BC 1030	HS	323	281	107
	IMMANUEL office@immanunlesheboygan.com www.immanuelsheboygan.com	1890	1634 ILLINOIS AVE	53081	SW	Donald T Johnson	(920)452-7266	WS 10 SS 845 BC 845	ED/MD/SN	263	208	97
	LUTHER MEMORIAL pastor.luthermemorial@gmail.com www.luthermemorialsheboygan.org	1948	1127 EISNER AVE	53083	SW	Adam P Barkley	(920)458-1322	WS 930 SS 1045 BC 1045		120	108	50
	OUR REDEEMER ourredeemersheboygan@gmail.com www.ourredeemersheboygan.org	1942	3027 WILGUS AVE	53081	SW	Bryan R Osladil	(920)452-0717 (920)452-2752	WS 8 1030 SS 915 BC 915	HS/ED/HC/ MD/SN	247	212	76
	OUR SAVIOR'S oslcsheboygan@gmail.com	1869	917 MEAD AVE	53081	SW	James R Schulz	(920)452-4005	WS 9 SS 1015 BC 1015	HS/ED/HC/ MD/SN	491	425	94
	ST MARK SHEBOYGAN office@stmarksheboygan.com www.stmarksheboygan.com	1853	1019 N 7TH ST	53081	EN	Tyler C Werner	(920)458-4343 (920)458-3484	WS 9 BC 1015	ED/HC/ MD/SN	153	153	59
	ST PAUL'S church@stpaulsheboygan.org stpaulsheboygan.org	1904	1810 N 13TH ST	53081	SW	Alan R Kretschmar Matthew D Shive	(920)452-6829 (920)452-2382	WS 815 1045 SS 930 BC 930	EL/HS/ED/ HC/MD/SN	941	738	168
	TRINITY stttwsecretary@gmail.com www.trinitytw.org	1853	6522 S BUSINESS DR	53081	SW	Shane R Cota	(920)458-8881 (920)803-5157	WS 1015 SS 9	HS/ED/MD	144	122	40
	TRINITY pastor@trinitysheboygan.org www.trinitysheboygan.org	1853	824 WISCONSIN AVE	53081	SW	Timothy J Mech John M Berg	(920)458-8246 (920)458-8267	WS 8 1045 SS 930 BC 930	EL/HS/ED/ HC/MD/SN	1574	1178	461
SHEBOYGAN FALLS	*ST PAUL* office@stpaulfalls.com stpaulfalls.com	1855	730 COUNTY ROAD PPP SHEBOYGAN FLS	53085	SW	Kyle L Backhaus Adam S Wolfe	(920)467-6449 (920)467-4239	WS 8 930 SS 930	EC/HS/ED/ HC/MD/SN	2111	1709	573
	ST THOMAS		See Waldo WI									
SHELDON	*TRINITY* trinitylutheransheldon@gmail.com ziontrinity-e.faithlifesites.com/?ssi=1	1919	W5568 Main St PO BOX 144	54766	NW		(715)452-5359	WS 1015 SS 1130 BC 1130	ED/SN	154	147	26
SHERRY	*ST LUKE* elvistcb@tds.net	1871	9297 3rd St PO BOX 96 AUBURNDALE	54454 54412	NW	Mark A Lundgren	(715)652-0256	WS 1030				
SHERWOOD	*ST LUKE*		See Chilton WI									
SHOREWOOD	*LUTHER MEMORIAL* lmcusc@lmcusc.org lmcusc.org	1916	3833 N MARYLAND AVE	53211	SW	Michael C Larson	(414)332-5732 (414)332-3696	WS 9 SS 1045 BC 1045	ED/HC/MD			
SLINGER	*LIVING WORD*		See Jackson WI									
SOLON SPRINGS	*CHRIST*		See Superior WI									
SOMERS	*GRACE*		See Racine WI									
SOUTH MILWAUKEE	*ST JOHN*		See Cudahy WI									
SOUTH RANGE	*CHRIST*		See Superior WI									
SPENCER	*TRINITY* trinity.spencer.wi@gmail.com www.trinitylutheranspencer.org	1882	109 W Clark St PO BOX 109	54479	NW		(715)659-4006	WS 1030 SS 915	HC/MD	183	165	68
SPOONER	*FAITH* spoonerfaithlutheran@gmail.com www.faithspooner.com	1912	W7148 LUTHER RD	54801	NW	Brent G Berkesch	(715)635-8167	WS 9 SS 915 BC 8	EC/ED/ MD/SN	309	268	90
STEVENS POINT	*BEAUTIFUL SAVIOR*		See Plover WI									
	ST PAUL office@splpoint.com www.stpaulequips.com	1872	1919 WYATT AVE	54481	NW	Steven A Hulke Joshua J Baumann Roger R Moldenhauer	(715)344-5660	WS 8 1045 SS 915 BC 915	EL/ED/HC/ MD/SN	1359	971	439
STOCKBRIDGE	*ST LUKE*		See Chilton WI									
STOUGHTON	*GOOD SHEP BY LK* gsoffice@tds.net www.goodshepherdbythelake.org	1976	1860 Hwy 51 1860 US HIGHWAY 51	53589	SW		(608)873-5924 (608)873-5924	WS 8 1030 SS 915 BC 915	ED/HC/ MD/SN			
STURGEON BAY	*PRINCE OF PEACE* office@princeofpeacesb.com princeofpeacesb.com	1974	1756 MICHIGAN ST	54235	NW	James F Gomez	(920)743-7750	WS 930 SS 830 BC 1030	ED/HC/MD	234	194	132
STURTEVANT	*FAITH* faithlutheranlcms@gmail.com faithsturtevant.org	1952	8500 DURAND AVE	53177	SW	Gerhard P Grabenhofer	(262)886-2522	WS 9 BC 1015	EL/HS/ED/ HC/MD	186	140	45
	GRACE		See Racine WI									
SUAMICO	*PILGRIM-SUAMICO SITE* Satellite Site of Pilgrim Green Bay WI	2007	2999 Lakeview Dr	54173				WS 9 SS 1015 BC 9 1015 3				

*Indicates a new church start. A new church start is an intentionally organized gathering which comes together on a regular basis for the purpose of worship and/or Bible study and is intended to grow into a member LCMS congregation. WS =Worship Service; SS = Sunday School; BC =Bible Class; EC = Early Childhood; EL = Elementary School; HS = High School; ED =Education Ministry; HC =Human Care Ministry; SN = Special Needs Ministry; MD = Media Ministry (PC)=Partner Church Pastor. See Page 53 for the Table of Abbreviations for key to additional abbreviations

CITY	CONGREGATION EMAIL WEBSITE	YEAR EST	LOCATION MAILING ADDRESS	ZIP CODE(S)	DIST.	PASTOR(S)	PHONE FAX	WS SS BC	SCHOOLS/ MINISTRIES	STATISTIC Bapt	Conf	Avg Attend
SULLIVAN	*ST JOHN* stjohnssullivan@centurytel.net www.stjohns-sullivan.com	1861	W407 Highway 18 W407 STATE ROAD 18	53178	SW	Gregory S Barto	(262)593-8630 (262)593-2741	WS 8 1015 SS 9 BC 9	ED/HC/ MD/SN	231	200	127
SUN PRAIRIE	*BETHLEHEM* office@bethlehemlc.org www.bethlehemlc.org	1964	300 BROADWAY DR	53590	SW	Rodney M Serbus Benjamin T Leeper	(608)837-7446 (608)825-2268	WS 8 1030 1045 SS 915 BC 915	ED/HC/MD	927	728	313
	CROSS		See Westport WI									
SUPERIOR	*CHRIST* clcoffice320@gmail.com christlutheran-superior.org	1892	320 N 28TH ST E	54880	MNN	Kirk W Schield	(715)398-3680	WS 9 SS 10 BC 10	ED/HC/MD	353	303	88
	PEACE CHRIST		See Hermantown MN									
SURING	*EMMANUEL*		See Breed WI									
	MOUNT OLIVE	1923	206 N Burk PO BOX 247	54174	NW	Michael A Paholke	(920)842-2488	WS 830 1015 SS 930	ED/HC	184	170	34
	ST JOHN stjohns@stjohnlutheranhayes.org stjohnlutheranhayes.org	1886	8905 SAINT JOHNS RD	54174	NW	Nicholas J Buchholz	(920)842-4443	WS 10 SS 9 BC 9	EL/HS/ED/ HC/MD			
	TRINITY mschuettpelz@hotmail.com	1877	8538 Trinity Church Rd 8905 SAINT JOHNS RD	54174	NW	Nicholas J Buchholz	(920)392-9335 (414)842-4443	WS 830	ED			
SUSSEX	*LAMB OF GOD*		See Pewaukee WI									
	PEACE office@peacesussex.org www.peacesussex.org	1962	W240 N6145 Maple Ave	53089	SW	Peter C Bender Gary V Gehlbach	(262)246-3200	WS 745 1030 SS 915 BC 915	EL/ED/ MD/SN	486	401	262
SYMCO	*ST MARK*		See Manawa WI									
TAYLOR	*ST JOHN*		See Black River Falls WI									
THERESA	*IMMANUEL*		See Mayville WI									
THORP	*ST PAUL* stpaulsthorp@gmail.com www.stpaulsthorpwi.com	1948	201 E RUSCH ST	54771	NW	Phillip L Beukema Jr	(715)669-5608	WS 830 SS 945 BC 945	ED/HC/MD			
THREE LAKES	*GRACE* gracelcms3l@gmail.com	1941	6948 East School PO BOX 216	54562	NW		(715)546-2262	WS 11 BC 12	ED/HC	27	27	15
TIGERTON	*ST JOHN*	1874	W13688 COUNTY ROAD M 514 HILLCREST DRIVE MARION	54486 54950	NW	Dean M Suehring	(715)851-1151	WS 730 1030 SS 9	ED/HC/MD	176	145	29
	ST JOHN stjohntigerton@gmail.com www.stjohntigerton.wixsite.com/home	1882	502 Cedar St PO BOX 68	54486	NW	Dean M Suehring	(715)535-2282	WS 9	ED/MD	421	317	104
TOMAH	*GOOD SHEPHERD* secretary@goodsheptomah.org www.goodsheptomah.org	1991	1221 LAGRANGE AVE	54660	SW	Noah J Rogness	(608)374-2444	WS 9 SS 1030 BC 1030	ED/HC/SN	153	112	75
	ST MATTHEW		See Warrens WI									
TOMAHAWK	*ST PAUL* saintpaultomahawk@gmail.com www.St-Pauls-church.org	1888	12 E WISCONSIN AVE	54487	NW	Stephen P Gillet	(715)453-5391	WS 9	ED/HC	485	394	60
	ST PAUL'S		See Irma WI									
TOWNSEND	*ST JOHN* sjoffice@granitewave.com www.stjohn-townsend.org/	1919	17963 State Road 32 PO BOX 78	54175	NW		(715)276-7214	WS 9 SS 1020	ED/HC/ MD/SN	420	256	51
TREVOR	*BEAUTIFUL SAVIOR*		See Antioch IL									
TURTLE LAKE	*ZION* zionlutherantlwi1@gmail.com	1889	300 Martin Ave W PO BOX 32	54889	NW		(715)986-4927	WS 850 SS 830		218	171	58
TWIN LAKES	*HOPE* secretary@hopetwinlakes.org hopetwinlakes.org	2000	876 LANCE DR	53181	SW	Dr Timothy J Oswald	(262)877-4381 (262)448-1159	WS 9 SS 1015 BC 1015	ED/MD	130	120	77
TWO RIVERS	*GOOD SHEPHERD* office@goodshepherdlcms.com goodshepherdlcms.com	1965	3234 MISHICOT RD	54241	SW	Joel M Brassfield David W Hintz	(920)793-1716	WS 915 SS 1030 BC 1030	ED/HC/ MD/SN	194	175	82
UNION GROVE	*ST PAUL* officeofstpauls@gmail.com www.stpaulsug.org	1924	1610 MAIN ST	53182	SW	David P Ramirez	(262)878-2600 (262)878-2600	WS 8 1030 SS 915	HS/ED/HC			
VAUDREUIL	*ST JOHN*		See Black River Falls WI									
VERONA	*CROSS*		See Westport WI									
VESPER	*ST PAUL*	1887	5065 SPRUCE RD	54489	NW		(715)569-4301	WS 9	HC			
	TRINITY trinityvesper-stjohnssigel@outlook.com	1898	6412 MICHIGAN ST	54489	NW	Ryan P Anderson	(715)569-4114	WS 1030 SS 915 BC 930	ED/HC/MD	206	184	58
WABENO	*ST JOHN*		See Laona WI									
WALDO	*ST THOMAS* revcota@yahoo.com stthomaswaldo.org	1858	N4097 County Trunk Hwy M PO BOX 223	53093	SW	Shane R Cota	(920)458-8881	WS 830	HS/MD	65	57	23
WALES	*BETHLEHEM* office@bethlehemfamily.org www.bethlehemfamily.org	1906	470 N OAK CREST DR	53183	SW	Aaron B Boerst	(262)968-2194 (262)201-4488	WS 9 SS 1030 BC 1030	EC/ED/HC/ MD/SN	348	288	180
WALWORTH	*TRIUNE*		See Sharon WI									
WARRENS	*ST JOHN*		See Black River Falls WI									
	ST MATTHEW office@stmatthewsonline.org www.stmatthewsonline.org		4285 US Hwy 12 PO BOX 432 TOMAH	54666 54660	SW	David C Weber	(608)378-3233	WS 915 SS 1015 BC 1015	ED/HC/ MD/SN	470	348	110

*Indicates a new church start. A new church start is an intentionally organized gathering which comes together on a regular basis for the purpose of worship and/or Bible study and is intended to grow into a member LCMS congregation. WS =Worship Service; SS = Sunday School; BC =Bible Class; EC = Early Childhood; EL = Elementary School; HS = High School; ED =Education Ministry; HC =Human Care Ministry; SN = Special Needs Ministry; MD = Media Ministry (PC)=Partner Church Pastor. See Page 53 for the Table of Abbreviations for key to additional abbreviations

CITY	CONGREGATION EMAIL WEBSITE	YEAR EST	LOCATION MAILING ADDRESS	ZIP CODE(S)	DIST.	PASTOR(S)	PHONE FAX	WS SS BC	SCHOOLS/ MINISTRIES	Bapt	Conf	Avg Attend
WATERFORD	*ST PETER* secretary@stpeterswaterford.com www.stpeterswaterford.com	1864	145 S 6TH ST	53185	SW	Joshua P Conradt	(262)534-3639	WS 930 SS 815 BC 815	EC/ED	461	364	188
WATERTOWN	*FAITH* faithlutheranchurchoffice@gmail.com www.faithlutheranwatertown.com	1987	626 MILFORD ST	53094	EN	Seth M Hoeppner	(920)261-8060 (888)275-0932	WS 9 SS 1015 BC 1015	EL/ED/HC/ MD/SN			
	GOOD SHEPHERD www.goodshepherdwi.org	1971	1611 E MAIN ST	53094	SW	Aaron J Reseburg	(920)261-2570 (920)261-2574	WS 8 1030 SS 915 BC 915	EL/ED/HC/ MD/SN	867	780	217
	ST PETER		See Lebanon WI									
WAUKESHA	*BEAUTIFUL SAVIOR* pastor@bsl-school.org www.beautifulsaviorwaukesha.org	1953	1205 S EAST AVE	53186	SW	Peter A Schmidt	(262)542-2496	WS 8 10 BC 915	EL/ED/HC/ MD/SN	399	340	150
	BLESSED SAVIOR		See New Berlin WI									
	CHRIST THE LIFE office@christthelife.com www.christthelife.com	1991	3031 SUMMIT AVE	53188	SW	Christopher T Bushre	(262)547-1817 (262)547-7394	WS 9 BC 1015	EC/HS/ED/ HC/MD/SN	133	113	57
	LAMB OF GOD		See Pewaukee WI									
WAUNAKEE	*BETHLEHEM*		See Sun Prairie WI									
	CROSS		See Westport WI									
WAUPACA	*CALVARY* calvary.lutheran@yahoo.com www.calvarywaupaca.org	1986	E1887 KING RD	54981	NW	Brian S Roehrborn	(715)258-3530 (715)258-3530	WS 1030	ED/MD	97	85	37
	EMMAUS EmmausLutheranTOL@gmail.com EmmausLutheranChurchWaupaca.com	1910	N180 COUNTY ROAD A	54981	NW	Kurt A Schilling	(715)258-3193	WS 10 SS 9	ED/HC/ MD/SN	344	277	73
WAUPUN	*PELLA* tknuth@pellalutheran.org www.pellalutheran.org	1899	315 S MADISON ST	53963	SW	David F Knuth	(920)324-3321 (920)324-9734	WS 9 SS 1015 BC 1015	EC/ED/HC/ MD	329	277	110
WAUSAU	*CHRIST* secretary@clc-wausau.org www.clc-wausau.org	1978	1300 TOWNLINE RD	54403	NW	David L Wetmore	(715)848-2040	WS 9 SS 1030 BC 1030	ED/HC/MD	186	155	100
	RIB MOUNTAIN rmlcwausau@gmail.com rmlcwausau.org	1964	227150 HARRIER AVE	54401	NW		(715)845-2313	WS 9 BC 1030	ED/MD/SN	163	145	92
	ST JOHN church.secretary@stjohnofwausau.org www.stjohnofwausau.org	1878	164923 COUNTY ROAD Z	54403	NW	John D Stransky	(715)842-5212 (715)849-9558	WS 745 1015 SS 9 1030 BC 9	EL/ED/HC/ MD	492	384	105
	ST MARK stmarkswausau.org	1950	600 STEVENS DR	54401	NW	Eric R Hauan	(715)848-5511	WS 8 1030 SS 915 BC 915	EC/ED/HC/ MD	1071	810	432
	ST PETER saintpeterstrinity@gmail.com	1877	238537 DEL RIO RD	54403	NW	Russell J Kampfer	(715)675-9901	WS 9 BC 10	ED/HC/ MD/SN	200	198	58
	TRINITY trinity@trinitynet.org www.trinitywausau.org	1908	501 STEWART AVE	54401	NW	James L Mayland Jr Paul D Sundbom Peter C Williamson Steven C Vaudt	(715)842-0769 (715)843-7278	WS 730 9 SS 1030 BC 1030	EL/ED/HC/ MD/SN	1235	863	351
	ZION zioneaston@hotmail.com www.zioneaston.com	1896	238145 STAR RD ANIWA	54408	NW		(715)845-2014	WS 10 SS 9 BC 9	ED/MD	367	338	50
WAUTOMA	*GRACE*		See Hancock WI									
	TRINITY wautomatrinity@gmail.com www.trinitywautoma.com	1904	121 W Elm St P. O. BOX 915	54982	SW	Brian D Rohde	(920)787-2891	WS 9 SS 1015 BC 1030	ED/MD/SN	149	125	54
WAUWATOSA	*OUR REDEEMER* church@orlctosa.org orlctosa.org	1930	10025 W NORTH AVE	53226	SW		(414)258-4555 (414)258-5775	WS 9 1030 SS 9 BC 9	EL/HS/ED/ HC/MD/SN	1566	1251	337
	PILGRIM info@pilgrimtosa.org www.pilgrimtosa.org	1929	6817 W Center St 2664 N 68TH ST	53210 53213	SW	Tod A Shouse	(414)476-0735	WS 930 SS 830 BC 11	EL/HS/ED/ MD	122	110	55
WAYSIDE	*ZION* church@zionwayside.org www.zionwayside.org	1863	8378 County Road W 8378 COUNTY RD W GREENLEAF	54126	NW	Kyle A Wangelin Jedidiah B McClellan	(920)864-2463 (920)864-2684	WS 745 930 SS 9	EL/HS/ED/ HC/MD/SN	1204	870	413
WEBSTER	*OUR REDEEMER* ourredeemer@centurytel.net	1893	26681 Lakeland Ave N PO BOX 715	54893	NW	Jody R Walter	(715)866-7191	WS 930 SS 830 BC 830	SN			
WEST ALLIS	*BLESSED SAVIOR*		See New Berlin WI									
	EMMANUEL DEAF wpalmer182@gmail.com	1898	2306 S 98TH ST	53227	SW	William C Palmer	(414)321-8430 (414)321-5379	WS 930				
	GREENFIELD PARK gplc@wi.rr.com www.gplcwestallis.org	1939	1236 S 115TH ST	53214	EN	Frederic J Reaman	(414)774-3019 (414)774-4979	WS 9 SS 9 BC 1015	ED/HC/ MD/SN			
	ST PAUL www.splcwa.org	1926	7821 W LINCOLN AVE	53219	SW	Harold J Bender Jr	(414)541-6250 (414)541-2205	WS 8 1030 SS 915 BC 915	EL/HS/ED/ HC/MD/SN	1142	934	248
	TRINITY office@trinitywa.org www.trinitywa.org	1942	2500 S 68TH ST	53219	SW	Silas M Hasselbrook	(414)321-3640 (414)321-6470	WS 8 SS 945 BC 945	ED/HC/ MD/SN	93	78	49

*Indicates a new church start. A new church start is an intentionally organized gathering which comes together on a regular basis for the purpose of worship and/or Bible study and is intended to grow into a member LCMS congregation. WS =Worship Service; SS = Sunday School; BC =Bible Class; EC = Early Childhood; EL = Elementary School; HS = High School; ED =Education Ministry; HC =Human Care Ministry; SN = Special Needs Ministry; MD = Media Ministry (PC)=Partner Church Pastor. See Page 53 for the Table of Abbreviations for key to additional abbreviations

CITY	CONGREGATION EMAIL WEBSITE	YEAR EST	LOCATION MAILING ADDRESS	ZIP CODE(S)	DIST.	PASTOR(S)	PHONE FAX	WS SS BC	SCHOOLS/ MINISTRIES	STATISTIC Bapt	Conf	Avg Attend
WEST BEND	*LIVING WORD*		See Jackson WI									
	PILGRIM pilgrimsecretary63@gmail.com www.pilgrimlutheran-westbend.org	1954	462 MEADOWBROOK DR	53090	SW	Joseph M Fisher Christopher L Raffa	(262)334-0375 (262)334-2424	WS 8 1030 SS 915 BC 915 1230	HS/ED/HC/ MD/SN	430	249	155
	ST ANDREW standrewchurchwb@gmail.com www.standrew-westbend.org	1989	7750 North Hwy 144 7750 STATE ROAD 144 N	53090	SW	Jonathan A Vierkant	(262)335-4200 (262)335-4175	WS 9 SS 1015 BC 1015	EC/HS/ED/ MD	259	226	105
	ST JOHN stjohns@stjohnswestbend.org www.stjohnswestbend.org	1858	809 S 6TH AVE	53095	SW	Christopher L Bruskiewicz Jeffrey J Hesse Stephen P Reynolds	(262)334-4901 (262)334-3094	WS 8 930 11 SS 930 BC 930	EC/EL/HS/ ED/HC/ MD/SN	1471	1123	712
WEST BLOOMFIELD	*CHRIST*		See Weyauwega WI									
WEST SALEM	*PRINCE OF PEACE* office@wspop.org www.wspop.org	1998	1901 E CHURCH RD	54669	SW	Peter T Adelsen	(608)786-3938 (608)786-4251	WS 9 SS 1015 BC 1015	ED/HC/MD	128	96	49
WESTFIELD	*IMMANUEL* pastor@ielcw.org www.ielcw.net	1886	210 S Charles St PO BOX 397	53964	SW	Jesse L Davis Rodney A Armon	(608)296-2088 (608)296-2088	WS 10 SS 845 BC 9	EC/ED/HC/ MD/SN	514	354	114
	ST PAUL	1856	W4704 10th Rd N5971 18TH DR MONTELLO	53964 53949	SW		(920)293-4312	WS 8	ED/HC	10	10	8
WESTON	*MOUNT OLIVE* gregg@mtoliveweston.org mtoliveweston.org	1972	6205 ALDERSON ST	54476	NW	Lance M Hoelscher Jordan D Balk	(715)359-5546 (715)359-9245	WS 8 9 1030 630 SS 9 BC 9	EC/ED/HC/ MD/SN	4195	2744	1120
	ZION		See Wausau WI									
WESTPORT	*CROSS* office@crosslutheran.church www.crosslutheran.church	2018	5062 TEXAS LONGHORN DR.	53597	SW	Joel T Brandt	(608)827-9600	WS 9 SS 1015 BC 1015	ED/HC/MD	230	186	133
WEYAUWEGA	*CHRIST* Secretary@christlutheranwest bloomfield.com www.christlutheranwestbloomfield.com	1861	N6412 STATE ROAD 49	54983	SW	Brian G Weber	(920)867-3263 (920)867-3263	WS 815 BC 930	EL/ED/HC/ MD/SN	329	272	65
WHITE LAKE	*ST MATTHEW* smlcwhitelake@gmail.com stmatthew-whitelake.360unite.com/	1917	138 Bissell St PO BOX 238	54491	NW	Kelly D Smith Jr	(715)882-3111	WS 10 SS 845 BC 845	ED/HC/ MD/SN	162	147	57
WHITEFISH BAY	*OUR SAVIOR* oursaviorlutheranwfb@gmail.com oursaviorwfb.com	1933	6021 N SANTA MONICA BLVD	53217	SW	Michael W Henrichs Dr John C Wohlrabe Jr	(414)332-4458 (414)332-2569	WS 9 SS 1030 BC 1030		198	181	105
WHITEHALL	*ST PAUL* st.paul.54758@gmail.com	1895	N40558 Cty Rd O C/O SAINT PETER LUTHERAN CHURCH E11770 COUNTY ROAD HH OSSEO	54773 54758	NW	David J Knefelkamp	(715)597-2431	WS 11	ED/HC	79	60	14
WILD ROSE	*IMMANUEL*	1885	N4514 24th Ave N 4506 25TH LANE	54984	SW		(920)622-5919			51	43	25
	ST PAUL'S saintpaulwildrose@gmail.com saintpaulslutheran.com	1912	420 Park Ave PO BOX 240	54984	SW	Brian S Roehrborn	(920)622-3280	WS 830 SS 945	MD	63	54	27
WINCHESTER	*TRINITY*		See Boulder Junction WI									
WIND POINT	*GRACE*		See Racine WI									
WISCONSIN DELLS	*TRINITY* office@trinitydells.org www.trinitydells.org	1918	728 CHURCH ST WISC DELLS	53965	SW	Matthew J Gehrke	(608)253-3241 (608)254-7585	WS 945 SS 945 BC 830	EL/ED/HC/ MD/SN	481	397	120
WISCONSIN RAPIDS	*IMMANUEL* ilcoffice@immanuelrapids.com www.immanuelrapids.com	1881	160 8th St N 111 11TH ST N WISC RAPIDS	54494	NW	Timothy M Ritter Bryce A Clayton	(715)423-3260 (715)423-2853	WS 8 1030 BC 915	EL/ED/HC/ MD	1512	1274	279
	ST JOHN office@stjohnkellner.org www.stjohnkellner.org	1865	8020 South Park Rd 8020 SOUTHPARK RD WISC RAPIDS	54494	NW	Matthew D Lorfeld	(715)423-7788	WS 930	ED/MD/SN	405	308	106
	ST JOHN SIGEL trinityvesper-stjohnssigel@outlook.com	1865	3805 SAINT JOHNS RD WISC RAPIDS	54495	NW	Ryan P Anderson		WS 815	ED/HC/ MD/SN	45	35	26
	ST LUKE'S mail@stlukeslutheran.com www.stlukeslutheran.com	1949	2011 10TH ST S WISC RAPIDS	54494	NW		(715)423-5990 (715)423-5936	WS 815 1030 SS 915 BC 915	EC/ED/HC/ MD/SN	1062	830	239
WITHEE	*ST JOHN* stjohnswithee@gmail.com www.stjohnswithee.com	1890	204 Division St PO BOX 354	54498	NW	Phillip L Beukema Jr	(715)229-4211	WS 1015 SS 915	ED	327	291	75
WITTENBERG	*ST PAUL* stpaulwi@gmail.com www.stpaulwittenberg.com	1881	701 S HOME ST	54499	NW	Matthew J Christians	(715)253-2790	WS 830 SS 945 BC 945	ED/HC/ MD/SN	448	394	80
WOODRUFF	*PEACE*		See Arbor Vitae WI									
WRIGHTSTOWN	*ALLELUIA*		See Greenleaf WI									
YORKVILLE	*GRACE*		See Racine WI									
ZACHOW	*ZION*		See Bonduel WI									

*Indicates a new church start. A new church start is an intentionally organized gathering which comes together on a regular basis for the purpose of worship and/or Bible study and is intended to grow into a member LCMS congregation. WS =Worship Service; SS = Sunday School; BC =Bible Class; EC = Early Childhood; EL = Elementary School; HS = High School; ED =Education Ministry; HC =Human Care Ministry; SN = Special Needs Ministry; MD = Media Ministry (PC)=Partner Church Pastor. See Page 53 for the Table of Abbreviations for key to additional abbreviations

WYOMING

CITY	CONGREGATION EMAIL WEBSITE	YEAR EST	LOCATION MAILING ADDRESS	ZIP CODE(S)	DIST.	PASTOR(S)	PHONE FAX	WS SS BC	SCHOOLS/ MINISTRIES	Bapt	Conf	Avg Attend
AFTON	*CHRIST OUR SAVIOR*		See Nordic Ranches WY									
ALPINE	*CHRIST OUR SAVIOR*		See Nordic Ranches WY									
ARVADA	*IMMANUEL*		See Sheridan WY									
BIG PINEY	*PEACE*		See Marbleton WY									
BONDURANT	*REDEEMER*		See Jackson WY									
BUFFALO	*PRINCE PEACE* revrenecastillero@gmail.com princeofpeacebuffalo.org	1972	1200 Fort St PO BOX 65	82834	WY	Roger M Mullet	(307)684-5470	WS 9 SS 1015 BC 1015	ED/HC/SN	50	43	40
BURNS	*IMMANUEL* Pastor.Steffensen@protonmail.com wyobraskalcms.org	1908	203 Washington Ave PO BOX 105	82053	WY	Ellery J Steffensen	(308)235-2582	WS 8		73	58	27
BYRON	*ST JOHN*		See Lovell WY									
CASPER	*MOUNT HOPE* mounthopecasper@aol.com www.mounthopecasper.com	1962	2300 HICKORY ST	82604	WY	Christian A Preus Andrew P Richard Harold Ristau	(307)234-8428	WS 9 SS 930 BC 930	EL/HS/ED/ HC/MD	380	285	208
	TRINITY trinitysecretary1240@gmail.com tlc-casper.com/	1917	1240 S MISSOURI AVE	82609	WY	Jon C Olson Jacob H Benson Joshua J Hayes	(307)234-0568 (307)577-5778	WS 9 SS 1045 BC 1045	ED/HC/SN	266	219	140
CHEYENNE	*KING OF GLORY* kogcheyenne1@gmail.com www.kingofglorylutheranchurch.org	1989	8806 Yellowstone Rd PO BOX 2195	82009 82003	WY	Mark J Maas Andrew W Dimit	(307)632-1247	WS 9 SS 1030 BC 1030	ED/HC/ MD/SN	191	169	98
	OUR SAVIOR office@oursaviorcheyenne.org www.oursaviorcheyenne.org	1957	5101 DELL RANGE BLVD	82009	WY	Marcus J Baikie	(307)632-2580 (307)433-8348	WS 8 1045 SS 930 BC 930	ED/HC/ MD/SN	404	344	199
	TRINITY secretary@trinitycheyenne.org trinitycheyenne.org	1892	1111 E 22ND ST	82001	WY	John C Preus	(307)635-2802	WS 9 BC 1030	EL/HS/ED/ MD	163	141	90
CLEARMONT	*IMMANUEL*		See Sheridan WY									
	PRINCE PEACE		See Buffalo WY									
CODY	*CHRIST THE KING* church@ctkcody.org www.ctkcody.org/	1961	1207 Stampede Ave PO BOX 355	82414	WY	Kenneth R Mars Dr Ronald M Garwood	(307)587-3025	WS 9 SS 1030 BC 1030	EC/ED/ MD/SN	419	343	118
COWLEY	*ST JOHN*		See Lovell WY									
DAYTON	*IMMANUEL*		See Sheridan WY									
DEAVER	*ST JOHN*		See Lovell WY									
DOUGLAS	*ZION* zionlcms@qwestoffice.net www.zion-lcms.org	1947	601 S 9TH ST	82633	WY	Jonathan R Durkopp	(307)358-2810	WS 830 1045 SS 945	ED/HC/SN			
DUBOIS	*MOUNT CALVARY* mtcalvary@dteworld.com	1955	516 W Ramshorn Ave PO BOX 707	82513	WY	Gregory A Sonnenschein	(307)349-3736	WS 9 BC 1030	ED	40	40	24
EVANSTON	*OUR SAVIOUR* jlange64@protonmail.com god-the-crucified.blogspot.com	1982	49 STRAIGHT AND NARROW DR	82930	WY	Jonathan G Lange	(307)727-7095	WS 9 1130 BC 8 1230	ED/HC/MD	23	18	17
FORT BRIDGER	*SHEP OF VALLEY*	1982	306 Uinta County Road 224 PO BOX 280	82933	WY	Daniel L Mulholland	(307)782-6802	WS 1030 SS 9 BC 9	ED/HC/ MD/SN			
FRANNIE	*ST JOHN*		See Lovell WY									
GILLETTE	*TRINITY* trinity@vcn.com www.trinitygillette.com	1929	1001 E 9TH ST	82716	WY	Zachary T Viggers	(307)682-4886	WS 9 SS 1030 BC 1030	ED/HC/ MD/SN	421	294	104
GLENROCK	*OUR REDEEMER*	1972	939 W Birch PO BOX 884	82637	WY	Jonathan R Durkopp	(307)436-8691	WS 1045 SS 1130	HC	57	48	30
GREEN RIVER	*EMMANUEL*	1965	901 TRONA DR	82935	WY	Andrew R Hill	(307)875-2598 (307)875-2598	WS 9 SS 8 BC 8	ED/HC/SN	52	48	29
GREYBULL	*GRACE* gracegreybull.ctshost.org	1947	501 6th Ave N PO BOX 309	82426	WY		(307)765-2865	WS 8 1030 BC 915 1145	ED/HC	29	29	18
	ZION zionemblem.ctshost.org	1899	3390 Rd 11 409 5TH AVE N	82426	WY			WS 8 1030 BC 915 1145		35	34	12
HOBACK	*REDEEMER*		See Jackson WY									
JACKSON	*REDEEMER* redeemer@wyoming.com www.westernwyominglutherans.wordpress.com		175 N Willow PO BOX 1016	83001	WY	David C Bott	(307)733-3409 (307)733-3409	WS 3 SS 9 BC 9	ED	28	20	23
JACKSON HOLE	*REDEEMER*		See Jackson WY									
KELLY	*REDEEMER*		See Jackson WY									

*Indicates a new church start. A new church start is an intentionally organized gathering which comes together on a regular basis for the purpose of worship and/or Bible study and is intended to grow into a member LCMS congregation. WS =Worship Service; SS = Sunday School; BC =Bible Class; EC = Early Childhood; EL = Elementary School; HS = High School; ED =Education Ministry; HC =Human Care Ministry; SN = Special Needs Ministry; MD = Media Ministry (PC)=Partner Church Pastor. See Page 53 for the Table of Abbreviations for key to additional abbreviations

CITY	CONGREGATION EMAIL WEBSITE	YEAR EST	LOCATION MAILING ADDRESS	ZIP CODE(S)	DIST.	PASTOR(S)	PHONE FAX	WS SS BC	SCHOOLS/ MINISTRIES	STATISTIC Bapt	Conf	Avg Attend
KEMMERER	*ST PAUL* jlange64@protonmail.com god-the-crucified.blogspot.com	1944	501 Opal St PO BOX 472	83101	WY	Jonathan G Lange	(307)727-7095	WS 9 1130 BC 8 1230	ED/HC/ MD/SN	40	32	15
LANDER	*BETHEL* bethelchurchlander@gmail.com www.lander-bethel.org	1952	626 SHOSHONE ST	82520	WY	Travis L Berg	(307)332-4320	WS 930 SS 830	ED/HC/MD	142	117	51
LARAMIE	*SPRING WIND ASSISTED LIVING* Satellite Site of Zion Laramie WY	2018	1072 N 22 & 57	82070								
	ST ANDREW pastor@standrewslaramie.org www.standrewslaramie.org	1963	1309 E GRAND AVE	82070	WY	Mark A Preus	(307)745-5892 (307)745-5892	WS 1030 BC 9	ED/MD			
	ZION lcmszion@gmail.com www.lcmszion.org	1926	406 S 19TH ST	82070	WY	Mark W Mumme	(307)745-9262	WS 9 1115 SS 1030 BC 1030	ED/HC/ MD/SN	169	141	48
LOVELL	*NEW HORIZONS* Satellite Site of St John Lovell WY	1995	1115 Lane 12	82431								
	ST JOHN stjohnslovell@gmail.com www.stjohnslovell.org	1916	520 MONTANA AVENUE	82431	WY		(307)548-7127 (307)548-7127	WS 1030 BC 915	ED/HC/SN	169	115	47
LUSK	*ST PAULS* stpauls@wyoming.com	1913	501 S Linn St PO BOX 1245	82225	WY	Darren M Pflughoeft	(307)334-2336	WS 1030 SS 915 BC 915	ED/HC/ MD/SN	78	60	20
MARBLETON	*PEACE* oursaviors172@centurytel.net	1965	19 Winkelman Ave PO BOX 674 BIG PINEY	83113	WY	Nathan D Raugutt	(307)276-3843	WS 1115	ED/HC/MD			
MOORCROFT	*BETHLEHEM*	1974	200 W Goshen St PO BOX 190	82721	WY	Norman A Wacker		WS 11	MD	39	29	15
MOOSE	*REDEEMER*		See Jackson WY									
MORAN JCT.	*REDEEMER*		See Jackson WY									
NORDIC RANCHES	*CHRIST OUR SAVIOR* redeemer@wyoming.com www.westernwyominglutherans. wordpress.com		1011 Lariat Dr PO BOX 5101 ETNA	83118	WY	David C Bott	(307)690-8697	WS 4 BC 3	ED/HC/MD	5	5	5
PINE BLUFFS	*GRACE ENGLISH*	1951	417 W 8th St PO BOX 670	82082	WY	Lincoln C Winter	(307)245-3390	WS 2	ED/HC/MD	40	30	10
PINEDALE	*OUR SAVIOR* oursaviorspinedale@gmail.com www.oursaviorspinedale.org	1960	512 North Tyler PO BOX 148	82941	WY	Nathan D Raugutt	(307)367-2612	WS 9 BC 1015	ED/HC/MD	54	51	23
POWELL	*IMMANUEL* ilcoffice3168@gmail.com www.immanuellutheranpowellwy.org	1936	675 Ave D 675 AVENUE D	82435	WY	Daniel R Harrington	(307)754-3168	WS 9 SS 1015 BC 1015	EC/ED/SN	207	172	91
RANCHESTER	*IMMANUEL*		See Sheridan WY									
RAWLINS	*CHRIST* rawlinslcms@outlook.com christlutheranrawlins.com	1948	311 Kendrick PO BOX 397	82301	WY	Patrick M Baldwin	(307)324-4168	WS 930 SS 1045 BC 1045	ED/HC/MD	136	102	35
RIVERTON	*TRINITY* trinitylutheranchurch@wyoming.com www.tlcriverton.org/home	1918	419 E PARK AVE	82501	WY	Stephen W Kieser	(307)856-9340	WS 8 11 SS 930 BC 930	EL/ED/ MD/SN	260	225	132
ROCK SPRINGS	*EMMANUEL*		See Green River WY									
	TRINITY trinitylcrs@qwestoffice.net www.trinityrocksprings.com/	1950	3101 COLLEGE DR	82901	WY	Andrew R Hill	(307)362-5088 (307)333-0323	WS 1030 SS 1130 BC 1130	ED/HC/ MD/SN	115	90	65
SARATOGA	*PLATTE VALLEY* plattevalleylutheran@gmail.com plattevalleylutheran.org	1956	513 S 1st PO BOX 385	82331	WY	Randolph J Schnack	(307)326-5449	WS 9 SS 10 BC 10	ED/HC	62	52	16
SHERIDAN	*IMMANUEL* immanuellutheran82801@gmail.com immanuelsheridan.blogspot.com	1903	1300 W 5TH ST	82801	WY	Paul J Cain Jr	(307)674-6434 (307)655-8243	WS 9 SS 915 BC 915	EL/ED/HC/ MD	528	389	136
STAR VALLEY	*CHRIST OUR SAVIOR*		See Nordic Ranches WY									
STORY	*IMMANUEL*		See Sheridan WY									
SUNDANCE	*MOUNT CALVARY* wackerna@gmail.com	1965	706 S 4th St PO BOX 6	82729	WY	Norman A Wacker	(307)281-2622	WS 9	ED/HC/MD	52	49	25
THAYNE	*CHRIST OUR SAVIOR*		See Nordic Ranches WY									
THERMOPOLIS	*ST PAUL*	1947	288 US Hwy 20 S 288 US HIGHWAY 20 S	82443	WY	Samuel J Needham	(307)864-2205	WS 9 SS 1030 BC 1030	ED/SN	57	50	36
TORRINGTON	*OUR SAVIOR* oslcoffice12@gmail.com oursaviortorrington.org	1935	2973 East B St 2973 E B ST	82240	WY	Scott G Firminhac	(307)532-5801	WS 9 SS 1030 BC 1030	ED/HC/ MD/SN	277	221	98
	TRINITY		See Morrill NE									
UCROSS	*IMMANUEL*		See Sheridan WY									
WHEATLAND	*TRINITY* TrinityWheatlandWY@gmail.com www.TrinityWheatland.church	1913	1004 Willow St PO BOX 216	82201	WY	Lincoln C Winter	(307)322-3291	WS 8 SS 1030 BC 1030	MD/SN	80	35	35
WILLSON	*REDEEMER*		See Jackson WY									
WORLAND	*ST LUKE'S* stlukesworland@gmail.com www.stlukesworland.com	1950	525 S 6TH ST	82401	WY	Jared A Korb	(307)347-2293	WS 1015 SS 9 BC 9	ED/MD	134	115	44

*Indicates a new church start. A new church start is an intentionally organized gathering which comes together on a regular basis for the purpose of worship and/or Bible study and is intended to grow into a member LCMS congregation. WS =Worship Service; SS = Sunday School; BC =Bible Class; EC = Early Childhood; EL = Elementary School; HS = High School; ED =Education Ministry; HC =Human Care Ministry; SN = Special Needs Ministry; MD = Media Ministry (PC)=Partner Church Pastor. See Page 53 for the Table of Abbreviations for key to additional abbreviations

BAHAMAS

CITY	CONGREGATION EMAIL WEBSITE	YEAR EST	LOCATION MAILING ADDRESS	ZIP CODE(S)	DIST.	PASTOR(S)	PHONE FAX	WS SS BC	SCHOOLS/ MINISTRIES	STATISTIC Bapt	Conf	Avg Attend
NASSAU	*NASSAU*	1962	119 John F Kennedy Dr PO BOX N-4794		FG	Samuel M Boodle Sr	(242)323-4107	WS 11 SS 945				

CANADA, ONTARIO

CITY	CONGREGATION EMAIL WEBSITE	YEAR EST	LOCATION MAILING ADDRESS	ZIP CODE(S)	DIST.	PASTOR(S)	PHONE FAX	WS SS BC	SCHOOLS/ MINISTRIES	STATISTIC Bapt	Conf	Avg Attend
AURORA	*CHRIST* blessaurora@gmail.com www.blessaurora.com	1960	7 LACEY CT	L4G 5H2	EN		(905)727-3311	WS 1030	ED/HC/MD	76	62	32
CHATHAM	*OUR SAVIOUR'S* oslcchatham@gmail.com www.lutheranchurchchatham.com	1946	445 MC NAUGHTON AVE W	N7L 4K3	EN		(519)352-1860	WS 11	HC/SN	61	51	33
GOLDEN LAKE	*ST JOHN* pastorklein1@gmail.com		1986 LAKE DORE RD	K0J 1X0	EN	Paul D Douglas	(613)625-2533	WS 930 SS 930	ED/MD			
KINGSVILLE	*FIRST* kingsvillefirstlutheran@gmail.com www.reachingchurch.org		27 SPRUCE ST N	N9Y 1G2	EN		(519)733-2127					
	NATIVITY pavel6057@hotmail.com		27 SPRUCE ST N	N9Y 1G2	S		(519)792-9459			25	25	11
KITCHENER	*HOPE* hlcoffice@hopelc.ca www.hopelc.ca	1964	30 SHAFTSBURY DR	N2A 1N6	EN		(519)893-5290	WS 10 SS 1115 BC 1115	ED/HC/MD	391	283	40
MISSISSAUGA	*ST MARK'S* office@saintmarks.ca www.saintmarks.ca	1953	130 MINEOLA RD E	L5G 2E5	EN	Jeffrey G Miskus Dr Matthias W Benfey Philip M Gai J D Mathers	(905)278-2122	WS 9 11 SS 9	ED/HC/SN			
MITCHELL	*GRACE* glchurch@bellnet.ca gracemitchell.ca	1862	108 St David St PO BOX 607	N0K 1N0	EN	Gerald B Andersen	(519)348-9082	WS 10 SS 9		552	408	44
NORTH YORK	*ST LUKE* office@stluketoronto.com www.stluketoronto.com	1954	3200 BAYVIEW	M2M 3R7	EN	Justin D Laughridge Gregory R Lutz Jung Hun Park Dr Dusan Tillinger	(416)221-8900 (416)221-8685	WS 10	ED/HC/ MD/SN			
PEMBROKE	*ST JOHN'S* office@stjohnspembroke.ca www.stjohnspembroke.ca	1891	357 MILLER ST	K8A 5Y8	EN	Stephen C Alles	(613)735-6332 (613)735-6741	WS 10 SS 9 BC 9	ED/HC/ MD/SN	514	426	136
PORT CREDIT	*ST MARK'S*		See Mississauga ON									
SARNIA	*REDEEMER* secretary.redeemersarnia@gmail.com www.redeemerlutheran-sarnia.ca	1929	429 Indian Road N 429 INDIAN RD N	N7T 7G3	EN	Colton J LaMay	(519)337-6615	WS 10 SS 1030 BC 9	ED/HC/ MD/SN	262	230	88
SCARBOROUGH	*ST MATTHEW* st.matthews@on.aibn.com www.saintmatthewlutheran.org	1954	3159 LAWRENCE AVE E	M1H 1A1	EN	Dereck Pillay	(416)431-9252 (416)431-4729	WS 1030 SS 930 BC 930	ED/MD	140	116	50
TORONTO	*ST LUKE*		See North York ON									
	ST PAUL	1942	1442 DAVENPORT RD	M6H 2H8	S		(416)656-5259					
WINDSOR	*GETHSEMANE* glcwindsor@gmail.com www.glcwindsor.org	1961	1921 CABANA RD W	N9G 1C7	EN	Jordan R Simon	(519)969-7561 (519)969-0747	WS 1030 SS 930	ED/HC/MD			
	PEACE church@peacewindsor.com www.peacewindsor.com	1942	1985 ROSSINI BLVD	N8W 4P6	EN	James A Leistico	(519)945-1344 (519)945-5811	WS 1030 SS 1030 BC 930	ED/HC/ MD/SN			

CANADA, QUEBEC

CITY	CONGREGATION EMAIL WEBSITE	YEAR EST	LOCATION MAILING ADDRESS	ZIP CODE(S)	DIST.	PASTOR(S)	PHONE FAX	WS SS BC	SCHOOLS/ MINISTRIES	STATISTIC Bapt	Conf	Avg Attend
MONTREAL	*ASCENSION* pastor@ascensionlutheran.ca www.ascensionlutheran.ca	1929	865 JARRY ST W	H3N 1G8	S	Charles P St Onge	(438)490-3698	WS 1030 SS 1130	ED/HC/MD	90	81	43

HONG KONG

CITY	CONGREGATION EMAIL WEBSITE	YEAR EST	LOCATION MAILING ADDRESS	ZIP CODE(S)	DIST.	PASTOR(S)	PHONE FAX	WS SS BC	SCHOOLS/ MINISTRIES	STATISTIC Bapt	Conf	Avg Attend
REPULSE BAY	*CAN HK* office@can.org.hk www.can.org.hk	1962	8 South Bay Close 23 SOUTH BAY CLOSE		NOW	Joel M Scheiwe Kevin S Kong	011-852-2812-5151	WS 1030 5 BC 930	ED/HC/MD			
SZ	*ML ENGLISH WORSHIP* Satellite Site of CAN HK Repulse Bay	2012	ML					WS 7				
	NS ENGLISH WORSHIP Satellite Site of CAN HK Repulse Bay	2016	NS					WS 2 SS 330				

MEXICO

CITY	CONGREGATION EMAIL WEBSITE	YEAR EST	LOCATION MAILING ADDRESS	ZIP CODE(S)	DIST.	PASTOR(S)	PHONE FAX	WS SS BC	SCHOOLS/ MINISTRIES	STATISTIC Bapt	Conf	Avg Attend
CIUDAD ACUÑA. COAHUILA	*IGLESIA LUTERANA RÍOS DE AGUA VIVA* Satellite Site of Cristo el Salvador Del Rio TX	1996	Colima #350 Colonia Luis Donaldo Colosio					WS 11 BC 1030				

*Indicates a new church start. A new church start is an intentionally organized gathering which comes together on a regular basis for the purpose of worship and/or Bible study and is intended to grow into a member LCMS congregation. WS =Worship Service; SS = Sunday School; BC =Bible Class; EC = Early Childhood; EL = Elementary School; HS = High School; ED =Education Ministry; HC =Human Care Ministry; SN = Special Needs Ministry; MD = Media Ministry (PC)=Partner Church Pastor. See Page 53 for the Table of Abbreviations for key to additional abbreviations

LCMS ROSTER OF MINISTERS OF RELIGION—ORDAINED

Corrected to September 18, 2025

Individuals on this listing were on the official Ordained Minister member roster of the Synod as of the above date, i.e., held membership in the Synod in conformity with Articles V and VI of the Constitution of The Lutheran Church–Missouri Synod. Qualified individuals who are not listed should contact their respective district president. Any congregation or other calling entity must contact the appropriate district president to find out whether an individual whose name is listed in this section is currently eligible for a call or service in the church. A candidate member is one who is eligible to perform the duties of any of the offices of ministry specified in Bylaw 2.11.1 but who is not currently an active or emeritus member. For further detailed information visit the LCMS Website at http://www.lcms.org and select Directories.

NAME	TELEPHONE NUMBER EMAIL	STREET ADDRESS CITY/STATE/ZIP	DISTRICT	POSITION/ STATUS**	WHERE SERVING	OFFICE PHONE	SEM/ PROGRAM	YR GRAD
Aadland Thomas V	(612)806-9531 thomas.v.aadland@gmail.com	13986 Dallas Ave Rosemount MN 55068	MNS	EM			CQ	2014
Aarsvold Paul J	(507)923-1494 pjaarsvold@gmail.com	3245 W 31st Ave Denver CO 80211	RM	Assoc	St Johns Denver CO	(303)733-3777	SL	2022
Abatelli Kirk W	pastor_abatelli@yahoo.com	c/o St Mark Lutheran Church 2565 N Miller Rd Saginaw MI 48609	MI	SP	St Mark Saginaw MI	(989)781-3205	SL	2006
Abbott Kenton L	(620)617-6833 kenton.abbott@outlook.com	400 N. Humboldt Ellinwood KS 67526	KS	SMP	St John Ellinwood KS	(620)564-2044	SL-SMP	2018
Abbott William A	(310)344-3439 waabbott@sbcglobal.net	135 Comstock Rd Dayton NV 89403	CNH	EM			CQ	2019
Abdelmalek Nader H	(714)724-2985 pastornader@gmail.com	7559 Hershey Dr Buena Park CA 90620	PSW	C03/2023			CQ	2021
Abel Alan E	abelalan44@gmail.com	111 Ralynn Drive Lorena TX 76655	TX	EM			SL	1970
Abel Nathan A	naabel12@gmail.com	c/o St Paul Lutheran Church 1800 West Fwy Fort Worth TX 76102	TX	Assoc	St Paul Fort Worth TX	(817)332-2281	SL	2017
Abel Scott F	(407)462-0105 sabel@oflc.net	924 W Peakview Cir Littleton CO 80120	RM	Sn/Adm	Our Father Centennial CO	(303)779-1332	SL	2005
Abendschoen Geoffrey S	(717)515-6485 geoffabendschoen@gmail.com	1430 Brittany Drive York PA 17404	SE	SMP	St Paul* Columbia PA	(717)764-4746	FW-SMP	2024
Abernathy Roger G	(573)517-8756 ra2-3845ol@outlook.com	14134 Highway C Frohna MO 63748	MO	EM			FW	1992
Abernethy Ralph A III	(828)464-0026 seagullx4@gmail.com	2987 Kay St Conover NC 28613	SE	SP	Mount Olive Newton NC	(828)464-2407	FW	1996
Abraham Andrew J	andrewtroutman71@gmail.com		MDS	Sn/Adm	Emmanuel Hermitage TN	(615)883-7533	CQ	2008
Abraham Stanley R	(831)685-3052 sabraham@cruzio.com	3005 Mar Vista Dr Aptos CA 95003	CNH	SP	Mount Calvary Soquel CA	(831)475-6962	SL	1972
Abrahams Dan C	(218)841-8130 revabe@arvig.net	1348 Pelican Ln Detroit Lakes MN 56501	MNN	SP	Immanuel Dent MN	(218)841-8130	SL	1971
Abram Mark H I			EN	EM			SL	1982
Abram Michael R	(310)793-0071 churchoffice@ascensiontorrance. org	18009 Amie Ave Torrance CA 90504	PSW	SP	Ascension Torrance CA	(310)793-0071	SL	1998
Acers Shane D	(402)669-0721 shane.acers@gmail.com	2206 3rd Ave SW Altoona IA 50009	IW	SMP	Hope Des Moines IA	(515)265-2057	SL-SMP	2024
Acton Thomas R Dr	(779)537-2051 thomas.acton@outlook.com	5495 W Bajada Dr Marana AZ 85658	EN	EM			FW	1979
Ada Michael	(913)669-0460 madakufan@hotmail.com	c/o Beautiful Savior Lutheran 13145 S Blackbob Rd Olathe KS 66062	KS	Assoc	Beautiful Savior Olathe KS	(913)780-6023	SL	2006
Adair Clifford	(618) 417-5900	205 West Pine Street Baldwin IL 62217	SI	EM			SL	1987
Adams Daniel J	(360)600-8654 dan@mlc.org		NOW	Sn/Adm	Memorial Vancouver WA	(360)695-7501	Other	1984
Adams Shaun P	(509)385-4963 pastorshaunadams@gmail.com	9027 W 72nd Ave Cheney WA 99004	NOW	SMP	Holy Cross Spokane WA	(509)483-4218	SL-SMP	2022
Adams Ricky L	(510)909-6798 rn_adams@comcast.net	2513 Legends Dr Southern Pines NC 28387	SE	EM			SL	1985
Adams Mark E	(541)567-6811 pastor.bethlehemhermiston@ gmail.com	596 E Heather Ave Hermiston OR 97838	NOW	SP	Bethlehem Hermiston OR	(541)567-6811	FW	1989
Adams Joseph M II	(260)410-6996 jnjadams@hotmail.com	1560 4th Ct Apt A Vero Beach FL 32960	FG	SP	Redeemer Vero Beach FL	(772)567-8193	FW	2001
Adams Douglas M	(517)320-3249 pastordouglasadams@yahoo.com	23000 Gratiot Ave Eastpointe MI 48021	MI	Sn/Adm	Saint Peters Eastpointe MI	(586)777-6300	SL	2001
Adams David L Dr	(314)505-7144 adamsd@csl.edu	801 Seminary Pl Saint Louis MO 63105	MO	S HS/C	Concordia Seminary Saint Louis MO	(314)505-7000	SL	1981
Adams Curtis W	(517)317-2303 curjoy2054@gmail.com	6064 Fairway Ln Bradenton FL 34210	FG	EM			SL	2009
Adams Charles W	(785)893-4387 revcwa@aol.com	4217 S 179th St Omaha NE 68135	NEB	EM			SL	1986
Adams Caleb M	(541)382-1832 caleb.adams@saints.org	3783 NE Petrosa Ave Bend OR 97701	NOW	Sn/Adm	Trinity Bend OR	(541)382-1832	SL	2011
Adams David C	(260)312-6294 pdandkim@gmail.com	10429 Bitterroot Ct Fort Wayne IN 46804	EN	SP	Jacobs Well Fort Wayne IN	(260)312-6294	SL	1991
Adamson Terrance S	(440)506-1075 tadamson1@msn.com	518 Circle Way St Lake Jackson TX 77566	TX	SP	St Mark Lake Jackson TX	(979)297-2667	SL	1992
Adelsen Peter T	peter.adelsen@gmail.com	505 Hill St Sparta WI 54656	SW	SP	Prince Of Peace West Salem WI	(608)786-3938	SL	2017
Adema Gemedo E	(503)704-5035 gemedo2013@gmail.com	1321 Kipling Ct SE Salem OR 97302	NOW	SP	Ebenezer Portland OR	(971)344-9437	SL	2008
Adle Scott T	scottadle@gmail.com	211 E 14th St Imperial NE 69033	NEB	SP	Zion Imperial NE	(308)882-5655	FW	2008
Adler David L	(903)363-6817 revadler@outlook.com	3212 An County Road 118 Elkhart TX 75839	TX	EM			SL	1979

*Multiple Assignments (See Church Worker Locator for Additional Details)

See Page 53 for the Table of Abbreviations for key to District, Position, and Seminary abbreviations

**C =Candidate; EM = Emeritus; the date following the C is the month and year the Candidate status began

NAME	TELEPHONE NUMBER EMAIL	STREET ADDRESS CITY/STATE/ZIP	DISTRICT	POSITION/ STATUS**	WHERE SERVING	OFFICE PHONE	SEM/ PROGRAM	YR GRAD
Adolf Donald E	(208)539-9079 gngadolf@hotmail.com	663 Alturas Dr N Twin Falls ID 83301	NOW	EM			FW	1989
Adrian Mark J Jr	pastormark@messiahtampa.com		FG	Sn/Adm	Messiah Carrollwood FL	(813)961-2182	SL	2011
Afamefuna Afam Ikanih	(414)339-7780 afam.ikanih@milwaukeecountywi.gov	4540 N 71st St Milwaukee WI 53218	SW	SP	Bethany Milwaukee WI	(414)444-3131	SL	2013
Agne Paul C	(314)810-2514 pastoragne@yahoo.com	2110 Penfield Ln Bowie MD 20716	SE	SP	Ascension Landover Hills MD	(301)577-0500	SL	2007
Aguilar Juan E	(303)383-0513 aguilar.pastorjuan@gmail.com	1140 N Broad St Fremont NE 68025	NEB	C07/2016			SL	2013
Ahlborn Marvin J	(920)410-2435 mahl8@yahoo.com	5501 Pennsylvania Ave Appleton WI 54914	SW	EM			CQ	1983
Ahlemeyer Eric M	reveric71@gmail.com	2522 Winding Oak Dr Plymouth IN 46563	IN	Sn/Adm	Calvary Plymouth IN	(574)936-2903	FW	2000
Ahlemeyer Michael D	(205)201-8866 pastor@vestavialutheran.org	2168 Bailey Brook Dr Hoover AL 35244	SO	SP	Vestavia Hills Vestavia Hills AL	(205)823-1883	FW	2002
Ahlemeyer Terry L	(920)530-6090 tahlemeyer@excite.com	2211 Hillcrest Ave Unit H Plymouth IN 46563	SO	EM			CQ	1979
Ahlersmeyer Thomas R Dr		3425 Crescent Ave Fort Wayne IN 46805	IN	Sn/Adm	Holy Cross Fort Wayne IN	(260)483-3173	FW	1979
Ahlersmeyer Benjamin T		4014 Manito Blvd Fort Wayne IN 46809	IN	SP	Bethlehem Fort Wayne IN	(260)744-3228	SL	2013
Ahlersmeyer Peter C	(260)580-3519 pastor@tlcfenton.org	7105 Primrose Lane Grand Blanc MI 48439	MI	SP	Trinity Fenton Fenton MI	(810)629-7861	FW	2014
Ahlersmeyer Steven M	(260) 602-5035 steve@thelutheranfoundation.org		IN	Asst	Concordia Fort Wayne IN	(260)422-2429	FW	1989
Ahlman Timothy P	(303)887-0507 tahlman@cglchurch.org	4097 E Palo Verde St Gilbert AZ 85296	PSW	Sn/Adm	Christ Greenfield Gilbert AZ	(480)892-8521	SL	2008
Ahlman Christopher S Dr	(713)998-0729 cahlman@mlchouston.org	5800 Westheimer Rd Houston TX 77057	TX	Assoc	Memorial Houston TX	(713)782-6079	SL	2006
Ahlman David J	(303)902-8113 daveahlman77@gmail.com	10101 Bradbury St Firestone CO 80504	RM	SP	Mount Hope Boulder CO	(303)499-9800	FW	1983
Ahlschwede Dale C	(989)652-6852 jdahlschwede@yahoo.com	8845 Gera Rd Birch Run MI 48415	MI	EM			SPR	1972
Ahrendt Anthony W	awahrendt@gmail.com	410 Main Ave S P.O. Box 104 Hankinson ND 58041	ND	EM			FW	2005
Airey Mark W	(636)399-5114 airey@att.net	1713 Northshore Dr. c/o Cor 1900 Pine St Sandpoint ID 83864	NOW	SP	Christ Our Redeemer Sandpoint ID	(208)263-7516	SL	2007
Aizenberg Samuel J	(702)481-3736 samaizenberg@gmail.com	31007 CR 141 Norborne MO 64668	MO	SP	Immanuel Carrollton MO	(660)542-2064	SL	2024
Ajak Simon A Jr	(517)507-6847 simon.ajak90@gmail.com	1108 W Ottowa St Lansing MI 48915	MI	C07/2016			FW	2005
Aker Corey W	pastoraker@faithlutheransiouxfalls.org	601 N Cliff Ave Sioux Falls SD 57103	SD	Sn/Adm	Faith Sioux Falls SD	(605)332-3401	SL	2007
Akers Barry A	(262)278-7669 PastorBarry@divineshepherdlc.org	14511 West Beloit Rd New Berlin WI 53151	SW	SP	Divine Shepherd Milwaukee WI	(414)321-0730	SL	1991
Akers Benjamin M	(207)509-6092 revakers20@gmail.com	10 Edgewood St Waterville ME 04901	NE	SP	Hope* Hampden ME		SL	2020
Akey Bradley D	(414)852-3469 houseakey@gmail.com	413 Meadowlark Lane Arlingt MN 55307	MNS	SP	Immanuel Gaylord MN	(507)237-2380	FW	2017
Alb Larry A Dr	(714)588-1731 eurocanam@doctor.com	7220 Greenwater Cr. Castle Rock CO 80108	PSW	EM			FW	1982
Albers Paul A	(303)659-9030 paul.albers@rm.lcms.org	Rocky Mountain District Office 88 Inverness Cir E Unit A210 Englewood CO 80112	RM	SMP	Rocky Mountain District Englewood CO	(303)695-8001	SL-SMP	2015
Albers Steven H	(314)965-6578 stevealbers@charter.net	2250 Ferncliff Ln Kirkwood MO 63122	MO	Assoc	Trinity Saint Louis MO	(314)231-4092	SL	1970
Albers Paul F		7301 N 28th Ave Omaha NE 68112	NEB	SP	Mount Olive Omaha NE	(402)455-8700	SL	2016
Albers David P	pastoralbers@yahoo.com		FG	EM			SL	1984
Albers John M	(219)462-4029 albers.john.m@gmail.com	401 Lafayette St Valparaiso IN 46383	IN	Sn/Adm	Saint Johns Laporte IN	(219)362-3726	SL	1989
Albers Grayson E	(254)654-2488 pastorgrayson@ilmtexas.org	1408 Cedar Oaks Cir Temple TX 76502	TX	Sn/Adm	Immanuel Temple TX	(254)773-3898	SL	2011
Albers James W Dr	(219)462-4640 jim.albers@valpo.edu	404 Andover Dr Valparaiso IN 46383	IN	EM			SL	1963
Alberson Davin J	(501) 593-3429 albersond@csl.edu	937 Maple Ave Holtville CA 92250	PSW	SP	St Paul Holtville CA	(760)356-4315	SL	2025
Albert Gary M	(715)384-2855 gmalbert@charter.net	1125 Ridge Rd Marshfield WI 54449	NW	EM			CQ	1982
Albertin David M Dr	(219)921-9317 davidmalbertin@gmail.com	106 Pontiac Dr Michigan City IN 46360	IN	SP	Immanuel Hamlet-Tracy IN	(219)921-9378	SL	1965
Alberts Andrew W	(330)203-5474 pastorandy@tlcoh.org	759 East Ave Tallmadge OH 44278	OH	SP	Tallmadge Tallmadge OH	(330)633-4775	SL	2002
Alberts Bruce A	(321)289-7232 revbrucealberts@gmail.com	380 Crown Dr SE Unit 8108 Cartersville GA 30120	FG	SP	Savior Of All Cartersville GA	(770)387-0379	SL	1999
Albertson Thomas J	(308)737-6657 rev.albertson@gmail.com	5310 Ramblin Rose Rd Colorado Springs CO 80908	RM	EM			SL	2009
Albrecht Martin K	(785)230-3034 mkalbrecht77@gmail.com	3121 SW Tutbury Town Rd Topeka KS 66614	KS	SMP	Faith Topeka KS	(785)272-4214	SL-SMP	2015
Albrecht Luther G		632 Driftwood Ave Romeoville IL 60446	NI	Asst	Trinity Burr Ridge IL	(708)839-1200	SL	1967

*Multiple Assignments (See Church Worker Locator for Additional Details)
See Page 53 for the Table of Abbreviations for key to District, Position, and Seminary abbreviations
**C =Candidate; EM = Emeritus; the date following the C is the month and year the Candidate status began

NAME	TELEPHONE NUMBER EMAIL	STREET ADDRESS CITY/STATE/ZIP	DISTRICT	POSITION/ STATUS**	WHERE SERVING	OFFICE PHONE	SEM/ PROGRAM	YR GRAD
Albrecht Brian A	pastortlcswfl@gmail.com	3138 Holcomb Road Port Charlotte FL 33981	FG	SMP	Trinity SW FL Port Charlotte FL	(941)828-1910	FW-SMP	2011
Albrecht Ardon D Dr	(805)522-9677 a-albrecht@sbcglobal.net	2085 Alscot Ave Simi Valley CA 93063	PSW	EM			SL	1962
Albrechtsen Henry III	(518)488-4991 revalbrechtsen@outlook.com	55 Southern Ln Warwick NY 10990	AT	SP	Good Shepherd Warwick NY	(845)986-3040	SL	2012
Albright Matthew L	(402)910-2670 albright82@gmail.com	216 Copper Way Little Rock AR 72223	MDS	Sn/Adm	Christ Little Rock AR	(501)663-5232	SL	2019
Aldrich Paul J	pauljaldrich@gmail.com	350 Myers Ct San Leandro CA 94577	CNH	EM			SL	1985
Alemayehu Fasil G	(615)693-8557 fagetahun@yahoo.com	308 Plus Park Blvd Apt L6 Nashville TN 37217	MDS	Assoc	Faith Thompsons Station TN	(615)791-1880	CQ	2014
Alemu Girma B	(919)345-8578 girmaandfele@yahoo.com	144 Bikram Dr Holly Springs NC 27540	SE	EM			CQ	2017
Alexander Phillip J	(978)514-3231 pastor2p@gmail.com	11992 SW Royalty Ct Apt 26 Portland OR 97224	NOW	EM			FW	1999
Alexander Robert D	(785)462-2497 bob_o_link_packerpastor@ reagan.com	33 Sable Dr Bella Vista AR 72715	MDS	EM			SL	1985
Alexander Peter C	(619)226-0939 pca676@gmail.com	2902 Laning Rd San Diego CA 92106	PSW	SP	University La Jolla CA	(858)453-0561	SL	1973
Alexander Howard M	(215)200-2855 saint4ever215x@yahoo.com	16 Dewey Rd Cheltenham PA 19012	EN	EM			CQ	1997
Alexander Arul J	(586)838-0062 arulalex@yahoo.co.in	15307 Drew Ct Macomb MI 48044	MI	SP	Faith Tamil Troy MI	(248)689-4664	CQ	2005
Alkire Bruce C	(385)365-2446 pastorbruce@va.metrocast.net	103 Freedom Way Warsaw VA 22572	SE	EM			CQ	1989
Allen Michael S	(989)971-4320 pastora01.stpaul@gmail.com	1907 Borton Ave Essexville MI 48732	MI	EM			FW	1984
Allen Stanley E Jr	(772)283-1717 Lt.SEA@hotmail.com	5518 SE Major Way Stuart FL 34997	FG	SMP	Redeemer Stuart FL	(772)286-0911	SL-SMP	2018
Alles Stephen C	(613)635-4737 pastor.stephen@ stjohnspembroke.ca	544 Isabella St Pembroke ON K8A 5 CANADA	EN	Sn/Adm	St John's Pembroke ON	(613)735-6332	CQ	2003
Alliet Paul W Dr	(920)993-0781 paul.alliet@gmail.com	1112 W Roberts Ave Appleton WI 54914	NW	EM			CQ	2000
Allison William S	billallison68@yahoo.com	380 Paymaster Dr Greenfield IN 46140	IN	EM			SL	1981
Allman Phillip J	(432)288-2201 pastorphilallman@gmail.com	12845 Springhill Dr Winnebago IL 61088	NI	SP	St John Pecatonica IL	(815)239-2400	FW	2017
Allmann Robert F	(989)600-1796 bob.allmann@gmail.com	2217 Post Ave Dodge City KS 67801	KS	SP	Holy Cross Dodge City KS	(620)227-6204	SPR	1972
Allshouse William N	(720)971-1907 ltcch@comcast.net	891 14th St Ut 4207 Denver CO 80202	RM	EM			FW	1978
Allsing Richard C	(619)672-5885 rcalls626@gmail.com	6100 Samuel St La Mesa CA 91942	PSW	EM			SL	1966
Allstaedt Jacob C	(253)720-6893 pastor@stjohns-wp.org	39 Winthrop St Williston Pk NY 11596	AT	SP	Saint John's Williston Park NY	(516)742-5858	SL	2011
Allwardt William H	(989)239-6810 pastorbill65@gmail.com	105 Twelve Oaks Dr Saint Peters MO 63376	MO	EM			SPR	1973
Allyn Eric F	ericallyn2844@sbcglobal.net	44 N Cornell Ave Villa Park IL 60181	NI	EM			FW	1978
Alms Maurice H Dr	(618)505-5009 mauricealms@gmail.com	122 Wild Rose Dr Belleville IL 62221	SI	EM			SL	1972
Alms Paul G	(828)324-8534 almspg@gmail.com	214 Rosewood Ave Catonsville MD 21228	SE	SP	Saint Paul Catonsville MD	(410)747-1897	FW	1992
Alsleben Robert L	(952) 207-1170 robuanals65@gmail.com	1165 Greenfield Cir Waconia MN 55387	MNS	EM			SL	1968
Altenberger Roger K	(636)368-6377 revrog427@att.net	2575 Hickory Manor Dr Wildwood MO 63011	MO	EM			FW	1995
Alter Anthony A	(573) 338-4602	1407 Pleasant Valley Dr Jefferson City MO 65109	MO	EM			SL	1991
Althoff Albert F Jr	(605)830-0411 revontrack@gmail.com	602 E 3rd St Crooks SD 57020	SD	Asst	Trinity Hartford SD	(605)526-3571	CQ	1989
Althoff Charles E	(419)388-5754 ce.althoff@gmail.com	5430 Lacour Monique St New Orleans LA 70131	SO	EM			FW	1979
Alvarado Luis A	(707)338-8939 merlui@comcast.net	7338 Hayward Dr Sacramento CA 95828	CNH	EM			HITSL	2000
Alvey Ryan C	(916)969-7582 ryan.alvey@yahoo.com	2918 87 1/2 St Bloomington MN 55431	MNS	Assoc	St Michaels Bloomington MN	(952)831-5276	SL	2009
Alwood John M	(562)412-1334 john@coastalmission.org	3319 Lemon Ave Signal Hill CA 90808	PSW	Assoc	Bethany Long Beach CA	(562)421-4711	CQ	2025
Alzate Edilberto M	(214)529-7511 balzate@hcdallas.org	1913 Glen Hill Dr Carrollton TX 75007	TX	Assoc	Holy Cross Dallas TX	(214)358-4396	SL	2014
Ameiss William H Dr	(630)855-8398	1643 Colfax Ct Unit 4 Bartlett IL 60103	NI	EM			SPR	1963
Amen Christopher M	(507)562-4851 pastorcamen@gmail.com	621 W Main St Pipestone MN 56164	MNS	SP	St Paul Pipestone MN	(507)825-5271	FW	2010
Ancira Mario E Jr	(253)778-5205 me_ancira@comcast.net	74 Anna St Watsonville CA 95076	MO	M Chap	Office of International Mission Saint Louis MO		FW	1997
Anderegg Richard M	(573)528-4597 rickanderegg87@gmail.com	316 Albany Dr Lake Ozark MO 65049	MO	EM			SL	1996
Andermann David J		24289 Fulfs Rd Sterling IL 61081	NI	SP	Christ Our Savior Dixon IL	(815)284-4554	SL	2001

*Multiple Assignments (See Church Worker Locator for Additional Details)
See Page 53 for the Table of Abbreviations for key to District, Position, and Seminary abbreviations
**C =Candidate; EM = Emeritus; the date following the C is the month and year the Candidate status began

NAME	TELEPHONE NUMBER EMAIL	STREET ADDRESS CITY/STATE/ZIP	DISTRICT	POSITION/ STATUS**	WHERE SERVING	OFFICE PHONE	SEM/ PROGRAM	YR GRAD
Andersen Neil E	(623)977-2910	10419 W Floriade Dr Sun City AZ 85351	PSW	EM			SL	1981
Andersen Carlton S	(715)421-4071 prcandersen@aol.com	540 Elm St Wisconsin Rapids WI 54494	NW	EM			CQ	2011
Andersen Shawn W	(715)681-0464 pswandersen@yahoo.com	265 S 3rd St Dorchester WI 54425	NW	SP	St Peter Dorchester WI	(715)654-5055	FW	2004
Andersen Eric N	rev.ena40@gmail.com	5859 S Archer Rd Summit IL 60501	NI	SP	Immanuel* Hodgkins IL	(708)354-0692	SL	2008
Andersen Gerald B	(519) 276-9091 vykingdane@hotmail.com	P.O. Box 736 114 St David St Mitchell ON N0K 1 CANADA	EN	SP	Grace Mitchell ON	(519)348-9082	ED	2003
Anderson Steven P	(941)400-7989 pastor@goodshepherdsarasota.org	7470 Featherstone Blvd Sarasota FL 34238	FG	SP	Good Shepherd Sarasota FL	(941)921-3673	SL	2003
Anderson Timothy W	(480)536-2256		PSW	SP	Beautiful Savior Tempe AZ	(480)967-2660	SL	2015
Anderson Ray N	(605)380-3710 rnanderson@nrctv.com	13867 390th Ave Aberdeen SD 57401	SD	SMP	St Paul* Aberdeen SD	(605)225-1847	SL-SMP	2021
Anderson Robert D	(865)469-7472 pastordanny@visitgrace.org	213 Norfolk Drive Knoxville TN 37922	MDS	Sn/Adm	Grace Knoxville TN	(865)691-2823	SL	2008
Anderson Robert L	(605)673-3077 bla@goldenwest.net	253 Boot Hill Rd Custer SD 57730	SD	EM			SPR	1974
Anderson Russell A	(386)864-3803 ra7207451@gmail.com	13 Wedge Ln Palm Coast FL 32164	FG	SP	Trinity Holly Hill FL	(386)255-7580	FW	1977
Anderson Ryan P	(715)540-8595 revryananderson2019@gmail.com	410 Witter St Wisconsin Rapids WI 54494	NW	SP	St John Sigel* Wisconsin Rapids WI		SL	2018
Anderson Steven L	(309)269-5276 rev@focusonthegospel.com	1723 Knoxville Rd Sherrard IL 61281	IE	EM			FW	1985
Anderson Paul W	(773)960-2895 panderson9@aol.com	33504 Boardwalk Dr. Spanish Fort AL 36527	EN	EM			CQ	1982
Anderson Timothy A		S1256 State Rd 58 La Valle WI 53941	SW	SP	St John* Loganville WI	(608)727-2000	FW	1993
Anderson Wayne A	pawaanderson@gmail.com	862 Mariners Pt Rodeo CA 94572	CNH	EM			SPR	1975
Anderson Timothy P	(260)416-1871 revdup01@msn.com	2732 Old Orchard Rd Fort Wayne IN 46804	IN	SP	Trinity Culver IN	(574)842-3175	CQ	1980
Anderson Paul N	(225)803-9636 revdranderson@cox.net	4773 Cottage Oaks Dr Gonzales LA 70737	SO	SP	Good Shepherd Baton Rouge LA	(225)766-4610	SL	1991
Anderson Wayne B	(661)946-0266 cavaleaf@verizon.net	43744 San Francisco Ave Lancaster CA 93535	PSW	EM			FW	1981
Anderson Steven J	(773)284-0926	5243 S Major Ave Chicago IL 60638	NI	SP	Hope* Countryside IL	(708)354-6176	SL	1999
Anderson Darryl A	(314)913-6318 darryla62@gmail.com	3715 Southern Manor Dr Saint Louis MO 63125	MO	EM			SPR	1972
Anderson Quinton B	(949)214-3111 quinton.anderson@cui.edu	1530 Concordia Dr W Irvine CA 92612	PSW	Cmp P	Concordia University Irvine Irvine CA	(949)854-8002	SL	2006
Anderson Allen D	303-433-4151 pastor@mtzionboulder.org	c/o Mount Zion 1680 Balsam Ave Boulder CO 80304	RM	SP	Mount Zion Boulder CO	(303)443-4151	FW	1981
Anderson Daniel A	(608)215-9526 boxcardan@gmail.com	8201 Mayo Dr Unit 302 Madison WI 53719	SW	C01/2023			SL-SMP	2015
Anderson Darren A	(719)491-5180 darrenanderson29@hotmail.com	10129 Thrive Ln Colorado Springs CO 80924	RM	C07/2016			SL	2005
Anderson David C	(309)737-1312 uacxiv@gmail.com	5944 Crow Valley Park Drive Davenport IA 52807	CI	SP	Trinity Coal Valley IL	(309)799-5650	FW	1993
Anderson David L	(307)286-9191 skypilotdave28@yahoo.com	3214 Plateau Ct Cheyenne WY 82009	WY	EM			FW	1990
Anderson David P	(507)399-1230 pastoranderson@yahoo.com	513 East Broadway Newport TN 37281	MDS	EM			Other	1981
Anderson Paul D	(763)689-4735 pda76@q.com	2765 Maple Dr S Cambridge MN 55008	MNN	SP	St John North Branch MN	(763)444-5988	FW	2002
Anderson Jeffrey M	(309)276-7650 pastorjeff@bethelmorton.org	520 North Ohio Street Morton IL 61550	CI	Sn/Adm	Bethel Morton IL	(309)263-2417	SL	1988
Anderson Jeffrey O	(216)496-1903 janderson@sbstone.com	2921 Hastings Rd Silver Lake OH 44224	EN	EM			SL	1972
Anderson Jon K Dr	(260) 416-8396 thrive70@gmail.com	8302 Redstone Dr Fort Wayne IN 46835	IN	EM			FW	1990
Anderson Jonathan M	(864)884-3095 jonathan.anderson@lcms.org	607 E Airport Rd Greer SC 29651	MO	S Miss	Office of International Mission Saint Louis MO		FW	2024
Anderson Luke J	(414)551-7500 pastor.anderson@splgrafton.org	1021 1st Ave Grafton WI 53024	SW	Assoc	St Paul Grafton WI	(262)377-4659	SL	2013
Anderson Mark A	mark@livingwateromaha.org	16305 Spring Cir Omaha NE 68130	NEB	Assoc	Living Water Omaha NE	(402)431-2593	SL	2011
Anderson Dustin L	(309)830-3322 revdustinlanderson@me.com	W156 N7534 Pilgrim Rd Menomonee FLS WI 53051	SW	Sn/Adm	St Johns Port Washington WI	(262)284-2131	FW	2007
Andrada Edward B	(224)567-9808 revted4@gmail.com	53 Grace Ln Uniontown MO 63783	MO	SP	Zion* Perryville MO	(573)788-2432	SL	1993
Andrae Eric R	(412)266-6719 ericandrae@gmail.com	1405 N Negley Ave Pittsburgh PA 15206	EN	Assoc	First Trinity Pittsburgh PA	(412)683-4121	SL	1997
Andrajack Joseph P Jr	pastorandrajack@sbcglobal.net	7106 Pace St Amarillo TX 79108	TX	EM			SL	1999
Andreasen Phill E	(712)330-0472 phill.andreasen@gmail.com	3911 East 68th Street Sioux Falls SD 57108	SD	EM			SPR	1975
Andreasen Jordon M	revandreasen@gmail.com		SD	S Miss	Office of International Mission Saint Louis MO		SL	2012

*Multiple Assignments (See Church Worker Locator for Additional Details)
See Page 53 for the Table of Abbreviations for key to District, Position, and Seminary abbreviations
**C =Candidate; EM = Emeritus; the date following the C is the month and year the Candidate status began

NAME	TELEPHONE NUMBER EMAIL	STREET ADDRESS CITY/STATE/ZIP	DISTRICT	POSITION/ STATUS**	WHERE SERVING	OFFICE PHONE	SEM/ PROGRAM	YR GRAD
Andrews Steven P Jr	(816)678-9152 andrews@gracefaithlove.org	1409 NE Bluff St Lee's Summit MO 64086	MO	Assoc	St Matthew Lees Summit MO	(816)524-7068	SL	2013
Andrews Arthur F	(714)637-0887 aandrews@hephatha.net		PSW	SP	Hephatha Anaheim CA	(714)637-0887	CQ	2004
Andrix Donald L	(952)457-0093 donandrix@gmail.com	16980 County Road 31 Nya MN 55368	MNS	EM			SL	1973
Andrus Richard W	(620)628-4866	6828 SW 150th St Augusta KS 67010	KS	EM			SL	1997
Andrus David S	(314)458-4561 dave.andrus@not-alone.net	4419 Butler Hill Saint Louis MO 63128	MO	Asst	Abiding Savior Saint Louis MO	(314)894-9200	SL	1985
Andrzejewski Jakob A	(248)541-0613 revjski@stpaulroyaloak.org	513 S Troy St Royal Oak MI 48067	MI	Sn/Adm	St Paul Royal Oak MI	(248)541-0613	FW	2020
Andrzejewski Darryl L	(313) 770-4333 revdski@historictrinity.org	58827 Frost Rd. Lenox MI 48048	MI	Sn/Adm	Hist Trinity Detroit MI	(313)567-3100	FW	1993
Angerman Melvin R	(850)598-3186 revray@gslcshalimar.org	206 Devon Ct Ft Walton Bch FL 32547	SO	SP	Good Shepherd Shalimar FL	(850)651-1022	FW	2002
Angland Dennis W	(320)760-5328 dwangland@gmail.com	771 Hidden Oaks Dr NW Alexandria MN 56308	MNN	SP	Zion Parkers Prairie MN	(320)760-5328	SPR	1974
Anglin David W	(516)725-1368 mysterium732@gmail.com	9191 Garrison Dr Apt 107c Indianapolis IN 46240	AT	EM			SL	1983
Angon Jose Tomas	(219)477-5805 tangon@immanuelvalpo.org	1300 Carriage Dr Valparaiso IN 46383	IN	Asst	Immanuel Valparaiso IN	(219)462-8207	HITSL	2005
Ankersen Ryan J	(314)630-7181 rankersen@hcwichita.net	7029 E 40th Cir N Wichita KS 67226	KS	Assoc	Holy Cross Wichita KS	(316)684-5201	SL	2014
Ankney Rueben J			SI	EM			FW	1989
Ansorge Bernard H	(256)361-6732 ansorgebh@aol.com	2000 Joseph Cir NE Huntsville AL 35811	SO	EM			SL	1963
Anthony James W	(218)259-0115 janthony@paulbunyan.net	516 4th St SE Deer River MN 56636	MNN	SP	Redeemer* Deer River MN	(218)259-0115	FW	1987
Anthony Donald E	(704)782-7620 lebuick@aol.com	37 Tribune Ave SW Concord NC 28025	SE	SP	Grace Concord NC	(704)782-7620	SL	1988
Anthony Edgar O	(440)458-8605 phoenixea@juno.com	18 Waterfall Dr Grafton OH 44044	S	SP	SS Peter and Paul Lorain OH	(440)233-5166	CQ	1995
Antonetti Christopher O	(847)971-0848 pastor.antonetti@gmail.com	1512 S Briggs St Lockport IL 60441	NI	SP	St Paul Lockport IL	(815)838-1832	FW	2020
Antor Donald M Dr		207 Raymond Ave Barrington IL 60010	NI	Assoc	Immanuel Palatine IL	(847)359-1549	SL	2011
Apfel Michael A	apfelpastor@gmail.com	2824 S Horton St Fort Scott KS 66701	KS	SP	Trinity Fort Scott KS	(620)223-3596	SL	2018
Appel Anthony E		2925 E 700 S Wolcottville IN 46795	IN	SP	Messiah Wolcottville IN	(260)854-3129	SL	2010
Appel Timothy A	timothyappel@gmail.com	862 Marc Dr Alton IL 62002	SI	SP	Faith Godfrey IL	(618)466-3833	SL	2010
Apple Andrew D	aapple@flcclearwater.org	3123 62nd Street North Saint Petersburg FL 33710	FG	SP	First Clearwater FL	(727)462-8000	SL-SMP	2018
Appold David R	pastorappold@stpaulpaducah.org	226 Minerva Pl Paducah KY 42001	MDS	SP	St Paul Paducah KY	(270)442-8343	FW	2014
Appold Mark L Dr	(660)665-7344 mappold@truman.edu	27 Overbrook Dr Kirksville MO 63501	MO	EM			SL	1961
Appold Paul C	(231)215-7968 revpappold@comcast.net	2351 Norcrest Dr Norton Shores MI 49441	MI	SP	Trinity Muskegon MI	(231)755-1292	SL	2001
Appold Robert B	(616)813-0420 revrba@me.com	3000 Northville Dr NE Grand Rapids MI 49525	MI	Asst	Mount Calvary Greenville MI	(616)754-4886	SL	1983
Arand Charles P	(314)391-2810 arandc@csl.edu	597 Woodlyn Xing Ballwin MO 63021	MO	S HS/C	Concordia Seminary Saint Louis MO	(314)505-7000	SL	1984
Arbogast Jon D	(210) 660-1577 jon78m@gmail.com	25923 Stone Cyn San Antonio TX 78260	TX	EM			SL	1998
Archbold Gary E	(337)462-6204 garchbold@yahoo.com	307 Meadow Wood Cir Long Beach MS 39560	SO	EM			SPR	1975
Archer Adam K	(360)584-0140 pastor@stjohnsord.com	1406 T St Ord NE 68862	NEB	SP	St John Ord NE	(308)728-5111	SL	2016
Arendell Mark W	(313)969-4075 cherrieandmark@sbcglobal.net	7664 Amanda Cir Washington Twp MI 48094	MI	EM			SL	2009
Arends Tyler R	(217)379-1031 tyler.arends@ctsfw.edu	1209 N. Ellison Guymon OK 73942	OK	SP	Trinity Guymon OK	(580)338-3820	FW	2020
Argueta Jose R	(713)514-4371 argueta-joser@outlook.com	12219 Hillcroft St Houston TX 77635	TX	Assoc	Saint Peter Houston TX	(713)485-6889	SL	2022
Arias Anthony A	(863)444-1045 allbbarias@gmail.com	3101 W Osborne Ave Tampa FL 33614	FG	SMP	Peace Valley* Wauchula FL	(863)773-2858	SL-SMP	2017
Arle Edward J Dr	(314)497-3115 Revedarle1970@gmail.com	2038 Beau Ct Saint Charles MO 63303	MO	EM			SL	1970
Armao Robert W	(317)749-5116 midnightclear1@hotmail.com	6825 Southpine Ct Maumee OH 43537	OH	EM			FW	2007
Armbrecht Isaiah A	(319)660-0162 pastor.armbrecht@gmail.com	114 Guetzko Ct Manchester IA 52057	IE	SP	Our Savior Manchester IA	(563)927-4860	FW	2024
Armon Rodney A	(308)380-4017 ch67bde@msn.com	W8214 Cnty Rd E Oxford WI 53952	SW	Assoc	Immanuel* Westfield WI	(608)296-2088	SL	1984
Armstrong Brandon J	(580)471-9237 bj.armstrong@lutheranok.com	P.O. Box 404 Blair OK 73526	OK	SP	St Johns* Lone Wolf OK	(580)471-9237	CQ	2022
Armstrong John W	jwarmstrong@gracecolumbus.org		IN	EM			SL	1986
Armstrong Clinton J Dr	(714)458-4567 clinton.armstrong@cui.edu	19140 Pilario St Rowland Heights CA 91748	PSW	Assoc	Holy Trinity* Hacienda Heights CA	(626)333-9017	SL	2001

*Multiple Assignments (See Church Worker Locator for Additional Details)
See Page 53 for the Table of Abbreviations for key to District, Position, and Seminary abbreviations
**C =Candidate; EM = Emeritus; the date following the C is the month and year the Candidate status began

NAME	TELEPHONE NUMBER EMAIL	STREET ADDRESS CITY/STATE/ZIP	DISTRICT	POSITION/ STATUS**	WHERE SERVING	OFFICE PHONE	SEM/ PROGRAM	YR GRAD
Armstrong Roy R Jr Dr	rrarms@aol.com	756 River Boat Cir Orlando FL 32828	FG	Pro Stf	Luth Counseling Services Inc Winter Park FL	(407)644-4692	SL	1979
Arndt Joshua B	(507)381-6577 josh.b.arndt@gmail.com	90 Kennedy Avenue South Lester Prairie MN 55354	MNS	SP	St Peter Lester Prairie MN	(320)395-2811	FW	2018
Arndt Dennis A	(563)732-2282 revdaa@netwtc.net	1132 W 53rd St Apt B1 Davenport IA 52806	IE	EM			SPR	1969
Arndt Paul W	(586)864-4117 paul@paulwarndt.com	39389 Dodge Park Sterling Heights MI 48313	MI	D Miss	East Bethlehem Detroit MI	(313)892-2670	FW	1992
Arndt Richard L	(727)264-6498 acastnet@aol.com	9706 Oakwood Hills Ct New Prt Rchy FL 34655	FG	EM			SL	1965
Arnholt Bradley P		5141 Yosemite Dr Columbus GA 31907	FG	SP	Bethlehem Columbus GA	(706)327-8756	FW	1996
Arnold Ronald L	(775)359-0198 ronnilarn@sbcglobal.net	2730 Springland Dr Sparks NV 89434	CNH	EM			SL	1972
Arnold Jefferson M	(812)322-0886 jefferson.arnold@comcast.net	3504 E Winston St Bloomington IN 47401	IN	SP	Christ the King Mooresville IN	(260)750-8198	FW	2024
Arnold Todd W	(415)405-6196	245 E Los Rincones Green Valley AZ 85614	EN	Sn/Adm	Risen Savior Green Valley AZ	(520)625-2612	SL	1996
Arnold Thomas E	(503)312-2512 dogbox7@msn.com	5955 SE Milwaukie Ave Portland Or OR 97202	NOW	EM			FW	2010
Arp Wally M Dr	(407)310-0349 wally.arp@gmail.com	1209 Winter Springs Blvd Winter Springs FL 32708	S	EM			FW	1988
Arrasmith Brett A	(417) 592-1854		MO	SP	Our Redeemer Marshall MO	(660)886-2270	SL	2025
Arroyo Edgar O	(714)277-8476 masterarroyo@aol.com	1109 S. Parton St Santa Ana CA 92707	PSW	C01/2019			SL	2008
Arsse Berhanu D	(614)377-8350 arsseber@gmail.com	477 Fallriver Dr Reynoldsburg OH 43068	OH	SP	Ebenezer Whitehall OH	(614)377-8350	CQ	2010
Artelt Thomas A Dr	(706)850-0009 tartelt@uga.edu	322 Georgetown Dr Athens GA 30605	FG	EM			CQ	1988
Arthur Joseph L IV	(985)264-7642 joearthuriv@bellsouth.net	441 Starlin Dr Sulphur LA 70663	SO	SP	Trinity Sulphur LA	(337)625-3276	SL	2004
Artigas Cristiano	(623)742-5067 vdeluna@asu.edu	P.O. Box 37065 Phoenix AZ 85069	PSW	D Miss	Pacific Southwest Di Irvine CA	(949)854-3232	CQ	1980
Asburry Randy K	(314)853-4714 rasburry@hopelutheranstl.org	5218 Neosho St Saint Louis MO 63109	MO	Sn/Adm	Hope Saint Louis MO	(314)352-0014	SL	1990
Asbury Christopher P	(402)302-4232 revchristopherasbury@yahoo.com	2800 Rolling Hills Dr Norfolk NE 68701	NEB	Sn/Adm	Grace Norfolk NE	(402)371-1044	SL	2008
Asche Stephen E	(661)747-7466 sasche@bak.rr.com	3117 Melrose Ave Bakersfield CA 93308	CNH	SMP	Bethany Bakersfield CA	(661)399-3532	CQ	2021
Aschenbeck Keith D Dr	(979)716-9910 pastor@gracelutheran-tx.org	109 Biltmore Dr Victoria TX 77904	TX	SP	Grace Victoria TX	(361)573-2232	SL	1999
Ascher Christopher D Dr	(605)759-3062 cascher76@gmail.com	6205 W Westminster Dr Sioux Falls SD 57106	SD	Sn/Adm	Resurrection Sioux Falls SD	(605)361-6631	SL	2003
Ash Eric D Sr	(412)841-9359 rev.ericash@gmail.com	9170 Oquendo Rd Unit 252 Las Vegas NV 89148	EA	EM			CQ	2011
Ashcraft Karl A	(972)948-2801 karl.ashcraft@gmail.com	2318 Aberdeen Bnd Carrollton TX 75007	TX	SMP	Waters Edge Frisco TX	(972)712-7377	SL-SMP	2015
Asher Joseph G	(320)583-4204 spartancoach2008@fastmail.com	3490 Brookwood Cir Saint Charles MO 63301	MO	EM			FW	1984
Ashley Jeremy R	(217)454-4080 ashleyfamily5@gmail.com	38530 Long St Harrison Twp MI 48045	MI	SMP	Trinity Clinton Township MI	(586)463-2921	SL-SMP	2022
Ashmon Scott A	scott.ashmon@cui.edu	10 Via Menta Rancho Santa Margarita CA 92688	PSW	S HS/C	Concordia University Irvine Irvine CA	(949)854-8002	SL	1996
Askins Roy S	(314)996-1227 roy.askins@lcms.org	c/o Lutheran Church-Missouri Synod 1333 S Kirkwood Rd Saint Louis MO 63122	MO	S Ex/S	The LCMS Corporate Saint Louis MO	(314)965-9000	FW	2009
Asmus Aaron J	(605)254-8471 asmuspa@yahoo.com	6509 S Mogen Ave Sioux Falls SD 57108	SD	EM			SL	1986
Asmus Bradley C	(612)720-5567 bradley@ehlc.org	1121 Bergmann Dr Stillwater MN 55082	MNS	SMP	Eastern Hghts Saint Paul MN	(651)735-4202	SL-SMP	2025
Asmus Erland H	(651)308-8492 weasmus@q.com	8963 Jasmine Ln S Cottage Grove MN 55016	MNS	EM			CQ	1981
Asmus Gerhardt C	glasmus@gmail.com	9070 W Hwy 86 Neosho MO 64850	MO	EM			SL	1956
Asp Andrew M Jr	612-309-6608 andrew.asp@concordiaacademy.com	1156 Benton Way Arden Hills MN 55112	MNS	Cmp P	Concordia Academy Roseville MN	(651)484-8429	SL	2022
Astorga Jesus	(260)433-5282 astorgaj612@hotmail.com	6528 High Point Run Fort Wayne IN 46825	IN	EM			FW	2002
Astrowski Leonard A Jr	(989)326-0199 pastrowski@gmail.com	14 Foxwood Ct Rock Island IL 61201	CI	SP	Immanuel Rock Island IL	(309)786-3391	FW	2004
Athey James B	(920)784-5736 off2sem@yahoo.com	315 Oak Grove Ave Green Bay WI 54302	NW	C11/2022			SL	2010
Atkinson Dustin C	(719)352-1060 revatkinson@icloud.com	35 Tee Ct Pagosa Springs CO 81147	RM	Sn/Adm	Our Savior Pagosa Springs CO	(970)731-4668	SL	2017
Au Buchon Stanley R	(734)770-1687 stanaubuchon@gmail.com	23875 Higgins Way Brownstown MI 48134	MI	EM			SL	1972
Aubey Dennis A Dr	(847)951-2178 docaubey@juno.com	1340 Ironwood Ct Aurora IL 60506	NI	SP	Faith Geneva IL	(630)232-8420	SL	1974
Audette Andrew A	(763)498-3388 andy@remedymn.com	4780 Grapevine Ter Fort Worth TX 76123	TX	Sn/Adm	St Paul Fort Worth TX	(817)332-2281	SL	2015
Auernhamer Mark E	716-417-1272 marka5149@verizon.net	6838 Herzog Rd Bridgeport MI 48722	MI	EM			SL	1995

*Multiple Assignments (See Church Worker Locator for Additional Details)

See Page 53 for the Table of Abbreviations for key to District, Position, and Seminary abbreviations

**C =Candidate; EM = Emeritus; the date following the C is the month and year the Candidate status began

NAME	TELEPHONE NUMBER EMAIL	STREET ADDRESS CITY/STATE/ZIP	DISTRICT	POSITION/ STATUS**	WHERE SERVING	OFFICE PHONE	SEM/ PROGRAM	YR GRAD
Aufdenkamp William M	(218)234-8026 william.aufdenkamp@outlook.com	117 6th Ave SE Elbow Lake MN 56531	MNN	SP	Zion* Hoffman MN	(320)986-2897	SL	1987
Aufderheide Stan M	(507)766-4674 aufderheide@yahoo.com	2311 W Houston Ave Spokane WA 99208	NOW	EM			CQ	1983
Auger Edmund D	(817)653-2115 ecauger@yahoo.com	7504 Belcross Ln Fort Worth TX 76133	TX	EM			FW	1985
Augustin Horst W	(480)704-3011 hjaugustin@cox.net	9046 E Corrine Dr Scottsdale AZ 85260	PSW	EM			SL	1969
Augustine John P	(507)884-7390 rev.paugustine@gmail.com	280 4th Ave SE Plainview MN 55964	MNS	SP	Immanuel Plainview MN	(507)534-3700	FW	2009
Aumann Bradley S	(985)788-2154 bradleysaumann@yahoo.com	419 Country Club Blvd Slidell LA 70458	SO	SP	St Paul Picayune MS	(601)798-4586	SL	1997
Auringer Jason P	(636)698-5087 jauringer@ilcsw.net	712 Buckner Rd Wentzville MO 63385	MO	Sn/Adm	Immanuel Wentzville MO	(636)327-4416	SL	1995
Ausra Valdas Dr	(708)422-1433 zionlithlutheran@aol.com	9000 Menard Ave Oak Lawn IL 60453	NI	SP	Zion Oak Lawn IL	(708)422-1433	Other	1994
Austin Kevin W Dr	(480)276-2198 kevin.austin@risensavioraz.org	5411 S Wilson Dr Chandler AZ 85249	PSW	Assoc	Risen Savior Chandler AZ	(480)895-6782	SL	2007
Austin John R	(817)736-5156 jraustin47@gmail.com	8415 Lucinda Dr Elgin TX 78621	TX	EM			FW	1986
Avers Harold A	(313)673-5963 today1yes@yahoo.com	218 Kerby Rd Grosse Pt Frm MI 48236	MI	EM			SL	1968
Awe Michael A	(531)218-5793	3018 Julia Cir S Sioux City NE 68776	NEB	Sn/Adm	Hope South Sioux City NE	(402)494-1847	SL	1989
Ayers Raymond L		13233 W Elmspring Dr Boise ID 83713	NOW	C06/2024			SL	2006
Azzam Timothy P	(989)305-9335 timothyazzam@gmail.com	6098 Stagecoach Trl Oscoda MI 48750	MI	EM			SL	1982
Baade Eugene W	(425)271-6481 gjbaade@q.com	824 Lynnwood Ave NE Renton WA 98056	NOW	SP	Redeemer Mercer Island WA	(206)232-1711	SPR	1970
Babbitts John J	(570)409-6323 babbittj@csp.edu	107 Lynric Ct Shohola PA 18458	NJ	SMP	Prince Peace Hamburg NJ	(973)827-5080	CQ	2018
Bach James F Dr		5237 W Montrose Ave Chicago IL 60641	NI	Asst	Trinity Roselle IL	(630)894-3263	SL	1968
Bach Philip L	bach.p@frontier.com	408 Antelope St Tilden NE 68781	NEB	EM			FW	1989
Bachert Alan H Dr	(636)375-4835 vintageviewstables@gmail.com	4739 Chateau Ln Wildwood MO 63069	MO	EM			SPR	1969
Bachman Karl D	(808)492-9806 karlbachman@me.com	1221 Victoria St Apt 3003 Honolulu HI 96814	CNH	EM			SL	1974
Bacic Ronald J	(501)410-2944 pastorbacic062809@gmail.com	10219 Raymond Dr Little Rock AR 72205	MDS	SP	First Little Rock AR	(501)372-1023	FW	2009
Backhaus Kyle L	(920)946-4251 kyleb@stpaulfalls.com	4715 Superior Ave Sheboygan WI 53083	SW	Sn/Adm	St Paul Sheboygan Falls WI	(920)467-6449	FW	2014
Backhus Robert J	(217)347-7275 rbackhus@mchsi.com	1003 N Martin St Effingham IL 62401	CI	EM			SPR	1969
Backs Ronnie W	(417)840-1610 r_backs@hotmail.com	1044 W Dade 182 Lockwood MO 65682	MO	EM			CQ	2012
Bacon Paul E Dr	(847)982-3909 pebacon@aol.com	5039 Mulford St Skokie IL 60077	EN	Sn/Adm	Bethesda Chicago IL	(773)743-6460	SL	1967
Bacon Arthur D Dr	(571)345-8301 bacon.arthur@gmail.com	1562 Mule Rd Columbia IL 62236	MO	EM			SPR	1976
Baden Thomas W	(325)384-7626 tbaden@aol.com	3217 Cumberland Dr San Angelo TX 76904	TX	SP	Faith* Ozona TX	(325)942-9275	CQ	2001
Bader Albert J	(308)380-3625 rev.bader20@gmail.com	466 Road East G South Ogallala NE 69153	NEB	SP	St John Ogallala NE	(308)284-6015	FW	2020
Bader Rick L	bader@mchsi.com		NI	EM			SL	1980
Baerwolf Phillip A			MI	SP	Zion Bay City MI	(989)894-2611	SL	1995
Baggor Elamin M	(517)333-2960 pastorebanjor@KnowingJesus.org	2638 Raphael Rd East Lansing MI 48823	MI	Asst	St Luke Haslett MI	(517)339-9119	SL	2008
Bagnall George S	(989)559-9740 prbagnall@yahoo.com	4283 Maple St Cass City MI 48726	MI	SP	Good Shepherd Cass City MI	(989)872-2770	FW	1998
Bagnall Michael R	(605)354-3703 revbag@msn.com	40 S Greenleaf Ave Staten Island NY 10314	AT	SP	St John Staten Island NY	(718)761-1600	FW	2002
Bahkou Abjar	(817)680-1794 bahkoua@csl.edu	1565 Summer Chase Ln Fenton MO 63026	MO	S HS/C	Concordia Seminary Saint Louis MO	(314)505-7000	CQ	2012
Bahls Dale W	(715)249-3043 grceluth@gmail.com	W10801 County Highway C Hancock WI 54943	SW	SP	Grace Hancock WI	(715)249-3043	FW	1987
Bahn Stanley G	(262) 421-8637 sabahn245@gmail.com	W76 N629 Wauwatosa Road Apt. #124 Cedarburg WI 53012	SW	EM			SL	1965
Bahn David L Dr	(713)492-8308 david@bahnfamily.com	18414 Florence Knoll Dr Cypress TX 77429	TX	EM			FW	1979
Bahn Daryn A	(715)305-8667 bahnd@trinitycr.og	48 Clive Dr NW Cedar Rapids IA 52405	IE	Assoc	Trinity Cedar Rapids IA	(319)366-1569	SL	1992
Bahn Charles A	(309) 826-4742 cab1@trinluth.org	2808 Rutherford Dr Bloomington IL 61705	CI	SMP	Trinity Bloomington IL	(309)828-6265	SL-SMP	2017
Bahr Benjamin G			EA	SP	Grace* Niagara Falls NY	(716)283-1843	SL	2008
Bahr Michael J	bahrfam@juno.com	4716 Indiana Ave Fort Wayne IN 46807	IN	C07/2022			SL	2008
Baikie Marcus J	(307)214-3763 marcusbaikie@gmail.com	1019 Diamond Ave Cheyenne WY 82001	WY	Assoc	Our Savior Cheyenne WY	(307)632-2580	FW	2009
Bailes David R	(936)521-9389 drbailes@livingsaviortexas.org	310 Louisa St Montgomery TX 77356	TX	Sn/Adm	Living Savior Montgomery TX	(936)597-8013	FW	1996

*Multiple Assignments (See Church Worker Locator for Additional Details)
See Page 53 for the Table of Abbreviations for key to District, Position, and Seminary abbreviations
**C =Candidate; EM = Emeritus; the date following the C is the month and year the Candidate status began

NAME	TELEPHONE NUMBER EMAIL	STREET ADDRESS CITY/STATE/ZIP	DISTRICT	POSITION/ STATUS**	WHERE SERVING	OFFICE PHONE	SEM/ PROGRAM	YR GRAD
Bailey Michael P	ret.texaspastor@gmail.com	176 Texas Mulberry San Antonio TX 78253	TX	SP	Redeemer San Antonio TX	(210)732-4112	FW	1986
Bailey Robert A Jr	(281)628-4199 rbailey@southlakelc.org	204 Civil Dr League City TX 77573	TX	SP	South Lake League City TX	(346)708-1202	SL	2017
Bailey Robert G	(507)373-1346 robert-g-bailey@msn.com	435 E 3rd St Albert Lea MN 56007	MNS	EM			SPR	1969
Bain Vincent A	(320)217-9918 bainfamily66@yahoo.com	189 Norwich Ln Gaithersburg MD 20878	MNN	M Chap	Office of International Mission Saint Louis MO		SL	2003
Baisch Arthur H	(501)253-8292 CTSFW93@yahoo.com	4256 Meadowview Blvd. New Castle PA 16105	S	EM			CQ	1991
Bakat Albert T		5500 West 26th Sioux Falls SD 57106	SD	Asst	Resurrection Sioux Falls SD	(605)361-6631	Other	2021
Baker David W	(303)255-8993 bakerdw@reagan.com	4975 E 117th Ave Thornton CO 80239	RM	SP	Our Saviour* Commerce City CO	(303)288-9577	FW	1986
Baker Garth L	(850)329-6787 glbaker54mhs@gmail.com	1843 Newman Ln Tallahassee FL 32312	FG	EM			SPR	1963
Baker Jesse C	(763)228-5435 pastorjessebaker@gmail.com	108 French Court Roberts WI 54023	MNS	SP	Family Of Christ Houlton WI	(715)549-6140	SL	2019
Baker Matthew J	(319) 300-0995 pastorbaker@theforgiveness-place.org	922 Bluff St. Cedar Falls IA 50613	IE	Sn/Adm	Our Redeemer Cedar Falls IA	(319)266-2509	FW	2025
Baker Otto E	(570)992-0679 rbob@ptd.net	321 Switzgabel Dr Brodheadsvlle PA 18322	S	EM			SPR	1963
Baker Ronald M	(719)471-4485 baker0268@msn.com	910 Valley Rd Colorado Spgs CO 80904	RM	EM			FW	1987
Baker Sean M	(331)999-5022 sbaker@bethany-joco.org	10424 Bales Ave Kansas City MO 64137	KS	Sn/Adm	Bethany Overland Park KS	(913)648-2228	SL	2021
Baker William C	(760)703-0743 pastorbillbaker@aol.com	c/o Mt Olive Lutheran Church 206 E Wyandotte Ave Shelton WA 98584	NOW	SP	Mount Olive Shelton WA	(360)426-6353	SL-D	2008
Baker David G	(920)987-5454 david.baker@lansintl.org	P.O. Box 305 Poy Sippi WI 54967	SW	S Miss	Office of International Mission Saint Louis MO		SL	2005
Bakker Jonathon J	jonathon.bakker@cuw.edu	8053 N 45th St Brown Deer WI 53223	SW	S HS/C	Concordia University Wisconsin Mequon WI	(262)243-5700	FW	2005
Baldauf Steven A	(847)526-6825 stevebaldauf73@gmail.com	172 Parkview Dr Wauconda IL 60084	NI	C07/2016			SL	1986
Baldinger Timothy L	uofm1970@gmail.com	5631 Regal Way Indian Land SC 29707	SE	EM			SPR	1975
Balduc Robert A	(972)998-4257 rbalduc@stpeterfw.org	2613 Avenel Ct Fort Worth TX 76177	TX	SP	St Peter Roanoke TX	(817)491-2010	SL	2005
Baldwin Charles S Dr	(336)882-5672 concordia1963@yahoo.com	2104 Setliff Dr High Point NC 27265	SE	EM			SL	1963
Baldwin Harold R	(719)334-1048 revhrbaldy@msn.com	559 W Slice Dr Pueblo West CO 81007	RM	EM			CQ	1995
Baldwin Mark J	(608) 239-0406 mjbaldwin73@gmail.com	312 Lucille St Verona WI 53593	SW	EM			FW	1984
Baldwin Patrick M	(307)324-4168 rawlinslcms@outlook.com	1305 Ritter St Rawlins WY 82301	WY	SP	Christ Rawlins WY	(307)324-4168	FW	2020
Balfour Brett i	(207)229-6279 fortwilliams09@gmail.com	35 Douglas Ave Saco ME 04072	NE	C07/2016			FW	2003
Balgeman Donald E	(815) 621-7223 donbalgeman@gmail.com	6 N 318 Knollwood Dr St Charles IL 60175	NI	EM			SPR	1975
Balgeman Frank J	(719)574-6727 fvcb@juno.com	4250 Thornbury Way Colorado Spgs CO 80922	CNH	Asst	Grace San Mateo CA	(650)345-9068	FW	2002
Balk Jordan D	(715)370-4303 jordan@mtoliveweston.org	2311 Mystic Meadow Dr Kronenwetter WI 54455	NW	SMP	Mount Olive Weston WI	(715)359-5546	SL-SMP	2014
Balke James W Dr	(904)631-4906 drjimbalke@gmail.com	404 Albemarle Ln Greer SC 29650	SE	EM			SL	1971
Ball Mark D	(585) 773-8794 pastorball@stpaulhilton.org	34 Turtle Creek Ln Hilton NY 14468	EA	SP	St Paul Hilton NY	(585)392-4000	SL	2018
Ball Joshua T	(810)392-2392 pastorjtball@gmail.com	3306 Gratiot Ave Port Huron MI 48060	MI	Sn/Adm	St John Ray MI	(586)749-5286	SL	2000
Ball Benjamin T	(618)979-4587 bball@stpaulhamel.org	6969 W Frontage Rd Worden IL 62097	SI	Sn/Adm	St Paul Worden IL	(618)633-2209	SL	1999
Balla David P Dr	davidballa@gmail.com	2711 Lindgren Trl Aurora IL 60503	NI	SP	Peace Plainfield IL	(815)436-9847	SL	1992
Ballard Sean R	(850) 307-8121 ballardsr@protonmail.com	8 Pembrooke Ct Niceville FL 32578	SO	SP	First Florala AL	(334)858-3515	FW	2003
Ballas Kenneth M	(440)886-6462 kenlob4455@aol.com	12965 W Linden Ln Parma OH 44130	S	EM			SL	1960
Balvanz Richard L	(319)350-3276 rlbalvanz@gmail.com	1375 Echo Ridge Ln Marion IA 52302	IE	EM			SL-SMP	2015
Balzer Martin W	(847)502-8439 martywb@comcast.net	41 N Wisconsin Ave Addison IL 60101	NI	EM			SL	1974
Bamsch Duane R	duane.bamsch@icloud.com	c/o Our Redeemer Lutheran Church 4605 Cypress Ave Wichita Falls TX 76310	TX	SP	Our Redeemer Wichita Falls TX	(940)692-3690	FW	1998
Banach James L Dr	717-817-0836 jlbanach@comcast.net	112 Marwood Road Apt. 4239 Cabot PA 16023	SE	EM			FW	1979
Banarsi Edward	(512)439-9963 edwardbanarsi@sbcglobal.net	18208 Mammoth Cave Blvd Pflugerville TX 78660	TX	Inst C	Luth Social Services South Inc Austin TX	(512)459-1000	CQ	2001

*Multiple Assignments (See Church Worker Locator for Additional Details)
See Page 53 for the Table of Abbreviations for key to District, Position, and Seminary abbreviations
**C =Candidate; EM = Emeritus; the date following the C is the month and year the Candidate status began

NAME	TELEPHONE NUMBER EMAIL	STREET ADDRESS CITY/STATE/ZIP	DISTRICT	POSITION/ STATUS**	WHERE SERVING	OFFICE PHONE	SEM/ PROGRAM	YR GRAD
Baneck James A Dr	(701)226-9136 james.baneck@lcms.org	c/o Lutheran Church-Missouri Synod 1333 S Kirkwood Rd Saint Louis MO 63122	MO	S Ex/S	The LCMS Corporate Saint Louis MO	(314)965-9000	FW	1987
Bangert Justin R	(678) 672-9862 bangertjustin@gmail.com		NEB	Sn/Adm	Peace Grand Island NE	(308)384-5673	S	2009
Bangert Joseph L	(810)444-9616 jacbang@gmail.com	336 W Erie St Rogers City MI 49779	MI	SP	Immanuel* Rogers City MI	(989)474-4032	FW	2016
Bangert Mark A Dr	(636)399-0828 pastormark@imlutheran.org	114 E 2nd St Washington MO 63090	MO	EM			SL	1985
Bangert David J	(414)510-7342 dbangert@tx.rr.com		MO	C06/2025			SL-SMP	2022
Banke Brian B	(253)365-3985 brian@thepathwaygrp.org	430 Cox Rd Greer SC 29651	NOW	C07/2021			SL	2002
Banken Robert E	(253)845-0350 banken@comcast.net	1305 N Highlands Parkway Unit #e5 Tacoma WA 98406	NOW	EM			SPR	1962
Banks Martin C	(734)394-8220 martin.banks05@gmail.com	36730 Thinbark Ct Wayne MI 48184	MI	SMP	St Michael Wayne MI	(734)728-1950	SL-SMP	2025
Barber Timothy D	(224)616-8015 rev.tbarber@gmail.com	1524 Chadwick Way Tallahassee FL 32312	FG	SP	Epiphany Tallahassee FL	(850)385-7373	SL	2022
Barber Alan J	(765)720-2256 alanjbarber@hotmail.com	500 Oak Leaf Dr Greencastle IN 46135	IN	EM			FW	1983
Barber David E	(847)657-0987 revsr75@aol.com	17439 Ohara Dr Pt Charlotte FL 33948	FG	EM			SL	1991
Barber Robert G Jr	rbarber626@gmail.com	1801 G St Washoughal WA 98671	NOW	SP	St Matthew Washougal WA	(360)835-5533	SL	1988
Barbey Daniel C	dan1397@frontier.com	834 N 3rd St Hampton NE 68843	NEB	SP	St Peter Hampton NE	(402)725-3234	SL	1986
Barbey James A	(815)786-8772 barbey4@comcast.net	1116 Anthony Ln Sandwich IL 60548	NI	SP	Immanuel Hinckley IL	(815)286-3885	FW	2002
Barcelos Miguel A	(260)564-3344 miguel.barcelos@flc-boston.org	299 Berkeley St Boston MA 02116	NE	Assoc	First Boston MA	(617)536-8851	FW	2019
Barckholtz Steven A	(208)788-3034	P.O. Box 218 Hailey ID 83333	NOW	SP	Clover Trinity Buhl ID	(208)326-4950	SL	1992
Barcott Adam L	(407)288-4977 abarcott@gmail.com	3449 Brixford Lane West Lafayette IN 47906	IN	Assoc	Saint James Lafayette IN	(765)423-1616	CQ	2017
Bard Randall C	(979)822-2742 fastpastor@hotmail.com	4221 Boonville Rd Bryan TX 77802	TX	Sn/Adm	Bethel Bryan TX	(979)822-2742	SL	1997
Barkdull Scott A	sbarkdull@gmail.com	3716 Swenson Ave Fairbanks AK 99709	NOW	SMP	Zion Fairbanks AK	(907)456-7660	CQ	2018
Barker Robert L III	barker@tlcsimi.com	2738 Ophelia Ct Simi Valley CA 93063	PSW	SMP	Trinity Simi Valley CA	(805)526-2429	SL-SMP	2015
Barkett Timothy A	timbarkett22@gmail.com	3020 Dogwood Dr Lake Havasu City AZ 86404	PSW	SP	Good Shepherd Kingman AZ	(928)757-3525	SL	2010
Barklage Richard C	(916)765-7687 rbelkhunter@aol.com	8670 Camino Colegio Apt 146 Rohnert Park CA 94928	CNH	EM			Other	2016
Barkley Adam P	(847)840-1351	1117 Eisner Ave Sheboygan WI 53083	SW	SP	Grace* Haven WI	(920)565-2186	FW	2017
Barkley Andrew K	(847)840-1296 claychaser@gmail.com	11906 250th Ave Trevor WI 53179	SW	EM			FW	1985
Barlau Joseph J	barlaujoseph@gmail.com	P.O. Box 172 Lester Prairie MN 55354	MNS	SP	Saint Paul Lester Prairie MN	(320)395-2573	SL	2014
Barlow William E	bnmbar@aol.com	5217 Goldfinch Ln Fort Wayne IN 46818	IN	EM			CQ	1982
Barlow Brian F	(949)872-6985 pastorbrian.glcbanning@gmail.com	35251 Hogan Dr Beaumont CA 92223	PSW	SP	Grace Banning CA	(951)849-3232	SL	2021
Barnes Ryan E	revrebarnes@gmail.com		TX	C08/2019			SL	2007
Barnes Michael W	(515) 322-6233 pastorbarnes1984@outlook.com	62361 Arlington Circle Unit 2 South Lyon MI 48178	MI	EM			FW	1984
Barnett Ryan E	(208)559-2919 revryanB24@gmail.com	8096 Crainmont Dr Glen Burnie MD 21061	SE	Assoc	St Paul's Glen Burnie MD	(410)766-2283	SL	2024
Barnett Douglas B	(702)449-6702 sandiahots@embarqmail.com	12920 Sandia Point Rd NE Albuquerque NM 87111	RM	EM			SL	1979
Barnett Shawn T	(314)556-4803 shawn.t.barnett@gmail.com	1829 Curdes Ave Fort Wayne IN 46805	EN	Assoc	Redeemer Fort Wayne IN	(260)744-2585	FW	2024
Baroi Isaac	404-294-7207 isaac.baroi@att.net	1093 Clydesdale Dr Clarkston GA 30021	FG	EM			SL	2022
Barone Timothy J	Tbarone@hclk.org	3606 11th Ave Kearney NE 68845	NEB	Assoc	Holy Cross Kearney NE	(308)237-2944	SL	2013
Barreto Lugo Luis E	(951)813-6611 leblugo@yahoo.com	39560 Meadow View Cir Temecula CA 92591	PSW	SP	Prince of Peace Hemet CA	(951)925-6121	CQ	2010
Barringer Vincent W	(928) 671-1500 pastorvincebarringer@yahoo.com	450 Rose Ln Wickenburg AZ 85390	PSW	SP	Redeemer Wickenburg AZ	(928)684-2729	Other	2014
Barron Kevin D	(410)610-3159 pastorkbarron@gmail.com	2625 East Northern Parkway Baltimore MD 21214	SE	SP	Calvary Baltimore MD	(410)426-4301	SL	2018
Barry Matthew A	pastor.barry@stjohns-chaska.org	321 Oak St N Chaska MN 55318	MNS	Assoc	Saint Johns Chaska MN	(952)448-2433	SL	2012
Bartell Steven D	(603)793-2124 steven.bartell@gmail.com	3 Clara St Exeter NH 03833	NE	EM			FW	1983
Bartels Dennis L	(786)859-2826 fasterpastorb@yahoo.com	5761 NW 201st Ln Hialeah FL 33015	FG	EM			SL	1982
Bartels Jonathan M	(402)319-9842 pastorjon@therockseward.org	227 N 4th St Seward NE 68434	NEB	SP	The Rock Seward NE	(402)643-6624	SL	2024
Bartels Mark L	(774)413-5384 mlbartels@aol.com	3 Chandler Rd East Sandwich MA 02537	NJ	EM			CQ	1980

*Multiple Assignments (See Church Worker Locator for Additional Details)
See Page 53 for the Table of Abbreviations for key to District, Position, and Seminary abbreviations
**C =Candidate; EM = Emeritus; the date following the C is the month and year the Candidate status began

NAME	TELEPHONE NUMBER EMAIL	STREET ADDRESS CITY/STATE/ZIP	DISTRICT	POSITION/ STATUS**	WHERE SERVING	OFFICE PHONE	SEM/ PROGRAM	YR GRAD
Bartelt Stephen R	(402)496-6140 stephenrbartelt@yahoo.com	15005 Tibbles St Omaha NE 68116	NEB	EM			SL	1971
Bartelt Philip D	(707)287-7649 philip.bartelt@gmail.com	c/o Lutheran Church Of The Good Shepherd 2 Colonial Rd New Fairfield CT 06812	NE	SP	Good Shepherd New Fairfield CT	(203)746-9022	FW	2021
Bartelt Andrew H Dr	(314)255-6114 barteIta@csl.edu		NW	EM			SL	1976
Bartens Norlyn D	(618)553-9932 norlynbartens@gmail.com	311 W. Meyers St. P.O. Box 127 Campbell Hill IL 62916	SI		Southern Illinois District Belleville IL	(618)234-4767	FW	2020
Bartens Emmett A	(618) 421-5219 bartens.emmett@gmail.com	17682 E. 1st Ave. Louisville IL 62858	CI	SP	St John Louisville IL	(618)686-2971	FW	2022
Barth Robert L	(217)488-2073 rlb47@juno.com	702 E Gibson St New Berlin IL 62670	CI	EM			SPR	1973
Barth Howard C Jr	howcbar@gmail.com	4401 S Redhawk Way Boise ID 83716	NOW	EM			CQ	1995
Barth Gregory J	(818)341-3460	3274 Hereford Ct Simi Valley CA 93063	PSW	Sn/Adm	Our Redeemer Winnetka CA	(818)341-3460	SL	1978
Barthel William L Jr	(865)657-9325 11barthel@gmail.com	204 Oakmont Court Sunset SC 29685	SE	EM			SL	1971
Bartholomew Andrew P	revabart@outlook.com	1694 Plateau Dr SW Wyoming MI 49519	MI	Sn/Adm	St Mark Kentwood MI	(616)455-5320	SL	2014
Bartholomew Richard O	(414)915-7832 richardbartholomew@reagan.com	1169 County Rd D Almond WI 54909	NW	SP	St John Almond WI	(715)366-2480	CQ	1993
Bartlett William C	(949)394-8849 bbartlett318@gmail.com	15221 N Clubgate Dr Unit 1046 Scottsdale AZ 85254	PSW	C07/2016			CQ	2007
Bartley Daniel A	(561)889-4835 julienne7@comcast.net	10303 Cypress Lake Preserve Dr Lake Worth FL 33449	FG	SP	Emmanuel Haitian Delray Beach FL	(561)889-4835	CQ	2007
Bartling Frederick A Dr	(612)590-8753 a_pydych@hotmail.com	678 Snelling Ave S Apt. 407 Saint Paul MN 55116	MNS	EM			SL	1953
Barto Gregory S	(656)465-5271 gregory.barto@gmail.com		SW	SP	St John Sullivan WI	(262)593-8630	SL	2020
Bartok James L	(734)624-3422 jimlbartok@gmail.com	2610 S Lilac St Ozark MO 65721	MO	Asst	Faith Springfield MO	(417)833-3749	SL	2019
Barton Thomas M	(505)401-8212 pastorthomas3@yahoo.com	704 4th St Lamar CO 81052	RM	SP	Grace* Lamar CO	(719)336-5500	SL	2005
Barton James P	(765)418-0003 jpbarton47@gmail.com	755 Cumberland Ave W Lafayette IN 47906	IN	EM			SPR	1973
Bartzsch Thomas W	(616)490-7315 BARCHYMAN@GMAIL.COM	47 White Dr Clarksville AR 72830	MDS	SP	River Valley Grace Lamar AR	(479)754-2769	FW	2011
Barz Mark D	(210)413-8077	801 Seminary Place St Louis MO 63105	MO	S HS/C	Concordia Seminary Saint Louis MO	(314)505-7000	SL	1982
Barz Marvin L	(316)542-5063 mnm61453@sbcglobal.net	2050 N Webb Rd Apt 202 Wichita KS 67206	KS	EM			SPR	1957
Barz Daniel S	(269)429-7521 buchsmp@gmail.com	5648 Mohican Dr Stevensville MI 49127	MI	SMP	St Paul Buchanan MI	(269)695-9061	FW-SMP	2013
Baseley Joel R	(313)565-4022 j_baseley@hotmail.com	2000 N York St Dearborn MI 48128	MI	Assoc	Emmanuel Dearborn MI	(313)565-4002	SL	1988
Baseley John C	(406)488-7139 revbaseley@gmail.com	817 4th St SW Sidney MT 59270	MT	SP	St John* Fairview MT	(406)742-5332	FW	2022
Bashir Sabir N	(972)294-0236 sabir.bashir@princeofpeace.org	1060 Ponderosa Rdg Little Elm TX 75068	TX	Assoc	Prince Peace Carrollton TX	(972)447-9887	SL	2014
Bass David J	(224)558-7152 pastordbass@aol.com	7506 Sika Deer Way Fort Myers FL 33966	FG	Sn/Adm	St Michael Fort Myers FL	(239)939-1218	SL	2007
Bass David R	(559)642-3139 basses2@sti.net	28530 Creek Rd Coarsegold CA 93614	CNH	EM			SL	1974
Bassett Carl W	(630)204-1570 fedrev@sbcglobal.net	1613 Lykins Ln Niles MI 49120	MI	EM			FW	1987
Batchelder Thomas C	(952)381-4093 pastorbatchelder@gmail.com	1300 Providence Pl Orange City IA 51041	IW	SP	Faith Orange City IA	(712)737-2112	FW	2018
Batchelder David A	(207)363-8016 lynndavid1997@gmail.com	P.O. Box 537 York Beach ME 03910	NE	EM			FW	1990
Batchelor James T	(309)349-0229 batchelorjt@gmail.com	1857 Stagecoach Ln Muscatine IA 52761	IE	EM			FW	2005
Bato Dinku L Dr	(651)468-9183 dinkubato@gmail.com	7361 Craig Ave Inver Grove Heights MN 55076	MI	RSO	Lutheran Heritage Foundation Macomb MI	(800)554-0723	CQ	2017
Batsky Thomas E	(269)428-7243 bemalt510@gmail.com	3790 Blenheim Rd Saint Joseph MI 49085	MI	EM			FW	1981
Bauch Alan J	(716)225-1279 alanjbauch@gmail.com	484 Walnut Street Lockport NY 14094	EA	EM			NESC	2005
Bauch Gregory D	(904)553-7066	337 Parmley Ln Nashville TN 37207	MDS	SP	Ascension Madison TN	(615)868-2346	FW	2016
Baue Frederic W Dr	fredbaue@gmail.com	908 Brownell Ave Saint Louis MO 63122	EN	EM			SL	1981
Bauer Allen J	(832)216-3417 allenbauer1950@hotmail.com	3313 Count Dr Fort Worth TX 76244	TX	EM			CQ	1980
Bauer Dennis D	(406)477-6791 circleoflife@rangeweb.net	628 Cooney Rd Roberts MT 59070	MT	EM			SL	1982
Bauer James D	(303)358-8362 pastorbauer@gototrinity.com	1811 S Harlan Cir Apt. 322 Lakewood CO 80232	RM	Assoc	Trinity Denver CO	(303)406-3143	SPR	1976
Bauer Steven M	(303) 619-7018 bauer_sm@msn.com	1421 Castleton Rd Libertyville IL 60048	NI	EM			SL	1981
Bauer Micah L	pastormicahbauer@gmail.com	1853 Burlewood Dr Saint Louis MO 63146	SD	C06/2025			SL	2015
Bauer Louis E	(503)348-9680 loubauer@comcast.net	7303 NE 43rd St Vancouver WA 98662	NOW	EM			CQ	2017

*Multiple Assignments (See Church Worker Locator for Additional Details)
See Page 53 for the Table of Abbreviations for key to District, Position, and Seminary abbreviations
**C =Candidate; EM = Emeritus; the date following the C is the month and year the Candidate status began

NAME	TELEPHONE NUMBER EMAIL	STREET ADDRESS CITY/STATE/ZIP	DISTRICT	POSITION/ STATUS**	WHERE SERVING	OFFICE PHONE	SEM/ PROGRAM	YR GRAD
Bauer Jeremiah A	(561)405-5241 jeremiahdce@gmail.com	21 Founders Way Unit A Saint Louis MO 63105	TX	SMP	Prince Peace Carrollton TX	(972)447-9887	SL-SMP	2023
Bauer Jeffery R	(605)323-9410 j_r_bauer@hotmail.com	1004 Clayton St P.O. Box 67 Lake Park IA 51347	IW	EM			FW	2002
Bauer Erhart L	(971)295-0312 aeb503@aol.com	6125 SE Division St Apt 114 Portland OR 97206	NOW	EM			SL	1959
Bauer Jason C	(231)929-0283 jason@redeemerofinterlocken.com	7511 Secor Rd Traverse City MI 49685	MI	SMP	Redeemer Interlochen Grawn MI	(231)276-6372	FW-SMP	2011
Bauernfeind Peter A	(201)944-2107 kuras@aol.com	9 E Homestead Ave Palisades Pk NJ 07650	EN	SP	Grace Palisades Park NJ	(201)944-2107	SL	1995
Baughman Terry A	(317)407-8464 tbaughman70@gmail.com	3951 Fieldview Rd Lake Orion MI 48360	MI	SMP	Crown Of Life Rochester Hills MI	(248)652-7720	SL-SMP	2020
Bauknecht Jamie D	(715)889-4610 jamie.bauknecht@gmail.com	11520 County Rd M Crandon WI 54520	NW	SMP	St John* Laona WI	(715)674-3836	SL-SMP	2024
Baum Henry E Jr Dr	(440) 315-2821 drhebaum@verizon.net	1814 Kentfield Way Goshen IN 46526	FG	EM			FW	1980
Bauman Gene D	baumangene@gmail.com	2 Swan Ln Spearfish SD 57783	SD	EM			SL	1979
Bauman James G	therev21@aol.com	1112 E Devon Ave Bartlett IL 60103	NI	SP	Immanuel Bartlett IL	(630)837-1166	SL	1970
Bauman Douglas D	(812)350-4115 pastorbauman@stpaulcolumbus.org	3019 Revere Ct Columbus IN 47203	IN	Sn/Adm	St Paul Columbus IN	(812)376-6504	FW	2002
Baumann Jacob T	(602)750-0096 jacob@thecross.family	1079 Vanderbilt Dr Eustis FL 32726	S	SMP	The Cross Mount Dora FL	(352)602-4635	SL-SMP	2019
Baumann Joshua J	(605)220-1908 jbaumann@stpaulequips.com	3117 Jefferson St Stevens Point WI 54481	NW	Assoc	St Paul Stevens Point WI	(715)344-5660	SL	2012
Baumann Paul G	(870)202-8724 paul.baumann@ymail.com	3404 Timber Ridge Trl McKinney TX 75071	TX	EM			SPR	1972
Baumann Ronald W	(317)861-6855 rwbvlf@sbcglobal.net	106 Church Ave Seymour IN 47274	IN	EM			SL	1964
Baumann Adam P	(402)860-5644 adam.p.baumann@gmail.com	302 2nd St SE Hampton IA 50441	IE	Tchr	St Pauls Latimer IA	(641)579-6046	FW	2022
Baumbach Mark H	(714)491-0388 pastorbaumbach@gmail.com	9722 Kennelly Ln Anaheim CA 92804	PSW	SP	Messiah Buena Park CA	(714)752-6040	SL	2001
Baumeister Wesley D	(906)364-9110 bo.baumeister63@gmail.com	W3868 Sylvan Acres E Lily WI 54491	NW	EM			SL	1998
Baumgarn David H	(507)227-5646 dhbaumgarn@yahoo.com	414 15th St N Benson MN 56215	MNN	SP	St Mark Benson MN	(320)843-4131	FW	1996
Baumgarn Jack R	(320)276-8215 revjrb67@gmail.com	15653 154th St NE Hawick MN 56273	MNN	EM			SPR	1967
Baumgartel Allan P	(949)637-1863	P.O. Box 4970 Irvine CA 92616	PSW	D Miss	Faith Irvine CA	(213)700-3504	SL	1970
Baumgarten Joseph M	(907)687-1189 pastor@glchurch.org	3930 Pearl St Eugene OR 97405	NOW	SP	Grace Eugene OR	(541)342-4844	SL	2007
Baumgartner James S	(907)310-0342 notforsaken@gmail.com	1333 S. Kirkwood Road St. Louis MO 63122	MO	S Ex/S	Office of International Mission Saint Louis MO		SL	2009
Baye Matthew D	(586)495-0253 baye733@gmail.com	715 S Superior St De Pere WI 54115	NW	SP	Hope De Pere WI	(920)336-9843	SL	2010
Bayens Patrick J Dr		712 Holland Ln Romeoville IL 60446	NI	S HS/C	Concordia University Chicago River Forest IL	(708)771-8300	FW	1977
Bayer Robert F	skipper22937@gmail.com	1261 W 12th St Wahoo NE 68066	NEB	EM			FW	1977
Bayer Timothy A	(585)402-2807 pastorbayer@gmail.com	8964 Church Rd Saint Johns MI 48879	MI	SP	St Peter Saint Johns MI	(989)224-3178	FW	2019
Bayer Timothy R	(509)332-9935 pastortim@oslc.com	9529 175th St Ct E Puyallup WA 98375	NOW	Sn/Adm	Our Savior Tacoma WA	(253)531-2112	SL	2009
Bayless Andrew C	(314)201-8815 andrewbayless@gmail.com	15326 E. 22nd Ave Spokane Valley WA 99037	NOW	Assoc	Redeemer Spokane WA	(509)926-6363	SL	2014
Beabout John L	(812)569-4463 johnbeabout71@gmail.com	13 Bingham Way Crossville TN 38558	MDS	Assoc	Shep Of The Hills Crossville TN	(931)484-3461	SL	2005
Beagley David R	(515)292-7542 drbeagley@gmail.com	2930 Eisenhower Ave Ames IA 50010	IW	Assoc	Memorial Ames IA	(515)292-5005	SL	2007
Bean Matthew D Dr	(804)272-7973 mbean@redeemerric.org	9400 Redbridge Rd N Chesterfld VA 23236	SE	Sn/Adm	Redeemer Richmond VA	(804)272-7973	SL	2000
Beane Larry L II	(504)256-3440 larrybeane@gmail.com	621 4th St Gretna LA 70053	SO	SP	Salem Gretna LA	(504)367-5126	FW	2004
Bear Eric R	(760) 880-7525 erbear2002@hotmail.com	7031 E Moreland St Scottsdale AZ 85257	MO	M Chap	Office of International Mission Saint Louis MO		SL	2025
Beardsley Brian M	(920)789-9252 pastor252015@gmail.com		SW	SP	St John Adams WI	(608)339-7869	SL	1991
Bearman Dean R	(317)967-7920 laurapbearman@gmail.com	1396 Evergreen Dr Greenfield IN 46140	IN	EM			SL	1967
Beasley Derrick K	(540)580-5361 pastor@gslcp.org	1887 Electric Rd Roanoke VA 24018	SE	SP	Good Shepherd Roanoke VA	(540)774-8746	SL	1998
Beaton Craig S	(864)380-6108 csbeaton@gmail.com	226 Waverton Dr Greer SC 29650	SE	C05/2021			CQ	2019
Beaumont Donald P	(216)299-3740 pastor@bethelwillowick.org	30540 Willowick Dr Willowick OH 44095	OH	SP	Bethel Willowick OH	(440)943-5000	FW	2005
Beaverson Thomas R	(352)201-0079 1stlutheranpastor@gmail.com	3736 E Limestone Ln Inverness FL 34452	FG	SP	First Inverness FL	(352)726-1637	SL-D	2003
Beck Gary L Dr	(810)736-2981 pastorbeck@sbcglobal.net	5415 N Belsay Rd Flint MI 48506	MI	EM			FW	1983

*Multiple Assignments (See Church Worker Locator for Additional Details)
See Page 53 for the Table of Abbreviations for key to District, Position, and Seminary abbreviations
**C =Candidate; EM = Emeritus; the date following the C is the month and year the Candidate status began

NAME	TELEPHONE NUMBER EMAIL	STREET ADDRESS CITY/STATE/ZIP	DISTRICT	POSITION/ STATUS**	WHERE SERVING	OFFICE PHONE	SEM/ PROGRAM	YR GRAD
Beck William V	(719)375-4763 bill.beck@roalcms.org	18115 Martingale Rd Monument CO 80132	RM	SMP	Rock Of Ages Colorado Springs CO	(719)632-9394	SL-SMP	2024
Beck Timothy E	(513)630-1010 pastorbecx@gmail.com	1096 Falls Church Road Milford OH 45150	OH	SP	St Paul Cincinnati OH	(513)271-4147	FW	2003
Beck John L	(203)346-4615 dreselbeck@sbcglobal.net	52 Missionary Rd 5322 Cromwell CT 06416	NE	EM			SL	1959
Beck James W	(503)812-5327 jwesleybeck27@gmail.com	3325 Northwood Way N Tillamook OR 97141	NOW	EM			SL	2007
Beck Dustin M	(940)337-1608	P.O. Box 15 Warda TX 78960	TX	SP	Holy Cross Giddings TX	(979)242-3333	SL	2011
Beck Christopher D	cbeck002@gmail.com	5060 W Hanks Xing Bloomington IN 47403	IN	C06/2025			FW	2014
Beck John E	john6beck@gmail.com	1412 9th Ave N Sauk Rapids MN 56379	MNN	EM			FW	1979
Beckendorf Timothy P	(618)282-8241 tim.beckendorf@lbt.org	380 Willow Oak Dr Red Bud IL 62278	MNS	RSO	Lutheran Bible Translators Inc Concordia MO	(660)225-0810	SL	2003
Becker Robert	(260)724-4977 brbecker62@msn.com	2411 West Deer Run Trl Decatur IN 46733	OH	EM			FW	1984
Becker Wallace M Dr	(314)378-7698 revwbecker@gmail.com	2396 Daisy Tree Rd Saint Cloud FL 34771	S	EM			SL	1988
Becker Vance G	(620)601-8084 vance.becker@lcms.org	2500 North Anderson Rd Garden City KS 67846	KS	EM			SL	1982
Becker Thomas E	(410)714-1772 onesabre@aol.com	312 Lochbridge Dr New Bern NC 28562	SE	EM			CQ	1979
Becker Steven A	(217)825-9853	9841 E 1600th Avenue Effingham IL 62401	CI	EM			SL	1978
Becker Stephen H Dr	(916)291-1111 sbecker@tls-hawaii.org	95-510 Wikao Street # J201 Mililani HI 96789	CNH	SP	Trinity Wahiawa HI	(808)621-6033	CQ	2011
Becker Richard A	(217)691-9315 rvrnd335d@protonmail.com	23993 Indian Point Ave Petersburg IL 62675	CI	SP	Immanuel Athens IL		SL	1975
Becker Paul F	(423)863-5630	2020 Malvern Dr Kingsport TN 37660	MDS	EM			SL	1985
Becker Gregory H	(715)986-2955	117 155th Ave Turtle Lake WI 54889	NW	EM			FW-SMP	2010
Becker David L	(218) 527-0021 dtcbeckr@charter.net	P.O. Box 598 Deerwood MN 56444	MNN	EM			SL	1982
Becker Andrew J	(314)996-1287 andy.becker@lcms.org		MO	S Ex/S	Office of National Mission Saint Louis MO		SL	2010
Becker Dale A	abeckers@icloud.com	4178 Heitz Ave Jeffersonville IN 47130	IN	SP	Shepherd Hills Georgetown IN	(812)945-2101	FW	2003
Beckett Garrick S	(734)620-8902 revbeckettg@gmail.com	300 Silver Pine Circle Unit 27 Gaylord MI 49735	MI	C01/2024			SL	2021
Beckman Aaron J	(952)353-2151 beckmanstmark@gmail.com	151 Jefferson Ave N New Germany MN 55367	MNS	SP	St Mark New Germany MN	(952)353-2464	SL	2022
Beckman Bradley P	(402)802-1896 bpbeckman@yahoo.com	353 E Bonneville Ave Unit 573 Las Vegas NV 89101	PSW	SP	First Good Shep Las Vegas NV	(702)384-6106	SL	1992
Beckstrom Robert	(253)517-5204 beckstromrobert@comcast.net	1240 SW 354th Pl Federal Way WA 98023	NOW	EM			CQ	1978
Beckwith Carl L Dr		4428 Wyndemere Ln Fort Wayne IN 46835	IN	S HS/C	Concordia Theological Seminary Fort Wayne IN	(260)452-2100	CQ	2009
Bednash Eric Z	(443)844-8378 pastorstjamesevluthchurch@gmail.com	710 Springbok Dr Aberdeen MD 21001	SE	SP	St James of Overlea Overlea MD	(410)668-0158	FW	2018
Beffrey Ryan D	(216)965-5959	2853 122nd Ave Allegan MI 49010	EN	SP	Epiphany Dorr MI	(616)681-0791	FW	2012
Behling David H	(920)419-2083 ddbehling@plbb.us	116 North Center Street P.O. Box 184 Suring WI 54174	NW	EM			SPR	1969
Behm David M	(701)572-9021 pastorbehm@gmail.com	c/o Concordia Lutheran Church 1805 Main St Williston ND 58801	MT	SP	Concordia* Williston ND	(701)572-9021	FW	2012
Behmlander Daniel M	(815)441-4560 rev84@live.com	10543 Pinetree Ct Covington KY 41015	NI	EM			FW	1984
Behnke Joseph C	(651)769-5185 jbehnke@beautifulsaviorlc.org	3716 Gettysburg Ave N Minneapolis MN 55427	MNS	Sn/Adm	Beautiful Savior Plymouth MN	(763)550-1000	SL	2010
Behnke Timothy J	(989)401-8537 heiditim@netzero.net	4235 Williamson Rd Saginaw MI 48601	MI	SP	Faith Bridgeport MI	(989)777-2600	SL	2008
Behnke James E	(520)803-6810 jimbehnke76@gmail.com	4964 S Laguna Ave Sierra Vista AZ 85650	PSW	EM			SL	1981
Behnke Allen L	(920)387-2058 behnkeallen@gmail.com	W1946 Hochheim Rd Mayville WI 53050	SW	SP	St John Horicon WI	(920)387-3775	SL	1973
Behnken Larry R	(651) 274-5106 lrbehnken@gmail.com	598 Yankton College Ln New Brighton MN 55112	MNS	EM			SL	1973
Behrens Matthew J	(510)278-2555 mbehrens@calvarysanlorenzo.com	15832 Via Cordoba San Lorenzo CA 94580	CNH	SP	Calvary San Lorenzo CA	(510)278-2555	SL	2012
Behrhorst Wallace D	(512)261-6968 wdbehrhorst@gmail.com	12501 Longhorn Pkwy A376 Austin TX 78732	TX	EM			SL	1950
Beilstein W J	(775)790-5180 jbeilstein@juno.com	1011 Silveranch Dr Gardnerville NV 89460	CNH	EM			CQ	2002
Beinke Robert D	(413)783-0131 RBeinke@ned-lcms.org	29 Cornell St Plainville CT 06062	NE	DP	New England District* Springfield MA	(413)783-0131	FW	1986
Beisel Paul L	(217)617-1442 revbeisel@hotmail.com	323 Lee Ln Iowa Falls IA 50126	IE	SP	Immanuel Iowa Falls IA	(641)648-3756	FW	2001
Bekele Mekru	(972)974-5156 mekru4@gmail.com	1717 Northampton Dr Rowlett TX 75089	TX	SP	Emmanuel Ethiopian Dallas TX	(972)674-7914	SL	2008

*Multiple Assignments (See Church Worker Locator for Additional Details)

See Page 53 for the Table of Abbreviations for key to District, Position, and Seminary abbreviations

**C =Candidate; EM = Emeritus; the date following the C is the month and year the Candidate status began

NAME	TELEPHONE NUMBER EMAIL	STREET ADDRESS CITY/STATE/ZIP	DISTRICT	POSITION/ STATUS**	WHERE SERVING	OFFICE PHONE	SEM/ PROGRAM	YR GRAD
Belay Belete D	(703)400-7955 beletedemessew@gmail.com	2710 Cecil Dr Chester MD 21619	SE	SP	Galilee Chester MD	(410)643-6545	CQ	2016
Belcher Nicholas R	(785)559-0015 nicholas.belcher@outlook.com	34 Suncrest Dr Cabot AR 72023	KS	C06/2025			FW	2023
Belinsky Michael G Sr	pastormike01@gmail.com	330 Lambrecht St Beemer NE 68716	NEB	SP	St John* Beemer NE	(402)528-7278	FW	2009
Belisle Russell S	belisler@bellsouth.net	10439 Pilot Rock Rd Collierville TN 38017	MDS	SP	Cross Of Calvary Memphis TN	(901)396-5566	FW	1988
Belknap Robert H Dr	(985)863-2878 rbobbelknap@gmail.com	37148 W Powerline Rd Pearl River LA 70452	SO	SP	Zion New Orleans LA	(504)524-1025	SL-D	2005
Bell Larry E	(314)941-3742 larry_e_bell@yahoo.com	401 E Evergreen St Payson AZ 85541	EN	EM			SL	1993
Bell Michael J	(786) 405-2367 michaelbell@live.com	12 Van Riper Rd Unit 123 Montvale NJ 07645	CNH	EM			CQ	2011
Bell Justin A		20275 Honeysuckle Drive Suite 110 Elkhorn NE 68022	NEB	Sn/Adm	GraceHill Elkhorn NE	(402)403-4941	SL	2011
Bell Daniel C	(614)457-9030 dbell2@columbus.rr.com	4236 Waddington Rd Columbus OH 43220	OH	EM			SPR	1965
Bell Charles	(631)236-5716 chuckkaryn@hotmail.com	97 Canterbury Dr Wading River NY 11792	AT	EM			SL	1975
Bell Aaron M	(651)769-7396 naphshi@gmail.com	4978 Jamestown Ct Columbus OH 43220	MNN	M Chap	Office of International Mission Saint Louis MO		SL	2010
Bell Randall D	(636)228-4773 prbell86@gmail.com	123 Church Rd Augusta MO 63332	MO	SP	Christ Augusta MO	(636)228-4642	FW	1986
Bellas Richard J	(815) 715-4573 rjbellas@gmail.com	1342 Acorn Dr Crest Hill IL 60403	NI	C07/2016			SL	1998
Belles James E	bellesj@comcast.net	6054 Daybreak Dr Bartlett TN 38135	MDS	SMP	Grace Celebration Cordova TN	(901)737-6010	CQ	2018
Bellinghausen Jake B	revjakebell@gmail.com		MI	SP	Cross Christ South Lyon MI	(248)437-8810	SL	2021
Below Mark G	(801) 487-6283 mbelow@rlcs-slc.org	5898 S Ragsdale Dr Murray UT 84121	RM	SP	Redeemer Salt Lake City UT	(801)467-4352	FW	1990
Belt Andrew D	(715)384-3535 revbelt18@gmail.com	1208 W 14th St Marshfield WI 54449	NW	SP	Christ Marshfield WI	(715)384-3535	SL	2018
Belter Kevin P	(925) 791-0914 westfarthinger@gmail.com	5022 Lakeview Dr Unit 202 San Ramon CA 94582	EN	SP	Messiah Danville CA	(925)736-2270	FW	2017
Belton Victor J	(678) 662-7989 vjbelton@gmail.com	P.O. Box 20128 St Simons Island GA 31522	FG	EM			SL	1986
Beltz Terry D	terry.beltz@gmail.com	5544 E Aspen Ave Castle Rock CO 80104	RM	EM			SL	1981
Beltz Samuel G	(870)476-0028 samuel.beltz@gmail.com	2368 Merino Ave Oskaloosa IA 52577	IE	SP	St John Oskaloosa IA	(641)673-6546	SL	2011
Benavides Oscar O	(972)754-2830 oscbenavides@gmail.com	6445 Branchwood Trl The Colony TX 75056	TX	Assoc	Waters Edge Frisco TX	(972)712-7377	CQ	2004
Bender Kevin J	(906)281-5089 pastorbender@copperluth.org	21567 Chassell Painesdale Rd Chassell MI 49916	NW	Assoc	SS Peter and Paul Houghton MI	(906)482-4750	SL	2020
Bender Peter C	(262)370-1189 prbender@peacesussex.org	4200 Elmwood Rd Colgate WI 53017	SW	Sn/Adm	Peace Sussex WI	(262)246-3200	FW	1987
Bender James W	(785)806-7590 bender.jimsally@gmail.com	5826 Walmer St Mission KS 66202	KS	SP	Our Saviour Kansas City KS	(913)236-6228	SL	1991
Bender Harold J Jr	(217)779-7985 harold@splcwa.org	2367 S 118th St West Allis WI 53227	SW	Sn/Adm	St Paul West Allis WI	(414)541-6250	SL	1993
Bender Gary L	(989)770-0005 rev.gary.bender@gmail.com	5640 Cortland Cir Bay City MI 48706	MI	SP	Bethlehem Saginaw MI	(989)755-1144	SPR	1976
Bender Douglas J	(262)277-1914 dbender@immlutheran.org	c/o Immanuel Lutheran Church 47120 Romeo Plank Macomb MI 48044	MI	Assoc	Immanuel Macomb MI	(586)286-4231	SL	2014
Bendewald Jon D	jonbendewald@gmail.com	4741 Beechnut Dr Saint Joseph MI 49085	MI	EM			CQ	1997
Bendix Leland D	(763)516-8024 bendixlb@aol.com	19104 Lincoln St NW Elk River MN 55330	MNN	EM			FW	1977
Benedix Gary S	(208)326-3182 jeddyybicki@gmail.com	3713 Buhler Rd Filer ID 83328	NOW	EM			SL	1968
Benedum Thomas J	(314)322-4380 tjbenedum@gmail.com	711 S Laclede Station Rd Apt 1105 Webster Groves MO 63119	MO	EM			SL	1969
Benfey Matthias W Dr	(905)822-6141	1111 Gorled Ct Mississauga ON L5J4S CANADA	EN	SMP	St Mark's Mississauga ON	(905)278-2122	SL-SMP	2017
Benham John V III	(919)943-7082 pastorjohn@royalredeemer.org	c/o Royal Redeemer 7127 Dutchland Pkwy Liberty Twp OH 45044	OH	Assoc	Royal Redeemer Liberty Township OH	(513)779-4740	SL	2008
Benish Joshua A	(608)377-3748 benish@swd.lcms.org	1606 Fayette Rd Darlington WI 53530	SW	D Miss	South Wisconsin District Milwaukee WI	(414)464-8100	FW	2023
Benjamin Richard L	(301)695-7496 pastorrb@peaceinchrist.org	7124 Autumn Leaf Ln Frederick MD 21702	SE	SMP	Peace In Christ Walkersville MD	(301)845-6300	CQ	2019
Benjamin Scott E	(586)322-5365 revsebenjamin@yahoo.com	218 Mason St Spring Lake MI 48456	EN	EM			FW	1989
Benke David H Dr	(914)497-9676 dhbad@aol.com	61-26 211th Street Oakland Gdns NY 11364	AT	Sn/Adm	St Peters Brooklyn NY	(718)647-1014	SL	1972
Benke Michael R	(775)772-7067 revofreno@aol.com	4190 Inwood Ln Reno NV 89502	CNH	EM			SL	1973
Benke Robert J	(651)214-4027 pastorbobbenke@sbcglobal.net	c/o Faith Lutheran Church 1196 Desoto Blvd Hot Springs AR 71909	MDS	SP	Faith Hot Springs Village AR	(501)922-5700	SL	1985
Benkendorf Rodney A	(314)704-8202 revbenkendorf@gmail.com	2030 Allen Dr Cape Girardeau MO 63701	MO	SP	Hanover Cape Girardeau MO	(573)335-8583	SL	2002
Bennai Nourreddine	(405)664-5389 bennai@sbcglobal.net	6609 Cove Hollow Rd Oklahoma City OK 73132	OK	D Miss	Oklahoma District Norman OK	(405)321-3443	FW	2005

*Multiple Assignments (See Church Worker Locator for Additional Details)
See Page 53 for the Table of Abbreviations for key to District, Position, and Seminary abbreviations
**C =Candidate; EM = Emeritus; the date following the C is the month and year the Candidate status began

NAME	TELEPHONE NUMBER EMAIL	STREET ADDRESS CITY/STATE/ZIP	DISTRICT	POSITION/ STATUS**	WHERE SERVING	OFFICE PHONE	SEM/ PROGRAM	YR GRAD
Bennett John C	(507)327-7383 pastorjbennett@gmail.com	13128 499th Ave Vernon Center MN 56090	MNS	SP	St John Vernon Center MN	(507)549-3760	FW	2005
Bennett Robert H Dr	(989)868-4857 robert.bennett@ctsfw.edu	733 Ivy Creek CV Fort Wayne IN 46804	IN	S HS/C	Concordia Theological Seminary Fort Wayne IN	(260)452-2100	FW	2002
Bennett Dennis H	(828) 455-3055 stangrev@gmail.com	1173 Mine Rd New Market TN 37820	MDS	EM			FW	1984
Bennett Robert M	(801)856-7040 robbennett2000@yahoo.com	2174 E High Mesa Dr Sandy UT 84092	RM	SMP	Good Shepherd Richfield UT		FW-SMP	2020
Benning David E	(217)697-9567	633 W Walnut St Nashville IL 62263	SI	SP	Trinity Nashville IL	(618)327-3311	SL	2010
Benning Mark W	(608)387-9401 markandemilyb@yahoo.com	376 Prairie Ave Mondovi WI 54755	NW	EM			FW	1982
Benscoter Randall K	(208)634-9516	4371 E Brooklyn Dr Nampa ID 83686	NOW	EM			FW	1979
Benson Robert L Dr	(608)495-9823 bensonnorway@gmail.com	2113 Ridgeview Dr Reedsburg WI 53959	SW	EM			CQ	1983
Benson Steven M	(651)735-4202 steve@ehlc.org	2127 Margaret St Saint Paul MN 55119	MNS	Sn/Adm	Eastern Hghts Saint Paul MN	(651)735-4202	SL	1985
Benson Steven K	(515)657-1292 chaplain.benson@gmail.com	849 N 22nd St Fort Dodge IA 50501	IW	EM			FW	1987
Benson Thayer K	ted@churchthatcares.org	1612 Meadow Edge Ln Spring TX 77388	TX	Sn/Adm	Resurrection Spring TX	(281)353-4413	SL	2009
Benson Jacob H	(307)254-9541 jacob.henry.benson@gmail.com	570 Granite Peak Dr Apt 201 Casper WY 82609	WY	Asst	Trinity Casper WY	(307)234-0568	FW	2019
Benson David M Dr	(573)356-1118 pastordavebenson@gmail.com	2171 E Richmond St Springfield MO 65804	MO	EM			SL	1979
Benson Burt P	(701)640-8133 burtpbenson@gmail.com	9815 Ravenswood Rosd Granbury TX 76049	TX	EM			FW	1980
Benson Steven A	(218) 821-9784 pastorsteve@mtolivelutheran.com	1912 S. Trainer Rd. Rockford IL 61108	NI	SP	Concordia* Machesney Park IL	(815)633-4983	SL	2009
Benson Ronald J	(402)350-1918	943 Redwood Ave Crete NE 68333	NEB	SP	Bethlehem Crete NE	(402)826-4359	FW	2001
Bentz Todd A	(612)597-8362 todd.bentz@yahoo.com	18165 County Road 50 Hamburg MN 55339	MNS	SMP	Emanuel Hamburg MN	(952)467-2788	SL-SMP	2023
Bentz Tyson V	231-796-6684 bentz.tyson@gmail.com		MI	Sn/Adm	St Peter's Big Rapids MI	(231)796-6684	SL	2018
Benzinger Timothy D	benzingertd@outlook.com	6158 Oakbay Ct Indianapolis IN 47237	IN	Cmp P	Indianapolis Indianapolis IN	(317)787-5474	FW	2022
Beran Joseph M	(402)730-5011 joe.beran@gmail.com	c/o Christ Lutheran Church - 4325 Sumner St. Lincoln NE 91351	NEB	Assoc	Christ Lincoln NE	(402)483-7774	SL	2017
Berauer Peter W		30 N Donald Ave Arlington Heights IL 60004	NI	Assoc	St Paul Mount Prospect IL	(847)255-0332	SL	2016
Bereuter Bryce A	(816)517-7946 bbereuter@calvarykc.com	9909 Wayne Ave Kansas City MO 64131	MO	Assoc	Calvary Kansas City MO	(816)444-6908	SL	1988
Berg John M	(920)254-9347 revberg@me.com		SW	Assoc	Trinity Sheboygan WI	(920)458-8246	FW	1993
Berg Travis L	(320)305-9476 berg.travis@proton.me	648 Shoshone St Lander WY 82520	WY	SP	Bethel Lander WY	(307)332-4320	FW	2013
Berg John W	(510)565-6096 jwhberg@gmail.com	9303 Gilcrease Ave Unit 1107 Las Vegas NV 89149	PSW	SP	Mount Calvary Beverly Hills CA	(310)277-1164	CQ	2008
Berg Henry F	(815)893-4774 berghank@hotmail.com	50 Hastings Ave Crystal Lake IL 60014	CI	EM			SL	1966
Berg Chad S	(701)893-6963 pastorcsberg@gmail.com	311 1st St NE Menahga MN 56464	MNN	Assoc	St John Park Rapids MN	(218)732-9783	SL	2023
Berg Brent W	(402) 883-0086 pastorbb22@gmail.com	1721 L St Auburn NE 68305	NEB	SP	Trinity Auburn NE	(402)274-4210	SL	2022
Berg Andrew G	(360)931-9979 aberg@ourshepherd.org	873 Hollowood Ln Avon IN 46123	IN	Sn/Adm	Our Shepherd Avon IN	(317)271-9103	SL	2022
Berg Donald A	(972)271-1714 daberg14@yahoo.com	2409 Country Club Pkwy Garland TX 75041	TX	EM			SPR	1968
Berg Peter M		31585 W Bell Vine Trl Beverly Hills MI 48025	EN	EM			CQ	2004
Bergelin Darrell L	(920)889-8809 dbergelin@tds.net	W3969 Skyline Rd Elkhart Lake WI 53020	SW	EM			SPR	1976
Bergelin David A	(309)824-8421 revbergelin@yahoo.com	c/o Mount Calvary Lutheran 2940 Mineral Point Ave Janesville WI 53548	SW	SP	Mount Calvary Janesville WI	(608)754-4145	SL	2005
Bergelin Douglas J			SW	SP	St Peter Lebanon WI	(920)925-3547	SL	2007
Bergen Ronald L	(330)612-7284 RonBCF36@gmail.com	1695 Queens Gate Cir Apt 311 Cuyahoga Falls OH 44221	OH	EM			SL	1961
Bergen Edward B	(815)459-1956	141 Maple St Crystal Lake IL 60014	NI	EM			SL	1969
Berger Warrens E	(425)471-9970 rev.weberger@gmail.com	12802 218th Pl SE Snohomish WA 98296	NOW	SP	Shepherd Hills Snohomish WA	(360)668-7881	FW	2007
Berger Hugo E	(646)267-5643 hugoeberger@hotmail.com	2142 New York Ave Brooklyn NY 11210	AT	SP	Good Shepherd Brooklyn NY	(718)338-6424	CQ	2006
Berger Jakob D	(406)598-8896 pastorjakeberger@gmail.com	P.O. Box 2462 Thompson Falls MT 59873	MT	SP	Shep of the Valley Thompson Falls MT	(406)827-9570	FW	2015
Bergman David R	(903)724-2908 dandsberg@hotmail.com	805 Stoneridge Dr Hewitt TX 76643	TX	EM			SL	1979
Bergman Larry W	(360)978-6389	470 Dluhosh Rd Onalaska WA 98570	NOW	Asst	Peace Chehalis WA	(360)748-4108	SPR	1972
Bergmann Kevin Dr	(219)838-5177 kevin.bergmann313@gmail.com	1102 Fran Lin Pkwy Munster IN 46321	S	C07/2016			FW	1988

*Multiple Assignments (See Church Worker Locator for Additional Details)
See Page 53 for the Table of Abbreviations for key to District, Position, and Seminary abbreviations
**C =Candidate; EM = Emeritus; the date following the C is the month and year the Candidate status began

NAME	TELEPHONE NUMBER EMAIL	STREET ADDRESS CITY/STATE/ZIP	DISTRICT	POSITION/ STATUS**	WHERE SERVING	OFFICE PHONE	SEM/ PROGRAM	YR GRAD
Bergquist David H	(361)857-3738 david.bergquist@cune.org	3741 Wl Breeding Dr Corpus Chrsti TX 78414	TX	SP	Faith Aransas Pass TX	(361)758-3145	FW	1985
Bergson John A	(262)354-4537 johnabergson@gmail.com	P.O. Box 143 Haugen WI 54841	NW	C01/2018			Other	1991
Bergstrazer Allen C	(843)212-5753 pastor@goodshepherdcharles-ton.org	8176 Long Shadow Ln N Charleston SC 29406	SE	SP	Good Shepherd Mount Pleasant SC	(843)814-7221	SL	1999
Bergstresser Edwin L II	(614)808-1663 predwinlot@gmail.com	2412 Sunladen Drive Grove City OH 43123	OH	SP	Holy Cross Of/Deaf Columbus OH	(614)429-1351	SL	1984
Bergstresser Matthew W	(614)949-9223 PrMatthewBergstresser@gmail.com	c/o Good Shepherd Of The Deaf Lutheran Church 5845 Elmer Dr Toledo OH 43615	OH	SP	Immanuel* Toledo OH	(419)726-3991	SL	2019
Berkesch Brent G	(715)635-8167 pastorbgb@hotmail.com	W7148 Luther Rd Spooner WI 54801	NW	SP	Faith Spooner WI	(715)635-8167	SL	1985
Berkesch Dennis M Dr	(702)306-5888 dberkesch@gmail.com	2452 Jada Dr Henderson NV 89044	PSW	EM			SPR	1975
Berkesch Wayne C	(260)437-7645 wcberkesch@gmail.com	481 Rabbit Run Rd W Lafayette IN 47906	EN	EM			FW	1987
Berlin Mark E	(231)709-1602 pastorberlin@hotmail.com	19813 Pine Woods Dr Lake Ann MI 49650	MI	EM			FW	2002
Berlinski Jacob M	(407)488-4815 pastorberlinski@rivercliff.org	3024 Lake Park Trl Aceworth GA 30101	FG	Assoc	Rivercliff Sandy Springs GA	(770)993-4316	SL	2018
Bernard David E	(585) 531-4155 revdbernard@pm.me	11139 Yocum Rd Wayland NY 14572	EA	EM			CQ	2000
Bernath Gary D	(419)906-0813 gncbernath@yahoo.com	1142 Bales Rd Napoleon OH 43545	OH	EM			SL	1968
Bernau Joshua P	(952)529-8755 pastorb@stjohnsnya.org	206 2nd Ave SE Norwood Young America MN 55397	MNS	Sn/Adm	St John Norwood Young America MN	(952)467-2740	SL	2008
Bernau Wayne A	bernauwd@gmail.com	1414 Hampton Ct Madison SD 57042	SD	EM			SL	1981
Berndt Jeffry D	(573)590-1498 jberndt214@gmail.com	1850 Lake Dr Fulton MO 65251	MO	EM			SL	1990
Berndt Lance D	(402)493-1744	14205 Ida St Omaha NE 68142	NEB	Sn/Adm	Zion Omaha NE	(402)493-1744	SL	2003
Berndt Leander P	(502) 905-8146 panchob38@yahoo.com	7518 Dudley Garden Way Louisville KY 40222	IN	EM			SL	1965
Berndt Matthew C	(308)214-1089 mcberndt1973@gmail.com	c/o Trinity Lutheran Church 110 S Park Ave Manito IL 61546	CI	SP	St Paul* Manito IL	(309)968-2872	SL	2001
Berndt Steve C	(440)428-3759 steve.berndt@oh.rr.com	4696 Spinnaker Ct Mentor OH 44060	OH	SMP	Holy Cross* Madison OH	(440)812-1635	FW-SMP	2019
Berndt Bruce E	(916)835-6836 lhsbberndt@gmail.com	8721 Armagh Ct Elk Grove CA 95624	CNH	SP	Redeemer* Lodi CA	(209)368-2288	FW	1982
Bernecker Gerald L	(218) 608-8310 janejerry3@gmail.com	325 West Toledo Street Duluth MN 55811	MNN	EM			SL	1983
Berner Carl R	(320)287-0915 candhberner@yahoo.com	330 W South St Vesta MN 56292	MNN	EM			SL	1993
Berner Timothy A Dr	(651)484-8429 tim.berner@concordiaacademy.com	2354 Auerbach St Roseville MN 55113	MNS	Tchr	Concordia Academy Roseville MN	(651)484-8429	SL	1994
Berner Milton T	(513)231-0267 mberner98@yahoo.com	7682 Clough Pike Cincinnati OH 45244	OH	EM			SL	1965
Bernhardt Robert K	pastorbob612@gmail.com	5375 Georgia Creek Road House Springs MO 63051	MO	Sn/Adm	Holy Cross Saint Louis MO	(314)772-8633	SL	2012
Bernstein John I	(419)953-6069 johnbern45@aol.com	11504 Dove Ln Saint Marys OH 45885	OH	EM			SL	1971
Bernthal Hubert L	(479)268-4801 thebernthals@yahoo.com	23 Sandhurst Dr Bella Vista AR 72714	MDS	EM			SL	1956
Bernthal Kenneth G	(989)448-8217 kbern582@live.com	3305 Glen Meadows Dr Gaylord MI 49735	MI	EM			SL	1970
Berquist Roy W	pastor.trinity.hayward@gmail.com	16544 W Ridgerock Rd. Hayward WI 54843	NW	SP	Trinity Hayward WI	(715)634-2260	FW	2011
Berry Matthew C	(734)770-4664 pastormatthewberry@gmail.com	836 Park Ave Sikeston MO 63801	MO	SP	Concordia Sikeston MO	(573)471-5842	SL	2021
Berry Sean G	(303)898-6268 sean.berry@cune.org	16431 52nd Ave W Edmonds WA 98026	NOW	SP	Saint Timothy Edmonds WA	(425)743-2323	SL	2019
Berry Fred L Jr	(515)509-3305 flberry@heartofiowa.net	2702 Dillon Rd Marshalltown IA 50158	IE	SP	Christ* Gladbrook IA	(641)473-2527	SL	1990
Bersche Mark L	(405)464-5848 pastor@stjohnsmoore.org	1696 Bloomington Ct Newcastle OK 73065	OK	Sn/Adm	St John Moore OK	(405)794-5462	FW	2003
Bersche Kenneth J	(979)398-0762 pastorken@tlcsealy.org	5622 Wild Flower Rd Sealy TX 77474	TX	SP	Trinity Sealy TX	(979)885-2211	SL	1994
Berteau Benjamin C	(757)333-2437 bberteau@sjlarnold.org	c/o St Johns Lutheran Church 3517 Jeffco Blvd Arnold MO 63010	MO	Assoc	St Johns Arnold MO	(636)464-0096	SL	2018
Berteau Daniel C	(757)318-1449 danielberteau@gmail.com	534 Holmes Ave N Forked River NJ 08731	S	Sn/Adm	Redeemer Manchester NJ	(732)657-2828	SL	1996
Bertels Gary L Sr	(630)333-2466 gary.bertels@cuchicago.edu	859 Princeton Ct Elmhurst IL 60126	NI	EM			CQ	1976
Bertels Ricky D	(660)262-8080 rick1janice2@gmail.com	1305b Sandra Ave. Warrensburg MO 64093	MO	EM			SL	1986
Bertermann Mark C	(509)531-5270 markbertermann@gmail.com	1322 Rathwood Ave Richland WA 99352	NOW	EM			SPR	1972
Bertram Anthony T	(507) 399-6293 abertram@splpastor.org	819 Reiman Ct Fairmont MN 56031	MNS	Sn/Adm	St Paul Fairmont MN	(507)238-9491	FW	1989
Bertram Peter W	pctsfw81b@outlook.com	704 E Nebraska St Le Roy KS 66857	KS	EM			FW	1981

*Multiple Assignments (See Church Worker Locator for Additional Details)

See Page 53 for the Table of Abbreviations for key to District, Position, and Seminary abbreviations

**C =Candidate; EM = Emeritus; the date following the C is the month and year the Candidate status began

NAME	TELEPHONE NUMBER EMAIL	STREET ADDRESS CITY/STATE/ZIP	DISTRICT	POSITION/ STATUS**	WHERE SERVING	OFFICE PHONE	SEM/ PROGRAM	YR GRAD
Bertram Craig C	(651)470-3028 lotlpastor@gmail.com	5000 261st Ln Wyoming MN 55092	MNN	SP	Lord Of Lakes Forest Lake MN	(651)462-3535	SL	1993
Bertrand William R	(402)584-2408 willie.bertrand@gmail.com	86628 580 Ave Concord NE 68728	NEB	SP	St John* Wakefield NE	(402)287-2385	SL	1979
Bertsch Arie D	(701)720-2232 lcms.nd.dp@outlook.com	1010 72nd St SE Minot ND 58701	ND	EM			FW	1998
Bertsch Dean S Dr	(715)298-3052 bertschdean1@yahoo.com	2215 Rosalind Ct Fort Wayne IN 46818	NW	EM			FW	2007
Berus Jean-Enock	jeanenockberus@gmail.com	954 West Vernon Ave # 5 Los Angeles CA 90037	PSW	Assoc	St Paul Los Angeles CA	(323)731-8384	SL	2023
Besel Gordon W	(479)531-5079 gwbesel@gmail.com	1016 Oak Hollow Ln Anna TX 75409	TX	EM			SL	1979
Besel Keith L	pastor@mtcalvaryluth.org	3137 W 132nd Ct Broomfield CO 80020	RM	SP	Mount Calvary Fort Lupton CO	(303)857-6827	SL	1996
Bessette Randall T Sr	(413)313-1775 capedpreacher@gmail.com	1 Drake Ln Holyoke MA 01040	NE	SP	First Holyoke MA	(413)534-7071	FW	2005
Bestian Brian R	(915)328-9762 bbestian@gmail.com	42048 Mystical Bend Rd Magnolia TX 77354	TX	SP	St Mark Conroe TX	(936)756-6335	SL	1987
Bestul John C	(408)899-4847 pastorjbestul@lcos.org	10785 Carver Dr Cupertino CA 95014	CNH	Sn/Adm	Our Savior Cupertino CA	(408)252-0345	FW	2005
Bestul Mark C	(630)337-9342 pastor@clce.org	307 Gregory M Sears Dr Gilberts IL 60136	NI	SP	Calvary Elgin IL	(847)741-5433	FW	2007
Bestul Dennis E		1191 Cordelia Ave San Jose CA 95129	CNH	Assoc	Our Savior Cupertino CA	(408)252-0345	SPR	1974
Betker Bruce R	(808) 285-2118 btbetker@hotmail.com	7400 Crestway Apt 904 San Antonio TX 78239	CNH	EM			SL	1973
Bettcher Brandon M	(586)850-9878 pastorbettcher@stpaulnapoleon.org	c/o Saint Paul Lutheran Church 1075 Glenwood Ave Napoleon OH 43545	OH	Assoc	St Paul Napoleon OH	(419)592-3535	SL	2023
Betten Brady W	(402)469-5876 brady@gracehillomaha.com	18210 Corby St Elkhorn NE 68022	NEB	SMP	GraceHill Elkhorn NE	(402)403-4941	SL-SMP	2023
Bettermann James A	(270)320-6718 rbetterso@yahoo.com	201 Abby Deeann Dr Nicholasville KY 40356	IN	EM			FW	1983
Bettin Charles R	(712)657-2582 cboljbet@netins.net	2553 310th St Lake View IA 51450	IW	SP	Zion* Auburn IA		SL-D	2003
Betzner David J	(301)514-1781 davidjbetzner@gmail.com	6958 Sundays Ln Frederick MD 21702	SE	EM			SL	1969
Beukema Phillip L Jr	(715)614-4123 pastorphilbeukema@gmail.com	202 E Rusch St Thorp WI 54771	NW	SP	St John* Withee WI	(715)229-4211	FW	2016
Beuster Alan R	(309)507-2117 hopelutherangc@gmail.com	3309 Bluebird Ln Granite City IL 62040	SI	SP	Hope Granite City IL	(618)876-7568	SL	2015
Beutel Gregory D Dr	(817)750-0444 pastorgreg@lotwchurch.org	8750 North Riverside Dr Fort Worth TX 76244	TX	SP	Light Of The World Fort Worth TX	(817)750-0444	SL	1998
Beverly Henry H Jr	(817)905-9257 budwiser.bb@gmail.com	320 Marseille Dr Hurst TX 76054	TX	EM			CQ	2001
Beversdorf James A	(219)477-0931 jimbeversdorf69@gmail.com	1100 Fountain Hills Dr Apt 233c Mount Pleasant WI 53406	SW	EM			SL	1969
Beyer Jay B	(806)787-9569 jaybeyer82@gmail.com	417 Pin Cherry Pass San Marcus TX 78666	TX	EM			SL	1993
Beyer William D	(919)553-4784 william.beyer@earthlink.net	2920 NC Highway 42 W Clayton NC 27520	SE	Sn/Adm	Holy Cross Clayton NC	(919)553-4784	SL	1996
Beyer Timothy P	(562)694-6437 beyertimothy@aol.com	1351 Yerba Verde Dr El Cajon CA 92020	PSW	EM			FW	1983
Beyer Philip J	(808)888-9293 philipjbeyer@gmail.com	1704 Canyon Run Healdsburg CA 95448	CNH	SP	Good Shepherd Healdsburg CA	(707)433-3835	FW	1983
Beyer Paul J	(307)333-6531 pjbeyer93@gmail.com	3379 Linden Way Casper WY 82604	WY	EM			FW	1993
Beyer Michael R	(619)850-3900	1205 Santa Lucia Rd Chula Vista CA 91913	PSW	C01/2022			SL	1991
Beyer Mark E	boomerbeyer@gmail.com	2202 Desert Forest Ct Oxnard CA 93036	PSW	EM			SPR	1976
Beyer Joel A			NOW	SP	Kuna Kuna ID	(208)860-1274	SL	2013
Beyer James D	(707)486-2741 jimbeyer2021@outlook.com	556 Saint Mary Dr Santa Rosa CA 95409	CNH	EM			FW	1977
Beyer Charles E	(989)684-0545 chuckby63@gmail.com	3314 Boy Scout Rd Bay City MI 48706	MI	EM			SL	1963
Beyer Jonathan M	(501)318-7109 pastorjon@flchsar.com	208 Brentwood St Hot Springs AR 71901	MDS	Sn/Adm	First Hot Springs AR	(501)525-0322	SL	1985
Beyersdorf Philip J	(281)799-0550 christusrex87@gmail.com	30 Harmony Blvd Surrey ND 58758	ND	SP	St Mark Minot ND	(701)839-4663	FW	2014
Biar Henry H II	(512)581-1185 pastorbiar@stpaulskokie.org	7860 Niles Center Rd Skokie IL 60077	NI	SP	St Paul Skokie IL	(847)673-5030	SL	1992
Biar Chad A	(480)567-8663 chad.biar@gmail.com	1292 Tommy Trail Fallon NV 89406	CNH	SP	St John Fallon NV	(775)423-4146	SL	2020
Bibb Tysen L	(816) 387-3694 revbibb@gmail.com	202 N Pine St Norborne MO 64668	MO	SP	Trinity Norborne MO	(660)593-3721	FW	2016
Biber Paul R Dr	(989)327-1185 nesiahl@yahoo.com	1591 Briarson Dr Saginaw MI 48638	MI	SP	Good Shepherd Saginaw MI	(989)793-8201	SL	2001
Biberdorf Nathanael R	(605)419-7830 biberdorfnathanael@gmail.com		RM	SP	Zion Farmington NM	(505)325-3420	SL	2020
Biberdorf Richard W	henry1929@hotmail.com		PSW	EM			SL	1983
Bibler Brian L	rommans8.31@gmail.com	27 Fountainhall Dr Bella Vista AR 72715	MDS	EM			FW	1986

*Multiple Assignments (See Church Worker Locator for Additional Details)

See Page 53 for the Table of Abbreviations for key to District, Position, and Seminary abbreviations

**C =Candidate; EM = Emeritus; the date following the C is the month and year the Candidate status began

NAME	TELEPHONE NUMBER EMAIL	STREET ADDRESS CITY/STATE/ZIP	DISTRICT	POSITION/ STATUS**	WHERE SERVING	OFFICE PHONE	SEM/ PROGRAM	YR GRAD
Bickel Lloyd A	(260)908-4440 lloydbickel@yahoo.com	12015 Fallen Leaf Ct Fort Wayne IN 46845	IN	EM			SL	1971
Bickel Paul V	(443)640-6049 paulbickel@gmail.com	2430 Johnson Mill Rd Forest Hill MD 21050	SE	EM			CQ	1982
Bickel Craig L	(616)805-3940 pastorcraigb@yahoo.com	4675 Oakwright Dr NE Ada MI 49301	MI	Sn/Adm	Immanuel Grand Rapids MI	(616)454-3655	FW	1992
Bickel Timothy A	(419)377-7506 tbickel79@gmail.com	5120 Mesa Dr Shelby Township MI 48316	MI	EM			SL	1998
Bicknase Keith W	(605)467-1059 bicnbec2@gmail.com	13364 Beach Blvd Unit 131 Jacksonville FL 32224	FG	EM			SL	1998
Bickner Gary A	(505) 399-8387 gary.bickner@gmail.com	711 S Navajo Dr Gallup NM 87301	RM	EM			SL	1983
Bidinger Richard M	(920)528-8881 rbidinger@wi.rr.com	507 Milwaukee Ave Cascade WI 53011	SW	SP	St Pauls Cascade WI	(920)528-8094	SL	1986
Biebighauser Mark A	(507)676-4275 pmbiebighauser@gmail.com	30 Caroletta Ct Mankato MN 56001	MNS	Sn/Adm	Hosanna Mankato MN	(507)388-1766	SL	2008
Biebighauser Paul F	(952)500-0090 pbiebig@gmail.com	732 Lenox Dr Waconia MN 55387	MNS	EM			SL	2002
Biegner Paul R	(218)828-1313 riverev207@hotmail.com	207 Hawkins Dr Brainerd MN 56401	MNN	EM			SL	1957
Biel Ronald D	ronbiel1651@gmail.com	1664 Sarakinis Path The Villages FL 32163	FG	EM			SL	1969
Bielefeldt Douglas L	(210)639-7065 dougb1315@gmail.com	26316 Jason Avenue San Antonio TX 78255	TX	EM			SL-SMP	2012
Bielenberg Steven M	(320)905-0053 sbielenberg@kingofkingsroseville.org	2541 Pascal Street Roseville MN 55113	MNS	Sn/Adm	King Of Kings Roseville MN	(651)484-5142	SL	1988
Bier Louis H	(781)326-5774 hbier@verizon.net	23 Rainbow Pond Dr - A1 Walpole MA 02081	NE	EM			SPR	1959
Bierlein Albert R	(260)486-0095 albierlein@hotmail.com	9615 Stowaway CV Fort Wayne IN 46835	IN	EM			SL	1971
Bierman Bret R	(605)887-3696 thatchurchguy@yahoo.com	14912 377th Ave Mansfield SD 57460	SD	SMP	St Johns* Aberdeen SD	(605)228-4032	SL-SMP	2012
Biermann John C	(253) 604-4003 jcbiermann01@gmail.com	2517 14th Street Pl SE Puyallup WA 98374	NOW	EM			SPR	1973
Biermann Todd A Dr	(810)771-8837 tabiermann@gmail.com	1008 S Gettysburg Loop Republic MO 65738	MI	RSO	Concordia Center for the Family Ann Arbor MI	(888)553-5133	SL	1990
Biermann Joel D Dr	(314)505-7567 biermannj@csl.edu	7663 Terri Lynn Dr Saint Louis MO 63123	MO	S HS/C	Concordia Seminary Saint Louis MO	(314)505-7000	SL	1987
Biermann Jess R	(314)255-8066 biermannjess@gmail.com	6038 St James Dr Edwardsville IL 62025	SI	Assoc	Trinity Edwardsville IL	(618)656-2918	SL	2021
Biermann Herbert L	(402)518-8379	401 S Moreland Rd Apt 238 Bethalto IL 62010	SI	EM			SPR	1962
Biernacki Christopher L	(931)252-1536 christopher.biernacki@cuw.edu	955 Hwy 109 Wildwood MO 63038	MO	SP	St Pauls Wildwood MO	(636)273-6239	SL	2015
Biesenthal Bruce W	(314)223-6627 biesenthal234@gmail.com	12625 Lockhart Dr Denton TX 76207	TX	EM			SL	1976
Biggs Luther C Dr	bbqrev@gmail.com	2120 Stone Creek Loop N. Lincoln NE 68512	NEB	EM			SL	1984
Bijjiga Jaya P	(314)482-6586 bijaimna@aol.com	2465 Cecelia Ave Saint Louis MO 63144	MO	C07/2016			CQ	1995
Bilgreen David A Dr	dbilgreen77@gmail.com	10888 NE Packard Lane Cameron MO 64429	MO	EM			FW	1983
Billings Steven S	(920)385-8170 sbillings@trinitymenasha.com	4909 Sherman Rd Oshkosh WI 54901	SW	Sn/Adm	Trinity Menasha WI	(920)722-2662	FW	1991
Bingenheimer Michael R Dr	(316)258-4240 gobing@hotmail.com	3114 N Ridge Port Ct Wichita KS 67205	KS	Sn/Adm	Ascension Wichita KS	(316)722-4694	SL	2011
Bingue Jean A	(773)313-3628 binguej@yahoo.com	1619 W Sherwin Ave Unit C Chicago IL 60626	EN	Asst	Bethesda Chicago IL	(773)743-6460	SL	2010
Binz Curtis A	(707)479-6407 pastorcbinz@wplsf.com	495 Lakeshore Dr. San Francisco CA 94132	EN	Sn/Adm	West Portal San Francisco CA	(415)661-0242	SL	1999
Bira Clifford F	(810)240-1445 onthejourney.316@comcast.net	6356 Queens Ct Flushing MI 48433	MI	EM			FW	1981
Bird Aaron T	(217)621-3912	2727 N Union Blvd Decatur IL 62526	CI	Assoc	St John Decatur IL	(217)875-3656	SL	2017
Birkholz Mark W Dr	(779)279-4582 birchholz@hotmail.com	16035 S George Ct Plainfield IL 60586	NI	SP	Zion Naperville IL	(630)904-1124	SL	2004
Birner Charles R Dr	chuck.birner@gmail.com	23442 El Toro Rd Apt Hc230 Lake Forest CA 92630	PSW	EM			SL	1947
Birner David C Dr	(314)740-1418 david.birner@gmail.com	947 Market House Way Cary NC 27518	SE	EM			CQ	1986
Birner Paul D	(828)310-6606 pastor@king-of-kings.org	19635 122nd Pl SE Kent WA 98031	NOW	Sn/Adm	King Of Kings Renton WA	(425)226-1480	SL	1985
Birtell Kenton J	(308)995-2208 mtcalpastor@gmail.com	1415 Pamela Dr Holdrege NE 68949	NEB	Sn/Adm	Mount Calvary Holdrege NE	(308)995-2208	SL	1995
Birtell Brad E	bbirtel@telebeep.com	715 2nd St NE Watertown SD 57201	SD	SP	Mount Olive Watertown SD	(605)886-5671	SL	1992
Biru Gugssa	(301)346-0477 gugssa@yahoo.com	10302 College Sq Columbia MD 21044	SE	Assoc	Trinity Mount Rainier MD	(301)864-4340	CQ	2005
Bischof Jon C	(870)236-0839 jonbischof@hotmail.com	311 N 62nd St Paragould AR 72450	MDS	SP	St Matthew Corning AR	(870)323-0338	SL	1991
Bischoff Clifford L	(314)921-1107 cliffordbischoff@sbcglobal.net	3914 Almara Ct Florissant MO 63034	MO	EM			SL	1971
Bishop Daniel J	(309)382-1106 prbishop@frontiernet.net	301 Beloit Road Marquette Heights IL 61554	CI	Sn/Adm	St John Pekin IL	(309)347-2136	FW	1992

*Multiple Assignments (See Church Worker Locator for Additional Details)

See Page 53 for the Table of Abbreviations for key to District, Position, and Seminary abbreviations

**C =Candidate; EM = Emeritus; the date following the C is the month and year the Candidate status began

NAME	TELEPHONE NUMBER EMAIL	STREET ADDRESS CITY/STATE/ZIP	DISTRICT	POSITION/ STATUS**	WHERE SERVING	OFFICE PHONE	SEM/ PROGRAM	YR GRAD
Bitely Rodney E	Rodney.Bitely@saintpaul-lcms.com	8100 Shady Grove Rd Mechanicsvlle VA 23111	SE	SP	St Paul Mechanicsville VA	(804)427-7500	SL	1999
Bitz Micheal J	(320)250-0380 bitzm2000@yahoo.com	17027 State 287 Grey Eagle MN 56336	MNN	SP	St John Grey Eagle MN	(320)285-2902	SL	2008
Bjoraker Alexander D	(231)313-2352 abjoraker@gmail.com	2249 Co Rd 400 Tobias NE 68453	NEB	SP	Immanuel* Daykin NE	(402)446-7357	SL	2024
Bjorgaard Jon A	(408)323-6848 jonabjorgaard@gmail.com	7350 N Via Paseo Del Sur Unit N106 Scottsdale AZ 85258	PSW	SP	Holy Cross Scottsdale AZ	(480)994-4848	SL	1986
Bjornstad Kristian G	(507)369-8705 fysherofmen@gmail.com	1010 Baker Ave Mankato MN 56001	MNS	C05/2018			ED	1994
Bjornstad Robert M	yasurebjorn@comcast.net	2387 North Fork Rd Seaside OR 97138	NOW	EM			CQ	1981
Black Donald G	(713)782-6307 dblack@trinitydt.org	c/o Atria-Westchase 11424 Richmond Ave #213 Houston TX 77082	TX	Assoc	Trinity Houston TX	(713)224-0684	SL	1958
Black Eric S	pastor.black@messiahgr.org	9300 Button Rd Belding MI 48809	MI	SP	Messiah Grand Rapids MI	(616)363-2553	SL	2015
Black Ricky C	(713)806-2197 rblack@trinityama.org	11950 E Fm 1151 Amarillo TX 79118	TX	SMP	Trinity Amarillo TX	(806)352-5629	SL-SMP	2019
Blackford Matthew D	matt@lolchurch.net	40w728 White Fence Way St Charles IL 60175	NI	Sn/Adm	Lord of Life Elburn IL	(630)513-5325	SL	2007
Blackwell Michael C	716-713-7305 blackwellmichael6@gmail.com	29 Gardenville On The Grn West Seneca NY 14224	EA	EM			SL	1971
Blain James H	(616)288-5594 blainlm@yahoo.com	400 Sligh Blvd NE Grand Rapids MI 49505	MI	EM			SL	1977
Blair David W	(206)291-4237 blairhouse6@live.com		NOW	EM			SL	1981
Blake Kyle H	rev.kblake@gmail.com		TX	Cmp P	Concordia Tomball TX	(281)351-2547	Other	2015
Blakeman Mark J	(281)455-5071 rev.mark.blakeman@gmail.com	507 Fairmont Rd Fairmont OK 73736	OK	SP	Zion Fairmont OK	(580)358-2291	FW	2017
Blakey Charles B	(219)816-0984 cblakey422@yahoo.com	430 E Hillside Dr Reynolds IN 47980	IN	EM			FW	2002
Blanchard Dale R	(262)581-6908 pastor@triunelutheranchurch.com	N1584 County Road K Sharon WI 53585	SW	SP	Triune Sharon WI	(262)882-4000	FW	2011
Blanco Charles W	cwb.blanco@gmail.com	1175 Rainbow Ave Seward NE 68434	NEB	EM			SL	1983
Blank Rudolph H Dr		5930 Cates Ave Saint Louis MO 63112	NI	S Miss	Office of International Mission Saint Louis MO		SL	1971
Blanke Jonathan A Dr	(919) 851-7248 jonathan.blanke@rlcary.org	5761 Brushy Meadows Dr Fuquay-Varina NC 27526	SE	Sn/Adm	Resurrection Cary NC	(919)851-7248	SL	1992
Blanke Neal R	(760)793-3582 nrblanke@gmail.com	581 Claremont Pl Pomona CA 91767	PSW	SP	St Pauls Pomona CA	(909)623-6368	FW	1988
Blanken Alexander J	(402) 518-1602 revblanken@gmail.com	218 Miner St. P.O. Box 98 Winside NE 68790	NEB	SP	St Paul* Carroll NE	(402)375-1291	FW	2021
Blankenship William O	(573)221-0139 imhos3@charter.net	312 Columbus Rd Hannibal MO 63401	MO	SMP	Trinity Center MO		CQ	2020
Blankschaen Randy M	(850)291-2069 pastor@immlu.com	4952 Forest Creek Dr. Pace FL 32571	SO	SP	Immanuel Pensacola FL	(850)438-8138	FW	2007
Blas David	(630)229-2455 pastordblas@yahoo.com	2627 Center Ave Sheboygan WI 53081	SW	Assoc	Good Shepherd Sheboygan WI	(920)452-8759	SL	2018
Blasdel Brady W	(832)345-8007		TX	SP	Zion Pasadena TX	(281)991-8600	SL	1998
Blau Timothy A	(928)713-3282 pastortimblau@yahoo.com	2400 Oxford Way Lodi CA 95242	CNH	SP	St Peter Lodi CA	(209)333-2223	SL	1992
Blazek Scott R	(575)769-0693 blazek.scott.r@gmail.com	5 Pineway Blvd Clovis NM 88101	RM	EM			SL	1975
Blemaster Richard E	(716) 288-7840 rbcbakron@aol.com	5951 Broadway Apt 165 Lancaster NY 14086	EA	EM			SL	1958
Bless Matthew A	(641)832-7253	11 S University St Vermillion SD 57069	SD	SP	Concordia Vermillion SD	(605)624-3459	FW	2018
Blevins Scott L	(734)947-4707 blevinsscott7575@gmail.com	37002 Ellis St New Boston MI 48164	MI	SMP	St Paul New Boston MI	(734)753-9048	CQ	2020
Blickhahn Henry A III	(620) 664-1406 dce@orlhutch.org	306 Crescent Blvd Hutchinson KS 67502	KS	SMP	Our Redeemer Hutchinson KS	(620)662-5642	SL-SMP	2015
Bliese Karl H	(707)513-6249 kbliese@icolud.com	17705 S Western Ave Spc 33 Gardena CA 90248	CNH	EM			CQ	1984
Bloch Philip E	(812)523-8415 pmbloch@me.com	1237 Hickory Hill Rd Seymour IN 47274	IN	Assoc	Immanuel Seymour IN	(812)522-3118	SL	1990
Block Harold H	(660) 238-9279 harolb375@gmail.com		MO	EM			CQ	1991
Block John E	(319)440-1044	8900 C Ave Unit 255 Marion IA 53202	IE	EM			CQ	2010
Block Kenneth B Dr	(402)310-7620 blockk36@hotmail.com	1261 N 1st St Seward NE 68434	NEB	EM			SL	1963
Block Larry H	(816)858-2994 block6dad@kc.rr.com	1720 Todd St Platte City MO 64079	MO	Assoc	Our Savior Platte City MO	(816)335-4049	SL	1996
Block Thomas E	(863)853-9792 teb1951@gmail.com	1434 Timberidge Loop N Lakeland FL 33809	FG	EM			SL	1977
Block David L Dr	(402)215-3353 dlbceb@gmail.com	100 W. Queen Creek Rd. Apt. 217 Chandler AZ 85248	PSW	EM			SL	1969
Blocker Bruce L	(218)401-3220 hblocker@new.rr.com	743 Lomond Dr NW Bagley MN 56621	MNN	SP	Immanuel Mc Intosh MN	(218)563-2121	FW	1990
Blodgett Michael S	(260)402-1599 mike.s.blodgett@gmail.com	13108 Perry Lake Ct Fort Wayne IN 46845	IN	SP	St Paul New Haven IN	(260)749-5444	FW	2012

*Multiple Assignments (See Church Worker Locator for Additional Details)
See Page 53 for the Table of Abbreviations for key to District, Position, and Seminary abbreviations
**C =Candidate; EM = Emeritus; the date following the C is the month and year the Candidate status began

NAME	TELEPHONE NUMBER EMAIL	STREET ADDRESS CITY/STATE/ZIP	DISTRICT	POSITION/ STATUS**	WHERE SERVING	OFFICE PHONE	SEM/ PROGRAM	YR GRAD
Bloedel David L	(805)566-1806 davebarbca@frontier.com	1480 Manzanita St Carpinteria CA 93013	PSW	EM			SL	1967
Blomenberg Ralph Dr		580 Nottingham Dr Seymour IN 47274	IN	Sn/Adm	Immanuel Seymour IN	(812)522-3118	SL	1981
Blomquist Rodney G	(217) 825-6160 prgb@ctitech.com	717 Glacier Dr Taylorville IL 62568	CI	EM			FW	1980
Blonski Edward A Sr	(909)373-7936 revedblonski@gmail.com	518 W. Cambria Dr Round Lake IL 60073	NI	Sn/Adm	St Matthew Hawthorn Woods IL	(847)438-7709	SL	1995
Bloom Jeffrey L		3420 Cooper Ave Lincoln NE 68506	NEB	SP	Immanuel Lincoln NE	(402)474-6275	SL	1998
Bloom Neil D	(208)215-9702 neilbloom203@gmail.com	10472 N Barcelona St Hayden ID 83835	NOW	EM			CQ	1993
Bluege Joseph R	joebluege@gmail.com		MO	Assoc	Faith Branson MO	(417)334-2469	SL	2022
Blythe Richard J Dr			SE	EM			SL	2001
Boarts Matthew A	(310)849-4750 boarts1234@me.com	308 Taylor Elaine Dr Warner Robins GA 31088	FG	EM			FW	1995
Boateng William A	(715)483-1186 rev.boateng@gmail.com	501 E Kentucky St St Croix Falls WI 54024	NW	Assoc	Shep Of Valley Saint Croix Fls WI	(715)483-1186	FW	2013
Bobby Jacob C Dr	(605)760-5838 jake.bobby1981@gmail.com	1009 Jackson Yankton SD 57078	SD	Assoc	St John Yankton SD	(605)665-7337	SL	2009
Bobby Samuel L	(605)415-5578 pastor.bobby@redeemerlincoln.org	706 Westminster Dr Lincoln NE 68510	EN	Sn/Adm	Redeemer Lincoln NE	(402)477-1710	SL	2008
Boche Richard O	(307) 259-1870 boche.rev.richard@gmail.com	8825 Ridge Rd Cheyenne WY 82009	WY	EM			SL	1973
Bocian Brian C	(724)822-3842 bbocian@stlukecabot.org	133 Hampton Ct Butler PA 16002	EA	SMP	St Luke Cabot PA	(724)352-2777	SL-SMP	2020
Bock Douglas P	(928)302-9297 dpbock@gmail.com	13024 SE 91st Ct Summerfield FL 34491	FG	EM			CQ	1994
Bock Gordon E	(320)563-4522 ruthbock@yahoo.com	607 11th St N Wheaton MN 56296	MNN	EM			SPR	1973
Bockelmann Neil M	(979)777-4432 nsbock50@gmail.com	311 Brookside Dr E Bryan TX 77801	TX	EM			SL	1972
Bocklage Stephen F	(434)594-8512 stannabock@gmail.com	842 E Wheel Rd Bel Air MD 21015	S	EM			SL	2005
Bode Gerhard H Jr Dr	(314) 505-7931 bodeg@csl.edu	3372 Whitsetts Fork Rd Glencoe MO 63038	MO	S HS/C	Concordia Seminary Saint Louis MO	(314)505-7000	SL	1995
Bode Grant T	(507)766-6483 rev.bode@newulmtel.net	57034 Brookview Ln New Ulm MN 56073	MNN	SP	St Stephens* Braham MN	(320)396-3103	FW	1994
Bode Gerhard H Sr	(320)587-7929 gerhardhbode@gmail.com	22543 Unit Ave Hutchinson MN 55350	MNS	EM			SPR	1966
Bode David A	(218)346-6409 boswell@arvig.net	43650 Boedigheimer Dr N Perham MN 56573	MNN	EM			SL	1963
Bode Christian D	(585)964-2550 pastorchris_@hotmail.com	446 Curtis Rd Hilton NY 14468	EA	SP	St John Hamlin NY	(585)964-2550	SL	1996
Bode Craig H	(772)353-1633 craig.bode@gmail.com	214 Brazillian Cir Port Saint Lucie FL 34952	FG	EM			FW	1980
Bode Edgar W	(719)576-3381 charis605@gmail.com	1264 Gumwood Dr Colorado Spgs CO 80906	RM	EM			SL	1968
Bodin Daniel E	(612)242-1743 pastordanbodin@gmail.com	819 7th St E West Fargo ND 58078	ND	Assoc	Beautiful Savior Fargo ND	(701)293-1047	SL	2016
Bodkins Michael D	(515)238-5446 bodkinsm@gmail.com	1518 5th Ave SW Altoona IA 50009	IW	SMP	St John* Audubon IA	(712)563-3333	SL-SMP	2010
Bodley Christopher R	(321)947-3433 christopherbodley8@gmail.com	31275 Broderick Dr Chesterfield MI 48051	MI	D Miss	Michigan District Ann Arbor MI	(888)225-2111	FW	1992
Bodling Kurt A	(301)751-8628 bodling@gmail.com	32 Pine Street Dillsburg PA 17019	AT	EM			SL	1980
Boeche Raymond W Dr	(402)770-8237 rayboeche@neb.rr.com	727 Marshall Ave Lincoln NE 68510	NEB	EM			CQ	2009
Boeck Thomas R	(501) 329-3854 pastortom@peaceconway.org	800 S Donaghey Conway AR 72034	MDS	SP	Peace Conway AR	(501)329-3854	SL	2021
Boeck Alan G	(608)742-8441 alanboeck@gmail.com	214 Highland Ave Portage WI 53901	SW	SP	St Luke Lyndon Station WI	(608)666-4091	FW	1981
Boedecker David E	(269)275-8500 davidboedecker@gmail.com	2018 Clark Drive Washington MO 63090	MO	EM			SL	1979
Boeder Royal E	(618)340-9911 royal.boeder@yahoo.com	1127 Franklin Maeystown IL 62256	SI	EM			SL	1989
Boegl Sigmund W	(360)275-0877 sboegl@q.com	9105 Fortuna Dr Apt 8419 Mercer Island WA 98040	NOW	EM			SL	1958
Boehler Robert A	(914)364-1618 pastor@stmarkslutheranyon-kers.org	27 Saint Marks Pl Yonkers NY 10704	AT	SP	St Mark Yonkers NY	(914)237-8199	FW	1984
Boehlke Craig R	(321)261-1749 craig.boehlke@gmail.com	508 Crest Hill Dr Fountain Inn SC 29644	SE	EM			SL	1990
Boehme Armand J Dr	(507)301-5299 armandboehme@yahoo.com	1106 Sunset Ct Northfield MN 55057	MNS	Assoc	Trinity Northfield MN	(507)645-4438	SPR	1974
Boehne Jonathan P	(309) 361-7578 jonboehne@hotmail.com	595 W 3rd St El Paso IL 61738	CI	SP	Trinity El Paso IL	(309)527-4333	FW	2006
Boehnke Christopher M	(616)843-6128 cboehnke@lakeshorefellowship.com	13477 Ravine View Dr Grand Haven MI 49417	MI	SP	Lakeshore Spring Lake MI	(616)846-8556	SL	2000
Boehnke David A	(970) 988-3454 dab.well@gmail.com	2578 Rainbow Dr Casper WY 82604	WY	EM			SL	1968
Boehnke Richard A	(218)346-4666 r.g.boehnke@gmail.com	202 Mark Dr Ortonville MN 56278	MNN	EM			SL	1965

*Multiple Assignments (See Church Worker Locator for Additional Details)
See Page 53 for the Table of Abbreviations for key to District, Position, and Seminary abbreviations
**C =Candidate; EM = Emeritus; the date following the C is the month and year the Candidate status began

NAME	TELEPHONE NUMBER EMAIL	STREET ADDRESS CITY/STATE/ZIP	DISTRICT	POSITION/ STATUS**	WHERE SERVING	OFFICE PHONE	SEM/ PROGRAM	YR GRAD
Boelte Ronald E	(580)846-5794 ronaldboelte@yahoo.com	P.O. Box 444 Hobart OK 73651	OK	EM			CQ	2005
Boelter Randy S	rsboelter@christthekinggp.org	4717 Avila Lakes Dr Wimauma FL 33598	EN	EM			SL	1983
Boerger Charles P	(210)259-6598 carlosboerger@gmail.com	2627 Sally Gay Dr San Antonio TX 78223	TX	EM			FW	1977
Boerger Timothy M	(203)415-7943 timboerger@sbcglobal.net	1004 South Main St Mount Airy MD 21771	SE	SP	Good Shepherd Olney MD	(301)774-9125	CQ	2009
Boerger Gerald L	(806)292-0139 geraldboerger@gmail.com	201 Cedarcrest Ln Double Oak TX 75077	TX	EM			FW	1977
Boerger Paul M	(989)351-0495 pbbrrgrr@gmail.com	793 N Bradley Hwy Rogers City MI 49779	MI	SP	St Michael Rogers City MI	(989)734-3007	SL	1979
Boernke Dean H	(303)514-8963 boernkezion@gmail.com	221 S 22nd Ave Brighton CO 80601	RM	EM			SPR	1973
Boerst Aaron B	(262)347-6971 pastoraaron@bethlehemfamily.org	450 N Oak Crest Drive Wales WI 53183	SW	SP	Bethlehem Wales WI	(262)968-2194	SL	2013
Boeschen Donald E	(515) 339-9156 dsboeschen@msn.com	6817 Aubrey Ct Johnston IA 50131	IW	EM			SL	1968
Boessling Jacob A	(480)747-3280 jnboessling@gmail.com	1509 Deering Run Leander TX 78641	TX	D Miss	Texas District Round Rock TX	(800)951-3478	Other	2017
Boester Ethan M	(618) 314-0808 pastorboester@stjames-lutheran. org	3040 N Kilbourn Ave Chicago IL 60641	NI	Assoc	Saint James Chicago IL	(773)549-1615	SL	2025
Boetcher Jason D	(321)591-7045 enoch34@yahoo.com	7545 McCormick Dr Shawnee KS 66227	KS	SP	Trinity Family Faith Basehor KS	(913)724-4441	SL	2004
Boetcher Kenneth F	boetcher.kenneth@yahoo.com	P.O. Box 5149 Spanaway WA 98387	NOW	EM			SL	1955
Boettcher Darold F	(303)366-1827 bvdpadre@msn.com	2101 S Garfield Ave Apt 429 Loveland CO 80537	RM	EM			SL	1961
Boettcher Dennis L	(920)316-2882 revdennisb@gmail.com	1530 Falcon Way Sheboygan FLS WI 53085	SW	EM			FW	1993
Boettcher Frederick N Dr	(262)783-6712 fritz0069@sbcglobal.net	N50w16326 Pin Oak Ct Menomonee FLS WI 53051	SW	EM			SL	1952
Boettcher Loren A	(573)339-0365	1419 N Clark St Cpe Girardeau MO 63701	MO	EM			SL	1958
Boettcher Mark A	(573)204-4700 pastormab5@gmail.com	490 State Highway F Jackson MO 63755	MO	SP	Immanuel Jackson MO	(573)204-4700	SL	1985
Bogardus Larry D	(714)932-7381 lbb.bogardus@gmail.com	37695 Townsville Ct Murrieta CA 92563	PSW	SP	Good Shepherd Sun City CA	(951)672-6675	CQ	1999
Bogda David W	(269)273-2700 bogdald@hotmail.com	13256 Spence Rd Three Rivers MI 49093	MI	EM			FW	1999
Boggs Chad U	boggs4x4@hotmail.com	711 S California St Tilden NE 68781	NEB	SP	St Matthew* Meadow Grove NE	(402)368-5690	SL	2010
Bogs Ronald A Dr	(832)515-4830 ronbogs58@gmail.com	1510 Anvil Dr Houston TX 77090	TX	Sn/Adm	St Matthew Westfield Houston TX	(281)443-2304	SL	1992
Boheim Keith D	(314) 277-2729 kdboh@aol.com	42 S Weston Ct Saint Charles MO 63303	MO	EM			SL	1979
Bohler Steven W	(218)289-2830 pastor.oslds@midconetwork.com	800 Washington Ave Crookston MN 56716	MNN	Sn/Adm	First English* Eldred MN	(218)281-1239	FW	1993
Bohlken Daniel C	(503)359-3585 pastordan611@gmail.com	3112 Mahonia Ct Forest Grove OR 97116	NOW	EM			SPR	1976
Bohlken Philip J	pbohlken64@comcast.net	209 Drummer Ln Knoxville TN 37924	MDS	EM			SL	1972
Bohlmann Timothy P	(540)471-4824 pastortb@bethanylcw.org		SE	SP	Bethany-Trinity Fishersville VA	(540)942-4361	SL	1992
Bohlmann Robert E	(765) 480-7975 rbsl67@usa.net	747 Montogomery Custer SD 57730	SD	EM			SL	1967
Bohlmann Gordon P	(540)256-2462 g_bohlmann08@comcast.net	312 Westminister Dr Fishersville VA 22939	SE	EM			SL	1964
Bohlmann Eric C	(503)867-5120 paprika.bohlmann@gmail.com	P.O. Box 329 Molalla OR 97038	NOW	SP	Shepherd Of Valley Corvallis OR	(541)753-2816	Other	2013
Bohlmann Matthew H	(314)960-9884 matthew.bohlmann210@gmail.com	1049 Tompkins St Saint Charles MO 63301	MO	Asst	Immanuel Saint Charles MO	(636)946-2656	SL	2020
Bohm Dale E	(512)253-6933 stjohnlincoln@yahoo.com	1012 Private Road 8012 Giddings TX 78942	TX	SP	St John Lincoln TX	(512)253-6350	SL	1989
Bohmer Glenn S	(712)209-1213 gsbohmer@gmail.com	915 3rd Ave N Estherville IA 51334	IW	EM			FW	1986
Bohn Daniel L	(920)341-2025 shepherdatzion@gmail.com	c/o Zion Lutheran Church 700 Main Street P.O. Box 220 Clyman WI 53016	SW	SP	Zion Clyman WI	(920)341-2025	FW	1987
Bohren Dennis M	(503)460-7733 dennis.bohren@comcast.net	2321 Timber Trail E Maplewood MN 55119	MNS	EM			FW	1984
Boisclair David R	(314)853-9904 clearwoodlouis@hotmail.com	14249 Oak Dr Desoto MO 63020	MO	Sn/Adm	Our Redeemer Overland MO	(314)427-3444	SL	1982
Bojens Donald L	(224)569-2698 bojensdon@comcast.net	13416 Cadence Dr Huntley IL 60142	NI	EM			CQ	1991
Bok Vern L	(216)374-2858 vern.bok@gmail.com	3223 Forest Overlook Dr Seven Hills OH 44131	OH	EM			SL	1971
Bokre Dawit A	(510)781-0317	c/o Good Shepherd Lutheran 166 W Harder Rd Hayward CA 94544	CNH	Sn/Adm	Good Shepherd Hayward CA	(510)782-0872	SL	2016
Boldt Louis A	(985)956-1766 pastor@stpaulhammond.org	11143 Martin Ln Tickfaw LA 70466	SO	SP	St Paul Hammond LA	(985)345-6008	SL	2010
Boldt Gerald L	(281)460-7002 boldtl@hotmail.com	2378 Seahurst Ct League City TX 77573	TX	EM			CQ	1996
Bollhagen James G Dr	(407)593-1440 docbollhagen@gmail.com	2920 Elbib Dr Saint Cloud FL 34772	FG	EM			SL	1971

*Multiple Assignments (See Church Worker Locator for Additional Details)
See Page 53 for the Table of Abbreviations for key to District, Position, and Seminary abbreviations
**C =Candidate; EM = Emeritus; the date following the C is the month and year the Candidate status began

NAME	TELEPHONE NUMBER EMAIL	STREET ADDRESS CITY/STATE/ZIP	DISTRICT	POSITION/ STATUS**	WHERE SERVING	OFFICE PHONE	SEM/ PROGRAM	YR GRAD
Bollhagen Karl C	(641)456-4060 kjbollhagen@msn.com	816 2nd Avenue Dr SE Hampton IA 50441	IE	SP	Bethlehem* Mason City IA	(641)423-0438	FW	1998
Bolling Gerard I Dr	(347)257-7599 Pastor.Bolling@BethlehemStLouis.org	6974 Lindenwood Pl Saint Louis MO 63109	MO	Sn/Adm	Bethlehem Saint Louis MO	(314)231-4702	SL	2016
Bolling Robert W	(262)492-0965 r.bolling1@gmail.com	5625 Kinsale Dr Fitchburg WI 53711	SW	EM			FW	1981
Bollinger Timothy R	(586)731-4544 tim@sgatechurch.org	17733 Crystal River Dr Macomb MI 48042	MI	Sn/Adm	Shepherd's Gate Shelby Township MI	(586)731-4544	CQ	2011
Bolosan Chad R	(630)363-8221 revchadbolosan@yahoo.com	614 W 16th St Sterling IL 61081	NI	SP	Messiah Sterling IL	(815)625-2284	SL	2021
Bolstad Arthur C	(314)494-6269 tolonaro@gmail.com	801 Delwood Ct Arnold MO 63010	MO	C07/2016			FW	1981
Bolt Randy G	(719)671-4853 boltlutzl@juno.com	991 W Stallion Dr Pueblo West CO 81007	RM	EM			SL	1983
Bolte David J	djbolte@gmail.com	615 Fairway Dr Litchfield Park AZ 85340	PSW	Sn/Adm	Trinity Litchfield Park AZ	(623)935-4665	FW	1990
Bombaro John J Dr	(619) 987-5865 seniorpastor@stjameslaf.org	3600 Cedar Lane Lafayette IN 47905	IN	Sn/Adm	Saint James Lafayette IN	(765)423-1616	FW	2007
Bomberger Gary D	(352)263-2014 gbomberger@tampabay.rr.com	1536 Overland Dr Spring Hill FL 34608	FG	EM			SPR	1975
Bomberger Kenneth J	(616)485-0478 pastorbomberger@gmail.com	1109 Ferebee Ave Chesapeake VA 23324	MO	M Chap	Office of International Mission Saint Louis MO		FW	2008
Bond Dale A Sr	(417)861-7306 kodiak4272tango@gmail.com	504 Hightower St Nixa MO 65714	MO	EM			SL	1976
Bongard Stephen H	(219)921-3788 sbongard@ckhome.org	3473 Cambridge Ave Maplewood MO 63143	MO	Sn/Adm	Concordia Kirkwood MO	(314)822-7772	SL	1989
Bonine Russell D	russellbonine@gmail.com	323 Buell Ave Ravenna NE 68869	NEB	SP	Bethlehem Ravenna NE	(308)452-3685	FW	2009
Bonine Jonathan R	(701)389-9033 pastorbonine@mill-iron.com	8489 9th Ave NW Newburg ND 58762	ND	SP	Zion* Kramer ND	(701)359-4461	SL	2008
Bonk John C	(218)290-1144 loghome42@yahoo.com	P.O. Box 323 Two Harbors MN 55616	MNN	SP	Shep Of The Lake Two Harbors MN	(218)834-5345	SL	1987
Bontke Jonathan C	revbontke@msn.com	2504 Highland Haven Dr Austin TX 78725	TX	SP	Beautiful Savior Austin TX	(512)443-4947	SL	1997
Boodle Samuel M Sr	(242)323-4107 lutheranchurch@coralwave.com	P.O. Box N-4794 Nassau BAHAMAS	FG	SP	Nassau Nassau	(242)323-4107	FW	2000
Booe Phillip E Dr	(860)837-3188 pastorbooe@gmail.com	819 N Cedar St Luverne MN 56156	MNS	SP	St John Luverne MN	(507)283-2316	SL	2010
Booher Lucas W	(712)330-9977 pastorbooher@gmail.com	1727 555th St Storm Lake IA 50588	IW	SP	Zion Storm Lake IA	(712)732-5223	FW	2016
Booker Tony R	(720)317-0599 tonyrbooker@gmail.com	464 Putney Ln Newport News VA 23602	SE	EM			FW	2011
Bookshaw John A	(231)250-1971 jabookshaw@gmail.com	13701 New Millpond Rd Big Rapids MI 49307	MI	EM			SL	1982
Boomhower Patrick J	(630)656-3336 pittypat72@outlook.com	51 Wilshire Dr Frankenmuth MI 48734	MI	EM			FW	1993
Boone Arthur E	(215) 435-6417 booneart@comcast.net	3 Regency Ct Lehigh Acres FL 33936	FG	EM			SL	1984
Boone David K	(915)309-6610 kerry@crosspointelpaso.com	14601 Friesian Trl El Paso TX 79938	RM	SMP	CrossPoint El Paso TX	(915)857-7492	SL-SMP	2021
Boos Antonio C	(618)288-3700 Tony.Boos@lssliving.org	540 Susan Rd Saint Louis MO 63129	MO	Inst C	Lutheran Senior Services DBA EverTrue Brentwood MO	(314)968-9313	SL	2002
Boos Brandon J	(586)381-2832 brandonjboos@gmail.com	540 Susan Rd Saint Louis MO 63129	MO	SMP	Faith Oakville MO	(314)846-8612	SL-SMP	2022
Boos Werner K Dr	(303)973-0411 buddykb@mindspring.com	7364 W Walden Dr Littleton CO 80128	RM	EM			SL	1971
Booth Timothy D	(402)640-5115 ltbooth2@gmail.com	121 2nd St Westphalia KS 66093	KS	SP	St John Aliceville KS		FW	1991
Boothby Michael J	(712)278-2207 michael.boothby@gmail.com		IW	SP	St John* Ireton IA		SL	2009
Borchardt Edwin J	(218)535-0283 borchardted@gmail.com	P.O. Box 36 Hardwick MN 56134	MNS	SP	Zion Hardwick MN	(507)669-2855	SL-D	2003
Borchelt Ray L	(678)232-9931 praybor@juno.com	4305 Sandy Pointe Acworth GA 30101	FG	EM			CQ	1995
Borcher Alan D	(801)860-6412 pastor@holytrinityut.org	13249 S Redwood Rd Riverton UT 84065	RM	Sn/Adm	Holy Trinity Riverton UT	(801)860-6412	FW	2004
Borcherding Alan W	(314)505-7763 borcherdinga@csl.edu	1445 S 18th St Apt 210 Saint Louis MO 63104	MO	S HS/C	Concordia Seminary Saint Louis MO	(314)505-7000	SL	1982
Borcherding Kyle D	(317)987-6553 kyle.borcherding@gmail.com	108 Golden Bear Dr Georgetown TX 78628	TX	SMP	Zion Georgetown TX	(512)863-3065	SL-SMP	2020
Borchers Dennis R	(260)485-9265 dborchers7353@gmail.com	5208 Blum Dr Fort Wayne IN 46835	IN	EM			SPR	1973
Borchers Eric E	(512)836-9600 pastor.borchers@oslaustin.org	3613 Del Payne Ln Pflugerville TX 78660	TX	SP	Our Savior Austin TX	(512)836-9600	SL	2007
Borchert Mark J	(314)885-6736 Mark.Borchert@ConcordiaPlans.org	11 Wheeler Ct Saint Charles MO 63303	MO	Pro Stf	Concordia Plans Services Saint Louis MO	(314)965-7580	SL	2005
Borg Paul M	(317)727-0024 paul@paullutheran.com	5837 E 81st St Indianapolis IN 46250	IN	EM			CQ	2014
Borgelt Larry G	(715)559-4804 revlborgelt@gmail.com	14970 N 140th Ave Surprise AZ 85379	PSW	EM			FW	1980
Borger Bryan G	(574)255-5585	437 E Dragoon Trl Mishawaka IN 46544	IN	Assoc	St Peter Mishawaka IN	(574)255-5585	SL	1990

*Multiple Assignments (See Church Worker Locator for Additional Details)

See Page 53 for the Table of Abbreviations for key to District, Position, and Seminary abbreviations

**C =Candidate; EM = Emeritus; the date following the C is the month and year the Candidate status began

NAME	TELEPHONE NUMBER EMAIL	STREET ADDRESS CITY/STATE/ZIP	DISTRICT	POSITION/ STATUS**	WHERE SERVING	OFFICE PHONE	SEM/ PROGRAM	YR GRAD
Borges Adolfo	(407) 777-5119	2727 Lake Margaret Dr Orlando FL 32806	FG	Assoc	Prince Of Peace Orlando FL	(407)277-3945	CQ	2004
Borglum Kent A	(605)999-5591 kborglum5@gmail.com	4005 40th St SW Montevideo MN 56265	MNN	SP	Trinity* Montevideo MN	(605)999-5591	FW	2007
Borgstede Michael R	(303)667-1350 pastormike@stjohnnt.com	121 William St Tonawanda NY 14150	EA	SP	St John North Tonawanda NY	(716)693-9677	SL	1997
Borhart Glen W Dr	(815)568-6738	1915 Seminole Blvd Lot 8 Largo FL 33778	NI	EM			FW	1979
Boriack Mark L	(571)228-2671 mark.boriack@poplc.org	10822 Broadwater Dr Fairfax VA 22032	SE	SMP	Prince Of Peace Springfield VA	(703)451-5855	SL-SMP	2018
Boring Richard D	(402) 641-3014 rboring55@gmail.com	5870 N 21st St Lincoln NE 68521	NEB	EM			SL	1993
Borkenhagen Daniel G	(214)440-7512 danborkenhagen@yahoo.com	636 12th St SE Owatonna MN 55060	MNS	Assoc	Good Shepherd Owatonna MN	(507)451-4125	SL	2006
Borntrager Phillip A	(951)306-2355 phillip.borntrager@gmail.com	101 Rainbow Dr PMB 5867 Livingston TX 77399	TX	EM			FW	2011
Borrasso Matthew E Dr	(630)725-8025 pastor@trinitylutheranlp.org	46707 S. Shangri-La Dr. Lexington Park MD 20653	SE	SP	Trinity Lexington Park MD	(301)863-9512	SL	2014
Borst Steven B	(714)742-9524 steven.borst@immanuelriverside. com	1133 Brasado Way Riverside CA 92508	PSW	Sn/Adm	Immanuel Riverside CA	(951)682-7613	SL	1992
Bose Kenneth A	(515)465-5447 kenbose@gmail.com	103 S Maple St Jefferson IA 50129	IW	SP	Trinity Perry IA	(515)465-3272	SL	2012
Boshoven Richard L	(219)669-0877 pastorbosh@gmail.com	1007 Falkirk Rd Alma MI 48801	MI	SP	St Paul Caro MI	(989)673-4214	SL	2000
Bossard Gerald E Dr	(256) 783-9125 mjbossard@aol.com	22610 Forrester Ln Glenwood IA 51534	IW	EM			FW	1999
Bostelman Kermit C	(936)870-5636 kermitb59@gmail.com	740 Planer Mill Rd Deridder LA 70634	SO	SP	Trinity* Leesville LA	(337)239-2457	FW	2012
Bostelmann Wallace L	(901)603-9448 wjbost@bellsouth.net	340 W Chulahoma Ave Holly Springs MS 38635	SO	SMP	Zion Holly Springs MS	(662)252-4513	CQ	2019
Boster Kory B	(918)208-9425 kboster@sbcglobal.net	32814 Waterfowl Dr Fulshear TX 77441	TX	SP	Christ Brookshire TX	(281)934-8218	SL	2003
Bostwick Eugene	(240) 412-5936 pastor@peacekg.com	14092 Beverly Dr Hughesville MD 20637	SE	SMP	Peace King George VA	(540)775-9131	SL-SMP	2025
Both Matthew W	(206)669-3195 pastormatthew@king-of-kings.org	18207 108th Ave SE Renton WA 98055	NOW	C06/2025			SL	2009
Bothwell James R	(415)488-9848 pjrbothwell@gmail.com	P.O. Box 174 San Geronimo CA 94963	CNH	EM			FW	1983
Bott David C	(307)733-6629 dcbott@charter.net	P.O. Box 1624 Jackson WY 83001	WY	SP	Christ Our Savior* Nordic Ranches WY	(307)690-8697	FW	2003
Bottoms Dennis W	(856)341-0548 denniswbottoms@gmail.com	246 Cedar Rd Mullica Hill NJ 08062	NJ	EM			SPR	1972
Bottorff David M	(815)304-4553	1573 Surrey Dr Bourbonnais IL 60914	NI	EM			SL	1979
Boudreau Kenneth J	(612)380-5417 pastor@hopeofhastings.com	4181 Starling Dr Hastings MN 55033	EN	SP	Hope Hastings MN	(651)480-2273	SL	2007
Bourret Ted A	(308)249-5262 luther2@vistabeam.com	4470 Road 89 Potter NE 69156	WY	EM			FW	2001
Bowder Russell E Jr	(573)645-4629 rbowder@icloud.com	1837 Hawk Pointe Dr. Festus MO 63028	MO	EM			SL	2000
Bowditch Mark A Dr	mark.bowditch@gmail.com	879 W M-20 Highway New Era MI 49446	MI	C11/2023			FW	1990
Bowen Gregg W	deanochado@yahoo.com	2026 Thornwood Cir St Charles IL 60174	NI	C07/2016			SL	1989
Bowes James F	(951)553-8500 pastorjamesbowes@gmail.com	39928 Candy Apple Way Murrieta CA 92562	EN	SP	Peace/Desert Palm Desert CA	(760)776-7100	SL	2023
Bowes Brian	(509)429-1567 deacon@ncidata.com	P.O. Box 214 Okanogan WA 98840	NOW	SP	Hope* Tonasket WA	(509)486-2254	CQ	2015
Bowlds John B	bradbowlds@gmail.com	3314 Snaffle Rd Lexington KY 40513	IN	C07/2016			SL	1997
Bowman Keith E Jr	rev.aggie.98@gmail.com	P.O. Box 505 Centerville TX 75833	TX	SP	Our Savior Centerville TX	(903)536-2019	SL	2005
Bowman Gary V	(404)557-9541 garybowman42@yahoo.com	251 Asa Mosely Rd Stockbridge GA 30281	FG	SP	Trinity Albany GA	(229)436-5272	CQ	2024
Boxman Mark D	(620)441-8342 markdboxman@gmail.com	435 Claremont Dr Salina KS 67401	KS	Sn/Adm	Trinity Salina KS	(785)823-7151	FW	1987
Boyce Bruce A	(319)332-1303 bruceaboyce@gmail.com	413 12th Ave NW Independence IA 50644	IE	EM			FW	1988
Boyd David A	(760)822-7712 revdboyd50@msn.com	5807 S Florence Ave Tulsa OK 74105	SE	EM			SL	1991
Boyd Michael B	revmbboyd@gmail.com	2614 Pinehurst Ct New Albany IN 47150	IN	EM			FW	1997
Boyd Richard A	(850)566-3553		FG	EM			CQ	2018
Boye Gary P	(480)252-4821 pastorboye@cox.net	7225 Promise Land Rd Mountain Home AR 72653	FG	SP	Trinity Delray Beach FL	(561)278-1737	SL	1976
Boye Lawrence C	larryboye@hotmail.com	1133 Meadowbrook Ln Manhattan KS 66503	KS	EM			SL	1972
Boyer Brad H	pastorboyer@gmail.com	812 E Lake Rd Lawton OK 73507	NEB	M Chap	Office of International Mission Saint Louis MO		SL	2003
Boyer Michael D	(989)640-0231 mboyer@ilcmi.org	816 E Bay St Sebewaing MI 48759	MI	Sn/Adm	Immanuel Sebewaing MI	(989)883-3050	FW	2007
Boykin Doyle W	(505)681-4408 doyle.boykin@icloud.com	61 Berta Dr Edgewood NM 87015	RM	SMP	Prince Of Peace Cedar Crest NM	(505)596-6142	SL-SMP	2015

*Multiple Assignments (See Church Worker Locator for Additional Details)
See Page 53 for the Table of Abbreviations for key to District, Position, and Seminary abbreviations
**C =Candidate; EM = Emeritus; the date following the C is the month and year the Candidate status began

NAME	TELEPHONE NUMBER EMAIL	STREET ADDRESS CITY/STATE/ZIP	DISTRICT	POSITION/ STATUS**	WHERE SERVING	OFFICE PHONE	SEM/ PROGRAM	YR GRAD
Boykin Michael C Dr	(205)246-1751 scipio18@pm.me	3914 38th Ave Northport AL 35473	SO	EM			FW	1983
Boylan Shawn V	(217)379-7443 pastorshawn@boylansweb.net	472 E Summer St Paxton IL 60957	CI	EM			SL	2001
Boyle Geoffrey R Dr	geoffrey.boyle@ctsfw.edu	3770 Kirkwood Dr Fort Wayne IN 46805	IN	S HS/C	Concordia Theological Seminary Fort Wayne IN	(260)452-2100	FW	2009
Boymah William Y	(610)241-6532		EA	SP	Christ Assembly Philadelphia PA	(610)241-6532	CQ	2015
Bozarth James S	(478) 919-7300	526 Madison Ave Blackwell OK 74631	OK	SP	Trinity Blackwell OK	(580)363-4026	SL	2023
Braaten Jason M	(217)460-2077 pastor.braaten@gmail.com	706 E Northline Rd Tuscola IL 61953	CI	SP	Immanuel Tuscola IL	(217)253-4341	FW	2006
Braband Charles A	(410)482-2802 brabands@verizon.net	25884 Spring Branch Dr Greensboro MD 21639	SE	EM			SL	1971
Brackman Matthew S	(409)789-5869 mbintexas@gmail.com	8001 Larkspur Dr Texas City TX 77591	TX	SP	Peace Texas City TX	(409)938-1277	FW	2003
Brademeyer Christopher W	(701)742-2595 cbrademeyer@gmail.com	109 S 10th St Oakes ND 58474	ND	SP	St Johns Oakes ND	(701)742-2595	CQ	2017
Braden Mark P	(313)894-7450 frbraden@ziondetroit.onmicrosoft.com	24942 Newton St Dearborn MI 48124	EN	Sn/Adm	Zion Detroit MI	(313)894-7450	FW	2003
Bradley Richard E Dr	(727)599-9619 bookearth@aol.com	2013 Nantucket Dr Sun City Center FL 33573	FG	EM			FW	1981
Bradshaw Dennis N	(805) 444-8687 pastordennis@centrocristianohispano.com	1200 Maria Way Oxnard CA 93030	PSW	EM			SL	1983
Brady Charles N	(323)636-3510 cnbrady007@aol.com	8145 San Miguel Ave South Gate CA 90280	PSW	EM			FW	1978
Bragdon Dennis J	(979)966-2242 djb75601@gmail.com	4706 Via Verde Way Bryan TX 77807	TX	EM			SL	1982
Brakhage Joshua	(918) 706-1632 joshua411@gmail.com	308 NW 164th St Edmond OK 73013	OK	Assoc	Holy Trinity Edmond OK	(405)348-3292	SL	2020
Bramich Christopher J	(817)439-2100 cb2890@att.net	1500 Fm 156 S Haslet TX 76052	TX	SP	Holy Shepherd Haslet TX	(817)439-2100	SL	1999
Brammeier Arnold H	(313)885-7923 abrammeier@aol.com	4141 Audubon Rd Detroit MI 48224	MI	EM			SL	1965
Brammeier Daniel G	(813)330-6569 danielbrammeier@gmail.com	8067 Whitney Ct Canton GA 30115	FG	SP	Timothy Woodstock GA	(770)928-2812	FW	1994
Brammeier James E	(515)276-3571 jebrammeier@msn.com	6814 Jules Verne Ct Johnston IA 50131	IW	EM			SL	1968
Bramstadt Allen H	(920)923-1532 ahbramstadt@att.net	1081 Prospect Ave N Fond Du Lac WI 54937	SW	SP	Divine Savior North Fond Du Lac WI	(920)923-1532	SL	1997
Bramstedt Terrill F	(507)696-3566 tbramstedt@icloud.com	104 Acorn Avenue NW New London MN 56273	MNN	EM			SL	1973
Bramwell Tyrel E	(707)382-7548 rev.ty.bramwell@gmail.com	P.O. Box 1016 Ferndale CA 95536	EN	SP	St Mark Ferndale CA	(707)786-9353	FW	2014
Brand Donald L	(610)438-1205 pastorchap2222@yahoo.com	657 Rosecliff Dr Easton PA 18040	NJ	EM			FW	1977
Brand Timothy J	(231)360-4493 pastorbrand@att.net	P.O. Box 348 Mayfield MI 49666	MI	SP	Trinity Conklin MI	(616)899-2167	FW	1996
Brandenburg Jonathan L Dr	(979)398-0216 jonpreach@yahoo.com	32338 Sea Raven Dr Rancho Palos Verdes CA 90275	PSW	SP	Christ Rancho Palos Verdes CA	(310)831-0848	SL	2007
Brandmahl Joshua J	(785)307-1381 joshuabrandmahl@gmail.com	566 S Main St Brillion WI 54110	SW	SP	Saint Bartholomew Brillion WI	(920)756-3031	FW	2022
Brandon Kurt A	pastorkurt14@gmail.com		MI	SP	Holy Cross Saginaw MI	(989)793-9723	SL	2014
Brandt Edward E	(208)901-0297 eebrandtfamily@gmail.com	934 W Creekbury St Meridian ID 83646	NOW	EM			SL	1994
Brandt Warren P	(573)645-1888 wbran64.ord85@gmail.com	609 Memory Ln Jefferson City MO 65101	MO	EM			FW	1985
Brandt Wade M	(515)290-7469 wade.brandt@gmail.com	1614 P Ave Clarinda IA 51632	IW	SP	Immanuel* Clarinda IA	(712)542-3283	SL	2012
Brandt Phillip L	(503) 358-8411 pbrandt@stmikeslutheran.org	4736 NE Holman St Portland OR 97218	NOW	SP	Saint Michael's Portland OR	(503)493-6333	SL	1991
Brandt Nathan M	(503)504-9587 nbrandt1980@gmail.com	4790 NW Anthony Pl Albany OR 97321	NOW	SP	All Nations Newport OR	(541)265-2503	SL	1980
Brandt Mark D	(989)284-5619 mbrandt14@gmail.com	9042 Tuscola Frankenmuth MI 48734	MI	D Ex/S	Michigan District Ann Arbor MI	(888)225-2111	SL	1980
Brandt Joel T	(608)999-0631 brandtj@crosslutheran.church	800 Lochmoore Dr Waunakee WI 53597	SW	SP	Cross Westport WI	(608)827-9600	SL	2008
Brandt Dwaine T	(509)991-1447 cavaliertim@gmail.com	22016 Airport Road NE Aurora OR 97002	NOW	EM			SL	1991
Brandt David T	(641)236-3688 revdtb@gmail.com	819 9th Ave Grinnell IA 50112	IE	EM			SL	1982
Brandt Christopher A	(307)431-2222 rockingck800@gmail.com	11 Rolys Rd Roberts MT 59070	MT	EM			SL	1981
Brandt Charles E	(608)630-5511 brandtc@crosslutheran.church	261 White Tail Dr Sun Prairie WI 53590	SW	EM			FW	1980
Brandt Gary R	(580)421-8108 garybrandt49@gmail.com	P.O. Box 823 Lake Ozark MO 65049	MO	EM			SL	1995
Brandvold Joel L	(701)244-9746 joel.brandvold@k12.nd.us	604 Wilderness Loop Saint John ND 58369	ND	SP	Trinity Tolley ND	(701)386-2246	FW	1988
Brann Johannes W	(417)321-5564	813 N Ash St Nevada MO 64772	MO	SP	Trinity Nevada MO	(417)667-5676	CQ	1994

*Multiple Assignments (See Church Worker Locator for Additional Details)
See Page 53 for the Table of Abbreviations for key to District, Position, and Seminary abbreviations
**C =Candidate; EM = Emeritus; the date following the C is the month and year the Candidate status began

NAME	TELEPHONE NUMBER EMAIL	STREET ADDRESS CITY/STATE/ZIP	DISTRICT	POSITION/ STATUS**	WHERE SERVING	OFFICE PHONE	SEM/ PROGRAM	YR GRAD
Brase Mark H	(641)919-5457 revilcms02@gmail.com	32105 232nd St Garnavillo IA 52049	IE	EM			FW	2002
Brashier Forrest E Jr	(205)296-3714 shepherdsheartministry@yahoo.com	8895 Stouts Rd Kimberly AL 35091	SO	Assoc	Good Shepherd Gardendale AL	(205)631-6590	FW	2002
Brassfield Joel M	(920) 246-2587 jm.brassfield@gmail.com	2322 Jackson St Two Rivers WI 54241	SW	Sn/Adm	Good Shepherd Two Rivers WI	(920)793-1716	FW	2012
Brath William A	(321) 287-7742 billybrath@gmail.com	235 W 56th St Apt 12e New York NY 10019	FG	Pro Stf	Lutheran Church Extension Fund Saint Louis MO	(314)965-9000	SL	2009
Brauer James L Dr	(314)755-1825 jlbrauer@aol.com	757 Eckrich Pl Saint Louis MO 63119	MO	EM			SL	1964
Brauer Martin J Dr	(512)789-8374 dr.martybrauer@gmail.com	197 Left Fork Dr Kyle TX 78640	TX	EM			SL	1994
Brauer Ronald A	brauerra@yahoo.com	1513 L St La Porte IN 46350	IN	EM			FW	2002
Braun Benjamin A	(512)709-1730 benjamin.braun82@gmail.com	9208 E 76th Pl Tulsa OK 74133	OK	SP	Immanuel Broken Arrow OK	(918)258-5506	SL	2012
Braun Wayne M Dr	(713)903-6316 pastorbraun58@gmail.com		TX	EM			SL	1984
Braun Timothy P	(515)979-5740 pastorbraun@hopelutheran-dsm.org	1114 Sandalwood Ct SW Altoona IA 50009	IW	Sn/Adm	Hope Des Moines IA	(515)265-2057	FW	1982
Braun Thomas P	(520)638-7881 t.braun@alcs-az.org	187 E Woolystar Ct Oro Valley AZ 85755	EN	Sn/Adm	Ascension Tucson AZ	(520)297-3095	FW	1982
Braun Allen L	(660)668-9981 mthuldapastor@gmail.com	22303 Mt Hulda Ave Cole Camp MO 65325	MO	SP	Mount Hulda Cole Camp MO	(660)668-9981	SL	2000
Braun Alan J	(651)483-3157 alrosiebraun@gmail.com	2975 Highpointe Curv Roseville MN 55113	MNS	EM			SL	1968
Braun Steven M	(863) 293-8447 sbraun@glwh.org		FG		Florida-Georgia District Orlando FL	(407)857-5556	FW	2019
Brauner Douglas P	(719)822-0830 dougbrauner@yahoo.com	8360 Avens Cir Colorado Spgs CO 80920	RM	EM			SL	1982
Braunersreuther Jon M Dr	(314)471-1072 jon.braunersreuther@txlcms.org	23334 E Pine Ivy Ln Tomball TX 77375	TX	DP	Texas District Round Rock TX	(800)951-3478	SL	1989
Bray Mark C	(214) 326-6264 mcbray03@gmail.com	1727 Boxwood Ln Wylie TX 75098	TX	SMP	Our Savior McKinney TX	(972)562-9944	SL-SMP	2021
Brazeal John	(773)536-1984	3701 S Lake Park Ave Chicago IL 60653	NI	SP	Christ King Chicago IL	(773)536-1984	CQ	1994
Brazinsky Thomas R	(616)915-5723 ptbrazinsky@yahoo.com	232 Plum Ln Coopersville MI 49404	MI	EM			CQ	1985
Breach Michael E	(641)344-2158 breachbunch@gmail.com	404 10th St N Wheaton MN 56296	MNN	EM			FW	1992
Brech Dennis E	(507)763-3699 djbrech@gmail.com	32 N Foreman Rd Currie MN 56123	MNS	EM			SPR	1973
Brechbuhl Peter R	(217)245-0289 pbrechbuhl3@gmail.com	80 Alice Dr Jacksonville IL 62650	CI	EM			SL	1984
Bredeson Jason J	(916)456-8701 revbred@gmail.com	1500 27th St Sacramento CA 95816	CNH	SP	Trinity Sacramento CA	(916)456-8701	SL	2006
Brege Daniel J Dr	(260)547-4256 djbrege@hotmail.com	8369 N 300 W Decatur IN 46733	IN	Assoc	St Paul Decatur IN	(260)547-4176	FW	1982
Brehmer Steven J	(509)276-9575 sbrehmer9575@msn.com	214 S Weber Rd Deer Park WA 99006	NOW	SP	Faith Deer Park WA	(509)276-5268	SL	1999
Brei Jamie S	(715)574-8696 jsbrei@gmail.com	803 N 29th Ave Wausau WI 54401	NW	C07/2016			CQ	2005
Breight Ronald M	(412)926-7811 pastor@christlutheranth.org	400 Barclay Ave Pittsburgh PA 15221	EA	SP	Trinity Deaf* Pittsburgh PA	(412)727-7632	SL	1990
Breitbarth Marcus A		325 Courthouse Rd Stafford VA 22554	SE	SP	Living Hope Stafford VA	(540)657-4105	SL	2011
Breitbarth Steven E	(218)440-1005 s.breitbarth@mchsi.com	3535 7th Ave E Hibbing MN 55746	MNN	EM			FW	1980
Breitbarth Robert C	(219)661-1726 resurrectionlutheranchurch@usa.net	3634 Saint Andrews Ct Crown Point IN 46307	S	EM			FW	1980
Breite Douglas C	(573)576-0764 dcb@t-lutheran.org	2127 Derbyshire Ln Cape Girardeau MO 63701	MO	Sn/Adm	Trinity Cape Girardeau MO	(573)335-8224	SL	1988
Brelje Larry E	(269)375-8223 lkbrelje@sbcglobal.net	6387 Saybrook Dr Kalamazoo MI 49009	MI	EM			SL	1960
Bremer Daniel G	(308)382-1190	545 Memorial Dr Grand Island NE 68801	NEB	Sn/Adm	Grace Grand Island NE	(308)382-1190	SL	1984
Bremer Nolan R	(503)281-2026	6315 NE 27th Ave Portland OR 97211	NOW	EM			SL	1964
Bremseth Richard L	(507)236-7165 rickbremseth@gmail.com	213 7th St N Mountain Lake MN 56159	MNS	SP	Trinity* Alpha MN	(507)639-5645	SL	2002
Bren Donald J	(406) 535-3654 brenranch@midrivers.com	1104 W Main St Lewistown MT 59457	MT	EM			SPR	1965
Brenner Donald J Dr	(619)596-0750 djbrenner@cox.net	2363 Grafton St El Cajon CA 92020	PSW	EM			SL	1966
Brenner Karl A	brenner3@sbcglobal.net	17432 Battles Rd South Bend IN 46614	IN	EM			SL	1969
Brese Erwin A Jr Dr	(716)297-5764 Erv.brese@gmail.com	8366 Ziblut Ct Niagara Falls NY 14304	EA	EM			SL	1961
Bresson Chad R	(937)974-7818 chad@thetableoflf.org	111 E 7th St Los Fresnos TX 78566	TX	SMP	Table of Los Fresnos Los Fresnos TX	(956)254-0294	SL-SMP	2021
Bretscher David J	(314)729-0310 breachbabe@yahoo.com	7231 General Sherman Ln Saint Louis MO 63123	MO	EM			SL	1992

*Multiple Assignments (See Church Worker Locator for Additional Details)

See Page 53 for the Table of Abbreviations for key to District, Position, and Seminary abbreviations

**C =Candidate; EM = Emeritus; the date following the C is the month and year the Candidate status began

NAME	TELEPHONE NUMBER EMAIL	STREET ADDRESS CITY/STATE/ZIP	DISTRICT	POSITION/ STATUS**	WHERE SERVING	OFFICE PHONE	SEM/ PROGRAM	YR GRAD
Bretthauer James A II	(830)285-1196 James.Bretthauer@ctx.edu	17423 Aspen Oak Court Spring TX 77379	TX	SMP	Trinity Klein Klein TX	(281)376-5773	SL-SMP	2022
Breudigam Bruce C	(330)345-5673 bhbreud@sssnet.com	2552 Fox Lake Rd Wooster OH 44691	OH	C07/2016			FW	1994
Brewer Carl A III	(920)536-1041 pastorbrewer@stjohnlux.com	N5578 Henry Ct Luxemburg WI 54217	NW	Sn/Adm	St John Luxemburg WI	(920)845-5250	SL	2005
Brewer Thomas R	(913)248-1497 ptombrewer@aol.com	5010 Widmer Rd Shawnee KS 66216	KS	EM			SL	2002
Brezina David E	(781) 258-0087 davidb027@gmail.com	9 Atwood St Wakefield MA 01880	NE	SMP	Messiah Lynnfield MA	(781)334-4111	SL-SMP	2012
Breznen Jack	203-966-3070 revjbrez@optonline.net	148 Farm Rd New Canaan CT 06840	S	EM			SPR	1976
Bridgman Richard A	(217)685-3153 rab1865@yahoo.com	933b E. Windfield Place Appleton WI 54911	NW	Assoc	Faith Appleton WI	(920)739-9191	SL	2019
Briel Steven C Dr	(763)213-7959 scbriel49@gmail.com	17425 83rd Ave N Maple Grove MN 55311	MNS	Asst	St John's Corcoran MN	(763)420-2426	SPR	1975
Briggs Robert T	(314)972-1784 revbobbriggs@msn.com	3745 Seville Dr Florissant MO 63033	MO	Inst C	Lutheran Senior Services DBA EverTrue Brentwood MO	(314)968-9313	SL	2004
Brighton Mark A	(949)584-8176 mark.brighton@cui.edu	13 Elderwood Irvine CA 92614	PSW	EM			SL	1986
Brimer William R	(940)453-4393 bill@soulthirstchurch.com	3942 Navarro Way Frisco TX 75034	TX	SMP	SoulThirst The Colony TX	(469)353-8655	SL-SMP	2014
Brindle Murray W	(570)240-1520 brindle.murray@gmail.com	3258 Buckland St Deltona FL 32738	FG	EM			CQ	1991
Bringewatt Richard P	richbring2006@yahoo.com	3305 Piney Creek Dr. Elkhorn NE 68022	NEB	EM			SL	1986
Brink Paul W Dr	(702)539-1576 bo.brink18@gmail.com	10010 San Gervasio Ave Las Vegas NV 89147	PSW	EM			FW	1978
Brink Wilbur F	(402)316-7076 pastorbrink@oursav.org	2615 Crestview Rd Norfolk NE 68701	NEB	EM			CQ	1994
Brinkley Thomas J	(218)343-2080 brinkley57@yahoo.com	3214 Bobs Dr Cloquet MN 55720	MNN	EM			FW	1996
Brinkley Weldon D	(662)719-2998 wbrinkley1@gmail.com	775 Gulf Shore Dr Unit 9119 Destin FL 32541	SO	EM			CQ	1994
Brinkley David R	(980)229-5921 davidrushbrinkley@gmail.com	919 Elwick Pl Murrells Inlet SC 29576	PSW	EM			CQ	1999
Brinkman Bruce A	(239)699-4576 bruceabrinkman@yahoo.com	500 Heritage Ct Apt 118 Waite Park MN 56387	FG	EM			SL	1966
Brinkman Paul R	(920)731-2729 brinksjp@jbcglobal.net	4809 N Gardenwood Ln Appleton WI 54913	NW	EM			SL	1967
Brinkmann Wayne O	(309)229-4056 revwbwb@gmail.com	1506 Brookcrest Ave Morton IL 61550	CI	EM			SL	1973
Brinkmeyer David A	revbrinkmeyer@yahoo.com	9540 W Panama Rd Hallam NE 68368	NEB	C08/2016			SL	2004
Brinkmeyer Arthur	(402)641-9855 revart@diodecom.net	9540 W Panama Rd Hallam NE 68368	NEB	EM			CQ	1978
Brisbois Timothy R	trbrisbois@gmail.com	1110 N 17th St Beatrice NE 68310	NEB	EM			FW	1990
Bristol Edward M	765-361-1681 jeanandmike@virtualbristol.net	6723 S. Anthony Blvd. Apt E420 Ft. Wayne IN 46816	IN	EM			SPR	1970
Britton Joshua D	(989)395-3922 jshbritton@gmail.com	17950 Red Oaks Dr Macomb MI 48044	MI	SMP	Trinity Utica MI	(586)731-4490	SL-SMP	2024
Broaddus Daniel S	pastorbroaddus@gmail.com	1413 Nebraska St Mound City MO 64470	MO	SP	Holy Trinity Mound City MO	(660)442-1029	FW	2018
Broadwell Alan L	(507)528-2643 sjlcpastor@frontiernet.net	4489 SE 84th Ave Claremont MN 55924	MNS	SP	St John Claremont MN	(507)528-2404	FW	2005
Brock Peter J	(260)301-1640 pastorbrock@gmail.com	11741 N 350 W Decatur IN 46733	IN	Sn/Adm	St John Decatur IN	(260)639-6178	FW	2010
Brockhoff David D Dr	(352)796-4066 htpastor@tampabay.rr.com	4516 Lake In The Woods Dr Spring Hill FL 34607	FG	SP	Holy Trinity Masaryktown FL	(352)796-4066	SL	1985
Brockhoff Mark J	(847)895-0088 kwelectric@aol.com	1038 Carpenter Ct Elk Grove Village IL 60007	NI	EM			SL	1982
Brockhouse David A	(210) 216-1114 dbhouse47@att.net	330 Threadneedle Ln San Antonio TX 78227	TX	Sn/Adm	Mount Olive San Antonio TX	(210)675-6394	SL	2012
Brockman Wayne R	(510)237-9432 wayne9363@att.net	5838 N Arlington Blvd San Pablo CA 94806	CNH	EM			SL	1973
Brockman Justin J	(920)716-4761 brockmanjustin71@gmail.com	502 Hammen Ct Kaukauna WI 54130	NW	C11/2024			SL	2024
Brockman Michael C	(316)249-3377 fathermichaelc@gmail.com	5416 N Saint Paul St Wichita KS 67204	KS	Cmp P	Concordia Academy Wichita KS	(316)202-8989	FW	1984
Brockmann James E	(602)684-8678 azrevjeb@cox.net	2152 N Stockton Pl Mesa AZ 85215	PSW	EM			SL	1959
Broecker Mark F	(847)328-3115 pastorbroecker@aol.com	1406 Wilder St Evanston IL 60202	NI	SP	Bethlehem Evanston IL	(847)328-9454	SL	1972
Broge Jason E Dr	(314)629-2022 jason.broge@lhm.org	25 Heather Dr Saint Louis MO 63123	MO	Aux	LLL/Lutheran Hour Ministries Saint Louis MO	(314)317-4100	SL	2010
Bromm Glen W	(989)329-5584 glenbromm@yahoo.com	P.O. Box 765 Prudenville MI 48651	MI	SMP	Our Savior* Glennie MI	(989)735-2710	CQ	2020
Brondos Joel A	(708)341-4819 jbrondos@gmail.com	234 Meadowbrook Ct Geneseo IL 61254	CI	EM			SL	1984
Brones Dana A	(904)859-3441 blcdana@bellsouth.net	2759 Canyon Falls Dr Jacksonville FL 32224	FG	Sn/Adm	Bethlehem Jacksonville Beach FL	(904)249-5418	SL	1983
Bronner Michael A	(253)263-2687 mabronner@aol.com	581 Shiloh Overlook Hayesville NC 28904	SE	EM			CQ	1996

*Multiple Assignments (See Church Worker Locator for Additional Details)

See Page 53 for the Table of Abbreviations for key to District, Position, and Seminary abbreviations

**C =Candidate; EM = Emeritus; the date following the C is the month and year the Candidate status began

NAME	TELEPHONE NUMBER EMAIL	STREET ADDRESS CITY/STATE/ZIP	DISTRICT	POSITION/ STATUS**	WHERE SERVING	OFFICE PHONE	SEM/ PROGRAM	YR GRAD
Brons Ryan M			NEB	C10/2024			SL	2007
Brooks John W	(231)578-7024	660 N Wythe St Pentwater MI 49449	MI	EM			FW	1985
Brooks Patrick J	(734) 285-9695 pj@ctk.me	15600 Trenton Road Southgate MI 48195	MI	SMP	Christ The King Southgate MI	(734)285-9695	SL-SMP	2024
Brooks Micah J	(616)375-9498 pastorbrooks23@gmail.com	11261 South St Nunica MI 49448	MI	SP	St Luke Nunica MI	(616)837-6059	FW	2023
Brooks M T	(417) 251-0140 tomarty55@cox.net	7700 E 13th St N Unit 41 Wichita KS 67206	KS	EM			SL	1963
Brooks David H	(919) 682-6030 pr.dave.brooks@zoho.com	P.O. Box 37188 Raleigh NC 27627	SE	Sn/Adm	Grace Durham NC	(919)682-6030	CQ	2019
Brooks Corey S	(252) 820-4519	1307 Beverly Ave Odenton MD 21113	SE	SMP	First Odenton MD	(410)672-3352	SL-SMP	2016
Brooks Gary D	(623)226-8296 garydebrooks@gmail.com	10304 E Alpha Ave Mesa AZ 85212	PSW	EM			SPR	1975
Brooks Dana A	(208)459-4191 pastordbrooks@gmail.com	2811 Willow Falls Ave Caldwell ID 83605	NOW	EM			SL	1988
Brouwer Jack	(949)338-5953 jb@apep.uci.edu	24 Harvey Ct Irvine CA 92617	PSW	Assoc	Christ Costa Mesa CA	(949)631-1611	SL	2018
Brown Scott D	(309)231-4878 scottbrown315@gmail.com	5393 County Road 5 NW Alexandria MN 56308	MNN	SP	Ebenezer* Alexandria MN	(309)231-4878	SL	2020
Brown Luther C	(620)786-5001	P.O. Box 218 Ellsworth KS 67439	KS	SP	Immanuel Ellsworth KS	(785)472-4045	SL	2009
Brown Hayden A	(309)231-2183 hayden.august.brown@gmail.com	5393 County Rd 5nw Alexandria MN 56308	MNN	Assoc	Zion Alexandria MN	(320)763-4842	SL	2025
Brown Mark P	(585)524-7909 brownmp@agricolae.net	20454 N 90th Lane Peoria AZ 85382	PSW	SP	Mount Zion Peoria AZ	(623)825-9221	SL	2009
Brown Micah R	(309) 231-4897 mrbrown5462@gmail.com	22w340 Turner Ave. Roselle IL 60157	NI	Assoc	Immanuel Batavia IL	(630)879-7163	SL	2025
Brown Michael A	(847)382-7002 pastorbrown@stmatthew barrington.org	c/o Saint Matthews 720 Dundee Ave Barrington IL 60010	NI	Sn/Adm	St Matthew Barrington IL	(847)382-7002	SL	2009
Brown Robert M	(618)580-8817 Pastor.Brown@peacelutheranstl.org	324 Magoffin Trails Ct Saint Louis MO 63129	MO	Assoc	Peace Saint Louis County MO	(314)892-5610	SL	2020
Brown Thomas C Dr	(605)920-9625 tbrown80@gmail.com		SD	SP	St Paul Spearfish SD	(605)642-2929	FW	2010
Brown Timothy C	(636)744-9044 revtcbrown@att.net	16004 Magnolia Hill St Clermont FL 34714	FG	SP	Christ King Orlando FL	(407)876-2771	SL	1989
Brown Kyle E	(260)615-9619 kyle.ev.brown@gmail.com	8811 Nicole Dr Fort Wayne IN 46806	IN	SP	Martini New Haven IN	(260)749-0014	FW	2019
Brown Nathaniel W	(605)593-2745 revnathanielbrown@protonmail.com	3197 141st Ave Bellingham MN 56212	MNN	SP	Grace* Correll MN	(320)568-2551	SL	2021
Brown Earl G III	(217)342-3593 rev_earl@msn.com	600 Norwood Ave Effingham IL 62401	CI	EM			FW	2006
Brown Keith E Jr	(803)448-1725 keith6400@aol.com	1566 Crestdale Rd Rock Hill SC 29732	SE	EM			CQ	2000
Brown Derrick C	(435)790-4528 pastor.dcbrown@gmail.com	2384 West 1000 North Vernal UT 84078	RM	SP	Our Saviour Vernal UT	(435)789-1421	FW	2010
Brown Eric J	(815)421-0297 pastorbrown.trinity@comcast.net	c/o Trinity Lutheran 255 E 3rd St Herscher IL 60941	NI	SP	Trinity Herscher IL	(815)426-2262	FW	2004
Brown Gary M	(520)508-5669 garynkim5@gmail.com	908 Plaza Encanto Sierra Vista AZ 85635	PSW	SP	Immanuel Sierra Vista AZ	(520)458-3883	SL	1994
Brown Gregory W	(580)571-4288 revgreg88030@yahoo.com	118 N Pine St Momence IL 60954	NI	SP	Our Savior Momence IL	(580)571-4288	FW	1991
Brown James P Sr	jamtwo02@hotmail.com	8595 Untreiner Ave Pensacola FL 32534	SO		Southern District Slidell LA	(504)282-2632	SPR	1973
Brown J D	(260)460-7725 usa1988ma@gmail.com	P.O. Box 2546 Cedar Park TX 78630	TX	EM			FW	2008
Brown Joshua D	(870)321-6157	8275 Opal Glen Ct Reno NV 89506	CNH	C08/2025			SL	2011
Brown Brad A	(319)423-5671 pastorbrown@imonmail.com	4220 Johnson Ave NW Cedar Rapids IA 52405	IE	SP	King Of Glory* Swisher IA	(319)431-5431	SL	2008
Browne Christopher C	(773)827-2469 c2browne@gmail.com	c/o Lutheran Church Of Our Savior 26 Brunswick Blvd Buffalo NY 14208	EA	SP	Our Savior Buffalo NY	(716)885-1108	SL	2000
Browning Jeffrey S	(516)746-4426 jeff@resgc.org	7 Devereaux Pl Garden City NY 11530	AT	Sn/Adm	Resurrection Garden City NY	(516)746-4426	SL	2003
Browning Richard L	(239)992-6952 pastorrichard@hopebonita.org	25999 Old 41 Rd Bonita Spgs FL 34135	FG	Sn/Adm	Hope Bonita Springs FL	(239)992-6952	SL	1998
Brownlee Jerome A Sr Dr	(913)908-3359 drjer09@live.com	402 Cheyenne Dr. Holton KS 66436	KS	SP	Trinity Holton KS	(785)364-2206	FW	1978
Brubaker Jesse L	(909)896-5837 jesse.brubaker@hotmail.com	2440 SE Wendy Dr Gresham OR 97080	NOW	SP	Christ The Vine Damascus OR	(503)658-5650	FW	2024
Brubaker James A	(360)489-4724 loisjimbru@gmail.com	5933 Cotton Dr SE Lacey WA 98513	NOW	EM			SL	1976
Bruce Gordon W	(402)649-3498	7144 Harvest Hills Dr Lavista NE 68128	NEB	EM			FW	1987
Bruce Donald	donald.bruce@ctsfw.edu	W3120 State Highway 29 Curtiss WI 54422	NW	SP	Christ* Abbotsford WI	(715)223-4315	FW	2016
Bruckner Robert A	pillowpack@centurylink.net	5134 Halley View Run Fort Wayne IN 46814	IN	EM			SPR	1972
Brueckner Peter R	(586)773-5344 peter.brueckner@sbcglobal.net	20840 Maple St St Clair Shrs MI 48081	MI	EM			CQ	1993

*Multiple Assignments (See Church Worker Locator for Additional Details)

See Page 53 for the Table of Abbreviations for key to District, Position, and Seminary abbreviations

**C =Candidate; EM = Emeritus; the date following the C is the month and year the Candidate status began

NAME	TELEPHONE NUMBER EMAIL	STREET ADDRESS CITY/STATE/ZIP	DISTRICT	POSITION/ STATUS**	WHERE SERVING	OFFICE PHONE	SEM/ PROGRAM	YR GRAD
Bruenger Richard W	(785)632-1515 rdbruenger@att.net	937 SW Woodbridge Pl Topeka KS 66606	KS	EM			SPR	1972
Bruening William P Dr	(804)690-8214 pbrue@comcast.net	307 Piping Rock Rd Manakin Sabot VA 23103	SE	EM			SL	1968
Bruer Robert L	(217)791-5675 rbruer@comcast.net	3070 E Lynnwood Dr Decatur IL 62521	CI	SP	Mount Zion Mount Zion IL	(217)864-4958	FW	1982
Brueske Robert E	(320)759-1985 merabrue@hotmail.com	4200 40th Ave N Apt 210 Minneapolis MN 55422	MNN	EM			SL	1963
Bruggeman Robert Q	(702)343-7070 pastorbobbruggeman@gmail.com	c/o Prince Of Peace Lutheran Church 350 Falcon Ridge Pkwy Ste 600 Mesquite NV 89027	EN	SP	Prince of Peace Mesquite NV	(702)345-2160	FW	2017
Bruhn Gerald J	(712)389-2187 bruhngerald01@gmail.com	7070 153rd St W Apt 207 Apple Valley MN 55124	MNS	EM			CQ	1999
Bruick Scott D	(402)641-7961 scott.bruick@stjohnseward.org	9901 W Mill Road Malcolm NE 68402	NEB	Sn/Adm	St John Seward NE	(402)643-2983	SL	1995
Brummer H D	dbrummer@comcast.net	798 N Emroy Ave Elmhurst IL 60126	NI	EM			SPR	1965
Brummet Daniel T	(574) 584-4640 brummetd@csl.edu	1612 Meadow Edge Ln Spring TX 77388	TX	Assoc	Resurrection Spring TX	(281)353-4413	SL	2025
Brummett Steven R	(940)552-7164 zionlockettpastor@gmail.com	14570 Fm 2074 Vernon TX 76384	TX	SP	Zion Vernon TX	(940)552-7164	FW	2011
Brumwell Tyrone S	(319)573-2066 tyronebrumwell@gmail.com	204 Hawthorne Dr SW Cedar Rapids IA 52404	IE	C07/2016			FW	2008
Bruner James R	(989)871-2407 pastor.bruner@spmill.org	8843 Fulmer Rd Millington MI 48746	MI	Sn/Adm	St Paul Millington MI	(989)871-4581	SL	1991
Brunette Mark D	(832)233-1098	11108 Avilla West Alexander AR 72002	TX	EM			SL	1983
Brunette Luther C	(317)345-4252 lbrunette1128@gmail.com	5147 Puffin Place Carmel IN 46033	IN	EM			SL	1980
Brunette John S	(314) 375-1107 jbrunette@aol.com	7020 Briar Bluff Dr Saint Louis MO 63129	MO	EM			SL	1987
Bruning Edward V Jr	(702)580-6589 ed-bruning@msn.com	580 Mona Ln Henderson NV 89015	PSW	SP	Our Savior Henderson NV	(702)565-9154	SL	1985
Brunner John G Dr	(828)349-0657 jgbrunnerdp@aol.com	178 Onion Mountain Br Franklin NC 28734	SE	EM			SL	1972
Brunold William L	(818)620-8008 dutch1913@gmail.com	11833 Larrylyn Dr Whittier CA 90604	PSW	EM			FW	1978
Brunow Eugene W Dr	(260)443-9627 genebrunow@comcast.net	6612 Durango Dr Fort Wayne IN 46815	IN	EM			CQ	1982
Bruns Benjamin R	(810)599-2213 pastorbenbruns@gmail.com	8905 Belmont Woods Blvd Fort Wayne IN 46835	IN	C04/2023			FW	2010
Brunworth Todd J	(989)370-9198 tjbrunworth@gmail.com	515 Wilson Rd Spring Lake MI 49456	MI	EM			SL	1976
Bruskiewicz Christopher L	(262)719-3754 cbrusky@sbcglobal.net	764 S 6th Ave West Bend WI 53095	SW	SMP	St John West Bend WI	(262)334-4901	SL-SMP	2012
Bruss Timothy J	(262)225-9174 tlbruss1@wi.rr.com	1918 E Sunset Dr Waukesha WI 53189	SW	EM			SL	1971
Bruss Eldor A	(636)464-7127 bruss-2@att.net	1643 Shadwell Dr Barnhart MO 63012	MO	EM			SL	1956
Bruss Jon S Dr	jon.bruss@ctsfw.edu	1137 Illsley Drive Fort Wayne IN 46807	IN	S HS/C	Concordia Theological Seminary Fort Wayne IN	(260)452-2100	CQ	2013
Brustuen Keith A	(320)321-2227 prbrustuen@gmail.com	4461 W Highway 212 Montevideo MN 56265	MNN	SP	St Paul Montevideo MN	(320)269-7145	SL	1988
Brutlag Joel R	(320) 815-3662 jcbrutlag@yahoo.com	22 England Ave Duluth MN 55808	MNN	EM			FW	1992
Brutlag Keith W	(612) 599-2506 kbrutlag@comcast.net	1328 Hillcrest Dr NE Fridley MN 55432	MNS	EM			SPR	1975
Bruzek Scott A Dr	(630)747-4229	2s065 Burning Trl Wheaton IL 60189	NI	Assoc	St John Wheaton IL	(630)668-0701	SL	1985
Brynestad Dale L	(830)743-2559 revdale00@gmail.com	1963 Venezia New Braunfels TX 78132	TX	Sn/Adm	Cross New Braunfels TX	(830)625-3969	SL	2000
Brynestad Christopher P	(979)639-1221 cbrynestad@kingofkingstx.org	c/o King Of Kings Lutheran 17000 Smyers Ln Round Rock TX 78681	TX	SP	King Of Kings Round Rock TX	(512)255-0829	SL	2009
Buchholz Nicholas J	(920)392-9335 pastorbuchholz@gmail.com	8903 Saint Johns Rd Suring WI 54174	NW	SP	St John* Suring WI	(920)842-4443	SL	2008
Buchholz Gordon A	(712)265-0245	916 Broadway St Audubon IA 50025	IW	EM			CQ	2002
Buchhop Mark J Dr	(218)779-6207 pastor.buchhop@gmail.com	17590 Otto Zeck Rd Detroit Lakes MN 56501	MNN	EM			FW	1979
Buchhorn Michael G	pastorbuchhorn@gmail.com	3417 Utah Ct Bryan TX 77808	TX	EM			FW	1989
Buchhorn Ralph H	clothcop@aol.com	25273 Ridgemoor Rd Menifee CA 92586	PSW	EM			FW	1982
Buchmueller Barrett R	(319)270-4532 pastorb@splcc.org	3611 Emerald Ln Country Club MO 64506	MO	Assoc	St Paul Saint Joseph MO	(816)279-1110	SL	2001
Buchs David M			MDS	Sn/Adm	Grace Little Rock AR	(501)663-3631	FW	2014
Bucka John D		Victoria Village 12600 Renaissance Ct #108 Homer Glen IL 60491	NI	EM			SPR	1964
Buckert Mark P	(989)996-1170 revmpb@yahoo.com	1861 Captain Mathes Dr Powder Spgs GA 30127	FG	EM			SL	1977
Buckhahn Charles F	(989) 780-2259 cbuckhahn@gmail.com	1109 Elmdale Dr Saginaw MI 48602	MI	EM			SL	1978
Bucklew Christopher B	(605)682-1850 bucklews@gmail.com	1505 Sheridan Dr Norfolk NE 68701	NEB	C02/2022			FW	2011

*Multiple Assignments (See Church Worker Locator for Additional Details)

See Page 53 for the Table of Abbreviations for key to District, Position, and Seminary abbreviations

**C =Candidate; EM = Emeritus; the date following the C is the month and year the Candidate status began

NAME	TELEPHONE NUMBER EMAIL	STREET ADDRESS CITY/STATE/ZIP	DISTRICT	POSITION/ STATUS**	WHERE SERVING	OFFICE PHONE	SEM/ PROGRAM	YR GRAD
Buckman Allan R Dr	(314)249-8340 albuckman65@gmail.com	790 Eckrich Pl Saint Louis MO 63119	MO	EM			SL	1965
Buckman James D	jbuckman007@cs.com	1001 Franklin St Mundelein IL 60060	NI	Sn/Adm	Faith Lake Forest IL	(847)234-1868	SL	1996
Budenholzer Mark D	(718)757-6725 markbudenholzer@gmail.com	4410 Cayuga Ave Bsmt B3 Bronx NY 10471	AT	Asst	The Village Bronxville NY	(914)337-0207	SL	2015
Budewig Robert L	(325)656-4302 rbudewig@gmail.com	243 Loch Ness Rd San Angelo TX 76901	TX	EM			CQ	1975
Buecheler Randall A	randallbuecheler4@gmail.com	P.O. Box 665 Lake Arrowhead CA 92352	PSW	EM			FW	1987
Buechner Quinten A	(715)307-4448 qabuech@gmail.com	1070 2nd Ave Cumberland WI 54829	NW	EM			CQ	2017
Buegel John E V	(651)683-0191 buegel@csp.edu	2250 Fieldstone Dr Mendota Hts MN 55120	MNS	EM			SL	1960
Buegler David D Dr	(440)281-7942 buegler.david@gmail.com	4321 Jaycox Rd Avon OH 44011	OH	EM			SPR	1972
Bueltmann Aaron J	(419)267-5266 pastoraaronbueltmann@gmail.com		OH	SP	St John Stryker OH	(419)267-5266	SL	2016
Bueltmann David J Dr	(217)364-4513 dj_bueltmann@hotmail.com	602 S Main St Buffalo IL 62515	CI	SP	Concordia Decatur IL	(217)428-6421	SPR	1968
Bueltmann Keith A	keith@bueltmann.org		CI	SP	St Paul Pana IL	(217)562-4731	SL	2001
Bueltmann Kevin J	480-588-8837 kevin@shepherdscanyon.org		PSW	RSO	Shepherd's Canyon Retreat Inc Wickenburg AZ	(480)588-8837	SL	2011
Bueltmann Kurtis A	(920)299-6912 kurtis@bueltmann.org	150 Lawrence Cir Abilene TX 79605	IN	M Chap	Office of International Mission Saint Louis MO		FW	2008
Buescher Jonathan W	(217)761-6907 buescher@gmail.com	203 S Vine St Mount Pulaski IL 62548	CI	SP	Zion Mount Pulaski IL	(217)792-5965	SL	2011
Buetow Mark T	(618)318-3680 buetowmt@gmail.com	1406 North Dr McHenry IL 60050	NI	Assoc	Zion McHenry IL	(815)385-0859	SL	1998
Buettner Lyle E	(618)696-2649 lylebuettner@yahoo.com	900 Belsha St New Athens IL 62264	SI	SP	Trinity* Darmstadt IL	(618)696-2649	FW	2020
Bugtong Leonardo R	(702)292-4070 bugtong1980@gmail.com	8113 Lilac Harbor Ct Las Vegas NV 89143	CNH	EM			CQ	1973
Buhrke Richard R	(414)807-5571 pb@familycrossfires.org	N6753 Black Oak Cir Shawano WI 54166	NW	SP	Zion Bonduel WI		SL	1978
Bultemeier Zachary N	(260) 452-4025 zbultemeier@tlcrva.org	3409 Broad Branch Cir Richmond VA 23238	SE	SMP	Trinity Richmond VA	(804)270-4626	SL-SMP	2025
Bultman William J Dr	(301)509-1431 bultmanw@gmail.com	9004 Chestnut Ave Bowie MD 20720	SE	C07/2016			CQ	2010
Bumby Norman A	(828)356-4351 normanbumby886@gmail.com	407 Villa Ridge Dr Paducah KY 42003	EN	EM			SPR	1964
Bumgardner John C	(218)230-8070 pastorbumgardner@yahoo.com	1700 Fountain Ct 104 Columbus GA 31904	FG	SP	Redeemer Columbus GA	(706)322-5026	FW	2011
Bunge Kenneth L	(218)640-7032 kenbunge@yahoo.com	1001 Atkinson Dr Lufkin TX 75901	TX	SP	First Lufkin TX	(936)634-7468	SL	2006
Bunge Todd A	(712)551-6510 pastorbunge@gmail.com	218 Phillips St Cookeville TN 38506	MDS	SP	Heavenly Host Cookeville TN	(931)526-3423	FW	2002
Bunnett Robert W	(562)420-7366	4843 Adenmoor Ave Lakewood CA 90713	PSW	EM			SL	1959
Bunzel F Christian J	(860)355-2630 chrisbunz@charter.net	40 Twin Oaks New Milford CT 06776	NE	SP	Trinity New Milford CT	(860)354-3450	SL	1977
Buono Neil F Dr	(785)633-4857 revneilbuono@gmail.com	2510 SW Staffordshire Rd Topeka KS 66614	KS	EM			SL	1999
Burakowski Jonah P	(262)901-8653 jonahburakowski@gmail.com	124 Evergreen St Delaven WI 53115	SW	Pro Stf	Martin Luther Greendale WI	(414)421-4000	SL	2009
Burch Herbert W Jr	herb.burch@lcms.org	3916 N Potsdam Ave #4948 Sioux Falls SD 57104	CNH	S Miss	Office of International Mission Saint Louis MO		FW	1998
Burch James R II	(607)838-3157 revjburch@gmail.com	730 Old Stage Rd Groton NY 13073	EA	SMP	Grace Canastota NY	(315)697-2128	CQ	2018
Burch Peter J	(734) 355-3481 rev.peter.burch@emmanuelon-theridge.com	10925 Welch Rd Britton MI 49229	MI	SP	Emmanuel Britton MI	(517)451-8148	SL	2025
Burcham Ronald D	(480) 895-6782 ron.burcham@risensavioraz.org	23914 S Alma School Rd Sun Lakes AZ 85248	PSW	Sn/Adm	Risen Savior Chandler AZ	(480)895-6782	SL	1988
Burdick Michael H	(309)255-5580 mike.burdick@stjohnslcms.net	717 S First St Effingham IL 62401	CI	Sn/Adm	St John Effingham IL	(217)342-4334	SL	1988
Burfeind Peter M	(419)324-5535 cyril9@aol.com	207 South St Marshall MI 49094	EN	SP	Our Savior* Union City MI	(517)741-7643	SL	1996
Burfiend Daniel L	(631)605-3308 daniel.burfiend@ctsfw.edu	323 Bittersweet Ln Ossian IN 46777	IN	S HS/C	Concordia Theological Seminary Fort Wayne IN	(260)452-2100	FW	2015
Burg Christian G	(715)851-7259 darkforestpella@yahoo.com	453 Rose Hill Dr Oneida WI 54155	NW	SP	Zion Lutheran Church Oneida WI	(920)869-9466	SL	1998
Burgdorf Noah E	(660)728-0441 noah@theburgdorfs.com	36157 Salem Ave Salisbury MO 65281	MO	SP	Salem Salisbury MO	(660)481-2249	FW	2016
Burgdorf Zachariah E	(636)328-2610 revburgdorf@gmail.com		KS	Assoc	Risen Savior Basehor KS	(913)724-2900	FW	2021
Burge Benjamin R	(513)571-3533 benjaminrburge@gmail.com	c/o Trinity Lutheran Church 38900 Harper Ave Clinton Twp. MI 48036	MI	Sn/Adm	Trinity Clinton Township MI	(586)463-2921	FW	2019
Burge David M	(417)593-0706 dmburge1953@gmail.com	766 Mica Rd Kirbyville MO 65679	MO	EM			FW	1978
Burgell Nathan A	(573)450-8037 nburgell@me.com	421 Charlestowne Place Dr Saint Charles MO 63301	MO	C07/2016			SL	2006

*Multiple Assignments (See Church Worker Locator for Additional Details)
See Page 53 for the Table of Abbreviations for key to District, Position, and Seminary abbreviations
**C =Candidate; EM = Emeritus; the date following the C is the month and year the Candidate status began

NAME	TELEPHONE NUMBER EMAIL	STREET ADDRESS CITY/STATE/ZIP	DISTRICT	POSITION/ STATUS**	WHERE SERVING	OFFICE PHONE	SEM/ PROGRAM	YR GRAD
Burger Mark M	(918) 629-7989 markburger1951@gmail.com	2710 Parkwood Ct Claremore OK 74017	OK	EM			CQ	1993
Burger Christopher A	rev.burger@gmail.com	P.O. Box 5692 Columbia SC 29250	SE	Sn/Adm	Holy Trinity Columbia SC	(803)799-7224	FW	2006
Burgess Jeffrey S	(440)503-2136 pastor@stpaulhamburg.com	1001 Wright Rd Howell MI 48843	MI	SP	St Paul Hamburg Whitmore Lake MI	(810)231-1033	SL	2016
Burgess David F	(586)739-2804 shibboleth77@yahoo.com	4243 Sundance Mdws Howell MI 48843	MI	EM			FW	1981
Burgett William R Dr	(804)627-3562 revdrburg@comcast.net	2705 Buckstone Dr Powhatan VA 23139	SE	EM			SL	1989
Burgland Lane A Dr	(260)417-6753 laburgland@gmail.com	323 Windsor Dr Churubusco IN 46723	IN	EM			SL	1979
Burhop Charles B	(906)440-5858 cbburhop@att.net	765 Kimball St Sault S Marie MI 49783	MI	SP	St Paul* Kincheloe MI	(906)635-2940	FW	1980
Burhop Daniel G	(260)312-7396 burhopdgo@gmail.com	7625 North Portsmouth Rd Saginaw MI 48601	MI	SP	Trinity Reese MI	(989)868-9901	FW	2007
Burk Keith H	khburk58@gmail.com	1140 E 13th St Crete NE 68333	NEB	SP	Faith Of Our Fathers Roca NE	(402)421-2222	NESC	1998
Burke Adam M	(928)575-0172 amb528@gmail.com	7813 E Painted Wagon Path Prescott Valley AZ 86315	PSW	SP	Shepherd Hills Prescott AZ	(928)778-9122	SL	2012
Burke Robert F	(708)837-3307 rfburke38@gmail.com	203 N Kenilworth Ave Apt 3h Oak Park IL 60302	EN	EM			SL	1965
Burke James D	(507)519-1204 pastor@immanuelclifton.org	911 W. 3rd Clifton TX 76634	TX	SP	Immanuel Clifton TX	(254)675-3281	SL	2023
Burke Kenneth O Dr	(337)364-2239 kennethoburke@bellsouth.net	1111 Honey Comb Dr St Martinvlle LA 70582	SO	EM			CQ	2015
Burkee Jonathan R	(520) 836-2451 jonathan.burkee@tlcscg.org	1515 N Trekell Rd Casa Grande AZ 85222	PSW	SP	Trinity* Casa Grande AZ	(520)836-2451	SL	2009
Burkhard Kenneth M	(832)287-2011 kmburkhard@gmail.com	26230 Raphael Dr Magnolia TX 77355	TX	SP	St Paul Magnolia TX	(281)259-7818	FW	1982
Burkman Arthur R	(219)922-4546 art.burkman@juno.com	455 O Hagan Dr Crown Point IN 46307	IN	EM			SPR	1971
Burma Cory W	(402)860-0443 cburma@peacecolumbus.org	2564 Pershing Rd Columbus NE 68601	NEB	Sn/Adm	Peace Columbus NE	(402)564-8311	SL	2004
Burmeister Scott E	(918)688-1390	420 S Main St Apt 1003 Tulsa OK 74103	OK	SP	Christ The Redeemer Tulsa OK	(918)492-6451	SL	2003
Burmeister Robert J	(952) 432-7291 svchaplain@yahoo.com	12574 Everest Ct E Apple Valley MN 55124	MNS	EM			SL	1973
Burmeister Devin J	(636)284-6061 revdev@beautifulsavior-lsmo.org		EN	Assoc	Beautiful Savior Lees Summit MO	(816)524-7288	SL	2020
Burmeister Clyde J	(763) 498-1630 cpburmeister@msn.com	8200 Main St N Apt 470 Maple Grove MN 55369	MNS	EM			SPR	1962
Burns James D	(501)231-8329 jburns7165@sbcglobal.net	2139 Helmich Dr Benton AR 72019	MDS	SP	First Benton AR	(501)231-8329	SL	1990
Burns Jesse A	(641)829-3030 pastorburns10@protonmail.com	P.O. Box 306 Ventura IA 50482	IE	SP	Redeemer Ventura IA	(641)829-3650	FW	2010
Burns Joseph G	(309)339-1719 pastorjburns@mchsi.com	110 N Grimm Rd Goodfield IL 61742	CI	SP	Our Redeemer Eureka IL	(309)467-5477	FW	2005
Burns Daniel R	rev.dburns@gmail.com	14321 Tungsten Way NW Ramsey MN 55303	MNS	SP	St Paul Osseo MN	(763)425-2238	FW	2002
Burow Gaylen A	(913)271-0866 pastorgburow@gmail.com	7601 Lyndale Ave S Apt 34a Minneapolis MN 55423	MNS	EM			SL	1973
Burreson Kent J Dr	(314)413-6309 burresonk@csl.edu	2500 Hartland Ave Saint Louis MO 63114	MO	S HS/C	Concordia Seminary Saint Louis MO	(314)505-7000	SL	1992
Burt Michael F	(252)633-0256 murtmb@suddenlink.net	1225 Pine Valley Dr New Bern NC 28562	SE	EM			SL	1969
Burt Stuart V	(850)549-6436 sburt@gmail.com	6608 Lake Charlene Dr Pensacola FL 32506	SO	EM			FW	2006
Burton Thomas R	(920)893-8271	420 Wilson St Plymouth WI 53073	SW	EM			SL	1969
Burton Kenneth W III		329 S Mill St Tehachapi CA 93561	PSW	SP	Good Shepherd Tehachapi CA	(661)822-6817	SL	1999
Burtzlaff Paul S Dr	paulburtzlaff@icloud.com		FG	SP	Amazing Grace Oxford FL	(352)748-1201	SL	1993
Busacker Scott M Dr	hopelutheranchurchlcms@ gmail.com	2745 Broadway Highland IL 62249	SI	SP	Hope Highland IL	(618)654-7891	SL	2009
Busch Lewis M	(562)522-0981 busl@juno.com	18724 Munsee Rd Apple Valley CA 92307	PSW	SP	Zion Victorville CA	(760)245-9725	SL	1992
Bush John L	(734)925-3220 cubsrev699@gmail.com	4355 Bristol View Ct Saint Louis MO 63129	MO	EM			SL	2000
Bush Julius B	(314)822-3630 julesbush@att.net	711 S Laclede Station Rd Apt G108 Saint Louis MO 63119	MO	EM			SL	1955
Bushre Christopher T	(309)945-5017 pastorbushre@christthelife.com	2332 Judith Ln Waukesha WI 53188	SW	SP	Christ The Life Waukesha WI	(262)547-1817	SL	2003
Bushuiakovish Mark R	(734)626-7679 markbushuiakovish@gmail.com	5110 Franklin Pike Nashville TN 37220	MDS	Assoc	Our Savior Nashville TN	(615)833-1500	SL	2012
Bushur James G Dr	(260)625-5637 james.bushur@ctsfw.edu	14521 Bitternut Ln Fort Wayne IN 46814	IN	S HS/C	Concordia Theological Seminary Fort Wayne IN	(260)452-2100	FW	1993
Buss Allan R Dr		Lcms Northern Illinois District 1107 Monroe Ave River Forest IL 60305	NI	DP	Northern Illinois District River Forest IL	(708)449-3020	FW	1990
Buss David M	(225)205-1639 davebuss@yahoo.com	6352 Feather Nest Ln Baton Rogue LA 70817	SO	D Ex/S	Southern District Slidell LA	(504)282-2632	SL	2004
Busse Robert M	(920)295-6896 revbusse@gmail.com	W4826 Village Acres Ln Princeton WI 54968	SW	EM			FW	2003

*Multiple Assignments (See Church Worker Locator for Additional Details)

See Page 53 for the Table of Abbreviations for key to District, Position, and Seminary abbreviations

**C =Candidate; EM = Emeritus; the date following the C is the month and year the Candidate status began

NAME	TELEPHONE NUMBER EMAIL	STREET ADDRESS CITY/STATE/ZIP	DISTRICT	POSITION/ STATUS**	WHERE SERVING	OFFICE PHONE	SEM/ PROGRAM	YR GRAD
Bussert Mark P	bussertm@yahoo.com	440 S Church Rd Bensonville IL 60106	NI	EM			SL	1981
Busskohl Kurtis R	(308)730-1913	4164 Norwood Dr Grand Island NE 68803	NEB	EM			SL	2006
Bussman John M	(256)734-3575 revbussman@stpaulscullman.com	513 4th Ave SE Cullman AL 35055	SO	Sn/Adm	St Paul Cullman AL	(256)734-3575	SL	2012
Butcher John W Dr	(573)489-3286 pastorjohnbutcher@gmail.com	9500 E Little Creek Rd Centralia MO 65240	MO	EM			SL	2009
Buth Frederick P	(715)353-2540 quilts@bevcomm.net	N4282 County Highway F Weyerhaeuser WI 54895	NW	EM			SL	1970
Butler James E	(781)636-8415 jamesbutler60@icloud.com	6 Crawford St Randolph MA 02368	NE	SP	St Lukes Dedham MA	(781)326-1346	SL	1985
Butler Robert W	(608)415-7241 grandpabutler@rocketmail.com	2068 Willow Run Reedsburg WI 53959	SW	EM			SPR	1974
Buttke Kerry D	(575)921-7921 buttkekr@yahoo.com	122 Morningside Dr Valparaiso IN 46383	RM	EM			FW	1985
Buuck David P	(952)939-9173 pastordavidpb@gmail.com	12201 Minnetonka Blvd Unit 102 Minnetonka MN 55305	MNS	EM			SL	1971
Buuck R J Dr	(414)581-1235 1jbuuck@gmail.com	N112w17500 Mequon Rd Apt. 316 Germantown WI 53022	FG	EM			CQ	1990
Buvinghausen Garrett K	(832)878-4532 pastor.buvinghausen@icloud.com	c/o Bethany Lutheran Church 231 E Hamilton St Wellington OH 44090	OH	SP	Bethany Wellington OH	(440)647-5300	FW	2019
Byars Andrew K	(623)341-9553 pastorbyars@phxcoxmail.com	7020 W Cactus Rd Peoria AZ 85381	PSW	Sn/Adm	Apostles Peoria AZ	(623)979-3497	SL	1990
Byer Charles R	(631)727-2510 pastorbyer@aol.com	102 Timber Dr Calverton NY 11933	AT	SP	Our Redeemer Aquebogue NY	(631)722-4000	SL	1983
Byers Gary W	(618)235-0612 SAIL97@AOL.COM	805 Penhurst Pl Belleville IL 62221	SI	EM			SPR	1974
Bynum Gordon W Dr	(612)321-8331 chaplain@sainttimothysociety.org	2355 Fairview Ave N # 161 Roseville MN 55113	MNS	Inst C	Saint Timothy Society Roseville MN	(307)242-5400	SL	1986
Byork James R	(804) 714-1608 jbyork1@verizon.net	5807 Portrait Pl N Chesterfld VA 23234	SE	EM			SL	1970
Byrd Joseph A	(805)268-2806 pastor.byrd@gmail.com	916 W. Loquat Ct Lompoc CA 93436	CNH	SP	Bethany Lompoc CA	(805)736-8615	SL	2006
Byrd Otis L	(415)468-3517 obyrd@comcast.net	176 Nueva Ave San Francisco CA 94134	CNH	SMP	Shepherd Hills San Francisco CA	(415)859-9603	CQ	2019
Byrd Toby O	(972)741-5485 pastortob@therookery1999.com	3173 County Road 3455 Honey Grove TX 75446	EN	SP	St Paul Paris TX		FW	2001
Cabrales Ramon	preacherrc@hotmail.com	9414 N 97th Dr Peoria AZ 85345	PSW	Assoc	Apostles Peoria AZ	(623)979-3497	SL	2016
Cage Peter C	(260) 450-9914	2929 Buckhurst Run Fort Wayne IN 46815	IN	Assoc	St Pauls Fort Wayne IN	(260)423-2496	FW	1991
Cahill Christopher T Dr	(330)421-6805 revcahill@gmail.com	656 Wooster St Lodi OH 44254	S	SP	Christ King Lodi OH	(330)948-3000	SL	1980
Cain Brock A	(228)239-3414 lohengrin4001@yahoo.com	108 York Dr Long Beach MS 39560	SO	SMP	Of The Pines Waveland MS	(228)467-6771	SL-SMP	2013
Cain Paul J Jr	(307)461-7643 revpaulcain@gmail.com	910 Idaho Ave Sheridan WY 82801	WY	Sn/Adm	Immanuel Sheridan WY	(307)674-6434	SL	2000
Cain John W	(281)844-3984 cain1020@sbcglobal.net	483 County Road 2041 Nacogdoches TX 75965	TX	SP	Redeemer Nacogdoches TX	(936)564-6729	SL	1996
Cain Lawrence E	(218)644-3289 lrptcain@frontier.com	2020 Highway 73 Cromwell MN 55726	MNN	EM			CQ	1989
Caithamer Jeffrey E	(217)359-1123 revcaithamer@stjohn-lcms.church	c/o St John Lutheran Church 509 S Mattis Ave Champaign IL 61821	CI	Assoc	St John Champaign IL	(217)359-1123	SL	2006
Callahan Phillip J			EA	SP	Faith Corning NY	(607)962-4970	FW	2011
Callies Arthur D	(920)904-5064 artcallies@gmail.com	402 Nelson St Fond Du Lac WI 54935	SW	EM			CQ	2004
Callies David W	(615)661-6455 d.callies2@comcast.net	5601 Cloverland Dr Apt 115 Brentwood TN 37027	MDS	EM			SL	1965
Cameron Philip J	(303)981-0103 philipjcameron@gmail.com	1384 Shadow Mountain Dr Highlands Ranch CO 80126	RM	EM			SL	1983
Cameron Bruce A	(314)443-5510 brucethecameron@gmail.com	1502 Wexford Ave Webster Groves MO 63119	MO	EM			SL	1979
Camin Baldwin A	(208)731-9772 pastorbc2j@gmail.com	39 W 600 S Jerome ID 83338	NOW	EM			SPR	1967
Campbell Braun C	(815) 544-8058		NI	Sn/Adm	Immanuel Belvidere IL	(815)544-8058	SL	2006
Campbell Delwyn X Sr	(517)410-4183 pastordxc@outlook.com	1410 Loraine Ave Lansing MI 48910	MI	Sn/Adm	Trinity* Lansing MI	(517)372-1631	Other	2015
Campbell Gunnar G	(217) 722-9542 prcampbell@christjacob.org	206 W Jacob Rd Jacob IL 62950	SI	SP	Christ Jacob IL	(618)763-4663	FW	2023
Campbell Jeffrey	(732)766-7362 campbell.jeffrey@ymail.com	14 Siedler Ln Sayreville NJ 08872	NJ	SMP	Good Shepherd Old Bridge NJ	(732)679-8883	SL-SMP	2023
Campbell Phillip A Dr	(314)614-0768 princepa@aol.com	114 Lillians Way Madison AL 35758	MO	EM			SL	1971
Campbell W C Jr	(281)351-1959 revwcc@sbcglobal.net	13503 Lost Creek Rd Tomball TX 77375	TX	EM			FW	1994
Canaday Matthew W	pastormatt@branson.church	185 Sunrise Villa Dr Branson MO 65616	MO	SP	Praise and Worship Branson West MO	(417)386-2422	SL	2009
Candreva Peter D	(412)999-4856 pastor@stpeterlutheranchurch.com	319 E. Center St. Petersburg MI 49270	MI	SP	St Peter Petersburg MI	(734)279-1949	FW	2025
Canion Matthew J	(320)444-4853 matthewlcms@hotmail.com	200 Barker Rd Whitmore Lake MI 48189	MI	SP	Living Water Whitmore Lake MI	(734)426-4006	SL	2005

*Multiple Assignments (See Church Worker Locator for Additional Details)
See Page 53 for the Table of Abbreviations for key to District, Position, and Seminary abbreviations
**C =Candidate; EM = Emeritus; the date following the C is the month and year the Candidate status began

NAME	TELEPHONE NUMBER EMAIL	STREET ADDRESS CITY/STATE/ZIP	DISTRICT	POSITION/ STATUS**	WHERE SERVING	OFFICE PHONE	SEM/ PROGRAM	YR GRAD
Canion Daniel A	(830)620-1018 dcanion2@aol.com	260 Bonner Blvd New Braunfels TX 78130	TX	EM			SPR	1966
Canjura Hector A		3716 S 60th Ct Cicero IL 60804	NI	EM			Other	1978
Cantwell Francis J Jr	(912)674-3358 fjcantwell@gmail.com	1237 Bella Vista Dr Jackson MO 63755	MO	EM			SL-SMP	2011
Carabotta Robert A	robert.carabotta@mail.com	1956 South Woodruff Avenue Apt. 325 Idaho Falls ID 83404	NOW	Assoc	Hope Idaho Falls ID	(208)529-8080	FW	2001
Carey Ralph W	(616)667-1522	259 Covington Ct SW Grandville MI 49418	MI	EM			SL	1957
Cario Matthew J	(512)964-4354 mattcario@gmail.com	8904 119th Street Ct E Puyallup WA 98373	NOW	SMP	Our Savior Tacoma WA	(253)531-2112	SL-SMP	2019
Carlisle Roger P	(712)790-2732 peacecar@netins.net	2965 300th St Sac City IA 50583	IW	EM			FW	1983
Carlone Brandon M	(985)502-6200 pastorcarlone@gmail.com	104 Rue Fontaine Lafayette LA 70508	SO	SP	Faith Lafayette LA	(337)216-9658	SL	2015
Carlson Matthew G	(630)726-8575 matt.carlson52@gmail.com	501 Bevan Dr W Joliet IL 60435	NI	SP	Our Savior Joliet IL	(815)725-1606	FW	2023
Carlson Steven C	(406)317-1431 oldfolkshome64@yahoo.com	5105 Village View Way Apt 1 Missoula MT 59803	MT	Assoc	First Missoula MT	(406)549-3311	FW	1982
Carlson Paul A	(715)214-7349 karenmarriedbutch@yahoo.com	713 N 4th St P.O. Box 207 Bruce WI 54819	NW	EM			FW	2001
Carlson Patrick K Dr	(301)742-0690 patcarlson240@gmail.com	1102 Legacy Farm Dr SE Huntsville AL 35802	SO	EM			SPR	1975
Carlson Neil L	(308)254-3062 rev.carlson@ymail.com	12108 Road 6 Sidney NE 69162	WY	SP	Zion* Chappell NE	(308)874-2533	FW	2011
Carlson Mark E	(765)618-2753 mcarlson@emmanuellc.org	c/o Emmanuel Lutheran Church 4865 Wilmington Pike Kettering OH 45440	OH	Sn/Adm	Emmanuel Kettering OH	(937)434-1798	SL	1983
Carlson Kenneth G	(301)279-2868 kencarlson@aol.com	11501 Brandy Hall Ln North Potomac MD 20878	SE	EM			SL	1967
Carlson Jeffrey H	(715)212-2088 pastorjeff@orlcms.net	6422 Prairie Park Dr Eau Claire WI 54701	NW	SP	Our Redeemer Eau Claire WI	(715)835-5239	SL	2015
Carlson Eric S	(573)822-5164 pastor@stjohnshannibal.org	12923 Green Meadows Pl New London MO 63459	EN	SP	St Johns Hannibal MO	(573)221-0615	SL	2011
Carlson Andrew J Sr	(907)513-9431	2982 Davis Rd Fairbanks AK 99709	NOW	Sn/Adm	Zion Fairbanks AK	(907)456-7660	SL	1997
Carlson Daniel R	(320) 362-8776 pastor@stpaulsmilaca.org	13734 127th Ave Milaca MN 56353	MNN	SP	St Paul's Milaca MN	(320)982-6703	FW	2013
Carlton Richard C Dr	(404)823-2062 rcarltoncc@gmail.com	370 River Trl Dahlonega GA 30533	FG	EM			FW	1980
Carnahan David A	(541)610-2577 cearn8ch@gmail.com	P.O. Box 189 Seabeck WA 98380	NOW	SP	Evergreen Seabeck WA	(360)830-4180	SL	1985
Carnahan Mark D	revsjlcs@gmail.com	1701 Elm View Dr Corpus Christi TX 78418	TX	EM			FW	1985
Carnehl Adam E	(630)439-5777 adamcarnehl@gmail.com	319 Quaker Church Rd Randolph NJ 07869	NJ	SP	Good Shepherd Randolph NJ	(973)366-4267	SL	2016
Carner Richard D	(724)387-1035 pastorcarner@yahoo.com	20023 Ideal Way Lakeville MN 55044	EA	EM			SL	1990
Carney William M	(808)227-9378 billcarney137@hotmail.com	204 Rowland Ave Leesburg IN 46538	IN	SP	Redeemer Warsaw IN	(574)267-5656	NESC	1986
Carney Michael R	(913)426-1455 trinityatchisonad@yahoo.com	711 Mound St Atchison KS 66002	KS	SMP	Trinity Atchison KS	(913)367-2837	Other	2022
Carnicom Ronald R	(218)675-6532 carnicom@tds.net	4483 Poquet Dr NW Apt F Hackensack MN 56452	MNN	EM			FW	1989
Carpenter Jon C	(740)610-7225 jccarpenter11@gmail.com	1573 Maple St Barberton OH 44203	S	SP	St Matthew Norton OH	(330)825-4100	FW	2020
Carr William W Jr	(314)809-7627 revbillcarr@gmail.com	1350 Ambrose Rucker Rd Monroe VA 24574	SE	EM			SL	1983
Carretto James P	(402)640-6529 jcarretto@hotmail.com	2002 Skyline Dr Norfolk NE 68701	NEB	Asst	Christ Norfolk NE	(402)371-1210	FW	1981
Carretto Stephen P	(561)400-8689	744 SW 7th St Boca Raton FL 33486	FG	Sn/Adm	St Paul Boca Raton FL	(561)395-0433	SL	2010
Carrier John S	(810)887-0363 pastorjcarrier@gmail.com	4115 Surrey Ln Fort Gratiot MI 48059	MI	Sn/Adm	St Paul Trenton MI	(734)676-1565	SL	1983
Carstens Gary J Dr	(765)602-3610 pastorgjc@gmail.com	1207 Smokey Ridge Rd Ardmore OK 73401	OK	EM			CQ	1982
Carstensen George D	george@ad-lcms.org	137 Front St Apt 207 Schenectady NY 12305	AT	SP	Immanuel* Niskayuna NY	(518)346-1958	SL	2010
Carter Mark E	(918)331-6753 mcarter565@gmail.com	2201 Woods Loop Driftwood TX 78619	TX	EM			CQ	1999
Carter Tyler D	(402)547-8515 pastortylercarter@gmail.com	1320 Alberta St NE Grand Rapids MI 49505	MI	Assoc	St Peter's Big Rapids MI	(231)796-6684	SL	2016
Carter Timothy R	tjcarter72592@gmail.com	16270 S 300 W Columbus IN 47201	IN	SMP	St Peter Columbus IN	(812)372-1571	SL-SMP	2013
Carter Stephen J	(314)846-7473 carterstephenj@aol.com	6240 Kings Ferry Pl Saint Louis MO 63129	MO	EM			SL	1966
Carter Richard E Dr	(763) 340-9135 carter@csp.edu	1175 Englewood Ave Saint Paul MN 55104	MNS	EM			SL	1980
Carter Robert T Jr Dr	(540)656-3154 robert.t.carter.jr@gmail.com	8 Revolutionary Rd Highland FLS NY 10928	AT	D Miss	Atlantic District Hastings-On-Hudson NY	(914)337-5700	SL	2009
Cartwright Timothy C	(828)569-9291 benhoss435@gmail.com	483 Church Street Seward NE 68434	NEB	EM			SL	1985
Cary Bryan S	(719)849-0586 bsatcary2@gmail.com	1908 Leila Dr Loveland CO 80538	RM	EM			FW	1988

*Multiple Assignments (See Church Worker Locator for Additional Details)
See Page 53 for the Table of Abbreviations for key to District, Position, and Seminary abbreviations
**C =Candidate; EM = Emeritus; the date following the C is the month and year the Candidate status began

NAME	TELEPHONE NUMBER EMAIL	STREET ADDRESS CITY/STATE/ZIP	DISTRICT	POSITION/ STATUS**	WHERE SERVING	OFFICE PHONE	SEM/ PROGRAM	YR GRAD
Casachahua Oscar D	(201)770-0960 osdicamna63@gmail.com	1819 Melvin Dr Gastonia NC 28054	NJ	EM			FW	1981
Casaday Timothy A	(609)758-3081 nickykat@comcast.net	1 Shevchenko Ave Cream Ridge NJ 08514	NJ	SMP	Immanuel East Rutherford NJ	(201)939-2386	CQ	2019
Casci Arthur M	(937)219-9559 amcasci@gmail.com	820 Autumn Leaf Dr Beavercreek OH 45430	OH	EM			SL	1984
Case Jan C	(985)847-9588 jccase123@bellsouth.net	123 Honeywood Dr Slidell LA 70461	SO	EM			SL	1984
Casey-Motley David D	(410)673-7107 pastordavid.immanuel@gmail.com	224 Apple Ln Preston MD 21655	SE	SP	Immanuel Preston MD	(410)673-7107	FW	2017
Cashmer Jason D	(734)281-2388	6970 Lakeshore Dr Newport MI 48166	MI	Sn/Adm	Christ The King Southgate MI	(734)285-9695	SL	1993
Cashmer Terry L	(734)281-3773 carol@@ctk.me	13690 Argyle St Southgate MI 48195	MI	EM			SPR	1971
Casiglia Joseph A	586-530-8433 jcasiglia@faithtroy.org	39434 Lakeshore Dr Harrison Township MI 48045	MI	Sn/Adm	Faith Troy MI	(248)689-4664	SL	2018
Casillas Mario	(832)262-5355 marioandres2525@gmail.com	P.O. Box 8406 Baytown TX 77522	TX	C01/2020			SL	2010
Caspersen David A	(307)637-4947 annmcaspersen@hotmail.com	221 Fort Hall Ave American Falls ID 83211	WY	EM			SPR	1969
Castaneda Trinidad	(405) 818-3278 josetrini1217@gmail.com	628 E Suera Ter. Mustang OK 73064	OK	EM			SL	2006
Castens Kyle D	(314)695-2235 pastor@ilcfestus.org	221 Brierton Lane Festus MO 63028	MO	Sn/Adm	Immanuel Crystal City MO	(636)937-5525	SL	2000
Castillero Rene G	(307)752-7957 rcastillero@stpaulhamel.org	319 W Wall St Worden IL 62097	SI	Assoc	St Paul Worden IL	(618)633-2209	FW	2017
Castor Kenneth R	(937)726-2677 kcastor@woh.rr.com	5164 Summerset Dr Tipp City OH 45371	OH	SP	Wilmington Wilmington OH	(937)366-6108	FW	1998
Catalan Carlos	(847)899-6012 revcatalan@aol.com	1297 Thorndale Ct Elgin IL 60120	NI	Asst	Faith Carpentersville IL	(847)428-2079	Other	1999
Cate William C	(719)221-8069 wcate@icloud.com	17468 Dunewood Ct Unit C Spring Lake MI 49456	MI	EM			SL	2005
Catherwood Robert Jr	(315)336-8090 pastor@stjohnslutheranrome. onmicrosoft.com	6397 Anderegg Dr Rome NY 13440	EA	SP	St John Rome NY	(315)336-8090	FW	2003
Caughey William F	(316)452-1300 wfcaughey@gmail.com	5109 Cottage Dr Unit C Pleasant Hill IA 50327	IW	EM			FW	1997
Causton Paul R	(763)340-9135 pcauston@gmail.com	315 River St Unit 207 River Falls WI 54022	MNS	C07/2016			SL	2001
Cave Andrew L	(870)847-5110 caveman0861@yahoo.com	c/o Mission Lutheran Church 2752 N Roadrunner Pkwy Las Cruces NM 88011	RM	Sn/Adm	Mission Las Cruces NM	(575)522-0465	SL	2016
Cavener James H	(530)841-1277 pastor@beautifulsaviorreedsport.org	c/o Beautiful Savior Lutheran Church 2160 Elm Ave Reedsport OR 97467	NOW	SP	Beautiful Savior Reedsport OR	(541)271-2633	FW	1988
Cearlock Jesse K	(563)583-1593 pastorcearlock@gmail.com	420 Maplewood Ct Dubuque IA 52001	IE	Sn/Adm	Our Redeemer* Dubuque IA	(563)588-1247	FW	2006
Cecil David C	(713)261-0868 djcecil71@att.net	21922 Whispering Daisy Ct Cypress TX 77433	TX	SP	Cross of Christ Waller TX	(979)702-0658	FW	1996
Celia Anthony M	(818)271-9022 anthony.celia529@gmail.com	41 Easton Rd Westport CT 06880	S		SELC District Macungie PA	(610)965-3265	SL	2023
Cenat Jean G	(347)499-5467 jcenat79@hotmail.com	1005 E 57th St Brooklyn NY 11234	AT	IndC P	Atlantic District Hastings-On-Hudson NY	(914)337-5700	Other	2004
Cephus Matthew A	(612)227-3974 mattcephus7@yahoo.com	1312 Dayton Rd Champlin MN 55316	MNS	SP	Gloria Dei Minneapolis MN	(612)781-1989	SL	2023
Cerchez Marin	(616)201-7305 marin.cerchez@ctsfw.edu	104 Labrador Ct Summerville SC 29485	SE	SP	Calvary Charleston SC	(843)766-3113	FW	2018
Cervantes Jose L	408-377-4411 trinity1500@att.net	267 San Antonio Ct San Jose CA 95116	CNH	Assoc	Trinity San Jose CA	(408)377-4411	SL	2009
Chadburn Pierce H	pastor@zionemmanuel.org	4498 State Route 21 N Odessa WA 99159	NOW	SP	Zion-Emmanuel Odessa WA	(509)982-2402	FW	2018
Chaffee Phillip W	(616)970-9373 phil.chaffee@ymail.com	16525 Bailey Rd Bailey MI 49303	MI	SMP	Resurrection Sand Lake MI	(616)636-5502	SL-SMP	2015
Chai Albert T	2albert.chai@gmail.com	4825 Agnes Ave Unit B Temple City CA 91780	PSW	C05/2024			Other	2015
Chamberlain Thomas J	(740) 721-5333 thmschamberlain398@gmail.com	c/o Emmanuel Lutheran Church 705 S Washington St Van Wert OH 45891	OH	SP	Emmanuel* Van Wert OH	(419)238-4992	FW	2024
Chan David T	(415)309-3015 dtchan@comcast.net	87 Montebello Dr Daly City CA 94015	CNH	EM			SL	1996
Chan Terrence C Dr	(650)438-7370 sfmissions@gmail.com		CNH	SP	Christ All Nations* San Francisco CA	(415)468-2937	CQ	1987
Chanderdatt Henry D	(347)804-5896 henrychand@gmail.com	129-33 134th St South Ozone Park NY 11420	AT	Assoc	St Peters Brooklyn NY	(718)647-1014	SL	2023
Chandler Christopher L	(314)755-5187 revchrisft2023@gmail.com	298 Baxter St Milford CT 06460	NE	SP	Faith* Groton CT	(860)445-0483	SL	2016
Chandler Thomas B	(817)223-4238 trinitypastortom@gmail.com	P.O. Box 2378 Albany TX 76430	TX	SP	Trinity Albany TX	(325)762-2557	FW	2011
Chang Corey J	(650)201-6680 corey.chang@hopedalycity.org	6564 Deerfield Dr Vallejo CA 95491	CNH	Assoc	Hope Daly City CA	(650)991-4673	SL	2024
Chanthaphon Pon	(209)373-3408 pondotcom1@hotmail.com	2079 Simpson St Honolulu HI 96819	FG	M Chap	Office of International Mission Saint Louis MO		SL	2006
Chapa Jonathan T	(763) 242-1669 pastorjon@trinitymerrill.com	1002 Rock Ridge Court #3 Merrill WI 54452	NW	Assoc	Trinity Merrill WI	(715)536-5482	SL	2025
Chapman Sean C	(402)210-9956 chapman.sean@gmail.com	2301 5th St East Meadow NY 11554	AT	SMP	Calvary East Meadow NY	(516)735-1473	SL-SMP	2015

*Multiple Assignments (See Church Worker Locator for Additional Details)

See Page 53 for the Table of Abbreviations for key to District, Position, and Seminary abbreviations

**C =Candidate; EM = Emeritus; the date following the C is the month and year the Candidate status began

NAME	TELEPHONE NUMBER EMAIL	STREET ADDRESS CITY/STATE/ZIP	DISTRICT	POSITION/ STATUS**	WHERE SERVING	OFFICE PHONE	SEM/ PROGRAM	YR GRAD
Charelus Saint-Luc L	Saintluccharelus@yahoo.com	14522 Abiaka Way Naples FL 34114	FG	C03/2018			SL	2015
Chase Eugene C Jr Dr	(507)491-6711 eccjrdr@juno.com	1316 Merrywood Ct Faribault MN 55021	MNS	EM			FW	1981
Chase Timothy A	(260)387-2146 timachase@gmail.com	404 Central Ave N Dodge Center MN 55927	SI		Southern Illinois District Belleville IL	(618)234-4767	FW	2011
Chelmo Walter P	chelmowalter92@gmail.com	274 Cedar Canyon Rd Crawford TX 76638	TX	EM			SPR	1955
Chen Timothy C	timchenclc@gmail.com	5600 Orangethorpe Ave #1114 La Palma CA 90623	PSW	C09/2021			CQ	2019
Chen Wen-Fu	(626)442-7191	5403 Robinhood Ave Temple City CA 91780	PSW	EM			CQ	1998
Chen Lesley W	(617)651-7890 lesleychen21@gmail.com	130 Spitbrook Rd Nashua NH 03062	NE	Assoc	Grace Nashua NH	(603)888-7579	SL	2022
Cheney Robert E	(936) 232-3232 jp@thewellway.com	11740 Northpointe Blvd Apt 1004 Tomball TX 77377	TX	EM			CQ	1980
Chepulis Mark A	(701)520-8836 pastor.chepulis@nodaklcms.org	299 Redwood Dr Mapleton ND 58059	ND	DP	North Dakota District Fargo ND	(701)293-9001	FW	2010
Chester Justin M	(425)382-9256 justin.chester@ctsfw.edu	5210 S Stone Ln Spokane WA 99223	NOW	SP	Beautiful Savior Spokane WA	(509)747-6806	FW	2025
Chestnutt Bryan J	(828)260-1732 pastorbryan.mtnsideluth@ gmail.com	5290 NC Hwy 105 S Banner Elk NC 28604	SE	SP	Mountainside Linville NC	(828)733-4404	CQ	2003
Childers Jacob L	(734)931-2013 jcchilers20@gmail.com	7116 W Arbor Trace Dr Apt 920 Knoxville TN 37909	MDS	Assoc	Grace Knoxville TN	(865)691-2823	SL	2023
Chinberg Douglas W	(314)469-2224 dchinberg@kokstl.org	13765 Olive Blvd Chesterfield MO 63017	MO	Sn/Adm	King Of Kings Chesterfield MO	(314)469-2224	SL	1989
Chinery James D	(989)248-7862 pastorchinery@yahoo.com	148 W Jefferson Frankenmuth MI 48734	MI	SP	Faith Bay City MI	(989)684-3430	CQ	2010
Chisamore Brian E	(417)574-6169 chisamorebe@yahoo.com	26247 State Highway 248 Aurora MO 65605	MO	Inst C	Missouri District Saint Louis MO	(314)590-6200	FW	2004
Chittick Aaron B	(407)925-9025 abchitti@gmail.com	286 Narrows Rd Coldwater MI 49036	MI	SP	St Paul Coldwater MI	(517)278-8061	SL	2013
Chitwood Kenneth W Dr	4915228269943		PSW	C05/2019			Other	2015
Cho Joseph E		1440 S Indiana Ave Apt 1002 Chicago IL 60605	NI	C07/2016			KO	1978
Cho Man O		16841 Morse Circle Huntington Beach CA 92649	PSW	EM			CQ	1999
Cho Ung W	(213)663-0205 revungwoncho777@hotmail.com	2207 W. 11th St. #309 Los Angeles CA 90006	PSW	Assoc	Ark Of Noah Los Angeles CA	(310)836-8342	CQ	2012
Choate Robert E	(713)412-9994 choater@csl.edu	7508 E 83rd St Kansas City MO 64138	KS	Assoc	Bethany Overland Park KS	(913)648-2228	SL	2025
Choi Young C	(469)269-8077 pastorisaacchoi@gmail.com	2974 Hickory Run Cir NW Duluth GA 30096	FG	O-Miss	St Mark Tucker GA	(770)938-4546	CQ	2015
Choi Nam J Dr	(949)307-3891 njinchoi@gmail.com	83 Goldenrod Irvine CA 92614	PSW	C05/2024			CQ	2017
Choi Sang J	(949)659-9939 sangjchoi@gmail.com	2 Seawind Irvine CA 92614	PSW	EM			CQ	2002
Cholak Steven T	(314)807-2259 revcholak@me.com	5607 Deepcreek Ln Houston TX 77091	TX	Asst	Our Savior Houston TX	(713)290-9087	FW	2004
Chrismer Daniel J Sr	(928)758-2301 pastordajochris@gmail.com		PSW	SP	St John Bullhead City AZ	(928)758-2301	SL	2017
Christ Dean E	(316)371-6893 deanchrist@gmail.com	4705 E Eagles Landing St Wichita KS 67220	KS	EM			FW	2010
Christ Jason A	(716) 860-5007 jchrist@firsttrinity.com	2501 Eggert Rd Tonawanda NY 14150	EA	SMP	First Trinity Tonawanda NY	(716)835-2220	SL-SMP	2021
Christ Mark E	(801)940-4903 mechrist89@gmail.com	4711 S 3025 W Roy UT 84067	RM	SP	St Paul Ogden UT	(801)392-6368	SL	1989
Christensen Lynn W	(307)365-3151 lcmschap@gmail.com	655 W Dawes St Ainsworth NE 69210	NEB	SP	Zion Ainsworth NE	(402)387-1512	FW	1994
Christensen Sam J	(307)450-3029 mclcms82513@yahoo.com	939 Moose Dr Riverton WY 82501	WY	EM			SPR	1976
Christensen Trenton D	(970)580-1864 pcstpaul@hotmail.com	911 Walnut St Julesburg CO 80737	RM	SP	Zion* Big Springs NE	(970)474-4757	FW	1995
Christensen Mark F	(406)239-7642 pastormarkchristensen@gmail. com	2951 Manitoba Ln Bismarck ND 58503	ND	C10/2017			FW-SMP	2011
Christensen John M	(307)286-1446 loonlakelover@yahoo.com	127 Cedar Ridge Dr Thermopolis WY 82443	WY	EM			FW	1987
Christensen Erik M	(907) 522-3899 pastorerik@bslc.org	8100 Arctic Blvd Anchorage AK 99518	NOW	SP	Beautiful Savior Anchorage AK	(907)522-3899	SL	2016
Christensen Matthew C Dr	(785)307-0288 chaplainchristensen@gmail.com	P.O. Box 534 Forsyth MT 59327	MT	SP	Concordia Forsyth MT	(406)346-7614	SL	2007
Christensen Jonathan K	(920)530-8606 mplc.pastor@gmail.com	2606 Chimney Rock Rd Hendersonville NC 28792	SE	SP	Mount Pisgah Hendersonville NC	(828)692-7027	SL	2012
Christenson Scott E	(714)501-1001 pastorc@soth.org	2218 N Mantle Ln Santa Ana CA 92705	PSW	Sn/Adm	Shepherd Hills Rancho Cucamonga CA	(909)989-6500	FW	1996
Christenson Timothy J	(406) 309-0958 tim.chris@yahoo.com	150 Granite Dr Whitefish MT 59937	MT	EM			SL-D	2012
Christian Douglas M	(260)515-3293 dmchristian1984@gmail.com	12912 Franke Rd Monroeville IN 46773	IN	SP	St John Monroeville IN	(260)639-6404	FW	1983
Christian Matthew J	(260)446-7953 mchristian@immanuelmurphy.com	215 S. 20th St. Murphysboro IL 62966	SI	SP	Immanuel Murphysboro IL	(618)684-3012	FW	2022
Christians Corey J	(828)838-5745 coreyjchristians@hotmail.com	19519 Crystal Oak San Antonio TX 78258	TX	Assoc	Concordia San Antonio TX	(210)479-1477	SL	2022

*Multiple Assignments (See Church Worker Locator for Additional Details)

See Page 53 for the Table of Abbreviations for key to District, Position, and Seminary abbreviations

**C =Candidate; EM = Emeritus; the date following the C is the month and year the Candidate status began

NAME	TELEPHONE NUMBER EMAIL	STREET ADDRESS CITY/STATE/ZIP	DISTRICT	POSITION/ STATUS**	WHERE SERVING	OFFICE PHONE	SEM/ PROGRAM	YR GRAD
Christians Matthew J	(715) 302-5420 wittbirnpastor@gmail.com	176001 Wodora Acres Rd Hatley WI 54440	NW	SP	St Paul* Wittenberg WI	(715)253-2790	SL	2002
Christiansen Joel T	(314)849-9852 joel@webstergardens.org	9129 Rusticwood Trl Saint Louis MO 63126	MO	EM			SL	1982
Christiansen Keaton G	(262)355-8860	1351 S Randolph St Garrett IN 46738	IN	SP	Zion* Garrett IN	(260)553-4202	FW	2014
Christiansen Keith P	(712)461-1904 christiansenkeith199@gmail.com	P.O. Box 171 Fenton IA 50539	IW	SP	St Paul* Emmetsburg IA	(712)852-2367	FW	1983
Christiansen Brennick T			TX	Asst	Messiah Keller TX	(817)431-2345	FW	2022
Christie Ronald E	(405)615-1292 zionluthokc@hotmail.com	12028 Surrey Ln Yukon OK 73099	OK	SP	Zion Oklahoma City OK	(405)615-1292	FW	1987
Christopher Thomas D	(605)239-4754 lutheranpreacher@gmail.com	P.O. Box 126 Alexandria SD 57311	SD	SP	St Martin* Alexandria SD	(605)239-4421	FW	1990
Chryst Thomas E	(262)744-3858 tomchryst@yahoo.com	9858 Gessner Dr Fort Worth TX 76244	TX	Sn/Adm	Messiah Keller TX	(817)431-2345	SL	1999
Chu Bill S	(510)757-7805 revbchu@aol.com	115 Lilac Cir Hercules CA 94547	CNH	C08/2019			SL	1996
Chung Paul J	(804)763-1941 pworldmm7@yahoo.com	431 Grandview Pl # 1 Fort Lee NJ 07024	SE	EM			CQ	1997
Chuol Paul R	801-548-9212 chuolp10@gmail.com	1125 Shirley Lane Storm Lake IA 50588	IW	C10/2023			SL	2021
Cigelske Brian A	(920)286-2635 azor_99@hotmail.com	1710 Van Buren St New Holstein WI 53061	SW	SP	Zion New Holstein WI	(920)898-5250	SL	2021
Cima John P II Dr	(804)404-5123 john.cima@lcms.org	4912 Monumental St Richmond VA 23226	SE	S Miss	Office of International Mission Saint Louis MO		SL	2009
Cizmar Thomas J	thomas119@gmail.com	4125 W Stone House St Eagle ID 83616	NOW	EM			CQ	1998
Clancy Bryant E Jr	(636)394-6713 bryantclancy@icloud.com	643 Highland Glen Dr Ballwin MO 63021	MO	EM			Other	1961
Clancy Robert A	(973)423-0756 revrobclancy62@gmail.com	165 Cedar Ave Hawthorne NJ 07506	NJ	C07/2016			SL	1988
Clark Thomas J	(701)242-7189 pastortomclark@gmail.com	301 2nd St NE Hankinson ND 58041	ND	SP	Immanuel* Hankinson ND	(701)242-7834	FW	2005
Clark William R	(515)491-8543 pastorbillclark.tlc@gmail.com	1792 Blackthorn St Council Bluffs IA 51503	IW	SP	Timothy Council Bluffs IA	(712)323-0693	SL	2022
Clark Ryan M	ryanjesuskatherine@yahoo.com	302 2nd St NE Buffalo MN 55313	MNS	Sn/Adm	St John Buffalo MN	(763)682-1883	SL	2002
Clark Paul M	(517)420-4826 revpmclark@gmail.com	P.O. Box 317 Fowler MI 48835	MI	Sn/Adm	St Paul Fowler MI	(517)420-4826	FW	1988
Clark Matthew J Dr	(314)832-5600 pastor@ascensionstl.com	5347 Donovan Ave Saint Louis MO 63109	MO	Sn/Adm	Ascension Saint Louis MO	(314)832-5600	SL	2007
Clark John B Jr	(256)520-2153 bkclark23@hotmail.com		FG	EM			SL	1987
Clark Gary L	(541)531-4100 glclark4650@gmail.com	465 Yew Wood Dr Shady Cove OR 97539	NOW	SP	St John Eagle Point OR	(541)826-4334	CQ	2002
Clark David E	(314)919-6226 declark07@gmail.com	616 S Dewey St Odebolt IA 51458	IW	SP	Trinity Odebolt IA	(712)668-4201	FW	2025
Clark Christopher R	(256)734-3575 revclark@stpaulscullman.com	513 4th Avenue SE Cullman AL 35055	SO	Assoc	St Paul Cullman AL	(256)734-3575	FW	2017
Clark Adam C Dr	(574)323-0654 adamclarknd@gmail.com	437 E Dragoon Trail Mishawaka IN 46544	IN	Sn/Adm	St Peter Mishawaka IN	(574)255-5585	SL	2007
Clark Lee S	(774)521-3388 lee.s.clark@comcast.net	248 Wheeler Rd Mashpee MA 02649	NE	EM			SL	1969
Clarke Justin C	(619)207-1436 pastorjustinclarke@gmail.com	c/o 240 E 5600 South Murray UT 84107	RM	SP	Christ Murray UT	(801)266-8714	FW	2021
Claus Terry A	(248)684-4839 pastorclaus@comcast.net	250 Jeni Ln Milford MI 48380	MI	EM			SL	1971
Clausen Eric K	(208)608-3949 eclausen@christbrea.org	593 N Milford Rd Orange CA 92867	PSW	Assoc	Christ Brea CA	(714)529-2984	SL	2015
Clausen George H	gclausen48@gmail.com		IW	SP	Our Savior Sheldon IA	(712)324-9725	FW	1983
Clausing Dean F	dfclausing@gmail.com	2222 Irondale Dr Benton AR 72019	MDS	EM			CQ	1979
Clausing Jonathan E	(636)922-4596 jonathan.clausing@lcms.org	613 Henry St Washington MO 63090	MO	S Miss	Office of International Mission Saint Louis MO		SL	2004
Clay Samuel P	(912)842-9674 stpaulstatesboro@frontiernet.net	7014 Rushing Rd Statesboro GA 30461	FG	SP	St Paul Statesboro GA	(912)681-2481	SL	2004
Clayton Bryce A	(715)423-3260 bclayton@immanuelrapids.com	111 11th St. N. Wisconsin Rapids WI 54494	NW	Assoc	Immanuel Wisconsin Rapids WI	(715)423-3260	SL	2024
Clayton Kirk M	(618)566-9093 kmcljcuac@yahoo.com	806 N 4th Ave Maywood IL 60153	NI	S HS/C	Concordia University Chicago River Forest IL	(708)771-8300	SL	2000
Cleland James S	(972)890-6575 jscleland@gmail.com	3680 Highway 395 South Carson City NV 89705	CNH	SP	Shepherd Of Sierra Carson City NV	(775)267-3680	SL	2022
Clemens Daniel J	(816) 805-1355 Daniel.Clemens@kokkc.org	7807 N College Ave Kansas City MO 64119	MO	Asst	King Of Kings Kansas City MO	(816)436-7680	SL	2018
Clemens Edward E	(320)291-6208 edclemm14@gmail.com	610 Keller Ave S Amery WI 54001	NW	SP	Redeemer Amery WI	(715)268-7283	SL	1991
Clemmer Seth M		1319 Pamela Ct Naperville IL 60540	NI	Sn/Adm	Bethany Naperville IL	(630)355-2198	FW	2011
Clocker Thomas R	(301)732-9203 revclocker@gmail.com	7336 Vincenzo Dr Moseley VA 23120	SE	EM			FW	1991

*Multiple Assignments (See Church Worker Locator for Additional Details)
See Page 53 for the Table of Abbreviations for key to District, Position, and Seminary abbreviations
**C =Candidate; EM = Emeritus; the date following the C is the month and year the Candidate status began

NAME	TELEPHONE NUMBER EMAIL	STREET ADDRESS CITY/STATE/ZIP	DISTRICT	POSITION/ STATUS**	WHERE SERVING	OFFICE PHONE	SEM/ PROGRAM	YR GRAD
Cloeter Jeffrey P	(314)631-0304 jeff.cloeter@cmstl.org	5322 Murdoch Ave Saint Louis MO 63109	MO	Sn/Adm	Christ Memorial Saint Louis MO	(314)631-0304	SL	2005
Cloeter Paul E	(320)333-6319 pecloeter@gmail.com	2045 E Highview Dr Sauk Rapids MN 56379	MNN	EM			FW	1982
Cloeter David R	(918)694-1364 drcloeter7@gmail.com	1 Blenheim Ln Bella Vista AR 72715	MDS	EM			FW	1980
Cloeter Carl D	(319)668-2352 carlcloeter@yahoo.com	400 S 8th Ct Unit 63 Indianola IA 50125	IW	EM			SL	1979
Cloeter Erik K	(810)265-9207 pc@messiahclio.org		MI	Sn/Adm	Messiah Clio MI	(810)686-0740	SL	1998
Cloose Anthony C	(320)674-0580 tonycloose@gmail.com	518 Morrison St Mora MN 55051	MNN	SP	Zion Mora MN	(320)679-1094	FW	1995
Clow Keith M	(573)386-5652 kmclow@yahoo.com	P.O. Box 42 Auxvasse MO 65231	MO	C10/2020			SL	2005
Clow Mark R	(860)346-2641 mrclow@snet.net	24 Arbutus St Middletown CT 06457	NE	SP	Grace Middletown CT	(860)346-2641	SL	1998
Cluppert Jonathan D	(715)719-0167 jcluppert@firstlutheranricelake. com	1905 22 1/2 St Rice Lake WI 54868	NW	SP	First Rice Lake WI	(715)234-7505	SL	2001
Cluver Steven P	(702)371-2167 pastorcluver@yahoo.com	1446 Bronco Rd Boulder City NV 89005	PSW	EM			SPR	1969
Cluver Joel A	(217)674-3405 jacluver17@yahoo.com	P.O. Box 48 Latham IL 62543	CI	EM			SPR	1975
Coats Roy A	(443)745-9200 royaxel@gmail.com	4213 Vermont Ave Baltimore MD 21229	SE	SP	Redeemer Baltimore MD	(410)644-0544	FW	2010
Coble Jeffrey L	(404)925-2416 jeffreycoble23@gmail.com	2787 Charlotte Hwy York SC 29745	SE	SMP	Emmanuel Rock Hill SC	(803)324-2283	SL-SMP	2020
Cobos John F	813-961-2182 jfcobos26@gmail.com	13723 Pimberton Dr Hudson FL 34669	FG	Assoc	Messiah Carrollwood FL	(813)961-2182	SL	2018
Cockey Joseph H	(941)350-7415 windward.cockey@gmail.com	3 Shoreland Dr Osprey FL 34229	FG	EM			FW	2003
Cockran Kurt R	(580)465-6498 kurtcockran@gmail.com	136 Phoenix Terre Haute IN 47803	IN	SP	Immanuel Terre Haute IN	(812)232-4972	FW	2017
Cody Jason K	(719)580-5084 pastorjasontlc@gmail.com	2924 County Road 12 S Alamosa CO 81101	RM	Sn/Adm	Trinity Alamosa CO	(719)589-4611	FW	2015
Cody Richard S	(832)745-3314 revcody11@gmail.com	3524 Saint Joseph Ave Saint Joseph MO 64505	MO	SP	St Peter Saint Joseph MO	(816)279-8190	SL	1996
Cody William M	(940)631-5219 pastormikecody@gmail.com	13 Freedom Cir. Wichita Falls TX 76306	TX	SMP	Grace* Burkburnett TX	(940)569-2706	SL-SMP	2014
Coe David L Dr	davidlawrencecoe@gmail.com	2468 N Columbia Ave Seward NE 68434	NEB	S HS/C	Concordia University Nebraska Seward NE	(402)643-3651	SL	2011
Coerber Scott M	(407)365-3408 scoerber@sllcs.org	1537 Chipmunk Lane 207a Oviedo FL 32765	S	SMP	St Luke Oviedo FL	(407)365-3408	SL-SMP	2010
Cofer Michael D	michael@missionlibertyhill.com	15725 Highway 29 W Suite 7 Liberty Hill TX 78642	TX	SP	Liberty Hill Liberty Hill TX	(512)778-9310	SL	2008
Coffey Daniel K	317-883-3165 fatherdaniel@comcast.net	79 Virgil Dr Greenwood IN 46142	IN	Asst	Our Shepherd Avon IN	(317)271-9103	FW	2001
Coffman George M	(864)247-5146 georgemcoffman@yahoo.com	P.O. Box 1 Walhalla SC 29691	SE	EM			SL	1988
Cohn Daniel F	(518)721-8313 prdan0212@gmail.com	P.O. Box 17 Stuyvesant Fl NY 12174	AT	SP	St Marks Second Hudson NY	(518)828-9514	SL	2012
Colageo Donald L	(207)735-7928 dcolageo@gmail.com	63 Broadway Pembroke NH 03275	NE	SP	Immanuel Manchester NH	(603)622-1514	FW	2003
Cole Thomas O	tom.lois.cole@gmail.com	9516 Fir Ln Johnston IA 50131	NEB	EM			FW	1985
Coles David Dr	(260)486-8252 david.coles@ctsfw.edu	5414 River Run Trl Apt C Fort Wayne IN 46825	NE	S Miss	Office of International Mission Saint Louis MO		FW	1986
Colgrove R T	(763)614-9622 rtcole@live.com	6899 Crosby Ct Excelsior MN 55331	MNS	EM			FW	1981
Collin Richard W	(231)942-1495 rev.rwcollin@gmail.com	13076 3 Mile Rd Evart MI 49631	MI	EM			SPR	1971
Collins Robin A	snilloc_1@yahoo.com	1021 5th St NE Staples MN 56479	MNN	EM			FW	1994
Collver Albert B III Dr	(636)751-3970 abc3@collver.net	474 Lindy Blvd Manchester MO 63021	SI	SP	St Paul Troy IL	(618)667-6681	SL	1997
Comer Larry E	(208)661-0244 larry@ctkcda.com	6216 W Meadowbrook Lp Coeur D' Alene ID 83814	NOW	SMP	Christ King Coeur D Alene ID	(208)664-9231	CQ	2018
Compton Dane W	(320)834-2184 dccompton@gctel.com	6517 County Road 22 NW Garfield MN 56332	MNN	EM			SPR	1968
Conger Kevin R	hopelutheranchurch@ymail.com	1204 Hill St Jacksonville AR 72076	MDS	SP	Hope Jacksonville AR	(501)982-1333	FW	2001
Conkling Christopher M	(571) 267-7433 cconkling@vablc.org	25615 Lennox Hale Dr Aldie VA 20105	SE	SP	Vine and Branches Aldie VA	(571)267-5900	SL	2019
Conkling Martin E Dr	(914)621-8287 thirdmartin@hotmail.com	307 Northshore Ct Saint Peters MO 63376	MO	EM			SL	1996
Conner Jonathan E	(712)655-2351 connerjonathanidw@gmail.com	1204 Center St Manning IA 51455	IW	SP	Zion Manning IA	(712)655-2352	SL	2004
Connor Raymond R	(715)302-1350 pastorray@mtoliveweston.org	5104 Quirt Sann Dr Schofield WI 54476	NW	EM			FW	1981
Conrad Matthew J	(630)538-2195 conrad.matt@gmail.com	495 Parkside Ln Yorkville IL 60560	NI	Assoc	Cross Yorkville IL	(630)553-7335	SL	2005
Conrad Dennis T	(360)378-1123 dandb1010@yahoo.com	1010 Miller Rd Friday Harbor WA 98250	NOW	EM			SL	1972

*Multiple Assignments (See Church Worker Locator for Additional Details)

See Page 53 for the Table of Abbreviations for key to District, Position, and Seminary abbreviations

**C =Candidate; EM = Emeritus; the date following the C is the month and year the Candidate status began

NAME	TELEPHONE NUMBER EMAIL	STREET ADDRESS CITY/STATE/ZIP	DISTRICT	POSITION/ STATUS**	WHERE SERVING	OFFICE PHONE	SEM/ PROGRAM	YR GRAD
Conrad Daniel E	(809)669-4798 uofm49@hotmail.com	530 Main St Ste 3a #305 Chester NJ 07930	CNH	S Miss	Office of International Mission Saint Louis MO		FW	1984
Conradt Robert J	rjamescon@aol.com	6434 Leeway Road Apt D Norton Shores MI 49441	MI	EM			FW	1979
Conradt Steven T	(715)526-5507 pastor.conradt@yahoo.com	N4793 Willow Creek Rd Shawano WI 54166	NW	EM			FW	2014
Conradt Joshua P	(262)534-3639 pastorconradt@stpeterswaterford.com	c/o St Peter Lutheran Church 145 S 6th St Waterford WI 53185	SW	SP	St Peter Waterford WI	(262)534-3639	FW	2012
Constien David P	(815)409-1156 pastor@mesquitelutheran.org	1616 Lime Wood St Mesquite NV 89027	PSW	SP	Mesquite Mesquite NV	(702)346-5811	SL	1989
Constien Stephen J	(678)296-9195 sjconstien@juno.com		MO	EM			SL	1989
Contreras Ramon	ramcon@hotmail.com	3060 54th St San Diego CA 92105	PSW	Assoc	Saint James Imperial Beach CA	(619)424-6166	SL	2004
Contreras Timothy D	(734) 489-5716 pastorcontreras@trinityjanesville.com	509 E. 1st St. Janesville MN 56048	MNS	Assoc	Trinity Janesville MN	(507)231-5189	SL	2025
Cook Joshua H Dr	(502)294-2615 cook.theophilus@gmail.com	515 E. Alton St. Marine IL 62061	MO	Pro Stf	Concordia Publishing House Saint Louis MO	(314)268-1000	FW	2008
Cook Theodore E Sr	(620)231-0492 zionpitt@ckt.net	783 S 196th St Pittsburg KS 66762	KS	SP	Trinity* Parsons KS		SL	1987
Cook Steven T	(253)472-1010 stevencook1010@msn.com	4530 S J St Tacoma WA 98418	NOW	SP	In Faith Dependent Anderson Island WA	(253)884-4974	FW	1980
Cook Richard P	(573)341-9463	10300 County Road 5160 Rolla MO 65401	MO	EM			FW	1987
Cook Kevin A	(618) 972-2138 pastorchaplainkevincook@gmail.com	500 E Tremont St Hillsboro IL 62049	SI	C01/2023			SL	2005
Cook Anthony A Dr	(314)363-7974 anthony.cook@lhm.org	1015 Washington Ave 707 Saint Louis MO 63101	MO	Aux	LLL/Lutheran Hour Ministries Saint Louis MO	(314)317-4100	SL	1994
Cook Philip E	(972)955-8801 phil.cook@lumakc.org	4606 Aminda St Shawnee KS 66226	MO	RSO	Lutheran Urban Mission Agency Kansas City MO	(816)844-5900	SL	2006
Cooksey Jared A	(612) 496-9300 pastorjared.clc@outlook.com		MNS	SP	Christ Eagan MN	(651)454-4091	FW	2020
Coons Michael J	(860)749-9748 revmcoons@gmail.com	65 N Maple St Enfield CT 06082	NE	SP	Our Redeemer Enfield CT	(860)749-3167	SL	2001
Coop Greggory S	(218)232-0846 pastor@princeofpeacelutheran.church	6819 Medford Rd Baxter MN 56425	MNN	SP	Prince Of Peace Baxter MN	(218)829-7092	SL	1989
Cooper Paul E	(714)257-9537 revpec@sbcglobal.net	712 Lantana Ave Brea CA 92821	PSW	EM			SPR	1969
Cooper Loren D	(402)604-0160 blackhills5052@hamilton.net	1436 State Rd 46 West Nashville IN 47448	IN	EM			FW	1990
Cooper Donald E	gcooper1023@gmail.com	2011 W Rokeby Rd Lincoln NE 68523	NEB	EM			FW	1980
Cooper Adam Jr	(228)896-9243 msyatlin@aol.com	2320 Farrell Cir Gulfport MS 39507	SO	EM			SL	1966
Copley Donald	(620)473-0296 copley1@cox.net	1300 S 8th St Humboldt KS 66748	KS	SMP	St Peter Humboldt KS	(620)473-2343	CQ	2018
Coppersmith Michael J Dr	(760)567-7684 coppersmith.mike@gmail.com	507 Dove Hollow Trl Georgetown TX 78633	TX	EM			SL	1980
Coppersmith Timothy J	(715)297-9025 tccusmith@yahoo.com	5804 Decker St Weston WI 54476	NW	C07/2016			SL	2000
Copus William P Jr	(660)232-3024 perry.copus@gmail.com	1318 Hollandale Dr Warrensburg MO 64093	MO	SP	St Matthew Ernestville MO	(660)463-2717	FW	2007
Corbett Gerald H Jr	(586)662-7094 jcvc1218@yahoo.com	16781 Country Club Dr Macomb MI 48042	MI	SMP	St Paul Pontiac MI	(248)758-9019	CQ	2018
Corder Jeffrey J	(419)551-9606 pastorcorder@gmail.com	302 Liberty Ln West Unity OH 43570	IN	SP	Clear Lake Fremont IN	(260)495-9219	SL	1986
Cordes Robert C	(651) 788-9718 susan.young.wi@gmail.com	3300 Rice St Unit 103 Saint Paul MN 55126	MNS	EM			SL	1960
Cordrey John	(314)422-6025 jcordrey@stpeters-columbus.org	2819 Grimes Way Columbus IN 47201	IN	Sn/Adm	St Peter Columbus IN	(812)372-1571	SL	2006
Cordt Nicholas R	(316)214-6407 pastornick@bethanylutheran-wichita.org	1216 N Oak Ridge Cir Goddard KS 67052	KS	SP	Bethany Wichita KS	(316)265-7415	SL	2023
Cordts Frederick T	(989)254-0409 timberguy1954@gmail.com	203 N Court St Au Gres MI 48703	MI	EM			FW	2009
Cormeny Randall D	(712)365-2520 cormenyzoo@frontiernet.net	600 5th St P.O. Box 212 Battle Creek IA 51006	IW	SP	St John Battle Creek IA	(712)365-4477	SL	1994
Cornelius Brett E	(740)244-2053 bcornelius62@gmail.com	612 W Edwards St Vandalia IL 62471	CI	Sn/Adm	Holy Cross Vandalia IL	(618)283-1133	CQ	2004
Cornelius William L	(402)921-8090 wlcorny@gmail.com	62292 Highway 62 Elk Creek NE 68348	NEB	EM			CQ	2014
Cornes Martin D	(952)917-9368 martin@thealley.org	10612 Yosemite Rd Bloomington MN 55437	MNS	SMP	theAlley Cottage Grove MN	(651)459-2063	SL-SMP	2021
Cornwell Steven J	(708)227-5279 sjcornwell@cs.com	13505 S Butternut Ct Plainfield IL 60544	NI	EM			FW	1986
Cornwell Simeon J	(708)738-0829 cornwellsimeon@gmail.com	22134 Colony St. St. Clair Shores MI 48080	EN	SP	St Paul Saint Clear Shores MI	(586)777-0215	FW	2020
Corrigan Jacob R	(509)362-3829 jacob.corrigan@ctsfw.edu	801 E Park St Livingston MT 59047	MT	SP	Emmaus MT Livingston MT		FW	2025

*Multiple Assignments (See Church Worker Locator for Additional Details)
See Page 53 for the Table of Abbreviations for key to District, Position, and Seminary abbreviations
**C =Candidate; EM = Emeritus; the date following the C is the month and year the Candidate status began

NAME	TELEPHONE NUMBER EMAIL	STREET ADDRESS CITY/STATE/ZIP	DISTRICT	POSITION/ STATUS**	WHERE SERVING	OFFICE PHONE	SEM/ PROGRAM	YR GRAD
Corson David B	(314)603-4821 jacobswellstl@yahoo.com	1916 Bookbinder Dr Saint Louis MO 63146	S	SP	Jacobs Well* Saint Louis MO	(314)603-4821	SL	2007
Cortright Charles L Dr	(636)253-6663 cortrightc54@gmail.com	4927 Connemara Ct Apt 5 Sheboygan WI 53083	SW	EM			CQ	2016
Corzine Jacob A Dr	jacob.corzine@cph.org		MO	Pro Stf	Concordia Publishing House Saint Louis MO	(314)268-1000	FW	2008
Cosby Samuel	pastorcosby@gmail.com		SE	EM			SL	1971
Cosgrove Tab E	(717)840-0382 pstrcosgrove@comcast.net	2580 Mount Rose Ave York PA 17402	SE	Sn/Adm	St John York PA	(717)840-0382	SL	2005
Cota Shane R		6502 S Business Dr Sheboygan WI 53081	SW	SP	Trinity* Sheboygan WI	(920)458-8881	FW	2002
Cotner John S	(737)285-7885 cotnerjs@outlook.com	10113 Up River Rd Apt 12303 Corpus Christi TX 78410	TX	SMP	Messiah Corpus Christi TX	(361)387-7748	SL-SMP	2024
Cottam Bertrand J	(810)624-4227 ncjc69@att.net	4243 Maplewood Meadows Ave Grand Blanc MI 48439	MI	EM			FW	1987
Cotter James R Dr	(260)493-0174 jcotter9@frontier.com	8017 Sedgewick Pl Fort Wayne IN 46835	IN	EM			FW	1980
Cottrell Bruce C	(918)665-0138 bcc45@att.net	8235 E 32nd Pl Tulsa OK 74145	OK	SP	Messiah Vinita OK	(918)256-3223	SL	1971
Couch Mark T	(269)598-8167 pastormarksg@gmail.com	1025 Royce Ave Kalamazoo MI 49001	MI	Assoc	Zion Kalamazoo MI	(269)382-2360	SL	1995
Couchman David M	(361)212-6664 duclie06@aol.com	8143 S Soltero Mine Dr Tucson AZ 85747	TX	EM			CQ	2010
Coulter Donald G	dcoulter@dgcoulter.com	6803 Pine Dr Chattanooga TN 37421	MDS	EM			SL	2007
Countryman Troy A	(217)294-3842 pastorcountryman@faithviera.org	c/o Faith Viera Lutheran Church 5550 Faith Dr. Rockledge FL 32955	S	Sn/Adm	Faith Viera Rockledge FL	(321)636-5504	SL	2008
Courie Zachary A	(402)277-0399 pastorcourie@gmail.com	1214 N Birch St Wahoo NE 68066	NEB	SP	Our Redeemer Wahoo NE	(402)443-4450	FW	2019
Courson Larry G	lgcourson@gmail.com	4701 Birch Ln Dexter MI 48130	MI	EM			CQ	1979
Couser Peter T	(817)992-1708 petercouser@newthing.live	40 E Burke Ave Towson MD 21286	SE	SMP	New Thing* Towson MD	(410)825-8770	SL-SMP	2010
Couser Mark T	(214)908-0242 mark.couser@gmail.com	1689 Timpson Dr Forney TX 75126	TX	SMP	Tree Of Life Garland TX	(972)226-6086	SL-SMP	2010
Cowell Thomas J	(319)464-5548 pastor.cowell@gmail.com	6666 NW 72nd St Platte Woods MO 64151	MO	Assoc	Christ Platte Woods MO	(816)741-0483	FW	2017
Cox Patrick M II	(541)988-5430 pastorcox@cocluth.com	429 Kingsridge Dr Hixson TN 37343	MDS	SP	Cross Of Christ Chattanooga TN	(423)877-7447	FW	2024
Cox Ronald L	(231)557-6074 pcox@concordialm.org	320 Questend Ave Mt Lebanon PA 15228	EA	SP	Concordia* Brentwood PA	(412)881-3005	SL	1988
Cox Raymond B	(228) 388-5767 raymond.cox@ctsfw.edu	2004 Pass Rd Biloxi MS 39531	SO	SP	Good Shepherd Biloxi MS	(228)388-5767	FW	2023
Cox Patrick J	(636)697-2290 pastorpjc@yahoo.com	836 Du Pre Ct Saint Peters MO 63376	MO	C06/2018			SL	1999
Cox Joseph L	(636)699-9472 jcox@lslancers.org	8973 Belmar Ct Saint Louis MO 63126	MO	Cmp P	Lutheran South Saint Louis MO	(314)631-1400	SL	2000
Cox Duncan M	(501)472-1269 duncanmcox@msn.com	P.O. Box 644 Pea Ridge AR 72751	MDS	EM			SL	1984
Cox Caleb C	(602)826-7061 Calebccox@gmail.com	2121 Lager St Fort Collins CO 80524	RM	Assoc	Redeemer Fort Collins CO	(970)225-9020	SL	2017
Cox Richard	(240)440-9960 pastor.richardcox3@gmail.com	2011 S 13th St Fort Pierce FL 34950	FG	C12/2024			CQ	2019
Coyne Tyler R	(248)872-8758 tyler@crosspointlakewood.org	916 Essex Ct McHenry IL 60050	NI	SMP	Crosspoint Lakewood Lakewood IL	(815)893-0888	SL-SMP	2024
Crabbe Kelly J	(303)502-7390 crabbekelly@yahoo.com	1844 S Jay Way Lakewood CO 80232	RM	EM			FW	1984
Craig Christopher M	(734)790-1992 rev.c.m.craig@gmail.com	300 N Indiana Ave Sylvan Grove KS 67481	KS	SP	Bethlehem Sylvan Grove KS	(785)526-7152	FW	2016
Craig Kenneth L	(716)946-5725 pastorklc@verizon.net	244 Rumbold Ave N Tonawanda NY 14120	EA	SP	Immanuel Lockport NY	(716)434-0521	NESC	2008
Craig Russell J	(518) 369-7631 rjcraig@gmail.com	9 Lexington Ct Voorheesville NY 12186	AT	EM			FW-D	2005
Cramer Ryan A	(251)923-7242 ryancramer2010@gmail.com	517 Jeraldean Ct Foley AL 36535	SO	SP	St Paul Foley AL	(251)943-6931	FW	2010
Crandall Ted L	(843)941-9591 pastorcrandall@gmail.com	2614 Boyer Street Beaufort SC 29902	SE	EM			FW	1990
Crane Brian T	(608)567-9029 revbriancrane@yahoo.com		EN	Sn/Adm	Eternal Life Mesa AZ	(480)985-0224	FW	2007
Crane Robert C	(585)506-2740 brotherbob316@outlook.com	6979 S Old West Lake Rd Honeoye NY 14471	EA	SMP	St Pauls Cohocton NY	(585)384-5667	CQ	2019
Crawford Jonathan T	(631)335-4019 revjcrawford@gmail.com	705 Wilson Ave Dubuque IA 52001	IE	SP	St Paul Dubuque IA	(563)556-7636	SL	2013
Crawford King M	(785)556-2324 kcrawf1014@aol.com	3232 Ella Ln Manhattan KS 66502	KS	EM			SL	2012
Creighton Gerald A	(320)468-0384 jpcr8on@midco.net	306 1st Ave SE P.O. Box 69 Pierz MN 56364	MNN	EM			SL	1971
Cripe Terry L	(419)769-1230 1969tcripe@gmail.com	1969 Redwood Dr Defiance OH 43512	OH	EM			SPR	1974
Critchett Daniel W Dr	(503)358-7762 dan@lifeteam.org	7138 SE Terrace Trails Dr Portland OR 97266	NOW	EM			SL	1981
Critchley Dale R	(651)689-3253 doulos12@gmail.com	317 Mount Columbia Dr Leadville CO 80461	RM	RSO	The Summit Mission Alliance Breckenridge CO	(303)902-6370	SL	1998

*Multiple Assignments (See Church Worker Locator for Additional Details)

See Page 53 for the Table of Abbreviations for key to District, Position, and Seminary abbreviations

**C =Candidate; EM = Emeritus; the date following the C is the month and year the Candidate status began

NAME	TELEPHONE NUMBER EMAIL	STREET ADDRESS CITY/STATE/ZIP	DISTRICT	POSITION/ STATUS**	WHERE SERVING	OFFICE PHONE	SEM/ PROGRAM	YR GRAD
Crocitto Brian M	(631)804-4857 crocitto@thelifeny.org	P.O. Box 348 Point Lookout NY 11569	AT	SMP	The Life Old Westbury NY	(516)333-3355	SL-SMP	2021
Crockett Dell J	(314)610-0098 revdellcrockett@yahoo.com	6948 Winona Ave Saint Louis MO 63109	MO	EM			SL	1957
Crolius Paul M	(608)524-3736 paulcrolius@ymail.com	445 3rd St Reedsburg WI 53959	SW	Sn/Adm	St Peter Reedsburg WI	(608)524-4512	SL	1993
Cronkright Tyler R	(810)240-4434 PastorTyler@stjohnrochester.org	109 Moross St Mt Clemens MI 48043	MI	SMP	St John Rochester MI	(248)402-8000	SL-SMP	2019
Croom Michael L II	(270)348-2849 pastorcroom@trinitymemphis.org	4375 Wind Tree Dr Bartlett TN 38135	MDS	Sn/Adm	Trinity Memphis TN	(901)525-1056	SL	2010
Croon Michael A Sr	(773)747-0160 meitman@aol.com	4825 N Ridgewood Norridge IL 60706	S	SP	Zion Norridge IL	(773)747-0160	FW	1996
Cross Corbie E	(907)394-8760 pastorcorbie@gmail.com	P.O. Box 874455 Wasilla AK 99687	NOW	EM			CQ	2007
Crossan Robert D II	(562)682-1758 robert.crossan@icloud.com	1807 E Alvarado St Fallbrook CA 92028	PSW	EM			CQ	1982
Crossman Mark	(602)803-0500 mark@thecross.family	25429 Rollong Oak Road Sorrento FL 32776	S	SMP	The Cross Mount Dora FL	(352)602-4635	SL-SMP	2019
Crosswhite Joseph E III	(320) 749-2059 joeddy3@outlook.com	121 E 6th St Randall MN 56475	MNN	SP	St Paul* Royalton MN	(320)584-8367	SL	2000
Croucher Douglas E	pastordoug@concordiachurch.org	6422 Oak Bridge Pl Fort Wayne IN 46835	IN	Sn/Adm	Concordia Fort Wayne IN	(260)422-2429	FW	2003
Croucher Mark H II		124 North Oxford Drive Raymore MO 64083	KS	Tchr	Bethany Overland Park KS	(913)648-2228	SL	2007
Crowe William L	(210) 617-3451 wlcrowe@gmail.com	15160 S Harrell's Ferry Rd Baton Rouge LA 70816	SO	SP	Trinity Baton Rouge LA	(225)272-3110	SL	2016
Crown Stewart D	(650)799-7179 pastorcrown@gmail.com	1230 Fulton St Palo Alto CA 94301	CNH	SP	Trinity Palo Alto CA	(650)853-1295	SL	1989
Crume Christopher D	(610)417-7837	15984 W Honeysuckle Dr Surprise AZ 85387	PSW	Sn/Adm	Life in Christ Peoria AZ	(623)773-1234	SL	2006
Cruz Evelio	(512)924-6343 eveliocruz047@gmail.com	505 Riverway Ln Leander TX 78641	TX	C05/2019			SL	2008
Cuen Eduardo	(562)639-6710 ecuen@tcstigers.net	9502 Millergrove Dr Santa Fe Springs CA 90670	PSW	SMP	Trinity Norwalk CA	(562)864-3713	SL-SMP	2014
Culbertson Tige A Dr	(989)465-7000 tige75@gmail.com	666 Cheoy Lee Cir Winter Spgs FL 32708	S	Sn/Adm	St Luke Oviedo FL	(407)365-3408	SL	2001
Cullen D L Jr	(734)652-4373 lee.cullen@holyghostmonroe.org	29674 Tamarack Dr Flat Rock MI 48134	MI	SP	Holy Ghost Monroe MI	(734)242-0509	FW	1992
Cullen Justin W	(804)694-6665 pastor@faithsullivan.org	P.O. Box 109 Sullivan IL 61951	CI	SP	Faith* Sullivan IL	(217)728-7711	SL	2021
Culver Perry A	(318)518-8767 pastor@christlutheranlcms.org	3440 Beverly Pl Shreveport LA 71105	SO	SP	Christ Shreveport LA	(318)671-1363	FW	2004
Cumbee Gregory J II	(540)667-1459 pastor.cumbee@gmail.com	110 Branch Ct Stephens City VA 22655	SE	SP	Our Savior Winchester VA	(540)667-1459	CQ	2014
Cumming James T	(608)788-0915 jtcumming@charter.net	2147 Hoeschler Dr La Crosse WI 54601	SW	EM			SPR	1964
Cummings Raymond D Sr	(845)778-7077 rdcummings62@gmail.com	25 Highland Ave Walden NY 12586	AT	EM			SPR	1965
Cummins Brian K	briancummins@att.net	2123 Tiburon Dr Redding CA 96003	CNH	SP	Trinity Redding CA	(530)221-6686	FW	1998
Cundiff Quintin M	pastorcundiff@gmail.com	5224 Camelot Estates Dr Saint Louis MO 63129	MO	S Ex/S	Office of National Mission Saint Louis MO		SL	2011
Cundiff Joel E	(457)328-0308 joelcundiff@gmail.com	129 Route 39 S Sherman CT 06784	KS	C10/2024			SL	2009
Cunningham Kirk R	(217)894-7717 barf.8868@yahoo.com	101 E Morgan St Clayton IL 62324	CI	SP	Good Shepherd Clayton IL	(217)894-7717	SL	1994
Cunningham Joseph R	(219)476-0054 jrcunning@comcast.net	2711 White Pine Cir Valparaiso IN 46383	IN	EM			FW	1984
Curley Patrick W	(626)475-5425 revcurley@hotmail.com	1354 E Dexter St Covina CA 91724	PSW	SP	Immanuel Chino CA	(909)628-2823	FW	1989
Currao Andrew J	revandyc@yahoo.com	1508 New Ford Rd Seymour IN 47274	IN	Sn/Adm	Redeemer Seymour IN	(812)522-1837	SL	1991
Curry Chris W	(541) 912-0628 chriscurry490@gmail.com	3700 Carmel Drive Casper WY 82604	WY	EM			FW	2001
Curtis Heath R	pastorcurtis@gmail.com	515 Main St Worden IL 62097	SI	DP	Southern Illinois District Belleville IL	(618)234-4767	SL	2004
Curtis Michael S	(630)964-1272 mikecurtis777@gmail.com	1514 Harpendon Ct Windsor CO 80550	RM	Assoc	Redeemer Fort Collins CO	(970)225-9020	SL-SMP	2016
Cusanelli Thomas W	(631)860-1356 pastorcusanelli@gmail.com	16 Media Ln Stony Brook NY 11790	AT	SMP	Saint Paul's Amityville NY	(631)264-0763	SL-SMP	2015
Cusson Bradley G	(916)784-9784	1520 Carbury Way Roseville CA 95747	CNH	Sn/Adm	St Matthew Rocklin CA	(916)435-0330	FW	1987
Cutler Mark G Dr	(920)387-3568 pastor.cutler@stjohnsmayville.com	N7146 County Rd Tw Horicon WI 53032	SW	Sn/Adm	St John Mayville WI	(920)387-3568	SL	1988
Cutler Paul J	(847)338-2070	1210 Sebring Cir Elgin IL 60120	NI	SP	Grace Streamwood IL	(630)289-3996	CQ	1998
Cwirla William M	(626)848-6325 wcwirla@gmail.com	21 Guy Kelly Rd Port Angeles WA 98362	NOW	EM			SL	1990
Cwynar Paul D	(724) 498-3961 paulcwynar@gmail.com	104 Mowry Rd Monaca PA 15061	EA	EM			CQ	2020
Czaplewski Daniel P Dr	(414)873-3931 pastorc@mtcalvary-mke.org	2862 N 53rd St Milwaukee WI 53210	SW	Sn/Adm	Mount Calvary Milwaukee WI	(414)873-3931	SL	1990
Czech Daniel D	(414)940-2225 pastordan51@aol.com	4920 S 84th St Greenfield WI 53228	SW	EM			SL	1989
Czischke Chad T	(313)378-5833 chadczischke@gmail.com	2140 NE 63rd Ct Fort Lauderdale FL 33308	FG	SP	Shep of the Coast Fort Lauderdale FL	(954)772-8010	SL	2006

*Multiple Assignments (See Church Worker Locator for Additional Details)
See Page 53 for the Table of Abbreviations for key to District, Position, and Seminary abbreviations
**C =Candidate; EM = Emeritus; the date following the C is the month and year the Candidate status began

NAME	TELEPHONE NUMBER EMAIL	STREET ADDRESS CITY/STATE/ZIP	DISTRICT	POSITION/ STATUS**	WHERE SERVING	OFFICE PHONE	SEM/ PROGRAM	YR GRAD
Dabsu Temesgen M	(510)754-1494 teme_meng@yahoo.com	354 Wildrose Cir Pinole CA 94564	CNH	SP	Grace El Cerrito CA	(510)525-9004	CQ	2019
Daene Roger W	(601)638-3542 tobruk1942@yahoo.com	109 2nd St Shelbyville IN 46176	IN	SP	Good Shepherd Franklin IN	(317)736-7849	NESC	1995
Daenzer Sean C	(701)640-5633 sean.daenzer@lcms.org	c/o Lutheran Church-Missouri Synod 1333 S Kirkwood Rd Saint Louis MO 63122	MO	S Ex/S	The LCMS Corporate Saint Louis MO	(314)965-9000	FW	2012
Dahl David C	(970)565-7433 dakdahl@yahoo.com	214 Lakeside Dr Cortez CO 81321	RM	EM			SL	1967
Dahl Jack E	(507)835-3211 bdahl41@gmail.com	14506 Bunker Dr Waseca MN 56093	MNS	EM			CQ	1985
Dahling Daniel F	(260)223-0903 dandahling@gmail.com	9406 Newgate Ct New Haven IN 46774	IN	EM			FW	1983
Dahlke David J	(941)493-5102 pastordavid@lakesidelutheran.net	2050 Mesic Hammock Way Venice FL 34292	FG	SP	Lakeside Venice FL	(941)493-5102	SL	1992
Dahlke James E	revjed@yahoo.com	11 Roberts St Seward NE 68434	NEB	EM			FW	1981
Dahmann Roy L	(830)496-3341 dahmannro@aol.com	134 Caribou Ln Kerrville TX 78028	TX	EM			SPR	1975
Dahn Mark D	markdahn7@gmail.com	113 Colonnade Dr Peachtree City GA 30269	FG	Sn/Adm	St Paul Peachtree City GA	(770)487-0339	SL	2001
Dailey Richard M	(254)681-0288 Richard.dailey1@yahoo.com	7735 Locust Rd Weleetka OK 74880	OK	SP	Trinity Okmulgee OK	(918)756-6046	FW	2021
Dallman Roger H Dr	(425)301-5089 royalrev@hotmail.com	1961 Newark Rd Lincoln University PA 19352	EA	EM			SPR	1976
Daly Thomas R	(480)522-0777	9210 N Firebrick Dr Fountain Hills AZ 85268	PSW	EM			FW	1984
Damery Michael	(217) 972-0971 Pastordamery@aol.com		CI	EM			SL	1998
Dancy Paul B Dr	(260)494-9970 pbdancy@yahoo.com	10503 Lagoon Dr Grabill IN 46741	IN	EM			FW	1980
Dandy Jacob W	(281)795-0151 jacob.dandy@gmail.com	818 N 6th St Atchison KS 66002	KS	Sn/Adm	Trinity Atchison KS	(913)367-2837	SL	2013
Dangba Moses G	(517)614-2098 mdangba@gmail.com	2316 Webster St Lansing MI 48944	MI	SP	Living Word Lansing MI	(517)490-5135	EIITSL	2023
Daniel David E	(815)343-4788 revddaniel@mail.com	621 Guthrie St Ottawa IL 61350	CI	SP	Faith Monticello IL	(217)762-9235	SL	2007
Daniels David M	(828)455-0422 pastor@redeemercatawba.com	1166 Stowehill Ln Catawba NC 28609	SE	SP	Redeemer Catawba NC	(828)241-2371	FW	2016
Danielsen Gary L Dr	(404)862-3345 garyldan@bellsouth.net	34 Bunker Hill Cir Shelton CT 06484	S	EM			SL	1973
Dankis Mark J Dr	(512)567-0300 mark.dankis@sbcglobal.net	2503 Donner Path Round Rock TX 78681	TX	EM			SL	1983
Dannenberg Donald G	(208)660-4345 dgdann@hotmail.com	3882 N Palmer Dr Coeur D Alene ID 83815	NOW	EM			SPR	1962
Dannenbring Richard A	(714) 747-6562 putt2@sbcglobal.net	1431 Cheltenham Ln La Habra CA 90631	PSW	EM			SL	1973
Danner Joel S	(715)539-9598 pastordanner@aol.com	N2965 Lokemoen Rd Merrill WI 54452	NW	SP	St Paul Evangelical * Hamburg WI	(715)536-7242	SL	1988
Danner Martin D	(817)372-0335 pastordanner@bethanyaustin.com	3701 W Slaughter Ln Austin TX 78749	TX	Sn/Adm	Bethany Austin TX	(512)292-8778	SL	2008
Danowski William F	william20418@yahoo.com	8680 Evergreen Ave Detroit MI 48228	MI	SP	Evergreen Detroit MI	(313)584-0450	SL	1991
Danzis Marc	(718)607-2141 aplohiseye@aol.com	8904 Willow Trace Ct Apex NC 27539	AT	EM			FW	2002
DaPena Jeremy J	(949)838-4021 jeremy.dapena@dflc.org	10758 E Tamarisk Way Scottsdale AZ 85262	PSW	SMP	Desert Foothills Scottsdale AZ	(480)585-8007	SL-SMP	2013
Dare Paul W	pastordareilc@gmail.com	1300 30th St Spirit Lake IA 51360	IW	SP	Immanuel Spirit Lake IA	(712)336-1010	SL	2000
Dargatz Robert A	ownerofbooks2@gmail.com	2534 Burly Ave Orange CA 92869	PSW				SPR	1976
Darnstaedt Mark L	(812)951-0005 revdarnstaedt@gmail.com	1230 Oakes Rd Georgetown IN 47122	IN	EM			SL	1981
Dart Jason S	(910) 353-4016 pastor@clcms.org	206 Pine Valley Rd Jacksonville NC 28546	SE	SP	Calvary Jacksonville NC	(910)353-4016	SL	2005
Dasch William E Dr	(817)319-0129 bill@billdasch.com	2503 Pepper Mill Trl Mansfield TX 76063	TX	EM			SPR	1973
Dass Allen S	(347)852-6702 pastorallendass@gmail.com	559 Raritan Rd Clark NJ 07066	S	SP	Zion Clark NJ	(732)382-7320	SL	2024
Dassow Eugene C	(608)481-1162 dassowg@gmail.com	1603 Burton St Beloit WI 53511	NI	SMP	Christ Our Savior Roscoe IL	(608)481-1162	SL-SMP	2018
Daub James M	(252) 349-5911 saintpaulpastor@gmail.com	702 Lee Dr Havelock NC 28532	SE	SP	St Paul Havelock NC	(252)447-3826	SL	1999
Daugherty Ervin A Jr	(913)660-3113 ervind1944@yahoo.com	33670 SE Hwy 31 P.O. Box 39 Kincaid KS 66039	KS	EM			FW	1984
Daugherty Shaun M	(214)514-3288 shaun.daugherty@gmail.com	1302 Milstead Trce NE Marietta GA 30066	FG	SP	Faith Marietta GA	(770)973-8877	CQ	2010
Dauk David A	(320)354-4103 pastor@livingwordlutheran.net	5126 County Road 40 NE New London MN 56273	MNN	SP	Living Word New London MN	(320)354-4637	SL	1994
Daul Wade A	(507)236-0095 pastordaul@yahoo.com	1200 N North Ave Fairmont MN 56031	MNS	Sn/Adm	Immanuel Fairmont MN	(507)238-1387	SL	1993
Daumer David H	(712)540-4754	4715 Ramsgate Ln Bowie MD 20715	SE	SP	Trinity Bowie MD	(301)262-5475	FW	1983
Dautenhahn John C	(573)280-0319	6230 Baydy Peak Rd Osage Beach MO 65065	MO	EM			SPR	1963

*Multiple Assignments (See Church Worker Locator for Additional Details)
See Page 53 for the Table of Abbreviations for key to District, Position, and Seminary abbreviations
**C =Candidate; EM = Emeritus; the date following the C is the month and year the Candidate status began

NAME	TELEPHONE NUMBER EMAIL	STREET ADDRESS CITY/STATE/ZIP	DISTRICT	POSITION/ STATUS**	WHERE SERVING	OFFICE PHONE	SEM/ PROGRAM	YR GRAD
Davenport Richard A Dr			MDS	SP	Our Redeemer Fort Smith AR	(479)646-7611	SL	2009
Davenport Dean M	(734)522-6830 pastord@christoursavior.org	14175 Farmington Rd Livonia MI 48154	MI	Sn/Adm	Christ Our Savior Livonia MI	(734)522-6830	FW	2002
Davenport John M	(512)635-6038 zlcsdavenport@yahoo.com	11027 La Paloma Loop W Salado TX 76571	TX	EM			SL	1983
Davidson Anders M	anders@holycrossnorthcanton.org	9164 Brookledge Ave NW North Canton OH 44720	OH	Sn/Adm	Holy Cross North Canton OH	(330)499-3307	SL	2010
Davidson John C Dr	(740)215-3295 1400redeemerpastor@gmail.com	420 Sells Rd Lancaster OH 43130	OH	SP	Redeemer Lancaster OH	(740)653-4083	FW	1982
Davidson Kenneth J	(812)523-8234	2174 S County Rd 750 E Seymour IN 47274	IN	SP	Emanuel Dudleytown IN	(812)523-8234	SL	1987
Davidson Seth T Dr	(903)675-9598 pastorsethd@gmail.com	451 Lila Ln Athens TX 75751	TX	SP	St John Athens TX	(903)675-9598	SL	2012
Davies Brian K	pastorbrian@lordofglory.org	799 Alleghany Rd Grayslake IL 60030	NI	SP	Lord Of Glory Grayslake IL	(847)548-5673	SL	2006
Davies Herbert J Dr	(949)335-9675 hjdavies7@gmail.com	8565 Trinity Cir Unit 825a Huntington Beach CA 92646	PSW	S Miss	Office of International Mission Saint Louis MO		FW	2003
Davies Karl C	(219)924-7123 krcleven@aol.com	3710 43rd St Highland IN 46322	IN	EM			SPR	1971
Davis William R	(940)872-0880 ross.davis@stpaulaustin.org	1207 Ritter Dr Cedar Park TX 78613	TX	SMP	St Paul Austin TX	(512)472-8301	FW-SMP	2023
Davis Joshua P	(402)462-5044 pastorjoshdavis@yahoo.com	837 Chestnut Ave Hastings NE 68901	NEB	Assoc	Faith Hastings NE	(402)462-5044	SL	2010
Davis Larry F	(352)318-0165 LDavis2645@aol.com	3301 SW 13th St Apt U287 Gainesville FL 32608	FG	EM			SPR	1968
Davis Martin W	pastormartydavis@gmail.com	c/o St Paul Lutheran Church 2326 Story Ave Battle Creek IA 51006	IW	SP	St Paul* Battle Creek IA	(712)365-4328	FW	2004
Davis Richard J Dr	(208)807-0741 skypilot_1@hotmail.com	935 W Crescent St Meridian ID 83646	NOW	SP	Faith Mountain Home ID	(208)587-4127	Other	2004
Davis David A	(517)243-1175 david.davis@michigandistrict.org	1242 Naples Ct. Ann Arbor MI 48103	MI	DP	Michigan District Ann Arbor MI	(888)225-2111	SL	1983
Davis Robert S	(813)447-6199 revrdavis79@yahoo.com	2102 SE 8th Terr Cape Coral FL 33990	FG	SP	Good Shepherd North Fort Myers FL	(239)995-7711	SL	1998
Davis Shawn P	(314)800-8419 pastordavis@stmfw.org	1923 Sherman Blvd Fort Wayne IN 46808	IN	Assoc	St Michael Fort Wayne IN	(260)432-2033	SL	2017
Davis Terrell L Sr	(770)679-9306 revterrell@peacelcmsdecatur.com	3347 Westborough Ln Conyers GA 30094	FG	SP	Peace Decatur GA	(404)289-1474	FW	2022
Davis Warren H Dr	(850)476-5725 wdavis0919@aol.com	7041 Kelvin Ter Pensacola FL 32503	SO	EM			SPR	1973
Davis Joseph B	(703)843-3573 davis301@verizon.net	12817 Prestwick Dr Ft Washington MD 20744	SE	Asst	Bethany Alexandria VA	(703)765-8255	EIITSL	2011
Davis Timothy P	(970)630-5191 kleros91@gmail.com	2535 Jefferson Rd Athens GA 30607	FG	SP	Trinity Athens GA	(706)546-0670	SL	1998
Davis Jesse L	pastorjldavis@gmail.com	210 S Charles St P.O. Box 397 Westfield WI 53964	SW	Sn/Adm	Immanuel Westfield WI	(608)296-2088	FW	2015
Davis Jeremy A	(678) 492-9963 jdbigcat@hotmail.com	6803 E Amarok Ave Wasilla AK 99654	NOW	SP	St John Palmer AK	(907)745-3338	SL	2009
Davis Isaac J	(808)219-9620 idavis@stpaulspb.com	6530 Reflection Dr Apt 2285 San Diego CA 92124	PSW	SMP	St Pauls San Diego CA	(858)272-6363	SL-SMP	2023
Davis Howard A	(440)428-5144 howardandbonnie4@gmail.com	2140 Green Rd Madison OH 44057	OH	EM			SPR	1962
Davis Eli T	(541)244-8413 pastorelidavis@gmail.com	865 NW 5th St Grants Pass OR 97526	NOW	SP	St Paul Grants Pass OR	(541)476-2565	FW	2010
Davis Douglas L	(703)992-5536 alabamapastor@gmail.com	1948 W Wayzata Blvd Apt 113 Long Lake MN 55356	MNS	EM			SL	2006
Davis Edward A	(812)530-9427 reveddavis@gmail.com	729 Hadleigh Pass Westfield IN 46074	IN	EM			SL	1980
Davis Clark M	(785)965-2234 norsk58@hotmail.com	102 W 5th Tampa KS 67483	KS	SP	Trinity* Ramona KS	(785)965-2234	FW	1980
Davis Christopher M	(262)894-5498 pastor.davis@mylivingword.com	N112 W12808 Mequon Rd Germantown WI 53022	SW	SP	Living Word Jackson WI	(262)677-1685	SL	2012
Davis Christopher B Dr	brownbassriver@gmail.com	701 S 1st St Millbank SD 57252	SD	SP	Emanuel Milbank SD	(605)432-9555	FW	2004
Davis Benjamin R	(575)376-5381 b.rankindavis@gmail.com	P.O. Box 268 Eagle Nest NM 87718	RM	SMP	Sangre de Cristo* Taos NM	(575)758-5944	SL-SMP	2025
Davis John F Jr Dr	(832)451-7248 pastordavis@mlckaty.com	5810 3rd St Katy TX 77493	TX	Sn/Adm	Memorial Lutheran Katy TX	(281)391-0171	SL	1993
Davison Tony Dr	(847)299-4593	1477 E Thacker St Apt 203 Des Plaines IL 60016	NI	Asst	Immanuel Des Plaines IL	(847)824-3652	SPR	1964
Davison Frederick E	pastordavison@gmail.com	7280 Noble Rd Windsor OH 44099	OH	Assoc	Lighted Cross Ashtabula OH	(440)466-6890	FW	1999
Dawson John K Jr	(605)521-8210 johnny.boy61@hotmail.com	1401 N Dubuque Ave Sioux Falls SD 57110	SD	C07/2016			FW	1988
Day J B	(314)604-1866 bart.day@lcef.org	12910 Baalbek Dr Saint Louis MO 63127	MO	Pro Stf	Lutheran Church Exten- sion Fund Saint Louis MO	(314)965-9000	SL	1997
De Beir Jerome A Jr	(636)549-3694 jdebeir@charter.net	1137 Zelda Hurst TX 76503	TX	SMP	Peace Hurst TX	(817)284-1677	SL-SMP	2013
De Giovanni Terry L	(785)396-4411 vicardegiovanni@yahoo.com	131 Railroad St Wheaton KS 66521	KS	SP	St Luke Wheaton KS	(785)396-4411	FW	2006
de la Rosa Victor M	(818)392-9067 mannyd1966@aol.com	10009 Columbus Ave Mission Hills CA 91345	EN	Asst	The Cross Mission Hills CA	(818)892-8490	SL	2017
De Lassus Mark J	delassusm@yahoo.com	1833 Traders Xing Fort Wayne IN 46845	IN	EM			FW	2009

*Multiple Assignments (See Church Worker Locator for Additional Details)
See Page 53 for the Table of Abbreviations for key to District, Position, and Seminary abbreviations
**C =Candidate; EM = Emeritus; the date following the C is the month and year the Candidate status began

NAME	TELEPHONE NUMBER EMAIL	STREET ADDRESS CITY/STATE/ZIP	DISTRICT	POSITION/ STATUS**	WHERE SERVING	OFFICE PHONE	SEM/ PROGRAM	YR GRAD
De Meritt Carl F Jr	(734)879-0488 Fuzzy_sergeant@yahoo.com	7226 Spy Glass Ln Ypsilanti MI 48197	MI	EM			FW	1983
De Mik Peter T	pastorpeter@blcmail.org	c/o Bethlehem Lutheran Church 155 Linwood Ave Ridgewood NJ 07450	NJ	SP	Bethlehem Ridgewood NJ	(201)444-3600	SL	2001
De Rosa Rudy A	(828)461-3899 patmosrev@live.com	816 Bales Chapel Rd Jamestown NC 27282	SE	EM			FW	1993
De Santo Steven A	(928)600-8270	22617 Respite Ln Foley AL 36535	SO	EM			SL	2008
De Vore Gregory D	(850)842-2411 gnldevore@aol.com	1633 Sardina CV Niceville FL 32578	SO	EM			CQ	2007
De Young John E	(214) 514-4954 johndeyoung@hotmail.com	512 N Cockrell Hill Rd Desoto TX 75115	TX	SP	Cross Christ Desoto TX	(972)223-9340	SL	1989
De Young Mark K	(512)470-1003 stpetertex@gmail.com	1406 Jackson St Bowie TX 76230	TX	SP	St Peter Bowie TX	(940)872-1886	FW	2022
Deal Jacob T	(724)977-1682 pastordeal@saintspeterandpaul.net	695 Crowder Ave Sharon PA 16146	S	SP	SS Peter and Paul Sharon PA	(724)347-3620	FW	2016
Deardoff Daniel H Sr	(605)261-7465 pastorbrlc@alliancecom.net	405 E Beechnut St Brandon SD 57005	SD	EM			SL	1984
Deardoff Robert E Jr	(308) 530-9267 revbob@bslcnp.com	820 W Philip Ave North Platte NE 69101	NEB	EM			SL	1982
DeArmond Zachary M	(920)629-4833 pastordearmond@gmail.com	3665 Madison St. Waukesha WI 53188	SW	SP	Blessed Savior New Berlin WI	(262)786-6465	SL	2011
DeBartolo Seth T	seth.debartolo@gmail.com	11470 Persimmon Ct Fort Myers FL 33913	FG	SP	Faith* Clewiston FL	(863)983-7302	FW	2018
Deberny Peter J	(716) 200-8207 pdebernycca2015@gmail.com	216 Mastic Rd Mastic Beach NY 11951	AT	SP	Grace Mastic Beach NY	(631)281-8196	SL	2022
DeBlieck Jared S		3431 Plymouth Dr Lafayette IN 47909	IN	Sn/Adm	University West Lafayette IN	(765)743-2472	FW	2014
Debner Adam M	(408)252-0345 pastoradebner@lcos.org	14950 Vickery Ave #19 Saratoga CA 95070	CNH	Assoc	Our Savior Cupertino CA	(408)252-0345	FW	2018
DeBoer Jordan L	(218) 289-1244 felc.pastor@paulbunyan.net	20268 State 226 Park Rapids MN 56470	MNN	SP	First English Dorset MN	(218)732-9466	FW	2024
Debowey Darrell L	(217)638-1023 ddebowey@aol.com	24 Corthell Rd Laramie WY 82070	WY	EM			FW	2003
Decker Daniel J	(608)322-5839 ed424261@gmail.com	4242 Saratoga Dr Janesville WI 53546	SW	EM			FW	1983
Decker Thomas R	(562)225-9812 tomdecker2010@yahoo.com	1290 Santa Rosa Drive No 220 Chula Vista CA 91913	PSW	EM			SL	1969
Decker Wayne D	(440)937-5765 wddadecker@hotmail.com	34509 Heatherwood Ave Avon OH 44011	OH	EM			SL	1981
Deddeh Suah S	(240)413-2610 deddehsuahs@yahoo.com	9116 Briarchip St Laurel MD 20708	SE	SP	Crosswalk Columbia MD	(410)730-8765	EIITSL	2007
Deebrah Peter A	(907)335-5801	4513 Carpenter Ave Bronx NY 10470	AT	SP	St Matthew New York NY	(212)567-5948	FW-D	2005
Deen Keffie A II	(779)772-2603 revkdeen@gmail.com		SE	SP	Trinity Chestertown MD	(410)778-2744	SL	2008
DeForest Brennan T	(801)910-6937 pastorbd4est@gmail.com	5 McKinley Lane Chico CA 95973	CNH	SP	Redeemer Chico CA	(530)342-6085	FW	2023
Degner Robert P	(608)772-5313 degner2000@aol.com	2137 County Rd Mm Fitchburg WI 53575	SW	EM			SPR	1965
DeGroot Adam J	(267)591-8920 adamdegroot78@gmail.com	5804 San Miguel Dr NE Rio Rancho NM 87144	RM	SP	Calvary Rio Rancho NM	(505)892-9407	FW	2010
Dehne James A	(580)716-5687 jimdehne@yahoo.com	2668 Calvalry Ln Neenah WI 54956	SW	EM			FW	2004
Dehne John A	(573)270-7500 john@lglomd.org	1561 Greenbrier St. Cape Girardeau MO 63701	MO	Sn/Adm	St Andrew Cape Girardeau MO	(573)334-3200	SL	2014
Dehning K C	(574)933-3126 pastor.dehning@gmail.com	1302 N Courtland Ave Kokomo IN 46901	IN	EM			FW	1991
Dehnke David R	drdehnke@gmail.com	1676 Bryn Mawr Ct New Albany IN 47150	IN	EM			FW	2001
DeHope Kevin G	(209)840-0289 galaxie65s@gmail.com	5543 SW Auburn Rd Topeka KS 66610	KS	SP	Prince Of Peace Topeka KS	(785)271-0808	FW	2008
Deinert Allen R	(951)233-7635 deinert@aol.com	2933 Diver Loop The Villages FL 32163	FG	EM			FW	1977
Deitemeyer Leo R	(952)456-1728 leodeitemeyer@gmail.com	2528 18th St South Fargo ND 58103	ND	EM			SPR	1971
Deitz John A	(715)769-3127 deitzjnl@yahoo.com	P.O. Box 158 Butternut WI 54514	NW	SP	St Paul Butternut WI	(715)769-3731	FW	1994
Deknatel Chris D	(760)224-8120	373 Rocky Top Dr Monterey TN 38574	MDS	EM			SL	2004
Deknatel Arnold W Dr	(585)507-6334 deknatelarnold@gmail.com	21 Bridgewood Dr Fairport NY 14450	EA	EM			FW	1979
DelCol Christopher R	(707)472-7971 cdelcol@yahoo.com	1510 Cannon Dr Fort Oglethorpe GA 30742	CNH	EM			Other	2005
Delin Benjamin J	(970)529-6829 pastorbendelin@gmail.com	328 Clear Spring Ave. Durango CO 81301	RM	SP	St Paul's Durango CO	(970)247-0357	SL	2013
DeLoach James H	(308) 627-5260 james.deloach@zionkearney.org	3510 14th Ave Kearney NE 68845	NEB	Sn/Adm	Zion Kearney NE	(308)234-3410	SL	1991
DeLoye Gerald J Jr Dr	(612)819-0541	5001 East Main St. #1323 Mesa AZ 85205	PSW	EM			SPR	1967
Demchuk Robert W Sr	(815)258-6858 rwdsrrev@comcast.net	1633 Waterberry Dr Bourbonnais IL 60914	NI	EM			SL	1991
Demel Mark W	(760)468-2712 mcdemel76@gmail.com	1544 Linda St Fallbrook CA 92028	PSW	EM			FW	1982

*Multiple Assignments (See Church Worker Locator for Additional Details)
See Page 53 for the Table of Abbreviations for key to District, Position, and Seminary abbreviations
**C =Candidate; EM = Emeritus; the date following the C is the month and year the Candidate status began

NAME	TELEPHONE NUMBER EMAIL	STREET ADDRESS CITY/STATE/ZIP	DISTRICT	POSITION/ STATUS**	WHERE SERVING	OFFICE PHONE	SEM/ PROGRAM	YR GRAD
Demera David G	(917)604-9223 dave31dd@yahoo.com	P.O. Box 93 Neffs PA 18065	AT	EM			SL	1980
DeMik Stephen R	(713)825-9002 stephendemik@yahoo.com	5700 98th St Lubbock TX 79424	TX	Assoc	Hope Lubbock TX	(806)798-2747	SL	2008
Deming Sean K	(347) 414-1971		PSW	SP	Faith Moorpark CA	(805)532-1049	SL	2025
Demski Merritt M	(847)254-9666 pastor.demski@gmail.com	165 630th St Alta IA 51002	IW	SP	St John Alta IA	(712)284-1450	SL	2016
DeMuth Gregory A	(218)256-9899 gademuth@yahoo.com	211 3rd St NE Barnesville MN 56514	MNN	SP	Saint Johns Barnesville MN	(218)354-7158	FW	2008
Den Ouden Robert P	(909)224-1420 rdenouden@verizon.net	9801 W Pineaire Dr Sun City AZ 85351	PSW	EM			SL	1985
Deneen Christopher M	(989)598-0679 revdeneen@gmail.com	2907 Deltas St Lansing MI 48906	MI	Assoc	Our Savior Lansing MI	(517)882-8665	SL	2021
Deng Bafel P	(402) 937-5781 dengbafel@gmail.com	5600 Roose St Apt 1 Lincoln NE 68506	EN	C06/2018			SL	2008
Denholm George A	(812)374-4586 pastor@jamstl.org	2737 Wyoming St Saint Louis MO 63118	MO	SP	Emmaus Saint Louis MO	(314)782-7678	SL	2021
Denke Glenn R	(605)842-3790	1006 E 6th St Winner SD 57580	SD	EM			FW	1982
Denninger John R Dr	(703)627-1863 john.denninger@lfnd.org	7209 Trappers Pl Springfield VA 22153	SE	Pro Stf	LCMS Foundation Saint Louis MO	(314)965-9000	SL	1980
Dennis Mark	(503)810-5986 scapfig@gmail.com	33729 SE Elm St Scappoose OR 97056	NOW	SMP	Calvary Saint Helens OR	(503)397-1739	CQ	2019
Dennis Marshall H	mhd721@juno.com	11556 Vermont St Crown Point IN 46307	IN	EM			CQ	1985
Dent Matthew T	(989)313-2525 dentm42@gmail.com	5606 Johnsfield Rd Standish MI 48658	MI	SP	Bethlehem Standish MI	(989)846-4972	FW	2009
d'Entremont James A III	(573)723-0339 jim_dentremont@hotmail.com	11265 State Route 177 Okawville IL 62271	SI		Southern Illinois District Belleville IL	(618)234-4767	SL	2016
Deombeleg Steve C	deombeleg@gmail.com	1255 N Sterling Ave Unit 109 Palatine IL 60067	NI	SP	Immanuel Hillside IL	(708)562-5590	SL	2004
DePaoli David M	(715)368-1075 rev.depaoli@gmail.com	1425 E 6th St Findlay OH 45840	OH	SP	Concordia Findlay OH	(419)422-4209	FW	2000
Deressa Samuel Y Dr	(651)621-9866 deressa@csp.edu	3305 Edgemere Ave Saint Anthony MN 55118	MNS	S HS/C	Concordia University St Paul Saint Paul MN	(651)641-8278	CQ	2018
Derong Wynn T	(713)471-0907 wynn.derong@gmail.com	4206 Gillespie St Houston TX 77020	TX	SMP	St Andrew Houston TX	(713)468-9565	SL-SMP	2020
DeSoto Kenneth J	(505)410-8233 revkendesoto@gmail.com	2637 Elm Lawn Dr. Marrero LA 70072	SO	SP	Trinity* New Orleans LA	(504)368-0411	FW	1989
Deterding Curtis L Dr	(239)810-0057 curtisdeterding@hotmail.com	16700 Wellington Lakes Cir Fort Myers FL 33908	FG	SP	Zion Fort Myers FL	(239)481-4040	SL	1987
Deterding Shawn L	pastorshawn@wateroflifelc.org	1439 Davis Ln Terrell TX 75160	TX	SP	Water of Life Forney TX	(972)552-9393	SL	2003
Deterding Paul E Dr	(321) 208-8177 deterdingpaul@gmail.com	4006 Meander Pl #207 Rockledge FL 32955	S	EM			SL	1978
Detrie Jace C	(423)507-7198 pastordetrie@gmail.com	2706 Hillside Dr Wylie TX 75098	TX	Assoc	Messiah Plano TX	(972)398-7500	SL	2008
Dettmer Linsey H	(865)850-5248 dettmer38@outlook.com	331 Lane Hollow Rd Sevierville TN 37876	MDS	EM			SPR	1970
Detviler Timothy J	(714)726-4495 tim.detviler@lhsoc.org	1423 E Lael Dr Orange CA 92866	PSW	Cmp P	Orange County Orange CA	(714)998-5151	SL	1996
Deuel Daniel D	(209)915-3118 dddeuel@gmail.com	Christ The King Lutheran Church 1700 E Pennsylvania Ave Coeur D Alene ID 83814	NOW	Sn/Adm	Christ King Coeur D Alene ID	(208)664-9231	CQ	2006
Devantier Paul W Dr	(571)235-1616 pauldevantier@gmail.com	2145 W. Twin Willows Drive Appleton WI 54914	NW	EM			SL	1972
DeVries Phillip M	(989)293-4032 hillhome21@yahoo.com	4035 E Munkwitz Ave Cudahy WI 53110	S	SP	St John Cudahy WI	(414)481-0520	SL	2007
DeVries Michael D	(248)394-0250 manirish17@hotmail.com	8098 W Circle Dr Clarkston MI 48348	MI	SMP	St Trinity Clarkston MI	(248)625-4644	CQ	2018
Dewell Russell L	(260)580-0124 russdewell@hotmail.com	243 W 2nd Ave N Columbus MT 59019	MT	SP	St Paul's Park City MT	(406)633-2356	FW	2007
DeWerff Robert E Dr	(651)482-1840 dewerffra@msn.com	1087 Westcliff Curve Saint Paul MN 55126	MNS	EM			SL	1973
DeWitt Douglas A	(931)796-7801 immanuelpastor@bright.net	600 Edgefield Dr Hohenwald TN 38462	MDS	Assoc	Faith Thompsons Station TN	(615)791-1880	FW	1998
DeWitt Edward J	(407)322-3552 pastor@redeemersanford.org	911 Millshore Dr Chuluota FL 32766	FG	SP	Redeemer Sanford FL	(407)322-3552	SL	1995
Dexheimer Larry J	(352)351-8539	2152 SE 7th Terr Ocala FL 34471	FG	EM			CQ	2019
DeYoung Joshua K	deyoung@stjohnsracine.org		SW	Assoc	St John Racine WI	(262)637-7011	FW	2018
Di Gregorio Philip J	503-659-2049 phild57@msn.com	1839 SE Parkview Cir Milwaukie OR 97267	NOW	EM			FW	1977
Diamond Thomas E	(843)771-0599 tediamond49@gmail.com	105 Coosawatchie St Summerville SC 29485	SE	EM			SL	1976
Diaz Luis A	(561)670-9596 luisdiaz64@aol.com	4398 Fountains Dr Lake Worth FL 33467	FG	EM			SL	2010
Diaz John A	(210) 834-6561 mydiazfamily@yahoo.com	8412 8th St Converse TX 78109	TX	EM			FW	1995
Dickerhoff Jacob S	(314)852-3590 jakedickerhoff@gmail.com	c/o Lutheran Church Of The Way 110 Robinson St Raynham MA 02767	NE	SP	Of The Way Raynham MA	(508)822-5900	SL	2012

*Multiple Assignments (See Church Worker Locator for Additional Details)
See Page 53 for the Table of Abbreviations for key to District, Position, and Seminary abbreviations
**C =Candidate; EM = Emeritus; the date following the C is the month and year the Candidate status began

NAME	TELEPHONE NUMBER EMAIL	STREET ADDRESS CITY/STATE/ZIP	DISTRICT	POSITION/ STATUS**	WHERE SERVING	OFFICE PHONE	SEM/ PROGRAM	YR GRAD
Dickerson Aaron L	(618)416-5647 aaron-dickerson@att.net	2617 Autumn Harvest Ln Belleville IL 62221	SI	Prin	Unity East Saint Louis IL	(618)874-6605	EIITSL	2007
Dickerson Paul N	(314)631-0304 paul.dickerson@cmstl.org	5252 S. Lindbergh Blvd Saint Louis MO 63109	MO	Assoc	Christ Memorial Saint Louis MO	(314)631-0304	SL	2020
Dickinson Dwight E Sr	(314)952-9530 greatcommissionlcl@gmail.com	c/o Great Commission Lutheran 4364 Dr Martin Luther King Saint Louis MO 63113	MO	SP	Great Commission Saint Louis MO	(314)773-9182	SL-D	2009
Dickmander Jon M	pastordickmander@gmail.com	P.O. Box 144 Brule NE 69127	NEB	SP	Trinity* Ogallala NE	(308)352-4079	FW	2008
DiConti Marc G	(951)490-8680 marc.diconti@gmail.com	216 West 5th Street Cheney WA 99004	EN	Assoc	Blessed Sacrament Hayden ID	(406)262-3298	CQ	2002
Didanu Berhanu K	(916)949-8863 berhanukumalo@yahoo.com	2765 Forrest St Sacramento CA 95815	CNH	Assoc	St Paul Woodland CA	(530)662-1935	SL	2020
Dieckmann Anthony A	(630)235-7390 aadieckmann1@gmail.com	265 Rainbow Dr #16526 Livingston TX 77399	NI	EM			FW-SMP	2015
Diedrick Theodore J	(651)756-1548 pted@goodshepherdlink.org	7521 155th Ave NE Forest Lake MN 55025	MNS	SP	Good Shepherd Circle Pines MN	(763)784-8417	SL	2009
Diefenthaler Jon T Dr	jtdiefen@aol.com	713 Warren Dr Annapolis MD 21403	SE	EM			SL	1969
Diekelman William R Dr	(858)487-1332 wrdiekelman@gmail.com	16291 Gabarda Rd San Diego CA 92128	PSW	EM			SL	1973
Diekroger Walter E	(740)253-9532 floodwood65@gmail.com	32929 Catawba Dr Avon OH 44011	OH	EM			SL	1973
Diener John H	(616)350-3199 revjhdiener@gmail.com	2603 Golfbury Dr SW Wyoming MI 49519	MI	EM			FW	1994
Diener Michael J	(440)554-6430 revmjdiener@gmail.com	5331 Sheridan Dr Jefferson City MO 65109	MO	SP	Grace Holts Summit MO	(573)896-8824	FW	2010
Dierks Andrew P	(217)997-5534 pastor@trinityarenzville.org	P.O. Box 49 Arenzville IL 62611	CI	SP	St Paul* Chapin IL	(217)472-7891	FW	2013
Dierks Daniel P	(219)775-5690 dpd1086@icloud.com	653 Burnt Sienna Dr Middleton WI 53562	SW	EM			FW	1983
Dierks Robert O Jr	rdierks208@gmail.com	825 N Cotner Blvd Apt 109 Lincoln NE 68505	NEB	EM			CQ	2019
Dieterichs Joel T	(216) 972-4490 pastor_joel@live.com		RM	C02/2024			SL	2004
Dietrich Joel M Dr	(571)839-0251 jdietrich@stpaulptc.org	164 Ardenlee Dr Peachtree Cty GA 30269	FG	SMP	St Paul Peachtree City GA	(770)487-0339	SL-SMP	2019
Dietrich Chadric A	(712)887-1204 revdietrich@gmail.com	3012 270th St Rockwell City IA 50579	IW	SP	Trinity* Manson IA	(515)463-2244	FW	2003
Dietrich Joel A	(708) 308-6260 revdietrich@aol.com	102 South Railway Street Mascoutah IL 62258	SI	SP	Zion Mascoutah IL	(618)566-7345	FW	2005
Dietsche David W	(518)482-2334 dwdietsche@icloud.com	167 Sand Creek Rd Albany NY 12205	AT	Asst	Bethlehem Delmar NY	(518)439-4328	CQ	2006
DiLiberto Anthony J	(787)464-3166 dilibertoaj@gmail.com	2657 W Horizon Ridge Pkwy Ste 120 Henderson NV 89052	PSW	SP	Grace Henderson NV	(702)492-4701	SL	2018
Dill Terence M	(206)715-8793 revtmd1@gmail.com	11621 NW Swantown St Silverdale WA 98383	NOW	EM			FW	1977
Dille Trey R	(636)328-4216 dillet@csl.edu	109 S Oak St Effingham IL 62401	CI	Assoc	St John Effingham IL	(217)342-4334	SL	2024
Dimit Andrew W	(575)200-0704 andrew.dimit@gmail.com	3731 Sunrise Hills Dr Cheyenne WY 82009	WY	Asst	King of Glory Cheyenne WY	(307)632-1247	FW	1986
Dinger Andrew D	revdinger@gmail.com		MO	Sn/Adm	Timothy Saint Louis MO	(314)781-8673	SL	2007
Dinger Timothy J	(409)548-2143 revtdinger@gmail.com	1300 Shadowdale St Bridge City TX 77611	TX	EM			CQ	1982
Dinger Jonathan M	(208)237-0467 jdinger@gracepocatello.org	1350 Baldy Ave Pocatello ID 83201	NOW	Sn/Adm	Grace Pocatello ID	(208)237-0467	SL	1995
Dinger Matthias J	(936)825-2285 mdinger@tlcnavasota.com	130 Thane St Navasota TX 77868	TX	SP	Trinity Navasota TX	(936)825-6851	SL	2007
Dirasse Getabicha	(260)804-1683 getad01@gmail.com	5598 Mill Pond Ln Redding CA 96001	CNH	EM			FW	2009
Disbro Roger E	(309)685-8268 vegedibles@protonmail.com	c/o Dr. Lonny Lannert 7810 W Krause Ct Mapleton IL 61547	CI	EM			SL	1982
Dishop James L	jldishop@yahoo.com	7910 Beckett Ln Naples FL 34113	FG	EM			SL	1956
Disney James G	(763)233-2515 disneyjames4@gmail.com	86 Cascade Cir Chanhassen MN 55317	MNS	EM			SL	1985
Dissen David V	(573)334-5736 davidvdissen@gmail.com	2825 Bloomfield Rd Duplex 74 Cape Girardeau MO 63703	MO	EM			SL	1959
Dittloff Todd A	(830)896-5540 dittloff@ktc.com	310 Oak Wood Rd Kerrville TX 78028	TX	EM			SPR	1976
Dittmar David L	(314)599-7434 pastordavid1950@live.com	7316 Coronado Ave Saint Louis MO 63116	MO	SP	Saint Lukes Saint Louis MO	(314)352-1224	CQ	1995
Dittmer Terry K Dr	(314)482-1994 drtkdittmer@gmail.com	1509 Friar Ln Kirkwood MO 63122	MO	EM			SPR	1974
Dixon Michael W	mikewithfaith@aol.com	815 Oak Hurst Dr Hopkinsville KY 42240	SO	SMP	Prince Of Peace Corinth MS		FW-SMP	2015
Dobberstein Paul M	(630)484-1011 pauld1181@gmail.com	41 Concordia Dr Paris IL 61944	CI	C07/2016			SL	1981
Dobbertien David F	(402)643-9394 revddobb@yahoo.com	1145 N 2nd St Seward NE 68434	NEB	SP	Zion Garland NE	(402)588-2229	CQ	1996
Dobbins Dennis L	(937)623-4462 dennis_dobbins@att.net	1687 Sunset Canyon Court Fairborn OH 45324	OH	EM			FW	1999
Dobler Michael R	(815)980-3443 michael.dobler@valpo.edu	107 Scott St Tonawanda NY 14150	EA	SP	Immanuel Tonawanda NY	(716)692-6200	SL	2016

*Multiple Assignments (See Church Worker Locator for Additional Details)
See Page 53 for the Table of Abbreviations for key to District, Position, and Seminary abbreviations
**C =Candidate; EM = Emeritus; the date following the C is the month and year the Candidate status began

NAME	TELEPHONE NUMBER EMAIL	STREET ADDRESS CITY/STATE/ZIP	DISTRICT	POSITION/ STATUS**	WHERE SERVING	OFFICE PHONE	SEM/ PROGRAM	YR GRAD
Dobratz Gordon J	(920)676-7952 jeffdobratz@yahoo.com	1333 Mather St Green Bay WI 54303	NW	EM			FW	1995
Dobratz Wayne P	(608)834-4364 predigtamt35@gmail.com	6842 Starburst Dr Sun Prairie WI 53590	SW	EM			CQ	1985
Dock Jeffrey M	(573)560-2418 pastordock@gmail.com	1806 W. Main St. Bowling Green MO 63334	MO	SP	Trinity* Louisiana MO	(573)754-6120	FW	2011
Dockery Richard K	(541)844-9355 rk_dockery@juno.com	2210 Griffitts Mill Circle Maryville TN 37803	MDS	EM			SL	2009
Dodge Clayton E	(918)519-2931 delt.strike@yahoo.com	609 Arapaho St #59 Garber OK 73738	OK	SP	Immanuel Garber OK	(580)863-2722	FW	2025
Dodge David A	(989) 553-0057 drdodge@juno.com	105 Cresthaven Ln. Mt. Pleasant MI 48858	MI	SP	Saint John Port Hope MI	(989)428-4140	FW	1999
Dodge Christopher R	(952)913-1345 pastordodge.awakeusnow@ gmail.com	6713 Conestoga Drive Lansing MI 48917	MI	EM			SL	1979
Dodgers Anthony C	pastordodgers@gmail.com		IN	Assoc	Bethlehem Ossian IN	(260)597-7121	FW	2011
Doebler James M	(703)677-6395 pastor@tlcnorfolk.com	1029 Marietta Ave Norfolk VA 23513	SE	SP	Trinity Norfolk VA	(757)489-2551	SL	2024
Doede Mark R	mdoede@gmail.com	20285 Beechaven St Southfield MI 48076	MI	SP	Huntington Woods Huntington Woods MI	(248)542-3007	SL	2018
Doel Brian C	(913)449-7219 pastorbdoel@gmail.com	3137 Hickory St Portage IN 46368	IN	SP	St Peter Portage IN	(219)762-2673	SL	2020
Doellinger Paul M	(269)635-1078 paul.doellinger@gmail.com	22405 Shady Ln Cassopolis MI 49031	MI	SP	St Paul Cassopolis MI	(269)445-3950	FW	2010
Doellinger Paul D	(503)838-4884 revpauldd@gmail.com	295 Knox St S Monmouth OR 97361	NOW	EM			SL	1969
Doellinger Jerry W	(319)721-5445 revjd@icloud.com	6843 Waterview Dr SW Cedar Rapids IA 52404	IE	EM			SL	1972
Doellinger David D	(712)330-4944 pastorddd@gmail.com	712 560th St Cleghorn IA 51014	IW	C04/2023			FW	2006
Doering Allen F	(281)300-8006 ald@christ4u.net	3319 Redwood Lake Dr Kingwood TX 77345	TX	Sn/Adm	Christ King Kingwood TX	(281)360-7936	SL	1983
Doering Martin E	(512)917-8354 grampster1012@gmail.com	2974 Wolfcreek New Braunfels TX 78130	TX	EM			CQ	1976
Doering Theodore A	ted@narrative.church		TX	SP	Narrative Round Rock TX		SL	2014
Doerner Edward F	(989) 259-8000	2413 Thayer Rd Freeland MI 48623	MI	Sn/Adm	Messiah Midland MI	(989)631-5200	FW	1991
Dohanyos Franklin J	(248)399-1101 franklinpr91@gmail.com	3375 Loon Lake Shored Rd Waterford MI 48329	MI	SMP	Saint Augustine Troy MI	(248)879-6400	CQ	2021
Doka Kenneth J Dr	(845)462-5837 kndok@aol.com	85 Alda Dr Poughkeepsie NY 12603	AT	SP	Family of Faith* Middletown NY	(845)692-7075	SL	1973
Dolak George	(724) 715-4678 rn86mdiv@earthlink.net	105 McWilliams Dr Natrona Hts PA 15065	S	EM			SL	1957
Dolby Benjamin A	(248)924-7362	All Saints Lutheran Church 5501 148th Ave NE Bellevue WA 98007	NOW	SP	All Saints Bellevue WA	(425)881-2925	SL	2008
Dolde John M	(260)579-6604 pastordolde@gmail.com	702 Smith St Grand Mound IA 52751	IE	SP	Immanuel Grand Mound IA	(563)847-2631	FW	2022
Dollar Christian B	(573)353-6249 CDollar@TLBR.org	15w680 89th St Burr Ridge IL 60527	NI	Assoc	Trinity Burr Ridge IL	(708)839-1200	SL	2025
Domanski David A	(612)720-8898 lion_of_judah2@hotmail.com	3551 21st Ave S Minneapolis MN 55407	MNS	SP	St Peter Afton MN	(651)436-3357	SL	2005
Domenichelli Jonah J	Jonah.Domenichelli@lcms.org	3916 Potsdam Ave #1913 Sioux Falls SD 57104	SD	S Miss	Office of International Mission Saint Louis MO		FW	2020
Dominguez Pablo G	(309)738-6124 cristorey-em@sbcglobal.net	106 Orchard Ct Silvis IL 61282	CI	SP	Christ the King East Moline IL	(309)738-6124	HITSL	1993
Dominguez-Martinez Ruben	(956)278-9196 ruben.domm@yahoo.com	1401 Redbud Ave McAllen TX 78504	TX	EM			Other	1980
Domke Daniel M	(605)461-9362 acall2@outlook.com	23054 Treebark Dr Bemidji MN 56601	MNN	EM			SL	1983
Dommer Douglas W	(281)352-5665 dwdommer@icloud.com	17511 Seidel Rd Tomball TX 77377	TX	Sn/Adm	Living Word The Woodlands TX	(281)363-4860	SL	1981
Donahue Randall C	(630)280-9631 rbdonahue1981@yahoo.com	17720 W. Sandy Road Goodyear AZ 85338	PSW	EM			SL	1998
Donaldson Robert J	(805)234-8322 donaldsonr@gmail.com	908 W 17th St Houston TX 77008	TX	Assoc	Oikos Houston TX	(832)236-0645	SL	2008
Donley Bruce C	(716)371-0989 bren_donley@yahoo.com	4045 Seneca Pkwy Niagara Falls NY 14304	EA	EM			FW	1988
Donnan John M	(406)534-8640 kerka1924@yahoo.com	610 Wood Duck Dr Park City MT 59063	MT	Asst	Christ The King Billings MT	(406)252-9250	FW	1993
Donner Paul H	(270)442-5218 dpaulh@bellsouth.net	4137 Rustic Ave Paducah KY 42001	MDS	EM			SL	1957
Donofrio Craig J	(216)408-7439 reverendme@gmail.com	809 16th St SW Willmar MN 56201	MNN	SP	Redeemer Willmar MN	(320)235-4685	SL	1998
Donovan Robert B Jr	(773)719-1485 prbdonovan@gmail.com	1452 S Pembroke Dr South Elgin IL 60177	NI	EM			SL	1996
Doolittle John M	(707)774-5690 inhishand23@yahoo.com	505 Grant St Saint Paul NE 68873	NEB	SP	St Johns* Palmer NE	(308)894-3545	FW	1998
Doremus Dwaine D	(605)270-1406 dddmoses@gmail.com	72 3rd Ave S P.O. Box 385 Ellendale ND 58436	ND	Asst	Zion Ellendale ND	(701)349-4147	FW	1986
Doria Jeffrey S	(210)387-5413 pastordoria@stpaulthorndale.com	P.O. Box 369 Thorndale TX 76577	TX	SP	St Paul Thorndale TX	(512)898-5455	SL	2001
Dorn Hilbert H	(804)379-1249 vadorns1@verizon.net	630 Krim Point Loop Midlothian VA 23114	SE	EM			SL	1963

*Multiple Assignments (See Church Worker Locator for Additional Details)

See Page 53 for the Table of Abbreviations for key to District, Position, and Seminary abbreviations

**C =Candidate; EM = Emeritus; the date following the C is the month and year the Candidate status began

NAME	TELEPHONE NUMBER EMAIL	STREET ADDRESS CITY/STATE/ZIP	DISTRICT	POSITION/ STATUS**	WHERE SERVING	OFFICE PHONE	SEM/ PROGRAM	YR GRAD
Dorn Michael P	(832)752-5886 mdorn@trinitydt.org	800 Houston Ave Houston TX 77007	TX	Sn/Adm	Trinity Houston TX	(713)224-0684	SL	1991
Dorn Paul H	(936)273-4423 pbdorn6@gmail.com	6 Steep Trail Pl Conroe TX 77385	TX	EM			SL	1961
Dorn Peter B	(708)580-0177 pbdorn@aol.com	15 Key Ct Oakland CA 94605	CNH	SP	Zion Piedmont CA	(510)530-4213	SL	1982
Dorn Vernon H	(763)862-4989	11941 Terrace Rd NE Blaine MN 55434	MNS	EM			SPR	1969
Dorn Victor E	(320)217-8593	1355 10th Ave N Saint Cloud MN 56303	MNN	EM			SPR	1969
Dornan Thomas L	(781)989-0101 dornanclergy@gmail.com	23 Hall St Mansfield MA 02048	NE	EM			CQ	2004
Dorner Michael H Dr	(651)641-8811 dorner@csp.edu	1760 Yorkshire Ave Saint Paul MN 55116	MNS	S HS/C	Concordia University St Paul Saint Paul MN	(651)641-8278	SL	1995
Dorner James E II	(631)707-2365 jimdorner@gmail.com	3 Parkwood St Albany NY 12203	AT	SP	St Pauls* Albany NY	(518)464-2648	SL	2020
Doroh David A	(256) 740-7475 dadoroh@att.net	330 Reddoch Rd Florence AL 35633	SO	EM			CQ	1976
Doroh Gerhardt A	(586)727-2888 mkrital@comcast.net	8903 Bartel Rd Columbus MI 48063	MI	EM			SL	1971
Dorow Maynard W	(651)628-4934 dorow@csp.edu	2680 Lexington Ave N Apt 8 Saint Paul MN 55113	MNS	EM			SL	1956
Dorow William R Jr	(315)651-6553 wdorow@rochester.rr.com	9 Stark St Waterloo NY 13165	EA	SP	Calvary Waterloo NY	(315)539-8053	FW	1989
Dorr Paul H	(239)246-9209 pcdorrway@yahoo.com	4102 Olde Meadowbrook Ln Estero FL 34134	EN	EM			SPR	1965
Dorre Ralph O	(760)320-4130 ralphdorre@gmail.com	42778 Middle Ridge Pl Broadlands VA 20148	AT	EM			SL	1956
Dorsch Timothy D	(580)297-3516 tdorsch@msn.com	2800 E Oklahoma Ave Enid OK 73701	OK	EM			SL	1973
Dorsey Curtis R	(512)785-4769 dorsey.curtis@gmail.com	62-18 80th Ave Glendale NY 11385	AT	SP	Redeemer Glendale NY	(718)456-5292	SL	2009
Dorth Jeffrey D	(262)707-9197	4400 Main St Hilton Head Island SC 29926	SE	Sn/Adm	Island Hilton Head Island SC	(843)689-5200	FW	1988
Dose Benjamin J	pastordose@trinityalgona.org	605 North Church St Algona IA 50511	IW	Sn/Adm	St John* Burt IA	(515)924-3344	SL	2003
Dost Timothy P Dr	(314)420-8030 tpdost@msn.com	7564 Ahern Ave Saint Louis MO 63130	MO	S HS/C	Concordia Seminary Saint Louis MO	(314)505-7000	SL	1985
Doublestein Philip S	(210)846-8505 pdoublestein@gmail.com	2922 Vista Parkway New Braunfels TX 78130	TX	Assoc	Word of Life Cibolo TX	(210)566-2237	SL	2015
Doubrava Raymond T II	(316) 993-4821 raymond.doubrava@outlook.com	219 N Maple St P.O. Box 242 Leigh NE 68643	IN	SP	New Hope Ossian IN	(260)622-7954	FW	2019
Douches Anthony J	(863)698-7769 tonydcarod@verizon.net	1001 Carpenter's Way Apt C-416 Lakeland FL 33809	FG	EM			SL	1967
Doughty Robert M III	(505)850-2343 robdoughty3@gmail.com	1312 W. Chilton Ave. Gilbert AZ 85233	EN	Assoc	Eternal Life Mesa AZ	(480)985-0224	FW	2024
Douglas Kirk D	(218)298-2342 pastorkirk@nymtrinity.org	P.O. Box J New York Mls MN 56567	MNN	Sn/Adm	Trinity New York Mills MN	(218)385-2450	FW	1998
Douglas Timothy S Jr	(713)515-2003 timothy.s.douglas@gmail.com	2006 Graystone Hills Dr Conroe TX 77304	TX	SMP	Living Savior Montgomery TX	(936)597-8013	SL	2025
Douglas Paul D	(613)639-1825 mrpaul67@gmail.com	185 Golf Course Rd Pembroke ON K8A 7 CANADA	EN	SP	St John Golden Lake ON	(613)625-2533	CQ	2022
Douglas Matthew G	(317)213-4380 pastor@immanuelglenview.org	2731 N Ridge Ave Arlington Heights IL 60004	NI	SP	Immanuel Glenview IL	(847)724-1034	SL	2016
Douthwaite Adam N	(214) 368-1371 revand@orlcs.com	3613 Shelley Ln. Rowlett TX 75088	TX	Assoc	Our Redeemer Dallas TX	(214)368-1371	SL	2013
Douthwaite James A	(703)861-4359 revjdoc@gmail.com	7920 Saint Dennis Dr Springfield VA 22153	S	SP	Saint Athanasius Vienna VA	(703)455-4003	FW	1994
Douthwaite William III	(386)346-0181 padrebill57@gmail.com	48 Barkley Ln Palm Coast FL 32137	EN	EM			FW	1986
Dowding Robert G	(517)974-6163 dowdingbob70@gmail.com	311 N Smith Rd Eaton Rapids MI 48827	MI	EM			CQ	2019
Downs Brian E	(618)920-6657 bdowns316@gmail.com	3134 Rentchler Rd Belleville IL 62221	SI	EM			SL	2003
Doyal Odis W Jr	(830)355-7670 odisdoyal@gmail.com	641 Fm 573 S Mullin TX 76864	TX	EM			SL-D	2010
Draeger Harold S Dr	(650)740-3508 hdraeger@gmail.com	881 Chesterton Ave Redwood City CA 94061	CNH	EM			SPR	1971
Draeger Jeffrey G	(586)752-7250 jeffreygdraeger@gmail.com		MI	EM			SL	1988
Drankwalter Richard H	(352)799-8036 rdrankwa@tampabay.rr.com	270 Greenwich Circle Spring Hill FL 34609	FG	EM			SPR	1970
Drawbaugh Galen F	(574)265-6308 jg6309@centurylink.net	3438 N Berry Patch Ln Warsaw IN 46582	IN	EM			SL	1966
Drawbaugh Timothy G	(908)852-2156 tg_drawbaugh@outlook.com	409 E Baldwin Street Hackettstown NJ 07840	NJ	SP	Gethsemane Hackettstown NJ	(908)852-2156	SL	2002
Drebes Bryan E	(913)282-2908 bryandrebes@pacifichillslutheran. org	7816 Heritage Cir Ralston NE 68127	NEB	Sn/Adm	Pacific Hills Omaha NE	(402)391-9625	SL	2001
Drees D B	(512)755-2928 bandb863@gmail.com	402 Long Mountain Dr Burnet TX 78611	TX	EM			FW	1988
Drehman Arthur J	(260)739-2594 pastordrehman@gmail.com	P.O. Box 93 Corona SD 57227	SD	SP	Trinity* Corona SD		FW	2013
Dreier Timothy P	(918)836-3752 pastor@osltulsa.org	4901 S. 177th E. Ave. Tulsa OK 74134	OK	SP	Our Savior Tulsa OK	(918)836-3752	SL	1986

*Multiple Assignments (See Church Worker Locator for Additional Details)

See Page 53 for the Table of Abbreviations for key to District, Position, and Seminary abbreviations

**C =Candidate; EM = Emeritus; the date following the C is the month and year the Candidate status began

NAME	TELEPHONE NUMBER EMAIL	STREET ADDRESS CITY/STATE/ZIP	DISTRICT	POSITION/ STATUS**	WHERE SERVING	OFFICE PHONE	SEM/ PROGRAM	YR GRAD
Drengler Mark J	(715)851-0089 mdrengler@stpaulfremontwi.org	N5987 24th Ln Wild Rose WI 54984	NW	SP	St Paul Fremont WI	(920)446-3251	SL	1991
Drengler Micah J	(919) 741-7610 micahdrengler5@hotmail.com	131 Winding Brook Dr Lumberton TX 77657	TX	SP	Redeemer* Beaumont TX	(409)892-3286	SL	2021
Dressel David A	(517) 285-4166 dresseld@msu.edu	922 Whitman Dr East Lansing MI 48823	EN	EM			SL	1968
Dressler Martin B Dr	(828)206-4556 martinbdressler@gmail.com	c/o Salem Lutheran Church 5180 Parker Rd Black Jack MO 63033	MO	SP	Salem Black Jack MO	(314)741-6781	SL	2013
Dressler Steven L	steven.dressler1677@gmail.com	5660 Main St Frohna MO 63748	MO	EM			SL	1989
Drevlow Ryan A	(605)251-5243 pastordrevlow@gmail.com	214 7th Ave SW Aberdeen SD 57401	SD	Sn/Adm	St Paul's* Leola SD	(605)439-3531	SL	2009
Drew Bradley A	(504)833-4963 pbdrew89@gmail.com	315 Ridgelake Dr Metairie LA 70001	SO	SP	Mount Olive Metairie LA	(504)833-4963	FW	1989
Drewitz Glen A	(660)548-3621 pastordrewitz@outlook.com	701 E Harrison St Brunswick MO 65236	MO	EM			FW	1979
Drews Mark R	(701)390-6073	708 S 4th St Pekin IL 61554	CI	SP	Trinity Pekin IL	(309)346-1391	SL	2003
Drews Richard T	(843)706-2279 f029562@gmail.com	106 Blessing Dr Bluffton SC 29909	SE	EM			SL	1972
Drews Michael P	647-588-1558 drewsfamily848@gmail.com	848 Shaw St Toronto ON M6G 3 CANADA	EN	EM			SL	1967
Drews Dennis M	(952)886-0882 drews5255A@aol.com	11228 Vessey Cir Bloomington MN 55437	MNS	EM			SL	1971
Drews Richard D Dr	(630)833-4433 schafrhund@aol.com	318 Arlington Ave. Elmhurst IL 60126	EN	EM			SL	1962
Dreyer John M	(765) 453-0969	705 E Southway Blvd Kokomo IN 46902	IN	Sn/Adm	Our Redeemer Kokomo IN	(765)453-0969	FW	1992
Drinnon Roger A	(618)381-6775 drinnon.roger@gmail.com	2278 Monarch St Bourbonnais IL 60914	NI	Assoc	St Paul Bourbonnais IL	(815)932-0312	SL	2017
Driskell James A	(410)725-8052 bm2driskell@aol.com	790 State Route 208 Pulaski PA 16143	EA	SP	Christ New Castle PA	(724)658-8009	SL	2010
Driver Steven D	(219)462-2671 valpodriver@gmail.com	1006 Domke Dr Valparaiso IN 46383	IN	EM			SL-SMP	2010
Droegemueller Beryl D Dr	(760)724-1080 bdrags@aol.com	2836 Hutchison St Vista CA 92084	PSW	EM			SPR	1967
Droegemueller Timothy J	(470)302-4815 lflcpastor@gmail.com	7320 Lake Knoll Ct Cumming GA 30041	FG	Sn/Adm	Living Faith Cumming GA	(770)887-0184	SL	1999
Droegemueller Paul E	(217)828-0065 pdrgmlr43@yahoo.com	1530 P B Ln PMB 101 Wichita Falls TX 76302	CI	EM			SL	1969
Droegemueller Carl M	(660)582-3698 carld1941@yahoo.com	1817 N Alco Ave Maryville MO 64468	MO	EM			SL	1967
Drosendahl John C	(985)792-7451 john.drosendahl@gmail.com	c/o Redeemer Lutheran Church 22531 Hwy 1088 Mandeville LA 70448	SO	SP	Redeemer Mandeville LA	(985)674-0377	SL	1992
Droutz Paul N	(770)765-0933 pauldroutz@hotmail.com	215 Paper Mill Rd Apt 6g Lawrenceville GA 30046	FG	EM			SL	1979
Drummond James A	(260)437-7708 southbeach2066@yahoo.com	920 West Ave Kendallville IN 46755	IN	EM			FW	2001
Du Philip H	(571)332-5177 philipdu3128@hotmail.com	3128 Cedar Grove Dr Fairfax VA 22031	SE	EM			CQ	2001
Dub Joshua P	pastorjpdub@gmail.com	434 E Washington Ave Peru IN 46970	IN	SP	St John Peru IN	(765)473-6659	FW	2022
Dubbelde David V	(260)486-2867 daviddubbelde@gmail.com	1211 South Broadway Street Apt 6208 Joshua TX 76058	TX	EM			SPR	1969
Dubberke William K	wkdubberke@outlook.com	3623 Colonia Place Dr Apt D Saint Louis MO 63125	MO	EM			SL	1989
Dube Michael S	(916)996-2856 elkdubes@comcast.net	2912 Peppergrass Way Elk Grove CA 95757	CNH	SMP	Shepherd of Valley Galt CA	(209)745-1825	SL-SMP	2018
Dube Walter A	(409)771-6968 wadube@sbcglobal.net	3410 Donnell Ridge Rd Conway AR 72034	TX	EM			SPR	1963
Dubensky Matthew R	(847)885-3350 matthewdubensky@gmail.com	216 E Schaumburg Rd Schaumburg IL 60194	NI	Assoc	St Peter Schaumburg IL	(847)885-3350	SL	2020
Dubisar Douglas A	(660)815-3467 dubisardouglas55@gmail.com	905 S Grant Ave Marshall MO 65340	MO	EM			FW	1988
Dubke Dallas C	(503)881-1084 revdcrdubke@gmail.com	698 Moki Ave Rifle CO 81650	RM	SP	Emmanuel Rifle CO	(970)625-2369	SL	2011
Dubke Dallas D	(530)529-1773 thankful_to_be@yahoo.com	22865 Tuscan Ave Red Bluff CA 96080	CNH	SP	St Paul Red Bluff CA	(530)527-3414	FW	1979
DuBois Craig A Dr	(830)714-5351 craigdubois@live.com	102 Wonder World Dr #304217 San Macros TX 78666	TX	Sn/Adm	Grace San Marcos TX	(512)392-4241	SL	1981
DuBois David W	(810)278-3659 ddubois@immanuelsc.org	3832 Riverview Terrace South East China MI 48054	MI	SMP	Immanuel Saint Clair MI	(810)329-7174	CQ	2018
Duchene Michael G	(586)922-3539 mikeduchene@me.com	44325 Meadowlake Dr Sterling Heights MI 48313	MI	SP	St Paul Sterling Heights MI	(586)247-4645	AA	2012
Duchow Gilbert J Dr	(414)544-1132 duke3726@gmail.com	12455 W Janesville Rd Unit 410 Muskego WI 53150	EN	EM			SL	1968
Dudley Nathan S	(712)303-9758 rabbid59@gmail.com	8609 East Arlington Rd Haven KS 67543	KS	SP	St Paul's Haven KS	(620)465-3427	FW	1997
Dueker Jonathan A	(585)690-9012 jdueker20@gmail.com	c/o Peace Lutheran Church 1401 68 Hwy Rogers City MI 49779	MI	SP	Peace Rogers City MI	(989)734-7621	SL	2024
Dueker Kirk D	pastorkirk@sharethehope.org	47 El Mar Dr Rochester NY 14616	EA	Sn/Adm	Hope Rochester NY	(585)723-4673	SL	1993
Dueppen Michael J	(928)636-2970 mjdueppen@gmail.com		PSW	SMP	Saving Grace Chino Valley AZ	(928)636-9533	CQ	2019
Duer Mark W	(918)399-3830 dew095@yahoo.com	90 South 6th Ave Unit 209 La Grange IL 60525	NI	SP	Zion* Lyons IL	(708)447-4499	FW	2009

*Multiple Assignments (See Church Worker Locator for Additional Details)

See Page 53 for the Table of Abbreviations for key to District, Position, and Seminary abbreviations

**C =Candidate; EM = Emeritus; the date following the C is the month and year the Candidate status began

NAME	TELEPHONE NUMBER EMAIL	STREET ADDRESS CITY/STATE/ZIP	DISTRICT	POSITION/ STATUS**	WHERE SERVING	OFFICE PHONE	SEM/ PROGRAM	YR GRAD
Duerr Mark A	(661)706-6528 mduerr@trinitylutheranmonroe.org	3078 Appleblossom Way Monroe MI 48161	MI	Assoc	Trinity Monroe MI	(734)242-2308	SL	2017
Duerr William L Jr	(760)219-5830 durbilttwo@aol.com	26235 Chambers Ave Menifee CA 92586	PSW	EM			SPR	1967
Duerr Timothy S	(713)906-1627 tduerr81@gmail.com	4536 E Joan De Arc Ave Phoenix AZ 85032	PSW	Assoc	St Mark Phoenix AZ	(602)992-1980	SL	2009
Duerr Matthew W	lodiduerrs@comcast.com	120 N California St Lodi CA 95240	CNH	EM			CQ	2015
Duerr Kerwin L	(714)496-9872 pastorduerr@yahoo.com	1636 W Cris Ave Anaheim CA 92802	PSW	EM			FW	1977
Duerr John M	(586)491-4070 pjohnduerr@gmail.com	50729 Harbour View Dr S New Baltimore MI 48047	MI	EM			SL	1982
Duerr Nicholas T	(661)706-9190 nicholastduerr@gmail.com	45160 Van Dyke Ave Utica MI 48317	MI	Assoc	Trinity Utica MI	(586)731-4490	SL	2018
Duescher Steven J	(858)792-7691 livingwatersd7@gmail.com	19816 Centerville Ct Parker CO 80134	EN	EM			SL	1985
Duesenberg Timothy A	(608)386-7021 stmaximos@aol.com	W6729 Hilltop Dr Onalaska WI 54650	SW	SP	Gift of Grace Holmen WI	(608)668-1587	CQ	2022
Duey William E Jr	(803)578-4022 wemaduey@att.net	c/o Grace Lutheran Village 21 Concordia Dr Paris IL 61944	CI	EM			SL	1961
Duff Kevin D	(616)550-4373 kduff8@gmail.com	2017 Blakers Blvd Okatie SC 29909	SE	Assoc	Island Hilton Head Island SC	(843)689-5200	SL	2016
Duff Alexander L	alexduff6@aol.com	c/o Suburban Bethlehem Lutheran Church 6318 W California Rd Fort Wayne IN 46818	IN	Asst	Sub Bethlehem Fort Wayne IN	(260)484-7873	FW	2002
Duffy Paul S	(402)752-3536 pduffy@paulstephenduffy.com	P.O. Box 36 Kenesaw NE 68956	NEB	SP	St Paul Kenesaw NE	(402)752-3421	FW	1998
Duffy Michael F	(708)343-1000 pastorduffysp@gmail.com	c/o St Paul Lutheran Church 1025 Lake St Melrose Park IL 60160	NI	Sn/Adm	St Paul Melrose Park IL	(708)343-1000	SL	2022
Duffy Joshua P	(832)922-2327	4602 N Pine Brook Way Houston TX 77059	TX	Sn/Adm	Pilgrim Houston TX	(713)432-7082	SL	2015
Dufon Dennis L	(785)531-1662 dldufon@hotmail.com	P.O. Box 296 Drummond Island MI 49726	MI	SP	Drummond Island Drummond Island MI	(906)493-5982	SL	2005
Dugall Robin J Dr	(208)891-5608 rdugall@immanuelloveland.org	635 Callisto Dr. #104 Loveland CO 80537	RM	Assoc	Immanuel Loveland CO	(970)667-4506	CQ	2010
Dugan Sean L	(518)723-3273 sdungan6546@gmail.com	4 Stoney Creek Dr Clifton Park NY 12065	AT	EM			SL	1997
Duitsman John E	760-912-7888 jkduitsman@aol.com	P.O. Box 123 Hnkley CA 92347	PSW	EM			CQ	1995
Duke John D Jr	(716)946-9034 professorduke@nachmu.com	67 Walter Ave Tonawanda NY 14150	EA	SP	Salem Buffalo NY	(716)824-2787	SL	1999
Duke Teshome W	(202)417-4012 jiratubulla8@yahoo.com	1344 Kennedy St NW Washington DC 20011	SE	EM			CQ	2015
Duke Cullen A	(281)381-0987 cadman57@outlook.com	101 Greenwood Ln Kingsport TN 37663	MDS	EM			FW	2011
Dukeman Jeffrey A Dr	(864)244-5825 jeffreydukeman@gmail.com	208 Peaks Ct Taylors SC 29687	SE	SP	Good Shepherd Greenville SC	(864)244-5825	FW	2004
Dukovan David M			EN	SP	Christ Lake Mills WI	(262)804-1087	SL	1999
Duley Duane M	(406) 579-0718 dmd6109@gmail.com		NEB	EM			FW	1980
Duley Jason A	(402)478-4278 jduley@stpaulsarlington.org	8823 County Road 9 Arlington NE 68002	NEB	Assoc	St Paul Arlington NE	(402)478-4278	SL	2012
Duling Collin P	(507)251-5568 dulingcp@gmail.com	c/o Saint John Evangelical Lutheran Church 6630 Southeastern Ave Indianapolis IN 46203	IN	Sn/Adm	St John Indianapolis IN	(317)352-9196	FW	2013
Dumbrille Dean G	(810)750-1415 hatman1959@hotmail.com	14393 Appletree Ln Fenton MI 48430	MI	Assoc	Christ King* Flint MI	(810)239-6200	FW	1991
Dummer Dean A	(414)305-3365 dadummer1@gmail.com	W177n7479 Amethyst Dr Menomonee Falls WI 53051	SW	SP	Zion Menomonee Falls WI	(262)781-8133	SL	1981
Dumperth Dale A	(620) 241-1627 PrDumperth@att.net	521 South Hartup St Mc Pherson KS 67460	KS	SP	Grace McPherson KS	(620)241-1627	FW	1992
Dunavan Dean A	(651)263-6651 dean.dunavan@concordiaacademy.com	883 Colleen Ave Shoreview MN 55126	MNS	SMP	Woodbury Woodbury MN	(651)739-5144	SL-SMP	2020
Dunaway Michael J	(785)285-1714 revdunaway@gmail.com	1043 S 190th St Pittsburg KS 66762	KS	EM			SL	2007
Dunbar Jon M	(402)641-4813 pastor@stpeternj.org	1606 Harbourton Rocktown Rd Lambertville NJ 08530	NJ	SP	St Peter Hopewell Township NJ	(609)466-0939	SL	2005
Dunbar Paul T	(402)984-5843 pastorpaultdunbar@yahoo.com	846 Chestnut Ave Hastings NE 68901	NEB	Sn/Adm	Faith Hastings NE	(402)462-5044	SL	2001
Dunbar Thomas A	(260)463-3858 tdunbar3@embarqmail.com	4480 S 075 E Wolcottville IN 46795	IN	EM			FW	2005
Duncan Robert E	(740)993-9206	531 N Basil St Baltimore OH 43105	OH	EM			FW	1980
Duncan Dean H	(319)573-2366 pastorduncanflc@gmail.com	1525 Sunset Dr Belle Plaine IA 52208	IE	SP	St Paul* Luzerne IA	(319)444-2378	FW	1991
Duncan Owen D	(701)318-1045 owenduncan777@gmail.com	4150 Goodlette Rd N Naples FL 34103	EN	Assoc	Faith Naples FL	(239)434-5811	SL	2024
Duncan Randall S	(734)968-9339 randy@ulcannarbor.org	1426 Long Lake Dr Brighton MI 48114	MI	Cmp P	University Chapel Ann Arbor MI	(734)663-5560	FW	1993
Dunker Gary L	(402)486-1372 gandcdunker73@gmail.com	5511 Van Dorn St Lincoln NE 68506	NEB	EM			SL-SMP	2013
Dunlop David M	(586)484-1497 pastordunlop@gmail.com	600 W Leander St Clinton IL 61727	CI	SP	Christ* Clinton IL	(217)935-5808	FW	2014

*Multiple Assignments (See Church Worker Locator for Additional Details)

See Page 53 for the Table of Abbreviations for key to District, Position, and Seminary abbreviations

**C =Candidate; EM = Emeritus; the date following the C is the month and year the Candidate status began

NAME	TELEPHONE NUMBER EMAIL	STREET ADDRESS CITY/STATE/ZIP	DISTRICT	POSITION/ STATUS**	WHERE SERVING	OFFICE PHONE	SEM/ PROGRAM	YR GRAD
Dunn James A	prjimdunn@yahoo.com	433 E 63rd Ter Kansas City MO 64110	MDS	EM			SL	1984
Dunne Michael P	(973)334-0547 pastormike.holyspirit@gmail.com	P.O. Box 250 Montville NJ 07045	NJ	SP	St Paul Incarnation* Pompton Lakes NJ	(973)835-5537	FW	2008
Dunseth Thomas W	(616)634-1100 twdunseth@gmail.com	4465 Middle Rd Highland MI 48357	MI	Assoc	Christ King* Flint MI	(810)239-6200	FW	1993
Dupre Brian C	(313)683-3133 briandupre84@yahoo.com	23190 Halsted Rd Apt 117 Farmington Hills MI 48335	MI	SP	Shadow of the Cross Farmington Hills MI	(248)474-0675	SL	2007
Duran John M	(785)248-9544 johnmduran43@gmail.com	2904 North Leisure World Blvd. #517 Silver Spring MD 20906	SE	Sn/Adm	Peace King George VA	(540)775-9131	SPR	1970
Durance Matthew H Dr	(989)573-0182 pr.matthew.durance@gmail.com	216 N 3rd St Harbor Beach MI 48441	MI	SP	Zion Harbor Beach MI	(989)479-3615	CQ	2017
Durand Edward E III	durande@ymail.com	1195 Prairieview Ave Van Meter IA 50261	IW	SP	Trinity Van Meter IA	(515)996-2093	SL	2009
Durante Kenneth A	(954)473-6888	8001 NW 5th St Plantation FL 33324	FG	SP	Our Savior Plantation FL	(954)473-6888	SL	2012
Durham Christopher D	(260)804-0103 cdurhamxv@gmail.com	P.O. Box 582 Lisbon ND 58054	ND	SP	Redeemer Lisbon ND	(701)683-3462	FW	2022
Durham Dennis J	(707)228-9377 cadurhams@sbcglobal.net	10767 W Leilani Dr Boise ID 83709	NOW	SP	Beautiful Savior Boise ID	(208)336-3616	CQ	1999
Durkin John M	(317)966-1954 johnd@bslc.com	15123 SE Myra Ln Clackamas OR 97015	NOW	SMP	Beautiful Savior Portland OR	(503)788-7000	SL-SMP	2022
Durkopp Jonathan R	(701)210-2170 revdurkopp@gmail.com	1059 Durango Dr Douglas WY 82633	WY	SP	Our Redeemer* Glenrock WY	(307)436-8691	FW	2016
Duy Douglas M Sr	(520)297-6799 d.duy@alcs-az.org	13305 N Teal Blue Trl Tucson AZ 85742	EN	EM			CQ	2019
Dwyer Gregory	(860)924-2467 gregorydwyer@outlook.com	191 Bantam Lake Rd Bantam CT 06750	NE	SP	Zion Manchester CT	(860)649-4243	SL	1992
Dwyer Keith E	(734)717-5876 kdwyer@sotlchurch.com	550 Browning St Ypsilanti MI 48198	MI	SMP	Shep Lakes Brighton MI	(810)227-5099	SL-SMP	2023
Dwyer Curtis E	(517)974-8198 dwyerc@martinlutherchapel.org	15617 Chandler Rd Bath MI 48808	EN	Sn/Adm	Martin Luther Chapel East Lansing MI	(517)332-0778	SL	1996
Dye Lawrence J Sr	(970)774-3320 ljdye@pctelcom.net	233 N Wayne Ave Haxtun CO 80731	RM	EM			FW	1991
Dyer David L	(719)201-8811 ddyer@bethlehemdenver.com	c/o Bethlehem Lutheran Church 2100 Wad-sworth Blvd Lakewood CO 80214	RM	Assoc	Bethlehem Lakewood CO	(303)238-7676	SL	2003
Dzurovcik Andrew J	(732)535-0096 hope62681@aol.com	566 Oak Ridge Rd Clark NJ 07066	S	EM			SL	1973
Earhart George R	(954)257-8244 earhartgeorge@yahoo.com	10154 Freedoms Way Keithville LA 71047	SO	EM			SL	1983
Earl Brian S	(720)695-2023 brian.s.w.earl@gmail.com	6232 Hannett Ave NE Albuquerque NM 87110	RM	O-Sp Min	Rocky Mountain District Englewood CO	(303)695-8001	SL	2009
Easterday David A	(219)798-9591 daetrinity@gmail.com	10664 S 9 W Pendleton IN 46064	IN	EM			FW	1994
Easterling John D	(870)424-6777 jneasterling@earthlink.net	P.O. Box 1758 Bailey CO 80421	RM	EM			SL	2009
Easterling Derek W	(281)435-8693 dweasterling1976@gmail.com	15407 Soaring Mesa San Antonio TX 78253	TX	SMP	Mount Olive San Antonio TX	(210)675-6394	FW-SMP	2025
Eatherton Lawrence L	(636)861-3591 leatherton_osl@hotmail.com	1600 Valley Park Rd Fenton MO 63026	MO	SP	St John* Bismarck MO	(573)779-3820	CQ	1983
Eaton Steven A	(360)681-2073 deerpark@juno.com	92 McLaughlin Rd Sequim WA 98382	NOW	EM			SL	1986
Eaton Timothy E	(951)893-0224 teaton@zionanaheim.org		PSW	Sn/Adm	Zion Anaheim CA	(714)535-1169	SL	2003
Eaves Thomas E	(701)340-8324 pastor@stjohnsbarnesville.org	1253 Omega Circle Ct Dekalb IL 60115	NI	SP	St Peter's Hampshire IL	(847)464-5721	SL	2005
Ebel Alfred R	(406)425-4616 alfredebel@mac.com	627 S 38th St W Billings MT 59102	MT	EM			CQ	1988
Ebersole James H	jebersole@ziondallas.org	6121 Lovers Lane Dallas TX 75214	TX	Assoc	Zion Dallas TX	(214)363-1639	FW	2019
Ebert Mark H	(402)525-3583 ebertmark1@gmail.com	4315 Bingham Cir Lincoln NE 68516	EN	EM			SL	1983
Ebert Kurt A	(317) 783-2000 kebert@clcs.org	6847 Minnow Dr Indianapolis IN 46237	IN	Sn/Adm	Calvary Indianapolis IN	(317)783-2000	SL	2007
Eble Robert D	(980) 844-8104 roberteble47@gmail.com	6501 Ziegler Ln Charlotte NC 28269	SE	EM			FW	1986
Eckardt Burnell F Jr		3 Ramsgate Collinsville IL 62234	CI	EM			FW	1981
Eckart Lawrence M	(586)668-1302 larryeckart54@gmail.com	3453 S Pointe Dr Apex NC 27539	SE	EM			SL	1984
Eckelkamp Michael A Dr	(303)910-1633	6035 S 87th St Lincoln NE 68526	NEB	Sn/Adm	Christ Lincoln NE	(402)483-7774	SL	1991
Eckelman Robert D	(303)654-1021 bobeckzion@gmail.com	210 Aspen Dr Brighton CO 80601	RM	EM			SL	1958
Eckels Chad M	revecks@hotmail.com	2008 Joyce Ave Evansville IN 47714	IN	Sn/Adm	St Paul Evansville IN	(812)422-5414	SL	1998
Eckert Mark W	(262)483-2771 meckertnf@hotmail.com	N665 County Road S Kewaskum WI 53040	SW	SP	St John New Fane WI	(262)626-2309	FW	1986
Eckert Stephen A	(805)264-1822 saeckert@aol.com	19415 W 98th St Lenexa KS 66220	KS	EM			SL	1986
Eckert Michael L	(218)326-1666 revmleckert@gmail.com	328 NW 10th St Grand Rapids MN 55744	MNN	SP	Trinity Hill City MN	(218)398-0859	FW	1983
Eckert Andrew W	(405)414-1335 eckert123456@hotmail.com	186 Pine Hollow Rd Stevensville MT 59870	MT	SP	Our Savior Stevensville MT	(406)777-5625	SL	1996

*Multiple Assignments (See Church Worker Locator for Additional Details)
See Page 53 for the Table of Abbreviations for key to District, Position, and Seminary abbreviations
**C =Candidate; EM = Emeritus; the date following the C is the month and year the Candidate status began

NAME	TELEPHONE NUMBER EMAIL	STREET ADDRESS CITY/STATE/ZIP	DISTRICT	POSITION/ STATUS**	WHERE SERVING	OFFICE PHONE	SEM/ PROGRAM	YR GRAD
Eckert Allan C	(361)522-5410 allan.eckert@gmail.com	3302 Canyon Creek Dr San Angelo TX 76904	TX	Sn/Adm	Trinity San Angelo TX	(325)944-8660	FW	1999
Eckert Timothy C	(563)359-7105 deaflutheran@q.com	2550 E 32nd St Davenport IA 52807	IE	Sn/Adm	Word Of God Df Cedar Rapids IA	(319)450-7699	SL	1996
Eckert James A	(215)826-8038 jaestm96@aol.com	1105 Rosa Ave Croydon PA 19021	EA	SP	St Luke Croydon PA	(215)788-8951	SL	1983
Eckhardt Wilfred E	(319)338-3386 beckhardt31@gmail.com	1 Oaknoll Ct Iowa City IA 52246	IE	EM			SL	1963
Eckhoff Karl F	(309)712-4268 keckhoff@christlutheranpeo.org	130 Baker St East Peoria IL 61611	CI	Sn/Adm	Christ Peoria IL	(309)637-5309	SL	1990
Eckman Joseph V	(217)248-4237 joe_eckman@yahoo.com	1909 Sprucewood Way Port Orange FL 32128	CI	EM			FW	1991
Eckstein Thomas R	(701)419-5797 pastoreck@gmail.com	902 9th Ave NE Jamestown ND 58401	ND	SP	Trinity* Adrian ND	(701)778-5181	SL	1991
Eckstrom Cory J	(607)591-5919 coryecks@aol.com	49 Hamlin St Cortland NY 13045	EA	SP	Christ* Interlaken NY		SL	1996
Eddins Andrew J	(702)334-4249 andrew.eddins@psd-lcms.org	8310 E Candleberry Cir Orange CA 92869	PSW	D Ex/S	Pacific Southwest District Irvine CA	(949)854-3232	SL-SMP	2018
Eddy Mark R	(309)795-1472 markeddy@att.net	18225 134th Ave W Taylor Ridge IL 61284	CI	SP	Zion Taylor Ridge IL	(309)795-1063	FW	1983
Eddy Daniel C	(314)775-7371 dan.eddy@verizon.net	1531 Townline Ave Beloit WI 53511	SW	SP	Messiah Beloit WI	(608)365-3794	SL	2008
Eden Joel S			MI	Assoc	St Lorenz Frankenmuth MI	(989)652-6141	SL	2014
Eden Martin R	(217) 653-9159 meden68@yahoo.com	1516 Stone Creek Dr Quincy IL 62305	CI	Sn/Adm	Our Redeemer Quincy IL	(217)223-1769	FW	1995
Eden Roger D	(612)437-0084	2130 Harrison St Quincy IL 62301	CI	EM			SL	1965
Eden Ryan L	(507) 450-0214 pastor@rlcwinona.com	222 E. King St. Winona MN 55987	MNS	SP	Redeemer Winona MN	(507)452-3828	FW	2010
Eden Timothy P	(903)348-5981 pastortim@blcbcs.org	4221 Boonville Rd Bryan TX 77802	TX	Assoc	Bethel Bryan TX	(979)822-2742	SL	2012
Edenfield Harry N	(734)479-6337 edenfield2@comcast.net	19545 Wherle Dr Brownstown MI 48193	MI	EM			CQ	1983
Eder Ben C	(716)316-8776 beneder.be@gmail.com	239 Fayette Ave Buffalo NY 14223	EN	EM			FW	1985
Edge David A	(903)465-1016 davidalanedge@gmail.com	2411 Woodlake Dr. Denison TX 75021	TX	SP	Grace Denison TX	(903)465-1016	SL	2012
Edwards David C	pastordavidedwards@gmail.com	423 Shrike Dr Satellite Beach FL 32937	NEB	M Chap	Office of International Mission Saint Louis MO		SL	2019
Edwards Eric J	(812) 332-1668 pastoredwards@faithbtown.org	2200 S High St Bloomington IN 47401	IN	Sn/Adm	Faith Bloomington IN	(812)332-1668	SL	2008
Edwards James P Dr		36 Sunlight Irvine CA 92603	PSW	SMP	Gethsemane La Crescenta CA	(818)248-3738	FW-SMP	2011
Edwards Lucas W	(605)388-0032 luke1719@hotmail.com	633 Ken Ct Rapid City SD 57701	SD	SP	Our Redeemer Rapid City SD	(605)388-0032	SL	2012
Edwards Michael A	(417)812-4462 pastormedwards@gmail.com	4208 Fair Haven Dr Nixa MO 65714	MDS	C08/2023			SL	2010
Edwards Timothy L	260-632-4821 christpastor@frontier.com	P.O. Box 354 Woodburn IN 46797	IN	SP	Christ Woodburn IN	(260)632-4821	FW	2002
Eggebraaten Jared A	(916)545-0222 jeggebraaten@faithfairoaks.com	4000 San Juan Ave Fair Oaks CA 95628	CNH	Sn/Adm	Faith* Fair Oaks CA	(916)961-4252	SL	2006
Eggebrecht Thomas J	(414)418-4705 eggebrecht@aol.com	543 Buckhorn Dr Winter Spgs FL 32708	FG	Pro Stf	Lutheran Church Extension Fund Saint Louis MO	(314)965-9000	SL	1991
Egger Paul D	(712)210-0138 paul@iowadistrictwest.org	400 Monona St Galva IA 51020	IW	DP	Iowa West District Fort Dodge IA	(515)576-7666	FW	1990
Egger Thomas J Dr	(314)505-7011 eggert@csl.edu	1 McCall Ter Saint Louis MO 63105	MO	S HS/C	Concordia Seminary Saint Louis MO	(314)505-7000	SL	1997
Eggerman Joseph M	(414)795-8257 pastor.eggerman@gmail.com	500 W 5th St Aurelia IA 51005	IW	SP	St Paul Aurelia IA	(712)434-2331	SL	2025
Eggers Robert M	rmeandjhe@gmail.com	2159 Weigl Rd Saginaw MI 48609	MI	EM			SPR	1970
Eggert James F Dr	(517)703-6529 jimeggert44@gmail.com	4084 Pheasant Run Holt MI 48842	MI	EM			FW	2003
Eggert John C	(503)331-1884 pastor.j.eggert@gmail.com	12635 SE Lani Ln Boring OR 97009	NOW	SP	Holy Cross Portland OR	(503)254-8705	SL	1985
Eggold Daniel A	daneggold@hotmail.com	3504 Waverly Dr Lafayette IN 47909	IN	Sn/Adm	St Peter's Fort Wayne IN	(260)749-5816	SL	2004
Eggold Thomas A	taeggold@hotmail.com	915 Nelson St Fort Wayne IN 46802	IN	Sn/Adm	Emmanuel Fort Wayne IN	(260)423-1369	FW	2003
Ehlers Donald D	(217)356-3525 ddehlers@comcast.net	1701 Congressional Way Champaign IL 61822	CI	EM			SPR	1960
Ehlers Jeffery J Dr	(623) 202-1641 jcmje_ehlers@yahoo.com	11034 N. 36th Street Phoenix AZ 85028	PSW	RSO	The Garuna Foundation Phoenix AZ	(602)765-7613	SL	1985
Ehlers David M	(309)370-8488 ehlersdm@yahoo.com	113 Cheltenham Dr Normal IL 61761	CI	EM			CQ	2004
Ehlke John W	(619)251-9744 jgehlke@aol.com	3035 Tanglewood Dr Waukesha WI 53189	SW	EM			SL	1973
Ehrhard Jacob W	(773)690-9361 jacob.ehrhard@gmail.com	4933 W Montrose Ave Chicago IL 60641	NI	SP	St John Chicago IL	(773)736-1112	FW	2007
Ehrichs Randal G	(850)319-4312 rev.ehrichs@gmail.com	5001 Sharon Dr Panama City FL 32404	SO	SP	Good Shepherd Callaway FL	(850)871-6311	SL	1992
Ehrke Donald W Jr	dehrke@gmail.com	9727 North Vista Kingman AZ 86401	PSW	C02/2023			FW	2000

*Multiple Assignments (See Church Worker Locator for Additional Details)
See Page 53 for the Table of Abbreviations for key to District, Position, and Seminary abbreviations
**C =Candidate; EM = Emeritus; the date following the C is the month and year the Candidate status began

NAME	TELEPHONE NUMBER EMAIL	STREET ADDRESS CITY/STATE/ZIP	DISTRICT	POSITION/ STATUS**	WHERE SERVING	OFFICE PHONE	SEM/ PROGRAM	YR GRAD
Eichberger Timothy M	(810)824-8395 pastortim67@yahoo.com	1641 Stacey Pl The Villages FL 32163	FG	EM			SL	1972
Eichelberger Albert J	(865)693-9293 tennike@aol.com	2114 Scenic Ridge CV Knoxville TN 37923	MDS	EM			SPR	1960
Eichers Jacob J	(414)659-8379 pastoreichers@faithonmain.com	1301 31st Pl S La Crosse WI 54601	SW	SP	Faith La Crosse WI	(608)782-3696	FW	2017
Eichhorn Arthur D Dr	(314)882-1983 aeich53024@aol.com	7116 Mardel Ave Saint Louis MO 63109	MO	EM			SL	2008
Eichinger Kurt W	(989)280-3495 kurdiku@aol.com	5265 Fairway Dr Bay City MI 48706	MI	EM			FW-D	2008
Eichinger Eric T	(352)504-2269 pastoreich@oslcarcadia.org	512 W Duarte Rd Arcadia CA 91007	PSW	SP	Our Savior Arcadia CA	(626)447-7690	SL	2006
Eichler Mark P	(515)448-4668 emporiahusker@centurylink.com	811 Ohio St Webster City IA 50595	IW	SP	Mount Calvary* Eagle Grove IA	(515)448-4668	SL	1985
Eickhoff Benjamin P	(308)645-2530 beickho@nebnet.net	39341 Highway 2 Thedford NE 69166	NEB	SP	Trinity Thedford NE	(308)645-2254	CQ	1994
Eickmann Jerrold A	(636)448-7796 eickmannja@gmail.com	13198 South Outer 40 Rd Apt 130 Town And Country MO 63017	MO	EM			SL	1964
Eickmann Robert E Jr	reeickmann@yahoo.com	7088 County Rd 427 Auburn IN 46706	IN	SP	Prince Of Peace Grabill IN	(260)627-5621	SL	1981
Eilers Keith H	(253)649-4481 keitheilers@comcast.net	4334 Borgen Blvd Ut 6 Gig Harbor WA 98332	NOW	EM			SL	1970
Einem John A	pjeinem@gmail.com	1501 Cron St Augusta KS 67010	KS	EM			NESC	1989
Einertson Christian J Dr	(770) 283-9197 pastor@trinityfarmington.org	600 Walnut Street Farmington MN 55024	MNS	Sn/Adm	Trinity Farmington MN	(651)463-7225	SL	2020
Eisberg Clarence H	(209)725-9082 pastor@redeemerfresno.com	3856 N Gardner Ave Merced CA 95340	CNH	Sn/Adm	Redeemer Fresno CA	(559)439-8500	SL	1973
Eisenbacher Joseph R	joe@livingwateromaha.org	2013 S 141st Cir Omaha NE 68144	NEB	SMP	Living Water Omaha NE	(402)431-2593	SL-SMP	2022
Eisinger Alan P	(586)850-5253	43681 Perignon Dr Sterling Hts MI 48314	MI	EM			FW	1983
Eisinger Jacob W	(775)385-4153 jacob.eisinger@hotmail.com	279 Willow St. Elko NV 89801	CNH	SMP	St Mark Elko NV	(775)738-5436	SL-SMP	2025
Eisold Mark T	(239)307-7336 pastormarknaples@gmail.com	1072 Frank Whiteman Blvd Naples FL 34103	FG	SP	The Pelican Naples FL	(239)307-7336	SL	2003
Ek Yah Ruberto	(971)280-2932 rubastinoek@yahoo.com	16729 SE Alder Portland OR 97233	NOW	Asst	Trinity Portland OR	(503)288-6403	SL	2022
Ekong Hosea J	(330) 506-2456 ekongh@live.com	3311 Glenwood Ave Youngstown OH 44511	S	EM			SL	1999
Elam Carey P	(334)272-6214 cpelam@stpaulmontgomery.org	4475 Atlanta Hwy Montgomery AL 36109	SO	Sn/Adm	St Paul Montgomery AL	(334)272-6214	SL	1984
Elbert Thomas J Jr	tjelbertjr@gmail.com	c/o Divine Savior 1025 N Buckman St Shepherdsville KY 40165	IN	SP	Divine Savior Shepherdsville KY	(502)543-2905	SL	1988
Eldridge Christopher R	(480)540-5701 alivefromfaith@yahoo.com	7519 Harbour Town Dr Pickerington OH 43147	OH	Assoc	Prince of Peace Columbus OH	(614)863-3124	SL	2011
Elfe Chad R	(920)297-0711 pastor@lmcrf.org	858 Bradley Dr Hudson WI 54016	NW	SP	Luther Memorial River Falls WI	(715)425-2675	SL	2013
Eliason Carl A	(308)380-4271 celiason@peacegi.org	2410 Gateway Ave Grand Island NE 68803	NEB	SMP	Peace Grand Island NE	(308)384-5673	SL-SMP	2014
Elkins Dan D	(901)299-9733 53chevydan1944@gmail.com	12089 Thompson Dr Olive Branch MS 38654	MDS	EM			FW	1978
Ellerbrock Keith D	(636)940-9233 kdanielbrock@gmail.com	2913 N Kristopher Bnd Saint Charles MO 63303	MO	SP	Trinity Bridgeton MO	(314)739-0022	SL	1985
Ellingworth Jon M	(845)216-3300 pastorellingworth@gmail.com	107 16th St SW Waverly IA 50677	IE	SP	St John Waverly IA	(319)352-2314	FW	2002
Elliott Paul M Dr	(949)520-0456 paul.elliott@cui.edu	5076 Apple Tree Irvine CA 92612	PSW	S HS/C	Concordia University Irvine Irvine CA	(949)854-8002	SL	2009
Elliott Mark R	(972)955-6965 melliott75321@gmail.com	6982 Draper Ln Garland TX 75043	TX	SP	Our Savior Sulphur Springs TX	(903)885-5787	FW	1984
Elliott John M	(407)730-6388 jelliott@sllcs.org	5854 Manchster Bridge Dr Orlando FL 32829	S	SMP	St Luke Oviedo FL	(407)365-3408	SL-SMP	2018
Elliott Bruce H	(414)254-8524 bruce17@live.com	4103 E Four Ridge Road Imperial MO 63052	MO	SP	Immanuel Barnhart MO	(636)464-4114	SL	2021
Elliott Peter W Dr	(206) 512-9759 pastor.elliott@messiahseattle.org	c/o Messiah Lutheran Church 7050 35th Ave NE Seattle WA 98115	NOW	SP	Messiah Seattle WA	(206)524-0024	SL	2010
Ellis David W	(605)760-7836 djellis9163@gmail.com	123 Spring Meadow Rd Yankton SD 57078	SD	EM			FW	2001
Ellis Garet M	(517)643-7140 ellisg13@yahoo.com	109 W Riding Dr Bel Air MD 21014	SE	Sn/Adm	St Matthew Bel Air MD	(410)838-3178	SL	2015
Ellis Roger C Dr	(519)383-4397 rellis45@teksavvy.com	948 Dagan St Sarnia ON N7S 1 CANADA	EN	EM			SL	1972
Ellis William F	PastorEllis@comcast.net	4812 Porto Pino Way Antelope CA 95843	CNH	EM			SL	1984
Ellison Adam W	(405)205-4431 maelstrom13@gmail.com	4925 Tiffany Ln El Reno OK 73036	OK	SMP	Faith Oklahoma City OK	(405)632-5744	SL-SMP	2022
Ellsworth Adam G	(615)477-8461 pastoradamellsworth@gmail.com	808 Marstevan Dr NE Atlanta GA 30306	FG	SP	Grace Atlanta GA	(404)875-5411	SL	2015
Ellul Gary J Dr	(636)359-5782 pastorellul@gmail.com	21 Craven Dr Montgomery CY MO 63361	MO	EM			SL	2005
Elmore James A	(714)809-7777 jimelmore@tlcanaheim.com	7966 E Bauer Rd Anaheim CA 92808	PSW	SP	Trinity Anaheim CA	(714)637-8370	CQ	2024
Elowsky Earl W	(989)742-2070 lareelowsky@gmail.com	121 Lynn St P.O. Box 127 Hillman MI 49746	MI	EM			SPR	1960

*Multiple Assignments (See Church Worker Locator for Additional Details)

See Page 53 for the Table of Abbreviations for key to District, Position, and Seminary abbreviations

**C =Candidate; EM = Emeritus; the date following the C is the month and year the Candidate status began

NAME	TELEPHONE NUMBER EMAIL	STREET ADDRESS CITY/STATE/ZIP	DISTRICT	POSITION/ STATUS**	WHERE SERVING	OFFICE PHONE	SEM/ PROGRAM	YR GRAD
Elowsky Joel C Dr	(314)505-7106 elowskyj@csl.edu	11 Fleetwood Dr Saint Louis MO 63124	S	S HS/C	Concordia Seminary Saint Louis MO	(314)505-7000	SL	1990
Elowsky Luke D	(262)365-1081 lukelowsky@gmail.com	3 Jefferson Dr Spotswood NJ 08884	NJ	SP	Christ Memorial East Brunswick NJ	(732)251-5454	SL	2022
Elser John H	(806)463-9268 johnelser@yahoo.com	1606 Armstrong St Amarillo TX 79106	TX	Inst C	Office of International Mission Saint Louis MO		SL	1992
Elseroad Richard M	(865)705-0210 relseroad@gmail.com	1128 Terra Rosa Dr Knoxville TN 37932	MDS	EM			SL	1979
Elseroad David A Dr	(917)757-4749 rev.elseroad@gmail.com	31 Milford St Hawthorne NY 10532	AT	SP	Trinity Hawthorne NY	(914)769-2546	SL	1976
Elseroad Kevin P	(404)234-7515	3535 Goldenrod Drive Alpharetta GA 30005	EN	Sn/Adm	Christ Shepherd Alpharetta GA	(770)475-0640	SL	1981
Emberger Carl D Sr	(610)350-7104 carlemberger@gmail.com	1403 Price Ln Downingtown PA 19335	EA	Asst	Christ Memorial Malvern PA	(610)644-4508	CQ	2018
Emery Glen A	glen.emery.ge@gmail.com	1010 20th St Fairbury NE 68352	NEB	SP	Grace Fairbury NE	(402)729-5163	SL	2014
Emmel Paul W	(612)924-0444 paulsatter@aol.com	3430 List Pl Apt 1503 Minneapolis MN 55416	MNS	EM			SL	1965
Emmrich David N	(262)385-1127 davidemmrich@hotmail.com	W3524 Vannoy Dr Whitewater WI 53190	SW	SP	Living Savior Fort Atkinson WI	(920)563-8050	SL	1989
Emrick William C	(618)267-6310 wce46@hotmail.com	10948 Bellflower Ct Indianapolis IN 46235	IN	EM			FW	1986
Emshoff Keith E	(713)906-8003 Pastor.Emshoff@holytrinitylcms.org	719 Derby St Raymore MO 64083	MO	SP	Holy Trinity Grandview MO	(816)763-3211	FW	2020
Enderle Phillip M	penderle@lifeathope.org	260 Vincent St Fond Du Lac WI 54935	SW	Sn/Adm	Hope Fond Du Lac WI	(920)922-5130	CQ	2013
Endrihs James E	(334)806-5740 jendrihs@aol.com	103 Woodland Dr Enterprise AL 36330	SO	SP	Christ The King* Enterprise AL	(334)347-6716	SL	1996
Eng Edward G	(909)573-5269 engmarilyn@yahoo.com	30770 Palmetto Palm Ave Homeland CA 92548	PSW	EM			CQ	2001
Engblade August P	(231)690-0637 pengblade@yahoo.com	317 N Delia St Ludington MI 49431	MI		Michigan District Ann Arbor MI	(888)225-2111	FW-SMP	2020
Engebretsen William C	wcengebretsen@yahoo.com	500 Oak Dr. Wayne NE 68787	NEB	EM			FW	1994
Engebretson Donald V	(715)623-2680 frzeke@gmail.com	N2890 Cty S Antigo WI 54409	NW	SP	St Peter Antigo WI	(715)623-6921	FW	1987
Engel Brant A	(248)980-5741 baecoach@comcast.net	1860 Korte St Hartland MI 48353	MI	Sn/Adm	Christ King* Flint MI	(810)239-6200	FW	1985
Engel Richard S	legne@juno.com	12403 Running River Road S. Jacksonville FL 32225	FG	EM			SL	1977
Engel Ronald P	(772)359-6590 pastortlc@bellsouth.net	5509 Buchanan Dr Fort Pierce FL 34982	FG	EM			SL	1970
Engel Ross M	therevross@gmail.com	45272 Callesito Ordenes Temecula CA 92592	FG	M Chap	Office of International Mission Saint Louis MO		SL	2006
Engel Thomas E	(219)293-3574 tom.teefish@gmail.com	2454 W Bryn Mawr Ave Chicago IL 60659	NI	SP	St Philip North Chicago IL	(773)561-9830	SL	1994
Engel Timothy A	(219)921-3487 tengel1963@live.com	18215 Forest Town Dr. Houston TX 77084	TX	SP	Messiah Houston TX	(713)861-3072	SL	1989
Engelbrecht Edward A	(614) 398-2593 ed.engelbrecht6@gmail.com	c/o Emmanuel Lutheran Church 80 E Markison Ave Columbus OH 43207	OH	IndC P	Ohio District North Olmsted OH	(440)235-2297	SL	1993
Engelbrecht Theodore C Dr	(360)609-4896 Ted.Engelbrecht@gmail.com	15507 NE 9th Cir Vancouver WA 98684	NOW	EM			SL	2003
Engelhardt Marc T	(414)967-9195	5080 Pondsedge Lane Prior Lake MN 55372	MNS	SP	Holy Cross Prior Lake MN	(952)445-1779	SL	2009
Engfehr William F III	pastor@engfehr.com	19 Ramsgate Collinsville IL 62234	SI	EM			SL	1978
England Edward L	(937)878-3152 e.l.england@att.net	342 Bowman Dr Fairborn OH 45324	OH	EM			FW	2003
Engle Tristan A			MO	M Chap	Office of International Mission Saint Louis MO		SL	2013
Engler Albert G	(816)333-5880 pastage@sbcglobal.net	7220 Baltimore Ave Kansas City MO 64114	MO	EM			SL	1960
Engler Thomas E	(262)744-0858 tomengler@verizon.net	N84w14707 Menomonee Ave Menomonee FLS WI 53051	EN	SP	Prince Peace Menomonee Falls WI	(262)251-3360	SL	1990
Engwall John B	(865)206-1603 teffiee@aol.com	1417 Whiskey Rd Aiken SC 29803	SE	SP	Bethlehem Aiken SC	(803)649-6417	FW	2018
Enko Keith E	(615) 812-5955 keithenko@yahoo.com	3333 Nina Cir Lebanon TN 37087	MDS	EM			SL	1982
Ensley Steven C	(260) 750-2526	5540 S 980 E Wolcottville IN 46795	IN	EM			FW	2005
Ensor Lewis S	(314)578-5126 forthlew@gmail.com	3322 Greenwood Blvd Saint Louis MO 63143	MO	SP	St Matthew Sullivan MO	(573)468-4245	SL	2003
Enterline Gregory W	(260)403-1854 genterli@gmail.com	4163 W Fork Rd Cincinnati OH 45247	OH	SP	Grace Cincinnati OH	(513)661-5166	SL	2010
Eppen Alan D	(701)320-8531 aleppen37@gmail.com	1423 10th Ave NE Apt 7 Jamestown ND 58401	ND	EM			FW	1983
Epperson Gerald N	(940)799-1208 epperson_gerald@att.net	137 High Ridge Ct Decatur TX 76234	TX	SP	Trinity Bridgeport TX	(940)683-5604	FW	1993
Erbel David R	(612)799-9119 revdaviderbel@gmail.com	18158 Settlers Way Eden Prairie MN 55347	MNS	EM			SL	2009

*Multiple Assignments (See Church Worker Locator for Additional Details)
See Page 53 for the Table of Abbreviations for key to District, Position, and Seminary abbreviations
**C =Candidate; EM = Emeritus; the date following the C is the month and year the Candidate status began

NAME	TELEPHONE NUMBER EMAIL	STREET ADDRESS CITY/STATE/ZIP	DISTRICT	POSITION/ STATUS**	WHERE SERVING	OFFICE PHONE	SEM/ PROGRAM	YR GRAD
Erber David M	517-944-2678 david.erber@lcms.org	3809 Westchester Blvd Jackson MI 49203	MI	S Miss	Office of International Mission Saint Louis MO		FW	1986
Erdman Roger A	(920)312-2079	3145 White Tail Lane Unit D Oshkosh WI 54904	SW	SP	St Paul* New Miner WI	(608)565-7252	FW	2008
Erdman Michael J	(952)491-3191 pastor@immanuelmadison.org	174 Lakewood Gardens Ln Madison WI 53704	SW	SP	St Paul* Madison WI	(608)244-8077	SL	2013
Erdman Alan M	(314)808-4900 erdman834@hotmail.com	13261 Barrett Chase Cir Ballwin MO 63021	MO	RSO	Luth Family/Children Services Saint Louis MO	(314)787-5100	CQ	1979
Erhardt Martin K Dr	lcmprinceton@gmail.com	407 Nassau St Princeton NJ 08540	EN	SP	Messiah Princeton NJ	(609)924-3642	CQ	2010
Ericksen David E	(712)928-3200 revdave@tcaexpress.net	201 N 7th Ave W Hartley IA 51346	IW	EM			SPR	1976
Erickson Michael K	(806)486-2243	2132 Mary Ellen St Pampa TX 79065	TX	SP	Zion Pampa TX	(806)669-2774	SL	1993
Erickson Michael W	(319)538-1745 revmwe@gmail.com	2048 5th Ave SE Cedar Rapids IA 52403	IE	Sn/Adm	Bethany Cedar Rapids IA	(319)364-6026	SL	2002
Erickson Michael D	(831)236-1015 uwrev1@gmail.com	25595 Tierra Grande Dr Carmel CA 93923	CNH	EM			FW	1979
Erickson John B	(623)512-1891 jbecme@gmail.com	10237 N 110th Ave Sun City AZ 85351	PSW	EM			SPR	1976
Erickson James D	(989)590-2164 ericksonj@immanuelalpena.org	351 Wilson St Alpena MI 49707	MI	Sn/Adm	Immanuel Alpena MI	(989)354-3443	SL	1982
Erickson Donald E	(712)541-7403 pdon51046@gmail.com	106 Church St Alcester SD 57001	SD	SP	Peace Alcester SD	(605)934-2365	SL	1986
Erickson Bror M	(505)419-4101 bror0122@hotmail.com	222 Apache St. Fort Morgan CO 80701	RM	SP	Trinity Fort Morgan CO	(970)867-5721	FW	2004
Erickson Patrick T	(972)685-5290 patricktheron4@gmail.com	725 Brighton Ln Garland TX 75043	TX	EM			SL	1986
Erkkinen Eric J	erkk51@gmail.com	3230 Overlook Ct Columbus IN 47203	IN	EM			SL	1977
Erler Mark R	(405)205-5551 pastor@stmarkedmond.org	2817 W Creek Side Dr Edmond OK 73012	OK	SP	St Mark Edmond OK	(405)340-0192	SL	1991
Ermeling Vernon F	(623)476-5377 vermeling@juno.com	14154 W. Denny Blvd Unit # 5 Litchfield Park AZ 85340	PSW	EM			CQ	1982
Ernewein Paul M	(985)607-4332 giveblood2@yahoo.com	766 Fair Hill Loop Covington LA 70433	SO	Sn/Adm	The Village Lacombe LA	(985)882-5727	SL	2007
Ernst Michael S	(262)895-0148 mikeerns@wi.rr.com	26445 Malchine Rd Waterford WI 53185	EN	EM			SL	1973
Ernst David W	(262)349-9510	100 Corrina Blvd Apt 321 Waukesha WI 53186	SW	EM			CQ	1997
Ernst Eugene W	gernst46@hotmail.com	3357 Deerbrook Dr Columbus IN 47203	IN	EM			SL	1972
Errer Joshua S	(920)492-9835 pastor@flcgb.com	133 S Ontario St De Pere WI 54115	NW	Sn/Adm	Faith Green Bay WI	(920)435-5524	SL	2011
Ersland David P	(405)395-7193 davidpersland@gmail.com	1311 N Rutland Cir Wichita KS 67206	KS	SP	Zion Argonia KS	(620)435-6524	CQ	1995
Esala Daniel D	(440)668-0795 danesala@gmail.com	17886 Lost Trl Chagrin Falls OH 44023	OH	SP	Hope Aurora OH	(330)562-9660	SL	1982
Esala Luther P	(520)401-7849 lpesala@msn.com	P.O. Box 665 Cortaro AZ 85652	EN	SP	Messiah Tucson AZ	(520)401-7849	SL	1973
Esala Philip J	(937)239-9007 phil.esala@gmail.com	5745 Newbank Cir Ste 102 Dublin OH 43017	OH	Aux	LLL/Lutheran Hour Ministries Saint Louis MO	(314)317-4100	SL	1984
Eschelbach Michael A Dr	michael.eschelbach@cui.edu	c/o Concordia University 1530 Concordia Dr W Irvine CA 92612	PSW	S HS/C	Concordia University Irvine Irvine CA	(949)854-8002	FW	1985
Escher Christopher W	(770)328-5078 cris@gracelutheranpsl.com	514 SE Maple Ter Port St Lucie FL 34983	FG	SP	Grace Port Saint Lucie FL	(772)871-6599	SL	2011
Escue Douglas K	(505)670-8275 dkescue@aol.com	207 E Barcelona Rd Santa Fe NM 87505	RM	Sn/Adm	Immanuel Santa Fe NM	(505)983-7568	SL	1986
Esget Christopher S	(703)549-0155 pastor@immanuelalexandria.org	1801 Russell Rd Alexandria VA 22301	EN	Sn/Adm	Immanuel Alexandria VA	(703)549-0155	FW	1997
Espinosa Alfonso J	espinosaa@aya.yale.edu	22106 Pheasant St Lake Forest CA 92630	PSW	C11/2022			SL	2014
Espinosa Alfonso O Dr	(949)379-0883 revdrespinosa@saintpaulsirvine.com	21986 Mae CR Lake Forest CA 92630	PSW	Sn/Adm	St Paul Irvine CA	(949)599-4760	FW	1991
Estby Alan C	(785)579-6494 pastorestby@gmail.com	2211 Elk Ct Junction City KS 66441	KS	EM			FW	1998
Estby Cory A	(815)258-0537 pastorestby@yahoo.com	11468 N 11000e Rd Grant Park IL 60940	NI	SP	Zion Grant Park IL	(815)361-0056	FW	2005
Esterline Sean M	(812)431-1923 sesterline@msn.com	937 Chads Way Charlotte MI 48813	MI	Sn/Adm	First Charlotte MI	(517)543-4360	FW	2000
Estes Eric M	rev.ericestes@gmail.com	1127 E Broadway Louisville KY 40204	IN	SP	Concordia Louisville KY	(502)585-4459	SL	2008
Estes Kenneth A	(321)243-9878 kestes@oursavior.com	1244 W Army Trail Rd Carol Stream IL 60188	NI	SP	Our Savior Carol Stream IL	(630)830-4833	SL	2024
Etheridge Robert D	bobetheridge32@gmail.com	651 Hapsfield Ln Apt 304 Buffalo Grove IL 60089	NI	SP	St John Schaumburg IL	(847)524-9746	FW	2020
Ethridge Shawn P	(507)425-0081 stpaulslutheranpastor@yahoo.com	302 4th St NE Fulda MN 56131	MNS	SP	St Paul Fulda MN	(507)425-2258	SL	1998
Etter Mark R	(859)486-9059 pastoretter@hotmail.com	345 Jerlou Ln Edgewood KY 41017	OH	EM			SL	1983
Ettner Dann J	(602)740-1851 dann.j.ettner@gmail.com	2806 Zinnia Ct Union City CA 94587	CNH	EM			SL	1983

*Multiple Assignments (See Church Worker Locator for Additional Details)
See Page 53 for the Table of Abbreviations for key to District, Position, and Seminary abbreviations
**C =Candidate; EM = Emeritus; the date following the C is the month and year the Candidate status began

NAME	TELEPHONE NUMBER EMAIL	STREET ADDRESS CITY/STATE/ZIP	DISTRICT	POSITION/ STATUS**	WHERE SERVING	OFFICE PHONE	SEM/ PROGRAM	YR GRAD
Etzel Russell A	(281)492-7046 red1517@hotmail.com	4115 Blalock Rd Houston TX 77080	TX	SP	Concordia Houston TX	(713)462-4040	SL	1992
Etzler Andrew R	(573)682-4050 aretzler@gmail.com	612 E Tarr St Centralia MO 65240	MO	SP	Shep Of The Hills Fayette MO	(660)248-3486	FW	1995
Evans Derek M	(409)939-1432 evansd621@gmail.com	7691 River Village Dr Sacramento CA 95831	CNH	SP	Greenhaven Sacramento CA	(916)428-8449	SL	2010
Evans Thomas L	(651)434-3890 pastortom@emanuellutheran church.org	3129 Alden Pond Ln Eagan MN 55121	MNS	Sn/Adm	Emanuel Inver Grove Heights MN	(651)457-3929	SL	1989
Evans Timothy N	(816)668-6205 timothynevans915@gmail.com	6963 Albanese St Colorado Springs CO 80902	MO	M Chap	Office of International Mission Saint Louis MO		SL	2021
Evanson E D	(248) 770-9187	4496 Meigs Ave Waterford MI 48329	MI	EM			SL	1960
Evenson Douglas A	revevie@gmail.com	1619 Timber Trail Shawano WI 54166	NW	EM			FW	2006
Evers James P	(865)483-6444 jaevers@comcast.net	106 Beechwood Ln Oak Ridge TN 37830	MDS	EM			SL	1967
Evers Timothy C	(970)749-7527 timmarevers@gmail.com	492 Florida Meadows Ln Durango CO 81303	RM	EM			SL	1967
Everson Gale R	(406)227-8326 gever68@outlook.com	1891 Baron Dr New Braunfels TX 78130	MT	EM			FW	1978
Evertsen Theodore A	(207)873-7319 everts7319@icloud.com	4 Ursula St Waterville ME 04901	NE	EM			CQ	1979
Ewell Ronald K	(513)256-0675 christthehealer@gmail.com	3199 Highland Ave Cincinnati OH 45219	OH	Inst C	Ohio District North Olmsted OH	(440)235-2297	CQ	1997
Ewert Michael W	(414) 795-8257 mew3rt@gmail.com		MNS	Asst	First Glencoe MN	(320)864-5522	SL	2025
Ewoldt Virgil W	(712)330-3573 v.ewoldt@gmail.com	1819 190th St Milford IA 51351	IW	EM			FW	1986
Eyer John C	(414)551-7388 revjceyer@gmail.com	4933 N Newhall St Whitefish Bay WI 53217	SW	C06/2021			SL	2010
Eyer Richard C	(414)332-0649 reyer@milwpc.com	4933 N Newhall St Milwaukee WI 53217	SW	EM			SL	1965
Fabricius Howard O	(317)881-3899	7809 Broadview Dr Indianapolis IN 46227	IN	EM			SPR	1965
Fabrizius Karl F	(414)529-3999	7390 Hill Valley Ct Greendale WI 53129	SW	EM			FW	1984
Faile Timothy M	(502)689-6792 tfaile@textport.org	13 Poinsettia Dr Rome GA 30161	FG	SP	Prince Peace Douglasville GA	(770)942-4681	CQ	2017
Fair John W	(336)707-4144 fairjohnw@gmail.com	5118 Birnamwood Trail Greensboro NC 27407	SE	EM			FW	1982
Fair Stephen T	(386)515-5916 sfair52@yahoo.com	349 SW Oakwood Ct Lake City FL 32024	FG	SP	Our Redeemer Lake City FL	(386)755-4299	SL	2017
Fairbairn Christopher D	(248)349-3140 pastorchris@ameritech.net	201 Elm St Northville MI 48167	MI	Sn/Adm	St Paul Northville MI	(248)349-3140	FW	1995
Faith Gary J	(504)858-8872 garyfaith@aol.com	166 Northshore Cir Casselberry FL 32707	FG	EM			SL	1986
Faith Scott M	(231)557-7888 faithhouse@comcast.net	4597 Rood Rd Norton Shores MI 49441	MI	SMP	St Mark Muskegon MI	(231)798-2197	FW-SMP	2021
Fajardo Magdiel U	(805)621-9518 magdieluziel@hotmail.com	P.O. Box 485 Lakin KS 67860	KS	Assoc	Immanuel* Lakin KS	(620)355-7161	FW	2014
Fajardo-Ruiz Abiut	abiutfajardo@gmail.com	1140 SW 29th St Oklahoma City OK 73109	OK	SP	Cristo Rey Oklahoma City OK	(405)636-1783	CQ	2014
Fakih Mark I		5003 Windsor Oaks Dr. Fort Wayne IN 46835	IN	SP	St Paul Denham IN	(574)896-5090	FW	2008
Fale John A	(314) 346-1383 johnafale@gmail.com	9838 Vicksburg Siege Ct Saint Louis MO 63123	MO	EM			FW	1985
Fandrey James E	(402)419-3037 jefandrey@gmail.com	5612 Barrington Cir Lincoln NE 68516	NEB	EM			FW	1980
Fangmeier Timothy J	(704)641-5811 tim@giftedpeople.org	400 Avinger Lane Villa 707 Davidson NC 28036	SE	EM			SPR	1971
Fangmeyer Dennis L	(620) 886-0911 pastorfang@att.net	1050 Plum St Brownsburg IN 46112	IN	EM			FW	2002
Fantaye Dereje Dr	(510)415-7363 DFantaye@aol.com	17238 Via Del Rey San Lorenzo CA 94580	CNH	SP	Bethlehem Ethiopian Berkeley CA	(510)551-7450	CQ	2000
Faragalli Daniel	(503)250-1628	19295 Marlin Ct Lake Oswego OR 97035	NOW	EM			CQ	1996
Farden John W Jr	(605)228-7799 jwfarden@gmail.com	4506 W Graceland Pl Sioux Falls SD 57106	SD	EM			SPR	1969
Farhat Andrew W	(541)315-1021 pastor.andrew@sjdenver.org	1710 S. Newport Way Denver CO 80224	RM	Sn/Adm	St Johns Denver CO	(303)733-3777	SL	2009
Farley David J	(612)845-4259 dfarley01@comcast.net	777 Viking Drive East Saint Paul MN 55117	MNS	SP	Triune God Brooklyn Center MN	(763)561-6470	CQ	2024
Farney Case A	(812)305-8557 casefarney0@gmail.com	2305 Glenn Ave Evansville IN 47711	IN	Assoc	St Paul Evansville IN	(812)422-5414	SL	2024
Farrow Arthur B	artfarrow@gmail.com	P.O. Box 992 Whitewright TX 75491	TX	SMP	Saint James* Windom TX	(903)583-5155	SL-SMP	2022
Fast Thomas E	(507)236-3361 pastortfast@gmail.com	567 E 12th St Saint Charles MN 55972	MNS	SP	St Matthew Saint Charles MN	(507)932-4246	SL	1988
Faszholz Thomas O	(971)245-5293 faszholz@gmail.com	1916 NE Harewood Pl Hillsboro OR 97124	NOW	EM			SL	1964
Fausel Charles A	(502)214-0641 cafausel@aol.com	10620 Eagle Pines Ln Louisville KY 40223	IN	EM			FW	1993
Fay Karl R	pastorkarl@pop.church	1327 E Sanborn Dr Palatine IL 60074	NI	Sn/Adm	Prince Peace Palatine IL	(847)359-3451	SL	2009

*Multiple Assignments (See Church Worker Locator for Additional Details)

See Page 53 for the Table of Abbreviations for key to District, Position, and Seminary abbreviations

**C =Candidate; EM = Emeritus; the date following the C is the month and year the Candidate status began

NAME	TELEPHONE NUMBER EMAIL	STREET ADDRESS CITY/STATE/ZIP	DISTRICT	POSITION/ STATUS**	WHERE SERVING	OFFICE PHONE	SEM/ PROGRAM	YR GRAD
Fechner David W	(507)676-1240 dwfechner@gmail.com	12001 N 80th Apt 124 Maple Grove MN 55369	MNS	EM			SL	1971
Fedder Andrew M	(406)426-3619 amjfedder@gmail.com	3916 N Potsdam Ave Sioux Falls SD 57104	EN	S Miss	Office of International Mission Saint Louis MO		FW	2016
Feddern David A	(402)340-9405 revfed@hotmail.com	2229 19th Avenue Central City NE 68826	NEB	C06/2025			SL	2006
Federwitz David M	(731) 227-9140 dvfederwitz@gmail.com	7 SE 14th St Concordia MO 64020	NI	SMP	Lutheran Bible Translators Inc Concordia MO	(660)225-0810	SL-SMP	2015
Feeder David W	(970)203-4246 davidfeeder@msn.com	1213 Heather Dr Loveland CO 80537	RM	EM			SPR	1969
Fehlauer Donald G	(920)563-4038 dgfehlauer@gmail.com	1503 Montclair Pl Fort Atkinson WI 53538	SW	SP	Zion Center WI	(608)876-6667	SL	1989
Fehrmann John R	(612)940-1927 thebotw@comcast.net	3601 Sunset Rd N Brooklyn Park MN 55443	MNS	Asst	Glory Of Christ Plymouth MN	(763)478-6031	SPR	1976
Fehrmann Ryan J			NW	Sn/Adm	St Paul Bonduel WI	(715)758-8559	SL	2004
Fehskens Edward H	efehskens@gmail.com	2971 Broad St Apt 167 Bristol TN 37620	MDS	EM			FW	1981
Feicho Brian J	(618)876-0630 bchibear57@gmail.com	3407 Maryville Rd Granite City IL 62040	SI	SP	Concordia Granite City IL	(618)451-9925	FW	1984
Feickert Roland K	rkfeickert@gmail.com	911 Quincy St Apt 203 Lakeland FL 33815	FG	EM			SL	2000
Feiertag Thomas E Dr	profsllick@gmail.com	W200 N16480 Pine Dr Jackson WI 53037	SW	EM			FW	1978
Felcher Lonnie R	revfelcher@hotmail.com	P.O. Box 240 McCook NE 69001	NEB	SP	Peace McCook NE	(308)345-2595	SL	2010
Feldmann Duane S	(720)379-7919 dsfeldmann@comcast.net	2020 Sagerock Dr Castle Pines CO 80108	RM	EM			CQ	1980
Feldmann Michael W	(618)548-3190 pastormike@salemlc.org	c/o Salem Lutheran Church 1401 Hawthorne Rd Salem IL 62881	CI	Sn/Adm	Salem Salem IL	(618)548-3190	SL	2011
Feldscher Daniel R	(262)498-3458 danfeldscher@gmail.com	8812 Mary Dr Racine WI 53406	SW	EM			SL	1969
Feldt Larry L	(319)240-8817 larryfeldt@gmail.com	2610 Killdeer Ave Denver IA 50622	IE	EM			FW	1998
Felix Bradley N	vicarbrad_7@hotmail.com	6568 Dewey Pt. Rd. Chisholm MN 55719	MNN	SP	Grace* Chisholm MN	(218)254-3466	SL	2005
Felton Steven J	(719)646-5919 stjoyfelton@yahoo.com	1915 Pearl St Fremont NE 68025	NEB	EM			FW	1991
Femmel Mark D Dr	(314)739-6121 pastor@zionmh.org	12075 Dorsett Road Maryland Heights MO 63043	MO	SP	Zion Maryland Heights MO	(314)739-6121	SL	2006
Fenco Jose D	(908)922-7491 pastordan@caminodefe.church	64 Mercer St Somerville NJ 08876	NJ	SP	Somerset Hills* Basking Ridge NJ	(908)766-2858	SL	2018
Fenker William G	(513)444-7648 williamfenker@gmail.com	1367 Finch Ln Milford OH 45150	OH	EM			FW	1982
Fenker Aaron T Sr	(785)706-3966 pastorfenker@icloud.com	1527 W Goldcrest Ave Milwaukee WI 53221	SW	SP	Our Father's Greenfield WI	(414)282-8220	FW	2012
Fennacy James B	(805)550-3144 jfennacy@gmail.com	558 W Sample Ave Clovis CA 93612	CNH	SMP	Redeemer Fresno CA	(559)439-8500	CQ	2019
Fenske Aric A	(920)878-0403 aricfe@gmail.com	219 Riverview Dr Manawa WI 54949	NW	RSO	Lutherans for Life Nevada IA	(888)364-5433	FW	2011
Fenske Craig B	(701)741-0854 cbfenske56@gmail.com	203 Cleo Ct Grand Forks ND 58201	ND	EM			FW	1986
Fenske Jarod M	(906)231-4484 j.fenske@peaceantigo.org	300 Lincoln St Antigo WI 54409	NW	Assoc	Peace Antigo WI	(715)623-2200	SL	2023
Fenske Shawn D	(989)295-8214 sdfenske@msn.com	743 S Shade Ct Andover KS 67002	KS	Sn/Adm	Holy Cross Wichita KS	(316)684-5201	SL	2007
Fenster Kevin W	(503)427-8304 pastorkevin@living-savior.org	8740 SW Sagert St Tualatin OR 97062	NOW	Sn/Adm	Living Savior Tualatin OR	(503)692-3490	SL	2008
Fenton Eugene L Jr	(813)814-9092	3641 15th St Riverside CA 92501	RM	EM			CQ	1978
Fenton Charles S	(734)218-4829	1085 McKnight Rd S Saint Paul MN 55119	MNS	SMP	Eastern Hghts Saint Paul MN	(651)735-4202	SL-SMP	2016
Ferber Steven E	(763)777-2001 pastorferber@redeemer wayzata.org	9931 Kiwi Ave N Brooklyn Park MN 55443	MNS	Sn/Adm	Redeemer Wayzata MN	(952)473-1281	SL	1989
Ferch Bradley E	(563) 726-5459 pastorferch@immanueldaven port.org	3605 N Birchwood Ave Davenport IA 52806	IE	SP	Immanuel Davenport IA	(563)324-6431	FW	2016
Ferderer Paul A	(701)464-3130 pastorpaulferderer82@gmail.com	103 Circle Dr Lake City IA 51449	IW	SP	Pilgrim Lake City IA	(712)464-3130	FW	2015
Ferguson Louis P Jr	(972) 342-6001 revrunnin262@gmail.com	5053 Almanor Drive Discovery Bay CA 94505	CNH	D Ex/S	California/Nevada/Hawaii District Livermore CA	(866)264-6079	FW	1999
Ferguson Travis W	(619) 462-5211 tferguson@christlamesa.org	7929 La Mesa Blvd La Mesa CA 91942	PSW	Sn/Adm	Christ La Mesa CA	(619)462-5211	SL	2017
Ferguson Randall L	(262)377-4152 randall.ferguson@cuw.edu	N42 W5493 Spring St Cedarburg WI 53012	SW	S HS/C	Concordia University Wisconsin Mequon WI	(262)243-5700	SL	1987
Ferguson Jack D Dr	(989)884-4976 revferg@lhi.net	P.O. Box 92 Hawks MI 49743	MI	SP	Faith Hawks MI		SL	1972
Ferguson Eamonn M	(608)512-5075 eamonn.m.ferguson@gmail.com	468 Bristol Dr Carol Stream IL 60188	NI	Assoc	St John Wheaton IL	(630)668-0701	FW	2017
Ferguson Aaron J	(420)641-3264 pastoraaronferguson@gmail.com	1316 N 7th St Perry OK 73077	OK	SP	Christ Perry OK	(580)336-2347	FW	2025

*Multiple Assignments (See Church Worker Locator for Additional Details)

See Page 53 for the Table of Abbreviations for key to District, Position, and Seminary abbreviations

**C =Candidate; EM = Emeritus; the date following the C is the month and year the Candidate status began

NAME	TELEPHONE NUMBER EMAIL	STREET ADDRESS CITY/STATE/ZIP	DISTRICT	POSITION/ STATUS**	WHERE SERVING	OFFICE PHONE	SEM/ PROGRAM	YR GRAD
Ferguson Ryan M	(951)581-8111 ferguson@stmattsonline.com	24530 N Old McHenry Rd Hawthorn Woods IL 60047	NI	Assoc	St Matthew Hawthorn Woods IL	(847)438-7709	SL	2023
Fernandez James F	(720)233-9130 james.fernandez@hope-brevard.org	1538 Huff Ct Melbourne FL 32935	S	SP	Hope Viera Melbourne FL	(321)622-6126	SL	2009
Fernandez Rodrigo	(281)857-1878 rfernandez@txlcms.org	13618 Lynnville Dr Houston TX 77065	TX	RSO	Lutheran Inter-City Network Houston TX	(713)426-2451	SL	2010
Ferrero Salvador G	(619)249-6972 salvadorferrero@hotmail.com	3455 Sky Rdg Alpine CA 91901	PSW	C08/2019			IV	2009
Ferrier Kenneth M	(970) 966-0231 kmfkona@gmail.com	3393 White Buffalo Dr Wellington CO 80549	FG	EM			SL	1983
Ferry Joseph W	(260)436-4474 joe@southwestlutheran.org	5120 Homestead Rd Fort Wayne IN 46814	IN	Sn/Adm	Southwest Fort Wayne IN	(260)436-4474	SL	2015
Ferry Patrick T Dr	(262)391-8255 patricktferry@gmail.com	2733 Painted Sky Bend Leander TX 78641	TX	EM			FW	1987
Ferry Charles D	charles.ferry@lcms.org	Strada Miraslau 35 Asoc. Concordia Lutherana Confesionala Brasov NO 50007 ROMANIA	SW	S Miss	Office of International Mission Saint Louis MO		SL	2008
Feuer Michael O	(505)603-9492 pastormikefeuer@gmail.com	1 Olive Rd Sandia Park NM 87047	RM	Sn/Adm	Prince Of Peace Cedar Crest NM	(505)596-6142	FW	2007
Feusse Daniel J	(402) 370-0842 seelsorg@aol.com	4685 Century Dr Saginaw MI 48638	MI	EM			SL	1998
Fichtner Lesley J	rev.fichtner@yahoo.com	211 Caperiole Pl Fort Wayne IN 46825	IN	EM			FW	2007
Fick Steven J	(512)695-2087 pastorfick@gmail.com	1319 Piney Creek Ln Cedar Park TX 78613	TX	SP	Redeeming Grace Austin TX	(512)695-2087	SL	2002
Fickel Erich R	(219)926-1556	701 Oakwood Dr Chesterton IN 46304	IN	SP	St Paul Chesterton IN	(219)926-1556	FW	1999
Ficken Jock E Dr	(630)715-3401 jficken81@gmail.com	1029 Tower Hill Ln Hendersonville TN 37075	TX	EM			SL	1982
Ficken Paul D	(262)822-5410 fickenp@yahoo.com	728 Lathrop Ave Racine WI 53405	SW	SP	Chapel Cross Racine WI	(262)886-4755	SL	2008
Ficken David W	(615)601-9078 dficken@linc.org	4129 N Highland Ave Arlington Heights IL 60004	NI	Assoc	St Peter Arlington Heights IL	(847)259-4114	SL	2011
Ficken David E	(925) 875-8208 dmcficken@gmail.com	7592 Interlachen Avenue Dublin CA 94583	CNH	Sn/Adm	St Philip Dublin CA	(925)828-2117	SL	2007
Fickenscher Daniel P	(260)710-6750	6045 E State St Columbus IN 47201	IN	Assoc	St Paul Columbus IN	(812)376-6504	FW	2020
Fickenscher James W Dr	(314)505-7027 fickenscherj@csl.edu		MO	S HS/C	Concordia Seminary Saint Louis MO	(314)505-7000	SL	2012
Fickenscher Robert F	(916)342-0791 robertficken1@gmail.com	3939 Walnut Avenue Box 124 Carmichael CA 95608	CNH	EM			SL	1963
Fickenscher Carl C II Dr	(260)452-2131 carl.fickenscher@ctsfw.edu	c/o Concordia Theological Seminary 6600 N Clinton St Fort Wayne IN 46825	IN	S HS/C	Concordia Theological Seminary Fort Wayne IN	(260)452-2100	FW	1984
Fieberkorn Michael T Dr	(937)689-8410 mfieberkorn@zionharvester.org	30 Oak Leaf Branch Ct Saint Charles MO 63304	MO	Assoc	Zion Saint Charles MO	(636)441-7425	SL	2013
Fiebiger Craig A	blulincoln@aol.com	1164 Road 11 1/2 Lovell WY 82431	MDS	SMP	Faith Thompsons Station TN	(615)791-1880	CQ	2019
Fiechtner Gregory K	(574)855-3130 fiechtnergreg@gmail.com	51610 Trowbridge Ln South Bend IN 46637	IN	EM			FW	1977
Fiege Scott T Dr	(712)880-1226 revdocstf@gmail.com	605 N High St P.O. Box 209 Lake City MN 55041	MNS	EM			SL	1982
Fields Thomas M	(303)756-2932 fieldsthomas@comcast.net	5680 E Bates Ave Denver CO 80222	RM	EM			SL	1972
Fields George N	(703)674-6002 george.fields@ctsfw.edu	c/o Christ Lutheran Church 4423 I 55 N Jackson MS 39206	SO	Assoc	Christ Jackson MS	(601)366-2055	FW	2017
Fields Andrew T	afields@immanuelvalpo.org	224 W 406 N Valparaiso IN 46385	IN	Sn/Adm	Immanuel Valparaiso IN	(219)462-8207	SL	2002
Fiene Hans W	pastorfiene@gmail.com		MO	SP	Prince Of Peace Crestwood MO	(314)843-8448	FW	2008
Fiene John W Dr	(317)902-0045 fienefam@att.net	5279 El Arbol Dr. Carlsbad CA 92008	PSW	EM			FW	1980
Fienen Daniel H	(231)287-7964 graceluthbaldwin@att.net	8636 S M37 Baldwin MI 49304	MI	SP	Grace Baldwin MI	(231)745-7521	FW	1978
Figur Nilo L Dr	(512) 264-5646 nilo.figur@lhm.org	803 Brookvale Ter Manchester MO 63021	MO	Aux	LLL/Lutheran Hour Ministries Saint Louis MO	(314)317-4100	Other	1974
Filipek Adam T Dr	(701)680-3130 revfilipek@gmail.com	101 2nd Ave SE Lidgerwood ND 58053	ND	SP	Immanuel* Lidgerwood ND	(701)538-4688	SL	2009
Filipek Aaron M	pateraaron@gmail.com	637 S Erie St. Wichita KS 67211	KS	Sn/Adm	Trinity Wichita KS	(316)685-1571	SL	2006
Filter Edward W	(517)230-6417 edfilter54@gmail.com	6824 Maynard Rd Portland MI 48875	MI	EM			CQ	1989
Finch Thomas L	(623)466-5180 trfinc13ba@yahoo.com	25944 W Mohawk Ln Buckeye AZ 85396	PSW	EM			FW	2004
Finck Richard J	(804)305-7521 TheRev220@gmail.com	13530 Hickory Glen Rd Chester VA 23831	SE	EM			SL	1975
Finger Sylvan N	(530)685-0010 firstolive2018@gmail.com	971 N. Plumas St Willows CA 95988	CNH	SP	Mount Olive* Corning CA	(530)824-5530	SL	2019
Fink Roger W	(410)961-9537	6130 Allwood Ct Apt 311 Baltimore MD 21210	SE	EM			SL	1960
Fink Samuel V	(734)255-3493 sam@hostoftheshepherdchurch.org	1657 Layton Rd Fowlerville MI 48836	MI	SP	Heart of the Shep Howell MI	(517)552-7218	SL	2019
Finke Gregory A	(281)844-7644 finkeonthemove@aol.com	489 Grand Hill St Paul MN 55102	TX	Assoc	Trinity Houston TX	(713)224-0684	SL	1989

*Multiple Assignments (See Church Worker Locator for Additional Details)

See Page 53 for the Table of Abbreviations for key to District, Position, and Seminary abbreviations

**C =Candidate; EM = Emeritus; the date following the C is the month and year the Candidate status began

NAME	TELEPHONE NUMBER EMAIL	STREET ADDRESS CITY/STATE/ZIP	DISTRICT	POSITION/ STATUS**	WHERE SERVING	OFFICE PHONE	SEM/ PROGRAM	YR GRAD
Finnern Terry L	(320)852-7592 terryf@rea-alp.com	9311 Park Lane Dr NE Alexandria MN 56308	MNN	EM			SPR	1974
Finnern Brady L	(320)282-8550 brady.finnern@mnnlcms.org	914 15th St N Sartell MN 56377	MNN	DP	Minnesota North District Brainerd MN	(218)829-1781	SL	2006
Finney Adam C	adamfinney@hotmail.com		MNS	SP	St Peter Vernon Center MN	(507)549-3166	SL	2007
Firminhac Scott G	(307)689-1889 sgfirm@gmail.com	3642 Laramie St Torrington WY 82240	WY	SP	Trinity* Morrill NE	(308)247-2432	SL	1996
Fischaber Phillip J	(513)384-4651 phillip.fischaber@gmail.com	105 Fairview Ct Walnut IL 61376	NI	Sn/Adm	Holy Trinity Walnut IL	(815)379-2839	FW	2017
Fischer Ted L	(847)414-0715 justplainted@gmail.com	3500 N Rutherford Ave Chicago IL 60634	NI	Assoc	St Peter Arlington Heights IL	(847)259-4114	FW	2024
Fischer Thomas F	(248)495-3723 pastorgolf@gmail.com	503 Tulip Dr Three Oaks MI 49128	MI	EM			SL	1983
Fischer Robert F	(207)370-0355 fischer1483@gmail.com	100 Smith Rd Windham ME 04062	NE	EM			FW	1988
Fischer Randy J	(618)670-7736 rjfischer92@yahoo.com	15 Magnolia St Wood River IL 62095	SI	EM			SL	1992
Fischer Glenn E	(352)688-7864 pastrfisch@aol.com	11097 Montcalm Rd Spring Hill FL 34608	FG	SP	Forest Oaks Spring Hill FL	(352)683-9731	FW	1991
Fischer David A	(801)550-8724 revdave74@gmail.com	5138 S Gurene Dr Salt Lake Cty UT 84117	RM	EM			SPR	1974
Fischer Charles L	(812)366-3985 ChuckandElaine349@gmail.com	2140 Spring Branch Rd NE New Salisbury IN 47161	IN	EM			FW	2004
Fischer William C	(715)213-3870 bfischer194865@gmail.com		SE	EM			SL	1978
Fish Jack D	(262)903-6103 cjfish1@charter.net	619 Tudor Dr Janesville WI 53546	SW	EM			SL	2002
Fish Robin D Sr	(218)296-4012 robin.fish@hotmail.com	104 SW 6th Ave Verndale MN 56481	MNN	SP	Immanuel Verndale MN	(573)286-1009	FW	1980
Fisher Alexander R	(828) 358-6563 arfisher623@gmail.com	324 Second Ave. SE Hickory NC 28602	SE	Sn/Adm	Christ Hickory NC	(828)328-1483	SL	2016
Fisher Joseph M	(262)305-1663 revjfisher@charter.net	616 Meadowbrook Dr West Bend WI 53090	SW	Sn/Adm	Pilgrim West Bend WI	(262)334-0375	FW	1994
Fisher Maxx J	(812)216-5891 maxxjofish@gmail.com	2238 Paris Ave SE Grand Rapids MI 49507	MI	Assoc	St Matthew Grand Rapids MI	(616)942-9091	SL	2020
Fisk Jonathan M		4129 Ruskin Rd Rockford IL 61101	NI	Sn/Adm	St Paul Rockford IL	(815)963-5435	SL	2006
Fistler Trae L	(270)885-3969 pastor@faithhopkinsville.com	405 Sheila Dr Hopkinsville KY 42240	MDS	SP	Faith Hopkinsville KY	(270)885-3969	FW	2020
Fitch Russell E	(701)301-1506 pastorfitch@gmail.com	3724 Rattlesnake Dr Missoula MT 59802	MT	SP	Messiah* Missoula MT	(406)549-9222	FW	2009
Fitch LaVerne J Dr	(979)743-4812 fitchphd@gmail.com	1104 Summit St Schulenburg TX 78956	TX	EM			SPR	1960
Fitch Josiah J	(574)540-1083 josiahfitch@gmail.com	3971 S 550 W Columbus IN 47201	IN	SP	Faith Columbus IN	(812)342-3587	SL	2016
Fittje Kyle J	(417)232-4642 PFittje@ImmanuelLCMS.net	304 Sycamore St Lockwood MO 65682	MO	SP	Immanuel Lockwood MO	(417)232-4642	SL	2011
Fitzgerald Michael N	(989)652-4858 padrefitz@gmail.com	9135 Bender Rd Frankenmuth MI 48734	MI	EM			FW	1994
Fitzner Timothy J Dr	(507)327-5956 pr.fitzner@gmail.com	2504 Kara Xing Bloomington IL 61704	CI	SP	Christ Normal IL	(309)452-5609	FW	2008
Fitzpatrick Dennis G Jr	(620)640-6700 revfitz@icloud.com	c/o St Johns Lutheran Church P.O. Box 436 Yuma CO 80759	RM	SP	St John Yuma CO	(970)848-2210	SL	2006
Fitzpatrick Matthew W	(407)595-2299 mathfitz@gmail.com	516 Darkwood Ave Ocoee FL 34761	S	SMP	New City Orlando FL	(407)595-2299	SL-SMP	2021
Fitzpatrick Paul J	(828)413-7319 paul51fitz@gmail.com	11066 39th St N Unit A Lake Elmo MN 55042	SE	EM			CQ	1980
Fjordbotten Allan H	(703)729-5725 ahfjord@aol.com	45001 Audubon Sq Apt 526 Ashburn VA 20147	AT	EM			SL	1979
Fjordbotten Dale A	(646) 265-7532 dale.fjordbotten@gmail.com	1178 E 1000 North Rd Onarga IL 60955	CI	SP	Trinity* Cissna Park IL	(815)457-2739	SL	2019
Flachsbart Jack B	(503)313-8735 jjrevtek@gmail.com	8701 Bristol Way Yakima WA 98908	NOW	EM			SL	1974
Flahn John O	(240)350-7750 fjomar.vision@gmail.com	6045a Cecil Ave Gwynn Oak MD 21207	SE	Asst	Our Savior Laurel MD	(301)776-7670	SL	2011
Flamenco Julio C	(210)647-0992 jflamenco@satx.rr.com	9523 Clear Fls San Antonio TX 78250	TX	C07/2016			HITSL	2002
Flammann William H Dr	(703)657-9210 bill.flammann@gmail.com	62 Watkins Drive Sandy Hook CT 06482	NE	EM			CQ	1983
Flamme Anthony B	(317)201-5527 brianflamme@gmail.com	5106 W College Blvd Roswell NM 88201	RM	Sn/Adm	Immanuel Roswell NM	(575)622-2853	FW	2014
Flamme John A	(317)437-5023 johnflamme46@gmail.com	3300 Airport Rd Trlr D17 Alamogordo NM 88310	RM	EM			FW	1992
Flanick Adam R	(443)974-4281 pastoraflanick@protonmail.com	201 N Bowery Ave Gladwin MI 48624	MI	SP	Our Savior Gladwin MI	(989)426-9689	SL	2022
Flannery Michael L	(406)471-2698 michael.darlene.flannery@ gmail.com	377 Church Hill Rd Augusta ME 04330	RM	EM			SL	1976
Flanscha Marvin L	(970)219-1599 joyce.flanscha@gmail.com	1792 E 11th St Loveland CO 80537	RM	EM			SPR	1966
Flatau Aaron G	(515)890-7558 pastora@goldfieldaccess.net	7 River Oaks Humboldt IA 50548	IW	Sn/Adm	Zion Humboldt IA	(515)332-3279	SL	2007
Flath Richard E	pastor_r_flath@msn.com	1425 Lake View Ave Snohomish WA 98290	NOW	EM			SL	1976

*Multiple Assignments (See Church Worker Locator for Additional Details)
See Page 53 for the Table of Abbreviations for key to District, Position, and Seminary abbreviations
**C =Candidate; EM = Emeritus; the date following the C is the month and year the Candidate status began

NAME	TELEPHONE NUMBER EMAIL	STREET ADDRESS CITY/STATE/ZIP	DISTRICT	POSITION/ STATUS**	WHERE SERVING	OFFICE PHONE	SEM/ PROGRAM	YR GRAD
Flegel Helmut D	(414)466-5924 hflegel@peoplepc.com	5710 N 33rd St Milwaukee WI 53209	SW	EM			CQ	2011
Fleischhauer Harold L	(832)467-0320 hlfleisch@gmail.com	15722 Honolulu St Jersey Vlg TX 77040	TX	EM			SL	1964
Fleischmann John G II Dr	(631) 252-0613 resqrev@gmail.com	119 Ocean Ave Center Moriches NY 11934	AT	SP	Christ East Moriches NY	(631)878-2277	SL	1986
Fleischmann Thomas G	(920)892-2211 brotherskeeper99@yahoo.com	N5451 State Road 57 Plymouth WI 53073	SW	EM			FW	1993
Fleming David C	(616)516-2945 pastor@oursavior-gr.org	1888 Ridgemoor Dr SE Grand Rapids MI 49506	MI	Assoc	Our Savior* Grand Rapids MI	(616)949-0710	FW	1986
Flentgen Ronald B	(913)782-6279 rflentgen@gmail.com	1102 W Wabash Ter Olathe KS 66061	KS	EM			SPR	1964
Flesch William E Jr	(507)452-2560 wfles3638@gmail.com	720 49th Ave Winona MN 55987	MNS	EM			SPR	1972
Fletcher Ronald A	(252)521-5364 tbonesax@yahoo.com	1204 Meadowwood Dr Kinston NC 28501	SE	EM			SL	1964
Flick Seth T	(314) 456-3742 seth@kingofkings.org	14566 Potter Cir Bennington NE 68007	NEB	Assoc	King Of Kings Omaha NE	(402)333-6464	SL	2011
Flo Paul S	flop@csl.edu	801 Seminary Place St. Louis MO 63105	MO	S HS/C	Concordia Seminary Saint Louis MO	(314)505-7000	SL	2019
Flo Steven L	(314) 420-9870 stevenlflo@gmail.com	9827 E Vista Dr Hillsboro MO 63050	MO	EM			FW	1990
Flohrs Robert J	(540)656-7517 robert.flohrs@gmail.com	8813 Brown Thrasher Ct Gainesville VA 20155	PSW	EM			FW	1985
Flor Eugenio W	41- 987-38-4066 toderke@yahoo.com	6755 Birchwood Rd Grand Ridge FL 32442	FG	EM			Other	1973
Flores Jose	(402)321-6360	1366 Road 5600 Hebron NE 68370	NEB	SP	Trinity* Hebron NE	(402)365-4317	CQ	1996
Flores Gilberto B	(361)215-8505	3908 Mueller St Corp Christi TX 78408	TX	EM			HITSL	1996
Florez Luis J	(716)826-3790	240 Abbott Rd Buffalo NY 14220	EA	SP	La Santa Cruz Kenmore NY	(716)875-5485	HITSL	2005
Floyd David A	(707)334-6305 surfingpastor@hotmail.com	1063 W L St Benicia CA 94510	CNH	SP	Faith Pleasant Hill CA	(925)685-7353	FW	1997
Fluechtling Duane K	(708)895-5660 dfluechtling@gmail.com	2927 191st St Lansing IL 60438	NI	EM			CQ	1981
Fluegge Glenn K Dr	(949)244-6096 glenn.fluegge@cui.edu	21831 Zuni Dr Lake Forest CA 92630	PSW	S HS/C	Concordia University Irvine* Irvine CA	(949)854-8002	SL	2000
Flynn Alan J	(916)717-2731 revalanflynn@gmail.com	505 Ashwill Ct Rio Linda CA 95673	CNH	EM			SL	2001
Flynn Daniel J	(734)649-5247 danflynn73@yahoo.com	7580 Webster Church Rd Whitmore Lake MI 48189	MI	EM			SL	2008
Flynn Patrick A	pastorflynnstpeters@gmail.com		NEB	M Chap	Office of International Mission Saint Louis MO		FW	2013
Foelber John T Sr	(410)668-2922 jt.fs@verizon.net	9701 Harding Ave Parkville MD 21234	SE	EM			FW	1990
Foerster Barry C	(909)929-0603 barryteri@gmail.com	c/o Westminster Gardens 1420 Santo Domingo Duarte CA 91010	PSW	EM			SPR	1967
Fofana Lusienie	(651)216-9242 safieyatu@yahoo.com	674 Wheelock Pkwy W Saint Paul MN 55117	MNS	Assoc	Bethel Saint Paul MN	(651)300-2642	SL	2012
Fogi Teka O	(301)706-2423 teka.obsa@gmail.com	3323 Sir Thomas Dr Apt #41 Silver Spring MD 20904	SE	SP	Oromo Resurrection Kensington MD	(301)942-7759	CQ	2017
Foley Kevin M	(530)903-2120 kevin.foley.flc@gmail.com	7382 N 89th St Omaha NE 68122	NEB	Sn/Adm	River of Life Omaha NE	(402)558-6212	FW	2016
Folks Hayden M	419-965-8240 haydenm.folks@gmail.com	c/o Zion Lutheran Church 17434 Schumm Rd Willshire OH 45898	OH	SP	Zion Willshire OH	(419)495-2398	FW	2022
Folle Ronald G	(702)498-0061 follecarole@gmail.com	4883 S Buckingham Ln Springfield MO 65810	MO	EM			SPR	1968
Folwaczny Norbert	(631)830-5046 bert12350@hotmail.com	1172c Franklin Turnpike Danville VA 24540	SE	SP	Christ King Danville VA	(434)836-6888	FW	1977
Fondow Donald J Dr	(218)820-1364 dfondow@protonmail.com	18626 Estate Dr Park Rapids MN 56470	MNN	EM			SL	1979
Fontaine Raymond A	(219)981-4235	568 Rio Vista Dr NE Rio Rancho NM 87144	NI	EM			SL	1969
Foote Robert M	(607)273-5169 pastor@trinityithaca.org	129 Whitetail Dr Ithaca NY 14850	EA	SP	Trinity Ithaca NY	(607)273-9017	FW	1985
Foote Randy C	(580)216-1526 revrcfoote@gmail.com	538 Oklahoma St Lahoma OK 73754	OK	SP	Zion Lahoma OK	(580)796-2243	SL	2004
Forbes Conner E	(812)603-0503 connereforbes@gmail.com	200 7th St Saint James NY 11780	AT	Assoc	Saint James Saint James NY	(631)584-5212	SL	2024
Ford Colin E	(231)645-1920 colinford90@gmail.com	500 Harbison Blvd Apt 708 Columbia SC 29212	SE	Assoc	Mount Olive Columbia SC	(803)781-5845	FW	2019
Foreman Curtis L	(515)724-8555 curtforeman554@gmail.com	3219 SE Grant St. Ankeny IA 50021	IW	EM			SPR	1966
Forgione Anthony	(646)732-5030 aforgione@our-saviour.org	6313 Dieterle Cres Rego Park NY 11374	AT	SMP	Our Saviour New York Rego Park NY	(718)275-2825	SL-SMP	2019
Forke David L	(715)210-5352 davidf@mypeacechurch.com	1021 Bradley Ave Eau Claire WI 54701	NW	SMP	Peace Eau Claire WI	(715)834-2486	SL-SMP	2012
Forke Terry R	(406)670-1101 forke@mtdistlcms.org	759 Newman Lane Suite 2 Billings MT 59101	MT	SP	St Paul* Roundup MT	(406)947-2360	SL	1989
Forrest Jessie A	(580)574-7985 pastorjforest@gmail.com	462 Ketch Creek Dr Lawton OK 73507	OK	EM			SL	1995

*Multiple Assignments (See Church Worker Locator for Additional Details)
See Page 53 for the Table of Abbreviations for key to District, Position, and Seminary abbreviations
**C =Candidate; EM = Emeritus; the date following the C is the month and year the Candidate status began

NAME	TELEPHONE NUMBER EMAIL	STREET ADDRESS CITY/STATE/ZIP	DISTRICT	POSITION/ STATUS**	WHERE SERVING	OFFICE PHONE	SEM/ PROGRAM	YR GRAD
Forss Eric C	(517)545-0245 immanuel_lutheran_howell@juno.com	515 W Highland Rd Apt E7 Howell MI 48843	EN	SP	Immanuel Howell MI	(517)548-2066	CQ	1995
Fortkamp Gary D	(217) 690-9746 garfor@hotmail.com	1009 W Evergreen Ave Effingham IL 62401	CI	EM			SPR	1966
Foss Richard A Dr	(314)750-2394 revrick@mac.com	12046 Maryland Manor Dr Maryland Hts MO 63043	MO	EM			SL	1984
Fosse Kenneth	(908)670-3540 kenneth.fosse1@gmail.com	23923 NE 113th Ln Redmond WA 98053	NOW	EM			CQ	1980
Foster Anthony K	(424)675-0289 anthony_foster@sbcglobal.net	11126 S Harvard Blvd Los Angeles CA 90047	PSW	SMP	Faith Inglewood CA	(323)750-3552	CQ	2019
Foster Charles Y Dr	(586) 286-4231 cfoster@immlutheran.org	47120 Romeo Plank Rd Macomb MI 48044	MI	Sn/Adm	Immanuel Macomb MI	(586)286-4231	SL	2001
Found Philip J	(308)249-3843 foundphil@hotmail.com	P.O. Box 631 Bayard NE 69334	WY	EM			CQ	1996
Found Shawn J	(732)966-4447 FoundProf70@oulook.com	7501 Amherst Dr Little Rock AR 72205	MDS	EM			FW	2008
Fountain Douglas E Dr	(561)254-1254 drdouglasfountain@gmail.com	1675 S Fiske Blvd Apt 128-G Rockledge FL 32955	S	EM			FW	1983
Foust Paul M Jr	(407)889-5958 pastor@zionnewlife.com	6430 Lakeville Rd Orlando FL 32818	FG	EM			SPR	1973
Fouts Bart J	(402)768-1470 saintbjf@gmail.com	c/o Camp Concordia 13400 Pinewood St NE Gowen MI 49326	MI	RSO	Camp Concordia Inc Gowen MI	(616)754-3785	SL	2008
Fox Charles A	(415)963-2348 pastorchipfox@gmail.com	5505 Diamond Heights Blvd San Francisco CA 94131	EN	SP	New Life Chinese* San Francisco CA	(415)508-9552	SL	1981
Fox Michael P	(715)571-8375 foxmichael26@gmail.com	100 S Daisy St Ishpeming MI 48949	NW	SP	Christ King Ishpeming MI	(906)485-4432	SL	2020
Foy William E	(219)613-3496 reverendfoy@gmail.com	234 W Division Rd Valparaiso IN 46385	IN	SP	Prince Peace Valparaiso IN	(219)464-4911	FW	2003
Frahm John A III	(715) 904-0642 chemnitzian@gmail.com	31 Illinois St Racine WI 53405	SW	SP	Grace Racine WI	(262)633-4831	NESC	1998
Frahm John H Dr	(512)826-0969 jhfrahm@gmail.com	2500 Barton Creek Blvd Apt 3314 Austin TX 78735	TX	EM			SPR	1976
Frahm Russell G	(321)626-5134 rgfcounselor@yahoo.com	40 Mark Ave Merritt Is FL 32952	FG	EM			SL	1982
Fraker Donald D II	(830)643-4099 frakerfamily@sbcglobal.net	1107 River Rock New Braunfels TX 78130	TX	EM			SL	1983
Fraker Timothy D	(817)881-3650 timfraker@pilgrimluth.org	1731 St. Agnes Dr Green Bay WI 54304	NW	Assoc	Pilgrim Green Bay WI	(920)965-2233	SL	2014
Francik Douglas D	(760)519-9187 defrancik@gmail.com	4172 Garnet Cir Marion IA 52302	IE	EM			SL-D	2009
Francik Brian D	(402) 710-6679 pastorbfrancik@gmail.com	P.O. Box 69 Deshler NE 68340	NEB	SP	Faith* Hebron NE	(402)710-6679	SL	2008
Francis Grant	(503)759-4055 gfrancis23@hotmail.com	745 Zepher Way Molalla OR 97038	NOW	EM			SL	1983
Francisco Thurman O	(209)628-4880 timofrancisco@gmail.com	1344 Pine Bluff Dr Saint Charles MO 63304	MO	EM			SL	2007
Francisco Benjamin J	(308)289-2784 francisco.benjamin@gmail.com	1604 E 13th St York NE 68467	NEB	SP	Faith York NE	(402)362-3000	SL	2008
Franck Robert C	(218) 391-9984 revfranck@msn.com	3622 Crescent View Ave Duluth MN 55804	MNN	Sn/Adm	Mount Olive Duluth MN	(218)724-2500	FW	1991
Franckowiak Michael S	(530)771-5438 mikeagsim@gmail.com	9933 Bridlewood Ln Waco TX 76708	TX	EM			SL	1999
Franco-Arango Jose M Mauricio	(956) 200-9938 glamaur@yahoo.com	2631 Cypress Dr Harlingen TX 78550	TX	Assoc	St Paul Harlingen TX	(956)423-3924	Other	2018
Frank Robert A	(309)282-0753 revraf101@gmail.com	523 Stonecrest Savoy IL 61874	CI	EM			FW	1986
Frank Victor L	(832)623-0824 vfrank1136@att.net	2410 Sweetgum Hill Ct Spring TX 77388	TX	EM			SPR	1975
Frank Timothy A	(712)269-3683 frank1685@yahoo.com	19244 Hawthorne Ave Council Blfs IA 51503	IW	Assoc	St Pauls Council Bluffs IA	(712)322-4729	FW	2011
Frank Steven J	(320)226-6268 steven_frank_68@hotmail.com	321 E Scharf Ave Vergas MN 56587	MNN	SP	St Paul* Vergas MN	(218)342-2379	FW	2007
Frank Paul J	(480)984-1414 pfrank@hosanna-lcms.com	11209 E Adobe Rd Mesa AZ 85207	PSW	SP	Hosanna Mesa AZ	(480)984-1414	SL	2005
Frank Carl R	(303)838-1618 cr1frank@hotmail.com	P.O. Box 1423 Conifer CO 80433	RM	SMP	Mount Hope Evergreen CO	(303)670-1387	SL-SMP	2013
Frank Arnold W	(602)482-0335 awalfran@juno.com	1746 E Marconi Ave Phoenix AZ 85022	PSW	EM			SL	1968
Frank Peter A	(828) 256-2970 pfrank@stpetersconover.org	806 4th St NE Conover NC 28613	SE	Sn/Adm	Saint Peter's Conover NC	(828)256-2970	SL	2024
Franke Gilbert A	g.a.franke@gmail.com	130 N Harris St Bellville TX 77418	TX	EM			SL	1972
Franke Matthew P	(307)214-5282 mmrfranke@icloud.com	2290 Laguna Ct Unit 207 Fairborn OH 45324	OH	EM			SL	1996
Franson Jon T	(308)201-0926 jfranson12@gmail.com	510 W. 9th St Coffeyville KS 67337	KS	SP	St Paul Coffeyville KS	(620)251-2927	FW	2015
Franzmeier Alvin H Dr	(956)376-1535 alvinhenry@gmail.com	1404 S Border Ave Apt 731 Weslaco TX 78596	TX	EM			SL	1957
Franzmeier Wilbur C	(651)322-1560 wcfdgf@gmail.com	13872 Autumnwood Ct Rosemount MN 55068	MNS	EM			SL	1950
Frazee Joshua J	pastorjoshfrazee@gmail.com	450 Bridge St Mayville WI 53050	SW	Assoc	St John Mayville WI	(920)387-3568	SL	2013
Frazier Larry	(708)557-7672 thnkylrd@att.net	20231 Linda Drive Euclid OH 44117	OH	EM			CQ	1994

*Multiple Assignments (See Church Worker Locator for Additional Details)

See Page 53 for the Table of Abbreviations for key to District, Position, and Seminary abbreviations

**C =Candidate; EM = Emeritus; the date following the C is the month and year the Candidate status began

NAME	TELEPHONE NUMBER EMAIL	STREET ADDRESS CITY/STATE/ZIP	DISTRICT	POSITION/ STATUS**	WHERE SERVING	OFFICE PHONE	SEM/ PROGRAM	YR GRAD
Frechette Jeffrey D Sr	(586)441-1020 jfrechette_sr@yahoo.com	9466 Hickory Hollow Ct Davison MI 48423	MI	Sn/Adm	St Mark Flint MI	(810)736-6680	FW	2008
Frederich Clifford M	(847) 962-6017 cfrederich@aol.com	5228 Valkyrie Way Louisville KY 40272	IN	EM			SL	1981
Frederick Clarke E	czfred@severewx.com	1045 6th St SE Mason City IA 50401	IE	EM			SPR	1973
Fredericksen Wayne P	(703)892-4846 pastor@osva.org	825 S Taylor St Arlington VA 22204	SE	Sn/Adm	Our Savior* Arlington VA	(703)892-4846	SL	1991
Frederickson David L	(507)259-0146 oma.frederickson@gmail.com	407 8th St SW Plainview MN 55964	MNS	EM			SL	1987
Frederickson Bruce G	(612)719-6845 BruceF6300@gmail.com	6050 Blanchard Blvd Apt 123 Circle Pines MN 55014	MNS	EM			SPR	1972
Fredstrom William G	(309)846-1679 wfredstrom@immanuelseymour. com	2298 Locust Court Ctr Seymour IN 47274	IN	Assoc	Immanuel Seymour IN	(812)522-3118	SL	2022
Freeman Daniel L	(360)880-4103 pastor_freeman@juno.com	109 Germaine Dr Chehalis WA 98532	NOW	Sn/Adm	Peace Chehalis WA	(360)748-4108	SL	1999
Freeman Jeremy M	(660)473-6131 jeremymichaelfreeman@gmail. com	1523 N Hedge Apple Dr Sedalia MO 65301	MO	SP	St Paul Sedalia MO	(660)826-1164	SL	2007
Freese Stuart W	(402)230-8510 stuartfreese@yahoo.com	27068 Co Rd 12 Hooper NE 68031	NEB	SP	Immanuel Hooper NE	(402)654-3663	CQ	2015
Freiberg Marc L Sr	(320)674-0351 marc.freiberg.sr@gmail.com	73278 310th St Racine MN 55967	MNS	SP	Immanuel* Racine MN	(507)754-5782	FW	2000
Freitag James A	(253)297-8786 james.a.freitag4@gmail.com	18914 77th Avenue Ct E Puyallup WA 98375	NOW	O-Sp Min	Office of International Mission Saint Louis MO		SL	2001
Freitag John P	(714)270-5555 jpfreitag@mac.com	355 Lauderback Gap Trl Rogersville TN 37857	MDS	EM			SL	1970
Fremder Manfred W	(260)493-8522 mlfremder@gmail.com	8104 Watermark Ct West Chester OH 45069	OH	EM			FW	1990
Fremer Joseph	(616) 523-5803 joe@fremer.com	3525 Pinckney Rd Saranac MI 48881	MI	EM			SL	1982
Fremer Noah A	(260)715-2353 pastorfremer@gmail.com	W2780 Highway 32 Howards Grove WI 53083	SW	SP	Trinity Howards Grove WI	(920)565-3669	FW	2012
French David R	(765)474-2525 frenchd143@gmail.com	2301 Manitoba Dr Lafayette IN 47909	IN	EM			FW	1992
Frentz Steven N	(630)846-1909 pastorfrentz@hotmail.com	1158 Valley View Road Lake City MN 55041	MNS	SP	Bethany* Lake City MN	(651)345-2424	SL	2010
Frerichs Andrew P	(971)217-1905 andrew.frerichs@gls-hsv.org	3321 S Memorial Pkwy Huntsville AL 35801	SO	Assoc	Grace Huntsville AL	(256)881-0552	SL	2024
Frerichs Paul C	(971)226-6112 pfrerichs@redeemerlutheran.us	c/o Redeemer Lutheran Church 2141 Fifth St Cuyahoga Falls OH 44221	OH	Sn/Adm	Redeemer Cuyahoga Falls OH	(330)923-1445	SL	1994
Frerking John L	(561)252-5250 ejfrerking@yahoo.com	130 Cruiser Rd S N Palm Beach FL 33408	FG	EM			SL	1967
Frese Michael N	(913)547-2292 pastorfrese@gmail.com	4939 Stratford Rd Fort Wayne IN 46807	EN	S Ex/S	The LCMS Corporate Saint Louis MO	(314)965-9000	FW	2002
Frese Kenneth W	(310)398-3741 kenfrese@gmail.com	3778 Ashwood Ave Los Angeles CA 90066	PSW	EM			SL	1969
Fretham David G	(612)859-8550 dfretham@gmail.com	611 1st Ave NW Winnebago MN 56098	MNS	EM			CQ	2002
Freudenburg Allen P	(407)365-3943 alfreud@att.net	2013 Inner Circle Dr Oviedo FL 32765	FG	EM			CQ	1988
Freudenburg Trevor A	rev.freudenburg@gmail.com	15750 Baxter Road Chesterfield MO 63017	MO	SP	Lord Of Life Chesterfield MO	(636)532-0400	SL	2018
Frey Thurman L Jr	(410)274-6085 thurman_frey@hotmail.com	7910 32nd St Baltimore MD 21237	SE	EM			FW-SMP	2010
Frias Bartolome R		9101 Carol Leigh Dr Charlotte NC 28213	FG	EM			CQ	1993
Frick Roger P	(714)639-7430 PastorFrick@SalemOrange.com	6500 E Santiago Canyon Rd Orange CA 92869	PSW	SP	Salem Orange CA	(714)633-2366	SL	2005
Frick E T	(815)784-2362 etfrick@gmail.com	12109 Ellwood Greens Rd Genoa IL 60135	NI	EM			SPR	1974
Frick Michael A	(972)839-9529 michaelwillbe@gmail.com	4615 The Station Blvd #3307 Sachse TX 75048	TX	EM			CQ	1989
Fricke Gary H	(303)819-5702 gpasnurse@peoplepc.com	P.O. Box 635 Bailey CO 80421	RM	EM			FW	1980
Fricke Milton E	(808)870-4038 revmilt@aol.com	783 Makalii St Kahului HI 96732	CNH	EM			SL	1968
Friedmeyer A N	revnorman.june@gmail.com	2715 Docs Dr Lincoln NE 68507	NEB	EM			FW	1981
Friedrich Brian L Dr	(651)641-8211 friedrich@csp.edu	1277 Dayton Ave Saint Paul MN 55104	MNS	S HS/C	Concordia University St Paul Saint Paul MN	(651)641-8278	SL	1986
Friedrich Henry W	ehfried@netamumail.com	512 N Finn Dr #410 Algona IA 50511	IW	EM			SL	1953
Friedrich Mark D	(480)671-9092 pastormarkfriedrich@yahoo.com	2575 W Ironstone Ave Apache Jct AZ 85120	PSW	SP	Mountain View Apache Junction AZ	(480)982-8266	SL	1986
Friedrich Ronald E	(301)251-5953 ronfriedrich@verizon.net	814 Brice Rd Rockville MD 20852	SE	EM			SL	1976
Friedrichs Galen M	(417)681-0981 exdairyman@hotmail.com	210 Poplar St Lamar MO 64759	MO	SP	Grace Lamar MO	(417)682-2257	FW	1993
Fries John J	(785)492-0229 revjfries@gmail.com	P.O. Box 314 Alta Vista KS 66834	KS	SP	St Paul* Junction City KS		SL	2012
Frincke Karl A	(260)466-5121 kfrincke@frontier.com	7420 Holden Dr Fort Wayne IN 46835	IN	EM			SL	1975

*Multiple Assignments (See Church Worker Locator for Additional Details)
See Page 53 for the Table of Abbreviations for key to District, Position, and Seminary abbreviations
**C =Candidate; EM = Emeritus; the date following the C is the month and year the Candidate status began

NAME	TELEPHONE NUMBER EMAIL	STREET ADDRESS CITY/STATE/ZIP	DISTRICT	POSITION/ STATUS**	WHERE SERVING	OFFICE PHONE	SEM/ PROGRAM	YR GRAD
Frisque Marshal R	(608)449-6243 revfrisque@gmail.com	134 Edmaro St Fredonia WI 53021	SW	SP	Peace Neenah WI	(920)725-0510	FW	2018
Frith Mark T	(913)375-4181 mthomasfrith@outlook.com	213 S Singletree St Olathe KS 66061	MO	Pro Stf	Lutheran Center for Religious Liberty Kirkwood MO		SL	1990
Fritsch Bryan L	(920)748-3882 contact@messiah.lc	526 Mayparty Dr Ripon WI 54971	SW	SP	Messiah Ripon WI	(920)748-3882	SL	1985
Fritsch Lyle H	(507)319-0635 lhfritsch@outlook.com	410 E Ivy Rd Unit 4 Tea SD 57064	SD	EM			FW	1982
Fritsche Joel P	(314) 376-8577 joelfritsche@me.com	11 McCall Terr St. Louis MO 63105	MO	S HS/C	Concordia Seminary Saint Louis MO	(314)505-7000	SL	2000
Fritz Rodney D	(785)337-6030 sargefritz409@gmail.com	409 Hilltop Drive Hanover KS 66945	KS	EM			SL	1980
Fritz Ross M	(218)651-0180 pastor_r_fritz@outlook.com	501 Northland Ct Breckenridge MN 56520	MNN	SP	Grace Breckenridge MN	(218)643-5286	SL	2010
Fritz John A	(630)898-7782 hope4aurora@sbcglobal.net	1541 Reckinger Rd Aurora IL 60505	NI	SP	Hope Aurora IL	(630)898-6754	SL	1984
Fritzler Sergio A	(809)455-8289 sergio.fritzler@lcmsintl.org	Calle M Corta #7 Cerro Alto Ii Santiago De Los Caballeros 51000 DOMINICAN REPUBLIC	IN	S HS/C	Concordia Theological Seminary Fort Wayne IN	(260)452-2100	VB	2018
Froehlich Charles W	(631)987-5043 revfroe2@gmail.com	5515 Burlington Ln Williamsburg VA 23188	AT	EM			SL	1974
Froelich Kevin M	(651) 263-6846 kmfroelich@live.com	1957 English St #426 Maplewood MN 55109	MNS	EM			SL	1982
Froh Charles E	(650)349-8265 cled2froh@aol.com	1244 Mercedes Dr Roseville CA 95747	CNH	EM			SL	1977
Froiland Brandon J	(816)746-2407 prfroiland@christlc.com	7304 NW Maple Ln Platte Woods MO 64151	MO	Sn/Adm	Christ Platte Woods MO	(816)741-0483	FW	2008
Fruehauf David A	(763) 416-0086 fruehaufd36@gmail.com	12001 80th Ave N Unit 327 Maple Grove MN 55369	MNS	EM			CQ	1997
Frusti Martin J	(623)249-5525 martinfrusti@yahoo.com	16160 W Tohono Dr Goodyear AZ 85338	PSW	EM			FW	1992
Frusti Mark A	(630)464-3857 trusti1@msn.com	26 Ridge Cir Streamwood IL 60107	NI	Sn/Adm	Faith Carpentersville IL	(847)428-2079	FW	1983
Frusti Jonathan M	(386)409-1280	838 E 17th Ave New Smyrna Beach FL 32169	FG	EM			FW	1980
Frusti James M	(734)417-1014 deacon@stpaulnorthville.org	44159 Westminister Way Canton MI 48187	MI	SMP	St Paul Northville MI	(248)349-3140	CQ	2018
Frusti Todd I	(810)658-3000 tfrusti@trinitydavison.org	5360 Archers Way Gladwin MI 48624	MI	Sn/Adm	Trinity Davison MI	(810)658-3000	FW	1993
Fry Karl F Dr	+44 0785 679 2803 karlfry2012@gmail.com	6 Amarylis Close Fareham Hampshire PO15 UNITED KINGDOM	OH	EM			Other	1974
Fry Victor G	(952) 891-5222 beckyvicofmtn@frontier.com	14212 Heritage Ln Apple Valley MN 55124	MNS	EM			SPR	1962
Fryckman James R	(541)994-5979	7123 Clover Creek Dr. SE Salem OR 97306	NOW	SMP	St John Salem OR	(503)588-0171	CQ	2019
Frye Frank G	(970)441-0491 fgfrye@gmail.com	1017 Everest St Clermont FL 34711	FG	Asst	Zion Winter Garden FL	(407)743-5533	FW	1983
Fuchs John G Jr	(507)534-6565 jgjefuchs@yahoo.com	605 3rd Ave NE Plainview MN 55964	MNS	EM			SL	1965
Fuchs John M	(515)570-7598 jsfuchs@yahoo.com	245 E 2nd St Fond Du Lac WI 54935	SW	Inst C	Office of National Mission Saint Louis MO		SL	1993
Fuchs James R	(612)859-9686 jamesfuchs27@yahoo.com	1503 Golden Aspen Dr Ames IA 50010	IW	EM			CQ	2010
Fuhrmann Russell D	rfuhrmann@gmail.com	10039 N 550 W Decatur IN 46733	IN	SP	Peace Berne IN	(260)589-3848	FW	1982
Fuller Nicholas M Dr	(317) 313-0763 nicholasm.fuller@gmail.com	504 N Walnut St. Seymour IN 47274	IN	RSO	Concordia Counseling A Lutheran Outreach Ministry Inc Seymour IN	(812)671-8704	SL	2007
Fulmer Daniel R	(231)330-3889 pastorfulmer@gmail.com	4015 72nd Ave E Sarasota FL 34243	FG	EM			SL	2001
Funck Stephen H	(443)813-8077 signdovesf@mac.com	3201 Hiss Ave Baltimore MD 21234	SE	EM			SL	1968
Fundum James K	(260)632-3092		IN	EM			FW	1990
Funke Kenneth R	(573)418-0611 klfunke@hotmail.com	431 E 3rd St Sanborn IA 51248	IW	EM			FW	1980
Fuqua Thomas K Dr	(727)487-4885 kf6634@gmail.com	4308 Buckhorn Groves Ct Valrico FL 33596	FG	SP	Faith New Port Richey FL	(727)849-4418	CQ	1975
Furgeson Jon C Dr	(314)601-1039 Pastor.Furgeson@peacelutheranstl.org	2008 Telford Dr Saint Louis MO 63125	MO	Sn/Adm	Peace Saint Louis County MO	(314)892-5610	SL	2006
Furry Craig M	(505)228-4759 craig.furry@icloud.com	123 Shady Oak Cir Tijeras NM 87059	RM	EM			SL-SMP	2015
Futch Christopher Y	(727)698-5425 chris.futch@oursaviorfl.org	627 Florenz Cir NE Saint Petersburg FL 33703	FG	SMP	Our Savior Saint Petersburg FL	(727)344-2684	SL-SMP	2019
Futrell Richard K	(417) 366-3212 prfutrell3@gmail.com	24 Wildwood Ln Kimberling Cy MO 65686	MO	SP	Shepherd Hills Kimberling City MO	(417)739-2512	SL	2008
Fyler George F III	(440)867-3287 revgff3@roadrunner.com	184 Newport Dr Painsville Township OH 44077	OH	EM			SL	1972
Gabriel Gem	(860)938-2100 pastorgemgabriel@gmail.com	208 Newtown Ave Norwalk CT 06851	NE	SP	St Peter Norwalk CT	(203)847-1252	SL	2017
Gadbaw Daniel J			MNS	SP	Our Savior Hutchinson MN	(320)587-3318	FW	2003
Gadbaw David R	(870)421-4320 djgadbaw@gmail.com	58 Belle Cove Pl Mountain Home AR 72653	MDS	EM			FW	1991

*Multiple Assignments (See Church Worker Locator for Additional Details)

See Page 53 for the Table of Abbreviations for key to District, Position, and Seminary abbreviations

**C =Candidate; EM = Emeritus; the date following the C is the month and year the Candidate status began

NAME	TELEPHONE NUMBER EMAIL	STREET ADDRESS CITY/STATE/ZIP	DISTRICT	POSITION/ STATUS**	WHERE SERVING	OFFICE PHONE	SEM/ PROGRAM	YR GRAD
Gaddini David C	(779) 704-2822	14806 Il Route 173 Harvard IL 60033	NI	Sn/Adm	Fellowship Of Faith McHenry IL	(815)759-0739	SL	2000
Gade Dean W	(612)869-5150 dewilga@gmail.com	6615 Stevens Ave Richfield MN 55423	MNS	EM			SL	1995
Gadeken Robert G	(989)780-1721 robggad@gmail.com	4553 Mellowlight Dr Saint Louis MO 63129	MO	EM			SL	1985
Gaede Fred A	(630)606-1986 fredgaede1@gmail.com	331 George St West Chicago IL 60185	NI	SMP	Trinity West Chicago IL	(630)231-1175	FW-SMP	2013
Gaertner Evan P Dr	(810)355-6517 therevev@ourshepherd.net	4203 Seminole Dr Royal Oak MI 48073	MI	Sn/Adm	Our Shepherd Birmingham MI	(248)646-6100	SL	2001
Gaertner Mark H	(260)667-0034 revmhg@gmail.com	28855 Sugarberry Dr Chesterfield MI 48051	MI	EM			SL	1971
Gage Raymond W	(601)825-5410 raymondgage@bellsouth.net	172 Cedar Spring Cir Pearl MS 39208	SO	SP	Epiphany Jackson MS	(601)353-0504	FW	1977
Gai Philip M	(905) 819-1057 philip.gai@saintmarks.ca	#11-1455 Bristol Rd W Mississauga ON L5V 1 CANADA	EN	Assoc	St Mark's Mississauga ON	(905)278-2122	SL-SMP	2017
Gaines Lloyd D Sr Dr	(202)398-5503 pastorlloyd_plc@icloud.com	8309 Deerstill Way Clinton MD 20735	SE	Sn/Adm	Peace Washington DC	(202)398-5503	SL	1984
Gajadhar James T	(718)463-0190 jtgaj@aol.com	189-28 45th Rd Flushing NY 11358	AT	Assoc	St John* Flushing NY	(718)463-2959	CQ	2006
Galchutt Daniel M	(314) 996-1730 dan.galchutt@lcms.org	1333 S Kirkwood Rd. St. Louis MO 63122	MO	S Ex/S	Office of National Mission Saint Louis MO		SL	2004
Galik Karl E Dr	(248)561-3656 karl.galik@gmail.com	2245 Barret Lane The Villages FL 32162	FG	EM			SL	1982
Gall Timothy A	(217)821-4505 timg07@gmail.com	P.O. Box 127 Pleasant Dale NE 68423	NEB	SP	Bethlehem Pleasant Dale NE	(402)795-3885	SL	2017
Gallagher Frank M	(573) 508-7662 gallag2g@aim.com	4223 Hwy 89 N Chamois MO 65024	CI	SP	Our Savior Washington IL	(309)444-4030	SL	1986
Galler Jayson S Dr	(903)984-4333 pastor@pilgrimlc.org	713 Florey St Kilgore TX 75662	TX	SP	Pilgrim Kilgore TX	(903)984-4333	NESC	1998
Galligar Patrick J	(812)350-7820 patrick.galligar@gmail.com	561 W Twisted Oaks Dr Beverly Hills FL 34465	FG	SP	Faith Lecanto FL	(352)527-3325	SL	2008
Gallmeier Alfred E	(512)237-3293 Gallmeiera@gmail.com	118 Wigwam Smithville TX 78957	TX	EM			CQ	1982
Gallo Stephen F	(682)202-1751 sfgallo@yahoo.com	543 33rd Ave N Clinton IA 52732	IE	EM			SL	1983
Gallup Roger B	(708)495-7545 gallup57@juno.com	Bethlehem Lutheran Church 2624 Oak St River Grove IL 60171	NI	SP	Bethlehem River Grove IL	(708)453-1113	FW	1986
Ganas Scott U	(626)812-7240 sganas19@yahoo.com	254 W 10th St Azusa CA 91702	PSW	EM			CQ	2005
Gandy Amadeus L	(608)498-9571 amadeus.gandy@gmail.com	742 Saltair Ln Mary Esther FL 32569	EN	M Chap	Office of International Mission Saint Louis MO		FW	2018
Gann Jaim E	(856)275-9575 pastor@gracelutheranva.org	4613 Crossgate Rd Chester VA 23831	SE	SP	Grace Chester VA	(804)748-6058	SL	2001
Gano Dennis R	(323)463-6589 cmsdennis@aol.com	1826 N Harvard Blvd Apt 4 Los Angeles CA 90027	PSW	EM			SL	1978
Gapski Nicholas C	(586)943-9558 nickgapski@yahoo.com	15734 Charles R Ave Eastpointe MI 48021	MI	Assoc	St Stephen* Detroit MI	(313)841-7940	FW	2023
Garazin Kenneth W	(630) 697-1706 kgarazin@aol.com	268 Bass Ct Marco Island FL 34145	FG	EM			SL	1972
Garber Alexander C IV	(586)241-8658 acgacgacg@gmail.com	P.O. Box 1163 Livingston TX 77351	TX	SP	Trinity Livingston TX	(936)327-3239	FW	2017
Garcia Juan G	juanito605@hotmail.com	1300 Carriage Dr Valparaiso IN 46383	IN	C07/2016			HITSL	2005
Garcia Adan C	(734)945-3052 pastorg@immanuelbaycity.com	c/o Immanuel Lutheran 300 N Sheridan St Bay City MI 48708	MI	Sn/Adm	Immanuel Bay City MI	(989)893-4088	SL	2018
Garcia Albert L Dr	(414)702-4275 dr.al.garcia502@gmail.com	1779 Wilsons Crossing Dr Decatur GA 30033	FG	EM			SPR	1974
Gard Daniel L	(260)417-7143 garddl@aol.com	6807 Nighthawk Dr Fort Wayne IN 46835	IN	EM			FW	1984
Gardner Robert E	605-745-3722 b.d.gardnerprsd@gmail.com	11932 Sundance Dr Hot Springs SD 57747	SD	EM			SPR	1976
Garland Curtis D	(605)863-1761 khakiman@juno.com	6272 W Albain Rd Monroe MI 48161	MI	SP	Immanuel Monroe MI	(734)269-2961	SL	2009
Garnett James L	(228)334-2287 jlg.elg@gmail.com	624 N Poplar St Florence AL 35630	SO	SP	Our Redeemer Florence AL	(256)764-3902	SL	2015
Garrabrant Steven A	sgarrabrant@gdlc.org	15518 Pilgrim Hall Dr Friendswood TX 77546	TX	SMP	Gloria Dei Houston TX	(281)333-4535	SL-SMP	2023
Garred Matthew M	(330)998-3923 revmmg@pm.me	10061 Hazelton Rd Streetsboro OH 44241	OH	SP	Concordia Independence OH	(216)524-2188	SL	2001
Garrett Dion T	(314)225-6272 dgarrett@pathfinderstl.org	318 Fox Den Dr Ballwin MO 63021	MO	Sn/Adm	Pathfinder Ellisville MO	(636)394-4100	SL	2004
Garrett Morgan J	(810)423-1661 garrettm@csl.edu	178 Cherrywood Dr Davison MI 48423	MI	Assoc	St Mark Flint MI	(810)736-6680	SL	2024
Garrison Bradley G	(737)646-8206 bradgarrison52@gmail.com	8384 Riverwalk Dr Fenton MI 48430	MI	EM			FW	1984
Garrison Jacob T	(402)314-2493 jgarrison3131@gmail.com	837 N Dakota St Superior NE 68978	NEB	SP	St John* Chester NE	(402)324-8075	FW	2025
Garrison Thomas B	(989) 977-1044 thomgarrison@aol.com	c/o St Johns 9476 Kilmanagh Rd Sebewaing MI 48759	MI	SP	St Peter* Sebewaing MI	(989)977-1044	SL	2004
Garrity Corey R	(919)612-4923 corey@bridgecity.cc	400 Grand St Redwood City CA 94062	CNH	Sn/Adm	Bridge City Redwood City CA	(650)366-5892	SL	2022
Garwood Burt L			NEB	SP	Pilgrim Bellevue NE	(402)291-2848	SL	1999

*Multiple Assignments (See Church Worker Locator for Additional Details)
See Page 53 for the Table of Abbreviations for key to District, Position, and Seminary abbreviations
**C =Candidate; EM = Emeritus; the date following the C is the month and year the Candidate status began

NAME	TELEPHONE NUMBER EMAIL	STREET ADDRESS CITY/STATE/ZIP	DISTRICT	POSITION/ STATUS**	WHERE SERVING	OFFICE PHONE	SEM/ PROGRAM	YR GRAD
Garwood Ronald M Dr	(307)259-6045 drgandb@aol.com	3313 Appalachian Ave Cody WY 82414	WY	Asst	Christ the King Cody WY	(307)587-3025	FW	1983
Gaschler Mark	(308)414-1023 markpgaschler@gmail.com	8511 Oxford Ave Raytown MO 64138	KS	SP	Immanuel Linn KS	(785)348-5892	FW	2023
Gaschler Paul R	(308)882-6015 paulgaschler@gmail.com	4834 Cayuga Dr Saint Louis MO 63123	MO	Assoc	Holy Cross Saint Louis MO	(314)772-8633	FW	2019
Gatnoor Jenina P	(605)251-0155 gatwang2009@hotmail.com	1622 Washington St #2 Lincoln NE 68502	SD	C04/2025			SL	2006
Gatz William A	(517)784-8338 misslynnegatz@gmail.com	1631 Duguid Rd Jackson MI 49203	MI	EM			SPR	1961
Gatz Dale G Dr	(904)553-9182 dggatz@bellsouth.net	8936 Oakland Hills Cir Portage MI 49024	AT	EM			SL	1968
Gau James A	(740)405-4722 pastorjag27@gmail.com	4272 Hart Road Richfield OH 44286	EN	Sn/Adm	Fairlawn Fairlawn OH	(330)836-7286	SL	1989
Gaub Richard M	(707)775-5406 revbo58@protonmail.com	c/o Saint Johns Lutheran Church 217 N Freeman Dr Prt Washingtn WI 53074	SW	Assoc	St Johns Port Washington WI	(262)284-2131	FW	2001
Gauger William J	(217)853-7689 billgauger72@aol.com	30331 Pebble Beech Cir Genoa IL 60135	NI	C07/2023			SL	2008
Gaulke Stephen E	(941)228-5758 thegaulkes@yahoo.com	2185 Woods St Sarasota FL 34237	FG	EM			SL	1984
Gaunt Douglas A	(308) 455-0552 douggaunt33@att.net	2004 W 49th St Kearney NE 68845	NEB	Asst	Zion Kearney NE	(308)234-3410	FW	1986
Gaunt Micah R	(308)627-7238 revgaunt@gmail.com	306 Forest Blvd Hastings NE 68901	NEB	SP	Peace Hastings NE	(402)462-9023	SL	2007
Gause Mark E	(253)335-4032	1862 Harding St Enumclaw WA 98022	NOW	SP	New Hope Pacific WA	(253)351-0450	SL	1984
Gauss Erik A		8609 State Route 47 Yorkville IL 60560	NI	Sn/Adm	Cross Yorkville IL	(630)553-7335	SL	2003
Gauthier Brian A Dr	(402)803-0742 bgauthier@me.com	4405 Berkshire Estates Dr Saint Louis MO 63129	MO	Pro Stf	Office of International Mission Saint Louis MO		SL	2010
Gauthier Gerald A II	jerry946@yahoo.com	1704 Amelith Rd. Bay City MI 48706	MI	SP	St John Bay City MI	(989)686-0176	FW	2004
Gavin Jeff G	(847)593-7670	1100 S Linneman Rd Mt Prospect IL 60056	NI	SP	St John Mount Prospect IL	(847)593-7670	FW	1982
Gawura Eric R	(847)346-4344 egawura@gmail.com	c/o Atonement Lutheran 1621 Francisco Rd Columbus OH 43220	OH	SP	Atonement Columbus OH	(614)451-1880	SL	2000
Gawura Mark A	(517) 667-6853 mgawura@gmail.com	1049 N Crandell Dr Charlotte MI 48813	MI	SMP	First Charlotte MI	(517)543-4360	CQ	2019
Gboeah Lawrence W	(862)215-5583 jacon49@yahoo.com	11 Carteret St Newark NJ 07104	NJ	EM			SL	2007
Ge Rue Keith E	(217)725-8137 kgerue@trinitymenasha.com	1018 N Hawthorne Dr Appleton WI 54915	SW	Assoc	Trinity Menasha WI	(920)722-2662	FW	1994
Geach John T Dr	(510)881-6404	21117 Gary Dr Unit 307 Castro Valley CA 94546	CNH	EM			SPR	1963
Gearig Mark A	(217)423-6955 pastormark@spldecatur.org	c/o St Paul Lutheran Church 1 Bachrach Ct Decatur IL 62526	CI	Assoc	St Paul's Decatur IL	(217)423-6955	SL	2016
Geaschel Robert E	(708)846-4170 rgeaschel@tlbr.org	11480 German Church Rd Burr Ridge IL 60527	NI	Sn/Adm	Trinity Burr Ridge IL	(708)839-1200	SL	1996
Gebauer Victor E Dr	(651)890-9317 vgebauer@bitstream.net	2554 Hazelwood St Maplewood MN 55109	MNS	EM			SL	1964
Gebauer Ronald F	(360)644-8037 loving.sols@gmail.com	1039 Quail Run Duncanville TX 75116	TX	EM			FW	1985
Gebauer Ethan C	(530)251-2025 revethangebauer@gmail.com	925 Cameron Way Susanville CA 96130	CNH	EM			SPR	1969
Gebel Robert J	(414)517-8987 revrobtgebel@gmail.com	1900 Norhardt Dr Apt 104 Brookfield WI 53045	SW	EM			SL	1996
Gebhardt Leonhardt C	(402)643-6989 gebhardt2@windstream.net	1900 E Lark Ln Nixa MO 65714	NEB	EM			SPR	1970
Gebremichael Hiruy B	(404)552-5164	2146 Saren Ct Tucker GA 30084	FG	SP	St Mark Tucker GA	(770)938-4546	SL	2009
Gebrewold Haileselassi M	(904)725-4307	2540 Sandusky Ave E Jacksonville FL 32216	FG	O-Miss	Grace Jacksonville FL	(904)928-9136	SL	2008
Gehlbach Gary V	(262)372-4353 garygehlbach@hotmail.com	W247n7860 Jean Ct Lisbon WI 53089	SW	Asst	Peace Sussex WI	(262)246-3200	SL	1987
Gehlbach Daryl D	(612)386-4824 revgehlbach@aol.com	305 Liberty St NE Fridley MN 55432	MNS	SP	Prince Peace Df Spring Lake Park MN	(763)786-1706	SL	1983
Gehne David F	(262)488-5104 dgehne@trinityracine.com	2029 Geneva St Racine WI 53402	SW	Sn/Adm	Trinity Racine WI	(262)632-2900	SL	2005
Gehrke Matthew J	(618)447-0766 matthew.gehrke@cuw.edu	840 Bauer St. Wisconsin Dells WI 53965	SW	SP	Our Savior* Baraboo WI	(608)356-9792	SL	2006
Gehrke Robert J Dr	(651)503-7032 pastorgehrke@gmail.com	8885 Irving Blvd N Lake Elmo MN 55042	MNS	EM			SL	1982
Gehrke Wesley A	(573)769-2739 pastorwesgehrke@gmail.com	210 S Spring St Palmyra MO 63461	MO	SP	Zion Palmyra MO	(573)769-2739	SL	2012
Gehrke Wilbur L	(541)662-1045 wkgehrke@frontier.com	3230 Lavina Dr Forest Grove OR 97116	NOW	EM			SL	1971
Gehrke Aaron R	(906)482-4750 pastorgehrke@copperluth.org	1112 2nd St Hancock MI 49930	NW	Sn/Adm	SS Peter and Paul Houghton MI	(906)482-4750	SL	2010
Geil Allen E	(417)298-6358 alretozarks@gmail.com	3330 Highway Rb Bolivar MO 65613	MO	EM			CQ	1994
Geis William S	(314)478-5244 wsgeis314@outlook.com	4306 Von Talge Rd Saint Louis MO 63128	MO	EM			SL	1990
Geisler Jeffrey L	geisler@clhcadets.com	7019 Antebellum Dr Fort Wayne IN 46815	IN	EM			FW	1997

*Multiple Assignments (See Church Worker Locator for Additional Details)

See Page 53 for the Table of Abbreviations for key to District, Position, and Seminary abbreviations

**C =Candidate; EM = Emeritus; the date following the C is the month and year the Candidate status began

NAME	TELEPHONE NUMBER EMAIL	STREET ADDRESS CITY/STATE/ZIP	DISTRICT	POSITION/ STATUS**	WHERE SERVING	OFFICE PHONE	SEM/ PROGRAM	YR GRAD
Geisler Robert G	(313)460-2794 rgeisler@trinitydavison.org	5407 Swan Dr. Burton MI 48509	MI	SMP	Trinity Davison MI	(810)658-3000	CQ	2018
Geistlinger Jack A Dr	(608)230-3310	5565 Tancho Dr Madison WI 53718	CNH	EM			SL	1965
Geitz Timothy P	(712)541-2266 pastorofgrace@live.com	1531 3rd Ave SE Le Mars IA 51031	IW	Sn/Adm	Grace Le Mars IA	(712)546-5516	SL	1987
Geminn Scott F Dr	(914) 200-8421 sgeminn@fordham.edu	25885 Trabuco Rd Apt 309 Lake Forest CA 92630	PSW	SP	St John El Segundo CA	(310)615-1072	SL	2009
Geml Michael A	(517)395-8422 mikegeml@comcast.net	216 5th Ave SE Conover NC 28613	SE	Sn/Adm	Concordia Conover NC	(828)464-3324	FW	2003
Gemta Yoseph G	614-322-1184 y.gemta@yahoo.com	446 Pruden Dr Pickerington OH 43147	OH	Assoc	Oromo Columbus OH	(614)322-1184	CQ	2017
Genke Quentin M	(336)686-3132 qgenke@yahoo.com	53150 Kansas Ave Ste 122 McConnell Afb KS 67221	SE	Inst C	Office of International Mission Saint Louis MO		SL	1998
Gensch Jeremiah B	(319)215-9370 jeremiahbgensch@hotmail.com	111 Davis Rd Troy MO 63379	MO	C02/2024			SL	2019
Gensch Daniel W	hrprdan72@sbcglobal.net	16320 S Fieldstone Pl Lockport IL 60441	NI	EM			SL	1974
Genszler John W	(262)343-1045 genszj@gmail.com	4125 Pickle Rd Oregon OH 43616	OH	SP	Prince of Peace Oregon OH	(419)691-9407	SL	2017
Genter Lee H	(567)259-9996	378 College Ave Oakmont PA 15139	EA	RSO	Concordia Lutheran Ministries Cabot PA	(724)352-1571	FW	1987
Genter John N	(562)417-7211 jonathan.nathan.genter@gmail.com	1610 N Columbia Ave Seward NE 68434	NEB	S HS/C	Concordia University Nebraska Seward NE	(402)643-3651	SL	2010
Gentet Robert E	(210)387-4736 regentet@yahoo.com	305 Cloudmont Dr Windcrest TX 78239	TX	EM			SL	1993
Genthner Glenndon C Dr	drgnthnr@gmail.com	724 Piney Pl Saint Johns FL 32259	MO	EM			FW	1998
Genzen Gary C Dr	(352)314-0514 ggenzen@comcast.net	32523 Crystal Breeze Ln Leesburg FL 34788	FG	EM			SPR	1970
George Gus A III	(712)278-1045 prgg3@premieronline.net	702 Oak St P.O. Box 191 Ireton IA 51027	IW	EM			CQ	1977
Georgi Gary D	rgdg1971@gmail.com	36451 N Reserve Cir Avon OH 44011	OH	EM			SL	1971
Geraci Coleman K	(734)439-2806 pastor.stpaulsmilan@gmail.com	106 Dexter St Milan MI 48160	MI	SP	St Thomas* Ann Arbor MI	(734)663-7511	SL	2019
Gerber Anthony J	(402)469-0541 anthonygerber@gmail.com	2522 E 10 St Fremont NE 68025	NEB	Sn/Adm	Trinity Fremont NE	(402)721-5536	SL	2014
Gerberding Kieth A Dr	(734)285-0155 kagerb@aol.com	12713 Wesley St Southgate MI 48195	MI	EM			SL	1960
Gerdes Timothy A	tim.gerdes@victorysouthbay.org		PSW	SP	Victory Chula Vista CA	(619)262-4444	SL	1999
Gerike Andrew S	(402)551-0244		NEB	Sn/Adm	Mount Calvary Omaha NE	(402)551-0244	FW	2014
Gerke David K	pastorgerke1@aol.com	140 River Park Dr Middlebury IN 46540	IN	EM			FW	1982
Gerke Robert A	(616)281-2183 rgerke@aol.com	898 Tierra St SE Grand Rapids MI 49508	MI	SP	Bethel Grandville MI	(616)534-3364	FW	1986
Gerken Mark A	(515)570-2331 picksruth@gmail.com	2201 N 15th St Adel IA 50003	IW	EM			SL	1982
Gerken Daniel J	(253)770-9115 djgerken1950@gmail.com	6016 85th St E Puyallup WA 98371	NOW	EM			CQ	1979
Gerken Herbert M	herbert.gerken@gmail.com	6311 Treasure CV Fort Wayne IN 46835	IN	EM			SL	1966
Gerlach Fred H	(609)751-2546 fred_gerlach@hotmail.com	c/o Family Of Christ 3501 E Chandler Blvd Phoenix AZ 85048	EN	SP	Family Of Christ Phoenix AZ	(480)759-4047	SL	2005
Gerloff Gary M	(559)284-3967 pastorgerloff@gmail.com	2105 Crosspoint Ave Santa Rosa CA 95403	CNH	SP	St Mark Santa Rosa CA	(707)545-1230	SL	2016
German Brian T Dr	(262)536-5101 brian.german@cuw.edu	405 S Garfield Ave Prt Washingtn WI 53074	SW	S HS/C	Concordia University Wisconsin Mequon WI	(262)243-5700	FW	2010
Gerner Alvin L	(402)981-0938 leroygerner61@gmail.com	15813 Gertrude St Omaha NE 68136	NEB	EM			SL	1983
Gersch Fred C	(972)775-4374 fredcgersch@gmail.com	313 George Hopper Rd Midlothian TX 76065	TX	EM			SPR	1967
Gerzevske Matthew N	(314)781-8673 mgerzevske@gmail.com	4144 De Tonty St Apt 1a Saint Louis MO 63110	MO	Asst	Timothy Saint Louis MO	(314)781-8673	SL	2024
Geske Steven R	(585) 465-0620 pastorsteve@goodshepherdc-dga.org	320 S Pearl St Canandaigua NY 14424	EA	SP	Good Shepherd Canandaigua NY	(585)394-2760	SL	1996
Gettinger Stephen D	(502)345-4203 gettingersd@yahoo.com	10955 Covington Gettysburg Rd Bradford OH 45308	OH	SP	Mount Calvary Dayton OH	(937)836-2238	FW	2008
Gewecke Stephen A	geweckes@njdistrict.org		NJ	DP	New Jersey District Mountainside NJ	(908)233-8111	SL	1985
Geyer Larry I	(319)825-6600 geyer@gcmuni.net	1523 Cantebury Cir Grundy Center IA 50638	IE	EM			FW	1981
Ghebru Yohannes	(651)373-6796 yohanneso@yahoo.com	10470 Rane St NW Coon Rapids MN 55433	MNS	Assoc	St Stephanus Saint Paul MN	(651)228-1486	SL	2024
Gibbons Nikolai J	(970)372-8919 ngibbons@immlutheran.org	Immanuel Lutheran Church 47120 Romeo Plank Rd Macomb MI 48044	MI	Assoc	Immanuel Macomb MI	(586)286-4231	SL	2016
Gibbons Thomas A	(847)707-8077	529 S Park St Roselle IL 60172	NI	EM			SL-SMP	2010

*Multiple Assignments (See Church Worker Locator for Additional Details)
See Page 53 for the Table of Abbreviations for key to District, Position, and Seminary abbreviations
**C =Candidate; EM = Emeritus; the date following the C is the month and year the Candidate status began

NAME	TELEPHONE NUMBER EMAIL	STREET ADDRESS CITY/STATE/ZIP	DISTRICT	POSITION/ STATUS**	WHERE SERVING	OFFICE PHONE	SEM/ PROGRAM	YR GRAD
Gibbs Jeffrey A Dr	(557) 202-2271 gibbsj@csl.edu	6421 Lloyd Ave Saint Louis MO 63139	MO	EM			FW	1979
Gibbs Karl H	(314) 910-3905 pastorkarlgibbs@gmail.com	4531 Tweet Ct Scott Air Force Base IL 62225	MO	M Chap	Office of International Mission Saint Louis MO		SL	2011
Gibney Michael F	(225)347-8721 drmgibney@outlook.com	10486 Wade Dr Denham Springs LA 70726	SO	SP	Absolution Denham Springs LA	(225)347-8721	Other	1997
Gibson Michael E Dr	(949)854-3232 mike.gibson@psd-lcms.org	16355 Laguna Canyon Rd Suite 300 Irvine CA 92618	PSW	DP	Pacific Southwest District Irvine CA	(949)854-3232	SL	1984
Giddings Michael G	mggiddings@yahoo.com	7415 Hidden Valley Dr Lincoln NE 68526	NEB	D Ex/S	Nebraska District Seward NE	(402)643-2961	SL	2007
Giebel Franklin H	(920)295-5331 revfhg@juno.com	6723 S Anthony Blvd Apt S109 Fort Wayne IN 46816	NW	EM			SPR	1976
Gier James D Jr	(260) 492-0039	c/o Ascension Lutheran Church 8811 St Joe Rd Fort Wayne IN 46835	IN	Sn/Adm	Ascension Fort Wayne IN	(260)486-2226	FW	2002
Gierke Eugene V	(402)641-1485 genegret2@gmail.com	1126 Eastridge Dr Seward NE 68434	NEB	EM			SPR	1971
Gierke John P	(402)372-6807 jpgierke@stpaulwp.org	431 N Colfax St West Point NE 68788	NEB	SP	St Paul West Point NE	(402)372-2111	SL	1996
Gierke Timothy J	timgierke@gmail.com	2012 Phelps Ave Fremont NE 68025	NEB	EM			SL	1976
Gies Clark H	(605)654-9500 giescj@gwtc.net	P.O. Box 235 Fairfax SD 57335	SD	EM			SPR	1966
Gieschen Charles A Dr	(260)416-2235	8610 Oakcliff Ct Fort Wayne IN 46825	IN	S HS/C	Concordia Theological Seminary Fort Wayne IN	(260)452-2100	FW	1984
Giese Joel M	(434)315-3801 joel.giese@gmail.com	2851 Kanaku St Wahiawa HI 96786	SE	Inst C	Office of International Mission Saint Louis MO		SL	2007
Giese Gordon W	(715)347-1779 giesegm@yahoo.com	510 Lawrence Ave Rothschild WI 54474	NW	EM			SL	1961
Giese Edward P	830-456-1760 pastored@coslc.org	7201 Lower Crabapple Rd Fredericksbrg TX 78624	TX	SP	Christ Our Savior San Antonio TX	(210)732-7223	FW	1998
Giese Curtis P Dr	(512)296-7498 curtis.giese@concordia.edu	5406 Bull Run Cir Austin TX 78727	TX	C04/2023			SL	1989
Giesler Wayne H	(330)465-5954 wgiesler@gmail.com	2920 Snouffer Rd Apt 123 Columbus OH 43235	OH	EM			SPR	1962
Gifford Daniel G	(402)360-4081 dkgiff@gmail.com	1601 Broadway Wheaton MN 56296	MNN	SP	St John* Wheaton MN	(320)563-4143	SL	1996
Giger Scott W	sgiger@cornerstonelutheran.church	7912 Turkel Dr Fishers IN 46038	IN	Sn/Adm	Cornerstone Carmel IN	(317)814-4252	SL	2002
Gilbert Dan P	(708)305-0876 gilbertnid@gmail.com	3643 Castleman St. Louis MO 63110	MO	EM			SL	1977
Gilbert Jacob A	(262)822-4802 pastorjackgilbert@gmail.com	501 Augusta St Racine WI 53402	SW	Sn/Adm	St John Racine WI	(262)637-7011	SL	2009
Gilkey Walter K	(785)571-4019 gilkey.walter@gmail.com	1926 N. 10th Ave Apt 13 Wausau WI 54401	NW	SP	St Paul* Bowler WI	(715)793-4608	FW	2014
Gilkey Kraig B	(509)439-9081 kraiggilkey@gmail.com	631 Elwood St Sterling CO 80751	RM	EM			SL	2004
Gillard Jacob S			MNN	SP	Faith Community Zimmerman MN	(763)856-3600	SL	2001
Gillaspie Wesley S	(989)262-8011 wessgill@airadv.net	743 Country Ln Frankenmuth MI 48734	MI	Assoc	St Michael Richville MI	(989)868-4791	FW	1986
Gillespie Arthur L	(646)358-5659 algklg@msn.com	906 Rainbow Ln Hendersonvile NC 28791	SE	EM			SL	1970
Gillespie Christopher R	(920)994-2228 pastor@sjrl.org	W5407 County Road Ss Random Lake WI 53075	SW	SP	St John Random Lake WI	(920)994-2228	FW	2010
Gillet Stephen P	(715)499-2693 revgillet@gmail.com	N8766 Lake View Dr Tomahawk WI 54487	NW	SP	St Paul Tomahawk WI	(715)453-5391	FW	1995
Gilliland Martin S	(360)991-5763 martingilliland@msn.com	25 Navajo Drive Picayune MS 39466	SO	Inst C	Southern District Slidell LA	(504)282-2632	SL	1998
Gillmore Steven R	(417)825-5906		MO	SMP	First Neosho MO	(417)451-2464	SL-SMP	2015
Gilson Mark E	(231)329-4994 pastormgilson@yahoo.com	21308 Deans Vw Big Rapids MI 49307	MI	SP	Chapel Lakes Mecosta MI	(231)972-7891	FW	1997
Gimbel James R	(952)594-4535 stjohnskimball@gmail.com	1536 Poppy Rd St Cloud MN 56303	MNN	SP	St John Kimball MN	(320)398-7151	SL	1985
Gimbel Andrew J	(636) 485-1592 agimbel@hcross.com	8945 Veterans Memorial Pkwy O Fallon MO 63366	MO	Sn/Adm	Holy Cross O'fallon MO	(636)272-4505	SL	2009
Giordano Anthony J	516-444-2656 ajg0132@gmail.com	32 S Prospect St Verona NJ 07044	NJ	SP	Calvary Verona NJ	(973)239-0577	CQ	2019
Gipson Russ W	(256)682-4550 russwgipson@gmail.com	219 Spring Valley Ct SW Huntsville AL 35802	SO	Sn/Adm	Grace Huntsville AL	(256)881-0552	SL	2008
Girard Steven D	(330)288-7735 pastorgirard@gmail.com	3456 Abington Ct Brunswick OH 44212	OH	SP	St Mark Brunswick OH	(330)225-3110	FW	2006
Girardin Mark E	(618)203-3457 mgirardin73@gmail.com	700 E Ryder St Litchfield IL 62056	SI	EM			FW	1977
Girardin Philip D	(618)204-6550 pastorphil2017@gmail.com	307 S Elm St Staunton IL 62088	SI		Southern Illinois District Belleville IL	(618)234-4767	SL	2017
Gittner William Jr	(828)897-1672 wgittner@bellsouth.net	500 Laurel Ln Newland NC 28657	SE	EM			SPR	1966
Gizynski Richard G	(248)667-6764 richardgizynski@att.net	13740 Lincoln St Oak Park MI 48237	MI	C05/2024			FW	2003
Gladden Dietrick A	(248)719-2766 prayerisworship371@gmail.com	15361 Stephens Dr Eastpointe MI 48021	MI	Sn/Adm	St Thomas Eastpointe MI	(586)772-3370	SL	2013

*Multiple Assignments (See Church Worker Locator for Additional Details)
See Page 53 for the Table of Abbreviations for key to District, Position, and Seminary abbreviations
**C =Candidate; EM = Emeritus; the date following the C is the month and year the Candidate status began

NAME	TELEPHONE NUMBER EMAIL	STREET ADDRESS CITY/STATE/ZIP	DISTRICT	POSITION/ STATUS**	WHERE SERVING	OFFICE PHONE	SEM/ PROGRAM	YR GRAD
Glade Wilfred W	wwglade@protonmail.com	11936 Hartdale Ave La Mirada CA 90638	PSW	EM			SL	1971
Glander Randall L	(260)918-5777 glander392@gmail.com	3505 Pinto Ct Arlington TX 76017	TX	EM			FW	1990
Glander Dennis E	(407)409-1179 rev.glander@gmail.com	8021 Blue Marlin Way Orlando FL 32822	FG	EM			SPR	1965
Glander Karl P	(239)293-1489 pastorkarlglander@gmail.com	34 Newbury Pl Naples FL 34104	FG	SMP	Bethlehem Fort Myers FL	(239)694-3878	SL-SMP	2016
Glaspie James J	+46 73 222 0397 brooklynglass223@gmail.com	Aprikosgatan 23 Lgh 161 Hasselby Stockholm 16566 SWEDEN	CNH	EM			SL	1986
Gleason William L	(618)381-6195 bill@wlgleason.com	P.O. Box 491 Hamel IL 62046	SI	EM			SL	1985
Gledhill Eric A	(573)298-1501 gled_eric@yahoo.com	P.O. Box 312 Ridgecrest CA 93555	MO	M Chap	Office of International Mission Saint Louis MO		SL	2008
Gleitz Monty D		620 Winning Colors Blvd Elizabethtown KY 42701	IN	SP	Gloria Dei* Elizabethtown KY	(270)769-5910	CQ	2012
Glenn Micah A			CNH	Prin	Sierra Carson City NV	(775)267-1921	SL	2016
Glenn Ellory W	(314)369-8014 ellory.glenn@chapelofthecross.org	226 Hereford Ave Ferguson MO 63135	EN	SMP	Chapel Cross Saint Louis County MO	(314)741-3737	SL-SMP	2021
Gless Adam C	(616)516-6377 adam.gless@gmail.com	1440 Overo Cir Springdale AR 72762	MDS	Sn/Adm	Salem Springdale AR	(479)751-9500	SL	2007
Glock Peter M	(815) 252-5335 pmglock@frontier.com	206 W. Jacob Rd. Jacob IL 62950	CI	EM			SL	1991
Glock Richard C	629-246-7429 rrglock2831@icloud.com	1415 N San Benito Dr Unit 1028 Gilbert AZ 85234	PSW	EM			SL	1954
Gloe Ronald F	(316)469-9435 rfgloe@aol.com	2323 N Woodlawn Blvd Apt 518 Wichita KS 67220	KS	EM			FW	1980
Glombicki Joseph S		503 Regan Dr East Dundee IL 60118	NI	SMP	Bethlehem West Dundee IL	(847)426-7311	SL-SMP	2020
Glover Graham B	(352)494-4532 revgbg@gmail.com	515 S.w. 41st Street Gainesville FL 32607	FG	Sn/Adm	Abiding Savior Gainesville FL	(352)331-4409	SL	2003
Glover John E Jr	iamjohnglover@gmail.com		FG	Pro Stf	Lutheran Church Extension Fund Saint Louis MO	(314)965-9000	SL	1991
Glowinski James D	(317)460-1617 james.glowinski@gmail.com	c/o Trinity Lutheran Church 1401 West Boonville New Harmony Rd Evansville IN 47725	IN	SP	Trinity Darmstadt IN	(812)867-5279	SL	2008
Gnewuch Carl M	gnewuchc@gmail.com	5481 Waters Bend Dr Belvidere IL 61008	NI	Asst	Immanuel Belvidere IL	(815)544-8058	SL	1991
Goble Mark D	(901)751-1630 markgoble@comcast.net	1068 Fox Trace CV Cordova TN 38018	MDS	Sn/Adm	Christ the King Memphis TN	(901)682-8404	SL	1997
Goddard Paul E	(573)263-8689 smokeyskypilot@gmail.com	501 E Eldon St Saint James MO 65559	MO	EM			FW	1986
Goeglein Evan C	(970) 597-0373 egoeglein@hotmail.com	163 Brock Ln Grants Pass OR 97527	NOW	C07/2022			FW	2011
Goehmann David P	(402)860-8735 david.goehmann@gmail.com	c/o St John Lutheran Church P.O. Box 209 Ludington MI 49431	MI	Sn/Adm	St John Ludington MI	(231)843-9188	SL	2004
Goehring Irwin D		Md Senior Center 10571 N 96th Pl Scottsdale AZ 85258	PSW	EM			SL	1960
Goehring Matthew D	(585)713-4400 mgoehring283@gmail.com	14715 Washington Rd Norton KS 67654	KS	SP	Immanuel Norton KS	(785)877-2430	FW	2022
Goeke Jonathan A	(281)251-3820 jonathan.goeke@thirstyforjesus.org	11718 Lochberry Ct Tomball TX 77377	TX	SP	Community of Hope Spring TX	(281)716-2929	SL	1996
Goeke Paul A	(512)395-7061 paulgoeke@hotmail.com	2415 Nina Clare Rd Billings MT 59102	TX	C08/2024			SL	2005
Goers Michael M	(231)392-9324 mgoers@yahoo.com	4428 Silver Valley Ln. Traverse City MI 49684	MI	Sn/Adm	Trinity Traverse City MI	(231)946-2720	SL	2006
Goerss John M Dr	(609)632-1939 jmgoerss@princeton.edu	16 Meadow Lakes 30I East Windsor NJ 08520	EN	EM			SL	1970
Goetz Gerold W	redeemd@rea-alp.com	5327 University Dr S Unit B Fargo ND 58104	ND	EM			SPR	1966
Goetz Lawrence F	(812)243-2317 goetzfoods@aol.com	16007 David Rd Apt 323 Fort Myers FL 33908	FG	EM			SL	1994
Goetz Roger M	(785)273-0613 rogomel2@sbcglobal.net	1918 SW Arrowhead Rd Topeka KS 66604	KS	EM			SPR	1967
Goff Dennison J Dr	(763)614-9585 dgoff2911@gmail.com	5525 Pine Oak Ct Fort Wayne IN 46835	IN	Sn/Adm	St Michael Fort Wayne IN	(260)432-2033	SL	1986
Gogl George L	(503)257-4168 logogl@aol.com	1955 Salem Dallas Hwy NW Apt 321 Salem OR 97304	NOW	EM			SL	1960
Going Thomas A	tagoing8457@gmail.com	5047 Countess Dr Columbus IN 47203	IN	EM			SPR	1958
Goldammer Gordon L	(605)920-8512 goldmer@goldenwest.net	P.O. Box 24 Custer SD 57730	SD	EM			FW	1978
Goldberger Arthur J	(563)505-0994 jack.goldberger@gmail.com	12130 Sapphire River San Antonio TX 78245	TX	EM			CQ	1984
Golden Ryan N	rgolden13@hotmail.com	4240 E Morenci Rd Queen Creek AZ 85143	PSW	SMP	Saving Grace Queen Creek AZ	(480)888-9673	SL-SMP	2023
Golden Daniel S	(607)398-8354 pastordangolden@gmail.com	c/o 3500 Broad St Parkersburg WV 26104	OH	SP	St Paul Parkersburg WV	(304)428-5826	FW	2021
Golden Kevin S Dr	(314)229-9402 pastorkevingolden@gmail.com	530 Bonhomme Forest Dr Olivette MO 63132	MO	S HS/C	Concordia Seminary Saint Louis MO	(314)505-7000	SL	1999
Goldhammer Maurice W	(303)986-6904 msgoldy@comcast.net	21817 E Otero Pl Aurora CO 80016	RM	EM			SL	1965

*Multiple Assignments (See Church Worker Locator for Additional Details)

See Page 53 for the Table of Abbreviations for key to District, Position, and Seminary abbreviations

**C =Candidate; EM = Emeritus; the date following the C is the month and year the Candidate status began

NAME	TELEPHONE NUMBER EMAIL	STREET ADDRESS CITY/STATE/ZIP	DISTRICT	POSITION/ STATUS**	WHERE SERVING	OFFICE PHONE	SEM/ PROGRAM	YR GRAD
Golter Randall L	(303)618-4564 Randall.Golter@trinitydavenport.org	1005 W 57th Pl Davenport IA 52806	IE	Sn/Adm	Trinity Davenport IA	(563)323-8001	SL	1984
Goltl Matthew B	(316)204-8393 matthewgoltl@gmail.com	5332 E Ashton St Bel Aire KS 67220	KS	Assoc	Risen Savior Wichita KS	(316)683-5538	SL	2024
Goltl Scott L	(316) 207-3431 maplecampus@gmail.com	8211 W. Havenhurst Cir Wichita KS 67205	KS	Assoc	Ascension Wichita KS	(316)722-4694	SL	1993
Gomez Fernando		2310 N Ridgeway Ave Chicago IL 60647	NI	SP	Jehovah-El Buen Past Chicago IL	(773)342-5854	CQ	2015
Gomez Samuel Dr	(760)580-4323 samygo4@proton.me	701 N Sanderson Ave Hemet CA 92545	PSW	C03/2022			SL	2002
Gomez Marcello	(626)298-0193 prcellogmez@gmail.com	2730 Mataro St Pasadena CA 91107	PSW	SP	La Santa Cruz Los Angeles CA	(626)298-0193	HITSL	2002
Gomez Andrew D Jr	(510)516-9566 gomez.andylorena@sbcglobal.net	6535 Cedar Blvd Newark CA 94560	CNH	SMP	Memorial-Deaf Fremont CA	(510)499-8473	SL-SMP	2016
Gomez James F	(920)743-7750 pastor@princeofpeacesb.com	1756 Michigan St Sturgeon Bay WI 54235	NW	SP	Prince of Peace Sturgeon Bay WI	(920)743-7750	SL	2002
Gomez Jorge	(952)334-2768 socceru2121@gmail.com	1190 Menke Cir Shakopee MN 55379	MNS	SP	New Creation Shakopee MN		SL	2023
Gonzales Ben	(832)331-0951 bgonzales@txlcms.org		TX	D Ex/S	Texas District Round Rock TX	(800)951-3478	SL	2003
Gonzales Jesus M	(504)467-9296 gonzales.becky@icloud.com	735 Blair Ave Kenner LA 70062	SO	SP	Monte De Olive Metairie LA	(504)451-9172	CQ	1984
Gonzales Lonnie A	(281)851-2663 lgonzales@trinitydt.org	1634 Beachcomber Ln Houston TX 77062	TX	Assoc	Trinity Houston TX	(713)224-0684	SL	2000
Gonzalez Felipe D	(949)391-8942 fdgonzalez2005@yahoo.com	400 Limestone Apt 522 Irvine CA 92603	PSW	C04/2022			CQ	2016
Gonzalez Rigoberto E	rigogonzalez51@gmail.com	710 Hemlock Ave Imperial Beach CA 91932	PSW	EM			SL	2012
Gonzalez Nicholas O	(732)804-0874 pastorngonzalez@gmail.com	8004 Quail Rise Ln Laurel MD 20723	SE	Assoc	St Andrew Silver Spring MD	(301)384-4394	SL	2019
Gonzalez Jaime	(469)653-7086 jaimegdesantiago@gmail.com	108 Unbridled Trl Caddo Mills TX 75135	TX	SP	Comunidad Cristiana Rockwall TX	(214)395-6222	SL	2024
Gonzalez Eloy S	(210)379-6375 eloy@gonzes.net	2215 Sugar Ln Mission TX 78572	CNH	Sn/Adm	Trinity San Jose CA	(408)377-4411	HITSL	2001
Gonzalez Matthew R	(718)828-3532 pastor@trinitylutheranbronx.org	2125 Watson Ave Bronx NY 10472	AT	Sn/Adm	Trinity* Bronx NY	(718)828-3532	SL	2011
Gonzalez-Feliciano Miguel A	(224)508-8668 rev.miguelgf@gmail.com	211 Lobeck Ave Readlyn IA 50668	IE	SP	St Paul* Readlyn IA	(319)279-3961	SL	2021
Good Douglas A	(763)218-5073 streetjeep327@gmail.com	4622 W Lawrence Way New Palestine IN 46163	IN	EM			FW	1984
Goodfellow Kendall E	(509)638-3148 kengoodfellow@hotmail.com	8703 N James Dr Spokane WA 99208	NOW	EM			SPR	1969
Goodin William D Dr	(509)633-2767 lindaeegoodin@yahoo.com	702 Central Dr Coulee Dam WA 99116	NOW	EM			SPR	1970
Goodman Harrison A			IE	RSO	Higher Things Inc Lisbon IA	(888)482-6630	FW	2010
Goodroad Thomas E	thomasgoodroad@gmail.com	6007 S 25t St Lincoln NE 68512	NEB	Assoc	Good Shepherd Lincoln NE	(402)423-7639	FW	2023
Goodroad Joseph R	(816)645-0188 joseph.richard.goodroad@gmail.com	1407 N Kentucky St Iola KS 66749	KS	SP	Grace Iola KS	(620)365-6468	FW	2024
Goodwill Richard R	r.goodwill42@gmail.com	1521 Carlene Pruett St Leander TX 78641	TX	EM			FW	1987
Goodwin Alexander A	(507)432-9193 pastor.alexandergoodwin@gmail.com	726 Willow St Fairmont MN 56031	MNS	Assoc	Immanuel Fairmont MN	(507)238-1387	SL	2022
Goodwin Eric A	(716)592-4893 pastorgoodwin@salemspringville.org	91 W Main St Springville NY 14141	EA	SP	Salem Springville NY	(716)592-4893	SL	2001
Goodwin Robert L	(262)309-5821 pastorrob@spldecatur.org	1 Bachrach Ct Decatur IL 62526	CI	Sn/Adm	St Paul's Decatur IL	(217)423-6955	SL	2007
Gordish Timothy R	(316)858-0960 gordisht@me.com	1115 W River Blvd Wichita KS 67203	KS	EM			FW	1998
Gore John D	(574)583-3372 johndgore100@yahoo.com	1824 Pierce St Lafayette IN 47904	IN	EM			CQ	2003
Gorline Jeremy D	(636) 730-0842 jgorline@coglcs.com	650 Salt Lake Rd Saint Peters MO 63376	MO	Sn/Adm	Child of God Saint Peters MO	(636)970-7080	SL	2001
Gorlitz Larry R	(269) 861-0260 larrygorlitz@gmail.com	11 Garrison Ave Battle Creek MI 49017	MI	SP	St Paul Battle Creek MI	(269)968-3055	FW	2001
Gorobo Hailu H	(651)528-1262 hailuhatte@gmail.com	2476 Timber Ct E St. Paul MN 55119	MNS	SP	Mekane Yesus Saint Paul MN	(651)644-1421	CQ	2019
Gorshe Christopher L	(479) 295-1416 pastorgorshe@bvlutheran.com	c/o Bella Vista Lutheran Church 1990 Forest Hills Blvd Bella Vista AR 72715	MDS	Assoc	Bella Vista Bella Vista AR	(479)855-0272	SL	2007
Gossman Paul K Dr	(425)495-1164 paul@gossman.org	30610 114th Pl SE Auburn WA 98092	NOW	SP	Light Of Christ Federal Way WA	(253)874-2517	SL	1985
Gotfredson Larry L	(928) 308-5608 larrygotfredson@gmail.com	3131 Crooked Wash Drive Loveland CO 80538	CNH	EM			SL	1986
Gottel Yeddo A	011-55-44-3017-5948 yeddogottel@hotmail.com	Tr Jose De Lima Jr N 74 Campo Mourao Parana 87 30 BRAZIL	MNS	EM			CQ	1995
Goucher Mark A	(816)390-4207 gouchermarka@gmail.com	4764 S. Highway 33 Maysville MO 64469	MO	SP	Prince Peace Cameron MO	(816)632-7904	SL	2009
Gourlay Donald B Dr	dgourlay@aol.com	1111 Ontario St Apt 1216 Oak Park IL 60302	NI	EM			SL	1964
Gowen Mitchell W	(808)488-3654 misc@oursaviorhawaii.com	98-325 Koauka St Aiea HI 96701	CNH	Sn/Adm	Our Savior Aiea HI	(808)488-3654	FW	1988

*Multiple Assignments (See Church Worker Locator for Additional Details)

See Page 53 for the Table of Abbreviations for key to District, Position, and Seminary abbreviations

**C =Candidate; EM = Emeritus; the date following the C is the month and year the Candidate status began

NAME	TELEPHONE NUMBER EMAIL	STREET ADDRESS CITY/STATE/ZIP	DISTRICT	POSITION/ STATUS**	WHERE SERVING	OFFICE PHONE	SEM/ PROGRAM	YR GRAD
Grabau Russell J	(507)514-1336 russellgrabau@gmail.com	259 Winona St NE Chatfield MN 55923	MNS	EM			SL	1992
Grabau Ezra G	(507)995-9862 pr.ezra.grabau@gmail.com	951 Westerner Dr Akron IA 51001	IW	SP	Faith Sioux City IA	(712)258-4820	SL	2022
Grabenhofer Gerhard P	(262)456-2272 gpgrabenhofer@gmail.com	2880 E Fieldstone Way Sturtevant WI 53177	SW	SP	Faith Sturtevant WI	(262)886-2522	FW	1993
Grabowski Daniel M	(909)986-2615 pastordan@redeemer4me.com	920 W 6th St Ontario CA 91762	PSW	SP	Redeemer Ontario CA	(909)986-2615	Other	2011
Gradberg Eric T	ericg@oursav.org	1110 Angus Dr Norfolk NE 68701	NEB	Assoc	Our Savior Norfolk NE	(402)371-9005	SL	2021
Grady James M	(317) 372-6289 jgrady@msn.com		EN	EM			FW	2017
Graef David A	(219) 386-1047 BSGoreo@proton.me	2400 Silhavy Rd Valparaiso IN 46383	IN	EM			CQ	1975
Graef Russell P	(224)436-2703 rpgraef@yahoo.com	P.O. Box 9188 Chesapeake VA 23321	SE	EM			CQ	2020
Grafe Stephen D	(248)505-0662 pastorsteve@stjohnrochester.org	c/o St John Lutheran Church 1011 W University Dr Rochester MI 48307	MI	Assoc	St John Rochester MI	(248)402-8000	FW	2003
Graff Paul L	(651)492-5160 revplg@gmail.com	1618 Stilt Street Berthoud CO 80513	RM	EM			SL	1966
Graff Warren W	(505)280-1543 wwgraff@gmail.com	6229 Rosemary Rd Las Cruces NM 88012	RM	EM			SL	1991
Graham Bo G	(847)255-0332 pastorbo@saint-paul.org	100 S School St. Mount Prospect IL 60056	NI	Sn/Adm	St Paul Mount Prospect IL	(847)255-0332	SL	2010
Graham John H	(719)500-9241 jhgraham11@hotmail.com	101 Crestview Ln Bailey CO 80421	RM	SP	Shep Rockies Bailey CO	(303)838-2161	CQ	2024
Graham Johnny M	(870) 674-7216 pastorjmg@hotmail.com	P.O. Box 434 Heber Springs AR 72543	MDS	EM			CQ	2003
Graham Mel	(905)259-5420 mel.h.graham@gmail.com	27 Limosano St Seagrave ON L0C-1 CANADA	EN	EM			NESC	1992
Gramenz Stefan M	(845)855-3169	14 Pine Dr Pawling NY 12564	AT	SP	Christ The King Pawling NY	(845)855-3169	FW	2018
Gramit Paul E	(978)365-9571 pastorgramit@yahoo.com	125 Chace St Clinton MA 01510	NE	SP	Trinity Clinton MA	(978)365-6888	FW	1998
Grams Daniel E	(248)928-4659 daniel@kslcms.org	15737 South Central Street Olathe KS 66062	KS	D Ex/S	Kansas District Topeka KS	(785)357-4441	FW	2002
Grams Jeffery W	(308)641-2747 revgrams@gmail.com	2218 Broadway Scottsbluff NE 69361	WY	SP	St John Scottsbluff NE	(308)635-1722	SL	1995
Grams Craig N	(605)397-2449 grams@nvc.net	2007 S Cleveland Ave Sioux Falls SD 57103	SD	EM			FW	1978
Grana Peter D	(706)391-3388 friargrana@hotmail.com	111 Locust St Manteo NC 27954	SE	SP	Grace By Sea Nags Head NC	(252)441-1530	FW	2008
Granado Lizardo Jesus R	(901)520-5842 granadoricardo@mail.com	26969 Ann Arbor Trail # 104 Dearborn Heights MI 48127	MI	D Ex/S	Michigan District Ann Arbor MI	(888)225-2111	Other	2003
Grannis Michael J	(952)686-3046 revgrannis@gmail.com	904 10th Ave NW Waseca MN 56093	MNS	SP	St Paul Waseca MN	(507)835-2647	SL	2010
Grant Christopher R	(914)443-3020 cgrant2323@gmail.com	30 Abraham Dr Montgomery NY 12549	AT	C06/2022			SL-SMP	2017
Grant Corey M	(805)433-2440 corey.grant83@gmail.com	7723 188th Ave E Bonney Lake WA 98391	NOW	C02/2020			Other	2018
Grant Edward J	(843)730-4420 edgrant53@gmail.com	108 Chesterton Dr Goose Creek SC 29445	SE	EM			CQ	1987
Grant Karl M	(651)503-4955 kmartingrant@gmail.com	63924 240th St Gibbon MN 55335	MNS	SP	St Peter's Gibbon MN	(507)834-6676	CQ	2021
Grassinger Timothy L	(719)761-7198 tim.grassinger75@gmail.com	4135 Cordera Crest Ave Apt 210 Colorado Spgs CO 80924	RM	EM			SPR	1965
Grassley David A	(817)249-1539 grassley@charter.net	321 Sexton Ln Benbrook TX 76126	TX	EM			FW	1985
Gratz William H	(208)305-7907 Billwhg@hotmail.com	806 3rd St Clarkston WA 99403	NOW	EM			FW	1984
Graudin Kevin A	(828) 578-4682 kevingraudin@gmail.com	2515 27th Avenue Cir NE Hickory NC 28601	SE	EM			SL	1983
Graul Robert W	(218)999-4781 r.graul@sbcglobal.net	36752 Pincherry Rd Cohasset MN 55721	NI	EM			CQ	1980
Graumann Wayne E	(281)727-6989 wgraumann@icloud.com	123 Mountain Laurel Dr Montgomery TX 77316	TX	EM			SPR	1974
Gravelyn Timothy W	(574) 286-5682 transpotimothy@yahoo.com	5823 S Bridgeton Ln South Bend IN 46614	IN	C07/2016			FW	1991
Graves David W	(573)999-2648 rev.davegraves@gmail.com	P.O. Box 67 Wartburg TN 37887	MDS	SP	St Paul Wartburg TN	(423)346-3554	SL	2013
Graves K F Dr	(616)929-2267 revbev65@hotmail.com	2290 Christine Ct SE Grand Rapids MI 49546	MI	SP	Redeemer Fremont MI	(231)924-2707	SL	1972
Graves Richard P	(345)307-8460 richardgraves52@outlook.com	348 Medina Ct Loveland CO 80537	RM	EM			SL	1989
Gray Daniel L	(856) 665-0116 parson.dgray@gmail.com	8266 Corbett Road Pennsauken NJ 08109	EN	SP	Martin Luther Pennsauken NJ	(856)665-0116	FW	2022
Gray Roosevelt Jr	(734)417-2540 revgrayjr@gmail.com	25205 Waycross Southfield MI 48033	MI	EM			FW	1988
Gray Robert W	(618)203-9200 mgray4327@gmail.com	835 Thunderstorm Rd Carbondale IL 62901	SI	EM			SL	1973
Gray Andrew W	(319)855-9688		SI	Assoc	Good Shepherd Collinsville IL	(618)344-3151	FW	2012
Gray Adam H	(904) 496-1264 ahgray63@gmail.com	4365 Worth Drive E Jacksonville FL 32207	FG	SMP	Holy Trinity Kingsland GA	(912)729-6085	SL-SMP	2022

*Multiple Assignments (See Church Worker Locator for Additional Details)
See Page 53 for the Table of Abbreviations for key to District, Position, and Seminary abbreviations
**C =Candidate; EM = Emeritus; the date following the C is the month and year the Candidate status began

NAME	TELEPHONE NUMBER EMAIL	STREET ADDRESS CITY/STATE/ZIP	DISTRICT	POSITION/ STATUS**	WHERE SERVING	OFFICE PHONE	SEM/ PROGRAM	YR GRAD
Gray Amos O IV	(501)701-9920 amosspeaks@yahoo.com	200 Oakwood Ave Hot Springs AR 71913	MDS	RSO	High Impact Movement Inc Hot Springs AR	(501)693-8232	SL-SMP	2013
Grayl Samuel J	(406)586-3480 revgrayl@yahoo.com	47 Boxwood Dr Bozeman MT 59718	MT	Sn/Adm	First Bozeman MT	(406)586-5374	SL	2004
Grebing Barrett H	(713)859-9267 barrett.grebing@sharingnewlife.com	1800 West Freeway Fort Worth TX 76102	TX	Assoc	St Paul Fort Worth TX	(817)332-2281	SL	2015
Grebing Terry L	(618)458-7142 terry.grebing@gmail.com	2033 Kaskaskia Rd Renault IL 62279	SI	SP	Holy Cross Renault IL	(618)458-6680	SL	1982
Gredvig Rodger J	(858)571-7118 stnsinr@yahoo.com	1924 Hanford Dr. San Diego CA 92111	PSW	EM			SPR	1972
Green Andrew W	(254)702-2362 pastor.green@gracelcs.com	612 Pomegranate Cir Harker Hts TX 76548	TX	SP	Grace Killeen TX	(254)392-0717	SL	2000
Green Ernest R III	(716)693-7044 ltshortee@aol.com	1603 Master St N Tonawanda NY 14120	EA	Sn/Adm	St Paul North Tonawanda NY	(716)692-3255	NESC	2011
Green Francis T	(507) 696-1802 franrunner@gmail.com	975 Istas Ln SW Oronoco MN 55960	MNS	SP	Mount Hope Bloomington MN	(952)888-5059	CQ	2012
Green Kenneth D II	(703)338-4387 ken.green@poporlando.com	2499 Ridgemoor Dr Orlando FL 32828	FG	Sn/Adm	Prince Of Peace Orlando FL	(407)277-3945	SL	1994
Green Robert L	(440)292-5915 revrlgreen@aol.com	4925 Ocala Dr Parma OH 44134	OH	SP	Bethlehem Parma OH	(440)845-2230	FW	1996
Green Timothy S	(215)868-8956 green153@verizon.net	8656 Forrest Ave Philadelphia PA 19150	EA	SP	Holy Cross Philadelphia PA	(215)242-0530	FW	1984
Greene John H	(314)341-0972 jhgreene2011@yahoo.com	2006 S 11th St Saint Louis MO 63104	MO	Tchr	Grace Chapel Bellefontaine Nghbrs MO	(314)868-3232	SL	1994
Greene Frank N III	(816)436-7680	1701 NE 96th St. Kansas City MO 64155	MO	Sn/Adm	King Of Kings Kansas City MO	(816)436-7680	SL	2007
Greene Everette E	(513)403-3627 egreene1@fuse.net	6364 Cheviot Rd Apt 11 Cincinnati OH 45247	OH	SP	Trinity* Cincinnati OH	(513)385-7024	FW	2003
Greene Steven R	(505)788-2215	17 Quinones Rd La Luz NM 88337	RM	EM			FW	1980
Greenfield Henry G II	(301)452-6152 henrygreenfield33@gmail.com	2105 Ramblewood Dr District Hts MD 20747	SE	Assoc	Zion Praise Bowie MD	(301)442-6726	SL	2021
Greenhagen Chase M	(763)219-6301 chasegreenhagen@yahoo.com	18426 Wild Onion San Antonio TX 78258	TX	Assoc	Crown Of Life San Antonio TX	(210)490-6886	FW	2025
Greenhagen Jesse R	(763)219-6142 jessegreenhagen@yahoo.com	1509 E Bellows St Apt C Mount Pleasant MI 48858	MI	Assoc	Zion Mount Pleasant MI	(989)772-1516	FW	2024
Greenmyer Joseph R	(701)680-3749 revjosephgreenmyer@gmail.com	204 West Cherry Parkston SD 57366	SD	SP	St Peter* Emery SD	(605)825-4222	FW	2024
Greenseth Ray A	(605)516-0077 hirev13@live.com	304 Cedar Ave Murdo SD 57559	SD	SP	Zion* Presho SD	(605)895-2334	SL	1982
Greenwald Kenneth A	(765) 513-8493 kgpastor@yahoo.com	514 W 11th St Peru IN 46970	IN	EM			SL	1984
Greenwalt James H II	(248)396-3700 jgreenwalt@redeemerbirmingham.org	1565 Squirrel Rd Bloomfield Hills MI 48304	MI	SMP	Redeemer Birmingham MI	(248)644-4010	SL-SMP	2022
Greenway Berton L	(412) 445-0675 revgreenway@verizon.net	2931 Universal Rd Pittsburgh PA 15235	EA	SP	Grace Penn Hills PA	(412)793-1394	FW	1988
Greer Johnny L	(314)869-0477 jlgreer1120@gmail.com	2272 Luxmore Dr Saint Louis MO 63136	MO	SMP	St Peter Spanish Lake MO	(314)741-2485	SL-SMP	2012
Greer Andrew T	andy.greer@messiah.us	8925 Foxtail Dr Lincoln NE 68526	NEB	SMP	Messiah Lincoln NE	(402)489-3024	SL-SMP	2023
Greg Daniel K			NI		Northern Illinois District River Forest IL	(708)449-3020	SL	2021
Gregory Karl W	(605)254-2348 karlw.gregory@gmail.com	801 N Madison St Lebanon IL 62254	SI	SP	Messiah Lebanon IL	(618)537-2300	SL	2006
Gregory Peter F	(260)445-8572 pgregory@oursaviorlcms.com	17 Marshall Hill Rd Westminster MA 01473	NE	Sn/Adm	Our Savior Westminster MA	(978)874-2504	FW	2007
Greig John E	(586)863-7827 greigj@oh.lcms.org	8187 Callow Rd Painesville OH 44077	OH	D Ex/S	Ohio District North Olmsted OH	(440)235-2297	SL	2002
Greig Nycholas C	(716)336-1767 nycholasg@gmail.com	132 Reserve Rd West Seneca NY 14424	EA	SP	Trinity West Seneca NY	(716)674-9188	SL	2013
Grein John O	(320)583-7788 johngrein84@gmail.com	1391 Heritage Ave NW Hutchinson MN 55350	MNS	EM			FW	1983
Greiner Micah D	(847)531-0546 pastor.greiner@gmail.com	495 Bernard Dr Buffalo Grove IL 60089	NI	Sn/Adm	St Peter Arlington Heights IL	(847)259-4114	SL	2007
Greinke Kenneth W	(816) 416-8060 kengreinke@alliancecom.net	626 NW Shamrock Cir Apt A Lees Summit MO 64081	SD	EM			SL	1965
Grell David E	(518)605-6754 dgrell@hotmail.com	132 Jackson Ave Apt A Schenectady NY 12304	AT	EM			SL	1982
Gremminger Joshua A	(262)685-8739 jgremminger@stpaulwestlake.org	176 S Point Dr Avon Lake OH 44012	OH	Assoc	St Paul Westlake OH	(440)835-3050	SL	2020
Grenz Greyson D	(734)309-6092 grey.hound.grenz@gmail.com	865 Riverbank St Wyandotte MI 48192	MI	Sn/Adm	Trinity Monroe MI	(734)242-2308	SL	2011
Gress C S	(561)542-4472 scottgress@me.com	12573 Oak Run Ct Boynton Beach FL 33436	FG	C07/2024			SL	1988
Gretarsson Emil Y	(240)385-5096 pastor.gretarsson@gmail.com	c/o Open Arms Ministries 1340 8th St Slidell LA 70458	SO	SP	Bethany Slidell LA	(985)643-3043	SL	2010
Grether Howard F II	(330)928-1620 revgrether@juno.com	1913 W Steels Corners Rd Cuyahoga FLS OH 44223	OH	EM			FW	1999
Greunke Martin R	(402)660-7956 martingreunke@gmail.com	5486 Great Lakes Drive Apt. B Holt MI 48842	MI	EM			SPR	1969
Greve Johnny V	(847)658-4320 grevejv@comcast.net	9811 Arthur Rd Algonquin IL 60102	NI	EM			FW	2006

*Multiple Assignments (See Church Worker Locator for Additional Details)
See Page 53 for the Table of Abbreviations for key to District, Position, and Seminary abbreviations
**C =Candidate; EM = Emeritus; the date following the C is the month and year the Candidate status began

NAME	TELEPHONE NUMBER EMAIL	STREET ADDRESS CITY/STATE/ZIP	DISTRICT	POSITION/ STATUS**	WHERE SERVING	OFFICE PHONE	SEM/ PROGRAM	YR GRAD
Grewe Nathan R	(732)299-3570	5205 Warren St Davenport IA 52806	IE	RSO	Lutheran Family Service Fort Dodge IA	(515)573-3138	FW	2011
Griebel David W	(260)424-4245 rev.griebel@yahoo.com	P.O. Box 13215 Fort Wayne IN 46867	IN	SP	Trinity Fort Wayne IN	(260)422-7931	FW	2005
Griebel Kirk E	(507)213-0981 kirk.griebel@gmail.com	7317 N Wabash Ave Kansas City MO 64118	MO	EM			SL	1985
Griebel Paul B	(704)604-0923 griebelp@yahoo.com	7111 Kilcullen Dr Charlotte NC 28270	SE	EM			SL	1973
Griebenaw Douglas A	doug.griebenaw@kfuo.org		MO	S Ex/S	The LCMS Corporate Saint Louis MO	(314)965-9000	FW	2016
Grieser Winston P	(260)804-1087 winstongrieser@gmail.com	c/o St Pauls Lutheran Church 109 S Elm St Kewanee IL 61443	CI	SP	St Paul Kewanee IL	(309)852-2461	FW	2017
Griesse Mark E	(509)594-6866 markg713@gmail.com	381 Sinclair Ln Selah WA 98942	NOW	EM			SL	1992
Grieve Michael S	(217)257-0615 pastor@ziongwinner.org		ND	SP	Zion Gwinner ND	(701)678-2401	FW	2007
Grieves Herbert H Jr	herbertgrieves@att.net	c/o Cedarhurst Senior Living Of Yorkville 4040 Cannonball Trail Apt 202 Yorkville IL 60560	NI	EM			SPR	1968
Griffin Gary W	(417)299-3218 fasterpastor@hotmail.com	214 N Dade 81 Lockwood MO 65682	MO	SP	Trinity Sarcoxie MO		CQ	1991
Griffin Larry J Dr	(507)420-2236 pastorgriffin54@gmail.com	86 W Byrsonima Loop Homosassa FL 34446	FG	SP	Good Shepherd Chiefland FL	(352)493-4597	FW	1980
Griffin Marvin A Sr	(313)427-8154 marvingriffin1954@yahoo.com	1421 Tremont St Selma AL 36701	SO	EM			CQ	1981
Griffin Timm L Dr	(901)428-3150 griffintimm@netscape.net	190 Golf Course Dr Wrightstown WI 54180	NW	EM			SL	1982
Griffith Christopher C	(405)240-7896 pastorgriffith@gmail.com	P.O. Box 733 Wellston OK 74881	OK	Sn/Adm	St Paul Wellston OK	(405)356-4203	SL	2012
Griffith Greg S	(402)915-1922 gg@kingofkings.org	13427 Taylor St Omaha NE 68164	NEB	Sn/Adm	King Of Kings Omaha NE	(402)333-6464	SL	2004
Grills Willie T	(606)225-2122 pastorgrills@gmail.com	300 Avilla E Alexander AR 72002	MDS	SP	Zion Avilla AR	(501)408-4630	FW	2017
Grime Paul J Dr	(260)416-2310 paul.grime@ctsfw.edu	1121 Woodland Xing Fort Wayne IN 46825	IN	S HS/C	Concordia Theological Seminary Fort Wayne IN	(260)452-2100	FW	1986
Grimenstein Edward O Dr	(412)523-7896 pastor@zlcb.org	3199 Washington Pike Bridgeville PA 15017	EA	SP	Zion Bridgeville PA	(412)221-4776	FW	1999
Grimm Dale A	(734)922-2537 revdgrimm@yahoo.com	4791 Cottonwood Ln Chelsea MI 48118	MI	EM			FW	1980
Grimm David A	(269)689-7482 grimmcp@gmail.com	30321 Covey Rd Leonidas MI 49066	MI	C07/2020			SL	1992
Grimm Gerald E	(586)783-8354 geraldegrimm@aol.com	21628 Mary Rose Dr Macomb MI 48044	MI	EM			SL	1969
Grimm Gerald J	(570)403-6194 gjgrimm27@gmail.com	9 Glendale Dr Mountain Top PA 18707	EA	EM			SPR	1964
Grimm Keith H	(763)438-7217 kgrimm@foclutheran.org	15384 Wintergreen St NW Andover MN 55304	MNS	Sn/Adm	Family Christ* Ham Lake MN	(763)434-7337	SL	1991
Grimm Robert W	(785)765-3632 r.w.grimm@juno.com	706 Iowa St Alma KS 66401	KS	SP	St John Alma KS	(785)765-3632	FW	1985
Grimmer Daniel P	(605)999-3482 pastorgrimmer@zionmitchell.org	1431 Sawgrass Ave Mitchell SD 57301	SD	Sn/Adm	Zion Mitchell SD	(605)996-7530	FW	2015
Griser Louis E	(402)499-3051 legriser@windstream.net	P.O. Box 93 Pleasant Dale NE 68423	NEB	SP	Immanuel Seward NE	(402)795-3770	CQ	1974
Grissom Daniel J	(630)533-1238 dangrissom@me.com	1009 Buckingham Dr Naperville IL 60563	NI	EM			FW-SMP	2011
Grobelch Michael R	(949)632-8480 MGrobelc@Gmail.com	1436 Glacier Dr. Allen TX 75002	TX	EM			CQ	2019
Grobien Gifford A Dr	(260)452-2143 gifford.grobien@ctsfw.edu	6600 N Clinton St Fort Wayne IN 46825	IN	S HS/C	Concordia Theological Seminary Fort Wayne IN	(260)452-2100	FW	2005
Groeling Neal S	(505)850-6236 neal@groeling.org	5123 Rio Las Vacas Pl NW Albuquerque NM 87114	RM	EM			SL	1987
Groh Ryan M	(573)256-9896 ryan.groh@cune.org	4409 St. John's Rd Jefferson City MO 65101	MO	SP	St John* Jefferson City MO	(573)395-4591	FW	2025
Grohs John K	(715)410-4160 john.grohs@gmail.com	2495 Canabury Dr Unit 119 Little Canada MN 55117	MNS	EM			SL	2001
Groleau James H	(320)336-8149 shepherd@jamesplace.net	303 N 2nd St Colby WI 54421	NW	SP	Zion Colby WI	(715)223-2166	SL	2009
Groll Douglas R Dr	(773)622-1879 douglasgroll@sbcglobal.net	1724 N Rutherford Ave Chicago IL 60707	NI	S HS/C	Concordia Seminary Saint Louis MO	(314)505-7000	SL	1966
Gronewold Geoffrey D	(507)327-6854 gronewoldg@gmail.com	7 London Dr Fort Liberty NC 28307	MNN	M Chap	Office of International Mission Saint Louis MO		SL	2013
Gross Jeffrey A	(217)416-4729	120 W Monroe St Petersburg IL 62675	CI	SP	Bethlehem Petersburg IL	(217)632-2453	FW	1988
Gross John P	(805)540-9002 revjpgross@gmail.com	5606 Ponderosa Ct Mariposa CA 95338	CNH	EM			FW	1988
Gross Lloyd E	(216)459-0767 revleg@aol.com	5901 Graydon Dr Seven Hills OH 44131	OH	EM			SL	1968
Grosskopf Sol E	revsolgrosskopf@gmail.com		MNS	M Chap	Office of International Mission Saint Louis MO		SL	2013
Grotelueschen Joshua	(608)290-9838 ilckalamazoo@gmail.com	c/o Immanuel Lutheran Church 3000 W Main St Kalamazoo MI 49006	MI	SP	Immanuel Kalamazoo MI	(269)345-8090	SL	2019
Groth Terence R	(402)646-2067	1289 Augusta Dr Seward NE 68434	NEB	Assoc	St Paul Utica NE	(402)534-2200	SL	1979

*Multiple Assignments (See Church Worker Locator for Additional Details)

See Page 53 for the Table of Abbreviations for key to District, Position, and Seminary abbreviations

**C =Candidate; EM = Emeritus; the date following the C is the month and year the Candidate status began

NAME	TELEPHONE NUMBER EMAIL	STREET ADDRESS CITY/STATE/ZIP	DISTRICT	POSITION/ STATUS**	WHERE SERVING	OFFICE PHONE	SEM/ PROGRAM	YR GRAD
Groth Theodore W	(720)737-1283 grotht@trinitycr.org	1365 1st Ave SW Cedar Rapids IA 52405	IE	Sn/Adm	Trinity Cedar Rapids IA	(319)366-1569	SL	2002
Groth David K	(920)261-2570 dgroth@goodshepherdwi.org	1406 Beacon Dr Watertown WI 53098	SW	C08/2025			SL	1992
Groth Charles A	(859)619-6337 ghanagroth@yahoo.com	6304 Brook Ln Savage MN 55378	MNS	EM			SPR	1975
Groth Jason J	(269)329-8463 jasonjamesgroth@gmail.com	9911 Sappington Rd Saint Louis MO 63128	MO	S Miss	Office of International Mission Saint Louis MO		SL	2024
Grothe Robert L	(253)946-0957 rgrothe@tcmnet.com	31416 11th Pl S Federal Way WA 98003	NOW	EM			FW	1981
Grovenstein Phillip S	(307)899-3006 revpgwy@gmail.com	P.O. Box 564 Dayton WY 82836	WY	EM			FW	1985
Grubbs Travis S	(716)532-1953 revtgrubbs@msn.com	64 Buffalo St Gowanda NY 14070	EA	EM			FW	1981
Gruber James L	jlgruber0310@gmail.com	826 2nd St P.O. Box 355 Fullerton NE 68638	NEB	EM			FW	1978
Gruden Mark E	(309)431-1704 markgrudn@icloud.com	1108 Kingsbury Rd Washington IL 61571	CI	SP	Zion* Wenona IL	(815)853-4479	SL	2000
Gruel Michael R	(603)986-6138 mandd_gruel@msn.com	190 Pinellas Ln Apt 307 Cocoa Beach FL 32931	NE	EM			SL	1967
Gruen Darald A	(920)349-9141 pastordgruen@gmail.com	519 Island View Cir Hutisford WI 53034	SW	EM			CQ	1996
Gruen Jonathan P	(816)726-0377 pastorjon@beautifulsavior-lsmo.org	615 SE Todd George Pkwy Lees Summit MO 64063	EN	Sn/Adm	Beautiful Savior Lees Summit MO	(816)524-7288	SL	2005
Gruenbaum Philip L	(630)896-2430 philgruenbaum@gmail.com	901 Prairie St Aurora IL 60506	NI	EM			CQ	1989
Gruenhagen Andrew D	(734)560-1786 gruenhad@gmail.com	15001 Maplewood Ln Plymouth MI 48170	MI	Sn/Adm	St Michael Wayne MI	(734)728-1950	FW	2002
Gruenhagen David L	(541)270-1110 davemaggie1967@gmail.com	7111 E Grandview Dr Prescott Valley AZ 86314	PSW	EM			CQ	1988
Grueninger William D	(314)941-5090 grueningerbill@gmail.com	143 Nevada Dr Decatur IL 62526	CI	Assoc	St Paul's Decatur IL	(217)423-6955	SL	2018
Gruenwald Daniel J	(616)363-4005 dcgruen@comcast.net	2438 College Ave. NE Grand Rapids MI 49505	MI	EM			FW	1983
Gruenwald David A	(314)322-0913 dagruenwald@gmail.com	9907 Sappington Rd Saint Louis MO 63128	MO	Sn/Adm	Resurrection Sunset Hills MO	(314)843-6633	SL	2013
Gruetzner James M	(248)681-3831 jmgruetz32@att.net	32220 Valley View Cir Farmington MI 48336	MI	EM			SL	1956
Gruhn Michael V	(936)293-6440 revgruhn@gmail.com	3905 105th St Lubbock TX 79423	TX	EM			CQ	1981
Grulke Galen E	517-918-1378 grulkeg010@comcast.net	1952 Maggie Ln Ypsilanti MI 48198	MI	EM			CQ	1991
Grulke Carl M	+267 779 036 54 carl.grulke@lbt.org	P.O. Box Ha 137 Hak Maun BOTSWANA	MO	RSO	Lutheran Bible Translators Inc Concordia MO	(660)225-0810	SL	2013
Grummer Roger H Dr	(817)684-0370 rgrummer@flash.net	3305 Langley Hill Ln Colleyville TX 76034	TX	EM			SPR	1961
Grund Terry L	(314)492-4446 tgrund60@gmail.com	143 Lamplighter Way O Fallon MO 63368	MO	EM			SL	1990
Grunewald Richard J	(586)295-3025 rgrunewald@faithtroy.org	5405 Saint Richard Dr Shelby Twp MI 48316	MI	SMP	Faith Troy MI	(248)689-4664	SL-SMP	2015
Grunklee Corey J	(334)887-3901 pastorcorey@tlcauburn.org		SO	SP	Trinity Auburn AL	(334)887-3901	SL	2007
Grunst Mark P	(406)690-2368 m5p9g55@yahoo.com	117 Legends Way Billings MT 59106	MT	EM			FW	1981
Gruoner David F	(785)447-9138 davidgruoner@gmail.com	4550 Periwinkle Dr Manhattan KS 66502	KS	EM			SL	1979
Grzybowski Terry L	(763)528-0239 pastorterry.grzybowski@gmail.com	13560 Oakwood Rd Zimmerman MN 55398	MNN	SP	Emmanuel Elk River MN	(763)441-2555	SL	1982
Guagenti Andrew D	(502)655-0925 pastor@holycrosslutheran-ky.org	1117 Summit Dr Shelbyville KY 40065	IN	SP	Holy Cross Shelbyville KY	(502)647-3696	FW	2003
Guagenti Andrew V	(502)648-8475 pastorag@gentiweb.com	1023 Windsor Dr Shelbyville KY 40065	IN	EM			FW	2001
Gude George J Dr	(618)420-7967 drgjg@mindspring.com	5180 Loop Rd Dorsey IL 62021	SI	EM			SL	1967
Gudel Joseph P Dr	jpg2cts@aol.com	6305 Sawmill Woods Dr Fort Wayne IN 46818	IN	EM			CQ	1991
Gudgel Michael R	(708)253-5761	66 Timberline Dr Lemont IL 60439	NI	SP	St Matthew Lemont IL	(630)257-5000	SL	2001
Gudmundson Thomas P	(920)946-9067 ourelliedog@gmail.com		SW	EM			SL	1981
Gueldner Peter L	revgueldner@trinityfaribo.org	8959 Darlington Ave NE Monticello MN 55362	MNS	SP	Trinity Faribault MN	(507)331-6579	FW	2011
Guelzow David J	dguelzow@sslcms.org	1761 30th Ave Ct NE Hickory NC 28601	SE	EM			SL	1990
Guelzow James R	(813)963-3419 jlguelzow@aol.com	5513 Raven Ct Tampa FL 33625	FG	EM			SL	1974
Guelzow Nathan J	(901)634-3717 nate.guelzow@plileadership.org	7920 Oakview Ln Woodridge IL 60517	TX	O-Sp Min	Texas District Round Rock TX	(800)951-3478	SL	2000
Guerra Lincon Jr	(515)528-0025 lincon@txlcms.org	4115 124th St Lubbock TX 79423	TX	D Ex/S	Texas District Round Rock TX	(800)951-3478	SL	2010
Guetersloh Ralph A	(417)538-9119 rgueter@hotmail.com	7024 State Highway Y Galena MO 65656	MO	EM			SL	1967

*Multiple Assignments (See Church Worker Locator for Additional Details)

See Page 53 for the Table of Abbreviations for key to District, Position, and Seminary abbreviations

**C =Candidate; EM = Emeritus; the date following the C is the month and year the Candidate status began

NAME	TELEPHONE NUMBER EMAIL	STREET ADDRESS CITY/STATE/ZIP	DISTRICT	POSITION/ STATUS**	WHERE SERVING	OFFICE PHONE	SEM/ PROGRAM	YR GRAD
Guettler Ronald H	(586)924-4974 revguettler@gmail.com	235 Orchard View Dr Royal Oak MI 48073	MI	EM			SL	1957
Gugel Christian F	(920)254-7067 secretary@swd.lcms.org	1614 S 23 Sheboygan WI 53081	SW	Sn/Adm	Christ* Sheboygan WI	(920)457-9205	FW	1987
Gugsa Assefa Z Zelelew Dr	assefa.gugsa@yahoo.com	33183 Romance Pl Temecula CA 92595	PSW	SP	Faith San Diego CA	(619)582-1068	CQ	2007
Guirguis George N Naeem Dr	(303)859-5693 gnaeem@comcast.net	9609 S. University Blvd. P.O. Box 631402 Highlands Ranch CO 80130	RM	SP	Christ Redeemer Bennett CO	(303)644-3044	CQ	2004
Gullidge Jason E	(206)947-0553 jasongullidge@gmail.com	202 Parkland Way Caldwell ID 83605	NOW	SP	Grace Caldwell ID	(208)459-4191	FW	2016
Gullion Jesse R	rev.j.guillion@gmail.com	155 South St Juneau WI 53039	SW	SP	Peace Beaver Dam WI	(920)887-1272	FW	2016
Gullion Robert H		12021 Shearwater Run Fort Wayne IN 46845	IN	EM			FW	1999
Gulseth Matthew M	(509)332-2830 matt.gulseth@concordiapullman.org	1750 NE Lower Dr Pullman WA 99163	NOW	SP	Concordia Pullman WA	(509)332-2830	SL	2016
Gumz Patrick M	rev.gumz@outlook.com	1850 N Grand Ave W Springfield IL 62702	CI		Central Illinois District Springfield IL	(217)793-1802	SL	2013
Gundermann Thomas M	(612)244-7684 gundermann@csp.edu	1308 Hague Ave Saint Paul MN 55104	MNS	S HS/C	Concordia University St Paul Saint Paul MN	(651)641-8278	SL-D	2003
Gunderson David E	605-660-6312 chaplaingunderson@yahoo.com	1910 NE 83rd St Kansas City MO 64118	SD	EM			SL	1981
Gunia Matthew J	(773)255-9597 mj.gunia@gmail.com	707 Alice St Whitehall MI 49461	MI	SP	Faith Whitehall MI	(231)893-7722	SL	2006
Gurganious Brady D	(317)778-5682 bgurganious@gmail.com	7203 W Ivy Ln New Palestine IN 46163	IN	SMP	Zion New Palestine IN	(317)861-5544	SL-SMP	2024
Gurrala Vijay	(281)997-0757 pastorvg@linchouston.org	3903 Leanett Way Ct Pearland TX 77584	TX	SP	The Tegulu-Redeemer Houston TX		SL	2006
Guse Travis B Dr	(208)680-4928	3618 Irby Pond Dr Midlothian VA 23112	SE	D Ex/S	Southeastern District Henrico VA	(703)971-9371	SL	2004
Gusewelle Monte W	galliacomata13@gmail.com	525 Animas View Dr Apt 44 Durango CO 81301	RM	EM			SL	1973
Gustafson Charles	(203)910-4626 coachrev17@gmail.com	29397 Andrew Jackson Dr Millsboro DE 19966	SE	EM			SL	1979
Gustafson Thomas M	541-556-4264 pastorthomas@immanuelgr.org	1030 Kendalwood St NE Grand Rapids MI 49505	MI	Assoc	Immanuel Grand Rapids MI	(616)454-3655	SL	2022
Gustafson Scott A	(715)351-0016 scott.gustafson2@us.army.mil	615 W Main St Merrill WI 54452	NW	Sn/Adm	Trinity Merrill WI	(715)536-5482	SL	1996
Gustke George M	(405)615-6079	8501 NW 23rd St Oklahoma City OK 73127	OK	EM			SPR	1960
Gutema Wasihun	(202)718-7627 wasihunguutamaa@gmail.com	4204 Cedar Tree Ln Burtonsville MD 20866	SE	SP	El-Shaddai Greenbelt MD	(240)701-4196	CQ	2024
Gutz Glen E	glen.gutz@gmail.com	201 E 4th St Salisbury MO 65281	MO	SP	Immanuel Salisbury MO	(660)388-5192	SL	1998
Gutz John E	(815)673-1635 joh.gutz@gmail.com	101 Trinity Dr Streator IL 61364	S	SP	Holy Trinity Streator IL	(815)672-2393	SL	1988
Gutz Luther R Dr	(208)765-2560 gutz65@aol.com	2229 W Marlborough Ave Coeur D Alene ID 83815	NOW	EM			SPR	1968
Guynn Kevin L Dr	(440)974-9806 revguynn@gmail.com	6625 Ivana Ct Mentor OH 44060	OH	SMP	Faith Mentor OH	(440)255-2229	SL-SMP	2012
Gwaltney Jim B III	jimgwaltney3@hotmail.com		PSW	Sn/Adm	Light of Christ Irvine CA	(949)786-3326	SL	2004
Haack James R	jim@bslcomaha.org	16268 Orchard Cir Omaha NE 68135	NEB	SMP	Beautiful Savior Lavista NE	(402)331-7376	SL-SMP	2015
Haag Steven J	(715)927-3790 skjhaag@gmail.com	N7406 Left Foot Lake Rd Crivitz WI 54114	NW	EM			SL	1994
Haak Joel D	(507)250-0828 rev.2.10@gmail.com	16339 14 Mile Rd. Fraser MI 48026	MI	Assoc	St John Fraser MI	(586)293-0333	SL	2010
Haakana Jon T	(763)205-5406 jonhaakana@gmail.com	8333 Emery Pkwy N Champlin MN 55316	MNS	EM			SL	1983
Haake Charles W	(320)267-9992 cghaake@gmail.com	2623 Viola Heights Dr NE Rochester MN 55906	MNS	EM			SL	1968
Haara David M	(813)892-3003 dhaara@msn.com	5065 Southampton Cir Tampa FL 33647	S	Assoc	Family Of Christ Tampa FL	(813)558-9343	SL	1989
Haas Thomas P	(409)988-6026 haast_270@msn.com	2431 23rd St Orange TX 77630	TX	EM			FW-SMP	2010
Habedank Ronald R	(585)902-6005 cronh156@aol.com	24 S Shore Dr Alden NY 14004	EA	EM			FW	2002
Haberer David E	(646)309-1935 davidh1888@aol.com	120 Gates Ave Brooklyn NY 11238	AT	SP	Trinity Jamaica NY	(718)525-3689	CQ	2007
Haberkost Daniel R	pastordhaberkost@gmail.com	3 Washington Ave Mayville NY 14757	EN	EM			FW	1986
Haberoth Steven G	(830)755-6055 shaberoth@juno.com	30661 Sweetridge Cir Fair Oaks Ranch TX 78015	TX	EM			CQ	2001
Haberstock Paul J	revpaulhaberstock@gmail.com	800 S River Rd Apt 819 Des Plaines IL 60016	EN	EM			CQ	1972
Habrecht Richard A	(419)536-3348 rhabrecht@hotmail.com	2414 Kimberly Dr Toledo OH 43615	OH	EM			FW	1991
Habthemariam Beniam B	(206)681-4751 hbeniam@ymail.com	4017 Grand Ave Everett WA 98201	NOW	SP	Christ Son of God Seattle WA		CQ	2014
Hackbardt Donald M	bfree2@msn.com	2290 Keaton Chase Dr Orange Park FL 32003	FG	EM			FW	1986
Hackett Thomas S	(954)336-1875 hackett.tom@gmail.com	631 Maple Creek Dr Holland MI 49423	MI	EM			SPR	1976

*Multiple Assignments (See Church Worker Locator for Additional Details)
See Page 53 for the Table of Abbreviations for key to District, Position, and Seminary abbreviations
**C =Candidate; EM = Emeritus; the date following the C is the month and year the Candidate status began

NAME	TELEPHONE NUMBER EMAIL	STREET ADDRESS CITY/STATE/ZIP	DISTRICT	POSITION/ STATUS**	WHERE SERVING	OFFICE PHONE	SEM/ PROGRAM	YR GRAD
Hackmann Steven M	rev.hackmann@gmail.com	36501 Lakehurst Dr Eastlake OH 44095	OH	SP	Shore Haven Euclid OH	(216)731-4100	FW	2017
Haedge Randall S	(972)822-0526 rshaedge@gmail.com	822 Arrowhead Dr Garland TX 75043	TX	EM			SL	1982
Haeger Martin A Dr	(815)370-5706 haegermartin@gmail.com	1011 Geyer Grove Kirkwood MO 63122	MO	EM			FW	1981
Haenftling Peter J	(330)314-6075 goosey424@gmail.com	663 N Main St Wilkes Barre PA 18705	S	SP	St Matthew Wilkes-Barre PA	(570)822-8233	FW	1996
Haertling Daniel C	(520) 812-9020 haveahaert@aol.com	3045 Kildaire Dairy Way Apex NC 27539	SE	EM			SL	1958
Hafeman Gregory S	(970)396-4072 greg_hafeman@comcast.net	1440 Grand Ave Windsor CO 80550	RM	C09/2020			FW	1985
Hafer Michael A	(979)777-0071 pastor@holycrossbcs.org	1200 Foxfire Dr College Sta TX 77845	TX	SP	Holy Cross College Station TX	(979)764-3992	SL	1992
Hafermann John E	(217)853-2733 hafermannjg@live.com	1112 N Oak St Normal IL 61761	CI	EM			FW	1977
Hafner Wesley H	(507) 591-3226 weshafner@gmail.com	241 Main St Walnut Grove MN 56180	MNS	EM			FW	1994
Hagan Robert L IV Dr	(314)590-6210 lee.hagan@mo.lcms.org	c/o Lcms Missouri District 660 Mason Ridge Ctr Dr Ste 100 Saint Louis MO 63141	MO	DP	Missouri District Saint Louis MO	(314)590-6200	SL	1996
Hagebusch Michael C	(775) 434-3468 hagebum@gmail.com	2991 Lida Ln Sparks NV 89434	CNH	EM			SL	1971
Hageman James A	(406)939-4851 cuisapiunt@gmail.com	470 Red Hille Way Bentonville VA 22610	MO	EM			FW	1985
Hageman Michael S	hagmission@att.net	1010 Fleming St Garden City KS 67846	KS	Sn/Adm	Immanuel* Lakin KS	(620)355-7161	SL	2004
Hagen Gary M	(360)903-1581 garymhagen@comcast.net	2336 NE Everett St Camas WA 98607	NOW	EM			SL	1987
Hagen Jeffrey D	jeff@sjlsherburn.com	413 Fox Lake Ave P.O. Box 6 Sherburn MN 56171	MNS	SMP	St John Sherburn MN	(507)764-5312	FW-SMP	2023
Hagen Robert E	(309)799-7464 revhag1976@gmail.com	712 E 3rd St Coal Valley IL 61240	CI	EM			SPR	1976
Hagenow Martin J	(989)642-3772 mjkjhagenows@charter.net	484 Ault St Hemlock MI 48626	MI	EM			CQ	1980
Hagerman Nicholas L Dr	(417) 866-5878 nhagerman@trinitylutheranspfd.org	1415 S Holland Ave Springfield MO 65807	MO	Sn/Adm	Trinity* Springfield MO	(417)866-5878	SL	2011
Haggas Joseph C	(402)618-3439 blessedbehisname@outlook.com	5520 Poppleton Ave Omaha NE 68106	NEB	SMP	River of Life Omaha NE	(402)558-6212	SL-SMP	2023
Hahn Daniel A Jr	(989)977-0166 revdahjr@gmail.com	1632 Vistaview Dr Verona PA 15147	EA	SP	Saint Johns Millvale PA	(412)821-6266	SL	1995
Hahn Timothy R	(815)278-0949 revtrh2002@yahoo.com	305 N Wallace Ave Haxtun CO 80731	RM	SP	Immanuel Haxtun CO	(970)774-6236	FW	2002
Hahn Kevin E	pastor@goodshepherdfrankfort.org	c/o Good Shepherd Luth Church 177 Luther Ln Frankfort IL 60423	NI	SP	Good Shepherd Frankfort IL	(815)469-2549	SL	1995
Hahn Kenneth S	(818)256-9139 kshahn@live.com	125 Legacy Ridge West Springville AL 35146	SO	EM			SL	1972
Hahn Joshua R	(979)739-1137 joshuarodger@gmail.com	180 W Washington St Giddings TX 78942	TX	Asst	Immanuel Giddings TX	(979)542-2918	SL	2022
Hahn David G	(320)362-0788 drechahndad@gmail.com	1963 Driftwood Ave Worthington MN 56187	MNS	SP	St Matthew Worthington MN	(507)376-6168	SL	1995
Hahn Jerome W	(715)350-4847 jhahn@dwave.net	307 Virginia St Antigo WI 54409	NW	EM			SPR	1975
Halakhe John H	(559)977-8066 abbalakhe@yahoo.com	c/o First Lutheran Church 9075 12th Ave Hanford CA 93230	CNH	SP	First Hanford CA	(559)582-2463	Other	1998
Halamka Ronald F Dr	(940)550-5594 rhalamka@sbcglobal.net	101 Watermark Blvd Apt. 212 Granbury TX 76048	TX	EM			SL	1959
Halboth Timothy P	(313)532-2266 glcms41@gmail.com	25630 Grand River Ave Redford MI 48240	EN	Sn/Adm	Grace Redford Township MI	(313)532-2266	SL	1989
Halche Yared H	(260)415-5579 pastoryared@aol.com	10214 Tarpley Ct Ellicott City MD 21042	SE	D Ex/S	Southeastern District Henrico VA	(703)971-9371	CQ	1999
Hale William E	(630)726-0128 william.e.hale@gmail.com	2017 Saint Clair Ave Granite City IL 62040	S	SMP	St John Granite City IL	(618)451-7788	SL-SMP	2017
Hale Philip W	pastorhale@zionwest.org	14205 Ida St Omaha NE 68142	NEB	Assoc	Zion Omaha NE	(402)493-1744	FW	2007
Hales Henry J	(989)864-3663 hchales@hotmail.com	c/o St John Lutheran Church 6600 Ruth Rd N Palms MI 48465	MI	SP	Trinity* Forestville MI	(989)864-3745	SL	1991
Hall Christopher D	(918)592-2999 srpastor@glctulsa.org	2331 E 5th Pl Tulsa OK 74104	OK	Sn/Adm	Grace Tulsa OK	(918)592-2999	SL	2000
Hall Gary J Jr	gary.hall@cph.org		MO	Pro Stf	Concordia Publishing House Saint Louis MO	(314)268-1000	SL	2007
Hall Joel D	(254)900-6748 cruentasarmo@yahoo.com	158 Fm 147 Groesbeck TX 76642	TX	SMP	Faith Mexia TX	(254)562-7756	SL-SMP	2023
Hall Michael D	pastormikehall@yahoo.com	7060 Hemlock Ave Lancaster CA 93536	PSW	SP	Grace Lancaster CA	(661)948-1018	SL	2008
Hall Rodney N	(408)892-7534 rodhall196@aol.com	49700 Rancho San Francisquito La Quinta CA 92253	PSW	EM			FW	1990
Hallenbeck Dana L	(860)365-5070 pastor.dlh@gmail.com	22 Bull Hill Rd Marlborough CT 06447	NE	EM			SL-D	2009
Haller Joshua T	(248)794-3703 pastorhaller19@gmail.com	4818 Slack Rd Fairgrove MI 48733	MI	SP	Grace Fairgrove MI	(989)693-6322	FW	2015
Haller Mark J	(586)859-1947 pastorhaller@gmail.com	67831 Madeline St Richmond MI 48062	MI	SP	St Peter Richmond MI	(586)727-9693	FW	1998

*Multiple Assignments (See Church Worker Locator for Additional Details)

See Page 53 for the Table of Abbreviations for key to District, Position, and Seminary abbreviations

**C =Candidate; EM = Emeritus; the date following the C is the month and year the Candidate status began

NAME	TELEPHONE NUMBER EMAIL	STREET ADDRESS CITY/STATE/ZIP	DISTRICT	POSITION/ STATUS**	WHERE SERVING	OFFICE PHONE	SEM/ PROGRAM	YR GRAD
Hallman Gerhardt F	(765)461-5090 bjhallman@hotmail.com	106 Wilson St Alden MN 56009	MNS	EM			CQ	1981
Halvorson Mark W	(612)205-4104 markannh@gmail.com	1120 Preserve Blvd Nya MN 55397	MNS	EM			SL	1985
Hambleton Aaron M	(641)640-5686 pastor.hambleton@stpauleldora.org	1109 Washington St Eldora IA 50627	IE	SP	St Paul Eldora IA	(641)858-2464	FW	2015
Hamer Brian J	(718)791-3490 revhamer@verizon.net	96 Wahoo Ln Oceanside CA 92058	MO	M Chap	Office of International Mission Saint Louis MO		FW	1995
Hamilton George O	(616)566-9519 ghamil64@yahoo.com	540 E Greenwood Cir Ste 209 Holland MI 49423	MI	EM			SL	1986
Hamilton Morgan W	(817)751-1651 morganwhamilton@gmail.com	1308 Middlesex Dr New Port Richey FL 34655	FG	C05/2022			SL	2004
Hamit Charles W	972-355-3773 whamit@conqm.com	2550 Post Oak Dr Corinth TX 76210	TX	SP	Hope Corinth TX	(940)497-4753	FW	1988
Hammel Vincent S Sr	(410)242-7062 rev.vince1@verizon.net	1226 Leeds Terrace Halethorpe MD 21227	SE	EM			CQ	2001
Hammer David M	(864)882-3209 pastor@eternalshepherd.org	220 Carson Rd Seneca SC 29678	SE	SP	Eternal Shepherd Seneca SC	(864)882-3209	SL	2002
Hammes Paul S	(719)728-7618 paul.hammes23@gmail.com	801 E 4th St Apt 110 Wayne NE 68787	NEB	Assoc	Grace Wayne NE	(402)375-1905	SL	2024
Hamre Jason P	(469)583-3525 jphamre6@gmail.com	1225 Mockingbird Dr Grapevine TX 76051	TX	SMP	SoulThirst The Colony TX	(469)353-8655	SL-SMP	2018
Hanan Norman A	(320)274-1099 mhanan@lakedalelink.net	310 Brown Ave N Annandale MN 55302	MNN	EM			CQ	1982
Hand Stephen M	(302)604-3438 revhand@gmail.com	2613 Swan Dr McKinney TX 75072	AT	C07/2016			FW	2007
Handrich Brian W	(973)383-9303 sutherland1540@yahoo.com	21 Elm St Newton NJ 07860	NJ	SP	Redeemer Newton NJ	(973)383-3945	SL	1997
Handrick Timothy P	(813)380-9577 handricktim@gmail.com	32 Fieldstone Ln Blairsville GA 30512	FG	SP	All Saints Blairsville GA	(706)745-7777	SL	2025
Handrick Thomas V Sr	(573)517-2000	103 Meadowbrook Dr Perryville MO 63775	MO	EM			FW	1978
Handschke Samuel P	(314)489-9181 sam.handschke@gmail.com	814 W 3rd St Pierre SD 57501	SD	Sn/Adm	Faith Pierre SD	(605)224-2216	SL	2018
Hanel Michael H	(913)940-8817 michael.hanel@gmail.com	7517 Sloewood Dr Leesburg FL 34748	FG	SP	Bethany Leesburg FL	(352)787-7275	SL	2008
Haner James R Dr	(254)315-0900 drjim89@gmail.com	8502 Preston Rd. Apt 243 Dallas TX 75225	TX	EM			SL	1966
Haney Byrene K Dr	(515)573-0053 keith@iowadistrictwest.org	1318 17th Ave N Fort Dodge IA 50501	IW	D Ex/S	Iowa West District Fort Dodge IA	(515)576-7666	SL	1993
Hanft Adrian E II	(402)649-5775 ahanft2@gmail.com	2700 Rolling Hills Dr Norfolk NE 68701	NEB	EM			SL	1997
Hanke Karl W IV	(314)223-1352 will.hanke@mtcalvarylcms.org	206 Almentor Ave Saint Louis MO 63119	MO	SP	Mount Calvary Brentwood MO	(314)968-2360	SL	2007
Hannah John R	(718)892-7268 hannahj39@aol.com	2130 Watson Ave Bronx NY 10472	AT	Assoc	Our Saviour Bronx NY	(718)792-5665	SL	1965
Hannemann Mark T Dr	(402)319-3938 mthannemann@gmail.com	2085 140th Raymond NE 68428	NEB	RSO	GracePoint Institute for Relational Health Lincoln NE	(402)614-6287	SL	1984
Hannemann Phillip L	(402)853-0187 hannephil@yahoo.com	6043 Old Farm Cir Lincoln NE 68512	NEB	EM			SPR	1975
Hannemann Aaron J	(402)910-2495	2022 17th St Columbus NE 68601	NEB	SP	Trinity Schuyler NE	(402)352-2307	SL	2015
Hannemann Justin L	justin@relationalhealth.org	54 Lincoln St Seward NE 68434	NEB	D Ex/S	Nebraska District Seward NE	(402)643-2961	SL	2012
Hannenberg Darryl S	(970)323-6242 revdarh@aol.com	8953 6085 Rd Montrose CO 81401	RM	SP	Hope Montrose CO	(970)249-8811	FW	1989
Hans Richard J Dr	(218)821-2751 doctri901@nisswa.net	20701 Cadwell Ave Brainerd MN 56401	MNN	SP	Living Savior Lake Shore MN	(218)963-9733	FW	1986
Hansell George R Jr	(440) 829-9218 grh61655@roadrunner.com	4581 Ashbury Park Dr North Olmsted OH 44070	S	EM			FW	1981
Hansen David L	(319) 551-3989 dlhansen054@gmail.com	7530 Lexington Club Blvd #a Delray Beach FL 33446	FG	EM			SL	1981
Hansen John G	(231) 233-7703 revjohn.hansen@gmail.com	1655 E Sugar Grove Rd Scottville MI 49454	MI	SMP	Lighthouse Pentwater MI	(231)869-2527	FW-SMP	2011
Hansen Lyle D	(515)570-5602 revlh82456@gmail.com	1825 120th St Boone IA 50036	IW	EM			FW	1981
Hansen Mark A	(712)330-9457 plchans77@gmail.com	2031 Burr Oak Ln Humbolt IA 50548	IW	Assoc	Zion Humboldt IA	(515)332-3279	FW	2004
Hansen Michael A	(760)433-2770 ilcpastormichael@gmail.com	1900 S Nevada St Oceanside CA 92054	PSW	SP	Immanuel Oceanside CA	(760)458-6570	SL	2018
Hansen Sean D	(319)895-8772 pastor@splcmv.org	600 5th Ave SW Mount Vernon IA 52314	IE	SP	St Paul Mount Vernon IA	(319)895-8772	FW	2011
Hanson Mark T	(701)212-0744 pastormarkclc@gmail.com	2412 Williams Rd Oak Harbor WA 98277	NOW	SP	Concordia Oak Harbor WA	(360)675-2548	SL	2006
Hanson Michael B Dr	michaelhanson@pilgrimluth.org	2489 Shady Oak Dr Green Bay WI 54304	NW	Sn/Adm	Pilgrim Green Bay WI	(920)965-2233	SL	2010
Hanson Lynn A		1214 Hidden Creek Cove Fort Wayne IN 46845	IN	SP	Living Water Wolf Lake IN	(260)635-2336	FW	2002
Hanson Kale W	(913)284-4008 pastorhanson@zionbethalto.org	622 Church Dr Bethalto IL 62010	SI	Sn/Adm	Zion Bethalto IL	(618)377-8314	SL	2014
Hanson Jeremy C	(920) 452-4331 jeremy.hanson@ourbethlehem.com	892 Eisenhower Ct Howards Grove WI 53083	SW	Assoc	Bethlehem Sheboygan WI	(920)452-4331	FW	2023

*Multiple Assignments (See Church Worker Locator for Additional Details)
See Page 53 for the Table of Abbreviations for key to District, Position, and Seminary abbreviations
**C =Candidate; EM = Emeritus; the date following the C is the month and year the Candidate status began

NAME	TELEPHONE NUMBER EMAIL	STREET ADDRESS CITY/STATE/ZIP	DISTRICT	POSITION/ STATUS**	WHERE SERVING	OFFICE PHONE	SEM/ PROGRAM	YR GRAD
Hanson Dean A	(308)627-6200 gracelutheran@frontiernet.net	28005 310 Rd P.O. Box 211 Pleasanton NE 68866	NEB	SP	Faith* Hazard NE		SL	1992
Hanson Carl M	011-82-10-3671-6274 hancarl@gmail.com	148 Hannam-Daero Yongsan-Gu Seoul 04417 KOREA	IW	S Miss	Office of International Mission Saint Louis MO		SL	1996
Hanson Bruce C	(251)454-1169 bp_hanson@bellsouth.net	650 Waukegan Rd 241 Glenview IL 60025	NI	EM			SL	1971
Hanson Joseph D		723 N 9th St Missouri Valley IA 51555	IW	SP	First Missouri Valley IA	(712)642-2483	SL	2018
Happ Carl G III	(631)942-5647 pastorchapp@aol.com	8091 State Route 89 Interlaken NY 14847	EA	EM			SL	2003
Harbaugh Darren M	(415)676-9043 darrenmharbaugh@gmail.com	1136 Buena St Seaside CA 93955	CNH	SP	Faith Seaside CA	(831)394-1312	SL	2012
Harbin Robert N	(901)853-4673 pastor.flc@comcast.net	250 Schrader Ln Collierville TN 38017	MDS	Sn/Adm	Faith Collierville TN	(901)853-4673	SL	1998
Hardaway Matthew D	(254)723-2373 kerussein@gmail.com	810 West Rd Salem CT 06420	NE	SP	Christ Amston CT	(860)228-1152	SL	2012
Harder William L	(312)215-3702	834 W Exner Ct Palatine IL 60067	NI	SMP	Living Christ Arlington Heights IL	(847)577-7133	SL-SMP	2023
Harders Daniel E	(785)252-3689 deharders@hotmail.com	301 S County Rd Holyrood KS 67450	KS	SP	St Peter* Holyrood KS	(785)252-3275	FW	2011
Hardin David S	(530)662-1935 stpwoodland@gmail.com	625 W Gibson Rd Woodland CA 95695	CNH	Sn/Adm	St Paul Woodland CA	(530)662-1935	SL	2014
Harding Christopher P	(440)387-1897 stoneypine1@aol.com	20062 Twin Pond Dr Brownstown MI 48183	MI	SMP	St Paul Trenton MI	(734)676-1565	SL	2025
Hardy Jamison J Dr	(724)413-8511 pastorhardy72@yahoo.com	2070 West View Ct Lake Orion MI 48360	EN	Assoc	Our Savior* Hartland MI	(248)887-4300	FW	2000
Harger Burton M	(715)736-7017 mar.burt@icloud.com	c/o Cambridge Care Facility 820 Bear Paw Ave Ste W231 Rice Lake WI 54868	NW	EM			SPR	1960
Harkey Edwin T	reveddiet@yahoo.com	c/o Trinity 100 Maple Ave Keene NH 03431	NE	SP	Trinity Keene NH	(603)352-4446	SL	1987
Harkins Nathan A	(913)669-6410 pr.harkins_LCMS@outlook.com	1605 Spruceway St Abilene KS 67410	KS	SP	Faith Abilene KS	(785)263-1842	SL	2025
Harman Corey J	(906)249-3172 mqtman11@gmail.com	226 Jean St Marquette MI 49855	NW	SMP	Trinity Covington MI	(906)355-2534	SL-SMP	2022
Harman Michael D	(507)440-8473 pastorharman@yahoo.com	23633 491st Avenue Gaylord MN 55334	MNS	SP	St John Gaylord MN	(507)237-2782	FW	1987
Harman Vincent R	(928)210-8659 vharman@christyuma.org	2242 E San Marcos Dr Yuma AZ 85365	PSW	SP	Christ Yuma AZ	(928)726-0773	SL	1995
Harmelink Daniel N Dr	(314)505-7911 dharmelink@concordiahistoricalinstitute.org	2347 Park Ave Apt B Saint Louis MO 63104	MO	ExecDir	Concordia Historical Institute Saint Louis MO	(314)505-7900	SL	1993
Harmon William A Dr	bharmon@se.lcms.org		SE	DP	Southeastern District Henrico VA	(703)971-9371	SL	1998
Harmon Thomas E	(316)650-3223 pastortom21@gmail.com	2731 N Cranberry St Wichita KS 67226	SO		Southern District Slidell LA	(504)282-2632	FW	1983
Harmon Dennis L	(262)250-0850 aaharmon5@yahoo.com	W143n9622 Amber Dr Germantown WI 53022	SW	SMP	Miss Of Christ* Milwaukee WI	(414)264-4050	FW-SMP	2012
Harmon Robert D	(303)242-6778 robertdharmon@gmail.com	7415 S Norfolk St Aurora CO 80016	RM	Sn/Adm	Mount Olive Aurora CO	(303)755-9123	FW	2001
Harmon Steven L	pastorharmon@embarqmail.com	2730 Fern Valley Road Marrietta GA 30066	MDS	EM			SL	1987
Harms Gerhard W	(760)637-5005 gamahmepas@gmail.com	1088 Laguna Dr B 108 Carlsbad CA 92008	PSW	EM			CQ	1965
Harms Myron D	(405)728-1858 mharms@messiahokc.org	10605 Basswood Canyon Rd Oklahoma City OK 73162	OK	SMP	Messiah Oklahoma City OK	(405)946-0681	SL-SMP	2021
Harms Walter W	(512)282-2626 waltpast@aol.com	11303 Menodora Dr Austin TX 78748	TX	EM			SL	1959
Harnack Michael E	(818) 732-5495 pastor@firstlutheranburbank.org	12930 Kittridge St N Hollywood CA 91606	PSW	SP	First Burbank CA	(818)848-7432	SL	2009
Harper Walter J	(803)229-2154 walt.harper@mtolivesc.org	238 Cabin Dr Irmo SC 29063	SE	Sn/Adm	Mount Olive Columbia SC	(803)781-5845	SL	2000
Harr Wade M	(605)842-1352 pastorharr730@gmail.com	730 East 6th St Winner SD 57580	SD	SP	Zion* Hamill SD	(605)842-0780	SL	1993
Harre Richard R	randrharre@frontier.com	4101 W Isles Ave Apt 2205 Springfield IL 62711	CI	EM			SL	1968
Harre Richard D	richharre@yahoo.com	1149 Eastridge Dr Seward NE 68434	NEB	EM			SL	1993
Harrell Brenden M	(703)217-0849 brendenharrell1@gmail.com	5435 Del Norte Way Santa Maria CA 93455	CNH	SP	Our Savior Santa Maria CA	(805)937-1116	SL	2021
Harries Thomas H	(913)709-1590 harriesth51@gmail.com	12691 W 82nd Ter Lenexa KS 66215	KS	EM			CQ	1992
Harrington Daniel R	daniel.harrington@gmail.com		WY	SP	Immanuel Powell WY	(307)754-3168	FW	2022
Harris Brendan G	(231)675-2909 brenharris15@gmail.com	316 S White St Fall Creek WI 54742	NW	SP	St John* Fall Creek WI	(715)877-3150	FW	2022
Harris Mark A	(512)448-7713 harrisprojectmanagement@gmail.com	120 Hideway Heights New Braunfels TX 78132	TX	C04/2023			SL	2016
Harris Lawrence H	(419)353-1401 lhharris@wcnet.org	515 Hillcrest Dr Bowling Green OH 43402	OH	EM			SL	1964
Harris James C	(760)514-8991 pastor@ascensionav.org	P.O. Box 1645 Apple Valley CA 92307	PSW	SP	Ascension Apple Valley CA	(760)247-7392	SL	2011
Harris Andrew M	(715)216-4410 rev.amharris@gmail.com	208 High St Clinton WI 53525	SW	SP	Christ Clinton WI	(608)676-4994	FW	2018

*Multiple Assignments (See Church Worker Locator for Additional Details)
See Page 53 for the Table of Abbreviations for key to District, Position, and Seminary abbreviations
**C =Candidate; EM = Emeritus; the date following the C is the month and year the Candidate status began

NAME	TELEPHONE NUMBER EMAIL	STREET ADDRESS CITY/STATE/ZIP	DISTRICT	POSITION/ STATUS**	WHERE SERVING	OFFICE PHONE	SEM/ PROGRAM	YR GRAD
Harris Alexander Q	(314)546-8625 alexqharris@gmail.com	850 Quincy St NW Apt 509 Washington DC 20011	SE	SP	Calvary Silver Spring MD	(301)589-4001	SL	2018
Harris Jacob T	(301)262-5475 jakeharris_2002@yahoo.com	9429 Murkirk Rd Apt 203 Laurel MD 20708	SE	Sn/Adm	Zion Praise Bowie MD	(301)442-6726	EIITSL	2008
Harrison Christopher D	(712)730-3175 pr.christopher.harrison@gmail.com	18 Matthew Dr Fairmont WV 26554	EN	SP	St John's Bridgeport WV	(304)608-3597	FW	2015
Harrison Daniel H	(260)452-9180 rev.harrison93@gmail.com	35037 Windsor Dr New Baltimore MI 48047	MI	SP	Christ New Baltimore MI	(586)725-1431	FW	2021
Harrison Matthew C Dr	(314)996-1402 mch@lcms.org	c/o Lutheran Church-Missouri Synod 1333 S Kirkwood Rd Saint Louis MO 63122	MO	S Adm	The LCMS Corporate* Saint Louis MO	(314)965-9000	FW	1991
Harriss Mark E	(618)246-3246 pastormark@stmks.net	603 W Illinois Steeleville IL 62288	SI	SP	St Mark Steeleville IL	(618)965-3192	SL	2016
Harrmann Bruce W	(414)438-0853 bharrmann@gmail.com	3501 N 98th St Milwaukee WI 53222	SW	SP	Lamb Of God Pewaukee WI	(262)691-3828	SPR	1975
Harrow Gerald W	(970)405-6691 gwharrow@gmail.com	386 Frederick Dr Robinson TX 76706	TX	SMP	Texas District Round Rock TX	(800)951-3478	SL-SMP	2010
Harste Kenneth K	(612)964-3867 kharste@samaritanshill.com	20083 226th Ave NW Big Lake MN 55309	MNS	Sn/Adm	Samaritans Hill Albertville MN	(763)595-1199	FW	1983
Hart Erik J	(402)300-1294 erik.hart@cune.org	804 G Avenue Central City NE 68826	NEB	SP	St Pauls Central City NE	(308)946-2680	SL	2022
Hart Ethan D	(573) 616-9749 hartet@csl.edu	310 Woodland Dr Salem IL 62881	CI	Assoc	Salem Salem IL	(618)548-3190	SL	2025
Hart Henry F	(832)489-8971 newchurchtx@gmail.com	19751 Coppervine Ln Houston TX 77084	TX	SMP	NewChurch Katy TX	(832)786-8212	SL-SMP	2018
Hart Leigh G	(818)303-6371	301 N Isabel St Glendale CA 91206	PSW	SP	Zion Glendale CA	(818)243-3119	SL	1999
Harter Jeffrey M	(309)401-5702 jeffrey.harter@lssliving.org	1515 Seven Pines Rd Apt L Springfield IL 62704	CI	Inst C	Lutheran Senior Services DBA EverTrue Brentwood MO	(314)968-9313	FW	1983
Hartfield Robert L	(215)412-8757 bobhartfield@msn.com	911 Breezewood Ln Lansdale PA 19446	EA	EM			SPR	1967
Hartjen Travis M	(972)740-6033 travis.hartjen@me.com	15824 Caballero Dr Justin TX 76247	TX	SMP	Crown of Life Colleyville TX	(817)421-5683	SL-SMP	2011
Hartke Nathan C	(716)662-4747 nate@stjohnsop.com	4536 S Buffalo St Orchard Park NY 14127	EA	Sn/Adm	St John Orchard Park NY	(716)662-4747	SL	2005
Hartke Gerald C	(419)787-6953 gchartke@icloud.com	1922 S Freedom Dr Northwood OH 43619	OH	EM			SL	1976
Hartley William R	(480)388-2635 Bill@FOLLutheran.org	c/o Fountain Of Life 710 S. Kolb Rd Tucson AZ 85710	PSW	SP	Fountain of Life Tucson AZ	(520)747-1213	CQ	2018
Hartman Theodore E	(925) 366-2846 theodore.hartman1@gmail.com	8380 Fair Pines Ln #656 Garden Valley CA 95633	CNH	EM			SPR	1975
Hartman Jack L	(724)822-8513 jhar495886@aol.com	110 Dolphin Dr Butler PA 16002	EA	Inst C	Eastern District Williamsville NY	(716)634-5111	SL	1976
Hartman James L	(920)627-5495 hartman_5654@yahoo.com	2215 N 34th St Sheboygan WI 53083	SW	EM			FW	1982
Hartman Jared P	(317)691-5892 pastorjaredhartman@icloud.com		NEB	SP	St Paul Wisner NE	(402)529-6583	FW	2013
Hartman Paul A	(940)262-0346 poimensjlc@aol.com	126 Saint Francis Ln Mabank TX 75156	TX	EM			SPR	1965
Hartman Stephen E	(605)553-6781 stephenhartman@sio.midco.net	6602 E Twin Pines Drive Sioux Falls SD 57110	SD	EM			FW	1986
Hartner Timothy J	timhartner2424@gmail.com	6215 Hawkes Bluff Ave Davie FL 33331	FG	EM			CQ	1986
Hartsough Mark R	(734)658-1300 pastormark@newhopelicking county.org	1137 Sharonvalley Rd Newark OH 43055	OH	Sn/Adm	New Hope Newark OH	(740)366-6459	FW	2016
Hartung Bruce M Dr	(314)412-4911 hartungb@csl.edu	1615 -C Piccard Dr Unit 1701 Rockville MD 20850	SE	EM			SL	1967
Hartung David M	(662)694-9201 david@lemagroup.us	1211 18th Ave N Columbus MS 39701	SO	SMP	Our Savior* Columbus MS	(662)323-3050	FW-SMP	2012
Hartwell Robert E Dr	(914) 329-9182 revhartwel@gmail.com	35 Desmond Ave Bronxville NY 10708	AT	Sn/Adm	The Village* Bronxville NY	(914)337-0207	FW	1993
Hartwig Brent M	(319)338-5626 bhartwig@ourredeemer.org	512 S 1st Ave Iowa City IA 52245	IE	Sn/Adm	Our Redeemer Iowa City IA	(319)338-5626	SL	2009
Hartwig Brett D	(314)223-5839 pastorbhartwig@gmail.com	2800 30th St S Moorhead MN 56560	MNN	SP	Trinity Sabin MN	(218)789-7259	SL	2013
Hartwig Raymond L Dr	(314)835-7534 lcmssec@aol.com	2508 S Main Ave Sioux Falls SD 57105	SD	EM			SL	1971
Harvala Adam D	(701)936-1156	1137 5th Ave W West Fargo ND 58078	ND	SP	First American Mayville ND	(218)779-5620	SL	2007
Harvala Larry S Dr	(218)573-2203 larry.harvala@gmail.com	24220 McKinley Avenue P.O. Box 293 Osage MN 56570	MNN	EM			FW	1980
Hase Richard A	(410)991-1351 rahase@gmail.com	203 Prize Taker Ct Pasadena MD 21122	SE	EM			SPR	1975
Haselhuhn Don M	(620)364-8236 pastoreph2810@gmail.com	966 N Highway 14 Lincoln KS 67455	KS	SP	St John* Lincoln KS	(785)524-4039	SL	1994
Hashimoto Gen	(310)351-9717 genhashim1@gmail.com	10136 Girard Ave South Bloomington MN 55431	MNS	EM			CQ	2016
Haskell Kenneth F	kenhaskell35@gmail.com	5801 N Oakwood Rd Unit E202 Enid OK 73703	OK	EM			SL	1961
Hass Robert C	(203)239-6635 nrhavenct@aol.com	235 Pond Hill Rd Wallingford CT 06492	NE	SP	Zion Wallingford CT	(203)269-6847	FW	1980
Hass Mark C	(660)281-2221 pastormchass@gmail.com	102780 US 59 Sallisaw OK 74955	MDS	EM			FW	1996

*Multiple Assignments (See Church Worker Locator for Additional Details)
See Page 53 for the Table of Abbreviations for key to District, Position, and Seminary abbreviations
**C =Candidate; EM = Emeritus; the date following the C is the month and year the Candidate status began

NAME	TELEPHONE NUMBER EMAIL	STREET ADDRESS CITY/STATE/ZIP	DISTRICT	POSITION/ STATUS**	WHERE SERVING	OFFICE PHONE	SEM/ PROGRAM	YR GRAD
Hass Matthew C	(203)980-9288 pastormatt@villagelutheran church.net	703 Western Blvd Lanoka Harbor NJ 08734	NJ	SMP	Village Lanoka Harbor NJ	(609)693-1333	SL-SMP	2018
Hass Paul E Dr	(479)685-2416 pastor@bvlutheran.com	1990 Forest Hills Blvd Bella Vista AR 72715	MDS	Sn/Adm	Bella Vista Bella Vista AR	(479)855-0272	SL	2003
Hasse Donald E	(920)467-3042 pastorhasse@charter.net	628 Giddings Ave Sheboygan FLS WI 53085	SW	EM			SL	1965
Hasselbrook Preus A	(319)429-5686 preus1282@gmail.com	5800 Westheimer Rd Houston TX 77059	TX	Assoc	Memorial Houston TX	(713)782-6079	FW	2025
Hasselbrook Silas M	(920)658-5190 silas7283@gmail.com	3130 S 54th St Milwaukee WI 53219	SW	Sn/Adm	Trinity* West Allis WI	(414)321-3640	FW	2022
Hasselbrook David S Dr	(319) 300-4820 davehasselbrook@gmail.com	741 Central Ave Evansdale IA 50707	IE	SP	St Paul Evansdale IA	(319)232-7657	FW	2003
Hasskarl Leif R	(402)999-2252 hasskarl@msn.com	913 N State Highway 11 Atkinson NE 68713	NEB	SP	Immanuel* Butte NE	(402)775-2194	FW	1997
Hasz Luther N	(731)423-5383 lunicho@aol.com	380 Henderson Rd Jackson TN 38305	MDS	EM			SL	1966
Hasz Martin A	(573)979-2791 marty.hasz@mo.lcms.org	1705 Bel Air Dr Cape Girardeau MO 63701	MO	D Ex/S	Missouri District Saint Louis MO	(314)590-6200	SL	2012
Hatch David H	(920)609-0248 dave@oslc-gb.org	120 S Henry St Green Bay WI 54302	NW	Sn/Adm	Our Saviour Green Bay WI	(920)468-4065	FW	1982
Hatcher Joshua M Dr	(314)231-4092 pastorhatcher@trinitystlouis.com	812 Soulard St Saint Louis MO 63104	MO	Sn/Adm	Trinity Saint Louis MO	(314)231-4092	SL	2008
Hatesohl Andrew B	(847)669-5780 pastorhatesohl@trinityhuntley.org	11008 N. Church Street Huntley IL 60142	NI	SP	Trinity Huntley IL	(847)669-5780	SL	2018
Hatteberg Kurt T	(970)854-4310 stpaulcone@pctelcom.coop	P.O. Box 54 Amherst CO 80721	RM	SP	St Paul* Amherst CO	(970)854-4310	FW	2008
Hauan Eric R	(507)993-5564 erichauan@yahoo.com	325 S 52nd Ave Wausau WI 54401	NW	Sn/Adm	St Mark Wausau WI	(715)848-5511	SL	2016
Haug Eugene W	(828)288-4699 revhaug2@hughes.net	815 Cross Creek Dr Rutherfordton NC 28139	CI	EM			FW	2007
Haugen Paul J	(507)951-4595 pbhaugen@gmail.com	3121 S Newcastle Ct Sioux Falls SD 57110	SD	EM			SL	1990
Haugen Peter J	(507)867-4604 pastorhaugen@stpaulchatfield.org	116 Fillmore St SE Chatfield MN 55923	MNS	SP	St Paul Chatfield MN	(507)867-4604	FW	2013
Haugen Joshua A	(336)541-2806 jhaugen@trinitycougars.org	1057 Holly Dr Seymour IN 47274	IN	Pro Stf	Trinity Seymour IN	(812)524-8547	FW	2006
Haugen James A III	(419)264-2962 pastorhaugen3@gmail.com	421 North Wilhelm St Holgate OH 43527	OH	SP	St John Holgate OH	(419)264-4641	FW	2023
Haugen James A Jr	(440)376-6275 pastorhaugen@whitecreek.org	16150 S 300 W Columbus IN 47201	IN	SP	St John Columbus IN	(812)342-6832	FW	1998
Haugen Daniel J	(360)961-9000 idavike@gmail.com	15 Oak Dr Minot ND 58701	ND		North Dakota District Fargo ND	(701)293-9001	SL	2013
Haught David P	(623)337-4927 church@atonementlc.org	14871 N 174th Ln Surprise AZ 85388	PSW	EM			FW	1987
Haun Monte R	(314)971-9629 monte.haun@lssliving.org	10515 Hanford Dr Saint Louis MO 63128	MO	Inst C	Lutheran Senior Services DBA EverTrue Brentwood MO	(314)968-9313	SL	2001
Haupt Benjamin D	(678)989-7777 hauptben@hotmail.com	519 East Dr Saint Louis MO 63130	MO	Asst	Christ Memorial Saint Louis MO	(314)631-0304	SL	2005
Haupt Dieter E	(616)294-1855 pastorhaupt@gmail.com	954 Village Ct Holland MI 49423	MI	EM			SL	1975
Haupt Kenneth W	(214)717-8901 kenlinhaupt@verizon.net	3713 Sam Rayburn Trl Dallas TX 75287	TX	EM			SL	1970
Hauptmeier Tyler D	revhauptmeier@hotmail.com	302 N 4th St P.O. Box 72 Doniphan NE 68832	NEB	SP	St Paul Doniphan NE	(402)845-2340	SL	2004
Hausch Thomas J Dr	(208)860-1274	398 N Sierra View Way Eagle ID 83616	NOW	EM			SPR	1973
Hausch Nathan A	(916)997-8745 nhausch@stpaulspb.com	7957 Blue Lake Dr. San Diego CA 92119	PSW	Sn/Adm	St Pauls San Diego CA	(858)272-6363	SL	2010
Hauschild Daniel C	dahauschild@gmail.com	6718 Wilmont Ln Highland CA 92346	PSW	EM			SPR	1973
Hauser Aaron T	(262)573-0557 athauser@yahoo.com	643 Weiss St Allenton WI 53002	SW	Assoc	First Immanuel Cedarburg WI	(262)377-6610	SL	2017
Hauser Daniel L	dhauser@hclc.info	9724 Ridgecrest Ln McCordsville IN 46055	IN	Sn/Adm	Holy Cross Indianapolis IN	(317)823-5801	SL	2007
Hauser Larry A	(414)659-1578 lehauser1511@att.net	4737 Maplewood Dr Bay City MI 48706	MI	EM			SL	1971
Hauser Leon E	(563)332-9810 hauserleco@msn.com	5621 Cavan Crossing St Bettendorf IA 52722	IE	EM			SPR	1969
Hauser Matthew J	(989)714-1367 mhauser@peacesaginaw.org	458 Foxboro Rd Saginaw MI 48638	MI	SMP	Peace Saginaw MI	(989)792-2581	SL-SMP	2016
Hauser Patrick T	(714)270-0248 hauserp@csl.edu	651 Pine Ave Brea CA 92821	PSW	EM			SL-SMP	2017
Hauser Paul A	(989)770-3397 basepaul3@yahoo.com	5786 Knoll Ct Saginaw MI 48603	MI	EM			SL	1983
Hauss Robert E	(828)896-5180 pastor_e@stpetersconover.org	2995 Shell Hollar Rd Claremont NC 28610	SE	SMP	Saint Peter's Conover NC	(828)256-2970	CQ	2019
Hauter Robert W	(219)510-7288 treborhw@protonmail.com	357 Bronk St Monte Vista CO 81144	RM	SP	Trinity Pueblo CO	(719)544-3016	FW	2005
Hawkins Daniel D	pastor@gpcmunford.org	288 Wooten Oaks Cir Munford TN 38058	MDS	SP	GracePoint Atoka TN	(901)840-2086	SL	1994
Hawkinson Mark A	(573)619-1270 markhawkinson1948@gmail.com	3470 Boeuf Lutheran Rd New Haven MO 63068	MO	EM			SPR	1975
Hayden Steven J	(515)360-5081 revshayden@gmail.com	109 Oakwood Dr. Eatonton GA 31024	FG	SP	Lake Oconee Eatonton GA	(706)485-4600	SL	1986

*Multiple Assignments (See Church Worker Locator for Additional Details)

See Page 53 for the Table of Abbreviations for key to District, Position, and Seminary abbreviations

**C =Candidate; EM = Emeritus; the date following the C is the month and year the Candidate status began

NAME	TELEPHONE NUMBER EMAIL	STREET ADDRESS CITY/STATE/ZIP	DISTRICT	POSITION/ STATUS**	WHERE SERVING	OFFICE PHONE	SEM/ PROGRAM	YR GRAD
Hayden Steven L	(217) 220-2487 pastorsteveh@hotmail.com	3340 State St Quincy IL 62301	CI	Sn/Adm	St John Quincy IL	(217)222-8579	SL	2000
Haydon Kenneth C	(479)253-7835 kchaydon@cox.net	8 Thomas Dr Eureka Spgs AR 72632	MDS	EM			SL	1968
Hayes Joshua J	(720)897-6829 joshua.hayes@lutheranclassical.org	1581 Serenity Ln Casper WY 82601	WY	Asst	Trinity Casper WY	(307)234-0568	SL	2011
Hayes Michael E Dr	(703)451-5855 michael.hayes@poplc.org		SE	Sn/Adm	Prince Of Peace Springfield VA	(703)451-5855	SL	2003
Hayman Mark C	(504)715-6984 markchayman@gmail.com	208 S Lark St Oshkosh WI 54902	SO	EM			Other	1975
Haynes Jason M	(970)926-3550 jason.graciousaviorchurch@gmail.com	P.O. Box 250 Edwards CO 81632	RM	SP	Gracious Savior Edwards CO	(970)926-3550	SL	1999
Haynes James M	haynes1213@aol.com	1215 Gage St Eagle NE 68347	NEB	EM			SL-SMP	2015
Hays Jerry D	(847)764-0599 jerry.hays@stpeterlcms.org	202 E Schaumburg Rd Schaumburg IL 60194	NI	Sn/Adm	St Peter Schaumburg IL	(847)885-3350	SL	2009
Hayter Benjamin M	(734)625-1023	415 N Walnut St Chebanse IL 60922	NI	SP	Zion Chebanse IL	(815)697-2212	SL	2022
Hayter Mathew A	(734)625-4483 pastor.mat@outlook.com	295 Lillian Ave Union MO 63084	MO	SP	St Paul Union MO	(636)583-2209	SL	2010
Hazel Shawn F	(503)769-6144 pastorshawn@calvarystayton.com	c/o Pilgrim Lutheran Church 5650 SW Hall Blvd Beaverton OR 97005	NOW	SP	Pilgrim Beaverton OR	(503)644-8697	SL	1997
Hazzard Christopher A	(863)619-6649	5509 Beverly Rise Blvd Lakeland FL 33812	FG	SP	Christ Lakeland FL	(863)682-7802	SL	2001
Headley Steven M	(512)284-1117 sheadley@gstx.org	484 Perryville Loop Liberty Hill TX 78642	TX	SMP	Good Shepherd Cedar Park TX	(512)258-6227	SL-SMP	2019
Hearn Fredrick C	fredrickhearn7@hotmail.com	4525 S Wigger St Marion IN 46953	IN	SP	Saint James Marion IN	(765)662-3092	FW	1993
Heath Timmothy W Jr	pastorheath@pm.me	1808 Japonica Ln Plano TX 75074	TX	Assoc	Faith Plano TX	(972)423-7447	FW	2013
Heaton William C	(314)534-8174 chrisheaton72@hotmail.com	1701 Plaza Dr Fulton MO 65251	MO	SP	St Pauls Fulton MO	(573)642-2856	SL	2018
Heck Kyle D Dr	(425)231-7679	P.O. Box 217 Granite Falls WA 98252	NOW	EM			SL	1992
Heckert Peter P	(262)251-8250 faithlutheran@faithgtown.com	c/o Faith Lutheran Church W172 N11187 Division Rd Germantown WI 53022	SW	SP	Faith Germantown WI	(262)251-8250	SL	2015
Heckmann Michael A	(806)685-4602 pastormheckmann@gmail.com	P.O. Box 446 Grant NE 69140	NEB	SP	Zion Grant NE	(308)352-4107	SL	2014
Heckmann Robert E Dr	(605)951-5307 roberteheckmann@gmail.com	27509 482nd Ave Canton SD 57013	SD	EM			SL	1984
Heckmann Peter T	(512)203-1635 peter.heckmann84@gmail.com	3909 Post Oak Rd Tyler TX 75701	TX	EM			SL	1992
Heckmann Joel T	(605)929-4608 revheckmann@gmail.com	5612 Wickershire Ln St Louis MO 63129	MO	S HS/C	Concordia Seminary Saint Louis MO	(314)505-7000	SL	2017
Heckmann Gary W	(702)232-8936 gwheckmann@netscape.net	1010 E Spring St #101 Cookeville TN 38501	MDS	EM			SL	1972
Heckmann John M	(254)986-2607 pastor@stpaulthegrove.org	1110 County Road 341 Gatesville TX 76528	TX	SP	St Paul The Grove TX	(254)986-2607	SL	1985
Hecksel Shawn R	servinhim13@yahoo.com	18635 Goldwater Rd Westfield IN 46062	IN	SMP	Cornerstone Carmel IN	(317)814-4252	SL-SMP	2021
Hedberg Carl R	(641)430-9211 hedberg@cltel.net	205 N Yorktown Pike Mason City IA 50401	IW	EM			SL	1981
Hedstrom Dale R	(308)991-7074 dalehedstrom@gmail.com	87515 440th Ave Lakefield MN 56150	MNS	SP	Holy Trinity* Lakefield MN	(308)991-7074	SL	2007
Hedt Frederick T III	(301)459-0028 fredhedt65@gmail.com	265 Sweet Bay Pl #27510 Carrboro NC 27510	SE	EM			SL	1974
Hedtke Thomas E	(319)721-6769 tmj@hedtke.org	23932 Basham Ln Anamosa IA 52205	IE	EM			SPR	1972
Hedtke Robert C	robert.hedtke@gmail.com	9045 Earlmont Dr Fort Wayne IN 46835	IN	EM			SPR	1973
Hedtke Scott R	scott@promisefw.com	1220 E Gump Rd Fort Wayne IN 46845	IN	Sn/Adm	Promise Fort Wayne IN	(260)493-9953	FW	2020
Heermann William G	(402)750-2061 wgheermann@gmail.com	2703 Bunker Ct Fremont NE 68025	NEB	EM			SL	2013
Heffelfinger John C Jr	(505) 239-4250 heffelfingerjohn9@gmail.com	7208 Keel Ave NW Albuquerque NM 87120	RM	EM			FW	1979
Hefta Donald R	(405)596-0956 heftadonald@gmail.com	14 Pintuerero Way Hot Springs Village AR 71909	MDS	SP	Faith Fairfield Bay AR	(501)884-3375	FW	1984
Heggen Michael J	(952)236-8146 mkheggen@gmail.com	15073 Dutchman Way Apple Valley MN 55124	MNS	EM			SL	1973
Heide Volker S	(203)245-6227 lcofmadison@aol.com	90 Fawn Brook Cir Madison CT 06443	NE	SP	Madison Madison CT	(203)245-4145	SL	1990
Heide Zelwyn C	701-794-8700 zelwyn.heide@gmail.com	2095 Highway 31 Hannover ND 58563	ND	SP	St Peter* Hannover ND	(701)794-8705	FW	2014
Heiden Dennis L	(507)382-0043	3766 Sioux Ln Madison Lake MN 56063	MNS	EM			SL	1983
Heiden Michael L	(586) 244-3492 mheiden85@gmail.com	9745 E Axle Ave Mesa AZ 85212	PSW	Assoc	Christ Greenfield Gilbert AZ	(480)892-8521	SL	2013
Heidt Brian F	(989)723-7643 brianheidt@msn.com	205 W Oliver St Owosso MI 48867	MI	SP	St Philip Owosso MI	(989)723-6238	FW	1993
Heien Donald J	don.heien@saints.org	63080 Dickey Rd Bend OR 97701	NOW	SMP	Trinity Bend OR	(541)382-1832	CQ	2019

*Multiple Assignments (See Church Worker Locator for Additional Details)
See Page 53 for the Table of Abbreviations for key to District, Position, and Seminary abbreviations
**C =Candidate; EM = Emeritus; the date following the C is the month and year the Candidate status began

NAME	TELEPHONE NUMBER EMAIL	STREET ADDRESS CITY/STATE/ZIP	DISTRICT	POSITION/ STATUS**	WHERE SERVING	OFFICE PHONE	SEM/ PROGRAM	YR GRAD
Heilman Mark T	(515)292-5005 mkheilman@aol.com	2010 Stevenson Dr Ames IA 50010	IW	Sn/Adm	Memorial Ames IA	(515)292-5005	SL	1984
Heilmann Steven J	(573)552-0076 pastorsteveh@outlook.com	459 Multrees Pl Smyrna TN 37167	MDS	EM			SL	1982
Heim Vernon F	(920)869-2777 zionrev@new.rr.com	749 Silver Creek Dr Oneida WI 54155	NW	EM			SL	1971
Heimbuck Joshua J	(314)223-6246 josh.heimbuck@gmail.com	c/o Grace Lutheran Church 660 Frances Ln Ashland OR 97520	NOW	SP	Grace Ashland OR	(541)482-1661	SL	2010
Heimer Jessten P	(815)451-0221 heimer.pastor@gmail.com	434 Mamie Eisenhower Ave Boone IA 50036	IW	Sn/Adm	Trinity Boone IA	(515)432-5140	FW	2021
Heimer Karl P Dr	(915)330-9064 karlheimer@yahoo.com	716 Horncastle Rd El Paso TX 79907	RM	EM			SPR	1971
Heimer Stephen E	(314)709-1193 stephenheimer@gmail.com	5025 Bellarina Dr Saint Louis MO 63129	MO	S Ex/S	Office of National Mission Saint Louis MO		SL	2011
Heimgartner Gail R	(618)614-2902 pastorrobert.rh54@gmail.com	417 W Grand Ave Carterville IL 62918	CI	EM			FW	2010
Heimsoth Jeffrey E	(989) 640-2200 pastor.jeff58@gmail.com	1213 W Taft Rd Saint Johns MI 48879	MI	Sn/Adm	Faith Grand Blanc MI	(810)694-9351	SL	1987
Hein Matthew C	(734)545-6123 matt.hein@newlifelutheran.net	5110 Highpoint Dr Swartz Creek MI 48473	MI	Sn/Adm	NewLife Community Swartz Creek MI	(810)655-3336	SL	2006
Hein Mark H		106 Willowwood Dr N Oswego IL 60543	NI	EM			FW	1992
Hein Mark E	(509)860-2688 albhein56@gmail.com	26903 W Maple Dr Buckeye AZ 85396	PSW	EM			SL	1986
Hein Carlton K	(720)610-7049 pastor@mzlc.org	620 Cantril St Apt B Castle Rock CO 80104	RM	SP	Mount Zion Castle Rock CO	(303)688-9550	SL	1993
Hein Jerrell P	(512)497-6580 jerrellh@gmail.com	301 Water Tower Rd San Marcos TX 78666	TX	Asst	Grace San Marcos TX	(512)392-4241	CQ	2020
Heine Jacob P	(402)405-6485 pastorheine@faithlutheran topeka.com	7224 SW 23rd St Topeka KS 66614	KS	Sn/Adm	Faith Topeka KS	(785)272-4214	SL	2006
Heine Mark G	(707)738-7976 markheine57@gmail.com	7696 Somerset Alcove Woodbury MN 55125	CNH	EM			SL	1988
Heinecke Timothy N	(651)429-1975 revheinecke@gmail.com	6000 148th St N Hugo MN 55038	MNS	SP	New Life Hugo MN	(651)429-1975	SL	2010
Heinecke Gerald D	pastor.heinecke@gmail.com	45 Chism Trl Batesville AR 72501	MDS	SP	Shepherd Hills* Horseshoe Bend AR	(870)793-3078	FW	2010
Heinecke Bradley D	bhein@juno.com	457 Saddle Ridge Dr Davenport FL 33896	FG	Asst	Zion Winter Garden FL	(407)743-5533	FW	1982
Heiney Timothy M	011 224 625 88 10 10 tim@guineamission.com	2282 Ramsgate Dr Henderson NV 89074	MI	EM			FW	1983
Heining James W Dr	(507)282-6955 jheining68@gmail.com	3380 Jasper Ct NE Rochester MN 55906	MNS	EM			SL	1976
Heinlein Dale V	(715)661-3975 4daleheinlein@gmail.com	10540 E Apache Trail Lot 57 Apache Junction AZ 85120	PSW	EM			FW	1984
Heinlein Paul L	(971)219-6152 heinlein@madboa.com	160 E Clarendon St Gladstone OR 97027	NOW	EM			SL	1990
Heino Jack D	(937)537-6222 jheino@stjohnsmarysville.org	12809 State Route 736 Marysville OH 43040	OH	Sn/Adm	St John's Marysville OH	(937)644-5540	SL	1988
Heins John L	(734)944-3200	5985 Bellwether Dr Saline MI 48176	MI	EM			SL	1988
Heins Paul C	(443)604-7231 pcheins@gmail.com	127 Couper Way Cartersville GA 30120	FG	EM			SL	1968
Heinsen Steven R	steveh@nowlcms.org	3476 Edith Ave Enumclaw WA 98022	NOW	SP	Peace* Kent WA	(253)631-3454	SL	1996
Heinz Benjamin L	(832)727-3135 heinzb@csl.edu	Athens Lutheran Church 710 Forrest Ave Athens TN 37303	MDS	SP	Athens Athens TN	(423)745-9419	SL	2025
Heinz Richard A	(773)420-7177 revfrheinz@gmail.com	621 W Commercial Ave Lowell IN 46356	IN	SP	Trinity Lowell IN	(219)696-9338	SL	1995
Heinze Ian M	(217)617-7947 ian.heinze1@gmail.com	227 E Market Havana IL 62644	CI	SP	St Paul Havana IL	(309)543-4850	SL	2022
Heise Matthew W Dr	(586)292-4575 mheise@lhfmissions.org	50470 Lancelot Dr Macomb MI 48044	MI	RSO	Lutheran Heritage Foundation Macomb MI	(800)554-0723	SL	2003
Heise Scott R	(281)496-0182 scottheise@sbcglobal.net	718 Country Place Dr Apt B Houston TX 77079	TX	SP	St Luke Houston TX	(281)442-2180	FW	2003
Heisinger Hans-Juergen W	(314)737-1125	5177 N 28th Ave # 10 Wausau WI 54401	NW	EM			SL	1979
Heithold Donavon W Jr	heithold1@tularosa.net	9921 Fm 2625 Hallsville TX 75650	TX	EM			SL	1997
Heitner David D	(580)606-1752 ddheitner@gmail.com	405 Regatta Rd Yukon OK 73099	OK	EM			FW	1986
Heitshusen Daniel W	(832) 727-3135 daniel.heitshusen@gmail.com	507 Walton St Carl Junction MO 64834	MO	SP	Grace Aurora MO	(417)678-3603	SL	2025
Heitshusen Scott E	(713)965-6761 scott@heitshusen.com	2204 Settlers Way Dr Sealy TX 77474	TX	SP	LifeBridge Sealy TX	(979)885-7270	SL	1996
Helbig Russell K	(919)259-0010 russ.helbig@gmail.com	6412 State Route 15 Addieville IL 62214	SI	EM			SL	1994
Held Joel J	joel@edgewaterlutheran.org	7283 Cottage Grove Dr Eastvale CA 92880	PSW	SP	Edgewater Eastvale CA	(478)919-6187	SL	2025
Heller Brian R Dr	(847)477-4656 Brian.Heller@lcms.org	c/o Lutheran Church-Missouri Synod 1333 S Kirkwood Rd Saint Louis MO 63122	MO	S Ex/S	The LCMS Corporate Saint Louis MO	(314)965-9000	FW	2016
Heller David R	drheller2000@yahoo.com	65 Cross Rock Dr Blue Ridge GA 30513	FG	EM			FW	1979

*Multiple Assignments (See Church Worker Locator for Additional Details)

See Page 53 for the Table of Abbreviations for key to District, Position, and Seminary abbreviations

**C =Candidate; EM = Emeritus; the date following the C is the month and year the Candidate status began

NAME	TELEPHONE NUMBER EMAIL	STREET ADDRESS CITY/STATE/ZIP	DISTRICT	POSITION/ STATUS**	WHERE SERVING	OFFICE PHONE	SEM/ PROGRAM	YR GRAD
Heller Richard A	(847) 571-7015 richardheller59@gmail.com	1832 W Crescent Ave Park Ridge IL 60068	NI		Northern Illinois District River Forest IL	(708)449-3020	FW	1985
Heller Toby H	(701)873-4223 revheller@westriv.com	500 3rd Ave NW P.O. Box 189 Beulah ND 58523	ND	SP	Zion* Glen Ullin ND	(701)348-3172	FW	1990
Hellert Alfred J	(317)286-3374 giselah@juno.com	965 Ironwood East Dr Brownsburg IN 46112	IN	EM			SL	1961
Helling Melbourne F	(605)338-7134 meladort@icloud.com	315 N Washington St P.O. Box 368 Viborg SD 57070	SD	EM			SPR	1962
Hellmers Clifford N Jr	(205)422-4951 vestluth@juno.com	238 Crest Lake Dr Hoover AL 35244	SO	EM			SL	1972
Hellmers Dwight D	(303)986-7155 dwighthellmers@yahoo.com	8263 White Fish Way Colorado Springs CO 80908	RM	EM			SPR	1974
Hellwege Allen D	(805)746-2880 adhellwege@gmail.com	1551 Tewsbury St Valparaiso IN 46385	IN	EM			SL	1967
Hellwege John P Jr	(314)808-5499 johnphellwege@gmail.com	315 Pcr 328 Farrar MO 63746	MO	SP	Zion* Crosstown MO	(573)824-5728	SL	1999
Hellwig Kurt W	mclcphx@gmail.com	3677 W Bryce Ct Phoenix AZ 85086	PSW	SP	Mount Calvary* Phoenix AZ	(602)230-1600	SL	2022
Helmer David E	dmhelmer1940@gmail.com	1877 N 4th St Seward NE 68434	NEB	EM			CQ	1979
Helmer Paul G	(913)515-9140 pandch41@yahoo.com	621 E Dogwood St Gardner KS 66030	KS	EM			SL	1967
Helmkamp Earl W	(217)774-3353 hkamp_5@yahoo.com	2028 Avignon Ct Saint Charles MO 63303	CI	EM			SL	1987
Helmke John E Sr	Johnhelmke37@icloud.net	227 Elgin Ave Apt 5e Forest Park IL 60130	NI	EM			SL	1963
Helms James H Jr	(585)610-8986 james.h.helmsjr@gmail.com	623 Elfin Ave Capitol Heights MD 20743	SE	SP	Holy Cross Greenbelt MD	(301)345-5111	CQ	2023
Hemenway Paul C	(217)481-4891 rev.hemenway@gmail.com	15804 Harts Mill Rd Edmond OK 73013	OK	Sn/Adm	Holy Trinity Edmond OK	(405)348-3292	SL	2007
Hemingway Jeffrey L	(281)761-8885 pastorhemingway@aol.com	25409 Ramrock Dr Porter TX 77365	TX	EM			FW	2002
Hemler Jonathan A	(314)397-9769 jon_kat_hemler@att.net	8527 Maylor Dr Affton MO 63123	MO	C08/2020			SL	2012
Hemme Seth R	(989)600-5343 pastorhemme@yahoo.com	1816 Rapanos Dr Midland MI 48642	MI	Assoc	Zion Auburn MI	(989)662-4264	SL	2004
Hemmer Jeffrey B	(618)632-6906 jeffhemmer@gmail.com	400 Guy St Caseyville IL 62232	SI	SP	Bethany* Fairview Heights IL	(618)632-6906	SL	2007
Hemmingson Gerald	(951)265-1290 jerryhemm@yahoo.com	2115 Pennsylvania Ave Joplin MO 64804	MO	EM			CQ	2017
Hempe Kevin D	(650)359-1550 oursaviorspacificacom@gmail.com	847 Dell Rd Pacifica CA 94044	CNH	SP	Our Savior's Pacifica CA	(650)359-1550	FW	2024
Hempeck Matthew P	(503)396-1873 phemp16@gmail.com	147 Vista De Oeste Palm Springs CA 92264	PSW	EM			SL	1992
Hemsath Robert W		95 Mary Lake Ct Huntsville TX 77320	TX	Sn/Adm	Faith Huntsville TX	(936)295-5298	SL	1996
Henderson Stephen P	(563)650-8047 shenderson@immanuel brookfield.org	N70w27524 Shady Oak Court Hartland WI 53029	SW	Sn/Adm	Immanuel Brookfield WI	(262)781-7140	SL	2006
Hendricks Dwayne R	(716)208-6838 dwaynehend@gmail.com	11014 Unser Ct Bakersfield CA 93306	CNH	SP	Prayer Bakersfield CA	(661)871-1289	SL	2013
Hendrickson Gary L	(580)603-2554 revgaryhendrickson@yahoo.com	105 7th St SE Little Falls MN 56345	MNN	EM			SL	1990
Hendrickson John C	(507)385-2024 jchendrickson@hotmail.com	219 Woodhaven Ln Mankato MN 56001	MNS	EM			CQ	2015
Hendrickson John H	(863)602-1046 nnjhen@aol.com	1020 Roselawn Ave W Roseville MN 55113	MNS	EM			SL	1968
Hendrickson Raymond V	(218)255-3300 eacdogcat@gmail.com	39536 Highway 65 Nashwauk MN 55769	MNN	EM			SL	1981
Hendry Thomas E Dr	sierrakitty-caesar@yahoo.com	7962 Elk Trail Yucca Valley CA 92284	PSW	EM			SPR	1972
Hengst Adam M	(952)495-4489 adam.hengst@oslcs.org	5039 Boulder Ln Chaska MN 55318	MNS	Sn/Adm	Our Savior Excelsior MN	(952)474-5181	SL	2012
Henke Gene G	gene.henke2@gmail.com	247 Burberry Glen Blvd Nolensville TN 37135	MDS	EM			FW	1978
Henkell James D	jim.henkell@psd-lcms.org	190 E Bluejay Dr Chandler AZ 85286	PSW	D Ex/S	Pacific Southwest District Irvine CA	(949)854-3232	SL	1998
Henkes Thomas P	(480)862-5048 tm5316@aol.com	9420 E Wapiti Trail Flagstaff AZ 86004	RM	SP	Shepherd Of Desert Page AZ	(928)645-0078	FW	2003
Henn Michael B	michael.henn@gmail.com	87 E Orange St Chagrin Falls OH 44022	OH	SP	Valley Chagrin Falls OH	(440)247-0390	SL	2008
Hennig James L	(217)793-4164 jhennig@trinitycentralia.org	22915 N Aut Ln Centralia IL 62801	SI	SP	Trinity Centralia IL	(618)532-2614	SL	1993
Henning Josef J	(260)466-3747 pastoremmanuelsoest@gmail.com	9335 Barkley Rd Hoagland IN 46745	IN	SP	Emmanuel Fort Wayne IN	(260)447-3005	FW	2002
Henning Roger B	(402)430-0804 mjroghenning@gmail.com	4401 Waterbury Ln Lincoln NE 68516	NEB	EM			CQ	1986
Henning Timothy J	(479)280-8245 tjcad5@suddenlink.net	707 W 18th Ter Russellville AR 72801	MDS	SP	Trinity Mena AR	(479)394-1290	FW	1999
Henningfield Craig W Dr	(303) 725-6760 pastorcraighenningfield@gmail. com	750 W 148th Ave #4321 Westminster CO 80023	RM	EM			SL	1986
Hennings Kenneth M	hennings622@gmail.com	3235 S. Purple Sage Dr. Chandler AZ 85248	PSW	EM			SL	1973
Hennings Luke N	(623)910-3865 luke@stlukemesa.com	8704 E Inca St Mesa AZ 85207	PSW	SP	St Luke Mesa AZ	(480)969-4414	SL	2007

*Multiple Assignments (See Church Worker Locator for Additional Details)
See Page 53 for the Table of Abbreviations for key to District, Position, and Seminary abbreviations
**C =Candidate; EM = Emeritus; the date following the C is the month and year the Candidate status began

NAME	TELEPHONE NUMBER EMAIL	STREET ADDRESS CITY/STATE/ZIP	DISTRICT	POSITION/ STATUS**	WHERE SERVING	OFFICE PHONE	SEM/ PROGRAM	YR GRAD
Henrichs Michael W	(414)587-3617 pastorhenrichs@gmail.com	6029 N Santa Monica Blvd Whitefish Bay WI 53217	SW	Sn/Adm	Our Savior Whitefish Bay WI	(414)332-4458	SL	1995
Henrichs Robert M	(314)822-2387 rmhenrichs@hotmail.com	1350 Wilton Ln Saint Louis MO 63122	MO	EM			SL	1976
Henry Travis M	(716)223-0496 travis.henry.8@us.af.mil	4100 Rock Springs Street Bldg. 4 Unit B Cheyenne WY 82001	OH	M Chap	Office of National Mission Saint Louis MO		SL	2022
Henry Donald P		7426 Holden Dr Fort Wayne IN 46835	IN	EM			FW-SMP	2019
Henry John C III	(507)235-8811 john.henryiii85@gmail.com	1623 170th St Fairmont MN 56031	MNS	SP	Zion* Fairmont MN	(507)436-5289	FW	2013
Henry Matthew R Dr	(208)957-9364 mhenry@friendshipcelebration.org	P.O. Box 1625 Meridian ID 83680	NOW	Sn/Adm	Friendship Meridian ID	(208)288-2404	SL	2004
Henry Patrick D	(520)906-2558 everus4@outlook.com	7760 S Caesar Dr Tucson AZ 85747	EN	EM			FW	1989
Henschel Marvin A	(405)570-6449 marvinhenschel@att.net	7707 W Britton Rd Apt 3202 Oklahoma City OK 73132	OK	EM			SL	1960
Henschen Nathan P	(605)216-9248 nathanpreachersd@gmail.com	P.O. Box 306 Bancroft NE 68004	NEB	SP	St Paul* Bancroft NE	(402)648-7689	SL	1996
Hensler David H	(810) 429-1789 dhenryh39@gmail.com	7336 Crystal Lake Dr. Apt. 9 Swartz Creek MI 48473	MI	EM			FW	1991
Hensley Adam D	(314)556-1185 a.d.hensley174@gmail.com	2 McCall Ter Clayton MO 63105	MO	S HS/C	Concordia Seminary Saint Louis MO	(314)505-7000	CQ	2022
Henze Gary J	(928)710-5880 garyhenze@gmail.com	9374 E Manzanita Cir Prescott Valley AZ 86314	PSW	EM			CQ	2019
Henze Richard S	(954)384-9096 scotthenze@bellsouth.net	14141 Harpers Ferry St Davie FL 33325	FG	SP	St Paul Weston FL	(954)384-9096	SL	2015
Henze Steven H	(281)923-0526 stevehenze3@gmail.com	1338 Chelshurst Spring TX 77379	TX	EM			SL	1981
Her Joel V	(414)559-0998 pastor.joelher@gmail.com	678 Johnson Parkway Saint Paul MN 55106	MNS	Assoc	Cornerstone White Bear MN	(952)239-9136	SL	2024
Her Richard X	richard.xai@gmail.com	c/o Hmong Lutheran Church 784 Jackson St St Paul MN 55117	MNS	SP	Hmong Saint Paul MN		SL	2016
Her Faiv Neng B	(414)722-2024 faivneng@yahoo.com	5326 W Crawford Ave Milwaukee WI 53220	SW	SP	Hmong Hope Milwaukee WI	(414)722-2024	SL-D	2003
Herald David D	(620)660-0150 david.herald@gmail.com	P.O. Box 154 207 5th St Yorktown IA 51656	IW	SP	St Paul Clarinda IA	(712)542-1505	SL	2010
Herb Daniel J	(513)727-3732 dan_herb@core.com	405 Eastline Dr Middletown OH 45044	OH	SP	Messiah Middletown OH	(513)422-2441	FW	2007
Herbert Scott E	(469)693-9683 chirev59@gmail.com	2118 Christine Drive Granbury TX 76048	TX	SP	Zion Tomball TX	(281)351-5757	SL	1995
Herberts Dean Z	(217)500-1986 rev.herberts@gmail.com	13234 N 2300th St Wheeler IL 62479	CI	SP	St John* Dieterich IL	(217)739-2252	SL	2012
Herbrich Rudy C	(920)268-9488 rubin2.rh@gmail.com	3805 Northwater Trl Denton TX 76226	TX	EM			SL	1972
Hercamp Jacob R	(812)344-4542 pastorhercamp@gmail.com	15316 Brantley Ln Noblesville IN 46060	IN	SP	Christ Noblesville IN	(317)773-3669	FW	2017
Herd Clifford L	herd917@hotmail.com	6234 Amber Brook Dr Hixson TN 37343	MDS	EM			SL	1969
Heren Thomas L Dr	(309)265-7174 pastorheren@gmail.com	524 Driftwood Ln Atkins IA 52206	IE	C01/2023			SL	2005
Hering William T	(503)407-0722 pastorbill@sheridantlc.org	20303 SW Tremont Way Beaverton OR 97007	NOW	SP	Trinity Sheridan OR	(503)843-4747	FW	1991
Hering Jeffrey P	(716)359-4248 jphcpm@rit.edu	93 Elaine Dr Rochester NY 14623	EA	EM			CQ	1979
Herman Darvin A	(864)879-6534 darvanne2@gmail.com	70 Oak St Apt 502 Tryon NC 28782	SE	EM			SL	1956
Herman Justin A	(714)614-7835 pastorherman@icloud.com	275 Hattie Ln Hamilton MT 59840	MT	SP	Grace Hamilton MT	(406)363-1924	FW	2006
Herman Luther S	(660)537-9816 lutherherman1999@gmail.com	685 Rankin Mill Ln Apt B Boonville MO 65233	MO	EM			SL	1967
Hermann Rory M	(904)982-5989	121 De Haven St St Augustine FL 32084	FG	EM			FW	1979
Hernandez Carlos Dr	(314)956-2005 prcarlos1941@yahoo.com	4150 Golden Pond Way Rncho Cordova CA 95742	CNH	EM			SL	1969
Hernandez Nelson O	(713)351-9986 nelo1881@hotmail.com	542 Road 5251 Cleveland TX 77327	TX	C12/2017			SL	2014
Herndon James N	(419)832-6047 jnhlcms@hotmail.com	14223 Harrison Rd Grand Rapids OH 43522	OH	EM			SL	1973
Herr Noel A	(320)815-5917 ps118.24letusrejoice@outlook.com	317 Brown St Jackson MN 56143	MNS	EM			SL	2001
Herrera Juan D Dr	(951)665-3418 angelena1@verizon.net	186 W 5th St San Jacinto CA 92583	PSW	SP	Fuente De Vida Hemet CA	(951)654-8691	HITSL	2005
Herring Robert G	(973)248-5161 bherring@mac.com	25 White Oak Dr Holiday Island AR 72631	MDS	EM			SL	1978
Herrmann John V	(916)965-1192 johnh123@gmail.com	7773 Greenridge Way Fair Oaks CA 95628	CNH	EM			SPR	1975
Herrod J R	(586)770-7731 bobherrod@att.net	111 Slate Ln Greer SC 29650	SE	EM			FW	1992
Hertel Benjamin D	(301)746-8170 prhertel@centurylink.net	209 N Main St Accident MD 21520	EA	SP	St John* Accident MD	(301)746-8466	FW	2011
Herter Paul W	(517)263-4317 ppaul.hope@tc3net.com	5653 Forrister Rd Adrian MI 49221	MI	SP	Hope Adrian MI	(517)263-4317	FW	1981
Hertwig Frederick C	(660)668-2414 fchert@hotmail.com	25809 Highway H Lincoln MO 65338	MO	EM			SL	1976
Herzberg Andrew E	(515) 371-3301 pastor@stjohns-mattoon.org	2960 Whitetail Dr Charleston IL 61920	CI	SP	St Johns Mattoon IL	(217)234-4923	FW	2014

*Multiple Assignments (See Church Worker Locator for Additional Details)

See Page 53 for the Table of Abbreviations for key to District, Position, and Seminary abbreviations

**C =Candidate; EM = Emeritus; the date following the C is the month and year the Candidate status began

NAME	TELEPHONE NUMBER EMAIL	STREET ADDRESS CITY/STATE/ZIP	DISTRICT	POSITION/ STATUS**	WHERE SERVING	OFFICE PHONE	SEM/ PROGRAM	YR GRAD
Herzberg Martin J II	(580)484-1312 herzbergmartin@yahoo.com	P.O. Box 110 Corona SD 57227	SI	RSO	Ongoing Ambassadors for Christ Greenville IL	(618)664-4056	FW	2016
Herzing Keith A	(440)539-5642 kherzing@icloud.com	17101 Ridge Point Cir Strongsville OH 44136	OH	EM			CQ	2018
Hess Joel A	joelahess@gmail.com	c/o St James Lutheran Church 2101 N Fremont St Chicago IL 60614	NI	Sn/Adm	Saint James Chicago IL	(773)549-1615	SL	2001
Hess Karl R	(541) 213-4979 revkhess@gmail.com	3335 SW Antler Ridge Ln Redmond OR 97756	NOW	SP	Emmaus Redmond OR	(541)508-1927	FW	2006
Hess Russell I	(916)481-5743 prhess@msn.com	4832 Andrew Circle Carmichael CA 95608	CNH	EM			SL	1983
Hess Steven J	(239)834-2337 runrev@gmail.com	6441 Emerald Pines Cir Fort Myers FL 33966	FG	EM			SL	1980
Hesse Jeffrey J	(262)389-0119 jeff.hesse15@gmail.com	4280 Pleasant Hollow Rd Jackson WI 53037	SW	SMP	St John West Bend WI	(262)334-4901	SL-SMP	2012
Hesse Mark W		401 Maple St Aurora IN 47001	IN	SP	St John Aurora IN	(812)926-3337	FW	2010
Hesse George L	(970)324-9029 hessefam@gmail.com	2107 35th Avenue Ct Greeley CO 80634	RM	EM			FW	2001
Hesse Brian J Dr	(254) 799-3211 pastorhesse@splcwaco.com	10225 Creekside Lane Waco TX 76712	TX	Sn/Adm	St Paul* Bellmead TX	(254)799-3211	SL	2001
Hessel Kenneth N	(402)657-6164 knhessel@gmail.com	16905 M Cir Omaha NE 68135	NEB	SP	Our Redeemer Springfield NE	(402)253-2893	SL	1987
Hessler William W	(989)598-4072 pastorwwh@yahoo.com	3312 Wintergreen Dr E Saginaw MI 48603	MI	EM			SL	1977
Hesterman Jeffrey A	(904)535-3552 jahesterman@gmail.com	2001 Wynfield Dr Prattville AL 36067	SO	SMP	Bethlehem Prattville AL	(205)365-2088	SL-SMP	2016
Hesterman Justin T	justin.hesterman@gmail.com	2585 Cty Rd 8 SE Saint Cloud MN 56304	MNN	SP	Messiah Sartell MN	(320)252-5883	FW	2013
Hetherington Dale L	(317)605-5536 glcpastordale@gmail.com	8307 Sheffield Ave. Dyer IN 46311	IN	SP	Grace Dyer IN	(219)865-1137	CQ	2017
Hetzel Brian J	(816)699-2265 brianhetzel@pointeofhope.org	1108 SW Granite Creek Dr Blue Springs MO 64015	MO	SP	Pointe of Hope Blue Springs MO	(816)220-2609	SL	1992
Hetzner Mark W	(586) 854-5634 hetzmark16@gmail.com	26208 Captains Lndg Chesterfield MI 48051	MI	EM			CQ	1983
Heupel Timothy J Sr Dr	(402)968-0237 timothyheupel@gmail.com	812 Van Es Pkwy Apt 3 Eau Claire WI 54703	NW	EM			FW	1978
Heuser Philip M	(815)440-5511 philheuser@aol.com	20354 Hickory Hills Rd Sterling IL 61081	NI	SP	Our Savior Sterling IL	(815)772-4345	SL	1998
Heuser Stephen M	(630)766-5109 pastor@zionconcord.org	863 S Church Rd Bensenville IL 60106	NI	SP	Zion Bensenville IL	(630)766-1039	FW	2001
Hewitt Martin A	(509)466-8844	11916 N Stevens Ct Spokane WA 99218	NOW	EM			SL	1963
Heyliger Wilton E Dr	(404)936-6628	530 Dalrymple Rd Sandy Spgs GA 30328	FG	SP	Incarnate Word Stone Mountain GA	(404)936-0628	FW	2003
Hickey Aaron J			EN	Assoc	Hales Corners Hales Corners WI	(414)529-6700	SL	2021
Hicks Steven B	(646)339-9279 prazhm116@gmail.com	11612 204th St Saint Albans NY 11412	EN	SP	Redeemer Saint Albans NY	(718)525-3233	CQ	2015
Hiesterman Joel S	(785)543-2865 jhiesterman@juno.com	1000 Prospect St Phillipsburg KS 67661	KS	EM			FW	1979
Higgins Nathan W	(320)281-0715 pastorhiggins@emmlp.org	623 3rd Ave SE Long Prairie MN 56347	MNN	IndC P	Minnesota North District Brainerd MN	(218)829-1781	FW	2002
Highley Joseph C	(580)762-1111	1101 North 4th St Ponca City OK 74601	OK	SP	First Ponca City OK	(580)762-1111	SL	2020
Hildebrand Justin M	pastor.hildebrand@gmail.com		NEB	SP	Christ* Bazile Mills NE	(402)358-5298	FW	2017
Hildebrandt Bradford W	(239)293-3261 faithnaples.fl@naples.org	114 Northeast Dr Brick NJ 08724	EN	SMP	Faith Naples FL	(239)434-5811	SL-SMP	2012
Hildebrandt Russell C Dr	(817)475-8853 pastorrch@gmail.com	6939 Regatta Dr Grand Prairie TX 75054	TX	EM			FW	1985
Hildebrandt Barry C	(423)877-7954	16 Johnson Blvd Chattanooga TN 37415	MDS	EM			SL	1973
Hile John A	(586)872-4310 johnhile@epicchurch.com	42206 Jo Ed Dr Sterling Heights MI 48314	EN	SP	Epic Shelby Township MI	(248)606-4348	SL	2011
Hileman Joshua M	joshh@blcbls.org		NOW	SP	Bethlehem Kennewick WA	(509)582-5858	SL	2020
Hiles Adam R	(618)301-6303 ahiles076@duck.com	841 Southgate Dr Freeburg IL 62243	SI	SP	Christ Our Savior Freeburg IL	(618)539-5664	FW	2025
Hilgendorf William A	(907)740-3060 whilge@yahoo.com	280 Forest St Fredonia WI 53021	SW	EM			CQ	2018
Hilgert David W	(352)989-5768 dwhilgert@outlook.com	712 Barefoot Bay Loop Groveland FL 34736	FG	EM			SL	1984
Hilken Dennis R	(661)319-1650 drhilken@icloud.com	5687 Yerba Anita Dr San Diego CA 92115	PSW	EM			FW	1993
Hill Martin R	revmartinhill@gmail.com	5104 Douglas St Ponca NE 68770	NEB	SP	Trinity Martinsburg NE	(402)945-2160	FW	2021
Hill Robert T	(701)435-2305 stpaulw@daktel.com	305 Gibson St P.O. Box 195 Wimbledon ND 58492	ND	SP	St Paul* Kensal ND	(701)435-2873	FW	2005
Hill Robert B Jr	(301) 830-0271 RBurkHill@aol.com	1 Apple Orchard Ln Clover SC 29710	SE	EM			SPR	1971
Hill Richard L	(757)434-2786 hillrichl@aol.com	246 Mt Vernon Ave Portsmouth VA 23707	S	EM			SL	1970
Hill Nathaniel W	(979)966-8036 pastor@stmichaelswinchester.org	704 Frio St Winchester TX 78945	TX	SP	St Michael's Winchester TX	(979)242-3444	SL	2012

*Multiple Assignments (See Church Worker Locator for Additional Details)
See Page 53 for the Table of Abbreviations for key to District, Position, and Seminary abbreviations
**C =Candidate; EM = Emeritus; the date following the C is the month and year the Candidate status began

NAME	TELEPHONE NUMBER EMAIL	STREET ADDRESS CITY/STATE/ZIP	DISTRICT	POSITION/ STATUS**	WHERE SERVING	OFFICE PHONE	SEM/ PROGRAM	YR GRAD
Hill John E	(307)237-2829 jhill@wylcms.org	3630 Navarre Rd Casper WY 82604	WY	DP	Wyoming District Casper WY	(307)265-9000	FW	1990
Hill James M	(586)722-3996 pastorh@christoursavior.org	21 Kendrick St Mount Clemens MI 48043	MI	Sn/Adm	St Stephen* Detroit MI	(313)841-7940	FW	2005
Hill Hurshel D	(785)452-0760	Colwich Gardens 300 E Chicago Ave Colwich KS 67030	KS	EM			SPR	1962
Hill Gary E	(440)539-5306 revgehill@gmail.com	7941 Lime Lane Parma OH 44129	OH	EM			SL	1977
Hill Andrew R	pastorhill307@gmail.com	208 College Court Rock Springs WY 82901	WY	SP	Emmanuel* Green River WY	(307)875-2598	FW	2023
Hill Christopher T	(314)236-7498 christopherthill927@gmail.com	633 Rayburn Ave Saint Louis MO 63126	MO	Assoc	Salem Saint Louis MO	(314)352-4454	SL	2023
Hille Kirk A Dr	kirk.a.hille@gmail.com	1430 S Samson Trl McCall ID 83638	NOW	SP	Our Savior McCall ID	(208)634-5905	SL	1999
Hillenbrand Philip J	(414)531-2461 philip.hillenbrand@gmail.com	11331 N Riverland Rd Mequon WI 53092	SW	EM			SL	1985
Hillenbrand Richard P Dr	989-295-0014 RPHofMI@gmail.com	2507 Lindell Rd Sterling Heights MI 48310	MI	EM			SL	1982
Hiller Michael J	(303)693-8416 mhillclimb@aol.com	3075 S Quintero Way Aurora CO 80013	RM	EM			FW	1978
Hiller Robert M	bhiller@clcfamily.org	15880 Camino Conejo Valley Center CA 92082	PSW	Sn/Adm	Community Escondido CA	(760)739-1650	SL	2006
Hillmer J C	(612)385-4783 hillmerca@gmail.com	7555 Bailey Rd Apt 407 Saint Paul MN 55129	SW	EM			Other	1959
Hills Keith M Jr	(325)236-3422 keithmhills@gmail.com	1712 E 14th St Sweetwater TX 79556	TX	SMP	Faith Sweetwater TX	(325)235-2773	SL-SMP	2016
Hillyer William J	(612)723-2606 pastorhillyer@gmail.com	9086 Xenia St Loretto MN 55357	MNS	SP	Eternal Hope Brooklyn Park MN	(763)424-8245	SL	2004
Hilpert Matthew R	(808)347-2876 m.hilpert@glcpasadena.org	19 Milburn Circle Pasadena MD 21122	SE	SP	Galilee Pasadena MD	(410)255-8236	SL	2003
Hilsabeck Howard R	(713)812-1470	2121 Pinegate #2212 Houston TX 77008	TX	EM			SL	1957
Hilton Alan R	(775)426-8067 revhilton1@outlook.com	143 Denio Dr Dayton NV 89403	CNH	EM			FW	2007
Hinchey Donald F Dr	dfhinchey@aol.com	1961 Pikes Peak Dr Loveland CO 80538	FG	EM			SL	1969
Hinckley Robert M Jr	(605)413-5671 rmhjr2@gmail.com	825 Main St Deadwood SD 57732	SD	SP	Grace* Deadwood SD	(605)578-2219	SL	1996
Hiner Eric D	(817)863-0146 ehiner@hopelubbock.com	3206 Langford Ave Lubbock TX 79407	TX	Sn/Adm	Hope Lubbock TX	(806)798-2747	SL	2007
Hingst Carl D	pastorhingst@redeemerkokomo.org	206 Sandy Ct Kokomo IN 46901	IN	Assoc	Our Redeemer Kokomo IN	(765)453-0969	FW	2019
Hinkle Chris N Dr	(319)850-1395	300 Roy El Ct Wapello IA 52653	IE	EM			SL	1981
Hinkle Marvin R	(260)387-6851	2818 Hazelwood Ave Fort Wayne IN 46805	IN	EM			CQ	1979
Hinners Gregory S	(605)228-0407 gshenricus@gmail.com		SD	SP	Our Redeemer* Philip SD	(605)859-2721	FW	1998
Hinojosa Alexander J	(313)244-6324 alexander.hinojosa@ctsfw.edu	4332 Lanette Dr Waterford MI 48328	MI	SP	Prince Peace Farmington Hills MI	(248)553-3380	FW	2025
Hinrichs Brett M	(847)553-8296 pastor@mtcalvarydecatur.org	97 Pennsylvania Dr Decatur IL 62526	CI	SP	Mount Calvary Decatur IL	(217)428-0641	SL	2014
Hinrichs Daniel L	(715)445-2998 dp.hinrichs@att.net	E273 N Rollofson Lake Rd Scandinavia WI 54977	NW	EM			SPR	1972
Hinrichs Kenneth N	(715)558-1054 revkenhi@yahoo.com	5185 David Dr Oshkosh WI 54904	NW	EM			FW	1992
Hinton Daniel A	pr.hinton@christlutheranlubbock.org		TX	SP	Christ Lubbock TX	(806)799-0162	FW	2011
Hintz Gregory M	(847)764-0611 ghintz53@gmail.com	N2044 Manley Rd Hortonville WI 54944	SW	Sn/Adm	New Hope Neenah WI	(920)725-4354	SL	2009
Hintz Larry L	(626)210-8082 hintz2@hotmail.com	1870 N Margaret St Appleton WI 54913	NW	EM			SL	1980
Hintz David W	(920)227-7915 revdwhintz@hotmail.com	1707 Wood Ln Green Bay WI 54304	SW	Asst	Good Shepherd Two Rivers WI	(920)793-1716	FW	1994
Hintze David J	(512)820-7872 djhintze@msn.com	1105 Sedona Leander TX 78641	TX	EM			FW	1977
Hintze Kevin J	(817)455-1594 kevin.hintze@zionwalburg.org	6001 Fm 1105 Georgetown TX 78626	TX	Assoc	Zion Georgetown TX	(512)863-3065	SL	2009
Hintzman Harold R Jr	(307)426-4950 thefishingrev@outlook.com	2017 Carob Ave Cheyenne WY 82007	WY	EM			SL	1975
Hinz Paul R	(313) 349-9542 revpaulhinz@gmail.com	5765 Tittabawassee Rd Saginaw MI 48604	MI	EM			SL	1991
Hinz Timothy M	(757)293-8164 timhinz@aol.com	4028 E Providence Rd Williamsburg VA 23188	SE	C07/2016			SL	1991
Hinz Fredric G	(507)317-9634 fghinz1227@gmail.com	100 Lincoln Ave Gaylord MN 55334	MNS	D Ex/S	Minnesota South District Burnsville MN	(952)435-2550	CQ	2001
Hinz David W	(360)438-5281 hinzdj@comcast.net	1835 Circle Ln SE Apt 410 Lacey WA 98503	NOW	EM			SL	1956
Hinz David W	(320)763-6508 pastorhinz@trinitysr.org	32027 Northwood Ln Saint Cloud MN 56303	MNN	Sn/Adm	Trinity Sauk Rapids MN	(320)252-3670	SL	2006
Hinz Clarence R	(586)731-3495 ed_hnz@hotmail.com	Northpoint Village 45201 Northpointe Blvd Apt 402 Utica MI 48315	MI	EM			SPR	1976
Hinze Dennis A		528 W 13th St Traverse City MI 49684	MI	EM			FW	1979

*Multiple Assignments (See Church Worker Locator for Additional Details)
See Page 53 for the Table of Abbreviations for key to District, Position, and Seminary abbreviations
**C =Candidate; EM = Emeritus; the date following the C is the month and year the Candidate status began

NAME	TELEPHONE NUMBER EMAIL	STREET ADDRESS CITY/STATE/ZIP	DISTRICT	POSITION/ STATUS**	WHERE SERVING	OFFICE PHONE	SEM/ PROGRAM	YR GRAD
Hipenbecker Dennis W	(414)403-9012 dennis.hipenbecker@yahoo.com	12220 W Ripley Ave Wauwatosa WI 53226	SW	EM			SPR	1965
Hippe Victor V Dr	(253)838-7500 vichippe@msn.com	1871 Parkview Dr NE Tacoma WA 98422	NOW	EM			SL	1971
Hirsch Bradley W	(314)477-2471 bradhirsch61@gmail.com	421 Parkshire Place Dr Dardenne Pr MO 63368	MO	EM			SL	2003
Hirsch John M Dr	(512)769-6736 jhirsch0227@gmail.com	3700 Lenior St #202 Columbia MO 65201	TX	EM			SPR	1972
Hirsch Thomas W Dr	(541)974-6397 drtdub@hotmail.com	618 Bunker Rd Sutherlin OR 97479	NOW	EM			SL	1975
Hirssig Scott S	(920) 629-2949 schirssig@gmail.com	2216 Meadow Way Manitowoc WI 54220	SW	EM			SL	1999
Hirst John C	(863)763-5042 johnhirst26@gmail.com	PMB 6126 5753 Highway 85 N Crestview FL 32536	FG	EM			SL	1981
Hjulberg Avery E	(951)398-8037 avery.hjulberg@gmail.com	3509 SW Burlingame Rd. Topeka KS 66611	KS	SP	Christ Topeka KS	(785)266-6263	SL	2024
Hoag Samuel R	(253)275-8146 samhoag15@gmail.com	8507 Landsowne Rd Henrico VA 23229	SE	Assoc	Trinity Richmond VA	(804)270-4626	SL	2024
Hoag Douglas E	(815)485-6973 douglashoag@gmail.com	508 N Cedar Rd New Lenox IL 60451	EN	SP	Trinity New Lenox IL	(815)485-6973	FW	1993
Hobbie Ronald L	(320)226-8799 hobbieron@gmail.com	504 Main St Anamoose ND 58710	ND	EM			FW	2001
Hobratschk Donald M Dr	(813)634-5547 donhobscc@gmail.com	3824 Cardenal Ave Ruskin FL 33573	FG	EM			SL	1966
Hobratschk John A	(573) 659-3368 jahobratschk@gmail.com	1216 Jefferson St Jefferson Cty MO 65109	MO	EM			SL	1970
Hobratschk Ralph W	(713)899-5364 rhobratschk@gmail.com	2406 San Augustine Ln Friendswood TX 77546	TX	EM			SL	1976
Hobson Jay G	(620)238-3894 pastorjayhobson@gmail.com	320 Deer Creek Ln Skiatook OK 74070	OK	SP	Shepherd of the Hill Skiatook OK	(918)895-2611	FW	2011
Hochgrebe Ryan W	ryanh@timothylutheran.com		MO	Assoc	Timothy Blue Springs MO	(816)228-5300	SL	2013
Hodges Jonathan E	(518)755-6261	222 Skylands Rd Ringwood NJ 07456	NJ	SP	Christ King Ringwood NJ	(973)962-6384	SL	2011
Hodges Leon A	(712)243-2323 ljhodges@metc.net	1013 E 3rd Street Pl Atlantic IA 50022	IW	EM			SPR	1962
Hodson John L	(815)547-1128 cadfael44@frontier.com	6992 Cora Lee Dr Belvidere IL 61008	NI	EM			SL	1998
Hoech Kip J		1417 Hanson Dr Normal IL 61761	PSW	S Miss	Office of International Mission Saint Louis MO		SL	2002
Hoefer Herbert E	herbhoefer@gmail.com	2412 NE 163rd Ave Portland OR 97230	NOW	EM			SL	1974
Hoeferkamp Harold R	(410)474-3597 gskamphoefer@hotmail.com	1503 S Walnut St Apt 512 Seymour IN 47274	SO	EM			CQ	1980
Hoehler David J	(618)708-0652 davidjhoehler@gmail.com	1024 Primrose Dr Jefferson City MO 65109	MO	EM			SL	2010
Hoehne Ronald E	(660)395-9852 revron@cvalley.net	1106 Overbrook Dr Macon MO 63552	MO	EM			CQ	1978
Hoehner Mark R Dr	(636)922-2774 mark.hoehner@chapelofthecross lutheran.org	715 Napa Ln Saint Charles MO 63304	MO	Sn/Adm	Chapel of the Cross Saint Peters MO	(636)928-5885	SL	2000
Hoehner Robert P Dr	(314)303-3444 rphoehner@gmail.com	244 Strayhorn Dr Saint Peters MO 63376	MO	EM			SL	1972
Hoehner Matthew J Dr	(314)541-0072 matt.hoehner@gmail.com	230 W Glendale Rd Webster Groves MO 63119	MO	Pro Stf	Christ Community Kirkwood MO	(314)822-7774	SL	2002
Hoelscher Lance M	(715) 302-1351 pastorlance@mtoliveweston.org	2403 Edgewood Ave Weston WI 54476	NW	Sn/Adm	Mount Olive Weston WI	(715)359-5546	SL	2003
Hoelter Joel A	(715)462-9350 hoelternorth@gmail.com	11153 N Louies Landing Rd Hayward WI 54843	NW	EM			SL	1979
Hoelter Mark E	(503)936-4916 mark@hoelter.net	2139 NE 158th Pl Portland OR 97230	NOW	EM			SL	1972
Hoem Josemon T	(920)912-0825 jhoem@stpaulsfw.org	1910 Worthington Dr Fort Wayne IN 46845	IN	Sn/Adm	St Pauls Fort Wayne IN	(260)423-2496	FW	2012
Hoemann James P	hoemannj@csl.edu	4009 NW Sol Dr. Blue Springs MO 64015	MO	S HS/C	Concordia Seminary Saint Louis MO	(314)505-7000	SL	1999
Hoener Kenneth E	724-524-1928 kehoener@aol.com	148 Marwood Rd Apt 1201 Cabot PA 16023	EA	EM			SPR	1956
Hoeppner Seth M	(920)285-9879 shoeppner4faithlutheran@ gmail.com	1109 Louisa St Watertown WI 53098	EN	SMP	Faith Watertown WI	(920)261-8060	SL-SMP	2017
Hoerr Steven R	(810)420-0048 pastor@stpeterfairhaven.org	125 N Water Rd Marine City MI 48039	MI	SP	St Peter Fair Haven MI	(810)765-8161	FW	2010
Hoerth Jason A	(724) 816-9282 jhoerth@zionlc.org	c/o Zion Lutheran Church 1175 Birney Ln Cincinnati OH 45230	OH	Sn/Adm	Zion Cincinnati OH	(513)231-2253	SL	2003
Hoese Terry E	(616)361-1384 tehoese@yahoo.com	1435 Mayfield Ct NE Grand Rapids MI 49525	MI	EM			CQ	1979
Hoesman C W Dr	(734)645-5695 hoesmanbb@gmail.com	289 Block St Frankenmuth MI 48734	MI	EM			SPR	1970
Hoff Clinton S	(760)217-4188 hoffinsky@gmail.com	4416 E Holland Ave Fresno CA 93726	CNH	Sn/Adm	Peace Fresno CA	(559)222-2320	CQ	2006
Hofferber Mark J	(314) 798-3198 markhofferber@gmail.com	5503 Genesta Walk Saint Louis MO 63123	MO	EM			SL	1995
Hoffman Frederick H	(410)877-4096 fhoffman7@gmail.com		SE	SP	St John Blenheim Glen Arm MD	(410)592-8018	CQ	2015

*Multiple Assignments (See Church Worker Locator for Additional Details)
See Page 53 for the Table of Abbreviations for key to District, Position, and Seminary abbreviations
**C =Candidate; EM = Emeritus; the date following the C is the month and year the Candidate status began

NAME	TELEPHONE NUMBER EMAIL	STREET ADDRESS CITY/STATE/ZIP	DISTRICT	POSITION/ STATUS**	WHERE SERVING	OFFICE PHONE	SEM/ PROGRAM	YR GRAD
Hoffman Robert A	(847)857-8015 roberthoffman647@gmail.com	6010 Deguise Ct. Rochester Hills MI 48306	MI	SP	St Stephen Waterford MI	(248)673-6621	SL	2009
Hoffman Peter	(630)306-4010 pastorpete51@gmail.com	10552 Roxbury Ln Jacksonville FL 32257	FG	EM			CQ	1994
Hoffman Zachary E	(309)634-5976 Holy-Cross@hclutheranchurch.org	1536 18th St NE Sauk Rapids MN 56379	MNN	Sn/Adm	Holy Cross Saint Cloud MN	(320)251-8416	SL	2010
Hoffman Charles R	(231)582-9301 pastor.clcboyne@gmail.com	c/o Christ Lutheran Church 1250 Boyne Ave Boyne City MI 49712	MI	SP	Christ Boyne City MI	(231)582-9301	SL	2011
Hoffman Brandt E Sr	(541)252-5756	1404 NW Whipple Ave Roseburg OR 97471	NOW	SP	St Johns Sutherlin OR	(541)459-3701	SL	2008
Hoffman Paul W Dr	(440)885-4857 pjhoff49@gmail.com	7900 Hollenbeck Cir Parma OH 44129	OH	EM			SL	1975
Hoffman Joshua W	(715)891-2743 joshhoffman@stjohnsnya.org	700 Martingale Dr Nya MN 55368	MNS	SMP	St John Norwood Young America MN	(952)467-2740	SL-SMP	2023
Hoffmann Paul G	(408)723-3004 hoffmann.paul.45@gmail.com	5386 Southbridge Ct San Jose CA 95118	CNH	EM			SL	1971
Hoffmann Bruce A	(715)325-7737 maruce@solarus.net	1332 Apache Cir Nekoosa WI 54457	NW	EM			SPR	1972
Hoffmann Gregory E		N1577 Washington Ave Lake Geneva WI 53147	NI	EM			FW	1982
Hoffmann Mark J	(480)356-0777	20248 E Hummingbird Dr Queen Creek AZ 85142	PSW	SP	Christ Coolidge AZ	(520)723-7428	SL	2004
Hoffmann Matthew J		1100 Garden St Park Ridge IL 60068	NI	Sn/Adm	St Andrews Park Ridge IL	(847)823-6656	SL	2003
Hoffmeyer Alex W	(847) 848-5110 alex.hoffmeyer1@gmail.com	492 Park St Coloma MI 49038	MI	SP	Salem Coloma MI	(269)468-6567	SL	2017
Hoffstetter Gary R	(573)243-6651 ghoffstetter@charter.net	713 Wedge Ln Jackson MO 63755	MO	EM			SL	1976
Hofman Marion C	(970)835-7987 mchofman36@gmail.com	21203 Apple Ln Eckert CO 81418	RM	EM			SL	1961
Hofmann Hunter	(262)375-3819 hunterhofmann@sbcglobal.net	1731 12th Ave Grafton WI 53024	SW	EM			FW	1994
Hofmann Michael L	(915)500-2993 pastorhofmann@gmail.com	215 N Osage St Girard KS 66743	KS	SP	Trinity Girard KS	(620)724-8895	SL	2018
Hofmann Ronald F		7573 Jeffery Ave S Cottage Grove MN 55016	MNS	EM			SPR	1964
Hofmeister Jon F	(215) 570-3880 jon.hofmeister@comcast.net	26 Sugar Hill Dr Telford PA 18969	EA	Asst	Christ Memorial Malvern PA	(610)644-4508	CQ	2018
Hoft Peter D	revhoft@hotmail.com		IE	Sn/Adm	Park View* Eldridge IA	(563)285-9035	SL	2000
Hoger Allen C	(316)214-9511 gladispir617@proton.me	4649 Farmstead St Bel Aire KS 67220	KS	EM			CQ	1979
Hoham Theodore A	theodore.hoham@gmail.com	3810 Charles Ave Alexandria VA 22305	EN	Assoc	Immanuel Alexandria VA	(703)549-0155	FW	2019
Hohe John W	pastor@graceofstcloud.org	1520 Cypress Woods Circle Saint Cloud FL 34772	FG	SP	Grace Saint Cloud FL	(407)892-4653	SL	1982
Hohnstadt Kevin A	(248) 495-8405 pastorkevin@bslc.com	533 SW 6th Ct Gresham OR 97080	NOW	Sn/Adm	Beautiful Savior Portland OR	(503)788-7000	SL	2017
Hojnacki Scott E	(701)690-4697 trinitypastor@htc.net	10241 S Prairie Rd Red Bud IL 62278	SI	SP	Trinity Red Bud IL	(618)282-2883	FW	2004
Hokana Steven C Dr	(913)360-0396 steven.hokana@lcms.org	3916 Cambridge Crossing Dr Saint Charles MO 63304	MO	S Ex/S	The LCMS Corporate Saint Louis MO	(314)965-9000	SL	1987
Hoke James L Jr Dr	(402)261-5211 chaphoke@hotmail.com	7005 Shamrock Rd Unit 309 Lincoln NE 68506	EN	EM			FW	1980
Holaday Robert W Dr	(956)460-6913 revholaday@gmail.com	3303 Miami Ave Wichita Falls TX 76309	TX	SP	Peace Waco TX	(254)420-4729	CQ	2000
Holden Jason S	(618)521-8006 jholden@oslcdale.org	2113 W Sunset Dr Carbondale IL 62901	SI	Sn/Adm	Our Savior Carbondale IL	(618)549-1694	SL	2012
Holder Christopher S	(214)535-1894 rom58@sbcglobal.net	11520 Abston Ln Dallas TX 75218	TX	SMP	Bethel Dallas TX	(214)348-0420	SL-SMP	2015
Holder Scott Dr	(913) 708-4749 pastor.scott.holder@gmail.com	3105 W 135th St Leawood KS 66224	KS	SP	Lord Of Life Leawood KS	(913)681-5167	SL	2001
Holdorf Zachary J	(715)846-8108	3637 Spring Arbor Rd Jackson MI 49201	MI	SP	Redeemer Jackson MI	(517)750-3100	SL	2012
Holdorf Kenneth P	(972)377-5952 kbholdorf@gmail.com	9815 Asheboro St Frisco TX 75035	TX	EM			SL	1964
Holland Richard A	(407)542-1143	2133 Fox Sparrow Ct Oviedo FL 32765	FG	EM			SPR	1962
Holland Roger A	(612)730-7778 rogholland@aol.com	6348 156th St W Apple Valley MN 55124	MNS	EM			SL	1969
Hollar Eric C	(828)244-7201 hollar76@yahoo.com	5759 Bolick Rd Claremont NC 28610	SE	Sn/Adm	Bethel Claremont NC	(828)459-7378	SL	2003
Hollar William H Jr	(757)871-3540 hhollar@hotmail.com	420 Cypress View Ave Little River SC 29566	SE	EM			FW	1979
Holle Brian G	(618)585-3606 revholle@sbcglobal.net	615 S 1st St Hiawatha KS 66434	KS	SP	St Paul* Fairview KS	(785)742-3995	SL	2004
Hollender David E	(989)550-9998 dmh3738@gmail.com	4267 Casey Drive Lambertville MI 48144	MI	EM			SPR	1966
Holleway George D IV	(713)677-4141 george@forterra.church	18619 Admiration Dr Cypress TX 77433	TX	SMP	CrossRoad Katy TX	(281)398-6464	SL-SMP	2023
Hollibaugh Karl D	(402)309-0824 revdochollibaugh@gmail.com	c/o St James Church 1415 E Highway 30 Gonzales LA 70737	SO	SP	Saint James Gonzales LA	(225)644-2432	SL	1993
Holling Ronald E	reholling44@gmail.com	9715 Valley View Dr La Vista NE 68128	NEB	SP	St John Omaha NE	(402)451-2441	SL	1970

*Multiple Assignments (See Church Worker Locator for Additional Details)
See Page 53 for the Table of Abbreviations for key to District, Position, and Seminary abbreviations
**C =Candidate; EM = Emeritus; the date following the C is the month and year the Candidate status began

NAME	TELEPHONE NUMBER EMAIL	STREET ADDRESS CITY/STATE/ZIP	DISTRICT	POSITION/ STATUS**	WHERE SERVING	OFFICE PHONE	SEM/ PROGRAM	YR GRAD
Hollingsead Benjamin A	(651)323-3293 pastorbenh@gmail.com	404 4th St NW Aitkin MN 56431	MNN	SP	St Paul Eden Valley MN	(320)453-2472	CQ	2021
Hollmann Joshua D Dr	joshua.hollmann@mail.mcgill.ca	195 Worth St New York NY 10013	AT	SP	True Light* New York NY	(212)962-1482	SL	2005
Holls Joel M	(313)330-5008 joholls@aol.com	14555 Cleveland Ave Allen Park MI 48101	EN	SP	Christ Our Redeemer Allen Park MI	(313)429-3085	SPR	1976
Holm Daniel A	(951)837-5262 daniel_holm@yahoo.com	15319 Adobe Way Moreno Valley CA 92555	PSW	SMP	Grace Rialto CA	(909)875-3163	FW-SMP	2017
Holm Michael H	rvmicholm@outlook.com	4502 Chestnut Ridge Rd NE Cedar Rapids IA 52411	IE	EM			FW	1984
Holman Raymond D	pastor.rholman@gmail.com		IN	C08/2023			SL	2014
Holmen Michael G	(507)236-3605 rev.michael.holmen@gmail.com	302 Victoria St Fairmont MN 56031	MNS	Assoc	St Paul Fairmont MN	(507)238-9491	FW	2010
Holmes Jonathan E	(870) 509-3111 jonny.rev@icloud.com	813 E 2nd St De Witt AR 72042	MDS	SP	St Paul* Gillett AR	(870)548-2554	FW	2012
Holoubek Scott L	(715)780-7169 bgtfica@gmail.com	P.O. Box 22 Phillips WI 54555	NW	C10/2024			SL	2012
Holowach James R	(601)454-0686 jimorsusan@yahoo.com	311 N West St Lake City IA 51449	IW	EM			FW	2004
Holschuh Edward B III	817-614-2657 rev.holschuh@gmail.com	199 Kipahulu Dr. Bastrop TX 78602	TX	SP	Epiphany Bastrop TX	(512)907-0717	FW	2017
Holst Robert A	(651) 395-6573 holst@csp.edu	733 Selby Ave Apt 112 Saint Paul MN 55104	MNS	EM			SL	1961
Holstein Bruce E	holsteinbhm@gmail.com	635 Hummingbird Ln Whiteland IN 46184	IN	EM			SPR	1974
Holstein Gilbert J	(316)683-0489	2608 E Clover Ln Wichita KS 67216	KS	EM			SL	1961
Holsten Robert W	(201)727-4542 pstrbb@aol.com	417 High St Closter NJ 07624	NJ	EM			SL	1984
Holt Benjamin T	(618)645-2388 btholt3@gmail.com	1600 N Sycamore Ave Apt 307 Roswell NM 88201	SI		Southern Illinois District Belleville IL	(618)234-4767	FW	2012
Holt Paul V	510-295-3142 paulholt4722@yahoo.com	405 E 745 S Wolcottville IN 46795	CNH	EM			SPR	1975
Holt James A	(630)433-6712 jamie.holt@stmarkslife.org	355 N Lincoln St Batavia IL 60510	NI	Sn/Adm	St Mark Saint Charles IL	(630)584-8638	SL	2013
Holthus Allen D	(952)236-8036 alba.holt@charter.net	17875 Glasgow Way Lakeville MN 55044	MNS	EM			SL	2001
Holthus Daniel G	(307)262-2973 pastordanholthus@gmail.com	1037 Dundee Casper WY 82609	WY	EM			FW	1999
Holtman Steven D	(309)369-2975 SDHOLTMAN@gmail.com	1912 Freedom Dr Melbourne FL 32940	S	EM			SL-SMP	2019
Holtorf Paul C	(402)643-7495	1437 N 1st St Seward NE 68434	NEB	S HS/C	Concordia University Nebraska Seward NE	(402)643-3651	SL	1991
Holtzen Merlin D	merlinholtzen@gmail.com	5430 Stephanie Ct Lincoln NE 68516	NEB	EM			CQ	1994
Holyer John M	(419)784-6983 jmmh01@yahoo.com	31 Rowe Blvd Annapolis MD 21404	SE	SP	St Paul Annapolis MD	(410)268-2400	SL	2006
Holz Richard W	(952)443-4709 rwholz44@gmail.com	5527 Bourbeuse Cmn # 6 Weldon Spring MO 63304	MNS	EM			SL	1982
Holzer William H	(979)451-1648 pastorholzer@gracelutheran brenhamtx.org	3112 Wood Creek Rd Brenham TX 77833	TX	Assoc	Grace Brenham TX	(979)836-3475	SL	1989
Holzerland Timothy A	(313)885-7202 pastortim91@yahoo.com	4363 Kensington Ave Detroit MI 48224	EN	SP	Shepherd King West Bloomfield MI	(248)626-2121	SL	1991
Homan Martin J	revmjhoman@gmail.com	4160 N Emma Dr Bloomington IN 47404	IN	EM			SL	1980
Homan Timothy M	thecubfan@gmail.com	398 Mount Tom Rd Bishop CA 93514	PSW	SMP	Mammoth Lakes* Mammoth Lakes CA	(760)934-4051	SL-SMP	2023
Honeycutt Ryan L	(918)960-4328 revryanhoneycutt@gmail.com	23121 Bessie Blvd Claremore OK 74019	OK	SP	Redeemer Claremore OK	(918)341-1429	SL	2008
Hong Jason J	520-977-2638 pastorjason@crosspointlutheran church.org	575 N Pecan Canyon Ln Sahuarita AZ 85629	EN	SP	Crosspoint Sahuarita AZ	(520)977-2638	SL	2001
Hong Young H Dr	(213)384-2295 revyounghong@hotmail.com	107 Mustang Irvine CA 92602	PSW	EM			KO	1970
Hood John A	(614)607-3265 revjhood@att.net	1670 Holderby Rd Huntington WV 25701	OH	EM			SL	1994
Hood William E	bhood@genesisone.com	2383 N Waterberry St Orange CA 92865	PSW	S HS/C	Concordia University Irvine Irvine CA	(949)854-8002	SL-SMP	2013
Hoogerhyde Richard S	richardhoogerhyde@yahoo.com	105 E Youngs Ct Midland MI 48640	MI	EM			FW	1988
Hoogland Kevin J	(715)218-9819 kevinhoogland73@gmail.com	W5640 County Road Ff Merrill WI 54452	NW	SP	Trinity Boulder Junction WI	(715)385-2267	SL	1984
Hook David J	(520)777-4401 david@hookcentral.com	13599 E Cienega Creek Dr Vail AZ 85641	PSW	SP	Christ Vail AZ	(520)468-7075	SL	2007
Hoover Chad E		7205 Bayhead CV Fort Wayne IN 46835	IN	Tchr	Concordia Fort Wayne IN	(260)483-1102	FW	2004
Hoover Curtis R	pastorcurthoover@gmail.com	2879 Carters Creek Station Rd Columbia TN 38401	MDS	Sn/Adm	Faith Thompsons Station TN	(615)791-1880	FW	2006
Hoover Frederick M Jr	(219)617-3469 pastor@christmemorial.us	274 Paoli Pike Malvern PA 19355	EA	Sn/Adm	Christ Memorial Malvern PA	(610)644-4508	SL	1999
Hoover Kenneth D	(217)549-1739 kdhoover56@gmail.com	101 W Edgewood St Morton IL 61550	CI	EM			SL	1983

*Multiple Assignments (See Church Worker Locator for Additional Details)
See Page 53 for the Table of Abbreviations for key to District, Position, and Seminary abbreviations
**C =Candidate; EM = Emeritus; the date following the C is the month and year the Candidate status began

NAME	TELEPHONE NUMBER EMAIL	STREET ADDRESS CITY/STATE/ZIP	DISTRICT	POSITION/ STATUS**	WHERE SERVING	OFFICE PHONE	SEM/ PROGRAM	YR GRAD
Hopf Lee A	(478)284-5975 hopfl@trinityklein.org	5201 Spring Cypress Rd Spring TX 77379	TX	Sn/Adm	Trinity Klein Klein TX	(281)376-5773	SL	2016
Hopfensperger Bryan L	revhopfensperger@gmail.com	E8193 Sanders Rd Bessemer MI 49911	NW	SP	Trinity* Bergland MI		SL	2000
Hopkins James P	(617)536-8851 James.Hopkins@FLC-Boston.org	299 Berkeley Street Boston MA 02116	NE	Sn/Adm	First Boston MA	(617)536-8851	FW	2015
Hopkins Theodore J Dr	tedhopkins@stpaulannarbor.org	2704 Maize Loop Saline MI 48176	MI	Sn/Adm	St Paul Ann Arbor MI	(734)665-9117	SL	2011
Hopkins Paul G	(217)273-8430 paul.hopkins@ctsfw.edu	614 Wolverton Dr Fort Wayne IN 46825	IN	S HS/C	Concordia Theological Seminary Fort Wayne IN	(260)452-2100	FW	2005
Hopkins Robert D	(715) 313-2218 rev.robert.hopkins@gmail.com	P.O. Box 58 Cadott WI 54727	NW	SP	St John* Cadott WI	(715)289-4521	FW	2016
Hoppe Hector E Dr	(636)236-3514 hectorhoppe@gmail.com	717 Rockridge Dr Manchester MO 63021	MO	EM			VB	1977
Hoppe Paul T	(913)938-5495 pthoppe@msn.com	606 N Sycamore St Gardner KS 66030	KS	EM			SL	1972
Hoppe Philip C	pastor@ihoppe.com	825 E 5th St Colby KS 67701	KS	SP	Trinity Colby KS	(785)462-3497	SL	2003
Hormachea Juan L	(303)627-9358 pastorjuanh@comcast.net	16255 Plover Pl Parker CO 80134	RM	SP	Cordero de Dios Denver CO	(303)579-6564	CQ	1987
Hormann David L	(218)451-0541 revdaveh@gmail.com	10850 Grunwald Ave SW Howard Lake MN 55349	MNS	SP	St John Winsted MN	(320)485-2522	SL	2003
Horn Jeffrey P	(818)312-8586 revjeffhorn@gmail.com	1087 W Country Club Ln Escondido CA 92026	PSW	SP	Gloria Dei Escondido CA	(760)743-2478	FW	1996
Horn Russell L Dr	(360)698-7778 rlh@horn-net.com	3460 NE Arrowhead Dr Bremerton WA 98311	NOW	EM			SL	1993
Horn David K	(952)200-9724 davehorn@burningbushleague.com	321 E Michigan St #b Marquette MI 49855	FG	Assoc	Bethlehem Jacksonville Beach FL	(904)249-5418	SL	1986
Horne Brent S	(815)326-8176 pastor@parishmusic.org	20 Depot St Seward NE 68434	NEB	SP	St Paul Malcolm NE	(402)796-2396	FW	2016
Hornig Edward R	(334)821-4461 ehornig@earthlink.net	446 S Gay St Auburn AL 36830	SO	EM			SL	1970
Horsman Jonathan R	(863)512-3652 jonathanhorsman@gmail.com	2045 Charleston Lane Bartow FL 33830	FG	SP	Redeemer Bartow FL	(863)512-3652	SL	2002
Horstmeyer Kirk P	bchjen57@gmail.com	1925 Volkman Rd Evansville IN 47725	IN	SP	Immanuel Evansville IN	(812)867-5088	FW	1984
Horstmeyer Paul A	paulhorstmeyer@gmail.com	8205 Carolwood Ln Woodridge IL 60517	NI	Assoc	Trinity Lisle IL	(630)964-1272	SL	2020
Horton Christopher P	(651)423-2149 pastorhorton@frontier.com	14385 Blaine Ave E Rosemount MN 55068	MNS	SP	Saint John Rosemount MN	(651)423-2149	FW	2011
Hosch Edward III	(620)794-3191 edwardhosch@yahoo.com	520 West One St Kahului HI 96732	CNH	Sn/Adm	Emmanuel Kahului-Maui HI	(808)877-3037	FW	2011
Hotopp Mark A	(214)284-6539 pastormarkh@yahoo.com	1345 E. Fm 544 Wylie TX 75098	TX	Assoc	Tree Of Life Garland TX	(972)226-6086	SL	2005
Hotopp Roger A	(210)269-4805 chaplainrogerhotopp@yahoo.com	121 High Oak Universal Cty TX 78148	TX	SP	Grace Seguin TX	(830)379-1690	FW	1979
Houck Linford D	(352)600-9957 lhouck2@tampabay.rr.com	14001 Pimberton Dr Hudson FL 34667	FG	EM			CQ	2008
Hougard Donald T	(262)512-1310 pastor@benediction-lcms.org	N122 W12692 Westwood Rd Germantown WI 53022	SW	Sn/Adm	Benediction Milwaukee WI	(414)463-9158	FW	1988
Houge Claude G	(402)739-3491 claudehouge@msn.com	3656 Vermilion Ct N Eagan MN 55122	MNS	EM			SL	1996
Hough Ralph C	(330)417-2303 prchr44@gmail.com	c/o Ascension Lutheran 8888 County Road 64 Daphne AL 36526	SO	SP	Ascension Daphne AL	(251)626-7500	FW	2003
House Thomas W	(580)423-7353 revhouse1@yahoo.com	1607 N James St Guymon OK 73942	OK	SP	St Paul Texhoma OK	(580)423-7353	FW	1996
Houser Glenn D Dr	(509)843-7068 ghouser28@hotmail.com	P.O. Box 875 Pomeroy WA 99347	NOW	EM			FW	1986
Houser Philip G		23247 New Maple Ridge Rd Blackduck MN 56630	MNN	SP	Trinity Lake George MN	(218)699-3693	CQ	1996
Hovel Le Roy K	(913)980-1485 lee.hovel@gmail.com	13316 W 172nd St Overland Park KS 66221	KS	EM			SL	1972
Hovland G G	(608)571-3360 greg@pastorhovland.com	850 Armstrong St Portage WI 53901	SW	Sn/Adm	St Johns Portage WI	(608)742-9000	SL	1997
Howald Gregory J	(541)572-0156 howaldgreg@gmail.com	257 Miller Ln Myrtle Point OR 97458	NOW	SP	Saint James Myrtle Point OR	(541)572-5665	CQ	2016
Howard Daniel C	(586)549-6196 pastordan@hopewarren.com	31415 Saratoga Ave Warren MI 48093	MI	Sn/Adm	Hope Warren MI	(586)979-9055	SL	2020
Howard Joel R Dr	(815)347-5833 revjoelhoward@gmail.com		SW	Sn/Adm	Grace Menomonee Falls WI	(262)251-0670	SL	2005
Howe Andrew J	(989)798-4965 pastor.howe@mountcalvaryga.org	207 Ousley Way Perry GA 31069	FG	Sn/Adm	Mount Calvary Warner Robins GA	(478)922-1418	SL	2016
Howe Danlias F	(407)314-2961 danliashowe2018@gmail.com	3835 NE 13th Ave Ocala FL 34479	EN	SMP	Trinity Ocala FL	(352)840-0711	SL-SMP	2020
Howe Paul F	(512)517-6078 paulfhowe@icloud.com	30701 Berry Creek Dr Georgetown TX 78628	TX	EM			SPR	1972
Howell Jeffrey P		17340 Greenbay Ave Lansing IL 60438	NI	SMP	St Paul Chicago IL	(773)721-2350	FW-SMP	2011
Howell Christopher N	(510)520-9010 pastorchowell@gmail.com	21127 Military Road Seatac WA 98198	NOW	SP	Beautiful Savior Seattle WA	(206)246-9533	SL	2016
Howell Colby C	(208)599-3974 colbycharleshowell@gmail.com	N84 W16299 Donald Ave Menomonee Falls WI 53051	SW	Assoc	Immanuel Brookfield WI	(262)781-7140	SL	2022
Hower Joshua M			NOW	C08/2017			SL	2003

*Multiple Assignments (See Church Worker Locator for Additional Details)
See Page 53 for the Table of Abbreviations for key to District, Position, and Seminary abbreviations
**C =Candidate; EM = Emeritus; the date following the C is the month and year the Candidate status began

NAME	TELEPHONE NUMBER EMAIL	STREET ADDRESS CITY/STATE/ZIP	DISTRICT	POSITION/ STATUS**	WHERE SERVING	OFFICE PHONE	SEM/ PROGRAM	YR GRAD
Hower Stephen D	howerstl@gmail.com	1632 Misty Hollow Ct Wildwood MO 63038	MO	EM			FW	1978
Howlett Joseph F	(409)651-4751 howlettrev@gmail.com	115 N Mable Ave Apt 107 Sioux Falls SD 57103	SD	EM			FW	1985
Hoyer Benjamin	(407)371-2925 ben@hclm.org	960 Paul Hoyer Way Lake Mary FL 32746	S	Asst	Holy Cross Lake Mary FL	(407)333-0797	SL	2008
Hoyer Horst I	(216)398-5552 pfarrerhh@aol.com	1723 Tampa Ave Cleveland OH 44109	OH	EM			SL	1955
Hoyer Joel F	joelfhoyer@icloud.com	250 Cleveland St E Coopersville MI 49404	MI	SP	Grace Coopersville MI	(616)837-7831	SL	1985
Hricko Mark A	(301)384-4394 markhricko@yahoo.com	15300 New Hampshire Ave Silver Spring MD 20905	SE	Sn/Adm	St Andrew Silver Spring MD	(301)384-4394	FW	1985
Hromowyk Wesley T	(716)531-2700		OH	Sn/Adm	Zion Columbus OH	(614)444-3456	NESC	2014
Hsu Will C	(714)761-3517 willchsu@icloud.com	5445 Riva Ct Cypress CA 90630	PSW	EM			CQ	1998
Hsu Kenneth G	(712)898-2728 kghhsu@yahoo.com	19185 Colonial Trail Farmington MN 55024	MNS	SP	Our Savior Rosemount MN	(651)423-2580	SL	2002
Huang Luke S	(909)861-2740	23300 Golden Springs Dr Ste A Diamond Bar CA 91765	PSW	SP	Mt Calvary Diamond Bar CA	(909)861-2740	CQ	2005
Hubbard Bradley B	(269)832-7256 bhubbard@stlorenz.org	137 Kingsbrook Drive Frankenmuth MI 48734	MI	Sn/Adm	St Lorenz Frankenmuth MI	(989)652-6141	SL	2004
Hubbard Lloyd A	(660)382-5380 pastor_al@aol.com	17328 Destiny Loop Princeton MO 64673	MO	SP	St John Chillicothe MO	(660)646-5944	SL	1992
Hubbard Roger R	(515)661-7300 hoosierhub@aol.com	137 Kingsbrook Dr Frankenmuth MI 48734	MI	EM			FW	1984
Huber Timothy L	(209) 296-3161 trinitytim@aol.com	18901 Leona Ln Pine Grove CA 95665	CNH	EM			SPR	1974
Huber David G	(734)459-8464 dghuber@aol.com	46761 Strathmore Rd Plymouth MI 48170	MI	EM			SL	1967
Huber Edward R	(301)934-5365 edhuber51@verizon.net	9855 Bon Air Pl Faulkner MD 20632	SE	SMP	Grace La Plata MD	(301)932-0963	CQ	2018
Huber John G Dr	(619)507-0768 johngeorgehuber@aol.com	1111 Ontario St Apt 317 Oak Park IL 60302	NI	EM			SL	1958
Huber Terell O	(402)358-0771	42792 260th St Emery SD 57332	SD	EM			FW	1982
Hudak David P	davidphudak@gmail.com	150 W Evergreen St W Jefferson NC 28694	SE	EM			SPR	1976
Huddle Raymond C	(772)567-0329 rchuddle38@att.net	185 12th Ave Vero Beach FL 32962	SO	EM			CQ	1969
Hudson Daniel K	(262)229-7617 hudsondk6@sbcglobal.net	N73w26656 Thousand Oaks Dr Lisbon WI 53089	SW	C12/2021			SL	2003
Hudson Douglas	(904)704-7482 Doug.Hudson@SmithHudson.com	229 Willow Lake Dr. Leesburg GA 31763	FG	EM			SL	2017
Hudspith Allan E	(334)740-8650 spithal@aol.com	10219 Windtree Lane Charlotte NC 28215	SO	EM			SL	1994
Huebel Glenn E	(817)657-6621 gandmhueb@gmail.com	6812 Mesa Dr N RICHLND HLS TX 76182	TX	EM			FW	1980
Huebner Michael W	pastor.huebner@gmail.com		IN	SP	Our Redeemer Lexington KY	(859)299-9615	SL	2008
Huebner Wayne K	(314)352-4454 waynehuebner@slcas.org	8343 Gravois Rd Saint Louis MO 63123	MO	Sn/Adm	Salem Saint Louis MO	(314)352-4454	SL	1992
Huehn Jonathan P	(920) 684-3989 pastorhuehn@redeemermanty.com	1712 Menasha Ave. Manitowoc WI 54220	SW	Sn/Adm	Redeemer Manitowoc WI	(920)684-3989	FW	2009
Huelle Denis E	(360)509-4870 dhuelle@outlook.com	1340 Lakehurst Dr NW Bremerton WA 98312	NOW	EM			FW	2006
Huelsman Dale B	(440)935-4953 dbhuelsman@gmail.com	247 Forest Park Dr Lagrange OH 44050	OH	EM			FW	1983
Huenink James E	(708)205-3480 pastorhuenink@youhaveaplace.com	1005 Merritt Dr El Cajon CA 92020	EN	SP	First El Cajon CA	(619)444-7444	SL	2008
Hues Daniel J	(559)696-3861	11032 E Crown Ridge Clovis CA 93819	CNH	SP	Emmanuel Clovis CA	(559)298-0725	Other	2013
Hues Ronald W	(503)845-4300 huesrw@hotmail.com	620 St Marys Ave Mount Angel OR 97362	NOW	EM			FW	1976
Huesmann Bernhard J			SO	SP	Grace Pensacola FL	(850)476-5667	FW	1991
Huff Mark L	(513)284-2696 pastor@faithporthuron.org	825 Virginia Ave Marysville MI 48040	MI	SP	Faith Port Huron MI	(810)985-5733	SL	2015
Huffines Warren L	(618)604-3779 huffines43w@yahoo.com	6455 Nottingham Ave Saint Louis MO 63109	S	EM			SL	1999
Huffman Zachary R	(765) 860-7212	815 Sarasota Dr Seymour IN 47274	IN	Assoc	Redeemer Seymour IN	(812)522-1837	SL	2021
Hufford Steven M	(630)290-9773 marty@peacehome.org	1n138 Darling St Carol Stream IL 60188	NI	Sn/Adm	Peace Lombard IL	(630)627-1101	SL	1995
Huggins Marvin A	(314)401-5759 marvinh@pobox.com	3507 Clubland Dr Marietta GA 30068	FG	EM			SL	1970
Hughes Michael W	(419)571-9078 mikeandcory29@hotmail.com	3088 Plesantwood Dr Fruitport MI 49415	MI	SP	St Matthew Spring Lake MI	(616)846-2490	CQ	2023
Hughes Joseph W III Dr	(217)898-9063 j_w_hughes@hotmail.com	4460 Victor Point Rd NE Silverton OR 97381	NOW	SP	Calvary Stayton OR	(503)769-6144	CQ	2010
Hughey Barry S Dr	(314)640-4830 bstevehughey@gmail.com	10616 Hickory Crest Ln Columbia MD 21044	SE	EM			SL	1968
Hugo William D	(763)788-9427 rev.billhugo@gmail.com	4226 7th St NE Columbia Hts MN 55421	MNS	SP	St Matthew Columbia Heights MN	(763)788-9427	SL	1996

*Multiple Assignments (See Church Worker Locator for Additional Details)
See Page 53 for the Table of Abbreviations for key to District, Position, and Seminary abbreviations
**C =Candidate; EM = Emeritus; the date following the C is the month and year the Candidate status began

NAME	TELEPHONE NUMBER EMAIL	STREET ADDRESS CITY/STATE/ZIP	DISTRICT	POSITION/ STATUS**	WHERE SERVING	OFFICE PHONE	SEM/ PROGRAM	YR GRAD
Hulett Raymond A	(818)613-6012 raymondahulett@yahoo.com	34390 Thornhill Ct Fremont CA 94555	EN	SP	Hope Fremont CA	(510)793-8691	FW	2021
Hulke Steven A	(715)544-1142 stol@chartermi.net	3633 Prais St Stevens Point WI 54481	NW	Sn/Adm	St Paul Stevens Point WI	(715)344-5660	SL	1987
Hull Robert C	(704)787-4999 roberthull1687@yahoo.com	20 Kirkland Branch Rd Bryson City NC 28713	SE	SP	Good Shepherd Callao VA	(804)529-5948	FW	2008
Hull Christopher J	(309)287-5902 luther1546@gmail.com	1191 Stacy Ln Macomb IL 61455	CI	SP	Immanuel Macomb IL	(309)833-5483	FW	2010
Hull Deon L	(815)501-0433 dlhull5@gmail.com	3327 Homestead Dr Fort Pierce FL 34945	FG	SP	Peace Okeechobee FL	(863)763-5042	SL	2024
Hullinger Robert N	(513)641-1024 ohionews12@gmail.com	1739 Bella Vista St Cincinnati OH 45237	OH	EM			SL	1958
Hulvey Kirk S	(253)854-3240 pastor@lutheranchurchofthe cross.net	23810 112th Ave SE Kent WA 98031	NOW	SP	Of the Cross Kent WA	(253)854-3240	SL	2013
Hummel Edward M	(636)916-5222 ehummel768@gmail.com	3614 W Clay St Saint Charles MO 63301	MO	EM			SL	1968
Humphrey Kenneth L	(308)631-8431 kennethlhumphrey@outlook.com	2311 Stone St Falls City NE 68355	NEB	SP	St Paul* Falls City NE	(402)245-4643	FW	2009
Huner Kenneth A	(734)395-4945 ken.huner@michigandistrict.org	10715 Warner Rd Milan MI 48160	MI	SP	Trinity Pinckney MI	(734)878-5977	SL	1978
Hunsaker Mark A	(417)860-2504 mark@gospelers.org	7304 Bucknell Dr Austin TX 78723	TX	Assoc	Christ King Kingwood TX	(281)360-7936	SL	2015
Hunt Clifford D	(618)476-9221 candmhunt@gmail.com	813 M And O Station Rd Millstadt IL 62260	SI	EM			SPR	1963
Huntington Dennis E	(317)787-7571 dshuntington2053@gmail.com	2053 E Legrande Ave Indianapolis IN 46203	IN	EM			SPR	1975
Huntley Michael J	(251)635-4994 pastormike@epiphanylc.org	1946 Treetop Dr Castle Rock CO 80109	RM	Asst	Epiphany Castle Rock CO	(303)688-4435	CQ	2023
Hunze Timothy R	(615)414-1097 timhunze@gmail.com	7504 Thornwood Ct Mount Juliet TN 37122	MDS	SMP	Emmanuel Hermitage TN	(615)883-7533	CQ	2018
Hurley Thomas R	(415)752-7331 sfthurley@gmail.com	841 32nd Ave San Francisco CA 94121	CNH	SP	Resurrection San Rafael CA	(415)479-1334	CQ	2017
Hursh Terry N Dr	(260)304-3279 revhursh@gmail.com	7235 Pine Lake Rd Fort Wayne IN 46814	EN	EM			CQ	1993
Hurst Derrick N	(937)209-0321 pastord@livingwordgalena.com	4944 Township Rd 179 Marengo OH 43334	OH	SP	Living Word Galena OH	(740)965-3335	SL	2002
Huscher Frederick J	(951)928-9313 chaplainfred13@gmail.com	27650 Benigni Ave Romoland CA 92585	PSW	EM			SPR	1964
Huse Thomas N	(480)747-4557	13102 Marshall Ln Tustin CA 92780	PSW	SMP	Peace Santa Ana CA	(714)731-2226	SL-SMP	2019
Huss John A	(805) 489-2708 pastor@peacearroyogrande.com	244 N Oak Park Blvd Arroyo Grande CA 93420	CNH	SP	Peace Arroyo Grande CA	(805)489-2708	SL	2006
Huston Mark T	(903)603-5071 holycrosscanton@yahoo.com	c/o Holy Cross P.O. Box 851 Canton TX 75103	TX	SP	Holy Cross Canton TX	(903)603-5071	FW	2015
Hutson David L	(785)476-7532 1stjohn@ruraltel.net	P.O. Box 24 Kensington KS 66951	KS	SP	First St John Kensington KS	(785)476-2246	SL	1981
Hutter Erwin M	(313)539-4400 ehutter@sbcglobal.net	179 N Tuscola Rd Bay City MI 48708	MI	SP	Pilgrim Essexville MI	(989)893-7224	SL	2006
Hutton Aaron L	(920)664-1540 rev.hutton@gmail.com	521 Danville Dr Lincoln NE 68510	NEB	Assoc	Christ Lincoln NE	(402)483-7774	SL	2009
Hyatt Gregory D	(641) 218-4028 ghyatt12@gmail.com	211 N. Catherine St. Bay City MI 48706	MI	SP	St John Pinconning MI	(989)879-2377	FW	1994
Hyvonen Steven D	(715)584-6908 steve32749@hotmail.com	N 12025 Moore Rd Bessemer MI 49911	NW	EM			FW	1994
Iadicicco Augie J	(480)620-5170 pastoraugie@iadicicco.net	1757 Skimmer Ct Carlsbad CA 92011	PSW	EM			SL	2001
Iannelli Mike A Jr Dr	(636)947-8010 pastormikeossc@gmail.com	703 Hidden Lake Dr Saint Peters MO 63376	MO	SP	Our Savior Saint Charles MO	(636)947-8010	SL	2002
Iben Douglas A Dr	(425)999-1877 douglas.iben@gmail.com	23725 NE Salal Pl Redmond WA 98053	NOW	EM			CQ	1981
Ikanih Christian O Dr	(414)467-2642 chrisikanih4@gmail.com	3269 Burchhaven Trace Powder Springs GA 30127	FG	EM			CQ	2004
Ill Peter W	(618)615-7341 pastorpeterill@gmail.com	503 E Washington St Millstadt IL 62260	SI	Sn/Adm	Trinity Millstadt IL	(618)476-3101	SL	2010
Imlah Peter R		209 E Wilson Ave Lombard IL 60148	NI	SMP	St John Lombard IL	(630)629-2515	SL-SMP	2014
Ingle Chad M	(865)209-8357 cmingle2@yahoo.com	c/o Prince Of Peace 2454 Andrews Ave Ozark AL 36360	SO	SP	Prince Peace Ozark AL	(334)774-6758	FW	2012
Iovine Anthony J	(201)407-9563	100 Spring St Garfield NJ 07026	NJ	SP	St Matthew* New Milford NJ	(201)262-5092	FW	2005
Iqbal Vincent	(269)719-5353 vincentiqbal@comcast.net	7048 Rockford St Portage MI 49024	MI	C07/2016			CQ	2009
Irey Lance A	(714)337-2247 pastor.lance@gmail.com	1126 Coronado St Upland CA 91786	PSW	SMP	Trinity Montclair CA	(909)626-6552	FW-SMP	2011
Irmer Douglas D	(317)457-5391 pastor.irmer@gmail.com	6749 Woodland Heights Dr Avon IN 46123	IN	EM			FW	1985
Irwin James M	(402)214-4261 pastorjames@holysavior.org	7000 N 15th St Lincoln NE 68521	NEB	Sn/Adm	Holy Savior Lincoln NE	(402)434-3325	SL	1997
Isenberg Gerard E	(219)942-8049 gisenberg1234@gmail.com	9420 Sullivan Ln Crown Point IN 46307	IN	EM			SL	1958
Isler Albert C	(252)261-7331 Pasal600@yahoo.com	P.O. Box 569 Kitty Hawk NC 27949	SE	EM			SL	1967
Issak Kbrab	(281)235-7707 kbrabissak@gmail.com	685 Macabee Way Hayward CA 94541	PSW	Assoc	Good Shepherd Downey CA	(562)803-4459	CQ	2017

*Multiple Assignments (See Church Worker Locator for Additional Details)

See Page 53 for the Table of Abbreviations for key to District, Position, and Seminary abbreviations

**C =Candidate; EM = Emeritus; the date following the C is the month and year the Candidate status began

NAME	TELEPHONE NUMBER EMAIL	STREET ADDRESS CITY/STATE/ZIP	DISTRICT	POSITION/ STATUS**	WHERE SERVING	OFFICE PHONE	SEM/ PROGRAM	YR GRAD
Ista Myron W	(530)282-4650 mtista@sbcglobal.net	173 Lariat Loop Oroville CA 95966	CNH	EM			SL	1973
Iverson Erik J	(406)210-1262 lutefisk777@yahoo.com	P.O. Box 869 Seeley Lake MT 59868	MT	SP	Faith* Condon MT	(406)677-2281	FW	2006
Iwen Jason L	(260)418-6087 pastoriwen@zionwinnemucca.org	3205 N Highland Dr Winnemucca NV 89445	CNH	SP	Christ* Battle Mountain NV	(775)635-2290	FW	2024
Izzard Richard C	(973)875-1931 erizzard@embarqmail.com	22 Southfield Dr Sussex NJ 07461	NJ	EM			SPR	1969
Jacks Joseph L	(423)954-1322 jjacks6271@comcast.net	2413 Laurelton Creek Ln Chattanooga TN 37421	MDS	SP	St Philip Chattanooga TN	(423)267-1475	CQ	2012
Jackson Bruce W	(712) 870-1654 brucejackson433@gmail.com	P.O. Box 177 Lawton IA 51030	IW	EM			FW	1989
Jackson Christopher Dr	(920)365-2218 revcjackson@gmail.com	322 W Main St Forestville WI 54213	NW	SP	St Peter* Forestville WI	(920)856-6420	SL	2006
Jackson Meredith B	(314)330-6559 jaypbsig@gmail.com	500 Deepwoods Dr Valley Grande AL 36701	SO	SP	Holy Cross Camden AL	(334)682-9552	FW	1999
Jackson Paul H	970-356-0316 stpauljackson1952@gmail.com	1122 19th Avenue Greeley CO 80631	RM	EM			SL	1979
Jacob David K Dr	(862)242-0503 davidjacob61@yahoo.com	E5120 Margaret St Ironwood MI 49938	NW	SP	Trinity Ironwood MI	(906)932-3022	SL	1994
Jacob Luke A	(262)308-2486 luke@tlcms.org	7819 Oakview Lane Lenexa KS 66216	KS	Sn/Adm	Trinity Mission KS	(913)432-5441	SL	2008
Jacob Ricky A	(402)922-1540 joslopastor@proton.me	206 Conser St. P.O. Box 416 Winnebago NE 68071	NEB	D Miss	Nebraska District Seward NE	(402)643-2961	SL	1987
Jacobi Frederick C	(847)873-1928 fj85ej@verizon.net	1225 Luther Ln Apt 249-D Arlington Heights IL 60004	EA	EM			SL	1964
Jacobs Daniel P	(406)638-2331	P.O. Box 335 Crow Agency MT 59022	MT	EM			FW	1986
Jacobs Matthew P	(979)451-0328 matt.antlertrailranch@gmail.com	1929 CR 218 Weimar TX 78962	TX	EM			FW	1989
Jacobs Robert C	(386)843-1204 bobannfla@earthlink.net	1207 Crown Pointe Ln Ormond Beach FL 32174	FG	EM			SPR	1964
Jacobsen Lonnie R		5407 Venture Dr Lincoln NE 68521	NEB	D Ex/S	Nebraska District Seward NE	(402)643-2961	SL	2000
Jacobsen Scott A	(559)960-0994 bookwormjake@gmail.com	3743 Saginaw Way Fresno CA 93726	CNH	SMP	Our Saviour Caruthers CA	(559)864-3008	CQ	2019
Jacobsen Steven J	(217) 204-6576 revjacobsen@outlook.com	108 Greenbrier Ln Bethalto IL 62010	SI	SP	St John* Kampsville IL		SL	1995
Jacobsen Gary W	(605)745-5327 maxlukas@gwtc.net	28933 340th Ave Gregory SD 57533	SD	EM			CQ	2000
Jacobsen Adam E			MNS	SP	Concordia* Lake Park IA	(712)832-3503	FW	2013
Jacobsen Jon H	(712) 269-7554 pastorjon19@gmail.com	1410 S Main St Denison IA 51442	IW	EM			CQ	2019
Jacobson Dennis M	(310)625-5307 jacobson86@aol.com	100 Pecan Ave Fairhope AL 36532	SO	SMP	Grace Mobile AL	(251)433-2749	Other	2023
Jacoby David S	(978)516-6963 davidjacoby65@hotmail.com	706 Rindge Rd Fitchburg MA 01420	NE	SP	Messiah Fitchburg MA	(978)343-7397	FW	2015
Jacoby Jeremy M	(303)514-7612 lcmsjacoby@msn.com	4813 E 142nd Pl Thornton CO 80602	RM	Sn/Adm	Summit Peace Thornton CO	(303)452-0448	SL	1997
Jaeger James G	(815)632-0918	2104 22nd Ave Sterling IL 61081	NI	EM			FW	2001
Jaeger Jay A	(641)373-6860 revjaeger@hotmail.com	P.O. Box 326 Alden IA 50006	IE	SP	St Paul's* Alden IA	(515)859-3901	SL	1997
Jaeger Ralph	(307)760-9760 hunters_r_m@hotmail.com	2709 East Danforth Rd Apt 210 Edmond OK 73034	WY	EM			CQ	1991
Jaekel James A	(518)598-9346 jjaekel1@nycap.rr.com	24 Claire Pass Saratoga Spgs NY 12866	AT	EM			SL	1968
Jagow Wayne F	(716)434-2022 mwjagow@roadrunner.com	6310 Ridge Rd Lockport NY 14094	EA	EM			SL	1969
Jagow Andrew W	703-765-8255 pastor@bethany-lcms.org	3613 Ransom Pl Alexandria VA 22306	SE	Sn/Adm	Bethany Alexandria VA	(703)765-8255	SL	1998
Jagow Frederick W	(707)838-1666 fnljagow@att.net	152 Cornell St Windsor CA 95492	CNH	EM			SPR	1956
Jahn Wayne P		618 W Grove Ave Waukegan IL 60085	NI	SP	Redeemer Waukegan IL	(847)336-4891	SL	1999
Jahnke Clark H	(701)282-4195 pastorjahnke@standrewlcms.org	325 Cherry Ct West Fargo ND 58078	ND	Sn/Adm	St Andrew West Fargo ND	(701)282-4195	SL	1989
Jahnke Jonathan C	(701)306-2072 goodshepherdalexpastor@ gmail.com		MNN	SP	Good Shepherd Alexandria MN	(320)762-5152	SL	2020
Jahnke Randall L		2052 10th Rd Greenleaf KS 66943	KS	SP	Bethlehem* Greenleaf KS	(785)747-2407	SL	1984
Jakupciak John P	(301)432-2777 johnjakupciak@verizon.net	110 Conestoga Ct Boonsboro MD 21713	SE	SMP	Peace In Christ Walkersville MD	(301)845-6300	CQ	2019
James Christopher N Dr	(630)853-2927 cjames@ilcdg.org	5211 Carpenter St Downers Grove IL 60515	NI	Sn/Adm	Immanuel Downers Grove IL	(630)968-3112	SL	2001
James Gary B	(540)508-4614 mngo469@gmail.com	142 Towhee Dr Lk Frederick VA 22630	SE	SMP	Good Shepherd Herndon VA	(703)437-5020	CQ	2018
James Roger B	(269)589-5403	8121 Trentman Rd Fort Wayne IN 46816	IN	SP	Our Hope Huntertown IN	(260)637-3625	SL	1991
James Asaph A	(313)892-2670 asaphjames@yahoo.com	3510 E Outer Dr Detroit MI 48234	MI	SP	East Bethlehem Detroit MI	(313)892-2670	SL	2008
Jameson John A	jalexjam@gmail.com	115 Misty View Ln St. Peters MO 63376	IN	Sn/Adm	Christ Anderson IN	(765)642-2154	SL	1990

*Multiple Assignments (See Church Worker Locator for Additional Details)
See Page 53 for the Table of Abbreviations for key to District, Position, and Seminary abbreviations
**C =Candidate; EM = Emeritus; the date following the C is the month and year the Candidate status began

NAME	TELEPHONE NUMBER EMAIL	STREET ADDRESS CITY/STATE/ZIP	DISTRICT	POSITION/ STATUS**	WHERE SERVING	OFFICE PHONE	SEM/ PROGRAM	YR GRAD
Jameson Leon C	(636)795-6361 ljameson@hcl.org	W151s7808 Long Bow Ct Muskego WI 53150	EN	Sn/Adm	Hales Corners Hales Corners WI	(414)529-6700	SL	2022
Jander David L	(512)639-5019 PastorDJander@gmail.com	5105 Henwich Ct Columbia MO 65203	MO	Inst C	Lutheran Senior Services DBA EverTrue Brentwood MO	(314)968-9313	SL	2020
Jang Soon S	(714)717-9410 onnuree@gmail.com	5541 Kingman Ave Buena Park CA 90621	PSW	Assoc	Good News Korean Buena Park CA	(714)681-6770	CQ	2017
Jank Orville J	(715)574-3985 oajank@gmail.com	420 South 47th St #300 Lincoln NE 68510	NEB	EM			SL	1953
Jank Roland A Jr	(402)455-9711 rajankjr@msn.com	3319 N 130th Cir Omaha NE 68164	NEB	EM			SL	1974
Janke Ryan M	(402)394-7021 ryan.m.janke@gmail.com	220 Cherry St P.O. Box 47 Orchard NE 68764	NEB	SP	St Peter* Orchard NE	(402)893-2390	FW	2016
Janke Paul B Dr	(916)216-6984 apjanke@aol.com	8484 Madison Ave Apt 217 Fair Oaks CA 95628	CNH	EM			SL	1961
Jankens John D	(256)352-6442 seelsorger@att.net	1403 Clearwater Dr. NE Cullman AL 35055	SO	Sn/Adm	Trinity Hanceville AL	(256)352-6442	FW	2002
Janneke Kory A	(501)514-5177 pastor.stmatthewlcmsconway@gmail.com	2 Sherwood Dr. Conway AR 72034	MDS	SP	St Matthew Conway AR	(501)358-6252	SL	2012
Janneke Alan W Dr	(618)317-4416 ajanneke@egyptian.net	604 S Charles St Steeleville IL 62288	SI	SP	Emmanuel* Percy IL	(618)317-4416	SL	1981
Jans Gregory D	(318)820-9358 hiflite04@gmail.com	1630 Amwell Rd Somerset NJ 08873	NJ	SP	Holy Trinity Somerset NJ	(732)873-2888	SL	1988
Jansen Daniel L	(989)836-6132 2dan08@gmail.com	6273 Bobcat Trl Alger MI 48610	EN	SP	New Beginnings West Branch MI	(989)836-3042	SL	1992
Jansen Nathan R	(615)509-8597 njansen@mail.com	1035 Wiseman Farm Rd Fairview TN 37062	MDS	SP	St John Burns TN	(615)446-2332	SL	1994
Janssen Benjamin N	(765)346-2050 janssenb.lcms@gmail.com	4635 Parnell St Pittsburgh PA 15207	EN	Assoc	First Trinity Pittsburgh PA	(412)683-4121	FW	2023
Janssen Laverne A	(325)665-4903 laj15@suddenlink.net	2301 Darrell Dr Abilene TX 79606	TX	EM			SL	1977
Janssen Nathan L	(765)342-2004 poppastorlcms@hotmail.com		IN	SP	Prince Of Peace Martinsville IN	(765)342-2004	FW	1989
Janssen Samuel J	(217)416-7999 pastor.janssen@sbcglobal.net	902 E 2nd St Webster SD 57274	CI	SP	Good Shepherd Rochester IL	(217)498-7991	FW	2008
Janzen Mark J	(920)889-8986 janzen.mj@gmail.com	2305 Saddle Back Ct Fort Lupton CO 80621	RM	EM			SL	1995
Janzow Joel M	(519)238-8928 joeljanzow68@gmail.com	29 Wanda Ct Troy NY 12180	AT	Inst C	Atlantic District Hastings-On-Hudson NY	(914)337-5700	SPR	1976
Jarvis Robert W	(763)280-4904 robjarviskids@yahoo.com	1202 Folsom St Boulder CO 80302	RM	SP	University Boulder CO	(303)443-8720	SL	1990
Jasa Mark C	(626)794-2294 markjasa@gmail.com	3208 Glendon Ave Los Angeles CA 90034	PSW	SP	Mount Olive Pasadena CA	(626)794-2294	SL	2005
Jaseph Philip J	443-454-1698 pjjaseph@gmail.com	1053 Cayer Dr Glen Burnie MD 21061	SE	SP	Martini Baltimore MD	(410)752-7817	FW	2021
Jasper James W Dr	(216) 402-7383 pastorjazzper@gmail.com	1443 Dorsh Rd Cleveland OH 44121	EN	EM			CQ	1993
Jastram Daniel N Dr	+81 080 5459-4810 daniel.jastram@lcms.org	2-35-14-210 Jindaiji Mitaka-Shi Tokyo-To 181-0 JAPAN	MO	S Miss	Office of International Mission Saint Louis MO		FW	1983
Jastram Nathan R Dr	(414)856-7700 nathan.jastram@cuw.edu	3317 W Colette Ct Mequon WI 53092	SW	S HS/C	Concordia University Wisconsin Mequon WI	(262)243-5700	FW	1984
Jauss Marcus R	(660)422-1378 markjauss@icloud.com	59679 Walnut Pl New London MO 63459	CI	SP	St Paul's* Bowen IL	(217)430-9372	SL	1984
Javor Thomas R	(402)493-4595 pastorjavor@q.com	4912 N 139th Ave Omaha NE 68164	NEB	EM			FW	1987
Jay Eric L	(402)391-6148 ejay@stmarkomaha.org	c/o Saint Mark 1821 N 90th St Omaha NE 68114	NEB	Sn/Adm	St Mark Omaha NE	(402)391-6148	Other	2011
Jean Jacques Rochenel	(239)362-7911 rochenel0826@gmail.com	4496 28th Pl SW Naples FL 34116	FG	Assoc	Peace Naples FL	(239)354-9144	SL	2025
Jeffords Matthew K	(843)779-7084 pastor.jeffords@yahoo.com	1813 Hazel Dr Florence SC 29501	SE	SP	Incarnate Word Florence SC	(843)662-9639	FW	2007
Jenista John F	(814)733-0063	161 Fochtman Rd Berlin PA 15530	EA	EM			CQ	1994
Jenkins Graham J	(207)554-0042 graham.jenkins@drlc.org	2157 N 56th St Milwaukee WI 53208	SW	Assoc	Divine Redeemer Hartland WI	(262)367-8400	SL	2024
Jenkins Julius Dr	(334)875-2983	P.O. Box 1273 Selma AL 36702	SO	EM			FW	2001
Jenkins William J	405-590-7894 pj@rlcms.onmicrosoft.com	1907 32nd St Lubbock TX 79411	TX	C07/2025			SL	2019
Jenks Timothy A	(805)990-8841	7357 Jordan Ave Canoga Park CA 91303	PSW	SP	Canoga Park Canoga Park CA	(818)348-5714	FW	1990
Jenks Todd A Dr	pastor@saintpaulames.org	610 15th St Ames IA 50010	IW	SP	St Paul Ames IA	(515)232-5838	FW	1991
Jennings James R	(281)725-4247 jrjklj2000@gmail.com	15 Lucas Ln SW Rome GA 30165	TX	SMP	Gethsemane Houston TX	(713)688-5227	SL-SMP	2015
Jennings Stephen E	(262)752-1692 sjennings@trinityracine.com	2121 Autumn Dr Racine WI 53402	SW	Assoc	Trinity Racine WI	(262)632-2900	FW	1986
Jennings Matthew H	(760)953-4322 pastor@stpetershumboldt.org	901 N 10th St Humboldt KS 66748	KS	Sn/Adm	St Peter Humboldt KS	(620)473-2343	SL	2008
Jennings Jonathan P	(618)545-9543 pastor@bethlehemlutheranferrin.org		SI	SP	Bethlehem Ferrin IL	(618)545-9543	FW	2018
Jennings Kevin M	(361) 739-0701	4934 Eider Dr Corp Christi TX 78413	TX	SP	Mount Olive Corpus Christi TX	(361)991-3416	SL	1997

*Multiple Assignments (See Church Worker Locator for Additional Details)

See Page 53 for the Table of Abbreviations for key to District, Position, and Seminary abbreviations

**C =Candidate; EM = Emeritus; the date following the C is the month and year the Candidate status began

NAME	TELEPHONE NUMBER EMAIL	STREET ADDRESS CITY/STATE/ZIP	DISTRICT	POSITION/ STATUS**	WHERE SERVING	OFFICE PHONE	SEM/ PROGRAM	YR GRAD
Jensen William A	(217)836-9305 jensen.william.a@gmail.com	104 Gladys Dr Normal IL 61761	CI	D Miss	Central Illinois District Springfield IL	(217)793-1802	SL	2010
Jensen David C	(608)393-2849 baraboobishop@gmail.com	1083 Pendleton Park Way Unit #113 Neenah WI 54956	SW	EM			SL	1976
Jensen Jefrey S	(978)933-1443 jefreyjensen@gmail.com	45 Appalachian Circle Talking Rock GA 30175	FG	SP	King of Kings Jasper GA	(706)301-9191	SL	1995
Jensen Nathaniel S	+491622758381 Nathaniel.Jensen@lcms.org	Danziger Str.7 Landstuhl 66849 GERMANY	MO	S Miss	Office of International Mission Saint Louis MO		FW	2020
Jensen Scott A	(210)792-7758 scottj@concordia-satx.com	25002 Terlingua Bnd San Antonio TX 78261	TX	C01/2021			CQ	2011
Jensen Scott A	(715)821-9553 pastorjensen@gmail.com	5819 SE Wilsie Dr Stuart FL 34997	FG	SP	Bethel Hobe Sound FL	(772)546-5399	SL	2006
Jenson Willis C	(541)923-2784 w0wi@juno.com	136 SW 11th St Redmond OR 97756	NOW	EM			FW	1989
Jenson James B	(360)793-4321 w0lu65@outlook.com	15707 423rd Ave SE Gold Bar WA 98251	NOW	SP	Saint James Bothell WA	(425)745-9859	CQ	1981
Jenson Jens B	(605)724-2489 redeemarmour@unitelsd.com	P.O. Box 157 Armour SD 57313	SD	SP	Redeemer Armour SD	(605)724-2489	FW	2016
Jeon Kwang H	(470)522-9300	2602 Brookhaven Run Cir Duluth GA 30097	FG	EM			CQ	1997
Jeong Ernest C	(760)562-5961 prjeong@redeemer-lutheran.net		PSW	Sn/Adm	Redeemer Huntington Beach CA	(714)846-6330	FW	2012
Jeong Jin O Dr	(618)920-9311 korealuther92@gmail.com		FG	C09/2017			CQ	2012
Jeppesen Randal R	(715)965-0940 rj8808@gmail.com	5516 Newland Pl Fort Wayne IN 46835	IN	EM			FW	1988
Jerabek Todd R	(715)823-2593 tjerabek@frontiernet.net	P.O. Box 197 Embarrass WI 54933	NW	SP	St John* Clintonville WI	(715)851-5199	FW	1993
Jerez Guillermo	708-439-8839 revjerez@yahoo.com	3615 S 61st Ave Cicero IL 60804	NI	SP	Faith Cicero IL	(708)439-8839	HITSL	2002
Jermiya Lewi J	(314)309-1371 lewino21@yahoo.com	4410 Little Chief Dr Saint Louis MO 63123	MO	Assoc	St Trinity Saint Louis MO	(314)353-3276	SL	2023
Jeske Bruce E	(562)338-3812 bcjeske@verizon.net	19951 Felcliff Ln Huntington Beach CA 92646	PSW	EM			SL	1968
Jimenez Dimas	(281)467-7373 Jimenez.dimas@att.net	17003 Applecross Ln Houston TX 77084	TX	Assoc	Memorial Lutheran Katy TX	(281)391-0171	CQ	2010
Jimenez Jesus H	(760)655-0285 ginajmnz24@gmail.com	2021 N. 8th St. #112 El Centro CA 92243	PSW	EM			SL	2008
Jobe Ronald W	218-346-7923 rgjobe@msn.com	44678 Plentywood Rd Perham MN 56573	MNN	EM			SL	1974
Jobst James M	(612)615-2939 pjjobst@gmail.com	312 Fiddler Ct SE New Prague MN 56071	MNS	EM			SL	1995
Joeckel Ralph T Jr	(702)523-6210 pastortoby@outlook.com	660 Red Sky Dr Yakima WA 98903	PSW	EM			FW	1981
Joersz Jerald C Dr	(314)412-6910 jcjoersz@att.net	140 River Breeze Way Saint Louis MO 63129	MO	EM			SL	1968
Joesten Leroy B	(847)698-3045 lee.joesten@gmail.com	44 Park Ln Unit 329 Park Ridge IL 60068	NI	EM			SL	1967
Jofre Pedro G	(281)736-5851 pedro-jofre@hotmail.com	800 Clark St Sterling CO 80751	RM	Assoc	Trinity Sterling CO	(970)522-5942	SL	2010
Johann Jotham S	(703)815-5339 pastorjo@gslcva.org	13578 Plumbago Dr Centreville VA 20120	SE	Sn/Adm	Good Shepherd Herndon VA	(703)437-5020	FW-D	2005
Johann Simon S Dr	(917)992-3003	3200 N Leisure World Blvd Apt 117 Silver Spring MD 20906	EN	EM			CQ	1980
Johnson Mark D	(928)726-2391 mdjemeritus@yahoo.com	1931 E San Marcos Dr Yuma AZ 85365	PSW	EM			SL	2005
Johnson Norman L Dr	(732)740-9877 pastorj1121@yahoo.com	820 Klumac Rd Apt Ad2 Salisbury NC 28144	SE	EM			SL	1966
Johnson Michael A Sr	(901)218-2665 johnsonjohnmic@aol.com	3914 Watermelon Rd Apt 13a Northport AL 35473	EN	C07/2023			FW	1999
Johnson Matthew P	(763)772-7315 philipmn210@hotmail.com	9139 Brockton Lane Hamel MN 55340	MNS	Assoc	St John's Corcoran MN	(763)420-2426	FW	2003
Johnson Paul D	(208)352-0830 pastorpauljohnson@gmail.com	N3774 High Pointe Cir Rubicon WI 53078	SW	EM			SL	2004
Johnson Mark D	(218)270-3081 revmdj7@gmail.com	14194 Kimberlee Ct Baxter MN 56425	MNN	EM			FW	1977
Johnson Lohn M	lohn5184@gmail.com	653 Southpoint Dr Lexington KY 40515	IN	SP	Bread of Life Georgetown KY		SL	1984
Johnson Lee D	(517) 610-1834 pldj56@gmail.com	133 S Howell St Hillsdale MI 49242	MI	EM			SL	1981
Johnson Paul E	(712)735-4021 pcjohn@iowatelecom.net	6665 Frederick Ave P.O. Box 128 May City IA 51354	IW	EM			SL	1980
Johnson Kyle L	(763)843-3256 klucas.johnson@gmail.com	507 Glen Oaks Cir Big Lake MN 55309	MNS	SMP	Samaritans Hill Albertville MN	(763)595-1199	SL	2024
Johnson Russell D	(586)342-1384 givenforyou@gmail.com	2191 Arapahoe Rd Holland MI 49424	MI	SP	Christ Our Savior Holland MI	(616)738-0100	FW	2009
Johnson Kevin L	pastorj.holycross@yahoo.com	1040 Market St Carlisle IA 50047	IW	SP	Holy Cross Carlisle IA	(515)989-3841	SL	2004
Johnson Larry G	(605)345-3016 rjohn57274@itctel.com	P.O. Box 181 Webster SD 57274	SD	EM			FW	1979
Johnson Peter D	(585) 773-4475 peter@faithpenfield.org		EA	SMP	Faith Penfield NY	(585)381-3970	SL-SMP	2020
Johnson Randy L	(313)522-6424 randyrev1958@yahoo.com	13618 W Jackson Dr Tekonsha MI 49092	MI	D Ex/S	Michigan District Ann Arbor MI	(888)225-2111	SL	2002

*Multiple Assignments (See Church Worker Locator for Additional Details)

See Page 53 for the Table of Abbreviations for key to District, Position, and Seminary abbreviations

**C =Candidate; EM = Emeritus; the date following the C is the month and year the Candidate status began

NAME	TELEPHONE NUMBER EMAIL	STREET ADDRESS CITY/STATE/ZIP	DISTRICT	POSITION/ STATUS**	WHERE SERVING	OFFICE PHONE	SEM/ PROGRAM	YR GRAD
Johnson Richard D	(503)390-5192 rjrpastor@reagan.com	7666 Vallhalla Dr Colorado Spgs CO 80920	RM	EM			SL	2006
Johnson David	(406)549-3311 pastor.1stlutheran@gmail.com		MT	Sn/Adm	First Missoula MT	(406)549-3311	FW	1988
Johnson Ricky R	(951)660-3774 pastorrickj57@gmail.com	2335 N University Dr Waukesha WI 53188	SW	EM			CQ	2018
Johnson Ross E Dr	(314)278-7050 ross.johnson@lcms.org	30 Heritage Pointe Cir Fenton MO 63026	MO	S Ex/S	The LCMS Corporate Saint Louis MO	(314)965-9000	FW	2006
Johnson Scott E	(517)607-5650 scojoh65@gmail.com	3046 14th Ave S Moorehead MN 56560	ND	Assoc	Immanuel Fargo ND	(701)293-7979	FW	2014
Johnson Steven P	(509)891-0839 spjrev@yahoo.com	6805 N Crestline St Lot 32 Spokane WA 99217	NOW	EM			FW	1979
Johnson Thomas R	(316)305-7163 pastor_at_faith@yahoo.com	319 E Stone Creek St Derby KS 67037	KS	SP	Faith Derby KS	(316)788-1715	SL	1988
Johnson Thomas R Dr	(708)738-2512 tomjohnson1517@gmail.com	18 Candlewood Path Dix Hills NY 11746	AT	Sn/Adm	St Luke Dix Hills NY	(631)499-8656	CQ	2003
Johnson William S	wscjohnson@gmail.com	8 Wycliffe Pl Fort Wayne IN 46825	IN	S HS/C	Concordia Theological Seminary Fort Wayne IN	(260)452-2100	SL	2001
Johnson Zachary S	(515)850-6759 rev.zach.johnson@outlook.com	102 N Spruce Ave Garrison IA 52229	IE	SP	St Mark* Garrison IA	(319)477-5141	FW	2025
Johnson Kenneth P	(605)286-3256 zion@gwtc.net	P.O. Box 243 Avon SD 57315	SD	SP	Our Savior* Springfield SD	(605)369-2386	SL	1993
Johnson Robert E	(262)250-1987 rjohnson@trinityfreistadt.com	N111w16328 Catskill Ln Germantown WI 53022	SW	EM			SPR	1972
Johnson Chris E	(361)237-5755 pastorchrisej@yahoo.com	109 Hollygrove Dr Hewitt TX 76643	TX	EM			SL	1981
Johnson Keith J	(330)819-3298 rlcfisherman@gmail.com	2762 Cedar Hill Rd Cuyahoga FLS OH 44223	OH	SP	Zion Akron OH	(330)253-3136	CQ	1978
Johnson Andrew J	(402)750-5756 pastorajtx@gmail.com	9350 Overland Way San Antonio TX 78254	TX	Assoc	Shepherd Hills San Antonio TX	(210)614-3742	SL	2021
Johnson Andrew M Dr	(248)396-4341 pastor@christlutheranmilford.org	c/o Christ Lutheran Church 620 General Motors Rd Milford MI 48381	MI	SP	Christ Milford MI	(248)684-0895	SL	2012
Johnson Anthony M	(501)282-9938 keithj72570@hotmail.com	419 Lakeshore Drive Hot Springs AR 71913	MDS	Assoc	First Hot Springs AR	(501)525-0322	SL	2021
Johnson Benjamin C	(515) 650-0377 ben.johnson@gdlc.church	1250 Country Club Blvd Clive IA 50325	IW	Sn/Adm	Gloria Dei Urbandale IA	(515)276-1700	SL	2012
Johnson Charles D	eldoradolutheran@gmail.com	14712 S 94 Ave Orland Park IL 60462	NI	Sn/Adm	Christ Orland Park IL	(708)349-0431	SL	2005
Johnson Daniel S	(641)328-4605 danielsjohnson356@gmail.com	2905 Cooper Ln Marshalltown IA 50158	IE	EM			SL	1990
Johnson David M	(763)360-0464 gracepastor@sherbtel.net	11225 Julia Ln Becker MN 55308	MNN	SP	Grace Becker MN	(763)262-7782	FW	1987
Johnson David C	hotpeppers65@gmail.com	502 N Pleasant St Jackson MI 49202	MI	EM			FW	1986
Johnson Donald L	(920)287-1667 revdon.zionglen@gmail.com	609 Humboldt Ave Sheboygan WI 53081	SW	EM			FW	1978
Johnson Donald T	(715)498-7251 pastor@immanuelsheboygan.com	2211 S 8th St Sheboygan WI 53081	SW	SP	Immanuel Sheboygan WI	(920)452-7266	FW	2013
Johnson Eric C	(985)445-9339 augsburg1530@yahoo.com	c/o Southern District Office 100 Mission Dr Slidell LA 70460	SO	DP	Southern District Slidell LA	(504)282-2632	SL	2002
Johnson John F Dr	(202)667-5357 revjfjohnson@gmail.com	1310 Adams Dr Ft Washington MD 20744	SE	SP	Mount Olive Washington DC	(202)667-5357	SL	1988
Johnson Frank E Jr	(970)227-9102 frank.johnson@cune.org	444 Osceola Dr Loveland CO 80538	RM	EM			SL-SMP	2018
Johnson Frank E	(620)877-0284 pastorfrankejohnson@gmail.com	212 S Washington Hillsboro KS 67063	KS	SMP	Our Savior* Marion KS	(620)382-2432	SL-SMP	2024
Johnson Gary L	(979)864-7577 gjmail2@cvctx.com	5634 State Highway 159 La Grange TX 78945	TX	EM			SL-SMP	2022
Johnson Gene E	(772)834-8103 johnsong@trinityklein.org	22306 Larch Grove Ct Tomball TX 77375	TX	Assoc	Trinity Klein Klein TX	(281)376-5773	SL	2008
Johnson Isaac R	(563)726-5476 revisaacjohnson@gmail.com	607 7th Ave Charles City IA 50616	IE	SP	New Hope Charles City IA	(641)552-4831	FW	2016
Johnson James P	(805)687-9627 jimpjohnson57@gmail.com	1123 Crestline Dr Santa Barbara CA 93105	PSW	EM			SL	1965
Johnson John F Dr	(708)227-3129	641 W Willow St Apt 150 Chicago IL 60614	NI	EM			CQ	1975
Johnson Jeffrey J	(909)771-9303 johnsonjeff1990@yahoo.com	2030 Thistle Ct Riverside CA 92506	PSW	SP	Trinity San Bernardino CA	(909)882-2989	FW	2011
Johnson Jeremiah D	(816)716-2453 jeremiahdj@gmail.com	9706 Lily Pond Ln Corcoran MN 55340	MNS	Sn/Adm	Glory Of Christ Plymouth MN	(763)478-6031	SL	2005
Johnson John D	(561)385-5460 pastorjohnd@bellsouth.net	15739 64th Pl N Loxahatchee FL 33470	FG	EM			SL	1987
Johnson John E	(217) 871-8497 jakotal@comcast.net	1241 Richland Ave Lincoln IL 62656	CI	EM			SPR	1970
Johnson Erik L	(206)251-8129 lutheranerik@gmail.com	1742 McCready Ave Richmond Heights MO 63117	MO	SP	Concordia Maplewood MO	(314)647-1215	SL	2024
Johnson Brandon R	(715)347-6126 johnsonbr97@gmail.com	400 4th St NE Little Falls MN 56345	MNN	SP	Zion Little Falls MN	(320)632-5792	SL	2024
Johnston Dale R		43 S Main St Apt 2 Woodstown NJ 08098	NJ	EM			SPR	1971
Johnston Allan R Dr	(509)823-3808 avantiarj@gmail.com	714 39th St Washougal WA 98671	NOW	EM			SPR	1976
Johnston Brian C	(707)685-5993 trinitychurchpastor@ctitech.com	818 N Shawnee St Taylorville IL 62568	CI	SP	Trinity Taylorville IL	(217)824-8148	FW	2019

*Multiple Assignments (See Church Worker Locator for Additional Details)
See Page 53 for the Table of Abbreviations for key to District, Position, and Seminary abbreviations
**C =Candidate; EM = Emeritus; the date following the C is the month and year the Candidate status began

NAME	TELEPHONE NUMBER EMAIL	STREET ADDRESS CITY/STATE/ZIP	DISTRICT	POSITION/ STATUS**	WHERE SERVING	OFFICE PHONE	SEM/ PROGRAM	YR GRAD
Johnstone Douglas V	douglas.johnstone@sbcglobal.net	10660 Validus Dr Unit 3428 Jacksonville FL 32256	FG	EM			SL	1970
Jonas Scott E	(805)345-6658 scottjonas314@gmail.com	9754 Cambrook Dr St. Louis MO 63123	MO	SP	Glendale Glendale MO	(314)966-3220	SL	2014
Jones Kevin C	(989) 391-5077	2510 Mason St Bay City MI 48708	MI	SP	Nativity Saint Charles MI	(989)865-9964	SL	1988
Jones Todd A Dr	(479)644-5265 todd@the20.org	7 Marionet Cir. Bella Vista AR 72714	MI	C01/2025			SL	1989
Jones Timothy A	(715)723-6380 tckjones@hotmail.com	1109 Archer Ln Eau Claire WI 54703	NW	Assoc	Zion Chippewa Falls WI	(715)723-6380	FW	2004
Jones Andrew R	(925)671-9942 pastor@flcconcord.org	4000 Concord Blvd. Concord CA 94519	CNH	SP	First Concord CA	(925)671-9942	SL	2017
Jones Steven M	(314)537-3088	4305 Aquila Ave N Minneapolis MN 55428	MNS	SP	Peace Robbinsdale MN	(763)533-0570	SL	2007
Jones Stanley E	(479)640-1700 stanjones2@cox.net	5 Highland Parkway Bella Vista AR 72715	MDS	EM			SL	1956
Jones Robert M	(949)910-7422 rjjcbeliever@hotmail.com	2591 Laramie Rd Riverside CA 92506	PSW	Assoc	Immanuel Riverside CA	(951)682-7613	SL	2016
Jones Richard S	(701)509-3874 r.jones@dakotaranch.org	5801 19th Ave NW Minot ND 58703	ND	Inst C	Dakota Boys and Girls Ranch Minot ND	(701)839-7888	SL	2012
Jones Richard J	(252)564-2447 rjsouthcarolina@gmail.com	813 W Josephine St McKinney TX 75069	TX	EM			SL	1991
Jones Kyle E	(586)980-9308 kyle.jones@stjohnswaltz.org	1611 Ash St. Carleton MI 48117	MI	Assoc	St Johns Waltz MI	(734)654-6366	SL	2015
Jones Joshua H Dr	jones5412@yahoo.com	4807 Baldwin St Rapid City SD 57702	SD	SP	Bethlehem Rapid City SD	(605)343-2011	SL	2007
Jones Joseph A Dr	(785)217-7785 revdoc18@gmail.com	4202 S Goodall Pl Tucson AZ 85730	PSW	EM			SPR	1975
Jones Jarrett D	(817)714-0200 jet.jones@stjohnmansfield.org	2111 Melissa Diane St Mansfield TX 76063	TX	SMP	St John Mansfield TX	(817)473-4889	SL-SMP	2016
Jones Howard F	(564)376-3768 howardjones618@yahoo.com	618 Pinehollow Drive Anderson SC 29621	SE	EM			FW	1992
Jones Douglas D	(619)213-4763 djones562@msn.com	311 Red Fox Run Summerville SC 29485	SE	EM			FW	1988
Jones Daniel G	(208)365-7137 abishai55@yahoo.com	c/o Deb Jones 3460 Twin Tunnel Ln Emmett ID 83617	NOW	SP	Christ Meridian ID	(208)888-1622	SL	1982
Jones Christian M	(314)422-4572 pastorjonesfam@gmail.com	8215 Summers St Utica MI 48317	MI	Assoc	Trinity Utica MI	(586)731-4490	SL	2019
Jones Brett A	(920) 471-6993 bajones7368@outlook.com	8702 Huey Rd Hoffman IL 62250	SI	SP	Trinity Hoffman IL	(618)495-2545	SL	2022
Jones Bryan D	(816)244-7342 indybdj@hotmail.com	7494 Benjestown Rd Millington TN 38053	SO	EM			FW	2004
Jones Keith R	(805)967-1416 yopjgslc@hotmail.com	6520 Camino Venturoso Goleta CA 93117	PSW	SP	Good Shepherd Goleta CA	(805)967-1416	SL	1988
Jonker Shayne M	(260)418-2206 shaynejonker@yahoo.com	5101 W 1000 N Huntington IN 46750	IN	SP	Faith Roanoke IN	(260)672-1140	FW	2009
Jordan Donald A	(530)513-1284 1365jordan@gmail.com	3007 Boston Dr Chico CA 95973	CNH	EM			SL	1983
Jordan James D	(703)314-2064 daxjordan@gmail.com	c/o St James Lutheran Church 5660 Trabue Rd Columbus OH 43228	OH	Sn/Adm	Saint James Columbus OH	(614)878-5158	CQ	2014
Jordan Jeffrey W	(770)993-4316	245 Whisperwood Dr Roswell GA 30075	FG	Sn/Adm	Rivercliff Sandy Springs GA	(770)993-4316	FW	2002
Jording Jeremiah N	(217)430-7853 jordingjn@gmail.com	21211 Detroit Rd Rocky River OH 44116	OH	SP	St Thomas Rocky River OH	(440)331-2680	SL	2018
Jore Ben	(763)688-0489 pastorbenjore@gmail.com	136 Callado Cir San Marcos TX 78666	TX	SP	St John Uhland TX	(512)668-4542	CQ	2023
Jorg Robert B	(814)746-5566 ministry285@aol.com	394 Rosebrock St. North Tonawanda NY 14120	EA	SMP	St Matthew North Tonawanda NY	(716)692-6862	FW-SMP	2010
Jow Patrick	(626)863-2937 pejow777@gmail.com	1339 S Concord Ln Glendora CA 91740	PSW	EM			SL	1986
Jow Warren	(559)638-8268 wdkcrsw@gmail.com	2345 E Early Ave Reedley CA 93654	CNH	EM			SL	2004
Joynt Michael F	(928)261-6501 mfjmfj@yahoo.com	41 Calderwood Cir Crossville TN 38558	MDS	EM			FW	2007
Jud Kevin R	(513) 309-1550 pastor.jud@immanuelhamilton.com	1842 Del Rio Dr Hamilton OH 45013	OH	SP	Immanuel Hamilton OH	(513)893-6792	SL	2001
Judge Leslie L	(361)827-4469 oneninja4jesus@yahoo.com	362 Werner Egg Rd Meyersville TX 77974	TX	EM			FW	2002
Juedes John P	(909)795-9071 messiah7@empirenet.com	P.O. Box 372 Highland CA 92346	PSW	SP	Messiah Highland CA	(909)862-2923	SL	1981
Juengel Dennis R	(330)467-6162 pastordrj5@gmail.com	1143 Meadow Woods Dr Macedonia OH 44056	OH	EM			FW	1987
Juergensen Stephen P Dr	(509)525-2493 tlcwallawalla@gmail.com	109 S Roosevelt St Walla Walla WA 99362	NOW	SP	Trinity Walla Walla WA	(509)525-2493	SL	1985
Juhl David M	(815)263-1376 pastorjuhl@gmail.com	211 Curtis P.O. Box 197 Arlington WI 53911	SW	SP	St Peter Arlington WI	(608)635-4825	FW	2002
Jukola Matthew G	(720)903-0193 churchclan13@gmail.com	75 Ln 105d Turkey Lake Lagrange IN 62420	CI	C08/2018			FW	2016
Julmiste Bernard	(754)422-6723 christianmissionteam@hotmail.com	5501 SW 7th Pl Margate FL 33068	FG	SP	Grace Tabernacle Fort Lauderdale FL		EIITSL	2008
Jun Chimin	(949)759-4739 Lutheran1031@gmail.com	1 Longbourn Aisle Irvine CA 92603	PSW	Sn/Adm	Jesus Love Irvine CA	(949)878-1970	CQ	2010
Jung David S	(281)799-8274 zionjse@gmail.com	1111 S Conyer St Visalia CA 93277	CNH	Sn/Adm	Grace Visalia CA	(559)734-7694	SL	2008

*Multiple Assignments (See Church Worker Locator for Additional Details)
See Page 53 for the Table of Abbreviations for key to District, Position, and Seminary abbreviations
**C =Candidate; EM = Emeritus; the date following the C is the month and year the Candidate status began

NAME	TELEPHONE NUMBER EMAIL	STREET ADDRESS CITY/STATE/ZIP	DISTRICT	POSITION/ STATUS**	WHERE SERVING	OFFICE PHONE	SEM/ PROGRAM	YR GRAD
Jung Matthew P	(812)764-8664 matt.jung@att.net	13859 S 60 E Columbus IN 47201	IN	SP	St Paul Jonesville IN	(812)523-9994	FW	2015
Jung David R	(817)919-8058 DavidRJung@hotmail.com	6865 Dogwood Ct N RICHLND HLS TX 76182	TX	EM			FW	1984
Jung David A	(313)530-3639	1355 E Kitchen Rd Pinconning MI 48650	MI	EM			FW	1982
Jung Christopher D	(313)330-2863 pastorchrisjung@gmail.com	7165 Huron Ave Lexington MI 48450	MI	SP	St Matthew Lexington MI	(810)359-8411	SL	2016
Junkans Mark R	(281)513-8416 mjunkans71@gmail.com	212 Detering St Houston TX 77007	TX	C09/2018			FW	2002
Junkin Daniel E	(209)596-3079 baronvonbismark@gmail.com	1531 Canyon Creek Dr Newman CA 95360	CNH	SMP	Saint James Newman CA	(209)862-3438	CQ	2019
Junkin Mark R	(620)203-1756 storyteller077@hotmail.com	P.O. Box 4 Corder MO 64021	MO	SP	Zion* Corder MO	(660)394-2322	SL	2005
Jurchen Arnold H	arnold.h.jurchen@gmail.com	1211 N. 1st Street Seward NE 68434	NEB	EM			SPR	1973
Jurchen Peter L Dr	(515)490-0197 pjurchen@gmail.com	800 N. Columbia Ave Seward NE 68434	NEB	S HS/C	Concordia University Nebraska Seward NE	(402)643-3651	SL	2009
Jurischk Bradley W	(281)961-7609 brad@stlhouston.org	6810 Ashmore Dr Houston TX 77069	TX	Sn/Adm	St Timothy Houston TX	(281)469-2457	SL	2020
Just Christian F Dr	(216)789-6688 doctorjust@gmail.com	1567 Meadowlawn Dr Macedonia OH 44056	EN	EM			SL	1973
Just Arthur A Jr Dr	arthur.just@ctsfw.edu	2001 Kensington Blvd Fort Wayne IN 46805	IN	S Ex/S	Office of International Mission* Saint Louis MO		FW	1980
Kabel James A	(541) 826-4219 jkabel3@aol.com	911 St Andrews Way Eagle Point OR 97524	NOW	EM			SL	1967
Kabell Douglas R Dr	(940)636-7433 faithlutheran.graham@gmail.com	1618 Hwy 380 Byp Graham TX 76450	TX	SP	Faith Graham TX	(940)549-5155	FW	1982
Kachelmeier Brian L Dr	(505)412-9682 bkachelmeier@msn.com	16219 Robinwood Ln San Antonio TX 78248	TX	Sn/Adm	Crown Of Life San Antonio TX	(210)490-6886	FW	2005
Kachmarek Kasimir A	(503)260-0531 KAkachmarek@yahoo.com	3205 NE 2nd Ct Hillsboro OR 97124	NOW	EM			SL	1966
Kade Timothy P	(248)930-0587 timkade@yahoo.com	15063 W Heritage Oak Way Surprise AZ 85374	PSW	C08/2023			FW	1996
Kaelberer John H	(253)752-4171	1015 N Whitman St Tacoma WA 98406	NOW	EM			CQ	1985
Kaelberer Eric V	(951)660-8500 erickawai@yahoo.com	6909 Quail Pl Unit B Carlsbad CA 92009	PSW	EM			FW	1985
Kaelberer Erich E	(307) 250-5383 pkaelberer@gmail.com	1007 Stampede Ave Cody WY 82414	MT	EM			SL	2011
Kah John P III	(209)470-1781 jkah333@gmail.com	3506 Windy Ridge Ct San Antonio TX 78259	TX	EM			FW	1980
Kahle David A	(913) 764-2826	800 N Alder St Gardner KS 66030	KS	SP	Redeemer Olathe KS	(913)764-2359	FW	2005
Kaiser Seth C	(712)242-8089 bstrongandcourageous@yahoo. com	10340 Lakewood Dr Saginaw MI 48609	MI	SP	Trinity Bay City MI	(989)662-6093	SL	2010
Kaiser Benjamin J	(402)366-4309 bkaiser@efyork.org	19 Eastridge Dr S York NE 68467	NEB	Assoc	Emmanuel York NE	(402)362-3655	SL	2010
Kaiser David W	(580)614-1229 davewkaiser@gmail.com	3316 Mark Twain Drive Pinetop AZ 85935	EN	EM			CQ	2009
Kaiser Joel C	(989)652-4091 jkaiser@stlorenz.org	576 Franconian Dr E Frankenmuth MI 48734	MI	Assoc	St Lorenz Frankenmuth MI	(989)652-6141	FW	1993
Kaiser John C			MI	EM			FW	1980
Kaiser Kurt R	(712)269-8452 pastor.kaiser@ziondenison.org	1989 N Ave Denison IA 51442	IW	EM			CQ	1984
Kaiser Paul M	(361)781-4241 propterchr@aol.com	508 S Wells St Edna TX 77957	TX	SP	St Paul Edna TX	(361)782-3037	FW	1992
Kalb Jeffrey T	(605)359-6456 kalbjt@gmail.com	46590 118th St Browns Valley MN 56219	SD	C07/2016			FW	2008
Kalbas Aaron C	(512)430-2034	1212 E Boynton St Hamilton TX 76531	TX	SP	St John Hamilton TX	(254)386-3158	SL	2009
Kaldahl Alex J	(402)610-3909 alex.j.kaldahl@gmail.com	5290 C Ave Marcus IA 51035	IW	SP	Trinity* Marcus IA	(712)376-2666	FW	2024
Kaldahl Paul E Jr	(712)262-5598 kaldahlrev@gmail.com	815 6th Street SW Spencer IA 51301	IW	SP	First English Spencer IA	(712)262-5598	FW	1988
Kallesen Douglas L	(407)234-5296 pastordoug@trinitydowntown.com	3334 Honeysuckle Ln Belle Isle FL 32812	FG	Sn/Adm	Trinity Orlando FL	(407)488-1919	SL	1983
Kallio Harold N	(928)680-7784	3630 Blue Colt Dr Lk Havasu Cty AZ 86406	PSW	EM			SPR	1957
Kalthoff James W Dr	(314)956-1798 jwk@kalthoffs.com	8501 E Camino Real Scottsdale AZ 85255	PSW	EM			SPR	1963
Kalthoff Glenn D	(303)752-9700 glennkalthoff@gmail.com	2000 S Dayton St Apt 301 Aurora CO 80247	RM	EM			SL	1964
Kaltwasser Bruce J	revkaltwasser@gmail.com	1215 Fox Ridge Rd Dike IA 50624	IE	EM			FW	1983
Kampfer Russell J	(715)491-6894 RussellKampfer1@gmail.com	602 Maple Ridge Rd Mosinee WI 54455	NW	SP	St Peter Wausau WI	(715)675-9901	SL	1991
Kampia Rudolf	(301)614-0918 rudy.kampia@gmail.com	8800 58th Ave Berwyn Hts MD 20740	SE	EM			SL	1973
Kamprath Stephen P	(573)578-5066 sk81272@yahoo.com	1208 Casey Ln Rolla MO 65401	MO	EM			CQ	1981

*Multiple Assignments (See Church Worker Locator for Additional Details)
See Page 53 for the Table of Abbreviations for key to District, Position, and Seminary abbreviations
**C =Candidate; EM = Emeritus; the date following the C is the month and year the Candidate status began

NAME	TELEPHONE NUMBER EMAIL	STREET ADDRESS CITY/STATE/ZIP	DISTRICT	POSITION/ STATUS**	WHERE SERVING	OFFICE PHONE	SEM/ PROGRAM	YR GRAD
Kamps Hilbert C	(262)758-2563 hilbyandjaney@yahoo.com	585 North St Rt 741 Lebanon OH 45036	OH	EM			SL	2005
Kan Wesley T Dr	(850)774-4158 gnesiohamaptolos@yahoo.com	7615 Sweetbriar Rd Panama City FL 32404	SO	EM			FW	2003
Kandakai Zaza L	(718)954-1985 zakandakai86@gmail.com	74 Laurel Ave Staten Island NY 10304	AT	Assoc	Christ Assembly Staten Island NY	(718)556-2652	EIITSL	2023
Kane Justin D	(828)446-2521 revjustinkane@gracewaterloo.org	905 East Bremer Avenue Waverly IA 50677	IE	SP	Grace Waterloo IA	(319)235-6705	FW	2002
Kane Michael O	(828)324-8163 carpenter-shop@juno.com	429 19th Ave NE Hickory NC 28601	SE	EM			FW	1991
Kane David F	(740)649-7382 pastordavidkane@gmail.com	17 Unioto Dr Chillicothe OH 45601	OH	EM			FW	2009
Kanefke Charles J	(239)209-2542 pastork@stpeter-lutheran.org	14 Summerhouse Ct Dawsonville GA 30534	FG	SP	St Peter Dahlonega GA	(706)864-6001	SL	2007
Kang Man S	(714)739-1004 mankang1957@gmail.com	1521 W Orangethorpe Ave Fullerton CA 92833	PSW	Sn/Adm	True Love Fullerton CA	(714)992-5008	FW	1990
Kangar Bennego G	(651)410-8580 kangerben1215@gmail.com	W9894 State Rd 35 Hager City WI 54014	MNS	Assoc	theAlley Cottage Grove MN	(651)459-2063	SL	2023
Kangas Aaron G	revkangas@yahoo.com	34835 Acacia Ave Yucaipa CA 92399	PSW	SP	Good Shepherd Yucaipa CA	(909)790-1863	FW	2001
Kangas Carlton W	(715)514-7153 cwkfinn@hotmail.com	410 E Roosevelt Ave Fall Creek WI 54742	NW	EM			FW	1980
Kanoy Rick G	(402)478-4278 rkanoy@stpaulsarlington.org	8959 County Road 9 Arlington NE 68002	NEB	Sn/Adm	St Paul Arlington NE	(402)478-4278	SL	1997
Kapanka Gerald C Dr	(319)290-5642 gerrykapanka@gmail.com	854 Maucker Rd Cedar Falls IA 50613	IE	Sn/Adm	Immanuel Cedar Falls IA	(319)260-2000	FW	1989
Kapels Calvin R	(402) 515-6932 ckapels@bslcomaha.org	6310 N. 104th Street Omaha NE 68134	NEB	Assoc	Christ Norfolk NE	(402)371-1210	SL	2015
Kappel Marc A	(352)589-5433 mkappel@flcse.org	806 E Washington Ave Eustis FL 32726	FG	Sn/Adm	Faith Eustis FL	(352)589-5433	SL	2000
Kappler Stephen A	(623)237-2858 kapplers0566@yahoo.com	45323 Park Sierra Dr. #560 Coarsegold CA 93614	TX	EM			SL	1967
Karay John S	(608)515-3369 jskmak@mindspring.com	1655 S. Elm St Unit 407 Canby OR 97013	NOW	SMP	Trinity Mount Angel OR	(503)634-2437	SL-SMP	2012
Karch John D Jr	(706)232-5723 PASTORJ16@AOL.COM	27 Gowen Dr SW Rome GA 30165	FG	EM			FW	1980
Karg Rory C	(314)761-5523 rkarg@immanuelolivette.org	150 Forest Brook Ln Saint Louis MO 63146	MO	Sn/Adm	Immanuel Olivette MO	(314)993-2394	SL	2008
Karle John E	(318)332-3352 johnkarle17@gmail.com	P.O. Box 17 College Station TX 77841	TX	D Miss	Texas District Round Rock TX	(800)951-3478	SL	1994
Karle Mark E	(360)229-2320 revnbuzz@comcast.net	1104 N Hobble Strap St Prescott Valley AZ 86314	TX	EM			CQ	2010
Karlen Fred W	(707)538-7410 karlen@sonic.net	5743 Los Alamos Ct Santa Rosa CA 95409	CNH	SP	Grace Cloverdale CA	(707)894-2330	CQ	2017
Karner Kevin A	(765)749-9951 kkarner@juno.com	1623 N Leith Ct Green Valley AZ 85614	NE	Sn/Adm	Immanuel Bristol CT	(860)583-5649	FW	1989
Karolus John D	jkarolus@sotdaz.org		PSW	Assoc	Shepherd Desert Scottsdale AZ	(480)860-1188	SL	2021
Karolus David B	(715)350-9420 d.karolus@peaceantigo.org	300 Lincoln St Antigo WI 54409	NW	Sn/Adm	Peace Antigo WI	(715)623-2200	SL	1989
Karsten Darwin L	(314)221-6525 darkarsten4403@gmail.com	164 Hunters Run Ct Eureka MO 63025	MO	Assoc	Praise and Worship Branson West MO	(417)386-2422	SL	1969
Karsten Wilfred L Dr	(309)716-2375 wilfredkarsten@gmail.com	2203 F15 Blvd Marengo IA 52301	IE	EM			SL	1983
Kasaty Michael P	(619) 607-0758 pkasaty@christlincoln.org		NEB	SMP	Christ Lincoln NE	(402)483-7774	SL-SMP	2024
Kasongo Gui K	(414)889-6752 kasongoguy1000@gmail.com	6460 N 54th St Milwaukee WI 53223	SW	SP	Gospel* Milwaukee WI	(414)562-1890	SL	2011
Kaspar Donald L	(936)577-4809 kaspar.don@gmail.com	2119 Avenue R Huntsville TX 77340	TX	EM			SPR	1965
Kaspar Jason M	(970)201-7499 revkaspar@gmail.com	840 N Franklin St La Grange TX 78945	TX	SP	Mount Calvary La Grange TX	(979)968-3938	FW	2019
Kasper Garret A	(314)229-1819 garretkasper1@gmail.com	400 SW Hickory Gln Grimes IA 50111	IW	SP	Mount Olive Des Moines IA	(515)277-8349	SL	2018
Kasper Robert E Dr	(734)340-4447 robert.kasper@michigandistrict. org	8145 Starling Ct Ypsilanti MI 48197	MI	D Ex/S	Michigan District Ann Arbor MI	(888)225-2111	SL	1983
Kasper Robert G	(512)680-3648 gabekasper1@gmail.com	2451 Dayton Dr Ann Arbor MI 48108	MI	Sn/Adm	University Chapel Ann Arbor MI	(734)663-5560	SL	2012
Kasper Donald M	(936)870-5946 mdkasper1@gmail.com	5707 Wells Ln Salado TX 76571	TX	EM			SL	1982
Kass Stephen R	(630)903-8173 srkass@fifcc.org	507 Heather Ln Carol Stream IL 60188	NI	SP	Family In Faith Glendale Heights IL	(630)653-5030	FW	1994
Kassa Eyob B	(703)674-7108 eyob1k@gmail.com	7859 Dogue Indian Cir Lorton VA 22079	SE	SP	VA Mekane Yesus Annandale VA	(202)215-7269	CQ	2023
Kassen John E	(248)969-0242 johnkassen@icloud.com	721 Golf Villa Dr Oxford MI 48371	MI	EM			FW	1979
Kast Edward L Jr	(989)791-4172 edemkast@sbcglobal.net	4449 Windemere Dr Saginaw MI 48603	MI	EM			SL	1962
Kasten Albert L Sr	(308)225-6080 akast1995@yahoo.com	P.O. Box 627 Chappell NE 69129	WY	EM			FW	1995
Kastens Dennis A Dr	(314)892-0888 dennisakastens@gmail.com	5101 Kings Park Dr Saint Louis MO 63129	MO	EM			SL	1965
Kaster Dale W	(904)509-0274 dale.kaster@lcms.org	1620 Pitch Pine Ave St Johns FL 32259	EN	S Miss	Office of International Mission Saint Louis MO		SL	1989

*Multiple Assignments (See Church Worker Locator for Additional Details)

See Page 53 for the Table of Abbreviations for key to District, Position, and Seminary abbreviations

**C =Candidate; EM = Emeritus; the date following the C is the month and year the Candidate status began

NAME	TELEPHONE NUMBER EMAIL	STREET ADDRESS CITY/STATE/ZIP	DISTRICT	POSITION/ STATUS**	WHERE SERVING	OFFICE PHONE	SEM/ PROGRAM	YR GRAD
Kasting Michael D	(509)305-6189 mskasting@gmail.com	18918 Highland Dr Oregon City OR 97045	NOW	EM			SL	1972
Kastner John L	913-780-6023 john.kastner@bslc.org	13145 S Blackbob Rd Olathe KS 66062	KS	Assoc	Beautiful Savior Olathe KS	(913)780-6023	FW	2024
Kastner Luke W	(360)593-6332 lkastner@stjohnshemet.org	761 Pinehurst Dr Hemet CA 92544	PSW	SP	St John Hemet CA	(951)925-7756	CQ	2009
Kastner Mark S	(609)330-7942 markdebkastner@gmail.com	4100 Rocky Rd Lenoir NC 28645	SE	EM			FW	1982
Katari Shadrach Dr	(773)743-4415 katari06@hotmail.com	6803 N Campbell Ave Chicago IL 60645	EN	Asst	Bethesda Chicago IL	(773)743-6460	CQ	1997
Katiso Alemu E Dr	(517)285-0446 aslenxi@yahoo.co.uk	821 Camden Ave Salisbury MD 21801	SE	SP	Bethany Salisbury MD	(410)742-1737	CQ	2016
Kauffman Alexander C	alex@holycrossnorthcanton.org	981 Easthill St SE North Canton OH 44720	OH	Assoc	Holy Cross North Canton OH	(330)499-3307	SL	2025
Kaufmann Arthur M	(423)652-0550 pastog_k@yahoo.com	6038 Old Jonesboro Rd Bristol TN 37620	MDS	EM			SPR	1968
Kaufmann Martin J	(217)503-7865 martinkaufmann7@gmail.com	4630 Timberview Dr Auburn IL 62615	CI	Sn/Adm	Trinity Auburn IL	(217)438-6820	FW	1997
Kaufmann Reinald W	(734)306-9364 rennie@renniekaufmann.com	46210 Ann Arbor Road W Plymouth MI 48170	EN	SMP	Risen Christ Plymouth MI	(734)453-5252	FW-SMP	2011
Kaul Thomas C	(414)573-7588 pastortck@aol.com	9993 W North Ave Apt133 Milwaukee WI 53226	SW	EM			SL	1985
Kauth Roland C	AZKauths@gmail.com	1125 E Racine Dr Casa Grande AZ 85122	NOW	EM			SL	1956
Kavouras Dean	(216)252-4711	5948 West 24th Street Parma OH 44134	OH	SP	Christ Cleveland OH	(216)252-4711	SL	1978
Kay William L	(716)474-5321 wlkay49@gmail.com	234 Gina Way Brockport NY 14420	EA	EM			CQ	1980
Kaye Carl R IV	(626) 496-8764 revckaye@gmail.com	300 N 4th St Apt 3 Alhambra CA 91801	PSW	EM			FW	2004
Kayser Lowell N	(307)654-1084 kayser657@yahoo.com	2110 Summerset Dr Colorado Springs CO 80920	WY	EM			SPR	1972
Kazmierski Jeffrey M	(260)417-0523 rev.kazmierski@gmail.com	11730 Champagne Court Fort Wayne IN 46845	IN	S HS/C	Concordia Theological Seminary Fort Wayne IN	(260)452-2100	FW	2020
Keane David L	760-505-1474 pastordave@faithvista.org	2346 Vista Royal Vista CA 92084	PSW	Sn/Adm	Faith Vista CA	(760)724-7700	SL	2024
Kear Dustin K	(956)404-3369 dkear22@gmail.com	8516 Moon Eagle Dr NE Albuquerque NM 87113	RM	SP	Immanuel Albuquerque NM	(505)242-0616	SL	2013
Kearney Channing L	(702)885-5005 chapclk@comcast.net	9748 Loganberry Ln Indianapolis IN 46256	IN	C08/2023			FW	1991
Kearney Michael J	(641)373-3202 kearney.isu@gmail.com		IE	M Chap	Office of International Mission Saint Louis MO		FW	2014
Keat James D	(517)589-5239 jamesdkeat@gmail.com	5230 State Rd Leslie MI 49251	MI	EM			CQ	1990
Keating David T	david.keating.1995@gmail.com	57 Washington St N Tonowanda NY 14120	EA	SP	St Mark NT North Tonawanda NY	(716)693-3715	FW	2020
Keddington David	(907)306-3631 dnkeddington@gmail.com	7040 Tulugak Cir Anchorage AK 99507	NOW	SMP	Anchorage Anchorage AK	(907)272-5323	SL-SMP	2022
Kegley Casey T	kegleyct@gmail.com	405 Garfield Ave Valparaiso IN 46383	IN	Assoc	Immanuel Valparaiso IN	(219)462-8207	SL	2017
Kegley Noah A	(262)302-9575 nkegley@ilcsbatavia.org		NI	Sn/Adm	Immanuel Batavia IL	(630)879-7163	SL	2018
Keil David D	(760)484-1058 gmctruck54@gmail.com	4804 NE 155th Ave Vancouver WA 98682	NOW	EM			SPR	1975
Keilani Anthony M	(248)480-3635 anthony.keilani@ctsfw.edu	862 Bennaville Ave Birmingham MI 48009	MI		Michigan District Ann Arbor MI	(888)225-2111	FW	2023
Keily Kenneth G	(812)528-1094	12811 W County Road 100 N Norman IN 47264	IN	SP	Emmanuel Bedford IN	(812)797-3693	FW	1988
Keinath Edgar M	(812)522-8440	450 Manor Dr Seymour IN 47274	IN	RSO	Ambassadors of Recon-ciliation Billings MT	(844)447-2671	FW	1977
Keinath Joshua A	(712)267-1375 pastorkeinath@gmail.com	4078 Highway 554 Loris SC 29569	SE	Sn/Adm	Risen Christ Myrtle Beach SC	(843)272-5845	SL	2011
Keinath Daniel P	(406)245-3984 danielkeinath@trinitybillings.org	537 Grand Ave Billings MT 59101	MT	Sn/Adm	Trinity Billings MT	(406)245-3984	SL	2007
Keinbaum Santiago E	(402) 430-8685 pastorkeinbaum@gmail.com		FG	C05/2023			FW	2017
Keistman Herbert A	(979) 540-8781 keistman@yahoo.com	1224 Private Road 1033 Paige TX 78659	TX	EM			FW	1996
Keller Roger A Sr	(314)363-3654 n9aklr@msn.com	2113 Harbour Watch Dr Tarpon Spgs FL 34689	FG	EM			SL	2006
Keller Walter A	(586)219-4168	15022 Annapolis Dr Sterling Hts MI 48313	MI	EM			SL	1981
Keller Michael B	(940)390-3065 prbkeller@gmail.com	102 S River Park Dr Guttenberg IA 52052	IE	SP	St Paul* McGregor IA	(563)873-3341	FW	2018
Keller Martin E	revkeller219@gmail.com	1700 N Country Rd 180 E Brownstown IN 47220	IN	EM			CQ	1990
Keller James N	magisterjk@gmail.com	4011 Daner Dr Fort Wayne IN 46815	IN	Sn/Adm	New Life Fort Wayne IN	(260)420-3024	FW	2001
Keller Andrew P	(812)216-8850	104 N Kenton St Reynolds IN 47980	IN	SP	Saint James Reynolds IN	(219)984-5421	FW	2020
Keller Albert L Jr	(985)327-7417 2kellers2vws@reagan.com	701 Penwood Dr Covington LA 70433	SO	EM			FW	1983

*Multiple Assignments (See Church Worker Locator for Additional Details)
See Page 53 for the Table of Abbreviations for key to District, Position, and Seminary abbreviations
**C =Candidate; EM = Emeritus; the date following the C is the month and year the Candidate status began

NAME	TELEPHONE NUMBER EMAIL	STREET ADDRESS CITY/STATE/ZIP	DISTRICT	POSITION/ STATUS**	WHERE SERVING	OFFICE PHONE	SEM/ PROGRAM	YR GRAD
Keller William L II Dr	wlkeller@outlook.com	217 14th Avenue SW #1320 Rochester MN 55902	MNS	SP	Grace Rochester MN	(507)289-7833	SL	1996
Kellerman Craig W	(208)590-1621	1145 N 7th E Mountain Home ID 83647	NOW	EM			CQ	1998
Kellerman David M	(262)388-6266 kells5@juno.com	705 Vine St West Bend WI 53095	SW	EM			SL-SMP	2012
Kellerman Robert W	(520)431-4649 rakell@q.com	900 SW 31 #241 Topeka KS 66611	MDS	EM			CQ	1984
Kelling John T	(262) 549-2150 johnkelling1@gmail.com	9168 N Sacred Sky Pl Tuscon AZ 85743	EN	EM			SL	1995
Kellogg Christopher E	(505)721-9852 prkelloggosl@gmail.com	2633 NE 39th St Topeka KS 66617	KS	EM			SL	1982
Kelm Daniel W	(608)566-4442 dw54k@yahoo.com	22 Mahan Ln Waynesville NC 28786	SE	EM			CQ	1995
Kelm Virgil M	(314)766-7611 pastorvkelm@sbcglobal.net	P.O. Box 60 Pocahontas MO 63779	MO	SP	Trinity* Shawneetown MO	(573)833-6055	FW	1982
Kelm Harvey F Jr	(409)363-2346 harvey.kelm@gmail.com	5610 Garden Village Dr Lumberton TX 77657	TX	EM			SL	1985
Kelm Richard G	(402)200-0190 richardkelm@ymail.com	829 Issac St Bovery MN 55709	MNN	SP	Mount Olive* Bovey MN	(218)245-3983	FW	1999
Keltner James A	(913)837-0303 pastorandy4@yahoo.com	1507 N Broadway St Louisburg KS 66053	KS	Sn/Adm	Christ Our Savior Louisburg KS	(913)837-4502	SL	1984
Kelto Paul D	(906)439-5147 pjkelts@charter.net	E2994 Tunteri Rd P.O. Box 224 Chatham MI 49816	NW	EM			FW	1987
Kemp Calvin W	(802)279-3266 kempcw@aol.com	1330 Appleby Dr Woodland Park CO 80863	NE	EM			FW	1996
Kemp William R	(469)774-9359 will_kemp50@yahoo.com	6412 Landmark Trl The Colony TX 75056	TX	Assoc	Waters Edge Frisco TX	(972)712-7377	CQ	2014
Kempin Daniel A	(989)708-6845 kempin04@yahoo.com	3801 Wintergreen Dr Midland MI 48640	MI	Sn/Adm	St John's Midland MI	(989)835-5861	SL	1995
Kendall Chad D Dr	chad.kendall@cuchicago.edu	2682 Le Baron Ct. Geneva IL 60134	NI	S HS/C	Concordia University Chicago River Forest IL	(708)771-8300	FW	2002
Kennaugh Eric D Dr	revkennaugh@gmail.com	8948 Dancer Ave NW North Canton OH 44720	NI	Pro Stf	Lutheran Church Exten- sion Fund Saint Louis MO	(314)965-9000	SL	2001
Kennedy Christopher M Dr	(210)614-3742 ckennedy@shlutheran.org	6914 Wurzbach Rd San Antonio TX 78240	TX	Sn/Adm	Shepherd Hills San Antonio TX	(210)614-3742	SL	2008
Kennell Andrew C	prkennell@gmail.com	700 Sheilah Ln Monett MO 65708	MO	SP	St Johns Monett MO	(417)235-3416	SL	2002
Kenreich John A	(631)728-0418 ckenreich@aol.com	12 Norwood Rd Hampton Bays NY 11946	AT	SP	Christ Our Saviour Hampton Bays NY	(631)728-3288	SL	1965
Kent James E	(410) 257-3030 pastor@firstlutheranchurch.org	3080 Whispering Dr Prnc Frederck MD 20678	SE	SP	First Huntingtown MD	(410)257-3030	SL	2017
Keogh Charles L	(816)510-7837 charles.l.keogh@gmail.com	8871 151st St W Prior Lake MN 55372	MNS	EM			SL	1979
Kern Paul T	(402)598-1417 pk90413@yahoo.com	1613 E Lawn Plaza Dr York NE 68467	NEB	EM			SPR	1972
Kern Jonathan M	(719)600-1082 revkern@gmail.com	4639 Hotspur Dr Colorado Spgs CO 80922	RM	SP	Immanuel Colorado Springs CO	(719)636-5011	SL	2011
Kern David W	618-610-0669 salvationdwk@gmail.com	305 Garland St Moyock NC 27958	SE	EM			FW	2005
Kern Dale B	(567)444-4866 dkern@bright.net	217 Sylvanus St Archbold OH 43502	OH	EM			SL	1971
Kern Timothy D	(989)448-1160 timothy.kern@oslmarlette.com	9277 Slattery Rd Marlette MI 48453	MI	SP	Our Savior Marlette MI	(989)635-7994	FW	2021
Kerner James L Dr	(860)647-0136 bishopofsuffield@yahoo.com	193 Hawthorne St Manchester CT 06042	NE	EM			SL	1983
Kerns Devin M	(910)547-8524 swimtherhine@gmail.com	4932 Spicewood Dr Charlotte NC 28227	SE	SP	Augustana Hickory NC	(828)328-6706	CQ	2016
Kerns Douglas S II	(618)920-3479 kernsds@gmail.com	2012 Sullivan Trl Easton PA 18040	EA	SP	Faith Easton PA	(610)253-1625	FW	2013
Kerr Jonathan W	(415)994-3275 otterdude23@gmail.com	6701 Oleatha Ave Saint Louis MO 63139	MO	EM			SL	2021
Kerstein Noah R	(850)240-5156 nkersteinchurch@gmail.com	215 Mayfair Dr Lincoln IL 62656	CI	SP	Faith Lincoln IL	(217)732-4901	FW	2024
Kersten Alfred A	pak50mel@gmail.com	3445 E Shaw Rd Lincoln MI 48742	MI	EM			CQ	2018
Keseman Bruce E	(618)641-3475	c/o Christ Our Savior Lutheran Church 612 N State St Freeburg IL 62243	SI	SP	Christ Our Savior Freeburg IL	(618)539-5664	SL	1990
Kessen Clifford F	(715)535-2728	210 Liberty Ests Tigerton WI 54486	NW	EM			SPR	1966
Kessler Michael E	(928)783-3024 pastorkessleryuma@gmail.com	711 S 7th Ave Yuma AZ 85364	PSW	SP	Calvary Yuma AZ	(928)783-3024	FW	2001
Kessler Richard W	(254)629-2009 srfarms.rk@gmail.com	9418 Highway 6 Cisco TX 76437	TX	EM			SPR	1971
Ketcham Bradley W	(712)291-8164 bishopbk@mchsi.com	504 Gran Dr Storm Lake IA 50588	IW	Sn/Adm	Grace Storm Lake IA	(712)732-5005	FW	1989
Ketelsen Brian L	(402)678-2878 rbketelsen@yahoo.com	302 N 7th P.O. Box 349 Saint Edward NE 68660	NEB	SP	St John* Cedar Rapids NE		FW	2004
Ketelsen Joshua C	(989)306-2586 joshua.ketelsen@gmail.com	c/o Immanuel Lutheran Church 1001 Immanuel Dr Boonville MO 65233	MO	SP	Immanuel Boonville MO	(660)882-2208	SL	2009

*Multiple Assignments (See Church Worker Locator for Additional Details)
See Page 53 for the Table of Abbreviations for key to District, Position, and Seminary abbreviations
**C =Candidate; EM = Emeritus; the date following the C is the month and year the Candidate status began

NAME	TELEPHONE NUMBER EMAIL	STREET ADDRESS CITY/STATE/ZIP	DISTRICT	POSITION/ STATUS**	WHERE SERVING	OFFICE PHONE	SEM/ PROGRAM	YR GRAD
Kettner David L	(573)453-6162 salemlchpas@gmail.com	1106 Bay Ct Salem MO 65560	MO	Sn/Adm	Holy Cross* Houston MO	(417)967-2204	FW	1989
Kettner Michael A	(618)763-5741 mike.alice@juno.com	537 Crestline Dr Pittsburgh PA 15234	SI	EM			FW	1992
Kettner Keith A	(618)534-5731	117 E 6th St Beardstown IL 62618	CI	SP	St John Beardstown IL	(217)323-1288	FW	2022
Kettner Joel W	(910) 471-7902 jkett7445@yahoo.com	258 W Winding Way Wallace NC 28466	SE	EM			SL	1965
Kettner Edward G Dr	(913)808-5008 ekettner1972@gmail.com	13207 W 85th Ct Lenexa KS 66215	KS	EM			Other	1969
Keuning Jeffrey M	(515)789-4008 keuningjm@iowatelecom.net	313 Marshall St Dexter IA 50070	IW	SP	St John* Casey IA	(641)746-2734	FW	2008
Keurulainen Barry J	(724)996-2160 bjk5579@gmail.com	287137 Latonka Dr Mercer PA 16137	EA	EM			FW	1978
Keyes Dennis A Sr	(940)366-2507 dennykeyes00@gmail.com	243 Private Road 265 Bowie TX 76230	TX	EM			SL	2006
Khan Farrukh M	(586)275-0770 farrukh@poblo.org	3555 Garfield Rd Ste 1 Clintn Twnshp MI 48035	MI	Assoc	All Nations Clinton Township MI	(586)636-5688	FW	2005
Khan Khurram M	(248)250-6112 khurram@poblo.org	6902 Aurora Dr Troy MI 48098	MI	Sn/Adm	All Nations Clinton Township MI	(586)636-5688	EIITSL	2005
Kibler Ray F III			PSW	EM			CQ	1999
Kiefer Jason T	(908)735-0880 jasonkiefer@comcast.net	33 Maple Ave Annandale NJ 08801	NJ	SMP	Good Shepherd Blairstown NJ	(908)362-9405	FW-SMP	2025
Kiefer John M	kieferfamily@aol.com	5948 State Rd 106 Bremen IN 46506	IN	EM			FW	1983
Kieschnick Charles B	(314)221-8741 clkies@charter.net	136 Meramec Ridge Dr Fenton MO 63026	MO	Asst	Concordia Kirkwood MO	(314)822-7772	SL	1991
Kieschnick Clyde J	(325)864-1036 pastork@zion-abilene.org	189 Tempest Ln Abilene TX 79602	TX	Sn/Adm	Zion Abilene TX	(325)690-0121	SL	1990
Kieschnick Gerald B Dr	(512)578-6035 gbkies@gmail.com	1109 Eagle Point Dr Georgetown TX 78628	TX	EM			SPR	1970
Kieschnick John H	(713)598-7278 johnkieschnick1@comcast.net	1050 Cayman Bend Ln League City TX 77573	TX	EM			SPR	1970
Kiesel Martin E	(203)558-3304 iamyashar@aol.com	12312 Litchfield Ln Fort Myers FL 33913	NE	EM			SL	1979
Kieselowsky Robert J Jr	(215)992-9102 revrobert@phillyministries.org	1800 Ginnodo St Philadelphia PA 19130	EN	SP	St John* Springfield PA	(610)543-3100	FW	2011
Kieser Stephen W	(972)210-1160 swkieser@gmail.com	610 E Park Ave Riverton WY 82501	WY	SP	Trinity Riverton WY	(307)856-9340	FW	2006
Kiessling Mark R	(314)984-0745 mark.kiessling@lcms.org	445 Bethany Ct Valley Park MO 63088	MO	S Ex/S	Office of National Mission Saint Louis MO		SL	2006
Kiessling Richard E	(503)616-6122 rmkiessling@gmail.com	1283 SW 175th Ave Beaverton OR 97003	NOW	EM			SL	1967
Kietzman Harvey H	(218)652-3341 harvey.kietzman@gmail.com	30683 Honeycomb Dr Akeley MN 56433	MNN	EM			SPR	1972
Kilgo Sean R	(505)553-4829 kilgosr@gmail.com	3917 Harvard Rd Lawrence KS 66049	KS	SP	Redeemer Lawrence KS	(785)843-8181	FW	2016
Kilian Jason P	pastorjpkilian@sbcglobal.net		PSW	SP	Amazing Grace Corona CA	(951)433-0151	SL	2005
Kilian Marvin V	(254)933-3205 vkilian@sbcglobal.net	2610 Riverside Trl Temple TX 76502	TX	EM			SPR	1960
Killian Edward J	1580@protonmail.com	239 W Olive St #4 Inglewood CA 90301	PSW	SP	The Good Shepherd Inglewood CA	(310)671-7644	FW	2006
Kilmer Eric S	(989)635-2969 kilmerek@yahoo.com	304 N Concord Rd Albion MI 49224	MI	EM			CQ	1989
Kilponen Roger R	(810)252-7877 rogerkilponen@gmail.com	P.O. Box 104 Hessel MI 49745	MI	EM			FW	1978
Kilps William R		3504 Pierce Ct Two Rivers WI 54241	SW	EM			FW	1982
Kim Joshua Y	rev.joshua.y.kim@gmail.com	62 Pomelo Rancho Santa Margarita CA 92688	PSW	EM			KO	1975
Kim Theodore S	(562)665-0791 tedkim49@gmail.com	19 Cerrito Irvine CA 92612	PSW	Assoc	Jesus Love Irvine CA	(949)878-1970	CQ	2015
Kim Seung W	(714)274-3334 tptg76@hotmail.com	8162 Crowley Cir Buena Park CA 90621	PSW	Assoc	True Love Fullerton CA	(714)992-5008	Other	2013
Kim Yeong K	(310)836-8342 arkofnoahchurch@gmail.com	3735 Hughes Ave Los Angeles CA 90034	PSW	Sn/Adm	Ark Of Noah Los Angeles CA	(310)836-8342	CQ	2009
Kim Min S	samil2110@gmail.com	355 Oak Springs Rd Lawrenceville GA 30043	FG	C04/2025			CQ	2015
Kim John C	(951) 707-3925 sarangchkim@gmail.com	4114 Orin Privado Ontario CA 91761	PSW	EM			CQ	2010
Kim Dong J	(213)598-1196	1308 S New Hampshire Ave #403 Los Angeles CA 90006	PSW	SP	Light of Light Los Angeles CA	(213)598-1196	CQ	1997
Kim David S Dr	(713)494-3127 davidkim@glocalmission.org	2422 Jill Cir Spring TX 77388	TX	C10/2016			SL	2007
Kim Byung G	kimbg1212@gmail.com	c/o Good News Korean Lutheran 13082 Bowen St Garden Grove CA 92843	PSW	Sn/Adm	Good News Korean Buena Park CA	(714)681-6770	CQ	2012
Kim Philip S	(718)357-3788 phillip.kim21@verizon.net	249-21 64th Ave #2 Little Neck NY 11362	AT	EM			CQ	1993
Kim John H		11254 Pantheon St Norwalk CA 90650	PSW	Assoc	Good Shepherd Downey CA	(562)803-4459	CQ	2006
Kimari Wallace J	(619)788-9929 wallykimari@gmail.com	561 Live Oak Dr El Cajon CA 92020	PSW	SP	Bethany* San Diego CA	(619)222-7295	FW	1991
Kimball Les L	(407)907-0980 lesdianekimball@gmail.com	1383 Haven Dr Oviedo FL 32765	FG	EM			SPR	1968

*Multiple Assignments (See Church Worker Locator for Additional Details)

See Page 53 for the Table of Abbreviations for key to District, Position, and Seminary abbreviations

**C =Candidate; EM = Emeritus; the date following the C is the month and year the Candidate status began

NAME	TELEPHONE NUMBER EMAIL	STREET ADDRESS CITY/STATE/ZIP	DISTRICT	POSITION/ STATUS**	WHERE SERVING	OFFICE PHONE	SEM/ PROGRAM	YR GRAD
Kimmel Mike L	(903)305-3250 pastorkimmel@hotmail.com	21 County Road 4426 Mt Pleasant TX 75455	TX	SP	St John* Clarksville TX		FW	2008
Kimmel Roger A	(585)637-5638 vicark@yahoo.com	2227 Sweden Walker Rd Hilton NY 14468	EA	EM			FW	2003
Kinast Frank X Jr	(252) 525-8011 revkinast@gmail.com	704 Madison Ann Dr Lagrange NC 28551	SE	SP	Faith Kinston NC	(252)523-6033	SL	1995
Kincaid Kristian G Dr	(563)582-2157 pastorkincaid@gmail.com	9161 Pheasant Ln Dubuque IA 52003	IE	EM			FW	1987
Kind David A	(651)302-2164	11705 Arnold Palmer Trl Minneapolis MN 55449	MNS	SP	Univ Chapel Minneapolis MN	(612)331-2747	FW	1996
Kindschy Lowell B	(805)708-2481 locorush@gmail.com	1684 Sneffels St Montrose CO 81401	RM	EM			FW	1978
King James T	revjtking@yahoo.com	621 E. Warren St. Bunker Hill IL 62014	SI		Southern Illinois District Belleville IL	(618)234-4767	SL	1997
King Idonis M	(314)326-9561 iking827@gmail.com	3605 Archerton Dr Saint Louis MO 63044	MO	Assoc	St Trinity Saint Louis MO	(314)353-3276	SL	2024
King Wayne A	(414)429-5962 prwking@yahoo.com	125 N Lar Ann St Belgium WI 53004	SW	EM			SL	2007
King Harold L Jr	(402)984-2701 revhking.jr@gmail.com	2308 W 9th St Hastings NE 68901	NEB	EM			FW	1982
King Brian J	(314)961-5275 brian@webstergardens.org	c/o The Lutheran Church Of Webster Gardens 8749 Watson Rd Saint Louis MO 63119	MO	SMP	Webster Gardens Webster Groves MO	(314)961-5275	SL-SMP	2010
King Delrich O	(623)523-1303 revdel98@yahoo.com	6510 W Butler Dr Unit 109 Glendale AZ 85302	PSW	EM			CQ	1999
King Jeffrey W	pastorjeffreywking@gmail.com	98 CR 428 Jonesboro AR 72404	MDS	SP	Our Shepherd Searcy AR	(501)268-1613	SL	2007
Kinley Daniel A	(757)262-6815 dkinley@holycrossfw.org	5341 Brookfarm Pl Fort Wayne IN 46835	IN	Assoc	Holy Cross Fort Wayne IN	(260)483-3173	FW	2025
Kinnaman Scot A	(314)608-6842 prkinnaman@gmail.com	4110 Minnesota Ave Saint Louis MO 63118	MO	Pro Stf	Concordia Publishing House Saint Louis MO	(314)268-1000	FW	1995
Kinne Timothy L	(224)360-2629 timothy.kinne53@gmail.com	4641 Esther Ln Green Bay WI 54311	NW	EM			FW	1989
Kinnee L E	(309)690-8252 bugbug316@juno.com	123 N Charlton St Peoria IL 61605	CI	EM			SL	1988
Kinney Ian P	(260)348-1891 pastoripkinney@gmail.com	311 Cedar St Sabetha KS 66534	KS	SP	First Sabetha KS	(785)284-3566	FW	2021
Kinslow Keith	(773)651-2786 keithkinslow@yahoo.com	8555 S King Dr Chicago IL 60619	EN	SMP	Chatham Fields Chicago IL	(773)723-3661	SL-SMP	2012
Kintz Joshua A	(618)541-2099 joshua.kintz@gmail.com	114 Del Rio Ct Belleville IL 62221	SI	Assoc	Zion Belleville IL	(618)233-2299	SL	2023
Kirby Peter N	(314) 590-6221 peter.kirby@mo.lcms.org	7 Gandy Dr Saint Louis MO 63146	MO	D Ex/S	Missouri District Saint Louis MO	(314)590-6200	SL	1994
Kirchhoff Donald G	(734)470-6115 don.kirchhoff@hotmail.com	2100 Maple Creek Cir Ann Arbor MI 48108	MI	EM			SL	1968
Kirchner Donald G	(218)368-9560 donaldgk@hotmail.com	48268 229th Ave Bemidji MN 56601	MNN	EM			SL	1999
Kirchner Duane E	(417)230-7993 duanekirchner@centurytel.net	261 Angelwing Ln Blue Eye MO 65611	MO	EM			SL	1972
Kirchoff Chad A	(612)751-1300 chad@redofitness.com	18283 207th St E Welch MN 55089	MNS	SMP	Shep Valley Hastings MN	(651)437-7010	SL-SMP	2014
Kirchoff Scott W	s10kirchoff@gmail.com	1032 Linda Drive Conway SC 29526	SE	SP	Holy Lamb Myrtle Beach SC	(843)236-1344	FW	1995
Kirk James D	(636)222-7106 jim.kirk37@gmail.com	12 Parkville Ln Festus MO 63028	MO	EM			SL	1985
Kirk William K	(903)520-7110 smpkirk@gmail.com	2610 Brahman Dr Manvel TX 77578	TX	EM			SL-SMP	2012
Kirk John E Jack	(785)744-3429 cvsix@bluevalley.net	647 Bison Rd Marysville KS 66508	KS	EM			SPR	1975
Kirk James A	(262)853-7671 james@kirk.org	1348 Skyridge Dr Apt B Crystal Lake IL 60014	NI	Assoc	Immanuel Crystal Lake IL	(815)459-1441	SL	2023
Kirk Alston S	(361)813-6832 captkirk6@gmail.com	737 Brock Dr Corpus Christi TX 78412	TX	EM			SL	1964
Kirk Raymond V	(519)208-5581 nanc.ray@rogers.com	629 Pine Island Crescent Waterloo ON N2V-1 CANADA	EN	EM			SL	1972
Kirkeide Duwayne D	(791)591-9133 ddkirk45@comcast.net	7234 Bonnie Brae Ln Colorado Spgs CO 80922	RM	EM			SL	1971
Kirklen Donald L	(254)445-8188 donkirklen@yahoo.com	3870 County Road 344 Dublin TX 76446	TX	EM			CQ	1984
Kirkman James L Jr	(602)525-0882 minkapup@gmail.com	37918 Apache Plume Dr Murrieta CA 92563	PSW	SP	Trinity Temecula CA	(951)676-1492	FW	2005
Kirkup George A Dr	(631)355-6029 gckirkup@gmail.com	63 Loop Dr Sayville NY 11782	AT	C08/2025			FW	2009
Kirmsse William H	(952)240-9080 whkirmsse@me.com	8800 W 35th St St Louis Park MN 55426	MNS	SP	St Peter Watertown MN	(952)955-1679	SL	1970
Kirsch Donald W	(320)251-1951 ddjjjkir@aol.com	2688 14 1/2 Ave SE Saint Cloud MN 56304	MNN	EM			SPR	1970
Kirschenmann James E	(224)795-1055 james.kirschenmann@gmail.com	23147 Topeka St Vassar KS 66543	KS	SP	Zion Vassar KS	(785)828-4482	SL	2016
Kirschke Gary A	(715)498-3341 garykirschke@yahoo.com	454 Maethy St SE Wyoming MI 49548	MI	EM			CQ	2002
Kischnick Bruce R	(502)797-7407	1787 Klerner Ln New Albany IN 47150	IN	EM			CQ	1991
Kister Thaine L	(605)949-1353 nmhusker95@outlook.com	103 E Berry Dr Hobbs NM 88240	RM	SP	Our Savior* Lovington NM	(575)396-4549	FW	2007

*Multiple Assignments (See Church Worker Locator for Additional Details)
See Page 53 for the Table of Abbreviations for key to District, Position, and Seminary abbreviations
**C =Candidate; EM = Emeritus; the date following the C is the month and year the Candidate status began

NAME	TELEPHONE NUMBER EMAIL	STREET ADDRESS CITY/STATE/ZIP	DISTRICT	POSITION/ STATUS**	WHERE SERVING	OFFICE PHONE	SEM/ PROGRAM	YR GRAD
Kistler Daniel L	(650)207-0982 dankistler62@gmail.com	27449 Calle Rabano Romoland CA 92585	PSW	EM			SL	1997
Kitson Robert J	(254)640-9972 pastork@ctwa.com	73549 Long Lake Boat Landing Rd Mellen WI 54546	NW	EM			SL	2005
Kittel Charles W	(847)464-2626 opakittel43@gmail.com	922 Fairmont Rd Pingree Grove IL 60140	NI	Asst	St Peter Arlington Heights IL	(847)259-4114	SL	1970
Kitzing Shawn L		3731 Marysville Rd Staplehurst NE 68439	NEB	SP	Our Redeemer Staplehurst NE	(402)535-2251	SL	2000
Kitzmann Dennis M	(817)847-7383 dmkitz@swbell.net	405 Lottie Ln Saginaw TX 76179	TX	EM			CQ	1995
Klade Jeffrey H	(405)202-6638 vicarklade@aol.com	17851 N Alfadale Rd Okarche OK 73762	OK	EM			SL-SMP	2012
Klafehn Michael A	(269)503-3197 klafehnmichael84@gmail.com	500 Clubhouse Vista Rd Apt 504 Altonna FL 32702	FG	EM			SPR	1975
Klahn Timothy D	(716)570-5953 ashfordtrinitylutheranchurch@gmail.com	9930 Route 219 West Valley NY 14171	EA	SMP	Trinity* West Valley NY	(716)570-5953	CQ	2019
Klamer Lance D	(989)798-7187 ldklamer@gmail.com	256 N. Maple St. P.O. Box 471 Fowler MI 48835	MI	Assoc	St Paul Fowler MI	(517)420-4826	FW	2013
Klatt Donald M	(612)270-9468 klattdm63@aol.com	22847 Thompson Point Rd Deerwood MN 56444	MNN	SP	Zion* Crosby MN	(218)546-6910	FW	2006
Klatt Gary H	(605)582-2592 gklatt@alliancecom.net	524 N Maple Ave Brandon SD 57005	MNS	EM			FW	1985
Klatt Michael V	(507)943-3390 mvklatt@gmail.com	3900 420th Ave Elmore MN 56027	MNS	SP	St John Elmore MN	(507)943-3390	SL	1982
Klatt Zachary A	(913) 209-8622 zach.klatt@gmail.com	3030 W Greenfield Dr Freeport IL 61032	NI	SP	Immanuel Freeport IL	(815)235-1993	SL	2019
Klauck Roland M Dr	(207)219-8569 jklauck@twc.com	542 Desfosses Ave Scarborough ME 04074	NE	EM			SL	1964
Klaus Kurt R	pastorkurt@messiahonline.org	18125 Dunbury Ave Farmington MN 55024	MNS	Sn/Adm	Messiah Lakeville MN	(952)431-5959	SL	2004
Klausmeier Arthur P	(260)493-3174 14arsu@comcast.net	1529 Faulkner Ct Fort Wayne IN 46815	IN	EM			CQ	1981
Klaustermeier Jeremy R	(636)359-1061 revklaus@hotmail.com	2359 Santa Maria Dr Warrenton MO 63383	MO	SP	St John Warrenton MO	(636)456-2888	SL	2001
Kleidon Norbert H Dr	nrkleidon@comcast.net	2101 S Garfield Ave Apt 139 Loveland CO 80537	RM	EM			SPR	1967
Kleimola Dale M Dr	(517)745-6241 kleimoladmk@gmail.com	214 N Higby St Jackson MI 49202	MI	EM			SL	1979
Kleimola Ryan D	(567)395-0316 kleimr@gmail.com	126 Yale Dr Toledo OH 43614	OH	Assoc	Trinity Toledo OH	(419)385-2651	SL	2010
Klein Bert A	(512)653-3232 bklein6617@aol.com	6617 Bramber Ln Austin TX 78754	TX	EM			SL	1970
Klein Brent A Dr	(507)645-4438 pastor.klein@trinitynorthfield.org	2113 Johnson St Northfield MN 55057	MNS	Sn/Adm	Trinity Northfield MN	(507)645-4438	SL	1987
Klein Frederick G	(703)250-4658 fredncliz@verizon.net	Greenspring Retirement 7446 Spring Village Dr Gt 413 Springfield VA 22150	SE	EM			SL	1968
Klein Jay B	(630)589-7262 JayKlein@outlook.com	13824 S Balsam Ln Apt D Plainfield IL 60544	NI	EM			SL	1999
Kleinfelter James O	(443)622-5967 kleinfj@hotmail.com	8623 Jessica Ln Perry Hall MD 21128	SE	EM			SL	1983
Kleino Jeremy A	(248)925-8454 jeremykleino@yahoo.com	2634 Hartline Dr Rochester Hills MI 48309	OH	C09/2019			FW	2018
Kleinschmidt Eric A	eaklein27@gmail.com	1001 Roanoke Ct Dyer IN 46311	IN	SP	Redeemer Highland IN	(219)838-4898	FW	2007
Kleinschmidt Travis R	(217)369-8357 trkleinschmidt@gmail.com	W8089 County Road A Shawano WI 54166	NW	SP	Saint Jakobi* Shawano WI	(715)524-4347	FW	2008
Klemm David R	(586)318-6188 pastorklemm@peaceshelby.org	55714 Shelby Rd Apt 8108 Shelby Township MI 48316	MI	SP	Peace Shelby Township MI	(586)731-4120	SL	2001
Klemm Derek S	(702)360-8290 dklemm@mvlcs.org	9550 W. Cheyenne Las Vegas NV 89129	PSW	Sn/Adm	Mountain View Las Vegas NV	(702)360-8290	SL	2007
Klemme Eric E	(831)331-6678 ericklemme@gmail.com	c/o Good Shepherd Lutheran Church 1 Meigs Dr Shalimar FL 32579	SO	SP	Good Shepherd Shalimar FL	(850)651-1022	SL	1994
Klemp Stephen J	(414)364-6574 pastor@stjohnglendale.com	7864 N Chadwick Glendale WI 53217	SW	SP	St John Glendale WI	(414)352-4150	SL	2003
Klemsz Scott C	(831)422-6352	1072 University Ave Salinas CA 93901	CNH	SP	Our Savior Salinas CA	(831)422-6352	FW	1997
Kleppe Glen A	(320)629-2242		MNN	SP	Living Branch North Branch MN	(651)674-5576	FW	1994
Kletke Daniel B	(719)275-0111	1014 Phay Ave Canon City CO 81212	RM	SP	St John Canon City CO	(719)275-0111	SL	2008
Klettke William R	(302)956-6188 klett9@aol.com	1 Champions Dr Bridgeville DE 19933	NJ	EM			SL	1973
Klieve John E	(262)955-4351 jeklieve@protonmail.com	430 W Jefferson St Port Washington WI 53074	SW	EM			FW	1983
Kliewer Mark A		3215 S Highland Dr Winnemucca NV 89445	CNH	EM			FW	1987
Kline Steven G	(920)412-2463 revkline@shepherdhills.org	N2240 Cornhusk Dr Greenville WI 54942	NW	Sn/Adm	Shepherd Hills Greenville WI	(920)757-5722	SL	1992
Klingbeil Kurt C	(608)415-3942 pastorkurtklingbeil@yahoo.com	2635 Manorwood Dr Gaylord MI 49735	MI	SP	Trinity* Gaylord MI	(989)732-4816	FW	2004
Klinge David H	pastorklinge@gmail.com	2419 Lynch Ave Auburn NE 68305	NEB	EM			FW	2008
Klinkenberg Timothy M	tklinkenberg@stjohnsorange.org	154 S Shaffer St Orange CA 92866	PSW	Sn/Adm	Saint Johns Orange CA	(714)288-4400	SL	1991

*Multiple Assignments (See Church Worker Locator for Additional Details)
See Page 53 for the Table of Abbreviations for key to District, Position, and Seminary abbreviations
**C =Candidate; EM = Emeritus; the date following the C is the month and year the Candidate status began

NAME	TELEPHONE NUMBER EMAIL	STREET ADDRESS CITY/STATE/ZIP	DISTRICT	POSITION/ STATUS**	WHERE SERVING	OFFICE PHONE	SEM/ PROGRAM	YR GRAD
Kloepping Michael G	(618) 830-5712 mrailguy@gmail.com	11272 Oak Forest Ln Lebanon IL 62254	CI	EM			SL	1997
Kloha Mark A	(606)325-1919 padre1953@hotmail.com	326 Long St Ashland KY 41101	OH	SP	St Paul Ashland KY	(606)324-3515	SL	1979
Kloha Jeffrey J Dr	(314) 800-3505 klohaj@me.com	3409 Wilson Blvd Unit 807 Arlington VA 22201	SE	Assoc	Our Savior Arlington VA	(703)892-4846	SL	1992
Klopke Paul J	(847)529-8535 paulklopke@gmail.com	4601 Magnolia Dr Rolling Meadows IL 60008	NI	Assoc	St Peter Arlington Heights IL	(847)259-4114	SL	1991
Klotz Gregory D	(260)246-2595 ethnogruves@gmail.com	2929 Bluebonnet Ct Antioch CA 94531	CNH	EM			SL	1984
Klug James R	(262)323-9411 q471215b@protonmail.com	2098 Ottawa Ln Grafton WI 53024	SW	EM			SL	2007
Klug Jerry L	(217) 251-2352 jlKlug42@gmail.com	11407 Blackhawk Dr Paris IL 61944	CI	EM			SL	1968
Klug Timothy D	(307)250-7557	925 4th St W Kalispell MT 59901	MT	C07/2016			FW	1989
Kluge David T	(630)564-9350 fatherdtk@comcast.net	4033 Prescott Ave Lyons IL 60534	NI	EM			SL	1965
Klumpp Zachary T	(218)780-9693 pastorklumpp@gmail.com	6961 Hwy 169 Virginia MN 55792	MNN	SP	Redeemer* Aurora MN	(218)229-3208	FW	2023
Kluth David L Dr	(512)294-3920 david.kluth@gmail.com	2508 Plantation Dr Round Rock TX 78681	TX	EM			SL	1977
Kluzek Mark T	(712)265-1286 Godcares1000@gmail.com	321 Jefferson St Wapello IA 52653	IE	SP	St Paul Wapello IA	(712)265-1286	SL	1996
Knaack William L	(218)252-0199 pastorknaack@gmail.com	23433 Witter Ave Park Rapids MN 56470	MNN	EM			FW	1994
Knapp James D	(303)880-7288 karenmfk@yahoo.com	2700 W Mulberry St Fort Collins CO 80521	RM	EM			FW	1982
Knapp Robert C	(636)584-2747 revknapp@gmail.com	5385 St Johns Rd Villa Ridge MO 63089	MO	C09/2022			SL	2009
Knapp Stephen A	saknapp@comcast.net	P.O. Box 8 Forest Park IL 60130	NI	EM			SPR	1976
Knapp Timothy D	tim.knapp@comcast.net	13 Porter Lane Marlborough NH 03455	NE	EM			FW	1983
Knauft Jess M	jessmknauft@gmail.com	3552 Baseline Ave Santa Ynez CA 93460	PSW	SP	Shep Of Valley Santa Ynez CA	(805)688-8938	FW	1986
Knaus Nathan K	(641)203-7155 pastorknaus@gmail.com	302 S 4th St Chariton IA 50049	IE	SP	Trinity Chariton IA	(641)774-8335	FW	2019
Knauss-Behal Matthew A	(805)256-5793 mknauss@clcfamily.org	2045 Camino Dr Escondido CA 92026	PSW	Assoc	Community Escondido CA	(760)739-1650	SL	2018
Knea Keith E	(920)285-9719 pastorknea@gmail.com	3433 S Van Buren Rd Reese MI 48757	MI	Sn/Adm	St Michael Richville MI	(989)868-4791	FW	2008
Kneer Dennis C	(920)285-5596 astrokneer@gmail.com	205 N Monroe St Watertown WI 53094	SW	EM			FW	1986
Knefelkamp David J	(315)540-3317 pastorknefelkamp@gmail.com	E11775 County Road Hh Osseo WI 54758	NW	SP	St Paul* Whitehall WI	(715)597-2431	SL	2007
Knepel Robert J	(352)775-4964 rknepel@yahoo.com	2224 Margarita Dr Lady Lake FL 32159	EA	EM			SL	1973
Knepper Christopher D	314-231-4702 pastor.chris@bethlehemstlouis.org	2153 Salisbury St St. Louis MO 63107	MO	Assoc	Bethlehem Saint Louis MO	(314)231-4702	SL	2024
Knepper Grant A	(503)536-3331 gknep@frontier.com	1120 Eastridge Dr Modesto CA 95355	CNH	SP	Grace Modesto CA	(209)522-8890	FW	1998
Kneser Brian N Dr	(863)608-7579	1202 O'doniel Loop N Lakeland FL 33809	FG	EM			FW	1981
Knief Louis C	(309)637-3037 hlknief@netzero.net	724 S Pleasant St Peoria IL 61604	CI	EM			SL	1960
Knierim John H	(715)363-2004 knierim@chequenet.net	1200 Town Centre Dr Apt 219 Saint Paul MN 55123	MNN	EM			CQ	1997
Knill James R Dr	(703)618-0272 jknill1@verizon.net	4160 Eby Dr Dumfries VA 22026	SE	Sn/Adm	Concordia Triangle VA	(703)221-3703	SL	1964
Knippa Joshua A	(409)434-9598 texaspreach@mac.com	2711 Helena Ave Nederland TX 77627	TX	SP	Holy Cross Nederland TX	(409)722-1609	SL	2005
Knippa Kenneth C	(816)810-6940 knippa.dce@gmail.com	2817 Arabian Ln Celina TX 75009	TX	SMP	Concordia Garland TX	(972)495-4714	SL-SMP	2023
Knippa Michael S	(512) 459-1500 michael.knippa@redeemer.net	1500 W Anderson Ln Austin TX 78757	TX	Assoc	Redeemer Austin TX	(512)459-1500	SL	2015
Knippa William B Dr	(512)663-9200	12505 Red Mesa Holw Austin TX 78739	TX	EM			SL	1973
Knippa Colter A	coltpeacemaker1@gmail.com	c/o Cross And Crown Lutheran Church 2435 E 17th St Tucson AZ 85719	PSW	Assoc	Cross and Crown Tucson AZ	(520)222-7453	SL	2018
Knobloch Larry N	(936)204-4070 theknoblochs6@gmail.com	264 CR 143 Riesel TX 76682	TX	SP	Trinity Riesel TX	(254)896-6043	FW	2005
Knoche Ernest J Jr	(412)719-9512 revejk@hotmail.com	141 Mountain Vista Blvd Canton GA 30115	FG	EM			FW	1978
Knolhoff Wayne J Dr	(314)920-2594 way_kno@yahoo.com	1205 Arbor Trails Ct Ballwin MO 63021	MO	EM			SL	1983
Knorr Bradley D	402-679-5460 brad@1cchurch.com	6752 56th Avenue Place Columbus NE 68601	NEB		Nebraska District Seward NE	(402)643-2961	SL	2006
Knowles Alexander H	(716)417-9980 pastorknowles@outlook.com	8758 Jennings Rd Eden NY 14057	IN	C08/2025			NESC	2004
Knox Michael R	(319)231-9761 pastorknox@theforgiveness place.org	125 Magnolia Dr Cedar Falls IA 50613	IE	Assoc	Our Redeemer* Cedar Falls IA	(319)266-2509	FW	1987
Knudson Garrett L	(253)254-4705 GarrettKnudson@Comcast.net	272 Ticetown Road Old Bridge NJ 08857	NJ	Sn/Adm	Good Shepherd Old Bridge NJ	(732)679-8883	SL	2000

*Multiple Assignments (See Church Worker Locator for Additional Details)
See Page 53 for the Table of Abbreviations for key to District, Position, and Seminary abbreviations
**C =Candidate; EM = Emeritus; the date following the C is the month and year the Candidate status began

NAME	TELEPHONE NUMBER EMAIL	STREET ADDRESS CITY/STATE/ZIP	DISTRICT	POSITION/ STATUS**	WHERE SERVING	OFFICE PHONE	SEM/ PROGRAM	YR GRAD
Knupp Keith A	(585)507-5249 keithaknupp@gmail.com	190 Broom Rd Sparta TN 38583	MDS	EM			FW	1998
Knuteson Dale H	dbk@ccrtc.com	4918 Country Oaks Dr Johnsburg IL 60051	NI	EM			SPR	1965
Knuth David F	dknuth@pellalutheran.org	400 S Madison St Waupun WI 53963	SW	SP	Pella Waupun WI	(920)324-3321	FW	1996
Knutson Peter J	pastorpeterk84@gmail.com	3206 Summitview Ave Yakima WA 98902	NOW	SP	Mount Olive Yakima WA	(509)966-2190	FW	2015
Ko Chang S	224-392-4998	3112 Oaktree Ln Duluth GA 30096	FG	EM			CQ	1981
Kobak Anthony F	(573)373-5532 jetpastor@yahoo.com	1400 Bypass 3960 E Humble TX 77338	TX	Sn/Adm	Lamb Of God Humble TX	(281)446-8427	SL	2009
Koble Brandon W	(260)445-8557 brandon.koble@gmail.com	735 Legend Trail Wylie TX 75098	TX	Pro Stf	Faith Plano TX	(972)423-7448	FW	2017
Kobler Robert A	(254) 900-7352 rskobler@gmail.com	5508 Tama Dr Waco TX 76708	TX	EM			CQ	2001
Kobs Darrell C	(479)857-1967 darrell.kobs@gmail.com	1016 Lancelot Dr Russellville AR 72801	MDS	EM			SL	1975
Kobs Matthew C	(443)988-3789 kobsy@hey.com		MO	Asst	Ascension* Saint Louis MO	(314)832-5600	SL	2010
Koch Mark A Dr	revmkoch@gmail.com	205 Fox Hunt Ln Lebanon TN 37087	CNH	SP	Good Shepherd Turlock CA	(209)667-7712	FW	1992
Koch Timothy A	(785) 747-7633 revtimkoch@gmail.com	303 Church Street Linn KS 66953	KS	SP	Zion Linn KS	(785)348-5332	SL	2010
Koch Ronnie L	(319)269-2220 ronnie.l.koch@gmail.com	427 South Washington Fredericksburg IA 50630	IE	SP	St Paul Fredericksburg IA	(319)269-2220	FW	1996
Koch Aaron A	pastor.koch@gmail.com	3840 W Layton Ave Greenfield WI 53221	SW	SP	Mount Zion Greenfield WI	(414)282-4900	SL	1990
Koch Robert A	(303)842-2900 robertakoch78@gmail.com	624 Pinewood Ave Seward NE 68434	NEB	EM			SPR	1975
Koch Paul E	pastorkoch@hotmail.com	361 Hayes Ave Ventura CA 93003	PSW	SP	Grace Ventura CA	(805)642-2267	SL	2003
Koch Jerome R	(260)442-7114 newlifeJK@comcast.net	7336 Foxfield Dr Fort Wayne IN 46835	IN	EM			FW	1988
Koch J R Dr	(239)272-1799 docjrk259@gmail.com	2590 Hillside Heights Dr Green Bay WI 54311	NW	EM			SPR	1962
Koch Alan R	(321)848-3072 park_jmk@yahoo.com	528 Tarr Ave SW Palm Bay FL 32908	FG	EM			CQ	1994
Koch Danny R	papa_koch@yahoo.com	224 Postage Cir Pickerington OH 43147	OH	EM			SL	1981
Koch Karl W	(614)890-1898 ka6ko@aol.com	5445 Aqua St Columbus OH 43229	OH	EM			SL	1959
Kocsis Mark D	(334) 792-9745 tluthpastor@comcast.net	131 Waterford Pl Dothan AL 36303	SO	SP	Trinity Dothan AL	(334)792-9745	SL	1987
Koczman John R	(480)225-2285 jrkoczman@gmail.com	17013 E Malta Drive Fountain Hills AZ 85268	PSW	SP	Trinity Fountain Hills AZ	(480)837-0130	FW	1983
Koehler Douglas W	(405)343-4998 totallysaved@msn.com	1016 W Idylwild Dr Midwest City OK 73110	OK	EM			SL	1995
Koehler Timothy J	(816)519-2289 dcetim@gmail.com	346 Rockport Dr Cape Girardeau MO 63701	MO	SMP	St Andrew Cape Girardeau MO	(573)334-3200	SL-SMP	2022
Koehler Robert A	(540)846-6411 abkoehler@comcast.net	5045 Tara Dr Fredericksbrg VA 22407	SE	EM			SPR	1972
Koehler James A	(253)354-6024 jkoehler@wavecable.com	1305 N Highland Pkwy Unit C 103 Tacoma WA 98406	NOW	EM			SL	1957
Koehler Paul E	(218)281-3407 pkoehler67@yahoo.com	14729 Jewelwood Dr Baxter MN 56425	MNN	SMP	Trinity* Staples MN	(218)894-2372	SL-SMP	2013
Koehlinger Vernon D	(602)875-9477 vern.koehlinger@gmail.com	30566 W Whitton Ave Buckeye AZ 85396	PSW	EM			SL	1986
Koehn Paul R	(517)629-8379 pastor@stpaulalbion.org	712 Orchard Dr. Albion MI 49224	MI	SP	St Paul Albion MI	(517)629-8379	SL	1985
Koehneke Dale A	(971)301-1762 dale.koehneke@gmail.com	1353 Sundance St NW Salem OR 97304	NOW	EM			CQ	1978
Koehneke Richard M	(260)484-0923 richmart1@juno.com	2529 Springfield Ave Fort Wayne IN 46805	IN	EM			SL	1971
Koeller Martin E Dr	(920)843-1917 lkoeller@hotmail.com	1727 West Linda Ln Robertsville MO 63072	MO	EM			SL	1979
Koen Russell E	(618)282-1958 russellkoen01@gmail.com	911 Bayberry Ln Red Bud IL 62278	SI	EM			SL	1983
Koeneman David A	(260)223-1664 d.koeneman@yahoo.com	903 Woodland Ct. Decatur IN 46733	IN	EM			FW	1991
Koenig Clifford W	(816)832-8682 ckoenigkc@sbcglobal.net	1701 SE Oldham Pkwy Apt 3009 Lees Summit MO 64081	MO	EM			CQ	1972
Koenig Jarod P	(573)768-9781 jkoenig@rlcmail.org	5106 N Graybrooke Dr Ozark MO 65721	MO	Sn/Adm	Redeemer Springfield MO	(417)881-5470	SL	2018
Koenig Kevin A	(239)970-2275 pkmarco@comcast.net	728 Deerwood Dr Defiance OH 43512	FG	EM			SL	1978
Koenig Matthew L	matt@pop.church	105 S Arlene Ave Palatine IL 60074	NI	Assoc	Prince Peace Palatine IL	(847)359-3451	SL	2017
Koenig Stephen E	(601)955-3743 sekoenig2015@gmail.com	112 Arbor Ridge Clinton MS 39056	SO	EM			SL	1971
Koepp Joel G Dr	(507)829-3901 lcms.immanuelgrinnell@gmail.com	1840 Sunset St. Grinnell IA 50112	IE	SP	Immanuel Grinnell IA	(641)236-6691	FW	2010
Koeppen Karl J	(815)932-0312	1474 W Budd Blvd Kankakee IL 60901	NI	Sn/Adm	St Paul Bourbonnais IL	(815)932-0312	SL	1996
Koeppen Robert D	(989)832-7357	5010 Stephanie Dr Midland MI 48640	MI	EM			SPR	1968

*Multiple Assignments (See Church Worker Locator for Additional Details)
See Page 53 for the Table of Abbreviations for key to District, Position, and Seminary abbreviations
**C =Candidate; EM = Emeritus; the date following the C is the month and year the Candidate status began

NAME	TELEPHONE NUMBER EMAIL	STREET ADDRESS CITY/STATE/ZIP	DISTRICT	POSITION/ STATUS**	WHERE SERVING	OFFICE PHONE	SEM/ PROGRAM	YR GRAD
Koepsell Gregory A	(763)913-8445 alivepastor@tds.net	c/o Good Shepherd Luth Church 2450 W 9th Ave Oshkosh WI 54904	SW	SP	Good Shepherd Oshkosh WI	(920)231-0530	FW	2006
Koessel Eugene H	(586)445-6290 ekoessel@sbcglobal.net	15265 Grovedale St Roseville MI 48066	MI	EM			CQ	1982
Koester Kevin M	pastor@stpaulstover.com	405 W. 3rd St. Stover MO 65078	MO	SP	St Paul Stover MO	(573)377-2690	FW	2007
Koester Kevin W			SD		South Dakota District Sioux Falls SD	(605)361-1514	SL	2019
Koester Paul R	(414)429-5120 prkoester@yahoo.com	7313 W Cleveland Ave Milwaukee WI 53219	EN	EM			SL	1972
Koglin Adam B	(507)316-8181 akoglin@redeemer-rochester.com	1435 9th Ave SE Rochester MN 55904	MNS	Sn/Adm	Redeemer Rochester MN	(507)289-5147	SL	2012
Kogutkiewicz Chad A	(414)331-4360 ckogutkiewicz@hcl.org	16925 W Sundown Dr New Berlin WI 53151	EN	SMP	Hales Corners Hales Corners WI	(414)529-6700	SL-SMP	2016
Kohl Matthew P	(260)431-7506 matthew_kohl@yahoo.com	601 Pearl St Cloquet MN 55720	MNN	SP	Our Redeemer Cloquet MN	(218)879-3380	SL	2008
Kohlmeier Timothy M	(760)256-2036 concordialutheranbarstow@ gmail.com	420 Avenue E Barstow CA 92311	PSW	SP	Concordia Barstow CA	(760)256-2036	FW	2002
Kohlmeier Keith E	(785)249-9996 kekohlmeier@gmail.com	2146 S Sierra Hills Cir Wichita KS 67230	KS	EM			FW	1978
Kohlmeyer Marcel L	revkohlmeyer@hotmail.com	217 S 13th St Tecumseh NE 68450	NEB	SP	St John* Tecumseh NE	(402)335-3816	SL	2005
Kohlmeyer Phillip	(925)586-2575 phillip333@gmail.com	1306 Gragg Ln Concord CA 94518	CNH	EM			SL	1966
Kohm Jason P	(314)704-3064	1613 Savannah Cir O Fallon MO 63368	MO	Assoc	Holy Cross O'fallon MO	(636)272-4505	SL	2024
Kohn Daniel L	(715)610-2400 revkohn@gmail.com	289 Karen Dr Unit 337 Saint Paul MN 55129	NW	EM			SL-D	2010
Kohn Elden D	(660)415-7523 pastorkohn@gmail.com	1204 Highland St Macon MO 63552	MO	SP	Zion Macon MO	(660)385-4433	SL	2013
Kohnke Kevin J Dr	(402)641-6733 kjkohnke@yahoo.com	173 Morgan School Road Wellsville MO 63384	MO	SP	St Paul Jonesburg MO	(636)488-5235	FW	1991
Kohrs Dale R	(507) 525-3844 dalekohrs@gmail.com	1018 W Lyon Ave Lake City MN 55041	MNS	EM			SL	2005
Kois Darrel K	pastorkois@gmail.com	15124 Burdette St Omaha NE 68116	NEB	EM			SL	1986
Kolander Kevin L	(951)245-9728	22267 Osprey Ct Wildomar CA 92595	PSW	SP	First Lake Elsinore CA	(951)674-2757	FW	1989
Kolander Mark D	(509)885-2490 koly1759@gmail.com	126 Vera Lane South West Salem WI 54669	SW	EM			CQ	2021
Kolaskey Richard K	pastorkolaskey@yahoo.com	9900 Central Avenue P.O. Box 546 Dillsboro IN 47018	IN	SP	Trinity Dillsboro IN	(812)432-5406	FW	2004
Kolb Robert A Dr	(314)647-5865 kolbr@csl.edu	7110 Clayton Rd Saint Louis MO 63117	MO	EM			SL	1967
Kolb Barry L Dr	(630)842-7184 drbarrykolb@gmail.com	120 Oak Ridge Court Branson MO 65616	MO	EM			CQ	1986
Kolb John C	(219)616-4519 jochar@comcast.net	3020 Tapwood Ln Indianapolis IN 46217	IN	SP	Good Shepherd Kokomo IN	(765)457-4968	SL	1968
Kolb Peter C	(254)754-0644 pastor@stmarkwaco.com	2000 Clay Ave Waco TX 76706	TX	SP	St Mark Waco TX	(254)754-0644	SL	2000
Kolesar Michael J	(319)647-3375 stjlcv@netins.net	P.O. Box 217 Victor IA 52347	IE	SP	Calvary* Deep River IA		FW	2000
Kolk Charles G	(763)421-8377 iwm.cgk1218@gmail.com	10826 Austin St NE Apt # 319 Blaine MN 55449	MNN	EM			SL	1972
Koll Quincy D	pastorquincysd@gmail.com		PSW	SP	Mount Olive* Poway CA	(858)748-3871	SL	2021
Kollbaum Todd E	(660)221-8973 pttlcmadison@gmail.com	P.O. Box 371 Madison NE 68748	NEB	SP	Trinity Madison NE	(402)454-3532	SL	2004
Kollek Paul K	(989)277-3460 paulkkollek@aol.com	5240 Braden Rd Byron MI 48418	MI	SMP	Hope Linden MI	(810)735-4807	CQ	2018
Kollmann Christopher J	(914)325-7145	6802 NW 43rd Pl Gainesville FL 32606	FG	SP	First Gainesville FL	(352)376-2062	SL	2012
Kollmann Victor J Dr	(972)398-7500 victor@messiahlutheran.com	1801 W Plano Pkwy Plano TX 75075	TX	Sn/Adm	Messiah Plano TX	(972)398-7500	SL	1981
Kollmeyer David L	(618)790-4085 davidkollmeyer@yahoo.com	811 State St Chester IL 62233	SI	SP	Trinity* Pinckneyville IL	(618)357-2818	SL	1982
Koltz Gary E	(248)732-9161 slisten12@aol.com		FG	SP	Trinity Cape Coral FL	(239)772-0172	SL	2014
Kolupa Christopher J	(630) 965-8570 churchnote@aol.com	3138 Home Avenue Berwyn IL 60402	EN	SMP	Concordia Berwyn IL	(708)484-9784	SL-SMP	2021
Kolzow Calvin J Jr	(269)257-1737 calkolzow@gmail.com	69503 Franklin Cir Sturgis MI 49091	MI	EM			FW	1987
Kong Albino Y	(907)350-8377 akong04@yahoo.com	502 N Bragaw St Anchorage AK 99508	NOW	Assoc	Anchorage Anchorage AK	(907)272-5323	SL	2020
Kong Kevin S	85293058477		NOW	Assoc	CAN HK Repulse Bay	011-852-2812- 5151	SL	2025
Konkel Dennis R	(301)304-8483 dennis.konkel@gmail.com	6512 Springwater Ct Apt 4202 Frederick MD 21701	SE	EM			SL	2001
Konkel Nathaniel W	(734)778-2412 nate.konkel@gmail.com	2173 Hwy 18 P.O. Box 60 Finlayson MN 55735	MNN	SP	Peace* Finlayson MN	(320)233-6138	FW	2022
Konrad Allen E	(319)938-2946 onamission1939@gmail.com	P.O. Box 157 Rowley IA 52329	NW	EM			SPR	1966
Konz Thomas R	(608)206-4739 tom.konz@yahoo.com	204 Starry Ave Monona WI 53716	SW	EM			SL	1986

*Multiple Assignments (See Church Worker Locator for Additional Details)
See Page 53 for the Table of Abbreviations for key to District, Position, and Seminary abbreviations
**C =Candidate; EM = Emeritus; the date following the C is the month and year the Candidate status began

NAME	TELEPHONE NUMBER EMAIL	STREET ADDRESS CITY/STATE/ZIP	DISTRICT	POSITION/ STATUS**	WHERE SERVING	OFFICE PHONE	SEM/ PROGRAM	YR GRAD
Kooi Nickolas M	(651)424-6294 pastornkooi@gmail.com	2301 Shawnee Dr North St Paul MN 55109	MNS	SP	Emmaus Saint Paul MN	(651)489-9426	FW	2016
Koontz Adam C Dr	revkoontz@gmail.com	c/o Redeemer Lutheran Church 1261 Pennsylvania Ave Oakmont PA 15139	EN	SP	Redeemer Oakmont PA	(412)828-9323	FW	2014
Koopman John H	(712)852-6095 pastorjohnkoopman@gmail.com	128 Falcon Dr Mankato MN 56001	MNS	Assoc	Our Savior Mankato MN	(507)385-2180	FW	2016
Koopmann Henry J	(320)217-8645 hjkoopman5@yahoo.com	815 5th Ave S Waite Park MN 56387	MNN	EM			FW	1989
Kootz Dennis L	(785)577-9764 pastordennis.kootz@gmail.com	2841 Crystal Lake Dr Salina KS 67401	KS	Assoc	Trinity Salina KS	(785)823-7151	SL	2011
Kophamer Mark A	(402)643-5342 makophamer1@gmail.com	107 Cannon Ave Bristol TN 37620	MDS	SP	Redeemer Elizabethton TN	(423)543-1132	FW	1989
Kopitske Harley L	(715)758-8284 hdkopitske@gmail.com	W4962 State Highway 156 Bonduel WI 54107	NW	EM			SPR	1960
Koppel Alexander J Jr	(231) 288-2161 ajohnkoppel2@aol.com	1735 Winding Rd Apt 103 Muskegon MI 49444	MI	EM			CQ	2018
Kopper Glenn P	(616)717-0992 gpkopper@gmail.com	5466 Turkey Run Dr Apt A Holt MI 48842	MI	EM			SL	1984
Kopper Evandro Sr	(573) 462-6953	207 N Owen St California MO 65018	MO	Sn/Adm	St Paul's California MO	(573)796-2735	Other	1996
Korabandi Paul A	(202)981-4199 paul.korabandi@gmail.com	3223 Spring Cypress Rd Apt 1125 Spring TX 77388	TX	Assoc	Resurrection Spring TX	(281)353-4413	CQ	2022
Korb Jared A	(307)388-4044 jared.korb1@gmail.com	525 S 6th St Worland WY 82401	WY	SP	St Luke's Worland WY	(307)347-2293	FW	2013
Korinek Alan W Dr	(806) 787-3498 alankorinek55@gmail.com	1709 29th St Lubbock TX 79411	TX	EM			SL	1981
Kornacki Alan R Jr	(618)615-6993 revalkorn@gmail.com	5825 Robinwood Lane Marion IA 52302	IE	Assoc	St Paul Marion IA	(319)377-4687	NESC	2000
Korte Michael R	(989)921-4425 mckorte590@charter.net	3456 Spicer Dr Saginaw MI 48603	MI	EM			FW	1986
Korte Seth P	sethkorte@gmail.com	168 Bass Pro Dr Unit 4301 Kodak TN 37764	MDS	SP	St Paul Sevierville TN	(865)365-8551	SL	2011
Korytkowski Robert A	(262)349-4484 bob.korytkowski@gmail.com	2100 Laura Ln Waukesha WI 53186	SW	EM			CQ	1980
Kosberg Adam P	(623)824-1258 pastor.adam@nhlchurch.org	8742 Shadowbrook Dr Jenison MI 49428	MI	SP	New Hope Hudsonville MI	(616)669-2790	SL	2018
Kosberg Steven P	(507)317-8739 stevekosberg1@gmail.com	216 Woodhaven Ln Mankato MN 56001	MNS	EM			CQ	1985
Kosberg Kevin C	(623)910-5878 kevin@anthemcross.org	40847 N Majesty Ct Anthem AZ 85086	PSW	Sn/Adm	Cross of Christ Anthem AZ	(623)551-9851	SL	1989
Kosberg Charles T	(850)893-3270 c.t.kosberg@gmail.com	2601 Crestline Rd Apt 303 Tallahassee FL 32308	FG	EM			SPR	1971
Kosberg Jerry M	(480)460-2193 jmk61568@cox.net	1817 W Satinwood Dr Phoenix AZ 85045	PSW	EM			SL	1972
Kosberg Joel D	(623)824-9802 jdkosberg@gmail.com	928 Sundance Ct Sartell MN 56377	MNN	Sn/Adm	Love Of Christ Saint Cloud MN	(320)253-7453	SL	2021
Koschmann Andrew M	(630)740-4731 akosch57@aol.com	2431 Appley Way San Jose CA 95124	CNH	SP	Holy Cross Los Gatos CA	(408)356-3525	SL	1983
Koschmann Mark A Dr	(651)641-8254 koschmann@csp.edu		MNS	S HS/C	Concordia University St Paul Saint Paul MN	(651)641-8278	SL	2011
Koschmann Michael A	(217)629-9969 pk@gcctv.com	P.O. Box 380 Riverton IL 62561	CI	SP	Immanuel Riverton IL	(217)629-8415	SL	1981
Koschmann Nicholas W	(734)752-2056 nkoschmann@mtolivefg.org	1345 Hartford Dr Forest Grove OR 97116	NOW	SP	Mount Olive Forest Grove OR	(503)357-2511	SL	2007
Koss James M	(406)679-0733 jameskoss54@gmail.com	P.O. Box 515 Huntley MT 59037	MT	SP	Redeemer Hardin MT	(406)679-0733	FW	1996
Koss Noel D	(206)852-2112 noelkoss@comcast.net	7260 S Robert Trl Apt 115 Inver Grove Heights MN 55077	NOW	EM			SPR	1970
Kostizen Leo E	(765)558-6840 kostizen@me.com	404 Hibiscus Dr Lafayette IN 47909	IN	EM			SL	1972
Kostizen Erwin	(810)429-0509 ervkost@cs.com	1065 Saint Andrews Highland MI 48357	MI	EM			SL	1965
Koterba Matthew C	(440)313-8058 koterm86@gmail.com	1102 Court St Scott City KS 67871	KS	SP	Holy Cross Scott City KS	(620)872-2294	FW	2017
Kothe Kenneth P	(763)292-0980 kkothe5689@centurylink.net	11419 17th St NE St Michael MN 55376	MNS	EM			SPR	1976
Kothe Richard A	(308)940-0839 kothes@hotmail.com	1212 12th St Central City NE 68826	NEB	EM			SPR	1976
Kothe Richard W	rwkothe45@gmail.com	8989 E Escalante Rd #163 Tucson AZ 85730	PSW	EM			FW	1982
Kotila Aaron P	(314)814-6630 revkotila@gmail.com	400 S Country Club Rd El Reno OK 73036	OK	SP	Trinity El Reno OK	(405)262-7116	SL	2007
Kotila Joel D	(860)940-7876 pastorjdkht@att.net	W193n16340 Lea Fon Cir Jackson WI 53037	NE	SP	Holy Trinity Terryville CT	(860)582-0723	FW	1995
Kottlowski David P	(913)972-0622 matt.1032@yahoo.com	1424 NW 23rd Ln Ankeny IA 50023	IW	Assoc	St Paul Ankeny IA	(515)964-1250	FW	1996
Kovac Gerald L	(314) 210-8296 gkoovie@aol.com	3609 S. Banana River Blvd. Cocoa Beach FL 32931	S	EM			SL	1965
Kowert Daniel C	(608)225-2136 kowert@living-christ.org	110 N Gammon Rd Madison WI 53717	SW	SP	Living Christ Madison WI	(608)829-2136	SL	1984
Koy Norman A	(586) 323-6147 nakoygl@gmail.com	44750 Brockton Ave Sterling Hts MI 48314	MI	EM			CQ	1987
Koyn Daniel M	(985)789-8738 pastor@htlministries.org	205 Woodcrest Dr Covington LA 70433	SO	SP	Holy Trinity Covington LA	(985)892-6146	SL	2007

*Multiple Assignments (See Church Worker Locator for Additional Details)
See Page 53 for the Table of Abbreviations for key to District, Position, and Seminary abbreviations
**C =Candidate; EM = Emeritus; the date following the C is the month and year the Candidate status began

NAME	TELEPHONE NUMBER EMAIL	STREET ADDRESS CITY/STATE/ZIP	DISTRICT	POSITION/ STATUS**	WHERE SERVING	OFFICE PHONE	SEM/ PROGRAM	YR GRAD
Kozak Ladislav P	(416)658-9793 lpkozak@sympatico.ca	97 Government Rd Toronto ON M8X 1 CANADA	S	EM			CQ	1992
Kozak Jack A	(330)322-4160 jakozak@ameritech.net	999 Portage Lakes Dr Akron OH 44319	OH	SP	Hope Coventry Township OH	(330)644-3522	FW	1990
Kozisek Scott A	(641)530-4743 sakozisek@me.com	1585 290th St Garner IA 50438	IW	SP	St Paul Garner IA	(641)923-2261	FW	1994
Krach James M	(443)610-1347 jkrach1616@aol.com	2828 Pearly Banks Dr Bradenton FL 34208	FG	SP	Hope Bradenton FL	(941)755-3256	SL	2000
Kraemer Fred H	(618)960-3328 fkraemer@zionlutheranlitchfield. org	8056 N 13th Ave Butler IL 62015	SI	SP	Zion Litchfield IL	(217)324-2033	SL	1986
Kraft Austin D	(970)688-1100 austin@gracegypsum.com	P.O. Box 5661 Eagle CO 81631	RM	SMP	Grace Fellowship Gypsum CO	(970)445-3101	SL-SMP	2018
Kraft Robert E	pastorkraft@mac.com		RM	M Chap	Office of International Mission Saint Louis MO		FW	2003
Kraft Ronald A	(951)684-3549 rkos1@msn.com	2855 David St Riverside CA 92506	PSW	EM			SL	1961
Kramer Loren T	(949) 291-2857 revlorenkramer@gmail.com	32353 San Juan Creek Rd Apt 236 San Juan Capistrano CA 92675	PSW	EM			SL	1959
Kramer Nathan G	(219)706-5997 revnathankramer@gmail.com	5523 Redwood Ave Portage IN 46368	IN	SP	Trinity Hobart IN	(219)942-2589	SL	2007
Kramer Charles E	(567)277-1339 charleskramer999@gmail.com	5336 County Rd 6 Delta OH 43515	OH	SP	St Paul Liberty Center OH	(419)533-3041	FW	2002
Kramer Kenneth J	(520)991-3228 margegv26@gmail.com	2028 S Santa Carla Dr Green Valley AZ 85614	EN	EM			SL	1982
Kramer Thomas F	(618)240-3220 revtomkramer@yahoo.com	1504 N Cherry St Mount Carmel IL 62863	SI	SP	Hope Mount Carmel IL	(618)240-3220	SL	2008
Kramp Allen J	(701)430-7117	316 Green Manor Drive Sun City Center FL 33573	FG	EM			FW	1994
Krans Glen A Dr	(910)381-5563 grafec1@yahoo.com		SE	EM			SL	1973
Kranz Mark J	(308)390-2640 pastorkranz@gmail.com	305 Wisconsin St Excelsior Springs MO 64024	MO	SP	Mount Calvary Excelsior Springs MO	(816)637-9800	FW	2020
Krause Jason D	(308) 643-7647 pastorkrause@nebnet.net	16627 Galaxie Way Lakeville MN 55068	MNS	SP	Mount Calvary Richfield MN	(612)866-5405	SL	2008
Krause Thomas P	(913)638-8271 tommirkrause@gmail.com	11556 Carter St Overland Park KS 66210	KS	EM			SL	1972
Krause Ronald E	revron52@gmail.com	2524 W Anna St Grand Island NE 68803	NEB	EM			SL	1988
Krause Roger L	(303)929-0388 rlkbak57@gmail.com	8094 Inspiration Dr Parker CO 80138	RM	EM			SPR	1974
Krause Paul W	(815)814-1962 paulwk1942@gmail.com	2750 West Highland Ave Apt 208 Elgin IL 60124	NI	EM			SL	1968
Krause Mark E	(479)841-4898 mekrause56@gmail.com	8315 San Marco Ave Springdale AR 72762	MDS	EM			SL	1987
Krause Donald R	(563)608-1637 revkrause@gmail.com	1701 Mason St New Holstein WI 53061	SW	EM			FW	2009
Krause Daniel L	(231)633-7010 dnkrs59@yahoo.com	425 Webster St Traverse City MI 49686	MI	EM			SL	1992
Krause Matthew M	(515)314-6980 mattkrau23@gmail.com	1519 Greene St Adel IA 50003	IW	SP	Faith Adel IA	(515)993-3848	SL	2013
Krauss Edward L Dr	(727)475-9002 dredlk2021@outlook.com	8666 140th Way Seminole FL 33776	FG	EM			SL	1962
Krebs Adrian J	(812) 498-2161 adrian.krebs@yahoo.com	9530 Marigold Lane Munster IN 46321	IN	Assoc	St Paul Munster IN	(219)836-6270	FW	2015
Krebs John R	ilcmsaf@hotmail.com		SW	SP	Immanuel Adams WI	(608)339-6102	FW	1987
Kreft James W	(610)750-0878 jim.kreft@gmail.com		S	EM			SL	1981
Kreil Dennis J	(989) 708-1776 dennis@messiahmidland.org	2510 Hearthstone Cir Midland MI 48642	MI	SMP	Messiah Midland MI	(989)631-5200	CQ	2018
Kreitenstein Richard C	kreitrc@aol.com	9121 SW 91st Cir Ocala FL 34481	SO	EM			FW	1988
Kreitler Zachary A	(314)330-1550 zakreitler@gmail.com	6600 N Clayton St Box 306 Fort Wayne IN 46825	SW	SP	Saint Johns Beloit WI	(608)362-8595	FW	2025
Krengel Douglas A Dr		c/o Immanuel Lutheran Church 9650 N Church St Bridgman MI 49106	MI	SP	Immanuel Bridgman MI	(269)465-6031	SL	1991
Krentz Eugene L Dr	(847)254-1463 joygene16@gmail.com	12850 Pronghorn Oak San Antonio TX 78253	TX	EM			SPR	1958
Krentz Paul D	(952) 888-2345 pastork@holyemmanuel.org	c/o Holy Emmanuel Lutheran Church 201 E 104th St Bloomington MN 55420	MNS	SP	Holy Emmanuel Bloomington MN	(952)888-2345	SL	1989
Krenz Jonathon T	(208)892-9224 jkrenz98@hotmail.com	876 Fairview Dr Moscow ID 83843	NOW	Sn/Adm	Augustana Moscow ID	(208)892-9224	FW	2006
Krenz Stephen N Dr	(618)363-0121 pastork@splcolumbia.com	239 Elizabeth Drive Columbia IL 62236	SI	SP	St Paul's Columbia IL	(618)281-4600	SL	1994
Krepel David L	(405)596-7681 dlklcms@aol.com	514 S 8th St Kingfisher OK 73750	OK	EM			SL	1984
Krepel Joshua R	(405)496-7436 joshua.krepel@gmail.com	19514 East Hamilton Place Aurora CO 80013	RM	Sn/Adm	Peace W Christ Aurora CO	(303)693-5618	SL	2014
Kress James T Sr	(941)979-2976 revdupone@gmail.com	14118 Appleton Blvd Pt Charlotte FL 33981	FG	Asst	Zion Winter Garden FL	(407)743-5533	FW	2003
Kretschmar Alan R	(920)912-6334	1810 N 13th St Sheboygan WI 53081	SW	Sn/Adm	St Paul's Sheboygan WI	(920)452-6829	SL	1984

*Multiple Assignments (See Church Worker Locator for Additional Details)
See Page 53 for the Table of Abbreviations for key to District, Position, and Seminary abbreviations
**C =Candidate; EM = Emeritus; the date following the C is the month and year the Candidate status began

NAME	TELEPHONE NUMBER EMAIL	STREET ADDRESS CITY/STATE/ZIP	DISTRICT	POSITION/ STATUS**	WHERE SERVING	OFFICE PHONE	SEM/ PROGRAM	YR GRAD
Kretzschmar Aaron C Dr	(219)393-9730 pastork@stpaulsdec.com	c/o St Pauls Luth Church 1700 Carridale St SW Decatur AL 35601	SO	SP	St Paul's Decatur AL	(256)353-8759	SL	2004
Krey Theodore M	(809)917-1778 ted.krey@lcms.org	Calle E-2 Cerro Alto Santiago 51000 DOMINICAN REPUBLIC	EN	S Miss	Office of International Mission Saint Louis MO		FW	2001
Kribs Larry M	(971) 701-5894 lmkribs@aol.com	1696 Ozark St E Monmouth OR 97361	NOW	EM			SL	2001
Kriefall Daniel P Dr	(314)349-5700		MO	EM			CQ	1983
Kriefall Theodore A	(360)866-0661	3916 Hillview Ct NW Olympia WA 98502	NOW	EM			SL	1960
Krieg Kelly D	pastorkrieg@bethlehemwmpenn.org	10210 Fm 1935 Brenham TX 77833	TX	SP	Bethlehem Brenham TX	(979)836-7303	FW	2017
Krieg Raymond D	(865)982-1983 Ray_Krieg@Yahoo.com		MDS	SMP	Celebration Seymour TN	(865)579-2218	CQ	2019
Krieger Timothy O		2136 Fox Sparrow Ct Oviedo FL 32765	FG	EM			SL	1980
Krienke Dale R	(320) 583-0517 pastorkrienke@gmail.com	165 S Edgehill Ave Austintown OH 44515	OH	SP	Redeemer Austintown OH	(330)799-7823	FW	2023
Krienke Howard A	(612)709-5355 howie.krienke@zionhopkins.org	15302 Boulder Creek Dr Minnetonka MN 55345	MNS	Assoc	Zion Hopkins MN	(952)938-7661	SL	1972
Krikava James A	(314) 996-1341 jameskrikava@yahoo.com	50 Moldstad Ln Brewster MA 02631	MO	S Ex/S	The LCMS Corporate Saint Louis MO	(314)965-9000	CQ	2014
Kringel Arthur D	(757)566-3781 artkringel@yahoo.com	14040 Bagley Avenue N Seattle WA 98133	SE	EM			SL	1969
Kringel Ray R	(805)925-9679 rnkringel@comcast.net	416 E Fesler St Santa Maria CA 93454	CNH	EM			SL	1968
Krippner Kenneth M	(972)495-2545	3237 Creekbend Dr Garland TX 75044	TX	EM			SL	1988
Kristalyn Bruce R	(620) 228-0259 borikkoakhammer@gmail.com	2003 N Belmont Place Garden City KS 67846	KS	EM			FW	1989
Kritsch Paul E	paulkritsch@hotmail.com	400 Fishers Loop Sharps Chapel TN 37866	MDS	SP	Good Shepherd Sharps Chapel TN	(865)279-1279	SL	1973
Kritzer Kevin L	kkritzer@bethanylutheran.org	4644 Clark Ave Long Beach CA 90808	PSW	Sn/Adm	Bethany Long Beach CA	(562)421-4711	SL	1992
Kroemer James G Dr	(414)467-2716 jameskroemer@gmail.com	9440 N Bethanne Dr Brown Deer WI 53223	SW	EM			SL	1980
Krog Mitchell D	(218)831-7092 k9kyro@gmail.com	28602 510th Ave Henning MN 56551	MNN	EM			FW	2003
Krohe Wayne A	(573)987-8804 w_krohe@yahoo.com	2172 Horton Way Lewisburg TN 37091	MDS	EM			FW	1986
Kroll Micheal D	(231)557-6312 krwander@aol.com	5545 Park Lake Rd East Lansing MI 48823	MI	EM			FW	1990
Kroll Roland H	(208)890-2061 toniandrolandkroll@gmail.com	28055 Running River St Wilder ID 83676	PSW	EM			SPR	1966
Krolus Harry M	(410)871-0712 krol07@msn.com	668 Geneva Dr Westminster MD 21157	SE	SP	Christ King Owings Mills MD	(410)356-3400	SL	1984
Kroonblawd Cory J	(651)295-7590 pastorckroonblawd@gmail.com	410 South 11th St Sac City IA 50583	IW	SP	St Paul's Sac City IA	(712)662-7029	FW	2021
Kroonblawd James L	(651)454-7235 james.kroonblawd@gmail.com	1025 Wedgewood Ln S Eagan MN 55123	MNS	Sn/Adm	Trinity Lone Oak Eagan MN	(651)454-7235	SL	1986
Krueger Mark L	(920)871-4039 mlkrueger58@gmail.com	79 S 11th St Hilbert WI 54129	SW	EM			SL	1984
Krueger Thomas I	(920)818-0636 tikrueger@yahoo.com	12 N Columbia Ave Sturgeon Bay WI 54235	NW	EM			SL	1983
Krueger Brian L	(920)994-9060 bkprayhard@hotmail.com	W8497 Brazelton Dr Random Lake WI 53075	SW	SP	St Stephen* Batavia WI	(920)994-9060	SL	2010
Krueger Ray A	(815)756-2515	206 Timbers Trl Saint Charles IL 60174	NI	Asst	St Mark Saint Charles IL	(630)584-8638	SL	2007
Krueger Mark A	(715)305-2704	309 Meadow Ln Marshfield WI 54449	NW	EM			CQ	1976
Krueger Larry G	(254)715-1707 larrygkrueger@gmail.com	608 Willow Creek Rd Salado TX 76571	TX	EM			SL	1986
Krueger Kyle D	(763)203-1152 pastorkrueger@yahoo.com	9656 Winslow Chase Maple Grove MN 55311	MNS	Assoc	Glory Of Christ Plymouth MN	(763)478-6031	FW	2010
Krueger Kenneth J	(480) 528-5296 ken.krueger45@gmail.com	1716 Linkside Dr Columbia MO 65201	MO	RSO	The Foundation for Called Workers DBA Ministry FOCUS Columbia MO	(480)528-5296	SL	2015
Krueger John W Dr	(209)883-3521 jkrueger0130@yahoo.com	7700 Fox Rd Unit G216 Hughson CA 95326	CNH	EM			SL	1972
Krueger Joel A	(573)253-4680 revjkrueger@gmail.com	228 Trinity Rd Branson MO 65616	MO	Sn/Adm	Faith Branson MO	(417)334-2469	SL	1997
Krueger James F	(989)293-5335 revjfk@hotmail.com	104 Robin Ln Oconto WI 54153	NW	SP	Faith Marinette WI	(715)735-6506	SL	2003
Krueger George A	(701)476-0589 gakrueger2@q.com	2000 28th St SW Apt 213 Minot ND 58701	MNN	EM			SPR	1967
Krueger Eugene R	(515)226-1612 Eugene@sotv-wdm.org	904 57th Pl Wdm IA 50266	IW	Asst	Shep Of The Valley West Des Moines IA	(515)225-1623	SL-D	2009
Krueger Edwin A	(559)862-7042 edinclovis@me.com	2937 Browning Ave Clovis CA 93611	CNH	EM			SL	1971
Krueger Dennis J	(716)997-5666 tlckrueger@verizon.net		EA	SP	Faith* Elma NY	(716)652-2221	NESC	1986
Krueger Delmar O	(419)522-9516 delkru@yahoo.com	612 S Trimble Rd Apt B Mansfield OH 44906	OH	EM			SL	1954

*Multiple Assignments (See Church Worker Locator for Additional Details)
See Page 53 for the Table of Abbreviations for key to District, Position, and Seminary abbreviations
**C =Candidate; EM = Emeritus; the date following the C is the month and year the Candidate status began

NAME	TELEPHONE NUMBER EMAIL	STREET ADDRESS CITY/STATE/ZIP	DISTRICT	POSITION/ STATUS**	WHERE SERVING	OFFICE PHONE	SEM/ PROGRAM	YR GRAD
Krueger Daniel L	(319)329-4833 Revkkris@gmail.com	321 Carnaby Dr NE Cedar Rapids IA 52402	IE	EM			SL	1981
Krueger Carl H Jr Dr	(414)762-9257 selcpres@gmail.com	6240 S Elaine Ave Cudahy WI 53110	S	EM			SPR	1974
Krueger Rod M	(630)373-5220 pastorrodk@yahoo.com	124 10th St Kaukauna WI 54130	NW	SP	Bethany Kaukauna WI	(920)766-1452	SL	2006
Krueger Jeffrey D	(715)216-5914 jeffrey.krueger@aol.com	4635 Terraceview Ln N Minneapolis MN 55446	MNS	EM			CQ	1984
Kruger Roger A Dr	(402)215-1833 drrogerkruger@yahoo.com	806 S 121st St Omaha NE 68154	NEB	EM			SL	1968
Kruger David F Dr	(770)313-0554 dfkruger@comcast.net	3010 Heatherton Park Way Roswell GA 30075	FG	SP	Savior Of All Cartersville GA	(770)387-0379	SL	1972
Krumdieck Gary A	(541)378-7229 gkrumdieck@gmail.com	4 S. Garfield Ave. Wenatchee WA 98801	NOW	SP	Faith East Wenatchee WA	(509)884-7623	SL	2014
Krupski Philip J	(317)840-3202 philip.krupski@lfnd.org	982 Winter Lake Dr Fenton MO 63026	MO	Pro Stf	LCMS Foundation Saint Louis MO	(314)965-9000	FW	1989
Krupsky Justin A	jkrupsky@trinityutica.com	60429 Apache Ln Washington MI 48094	MI	Sn/Adm	Trinity Utica MI	(586)731-4490	SL	2008
Kruse Caleb J	pastorcaleb@lordoflifeelkhorn.org	3402 N 206th St Elkhorn NE 68022	NEB	Assoc	Lord Of Life* Elkhorn NE	(402)289-3437	SL	2014
Kruse Loren D	(320)220-0097 lodikruse@charter.net	209 15th Ave NW Willmar MN 56201	MNN	EM			SPR	1969
Kruse Paul G	(989)992-6030 paul@stjohnhl.com	3220 W Higgins Lake Dr Roscommon MI 48653	MI	SP	St John Houghton Lake MI	(989)366-5164	SL-D	2010
Kruse Scott D	(737)222-4781 pastor@peacelutheran.org	226 E Pier St Port Washington WI 53074	EN	SP	Peace New Berlin WI	(262)679-1441	SL	2000
Krusemark Jesse E	(507)567-2272 pastorkrusemark@yahoo.com	29952 570th Ave Austin MN 55912	MNS	SP	St Paul's* Hollandale MN	(507)567-2272	FW	2007
Krystowiak Dustin J	(608)395-8498 dustinkrystowiak@gmail.com	5430 Quercus Grove Rd Edwardsville IL 62025	SI	SP	Zion* Carpenter IL	(618)656-4492	SL	2010
Kubow Alan D	(920)918-2146 alankubow@yahoo.com	1929 S 16th St Sheboygan WI 53081	SW	EM			FW	1981
Kubowicz Andrew J	andrewkubowicz@gmail.com	23147 Sunfield Dr Boca Raton FL 33433	FG	C06/2023			SL	2018
Kucera Jan S Dr	(419)448-9477 dk1278@att.net	25 Orchard Park Tiffin OH 44883	OH	SP	Redeemer Tiffin OH	(419)447-7794	SPR	1974
Kucera Edward A	(724)342-6130 edwardal1@hotmail.com	13352 East Lane St. Louis MO 63128	S	EM			SL	1959
Kuchta David R	(814)964-8591 pastordrk@gmail.com	49 Robinson St North East PA 16428	EA	EM			S	1988
Kudart Larry R	(614)507-1680 kudart8@yahoo.com	3386 Joberryloop Grove City OH 43123	OH	EM			SL	1964
Kuddes Jeffrey M	(816)731-0029 prkuddes@gmail.com	1909 Sleepy Hollow Dr Lexington MO 64067	MO	SP	Grace Lexington MO	(660)259-2932	SL	1992
Kuder Adam F	(757)596-5808 news@rlcnn.org	765 J Clyde Morris Blvd Newport News VA 23601	SE	SP	Resurrection Newport News VA	(757)596-5808	SL	2007
Kudick Ronald J	(623)582-9882 grjkudick@cox.net	18828 N 20th Dr Phoenix AZ 85027	PSW	EM			SL	1960
Kuefner Robert C Jr	(308)746-2270 rkuefner@tlclex.org	211 E 7th St Lexington NE 68850	NEB	Sn/Adm	Trinity Lexington NE	(308)324-4341	SL	1995
Kuehl Kyle I	(262)689-7488 pastorkuehl@outlook.com	111 E Avenue B Newberry MI 49868	MI	SP	Bethlehem* Engadine MI		SL	2015
Kuehn Gilbert A	(813)629-6070 kuehn@ebuffalo.net	23920 Nene Cir Land O Lakes FL 34639	FG	EM			SL	1969
Kuehn Todd A	todd.kuehn@verizon.net	4732 Charles Partin Dr Parrish FL 34219	FG	SMP	Beautiful Savior Sarasota FL	(941)355-2798	SL-SMP	2011
Kuehn Richard R	(919)682-6960 rrkuehn@hotmail.com	918 Englewood Ave Durham NC 27701	SE	Asst	Grace Durham NC	(919)682-6030	SL	1969
Kuehn Aaron J	(952)443-2993 pastoraaron@christvictorious.org	1140 Pond Curv Waconia MN 55387	MNS	Sn/Adm	Christ Victorious Chaska MN	(952)443-2993	SL	2010
Kuehn Roger R	(925)757-5182 rrmikuehn@aol.com	1201 Saint Frances Dr Antioch CA 94509	CNH	Sn/Adm	St Andrew Antioch CA	(925)757-1672	SL	1969
Kuehne Jonathan D	kuehnej.jk@gmail.com	4016 Stockdale Drive Vadnais Heights MN 55127	MNS	SP	Trinity First Minneapolis MN	(612)870-9487	SL	2016
Kuehner Ronald K	(402)756-3703 revron@gtmc.net	530 N Willson St Blue Hill NE 68930	NEB	EM			SL	1986
Kuehnert John M Dr	jmarkkuehnert@yahoo.com	34 Launch Dr Ashville AL 35953	SO	EM			SL	1963
Kueker Jesse L	(573)768-5752 revkueker@gmail.com		MO	S HS/C	Concordia Seminary Saint Louis MO	(314)505-7000	SL	2015
Kueker Kenneth M	(513)304-3253 thekuekers@gmail.com	2701 Blue Rock Dr Beavercreek OH 45434	OH	EM			FW	1980
Kuerschner Victor H Sr	(920)923-6316 kuersch@charter.net	431 Austin Ln Fond Du Lac WI 54935	SW	EM			SL	1961
Kufahl Peter J	(507)822-3606 oursaviorpk@gmail.com	3395 Kaleta Dr Eagle River WI 54521	NW	SP	Our Savior Eagle River WI	(715)479-6226	SL	2006
Kufahl Mark C	mkufahl@cuw.edu	1733 Foxmoor Dr Fennimore WI 53809	SW	SP	St Luke* Richland Center WI	(608)334-2639	SL	1989
Kuhfal David P	(402)929-0201 dkuhfal@gmail.com	3908 SW Walnut St Ankeny IA 50023	IW	SP	Our Saviour Des Moines IA	(515)244-9347	SL	1992
Kuhl Charles W	(989)883-3471	486 9th St Sebewaing MI 48759	MI	EM			SPR	1965
Kuhlman Brent W	(402)867-2916 kuhlman.brent@gmail.com	31112 Church Rd Murdock NE 68407	NEB	SP	Trinity Murdock NE	(402)867-2916	SL	1990
Kuhlman Nathan A Dr	(573)612-9090 pastorkuhlman@gmail.com	10566 Butler Cir Rolla MO 65401	MO	SP	Redeemer Rolla MO	(573)364-7071	SL	2000

*Multiple Assignments (See Church Worker Locator for Additional Details)
See Page 53 for the Table of Abbreviations for key to District, Position, and Seminary abbreviations
**C =Candidate; EM = Emeritus; the date following the C is the month and year the Candidate status began

NAME	TELEPHONE NUMBER EMAIL	STREET ADDRESS CITY/STATE/ZIP	DISTRICT	POSITION/ STATUS**	WHERE SERVING	OFFICE PHONE	SEM/ PROGRAM	YR GRAD
Kuhlman Patrick J	pkuhlman@frontier.com	3013 Water Wheel Run Fort Wayne IN 46818	IN	SP	Immanuel Avilla IN	(260)897-2071	SL	2000
Kuhlmann Kurt P	(269)432-4306 burroak@juno.com		MI	SP	St John Burr Oak MI	(269)489-5539	SL	1995
Kuhn Dale R	(314)369-6617 Dale_Kuhn@icloud.com	119 Waverly Pl Saint Louis MO 63119	MO	EM			SL	1973
Kuhn Henry P	(712)284-2282 shkuhn85@gmail.com	310 Lake St Alta IA 51002	IW	EM			SL	1960
Kuhnke Gerald J	pastorgerryk@gmail.com	460 W. Church St. Evansville WI 53536	PSW	EM			CQ	2001
Kuhnle David R	(402)740-5038 drkuhnle07@gmail.com	1414 Oran Dr Council Blfs IA 51503	IW	EM			SL	1987
Kumfer Justin A	(507)606-1901 japanesefire@gmail.com	125 1st St E Stewartville MN 55976	MNS	Sn/Adm	St Johns Stewartville MN	(507)533-4420	SL	2016
Kumm Michael L Dr		4228 Fremar Drive Sioux City IA 51104	SD	Asst	Holy Cross Dakota Dunes SD	(605)232-9117	SL	2000
Kummer Carl M	(214)903-7070	1250 W Hwy 287 Bypass #227 Waxahachie TX 75165	TX	EM			SL	1961
Kummer David J	(302)547-7555 pastor@concordiade.com	3313 Altamont Drive Wilmington DE 19810	SE	SP	Concordia Wilmington DE	(302)478-3004	SL	2000
Kunkel Kristofer A	(360)490-9108 kris.kunkel@lcef.org	3108 SW Thistle St Seattle WA 98126	NOW	Pro Stf	Lutheran Church Extension Fund Saint Louis MO	(314)965-9000	SL	2005
Kunkel Lee R	(979)743-1500 LKUNKEL7@gmail.com	2200 Salem Cemetery Ln Brenham TX 77833	TX	EM			SL	1985
Kunkel Danny J	(509)707-0125 asempadan@gmail.com	615 S. Atlantic Moses Lake WA 98837	NOW	EM			SL	1973
Kunsman Jeffrey R	(416)265-0489 jkunsman23@gmail.com	1037 Propeller Dr Haliburton ON K0M 1 CANADA	EN	EM			SL-SMP	2010
Kuntz John P	(949)282-7238 jpk.kuntz@gmail.com	22972 Springwater Lake Forest CA 92630	PSW	EM			SL	1957
Kuntz Scott A	(412)992-0277 PastorKuntz@gmail.com	11 Pearl Ave Pittsburgh PA 15229	EA	SP	Mount Calvary West View PA	(412)931-4500	FW	1995
Kunz Siegfried J	(318)564-6657 SJKunz@aol.com	2410 Melrose Ave Bossier City LA 71111	SO	EM			SPR	1963
Kunze Jeffrey D	(913)954-1768 revkunze@gmail.com		KS	EM			SL	1991
Kunze John R	(402)770-8165	9237 Dargent Ct Lincoln NE 68526	NEB	Sn/Adm	Messiah Lincoln NE	(402)489-3024	SL	1996
Kunze Seth L	(281)299-1909 sethkunze@gmail.com	21554 Sullivan Forest Dr Porter TX 77365	TX	SP	The Dwelling Porter TX	(281)299-1909	SL	2016
Kuppler Robert A	(908)531-7266 bobkuppler@gmail.com	1625 Feldspar Ct Leland NC 28451	SE	EM			CQ	1980
Kurka Gerald E	(314) 757-8199 jerrykurka@gmail.com	1233 3rd St Troy MO 63379	MO	EM			SL	2014
Kurowski Peter M Dr	(605)471-0293 pastorpete067@gmail.com	20209 Ellis Davis Rd Booneville MO 65233	MO	SP	Immanuel* Jamestown MO	(605)471-0293	SL	1978
Kurth Richard E	(216)402-3674 smelc4464@gmail.com	4831 W Lawther Dr Apt 305 Dallas TX 75214	TX	EM			SL	1970
Kurz Erich L	(660)221-1854 kurzek2012@gmail.com	1801 Villa Dr Warrensburg MO 64093	MO	C07/2016			FW	1988
Kurz Joel R	(660)441-5710 pastor@blchurch.com	19 SE 240th Rd Warrensburg MO 64093	MO	Sn/Adm	Bethlehem Warrensburg MO	(660)747-6742	FW	1997
Kusch Matthew S	mskusch@gmail.com	2916 Darley Dr Montgomery IL 60538	NI	SP	King Of Glory Elgin IL	(847)931-1520	SL	2017
Kusel Ronald J Dr	(562)425-2186 ronaldkusel@verizon.net	3520 Ladoga Ave Long Beach CA 90808	PSW	EM			SL	1964
Kuster Theodore F	(612)387-6233 kuster.theodore@gmail.com	1320 Dakota St. SE Albuquerque NM 87108	RM	EM			CQ	1982
Kutter Frederick M	(320)597-2132 revkutter@arvig.net	26245 County Road 9 Richmond MN 56368	MNN	EM			FW	1986
Kuznik Rollin F	(317)354-3299 pastorkuz@yahoo.com	15962 Venito Trl Fishers IN 46037	IN	EM			SL	1968
Kwon Young M	(213)480-9945 revyoungmankwon@yahoo.com	1 Horizon Rd Apt 626 Fort Lee NJ 07024	PSW	EM			CQ	1995
Kyes James M	(425)367-3070 pastorkyes@gmail.com	c/o St Peter The Fisherman P.O. Box 169 Lincoln City OR 97367	NOW	SP	St Peter Fisherman Lincoln City OR	(541)994-8793	SL-D	2010
Kyle John R	(248)930-1070 johnkyle1953@gmail.com	550 First Ave S Apt 1403 Saint Petersburg FL 33701	FG	C07/2024			SL	2020
Kyler Jeffrey B	(417)309-3018 j.kyler.783@gmail.com	10100 SE Co Rd 9526 Rockville MO 64780	MO	SP	Zion Rockville MO	(660)598-6215	FW	2019
L Heureux Calvin L	(402)750-3465 blestbygrace1969@gmail.com	891 South 800 West Indianapolis IN 46239	IN	EM			FW	1991
La Dassor Larry D	(507)533-7895 ldlfishon@yahoo.com	905 Beachwood Ct NE Stewartville MN 55976	MNS	EM			SL	1967
Laabs Bruce H	(612) 457-6358 imsetfree@outlook.com	925 Airport Rd Apt 201 Waconia MN 55387	MNS	C01/2021			SL	1985
Laatsch James F	jklaatsch@gmail.com	600 Clark St #210 Lodi WI 53555	SW	EM			SL	1967
Laatsch John V	(920)598-0170 jvlaatsch@gmail.com	W2253 State Highway 22 Gillett WI 54124	NW	SP	Faith United Gillett WI	(920)855-6464	FW	1986
LaBore Richard D Dr	(314)960-5350 rglabore@sbcglobal.net	1421 Woodhue Dr Saint Louis MO 63126	MO	C05/2019			SL	1958
LaBoube Christopher J	(712)840-1652 pastorlaboube@immanueldp.org	1068 Hollywood Ave Des Plaines IL 60016	NI	Sn/Adm	Immanuel Des Plaines IL	(847)824-3652	FW	2008

*Multiple Assignments (See Church Worker Locator for Additional Details)
See Page 53 for the Table of Abbreviations for key to District, Position, and Seminary abbreviations
**C =Candidate; EM = Emeritus; the date following the C is the month and year the Candidate status began

NAME	TELEPHONE NUMBER EMAIL	STREET ADDRESS CITY/STATE/ZIP	DISTRICT	POSITION/ STATUS**	WHERE SERVING	OFFICE PHONE	SEM/ PROGRAM	YR GRAD
Labuhn David H	(571)436-1687 labuhnd@cs.com	820 Anthony Ct SE Leesburg VA 20175	SE	SMP	Our Savior Arlington VA	(703)892-4846	CQ	2018
Labuhn Hans T	(703)459-0518 tlabuhn@stjohnsws.org	675 Croston Dr Winston Salem NC 27104	SE	Sn/Adm	St John Winston-Salem NC	(336)725-1651	SL	2007
Lacey Stanley J	stanley.james.lacey@gmail.com	7334 Winter Song Dr Magnolia TX 77354	EN	SP	St Thomas Magnolia TX	(281)206-4043	FW	2021
Lach Noble P	(407)542-3460 dnlach@gmail.com	1378 Haven Dr Oviedo FL 32765	S	EM			SL	1963
Lackey Jonathan S			EN	SP	Grace Vine Grove KY	(270)877-2855	SL	2023
Lackey Travis T Jr	(205)956-6727 ptlack01@gmail.com	3548 Bermuda Dr Birmingham AL 35210	SO	EM			SL-D	2009
Laeder Richard P	(517)348-9587 revlaeder@gmail.com	207 Cadgewith E Lansing MI 48906	MI	EM			FW	1986
Laesch Theodore L Jr	(314)355-0688 revtheo@gmail.com	9 Deer Valley Ct Florissant MO 63034	EN	Sn/Adm	Chapel Cross Saint Louis County MO	(314)741-3737	SL	1998
LaFeve Joshua C Dr	(231)590-0233 joshua.lafeve@cuw.edu	1511 S 17th Street Sheboygan WI 53081	SW	S HS/C	Concordia University Wisconsin Mequon WI	(262)243-5700	SL	2010
LaFore David C	(253)394-3722 davelafore@gmail.com	c/o Saint John Lutheran Church 5810 E Meadowlane Rd Spokane WA 99224	NOW	SP	St John's Spokane WA	(509)747-0984	SL	2018
Lagoutine Anton G	(828)464-4071 pastorlagoutine@gmail.com	4110 54th Ave NE Hickory NC 28601	SE	Sn/Adm	St John Conover NC	(828)464-4071	FW	2002
LaGrave Tyler R		1621 Genoa Ct New Haven IN 46774	EN	C07/2024			CQ	2020
Lahners Kenneth W	715-264-3961 kennethlahners@yahoo.com		NW	SP	Trinity Glidden WI	(715)264-3961	CQ	2017
Lahrman William C	(616)402-1265 lahrmanw@gmail.com	2515 Fountain St Muskegon MI 49441	MI	EM			FW	1983
Lahue Alexander D	(314)560-1085 alexlahue3@gmail.com	14225 Hargrave Rd Houston TX 77070	TX	Assoc	St Timothy Houston TX	(281)469-2457	SL	2019
Lail Robert C	(636)541-9195 bob.lailfamily@gmail.com	7019 N Fischer Ct Spokane WA 99208	NOW	C01/2019			SL	2008
Lakies Chad D Dr	(314)317-4163 chad.lakies@lhm.org	1311 Whispering Ridge Ln Saint Peters MO 63376	MO	Aux	LLL/Lutheran Hour Ministries Saint Louis MO	(314)317-4100	SL	2006
Lakso Thomas E	(479)981-3061	5035 Griffins Gate Ln Knoxville TN 37912	MDS	EM			FW	1983
Lalljie Jimmy A	(917)915-8612 jimmylalljie@yahoo.com	9 Durham Rd New Hyde Park NY 11040	AT	SP	Trinity* New Hyde Park NY	(516)354-8883	CQ	2009
Lally Richard A Jr	(785)313-2434 pastor@stmatthewlcms.org	1171 Johnson Rd Nortonville KS 66060	KS	SP	St Matthew Nortonville KS	(913)886-6331	SL	2014
LaMay Colton J	(519) 918-7182 coltonlamay@gmail.com	357 Nash Dr Corunna ON N0N 1 CANADA	EN	SMP	Redeemer Sarnia ON	(519)337-6615	SL-SMP	2020
Lamb James I Dr	(641)751-4433 lambforlife@gmail.com	908 W Boone St Marshalltown IA 50158	IW	EM			SL	1982
Lamb Richard E	(432)385-4022 revrlamb@gmail.com	P.O. Box 409 Anderson TX 77830	TX	SP	Zion Anderson TX	(936)873-2175	SL	1996
Lambart Kurt E	(734) 560-9001 klambart@outlook.com	28484 Balmoral St Garden City MI 48135	MI	SP	Peace Ann Arbor MI	(734)424-0899	SL	1995
Lambrecht Jeffrey A	(262)215-3810 JeffreyALambrecht@gmail.com	10230 8th Avenue Pleasant Prairie WI 53158	NI	C09/2021			SL	2003
LaMie Julian A	(815)471-2221 pastorlamie@ourpeacelutheran.org	28054 S Yates Ave Beecher IL 60401	NI	Sn/Adm	Peace Beecher IL	(708)946-2271	SL	2019
LaMie Oliver Q	(815)471-1125 oliverlamie@gmail.com	7187 Renken Rd Dorsey IL 62021	SI	SP	St Peter Prairietown IL	(618)888-2250	SL	2023
Lamkin Timothy H Sr	(651)368-1153 revthlsr@hotmail.com	7495 269th Ave NW Saint Francis MN 55070	MNN	SP	Zion Saint Francis MN	(763)856-2099	FW	1995
Lammert Richard A	(260)484-2889 richard.lammert52@gmail.com	4743 Ashland Dr Fort Wayne IN 46835	IN	EM			FW	1998
Lamont Bruce B	(715)849-2441 bruceblamont@gmail.com	153000 Morning Glory Ln Wausau WI 54401	NW	EM			SL	1987
Lamont Jeremy D	(801)233-0090 church@gracesandy.org	8446 S 1330 E Sandy UT 84093	RM	SMP	Grace Sandy UT	(801)572-6375	SL-SMP	2024
Lampe Kendall M	kenlampe1941@icloud.com	26530 Greenbriar Ln Warsaw MO 65355	MO	EM			CQ	1988
Lampe Kenneth E	(417)366-3597 klampe@mid-southlcms.com	16875 Lawrence 1110 Mount Vernon MO 65712	MO	EM			SL	1973
Lampella Thomas A	(205)301-1040 tlampella@gmail.com	2651 S Juniper St Unit 2202 Foley AL 36535	SO	EM			SL	1984
Lampi Stephen A	(989)859-4312 lampi.steve@gmail.com	2115 Burlington Dr Midland MI 48642	MI	SMP	Messiah Midland MI	(989)631-5200	FW-SMP	2024
Lampitt Carl R	(256)352-5884 blackmacoco@bellsouth.net	109 1/2 Michelle St NW Hanceville AL 35077	SO	EM			SPR	1962
Lampman David P	(931)335-9163 dvdlampman51@gmail.com	P.O. Box 1264 Crossville TN 38557	MDS	EM			NESC	1995
Landes Logan P	(317)682-8697	1239 Summer Springs Dr Middleburg FL 32068	FG	SP	St Peter Middleburg FL	(904)282-8876	FW	2016
Landgraf Paul D	(314)791-6401 pjlandgraf@yahoo.com	107 S Edward Ct Eureka MO 63025	MO	SP	St John* Drake MO	(314)791-6401	SL	1990
Landskroener Timothy J	(330)204-4180 lawandgospel@hotmail.com	1295 E 900th Ave Shobonier IL 62885	CI	SP	Immanuel Shobonier IL	(618)846-8383	SL	1994
Landsmann Lon E	(402) 756-5723 prspnzn@gmail.com	P.O. Box 398 Kenesaw NE 68956	NEB	SP	St Paul* Holstein NE	(402)200-0078	FW	1994

*Multiple Assignments (See Church Worker Locator for Additional Details)
See Page 53 for the Table of Abbreviations for key to District, Position, and Seminary abbreviations
**C =Candidate; EM = Emeritus; the date following the C is the month and year the Candidate status began

NAME	TELEPHONE NUMBER EMAIL	STREET ADDRESS CITY/STATE/ZIP	DISTRICT	POSITION/ STATUS**	WHERE SERVING	OFFICE PHONE	SEM/ PROGRAM	YR GRAD
Lane Robert A	(406)671-0193 rev.pastorlane@gmail.com	3722 Chippewa Trl Billings MT 59106	MT	SP	Our Redeemer* Worden MT	(406)656-2860	SL	1998
Lane William J	(785)224-0971 lanejeff6850@yahoo.com	6850 SW 44th St Topeka KS 66610	KS	SMP	Faith Topeka KS	(785)272-4214	SL-SMP	2024
Lane Stephen S	(352)586-4468 suzannel119@outlook.com	1150 W Legion Ct Hernando FL 34442	FG	EM			FW	1983
Lane Jason D Dr	(314)505-7763 lanej@csl.edu	7045 Cornell Ave University City MO 63130	MO	S HS/C	Concordia Seminary Saint Louis MO	(314)505-7000	FW	2007
Lane Marcus J	(206)422-1774 lane.marcusj@gmail.com	2459 Nottingham Rd Ann Arbor MI 48104	MI	Assoc	University Chapel Ann Arbor MI	(734)663-5560	SL	2015
Lane Morgan S	(828) 228-2696 mstewartlane@gmail.com	2176 St James Church Rd Newton NC 28658	SE	SMP	Bethel Claremont NC	(828)459-7378	SL-SMP	2022
Lane Matthew D	(507)340-4744 mlane@kingofkingsroseville.org	1450 18th Ave NW Faribault MN 55021	MNS	Assoc	King Of Kings Roseville MN	(651)484-5142	SL	2013
Lange Harvey D Dr	(317)802-7112 REVHARVEYLANGE@GMAIL.COM	4923 Coventry Park Cir Indianapolis IN 46237	IN	EM			SL	1955
Lange Thomas M	(248)719-0196 tlange4x@gmail.com	c/o Saint Paul Lutheran High P.O. Box 719 Concordia MO 64020	MO	Tchr	Saint Paul Concordia MO	(660)463-2238	SL	1995
Lange Roger A	(218)770-0612 revnmrs@prtel.com	1506 N Park St Fergus Falls MN 56537	MNN	EM			SL	1961
Lange Peter K	(314)996-1408 peter.lange@lcms.org	c/o Lutheran Church-Missouri Synod 1333 S Kirkwood Rd Saint Louis MO 63122	MO	S Ex/S	The LCMS Corporate Saint Louis MO	(314)965-9000	FW	1988
Lange Peter A	(573)392-4603 faithpal@yahoo.com	1000 N Grand Ave Eldon MO 65026	MO	SP	Bethany Eldon MO	(573)392-4603	SL	2006
Lange Michael R	(925) 876-5621 mike@cnh-lcms.org	523 Escondido Cir Livermore CA 94550	CNH	DP	California/Nevada/Hawaii District Livermore CA	(866)264-6079	SL	1988
Lange Jonathan C	jon.lange7@gmail.com		CNH	EM			SL	1994
Lange George H	(260) 969-7079 langegeo@frontier.com	2209 St. Joe Center Road - Apt. 292SW Fort Wayne IN 46825	IN	EM			SPR	1960
Lange Eric T	(503)816-8558	261 SW Wallula Ave Gresham OR 97080	NOW	Sn/Adm	Redeemer Gresham OR	(503)665-5414	FW	1988
Lange Alvin H	(573)644-3126 alsylvia.lange@gmail.com	2133 Rivina Dr Austin TX 78733	TX	EM			SL	1962
Lange Alexander J	(503)737-8154 gracealone11@gmail.com	3325 22nd Ave SE Albany OR 97322	NOW	SP	Holy Cross Albany OR	(541)928-0214	SL	2015
Lange Jonathan G	(307)727-7095 jlange64@protonmail.com	221 Southridge Rd Evanston WY 82930	WY	SP	St Paul* Kemmerer WY	(307)727-7095	FW	1990
Langemo Martin S	(763)631-0710 pastor@langemo.com	926 Watson Ave Saint Paul MN 55102	MNN	EM			SPR	1964
Langewisch John E	(989)430-3031 pjlwisch@yahoo.com	3511 S 186th St Omaha NE 68130	NEB	EM			SL	1974
Langewisch David J	(303)887-0476 dlangewisch@bethlehemdenver.com	11230 West Ford Dr Lakewood CO 80226	RM	Sn/Adm	Bethlehem Lakewood CO	(303)238-7676	SL	1991
Langewisch Daniel J	(720)402-1330 langewischd@woodburylutheran.org	1848 Lamplight Dr Woodbury MN 55125	MNS	Assoc	Woodbury Woodbury MN	(651)739-5144	SL	2023
Langfeldt Jack E	jack.langfeldt@gmail.com	5269 Skyview Ln Apt 6 Battle Creek MI 49015	MI	EM			CQ	2018
Langhoff Donald H	(573)465-4128 revdhl@yahoo.com	1319 Whitney Lane Rolla MO 65401	MO	EM			SPR	1971
Langhorst Richard E	(218)273-6248 pastorlanghorst@yahoo.com	2808 Lund Rd Kettle River MN 55757	MNN	SP	Immanuel* Giese MN	(218)273-6248	FW	1979
Langness Richard D	(720)534-6563 pastorlangness@yahoo.com	2800 S Grant St Englewood CO 80113	RM	SP	Beautiful Savior Broomfield CO	(303)469-1785	SL	2004
Lanham Curtiss L	(713) 828-3025 curtiss@WeAreDogsmart.com	5635 Westerdale Dr Weston Lakes TX 77441	TX	EM			SL-SMP	2016
Lanning James R	(512)682-3941 pastorlanning@goodshepherd-centralia.org	15 Mays Meadows Centralia MO 65240	MO	SP	Good Shepherd Centralia MO	(573)682-3941	SL	2022
Lantz Paul L	(339) 203-2258 plantz@crosshanover.org	120 Karen Rd Hanover MA 02339	NE	SP	Of The Cross Hanover MA	(781)826-5121	Other	2009
Lapacka John T III Dr	(806)664-0525 lapackajt@aol.com	12635 Green Darner San Antonia TX 78253	TX	EM			FW	1998
LaPlant LeRoy J	(763)219-0692 revljlaplant@gmail.com	707 Lower Johnson Cir Saint Peter MN 56082	MNS	SP	Good Shepherd North Mankato MN	(507)388-4336	FW	2008
Lappe Dustin P	(402) 417-8467 dustin.lappe@messiah.us	916 Twin Ridge Rd Lincoln NE 68510	NEB	Assoc	Messiah Lincoln NE	(402)489-3024	SL	2002
Lark Devon H	devonlark65@gmail.com	18601 Midway Rd Walton NE 68461	NEB	EM			SL-SMP	2018
Larmi Eugene A	(907)602-4204 eugenelarmi@me.com	1031 W Nugget Ave Wasilla AK 99654	NOW	SMP	Lamb Of God Wasilla AK	(907)357-8077	SL-SMP	2015
Larsen Nicholas L	(208)290-4778 pastor.livingwater@gmail.com	P.O. Box 438 Clark Fork ID 83811	NOW	SP	Living Water Clark Fork ID	(208)266-1282	CQ	2020
Larsen Peter E Dr	(734) 660-3595 pel5765@gmail.com	5470 Albright Ave SW Wyoming MI 49418	MI	EM			SL	1965
Larsen James F	(559)325-7693 jameslar25@comcast.net	10751 E San Felipe Ave Clovis CA 93619	CNH	EM			FW	1986
Larsen Daniel C		702 Douglas Ave Henning MN 56551	MNN	SP	St Paul Henning MN	(218)583-2707	SL	2012
Larsen Steven M	(979)900-5911 stevenlarsen844@gmail.com	125 Spanish Moss Ln Lake Jackson TX 77566	TX	EM			FW	1983
Larsen Larry J	(402)369-4637 larry21168787@yahoo.com	104 South 8 Street Apt. 2 Norfolk NE 68701	FG	EM			SPR	1976

*Multiple Assignments (See Church Worker Locator for Additional Details)
See Page 53 for the Table of Abbreviations for key to District, Position, and Seminary abbreviations
**C =Candidate; EM = Emeritus; the date following the C is the month and year the Candidate status began

NAME	TELEPHONE NUMBER EMAIL	STREET ADDRESS CITY/STATE/ZIP	DISTRICT	POSITION/ STATUS**	WHERE SERVING	OFFICE PHONE	SEM/ PROGRAM	YR GRAD
Larson Eric G	eric.larson@gslcgretna.org	18031 Sunridge St Omaha NE 68136	NEB	Assoc	Good Shepherd Gretna NE	(402)332-3345	SL	2022
Larson Thomas W	(402)270-3237 pastorlarson@juno.com	2201 NE 110th St Vancouver WA 98686	NOW	EM			SL	1982
Larson Michael C	(414)530-5732 mlarson@lmcusc.org	2118 E Shorewood Blvd Shorewood WI 53211	SW	SP	Luther Memorial Shorewood WI	(414)332-5732	FW	2011
Larson Mark S	(314)546-0477 mlarson.54@gmail.com	810 W Main St Clarinda IA 51632	MO	EM			SL	2013
Larson Mark C Dr	(314)623-2410 markclarson0341@gmail.com	c/o St Lucas Lutheran Church 7100 Morgan Ford Rd Saint Louis MO 63116	S	SP	St Lucas Saint Louis MO	(314)351-2628	SL	1988
Larson Kurt R	(563)505-2342 krlarson19@gmail.com	4416 Warren St Davenport IA 52806	CI	SP	St Matthew Milan IL	(309)787-4295	FW	1992
Larson John R	(303)420-8918 pastorjohnlarson@aol.com	6308 S Chase Ct Littleton CO 80123	RM	SP	Ascension Littleton CO	(303)794-4636	SL	1983
Larson David N	(952)232-8134 pastordavelarson@gmail.com	7237 Janero Ave. S Cottage Grove MN 55016	MNS	SP	St John Woodbury MN	(651)436-6621	SL	2009
Larson Daniel J	(602)394-6685 avsfan81@yahoo.com	18402 N 66th Ln Glendale AZ 85308	PSW	Sn/Adm	Atonement Glendale AZ	(623)582-8785	FW	2010
Larson Brian T	revlarson.brian@gmail.com	2201 NE 110th St Vancouver WA 98686	NOW	SP	St John Vancouver WA	(360)573-1461	SL	2003
Larson Brandon D	(928)542-1902 b_larson@me.com	11112 Harvest Hill Ln Las Vegas NV 89135	PSW	Assoc	Faith Community Las Vegas NV	(702)921-2700	SL	2016
Larson Kenneth E	(561)346-8245 kenlarson42@hotmail.com	1130 Whitcombe Dr Royal Palm Beach FL 33411	FG	EM			FW	1977
Lasch Mark F Dr	mlasch@concordialutheran.org	535 Woodhill Ct Grapevine TX 76051	TX	SP	Concordia Bedford TX	(817)283-3560	SL	2000
Laska Gregory R	(715)536-1511 grlaska@yahoo.com	N1836 Monteray Dr Merrill WI 54452	NW	SP	Luther Memorial* Gleason WI	(715)873-4592	SL-D	2003
Laskowsky Kurt G	(605)667-0999 kurt.laskowsky@ctsfw.edu	P.O. Box 129 Centerville SD 57014	SD	SP	Zion* Hurley SD	(605)563-2904	FW	2020
Lassanske Dennis L	dennlass03@gmail.com	3042 Chapel Ct Muskegon MI 49441	MI	EM			SL	1972
Lassman Ernie V	(206) 526-8820 elassman@aol.com	15020 Bothell Way NE Apt 304 Lake Forest Park WA 98155	NOW	EM			FW	1978
Latham Mark E	(208)404-1673 mlrevswim@gmail.com	1030 Centre St Traverse City MI 49686	MI	SP	St Michael Traverse City MI	(231)947-5293	FW	1985
Lattimore Warren L Malueg-Lattimore	(504)944-5401 lattimorew@gmail.com	c/o Trinity Lutheran Church 2125 Watson Ave Bronx NY 10472	AT	Assoc	Trinity Bronx NY	(718)828-3532	SL	2013
Latzke Jeremy A	(217)653-9593 pastor@stjohnsalgonquin.org	719 Old Hunt Rd Fox River Grove IL 60021	NI	Sn/Adm	St John Algonquin IL	(847)658-9300	SL	2009
Latzke Steven D	(574)261-4427 stevenlatzke@gmail.com	5501 Dollar Hide South Dr Indianapolis IN 46221	IN	SP	Living Christ Plainfield IN	(317)839-4800	SL	2000
Lau Shiu M Dr	(650)455-8842 jlau128@yahoo.com	88 S Broadway Unit 3107 Millbrae CA 94030	CNH	Sn/Adm	Holy Spirit San Francisco CA	(415)661-1120	CQ	1999
Laue David E	(218)773-8775 dlegfmn@gmail.com	16 James Cir SE E Grand Forks MN 56721	MNN	SP	Redeemer* Grand Forks ND	(701)772-0706	SL	1991
Laue Ronald H	(814)882-8798 rhlaue@yahoo.com	5831 Forest Crossing Erie PA 16506	EN	EM			SL	1963
Lauer Paul A	(507)304-2402 palauer@gmail.com		MNS	SP	Trinity Lake Crystal MN		SL	1991
Laufer Ralph E	(618)340-6710	201 Eastlawn St New Athens IL 62264	SI	SP	Holy Cross Sugar Loaf Township IL	(618)538-5600	SL	1986
Laughridge Justin D		3202 Bayview Ave Toronto ON M2M 3 CANADA	EN	Sn/Adm	St Luke* North York ON	(416)221-8900	SL	2008
Lauterbach Travis E	pastortravisl@hotmail.com		MNN	SP	Emmanuel Backus MN	(218)947-4182	FW	2013
Laux John A	(217)521-3372 revjal87@yahoo.com	10520 Waltz San Antonio TX 78254	SW	EM			FW	1987
Lavrenz Mark E	(641)583-3861 rnssmo4@hotmail.com	507 W Main St P.O. Box 192 Steamboat Rock IA 50672	IE	EM			FW	1991
Law Richard M	pastorlaw@wlchurch.org	10 Mount Vernon St Quincy MA 02169	NE	EM			HK	1969
Law Steve T	(617)773-5482 steve@wlchurch.org	550 Hancock St Quincy MA 02170	NE	SP	Wollaston Quincy MA	(617)773-5482	FW	2017
Lawrence Wayne E	(314)727-3253 welawrence2002@yahoo.com	1401 N Hanley Rd University Cy MO 63130	MO	SP	Saint James University City MO	(314)727-3253	SL	1998
Laws Jonah Q	(541) 218-2046	P.O. Box 428 Rogue River OR 95737	NOW	Sn/Adm	Faith Rogue River OR		FW	2023
Lawson Jerrald B	(239)246-3256 jerrald.lawson@lcms.org		FG	S Miss	Office of International Mission Saint Louis MO		FW	2001
Lawson Timothy A	(480)486-0597	19422 E Via De Olivos Queen Creek AZ 85142	PSW	Sn/Adm	Saving Grace Queen Creek AZ	(480)888-9673	SL	2006
le Feber Gerard F	(716)372-9220 lefeeb@bluefrog.com	707 Main St Olean NY 14760	EA	EM			SL	1972
Le Pere Ronald P	(440)953-8350 fatherlepere@sbcglobal.net	8032 Brentwood Rd Mentor OH 44060	OH	EM			SL	1971
Le Sieur Gregory M	(321)750-7910 myjoynaomi@yahoo.com	625 Paula Ave Merritt Is FL 32953	FG	SP	Christ Cape Canaveral FL	(321)783-3303	SL	2005
Leach Le Roy H Jr Dr	(914)513-1767 leroy.leachphd@gmail.com	1210 Salem Rd Conway AR 72034	MDS	EM			FW	2004
Leary Kelly J	(920)216-8387 padre_oleary@me.com	10 Main St Apt 101 Menasha WI 54952	RM	C09/2018			SL	1995
Leavitt Roger G	(402)371-5043 rgleavitt1@gmail.com	2708 Cook Ct Plattsmouth NE 68048	NEB	EM			FW	1996

*Multiple Assignments (See Church Worker Locator for Additional Details)
See Page 53 for the Table of Abbreviations for key to District, Position, and Seminary abbreviations
**C =Candidate; EM = Emeritus; the date following the C is the month and year the Candidate status began

NAME	TELEPHONE NUMBER EMAIL	STREET ADDRESS CITY/STATE/ZIP	DISTRICT	POSITION/ STATUS**	WHERE SERVING	OFFICE PHONE	SEM/ PROGRAM	YR GRAD
Leavitt Rossetter T	(941)752-1393 pastor@beautifulsaviorlcms.com	4105 59th Pl E Bradenton FL 34203	FG	Sn/Adm	Beautiful Savior Sarasota FL	(941)355-2798	SL	1981
LeBlanc Robert E	(361)781-4226 word.boc4all@gmail.com	796 Texas Sage Loop Buda TX 78610	TX	C04/2025			FW	1996
LeBorious Joshua M Dr	(478)919-6187 jleborious@hope-lutheran.org	4208 Willow Bay Ct. League City TX 77573	TX	Sn/Adm	Hope Friendswood TX	(281)482-7943	SL	2021
LeBorious Peter J	(478)919-3723 dcepete91@gmail.com	413 Erin Way Warner Robins GA 31088	FG	SMP	Mount Calvary Warner Robins GA	(478)922-1418	SL-SMP	2020
Leckband Jerome P	(402)329-4262 revband@ptcnet.net	308 County Road 388 Jonesboro AR 72401	MDS	Assoc	All Saints Jonesboro AR	(870)935-2001	FW	2000
Leckband Mark T	(319)329-1944 mtleckband@proton.me	9 Nelson St P.O. Box 317 Ventura IA 50482	IE	EM			SL	1996
Lecke Josepha H Jr	(618)214-2766 jlecke@hotmail.com	1105 Lake Pointe Cir Roswell GA 30075	FG	EM			FW	1978
LeClair Edward P	(314)395-4421 eleclair@pathwayshospice.com	419 Cannonbury Dr Saint Louis MO 63119	MO	C04/2018			SL	2012
LeClair Timothy J	(586)536-8102 timothy1sg@aol.com	38964 Farmcrest Clinton Twp MI 48036	MI	SMP	Family of God Detroit MI	(586)722-3996	CQ	2021
Ledbetter Randy W	(713)818-7629 randy@ledbetter.net	1008 Margaret Drive McKinney TX 75071	TX	EM			FW	1986
Ledic Peter	(925)216-9950 pjl603@yahoo.com	4242 Nevis Pl El Dorado Hills CA 95762	EN	EM			FW	1982
Ledlow Landon M	(972)342-8800	17203 Keely Dr Tampa FL 33647	S	Sn/Adm	Family Of Christ Tampa FL	(813)558-9343	SL	2008
Lee Jeffrey A	(763)568-2318 Ptl4revlee@gmail.com	3000 Northwest Loop Stephenville TX 76401	TX	SP	Faith Stephenville TX	(254)968-2710	FW	1987
Lee Stephen C	(708)334-5883 revstevelee@gmail.com	1805 Fox Mead Cir Montgomery IL 60538	NI	EM			FW	1992
Lee Samuel Dr	(414)979-5503 samghlee@gmail.com	21915 Clearfield Rd Brookfield WI 53045	SW	SMP	Elm Grove* Elm Grove WI	(262)797-2970	FW-SMP	2024
Lee Matthew A	(972)398-7510 mlee@messiahlutheran.com	Messiah Lutheran Church 1801 W Plano Pkwy Plano TX 75075	TX	SMP	Messiah Plano TX	(972)398-7500	SL-SMP	2022
Lee Martin E Schroeder Dr	(517)755-8770	3148 Hagadorn Rd Mason MI 48854	PSW	SP	Palisades Pacific Palisades CA	(310)459-2358	FW	1997
Lee Kwang M		1151 N Madison Ave Apt 108 Los Angeles CA 90029	PSW	D Miss	Pacific Southwest Di Irvine CA	(949)854-3232	CQ	1995
Lee Kwang K	paullee712@hotmail.com	7632 21st St Apt 64 Westminster CA 92683	PSW	EM			CQ	2009
Lee Kirk E	(218)338-5351 ilcpp@midwestinfo.net	609 S Douglas Ave Parkers Pr MN 56361	MNN	SP	Immanuel Parkers Prairie MN	(218)338-2511	SL	1989
Lee Key J	(714)772-1140 usammission@yahoo.com	1919 W Coronet Ave Spc 25 Anaheim CA 92081	PSW	O-Miss	Pacific Southwest Di Irvine CA	(949)854-3232	CQ	1999
Lee James A II Dr	James.Lee@cuchicago.edu	7400 Augusta St Box 27n River Forest IL 60305	NI	S HS/C	Concordia University Chicago River Forest IL	(708)771-8300	FW	2010
Lee Ho J	(917)294-5416 lee.attorney77@gmail.com	3201 167th St Flushing NY 11358	EN	SP	Immanuel Korean Flushing NY	(718)460-5736	CQ	2022
Lee Esaias C Chunshick	(949)683-2244 chunshicklee@hotmail.com	12106 Barnwall St Norwalk CA 92603	PSW	EM			CQ	2015
Lee Donald W	(845)928-9644 thelees70@optonline.net	64 Midland Ave Central Vly NY 10917	AT	EM			FW-D	2003
Lee Chandara A	(562)595-0108 cdalee@verizon.net	2599 Walnut Ave Unit 120 Signal Hill CA 90755	PSW	EM			SL	2000
Lee Brian D	brian@trinitykalispell.org	c/o Trinity Lutheran Church 400 W California St Kalispell MT 59901	MT	Sn/Adm	Trinity Kalispell MT	(406)257-5683	SL	2010
Lee Tommy R Sr	(334)303-2089 pastor@mymessiahchurch.org	1713 Meadowbrook Dr Prattville AL 36066	SO	SMP	Messiah Prattville AL	(334)290-5215	SL-SMP	2024
Lee Khai N	(559)940-3494 khai.n.lee@gmail.com	11250 E McKinley Ave Sanger CA 93657	CNH	Assoc	Peace Fresno CA	(559)222-2320	SL	2012
Lee Suk H	703-978-5941 kkp2h@hotmail.com	5618 Rapid Run Ct Burke VA 22015	SE	C07/2016			CQ	1998
Lee Vue	(209)261-0510 vue.lee@mnsdistrict.org	7530 W River Rd Brooklyn Park MN 55444	MNS	D Ex/S	Minnesota South District Burnsville MN	(952)435-2550	SL	2016
Lee Yong M	(619)497-0524 yongmolee33@gmail.com	3955 Park Blvd Apt 212 San Diego CA 92103	PSW	EM			CQ	1995
Lee Yun S	(323)891-4113 laca.newthing@gmail.com	25330 Silver Aspen Way Apt 1227 Valencia CA 91381	PSW	EM			CQ	2018
Lee Sun Moon S	(832)202-7761 sun.lee.hou@gmail.com	1118 Barkston Dr Katy TX 77450	TX	EM			NESC	1989
Leech Joseph L	(570)687-4219	3160 Katherine Cir Plover WI 54467	NW	SP	Beautiful Savior Plover WI	(715)341-2898	SL	2017
Leeland David A	(281)345-7951 david.a.leeland@gmail.com	19011 Village Dogwood Ct Houston TX 77084	TX	Assoc	Epiphany Houston TX	(713)896-1773	SL	1981
Leem Sung Woo	swohsmsj@hotmail.com	105 Applegate Dr Central Islip NY 11722	AT	C09/2018			CQ	2009
Leeper Benjamin T	(314)920-1854 ben.leeper@cune.org	608 Benwood Dr Marshall WI 53559	SW	Assoc	Bethlehem Sun Prairie WI	(608)837-7446	SL	2023
Lefort Chase K	(919)610-9219 pastor@faithlutheranoakridge.org	790 Emory Valley Rd Apt 512 Oak Ridge TN 37830	MDS	Sn/Adm	Faith Oak Ridge TN	(865)483-5431	FW	2022
LeGreco Nathan P	(775)777-5224 pastorbucklegreco@gmail.com	2714 Staples Ave Key West FL 33040	FG	SP	Grace Key West FL	(305)296-5161	SL	2015
Lehenbauer Walter	(218)729-4600 wlehenbauer@gmail.com	6411 West Arrowhead Rd Cloquet MN 55720	MNN	Assoc	Emmanuel* Barnum MN	(218)389-6849	FW	1981
Lehenbauer Andrew A	(573)480-2043 andrew.lehenbauer@cune.org	404 S Saint Louis St Concordia MO 64020	MO	Assoc	St Paul Concordia MO	(660)463-2291	SL	2019

*Multiple Assignments (See Church Worker Locator for Additional Details)

See Page 53 for the Table of Abbreviations for key to District, Position, and Seminary abbreviations

**C =Candidate; EM = Emeritus; the date following the C is the month and year the Candidate status began

NAME	TELEPHONE NUMBER EMAIL	STREET ADDRESS CITY/STATE/ZIP	DISTRICT	POSITION/ STATUS**	WHERE SERVING	OFFICE PHONE	SEM/ PROGRAM	YR GRAD
Lehenbauer Carl W	(262)527-4402 clehenbauer@trinityfreistadt.com	10729 W Freistadt Rd Mequon WI 53097	SW	Sn/Adm	Trinity Mequon WI	(262)242-2045	SL	2008
Lehenbauer Joel D Dr	(314)996-1435 joel.lehenbauer@lcms.org	c/o Lutheran Church-Missouri Synod 1333 S Kirkwood Rd Saint Louis MO 63122	MO	S Ex/S	The LCMS Corporate Saint Louis MO	(314)965-9000	SL	1984
Lehenbauer John C	(478)397-5914 john@lehenbauer.us	213 Hearthwood Dr Kathleen GA 31047	FG	EM			FW	1986
Lehenbauer Ronald P	(573)480-0646 rlehenbauer@charter.net	13 Knox Point Cir Lake Ozark MO 65049	MO	Sn/Adm	Christ King Lake Ozark MO	(573)365-5212	SL	1991
Lehenbauer Ronald W Dr	(718)359-7022 psa23v6@aol.com	150-12 28th Ave Flushing NY 11354	AT	EM			SL	1968
Lehman Matthew L	(507)251-1698 lehman.mlr@gmail.com	1209 Foothills Cir Albert Lea MN 56007	MNS	SP	Zion Albert Lea MN	(507)373-8609	SL	1997
Lehman Andrew S	(251)214-4799	1812 Rains St Jonesboro AR 72401	MDS	Assoc	All Saints Jonesboro AR	(870)935-2001	FW	2014
Lehman Adam M	(314)965-9000 adam.lehman@lcms.org	D23 Calle Marlin Bahia Vistamar Carolina PR 00983	SO	S Miss	Office of International Mission Saint Louis MO		FW	2011
Lehmann Charles R			SO	SP	St John Lake Charles LA	(337)478-5666	FW	2007
Lehmann William H III	(541)772-4395 luth1020@gmail.com	1020 E Main St Medford OR 97504	NOW	SP	St Peter Medford OR	(541)772-4395	SL	1986
Lehmkuhl William K	(612) 269-5939 kurt@thelehmkuhls.com	301 7th St W Northfield MN 55057	MNS	EM			SL	1971
Lehr Gregory A	(605)338-5226 glehr@zionlutheransf.com	1400 S Duluth Ave Sioux Falls SD 57105	SD	Sn/Adm	Zion Sioux Falls SD	(605)338-5226	SL	2009
Lehrer Wayne J Dr	(703) 663-6056 wlehrer@verizon.net	7452 Spring Village Dr Apt 528 Springfield VA 22150	SE	EM			SL	1969
Leichman Jeffery H	(847)494-9494 leichman.jeffery@gmail.com	1905 Maple St Des Plaines IL 60018	NI	SP	Our Redeemer Prospect Heights IL	(847)537-4430	SL	1998
Leidich Kevin L	(606)759-6603 leid606@earthlink.net	5536 US Highway 62 Maysville KY 41056	OH	C01/2021			SL	1994
Leigeber Paul A	paulleigeber@gmail.com		MDS	SP	Trinity* Dyersburg TN	(731)285-9691	SL	1987
Leigeber Joshua P	(870)935-2001 pastor@allsaintsjonesboro.org	P.O. Box 141 Waldenburg AR 72475	MDS	Sn/Adm	All Saints Jonesboro AR	(870)935-2001	SL	2011
Leimer Weldon H	wjleimer@sbcglobal.net	1737 Timber Heights Dr Carmel IN 46280	IN	EM			FW	1983
Leinhos Steven J	sleinhos@verizon.net	31535 Cala Carrasco Temecula CA 92592	PSW	EM			SL	1985
Leininger Jeffrey W Dr	(708)606-5055 jleininger@fspauls.org	211 Augusta St Maywood IL 60153	NI	SP	First St Paul Chicago IL	(312)642-7172	SL	1995
Leiste Robert A	(785)766-8447 2197rlksole@gmail.com	3721 W 4th St Lawrenceville KS 66047	KS	EM			FW	1984
Leistico James A	pastor@peacewindsor.com	1797 Hickory Windsor ON N8Y 3 CANADA	EN	SP	Peace Windsor ON	(519)945-1344	FW	2001
Leiter Samuel K	(317)753-8295 pastorsamleiter@gmail.com	6056 Canterbury Ct Pittsboro IN 46167	IN	C02/2022			SL-SMP	2011
Leland Dale D	revdale98@aol.com	414 Morning Dove Trl Sealy TX 77474	TX	EM			SL	1980
LeMahieu Nathan S	(224)374-4453 nlemahieu@stjohnwheaton.org	2s061 Apache Ave Wheaton IL 60189	NI	Asst	St John Wheaton IL	(630)668-0701	CQ	2021
Lemcke Brian S	(605)572-8263 zionlutherandelmont@midstatesd.com	103 South Seaman Street P.O. Box 215 Delmont SD 57330	SD	SP	Zion* Delmont SD	(605)779-5181	FW	2003
Lemke Larry G	(712)221-1506 lgllemke@yahoo.com	517 Windsor Dr Solon IA 52333	IE	EM			CQ	1990
Lemke Layton L	(952)467-4496 laytonlarry@centurylink.net	17200 104th St Young America MN 55397	MNS	EM			SPR	1962
Lemley Andrew H	pastorlemley@gmail.com	8985 Fernwood Path Washington Twp MI 48094	RM	C07/2016			SL	2005
Lemley Keith H	(586)651-1040 pastorkeithlemley@gmail.com	8985 Fernwood Path Washington MI 48094	MI	SP	Our Redeemer Washington MI	(586)781-5567	FW	2010
Lentner Charles D	(330)592-7958 cde.lentner@gmail.com	3006 Burnbrick Rd Richfield OH 44286	EN	EM			SL	1967
Lentz Kevin D	(512)913-3974 pastorlentz@fullerheaven.com	2 Ritchie Rd Waco TX 76712	TX	SP	Trinity Woodway TX	(254)772-4225	SL	1990
Lentz Robert A	(507)258-4652 cheryllentz@hotmail.com	633 Fireside Ln SW Rochester MN 55902	MNS	EM			FW	1977
Lepley Daniel J	(317)402-9401 pastorlepley@gmail.com	3361 Rio Rogue Lane NE Belmont MI 49306	MI	Sn/Adm	Mount Calvary Greenville MI	(616)754-4886	FW	2007
Lepper George A	(805)459-2552 prgl7@sbcglobal.net	115 Mesa Rd Nipomo CA 93444	CNH	EM			FW	1984
Lescow John K	(843)795-6555 revjklescow@gmail.com	886 Kushiwah Creek Dr Charleston SC 29412	SE	EM			SL	1966
Lesemann Brian A	(309)256-6514 banblesemann@juno.com	13961 E CR 1100n Bath IL 62617	CI	SP	Salem* Chandlerville IL	(309)546-2434	SL	1993
Lesemann Bruce H	(712) 291-6424 revbruce003@gmail.com	215 Cayuga St Storm Lake IA 50588	IW	SP	St John Storm Lake IA	(712)732-2400	SL	1997
Lessing Robert R Dr	(651) 341-0475 lessing@csp.edu	1737 Jefferson Ave Saint Paul MN 55105	MNS	Assoc	Cross View* Edina MN	(952)941-1094	SL	1985
Letcher Kurt R	(402)631-8680 il55727@gmail.com	619 Rolling Hills Dr Newton KS 67114	KS	SP	Zion Newton KS	(316)283-1441	FW	1997
Letsche Jason M	pastor.letsche@gmail.com	412 Main St Kingsley IA 51028	IW	SP	First Kingsley IA	(712)378-2129	SL	2015

*Multiple Assignments (See Church Worker Locator for Additional Details)

See Page 53 for the Table of Abbreviations for key to District, Position, and Seminary abbreviations

**C =Candidate; EM = Emeritus; the date following the C is the month and year the Candidate status began

NAME	TELEPHONE NUMBER EMAIL	STREET ADDRESS CITY/STATE/ZIP	DISTRICT	POSITION/ STATUS**	WHERE SERVING	OFFICE PHONE	SEM/ PROGRAM	YR GRAD
Lett Randy D	(269)426-2388 rdltrinity@icloud.com	3416 Old Orchard Ln Lexington MI 48450	MI	SP	St John Port Sanilac MI	(810)425-3085	FW	1983
Lettieri Domenick A	(716)941-5419 rlcstmpastor@gmail.com	8740 Supervisor Ave Colden NY 14033	EA	SP	St Martin* Boston NY	(716)941-5419	NESC	2012
Leuthaeuser Larry L	(330) 620-3463	26 Bungalow Bay Blvd Chippewa Lake OH 44215	EN	EM			SL	1966
Levenhagen Aaron R	(847)857-9263 pastor@stjohnselgin.org	5n622 Lostview Ln Saint Charles IL 60175	NI	SP	Saint John's Elgin IL	(847)741-0814	SL	2024
Lewis David I II Dr	(314)898-5709 lewisd@csl.edu	5 McCall Ter Saint Louis MO 63105	MO	S HS/C	Concordia Seminary Saint Louis MO	(314)505-7000	SL	1994
Lewis William R	(262)210-0279 william.lewis1936@gmail.com	1932 448th Utica NE 68456	NEB	EM			SL	1963
Lewis Richard E	(989)971-3180 richelewis@gmail.com	8470 E Curtis Rd Frankenmuth MI 48734	MI	SMP	St John Marion Spr Brant MI	(989)715-4555	SL-SMP	2023
Lewis Randall C	(501)744-8095 randall9300@aol.com	2709 S Ringo St Little Rock AR 72206	MDS	SMP	Community of Faith Little Rock AR	(501)562-7704	CQ	2022
Lewis Nathan D	(920)559-7750 nlewishidingplace@gmail.com	2182 S Lake Michigan Dr Sturgeon Bay WI 54235	NW	C10/2023			SL	2001
Lewis Kyle A	(507)676-7052 klewlisaubr@gmail.com	469 Ronald Ave Winona MN 55987	MNS	Assoc	St Martin Winona MN	(507)452-6928	SL	2023
Lewis Johnathan C	314-437-1230 pastorlewis68@gmail.com	4066 Westminister Pl Apt F Saint Louis MO 63108	MO	SMP	St Matthew Saint Louis MO	(314)261-7765	SL-SMP	2012
Lewis Elstner C Jr	(773)476-0446 stphilpastor61@gmail.com	7501 S Saint Louis Ave Chicago IL 60652	NI	SP	St Philip Chicago IL	(773)493-3865	CQ	1998
Lewis David A	(314)202-8344 dave@sainttrinity.org	5612 Finkman St Saint Louis MO 63109	MO	Sn/Adm	St Trinity Saint Louis MO	(314)353-3276	SL	1988
Lewis Daniel J	(651)786-9523 dan.j.lewis@gmail.com		NEB	S HS/C	Concordia University Nebraska Seward NE	(402)643-3651	CQ	2016
Lewis Cleveland A	(317) 345-3540 pastor@firsttimothylcms.org	5085 Knollton Rd Indianapolis IN 46228	IN	SMP	First Timothy Indianapolis IN	(317)257-6383	CQ	2020
Lewis Bertram B Sr Dr	(734)796-3775	457 High Street Elyria OH 44035	OH	EM			CQ	1990
Lewis James M	(317)984-3651	9607 England Ct Noblesville IN 46060	IN	EM			FW	1996
Ley Bruce G	(541)812-0684 pastorley@leychalet.com	1800 47th Ave SE Albany OR 97322	NOW	EM			FW	1994
Li Xiaoyu J	(626)899-2800	2743 Sarandi Grande Dr Hacienda Heights CA 91745	PSW	C04/2025			SL	2007
Li Wenbin F	(831)889-0135 freeman2755@gmail.com	235 Spring St Santa Cruz CA 95060	CNH	C05/2018			CQ	2012
Licht Brian C	(712)790-9686 pastorlicht@rcicqc.org	c/o Risen Christ 6021 Northwest Blvd Davenport IA 52806	IE	SP	Risen Christ Davenport IA	(563)386-2342	FW	2006
Lieb Francis M	(816)229-1904 kflieb@att.net	2100 NW 4th Street Pl Blue Springs MO 64014	MO	EM			SL	1971
Liebich Dennis J	(239)272-6005 djliebich@gmail.com	2582 Thyme Way North Port FL 34289	FG	EM			SL	1986
Liebich Jonathan A	(860)319-7487 revliebich@gmail.com	1803 W Glendora Rd Buchanan MI 49107	MI	SP	Trinity Glendora MI	(269)422-2554	SL	2006
Liebmann Martin W Jr	(636)222-7598 bill.liebmann@gmail.com	7043 Forest Oak Dr Barnhart MO 63012	MO	EM			FW	1983
Liebmann Robert O	(314)229-4678 pastorbob@stmarkseureka.org	313 Wallach Dr Eureka MO 63025	MO	Sn/Adm	St Mark Eureka MO	(636)938-4432	SL	1999
Liebnau David A	(314)961-4151 herbiethehornet9@gmail.com	934 Briarton Dr Saint Louis MO 63126	MO	EM			SL	1973
Lieder Lawrence A	(281)351-9646 larry.elaine@frontier.com	P.O. Box 1129 Crockett TX 75835	TX	EM			FW	1987
Liefeld David R	(636)226-4788 drliefeld@charter.net	182 Ameren Way Apt 942 Ballwin MO 63021	EN	EM			Other	1975
Liefer Todd W	(636)887-6035 tliefer@hcl.org	14361 W Old Farm Rd New Berlin WI 53151	EN	Assoc	Hales Corners Hales Corners WI	(414)529-6700	SL	2011
Liermann Brian D	(262)573-6779 rev.brian.liermann@gmail.com	9075 Rapps Rd Woodruff WI 54568	NW	SP	Rock Of Ages Minocqua WI	(715)356-3848	SL	2011
Liersemann Frank P Jr	(410)610-6199 pastorfpl@gmail.com	2420 Abigail Ct Prnc Frederck MD 20678	SE	EM			SL	1973
Liese Michael D	(309)419-5354 mdliese@gmail.com	319 North Elm St Apt E Henderson KY 42420	IN	SP	Trinity Henderson KY	(270)826-4337	SL	1995
Lieske Mark A	(503)922-2960 mileske44@gmail.com	19326 2nd Dr SE #a Bothell WA 98012	NOW	EM			SL	1970
Lieske Christopher A	chris.lieske@gmail.com	609 N Lundys Ln Fergus Falls MN 56537	MNN	SP	Trinity Fergus Falls MN	(218)736-4869	SL	2008
Lieske David J Dr	(608) 201-7852 djlieske@gmail.com	3733 Huntington Ave. Janesville WI 53546	SW	EM			SL	1972
Lietzau Eli J			RM	SP	Wheat Ridge* Wheat Ridge CO	(303)424-3161	FW	2010
Likeness David A	(309)670-0247	2318 W Chandler Ct Peoria IL 61615	CI	EM			SL	1968
Likens James D	(314)308-5203 jim@jdlvideo.com	5425 Lindenwood Ave Saint Louis MO 63109	MO	EM			FW	1982
Lim Edmund T	(317)450-2211 revedlim@hotmail.com		MO	EM			CQ	1996
Lim Jubin	714-262-2661 jubinlim@hotmail.com	1521 W Orangethorpe Ave Fullerton CA 92833	PSW	Assoc	True Love Fullerton CA	(714)992-5008	SL	2007
Limmel Frederick B	(952)457-2630 fred.limmel@oslcs.org	205 Carver Sq Waconia MN 55387	MNS	SMP	Our Savior Excelsior MN	(952)474-5181	SL-SMP	2023

*Multiple Assignments (See Church Worker Locator for Additional Details)

See Page 53 for the Table of Abbreviations for key to District, Position, and Seminary abbreviations

**C =Candidate; EM = Emeritus; the date following the C is the month and year the Candidate status began

NAME	TELEPHONE NUMBER EMAIL	STREET ADDRESS CITY/STATE/ZIP	DISTRICT	POSITION/ STATUS**	WHERE SERVING	OFFICE PHONE	SEM/ PROGRAM	YR GRAD
Linck Stephen S	(850)525-1328 director@southerncef.org	120 Aiken Road Waveland MS 39576	SO	D Ex/S	Southern District Slidell LA	(504)282-2632	FW	1989
Lind Steven D	(260)418-9320 man_tech2000@hotmail.com	4022 Wayne Trce Fort Wayne IN 46806	IN	EM			FW	1994
Lind Maurice W	(262)215-4646 gslpastor@wi.rr.com	400 S Edwards Blvd Apt 211 Lake Geneva WI 53147	SW	EM			FW	1979
Lindau Robert H Jr	revlin01@msn.com	10607 Canyon Rd Omaha NE 68112	NEB	EM			CQ	1980
Lindeman Timothy J	(303) 358-6412 tlindeman@peacelutheran.net	6424 W 82nd Dr Arvada CO 80003	RM	SMP	Peace Arvada CO	(303)424-4454	SL-SMP	2011
Lindemann John D	(480)661-1381 winsomewordsjdl@aol.com	5617 Willow Crest Dr Shreveport LA 71119	PSW	EM			FW	1984
Lindemann Peter A	(585)798-5740	11530 Munzel Rd Medina NY 14103	EA	EM			SL	1972
Lindemann Rodney A	(816) 223-8977 lindemannra@gmail.com	1315 SE Scenic Dr Blue Springs MO 64014	MO	EM			SL-SMP	2011
Lindemood Bryan N	(208)312-8587 bryan.lindemood@gmail.com		NOW	C05/2020			SL	2000
Lindenberg David J	(605)716-3753	2112 Maple Ave Rapid City SD 57701	SD	SP	Peace Rapid City SD	(605)721-6480	SL	2001
Lindenmeyer William D	(760)977-1177 lindyrev@icloud.com	5115 Nichols Ct Flowery Branch GA 30542	FG	EM			FW	1981
Linderman Bruce E	(406)570-3850 lindermanloisbruce@gmail.com	3150 Prairie Smoke Rd Bozeman MT 59715	MT	EM			SL	1976
Lineberger Richard W	(352) 843-1536 RichardWLineberger@gmail.com	10620 SE 160th Court Road Ocklawaha FL 32179	FG	EM			SL	1985
Lineberger Lawrence R	(919)562-8835 lrline@nc.rr.com	10820 Sandy Oak Ln Unit 321 Raleigh NC 27614	SE	EM			SL	1961
Linehan Nathan D	(858)863-3291 nlinehan858@gmail.com	1752 Northfield Dr Yuba City CA 95993	CNH	SP	First Yuba City CA	(530)673-8894	SL	2024
Ling Timothy K	(510)919-4693 timklling@gmail.com	3621 W El Campo Grande Ave North Las Vegas NV 89031	CNH	EM			HK	1977
Lingard David C	(319)228-8324 david_lingard@hotmail.com	P.O. Box 414 Van Horne IA 52346	IE	SP	St Andrew Van Horne IA	(319)228-8325	FW	2008
Lingsch Keith A	(239)207-9571 pastor@graceofnaples.com	2500 River Reach Dr Naples FL 34104	FG	Sn/Adm	Grace Naples FL	(239)261-7421	FW	1996
Linkugel David H	(402)960-1386 PastorDavid@LordofLifeElkhorn.org	7423 N 175th Circle Bennington NE 68007	NEB	Sn/Adm	Lord Of Life Elkhorn NE	(402)289-3437	FW	1985
Linnell Shawn C	shawn.linnell@gmail.com		SE	Assoc	King of Glory Williamsburg VA	(757)258-9701	FW	2013
Linnemann Paul A Dr	pastorpaullinn@gmail.com	816 NE 154th Ave. Vancouver WA 98684	NOW	EM			CQ	1995
Linthicum Eric R	(301)213-8989 ericlinthicum@gmail.com	1715 W Caroline Path Lecanto FL 34461	EN	SP	Tree of Life Inverness FL	(352)419-4100	FW	1996
Lintner Joel W	(651)332-9736 joellintner@gmail.com	295 W 4th St Garner IA 56048	IW	EM			CQ	2008
Lippitt George D	(443)857-8924 gdlippitt@gmail.com	2514 Genito Rd Powhatan VA 23139	SE	SP	Good Shepherd Midlothian VA	(804)897-0262	SL	2001
Liss Joseph T	(517)740-2836 fearliss00@gmail.com	3445 Lincoln Ave Saint Joseph MI 49085	MI	SMP	Trinity Saint Joseph MI	(269)983-5000	FW-SMP	2014
Lissow Alexander G	(208)970-8057 alissow@ipatriots.us	c/o Zion Lutheran Church 2410 Miller Ave Burley ID 83318	NOW	SP	Zion Burley ID	(208)678-4167	CQ	2005
Lissy Andrew C	(703)830-8947 ott925@aol.com	6446 Battle Rock Dr Clifton VA 20124	SE	EM			SL	1985
Lissy Joel N	(480) 823-3533 office@stjohnsambridge.org	1326 Church St Ambridge PA 15003	EA	SP	Mount Olive* Beaver Falls PA	(724)650-5682	SL	2025
List David F	(402)599-9837 davidlist@hotmail.com	17106 Palisades Dr Omaha NE 68136	NEB	EM			SL	2001
Litke Arthur E	(412)427-8606 litke.art@gmail.com	5926 Vance Ave Fort Wayne IN 46815	IN	EM			FW	1981
Liu Samuel H Dr	(909)344-9747 hsiaoyungliu@gmail.com	1037 Canyon Springs Diamond Bar CA 91765	PSW	EM			CQ	2002
Liu Futao	(812)785-6388	100 E Michigan St Evansville IN 47711	IN	Assoc	St Paul Evansville IN	(812)422-5414	SL	2023
Llewellyn Joseph J	(989)727-2677 pastor.stpaulhl@gmail.com	14102 Sawmill Dr Hubbard Lake MI 49747	MI	SP	St Paul Hubbard Lake MI	(989)727-2496	SL	2014
Llewellyn Timothy J	tjllew4j@gmail.com	940 Central Ave Humboldt NE 68376	NEB	SP	Faith* Humboldt NE	(402)862-2437	SL	2003
Lo Fungchatou T Dr	lolegacy@gmail.com	10438 Lever St Northeast Circle Pines MN 55014	MNS	C09/2020			EIITSL	2007
Lobien George F Dr	(757)291-9393 globien@comcast.net	4247 Corbridge Course Williamsburg VA 23188	SE	EM			SL	1960
Lochner Daniel E	(231)250-6390 delochner@mac.com	15113 182nd Ave E Bonney Lake WA 98391	NOW	EM			SPR	1975
Lock Thomas E	(720)285-6648 kantorlock@gototrinity.com	2695 S Raleigh St Denver CO 80219	RM	Asst	Trinity Denver CO	(303)406-3143	FW	2002
Locke Lawrence R	(360)335-0311 lrmclocke@comcast.net	2302a NE 249th Ave Camas WA 98607	NOW	EM			FW	1984
Lockie Christopher K	(262)977-5077 pstrlockie@gmail.com	2713 4 1/2 Mile Rd Racine WI 53402	SW	SP	Prince Peace Racine WI	(262)639-1277	SL	2007
Loder Mark S	(320)282-2048 revloder@gmail.com	1004 7th Ave P.O. Box 745 Howard Lake MN 55349	MNS	Sn/Adm	Saint James Howard Lake MN	(320)543-2766	FW	2009
Lodholz Gary D	(715)762-4438 lodholz@centurytel.net	W7837 Simon Rd Fifield WI 54524	NW	EM			SL	1973

*Multiple Assignments (See Church Worker Locator for Additional Details)

See Page 53 for the Table of Abbreviations for key to District, Position, and Seminary abbreviations

**C =Candidate; EM = Emeritus; the date following the C is the month and year the Candidate status began

NAME	TELEPHONE NUMBER EMAIL	STREET ADDRESS CITY/STATE/ZIP	DISTRICT	POSITION/ STATUS**	WHERE SERVING	OFFICE PHONE	SEM/ PROGRAM	YR GRAD
Loehrke Kenneth L	(920)324-5264 kenloehrke@yahoo.com	605 Autumn Ave Waupun WI 53963	SW	EM			SPR	1971
Loesch Jeremy D	(443)466-3341 revloesch@gmail.com	10 Johnson Rd Newark DE 19713	SE	SP	Our Redeemer Newark DE	(302)737-6176	SL	1999
Loesch Keith W	(816)623-5909 kandjloesch@comcast.net	501 NW Shamrock Ave Apt 2015 Lees Summit MO 64081	MO	EM			SL	1967
Loeschen David P	(712)269-0245 debslpn@yahoo.com	10710 Crescent Moon Dr Lincoln NE 68527	NEB	Asst	Messiah Lincoln NE	(402)489-3024	FW	1984
Loeschen Donald P	(325)280-5246 dploeschen@outlook.com	3417 Summer Hill Cir Nacogdoches TX 75965	TX	EM			SL	1976
Loeschke David R	(970)580-0495 cdloeschke5@hotmail.com	528 East Donegal St Oneill NE 68763	NEB	EM			FW	1985
Loeschman Albert J	(979)574-3655 wd5iqr.al@gmail.com	1197 Lovers Ln Bastrop TX 78602	TX	EM			SL	1965
Loesel Andrew E	(989)324-7309 candloes@gmail.com	4115 N 9 Mile Rd Pinconning MI 48650	MI	EM			SPR	1969
Loeslie Ryan L	(605)928-3117 rlloeslie@outlook.com	40201 270th St Dimock SD 57331	SD	SP	Immanuel Dimock SD	(605)928-3117	FW	2009
Loeslie Travis J	(320) 582-5022 pastorloeslie@live.com	1204 Maple Ln Faribault MN 55021	MNS	EM			FW	2012
Loest Mark A	(989)752-6413 pastorloest@frankentrost.org	1220 S Mueller Rd Saginaw MI 48601	MI	Sn/Adm	Immanuel Saginaw MI	(989)754-0929	FW	1988
Loewe Timothy J	(734)224-0887 timothy.loewe@yahoo.com	1568 Indian Creek Dr Temperance MI 48182	MI	SP	Christ King Lambertville MI	(734)856-1461	FW	1993
Lofgren Richard S Dr	(260)417-9003 lofgrenrs@aol.com	P.O. Box 274 Hamler OH 43524	OH	SP	Immanuel Hamler OH	(419)274-4811	SL	1986
Lofthus David J	(504)296-1191 boharahan@gmail.com	1605 Mason Smith Ave Metairie LA 70003	SO	SP	Faith Harahan LA	(504)737-0448	FW	1989
Loftis Joseph N Dr	(219)575-0272 drloftis@hotmail.com	6 W Indiana Ave Hamlet IN 46532	IN	EM			FW	1993
Logid Mark J Dr	(760)212-7488 mark.logid@gmail.com	19548 W Marshall Ave Litchfield Park AZ 83540	PSW	EM			SL	1982
Lohman Richard S	(630)379-1477 scott_lohman@sbcglobal.net	202 Orange Drive Elon NC 27244	SE	SMP	Advent Chapel Hill NC	(919)968-7690	SL-SMP	2012
Lohman John R	(515)573-5114	2921 21st Ave N Fort Dodge IA 50501	IW	EM			CQ	1982
Lohmeyer Richard G Dr	(304)992-2365 revlohmeyer@hotmail.com	5753 Highway 85 N #3395 Crestview FL 32536	FG	EM			SL	1988
Lohrke Merlyn C	(620)298-2762 lohrman1@embarqmail.com	515 S Valley St Cunningham KS 67035	KS	EM			SL	1964
Loman Clifton R	(417)440-0281 lomancsl@live.com	25043 E 727 Rd Tahlequah OK 74464	OK	SP	First Tahlequah OK	(918)456-5070	SL	2009
Londenberg David L	(830)931-1911 rev.d.londenberg@gmail.com	P.O. Box 203 Mount Enterprise TX 75681	TX	EM			SPR	1969
Long Ray W III	(419)503-3518 digteeyah@yahoo.com	8342 Road 61 Payne OH 45880	IN	EM			FW	2006
Long Charles M Jr	(301)885-8309 longcharlesm@gmail.com	8266 Trudi Pl Mechanicsville VA 23111	SE	EM			SL	1992
Long Barry A	(309)243-2042 prblong@aol.com	1003 W Hiawatha Ct Dunlap IL 61525	CI	SP	Mount Calvary Peoria IL	(309)688-4321	CQ	1997
Longacre Randall D	longacrr@me.com	4 Lakeshore Dr Columbus NE 68601	NEB	SMP	1C The Sanctuary Columbus NE	(402)835-5511	SL-SMP	2022
Longden Daniel R	(248)802-2392 daniellongden@gmail.com	1052 Eaton Green Dr Charlotte MI 48813	MI	SMP	First Charlotte MI	(517)543-4360	SL-SMP	2020
Longman Eric A	(479)903-2600 elongman@proton.me	6508 W Coat Brg Rogers AR 72758	MDS	Sn/Adm	Holy Trinity Rogers AR	(479)636-1135	SL	2015
Longshore Hal R	(971) 222-7713 rexbonlong@gmail.com	500 3rd Ave NW Apt 110 Fairbault MN 55021	MNS	EM			SL	1966
Loock Lambert E Jr	(858)794-7684 loock57@san.rr.com	911 Taylor St Apt 173 Vista CA 92084	PSW	EM			SL	1959
Loos Bartholomew C	(716)472-9103		PSW	SP	First Manhattan Beach CA	(310)545-5653	SL	2016
Loos Donald A	(716)549-1062 donlo48@msn.com	1310 Seneca Creek Rd Buffalo NY 14224	EA	EM			SL	1976
Lopez Antonio J Dr	(323)594-6221 drbolskan@gmail.com	1716 N Ave 46 Los Angeles CA 90041	PSW	SP	Palabra De Dios Maywood CA	(323)404-8583	SL	2003
Lopez Pedro L	(571)606-7600 pedro@iowadistrictwest.org	311 11th St Manilla IA 50454	IW	D Miss	Iowa West District Fort Dodge IA	(515)576-7666	HITSL	1995
Lopez Zabdi	(530)713-1451 pastorzabdi@gmail.com	c/o Hope Lutheran Church P.O. Box 355 Woodburn OR 97071	NOW	SP	Hope Woodburn OR	(503)981-0400	SL	2004
Loppnow Henry H	(812)725-7774 henry.loppnow@twc.com	2714 Klerner Ct New Albany IN 47150	IN	EM			CQ	1993
Loppnow Richard E	(416)554-1275 richardloppnow@hotmail.com	N1137 Wendt Rd Columbus WI 53925	SW	C06/2023			SL	2007
Lor Yia S	(763)670-8551 naikhu76@hotmail.com	936 Hazel St N Saint Paul MN 55119	MNS	Assoc	The Gathering Place Arden Hills MN	(651)633-2402	SL	2015
Loree Larry K Sr	(989)550-9782 ironpadre@gmx.com	8514 Filion Rd Pigeon MI 48755	MI	EM			NESC	1990
Loree Larry K Jr	(724)996-2270	6138 Cheshire Park Drive Clarkston MI 48346	EN	SP	Ascension/Christ Beverly Hills MI	(248)644-8890	FW	2002
Lorenz Jonathan J	(812)802-4182 jonathan.j.lorenz.mil@mail.mil	502 Manor Dr Seymour IN 47274	EN	M Chap	Office of International Mission Saint Louis MO		FW	2009
Lorenz Matthew S	(586)876-6470 mlorenz@zionalex.org	2815 Crestwood Dr NE Alexandria MN 56308	MNN	Sn/Adm	Zion Alexandria MN	(320)763-4842	SL	2021

*Multiple Assignments (See Church Worker Locator for Additional Details)
See Page 53 for the Table of Abbreviations for key to District, Position, and Seminary abbreviations
**C =Candidate; EM = Emeritus; the date following the C is the month and year the Candidate status began

NAME	TELEPHONE NUMBER EMAIL	STREET ADDRESS CITY/STATE/ZIP	DISTRICT	POSITION/ STATUS**	WHERE SERVING	OFFICE PHONE	SEM/ PROGRAM	YR GRAD
Lorenz Benjamin G	lorenzbg@yahoo.com	322 E 550 S Columbus IN 47201	IN	EM			SL	1977
Lorenz Dennis L	(208)667-3599 djlorenz@earthlink.net	624 W Harrison Ave Apt 206 Coeur D Alene ID 83814	NOW	EM			SPR	1963
Lorenz Timothy J	(260)356-6528 pastorlorenz@pm.me	657 Polk St Huntington IN 46750	IN	SP	St Peter Huntington IN	(260)356-6528	FW	2010
Lorenz Gregory M	(956)682-2345 glorenz@stpaulmcallen.org	c/o St Paul Lutheran Church 300 Pecan Blvd McAllen TX 78501	TX	Sn/Adm	St Paul McAllen TX	(956)682-2345	SL	1989
Lorfeld Matthew D	(608)780-4620 mlorfeld@gmail.com	7010 Country Village Dr Wisconsin Rapids WI 54494	NW	SP	St John Wisconsin Rapids WI	(715)423-7788	SL	2009
Loudenback George D	(432)413-3323 loudenbackl@grandecom.net	5000 Conley Ave Odessa TX 79762	TX	EM			FW	1977
Loughran Kevin R	(727)612-9782 pastor.loughran@grace-lutheran. com	4301 16th St N St Petersburg FL 33703	FG	Sn/Adm	Grace Saint Petersburg FL	(727)527-6213	FW	1993
Louissaint Elie	(561)856-2536 elie1020@yahoo.com	2921 Donald Rd Lake Worth FL 33461	FG	O-Sp Min	Salem Haitian Lake Worth FL	(561)586-5691	CQ	1991
Loum Cyril D	(260)580-2575 Cyril.Loum@FaithSTL.org	11048 Cedarberry Pl Saint Louis MO 63123	MO	SMP	Faith Oakville MO	(314)846-8612	SL-SMP	2021
Loux Randy B	(920)740-7158 rbloux62@gmail.com	1227 Viewmont Dr Clarksville TN 37040	MDS	M Chap	Office of International Mission Saint Louis MO		CQ	2001
Love Donald G	(815)922-0397 dklove897@yahoo.com	601 Bramble Way Merrill WI 54452	NW	SP	St John* Athens WI	(715)536-1810	FW	1989
Love Mark W	(616)540-3137 mlove@trinitylutheran.org	7302 Woodsman Cir Holland OH 43528	OH	Sn/Adm	Trinity Toledo OH	(419)385-2651	FW	1992
Lovejoy Patrick S Dr	218-326-5453 pastorlovejoy@rocketmail.com	735 1st Ave NE Grand Rapids MN 55744	MNN	SP	First Grand Rapids MN	(218)326-5453	SL	2009
Lovett Mark D	(620)292-7098 pastor@ilchurch.org	7205 E Greenbriar Cir Wichita KS 67226	KS	SP	Immanuel Wichita KS	(316)264-0639	FW	2006
Lovick Richard N	(636)577-7667 rlovick1@gmail.com	101 Boltons Mill Pkwy Williamsburg VA 23185	SE	EM			SL	2001
Low Maurice R	(231) 942-1594 lowrobert200@yahoo.com	6339 W 16 Rd Mesick MI 49668	MI	EM			FW	1977
Lowe Joshua T Dr	(402)705-3826 joshua.lowe@cune.org	605 11th St Hawarden IA 51023	IW	SP	Trinity Hawarden IA	(712)551-2743	SL	2008
Lowrey George W Jr	pastorlowrey@gmail.com		PSW	SP	Immanuel Redondo Beach CA	(310)540-4435	SL	1994
Loy David W Dr	(949)214-3396 david.loy@cui.edu	4 Eccelstone Cir Irvine CA 92604	PSW	S HS/C	Concordia University Irvine Irvine CA	(949)854-8002	SL	2003
Loza David H	(913)262-7239 david4janel@peoplepc.com	6850 W 51st Ter Apt 1d Mission KS 66202	MO	EM			SL	1984
Loza Erik J	(747) 200-7034 erikjloza@hotmail.com	17311 Chatsworth St Unit 3 Granada Hills CA 91344	PSW	SP	First Van Nuys CA	(818)989-5844	SL	2007
Lozano Marco A	(805)766-5745 lozaccr@gmail.com	1853 Ives Ave Spc 134 Oxnard CA 93033	PSW	EM			HITSL	2005
Lubeck Thomas M	(248) 613-5507 tlubeck@ameritech.net	2786 Oyster Bay Dr Frisco TX 75036	TX	EM			FW	1982
Lubke Lewis L	(956)357-1493 pastor_lubke@yahoo.com	1411 S Pine St Brady TX 76825	TX	SP	Mount Calvary Brady TX	(325)597-2498	FW	2005
Lubkeman August H	(309)585-0125 adlubkeman@comcast.net	2025 E Lincoln St Bloomington IL 61701	CI	EM			SL	1957
Lucas Bruce K	(734)755-7676 brucelucas@gmail.com	3180 Paysage Pl Traverse City MI 49684	MI	Assoc	Trinity Traverse City MI	(231)946-2720	FW	1995
Lucas Frank E	(734)735-8613	8201 Main St Altenburg MO 63732	MO	SP	Immanuel Altenburg MO	(573)824-5636	FW	2016
Lucas Glenn A	(949)830-1460 glucas@abidingsavior.com		PSW	Sn/Adm	Abiding Savior Lake Forest CA	(949)830-1460	SL	1987
Lucas James A	(618)407-3709 jim.lucas@icloud.com	805 Powell Ave Collinsville IL 62234	SI	EM			FW	1980
Lucero Dennis F Dr	(719) 728-3705 dennis.lucero51@gmail.com	3105 E Whileaway Cir Colorado Spgs CO 80917	RM	SP	Resurrection Colorado Springs CO	(719)392-7045	SL	1985
Luchterhand Karl J	kluchterhand365@gmail.com	660 Hughes Rd Henderson TN 38340	SW	EM			FW	1984
Lucido Gregory J		702 N Meade Ave Glendive MT 59330	MT	SP	Our Savior* Glendive MT	(406)377-3890	SL	2000
Luck Gerald E	(519)229-8040 gluck1@quadro.net	3173 Perth Rd 163 Rr 1 Fullarton ON N0K 1 CANADA	EN	EM			CQ	2005
Lucke Jeremy N	(541)609-8057 pastorlucke@gmail.com	6206 SW Grand Oaks Dr Corvallis OR 97333	NOW	SP	Peace Philomath OR	(541)929-5504	SL	2008
Luckemeyer Joel A	(775)336-9680 luckemeyerj@gmail.com	212 Perennial Pl Fallbrook CA 92028	PSW	SP	Shep Of Valley Oceanside CA	(760)433-9250	SL	2016
Luckritz Harold S	(314)707-4145 pastorhal@sbcglobal.net	1829 Crosshaven Dr High Ridge MO 63049	MO	EM			SPR	1975
Ludwig Richard C	(847)915-4544 rcmm1955@gmail.com	2001 W Algonquin Rd Unit 2426 Algonquin IL 60102	NI	EM			SL	1961
Ludwig Alan G Dr	509-540-9083 lutheranprof@gmail.com		SD	Asst	Our Savior* Aberdeen SD	(605)225-7106	SL	1989
Ludwig Timothy J	(218)591-0446 picpastorludwig@gmail.com	5007 Maple Grove Rd Hermantown MN 55811	MNN	Sn/Adm	Peace Christ Hermantown MN	(218)729-9473	SL	1985
Ludwig William A	(206)524-2283	1410 225th St SW Bothell WA 98021	NOW	EM			SPR	1959
Ludwig David G Sr	(407)341-0814 dcludpud@aol.com	1308 Haven Dr Oviedo FL 32765	FG	EM			SL	1959

*Multiple Assignments (See Church Worker Locator for Additional Details)

See Page 53 for the Table of Abbreviations for key to District, Position, and Seminary abbreviations

**C =Candidate; EM = Emeritus; the date following the C is the month and year the Candidate status began

NAME	TELEPHONE NUMBER EMAIL	STREET ADDRESS CITY/STATE/ZIP	DISTRICT	POSITION/ STATUS**	WHERE SERVING	OFFICE PHONE	SEM/ PROGRAM	YR GRAD
Ludwig Eugene M	(503)434-5586 eugene.ludwig@comcast.net	3135 NE Cumulus Ave McMinnville OR 97128	NOW	EM			SL	1959
Ludwig David J	(828)302-4777 ludwig@lr.edu	1974 12th Street Pl NE Hickory NC 28601	SE	Assoc	Christ Hickory NC	(828)328-1483	SL	1965
Lueck Chad D	(309)838-0306 revicb@yahoo.com	2707 Essington St Bloomington IL 61705	CI	SP	Good Shepherd Bloomington IL	(309)662-8905	FW	1991
Lueck Dwayne M Dr	dmlueck@gmail.com		NW	EM			SL	1979
Luecke David L Dr	(703)943-4431 daveandmardiluecke@gmail.com	700 Lovers Ln Waynesboro VA 22980	SE	EM			SL	1956
Luecke David S	dsluecke@aol.com	9419 Misty Oakes Dr Broadview Hts OH 44147	OH	Assoc	Royal Redeemer North Royalton OH	(440)237-7958	SL	1967
Luecke Mark G	(330)704-1622 mluecke53@gmail.com	2140 Prestwick Dr Uniontown OH 44685	OH	EM			SL	1986
Luedemann Ronald S	(623)910-6749 ronannetx@gmail.com	9901 N Riverside Dr Apt 139 Fort Worth TX 76244	TX	EM			SL	1999
Luehmann Alfred J	(507)380-9876 revallaura@hotmail.com	1900 Ford Ave N Apt 210 Glencoe MN 55336	MNS	EM			SL	1960
Lueke Kenneth D	(989)269-6357 prlueke@gmx.com	513 Cleveland St. Bad Axe MI 48413	MI	EM			SL	1981
Luft Ethan W	(816)812-9227 ethan.luft@outlook.com	912 Elm St Park Ridge IL 60068	NI	Assoc	St Andrews Park Ridge IL	(847)823-6656	SL	2025
Luhman Eric M	(314)302-1965 pastor.luhman@gmail.com	530 Fernwood Dr Altamonte Springs FL 32701	FG	C09/2019			SL	2017
Luhman Ethan M	(608)214-3421 ethanl@mypeacechurch.com	501 E Fillmore Ave Eau Claire WI 54701	NW	Assoc	Peace Eau Claire WI	(715)834-2486	SL	2015
Lujang Isaac L	(817)308-1065 ilujang@yahoo.com	3320 Chapel Ridge Way Fort Worth TX 76116	TX	Asst	St Paul Fort Worth TX	(817)332-2281	SL	2023
Lukas Hayden M	(248)254-2306 lukash@csl.edu	100 S Clinton Ave Clintonville WI 54929	NW	Assoc	St Martin Clintonville WI	(715)823-6538	SL	2023
Luke Leo P	(407)558-0982 plepumbing@gmail.com	9627 Gotha Rd Windemere FL 34786	FG	SMP	Our Savior Orlando FL	(407)295-0261	SL-SMP	2021
Lukefahr David P	(660)342-3900 revluke@sbcglobal.net	19308 Orrick Trl Kirksville MO 63501	MO	EM			SL	1998
Lukomski John P	(618)550-8339 lukomski@icloud.com	905 South St New Athens IL 62264	SI	EM			FW	1978
Luley William T	(314)974-7797 billndfan77@att.net	769 Pecan Hill Dr Saint Charles MO 63304	MO	EM			CQ	2019
Lumpp David A	lumpp@csp.edu	2838 Lakeview Ave Saint Paul MN 55113	MNS	EM			SL	1979
Lund Mark P	(507)530-4724 pastormarklund@gmail.com	2405 260th St Garner IA 50438	IW	SP	St John Garner IA	(641)829-4493	CQ	2020
Lund Robert L	(651)324-9229 bltpbj@yahoo.com	104 Autumn Blaze Ct Mankato MN 56001	MNS	C03/2022			SL-SMP	2010
Lundgren Mark A	(715)383-4582 preacher000000@gmail.com	5472 Main St Auburndale WI 54412	NW	SP	St John* Auburndale WI	(715)652-2213	SL	1992
Lundquist Bryan G	(906)934-2570 bslundquist@charter.net	201 Tamarack St Laurium MI 49913	NW	SP	Saint Paul* Laurium MI	(906)337-3810	FW	1996
Lunneberg Allen D	(248)342-1045 allend@lunneberg.com	5534 S Rainbow Ln Waterford MI 48329	EN	EM			FW	1979
Luther John W	(541)988-1616 prluther@comcast.net	87752 Rendezvous Loop Veneta OR 97487	NOW	SP	Christ Veneta OR	(541)935-1335	SL	1988
Lutjens Robert W	pastor@revrwl.com	614 Pecan St Wharton TX 77488	TX	SP	St John Wharton TX	(979)532-4522	SL	2004
Luttinen Calvin W	(734)904-8294 calvinluttinen@gmail.com	140 N Old Manor Rd Wichita KS 67208	KS	Sn/Adm	Risen Savior Wichita KS	(316)683-5538	SL	2015
Luttmann John B	(503)362-6927 pastor_luttmann_sjlc@hotmail.com	4525 Sunland St SE Salem OR 97302	NOW	EM			SPR	1971
Luttmann Richard L	(763)486-0310 rbluttmann@gmail.com	119 N Marquette Ave Sioux Falls SD 57110	SD	EM			SPR	1969
Lutz Clinton J	(208)562-9902 clintlutz@gmail.com	1122 Paintbrush Ave Kimberly ID 83341	NOW	SP	XrossWay Twin Falls ID	(208)423-5139	SL	1997
Lutz Stephen H	(419)862-0015 trinityelmore@frontier.com	P.O. Box 22 Elmore OH 43416	OH	SP	Trinity Elmore OH	(419)862-3461	FW	1991
Lutz Michael J	(586)739-3568 lutzmichaelj04@gmail.com	115 Bramblewood Dr Youngsville NC 27596	SE	EM			SL	1972
Lutz Gregory R	(519) 995-0095 padre.lutz@outlook.com	843 Glacial Shores Manor Saskatoon SK S7W 0 CANADA	EN	Assoc	St Luke* North York ON	(416)221-8900	ED	1996
Lutz Thomas S	(716)818-9860 Clement9@aol.com	3487 N Boston Rd Eden NY 14057	EA	SP	St Paul Eden NY	(716)992-9112	FW	1993
Lutz Elliott M	(309)635-3656 elliottlutz@gmail.com	323 Hopkins Rd Kernersville NC 27284	SE	Sn/Adm	Fountain of Life Kernersville NC	(336)993-4447	SL	2011
Lutz Carl E Jr	carl8015@att.net	183 3rd Ave Room 615 Chula Vista CA 91910	PSW	EM			SL	1959
Lutz Bernhard W V Dr	(218)929-0447 br.lutz@hotmail.com	6309 Burnham Cir Apt 200 Inver Grove Heights MN 55076	MNN	EM			SPR	1967
Lutz Arleigh L Jr	(715)302-8465 alutzjr@gmail.com	1517 Severson Dr Stoughton WI 53589	NW	EM			SPR	1963
Lutz Craig E	(973)670-3993 clutz3@verizon.net	13 Sandlor Ter Oak Ridge NJ 07438	NJ	SP	Holy Faith Oak Ridge NJ	(973)697-6060	SL	1989
Lutz Donald H	(260) 447-3384 lannlutz@gmail.com	6723 S Anthony Blvd Apt S310 Fort Wayne IN 46816	IN	EM			SL	1954
Luu Tich H	tichhluu@msn.com	3120 Birdsong Ave Covington GA 30016	IN	EM			SL	1995

*Multiple Assignments (See Church Worker Locator for Additional Details)

See Page 53 for the Table of Abbreviations for key to District, Position, and Seminary abbreviations

**C =Candidate; EM = Emeritus; the date following the C is the month and year the Candidate status began

NAME	TELEPHONE NUMBER EMAIL	STREET ADDRESS CITY/STATE/ZIP	DISTRICT	POSITION/ STATUS**	WHERE SERVING	OFFICE PHONE	SEM/ PROGRAM	YR GRAD
Ly Kue	(920)496-1543 kue_ly@hotmail.com	415 S Fisk St Green Bay WI 54303	NW	SP	Hmong Pilgrim Green Bay WI	(920)965-2233	SL	2003
Lynch Matthew S	(832)687-8240 matthewlynch543@gmail.com	c/o Christ The King Lutheran Church 5296 Park Ave Memphis TN 38119	MDS	Assoc	Christ the King Memphis TN	(901)682-8404	SL	2024
Lyons David W	(712)749-0828 davidlyons2962@gmail.com	P.O. Box 368 Schaller IA 51053	IW	SP	St Paul Schaller IA	(712)275-4299	SL	2004
Lytikainen Matthew S	(616)560-5161 matt@messiahmidland.org		MI	Assoc	Messiah Midland MI	(989)631-5200	SL	2017
Lytle Jeffrey S	(218) 235-1797 jslytlemn@yahoo.com	P.O. Box 91 Red Lake Falls MN 56750	MNN	SP	Redeemer* Plummer MN		FW	1994
Lytle Aaron L	(832)236-0645	1517 Ovid St Houston TX 77007	TX	Sn/Adm	Oikos Houston TX	(832)236-0645	SL	2004
Lyvere Gary D	(989)642-8014 glyvere@yahoo.com	15105 Lakefield Rd Hemlock MI 48626	MI	SMP	Our Savior Midland MI	(989)832-3667	CQ	2018
Maack David R Dr	dr.dmaack@gmail.com	16240 Cape Coral Dr Wimauma FL 33598	SE	EM			SL	1983
Maack Roy A Dr	(410)371-3936 roymsed@aol.com	2102 Lark Ct Oviedo FL 32765	SE	EM			SL	1956
Maanum Edward J	(719)696-1487 ed.maanum@protonmail.com	2724 Minuteman Ln Knoxville TN 37920	MDS	SP	First Knoxville TN	(865)524-0308	SL	2008
Maas Mark J	(307)214-2067 mmaas@reagan.com	1301 Hackamore Rd Cheyenne WY 82009	WY	Sn/Adm	King of Glory Cheyenne WY	(307)632-1247	FW	1987
Maas Korey D Dr	(949)910-9934 kmaas@hillsdale.edu	4320 Reading Rd E Osseo MI 49266	MI	Asst	St Paul Hillsdale MI	(517)437-2762	SL	1998
Maas Duane N	(417)619-1536 duane@poblo.org	139 Riverdale Woods Cir O Fallon MO 63366	MO	EM			FW	1978
Maas Edward F	edwardmaas22@gmail.com	111 N Emerson St Apt 1742 Denver CO 80218	RM	EM			CQ	1991
Maaske Dennis M	(402)558-3446 dkmaaske@gmail.com	670 N 58th St Omaha NE 68132	IW	EM			SL	1968
Maass Robert W	(619)792-8035 rwm_sd@yahoo.com	8726 Tommy Dr San Diego CA 92119	EN	EM			SL	1968
Maassel Richard G	(260)489-0453 maasseldc@comcast.net	162 Ameren Way Apt 513 Ballwin MO 63021	IN	EM			SL	1957
Mably Martin W	(763)259-8168 pmabes70@gmail.com	46 Johnson Rd Esko MN 55733	MNN	SP	St Matthews* Esko MN	(218)879-3510	SL	2007
Mabry Robert R	(714)785-7617 bmabry@gmail.com	625e Kunawai Ln Honolulu HI 96817	CNH	Sn/Adm	Good Shepherd Honolulu HI	(808)523-2927	CQ	2023
Mac Kain David E	(662)842-0364 davidemackain@yahoo.com	4648 N Gloster Apt 4a Tupelo MS 38804	SO	SP	Holy Trinity Tupelo MS	(662)350-3679	FW	1995
Mac Lachlan Neal F	(715)492-0281 nealjanmac@gmail.com	30455 Lehigh Ave Unit 338 Lindstrom MN 55045	MNN	EM			SPR	1964
Maccenat Oslet	(954)735-0017 pastoroslet@hotmail.com	4361 NW 38th Terrace Lauderdale Lakes FL 33309	FG	SP	Mont Garizim Fort Lauderdale FL		EIITSL	2008
MacDonald Scott M	(203)238-2332 pastorsaintjohn@gmail.com	Saint John Lutheran Church 520 Paddock Ave Meriden CT 06450	NE	SP	St John Meriden CT	(203)238-2331	SL	2002
MacDougall Steven A	(618)443-8160 stevem53@gmail.com	2103 Heritage Park Dr Fort Wayne IN 46805	IN	EM			FW	1992
Machula Lynn A	(320) 252-5795 oxcart@charter.net	5150 15th St NE Sauk Rapids MN 56379	MNN	EM			SPR	1976
Macina Robert D Dr	(720)206-4366 koinonoi@juno.com	1311 Galactic Place Castle Rock CO 80108	RM	SP	Risen Christ Arvada CO	(303)421-5872	FW	1995
Maciupa Michael	mmaciupa@aol.com	4190 Becca Ln Kernersville NC 27284	SE	EM			FW	1981
Mackay Marcus J	(317)847-7215 mmackay@adventlutheran.org	6568 Hunters Ridge S Zionsville IN 46077	EN	Sn/Adm	Advent Zionsville IN	(317)873-6318	SL	2004
MacKenzie Cameron A	(260)452-2226	6 Tyndale Pl Fort Wayne IN 46825	IN	S HS/C	Concordia Theological Seminary Fort Wayne IN	(260)452-2100	CQ	1981
Mackereth James R	(805)291-3821 jimlynn1981@gmail.com	2664 Stephen Pl Santa Maria CA 93455	CNH	EM			CQ	1995
Mackey Daniel P	(660)492-3958 mackeydp@hotmail.com	13308 E Lieder Way Fishers IN 46037	IN	SP	Grace Muncie IN	(765)282-2537	FW	2004
Mackey Thomas R	(308)216-0563 tomrmackey@yahoo.com	W8509 Burbey St Niagara WI 54151	NW	EM			CQ	1998
Mackie Roger L	(507)351-8670 rogermackie@gmail.com	2022 Marlee Ln Green Bay WI 54304	NW	SP	Alleluia Greenleaf WI	(920)532-3892	SL	1982
Mackowiak John E	(608)572-0709 blanda463@gmail.com	2647 Privada Dr The Villages FL 32162	FG	EM			FW	1977
MacMillin Gregory C	(210)413-3686 therealcodymac@gmail.com	20915 Wilderness Oak Apt 4208 San Antonio TX 78258	TX	C07/2025			SL	2024
Maconachy Samuel O	(410)292-4055 sammacon@aol.com	3640 Morgan Way Imperial MO 63052	MO	Assoc	Faith Oakville MO	(314)846-8612	SL	2016
Maddox Richard L	(219)588-3794 dmaddox737681@gmail.com	2517 White Pine Circle Valparaiso IN 46383	SE	EM			SL	1981
Mader Robert J	(931)624-3554 r.j.mader1969@gmail.com	2307 Dogwood Ln Clarksville TN 37043	MDS	EM			SPR	1969
Madison Charles E	(315)594-9918 cmadison@live.com	5899 New Hartford Street Wolcott NY 14590	EA	SMP	Hope Community Red Creek NY	(585)690-1648	CQ	2018
Madsen Luke C	(817) 451-7561 pastorluke@holycrossarlington.org	4400 W Arkansas Ln Arlington TX 76016	TX	SP	Holy Cross Arlington TX	(817)451-7561	FW	2006
Madson Mark J Dr	(810)887-1953 markjmadson@gmail.com	3004 Wedgewood Dr Fort Gratiot MI 48059	MI	SP	Trinity Port Huron MI	(810)984-2993	SL	2007
Magarino Aurelio	(240)603-3371 amagarino62@gmail.com	3041 Dubarry Ln Brookeville MD 20833	SE	SP	Of the Cross Rockville MD	(301)762-7565	HITSL	1996

*Multiple Assignments (See Church Worker Locator for Additional Details)

See Page 53 for the Table of Abbreviations for key to District, Position, and Seminary abbreviations

**C =Candidate; EM = Emeritus; the date following the C is the month and year the Candidate status began

NAME	TELEPHONE NUMBER EMAIL	STREET ADDRESS CITY/STATE/ZIP	DISTRICT	POSITION/ STATUS**	WHERE SERVING	OFFICE PHONE	SEM/ PROGRAM	YR GRAD
Maggard William R Jr	(909)600-4917 wrmaggard@gmail.com	1950 N Willow Ave Rialto CA 92376	PSW	Sn/Adm	Grace Rialto CA	(909)875-3163	FW	2018
Magneson Scott S	(810)650-6996 magnesonscott@gmail.com	3519 Crimson Ct Port Huron MI 48060	MI	SMP	Light of Christ Marysville MI	(810)334-6756	SL-SMP	2020
Magruder David B	(307)840-0310 dulutheran@mac.com	1108 Aruba Dr Fort Collins CO 80525	RM	SP	Peace W Christ Fort Collins CO	(970)226-4721	SL	1990
Mahlburg Steven C	(989)310-0779 smahlburg@gmail.com	5160 Green Acres Dr Frederic MI 49733	MI	S Miss	Office of International Mission Saint Louis MO		SL	1995
Mahlum Dean E	(952)442-4882 djmahlum@embarqmail.com	632 E 2nd St Waconia MN 55387	MNS	EM			FW	1987
Mahmood Wilson I	(214)680-8967 Irfanwilson@yahoo.com	7314 Danridge Rd Rowlett TX 75089	TX	D Miss	Texas District Round Rock TX	(800)951-3478	SL	2014
Mahnken Merle F	(712)676-2235 immansch@iowatelecom.net		IW	SP	Immanuel Schleswig IA	(712)676-2235	SL	1991
Mahsman David L	dmahsman@gmail.com	142 Edwin Ave Saint Louis MO 63122	MO	EM			FW	1983
Mai Benjamin J	(858)527-2983 bjqmai05@gmail.com	3791 Lesser Dr Newbury Park CA 91320	PSW	SP	Christ King Newbury Park CA	(805)498-2217	SL	2018
Maier David P Dr			MI	EM			FW	1982
Maier Walter A III Dr	(260)483-7275 walter.maieriii@ctsfw.edu	5017 Lonesome Oak Trl Fort Wayne IN 46845	IN	S HS/C	Concordia Theological Seminary Fort Wayne IN	(260)452-2100	FW	1978
Main Raymond H	(317)786-7583 rmain1938@gmail.com	1002 E Bradbury Ave Indianapolis IN 46203	IN	EM			SL	1966
Maita Sergio E	sergio.maita@lcmsintl.org	Juan Luis Duquela Santo Domingo Este Santo Domingo 11501 DOMINICAN REPUBLIC	MO	S Miss	Office of International Mission Saint Louis MO		FW	2018
Majak Samuel G	(701)205-7150 majaksamuel5@gmail.com	6650 17th St S Fargo ND 58104	ND	Assoc	Beautiful Savior Fargo ND	(701)293-1047	SL	2017
Majeski Eric W	(586)557-4541 emajeski@sbcglobal.net	6532 Westridge Washingtn Twp MI 48094	MI	Sn/Adm	Grace Fellowship Romeo MI	(586)752-9800	FW	1993
Makelin Terry J	(402)336-7819 makelint60@gmail.com	301 W Schnieder St. Foster NE 68765	NEB	SP	Trinity* Foster NE	(402)329-4262	SL	2010
Makey Joshua A	(716)923-3815 jmky85@yahoo.com	8 Twin Dr Tunkhannock PA 18657	EA	SP	St Paul's Tunkhannock PA	(570)836-2301	SL	2022
Maland Randy C	(218)583-2237 rmaland@arvig.net	30066 491st Ave Henning MN 56551	MNN	EM			FW	1995
Malec Raymond A	(610)428-7825 malecr@aol.com	299 Allen Dr Northampton PA 18067	S	Sn/Adm	Concordia Northampton PA	(610)262-8500	SL	1983
Malinsky Michael A	(812)375-9575	3810 Waycross Dr Columbus IN 47203	IN	EM			SL	1977
Mallardi Rocco J Dr	(660) 223-8503 pastormallardi@gmail.com	28091 Heits Point Ave Lincoln MO 65338	MO	RSO	Heits Point Lutheran Camp Lincoln MO	(660)668-2363	FW	2011
Mallepalle Ebenezer C	(732) 977-6867 ebmallepalle@yahoo.com	5 Whitall Dr Sicklerville NJ 08081	NJ	SP	Luther Memorial Blackwood NJ	(856)227-2209	SL	2008
Mallett Larry G	(740)851-6646 ohioxav@hotmail.com	1920 N Bridge St Apt 701 Chillicothe OH 45601	OH	EM			FW	1985
Mallie Charles S	(832)584-8573 bluewaterhunter@earthlink.net	13144 Westridge Dr NW Silverdale WA 98383	TX	M Chap	Office of International Mission Saint Louis MO		FW	2002
Malm Elliott R	(507)633-2253 emalm@protonmail.com	306 Central Ave N Dodge Center MN 55927	MNS	SP	Grace Dodge Center MN	(507)633-2253	Other	2005
Malme Scott C	(920)494-4554 scottmalme@pilgrimluth.org	1705 Forest Glen Green Bay WI 54304	NW	Asst	Pilgrim Green Bay WI	(920)965-2233	SL	1992
Malmstrom Richard E	(252)876-1517 revmalmstrom@gmail.com		SE	Assoc	Our Savior Lynchburg VA	(434)384-6651	FW	2000
Malone Henry B	(385)234-1931 rev.dr.hankmalone@gmail.com	2045 E 3110 S Salt Lake Cty UT 84109	RM	SP	St Johns Salt Lake City UT	(801)364-2873	SL	1994
Malone Barry C	(208)705-9488 ablepastor555@gmail.com	1612 W Glendale Dr Marion IN 46953	IN	C11/2024			CQ	2013
Malone C R Sr	(816)761-9315 twenteegran@aol.com	9723 Lawndale Ave Kansas City MO 64137	MO	SP	Trinity* Creighton MO	(660)499-2205	SL	1980
Maltz Myron C	(405)321-7828 mcmaltz@hotmail.com	2010 Morren Dr Norman OK 73071	OK	EM			SPR	1967
Maltzahn Robert F Dr	(678)897-9757 malt2@aol.com	940 S Enota Dr NE Apt 122 Gainesville GA 30501	FG	EM			SL	1959
Malysz Piotr J Dr	205-324-2063 pmalysz@mail.harvard.edu	1216 Forest Brook Cir Birmingham AL 35226	SO	Asst	St Paul Birmingham AL	(205)324-2063	FW	2003
Mandel Warren G	(708)946-9530	1884 Monhegan Ave Beecher IL 60401	NI	EM			SL	1968
Mandile Anthony B III	(305)923-5148 abmnepa@gmail.com		FG	SP	Martin Luther Marathon FL	(305)289-0700	SL	2003
Mandile Anthony B IV	(860)573-6465 pastor@stjohnluth.org	c/o St John Lutheran Church 8888 Prospect Rd Strongsville OH 44149	OH	SP	St John Strongsville OH	(440)234-5806	FW	2022
Mandley Jason L	(989)742-4400 tubarev@speedconnect.com	22000 County Road 452 Hillman MI 49746	MI	SP	St John Hillman MI	(989)742-4400	FW	1996
Mangar Ratna B	(314)295-3467 ratnasama916@gmail.com	7125 Field Ave Saint Louis MO 63116	MO	Assoc	St Johns Saint Louis MO	(314)773-0126	SL	2024
Manila John K	(509)591-6114 charis_eis_christo@hotmail.com	813 E Paske Rd Colbert WA 99005	NOW	EM			FW	1989
Mankin Trevor A	(206)200-2993	4049 Marconi Ave Sacramento CA 95821	CNH	SP	Town and Country Sacramento CA	(916)481-2542	FW	2011
Manley Marcus G	(712)880-2452 bzaltamontpastor@gmail.com	6267 N 200th St Altamont IL 62411	CI	SP	Zion* Altamont IL		FW	2012

*Multiple Assignments (See Church Worker Locator for Additional Details)
See Page 53 for the Table of Abbreviations for key to District, Position, and Seminary abbreviations
**C =Candidate; EM = Emeritus; the date following the C is the month and year the Candidate status began

NAME	TELEPHONE NUMBER EMAIL	STREET ADDRESS CITY/STATE/ZIP	DISTRICT	POSITION/ STATUS**	WHERE SERVING	OFFICE PHONE	SEM/ PROGRAM	YR GRAD
Mann Dennis C	(734)731-1223 dmannrev@gmail.com	1027 Plum Grove Dr Monroe MI 48161	MI	EM			CQ	1992
Mann James K	(512)269-3843 prjimmann@hotmail.com	215 Glacier Dr Cedar Park TX 78613	TX	EM			CQ	1980
Mann Kevin D	pastor.kmann@gmail.com	8915 Sunflower Cove Fort Wayne IN 46819	IN	SP	Peace Fort Wayne IN	(260)744-3869	SL	2009
Mann Philip E	philmann@centurytel.net	26815 Scappoose Vernonia Hwy Scappoose OR 97056	NOW	EM			CQ	2009
Mann Robert A	(719)510-6931 mannboba@gmail.com	6950 Lost Springs Dr Colorado Spgs CO 80923	RM	EM			SL	2002
Mann William B V	(703)517-4352 billymann1956@gmail.com	126 Green Spring Rd Locust Grove VA 22508	SE	C01/2020			SL	1985
Manning Gregory T	(913)940-5713 gmanning1973@yahoo.com	3105 Milan St New Orleans LA 70125	SO	SP	Gloria Dei New Orleans LA	(504)822-7229	FW	2000
Manning Mark L	(714)342-2718 mark.manning@searchlight ministries.com	2710 N Gaff St Orange CA 92865	PSW	SP	Searchlight Fullerton CA	(714)871-1711	SL	1998
Manor Jonathan J	(860)491-0086 pastor.manor@gmail.com	c/o Lutheran Church-Missouri Synod 1333 S Kirkwood Rd Saint Louis MO 63122	MO	S Ex/S	The LCMS Corporate Saint Louis MO	(314)965-9000	SL	2005
Manteufel Thomas E	(913)232-9068 2bandt@charter.net	5832 W 87 Ter Overland Park KS 66207	KS	EM			SL	1968
Mantey Matthew R	(206)651-7991 matt.mantey@resurrection-lcms. org	20435 1st Pl S Des Moines WA 98198	NOW	SP	Resurrection Des Moines WA	(206)824-2978	SL	2011
Manthe Jeffrey D	(320)761-0715 jmanthe24@gmail.com	953 Hamlet Dr N Avon MN 56310	MNN	SMP	SonRise Avon MN	(320)761-0715	SL-SMP	2015
Manthei Jonathan M	(949)878-0046 jman856@hotmail.com	747 N 7th St Unit A Blythe CA 92225	PSW	SP	Zion Blythe CA	(760)922-7321	SL	2003
Manweiler John	(435)669-9012 coyotej@infowest.com	708 E Prairie Way Washington UT 84780	RM	SP	Trinity Saint George UT	(435)628-1850	FW	1988
Manz Stephen R	618-697-7934 stephenrmanz@gmail.com	581 S Proctor Ln Eagle ID 83616	NOW	EM			FW	2007
Manz Michael J	(417)876-7099 pastormanz@gmail.com	339 S 6th Ave W Newton IA 50208	IE	SP	Our Savior Newton IA	(641)792-1084	FW	2009
Mapur Daniel D	(712)898-4643 mapurdaniel@gmail.com	1982 Dogwood Dr SE Le Mars IA 51031	IW	Asst	Grace Le Mars IA	(712)546-5516	SL	2017
Mapus Michael A II	(419)357-6601 mapus@concordiatoledo.org	3717 Maple Ave Castalia OH 44824	OH	SP	Concordia Toledo OH	(419)382-0410	FW	2022
Marchetti Gino C II	(763)760-5595 revmarchetti@gmail.com	5336 Meadowbrook Dr Fort Wayne IN 46835	IN	SP	St John Columbia City IN	(260)244-3712	FW	2020
Marcis Peter C	(419)592-3535 pmarcis@yahoo.com	610 Cripple Creek Ct Napoleon OH 43545	OH	Sn/Adm	St Paul Napoleon OH	(419)592-3535	SL	1987
Marcis Thomas R Jr	tmarcisjr@gmail.com	1982 North 20th St Bismarck ND 58501	ND	Sn/Adm	St Matthew* Napoleon ND		SL	1986
Marcis Walther P Dr	(440)376-6296 walthermarcis@gmail.com	24227 Maple Ridge Rd North Olmsted OH 44070	OH	Sn/Adm	St John Cleveland OH	(216)531-1156	SL	1961
Marhenke Larry E	(501)204-4288 lsmarhenke@yahoo.com	50 Estremedura Dr Hot Springs AR 71909	MDS	EM			SPR	1965
Marin Thompson	thompsonmarin24@gmail.com	24 Park Ave Batavia NY 14020	EA	SP	St Paul Batavia NY	(585)343-0488	FW	2024
Marin Blaise E	pastorblaisemarin@gmail.com	424 N Bellflower Blvd Unit 116 Long Beach CA 90814	PSW	SP	Redeemer South Gate CA	(323)588-0934	FW	2014
Markel Jerry E	(219)210-2326 markelministry135@gmail.com	2232 E Livingston St Springfield MO 65803	MO	EM			SPR	1969
Marklevitz Zachary W	(616) 534-0805 zmarklevitz@gmail.com	4483 Chicory Ct Wayland MI 49348	EN	SP	Grace Wyoming MI	(616)534-0805	FW	2016
Marks Martin L	(815)754-5590	498 Wood St Dekalb IL 60115	NI	Sn/Adm	Immanuel Dekalb IL	(815)756-6669	SL	1997
Marks Matthew T	(573)768-2140 mmarkslcms@hotmail.com	4552 Highway B Perryville MO 63775	MO	Sn/Adm	Immanuel Perryville MO	(573)547-8317	SL	2000
Marks Paul W	(920)400-0425 pastor@emmanueladell.org	402 Central Ave Adell WI 53001	SW	SP	Emmanuel Adell WI	(920)994-9005	FW	2021
Markus James L	(541)767-9934 jimarkus@aol.com	1157 Bennett Creek Rd Cottage Grove OR 97424	NOW	EM			SL	1986
Markworth James A	(651)463-2501 jimmarkworth@charter.net	18236 Embers Ave Farmington MN 55024	MNS	EM			SL	1974
Markworth David J	(320)234-7103 revmarkworth@gmail.com	60883 110th St Hutchinson MN 55350	MNS	SP	St John Hutchinson MN	(320)587-4853	FW	2003
Markworth Gary L	(715)697-0498 revgarymarkworth@gmail.com	5378 6th Ave Pittsville WI 54466	NW	SP	St Paul* Pittsville WI	(715)884-2211	SL	2006
Marler William R	(417)840-1023 wmarler73@gmail.com	3642 W Greenwood St Springfield MO 65807	MO	EM			SL	1983
Maronde Christopher A	(402)802-4279 pastormaronde@protonmail.com	2049 G Ave Shenandoah IA 51601	IW	SP	St John* Hastings IA		FW	2010
Marquardt Clarence L	(509)741-9773 clarmarq@gmail.com	2335 NW Cascade Ave E Wenatchee WA 98802	NOW	EM			SL	1970
Marquardt Jeffrey D	(704)562-9104 jmarquardt@growingwithgrace. org	9325 Gunston Road Welcome MD 20693	SE	Sn/Adm	Grace La Plata MD	(301)932-0963	SL	1994
Marque Edward A	(513)403-0614 alexandermarque86@gmail.com	33-38 75th St Jackson Heights NY 11372	AT	SP	Christ Woodside NY	(718)639-3945	SL	2019
Marriott James F Dr	(972)741-5978 jim.marriott@concordia.edu	2503 Paden Cir Cedar Park TX 78613	TX	Assoc	Faith Georgetown TX	(512)863-7332	SL	2020
Marrs Richard W Dr	(314)780-5009 marrsr@csl.edu	9336 Litzsinger Rd Saint Louis MO 63144	MO	S HS/C	Concordia Seminary Saint Louis MO	(314)505-7000	SL	2001

*Multiple Assignments (See Church Worker Locator for Additional Details)

See Page 53 for the Table of Abbreviations for key to District, Position, and Seminary abbreviations

**C =Candidate; EM = Emeritus; the date following the C is the month and year the Candidate status began

NAME	TELEPHONE NUMBER EMAIL	STREET ADDRESS CITY/STATE/ZIP	DISTRICT	POSITION/ STATUS**	WHERE SERVING	OFFICE PHONE	SEM/ PROGRAM	YR GRAD
Mars Kenneth R	(308)241-0233 kenmars1997@gmail.com	902 37th St Cody WY 82414	WY	Sn/Adm	Christ the King Cody WY	(307)587-3025	FW	2005
Marschke Paul O Dr	(847)905-0198 paul.marschke@comcast.net	2333 Central St Apt 402 Evanston IL 60201	NI	EM			SL	1963
Marschner Larry D	(701)624-5341 mhase@staloisius.com	203 1st Ave E P.O. Box 196 Sawyer ND 58781	ND	EM			SPR	1972
Marsh Prentice D	(773)398-5152 pd1marsh@gmail.com	8448 S Indiana Ave Chicago IL 60619	EN	SP	Ephphatha-Deaf Chicago IL	(773)723-3232	CQ	1981
Marsh Benjamin D	(832)450-5182 b.d.marsh89@gmail.com	28806 Squire Dr Chesterfield MI 48047	MI	SMP	Shepherd's Gate Shelby Township MI	(586)731-4544	SL-SMP	2024
Marshall Ulmer Jr Dr	(251)456-7929 umarshall@trinitylutheranmobile.org	7210 Blakeley Forest Blvd Spanish Fort AL 36527	SO	SP	Bethel* Point Clear AL	(251)928-8327	SPR	1973
Marshall Blake A	(406)346-7614 blakemarshallrollf@gmail.com	P.O. Box 843 Forsyth MT 59327	MT	EM			CQ	2014
Marshall Frank T	(904)765-1133 fmarsh8925@aol.com	1503 Carbondale Dr N Jacksonville FL 32208	FG	EM			SPR	1973
Marshall Robert H Jr	(734)284-3685 robert2.marshall@gmail.com	1509 Chestnut Street Wyandotte MI 48192	MI	EM			FW	1987
Marshall Stewart A	(870) 592-4522 revsamarshall@gmail.com	4640 S Beech St Pine Bluff AR 71603	MDS	SP	Trinity Pine Bluff AR	(870)534-4316	SL	1982
Marshall Timothy J	(651)295-0938 marshallt@woodburylutheran.org	6573 Jocelyn Ave South Cottage Grove MN 55016	MNS	Assoc	Woodbury Woodbury MN	(651)739-5144	SL	1997
Marten William G	(303)745-6242 billmarten@juno.com	2560 S Sable Way Aurora CO 80014	RM	EM			SL	1961
Martens Dennis L	(515)370-4809 pastortlc@netins.net	201 Briarwood Bnd Jefferson IA 50129	IW	SP	Trinity Jefferson IA	(515)386-3517	SL	2008
Marth Cory W	(260)312-9204 pastor@corymarth.com	1205 Mount Isa Pl Fort Wayne IN 46845	IN	C03/2022			SL	2015
Marth Thomas J	(712)209-6421 marthstj@hotmail.com	623 17th Ave N Estherville IA 51334	IW	SP	Immanuel Estherville IA	(712)362-3237	FW	2011
Marth Walter D	(206)369-2202 deanmarth@hotmail.com	4800 Steiner Ranch Blvd Apt 3106 Austin TX 78732	TX	EM			SL	1959
Martin Kevin W	(919)696-8312 kmartinnc@gmail.com	1500 Glenwood Ave Raleigh NC 27608	SE	SP	Our Savior Raleigh NC	(919)832-8822	CQ	1992
Martin Stephen W	(520)979-8036 stephen.w.martin1@gmail.com	P.O. Box 826 Ridgeley WV 26753	EN	Asst	Ascension Tucson AZ	(520)297-3095	CQ	2022
Martin Ronald L	ronm1895@aol.com	1895 N Shattuck Pl Orange CA 92865	PSW	EM			SPR	1973
Martin Paul A	(951)676-7626 epfncl@aol.com	30998 Greensboro Dr Temecula CA 92592	PSW	SMP	Faith Vista CA	(760)724-7700	SL-SMP	2015
Martin Michael R	(517)579-0572 pastormartin@outlook.com	2744 Brentwood Ave East Lansing MI 48823	MI	EM			FW	1979
Martin Matthew J	(920)821-3368 felsenherr@yahoo.com	1606 S Westhaven Dr Oshkosh WI 54904	SW	C08/2023			CQ	2006
Martin Lannon R Dr	(202)855-8900 revlannonmartin@gmail.com	3605 Marigold Ct Toano VA 23168	SE	Sn/Adm	King of Glory Williamsburg VA	(757)258-9701	FW	2012
Martin Juan M	(954)495-0712 jmartin1934@yahoo.com	3000 N 75th Ave Hollywood FL 33024	FG	EM			CQ	1976
Martin James S	(931) 320-9023 james@martinnet.us	3124 Southpoint Dr Clarksville TN 30743	MDS	Assoc	Grace Clarksville TN	(931)647-6750	FW	2024
Martin James P	(440)376-4430 jim.martin1247@gmail.com	19 Blessings Ln Waynesville NC 28786	SE	EM			SPR	1973
Martin James C Sr	(210)789-3832 pastordude47@gmail.com	1334 Farm Rd 3357 Winnsboro TX 75494	TX	EM			FW	1989
Martin Gary E	(830)775-7375 gmartin4him@yahoo.com	126 Alta Vista Dr Del Rio TX 78840	TX	EM			SPR	1974
Martin Gabriel J	(586)876-3461 gabriel.martin@ctsfw.edu	720 2nd St Tawas City MI 48763	MI	SP	Zion Tawas City MI	(989)362-5712	FW	2017
Martin Frank H	(734)770-3455 pastorfrankmartin@sbcglobal.net	408 W Front St Apt 37c Monroe MI 48161	MI	EM			FW	1989
Martin David W Dr	(623)202-3926 pastordavewol@gmail.com	17525 W Bell Rd Surprise AZ 85374	PSW	SP	Word of Life Surprise AZ	(623)544-3000	FW	1987
Martin Clarence L	(901)299-6180 cmrt108@bellsouth.net	6605 Stephan Ridge Dr Bartlett TN 38135	MDS	EM			CQ	1997
Martin Brian D	(434)738-3353 martinbc71@gmail.com	9913 Fawnhope Court Midlothian VA 23112	SE	EM			SL-D	2010
Martin Brandon L	(828)315-0978 brandonmartin327@gmail.com	1800 W Emma Ave Springdale AR 72762	MDS	Assoc	Salem Springdale AR	(479)751-9500	SL	2008
Martin James R	(307)871-0357 mastorpastor@hotmail.com	2303 Steve Ave Cheyenne WY 82007	WY	EM			FW	1999
Martin Matthew A	(712)216-0079 mattm298@yahoo.com	P.O. Box 617 511 S Washington Remsen IA 51050	IW	SP	Christ Remsen IA	(712)786-2225	SL	2024
Martinal Timothy D	(402)672-9817	c/o St Paul Lutheran Church 4941 Center St Millington MI 48746	MI	Assoc	St Paul Millington MI	(989)871-4581	SL	2014
Martinek Robert W	(503)724-5596 retiredbob2021@outlook.com	1803 Imperial Palm Dr Largo FL 33771	FG	EM			FW	1988
Martinez Daniel J	(305)498-0205 daniel.jordan89@yahoo.com	5524 NE 58th St Kansas City MO 64119	KS	Assoc	Trinity Mission KS	(913)432-5441	CQ	2018
Martinez Eduardo M	(321)278-4612 revmartinezed@gmail.com	10742 Flycast Cir Orlando FL 32825	FG	SP	Esperanza Viva* Orlando FL	(321)278-4612	SL	2021
Martinez Luis G	(832)282-6203 luisgm79@sbcglobal.net	6730 Lilabrook Ct Spring TX 77379	TX	Assoc	Trinity Klein Klein TX	(281)376-5773	SL	2021
Martzowka Blake J	(989)372-5318 blakemartzowka@gmail.com	P.O. Box 737 10827 Main St Mantua OH 44255	EN	SP	Christ* Mantua OH	(330)274-2849	FW	2020

*Multiple Assignments (See Church Worker Locator for Additional Details)

See Page 53 for the Table of Abbreviations for key to District, Position, and Seminary abbreviations

**C =Candidate; EM = Emeritus; the date following the C is the month and year the Candidate status began

NAME	TELEPHONE NUMBER EMAIL	STREET ADDRESS CITY/STATE/ZIP	DISTRICT	POSITION/ STATUS**	WHERE SERVING	OFFICE PHONE	SEM/ PROGRAM	YR GRAD
Marwang Riek K	riek.marwang@yahoo.com	3007 Kansas Dr Bellevue NE 68005	NEB	C07/2016			SL	2010
Masaki Naomichi Dr	(260)452-3209	5710 Kinlock Pl Fort Wayne IN 46835	IN	S HS/C	Concordia Theological Seminary Fort Wayne IN	(260)452-2100	FW	1991
Maschke Jedidiah T Dr	pastormaschke@gmail.com	2288 Oak Ridge Dr. Carson City NV 89703	CNH	SP	Bethlehem Carson City NV	(775)882-5252	SL	2004
Maschke Timothy H Dr	pastor.maschke@splgrafton.org	378 B Prairie Run Grafton WI 53024	SW	Assoc	St Paul Grafton WI	(262)377-4659	SL	1974
Maser Ryan D	pastormaser@gmail.com	303 11th Ave Plattsmouth NE 68048	NEB	SP	First Plattsmouth NE	(402)296-2832	SL	2021
Mashburn Joe Q	(817)602-8575 jqmash@gmail.com	2317 W Park Row Blvd Corsicana TX 75110	TX	SP	Faith Corsicana TX	(903)874-8795	SL	2004
Masih George G	(972)351-9931 graceccir@yahoo.com	7217 Saturn Dr Rowlett TX 75089	TX	D Miss	Texas District Round Rock TX	(800)951-3478	FW-D	2005
Masih Afzal	(616)724-6944 mashiha@messiahgr.org	1704 Kingsland Dr Byron Center MI 49315	MI	C10/2021			FW	2005
Masinelli Anthony D	(239)248-7134 Rev.Masinelli@stpaulscheney.com	505 North Wolf Street Cheney KS 67025	KS	SP	St Paul Cheney KS	(316)540-0115	SL	2004
Maske Daniel S	(810)429-9144 dmaske@mightymessengers.org	2213 Springmont Ave Kalamazoo MI 49008	MI	Assoc	St Michael Portage MI	(269)327-7832	SL	2016
Maske Steven R	(810)429-3980 pastormaske@gmail.com	357 E Jackson Ave Hampshire IL 60140	NI	Sn/Adm	Good Shepherd Elgin IL	(847)741-7788	SL	2000
Mason Justin M	office@oursaviorlouisville.com	431 Silverbrook Dr Dansville KY 40422	IN	SP	Our Savior Danville KY	(330)432-2678	FW	2019
Mason Leroy W	(530)743-7754 lwmason@hotmail.com	6763 Penny Way Browns Valley CA 95918	CNH	EM			SPR	1960
Mason Joseph E Jr	(541)647-2699 revjmjr@gmail.com	18160 Cottonwood Rd #820 Bend OR 97707	NOW	EM			FW	1983
Mason John S III	(302)521-2734 jaymason48@mac.com	11999 Palba Way Apt 6404 Fort Myers FL 33912	FG	EM			SL	1997
Mason Patrick D	(620)356-4651 kpuwuibu@pld.com	P.O. Box 586 Ulysses KS 67880	KS	EM			FW	1983
Massey Justin D	(254)423-0405	230 E Donnewald St Worden IL 62097	SI	SP	Trinity Nokomis IL	(217)563-2718	FW	2017
Massey Steven M	stevemasseymich@outlook.com	4811 12th Street N St Petersburg FL 33703	FG	Assoc	Grace Saint Petersburg FL	(727)527-6213	SL	1988
Mast Michael W	(708)990-0972 hisjoy4u@gmail.com	608 Dogwood Run Bradenton FL 34212	FG	SP	Christ The King Largo FL	(727)595-2117	SL	1978
Mastic Andrew J	(636)779-2318 amastic@pathfinderstl.org	15800 Manchester Rd. Ellisville MO 63011	MO	Assoc	Pathfinder Ellisville MO	(636)394-4100	SL	2024
Mastin Tyson F	pastormastin@gmail.com	216 McLeod Ave N Plato MN 55370	MNS	SP	St John Plato MN	(320)238-2338	NESC	2014
Matarazzo Philip R	(732)929-9095 philipmatarazzo9@gmail.com	2007 Teakwood Rd Toms River NJ 08753	NJ	EM			SL	2000
Matasovsky Daniel V	(651)739-9301 dan.matasovsky@gmail.com	2711 Snowdrift Cir E Maplewood MN 55119	MNS	EM			SPR	1965
Matheny Mark T	(248) 881-7627 pastormarkPLB@gmail.com	495 S Newman Rd Lake Orion MI 48362	MI	SP	Pilgrim Burton MI	(810)744-1188	FW	2020
Matheny Adam M	(812)449-6866 matheny@oslcmankato.org	27 Westminster Rd Mankato MN 56001	MNS	Sn/Adm	Our Savior Mankato MN	(507)385-2180	SL	2016
Mather Elwood E III Dr	(845)649-7553 woodymather@gmail.com	4 Treefort Ct Selbyville DE 19975	EN	EM			SL	1979
Mather George A	(435)512-0819 pastorgeorgemthr@gmail.com	42 Tucker Terr Raynham MA 02767	NE	EM			FW	1989
Mathers J D	(416)320-6366 jd.mathers@outlook.com	3227 King Street East Unit 503 Kitchener ON N2A3Z CANADA	EN	Assoc	St Mark's* Mississauga ON	(905)278-2122	NESC	1984
Mathews Craig A	(941)527-5834 crgmthws@gmail.com	3790 Pinebrook Cir #508 Bradenton FL 34209	FG	SP	Redeemer Englewood FL	(941)475-2410	SL	2001
Mathews Michael W	(507)461-4720 mmathews1517@gmail.com	362 N Mark Pl Lakeside AZ 85929	EN	SP	Shep Mountains Pinetop AZ	(928)367-1183	SL	1993
Mathey Michael J	(715)330-5599 lcmsrevmike@gmail.com	119417 Huckelberry Rd Edgar WI 54426	NW	SP	St John Edgar WI	(715)352-2888	SL	2005
Mathis John W	(501)804-9407 jndmathis@sbcglobal.net	4 S Point Ct Little Rock AR 72223	MDS	EM			SL-SMP	2018
Mathison Ronald L	(320)864-5616 rmathison@firstglencoe.org	1420 Prairie Ave Apt 226 Glencoe MN 55336	MNS	EM			CQ	1988
Matlock Albert H	(561)248-3519 bert.matlock@gmail.com	P.O. Box 602 Sopchoppy FL 32358	FG	SP	Trinity Crawfordville FL	(850)926-7808	SL	2012
Maton Benjamin O	(434)806-0021 pastormaton@hotmail.com	1324 Delphi Ln Charlottesvle VA 22911	SE	SP	Immanuel Charlottesville VA	(434)295-4038	SL	2000
Matranga George J	(916) 801-1516 chapmat@outlook.com	6372 Driftwood St Sacramento CA 95831	CNH	EM			SL	1964
Matro Lawrence K	(231)866-1542 pastormatro@gmail.com	6148 Rawlins Rd The Villages FL 34762	FG	EM			FW	1984
Mattfeld William A	wam632@gmail.com	632 Road 8 Schuyler NE 68661	NEB	EM			SL-D	2009
Matthew Timothy C	(314)406-6357 revtimothymatthew@gmail.com	Stanton Nursing Home 301 17th Street Stanton NE 68779	NEB	EM			SL	2009
Matthews Michael A	(619)990-5868 kkuhfal@cox.net	11515 Fury Lane # 49 El Cajon CA 92019	EN	SMP	Borrego Borrego Springs CA		CQ	2020
Matthews James A	(360)701-6197 james@jam-mat.com	6602 76th St W Lakewood WA 98499	NOW	SP	Grace Lakewood WA	(253)472-7105	SL	2011
Matthews Frank L III	no1redder@gmail.com	3634 Wellington Rd Los Angeles CA 90016	PSW	EM			CQ	2019

*Multiple Assignments (See Church Worker Locator for Additional Details)
See Page 53 for the Table of Abbreviations for key to District, Position, and Seminary abbreviations
**C =Candidate; EM = Emeritus; the date following the C is the month and year the Candidate status began

NAME	TELEPHONE NUMBER EMAIL	STREET ADDRESS CITY/STATE/ZIP	DISTRICT	POSITION/ STATUS**	WHERE SERVING	OFFICE PHONE	SEM/ PROGRAM	YR GRAD
Matthews David H Jr	(417) 318-1021 rev.matthews@pm.me	221 W Southern St Sutherland IA 51058	IW	Assoc	Zion* Paullina IA	(712)949-3910	FW	2024
Matthias Ryan P	(402)646-5431 ryan.matthias@cune.edu	1142 Eastridge Dr Seward NE 68434	NEB	Cmp P	Concordia University Nebraska Seward NE	(402)643-3651	SL	2004
Matthis Christopher S	(303)688-4435 pastorchris@epiphanylc.org	550 E Wolfensberger Rd Castle Rock CO 80109	RM	Sn/Adm	Epiphany Castle Rock CO	(303)688-4435	SL	2007
Mattil Michael J	(903)421-1010 revmattil@gmail.com	2190 Hayden Hall Rd Bells TX 75414	TX	EM			SL	1984
Mattsfield Wade R	(402)826-9563 chemnitznsasse@yahoo.com	1614 Tiffany St West Plains MO 65775	MO	SP	Immanuel West Plains MO	(417)256-3407	SL	2003
Mattson Daniel L Dr	(314) 681-5254 mattson.daniel@gmail.com	4808 Laketon Ct Saint Louis MO 63128	MO	EM			SL	1968
Matyas Dennis W Dr			MI	Sn/Adm	St Paul Bay City MI	(989)684-4450	SL	2011
Matz Brett A	(920)226-4113 revguy66@gmail.com	c/o Bethany Lutheran Church 3501 Turkeyfoot Rd Erlanger KY 41018	OH	SP	Bethany Erlanger KY	(859)331-3501	SL	2010
Matzat Donald G Dr	(636)474-9151 donmatzat@hotmail.com	690 Springfield Dr O Fallon MO 63366	MO	EM			SL	1998
Matzat William A Dr	(636) 579-0379 billmatzat@gmail.com	15618 Coventry Farm Dr Chesterfield MO 63017	MO	EM			SL	1967
Matzke Bruce R	(303) 881-4792 brucermatzke@gmail.com	1449 Bismarck Ln Brentwood CA 94513	CNH	EM			FW	1990
Matzke Gerald D	(440)639-0415	514 Greenside Dr Painesville OH 44077	OH	EM			CQ	1981
Matzke Mark G	(740)297-9724 pastormatzke@hotmail.com	11900 Chillicothe Rd Chesterland OH 44026	OH	Sn/Adm	St Mark Chesterland OH	(440)729-1668	FW	1998
Mau Richard A	(847)391-9284 maushaus1780@sbcglobal.net	1780 E Algonquin Rd Des Plaines IL 60016	NI	EM			FW	1999
Mau Gerhard	(847) 962-9068 gerhardmau@sbcglobal.net	216 Alaska Jade St Henderson NV 89074	PSW	EM			FW	1983
Mau Jon C	(425)577-3075 jmau00@gmail.com	15173 E Lincoln Rd Spokane WA 99217	NOW	EM			SL	1994
Mau Matthew L	(402)363-1540	1409 Road S Waco NE 68460	NEB	SP	St John Waco NE	(402)728-5446	SL	2013
Maulella Robert J	(863)385-7848 pastor@faithlutheransebring.org	2740 Lakeview Dr Sebring FL 33870	FG	SP	Faith Sebring FL	(863)385-7848	SL	1997
Maunula Mark L	(320)676-3435 mskidsmn@yahoo.com		MNN	SP	Trinity Isle MN	(320)676-8774	SL	1989
Maurer Rudolph H Jr	(507)381-5394 rudymaurer@aol.com	220 1st St Northeast P.O. Box 113 New Richland MN 56072	MNS	EM			FW	1983
Maurer Timothy D	(208)346-2895 Pastor.Tim@yahoo.com	1273 N 3100 E Ashton ID 83420	NOW	EM			CQ	2019
Mauss Douglas E	(314)722-9690 dmauss@pathfinderstl.org	308 Bradford Estates Ct Ellisville MO 63011	MO	Assoc	Pathfinder Ellisville MO	(636)394-4100	SL	2017
Mavis James M	mavisjm@msn.com		MT	EM			FW	1993
Maxon Bradford C	(630)279-4775 maxonrev@aol.com	150 W Harrison St Elmhurst IL 60126	EN	SP	Messiah Elmhurst IL	(630)279-4775	CQ	1984
Maxwell James B	(303)695-8001 maxwell@rm.lcms.org	Rocky Mountain District Office 88 Inverness Cir E Unit A210 Englewood CO 80112	RM	DP	Rocky Mountain District* Englewood CO	(303)695-8001	SL	2009
Maxwell Ronnie D	(812)882-4662 revronfw97@gmail.com	707 N 8th St Vincennes IN 47591	IN	SP	St John Vincennes IN	(812)882-4662	FW	1997
Maxwell David R Dr	(314)229-1767 maxwelld@csl.edu	5214 Pernod Ave Saint Louis MO 63139	MO	S HS/C	Concordia Seminary Saint Louis MO	(314)505-7000	SL	1995
May Daniel P Dr	(260)432-2950 danielmay1905@gmail.com	6335 Dirwood Ct Fort Wayne IN 46804	IN	EM			SPR	1970
May Douglas C	(575)835-9648 dougmay@sdc.org	4000 25th E. Room 230 Idaho Falls ID 83404	RM	EM			SPR	1965
May Edward H	(608)931-6117 edhmay@gmail.com	2238 Brookside Drive Jackson WI 53037	SW	EM			SPR	1975
May George M	(314)775-6956 sidace99@yahoo.com	6811 110th Ave NE Lake Stevens WA 98258	NOW	SP	Lamb Of God Lake Stevens WA	(425)377-2173	SL	2013
May Jacob T	(314)616-8044 pastorjacobmay@gmail.com	P.O. Box 72 Gordonville MO 63752	MO	SP	Christ Gordonville MO	(573)243-5639	SL	2008
May James E Jr	(216)513-8139 proliturgy@icloud.com	526 Eastland Rd Berea OH 44017	MNS	C07/2016			FW	2006
May Jeremy D	(573)431-3442 jeremy.may@cune.org	309 Taylor Ave Park Hills MO 63601	MO	Sn/Adm	Trinity Park Hills MO	(573)431-3442	SL	2009
May Curtis A	(574)835-8355 akcamay@outlook.com	3358 Adele Dr Rochester IN 46975	IN	SP	St Johns Rochester IN	(574)223-6898	FW	2006
Mayer Richard H	mrs.mayer@yahoo.com	1210 Blue Quail Dr Bentonville AR 72712	MDS	SP	Messiah Pea Ridge AR	(479)451-0021	SL	1982
Mayer Ronald P	(775)727-4690	P.O. Box 2016 Pahrump NV 89041	PSW	EM			SL	1973
Mayerhoff Richard G	(214)802-0164 mandrmayerhoff@sbcglobal.net	4107 Chamberlain Cir Bryan TX 77802	TX	EM			SL	1969
Mayes Benjamin T Dr	(260) 452-2228 benjamin.mayes@ctsfw.edu	3 Coverdale Place Fort Wayne IN 46825	IN	S HS/C	Concordia Theological Seminary Fort Wayne IN	(260)452-2100	FW	2003
Mayes Robert J	(402)528-7253 revmayes@hotmail.com	1101 K Rd Beemer NE 68716	NEB	SP	Immanuel* Beemer NE	(402)528-7253	FW	2003
Mayes Theodore E	(260)750-1604 tedjomayes@gmail.com	8920 Greyhawk Dr Fort Wayne IN 46835	IN	EM			SL	1976

*Multiple Assignments (See Church Worker Locator for Additional Details)
See Page 53 for the Table of Abbreviations for key to District, Position, and Seminary abbreviations
**C =Candidate; EM = Emeritus; the date following the C is the month and year the Candidate status began

NAME	TELEPHONE NUMBER EMAIL	STREET ADDRESS CITY/STATE/ZIP	DISTRICT	POSITION/ STATUS**	WHERE SERVING	OFFICE PHONE	SEM/ PROGRAM	YR GRAD
Mayland James L Jr	(612)269-3812 jmayland97@gmail.com	312 S 68th Ave Wausau WI 54401	NW	Sn/Adm	Trinity Wausau WI	(715)842-0769	FW	2016
Maynard Arthur F	(830)535-2026 maynards70@gmail.com	443 Ewing Dr Pipe Creek TX 78063	TX	EM			CQ	1994
Mayo Brian P Sr	(708)602-0162 mayosenior54@att.net	3001 Kathleen Ct Homewood IL 60430	NI	SMP	Salem Homewood IL	(708)798-1820	FW-SMP	2012
Mazariegos Jorge	(331) 575-6238 jmazariegos@vidayfechurch.org	725 Morgan St Elgin IL 60123	NI	Assoc	San Pablo Aurora IL	(630)820-3450	SL	2014
Mazikas Joseph E Jr	(443)504-2242 jmazikas@gmail.com	113 Fitzpatrick Trail West Henrietta NY 14623	EA	EM			FW	2009
Mazzaferro Steven D	(601) 685-9190 reverendmazzaferro@gmail.com	4905 Shumate Rd Meridian MS 39305	SO	SP	Trinity Meridian MS	(601)483-5457	FW	2011
Mc Call George T	(785)513-0081 lcmspastortim@gmail.com	902 Mulberry St Junction City KS 66441	KS	SP	Immanuel Junction City KS	(785)238-6007	SL	2010
Mc Cants Jimmy Jr	(251)344-9182 jrmccants55@att.net	1508 Homestead Dr W Semmes AL 36575	SO	SP	Mount Calvary Mobile AL	(251)471-4200	FW	1982
Mc Cants Reholma	(724)327-6419 rmmccants@windstream.net	7830 Lakeside Oaks Dr Pensacola FL 32526	SO	SP	St Matthew Pensacola FL	(850)477-0567	FW	1979
Mc Clean Charles L	(410)554-9994 charlesmcclean1942@gmail.com	4 Upland Rd Apt 21 Baltimore MD 21210	SE	SP	Our Saviour Baltimore MD	(410)235-9553	SL	1967
Mc Clellan Gary W	(580)938-5208 garymc@pldi.net	P.O. Box 456 Shattuck OK 73858	OK	SP	Christ Shattuck OK	(580)938-5208	SL	1992
Mc Coid James W	pastorjim@ctrockford.org	3722 Foxborough Ln Rockford IL 61114	NI	SP	Christ The Rock Rockford IL	(815)332-7191	SL	2007
Mc Comack Paul M	(318)366-5185 pastor@tlcinmonroe.org	7297 Ellie B Dr Panama City FL 32404	SO	SP	Christ Our Sav* Panama City Beach FL	(850)233-6249	FW	1989
Mc Coy Michael L	(541)772-3381 mmccoy19@gmail.com	207 Rogue Ln Rogue River OR 97537	NOW	Asst	Faith Rogue River OR		FW	1984
Mc Dermott Lawrence J	(785)434-6846 twomax@ruraltel.net	406 S Cochran St Plainville KS 67663	KS	EM			CQ	1993
Mc Donald David P	(507)842-5667 mcdonald.david66@yahoo.com	1019 4th Ave P.O. Box 362 Brewster MN 56119	MNS	SP	St John* Rushmore MN	(507)478-4922	SL	1999
Mc Donald Gilbert K	(248)674-1564 g47mcd@hotmail.com	4770 Pine Knob Ln Clarkston MI 48346	MI	EM			SPR	1973
Mc Intyre David R	(225)244-3784 zionlutheran@bellsouth.net	12526 Cedar St Clinton LA 70722	SO	SP	Zion Clinton LA	(225)683-5592	SL	1979
Mc Lain Philip C	(615)396-7559 philmclain@gmail.com	29 Calm Sea Dr Salem SC 29676	SE	EM			FW	1984
Mc Manus Dennis J	(320)808-0624 revdmcmanus@gmail.com	8054 County Road 32 New Germany MN 55367	MNN	EM			SL	1987
Mc Mullin Clinton R	(405)210-3102		OK	EM			SL	1990
Mc Pherson Daniel P	(561)385-3237 mcphersondp@gmail.com	320 Granada Rd West Palm Beach FL 33401	FG	SP	Redeemer West Palm Beach FL	(561)832-8705	SL	1998
Mc Pike Jeffrey D	(312)650-9890 jmcpike@n9cqs.com	112 W Jefferson St Philo IL 61864	CI	SP	Immanuel Osman IL	(217)897-6170	FW	1988
Mc Quiggin Brian S	(507)519-1204 pastor@riveroflifelutheran.com	830 Sunrise Dr Saint Peter MN 56082	MNS	SP	River of LIFE Saint Peter MN	(507)934-0063	SL	2009
Mc Vey Daniel J	(517)375-2746 marge3172@yahoo.com	543 Wallace Rd NE Alden MI 49612	MI	EM			CQ	1982
McBee Kyle A	(712)249-9102 pastor.k.mcbee@gmail.com	401 E 8th St Atlantic IA 50022	IW	SP	Zion Atlantic IA	(712)243-2927	FW	2017
McBurney David L	(314)650-4380 pastordavid@trinluth.org	1204 Koch St Bloomington IL 61701	CI	Assoc	Trinity Bloomington IL	(309)828-6265	SL	2008
McCafferty Richard A	(907)229-8320 rickardo33@gmail.com	20221 N Broken Arrow Dr Sun City West AZ 85375	NOW	C05/2023			SL	2020
McCall Jonathan C	(216)618-1811 info@oursaviornorthroyalton.org	4000 Wallings Rd North Royalton OH 44133	EN	SP	Our Savior North Royalton OH	(216)381-2873	FW	2018
McCall Willis J	(406)200-3203 willismccall@gmail.com	1704 Squaw Creek Rd Huntley MT 59037	MT	Sn/Adm	Mount Olive Billings MT	(406)656-6687	SL	2010
McCalley Joseph M	(303)248-6426 pastormccalley@gmail.com	2201 West Rollins Rd Columbia MO 65203	MO	Assoc	Trinity Columbia MO	(573)445-2112	FW	2019
McCanless Robert E	412-523-6741 pr_mccanless@juno.com	32 D&N Road Apt. G-4 Stuggart AR 72160	MDS	C09/2022			CQ	2002
McCants Elder	(210)381-7699 elder0311@att.net	6302 Mission Hills Dr San Antonio TX 78244	TX	SP	Holy Cross San Antonio TX	(210)532-1300	FW	1977
McCarthy Christopher R	(605)218-1967	P.O. Box 327 Wall SD 57790	SD	SP	Emmanuel* Creighton SD	(605)457-3171	SL	2017
McCarthy David J	(406)260-2014 rev.mccarthy@outlook.com	P.O. Box 1284 Eureka MT 59917	MT	SP	Holy Cross Eureka MT	(406)297-2116	FW	2014
McCarty David J	(517)301-0456 ddaddyjmac@aol.com	1127 Lee Ave West Bend WI 53090	SW	EM			SL	2015
McCarty Nathan A	(423)322-4188 namccarty88@gmail.com		FG	Assoc	Bethlehem Jacksonville Beach FL	(904)249-5418	SL	2019
McCarty Timothy L	revtimmcc@gmail.com	c/o Emmanuel Lutheran 124 W Douglas Ave Kingfisher OK 73750	OK	SP	Emmanuel Kingfisher OK	(405)375-3431	SL	2007
McCaslin Gregg A	(303)619-8581 gregg.mccaslin@gmail.com	217 S Ripplerock Ln Star ID 83669	RM	C07/2025			SL-SMP	2015
McClean David R	(317)823-5801 dmcclean@hclc.info	830 Woodhill Dr Indianapolis IN 46227	IN	Assoc	Holy Cross Indianapolis IN	(317)823-5801	SL	1986
McClellan Jedidiah B	(920)562-2505 pastorjed@zionwayside.org	2420 Sycamore Dr Apt L182 Green Bay WI 54311	NW	Assoc	Zion Wayside WI	(920)864-2463	SL	2024
McClelland Philip D	(330)461-2734 pastor@faithwb.org	520 Miller Dr Medina OH 44256	OH	SP	Hosanna* Columbia Station OH	(440)328-7167	SL	2008
McCloskey David A	(949)712-0626 mccloskey.dave@gmail.com	415 S Poplar St Greensburg KS 67054	KS	SP	Peace Greensburg KS	(620)966-8845	SL	2008

*Multiple Assignments (See Church Worker Locator for Additional Details)
See Page 53 for the Table of Abbreviations for key to District, Position, and Seminary abbreviations
**C =Candidate; EM = Emeritus; the date following the C is the month and year the Candidate status began

NAME	TELEPHONE NUMBER EMAIL	STREET ADDRESS CITY/STATE/ZIP	DISTRICT	POSITION/ STATUS**	WHERE SERVING	OFFICE PHONE	SEM/ PROGRAM	YR GRAD
McClure Garry D Dr	gdmmac42@gmail.com	2012 E Monte Vista Dr Tucson AZ 85719	EN	EM			SL	1969
McCombs John W	(951)295-0193 jmccombs951@gmail.com	4465 Sixth St Riverside CA 92501	PSW	SMP	Immanuel Riverside CA	(951)682-7613	SL-SMP	2024
McCourt Craig T	(952)769-6348 pastor@peacearlington.org	518 E Elmwood Street Arlington MN 55307	MNS	SMP	Peace Arlington MN	(507)964-2959	SL-SMP	2019
McCoy Sean Q	pastor@ascensioneastlansing.org	1913 Dell Rd Lansing MI 48911	MI	SP	Ascension East Lansing MI	(517)337-9703	SL	2011
McCoy Shane D	(337)287-0705 pastormccoyclal@yahoo.com	121 Red Water Pt Lake Placid FL 33852	FG	C10/2021			SL	2013
McCracken Garry A	(314)348-2474 gmccracken@charter.net	1823 Packard Ct O Fallon MO 63368	MO	SP	Trinity Troy MO	(636)528-4999	SL	1998
McCrory Mark K Dr	(480)585-8007	29305 N Scottsdale Rd Scottsdale AZ 85266	PSW	Sn/Adm	Desert Foothills Scottsdale AZ	(480)585-8007	SL	2010
McCullam Perry L	(205)218-3474 mccullamp@aol.com	3717 Charles St Dolomite AL 35061	SO	SP	Ebenezer Atmore AL	(251)368-4719	FW	2004
McDaniels James A	(336)402-4150 revjmcdaniels@aol.com	1705 Stanley Rd Greensboro NC 27407	SE	SP	St Luke High Point NC		CQ	1977
McDonald Jeremy T	(901)734-1614 returnmeigs@yahoo.com	P.O. Box 108 Ulm AR 72170	MDS	SP	Our Savior* Brinkley AR		FW	2023
McDonald Robert A	(760)431-2245 revrobmcd@gmail.com	952 Jasmine Ct Carlsbad CA 92011	PSW	EM			FW	1978
McDougall Daniel T	(661)313-3457 pmac@suddenlinkmail.com	705 Keesee Benton AR 72019	MDS	EM			SL	1981
McDowell Adam M	(409)920-3019	8713 Edwardsberg Pl New Haven IN 46774	IN	Assoc	St Peter's Fort Wayne IN	(260)749-5816	FW	2019
McElvain John M	(540)288-1097 pastorjohn@concordialuther-anva.org	3404 Aquia Dr Stafford VA 22554	SE	SMP	Concordia Triangle VA	(703)221-3703	SL-SMP	2010
McFadden Dennis E	dmcfaddenfw@gmail.com	4919 S Wayne Ave Fort Wayne IN 46807	IN	EM			CQ	2014
McGhghy Paul G	(217)962-1123 4mcghghy@gmail.com	362 Autumn Creek Dr Apt C Manchester MO 63088	CI	EM			SL	1978
McGinley Michael J	(515)419-0865 revmcginley@protonmail.com	310 E 4th St Spencer IA 51301	IW	SP	Christ King Spencer IA	(712)262-2244	FW	2019
McGinley David M	(314)961-5275 dave@webstergardens.org	c/o The Lutheran Church Of Webster Gardens 8749 Watson Rd Saint Louis MO 63119	MO	Sn/Adm	Webster Gardens Webster Groves MO	(314)961-5275	SL	2016
McGladdery Kevin	(510) 480-6082 kevin@kmcg.io	780 Grassy Hill Rd Orange CT 06477	NE	SP	Zion Orange CT	(203)795-3916	FW	2024
McGuire Geoffrey B	(214)537-6933 brentmcguire@mac.com	3448 Purdue Ave Dallas TX 75225	TX	Sn/Adm	Our Redeemer Dallas TX	(214)368-1371	SL	2000
McGurer Lawrence W Jr	(303)902-6370 larry@summitmissionalliance.org	2091 Vining Dr Unit F Woodbury MN 55125	RM	SP	Christ Breckenridge CO	(970)453-8019	SL	2007
McIntosh Zachary	(210)260-7018 zachm@concordia-satx.com	123 Village Park Dr Georgetown TX 78633	TX	Sn/Adm	Zion Georgetown TX	(512)863-3065	SL	2004
McKee Terry L	(352)817-8161 terrymckee1957@gmail.com	17788 SW 40th St Dunnellon FL 34432	FG	SP	Peace Dunnellon FL	(352)489-5881	FW-D	2009
McKenney Mervin A III	(804)316-3182 mervin3rd@msn.com	4108 Roundtree Rd Richmond VA 23294	SE	C07/2016			SL	2007
McKenzie Mark L		1426 Wrightwood Dr San Bernrdno CA 92407	PSW	SP	Iglesia La Santisima San Bernardino CA	(909)999-8311	FW	1985
McKenzie Patrick C	(716)957-0470 kiltedrev@yahoo.com	5030 Bradford Rd Jacksonville FL 32217	FG	SP	Hope Jacksonville FL	(904)677-4506	SL	1984
McKillop Don C	(605)840-0554 prdomc5897@yahoo.com	109 W State St Plankinton SD 57368	SD	EM			FW	1982
McKinley Jordan J	(812)569-1020 pastor.jjmckinley@gmail.com	4385 S State Road 135 Vallonia IN 47281	IN	SP	Trinity Vallonia IN	(812)358-3225	FW	2012
McKnight David M	(970)846-4759 pdm552@msn.com	16614 Front Royal St San Antonio TX 78247	TX	EM			SL	1979
McLean Scott J	(863)446-0911 sjmclean@embarqmail.com	2300 Pinewood Blvd Sebring FL 33870	FG	SP	Christ Avon Park FL	(863)471-2663	Other	1985
McLellan Duncan B	(515)444-3140 duncan@minister.com	c/o Trinity Lutheran Church 601 E 2nd St Waconia MN 55387	MNS	Sn/Adm	Trinity Waconia MN	(952)442-4165	SL	2005
McLeod Kevin A	(330)312-7039 kamcleod99@yahoo.com	P.O. Box 644 Malvern OH 44644	S	SP	Resurrection Malvern OH	(330)312-7039	FW	2012
McMahan Daniel M	(402)304-7786	2501 Nancy Dr Lincoln NE 68507	NEB	SMP	Faith Lincoln NE	(402)466-6861	SL-SMP	2023
McMaughan Sean P	(469)994-2710 olarmy02@gmail.com	301 Ford Way Ferris TX 75125	TX	Cmp P	Dallas Lutheran Sch Dallas TX	(214)349-8912	CQ	2020
McMiller Tyler J	(314)348-1526 tyler.mcmiller@lcms.org	11128 Pam Ln Saint Louis MO 63146	MO	S Miss	Office of International Mission Saint Louis MO		FW	2021
McMiller Daniel F	lamolina1986@gmail.com	11128 Pam Lane Saint Louis MO 63146	MO	S Ex/S	Office of International Mission Saint Louis MO		CQ	1996
McMillian Ric L	(281) 851-6226 ric@churchthatcares.org	26018 Bearborough Dr Spring TX 77386	TX	EM			FW	1985
McMinn Theodore D III	(931)303-2439 pastor@sothlutheran.org	1891 Horton Road Quebeck TN 38579	MDS	SP	Shepherd Hills McMinnville TN	(931)815-7684	FW	2008
McNamara Jerome F	(832)576-6716 jerry@youmattertogod.com	519 Little River Ct Richmond TX 77469	TX	C07/2023			SL	1991
McNeil Sean R	(231)750-2294 sean.mcneil@ctsfw.edu	207 N Court St Au Gres MI 47803	MI	SP	St John Au Gres MI	(989)876-8910	FW	2025
McPherson Roderick G	prod-t@comcast.net	2568 Palentina St Henderson NV 89044	PSW	EM			FW	2001

*Multiple Assignments (See Church Worker Locator for Additional Details)
See Page 53 for the Table of Abbreviations for key to District, Position, and Seminary abbreviations
**C =Candidate; EM = Emeritus; the date following the C is the month and year the Candidate status began

NAME	TELEPHONE NUMBER EMAIL	STREET ADDRESS CITY/STATE/ZIP	DISTRICT	POSITION/ STATUS**	WHERE SERVING	OFFICE PHONE	SEM/ PROGRAM	YR GRAD
McReynolds Kevin S	(308)850-0810 rlcmhpastor@gmail.com	46 Georgia Ln Gassville AR 72635	MDS	SP	Redeemer Mountain Home AR	(870)425-6071	SL	2008
McReynolds Terry A	(847)301-7961 tmcreynolds@saintlukeitasca.org	325 Russellwood Ct Schaumburg IL 60193	NI	Sn/Adm	St Luke Itasca IL	(630)773-0396	SL	1985
McReynolds Lawrence J	(757)784-2170 ljmcreynolds@yahoo.com	4800 N Courthouse Rd Providence Forge VA 23140	SE	SP	King of Glory Providence Forge VA	(804)966-5525	SL-D	2012
McVey Todd J	(608)276-5793 pastortodd@tds.net	3043 Artesian Lane Madison WI 53713	SW	EM			SL	1984
Meador Nathan M Dr	(920)838-4709 meador@swd.lcms.org	455 E. Green Bay Avenue Saukville WI 53080	SW	DP	South Wisconsin District Milwaukee WI	(414)464-8100	SL	1996
Meadows Bryan W	(605)858-0015 bryan.meadows@zionrc.org	420 East Liberty St. Rapid City SD 57701	SD	Sn/Adm	Zion Rapid City SD	(605)342-5749	SL	2019
Meadows Phillip W	(812)374-4263 ac9bradio@gmail.com	114 Saint Anne St Rapid City SD 57701	SD	EM			FW	2002
Mease Van E	(913)758-7624 edmease@outlook.com	2300 E Gary St Park City KS 67219	KS	EM			FW	1984
Mease Rocky W	(316)765-5989 rockywmease@gmail.com	2900 N Button Bush St Derby KS 67037	KS	Assoc	Christ Overland Park KS	(913)345-9700	SL	1981
Measel Martin P	(269)369-6216 mmeasel@christstevensville.com	1593 S Teakwood Dr Stevensville MI 49127	MI	Sn/Adm	Christ Stevensville MI	(269)429-7222	FW	2009
Mech Timothy J	tjdjmech@gmail.com	4589 Hunters Glen Dr Sheboygan WI 53083	SW	Sn/Adm	Trinity Sheboygan WI	(920)458-8246	SL	1989
Mech Gregory A	(417)540-6354 pastormech@hotmail.com	4454 N Glenway St Wauwatosa WI 53225	SW	SP	Beautiful Savior Milwaukee WI	(414)871-6744	SL	1986
Meckes Daniel C	(989)545-8524 pastormeckes@yahoo.com	1920 Washington Road Rochester Hills MI 48306	MI	D Ex/S	Michigan District Ann Arbor MI	(888)225-2111	FW	1989
Meehan John S	(703)922-1833 pastor.meehan@sjlc.com	5606 Cornish Way Alexandria VA 22315	SE	Sn/Adm	St Johns Alexandria VA	(703)971-2210	SL	1988
Meggers David L	dvdmeggers@gmail.com	505 S Kirkwood Rd Saint Louis MO 63122	MO	Assoc	Concordia Kirkwood MO	(314)822-7772	SL	1988
MehdiKhan Amer	(586) 636-5688 church_allnations@yahoo.com	37635 Dequindre Rd Troy MI 48083	MI	Assoc	All Nations Clinton Township MI	(586)636-5688	FW	2005
Mehl Timothy L	352-629-1794 timothymehl@yahoo.com	3241 SE 56th Ter Ocala FL 34480	FG	Assoc	St John Ocala FL	(352)629-1794	SL	2024
Mehl Silas C	(417) 358-1325 mehlsilas@gmail.com	P.O. Box 257 Carthage MO 64836	MO	SP	Good Shepherd Carthage MO	(417)358-1325	SL	2013
Mehl John L Dr	(314)799-9176 john.mehl@att.net	1253 Plainview Ave Seward NE 68434	NEB	Pro Stf	Saint Paul Concordia MO	(660)463-2238	SL	1985
Mehl Paul M	(660)463-2238	213 S Main St Concordia MO 64020	MO	ExecDir	Saint Paul Concordia MO	(660)463-2238	SL	1986
Meier Ronald W	(920)589-4213 meierronald.meier@gmail.com	1130 N Westfield St Oshkosh WI 54902	SW	EM			SPR	1965
Meier William E	(920)787-4707	W6264 Retreat Cir Wautoma WI 54982	EN	EM			SL	1962
Meier Peter A Dr	(952)221-0362 peter.meier@frontiernet.net	8705 Ribault Ave Orlando FL 32832	FG	EM			FW	1982
Meier Mark R Sr	(608)341-6017 meierfam@gmail.com	806 Cedar Dr Unit A La Crescent MN 55947	MNS	SP	Messiah* La Crescent MN	(507)895-5673	FW	1994
Meier David E	(620)473-0205 pastormeier8@gmail.com	31412 Keene Eskridge Rd Maple Hill KS 66507	KS	EM			FW	1978
Meier Bruce K	(920) 319-0741 pastor.meier@gmail.com	313 E Hamilton St Fox Lake WI 53933	SW	EM			CQ	2008
Meier Austin D	revameier565@gmail.com	616 Meadowbrook Dr West Bend WI 53090	SW	C09/2023			FW	2022
Meilaender Gilbert C	(219)462-6984 gilbert.meilaender@valpo.edu	760 Verbena Ct Valparaiso IN 46385	EN	EM			SL	1972
Meilander Douglas H	(443)725-4740 dougmwwjd@comcast.net	2402 Perring Woods Rd Parkville MD 21234	SE	EM			SL	1972
Meilner William C	(507)218-6052 pastormeilner@gmail.com	30 Benson Drive South Lewiston MN 55952	MNS	EM			FW	1983
Meinhart Walter F Jr	(360)221-0764 wmeinh1438@aol.com	2688 Dreamland Ln Langley WA 98260	NOW	EM			SL	1971
Meissler Craig D	(210)491-9677 cmeissler@shlutheran.org	15726 Shell Creek St San Antonio TX 78232	TX	SMP	Mount Calvary San Antonio TX	(210)824-8748	SL-SMP	2012
Meissner Bruce W	(847)854-5761	1165 Holly Ln Algonquin IL 60102	NI	Asst	Immanuel East Dundee IL	(847)428-4477	SL	1963
Meissner Michael J	(832)628-0072 pastormichael@lifebridgecy press.org	16614 Mueschke Rd Cypress TX 77433	TX	SP	LifeBridge Cypress TX	(832)628-0072	SL	1996
Meissner Craig A Dr	revmeissc@sbcglobal.net	7807 NE 54th St Kansas City MO 64119	MO	SP	Holy Cross Kansas City MO	(816)452-9113	FW	2002
Meissner Duane P	(346)616-8090 duanepaulmeissner@gmail.com	3520 N Josephine St Apt A Denver CO 80205	RM	SP	Resurrection City Denver CO	(346)616-8090	SL	2011
Mekasha Eddie H	(402)917-2852 eddiemekasha@gmail.com	1312 Lombar St Raleigh NC 27610	SE	C12/2019			SL	2007
Mekonnen Berihun R	(714)995-7324 mountzionem@yahoo.com	11235 Oak Leaf Dr Apt 603 Silver Spring MD 20901	SE	C07/2020			CQ	2012
Melchior Edward F	(314)631-0301	8431 Weber Trail Dr Saint Louis MO 63123	MO	EM			SPR	1958
Melin Jaron P	(316)250-9324 jaronpmelin@protonmail.com	300 S H St Herington KS 67449	KS	SP	St John* Herington KS	(785)366-0270	SL	2022
Melinat Theodore C	(989)879-3195 tcmelinat@gmail.com	2770 N Garfield Rd Pinconning MI 48650	MI	EM			SL	1963
Melius Jared K	(303)325-3309 pastor@mtzionlcms.org	14781 Huron St Broomfield CO 80023	RM	Sn/Adm	Mount Zion Denver CO	(303)429-0165	FW	2006

*Multiple Assignments (See Church Worker Locator for Additional Details)

See Page 53 for the Table of Abbreviations for key to District, Position, and Seminary abbreviations

**C =Candidate; EM = Emeritus; the date following the C is the month and year the Candidate status began

NAME	TELEPHONE NUMBER EMAIL	STREET ADDRESS CITY/STATE/ZIP	DISTRICT	POSITION/ STATUS**	WHERE SERVING	OFFICE PHONE	SEM/ PROGRAM	YR GRAD
Meltzer Stephen N	(218)640-3081 stjohnwadenapastor@yahoo.com	710 Franklin Ave SW Wadena MN 56482	MNN	SP	St John Wadena MN	(218)631-3000	FW	2010
Menacher Mark D	(858)352-8337 pastor-mark@st-lukes-la-mesa.org	13823 Olive Grove Pl Poway CA 92064	EN	SP	St Lukes La Mesa CA	(619)463-6633	CQ	2023
Menagh Jason C	(406) 223-9382 jasonmenagh59@gmail.com	2221 Willow Dr Unit 107g Livingston MT 59047	MT	EM			FW	1987
Mendedo Tilahun M Dr	(251)751-1289 tilahunmm@yahoo.com		FG	C04/2025			CQ	2003
Mendez Arturo G	(832)883-1705 pastormendez@stmatthewlcms. com	1423 Hallcroft Ln Houston TX 77073	TX	Assoc	St Matthew Westfield Houston TX	(281)443-2304	SL	2015
Meneghello Peter C	(260)750-2229 pmeneghello@lutheranlifevil- lages.org	9405 Monique Dr Fort Wayne IN 46835	IN	RSO	Lutheran Homes Inc Fort Wayne IN	(260)447-1591	FW-SMP	2021
Menet David M	(847)951-5252 david.menet52@gmail.com	4112 Daina Dr Cedar Falls IA 50613	IE	SP	Faith Waterloo IA	(319)236-1771	FW	2006
Mengsteab Yohannes A Dr	(260)458-4825 ymengsteab@gmail.com	5012 Glen Springs Trl Fort Worth TX 76137	TX	EM			SL	1991
Menk Gerald R	(847)848-7698 grmenk133@gmail.com	458 Kevin Ln Grayslake IL 60030	NI	EM			CQ	1981
Menke James W	(254)405-0484 jamesmenke17@gmail.com	1903 Elkington Circle Conroe TX 77304	TX	EM			SL	1983
Menke Noah T	(512)736-2505 menk721@gmail.com	2227 Crockett Dr Carrollton TX 75006	TX	Sn/Adm	Holy Cross Dallas TX	(214)358-4396	SL	2025
Mennicke David G	(407)542-1329 djmenn99@earthlink.net	2024 Inner Circle Dr. Oviedo FL 32765	FG	EM			SL	1965
Mentz Stephen H Dr	(301)785-0800 stephen.mentz@gmail.com	8401 Triple Crown Rd Bowie MD 20715	SE	EM			SL	1979
Menz Andrew P	(989)513-0197 andrewmenz@gmail.com		MI	Sn/Adm	Zion Auburn MI	(989)662-4264	SL	2008
Meraz Jonathan R	(402)841-6113 pastormeraz@hotmail.com	551 Lancaster Rd Centerton AR 72719	MDS	C01/2022			SL	2003
Mercado Antonio	(281)739-8172 rev.antonio@yahoo.com	3914 Redell Rd Baytown TX 77521	TX	C10/2017			SL	2013
Mercer Ernest A	(609)442-1610 merceralan@aol.com	673 E Chancery Ln Galloway NJ 08205	S	EM			SL-SMP	2017
Mercer Dennis D	(443)980-7338 dslcvicar@divineshep.org	1002 Cobalt Dr Rapid City SD 57701	SD	SMP	Divine Shepherd Black Hawk SD	(605)787-6438	FW-SMP	2023
Merino Larry C Dr	(260)471-5603	2226 Lawndale Dr Fort Wayne IN 46805	IN	EM			FW	1992
Meritt Kelly-Ray	(646)387-0867 pyx2go2@gmail.com	2090 E Tremont Ave Apt 10h Bronx NY 10462	AT	EM			SL	1980
Merker Michael S	(919)303-1613 pastor@jordanapex.org	1905 Loganwood Dr Apex NC 27523	SE	SP	Jordan Apex NC	(919)303-1613	SL	2008
Merlo Alex L		673 Meadowsedge Ln Aurora IL 60506	NI	Sn/Adm	San Pablo Aurora IL	(630)820-3450	HITSL	1996
Merrell Gene E	(717)684-5510 blgem@earthlink.net	742 Prospect Rd Columbia PA 17512	SE	EM			SL	1957
Merrick Brandon P	(530)240-5133 revinparadise@gmail.com	6404 Pentz Rd Paradise CA 95969	CNH	SP	Our Savior Paradise CA	(530)877-7321	Other	2011
Merrill John E	john_m_48066@yahoo.com	401 S 17th Street Springs Hot SD 57747	SD	EM			CQ	1987
Merrill John F	jfrmerrill@gmail.com	c/o First Lutheran Church 1115 N D St Fort Smith AR 72901	MDS	SP	First Fort Smith AR	(479)785-2886	SL	2009
Merrill Richard C	(712)678-3618 stjohnpastor@frontiernet.net	P.O. Box 73 Charter Oak IA 51439	IW	SP	Immanuel* Charter Oak IA	(712)678-3630	FW	1991
Merrill Theodore H Dr	(541)990-2434	3230 15th Ave SE Albany OR 97322	NOW	EM			FW	1981
Merritt Glenn F Jr	merrittministries@gmail.com	14554 Nelsons Creek Dr Omaha NE 68116	NEB	EM			FW	1985
Mertz Robert C	(440)842-1208 revmertz@gmail.com	4410 Dawnshire Dr Cleveland OH 44134	EN	EM			Other	2002
Mertz Glenn A	(440)225-5683 glennamertz@gmail.com	313 Stanford Ave Elyria OH 44035	EN	SMP	Grace Elyria OH	(440)322-5497	FW-SMP	2025
Merz Daniel S	pastormerz@gmail.com		MT	C02/2025			SL	2016
Meseke Morris D	(660)723-3080 meseke@embarqmail.com	27477 Forest Ridge Ct Warrenton MO 63383	MO	EM			SL	1992
Meseke Paul R	(352)797-2882 pastormeseke@yahoo.com	10021 Weeks Dr Brooksville FL 34601	FG	SP	Christ Brooksville FL	(352)796-8331	FW	1998
Meseke Gilbert F	(260)452-4842 gmgilmeseke9@gmail.com	9210 Maysville Rd Apt 4 Ft Wayne IN 46815	IN	EM			SPR	1953
Messer Thomas C	(989)388-2037 pastormesser@gmail.com	8155 N Rich Rd Alma MI 48801	MI	SP	Calvary* Carson City MI	(989)584-6068	FW	2005
Messmann John A Dr	(817)915-0063 john.messmann@gmail.com	3987 Truman Dr Frisco TX 75034	TX	EM			SL	1982
Metcalf James E	(616) 915-4990 jim9654@me.com	3942 Ravines Dr Allendale MI 49401	MI	EM			SL	1978
Metcalf Brandon W	(573)286-1214	292 Westerholdt St East Alton IL 62024	SI	Assoc	Zion Bethalto IL	(618)377-8314	SL	2022
Mettala Eric M	(805)340-2283 emettala@gmail.com	435 Manzanita Ave Ventura CA 93001	PSW	EM			CQ	2019
Metz William E	wemetz@sbcglobal.net	1990 Wellsona Rd Paso Robles CA 93446	CNH	EM			SL	2002
Metzger Daniel J	(316)684-3415 pastor.metzger@gmail.com	2465 N Peckham St Wichita KS 67228	KS	Assoc	Trinity Wichita KS	(316)685-1571	FW	1990

*Multiple Assignments (See Church Worker Locator for Additional Details)
See Page 53 for the Table of Abbreviations for key to District, Position, and Seminary abbreviations
**C =Candidate; EM = Emeritus; the date following the C is the month and year the Candidate status began

NAME	TELEPHONE NUMBER EMAIL	STREET ADDRESS CITY/STATE/ZIP	DISTRICT	POSITION/ STATUS**	WHERE SERVING	OFFICE PHONE	SEM/ PROGRAM	YR GRAD
Metzger Marvin G		4083 S Center Rd Rochelle IL 61068	NI	EM			FW	1990
Metzger William L	(815)212-1250 billmetzger57@gmail.com	1654 N Pinnacle Ave Nixa MO 65714	MO	EM			SL	1983
Metzler Michael J		507 2nd St Glenwood IA 51534	IW	SP	Trinity Glenwood IA	(712)527-4667	SL	2018
Metzler Norman P Dr	(503) 833-2754 npjmetzler@gmail.com	1909 NE 107th Ave Vancouver WA 98664	NOW	EM			SL	1967
Mews David M	swemdivad@gmail.com	2116 Patricia Ln Billings MT 59102	MT	Assoc	Trinity Billings MT	(406)245-3984	FW	2015
Mews Kurt F			OH	Sn/Adm	St John Defiance OH	(419)782-5766	FW	2002
Meyer Lealand L	(480)292-1198 lealandmeyer@gmail.com	1250 E Mineral Rd Gilbert AZ 85234	PSW	EM			SL	1973
Meyer Paul E Dr	(512)554-9766 MeyerPEM@gmail.com	5103 Trail West Drive Austin TX 78735	TX	EM			SL	1981
Meyer Norman S	(815)568-5531	17106 Garden Valley Rd Woodstock IL 60098	NI	EM			SL	1970
Meyer Monte L	(507)420-0617 monte.meyer@gmail.com	8437 County Rd 123 Brainerd MN 56401	MNN	SP	Gloria Dei Pequot Lakes MN	(218)568-5668	FW	1987
Meyer Milferd J	(512)303-4046 revmick2@juno.com	144 Marjess Dr Cedar Creek TX 78612	TX	EM			CQ	1979
Meyer Michael W	(314)526-6421 pastormeyer727@gmail.com	41 Shady Valley Dr Chesterfield MO 63017	MO	S Ex/S	The LCMS Corporate Saint Louis MO	(314)965-9000	FW	2008
Meyer Michael J	(402)641-7636 michael.meyer0309@gmail.com	6 Mayfair Ln Bella Vista AR 72715	MDS	Assoc	Holy Trinity Rogers AR	(479)636-1135	SL-D	2006
Meyer Philip G	(812) 249-0042 philipgmeyer@gmail.com		IN	EM			SL	1971
Meyer Matthew J	(218)849-5031 matt@onenetfamily.com	P.O. Box 98 Callaway MN 56521	MNN	SP	Beautiful Savior Callaway MN	(218)375-2786	SL	2013
Meyer Terry L	(202)374-1165 bran_desi@hotmail.com	23606 Country Villa Rd Ramona CA 92065	PSW	SP	Ramona Ramona CA	(760)789-1367	SL	2001
Meyer Laurence L	(509)582-5368 lmeyer1016@charter.net	3419 W Canyon Lakes Dr Kennewick WA 99337	NOW	EM			SL	1966
Meyer Michael H	(603)759-0335 retiredpastormick@gmail.com	67 Robin Hood Rd Nashua NH 03062	NE	EM			FW	1984
Meyer Richard A	(319)668-2999 revmeyer@iowatelecom.net	180 Rogers Dr Williamsburg IA 52361	IE	SP	Hope* Sigourney IA	(319)668-2999	FW	1986
Meyer Richard Z	(310)454-3471 richzmeyer@aol.com		PSW	EM			SL	1952
Meyer Richard G Dr	mt317@sbcglobal.net	7560 Blairmore Dr Rockford IL 61107	NI	C09/2017			SL	1992
Meyer Seth A	(620)654-6682 revsahmeyer@gmail.com	515 Alexander Winfiield KS 67156	KS	Sn/Adm	Trinity Winfield KS	(620)221-9460	SL	2005
Meyer Thomas F	(442)999-5305 tlmeyer45@att.net	2124 Royal Lytham Glen Escondido CA 92026	PSW	EM			SPR	1972
Meyer Timothy K	(316)214-9638 tim89272@gmail.com	14923 E Plymouth Ct Wichita KS 67230	KS	EM			CQ	2021
Meyer Vernon J	(417)770-2344 meyervjim01@gmail.com	540 9th St W Apt 8 Thief Rvr FLS MN 56701	MNN	EM			SL	1988
Meyer Wade R	(320)760-7005 meyer.wade76@gmail.com	3255 S Pillsberry Ave Sioux Falls SD 57103	SD	EM			SL	1990
Meyer Willard V	(618)377-9815 revwilly@charter.net	4 Ridgewood Ct Bethalto IL 62010	SI	EM			SL	1969
Meyer William J	wmeyer4@comcast.net	80 Deaconess Rd Suite 439 Concord MA 01742	AT	EM			SL	1963
Meyer Kendall L	(515)306-9479 pastorkendall@stpaulfd.org	2954 22nd Ave N Fort Dodge IA 50501	IW	Sn/Adm	St Paul* Fort Dodge IA	(515)955-7285	SL	2005
Meyer Ryan W	(618)349-8321 revrmeyer@gmail.com	605 E. 3rd St. Saint Peter IL 62880	CI	SP	St Peter Saint Peter IL	(618)349-8321	SL	2007
Meyer Dylan K	(763)301-9193 dkmeyer827@gmail.com	1005 1st St West Fargo ND 58078	ND	Assoc	St Andrew West Fargo ND	(701)282-4195	SL	2025
Meyer Aaron M	(815)575-3556 pastoraaron@sothpewaukee.org	620 Coventry Ln Hartland WI 53029	SW	Sn/Adm	Shepherd/Hills Pewaukee WI	(262)691-0700	SL	2013
Meyer Benjamin C	(815)644-2314 pastorbenmeyer@gmail.com	11 Wildflower Dr Centerburg OH 43011	OH	SP	Hope Condit OH	(740)965-1685	SL	2005
Meyer Craig M	(586)255-5774 cmeyer711@gmail.com	14969 Clemson Dr Sterling Hts MI 48313	MI	EM			CQ	2003
Meyer Dale A Dr	(618)910-1676 meyerd@csl.edu	624 Tillotson Collinsville IL 62234	MO	EM			SL	1973
Meyer David M	(863)295-9361 davidmeyer@gmail.com	931 La Quinta Blvd Winter Haven FL 33881	MNN	EM			SL	1964
Meyer Delbert H	(218)385-3455 kochiern@gmail.com	53766 410th St New York Mls MN 56567	MNN	EM			SL	1971
Meyer Ronald E Dr	(262)784-5232 rmeyer141@wi.rr.com	14248 Waters Edge Trl New Berlin WI 53151	SW	EM			SL	1969
Meyer Douglas E	(618) 267-3420 dougmeyer811@gmail.com	408 Cottonwood Dr Salem IL 62881	CI	EM			FW	1981
Meyer Edward A	(989)751-1504 edmeyer5@hotmail.com	603 Prescott St Prescott MI 48756	MI	SP	Faith Prescott MI	(989)873-4506	FW	1997
Meyer Edward F	(315)752-3117	8469 Farm Gate Path Cicero NY 13039	EA	EM			SL	1957
Meyer Joseph M Dr	(515)346-7084 Joe.meyer@gdlc.church	8301 Aurora Ave Urbandale IA 50322	IW	Assoc	Gloria Dei Urbandale IA	(515)276-1700	SL	1995
Meyer Gerald A	snjest62@gmail.com	88 Cottage Cir Crossville TN 38558	MDS	EM			CQ	1985

*Multiple Assignments (See Church Worker Locator for Additional Details)
See Page 53 for the Table of Abbreviations for key to District, Position, and Seminary abbreviations
**C =Candidate; EM = Emeritus; the date following the C is the month and year the Candidate status began

NAME	TELEPHONE NUMBER EMAIL	STREET ADDRESS CITY/STATE/ZIP	DISTRICT	POSITION/ STATUS**	WHERE SERVING	OFFICE PHONE	SEM/ PROGRAM	YR GRAD
Meyer Jonathan D	(979)773-2634 revjmeyer@hotmail.com	P.O. Box 247 Lexington TX 78947	TX	SP	Holy Trinity* Lexington TX	(979)773-2634	SL	2004
Meyer Donald J	(712)376-1022 tlcrev.meyer@gmail.com	5752 C Ave Marcus IA 51035	IW	Sn/Adm	Bethel* Sutherland IA	(712)446-3630	FW	1997
Meyer Jonathan F	(281)785-5396 jfmeyer74@gmail.com	411 Waurika Enid OK 73701	OK	SP	Saint Paul's Enid OK	(580)234-6646	SL	2000
Meyer Glenn A	(918)916-4469 glennm794@gmail.com	502 Garden Ln McAlester OK 74501	OK	SP	Trinity McAlester OK	(918)426-4544	SL	2004
Meyer Jonathan C	(405)315-9400 jonathan.meyer924@gmail.com	c/o Saint Matthew Lutheran Church 5125 Cascade Rd SE Grand Rapids MI 49546	MI	Sn/Adm	St Matthew Grand Rapids MI	(616)942-9091	SL	2014
Meyer John-Paul	(916)960-3543 pastorjpmeyer@att.net	5445 5th St Rocklin CA 95677	CNH	EM			SPR	1974
Meyer John W	(313)205-5185 grandpameyer46@aol.com	222 Jackson Ave Seward NE 68434	NEB	EM			CQ	1978
Meyer Joel W	(816)889-8905 jwmeyer83@gmail.com	c/o St Paul Lutheran Church 1165 E County Rd 400 S Brownstown IN 47220	IN	SP	St Paul Brownstown IN	(812)358-2334	SL	2010
Meyer Jonathan V	(260)740-8116 meyerjv87@gmail.com		IN	Cmp P	Concordia Fort Wayne IN	(260)483-1102	FW	2014
Meyer Joel P Dr	(912)467-1993 joel8meyer@yahoo.com	74 Manatee Way Saint Marys GA 31558	FG	Sn/Adm	Holy Trinity Kingsland GA	(912)729-6085	SL	2012
Meyer Jeffrey S	(608)332-0580 jmeyer@livelifetogether.com	104 Melody Cir Verona WI 53595	SW	Sn/Adm	Christ Memorial Madison WI	(608)271-2811	SL	1992
Meyer Glenn D	(402)580-2929 glenn56@mac.com	12088 Elmwood Dr Bennington NE 68007	NEB	EM			FW	1981
Meyer John A	(507)236-7427 chmeyerj@gmail.com	6305 437th Ave. Janesville MN 56048	MNS	EM			SL	1989
Meyers Sawyer A			MDS	SP	Beautiful Savior Olive Branch MS	(662)890-7272	FW	2020
Meyers Jeffrey T	(913)522-8678 jeff.meyers@clcop.org	12831 W 173rd Ter Overland Park KS 66221	KS	Assoc	Christ Overland Park KS	(913)345-9700	SL	1989
Meyr Ronald K	(321)205-6014 rmeyr@faithviera.org	110 Frumenti Pl Rockledge FL 32955	S	EM			SL	1980
Mezilus Andre F	(239)657-3822 amezilus@aol.com	1936 45th Ter SW Naples FL 34116	FG	SP	Bethlehem Haitian Immokalee FL	(239)657-3822	SL	2013
Michael Gerhard C Jr Dr	(407)353-8420 gmjrflga@aol.com	7350 Cove View Ct Cumming GA 30041	FG	EM			SL	1965
Michael Gregory C Dr	(706)543-3801	140 Rock And Shoals Dr Athens GA 30605	FG	SP	Christus Victor* Athens GA	(706)543-3801	SL	2003
Michaelson Craig A	(702)921-2700 pastorcraig@faithlasvegas.org	3505 S Town Center Dr Las Vegas NV 89135	PSW	Sn/Adm	Faith Community Las Vegas NV	(702)921-2700	SL	1994
Michalk Michael E	(952)472-2756 pastor@mountolivelcms.org	5200 Bartlett Blvd Mound MN 55364	MNS	SP	Mount Olive Mound MN	(952)472-2756	SL	1990
Michalk Wilbern C	(512)863-8515 wbchalk@gmail.com	775 County Road 140 Georgetown TX 78626	TX	EM			SPR	1963
Micheel Benjamin P	(816)519-7917 benjamin.micheel@discovertrinity.org	c/o Trinity Lutheran Church 609 Court St St. Joseph MI 49085	MI	Assoc	Trinity Saint Joseph MI	(269)983-5000	SL	2016
Michel Gregory S	(309)269-4295 pastorgregsotc@gmail.com	11 Windsor Terrace Palm Coast FL 32164	EN	SP	Shepherd Coast Palm Coast FL	(386)446-2481	SL	1996
Middaugh Michael S	(202)316-1921 msm004@gmail.com	25516 Echo Terrace St San Antonio TX 78260	TX	Assoc	Mount Calvary San Antonio TX	(210)824-8748	SPR	2009
Middendorf Mark G	(308)245-4151 pastor@zionscotia.org	P.O. Box 248 Scotia NE 68875	NEB	SP	Zion Scotia NE	(308)245-4151	SL	1997
Middendorf Michael P Dr	(949)214-3404	40 Frontier St Trabuco Canyon CA 92679	PSW	S HS/C	Concordia University Irvine Irvine CA	(949)854-8002	SL	1987
Miedema David M	(317)289-4176		SE	SMP	Saint James Southern Pines NC		FW-SMP	2025
Mielke Spencer A	pastormielke@trinityl.org	30888 County Road 6 Elkhart IN 46514	IN	Sn/Adm	Trinity Elkhart IN	(574)674-8800	SL	1998
Miels John A	(715)822-8690 jmiels89@gmail.com	1227 26 1/2 Ave Rice Lake WI 54868	NW	SP	St Paul Cumberland WI	(715)822-8690	FW	2010
Mierow Seth A	(317)730-6769 prmierow@gmail.com	7115 Pluto Dr Indianapolis IN 46241	IN	SP	Saint Peters Indianapolis IN	(317)638-7245	FW	2007
Miesner Duane C	(712) 253-1478 duanemiesner@gmail.com	2273 180th Ave Milford IA 51351	IW	EM			FW	1998
Mietzner Kyle D	(336)944-2394 kyle.mietzner@gmail.com	80002a General Patton St Watertown NY 13603	NOW	M Chap	Office of International Mission Saint Louis MO		SL	2010
Miille Timothy C	(660)538-4688 revsmiley1011@hotmail.com	P.O. Box 85 Blackburn MO 65321	MO	SP	Zion Blackburn MO	(660)538-4688	FW	1996
Mikits Janis C	(314) 931-6003 1517mikits@gmail.com	P.O. Box 344 Salem IN 47167	IN	SP	Faith* Salem IN	(314)931-6003	SL	2024
Mikkelson Robert L	mikkelsonrl@gmail.com	9666 S Bass Ct Pinckney MI 48169	MI	EM			CQ	1996
Miklos Troy A	(817)905-8758 troy.miklos@sharingnewlife.com	128 Shadow Creek Ln Aledo TX 76008	TX	SMP	St Paul Fort Worth TX	(817)332-2281	SL-SMP	2017
Milas Rick R	(217)714-3880 rmilas7@gmail.com	2904 Garrison Ave Port St Joe FL 32456	CI	EM			FW	1979
Milash Bruce P	(815)263-1896 bmilash@stpeterlutheran.org	40w602 Barko Pkwy Huntley IL 60142	NI	SP	St Peter Dundee IL	(847)428-4054	FW	2008
Milbrandt Richard W	(605)222-3353 milbrandtrichard@gmail.com	1079 Pine St Ocheyedan IA 51354	IW	SP	St John* Ocheyedan IA	(712)735-4401	FW	1989
Miles Donald G Dr	(303)589-5253 secondmile@aol.com	9167 E Floyd Pl Denver CO 80231	RM	EM			CQ	1982

*Multiple Assignments (See Church Worker Locator for Additional Details)

See Page 53 for the Table of Abbreviations for key to District, Position, and Seminary abbreviations

**C =Candidate; EM = Emeritus; the date following the C is the month and year the Candidate status began

NAME	TELEPHONE NUMBER EMAIL	STREET ADDRESS CITY/STATE/ZIP	DISTRICT	POSITION/ STATUS**	WHERE SERVING	OFFICE PHONE	SEM/ PROGRAM	YR GRAD
Millard Ronald G Jr	(636)928-5100 millard@lhssc.org	5100 Mexico Rd St Peters MO 63376	MO	Pro Stf	St Charles Saint Peters MO	(636)928-5100	SL	2011
Miller Rick L	(303)709-7456 rlmtetelestai@yahoo.com	1005 Casa Del Sol Apt E La Junta CO 81050	RM	SP	Trinity La Junta CO	(719)384-6555	FW	1987
Miller Micah D	(402)416-1229 micah.miller@princeofpeace.org	3802 Keystone Ct Carrollton TX 75007	TX	Sn/Adm	Prince Peace Carrollton TX	(972)447-9887	SL	2013
Miller Michael A	(541)451-0099	434 E. Grant Street Lebanon OR 97355	NOW	SP	Bethlehem Lebanon OR	(541)258-6393	FW	2012
Miller Michael M	(865)882-1967 mixer50@comcast.net	324 Sunset Ln Harriman TN 37748	MDS	SP	Redeemer Harriman TN	(865)376-7647	SL	1987
Miller Paul E	(760)831-8715 ichthus123@icloud.com	65661 Avenida Dorado Desert Hot Springs CA 92240	PSW	EM			FW	1980
Miller Philip T	(785)304-4882 pastorphilipmiller@gmail.com	c/o Mt Calvary Lutheran 1710 Jenkins St Marysville KS 66508	KS	Sn/Adm	Mount Calvary Marysville KS	(785)562-2046	FW	2004
Miller William D Dr	wmiller@faithlincoln.org	8110 Oshel Ave Lincoln NE 68505	NEB	Sn/Adm	Faith Lincoln NE	(402)466-6861	SL	2008
Miller Wayne J	(251)230-1886 revwjm@outlook.com	10028 Briarcliff Dr S Mobile AL 36608	SO	SP	Grace Mobile AL	(251)433-2749	SL	2015
Miller Randy J	(931)626-3466 revrandymiller@gmail.com	3205 Windy Cape Lane League City TX 77573	TX	Assoc	Gloria Dei Houston TX	(281)333-4535	SL	2002
Miller Ronald C	(309)691-3616 revrmiller@hotmail.com	5414 W Flagstone Dr Peoria IL 61615	CI	EM			SPR	1970
Miller Stephen C	(715)931-0056 tekonshami@yahoo.com	306 Martin Ave W Turtle Lake WI 54889	NW	SP	Christ Comstock WI	(715)931-0056	FW	1977
Miller Stephen W	(314) 772-4474 steve.miller@messiahstl.org	2846 S Grand Blvd Saint Louis MO 63118	MO	Sn/Adm	Messiah Saint Louis MO	(314)772-4474	SL	2013
Miller Thomas R	(714)746-5235 occnslt@gmail.com	13242 Chestnut St Westminster CA 92683	PSW	SMP	Redeemer Huntington Beach CA	(714)846-6330	SL-SMP	2021
Miller Timothy P	(260) 667-4111 ptimmill@gmail.com	2035 Rough Gold Ct Gold River CA 95670	CNH	EM			SL	1981
Miller Warren E Dr	(636)734-9531 jactun@sbcglobal.net	6 Hurstfield Ct Fenton MO 63026	FG	EM			SL	1985
Miller Mark A	(309)267-0452 markamiller1955@gmail.com	2608 Haverford Rd Springfield IL 62704	CI	EM			FW	1983
Miller Richard C	(715)420-0076 816rmiller@gmail.com	816 Balsam St Rhinelander WI 54501	NW	SP	St Mark Rhinelander WI	(715)362-2470	SL	1971
Miller Donald L	(785)218-7115 whiteknight0841@gmail.com	233 Bramble Bend Court Lawrence KS 66049	KS	EM			SL	1967
Miller Richard D	(612)787-8412 nodmin48@gmail.com	303 Wrangler Ln Denton TX 76205	TX	EM			SPR	1974
Miller Alan J	(712)790-8251 alanbecky2000@yahoo.com	301 W 4th Street Alta IA 51002	IW	SP	St Paul Alta IA	(712)200-1133	FW	1991
Miller Bruce H	(641)530-0122 bhmklm1@aol.com	18682 330th St Mason City IA 50401	IE	SP	St Peter Elma IA	(641)393-2558	SL	1999
Miller Carl H	(618)742-8136 pschmqpb@att.net	216 McNiel Street Carterville IL 62918	SI	SP	St John Sparta IL	(618)443-3634	SPR	1974
Miller Chad M	(281)923-3873 lifeforyou@att.net	2414 Horseshoe Ln Richmond TX 77406	TX	SP	Spirit of Life Richmond TX	(281)238-5531	SL	1983
Miller Charles R	(337)526-1500 pastorcharlesm1@gmail.com	111 Orchard Dr Lake Charles LA 70605	SO	SP	St John Lake Charles LA	(337)478-5666	SL	1987
Miller David L III	(616)915-2055 pastormiller@stpaulcaledonia.org	4389 9th St Wayland MI 49348	MI	SP	St Paul Caledonia MI	(616)891-8688	FW	2024
Miller Lucas S	revlucasmiller@gmail.com	507 N 3rd St Plainview NE 68769	NEB	C11/2019			FW	2016
Miller David V	(708)710-4996 pastor@ascension-lcms.com	35 Coopers Glen Drive SW Mableton GA 30126	EN	SP	Ascension Atlanta GA	(404)255-0224	FW	2010
Miller Gary L	(269)313-3016 gary.n8wol@gmail.com	20679 Roberts Drive Sheridan IN 46069	IN	EM			FW	1990
Miller James P	(469)353-8655 patrickmillertx@gmail.com	200 Hayden Hall Rd Bells TX 75414	TX	Sn/Adm	SoulThirst The Colony TX	(469)353-8655	SL	2000
Miller Jeffrey J	(320)510-3674 jeff1812@aol.com	366 School Rd SW Hutchinson MN 55350	MNS	EM			SPR	1971
Miller Joshua C Dr	(651) 644-1421 pastorjoshuamiller@gmail.com		MNS	SP	Jehovah Saint Paul MN	(651)644-1421	CQ	2020
Miller Joshua M	pjmilleris@gmail.com	P.O. Box 1596 Leander TX 78646	TX	SP	ACTS Leander TX	(512)337-6524	SL	2012
Miller Kirk D	(303)868-0117 tinamillerpt@yahoo.com	9796 Teller Ct Westminster CO 80021	RM	EM			SL	1993
Miller Larry A	(406)431-8828 revelry.flc.057@gmail.com	3827 Chokecherry St East Helena MT 59635	MT	Sn/Adm	First Helena MT	(406)442-5367	FW	1983
Miller Louis J	(629) 237-0114 patriciamiller1623@gmail.com	1008 Eddystone Ct Nashville TN 37207	SE	EM			CQ	1994
Miller David P	(715)758-6580 revdpmiller@tds.net	420 Boettcher Ln Bonduel WI 54107	NW	EM			CQ	1990
Milligan John W	(216)392-8560 hlytrinity@aol.com	3711 Washington Park Blvd Newburgh Heights OH 44105	S	SP	Grace* Lakewood OH	(216)221-4959	SL	1980
Mills Jeremy H	(317)989-0403	175 Parkview Ct Carmel IN 46032	IN	SP	Epiphany Westfield IN	(317)815-3884	FW	2007
Mills Ryan E	(307)640-6645 therev2005@hotmail.com	5302 PSC 400 Apo AP 96273	WY	M Chap	Office of International Mission Saint Louis MO		FW	2005
Mills Peter E	(330)573-3842 millspe@earthlink.net	732 Newcastle Dr Akron OH 44313	EN	EM			FW	1996
Milo Frank V	(218)820-6978 frankvmilo@live.com	959 State 84 SW Pine River MN 56474	MNN	EM			SL	1979

*Multiple Assignments (See Church Worker Locator for Additional Details)
See Page 53 for the Table of Abbreviations for key to District, Position, and Seminary abbreviations
**C =Candidate; EM = Emeritus; the date following the C is the month and year the Candidate status began

NAME	TELEPHONE NUMBER EMAIL	STREET ADDRESS CITY/STATE/ZIP	DISTRICT	POSITION/ STATUS**	WHERE SERVING	OFFICE PHONE	SEM/ PROGRAM	YR GRAD
Milz David S	(320)492-2436 minnmilz@gmail.com		MNS	EM			SL	1994
Milz Norman W	(775)315-6740 revmilz@gmail.com	1534 Oreana Dr Carson City NV 89701	CNH	EM			SL	2007
Miner David B	(540)491-3469 pastor2@redeemerfxbg.org	15 Pennsbury Ct Fredericksburg VA 22406	SE	SMP	Redeemer Fredericksburg VA	(540)898-4748	CQ	2020
Minetola Victor J	(317)764-7424 victor.minetola@gmail.com	1425 N New Jersey St Indianapolis IN 46202	IN	C05/2023			SL-SMP	2019
Minetree Charles C III	(443)615-4852 cminetree@verizon.net	1911 Lydonlea Way Baltimore MD 21239	SE	SP	Immanuel Baltimore MD	(410)435-6861	SL	1987
Minnix Roy W III Dr	(914)588-1463 roy.minnix@gmail.com	11601 Autumnwood Way Glen Allen VA 23059	SE	Sn/Adm	Trinity Richmond VA	(804)270-4626	SL	2006
Minnix Roy W Jr	(609)709-3786 rwminnix@gmail.com	258 W 20th St Ship Bottom NJ 08008	NJ	EM			SL	1973
Minton Harold D Jr	(507)626-0202 wrestlingwiththeology@gmail.com	211 W Jones St Milford IL 60953	CI	SP	Our Savior Milford IL	(815)889-4121	SL	2007
Mirly Ray G Dr	(314)920-1103 rgmirly@gmail.com	27125 W Mohawk Ln Buckeye AZ 85396	PSW	EM			CQ	1977
Mirtschin Neville	(705)326-8666 neville@mirtschin.org	604 Moberley Ave Orillia ON L3V-6 CANADA	EN	EM			CQ	1972
Misch Jonathan Z	(602)582-7473 zach.misch@gmail.com	1120 Sulphur Springs Rd Waynesville NC 28786	SE	SP	Our Savior Clyde NC	(828)456-6493	SL	2013
Misch Stephen N	(361)728-9796 stephen.misch@gmail.com	1401 W 7th St Plainview TX 79072	TX	SP	St Paul Plainview TX	(806)293-1697	SL	2012
Misch Steven J	(806)433-4536 steven.misch@gmail.com	1511 Gawain St Borger TX 79007	TX	EM			SL	1982
Mischnick Mark R	(605)292-0263 themischnicks@midco.net	1418 Mitchell Blvd Mitchell SD 57301	SD	EM			CQ	1998
Miskus Jeffrey G	(647)825-7712 jmiskus@englishdistrict.org	3459 Caribou Crescent Windsor ON N8W5V CANADA	EN	DP	English District* Farmington MI	(248)476-0039	NESC	1994
Missling Scot D	(612) 845-1966 sdmissling@gmail.com	247 Ash St E South Saint Paul MN 55075	MNS	SP	Bethlehem Saint Paul MN	(651)776-4737	SL	2023
Mitchell John W Jr	(225)772-4120 jwmjr97@gmail.com	5071 Lord Alfred Ct Cincinnati OH 45241	OH	EM			SL	1987
Mitchell Lawrence W	(812)339-9275 lwm1974spfld@gmail.com	720 E Eddington Ct Bloomington IN 47401	IN	EM			SPR	1974
Mitchell Herbert D	1940borders@gmail.com		FG	EM			SL	1966
Mitchell Christopher W Dr	chris.mitchell@cph.org	8921 Westhaven Ct Saint Louis MO 63126	MO	Pro Stf	Concordia Publishing House Saint Louis MO	(314)268-1000	SL	1987
Mitchell Jerome K	(440)781-2898 jerry@joshuacalebleaders.org	10076 Barr Road Brecksville OH 44141	OH	C02/2020			FW	1990
Mitkos Leslie J Jr Dr	(217)851-5767 lmitkosjr@gmail.com	911 S Main St Concordia MO 64020	MO	EM			FW	1976
Mitschke Herman M	(760)944-6253	955 Sealane Dr Encinitas CA 92024	PSW	EM			SL	1950
Mitschke Kenneth R	(210)862-7629 Ken@WordofLife4u.com	1531 Jasmine Dr Schertz TX 78154	TX	Sn/Adm	Word of Life Cibolo TX	(210)566-2237	SL	1987
Mitschke William T	(815)725-1341	2500 Hacker Dr Joliet IL 60435	NI	SP	Trinity Dwight IL		SL	1958
Mitteis Kelly G	(618)979-7991 kmitteis55@gmail.com	17973 Staunton Bunker Hill Rd Staunton IL 62088	SI	SP	Trinity Girard IL	(217)697-0072	SL	2002
Mittelstadt Richard A	(830)433-1811 lutheranmittelstadt@hotmail.com	1401 First Street Brownwood TX 76801	TX	SP	Grace Brownwood TX	(325)646-2045	FW	2007
Mittelstaedt Neil A	(631)621-5072 pastorneil@stjlc.com	193 Woodlawn Ave Saint James NY 11780	AT	Sn/Adm	Saint James Saint James NY	(631)584-5212	NESC	1989
Mittwede Richard A	(512) 461-3425 richard@ulcaustin.com	3207 E 18th St Austin TX 78721	TX	EM			SL	2008
Mize Gaven M	(838)308-9765 pastormize@gmail.com	302 Frontier Cir China Grove NC 28023	SE	C11/2021			FW	2011
Mizel Christopher R Dr	(307)389-1340 christophermizel@gmail.com	3905 Goshawk Dr Rock Springs WY 82901	MO	D Miss	Missouri District Saint Louis MO	(314)590-6200	SL	2011
Moe John M	(651)271-4601 revmoe@mail.com	21340 County Road 1 Emily MN 56447	MNN	EM			SL	1982
Moe Soe	(260)316-2468 soemoe@southwestlutheran.org	3714 Congress Ave Fort Wayne IN 46806	IN	Assoc	Southwest Fort Wayne IN	(260)436-4474	EIITSL	2023
Moe Timothy E	(715)379-5898 timothymoe400@icloud.com	4818 Rye Ct Eau Claire WI 54701	NW	EM			SL	1990
Moehring Martin K	(260)223-0310 martin_moehring@comcast.net	2933 Old Orchard Rd Fort Wayne IN 46804	IN	EM			FW	1982
Moeller Randall J	(636)349-9458 rmoeller@oursaviorlcs.org	842 San Sebastian Dr Fenton MO 63026	MO	EM			SL	2006
Moeller Theodore C III Dr	(360)600-0274 pastor@vanflock.org	14621 NE 49th Cir Vancouver WA 98682	NOW	SP	Good Shepherd Vancouver WA	(360)254-5158	Other	1982
Moeller Robert E Jr	(605)321-1641 seelsorge8@aol.com	P.O. Box J Britton SD 57430	SD	SP	St Paul* Ferney SD	(605)395-6420	FW	2001
Moeller Eric J Dr	(956)884-5579 pastoreric60@gmail.com	1028 Chillem Dr Batavia IL 60510	NI	SP	Trinity West Chicago IL	(630)231-1175	SL	1989
Moeller Dwight F	(918)785-2994	10820 N 429 Rd Adair OK 74330	OK	SP	Bethlehem Adair OK	(918)785-2994	FW	2008
Moeller Daniel G	(715)866-4733 pdanmoeller@gmail.com	28515 Jensen Rd Danbury WI 54830	NW	EM			FW	1983
Moeller William F Jr	(218)634-2808 williamfm01@yahoo.com	P.O. Box 694 Baudette MN 56623	MNN	SP	Bethlehem* Warroad MN	(218)386-3555	SL	1993

*Multiple Assignments (See Church Worker Locator for Additional Details)

See Page 53 for the Table of Abbreviations for key to District, Position, and Seminary abbreviations

**C =Candidate; EM = Emeritus; the date following the C is the month and year the Candidate status began

NAME	TELEPHONE NUMBER EMAIL	STREET ADDRESS CITY/STATE/ZIP	DISTRICT	POSITION/ STATUS**	WHERE SERVING	OFFICE PHONE	SEM/ PROGRAM	YR GRAD
Moeller John S	(708)927-2434 jomamo1999@gmail.com	P.O. Box 224 Walcott IA 52773	IE	EM			SL	1999
Moen Darrel T	(716)432-0687 dtmoen@roadrunner.com	11173 Route 39 Gowanda NY 14070	EA	EM			FW	2003
Moerbe David C	(205)841-5325 dmoerbe2456@gmail.com	467 Gowins Dr Gardendale AL 35071	SO	Sn/Adm	Good Shepherd Gardendale AL	(205)631-6590	SL	2002
Moerbe Ned A	(580)262-9220 nmoerbe@mlchouston.org	12218 Rocky Knoll Dr Houston TX 77077	TX	Sn/Adm	Memorial Houston TX	(713)782-6079	FW	2009
Mohr Gary W	(510)538-0941 retiredgm2010@hotmail.com	23400 Mona Marie Ct Hayward CA 94541	CNH	EM			CQ	1991
Mohr Gerry W	(260)497-7959 gwm1217@yahoo.com	11515 Green Holly CV Fort Wayne IN 46845	OH	EM			FW	1977
Mohr Michael W	(217) 793-1802 mmohr@cidlcms.org	1850 N Grand Ave W Springfield IL 62702	CI	DP	Central Illinois District* Springfield IL	(217)793-1802	SL	1998
Mohr Richard A	(214)356-3402 richmohr@icloud.com	200 River Rd Coppell TX 75019	TX	EM			SPR	1974
Mokry Richard M Dr	(215)584-1262 richmokry@gmail.com	1040 Forest Lakes Dr Naples FL 34105	FG	SP	Peace Naples FL	(239)354-9144	CQ	2001
Mol Aaron J	aaronmolofficial@gmail.com	244 Mistwood Ln North Aurora IL 60542	NI	SP	St Luke Montgomery IL	(630)892-9309	SL	2017
Moldenhauer Joshua P	(605)759-8872 pastorjoshm08@gmail.com	25 First St NW Elgin MN 55932	MNS	SP	Trinity Elgin MN	(507)876-2671	SL	2008
Moldenhauer Mark A	(979)551-2293 mmoldenhauer1@gmail.com	660 Gillespie Rd Madison AL 35758	SO	SP	Faith Madison AL	(256)830-5600	SL	2004
Moldenhauer Paul M	(248)550-4855 pastorpaul@st-matthew.org	2020 S Commerce Rd Walled Lake MI 48390	MI	Sn/Adm	St Matthew Walled Lake MI	(248)624-7676	FW	1981
Moldenhauer Roger R	(715)574-1013 rogerm38@me.com	129099 Hillwood Rd Edgar WI 54426	NW	Assoc	St Paul Stevens Point WI	(715)344-5660	SL	1965
Moldenhauer Aaron M Dr	(262)243-4383 aaron.moldenhauer@cuw.edu	12800 N Lake Shore Drive Mequon WI 53097	SW	S HS/C	Concordia University Wisconsin Mequon WI	(262)243-5700	FW	2005
Moline Adam S	pastormoline@goodshepherd lincoln.org	2900 Crown Pointe Rd Lincoln NE 68506	NEB	Sn/Adm	Good Shepherd Lincoln NE	(402)423-7639	FW	2010
Molitoris Craig L	(714)308-9353 craigmolitoris@gmail.com	5414 Eau Claire Dr Rancho Palos Verdes CA 90275	PSW	EM			SL	1985
Molitoris Joseph	(904)230-1976 josephmolitoris@comcast.net	609 Sparrow Branch Cir Saint Johns FL 32259	EN	EM			SPR	1962
Moll James P	(402)365-4181 jemoll@gpcom.net	214 Crestview Dr Deshler NE 68340	NEB	SP	Zion Shickley NE	(402)366-5818	CQ	1977
Moll Robert L	(847)382-3292 mollcenter@aol.com	509 Park Barrington Way Barrington IL 60010	NI	EM			CQ	1981
Molnar Stephen C	(805)458-4686 scmolnar2010@gmail.com	1732 E Flame Bush St Kingman AZ 86409	CNH	EM			SL	1979
Molyneux Daniel R Dr	(707)330-2040 pastordanmolyneux@yahoo.com	18306 Cobblestone Dr Cypress TX 77429	TX	EM			CQ	2003
Mommens David R	(320)256-3840 pastor.mommens@gmail.com	519 4th Ave NE Melrose MN 56352	MNN	SP	Saint Pauls Melrose MN	(320)256-3847	SL	2015
Mommens David A	(260)750-2900 dmommens@icloud.com	5875 N Center St Columbia City IN 46725	IN	EM			FW	1984
Monday Dakota S	(336)596-0347 dakota.monday@ctsfw.edu	174 Pine Park Dr Lexington NC 27295	SE	SP	St Paul Whispering Pines NC	(910)949-2345	FW	2023
Mongeau Kevin A	(860)496-1392 kevin_mongeau@yahoo.com	220 Cedar Ln New Hartford CT 06057	NE	SMP	Saint Pauls New Hartford CT	(860)379-3172	SL-SMP	2014
Mons William M	(319)337-3652 wmaxmons@gmail.com	c/o Saint Paul's Lutheran Chapel 404 E Jefferson St Iowa City IA 52245	IE	SP	St Paul Iowa City IA	(319)337-3652	SL	1996
Monson John R	(248)526-1699	2380 Terova Dr Troy MI 48085	MI	EM			SL	1961
Monson Paul C	(248)879-0464 paul197251@msn.com	135 McKinley Dr Troy MI 48098	MI	Sn/Adm	Saint Augustine Troy MI	(248)879-6400	SL	1997
Monterastelli Michael S	(936)404-9660 michael.monterastelli@gmail.com	980798 S 3308 Road Wellston OK 74881	OK	Asst	St Paul Wellston OK	(405)356-4203	FW	2007
Montgomery John W Dr	01133-388610882 106612.1066@compuserve.com	2 Rue De Rome Strasbourg 67000 FRANCE	NOW	EM			CQ	1965
Montgomery Matthew J	(815)768-6469 matthew.montgomery@ctsfw.edu		IN	S HS/C	Concordia Theological Seminary Fort Wayne IN	(260)452-2100	FW	2015
Moody Richard A	(314)406-1082 revrmoody@aol.com	90 W Lakewood Dr Fenton MO 63026	MO	EM			SL	1979
Moog Mark A	(812)454-1575 mamoog52@gmail.com	1131 B Shooters Hill Ct Evansville IN 47725	IN	EM			CQ	2012
Moon Colin M	(414)870-6696 pastormoonshine@gmail.com	104 Redwood Ct Bonduel WI 54107	SW	C09/2025			SL	2020
Moon Harry H	(714)884-0481 harryhunmoon@gmail.com	2481 Via Castillo Tustin CA 92782	PSW	EM			CQ	1990
Moon Shang I	(949) 559-1881	13842 Typee Way Irvine CA 92620	PSW	EM			SL	1963
Moon Aidan M	(719) 653-1003 aidanmoon@foccs.net	675 W Baptist Rd Colorado Springs CO 80921	RM	Assoc	Family Of Christ Colorado Springs CO	(719)481-2255	SL	2023
Moore John M	(641)521-3000 pastor.jmmoore@gmail.com	21419 Russell Chase Dr Porter TX 77365	TX	SP	Our Shepherd Huffman TX		SL	1986
Moore Adam P	(860)368-1480 adam71992@gmail.com	54 Muddy Brook Road Ellington CT 06029	NE	SMP	Good Shepherd Suffield CT	(860)668-2790	FW-SMP	2020
Moore William T	(901)755-1576 bama3521@aol.com	8865 Quailwood Cove Cordova TN 38018	MDS	EM			CQ	2018

*Multiple Assignments (See Church Worker Locator for Additional Details)

See Page 53 for the Table of Abbreviations for key to District, Position, and Seminary abbreviations

**C =Candidate; EM = Emeritus; the date following the C is the month and year the Candidate status began

NAME	TELEPHONE NUMBER EMAIL	STREET ADDRESS CITY/STATE/ZIP	DISTRICT	POSITION/ STATUS**	WHERE SERVING	OFFICE PHONE	SEM/ PROGRAM	YR GRAD
Moore Tyler C	(407)761-9255 therevty@gmail.com	c/o Immanuel Lutheran Church 305 9th St Hood River OR 97031	NOW	SP	Immanuel Hood River OR	(541)386-3046	SL	2012
Moore Richard A	(507)474-0355 pastor.moore@stmartinswinona.org	272 Knopp Valley Dr Winona MN 55987	MNS	Sn/Adm	St Martin Winona MN	(507)452-6928	SL	1985
Moore Kevin D	(509)449-5572 bemusedkdm@gmail.com	221 E. 1st Street Redfield SD 57469	SD	SP	Redeemer* Doland SD	(605)472-0730	SL	1990
Moore Jeffery C Dr	(407)446-5638 revjcmoore@gmail.com	2 Fountainebleau Cir Daytona Beach FL 32118	FG	EM			SL	1980
Moore Jacob M	(636)582-0685 revjake23@outlook.com	300 E Gibson St New Berlin IL 62670	CI	SP	St John New Berlin IL	(217)488-3190	SL	2023
Moore Donald A Jr	(407)464-5967 stpaullcms@embarqmail.com	2266 Lake Marion Dr Apopka FL 32712	FG	SP	St Paul Apopka FL	(407)889-2634	SL	1999
Moore David W	(816)248-9646 pastorm@splcc.org	4814 S Lakewood Dr Saint Joseph MO 64506	MO	Sn/Adm	St Paul Saint Joseph MO	(816)279-1110	SL	2007
Moore Brendon T	(316)708-0688 bemoorebrendon@gmail.com	1660 E Winterset St Goddard KS 67052	KS	Assoc	Ascension Wichita KS	(316)722-4694	SL	2021
Moore David R Dr	(925)708-5127 drmoore4@gmail.com	250 Augustine Dr Martinez CA 94553	CNH	EM			FW	1986
Moorhead William G IV Dr	(402)651-2239 revhawk@cox.net	9521 West Center Road Omaha NE 68124	NEB	EM			SL	1973
Moorman Seth J	(562)307-6122 mrmoorman@yahoo.com	5852 E Pavo St Long Beach CA 90808	PSW	C07/2022			SL	2008
Moquin Eric M	(419)439-8470 emoquin@gmail.com	11984 Lockwood Rd Sherwood OH 43556	OH	SP	St John Sherwood OH	(419)899-2850	SL	2012
Morales Luis E	(830)522-5090 lemorales@cristoelsalvador.org	703 Pierce St Del Rio TX 78840	TX	D Miss	Texas District Round Rock TX	(800)951-3478	SL	2023
Morales Moises	52 741 122 0149 mm10517@gmail.com	1900 23rd St San Pablo CA 94866	CNH	Assoc	Mount Zion Richmond CA	(510)685-9662	Other	2020
Morales Oscar G	(260)214-0648	2732 Trudeau Ln Palmdale CA 93551	PSW	EM			HITSL	2005
Morales Eddie	(248)302-0037 odflc1@yahoo.com	22835 Lisa Ct Farmingtn Hls MI 48335	MI	SP	Outer Dr Faith Detroit MI	(313)341-4095	FW	1999
Morales Angel G	(630)715-8805 builders2x4@yahoo.com	807 S Edgelawn Dr Aurora IL 60506	NI	SP	New Song Aurora IL	(630)499-0542	SL	2013
Morales Jesus G	(312)522-3966 jesusmorales466@yahoo.com	807 S Edgelawn Dr Aurora IL 60190	NI	SP	Christ Our Savior Winfield IL	(630)665-5110	SL	2022
Moran David R	(269)967-7586 revdavidmoran@gmail.com	17328 G Dr N Marshall MI 49068	MI	SMP	Christ Marshall MI	(269)781-5842	CQ	2018
Mordhorst Robert L Dr	(302)212-9083 bob.mordhorst@gmail.com	9531-1 Veirs Dr Rockville MD 20850	SE	EM			SL	1965
Morehouse Michael A Dr	(520)349-8440 pastormorehouse@catalinalutheran.org	15879 N Twin Lakes Dr Tucson AZ 85739	EN	Sn/Adm	Catalina Tucson AZ	(520)825-9255	FW	1998
Moreno Jason A	(832)784-2349 lcmspastor@gmail.com	18230 Brightwood Park Ln Richmond TX 77407	TX	SP	Christ Memorial Houston TX	(281)497-0250	SL	2007
Moreno Mark C Dr	(321)242-1610 markmoreno@foccs.net		RM	Sn/Adm	Family Of Christ Colorado Springs CO	(719)481-2255	SL	2002
Moreno Michael P	(402)316-8873	1401 Homewood Dr Norfolk NE 68701	NEB	Sn/Adm	Christ Norfolk NE	(402)371-1210	FW	1990
Moretz Mark D	(828)781-2287 pastormarkmoretz@gmail.com		SE	SP	Concordia Hagerstown MD	(301)797-5955	SL	2018
Morey Jeffrey D	(209) 581-3463 jeffmorey@sbcglobal.net	2412 Van Layden Way Modesto CA 95356	CNH	SMP	Trinity Stockton CA	(209)464-1936	SL-SMP	2014
Morfitt David C	(224)627-6124 dmorfitt@aol.com	2711 West Oak Hill Dr Sioux Falls SD 57108	SD	EM			SL	2008
Morfitt Steven A	(956)548-0579 stevmorf@aol.com	1265 Bluebonnet Dr Brownsville TX 78521	TX	SP	Mount Calvary* Raymondville TX	(956)689-2224	SL	1982
Morgan Joel C	(513)300-5017 pastorjoel0410@gmail.com	5757 McCarthy Ct West Chester OH 45069	OH	SP	Prince of Peace Cincinnati OH	(513)621-7265	FW	1988
Moritz Ronald C	(269)858-8888 pasmoritz@dls.net	50470 Robin Way P.O. Box 92 Marcellus MI 49067	MI	EM			SPR	1972
Mork Joshua D	(218)303-6049	P.O. Box 607 Howard SD 57349	SD	SP	St John* Howard SD	(605)256-4483	SL	2020
Morner Dennis D	(907)529-6973 dennismorner@gmail.com	8710 Bell Pl Anchorage AK 99507	NOW	EM			FW	1981
Morris Robert H II	(978)500-4245 rcmorris727@hotmail.com	81 Mount Pleasant Rd Newtown CT 06470	NE	SP	Christ King Newtown CT	(203)426-6300	CQ	2012
Morris Timothy E	(573)499-0443 pastortim@aic.org	201 Southampton Dr Columbia MO 65203	MO	Sn/Adm	Alive in Christ Columbia MO	(573)499-0443	SL	1998
Morris George W II	(989)414-0817 pastorgeorgemorris@yahoo.com	P. O. Box 697 Watertown MN 55388	MNS	Sn/Adm	St Pauls Watertown MN	(952)955-1498	SL	2008
Morris Robert S	(480)521-3141 bsm911@live.com	1573 E Jeanne Ln San Tan Valley AZ 85140	PSW	EM			SL	1979
Morris William L Dr	(989)255-4922 william.morris@stpeterhemlock.org	933 Poplar Dr Saginaw MI 48609	MI	Sn/Adm	St Peter Hemlock MI	(989)642-8188	FW	1986
Morris Kristan J	(503)480-0889 pastor@christthevinelutheran.org	3611 SE Hillside Dr Milwaukie OR 97267	NOW	EM			FW	2005
Morris Alarik D	(860)428-7754	330 West Tipton St. Seymour IN 47274	IN	SP	Peace Seymour IN	(812)523-3838	SL	2022
Morris Kristopher M	(573)286-3862 kristopher.morris@cune.edu	800 N Columbia Ave Seward NE 68434	NEB	S HS/C	Concordia University Nebraska Seward NE	(402)643-3651	SL	2005
Morris Ralph C	(308)436-2662 rpmorris1936@gmail.com	1755 Flaten Ave Gering NE 69341	WY	EM			FW	1978

*Multiple Assignments (See Church Worker Locator for Additional Details)
See Page 53 for the Table of Abbreviations for key to District, Position, and Seminary abbreviations
**C =Candidate; EM = Emeritus; the date following the C is the month and year the Candidate status began

ORDAINED MINISTERS

NAME	TELEPHONE NUMBER EMAIL	STREET ADDRESS CITY/STATE/ZIP	DISTRICT	POSITION/ STATUS**	WHERE SERVING	OFFICE PHONE	SEM/ PROGRAM	YR GRAD
Morrow Edwin L	morrowelm@gmail.com	2020 Flamingo Way Franklin IN 46131	IN	EM			FW	1991
Morsching Samuel L	(507)272-9954 pastormorsching@gmail.com	1207 Ridgewood Cir Phillips WI 54555	NW	SP	Trinity* Phillips WI	(715)339-3495	SL	2007
Morten Carl R	(404)667-7668 mortencarl@yahoo.com	2544 Greenville Way Decatur GA 30034	FG	SMP	Lord Of Life Stockbridge GA	(470)278-5837	SL-SMP	2019
Mortenson Jeffrey E	(262)880-0614 threemofwi@netzero.net	1813 Cloverview St West Bend WI 53095	SW	EM			SL	1983
Mortenson Matthew C	mortenson1@gmail.com	29 Jadwin Dr Fort Leonard Wood MO 65473	NEB	M Chap	Office of International Mission Saint Louis MO		SL	2008
Morton R W	(928)242-5332 waynemorton53@gmail.com	8745 W 260n Shipshewana IN 46565	EN	EM			FW	1994
Morton Douglas V	(605)691-4576 dmorton@ilt.edu	5141 S 195th Cir Omaha NE 68135	NEB	EM			SL	1979
Mosemann Brian M	(605)387-5188 brianmosemann@icloud.com	P.O. Box 354 Menno SD 57045	SD	SP	Immanuel* Menno SD	(605)387-5188	Other	2008
Moser C D	(828)408-3969 cdavidmoser@gmail.com	822 2nd St NW Conover NC 28613	SE	C07/2016			Other	1979
Moser Stephen C	(417)755-0522 smoser1959@yahoo.com	5473 Twelve Oaks Rd Springfield MO 65810	MO	Assoc	Redeemer Springfield MO	(417)881-5470	FW	1988
Moshier James A	(308)962-7667 james_moshier@yahoo.com	1006 9th St Arapahoe NE 68922	NEB	SP	Trinity Arapahoe NE	(308)962-7667	FW	2010
Moskovites Nicholas	(239)470-4845	4495 Watercolor Way Fort Myers FL 33966	FG	EM			CQ	2016
Moss Matthew V	(763)496-5350 pastor.moss@stjlutheran.org	9671 97th Place N Maple Grove MN 55369	MNS	Sn/Adm	St John's Corcoran MN	(763)420-2426	FW	2012
Moss Mark E	(253)888-2610 mmoss@lhfmissions.org	13300 Elm Dr Burnsville MN 55337	MNS	RSO	Lutheran Heritage Foundation Macomb MI	(800)554-0723	FW	1986
Mossman Donald J Dr	(360)223-0164	4109 E Cortez St Phoenix AZ 85028	PSW	EM			SPR	1964
Moyer Gregory S	(402)301-7546	325 E Queenwood Rd Morton IL 61550	CI	Assoc	Bethel Morton IL	(309)263-2417	SL	2008
Moyer Jonathan J	(810)771-8177 pastormoyer@faithviera.org	443 Wenthrop Cir Rockledge FL 32955	S	Assoc	Faith Viera Rockledge FL	(321)636-5504	SL	2009
Moyer Thomas E	(248)795-8303 temgem@gmail.com	6394 Autumn Ridge Dr Madison OH 44057	OH	EM			FW	1985
Mozeik Mark A	(580)291-1480 pastor_mozeik@sbcglobal.net	P.O. Box 700 Meade KS 67864	KS	SP	St John Meade KS	(620)873-2966	FW	2011
Mrosko Robert A	(262)409-3958 rmrosko@goblc.org	N24w22431 Elmwood Dr Waukesha WI 53186	SW	Sn/Adm	Brookfield Brookfield WI	(262)783-4270	SL	1997
Mroz Vincent A	(412)298-5149 pghdeafoutreach@gmail.com	1616 Ardmore Blvd Pittsburgh PA 15221	EA	Df Min	Eastern District Williamsville NY	(716)634-5111	SL	2025
Muchow Donald K Dr	ambithor@yahoo.com	485 Faircrest Dr Buda TX 78610	TX	EM			SL	1962
Muchow Jeffrey A	(281)630-2431 jmuchow@elcsh.org	12514 Grove Hollow Ct Houston TX 77065	TX	Sn/Adm	Epiphany Houston TX	(713)896-1773	ED	1993
Muck Alan D	(314)517-0873 amuck726@yahoo.com	9828 Devils Lake Hwy Manitou Beach MI 49253	MI	EM			SL-SMP	2011
Mudge Ronald R Jr Dr	(314)505-7014 mudger@csl.edu	801 Seminary Place St. Louis MO 63105	MO	S HS/C	Concordia Seminary Saint Louis MO	(314)505-7000	SL	1996
Muecke Dan W	(719)966-9334 rev.d.muecke@gmail.com	104 Lakeview Dr Weare NH 03281	NE	EM			SL	2004
Muehler Craig G	(571)234-0073 craig.muehler@lcms.org	973 Villa Gran Way Fenton MO 63026	MO	S Ex/S	Office of International Mission Saint Louis MO		SL	1988
Muehler Gary A	(660)530-7882 efmuehler@gmail.com	202 S West St Concordia MO 64020	MO	EM			SPR	1966
Muehler Carl	(757)412-5410 carl.muehler@cvn70.navy.mil	1897 Cabrena St San Diego CA 92154	MO	M Chap	Office of International Mission Saint Louis MO		SL	2003
Mueller Robert B	(908)782-5120 bob@stpaulnj.com	201 State Route 31 Flemington NJ 08822	NJ	Sn/Adm	St Paul Flemington NJ	(908)782-5120	SL	2001
Mueller Michael L	(661)406-0659 pastormlmueller@sbcglobal.net	25326 Tether Ln Punta Gorda FL 33983	FG	EM			CQ	2011
Mueller Thomas P	(605) 467-1645 tpmueller59@gmail.com	100 West Kellam Avenue Chamberlain SD 57325	SD	SP	Zion* Waubay SD	(605)520-9919	SL	2022
Mueller Paul G	(715)423-8649 pgm@wctc.net	1710 Plum St Wisc Rapids WI 54494	NW	EM			SL	1964
Mueller Paul W Dr	(651)587-2705 PaulWMueller@gmail.com	4650 Links Village Dr N Unit B102 Ponce Inlet FL 32127	FG	EM			SL	1983
Mueller Peter C	(714)227-2484 pmueller@hopeseattle.org	4456 42nd Ave SW Seattle WA 98116	NOW	SP	Hope Seattle WA	(206)937-9330	CQ	2004
Mueller Peter E	(512)623-9867 pmuelleraustin@gmail.com	16116 Zagros Way Bee Cave TX 78738	TX	SP	Acts Austin TX	(512)263-8175	CQ	1998
Mueller Peter L	(732)754-5472 peteandadele@msn.com	30 Riverside Dr Elkton MD 21921	SE	EM			SL	1984
Mueller Randall F Dr	(352)584-3241 rfmueller2@gmail.com	530 N Silverbrook Dr #222 West Bend WI 53090	SW	EM			SL	1973
Mueller Richard C	(308)760-7213	1031 Dakota Ave Alliance NE 69301	WY	Sn/Adm	Immanuel Alliance NE	(308)762-4663	SL	1990
Mueller Robert R	(505)256-2735 robert.mueller5@va.gov	Nmvahcs Dept 125 Chaplains 1501 San Pedro Dr SE Albuquerque NM 87108	RM	Inst C	Office of National Mission Saint Louis MO		FW	1988
Mueller Ronald A	(937)848-2733 ronald.mueller@sbcglobal.net	2280 Byron View Dr SW Ste 907 Byron Center MI 49315	OH	EM			SL	1958

*Multiple Assignments (See Church Worker Locator for Additional Details)
See Page 53 for the Table of Abbreviations for key to District, Position, and Seminary abbreviations
**C =Candidate; EM = Emeritus; the date following the C is the month and year the Candidate status began

NAME	TELEPHONE NUMBER EMAIL	STREET ADDRESS CITY/STATE/ZIP	DISTRICT	POSITION/ STATUS**	WHERE SERVING	OFFICE PHONE	SEM/ PROGRAM	YR GRAD
Mueller Ronald R	(352)237-3162 ronrmueller@gmail.com	10700 SW 53rd Cir Ocala FL 34476	FG	EM			SL	1965
Mueller Ronald W	(715)931-0879 ron.kathy.mueller@gmail.com	18533 77th Ave N Chippewa FLS WI 54729	NW	EM			SPR	1973
Mueller Stephen M	(715)850-2789 smuellerixthus@gmail.com	5983 Edward Dr Sturgeon Bay WI 54235	NW	EM			SL	1982
Mueller Stephen M	(309)944-3993 pastor.smueller@yahoo.com	318 S Oakwood Ave Geneseo IL 61254	CI	SP	Concordia Geneseo IL	(309)944-3993	SL	2008
Mueller Marvin F	marvmuel36@yahoo.com	6853 Pine St Eight Mile AL 36613	SO	EM			SL	1961
Mueller Thomas H	(805)835-7887 thmpls@aol.com	225 Davenport Ct Sartell MN 56377	MNN	EM			SPR	1975
Mueller Jonathan R	(859)533-7411 jonrmueller@yahoo.com	1705 Leestown Rd Apt 301 Lexington KY 40511	IN	SP	Risen Lord Taylorsville KY	(502)477-6557	FW	2004
Mueller Timothy P	(618)478-5544 tpm@frontiernet.net	15516 State Route 127 Nashville IL 62263	SI	SP	St Luke* Okawville IL	(618)478-5544	SL	1987
Mueller William E	(260) 484-7873	6318 W California Rd Fort Wayne IN 46818	IN	Sn/Adm	Sub Bethlehem Fort Wayne IN	(260)484-7873	SL	1994
Mueller Steven P Dr	(949)214-3386 steve.mueller@cui.edu	1530 Concordia West Irvine CA 92612	PSW	Asst	St Paul* Irvine CA	(949)599-4760	FW	1990
Mueller Bart A	(660)463-1960 bart4c@frontier.com	510 S Travis St Concordia MO 64020	MO	EM			SL	1986
Mueller Aaron J	(618)670-1299 aaronjamesmueller@gmail.com	2124 Greenbriar Rd Springfield IL 62704	CI	Sn/Adm	Trinity Springfield IL	(217)787-2323	CQ	2015
Mueller Mark A	(518)369-5861 mmueller@ascensionlcms.org	831 Hillary Ct Longwood FL 32750	FG	Sn/Adm	Ascension Casselberry FL	(407)831-7788	SL	1999
Mueller Barry L	(586)883-3983 bjmueller@comcast.net	70521 Karen St Richmond MI 48062	MI	EM			FW	1988
Mueller Mark A		1784 Augusta Dr Apt 204 Ft Myers FL 33907	SW	EM			SL	1976
Mueller Charles S Jr Dr	(630)707-7707 csmuellerjr@gmail.com	479 Pintail Ct Bloomingdale IL 60108	NI	EM			SL	1982
Mueller Daniel G Dr	(210) 400-3328 dmuellerretired@gmail.com	8511 Fairway Trace Fair Oaks Ranch TX 78015	TX	EM			SL	1975
Mueller David L	(573) 826-0005 dmueller55146@gmail.com	146 Boulder Dr Dublin NH 03444	NE	SP	Good Shepherd Peterborough NH	(603)924-4019	SL	1981
Mueller David R		213 W Jasper St Goodland IN 47948	IN	SP	Trinity* Goodland IN	(219)297-3556	FW	2000
Mueller Herbert C III	(319)238-3518	22551 County Road 25 Lewiston MN 55952	MNS	SP	Immanuel Lewiston MN	(507)523-2228	SL	2004
Mueller Jacob T	(816)565-3728 rev.jacob.mueller@gmail.com	5734 Connell Dr Shawnee KS 66203	KS	Sn/Adm	Hope Shawnee KS	(913)631-6940	SL	2012
Mueller James L Dr	(512)351-5983 mueller0024@yahoo.com	c/o Messiah Lutheran Church 5911 MO-94 Weldon Spring MO 63304	MO	Sn/Adm	Messiah Weldon Spring MO	(636)926-9773	SL	2003
Mueller James P	(573)469-2983 jim.mueller@lssliving.org	1314 W Main St Jefferson Cty MO 65109	MO	Inst C	Lutheran Senior Services DBA EverTrue Brentwood MO	(314)968-9313	SL	2008
Mueller Jeffrey E	(541)645-0191 pastorjmueller@gmail.com	P.O. Box 384463 Waikoloa HI 96738	CNH	SP	Waikoloa Waikoloa HI	(808)883-9255	SL	1993
Mueller Jeffrey G	(414)416-2118 berea.pastor@sbcglobal.net	P.O. Box 125 Land O Lakes WI 54540	NW	SMP	Hope Watersmeet MI	(906)544-2259	FW-SMP	2010
Mueller John F Dr	(815)374-5057 revpm56@gmail.com	315 E Mazon Ave Dwight IL 60420	NI	SP	Emmanuel Dwight IL	(815)584-3433	SL	1982
Mueller John H	(209)918-1112 7jhmueller@comcast.net	3109 Highgate Rd Modesto CA 95350	CNH	EM			SL	1982
Mueller John W	(513)309-8771 pjwm6297@gmail.com	6297 Inverness Way Mason OH 45040	OH	EM			SL	1978
Mueller Marcus R	(361)433-1064 muellervtx@gmail.com	201 Angus St Victoria TX 77904	TX	EM			CQ	1985
Mueller Alan I	(770)548-8869	329 Waxmyrtle Way Perry GA 31069	FG	SP	Christ Perry GA	(478)987-6016	SL	2019
Mueller Jacob S	(949)510-8003 jacobstevenmueller@gmail.com	4107 238th Pl SE Apt 56c Bothell WA 98021	NOW	SP	Epiphany Kenmore WA	(425)488-9606	SL	2021
Muench David A	muenchda@gmail.com	17900 Mahoney Ct Ashland NE 68003	NEB	RSO	GracePoint Institute for Relational Health Lincoln NE	(402)614-6287	SL	1986
Muench Josef L	(218)350-2040 revjosefmuench@gmail.com	201 N Pine St. Nokomis IL 62075	SI	SP	Trinity Nokomis IL	(217)563-2718	FW	2021
Muenchow Mark R	(405)946-0681 mmuenchow@messiahokc.org	3600 NW Expressway Oklahoma City OK 73112	OK	Sn/Adm	Messiah Oklahoma City OK	(405)946-0681	SL	1990
Mugnolo William F	(585)472-0266 pastor.mugnolo@yahoo.com	323 Berlin Road Huron OH 44839	OH	SP	Zion Lorain OH	(440)282-8418	NESC	1990
Muhlbach Craig A	(812)523-3131 pastor@sjsauerslutheran.org		IN	SP	St John Seymour IN	(812)523-3131	SL	1992
Muhle Dean R	(989)728-7165	6951 Shellenbarger Rd Hale MI 48739	MI	SP	Saint Paul Hale MI	(989)728-4082	SL	1992
Muhly Jonathan T	(970)879-0175 jon@steamboatlutheran.com	c/o Concordia Lutheran Church 755 Concordia Ln Steamboat Springs CO 80487	RM	SP	Concordia Steamboat Springs CO	(970)879-0175	SL	2007
Muldowney Brian C	(313)418-3250	2780 Calariva Dr Stockton CA 95204	CNH	Sn/Adm	St Andrew Stockton CA	(209)957-8750	SL	2019
Mulholland Daniel L	(307)782-6882 mulholland@bvea.net	P.O. Box 280 Fort Bridger WY 82933	WY	SP	Shep Of Valley Fort Bridger WY	(307)782-6802	FW	1997
Mull John D	(817)521-9517 johndavid@sotv-wdm.org	4653 Timberline Dr West Des Moines IA 50265	IW	Sn/Adm	Shep Of The Valley West Des Moines IA	(515)225-1623	SL	2012

*Multiple Assignments (See Church Worker Locator for Additional Details)
See Page 53 for the Table of Abbreviations for key to District, Position, and Seminary abbreviations
**C =Candidate; EM = Emeritus; the date following the C is the month and year the Candidate status began

NAME	TELEPHONE NUMBER EMAIL	STREET ADDRESS CITY/STATE/ZIP	DISTRICT	POSITION/ STATUS**	WHERE SERVING	OFFICE PHONE	SEM/ PROGRAM	YR GRAD
Muller Robert J	(260)318-2595 pastorbobmuller@gmail.com	6519 Bennington Dr Fort Wayne IN 46815	IN	EM			SL	1971
Muller Donald M	(585)394-8825 pastordon1948@gmail.com	84 Arlington Park Canandaigua NY 14424	EA	EM			SL	1973
Muller Lyle D Dr	(407)542-3497 lylecubsfan@gmail.com	5111 Palmer Ranch Parkway #349 Sarasota FL 34238	FG	EM			SL	1961
Mullet Roger M	(307)621-0333 rev.mullet@gmail.com	141 Norma Dr Buffalo WY 82834	WY	SP	Prince Peace Buffalo WY	(307)684-5470	FW	2018
Mullins Kyle S	(812)870-4200 kylescotm@gmail.com	276 Oak Hill Dr Friedens PA 15541	EA	SP	Trinity Fairhope PA	(814)267-4474	FW	2022
Mulso Michael R	(651)755-4845 mrmulso@gmail.com	2602 15th Ave E North St Paul MN 55109	MNS	SMP	Emanuel Inver Grove Heights MN	(651)457-3929	SL-SMP	2015
Mumm David P	(815)315-2338 davidmumm@aol.com	2086 County Road 213 Giddings TX 78942	TX	SP	Christ Loebau TX		SL	1981
Mumme David C	(507)362-8133 pastormumme@gmail.com	415 Lake St W Waterville MN 56096	MNS	SP	Trinity Waterville MN	(507)362-4454	FW	1997
Mumme Jonathan W Dr	(262)546-6342 jonathanmumme@hotmail.com	1039 Markris Dr Hillsdale MI 49242	MI	C08/2022			SL	2011
Mumme Mark W	(307)851-1910 revmumme@gmail.com	1217 Canby St Laramie WY 82072	WY	SP	Zion Laramie WY	(307)745-9262	FW	2000
Mumme Paul G	(815)895-4477 pastormumme@stjohnsycamore.org	640 Walnut Ave Maple Park IL 60151	NI	Sn/Adm	St John Sycamore IL	(815)895-4477	FW	1998
Mundahl Robert L	(507)384-1171 ponderosascent@aol.com	301 Brady Dr Rolla MO 65401	MNS	EM			FW	1982
Mundinger Andrew P	(608)797-9163 office@holycrossconcord.org	1092 Alberta Way Concord CA 94521	CNH	SP	Holy Cross Concord CA	(925)686-2000	FW	2019
Mundinger Paul J	(608)797-9130 paul.mundinger55@gmail.com	2818 29 1/2 29 7/8 Ave Birchwood WI 54817	NW	EM			FW	1998
Mundorf Christian Q	989-753-7281 pastor@messiahcarrollton.org	4205 Lorraine Ave Saginaw MI 48604	MI	SP	Messiah Saginaw MI	(989)753-7281	FW	2023
Mundt Richard E	(989)642-8346 rmundt@stpeterhemlock.org	199 Norbert Ln Hemlock MI 48626	MI	EM			SPR	1973
Munnicha Khampheuy T	(770)823-1400	140 Creekwood Trl Fayetteville GA 30214	FG	EM			CQ	1991
Munz Jerold D	(863)937-6756 jerrymunz@yahoo.com	2833 Blush Dr Lakeland FL 33813	FG	EM			SL	1972
Murdaugh George E	(678)787-1173 georgeearl@hotmail.com	814 Bainbridge Way Irondale AL 35210	SO	EM			SL	1984
Murdock Cecil L	(573)746-1120 pjclmurdock@yahoo.com	P.O. Box 337 Hampton IL 61256	CI	EM			FW	1999
Murillo David J	(714)342-4734 davem@stpaulsa.org	10118 Silverwagon San Antonio TX 78254	TX	Sn/Adm	St Paul San Antonio TX	(210)532-7341	SL	2014
Murphy William M	(863)409-8491 will@webstergardens.org	8749 Watson Rd Webster Gardens MO 63119	MO	SMP	Webster Gardens Webster Groves MO	(314)961-5275	SL-SMP	2020
Murphy Max J	mmurphy@cornerstonelutheran.church	11215 Haverstick Rd Carmel IN 46033	IN	Assoc	Cornerstone Carmel IN	(317)814-4252	SL-SMP	2010
Murphy Brian W	(480)990-9674 pastor@scottsdaleholycross.org	256 E Gemini Pl Chandler AZ 85249	PSW	EM			SL	2001
Murphy Devin K	(954) 596-6966 dmurphy@hopelutheranwf.org	c/o Hope Lutheran Church 3525 Rogers Rd Wake Forest NC 27587	SE	Assoc	Hope Wake Forest NC	(919)554-8109	SL	2023
Murphy Joseph G	(303)596-7931 pastormurphy@glcparker.org	11521 Bent Oaks St Parker CO 80138	RM	SP	Grace Parker CO	(303)840-5493	FW	1994
Murr James O Jr	(224)829-8840 revmurr66@aol.com	3664 River Rd East China MI 48054	MI	Sn/Adm	Immanuel Saint Clair MI	(810)329-7174	SL	1992
Murray Daniel P	revdpm@gmail.com		MI	SP	Immanuel Dearborn Heights MI	(313)278-5755	FW	2013
Murray Scott R Dr	srmurray25@outlook.com	2525 Nantucket Dr Unit 10 Houston TX 77057	TX	EM			FW	1983
Musegades Michael A	(208)451-6239 h46pilot@sbcglobal.net	5 Miller Ln Salmon ID 83467	MT	SP	Christ Our Savior* Challis ID	(208)756-4429	SL	2012
Musick Michael D	(319)558-9083 ideuichaplain@live.com	103 Maple St Luzerne IA 52257	IE	Asst	Prince Of Peace Coralville IA	(319)338-1842	FW	2003
Musolf Gregory S	(612)805-0016 gmusolf@comcast.net	445 140th Ave NW Andover MN 55304	EN	SP	Messiah Forest Lake MN	(651)464-6842	FW	1991
Mussell Andrew C	(763)614-9827 aamussell@outlook.com	c/o Zion Lutheran Church 1100 Lake Ave Detroit Lakes MN 56502	MNN	Sn/Adm	Zion Detroit Lakes MN	(218)847-7630	SL	2021
Muther Paul D	(507)508-0153 paul.muther@gmail.com	381 S Kane St Burlington WI 53105	SW	Sn/Adm	Our Savior Burlington WI	(262)763-3281	SL	2012
Myers Daniel W	(316)619-1532 myers.danw@gmail.com	11212 E Tipperary St Wichita KS 67206	KS	EM			SL	1990
Myers James A	(317)902-3135 revjmyers@aol.com	1411 Colony Park Dr Greenwood IN 46143	IN	EM			FW	1999
Myers John W	(440)871-7067	2700 Whiteside Pl Springfield IL 62711	OH	EM			SPR	1971
Myhre Thomas E	(715)613-2687 ptom101@charter.net	613 W North St Owen WI 54460	NW	EM			FW	1982
Naasz Terry W	(605)216-8419 naasztan@gmail.com	8425 Kings Rd Rapid City SD 57702	SD	EM			FW	1981
Nack Jonathan C	revnack@gmail.com	1803 N Main St Auburn IN 46706	IN	SP	Trinity Auburn IN	(260)925-2440	SL	1994
Nadasdy Dean W Dr	(651)734-0673 dean.nadasdy@gmail.com	9255 Pinehurst Rd Woodbury MN 55125	MNS	EM			SL	1973
Nadeau William E	pastorbill4646@yahoo.com	2223 N Arena Del Loma Rd Lot 29 Camp Verde AZ 86322	PSW	EM			CQ	2018

*Multiple Assignments (See Church Worker Locator for Additional Details)
See Page 53 for the Table of Abbreviations for key to District, Position, and Seminary abbreviations
**C =Candidate; EM = Emeritus; the date following the C is the month and year the Candidate status began

NAME	TELEPHONE NUMBER EMAIL	STREET ADDRESS CITY/STATE/ZIP	DISTRICT	POSITION/ STATUS**	WHERE SERVING	OFFICE PHONE	SEM/ PROGRAM	YR GRAD
Nafzger Peter H Dr	(651)303-9248 nafzgerp@csl.edu	6 McCall Terrace Saint Louis MO 63105	MO	S HS/C	Concordia Seminary Saint Louis MO	(314)505-7000	SL	2004
Nafzger Samuel H Dr	(314)580-1672 samuel.nafzger@gmail.com	713 Eckrich Pl Saint Louis MO 63119	MO	EM			SL	1965
Nagler Stephen L	(315)629-4937 slnagler@twcny.rr.com	P.O. Box 59 Evans Mills NY 13637	CNH	M Chap	Office of International Mission Saint Louis MO		SPR	1973
Nagy Gary S	(219)688-3455 Gary1950Nagy@comcast.net	60 Meadow View Dr Trinity AL 35673	S	EM			FW	1978
Nagy Scott	(260)797-8064 scott.nagy@lhsoc.org	2253 E Belmont Pl Anaheim CA 92806	PSW	Tchr	Orange County Orange CA	(714)998-5151	FW	2018
Naibaho Tambatua	(909)256-1003 naibaho_pendeta@yahoo.com	16705 S Dalton Ave Apt A Gardena CA 90247	PSW	EM			SL	2007
Naito Uchel R	(808)386-8932 naitosan2@yahoo.com	1510 Evelyn Ln Honolulu HI 96822	CNH	SMP	Good Shepherd Honolulu HI	(808)523-2927	CQ	2021
Nare Limakatso	(504)352-5155 limakatsonare@gmail.com	3864 17th St Metairie LA 70002	SO	SP	Mount Zion New Orleans LA	(504)522-9951	FW	2002
Narring Dana A	(941)889-8688 faithlutheranpg@gmail.com	8608 Lake Front Ct Punta Gorda FL 33950	FG	SP	Faith Punta Gorda FL	(941)639-6309	SL	1996
Nash James R	(970)580-1824 pastor_nash@yahoo.com		RM	EM			SL	2003
NaThalang Pomprom	(636)936-1412 tnathalang@LHFmissions.org	51474 Romeo Plank Rd Macomb MI 48042	MO	RSO	Lutheran Heritage Foundation Macomb MI	(800)554-0723	SL	1991
Nathan Bruce A	(631)758-0964 banathan4@outlook.com	5008 W. Wedgewood Lane Muncie IN 47304	IN	EM			FW	1980
Natzke Royal W	(262)334-9811 rdnatzke@yahoo.com	107 Cedar Ridge Dr. Apt. N-320 West Bend WI 53095	SW	EM			SL	1960
Natzke William J	(507)206-3029 wjnatzke@gmail.com	3412 42nd St NW Rochester MN 55901	MNS	EM			SL	1968
Nauman Marc E	(727)808-7153 mcnauman5@yahoo.com	17901 Souter Ln Land O Lakes FL 34638	FG	SMP	Trinity Trinity FL	(727)364-4667	SL-SMP	2011
Naumann Paul R Dr	(269)491-7832 naumann@mightymessengers.org	1749 Greenbriar Dr Portage MI 49024	MI	Sn/Adm	St Michael Portage MI	(269)327-7832	SL	1984
Naumann Terrance A	(540)413-0093 terryanaumann@gmail.com	10405 Johnson Dr King George VA 22485	SE	EM			SPR	1976
Naumann William G	(818)346-5815 wgnaumann@aol.com	6626 Moorcroft Avenue Canoga Park CA 91303	EN	Sn/Adm	The Cross Mission Hills CA	(818)892-8490	SL	1959
Naumann Edward A Dr	edward.naumann@gmail.com	c/o St Pauls Lutheran Church 9035 Grant Ave Brookfield IL 60513	NI	SP	St Paul Brookfield IL	(708)485-6987	FW	2013
Naumann Gordon S	(917)900-7502 gordonnaumann@gmail.com	1032 W 20th St. Hazle Township PA 18202	S	SP	St John Hazleton PA	(570)459-6423	Other	2009
Naumann Jonathan C Dr	+18297417292 jonathan.naumann@lcms.org	782 15th St Oakmont PA 15139	EN	S Miss	Office of International Mission Saint Louis MO		FW	1982
Nava Jaime A	pastor.nava@gmail.com	46 Menusa Dr Oceanside CA 92058	MO	M Chap	Office of International Mission Saint Louis MO		SL	2011
Navurskis Christopher A	pcnavurskis@kingofkingscr.org	216 31st St NW Cedar Rapids IA 52405	IE	Sn/Adm	King Of Kings Cedar Rapids IA	(319)393-2438	SL	2004
Naylor George E	(308)672-0827 revgeorge@protonmail.com	P.O. Box 637 Bridgeport NE 69336	WY	SP	Saint James* Scottsbluff NE	(308)632-8001	SL	1998
Naylor Steven A	(727)992-7681 pastorsnaylor@gmail.com	316 W North 7th St Grangeville ID 83530	NOW	SP	Trinity Grangeville ID	(208)983-0562	NESC	2009
Ndon Elijah A		3334 N 46th St Milwaukee WI 53216	SW	SP	Holy Ghost Milwaukee WI	(414)264-0372	SL	2008
Neagley Richard L	(717)343-2417 hockey76@verizon.net	560 Oak Dr Apt 234 Harleysville PA 19438	EA	EM			SL	1976
Neal Randall A	(952)938-7661 randall.neal@zionhopkins.org	241 5th Ave N Hopkins MN 55343	MNS	Sn/Adm	Zion Hopkins MN	(952)938-7661	SPR	1976
Nebel Mark A	(660)463-2238 mnebel@splhs.org	P.O. Box 60 Concordia MO 64020	MO	Tchr	Saint Paul Concordia MO	(660)463-2238	SL	1989
Nedjo Daniel T	(614)772-5579 dantene2012@gmail.com		SE	C05/2025			CQ	2019
Nedrow Alan L	anedrow@myidahomail.com	1327 N 3786 E P.O. Box 726 Ashton ID 83420	NOW	SMP	Trinity Saint Anthony ID	(208)624-0357	CQ	2019
Needham Samuel J	(307)864-9354 gogobroncos2007@gmail.com	267 Lane 14 Thermopolis WY 82443	WY	SP	St Paul Thermopolis WY	(307)864-2205	FW	2009
Neel Jason D	(612)581-8786 soclcpastor@gmail.com	1076 122nd Ave NE Blaine MN 55434	MNS	SP	Spirit Christ Ham Lake MN	(763)755-7234	CQ	2006
Neels Dennis J	(701)397-5292 djneels@polarcomm.com	4722 26th Ave NE Niagara ND 58266	ND	EM			SPR	1973
Neff Bruce A	(805)458-8464 bneff09@gmail.com	986 Spring Street W Madera CA 93636	CNH	EM			FW	1983
Nehrenz David R	(405)306-8464 davidnehrenz@gmail.com	902 Carey Dr Norman OK 73069	OK	DP	Oklahoma District* Norman OK	(405)321-3443	FW	1982
Nehring Craig J	(715)944-6548 cnehring@yahoo.com	W3122 White Clay Lake Dr Cecil WI 54111	NW	SP	Immanuel* Cecil WI	(715)745-2364	CQ	2022
Nehring Gary L	(517)629-2075 gsnehring@outlook.com	132 Bushong Dr Albion MI 49224	MI	EM			SL	1997
Nehring Joseph M	(314)517-6393 joenehring@yahoo.com	18325 E Il Highway 15 Mount Vernon IL 62864	SI	SP	Faith Mount Vernon IL	(618)242-4330	SL	2020
Nehrt Jeffery D Dr	(618)292-4392 jeffnehrt84@gmail.com	1665 Hookdale Ln Smithboro IL 62284	SI	SP	Our Redeemer Greenville IL	(618)664-0223	SL	1993
Neider Erik D	(262)825-3136 erik.neider@gmail.com	21 Glenmore Street Saratoga Springs NY 12866	CNH	M Chap	Office of International Mission Saint Louis MO		SL	2010

*Multiple Assignments (See Church Worker Locator for Additional Details)
See Page 53 for the Table of Abbreviations for key to District, Position, and Seminary abbreviations
**C =Candidate; EM = Emeritus; the date following the C is the month and year the Candidate status began

NAME	TELEPHONE NUMBER EMAIL	STREET ADDRESS CITY/STATE/ZIP	DISTRICT	POSITION/ STATUS**	WHERE SERVING	OFFICE PHONE	SEM/ PROGRAM	YR GRAD
Neider Howard R	(715)889-1720 hsneider1971@gmail.com	2687 Trump Lake Rd Wabeno WI 54566	NW	EM			SL	1989
Neider Shawn F	ziongrandcoulee@gmail.com	328 Roosevelt Dr P.O. Box 4 Grand Coulee WA 99133	NOW	SP	Zion* Grand Coulee WA	(509)633-2566	SL	2011
Neidigk Donald H	revdhn@gmail.com	P.O. Box 45151 Rio Rancho NM 87174	RM	EM			CQ	1985
Neidow Michael P	mneidow@efyork.org	7937 Broadview Dr Lincoln NE 68505	NEB	Sn/Adm	Emmanuel York NE	(402)362-3655	SL	1984
Neigh Dennis J	(989)739-8828 dneigh@charter.net	4441 E Cedar Lake Dr Greenbush MI 48738	MI	EM			FW-D	2008
Neiswender Donald R	djneis@hotmail.com	35 Point Of Vw Paducah KY 42001	MDS	EM			SPR	1965
Nelson Mark J	(309)453-7231 pastornelson@trinitypeoria.com	3229 W Pilgrims Way Peoria IL 61615	CI	Sn/Adm	Trinity Peoria IL	(309)676-4609	SL	2007
Nelson Tracy T	(615)663-4890 ttn9767@netzero.net	2206 Eastview Dr Murfreesboro TN 37128	MDS	Assoc	Our Savior Nashville TN	(615)833-1500	SL	2002
Nelson Terry A	(248)880-0048 chris.terrynelson@yahoo.com	2853 Sycamore River Dr. Fowlerville MI 48836	MI	EM			FW	1980
Nelson Robert J	(248)804-3533 robertjnelson55@gmail.com	1219 Coachman Way Sanford NC 27332	MI	M Chap	Office of International Mission Saint Louis MO		SL	2004
Nelson Richard E	(703)895-6974 8sandrich23@gmail.com	1 Towers Park Ln Apt 1210 San Antonio TX 78209	TX	EM			FW	1983
Nelson Paul R	(701)626-7510	333 6th Ave NE Apt E5 Garrison ND 58540	ND	EM			FW	1981
Nelson David J	(320)202-0455 northwing@charter.net	1307 14th St N Saint Cloud MN 56303	MNN	EM			CQ	2004
Nelson Paul A	paulnelson@emanuellutheransb.org	1250 E. Mineral Road Gilbert AZ 85234	PSW	S Miss	Office of International Mission Saint Louis MO		SL	2008
Nelson Nathan R	(314)604-0236 nelsonn@csl.edu	401 N Charles St Steeleville IL 62288	KS	Assoc	Trinity Leavenworth KS	(913)682-7474	SL	2024
Nelson Matthew E	(406)871-5282 mdcnelson@hotmail.com	49 Waving Grass Way Columbia FLS MT 59912	MT	SP	Our Redeemer Columbia Falls MT	(406)892-4074	FW	2004
Nelson Victor H Jr	(518)622-3286 vhnelson@gmail.com	P.O. Box 563 Cairo NY 12413	AT	Assoc	Resurrection Cairo NY	(518)622-3286	FW	1984
Nelson Marcus J	(630)868-3275	410 N Cross St Wheaton IL 60187	NI	Sn/Adm	St John Wheaton IL	(630)668-0701	FW	2007
Nelson Kyle P	405-224-1552 pr.kpnelson@gmail.com	38 Ridgecrest Dr Chickasha OK 73018	OK	SP	First Chickasha OK	(405)224-1552	FW	2022
Nelson John E Sr	dad@nelsonville.org	4122 Rolling Green Dr Grand Island NE 68803	NEB	EM			SPR	1973
Nelson John E Jr	revnelson92@gmail.com	204 S Madison St O' Neill NE 68763	NEB	SP	Christ* Lynch NE	(402)589-1323	SL	1992
Nelson Jeffrey A	(314)471-4883 bombrod@socket.net	102 Heritage Hills Pl Arnold MO 63010	MO	EM			SL	2001
Nelson Dewayne R Jr	(972)679-4107 drnelson1947@gmail.com	110 Oakbend Trl Mabank TX 75147	TX	EM			SL	1973
Nelson Darrell P	(828) 302-9860 nelsondarrelpaul@gmail.com	2500 Penngate Dr Sherrills Frd NC 28673	SE	EM			SPR	1966
Nelson Carl E	(920)395-2681 carlenelson1@gmail.com	2748 Lisa Ave Sheboygan WI 53083	SW	EM			SL	1960
Nelson Briton J	(608)415-8228 pastornelson@trinityalgona.org	603 S Harlan St Algona IA 50511	IW	Assoc	St John* Burt IA	(515)924-3344	SL	2023
Nelson Andrew J	ajnelson6@gmail.com		SW	SP	St Paul's Janesville WI	(608)754-4471	SL	2023
Nelson Eric M	(231) 894-8471 pastornelson@stjamesmontague.com	6526 Terravita Dr Whitehall MI 49461	MI	SP	Saint James Montague MI	(231)894-8471	SL	1995
Nemec Charles E	(254) 205-3170 revcharlesnemec@gmail.com	2221 Avenue W Lubbock TX 79411	TX	SP	Redeemer Lubbock TX	(806)744-6178	FW	2022
Nemec Donald P	(906)440-2782 dcnemec@tds.net	1991 Pioneer Rd Gaylord MI 49735	MI	EM			FW	2004
Nemec Michael C	(254)266-0589 revmcnemec@hotmail.com	428 Alexander St. Hillsboro TX 76645	TX	SP	Christ Hillsboro TX	(254)582-5782	FW	2000
Nemera Chera H	(605)371-3501	4012 S Bedford Ave Sioux Falls SD 57103	SD	Assoc	Lord Of Life Sioux Falls SD	(605)371-3501	SL	2014
Nemoyer Robert J	(717)559-0340 rjnemoyer@gmail.com	2406 Ken James Ct Napoleon OH 43545	OH	EM			SL	1983
Nerud Timothy L	(815) 989-2025 pastor@stjohnsgeneseo.org	St. John's Lutheran Church 8948 N 1900th Ave. Geneseo IL 61254	CI	SP	St John Geneseo IL	(815)989-2025	FW	2005
Nesbit Michael A	(815)858-5621 pastormikenesbit@gmail.com	P.O. Box 262 Elizabeth IL 61028	NI	SMP	St Paul Elizabeth IL	(815)858-3334	SL-SMP	2012
Nestler Robert B	(785)286-2871 bobnest@gmail.com	6701 SW Scathelock Rd Topeka KS 66614	KS	EM			CQ	1978
Netland Lance A	(404)377-9730 jeffpl@bellsouth.net	203 Jefferson Pl Decatur GA 30030	FG	EM			SL	1971
Nettleton Shawn P	(970)305-2420 nettleton@stjohnsfc.org	3139 Bryce Dr Fort Collins CO 80525	RM	Sn/Adm	Saint John's Fort Collins CO	(970)482-5316	SL	2006
Nettling Kenneth J	(913)709-4417 revken1@msn.com	1439 S 33rd St Kansas City KS 66106	KS	SP	Faith Kansas City KS	(913)321-1326	CQ	1997
Neubacher Mark A	(260) 804-4422	7016 Brackenwood Ct Fort Wayne IN 46835	IN	EM			FW	2003
Neubauer James H	(218)732-5621 revneu@unitelc.com	803 First St W Park Rapids MN 56470	MNN	Sn/Adm	St John Park Rapids MN	(218)732-9783	SL	1994

*Multiple Assignments (See Church Worker Locator for Additional Details)

See Page 53 for the Table of Abbreviations for key to District, Position, and Seminary abbreviations

**C =Candidate; EM = Emeritus; the date following the C is the month and year the Candidate status began

NAME	TELEPHONE NUMBER EMAIL	STREET ADDRESS CITY/STATE/ZIP	DISTRICT	POSITION/ STATUS**	WHERE SERVING	OFFICE PHONE	SEM/ PROGRAM	YR GRAD
Neuberger Paul E	neubs61@gmail.com	3713 Montague Dr Amarillo TX 79109	TX	EM			SL	1987
Neuendorf Christopher J	(563)505-2033 oslcpastor@utma.com	315 13th St W Bottineau ND 58318	ND	SP	Our Savior's* Bottineau ND	(701)228-3021	FW	2010
Neuendorf Donald O	(734)646-3691 don@neuendorfs.com	1084 Darwin Road Pinckney MI 48169	MI	EM			FW	1985
Neuendorf James A	(734)277-6076 james.neuendorf@lcms.org	1428 Calle Aloa Buena Vista Ponce PR 00717	MI	S Miss	Office of International Mission Saint Louis MO		FW	2018
Neugebauer Charles J	(901)828-6928 pastorchuck@ctkmemphis.com	2082 Donnington Cove Germantown TN 38138	MDS	EM			FW	1983
Neugebauer Nathan T	(308)672-5831 pastor.ntn@pm.me	P.O. Box 14 Revillo SD 57259	SD	SP	Bethlehem* Milbank SD	(605)623-4280	FW	2014
Neugebauer Richard H	(308)672-1096 richardneugebauer7@gmail.com	1815 R St Gering NE 69341	WY	Sn/Adm	Faith Gering NE	(308)436-4307	SL	1987
Neugebauer Aaron J	aaronneuge@gmail.com	11530 Highway 135 N Lafe AR 72436	MDS	Sn/Adm	St John Lafe AR	(870)586-0319	SL	2008
Neugebauer Kirk C	(901)828-6930 kneugebr@gmail.com	c/o Redeemer Lutheran Church 829 W Kingshighway Paragould AR 72450	MDS	SP	Redeemer Paragould AR	(870)236-2162	SL	2016
Neugebauer John C	(815)514-6995 pastorjcn@hotmail.com	520 Twilight Dr Apt D Morris IL 60450	NI	EM			SL	1973
Neuhaus Ryan S	(512)295-3933 neuhauscrew@gmail.com	P.O. Box 457 La Grange TX 78945	TX	RSO	Lutheran Outdoors Min of TX La Grange TX	(979)968-1657	SL	2005
Neujahr Troy R Dr	(216)862-1088 pastortroy@stpeterslc.org	3625 Stoer Rd Shaker Hts OH 44122	OH	SP	St Peter Shaker Heights OH	(216)561-2511	SL	2005
Neuman Paul D	(812)797-3693 neumanp27@juno.com	616 Black Lion Dr NE Saint Petersburg FL 33716	FG	EM			FW	1984
Neumann Wilbur F	(218)732-7715 dneumann718@yahoo.com	17922 Dayspring Dr Park Rapids MN 56470	MNN	EM			SL	1959
Neumann Mark A	(918)200-5013 pastormarkflc@sbcglobal.net	14757 N 60th East Ave Collinsville OK 74021	OK	SP	Faith Owasso OK	(918)272-9858	SL	1984
Neumann Mark G	(715)316-8902 markandjoan.neumann@gmail.com	623 Macomber St Chippewa Falls WI 54792	NW	EM			FW	1980
Neustel Terry L II	(720)979-1327 pastorneustel@eoni.com	5282 Riverdale Ln Thornton CO 80229	RM	SP	Faith Denver CO	(303)455-5878	FW	2009
Nevis E E	(352)275-7539 pastor@sttimothyotisville.org	9527 Castle Ct Otisville MI 48463	MI	SP	St Timothy Otisville MI	(810)631-4730	SL	1999
Newberg Steven E	(715)218-8571 lcolpastor@gmail.com	1225 E Morehead St Charlotte NC 28204	SE	Sn/Adm	Ascension Charlotte NC	(704)372-7317	SL	2009
Newell William J	(309)665-2995 pastorbillyn@gmail.com	4924 S Kalen Pl Sioux Falls SD 57108	SD	Sn/Adm	Lord Of Life Sioux Falls SD	(605)371-3501	SL	2011
Newman Michael W	(210)633-4368 mike@mnewman.org	4527 Jarrell San Antonio TX 78253	TX	EM			SL	1987
Newman Drew A	(816)651-8047 gnuguy1946@gmail.com	1606 Lynn Rd Excelsior Spg MO 64024	MO	SP	Trinity Kearney MO	(816)628-6644	FW	1985
Newman Irvin M Jr	(217)417-5739 pmel2@icloud.com	2027 Lisa Ln San Marcos TX 78666	TX	EM			SPR	1972
Newton Steven M	(734)414-7422 stevenewt10@gmail.com	43937 Southampton Dr Canton MI 48187	MI	SP	Salem National* Westland MI	(734)422-5550	SL	2008
Newton Roger A	215-745-8922 rogeranewton@msn.com	3116 Derry Rd Philadelphia PA 19154	EA	EM			CQ	1997
Newton Alvin L	(410)866-4763	1815 Greencastle Dr Rosedale MD 21237	SE	EM			SL	1969
Newton Joel L	(815)222-1359 pastornewton@stpaulankeny.org	313 NW Waterview Ct Ankeny IA 50023	IW	Sn/Adm	St Paul Ankeny IA	(515)964-1250	SL	2018
Newton Robert D Dr	(408)644-4535 rdnewton461@gmail.com	3963 Raymond Rd. Frankfort MI 49635	MI	EM			FW	1977
Ng Christopher H	(415)661-1120 christopherng@gmail.com	2400 Noriega St San Francisco CA 94122	CNH	Assoc	Holy Spirit San Francisco CA	(415)661-1120	SL	2009
Ngare Philemon O	(763)222-4334 philemon.ngare@gmail.com	9204 NE 45th Place Vancouver WA 98665	NOW	SP	Triumphant King* Lake Oswego OR	(503)636-3436	Other	1998
Nguyen Dung C	(503)516-4660 nguyendungandrew@yahoo.com	24035 Buffalo Cove Ln Katy TX 77493	TX	SP	Vietnamese Houston TX	(503)516-4660	CQ	2019
Nguyen Ninh Huu	(832)859-2352 pastorninh@gmail.com	12714 Blanton Lane Sugar Land TX 77478	TX	EM			CQ	1992
Nicely Douglas A Dr	(618)566-8236 dougnicely81@gmail.com	514 W South St Mascoutah IL 62258	SI	SP	Jerusalem Collinsville IL	(618)346-1925	SL	1977
Nichols Jerrold L	(260)450-5123 jerryandmary132@gmail.com	7789b W Jefferson Blvd Fort Wayne IN 46804	IN	EM			SL	1961
Nicholson Paul E	(612)804-9852 nicholson.paul.e@gmail.com	3663 Park Center Blvd # 1315 St Louis Park MN 55416	MNS	EM			SPR	1963
Nicholson Harvey E	henicholson@yahoo.com	665 Mary Ln Saint Anne IL 60964	NI	EM			SPR	1974
Nicholson Isaac W	(606)923-5956 pastorikennicholson@gmail.com	301 Clinton Street South Almena WI 54805	NW	SP	St Matthew Almena WI	(715)357-3267	CQ	2022
Nicholus Robert H	(650)619-2700 bobnicholus@aol.com	247 Blair Mine Rd Angels Camp CA 95222	CNH	EM			SL	1969
Nickel Timothy M	(904)392-1534 timritanickel@gmail.com	6050 Las Nubes Ter Elkton FL 32033	FG	EM			SL	1970
Nickel Jeffrey D	(716)634-2332 pastornickel.holycross@gmail.com	6440 Conner Rd East Amherst NY 14051	EA	SP	Holy Cross Clarence NY	(716)634-2332	SL	2015
Nickel Joel T	(503)763-1922 joelnickel15@gmail.com	510 W Hills Way NW Salem OR 97304	NOW	EM			SL	1965

*Multiple Assignments (See Church Worker Locator for Additional Details)
See Page 53 for the Table of Abbreviations for key to District, Position, and Seminary abbreviations
**C =Candidate; EM = Emeritus; the date following the C is the month and year the Candidate status began

NAME	TELEPHONE NUMBER EMAIL	STREET ADDRESS CITY/STATE/ZIP	DISTRICT	POSITION/ STATUS**	WHERE SERVING	OFFICE PHONE	SEM/ PROGRAM	YR GRAD
Nickel Peter S	(248)935-7388 psnickel52@gmail.com	12762 Lasalle Ln Huntingtn Wds MI 48070	MI	EM			CQ	1982
Nickel Ronald P	(970)391-0714 nickel.ron70@gmail.com	16510 Grays Way Broomfield CO 80023	RM	EM			CQ	1978
Nickodemus Stephen E	smnick060896@yahoo.com	15320 E Marquam Rd NE Mount Angel OR 97362	NOW	EM			SL	1982
Nicolaus Jon R	(816)809-3664 jnicolaus@messiahlcms.net	1101 NW Persimmon Dr Grain Valley MO 64029	MO	EM			SL	1984
Niebling Todd M	(661)492-0110 tmniebling@gmail.com	2521 Wood Opal Way Oxnard CA 93030	PSW	SP	St John's Oxnard CA	(805)983-0330	SL	2006
Niebuhr Jon E	(507)210-0652 pastor@gslcglencoe.org	200 Edgewood Drive Glencoe MN 55336	MNS	SP	Good Shepherd Glencoe MN	(320)864-6157	SL	2012
Niederstadt Jeffrey W	stadt@earthlink.net	1412 Skyline Dr SW Rochester MN 55902	MNS	Sn/Adm	Holy Cross Rochester MN	(507)289-1354	SL	2003
Niedner Frederick A Jr Dr		1402 Cross Creek Rd Valparaiso IN 46383	IN	END	Valparaiso University Valparaiso IN	(219)464-5000	SL	1971
Niekerk Timothy R	(281)351-8223 tniekerk@salem4u.com	22601 Lutheran Church Rd Tomball TX 77377	TX	Sn/Adm	Salem Tomball TX	(281)351-8223	SL	1997
Nielsen Glenn A Dr	(314)651-4274 nielseng@csl.edu	13279 Gateroyal Dr Saint Louis MO 63131	MO	S HS/C	Concordia Seminary Saint Louis MO	(314)505-7000	SL	1981
Nielsen Michael J Dr	(218)280-0999 pastornielsen@stjohnsnp.org	1146 Downing Drive Waukesha WI 53186	SW	SP	St Johns North Prairie WI	(262)392-2170	SL	2010
Nielsen David G	(830)734-5132 pastor.nielsen@live.com	114 Rawhide Trl Del Rio TX 78840	TX	SP	Grace Del Rio TX	(830)308-3311	SL	2012
Nielsen Paul	(610)390-3912 inexile20@hotmail.com	2332 25th Ave. Ct. NE Hickory NC 28601	SE	EM			FW	1993
Nieman David S	(575)499-8016 davesnieman@gmail.com	116 S Grant St Hinsdale IL 60521	NI	SP	Zion Hinsdale IL	(630)323-0384	SL	2017
Nieman Ronald C	(810)706-5530 revronnieman@gmail.com	6090 Ada Van Dr Dryden MI 48428	MI	EM			CQ	2017
Niemann Glenn R	(309)267-7856 revgraniemann@gmail.com	1419 N Idaho St Peoria IL 61615	CI	EM			SL	1996
Niemeier Craig K	(308)687-6314 cniem@kdsi.net	1653 Worms Rd Saint Libory NE 68872	NEB	SP	Zion Saint Libory NE	(308)687-6314	SL	1998
Niemeier Nils P	nilswerks@yahoo.com	426 Davis Road Bedford MA 01730	NE	SP	Of The Savior Bedford MA	(781)275-6013	SL	2020
Nieminen Johannes	(505)709-7090 johannes_nieminen@hotmail.com	93 Mesa Verde St White Rock NM 87547	RM	SP	Redeemer Los Alamos NM	(505)662-0782	NESC	2014
Niemtschk Bobby G	(512)366-2933 niemtschk-4@msn.com	5 Hobbs Ml Saint Charles MO 63303	MO	M Chap	Office of International Mission Saint Louis MO		SL	2002
Nierman Mark J	(970)980-5584 pr_nierman@juno.com	3569 Harding Dr Loveland CO 80538	RM	SP	Mount Olive Loveland CO	(970)669-7350	SL	2003
Niermann Scott A	revniermann@outlook.com	10711 N 200th St Altamont IL 62411	CI	SP	Immanuel Altamont IL	(618)483-6395	SL	2008
Niermann Stephen J	(419)960-5193 sbniermann@gmail.com	U162 County Road 16 Napoleon OH 43545	OH	EM			FW	1985
Niermann Stephen M	(412)916-7597 stephenm15235@yahoo.com	1327 Eagles Nest Ln Monroeville PA 15146	EA	SP	Faith Pittsburgh PA	(412)363-8520	SL	1991
Niermann Thomas A		715 Wright Ave Elgin IL 60120	NI	D Ex/S	Northern Illinois District River Forest IL	(708)449-3020	SL	1969
Nies Jared R	(605)830-0919 pastornies@stpaul-lapeer.org	c/o St Paul Lutheran Church 90 Millville Rd Lapeer MI 48446	MI	Sn/Adm	St Paul Lapeer MI	(810)664-6653	SL	2011
Nietfeld Danny L	dnietfeld@cox.net	1719 Hillcrest Dr Bellevue NE 68005	NEB	EM			SL	1972
Nieting Robert M	(757)635-4046 mnieting@hotmail.com	1116 Norcova Ct Chesapeake VA 23320	SE	EM			CQ	1986
Nihiser James L	(231)590-5485 jandjnihiser@gmail.com	4945 Pinespar Trl Traverse City MI 49685	MI	SP	Bethlehem Glen Arbor MI	(231)334-4180	FW	2001
Nikl Robert L	(651)295-7682 blnkl@comcast.net	7709 Inskip Trl S Cottage Grove MN 55016	MNS	C02/2020			CQ	2012
Niles John P	(920)627-4729 pastorniles@gmail.com	2405 Saemann Ave Sheboygan WI 53081	SW	Sn/Adm	Bethlehem Sheboygan WI	(920)452-4331	SL	2008
Nilges Chris V	(636) 386-9006 chris.nilges@lssliving.org	837 Crescent Ridge Drive Valley Park MO 63088	MO	Inst C	Lutheran Senior Services DBA EverTrue Brentwood MO	(314)968-9313	SL	1985
Ninke John H	(706)662-1900 jhninke@gmail.com	918 Rock Hill Rd Jefferson City MO 65109	MO	EM			SL	2012
Nitzel Christopher A	(712)928-2890 chrisnitzel1@gmail.com	50 N Central Ave Hartley IA 51346	IW	SP	St Paul Hartley IA	(712)728-2711	SL	2006
Nix Joshua D	(253)882-9541 jnixtwin2@gmail.com	2229 SE Minter Bridge Rd Hillsboro OR 97123	NOW	SMP	Trinity Hillsboro OR	(503)640-1693	SL-SMP	2021
Nix Matthew W	(605)338-5267 mw_nix@yahoo.com	6205 N Purple Martin Ave Sioux Falls SD 57107	SD	SP	Christ* Sioux Falls SD	(605)338-3769	SL	1993
Nizinski Leonard R	(717) 654-9572 skipniz@gmail.com		PSW	SP	Lamb Of God Lake Havasu City AZ	(928)854-7170	SL	2004
Noack Brian B	(631)806-7119 stbnoack@aol.com	45 Greene Ave Sayville NY 11782	AT	SP	St John Sayville NY	(631)589-3202	FW	2004
Noack Richard C Dr	(281)813-5260 noacks@usa.net	6310 Elmgrove Rd Spring TX 77389	TX	EM			SL	1974
Noble Andrew C	(712)210-3543 andrewcarlnoble@gmail.com	200 W Tracy St Arcadia IA 51430	IW	SP	Zion Arcadia IA	(712)689-2441	SL	2015
Noble Carl L I	(218)298-1428 carlka0ibf@gmail.com	115 Connie Dr Gulfport MS 39503	SO	SP	Good Shepherd Slidell LA	(985)641-2109	SL	1983
Noennig Bruce E	(701)388-4740 pastornoennig@gmail.com	21704 E Height Of Land Dr Detroit Lakes MN 56501	MNN	Asst	Zion Detroit Lakes MN	(218)847-7630	CQ	1981

*Multiple Assignments (See Church Worker Locator for Additional Details)
See Page 53 for the Table of Abbreviations for key to District, Position, and Seminary abbreviations
**C =Candidate; EM = Emeritus; the date following the C is the month and year the Candidate status began

NAME	TELEPHONE NUMBER EMAIL	STREET ADDRESS CITY/STATE/ZIP	DISTRICT	POSITION/ STATUS**	WHERE SERVING	OFFICE PHONE	SEM/ PROGRAM	YR GRAD
Noh Jong W	(714)337-1761 jjwwnoh@gmail.com	828 Grand Canal Irvine CA 92620	PSW	Assoc	Good News Korean Buena Park CA	(714)681-6770	CQ	2000
Noland Martin R Dr	(812)573-3257 martin.r.noland@gmail.com	421 28th Ave San Mateo CA 94403	CNH	Sn/Adm	Grace San Mateo CA	(650)345-9068	FW	1983
Noll David C	(509)953-1425 dnoll@redeemeralive.org	12509 E 26th Ave Spokane Vly WA 99216	NOW	Sn/Adm	Redeemer Spokane WA	(509)926-6363	CQ	2010
Noll Thomas C	(224)735-7068 eliab1of7@aol.com	1282 Luther Ln Arlington Heights IL 60004	NI	Asst	St Peter Arlington Heights IL	(847)259-4114	CQ	1983
Nollet Joseph R	(860)478-2559 clcpastorjoe@gmail.com	478 Boston St Topsfield MA 01983	NE	SP	Our Savior Topsfield MA	(978)887-5701	FW	2003
Nolte Matthew T	(805)367-6390 pastormatt@stpaulagoura.com	2175 Calle Lila Thousand Oaks CA 91360	PSW	SP	Redeemer* Thousand Oaks CA	(805)498-4813	SL	2007
Nolting Dudley E		1138 Chardonnay Loop NE Keizer OR 97303	NOW	EM			SPR	1973
Noon Thomas R	(205)824-3811 noon4130@bellsouth.net	2243 N Sherrlyn Dr Hoover AL 35226	SO	EM			SPR	1971
Nordlie Robert L Dr	(210)560-6696 bobn@concordia-satx.com	26710 Sierra Hollow San Antonio TX 78261	TX	EM			SPR	1975
Nordling John G Dr	(260)413-9464 john.nordling@ctsfw.edu	6015 Countess Dr Fort Wayne IN 46815	IN	S HS/C	Concordia Theological Seminary Fort Wayne IN	(260)452-2100	SL	1985
Nordquist Wallace D	nordfam@att.net	700 W Fabyan Pkwy Apt 269d Batavia IL 60510	NI	EM			SL	1964
Noren Mark A	(763)259-8021 mark.noren@charter.net	1816 Lake Dr Northfield MN 55057	MNS	EM			CQ	2007
Norris Paul D	pd_norris@sbcglobal.net	5348 Austin Dr Monticello IN 47960	IN	SP	St Matthews Delphi IN	(765)564-3200	FW	2023
Norris Thomas G Jr	(208) 999-1058 norris.tg@gmail.com	1115 East Pastoral Court Eagle ID 83616	CNH	Assoc	Bethany Menlo Park CA	(650)854-5897	SL	1990
Norris Ronald T	norrisrt@yahoo.com	3915 64th Avenue Ct NW Gig Harbor WA 98335	NOW	EM			FW	1991
Norris Andrew S	(513) 385-8342 anorris@christ-lcms.org	2925 Parkwalk Dr Cincinnati OH 45239	OH	Sn/Adm	Christ Cincinnati OH	(513)385-8342	Other	1989
Norris Richard A	(863)441-4168 pastortrinitylp@gmail.com	114 McKinley Ave Lake Placid FL 33852	FG	Sn/Adm	Trinity Lake Placid FL	(863)465-5253	FW	1983
Northrop Andrew E Dr	(206)849-2397 atn1078@comcast.net	53994 Pine Grove Rd La Pine OR 97739	NOW	EM			FW	1981
Northwick Byron Dr	(641)420-6989 bnilsta@myomnitel.com	152 Brook Ter Mason City IA 50401	IE	SP	Messiah* Mason City IA	(641)423-2970	FW	1981
Norton William D	(360)681-8864 billn@olypen.com	3293 Lost Mountain Rd Sequim WA 98382	NOW	EM			CQ	1977
Norton Cody E	(512)703-0583 cody.norton@gmail.com	506 Lily Dr Apt 1 Fort Wainwright AK 99703	KS	Inst C	Office of International Mission Saint Louis MO		FW	2016
Norton James E	(715)514-5478 jenorton46@gmail.com	552 Windsor Forest Dr Altoona WI 54720	NW	SP	Bethlehem* Fall Creek WI	(715)877-3249	SL	1979
Norton Timothy P	(505)567-4316 timandheidinorton@gmail.com	411 E Logan Ave Gallup NM 87301	RM	SP	Shep of the Valley Navajo NM	(505)567-4316	Other	2017
Nour Nabil S Dr	(605)201-6998 preachermanfootwasher@gmail.com	7701 South Tuscan Club Cir Sioux Falls SD 57108	SD	EM			SL	1994
Novacek Mark D	(630)352-8987 marknovacek1138@comcast.net	6821 Main St Union IL 60180	NI	SMP	St John Union IL	(815)923-2733	SL-SMP	2021
Novack William J	(716) 581-5451 bflonovack@msn.com	123 Madaline Ln Depew NY 14043	EA	Assoc	St Paul North Tonawanda NY	(716)692-3255	SL-D	2010
Novelli German Jr	german.novelli@lhm.org	513 Winter Bluff Drive Fenton MO 63026	MO	Aux	LLL/Lutheran Hour Ministries Saint Louis MO	(314)317-4100	SL	2018
Nowak Brian L	(708) 369-7741 Pastorbriannowak@gmail.com	312 S 5th St P.O. Box 12 Baldwin IL 62217	SI	SP	St John* Baldwin IL	(618)785-2344	SL	2021
Nowak Robert W	(952)440-8095 mnnowaks@gmail.com	14339 Peninsula Point Dr Savage MN 55378	MNS	EM			FW	1979
Nowak Thomas M	nowakthomas52@yahoo.com	4411 Monona Dr Monona WI 53716	SW	SP	Monona Monona WI	(608)222-7071	SL	1989
Nuckols Mark S Dr	(512)466-3840 mark.nuckols@outlook.com	N173 W20585 Crestview Dr Jackson WI 53037	SW	EM			FW	1989
Nuerge Roger D	(724)869-1936 pnuerge@concordialm.org	675 Moonridge Dr Freedom PA 15042	EA	SP	St Paul* New Kensington PA	(724)339-2829	CQ	1974
Nuffer Richard T Dr	(260)438-9493 richard.nuffer@ctsfw.edu	6527 Deepwater Point Rd Williamburg MI 49690	MI	EM			FW	1993
Nunez Hiram	901-362-1395 revnunez@bellsouth.net	709 Neptune Dr Granbury TX 76049	MDS	EM			HITSL	1999
Nus Paul F	(260)246-1781 paul.nus@gmail.com	1026 Wenrick Dr Beavercreek OH 45434	OH	C07/2018			FW	2008
Nuttelman Christopher K	cnuttelman@me.com		EN	SP	Hope Grand Rapids MI	(616)459-2941	FW	2015
Nutter Martin S	(931)455-6756	202 Meadowbrook St Tullahoma TN 37388	MDS	SP	Faith Tullahoma TN	(931)455-3510	SL	1979
Nuttmann Quentin T	(989)640-7004	407 E 12th Ave Hutchinson KS 67501	KS	Sn/Adm	Our Redeemer Hutchinson KS	(620)662-5642	SL	2006
Nwokeneme Anthony	317-787-4464	3932 Mi Casa Ave Indianapolis IN 46237	IN	Assoc	St Pauls Indianapolis IN	(317)787-4464	FW	2013
Nye Ferry L Sr	(334)467-3548 nfmln@aol.com	3317 Cross Creek Dr Montgomery AL 36116	SO	SP	Jehovah Pensacola FL	(850)433-2091	FW	1999
Nygaard Brian J		11210 Fayette St Crown Point IN 46307	IN	SP	Trinity Memorial Merrillville IN	(219)769-5376	FW	2023

*Multiple Assignments (See Church Worker Locator for Additional Details)

See Page 53 for the Table of Abbreviations for key to District, Position, and Seminary abbreviations

**C =Candidate; EM = Emeritus; the date following the C is the month and year the Candidate status began

NAME	TELEPHONE NUMBER EMAIL	STREET ADDRESS CITY/STATE/ZIP	DISTRICT	POSITION/ STATUS**	WHERE SERVING	OFFICE PHONE	SEM/ PROGRAM	YR GRAD
O Brien Pat F	(727)530-9270 pfao242@gmail.com	2429 Harn Blvd Clearwater FL 33764	FG	EM			SPR	1970
O Connor James P	(757)752-0495 jocon76517@aol.com	151 Simon Ct Apt 211 Fogelsville PA 18051	SE	EM			SL	1965
Oakes Ryan J	(303)877-3864 revro79@gmail.com	c/o Immanuel Lutheran Church 18 Clapboard Ridge Rd Danbury CT 06811	NE	SP	Immanuel Danbury Danbury CT	(203)748-3320	SL	2006
Oatman Mark A	(510)303-0071 pastormarkflc@att.net	c/o First Lutheran Church 1200 Pinecrest Ct Placerville CA 95667	CNH	SP	First Placerville CA	(530)622-3022	SL	2002
Oberdeck John W Dr	(414)839-0695 joberdec402@gmail.com	4884 W Willow Rd Brown Deer WI 53223	SW	EM			SL	1979
Oberdieck David L	(417)532-1698 augsburguac@gmail.com	1300a Kent Dr Lebanon MO 65536	MO	SP	Trinity Lebanon MO	(417)532-2717	SL	1993
Obermann Eric P	(563)321-0032 eobermann76@gmail.com	511 Chicago St Lakefield MN 56150	MNS	SP	Immanuel Lakefield MN	(507)662-5718	SL	2016
Obermann Joshua P	(412)610-1919 rev.obermann@gmail.com	2 Nancy Drive Jeannette PA 15644	EA	SP	Calvary Murrysville PA	(724)327-2898	SL	2016
Obersat Thomas F Sr	(402)570-2180 obersat@obersat.net	2300 Hickory St Casper WY 82604	TX	SP	Trinity Eden TX	(325)869-4031	FW	1991
O'Brien Terrence E	(217)561-0544 obie1950@gmail.com	6642 Hancock Ave Saint Louis MO 63139	CI	EM			FW	2009
O'Brien Patrick E	(701)742-2305 aobrien@drtel.net	P.O. Box 3 Oakes ND 58474	ND	EM			SPR	1975
Ochner Douglas A	dochner@hotmail.com	1121 Hunters CV Evans GA 30809	MO	M Chap	Office of International Mission Saint Louis MO		SL	1998
Ochoa Gabriel S	(619)755-4409 fideigratia@hotmail.com	820 Caminito Estrella Chula Vista CA 91910	PSW	Assoc	Hope Linda Vista San Diego CA	(858)268-4688	SL	2018
Ochsner Timothy L	(512)734-2071 revtim@sbcglobal.net	8 Goldman Ln Lampasas TX 76550	TX	SP	Faith Lampasas TX	(512)556-3514	FW	2002
Ockree Benjamin R	(913)674-1051 bockree@gmail.com	4715 NW Hiawatha Pl Topeka KS 66618	KS	SP	Calvary Topeka KS	(785)286-1431	FW	2013
OConnor Bryan T	(262)844-4728 bd2010@sbcglobal.net	405 Cheviot Chase #2 Waukesha WI 53186	SW	EM			CQ	1991
O'Connor William D	pastorwdo@faithgreenfield.org	200 W McKenzie Rd Greenfield IN 46140	IN	SP	Faith Greenfield IN	(317)462-4609	FW	1994
Oddi David M	(816)351-0744 pastordave59@gmail.com	265 Buzz St Unit 15 Branson MO 65616	MO	SP	Shep Of The Lakes Forsyth MO	(417)546-2246	SL	2007
O'Dea Patrick K	pat490@hotmail.com	28565 Alden Drive North Olmsted OH 44070	OH	EM			FW	2003
Odom Weslie T	(507)838-8996 pastorweslieodom@gmail.com	405 Main St W Morristown MN 55052	MNS	SP	Bethlehem Morristown MN	(507)685-4338	FW	2012
ODonnell Lance A	(262)567-5001 revlao@gmail.com	N8052 Woody Ln Ixonia WI 53036	SW	Sn/Adm	St Paul Oconomowoc WI	(262)567-5001	FW	2001
Oedewaldt Zachary R	(619)905-2160 zoedewaldt@gmail.com	922 Hickory Ct Decatur IN 46733	IN	SP	Zion Decatur IN	(260)724-7177	FW	2020
Oehlert Conrad W	(580)652-2085 conradoehlert@gmail.com	P.O. Box 543 Hooker OK 73945	OK	SP	St John Hooker OK	(580)652-2683	FW	2008
Oehlerts Gary L	(702)401-1295 garyoehlerts@gmail.com	13 Amy Scott Ct Longview TX 75605	TX	EM			SL	2003
Oelschlaeger Benjamin G	(612)598-9571 benjamin.oelschlaeger@valpo.edu	1950 S Baldwin Rd Lake Orion MI 48360	MI	SP	Good Shepherd Lake Orion MI	(248)391-1170	SL	2021
Oesch Norbert C Dr	(714)585-1431 oeschnorbert@gmail.com	16611 Mosscreek St Tustin CA 92782	PSW	EM			SL	1966
Oesch Benjamin T	(425)876-5287 boesch@sothfamily.org	9079 E Panorama Cir #417 Englewood CO 80112	RM	Assoc	Shepherd Hills Centennial CO	(303)798-0711	SL	2025
Oester James A	(301)533-6978 bishop.accident@gmail.com	31275 Garrett Hwy Accident MD 21520	EA	EM			FW	1995
Oester David A	(814)516-3454 oesterda@verizon.net	1193 Grandview Rd Oil City PA 16301	EA	SP	Christ Oil City PA	(814)677-4484	FW	2008
Oetting Jonathan W	(308)458-7300 oetting.jon@gmail.com	208 S Dellinger Ave P.O. Box 303 Hyannis NE 69350	NEB	SP	Shepherd of Hills Hyannis NE	(308)458-2831	S	1987
Oetting Larry W Dr	larryoetting@gmail.com	202 Knotty Pine Lane Seward NE 68434	NEB	EM			SL-D	2009
Offermann Wray A	(217)423-6955 grammyoffermann@yahoo.com	5840 Heritage Ln Oakley IL 62501	CI	EM			SL	1971
Ofgaa Berhanu E	(614)239-8079 bofgaa1724@sbcglobal.net	1092 Ross Rd Columbus OH 43227	OH	D Miss	Ohio District North Olmsted OH	(440)235-2297	CQ	2002
Ogden Alexander R	(586)303-6255 alex@fogdetroit.com		MI	Assoc	Family of God Detroit MI	(586)722-3996	FW	2025
Ogne Christopher M	(301)655-0264 pcmogne@gmail.com	7365 Indian Head Hwy Bryans Road MD 20616	SE	SP	Our Savior Bryans Road MD	(301)375-7507	SL	2002
Ognoskie Daniel F	(815)260-1211 revdanognoskie@gmail.com	1010 Maurer Street Wilton IA 52778	IE	SP	Zion Wilton IA	(563)732-3651	SPR	1975
Ogrodowicz Ryan J	(682)540-7679 pastoro@glcsbren.org	1202 W Main St Brenham TX 77833	TX	Sn/Adm	Grace Brenham TX	(979)836-3475	FW	2011
Ohlman David D	(402)765-7255 FatherFarmer@protonmail.com	2404 E 26th Rd Polk NE 68654	NEB	SP	Immanuel Polk NE	(402)765-7252	FW	2004
Ohlmann William O	(308)325-0069 ohlmannw@outlook.com	4811 Parklane Dr Kearney NE 68847	NEB	EM			SL-SMP	2014
Ohlwine Arthur A	(217)791-4124 hardlutheran@yahoo.com	4725 N Martin Luther King Jr D Apt 107 Decatur IL 62526	CI	C07/2016			SL	2000
Oien Mark R	(603)664-7938 magoien73@outlook.com	49 Bow Lake Estates Rd Strafford NH 03884	NE	EM			SPR	1976
Ok Seungwoong	(281)723-8589 seungwoong@gmail.com	12633 Memorial Dr Apt 93 Houston TX 77024	TX	SP	Hilltop Houston TX	(713)463-5954	CQ	2010

*Multiple Assignments (See Church Worker Locator for Additional Details)
See Page 53 for the Table of Abbreviations for key to District, Position, and Seminary abbreviations
**C =Candidate; EM = Emeritus; the date following the C is the month and year the Candidate status began

NAME	TELEPHONE NUMBER EMAIL	STREET ADDRESS CITY/STATE/ZIP	DISTRICT	POSITION/ STATUS**	WHERE SERVING	OFFICE PHONE	SEM/ PROGRAM	YR GRAD
Okai Andrew T Dr	(301)379-0940 pastor@holy-nativity.com	4 Golden Grass Ct Owings Mills MD 21117	SE	SP	Holy Nativity Arbutus MD	(410)242-9441	EIITSL	2007
Okamoto Toshio	reo.motol@gmail.com	7222 Heritage Spring Dr Unit 2401 West Chester OH 45069	OH	EM			SL	1956
Okamoto Joel P	(314)505-7152 okamotoj@csl.edu	870 Atalanta Ave Saint Louis MO 63119	MO	S HS/C	Concordia Seminary Saint Louis MO	(314)505-7000	SL	1996
Okine Michael	mikejo03@sbcglobal.net	3543 Pestalozzi St Saint Louis MO 63118	MO	Assoc	Messiah Saint Louis MO	(314)772-4474	SL	2001
Okpisz Steven J	(331)442-7539 sjopies777@gmail.com	274 Streamside Ct Nixa MO 65714	MO	SP	Peace Shell Knob MO	(417)858-3900	SL	1994
Okubo Mason K Dr	pastorokubo@immanuelfirst.org	512 S Valinda Ave West Covina CA 91790	PSW	SP	Immanuel First West Covina CA	(626)919-1530	SL	1999
Olana Gemechu	(507)438-3888 g.olana@outlook.com	1617 1ave SE Austin MN 55912	MNS	SP	Holy Cross* Austin MN	(507)437-2107	CQ	2009
Olander Charles P	(217)416-8842 c-olander@msn.com	2041 1500th St Beason IL 62512	CI	EM			FW	1978
Olckers Marthinus J	(561)843-3775 kolckers@pstglobal.com	1012 W Oak St Arcadia FL 34266	FG	SMP	Trinity Lake Placid FL	(863)465-5253	CQ	2019
Oldenburg Donald R	(714)319-2236 droldenburg@yahoo.com	920 Chicago Friendship WI 53934	SW	EM			FW	1977
Oldenettel Ronnie L	appleredron@gmail.com	23 Newburgh Dr Bella Vista AR 72715	MDS	EM			FW	1981
Oliphant Anthony J	(630)834-1411 aoliphant@redeemerlcms.com	123 E St Charles Rd Elmhurst IL 60126	EN	SP	Redeemer Elmhurst IL	(630)834-1411	FW	2010
Oliver Larry L	lloliverdc@comcast.net	4744 SW Birdsong Dr Corvallis OR 97333	NOW	SMP	Immanuel Albany OR	(541)926-3495	CQ	2018
Oliver Stephen P Dr	(510)564-4061 ouqiren@gmail.com	15536 Montreal St San Leandro CA 94579	CNH	C07/2024			SL	1986
Oliver Harold H	(805)287-9185 rohhgo@gmail.com	608 Monterey Rd Santa Maria CA 93455	CNH	EM			SL	1969
Ollek Kenneth L	(503)393-0507 shalom2u1@q.com	3457 Lake Vanessa Cir NW Salem OR 97304	NOW	EM			SL	1961
Olsen Arthur R	(503)407-6869 olsenb1@gmail.com	4801 Pretty Lake Ave #403 Norfolk VA 23518	SE	EM			CQ	2000
Olsen Jeffrey A	(260)749-0887 jaglo1@comcast.net	3810 Sugarhill Ct New Haven IN 46774	IN	EM			SL	1972
Olsen Roy C III	revolsen@emmausfortwayne.org	14825 Deerberry Ct Fort Wayne IN 46814	IN	SP	Emmaus Fort Wayne IN	(260)459-7722	SL	2005
Olsen Steven W	(206)852-4027 seaolsen@gmail.com	7863 Wildwood Farms Lane Indianapolis IN 46239	IN	EM			CQ	1980
Olson Daniel A Dr	(217)781-3278 pastorolson@stpaullux.org	N4118 County Road Ab Luxemburg WI 54217	NW	SP	St Paul Luxemburg WI	(920)845-2095	FW	1995
Olson Jonathan T	(303)364-7416 pastorolson@hopeaurora.org	1345 Macon St Aurora CO 80010	RM	SP	Hope Aurora CO	(303)364-7416	FW	2020
Olson Thomas L	(828)817-5506 pto351@gmail.com	1540 Golf Course Rd Columbus NC 28722	SE	SP	Trinity Tryon NC	(828)859-0379	FW	1982
Olson Norman V	(510)558-9442 normanvo@comcast.net	760 Richmond St El Cerrito CA 94530	CNH	EM			SL	1979
Olson Marlow J	(518)356-2646 marlowolson@gmail.com	3570 Carman Rd Schenectady NY 12303	AT	C07/2016			SL	1972
Olson Kevin R		7224 Wimbledon Rd Machesney Park IL 61115	NI	SP	Redeemer Rockford IL	(815)397-2227	SL	2004
Olson Jon C	(307)337-7838 pastorolson@gmail.com	4418 East 21st St Casper WY 82609	WY	Sn/Adm	Trinity Casper WY	(307)234-0568	FW	2006
Olson Jeremiah F Dr	(651)503-8381 pastorolson@comcast.net	2014 6th Ave NE Beulah ND 58523	ND	EM			CQ	1997
Olson Gary C	(804)484-5648 golson9350@gmail.com	9350 Brundidge Rd N Chesterfld VA 23236	SE	EM			FW	1984
Olson Darren R	(605)421-8123 revdarrenolson@gmail.com	13115 W 70th St Juniata NE 68955	NEB	SP	Christ Juniata NE	(402)744-4991	SL	2003
Olson DuWayne H	(845)750-2196 revwayneolson@gmail.com	8 Robin Ln Hyde Park NY 12538	AT	C08/2025			SL	2012
Ommen Erik J	(956)693-7256 ejommen@hotmail.com	612 Longspur Ct Laredo TX 78045	TX	SMP	Faith Laredo TX	(956)602-0175	CQ	2018
Omtvedt Michael J	(507)381-4867 pastormike@hosanna.church	105 Hosanna Dr Mankato MN 56001	MNS	SMP	Hosanna Mankato MN	(507)388-1766	SL-SMP	2014
Ondov Daniel P	(906)228-9883 dondov@redeemermqt.org	1700 W Fair Ave Marquette MI 49855	NW	Assoc	Redeemer Marquette MI	(906)228-9883	SL	2018
Ondracka William J	(865)687-6622 wondracka@gmail.com	10421 Old Rutledge Pike Mascot TN 37806	MDS	SP	Christus Victor Knoxville TN	(865)687-6622	SL	2011
ONeal Patrick F	(507) 334-0717 patrick.oneal@state.mn.us	Minnesota Correctional Facility 1101 Linden Lane Faribault MN 55021	SE	C08/2021			SL	2004
ONeill Dennis B	(218)415-0023 dennisoneill3850@yahoo.com	50 Teton Ln Apt 230 Mankato MN 56001	MNS	EM			FW	1980
Onken Kurt D	(360)659-6038 pastor@messiah-lcms.org	8308 57th Pl NE Marysville WA 98270	NOW	SP	Messiah Marysville WA	(360)659-4112	FW	1996
Onken Luke W	(812)528-7342 lukeonken@gmail.com	306 7th St NE Mayer MN 55360	MNS	Pro Stf	Mayer Mayer MN	(952)657-2251	SL	2024
Onkka Jackson D	(850)529-3730 gracealone@bellsouth.nt	66 Blithewood Drive Pensacola FL 32514	SO	SMP	Trinity Cantonment FL	(850)607-9524	SL-SMP	2013
Onnen Timothy G	(417)593-6878 kim4tim@gmail.com	21750 Uncompahgre Road Montrose CO 81403	RM	SMP	Christ Montrose CO	(970)633-0226	SL-SMP	2024
Opper Allan E	(814)938-3398	679 Wachob Dr Punxsutawney PA 15767	EA	EM			FW	1983

*Multiple Assignments (See Church Worker Locator for Additional Details)

See Page 53 for the Table of Abbreviations for key to District, Position, and Seminary abbreviations

**C =Candidate; EM = Emeritus; the date following the C is the month and year the Candidate status began

NAME	TELEPHONE NUMBER EMAIL	STREET ADDRESS CITY/STATE/ZIP	DISTRICT	POSITION/ STATUS**	WHERE SERVING	OFFICE PHONE	SEM/ PROGRAM	YR GRAD
Oren Albert S	(904)315-5115 revasoren@bellsouth.net	829 River Fall Dr Jefferson GA 30549	FG	EM			FW	1999
Orman Richard L	(760)741-0676 richardorman2021@gmail.com	1325 Las Villas Way Apt 310 Escondido CA 92026	PSW	EM			SL	1964
Orozco Enrique A	(305)556-9260	596 W 65th St Hialeah FL 33012	FG	Assoc	St Andrew Hialeah FL	(305)821-3622	SL	2010
Orr Travis N	(580)402-0469 OrrT1222@gmail.com	2942 27th Rd Hanover KS 66945	KS	SP	Trinity Hanover KS	(785)713-2764	FW	2012
Orr William J	(708)485-8393 fatherorr@gmail.com	2038 Dawson Dr Saint Charles MO 63301	MO	SP	Hope Saint Ann MO	(314)429-3808	FW	2008
Ortega Nelson S	(469)386-3911 nelof50@hotmail.com	3017 W 11th St Irving TX 75060	TX	Asst	Our Redeemer Irving TX	(972)255-0595	SL	2020
Ortiz-Lugo Carlos A	(773) 719-6631 pastorcarlos60641@gmail.com	4921 West Cornelia Ave Chicago IL 60641	NI	SP	Holy Cross Chicago IL	(773)523-3838	CQ	2022
Osbun Michael J	(574)367-8942 pastorosbun@gmail.com	66354 State Road 331 Bremen IN 46506	IN	Sn/Adm	First Hanna IN	(219)797-4855	FW	2010
Oschwald Jeffrey A Dr	(314)505-7146 oschwaldj@csl.edu	1017 Fond Du Lac Ct Fenton MO 63026	MO	S HS/C	Concordia Seminary Saint Louis MO	(314)505-7000	FW	1983
O'Shoney Glenn R Dr	(512)468-4922 drglennos@gmail.com	251 White Heron Dr Georgetown TX 78628	TX	EM			SPR	1962
Osladil Bryan R	(920)452-0717 bosladil@wi.rr.com	542 Martin Ln Howards Grove WI 53083	SW	SP	Our Redeemer Sheboygan WI	(920)452-0717	FW	1988
Osslund Richard N Dr	(515) 708-9736 rnosslund@aol.com	1025 Lakeshore Dr Brooklyn IA 52211	IW	EM			SL	1970
Ostafinski Joseph A	(219) 241-7885 jostafinski0405@gmail.com	3307 Morgan Creek Ct Valparaiso IN 46385	IN	EM			FW	1988
Ostebee Merlene D	ostebeem@gmail.com	1553 155th Ln Audubon IA 50025	IW	SP	Trinity* Persia IA	(712)488-2023	SL-D	2003
Oster Kevin W	(320)582-0307 revoster@gmail.com	1069 3rd St Tillamook OR 97141	NOW	SP	Redeemer Tillamook OR	(503)842-4823	FW	1994
Ostermeyer Timothy J	(314)650-2997 timothyostermeyer@gmail.com	23 Great Lakes Dr Saint Charles MO 63376	MO	SP	Beautiful Savior Bridgeton MO	(314)291-2395	SL	2004
Ostlund Daniel A	(618)301-6358 wartburg.pastor@gmail.com	1221 Coral St Red Bud IL 62278	SI	SP	Holy Cross Waterloo IL	(618)939-7094	SL	2014
Oswald Drew R	(402)992-0804 pastor@stpaulutica.com	625 Indiana St Utica NE 68456	NEB	Sn/Adm	St Paul Utica NE	(402)534-2200	SL	2024
Oswald Mark A	(616)899-2426	2315 Silver Leaf Lane Sheboygan WI 53083	MI	EM			FW	1991
Oswald Timothy J Dr	(757)831-6948 oswald1@charter.net	c/o Hope Lutheran Church 876 Lance Dr Twin Lakes WI 53181	SW	SP	Hope Twin Lakes WI	(262)877-4381	Other	1992
Oswald Wallace C	(715)479-8707	5649 Silver Shore Ln Eagle River WI 54521	SW	EM			SL	1957
Ott Chad M	(906)273-0280 cott@redeemermqt.org	1700 W Fair Ave Marquette MI 49855	NW	Sn/Adm	Redeemer Marquette MI	(906)228-9883	SL	2000
Ott Gene A		2703 N Highland Dr Connersville IN 47331	IN	SP	Bethany Connersville IN	(765)338-6527	FW	1985
Ott Timothy M	(906)250-8649 cohotim@charter.net	1510 County Road 496 SE Ishpeming MI 49849	NW	EM			SL	1973
Otte Gregory A	(714)997-7878 gotte@socal.rr.com	553 S Shasta Way Orange CA 92869	PSW	EM			SPR	1967
Otte James E	(972)741-9407 jotte2554@gmail.com	4205 Sparkford Ct Arlington TX 76013	TX	EM			SL	1980
Otte William H	(507)529-0989 whotte@gmail.com	909 18th Ave NE Rochester MN 55906	MNS	EM			SL	1972
Otten David G	(605)765-9300 revdavidotten@gmail.com	601 E Logan Ave Gettysburg SD 57442	SD	Sn/Adm	Emmanuel* Gettysburg SD	(605)765-9201	FW	1996
Otten David L	(618)606-5674 otter59@hotmail.com	101 Constitution Blvd Jerseyville IL 62052	SI	SP	Hope Jerseyville IL	(618)498-3423	SL	1984
Otten Luke H	(920)287-6329 lukehotten@sbcglobal.net	3357 Lasalle St Racine WI 53402	SW	SP	Holy Cross* Racine WI	(262)554-7010	FW	2024
Otten Walter D	(708)485-7074 theottens1@juno.com	9044 Sheridan Brookfield IL 60513	NI	EM			SL	1959
Otten William H	586-871-9960	885 Augusta Dr Rochester Hls MI 48309	MI	EM			SPR	1965
Ottmers Tab C	(214)773-2567 pastor_tab_ottmers@att.net	2205 Dalhart Trl Mc Kinney TX 75070	TX	SP	Immanuel Fairview TX	(972)540-1036	FW	2010
Otto William H Dr	(262)242-2461 revwho@sbcglobal.net	205 Green Bay Rd Apt 222 Thiensville WI 53092	SW	EM			SL	1961
Otto Vincent J	(816)213-8049 rev.vincentotto@gmail.com	601 N. 32nd St. Bismarck ND 58501	ND	Assoc	Zion Bismarck ND	(701)223-8286	SL	2024
Otto Craig D	(816)916-4935 otto@gracefaithlove.org	1124 NE Clubhouse Ln Lees Summit MO 64086	MO	Sn/Adm	St Matthew Lees Summit MO	(816)524-7068	SL	1995
Otto Mitchell E Dr	popcoralville@msn.com	1025 20th Ave Coralville IA 52241	IE	Sn/Adm	Prince Of Peace Coralville IA	(319)338-1842	FW	1996
Otto Rodney D Dr	(616)724-7446 rod.phyl@gmail.com	2252 Hummingbird Ct SE Grand Rapids MI 49546	MI	EM			SL	1969
Ouellette Dennis E	deo1929@gmail.com	308 Gleneagles Way Versailles KY 40383	IN	EM			CQ	1997
Overway Kurt R	(231)239-0252 roborev@charter.net	8381 Old Channel Trail Montague MI 49437	MI	SP	St Stephen Shelby MI	(231)861-2952	SL	1987
Ovil Michel J	(561) 531-2296 revmichelovil@gmail.com	733 SW Sail Terrace Port St Lucie FL 34953	FG	SP	New Alliance Haitian West Palm Beach FL		SL	2008
Owen Richard N	(540)520-2231 pastorfaithlutheran@yahoo.com	W4460 Davey Lane Merrill WI 54452	NW	EM			FW	2020
Owens David L	themustardseed7@gmail.com	301 N Amethyst Way Mustang OK 73064	OK	EM			SL	2006

*Multiple Assignments (See Church Worker Locator for Additional Details)
See Page 53 for the Table of Abbreviations for key to District, Position, and Seminary abbreviations
**C =Candidate; EM = Emeritus; the date following the C is the month and year the Candidate status began

NAME	TELEPHONE NUMBER EMAIL	STREET ADDRESS CITY/STATE/ZIP	DISTRICT	POSITION/ STATUS**	WHERE SERVING	OFFICE PHONE	SEM/ PROGRAM	YR GRAD
Paape David B	(414)430-5030 repaa@aol.com	N71w23588 Homestead Rd Sussex WI 53089	SW	EM			FW	1977
Paavola Daniel E	(262) 377-6610 daniel.paavola@cuw.edu	1011 South Main St Cedar Grove WI 53013	SW	Assoc	First Immanuel Cedarburg WI	(262)377-6610	FW	1983
Paavola Roger C Dr	(931)510-9639 rpaavola@mid-southlcms.com	6062 Daybreak Dr Bartlett TN 38135	MDS	DP	Mid-South District Cordova TN	(866)373-1343	NESC	1997
Paavola Christopher K	(314)604-3353 chris.paavola@gmail.com	c/o St Mark Lutheran Church 114 E Minges Rd Battle Creek MI 49015	MI	Sn/Adm	St Mark Battle Creek MI	(269)964-0401	SL	2016
Pace Edward B	(509)570-4394 revedpace@yahoo.com	4716 S Sands Rd Spokane Vly WA 99206	NOW	EM			CQ	2011
Pacey Ian S	revpacey@yahoo.com	306 E 15th St Houston TX 77008	TX	Sn/Adm	Immanuel Houston TX	(713)864-2651	FW	2000
Packer Andrew L	(970)507-0773 pastorandrewpacker@gmail.com		SI	Sn/Adm	Good Shepherd Collinsville IL	(618)344-3151	FW	2012
Padilla Benseslado C	(530)528-2481 benpadilla@att.net	442 Jefferson St Red Bluff CA 96080	CNH	EM			CQ	1991
Paepke William A	605-484-4428 abpep42@rap.midco.net	P.O. Box 285 Piedmont SD 57769	SD	EM			SL	1968
Paetow Derek S	(314)580-7396 pastorpaetow@gmail.com	138 Robinson St Genoa IL 60135	NI	SP	Trinity Genoa IL	(815)784-2522	SL	2005
Pagan Richard		1515 Silver Linden Ct Fort Wayne IN 46804	IN	Sn/Adm	Aboite Fort Wayne IN	(260)436-5673	FW	1979
Page Fred L III	(208)264-5559 wltrkurtz@aol.com	P.O. Box 302 Hope ID 83836	NOW	EM			FW	1994
Pagel Peter	(541)536-7934 peterpagel727@gmail.com	P.O. Box 113 La Pine OR 97739	NOW	SP	Faith La Pine OR	(541)536-1198	ED	1989
Pahl Justin R	(757)344-3689 pastor.pahl@gmail.com	1503 Bering Rd Wesley Chapel FL 33543	FG	SP	Holy Trinity Lutz FL	(813)949-7173	SL	2013
Pahlkotter Henry G II	(507)993-6311 henry.pahlkotter@vlscrusaders.org	718 Spruce Needle Ln Cedar Falls IA 50613	IE	Prin	Valley Cedar Falls IA	(319)266-4565	SL-SMP	2021
Paholke Michael A	(920)842-2477 revmichael@plbb.us	P.O. Box 247 Suring WI 54174	NW	SP	Christ* Gillett WI		FW	1994
Paine Franklin W Jr	(206) 229-4900 fwpainejr@ieee.org	14570 SW Hart Rd. Apt 110 Beaverton OR 97007	NOW	EM			CQ	1982
Palach Craig M	(218)770-7191 pastor.revcmp@gmail.com	15972 County Highway 2 Fergus Falls MN 56537	MNN	SP	St Paul* Campbell MN	(218)630-5377	FW	1995
Palka John M	palka.john@gmail.com	4060 Glencoe Ave # 219 Marina Del Rey CA 90292	PSW	SP	First Venice CA	(310)821-2740	FW	1991
Palm Juan D	(507)685-2307 jhpalm@outlook.com	c/o Trinity Lutheran Churvch 10500 215th St W Morristown MN 55052	MNS	SP	Trinity Morristown MN	(507)685-2307	FW	1999
Palmer William C	(262)363-6897 wpalmer182@gmail.com	S110w26510 Craig Ave Mukwonago WI 53149	SW	SP	Emmanuel Deaf West Allis WI	(414)321-8430	FW	1984
Palmer Jonathan R	jon.palmer@theway618.church	7206 Becker Crossing Ct Saint Louis MO 63129	S	SP	The Way Columbia IL	(618)504-8585	SL	2007
Palmer Joshua S	(520)271-8157 pastor.joshua.palmer@gmail.com	9535 N Placita Roca De Bronce Tucson AZ 85704	PSW	Sn/Adm	Cross and Crown Tucson AZ	(520)222-7453	SL	2015
Palmer Mark R	(715)758-6589 m.palmer@stpaulbonduel.com	134 N. Church St. P.O. Box 97 Bonduel WI 54107	NW	Assoc	St Paul Bonduel WI	(715)758-8559	SL	1987
Palmer Nickalaus W	(319)560-9650 Stjohnnewhall5@southslope.net	306 2nd St E P.O. Box 341 Newhall IA 52315	IE	SP	St John Newhall IA	(319)223-5593	SL	2023
Palmer Stanley E	(620)789-0957 prpalmer52@gmail.com	13307 Jewell Rd Offerle KS 67563	KS	SP	Our Redeemer* Kinsley KS	(620)659-2262	FW	2013
Palmer Wayne H	(314)268-1080 wayne.palmer@cph.org	5207 Depaul Drive Fairview Heights IL 62208	MO	Pro Stf	Concordia Publishing House Saint Louis MO	(314)268-1000	FW	1992
Palomaki David W	(402)367-6136	880 M St David City NE 68632	NEB	SP	Redeemer* David City NE	(402)367-3859	SL	1987
Panning David J	(843)424-5300 panningdj@gmail.com	148 Zinnia Dr Myrtle Beach SC 29579	SE	EM			FW	2006
Panzer Justin A	kspres@kslcms.org	c/o Kansas District Office 1000 SW 10th Ave Topeka KS 66604	KS	DP	Kansas District Topeka KS	(785)357-4441	SL	2003
Panzigrau Jerome E	(724)594-8759 jpanzigrau@comcast.net	149 Glenview Dr New Kensingtn PA 15068	S	SP	John Huss Arnold PA	(724)334-2272	SL	2000
Pape Brian N	pastorbrian@stpeters-epil.com	604 Mickel Parkway Washington IL 61571	CI	SP	St Peters East Peoria IL	(309)699-5411	SL	1999
Pape Neil F Dr	(850)477-1792 neilfranpape@gmail.com	1698 Spalding Cir Pensacola FL 32514	SO	EM			SL	1960
Pape Richard E	(585)678-4647 richardpape@rochester.rr.com	9 Sablewood Cir Fairport NY 14450	EA	EM			SL	1975
Parent Raymond D II	frparent@att.net	6481 Welannee Blvd Laurel Hill FL 32567	SO	SP	Our Savior Crestview FL	(850)682-3154	FW	2001
Parent Jean A	(561)252-4368 jeanparent19@aol.com	2382 Mantilla Ave SE Palm Bay FL 32909	FG	SP	Zion Haitian Palm Bay FL	(321)984-8987	SL	2008
Parham Collis Sr	(504)431-3417 collispl@att.net	25 Larkspur Ln Westwego LA 70094	SO	SMP	Epiphany New Orleans LA	(504)861-7093	SL-SMP	2011
Park Jae H	(972)762-7495 pastorpark@log.org	1301 Meadow Cove Ct Carrollton TX 75007	TX	Assoc	Lamb Of God Flower Mound TX	(972)539-5200	EIITSL	2024
Park Jung Hun	(416) 993-3435 newhope@stluketoronto.com	311 Roywood Cres Newmarket ON L3Y1A CANADA	EN	Assoc	St Luke North York ON	(416)221-8900	CQ	2016
Park Thomas D Dr	(414)326-6490	24701 Raymond Way Space 225 Lake Forest CA 92630	PSW	S Miss	Office of International Mission Saint Louis MO		CQ	2011
Park Chan K	(949)786-3667 chankp112@yahoo.com	19032 Singingwood Cir Trabuco CA 92679	PSW	D Miss	Pacific Southwest Di Irvine CA	(949)854-3232	SL	2002
Parker Marion K	(936)441-7503 wolfparker1957@gmail.com	1901 N Thompson St Conroe TX 77301	TX	EM			SPR	1970

*Multiple Assignments (See Church Worker Locator for Additional Details)
See Page 53 for the Table of Abbreviations for key to District, Position, and Seminary abbreviations
**C =Candidate; EM = Emeritus; the date following the C is the month and year the Candidate status began

NAME	TELEPHONE NUMBER EMAIL	STREET ADDRESS CITY/STATE/ZIP	DISTRICT	POSITION/ STATUS**	WHERE SERVING	OFFICE PHONE	SEM/ PROGRAM	YR GRAD
Parker Dustin T Dr	(562)926-7416	1642 W Brookdale Pl Fullerton CA 92833	PSW	SP	Concordia Cerritos CA	(562)926-7416	CQ	2004
Parker Edwin L	(260)493-9041 edwinlparker@gmail.com	7009 Lake Valley Ct Fort Wayne IN 46815	IN	EM			FW	1994
Parker Harrison S	858-722-9445 magnifiedplaid10@gmail.com	366 Ivylawn Whitmore Lake MI 48189	MI	C10/2020			SL	2014
Parkhurst Aaron	lcmspastoraaron@gmail.com	P.O. Box 131 Cavalier ND 58220	ND	SP	Our Savior* Cavalier ND	(701)265-4408	NESC	2025
Parks David H	(785) 466-6126	32a Cherry St Liberty MO 64068	KS	EM			SPR	1968
Parks Steven R Dr	(626)335-5315 pastor@hopeglendora.org	15401 Beach Blvd Apt 232 Westminster CA 92683	PSW	SP	Hope Glendora CA	(626)335-5315	FW	2007
Parks Vincent S III	(936)449-5402 vparks@salem4u.com	259 Magnolia Reserve Loop Magnolia TX 77354	TX	SMP	Salem Tomball TX	(281)351-8223	SL-SMP	2011
Parodi Hector L Sr	(321)210-1959 hector.hector2@aol.com	2601 Brigg St Kissemmee FL 34743	FG	EM			HITSL	1999
Parris Michael J	(641)426-0348 msgr87@yahoo.com	309 E 2nd St Riceville IA 50466	IE	EM			FW	1987
Parrish Brent L Dr	(612)499-1135 pastorp@immanuel-fishlake.org	20200 Fairlawn Ave Prior Lake MN 55372	MNS	Sn/Adm	Immanuel Prior Lake MN	(952)492-6010	SL	1989
Parrish Joshua L	(612)499-0519 pastorjosh@redemptionmn.org	4540 W 131st 1/2 St. Savage MN 55378	MNS	SP	Redemption Bloomington MN	(952)881-0035	SL	2020
Parron Richard K	(443)912-8181 rkparron@yahoo.com	10405 Bird River Rd Baltimore MD 21220	SE	SMP	Living Water Rosedale MD	(410)391-0755	SL-SMP	2022
Parsch David H	(407)529-8829 revdhpar@gmail.com	78 Harvest Dr Maggie Valley NC 28751	FG	EM			SL	1968
Parshall Daniel W	dwparshall@aol.com	3812 SE 182nd Ct Vancouver WA 98683	NOW	EM			SPR	1964
Parsons Jacob D	(805) 835-1317 jjparsons@comcast.net	6880 Navajoa Ave Atascadero CA 93422	CNH	C07/2016			SL	2012
Parsons Joshua J	jparsons@sjlmidland.org	5315 Cortland St Midland MI 48642	MI	SMP	St John's Midland MI	(989)835-5861	FW-SMP	2017
Parsons William A III	(251)591-0602 redeemerfairhope@bellsouth.net	513 4th Ave SE Cullman AL 35055	SO	SP	Redeemer Fairhope AL	(251)928-8397	FW	1998
Parvey Adam D	(507)382-0458 aparvey@abidingsaviorlutheran. org	1024 Winter Lake Dr Fenton MO 63026	MO	Sn/Adm	Abiding Savior Saint Louis MO	(314)894-9200	SL	2008
Parviz Kevin D	(314)645-4456	6327 Clayton Ave Saint Louis MO 63139	MO	SP	Cong Chai v Shalom Saint Louis MO	(314)645-4456	SL	1998
Pasch Rodney W	(985)290-3508 rod_pasch@yahoo.com	609 Dockside Dr Slidell LA 70461	SO	EM			SL	1981
Pasche John A	(320)296-9877 jpasche@hutchtel.net	21377 Tetonka Lake Rd Waterville MN 56096	MNS	SP	Bethlehem* Elysian MN	(507)362-8381	SL	2002
Pase Robert J	pastorpase@gmail.com	3818 Purdue Ln Abilene TX 79602	TX	SP	Our Savior Abilene TX	(325)692-6163	SL	1989
Pater Paul M	(920)296-9630 pastor.pater@gmail.com	8257 Trinity Lane Iuka IL 62849	SI	SP	Trinity* Iuka IL	(618)323-6586	SL	2010
Patt Richard W	(414)839-6315 rpatt@wi.rr.com	9999 W North Ave Apt 107 Wauwatosa WI 53226	EN	EM			SL	1960
Patten Timothy R	(513)899-4380 patlehome@roadrunner.com	6186 Avebury Ct Morrow OH 45152	OH	EM			SL	1995
Patterson Zachary J	pastorpattersonlcms@gmail.com	90 Erin Dr Cary IL 60013	NI	SP	Holy Cross Cary IL	(847)639-1702	FW	2019
Patterson Christopher J	(305)378-6728 miamirev@gmail.com	15802 Country Lake Dr Tampa FL 33624	FG	C02/2022			FW	2005
Patterson Craig A	(720)314-2492 crgteg@hotmail.com	6108 Trailhead Rd Highlands Ranch CO 80130	RM	EM			FW	1978
Patterson Jeffery L	(719)396-4710 sslc.cos@gmail.com	6142 Rowdy Dr Colorado Springs CO 80924	RM	SP	Shep Springs Colorado Springs CO	(719)396-4710	FW	2008
Patterson Jeffrey D	(812) 569-2471 jdp0428@icloud.com		IN	Assoc	St Paul Columbus IN	(812)376-6504	FW	1986
Patton Steven B	(704)390-3784 pastorsteve@messiah-nc.org	8300 Providence Rd Charlotte NC 28277	SE	Sn/Adm	Messiah Charlotte NC	(704)541-1624	SL	2008
Paul Gerald A Dr	(345)926-5491 gerald.paul@lcms.org	P.O. Box 32324 Grand Cayman KY112 CAYMAN ISLANDS	MT	S Miss	Office of International Mission Saint Louis MO		FW	1998
Paul Mark A	(903)245-7628	21374 Southwind Dr Chandler TX 75758	TX	EM			SL	1975
Paul Michael J Dr		No. 21 5F-1 Xinrong Road Alley 35 Chiayi City NO 600 TAIWAN	IN	S Miss	Office of International Mission Saint Louis MO		SL	1996
Paul Preston A	(715)641-1426 prestonpaul@icloud.com		NW	SP	Zion Eleva WI	(715)878-4512	FW	2002
Paul Richard D Dr	(714)315-9938 revdrrdpaul@dslextreme.com	6004 E Bryce Ave Orange CA 92867	PSW	EM			SPR	1970
Paul Robert W	(575)910-6273 rpaul@mlchouston.org	c/o Memorial Lutheran Church 5800 Westheimer Rd Houston TX 77057	TX	Assoc	Memorial Houston TX	(713)782-6079	FW	2012
Paul Gary G Dr	(715)313-4052 bevnrev@gmail.com	6230 Lars Rd Eau Claire WI 54701	NW	EM			FW	1980
Paulison Michael E Dr	(303)249-0333 mike.e.paulison@gmail.com	19869 E Tufts Dr Centennial CO 80015	RM	Assoc	Peace W Christ Aurora CO	(303)693-5618	SL	1990
Pauls Timothy J	(208)343-7212 timothypauls@gslcboise.org	5009 Cassia Boise ID 83705	NOW	SP	Good Shepherd Boise ID	(208)343-7212	SL	1993
Paulson Charles E	(480)619-1269 ckpaulson11@gmail.com	2361 Appellation Dr New Braunfels TX 78132	TX	EM			SL	1982

*Multiple Assignments (See Church Worker Locator for Additional Details)
See Page 53 for the Table of Abbreviations for key to District, Position, and Seminary abbreviations
**C =Candidate; EM = Emeritus; the date following the C is the month and year the Candidate status began

NAME	TELEPHONE NUMBER EMAIL	STREET ADDRESS CITY/STATE/ZIP	DISTRICT	POSITION/ STATUS**	WHERE SERVING	OFFICE PHONE	SEM/ PROGRAM	YR GRAD
Pautz Jeffrey W	(563) 263-0347 oslcp@machlink.com	1103 Westwood Ln Muscatine IA 52761	IE	SP	Our Savior Muscatine IA	(563)263-0347	SL	2002
Pavel John D		332 Maple St Apt 9 Birnamwood WI 54414	NW	EM			SL	1981
Pavelski Gregory J	(719)582-1353 gpavelski1950@yahoo.com	44 Douglas Ln Pueblo CO 81001	RM	EM			SL	2009
Pavich Michael P	(562)447-7723 mikepavich67@yahoo.com	10334 Santa Gertrudes Ave #23 Whittier CA 90603	PSW	SMP	Trinity Central Los Angeles CA	(323)737-2790	CQ	2019
Pay Garen R	pastorpay@gmail.com	c/o Hope Lutheran Church 2071 12th St Idaho Falls ID 83404	NOW	Sn/Adm	Hope Idaho Falls ID	(208)529-8080	SL	2012
Payne Mark E	(972)539-5200 PastorPayne@log.org	1401 Cross Timbers Rd. Flower Mound TX 75028	TX	SMP	Lamb Of God Flower Mound TX	(972)539-5200	SL-SMP	2021
Payne Bryan D	(405)436-9741 bryan.d.payne@gmail.com	7204 S Douglas Ave Oklahoma City OK 73139	MO	S Miss	Office of International Mission Saint Louis MO		FW	2023
Payton Leonard R Dr	lrpayton@stjohnforestpark.org	3211 Vernon Ave Brookfield IL 60513	NI	Sn/Adm	St John Forest Park IL	(708)366-3226	FW	2005
Pearl James M	(269)275-4016 pastorjimpearl@gmail.com	108 S Oakland St Saint Johns MI 48879	MI	SP	St John's Saint Johns MI	(989)224-6796	CQ	2019
Pearson Charles W Jr	(818) 648-7798 cpearl@aol.com	958 Richardson Ave Simi Valley CA 93065	PSW	EM			SPR	1972
Peck Adam J	(616)350-0093 pastoradam@holycrossjenison.org	3555 Lenters Dr Hudsonville MI 49426	MI	Assoc	Holy Cross Jenison MI	(616)457-2420	SL	2010
Peck Jerome K	(913)424-3455 nflynrev1@gmail.com	709 Rosewood Ct Paola KS 66071	KS	EM			SL	1973
Peck Kent A	(720)456-5394 revkentpeck@gmail.com	270 Main St Westgate IA 50681	IE	SP	Grace* Fayette IA	(563)425-3544	FW	2008
Peckman Walter A	(816)632-2493 wapeckman@gmail.com	1106 Sam G Hiner Dr Cameron MO 64429	MO	EM			SL	1972
Peckman Paul H Dr	peckmfwi@yahoo.com	408 W Everwood Way Nixa MO 65714	MO	EM			SL	1975
Peckman Richard E	(620)252-9078 rcpeckman77@att.net	566 E Katella Cir Nixa MO 65714	MO	EM			SL	1975
Pederson Ronald D	(435)630-3527 rdpeders@gmail.com	387 W 500 S Vernal UT 84078	RM	EM			FW	1995
Pederson Joe E	(573)677-0171 eojde2@yahoo.com	11 Pin Oak Ct Cuba MO 65453	MO	EM			SL	1987
Peeples Matthew J	(865)765-2289 peeplesmatthew@gmail.com	5809 Pebble Oak Dr Saint Louis MO 63128	MO	Sn/Adm	Faith Oakville MO	(314)846-8612	SL	2009
Peffer Bruce A Dr	(562)454-7330 brucepeffer@sbcglobal.net	204 Daphne St Lakeside IA 50588	IW	EM			SL	1986
Peiser Jordan R	(847)409-3975 rev.j.peiser@gmail.com	314 E South First St Stewardson IL 62463	CI	SP	Faith Shumway IL	(217)868-5484	FW	2022
Peitsch Nathan A	(712)885-2221 pastornpeitsch@gmail.com	303 E 4th St P.O. Box 139 Ute IA 51060	IW	SP	St Paul Ute IA	(712)885-2221	SL	2010
Peitsch Peter M	(920)876-2341 triple.ppp@frontier.com	301 Moraine Dr Elkhart Lake WI 53020	SW	SP	Grace Elkhart Lake WI	(920)781-5076	FW	1985
Pekari Randall L	(860)810-0761 randallpekari@gmail.com	20 Aroda Dr South Windsor CT 06074	NE	Sn/Adm	Our Savior South Windsor CT	(860)644-3350	SL	1999
Pekari William J	(717)414-7102 wsp25@comcast.net	2716 St Joseph Ln Chambersburg PA 17202	SE	EM			SL	1972
Pekari Jeremy R Dr	(978)587-2621	5 Wayne Rd Peabody MA 01960	NE	Sn/Adm	Messiah Lynnfield MA	(781)334-4111	SL	2002
Pellegrino Joseph E	(505)538-9446 josephpellegrino47@yahoo.com	3210 N Ridge Crest Dr Silver City NM 88061	RM	SP	Messiah Silver City NM	(505)538-9446	SL	1995
Pellom Warren R	(901)216-7191 wrpellom@aol.com	9250 Plantation Rd Olive Branch MS 38654	SO	SP	Prince Of Peace Southaven MS	(662)393-3432	CQ	2001
Pelsue David C	(314)398-5488 dcpelse@gmail.com	6325 De Mara Dr Affton MO 63123	MO	EM			SL	1981
Pemberton James F	(330)464-6875 jamespem@earthlink.net	1340 Timothy Trail Oshkosh WI 54904	SW	Sn/Adm	Trinity Oshkosh WI	(920)235-7440	SL	1999
Pena Arturo	(210)725-7266 arturopena1@sbcglobal.net	4326 Stetson Vw San Antonio TX 78223	TX	SP	Abundant Grace San Antonio TX	(210)648-5509	SL	2007
Penhallegon Philip W Dr	(314)505-7165 penhallegonp@csl.edu	801 Seminary Place St Louis MO 63105	MO	S HS/C	Concordia Seminary Saint Louis MO	(314)505-7000	SL	1998
Penikis Michael A	(913)709-7220 patermap@yahoo.com	N4794 430th St Menomonie WI 54751	NW	SP	Holy Trinity* Boyceville WI		FW	2000
Pennekamp Ronald D	(863)398-0557 rpenne5253@aol.com	3135 Bellflower Way Lakeland FL 33813	FG	EM			CQ	1994
Pennington Shea R	(512) 925-0180 shea.r.pennington@gmail.com	220 19th Avenue Southeast Hickory NC 28602	SE	Assoc	St Stephen Hickory NC	(828)256-9865	SL	2016
Pennington Ryan W	(832)233-3392 ryan@fortress.today	19318 Fm 2484 Killeen TX 76542	TX	SMP	Fortress Harker Heights TX	(254)393-0669	SL-SMP	2023
Penny Roger	(980)229-8758 pastorroger@messiah-nc.org	8300 Providence Rd. Charlotte NC 28277	SE	SMP	Messiah Charlotte NC	(704)541-1624	SL-SMP	2021
Penrod Thomas	tpmarketed@gmail.com	32446 155th St Tolstoy SD 57475	SD	SMP	Emmanuel* Gettysburg SD	(605)765-9201	SL-SMP	2024
Peperkorn Todd A Dr	(262)705-3232 todd.peperkorn@ctsfw.edu	2624 Chichester Ln Fort Wayne IN 46815	IN	S HS/C	Concordia Theological Seminary Fort Wayne IN	(260)452-2100	FW	1996
Peperkorn Troy W	(515)291-3559 revtroypeperkorn@gmail.com	107 Outer Dr Silver Bay MN 55614	MNN	SP	Faith Silver Bay MN	(218)226-3908	FW	2014
Percy Herbert M Jr	(949) 981-2824 hpercyjr@gmail.com	101 Twin Creeks Xing Apt 5 Central Point OR 97502	NOW	SP	Gloria Dei Central Point OR	(541)664-3724	FW	2003
Peregoy Nathan F	(727) 501-3459 nate.peregoy@gmail.com	c/o Our Father Lutheran 6335 S Holly St Centennial CO 80121	RM	Assoc	Our Father Centennial CO	(303)779-1332	SL	2007

*Multiple Assignments (See Church Worker Locator for Additional Details)
See Page 53 for the Table of Abbreviations for key to District, Position, and Seminary abbreviations
**C =Candidate; EM = Emeritus; the date following the C is the month and year the Candidate status began

NAME	TELEPHONE NUMBER EMAIL	STREET ADDRESS CITY/STATE/ZIP	DISTRICT	POSITION/ STATUS**	WHERE SERVING	OFFICE PHONE	SEM/ PROGRAM	YR GRAD
Pereira Keith R	(217)435-9685 katco@speednet.com	181 E Tremont St Waverly IL 62692	CI	SP	Christ Waverly IL	(217)435-9685	SL	1985
Perez Claudio Sr	(713)926-4621 elisaperez57@yahoo.com	7439 Azalea St Houston TX 77023	TX	Asst	Immanuel Houston TX	(713)864-2651	CQ	1995
Perez-Arche Erwin	(305)607-5738	14520 SW 132 Ave Miami FL 33186	FG	SP	Bay Shore Miami FL	(305)758-1344	SL	1992
Perez-Lopez Benito	(305)227-4733 bperez6950@aol.com	10301 SW 45th St Miami FL 33165	FG	D Miss	Hospital del Alma Leisure City FL	(305)247-0459	HITSL	1995
Perkins Benjamin D	(636)328-5648 pbenmin@outlook.com	P.O. Box 36 Sergeant Bluff IA 51054	IW	SP	Shepherd Of Peace Sergeant Bluff IA	(712)943-4502	SL	2013
Perkins Timothy B	(817)875-2682 timothybperkins@gmail.com	1333 Bluff Springs Dr Haslet TX 76052	TX	Assoc	St John Mansfield TX	(817)473-4889	SL	2002
Perling John F	(573) 337-0253 pastor@felclcms.org	981 State Hwy Z Saint Robert MO 65584	MO	SP	Faith Saint Robert MO	(573)336-4464	SL	1997
Perry Scott D	(408)506-8234 soojiwei@gmail.com	5109 Adair Way San Jose CA 95124	CNH	Tchr	Prince Of Peace Fremont CA	(510)797-8186	SL	2001
Perry Andrew G	(956)330-6078 mor_perrya@yahoo.com	233 Cinnamon Loop Burnet TX 78611	TX	EM			SL	2021
Perry Milton K	(224)402-2535 chaplainkperry@gmail.com	325 Engler Blvd Apt 347 Chaska MN 55318	MNS	EM			CQ	1996
Perryman Dennis S	dsperryman@gmail.com	1037 Riviera Dr Elgin IL 60124	NI	EM			SPR	1975
Persaud Charles L	(917)570-3743 rev.persaud@yahoo.com	89-24 145th St Jamaica NY 11435	AT	SP	Grace Jamaica NY	(718)526-6290	CQ	2006
Persich Wayne T	(816)987-6114	903 Buckeye Ln Pleasant Hill MO 64080	MO	EM			SL	2001
Peske Mark I	(218)760-0909 mspeske@paulbunyan.net	1416 Aspen Dr Deer River MN 56636	MNN	EM			FW	1997
Petajan Andrew D	(202)459-6680 adpetajan@gmail.com	236 Beachwood Rd Pasadena MD 21122	SE	SP	Christ Deaf Silver Spring MD	(301)251-5953	SL	2021
Peter David J Dr	(314)909-0948 PeterD@csl.edu	559 Brookhaven Ct Kirkwood MO 63122	MO	S HS/C	Concordia Seminary Saint Louis MO	(314)505-7000	SL	1987
Petering Jonathan E	(281)725-4465 jpetering@immanuelmemphis.org	c/o Immanuel Lutheran Church 6325 Raleigh Lagrange Rd Memphis TN 38134	MDS	Sn/Adm	Immanuel Memphis TN	(901)373-4486	SL	2006
Peters Matthew D	(916)541-4663 matthewpeters1957@gmail.com	10617 Ambassador Dr Rancho Cordova CA 95670	CNH	SP	Cordova Rancho Cordova CA	(916)363-5687	SL	2014
Peters Roger A	(260)452-3146 roger.peters@ctsfw.edu		IN	S HS/C	Concordia Theological Seminary Fort Wayne IN	(260)452-2100	FW	2013
Peters Orval F	(405)550-7031 orval_peters@yahoo.com	1212 Regency Ct Kingfisher OK 73750	OK	SMP	St John* Hinton OK	(405)542-6472	CQ	2020
Peters Matthew D	(262)794-3905 mpeters715@gmail.com	3855 Mountain Dr Brookfield WI 53045	SW	SP	Trinity UAC Milwaukee WI	(414)271-2219	FW	2012
Peters Matthew A	(231)622-9210 mpeters@zionlutheranpetoskey.org	c/o Zion Lutheran Church 500 W Mitchell St Petoskey MI 49770	MI	SP	Zion Petoskey MI	(231)347-3438	SL	2007
Peters Mark D	(815)718-0780 peters.mark1954@gmail.com	2236 Chelsea Ave Freeport IL 61032	NI	EM			FW	1980
Peters Curtis H Dr	(812)948-8711 curtandpam@earthlink.net	1605 Hedden Ct New Albany IN 47150	IN	EM			SL	1969
Peters Larry A	(931) 801-2344	203 Rachel Ct Clarksville TN 37043	MDS	EM			FW	1980
Peters Michael J	(309)744-2256 michaelpeters@earthlink.net	P.O. Box 229 Secor IL 61771	CI	SP	St John Secor IL	(309)744-2255	FW	2014
Peters Kirk L	(307) 217-1041 klpeters35@gmail.com	8614 River Rd Suring WI 54174	NW	EM			FW	1998
Peters Gregory G	(303)973-1706 hosanna.lutheran@att.net	12095 W Bowles Pl Littleton CO 80127	RM	Sn/Adm	Hosanna Littleton CO	(303)973-1706	CQ	1981
Peters Mark J		7616 Bull Rapids Rd Woodburn IN 46797	IN	SP	Mount Calvary* Antwerp OH	(419)258-6505	FW	2022
Petersen Don M	(509)781-4746 pastor.don.petersen@gmail.com	12115 Paige Ln Prosser WA 99350	NOW	SP	Calvary* Sunnyside WA	(509)837-5662	CQ	2020
Petersen Thomas E	(512)452-1038	6709 Shoal Creek Blvd Austin TX 78757	TX	EM			SL	1956
Petersen David H Dr	(260)414-3083 prdhpetersen@gmail.com	4024 S Harrison St Fort Wayne IN 46807	EN	Sn/Adm	Redeemer Fort Wayne IN	(260)744-2585	FW	1996
Petersen Thomas E	(608)334-5718 sotlpastortom@gmail.com	36141 Barbour Ln Pine River MN 56474	MNN	EM			CQ	1988
Peterson Kevin M	(208)993-1125		KS	SP	Zion Independence KS	(620)332-3300	FW	1999
Peterson Ryan R Dr	(734)864-6528 petersor15@csp.edu	10613 Alison Way Inver Grove Heights MN 55077	MNS	S HS/C	Concordia University St Paul Saint Paul MN	(651)641-8278	SL	2007
Peterson Richard J	(360)532-4943 revpete2@yahoo.com	907 K St Apt 505 Hoquiam WA 98550	NOW	EM			SL	1964
Peterson Roy R Dr	(262)442-4090 roy.peterson@gsmlcs.org	10373 Fontanella Dr Ft Myers FL 33913	FG	Assoc	St Michael Fort Myers FL	(239)939-1218	CQ	1998
Peterson Wendell P	(224)227-8591 wendellpolly64@gmail.com	1697 Kelley Ln Pingree Grove IL 60140	NI	EM			SL	1966
Peterson Norman F	(612)382-8704 pztzrszn@gmail.com	2033 Carnelian Ln Eagan MN 55122	NW	EM			SPR	1972
Peterson Mark E	(920)340-4476 stpeterhilbert@gmail.com	37 N 3rd St Hilbert WI 54129	SW	SP	St Luke* Chilton WI	(920)483-0956	SL	2002
Peterson Kevin P	(507)779-4082 prkevinpeterson@gmail.com	3112 Thunderbird Court W Aurora IL 60503	NI	SP	St Paul Addison IL	(630)543-6909	SL	2021

*Multiple Assignments (See Church Worker Locator for Additional Details)
See Page 53 for the Table of Abbreviations for key to District, Position, and Seminary abbreviations
**C =Candidate; EM = Emeritus; the date following the C is the month and year the Candidate status began

NAME	TELEPHONE NUMBER EMAIL	STREET ADDRESS CITY/STATE/ZIP	DISTRICT	POSITION/ STATUS**	WHERE SERVING	OFFICE PHONE	SEM/ PROGRAM	YR GRAD
Peterson James M	(308) 442-1195 pastorpeterson8@hotmail.com	602 E 6th St Curtis NE 69025	NEB	SP	St John Curtis NE	(308)367-4238	FW	2019
Peterson Ivan E	(309) 291-1232 ipjp72@gmail.com	1112 11th St Bloomington IL 61704	CI	EM			SL	1971
Peterson Gary W	(630)809-7633 gwpete48@gmail.com	4622 W Lake Shore Dr Wonder Lake IL 60097	NI	EM			SL	2002
Peterson Gary I	(225)622-4629 chapelcrossluthbr@yahoo.com	43157 Highway 933 Prairieville LA 70769	SO	SP	Cross of Calvary Baton Rouge LA	(225)383-2962	SL	1993
Peterson Drake M	(262) 424-4779 dpeterson@sjsmarysville.org	c/o Saint Johns Lutheran Church 12809 State Route 736 Marysville OH 43040	OH	Assoc	St John's Marysville OH	(937)644-5540	SL	2024
Peterson Donald E III	(712)657-3056 donald_e_peterson@hotmail.com	P.O. Box 260 Lake View IA 51450	IW	SP	Emmanuel Lake View IA	(712)657-3324	FW	2005
Peterson David A	(858)279-4815 preachnpaint@gmail.com	3582 Chasewood Dr San Diego CA 92111	PSW	EM			FW	1987
Peterson Russell A	(810)547-6180 russ@hclm.org	867 Roseling Circle Unit 213 Lake Mary FL 32746	S	Sn/Adm	Holy Cross Lake Mary FL	(407)333-0797	SL	2003
Peterson Jason P	(616)866-1818 revjpeterson@yahoo.com		MI	SP	St Peter Rockford MI	(616)866-1818	FW	2006
Petrak Daniel G	(515) 971-7468 dgpetrak@gmail.com	3890 NW 77th Ln Ankeny IA 50023	IW	Assoc	Living Faith Clive IA	(515)987-4030	SL-SMP	2015
Petri Michael J	(712)329-8959 revpetri@hotmail.com	245 Canterbury Cir Council Blfs IA 51503	IW	EM			SL	1983
Petrich David J	(218)245-2762 petrichfamily44@hotmail.com		MNS	SP	Saint James Holland MN	(507)347-3357	FW	1985
Pett Paul K	pastorpett@gmail.com	205 Hudson St Green Bay WI 54303	NW	SP	Redeemer Green Bay WI	(920)499-1033	FW	1990
Pettey Ricky L	(573)944-4378 rpettey562@yahoo.com	P.O. Box 201 Barnhart MO 63012	MO	EM			FW	1991
Pettit Joshua M	(407)469-2525 pastorjosh@woodlandschurch.com	411 Sky Valley St Clermont FL 34711	FG	Sn/Adm	Woodlands Montverde FL	(407)469-2525	SL	2014
Petzke Karl G	(208)773-9160 kmpetzke@yahoo.com	515 N Garden Plz Ct Apt 324 Post Falls ID 83854	NOW	EM			SPR	1972
Petzold Carl R	(989) 233-8769 pastorpetzold@gmail.com	129 N Fairview St West Branch MI 48661	MI	SP	Hope* Saint Helen MI	(989)389-7715	FW	2023
Petzold Jonathan D	(847) 395-9400 pastor@bslcantioch.com		NI	SP	Beautiful Savior Antioch IL	(847)395-9400	SL	2016
Petzoldt Shirrel W	(419)654-9107 petz@accesstoledo.com	946 Hialea Ct Holland OH 43528	OH	EM			CQ	1976
Pevy James A	(916)767-4686 pastorpevy2020@gmail.com	5629 49th St Sacramento CA 95824	CNH	SMP	Peace Sacramento CA	(916)927-5934	SL-SMP	2020
Pezzica Daniel W	(818)540-8104	c/o Our Savior Lutheran Church 1515 S Main St Chelsea MI 48118	MI	SP	Our Savior Chelsea MI	(734)475-1404	FW	2008
Pfaff Robert D	(865)207-8530 robert_pfaff@hotmail.com	152 Cornerstone Dr Madison MS 39110	MDS	EM			SL	1983
Pfaff Richard C	(281)380-4737 txpfaff@gmail.com	711 Dresden Wood Dr Boerne TX 78006	TX	EM			SL	1983
Pfaffe Daniel M	(715)495-3896 pfaffe@nelson-tel.net	608 3rd Ave E Durand WI 54736	NW	SP	St Paul* Mondovi WI	(716)926-5973	FW	1990
Pfanstiel Barry L	(573)334-2870 bpfanstiel@me.com	1063 Stewart Dr Cpe Girardeau MO 63701	MO	EM			SL	1974
Pfeffer Dean R	(813)416-2373 hopepcpastor@gmail.com	2001 N Park Rd Plant City FL 33563	FG	Sn/Adm	Hope Plant City FL	(813)752-4622	SL	1994
Pfeil Robert A	(715)266-2187 pastorpfeil@yahoo.com	4291 W North Clover Rd Winter WI 54896	NW	EM			FW	1984
Pflueger James K	(408)274-9795 jimpflueger733@gmail.com	733 W Desert Seasons Dr San Tan Valley AZ 85143	PSW	EM			SL	1970
Pflug Jeffery D	(812)701-0498	323 Hillcrest Dr Madison IN 47250	IN	SP	Faith Madison IN	(812)273-1371	SL	1993
Pflug Mark R	(734)316-2858 mark.pflug669@gmail.com	669 Woodcreek Cir Saline MI 48176	MI	EM			SL	1966
Pflughoeft Darren M	(307)334-2287 pflughoeft@wyoming.com	P.O. Box 795 Lusk WY 82225	WY	SP	St Pauls Lusk WY	(307)334-2336	FW	1999
Pflughoeft Mark E	(219) 775-3928	311 Carnation Ave NE Demotte IN 46310	IN	EM			FW	1980
Pfotenhauer Paul J	(630)204-3234 pastorpj@messiah-lutheran.org	1479 Raymond Ave. Saint Paul MN 55108	MNS	SP	Messiah Mounds View MN	(763)784-1786	SL	1992
Pfotenhauer Thomas J	(651)739-5144 pastortom@woodburylutheran.org	2245 Vermillion Curve Woodbury MN 55129	MNS	Sn/Adm	Woodbury Woodbury MN	(651)739-5144	SL	2004
Pfotenhauer Paul J	(651)739-1522 pfotenhauer@juno.com	7217 Coachwood Rd Woodbury MN 55125	MNS	EM			SPR	1958
Phan Van C	(503)367-0377 mucsuvan@yahoo.com	2650 NE 102nd Ave Portland OR 97220	NOW	SP	The Master Portland OR	(503)257-9323	CQ	2003
Phanco Timothy J	(951)837-9360 tjphanco@gmail.com	1069 Brentford Pl Myrtle Beach SC 29579	SE	SMP	Risen Christ Myrtle Beach SC	(843)272-5845	SL-SMP	2024
Phifer Phillip L	(989)278-9817 surfpastorphil@gmail.com	835 Cherokee Ave Port Neches TX 77651	TX	SP	Peace Groves TX	(409)962-1133	SL	1998
Philipp John C	(847)336-8346 dianephilipp@att.net	825 Hickory St Waukegan IL 60085	NI	EM			SPR	1972
Phillips Max A	(515)465-5342 mphillips@lutheranfamilyser-vice.org	29399 140th St Woodward IA 50276	IW	Sn/Adm	Christ* Perry IA	(515)676-2289	SL-D	2006
Phillips Thomas P	(217)371-2122 Rev.Phillips.STL91@gmail.com	c/o St Paul Lutheran Church 2470 Beebe Rd NE Kalkaska MI 49646	MI	SP	St Paul* Kalkaska MI	(231)258-9258	SL	1991
Phillips Timothy J	(515)360-2470 tphillips@gloriadeionline.com	4901 Merced St Des Moines IA 50310	IW	Assoc	Gloria Dei Urbandale IA	(515)276-1700	SL	1989

*Multiple Assignments (See Church Worker Locator for Additional Details)
See Page 53 for the Table of Abbreviations for key to District, Position, and Seminary abbreviations
**C =Candidate; EM = Emeritus; the date following the C is the month and year the Candidate status began

NAME	TELEPHONE NUMBER EMAIL	STREET ADDRESS CITY/STATE/ZIP	DISTRICT	POSITION/ STATUS**	WHERE SERVING	OFFICE PHONE	SEM/ PROGRAM	YR GRAD
Phillips Eric G	aureliusaugustine@yahoo.com	2300 Peak Hill CV Nashville TN 37211	MDS	SP	Concordia Nashville TN	(615)292-0982	FW	2013
Phillips Michael G	(586)336-1888 mgp001@yahoo.com	75603 Peters Dr Bruce Twp MI 48065	MI	SMP	Grace Fellowship Romeo MI	(586)752-9800	SL-SMP	2016
Phillips Michael A	(419)236-4612 maphil@wcoil.com	1725 Wendell Ave Lima OH 45805	OH	SP	Immanuel Lima OH	(419)222-2541	SL	1992
Philp Paul A Dr	(314)226-4722	4792 Scharmen Rd Traverse City MI 49696	MI	S Ex/S	Concordia University System Saint Louis MO	(314)996-1252	SL	1999
Phiwthong Kham P	(515)835-7093	1024 Boone St Webster City IA 50595	IW	EM			CQ	2019
Piazza Adrian L	(317)490-7651 revpiazzaclc@gmail.com	1211 N Jefferson St Robinson IL 62454	CI	SP	Trinity* Casey IL	(217)932-2645	SL	1989
Pica Sean G	revpica@gmail.com	5564 Sultana Ave Temple City CA 91780	PSW	Sn/Adm	Good Shepherd Downey CA	(562)803-4459	Other	2011
Picard Jean C	(407)293-7096	8630 Valley Ridge Ct Orlando FL 32818	FG	Asst	Trinity Orlando FL	(407)488-1919	SL	2009
Picard Joel T	(641)842-4724 pastor.picard@gmail.com	1877 150th Pl Knoxville IA 50138	IE	SP	Trinity Knoxville IA	(641)842-4724	SL	1997
Pick Wayne T	(308)352-6353 wdjsp@gpcom.net		NEB	EM			SL	1979
Pieper Christian L	(763)516-3013 christian.pieper@gdlc.church	8301 Aurora Ave Urbandale IA 50322	IW	Assoc	Gloria Dei Urbandale IA	(515)276-1700	SL	2021
Pieper Wilfred L	(763)234-7799 papa_pieper@hotmail.com	5620 Royal Oaks Dr Shoreline MN 55126	MNS	EM			SL	1990
Piepkorn Gary A	(575)693-7899 prpiepkorn@yucca.net	8168 New Mexico 206 Portales NM 88130	RM	C07/2025			FW	1981
Pieplow Charles F	(205)591-7386 cpieplowlu@aol.com	931 42nd St S Birmingham AL 35222	SO	EM			SL	1967
Pieplow Richard E	(229)244-2831 pieplowrc@bellsouth.net	1803 S Sherwood Cir Valdosta GA 31602	FG	EM			CQ	1980
Pierce William J	(808)639-9166 kielesdad@gmail.com	5750 Kuamoo Rd Kapaa HI 96746	CNH	SMP	St Matthew Koloa HI	(808)639-9166	SL-SMP	2020
Pierce James R			NOW	SP	Messiah* Mesa WA	(509)492-7399	FW	2018
Pierce Earl J Dr	pastorpierce@me.com	1645 N First St Seward NE 68434	NEB	EM			SL	1987
Pierce Kent D Dr	(573)442-5942 kent.pierce@campuslutheran.org		MO	Sn/Adm	Campus Columbia MO	(573)442-5942	SL	1999
Pierce James R	(843)640-3214 jimpierce2006@bellsouth.net	2465 Shadowcreek Ct N Charleston SC 29406	SE	EM			SL	1970
Piering Arnold E	(727)359-2305 arnie.piering@gmail.com	2284 Oberon Ln Punta Gorda FL 33983	FG	EM			CQ	1996
Pierson Joseph B	(515)832-3043 revpierson@gmail.com	905 Beach St Webster City IA 50595	IW	SP	St Paul's Webster City IA	(515)832-3043	SL	2021
Pierson Mark A	(714)473-5158 markapierson@gmail.com	1766 Bahama Pl Costa Mesa CA 92626	EN	SP	St Paul Long Beach CA	(562)596-4409	FW	2011
Pies Frank J Jr Dr	(248)887-9695	4249 Fenton Rd Hartland MI 48353	EN	EM			SPR	1972
Piescer Michael A	011-81-80-4328-1555 mpiescer@yahoo.com	292 Nakayama Hanno-Shi Saitama-Ken 357-0 JAPAN	CNH	Inst C	California/Nevada/Hawaii District Livermore CA	(866)264-6079	SL	1998
Pietsch Stephen J Dr	(314)297-8662 drsjpietsch@outlook.com	18 McCall Terr Clayton MO 63105	MO	S HS/C	Concordia Seminary Saint Louis MO	(314)505-7000	CQ	2023
Pietsch Thomas D	(414)446-1260 thomas.pietsch@gmail.com	9263 N Waverly Dr Bayside WI 53217	SW	S HS/C	Concordia University Wisconsin Mequon WI	(262)243-5700	CQ	2025
Pillay Dereck	(416)669-4295 pastordereck@rogers.com	5 Angela Court Markham ON L3S 4 CANADA	EN	SP	St Matthew Scarborough ON	(416)431-9252	NESC	2013
Pilli Sagar Dr	(713) 815-5693	2614 Taos Trail Deer Park TX 77536	TX	C10/2023			SL	2005
Pillsbury Hugh A	(207)730-6339 hugh.pillsbury@gmail.com	Concordia Luther Haven 148 Marwood Rd Apt 1320 Cabot PA 16023	S	EM			FW	2001
Pineros Armenio Sr	(719)574-3463 armeniop@gmail.com	800 Clark St Sterling CO 80751	RM	EM			SL	2011
Pingel Gilbert H	gpingel322@bellsouth.net	8106 Carriage Xing Chattanooga TN 37421	MDS	EM			SL	1965
Pingel Dennis L	(608)362-1614 pingeldennis@yahoo.com	2740 N Wood Dr Beloit WI 53511	SW	EM			SL	1969
Pingel John L	(716)983-2319	135 Liberty Ln West Seneca NY 14224	EA	DP	Eastern District Williamsville NY	(716)634-5111	SL	1983
Pingel Richard W	(913)777-8228 rwpingel71@yahoo.com	305 S Canyon Dr Olathe KS 66061	KS	EM			SL	1971
Pingel Allen L	(308)482-0620 allenpingel@yahoo.com	P.O. Box 7 Fullerton NE 68638	NEB	SP	Mount Calvary Fullerton NE	(308)536-2635	SL	1985
Pingel Aaron A	(440)265-8108 chrysostom02@gmail.com	1405 E Fallbrook St Fallbrook CA 92028	PSW	SP	Zion Fallbrook CA	(760)728-8288	SL	2003
Pingel Dean T	(715)384-5153 immanuel.hewitt@gmail.com	7735 Yellowstone Dr Hewitt WI 54441	NW	SP	Immanuel Hewitt WI	(715)384-5153	SL	1985
Pinion Patrick D	patrickpinion@yahoo.com	P.O. Box 85 Burlington IL 60109	NI	SP	St John Hampshire IL	(847)683-2338	SL	2002
Pinkerton Van M	(714)554-1779 vpink@msn.com	St Paul's Lutheran Church 13082 Bowen St Garden Grove CA 92843	PSW	SMP	St Paul Garden Grove CA	(714)537-4245	CQ	2019
Piotter Alan G Dr	alanpiotter@gmail.com	474 Linda Dr Sonoma CA 95476	CNH	EM			SL	1969

*Multiple Assignments (See Church Worker Locator for Additional Details)

See Page 53 for the Table of Abbreviations for key to District, Position, and Seminary abbreviations

**C =Candidate; EM = Emeritus; the date following the C is the month and year the Candidate status began

NAME	TELEPHONE NUMBER EMAIL	STREET ADDRESS CITY/STATE/ZIP	DISTRICT	POSITION/ STATUS**	WHERE SERVING	OFFICE PHONE	SEM/ PROGRAM	YR GRAD
Piotter Keith A	(563)332-7046	3436 43rd Avenue Ct Bettendorf IA 52722	IE	Sn/Adm	Our Savior Bettendorf IA	(563)332-5141	SL	1991
Pirn Peeter	(216)215-5364 other.wood8672@pirn.us	4801 Burger Ave Cleveland OH 44109	OH	SP	Unity Cleveland OH	(216)741-2085	FW	2007
Pitcher John C	(360)778-2948 jypitcher@comcast.net	1220 Spruce Cir # A Lynden WA 98264	NOW	EM			FW	1990
Pitsch David S	(479)806-5001 PastorSamPitsch@outlook.com	203 7th St S Moorhead MN 56560	MNN	Sn/Adm	Our Redeemer Moorhead MN	(218)233-7569	SL	2015
Pitsch Alexander S	(636)317-8780 aspitsch@gmail.com	3023 Brentmoor Dr Saint Charles MO 63303	MO	Assoc	King Of Kings Chesterfield MO	(314)469-2224	SL	2018
Pittelko Dean D Dr	(224)645-3300 dr.deancounseling@gmail.com	344 Pembroke Ct Apt 2 Schaumburg IL 60193	NI	SP	Faith Oak Lawn IL	(708)424-1059	SL	1988
Pittock Travis A	(682)270-6340 pastortravisp@hotmail.com	3905 105th St Lubbock TX 79423	TX	SP	Emmanuel Littlefield TX		SL	2002
Plain Robert D Sr	(440)429-2069 pastorplain@icloud.com	3894 Clague Rd North Olmsted OH 44070	OH	C07/2023			FW-SMP	2012
Plautz William C	(715)226-0324 rev_81_@hotmail.com	13502 42nd Ave Chippewa FLS WI 54729	NW	EM			FW	1981
Pledger Phillip M Dr	(909)255-1054 philpledger@gmail.com	3216 W 200 N Peru IN 46970	IN	EM			FW	1984
Pless John T Dr	(260)452-2271	1 Wycliffe Pl Fort Wayne IN 46825	IN	S HS/C	Concordia Theological Seminary Fort Wayne IN	(260)452-2100	CQ	1983
Plump John T	(505)715-8968 johnplump70@yahoo.com	P.O. Box 61 Cedar Crest NM 87008	MI	EM			FW	1980
Pobanz Don F	dpobanz@gmail.com	P.O. Box 326 Shelton NE 68876	NEB	SP	St Paul* Shelton NE	(308)647-6733	FW	2011
Pockat Steven N Sr	715-526-5065 spockat53@yahoo.com	404 North Ave Box 22 Mattoon WI 54450	NW	SP	St John Mattoon WI	(715)489-3471	FW	2000
Podeszwa Michael A	(724)650-3427 mpodes24@gmail.com	10010 E. Monroe Rd Wheeler MI 48662	MI	SP	Immanuel Wheeler MI	(989)842-3459	SL	2010
Podoll Lynn A	(216)273-7185 allanlynn41@yahoo.com	2401 Silverdale Avenue Cleveland OH 44109	OH	EM			SL	1967
Poedel David G Dr	(602)402-6342 dave@padredave.com	8743 E Jaeger St Mesa AZ 85207	PSW	EM			CQ	2000
Poellet Dean R	(517)712-1798 holt683@outlook.com	956 Riverview Ct Williamston MI 48895	MI	SP	St Matthew Holt MI	(517)694-0978	FW	1999
Poganski David F	(916)591-3816 dfpogo@gmail.com	249 Nation Dr Auburn CA 95603	CNH	SP	St Paul Auburn CA	(530)885-5378	FW	1980
Pohanka John C	(989)631-6388 jpohanka@aol.com	2874 N Cedaridge Dr Midland MI 48642	MI	EM			SL	1973
Pohl Gary L	(512)341-0201 garylpohl@gmail.com	2904 Forest Meadow Dr Round Rock TX 78665	TX	EM			SPR	1971
Pohland Walter A	(512)869-5044	2423 Candle Ridge Trail Georgetown TX 78626	TX	EM			SL	1988
Polansky Roger W	(507)251-5171 repolansky@gmail.com	5520 Ballington Rd NW Apt 2029 Rochester MN 55901	MNS	EM			SL	1957
Polege Donald R	(651)238-4802 dpolege1@gmail.com	28359 Lakeside Way Lindstrom MN 55045	MNN	EM			SL	1988
Pollatz Paul A	313-565-9445 paulpollatz44@gmail.com	31543 Rosslyn Ave Garden City MI 48135	MI	SP	Mount Hope Allen Park MI	(313)565-9445	SPR	1969
Pollock Benjamin D	sawtooths@hotmail.com	4017 Hiawatha Blvd Fort Wayne IN 46809	IN	C07/2016			FW	2002
Pollock Roger J	(224)856-1277 rogerpo@aol.com	348 Copper Springs Ln Elgin IL 60124	NI	EM			SPR	1975
Polzin Joseph W	(734)429-9200 pastorpolzin@c-o-k.org		MI	Sn/Adm	Christ Our King Saline MI	(734)429-9200	SL	2016
Polzin Lewis R	(414)405-6262		SW	SP	St Mark Belgium WI	(262)285-3820	SL	2013
Pomplun Raymond L	(605)225-7099 rpomplun@abe.midco.net	1211 Pinewood Ln Aberdeen SD 57401	SD	EM			SL	1961
Pomrenke Gary R	(240) 424-2451 pastorgary.pomrenke@gmail.com	c/o New Hope Lutheran Church 14851 Hull St Rd Chesterfield VA 23832	SE	SMP	New Hope Chesterfield VA		CQ	2019
Ponseti Sidney J	(225)293-3176	12126 Excalibur Ave Baton Rouge LA 70816	SO	EM			SPR	1962
Poock Patrick W	(707)716-7598 revpoock@gmail.com	9608 US Hwy 301 N Parrish FL 34219	FG	SP	Faith Parrish FL	(941)776-1395	SL	2001
Pool Daniel P Dr	(563)593-2502 dpool@stjohn-clinton-ia.org	422 Main Ave Clinton IA 52732	IE	Sn/Adm	St John Clinton IA	(563)242-5588	SL	2009
Poole Donnie L	(806)576-1216 dondacleric@gmail.com	802 S Avenue O Clifton TX 76634	TX	EM			FW	1990
Pope Addison V	(501)605-8082 avpope@protonmail.com	301 S Pine St Cabot AR 72023	MDS	SP	Our Savior Cabot AR	(501)605-8082	FW	2025
Pope John F	(602)819-4126 johnfpope@cox.net	38632 N Donovan Ct Anthem AZ 85086	PSW	EM			SL	1969
Pope Stephen D	(920)931-5299 popestephen1955@gmail.com	801 Plymouth Rd Wakefield MI 49968	NW	EM			CQ	2003
Popovits Matthew L	(713)548-4513 mlpopovits@gmail.com	11310 Pecan Creek Dr Houston TX 77043	TX	Sn/Adm	St Mark Houston TX	(713)468-2623	SL	2006
Popp Michael S	(904)254-3135 michael_popp@gracelutheraneagles.org	1502 Arden Way Jacksonville Beach FL 32250	FG	SMP	Grace Jacksonville FL	(904)928-9136	SL-SMP	2017
Poppe Randal A	(262)633-9592 revrpoppe@gmail.com	4820 County Road P Highland WI 53543	SW	EM			FW	1983
Poppe Clint K	(402)499-3631 pastorpoppe1@gmail.com	705 Glenarbor Cir Lincoln NE 68512	NEB	EM			SL	1998

*Multiple Assignments (See Church Worker Locator for Additional Details)
See Page 53 for the Table of Abbreviations for key to District, Position, and Seminary abbreviations
**C =Candidate; EM = Emeritus; the date following the C is the month and year the Candidate status began

NAME	TELEPHONE NUMBER EMAIL	STREET ADDRESS CITY/STATE/ZIP	DISTRICT	POSITION/ STATUS**	WHERE SERVING	OFFICE PHONE	SEM/ PROGRAM	YR GRAD
Poppe John C	(651)252-5060 reverend.poppe@gmail.com	9590 Hudson Blvd. Apt 715 Lake Elmo MN 55042	NW	EM			SPR	1970
Poppen Tyler P	(605)695-8043 colecamplutheran@gmail.com	14547 Klink Ave Cole Camp MO 65325	MO	SP	Holy Cross* Cole Camp MO	(660)668-0117	SL	2013
Porath Norman E	(402) 615-0938 porathne@gmail.com	8331 SW 98th St Denton NE 68339	NEB	EM			SPR	1965
Porath Scott T	(402)781-2776 immanuelpastor@windstream.net	100 S 4th St Eagle NE 68347	NEB	SP	Immanuel Eagle NE	(402)781-2190	FW	1991
Porter Marty L	(320)352-5240 pastor.porter@gmail.com	331 Maple St Sauk Centre MN 56378	MNN	SP	Zion Sauk Centre MN	(320)352-3447	FW	2007
Porter Arthur L	(205)821-1906 artandjan1@comcast.net	1015 River Plantation Dr Woodstock GA 30188	FG	EM			FW	2000
Porter Donald C	(260)443-5776 revdcporter@msn.com	200 Bluff Valley Dr Lot 219 Fredericksbrg TX 78624	TX	EM			FW	1980
Porterfield Robert L Sr	(425)629-3241 oneshepherd.porterfield@gmail.com	23600 Marine View Dr S Des Moines WA 98198	NOW	EM			SL	1982
Portier Robert M	(865)771-2118 revrobertportier@gmail.com	c/o Immanuel Lutheran Church 2565 Airline Dr Bossier City LA 71111	SO	Sn/Adm	Immanuel Bossier City LA	(318)746-2215	FW	2007
Possehl Iver L	(605) 520-3174 ipossehl@mchsi.com	1721 Orchard Dr Brookings SD 57006	SD	EM			FW	1982
Post Alexander C	(641)758-1915 alexpost1226@gmail.com	1603 S 2nd Ave Marshalltown IA 50158	IE	SP	Redeemer Marshalltown IA	(641)753-9565	FW	2013
Post Mark D	(630)832-2685 revmarkdpost@yahoo.com	304 E Highland Ave Villa Park IL 60181	NI	SP	St Michael* Chicago IL		SL	2000
Post Tanner B	(319)327-4853 Rev.tpost@protonmail.com	218 S Divison St Sumner IA 50674	IE	SP	St John* Sumner IA	(563)578-3315	FW	2021
Postel William E	(913) 388-1282 billpostel784@gmail.com	784 S Poplar Gardner KS 66030	KS	EM			CQ	1981
Potter Jeffrey R	(406)210-0225 jpotter777@yahoo.com	55 Spring Mountain Dr Kalispell MT 59901	MT	C07/2016			FW	1987
Potthoff Timothy C	(949)351-6821 mrpotthoff11@gmail.com	309 N Sweetwater St Anaheim CA 92807	PSW	SP	Bethel Buena Park CA	(714)527-4776	SL	2023
Potthoff William F	(253)318-2702 revwmpotthoff@gmail.com	P.O. Box 731222 Puyallup WA 98373	NOW	EM			SL	1960
Potts Daniel A Dr	potts.da@gmail.com	6531 Tanglewood Ln Lincoln NE 68516	NEB	Assoc	Christ Lincoln NE	(402)483-7774	SL	2014
Potts Chadwick L	(260)573-7736 pottscl@gmail.com	8850 Echelon Point Dr Unit 2007 Las Vegas NV 89149	TX	M Chap	Office of International Mission Saint Louis MO		FW	2012
Pottschmidt Michael T	(804)543-8865 mtpottschmidt@stpaulsconcordia.org	514 S Magdalena St Concordia MO 64020	MO	Sn/Adm	St Paul Concordia MO	(660)463-2291	SL	2005
Poulos George E Jr	(954)585-3836 gepoulosjr@aol.com	5801 Peppertree Cir E Davie FL 33314	FG	Sn/Adm	Gloria Dei Davie FL	(954)475-0683	CQ	1997
Poulson Quentin G	(704)491-0126 qgirard@bellsouth.net	4324 Garvin Dr Charlotte NC 28269	SE	EM			NESC	1993
Powell Samuel M	(573)632-0206 spowell@trinityjc.org	2016 Saint Louis Rd Jefferson City MO 65101	MO	Sn/Adm	Trinity Jefferson City MO	(573)636-6750	SL	2010
Powers Jerry D	(480)710-6825 revjerr@gmail.com	2377 Fieldstone Ct Ammon ID 83401	NOW	EM			FW	1992
Powers Michael E	(626)233-2313 michael.powers@lutheranmonrovia.org	1015 E Grandview Ave Sierra Madre CA 91024	PSW	SMP	First Monrovia CA	(626)357-3543	CQ	2019
Powers Gregory J	(219)836-0805 gregpfw@hotmail.com	8750 Harrison Ave Apt 201 Munster IN 46321	IN	EM			FW	1992
Powers Marcus H	(920)917-7358 mhpowers@hotmail.com	787 W Willis Rd Tahlequah OK 74464	OK	EM			SL	1993
Powers Lloyd D	(480)471-7727 lpowers5@cox.net	25232 N Abajo Dr Rio Verde AZ 85263	PSW	EM			SL	1960
Poynter Michael J	masappoynter@reagan.com	5556 Anstaett Rd Batavia OH 45103	OH	SP	Good Shepherd Florence KY	(859)746-9066	FW	2003
Prada Alfonso J	(414)233-0569 alfonsorosmy@yahoo.es	2841 S 44th St Milwaukee WI 53219	SW	SP	St Martini Milwaukee WI	(414)645-4094	Other	2013
Praeuner Daniel C	(575)910-6181 daniel.praeuner@gmail.com	P.O. Box 508 Ranchester WY 82839	WY	EM			FW	1993
Prahl Larry J	(262)375-2049 ljprahl@aol.com	2379 Stoney Ln Grafton WI 53024	SW	EM			CQ	1983
Pralle Leroy H	(785)825-6210 l.pralle@att.net	2657 Quail Hollow Dr Salina KS 67401	KS	EM			CQ	1982
Prange Anton A	(831)293-8305 antonprange@comcast.net	3850 Rio Rd Apt 82 Carmel CA 93923	CNH	EM			SL	1967
Prange Paul T	(314)739-7301 pastorp@charter.net	11452 Nora Ct Bridgeton MO 63044	MO	EM			SL	1963
Pranschke Thomas J	(201)358-9132 pastortjp@zionwestwoodnj.org	149 2nd Ave Westwood NJ 07675	NJ	Sn/Adm	Zion Westwood NJ	(201)664-1325	CQ	2006
Pratt Brian V	(260)442-8039 brianpratt23@gmail.com	10305 E 550 S Hudson IN 46747	EN	SP	Prince Peace Hudson IN	(260)351-2144	FW	2004
Prauner Gregory J	(314)413-6813 gregoryprauner@gmail.com	P.O. Box 365 Battle Creek NE 68715	NEB	C02/2021			SL	2008
Precht Stephen F	revprecht@aol.com	1040 Appaloosa Drive Freeport IL 61032	NI	EM			SL	1980
Precup J L	(858)270-7874 chaps05@yahoo.com	5112 New Haven Rd San Diego CA 92117	PSW	EM			SL	1972
Predoehl Theodore G	(520)393-0082 tpredoehl@cox.net	2303 S Cliff Dr Green Valley AZ 85614	EN	EM			SL	1964

*Multiple Assignments (See Church Worker Locator for Additional Details)
See Page 53 for the Table of Abbreviations for key to District, Position, and Seminary abbreviations
**C =Candidate; EM = Emeritus; the date following the C is the month and year the Candidate status began

NAME	TELEPHONE NUMBER EMAIL	STREET ADDRESS CITY/STATE/ZIP	DISTRICT	POSITION/ STATUS**	WHERE SERVING	OFFICE PHONE	SEM/ PROGRAM	YR GRAD
Preece Robert C Dr	(214)477-9057 rpreece@revpreece.org	10334 Cimmaron Trl Dallas TX 75243	TX	EM			SL	1973
Prentice David L Jr	(708) 650-4082 pastor.prentice@comcast.net	231 W 17th St Lombard IL 60148	NI	SP	Faith Westchester IL	(708)885-0001	SL-D	2006
Presley Thomas T	(256)698-5204 thomas.presley13@gmail.com	c/o First Lutheran Church 2507 Highland Ave S Birmingham AL 35205	SO	SP	First Birmingham AL	(205)933-0380	FW	2017
Press Mark G Dr	mgpckp@yahoo.com	1157 Yorktown Ln Bowling Green KY 42104	MDS	Assoc	Holy Trinity Bowling Green KY	(270)843-9595	FW	1977
Presuhn Gerald E	(262)629-9459 HPresuhn@wauknet.com	5474 E Moraine Hills Dr West Bend WI 53095	SW	EM			SL	1964
Pretznow Mark E	(248)736-8639 pastor.mark.log@gmail.com	2061 W Maple Ave Flint MI 48507	MI	SP	Lamb of God Flint MI	(810)234-2423	SL	2018
Preus James A	(641)814-3292 jamespreus@gmail.com	297 Shaul Ave Ottumwa IA 52501	IE	SP	Trinity Ottumwa IA	(641)684-7279	NESC	2015
Preus Stephen K	(319)457-0638 stephenpreus@gmail.com	1503 H Ave Vinton IA 52349	IE	SP	Trinity Vinton IA	(319)472-5571	FW	2011
Preus Rolf D	(218)388-0405 rolfpreus@msn.com	617 S Gunflint Lk Grand Marais MN 55604	MNN	EM			FW	1979
Preus Peter E	(612)308-5394 pjpreus@gmail.com	7755 Polaris Ln N Maple Grove MN 55311	MNS	EM			FW	1982
Preus Peter D	(307)460-1302 pastorpeterpreus@gmail.com	P.O. Box 584 Bridgeport NE 69336	WY	SP	St Paul Bridgeport NE	(308)262-0424	FW	2024
Preus Paul O	(701)349-4465 oleseverinpreus@gmail.com		ND	Sn/Adm	Zion Ellendale ND	(701)349-4147	NESC	2014
Preus John C	(563)249-6357 pr.preus@trinitycheyenne.org		WY	SP	Trinity Cheyenne WY	(307)635-2802	FW	2011
Preus David R	(406)694-6906 davidrpreus@gmail.com	606 Joyce St Cheyenne WY 82009	MT	S Miss	Office of International Mission Saint Louis MO		FW	2007
Preus Daniel Dr	(314)809-8418 dospreus@gmail.com	P.O. Box 986 Grand Marais MN 55604	MNN	EM			SPR	1975
Preus Christian A	(307)262-8571 capreus7@gmail.com	3721 W 46th St Casper WY 82604	WY	Sn/Adm	Mount Hope Casper WY	(307)234-8428	FW	2016
Preus Andrew J	(563)329-0943 ajpreus@gmail.com	9691 Highway 100 New Haven MO 63068	MO	SP	Trinity New Haven MO	(573)237-3026	NESC	2013
Preus Mark A	(307)343-3147 markpreus@gmail.com	4611 Oriole Ln Laramie WY 82070	WY	SP	St Andrew Laramie WY	(307)745-5892	FW	2008
Preuss David H Dr	(507)545-9907 davidpreuss@juno.com	1072 Bush Ct SW Eyota MN 55934	MNS	EM			SL	1965
Prewitt Jeffery S	(920)725-1445 jeff.prewitt@missionofchrist.org	1712 Mill Pond Ln Neenah WI 54956	SW	EM			FW	1983
Price Nicholas M	(630)390-3079	2866 Garden Dr Lisle IL 60532	NI	Sn/Adm	Trinity Lisle IL	(630)964-1272	SL	2016
Price James M	(254)716-0166 jim.price86@aol.com	c/o Mount Calvary Lutheran Church 17535 Say Rd Wamego KS 66547	KS	SP	Mount Calvary Wamego KS	(785)456-2444	SL	1997
Priem Matthew D Dr	(816)322-3606 mpriem@bethlehem-raymore.org	300 N High Dr Raymore MO 64083	MO	Assoc	Bethlehem Raymore MO	(816)322-3606	SL	2009
Priest John E	(607)287-0870 jpriest2@att.net	1204 Williamsburg Dr Anderson SC 29621	SE	EM			CQ	2009
Priest Jonathan P	(206)280-2292 rev.j.priest@gmail.com		CNH	D Ex/S	California/Nevada/Hawaii District Livermore CA	(866)264-6079	SL	2002
Prieto Ely Dr	(210)365-9217 elyprieto83@gmail.com	8 McCall Terrace Saint Louis MO 63105	MO	S HS/C	Concordia Seminary Saint Louis MO	(314)505-7000	Other	1983
Prigge Brendan S	(612)616-0313 revbprigge@victorylcms.org	15290 Village Woods Dr Eden Prairie MN 55347	MNS	SP	Victory Eden Prairie MN	(952)934-0956	SL	1991
Prill David J	(925)354-6934 prilldavid@hotmail.com		MO	Assoc	Alive in Christ Columbia MO	(573)499-0443	SL	2009
Prince James M	(636)734-4159 james.m.prince@charter.net	1321 Avondale Spring Dr O Fallon MO 63368	MO	Asst	Chapel of the Cross Saint Peters MO	(636)928-5885	SL	2007
Prince Matthew G Dr	msprince97@yahoo.com	2624 Wingfield Rd Norfolk VA 23518	IN	Inst C	Office of International Mission Saint Louis MO		SL	2002
Prince Timothy A Dr	(402)217-5218 revprince@hotmail.com	3242 Superior Ave East Troy WI 53120	SW	SP	Good Shepherd East Troy WI	(262)642-3310	SL	1996
Prinz David C	(707)554-2161 koyemsi@sbcglobal.net	224 Lexington Dr Vallejo CA 94591	CNH	EM			CQ	1982
Pritchard Donald F	(217)626-1444 revdfp@aol.com	P.O. Box 25 Pleasant Plains IL 62677	CI	SP	Zion Pleasant Plains IL	(217)626-1282	FW	1988
Pritchard Griffith F	(719)298-1615 griff.pritchard@yahoo.com	380 Soubry Pl Fort Garland CO 81133	RM	EM			FW	2000
Proctor Jeffrey J	(260)494-7622 jeffreyjohnproctor@gmail.com	8508 Elmont CV Fort Wayne IN 46835	IN	C07/2025			FW	2015
Prohl Benjamin T	(614)599-8537 12tribeprohl@gmail.com	20230 Bluegrass Cir Flint TX 75762	TX	Assoc	Trinity Tyler TX	(903)593-1526	SL	2022
Prohl John R	(630)251-6578 john.prohl@nidlcms.org	4101 Main St Downers Grove IL 60515	NI	D Ex/S	Northern Illinois District River Forest IL	(708)449-3020	CQ	1977
Prok Myron K	(440)748-0776	33073 Cobblestone Cir N Ridgeville OH 44039	EN	EM			SPR	1967
Pronsati Dante B	610-574-4978 dpronsati@splcs.net	c/o Saint Peter Lutheran Church 17051 24 Mile Rd Macomb MI 48042	MI	Assoc	St Peter Macomb MI	(586)781-3434	SL	2024
Pronsati Andrew M	(651)249-5919 andypronsati@gmail.com	5949 Redbud Ln NW Rochester MN 55901	MNS	Assoc	Redeemer Rochester MN	(507)289-5147	SL	2017
Prostka Carl A	(315)986-3968 ceprostka@gmail.com	109 Creekside Dr Farmington NY 14425	EA	EM			SL	1971

*Multiple Assignments (See Church Worker Locator for Additional Details)
See Page 53 for the Table of Abbreviations for key to District, Position, and Seminary abbreviations
**C =Candidate; EM = Emeritus; the date following the C is the month and year the Candidate status began

NAME	TELEPHONE NUMBER EMAIL	STREET ADDRESS CITY/STATE/ZIP	DISTRICT	POSITION/ STATUS**	WHERE SERVING	OFFICE PHONE	SEM/ PROGRAM	YR GRAD
Prout David L Dr	(248)879-7361 dlawprout@gmail.com	1164 Nicklaus Dr Troy MI 48085	MI	SP	GoodLife Rochester MI	(248)852-5510	SL	1983
Provost Daniel M	(507)440-3147 pastorprovost@hotmail.com	2423 Pembrooke Drive Grand Forks ND 58201	ND	SP	Trinity* Drayton ND		FW	2004
Prugh Daniel R Dr	(804)836-4126 danprugh@gmail.com	3705 W Kensington Ave Tampa FL 33629	FG	SP	Holy Trinity Tampa FL	(813)839-6847	SL	2008
Prumm Christen E	stpaulnokomis@gmail.com	22009 E 19th Rd Nokomis IL 62075	SI	SP	St Paul's Nokomis IL	(217)563-2487	FW	2006
Pudell Robert A	bobp@mac.com	760 Duxbury Ln Bartlett IL 60103	NI	C07/2021			FW-SMP	2010
Pueschel Alec E	(904)998-9711 ADPueschel@gmail.com	7645 Sentry Oak Cir E Jacksonville FL 32256	FG	EM			FW	1997
Puffe Paul J Dr	512-244-7750 paulpuffe@gmail.com	13207 Rampart St Austin TX 78727	TX	EM			SL	1979
Puffe Thomas L	(218)689-6961 pastorpuffe@gmail.com		MNN	SP	St John Madison MN	(320)598-7550	FW	1993
Pulliam Mark T	(210)643-4319 pulliammarkt@gmail.com	1918 Creston Dr Spring TX 77386	TX	SP	Lazarus Spring TX	(210)643-4319	Other	2014
Pullmann Arlo W	anpullmann@gmail.com	908 5th Ave Laurel MT 59044	MT	SP	St John Laurel MT	(406)628-4775	SL	1987
Pullmann Gideon J	(402)243-3185 gideonpullmann@gmail.com	317 S Main St P.O. Box 586 Boulder MT 59632	MT	SP	Faith Boulder MT	(402)243-3185	FW	2018
Puls Wayne D	(919)741-7007 wayne.puls@gmail.com	485 Harbor Side St #801 Woodbridge VA 22191	SE	Sn/Adm	Grace Woodbridge VA	(703)494-4600	FW	1984
Puls Arthur H	(619)659-3275 artbeth@icloud.com	2666 Columbine Rd Alpine CA 91901	PSW	EM			SPR	1962
Puls Kenton A	(760)258-6930 revkpuls@gmail.com	29406 Fawn Way Tehachapi CA 93561	PSW	EM			FW	1987
Puls Timothy R Dr	(260)602-2375 timothy.puls@ctsfw.edu	4 Tyndale Pl Fort Wayne IN 46825	IN	S HS/C	Concordia Theological Seminary Fort Wayne IN	(260)452-2100	FW	1989
Pulse Jeffrey H Dr	jeffrey.pulse@ctsfw.edu	2320 Forest Park Blvd Fort Wayne IN 46805	IN	S HS/C	Concordia Theological Seminary Fort Wayne IN	(260)452-2100	FW	1984
Pummill Brian L	(870)257-4169 bkpummill@hotmail.com	55 Wahoo Dr Cherokee Vlg AR 72529	MDS	SP	Peace Cherokee Village AR	(870)257-3957	SL	1989
Pumphrey Ryan J	(260)479-9968 ryan.j.pumphrey@gmail.com	P.O. Box 36 Villard MN 56385	MNN	SP	Trinity* Grove Lake MN	(320)554-2161	FW	2021
Punke Douglas D	dpunke@zionfw.org	6114 Hunter Wood Dr Fort Wayne IN 46835	IN	Sn/Adm	Zion Fort Wayne IN	(260)744-1389	FW	1998
Purpura Galen M Jr	(716)474-6418 pastor.galenp@gmail.com	205 Gould Ave Depew NY 14043	EA	SP	St Johns Depew NY	(716)683-3947	NESC	2008
Puscheck John E	(805)698-9846 jpuscheck@clearpromise.com		CNH	SMP	Clear Promise Lompoc CA	(805)698-9846	CQ	2019
Putnam Vincent W	pastorputnam@hotmail.com	1057 12th Ave Grafton WI 53024	SW	Sn/Adm	First Immanuel Cedarburg WI	(262)377-6610	SL	2006
Putnam Aaron D	(510) 731-7050 aputnam@linc.org	26270 Stanwood Ave Hayward CA 94544	CNH	Pro Stf	California/Nevada/Hawaii District Livermore CA	(866)264-6079	SL	2008
Putnam George B	(503)842-7740 gputnam38@gmail.com	4140 Sandy Way Tillamook OR 97141	NOW	EM			FW	1982
Puttler James D	(757)560-6435 jputtler@hotmail.com	19689 7th Ave NE # 345 Poulsbo WA 98370	NOW	EM			SPR	1976
Putz David L	dlputz89@gmail.com	121 Peacock Ct W Lafayette IN 47906	IN	SP	Holy Cross Crawfordsville IN	(765)362-5599	FW	1999
Quackenboss Dennis C	(828)260-2033 revdq801LXX@gmail.com	1644 Shady Grove Ct Newton NC 28658	SE	EM			SL	1970
Quail David C	(936)443-6679 revquail@gmail.com	1938 Parnevik Pl Conroe TX 77304	TX	EM			SPR	1976
Quandt Walter H	(949) 317-0777 wquandt@earthlink.net	27012 Mariscal Ln Mission Viejo CA 92691	PSW	EM			SL	1965
Quardokus Philip G Dr	(269)429-9309 pquardokus@gmail.com	1448 Castle Ct Saint Joseph MI 49085	MI	EM			SL	1977
Quarles Phillip L	(505)235-7265 phil.quarles@mac.com	19761 Hunters Loop Fairhope AL 36532	SO	EM			FW-D	2011
Queck Thomas J	(320)237-7851 tjqueck@gmail.com	611 Morrison Ave S Annandale MN 55302	MNS	EM			FW	1983
Quick Terry L	(507)837-9552 pastor.quick@holycrossdav.org	2615 Western Ave Davenport IA 52803	IE	SP	Holy Cross* Davenport IA	(563)322-2654	FW	2004
Quill Timothy C Dr		9509 Courtyard CV Fort Wayne IN 46825	IN	EM			SL	1980
Quiram Daniel H	(804)379-2311 daniel.quiram@yahoo.com	14428 Tanager Wood Trail Midlothian VA 23114	SE	EM			SL	1968
Quiring Craig A	(612)910-1721 cquiring@foclutheran.org	830 117th Ln NW Coon Rapids MN 55448	MNS	SMP	Family Christ Ham Lake MN	(763)434-7337	CQ	2019
Quoss Albert F	pastorquoss@hotmail.com	39 Metfield Dr Bella Vista AR 72714	MDS	EM			SPR	1974
Raab Klaus W Dr	(402)404-4810 raabdr155@yahoo.com	29016 Lake Ave Hinton IA 51024	IW	EM			CQ	2006
Raabe Paul R	(602)413-7790 paul.raabe@gcu.edu	4813 N 73rd St Apt 36 Scottsdale AZ 85251	PSW	EM			SL	1979
Raabe Richard G Jr	(414)861-2060 rraabe1@wi.rr.com	2420 Lefeber Ave Wauwatosa WI 53213	SW	EM			CQ	2007
Raasch Randolph H	(414)412-6610 rraasch@fils.org	W 71 N1706 Harrison Ave Cedarburg WI 53012	SW	EM			SL	1982

*Multiple Assignments (See Church Worker Locator for Additional Details)

See Page 53 for the Table of Abbreviations for key to District, Position, and Seminary abbreviations

**C =Candidate; EM = Emeritus; the date following the C is the month and year the Candidate status began

NAME	TELEPHONE NUMBER EMAIL	STREET ADDRESS CITY/STATE/ZIP	DISTRICT	POSITION/ STATUS**	WHERE SERVING	OFFICE PHONE	SEM/ PROGRAM	YR GRAD
Rabe Mark A Dr	(314)680-8805 mark.rabe@lcms.org	5367 Glencullen Way St Louis MO 63128	MO	S Ex/S	The LCMS Corporate Saint Louis MO	(314)965-9000	SL	2001
Rachuy Gregory S	pstr1999@aol.com	233 S London Station Rd Tucson AZ 85748	PSW	EM			CQ	1999
Raddatz Mark R	mrraddatz@juno.com	420 N Maple St Lancaster OH 43130	OH	EM			SL	1983
Raddatz Simeon D	(773)634-0082 simeon.raddatz@cuchicago.edu	1s309 Windsor Ln Villa Park IL 60181	NI	S HS/C	Concordia University Chicago River Forest IL	(708)771-8300	SL	2017
Raddatz John F	(832)287-6500 raddatz.john@gmail.com	7501 E 80th St Tulsa OK 74133	OK	EM			FW	1982
Radde Donn H	(715)486-8301 pastorradde@gmail.com	1112 Briarwood St Marshfield WI 54449	NW	Assoc	Immanuel Marshfield WI	(715)384-5121	SL	1970
Radke Edward F	(519)381-3951 ted.radke@quadro.net	c/o River Gardens Retirement Residence 10 Romeo St N Suite 317 Stratford ON N545M CANADA	EN	EM			SL	1969
Radke Paul C	(262)349-3393	N5674 County Road E Deerbrook WI 54424	NW	SP	St Luke* Elcho WI	(715)275-3152	FW	2019
Radkey Timothy M	tim.radkey@oslmckinney.org	2821 Fair Timber Way McKinney TX 75071	TX	SP	Hosanna Kerrville TX	(830)257-6767	SL	2002
Radloff Alan L	(928)533-2659 Paalan731@gmail.com	1616 Allerton Way Chino Valley AZ 86333	PSW	EM			CQ	2020
Radtke Thomas G Dr	(217)698-7569 rev.radtke@radmen3.com	402 Oxley Dr Springfield IL 62711	CI	EM			FW	1978
Radtke Gerald T	(785)201-4763 ginnyjerry@cox.net	4808 Brandon Woods Pl Lawrence KS 66047	KS	EM			SL	1970
Radtke Richard S	(260)483-0650 RadCar1969@comcast.net	8128 Covenant Ln Fort Wayne IN 46835	IN	EM			SPR	1968
Raebel Jared M	(972) 938-1633 lutheran987@gmail.com	301 Hwy 287 W Waxahachie TX 75165	TX	SP	Christ King Waxahachie TX	(972)938-1633	SL	1987
Raedeke Frederick A	(314)609-1916 fritz@zion-lcms.com	2000 Benton St Saint Louis MO 63106	MO	SP	Zion Saint Louis MO		SL	1982
Raess John K	(505)296-2377 raess@comcast.net	14312 Arcadia Rd NE Albuquerque NM 87123	RM	EM			SL	1964
Raether Jerry K	(515)332-1303 jerry.raether@yahoo.com	802 9th Ave S Humboldt IA 50548	IW	EM			FW	1977
Raffa Christopher L	revcraffa@gmail.com	440 Meadowbrook Dr West Bend WI 53090	SW	Assoc	Pilgrim West Bend WI	(262)334-0375	FW	2007
Rafferty Charles R	(563)503-2855 revrafferty@gmtel.net	22805 E 98th St S Broken Arrow OK 74014	OK	SP	Our Redeemer Cushing OK	(918)225-4646	FW	1991
Ragazinskas Nathan P	(850)495-1075 revr2011@gmail.com	6305 N Blue Angel Pkwy Pensacola FL 32526	SO	SP	Resurrection Pensacola FL	(850)944-3777	FW	2011
Rager Dean G	(281)389-4872 brotherdean2017@gmail.com	P.O. Box 143 Canby MN 56220	MNN	SP	Nicolai* Canby MN	(507)223-5223	FW	2017
Rahe Gary A	(970)809-3315 zion@pctelcom.coop	240 S High School Ave Holyoke CO 80734	RM	SP	Zion Holyoke CO	(970)854-2615	SPR	1975
Rahn Dennis D	(231)723-5149 drahn@trinitymanistee.com	420 Oak St Manistee MI 49660	MI	SP	Trinity Manistee MI	(231)723-5149	FW	1996
Rahn Robert L Dr	(586)201-3856 rrahn@lhfmissions.org	21247 Raintree Dr Macomb MI 48044	MI	RSO	Lutheran Heritage Foundation Macomb MI	(800)554-0723	SL	1961
Rains William R	(405)728-8330 faithokc@aol.com	11908 Sundance Mountain Rd Oklahoma City OK 73162	OK	EM			SL-D	2005
Raj Victor A Dr	(314)518-3142	10216 Jubil Dr Saint Louis MO 63123	MO	EM			SL	1976
Rajamony Prince V Dr		16-18 Samathanapuram Kovalam Po Kanyakumari 62970 INDIA	S	D Miss	SELC District Macungie PA	(610)965-3265	CQ	2015
Rajek Cory J Dr	(608)359-2646 cory.rajek@lcms.org	93 Lamar Pkwy Pacific MO 63069	MO	S Ex/S	Office of International Mission Saint Louis MO		SL	2001
Raji Udhayanesan	(317)916-0222 revudhay@hotmail.com	6643 Locust Grove Dr Indianapolis IN 46237	IN	Assoc	Calvary Indianapolis IN	(317)783-2000	Other	1989
Rakotonirina Solomona J	(262)208-0810 solomona.jaona@gmail.com	72 Coyote Rd Las Vegas NM 87701	RM	SP	Immanuel Las Vegas NM	(505)652-2562	FW	2025
Rakow Gordon W	(302)276-5310 impart22@aol.com	252 Avon Bridge Dr Towsend DE 19734	AT	EM			SPR	1973
Rall Bart P	(651)216-7022 bartprall@gmail.com	318 Branner Avenue Monterey CA 93940	CNH	C08/2021			SL	2013
Rall Ronald D Dr	(314)443-6659 pastorrall@timothystl.org	6949 Pernod Avenue Saint Louis MO 63139	MO	S Miss	Office of International Mission Saint Louis MO		SL	1973
Rallison John C	(407)923-7251 Johncrallison@gmail.com	4759 Apollo Ave NE Salem OR 97305	NOW	SP	Redeemer Salem OR	(503)393-7121	SL	1995
Ralston Joshua A	rev.jralston@gmail.com	8 Wedgewood Dr Russellville AR 72802	MDS	SP	Zion London AR	(479)331-3277	FW	2019
Ramey John M Dr	(443)655-1485 rev.mikeramey@gmail.com	3700 N Edwards St #0927 Midland TX 79705	TX	SP	Grace Midland TX	(432)697-3221	SL	1984
Ramey Scott A	(701)278-3176 pastor_scott_ramey@hotmail.com	c/o Immanuel Lutheran Church P.O. Box 37 Rolla ND 58367	ND	SP	Zion* Munich ND	(701)682-5126	FW	2001
Ramirez David P	david.p.ramirez@gmail.com	1618 Main St Union Grove WI 53182	SW	SP	St Paul Union Grove WI	(262)878-2600	FW	2008
Ramirez Walter J	wramir45@hotmail.com	4516 N Drake Avenue Unit 2 Chicago IL 60625	NI	Assoc	Tabor Chicago IL	(773)588-4040	SL	2015
Ramirez Richard L	(440)360-0390 dadchilos@gmail.com	5344 S Francisco Ave Chicago IL 60632	S	SP	Dr Martin Luther Chicago IL	(440)360-0390	CQ	2013
Ramirez Orlando	(239)821-0660 orlandorapa@gmail.com	4475 25th Ave SW Naples FL 34116	FG	SP	Conexion Naples FL	(239)821-0660	CQ	2024

*Multiple Assignments (See Church Worker Locator for Additional Details)

See Page 53 for the Table of Abbreviations for key to District, Position, and Seminary abbreviations

**C =Candidate; EM = Emeritus; the date following the C is the month and year the Candidate status began

NAME	TELEPHONE NUMBER EMAIL	STREET ADDRESS CITY/STATE/ZIP	DISTRICT	POSITION/ STATUS**	WHERE SERVING	OFFICE PHONE	SEM/ PROGRAM	YR GRAD
Ramirez Eliexer	(305)803-5988 reveliexer@yahoo.com	8254 NW 192 Terr Hialeah FL 33015	FG	SP	Prince Peace Hollywood FL	(954)495-0712	CQ	2023
Ramirez Gregg S	revram420@gmail.com	1454 Ashland Ave Apt 401 Des Plaines IL 60016	NI	EM			SL	1985
Ramming Michael E	(804)456-6554 meramming@gmail.com	171 Merganser St Montross VA 22520	SE	EM			SL	1969
Ramsbacher John A	jbbacher@hotmail.com	160 N Bordson St Appleton MN 56208	MNN	SP	Trinity Appleton MN	(320)289-1342	SL	1996
Ramsey Charles M III	(402)641-3761 chckrmsy@aol.com	330 Stockton St P.O. Box 51 Bradshaw NE 68319	NEB	SP	Peace Waco NE	(402)728-5227	SL	1988
Ramsey Mc Nair Jr Dr	(334)875-8972 mcnairramsey@gmail.com	176 Deepwoods Cir Valley Grande AL 36701	SO	EM			FW	2001
Ramsey John C II	(330)321-3225 revjcr2@gmail.com	519 Arlington Dr Destrehan LA 70047	SO	SP	First English Metairie LA	(504)455-5562	SL	2012
Ramsey Daniel J	(308)532-4753 PastorRamsey@mac.com	1400 East E St North Platte NE 69101	NEB	SP	Our Redeemer North Platte NE	(308)532-4753	SL	1994
Ramstad Christopher M	(417)414-8595 cramstad@immanueljoplin.com	2605 Vermont Joplin MO 64804	MO	SP	Immanuel Joplin MO	(417)624-0333	SL	2018
Ramsudh George R	(646)938-2966 georam125@cs.com	305 Convent Ave Apt 26 New York NY 10031	AT	SP	Mount Zion Manhattan NY	(646)370-3940	FW-D	2005
Ramthun Benjamin H	(715)297-5170 ben994@gmail.com	2401 N Lincoln Rd Escanaba MI 49829	NW	SP	Our Savior Escanaba MI	(906)789-9350	SL	2022
Ramthun Daniel W	(734)637-8552 pastorramthun@guardianluther-an.org	22804 Law St Dearborn MI 48124	MI	SMP	Guardian Dearborn MI	(313)274-1414	FW-SMP	2010
Ramthun Marvin W	(810)664-7830	1677 Woodbridge Park Ave Apt 109 Lapeer MI 48446	MI	EM			SPR	1969
Rand Neil E Dr	nrand@wi.rr.com	N8w31265 Concord Ln Delafield WI 53018	EN	EM			CQ	2012
Randall William R	(812)985-0685 bill.toni.randall@gmail.com	11711 Upper Mount Vernon Rd Evansville IN 47712	IN	EM			FW	1982
Randolph Patrick W	(567)342-4037 pwre208@gmail.com	6600 N Clinton St Box 139 Fort Wayne IN 46825	SW	SP	Grace Milwaukee WI	(414)384-3520	FW	2024
Rangel Bernardo Sr	(918)622-2905 revrangelbernardo64@yahoo.com	3203 S Memorial Dr Tulsa OK 74145	OK	SP	Good Shepherd Tulsa OK	(918)622-2905	CQ	2005
Rankin Kenneth C III	(262)527-1688 revrankin@att.net	29 Reverie Dr N Palm Coast FL 32137	EN	EM			FW	2002
Ransdell Charles E Jr Dr	(810)824-2424 cjransdell@gmail.com	35 Pilgrim Ct Felton DE 19943	SE	SP	St John Dover DE	(302)734-7078	SL	2005
Rapp Eric W	(507)326-5979 erapp_99@yahoo.com	P.O. Box 24 Green Isle MN 55338	MNS	SP	St Paul* Green Isle MN	(507)326-3451	FW	2013
Rapp Victor J	(516)655-3952 vjrapp@aol.com	95 Sunrise Ln Levittown NY 11756	AT	EM			SPR	1973
Rappe Tod R	(910)488-6010 orlc_pastor@ncrrbiz.com	1605 Van Buren Ave Fayetteville NC 28303	SE	SP	Our Redeemer Fayetteville NC	(910)488-6010	FW	1991
Rasch Arthur C	(509)586-8551 revrasch@yahoo.com	2802 W 35th Ave W #128 Kennewick WA 99337	NOW	EM			SL	1966
Rasmussen Matthew G	(802)578-1300 matthewg.rasmussen@ protonmail.com	28 Barber Ter S Burlington VT 05403	NE	SP	Community South Burlington VT	(802)864-5537	FW	2011
Rasmussen Steven C	(319)371-9472 oldbutstillkickin@gmail.com	533 Avenue C Fort Madison IA 52627	IE	EM			FW	1990
Rasmussen Victor J	(308)627-6263 vicandrogene@gmail.com	20832 Riverdale Rd Riverdale NE 68870	NEB	SP	Grace* Sumner NE		SL-D	2010
Rasmussen John W Dr	(308)233-1304 jrasmussen@hclk.org	1020 13th Ave Kearney NE 68845	NEB	Sn/Adm	Holy Cross Kearney NE	(308)237-2944	SL	2012
Rasmussen John A	(307)286-6790 jarcj19@gmail.com	6206 Shaun Ave Cheyenne WY 82009	WY	EM			SPR	1968
Rasmussen Christian J	(970)406-1071 cjrasmussn@aol.com	c/o Saint Paul Lutheran Church 2624 Burgundy St New Orleans LA 70117	SO	SP	St Paul New Orleans LA	(504)945-3741	SL	2001
Rasmussen James D	jim@dsomaha.org	6105 S 102nd Ter Omaha NE 68127	NEB	Assoc	Divine Shepherd Omaha NE	(402)895-1500	SL	2004
Rast Lawrence R Jr Dr	lawrence.rast@ctsfw.edu	c/o Concordia Theological Sem 6600 N Clinton St Fort Wayne IN 46825	IN	S HS/C	Concordia Theological Seminary Fort Wayne IN	(260)452-2100	FW	1990
Rastl Nathan P	(812)886-9965 nprastl@gmail.com	6926 S Decker Rd Vincennes IN 47591	IN	SP	St Peter Vincennes IN	(812)882-8229	FW	1988
Ratcliffe Andrew B	(218)457-3916 andrew.ratcliffe@stpaulsperham.org	530 3rd Ave SW Perham MN 56573	MNN	SP	St Paul Perham MN	(218)346-7725	SL	2007
Ratcliffe Keith B	(816)419-8926 revratcliffe@gmail.com	22001 County Highway 10 Fergus Falls MN 56537	MNN	SP	Immanuel Fergus Falls MN	(218)736-6228	SL	1979
Ratcliffe Kermit H Dr	(414)365-1288 kermit01@att.net	9119 N 70th St Milwaukee WI 53223	SW	EM			SPR	1966
Rather Ronald S	(620)899-6339 nuclearev@gmail.com	709 High St Clinton WI 53525	SW	EM			SL	2008
Rathgeber Benjamin G	lois.rathgeber@yahoo.com	1209 Wedgewood Dr Cleburne TX 76033	TX	EM			SL	1958
Rathje John R	(314)255-4453 jrathje62@gmail.com	609 Rosewood Ave. Ypsilanti MI 48198	MI	EM			SL	2008
Rathjen Jonathan C	(308)470-1429 jonathancrathjen@gmail.com	1961 Capman Rd P.O. Box 442 Saint Germain WI 54558	NW	SP	Peace Arbor Vitae WI	(715)358-8338	SL	1995
Rathke Greg D	(402)316-0094 greg.rathke@trinityfremont.org	3239 N Armour Dr Fremont NE 68025	NEB	SMP	Trinity Fremont NE	(402)721-5536	SL-SMP	2024
Rattelmuller George H	(573)529-0691 glrattelmuller@gmail.com	13198 S Outer 40 Rd Apt 104 Town And Country MO 63017	MO	EM			SL	1956

*Multiple Assignments (See Church Worker Locator for Additional Details)
See Page 53 for the Table of Abbreviations for key to District, Position, and Seminary abbreviations
**C =Candidate; EM = Emeritus; the date following the C is the month and year the Candidate status began

NAME	TELEPHONE NUMBER EMAIL	STREET ADDRESS CITY/STATE/ZIP	DISTRICT	POSITION/ STATUS**	WHERE SERVING	OFFICE PHONE	SEM/ PROGRAM	YR GRAD
Rau Carl R	(719)482-8234 ceokatz@gmail.com	1908 Shearwater Pl Van Alstyne TX 75495	TX	EM			FW	1984
Rau Harold M	(314)780-8625	182 Ameren Way Apt 453 Ballwin MO 63021	MO	EM			FW	1982
Raugutt Nathan D	(307) 367-2612 rev_raugutt@pm.me	c/o Our Savior Lutheran Church 512 N Tyler #148 Pinedale WY 82941	WY	SP	Peace* Marbleton WY	(307)276-3843	FW	2025
Rauh John W	(636)698-4921 jwljsooners@gmail.com	124 Cypress Meadows Dr Wentzville MO 63385	MI	EM			SL	1964
Rauhut Donald E	830-895-4398 dbrau@ktc.com	15126 Brookfield St Livonia MI 48154	IN	EM			SL	1960
Rauscher Paul N	(386)717-2506 pastorpnr@yahoo.com	50 Lake Fairgreen Cir New Smyrna FL 32168	FG	EM			FW	1980
Ravell Robert J	(603)539-3388 bobravell@yahoo.com	94 Rumney Hill Rd Effingham NH 03882	NE	EM			FW	1982
Rawlings David A Sr	(573)590-2217 dakrawlings@yahoo.com	113 Hidden Bluff Dr Lake Saint Louis MO 63367	MO	EM			SL	2006
Ray Adam M	(708)601-5015 aray4848@gmail.com	2834 S Forrest Ln Decatur IL 62521	CI	Sn/Adm	St John Decatur IL	(217)875-3656	SL	2013
Ray Donald E Dr	(509) 906-2694 dr@donalderay.com	P.O. Box 2091 Wenatchee WA 98807	NOW	SP	St Paul Wenatchee WA	(509)662-8790	SL	2011
Raynor LeRoy D	(928)514-1599 lraynor20@gmail.com	4409 Bellows Dr Ontario OR 97914	NOW	SP	Pilgrim Ontario OR	(541)889-5458	SL	2019
Reagan Kelly	(614)564-7317 k_w_reagan@yahoo.com	P.O. Box 131 Marysville OH 43040	OH	SP	St Matthew Huber Heights OH	(937)233-4632	FW	2010
Reaman Frederic J	f.reaman@live.com	560 E Ravenswood Hills Cir Brookfield WI 53045	EN	SP	Greenfield Park West Allis WI	(414)774-3019	SL	2005
Reat Gatluk L	(613)993-3959 gatluklul@yahoo.com	725 Willow St Faribault MN 55021	MNS	Assoc	Sudanese Mankato MN	(507)385-2186	SL	2019
Rebensal Robert F	(805)284-2129	2721 Los Pinos Cir Santa Rosa Valley CA 93012	PSW	EM			FW	1997
Reber David H Jr	(918)625-5876 dreberjr@gmail.com	701 W 101st Pl S Apt 523 Jenks OK 74037	OK	EM			SL	2013
Reber Joshua S	(817)789-3516 pastorjoshuareber@gmail.com	1430 10th Ave N Saint Cloud MN 56303	MNN	SP	Trinity* Clear Lake MN	(320)743-2919	FW	2020
Reckling Roger C Dr	roger@reckling.com	9701 Grove Lake Way 202 Knoxville TN 37922	MDS	EM			SPR	1970
Redeker Michael J	(314)608-5538 pstrredeker@aol.com	209 W Sunset Dr Fruita CO 81521	RM	Sn/Adm	Messiah Grand Junction CO	(970)245-2838	SL	1995
Redhage Daniel T	(563)941-7464 pastorredhage@gmail.com	805 Washington Ave 474 Lowden IA 52255	IE	Sn/Adm	Trinity Lowden IA	(563)941-5853	FW	2006
Redhage Lloyd W	(605)949-9423 sheepcircles@hotmail.com	P.O. Box 239 233 1st St Charlotte IA 52731	IE	SP	Immanuel Charlotte IA	(563)677-2756	FW	1983
Redmann James C	(231)938-3328 jrlr.redmann@gmail.com	4656 Arthur Ct Williamsburg MI 49690	MI	SP	Grace Elk Rapids MI	(231)264-5312	SPR	1975
Redmann Kenneth P	(941)457-7576 revredmann@gmail.com	18935 Henequen Ln Spring Hill FL 34610	FG	EM			FW	1996
Reed Marty E	(573)300-9215 rev.mreed@gmail.com	713 Laramie Atchison KS 66002	KS	Assoc	Trinity Atchison KS	(913)367-2837	SL	1993
Reed Russell A	(320) 510-0053 rallanreed@gmail.com	P.O. Box 147 Brownton MN 55312	MNS	SP	Immanuel Brownton MN	(320)328-5522	SL	1995
Reed Jason A	(260)993-2223 jason@jasonadamreed.net	1614 Fitzgerald Ct Lagrange KY 40031	IN	SP	Holy Trinity La Grange KY	(502)222-5827	FW	2006
Reed James W	(916)799-2611 revmagg@gmail.com	8640 Graybill Ln Elk Grove CA 95624	CNH	Sn/Adm	Light Of The Valley Elk Grove CA	(916)691-3568	SL	2004
Reed David H	(989)600-2264 pastordavereed@gmail.com	683 Hickory Ct Sebewaing MI 48759	MI	EM			FW	1983
Reeder Thomas N Jr	(575)763-4526 ilcpastorclovis@gmail.com	2549 Fred Daugherty Ave. Apt B Clovis NM 88101	RM	SP	Immanuel Clovis NM	(575)763-4526	SL	1999
Reeder David K	(208)365-5231 revdkreeder@gmail.com	403 S Hayes Ave Emmett ID 83617	NOW	SP	Our Redeemer Emmett ID	(208)365-5231	FW	2006
Reedy David D	(210)612-0571 pastorreedy@lutheran-resources.org	2103 Vernice Dr Copperas Cove TX 76522	TX	SP	Trinity* Copperas Cove TX	(254)547-2225	SL	1996
Reek John D Dr	dirk.reek@cune.edu	5552 Blackpool Rd Lincoln NE 68516	NEB	EM			SPR	1974
Rees James R	(309)830-0914 rjrrees@hotmail.com	25092 N 2200 East Rd Lexington IL 61753	CI	C07/2016			FW	1982
Reese Ryan D	(586)601-6619 heishe001@yahoo.com	15437 Dobson Ave Dolton IL 60419	NI	SP	Trinity Lansing IL	(708)474-7997	SL	2006
Reese David A	(925)457-7720 revdave47@gmail.com	P.O. Box 929 Van Alstyne TX 75495	TX	EM			SL	1991
Reese Kerry D	rev.kdreese@icloud.com	12618 47th Dr SE Everett WA 98208	NOW	EM			SL	1980
Reetz Peter R		5814 Knob Creek Dr Westerville OH 43081	OH	EM			SPR	1972
Reeves Bryan A	(708)941-5469	10334 Nicklaus St Crown Point IN 46307	NI	SP	Immanuel Richton Park IL	(708)748-0558	FW	2007
Reeves James V	(601)928-9481 jimvreeves@gmail.com	378 Clark Batson Road Perkinston MS 39573	SO	EM			FW	2002
Reeves Sean D	(940)564-0030 pastor.reeves@gmail.com	303 N Avenue O Olney TX 76374	TX	SP	St Luke Olney TX	(940)564-5466	FW	2002
Reh Daniel	262-242-2045 dreh@trinityfreistadt.com	11856 N Church Place Mequon WI 53097	SW	Assoc	Trinity Mequon WI	(262)242-2045	FW	2023
Rehborg Gary R	(763)370-3441 drwho270@yahoo.co.uk	56540 Frazier St Park Rapids MN 56470	MNN	EM			FW	1985

*Multiple Assignments (See Church Worker Locator for Additional Details)
See Page 53 for the Table of Abbreviations for key to District, Position, and Seminary abbreviations
**C =Candidate; EM = Emeritus; the date following the C is the month and year the Candidate status began

NAME	TELEPHONE NUMBER EMAIL	STREET ADDRESS CITY/STATE/ZIP	DISTRICT	POSITION/ STATUS**	WHERE SERVING	OFFICE PHONE	SEM/ PROGRAM	YR GRAD
Rehwaldt Carl H Dr	(402)462-9460 crehwaldt@gmail.com	133 Lakeside Dr Hastings NE 68901	NEB	EM			SL	1969
Rehwaldt Timothy J Dr	(651)231-5934 pastortj@live.com	1120 Garden Brook Dr Sauk Rapids MN 56379	MNN	SP	St John Sauk Rapids MN	(320)968-7047	FW	1984
Reich Charles T	(863)293-8447 creich@glwh.org	327 Avenue C SE Winter Haven FL 33880	FG	Sn/Adm	Grace Winter Haven FL	(863)293-8447	SL	1996
Reich Keith A	(254)784-0055	1610 Conrad Hilton Blvd Cisco TX 76437	TX	SP	Redeemer Cisco TX	(254)442-2090	SL	2005
Reichart Adam W	(620)767-3260 revreichart@yahoo.com	715 E Main St Council Grove KS 66846	KS	SP	Faith* Emporia KS	(620)342-3590	FW	2003
Reichle Nathan A	(920)475-8618 natereichle@gmail.com	N7625 Swamp Rd Manawa WI 54949	NW	SP	St Paul Manawa WI	(920)596-2837	SL	2006
Reichmann Wilmer H	(262)376-1942 wilreichmann@fil.org	N27w6565 Alyce St Cedarburg WI 53012	SW	EM			SL	1969
Reicks Timothy M	(402)360-3578 st.paulandst.johnspastorsoffice@ gmail.com	727 H Street P.O. Box 623 Burwell NE 68823	NEB	SP	St Johns* Burwell NE	(308)346-5060	SL	2025
Reifsteck Joshua P	(630)450-3998 joshua.reifsteck@gmail.com	1708 Doran Rd S Murray KY 42071	MDS	SP	Immanuel Murray KY	(270)753-6712	SL	2015
Reimers Russell D	russellreimers@frontiernet.net		MNS	EM			FW	1993
Reimnitz Elroi Dr	(760)669-0219 elroi.reimnitz@gmail.com	11649 Halter St Victorville CA 92392	PSW	SP	Faith Hesperia CA	(760)244-5943	SL	1971
Reimnitz Stewart N	(858)344-3965 sreimnitz@san.rr.com	7971 Calico St San Diego CA 92126	PSW	EM			SL	1964
Reimnitz Wesley E	(217)816-9533 wer_cid@hotmail.com	2704 Buckskin Trl Springfield IL 62711	CI	EM			FW	1980
Reimnitz David M	(816)456-6662	215 Hillcrest Rd Belton MO 64012	MO	EM			SL	1986
Rein Karl H	(330)519-9950 karlrein@yahoo.com	4906 Logsdons Meadow Drive Liberty Twp OH 45011	OH	C07/2016			FW	1995
Rein Mark A	(216)386-1008 mrein@royred.org	10114 Highland Dr Brecksville OH 44141	OH	SMP	Royal Redeemer North Royalton OH	(440)237-7958	CQ	2020
Reina Andres L	(512)876-0389 encristo32@yahoo.com	542 Greenfield Dr Grafton WI 53024	TX	C11/2020			CQ	2018
Reinbacher Otto A	(908)625-4224 oarrock@aol.com	3440 S Jefferson St Apt 1376 Falls Church VA 22041	SE	EM			SL	1961
Reinders Douglas R	(920)667-4301 pastordoug@zion-fremont.com	E9016 Marsh Rd Fremont WI 54940	NW	SP	Zion Fremont WI	(920)667-4301	FW	1995
Reineke Joseph D	(715)610-0674 josephreineke@gmail.com	2007 California Ave Fort Wayne IN 46805	IN	Assoc	Concordia Fort Wayne IN	(260)422-2429	SL	2022
Reiner Darold A	(406)890-1149 imhis38@gmail.com	2457 Mission Trl Kalispell MT 59901	MT	EM			CQ	1972
Reiner Mark W	(719)648-0031 pastorreiner@icloud.com	340 Minnesota St. Rapid City SD 57701	SD	EM			CQ	2006
Reiners Michael E	luvtobike@gmail.com	11607 Bayview Dr Papillion NE 68133	NEB	EM			FW	1988
Reinhard Sam C	pastorsam@faithlasvegas.org	9550 W Sahara Ave Apt 2146 Las Vegas NV 89117	PSW	Assoc	Faith Community Las Vegas NV	(702)921-2700	SL	2020
Reinhardt Frederick M	(850)495-4209 togo_fred@yahoo.com	1205 W Romana St Pensacola FL 32502	SO	EM			SL	2002
Reinhardt Larry L	(702) 501-5396 dreinhardt1944@gmail.com	490 S Hualapai Way Unit 2114 Las Vegas NV 89145	PSW	EM			CQ	1973
Reinhardt Robert C	(812)459-6476 bobjoarein@gmail.com	302 Medical Parkway Apt. 303 Lakeway TX 78738	TX	EM			SL	1960
Reinhardt William B	(407)221-2397 reinclergy2@att.net	1451 Haven Dr Apt 211 Oviedo FL 32765	FG	EM			SL	1956
Reinke Clarence F Jr	cfreinke@yahoo.com	6421 Huntington Dr Zephyrhills FL 33542	FG	EM			SL	1995
Reinke John P Dr	(608)436-9600 revreinke@gmail.com	115 Dark Horse Ct Wentzville MO 63385	TX	D Miss	Texas District Round Rock TX	(800)951-3478	SL	1989
Reinke Joshua C	(218)330-7575 jcreinke@gmail.com	409 Clearwater Ct Great Falls MT 59405	MT	SP	First* Fort Benton MT		SL	2014
Reinke Chris J Dr	chrisjreinke@gmail.com	1139 N College Rd W Twin Falls ID 83301	NOW	EM			SPR	1969
Reinke Gerald R	(208)221-4114 greinke13@gmail.com	P.O. Box 218 Hailey ID 83333	NOW	SP	Valley Of Peace Hailey ID	(814)251-2852	SL	1992
Reinke David E	(206)850-1540 davidereinke@aol.com		NOW	EM			SL	1971
Reinking Aaron M	(706)207-3110 amreinking@hotmail.com	5625 Highway 106 S Hull GA 30646	FG	C11/2024			FW-SMP	2012
Reinsch Mark C	(906)458-0278 pegreinsch28@gmail.com	14411 E Woolsey Lake Rd Northport MI 49670	MI	SP	St Paul Good Harbor MI	(231)228-6888	FW	1997
Reiser Gregg A	gareiser63@gmail.com	98 Main St P.O. Box 88 Farley MO 64028	MO	SP	St John Farley MO	(816)330-3314	FW	1991
Reister William P	(904)608-9174 revbillreister@aol.com	3845 Dexter Dr N Jacksonville FL 32218	FG	SP	Our Redeemer Jacksonville FL	(904)766-4728	SL	1981
Reiter Craig J	(414)916-0546 reiterc@csl.edu	10635 State Route O Sainte Genevieve MO 63670	MO	S HS/C	Concordia Seminary Saint Louis MO	(314)505-7000	SL	2017
Reiter Ahren L	(580)357-7684 rev.reiter@outlook.com	1545 NW 31st St. Lawton OK 73505	OK	SP	Holy Cross Lawton OK	(580)357-7684	SL	2020
Reith Samuel B	(989)775-6228 sbreith@juno.com	2152 Lynn Sanford MI 46857	MI	EM			SL	1983
Reitz Jason E	(801)389-2227 pastor.jason@blcwh.org		NE	SP	Bethany West Hartford CT	(860)521-5076	SL	2007

*Multiple Assignments (See Church Worker Locator for Additional Details)
See Page 53 for the Table of Abbreviations for key to District, Position, and Seminary abbreviations
**C =Candidate; EM = Emeritus; the date following the C is the month and year the Candidate status began

NAME	TELEPHONE NUMBER EMAIL	STREET ADDRESS CITY/STATE/ZIP	DISTRICT	POSITION/ STATUS**	WHERE SERVING	OFFICE PHONE	SEM/ PROGRAM	YR GRAD
Rekstad Roger A	(480)532-5818 rekstad2003@gmail.com		SE	EM			SL	1971
Rellstab Theodore L	(419)966-4517 rellstab@yahoo.com	E 324 County Road 16c Holgate OH 43527	OH	EM			FW	1980
Rempfer David P	david.rempfer@stjohnseward.org	1350 N 2nd St Seward NE 68434	NEB	Asst	St John Seward NE	(402)643-2983	SL	1982
Rempfer Marlin R	(217)685-3315 revremp@yahoo.com	2721 Ken Ray Dr Quincy IL 62301	CI	Asst	Saint James Quincy IL	(217)222-8447	SL	1979
Rempfer Paul D	paul.rempfer@cune.org	206 Oak Street P.O. Box 121 Creston NE 68631	NEB	Assoc	St John Columbus NE	(402)285-0335	SL	2021
Rempfer Steven W	rempfernew@yahoo.com		IE	EM			SL	1986
Rendahl Craig S	(520)241-1572 ckrendahl@gmail.com	c/o Saint Paul Lutheran Church 4405 Hospital Dr Vernon TX 76384	TX	SP	St Paul Vernon TX	(940)552-2495	FW	2025
Renfro David W	(319)389-9115 pastordrenfro@aol.com	1300 Centennial Dr Thief River Falls MN 56701	NI	EM			FW	1986
Renken Gerald L	(217)251-4112 geraldre4@gmail.com	2080 Woodpecker Ln Ovideo FL 32765	FG	EM			SPR	1963
Renner Mark J	(419)957-9511 markjrenner87@gmail.com	c/o St James Lutheran Church 4771 Broadview Rd Cleveland OH 44109	OH	SP	Saint James Cleveland OH	(216)351-6499	SL	2020
Renning Wayne A Dr	(903)572-8268 9328home@suddenlink.net	3005 Old Paris Rd Mt Pleasant TX 75455	TX	EM			SPR	1966
Rensner Jason E	(217)343-2246 rensner@juno.com	601 North Cliff Ave Sioux Falls SD 57103	SD	Assoc	Faith Sioux Falls SD	(605)332-3401	SL	1991
Renstrom Tim J	(320)297-0382 tjrenstrom@icloud.com	7130 153rd Ave NE Spicer MN 56288	MNN	EM			SL	1997
Resch Richard C	(260)267-2140 reschr@aol.com	2221 Youngman Ave Apt 401 Saint Paul MN 55116	MNS	EM			FW	1988
Reschke Mark C	(949)874-4753 greenchap_2000@yahoo.com		PSW	C03/2018			SL	1989
Reseburg Aaron J	(920)917-0691 reseburgaaron@gmail.com	c/o Good Shepherd Lutheran Church 1611 E Main St Watertown WI 53094	SW	Assoc	Good Shepherd Watertown WI	(920)261-2570	SL	2021
Resner Steven J	(574)780-0925 prresner@hotmail.com	6001 E Southern Ave Unit 64 Mesa AZ 85206	EN	EM			FW	1991
Resner Steven A	(573)893-5330 sresner@midmoimmanuel.com	2313 Colonial Hills Rd Jefferson Cty MO 65109	MO	SP	Immanuel Jefferson City MO	(573)496-3451	SL	2023
Resner Mark A	(515)200-9398 pastor.resner@gmail.com	502 Clay St P.O. Box Whittemore IA 50598	IW	SP	St Paul Whittemore IA	(515)884-2629	FW	2014
Resner Matthew T	(573) 301-2600 resner.mk@gmail.com	311 W Urbandale Dr Moberly MO 65270	MO	SP	Zion Moberly MO	(660)263-3256	SL	2015
Ressler Philip W	(813) 294-4947 phil@immanuelbrandon.com	2439 Cedarcrest Pl Valrico FL 33596	FG	Sn/Adm	Immanuel Brandon FL	(813)689-1787	SL	2000
Rethinasamy Johnson E Dr	(917)553-9379 pastorejr@gmail.com	97 W Nicholai St Apt B Hicksville NY 11801	AT	SP	Trinity Hicksville NY	(516)931-2225	CQ	2005
Rethwisch Stuart A	(618)792-2238 stuartrethwisch@yahoo.com	2653 Cc Ave Victor IA 52347	IE	SP	Saint Johns Victor IA	(319)685-4400	SL	2003
Retzlaff Brady N	(920)655-7917 Retzlaffb13@gmail.com	3221 Shortridge Dr Caledonia WI 53402	S	SP	Pentecost Racine WI	(262)633-9674	SL	2020
Reuning Daniel G Dr	(260)485-2143 dbreuning1935@gmail.com	6218 Stony Brook Dr Fort Wayne IN 46835	EN	EM			SL	1960
Reusch Jon W	(248)932-5374 bettyjr47@sbcglobal.net	4435 Westover Dr W Bloomfield MI 48323	MI	EM			CQ	1981
Reuscher Elmer A	(407) 604-3535 ereuscher@yahoo.com	2101 Lark Ct. Oviedo FL 32765	FG	EM			SL	1963
Reuter Jeffrey A	(585)723-4673 pastorjeffrey@sharethehope.org	124 Long Park Dr Rochester NY 14012	EA	Assoc	Hope Rochester NY	(585)723-4673	SL	2023
Reuter Lane B	(615)833-1500 pastorlane@oslcnashville.org	2810 Kaye Dr Thompsons Station TN 37179	MDS	Sn/Adm	Our Savior Nashville TN	(615)833-1500	SL	1996
Rey Philip Sang S	(201)852-3600 goaheadinc@gmail.com	9 East Homestead Ave Palisades Park NJ 07650	EN	SP	Korean Cho Won Palisades Park NJ	(201)852-3600	CQ	2013
Reynolds John D Dr	(256) 485-1201 johndalereynolds@gmail.com	1847 Lauren Cir Southside AL 35907	SO	SP	Trinity Gadsden AL	(256)546-1712	FW	1998
Reynolds Stephen P	(954)330-8551 sreynolds@stjohnswestbend.org	1315 Royal Dr West Bend WI 53090	SW	Assoc	St John West Bend WI	(262)334-4901	SL	2014
Reynolds Terrence P	703-597-0210 reynoldt@georgetown.edu	11776 Stratford House Pl. #704 Reston VA 20190	SE	EM			SPR	1972
Rhiver James W	(314)659-9424 rhiverjw@att.net	5200 Nottingham Estates Dr Saint Louis MO 63129	MO	EM			CQ	1981
Rhoads Mark R	(865)202-5795 pastorrhoads260@gmail.com	1060 W Glenview Dr Lenoir City TN 37771	MDS	SP	Christ Our Savior Loudon TN	(865)458-9407	SL	2008
Rhoads Dennis E	(757)525-6236 dennisrhoads1945@gmail.com	1125 Clay St Franklin VA 23851	SE	EM			SL	2002
Rhoads John H	(314) 647-7125 jhrhoads1212@gmail.com	1212 Sunset Ave Richmond Hts MO 63117	MO	C08/2017			SL	2002
Rhode Jeremy D	(949)496-1901	26221 Beachcomber Ln San Juan Capistrano CA 92675	PSW	SP	Faith Capistrano Beach CA	(949)496-1901	FW	2007
Rhode Paul G	(303)665-0266 pgrhode@comcast.net	2828 Mountain View Ave Longmont CO 80503	RM	SP	Mount Calvary Estes Park CO	(970)586-4646	FW	1981
Rhodes Jacob W	(686)875-0185 jakobwr@bu.edu	187 Strathmore Rd Boston MA 02135	NE	Asst	First Boston MA	(617)536-8851	SL	2023
Rhodes Thomas A	(417)770-7655 rvtrhodes@gmail.com	245 Abbi Ln Bolivar MO 65613	MO	EM			FW	2004
Riang James C	(402)770-3124 riangjames43@gmail.com	8634 Delphinium Ln Lincoln NE 68505	NEB	Asst	Christ Lincoln NE	(402)483-7774	SL	2010

*Multiple Assignments (See Church Worker Locator for Additional Details)

See Page 53 for the Table of Abbreviations for key to District, Position, and Seminary abbreviations

**C =Candidate; EM = Emeritus; the date following the C is the month and year the Candidate status began

NAME	TELEPHONE NUMBER EMAIL	STREET ADDRESS CITY/STATE/ZIP	DISTRICT	POSITION/ STATUS**	WHERE SERVING	OFFICE PHONE	SEM/ PROGRAM	YR GRAD
Ricard Robert W	(321)848-4510 revrobertricard@gmail.com		IE	SP	Trinity State Center IA	(641)483-2682	FW	2019
Rice James W	(413) 588-7826 bjrinshore@gmail.com	779 Ryan Rd Florence MA 01062	NE	SP	Trinity Easthampton MA	(413)527-3311	FW	2002
Rice Richard R	revrrice@aol.com	801 High St Santa Cruz CA 95060	CNH	SP	Messiah Santa Cruz CA	(831)423-8330	SL	1985
Rich Martin M	920-427-7424 grandcrazies@gmail.com	N4548 County Road G Wild Rose WI 54984	NW	EM			FW	2006
Richard Andrew P	(307) 439-3542 andpaulrich@gmail.com	1755 W 15th St Casper WY 82604	WY	Asst	Mount Hope* Casper WY	(307)234-8428	FW	2012
Richard Donald F	hu16albatross@outlook.com	21190 SW Ladyfern Dr Sherwood OR 97140	NOW	SP	St Paul Sherwood OR	(503)625-6648	SL	2010
Richard Gary L	(440)309-8252 revgrichard@gmail.com	1300 W Southfield Dr Jackson MI 49203	MI	EM			FW	2004
Richard Keith R	(815)765-0088 klcarichard@gmail.com	303 Sherman Ln Poplar Grove IL 61065	NI	SMP	Immanuel Belvidere IL	(815)544-8058	SL-SMP	2015
Richard Matthew R Dr	(701)389-0418 stpaulsrev@srt.com	4401 42nd St SE Minot ND 58701	ND	Sn/Adm	St Paul Minot ND	(701)852-2821	CQ	2013
Richardson Bruce H	(715)214-7900 brich6@gmail.com	3546 E Meadows Pl Apt 4 Eau Claire WI 54701	NW	EM			SL	1996
Richardson Kyle J	(317) 642-6522 pastorkylerichardson@gmail.com	2306 E Banta Rd Indianapolis IN 46227	IN	C06/2025			FW	2019
Richardson James S	(334)272-6214 steve4christ@icloud.com	232 Lakeshore Dr Pike Road AL 36064	SO	SMP	St Paul Montgomery AL	(334)272-6214	SL-SMP	2011
Richardson James M Jr	(817)901-1813 mrichardson@crownoflife.org	8432 Stephanie Dr North Richland Hills TX 76182	TX	Sn/Adm	Crown of Life Colleyville TX	(817)421-5683	SL	2010
Richardson Glenn W	(716)807-2538 Glenn7881@aol.com	7881 Moore Rd Akron NY 14001	EA	EM			SPR	1976
Richardson Christopher D	(936)870-5279 chrisdrich@aol.com	810 Parkview Cir Harlingen TX 78550	TX	EM			FW	2009
Richardson Gale D Jr	(231)848-4202 aquaticplantlady@gmail.com	13428 Caberfae Hwy Wellston MI 49689	MI	EM			CQ	2018
Richard-Wokoma P A	(262)599-3314 wokoma@mlchouston.org	18431 Brenwood Manor Dr Katy TX 77449	MO	C06/2021			FW	1997
Richert Cary M	richert.k@yahoo.com	7547 Shagwood St SE Caledonia MI 49316	MI	EM			CQ	2001
Richert Jeremy D	pastorjrichert@gmail.com	476 Prairie Blvd Dakota Dunes SD 57049	SD	Sn/Adm	Holy Cross Dakota Dunes SD	(605)232-9117	NESC	2014
Richert Peter A	(570)839-1428 richertp@yahoo.com	675 Belmont Ave Mount Pocono PA 18344	EA	SP	Our Savior Mount Pocono PA	(570)839-9868	FW	2007
Richert Aaron M	(248)786-7486 aaronmrichert@gmail.com	c/o Grace Lutheran Church 7550 Eubank Blvd NE Albuquerque NM 87122	RM	SP	Grace Albuquerque NM	(505)823-9100	FW	2008
Richeson Ronald L	(502)995-0499 ronr129@twc.com	2108 Ann Marie Dr Louisville KY 40299	IN	EM			SL	1991
Richter James F	pastorjimvine@gmail.com	2115 Arbor Trail NW Walker MI 49534	MI	SP	The Vine Grand Rapids MI	(616)202-1540	SL	1995
Richter Jon D	(803)260-1418 jonr828@gmail.com	146 Roan Drive Garner NC 27529	SE	EM			SL-SMP	2015
Richter Kevin C	(641)740-0865 pastorkevinrichter@gmail.com	103 Upper Ridge Reinbeck IA 50669	IE	SP	St John's* Reinbeck IA	(319)345-2766	SL	2015
Richter Paul W	410-456-2018 paulrichter728@gmail.com	34159 Gooseberry Ave Ocean View DE 19970	SE	EM			SL	1976
Richy John M Dr	jrichy@comcast.net	18062 Wentworth Ave Lansing IL 60438	NI	SP	StJohns Lansing IL	(708)895-9240	CQ	1985
Rick Paul B	(308)278-2355 rickfamily@gpcom.net	606 Ivey St Culbertson NE 69024	NEB	SP	St John's* Oberlin KS	(785)475-2333	FW	1987
Rickbeil Blake A	(218)371-6266 rickbeilb@gmail.com	P.O. Box 296 Bertha MN 56437	MNN	SP	St Paul Bertha MN	(218)924-4051	FW	2002
Rickenberg Kermit P	(863)877-6702 pastorrickenberg@yahoo.com	321 Country World Dr W Davenport FL 33897	MO	RSO	Lutherans in Jewish Evangelism Saint Louis MO	(314)645-4456	FW	2007
Rickert John R Dr	(864)357-5736 pastorrickert@hotmail.com	911 Freestyle Ct Longs SC 29568	SE	EM			FW	1987
Rickman Arthur A Dr	562-805-6248 arthurandeva@gmail.com	c/o Doug Morlok 9030 Parrot Ave Downey CA 90240	IE	S Miss	Office of International Mission Saint Louis MO		SL	2008
Rickman Robert P	(262) 745-6392 pastororlcs1@gmail.com	209 Meadow Ct Delavan WI 53115	SW	EM			SL	1978
Riddering Wayne W	(864)888-7422 wayneriddering@gmail.com	263 Adventure Trail Westminster SC 29693	FG	EM			FW	1978
Riddle J D	(517) 784-3135 pastorjdriddle@gmail.com	1007 W Washington Ave Jackson MI 49203	MI	SP	Trinity Jackson MI	(517)784-3135	SL	1998
Ridings Dustin E	(920)609-2588 ridingsdustin@gmail.com	1401 McDonald St Ocouto WI 54153	NW	SMP	Zion Oconto WI	(920)834-5037	FW-SMP	2023
Ridley Charles E	(832)941-7532 ceridley@gmail.com	2011 Austin Parkway Sugar Land TX 77479	TX	Sn/Adm	Fishers Of Men Sugar Land TX	(281)242-7711	SL	2022
Ridulph Charles M	(815) 751-7208 revridulph@gmail.com	129 N Cross St Sycamore IL 60178	NI	EM			CQ	2018
Riebau Robert O	(240) 321-4947 revriebau@gmail.com	P.O. Box 688 Eureka MO 63025	MO	SP	Reformation Affton MO	(314)352-1355	SL	2006
Riebhoff John W	(712)539-8801 jgrieghoff@yahoo.com	417 Clarendon St Kingsley IA 51028	IW	EM			FW	1981
Riege Lynn A	geranium2010@gpcom.net	50114 868th Rd Page NE 68766	NEB	EM			CQ	1999
Rieger Paul L	(636)751-4784 pauli.rieger@gmail.com	206 SW Flynn Dr Ankeny IA 50023	IW	SP	Christ Ankeny IA	(515)261-2131	SL	2015

*Multiple Assignments (See Church Worker Locator for Additional Details)

See Page 53 for the Table of Abbreviations for key to District, Position, and Seminary abbreviations

**C =Candidate; EM = Emeritus; the date following the C is the month and year the Candidate status began

NAME	TELEPHONE NUMBER EMAIL	STREET ADDRESS CITY/STATE/ZIP	DISTRICT	POSITION/ STATUS**	WHERE SERVING	OFFICE PHONE	SEM/ PROGRAM	YR GRAD
Rieger Ronald S	(303)845-0430 revrond@gmail.com	1351 Francis St Longmont CO 80501	RM	SP	Messiah Longmont CO	(303)776-2573	SL	2009
Rieker Eric A	(201)362-0891 ourcrew@aol.com	646 Lincoln Ave Pompton Lakes NJ 07442	NJ	EM			FW	1981
Rieker John M	(973)650-1253 john213a@aol.com	792 Route 145 Cairo NY 12413	NJ	EM			FW	1979
Rieman Donald A	(716)714-5134 darieman413@gmail.com	100 Weiss Ave Apt 137 West Seneca NY 14224	WY	EM			FW	1978
Riemer Leroy E	(262)204-6965	Village Pointe Community Rm 2212 101 Walnut Cir Grafton WI 53024	IW	EM			SL	1970
Riemer Carlton L	(405)338-8379 carltonriemer@gmail.com	410 N Manning St Stillwater OK 74075	OK	EM			SL	1967
Riemer Hilbert W Dr	(651)714-3802 koreariemers@gmail.com	7919 15th St N Oakdale MN 55128	MNS	EM			SL	1961
Rienstra Jan G III	(903)390-7735 pastortreyrienstra@yahoo.com		TX	EM			SL	2008
Ries Jeffrey E	(253)752-1264 lcmspastor896@gmail.com	3410 6th Ave Tacoma WA 98406	NOW	Sn/Adm	Zion Tacoma WA	(253)752-1264	SL	2006
Ries Thomas K Dr	(952)484-2964 ries@csp.edu	14095 1st S Ave Burnsville MN 55306	MNS	EM			SL	1980
Riethmeier Hubert G	revhgr@yahoo.com	5018 Nicholas Ridge Dr Saint Louis MO 63129	SE	EM			SL	1972
Rigdon Philip J Dr	curf1996@yahoo.com	906 Eagle Trace Kendallville IN 46755	IN	Sn/Adm	St John Kendallville IN	(260)347-2158	FW	2008
Riggert Jerry A	(660)537-2727 rev78@sbcglobal.net	3702 Bedford Dr Columbia MO 65203	MO	EM			FW	1978
Riggert Robert D	(515)570-3137 bob.riggert@gmail.org	1002 Magnolia Drive Manning IA 51455	IW	EM			CQ	1982
Riggert Richard L	(661)965-2448 rich.riggert@gmail.com	875 Whispering Pines Dr # B Scotts Valley CA 95066	NOW	EM			CQ	1997
Riggert Jonathan R	(712)221-4050 pastorriggert@trinitycherokee.org	725 N Roosevelt Ave Cherokee IA 51012	IW	SP	Trinity Cherokee IA	(712)225-4332	SL	2005
Riggs Robert V	(614) 562-9222 dkmriggs2@aol.com	220 S 7th St Carson City MI 48811	MI	EM			SL	1983
Rigobert Francis S	(845)642-9048 franzorigzo@gmail.com	221 Green St Schenectady NY 12305	AT	SP	Zion Schenectady NY	(518)374-1811	CQ	2014
Rikli Richard L	riklirev@gmail.com	2311 Karne Vandalia IL 62471	CI	EM			SL	2009
Riley Douglas E	(330)297-1939 djriley6664@aol.com	3218 Shawnee Trl Ravenna OH 44266	OH	EM			SL	1964
Riley Roney C	708-681-1117 rcrileymyha@sbcglobal.net	1935 S 8th Ave Maywood IL 60153	NI	SMP	St John Forest Park IL	(708)366-3226	FW-SMP	2015
Riley Patrick J	(843)812-8238 psriley7@yahoo.com	852 Olsen Dr Sidney NE 69162	NEB	EM			SL	1983
Riley Nathan R	(714)401-3685 nathanralph3685@gmail.com	1414 E Concord Ave Orange CA 92867	PSW	EM			SPR	1975
Riley Matthew E	(605)519-3488 mriley@stjamesquincy.org	938 S 24th St Quincy IL 62301	CI	Sn/Adm	Saint James Quincy IL	(217)222-8447	SL	2023
Riley Dwight D	(870)814-4828 dvsriley@suddenlink.net	125 Glenwood Dr Westfield MA 01085	NE	SP	St John's* Westfield MA	(413)568-1417	FW	1993
Riley Donavon L	(651)894-3642 elleon713@gmail.com	4396 41st St W Webster MN 55088	MNS	SP	St John Webster MN	(952)652-2844	CQ	2009
Riley Benjamin P	(631)255-2773	7163 Beale Ln Colorado Springs CO 80916	CNH	M Chap	Office of International Mission Saint Louis MO		SL	2016
Riley Jimmy K	(440)667-9655 tsjpastorriley@gmail.com	P.O. Box 156 Munger MI 48747	MI	SP	Trinity-St James Munger MI	(989)659-2506	SL-D	2009
Rinderknecht Daniel W	(406)373-9340 drinderknecht@hotmail.com	5032 McIntyre Dr Billings MT 59105	MT	EM			SL	1983
Rinehard Roy W Dr	(715)526-5280	N6927 River Dr Shawano WI 54166	NW	SP	Our Savior Gresham WI	(715)526-5280	SL	1964
Rinehart Royce E	(319)753-1140 revroyce73@gmail.com	P.O. Box 211 Danville IA 52623	IE	EM			SPR	1973
Ring Robb C Dr	(714)624-0693 robb.ring@cui.edu	377 Pineridge St Brea CA 92821	EN	Sn/Adm	Immanuel Orange CA	(714)538-2373	CQ	2014
Ring Marcus J	revmring@gmail.com	c/o St. John Lutheran Church 211 Church Ave Gregory SD 57533	SD	SP	St John Gregory SD	(605)835-9214	FW	2011
Ringer William N	ringerw@gmail.com	27 Robinson St North East PA 16428	EA	SP	St Paul North East PA	(814)725-4395	FW	2013
Ringers Keith J	(251)986-5782 kringers@gulftel.com	12521 Chicago St Elberta AL 36530	SO	SP	St Mark Elberta AL	(251)986-8133	SL	1984
Rinker Craig W Dr	(504)305-6966 rinkercw@aol.com	157 Avant Garde Cir Kenner LA 70065	SO	EM			SL	1971
Rinne Rex A	(920)815-3716 rexrinne@gmail.com	1028 W Bent Oak Ln Appleton WI 54914	NW	EM			SPR	1975
Riordan Todd C	pastor@gracecolumbus.org		IN	SP	Grace Columbus IN	(812)372-4859	SL	1996
Ripke Jonathan M	(779)901-9568 pastor.ripke@zionmarengo.net	115 S East St Marengo IL 60152	NI	Sn/Adm	Zion Marengo IL	(815)568-6564	SL	2011
Ripke Joel D	(402)942-1886 jripke@peacecolumbus.org	2053 37th Avenue Columbus NE 68601	NEB	SMP	Peace Columbus NE	(402)564-8311	SL-SMP	2025
Rippy Sean L	(208)455-6274 oratiocredendi@aol.com	11935 Virginia Pkwy Caldwell ID 83605	NOW	SP	Mount Calvary Homedale ID	(208)337-4248	SL	1998
Rische Scott F Dr	(619)890-7278 scottrische@yahoo.com	14370 N. Samhill Trail Hayden ID 83835	TX	O-Sp Min	Texas District Round Rock TX	(800)951-3478	SL	1988

*Multiple Assignments (See Church Worker Locator for Additional Details)
See Page 53 for the Table of Abbreviations for key to District, Position, and Seminary abbreviations
**C =Candidate; EM = Emeritus; the date following the C is the month and year the Candidate status began

NAME	TELEPHONE NUMBER EMAIL	STREET ADDRESS CITY/STATE/ZIP	DISTRICT	POSITION/ STATUS**	WHERE SERVING	OFFICE PHONE	SEM/ PROGRAM	YR GRAD
Rische Henry R	(970)646-5078 lpkhenry36@gmail.com	1600 Wapiti Cir Unit 27 Estes Park CO 80517	RM	EM			SL	1961
Rist Paul L	(704)497-3108 pmrist@outlook.com	961 Sedgefield Circle Grovetown GA 30813	SE	EM			SL	1979
Ristau Harold	(307) 301-9040 harold.ristau@lutherclassical.org	3201 Hawthorne Casper WY 82604	WY	Asst	Mount Hope Casper WY	(307)234-8428	NESC	2001
Ristow Neil G	(651)206-8365 neilristow@gmail.com	14980 Diamond Path W Rosemount MN 55068	MNS	EM			SL	1986
Ritchie Andrew J	(907)529-5644	6101 Quail Ridge Drive Lakeland FL 33813	FG	Sn/Adm	St Paul Lakeland FL	(863)644-7710	SL	2002
Ritchie William R	(859)466-9224 bill.ritchie61@gmail.com	9110 Kenlock Dr Louisville KY 40242	OH	SP	Amazing Grace Harrison OH	(513)367-5094	Other	2007
Ritt David H Dr	(248) 444-9599 pgarev@gmail.com	2501 Westminster Ln Aurora IL 60506	EN	EM			SPR	1969
Rittenbach Leroy C	leroy.rittenbach@att.net	106 Red Hawk Rd Novato CA 94949	NOW	EM			SPR	1969
Ritter Daniel R	pdr9498@gmail.com	11820 Little River Way Parrish FL 34219	FG	Sn/Adm	Our Savior Saint Petersburg FL	(727)344-2684	SL	1985
Ritter James F	(618)343-0761 revjfritter@hotmail.com	601 E 3rd South St Mount Olive IL 62069	SI	SP	Immanuel Mount Olive IL	(217)999-7442	SL	1984
Ritter James P	(952)426-5806 jimritter1@outlook.com	4123 Blakewood Dr Shakopee MN 55379	MNN	SP	Joy Cambridge MN	(763)689-4355	CQ	2019
Ritter Philip K	(712)829-2986 revritter75@gmail.com	709 Halland Ave Stanton IA 51573	IW	EM			SL	1975
Ritter Timothy M	(715)558-4054 tritter@immanuelrapids.com	5211 Hunters Ridge Dr Wisconsin Rapids WI 54494	NW	Sn/Adm	Immanuel Wisconsin Rapids WI	(715)423-3260	SL	2011
Rittner Philip R II		3415 W Shoreline Dr Columbia City IN 46725	MI	SP	St Paul Centreville MI	(269)467-4355	FW	2011
Riveness Rodney D	(253)249-9984 rdriveness@hotmail.com	4301 Norpoint Way NE Apt 12d Tacoma WA 98422	NOW	EM			CQ	1983
Rivera Wilfredo C Sr Dr	revrivera@hotmail.com	307 S Lake Mariam Dr Winter Haven FL 33884	FG	EM			CQ	1988
Rivkin Dominic J	(310)498-2978	3141 N Atlas Rd Coeur D Alene ID 83814	PSW	D Ex/S	Pacific Southwest District Irvine CA	(949)854-3232	SL	2006
Roach John F	(660)888-3250 roach605@sbcglobal.net	1030 Dogwood Ln Sullivan MO 63080	MO	EM			SL	2001
Robarge Philip D	(773)484-6991 phil.robarge@taborchicago.org	c/o Concordia Lutheran 2645 W Belmont Ave Chicago IL 60618	NI	Sn/Adm	Tabor Chicago IL	(773)588-4040	SL	2009
Robb Joseph E	robb.joseph@gmail.com	1163 Caroline Ct Livermore CA 94551	CNH	Sn/Adm	Our Savior Livermore CA	(925)447-1246	SL	2009
Robbins Phillip L	(760)518-0704 plrobbins@cox.net	5917 W La Polma Dr Surprise AZ 85374	PSW	EM			SL	2006
Roberts Robert R	(989)686-0376 rrrlakin@hotmail.com	P.O. Box 1428 Bay City MI 48706	MI	EM			SPR	1973
Roberts William J	(248)820-8840 radio8dxxwjr@gmail.com	4308 Mercedes St Sebring FL 33872	FG	EM			SL-SMP	2021
Roberts Todd W		1502 S 58th Ct Cicero IL 60804	NI	SP	St Paul Norwood Park Twp IL	(708)867-5044	SPR	1975
Roberts Scott P	scottroberts60@sbcglobal.net	422 Emerson Dr Seymour IN 47274	IN	SP	Shepherd Hills Bean Blossom IN	(812)988-8057	SL	2008
Roberts Sammy G	(817)404-7539 minroberts1@yahoo.com	9921 Little Tree Ln Fort Worth TX 76179	TX	SP	Grace Divine Hurst TX	(817)404-7539	EIITSL	2024
Roberts Robert R	(530)519-2566 rrrcar@sbcglobal.net	2801 Cohasset Rd #213 Chico CA 95973	CNH	EM			CQ	1982
Roberts Derek A	(865) 421-9988 revderekroberts@gmail.com	1813 Oxford Dr Maryville TN 37803	MDS	SP	Praise Maryville TN	(865)977-5810	FW	2005
Roberts Leon M Dr	(954)649-4787 Pastor19621962@gmail.com	6511 Ava Dr Jacksonville FL 32211	FG	SP	Holy Cross Jacksonville FL	(904)477-0800	CQ	2020
Roberts Guy W	(218)850-1239 groberts@peacelutheran.net	19012 W 84th Ave Arvada CO 80007	RM	Sn/Adm	Peace Arvada CO	(303)424-4454	SL	2008
Roberts Bryan L	(636)524-9469 bryanroberts@email.com	1411 Farnman Dr Herculaneum MO 63048	MO	SP	Zion Pevely MO	(636)475-4486	SL	2018
Roberts Brian D	(407)230-8659 broberts851@gmail.com	14617 Kristenright Ln Orlando FL 32826	S	EM			FW	1988
Roberts Benjamin A	(720)357-5626 pastorbenroberts@gmail.com	2685 Edsel St Trenton MI 48183	MI	Assoc	St Paul Trenton MI	(734)676-1565	SL	2007
Roberts Kenneth H	(858)231-5719 kroberts1@prodigy.net	249 Flip Side Ln Daytona Beach FL 32124	FG	EM			SL	1981
Robertson Elliott M	(410)752-5149 PastorElliottBalto@gmail.com	1338 S Hanover St Baltimore MD 21230	SE	EM			FW	1985
Robertson Gregory L	2PastorGreg@gmail.com	2686 W Mill St Spc 51 San Bernardino CA 92410	PSW	EM			CQ	2004
Robinson Richard E	(313)461-9649 eric7935@gmail.com	P.O. Box 37303 Oak Park MI 48237	MI	SP	St John Detroit MI	(313)933-9360	CQ	1994
Robinson Anthony I Sr	(334)413-3231 arobinson5@hotmail.com	717 Genetta Ct Montgomery AL 36104	SO	SP	Epiphany* Arlington AL	(334)385-2435	CQ	2013
Robinson Eric W	(650)722-6789 ericwalterrobinson@gmail.com	6704 Esther Ave NE Albuquerque NM 87109	RM	SP	Christ Albuquerque NM	(505)884-3876	SL	2009
Robinson Geoffrey L Dr	(260)409-4963 geoff.robinson@in.lcms.org	P.O. Box 85 Leo IN 46765	IN	D Ex/S	Indiana District Fort Wayne IN	(800)837-1145	SL	1982
Robinson James B	(517) 332-0778 robinsonj@martinlutherchapel.org	444 Abbot Rd East Lansing MI 48823	EN	Assoc	Martin Luther Chapel East Lansing MI	(517)332-0778	FW	2019
Robinson James W	(303) 210-4086 chaprobinson@earthlink.net	9254 Ritenour Ct Lone Tree CO 80124	RM	EM			SL	1972
Robinson Paul W Dr	(314)505-7133 robinsonp@csl.edu	8953 Forestate Dr Affton MO 63123	MO	S HS/C	Concordia Seminary Saint Louis MO	(314)505-7000	SL	1989

*Multiple Assignments (See Church Worker Locator for Additional Details)
See Page 53 for the Table of Abbreviations for key to District, Position, and Seminary abbreviations
**C =Candidate; EM = Emeritus; the date following the C is the month and year the Candidate status began

NAME	TELEPHONE NUMBER EMAIL	STREET ADDRESS CITY/STATE/ZIP	DISTRICT	POSITION/ STATUS**	WHERE SERVING	OFFICE PHONE	SEM/ PROGRAM	YR GRAD
Robson Kevin D	kevindrobson@gmail.com		MO	C08/2025			FW	2001
Robson Falak	(410)446-4528 revrobson@live.com	3401 Bank St Baltimore MD 21224	SE	Asst	Emmanuel Catonsville MD	(410)744-0016	SL	2016
Rock Ronald D	(708)363-9863 rdrock33@gmail.com	1739 E Indiana Ave Beecher IL 60401	NI	EM			FW	1993
Rockemann Joel D	(209)241-6723 jrockemann@stpaulstracy.org	37651 S Bird Rd Tracy CA 95304	CNH	Assoc	St Paul Tracy CA	(209)835-7438	SL	2022
Rockemann Larry W	(847)754-8729	8600 N Liston Avenue Kansas City MO 64154	MDS	EM			SL	1978
Rockenbach Mark D Dr	(314)505-7109 rockenbachm@csl.edu	33 Franjoe Ct Saint Charles MO 63304	MO	S HS/C	Concordia Seminary Saint Louis MO	(314)505-7000	SL	1998
Rockett Dennis W	(201)916-2455 revrockett54@gmail.com	87 Easedale Rd Wayne NJ 07470	NJ	EM			SL-D	2008
Rockey James H	(877)457-5556 jrockey@flgadistrict.org	11227 Roz Way Oxford FL 34484	FG	DP	Florida-Georgia District Orlando FL	(407)857-5556	SL	1998
Rockey Jonathan R	(907) 841-4066 jonrock53@mtaonline.net	P.O. Box 1994 Palmer AK 99645	NOW	EM			SL	1979
Rockhill James L	(641) 732-4771 pastor@trinityosage.org	415 State St Osage IA 50461	IE	SP	Trinity Osage IA	(641)732-4771	FW	2016
Rockrohr Carl E Dr	carl.rockrohr@gmail.com		OH	EM			SL	1990
Rockrohr Paul E	(720)517-0666 paul.rockrohr@gmail.com	8745 33rd Ave Kenosha WI 53142	SW	M Chap	Office of International Mission Saint Louis MO		FW	2015
Rodencal Larry J	(513)824-9865 plarry04@hotmail.com	5367 Rawhide Ct Cincinnati OH 45238	OH	EM			SL	1981
Rodgers David A	(443)515-7639 samdavid@smlc.org	625 Lochern Terrace Bel Air MD 21015	SE	SMP	St Matthew Bel Air MD	(410)838-3178	SL-SMP	2022
Rodriguez Manny	(660)287-7894 mrmanny1@sbcglobal.net	2103 Schorn Dr Apt B Killeen TX 76542	TX	EM			SL	2006
Rodriguez Moises E	(562)359-9170 moises.rodriguez@eagles.cui.edu	6475 Harvey Pt Unit 64 Chino Hills CA 91709	PSW	C06/2024			SL	2023
Rodriguez James A Jr	(812)522-6569 jrodriguez@immanuelseymour.com	1449 Robin Hood Dr Seymour IN 47274	IN	Assoc	Immanuel Seymour IN	(812)522-3118	SL	2003
Rodriguez James A	(812)707-9644 dceadam@gmail.com	3610 Sandy Hook Dr Columbus IN 47203	IN	Assoc	St Peter Columbus IN	(812)372-1571	SL	2019
Rodriguez Nelson	(281)974-1946 nelson.rodriguez-garcia@kuraray.com	2311 Churchill Cove Ln Pearland TX 77089	TX	Assoc	Gloria Dei Houston TX	(281)333-4535	SL	2011
Rodriguez Jose J Jr	(816)518-7574 pastorjoe@teamjesusliberty.org	9030 NE 103rd Ter Kansas City MO 64157	MO	Sn/Adm	St Stephen Liberty MO	(816)781-3377	SL	2007
Roedemeier Dennis D	(573)885-7960 ddrcubadev@gmail.com	602 S Bond St Cuba MO 65453	MO	SMP	Salem Salem MO	(573)729-5512	SL-SMP	2012
Roedsens Jacob J	jroedsens@gmail.com	7799 Bishopwood Rd Lake Worth FL 33467	FG	Sn/Adm	Trinity Delray Beach FL	(561)278-1737	SL	2018
Roeglin Matthew D	(314)222-9117 pastor@blessedsavior-lcms.org	1841 Charleston Estates Dr Florissant MO 63031	MO	SP	Blessed Savior Florissant MO	(314)831-1300	SL	2000
Roegner Robert M Dr	(314)640-9558 Pastorbob@woodlandschurch.com	230 Puma Loop St Groveland FL 34736	FG	Asst	Woodlands Montverde FL	(407)469-2525	FW	1981
Roehrborn Brian S	(715)366-4644 revroehrborn@gmail.com	1312 Elm St Almond WI 54909	SW	SP	Calvary* Waupaca WI	(715)258-3530	SL	2012
Roehrig Ryan K	(631)456-2875 pastor.roehrig@stpaul-ia.com	1321 N Main St Carroll IA 51401	IW	SP	St Paul Carroll IA	(712)792-4354	SL	2016
Roehrs Stephen P	(904)349-3620 dadroehrs@aol.com	608 Northlake Dr Anderson SC 29625	FG	EM			SL	1971
Roemer Carl E Dr	(410)573-5315 ceroemer@gmail.com	719 Maiden Choice Ln Apt Hr203 Catonsville MD 21228	SE	EM			SPR	1964
Roemke James A	(262)455-0255	2026 22nd Ave Kenosha WI 53140	SW	SP	Messiah Kenosha WI	(262)551-8182	SL	2007
Roepke Christopher A	(319)750-0659 roepkeca@msn.com	2228 Madison Ave Burlington IA 52601	IE	SP	Our Savior* Fort Madison IA	(319)372-7952	SL	1989
Roeske Todd E	(907)259-5115 todd@peacemonroe.org	695 Park Lane Monroe WA 98272	NOW	SP	Peace Monroe WA	(360)794-2082	CQ	2007
Roethemeyer Robert V	(260)452-2146 robert.roethemeyer@ctsfw.edu	223 Eagle Point Ct Fort Wayne IN 46845	IN	S HS/C	Concordia Theological Seminary Fort Wayne IN	(260)452-2100	SL	1986
Roettjer Andrew D	(303)204-7642 aroettjer@zionbrighton.org	2191 Broadleaf Loop Castle Rock CO 80109	RM	Assoc	Zion Brighton CO	(303)659-2339	SL	2012
Roever Robert C	(432)270-1383 bjroever@suddenlink.net	4020 Vicky Big Spring TX 79720	TX	SMP	Alive in Christ Big Spring TX	(432)264-7818	FW-SMP	2023
Rogers Ray M	(443)523-8579 revraymrogers@hotmail.com	303 Poplar St Delmar MD 21875	SE	EM			SL	1982
Rogers Robert A	(630)439-6176 pastor@trinityvp.com	43 S Craig Pl Lombard IL 60148	EN	Sn/Adm	Trinity Villa Park IL	(630)834-3440	SL	1990
Rogers Charles F Dr	(903)681-3285 charlesfrogers47@gmail.com	13716 County Road 2858 Eustace TX 75124	TX	EM			SL	1973
Rogers Clarence O III	(217)691-8654 rogersco3@gmail.com	319 Butler Ln Chatham IL 62629	CI	EM			FW	2005
Rogers Thomas J Dr	(949)275-8644 emeritus1952@gmail.com	24411 Corta Cresta Dr Lake Forest CA 92630	PSW	EM			CQ	1980
Roggow Aaron W	(734)395-3059 aroggow@stpaulannarbor.org	8278 S Warwick Ct Ypsilanti MI 48198	MI	Assoc	St Paul Ann Arbor MI	(734)665-9117	SL	2010
Roggow Gerald W	(580)446-5740 gwrjar@sbcglobal.net	105 Red Cedar St Enid OK 73701	OK	EM			CQ	1992

*Multiple Assignments (See Church Worker Locator for Additional Details)
See Page 53 for the Table of Abbreviations for key to District, Position, and Seminary abbreviations
**C =Candidate; EM = Emeritus; the date following the C is the month and year the Candidate status began

NAME	TELEPHONE NUMBER EMAIL	STREET ADDRESS CITY/STATE/ZIP	DISTRICT	POSITION/ STATUS**	WHERE SERVING	OFFICE PHONE	SEM/ PROGRAM	YR GRAD
Roggow Timothy C	(618)477-7088 taroggow@gmail.com	826 3rd St Alva OK 73717	OK	SP	Zion Alva OK	(580)327-0510	SL	2020
Rogness Noah J	(612)385-1183 pastor.rogness@goodsheptomah.org	20025 Blackberry Ave Warrens WI 54666	SW	SP	Good Shepherd Tomah WI	(608)374-2444	FW	2016
Rohde Roger E	prerohde@gmail.com	325 Gumwood Rd Bremen IN 46506	IN	Asst	Calvary Plymouth IN	(574)936-2903	FW	1977
Rohde Brian D	(608)853-2125 revrohde@outlook.com	120 West Division St Wautoma WI 54982	SW	SP	Trinity Wautoma WI	(920)787-2891	FW	2004
Rohde David W	(806)789-7611 rohdedw@aol.com	3012 Peadittle Road Moatsville WV 26405	TX	EM			FW	1984
Rohlfs Raymond M	(708)308-3460 rohlfsrj@icloud.com	6441 Forestview Dr Oak Forest IL 60452	NI	EM			SL	1983
Rohrberg Kenton G	(785)215-6008 rohrberg2@gmail.com	1009 S Sandalwood St Wichita KS 67230	KS	EM			Other	1974
Rohrs Raymond H	(443)752-7639 revray12@yahoo.com	1203 Talbott Sq Belcamp MD 21017	SE	SP	Faith Middle River MD	(410)687-7500	SPR	1975
Rohwer Gary E Dr	(818)281-1340 pastor@oursaviorokc.org	2133 NW 25th St Oklahoma City OK 73107	OK	SP	Our Savior Bethany OK	(405)495-1605	FW	1986
Rojas Roberto E Jr	pastorrojas@zionwg.org		FG	Sn/Adm	Zion Winter Garden FL	(407)743-5533	FW	2014
Rojas Roberto E Sr	(407)967-5517 elrancho214@gmail.com	214 N Dean Rd Orlando FL 32825	FG	EM			CQ	1981
Rokke Ralph M Dr	rokke@aol.com	5837 Pleasant Ave Minneapolis MN 55419	MNS	EM			CQ	1997
Roland Ronald B	(586)749-9804 rev.ronaldroland@gmail.com	28140 26 Mile Rd Chesterfield MI 48051	MI	SP	St Andrew Memphis MI	(810)392-2392	FW	2003
Rolf Richard R	(716) 432-1360 richardrolf32@gmail.com	7220 E Genesee St Apt 138 Fayetteville NY 13066	EA	EM			SL	1958
Rolf John D	(303)422-5362 jdrolf@aol.com	9153 Yarrow St Apt 1516 Westminister CO 80021	RM	EM			SPR	1955
Rolf David M	(816) 730-8923 pastorrolf@att.net	14250 Oakland Ct Grandview MO 64030	MO	Sn/Adm	Peace Kansas City MO	(816)353-3813	SL	2015
Rolf James E	(248)891-6027 pastorjimrolf@gmail.com	223 Pine St Rochester MI 48307	MI	EM			FW	2012
Roll Zachary H	(970)520-1456 revroll@ourglc.org	1110 N Salem Warren Rd North Jackson OH 44451	OH	SP	Gethsemane North Jackson OH	(330)538-2630	SL	2023
Rollefson Stacy D Dr	(530)209-0066 rollefson@juno.com	11 Duskview Ln. Fort Worth TX 76134	TX	SP	Christ Fort Worth TX	(817)370-6242	FW	1992
Rollings Deral E	(251)550-5833 st.judeslutheranchurch@yahoo.com	P.O. Box 791 Gulf Shores AL 36547	SO	SP	St Jude By Sea Gulf Shores AL	(251)968-JUDE	SL	1981
Rollins Ronald W	(216)701-5964 ronroll1990@gmail.com	17619 Nottingham Rd Cleveland OH 44119	OH	SMP	St John Cleveland OH	(216)531-1156	CQ	2018
Roloff Robb W Dr	(317)385-9017 robbroloff@aol.com	167 Verdant Drive Cicero IN 46034	IN	Sn/Adm	Emanuel Tipton IN	(765)675-4090	SL	2008
Roluffs Charles J	(503)538-8230 candenewberg@comcast.net	3130 Ivy Dr Newberg OR 97132	NOW	EM			SPR	1960
Roma Thomas R	(919)437-8065 troma@ilcsw.net	c/o Immanuel Lutheran Church 632 East Highway N Wentzville MO 63385	MO	Assoc	Immanuel Wentzville MO	(636)327-4416	SL	2012
Roma Ron T	(314)849-8488 ronroma01@gmail.com	5137 Suson Way Ct Saint Louis MO 63128	MO	Inst C	Lutheran Church Extension Fund Saint Louis MO	(314)965-9000	SL	1980
Roma Stephan A	steveroma88@gmail.com	2338 Park Ave Santa Clara CA 95050	CNH	Sn/Adm	Redeeming Grace Santa Clara CA	(408)736-6605	SL	2016
Ronchetto Kyle C	(815)450-1556 kyle.ronchetto@gmail.com	404 Davis St Chenoa IL 61726	CI	SP	St Paul* Chenoa IL	(815)945-5331	SL	2021
Ronsick Eric S	(573)270-7032 rick.ronsick@gmail.com	143 Sun Valley Ct Jackson MO 63755	MO	SMP	Trinity Cape Girardeau MO	(573)334-4549	SL-SMP	2024
Rooney Patrick M	(541)639-6832 patrickmrooney@gmail.com	15790 SW Misty Ct Beaverton OR 97007	NOW	SP	Our Redeemer Tigard OR	(503)524-6646	SL	2011
Roop Larry K	(712)376-4826 roop50216@yahoo.com	207 N Oak St P.O. Box 482 Marcus IA 51035	IW	SP	Peace Marcus IA	(712)376-4818	SL	2006
Roper R W	(517)795-4433 ropes4@comcast.net	124 Holly Ridge Dr Mooresville NC 28115	SE	EM			CQ	1977
Rosche Bryce S	(810)650-1978 pastorbryce@stmatthew.info	42420 Gateway Dr Plymouth MI 48170	MI	Sn/Adm	St Matthew Westland MI	(734)425-0260	SL	2021
Roschke Paul N	(808)446-6618 proschke@gmail.com	836 N Rosemary Dr Bryan TX 77802	CNH	EM			CQ	2009
Rose David R	(707)263-4742 drrose@xprs.net	1290 Big Valley Rd Lakeport CA 95453	CNH	EM			SL	1974
Rose Karl A	(715)861-3962 kpjrose@charter.net	834 Stanley St Chippewa FLS WI 54729	NW	EM			SPR	1974
Rose Kevin S	(307)350-0339 ksc4rose@gmail.com	351 Sunset St Green River WY 82935	WY	EM			SL	2012
Rose William D	(940)765-1112 revwillrose@gmail.com	727 Country Rd Dd Farwell TX 79325	TX	SP	St John Lariat TX	(806)825-2409	ED	2017
Rosebrock Matthew D Dr	pastor@immanuel-lindenwood.org	1101 Forest Ct Rochelle IL 61068	NI	SP	Immanuel Lindenwood IL	(815)393-4500	SL	2010
Rosebrock Stephen M	(414)774-2200 stephen.rosebrock@mtolivemke.org	5327 W Washington Blvd Milwaukee WI 53208	SW	Asst	Mount Olive Milwaukee WI	(414)774-2200	FW	2002
Roseman James N Dr	(941)806-8474 barjrose@aol.com	16 Rustling Pine Trl Black Mtn NC 28711	SE	EM			SPR	1961
Roseman Glenn A Sr	(828) 302-9305 glennroseman5@gmail.com	392 Old Homestead Lane Hayesville NC 28904	SE	SMP	Resurrection Franklin NC	(828)524-5996	CQ	2018

*Multiple Assignments (See Church Worker Locator for Additional Details)
See Page 53 for the Table of Abbreviations for key to District, Position, and Seminary abbreviations
**C =Candidate; EM = Emeritus; the date following the C is the month and year the Candidate status began

NAME	TELEPHONE NUMBER EMAIL	STREET ADDRESS CITY/STATE/ZIP	DISTRICT	POSITION/ STATUS**	WHERE SERVING	OFFICE PHONE	SEM/ PROGRAM	YR GRAD
Rosenau Mark W	pastorrosenau@msn.com	3830 S 32nd Pl Lincoln NE 68502	NEB	EM			CQ	1997
Rosenau Aaron M	(920)358-4080 aaron.rosenau@faithfv.org	601 E Glendale Ave Appleton WI 54911	NW	Assoc	Faith Appleton WI	(920)739-9191	SL	2002
Rosenau Graeme M Dr	(562)941-4658 gmr07@verizon.net	14717 Fairvilla Dr La Mirada CA 90638	PSW	EM			SL	1959
Rosenkaimer Robert R II	(712)256-0128 prron13@gmail.com	705 Oak Ridge Dr Glenwood IA 51534	IW	SP	Faith Council Bluffs IA	(712)323-6445	FW	1992
Rosenkoetter Brian J	(410)757-3293 brosenkoetter@gmail.com	1148 Riverboat Ct Annapolis MD 21409	SE	C02/2022			SL	2012
Rosenthal Edwin H Jr	(971)339-3963 ehrjr71050@gmail.com	119 E Clifford Ct Newberg OR 97132	NOW	EM			CQ	1992
Rosenthal Leon G Dr	rosenthalleon@yahoo.com	2900 Mach 1 Dr Norfolk NE 68701	NEB	EM			CQ	2005
Rosenthal Timothy S	(512)905-8456 drtrose@yahoo.com	P.O. Box 699 Menard TX 76859	TX	SP	Grace Menard TX	(325)456-1875	SL	1988
Rosenvinge Douglas A	acolyte@juno.com	400 Prince Of Wales Dr Virginia Bch VA 23452	SE	EM			FW	1981
Roser Timothy W Dr	(715)457-2405 twroser@yahoo.com	1225 Main St Junction City WI 54443	NW	SP	St Paul* Junction City WI	(715)457-2405	SL	1989
Roser Dennis M	(414)881-4311 dennismroser@gmail.com	8652 N 52nd St Brown Deer WI 53223	SW	SP	St Paul Brown Deer WI	(414)355-5030	CQ	2015
Rosin Robert L Dr	(314)757-1101 renref@me.com	723 Castle Pines Dr Ballwin MO 63021	MO	EM			SL	1976
Roskowic David G	(815) 904-3731 davidroskowic@gmail.com	1026 McKnight Cir Apt 4 Rockford IL 61107	NI	C04/2021			SL-SMP	2014
Rosnau Alan P	(602)909-6309 arosnau@sotdaz.org	5959 E Phelps Rd Scottsdale AZ 85254	PSW	Assoc	Shepherd Desert Scottsdale AZ	(480)860-1188	SL	1985
Ross Daniel C	(405)376-3116 ross.c.daniel@gmail.com	501 N Clear Springs Rd Mustang OK 73064	OK	SP	Christ Mustang OK	(405)376-3116	SL	2011
Ross Richard	(714)334-1252 newredshoe@gmail.com	4659 Texas St. Unit 5 San Diego CA 92116	PSW	SP	Morning Star Lakeside CA	(619)443-6032	SL	2003
Ross Jeffrey C	(248)321-2982 jeffreyross83@gmail.com	408 East St N P.o 153 Garfield MN 56332	MNN	SP	St John Garfield MN	(320)834-2248	FW	2012
Ross Hal G	(360)620-8663 umgriz76@msn.com	1036 Sedonia St Bremerton WA 98310	NOW	EM			FW	1996
Ross Brandon W	(719)963-2881 concord.1580@yahoo.com		RM	Sn/Adm	Faith Johnstown CO	(970)587-6460	FW	2014
Ross Bernard M III	(660)641-0051 pastor.trinity@almanet.net	304 Waverly Ave P.O. Box 257 Alma MO 64001	MO	SP	Trinity Alma MO	(660)674-2376	SL	2014
Ross Andrew B	(949)734-9032 drew.ross@christcm.org	c/o Christ Lutheran Church 760 Victoria St Costa Mesa CA 92627	PSW	Sn/Adm	Christ Costa Mesa CA	(949)631-1611	SL	2006
Ross Harold E	(708)901-0217 rosshe@comcast.net	311 N Airlite St Apt B Elgin IL 60123	NI	EM			SL	1961
Rosser Edward K Dr	rwwjdgrace@aol.com	310 County Road 832 Flat Rock AL 35966	MDS	Asst	Good Shepherd Chattanooga TN	(423)629-4661	SL-D	2009
Rossington Mark W	pastormark@epiphanychandler.org	Epiphany Lutheran Church 800 W Ray Rd Chandler AZ 85225	PSW	SP	Epiphany Chandler AZ	(480)963-6105	FW	1993
Rossow Jerome W	(402)328-9509 jeromerossow@yahoo.com	2915 Coronado Dr Lincoln NE 68516	NEB	EM			SPR	1968
Rossow Robert F	(714) 356-9031 bobfrossow@gmail.com	1521 Wood Lk Santa Ana CA 92705	PSW	EM			SL	1986
Rossow Richard H	(314)623-6775 richardhrossow@gmail.com	1260 Crystal Pointe Cir Fenton MI 48430	MI	EM			CQ	1989
Rossow Timothy A Dr	(630)362-7535 rossow.tim@gmail.com	P.O. Box 121 Ocean Shores WA 98569	NOW	EM			SL	1985
Rossow Francis C	(314)325-5833	211 Innisfail Dr Webster Grvs MO 63119	MO	EM			SL	1948
Rossow David E	(810)814-3816 daviderossow@gmail.com	5091 Nichols Rd Swartz Creek MI 48473	MI	EM			FW-SMP	2013
Rossow Lowell D	(417)276-2561 rossow44@hotmail.com	15060 E 2030 Rd Stockton MO 65785	MO	EM			SL	1970
Rossow Justin P Dr	justinrossow@gmail.com	6620 Memory Ln Ann Arbor MI 48105	MI	SP	Trinity Arcadia MI	(231)889-3620	SL	2003
Rostek Wayne F Jr	circuit15delegate@gmail.com	1212 Deer Creek Rd Pryor OK 74361	OK	EM			SL	2001
Roth Delbert R	(828)256-5070 delroth@twave.net	3120 44th Avenue Dr NE Hickory NC 28601	SE	EM			SPR	1958
Roth Timothy L	(314)650-1745 pastor.troth@gmail.com	1031 Highway K 68 Pomona KS 66076	KS	SP	Faith Ottawa KS	(785)242-1906	SL	2016
Roth Steven M	(972) 637-3403 steveroth49@aol.com	450 Rainier St Cedar Hill TX 75104	TX	Assoc	Grace Arlington TX	(817)274-1626	CQ	1996
Roth John D Dr	(239)405-8638 johndavidroth@gmail.com	20252 Black Tree Ln Estero FL 33928	FG	SP	Thrive Community Estero FL	(239)687-3430	SL	1987
Roth David J Jr	(573)437-2085 pr.david.roth@gmail.com	P.O. Box 153 Owensville MO 65066	MO	SP	Mount Calvary* Belle MO	(573)207-4148	SL	2015
Roth Carlyle L	(701)838-6352 croth@srt.com	1511 Glacial Dr Minot ND 58703	ND	Assoc	St Paul Minot ND	(701)852-2821	SPR	1975
Roth Carl D	(512)229-8899 pastor.roth@gmail.com	17805 Floribundas Elgin TX 78621	TX	SP	Grace Elgin TX	(512)281-3367	FW	2006
Roth Michael J	(269)932-8456 michael.roth@discovertrinity.org	3460 Kedzie St Saint Joseph MI 49085	MI	Sn/Adm	Trinity Saint Joseph MI	(269)983-5000	FW	1986
Rothchild Daryl G	(701)263-2288 revdgr1984@gmail.com	1247 15th Ave SW Minot ND 58701	ND	EM			FW	1984
Rothchild Dean F Dr	(319)350-9564 deanrothchild@peoplepc.com	512 Greenfield St NE Cedar Rapids IA 52402	IE	EM			FW	1982

*Multiple Assignments (See Church Worker Locator for Additional Details)

See Page 53 for the Table of Abbreviations for key to District, Position, and Seminary abbreviations

**C =Candidate; EM = Emeritus; the date following the C is the month and year the Candidate status began

NAME	TELEPHONE NUMBER EMAIL	STREET ADDRESS CITY/STATE/ZIP	DISTRICT	POSITION/ STATUS**	WHERE SERVING	OFFICE PHONE	SEM/ PROGRAM	YR GRAD
Rottmann Erik J	(573)378-5512 erottmann@gmail.com	11439 Great Oaks Rd Versailles MO 65084	MO	SP	Grace Versailles MO	(573)378-5512	FW	1996
Rouland Mark A	(636)441-7425 mrouland@zionharvester.org	3866 S Old Hwy 94 Saint Charles MO 63304	MO	Sn/Adm	Zion Saint Charles MO	(636)441-7425	SL	2005
Rouse Adam L	(520)869-9185 rousea@csl.edu	2032 Stonehenge Rd Springfield IL 62702	CI	SP	Immanuel Springfield IL	(217)528-5232	SL	2024
Rowe Daniel	danielrowe@rocketmail.com	39835 Grove Hts Lady Lake FL 32159	CNH	EM			SL	1985
Rowland Robert C II	(510)230-5410 aresee.rcrii@gmail.com	1074 View Dr Richmond CA 94803	CNH	EM			SPR	1974
Rowland William D	(501)413-1376 william@peacechurch.org	5708 Greenfield Dr Watauga TX 76148	TX	SMP	Peace Hurst TX	(817)284-1677	SL-SMP	2024
Rowold David P Dr	(203)800-5495 pastor@cheshirelutheran.org	312 Sharon Drive Cheshire CT 06410	NE	SP	Cheshire Cheshire CT	(203)272-5106	SL	2003
Rowold Henry L	(314)425-9937 rowoldh@csl.edu	718 Imse Drive Apt 204 Saint Louis MO 63119	MO	EM			SL	1964
Roy James S	(917)605-4566 roy_js52@yahoo.com	12706 89th Ave Richmond Hill NY 11418	AT	SP	United Bengali Woodside NY	(718)639-3945	CQ	2005
Rozelle Randall L Dr	(630) 373-3952 pastorrandy8900@gmail.com	400 Orchard Ter Roselle IL 60172	NI	Cmp P	St Peter Arlington Heights IL	(847)259-4114	SL	2005
Rub Robert H Jr	(815)988-4673 rhrubjr@aol.com	4863 Alpine Park Dr Rockford IL 61108	NI	EM			SPR	1966
Ruback Nathan A	(314)496-5865 nruback@gracechapelstl.org	1450 Washington St Florissant MO 63033	MO	Sn/Adm	Grace Chapel Bellefontaine Nghbrs MO	(314)868-3232	SL	2007
Rubeck Larry D	lrubeck33@gmail.com	907 Hawthorne Dr Crystal Lake IL 60014	NI	Sn/Adm	Prince Peace Crystal Lake IL	(815)455-3200	SL	1994
Rubino Chris J	(616)648-6451 crubino50@gmail.com	1268 Jakarta Dr SW Byron Center MI 49315	MI	EM			CQ	2018
Rubino Alessandro A	(516)582-4647 rubino@thelifeny.org	1860 Chester Dr East Meadow NY 11554	AT	SMP	The Life Old Westbury NY	(516)333-3355	SL-SMP	2024
Rucker Benjamin K	(507)441-2257 ruckebe@yahoo.com	318 N Jefferson St New Ulm MN 56073	MNS	SP	Zion* Springfield MN	(507)723-5609	FW	2006
Ruckman Gary L	(952)994-9695 roseann.gary@gmail.com	c/o St John Lutheran Church 38597 State Highway 19 Arlington MN 55307	MNS	SP	St John Arlington MN	(507)964-2400	FW	1986
Rudloff Dean H	(218)353-7361 djrudloff74@yahoo.com	5736 Lax Lake Rd Silver Bay MN 55614	MNN	EM			SL	2003
Rudnik Richard D	(985)226-1043 pastor@gracehouma.org	183 Evangeline Heights St Houma LA 70364	SO	SP	Grace Houma LA	(985)879-1865	SL	2007
Rudolf Bruce E	(772)321-8692 barefootrev1@gmail.com	P.O. Box 54 Brant Lake NY 12815	AT	Assoc	SonRise Pottersville NY	(772)321-8692	SL	1966
Rudolph Jared E	(260) 495-4306 pastorrudolph@plcms.org	711 Carlin Dr Angola IN 46703	EN	Assoc	Peace Fremont IN	(260)495-4306	FW	2024
Rudow Allen A	(623)760-5131 allen@rudowgroup.com	44 N Vail Ave #209 Arlington Heights IL 60005	PSW	EM			SL	1960
Rudowske Richard C Jr Dr	(269) 277-2326 rich.rudowske@lbt.org	2208 W Chesterfield Blvd Apt 307 Springfield MO 65807	MO	RSO	Lutheran Bible Translators Inc Concordia MO	(660)225-0810	SL	2005
Rudsenske Eric M	(601)665-0183	637 Wallace Rd Jackson TN 38305	MDS	SP	Concordia Jackson TN	(731)668-0757	FW	2017
Rueger Matthew W Dr	(641)373-8727 mrueger@netins.net	P.O. Box 545 Hubbard IA 50122	IE	SP	St John Hubbard IA	(641)864-2672	FW	1990
Ruehs Jonathan B	(818)426-6738 jbruehs@yahoo.com		PSW	Assoc	Light of Christ Irvine CA	(949)786-3326	SL	2015
Ruesch Matthew D	(906)396-7401 revruesch@gmail.com	696 Osterberg Pkwy Niagara WI 54151	NW	SP	Our Redeemer Kingsford MI	(906)774-1844	SL	2005
Rueter Gary D	(540)841-8673 gdrueter@mac.com	42 Boulder Dr Stafford VA 22554	SE	EM			SPR	1972
Ruey James N	(507)387-7198 jamesruey1205@yahoo.com	105 Emily Ln Mankato MN 56001	MNS	Sn/Adm	Sudanese Mankato MN	(507)385-2186	SL	2008
Ruff Daniel J	(740)587-3453 deej49@gmail.com	10 Samson Pl Granville OH 43023	OH	EM			FW	1984
Ruff Roger O	(314) 395-3397 rogerruff@hotmail.com	789 Eckrich Pl Webster Grvs MO 63119	SE	EM			SL	1965
Ruffatto Frank C	(704)608-4200 revfrank1745@gmail.com	116 Hickory Rd Charleston WV 25314	OH	SP	Redeemer Charleston WV	(304)345-6251	SL	2009
Rufner David J	drufner@gmail.com	P.O. Box 1959 Big Bear City CA 92314	PSW	C06/2020			SL	2004
Ruger Lawrence M	(630)742-7824 lruger@stpaulsonline.org	3515 E Brunswick Rd Beecher IL 60401	NI	SMP	St Paul Matteson IL	(708)720-0880	SL-SMP	2024
Ruhbusch William H	(715)359-9757	6209 Alta Verde St Schofield WI 54476	NW	EM			SPR	1963
Ruhl Michael R	(734)678-9358 mrrmultiply21@gmail.com	10738 S Splitstone Pinckney MI 48169	MI	EM			SL	1971
Ruhlig Michael J	(940)282-0822 revmjr3168@gmail.com	111 W Woodworth Rd Milford IL 60953	CI	SP	St Paul Milford IL	(815)889-4209	FW	1995
Ruiz Francisco	(760)831-6631 franciscoruiz7@gmail.com	5985 Paradise East Dr Apt A La Quinta CA 92253	PSW	C07/2016			SL	2010
Ruland Warren J	(504)524-1025 warrenruland1012@gmail.com	1004 Section Line Rd NE Hanceville AL 35077	SO	SP	Christ Albertville AL	(256)891-0608	CQ	1988
Rumsch Bruce A	(503)341-9542 padre19@comcast.net	3668 SE Smith Dr Hillsboro OR 97123	NOW	EM			FW	1978
Rumsey John C III	(405)434-1985 jrumsey3@yahoo.com	2201 Edwards Dr Guthrie OK 73044	OK	SP	Our Savior Guthrie OK	(405)282-5144	CQ	2018
Runge Brian E	(713)870-4830 brunge358@gmail.com	9107 Rippling Fields Dr Houston TX 77064	TX	EM			SL	1985

*Multiple Assignments (See Church Worker Locator for Additional Details)

See Page 53 for the Table of Abbreviations for key to District, Position, and Seminary abbreviations

**C =Candidate; EM = Emeritus; the date following the C is the month and year the Candidate status began

NAME	TELEPHONE NUMBER EMAIL	STREET ADDRESS CITY/STATE/ZIP	DISTRICT	POSITION/ STATUS**	WHERE SERVING	OFFICE PHONE	SEM/ PROGRAM	YR GRAD
Runge Richard H	(704)552-7719 dlrunge@bellsouth.net	10153 Bishops Gate Blvd Pineville NC 28134	SE	EM			SPR	1969
Runk Patrick D	(386)864-0498 patrickrunk@gmail.com	96 Beechwood Ln Palm Coast FL 32137	FG	C11/2022			SL	2007
Runtsch Timothy D	(970)225-9020 pt@redeemerconnect.com	7755 Greenstone Trl Fort Collins CO 80525	RM	Sn/Adm	Redeemer Fort Collins CO	(970)225-9020	SL	1990
Rupe Ryan R Dr	(414)336-9522 ryanrupe@yahoo.com	57 Windswept Dr Arnold MO 63010	MO	Assoc	Our Savior Fenton MO	(636)343-2192	SL	1998
Rupert Lee E	(307)431-9636 leerupert@yahoo.com	3325 Greenbrier St Saint Paul MN 55127	WY	EM			SL	1991
Rupp Robert G	(850)456-6428 bobruppmel3@gmail.com	1500 N 52nd Ave Pensacola FL 32506	SO	EM			SPR	1969
Ruppert Mark A	(412)216-0203 revmarkruppert@comcast.net	6371 Windrush Ln Blacklick OH 43004	S	EM			FW	1997
Rusche Jonathon H	(812)483-6663 jon.rusche@gmail.com	333 Jackson St Apt 1f Marengo IL 60152	NI	Assoc	Zion Marengo IL	(815)568-6564	SL	2020
Rusert Joshua D	(262)389-2839 jd8323777@gmail.com	7448 Westlake Terrace Bethesda MD 20817	SE	SP	Pilgrim Bethesda MD	(301)229-2800	SL	2014
Rusert Matthew L	(507)375-4228 sbsquire@hotmail.com	41486 760th Ave Saint James MN 56081	MNS	SP	St John* Saint James MN	(507)375-4228	FW	1985
Rusert Nathan J	(507)236-2779 njrusert@juno.com	1105 Pestalozzi St Tell City IN 47586	IN	SP	Emmanuel Tell City IN	(812)547-4215	FW	1987
Rushton John S	(585)286-2600 revjohnrushton@gmail.com	1830 Chili Ave Rochester NY 14624	EA	SMP	Alpha Deaf Rochester NY	(585)286-2600	CQ	2019
Rusnak Jonathan W	(414) 704-6724 jonathanrusnak@outlook.com	141 Struthers Place Seward NE 68434	NEB	S HS/C	Concordia University Nebraska Seward NE	(402)643-3651	SL	2010
Rusnak Joshua W	(314)277-5192	544 Orchard Ln Eureka MO 63025	MO	Assoc	St Mark Eureka MO	(636)938-4432	SL	2019
Russell Noah A	pnrussell@kingofkingscr.org		IE	Assoc	King Of Kings Cedar Rapids IA	(319)393-2438	SL	2025
Russert Luke D	LukeRussert56@gmail.com	5548 S 38th St Lincoln NE 68516	NEB	EM			FW	1984
Russert David J	(201)746-0261 dsaaa946@aol.com	37 Old Chestnut Rd Montvale NJ 07645	NJ	SP	Trinity Morris Plains NJ	(973)538-7606	CQ	2009
Russow James R	(209)478-4228 jnbrussow@att.net	1986 Angelico Cir Stockton CA 95207	CNH	EM			SPR	1973
Rust Jason S	(314)420-4546 pastorrust@shlcruidoso.org	1120 Hull Rd Ruidoso NM 88345	RM	SP	Shepherd Hills Ruidoso NM	(575)258-4191	SL	2007
Rutherford Stephen W	rev.srutherford@gmail.com	21037 Rotermund Ave Lincoln MO 65338	MO	SP	Immanuel* Lincoln MO	(660)547-3399	SL	2014
Rutt Douglas L Dr	(314) 505-7019 ruttd@csl.edu	261 S Old Orchard Ave Webster Groves MO 63119	MO	EM			FW	1986
Rutter David A	(586)863-8795 rutter5@sbcglobal.net	4941 Dusk Dr Shelby Township MI 48316	MI	Asst	Trinity Saint Joseph MI	(269)983-5000	FW	1993
Rutz John M	(419)873-8174 jnrutz@att.net	601 Louisiana Ave Perrysburg OH 43551	OH	SP	Shep Of Valley Perrysburg OH	(419)874-6939	SL	1987
Rutz Kurt G	(254)876-3175 krutz.glc@gmail.com	104 S Carpenter St Mart TX 76664	TX	SP	Grace* Marlin TX	(254)803-2475	FW	1984
Rutz John B	(712)621-5971 pastorrutz@hotmail.com	800b N Sumner Ave Creston IA 50801	IW	SP	Trinity Creston IA	(641)782-5095	FW	2009
Ruwisch George A V	(703)994-0077 GeorgeRuwisch@gmail.com		NE	Sn/Adm	Grace Nashua NH	(603)888-7579	FW	2012
Rux Jarold D	(636)933-0512 jaroldrux@gmail.com	116 Gran Vista Dr Festus MO 63028	MO	EM			SPR	1976
Ryan Christopher A	(440)264-3825 christopher.ryan@gmail.com	6487 Meadowbrook Dr Mentor OH 44060	OH	SMP	St Mark Chesterland OH	(440)729-1668	SL-SMP	2021
Ryan Christopher M	(612)704-5255 christophermryan2@gmail.com	1710 County Rd 35 W Buffalo MN 55313	MNS	SMP	St John Buffalo MN	(763)682-1883	SL-SMP	2021
Ryden William C	(708)479-5655 williamcryden@yahoo.com	1811 Flagstone St Joliet IL 60431	NI	SP	Hope Shorewood IL	(815)741-2428	SL	1998
Ryherd Brian D	(314)892-4408 ryherdbrian@gmail.com	3490 Brookstone View Dr Saint Louis MO 63129	MO	Prin	Abiding Savior Saint Louis MO	(314)894-9200	SL-SMP	2022
Rynearson Timothy J	(605)692-1894 peacelut@brookings.net	3104 Sunnyview Dr Brookings SD 57006	SD	Sn/Adm	Zion* White SD	(605)629-2951	SL	1985
Sabel Thomas A Dr	(260)438-6057 revtsabel@gmail.com	1126 Northlawn Dr Fort Wayne IN 46805	IN	EM			SL	1993
Sabol Alexander W	(412)266-1354 asabol9117@gmail.com	8892 Tamarack Rd Lakeview MI 48850	EN	SP	Holy Trinity* Lakeview MI	(989)352-6374	FW	2017
Sackschewsky Ralph A	(281)702-9040 ralphasack@yahoo.com	18414 Memorial Mist Ln Tomball TX 77375	TX	EM			CQ	1981
Saddler Thomas W	(402)435-0266 csaddler@gmail.com	c/o Melissa Sadler 5274 Watson St NW Washington DC 20016	NEB	EM			SL	2007
Sadlo Christopher N	(732)738-7073 pastorsadlo@yahoo.com	18 Izola Ave Fords NJ 08863	NJ	SP	Our Redeemer Fords NJ	(732)738-7470	SL	2010
Safarik Andrew C	(308)458-8231 josafarik4@gmail.com	1830 Waterhole Canyon Ave Pahrump NV 89048	PSW	SP	Shep/Valley Pahrump NV	(775)727-4098	SL-D	2009
Sage Jeffery J	(507)438-4006 sgjjff@yahoo.com	38854 800th St Lakefield MN 56150	MNS	SP	St Paul* Lakefield MN	(507)853-4512	SL	2008
Sager William A	(254)444-0091 william.a.sager@gmail.com	153 Eagle Landing Dr Belton TX 76513	TX	EM			FW	1985
Sagissor George W III	(320)743-3641 revsag@hotmail.com	11519 59th Ct Clear Lake MN 55319	MNN	EM			SPR	1975
Sahlberg Eric S Jr		14057 Helsby Street Orlando FL 32832	NE	SP	Mount Calvary Acton MA	(978)263-5156	SL	2010

*Multiple Assignments (See Church Worker Locator for Additional Details)
See Page 53 for the Table of Abbreviations for key to District, Position, and Seminary abbreviations
**C =Candidate; EM = Emeritus; the date following the C is the month and year the Candidate status began

NAME	TELEPHONE NUMBER EMAIL	STREET ADDRESS CITY/STATE/ZIP	DISTRICT	POSITION/ STATUS**	WHERE SERVING	OFFICE PHONE	SEM/ PROGRAM	YR GRAD
Saie Peter N	(215)839-4408 nuahnsaie10@gmail.com	15 Bonnie Brae Utica NY 13501	EA	SP	Redeemer* Canastota NY	(315)697-3332	SL	2018
Sailer Scott C	(605)212-2706 scottsailer@aol.com	2105 S Lincoln Ave Sioux Falls SD 57105	SD	EM			SL	1985
Sailer Armand D	(423)591-2671 adsailer43@gmx.com	2508 Myron Avenue North Chesterfield VA 23237	SE	EM			SL	1968
Sajban Paul M	pastorps@windomnet.com	769 16th St Windom MN 56101	MNS	SP	Our Savior Windom MN	(507)831-3522	FW	1994
Sakach Randy K	rmsak@comcast.net	904 Tyree Spring Rd White House TN 37188	MDS	SMP	Prince Of Peace White House TN	(615)362-1902	CQ	2018
Salcido Richard A	(712)371-2573 rich.salcido@gmail.com	24 Concordia Dr Paris IL 61944	CI	EM			CQ	1991
Salemink Michael W	(765)418-2342 michael.salemink@ctsfw.edu	6600 N Clinton St Fort Wayne IN 46825	IN	S HS/C	Concordia Theological Seminary Fort Wayne IN	(260)452-2100	FW	2003
Salemink Raymond J	rundershepherd@gmail.com	501 W. Walnut Street Pierceton NO 46562 EUROPE	IN	SP	St Paul Woodland IN	(574)633-4888	FW	2000
Saleska Timothy E Dr	(314)646-0620 saleskat@csl.edu	7441 Wise Ave Saint Louis MO 63117	MO	S HS/C	Concordia Seminary Saint Louis MO	(314)505-7000	SL	1982
Salinas Adam C	(406)750-8723 adaminas@yahoo.com	317 Market St. Freeport PA 16229	EA	Inst C	Concordia Lutheran Ministries Cabot PA	(724)352-1571	FW	2010
Saling Loucan E	972-351-1040 loucan.saling@gmail.com	202 Reel Rd Longview TX 75604	TX	SP	Our Redeemer Longview TX	(903)758-2019	FW	2019
Sallach Philip N	(716)264-5876 pnsesox@aol.com	3125 Krueger Rd North Tonawanda NY 14120	EA	EM			SPR	1975
Sallach Timothy L	(920)251-0170 timsallach@yahoo.com	W7201 Cty Rd C Burnett WI 53922	SW	SMP	Zion Burnett WI	(920)689-2280	FW-SMP	2015
Salminen Jon D	(281)743-3242 pastor_jon@epiphanypearland.org	4010 Crystal Lake Cir N Pearland TX 77584	TX	Sn/Adm	Epiphany Pearland TX	(281)485-7833	SL	1989
Salo Scott A	(313)600-6638 salscott1@gmail.com	6508 County Road 263 Hannibal MO 63401	MO	SP	Our Savior* Monroe City MO	(573)221-7051	FW	2017
Salomon Jeffrey A	(214)789-4115 salomon1402@gmail.com	4618 Sky Harbor Drive Rockwall TX 75087	TX	C12/2021			SL-SMP	2018
Samal Nabin	(314)814-4835 nabinsamal8@gmail.com	4100 Weber Rd Saint Louis MO 63123	MO	Assoc	St Johns Saint Louis MO	(314)773-0126	SL	2024
Sampson Charles M Jr	(815)496-2284 cms21749@sbcglobal.net	P.O. Box 251 Serena IL 60549	NI	SP	Lord of Life Millbrook IL	(815)496-2284	CQ	2015
Samuel Victor	(502)893-7469	4325 Cara Way Louisville KY 40299	MO	EM			CQ	1997
Sanabria Miguel D Sr	813-406-5028 migueldarios@hotmail.com	7217 Ashwood Dr Port Richey FL 34668	FG	D Miss	Florida-Georgia District Orlando FL	(407)857-5556	SL	2010
Sanabria Miguel A Jr	(813)406-9174 Miguelk0710@gmail.com	7212 Alafia Dr Riverview FL 33578	FG	Assoc	Immanuel Brandon FL	(813)689-1787	SL	2018
Sanchez Leopoldo A Dr	(314)505-7273 sanchezl@csl.edu	2537 Annalee Ave Brentwood MO 63144	MO	S HS/C	Concordia Seminary Saint Louis MO	(314)505-7000	FW	1999
Sanchez-Zapata Vicente	(816)988-1747 pastorsanchez@ourredeemerkc.com	3448 NW Pink Hill Cir Blue Springs MO 64015	MO	SP	Our Redeemer Kansas City MO	(816)241-2334	SL	2009
Sandeno Timothy E	(843)814-7992 timothy@sandeno.us	4238 Eastwood Rd SE Rochester MN 55904	MNS	EM			FW	2005
Sander Martinho Q	(414)630-6802 revsander@gmail.com	15300 W Glendale Ave New Berlin WI 53151	SW	EM			CQ	1984
Sanders Thomas J	pastomgr@gmail.com	715 S McKinley Ave Freeport IL 61032	NI	EM			FW	1978
Sanders Randall C	(325)518-9255 craig.sanders@suddenlink.net	5 Lake Point Cir Abilene TX 79606	TX	SMP	Zion Abilene TX	(325)690-0121	SL-SMP	2023
Sandersfeld Vernon G	(406)214-4290 vsandds@gmail.com	P.O. Box 405 Hamilton MT 59840	MT	EM			SL	1983
Sandersfeld Kyle J	(618)939-4268 kylek3@yahoo.com	216 Norma Ave Waterloo IL 62298	SI	C07/2016			FW	1997
Sandfort Stephen D	(817)213-7703 stevesandfort@me.com	1425 Florence Dr Azle TX 76020	TX	SP	The Edge Azle TX	(817)237-4822	FW	2011
Sandmann Donald W Dr	(260)433-2967 donsand2@msn.com	8212 Covenant Ln Fort Wayne IN 46835	IN	EM			SL	1963
Sandoval Carlos R	(811)979-9658 sandoval.carlos.r@gmail.com	1915 Victoria Dr Brownsville TX 78521	TX	SMP	Zion Alamo TX	(956)787-1584	FW-SMP	2025
Sanger David J	(760)832-4452 pastordavidsanger@live.com	601 Bali Dr Palm Springs CA 92264	PSW	C07/2016			CQ	2006
Sansom James C	(309)306-1170 pastor.chris@stjsp.org	13441 Townline Rd Green Valley IL 61534	CI	Assoc	St John Green Valley IL	(309)348-3180	SL	2008
Sansom Vernon J III	(865)456-4023 trey@project242church.com	9926 Chimney Swift Ln Conroe TX 77385	TX	SP	Joy Houston TX	(832)850-5070	SL	2020
Santana Luis M	(305)642-2860 pastorlsantana1@gmail.com	1005 NW 127th Path Miami FL 33182	FG	SP	St Matthew Miami FL	(305)642-2860	FW	1988
Santos David	(631)633-1772 pastor@htlcny.org	6 East Street Shoreham NY 11786	AT	SMP	Holy Trinity Middle Island NY	(631)924-6991	SL-SMP	2022
Santos Jesus	(713)826-6573 jesus@glocalmission.org	1001 Knowlton Rd Baytown TX 77520	TX	SP	Christ Redeemer La Porte TX	(281)479-2201	Other	2022
Sarrault Joel H	(517)263-5012 pastor@stjohnsadrian.org	3448 N Adrian Hwy Adrian MI 49221	MI	SP	St John Adrian MI	(517)265-6998	SL	1988
Sarrault Zachery R	(517)215-0479 zach.sarrault@rlcary.org	7529 Faith Haven Ct. Willow Spring NC 27592	SE	Assoc	Resurrection Cary NC	(919)851-7248	SL	2021
Sathyaraj Vijendran	(503)645-5487 vsathyaraj@gmail.com	13555 NW Stonebridge Dr Portland OR 97229	NOW	EM			CQ	2005

*Multiple Assignments (See Church Worker Locator for Additional Details)

See Page 53 for the Table of Abbreviations for key to District, Position, and Seminary abbreviations

**C =Candidate; EM = Emeritus; the date following the C is the month and year the Candidate status began

NAME	TELEPHONE NUMBER EMAIL	STREET ADDRESS CITY/STATE/ZIP	DISTRICT	POSITION/ STATUS**	WHERE SERVING	OFFICE PHONE	SEM/ PROGRAM	YR GRAD
Satkowiak Brett A	(586)850-5624 brett.satkowiak@gmail.com	121 16th Place SW Demotte IN 46310	IN	SP	Faith Demotte IN	(219)987-3730	SL	2016
Sattelmeier Glenn O	(248)853-8684 pastorsattelmeier@gmail.com	2532 Eastern Ave Rochester Hls MI 48307	MI	EM			SPR	1962
Sattgast Dale L Dr	(605)352-7824 dale.sattgast@gmail.com	20723 396th Ave Huron SD 57350	SD	EM			SL	1980
Sattler John W	(317) 829-4495 jwsattler@att.net	8554 N Deer Hill Dr McCordsville IN 46055	IN	EM			SL	1979
Sauder Frederick C	(715)832-6271 alfreds7@sbcglobal.net	2217 Vienna Ter Eau Claire WI 54703	NW	EM			SPR	1963
Sauer David M	(510)793-3366 dsauer@popfremont.org	38451 Fremont Blvd Fremont CA 94536	CNH	Assoc	Prince of Peace Fremont CA	(510)793-3366	SL	1973
Sauer Paul R	(718)213-3070 prsauer@hotmail.com	1444 5th Ave # B Fort Knox KY 40121	AT	M Chap	Atlantic District Hastings-On-Hudson NY	(914)337-5700	SL	2000
Sauls Donald A	(260)525-4300 donald.sauls@aol.com	765 Bryan Street Berne IN 46711	IN	EM			FW	1984
Saunders Brian S Dr	(319)389-5526 bsaunders@lcmside.org	3318 Emerson Ave NE Cedar Rapids IA 52411	IE	DP	Iowa East District* Marion IA	(319)373-2112	FW	1990
Saunders Erik D	(414)248-8040 erik.saunders@ctsfw.edu	205 S Center Ave Miles City MT 59301	MT	SP	Trinity Miles City MT	(406)234-4983	FW	2024
Sawah Robert W	(240)408-9863 robertsawah52@gmail.com	958 Jubal Way Frederick MD 21701	SE	SP	Lamb of God Landover Hills MD	(202)394-0356	SL	2020
Sawhill David L	(713)553-8034 davesawhill@hotmail.com	2224 Walnut Ln Pasadena TX 77502	TX	EM			SL	1981
Sawyer Gregory L	(631)408-8785 greg@gregsawyer.net	3151 Sun Lake Ct Apt A Kissimmee FL 34747	FG	Prin	St Paul Lakeland FL	(863)644-7710	SL	1991
Sawyer James R Jr	(601)259-9746 seelsorge@aol.com	P.O. Box 5013 Brandon MS 39047	SO	SP	Holy Cross* Hattiesburg MS	(601)402-8147	SL	1987
Saxe Steven M	(864)313-4891 lcgs1601@aol.com	319 Longstreet Dr Greer SC 29650	SE	EM			SL	1987
Saylor Kevin K	(641)777-7670 saylor.kevin@gmail.com	6848 Day Dr Parma OH 44129	EN	EM			FW	1981
Saylor Michael W	(419)203-6770 saymike65@gmail.com	c/o Zion Lutheran Church 2122 Bronson Blvd Kalamazoo MI 49008	MI	Sn/Adm	Zion Kalamazoo MI	(269)382-2360	FW	1999
Sayre Roger B	(740)416-9586 rsayre99@live.com	42765 Cook Rd Pomeroy OH 45769	OH	EM			FW	1988
Sayre Thomas M	revsaytom@yahoo.com	101 Brannan Place #102 St John's FL 32259	MDS	EM			FW	1986
Saywrayne Philip S	(718)490-8314 calclcms1@gmail.com	27 Hudson St Staten Island NY 10304	AT	SP	St Matthew* Staten Island NY	(718)351-0866	CQ	2003
Scaer Peter J Dr	(260)338-2510	1412 Chanterelle Dr Fort Wayne IN 46845	IN	S HS/C	Concordia Theological Seminary Fort Wayne IN	(260)452-2100	FW	1992
Scaer David P Dr	(260)354-1744 dpscaer@gmail.com	5 Tyndale Pl Fort Wayne IN 46825	IN	EM			SL	1960
Scamman Evan P	(203)962-8700	292 Devalan Ave Greenwich CT 06830	NE	SP	St Paul Greenwich CT	(203)531-8466	FW	2018
Scar William C Dr	(310)487-7236 goodsamctr@aol.com	374 Bridle Creek Tr Aiken SC 29803	SE	EM			SL	1971
Scarbeary Bruce W	(309)472-5984 revbear@frontier.com	704 N Jefferson St Po 687 Roanoke IL 61561	CI	Sn/Adm	Trinity Roanoke IL	(309)923-5251	FW	1989
Schaaf Kent R		13387 Congo Ferndale Rd Alexander AR 72002	MDS	C08/2024			FW	2002
Schaar Christopher G	(626)793-1139 Firstpasa@aol.com	808 N Los Robles Ave Pasadena CA 91104	PSW	SP	First Pasadena CA	(626)793-1139	SL	1994
Schaarschmidt Mark F Dr	(860)922-2727 mark.schaarschmidt@omh.ny.gov	23 Meadow Crest Dr Woodbury CT 06798	AT	Inst C	Atlantic District Hastings-On-Hudson NY	(914)337-5700	FW	1979
Schack Gary R	(314)578-4343 gschack@sbcglobal.net	128 Cabot Ct Wentzville MO 63385	MO	EM			CQ	1996
Schade Allen W	(314)308-4146 dial8269@gmail.com	2381 Chemin Ave Saint Charles MO 63301	MO	EM			SPR	1973
Schaedel Robert C	(402) 310-8364 revrobcs@aol.com	5610 Pioneers Blvd Apt 183 Lincoln NE 68506	NEB	EM			SL	1972
Schaedig Michael W	(989)539-0680 mjschaedig@hotmail.com	534 E Lincoln Ave Cheboygan MI 49721	MI	SP	St John Cheboygan MI	(231)627-5149	FW	2003
Schaefer Larry A	(717)515-3099 lcschaefer@aol.com	1932 Outer Circle Dr Oviedo FL 32765	FG	EM			CQ	1996
Schaefer Mark A	(805)908-5525 kingterp@aol.com	15560 Durango Dr Frisco TX 75035	TX	C03/2024			SL	2000
Schaefer Theodore P	tedandnancy@q.com	1972 Marten Ave SW Albany OR 97321	NOW	SP	Zion Corvallis OR	(541)757-0946	SL	1991
Schaefer Donald C	(302)945-6284 donalds807@aol.com	1 Beebe Dr Lewes DE 19958	SE	EM			CQ	1975
Schaeffer Glenn E Dr	(616) 363-7718 glenn.schaeffer@stjamesgr.com		MI	SP	Saint James Grand Rapids MI	(616)363-7718	FW	2002
Schaeffer Kendall L	(248)767-2239 revkenschaeffer@aol.com	1306 K St Laporte IN 46350	IN	Assoc	First Hanna IN	(219)797-4855	FW	1989
Schaeffer Norman W	(402)304-2487 nschaeffer@enkadia.com	1628 Sunset Rd Lincoln NE 68506	NEB	EM			SL	1982
Schaekel Timothy H	(605)408-4008 schaekelt@gmail.com	1991 Waterford Ln Chaska MN 55318	MNS	C09/2018			SL	2014
Schaetzle George D	(920)783-8132 schrev@att.net	1953 N 10th St Sheboygan WI 53081	EN	EM			CQ	1981
Schafer Edmund E	(414)464-9934 pastor@benediction-lcms.org	N122w12692 Westwood Rd Germantown WI 53022	SW	EM			CQ	1987

*Multiple Assignments (See Church Worker Locator for Additional Details)
See Page 53 for the Table of Abbreviations for key to District, Position, and Seminary abbreviations
**C =Candidate; EM = Emeritus; the date following the C is the month and year the Candidate status began

NAME	TELEPHONE NUMBER EMAIL	STREET ADDRESS CITY/STATE/ZIP	DISTRICT	POSITION/ STATUS**	WHERE SERVING	OFFICE PHONE	SEM/ PROGRAM	YR GRAD
Schafer Stephen B	(410)456-2610 revschaf@comcast.net	858 Honeysuckle Drive Rockledge FL 32955	FG	EM			SL	1985
Schaffer Gregory A	(402)364-3239 revgregschaffer@gmail.com	203 W 10th St P.O. Box 58 Davenport NE 68335	NEB	SP	St Peters Davenport NE	(402)364-2182	SL	2018
Schalk Gerald P Dr	(847)516-3390	217 Lexington Ave Fox River Grove IL 60021	NI	EM			CQ	1980
Schaller Jordan E	(269)487-6795 pastorschallerlcms@gmail.com	c/o Redeemer Lutheran Church 1000 Pioneer Rd Delta CO 81416	RM	SP	Redeemer Delta CO	(970)874-3052	FW	2019
Schaller Scott A	(512)429-5171 pastorschaller@yahoo.com	2142 County Road 455 Thorndale TX 76577	TX	SP	Trinity Taylor TX	(512)352-6958	SL	2000
Schallhorn Robert G Jr	robertschallhorn@comcast.net	433 Aspin Dr Elkhart IN 46514	IN	EM			SL	1977
Schalow Douglas A	(715)569-4878 dschalow@tds.net	5059 Sunset Cir Vesper WI 54489	NW	EM			CQ	1993
Schamber Kenneth G	(573)248-6201 kenschamber@gmail.com	615 Clover Rd Hannibal MO 63401	MO	EM			SL	1974
Schamens Kenneth W	(352)387-7744 kenschamens@yahoo.com	9911 SW 63rd Loop Ocala FL 34481	FG	EM			CQ	1982
Schanbacher Jeffrey A	(573)298-0056 gracebtown@gmail.com	P.O. Box 156 Blairstown IA 52209	IE	SP	Grace Blairstown IA	(319)454-6941	SL	2005
Schaper Gary G Dr	(314)223-4409 gschaper40@gmail.com	1101 Pasatiempo Dr Frisco TX 75036	TX	EM			SL	1966
Scharlemann John P	(909)283-4308 jpczhar@aol.com	259 Candy Ln Redlands CA 92373	PSW	EM			SL	1982
Scharnitzke Philip J	(602) 686-6768 PJS107@pm.me	16601 S 37th Way Phoenix AZ 85048	CNH	EM			SL	1993
Scharr Timothy J	tjscharr@gmail.com	890 W 4th St P.O. Box 15 Aviston IL 62216	SI	Asst	Messiah* Carlyle IL	(618)594-3912	FW	1984
Scharrer Gary J	belikesalt@yahoo.com	615 Highland Ave Antioch IL 60002	NI	C12/2019			SL	2003
Schatte David E	(817)219-0315 schatted1@gmail.com	901 Mallard Pointe Dr Granbury TX 76049	TX	SP	Our Savior Granbury TX	(817)573-5011	SL	2006
Schatz John W	(541)343-3509	1314 Buck St Eugene OR 97402	NOW	SMP	Shep Of Valley* Junction City OR	(541)998-6659	CQ	2019
Schatz Donald D Dr	(206)769-8225 donald.d.schatz@protonmail.com	18519 Blue Ridge Dr Lynnwood WA 98037	NOW	EM			FW	1980
Schauder Steven R	(715)853-2566 gbpastorhc@yahoo.com	N2665 Rustic Dr Clintonville WI 54929	NW	EM			SL	1981
Schauer Arthur P	(402)366-6283 arthurschauer@windstream.net	1441 Crestwood Dr Seward NE 68434	NEB	EM			SL	1970
Schauer Caleb J	(815)923-2733 pastorcaleb@stjohnsluth.org	6305 Main St Union IL 60180	NI	Sn/Adm	St John Union IL	(815)923-2733	SL	2006
Schauer John E	(712)292-4254 johnschauerpma@gmail.com	1007 Monterey Dr Carroll IA 51401	IW	EM			SL	1969
Schauer Kenneth E	(509)775-0657 ksschauer@rcabletv.com	P.O. Box 615 Republic WA 99166	NOW	SP	Trinity Republic WA	(509)775-2617	SL	1968
Schauer Richard V	(708)567-5135 rschauer@tlcs.org	7900 Belle Rive Ct Tinley Park IL 60477	NI	Assoc	Trinity Tinley Park IL	(708)532-9395	SL	1991
Schaum Charles P	(256)349-8268 charles.schaum@comcast.net	223 Colorado Ave Muscle Shoals AL 35661	SO	SP	Christ King Tuscumbia AL	(256)381-3560	SL	1998
Schaus Nathan E	(623)535-0251 pastornate@summitcc.org	20409 W Terrace Ln Buckeye AZ 85396	PSW	SP	Summit Community Buckeye AZ	(623)535-0251	SL	2000
Schave Steven D Dr	(314)707-7248 steveschave@hotmail.com	126 Peine Valley Ct Wentzville MO 63385	MO	RSO	Lamp Ministries New Haven MI	(800)307-4036	FW	2006
Scheblein Adam L		14300 Pine Valley Rd Orlando FL 32826	SW	EM			SL	1992
Scheck Benjamin I	(817)975-7511 Ben@GroveChurchNTX.org	129 Gannet Trl Argyle TX 76226	TX	SMP	The Grove Argyle TX	(817)709-9401	SL-SMP	2012
Scheck Jonathan A	(240)475-5207 pastor.scheck@icloud.com	9400 Stanmore Ct Chesterfield VA 23236	SE	SP	Bethlehem Richmond VA	(804)353-4413	FW	2016
Scheck Nathan D	(678)372-0733 nkscheck@gmail.com	441 Bader Ave Seward NE 68434	NEB	Assoc	St John Seward NE	(402)643-2983	SL	2016
Schedler Donald E Dr	(530)957-3944 donsched@gmail.com	1408 W Business Loop 70 Apt N 213 Columbia MO 65202	MO	EM			SL	1954
Schedler Marvin J	(910)262-0562 mjoelsched@yahoo.com	71 Cavalier Dr Apt 1304 Wilmington NC 28405	SE	EM			SPR	1961
Schedler Walter J	(408)431-1660 waltschedler@yahoo.com	1140 3rd St Colusa CA 95932	CNH	EM			FW	1992
Scheele Luke P	(303)332-8971 PastorScheele@gmail.com	c/o Trinity Lutheran Church 208 N Dolores Rd Cortez CO 81321	RM	SP	Trinity Cortez CO	(970)565-9346	SL	2019
Scheele Pete A	(303)838-7111 ppascheele@gmail.com	48 Wells Fargo Ct Bailey CO 80421	RM	EM			FW	1996
Scheer Harold A	(319)321-7442	117 S 3rd St Box 220 Hills IA 52235	IE	EM			SPR	1970
Scheer Jeffery J	(314)703-3774 jefferyscheer2013@gmail.com	6315 S Spring Rd Cheney WA 99004	NOW	C12/2019			SL	2004
Scheer Joshua V	(307)630-1242 pastorscheer@gmail.com		WY	C06/2025			FW	2008
Scheer Michael D Dr	reverendscheer@aol.com	8144 Loon Ln Grand Blanc MI 48439	EN	Prin	Our Savior Hartland MI	(248)887-4300	FW	2002
Scheer Ronald P	(352) 286-8337 scheerclr@gmail.com	1300 Haven Dr Oviedo FL 32765	FG	EM			CQ	1979
Scheer Scott C	(559)359-2022 scottscheeremt@aol.com	1161 W Merrill Ave Porterville CA 93257	CNH	SMP	Mount Olive Lindsay CA	(559)359-2022	CQ	2019
Schefelker Perry W	PSchefelker@gmail.com	1816 Riviera Lane O'fallon IL 62269	SI	EM			SL	1973

*Multiple Assignments (See Church Worker Locator for Additional Details)
See Page 53 for the Table of Abbreviations for key to District, Position, and Seminary abbreviations
**C =Candidate; EM = Emeritus; the date following the C is the month and year the Candidate status began

NAME	TELEPHONE NUMBER EMAIL	STREET ADDRESS CITY/STATE/ZIP	DISTRICT	POSITION/ STATUS**	WHERE SERVING	OFFICE PHONE	SEM/ PROGRAM	YR GRAD
Scheich Jeffrey L	(402)483-7774 jscheich@christlincoln.org	6700 Chatsworth Lane Lincoln NE 68516	NEB	Assoc	Christ Lincoln NE	(402)483-7774	SL	1985
Scheidt Theodore L	(937)275-4960 tjscheidt@sbcglobal.net	1735 Benson Dr Dayton OH 45406	OH	EM			SL	1964
Scheiwe Logan B	(214)232-3358 pastor.scheiwe@gmail.com	582 Becklee Dr Napoleon OH 43545	OH	Assoc	St Paul Napoleon OH	(419)592-3535	SL	2011
Scheiwe Joel M			NOW	Sn/Adm	CAN HK Repulse Bay	011-852-2812-5151	SL	2006
Scheler Eddie R Jr	(256)221-5432 scheler@bellsouth.net	205 S Ridgeway Dr Cleburne TX 76033	TX	SP	Ascension Cleburne TX	(817)645-9452	FW	1991
Scheler Jacob R	(561) 395-0433 Pastorjacob@stpaulboca.com	701 W Palmetto Park Rd Boca Raton FL 33486	FG	Assoc	St Paul Boca Raton FL	(561)395-0433	SL	2025
Scheler Jason J	(850)520-0800 schelerj@gmail.com	199 Wayne Trl Santa Rsa Bch FL 32459	SO	SP	Hope on the Beach Santa Rosa Beach FL	(850)267-0322	SL-D	2008
Schellhas Aaron M	(815)861-8200 aaron@immanuelmokena.org	19946 Arden Ln Mokena IL 60448	NI	SP	Immanuel Mokena IL	(708)479-5600	SL	2008
Scheltens Henry S	(309)824-5903 henry.sam.scheltens@gmail.com	562 Harmony Dr Greenwood IN 46143	IN	SP	Concordia Greenwood IN	(317)881-4477	FW	2025
Schemm David G	(785)408-6164 pastordgs7@gmail.com	14415 Front Beach Road Unit 904 Panama City Beach FL 32413	FG	EM			SPR	1974
Schempf Michael D	(920)342-1578 mschempf@gmail.com	7 Olde Coventry Ct Saint Charles MO 63301	MO	EM			FW	1982
Schenck John W	(515)494-7440 jschenck2008@gmail.com	5822 S Glenstone Ct Johnston IA 50131	IW	EM			SL	1973
Schenk Allen E	(321)370-3561 alschenk47@gmail.com	1308 Rockwood Forest Dr Arnold MO 63010	MO	EM			SL	1973
Scheperle Gerald R	rev.mrs.schep@hotmail.com	7707 Stringtown Station Rd Lohman MO 65053	MO	EM			FW	1980
Schepman Timothy W	(860)857-2369 timschepman@gmail.com	1526 E Cartagena St Long Beach CA 90807	CNH	SP	Rollingwood* San Pablo CA	(510)223-1932	FW	1983
Schepmann Daniel W	dschepmann@gdlc.org	919 Elm Pointe League City TX 77573	TX	Sn/Adm	Gloria Dei Houston TX	(281)333-4535	SL	1996
Schepmann Roger D	rschepmonk@hotmail.com	10720 S Appleridge Ln Olathe KS 66061	KS	EM			CQ	1982
Scherbarth Chet L	(619) 385-2094 pastorscherbarth@att.net	c/o St John Lutheran Church 2001 Hardy St Hattiesburg MS 39401	SO	SP	St John Hattiesburg MS	(601)583-4898	SL	2011
Scherer Henry A	(530)662-1122 pastorhank@wavecable.com	387 Quail Dr Woodland CA 95695	CNH	EM			CQ	1979
Scherer Kenneth R	(815)388-1957 kenscherer@att.net	903 Wiltshire Dr Apt 3 McHenry IL 60050	NI	EM			SPR	1965
Schermbeck Andrew D	(813)399-0048 ascherm@hotmail.com	1275 Leslie Dr Merritt Island FL 32952	FG	SP	Faith Merritt Island FL	(321)452-4080	SL	2009
Schettler Matthew C	(716)861-7721 mcschettler@gmail.com	334 Temple Street Fredonia NY 14063	EA	SP	St Paul Fredonia NY	(716)672-6731	FW	2019
Scheuermann John H Jr	(775)848-5835 johnscheuermannjr@gmail.com	4907 Trailwood Dr Greensboro NC 27407	SE	SP	Ebenezer Greensboro NC	(336)272-5321	Other	2014
Scheunemann Paul A	(920)246-7759 sch-mann@juno.com	807 W Lincoln Ave Port Washington WI 53074	SW	EM			SL	1980
Scheusner John L	(817)296-8670 johnscheusner@hotmail.com	5805 Churchill Dr. Tyler TX 75701	TX	Sn/Adm	Trinity Tyler TX	(903)593-1526	CQ	2021
Schewe Caleb W	(319)480-7427 calebschewe@gmail.com	18925 Highway 38 Monticello IA 52310	IE	SP	St John Monticello IA	(319)465-4842	FW	2012
Schey Bernard J	(254)368-0261 bernardschey@gmail.com	4402 Buckskin Trl Temple TX 76502	TX	SP	Trinity Dime Box TX	(979)884-1471	FW	1985
Scheyder Paul L	(860)501-8021 pastor@clcniantic.org	42 Corey Ln Niantic CT 06357	NE	Sn/Adm	Christ Niantic CT	(860)739-6849	FW	1990
Schian Aaron T	(607)972-5792 aaronschian@yahoo.com	c/o Grace Lutheran Church 303 Ruth St Auburn MI 48611	MI	SP	Grace Auburn MI	(989)662-6161	FW	2011
Schiebel Peter A	(301)864-4340 trinity-elc-pastor@verizon.net	7803 Somerset Ct Greenbelt MD 20770	SE	Sn/Adm	Trinity Mount Rainier MD	(301)864-4340	FW	1997
Schieber Nathan D	(701)460-9325 schieber.nathan@gmail.com	215 Forrest Ave Wabash IN 46992	IN	SP	Zion Wabash IN	(260)563-1886	FW	2015
Schiefer Elmer B	(573)529-0584 elmer@myglobalemail.com	719 Kennely Rd Unit E68 Saginaw MI 48609	MO	EM			SL	1950
Schield Kirk W	(218)834-4707 schieldofarmor@gmail.com	574 Valley Rd Two Harbors MN 55616	MNN	SP	Christ Superior WI	(715)398-3680	FW	2005
Schielke Philip J Dr	(512)629-8507 phisch2@mac.com	501 E Saunders St Decatur TX 76234	TX	SP	Victory in Christ Newark TX	(817)489-5400	FW	2009
Schiemann Matthew P	(314)365-9583 mpschiemann@gmail.com	16561 Fox Cross Dr Granger IN 46530	IN	SP	St Paul South Bend IN	(574)271-1050	SL	2016
Schierlinger Joseph S	(810)441-2977 deaconjoe57@yahoo.com	3814 Mill St North Branch MI 48461	MI	SP	New Life In Christ North Branch MI	(810)688-2747	CQ	2019
Schiff Joshua J	(618)638-2862 schiff.joshua@gmail.com	6910 McMahon St Apt B Colorado Springs CO 80902	NE	M Chap	Office of International Mission Saint Louis MO		FW	2021
Schilbe Scott R	(507)884-2589 pastorschilbe@hotmail.com	2703 Hunters Crossing Drive Edwardsville IL 62025	SI	Asst	Our Redeemer* Overland MO	(314)427-3444	SL	2003
Schild Mark A	(704)519-6403 officelnlc@gmail.com	1686 Verdict Ridge Dr Denver NC 28087	SE	SMP	Lake Norman Denver NC	(704)483-2130	CQ	2019
Schildwachter John C Sr	(651)429-7779 johnschildwachter@gmail.com	14602 Finale Ave N Apt 115 Hugo MN 55038	MNS	EM			SPR	1972
Schilf Warren K	wschilf@hotmail.com	1400 Yellowstone Pkwy Algonquin IL 60102	NI	Sn/Adm	Immanuel Palatine IL	(847)359-1549	FW	2010
Schilke Stephen E	(989)619-3776 schilkes1815@gmail.com	1815 Kloha Rd Bay City MI 48706	MI	SP	Trinity Oscoda MI	(989)739-9292	CQ	1998

*Multiple Assignments (See Church Worker Locator for Additional Details)
See Page 53 for the Table of Abbreviations for key to District, Position, and Seminary abbreviations
**C =Candidate; EM = Emeritus; the date following the C is the month and year the Candidate status began

NAME	TELEPHONE NUMBER EMAIL	STREET ADDRESS CITY/STATE/ZIP	DISTRICT	POSITION/ STATUS**	WHERE SERVING	OFFICE PHONE	SEM/ PROGRAM	YR GRAD
Schiller Evan G	(507)820-0795 eschiller@iw.net	1105 7th Ave SW Pipestone MN 56164	MNS	EM			CQ	1982
Schiller Timothy D	ptschiller@gmail.com	1950 125th St NW Rice MN 56367	MNN	SP	Shepherd Pines Rice MN	(320)393-4295	SL	1995
Schilling David D	chapsschilling@yahoo.ca	4701 Crestone Peak St Brighton CO 80601	RM	EM			SL	1988
Schilling Matthew B	(812)202-3272 pastorschilling@gmail.com	2616 Crystal Creek Dr Davenport IA 52804	IE	Assoc	Trinity Davenport IA	(563)323-8001	SL	2008
Schilling Robert G	(402)385-2506 revbobschilling@yahoo.com	2171 15th Rd Pender NE 68047	NEB	SP	St John Pender NE	(402)385-2447	SL	1983
Schilling David A	ndschilling@msn.com	4563 E 75 N Rigby ID 83442	NOW	EM			CQ	2018
Schilling Kurt A	(217)971-3746 schilling.kurt@gmail.com	N184 County Road A Waupaca WI 54981	NW	SP	Emmaus Waupaca WI	(715)258-3193	FW	2006
Schilling David E	(623)248-5083 germanshepherd-39@hotmail.com	20648 W College Dr Buckeye AZ 85396	PSW	EM			SL	1965
Schillinger David R Sr	(386)239-5132 drs0516@aol.com	724 Big Tree Rd South Daytona FL 32119	FG	Sn/Adm	Holy Cross South Daytona FL	(386)767-6542	CQ	1980
Schillo Eric L	(515)570-5818 eschillo@gmail.com	156 Crossroads Ct Polk City IA 50226	IW	EM			SPR	1975
Schimm Benjamin T	(414)687-8171 bentschimm@gmail.com	5237 N 108th Ct Milwaukee WI 53225	SW	SP	Sherman Park Milwaukee WI	(414)445-5185	FW	2012
Schinbeckler David L	(260)437-1288 schinbecklerdl@gmail.com	6594 S Timberidge Dr Youngstown OH 44515	OH	EM			FW	2014
Schindel Bryan K	(734)474-1626 pastorbryan@crossandres.org	812 Ann St Ypsilanti MI 48197	MI	Sn/Adm	St Mark* Brooklyn MI	(517)467-7565	ED	1994
Schindler Vernon L Dr	(520)243-0284 belvaschin@aol.com	2001 W Rudasill Rd Apt 1211 Tucson AZ 85704	EN	EM			SL	1967
Schinkel John A	(517)896-8779 jcschinkel@bex.net	7567 Willow Pointe Dr Temperance MI 48182	MI	EM			SL	1979
Schinnerer Craig R	(817)874-8736 crschinn@aol.com	8344 Horse Whisper Lane Fort Worth TX 76131	TX	EM			SL	1983
Schipul Robert F	(781)875-3900 robert.schipul@comcast.net	204 Linden Ponds Way Unit 522 Hingham MA 02043	NE	EM			SPR	1975
Schkade Landon L Jr	(682)300-7969 llschkade@outlook.com	3822 Lucena Ct Grand Prairie TX 75052	TX	EM			FW	1984
Schlak Randall J	rschlak@redeemerbirmingham.org	785 Westwood Dr Birmingham MI 48009	MI	Sn/Adm	Redeemer Birmingham MI	(248)644-4010	FW	1990
Schlak Richard K	(915)238-3278 rschlak@hotmail.com	6317 Franklin Vista Dr El Paso TX 79912	RM	SP	Ascension El Paso TX	(915)833-1009	SL	1986
Schlamann Mark A	(435)840-5569 quia.concordia.1580@gmail.com	P.O. Box 39 Elkhart KS 67950	OK	SP	Christ* Elkhart KS	(620)697-2284	FW	2001
Schlecht Glen A Dr	(970)203-4810 gschlecht@immanuelloveland.org	3306 N Franklin Ave Loveland CO 80538	RM	Sn/Adm	Immanuel Loveland CO	(970)667-4506	SL	1989
Schlechte Roger E	(303)590-8317 reschl@aol.com	2664 Taft Ct Lakewood CO 80215	RM	EM			FW	1977
Schleicher Jason P	(281)825-1944 jschleicher@salem4u.com	22419 Willow Creek Bridge Ln Tomball TX 77375	TX	SMP	Salem Tomball TX	(281)351-8223	SL-SMP	2019
Schleicher John C	(616)212-9086 jcschleichermn@gmail.com	21831 Glade Canyon Dr Spring TX 77388	TX	EM			SPR	1975
Schleider Michael J	(414)232-2919 pastorschleider@yahoo.com	1715 N 53rd St Milwaukee WI 53208	SW	Sn/Adm	Mount Olive Milwaukee WI	(414)774-2200	FW	2009
Schlensker Daniel A	pastordan1999@hotmail.com	16 Fussel St P.O. Box 904 Bodfish CA 93205	CNH	SP	Shepherd Hills Lake Isabella CA	(760)379-2343	SL	1999
Schleusener David S Dr	(919) 302-8932 davidschleusener45@gmail.com	578 S 1st Ave Apt B Yuma AZ 85364	PSW	M Chap	Office of International Mission Saint Louis MO		CQ	2004
Schleusener Timothy M	(313)850-2274 rev.schleus@gmail.com	660 N 4th Ave Canistota SD 57106	SD	SP	Zion* Canistota SD	(605)296-3166	FW	2025
Schlicker Gregory A	(507)444-4078 pastorschlicker@msn.com	527 Agnes St Owatonna MN 55060	MNS	Sn/Adm	Good Shepherd Owatonna MN	(507)451-4125	SL	1988
Schlie Joseph E	(260)750-5314 pastor.j.schlie@gmail.com	453 N West St Perryville MO 63775	MO	Assoc	Immanuel Perryville MO	(573)547-8317	FW	2019
Schlie Charles S	(636)441-4221 cschlie@messiahnetwork.org	109 Starlight Ridge Ct Saint Charles MO 63304	MO	Assoc	Messiah Weldon Spring MO	(636)926-9773	SL	2001
Schlie Jesse S	(260)750-0061 Jesse.s.schlie@gmail.com	641 Fairview St Denver IA 50622	IE	SP	St John Denver IA	(319)984-5351	FW	2019
Schliepsiek Richard S	rick.schliepsiek@gmail.com	1035 Scott Dr Apt 132 Prescott AZ 86301	PSW	EM			SL	1968
Schloeman Karl E	(928)634-8214 karl1092@aol.com	1216 S Settlers CR Cottonwood AZ 86326	PSW	SP	Faith Cottonwood AZ	(928)634-7876	SL	2008
Schlote Loy G	yoursavior2@comcast.net		NI	EM			SL	1983
Schlueter Paul R Dr	(937)594-1575 pastorschlueter@gmail.com	7978 State Route 38 Milford Ctr OH 43045	OH	SP	St Paul Milford Center OH	(937)349-2405	SL	1999
Schlund Andrew C	(504)401-2242 paschlund86@gmail.com	2941 Westerland Ct Saint Charles MO 63301	MO	Inst C	Lutheran Senior Services DBA EverTrue Brentwood MO	(314)968-9313	SL	2015
Schlund Steven R	(308)440-0128 sschlund56@gmail.com	6806 Belle Plain CV Fort Wayne IN 46835	IN	EM			SL	1983
Schlund Thomas S	tom.s@lutheranfcu.org	10733 Sunset Office Dr. Suite 406 St. Louis MO 63127	MO	C03/2025			SL	2015
Schmalz Daniel M	(973)697-6899 latte972004@yahoo.com	10 Merganser St Westbrook ME 04092	NJ	EM			SL	1968
Schmeisser Kirk R	(816)261-8538 rev.kirk.schmeisser@gmail.com	714 W Stonecrest Cir Saint Joseph MO 64506	MO	EM			FW	1984

*Multiple Assignments (See Church Worker Locator for Additional Details)
See Page 53 for the Table of Abbreviations for key to District, Position, and Seminary abbreviations
**C =Candidate; EM = Emeritus; the date following the C is the month and year the Candidate status began

NAME	TELEPHONE NUMBER EMAIL	STREET ADDRESS CITY/STATE/ZIP	DISTRICT	POSITION/ STATUS**	WHERE SERVING	OFFICE PHONE	SEM/ PROGRAM	YR GRAD
Schmeisser Timothy D	(816)261-7865 rev.tschmeisser@gmail.com	500 Berkey Ave Swanville MN 56382	MNN	SP	St Peter Swanville MN	(320)547-2928	FW	2021
Schmeling Brock W	(701)426-5465 bwschmeling@gmail.com	316 Iowa Ave Barney ND 58008	ND	SP	Peace* Barney ND	(701)439-2429	FW	2020
Schmeltz Rodney L	(812)686-6054 pastorschmeltz@gmail.com	2179 Rainbow Trail P.O. Box 2904 Overgaard AZ 85933	EN	SP	Faith Overgaard AZ	(928)535-9575	FW	2009
Schmid Michael A	(707)255-0119 pastormike@stjohnsnapa.org	3521 Linda Vista Ave Napa CA 94558	CNH	Sn/Adm	St John's Napa CA	(707)255-0119	FW	1990
Schmidlin Paul R	(419)350-4347 paul.schmidlin@gmail.com	11461 Sylvania Ave Berkey OH 53504	EN	SP	King Of Glory Sylvania OH	(419)882-6488	CQ	2018
Schmidt Peter A	pastorschm@gmail.com	650 S Greenfield Ave Waukesha WI 53186	SW	SP	Beautiful Savior Waukesha WI	(262)542-2496	SL	1989
Schmidt Larry O	(701)403-4256 schmidtlarry46@gmail.com	c/o Janella Schmidt 1403 7th St N Wahpeton ND 58075	ND	EM			FW	1990
Schmidt Larry W	(410)647-1407 larsue35@verizon.net	600 McKinsey Park Dr Apt 304 Severna Park MD 21146	SE	EM			SL	1962
Schmidt Lawrence A	(319)651-8400 lschmidt@southslope.net	6837 Waterview Dr SW Cedar Rapids IA 52404	IE	EM			CQ	1977
Schmidt Micah D	pastormicahschmidt@gmail.com	515 Pasadena Dr Lexington KY 40503	IN	SP	St John Lexington KY	(859)277-6391	SL	2014
Schmidt Michael J	(785)370-9790 srpastor@stlukesmanhattan.org	1800 Little Kitten Ave Manhattan KS 66503	KS	SP	St Lukes Manhattan KS	(785)539-2604	SL	1995
Schmidt Michael J	(785)885-4821 revschmidt@yahoo.com	P.O. Box 282 Natoma KS 67651	KS	SP	First* Plainville KS	(785)434-2874	SL	2007
Schmidt William H Sr	(201)370-6344 pastorwhs@zionwestwoodnj.org	291 N Farview Ave Paramus NJ 07652	NJ	SMP	Zion Westwood NJ	(201)664-1325	CQ	2019
Schmidt Nathan E	(503)351-1587 pottedplantproduction@yahoo.com	31399 SE Strubhar Ln Estacada OR 97023	NOW	O-Miss	Lamp Ministries New Haven MI	(800)307-4036	SL	2025
Schmidt John A	(920)723-6794 johnsueschmidt@yahoo.com	W9072 Ripley Rd Cambridge WI 53523	SW	EM			FW	1979
Schmidt Paul R Jr	(443)474-0853 pastor.paul8@hotmail.com	20276 Bay Vista Rd Rehoboth Bch DE 19971	SE	Assoc	St Matthew Bel Air MD	(410)838-3178	SL	1988
Schmidt Ralph G	ralphschmidt1947@gmail.com	2807 Cliffwood Ln Fort Wayne IN 46825	IN	EM			SL	1973
Schmidt Richard W Jr	(619)370-5699 pastor@concordiachurch.com	744 Cholla Rd Chula Vista CA 91910	PSW	SP	Concordia Chula Vista CA	(619)656-8100	SL	1993
Schmidt Robert F Dr	(612)554-2491 robert.f.schmidt@comcast.net	1052 Hamer Loop Sequim WA 98382	NOW	EM			SL	1960
Schmidt Tobias P	(952) 923-4032 pastortoby@christvictorious.org	6780 Chaparral Ln Chanhassen MN 55317	MNS	Assoc	Christ Victorious Chaska MN	(952)443-2993	SL	2016
Schmidt Travis J	(414)313-1522 pastorschmidt@yahoo.com	603 Kahkwa Blvd Erie PA 16505	EN	SP	Trinity Erie PA	(814)452-4888	FW	1989
Schmidt Troy M	(480)839-4891 tschmidt@watersedgefrisco.com	P.O. Box 894 Frisco TX 75034	TX	Sn/Adm	Waters Edge Frisco TX	(972)712-7377	SL	2004
Schmidt Walter C	(469)338-5218 wschmidt13@att.net	1356 Petaluma Dr Rockwall TX 75087	TX	EM			SL	1965
Schmidt Kenneth A	(712)251-1791	1530 Ennen Dr Rapid City SD 57703	SD	EM			SL	2005
Schmidt Neldo	(651)492-8369 pastorschmidt@satx-kingofkings.church	6059 Akin Circle San Antonio TX 78261	TX	Sn/Adm	King Of Kings San Antonio TX	(210)656-6508	Other	1983
Schmidt Dennis W	(314)892-0653 dwsjeschmidt@att.net	4616 Longspur Dr Saint Louis MO 63128	MO	EM			SL	1986
Schmidt Charles O	(402)429-7053 rev.charles.schmidt@gmail.com	7420 Exbury Rd Lincoln NE 68516	NEB	EM			CQ	1981
Schmidt David H	(253) 441-8459 mariner4fan@yahoo.com	491 Goldon Trophy Trail Lexington KY 40514	IN	EM			SL	1966
Schmidt David P	(479)268-0086 revdavidpschmidt@gmail.com	610 Arkansas Black Bentonville AR 72712	MDS	SP	Faith Bentonville AR	(479)273-9419	SL	2005
Schmidt John E	schmidtjoho072@gmail.com	5338 Fairview Dr Stevens Point WI 54482	NW	EM			SL	1962
Schmidt David R		15445 N 23rd Ln Phoenix AZ 85023	PSW	Assoc	Christ Phoenix AZ	(602)955-4830	Other	2010
Schmidt Karl K	(478)957-2760 karl.k.schmidt@gmail.com	5927 W Copper Mountain Dr Spotsylvania VA 22553	SE	EM			SL	1961
Schmidt Earl R	(651)357-6210 sch7345@gmail.com	5800 Saint Croix Ave N Apt C507 Golden Valley MN 55422	FG	EM			SL	1966
Schmidt Edward H	(970)379-0105 smtnfam@aol.com	9511 Castle Ridge Ct Highlands Ranch CO 80129	RM	SP	St Luke Golden CO	(303)233-5658	FW	1989
Schmidt Erik R	(734)846-1623 RevErik7@gmail.com	3 Five Oaks Dr Saginaw MI 48638	MI	Sn/Adm	Peace Saginaw MI	(989)793-9025	SL	2011
Schmidt Karl E	(716)310-2076 keschmidt184@gmail.com	184 Grandview Ave Town Of Tonawanda NY 14223	EN	EM			FW	1985
Schmidt John D	(253)906-6813 jubilate@comcast.net	P.O. Box 99967 Lakewood WA 98496	NOW	EM			SL	1969
Schmidt John E	(979)366-9650 revjes@stpaulserbin.org	1572 County Road 211 Giddings TX 78942	TX	SP	St Paul Serbin TX	(979)366-9650	SL	1992
Schmidt John H	(712)730-1010 vdma824jhs@gmail.com	5024 Cresthaven Dr Lincoln NE 68516	NEB	EM			FW	1986
Schmidt John L	(402)575-8200 Revjls@aol.com	3033 Ems Glen Ln Arnold MO 63010	MO	EM			FW	1977
Schmidt Joshua A			CNH	SP	Bethlehem Monterey CA	(831)373-1523	SL	2018
Schmidt Joshua W	(573)270-2119 jschmidt@stpauljackson.com	225 W Main St Jackson MO 63755	MO	Assoc	St Paul Jackson MO	(573)243-2236	SL	2010

*Multiple Assignments (See Church Worker Locator for Additional Details)
See Page 53 for the Table of Abbreviations for key to District, Position, and Seminary abbreviations
**C =Candidate; EM = Emeritus; the date following the C is the month and year the Candidate status began

NAME	TELEPHONE NUMBER EMAIL	STREET ADDRESS CITY/STATE/ZIP	DISTRICT	POSITION/ STATUS**	WHERE SERVING	OFFICE PHONE	SEM/ PROGRAM	YR GRAD
Schmidt Justin R	justinschmidt40@hotmail.com	313 Casa Dr Pittsburgh PA 15241	EN	Sn/Adm	Peace McMurray PA	(724)941-9441	SL	2002
Schmidt Gale D	(602)326-7838 gschmidt2@yahoo.com	1111 Ontario St Apt #1104 Oak Park IL 60302	PSW	EM			SL	1962
Schmidt David P	(636)226-4196 daveschmidt14@aol.com	162 Ameren Way Apt 429 Ballwin MO 63021	MO	EM			SL	1963
Schmidtke Richard L	(503)257-3460 RLSCH3334@aol.com	3363 NE 133rd Ave Portland OR 97230	NOW	EM			SL	1971
Schmidtke Gary R	(219)374-0037 gardor@sbcglobal.net	6823 W 142nd Ln Cedar Lake IN 46303	IN	EM			SL	1972
Schmieding Scott A	(225)802-8602 sschmieding@immanuelstcharles.org	3593 Compton Pkwy Saint Charles MO 63301	MO	Sn/Adm	Immanuel Saint Charles MO	(636)946-2656	SL	1991
Schmiege Donald R	(952)237-9688 drschmiege@comcast.net	11906 River Hills Cir Burnsville MN 55337	MNS	EM			SPR	1975
Schmitt David E	(573)315-8287 meschmd@hotmail.com	215 Timberfield Dr Farmington MO 63640	MO	SMP	Trinity Park Hills MO	(573)431-3442	SL-SMP	2021
Schmitt David R Dr	(314)729-0122 schmittd@csl.edu	77 Flamingo Dr Saint Louis MO 63123	EN	S HS/C	Concordia Seminary Saint Louis MO	(314)505-7000	SL	1988
Schmitt Frederick A	(586)819-9386 fritz_schmitt@wowway.com	38748 Trafalgar Way Sterling Hts MI 48312	MI	EM			FW	1982
Schmitt Thomas K	(920)418-1559 pastorschmitt@gmail.com		SW	SP	St Martin Chilton WI	(920)849-4421	SL	1991
Schmoock Norman W	(970)587-4046 nrschmoock@hotmail.com	3651 Claycomb Ln Johnstown CO 80534	RM	EM			Other	1974
Schnack Randolph J	rjs52@priest.com	P.O. Box 723 Saratoga WY 82331	WY	SP	Platte Valley Saratoga WY	(307)326-5449	FW	1981
Schnackenberg James F	(417)451-3819 jschnack@ecarthage.com	1346 E McKinney St Neosho MO 64850	MO	SP	St John Purdy MO	(417)442-3836	SL	1971
Schnake Luke R Dr	(402)429-8919 lschnake@christlincoln.org	5011 S 71st St Lincoln NE 68516	NEB	Assoc	Christ Lincoln NE	(402)483-7774	FW	1978
Schnake Ryan K	81 0 80 9850 9651 revschnake@gmail.com	PSC 80 Box 20699 Apo Ap NO 96367 JAPAN	S	M Chap	Office of International Mission Saint Louis MO		SL	2021
Schnakenberg Kevin L	(816)761-5397 klschnak@yahoo.com	991 SW Perth Shire Dr Lees Summit MO 64081	MO	C07/2016			SL	1996
Schnare Martin T	(618)623-5990 altarboylcms@gmail.com	P.O. Box 493 237 Hamel Ave. Hamel IL 62046	SI	EM			SL	1984
Schneeflock Edward C	(978)827-5253 ed@schneeflock.com	44 Sherbert Rd Ashburnham MA 01430	NE	SMP	Our Savior Westminster MA	(978)874-2504	FW-SMP	2022
Schneekloth Larry G Dr	(708)596-5398 RevLarrySchneek@gmail.com	3332 W 160th St Markham IL 60428	EN	SP	Markham Markham IL	(708)331-4885	SPR	1967
Schnegelberger Kent E	(308)587-5271 ckschnege@msn.com	1526 Mallard Dr Johnstown CO 80534	RM	EM			SL	1975
Schneider Joshua V	(808) 205-1787 joshua.v.schneider.mil@army.mil	15221 Windy Ridge Road Midlothian VA 23112	CNH	M Chap	Office of National Mission Saint Louis MO		FW	2006
Schneider Ryan B	(812)521-2283 schneidomite@hotmail.com	402 W Bridge St Brownstown IN 47220	IN	SP	St Peter Brownstown IN	(812)358-2539	FW	2017
Schneider Robert W	schneiderrobert56@gmail.com	3320 N Stockwell Rd Evansville IN 47715	IN	EM			FW	1990
Schneider Richard J Jr	(864)915-4056 PastorSchneider00@gmail.com	c/o Redeemer Lutheran Church 808 S 1st St Atwood KS 67730	KS	SP	Redeemer Atwood KS	(785)626-3178	FW	2016
Schneider Matthew M	(785)524-4039 mattschneider63@gmail.com	1993 County 671 Ave Waldo KS 67673	KS	SP	Trinity Hunter KS	(785)529-2715	SL	2008
Schneider Paul H	(231)329-6397 cllc1pastorpaul@me.com	2065 Pauls Ct. Marysville MI 48040	MI	EM			SL	1995
Schneider Matthew L	m.l.schneider412@gmail.com	109 S English Ave Springfield IL 62704	CI	Sn/Adm	Good Shepherd Sherman IL	(217)496-3149	SL	2009
Schneider Terrell J	(715)544-4647	2900 Porter Ct Plover WI 54467	NW	EM			SPR	1966
Schneider Eugene W III Dr	(580)353-0556 pastor_schneider@sbcglobal.net	102 SW 7th St Lawton OK 73501	OK	Assoc	St John Lawton OK	(580)353-0556	SL	1982
Schneider Richard E	(414)331-5067 schneider1277@yahoo.com	c/o Brookfield Lutheran Church 18500 W Burleigh Rd Brookfield WI 53045	SW	Assoc	Brookfield Brookfield WI	(262)783-4270	SL	2008
Schneider Edward L	(210) 416-7050 ssaulnier@sbcglobal.net		TX	EM			SL	1949
Schneider Donald D	(831)600-5869 pstrdon2003@me.com	2931 Leotar Cir Santa Cruz CA 95062	CNH	EM			SL	1994
Schneider Daniel S	(414)614-7126 schneid6@sbcglobal.net	N77w15511 Crossway Dr Menomonee Falls WI 53051	SW	EM			FW	1980
Schneider Curtis W	(325)200-6749 lioncurt@astound.net	9 Canyon Creek Dr Brownwood TX 76801	TX	EM			CQ	1977
Schneider Christopher W	(269) 275-1945 chriswschneider2911@gmail.com	c/o Beautiful Savior Lutheran Church 3924 Home Rd Powell OH 43065	OH	SP	Beautiful Savior Powell OH	(740)938-4248	SL	2015
Schneider Carl W	pastorcarlschneider@gmail.com	10136 Corona Ln Plain City OH 43064	OH	EM			SL	1981
Schneider Jack A	(469)855-0783 jackthevicar1@aol.com	520 High Desert Dr Fort Worth TX 76131	TX	EM			SL	1974
Schnelle Aaron D	(217)416-6972 rev.schnelle@gmail.com	c/o Bethel Lutheran Church 3166 McMullen Booth Rd Clearwater FL 33761	FG	SP	Bethel Clearwater FL	(727)799-3010	SL	2007
Schnepp Kenneth E Jr	(410)530-6015 pkrailshep1@gmail.com	112 Fire Island Ave Babylon NY 11702	AT	EM			SL	1973

*Multiple Assignments (See Church Worker Locator for Additional Details)
See Page 53 for the Table of Abbreviations for key to District, Position, and Seminary abbreviations
**C =Candidate; EM = Emeritus; the date following the C is the month and year the Candidate status began

NAME	TELEPHONE NUMBER EMAIL	STREET ADDRESS CITY/STATE/ZIP	DISTRICT	POSITION/ STATUS**	WHERE SERVING	OFFICE PHONE	SEM/ PROGRAM	YR GRAD
Schober John H II	(817)975-1651 reverend.schober@gmail.com	c/o Risen Savior Lutheran Church 9501 W Drexel Ave Franklin WI 53132	SW	SP	Risen Savior Franklin WI	(414)529-5647	FW	2024
Schockman Jason A	(608)774-5618	N55w37144 Roland St Oconomowoc WI 53066	SW	Assoc	St Paul Oconomowoc WI	(262)567-5001	SL	2007
Schoech Thomas K	(575)937-9584 schoecht@yahoo.com	205 Pigeon Dr Lake Saint Louis MO 63367	MO	EM			SL	1979
Schoech Eric W	(219)242-9139	753 N Calumet Ave Valparaiso IN 46383	IN	Sn/Adm	Faith Memorial Valparaiso IN	(219)462-7684	SL	2008
Schoedel John F	(314)803-2096 johnschoedel108@aol.com	286 Bridgewater Heights Dr Villa Ridge MO 63089	MO	SMP	St Johns Beaufort MO	(573)484-3575	FW-SMP	2019
Schoemann Randal W	(920)304-2591 Showboat41@gmail.com	903 County Rd C Hancock WI 54943	SW	EM			CQ	2010
Schoen Mark K	(715)483-1186 revschoen@yahoo.com	1634 State Hwy 87 St Croix Flls WI 54024	NW	Sn/Adm	Shep Of Valley Saint Croix Fls WI	(715)483-1186	FW	1985
Schoenback Donald E Jr	(623)337-2568 dschoenback@gmail.com	5884 Coriander Ct Prescott AZ 86305	PSW	EM			SL	1982
Schoenfeld King K	(314)610-1077 kingschoenfeld@icloud.com	1617 Division Ave #3 Tacoma WA 98403	MO	EM			SL	1967
Schoenfeld Martin T	(651)459-3551 pastor@roseofsharonlutheran.org	8187 Johansen Ave S Cottage Grove MN 55016	MNS	SP	Rose Of Sharon Cottage Grove MN	(651)459-3551	SL	1995
Schoenfuhs Walter P Jr	(630)422-5098	143 Prospect Ave Wood Dale IL 60191	NI	EM			FW	1979
Schoenherr Philip H	(541)484-6362 phil@schoenherrs.us	2365 Chambers St Eugene OR 97405	NOW	EM			SL	1973
Schoepflin Adam R	(631) 944-1808 AdamSchoepflin@gmail.com	91 Ocean Ave Massapequa Park NY 11762	AT	SMP	The Life Old Westbury NY	(516)333-3355	SL-SMP	2020
Schoessow Daniel R	(715)238-7422 lutheranpastor@gmail.com	W2880 Granton Rd Granton WI 54436	NW	SP	Christ* Chili WI	(715)238-7422	FW	1992
Schoessow David G		14 Kilner Bay Dr Superior WI 54880	MNN	EM			SL	1981
Scholl Louis N Dr	(519)735-9524 1scholl1@cogeco.ca	512 Cambridge Ct Tecumseh ON N8N 4 CANADA	EN	EM			SL	1959
Scholl Travis J Dr	314-262-8231 travis.scholl@evertrueliving.org	7237 Cornell Ave University City MO 63130	MO	O-Sp Min	Lutheran Senior Services DBA EverTrue Brentwood MO	(314)968-9313	CQ	2007
Scholle Raymond W Jr	(636)949-2086 rcctscholle@aol.com	1820 Willow Oak Dr Saint Charles MO 63303	EN	EM			SL	1994
Schomburg Dell B	dellsmailbox@gmail.com	15811 NE 42nd St Vancouver WA 98682	NOW	EM			CQ	1980
Schonberg Christian L	(732) 948-9182 clschonberg@gmail.com	21 Pine Rd Howell NJ 07731	NJ	EM			SL	1984
Schonkaes John R	(515)779-5355 revschonkaes@gmail.com	3701 Brook Ridge Ct Unit 1102 Des Moines IA 50317	IW	SP	Christ King Altoona IA	(515)967-3349	SL	1997
Schoon Joshua A	(330)701-3123 josh_schoon@yahoo.com	3177 Buchanan Ln Montgomery IL 60538	NI	SP	Word Of Life Naperville IL	(630)355-9655	SL	2003
Schoop David A	(712)239-3655 annelie@att.net	2447 Pueblo Dr Sioux City IA 51104	IW	SP	St John Climbing Hill IA	(712)239-3655	CQ	1980
Schooping Joshua K	(407)928-1897 joshuaschooping@gmail.com	1410 N Cleveland Ave Russellville AR 72801	MDS	SP	St John Russellville AR	(479)968-1309	CQ	2023
Schopp Chad C	(605) 380-2545 cschopp@protonmail.com	1519 S. Lincoln St. Aberdeen SD 57401	SD	Sn/Adm	Our Savior* Aberdeen SD	(605)225-7106	FW	2013
Schornhorst Ronald L	(706)484-9855 ronsamwise1946@gmail.com	107 Kathryn Ct Eatonton GA 31024	FG	EM			SL	1972
Schotte Michael L	(620)672-5354 mslcms@sctelcom.net	40307 NE 40th Ave Preston KS 67583	KS	SP	St Paul Preston KS	(620)672-5354	FW	1991
Schouweiler James A	(231)924-3158 pneumaj@comcast.net	650 Seminole Dr Fremont MI 49412	MI	EM			SL	1984
Schrader Alexander A	(313) 569-6572 alex@alexschrader.com	35615 Orchard Lane Richmond MI 48062	MI	SP	Our Saviour Armada MI	(586)784-9088	SL	2019
Schrader Darwin P Dr	(618)206-8761 kardarschrader@yahoo.com	12 Bernhardt Rd Lebanon IL 62254	SI	C07/2016			SL	1973
Schrader Robert M	(920) 539-4603 pastor@stjohnberlin.org	363 E Cumberland St Berlin WI 54923	SW	SP	St John Berlin WI	(920)361-9935	FW	2021
Schrader Stephen W	(256)997-8033 possumcop@earthlink.net	901 Holmes Ave. Foley AL 36535	SO	EM			FW	2002
Schram Michael J	(715)851-8400 rev_schram@hotmail.com	W5655 Country Meadows Dr Campbellsport WI 53010	SW	EM			SL	1999
Schram Nicholas A	(989)295-0414 schram@lcrstl.org	1858 Marriott Ln Barnhart MO 63012	MO	Assoc	Resurrection Sunset Hills MO	(314)843-6633	SL	2020
Schramm Frederick J Dr	(907)388-3487 fjschramm@gmail.com	2725 Stony Creek Rd Broomall PA 19008	NOW	EM			SL	1970
Schramm Verdell D	(402)488-9648 spanave6@gmail.com	6933 Sumner St Lincoln NE 68506	NEB	EM			CQ	1997
Schrank Benjamin J	(210)601-3246 bschrankly@gmail.com	c/o Saint John Lutheran Church 4500 Buena Vista Rd Bakersfield CA 93311	CNH	Assoc	St John Bakersfield CA	(661)665-7815	SL	2013
Schrank Jeffery T Dr	(602)955-4830	3901 E Indian School Rd Phoenix AZ 85018	PSW	Sn/Adm	Christ Phoenix AZ	(602)955-4830	FW	1988
Schreibeis Howard D	(406)234-2985 hojos@midrivers.com	1007 S Earling Ave Miles City MT 59301	MT	EM			FW	1985
Schreiber Iromar	(417)414-9933 iromar78@hotmail.com	1831 Brett Ct Annapolis MD 21401	SE	SP	St Paul Gambrills MD	(410)721-2332	Other	2005
Schreiber Mark A	(715)377-5661 pastorschreiber@yahoo.com	706 12th St Hudson WI 54016	MNS	Sn/Adm	Trinity Hudson WI	(715)386-9313	FW	2002

*Multiple Assignments (See Church Worker Locator for Additional Details)

See Page 53 for the Table of Abbreviations for key to District, Position, and Seminary abbreviations

**C =Candidate; EM = Emeritus; the date following the C is the month and year the Candidate status began

NAME	TELEPHONE NUMBER EMAIL	STREET ADDRESS CITY/STATE/ZIP	DISTRICT	POSITION/ STATUS**	WHERE SERVING	OFFICE PHONE	SEM/ PROGRAM	YR GRAD
Schreiber Mark J Dr	(386)627-5674 mjsch767@outlook.com	3 Creekside Dr Palm Coast FL 32137	FG	EM			FW	1977
Schrepferman Cody A	(630)457-0190 codyschrepferman@gmail.com	708 1/2 E Center St Marion OH 43302	OH	SP	Gethsemane Marion OH	(740)375-0599	FW	2025
Schrieber Paul L Dr	(618)282-4807 schrieberp@hotmail.com	351 Lockwood Dr Apt 4 Red Bud IL 62278	MO	EM			SPR	1975
Schriever Henry R	(516)742-3964 hrsdds@juno.com	28 Moore St New Hyde Park NY 11040	AT	EM			SL	1957
Schroder David N	(512)468-3785 davesandyschroder@gmail.com	4008 Palomar Ln Austin TX 78727	TX	EM			SL	1972
Schroeder Stephen E	(407)296-2215 StephenESchroeder@gmail.com	6114 Buford St Orlando FL 32835	FG	EM			SL	1970
Schroeder Ricky P	(262)224-4992 ricracl223@yahoo.com	1623 Palisades Dr Appleton WI 54915	SW	EM			FW	1986
Schroeder Richard W	(936)890-1448 rmschroeder81@gmail.com	12662 Lake Vista Dr Willis TX 77318	TX	EM			SL	1967
Schroeder Robert J	(562)857-3981 revbob531@yahoo.com	10323 Larrylyn Dr Whittier CA 90603	PSW	EM			SL	1975
Schroeder Ryan M	(262)224-8482	214 W Spooner Rd Milwaukee WI 53217	SW	Tchr	Milwaukee LHS Milwaukee WI	(414)461-6000	SL	2012
Schroeder Thomas L	734-323-3675 pastortom10700@gmail.com	214 County Street Milan MI 48160	MI	EM			CQ	1984
Schroeder Todd E	(509)943-4967 revtodd@mac.com		NOW	SP	Redeemer Richland WA	(509)943-4967	SL	2001
Schroeder Wayne C	(414)839-9445 wayne-bev@sbcglobal.net	N56w19517 Deer Park Ct Menomonee FLS WI 53051	SW	EM			SL	1969
Schroeder Albert H	(970)587-2366 Schroeder.alfloco@gmail.com	1003 N 2nd St Johnstown CO 80534	RM	EM			SL	1958
Schroeder Randall A Dr	drrandy@drrandyschroeder.com	13481 Mosel Ct Fishers IN 46037	IN	EM			FW	1986
Schroeder William C	(816)377-9504 schroederbiz@hotmail.com	1290 Oakholt Ct Herculaneum MO 63048	MO	EM			SL	1976
Schroeder Douglas W	(414)421-6016 dougs@ourshepherdlutheran.org	7611 Overlook Dr Greendale WI 53129	SW	Sn/Adm	Our Shepherd Greendale WI	(414)421-2060	SL	1988
Schroeder Andrew L	(561)512-4844 Beowulfvu@netscape.net	1270 Flat Rock Church Rd White Plains GA 30678	FG	C04/2022			CQ	2001
Schroeder Mark A Dr	markaschroeder@outlook.com	1525 Seneca Ave Cumming GA 30041	FG	EM			SL	1984
Schroeder Dean F	(605)464-8906 pastorschroeder@hcinet.net	30825 417th Ave Tyndall SD 57066	SD	SP	Martinus* Utica SD	(605)589-3195	FW	2004
Schroeder Dwayne J	(405)306-2007 Dwayne.Schroeder.70@gmail.com	2906 W. Maine Ave Enid OK 73703	OK	EM			SL	1991
Schroeder James E	(231)757-9311	4353 N US Highway 31 Scottville MI 49454	MI	EM			SPR	1976
Schroeder Jonathan C	(440)466-4026 jnthnschroeder@yahoo.com	1070 Sherman St Geneva OH 44041	OH	SP	St John Geneva OH	(440)466-2473	SL	1999
Schroeder Kenneth O	(989)652-4516 k.o.schroeder@att.net	662 Willow Ln Frankenmuth MI 48734	MI	EM			SL	1969
Schroeder Leo G	(918)801-5343 sidekick4350@aol.com	60245 E 200 Rd Fairland OK 74343	OK	EM			CQ	2003
Schroeder Marc D	(614)397-8451 schroeder.m.d@gmail.com	132 Northview Dr SW Reynoldsburg OH 43068	OH	EM			CQ	2002
Schroeder Benjamin E	(561)207-0532 prschroeder@live.com	416 High St Waupaca WI 54981	NW	Inst C	North Wisconsin District Wausau WI	(715)845-8241	SL	2001
Schroter John H	(201)941-4161 revjohnnys@aol.com	248 Columbia Ave Cliffside Pk NJ 07010	NJ	SP	Trinity Cliffside Park NJ	(201)943-0088	SL	1992
Schruhl Joe E	(703)250-0206 revjoe@earthlink.net	6443 Lake Meadow Dr Burke VA 22015	SE	EM			SPR	1969
Schubert John R	573-352-0027 john@livinghopega.com	2146 Merrimac Ct Acworth GA 30101	FG	SP	Living Hope Kennesaw GA	(770)425-6726	SL	1999
Schubert Alfred W III	(906) 280-7039 schube3@gmail.com	3 Oakwood Glen Dr Clinton MS 39056	SO	SP	Our Redeemer Clinton MS	(601)924-9999	SL	1989
Schubert Jeffery S	jschub9516@aol.com	W310 N4932 Old Steeple Rd Hartland WI 53029	SW	EM			SL	1981
Schubkegel Kevin L	(360)428-0290 pastor@tlcmv.com	301 S 18th St Mount Vernon WA 98274	NOW	SP	Trinity Mount Vernon WA	(360)428-0290	CQ	2004
Schuchard Bruce G Dr	(314)725-5232 schuchardb@csl.edu	3960 Federer Pl Saint Louis MO 63116	MO	S HS/C	Concordia Seminary Saint Louis MO	(314)505-7000	FW	1984
Schudde Albert M	(443)540-4292 mschudde@gmail.com	107 Lilac Blossom Dr Cottleville MO 63304	MO	EM			SL	1985
Schudde Arthur I	(303)728-9017 aschudde@msn.com	828 Mapleton Ct Castle Rock CO 80104	RM	EM			SL	1965
Schueler Wayne A	(281)731-1617 waysch52@gmail.com	4518 Meadowbend Dr Richmond TX 77469	TX	EM			FW	1982
Schuermann Michael P	(217)344-1558 pastor@uniluchampaign.org	1507 W. Clark St. Champaign IL 61821	CI	SP	University Champaign IL	(217)344-1558	FW	2010
Schuessler Mitchel E	(618)553-3133 revmitchel@yahoo.com	209 W Main St Clarinda IA 51632	IW	SP	St John Clarinda IA	(712)542-3708	SL	1987
Schuett Fred P	(541)889-5674 schuetts@yahoo.com	4404 Bellows Dr Ontario OR 97914	NOW	EM			SL	1965
Schuett Scott R	(860)642-6191 fm106retired@gmail.com	269 Babcock Hill Rd Lebanon CT 06249	NE	EM			FW	1980
Schuett Wayne M	(918)360-5083	1803 East L St Apt D Russellville AR 72801	MDS	EM			FW	1985
Schuette Michael L	(952)457-6973 mls7593@aol.com	2429 River Bend Trail Mayer MN 55360	MNS	C07/2017			FW	2012

*Multiple Assignments (See Church Worker Locator for Additional Details)
See Page 53 for the Table of Abbreviations for key to District, Position, and Seminary abbreviations
**C =Candidate; EM = Emeritus; the date following the C is the month and year the Candidate status began

NAME	TELEPHONE NUMBER EMAIL	STREET ADDRESS CITY/STATE/ZIP	DISTRICT	POSITION/ STATUS**	WHERE SERVING	OFFICE PHONE	SEM/ PROGRAM	YR GRAD
Schuetz Daniel M			TX	SP	Redeemer Baytown TX	(281)422-2207	FW	2020
Schuetz John A	revjaschuetz@gmail.com	400 Morrison Ave Jackson MN 56143	MNS	SP	Our Redeemer Jackson MN	(507)847-3693	FW	2006
Schuetze Nathaniel A	(573)825-7724 naschuetze@yahoo.com	3700 Chatham Dr Columbia MO 65203	MO	C02/2019			SL	2004
Schuetzler Michael J	(915)637-6436 mjschuetzler@yahoo.com	1812 Pueblo Alegre Dr El Paso TX 79936	RM	C09/2022			SL	2021
Schufreider Jeffrey L	(650)273-1202 schufreider@gmail.com	37 Lilac Ln South San Francisco CA 94080	CNH	SP	Trinity* Burlingame CA	(650)347-4100	FW	1979
Schuldheisz Joel M Dr	(503)572-9733 pastorjoel@goodshepherdluth.com	917 23rd St NW Puyallup WA 98371	NOW	SMP	Good Shepherd Tacoma WA	(253)473-4848	SL-SMP	2022
Schuldheisz Samuel P	(253)922-6977 sschuldheisz@mybslc.com	2306 Milton Way Milton WA 98354	NOW	SP	Beautiful Savior Milton WA	(253)922-6977	FW	2008
Schuler Karl G	(703)978-3205 kgschuler@yahoo.com	5104 Richardson Dr Fairfax VA 22032	SE	C07/2016			SL	2008
Schuler Mark T Dr	(651)210-2660 mark@markschuler.com	1288 Marshall Ave Saint Paul MN 55104	MNS	EM			SL	1981
Schuler Matthew G	schulermatt@gmail.com	13201 Churchill St. Sterling Heights MI 48313	MI	Assoc	Faith Troy MI	(248)689-4664	SL	2015
Schuler Robert D	(440)579-5133 barbbob2019@gmail.com	7882 Hunting Lake Dr Concord Twp OH 44077	OH	EM			SL	1969
Schulingkamp Warren J II	(225)287-0147 warrenii@yahoo.com	1511 Park Dr McComb MS 39648	SO	SP	Trinity* McComb MS	(769)276-1897	FW	1992
Schuller Isaac S	(408)817-0358 pastorschuller@glsbrenham.com	2601 Brookbend Dr Brenham TX 77833	TX	Assoc	Grace Brenham TX	(979)836-3475	FW	2013
Schuller Richard L	(832)523-4513 missionoverhills@gmail.com	412 Kelley St Houston TX 77009	TX	EM			FW	1982
Schult Paul E	(816)898-9510 pes5076@hotmail.com	8546 N Britt Ave Kansas City MO 64154	MO	EM			FW	1983
Schult Paul T	(636)922-7030 pschult@redeemerrwc.org	c/o Redeemer Luth Church 468 Grand St Redwood City CA 94062	CNH	Assoc	Bridge City Redwood City CA	(650)366-5892	SL	1995
Schulte Gary R	(605)858-4125 gschulte06@gmail.com	2607 W Saint Patrick St Rapid City SD 57702	SD	Assoc	Zion Rapid City SD	(605)342-5749	SL	2006
Schulte Timothy M	(314)285-6231 tms8777@gmail.com	2607 W Saint Patrick St Rapid City SD 57702	MO	RSO	Lutheran Bible Translators Inc Concordia MO	(660)225-0810	SL	2022
Schultheis Martin J	(410)499-1268 mschultheis@se.lcms.org	2910 Griffin Ave Richmond VA 23222	SE	D Ex/S	Southeastern District Henrico VA	(703)971-9371	SL	1998
Schultz Leon W	(401)595-1561 lschultz216@verizon.net	445 Elmwood Ave Providence RI 02907	NE	EM			SL	1983
Schultz Jonathan G	(406)402-2081 pastor.jschultz@gmail.com	1000 45th Ave NE Great Falls MT 59404	MT	SP	Trinity Great Falls MT	(406)452-2121	SL	2008
Schultz Joshua M	(989)310-3525 schultzjm@immanuelalpena.org	1015 Golf Course Rd Alpena MI 49707	MI	Assoc	Immanuel* Alpena MI	(989)354-3443	FW	2014
Schultz Robert J Dr	revdocbob8@gmail.com		MI	EM			SL	1971
Schultz Josiah J	(913)223-8261 pastorschultzsjl@outlook.com	203 4th Ave Keystone IA 52249	IE	SP	St John Keystone IA	(319)442-3514	SL	2024
Schultz Jonathan D	(918)694-2980 jdsmlbna@yahoo.com	1318 W Pittsburg Pl Broken Arrow OK 74012	OK	EM			SL-SMP	2011
Schultz William K	(408)315-7930 Revwks@gmail.com	229 Covington Ct Sequim WA 98382	NOW	EM			FW	1985
Schultz Kurt D	(716)342-4494 kurt.schultz2@gmail.com	3229 Upper Mountain Rd Sanborn NY 14132	EA	SP	Our Savior* Niagara Falls NY	(716)297-3880	NESC	2016
Schultz Frederick W	(386)677-3146 ricdelsch23@yahoo.com	39 China Moon Dr Ormond Beach FL 32174	FG	EM			FW	1984
Schultz Kurtis D	(205)533-0444 kurtis.schultz71@gmail.com	4743 Cotswold Ln Birmingham AL 35242	SO	SP	First Birmingham AL	(205)933-0380	FW	1979
Schultz Mark A	(406)404-2021 thaischultz2@yahoo.com	11 Teton Ave Bozeman MT 59718	MT	EM			FW	1983
Schultz Matthew C	(314)440-2168 pastormcschultz@gmail.com	c/o Ascension Lutheran Church P.O. Box 846 Pratt KS 67124	KS	SP	Ascension Pratt KS		SL	2006
Schultz Myles R	(918)885-2816 mylesschultz@gmail.com	12 Appaloosa Dr Holiday Island AR 72631	MDS	SP	Grace Holiday Island AR	(479)253-9040	FW	1990
Schultz Nathan E	(734)770-4181 nathan.e.schultz@gmail.com	c/o Christ Memorial Lutheran Church 5252 S Lindbergh Blvd Saint Louis MO 63126	MO	Assoc	Christ Memorial Saint Louis MO	(314)631-0304	SL	2018
Schultz Phillip R	(716)276-3949 philliprschultz@gmail.com	150 Unionvale Rd Cheektowaga NY 14225	EA	SP	St Luke Cheektowaga NY	(716)633-6752	CQ	2013
Schultz Richard O			NW	M Chap	Office of International Mission Saint Louis MO		SL	2008
Schultz Roderick D	(517)420-7614 revschultz1@gmail.com	13562 Milton Dr Belleville MI 48111	MI	SP	St Luke Clinton Township MI	(586)791-1150	FW	2008
Schultz Ronald C	(734) 755-3202 ronschultz08@gmail.com	1011 College Ave Holland MI 49423	MI	EM			FW	1983
Schultz Jonah J	(913)339-8515 jonah.schultz@gmail.com	18 Newland Ln Jacksonville IL 62650	CI	SP	Salem Jacksonville IL	(217)243-3419	SL	2024
Schultz Randall P	(810)730-7071 revrand.schultz@gmail.com		MI	EM			SL	1979
Schultz Craig D	(907)502-0120 cdschultz1949@gmail.com	8651 N Michaelson St Palmer AK 99645	NOW	EM			SL	1975
Schultz John M	(618)972-3914 jschultz1986@gmail.com	223 Stafford St Plymouth WI 53073	SW	Sn/Adm	St John Plymouth WI	(920)893-3071	SL	2012

*Multiple Assignments (See Church Worker Locator for Additional Details)

See Page 53 for the Table of Abbreviations for key to District, Position, and Seminary abbreviations

**C =Candidate; EM = Emeritus; the date following the C is the month and year the Candidate status began

NAME	TELEPHONE NUMBER EMAIL	STREET ADDRESS CITY/STATE/ZIP	DISTRICT	POSITION/ STATUS**	WHERE SERVING	OFFICE PHONE	SEM/ PROGRAM	YR GRAD
Schultz Gary H	(608)403-8250 revghschultz@hotmail.com	1170 Reading Dr Montgomery IL 60538	NI	SP	St Paul Aurora IL	(630)896-3250	SL	2005
Schultz Aaron A	(559)920-0476 aschultz@adventlutheran.org	7846 Clarendon Rd Indianapolis IN 46260	EN	Assoc	Advent Zionsville IN	(317)873-6318	FW	2022
Schultz Anthony J Sr	(907)301-3378 tminton143@gmail.com	1407 O St Anchorage AK 99501	NOW	EM			SL	1979
Schultz Charles P	(314)779-4714 pastorschultz@yahoo.com	219 N State St Neskoro WI 54960	SW	SP	Calvary* Princeton WI	(920)295-4747	SL	2009
Schultz Christian F	(785)458-9852 chris@cwtemail.com	4400 Rockenham Rd Saint George KS 66535	KS	EM			SL	2012
Schultz Daniel E	(952)938-7661 dan.schultz@zionhopkins.org	241 5th Ave N. Hopkins MN 55343	MNS	SMP	Zion Hopkins MN	(952)938-7661	SL-SMP	2013
Schultz David M Dr	(618)972-4804 schultz137@gmail.com	1301 Vaughn Rd Wood River IL 62095	SI	SP	St Paul Wood River IL	(618)259-0257	SL	2015
Schultz David M	(989)450-2516 davidatchurch@juno.com	6116 Westside Saginaw Rd Bay City MI 48706	MI	SMP	St Paul Bay City MI	(989)684-4450	SL-SMP	2024
Schultz Jacob M	(618)972-1292 jacobmaschultz@gmail.com		SW	Assoc	St Paul Grafton WI	(262)377-4659	SL	2017
Schultz Joel S	(913)660-3946 pastorschultz@bslcks.org	12915 W 104th Ter Overland Park KS 66215	KS	Sn/Adm	Beautiful Savior Olathe KS	(913)780-6023	SL	2000
Schultz Christian D	(785)313-4633 christian.schultz@ctsfw.edu	1 Coverdale Dr Fort Wayne IN 46825	IN	S HS/C	Concordia Theological Seminary Fort Wayne IN	(260)452-2100	FW	2021
Schultz Jeremy J	(636)212-5608 jschultz@sjlarnold.org	1808 Adyn Ave Arnold MO 63010	MO	Sn/Adm	St Johns Arnold MO	(636)464-0096	SL	1998
Schultz David P	(507)848-0816 lcmspastorschultz@hotmail.com	137 Linden Ave Fairmont MN 56031	IW	SP	Our Savior Swea City IA	(515)538-0620	FW	1999
Schultz Glenn A		2205 Meadow Ln Rapid City SD 57703	SD	EM			SL	1970
Schultz Gary W	(260)206-4443 pastor.gwschultz@gmail.com	101 S Harding St Apt 102 Indianapolis IN 46222	EN	C07/2016			FW	2008
Schultz Gary G	(715)574-1650 schultzg8115@gmail.com	233202 Sunnyvale Ln Wausau WI 54401	NW	EM			SL	1987
Schultz Dennis L	(320)564-9239 dpschultz@mchsi.com	93 Primrose Ln Granite Falls MN 56241	MNN	EM			SL	1968
Schultz David V	(713)828-8347 dvs@schultzllc.com	6822 Queensclub Dr Houston TX 77069	TX	SP	St John Cypress TX	(281)373-0503	CQ	1988
Schultze Michael A	mike@peacecamarillo.com	412 Lakeview Ct Oxnard CA 93036	PSW	Assoc	Peace Camarillo CA	(805)482-3313	CQ	2019
Schultze Edwin L Dr	(253)397-9308 e_schultze@hotmail.com	12739 E Apache Pass Rd Spokane WA 99206	NOW	EM			SPR	1965
Schulz Mark R Dr	(913)231-9726 markschulz52@gmail.com	8405 W 98th Cir Overland Park KS 66212	KS	EM			SL	1986
Schulz Michael P	(608)580-0157 Mp.schulz@icloud.com	4301 Huntington Ave Janesville WI 53546	SW	EM			SL	1973
Schulz Wallace R Dr	(314)504-9696 wrs.gn@outlook.com	532 S High Post Rd Augusta MO 63332	MO	EM			SPR	1973
Schulz Stewart G	(847)899-3506 pastorstewartschulz@gmail.com	4 Doral Ct Lake In The Hills IL 60156	NI	EM			SL	1977
Schulz Paul A	(314)374-1590 p.schulz571@gmail.com	810 Inman St Mallard IA 50562	IW	SP	Trinity* Mallard IA	(712)425-3328	NESC	2017
Schulz Maynard L	(707) 355-4444 ribodar2@gmail.com	21271 Hidden Bend Loop Magnolia TX 77354	TX	EM			SL	1991
Schulz Mark W Dr	(715)834-2486 marks@mypeacechurch.com	820 Pamela Pl Eau Claire WI 54701	NW	Sn/Adm	Peace Eau Claire WI	(715)834-2486	SL	1982
Schulz Charles R Dr	concordiaschulz@gmail.com	20 Princess Ct Westchester IL 60154	NI	S HS/C	Concordia University Chicago River Forest IL	(708)771-8300	SL	1996
Schulz Mark C	(630)983-2535 schulzmc@me.com	3 Steck Ct Bolingbrook IL 60440	NI	EM			CQ	1995
Schulz Klaus D Dr	(260)452-3131 detlev.schulz@ctsfw.edu	4109 S Harrison St Fort Wayne IN 46807	IN	S HS/C	Concordia Theological Seminary Fort Wayne IN	(260)452-2100	SL	1994
Schulz Jeffrey P		5614 Gatewood Ln Greendale WI 53129	SW	EM			SL	1997
Schulz Steven M	steve.schulz@lcms.org	40052 County Hwy E16 Mapleton IA 51034	IW	S Ex/S	The LCMS Corporate Saint Louis MO	(314)965-9000	SL	1991
Schulz James R	(920)240-5020 jimschulz50@gmail.com	4029 Hazelnut Ct Sheboygan WI 53081	SW	SP	Our Savior's Sheboygan WI	(920)452-4005	CQ	2013
Schulz Gregory P Dr	(262)247-6969	5338 Kettle View Ct Slinger WI 53086	SW	EM			CQ	2013
Schulz Donald R	(719) 740-0868 frdons@gmail.com	1805 Bluff St Bellevue NE 68005	NEB	EM			FW	1991
Schulz Mark E	(850)728-2597 pastorschulz@gmail.com	34 Jb Ivey Ln Lk Junaluska NC 28745	FG	EM			NESC	1984
Schulze Robert A	(952)687-1586 jaschulze07@gmail.com	12397 74th Ave N Maple Grove MN 55369	MNS	EM			SPR	1975
Schulze Christoph M	(646)249-3836 tentinasia@aol.com	1182 E 93rd St Brooklyn NY 11236	AT	SP	St Matthew* Brooklyn NY	(347)659-7562	FW	2000
Schulze Mark E	(208)432-2544 vwpastor.eden@gmail.com	1602 E 1100 S Eden ID 83325	NOW	SP	Trinity Eden ID	(208)825-5277	SL	2008
Schumacher Michael D	(208)922-8299 rev0466@aol.com	10145 W Plum Tree Cir Apt 103 Hales Corners WI 53130	SW	C08/2023			SL	1987
Schumacher Stephen O	(630)362-7548 soschumacher@gmail.com	1122 Catalpa Ln Naperville IL 60540	NI	Assoc	Bethany Naperville IL	(630)355-2198	SL	1985

*Multiple Assignments (See Church Worker Locator for Additional Details)
See Page 53 for the Table of Abbreviations for key to District, Position, and Seminary abbreviations
**C =Candidate; EM = Emeritus; the date following the C is the month and year the Candidate status began

NAME	TELEPHONE NUMBER EMAIL	STREET ADDRESS CITY/STATE/ZIP	DISTRICT	POSITION/ STATUS**	WHERE SERVING	OFFICE PHONE	SEM/ PROGRAM	YR GRAD
Schumacher Steven R Dr	(260)633-0328 rev.schumacher@gmail.com	1109 Dakota Dr Fort Wayne IN 46845	IN	EM			FW	1987
Schumacher Warren W Dr	(503)816-2030 wshoebox@comcast.net	2254 NE 13th Ave Hillsboro OR 97124	NOW	EM			SPR	1965
Schumacher William W Dr	(314)505-7112 schumacherw@csl.edu	2929 Collier Ave Saint Louis MO 63144	MO	S HS/C	Concordia Seminary Saint Louis MO	(314)505-7000	SL	1985
Schumm Mark E Dr	(920)445-6021 mark.schumm@gmail.com	4038 Oak Trail Drive Indianapolis IN 46237	IN	Assoc	Calvary Indianapolis IN	(317)783-2000	SL	1998
Schumm William E Sr	(360)679-9459	2047 Pine Wood Way Oak Harbor WA 98277	NOW	EM			SL	1959
Schumm Daniel D	(317)514-4252		IN	EM			SL	1983
Schumm Herbert L	herbschumm@gmail.com	1816 Broken Oak Rd Fort Wayne IN 46818	IN	EM			FW	1979
Schurb Ken R Dr	(217)793-1802 kschurb@cidlcms.org	c/o Lcms Central Il District 1850 N Grand Ave W Springfield IL 62702	CI	D Ex/S	Central Illinois District Springfield IL	(217)793-1802	FW	1982
Schuschke Gary S	+491738937656 gsschuschke@gmail.com	c/o Faith Lutheran Church 1310 Evergreen Heights Dr Woodland Park CO 80863	RM	SP	Faith Woodland Park CO	(719)687-2303	SL	2000
Schut Bruce L	(402)719-8336 blschut_55@gpcom.net	600 Bridge St Scribner NE 68057	NEB	SP	St Peter Scribner NE	(402)664-3462	FW	1984
Schut Jordan B	(402) 317-4727 schut.jordan@gmail.com	120 N 7th St O Neill NE 68763	NEB	Assoc	Christ O'neill NE	(402)336-1884	SL	2022
Schutt Timothy E	(504)462-1478 tim.schutt1983@gmail.com	9664 Mirada Blvd Fort Myers FL 33908	FG		Florida-Georgia District Orlando FL	(407)857-5556	SL	2009
Schutte Dennis C	(218)663-7700 schuttes@boreal.org	812 4th Ave SE Hampton IA 50441	MNN	EM			SL	1993
Schutte William B	(870)404-2925 outbackbanners@yahoo.com	906 Brassie Dr Mountain Home AR 72653	MDS	EM			CQ	2018
Schutz Roland D Dr	(501)909-6531 dr.rds77@yahoo.com	618 Purdue Dr Tyler TX 75703	TX	EM			FW	1977
Schwab Guenter	(410) 657-9954 guenter_schwab@aol.com	8810 Walther Blvd Apt 3212 Parkville MD 21234	SE	EM			SL	1965
Schwalenberg Mark L	(715)218-8814 athenspastor@gmail.com	637 Faith St Athens WI 54411	NW	EM			SL	1991
Schwalenberg Dennis D	(715)909-0041 god4usx4@yahoo.com	464 Fairview Ln Nekoosa WI 54457	NW	Sn/Adm	Bethlehem Nekoosa WI	(715)886-4081	SL	1980
Schwan David E	deschwan51@gmail.com	1846 S Foxcove Blvd New Palestine IN 46163	IN	EM			FW	1977
Schwandt Richard L	(828)322-5078 rjschwandt@charter.net	4532 1st St NW Hickory NC 28601	SE	EM			SL	1982
Schwanke Gerald A	(320)282-9838 schwanke5@yahoo.com	1790 Sunrise Cir Mayer MN 55360	MNS	Asst	St Pauls Watertown MN	(952)955-1498	FW	1989
Schwanke Wayne L	(715)256-9668 wlschwanke2@aol.com	E2748 Catherine Ct Waupaca WI 54981	NW	EM			FW	1987
Schwanz Chris A	(715)340-9070 pastor@immanuelmarshfield.org	P.O. Box 326 Marshfield WI 54449	NW	Sn/Adm	Immanuel Marshfield WI	(715)384-5121	FW	1989
Schwartz Roger A	roger.schwartz@orlcaugusta.com	464 Cambridge Way Martinez GA 30907	FG	SP	Our Redeemer Augusta GA	(706)733-6076	SL	2000
Schwartz John W	(586)850-9960 revjwschwartz@gmail.com	120 Woodcliff Cir Pineville LA 71360	SO		Southern District Slidell LA	(504)282-2632	FW	2003
Schwartz Nathaniel R	(816)806-6797 pastorschwartz@trinitylutheran-church.org	1010 Double Eagle Ave SE Rochester MN 55904	MNS	Sn/Adm	Trinity Rochester MN	(507)289-1531	SL	1989
Schwarz Mark L	(320)460-0282 markschwarz@trinityathens.net	616 Elm St Athens WI 54411	NW	SP	Trinity Athens WI	(715)257-7526	SL	2018
Schweigert Jon-Michael	(660)563-5973 faithknobnoster@gmail.com	P.O. Box 42 Knob Noster MO 65336	MO	SP	Faith Knob Noster MO	(660)563-5973	SL	2015
Schweitzer Keith W Dr	(641)743-8443 keithlcms@gmail.com	P.O. Box 185 608 NE 5th St Greenfield IA 50849	IW	SP	Faith* Winterset IA	(641)745-5143	SL	1989
Schwenk Arthur Jr	(812)350-0986 schwenk.a@hotmail.com	10990 N County Road 900 E Hope IN 47246	IN	EM			FW	2006
Schwichtenberg Marc N	(847)208-7686 pastormarc@stjohnrochester.org	1283 Thames Ct Rochester Hls MI 48307	MI	Sn/Adm	St John Rochester MI	(248)402-8000	FW	1997
Schwichtenberg Willis R Dr	(815)266-9370 pastorswitz@gmail.com	321 N Holly Ave Freeport IL 61032	NI	SP	Our Redeemer Freeport IL	(815)232-6934	SPR	1972
Schwieger Alan J	(810)329-4502 Ajs5067@icloud.com	5067 Pointe Dr East China MI 48054	MI	EM			FW	1979
Schwiesow Barry R	pastorbarry5357@gmail.com	617 Twin Creeks Ln Pryor OK 74361	OK	EM			SL	2005
Schwiesow Wayne W	(573)986-8097 wndsch@clas.net	2079 Flowline Rd Levelland TX 79336	MO	EM			FW	1992
Scicluna Jon D	(469) 891-6414 jon.scicluna@gmail.com	1280 Crestcove Dr Rockwall TX 75087	TX	EM			FW	2007
Scofield Jackson R	(708)373-0165 jacksonryanscofield@gmail.com	4905 Cross St Downers Grove IL 60515	NI	SP	River Of Life* Channahon IL	(815)467-0641	FW	2025
Scoles Brian R	(651) 280-7657 brscoles@gmail.com	717 S State St New Ulm MN 56073	MNS	SP	Redeemer New Ulm MN	(507)233-3470	SL	2007
Scott John W	(571)508-8670 john@oswlc.org		SE	Sn/Adm	Our Savior's Way Ashburn VA	(703)858-9254	SL	2006
Scott Tobin L	(325)340-0518 tobinlscott@gmail.com	134 3rd St Barnett MO 65011	MO	C12/2020			SL	2017
Scott Robert G	(810)845-5697 rscott1865@aol.com	8307 Sherwood Dr Grand Blanc MI 48439	MI	SMP	Faith Grand Blanc MI	(810)694-9351	FW-SMP	2014

*Multiple Assignments (See Church Worker Locator for Additional Details)

See Page 53 for the Table of Abbreviations for key to District, Position, and Seminary abbreviations

**C =Candidate; EM = Emeritus; the date following the C is the month and year the Candidate status began

NAME	TELEPHONE NUMBER EMAIL	STREET ADDRESS CITY/STATE/ZIP	DISTRICT	POSITION/ STATUS**	WHERE SERVING	OFFICE PHONE	SEM/ PROGRAM	YR GRAD
Scott Jacob A	(314)808-4446 j.arthur.scott@gmail.com	5243 Launch St NE Salem OR 97305	NOW	M Chap	Office of International Mission Saint Louis MO		SL	2010
Scott Edward A	(772)546-7626 edscott1@bellsouth.net	6236 SE Charleston Pl Apt 104 Hobe Sound FL 33455	FG	EM			CQ	1980
Scott Charles R	(620)342-1929 revcabscott@hotmail.com	1 S Constitution St Emporia KS 66801	KS	EM			FW	1992
Scott Bradford E	(567)868-9936 ixthus@bex.net	581 Webber Dr Temperance MI 48182	EN	SP	Good Shepherd Toledo OH	(419)474-0529	SL	1982
Scott Alan D Dr	alan@3ccw.com		IN	EM			FW	1983
Scott Kevin M	(757)268-5735 kevinscott@kogva.org	616 Newfield Rd Glen Burnie MD 21061	SE	Sn/Adm	St Paul's Glen Burnie MD	(410)766-2283	SL	2020
Scroggins Troy D	(806)930-1476 troy_scroggins@hotmail.com	512 Belmont Dr Dumas TX 79029	TX	SP	St John Dumas TX	(806)935-2974	FW	2007
Scruggs Darren K	(507)382-3981 pastordarren@hosannamankato.com	43168 Reeds Lake Rd Janesville MN 56048	MNS	SMP	Hosanna Mankato MN	(507)388-1766	SL-SMP	2013
Scudder Michael R	(319) 385-2080 pastorscuddermr@gmail.com	906 E Mapleleaf Dr Mt Pleasant IA 52641	IE	SP	Faith Mount Pleasant IA	(319)385-8427	FW	1994
Scudieri Robert J Dr	(239)776-5397 bscudieri@gmail.com	4954 Lindell Blvd Apt 2w 2w Saint Louis MO 63108	FG	EM			SL	1971
Seabaugh David W	pastorseabaugh@immanuelelmhurst.org	770 N Howard Ave Elmhurst IL 60126	NI	Sn/Adm	Immanuel Elmhurst IL	(630)832-1649	SL	2005
Seabaugh Timothy M	(920)257-1940 tseabaugh@gslchurch.net	2220 E College Ave Appleton WI 54915	NW	Sn/Adm	Good Shepherd Appleton WI	(920)734-9643	SL	2000
Sealey Herman A	(925)777-1974 hermsings@aol.com	5119 Sundance Ct Antioch CA 94531	CNH	SMP	St Andrew Antioch CA	(925)757-1672	CQ	2019
Seals Timothy L	(951)233-8739 tjseals@aol.com	6369 Daylily Ct Alta Loma CA 91737	PSW	SP	St Luke Claremont CA	(909)624-8898	FW	1984
Seaman Gerald W	(407)687-0644 seamang001@cfl.rr.com	1326 Haven Dr Oviedo FL 32765	FG	EM			SL	1964
Seaman Mark M	(828)243-5386 mkseaman@yahoo.com	3420 21st Street Dr NE Hickory NC 28601	SE	SP	Our Savior Hickory NC	(828)256-5469	SL	2004
Seaman William D Dr	(919)610-1392 wseaman@bellsouth.net	5101 Duckdown Ct Raleigh NC 27604	SE	EM			SL	1971
Sears Richard G II	(608)346-1531 ricksears7@gmail.com	10501 W State Highway 81 Beloit WI 53511	SW	SMP	Our Savior Janesville WI	(608)563-2912	FW-SMP	2020
Sears Gary L	(319)662-4108 glsears@iowatelecom.net	P.O. Box 66 Conroy IA 52220	IE	SP	St John* Homestead IA	(319)662-4286	FW	1987
Seat Stanley F Dr	(214)766-0054 stan@seatcpa.com	916 Alvero Pl Mansfield TX 76063	TX	EM			CQ	2021
Seaton Robert G		2825 Julian Ave NE Cleveland TN 37312	MDS	SP	First Cleveland TN	(423)472-6811	SL	1982
Seaver Todd A	(419)376-3992 seaverta@icloud.com	4981 Kay Dr Monroe MI 48161	EN	EM			FW	2000
Seaver Wade M	(231)533-8129 HopeInBellaire@gmail.com	c/o Hope Lutheran Church P.O. Box 160 Bellaire MI 49615	EN	SP	Hope Bellaire MI	(231)533-8129	FW	1999
Seban Calvin F	(262)255-7656 calseban@gmail.com	N86 W15852 Riverside Bluff Rd Menomonee FLS WI 53051	SW	EM			SL	1968
Seban Timothy R	(262)665-8090 tseban@stpaulskingsville.org	12028 Jerusalem Rd Kingsville MD 21087	SE	SP	St Pauls Kingsville MD	(410)592-8100	SL	2003
Sedlmayr Roger M	(208)308-7993 pastor.sedlmayr@gmail.com	527 Stonehedge Loop Twin Falls ID 83301	NOW	Sn/Adm	Immanuel Twin Falls ID	(208)733-7820	SL	1986
Sedney Blaise C	(410)838-3178 blaisesedney@aol.com	334 W Gordon St Bel Air MD 21014	SE	Assoc	St Matthew Bel Air MD	(410)838-3178	SL-D	2010
Sedotto Anthony C	(518)944-3494 acsedotto@gmail.com	W167 N8923 Grand Ave #325 Menomonee Falls WI 53051	SW	Assoc	Grace Menomonee Falls WI	(262)251-0670	SL	2024
Sedwick John M	(618)767-4682 john.m.sedwick@gmail.com	11854 Wine Hill Rd Steeleville IL 62288	SI	SP	Immanuel* Campbell Hill IL	(618)426-3154	FW	2004
See Soun	(559)563-2140 sounsoun@att.net	331 Chandler St Farmersville CA 93223	CNH	Asst	Grace Visalia CA	(559)734-7694	SL	2012
Seeber Timothy W	(269)382-2360 pastortim@zionkazoo.org	6148 Rothbury St Portage MI 49024	MI	Asst	Zion Kalamazoo MI	(269)382-2360	CQ	1984
Seeger Carl W	(608)884-3324 revcarlseeger@hotmail.com	205 E High St Edgerton WI 53534	SW	Sn/Adm	St John Edgerton WI	(608)884-3515	SL	2000
Seeger David M	(301)916-2227 romans32024@msn.com	11215 Seven Locks Rd Potomac MD 20854	SE	Asst	Messiah Germantown MD	(301)972-2130	FW	1980
Seeger Mark W	(512)251-3125 markjlcd@aol.com	2000 Magic Hill Dr Pflugerville TX 78660	TX	EM			FW	1979
Seehafer Daniel J	(920)382-9655 danseehafer@gmail.com	W7550 Shady Ln Beaver Dam WI 53916	SW	Sn/Adm	St Stephen Horicon WI	(920)485-6687	FW	1997
Seel Martin A Jr	(607)239-2196 tseel12@gmail.com	817 Taylor Dr Vestal NY 13850	EA	SP	Holy Trinity Binghamton NY	(607)204-0704	CQ	2024
Seetin Lee D		2320a Highway 69 Gresham NE 68367	NEB	SP	St Peter Gresham NE	(402)735-7333	SL	1985
Seger Jeremy B	(812) 454-0198 jeremy@redeemerchurch.org	4011 Chappell Drive Evansville IN 47725	IN	SMP	Our Redeemer Evansville IN	(812)476-9991	SL	2024
Seible Robert D II	(720)379-3132 sailorpb@sbcglobal.net	6757 W Kingsley Ave Littleton CO 80128	RM	EM			SL	1983
Seidenstricker Michael R	(618)783-3923 seideyl@yahoo.com	101 E Rickelman Ave Apt 20 Effingham IL 62401	CI	EM			SL	2007
Seidler Scott K Dr	pastorscott@sotdaz.org	15203 Vista Dr Fountain Hills AZ 85268	PSW	Sn/Adm	Shepherd Desert Scottsdale AZ	(480)860-1188	SL	1996

*Multiple Assignments (See Church Worker Locator for Additional Details)
See Page 53 for the Table of Abbreviations for key to District, Position, and Seminary abbreviations
**C =Candidate; EM = Emeritus; the date following the C is the month and year the Candidate status began

NAME	TELEPHONE NUMBER EMAIL	STREET ADDRESS CITY/STATE/ZIP	DISTRICT	POSITION/ STATUS**	WHERE SERVING	OFFICE PHONE	SEM/ PROGRAM	YR GRAD
Seifert Joseph A Jr	(316)542-0170 pastor.seifert@gmail.com	5322 PSC 559 Fpo AP 96377	KS	M Chap	Office of International Mission Saint Louis MO		SL	2011
Seiferth Larry G Sr	(501)766-6824 preacher-larry@sbcglobal.net	10762 W Bronco Trl Peoria AZ 85383	MDS	EM			SL	1982
Seifferlein Christopher M	(920)918-7200 pastorcms@lancasterlutheran.com	375 Camp Meeting Rd Landisville PA 17538	EN	SP	Mount Calvary Lititz PA	(717)560-6751	FW	2003
Seifrid Mark A	(502)473-0496 seifridm@csl.edu	2562 Dell Rd Louisville KY 40205	MO	S HS/C	Concordia Seminary Saint Louis MO	(314)505-7000	CQ	2015
Seim Carl J	(651)233-7755 hockey4434@gmail.com	9900 166th Ct SE Becker MN 55308	MNN	SMP	Lord Of Glory Elk River MN	(763)263-3090	SL-SMP	2021
Seitz Lane R Dr	(612)865-0939 lane.seitz@outlook.com	8109 - 139th Street West Savage MN 55378	MNS	EM			SPR	1974
Selbana Abdi M	(816)672-9902 abdimegeressa@gmail.com	3527 NW 69th Terrace Apt 11 Kansas City MO 64151	MO	Asst	Christ Platte Woods MO	(816)741-0483	CQ	2020
Seletzky Douglas S	(440)570-8441 pastordoug@cohchurch.com	236 Jananna Dr Berea OH 44017	OH	SP	Community Hope Broadview Heights OH	(440)457-2296	CQ	2009
Self Les H	(623)271-0809 lesself6@gmail.com	12946 W Vista Paseo Dr Litchfield Pk AZ 85340	CNH	EM			FW	1986
Self Luke W	(828)578-1296 lukefromthehomestead@gmail.com	149 Liz Dr Statesville NC 28625	SE	SMP	St John Conover NC	(828)464-4071	FW-SMP	2021
Selim Timothy C	(231)884-8193 rev.selim@gmail.com	11809 E 20 Rd Manton MI 49663	MI	SMP	Faith Mesick MI	(231)885-1072	FW-SMP	2016
Sell Mark E	(314)807-9570	546 Stoddards Mill Dr Ballwin MO 63011	MO	Sn/Adm	Our Savior Fenton MO	(636)343-2192	FW	1988
Selle Robert V	(239)281-1664 robert.selle@aol.com	10810 John Randolph Drive Jacksonville FL 32257	FG	EM			SL	1983
Selle Robert F	(920)987-5454 selle@athenet.net	P.O. Box 305 Poy Sippi WI 54967	NW	EM			SL	1970
Selle John F	(512)863-3634 jselle@flcms.org	124 Melissa Ct Georgetown TX 78628	TX	Assoc	Faith Georgetown TX	(512)863-7332	SL	1971
Sellers Justin C	(512)845-2746 csellers06@gmail.com	191 Glen Echo Rd Collierville TN 38017	MDS	Assoc	Faith Collierville TN	(901)853-4673	SL	2013
Seltz Gregory P Dr	gregory.seltz@lcrlfreedom.org	17624 Myrtlewood Dr Wildwood MO 63005	MO	Pro Stf	Lutheran Center for Religious Liberty Kirkwood MO		SL	1986
Senkbeil Harold L Dr	(262)716-8575 hsenkbeil@doxology.us	2125 Broken Hill Rd Unit 2 Waukesha WI 53188	SW	EM			SPR	1971
Senn Randall B	(608)436-1355 baldingpastor@gmail.com	1 Plum Tree Village Beloit WI 53511	SW	EM			SL	1996
Senne Edgar P	ed.senne@valpo.edu	3303 Pines Village Cir Apt 151 Valparaiso IN 46383	IN	EM			SL	1957
Senstad Russell C	(712)276-9498 imsenstad@yahoo.com	4211 Eldorado Ct Sioux City IA 51106	IW	Sn/Adm	Redeemer Sioux City IA	(712)276-1125	SL	1992
Serbus Rodney M	(630)512-7023 pastorrodserbus@gmail.com	c/o Bethlehem Lutheran Church 300 Broadway Dr Sun Prairie WI 53590	SW	Sn/Adm	Bethlehem Sun Prairie WI	(608)837-7446	SL	2009
Serina Richard J Jr Dr	(314)996-1432 richard.serina@lcms.org	11044 Cedarberry Pl Saint Louis MO 63123	MO	S Ex/S	The LCMS Corporate Saint Louis MO	(314)965-9000	CQ	2004
Sernessa Alemu	(614)519-6256 lubaalemu@aol.com	705 Salisbury St Pickerington OH 43147	OH	C06/2019			CQ	2016
Serr Kenneth R		2334 Weeden Creek Rd Sheboygan WI 53081	SW	EM			SL	2009
Serr William C	(605)835-8351 jserr@hotmail.com	32949 298th St Dallas SD 57529	NEB	SP	Grace* Burton NE	(402)497-2507	SL-D	2010
Sessa Samuel J	sessasamuel@gmail.com	20 John Peter Dr Acra NY 12405	AT	Sn/Adm	Resurrection Cairo NY	(518)622-3286	SL	2018
Sestak Peter J	(507)696-4684 rev.peter.sestak@gmail.com	5012 E Brennan Dr Sioux Falls SD 57110	SD	EM			SL	1977
Seto Lester T	(808)345-1712 lesterseto@gmail.com	68-1898 Eha Ko Pl Waikoloa HI 96738	CNH	EM			SL	1985
Settle Rance A Dr	pastorsettle@log.org	1401 Cross Timbers Rd Flower Mound TX 75028	TX	Sn/Adm	Lamb Of God Flower Mound TX	(972)539-5200	SL	2006
Sewing David M	(712)269-8469 dsewing57@gmail.com	1362 State Route 121 Lincoln IL 62656	IW	EM			SL	1997
Seyboldt David A	(574)304-4559 dave.seyboldt@gmail.com	313 Haney Ave Apt 2 South Bend IN 46613	IN	EM			FW	1988
Seyoum Berhanu	(206)371-2938 berhanusg@gmail.com	16626 6th Ave W Apt F101 Lynnwood WA 98032	NOW	SP	Mekane Yesus Mountlake Terrace WA	(206)371-2938	CQ	2009
Shackel Paul L	(920)722-6686 plshackel@aol.com	1140 Pomer Way Menasha WI 54952	NW	EM			SL	1973
Shadday David A	(317)784-9872	660 Bluestem Circle New Whiteland IN 46184	IN	Sn/Adm	St Pauls Indianapolis IN	(317)787-4464	FW	2004
Shaffer Corey A	(715)315-4919 corey.shaffer@undershepherd.org	5711 Patrick Henry Ct. Wisconsin Rapids WI 54494	NW	C10/2024			SL	2021
Shaltanis Joel A	(909)210-7309 pastorshaltanis@yahoo.com	1904 Vantage Dr Plano TX 75075	TX	SP	Lord of Life Plano TX	(972)867-5588	SL	2000
Shaltanis Mark A	(703)573-6008 pastormark@stpaulsfallschurch.org	2336 Morgan Ln Dunn Loring VA 22027	SE	Sn/Adm	St Paul Falls Church VA	(703)573-0295	SL	1993
Shamburger Douglas M	(619)370-2446 shamburg3@aol.com	P.O. Box 440146 Aurora CO 80044	RM	EM			SPR	1967
Shamburger William M III	(505)681-0922 pastor@holycrossrocklin.org	4453 Sierra Pine Way Rocklin CA 95677	CNH	SP	Holy Cross Rocklin CA	(916)624-8185	FW	2023
Shanburn Eric J	(586) 751-2550 pastor@holycrosswarren.com	30003 Ryan Rd Warren MI 48092	MI	SP	Holy Cross Warren MI	(586)751-2550	CQ	2023

*Multiple Assignments (See Church Worker Locator for Additional Details)
See Page 53 for the Table of Abbreviations for key to District, Position, and Seminary abbreviations
**C =Candidate; EM = Emeritus; the date following the C is the month and year the Candidate status began

NAME	TELEPHONE NUMBER EMAIL	STREET ADDRESS CITY/STATE/ZIP	DISTRICT	POSITION/ STATUS**	WHERE SERVING	OFFICE PHONE	SEM/ PROGRAM	YR GRAD
Shane Brian T	(314)532-0012 brtshane@gmail.com	2606 4th Avenue A Canyon TX 79015	TX	SP	St Paul Canyon TX	(806)655-4086	SL	2019
Shane Howard O	(605)271-5532 hshane101@gmail.com	3220 W 57th St Apt 213 Sioux Falls SD 57108	SD	EM			CQ	1978
Shank John C	(618)407-1067 jshank@trinitylutheran ministries.org	2012 Stanford Pl Edwardsville IL 62025	SI	Sn/Adm	Trinity Edwardsville IL	(618)656-2918	FW	2010
Shank Steven A	(260)402-3099	15445 Outback Ln Leopold IN 47551	IN	SMP	St John Evanston IN	(812)547-2007	SL-SMP	2011
Shanks Jeffrey P	(402)658-2098 pastor.jeff@stjohnocala.org	644 SW 48th Ln Ocala FL 34471	FG	Sn/Adm	St John Ocala FL	(352)629-1794	FW	1989
Shannon Michael K	(318)780-0652 mkshannon0251@gmail.com	9833 E Chase Cir Shreveport LA 71118	SO	SMP	Faith Shreveport LA	(318)635-8084	FW-SMP	2013
Sharp John W	(217)493-4632 pastor@gslcrf.org	c/o Good Shepherd Lutheran Church 435 Martin Rd Rock Falls IL 61071	NI	SP	Good Shepherd Rock Falls IL	(815)625-3376	SL	1998
Sharp William B	979-533-8152 wbsharp1@gmail.com	1176 Fm 431 Rosebud TX 76570	TX	EM			FW	1992
Sharp Robert A	(435)233-8085 pbob022212@cedarlutheran.org	3987 West 225 North Cedar City UT 84720	RM	SP	Trinity Cedar City UT	(435)586-7103	SL	1996
Sharp Michael D	(712)363-0868	17 18th St SE Spencer IA 51301	IW	EM			FW	1982
Sharp Kevin G	(810) 813-0051 pastorsharp@hope4sandiego.org	6548 Alcalla Knolls Dr San Diego CA 92111	PSW	Sn/Adm	Hope Linda Vista San Diego CA	(858)268-4688	SL	2024
Sharp James T	(443)421-6531 pastor.sharp@gmail.com	203 Avenue A Denison IA 51442	SE	S Miss	Office of International Mission Saint Louis MO		SL	2004
Sharp Jonathan M	(816)728-5582 revjohnsharp@gmail.com	2221 West Road Dr Springfield IL 62711	CI	Assoc	Trinity Springfield IL	(217)787-2323	SL	2023
Sharpe Thomas M	(209)770-5195 pastortomsharpe@gmail.com	17591 Twin Oak Dr Jamestown CA 95327	CNH	SP	St Matthew Sonora CA	(209)532-4639	SL	1992
Shaver Ross P Dr	(208)936-8556 Ross.Shaver@lcms.org	9713 Kingsport Place Bakersfield CA 93306	NOW	S Miss	Office of International Mission Saint Louis MO		SL	2007
Shaw Jonathan E Dr	(703)317-7793 jonathan.shaw@lcms.org	2335 Lake Ridge Drive Fort Wayne IN 46804	EN	S Ex/S	The LCMS Corporate Saint Louis MO	(314)965-9000	FW	1984
Shaw Vincent X	(702)810-7305 pastor.shaw@gmail.com	Chaplain 55th Wing Offutt Afb NE 68113	CNH	M Chap	Office of International Mission Saint Louis MO		FW	2009
Shaw Paul E	(740)603-7874 pastor.bethany25@gmail.com	6565 Hemmingford Dr Canal Winchester OH 43110	OH	SP	Bethany Columbus OH	(614)866-7755	FW	2021
Shaw Kenneth B	kbs615@gmail.com	1117 Pinnacle Way Castalian Springs TN 37031	MDS	SP	Trinity Gallatin TN	(615)452-3352	FW	2002
Shaw Jason A	(573)987-8420 jshaw@stjohnslena.org	10099 E Chelsea Rd Stockton IL 61085	NI	Sn/Adm	St John Lena IL	(815)369-4035	SL	2004
Shaw Alan C	(414)574-1035 shawihs@icloud.com	1405 Hopson Downs Ct Holly Springs NC 27540	SE	SMP	Resurrection Cary NC	(919)851-7248	SL-SMP	2021
Shaw Paul C Dr	paulbeckyshaw@yahoo.com	17 Friese Dr Olivette MO 63132	MO	EM			HK	1988
Sheafer Daniel M	(260)416-2590	14915 Bristlecone Ct Fort Wayne IN 46814	IN	Assoc	Emmanuel Fort Wayne IN	(260)423-1369	FW	2016
Sheafer Mark C		8809 Hunters Knoll Run Fort Wayne IN 46825	IN	EM			FW	1988
Shearier Jeffrey E Dr	(503)746-3077 jeff.shearier@gmail.com	8061 Capt Meriwether Lewis Dr Parker CO 80134	RM	EM			SL	1984
Shearman Christopher D	(314)518-6698 chris@ldgstl.org	3100 Chippewa Street Saint Louis MO 63118	MO	RSO	Lutheran Development Group Saint Louis MO		SL	2025
Sheek Darrin D	pastorsheek@princeofpeaceana heim.org	c/o Prince Of Peace Lutheran Church 1421 W Ball Rd Anaheim CA 92802	PSW	SP	Prince Peace Anaheim CA	(714)774-0993	Other	2015
Sheets Harry C	(815)545-2091 chrissheets7040@gmail.com	6239 Micasa Ln Ooltewah TN 37363	MDS	Sn/Adm	Good Shepherd Chattanooga TN	(423)629-4661	SL	1987
Sheffler Charles	(701)256-2336 the.rev@frontier.com	1654 Forest Dr Saint Germain WI 54558	NW	SP	St Pauls Iron River MI	(906)265-4750	SL	1991
Shehab Hesham A	hicham.chehab@gmail.com	305 Pinecroft Dr Roselle IL 60172	NI	Assoc	Peace Lombard IL	(630)627-1101	FW	2009
Sheldon Barry C		247 Forest Ln Marysville MI 48040	MI	EM			FW	1983
Sheldon Michael B	(480)266-1377 pastormike@stmarkphx.org	8643 E Sells Dr Scottsdale AZ 85251	PSW	Sn/Adm	St Mark Phoenix AZ	(602)992-1980	SL	1997
Shelton Glenn M	714-864-1090 gshelton1014@gmail.com	1424 Shamrock Ln Costa Mesa CA 92626	PSW	EM			FW	1986
Shemwell Charles V	revshemwell@blcjc.org	107 W Pine St Johnson City TN 37604	MDS	SP	Bethlehem Johnson City TN	(423)926-5261	FW	2023
Sheppard Larry G	(608)586-6415 sheepdawg7@hotmail.com	227 West Ormsby St P.O. Box 273 Oxford WI 53952	SW	SP	St John* Oxford WI	(608)586-5877	FW	1999
Sheppard Sean W	(248)918-7341 sean.w.sheppard@gmail.com	4906 Fall Brook Ln Fort Wayne IN 46835	IN	Assoc	Promise Fort Wayne IN	(260)493-9953	SL	2025
Sheridan Timothy J	pastortimothysheridan@gmail.com	c/o Saint Luke Lutheran Church 616 South Fourth St Harrison MI 48625	MI	SP	St Luke Harrison MI	(989)539-6312	FW	2020
Sherman Kenneth	(386)576-3815 kensherman@stpaullakeland.org	6526 Evergreen Park Dr Lakeland FL 33818	FG	SMP	St Paul Lakeland FL	(863)644-7710	SL-SMP	2024
Sherman Travis W	(308)282-0254 pastorsherman@hotmail.com	622 Fairview Dr Gordon NE 69343	WY	SP	Our Savior* Chadron NE	(308)432-5698	SL	2012

*Multiple Assignments (See Church Worker Locator for Additional Details)
See Page 53 for the Table of Abbreviations for key to District, Position, and Seminary abbreviations
**C =Candidate; EM = Emeritus; the date following the C is the month and year the Candidate status began

NAME	TELEPHONE NUMBER EMAIL	STREET ADDRESS CITY/STATE/ZIP	DISTRICT	POSITION/ STATUS**	WHERE SERVING	OFFICE PHONE	SEM/ PROGRAM	YR GRAD
Sherouse Paul L	(850)341-3906 paulsherouse@hotmail.com	1023 Bucyrus Ln Cantonment FL 32533	SO	EM			SL	1983
Sherrill Adrian N	(303)936-8707 pastorsherrill@go2trinity.com	2518 S Dover Way Lakewood CO 80227	RM	Sn/Adm	Trinity Denver CO	(303)406-3143	FW	2001
Sherrill Nathan A	(712) 310-4248 nathansherrill1978@gmail.com	19232 Garner Ave Council Bluffs IA 51503	IW	Sn/Adm	St Pauls Council Bluffs IA	(712)322-4729	FW	2005
Sherrill North P Jr	(616)581-8353 north.sherrill@att.net		RM	Assoc	Trinity Denver CO	(303)406-3143	FW	1979
Sherry Jacob T	(231)655-2680 trinityonekama@gmail.com	5472 Fairview St Onekama MI 49675	MI	SP	Trinity Onekama MI	(231)889-4429	FW	2013
Shewmaker Russell L	(870)897-4443 russellshewmaker55@gmail.com	904 Rocky Dell Rd NE Gravette AR 72736	MDS	SP	Christ Siloam Springs AR	(870)897-4443	SL	1987
Shick Samuel A	(231)260-2943 sshick@sllcs.org	117 Bent Oak Ct Sanford FL 32773	S	Assoc	St Luke Oviedo FL	(407)365-3408	SL	2022
Shields Scott L	navychaps15@gmail.com	1360 Muskrat Way Kenai AK 99611	NOW	SP	Star Of The North Kenai AK	(907)283-4153	FW	2001
Shifflett Wallace H Jr	(434)294-9277 wsredeemed@aol.com	665 Tomlinson Rd Victoria VA 23974	SE	EM			FW	1994
Shimkus William E	(808) 384-0093 pastorrredeemer@hotmail.com	1010 NE 126th Ave Portland OR 97230	NOW	EM			CQ	1978
Shin Dong S	(206)476-3333 shalomshinn74@gmail.com	15232 Foothills Blvd #131 Sylmar CA 91342	PSW	C07/2016			SL	2006
Shirley Luke M	(478)365-6125 luke.shirley@ctsfw.edu	2810 W 10th St The Dalles OR 97058	NOW	SP	Faith The Dalles OR	(541)296-3586	FW	2025
Shive Matthew D	(419)420-4973 matt.shive81@gmail.com	2524 S 12th St Sheboygan WI 53081	SW	Assoc	St Paul's Sheboygan WI	(920)452-6829	FW	2007
Shoaff Reed T	(828)632-5311 pastorshoaff@gmail.com	4046 NC Highway 16 N Taylorsville NC 28681	SE	SP	Salem Taylorsville NC	(828)632-4863	FW	2016
Shockey Mark W	(612)799-0512 mshockey@stpetersedina.org	2827 Spy Glass Drive Chaska MN 55318	MNS	Sn/Adm	St Peters Edina MN	(952)927-8400	SL	1989
Shockley Robert M	(903)922-8217 bobshockley1@gmail.com	1502 Meadowhill Drive Jacksonville TX 75766	TX	EM			CQ	2019
Shoemaker Paul E	(260)615-9580 pastorshoemaker@emanuelnh.org	13165 Malfini Trail Fort Wayne IN 46845	IN	SP	Lake George Fremont IN	(260)615-9580	FW	1978
Shorey Ralph C III	(712)204-6748 pastoroffaithsc@gmail.com	W5334 Dassow Ave Medford WI 54451	NW	SP	Trinity* Chelsea WI	(715)748-4181	SL	1995
Short Lawson K	lshort190@gmail.com	920 Linden Dr P.O. Box 496 North Bend NE 68649	NEB	SP	St Peter North Bend NE	(402)652-8215	FW	2019
Short Paul J	(573)579-4980 pjshort6548@sbcglobal.net	1563 Bunker Hill Cape Girardeau MO 63701	MO	EM			SPR	1974
Shoup Timothy J	(715)758-7303 tim@nwdlcms.org	N3969 Highline Rd P.O. Box 543 Bonduel WI 54107	NW	DP	North Wisconsin District Wausau WI	(715)845-8241	SL	1987
Shouse Tod A	(262)227-6795 tosa2655@gmail.com	14900 W Library Ln Unit 228 New Berlin WI 53151	SW	SP	Pilgrim Wauwatosa WI	(414)476-0735	FW	2010
Shreckhise Robert			MO	EM			CQ	2016
Shriner Robert W Dr	(260)343-0071 bshriner@sjlc.net	6233 E Beck Lake Rd N Kendallville IN 46755	IN	EM			FW	1987
Shrum Stephen O	(216)551-1334 pastorsteve4464@gmail.com		OH	Sn/Adm	Redeemer Convoy OH	(419)749-2167	SL	2010
Shudy David F	(715)299-0314 PastorShudy@gmail.com	c/o St John Lutheran Church 351 W Jefferson St Black River Falls WI 54615	NW	SP	St John Black River Falls WI	(715)284-7003	SL	2018
Shults Nicholas R	nick.shults@gmail.com	5308 Avocet Ct Pueblo CO 81008	RM	SP	Bethany* Pueblo CO	(719)544-5269	SL	2017
Shumate John A	(847)244-3234	10182 W Bairstow Ave Beach Park IL 60087	NI		Northern Illinois District River Forest IL	(708)449-3020	SPR	1976
Shupe Paul R	(406)662-3776 shupepr@outlook.com	P.O. Box 310 Bridger MT 59014	MT	SP	St Paul* Bridger MT	(406)662-3776	FW	2011
Shupe William J Dr	(918)331-3811 pastorshupe@rlcbvl.org	1100 Ridgewood Rd Bartlesville OK 74006	OK	SP	Redeemer Bartlesville OK	(918)333-6022	FW	2013
Sias John W Dr	(314)996-1415 john.sias@lcms.org	c/o Lutheran Church-Missouri Synod 1333 S Kirkwood Rd Saint Louis MO 63122	MO	S Ex/S	The LCMS Corporate Saint Louis MO	(314)965-9000	FW	2009
Sidwell David H III	(269)808-1705 dhsidwell19@gmail.com	3036 Valley Glenn Cir Kalamazoo MI 49004	MI	EM			SL	1997
Siebert Benjamin R	(785)262-7448 schranke@gmail.com	1228 Heritage Dr Hastings NE 68901	NEB	SP	Zion Hastings NE	(402)469-2133	FW	2013
Siedenburg Dan L	(952)567-1941 isaiah43one@hotmail.com	9700 Portland Ave S Unit 327 Bloomington MN 55420	MNS	EM			FW	1980
Siefert Gary L	pastorsiefert@comcast.net	256 Monroe Creek Dr. Midway FL 32343	FG	EM			FW	1996
Sieg David C	(706)258-3813 dcsieg@yahoo.com	P.O. Box 2402 Gainesville GA 30503	FG	EM			FW	2002
Siegel Jeffrey A	(515)868-7456 pr.jsiegel@gmail.com	3933 Richmond Ave Des Moines IA 50317	IW	EM			FW	2007
Siegert Mark W	(949)278-8805 marksiegert60@gmail.com	160-G N Mine Canyon Rd Orange CA 92869	PSW	Tchr	Crean Irvine CA	(949)387-1199	Other	2011
Siegfried Arthur W	(509)662-2464	3685 School St Wenatchee WA 98801	NOW	EM			SL	1958
Sielaff Ralph L	RLSielaff@aol.com	1014 Glenn Ct Roanoke IN 46783	IN	EM			FW	2002
Sielk William A	(786)399-8765 pastorsielk@yahoo.com	9810 SW 84th St Miami FL 33173	FG	SP	San Pablo Apostol* Miami FL	(305)271-3171	FW	1985
Siepert Dagan W	(254)206-0258 parsonsiepert@gmail.com	51 Hakala Dr New Ipswich NH 03071	NE	SP	Our Redeemer New Ipswich NH	(603)878-1837	FW	2019
Sieveking Paul G Dr	(515)570-3144 sievekingpg@gmail.com	1539 Bent Oak Ridge Dr Fenton MO 63026	IW	EM			SL	1976

*Multiple Assignments (See Church Worker Locator for Additional Details)
See Page 53 for the Table of Abbreviations for key to District, Position, and Seminary abbreviations
**C =Candidate; EM = Emeritus; the date following the C is the month and year the Candidate status began

NAME	TELEPHONE NUMBER EMAIL	STREET ADDRESS CITY/STATE/ZIP	DISTRICT	POSITION/ STATUS**	WHERE SERVING	OFFICE PHONE	SEM/ PROGRAM	YR GRAD
Sievers Kenneth W	(314)846-1674 pastorsievers@yahoo.com	5840 Hunter Brook Ct Saint Louis MO 63129	MO	EM			SL	1972
Sievers Philip D	(219) 929-8030 philip73@comcast.net	201 Andover Dr Valparaiso IN 46383	IN	EM			FW	2010
Sifuentes Cesar G	(312)636-6496	620 Newbury Ln Schaumburg IL 60173	NI	SP	St Matthew Chicago IL	(312)636-6496	CQ	1982
Sigmon Chris L	(260)416-8634 sigmonchris5@gmail.com	1640 State Route 108 Wauseon OH 43567	OH	SP	St Luke Wauseon OH	(419)335-9170	FW	2003
Signore Joseph D III	(352)237-2233 pastorsignore@gmail.com	5200 SW College Rd Ocala FL 34474	FG	SP	Our Redeemer Ocala FL	(352)237-2233	SL	2013
Siikavirta M S	(260)452-2100 samuli.siikavirta@ctsfw.edu	1 Martin Luther Dr Fort Wayne IN 46825	IN	S HS/C	Concordia Theological Seminary Fort Wayne IN	(260)452-2100	Other	2015
Sikora Edward A Sr Dr	(517)669-3930 revsikora@gmail.com	7210 W Howe Rd Dewitt MI 48820	MI	Sn/Adm	Hope Dewitt MI	(517)669-3930	SL	1999
Silber Timothy P		1211 Eagleshire Dr Manchester MO 63021	NI	EM			SL	1984
Simek Brett E	(618)410-9827 rev.simek@gmail.com	5921 S Hosta Ave Sioux Falls SD 57108	SD	SP	Our Redeemer Sioux Falls SD	(605)338-6957	FW	2015
Simmerman Jerrell S Dr	(317)418-5509 simmerman.js@gmail.com	7806 Hardwick Pl Fishers IN 46038	IN	SP	Emanuel Arcadia IN	(317)418-5509	FW-D	2007
Simmons Arthur G	(573)825-3552 revart2013@gmail.com	3700 S Lenoir St Apt G27 Columbia MO 65201	MO	EM			SL	1970
Simmons Christopher M	(630)670-9064 pastor@trinitypaso.com	940 Moran Ct Paso Robles CA 93446	CNH	Sn/Adm	Trinity Paso Robles CA	(805)238-3702	SL	2021
Simmons Patrick S	(952)451-0940 pastorpat@smlcb.org	10608 Wyoming Rd S Bloomington MN 55438	MNS	Sn/Adm	St Michaels Bloomington MN	(952)831-5276	SL	2008
Simmons Ronald C	(573)701-7781 datasimmons@hotmail.com	504 E 3rd St Stover MO 65078	MO	EM			FW	1985
Simmons William T	wtsimmons524@gmail.com	3025 Woodbridge Creek Dr Saint Louis MO 63129	MO	EM			FW	1979
Simon Fredrick A	(402)670-0522 simonfred2007@gmail.com	2205 Pilgrim Dr Bellevue NE 68123	NEB	EM			SL	1984
Simon Steven D Dr	(713)480-3191 mrnkp1@yahoo.com	735 Weidner Rd Buffalo Grove IL 60089	SO	EM			FW	1983
Simon Jordan R	(519)564-9955 jordansimon82@yahoo.ca	3627 Wells Windsor ON N9C 1 CANADA	EN	Asst	Gethsemane Windsor ON	(519)969-7561	SL	2012
Simon Henry A	(239)208-2260 hsimon8100@comcast.net	10129 Crepe Myrtle Fort Myers FL 33913	FG	EM			SL	1972
Simoneaux Brandon J	(504)812-8445 brandon84@aol.com	2545 Cedarlawn Dr Marrero LA 70072	SO	SP	Christ Our Savior Harvey LA	(504)348-1212	FW	2002
Simonson David L	(515)297-2046 davesimonson@netins.net	1211 Lake Drive Avenue Spirit Lake IA 51360	IW	EM			SL	1985
Simpson Andrew M	(586)907-2564 andrews48093@gmail.com	134 W Butler St Bad Axe MI 48413	MI	SP	Our Savior Bad Axe MI	(989)269-7642	SL	2021
Simpson Ronald L	(405)230-0835 pastor@gslok.org	2413 SW 113th Ter Oklahoma City OK 73170	OK	SP	Good Shepherd Midwest City OK	(405)732-2585	SL	1988
Simpson Scott E	(910)987-2619 scottsimpson1931@gmail.com	112 Walnut Wood Trl Blythewood SC 29016	SE	Asst	Holy Trinity Columbia SC	(803)799-7224	SL	1999
Sims Timothy A	(414)202-6165 timoteosims@hotmail.com	637 White Oak Dr Chester IL 62233	SI	Sn/Adm	St John Chester IL	(618)826-3545	SL	2006
Sims Timothy E	(260)493-1153 simsftw@myyahoo.com	925 Koehlinger Dr New Haven IN 46774	IN	EM			SL	1964
Sims Raleigh N	(407)327-4333 raleigh.sims@gmail.com	638 Blenheim Loop Winter Spgs FL 32708	FG	SMP	Ascension Casselberry FL	(407)831-7788	SL-SMP	2013
Sinatra Nicholas J	(712)344-9218 pastorsinatra@pm.me		IW	SP	St John Sanborn IA	(712)729-3800	FW	2025
Sinclair Kenneth E	(713)269-4070 pastorken@faithsugarland.org	8130 Blase Rd Rosenberg TX 77471	TX	EM			SL	1971
Singer Bradley J	(301)304-5773 pastor@peaceinchrist.org	8798 Adventure Ave Walkersville MD 21793	SE	Sn/Adm	Peace In Christ Walkersville MD	(301)845-6300	SL	2021
Singer Christopher M	(224)813-2411 csinger@lutheranchurchchari-ties.org	3020 Milwaukee Ave Northbrook IL 60062	NI	RSO	Lutheran Church Charities Northbrook IL	(866)455-6466	SL	2003
Singh Mohan P	(917)254-2597 patrick204642003@yahoo.com	14 Division St Schenectady NY 12304	AT	SP	Trinity Schenectady NY	(518)346-5646	SL	2011
Singh Sam S	(917)402-1928 pastorsamssingh@yahoo.com	107 Crest Ave Elmont NY 11003	AT	EM			CQ	2007
Sipe Larry R Jr	(507)835-2621 revsipe@gmail.com	31184 W Wilton River Rd Waseca MN 56093	MNS	SP	St John* Minnesota Lake MN		FW	1996
Sipes Timothy A	(562)435-3265 timsbeach67@gmail.com	619 Cedar Ave Apt 12 Long Beach CA 90802	PSW	EM			SL	1984
Sipes Jacob A	(812)569-3365 jacob.sipes@imlutheran.org	713 Sydney Ct Washington MO 63090	MO	Assoc	Immanuel Washington MO	(636)239-4705	SL	2023
Sipes Phillip L	(714)282-8003 pastorsipes@hotmail.com	306 E Riverdale Ave Orange CA 92865	PSW	EM			FW	1979
Sippy Jeffrey E	(417)444-3632 sippy091208@gmail.com	P.O. Box 5 Bolivar MO 65613	MO	SP	Zion* Bolivar MO	(417)326-5506	SL	1988
Sirek Steven B	(402)488-4390 sbsirek@gmail.com	5625 La Salle St Lincoln NE 68516	NEB	EM			CQ	1997
Sizemore Paul C	(386)882-5267 paulsizemore5@gmail.com	517 Thornewood Ct Columbia SC 29212	FG	EM			SL	1981
Skarda Michael A	(603) 913-4208 mskarda@rlclebanon.org	321 Village Hill Road Lebanon CT 06249	NE	SP	Redeemer Lebanon CT	(860)423-4320	FW	2024
Skeesick Dale A	(618)792-2685 daleskeesick@yahoo.com	1315 Lexington Dr Collinsville IL 62234	SI	Asst	Holy Cross Collinsville IL	(618)344-3145	SL	1992

*Multiple Assignments (See Church Worker Locator for Additional Details)

See Page 53 for the Table of Abbreviations for key to District, Position, and Seminary abbreviations

**C =Candidate; EM = Emeritus; the date following the C is the month and year the Candidate status began

NAME	TELEPHONE NUMBER EMAIL	STREET ADDRESS CITY/STATE/ZIP	DISTRICT	POSITION/ STATUS**	WHERE SERVING	OFFICE PHONE	SEM/ PROGRAM	YR GRAD
Skelton Bruce A	(303)683-1300 holycrosspastor@aol.com	3617 Seramonte Dr Hghlnds Ranch CO 80129	RM	SP	Holy Cross Highlands Ranch CO	(303)683-1300	FW	1992
Skopak Jeffrey E Dr	(520)247-9045 rvskopak@aol.com	46 Mayday St Asheville NC 28806	SE	Sn/Adm	Emmanuel Asheville NC	(828)252-1795	SL	1992
Skov Clare B Dr	(719)375-4771 pastorc_skov@hotmail.com	17415 N 99th Dr Sun City AZ 85373	PSW	EM			CQ	1982
Skov Stephen E	skovstephen@gmail.com		IN	EM			SPR	1968
Skovgaard Eric C	(262)352-1461 eskovgaard@egl.org	945 Terrace Dr Elm Grove WI 53122	SW	Sn/Adm	Elm Grove Elm Grove WI	(262)797-2970	SL	2000
Skurla Dale G	(301)481-7200 revdgs2001@yahoo.com	971 Custer Ln Prescott AZ 86305	KS	SP	St Paul Leavenworth KS	(913)682-0387	SL	2000
Slater Troy L	(785) 512-9505 slatertroy@outlook.com	703 26th Ave Canton KS 67428	KS	SP	Immanuel Canton KS	(620)628-4801	SL	2003
Slavens Douglas J	(314)348-5487 djslavens@yahoo.com	5000 S Western Ave Sioux Falls SD 57108	SD	Assoc	Memorial Sioux Falls SD	(605)334-7133	SL	2019
Sletten Jacob E	(310)483-2280 waterandtheword@outlook.com	c/o Trinity 207 N Main St Freistatt MO 65654	MO	SP	Trinity Freistatt MO	(417)235-7300	SL	2009
Sloter John A	(515)230-1362 alexsloter@hotmail.com	910 S Carroll St Rock Rapids IA 51246	IW	SP	English* Larchwood IA	(712)477-2387	SL	2020
Sluder Jason B	(864)784-0691 jason.sluder328@gmail.com	P.O. Box 63083 Mcbh Kaneohe Bay HI 96863	SE	M Chap	Office of International Mission Saint Louis MO		CQ	2023
Small David C	(609) 975-9751 dsmall@calvary-medford.org	3 Eayrestown Rd Calvary Lutheran Church Medford NJ 08055	NJ	SP	Calvary Medford NJ	(609)654-2489	SL	2018
Small Terry S	(319)594-6392 smallts@gmail.com	13486 211th Ave NW Elk River MN 55330	MNS	EM			SL	1995
Smidt Donald D	(602)548-8536 ssninaz@cox.net	1535 E Meadow Ln Phoenix AZ 85022	PSW	EM			SPR	1968
Smiles Jeffrey A	(920) 407-1094 revjasmiles@yahoo.com	N7530 Church St Manawa WI 54949	NW	SP	St Luke* Big Falls WI	(920)596-3241	SL	1994
Smith Robert E	cosmithb@msn.com	315 Carroll Rd. Fort Wayne IN 46845	IN	EM			SL	1985
Smith Kelly D Jr	(605)299-2559 smith.kjr@gmail.com	140 Bissell St White Lake WI 54491	NW	SP	St Matthew White Lake WI	(715)882-3111	FW	2010
Smith Kelly D Sr	(720)527-6731 heavenl@gmail.com		RM	C09/2017			FW	1991
Smith Logan S	(314)406-6761 loganssmith57@gmail.com	61 W Main St Trimont MN 56176	MNS	SP	Trinity* Trimont MN	(507)639-4111	FW	2025
Smith Garrett L	(979)209-9304 glsiv54@gmail.com	1000 Steamboat Dr Hewitt TX 76643	TX	C03/2025			SL	2015
Smith Mark D	(260)775-0140 mdsmith2038@msn.com	P.O. Box 424 Sequim WA 98382	NOW	EM			FW	2009
Smith Mark S Dr	(636)220-1244 barbarajsmith@charter.net	1044 Medoc Ct Chesterfield MO 63017	MO	EM			SL	1979
Smith Randall J	(979)220-4439 randall_j_smith@juno.com	5013 Church Ln North Zulch TX 77872	TX	SP	Bethlehem North Zulch TX	(936)399-5563	FW	2006
Smith Ray L Jr	(405)820-5256 dropset54@hotmail.com	29270 N 2840 Road Okarche OK 73762	OK	EM			SL	2003
Smith William P		4335 Van Dyke Ave. San Diego CA 92105	PSW	SP	Good Shepherd San Diego CA	(619)284-7228	CQ	2017
Smith Robert E	(760)485-5171 revs455@verizon.net	43-629 Hollyhock St Indio CA 92201	PSW	SP	Trinity Indio CA	(760)347-3971	FW	1985
Smith Robert W	(989)295-8494 rwsmith316@yahoo.com	535 W Genesee St Unit E Frankenmuth MI 48734	MI	EM			FW	1986
Smith Ronald E	570-956-5623 resrev61@pa.metrocast.net	657 Winterthur Way Easton PA 18040	EA	EM			SL	1961
Smith Samuel S	(217)260-1708 samuel.smith@ctsfw.edu	931 Woodbury Ln Charleston IL 61920	CI	SP	Immanuel Charleston IL	(217)345-3008	FW	2025
Smith Sean R	revseansmith@icloud.com	1145 Presto Ct Adams TN 37010	MDS	Sn/Adm	Grace Clarksville TN	(931)647-6750	SL	2011
Smith Steven N	(262)375-4325 steve.smith@cuw.edu	1661 Devonshire Dr Cedarburg WI 53012	SW	EM			SL	1989
Smith Timothy D	(715)216-0754 smitht@trinitynet.org	1407 26th St NW Rochester MN 55901	MNS	Assoc	Trinity Rochester MN	(507)289-1531	SL	2019
Smith Wiley J	(909)794-0402 ctklutheranpax@verizon.net	1566 Campus Ave Redlands CA 92374	PSW	SP	Christ King Redlands CA	(909)793-5703	FW	1995
Smith William G Jr	(417)309-1826 javaswiller@gmail.com	308 E 1st St Appleton City MO 64724	MO	SP	Trinity Appleton City MO	(660)476-5438	FW	2019
Smith Justin M	(475)414-1199 smith.justinmatthew@gmail.com	5155 Park Ave Minneapolis MN 55417	MNS	C10/2021			SL	2015
Smith Richard K	(330)413-4865 pastorkip@comcast.net	9548 Carriage Ln Fort Wayne IN 46804	IN	EM			SL	1981
Smith Brent D Dr	(703)713-2851 brent.d.smith@gmail.com	9904 S 175th Cir Omaha NE 68136	NEB	Sn/Adm	Divine Shepherd Omaha NE	(402)895-1500	SL	2001
Smith Aaron R	(702)374-3939 arsmith40@gmail.com	1525 N Elm St Escondido CA 92026	PSW	Sn/Adm	Grace Escondido CA	(760)745-0831	SL	2006
Smith Alexander K	(262)353-1050 aksmithcuw@gmail.com	11087 Gravois Rd Apt 302 Saint Louis MO 63126	MO	Tchr	Lutheran South Saint Louis MO	(314)631-1400	SL	2022
Smith Alexander L	(712)267-0747 revalexsmith24@gmail.com	3800 Glen Oaks Blvd #133 Sioux City IA 51104	IW	Assoc	Calvary Sioux City IA	(712)239-1575	SL	2024
Smith George E	(865)482-6695 surgeon@gesmithmd.com	12 Presidential Dr Oak Ridge TN 37830	MDS	SMP	Faith Oak Ridge TN	(865)483-5431	CQ	2018
Smith Bradley A	(586)264-1320 bsmith@stjohnfraser.org	36350 Clifford Dr Sterling Hts MI 48312	MI	Sn/Adm	St John Fraser MI	(586)293-0333	FW	1988

*Multiple Assignments (See Church Worker Locator for Additional Details)
See Page 53 for the Table of Abbreviations for key to District, Position, and Seminary abbreviations
**C =Candidate; EM = Emeritus; the date following the C is the month and year the Candidate status began

NAME	TELEPHONE NUMBER EMAIL	STREET ADDRESS CITY/STATE/ZIP	DISTRICT	POSITION/ STATUS**	WHERE SERVING	OFFICE PHONE	SEM/ PROGRAM	YR GRAD
Smith Jeffery M	(479)422-2840 jsmith@stpaulwestlake.org	2050 Ridgeland Dr Avon OH 44011	OH	Sn/Adm	St Paul Westlake OH	(440)835-3050	SL	2015
Smith Brian K	(585)301-8564 yorkshepherd@verizon.net	65 Hagarman Dr York PA 17408	SE	SP	Good Shepherd York PA	(717)764-4746	SL	1995
Smith Bruce W	(908)812-2567 smithbrucew@msn.com	193 Milltown Rd E Brunswick NJ 08816	NJ	EM			FW-D	2003
Smith Charles A Jr	(252) 269-0024 charlessmithsmith69@gmail.com	5100 Paw Paw Crossing Apt 5111 New Bern NC 28562	SE	EM			FW	1977
Smith Jacob E	(586)556-6077 jacobsmith798@yahoo.com	214 7th Ave SW Aberdeen SD 57401	SD	Assoc	St Paul Aberdeen SD	(605)225-1847	SL	2021
Smith David S Dr	(314)365-2040 pastorsmith1111@gmail.com	1834 Ridgeview Circle Dr Ballwin MO 63021	MO	EM			SL	1978
Smith Donald G	(360)452-5893 jdsmith3w7@yahoo.com	13013 Woodside Ln SW Port Orchard WA 98367	NOW	EM			FW	1993
Smith Eugene N	(909)633-2374 g34793479@gmail.com	27250 Murrieta Rd Spc 99 Sun City CA 92586	PSW	SP	Faith Riverside CA	(951)689-2626	SL	2001
Smith Frederick V	(423)886-0705 adsconsult@hotmail.com	Seyler Str 5 Berlin 14109 GERMANY	KS	EM			SL	1979
Smith Andrew D	(984)214-1422 smithad19@gmail.com	1810 Glenbridge Rd Bloomington IL 61704	CI	SP	Our Redeemer Bloomington IL	(309)662-3935	SL	1997
Smith Gary L	(602)717-0427 glnbjsmith@cox.net	8941 W Wedgewood Dr Peoria AZ 85382	PSW	EM			SL-SMP	2012
Smith Gordon L	way2appy@yahoo.com	524 Shields Crossing Dr. Bean Station TN 37708	MDS	SP	Our Savior* Morristown TN	(423)586-8818	SL	2008
Smith Harry R	(703)687-7333 harryreedsmith@gmail.com	1200 Fuller Wiser Rd Apt 732 Euless TX 76039	TX	Sn/Adm	Our Redeemer Irving TX	(972)255-0595	SL	2014
Smith Daniel M	(217)466-1215 revdms@gmail.com	10 Poplar Dr Paris IL 61944	CI	SP	Grace Paris IL	(217)466-1215	SL	1992
Smithley Jon W	(580)540-4694 jwsmithley@yahoo.com	3 Custer Ct Ellsworth Afb SD 57706	SI	M Chap	Office of International Mission Saint Louis MO		FW	2003
Snashall Gleason G	(619)246-8796 gleason.snashall@gmail.com	811 4th St Coronado CA 92118	EN	C06/2020			FW-SMP	2015
Sneath Michael W	(901)530-1575 msneath@aol.com	12 Nugent Dr Stafford VA 22554	NI	M Chap	Office of International Mission Saint Louis MO		SL	1998
Snider Brett N	(386)562-7057 mrpreacherman@gmail.com	15 Bird Tree Pl Palm Coast FL 32137	FG	Assoc	Holy Cross South Daytona FL	(386)767-6542	SL	2007
Snider Merelyn R	(734) 680-6260 pstrsnider@yahoo.com	13817 Gilbert Dr Peyton CO 80831	RM	EM			CQ	1998
Snoberger Adam J	pastoradam@tlcgi.org	212 W 12th St Grand Island NE 68801	NEB	Sn/Adm	Trinity Grand Island NE	(308)382-0753	SL	2012
Snow Scott A	(316)927-3046 ps@holycrosslutheran.net	15320 E Windham Ct Wichita KS 67230	KS	Assoc	Holy Cross Wichita KS	(316)684-5201	SL	1983
Snow Gregory J	(952)361-0186 pastor.snow@stjohns-chaska.org	3105 Bluegrass Rd Chaska MN 55318	MNS	Sn/Adm	Saint Johns Chaska MN	(952)448-2433	SL	2000
Snow Richard L	(402)675-1444 richs@ndlcms.org	P.O. Box 407 Seward NE 68434	NEB	DP	Nebraska District Seward NE	(402)643-2961	SL	1987
Snyder William S	(850) 293-4705 snyderhouse1@gmail.com	3058 Creekwood Dr Cantonment FL 32533	SO	EM			SL-D	2009
Snyder Walter P	(660)463-7553 xrysostom@xrysostom.com	311 S Gordon St Concordia MO 64020	MO	SP	Peace* Slater MO	(660)529-2248	SL	1992
Snyder Dale O	(940)257-7340 pastorsnyder@sbcglobal.net	2616 Amherst Dr Wichita Falls TX 76308	TX	EM			SL	1998
Snyder Damian M Dr	tlcsp@inbox.com		KS	Sn/Adm	Trinity Leavenworth KS	(913)682-7474	SL	2002
Snyder Richard H	(830)522-1917 rheadleys@indian-creek.net	P.O. Box 1684 Bandera TX 78003	TX	EM			SL	1981
Sobocinski Anthony D	(937)361-3752 1sam1623@gmail.com	4164 Braewick Cir Dayton OH 45440	OH	SP	Concordia Dayton OH	(937)299-1912	CQ	1986
Soenksen Jason R Dr	(414)357-6281 jason.soenksen@cuw.edu	1724 17th Ave Grafton WI 53024	SW	S HS/C	Concordia University Wisconsin Mequon WI	(262)243-5700	SL	2001
Sohns Stephen J Dr	(832)656-5628 stephensohns@gmail.com	511 Tanguey Ct Spring TX 77388	TX	EM			FW	1984
Sohns Wilbert J Dr	(254)709-6474 sohnswill@gmail.com	110 Chicktown Rd Gatesville TX 76528	TX	EM			SL	1959
Sollberger Jon J	(402)234-5980 revsoll77@gmail.com	36712 Church Rd Louisville NE 68037	NEB	Sn/Adm	Immanuel Louisville NE	(402)234-5980	FW	2002
Sollie Galen R	grsollie@gmail.com	13918 Davis Rd Woodstock IL 60098	NI	EM			FW	1978
Soltis Thomas	(440)212-1651 tomsoltis1231@att.net	Pleasant Lake Villa 7260 Ridge Rd Parma OH 44129	S	EM			SL	1956
Solum David R	(219)873-6443 solumdr@gmail.com	2656 N Jongkind Park Rd La Porte IN 46350	IN	SP	Immanuel Michigan City IN	(219)872-4419	FW	2010
Sommer Alan J	(530)677-9536 pastor.sommer@loth.org	3100 Rodeo Rd Cameron Park CA 95682	CNH	Sn/Adm	Light of the Hills Cameron Park CA	(530)677-9536	SL	1990
Sommer Christopher	csommer@lslancers.org	5562 Fireleaf Dr Saint Louis MO 63129	MO	Cmp P	Lutheran South Saint Louis MO	(314)631-1400	SL	2016
Sommerer Steven L	(309)341-4430 revsommerer@sbcglobal.net	1346 W Fremont St Galesburg IL 61401	CI	SP	Mount Calvary Galesburg IL	(309)342-7083	SL	1997
Sommerfeld Russell L Dr	(402) 641-0333 russell.sommerfeld@cune.edu	535 S Evergreen Dr Seward NE 68434	NEB	S HS/C	Concordia University Nebraska Seward NE	(402)643-3651	SL	1980
Sommerfeld Scott G Dr	(616)669-5163	9169 Lakewood Drive Whitmore Lake MI 48189	MI	Sn/Adm	Shep Lakes Brighton MI	(810)227-5099	SL	1987

*Multiple Assignments (See Church Worker Locator for Additional Details)
See Page 53 for the Table of Abbreviations for key to District, Position, and Seminary abbreviations
**C =Candidate; EM = Emeritus; the date following the C is the month and year the Candidate status began

NAME	TELEPHONE NUMBER EMAIL	STREET ADDRESS CITY/STATE/ZIP	DISTRICT	POSITION/ STATUS**	WHERE SERVING	OFFICE PHONE	SEM/ PROGRAM	YR GRAD
Son DongSu	(972)835-0938 grace42church@gmail.com	1404 Limestone Creek Dr Keller TX 76248	TX	SP	Grace Korean Watauga TX	(817)427-2909	CQ	2018
Song Joseph C	(404)429-9072 jchsong@hotmail.com	2637 Ashley Oaks Ct Duluth GA 30096	FG	RSO	Stepping Stone Mission Inc Duluth GA	(404)429-9072	CQ	1999
Song C B Dr	(253)838-4599 cbensong@hotmail.com	34950 7th Ave SW Federal Way WA 98023	NOW	EM			CQ	1980
Song Jin Y	(714)403-6803 danisong99@naver.com	8781 Walker St #5 Cypress CA 90630	PSW	Assoc	Good News Korean Buena Park CA	(714)681-6770	CQ	2016
Sonnenberg Roger R	(626) 232-0797 sonnenr5@gmail.com	31 N Olympic View Ave Sequim WA 98382	PSW	EM			SL	1971
Sonnenschein Gregory A	(307)349-3736 lcmsman@hotmail.com	P.O. Box 707 Dubois WY 82520	WY	SP	Mount Calvary* Dubois WY	(307)349-3736	FW	2009
Sonntag Donaldo	(573)253-1594 pastorsonntag@gmail.com	3785 Lynnwood Dr Mexico MO 65265	MO	SP	St John Mexico MO	(573)581-5655	Other	1984
Sorensen Robert A Dr	(708)712-9678 robert.sorensen@cuchicago.edu	11114 84th Pl Willow Springs IL 60480	NI	S HS/C	Concordia University Chicago River Forest IL	(708)771-8300	SL	1989
Sorensen David E	(414)813-9072 desor1119@gmail.com	8073 S Chapel Hill Dr Franklin WI 53132	SW	EM			FW	1977
Sorensen James T	(402)432-5090 jtsorensen1@gmail.com	132 Starbuck Circle Box 4 Salida CO 81201	RM	SP	Faith* Buena Vista CO	(719)395-2039	SL	2014
Sorenson Robert H	(434) 390-6321 bs.sorenson@gmail.com	307 First Ave Farmville VA 23901	SE	EM			SPR	1965
Sorenson Matthew D	(434)392-1875 pastor@stjohnsfarmville.org	1003 2nd Avenue Ext Farmville VA 23901	SE	SP	St John Farmville VA	(434)392-1875	NESC	2009
Sorenson Lowell S Dr	(651)388-4577 immanuellcms@yahoo.com	24686 Old Church Rd Red Wing MN 55066	MNS	SP	Immanuel Hay Creek MN	(651)388-4577	FW	2004
Sorenson Grant A	(317)690-5204 gsorenson13@sbcglobal.net	2103 Walden Dr Bedford IN 47421	IN	SP	Calvary Bedford IN	(812)275-5488	FW	2020
Sorenson Erik J	(812)371-1151	11750 W 930 S Columbus IN 47201	IN	SP	St Peter Waymansville IN	(812)343-1688	FW	2018
Sorenson Adam L	(440)375-1008 pastor.adam.sorenson@gmail.com		IN	SP	Faith Churubusco IN	(260)693-6254	FW	2009
Sorenson Andrew J	(727)729-2576 rev.a.sorenson@paxdeo.org	1620 Pinehurst Rd Dunedin FL 34698	FG	SP	Faith Dunedin FL	(727)733-2657	SL-D	2012
Souer Eric D	(704)491-7671 ericsouer@gmail.com	P.O. Box 68 Oxford NE 68967	NEB	SP	St John Oxford NE	(308)824-3269	FW	2022
Sound John S Dr	(540)868-2582 prsound@msn.com	100 Glasgow Ct Stephens City VA 22655	SE	EM			FW	1991
Sovitzky Richard IV	(260)804-2489 richard.sovitzky@ctsfw.edu	c/o Trinity Lutheran Church 7120 Sponagle Rd Sugar Grove OH 43155	OH	SP	Trinity Sugar Grove OH	(740)281-7593	FW	2024
Sowers Timothy E	(850)781-9159 timothy.e.sowers@live.com	4200 Griffis Rd Milton FL 32583	SO	EM			SL	1985
Soyk Kenneth A		824 W Birch Ave Mitchell SD 57301	SD	EM			FW	2004
Spaeth David M	(309)620-9987 chapcptdave@hotmail.com	1604 Summit Dr Pekin IL 61554	CI	EM			CQ	1986
Spaeth Marc D	(352)272-2005 pastormarcspaeth@aol.com	19807 E Fifth St Umatilla FL 32784	FG	EM			SL	1984
Spallek Peter J	(928)660-8675 spallek1@msn.com	1021 S. Greenfield Rd #1157 Mesa AZ 85206	PSW	EM			SL	2007
Spang Bryan J	(814)308-3417 pastorbspang@gmail.com	946 Kathryn St Boalsburg PA 16827	EA	SP	Good Shepherd State College PA	(814)234-8177	FW	2004
Spangler Solomon K	(810)923-6489 Sol.Spangler@gmail.com	25705 Ronald St Roseville MI 48066	EN	SP	Christ King Grosse Pointe Woods MI	(313)884-5090	FW	2024
Spangler Isaac M	(740)304-4709 revspangler@purelymail.com	1018 Cicero Rd Edgerton OH 43517	OH	SP	Zion Edgerton OH	(419)298-2594	FW	2025
Sparling Daniel P	(609)500-5027 daniel.sparling@gmail.com	224 Fairview Rd Blairsville GA 30512	FG	SP	Good Shepherd Gainesville GA	(770)532-2428	SL	2005
Sparling Patrick R	(402)276-4137	3352 36th Ave Columbus NE 68601	NEB	Sn/Adm	Immanuel Columbus NE	(402)564-0502	SL	1993
Spaulding Benjamin A	(585)588-1756	136 S Washington St Oxford MI 48371	MI	SP	Journey Oxford MI	(248)628-2011	SL	2020
Spaulding Nathan W	(586)588-1753 brokenbeloved33@gmail.com	810 South Roosevelt St - Upper Green Bay WI 54301	NW	C08/2019			SL	2017
Speaks Keith A	(224) 573-8985 pastorkeith@trinityroselle.com	12374 W. Virginia Cir. Unit 2 Franklin WI 53132	NI	Sn/Adm	Trinity Roselle IL	(630)894-3263	SL	1990
Speckhard Peter A	(219)741-6270 pspeckhard@hotmail.com	8434 Jackson Ct Munster IN 46321	IN	Sn/Adm	St Paul Munster IN	(219)836-6270	SL	1997
Speckhard Daniel A	(219)508-6043 speckhard@stpeternorthjudson.org	2340 E 800 S North Judson IN 46366	IN	SP	St Peter North Judson IN	(574)896-2025	FW	2015
Speckhard Michael P	(219)252-7941 michael.speckhard@stpeterhemlock.org	320 Sandridge Dr Hemlock MI 48626	MI	Assoc	St Peter Hemlock MI	(989)642-8188	FW	2025
Speerbrecker Paul E	(608) 774-9720 pespeer1@juno.com	3805 Old Klerner Ln New Albany IN 47150	IN	EM			SL	1979
Speerbrecker Nathan D	(763)234-6739 nathanspeerbrecker@gmail.com	1204 Roble Ct Chesapeake VA 23322	SE	SP	Community of Hope Chesapeake VA	(757)436-0079	SL	2021
Speerbrecker David W Dr	(708)539-8236 speerbrecker@att.net	2727 South Lakeshore Dr Apt 30 Saint Joseph MI 49085	MI	EM			SL	1980
Speers David R	(618)483-6993 dspeers@altamont.net	5088 E 1400th Ave Altamont IL 62411	CI	SP	St Paul Altamont IL	(618)483-6993	FW	1989
Spelbring Christopher A	(618)233-2299 cspelbring@zionbelleville.org	2292 Birmingham Dr Belleville IL 62221	SI	Sn/Adm	Zion Belleville IL	(618)233-2299	SL	2011

*Multiple Assignments (See Church Worker Locator for Additional Details)
See Page 53 for the Table of Abbreviations for key to District, Position, and Seminary abbreviations
**C =Candidate; EM = Emeritus; the date following the C is the month and year the Candidate status began

NAME	TELEPHONE NUMBER EMAIL	STREET ADDRESS CITY/STATE/ZIP	DISTRICT	POSITION/ STATUS**	WHERE SERVING	OFFICE PHONE	SEM/ PROGRAM	YR GRAD
Spelzhausen Mark H	(910)616-9532 spelznc@yahoo.com	914 Fitzgerald Dr Wilmington NC 28405	SE	EM			SL	1972
Spence Kenneth M	(734)775-8337 kenneth.spence0412@gmail.com	109 Greenridge Dr Monongahela PA 15063	EA	EM			FW	2000
Spencer Steven D	(971) 372-1430 pastorsdspencer@outlook.com	1895 Corina Dr SE Salem OR 97302	NOW	EM			FW	2003
Spencer Lynn E	(402)525-8552	3506 SW Briar Creek Ave Bentonville AR 72713	MDS	EM			FW	1981
Sperb Christopher N	(410)852-4478 sperbc@gmail.com	6412 Bonnie Brae Rd Sykesville MD 21784	SE	Sn/Adm	Faith Eldersburg MD	(410)795-8082	SL	2006
Spicer George A	(623)547-6601 gspicer2@cox.net	9656 W Kimberly Way Peoria AZ 85382	PSW	EM			SL	1997
Spiehs Leonard S	(605)354-1771 rev1spiehs@aol.com	P.O. Box 327 Wolsey SD 57384	SD	Sn/Adm	Mount Olive* Woonsocket SD	(605)796-4141	FW	1991
Spilker Gaylord J	(618)267-5673 gspilker@onemain.com	P.O. Box 259 Edinburg IL 62531	CI	SP	Trinity Edinburg IL	(618)267-5673	SL	2002
Spilman Robert C	(716)839-4316 rcspilman@roadrunner.com	363 Darwin Dr Amherst NY 14226	EA	EM			SL	1972
Spira Ethan P			IN	SP	Lord of Life Westfield IN	(317)867-5673	FW	2018
Spittel Douglas H Dr	(412)606-1151 dspittel@gmail.com	6216 Quillen Dr Chincoteague VA 23336	EN	S Ex/S	Concordia University System Saint Louis MO	(314)996-1252	FW	1990
Spitzenberger Raymond D Dr	(979)335-6170 rspastorpal405@gmail.com	P.O. Box 575 East Bernard TX 77435	TX	EM			CQ	2000
Splett David L	(319)830-3022 revdav1950@gmail.com	505 25th St Ames IA 50010	IW	EM			SL	1977
Splitgerber William F	(352)243-5754 billsplit@mac.com	4114 Hammersmith Dr Clermont FL 34711	FG	EM			SL	1960
Spomer Arthur J Dr	(918) 724-4707 aspomer@cox.net	3708 N Battle Creek Dr Broken Arrow OK 74012	OK	EM			SL	1964
Spomer Charles W Dr	(314)704-1732 spo.mer@sbcglobal.net	238 Collinwood Dr Burlington NC 27215	SE	SP	Redeemer Burlington NC	(336)227-7092	SL	1973
Spomer Philip T	(505)379-1207 pastorspomer@msn.com	3115 Egret Ter Safety Harbor FL 34695	RM	EM			FW	1987
Sponaugle Justin C	(573)625-0709 jsponaug@gmail.com	14501 Pinnon Ln Dexter MO 63841	MO	SP	Zion* Poplar Bluff MO	(573)785-3936	SL	2011
Spooner Dean H	(618) 384-5291 OurSaviorLutheran@protonmail.com	1102 Jill St Carmi IL 62821	SI	Sn/Adm	Our Savior Carmi IL	(618)384-5291	FW	1995
Spratt Aaron D	(360)969-6869 aaron.d.spratt@gmail.com	2512 Sunset Dr Juneau AK 99881	NOW	SP	Faith Juneau AK	(907)789-7568	FW	2017
Sprehe Ronald R	(716)200-7867 revrsprehe@gmail.com	169 Amber Trail Sun Prairie WI 53590	EA	EM			CQ	1980
Sprengle James J	pastor@sprengle.com	1440 SE 182nd Ave Portland OR 97233	NOW	SP	Ascension Portland OR	(503)665-8821	SL	2008
Sprick Donovan J	(636)226-4698 desprick@gmail.com	40 Meramec Trail Dr Apt 100 Ballwin MO 63021	MO	EM			SL	1962
Sprick Lloyd E	(785)252-3317 lsprick@hbcomm.net	P.O. Box 147 Holyrood KS 67450	KS	EM			SL	1962
Springer Jeffrey D	jeff.springer@icloud.com	4340 Doenges Dr Fort Wayne IN 46815	IN	EM			FW	2006
Springer Joel W	(248)818-0742 joelspringer20@gmail.com	3209 Dorchester Dr Springfield IL 62704	CI	SMP	Our Savior's Springfield IL	(217)546-4531	SL-SMP	2024
Springer Martin R	(815)529-3884 marspring1957@gmail.com	1314 Evergreen Parkway SW Unit X Olympia WA 98502	NOW	EM			SL	2000
Sproul John M Dr	(314)795-9539 johnsproul3@gmail.com	7966 Lake Crest Dr Ypsilanti MI 48197	MI	EM			NESC	1988
Squire Mark R	(641)713-4753 pastorsquire@myomnitel.com	312 W 5th St P.O. Box 78 Saint Ansgar IA 50472	IE	SP	Immanuel Saint Ansgar IA	(641)713-4782	SL	2011
Squires Benjamin C Dr	(224)419-5519	Bethel Lutheran Church 5110 Grand Avenue Gurnee IL 60031	NI	SP	Bethel Gurnee IL	(847)244-9647	SL	2000
St Jean Thomas R	(562)305-7225 tstjean@ymail.com	64 Westwood Village Dr Trinity TX 75862	TX	SP	Grace Crockett TX	(936)544-3508	CQ	1983
St John Samuel M	(520) 297-3095 s.stjohn@alcs-az.org	1220 W Magee Rd Tucson AZ 85704	EN	Assoc	Ascension Tucson AZ	(520)297-3095	SL	2022
St Onge Charles P	charles.p.stonge@gmail.com	244 21e Ave Deux-Montagnes QC J7R 4 CANADA	S	Sn/Adm	Ascension* Montreal QC	(438)490-3698	FW	2003
St Pierre Marvin F			CNH	SMP	St John Bakersfield CA	(661)665-7815	SL-SMP	2022
Stacy Eric T	(515)343-0946 stacye@csl.edu	10015 Lance Dr Bellefontaine Neighbors MO 63137	MO	Assoc	Grace Chapel Bellefontaine Nghbrs MO	(314)868-3232	SL	2020
Stadler Erik W	(281)703-7686 aggie0108@gmail.com	824 E 18th St Odessa TX 79761	TX	SP	Redeemer Odessa TX	(806)416-0951	FW	1998
Stadler Richard H	(651)338-8621 ps007@hushmail.com	1684 Oakbrooke Ct Eagan MN 55122	MNS	EM			CQ	2020
Staehr Zachary A	(308)218-9705 zstaehr@gmail.com	373 7th St Manilla IA 51454	IW	SP	Trinity Manilla IA	(712)654-3031	FW	2024
Staffeld Timothy W	(314)752-7065 pastortim@elcstl.org	4045 Holly Hills Blvd Saint Louis MO 63116	MO	SP	Epiphany Saint Louis MO	(314)752-7065	SL	2017
Stahl Martin R	(401)841-2557 martystahl@msn.com	42954 Corte Cabello Temecula CA 92592	IN	EM			SPR	1976
Stahl Michael G	(989)980-6051 mgstahl@yahoo.com	5984 Birchcrest Dr Saginaw MI 48638	MI	Pro Stf	Valley Saginaw MI	(989)790-1676	SL	2007
Stahlecker Alan R	revalanstahlecker@hotmail.com	P.O. Box 187 Lincolnville KS 66858	KS	SP	St John Lincolnville KS	(620)924-5236	FW	1993

*Multiple Assignments (See Church Worker Locator for Additional Details)
See Page 53 for the Table of Abbreviations for key to District, Position, and Seminary abbreviations
**C =Candidate; EM = Emeritus; the date following the C is the month and year the Candidate status began

NAME	TELEPHONE NUMBER EMAIL	STREET ADDRESS CITY/STATE/ZIP	DISTRICT	POSITION/ STATUS**	WHERE SERVING	OFFICE PHONE	SEM/ PROGRAM	YR GRAD
Stahlhut Stephen C	(810)735-4707 revstahlhut@yahoo.com	410 Riverside Dr Linden MI 48451	MI	EM			SL	1974
Stainbrook Michael S	(517) 599-1378 pastormstainbrook@knowing jesus.org	2594 Mount Hope Rd Okemos MI 48864	MI	Assoc	St Luke Haslett MI	(517)339-9119	SL	2022
Stallings Cory S	(573)605-9225 cstal001@yahoo.com	219 N Hope St Jackson MO 63755	MO	SMP	The Exchange Jackson MO		SL-SMP	2019
Stallings Stephen S		6907 Glen Rosa Drive Katy TX 77494	TX	EM			SPR	1970
Stallworth Benjamin F Sr	(334)928-1069 bfstallworth60@gmail.com	P.O. Box 1927 Fairhope AL 36533	SO	SP	Ebenezer* Atmore AL	(251)368-4719	FW	1988
Stallworth Willie P Sr Dr	(314)724-9949 stallwortwillie@gmail.com	6160 Lucille Ave Saint Louis MO 63033	SI	SP	Unity East Saint Louis IL	(618)874-6600	SL-D	2011
Stam Bruce L	(651)345-5789 blcjstam@gmail.com	909 S 6th St Lake City MN 55041	MNS	EM			SL	1973
Stamm Shawn O	(661)917-1280 sostamm@aol.com	10921 Shoshone Ave Granada Hills CA 91344	PSW	C03/2017			FW	1996
Standfest Michael R	(515)432-8022 pastor@stpaulboone.org	295 Spruce Ln Boone IA 50036	IW	SP	Saint Paul* Boone IA	(515)432-4470	FW	2008
Standley John M	(916)801-2437 revstandley@sbcglobal.net	10067 Kern River Court Rancho Cordova CA 95670	CNH	EM			SL	2000
Staneck Matthew O	(718)847-3188 pastormstaneck@gmail.com	78-31 76th St Glendale NY 11385	AT	SP	St John Glendale NY	(718)847-3188	SL	2013
Staneck Michael C	(631)872-6331 pastormcstaneck@trinityislip.org	250 Grant Ave Islip NY 11751	AT	SMP	Trinity Islip NY	(631)277-1555	SL-SMP	2011
Stanley Stanish	(314)371-6312 sstanley@cfna-stl.org	c/o Christian Friends Of New Americans 4019 S Grand Blvd Saint Louis MO 63118	MO	RSO	Christian Friends Saint Louis MO	(314)351-1740	SL	2016
Stanley Vincent C		11120 Golf Crest Dr Saint Louis MO 63126	MO	EM			SL	2000
Stano Lester P	(301)806-1726 lessp@aol.com	7772 James Blair Ln New Kent VA 23124	SE	EM			SPR	1973
Stanton Gregg A	(414)327-1239 gregg2327@yahoo.com	3240 S 106th St West Allis WI 53227	SW	EM			FW	1989
Stanton Sanford D	(850)516-7556 sspoohbear29@gmail.com	3315 Pursell Ln Pensacola FL 32526	SO	SP	Trinity Cantonment FL	(850)607-9524	SL	1992
Stapleton Mark R	mstapleton1@comcast.net	21 N Warwick Ave Westmont IL 60559	NI	SMP	Saint Johns La Grange IL	(708)354-1690	CQ	2017
Starfeldt Chad J	(920)659-9591 chadstarfeldt@sbcglobal.net	N1467 Ellen Ln Greenville WI 54942	NW	Assoc	Shepherd Hills Greenville WI	(920)757-5722	SL	2012
Stark Brian T	(785)851-8497 brian.stark@ctsfw.edu	10532 River Rapids Run Fort Wayne IN 46845	IN	SP	Zion* Corunna IN	(260)668-0250	FW	2007
Stark Richard P	(619)318-0533 pastorrick@tlcsd.org	797 River Rock Rd Chula Vista CA 91914	PSW	SMP	Trinity San Diego CA	(619)262-1089	CQ	2019
Stark Thomas C	(972)802-0444 pastor@sjlcfrisco.com	6960 Parkwood Blvd Ste 200 Frisco TX 75034	TX	SP	Saint John The Colony TX	(469)573-0885	FW	2007
Starke Stephen P	(989)860-2441 spstarke5678@gmail.com	1693 Amelith Rd Bay City MI 48706	MI	EM			FW	1983
Starr Frank D	936-465-8611 frankstarr01@gmail.com	8 East Maple St Easthampton MA 01027	NE	EM			SL	1967
Staub Aaron J	(402) 769-9692 stauba@concordiaomaha.org	4314 N 158th Ave Omaha NE 68116	NEB	SMP	Concordia Omaha NE	(402)445-4000	SL-SMP	2018
Stauffer W R	(989)859-7571 rcstauffer@gmail.com	991 W Walter Rd Sanford MI 48657	MI	EM			SL	1982
Stauty Donald M	dpstauty@gmail.com	7606 Highway 68 Virginia MN 55792	MNN	EM			SL-D	2003
Stavig Wendell C	(832)257-2659 stavigw@trinityklein.org	184 Chestnut Bay The Woodlands TX 77382	TX	EM			SL	2008
Stebbins John T	jstebbins1105@gmail.com	4502 Walsh Dr Louisville KY 40272	IN	SP	Faith Louisville KY	(502)367-8513	FW	2016
Stechholz David P Dr	(248)470-6298 bpem1948@gmail.com	14374 Pere St Livonia MI 48154	EN	EM			FW	1978
Stecker Bryan D	(313)804-0201 bdstecker@gmail.com	1512 Pond View Ct Cologne MN 55322	MNS	Assoc	Trinity Waconia MN	(952)442-4165	FW	2018
Stecker David O	(219)493-1899 pastorstecker@emanuelnh.org	9910 N Country Knl New Haven IN 46774	IN	Assoc	Emanuel New Haven IN	(260)749-2163	FW	1998
Stecker Jerome A	(414)899-6193 martinimilw@hotmail.com	P.O. Box 72 Sherwood WI 54169	SW	EM			SL	1976
Steckling Larry L	(920)460-6200 lsteckling@yahoo.com	424 S. Raspberry Lane Apt. #10 Eagle River WI 54521	NW	EM			SL	1982
Steckling Timothy J	(906)285-3452 timothysteckling@gmail.com	1900 E Lark Ln Nixa MO 65714	MO	SP	Faith Springfield MO	(417)833-3749	SL	1998
Steeb Daniel P	(317)908-1874 daniel.steeb@ctsfw.edu	212 N 3rd Ave Logan IA 51546	IW	SP	Immanuel Logan IA	(712)644-2384	FW	2016
Steege David L	(319)215-2513 revsteg@outlook.com	1 Riverside Cir Monticello MN 55362	MNN	SP	Immanuel Albany MN	(320)845-2620	SL	1998
Steeh Edward J	(586)610-8747 edwsteeh@gmail.com	31970 Carlelder Street Beverly Hills MI 48025	EN	EM			FW	1995
Steele Walter R Dr	(214)316-1315 walter.steele@lcms.org	4916 Rushden Rd McKinney TX 75070	TX	S Miss	Office of International Mission Saint Louis MO		FW	1994
Steele Cameron K	(989)550-3355 revcameron.steele@gmail.com	1445 Eudora Dr Caro MI 48723	MI	EM			FW	1993
Steele Robert W	(920)918-9915 revrsteele@me.com	2338 Weeden Creek Rd Sheboygan WI 53081	SW	EM			FW	1997

*Multiple Assignments (See Church Worker Locator for Additional Details)
See Page 53 for the Table of Abbreviations for key to District, Position, and Seminary abbreviations
**C =Candidate; EM = Emeritus; the date following the C is the month and year the Candidate status began

NAME	TELEPHONE NUMBER EMAIL	STREET ADDRESS CITY/STATE/ZIP	DISTRICT	POSITION/ STATUS**	WHERE SERVING	OFFICE PHONE	SEM/ PROGRAM	YR GRAD
Steele Timothy C	(910)791-7040 timothycsteele@hotmail.com	6624 Wedderburn Dr Wilmington NC 28412	SE	SP	Messiah Wilmington NC	(910)791-7040	SL	2004
Steele Timothy D II	(402) 630-1047 rev.steele92@gmail.com	1520 Highland Dr Ogallala NE 69153	NEB	SP	St Paul Ogallala NE	(308)284-2944	FW	2022
Steele-Steeber Jeffrey B	(440)241-1375 jsteele-steeber@lutheranwest.com	473 Walleyford Dr Berea OH 44017	OH	Cmp P	Cleveland LHS Association Rocky River OH	(440)356-7155	CQ	2024
Steensma Richard D Jr	(816)274-2201 pastorrichsteensma@gmail.com	4670 Ambassador Rd Ashland MO 65010	MO	Sn/Adm	Faith Jefferson City MO	(573)636-4602	SL	2008
Stefanic James J	(414)305-8565 pastor@gslcmarshall.org	604 Roosevelt St Marshall MN 56258	MNS	SP	Good Shepherd Marshall MN	(507)532-4857	SL	2013
Steffen Berett J	churchoffice@stjohnbingen.com	329 N 4th St Decatur IN 46733	IN	Assoc	St John Decatur IN	(260)639-6178	FW	2022
Steffens Earl L	(229)469-7269	2828 Bud McKey Cir Valdosta GA 31602	FG	EM			SL	1974
Steffensen Ellery J	(308) 235-2582 Pastor.Steffensen@protonmail.com	615 S Locust St Kimball NE 69145	WY	SP	Immanuel* Burns WY	(308)235-2582	FW	2023
Steffenson Jason A	630-962-4044 jason.steffenson@lcms.org	c/o Lcms Office Of International Mission 1333 S Kirkwood Rd Saint Louis MO 63122	OK	S Miss	Office of International Mission Saint Louis MO		SL	2019
Stehr Ronald E	(651) 388-3792 oldtownt1@hotmail.com	33300 Kolshorn Rd Red Wing MN 55066	MNS	EM			SL	1972
Stein Donald C	(815) 624-6051 pastor@standrewrockton.com	511 W Rockton Rd Rockton IL 61072	NI	SP	St Andrew Rockton IL	(815)624-6051	SL	2022
Stein Timothy A	(715)832-9953 PastorTim@blcaltoona.org	1419 Edgewood Drive Altoona WI 54720	NW	SMP	Bethlehem Altoona WI	(715)832-9953	SL-SMP	2012
Stein Donald M Dr	(608)769-0305 revdms78@hotmail.com	217 Fiddlecreek Ridge Road Wentzville MO 63385	MO	EM			FW	1978
Stein Michael L	mlstein76@gmail.com	N89w15769 Cleveland Ave Menomonee Falls WI 53051	SW	SP	Beautiful Savior Mequon WI	(262)242-6650	SL	2020
Steinbach Walter A	(920)766-5882 wsteinb727@aol.com	1707 Fieldcrest Dr Kaukauna WI 54130	NW	EM			SL	1971
Steinbauer William J	(402)889-2965 bsteinbauer@christlincoln.org	1201 Twin Ridge Rd Lincoln NE 68510	NEB	Assoc	Christ Lincoln NE	(402)483-7774	SL	1992
Steinbeck Allen L	(805)591-9883 allensteinbeck@gmail.com	4950 Union Rd Paso Robles CA 93446	CNH	C10/2024			SL	1988
Steinberg Donald E	(920)927-5734 immanuellc@tds.net	212 Lincoln Ave P.O. Box 451 Reeseville WI 53579	SW	SP	Immanuel Reeseville WI	(920)927-5734	FW	1986
Steinbrenner Adam J	(586)246-7463 adam.steinbrenner@stjohndublin.org	6135 Rings Road Dublin OH 43016	OH	Sn/Adm	St John Dublin OH	(614)889-2284	SL	2015
Steinbronn Anthony J Dr	(908)839-2973 anthony.steinbronn@gmail.com	1382 Haven Dr Oviedo FL 32765	FG	EM			SL	1982
Steinbrueck Roger C	(573)768-1847 drsteinbrueck@yahoo.com	801 Scott St Beaver Dam WI 53916	SW	EM			SL	2004
Steinbrueck Kurt R	(813)326-5255 kurt@faithwesleychapel.com	4414 Crystal Downs Ct Wesley Chapel FL 33543	S	SP	Faith Wesley Chapel FL	(813)602-1104	SL-SMP	2014
Steiner Mark G Dr	(760)299-3041 m.g.steiner@cox.net	5206 Commonwealth Ct Fairfax VA 22032	SE	EM			SL	1982
Steiner Mark H	fwasteiner@gmail.com	6707 Charlottesville Row Fort Wayne IN 46804	IN	EM			FW	2009
Steiner Micah P	(303)506-1796 msteiner@oflc.net	3825 E Easter Pl Centennial CO 80122	RM	SMP	Our Father Centennial CO	(303)779-1332	SL-SMP	2019
Steinke Robert C	(727)808-9398 revstein@verizon.net	8665 Cypress Lakes Blvd New Prt Rchy FL 34653	FG	EM			SL	1969
Steinke Alan F	(516)799-0137 afs516@cs.com	4 E Lincoln Ave Massapequa NY 11758	AT	EM			SL	1971
Steinke Jeremy A	jsteinke2488@gmail.com	149 E Elmhurst Ave Elmhurst IL 60126	NI	Assoc	Immanuel Elmhurst IL	(630)832-1649	SL	2020
Steinke Richard G	(407)223-6416 richsteinke@hotmail.com	1357 Haven Dr Oviedo FL 32765	FG	EM			SL	1973
Steinmann Andrew E Dr	andrew.steinmann@cuchicago.edu	2144 Heritage Ln Westlake OH 44145	OH	EM			FW	1981
Stelling John F	(512)581-0232 stellingjk@yahoo.com	12501 Longhorn Pkwy Apt A400 Austin TX 78732	TX	EM			SL	1965
Stelzer Ronald W	(631)816-1220 rwstelzer@optonline.net	28 Belair Rd Selden NY 11784	AT	Sn/Adm	Our Savior Centereach NY	(631)588-2757	SL	1980
Stenbeck Mark C	mstenbeck@comcast.net	1056 Taborlake Dr Lexington KY 40502	IN	EM			SPR	1976
Stennett Arthur R Dr	(330)794-2822 ag_stennett@msn.com	135 Goodview Ave Akron OH 44305	EN	EM			SPR	1961
Stennfeld John C	(512)442-5844 jcs442@hotmail.com	4607 Yellow Rose Trl Austin TX 78749	TX	SP	Christ Austin TX	(512)442-5844	SL	1989
Stenson Sherman D	(512)963-6290 sdstenson@yahoo.com	1015 Blunt Street Downs KS 67437	KS	SP	Zion Downs KS	(785)454-3733	FW	2007
Stensrud Kenneth O	(406)684-5153 stensrud@3rivers.net	102 Stone Ln Twin Bridges MT 59754	MT	SP	Living Water* Dillon MT	(406)684-5153	FW-D	2008
Stenzel Carl B	(712)229-4203 cbstenzel@hotmail.com	5086 480th St Paullina IA 51046	IW	SP	St John Germantown IA	(712)448-2630	SL	1994
Stephan Merlin E	(507)459-1291 unclemer@yahoo.com	30 Delafield Dr Fort Leonard Wood MO 65473	MNS	M Chap	Office of International Mission Saint Louis MO		SL	2007
Stephan Luke F	(734)276-7553 lukestephan7@gmail.com	5297 N Via Sempreverde Tucson AZ 85750	PSW	EM			SL	1967
Stephanos Francis B	(612)310-1822 franandfetle@yahoo.com	4537 Cinnamon Ridge Trl Eagan MN 55122	MNS	EM			CQ	2006

*Multiple Assignments (See Church Worker Locator for Additional Details)
See Page 53 for the Table of Abbreviations for key to District, Position, and Seminary abbreviations
**C =Candidate; EM = Emeritus; the date following the C is the month and year the Candidate status began

NAME	TELEPHONE NUMBER EMAIL	STREET ADDRESS CITY/STATE/ZIP	DISTRICT	POSITION/ STATUS**	WHERE SERVING	OFFICE PHONE	SEM/ PROGRAM	YR GRAD
Stephens Curtis D	(570)578-0047 curtisstephens001@gmail.com	23 Crane Rd Scarsdale NY 10583	EN	SP	Trinity Scarsdale NY	(914)723-1998	FW	2014
Stephens Jeffrey B Dr	(330)659-6221 jbswio@gmail.com	3266 Ashby Ln Richfield OH 44286	OH	EM			FW	1983
Stephens Morris W Jr	(701)899-0290 stephensrev@gmail.com	1404 Blanchard Drive Woodland CA 95776	CNH	SP	Messiah Citrus Heights CA	(916)725-4550	FW	2002
Stephens Richard C	(308)380-6738 revrcstephens@gmail.com	4513 Williams Rd Benbrook TX 76116	TX	SP	Redeemer Fort Worth TX	(817)560-0030	FW	2018
Stephens Ronald A	(201)572-6832 rstephens82@aol.com	59886 Red Fox Ct South Bend IN 46614	IN	Sn/Adm	Emmaus South Bend IN	(574)287-4151	FW	2008
Stephenson John R Dr	(319)318-5138 jrstephenson@protonmail.com	1305 Donels Dr Vinton IA 52349	IE	RSO	The Lutheran Home for the Aged Assoc East Vinton IA	(319)472-4211	Other	1982
Sterle Roger D	(319)830-2598 rdsterle@gmail.com	5 Green Circle Bella Vista AR 72715	MDS	SP	Living Savior Springdale AR	(479)770-2124	SPR	1976
Sterling Aaron D	(314)956-6187 aaron.sterling7633@gmail.com		EN	Assoc	Christ Shepherd Alpharetta GA	(770)475-0640	SL	2018
Stern John T	(952)997-7752 JTStern@frontiernet.net	14656 Hanover Ln Apple Valley MN 55124	MNS	EM			SL	1970
Sternquist Adam A	(224) 678-2048	2604 Bittel Rd Owensboro KY 42301	IN	SP	Peace Owensboro KY	(270)685-0249	FW	2021
Stetson Adam	adam.stetson@eagles.cui.edu	1401 5th St Boulder City NV 89005	PSW	SP	Christ Boulder City NV	(702)293-4332	SL	2017
Stevens Arthur J	aj.stevens@att.net	4932 W 139th St Hawthorne CA 90250	PSW	SMP	Grace Los Angeles CA	(213)359-5740	SL	2021
Stevens Robert J	(828)579-0114 stevensclan2004@yahoo.com	5360 37th St Dr NE Hickory NC 28601	SE	SP	Immanuel Conover NC	(828)464-4050	FW	1994
Stewart Scott A	(281)993-6702 beefstew83@gmail.com	702 Flamingo Ct Friendswood TX 77546	TX	C07/2016			SL	1991
Stewart Rod D Jr	(303)845-2718 rodstewart446@gmail.com		NW	SP	Immanuel Mellen WI	(715)274-2751	FW	2025
Stiegemeyer Scott E	(949)214-3406 scott.stiegemeyer@cui.edu	21041 Berry Gln Lake Forest CA 92630	PSW	S HS/C	Concordia University Irvine Irvine CA	(949)854-8002	FW	1995
Stier Donald L	(612)720-4600 stierdon@aol.com	120 Ocean Dr Tavernier FL 33070	FG	SP	Immanuel Plantation Key FL	(305)852-8711	FW	1987
Stier Lewis W	(260) 579-1087 pastorlewistier24@gmail.com	22943 Glenbrook St St Clair Shores MI 48082	MI	EM			FW	2003
Stieve John W Dr	(520)403-8969 pex63@hotmail.com	68 W Aliso Dr Green Valley AZ 85614	EN	EM			SL	1970
Stillman Mark G	(609)314-2520 mstillman@faithnpb.com	4501 Central Gardens Way Apt 201 Palm Bch Gdns FL 33418	FG	SP	Faith North Palm Beach FL	(561)848-4737	SL	1986
Stinnett Aaron A	(985)302-2198 pastorstinnett@yahoo.com	2970 Mendon Rd Unit 119 Cumberland RI 02864	NE	SP	Our Redeemer Smithfield RI	(401)232-7575	FW	2005
Stinnett Eric A	406566-2723 eric.stinnett@lcms.org	625 6th Ave Havre MT 59501	MO	S Miss	Office of International Mission Saint Louis MO		FW	2004
Stinnette Eric A	(254)631-9715 ericstinnette@icloud.com	1652 Victory Ave Wichita Falls TX 76301	TX	SP	St Paul Wichita Falls TX	(940)322-6112	SL	2010
Stirdivant Mark B	(816)769-2277 revhollowleg@gmail.com	21 Milton St Saint Augustine FL 32084	FG	SP	Christ Our Savior Saint Augustine FL	(904)829-6823	FW	2001
Stites Jonathan R	revstites@gmail.com	14257 E 31st Pl Yuma AZ 85367	PSW	SP	Shep of the Hills Yuma AZ	(928)345-9694	SL	2008
Stites Roger E Jr	revstites@hotmail.com	P.O. Box 1021 Sequim WA 98382	NOW	Assoc	Faith Sequim WA	(360)683-4803	SL	2005
Stobaugh Gerald	kmaster9@hotmail.com	315 Oakwood Rd Arlington TN 38002	MDS	SMP	Holy Spirit Oakland TN	(901)465-6103	CQ	2018
Stock Donald E	(219)384-3718 donstock92@hotmail.com	29523 Walnut Hollow Dr Wright City MO 63390	MO	EM			SL	1992
Stocker Todd D	(651)280-7937 stockertodd@gmail.com	6900 Stratford Draw Woodbury MN 55125	MNS	SP	Living Christ Chanhassen MN	(952)934-5110	SL	1998
Stockland James B	(479)236-5964 pastorstockland@gmail.com	1267 E Highway 7 Clinton MO 64735	MO	SP	Trinity Clinton MO	(660)885-4728	SL	2025
Stockman Reed J	revstockman@gmail.com	311 S Columbia Ave Morris MN 56267	MNN	SP	Zion Morris MN	(320)589-2744	SL	1986
Stockman Robert E	(480)983-2224 robearuno@gmail.com	619 S Copper Dr Apache Jct AZ 85120	PSW	EM			SL	1960
Stoebig Thomas K	(612)210-5320 tkstoebig@gmail.com	11900 44th Pl N Plymouth MN 55442	MNS	EM			SL	1982
Stoerger Michael W	(217) 560-4473 revstoerger@icloud.com	307 N 1st St Fisher IL 61843	CI	SP	Peace Thomasboro IL	(217)643-3265	SL	2006
Stoever Caleb D	(620)238-3240 Rev.Stoever@proton.me	673 W 680th Ave Hepler KS 66746	KS	SP	Good Shepherd* Erie KS	(620)244-5555	FW	2021
Stogdill James A	(515)240-7700 pastor@messiahjohnston.com	8151 NW 37th St Ankeny IA 50023	IW	SP	Messiah Johnston IA	(515)270-6268	SL-D	2008
Stohlmann David H Dr	(707)528-4122	2289 Valley West Ct Santa Rosa CA 95401	CNH	EM			SL	1970
Stohlmann John S	(718)894-4000 rjsnyc@hotmail.com	56-64 59th St Maspeth NY 11378	AT	SP	Redeemer Bayside NY	(718)229-5770	SL	1999
Stohlmann Philip J	pjstohlmann@gmail.com		RM	C04/2018			SL	2013
Stohlmann Robert V	(507) 279-7068 robert.stohlmann@gmail.com	1450 Bidwell St Apt 206 Saint Paul MN 55118	MNS	EM			SL	1963
Stohs Delton G	(701)367-7832 pastord1@arvig.net	812 7th Ave SW Perham MN 56573	MNN	EM			SL-D	2003

*Multiple Assignments (See Church Worker Locator for Additional Details)
See Page 53 for the Table of Abbreviations for key to District, Position, and Seminary abbreviations
**C =Candidate; EM = Emeritus; the date following the C is the month and year the Candidate status began

NAME	TELEPHONE NUMBER EMAIL	STREET ADDRESS CITY/STATE/ZIP	DISTRICT	POSITION/ STATUS**	WHERE SERVING	OFFICE PHONE	SEM/ PROGRAM	YR GRAD
Stojkovic Larry S	pastorlarry@sharethehope.org	1301 Vintage Ln Rochester NY 14626	EA	Assoc	Hope Rochester NY	(585)723-4673	NESC	1987
Stolarczyk Raymond B Dr	(941)979-7490 pastor-s@lccross.org	478 Gallegos St Punta Gorda FL 33983	FG	SP	Of The Cross Port Charlotte FL	(941)627-6060	SL	2005
Stolarczyk Steven M		3040 Bay St P.O. Box 272 Unionville MI 48767	MI	SP	St Paul Unionville MI	(989)674-8681	FW	2004
Stoll Steven E	(712)947-4435 1soulman@live.com	P.O. Box 68 Mountain WI 54149	NW	SP	Tabor* Mountain WI	(715)276-7707	SL	2002
Stolle Gary D	(816)582-5649 jag5219st@comcast.net	15805 E 45th Pl S Independence MO 64055	MO	EM			SL	1977
Stoltenberg James G Dr	(443)340-4378 celide1947@gmail.com	219 Daniel Dr Hendersonvlle NC 28739	SE	EM			SPR	1974
Stoltenow Bradley R Dr	(303)503-7731 bstoltenow@sothfamily.org	1371 Beacon Hill Dr Hghlnds Ranch CO 80126	RM	Sn/Adm	Shepherd Hills Centennial CO	(303)798-0711	FW	1988
Stoltzman Jacob A	(224)715-3590 jastoltzman@comcast.net		NI	SP	Emmanuel Aurora IL	(630)851-2200	FW	2021
Stone Jeffrey A	(317)678-8833 revjeff2003@gmail.com	11457 Flynn Pl Noblesville IN 46060	IN	C02/2022			SL	2003
Stoppenhagen Norman W	(512)712-4453 normstop@att.net	9513 Graceland Trl Austin TX 78717	TX	EM			SL	1967
Storck Timothy D	(586)212-0405 tdstorck@yahoo.com	25566 Norvell St. Chesterfield MI 48051	MI	SP	Good Shepherd Chesterfield MI	(586)949-9440	FW	2007
Stork Steven D	(715) 896-1453 stevestork101@gmail.com	3033 Acorn Ave Sparta WI 54656	SW	EM			FW	1982
Storm Harold A	(507)779-8844 Harold@GSOwatonna.com	411 2nd St SW Medford MN 55049	MNS	Assoc	Good Shepherd Owatonna MN	(507)451-4125	FW	1983
Storteboom Fred A	(360)783-2750	c/o Charlotte Wiseman 2115 1st St Lagrande OR 97850	NOW	EM			CQ	1982
Stoterau Larry A Dr	(949)433-4131 pastorstoterau@splsorange.org	2230 E Vista Canyon Rd Orange CA 92867	PSW	Sn/Adm	St Paul Orange CA	(714)637-2640	SL	1973
Stottlemyer William J	(419)395-1507 willstottlemyer@gmail.com	30316 New Bavaria Rd Defiance OH 43512	OH	SP	St Stephen Defiance OH	(419)395-1507	FW	1990
Stottlemyer William K	(301)678-5648 pcman76@yahoo.com	3740 Resley Rd Hancock MD 21750	SE	SP	St Paul Hancock MD	(301)678-7180	FW	2004
Stoudt John A	(718)366-9231 johnastoudt@aol.com	77-02 82nd St Glendale NY 11385	AT	SP	Emmaus Ridgewood NY	(718)821-5253	NESC	1992
Stout David L	davidstout56@icloud.com	803 West Sherman Windfall IN 46076	IN	Assoc	Emanuel Tipton IN	(765)675-4090	CQ	2017
Stout Timothy L	(701)381-9380 revstout@mail.com	120 5th St SW Sawyer ND 58781	ND	SP	St John* Kongsberg ND	(701)626-7510	FW	2007
Stout Christopher T	(812)827-9134 pastorstout@yahoo.com	1699 Barbara Ann Cir Kannapolis NC 28083	SE	SP	Center Grove* Kannapolis NC	(704)750-1463	FW	2012
Stowe Douglas J Dr	(262)224-3840 pastor.stowe@divinesavior lutheran.com	869 Spruce St Hartford WI 53027	SW	Sn/Adm	Divine Savior Hartford WI	(262)673-5140	SL	1997
Strable David F	(260)416-4990 david.strable@gmail.com	507 S Main St Onida SD 57564	SD	SP	Immanuel* Harrold SD		FW	2009
Strade Bruce B	(503)241-7797 brstrade@aol.com	6315 NE 35th Ave Portland OR 97211	NOW	EM			SL	1970
Strand Gregory A	(541)231-8166 pastorgreg@flschool.org	1442 91st Ave SE Tumwater WA 98501	NOW	SP	Faith Lacey WA	(360)491-3552	SL	2000
Strand Noah O	262-691-0700 strandn@csl.edu	N36 W23309 Main St #201b Sussex WI 53089	SW	Assoc	Shepherd/Hills Pewaukee WI	(262)691-0700	SL	2023
Strand Paul O	(708)567-5134 pstrand@tlcs.org	6851 W 157th Pl Tinley Park IL 60477	NI	Sn/Adm	Trinity Tinley Park IL	(708)532-9395	FW	1979
Stransky John D	(715)870-1700 pastor.john@stjohnofwausau.org	2123 Meadowbrook Way Wausau WI 54403	NW	SP	St John Wausau WI	(715)842-5212	SL	2017
Stratmann David T	(636)579-4687 david.stratmann@lssliving.org	2 Elk Ridge Ct Saint Charles MO 63304	MO	Inst C	Lutheran Senior Services DBA EverTrue Brentwood MO	(314)968-9313	SL	2010
Strattman Gene A	(217)472-7651 grcvststmnn@irtc.net	6 Pine Cone Dr Jacksonville IL 62650	CI	EM			CQ	1994
Stratton Harry M	(503)881-2323 hmsaved@aol.com	1189 E Burnett St Stayton OR 97383	NOW	SMP	St John Salem OR	(503)588-0171	CQ	2020
Straub John A	(734)285-2601 pastorstraub@gmail.com	11900 Fordline St Southgate MI 48195	MI	EM			FW	2004
Straub Roger K	(517)230-3872 revrkstraub@hotmail.com	9960 W Herbison Rd Eagle MI 48822	MI	SP	St Andrew Portland MI	(517)647-4473	SL	1977
Strawn Allen K	astrawn@calvarymadison.org	701 State St Madison WI 53703	SW	SP	Calvary Madison WI	(608)255-7214	SL	2002
Strawn Gabriel	(260)458-7937 pastorgstrawn@gmail.com	22 Jean St Lewiston ME 04240	NE	SP	Redeemer Gorham ME	(207)839-7100	FW	2024
Strawn James C	(419)446-2217 atlastrawn@yahoo.com	22881 Monroe St Archbold OH 43502	OH	SP	Saint James Archbold OH	(419)445-4750	FW	1988
Strawn Paul M	(763)786-1706 pstrawn@ppslp.org	7835 Monroe St NE Spring Lake Park MN 55432	MNS	SP	Prince Of Peace Spring Lake Park MN	(763)786-1706	FW	1992
Strenge Karl N	(269)275-0567 knordstrenge@hotmail.com	141 Garrison Ave Battle Creek MI 49017	MI	SP	Redemption Battle Creek MI	(269)964-2321	SL	2003
Stresman Glenn D	(519)566-0009 glennstresman@gmail.com	314-1885 Westview Park Blvd Lasalle ON N9H-2 CANADA	EN	EM			CQ	2000
Streufert Philip E	206-623-8193 philstreufert@aol.com	11918 61st Ave SE Snohomish WA 98296	NOW	EM			CQ	1976
Streufert Stephen C	(816)739-6820 sstreufert5377@gmail.com	613 Gentry St Liberty MO 64068	MO	EM			SL	1972
Streufert Daniel A	(903)805-8635 djs3121@yahoo.com	The Whitcomb Apt 202 509 Ship St Saint Joseph MI 49085	MI	EM			SL	1966

*Multiple Assignments (See Church Worker Locator for Additional Details)

See Page 53 for the Table of Abbreviations for key to District, Position, and Seminary abbreviations

**C =Candidate; EM = Emeritus; the date following the C is the month and year the Candidate status began

NAME	TELEPHONE NUMBER EMAIL	STREET ADDRESS CITY/STATE/ZIP	DISTRICT	POSITION/ STATUS**	WHERE SERVING	OFFICE PHONE	SEM/ PROGRAM	YR GRAD
Strickland John C	(320)469-1366 jyodacs@gmail.com	19921 56th Ave NE Atwater MN 56209	MNS	SP	St John Atwater MN	(320)974-8984	SL	2007
Strimple Russell M	(713)878-8237 pastorstrimple@gmail.com	29420 Graceful Path Way Spring TX 77386	TX	SP	Savior Redeemer Houston TX	(713)691-2203	SL	2009
Stringer Gregory S	(510)468-7181 gregsstringer@sbcglobal.net	6025 Apex Way Lady Lake FL 32159	FG	EM			SL	1982
Strohschein Glenn L	(217)836-4003 gstroh1126@gmail.com	16 Bradford Hills Sullivan IL 61951	CI	EM			SPR	1972
Strohschein John A	(651)271-0869 jstrohs57_@hotmail.com	908 Summerlake Fort Mill SC 29715	EN	EM			SL	1969
Strohschein Martin D	(623)551-9851 marty@anthemcross.org	39808 N. Gavilan Peak Pkwy Phoenix AZ 85086	PSW	Assoc	Cross of Christ Anthem AZ	(623)551-9851	SL	2006
Strohschein David P	(320) 241-5806 dpstrohs@gmail.com	2492 65th St NE Sauk Rapids MN 56379	MNN	EM			SL	1977
Strom Terry A	(309)533-6687 pastorterrystrom@yahoo.com	442 North 4th Street Cissna Park IL 60924	CI	EM			SL	1995
Stroming Carl R	(763)350-3105 revrand55@gmail.com	27023 Ingrid Dr Park Rapids MN 56470	MNN	EM			SL-D	2012
Strong Micheal M Dr	(217)725-1717 strong@eosinc.com	675 Centerwood Dr Springfield IL 62711	SI	SP	Zion Farmersville IL	(217)725-1717	SPR	1971
Stroud Kenyon L	(979)209-4060 kenyonstroud@gmail.com	9732 Weedon Loop Bryan TX 77808	TX	EM			SL	1987
Stroud Robert C Dr	(360)434-2575 chaplainstroud@gmail.com	5965 Squirrel Pl NW Seabeck WA 98380	NOW	EM			CQ	2005
Strubbe Joseph H	(714) 401-5891 josephstrubbe@yahoo.com	3473 Venetian Dr Costa Mesa CA 92626	PSW	EM			CQ	1994
Struecker Steven M	(515)887-8521 skafarms@ncn.net	204 160th St West Bend IA 50597	IW	SMP	Zion* Lu Verne IA	(515)882-3347	SL-SMP	2015
Strum Loren W	(701)333-8912 lorensmaa@gmail.com	1017 N 29th St Bismarck ND 58501	ND	EM			SL	1988
Strussenberg Daniel P	(412)780-5252 dstruss@yahoo.com	1050 Springdale Dr Pittsburgh PA 15236	EA	EM			CQ	1983
Struve John W	(414)791-8909 john@struve.us	1910 Norhardt Dr Apt 300 Brookfield WI 53045	SW	EM			SL	1974
Stubbs Robert G Jr	(845)226-6690 rgstubbsjr@gmail.com	36 Doran Dr Hopewell Jct NY 12533	AT	C04/2017			FW	2005
Stubenrouch John J Jr	(308)289-3897 pstubenrouch@yahoo.com	1430 E 8th St Ogallala NE 69153	NEB	EM			SL	1998
Stuckwisch Jeffrey L	jstuckwisch@zionseymour.org	1501 Gaiser Dr Seymour IN 47274	IN	Sn/Adm	Zion Seymour IN	(812)522-1089	SL	1991
Stuckwisch Allen D	(479)650-0037 pastor@messiahgrh.org	315 Meadowcrest Rd Cincinnati OH 45231	OH	SP	Messiah Greenhills OH	(513)825-4768	SL	1987
Stuckwisch Don R Jr Dr	richard.stuckwisch@in.lcms.org		IN	DP	Indiana District* Fort Wayne IN	(800)837-1145	FW	1993
Stuckwisch Gregory L	schwisch@diodecom.net	P.O. Box 55 Odell NE 68415	NEB	SP	Zion* Harbine NE	(402)754-4522	SL	2001
Stuehrenberg Lyle R	(719)315-2869 lrst26@yahoo.com	3051 Sherrelwood Dr S Canon City CO 81212	RM	EM			SL	1970
Stuenkel Jacob A	(715)663-1845 jacobstuenkel@ctsfw.edu	107 E School St Napoleon OH 43545	OH	SP	St Peter* Napoleon OH	(419)762-5075	FW	2013
Stuenkel James A	(217)622-7266 revstuenkel@gmail.com	2659 Windfall Dr Sherman IL 62684	CI	EM			CQ	1982
Stuenkel Robert E	(303)514-3494 jhstuenkel@aol.com	2775 Emerson Ave Boulder CO 80305	FG	EM			SL	1964
Stuenkel Roger R	(520)393-3639 rstuenkel@aol.com	1460 N Rio Sonora Green Valley AZ 85614	EN	EM			SL	1970
Stuenkel William H	(360)535-9925 gstuenkel@gmail.com	4164 Sutherland Ct Gig Harbor WA 98332	NOW	EM			CQ	1986
Stueve Eugene H	(660)349-6506 imarev@cvalley.net	1112 Rustic Dr Macon MO 63552	MO	EM			CQ	1976
Stueve Barry J	(425)261-4554 barry.stueve@providence.org	1700 13th St Everett WA 98201	NOW	Inst C	Northwest District Portland OR	(503)288-8383	SL	1988
Stueve Dennis W	(951)719-6311 stueve2@gmail.com	4382 SE Jetty Ave Lincoln City OR 97367	NOW	EM			SL	1980
Stuhr Lloyd R	(402)770-5671 lloydstuhr53@gmail.com	1948 County Road 6 Yutan NE 68073	NEB	EM			SL	2008
Stults Don A	(425)243-9582 god_rules@email.com	815 103rd Drive SE Lake Stevens WA 98258	NOW	SP	Zion Snohomish WA	(360)568-2700	SL	1996
Stumpf Eric C Dr	estumpf21@gmail.com	10348 Marlou Dr Munster IN 46321	IN	EM			SL	1973
Stumpf Karl E Dr	(267)994-2420 karlstu@comcast.net	112 Walden Rd New Bern NC 28562	SE	EM			SPR	1972
Sturges Christopher J	(248)875-3749 christopher.sturges@drlc.org	148 Morningside Orchard Dr. Apt. 8 Oconomowoc WI 53066	SW	Assoc	Divine Redeemer Hartland WI	(262)367-8400	SL	2024
Sturgis James E Sr	(361)643-1526 sturgis.jim@gmail.com	1001 Bayview Blvd Unit 1 Portland TX 78374	TX	EM			CQ	1994
Sturtz Arlyn L Dr	(251)533-7686 arlyn.sturtz@gmail.com	889 County Rd 326 Orrville AL 36767	SO	EM			SL	1973
Sturzenbecher Randy R	(605)391-0428 dslcpsturz@divineshep.org	8605 Woodland Dr Black Hawk SD 57718	SD	DP	South Dakota District Sioux Falls SD	(605)361-1514	SL	2001
Suehring Dean M	(715) 851-1151 dean.suehring@gmail.com	N4638 Weasel Dam Rd Tigerton WI 54486	NW	SMP	St John* Tigerton WI	(715)535-2282	FW-SMP	2016
Suelflow John G	(262)377-3785 jjsilfo@sbcglobal.net	1406 Fox Ln Grafton WI 53024	SW	EM			SL	1962
Suelzle Daniel P	(701)215-2592 dsuelzle@icloud.com	2704 Greenbriar Dr Jonesboro AR 72401	MDS	Assoc	All Saints* Jonesboro AR	(870)935-2001	SL	2011

*Multiple Assignments (See Church Worker Locator for Additional Details)

See Page 53 for the Table of Abbreviations for key to District, Position, and Seminary abbreviations

**C =Candidate; EM = Emeritus; the date following the C is the month and year the Candidate status began

NAME	TELEPHONE NUMBER EMAIL	STREET ADDRESS CITY/STATE/ZIP	DISTRICT	POSITION/ STATUS**	WHERE SERVING	OFFICE PHONE	SEM/ PROGRAM	YR GRAD
Suelzle David K	(701)388-1549 revsuelzle@gmail.com	4288 Russet Ave S Fargo ND 58104	ND	EM			SL	1982
Suelzle Michael D	(701)807-2009 michaelsuelzle@live.com		ND	SP	Grace Fargo ND	(701)232-1516	SL	2010
Suggitt Christopher S	(989)551-3976 suggitt1@hotmail.com	c/o St. Paul Lutheran Church 7292 Kilmanagh Rd Pigeon MI 48755	MI	SP	St Paul* Linkville MI	(989)453-2271	FW	2015
Sui Liwei	liweisui@gmail.com	4592 E Compton Blvd Bloomington IN 47401	IN	Asst	Faith Bloomington IN	(812)332-1668	FW	2014
Sukhdeo Desmond A	(718)450-1110 desmond@deslaw1.com	123-07 22nd Ave College Point NY 11356	AT	SP	St Johns College Point NY	(718)463-4790	CQ	2014
Sukstorf Perry T	(504) 482-2118 pts2000@msn.com	3501 Inwood Ave New Orleans LA 70131	SO	SP	St John New Orleans LA	(504)482-2118	SL	2006
Sullivan Brandon M	(815) 909-9291 revbsullivan@gmail.com	406 N Tonica St Mason City IL 62664	CI	SP	Christ* Mason City IL	(217)482-5168	FW	2024
Sullivan Joseph D	(636)257-4455 joe.sullivan@nblc.net	604 Williams Dr Eureka MO 63025	MO	Sn/Adm	New Beginnings Pacific MO	(636)257-4455	SL	1999
Sultze Stuart A	(661)487-4853 ssultze@hotmail.com	c/o Faith Lutheran Church 560 Park Blvd Ukiah CA 95782	CNH	SP	Faith Ukiah CA	(707)462-2618	FW	2021
Sund Joel E	(763)233-8894 revjes@msn.com	10364 Quaker Ln N Maple Grove MN 55369	MNS	C07/2016			SL	1993
Sundbom Paul D	(910)382-8725 paulsundbom@gmail.com	3804 Mount View Ave Apt 24 Schofield WI 54476	NW	Assoc	Trinity Wausau WI	(715)842-0769	FW	2000
Sundbye Scott A	(940)902-4039 scottsundbye@gmail.com	3 Overcup St Texarkana TX 75503	TX	SP	First Texarkana TX	(903)792-5253	FW	1995
Sundell Dennis D	(920) 286-2693 packerpair1@gmail.com	803 Tallgrass Ln Plymouth WI 53073	SW	EM			FW	1985
Sundquist Robert P	(702)274-8900	9905 Ranch Hand Ave Las Vegas NV 89117	PSW	Assoc	Faith Community Las Vegas NV	(702)921-2700	SL	2008
Surburg Mark P	(618)751-9138 pastormarksurburg@frontier.com	1801 Westminster Dr Marion IL 62959	SI	SP	Good Shepherd Marion IL	(618)993-3649	SL	1999
Susan David J	(224)458-7194 davidjsusan45@gmail.com	2210 Lakeland Ave Madison WI 53704	SW	EM			SL	1971
Susskraut Kenneth J			AT	EM			CQ	1978
Sutcliffe Tanner T	(623)414-2509 sutcliffet@csl.edu	1401 N Main Ave Tea SD 57064	SD	SP	Risen Savior Tea SD	(605)498-5050	SL	2025
Sutherlin Jeffrey W	jeffsutherlin@gmail.com	352 E Mary Ln Gilbert AZ 85295	PSW	SMP	Christ Greenfield Gilbert AZ	(480)892-8521	SL-SMP	2019
Sutterer Paul R	(352)233-9669 psutterer1@gmail.com	10340 SE 177th Pl Summerfield FL 34491	EN	EM			SPR	1966
Sutterer Steven E	(517)243-5167 ssutterer@gmail.com	P.O. Box 665 Eastport MI 49627	EN	EM			SL	1984
Sutton Jacob R	(972)922-7275 rev.jsutton@gmail.com	701 W 7th St Seymour IN 47274	IN	Inst C	Lutheran Community Home Inc Seymour IN	(812)522-5927	FW	2007
Sutton Joel L	(937)542-9542 jlsut78@gmail.com	1316 Stoney Springs Rd Vandalia OH 45377	OH	EM			FW	2012
Sutton David J	(715)966-5591 revsutton@outlook.com	P.O. Box 7 W4815 Kemp Ave Irma WI 54442	NW	SP	St Paul's* Irma WI	(715)536-5069	FW	2014
Sutton August T Dr	(517)256-3460 pastortsutton@knowingjesus.org	4392 Elmwood Dr Okemos MI 48864	MI	Sn/Adm	St Luke Haslett MI	(517)339-9119	SL	2012
Sutton Albert G	(605)391-1566 alsutton@midconetwork.com	12648 Campfire Dr Rapid City SD 57702	SD	D Miss	South Dakota District Sioux Falls SD	(605)361-1514	SL-SMP	2012
Sveom Dale D	(816)322-8327 dsveom3@yahoo.com	810 Minnie Ave Belton MO 64012	MO	EM			SL	1981
Swan Jason A	(208) 466-6746 pastorswan@zionlutherannampa. com	404 Nectarine St Nampa ID 83686	NOW	SP	Zion Nampa ID	(208)466-6746	SL	2013
Swanson Douglas R	(708)310-2400 pastor.doug@koklcms.org	3621 Socialville Foster Rd Mason OH 45040	OH	SP	King Of Kings Mason OH	(513)398-6089	SL	2007
Swanson Herbert C	(479)979-2425 mtkilimanjaro7@yahoo.com	225 W Cobblestone Ct Russellville AR 72801	MDS	EM			SPR	1969
Swanson Richard M	(480)816-5757 riclindas@hotmail.com	15504 E Cavern Dr Fountain Hills AZ 85268	PSW	EM			SL	1971
Swanson Timothy R	(715)432-5563 tswanson815@gmail.com	217 Orourke Dr Platte City MO 64079	MO	Sn/Adm	Our Savior Platte City MO	(816)335-4049	SL	2015
Sward Steven H	(847)208-9451 steven.sward@yahoo.com	6403 38th Ave Kenosha WI 53142	SW	EM			CQ	2012
Sweet Robert L	(713) 418-0015 robsweet2020@netscape.net	15810 Brookford Dr Houston TX 77059	TX	SP	Good Shepherd Angleton TX	(979)849-2223	SL	1992
Swem Jeremy M	(616)644-8338 swemjm@gmail.com	2317 Ridgewood Ave SE Grand Rapids MI 49546	MI	Sn/Adm	Our Savior Grand Rapids MI	(616)949-0710	FW	2011
Swenson Jacob D	(651)331-1014 pastorswenson@wplsf.com	136 Sloat Boulevard San Francisco CA 94132	EN	Assoc	West Portal San Francisco CA	(415)661-0242	FW	2014
Sweyko Stephen C	(620) 644-9158 ssweyko@gmail.com	2846 Graniteville Rd Graniteville VT 05654	NE	SP	Williamstown Graniteville VT	(802)479-1164	SL	1998
Swinford James S	pastor.jim.nlm@outlook.com	1880 S 236th Dr Buckeye AZ 85326	PSW	C06/2025			FW	1989
Switzer Matthew D	(415)460-7735 Somedayson@gmail.com	1044 Lea Dr San Rafael CA 94903	CNH	C01/2022			FW	2000
Swords Jeffrey F	j.swords@hotmail.com	444 Doans Ridge Rd Welland ON L3B5N CANADA	EA	EM			NESC	2016
Swyres Eric D	(660)572-9879 rev.swyres@proton.me	907 Cypress Dr Rolla MO 65401	MO	SP	Immanuel Rolla MO	(573)364-4525	SL	1996
Sylwester Roger O	(206)935-4135 rogersylwester@gmail.com	1501 California Ave SW Apt 407 Seattle WA 98116	NOW	EM			SL	1965

*Multiple Assignments (See Church Worker Locator for Additional Details)
See Page 53 for the Table of Abbreviations for key to District, Position, and Seminary abbreviations
**C =Candidate; EM = Emeritus; the date following the C is the month and year the Candidate status began

NAME	TELEPHONE NUMBER EMAIL	STREET ADDRESS CITY/STATE/ZIP	DISTRICT	POSITION/ STATUS**	WHERE SERVING	OFFICE PHONE	SEM/ PROGRAM	YR GRAD
Symm David V	(806)206-4732 davidsymm@gmail.com	420 W Orange St Girard KS 66743	KS	EM			FW	1983
Symmank Joel E	(651)739-5144 symmankj@wlc.church	1921 59th Ct E Inver Grove Heights MN 55077	MNS	SMP	Woodbury Woodbury MN	(651)739-5144	S	1992
Symmank Clarence L	(720)556-5265 familyjsjj@gmail.com	10536 Kalahari Ct Littleton CO 80124	TX	EM			SL	1953
Symmank Herman M	(972)754-6878 melsymmank@gmail.com	4831 W Lawther Dr Apt 306 Dallas TX 75214	TX	EM			SL	1965
Synnott Matthew B	(713)302-6908 synnott.matthew@gmail.com	2528 N Woodbine Ter Peoria IL 61604	CI	Assoc	Trinity Peoria IL	(309)676-4609	SL	2012
Sype Kenneth O	(402)328-2712 kennethosype@yahoo.com	9011 S 72nd St Lincoln NE 68516	NEB	EM			SL	1970
Syth Gary A Jr	pastor@gracevancouver.org		NOW	SP	Grace Vancouver WA	(360)892-7850	SL	2009
Szczesny Jonathan D	(920)344-8213 jonathan.szczesny@yahoo.com	N6199 Neda Rd Iron Ridge WI 53035	SW	EM			FW	1997
Szedlak Erno L	(715)492-6673 doreenaszedlak@gmail.com	5512 Renee Dr #213 Eau Claire WI 54703	NW	EM			SPR	1964
Szeto Lenny	(510)580-6756 revszeto@yahoo.com	c/o Zion Lutheran Church 495 9th Ave San Francisco CA 94118	CNH	SP	Zion San Francisco CA	(415)221-7500	SL	1999
Szeto David K	(516) 592-1558 daveszeto012@gmail.com	4930 Douglas Road Downers Grove IL 60515	NI	SP	Bethel Westmont IL	(630)968-3232	SL	2006
Tabbert Christopher J	(406)291-2099 revctab51@gmail.com	2007 Tammany St. Anaconda MT 59711	MT	EM			FW	1998
Taber Jason A	jasontaber2010@gmail.com	875 SE Tamango St Hillsboro OR 97123	NOW	Sn/Adm	Trinity Hillsboro OR	(503)640-1693	SL	2015
Tabisz Richard	(918)640-1423 RevRickT@gmail.com	17400 S 97th West Ave Mounds OK 74047	OK	EM			SL	2005
Tafel Gregory S	(610)417-0619 revgtafel@outlook.com	179 Park Ridge Dr Easton PA 18040	EA	EM			NESC	1997
Taggatz John M	(715) 467-1231 jtaggatz@yahoo.com	5419 Citation Ln Racine WI 53402	SW	SP	Grace Oak Creek WI	(414)762-8990	SL	2007
Taglauer Kenneth C	(870)424-4382	148 University Rd Brookline MA 02445	MDS	EM			SPR	1970
Takagi Jun	(714)307-7803 samuraifaith2012@att.net	15911 S Harvard Blvd Apt D Gardena CA 90247	PSW	EM			SL	2010
Takele Hunde G	(952)831-5276 takelemeseret5@gmail.com	9201 Normandale Blvd Bloomington MN 55437	MNS	Asst	St Michaels Bloomington MN	(952)831-5276	SL	2023
Talsma Dale A	(260)804-8460 datalsma@gmail.com	128 S. Quarterline Rd. Scottville MI 49454	MI	C07/2016			SL	1985
Tanksley Leonard E	(260)246-7470		IN	SP	St Peter Decatur IN	(260)724-7533	FW	2018
Tannahill David S			EN	EM			NESC	1986
Tanney Adam L	(262)269-2979 adam.tanney@gmail.com	26 Hickory Ln Cary IL 60013	NI	Assoc	Immanuel East Dundee IL	(847)428-4477	SL	2024
Tanney Michael H	(314)616-2762 tanney722@gmail.com	c/o Saint John Lutheran Church 405 West State Rd Island Lake IL 60042	NI	SP	St John Island Lake IL	(847)526-7614	SL	2011
Tanz Jared L	(573)846-7474 jared@lglomd.org	3217 Lakewood Dr Cape Girardeau MO 63701	MO	SMP	St Andrew Cape Girardeau MO	(573)334-3200	SL-SMP	2022
Tape John W Dr	drjohntape@gmail.com	8585 Laurel Ct Fishers IN 46038	IN	EM			FW	1980
Tapken Grant P	(319)215-2836 pastortapken@gmail.com	206 N 4th St Fairbank IA 50629	IE	SP	Grace* Jesup IA	(319)827-1257	FW	2025
Tasler Robert L	bobncarol@ecentral.com	16615 Las Ramblas Ln Unit G Parker CO 80134	RM	EM			SL	1971
Tassey Matthew W	pastortassey@gmail.com	39307 W Macarthur Dr Shawnee OK 74804	OK	SP	Redeemer Shawnee OK	(405)273-6286	FW	2011
Tatkenhorst Kenneth L	(660)619-1164 stpaultat@yahoo.com	14368 184th Ln NW Elk River MN 55330	MNS	SP	Immanuel Silver Creek MN	(763)878-2820	CQ	1992
Tauscher Robert W Jr	(330)807-4643 btauscher@aol.com	428 Sheraton Dr NW North Canton OH 44720	EN	EM			FW	1980
Tausz Ralph G	(847)455-0903 pastortausz@comcast.net	427 N Regal Ct Addison IL 60101	NI	SP	Hope* Hillside IL	(708)449-8688	FW	2000
Taye Muluneh	(650)796-7695 mulunehtaye@gmail.com	350 Bryant Ave Alameda CA 94501	CNH	Assoc	Redeeming Grace Santa Clara CA	(408)736-6605	SL	2020
Taylor Douglas J	(253)720-0067 rev.douglas.j.taylor@gmail.com	1005 NE Lake St Apt 4 Pullman WA 99163	NOW	Assoc	Augustana Moscow ID	(208)892-9224	FW	2009
Taylor Samuel D	(763)370-2423 dtaylor@stjohnsbuffalo.org	702 Lawrence Pkwy Buffalo MN 55313	MNS	EM			CQ	2012
Taylor Ryan S	(636)734-9351 rtaylor@immanuelstcharles.org	115 S 6th St Saint Charles MO 63301	MO	Assoc	Immanuel Saint Charles MO	(636)946-2656	SL	2014
Taylor Michael S	(216)832-0046 mikestst@gmail.com	102 Norton Rd Albion PA 16401	EN	SP	Holy Trinity Albion PA	(814)756-3426	FW	1984
Taylor Mark M	(972)632-0902 pastor.taylor@faithplano.org	1311 Periwinkle Dr Wylie TX 75098	TX	Sn/Adm	Faith Plano TX	(972)423-7447	FW	2009
Taylor M A	(409)795-0608 patmostx@gmail.com	1100 Redfish St Bayou Vista TX 77563	TX	SP	St John Galveston TX	(409)762-2702	FW	1993
Taylor Jason W	jtaylor@zionnewpal.org	6513 W 300 S New Palestine IN 46163	IN	Sn/Adm	Zion New Palestine IN	(317)861-5544	SL	2004
Taylor Donald L	(952)445-6955 revdont@aol.com	433 W 5th St Apt 321 Waconia MN 55387	MNS	EM			SL	1964
Taylor Dien A Dr	(718)324-1288 dien.taylor@ad-lcms.org	c/o Rev. Theo. Wittrock Cros. 4360 Boyd Ave The Bronx NY 10466	AT	DP	Atlantic District* Hastings-On-Hudson NY	(914)337-5700	SL	2000

*Multiple Assignments (See Church Worker Locator for Additional Details)

See Page 53 for the Table of Abbreviations for key to District, Position, and Seminary abbreviations

**C =Candidate; EM = Emeritus; the date following the C is the month and year the Candidate status began

NAME	TELEPHONE NUMBER EMAIL	STREET ADDRESS CITY/STATE/ZIP	DISTRICT	POSITION/ STATUS**	WHERE SERVING	OFFICE PHONE	SEM/ PROGRAM	YR GRAD
Taylor Deric A	(201)388-1620 dtaylor92@verizon.net	31-06 Morlot Ave Fair Lawn NJ 07410	NJ	SP	Our Savior Fair Lawn NJ	(201)796-3007	SL	1992
Taylor Kurt S Dr	(734)625-3200 kurt.taylor@cuw.edu	c/o Concordia University 12800 N Lake Shore Dr Mequon WI 53097	SW	S HS/C	Concordia University Wisconsin Mequon WI	(262)243-5700	SL	1992
Teasdale James R Dr	jimteasdale@comcast.net	245 E Pettit Ave Fort Wayne IN 46806	IN	EM			FW	1983
Teeple Jeffrey S	(260)495-4306 pastort@plcms.org	2025 N 110 W Angola IN 46703	EN	Sn/Adm	Peace Fremont IN	(260)495-4306	FW	2003
Teferi Adam K	(617)892-0066 ateferi2004@gmail.com	P.O. Box 2149 Acton MA 01720	NE	SP	Bethel Oromo Acton MA		CQ	2022
Teggatz Joshua D	(309)203-9052 jteggatz@egl.org	945 Terrace Dr Elm Grove WI 53122	SW	Assoc	Elm Grove Elm Grove WI	(262)797-2970	SL	2025
Tegtmeier Dennis H Dr	(512)964-6741 drdennisteg@gmail.com	4833 Eck Ln Austin TX 78734	TX	EM			SPR	1966
Tegtmeier Norbert D	(620)343-4371 norbert.tegtmeier1953@gmail.com	148 Walnut Creek Rd Wellsville KS 66092	KS	EM			FW	1979
Tegtmeier Victor D	(920)262-9188 vtegtmeier2@gmail.com	317 S Water St #408 Watertown WI 53094	SW	EM			SL	1962
Teichmiller Robert J	(832)717-4957 revtike@juno.com	13222 Chriswood Dr Cypress TX 77429	TX	EM			SPR	1973
Teigen Martin A	(507)344-8087 martinteigen@gmail.com	208 Wilson Way Mankato MN 56001	MNS	EM			CQ	1997
Teike Mark R	(812)350-0609	1032 Coles Dr Columbus IN 47201	IN	EM			SL	1983
Teklegiorgis Tuquabo H	(610)623-8401 tuquabo37@hotmail.com	401 Netherwood Rd Apt 1 Upper Darby PA 19082	EA	EM			FW	1989
Teller Nickolas E		1241 Marionola Way Pinole CA 94564	CNH	SP	Our Savior Pinole CA	(510)275-3494	SL	2017
Telloni John L	jlt3750@aol.com	7122 Wales View Cir NW Apt C North Canton OH 44720	S	Sn/Adm	St John* Massillon OH	(330)837-4645	FW	1977
Temme Marvin L	(307)534-5490 mtme45@gmail.com	611 Sterling Dr Cheyenne WY 82009	WY	EM			SL	1973
Temme Stanton J Dr	(219) 615-9362 pastortemme@gmail.com	2604 Estero Parkway Valparaiso IN 46383	IN	SP	Heritage Valparaiso IN	(219)464-2810	FW	2008
Temple John F	(636)357-1870 temple1946@gmail.com	1358 Timothy Ridge Dr Saint Charles MO 63304	MO	EM			SPR	1973
Terhune Paul C	(626)512-8457 pcterhune@yahoo.com	1419 E Dalton Ave Glendora CA 91741	PSW	EM			CQ	1977
Terjesen William P	(914)293-0081 prwpt@optonline.net	714 Hudson Ave Peekskill NY 10566	AT	SP	Our Redeemer Peekskill NY	(914)293-0081	CQ	1991
Terkula Michael D	mdterkula@outlook.com	1440 Saint Johns Church Road NE Lanesville IN 47136	IN	SP	Saint John Lanesville IN	(812)952-3711	FW	2019
Terral Paul Q	(979)250-3084 rev.paulterral@gmail.com	1349 Greenfield St Gainesville TX 76240	TX	SP	Faith Gainesville TX	(940)668-7147	SL	2019
Terry Jerome N	(504)812-6881 iamapreacherman@att.net	153 Tammy Dr La Place LA 70068	SO	SP	Bethel New Orleans LA	(504)941-5888	SL-D	2006
Tesch Philip C	(916)281-4483 tesch132@gmail.com	1863 William Bird Ave. Sacramento CA 95835	CNH	EM			SPR	1975
Tesema Tesfai Z	(408)227-8260	2557 Alemany Blvd San Francisco CA 94112	CNH	D Miss	California/Nevada/Hawaii District Livermore CA	(866)264-6079	CQ	2004
Teshome Alebachew E	aleteshome7@gmail.com	5558 Oak Chase Dr. Antioch TN 37013	MDS	Assoc	Faith Thompsons Station TN	(615)791-1880	CQ	2015
Teske Walter W	(231)886-0213 wwteske@gmail.com	6117 Ivanhoe St Ludington MI 49431	MI	EM			SL	1972
Teske Herbert J Jr	(708)502-1330	174 Linden Ln Chicago Heights IL 60411	NI	EM			SPR	1955
Teske Martin E	(713)205-6315 martinteske66@gmail.com	95 Danforth Crescent Rochester NY 14618	SE	EM			SL	1966
Teske Paul N	(203)858-8967 info@paulteskeministries.com	6441 Norway Rd Dallas TX 75230	TX	EM			SPR	1976
Teske Steven W	(501)400-6742 srteske@att.net	7613 Yuma Ct Little Rock AR 72116	MDS	SP	Immanuel Alexander AR		FW	1988
Tessaro Charles R		c/o Lutheran Bible Translators 107 S Main St Concordia MO 64020	NI	RSO	Lutheran Bible Translators Inc Concordia MO	(660)225-0810	FW	1984
Tessaro Paul D	(785)632-5301 revpt@juno.com	816 9th St Clay Center KS 67432	KS	Sn/Adm	St Paul Clay Center KS	(785)632-5301	SL	1992
Tessmann David H	(336)662-5283 revdht@aol.com	915 Edgewater Rd Gibsonville NC 27249	SE	EM			SPR	1969
Tessone Andrew T	(660)619-2055 prtessoneosl@gmail.com	1320 W 4th St Sedalia MO 65301	MO	Sn/Adm	Our Savior Sedalia MO	(660)827-0226	SL	2011
Teuscher Daniel J	(636)375-4344 danjudy@aol.com	958 Shire Ln Eureka MO 63025	MO	EM			SPR	1963
Tewes Mark S	(952)200-2954 80pmt1957@gmail.com	21055 62nd St NW Sunburg MN 56289	MNN	EM			SL	1989
Tews Thomas H	(815)459-1447	163 Pomeroy Ave Crystal Lake IL 60014	NI	EM			SL	1971
Tews David E	(870)670-4814	1703 N Spring Dr Horseshoe Bnd AR 72512	MDS	EM			SL	1968
Tews Mark W	(832) 630-8743 mazk2s@aol.com	1334 CR 850-B Alvin TX 77511	TX	EM			SL	1992
Thackery Nicholas J	(515) 573-3174 pastor@goodshepfortdodge.org	1464 21st Ave N Fort Dodge IA 50501	IW	SP	Good Shepherd Fort Dodge IA	(515)573-3174	FW	2009

*Multiple Assignments (See Church Worker Locator for Additional Details)
See Page 53 for the Table of Abbreviations for key to District, Position, and Seminary abbreviations
**C =Candidate; EM = Emeritus; the date following the C is the month and year the Candidate status began

NAME	TELEPHONE NUMBER EMAIL	STREET ADDRESS CITY/STATE/ZIP	DISTRICT	POSITION/ STATUS**	WHERE SERVING	OFFICE PHONE	SEM/ PROGRAM	YR GRAD
Thai An B	(909)282-9437 anthaishalom7@gmail.com	?1777 Sun Ridge Dr Apopka FL 32703	FG	EM			SL	2002
Thao Chia	(920)819-3540 chiathao57@gmail.com	1781 Susan Ln Green Bay WI 54303	NW	EM			EIITSL	2007
Thao Daniel	(952)239-9136 daniel.thao@cllc.church	809 New Century Blvd S Saint Paul MN 55119	MNS	Sn/Adm	Cornerstone White Bear MN	(952)239-9136	Other	2024
Thao Moses	(414)897-4082 mosesthao@yahoo.com	7119 W Lima St Milwaukee WI 53223	SW	C08/2021			SL	2014
Thayer Edward B	(845)239-9636 deacontad@gmail.com	15440 Pemberton Way Milton DE 19968	SE	EM			SL-SMP	2013
Theil Stephen L	(480)586-5034 stheil@cox.net	9427 E Via De Vaquero Dr Scottsdale AZ 85255	PSW	EM			SPR	1970
Theilen Joshua W	(217)415-2311 theilenjoshua@gmail.com	4124 Camp Cilca Rd Cantrall IL 62625	CI	Asst	Good Shepherd Sherman IL	(217)496-3149	SL	2008
Theimer Doyle J	(832)233-7837 doylet@christ4u.net	3315 Maple Park Dr Kingwood TX 77339	TX	Assoc	Christ King Kingwood TX	(281)360-7936	SL	1990
Theimer Roger P Dr	(402)960-3474	36889 Quail Ridge Rd Louisville NE 68037	NEB	Assoc	King Of Kings Omaha NE	(402)333-6464	SL	1984
Theiss Benjamin J	(660) 414-7958 benjamin_theiss@live.com	27959 Steamboat Ave Brunswick MO 65236	MO	SP	St John Brunswick MO	(660)548-3642	SL	2016
Theiss Steven C	(618)977-1678 steven.c.theiss@hotmail.com	227 623 Perry County Rd 346 Frohna MO 63748	SI	EM			SL	1981
Theiss Terry L	(815)222-9731 pastortheiss@hotmail.com	1806 Maxwell St Rolla MO 65401	MO	EM			SL	1981
Thelen James E	jthelen61@gmail.com	c/o Marco Lutheran Church 525 N Collier Blvd Marco Island FL 34145	FG	SP	Marco Marco Island FL	(239)394-0332	SL	1989
Thews Daniel P	(920)739-9191 dan.thews@faithfv.org	601 E Glendale Ave Appleton WI 54911	NW	Sn/Adm	Faith Appleton WI	(920)739-9191	SL	1989
Thiagarajan Alfred R	(212)363-0524 pastoralfy@gmail.com		EN	SP	Our Saviour Valley Stream NY	(516)825-5453	CQ	2013
Thiel Steven E	sethiel54@gmail.com	5020 N River Rd Freeland MI 48623	MI	EM			FW	1992
Thiel Grant E	(920)412-1707 grant.thiel@shepherdhills.org	3327 N Casaloma Dr Apt 168 Appleton WI 54913	NW	Assoc	Shepherd Hills Greenville WI	(920)757-5722	SL	2024
Thieme Brian K	(573)268-3241 revthieme@trinity-lcms.org	520 N Crater Lake Dr Columbia MO 65201	MO	Sn/Adm	Trinity Columbia MO	(573)445-2112	SL	1993
Thieme John A	(303)776-1789 jthieme@comcast.net	640 Alpine St Longmont CO 80504	RM	SP	Christ Our Savior Longmont CO	(303)776-1789	SL	1988
Thierfelder David F	(214)883-6139 dthierfelder@msn.com	1354 Haven Dr Oviedo FL 32765	S	EM			SPR	1962
Thierfelder Thomas J	(620)797-1518 pastorth@gmail.com	815 S 10th St Kingsville TX 78363	TX	SP	St Paul* Bishop TX	(361)584-2778	FW	1993
Thies Daniel E Dr	(850)626-5626 dethies@gmail.com	5733 Loring Dr Milton FL 32583	SO	SP	Eternal Trinity Milton FL	(850)623-5780	FW	2000
Thoe Alan M	(615)542-7703 athoe@comcast.net	1514 Maymont Dr Murfreesboro TN 37130	MDS	SMP	Grace Murfreesboro TN	(615)893-0338	FW-SMP	2013
Thoelke Hermann L	(219)213-2064 thoelke@juno.com	532 O Hagan Dr Crown Point IN 46307	IN	EM			SL	1965
Thole Samuel R	(971)344-2552 samuel.thole@gmail.com	505 20th Ave Brookings SD 57706	SD	Asst	Zion* White SD	(605)629-2951	SL	2017
Thoma Christopher I Dr	(248)887-4300 pastorthoma@oursaviorhartland.org	555 Tania Trl Linden MI 48451	EN	Sn/Adm	Our Savior Hartland MI	(248)887-4300	FW	2007
Thomas Howard L III	(931)472-5999 howardlee58@yahoo.com	1200 N 62nd St Apt 325 Milwaukee WI 53213	SW	Assoc	Mount Calvary Milwaukee WI	(414)873-3931	CQ	2020
Thomas Steven E	(608)844-9503	W3801 W Lemonweir Ct Mauston WI 53948	SW	EM			FW	1978
Thomas Steven C	snlthomas72@gmail.com	403 Reserve Rd Libby MT 59923	MT	SP	St John Libby MT	(406)293-4024	SL	1999
Thomas Jonathan R	(407)902-9362 jon@stjohnmansfield.org	2046 W Belt Line Rd Cedar Hill TX 75104	TX	Sn/Adm	St John Mansfield TX	(817)473-4889	SL	1994
Thomas James M	(314)799-8746 jthomas@trinityof.org	701 N Mosley Rd Saint Louis MO 63141	MO	SP	Trinity Saint Charles MO	(636)250-3350	SL	2015
Thomas Eli J	(360)836-0292 eli@ccridgefield.com	c/o Christ Community 202 S 4th Ave Ridgefield WA 98642	NOW	SP	Grace* Longview WA	(360)423-2114	CQ	2013
Thomas Craig B	(303)679-1423 cbthomas32@gmail.com	30183 Arena Dr Evergreen CO 80439	RM	EM			FW	1992
Thomas Brian W	brianwilliamthomas@gmail.com	3993 Park Blvd San Diego CA 92103	PSW	SP	Grace San Diego CA	(619)299-2890	Other	2012
Thomas Brad	(715)864-0873 revbradthomas@gmail.com	621 Rand Street Chippewa Falls WI 54729	NW	Sn/Adm	Zion Chippewa Falls WI	(715)723-6380	SL	2008
Thomas Glen D Dr	glenthomaslcms@gmail.com	1069 Big Bend Station Dr Manchester MO 63088	MO	EM			SL	1982
Thompson Mark A	(217)737-3894 pastort@zlclinc.org	205 Pulaski St Lincoln IL 62656	CI	Sn/Adm	Zion Lincoln IL	(217)732-3946	SL	1998
Thompson William M I Dr	(314)608-7004 thompsonw@csl.edu	c/o Concordia Seminary 801 Seminary Place Saint Louis MO 63105	MO	S HS/C	Concordia Seminary Saint Louis MO	(314)505-7000	SL	1988
Thompson Stafford L	(218) 729-6380 stafford.thompson225@gmail.com	6310 Maple Grove Rd Cloquet MN 55720	MNN	SP	Hope Cloquet MN	(218)729-6380	FW	2021
Thompson Richard L Dr	(406)696-5107 rchrd.thompson@gmail.com	W5572 County Road C W Unit 2a Watertown WI 53098	SW	EM			SPR	1973
Thompson Adam R	(314)691-0625 semtennis0420@gmail.com	c/o Ascension Lutheran Church 8225 Peebles Rd Pittsburgh PA 15237	EA	SP	Ascension Pittsburgh PA	(412)364-4463	SL	2016
Thompson Matthew E	(707)756-0404 matthewphmt@gmail.com	W5572 County Rd CW Watertown WI 53098	SW	EM			FW	1985

*Multiple Assignments (See Church Worker Locator for Additional Details)

See Page 53 for the Table of Abbreviations for key to District, Position, and Seminary abbreviations

**C =Candidate; EM = Emeritus; the date following the C is the month and year the Candidate status began

NAME	TELEPHONE NUMBER EMAIL	STREET ADDRESS CITY/STATE/ZIP	DISTRICT	POSITION/ STATUS**	WHERE SERVING	OFFICE PHONE	SEM/ PROGRAM	YR GRAD
Thompson Lawton D	(321)377-8207 ldthompson113@gmail.com	8 Banbury Ct St. Louis MO 63126	MO	Assoc	St Paul Des Peres MO	(314)822-0447	SL	2022
Thompson Henry H Jr	(501)617-1702 henryhthompsonjr@gmail.com	4709 Willow Ridge Way Rogers AR 72758	MDS	EM			CQ	2018
Thompson Gregory N	(303) 518-5297 gnthompson66@gmail.com	10086 Zenobia Ct Westminster CO 80031	RM	Assoc	Mount Zion Denver CO	(303)429-0165	FW	1992
Thompson Douglas S	(406) 670-1673 doug.thompson3737@gmail.com	P.O. Box 14 Fisher MN 56723	MNN	SP	St Paul* Euclid MN		SL	1997
Thompson Dennis L	dennis95@aol.com	11648 Maryland St Crown Point IN 46307	NI	EM			SL	1977
Thompson David R	(214)282-9229 david.thompson@oslmckinney.org	2809 Cobre Valle Ln Plano TX 75023	TX	SMP	Our Savior McKinney TX	(972)562-9944	SL-SMP	2015
Thompson David B	(405)574-6835 wctltr@gmail.com	872 County Rd 1400 Chickasha OK 73018	OK	EM			FW	1996
Thompson Calvin J	(256)461-0352 pastorcjt@comcast.net	28 Forest Valley Dr Albertville AL 35950	SO	EM			FW	1977
Thompson Bert A	(586)219-4262 amcgremlin232@yahoo.com		SW	EM			FW	1996
Thompson Andrew S	(319)213-1199 asthomp10@gmail.com	216 Division St Plymouth WI 53073	SW	Assoc	St John Plymouth WI	(920)893-3071	SL	2022
Thompson Andrew P	(612)208-7388 pastor@saintstephanus.org	1573 Fernwood St Saint Paul MN 55108	MNS	Sn/Adm	St Stephanus Saint Paul MN	(651)228-1486	SL	2005
Thompson Andrew L	(214)280-3061 drewacet@gmail.com	P.O. Box 4973 Lago Vista TX 78645	TX	SP	Christ Our Savior Lago Vista TX	(512)267-7121	SL	2022
Thompson Matthew R	(701)426-4877 mt@midco.net	928 Arthur Dr Bismarck ND 58501	ND	SP	St John* McClusky ND	(701)363-2636	SL	2001
Thompson Donald F Jr	(504)841-7470 dontomp2000@yahoo.com	5445 Provine Pl Apt 609 Alexandria LA 71303	SO	SP	Redeemer Alexandria LA	(318)442-4325	FW	1990
Thoms Leo G	(810)710-1773 leothoms@juno.com	3080 N Lakeshore Rd Port Hope MI 48468	MI	EM			FW	2002
Thomsen Dwain J	(906)250-2132 pastorthomsen@gmail.com	1376 168th Ave New Richmond WI 54017	NW	SP	St Luke New Richmond WI	(715)246-4861	SL	2010
Thomson John M	(218) 900-7164 jazzman712@hotmail.com	120 3rd St S McGregor MN 55760	MNN	SP	Our Savior* Mc Gregor MN	(218)768-3198	FW	1993
Thomson Kevin C	(314)365-3521 kevint1717@gmail.com	12215 Southcreek Ct Indianapolis IN 46236	IN	Assoc	Cornerstone Carmel IN	(317)814-4252	SL	2016
Thormodson Ian O	(715)533-0386 ian.thormodson@gmail.com	404 3rd Ave. SE Medford MN 55049	MNS	SP	Trinity Medford MN	(507)451-0447	SL	2021
Thormodson Jeffrey L	(314)505-7108 thormodsonj@csl.edu	14100 Sunland Dr. Florissant MO 63034	MO	S HS/C	Concordia Seminary Saint Louis MO	(314)505-7000	SL	1995
Thorson Brian J	(816)934-1741 pastor@bethlehemlutheran-churchmn.org	7809 County Rd 35w Annandale MN 55302	MNS	SP	Bethlehem* Annandale MN	(320)963-3592	FW	2005
Thorson Clint O	(605)270-0059 rev.thorson@gmail.com	c/o Eternal Savior 2688 N Park Dr Lafayette CO 80026	RM	SP	Eternal Savior Lafayette CO	(303)665-6105	SL	2014
Thress Michael P	(302)540-9737 revthress@gmail.com	154 Kirkcaldy Dr Elkton MD 21921	SE	SP	Faith Bear DE	(302)834-1214	SL	1997
Thur Richard F	(314)706-6230 dickandjanethur2@hotmail.com		MO	EM			SL	1967
Thurau Michael R	(727)542-9912 mrtministry@gmail.com	439 Christan Bend Rd Church Hill TN 37642	FG	EM			SL	1987
Tiaden Kevin N	pastor.tiaden@berealutheran.org	9632 Elliot Ave S Bloomington MN 55420	MNS	SP	Berea Richfield MN	(612)861-7121	SL	1998
Tibben Kent A	(217)446-2321 danetibb@aol.com	1429 Woodridge Dr Danville IL 61832	CI	Sn/Adm	Trinity Danville IL	(217)446-4300	FW	1992
Tieken Russell W	(940)453-8361 rtiecken@yahoo.com	2009 Lake Fork Cir Denton TX 76210	TX	EM			SL	1981
Tieman Larry W Dr	(815)459-1441	409 Reserve Dr Crystal Lake IL 60012	NI	Sn/Adm	Immanuel Crystal Lake IL	(815)459-1441	SL	1991
Tieman Terry D Dr	terry.tieman@gmail.com	8601 Trinity Rd Cordova TN 38018	MDS	Sn/Adm	Grace Celebration Cordova TN	(901)737-6010	SL	1983
Tietjen Richard H	(253)564-2028 uptietjen@gmail.com	4416 61st Ave W Tacoma WA 98466	NOW	EM			SL	1965
Tietjen Walter C Dr	(916)832-5955 wctietjen@icloud.com	Carlton Senior Living 6915 Elk Grove Blvd Apt 131 Elk Grove CA 95758	CNH	EM			SL	1961
Tietz Ryan M Dr	(260)206-5833	2514 Florida Dr Fort Wayne IN 46805	IN	S HS/C	Concordia Theological Seminary Fort Wayne IN	(260)452-2100	SL	2003
Tietze Sean M	(757)376-7386 pastorseantietze@gmail.com	4704 Jardin Cove Chesapeake VA 23321	SE	SMP	Christ Norfolk VA	(757)853-5655	SL-SMP	2022
Tiews Christian C Dr	+49-176-7236-7504 christian.tiews@lcms.org		OK	S Miss	Office of International Mission Saint Louis MO		SL	2009
Tillinger Dusan Dr	(519)300-2710 dusan.tillinger@gmail.com	1842 Rd 3 West Kingsville ON N9Y 2 CANADA	EN	Assoc	St Luke North York ON	(416)221-8900	CQ	2012
Tillmann Gary W	(920)474-4749 pastor@stjohnashippun.com	N 1247 St Johns Way Oconomowoc WI 53066	SW	SP	St John Oconomowoc WI	(920)474-4749	SL	2000
Tilney David M	(218)206-5825 dmtilney@hotmail.com		MNN	SP	St Luke Wood Lake MN	(507)485-3527	SL	2002
Timm Luke R	(515) 987-4030 luke@livingfaithclive.com	2180 NW 142nd St Clive IA 50325	IW	Sn/Adm	Living Faith Clive IA	(515)987-4030	SL	2004
Timm Gary M	(720)980-0530 exracer327b@gmail.com	4165 Aspen Hills Dr Bettendorf IA 52772	IE	Assoc	Our Savior Bettendorf IA	(563)332-5141	SL	2010
Timm Bruce A	(320)252-8171 pastortimm@redeemerstcloud.org		MNN	Sn/Adm	Redeemer Saint Cloud MN	(320)252-8171	SL	1988

*Multiple Assignments (See Church Worker Locator for Additional Details)
See Page 53 for the Table of Abbreviations for key to District, Position, and Seminary abbreviations
**C =Candidate; EM = Emeritus; the date following the C is the month and year the Candidate status began

NAME	TELEPHONE NUMBER EMAIL	STREET ADDRESS CITY/STATE/ZIP	DISTRICT	POSITION/ STATUS**	WHERE SERVING	OFFICE PHONE	SEM/ PROGRAM	YR GRAD
Timm David H	(440)241-4779 dtimm@royred.org	10390 Rock Ledge Way N Royalton OH 44133	OH	Assoc	Royal Redeemer North Royalton OH	(440)237-7958	CQ	2008
Timmermann Norman A	pr.norm@yahoo.com	W148n7346 Woodland Dr Menomonee FLS WI 53051	EN	EM			CQ	1980
Timmons James G	(407)402-2530 jtimm52@aol.com	519 E 1st St Sanford FL 32771	FG	EM			SL	2004
Tiner Robert J	(979)542-8304 rtiner@ilgtx.com	1090 E Hempstead St Giddings TX 78942	TX	Sn/Adm	Immanuel Giddings TX	(979)542-2918	SL	2005
Tinetti Ryan P Dr	(231) 970-0883 r.tinetti@gmail.com	9 McCall Ter Saint Louis MO 63105	MO	S HS/C	Concordia Seminary Saint Louis MO	(314)505-7000	SL	2010
Tinglund Jais H	(605)228-9216 tinglund@nvc.net	10308 W Kingswood Cir Sun City AZ 85351	PSW	Assoc	Atonement Glendale AZ	(623)582-8785	CQ	2002
Tino James C Dr	(305)333-0156 revtino@hotmail.com	6709 Ficus Dr Miramar FL 33023	FG	SP	Faith Hialeah FL	(305)888-6706	FW	1988
Tischer Steven L	(763)923-3830 tisch_62@hotmail.com	6971 330th Ln NW Princeton MN 55371	MNN	SP	Zion Princeton MN	(763)389-1286	FW	1993
Tkac Russell S	(248)821-2727 peacetkac@gmail.com	2210 Highfield Rd Waterford MI 48329	MI	SMP	Peace Waterford MI	(248)681-9360	FW-SMP	2012
Todd Gerald E	(443)562-0579 pastorflc02@verizon.net	302 E Joppa Rd Apt 1803 Towson MD 21286	SE	EM			SL	1977
Todd Gregory N Dr		632 Warrington Ave SE Washington DC 20003	SI	M Chap	Office of International Mission Saint Louis MO		SL	1988
Todd Kelly D	(810)444-3006 revkellytodd@icloud.com	5225 Hadley Rd Goodrich MI 48438	MI	SP	Christ Goodrich MI	(810)255-1185	FW	2000
Toenjes Alan M	(920)360-5094 htoenjes@trinitycp.org	1206 Troutwine Rd Crown Point IN 46307	IN	Sn/Adm	Trinity Crown Point IN	(219)663-1578	SL	1991
Toensing Maynard L Jr	pastortoensing@gmail.com	11440 W Panama Rd Crete NE 68333	NEB	SP	St John Crete NE	(402)826-3883	SL	1992
Toepke Ival L	(256)726-0011 iltoepke@gmail.com	920 Martin Rd Mogadore OH 44260	SO	SMP	Trinity Scottsboro AL	(256)574-4927	FW-SMP	2016
Tolzman Brion P	(402)846-5935 tolzie@abbnebraska.com	P.O. Box 252 Walthill NE 68067	NEB	SP	Trinity* Decatur NE	(402)349-5541	SL	1986
Toma James B	(714)676-6190 jimtoma54@yahoo.com	1378 E 10th Pl Casa Grande AZ 85122	PSW	EM			SL	2018
Tomac Steven B	(775)750-1579 trc.nev@gmail.com	13 Nordyke Rd Yerington NV 89447	CNH	SMP	Faith Yerington NV	(775)463-5675	SL-SMP	2024
Toman Jason D	(269) 271-6588 jasontoman@yahoo.com	10577 W Tu Ave Lawton MI 49065	MI	C01/2025			SL-SMP	2012
Tomesch Harald G Dr	(414)247-8622 hgt@cuw.edu	150 Patriot Ct Slinger WI 53086	SW	S HS/C	Concordia University Wisconsin Mequon WI	(262)243-5700	NESC	1981
Tomesch Jordan H	(414)331-8825 jtomesch@gmail.com	150 Patriot Ct Slinger WI 53086	MO	C02/2017			SL	2016
Tomhave Gregory J	(320)223-3836 revgjtomhave@gmail.com	1867 Eastern Star Loop Sauk Rapids MN 56379	MNN	SP	Good Shepherd Sauk Rapids MN	(320)259-3474	FW	1987
Tompkins Daryl G	(712)542-0298 countrypreacher@reagan.com	560 W Oak St Clarinda IA 51632	IW	EM			SL	1997
Toms Richard E	(916)316-0688 reliablerich@yahoo.com	4085 Clover Valley Rd Rocklin CA 95677	CNH	SMP	Trinity Georgetown CA	(530)333-0798	CQ	2019
Tonack Donald P	(541)259-2820 donanita@centurytel.net	34711 Bond Rd P.O. Box 524 Lebanon OR 97355	NOW	EM			SL	1980
Tonn Paul A	pastorpaultonn@gmail.com	c/o Trinity Lutheran Church 19778 US Highway 10 Reed City MI 49677	MI	SP	Trinity Reed City MI	(231)832-5186	SL	2009
Tooley Mark D	(501) 339-7866 marktooley3600@gmail.com	101 Mako Dr Cambridge MD 21613	SE	SMP	Immanuel Easton MD	(410)822-5665	SL-SMP	2015
Tooman Matthew M	(701)640-9594 looktoxp@reagan.com	402 3rd Ave N Wahpeton ND 58075	IW		Iowa West District Fort Dodge IA	(515)576-7666	SL	2005
Toombs Jason W	(281)330-8282 jason.toombs@gmail.com	2510 Cheyenne Rd Liberal KS 67901	KS	SP	Grace* Liberal KS	(620)624-5900	FW	2014
Toopes Andrew W	(870)672-2117 toopes57@gmail.com	334 Sylvan Cir Bowling Green KY 42101	MDS	EM			FW	1983
Torea Eduardo J	(469)867-3477 pastortorea@gmail.com	2705 S Cypress Cir Plano TX 75075	TX	C01/2021			SL	2016
Torkelson Daniel T	(920)342-0459 revtork70@gmail.com		SW	SP	Mount Olive Madison WI	(608)238-5656	SL	1997
Torneire Miguel A	(636)793-1300 miguel@torneire.com	8 Cambourne Court St. Peter's MO 63376	S	D Miss	SELC District Macungie PA	(610)965-3265	Other	2003
Torreson Jonathan A	(616)802-2841 jonathantorreson@gmail.com	c/o Our Redeemer Lutheran Church 7196 Som Center Rd Solon OH 44139	OH	SP	Our Redeemer Solon OH	(440)248-4066	SL	2018
Torreson Theodore D	(573) 579-1305 tdtorreson@gmail.com	2697 Highway 59 Denison IA 51442	IW	SP	Christ Denison IA		SL	2009
Torske Kerry E	(509)226-3042 kerrytorske60@gmail.com	5715 N Vincent Rd Newman Lake WA 99025	NOW	SMP	Hope Spokane Valley WA	(509)924-1630	CQ	2019
Toth Dusan Dr	(416)221-0418 dusanto38@gmail.com	c/o Pent House 106 8 Hillcrest Ave Toronto ON M2N 6 CANADA	EN	EM			Other	1961
Totsky David W	(262)894-3614 davidtotsky@sbcglobal.net	709 Prestiage St Joliet IL 60435	NI	SP	St Peter* Joliet IL	(815)722-3567	FW	1989
Townes Richard A Jr	(760)285-6380 sermonator1960@live.com	13947 Wintervalley NE Cedar Springs MI 49319	MI	SP	Bethel Howard City MI	(231)937-4921	FW	1994
Townley Jared C	(989)860-9030 pastorjared@lambofgodlv.org	5521 Raven Creek Ave Las Vegas NV 89130	PSW	SP	Lamb Of God Las Vegas NV	(702)645-4998	SL	2020
Townsend Larry W	(770)280-5125 townsend949870@bellsouth.net	115 Tara Trace McDonough GA 30252	FG	EM			SL	2001

*Multiple Assignments (See Church Worker Locator for Additional Details)
See Page 53 for the Table of Abbreviations for key to District, Position, and Seminary abbreviations
**C =Candidate; EM = Emeritus; the date following the C is the month and year the Candidate status began

NAME	TELEPHONE NUMBER EMAIL	STREET ADDRESS CITY/STATE/ZIP	DISTRICT	POSITION/ STATUS**	WHERE SERVING	OFFICE PHONE	SEM/ PROGRAM	YR GRAD
Townsend Joseph E	(765)409-3744 revjet54@frontier.com	2512 McShay Dr W Lafayette IN 47906	IN	SP	Redeemer West Lafayette IN	(765)463-5851	FW	1980
Trampe Heath A Dr	heath.trampe@lcms.org		MO	S Ex/S	Office of National Mission Saint Louis MO		FW	2010
Traphagan William J	(641)373-4128 christcrucifiedforus@gmail.com	14321 Shafer Rd Crosslake MN 56442	MNN	SP	Mission Of The Cross Crosslake MN	(218)692-4228	FW	2014
Trapp Allen R	(440)667-9513 jo777al@aol.com	7523 Pinnacle Ct Indian Trail NC 28079	SE	EM			SL	1972
Trapp Thomas H Dr	(952)835-2223 ttrapp@csp.edu	10220 Chowen Ave S Bloomington MN 55431	MNS	EM			SL	1971
Trask Michael A	(763)350-3791 mitrask@embarqmail.com	14010 Hillcrest Pl Rogers MN 55374	MNS	SP	Life In Christ Albertville MN	(763)497-3799	SL	1986
Travis Howard S	(989)343-9088 hstravis@zohomail.com	2591 Holiday House Rd Saint Joseph MI 49085	MI	EM			FW	2006
Travis James W	(712)202-8516 rev.travis@hotmail.com	3622 Pierce Pl Sioux City IA 51104	IW	Sn/Adm	Calvary Sioux City IA	(712)239-1575	SL	2002
Traxel Joshua T	(217)546-4531 joshua.traxel@oursaviors-church.org	79 Bellerive Rd Springfield IL 62704	CI	Sn/Adm	Our Savior's Springfield IL	(217)546-4531	SL	2013
Trebus Louis R	ltrebus@gmail.com	804 Shannondale Way Apt 317 Maryville TN 37803	MDS	EM			CQ	2006
Treglown Donald E	(239)598-1945 revdet@flcnaples.com	1260 Shady Rest Lane Apt 101 Naples FL 34103	EN	Sn/Adm	Faith Naples FL	(239)434-5811	FW	1987
Tremain Richard D	(812)350-4485 r.tremain@sbcglobal.net	4151 W 200 S Columbus IN 47201	IN	EM			SL	1955
Tremain Peter D Dr	(785)220-2719 petertremain@gmail.com	203 Willoughby Court Louisville KY 40245	KS	EM			SL	1969
Trempala Daniel S	(314)971-9340 jdtrempala@yahoo.com	101 Rainbow Dr #6108 Livingston TX 77399	TX	EM			SL	2016
Treude John M	(479)646-2506 mostrightrev@juno.com	3108 Canongate Way Fort Smith AR 72908	MDS	EM			SL	1985
Trewyn John I Sr	(715)820-3445 greenbay43@hotmail.com	884 Pinecrest Ave Phillips WI 54555	NW	EM			SL	1998
Trieglaff Eugene E Dr	(920)622-3603	W6401 Aniwa Rd Wild Rose WI 54984	NI	EM			SL	1961
Trier Orlando E	(503)705-7528 h2ofallman1@comcast.net	703 E Sierra Vista Dr Newberg OR 97132	NOW	EM			SL	1971
Trinklein John K Dr	(602)550-2548	c/o Concordia University 800 N Columbia Ave Seward NE 68434	NEB	S HS/C	Concordia University Nebraska Seward NE	(402)643-3651	SL	1995
Trinklein Jonathan B	(586)201-9217 jontrinklein6262@gmail.com	1619 Claystone Ct Zeeland MI 49464	MI	EM			SL	1981
Triplett Glen M	(260)498-4054 revtriplett@gmail.com	3601 S Duncan Rd Champaign IL 61822	CI	SP	Friendship/Joy Champaign IL	(217)355-0454	FW	2016
Triplett Kirk E Dr	(530)306-0712 kirktrip@gmail.com	104 New Orleans Dr El Paso TX 79912	RM	SP	Zion El Paso TX	(915)566-4667	CQ	2021
Triplett David S	(440)241-2457 pastordavesue@yahoo.com	6471 Forest Park Drive North Ridgeville OH 44039	S	EM			FW	1980
Tritten Eric E Dr	(330)322-0534 pastort@gloriadeihudson.org	4258 Newcomer Rd Stow OH 44224	OH	SP	Gloria Dei Hudson OH	(330)650-6550	SL	1998
Troemel Samuel R	stroemel@clcs.org	7146 Chandler Ct Indianapolis IN 46217	IN	SMP	Calvary Indianapolis IN	(317)783-2000	SL-SMP	2020
Troester Jerome A	(801)803-0901 jerometroester@hotmail.com	12097 S Window Arch Ln Herriman UT 84096	RM	EM			SL	1983
Troester Matthew D	(708) 720-0880 rtroester@stpaulsonline.org	19555 Willowfield Ct Mokena IL 60448	NI	Sn/Adm	St Paul Matteson IL	(708)720-0880	SL	1984
Trombley Michael W	pastortrombley@gmail.com	7821 Decatur Rd Fort Wayne IN 46816	IN	SP	Trinity Fort Wayne IN	(260)447-2411	FW	2008
Trosien Carl F	(989)450-0502 pastort48@yahoo.com	375 Norbert Ln Hemlock MI 48626	MI	SP	Lord/New Life Midland MI	(989)837-2856	SL	1978
Trosien William J	(715)479-6757 trosien@newnorth.net	1379 Bluebird Ln Eagle River WI 54521	NW	EM			SL	1980
Trost Edward W	(913)768-4288 pastortrost@gmail.com	26799 W Shadow Cir Olathe KS 66061	KS	EM			SL	1967
Troup Antonin C Dr	(618)340-8375 pastortonytroup@gmail.com	5876 J Rd Waterloo IL 62298	SI	Assoc	Immanuel Waterloo IL	(618)939-6480	SL	1984
Trouten Chad D	(260)494-6592	2435 Engle Rd Fort Wayne IN 46809	EN	Sn/Adm	Bethany Fort Wayne IN	(260)747-0713	FW	1995
Trower Charles T	(727)422-6524 charles.trower@aol.com	353 Woodlander Dr Blythewood SC 29016	FG	EM			SL-D	2005
Troxel Christopher D	(810)990-7572 troxel@me.com	20333 Weyher St Livonia MI 48152	MI	Assoc	University Chapel Ann Arbor MI	(734)663-5560	SL	2016
Troyke James F	(417)320-2099 troyke@live.com	4349 S Kansas Ave Apt B206 Springfield MO 65810	MO	EM			SL	1972
Truax Charles J	(985)502-7088 candcin@hotmail.com	P.O. Box 5761 Slidell LA 70469	SO	EM			SL	1972
Truelsen Christopher D		1363 Northern Valley Trl Avon IN 46123	IN	SP	Christ Brownsburg IN	(317)852-3343	SL	2001
Truenow David L	(602)799-3299 ydavetrue@gmail.com	1447 Allison Dr New Braunfels TX 78130	TX	SP	Evangelists Kingsbury TX	(830)639-4906	SL	1996
Truesdell Daniel B	(808)227-3030 PastorDan@StMarkHawaii.Org	1151 Kahili St Kailua HI 96734	CNH	SP	St Mark Kaneohe HI	(808)227-3930	CQ	2016
Trump Shauen T	(314)585-6271 shauen.trump@lcms.org	P.O. Box 22 Karen 00502 KENYA	NOW	S Miss	Office of International Mission Saint Louis MO		SL	2010

*Multiple Assignments (See Church Worker Locator for Additional Details)
See Page 53 for the Table of Abbreviations for key to District, Position, and Seminary abbreviations
**C =Candidate; EM = Emeritus; the date following the C is the month and year the Candidate status began

NAME	TELEPHONE NUMBER EMAIL	STREET ADDRESS CITY/STATE/ZIP	DISTRICT	POSITION/ STATUS**	WHERE SERVING	OFFICE PHONE	SEM/ PROGRAM	YR GRAD
Trunkhill Chad A	(712)571-9249 chad@trunkhill.org	110 Logan St P.O. Box 167 Dow City IA 51528	IW	Sn/Adm	Our Savior* Denison IA	(712)263-3282	SL	2008
Truog Brian M	(865)250-8334		MDS	EM			SL	1982
Truwe Gregory R Dr	(660)234-2885 pastortruwe@gmail.com	102 E Jefferson St Cole Camp MO 65325	MO	Sn/Adm	Trinity Cole Camp MO	(660)668-2364	SL	2007
Tsang James T	(419)866-1772	5666 Knightsbridge Dr Toledo OH 43614	OH	D Miss	Ohio District North Olmsted OH	(440)235-2297	CQ	1980
Tucher Jared C	(307)689-5322 revtucher@gmail.com	7291 Sr 62 Dillsboro IN 47018	IN	SP	St Paul's* Cross Plains IN	(812)667-5700	FW	2005
Tucker Jeffrey D	(210)216-7861 jmambatucker@gmail.com	c/o Concordia Lutheran Church 16801 Huebner Rd San Antonio TX 78258	TX	Assoc	Concordia San Antonio TX	(210)479-1477	SL	2021
Tucker Richard J Sr	(828)781-5263 richard@commfab.com	1336 6th St NW Hickory NC 28601	SE	SMP	Christ Hickory NC	(828)328-1483	CQ	2018
Tucker William H	(210)287-8825 friartuc@concordia-satx.com	19031 La Verita San Antonio TX 78258	TX	Sn/Adm	Concordia San Antonio TX	(210)479-1477	FW	1987
Tuell James A	(303) 594-2556 jamestuell@aol.com	3695 S Acoma Street Englewood CO 80110	RM	SMP	Immanuel Englewood CO	(303)781-5887	FW-SMP	2019
Tuft Jeffrey W	(719)447-7219 jeff.tuft@comcast.net	527 Hillcrest Ave Oroville CA 95966	CNH	SMP	Grace* Gridley CA	(530)846-4736	SL-SMP	2022
Tuma Brian D	(402)576-3036	P.O. Box 17 Cordova NE 68330	NEB	SP	Saint John Cordova NE	(402)576-3211	SL	2005
Tuma Jacob B	(402)710-2977 pastorjtuma@gmail.com	55205 854th Rd Pierce NE 68767	NEB	SP	St John's Pierce NE	(402)329-4298	SL	2020
Tumbuan Dino F	(562)480-2834 metalboy50@yahoo.com	7952 Stewart And Gray Rd Apt 5 Downey CA 90241	PSW	EM			CQ	1988
Turanski Ted N	(231)839-4746	4940 River Woods Rd Lake City MI 49651	MI	EM			SL	1972
Turner Wallace B Dr	(619) 850-6072 revbevturner@aol.com	10858 Rueda Ct San Diego CA 92124	PSW	EM			SL	1962
Turner Steven D Dr	(515) 341-3602 sdturner58@gmail.com	1500 Crown Colony Court Unit 240 Des Moines IA 50315	IW	EM			FW	1985
Turner Richard T Jr	(832)746-2065 pastorturner@gmail.com	407 Doris St El Campo TX 77437	TX	EM			FW	1988
Turner John S	(970)629-8538 johnjsturner@aol.com	P.O. Box 1310 Craig CO 81626	RM	SP	Faith Craig CO	(970)824-3043	FW	2007
Tutwiler Danny W	(630)777-4167	1831 Ness Way Montgomery IL 60538	NI	EM			SL	1982
Twenhafel Ricky J	(913)370-3926 ricktwenhafel@gmail.com	1717 Haskell Rd Nortonville KS 66060	KS	SP	St Pauls Duluth KS	(785)456-4606	SL	1994
Twietmeyer Andrew R	(262)389-6562 pastor.twietmeyer@gmail.com	5200 Cronk Rd Jonesville MI 49250	MI	Assoc	St Paul Hillsdale MI	(517)437-2762	FW	2021
Twietmeyer Philip W	(267)738-8103 ptwietm1@comcast.net	55 Fern Dr Yardley PA 19067	EA	SMP	Hope Levittown PA	(215)946-3467	SL-SMP	2024
Tyce Martin A	(845)269-9114 mtyce@hvc.rr.com	36 Walnut Ave Highland FLS NY 10928	AT	SP	Atonement Stony Point NY	(845)942-0121	SL	2012
Tyler Marty L	(408)310-3349 revmltyler@yahoo.com	118 Red Hawk Ln Crescent City CA 95531	CNH	SP	Grace Crescent City CA	(707)464-4712	SL	2004
Ude Stephen C	(515)291-9499 revsude1@netins.net	1239 Jasmine Pl Ogden IA 50212	IW	Asst	Christ* Perry IA	(515)676-2289	SPR	1971
Udoekong Michael D		3823 Fox Hunt Way Grayslake IL 60030	NI	EM			SL	1996
Uecker Warren W	(605)480-2908 black.hills.hermit@gmail.com	12440 Willow Creek Rd Custer SD 57730	SD	EM			SL	1981
Uglum James R	(636)577-7539 james.uglum@chapelofthecross lutheran.org	305 Booth Bay Ct Saint Charles MO 63304	MO	Assoc	Chapel of the Cross Saint Peters MO	(636)928-5885	SL	2010
Uhrinak Leslie H	(218)820-2792	30641 Hornet Rd. NE Blackduck MN 56630	MNN	EM			CQ	2008
Ulledalen Benjamin J Sr	pastor.ulledalen@protonmail.com	13541 W. Highway 53 Rathdrum ID 83858	NOW	SP	Shepherd Hills Rathdrum ID	(208)687-1809	FW	2015
Ullman Walter W	ullmanwalter@hotmail.com	1057 Maryport Dr Westfield IN 46074	IN	EM			SL	1973
Ulm Joshua R	(330)419-2720 pastorulmascension@gmail.com	23541 Marion Rd North Olmsted OH 44070	EN	SP	Ascension North Olmsted OH	(440)777-6365	SL	2018
Ulmer Kurt A	(972)955-4465 pastorulmer@gmail.com	423 Da Vinci Ln Wylie TX 75098	TX	SP	Faith Wylie TX	(972)461-2777	FW	2010
Ulmer Matthew T		10653 N 550 W Decatur IN 46733	IN	SP	Zion Decatur IN	(260)547-4248	SL	2010
Ulrich Daniel M	(931) 494-3100 pastordanulrich@gmail.com	1100 Unique Ct Mattoon IL 61938	CI	SP	St Pauls Mattoon IL	(217)234-9880	FW	2015
UmaShankar Kanagasabai	(971)322-8177 umak@trinityklein.org	91-679 Ft Weaver Rd Ewa Beach HI 96706	CNH	SP	Messiah Ewa Beach-Oahu HI	(808)321-3941	SL	2025
Umbach Arthur M	(804)512-0723 art.umbach@gmail.com	13319 Langford Dr Midlothian VA 23113	SE	EM			SL	1969
Umbarger Kent A	(309)738-9249 kentumbarger@gmail.com	6655 Primrose Ct. Bettendorf IA 52722	CI	EM			FW	1987
Undlin Paul J	(248)625-4644 pundlin@sainttrinitylutheran.com	811 Island Lake Dr Oxford MI 48371	MI	Sn/Adm	St Trinity Clarkston MI	(248)625-4644	SL	2008
Ungrodt Richard J	(219)393-5287 rungrodt@idoc.in.gov	3645 S Wayne Dr La Porte IN 46350	IN	Inst C	Indiana District Fort Wayne IN	(800)837-1145	FW	1981
Unke Timothy A	(949)294-4284 teknorev@msn.com	27971 Calle Casal Mission Viejo CA 92692	PSW	Cmp P	Crean Irvine CA	(949)387-1199	CQ	2017
Unseth Aaron J	(314)497-0339 aaron@twhmn.org	255 Capitol View Cir Roseville MN 55113	MNS	C06/2019			SL	2007

*Multiple Assignments (See Church Worker Locator for Additional Details)
See Page 53 for the Table of Abbreviations for key to District, Position, and Seminary abbreviations
**C =Candidate; EM = Emeritus; the date following the C is the month and year the Candidate status began

NAME	TELEPHONE NUMBER EMAIL	STREET ADDRESS CITY/STATE/ZIP	DISTRICT	POSITION/ STATUS**	WHERE SERVING	OFFICE PHONE	SEM/ PROGRAM	YR GRAD
Upchurch Lewis M III	(949)933-3595 lew.upchurch@gmail.com	2113 Monrovia Ave Costa Mesa CA 92627	PSW	C05/2024			SL-SMP	2013
Uphoff Aaron D	(815)432-4136 aduphoff@gmail.com	419 N 4th St Watseka IL 60970	CI	SP	Calvary Watseka IL	(815)432-4136	FW	2014
Urbach Jon B	(605)280-2838 jburbach@faithluth.com	803 N Grand Ave Pierre SD 57501	SD	EM			SL	1971
Urena Aguilar Martin	(559) 481-2291 martintheluther7@gmail.com	2190 N Schnoor Ave Apt 122 Madera CA 93637	CNH	C07/2016			SL	2009
Urlaub Bradley P	(585) 348-1545 pastorbradurlaub@gmail.com	17 Rollingwood Dr Pittsford NY 14534	EA	SP	St Mark Mendon NY	(585)624-1766	SL	2012
Urvan John R	(440)632-8044 john_urvan@yahoo.com	15388 Knox Cir Middlefield OH 44062	OH	EM			SL	2007
Utech William G Dr	(314)703-8071 utechw@gofast.am	3678 120th Ct W Faribault MN 55021	MNS	EM			SL	1985
Utecht Andrew E	(605)747-2448 chiefsin2@gmail.com	P.O. Box 558 Rosebud SD 57570	SD	SP	Our Savior* Valentine NE	(605)828-2695	FW	1997
Utecht Titus A	(402)389-0621 titus.utecht@gmail.com	15117 Greenleaf St Sherman Oaks CA 91403	EN	SP	Sherman Oaks Sherman Oaks CA	(818)789-0215	FW	2019
Utecht Peter M	605-460-1307 3nails@abe.midco.net	1537 Baltimore Ave Hot Springs SD 57747	SD	SP	Bethesda Hot Springs SD	(605)745-4834	FW	1994
Uttech Gary R Dr	(715)453-5865 ventriloquistsdummy@charter.net	104 S 2nd St Tomahawk WI 54487	NW	EM			CQ	1994
Uttenreither Matthew J	(262)305-2600 uttenreither18@gmail.com	7423 N Milwaukee Ave Niles IL 60714	NI	SP	Ascension Niles IL	(847)647-9867	FW	2002
Utton Timothy A	(757)567-2772 timothyutton@gmail.com	1132 Rollingwood Arch Virginia Beach VA 23464	SE	C01/2021			SL	2002
Vail Clayton G	(618)483-9825 vailfamily@hotmail.com	5600 Powell Rd Huber Heights OH 45424	OH	EM			FW	1978
Valencia Erwin A	(847)767-3656 avalencia@saint-paul.org	113 S School St Mount Prospect IL 60056	NI	Assoc	St Paul Mount Prospect IL	(847)255-0332	SL	2022
Valigorsky Mark S	(860)223-3503 msvaligorsky@hotmail.com	456 W. Rutland Rd Milford CT 06461	NE	SP	St Matthew New Britain CT	(860)223-3503	CQ	2013
Vallejo Gabriel E	(408)406-1715 gabrielvallejo417@gmail.com	2011 McCloud River Rd Chula Vista CA 91913	CNH	EM			HITSL	1996
Vallejo Juan G	(408)410-9771 jvallejo11@netzero.com		CNH	SP	Trinity Watsonville CA	(831)724-0176	SL	2015
Vallie John C	(406)650-2289 triparishpastor@gmail.com	505 W Laurel Ave Plentywood MT 59254	MT	EM			SL	2000
Van Blarcom Trevor E	(714)345-5084 tvanblarcom@stjohnsorange.org	600 E Moreland Dr Orange CA 92866	PSW	Assoc	Saint Johns Orange CA	(714)288-4400	Other	2017
Van Buskirk Raymond J	(281)838-5875 pastor.raymond@stpeterdown-townhouston.org	2514 Alan Lake Ln Spring TX 77388	TX	Sn/Adm	Saint Peter Houston TX	(713)485-6889	SL	2004
Van Dellen James H	(248)736-1891 pastorvan44@gmail.com	940 Schloemer Dr West Bend WI 53095	SW	EM			SPR	1970
Van Duzer Thomas N	(760)238-7853 tomvanduzer@yahoo.com	219 Meir Ln College Station TX 77845	TX	EM			SL	1979
Van Fossan Kurt A	(970)238-6551 uskav34@protonmail.com	1280 Sunrise Dr Delta CO 81416	RM	SP	Immanuel Paonia CO	(970)238-6551	SL	1987
Van Gorder Laird W	(478)951-3397 l.jvangorder@cox.net	203 Squires Ct Warner Robins GA 31093	FG	SMP	Holy Trinity Macon GA		SL-SMP	2019
Van Hemert Thomas C	(563)607-3737 prtcvanhemert@gmail.com	287 Roberts Avenue Marengo IA 52301	IE	SP	St Johns Marengo IA	(319)642-5452	FW	2020
Van Meter Chad M	(260)739-6524 cvanmeter@holycrossfw.org	c/o Holy Cross 3425 Crescent Ave Fort Wayne IN 46805	IN	Assoc	Holy Cross Fort Wayne IN	(260)483-3173	FW	2025
Van Nostrand Carl W	(515)231-1564 h808rx@gmail.com	2665 390th St Story City IA 50248	IW	EM			SL	1992
Van Patten Paul L Jr Dr	(580)478-7198 drplvpjr@gmail.com	6701 S. Anthony Blvd. #116a Fort Wayne IN 46816	OK	EM			FW	1996
Van Scharrel Eric J	(918)284-0409 evanscharrel@sjlchurch.org	1706 Classen St Bakersfield CA 93312	CNH	Sn/Adm	St John Bakersfield CA	(661)665-7815	SL	2007
Van Scyoc Eric L	(440)488-3191 escyoc@sbcglobal.net		OH	EM			SL	1987
van Sliedrecht Jonathan	(407)489-7727 jvansliedrecht@yahoo.com	10044 Deering St Fishers IN 46037	IN	SP	Journey Fishers IN	(407)489-7727	SL	2004
VanBriggle Richard A	(586)925-3260 rick@gencen.org	52104 Elizabeth Ln New Baltimore MI 48047	MI	SMP	St Thomas Eastpointe MI	(586)772-3370	SL-SMP	2012
Vanderbilt Thomas W	(615)557-6802 tom.vanderbilt@icloud.com	1603 W. Girard Ave. Indianola IA 50125	IW	SP	Mount Calvary Indianola IA	(515)961-4321	SL	1997
Vanderbush Neil S	n.vanderbush@icloud.com	25040 Black Creek San Antonio TX 78257	TX	SP	Messiah Boerne TX	(830)755-4300	SL	2007
Vandercook David D Sr	(501)800-2069 david.vandercook@protonmail.com	914 2nd St. Crawford NE 69339	WY				SL	2007
Vanderhyde Benjamin D	(720)394-8651 vanderhydeb@csl.edu	514 Dexter St Wray CO 80758	RM	SP	Calvary Wray CO	(970)630-5636	SL	2021
Vanderhyde David R Jr	(720)484-5631 pastorvanderhyde@uhillslutheran.org	4734 E Dartmouth Ave Denver CO 80222	RM	SP	University Hills Denver CO	(303)759-0161	SL	2013
Vanderhyde Joshua S	(970)340-9221 jvanderhyde@tgreeley.com	2160 26th Ave Greeley CO 80634	RM	SP	Trinity Greeley CO	(970)330-2485	SL	2018
Vanek James A	(715)338-7792	400 E 19th St Monahans TX 79756	NW	EM			SL	1965
Vang Johnny	(763)213-7991 nomtsa@gmail.com	5316 76th Pl N Brooklyn Park MN 55443	MNS	Assoc	The Gathering Place Arden Hills MN	(651)633-2402	SL	2015
Vang Yia Z	(651)242-9366 ntxoov36@gmail.com	4612 N 24th Place Milwaukee WI 53209	EN	EM			SL	1993

*Multiple Assignments (See Church Worker Locator for Additional Details)
See Page 53 for the Table of Abbreviations for key to District, Position, and Seminary abbreviations
**C =Candidate; EM = Emeritus; the date following the C is the month and year the Candidate status began

NAME	TELEPHONE NUMBER EMAIL	STREET ADDRESS CITY/STATE/ZIP	DISTRICT	POSITION/ STATUS**	WHERE SERVING	OFFICE PHONE	SEM/ PROGRAM	YR GRAD
Vang Daniel X	(414)292-7283 pastor.molc@gmail.com	104 Picasso Way Folsom CA 95630	CNH	SP	Mount Olive Folsom CA	(916)985-2984	SL	2016
Vang Chou	(612)840-1364 kxfchouvang@gmail.com	13420 36th Ave N Minneapolis MN 55441	MNS	SP	Shepherd Grove Maple Grove MN	(763)425-5941	SL	2016
Vang Chang T	(651)772-3454 vaajtsaav@yahoo.com	1586 Hazel St N Saint Paul MN 55119	MNS	EM			SL-D	2003
Vang Blong	(920)303-1438 tbvang@yahoo.com	161 Johnson Ave Oshkosh WI 54902	SW	SP	Hmong Oshkosh WI	(920)267-3305	EIITSL	2007
Vang Moua	(414)324-3945 mvkt05@gmail.com	8435 W Brentwood Ave Milwaukee WI 53224	SW	Assoc	Benediction Milwaukee WI	(414)463-9158	SL	2012
Vangen Philip M	(336) 825-3417 pmvangen@gmail.com	522 Claridge Cir Winston Salem NC 27106	FG	EM			CQ	1988
Vangor William M	(914)886-2460 bvangor@gmail.com	5 Carey St Mahopac NY 10541	AT	SMP	St Luke Putnam Valley NY	(845)528-8858	SL-SMP	2011
Vano Joel M	(952)999-2025 pastorjoel@ascensionburnsville.org	4269 Joppa Cir Savage MN 55378	MNS	SP	Ascension Burnsville MN	(952)890-3412	SL	2003
VanOsdol Jeffrey M	(864)607-3496 revjvan29681@yahoo.com	112 Five Gait Turn Simpsonville SC 29681	SE	SP	Immanuel Simpsonville SC	(864)297-5815	FW	1992
VanPay Craig J	(920)255-3267 pastorvanpay@stjohnlux.com	414 East Ave Casco WI 54205	NW	SMP	St John Luxemburg WI	(920)845-5250	SL-SMP	2021
Varblow Bryan S	(734)355-7389 bvarblow@stmarksih.org	11730 Lakeview Ct Onsted MI 49265	MI	SMP	St Mark Brooklyn MI	(517)467-7565	SL-SMP	2024
Varns Jonathan J	(218) 235-8493 shepherdofthecross@gmail.com	P.O. Box 318 Browns Valley MN 56219	MNN	SP	Zion* Claire City SD	(320)695-2354	SL	2015
Varsogea Charles E	(260)704-0566 cvarsogea@gmail.com	16 Cimarron Ct Portsmouth RI 02871	EN	M Chap	Office of International Mission Saint Louis MO		FW	1995
Varvaris Peter W	(704)928-5390 peter.varvaris@gmail.com	1807 Brookgreen Ct SE Bolivia NC 28422	SE	EM			SL	1997
Vasconcellos Allan P Dr	(402)643-4095 paul.edna.vasco@gmail.com	1480 Karol Kay Blvd Seward NE 68434	NEB	EM			SL	1964
Vatthauer Matthew E	(817)917-6288 m.vatthauer@yahoo.com	St Paul Lutheran Church 816 9th St Clay Center KS 67432	KS	Assoc	St Paul Clay Center KS	(785)632-5301	SL	2025
Vaudt Steven C	(715)610-2920 svaudt1949@yahoo.com	5904 Fieldcrest Ln Weston WI 54476	NW	Asst	Trinity Wausau WI	(715)842-0769	CQ	1982
Vaughan Timothy B	(763)331-1905 tvaughan@trinitysf.org	22830 Zion Parkway NW Oak Grove MN 55005	MNS	Sn/Adm	Trinity Saint Francis MN	(763)753-1234	FW	1992
Vaughn David J	(636)394-2935 david.vaughn@coreconceptsllc.com	632 Golfview Dr Ballwin MO 63011	MO	Assoc	Christ Memorial Saint Louis MO	(314)631-0304	SL	2007
Vaughn John P Jr	(612)269-4478 pastorjpv@gmail.com	1658 Tanya Ter The Villages FL 34762	FG	EM			FW	1978
Vedder Lawrence M	(208)421-6703 lawved123@outlook.com	1339 Evergreen Dr Twin Falls ID 83301	NOW	EM			CQ	1988
Veen Evan C	(574)612-8980 evanveen@msn.com	4570 Dryden Road Dryden MI 48428	MI	SP	Holy Redeemer Dryden MI	(810)796-3951	SL	2021
Vega Roland D	rolandvega@att.net	160 Millstone Trl Clarkesville GA 30523	FG	SP	Trinity Eastanollee GA	(706)886-6723	SL	2007
Vega-Ayala Luciano	(832)212-3515 luciano@vega-ayala.com	1898 Longmire Rd Unit 7 Conroe TX 77304	TX	RSO	LINC Houston Houston TX	(713)426-2451	CQ	2010
Vehling James J	(651)501-5611 vehlingj@msn.com	1008 Farrell St S Maplewood MN 55119	FG	EM			SL	1966
Veitengruber Donald P	(616)754-1853 don.veitengruber@sbcglobal.net	912 Colleen St Greenville MI 48838	MI	EM			SL	1964
Vekasy Stephen A	(603)358-0892 stevevkc@gmail.com	95 Wyman Rd. Unit 1407 Keene NH 03431	NE	SMP	Trinity West Roxbury MA	(617)327-5155	CQ	2019
Velasco Marcelino	(805)727-0127 marvel2772@me.com	234 W Harvard Blvd #23 Santa Paula CA 93060	PSW	SP	Centro Cristiano Santa Paula CA	(805)525-5911	SL	2010
Velazquez Carlos V	(714)408-3948 carlos.velazquez@splsorange.org	2465 N Hayford St Orange CA 92865	PSW	Assoc	St Paul Orange CA	(714)637-2640	Other	2020
Vera Steven R	pastor@kofkluther.com	22 Trafalgar Ct Sparta NJ 07871	NJ	SP	King Of Kings Mountain Lakes NJ	(973)334-8333	SL	2010
Verage Kyle T	(715)889-3474 kverage@gmail.com		SW	SP	Good Shepherd Pleasant Prairie WI	(262)694-4405	FW	2013
Vergin Aaron H	(248)742-5906 pastor.vergin@gmail.com	521 Marion Avenue Grand Haven MI 49417	MI	SP	St John Grand Haven MI	(616)842-4510	FW	2014
Verity Timothy M	(616)238-8706 tverity@yahoo.com	737 Covell Ave NW Grand Rapids MI 49504	MI	EM			FW	1982
Vernava Michael N	(559)707-8557 pastorvernava@gmail.com	3779 W. River Rock Street Springfield MO 65807	MO	EM			FW	1989
Versemann Matthew O	(217) 454-6630 pastorversemann@msn.com	c/o Trinity Lutheran Church 1960 E Johns Ave Decatur IL 62521	CI	SP	Trinity Decatur IL	(217)422-3630	SL	1991
Vesey Matthew W	(414)712-0293 vesey99@gmail.com	211 Adams St Delaware IA 52057	IE	SP	St Paul Delaware IA	(563)922-2364	FW	1993
Vetrano Justin K	(516)902-7602 pastor@thelifeny.org	1 Old Westbury Rd Old Westbury NY 11568	AT	Sn/Adm	The Life Old Westbury NY	(516)333-3355	SL-D	2010
Vician Louis R	Lvician@hotmail.com	1142 Robert Dr Apt A Columbus IN 47201	IN	EM			FW	2000
Vieker Jon D Dr	viekerj@csl.edu	3 McCall Ter Clayton MO 63105	MO	S HS/C	Concordia Seminary Saint Louis MO	(314)505-7000	SL	1987
Vieregge Michael S	(248)595-9556 churchoffice@ourshepherd.net	2677 Burnham Rd Royal Oak MI 48073	MI	SMP	Our Shepherd Birmingham MI	(248)646-6100	SL-SMP	2014
Viergutz William H	(719)346-7401 trinityburlington@hotmail.com	365 9th St Burlington CO 80807	RM	SP	Trinity Burlington CO	(719)346-7401	SL	1987

*Multiple Assignments (See Church Worker Locator for Additional Details)

See Page 53 for the Table of Abbreviations for key to District, Position, and Seminary abbreviations

**C =Candidate; EM = Emeritus; the date following the C is the month and year the Candidate status began

NAME	TELEPHONE NUMBER EMAIL	STREET ADDRESS CITY/STATE/ZIP	DISTRICT	POSITION/ STATUS**	WHERE SERVING	OFFICE PHONE	SEM/ PROGRAM	YR GRAD
Vierkant Jonathan A	(262)808-7974 jatvierkant@outlook.com	721 Orchard St West Bend WI 53095	SW	SP	St Andrew West Bend WI	(262)335-4200	SL	2005
Vieth Mason W			IN	Assoc	Trinity Elkhart IN	(574)674-8800	SL	2021
Viets Mark L	(440)915-1451 markviets@aol.com	394 Gulf St. Milford CT 06460	EN	EM			SL	1970
Viggers Zachary T	(515)371-2102 rev.viggers@gmail.com	4102 Silver Spur Ave Gillette WY 82718	WY	SP	Trinity* Gillette WY	(307)682-4886	FW	2018
Viken Bradley D	(760)792-2879 basicfaith@hotmail.com	2007 Avon Dr Beavercreek OH 45431	OH	SP	Risen Christ Springfield OH	(937)323-3688	SL	1992
Villalobos Jose S	(714)675-5462 jsvillalobos1517@gmail.com	13128 Edwards Rd La Miranda CA 90638	PSW	SP	First Fontana CA	(909)823-3457	Other	2023
Vilsaint Josue J	(954)463-2450	11 SW 11th St Ft Lauderdale FL 33315	FG	O-Miss	Trinity Fort Lauderdale FL	(954)463-2450	EIITSL	2008
Vines Daniel D	(360)580-3390 dvinesco@gmail.com	510 Simpson Ave Aberdeen WA 98520	NOW	SMP	Calvary Aberdeen WA	(360)532-3980	SL-SMP	2010
Vineyard Benjamin M	(402)326-0389 benjamin.vineyard@gmail.com	2748 Franklin St Lincoln NE 68502	NEB	SP	Calvary Lincoln NE	(402)476-1567	SL	2023
Vinovskis Waldemar R	(610)965-3265 wrvinovskis@gmail.com	68 Willow St Macungie PA 18062	S	DP	SELC District* Macungie PA	(610)965-3265	SL	1992
Vitello John T	(216)475-2618	6009 E 135th St Garfield Hts OH 44125	OH	EM			FW	1983
Vo Minh Chau N	(314)835-0063 pastorvo@yahoo.com	17 Ponca Trl Kirkwood MO 63122	MO	Asst	Timothy Saint Louis MO	(314)781-8673	SL	1992
Voelker William J	pastorvoelker@gmail.com	32392 122nd Ave Columbus NE 68601	NEB	SP	Christ Columbus NE	(402)563-1314	SL	2004
Voelker Steven M	(989)818-0786 stevevoelker@hotmail.com	9922 Flag Stone Pl Fort Wayne IN 46804	IN	EM			FW	2006
Voelker Robert E	(507) 589-8528 robertevoelker@gmail.com	1000 9th St NW Austin MN 55912	EN	EM			FW	1984
Voelker John C II	(330)808-1244 jvoelker@kent.edu	6294 Marteney Ave Kent OH 44240	OH	Sn/Adm	St John Akron OH	(330)773-4128	SL	2012
Voelz James W	(314)505-7138 voelzj@csl.edu	8827 Dune Creek CV Fort Wayne IN 46835	MO	S HS/C	Concordia Seminary Saint Louis MO	(314)505-7000	SL	1971
Vogel Benjamin W	(517)376-8851 Benvog@gmail.com	c/o Bethany Luth Church 6041 Ridge Rd Parma OH 44129	OH	Sn/Adm	Bethany Parma OH	(440)884-1230	SL	2011
Vogel Daniel J	(712)309-1292 daniel.1951vogel@gmail.com	32678 Aspen Ave Manning IA 51455	IW	EM			FW	1982
Vogel Guy A	(608)718-8603 birdguy4025@gmail.com	4025 Hearthstone Dr Janesville WI 53546	EN	EM			SL	1963
Vogel Larry M	(856)265-7275 revogelnj@juno.com	3116 Victor Ave Tom's River NJ 08753	EN	S Ex/S	The LCMS Corporate Saint Louis MO	(314)965-9000	SL	1981
Vogel Leroy E	(507)346-2614 vogel@centurytel.net	1864 First Minnesota Preston MN 55965	MNS	EM			SL	1961
Vogel Robert H	(972)363-0650 vogelrh@grandecom.net	410 Branding Iron Way Fairview TX 75069	NJ	EM			FW	1999
Vogeler Richard P	(716)380-8546 poimenvog@roadrunner.com	6035 S Transit Rd Lot 490 Lockport NY 14094	EA	EM			FW	2001
Vogeli Mitchell R		8381 Volkmer Rd Chesaning MI 48616	MI	EM			SL	2013
Vogelsang William R Jr	(760)207-0410 wrvogcmvog@cox.net	2335 Amber Ln Escondido CA 92026	PSW	EM			FW	1978
Voges Carl A	(803)269-6656 carl.voges4@icloud.com	129 Pond Ridge Rd Columbia SC 29223	SE	EM			SPR	1966
Voges Jordan R	(218)251-2340 Jordan.r.voges@gmail.com	438 Bernard St E Saint Paul MN 55118	MNS	Assoc	Saint James West Saint Paul MN	(651)457-9232	SL	2018
Vogler Loren L	(515)201-3328 rvshepherdvogler@gmail.com	300 Commercial Ave N Apt 312 Sandstone MN 55072	MNN	EM			SL	1966
Vogt Bradley A	(218)389-6266 pastorbradvogt@hotmail.com	3826 Main St Barnum MN 55707	MNN	Sn/Adm	Emmanuel* Barnum MN	(218)389-6849	FW	2007
Vogt Stephen	(973)919-5539 rev.poplc@gmail.com	412 Rowells Ct Conway SC 29526	NJ	EM			SL	1982
Vogts Kevin D	(913)594-9865 pastorvogts@gmail.com	4908 NE 78th Ter Kansas City MO 64119	MO	EM			SL	1986
Voigt Arnold J	(303)798-7887 arnievoigt@msn.com	9153 Yarrow St Apt 1403 Broomfield CO 80021	RM	EM			SL	1965
Voigt Steven J	(414)520-0141 pastorvoigt@sbcglobal.net	2970 S 128th St New Berlin WI 53151	SW	Sn/Adm	Covenant Milwaukee WI	(414)464-2410	SL	1991
Voigt Eric W	(989)351-6040 voigtlcms@yahoo.com		MNS	SP	St John Nowthen MN	(763)441-3646	SL	2005
Voigt Eli B	eli.voigt1@gmail.com	340 Claymore Rd Unit 1d Hindsale IL 60521	NI	SP	St John Darien IL	(630)969-7987	FW	2018
Volbrecht Gregory H	(507)642-8414 pastorvolbrecht@gmail.com	80837 420th St Truman MN 56088	MNS	SP	Trinity* Lewisville MN	(507)642-8414	FW	2011
Volk Michael F	(513)260-8008 mvolk5@aol.com	7123 S Harrison Hills Dr Apt 108 La Vista NE 68128	NEB	EM			SL	1971
Volker Thomas G	(612)866-1814 astro4919satch@gmail.com	31543 State Highway 43 Rushford MN 55971	MNS	SP	St John* Rushford MN	(507)864-2585	SL	1997
Volkert George A	(563)578-8841 gavolkert@gmail.com	315 N Guilford St Sumner IA 50674	IE	EM			SL	1980
Voll Theodore E	(989)980-1750 thevolls@gmail.com	1927 S Gray Rd West Branch MI 48661	MI	EM			SL	1975
Vollrath Jonathan H	(507)272-3104 pastorjonvollrath@yahoo.com	237 Pearl St S Dover MN 55929	MNS	SP	Our Savior Eyota MN	(507)545-2067	SL	1998
Volm William P	(715)610-4680 wpvolm@mac.com	711 N 12th Ave Wausau WI 54401	NW	EM			SPR	1973

*Multiple Assignments (See Church Worker Locator for Additional Details)
See Page 53 for the Table of Abbreviations for key to District, Position, and Seminary abbreviations
**C =Candidate; EM = Emeritus; the date following the C is the month and year the Candidate status began

NAME	TELEPHONE NUMBER EMAIL	STREET ADDRESS CITY/STATE/ZIP	DISTRICT	POSITION/ STATUS**	WHERE SERVING	OFFICE PHONE	SEM/ PROGRAM	YR GRAD
Volzke Gregory R	gregvolzke@gmail.com	604 N 5th Ave Kenesaw NE 68956	NEB	SP	Trinity Campbell NE	(402)756-8552	CQ	1993
Von Behren Michael T Dr	mikevb@nowlcms.org	619 E Cascade Pl Spokane WA 99208	NOW	DP	Northwest District Portland OR	(503)288-8383	SL	2005
Von Busch James A Dr	(208)339-6679 vonbusch.james@gmail.com	1034 W 74 Ln S Paul ID 83347	NOW	SP	Trinity Rupert ID	(208)436-3413	CQ	2013
von der Lage Jason D	(810)252-6054 vonderlage@gmail.com	3311 Compton Cincinnati OH 45251	OH	Assoc	Christ Cincinnati OH	(513)385-8342	FW	2025
Von Hagel Thomas A	(773)494-1940 tvonhagel@yahoo.com	635 Faxon St Superior WI 54880	MNN	EM			FW	1985
von Hindenburg Bruce J	(559)285-8972 prbjvh@catalinalutheran.org	39568 S Cinch Strap Pl Tucson AZ 85739	EN	Asst	Catalina Tucson AZ	(520)825-9255	CQ	2007
Von Rentzell Marion W	(308)660-3473 gmvonrentzell@gmail.com	4120 Rolling Green Dr Grand Island NE 68803	NEB	EM			SL	1964
Von Schmidt Aleksandr A	(805)570-0257 a.von.schmidt@gmail.com	1010 E Foothill Blvd San Luis Obispo CA 93405	CNH	SP	Zion San Luis Obispo CA	(805)543-8327	Other	2018
von Steinman Richard	(970)522-7096 vonsteinmans@gmail.com	725 Fairhurst St Sterling CO 80751	RM	SP	First English Sterling CO	(970)522-5142	FW	2001
Von Stroh C Dean	(316) 734-2501 cdeanvonstroh@aol.com	425 E Lexington Ln Andover KS 67002	KS	EM			SPR	1968
vonSeggern Arleigh F Dr	(715)339-3187 arleigh.f.vonseggern@gmail.com	W7319 County Rd W Phillips WI 54555	NW	SP	St Paul* Marengo WI	(715)278-3271	FW	1992
vonWerder Paul W	(407)312-4556	11165 Sylvan Pond Cir Orlando FL 32825	FG	SP	Hope Orlando FL	(407)657-4556	SL	1994
Voorman Duane R Jr	(402)580-7553 rev.voorman@gmail.com	218 Hampshire Dr Cranberry Twp PA 16066	EA	Inst C	Concordia Lutheran Ministries Cabot PA	(724)352-1571	FW	1983
Voorman James L	(260)403-0947 jvoorman@lutheranlifevillages.org	3914 Scarborough Dr New Haven IN 46774	IN	RSO	Lutheran Homes Inc Fort Wayne IN	(260)447-1591	FW	2010
Voss Laerte Tardelli H Dr	858-273-2886 ltvoss@hotmail.com	836 Makani St Unit 4 Chula Vista CA 91911	PSW	Assoc	Hope Linda Vista San Diego CA	(858)268-4688	Other	2004
Voss Zachary M	(605)651-0699 revzmv@gmail.com	541 Stephens Ave Ortonville MN 56278	MNN	C08/2025			FW	2017
Voss Kevin E Dr	(262)339-0459	31764 Griffin Sands Ln San Antonio FL 33576	SW	EM			SL	1999
Voss Dennis L	(715)491-2332 rev.af.col@gmail.com	4703 Nova Ave NW Mandan ND 58554	ND	EM			FW	1999
Vossler Lawrence R Jr Dr	(973)303-8250 rvossler@minister.com	38 Furnace Ave Wanaque NJ 07465	NJ	SP	Grace Livingston NJ	(973)992-0145	SL	1985
Vossler Christopher P	(973)303-8252 cpvossler@gmail.com	172 W. Saginaw Rd. Sanford MI 48657	MI	SP	St Paul Sanford MI	(989)687-2824	SL	2013
Voth Daniel C	(701)509-5641 voth@immanuelgf.org	2229 Fallcreek Ct Grand Forks ND 58201	ND	Sn/Adm	Immanuel* Grand Forks ND	(701)775-7125	FW	1999
Vrudny Matthew J	(612)390-4935 pastorvrudny@gmail.com	4656 State 200 NW Walker MN 56484	MNN	SP	Immanuel Walker MN	(218)547-3156	SL	1990
Vu Kinh T	(714)633-5549 vukinh@yahoo.com	3331 E Casselle Ave Orange CA 92869	PSW	Sn/Adm	St Paul Garden Grove CA	(714)537-4245	FW	1995
Wachholz Dean C	(734)944-6722 bmww2@frontier.com	552 Woodland Dr Saline MI 48176	MI	EM			SPR	1972
Wachholz William H Dr	(402)643-0408 bill.wachholz@cune.org	3600 Zanzibar Ln N Minneapolis MN 55446	MNS	EM			SL	1972
Wachter Brian C	(314)341-6444 bwachter43@yahoo.com	4645 Pine Isle Way Sugar Hill MO 30518	FG	SMP	St John the Apostle Hoschton GA	(678)858-4961	FW-SMP	2024
Wachter Keith D	(636) 233-1318 kdskwachter@gmail.com	643 Zumwalt Xing O Fallon MO 63366	MO	EM			SL	1980
Wackenhuth David G			AT	EM			CQ	1986
Wacker Norman A	(307)281-2622 wackerna@gmail.com	P.O. Box 1410 Sundance WY 82729	WY	SP	Bethlehem* Moorcroft WY		FW	2012
Wacker Robert J	(708)203-5443 robert.j.wacker@me.com	211 N. Colonial Dr. Cortland OH 44410	OH	SP	Trinity Warren OH	(330)647-6402	FW	2016
Wackett Kevin D	(443)614-0074 86kevinw@gmail.com	307 Hunt Ct Salisbury MD 21804	SE	EM			FW	1986
Wackler John E	(405)743-1831 mightywack1@gmail.com	4407 E Zachary Ln Stillwater OK 74074	OK	SP	Zion Stillwater OK	(405)372-3703	FW	2005
Waddell James A Dr	(517)262-2148 ja.waddell@yahoo.com	c/o Faith Lutheran Church 1255 E Forest Ave Ypsilanti MI 48198	MI	SP	Faith Ypsilanti MI	(734)482-9412	SL	1991
Wade Jeffrey E	(586)419-6166 jeffrey.wade@ziondenison.org	2606 Idlewood Dr Denison IA 51442	IW	SP	Zion Denison IA	(712)263-2235	SL	2014
Wade Kenneth E	(580)484-6666 kewade@suddenlink.net	3602 W Purdue Ave Enid OK 73703	OK	EM			SL	1968
Wade Tanner S	(714)222-2989 TWade@StPaulsDP.org	126 Caravel Ct Ballwin MO 63021	MO	Assoc	St Paul Des Peres MO	(314)822-0447	SL	2020
Waetzig Kalvin L	(209)834-4574 kwaetzig@stpaulstracy.org	1460 Divine Ln Tracy CA 95376	CNH	Sn/Adm	St Paul Tracy CA	(209)835-7438	SL	1986
Waffel Derek C	(256) 536-6083	c/o Ascension Lutheran Church 3801 Oakwood Ave. NW Huntsville AL 35810	SO	SP	Ascension Huntsville AL	(256)536-9987	SL	2015
Wagener Kenneth C	(317)650-5843 KennethCWagener@gmail.com	74 Jackson Farm Rd Cartersville GA 30120	FG	EM			SL	1986
Wagenknecht Nicholas M	(651) 274-7432 pastornick@stjohnsandweecare.org	304 Fairway Ct South Stewartville MN 55976	MNS	Assoc	St Johns Stewartville MN	(507)533-4420	SL	2023
Wagley Douglas L	(509)499-0121 dougwagley@outlook.com	3307 W Rowan Ave Spokane WA 99205	NOW	SP	New Vision Spokane WA	(509)499-0121	CQ	2004

*Multiple Assignments (See Church Worker Locator for Additional Details)

See Page 53 for the Table of Abbreviations for key to District, Position, and Seminary abbreviations

**C =Candidate; EM = Emeritus; the date following the C is the month and year the Candidate status began

NAME	TELEPHONE NUMBER EMAIL	STREET ADDRESS CITY/STATE/ZIP	DISTRICT	POSITION/ STATUS**	WHERE SERVING	OFFICE PHONE	SEM/ PROGRAM	YR GRAD
Wagner Norman R	(907)982-9956 pastornormlcms@gmail.com	18 Beith Lane Bella Vista AR 72715	MDS	EM			SL	2004
Wagner William B Jr	(931)982-8932 pastorbillwagner@gmail.com	2800 Kaye Dr Thompsons Station TN 37179	MDS	SP	Trinity Columbia TN	(931)388-0790	SL	1988
Wagner Timothy W	(402)520-1818 tcwagner2000@yahoo.com	116 N. Jefferson Plymouth NE 68424	NEB	SP	First Trinity Beatrice NE	(402)228-0216	FW	1995
Wagner Ronald A	(309)923-7542 fish61561@yahoo.com	508 W Smith St Roanoke IL 61561	CI	EM			SL	1983
Wagner Stephen A	(469)585-0023 stevew@concordia-satx.com	18706 Wild Onion San Antonio TX 78258	TX	EM			SL	1973
Wagner Robert W	juniperwoodbob@gmail.com	904 E Clayton St Cuero TX 77954	TX	EM			SL	1984
Wagner Robert V	(616)712-6200 bobkat6103@gmail.com	6103 Shearer Rd Greenville MI 48838	MI	SP	Holy Cross Belding MI	(616)794-1310	FW	1980
Wagner Richard F	(832)698-2858 richard0626@sbcglobal.net	5600 Cypress Wood Dr Unit 129 Spring TX 77379	TX	EM			SL	1953
Wagner Richard A		10423 Ray Dr Roscoe IL 61073	NI	EM			SL	1973
Wagner Preston E	(919)556-4658 pwagner9@nc.rr.com	3904 Sanford Creek Ave Wake Forest NC 27587	SE	EM			SPR	1972
Wagner Philip P	(612)816-9635 ppwtrin@gmail.com	14830 41st Ave N Plymouth MN 55446	MNS	EM			SL	1982
Wagner Paul R	(518)792-7971	40 Coolidge Ave Glens Falls NY 12801	AT	SP	Good Shepherd Glens Falls NY	(518)792-7971	SL	1992
Wagner Daniel E	(712)540-9719 revdwagner@gmail.com	604 Kendall Ct Sartell MN 56377	MNN	EM			SL	1984
Wagner Merlyn D	(801)255-4739 binksu@juno.com	625 E Pioneer Ave Sandy UT 84070	RM	EM			SPR	1962
Wagner Ainslie B	(980)231-5284 lamsadie2@yahoo.com	20901 Sterling Bay Ln E Apt C Cornelius NC 28031	SE	EM			FW	1983
Wagner David S	(701)232-1215 pastor@trinitybellingham.org	2505 Elmhurst Ct Bellingham WA 98229	NOW	SP	Trinity Bellingham WA	(360)734-2770	SL	1987
Wagner Steven E	(936)203-0240 pastorwagner@trinitylombard.org	1008 E Roosevelt Rd Lombard IL 60148	NI	Sn/Adm	Trinity Lombard IL	(630)629-8765	FW	2009
Wagner Donald R	(320)766-1002 wagsdw@gmail.com	P.O. Box 314 Deer Creek MN 56527	MNN	SP	Trinity Deer Creek MN	(218)462-2465	SL	1990
Wagner Geoffrey A	(303)656-3430 pastor@cos-lutheran.org	P.O. Box 1981 Elizabeth CO 80107	RM	SP	Christ Our Savior Elizabeth CO	(303)646-1378	SL	2003
Wagner Jacob D	(218)275-9384 revjacobwagner@gmail.com	604 Kendall Ct Sartell MN 56377	MI	C06/2023			SL	2016
Wagner Jason M Dr	(636)222-4303 pastorwagner@email.com	816 Winter Top Ct Fenton MO 63026	MO	SP	Hope High Ridge MO	(636)677-8788	SL	2004
Wagner Aaron D	(580)748-2378 revaaronwagner@gmail.com	2045 Queens Rd Salina KS 67401	KS	Sn/Adm	Christ King Salina KS	(785)827-7492	SL	2011
Wagner Joel P	(320)279-2033 joelpeterwagner@gmail.com	318 W Main St Latimer IA 50452	IE	SP	St Paul Latimer IA	(641)579-6281	FW	2023
Wagner Mark E	markewagnr@aol.com	3928 Saint Simons Ct Indianapolis IN 46237	IN	SP	Ascension Beech Grove IN	(317)788-1118	FW	1996
Wagner Eugene F	(269)445-2435 efw@wagnercares.com	202 N Broadway St Cassopolis MI 49031	IN	EM			FW	1986
Wagnitz Michael G	(319)350-1339 a4adelphos@yahoo.ca	228 W Clay Brimfield IL 61517	CI	SP	St Paul Brimfield IL	(309)446-3233	CQ	2012
Wagoner Jerome	(712)542-4241 jeromewagoner@gmail.com	1860 N Ave Clarinda IA 51632	IW	SP	Mount Calvary Villisca IA	(712)826-7202	SPR	1971
Wagstaff Thomas L	(361)727-7287 wforgiven@juno.com	308 Daisy Ln Waco TX 76706	TX	EM			SL	2004
Wahl Randolph C	(402)560-3558 rnrwahl@gmail.com	10810 W Manzanita Dr Sun City AZ 85373	PSW	EM			FW	1997
Waiser Walter E	(817)797-8974 wwaiser@yahoo.com	6220 Lake Way Mews N RICHLND HLS TX 76180	TX	EM			CQ	1975
Wait Matthew	(310)488-4585 matt@firstlutherancc.org	c/o First Lutheran Church 3735 Hughes Ave Los Angeles CA 90034	PSW	SP	First Los Angeles CA	(310)838-6076	SL	2013
Waite Wallace J	(920)284-5620	157 Congress Dr Valparaiso IN 46383	IN	EM			SL	1980
Wakeland Michael S	(260) 363-8821 mikewakeland@gmail.com	3606 Oak Park Dr Fort Wayne IN 46815	IN	EM			FW	1987
Walburg James S	(763)732-2781 walb3115@rea-alp.com	3115 Crestwood Dr NE Alexandria MN 56308	MNN	SP	Trinity Evansville MN	(320)876-4021	SPR	1975
Waldvogel Christopher C	(701)893-6995 pastorchrisbslc@gmail.com	4795 47th Ave S Fargo ND 58104	ND	Sn/Adm	Beautiful Savior Fargo ND	(701)293-1047	SL	2008
Walker Andrew J	awalker@txlcms.org	117 Johnny Hall Dr Kyle TX 78640	TX	C01/2021			SL	2013
Walker David F	(847)956-4628 dewalker6@att.net	811 E Central Rd Apt 419 Arlington Heights IL 60005	NI	EM			SL	1958
Walker John F	(319)695-5139	1158 140th St Hedrick IA 52563	IE	EM			FW	1994
Walla Jonathan J	pastor@bethelbismarck.com	517 E Turnpike Ave Bismarck ND 58501	ND	Sn/Adm	Bethel Bismarck ND	(701)255-1433	SL	2010
Wallace Michael S	(440)759-2115 wallace3mdj@yahoo.com	2129 Lorimer Rd Parma OH 44134	OH	SP	Gethsemane Lakewood OH	(216)521-0434	FW	1994
Wallingsford Jason D	(832)577-3287 dce@connectwithJesus.org	11629 Cherisse Dr Austin TX 78739	TX	SMP	Mount Olive Austin TX	(512)288-2370	SL-SMP	2021
Wallis Matthew J	(407) 754-8035 first_brother@yahoo.com	2301 Lucretia Ct Sanford FL 32771	S	EM			SL	2000
Wallschlaeger Joel D	(434)610-1526 wallschlaegerj@hotmail.com	10391 Sudley Manor Dr Manassas VA 20109	SE	SP	Hope Manassas VA	(703)361-8732	SL	2004

*Multiple Assignments (See Church Worker Locator for Additional Details)

See Page 53 for the Table of Abbreviations for key to District, Position, and Seminary abbreviations

**C =Candidate; EM = Emeritus; the date following the C is the month and year the Candidate status began

NAME	TELEPHONE NUMBER EMAIL	STREET ADDRESS CITY/STATE/ZIP	DISTRICT	POSITION/ STATUS**	WHERE SERVING	OFFICE PHONE	SEM/ PROGRAM	YR GRAD
Walquist Randy W	(505)503-5054 prwalquist@aol.com	9407 Empress Crossing Dr Spring TX 77379	TX	EM			SL	1978
Walsh David J	(585)747-1507 revdavidjwalsh@gmail.com	299 Kaymar Dr Amherst NY 14228	EN	SP	Pilgrim Kenmore NY	(716)875-5485	FW	2017
Walston Robert W	(817)874-0983 bawalston@gmail.com	17857 Domingo Dr Parker CO 80134	RM	SP	Trinity Franktown CO	(303)841-4660	SL	2015
Walta Arnold H	(253)334-7662 ahw6@juno.com	37601 37th Ave S Auburn WA 98001	NOW	EM			SL	1958
Walter Jody R	(715)866-4622 voneisenach@gmx.com	7421 Maple St W Webster WI 54893	NW	SP	Our Redeemer Webster WI	(715)866-7191	FW	1992
Walter John W		350 E Dundee Rd Apt 205 Buffalo Grove IL 60089	NI	EM			SPR	1973
Walters Christopher M	(309)966-1010 revwalters5@gmail.com	929 320th St Woodward IA 50276	IW	Assoc	Christ* Perry IA	(515)676-2289	FW	2022
Walters David L	(440)390-1340 dave@crossroadscle.com	8306 Ridge Rd North Royalton OH 44133	OH	SMP	Crossroads CLE Brook Park OH	(216)816-1615	CQ	2019
Walters Lewis J	(405)481-5730 lewisjwalters@yahoo.com	10 Robinette St Shawnee OK 74801	OK	EM			SL	2005
Walters Mark R	(920)850-9179 4bigrace@gmail.com	5231 Briarwood Cir Caledonia WI 53402	SW	Cmp P	Lutheran High School Racine WI	(262)637-6538	CQ	2017
Walters Sean G	(724)856-8584 pastorseangw@gmail.com	108 Oticon Dr. New Castle PA 16105	EA	SP	Prince Peace Freedom PA	(724)728-3881	SL	2009
Walther Michael P	(618)960-5723 michaelpwalther@gmail.com	5111 Kirkland Trail Sorento IL 62086	SI	Sn/Adm	Good Shepherd Collinsville IL	(618)344-3151	SL	1984
Walther Galan D	gwalther2022@gmail.com	1100 Larchmount Dr Waukesha WI 53186	SW	EM			SL	1980
Walther John D	(972)804-9865 johnwalther@hotmail.com	2824 Macdonald St Oceanside CA 92054	PSW	EM			FW	1990
Walton Gregory S Dr		423 Grafton Walk Woodstock GA 30188	FG	Pro Stf	Lutheran Church Exten- sion Fund Saint Louis MO	(314)965-9000	SL	1987
Walworth Tyler A	(816) 590-1692 tyler.walworth@gmail.com	3 Adams Ln Dearborn MI 48120	MI	SP	Our Savior Df* Beverly Hills MI	(816)590-1692	FW	2015
Walz Arden D	(541)926-2380 arden.walz@hotmail.com	2311 Gale St NW Albany OR 97321	NOW	EM			SL	1968
Walz Orville C	(402)315-9586 orville.walz@cune.org	14718 Black St Bennington NE 68007	NEB	EM			CQ	1982
Wampfler Jacob D	(715)558-2643 jacob.wampfler@gmail.com	14000 North 94th Street Unit 1010 Scottsdale AZ 85260	PSW	SP	The Master Phoenix AZ	(602)997-7439	SL	2014
Wanderer Douglas C	(651)235-7992 dlplanatas@outlook.com	2309 Cottage Dr Stillwater MN 55082	MNS	EM			FW	1995
Wang Harry H	626-215-1765 harrymymail@gmail.com	1707 Flag Pin Dr Corona CA 92883	PSW	Assoc	Shepherd Hills Rancho Cucamonga CA	(909)989-6500	CQ	2014
Wang Isaac K	(909)597-7525 kehruwang@yahoo.com	3723 Terrace Dr Chino Hills CA 91709	PSW	EM			CQ	2006
Wangelin Kyle A	(586)651-9721 kylewangelin@yahoo.com	2948 Meadowview St Kaukauna WI 54130	NW	Sn/Adm	Zion Wayside WI	(920)864-2463	SL	2019
Wangelin William R	pastorw@oursaviorlansing.org	7006 Captiva Dr Lansing MI 48917	MI	Sn/Adm	Our Savior Lansing MI	(517)882-8665	SL	2007
Wangerin Timothy P	(405)887-5949 timothy.wangerin57@gmail.com	408 W Cloud St Salina KS 67401	KS	Assoc	Christ King Salina KS	(785)827-7492	ED	1990
Wangerin Mark E	(414)259-9837 pastor.wangerin@gmail.com	1821 W Daisy Ln Glendale WI 53209	SW	EM			SL	1978
Wanner Michael D	(417)335-1602 mikewanner92@gmail.com	2675 Lachar Dr. Holts Summit MO 65043	MO	EM			FW	1985
Ward Dale B	(636)249-3973 dward@cornerstonelutheran. church	c/o Cornerstone Lutheran Church 4850 E Main St Carmel IN 46033	IN	SMP	Cornerstone Carmel IN	(317)814-4252	SL-SMP	2021
Ward Douglas C	(802)863-8014 dc3ward@yahoo.com	1510 Williston Rd Apt 212 South Burlington VT 05403	NE	EM			SPR	1974
Ward William W	(443)655-6446 wward626@verizon.net	1201 Fergus Ct Bel Air MD 21014	SE	SMP	St Matthew Bel Air MD	(410)838-3178	SL	2025
Ware Steven L	(845)978-4597 drsware598@gmail.com	330 W Presnell St Apt 40 Asheboro NC 27203	AT	EM			CQ	2021
Ware Jeffrey W			SE	SP	All Saints Charlotte NC	(704)752-4287	FW	2007
Wareham Christopher E	(406)491-1215 cwareham007@gmail.com	3002 Irene St Butte MT 59701	MT	EM			SL	1980
Wareham Stephen D	(404)951-6336 warehams@csl.edu	3914 Robin Ct Acworth FL 30101	FG	SP	Messiah Valdosta GA	(229)244-0143	SL	2025
Wargo Paul E	(586)943-3155 paulwargo3@gmail.com	8086 S Channel Dr Harsens Is MI 48028	MI	EM			CQ	1980
Warmann Douglas R		323 Orchard Ter Roselle IL 60172	NI	Asst	Trinity Roselle IL	(630)894-3263	CQ	1995
Warmbier Matthew G	pastor@lcspgraham.org	11409 92nd Ave. E. Puyallup WA 98373	NOW	SP	St Paul Graham WA	(253)847-3084	SL	2014
Warmbier Michael G	(503)522-2611 mwarmbier49@outlook.com	4373 SW Golf Course Rd Cornelius OR 97113	NOW	SP	St Peter Cornelius OR	(503)357-3863	SL	1985
Warneck Walter J Jr Dr	(843) 686-3665 wwarneckjr@gmail.com	4 Leeward Psge Hilton Head Island SC 29926	FG	O-Sp Min	Florida-Georgia District Orlando FL	(407)857-5556	SL	1971
Warneke Paul M	pastorwarneke@hotmail.com	2221 2nd Ave Nebraska City NE 68410	NEB	SP	St Paul* Weeping Water NE	(402)267-5206	FW	1996
Warneke Christopher W	(402)705-1709 cwarneke3@gmail.com	312 W Central Ave Arkansas City KS 67005	KS	SP	Redeemer* Arkansas City KS	(620)442-5240	FW	2024
Warner Jeffery P	(402)922-3017 warnermac@mac.com	303 Alma St Laurel NE 68745	NEB	SP	Immanuel Laurel NE	(402)256-3314	SL	1995

*Multiple Assignments (See Church Worker Locator for Additional Details)

See Page 53 for the Table of Abbreviations for key to District, Position, and Seminary abbreviations

**C =Candidate; EM = Emeritus; the date following the C is the month and year the Candidate status began

NAME	TELEPHONE NUMBER EMAIL	STREET ADDRESS CITY/STATE/ZIP	DISTRICT	POSITION/ STATUS**	WHERE SERVING	OFFICE PHONE	SEM/ PROGRAM	YR GRAD
Warner Howard H III	(716)668-5194 hw2030466@gmail.com	14 Slate Creek Dr Apt 9 Cheektowaga NY 14227	EA	EM			NESC	2011
Warner David M	(605) 673-4361 pastorwarner@outlook.com	P.O. Box 907 Custer SD 57730	SD	SP	Our Redeemer* Custer SD	(605)673-4361	FW	2004
Warner Daniel E	(812)608-0286 pastorwarner@zlcgordonville.org	138 Co Rd 226 Cape Girardeau MO 63701	MO	SP	Zion* Gordonville MO	(573)204-1944	FW	2023
Warner Daniel M		5803 Wisteria Dr Colorado Springs CO 80919	RM	Sn/Adm	Rock Of Ages Colorado Springs CO	(719)632-9394	SL	2018
Warnier Paul A	(605)237-1989 revpaw83@gmail.com	310 Park Ave Alcester SD 57001	SD	EM			SL	1981
Warnke Joseph M	(706)974-8932 pastorwarnke@gmail.com	7516 Watson Cir Locust Grove GA 30248	FG	SP	Christ Our Savior Griffin GA	(770)227-4082	SL	2017
Warnke Matthew L	(712)337-4027 mlwarnke@aol.com	1052 Emerald Pines Dr Arnolds Park IA 51331	IW	EM			FW	1983
Warnsholz Merle T	(563)271-3977 warnmerle@gmail.com	26 Madison Cir Davenport IA 52806	IE	EM			SL	2007
Warren Steven D	(312)241-5635 steve_warren67@yahoo.com	10855 S Calumet Ave Chicago IL 60628	NI	SP	Salem Blue Island IL	(708)388-1830	FW-SMP	2013
Warsinski Larry A	(810)432-1804 revlarry@ispmgt.com	5371 Beard Rd Clyde MI 48049	MI	SP	Zion Hemlock MI	(989)642-5909	FW	1978
Warther John B Dr	(443)996-1653 jbwarther@gmail.com	220 Hickory Ridge Circle York PA 17404	SE	EM			SL	1988
Washington Oliver C Jr	(313)516-2752 pointmanxp@yahoo.com	3449 Yorkshire Rd Detroit MI 48224	EN	EM			FW	2002
Washington Steven	(334)467-5840 trinitylutheran1900@gmail.com	261 Speir Dr Valley Grande AL 36703	SO	SP	Immanuel* Vredenburgh AL	(251)789-2388	CQ	1982
Wasmuth James S	(765)626-3034 wbears4jesus@gmail.com	1837 Carol Lynn Dr Kokomo IN 46901	IN	EM			FW	1998
Wassman Darwin D		6201 Normal Blvd Apt 324 Lincoln NE 68506	NEB	EM			SL	1963
Waterman Steven M Dr	(541)563-7729 steveandsuew@hotmail.com	P.O. Box 2629 Waldport OR 97394	NOW	SP	Resurrection Florence OR	(541)997-8038	CQ	2001
Watkins Andrew C Dr	(302)858-2851 andrewwatkins00@yahoo.com	P.O. Box 207 Bennett IA 52721	IE	SP	St Paul* Bennett IA	(563)890-6619	SL	1998
Watkins Lindsay W Dr		4009 NE Bittersweet Dr Lees Summit MO 64064	IW	EM			SL	1979
Watson Edward L Sr	(314)405-7945	2521 Nathan Dr Saint Louis MO 63136	MO	EM			CQ	1984
Watson James C	(865)368-2813 chapwat@aol.com	7723 Bebe Branch Ooltewah TN 37363	MDS	EM			SL	1981
Watson Jay W	(785)331-3890 paterjww@sbcglobal.net	2925 Kensington Rd Lawrence KS 66046	KS	SP	Augsburg Shawnee KS	(913)403-6194	FW	1995
Watson Joseph M	(719)650-5195 chjmwatson@hotmail.com	9162 Sugarstone Circle Highlands Ranch CO 80130	TX	EM			SL	1996
Watson Kenneth R	(979)421-8282 kwatson67@att.net	2903 Oakwood Dr Brenham TX 77833	TX	EM			SL	1994
Watson Aubrey J Jr	(504)913-7332 ajwatsonjr@cox.net	7030 Coventry St New Orleans LA 70126	SO	SP	Holy Cross New Orleans LA	(504)288-3437	FW	2002
Watt Luke J	(402)853-3514 trinitywaltonpastor@gmail.com	5373 S 162nd St Walton NE 68461	NEB	SP	Trinity Walton NE	(402)782-6515	SL	2018
Watt Rex E	rewatt@comcast.net	1409 Myers Dr Ferndale WA 98248	NOW	SMP	Redeemer Bellingham WA	(360)384-5923	SL-SMP	2021
Watt Jonathan C	(515)462-0566 pastor@licgm.org	P.O. Box 765 Grand Marais MN 55604	MNN	SP	Life In Christ Grand Marais MN	(515)462-0566	SL	2001
Watters Samuel P	(734)664-4489 slswatters@sbcglobal.net	50526 Steed Dr Canton MI 48187	MI	SMP	St Matthew Westland MI	(734)425-0260	FW-SMP	2015
Waynick Thomas C	tomwaynick@gmail.com	5031 Wellington Way Midland GA 31820	FG	S Miss	Office of International Mission Saint Louis MO		FW	1982
Weander Kenneth L Jr	(402)649-4898	83853 561st Ave Norfolk NE 68701	NEB	Sn/Adm	Our Savior Norfolk NE	(402)371-9005	SL	1994
Weatherell Joseph P	(732)429-7090 pastorweatherell@trinitylutheranwellsboro.org	9 Calkins Ln Wellsboro PA 16901	EA	SP	Trinity Wellsboro PA	(570)724-2316	SL	2004
Weaver Brian S	(828)695-7555 pastorbrian@peacechurch.org	941 Bedford-Euless Rd Hurst TX 76053	TX	Sn/Adm	Peace Hurst TX	(817)284-1677	SL	2012
Weaver David J	(402)750-1629 revdavidweaver@gmail.com	P.O. Box 328 Stewardson IL 62463	CI	SP	Trinity Stewardson IL	(217)682-5722	FW	2002
Webb Jeffrey N	(717)333-6263 pastorjeffwebb@yahoo.com	208 Mosswood Dr Savannah GA 31405	FG	SP	Trinity Savannah GA	(912)925-4839	SL	1992
Webb Charles W Dr	(231)499-2139 weswebb30@gmail.com	600 Cottageview Dr Room 414 Traverse City MI 49684	MI	EM			SPR	1962
Weber James E	(989)652-4083 dajweb1@gmail.com	865 W Tuscola Frankenmuth MI 48734	MI	EM			CQ	1998
Weber Jason M			CNH	SMP	Zion Lodi CA	(209)369-1919	SL-SMP	2013
Weber Karl A	(218)367-2473 pa5wk47@arvig.net	31957 County Highway 61 Ottertail MN 56571	MNN	SP	St Paul* Richville MN		FW	1991
Weber Wilhelm Dr	+49-341-420-290 kppwweber@gmail.com		MI	NILE	International Lutheran Society of Wittenberg Wittenberg GERMANY		Other	1976
Weber Mark W	(402)719-8324 pastmarkw@gmail.com	575 Nighthawk Rd Lincoln NE 68521	NEB	EM			SL	2007
Weber Kurt A	(989)430-6585 kweber1764@gmail.com	445 Glen St SW Hutchinson MN 55350	MNS	SP	Peace Hutchinson MN	(320)587-3031	SL	2004

*Multiple Assignments (See Church Worker Locator for Additional Details)

See Page 53 for the Table of Abbreviations for key to District, Position, and Seminary abbreviations

**C =Candidate; EM = Emeritus; the date following the C is the month and year the Candidate status began

NAME	TELEPHONE NUMBER EMAIL	STREET ADDRESS CITY/STATE/ZIP	DISTRICT	POSITION/ STATUS**	WHERE SERVING	OFFICE PHONE	SEM/ PROGRAM	YR GRAD
Weber Roberto A	18495172103 roberto.weber@lcms.org	Calle F #46 Cerro Alto Santiago De Los Caballeros NO 51062 DOMINI-CAN REPUBLIC	MO	S Miss	Office of International Mission Saint Louis MO		VB	2014
Weber Glenn A	(915)861-6543 rockysusan@sbcglobal.net	543 La Melodia Dr Las Cruces NM 88011	RM	EM			SL	1970
Weber Paul M	(309) 755-4511 paulmweber17@gmail.com	3105 15th St A Moline IL 61265	CI	SP	Faith Kewanee IL	(309)852-2787	FW	1997
Weber Brian G	(517)614-4236 pastor.weber@hotmail.com	N6404 State Rd. 49 Weyauwega WI 54983	SW	SP	Christ* Weyauwega WI	(920)867-3263	FW	2012
Weber Edmund J	956-565-4678 eweber10@aol.com	27236 McLelland Rd Harlingen TX 78552	TX	SP	Immanuel Mercedes TX	(956)565-1518	FW	1990
Weber Paul A	(906)226-6195 pcweber@charter.net	13 Oak Hill Dr Marquette MI 49855	NW	EM			SL	1973
Weber Christopher J	(314)681-4906 perhapstoday3@gmail.com	849 Armstrong Ave St Paul MN 55102	MNS	SP	St Peter Saint Paul MN	(651)228-1482	SL	2013
Weber Daniel J	(253) 941-3000		NOW	SP	St Lukes Federal Way WA	(253)941-3000	SL	2008
Weber David A	(619)301-8545 davidarthurweber@gmail.com	1440 Connecticut St Imperial Beach CA 91932	PSW	SP	Our Redeemer San Diego CA	(619)262-0757	SL	2003
Weber David C	(608)378-3384 pastor@stmatthewsonline.org	4281 US Highway 12 Warrens WI 54666	SW	SP	St Matthew Warrens WI	(608)378-3233	SL	1991
Weber David J	(906)482-3561	49610 Blessent Rd Hancock MI 49930	NW	EM			SL	1979
Weber David K Dr	david.weber@valpo.edu	2325 W Giddings St Apt 3d Chicago IL 60625	IN	EM			FW	1982
Weber Dillon M	(253)205-9086 pastorweber@tlcseattle.org	1210 10th Ave E Seattle WA 98102	NOW	SP	Trinity Seattle WA	(206)324-1066	SL	2024
Webster Stanley D	(518)943-5888 stankim@mhcable.com	9 Cottontail Ln Catskill NY 12414	AT	Inst C	Atlantic District Hastings-On-Hudson NY	(914)337-5700	CQ	1988
Weden Andrew L	(715)347-1973 aweden@uwsp.edu	8056 County Road Cc Rosholt WI 54473	NW	Cmp P	North Wisconsin District Wausau WI	(715)845-8241	SL	2011
Wee Peter	(732) 252-9550 peterkhwee@gmail.com	151 Shinnecock Dr Manalapan Township NJ 07726	NJ	SP	St Thomas Manalapan NJ	(732)252-9550	CQ	2020
Weedon William C	weedon@mac.com	P.O. Box 484 Hamel IL 62046	SI	Asst	St Paul Worden IL	(618)633-2209	SL	1986
Weeks David L	(412)601-0164 revdlw@gmail.com	9380 Barnes Lake Rd Irwin PA 15642	EA	EM			FW	1980
Weeks Kyle T	(530)647-6498 ktweeks2015@gmail.com	c/o St. Luke Lutheran Church 4205 Washtenaw Ave Ann Arbor MI 48108	MI	SP	St Luke Ann Arbor MI	(734)971-0550	SL	2019
Weeks Peter J	(618) 517-4475 pastorpeter42@gmail.com	3105 W Striegel Rd Carbondale IL 62901	SI	Assoc	Our Savior Carbondale IL	(618)549-1694	SL	2008
Weeman Richard D	(605)925-4004 revrdwbun@goldenwest.net	P.O. Box 566 Freeman SD 57029	SD	Asst	St John* Wolsey SD	(605)883-4972	FW	1990
Weems Stephen B	(303)408-4409 pastorstephen83401@gmail.com	1415 Whitewater Dr Apt 7202 Idaho Falls ID 83402	NOW	SMP	St John Idaho Falls ID	(208)522-5650	SL-SMP	2010
Wegener John H	(319)427-3098 prwegener@cfu.net	32147 160th St Dike IA 50624	IE	SP	College Hill Cedar Falls IA	(319)266-1274	FW	2004
Wegener Thomas C	(319)231-2848 tcrawegener@gmail.com	914 Bluegrass Cir Unit 205 Cedar Falls IA 50613	IE	EM			SPR	1967
Wegner Mark A	(907)980-2824 marah1523@gmail.com	1707 Hawthorne Ln Billings MT 59105	MT	EM			SL	1982
Wegrzyn Daniel J Dr	revdan13@stjohnslombard.org	1158 Michelle Ln Lombard IL 60148	NI	Sn/Adm	St John Lombard IL	(630)629-2515	SL	1989
Wehling Andrew A	(620)655-2624 revwehling@hotmail.com	2108 E 29th St Lawrence KS 66046	KS	SP	Immanuel Lawrence KS	(785)843-0620	SL	1993
Wehling Caleb J	(620)655-9152 calebw@oursav.org	803 S Boxelder St Norfolk NE 68701	NEB	Assoc	Our Savior Norfolk NE	(402)371-9005	SL	2024
Wehmas Neil E	(515)201-3753 pastorwehmas@gmail.com	1101 Park Ln Ida Grove IA 51445	IW	SP	St Paul Ida Grove IA	(712)364-2918	SL	2012
Wehmeier Daniel L	pastor@kingofkingsks.org	18400 Hickory St Gardner KS 66030	KS	SP	King Of Kings Gardner KS	(913)856-2500	SL	1993
Wehmeier Waldemar W Dr	(832)814-2749 wwehmeier@att.net	11107 Brandon Gate Houston TX 77095	TX	EM			SL	1959
Wehmeyer Randall C	rcwehmeyer@yahoo.com	405 Ingram Rd Devine TX 78016	TX	SP	Divine Savior Devine TX	(830)663-3735	SL	2005
Wehmeyer Craig B	craig.wehmeyer@imlutheran.org	214 W 5th St Washington MO 63090	MO	Sn/Adm	Immanuel Washington MO	(636)239-4705	SL	2020
Wehrmeister Arthur H	awehrmeister@clcs.org	5542 Blairwood Dr Indianapolis IN 46237	IN	EM			CQ	1980
Wehrspann Noah J	(320)533-0387 boatmaninc@gmail.com	610 2nd Ave SE Long Prairie MN 56347	MNN	SP	Trinity Long Prairie MN	(320)732-2238	SL	2006
Weibel Dean J	(952)473-0171 ddweib@gmail.com	215 Barry Ave S Apt 122 Wayzata MN 55391	MNS	EM			FW	1980
Weideman Jay R	(218)770-1279 weidemanjay433@gmail.com	700 3rd St SW Oelwein IA 50662	IE	SP	Our Redeemer* Independence IA	(319)334-2745	FW	2020
Weider Michael J Dr	(636)577-0458 mike@crossroadkaty.org	5338 Baronet Dr Katy TX 77493	TX	Sn/Adm	CrossRoad Katy TX	(281)398-6464	SL	2015
Weidler Ronald W	(630)761-8830 rweidler@sbcglobal.net	1073 Ponca Dr Batavia IL 60510	NI	EM			SPR	1976
Weidmayer Robert C	(616)443-9053 revbob@pumpkinhook.org	153 Church Ave Farmington NY 14425	EA	SP	St John Farmington NY	(315)986-3045	SL	1996
Weier Gary W	(228) 256-2791 garyweier@yahoo.com	13704 Hidden Oaks Dr Gulfport MS 39503	SO	EM			SL	1969
Weight Caleb P	(218) 729-9473	5007 Maple Grove Road Hermantown MN 55811	MNN	Assoc	Peace Christ Hermantown MN	(218)729-9473	SL	2019

*Multiple Assignments (See Church Worker Locator for Additional Details)

See Page 53 for the Table of Abbreviations for key to District, Position, and Seminary abbreviations

**C =Candidate; EM = Emeritus; the date following the C is the month and year the Candidate status began

NAME	TELEPHONE NUMBER EMAIL	STREET ADDRESS CITY/STATE/ZIP	DISTRICT	POSITION/ STATUS**	WHERE SERVING	OFFICE PHONE	SEM/ PROGRAM	YR GRAD
Weikart Robert C Dr	(352)429-5596 isettabob@aol.com	12952 Mascotte Empire Rd Groveland FL 34736	FG	EM			SPR	1969
Weiler John S	(314)440-3886 jswknock2007@gmail.com	617 Marian Dr Dupo IL 62239	MO	SP	Zion Valley Park MO	(636)225-7780	SL	2007
Weinhold Robert W	rww1222@comcast.net	604 Pimlico Way Unit C Epworth IA 52045	NI	EM			SL	1982
Weinhold Terry E	(636)244-2316 weinhold801@gmail.com	540 Rolling Hills Dr Saint Charles MO 63304	MO	EM			SL	1977
Weinkauf Robert C	(913)724-2900 pastor@risensaviorlcms.org	c/o Risen Savior Lutheran Church 14700 Leavenworth Rd Basehor KS 66007	KS	Sn/Adm	Risen Savior Basehor KS	(913)724-2900	FW	2007
Weinrich Charles A	(570)551-6871 chuck.carol.1941@gmail.com	19 Tressler Blvd Lewisburg PA 17837	EN	EM			SL	1967
Weinrich William C	(260)417-2555 wmwein@aol.com	3 Wycliffe Pl Fort Wayne IN 46825	IN	S HS/C	Concordia Theological Seminary Fort Wayne IN	(260)452-2100	SL	1972
Weir David	(541)430-5072 davew@stpaulroseburg.org	692 Elkhorn Ln. Glide OR 97443	NOW	SMP	St Paul Roseburg OR	(541)673-7212	CQ	2019
Weirauch David M	(937)658-8462 weirauchdm@gmail.com	7107 Pointe Inverness Way Fort Wayne IN 46804	IN	C02/2022			FW	2017
Weise Robert W Dr	(618)444-2625 weiser@csl.edu	224 Belden Dr Edwardsville IL 62025	SI	EM			SL	1982
Weise Russell J Dr	(217)521-0352 gofishruss.w@gmail.com	8957 Grand Ave North Richland Hills TX 76180	TX	EM			CQ	1982
Weisenborn Paul C	(660)838-6428 pryzborn@hotmail.com	9195 B Hwy Bunceton MO 65237	MO	SP	Zion Bunceton MO	(660)838-6428	FW	1997
Weiser Delton R	(512)497-1212 deltonweiser@hotmail.com	500 Windmill Rdg Hutto TX 78634	TX	SP	Point Of Grace Pflugerville TX	(512)251-9095	SL	1991
Weiser Tim W	(618)614-3961 weisertim@yahoo.com	703 Oriole Ln Washington MO 63090	MO	EM			SL	2007
Weishaupt Theodore F Jr	pastorted1993@gmail.com	704 Maple St Anita IA 50020	IW	SP	Holy Cross Anita IA	(712)249-0240	CQ	1995
Weispfennig Steven A	steve.stjohnsyankton@gmail.com	701 Green St Yankton SD 57078	SD	Sn/Adm	St John Yankton SD	(605)665-7337	SL	2008
Weiss David E	pastorsttimothy@gmail.com	1910 Big Bend Rd Waukesha WI 53189	SW	EM			SL	1993
Weiss Donald E	(419) 509-0340 dweiss1942.dw@gmail.com	5211 Eagles Landing Dr Oregon OH 43616	OH	EM			SPR	1973
Weiss Donald P	(414)719-7008 dpweissrev@yahoo.com	8744 W Magnolia St Milwaukee WI 53224	SW	EM			SL	1973
Weiss Stephen T	(970)301-9097 stevetweiss@yahoo.com	652 54th Ave Greeley CO 80634	RM	SP	Gloria Christi Greeley CO	(970)353-2554	NESC	1999
Weiss William M Jr	(515)720-7937 weissone77@gmail.com	c/o Peace Lutheran Church 3430 N 4th St Flagstaff AZ 86004	PSW	SP	Peace Flagstaff AZ	(928)526-9578	SL	2008
Weist James D	(810)210-4540 pastorjimw2017@gmail.com	c/o Lutheran Church Of The Lakes 8800 N Rollin Hwy Addison MI 49220	MI	SP	Of the Lakes Addison MI	(517)547-4261	FW	1997
Welch Daniel J	(612) 214-8912 dwelch@1stglencoe.org	1712 Cedar Ave N Glencoe MN 55336	MNS	Sn/Adm	First Glencoe MN	(320)864-5522	SL	1998
Weldon John H	(412)999-4226 weldjonshar@yahoo.com	1818 Fairfield St Saginaw MI 48602	MI	EM			SL	1971
Weldon Robert F Sr	(270)792-0570 RFWdesign1@aol.com	170 Brentview Dr Grafton OH 44044	EN	Sn/Adm	Grace Elyria OH	(440)322-5497	FW	2004
Weldtensai Benyam	(619)841-8030 benaflus@gmail.com	8260 Meadow Rd Apt 3102 Dallas TX 75231	TX	Asst	Zion Dallas TX	(214)363-1639	CQ	2023
Weller Robert D	(408)997-4848 pastor@sanjoselutheran.org	1281 Redmond Ave San Jose CA 95120	CNH	SP	Shep Of Valley San Jose CA	(408)997-4848	FW	1994
Wellhousen Austin M	(248)758-8688 pastoraustin@hosanna.church	100 Bunker Ct Mankato MN 56001	MNS	Assoc	Hosanna Mankato MN	(507)388-1766	SL	2020
Wellik Bradley M	(520)256-4783 bwellik@mvlcs.org	10621 Capitol Peak Ave Las Vegas NV 89166	PSW	Assoc	Mountain View Las Vegas NV	(702)360-8290	SL	2019
Wellman Keith B	(308)394-5562 02beth10@vistabeam.com	33851 Road 726 Wauneta NE 69045	NEB	SP	Redeemer* Wauneta NE	(308)394-5522	SL	1974
Wellnitz Karl A	(920)450-2455 pstrkarl@gmail.com	P.O. Box 793 Ashland WI 54806	NW	C10/2022			FW	1992
Wells Timothy M		1820 E Condon Ave Aurora NE 68818	NEB	SP	Cross of Christ Aurora NE	(402)694-4209	SL	2016
Welmer Donald N	pastor@first4u.org	2800 McCallie Ave Chattanooga TN 37404	MDS	SP	First Chattanooga TN	(423)629-5990	FW	2012
Welton Adam J	(307)221-1256 adwelton@gmail.com	163 1st Ave S Apt 6 Brookings SD 57006	SD	C09/2024			FW	2013
Wenck Carl R	carlwenck22@gmail.com	331 Braxton Dr Murfreesboro TN 37130	MDS	EM			FW	1981
Wende John D	(651)330-6981 johnwende7201@comcast.net	1219 Gresham Ave N Oakdale MN 55128	MNS	EM			SPR	1970
Wendelin Timothy J	(303)884-2839 timwendelin@gmail.com	12429 W 17th Ave Lakewood CO 80215	RM	SMP	Bethlehem Lakewood CO	(303)238-7676	SL-SMP	2015
Wendorf Kenton G	(262)573-9532 kgwendorf@gmail.com	794 Milkweed Ct Neenah WI 54956	SW	EM			CQ	1979
Wendorf Kevin C	kcwendorf@hotmail.com	49 Partridge Chatham IL 62629	CI	Sn/Adm	St John Chatham IL	(217)483-2612	FW	2005
Wendorf Nathan M	(956)423-3924 nw@splch.com	602 Morgan Blvd Harlingen TX 78550	TX	Sn/Adm	St Paul Harlingen TX	(956)423-3924	SL	2005
Wendorff Carl E	(515)721-8222 pastor.wendorff@gmail.com	1523 18th St West Des Moines IA 50265	IW	SP	Trinity Des Moines IA	(515)279-3609	FW	2019

*Multiple Assignments (See Church Worker Locator for Additional Details)

See Page 53 for the Table of Abbreviations for key to District, Position, and Seminary abbreviations

**C =Candidate; EM = Emeritus; the date following the C is the month and year the Candidate status began

NAME	TELEPHONE NUMBER EMAIL	STREET ADDRESS CITY/STATE/ZIP	DISTRICT	POSITION/ STATUS**	WHERE SERVING	OFFICE PHONE	SEM/ PROGRAM	YR GRAD
Wendorff Aaron N	(507)766-2165 pr.awendorff@gmail.com	106 E View Pl Osceola IA 50213	IW	SP	Our Savior's* Leon IA	(507)766-2165	FW	2022
Wendt Vernon E Jr Dr	(616)717-0882 vernwendt@aol.com	1641 North 78th Avenue Elmwood Park IL 60707	NI	SP	St Paul* Chicago Heights IL	(708)754-4493	FW	1990
Wendt Ryan D	(406)860-9540 pastorwendt@gmail.com	5176 Bridle Creek Trl Billings MT 59106	MT	DP	Montana District* Billings MT	(406)259-2908	FW	2004
Wendt Ernest C	(734)905-7861	7062 Creekway Ct Ypsilanti MI 48197	MI	EM			CQ	1985
Wendt Kevin M Dr	(850)240-3753 pastorkevin@gracedestin.com	4071 Drifting Sand Trail Destin FL 32541	SO	SP	Grace Destin FL	(850)353-2996	SL	1993
Wendzel Linden B	(515)443-0925 revlbwendzel@hotmail.com	115 W 5th St P.O. Box 115 Bagley IA 50026	IW	EM			FW	1977
Wenger Eric R	(715)325-5475 ewenger@lacfchurch.com	479 Duffers Trail Nekoosa WI 54457	NW	SP	Lakes Area Nekoosa WI	(715)325-5475	SL	1997
Wenholz Dennis A	(314)610-7838 pastordw.2006@gmail.com	3628 S Pacific Hwy Spc 13 Medford OR 97501	NOW	Inst C	Board for National Mission Saint Louis MO		FW	2006
Wenig Thomas D Dr	(812)476-9991 pastor@redeemerchurch.org	229 Plaza Dr Evansville IN 47715	IN	Sn/Adm	Our Redeemer Evansville IN	(812)476-9991	SL	1991
Wenker Kevin L	(623)910-4978 winks147@gmail.com	15127 N 86th Dr Peoria AZ 85381	PSW	EM			SPR	1976
Wenndt David L	(260)440-6807 peacewalllakepastor@gmail.com	P.O. Box 189 405 Center St Wall Lake IA 51466	IW	SP	Peace Wall Lake IA	(712)664-2961	FW	2024
Wenskay Lee C	(989)453-2382 leeandsheryl75@gmail.com	104 Clara St Pigeon MI 48755	MI	EM			FW	2000
Wenthe Dean O Dr	(260)471-6054 dean.wenthe@ctsfw.edu	2919 Foxchase Run Fort Wayne IN 46825	IN	EM			SL	1971
Wentzel Robert W	(218)760-3417 revwentzel@gmail.com	8574 Esther Ln NE Bemidji MN 56601	MNN	EM			SL	2001
Wentzel Wayne H Dr	(810)964-2184 whwentz@aol.com	6998 Langle Dr Clarkston MI 48346	MI	EM			FW	1977
Wenz Paul G Dr	paulgwenz@yahoo.com	2127 Monterey St Santa Barbara CA 93101	PSW	SP	Emanuel Santa Barbara CA	(805)687-3734	SL	1993
Wenzel Mark A	(920)296-5206 revpastormark@gmail.com	7247 Meadowridge Drive Pickett WI 54964	SW	SP	Grace Omro WI	(920)685-2621	SL	1996
Wenzel Michael D	mdwenzel@comcast.net	1501 Arab Dr SE Tumwater WA 98501	NOW	SP	Trinity Olympia WA	(360)357-6574	SL	2002
Wenzelburger Mark E	(479)359-2674 mkmkwenz@gmail.com	14607 Ravenwood Lane Garfield AR 72732	MDS	EM			SL	1998
Wenzelburger Kurt R	(414)736-1772 kwenzelburger@splcs.net	52910 Romeo Plank Rd Macomb MI 48042	MI	Sn/Adm	St Peter Macomb MI	(586)781-3434	SL	2005
Werfelmann Arthur H	(509)492-1161 revwolfman@msn.com	5809 95th Dr SE Snohomish WA 98290	NOW	EM			CQ	1984
Werfelmann Theodore P	(253)653-5373 rev.ted@comcast.net	5307 Nathan Loop SE Auburn WA 98092	NOW	EM			SL	1976
Werk Allen A	(585)721-4218 allenwerk@gmail.com	36 Trailside Dr Winona Lake IN 46590	IN	EM			SL	1982
Werling Gary W	(402)880-8864 gwwerling@yahoo.com	425 Devonshire Dr Gretna NE 68028	NEB	EM			FW	1979
Werly David C	(607)221-8141 dcwrev3@gmail.com	P.O. Box 525 Chenango Brg NY 13745	EA	EM			FW	1999
Wernecke John W	jwwpastor@gmail.com	4259 Zander Dr Bay City MI 48706	MI	EM			FW	1985
Werner Joel A	(609)450-3502 joelwerner10@gmail.com	c/o Christ Our Savior Lutheran Church 14175 Farmington Rd Livonia MI 48154	MI	Assoc	Christ Our Savior Livonia MI	(734)522-6830	SL	2023
Werner Paul G	(586)201-3302 wernerpaul@sbcglobal.net	4150 Jenee Drive Lorain OH 44053	OH	SP	St Paul Amherst OH	(440)988-4157	SL	1987
Werner Tyler C	(920)458-4343 pastor@stmarksheboygan.com	1019 N 7th St Sheboygan WI 53081	EN	SP	St Mark Sheboygan Sheboygan WI	(920)458-4343	SL	2020
Werner Mark A	(906)202-3624 rev.mark.werner@gmail.com	122 S Walnut Ct Mason MI 48854	MI	SP	Messiah Holt MI	(517)694-1280	FW	2014
Werner David W	(260)485-3586 pastordww@hotmail.com	2924 S Broadway St Yorktown IN 47396	IN	EM			CQ	1978
Werner Kevin L	(815)468-7224 kevinwerner813@gmail.com	689 Marquette Dr Manteno IL 60950	NI	SP	Risen Savior Manteno IL	(815)468-2011	FW	1991
Werner John T	(612)716-4753 revjohnwerner@gmail.com	P.O. Box 155 Linn KS 66953	KS	SP	St John Palmer KS	(785)692-4228	SL	2016
Werth Alan R	(701)899-3916 alrwerth@gmail.com	417 4th St S Wahpeton ND 58075	ND	EM			FW	1993
Werzner Arthur L	(425) 445-9115 pastorawerzner@hotmail.com	1709 Glennwood Ave SE Renton WA 98058	NOW	RSO	Lutheran Ministry Services Northwest Seattle WA	(206)450-7128	SL	2001
Wesche David P	(706) 970-8869 davewoohoo705@gmail.com	2720 Bradley Rd Blairsville GA 30512	FG	EM			SL	2005
Wescoatt Mark A	(580)651-9101 wescoattmd@gmail.com	1701 N Oklahoma St Guymon OK 73942	OK	EM			FW	1991
Wescoatt Benjamin M	(229)444-2093 ben.wescoatt@gmail.com	5825 S Grand Blvd Saint Louis MO 63111	MO	Sn/Adm	St Johns Saint Louis MO	(314)773-0126	SL	2025
Weseloh Melvin L	(309)392-1721 revpepsimel@aol.com	P.O. Box 772 Minier IL 61759	CI	EM			SL	1957
Wesolik Larry F	(612)413-0309 lwesolik@gmail.com	20587 Kearney Path Lakeville MN 55044	MNS	EM			SPR	1970
Wessel Jonathan A	(715)533-9662 gracerev@plbb.us	707 W Brown St P.O. Box 408 Augusta WI 54722	NW	SP	Grace Augusta WI	(715)286-2116	FW	1988

*Multiple Assignments (See Church Worker Locator for Additional Details)

See Page 53 for the Table of Abbreviations for key to District, Position, and Seminary abbreviations

**C =Candidate; EM = Emeritus; the date following the C is the month and year the Candidate status began

NAME	TELEPHONE NUMBER EMAIL	STREET ADDRESS CITY/STATE/ZIP	DISTRICT	POSITION/ STATUS**	WHERE SERVING	OFFICE PHONE	SEM/ PROGRAM	YR GRAD
Wessel Loel A	(507)346-1073 loelwessel@msn.com	503 W Fremont St Spring Valley MN 55975	MNS	SP	First English Spring Valley MN	(507)346-2793	FW	1993
Wessel Zachary T	(507) 441-9592 zachary.wessel@ctsfw.edu	46448 263rd St Hartford SD 57033	SD	Sn/Adm	Trinity Hartford SD	(605)526-3571	FW	2025
West Aaron M		1219 S Michigan Ave Greensburg IN 47240	IN	SP	Holy Trinity Greensburg IN	(812)663-8192	FW	2014
West Brian D	(713)213-7193 pastorbrian@holycrossjenison.org	7100 Jasper Dr Hudsonville MI 49426	MI	Sn/Adm	Holy Cross Jenison MI	(616)457-2420	SL	2007
Westad Robert C	(320)593-1860 karbert@hutchtel.net	427 Tischler Ave SE Faribault MN 55021	MNS	EM			SL	1965
Westby Charles W Dr	(303)503-6581 pastorwestby@gmail.com	14936 E. Crestridge Place Aurora CO 80015	RM	Asst	Trinity Denver CO	(303)406-3143	CQ	1992
Westergren Kevin T		7904 Tisdale Dr Austin TX 78757	TX	Sn/Adm	Redeemer Austin TX	(512)459-1500	SL	1987
Westfall John H	(574)297-4477 jhblwestfall@gmail.com	5749 E Indian Creek Rd Monticello IN 47960	IN	EM			CQ	2016
Westgate Brian P	(724)487-1017 brian_westgate@hotmail.com	305 E. Indiana St. Kouts IN 46347	IN	SP	St Paul Kouts IN	(219)766-2395	FW	2011
Westhafer John A	(458)562-9127 westhafer@wavecable.com	1913 NW Bayshore Dr Waldport OR 97394	NOW	SP	Our Savior Waldport OR	(541)563-7729	SL	1985
Wetmore David L	(715)581-6084 pastordave@clcwausau.org	2502 Windsong Cir Kronenwetter WI 54455	NW	Sn/Adm	Christ Wausau WI	(715)848-2040	FW	1999
Wetnyangran Wichieng T	(817)335-2915 wichieng@peacechurch.org	5505 Finian Ln N RICHLND HLS TX 76180	TX	Assoc	Peace Hurst TX	(817)284-1677	EIITSL	2007
Wetzel Oliver H	(847)549-0713	14595 W Rockland Rd Apt 210 Libertyville IL 60048	NI	EM			SL	1956
Wetzel Ralph M Jr Dr	(260)493-3695 chattychaplain@gmail.com	4310 Ara Dr Woodburn IN 46797	IN	EM			SPR	1964
Wetzstein James A	(219)464-5096 james.wetzstein@valpo.edu	1600 Chapel Dr Helge Center #117 Valparaiso IN 46383	IN	Assoc	Faith Memorial Valparaiso IN	(219)462-7684	SL	1989
Whaley Andrew D	(214)417-5950 andy.whaley@yahoo.com	1217 Rio Grande Dr Allen TX 75013	TX	Assoc	Waters Edge Frisco TX	(972)712-7377	SL	2005
Whaley Kyle T	(406)890-4851 pastor.whaley@bresnan.net	24 A Ave Polson MT 59860	MT	SP	MT Calvary* Polson MT	(406)883-4041	SL	2010
Whan David J	(260)633-6535 pastorwhan@gmail.com	3880 E Cider Mill Rd Columbia City IN 46775	IN	SP	Zion Columbia City IN	(260)244-5513	FW	2010
Wheeler Jay R	(641)414-8252 jrwheeler@iowatelecom.net	260 Country Club Dr Osceola IA 50213	IW	EM			FW	1983
Wheeler Neil D	(402)617-4100 pastor@peacewaverly.org	10310 N 149th Cir Waverly NE 68462	NEB	SP	Peace Waverly NE	(402)786-2345	SL	2005
Wheeler Steven J	(952)941-1094	9633 Xerxes Cir S Bloomington MN 55431	MNS	Sn/Adm	Cross View Edina MN	(952)941-1094	SL	1995
Whitby Kristopher R	(708)223-3112 kris.whitby@nidlcms.org	140 W Wood St Unit 329 Palatine IL 60067	NI	D Ex/S	Northern Illinois District River Forest IL	(708)449-3020	SL	1996
White Virgil R	(253)564-4238 vroywhite@hotmail.com	4225 Juniper Dr W University Place WA 98446	NOW	EM			Other	1969
White Laurence L	(713)686-5928 paswhite@osl.com	1008 Richelieu Ln Houston TX 77018	TX	Sn/Adm	Our Savior Houston TX	(713)290-9087	SPR	1974
White Donald R	(870)674-4836 bobbiekazoo@gmail.com	33 Clark Rd Lakeview AR 72642	MDS	EM			SL	1991
White Denton W	(716) 545-5281 dentonlhva@gmail.com	6637 Luther St Niagara Falls NY 14304	EA	SP	Holy Ghost Bergholtz NY	(716)731-3030	CQ	2010
Whited Charles E Jr Dr	(716)835-2220 cwhited@firsttrinity.com	1570 Niagara Falls Blvd Tonawanda NY 14150	EA	Sn/Adm	First Trinity Tonawanda NY	(716)835-2220	SL	1993
Whitehead William K	(813)681-1903 billwhitehead@verizon.net	2948 Forest Circle Seffner FL 33584	FG	SMP	Lake Wales Lake Wales FL	(863)676-4715	SL-SMP	2014
Whitfield Alexander Dr	(757) 318-9400 pastorwhitfield@gmail.com	2352 Haversham Close Virginia Beach VA 23454	SE	Sn/Adm	Hope Virginia Beach VA	(757)424-4848	SL	1997
Whitmore Justin D	pastorwhitmore@hotmail.com	49594 County Highway 53 Perham MN 56573	MNN	SP	St John Perham MN	(218)346-4302	SL	2012
Whitney Nicholas K	(308) 826-3421	P.O. Box 157 Amherst NE 68812	NEB	SP	Trinity Amherst NE	(308)826-3421	FW	2022
Whitsett Mark D Dr	(502) 438-7260 culture.doctor55@gmail.com	12113 Briargate Ln Goshen KY 40026	IN	EM			SL	1979
Whitson Craig E	(402)430-1721 cwhitson1517@hotmail.com	91 Lakeview Shores Dr. Coldspring TX 77331	TX	EM			SL	1984
Whittaker Mark C	(269)366-9746 markcwhittaker@gmail.com	677 Springwood Dr Kalamazoo MI 49009	MI	SP	St Johns Taylor MI	(734)287-2080	SL	1984
Whittaker Nathan C	(206)325-2733 whittaker.82@gmail.com	2719 S King Seattle WA 98144	NOW	SP	Good Shepherd Seattle WA	(206)325-2733	SL	2017
Whittenburg Scott M	(580)395-0221 scott@whittenburgfamily.net	18709 E. 42nd Street Tulsa OK 74134	OK	EM			SL	2007
Whittle Brian C	(417)343-6461 pastorwhittle@pm.me	4422 Stringtown Rd Lohman MO 65053	MO	SP	St John Lohman MO	(573)782-3191	SL	1998
Whybrew Kene A	(815)383-1148		CI	SP	St Paul's* Strasburg IL	(217)644-2661	FW	1990
Wicher Chris C Dr	(716)951-0222 chriscwicher@gmail.com	19 Vernon Dr Cheektowaga NY 14225	EA	EM			SL	1982
Wichner Erwin	(503)523-7919 swichner@yahoo.com	933 Harvest Dr SE Tumwater WA 98501	NOW	EM			SPR	1968
Wichtendahl Steven D	(641)757-0593 papawick@aol.com	2708 50th Ave Lone Rock IA 50559	IW	SP	St Thomas* Panora IA	(641)755-2051	FW	2007
Wickert Garry E	gewickert@gmail.com	3260 S. 850 W San Pierre IN 46374	IN	EM			FW	1986
Widener Nathan C		206 Passier Ct Fort Wayne IN 46825	IN	Assoc	St Peter's Fort Wayne IN	(260)749-5816	FW	2022

*Multiple Assignments (See Church Worker Locator for Additional Details)
See Page 53 for the Table of Abbreviations for key to District, Position, and Seminary abbreviations
**C =Candidate; EM = Emeritus; the date following the C is the month and year the Candidate status began

NAME	TELEPHONE NUMBER EMAIL	STREET ADDRESS CITY/STATE/ZIP	DISTRICT	POSITION/ STATUS**	WHERE SERVING	OFFICE PHONE	SEM/ PROGRAM	YR GRAD
Widger Douglas D	(817)922-0015 widger4@sbcglobal.net	2735 5th Ave Fort Worth TX 76110	TX	SMP	Grace Arlington TX	(817)274-1626	SL-SMP	2012
Widger Donal C	(719)375-0231 pastorwidger@gmail.com	2221 N Wahsatch Ave Colorado Spgs CO 80907	RM	SP	Redeemer Colorado Springs CO	(719)633-7661	SL	2000
Widmer John G	(970)946-4740 widmerjg@gmail.com	614 Antelope Ave Pagosa Spgs CO 81147	RM	SMP	Our Savior Pagosa Springs CO	(970)731-4668	FW-SMP	2019
Wiebel James R	(920)277-4851 jwiebel45@gmail.com	4812 N Stargaze Dr Appleton WI 54913	NW	EM			SL	1971
Wiechman Steven L	(832)524-3016 freewish72@gmail.com	7810 Deep Green Dr Rosenberg TX 77469	TX	SP	Trinity Rosenberg TX	(281)341-1451	SL	2003
Wiechman Terry F	(316)393-0374 vcpastor4@gmail.com	7000 Chaparral St Valley Center KS 67147	KS	EM			CQ	2010
Wiechmann Ralph E	(703)622-5480 mjwiec@gmail.com	21160 Maple Branch Terrace Ashburn VA 20147	SE	EM			SL	1962
Wiegand Adam C	(518)584-0904 pastoradam@spalutheran.org	10 Judys Way Saratoga Springs NY 12866	AT	Sn/Adm	St Paul Saratoga Springs NY	(518)584-0904	SL	1996
Wiegert Raymond P	(406)549-2705 rdwiegert@bresnan.net	4007 Lincoln Rd Missoula MT 59802	MT	EM			SPR	1959
Wiegert Mark R	(406)350-0898 mark.wiegert@outlook.com	1446 Casino Creek Rd Lewistown MT 59457	MT	SMP	Our Savior* Denton MT	(406)535-8563	SL-SMP	2018
Wiegert Paul H	(407)542-4312 plwiegert@comcast.net	1918 Outer Circle Dr Oviedo FL 32765	FG	EM			CQ	1979
Wielert Cory A	(219)688-5201 cwielert@trinitycp.org	11170 Ohio St Crown Point IN 46307	IN	Assoc	Trinity Crown Point IN	(219)663-1578	SL	2006
Wielgos Thaddeus S	(847)254-4431 twielgos@fellowshipoffaith.org	736 Weston Dr Crystal Lake IL 60014	NI	SMP	Fellowship Of Faith McHenry IL	(815)759-0739	SL	2025
Wierschke Allan D	(308)327-3103 blackduckwierschke@yahoo.com	P.O. Box 546 Rushville NE 69360	WY	SP	Zion* Hay Springs NE	(308)638-7575	FW	1994
Wiese Ronald J Dr	(803)448-1007 pastorronwiese@gmail.com	14000 Albert Ct Fort Mill SC 29707	SE	EM			SL	1969
Wiese Daniel T	(308)991-6289 danieltwiese@gmail.com	1202 Hancock St Holdrege NE 68949	NEB	SMP	St Paul Cambridge NE	(308)697-3725	SL-SMP	2015
Wiese James M	(413)250-2821 trinityem@yahoo.com	35 Croft Ct Pawcatuck CT 06379	NE	C06/2019			FW	1988
Wiesenborn Mark R	(832)693-8310 mark.wiesenborn@gmail.com	2516 Sunfish Dr Pearland TX 77584	TX	SP	St Matthew Houston TX	(713)526-5731	SL	2004
Wiesner David E	(314)892-3477 davidwiesner@charter.net	723 Woodward Dr Saint Louis MO 63125	SI	EM			CQ	1985
Wiesner Mark D	(618)397-1407 mdwiesner@charter.net	8100 W Main St Belleville IL 62223	SI	Sn/Adm	Signal Hill Belleville IL	(618)397-1407	SL	1984
Wiest Robert D	(402)643-0421 revmeisterorlcs@gmail.com	1212 Crown Rd Norfolk NE 68701	NEB	SP	Mount Olive Norfolk NE	(402)371-1238	SL	2004
Wietfeldt Matthew J	(260)452-5912 matthew.wietfeldt@ctsfw.edu	9317 Skyhill Dr Fort Wayne IN 46804	IN	S HS/C	Concordia Theological Seminary Fort Wayne IN	(260)452-2100	FW	2011
Wieting Kenneth W Dr	(262)725-6345 kwieting2@gmail.com	628 Westbury Ln Unit 1 Delavan WI 53115	SW	EM			SL	1982
Wiggins Stephen A Sr	(404) 710-4662 pastorsawiggins@gmail.com	6529 Hannah Stables Dr Jacksonville FL 32244	FG	SP	St Paul Jacksonville FL	(904)765-4219	FW	1988
Wiggins James Sr	(850)505-4905 wigjames@aol.com	8505 Rawls Ave Pensacola FL 32534	SO	EM			Other	1959
Wiggins La Vaughn	(334)419-7262 lw0009@bellsouth.net	c/o United Lutheran 1104 Rosa L Parks Ave Montgomery AL 36108	SO	SP	United Montgomery AL	(334)262-4326	FW	2002
Wiist David E	(812)461-8171 concordiachurch@juno.com	7015 Darmstadt Rd Evansville IN 47710	IN	SP	Concordia Evansville IN	(812)422-0384	SL	1997
Wikstrom Mark J	(559) 304-8902 helen.wikstrom@sbcglobal.net	1550 Kamm Ave Apt 104 Kingsburg CA 93631	CNH	EM			CQ	1997
Wilber James G	(360)460-2184 jgwwa@olypen.com	P.O. Box 3632 Sequim WA 98382	NOW	EM			SPR	1972
Wilch Gerhard	(715) 807-7207 pastor@stpaulsamherst.org	3324 Teton Dr Stevens Point WI 54481	NW	SP	St Paul Amherst WI	(715)824-3314	NESC	1996
Wilcoxen Timothy J		902 Kennedy St Burlington KS 66839	KS	SP	Trinity Burlington KS	(620)364-2283	FW	2017
Wildauer Leonard P	lwildauer@centurytel.net	259 River Pine Dr Shawano WI 54166	NW	EM			FW	1995
Wildauer Micah J	(414)758-4477 micah.wildauer@lcms.org	118 Pine Crest Dr Bremen IN 46506	MO	S Miss	Office of International Mission Saint Louis MO		FW	2006
Wildauer Weston J	(573)270-6925 weston.wildauer@gmail.com	1919 Sherwood Dr. Cape Girardeau MO 63701	MO	SP	Good Shepherd Cape Girardeau MO	(573)335-3974	SL	2014
Wilder William B	(505)220-3781 wbw108@comcast.net	13001 Cedarbrook Ave NE Albuquerque NM 87111	RM	SP	Christ Our Redeemer Albuquerque NM	(505)256-9881	CQ	2023
Wildermuth Dennis J	(360)371-7365 pastordennis2@gmail.com	P.O. Box 2193 Blaine WA 98231	NOW	EM			SL	1972
Wiley Don C Dr	(260)452-3203	10825 Oakbriar Ct Fort Wayne IN 46845	IN	S HS/C	Concordia Theological Seminary Fort Wayne IN	(260)452-2100	FW	1992
Wiley Joshua C	pastor@gracescappoose.org	33966 SE Uhlman Lane Scappoose OR 97056	NOW	SP	Grace Scappoose OR	(503)543-6555	SL	2018
Wiley Terry W	(307)321-0669 kidwiley@hotmail.com	1320 Clark Street Thermopolis WY 82443	WY	EM			SL	1993
Wilhelm Jeffrey M		11 SW 11th St Trinity Lutheran Fort Lauderdale FL 33315	FG	Sn/Adm	Trinity Fort Lauderdale FL	(954)463-2450	SL	2001
Wilhelmsen Dana	(254)217-3763 pneuagex@outlook.com	2709 Olympia Dr Temple TX 76502	TX	EM			FW	1992

*Multiple Assignments (See Church Worker Locator for Additional Details)
See Page 53 for the Table of Abbreviations for key to District, Position, and Seminary abbreviations
**C =Candidate; EM = Emeritus; the date following the C is the month and year the Candidate status began

NAME	TELEPHONE NUMBER EMAIL	STREET ADDRESS CITY/STATE/ZIP	DISTRICT	POSITION/ STATUS**	WHERE SERVING	OFFICE PHONE	SEM/ PROGRAM	YR GRAD
Wilk Max W	(719)314-7470	15339 S Lakecrest Dr Olathe KS 66061	NJ	EM			SL	1960
Wilke John M	(918)289-9707 jwilke@tlcba.org	20215 E 141st S Broken Arrow OK 74014	OK	SP	Trinity Broken Arrow OK	(918)455-5750	SL	2004
Wilke Ray S	(402)841-1785	84607 Hadar Rd Norfolk NE 68701	NEB	Assoc	Grace Norfolk NE	(402)371-1044	SPR	1970
Wilke Donald L	revrup2u@gmail.com	1415 Lake St Apt 113 Alexandria MN 56308	MNN	EM			SL	1978
Wilke Wayne W Dr	wilkew@yahoo.com	808 E Rose Marie Ln Phoenix AZ 85022	PSW	EM			SL	1974
Wilken Todd A	(618)939-9064 talkback@issuesetc.org	1437 Jamie Ln Waterloo IL 62298	SI	Asst	Trinity Millstadt IL	(618)476-3101	SL	1990
Wilkens Mark C	(920)698-2246 mcwilkens1@gmail.com	514 Washington St Kohler WI 53044	SW	SP	Our Redeemer Delavan WI	(262)728-4266	SL	1994
Wilkey Mickey D	mick_wilkey@yahoo.com	143 Mounds St P.O. Box 655 Forsyth MO 65653	MO	EM			FW	1983
Wilkie Dana M	dwilkie595@aol.com	125 N Iowa St Muscoda WI 53573	SW	SP	Christ* Highland WI	(608)739-4017	FW	1995
Wilkins Timothy M	(314)435-1025 timwilkins.sanctus@gmail.com	8517 Elgin Ave Saint Louis MO 63123	MO	EM			SL	2004
Will Kyle J	kjw1206@gmail.com	505 Wilmuth St Monroe LA 71201	SO		Southern District Slidell LA	(504)282-2632	SL	2020
Will Theodore W Jr	(360)828-8405 twilljr@gmail.com	9615 NE 7th St Vancouver WA 98664	NOW	EM			SL	1973
Willadsen Joshua J	(901)581-1269 jjwilladsen@gmail.com	8012 Williamsburg Rd Fort Smith AR 72903	MDS	SP	Trinity* Sallisaw OK	(918)775-6753	SL	2004
Wille Nathan J	(319)930-2259 rev.wille@gmail.com	919 7th Ave N Clinton IA 52732	IE	SP	Trinity Clinton IA	(563)242-5328	FW	2020
Williams Marcus A	(406)262-3298 pastormawilliams@gmail.com	8989 N Huetter Rd Rathdrum ID 83858	EN	Sn/Adm	Blessed Sacrament Hayden ID	(406)262-3298	FW	2017
Williams Richard F	(715)209-0479 rwilli6767@gmail.com	63611 Philaja Rd Ashland WI 54806	NW	SMP	Zion Ashland WI	(715)682-6075	SL-SMP	2015
Williams Jeffrey B Dr	(720)234-9980 pastor@trinityslayton.info	2010 Broadway Ave P.O. Box 215 Slayton MN 56172	MNS	SP	Trinity Slayton MN	(507)836-8129	FW	1992
Williams Isaac T	(651)890-6708 isaacnbrenda@aol.com	612 Spring Hill Bay Woodbury MN 55125	MNS	SP	Grace International Robbinsdale MN	(651)890-6708	SL	2013
Williams Guillaume J Sr	johnthree17@gmail.com	6249 Shadow Cir Osage Beach MO 65065	MO	SP	Hope Osage Beach MO	(573)348-2108	SL	1995
Williams Gary C	(616)819-9796 nutsforicecream@yahoo.com	5230 Storm Branch Leg Aiken SC 29803	SE	EM			FW	1983
Williams Byron R Sr	972-291-1643 pastorray2@yahoo.com	1368 Ridgeview Dr Cedar Hill TX 75104	TX	Sn/Adm	St Paul Dallas TX	(214)371-9429	CQ	1996
Williams Barry A	(402)454-2823 stjohngg@telebeep.com	82660 547 Ave Madison NE 68748	NEB	SP	St Paul* Tilden NE	(402)454-2823	SL	2003
Williamson Gregory R	(847)420-1411 revgrw@gmail.com	5640 Lucore Rd Marion IA 52302	IE	EM			FW	1983
Williamson Jay D	(785)562-8299 deaconmarine@att.net	1404 Spring St Marysville KS 66508	KS	SMP	Mount Calvary Marysville KS	(785)562-2046	CQ	2021
Williamson Kenneth L	(989)292-2392 pastorken73@gmail.com	c/o Our Savior Lutheran Church P.O. Box 66 Scottville MI 46454	MI	SP	Our Savior Scottville MI	(231)757-2271	SL	1994
Williamson Mark E	(402)782-1802 stillruntrains@gmail.com	488 Spencer Rd Rochester NY 14609	EA	EM			SL	2006
Williamson Peter C	(805)551-9148 pwilliamson4555@gmail.com	6711 Cavin Dr Wausau WI 54401	NW	Assoc	Trinity Wausau WI	(715)842-0769	SL	2017
Williamson Gregory K	(910)644-3480 abncmo@gmail.com	105 Saint Marys Pkwy Fayetteville NC 28303	SE	EM			SL	1983
Williamson-Link Steven J	steven.williamsonlink@yahoo.com	26 Rose Ave Patchogue NY 11772	AT	SP	Emanuel Patchogue NY	(631)758-2240	FW	2013
Willig Mark S	(815)585-4741 markwillig@me.com	4892 Cedar Point Ln Pinckneyville IL 62274	NI	EM			SL	1981
Willis Ryan S Sr			SW	SP	Immanuel Auroraville WI	(920)361-1812	SL	2001
Willman Sean A	(262)891-2697 pastorwillman@gmail.com	2651 W Bacon Rd Hillsdale MI 49242	MI	Sn/Adm	St Paul Hillsdale MI	(517)437-2762	FW	2013
Willms Levi R	(605)760-9299 willmslevi@gmail.com	5282 West Oakes Dr Saint Cloud MN 56303	MNN	Assoc	Trinity Sauk Rapids MN	(320)252-3670	SL	2006
Willsea Wendell R III	(404)290-4844 pastor@gracesummerville.org	303 Mayfield St Summerville SC 29485	SE	SP	Grace Summerville SC	(843)871-5444	SL	2001
Willson William C	(585)268-5326 kb3wl@localnet.com	5761 County Rt 31a Scio NY 14880	EA	EM			SPR	1973
Willweber Paul L		2025 Flying Hills Ct El Cajon CA 92020	PSW	SP	Prince Peace San Diego CA	(619)583-1436	SL	1995
Willweber Stephen K	(805)286-2789 pastor@kingofglorygh.org	7310 Glenwood Rd SW Port Orchard WA 98367	NOW	SP	King Of Glory Gig Harbor WA	(253)857-4574	SL	1998
Willweber Lloyd H	(559)310-9092 lloyd@willweber.net	10328 Road 256 Terra Bella CA 93270	CNH	EM			CQ	1996
Wilman John A	(715)790-1558 jjwilman@amerytel.net	318 Johnson St Amery WI 54001	NW	EM			FW	1999
Wilshek David E	(636)212-0434 dgmwilshek@aol.com	5160 Country Club Dr High Ridge MO 63049	MO	EM			SL	1984
Wilshusen James M	(314)239-9574 jameswilshusen@gmail.com	9100 Hwy. Yy Leslie MO 63056	MO	SP	Bethlehem* New Haven MO	(573)237-2602	SL	2014
Wilson Richard G	(616)916-9284 rgw456@hotmail.com	3859 N. Lakeshore Rd. Port Hope MI 48468	MI	EM			FW	1990
Wilson Winston	(360)928-9619 wincon9619@gmail.com	143 Bald Eagle Way Port Angeles WA 98363	NOW	EM			EIITSL	2015

*Multiple Assignments (See Church Worker Locator for Additional Details)
See Page 53 for the Table of Abbreviations for key to District, Position, and Seminary abbreviations
**C =Candidate; EM = Emeritus; the date following the C is the month and year the Candidate status began

NAME	TELEPHONE NUMBER EMAIL	STREET ADDRESS CITY/STATE/ZIP	DISTRICT	POSITION/ STATUS**	WHERE SERVING	OFFICE PHONE	SEM/ PROGRAM	YR GRAD
Wilson William G	pstor123@gmail.com	16100 Bridle Ridge St Port Charlotte FL 33953	FG	EM			SL	2003
Wilson Steven D	(507) 236-1181 pastor@sjlsherburn.com		MNS	Sn/Adm	St John Sherburn MN	(507)764-5312	FW	1989
Wilson Robert C	(845)537-1442 mrrwilson83@gmail.com	205 County Highway 18 Delhi NY 13753	AT	SMP	Immanuel* Delhi NY	(607)746-2098	SL-SMP	2017
Wilson Kevin A Dr	(614)440-5054 wilsonk@oh.lcms.org	12030 State Route 736 Marysville OH 43040	OH	DP	Ohio District North Olmsted OH	(440)235-2297	SL	1992
Wilson Jessy J	(518) 439-4328 wilson@blcdelmar.com	638 Elm Ave Selkirk NY 12158	AT	SMP	Bethlehem Delmar NY	(518)439-4328	SL-SMP	2021
Wilson Jeffrey J	(541)554-5541 pastorwilson.jw@gmail.com	152 Cardinal CV Irmo SC 29063	SE	C07/2016			SL	2008
Wilson Andrew J	(740)618-0931 awilson@cclphoenix.org		PSW	Assoc	Christ Phoenix AZ	(602)955-4830	SL	2014
Wilson Lynn J Dr	(605)381-8387 chappyljwilson@gmail.com	815 SW Bishop Dr Blue Springs MO 64015	MO	C01/2020			CQ	2006
Winckler Michael T	(402)909-2386 wincklerint@gmail.com	3700 County Rd 415 Friedheim MO 63747	MO	SP	Trinity Friedheim MO	(573)788-2536	SL	2024
Winckler Paul M	(605)939-4971 paul.winckler@sddlcms.org	603 Brannon Dr Harrisburg SD 57032	SD	D Ex/S	South Dakota District Sioux Falls SD	(605)361-1514	SL	2012
Windoloski Jeffrey M	jeffrey.windoloski@gmail.com		NE	Assoc	St John's Westfield MA	(413)568-1417	Other	2014
Winegarden Jerry D Dr	(574)275-1353 office@sbtl-lcms.com	7449 E 1000 N Syracuse IN 46567	IN	SP	Shep by Lakes Syracuse IN	(574)528-6137	FW	2003
Wing Daniel S	(660)851-3810 pastorwing@trinityoflincoln.org	1955 Gunnison Dr Lincoln NE 68521	NEB	Sn/Adm	Trinity Lincoln NE	(402)474-0606	SL	2006
Wingfield William R	(620)507-7340 pastorwingfield@outlook.com	704 Horizon Cir Linn KS 66953	KS	EM			SL	2014
Wink Thomas R	(414)581-7413 tlwinker49@gmail.com	718 Cameron Cir Hartland WI 53029	SW	EM			SL	1976
Winkel Randy Dr	(941)716-5432 rwinkel614@aol.com	6149 Manasota Key Road Englewood FL 34223	FG	EM			CQ	1979
Winkelman Michael L	mwinkelman7998@gmail.com	15290 Norrish Rd Morrison IL 61270	NI	EM			SL	1972
Winkelman Mark P	mwinkelman@stjohnsredbud.org	311 N Main St Red Bud IL 62278	SI	Sn/Adm	St John Red Bud IL	(618)282-3873	SL	2009
Winningham David C	(989)391-4545 dcwinningham@gmail.com	82 Tobico Beach Rod Bay City MI 48706	MI	EM			SL	1977
Winningham Paul R Dr	(573) 517-8250 winninghampaul135@gmail.com	964 Pcr 410 Frohna MO 63748	MO	EM			SL	1990
Winningham Ryan A	(616)392-7151 ryan@zionholland.org	1109 Colonial Ct Holland MI 49423	MI	Sn/Adm	Zion Holland MI	(616)392-7151	SL	2009
Winslett Timothy E	(865)406-6540 twinslett@winslettit.com	P.O. Box 204 Glade Spring VA 24340	SE	SMP	Holy Trinity Bristol TN		FW-SMP	2024
Winston Robert D	(703)789-3208 robnkimwinston@hotmail.com	7840 Belleflower Dr Springfield VA 22152	SE	SMP	Prince Of Peace Springfield VA	(703)451-5855	FW-SMP	2019
Winter Lincoln C	(307)331-0091	809 12th St Wheatland WY 82201	WY	SP	Zion* Grover CO	(307)245-3390	FW	1998
Winter William C	(989)329-0164 revwmwinter@gmail.com	302 Kimberly Dr Prudenville MI 48651	MI	EM			SL	1973
Winter William J	(541)538-1061 william.winter@ctsfw.edu	323 Gettysburg Coatesville IN 46121	IN	SP	Peace Greencastle IN	(765)653-6995	FW	2022
Winter Thomas W	(830)267-0827 thomaswwinter@gmail.com	807 E Brazos St Pearsall TX 78061	TX	SP	St Peter Pearsall TX	(830)334-2336	FW	2007
Winter Frank E III	(402)750-1592 chipjami@juno.com	5600 N Mooring Way Peoria IL 61615	CI	Sn/Adm	Redeemer Peoria IL	(309)691-2333	SL	1988
Winter Frank E Sr	(309)966-2234 mtcabin20@yahoo.com	5308 N Stenning Dr Peoria IL 61615	CI	EM			SL	1961
Winter Clifford A	cliffwinter@yahoo.com	4700 W 13th St N Apt 1106 Wichita KS 67212	KS	EM			SL	1965
Winter David W	(952)200-8177 winterflake16@gmail.com	13505 485th Ave Parkers Pr MN 56361	MNN	EM			FW	1984
Winter Kyle C	kylecwinter@gmail.com	71 Aspen Grove Way Kalispell MT 59901	MT	SP	Creston Kalispell MT	(406)752-1205	SL	2016
Winterfeldt Jonathan C	(618) 830-6762 jwinterfel@aol.com	803 Champlain Dr Cahokia IL 62206	SI	SP	St Peter Caseyville IL	(618)398-2646	SL	1998
Winterhoff Warren F	(757)565-2651 wwinterhoff@msn.com	106 Starboard Ct Williamsburg VA 23185	AT	EM			SPR	1969
Winters Jay A	(850)284-9507 pastor@universitylutheranchurch.org	2207 Monticello Dr Tallahassee FL 32303	FG	SP	University Tallahassee FL	(850)778-5854	SL	2007
Winters Thomas J	(210)479-1477 winters.tj@gmail.com	5802 Pheasant Ridge Ln Houston TX 77041	TX	SMP	St Mark Houston TX	(713)468-2623	SL-SMP	2015
Winters Walter A Dr	(314)749-0024 walt@jigabyte.com	6986 Mardel Ave Saint Louis MO 63109	MO	EM			SL	1975
Winterstein Paul E	(206)762-1362 paulwinterstein.pw@gmail.com	8108 11th Ave SW Seattle WA 98106	NOW	SP	Lamb of God Seattle WA	(206)363-0110	SL	1967
Winterstein Timothy J	(509)885-8275 pastorwinterstein@gmail.com	5760 S Handy Rd Bloomington IN 47401	IN	SP	University Bloomington IN	(812)336-5387	SL	2006
Wipperman Matthew P	(608)444-5660 mwipperman@livelifetogether.com	837 Royster Oaks Dr. Madison WI 53714	SW	SMP	Christ Memorial Madison WI	(608)271-2811	SL-SMP	2013
Wipperman Stephen K	(316)749-7767 skwipp@gmail.com	141 N Brookside St Witchita KS 67208	KS	SP	Peace Andover KS	(316)733-2633	SL	1978
Wirgau Samuel S	(260)273-7595 samuel.wirgau@gmail.com	6514 E 750 N Ossian IN 46777	IN	Sn/Adm	Bethlehem Ossian IN	(260)597-7121	FW	2011

*Multiple Assignments (See Church Worker Locator for Additional Details)
See Page 53 for the Table of Abbreviations for key to District, Position, and Seminary abbreviations
**C =Candidate; EM = Emeritus; the date following the C is the month and year the Candidate status began

NAME	TELEPHONE NUMBER EMAIL	STREET ADDRESS CITY/STATE/ZIP	DISTRICT	POSITION/ STATUS**	WHERE SERVING	OFFICE PHONE	SEM/ PROGRAM	YR GRAD
Wirsing Thomas C	(309)454-2015 tcw1@trinluth.org	1402 Henry Normal IL 61761	CI	EM			SL	1979
Wirtz Isaac H	(909)538-1078 isaac.h.wirtz@gmail.com	13136 East Kahlua Rd Vail AZ 85641	EN	SP	Mount Olive Tucson AZ	(520)298-0996	FW	2020
Wirtz Nicholas D	(323)717-4390 revnwirtz@yahoo.com	13136 E Kahlua Rd Vail AZ 85641	EN	IndC P	Risen Savior Green Valley AZ	(520)625-2612	FW	1994
Wise Kenneth M	(586)871-4891 amskwise@gmail.com	20325 Dunham Rd Clinton Twp MI 48038	MI	EM			SL	1988
Wiseman Samuel C	(541)963-2831 flglcmspastor@gmail.com	104 S 12th St La Grande OR 97850	NOW	SP	Faith La Grande OR	(541)963-2831	CQ	2002
Wismar Adolph H Jr Dr	(617)529-2203 a.wismar@rcn.com	362 Music Mountain Rd Falls Village CT 06031	NE	EM			SL	1969
Wismar Eric A	(203)240-7906 chapwismar@gmail.com	72 Laurel Ln Simsbury CT 06070	NE	Inst C	Office of International Mission Saint Louis MO		SL	2004
Wismar Gregory J Dr	(203)405-1135 wismar@prodigy.net	979b Heritage Vlg Southbury CT 06488	NE	EM			SL	1971
Wismar Stefan K	(612)791-4678 stefan.wismar@mnsdistrict.org	674 Ravencroft Rd Waconia MN 55387	MNS	D Ex/S	Minnesota South District Burnsville MN	(952)435-2550	SL	2001
Wisroth Lee A	(307) 254-2240 wizzylee44@gmail.com		WY	EM			FW	1983
With Jacob A	(970)765-4028 jwith@lawoftherockies.com	497 Kokanee Ct Gunnison CO 81230	RM	SMP	Mount Calvary Gunnison CO	(970)641-1860	FW-SMP	2022
Witmer Brett P	(717)514-9825 pastor.bwitmer@gmail.com	711 Chestnut St Johnstown PA 15906	EA	SP	Holy Cross* Johnstown PA	(814)539-0123	FW	2020
Witschy Emil A	(203)526-8708 wits.end@me.com	75 Marlborough St Apt 327 Portland CT 06480	SE	EM			SL	1981
Witt Aaron M	revwitt@gmail.com	702 Smith Ave P.O. Box 343 Elwood NE 68937	NEB	SP	Our Redeemer Elwood NE	(308)785-2875	SL	2000
Witt David L	david.witt@ctsfw.edu	8110 N 500 W Decatur IN 46733	IN	S HS/C	Concordia Theological Seminary Fort Wayne IN	(260)452-2100	FW	2015
Witt James E	(402)469-5957 revwittsr@gmail.com	2005a Old Rothsville Rd Lititz PA 17543	EN	EM			SL	2000
Witt Lucas D	LWitt@CompassionPlace.org	1001 E Cold Spring Ln Baltimore MD 21212	SE	RSO	Lutheran Mission Society of MD Linthicum MD	(410)636-0123	SL	2014
Witt Duarte Alvaro J	(630) 668-0701 alvaro@stjohnwheaton.org	410 N Cross St. Wheaton IL 60187	NI	Assoc	St John Wheaton IL	(630)668-0701	SL	2023
Witte Mark K	mwitte@gracelutheranmonroe.org	630 N Monroe St Monroe MI 48162	MI	Sn/Adm	Grace Monroe MI	(734)242-1401	FW	2006
Witte David R	drwitte@gmail.com	63 Belle Meadow Ln Little Rock AR 72210	MDS	Asst	Grace Little Rock AR	(501)663-3631	CQ	2014
Witte Henry F	(712)202-4751 handrwitte@gmail.com	1013 S Newton St Sioux City IA 51106	NEB	Asst	Hope South Sioux City NE	(402)494-1847	FW	1979
Witte Keith F	(419)966-3499 pastorwitte1@gmail.com	76 Waterford Blvd Fairborn OH 45324	OH	SP	Bethlehem Fairborn OH	(937)878-0651	FW	2009
Witten David M	(859) 324-5560 witten.david@yahoo.com	581 Pin Oak Hill Rd Stanford KY 40484	IN	EM			FW	1981
Wittenberg Paul F	(407)359-9790 dotwittenberg@yahoo.com	1323 Haven Dr Oviedo FL 32765	FG	EM			Other	1960
Wittenberger Denis J	(636)385-6335 bbjwit@aol.com	208 Barrington Ridge Ln Wentzville MO 63385	MO	EM			CQ	1983
Wittig Brandon M	(989)996-5353 wittigb@csl.edu	12762 Flynn Rd Sawyer MI 49125	MI	SP	Trinity Sawyer MI	(269)426-3937	SL	2021
Witt-Jablonski Jerry	(440)317-0695 revjablonskilutheran@gmail.com	4986 Donovan Dr Garfield Hts OH 44125	OH	SP	Immanuel Cleveland OH	(216)781-9511	FW	2017
Wittmayer Garland R	(314)631-3239 gmwittmayer@sbcglobal.net	9620 Labette Dr Saint Louis MO 63123	MO	EM			SL	1963
Witto Lawrence E	(810)344-7029 lwitto@att.net	3165 Ivy Ln Grand Blanc MI 48439	MI	EM			SL	1963
Wittrock Michael C	(308)360-1445 mcwittrock.wittrock3172@gmail.com	P.O. Box 858 Chadron NE 69337	WY	EM			FW	2001
Wixon Justin W	(520)401-3989 Wixonjustin@gmail.com	1111 W Graythorn Pl Tucson AZ 85737	PSW	SMP	Alive in Christ Marana AZ	(520)401-3989	SL-SMP	2019
Wobrock David E	(805)270-4270 ddwobrock@gmail.com	521 S Oak Park Blvd Arroyo Grande CA 93420	PSW	EM			SL	1973
Wodtke Norbert R	(785)478-4939 MJW2628@aol.com	3124 SW Landsdown Apt 46 Topeka KS 66614	KS	EM			SL	1954
Woebbeking Paul S	(715)926-6464 pswebbs@nelson-tel.net	497 N Washington St Mondovi WI 54755	NW	EM			SL	1979
Woell Brennan A	(517)899-2940 pastorwoell@gmail.com	127 Evart Street Cadillac MI 49601	MI	SP	Emmanuel Cadillac MI	(231)775-3261	SL	2015
Woelmer Richard L	(812)361-4504	1112 S Chaseway Ct Bloomington IN 47401	IN	EM			FW	1988
Woelmer Joshua J	(785)893-3960 joshua.woelmer@gmail.com	34838 Block Rd Paola KS 66071	KS	SP	Trinity* Paola KS	(913)849-3344	FW	2015
Woelmer James D	(972)704-6722 jwoelmer@verizon.net	4440 Brookes Ct Manhattan KS 66502	KS	SP	Christ Manhattan KS	(785)776-2227	FW	1990
Woelmer David C	(214)218-8354 rev.davidwoelmer@gmail.com	308 Byrne St. Smithville TX 78957	TX	SP	Grace Smithville TX	(512)237-2108	FW	2023
Woelzlein Allen J	(620)669-7298 woe52001@yahoo.com	1901 N Monroe St Hutchinson KS 67502	KS	EM			SPR	1976
Woerner Emil L	emilwoerner63@gmail.com	1212 Nature Way Benton AR 72019	MDS	SP	Friends In Christ Bryant AR	(501)749-4574	FW	2009

*Multiple Assignments (See Church Worker Locator for Additional Details)

See Page 53 for the Table of Abbreviations for key to District, Position, and Seminary abbreviations

**C =Candidate; EM = Emeritus; the date following the C is the month and year the Candidate status began

NAME	TELEPHONE NUMBER EMAIL	STREET ADDRESS CITY/STATE/ZIP	DISTRICT	POSITION/ STATUS**	WHERE SERVING	OFFICE PHONE	SEM/ PROGRAM	YR GRAD
Woerth Warren R	(636)296-1292 goodsheparnold@sbcglobal.net	2211 Tenbrook Rd Arnold MO 63010	MO	SP	Good Shepherd Arnold MO	(636)296-1292	FW	1979
Wohlers Richard L	(262)613-8383 richard.wohlers@cuw.edu	449 Green Bay Rd Cedarburg WI 53012	SW	EM			SL	1968
Wohletz Roger C	(720)283-8128 theophilus4@hotmail.com	7191 S Vine Cir W Centennial CO 80122	RM	Sn/Adm	Christ Denver CO	(303)722-1424	SL	1998
Wohlrabe John C Jr Dr	(207)400-2017 chapsjcw@yahoo.com	3832 S Lake Dr St Francis WI 53235	SW	Asst	Our Savior Whitefish Bay WI	(414)332-4458	SL	1982
Woita Steven R	stevewoita67@gmail.com	814 15th St Rockford IL 61104	NI	EM			CQ	2006
Wojtowicz Daniel A	(989)714-9469 danielwojo417@gmail.com	4050 Curtis Rd Birch Run MI 48415	MI	SMP	Immanuel Saginaw MI	(989)754-0929	FW-SMP	2017
Woldt Adam T	pastoradam@thepointknox.com		MDS	SP	The Point Knoxville TN	(402)681-5708	SL	2017
Wolf Gary C	(620)292-6161 gapswolf@sbcglobal.net	367 W. 10th Hoisington KS 67544	KS	SP	Concordia Hoisington KS	(620)653-4644	SL	1982
Wolf Philip B	(660)200-6488 mrchurch@juno.com	208 E Illinois St Highland KS 66035	KS	SP	Christ Wathena KS	(785)989-3348	SL	1986
Wolf Richard P	585-659-9175 rwolf39@rochester.rr.com	17192 Roosevelt Hwy Kendall NY 14476	EA	SMP	Holy Cross Middleport NY	(716)735-7209	SL-SMP	2015
Wolfe Adam S	(262)367-8400 adamw@stpaulfalls.com	2111 Creekside Ct Sheboygan WI 53081	SW	Assoc	St Paul Sheboygan Falls WI	(920)467-6449	SL	2020
Wolff Michael D	mdwolff@yahoo.com		NI	EM			SL	1989
Wolff Paul A	(248)424-9499 pawolff@aol.com	27356 Pierce St Southfield MI 48076	MI	Asst	Emmanuel Dearborn MI	(313)565-4002	SL	1996
Wolff Robert P	(262)320-3529 wolfma419@gmail.com	5215 Douglas Ave Apt 211 Racine WI 53402	SW	EM			SPR	1958
Wolfgram Andrew C	revandrewwolfgram@gmail.com	803 Catherine St Point Pleasant Boro NJ 08742	NJ	SP	Good Shepherd Point Pleasant NJ	(732)892-4492	SL	2018
Wolfgram Lester J	(701)400-0646 pastor.wolfgram@gmail.com	4601 Rolling Ridge Rd Bismarck ND 58503	ND	Sn/Adm	Shep Valley Bismarck ND	(701)258-4231	SL	1992
Wolfmueller C B	(303)525-4991 bwolfmueller@gmail.com	2230 Fernspring Dr Round Rock TX 78665	TX	Sn/Adm	Jesus of the Deaf* Austin TX	(512)442-1715	FW	2005
Wolfram Michael C	(515)988-4324 mcwolfram25@gmail.com	2914 Center Lake Dr Spirit Lake IA 51360	IW	EM			FW	1977
Wolfram Richard J Dr	(734)645-4792 richardwolfram@sbcglobal.net	3057 Wheat Valley Dr Howell MI 48843	MI	EM			SL	1982
Wollberg Jeffrey N	(269)598-8505 wollbergjn@yahoo.com	8463 Wolf Rd Bellevue MI 49021	MI	EM			FW	1989
Wollberg Matthias C	(308)293-4063 matthias.wollberg@ctsfw.edu	103 W 6th St Riceville IA 50466	IE	SP	St Peter Riceville IA	(641)985-2421	FW	2019
Wollberg Trenton N			MI	SP	Holy Cross Onaway MI	(989)733-8412	FW	2017
Wollenberg Nathan T	(618)335-4155 wollenbergn@gmail.com	191 N Main St Hoyleton IL 62803	SI	SP	Trinity Hoyleton IL	(618)493-6226	SL	2012
Wollenburg Alan J	(573)380-0752 ajwrev@gmail.com	104 Linda Dr Sikeston MO 63801	MO	EM			SL	1979
Wollenburg David W Dr	(618)910-2856 djwoll@charter.net	2340 Fourlakes Dr Belleville IL 62220	SI	EM			SL	1971
Wollman Michael W Dr	(410)569-9237 pmike2@verizon.net	1004 Old Joppa Rd # A Joppa MD 21085	SE	EM			FW	1990
Wollman Andrew J	(574)533-7705 pastorajw@gmail.com	18548 County Road 18 Goshen IN 46528	IN	SP	Prince Peace Goshen IN	(574)533-7705	FW	2002
Woltemath Douglas M	(319)521-8201 pastor@sslchurch.org	311 3rd Ave Atkins IA 52206	IE	SP	Saint Stephens Atkins IA	(319)446-7675	CQ	1999
Wolter Derek M	(636)634-6656 derek.wolter2710@gmail.com	7500 W North Ave Wauwatosa WI 53213	SW	Inst C	The Lutheran Home Inc Wauwatosa WI	(414)258-6170	FW	1989
Wolter Jason M	(402)335-7518 jwolter78@hotmail.com	406 N Main St Janesville MN 56048	MNS	Sn/Adm	Trinity Janesville MN	(507)231-5189	SL	2002
Wolters Luke B	(314)956-8664 gracelcms@sbcglobal.net	528 W Hudson St Wellsville MO 63384	MO	SP	Grace Wellsville MO	(573)684-2106	SL	2012
Wolters Michael D	(701)483-8876 rlcrev@ndsupernet.com	1068 7th St W Dickinson ND 58601	ND	SP	Redeemer Dickinson ND	(701)483-4463	SL	1987
Wonderly Daniel A Dr	danwonderly@yahoo.com	5751 Stone Briar Ln S Freeland MI 48623	NW	SP	Faith Chippewa Falls WI	(715)723-7754	FW	1985
Wondrasch Connor L	(507)696-5181 connor.wondrasch@gmail.com	4110 Wenzel Ln Saint Louis MO 63129	MO	Tchr	Luth High School Assn St Louis Saint Louis MO	(314)833-2904	SL	2024
Wong Larry L	(281) 865-3288 larrywong0752@gmail.com	7202 Barker Cypress Rd Apt 4104 Cypress TX 77433	TX	EM			SL	2008
Wonnacott Neil K	ncwonnacott@yahoo.com	126 E South St Bremen IN 46506	IN	SP	St Paul Bremen IN	(574)546-2332	FW	1993
Wonnacott James M	jmwpc@cableone.net	917 Blaine St Norfolk NE 68701	NEB	Inst C	Nebraska District Seward NE	(402)643-2961	SL	1982
Woo Daniel K	(415)990-0324 pastordwoo@comcast.net	41 Ina Ct San Francisco CA 94112	CNH	Sn/Adm	Hope Daly City CA	(650)991-4673	SL	1998
Wood Mark A Dr	(623)377-6856 pastorwood@shepherdofthecan-yon.org	18019 E La Posada Ct Gold Canyon AZ 85118	EN	SP	Shepherd of Canyon Gold Canyon AZ	(623)396-5262	FW	2000
Wood Mark C			KS	Assoc	Trinity Mission KS	(913)432-5441	SL	2011
Wood Justin S	(415)680-7148 revjswood@gmail.com	c/o 304 E Covina Blvd Covina CA 91722	PSW	SP	St John Covina CA	(626)332-3142	SL	2025
Wood Eric R	(618)243-2846 myhomeontherange@juno.com	204 E Schumacher St Okawville IL 62271	SI	SP	Immanuel Okawville IL	(618)243-6216	SL	2000

*Multiple Assignments (See Church Worker Locator for Additional Details)

See Page 53 for the Table of Abbreviations for key to District, Position, and Seminary abbreviations

**C =Candidate; EM = Emeritus; the date following the C is the month and year the Candidate status began

NAME	TELEPHONE NUMBER EMAIL	STREET ADDRESS CITY/STATE/ZIP	DISTRICT	POSITION/ STATUS**	WHERE SERVING	OFFICE PHONE	SEM/ PROGRAM	YR GRAD
Wood David A	(507) 206-7057 padredawood@yahoo.com	412b Pleasant St NE Preston MN 55965	MNS	EM			SL	1968
Wood Christian R Dr	(414)529-6700 cwood@hcl.org	3960 S 41st Street Milwaukee WI 53221	EN	Assoc	Hales Corners Hales Corners WI	(414)529-6700	SL	2008
Wood Matthew J	(952)491-0762 revwoodm@gmail.com		MO	S Miss	Office of International Mission Saint Louis MO		SL	2011
Woodfin Stephen W	(248)646-6100 woodfins@ourshepherd.net	2200 Dunstable Rd Birmingham MI 48009	MI	SMP	Our Shepherd Birmingham MI	(248)646-6100	SL-SMP	2010
Woodford Lucas V Dr	(952)223-2165 lucas.woodford@mnsdistrict.org	4517 199th St W Farmington MN 55024	MNS	DP	Minnesota South District* Burnsville MN	(952)435-2550	SL	2003
Woodhouse Scott A	(260)229-5323 RevWoodhouse@gmail.com	422 9th St Logansport IN 46947	IN	SP	Saint James Logansport IN	(574)753-4227	FW	2024
Woodley Thomas A	(574)205-2274 deactom1@msn.com	2513 S 400 W Winamac IN 46996	IN	EM			FW	2004
Woodrow Joshua M	(423)321-4364 joshuamwoodrow@gmail.com	22154 Montgomery St Hayward CA 94541	CNH	Assoc	Good Shepherd Hayward CA	(510)782-0872	SL	2012
Woodruff Brandon D	(701)463-2004 edgeleylcms@gmail.com	P.O. Box 93 Edgeley ND 58433	ND	SP	Zion* Edgeley ND	(701)493-2537	CQ	2011
Woods Vernon P	(440)319-0451 vipwoods@gmail.com	8158 Westhill Dr Chagrin Falls OH 44023	OH	EM			CQ	1994
Woods Matthew B		9325 Arthur Coffman Rd Greenville IN 47124	IN	Assoc	Grace New Albany IN	(812)944-1267	SL	1996
Woodside Justin E	(951)217-3385 pastorwoodside@gmail.com	2518 Atlas Dr Bismarck ND 58503	ND	Asst	Shep Valley* Bismarck ND	(701)258-4231	FW	2020
Woodward Peter C	(925)998-7420 woodturnpete@gmail.com	208 E Colorado Ave Berthoud CO 80513	RM	EM			SL	2009
Woolery Nathan P	(309)648-5357 n_woolery@yahoo.com	1901 E 1525 North Road Shelbyville IL 62565	CI	SP	Holy Cross Shelbyville IL	(217)774-2952	FW	2006
Woolery Wayne N	(319)899-2718 wayne.woolery@gmail.com	7100 Xavier St Westminster CO 80030	RM	EM			CQ	1992
Woolsey Bill R	(713)854-3983 bwoolsey@fivetwo.com	100 CR 139a Burnet TX 78611	TX	Asst	Bethany Austin TX	(512)292-8778	SL	1987
Woolsey David C	(440)281-0991 pastorwoolsey@gmail.com	2238 Garden Dr Avon OH 44011	OH	SP	Faith Avon OH	(440)934-4710	SL	1998
Woolweber Donn E	(747) 232-4911 pastor_bethel_zion@yahoo.com	3672 Saxonburg Blvd Pittsburgh PA 15238	EA	SP	Bethel* Glenshaw PA	(412)486-5777	SL	2021
Worral Caleb J	(701)866-9684 caleb.worral@gmail.com	300 5th St W Ada MN 56510	MNN	SP	Zion* Ada MN	(218)784-7103	SL	2022
Worral Bernard M	(701) 866-1163	2814 Hickory St Fargo ND 58102	ND	Sn/Adm	Immanuel Fargo ND	(701)293-7979	SL	1986
Worst Terry J	(740)404-9151 terryworst@roadrunner.com	1708 W Main St Newark OH 43055	OH	SMP	New Hope Newark OH	(740)366-6459	FW-SMP	2019
Wottrich Philip C	(254)694-8620 pwottrich@aol.com	P.O. Box 365 Whitney TX 76692	TX	SP	Our Savior Whitney TX	(254)694-3234	SL	1992
Wrasman Andrew J	(949)616-8182 andy@islandlutheran.org	4400 Main St Hilton Head Island SC 29926	SE	Assoc	Island Hilton Head Island SC	(843)689-5200	SL	2021
Wrede William F	(718)902-8114 mgobluewrede@gmail.com	4181 Church Rd. Lockport NY 14094	EA	SP	St Peter* Lockport NY	(716)433-9014	SL	2000
Wright Clarence J Sr	(708)269-8051 asenath@aol.com	2125 Parkview Dr South Holland IL 60473	EN	SP	Christ English Chicago IL	(773)637-4800	FW	1999
Wright Larry D		2683 E Monroe Rd Midland MI 48642	MI	EM			FW	2007
Wright Kyle J II	rev.kylewrightii@gmail.com	1 Glenwood Ct Troy IL 62294	MO		Missouri District Saint Louis MO	(314)590-6200	FW	2006
Wright Karl F	(719)588-5856 wrightktlcs@yahoo.com	905 N Halaqueno St Carlsbad NM 88220	RM	SP	Immanuel Carlsbad NM	(575)885-5780	SL	1987
Wright Richard T	(850)718-6178 r.thomas.wright@gmail.com	3975 Highway 90 Marianna FL 32446	SO	SP	Grace* Bonifay FL	(850)547-9898	SL	2006
Wright Jimmie L Dr	(325)206-3793 jimwright5509@gmail.com	5509 Cedar Creek Dr Snyder TX 79549	TX	SP	Grace Snyder TX	(325)436-0414	CQ	2011
Wright Edward W Jr	(948)209-0770 thewrightrev@gmail.com	200 Colorado Ave Whitefish MT 59937	MT	SP	St Peter Whitefish MT	(406)862-3008	FW	2006
Wright Chad E	(586) 731-4490 cwright@trinityutica.com	45160 Van Dyke Utica MI 48317	MI	Assoc	Trinity Utica MI	(586)731-4490	CQ	2012
Wright Brian L	(303)506-6481 iamwings@msn.com	501 W Medina St P.O. Box 272 Cairo NE 68824	NEB	SP	Christ Cairo NE	(308)485-4863	SL	2016
Wright Boyd A	(319)488-0758 awright@stjlcms.org	6114 SW 39th St Topeka KS 66610	KS	Sn/Adm	Saint Johns Topeka KS	(785)354-7132	FW	2011
Wright Gary A	(309)236-3882 pastorwright@mchsi.com	17618 Hubbard Rd East Moline IL 61244	CI	SP	Zion East Moline IL	(309)496-2186	FW	1987
Wright James F Dr	j.wright@trinityberrien.org		MI	SP	Trinity Berrien Springs MI	(269)473-1811	SL	1988
Wu Andy	pastorandywu@gmail.com	14816 Peyton Dr Chino Hills CA 91709	PSW	SP	Loving Savior Chino Hills CA	(909)597-4668	CQ	2005
Wuerffel Jon L	(850)654-1174 wuerffelfl@cox.net	713 Sixth St Destin FL 32541	SO	EM			SL	1972
Wuerffel Theodore L	(314)729-1568 wuerffta@gmail.com	8820 Rock Forest Dr Saint Louis MO 63123	MO	EM			SL	1972
Wuertz Jeffrey G	(757)407-9273 pj@flcsl.org	21822 Juniper Wood Ln Richmond TX 77469	TX	SP	Faith Sugar Land TX	(281)242-7729	SL	1992
Wuggazer Mark T	(248)767-4649 marktwuggazer@gmail.com	14206 Spyglen Ln Cypress TX 77429	TX	C06/2024			SL	2009
Wulf Craig M	(509)926-7707 pastorwulf@hlcms.org	17909 E Broadway Ave Spokane Vly WA 99016	NOW	Sn/Adm	Hope Spokane Valley WA	(509)924-1630	FW	1980
Wunrow Donald N	dn1row@aol.com	3425 W Shady Side Rd Angola IN 46703	IN	EM			SL	1967

*Multiple Assignments (See Church Worker Locator for Additional Details)
See Page 53 for the Table of Abbreviations for key to District, Position, and Seminary abbreviations
**C =Candidate; EM = Emeritus; the date following the C is the month and year the Candidate status began

NAME	TELEPHONE NUMBER EMAIL	STREET ADDRESS CITY/STATE/ZIP	DISTRICT	POSITION/ STATUS**	WHERE SERVING	OFFICE PHONE	SEM/ PROGRAM	YR GRAD
Wurdeman David L	(317)410-2271 dlwurdeman@gmail.com	6585 Bismark Rd Colorado Springs CO 80922	RM	M Chap	Office of International Mission Saint Louis MO		FW	2019
Wurdeman Glen D	(317)850-0592 glenwurdeman@gmail.com	309 N. Pine Street Blue Hill NE 68930	NEB	SP	Trinity* Blue Hill NE	(402)756-2102	SL	1990
Wurm Matthew E	(605)692-2678 pastormc@swiftel.net	629 9th Ave Brookings SD 57006	SD	Sn/Adm	Mount Calvary Brookings SD	(605)692-2678	SL	2008
Wurst John F	(231)944-9982 navychief98@gmail.com	4791 N Reynolds Rd Lake Ann MI 49650	MI	EM			FW	2008
Wurst Robert W Jr	rwurstjr@gmail.com	c/o Good Shepherd Lutheran Church 908 W. Main St. Middleville MI 49333	MI	SP	Good Shepherd Middleville MI	(269)795-2391	FW	1995
Wurster Daniel A	pastordankaylyn71@gmail.com	29989 N Red Fish St Athol ID 83801	NOW	SP	First Spirit Lake ID	(208)623-2275	SL	1973
Wurster David F Dr	(716)649-0796 dfcrew@verizon.net	4646 Abbott Rd Orchard Park NY 14127	EA	EM			SL	1969
Wyckoff Jon K	(217)394-2495 jkevinw@frontier.com	P.O. Box 464 Buckley IL 60918	CI	SP	St Johns Buckley IL	(217)394-2444	SL	1995
Wyeth Dwight D	d.wyeth@outlook.com	11544 W Il-17 Bonfield IL 60913	NI	SP	Zion Bonfield IL	(815)426-2650	SL	2020
Wyneken Alan A Dr	(619)495-6346 judyalan2@cox.net	2529 Whispering Palms Loop Chula Vista CA 91915	PSW	EM			SL	1961
Wyneken Kenneth M	kenmarw@gmail.com	14507 189th Ave E Bonney Lake WA 98391	NOW	EM			SL	1971
Wyppich Raymond W	(610)543-5323 wwypp@aol.com	307 Gleaves Rd Springfield PA 19064	EN	EM			SL	1957
Wyss James M Dr	(205)934-6086 jmwyss@uab.edu	1925 Old Creek Trl Vestavia AL 35216	SO	SP	Trinity Birmingham AL	(205)923-6494	CQ	2006
Wyssmann Gene A	(417)766-2183 gawyssmann@hotmail.com	5720 Kingfisher Dr. Ashland MO 65010	MO	EM			FW	1978
Wyssmann Kevin L Dr	(480)250-5201	608 S. Riata St Gilbert AZ 85296	PSW	EM			SL	1982
Xiong Doua	(209)383-3301 dxiong@stpaulmerced.com	6537 Aggies Ct Winton CA 95388	CNH	Assoc	St Paul Merced CA	(209)383-3301	SL	2016
Xiong Neal C	(608)515-7726 neal_xiong@yahoo.com	3019 Kohlhepp Rd Eau Claire WI 54703	SW	EM			EIITSL	2007
Yadessa Solomon E Dr	(214)326-5969 syadessa@gmail.com	1517 Evergreen Dr Allen TX 75002	TX	D Miss	Texas District Round Rock TX	(800)951-3478	CQ	2015
Yaeger Aaron E	(434)384-6651 pastor.yaeger@oursaviorlynchburg.org	c/o Our Savior Lutheran Church 2940 Link Rd Lynchburg VA 24503	SE	Sn/Adm	Our Savior Lynchburg VA	(434)384-6651	FW	2017
Yaeger Kaleb J	(989)274-8037 portal@yaeger.biz	400 S Lakeview Ave Sturgis MI 49091	MI	SP	Trinity Sturgis MI	(269)651-6511	FW	2024
Yahr Terry L	(304)982-8249 terry.yahr@gmail.com	133 1st St SW Menahga MN 56464	MNN	SP	Redeemer* Menahga MN	(218)564-4931	CQ	2000
Yahr Karl J	(218) 536-9429 rev.yahr@gmail.com	3914 State 371 NW Hackensack MN 56452	MNN	SP	St John Akeley MN	(218)652-3779	FW	2013
Yakimow Scott E Dr		6095 Sundance Trl Brighton MI 48116	MI	D Ex/S	Michigan District Ann Arbor MI	(888)225-2111	SL	2004
Yamamoto Koh M	koh.yamamoto@ctsfw.edu	c/o Christ Lutheran Church 3235 Hwy 79 S Paris TN 38242	MDS	SP	Christ Lutheran Paris TN	(731)642-6620	FW	2024
Yang Chris X	xinhongy@yahoo.com	3217 White Flint Ct Oakton VA 22124	SE	Assoc	St Paul Falls Church VA	(703)573-0295	FW	2009
Yang Lang Dr	(989)239-4758 numlaaj@yahoo.com	236 Arbunoth St. Winter Haven FL 33881	FG	C04/2025			SL	2008
Yang Zang	(336)325-5268 hmonglutheranmission@gmail.com	218 Rowal St SE Conover NC 28613	SE	SP	Trinity Hmong Newton NC	(336)325-5268	SL	2014
Yang Zong H	(863)513-2543 zyang@stpaullakeland.org	5960 County Line Rd Lakeland FL 33811	FG	D Miss	Florida-Georgia District Orlando FL	(407)857-5556	CQ	1993
Yanke Paul E	814-267-4474 paulyanke@gmail.com	486 N Belle River Ave Marine City MI 48039	MI	SP	Living Faith Marine City MI	(810)765-8440	FW	1999
Yarrington David L	(815)595-4134 dly652003@yahoo.com	5548 Spring Brook Rd Apt 309 Rockford IL 61114	NI	EM			SL	1963
Yates Mark B	(608) 367-2191 radarphos@gmail.com	1006 Olympian Blvd Beloit WI 53511	SW	EM			FW	1980
Yates William T	(317)440-2561 pbyates@gmail.com	23 Glendale Rd Ext P.O. Box 87 Pottersville NY 12860	AT	EM			SL	1982
Yaw Larry R	pastor.yaw@netnet.net	733 Johnson St Pulaski WI 54162	NW	SP	St John Pulaski WI	(920)822-3511	FW	2007
Yeadon Jeremy T	yeadonjt@yahoo.com	P.O. Box 348 Groton SD 57445	SD	SP	Zion* Andover SD		FW	2010
Yeager Andrew T I	(260)226-0375 andrewtyeager@gmail.com	7535 N 450 W Decatur IN 46733	IN	Sn/Adm	St Paul Decatur IN	(260)547-4176	FW	2010
Yeager Christopher J	(260)580-4078 chryeager@gmail.com	1503 Williamsburg Dr Bossier City LA 71112	SO	Assoc	Immanuel Bossier City LA	(318)746-2215	FW	2017
Yeager Mark A	(951)501-9175 revmyeager@gmail.com	3225 Pachappa Hill Dr Riverside CA 92506	PSW	EM			SL	2004
Yearyean Anthony P	(951)924-4688 pastor@svlcmoval.net	11650 Perris Blvd Moreno Valley CA 92557	PSW	SP	Shep Of The Valley Moreno Valley CA	(951)924-4688	SL	2009
Yearyean Timothy N	(218)263-3955 thirdinlife@yahoo.com	3841 2nd Ave E Hibbing MN 55746	MNN	SP	Grace Hibbing MN	(218)263-3955	SL	2012
Yee Travis J	(845)772-2586 pastoryee22@gmail.com	11-10 150th St Whitestone NY 11357	AT	SP	Immanuel Whitestone NY	(718)767-5656	SL	2008
Yi Kyu D	(215)853-3927 YANGMUN91@GMAIL.COM	455 Highland Dr Apt 2211 Lewisville TX 75067	TX	D Miss	Texas District Round Rock TX	(800)951-3478	CQ	2017
Yoakum Kevin L	(813)385-1951		FG	SP	Christ The King Riverview FL	(813)677-1332	SL	1998

*Multiple Assignments (See Church Worker Locator for Additional Details)
See Page 53 for the Table of Abbreviations for key to District, Position, and Seminary abbreviations
**C =Candidate; EM = Emeritus; the date following the C is the month and year the Candidate status began

NAME	TELEPHONE NUMBER EMAIL	STREET ADDRESS CITY/STATE/ZIP	DISTRICT	POSITION/ STATUS**	WHERE SERVING	OFFICE PHONE	SEM/ PROGRAM	YR GRAD
Yoder Roger W	(928)581-2408 kayrog2003@aol.com	621 West Riverside Dr Apt 101 Parker AZ 85344	EN	EM			CQ	2019
Yogerst Jared D Dr	(715)307-1959 jyogerst001@luthersem.edu	620 California Ave E St Paul MN 55130	MNS	SP	Faith Minneapolis MN	(612)729-5463	CQ	2015
Yohannes Zerehaimanot Z	(517)203-0102 zerityohan@hotmail.com	858 Ramblewood Dr East Lansing MI 48823	MI	Assoc	St Luke Haslett MI	(517)339-9119	CQ	1990
Yonker William P	(847)844-3320 pastoryonker@hotmail.com	460 Tartans Dr West Dundee IL 60118	NI	Sn/Adm	Immanuel East Dundee IL	(847)428-4477	SL	1986
Yonkers James E	(260)413-8375 pastoryonkers@outlook.com	1029 Hillside Danville IL 61832	CI	Sn/Adm	Immanuel Danville IL	(217)442-5675	FW	2011
Yops Bradley J Dr	(810)423-0493 yops.brad@gmail.com	2822 Pittsfield Blvd Ann Arbor MI 48104	MI	EM			FW	1984
York Ronald K	(520)869-5299 ryork1952@gmail.com	666 W Calle El Teclado Sahuarita AZ 85629	PSW	SMP	Peace Valley Benson AZ	(520)586-3171	SL-SMP	2011
Yoseph Demelash O	(651)468-9679 demoyd@yahoo.com	13157 Avery Way Rosemount MN 55068	TX	O-Miss	LINC Houston Houston TX	(713)426-2451	CQ	2014
Young John M	(914)204-1700 revjmyoung@gmail.com	1410 Route 52 Fishkill NY 12524	AT	SP	Our Savior Fishkill NY	(845)897-4423	SL	1996
Young Ronald L	(440)292-6211 ronyoung101@gmail.com	37080 Tail Feather Dr N Ridgeville OH 44039	OH	EM			FW	1981
Young Victor P	(720)456-9087 victorpyoung@comcast.net	5856 Canyon Cir Frederick CO 80504	RM	Asst	Faith Johnstown CO	(970)587-6460	FW	1982
Young Philip H	(615)513-6918 revphyoung@protonmail.com	7080 Asberry Dr Nashville TN 37221	MDS	SP	Redeemer Nashville TN	(615)646-3150	SL	1998
Young Gregory S	(559) 779-0573 windwood41132@gmail.com	1621 N Magnolia Ave Clovis CA 93619	CNH	EM			SL	1982
Young David R	(716)639-1169 mamydry@roadrunner.com	45 Woodshire N Getzville NY 14068	EA	EM			SL	1961
Young Virtus E	(509)443-0602 youngdv@comcast.net	4015 S Rebecca Ln Spokane WA 99223	NOW	EM			SL	1959
Young David M	(610)247-3979 dmyrev@comcast.net	6024 Butler Pike Blue Bell PA 19422	EN	SP	Grace* Warminster PA	(215)442-5500	FW	2001
Young Alvin P	(805)522-7782 airrev@sbcglobal.net	2047 Potter Ave Simi Valley CA 93065	PSW	EM			SL	1964
Young James P	(951)764-0509 pastorjimy@outlook.com	44120 Quiet Meadow Rd Temecula CA 92592	PSW	EM			CQ	1979
Youngdale Ronald A	(209)404-4817 praydale@gmail.com	4246 Piro Ct Turlock CA 95382	CNH	EM			SL	1981
Younger Melvin F	(937)233-5222 mygolf@earthlink.net	4949 Bath Rd Dayton OH 45424	OH	EM			SL	1962
Yount Andrew T	(314)974-9833 newchurchplanter@gmail.com	370 Country Club Bluffs Ln Washington MO 63090	MO	SMP	A Bridge to Faith Washington MO	(314)974-9833	SL-SMP	2012
Yount Allen	(970)630-5601 revallenyount@yahoo.com	400 16th Avenue Ct Greeley CO 80631	RM	C07/2016			SL	2005
Yue James H	(626)863-8397 jameshoiyue@rocketmail.com	9250 Isora St Pico Rivera CA 90660	PSW	Assoc	Emmaus Alhambra CA	(626)289-3664	CQ	2019
Yun Young S Dr	(703)580-5815 youngsyun@yahoo.com	14339 Westminister Ln Apt 14 Woodbridge VA 22193	SE	Asst	Grace Woodbridge VA	(703)494-4600	CQ	1999
Yunker Arthur D	(228)219-1754 agyunker@aim.com	P.O. Box 4057 Sanford NC 27331	SE	EM			SL	1972
Yunker Jason P	(812) 568-5595 JPYunker@ymail.com	9160 Halston Cir Newburgh IN 47630	IN	SMP	Our Redeemer Evansville IN	(812)476-9991	SL-SMP	2024
Zabell Philip W	(530) 520-1458 pzcard@hotmail.com	881 Brennan Pl Willows CA 95988	CNH	EM			SL	1972
Zabrocki Lee H	(231)903-8491 leezab39@yahoo.com	10232 Long Home Rd Louisville KY 40291	IN	EM			SPR	1970
Zacharias Eric L	(952)843-3678 revez123@juno.com	14725 County Road 153 Cologne MN 55322	MNS	SP	Zion Cologne MN	(952)466-3379	SL	1987
Zachrich David R Dr	(330)958-3159 dzachric@kent.edu	1573 Timbertop Dr Tallmadge OH 44278	OH	EM			SPR	1975
Zagel Bruce R Dr	(406)901-7454 brzagel2113@gmail.com	5440 Vardon Pl Billings MT 59106	MT	EM			SL	1985
Zagore Robert M	(231)360-9370 bob@zagore.com	314 Winters Rd Butler PA 16002	EA	Inst C	Concordia Lutheran Ministries Cabot PA	(724)352-1571	FW	1990
Zahn Carleton E	(612) 554-4730 c.zahn@comcast.net	8800 45th Ave N New Hope MN 55428	MNS	EM			SL	1964
Zahner Douglas J	(920)763-2569 pastorzahner@gmail.com	N8092 County Road Ay Mayville WI 53050	SW	SP	Immanuel Mayville WI	(920)387-5363	NESC	2010
Zahrte John C	(612)418-4744 jzahrte@royred.org	746 Seasons Pass Dr Brunswick OH 44212	OH	Sn/Adm	Royal Redeemer North Royalton OH	(440)237-7958	SL	1988
Zakian Gary W Dr	garyzakian@gmail.com	5730 207th Pl SW Lynnwood WA 98036	NOW	EM			SL	1982
Zamora Juan A	(817)751-0583 pastor.juan@t2c2.org	519 Garden Ave Euless TX 76039	TX	Assoc	Our Redeemer Irving TX	(972)255-0595	SL	2011
Zandi Craig S	(715)532-5780 pastorstjohn@centurylink.net		NW	SP	Saint Johns Ladysmith WI	(715)532-5780	FW	2010
Zandstra Steven C	(719)342-2717 zandstras@yahoo.com	P.O. Box 624 Cheyenne Wells CO 80810	RM	SMP	Grace Cheyenne Wells CO	(719)767-5913	SL-SMP	2021
Zang James T III	(727)863-6446 pastorjameszang@gmail.com	8601 Stonehedge Way Hudson FL 34667	FG	SP	Hope Hudson FL	(727)863-6446	SL	2004
Zank Steven E	(805)444-3768 stevezank@gmail.com	12295 Marlow Ave Tustin CA 92782	PSW	S HS/C	Concordia University Irvine Irvine CA	(949)854-8002	SL	2011
Zarate Martin M		2812 S 10th Ave Broadview IL 60155	NI	Assoc	St Paul Melrose Park IL	(708)343-1000	SL	2012

*Multiple Assignments (See Church Worker Locator for Additional Details)

See Page 53 for the Table of Abbreviations for key to District, Position, and Seminary abbreviations

**C =Candidate; EM = Emeritus; the date following the C is the month and year the Candidate status began

NAME	TELEPHONE NUMBER EMAIL	STREET ADDRESS CITY/STATE/ZIP	DISTRICT	POSITION/ STATUS**	WHERE SERVING	OFFICE PHONE	SEM/ PROGRAM	YR GRAD
Zastrow William F	(314)623-3588 williamfzastrow@gmail.com	804 Meadowlark Dr Washington MO 63090	MO	EM			SL	1986
Zavala Alex	(562)382-4561 zavala17@yahoo.com	12310 Corley Dr Whittier CA 90604	PSW	SMP	Peace Pico Rivera CA	(562)949-5203	CQ	2019
Zech Rako D	(716)529-9201 rakozech@gmail.com	4348 Sunset Dr Lockport NY 14094	EA	SP	St Paul Clarence Center NY	(716)741-2500	SL	2021
Zechiel Timothy B	(260)223-8374 tbz1951@yahoo.com	23303 Harvest Ln Woodburn IN 46744	IN	EM			FW	1995
Zeckzer Scott A	(219)493-2143	4016 Bridgewood Ct New Haven IN 46774	IN	Sn/Adm	Emanuel New Haven IN	(260)749-2163	FW	1996
Zehnder Zachary A	zach@kingofkings.org	2006 S 214th Ave Elkhorn NE 68022	NEB	Assoc	King Of Kings Omaha NE	(402)333-6464	SL	2010
Zehnder George P	revgeozeh@yahoo.com	12104 Parker Dr Chesterland OH 44026	OH	EM			FW	1984
Zehnder Jon H	(239)910-4978 jon56.zehnder@gmail.com	1470 Grace Ave Fort Myers FL 33901	FG	EM			SL	1982
Zehnder Mark P Dr	(402)689-8425 mark@alwaysforwardministries.com	14909 Dorcas Cir Omaha NE 68144	NEB	EM			SL	1981
Zehnder Michael J	(480)861-5000 mjzehnder@aol.com	6053 W Adriatic Pl Lakewood CO 80227	RM	EM			CQ	1993
Zehnder Thomas R	(920)256-9563 tomrz@aol.com	1347 Haven Dr Oviedo FL 32765	FG	EM			SL	1961
Zeige William C	(701)936-1161 suebillz@msn.com	824 North Pokegama Ave Grand Rapids MN 55744	MNN	EM			SL	1973
Zeigler Paul E	pez.zeigler@gmail.com	105 Grove Isle Blvd Panama City Beach FL 32408	SO	Assoc	Trinity* Panama City FL	(850)763-2412	FW	2011
Zeigler Michael W Dr	(417)425-8424 michael.zeigler@lhm.org	4247 Flad Ave Saint Louis MO 63110	MO	Aux	LLL/Lutheran Hour Ministries Saint Louis MO	(314)317-4100	SL	2012
Zeile John C	(407)977-2045 jczstm@gmail.com	2124 Toucan Ct Oviedo FL 32765	FG	EM			SL	1971
Zeile Richard A Dr	(313)802-1146 martinlutherseveningprayer@gmail.com	11500 Skyline Dr. Fenton MI 48430	MI	EM			FW	1986
Zeleke Mitiku Woldegeberal Dr	(703)888-3872 mitikuzeleke22@gmail.com	11 Gray Birch Ln Stafford VA 22554	SE	SP	Shalom Ethiopian Alexandria VA	(571)422-7930	CQ	2015
Zell Jeffrey S	jeff.zell@yahoo.com	725 E. Emilie St. Rensselaer IN 47978	IN	SP	Our Saviour* Monticello IN	(574)583-5005	CQ	2022
Zell Loren C	(920)878-0994 zellloren@gmail.com	207 E Hancock St New London WI 54961	NW	EM			FW	1994
Zellers Kevin C	(701)712-1981 pastorzellers@live.com	601 Yorkshire Lane Bismarck ND 58504	ND	SP	Messiah Mandan ND	(701)663-8545	FW	1991
Zellers Kevin C Jr	(701)306-4016 kevin.zellers@hotmail.com	7803 Crossroads Dr SW Cedar Rapids IA 52404	IE	SP	Zion Hiawatha IA	(319)393-2013	FW	2013
Zellmer Robert J	(515)351-7246		IW	SP	Bethel Lawton IA	(712)944-5580	SL	2008
Zellmer John W	(920) 344-2203 zelljw@hotmail.com	P.O. Box 414 Lowell WI 53557	SW	EM			SPR	1973
Zelt Thomas J Dr	(510)429-1905 tzelt@popfremont.org	38451 Fremont Blvd Fremont CA 94536	CNH	Sn/Adm	Prince of Peace Fremont CA	(510)793-3366	SL	1984
Zemke David M	(509)844-3665 pastorzemke@gmail.com	308 SW 3rd Ave Battle Ground WA 98604	NOW	SP	Prince Of Peace Battle Ground WA	(360)687-7455	SL	2009
Zemple Dean D	(920)723-6955 dzemple@hotmail.com	7134 Hwy 247 NE Elgin MN 55932	MNS	SP	St John* Hammond MN	(507)753-2388	CQ	2004
Zerkel Bradley G	(816)510-0075 brad4862@att.net		MNS		Minnesota South District Burnsville MN	(952)435-2550	SL	2001
Zersen David J Dr	(414) 727-3890 zersendj@gmail.com	8220 Harwood Ave Apt 132 Wauwatosa WI 53213	EN	EM			SPR	1964
Zeuschner David W	(414)808-8518 davidzeuschner@aol.com	329 W Bolivar Ave Apt 6 Milwaukee WI 53207	SW	SP	Chapel of the Cross Milwaukee WI	(414)481-1880	SL	2001
Zick Robert C	rczick@yahoo.com	2844 Georgia Ave Sheboygan WI 53081	SW	EM			FW	1979
Zickler Matthew L		4121 Wolf Rd Western Springs IL 60558	NI	SP	Grace Western Springs IL	(708)246-0536	FW	2011
Ziegler Karl P	(402)339-3668 pkz@1st-lutheran.org	420 N Washington St Papillion NE 68046	NEB	Sn/Adm	First Papillion NE	(402)339-3668	CQ	1994
Ziegler Larry E	(303)688-5986 ZLCKEM@gmail.com	202 Elm Ave Castle Rock CO 80104	RM	EM			SPR	1973
Ziegler Roland F Dr	(260)452-2282		IN	S HS/C	Concordia Theological Seminary Fort Wayne IN	(260)452-2100	Other	1993
Ziehr David W	(828)291-0582	2304 Springs Rd NE Hickory NC 28601	SE	Sn/Adm	St Stephen Hickory NC	(828)256-9865	SL	1992
Zielinski Philip E	(440)458-0189 pastorzielinski@spvc.org	524 W 130th St Brunswick OH 44212	OH	SP	St Paul* Valley City OH	(330)483-3883	FW	2004
Ziemann Kurt R Dr	kziemann63@gmail.com	508 Mentor Ave Painesville OH 44077	OH	Sn/Adm	Zion Painesville OH	(440)357-5174	FW	2003
Zier Mark A	(253)307-4541 mzier01@aol.com	1106 University Avenue West Minot ND 58703	CNH	EM			CQ	2014
Zieroth Gary W Dr	gary.zieroth@ctsfw.edu	5109 Millers CV Fort Wayne IN 46835	IN	Assoc	Ascension* Fort Wayne IN	(260)486-2226	FW	1990
Zieroth Mark G	(612)834-5169 zierothmark@gmail.com	3467 Glencove Ln Dubuque IA 52002	IE	Assoc	Our Redeemer* Dubuque IA	(563)588-1247	FW	2023
Zill M T	(520)400-3470 toddzillarising@gmail.com	509 W Wade Ln Payson AZ 85541	EN	Cmp P	Faith Tucson AZ	(520)326-2262	FW	1996
Zillinger Gregory A	(303)859-8886 zillinger@gmail.com	2680 Emerald Ridge Dr Colorado Springs CO 80920	RM	Sn/Adm	Holy Cross Colorado Springs CO	(719)596-0661	SL	2000

*Multiple Assignments (See Church Worker Locator for Additional Details)

See Page 53 for the Table of Abbreviations for key to District, Position, and Seminary abbreviations

**C =Candidate; EM = Emeritus; the date following the C is the month and year the Candidate status began

NAME	TELEPHONE NUMBER EMAIL	STREET ADDRESS CITY/STATE/ZIP	DISTRICT	POSITION/ STATUS**	WHERE SERVING	OFFICE PHONE	SEM/ PROGRAM	YR GRAD
Zimmer David C	pastorzimmer@gmail.com	251 Abbotsford Ct Glen Ellyn IL 60137	NI	SP	Divine Shepherd Bolingbrook IL	(630)759-5300	FW	2004
Zimmer Giles H Dr	(507)201-7008 gzzimmer@protonmail.com	29125 28th St Pemberton MN 56078	MNS	EM			SL	1982
Zimmerman Frank W	(309)963-4825 fwz@frontiernet.net	204 W North St Danvers IL 61732	CI	SP	Good Shepherd* Minier IL	(309)963-4825	FW	1992
Zimmerman Theodore B Jr	(707)294-2033 revtbz@comcast.net	2520 Trower Ave Napa CA 94558	CNH	EM			SL	1967
Zimmerman Russell E	(989)391-4068 pastorrusszimmerman@gmail.com	210 Fitzhugh St Apt 112 Bay City MI 48708	MI	EM			SPR	1975
Zimmerman Mark E	(231) 557-0756 revmez@aol.com	17932 Wildwood Springs Pkwy Spring Lake MI 49456	MI	EM			SPR	1972
Zimmerman Thomas P	tpzimm@me.com	3414 Walden Run Fort Wayne IN 46815	IN	EM			CQ	1984
Zimmerman David P Dr	drzimmerman@rentonprep.org	7003 S 132nd St Seattle WA 98178	NOW	SP	Amazing Grace Renton WA	(206)723-5526	FW	1988
Zimmerman Darrell W Dr	(314)580-4608 darrellz23@gmail.com	13259 Bonroyal Dr Des Peres MO 63131	MO	SP	Cedar Hill Cedar Hill MO	(636)274-4802	SL	1982
Zimmerman Aaron A	(952)797-2307 ajzimmerman2012@gmail.com	3670 350th St Farnhamville IA 50538	IW	SP	Holy Trinity Farnhamville IA	(515)544-3264	FW	2019
Zimmerman Luke T	(717)636-1545 revzimmerman@gmail.com	6386 Galleon Dr Mechanicsburg PA 17050	EN	SP	Calvary Mechanicsburg PA	(717)697-9771	FW	2003
Zimmerman John M	(570) 507-6138 revzim@icloud.com		EA	SP	St John* Pittston PA	(570)655-2505	FW	2016
Zimmermann James W	(209) 401-6836 soquelzimm@sbcglobal.net	1251 E Lugonia Ave Spc 5 Redlands CA 92374	CNH	EM			SL	1960
Zimmermann Lawrence J Dr	lzvab@hotmail.com	51 Evans Dr Palm Coast FL 32164	FG	EM			SPR	1975
Zimmermann Fred T	(608)228-4453 pzjerusalem@yahoo.com	9312 Braun Rd Cross Plains WI 53528	SW	EM			SL	1978
Zimmermann Bruce L	(641)869-3838 pastorz@iowatelecom.net	P.O. Box Q Wellsburg IA 50680	IE	SP	St John Wellsburg IA	(641)869-3838	SL	1968
Zimmermann B C	z.idaho@yahoo.com	321 N Yellowpine Place Eagle ID 83616	NOW	EM			SL	1980
Zimmermann Paul S	(843)227-1907	12 Screven Court Bluffton SC 29909	SE	EM			FW	1987
Zinkowich James R	(440)357-1713 jz.lz@sbcglobal.net	2043 Marsh Ln Painesville OH 44077	OH	EM			SPR	1969
Zipay Joel S	jlzip5@msn.com	c/o St John Lutheran Church 15496 S 900 W Wanatah IN 46390	IN	SP	St John* Lacrosse IN	(219)754-2296	SL	1988
Zirbel Frank J	frankzirbel34@icloud.com	3917a Sansing Hollow Rd Harrison AR 72601	MDS	EM			SL	1960
Zirbel Jason P	pastorzirbel@gmail.com	610 Forrest Park Way Greenwood AR 72936	MDS	SP	Grace Greenwood AR	(479)996-7747	FW	2008
Zirpel David N	(712)253-8751 davidzirpel@yahoo.com	2911 S Cedar St Sioux City IA 51106	IW	Assoc	Redeemer Sioux City IA	(712)276-1125	SL	1991
Zischke John David K	(210)601-0682 jd.zischke@gmail.com	3526 Foxtail Lily Ln Fayetteville AR 72704	MDS	SP	Restoration Fayetteville AR	(210)601-0682	SL	2017
Zitsch Kenneth E Jr	(814)345-5861 kzitsch@hotmail.com	P.O. Box 162 Lanse PA 16849	EA	SP	St John Munson PA	(814)345-5741	CQ	2013
Zittlow Todd D	(920)562-1323 tzittlow@concordiahistorical institute.org	1408 Plantation Manor Ct Saint Peters MO 63303	MO	Pro Stf	Concordia Historical Institute Saint Louis MO	(314)505-7900	SL	2008
Zobel Andrew J	(715)853-8433 azobel@stjamesshawano.org	100 Hillside Ln Shawano WI 54166	NW	Sn/Adm	Saint James Shawano WI	(715)524-4815	SL	2021
Zobel Jason W	(608)228-4134 jzobel@stmlc.org	W8955 Oak Ln W Clintonville WI 54929	NW	Sn/Adm	St Martin Clintonville WI	(715)823-6538	SL	1997
Zoch Jonathan R	(832)748-1400 pastor@trinitygv.com	1852 Bougainvillea Dr Minden NV 89423	CNH	SP	Trinity Gardnerville NV	(775)782-8153	SL	2024
Zoeller Kenneth H	(406)651-2064 kenzoeller@gmail.com	4403 Palisades Park Dr Billings MT 59106	MT	SP	Our Savior Billings MT	(406)252-5141	FW	1999
Zoller Albert P	(585)747-2134 albertzoller@hotmail.com	4703 E Dragoon Ave Mesa AZ 85206	EA	EM			SPR	1966
Zolue Borbor A	(862)224-4938 abitu1968@gmail.com	11 Carteret St Newark NJ 07104	NJ	SP	Christ Assembly Newark NJ	(973)485-7096	SL	2023
Zoske Jason B	(260)413-7253 stpaullcmspastor@gmail.com	503 Hampton Ct Williamsburg IA 52361	IE	SP	St Paul Williamsburg IA	(319)668-1266	FW	2022
Zuber Clayton G	(585)738-8865 czuber1@rochester.rr.com	252 Taylor Rd Honeoye Falls NY 14472	EA	SP	Epiphany Avon NY	(585)226-2200	SL-D	2010
Zucconi Thomas A	(248) 259-2649 zucconit@gmail.com	5908 Loch Maree Dr Plano TX 75093	TX	C01/2025			SL	2003
Zuch Aaron T	(360)332-6589 zucha38@yahoo.com	1260 Blaine Ave Blaine WA 98230	NOW	SP	Grace Blaine WA	(360)332-6589	SL	2006
Zucker Tyge C	(414)477-8816 ty.zucker@gmail.com	3191 Woodvalley Dr Flushing MI 48433	MI	SP	Holy Cross Flushing MI	(810)659-5926	SL	1997
Zuehsow Mark J	mzuehsow@yahoo.com	5118 N Oconto Ave Harwood Hts IL 60706	S	C07/2016			SL	2002
Zutz Alfred E	(707)366-2221 azutz@juno.com	261 Paseo Gregario Palm Desert CA 92211	CNH	EM			SPR	1968
Zwemke Michael G	zwemkega@comcast.net	125 Mercer Ln Cartersville GA 30120	FG	EM			SL	1999
Zwick William F	revzwick@gmail.com	228 N Colorado Minden NE 68959	NEB	SP	St Paul Minden NE	(308)832-1343	FW	2019
Zwonitzer Rodney E	(313)610-9933 rod.zwonitzer@gmail.com	12423 Sugar Maple Drive Fenton MI 48430	EN	EM			SL	1988
Zyskowski Stanley J Jr	(920)847-2576 sjpl21zyskowski@gmail.com	1870 Dock Rd Washington Is WI 54246	NI	EM			FW	1979

*Multiple Assignments (See Church Worker Locator for Additional Details)
See Page 53 for the Table of Abbreviations for key to District, Position, and Seminary abbreviations
**C =Candidate; EM = Emeritus; the date following the C is the month and year the Candidate status began

LCMS ROSTER OF MINISTERS OF RELIGION—COMMISSIONED

Corrected to September 18, 2025

Individuals on this listing were on the official Commissioned Minister member roster of the Synod as of the above date, i.e., held membership in the Synod in conformity with Articles V and VI of the Constitution of The Lutheran Church–Missouri Synod. Qualified individuals who are not listed should contact their respective district president. Any congregation or other calling entity must contact the appropriate district president to find out whether an individual whose name is listed in this section is currently eligible for a call or service in the church. A candidate member is one who is eligible to perform the duties of any of the offices of ministry specified in Bylaw 2.11.1 but who is not currently an active or emeritus member. For further detailed information please visit the LCMS Website at http://www.lcms.org and select Directories. With the adoption of Resolution 9-05 by the 67th Regular Convention of the LCMS and its subsequent ratification by the member congregations of the Synod, the Commissioned Minister roster classification previously titled "Commissioned Lay Minister" (Lay Minister) has been replaced with the title "Commissioned Director of Church Ministries" (DCM).

NAME	TELEPHONE NUMBER EMAIL	STREET ADDRESS CITY/STATE/ZIP	DISTRICT	CLASS.	POSITION/ STATUS**	WHERE SERVING	OFFICE PHONE	COLLEGE/ UNIV/CQ	YR GRAD
Aadsen Lori A Hall	(830)733-0043 57loriann@gmail.com	4137 Trapper Lake Dr Loveland CO 80538	RM	Teacher	EM			CQ	1997
Aarhus Deborah G Dr	(949)656-0634 dgaarhus@gmail.com	431 Cantor Irvine CA 92620	PSW	Teacher	C08/2017			CQ	2009
Abate Amarech G Deac	(949)307-4955 amarechg@hotmail.com	60 Wetstone Irvine CA 92604	PSW	Deaconess	S HS/C	Concordia University Irvine Irvine CA	(949)854-8002	CQ	2016
Abban Mary J Moore Klaustermeier	(913)671-0202 maryjkabban@gmail.com	7624 Brooklyn Park Dr Minneapolis MN 55444	MNS	Teacher	Tchr	Trinity First Minneapolis MN	(612)871-2353	S	2002
Abbott Amanda A			PSW	Teacher	Tchr	Faith Las Vegas NV	(702)804-4400	S	2017
Abbott Phillip G	(214)695-7222 djc.gabbott@gmail.com	530 Wentworth Dr Richardson TX 75081	TX	Teacher	EM			CQ	1985
Abbuhl Nancy J	(660)641-2925 nancyabbuhl@yahoo.com	1030 N. 4th Ponca City OK 74601	OK	Teacher		Oklahoma District Norman OK	(405)321-3443	S	1994
Abel Carla Gennrich	(262)417-5169 jabel2@wi.rr.com	7233 Douglas Ave Racine WI 53402	SW	Teacher	ExecDir	Prince Of Peace Racine WI	(262)639-1277	CQ	2021
Abel Joan K Nehrbass	(507)236-9521	625 W Interlaken Rd Fairmont MN 56031	MNS	Teacher	EM			SP	1981
Abel Leah A Helmrichs	(407)716-1606	924 W Peakview Cir Littleton CO 80120	RM	DCE	C07/2016			S	2002
Abercrombie Janet K Moeller			NOW	Teacher	C07/2016			PO	1993
Abernathy John F	(828)781-6595 johnabernathy@yahoo.com	3974 Brickfield St Hickory NC 28601	RM	Tch/DCE	C09/2020			S	1988
Abernathy Judye A Ambrose	(724)954-2674 jabernat@stlukecabot.org	330 Hannahstown Rd Cabot PA 16023	EA	Teacher	Tchr	St Luke Cabot PA	(724)352-2221	BR	1999
Abijay Rachel Young	youngr@lhsoc.org	24149 Grayston Dr Lake Forest CA 92630	PSW	Teacher	Tchr	Orange County Orange CA	(714)998-5151	SP	2002
Abraham Caleb J	(989)225-6239 caleb.j.g.abraham@gmail.com	5487 Katherine Ct. Saginaw MI 48603	MI	Teacher	Tchr	Valley Saginaw MI	(989)790-1676	AA	2009
Abraham Jennifer L Marter	(989)980-0093 jennifer.abraham@frankentrost.org	5090 McGrandy Rd Bridgport MI 48722	MI	Teacher	Tchr	Immanuel Saginaw MI	(989)754-0929	CQ	2019
Abraham Rachel M	(989)928-0838 missahasclass@gmail.com	1760 S Airport Rd Saginaw MI 48601	MI	Teacher	P/Tchr	Immanuel Saginaw MI	(989)754-4285	AA	2004
Abramowski Meredith D Rossow	(847)594-2579 meredithabramowski@yahoo.com	16645 Martha Dr Brookfield WI 53005	SW	Teacher	C07/2016			S	1999
Abresch Mark T	(678)416-6422 mabr1@yahoo.com	201 Beacon Tree Way Peachtree Cty GA 30269	FG	Teacher	Tchr	St Paul Peachtree City GA	(770)487-0339	S	1982
Abresch Vera K Fowler	(505)400-0453 vkabresch@yahoo.com	518 Elm Street Crawford NE 69339	IN	Teacher	EM			S	1991
Acamo Jens E	(402)332-9676	17010 Redman Avenue Omaha NE 68116	NEB	DCE	C09/2023			S	2018
Acers Gina M Wroge	(952)334-5415 wrogeg@csp.edu	3857 E. 42nd St Des Moines IA 50317	IW	DCE	Mem C	Hope Des Moines IA	(515)265-2057	SP	2011
Aceto Alfred A Jr	(863)324-5854 coacha22@gmail.com	60 Enclave Dr Winter Haven FL 33884	FG	Teacher	EM			RF	1969
Achong Angela S McKenzie	(620)779-3801 lcmsteacher@hotmail.com	1208 W Beech St Independence KS 67301	KS	Teacher	Tchr	Zion Independence KS	(620)332-3300	S	2012
Achong Robert D	(620)779-3781 ke.pilikia@gmail.com	1208 W Beech St Independence KS 67301	KS	DCE	C07/2016			IV	1999
Achterberg Kathleen R Kirchner	(512)350-5265 kraberg70@gmail.com	12503 Terra Nova Ln Austin TX 78727	TX	Teacher	EM			S	1970
Achterberg Robert A Dr	(512)837-0051 raachterberg@hotmail.com	12503 Terra Nova Ln Austin TX 78727	TX	Teacher	EM			S	1970
Ackermann Kelly J Huck	(507)840-0138 ent@frontiern.net	80884 State Highway 86 Lakefield MN 56150	MNS	Teacher	EM			S	1979
Ackmann Jennifer Hille	(260)450-3466 jackmann@esmeagles.com	2870 E 950 N Roanoke IN 46783	IN	Teacher	Pro Stf	Emmanuel-St Michael Fort Wayne IN	(260)422-6712	CQ	2023
Acord Deanna L Schultz	(319)396-8960	2614 29th St SW Cedar Rapids IA 52404	IE	Teacher	EM			SP	1965
Adam David J	(303)756-3843 djadam1749@gmail.com	2820 S Franklin St Denver CO 80210	RM	Teacher	EM			RF	1961
Adamec Margo M	(832)451-5441 mar.m.adamec@gmail.com	6680 Boxwood Ln Apt B Liberty Township OH 45044	OH	DCE	Mem C	Royal Redeemer Liberty Township OH	(513)779-4740	IV	2024
Adams Amanda M Knox	(785) 266-6263 amanda.adams.dce@gmail.com	c/o Christ Lutheran Church 3509 SW Burlingame Rd Topeka KS 66611	KS	DCE	Mem C	Christ Topeka KS	(785)266-6263	S	2012
Adams Carla M Wills	(727)343-3206 carla.adams@oursaviorfl.org	2756 61st Ln N St Petersburg FL 33710	FG	Teacher	Tchr	Our Savior Saint Petersburg FL	(727)344-1026	RF	1991
Adams Chelsea A	(405)202-6194 caadams1086@gmail.com	5625 Franklin Ave Des Moines IA 50310	IW	Teacher	Tchr	Mount Olive Des Moines IA	(515)277-8349	S	2009
Adams Donald W	(828)455-1254 roverbee7@gmail.com	1503 Noble Park Dr Missouri City TX 77459	SE	Teacher	EM			RF	1961
Adams Elyse M Baschal Ahlgrimm	(262)632-0219 emahlgrimmadams@gmail.com	913 Perry Ave Racine WI 53406	SW	Teacher	EM			CQ	1978

*Multiple Assignments (See Church Worker Locator for Additional Details)

See Page 53 for the Table of Abbreviations for key to District, Classification, Position, and College abbreviations.

**C =Candidate; EM =Emeritus; the date following the C is the month and year the Candidate status began

NAME	TELEPHONE NUMBER EMAIL	STREET ADDRESS CITY/STATE/ZIP	DISTRICT	CLASS.	POSITION/ STATUS**	WHERE SERVING	OFFICE PHONE	COLLEGE/ UNIV/CQ	YR GRAD
Adams Forrest E	(619)559-9970 trees510@yahoo.com	487 Quinault Ave SE Ocean Shores WA 98569	NOW	Teacher	EM			S	1969
Adams Garnet M	(815)382-1917 gmadams51@yahoo.com	4389 Memorial Cir Windsor WI 53598	NI	Teacher	EM			CQ	2009
Adams Grace K	(269)313-1479 graciekate99@gmail.com	44316 Highgate Dr Clinton Township MI 48038	MI	Teacher	Tchr	Christ The King Southgate MI	(734)285-9697	AA	2021
Adams Jacob A	(269)313-7760 jake12adams@yahoo.com	11 Village West Ct Apt 301 Washington MO 63090	MO	DFLM	Mem C	Immanuel Washington MO	(636)239-4705	AA	2021
Adams Joyce A Schmidt	curjoy2@gmail.com	6064 Fairway Ln Bradenton FL 34210	FG	Teacher	EM			S	1972
Adams Melissa K Roth	(573)979-3087 madams@saxonylutheranhigh.org	2657 Watson Dr Jackson MO 63755	MO	Teacher	Prin	Saxony Jackson MO	(573)204-7555	CQ	2016
Adams Richard J	(414)801-6690 radams111161@gmail.com	N3971 Arden Drive Wautoma WI 54982	SW	Teacher	EM			MQ	1984
Adcock Kelsey	(785)844-3032 adcock@hopelutheran.org	4205 Taneil Dr Manhattan KS 66502	KS	Teacher	C05/2022			S	2018
Adelmann Cara L Schmidtke	(218)252-5024 woodlandcara28@yahoo.com	25851 Skyline Cir Elko MN 55020	MNS	Teacher	C07/2022			SP	2020
Adle Rose E Gilbert Deac	(314)591-7313 reg1219@yahoo.com	211 E. 14th St Imperial NE 69033	IN	Deaconess	S HS/C	Concordia Theological Seminary Fort Wayne IN	(260)452-2100	SL-DEAC	2006
Adler Clinton J	(314)757-6897 cadler@ccls-stlouis.org	49 Winter Valley Dr Fenton MO 63026	MO	Teacher	Tchr	Christ Community Kirkwood MO	(314)822-7774	RF	1993
Adler Denise L Gehrke	(262)893-9044 deniselynnadler@yahoo.com	W349N5924 Sunflower Ct Oconomowoc WI 53066	SW	Teacher	Tchr	Divine Redeemer Hartland WI	(262)367-3664	MQ	1996
Aeikens Madison R Schellack	(701)238-5222 madiaeikens@gmail.com	1061 Dolores Pl Waukee IA 50263	IW	DCE	Mem C	Faith Adel IA	(515)993-3848	SP	2020
Affeldt Denise E Affeldt-Boetcher	(218)281-1108 dathesecond@yahoo.com	509 Holly Ave Crookston MN 56716	MNN	Tch/DCE	EM			SP	1981
Agard Jennifer L Kumm	(217)414-1624 jennifer.agard@gmail.com	3521 Ivanhoe Dr Springfield IL 62703	CI	Teacher	C07/2024			S	1990
Agee Sara A	(336)422-9722 sara.agee27@gmail.com		CNH	DCE	Mem C	Our Savior Livermore CA	(925)447-1246	S	2012
Agner Laura E Ray	bagner@hopelutheranwf.org	1416 Main Divide Dr Wake Forest NC 27587	SE	DCE	Mem C	Hope Wake Forest NC	(919)554-8109	IV	2006
Agnew Elizabeth A Lehl	bagnewteach@aol.com	7687 Garrick St Fishers IN 46038	IN	Teacher	Tchr	Holy Cross Indianapolis IN	(317)823-5801	S	1985
Ahlers Erich	(573)896-4688 erichahlers@yahoo.com	1140 Branch Rd Holts Summit MO 65043	MO	Teacher	P/Tchr	Calvary Jefferson Cty MO	(573)638-0228	MQ	1998
Ahlers Melisa A Duensing	(573)896-4688 melisaahlers@yahoo.com	1140 Branch Rd Holts Summit MO 65043	MO	Teacher	Tchr	Calvary Jefferson Cty MO	(573)638-0228	S	1999
Ahlman Elizabeth C Meckler Deac	(713)575-7420 elizabeth.ahlman@gmail.com	5607 Dolores St Houston TX 77057	TX	Deaconess	Tchr	Memorial Houston TX	(713)782-6079	SL-DEAC	2007
Ahlschwede Gordon E	(909)437-8381	127 E Harvard Pl Ontario CA 91764	PSW	Teacher	EM			S	1964
Aho Timothy J	(970)663-6384 tandcaho@gmail.com	3815 Steelhead St Unit F Fort Collins CO 80528	RM	Teacher	EM			SP	1975
Ahrens Linda A Sayer	(402)430-0748 lindaahrens67@gmail.com .	7538 Kentwell Lane Lincoln NE 68516	NEB	Teacher	Tchr	Christ Lincoln NE	(402)483-7774	S	1990
Aiello Katherine F Engebrecht Deac	(309)230-1535 katie.engebrecht97@gmail.com	4 Wycliffe Pl Fort Wayne IN 46825	IN	Deaconess	S HS/C	Concordia Theological Seminary Fort Wayne IN	(260)452-2100	FW-DEAC	2021
Ailts Dixie J Ketola	(651)210-6257 happydixiechick@hotmail.com	606 Derringer Ct Gillette WY 82718	WY	Teacher	C07/2016			SP	2005
Aitken Mary E	(314)240-0528 mary.aitken@cune.org	205 Runyon Ave Saint Louis MO 63125	MO	Teacher	Tchr	Lutheran South Saint Louis MO	(314)631-1400	S	2014
Akers Caleb J	(765)432-9702 akers.caleb@gmail.com	19966 Evelyn Ct Sonora CA 95370	CNH	DCE	C09/2019			RF	2017
Akers Kaila L Claucherty	(765)513-6619 kakers@bsl-school.org	14511 W Beloit Rd New Berlin WI 53151	SW	Teacher	Tchr	Beautiful Savior Waukesha WI	(262)542-2496	CQ	2015
Akerson Brian S	(314)629-7509 scottakerson@gmail.com	3806 Rock Bluff Ct Saint Louis MO 63129	MO	Teacher	Tchr	Lutheran South Saint Louis MO	(314)631-1400	CQ	2013
Akey Alyson E Bellis	(260)479-5427 iucolts@gmail.com	10272 E Swan Rd Laotto IN 46763	IN	Teacher	Tchr	Concordia Fort Wayne IN	(260)422-2429	CQ	2012
Albachten Sarah J	sjalbachten@gmail.com	986 Redstone Ct Rougemont NC 27572	SE	Teacher	C08/2023			SP	2019
Albers Bethany		617 Knierim Pl Saint Louis MO 63122	MO	Teacher	Tchr	Christ Community Kirkwood MO	(314)822-7774	RF	2005
Albers Deborah M Lehmann	(813)361-4433 dm_albers@hotmail.com	2403 Stirrup Dr Round Rock TX 78681	FG	Teacher	Tchr	Immanuel Brandon FL	(813)685-1978	RF	1980
Albers Jessica L Grothaus	(248)310-8583 jessica_albers@live.com	21719 Rose Maris Ln Tomball TX 77377	TX	DCM	RSO	Lutheran Bible Translators Inc Concordia MO	(660)225-0810	MQ	2022
Albers Mike R	(314)956-9240 malbers2323@gmail.com	9718 Lenor Dr Saint Louis MO 63123	MO	Teacher	EM			S	1972
Albert Janine M Bienz	(260)223-7734 childcare@wyneken.org	7030 N 450 W Decatur IN 46733	IN	Teacher	Tchr	Wyneken Memorial Decatur IN	(260)639-6177	AA	1985
Albert Jolene K Juedes	(715)384-2855 jolenekalbert@gmail.com	1125 Ridge Rd Marshfield WI 54449	NW	Teacher	EM			SP	1970
Albert Raymond A	(708)484-8225	6946 W 30th St Berwyn IL 60402	NI	Teacher	EM			RF	1956
Albertin Daniel A	(260)750-1059 dalbertin@frontier.com	8225 Meadow Hills Dr Fort Wayne IN 46835	IN	Teacher	EM			S	1974
Albertin Matthew P	(219)246-9312 malbertin88@hotmail.com	22575 Arbor Pointe Dr South Bend IN 46628	IN	Teacher	Tchr	Trinity Elkhart IN	(574)674-8800	CQ	2012
Alberts Jacqualyn M Berg	(605)261-7289 jacqualyn.alberts@gmail.com	7407 North Cliff Ave Sioux Falls SD 57104	SD	Teacher	Tchr	Blessed Redeemer Brandon SD	(605)582-2396	S	2020

*Multiple Assignments (See Church Worker Locator for Additional Details)

See Page 53 for the Table of Abbreviations for key to District, Classification, Position, and College abbreviations.

**C =Candidate; EM =Emeritus; the date following the C is the month and year the Candidate status began

NAME	TELEPHONE NUMBER EMAIL	STREET ADDRESS CITY/STATE/ZIP	DISTRICT	CLASS.	POSITION/ STATUS**	WHERE SERVING	OFFICE PHONE	COLLEGE/ UNIV/CQ	YR GRAD
Albrecht Beth	(509)995-8013 balbrecht@shepherdofthecoast.org	5530 NW 44th St Apt 213c Lauderhill FL 33319	FG	Teacher	C07/2016			SP	2014
Albrecht Daniel R	(815)547-7503 musicman0323@aol.com	424 W Boone St Belvidere IL 61008	NI	Teacher	Tchr	Immanuel Belvidere IL	(815)547-5346	RF	1983
Albrecht Dorothy A Theiss	dalbrecht@albrechtstudios.com	6105 Farmview Ct Imperial MO 63052	MO	Teacher	Tchr	St John Arnold MO	(636)464-7303	S	1987
Albright Janice M Ritt	(414)745-8940 janicealbright@mac.com	1813 Tiffany Dr Racine WI 53402	SW	Teacher	EM			RF	1958
Aleithe Matthew P	(262)457-4901 matta3479@yahoo.com	4203 Hidden Creek Ct Jackson WI 53037	SW	Teacher	Tchr	Living Word Jackson WI	(262)677-9353	MQ	2002
Alexander James L	(309)696-0940 jima1946@yahoo.com	10 Timberlane Dr Morton IL 61550	CI	Teacher	EM			S	1969
Alexander Katie J	(414)412-5978 kalexander@wauwatosa lutheran.org	11828 W North Ave #1 Wauwatosa WI 53226	SW	Teacher	Tchr	Wauwatosa Wauwatosa WI	(414)258-4558	MQ	2010
Alle Bonnie Jo	(808)220-6181	P.O. Box 11455 Honolulu HI 96828	CNH	Teacher	C07/2016			RF	1982
Allen Jeffrey A	(206)228-3724 jeff.a.allen@comcast.net	17072 SE Pagoda Ct Milwaukie OR 97267	NOW	Teacher	EM			S	1979
Allen Johanna R Miller	(760)220-7025 johannarmiller@gmail.com	18720 Munsee Rd Apple Valley CA 92307	PSW	Teacher	Tchr	Zion Victorville CA	(760)243-3074	S	2009
Allen Marcail J Clark	(217)827-2756 marcail425@gmail.com	2483 E 850 North Rd Strasburg IL 62465	CI	Teacher	Tchr	Altamont Altamont IL	(618)483-6428	CH	2021
Allen Marianne Hamilton	(605)891-1274 mariannemarieallen@gmail.com	12578 West Cascade Mtn. Rd. Hot Springs SD 57747	SD	Teacher	EM			S	2008
Allen Ronald M Dr	(734)972-6154 allenr@cuaa.edu	475 Pine Brae St Ann Arbor MI 48105	MI	Teacher	EM			RF	1972
Allen Timothy W	(206)227-9786 timallen0504@gmail.com	7149 Woodside Pl SW Seattle WA 98136	NOW	Teacher	C07/2024			PO	2012
Alles Brad A Dr	(262)502-9698 bkalles@att.net	W168 N10503 Deer Xing Germantown WI 53022	SW	Teacher	S HS/C	Concordia University Wisconsin Mequon WI	(262)243-5700	S	1987
Alles Cheryl M Buuck	(414)559-2148 cherylalles90@gmail.com	W225N2599 Alderwood Ln Waukesha WI 53186	SW	Teacher	EM			MQ	1990
Alliger Luke M	(260)452-0185 luke.alliger@gmail.com	28023 Terrace Dr North Olmsted OH 44070	MNS	Teacher	Tchr	Mayer Mayer MN	(952)657-2251	CQ	2022
Allmon Richard L	(630)989-0003 rick.allmon@yahoo.com	8758 N Avalanche Ln Hayden ID 83835	NOW	Teacher	EM			RF	1973
Allmon Steven A	(214)334-5049 sallmon5@aol.com	10907 Villa Haven Dr Dallas TX 75238	TX	Teacher	EM			RF	1972
Allor Cindy A Lemke	(630)849-7802 callor@aol.com	6n451 Cedar Ave Wood Dale IL 60191	NI	Teacher	Tchr	St Peter Schaumburg IL	(847)885-3350	RF	1984
Alsin Kristine L Urbach	(913)488-6111 kris.alsin@gmail.com	7138 Caenen Ave Shawnee KS 66216	KS	Teacher	EM			CQ	1994
Altevogt Lester L	(989)447-0439 a6422788@aol.com	189 Golfview Dr Brooklyn MI 49230	MI	Teacher	EM			S	1968
Altevogt Orville C	(785)765-3461 ocaltevogt49@gmail.com	P.O. Box 306 Alma KS 66401	KS	Teacher	EM			S	1971
Althage Richard A	(504)362-7439 ralthage@salemls.org	2656 Centaur St Harvey LA 70058	SO	Teacher	EM			S	1965
Altis Marvin R	(715)423-2982 mcaltis@tznet.com	3221 44th St S Wisc Rapids WI 54494	NW	Tch/DPM	Mem C	St Paul Stevens Point WI	(715)344-5660	RF	1978
Alvarado Lauren B Serrano	(714)383-0342 lauren.serrano@eagles.cui.edu	16390 Springdale St Huntington Beach CA 92647	PSW	Teacher	Tchr	Loving Savior Chino Hills CA	(909)597-4668	IV	2012
Alviani Cynthia D Green	(814)221-8696 cyndialviani59@gmail.com	72 Campbell Ave Clarion PA 16214	EA	Tch/DCE	EM			RF	1982
Alyea-Brooks Elizabeth F Alyea	(281)794-4658 lbrookstls@yahoo.com	169 F County Road 421 W Buffalo TX 75831	TX	Teacher	EM			AU	1982
Amendt Melissa K Owens Deac	(405) 596-4113 mkay315@hotmail.com	1721 Silver Oaks Dr Edmond OK 73025	OK	Deaconess	C08/2021			RF	2004
Amereller Rebekah R Heuer	(720)448-4992 rebekah.amereller@gmail.com	6534 Leathers Ln Parker CO 80134	RM	Teacher	C01/2024			S	2009
Amey Betty A Wiese	(316) 737-2973 bamey@sbcglobal.net	4170 N Parkwood Ln Bel Aire KS 67220	KS	Teacher	EM			S	1968
Amey Brian D	(316)682-1318 dcebda@yahoo.com	1824 S Stoneybrook St Wichita KS 67207	KS	DCE	Mem C	Holy Cross Wichita KS	(316)684-5201	S	2004
Amey Edward R	(661)803-6557 ed@amey.net	22302 Claibourne Ln Santa Clarita CA 91350	PSW	Teacher	Mem C	Bethlehem Santa Clarita CA	(661)252-0622	CQ	2009
Amey Pamela D Wilkening	(316) 737-9559 pamey@hcwichita.net	1824 S Stoneybrook St Wichita KS 67207	KS	DCE	C07/2016			S	2003
Amick Deborah L	(408)489-5298 amickdebby@gmail.com	32104 Via Buena San Juan Capistrano CA 92675	PSW	Teacher	Tchr	Abiding Savior Lake Forest CA	(949)830-1460	S	1976
Amling Albert J III	(414)617-4454 aamling@englishdistrict.org	5908 N River Bay Rd Waterford WI 53185	EN	Teacher	D Ex/S	English District Farmington MI	(248)476-0039	S	1981
Amling Albert J IV	(414)467-7943 ajamling4@gmail.com	9740 E Seismic Ave Mesa AZ 85212	PSW	Teacher	Prin	Christs Greenfield Gilbert AZ	(480)892-8314	MQ	2010
Amling Christa P Meinzen	(262)707-4618 christaamling4@gmail.com	9740 E Seismic Ave Mesa AZ 85212	PSW	Teacher	Tchr	Christs Greenfield Gilbert AZ	(480)892-8314	MQ	2009
Amling Grace I	(414)336-9301 grace.amling@cuw.edu	9745 E Hampton Ave Unit 1097 Mesa AZ 85209	PSW	Teacher		Pacific Southwest District Irvine CA	(949)854-3232	MQ	2021
Ampt Kimber L Wilkie	(812)926-4729	5920 Melody Dr Aurora IN 47001	IN	Teacher	Tchr	St John Aurora IN	(812)926-3337	SP	1989
Amt Philip M	(260)482-6516 philipamt@aol.com	3402 Kirkland Ave Fort Wayne IN 46805	IN	Teacher	EM			RF	1969
Anders Brian L	(586)703-0074 bandersinsurance@gmail.com	P.O. Box 223 Buckley MI 49620	MI	Tch/DCE	EM			S	1984

*Multiple Assignments (See Church Worker Locator for Additional Details)
See Page 53 for the Table of Abbreviations for key to District, Classification, Position, and College abbreviations.
**C =Candidate; EM =Emeritus; the date following the C is the month and year the Candidate status began

NAME	TELEPHONE NUMBER EMAIL	STREET ADDRESS CITY/STATE/ZIP	DISTRICT	CLASS.	POSITION/ STATUS**	WHERE SERVING	OFFICE PHONE	COLLEGE/ UNIV/CQ	YR GRAD
Anders Karen L Bevirt	(618)344-3620 chocolatemom3620@gmail.com	478 S Mulberry Rd Collinsville IL 62234	SI	Teacher	C07/2016			S	1979
Andersen Cynthia L Huggins	(507)252-9852 canb9@charter.net	4608 Acorn Ln NW Rochester MN 55901	MNS	Teacher	Tchr	Rochester Central Rochester MN	(507)289-3267	CQ	1988
Andersen Rhonda J Klug	(660)553-7053 mrs.andersen@embarqmail.com	2842 S Springfield Farms Blvd Brrokline MO 65619	MO	Teacher	EM			SP	1986
Anderson Aislinn R	(763)245-2477 aislinnanderson@yahoo.com	13885 Iris Ave Rogers MN 55374	MNS	Teacher	Mem C	Shepherd Grove Maple Grove MN	(763)425-5941	CQ	2015
Anderson Ann M Warner	(308)991-5855	918 McMillan St Holdrege NE 68949	NEB	Teacher	Mem C	Mount Calvary Holdrege NE	(308)995-2208	S	1996
Anderson Anne E Tiberg	(530)919-6968 annie.dce@gmail.com	1250 S Rialto Unit 1 Mesa AZ 85209	PSW	DCE	Mem C	Hosanna Mesa AZ	(480)984-1414	SP	2007
Anderson Dorothy I Fick	(612)916-1106 warrenanderson84@frontier.com	1104 Saint Paul Dr Merrill WI 54452	MNS	Teacher	EM			RF	1962
Anderson Eloise M	(559)535-7294	10313 Road 256 Terra Bella CA 93270	CNH	Teacher	EM			S	1970
Anderson Emily J Rausch	(937)303-2164 emmyjane819@yahoo.com	17501 Paris Darby Line Rd Marysville OH 43040	OH	Teacher	Tchr	St Johns Marysville OH	(937)644-5540	AA	2006
Anderson Emily J Tews	(507)358-6086 mrs.emilyanderson@gmail.com	215 2nd Ave NW Altura MN 55910	MNS	Teacher	Tchr	Immanuel Lewiston MN	(507)523-2228	CQ	2009
Anderson G P	(541)295-0014 panderson86@yahoo.com	321 Appalachian St Caldwell ID 83607	NOW	Teacher	EM			S	1976
Anderson Heather E			RM	Teacher	Tchr	Messiah Grand Junction CO	(970)245-2838	PO	2008
Anderson James C	(517)652-3119 canderson@stlorenz.org	8720 Gera Rd Birch Run MI 48415	MI	Tch/DCE	EM			RF	1980
Anderson James W	(612)760-4820 7755jwa@gmail.com	14280 Enclave Ct NW Prior Lake MN 55372	MNS	Tch/DCE	EM			SP	1978
Anderson Jasmine J Toole	(949)370-7706 jasmine.j.anderson@gmail.com	9625 West Wind Cir Woodbury MN 55129	MNS	Teacher	Prin	Concordia Academy Roseville MN	(651)484-8429	CQ	2019
Anderson Jean E Behrens	(541)295-5455 panderson86@yahoo.com	321 Appalachian St Caldwell ID 83607	NOW	Teacher	EM			S	1976
Anderson Jessica A Baumann	(720)955-7154 jessicabaumann9@hotmail.com	711 88th St NW Bradenton FL 34209	FG	Teacher	C07/2016			RF	2000
Anderson John A	(812)707-9072 jandrewanderson@hotmail.com	1220 Starlit Dr Laguna Beach CA 92651	PSW	Teacher	EM			S	1980
Anderson Kathleen E Schulenburg	(317) 502-1590 jewelryladykathya@gmail.com	6249 Amber Valley Ln Indianapolis IN 46237	IN	Teacher	C07/2016			AA	1998
Anderson Laurie S Bogenpohl	(307)286-0677 lauriesue0428@gmail.com	314 State Hwy E Jackson MO 63755	MO	Teacher	Tchr	United in Christ Frohna MO	(573)824-5218	RF	1984
Anderson Linda L Albers	(678)471-2637 anson6520@gmail.com	408 Keota Ln Loudon TN 37774	FG	Teacher	EM			RF	1970
Anderson Lisa M Klute	(517)652-3119 landerson@stlorenz.org	8720 Gera Rd Birch Run MI 48415	MI	Teacher	Tchr	St Lorenz Frankenmuth MI	(989)652-6141	SP	1977
Anderson Lori A Pethes	(847)987-0560 livingbyprayer@sbcglobal.net	488 Rosewood Dr Carpentersvle IL 60110	NI	Teacher	Tchr	Immanuel East Dundee IL	(847)428-4477	RF	1993
Anderson Margaret L Deac	(205)520-9376 dcs.margaretanderson@yahoo.com	4744 Cheshire Cir Birmingham AL 35235	SO	Deaconess	EM			CQ	2000
Anderson Marisa L	(734)770-8522 m.anderson_15@hotmail.com	512 Live Oak Ln Boynton Beach FL 33436	FG	Teacher	Tchr	Trinity Delray Beach FL	(561)278-1737	CH	2014
Anderson Mark C	(651)341-2601 dcemark1989@gmail.com	1512 Selby Ave St Paul Park MN 55071	MNS	DCE	C07/2016			PO	1989
Anderson Marlene J Hedrich Deac	(262)424-1423 stemara2@sbcglobal.net	W161 N11064 Meadow Dr Germantown WI 53022	SW	Deaconess	EM			CQ	2003
Anderson MaryJane	(952)927-8400	c/o St Peters Luth Church 5421 France Ave S Edina MN 55410	MNS	Teacher	EM			S	1982
Anderson Patricia L Deac	(714)824-0027 ms.dingaling@yahoo.com	16171 Springdale St # 108 Huntington Beach CA 92649	PSW	Deaconess	Mem C	Redeemer Huntington Beach CA	(714)846-6330	FW-DEAC	2017
Anderson Robert C	(414)578-0722 banderson080655@gmail.com	336 N 115th St Milwaukee WI 53226	SW	Teacher	EM			RF	1978
Anderson Ruth A Schupmann	randerson3161@gmail.com	2973 E Highway 47 Old Monroe MO 63369	MO	Teacher	EM			S	1995
Anderson Sarah J Schroeder	(414)412-8898 sja8988@yahoo.com	336 N 115th St Wauwatosa WI 53226	SW	Teacher	Tchr	Our Father's Greenfield WI	(414)282-8220	RF	1979
Anderson Sarah N	(260)409-9172 spotter08@frontier.com	14607 Bremer Rd New Haven IN 46774	IN	Teacher	Tchr	Wyneken Memorial Decatur IN	(260)639-6177	CH	2012
Anderson Summer C Silsby	(303)431-1003 summersilsby@hotmail.com	1530 Concordia Irvine CA 92612	RM	Teacher	C07/2016			IV	2001
Anderson Teresa L	(414)258-3691 tanderson@egl.org	2925 N 89th St Milwaukee WI 53222	SW	Teacher	Tchr	Divine Redeemer Hartland WI	(262)367-3664	S	1985
Anderton Kristina L Zellar-Pluard	(907)315-0585 kristylanderton@gmail.com	2873 N Kalmbach Lake Dr Wasilla AK 99623	NOW	Teacher	C07/2016			IV	2001
Andreasen Alison T Tyhurst	(605)401-2727 jaandreasen1517@gmail.com	3911 E 68th St Sioux Falls SD 57108	SD	Teacher	C11/2020			S	2007
Andreasen Angela M Orne	(210)313-2792 angelamandreasen@gmail.com	413 E Park Ave Norfolk NE 68701	NEB	Teacher	C03/2018			S	2012
Andreasen Dennis C	(608)768-7543 dbandreasen@rucls.net	2381 Ernstmeyer Rd Reedsburg WI 53959	SW	Teacher	EM			S	1963
Andrelczyk Jennifer E Vaughn			FG	Teacher	C07/2016			CH	2010
Andrew Ashlie J Siefkes	(714)469-1085 ashlie.andrew@cui.edu	1402 Columbine Way Livermore CA 94551	PSW	Teacher	S HS/C	Concordia University Irvine Irvine CA	(949)854-8002	CQ	2012
Andrews Bethany J		1596 S 150 W Albion IN 46701	IN	DCE	C09/2025			S	2015
Andrews Marie A Webb	(913)827-2705 zmandrews18@gmail.com	914 Carpathian Dr Lake Saint Louis MO 63367	MO	Teacher	C07/2021			S	2017

*Multiple Assignments (See Church Worker Locator for Additional Details)
See Page 53 for the Table of Abbreviations for key to District, Classification, Position, and College abbreviations.
**C =Candidate; EM =Emeritus; the date following the C is the month and year the Candidate status began

NAME	TELEPHONE NUMBER EMAIL	STREET ADDRESS CITY/STATE/ZIP	DISTRICT	CLASS.	POSITION/ STATUS**	WHERE SERVING	OFFICE PHONE	COLLEGE/ UNIV/CQ	YR GRAD
Andrich Janie L Turner	(310)650-8871 janie.andrich@concordia shanghai.org	1618 Miracosta St San Pedro CA 90732	PSW	Teacher	S Miss	Office of International Mission Saint Louis MO		CQ	1993
Andrzejewski Rachel M	(734)447-6955 rachiemoski@gmail.com	24345 Grove Ave Eastpointe MI 48021	MI	Teacher	Tchr	St Peter Macomb MI	(586)781-9296	CQ	2024
Angell Jeffrey W	(612)877-2112 jeffwillangell@gmail.com	9340 Rhoy Ave Chaska MN 55318	MNS	Teacher	Tchr	Trinity Waconia MN	(952)442-4165	CQ	2024
Angell Paul M	(505)554-1428 gangell5256@gmail.com	1044 Monte Largo Dr NE Albuquerque NM 87123	RM	Teacher	EM			S	1974
Angerman Austin	(850)582-3186 austin@flcms.org	304 Majestic Cedar Ct Liberty Hill TX 78642	TX	DCE	Mem C	Faith Georgetown TX	(512)863-7332	AU	2018
Angerman David M	(512)658-5114 david.angerman@bethanyaustin. com	340 Grafton Ln Austin TX 78737	TX	DPM	Mem C	Bethany Austin TX	(512)292-8778	CQ	2013
Angerman Kimberly K	(512)428-4191 kimangerman@austin.rr.com	340 Grafton Ln Austin TX 78737	TX	DPM	Mem C	Bethany Austin TX	(512)292-8778	CQ	2013
Angerman Michaelle J Karlin	(408)930-4077 mjangerman@sbcglobal.net	303 N Broadway Avenue Spring Valley MN 55975	MNS	Teacher	P/Tchr	St Johns Wykoff MN	(507)352-2296	S	1980
Angers Kristine A Martz	(616)340-8046 kristine.a.angers@gmail.com	811 Den Hertog St SW Wyoming MI 49509	MI	Teacher	P/Tchr	WMLHS Wyoming MI	(616)455-2200	AA	2004
Angott Donna L Renkert	(586) 246-2020 donna.angott@gmail.com	2025 Barberry Dr Shelby Twp MI 48316	MI	Teacher	Tchr	Trinity Utica MI	(586)731-4490	CQ	1978
Ankerberg Erik P Dr	erik.ankerberg@gmail.com	1112 Sunset Ct Grafton WI 53024	SW	Teacher	S HS/C	Concordia University Wisconsin Mequon WI	(262)243-5700	RF	1992
Annas Michelle L Platts	(810)599-0640 cannas6@comcast.net	4511 Argenta Dr Brighton MI 48116	MI	Teacher	EM			AA	1984
Anschutz Mark D	(402)570-7271 mark.anschutz@cune.edu	221 Locust Ave Seward NE 68434	NEB	Teacher	EM			S	1977
Anson Harlan D	(402)641-0757 harlan.anson@orlcne.org	635 South St Staplehurst NE 68439	NEB	Teacher	P/Tchr	Our Redeemer Staplehurst NE	(402)535-2251	S	2005
Anthony Jill Kline Dr	(440)458-8605 docantony@aol.com	18 Waterfall Dr Grafton OH 44044	S	Teacher	EM			RF	1968
Antonacci Jill A Beilke	(815)904-3963 jaantonacci@hotmail.com	521 Carleton Ave Glen Ellyn IL 60137	NI	Teacher	C07/2016			RF	2002
Antonetti Karin L Nalefski	(309)826-0589 karin.antonetti@gmail.com		NI	Teacher	C05/2018			RF	2011
Anwyl Evan S	(916)300-9995 eanwyl@sjlschool.org	9820 Sentinel Peak Pl Bakersfield CA 93311	CNH	Teacher	Prin	St John Bakersfield CA	(661)665-7815	CQ	2005
Appel Kimberly A Winslow	(210)722-8255 pmla1@yahoo.com	P.O. Box 575 Giddings TX 78942	TX	Teacher	Tchr	Immanuel Giddings TX	(979)542-2918	AU	1982
Appelquist Melanie R Beier	(612)834-9822 small_peach_17@yahoo.com	8655 Dunkirk Ct NE Blaine MN 55449	MNS	DCE	Mem C	Good Shepherd Circle Pines MN	(763)784-8417	SP	2005
Appold Patrice M	(661)205-4549 pmappold2@bak.rr.com	408 Hollyhill Dr Bakersfield CA 93312	CNH	Teacher	Tchr	St John Bakersfield CA	(661)665-7815	AA	1983
Aquino Angela M Krentz	(219)221-0236 aquinoteacher@yahoo.com	11301 W 100 S Wanatah IN 46390	IN	Teacher	Tchr	St John's La Porte IN	(219)362-6692	CQ	2024
Arambel Sally A Schwarz	(314)540-7195 sally.schwarz@me.com	13219 Adonis Dr Austin TX 78729	TX	Teacher	C06/2023			Other	2011
Arbeiter Arlin A	(863)293-8156 arlin3@verizon.net	19 Lake Link Dr SE Winter Haven FL 33884	FG	Teacher	EM			RF	1966
Arden Brenda K Krause	(765)491-8969 mikeandbrenda05@gmail.com	197 Turkey Creek Alachua FL 32615	FG	Teacher	Prin	Abiding Savior Gainesville FL	(352)331-7770	S	1998
Arfsten Debra J Dr	(708)308-1942 debra.arfsten@cuchicago.edu	610 W Moreland Ave Addison IL 60101	NI	DCE	S HS/C	Concordia University Chicago River Forest IL	(708)771-8300	S	1990
Argue Joanne R Prudek	(616)465-5027	4023 Popalardo St Bridgman MI 49106	MI	Teacher	EM			RF	1958
Arguto Pamela J Erickson	(719)242-4154 pjarguto@yahoo.com	512 Whitewater Way Elgin MN 55932	MNS	Teacher	C05/2025			S	1989
Aring Elizabeth R Brott	(217)473-5881 aringlisa07@gmail.com	1227 N 5th St Seward NE 68434	NEB	Teacher	Mem C	St John Seward NE	(402)643-2983	RF	1980
Armao Ruth A Heider	(317)373-9191 raharmao@att.net	6825 Southpine Ct Maumee OH 43537	OH	Teacher	EM			S	1982
Armbrecht Andy P	(319)668-1562 aarmbrecht@lutheraninter parish.com	2677 230th St Williamsburg IA 52361	IE	Teacher	Tchr	Lutheran Interparish Williamsburg IA	(319)668-1711	S	1989
Armbrecht Carol M Jeske	(815)382-2466 arminarm3@gmail.com	4282 Scenic Dr E Saginaw MI 48603	MI	Teacher	Mem C	Peace Saginaw MI	(989)793-9025	RF	1984
Armbrecht Deanna J Zobel	(319)279-3237 tarmbrecht@rtc279.com	2515 Quail Ave Readlyn IA 50668	IE	Teacher	C08/2019			MQ	1991
Armbrecht Donna J Spomer	(319)660-0913 darmbrecht@lutheraninter parish.com	2677 230th St Williamsburg IA 52361	IE	Teacher	Tchr	Lutheran Interparish Williamsburg IA	(319)668-1711	S	1991
Armbrecht Louis W	louis.armbrecht@gmail.com	205 N Denwood St Dearborn MI 48128	MI	Teacher	Tchr	Guardian Dearborn MI	(313)274-1414	CQ	2017
Armbrust Anna G	(262)242-2045 aarmbrust@trinityfreistadt.com	N169W19942 Georgetown Dr Apt F Jackson WI 53037	SW	Teacher	Tchr	Trinity Mequon WI	(262)242-2045	S	2020
Armbrust Robyn L Hemler	(785)341-3575 robyn.armbrust@lcms.org	1208 Holgate Dr Manchester MO 63021	MO	Tch/DCE	S Ex/S	The LCMS Corporate Saint Louis MO	(314)965-9000	RF	1990
Armbrust Steven D	(678)849-8862 sa4903@aol.com	1700 Wynridge Path Alpharetta GA 30005	FG	DCE	EM			S	1981
Armbruster Deborah A Fitzpatrick	(314)280-7630 darmbruster@stmarkseureka.org	1449 Palisades Rd Wildwood MO 63021	MO	Teacher	EM			S	1978
Armer Faith A	(918)289-4585 farmer@hopelcs.org	7 Mary Ln Levittown PA 19057	EA	DCE	Mem C	Hope Levittown PA	(215)946-3467	S	2023
Armstrong Angelia D Wiley Deac	(504)324-5785 deaconessangie@cox.net	77589 Roubion Rd Folsom LA 70437	SO	Deaconess	C07/2016			RF	2001

*Multiple Assignments (See Church Worker Locator for Additional Details)
See Page 53 for the Table of Abbreviations for key to District, Classification, Position, and College abbreviations.
**C =Candidate; EM =Emeritus; the date following the C is the month and year the Candidate status began

NAME	TELEPHONE NUMBER EMAIL	STREET ADDRESS CITY/STATE/ZIP	DISTRICT	CLASS.	POSITION/ STATUS**	WHERE SERVING	OFFICE PHONE	COLLEGE/ UNIV/CQ	YR GRAD
Armstrong Debra S Schmidt	(713)898-8010 darmstrong82@comcast.net	5002 Bayou Vista Dr Houston TX 77091	TX	Teacher	Tchr	Our Savior Houston TX	(713)290-9087	IV	1986
Armstrong Jeffery S	(713)849-5237 jeffarm@osischool.org	5002 Bayou Vista Dr Houston TX 77091	TX	DCE	Mem C	Our Savior Houston TX	(713)290-9087	IV	1995
Armstrong Leah A Euper	leah.armstrong@mtolivemke.org		SW	Teacher	Tchr	Mount Olive Milwaukee WI	(414)774-2200	MQ	2014
Armstrong Sandra A Sunderman	(308)379-9635 sandraarmstrong1155@gmail.com	3425 Graham Ave Grand Island NE 68803	NEB	Teacher	EM			CQ	1993
Armstrong Sandy E Volz	(314)604-4340 sdjjcel@yahoo.com	576 Summit Downs Ct Fenton MO 63026	MO	Teacher	EM			CQ	2010
Armstrong Sara J Birmingham	(972)746-9881 sarabirmingham@yahoo.com	4529 Shady Lake Dr N Richlnd Hls TX 76180	TX	Teacher	Tchr	St Paul Fort Worth TX	(817)332-2281	AA	2004
Arndt Ann L Osborn	(816)225-6524 annarndt@me.com	400 N Kirk Ave Independence MO 64050	MO	Teacher	EM			S	1970
Arndt John E	(816)833-0957 arndtresidence@aol.com	400 N Kirk Ave Independence MO 64050	MO	Tch/DCE	EM			S	1966
Arndt Karen D Ferguson	(770)924-6977 pkarndt@msn.com	4899 Raven Ct NE Marietta GA 30066	FG	Teacher	EM			CQ	2001
Arndt Richard E	(219)836-2395 reamac@sbcglobal.net	220 W. Division Street Manteno IL 60950	IN	Teacher	Tchr	St Paul Munster IN	(219)836-6270	RF	1992
Arndt Sharon L Polubinski	(219)741-9985 sharonarndt72@gmail.com	557 Dunewood Dr Chesterton IN 46304	IN	Teacher	C07/2016			RF	1994
Arneson Janice L Hesemann Rusnak	(314)606-5703 jarneson119@gmail.com	164 S Coeur Dalene St Unit C107 Spokane WA 99201	NOW	Teacher	EM			RF	1977
Arnett Beverly L	bevarnett@yahoo.com	1551 Red Bud Ln Apt 332 Round Rock TX 78664	TX	Teacher	EM			RF	1965
Arnett Gregory S	(989)672-9672 manland2319@icloud.com	2500 Van Wormer Rd. Saginaw MI 48609	MI	Tch/DCE	EM			RF	1987
Arnholt Philip J Dr	(262)241-4419 philip.arnholt@cuw.edu	10910 N San Marino Dr Mequon WI 53092	SW	Teacher	EM			CQ	1982
Arnholz Donald R	dsarnholz@msn.com	3934 Parkway Blvd Land O Lakes FL 34639	FG	Teacher	EM			RF	1964
Arnold Joel F	arnoldj@flhsemail.org	4112 Bennett Mountain St Las Vegas NV 89129	PSW	Teacher	Tchr	Faith Las Vegas NV	(702)804-4400	SP	2001
Arnold Kimberly D Edwards	(760)546-5012 karnold@gracelcms.net	1631 Bay Hill Dr San Marcos CA 92069	PSW	Teacher	Tchr	Grace Escondido CA	(760)745-0831	CQ	2018
Arnold Larry J	(571)684-0431	c/o Our Savior Lutheran School 13667 Highland Rd Hartland MI 48353	EN	Teacher	Tchr	Our Savior Hartland MI	(248)887-3836	AA	1992
Arnold Linda S Phillips	(630)430-8610 linda.arnold726@gmail.com	205 Isleview Dr Oswego IL 60543	NI	DCM	EM			MQ	2001
Arnold Richard J	(314)803-4324 rarnold404@gmail.com	1440 Summerhill Dr Mundelein IL 60060	NI	Teacher	EM			S	1968
Arntson Devan G	(218)491-4978 darnston@racinelutheran.org	2328 Indiana St Racine WI 53405	SW	DCE	Tchr	Lutheran High School Racine WI	(262)637-6538	SP	2021
Arp Woodrow A	(512)837-6857	9606 Chukar Cir Austin TX 78758	TX	Teacher	EM			S	1965
Arrick Mary S Petzold	(517)518-0613 mary@arrick.net	1317 Maple Leaf Ln Howell MI 48843	MI	Teacher	C06/2025			AA	1988
Arturi Jeanne M O Toole	jeannearturi@gmail.com	8000 Archer Ave Apt A106 Willow Spgs IL 60480	NI	Teacher	EM			CQ	2003
Aschbrenner Henry J	(714)747-8179 hank.aschbrenner@cui.edu	209 N Avenida Veracruz Anaheim CA 92808	PSW	Teacher	EM			S	1960
Aschemeier Susan K Hammon	(419)267-5585 basch@bright.net	1800 Walnut Grove Rd Defiance OH 43512	OH	Teacher	EM			RF	1975
Ash Margaret R Bohne	(208) 520-4377 peggy12bill@gmail.com	3241 Wexford Cir Idaho Falls ID 83404	NOW	Teacher	EM			RF	1970
Ash Randall W	(952)220-4530 ashrw10@gmail.com	1411 McKnight Cir Victoria MN 55386	MNS	Teacher	EM			RF	1975
Ashbaugh Megan R Megan Franz	(260)433-0190 cuaaredhead@gmail.com	3636 W 800 S South Whitley IN 46787	IN	Teacher	C07/2016			AA	2009
Ashby Lisa A Dr	(402)643-7419 lisa.ashby@cune.edu	P.O. Box 75 Seward NE 68434	NEB	Teacher	S HS/C	Concordia University Nebraska Seward NE	(402)643-3651	S	1987
Ashcraft Ashley N Biggs	(214)536-3078 ashley.ashcraft@popcs.org	2318 Aberdeen Bnd Carrollton TX 75007	TX	Teacher	Tchr	Prince Of Peace Carrollton TX	(972)447-0532	AU	2006
Asher Jennie J Waters Deac	(320)583-2625 mrsdrjash@fastmail.com	2457 Castle Pines Dr Imperial MO 63052	MO	Deaconess	S HS/C	Concordia Seminary Saint Louis MO	(314)505-7000	RF	1993
Ashford Julie L Burns	(405)733-1519 jjashford@aol.com	1326 Damron Dr Midwest City OK 73110	OK	Teacher	Tchr	Good Shepherd Midwest City OK	(405)732-2585	S	1990
Asmus Eunice E Harms	(612)237-2082 walterandeunice@yahoo.com	28241 505th Ave Winthrop MN 55396	MNS	Teacher	EM			S	1960
Asplin Laura D	(402)643-0271 laura.asplin@cune.org	438 Grand Ave Seward NE 68434	NEB	Teacher	EM			S	1991
Atkinson Ashley R Willoughby	(515)537-4216 aatkinson.tle@gmail.com	35 Tee Ct Pagosa Springs CO 81147	SI	Teacher	Tchr	Trinity Edwardsville IL	(618)656-2918	S	2013
Atkinson Joshua J	(414)975-8955	2027 S East Ln New Berlin WI 53146	SW	Teacher	Tchr	Milwaukee LHS Milwaukee WI	(414)461-6000	MQ	2009
Attenberger David F	(586)214-0083	482 1st St Lupton MI 48635	MI	Teacher	EM			RF	1973
Au Buchon Barbara A Hoeft	(734)755-7650 barbaubuchon@att.net	23875 Higgins Way Brownstown MI 48134	MI	Teacher	EM			RF	1968
Auer Anna M Frank	(314)302-9140 aauer@sjlarnold.org	2279 Aileswick Dr Saint Louis MO 63129	MO	Teacher	Tchr	St John Arnold MO	(636)464-7303	S	1999
Auer Donna K Calvin	(314)740-5151 calvindk99@hotmail.com	2938 Hubert Dr Saint Louis MO 63125	MO	Teacher	Tchr	Green Park Saint Louis MO	(314)544-4248	S	1999

*Multiple Assignments (See Church Worker Locator for Additional Details)

See Page 53 for the Table of Abbreviations for key to District, Classification, Position, and College abbreviations.

**C =Candidate; EM =Emeritus; the date following the C is the month and year the Candidate status began

NAME	TELEPHONE NUMBER EMAIL	STREET ADDRESS CITY/STATE/ZIP	DISTRICT	CLASS.	POSITION/ STATUS**	WHERE SERVING	OFFICE PHONE	COLLEGE/ UNIV/CQ	YR GRAD
Aufdemberge Erwin J	(586)949-2961 ejaufdem@comcast.net	23805 24 Mile Rd Macomb MI 48042	MI	Teacher	EM			S	1957
Aufdemberge Theodore P Dr	(734)808-1126 aufdet@gmail.com	913 Ruddy Duck Ln Chelsea MI 48118	MI	Teacher	EM			S	1956
Aufdembrink Fredrick L	(402)750-4365 faufdembrink@lhne.org	1204 E Sycamore Ave Norfolk NE 68701	NEB	Tch/DCE	Pro Stf	Northeast Norfolk NE	(402)379-3040	S	1987
Aufdenberg Ann M Stevenson	(417)260-4511 aaufdenberg@saxonylutheran high.org	6813 State Hwy Oo Jackson MO 63755	MO	Teacher	Tchr	Saxony Jackson MO	(573)204-7555	CH	2022
Auger Cherie L Crossman Deac	(817)925-7233 auger_cl@yahoo.com	7504 Belcross Ln Fort Worth TX 76133	TX	Deaconess	EM			FW-DEAC	2014
Auger Christopher P	(989)553-1036 cauger@splcc.org	3932 N Spruce Ave Kansas City MO 64117	MO	Teacher	Tchr	St Paul Saint Joseph MO	(816)279-1118	Other	2016
Auger Emma C Otto	(816)332-7687 emma.casie777@gmail.com	3932 N Spruce Ave Kansas City MO 64117	MO	DCE	Mem C	Christ Platte Woods MO	(816)741-0483	CH	2017
Auger Noah R	(989)975-2134 nrauger@hotmail.com	2606 Parallel Ave. Apt F8 Saint Joseph MO 64506	MO	Teacher	Tchr	St Paul Saint Joseph MO	(816)279-1110	CH	2016
Auger Robert G Jr	(989)269-7756 augerfamily45@gmail.com	2606 Parallel Ave Saint Joseph MO 64506	MO	Tch/DCE	EM			SP	1984
Aughe Kent J	(248)376-7477 chappie81@wowway.com	420 S Stephenson Hwy Royal Oak MI 48067	MI	DCM	EM			MQ	1986
Augustine Erika J Ebel	erikaaugustine@yahoo.com	208 Princeton Dr Costa Mesa CA 92626	PSW	Teacher	Tchr	Christ Brea CA	(714)529-2984	IV	1996
Augustine Jennifer L Wendling Deac	(507)438-9984 dcs_flute@yahoo.com	55 Tews Ave Lewiston MN 55952	MNS	Deaconess	C09/2023			RF	2000
Aumann James C	(262)633-8653 jcaumann@att.net	5705 Castleton Dr Racine WI 53406	SW	Teacher	EM			RF	1982
Aumick James T	(260)312-5639 jaumick@cluth.org	1018 Straford Rd New Haven IN 46774	IN	Teacher	Tchr	Central New Haven IN	(260)493-2502	RF	1983
Aurich Dean R	(952)564-0491 draurich@hotmail.com	6051 County Road 30 SW Waverly MN 55390	MNS	Teacher	EM			S	1979
Aurich John B		N485 Ford Dr Geneva IL 60134	NI	Teacher	EM			S	1976
Aurich Michael A	(651)247-4442 beaconfb@gmail.com	1773 Quie Ln Northfield MN 55057	MNS	Teacher	EM			S	1975
Aurich Rebecca R Pennekamp	(952)564-1445 aurich7@hotmail.com	6051 County Road 30 SW Waverly MN 55390	MNS	Teacher	Tchr	Zion Mayer MN	(952)657-2339	S	1980
Aurich Shannon J Oelfke	(952)334-0079 saurich4@gmail.com	1388 Pinecone Cir Mayer MN 55360	MNS	Teacher	Tchr	Zion Mayer MN	(952)657-2339	SP	2003
Austin Kimberly D Mueller	(816)507-9910 kimdaustin14@gmail.com	7501 Berrenda Dr Fort Worth TX 76131	TX	DCE	Mem C	Peace Hurst TX	(817)284-1677	S	2011
Avery Ryan J	(708)334-6828 crossrock7@gmail.com	23708 Whitley Drive Clinton Township MI 48035	MI	DCE	Mem C	Immanuel Macomb MI	(586)286-4231	CH	2007
Axtell Virginia D Devall	(210)912-0188 vaxtell@shlutheran.org	6103 Ashley Springs San Antonio TX 78244	TX	Teacher	Tchr	Shep Of The Hills San Antonio TX	(210)614-3741	AU	1982
Baack Laura L Modlin	(913)268-0252 lb_dce@hotmail.com	12601 W 66th St Shawnee KS 66216	KS	DCE	C07/2016			S	1997
Baacke Bruce M		143 Mountain Laurel Dr Montgomery TX 77316	TX	Teacher	EM			S	1970
Baacke Deborah J Snyder	(832)372-5331	4711 Cavern Dr Friendswood TX 77546	TX	Teacher	EM			S	1973
Baacke Mark L	(832)721-9907 mlbaacke@gmail.com	4711 Cavern Dr Friendswood TX 77546	TX	Teacher	EM			S	1973
Baarck Stephanie L Kroeger	(989)652-6141 sbaarck@stlorenz.org	932 Eastgate Ct Frankenmuth MI 48734	MI	Teacher	Tchr	St Lorenz Frankenmuth MI	(989)652-6141	RF	1990
Baars Marilyn J Riess Friese	(608) 576-4453 marilynbaars27@gmail.com	1120 Prospect Ave Unit 3 Portage WI 53901	SW	Teacher	EM			RF	1969
Babchak Elizabeth A	(573)335-0857	1236 W Cape Rock Dr Apt 42 Cpe Girardeau MO 63701	MO	Teacher	EM			RF	1976
Babisak Matthew D	(469)358-8621 mbabisak@ordallas.org	401 Tallowtree Dr Fate TX 75087	TX	Teacher	Tchr	Our Redeemer Dallas TX	(214)368-1465	CQ	2023
Bach Gary D	(218)640-3770 dcegaryb@gmail.com	320 N Broadway Ave New York Mills MN 56567	MNN	DCE	EM			SP	1982
Bach Lisa A Rude	(989)550-2558 coachbach1989@gmail.com	3842 Swaffer Rd Millington MI 48746	MI	Teacher	Tchr	St Johns Midland MI	(989)835-7041	AA	1989
Bachert Zina M Decker	(708) 932-1214 gkatz@comcast.net	10136 Margo Ln Munster IN 46321	IN	Teacher	Tchr	St Paul Munster IN	(219)836-6270	RF	1986
Bachman Joshua K	(219)916-1112 joshkarl@yahoo.com	1115 Ohio St Valparaiso IN 46383	IN	Teacher	Prin	Immanuel Valparaiso IN	(219)462-8207	CQ	2014
Bachmann Charlene K	(618)493-7596 ckbachmann2000@yahoo.com	P.O. Box 192 Hoyleton IL 62803	SI	Teacher	Tchr	Trinity Hoyleton IL	(618)493-7754	S	1980
Bachmann Raymond E	(812)358-4461	621 S Sugar St Brownstown IN 47220	IN	Teacher	EM			RF	1956
Bacic Frances M Kline	(501)410-2945 francesbacic@yahoo.com	10219 Raymond Dr Little Rock AR 72205	MDS	Teacher	Tchr	Zion Avilla AR	(501)408-4630	AA	1993
Backs Diane K Goebel	(618)824-6492 cdkbacks@egyptian.net	1497 Grouse Rd Venedy IL 62214	SI	Teacher	Tchr	Trinity-St John Nashville IL	(618)327-8561	RF	1983
Bacon Annette L Voth	(847)982-3909 pebacon@aol.com	5039 Mulford St Skokie IL 60077	EN	Teacher	EM			RF	1963
Bacon Harold L	(859)586-1117 baconstation@fuse.net	2663 Sterling Trce Burlington KY 41005	IN	Teacher	EM			RF	1965
Badciong Ruth E Bauman Dr	(507)450-8816 badciong@hbci.com	1419 Homer Rd Winona MN 55987	MNS	Teacher	C06/2024			MQ	1987
Bade Barbara L Senechal	(480)254-3783 wlb7939@gmail.com	25850 S Eastlake Dr Sun Lakes AZ 85248	PSW	Teacher	EM			S	1963

*Multiple Assignments (See Church Worker Locator for Additional Details)
See Page 53 for the Table of Abbreviations for key to District, Classification, Position, and College abbreviations.
**C =Candidate; EM =Emeritus; the date following the C is the month and year the Candidate status began

NAME	TELEPHONE NUMBER EMAIL	STREET ADDRESS CITY/STATE/ZIP	DISTRICT	CLASS.	POSITION/ STATUS**	WHERE SERVING	OFFICE PHONE	COLLEGE/ UNIV/CQ	YR GRAD
Bade William L	(480)932-3298 wlb7939@gmail.com	25850 S Eastlake Dr Sun Lakes AZ 85248	PSW	Teacher	EM			S	1963
Baden Corwin R Dr	corwinbaden@gmail.com	466 10th Ave San Francisco CA 94118	CNH	Teacher	Tchr	Zion San Francisco CA	(415)221-7500	CQ	2002
Baden Marian J Pfeiffer Dr	(714)974-8928 paradox59@earthlink.net	1796 N Shattuck Pl Orange CA 92865	PSW	Teacher	EM			S	1959
Bader Gretyl A Bremer	(308)390-2527 gretylb@gmail.com	466 Rd East G South Ogallala NE 69153	NEB	Teacher	C05/2020			S	2014
Bader Joanne E Sandfort	(636)244-3390 joannesbader@gmail.com	600 Breeze Park Dr Apt 314 Saint Charles MO 63304	MO	Teacher	EM			RF	1958
Bader Judith J Janzow	(818) 620-8464 nordylvr@aol.com	120 Helecho Ct Thousand Oaks CA 91362	PSW	Teacher	Mem C	St Paul Agoura Hills CA	(818)889-1620	S	1978
Bady Melissa K Rossow		632 E Highway N Wentzville MO 63385	MO	Teacher	Tchr	Immanuel Wentzville MO	(636)327-4416	CQ	2003
Baehr Carrie Lemm	(832)326-0726 baehrc@trinityklein.org	4418 Countrycrossing Dr Spring TX 77388	TX	Teacher	Tchr	Trinity Spring TX	(281)376-5810	CQ	2024
Baerenklau James C	(630)254-0785 jambaer@aol.com	220 E Madison St Villa Park IL 60181	NI	Teacher	Tchr	Trinity Lombard IL	(630)629-8765	RF	1990
Baertlein Kalen A Kleinberg	(661)505-5667 kalen.baertlein@creanlutheran.org	909 Sunset Ridge Lake Forest CA 92610	PSW	Teacher	Tchr	Crean Irvine CA	(949)387-1199	CQ	2016
Baerwolf Paul R	(313)580-7734 cbaerwolf@sbcglobal.net	22726 Arlington St Dearborn MI 48128	MI	Teacher	P/Tchr	Emmanuel Dearborn MI	(313)565-4002	AA	1992
Baez Hillary J Hillary Snyder	(402)430-4558 hillyface09@gmail.com	1804 1/2 Hart Ave Dodge City KS 67801	KS	Teacher	C06/2020			S	2013
Baganz Chad D	(630)696-4034 cdbaganz@hotmail.com	485 De Lasalle Ave Naperville IL 60565	NI	Teacher	Tchr	Bethany Naperville IL	(630)355-6607	RF	1996
Baganz Mark J	(920)206-0135 mbaganz@att.net	W1797 Fox Rd Ixonia WI 53036	SW	Teacher	EM			RF	1965
Baganz Micah A	(262)613-8327 micah21us@yahoo.com	31385 W Hill Rd Hartland WI 53029	SW	Teacher	Tchr	Divine Redeemer Hartland WI	(262)367-3664	MQ	2003
Baginski John C	(618)420-4275 jcbag@yahoo.com	4 E Meadows Dr Altamont IL 62411	CI	Teacher	EM			RF	1969
Baglow Ryan T	(248)408-8460 rbaglow@lhsa.com	50716 Steed Dr Canton MI 48187	MI	Teacher	Tchr	LHS Assn Of Greater Detroit Rochester Hls MI	(248)856-0240	MQ	2013
Bagnara Alexander V			PSW	DCE	Tchr	Faith Las Vegas NV	(702)804-4400	IV	2015
Bahn Karen E Houck Dr	(715)305-8668 bahnk@trinitycr.org	48 Clive Dr NW Cedar Rapids IA 52405	IE	Teacher	Prin	Trinity Cedar Rapids IA	(319)362-6952	MQ	1988
Bahr Amber D Ockree	(217)883-7019 abahr@lsusfw.org	4716 Indiana Ave Fort Wayne IN 46807	IN	Teacher	Prin	South Unity Fort Wayne IN	(260)744-0459	CQ	2015
Bahr Angela	(217)553-9727 taabahr@yahoo.com	1210 S 115th St West Allis WI 53214	SW	Teacher	C08/2022			Other	2017
Bahr David M	(262)490-8104 davidbahr711@gmail.com	W233N6730 Nancy Dr Sussex WI 53089	SW	Teacher	C04/2024			RF	1987
Bahr Donald G	(512)925-5633 bahrdonald1@gmail.com	2101 Tall Withers CV Austin TX 78754	TX	Teacher	EM			S	1977
Bahr Janet L Young	(262)490-8101 janet.bahr@drlc.org	W233 N6730 Nancy Dr Sussex WI 53089	SW	Teacher	Prin	Divine Redeemer Hartland WI	(262)367-3664	RF	1987
Bahr Joel M	(616)350-3578 principal@fils.org	105 Charolais Dr Slinger WI 53086	SW	Teacher	EM			BR	1977
Bahr Joel S	(262)312-0608	4028 Fielding Dr North Olmsted OH 44070	OH	Teacher	Tchr	Cleveland LHS Association Rocky River OH	(440)356-7155	MQ	2010
Bahr Kenneth E	(262)255-4643 kenbet@twc.com	W158N9752 Broadleaf Ln Germantown WI 53022	SW	Teacher	EM			RF	1956
Bahr Kimberly A Fetz Deac	(320)497-0868 deac.kimberly@proton.me	11817 Monroe St NE Blaine MN 55434	MNN	Deaconess	C03/2017			FW-DEAC	2009
Bahr Lindsey M	(262)490-2637 lindsey.bahr294@gmail.com	W233N6730 Nancy Dr Sussex WI 53089	SW	Teacher	Tchr	Lake Country Hartland WI	(262)367-8600	SP	2022
Bahr Lisa A Banks	(913)486-3330 lbahr@lhskc.com	15553 W 163rd Ter Olathe KS 66062	MO	Teacher	Tchr	Kansas City Kansas City MO	(816)241-5478	CQ	2023
Bahr Mark M	(414)870-4097 mbahr@weteachtruth.org	403 Park Ct Hartland WI 53029	SW	Teacher	Tchr	LHS Assn of Greater Milwaukee West Allis WI	(414)421-9100	RF	1982
Bahr Natalie	(512)944-5911 nataliembahr@gmail.com	1207 N. Broadway Knoxville TN 37917	SE	Teacher	Tchr	Emmanuel Catonsville MD	(410)744-0015	AU	2016
Bahr Nathan D	(262)337-0408 nathan.bahr@lutheransouth.org	12555 Ryewater Dr # 1233 Houston TX 77089	TX	Teacher	Tchr	South Houston TX	(281)464-8299	CH	2012
Bahr Paul M	(414)462-6789 paulbahr@execpc.com	2865 Woodland Dr Jackson WI 53037	SW	Teacher	EM			RF	1973
Bahr Rachel A	(616)560-5395 rachelabahr@gmail.com	7005 Embers Ct Fort Wayne IN 46815	IN	Teacher	Tchr	Concordia Fort Wayne IN	(260)422-2429	MQ	2016
Bahr Timothy D	(262)490-8040 tbahr123@yahoo.com	1210 S 115th St West Allis WI 53214	SW	Teacher	Tchr	Martin Luther Greendale WI	(414)421-4000	CH	2017
Bahrns Elizabeth M	(217)821-2556 ebethie@gmail.com	225 W Calumet St Apt 8 Appleton WI 54915	SW	Teacher	Tchr	Trinity Menasha WI	(920)886-1083	MQ	2005
Bailes Cheryl G Wilkie	(281)513-8686 cgbailes@hotmail.com	9346 Amelia Dr Anderson TX 77830	TX	Teacher	Prin	Faith Huntsville TX	(936)291-1706	AU	1993
Bailey Bonnie J Banash	(931)210-4964 bonjon1968@gmail.com	52 Heather Glen Ct Crossville TN 38558	MDS	Teacher	EM			CQ	1986
Bailey Enith C Degler	(608)254-7793 enithbailey@hotmail.com	N9458 Pine Valley Ln Wisc Dells WI 53965	SW	Teacher	EM			SP	1969
Bailey Hayley G Carlove	(214)493-0733 hayleycarlove@yahoo.com	2826 Rosewood Blvd McKinney TX 75071	TX	Teacher	Tchr	Prince Of Peace Carrollton TX	(972)447-0532	AU	2018
Bailey Jonathon W	(620)655-5395 jonathon.bailey35@gmail.com	34 Deer Run Trail Climbing Hill IA 51015	IW	DCE	Mem C	Redeemer Sioux City IA	(712)276-1125	S	2019

*Multiple Assignments (See Church Worker Locator for Additional Details)

See Page 53 for the Table of Abbreviations for key to District, Classification, Position, and College abbreviations.

**C =Candidate; EM =Emeritus; the date following the C is the month and year the Candidate status began

NAME	TELEPHONE NUMBER EMAIL	STREET ADDRESS CITY/STATE/ZIP	DISTRICT	CLASS.	POSITION/ STATUS**	WHERE SERVING	OFFICE PHONE	COLLEGE/ UNIV/CQ	YR GRAD
Bailey Linda M Sund	lindabaileytlc@gmail.com	5512 Riverview Dr Lisle IL 60532	NI	Teacher	C10/2022			SP	1983
Bailey Pamela L Scheer	scheer33bailey@hotmail.com	10215 Dean Point Pl Orlando FL 32825	S	Teacher	Tchr	St Luke Oviedo FL	(407)365-3408	AA	1998
Bailey Susan E Neisch	(920)221-2049 baileysen@gmail.com	N3531 Fairground Ave Neillsville WI 54456	NW	Teacher	EM			RF	1980
Bailey-Mc Cray Kelly A Bailey	(541)480-8314 kbmccray@msn.com	2766 Glenview Drive Sierra Vista AZ 85650	NOW	DCE	EM			IV	1983
Bain Janeen A Schudde	(414)352-3759 janeen.bain@stjohnglendale.com	2208 W Mill Rd Glendale WI 53209	SW	Teacher	Tchr	St Johns Glendale WI	(414)352-4150	MQ	1989
Bain La Vaun M Lee Messer	(541)754-1514 bainlv@peak.org	3253 NW Harrison Blvd Corvallis OR 97330	NOW	Teacher	EM			RF	1971
Bair Cori M Lotz	(404)824-5858 baircori@gmail.com	625 High School St Collinsville IL 62234	MO	Teacher	Tchr	Salem Saint Louis MO	(314)352-4454	CQ	2007
Baird Barbara K Hall	(608)432-2129 bkbthreads@hotmail.com	717 Park St Baraboo WI 53913	SW	Teacher	EM			S	1969
Baisch Evelyn J Netz	(501)253-8393 ejbaisch@hotmail.com	4256 Meadowview Boulevard Ext New Castle PA 16105	S	Teacher	EM			RF	1969
Bajda Kaylyn A Anderson	(219)781-0175 kayanderson0329@gmail.com	5621 Homerlee Ave East Chicago IN 46312	IN	Teacher	Tchr	St Paul Munster IN	(219)836-6270	Other	2017
Bajus Luther J II	(920)457-9519 ljbsheb@charter.net	3210 S 11th Pl Sheboygan WI 53081	SW	Teacher	EM			RF	1977
Bajwa Rebekah A Beal	(408)930-4837 rebekahbajwa@gmail.com	59 Wrenwood Dr Clayton NC 27527	SE	DCE	Mem C	Holy Cross Clayton NC	(919)553-4784	S	2010
Bakalyar Judith A Samuel	(562)926-1752 judybakalyar@gmail.com	17914 Gerritt Pl Cerritos CA 90703	PSW	Teacher	EM			RF	1969
Bakalyar Kenneth W	(320)766-1719 dceandmrsb@gmail.com	3221 Reeds Villa Ct SW Alexandria MN 56308	MNN	DCE	EM			SP	1982
Baker Alissa A Asmus	(605) 254-0726 alissa.asmus2@gmail.com	108 French Ct Roberts WI 54023	MNS	Teacher	C07/2016			MQ	2010
Baker Jodene A Kabisch	(605)323-7849 gigi_n_me@hotmail.com	317 Brandon St Kingsley IA 51028	IW	DCE	EM			S	2000
Baker Kevin C	01-402-210-2840 kcbaker63@gmail.com	50 Gijangdaero Busan 619-9 KOREA	TX	Teacher	S Miss	Office of International Mission Saint Louis MO		S	1986
Baker Leah A Fuller	(405)822-0813 leahbaker498@yahoo.com	10312 NE 144th St Jones OK 73049	OK	Teacher	EM			CQ	2019
Baker Molly Goltl	(316)214-7155 Molly.Goltl@cune.org	9101 Lamar Ave Overland Park KS 66207	KS	Teacher	Tchr	Bethany Overland Park KS	(913)648-2228	S	2018
Baker Rachel P Selle	(920)987-5454 davidandrachel1@mac.com	P.O. Box 305 Poy Sippi WI 54967	SI	Teacher	C07/2016			S	1998
Bakker Anne E Anne Elizabeth Kosche Deac	(414)339-3759 annekbakker@gmail.com	8053 N 45th St Brown Deer WI 53223	SW	Deaconess	C04/2024			FW-DEAC	2017
Baldwin Alice F Houge	(719)269-1236 mommy_net@msn.com	559 W Slice Dr Pueblo West CO 81007	RM	Teacher	EM			S	1965
Baldwin Lana M Tobias	(813)716-1387 lanabaldwin1947@gmail.com	1994 Outer Circle Dr Oviedo FL 32765	FG	Teacher	EM			S	1969
Baldwin Thomas D	(336)971-1690 tbaldwin@stjohnsws.org	3212 Grouse Hollow Rd Winston Salem NC 27106	SE	DCM	Mem C	St John Winston-Salem NC	(336)725-1651	MQ	2012
Bales William	(865)363-9649 williambales76@gmail.com	1505 W Cottonwood Ln Mount Prospect IL 60056	NI	Teacher	Tchr	St John's Lombard IL	(630)932-3196	RF	2023
Balke William H	(503)805-7837 whbalke3@gmail.com	12154 SE 114th Ct Apt 321 Happy Valley OR 97086	NOW	Teacher	EM			S	1959
Ball Carol M Suhr	(630)251-0360 randyball@juno.com	9035 Skyline Dr Burr Ridge IL 60527	NI	Teacher	EM			CQ	1997
Ball Grace C Stults	(719)849-1001 grace.stults@cune.org	775 Wayne Ave Pocatello ID 83201	NOW	Teacher	Tchr	Grace Pocatello ID	(208)237-4142	S	2018
Ball Jared E	(208)915-7445 jball@gracepocatello.org	775 Wayne Ave Pocatello ID 83201	NOW	Teacher	Tchr	Grace Pocatello ID	(208)237-4142	PO	2017
Ball Rebecca Bierlein	(989)798-5301 rball@stlorenz.org	3406 S Reese Rd Frankenmuth MI 48734	MI	Teacher	Tchr	St Lorenz Frankenmuth MI	(989)652-6141	AA	2010
Ballard Erin C Wilson	(414)807-9789 emer54956@gmail.com	3170 N 81st St Milwaukee WI 53222	SW	Teacher	Prin	Mount Olive Milwaukee WI	(414)774-2200	MQ	2007
Ballard Lisa C Rocheleau	(503)577-2141 lisa.ballard.2011@gmail.com	17240 S Radfords View Ln Oregon City OR 97045	NOW	DCE	C09/2021			PO	2010
Ballard Nathan C	nathancballard@gmail.com		SW	DCM	C07/2022			MQ	2011
Ballesteros Kristine Zschernitz	(715)218-5049 kballesteras@immanuelbrookfield.org	N115W19680 Woodland Dr Germantown WI 53022	SW	Teacher	Tchr	Immanuel Brookfield WI	(262)781-7140	CQ	2018
Ballman Heather M Donnan	(507)330-2397 jhballman@gmail.com	47243 221st Ave Waterville MN 56096	MNS	DCE	C07/2016			PO	2002
Balsman Benjamin M	(815)298-7244 benjamin.balsman@gmail.com	9617 W Hampton Ave Wauwatosa WI 53225	SW	Teacher	Tchr	St Pauls West Allis WI	(414)541-6251	MQ	2012
Balsman Kate Yahr	(262)707-0428	W207 N17295 Parkview Dr Jackson WI 53037	SW	Teacher	Tchr	Living Word Jackson WI	(262)677-9353	MQ	2006
Balsters Sandra M Nieman	(618)377-9077 sbalsters@pv-farms.com	905 S Moreland Rd Bethalto IL 62010	SI	Teacher	EM			S	1975
Balzer Jo Ann Grote	(269)651-1418 joannbalzer@trinitysturgis.com	901 Canterbury Dr Sturgis MI 49091	MI	Teacher	Tchr	Trinity Sturgis MI	(269)651-4245	AA	1984
Balzum Mary J Prochnow	(612)735-1901 mjbalzum@hotmail.com	114 Reform St N Apt 211 Nya MN 55368	MNS	Teacher	EM			SP	1974
Bame Kelly J	kellyb@blcbls.org	10251 Ridgeline Dr #a266 Kennewick WA 99338	NOW	Teacher	Tchr	Bethlehem Kennewick WA	(509)582-5858	PO	2018
Bamesberger JoAnn Kitchen	(402)326-6607 jobames@icloud.com	8721 S Rivera Ct Aurora CO 80016	RM	Teacher	EM			CQ	1985

*Multiple Assignments (See Church Worker Locator for Additional Details)
See Page 53 for the Table of Abbreviations for key to District, Classification, Position, and College abbreviations.
**C =Candidate; EM =Emeritus; the date following the C is the month and year the Candidate status began

NAME	TELEPHONE NUMBER EMAIL	STREET ADDRESS CITY/STATE/ZIP	DISTRICT	CLASS.	POSITION/ STATUS**	WHERE SERVING	OFFICE PHONE	COLLEGE/ UNIV/CQ	YR GRAD
Bamsch Abigail Schaffer	(734)787-5543 abigailbamsch@gmail.com	3008 Albany Dr Mesquite TX 75150	TX	Teacher	Tchr	Prince Of Peace Carrollton TX	(972)447-0532	CH	2020
Bandelow Denise E Long	(217)624-2308	10499 Mansion Rd Loami IL 62661	CI	Teacher	EM			RF	1976
Baney Kara J Dunn	(308)370-1624 kara.baney@gmail.com	5805 N 128th St Omaha NE 68164	NEB	Teacher	C10/2022			S	2014
Baney Ryan H	(605)413-7707 ryan.h.baney@gmail.com	5805 N 128th St Omaha NE 68164	NEB	Teacher	Tchr	Concordia Omaha NE	(402)445-4000	S	2015
Bangert Amanda G Danek	(678)699-2345 amanda.bangert@cune.org	320 Mallard Ln Grand Island NE 68801	NEB	Teacher	Tchr	Trinity Grand Island NE	(308)382-5274	S	2006
Bangert Jason T	(832)270-7095 jbangert@lslancers.org	4663 Forest Valley Dr Saint Louis MO 63128	MO	Teacher	Tchr	Lutheran South Saint Louis MO	(314)631-1400	CH	2007
Bangert Jean M Hessenthaler	mamajean429@yahoo.com	532 Beneficial Way Saint Charles MO 63304	TX	Teacher	EM			RF	1978
Bangert Jessica E Theilen	jbangert86@gmail.com	4663 Forest Valley Dr Saint Louis MO 63128	MO	Teacher	Pro Stf	St Pauls Des Peres MO	(314)822-9219	RF	2008
Bangert Sandra J Buelow	(402)643-6340 sandy.bangert@messiah.us	1542 Plainview Ave Seward NE 68434	NEB	Teacher	Tchr	Messiah Lincoln NE	(402)489-3024	S	1982
Banholzer Eileen J Lierman	(208)326-5303	2020 E 3550 N Filer ID 83328	NOW	Teacher	EM			S	1964
Banks Erin K	(507)413-2067 erinbanks27@gmail.com	521 5th St E Wanamingo MN 55983	MNS	Teacher	Tchr	Faribault Faribault MN	(507)334-7982	CQ	2018
Banks-Ritter Laura L Banks	(812)522-6340 laurieritter@juno.com	833 Phillips Ln Seymour IN 47274	IN	Teacher	Tchr	St Peter Columbus IN	(812)372-5266	RF	1998
Banta Katharine E Pratt	(260)414-4951 kbanta85@gmail.com	10 Madera Dr Rochester NY 14624	EA	Teacher	C07/2016			RF	2008
Banwart Randolph J	(828)387-2854 rbanwart@charter.net	105 N Pinnacle Ridge Rd Apt 8 Beech Mtn NC 28604	SE	Teacher	EM			RF	1966
Baranski Leah E Mueller	(619)403-7226 leahbaranski@gmail.com	12248 Langley Hill Dr Fort Worth TX 76244	TX	Teacher	Tchr	Crown Of Life Colleyville TX	(817)251-1881	IV	2019
Barber Anna E Lange	(847)877-1011 dce85@aol.com	17439 Ohara Dr Pt Charlotte FL 33948	FG	Tch/DCE	EM			S	1985
Barber Sarah L Frank	(816)277-5460 sarahlovesdanbarber@gmail.com	6908 Hickory View Ln Chattanooga TN 37421	MDS	Teacher	Tchr	Belvoir Chattanooga TN	(423)622-3755	S	2006
Barckholtz Margaret L Mroch	(208)733-9492 mlbarckholtz@gmail.com	614 N Pointe Dr Twin Falls ID 83301	NOW	Teacher	EM			RF	1962
Barcus Kaylie J Scott	(657)243-7244 kbarcus93@gmail.com	245 E Lincoln Ave Apt 15 Orange CA 92865	PSW	Teacher	Tchr	St Johns Orange CA	(714)288-4406	IV	2016
Bardeleben Alan	(217)855-5980 abardeleben@yahoo.com	2423 W Forest Ave Decatur IL 62522	CI	Tch/DCE	EM			RF	1982
Bardeleben Angela Y Curry	(765)714-5949 angelabardeleben@gmail.com	2510 Kingsbury Dr Charlotte NC 28205	PSW	Teacher	C09/2022			CQ	2020
Barefoot Joy G Malchow	(402)637-9962 joy.barefoot@zionkearney.org	1832 W 50th Street Kearney NE 68845	NEB	Teacher	Tchr	Zion Kearney NE	(308)234-3410	S	1989
Bargen Christine A Kiehl	(636)940-9005 chris.bargen@sbcglobal.net	3286 Principia Ave Saint Charles MO 63301	MO	Teacher	EM			S	1976
Baringer Brooke A Kabobel	(507)206-6797 brooke.baringer@gmail.com	6030 Woodcock Cir Roanoke VA 24018	MNS	Teacher	C06/2022			AA	1997
Baringer Todd R	(614)406-5201 todd.baringer@gmail.com	6030 Woodcock Cir Roanoke VA 24018	MNS	Teacher	C07/2022			CQ	2011
Barker Autumn M Carter	(810)824-2975 autumn.barker95@gmail.com	12107 Sharp Rd Linden MI 48451	MI	Teacher	C04/2022			AA	2018
Barkhau Alvin L	(847)659-8663	4141 N Rockton Ave Rockford IL 61103	NI	Teacher	EM			RF	1958
Barkley Sarah J Bode Deac	(224)430-3323 sfootloser@gmail.com	1117 Eisner Ave Sheboygan WI 53083	NW	Deaconess	C07/2016			FW-DEAC	2010
Barlau Amanda K Kaisler	(812)968-9138 amakayek@gmail.com	P.O. Box 172 Lester Prairie MN 55354	MNS	Teacher	C03/2017			MQ	2007
Barlow Emily M Guynn	(440)749-1594 guynne@gmail.com		SO	Teacher	C06/2025			AA	2007
Barlow Susan	(515)333-1607 sue.barlow@molcs.org	5920 Aspen Cir Johnston IA 50131	IW	Teacher	Tchr	Mount Olive Des Moines IA	(515)277-8349	S	2010
Barnard Anne L Wahnefried	(501)626-8834 abarnard@flsbenton.com	916 Country Estates Rd Benton AR 72019	MDS	Teacher	Tchr	First Benton AR	(501)317-1325	AA	2001
Barnes Audrey J Peterson		919 County Road 123 Wharton TX 77488	TX	Teacher	EM			S	1970
Barnes Katrina L Hack	(360)566-5914	3304 W St Vancouver WA 98663	NOW	DCE	C07/2016			SP	1988
Barnes Richard M	(901)757-3815 rbarnes@immanuelmemphis.org	4202 Cedar Point Rd Lakeland TN 38002	MDS	Teacher	EM			SP	1978
Barnes Susan M	(586)228-9390	47898 Lexington Dr Macomb MI 48044	MI	Teacher	Tchr	Immanuel Macomb MI	(586)286-7076	CQ	2013
Barnett Michelle D Bode	(812)522-8574 mbarnett@whitecreek.org	11980 Moores Vineyard Columbus IN 47201	IN	Teacher	Tchr	White Creek Columbus IN	(812)342-6832	CQ	2014
Barney Mary L Barretta Deac	(260)445-9249 barneymary70@yahoo.com	4911 Fairington Dr Apt 121 Fort Wayne IN 46825	IN	Deaconess	EM			CQ	2001
Barnholt Aaron M	(260)403-5661 aaron@deeplyrootedtogrow.org	7316 Abington Dr Fort Wayne IN 46835	IN	Teacher	Tchr	Sub Bethlehem Fort Wayne IN	(260)484-7873	CQ	2012
Barnhouse Krista K Radke	(402)477-6461 kbarnhouse@faithlincoln.org	1809 SW 32nd St Lincoln NE 68522	NEB	Teacher	Prin	Faith Lincoln NE	(402)466-7402	S	1995
Barningham Nola L Losser		1259 Saint James Ct Middleton ID 83644	NOW	Teacher	EM			PO	1981
Baron Ananda C Smallwood	(618)567-0045 abaron80@sbcglobal.net	9101 Avebury Ct Columbia IL 62236	SI	Teacher	Tchr	Zion Belleville IL	(618)234-0275	S	2002
Barone Megan M Geu	(308)455-0083 megan@weservestrong.com	3606 11th Ave Kearney NE 68845	NEB	DCE	Mem C	Holy Cross Kearney NE	(308)237-2944	S	2009

*Multiple Assignments (See Church Worker Locator for Additional Details)

See Page 53 for the Table of Abbreviations for key to District, Classification, Position, and College abbreviations.

**C =Candidate; EM =Emeritus; the date following the C is the month and year the Candidate status began

NAME	TELEPHONE NUMBER EMAIL	STREET ADDRESS CITY/STATE/ZIP	DISTRICT	CLASS.	POSITION/ STATUS**	WHERE SERVING	OFFICE PHONE	COLLEGE/ UNIV/CQ	YR GRAD
Barr Andrew K	(815)439-5930 aknaebarr@aol.com	1814 Olde Mill Rd Plainfield IL 60586	NI	Teacher	EM			RF	1962
Barr Jennifer Cannon	(817)228-2292	7801 Blossom Dr Fort Worth TX 76133	TX	Teacher	Tchr	St Paul Fort Worth TX	(817)332-2281	CQ	2012
Barreto Blythe A Harkennder	(346)293-6306 blytheann13@gmail.com	259 SW Panther Trce Port Saint Lucie FL 34953	FG	DCE	C07/2022			CH	2014
Barrie Pamela M Wilson	(989)742-4049 barriep@immanuelalpena.org	24055 Hunt Rd Hillman MI 49746	MI	Teacher	EM			S	1975
Barrington Abigail	(217)622-2214 barringtona3@gmail.com	618 Hayes Ave Racine WI 53405	SW	Teacher	Tchr	Lutheran High School Racine WI	(262)637-6538	SP	2023
Barrington Madelyn	(217)622-2987 madelynbarrington@gmail.com	5 San Miguel Dr Saint Charles MO 63303	MO	Teacher	Tchr	Immanuel Saint Charles MO	(636)946-0051	CH	2021
Barron Sarah A Linde	(651)428-9474 linde@csp.edu	1468 129th St New Richmond WI 54017	MNS	Teacher	Tchr	Hand In Hand Saint Paul MN	(651)641-8491	SP	2004
Barron Valadez Maria E Deac	(214)431-6009 maryebarron07@gmail.com	534 Santa Fe Ln Royse City TX 75189	TX	Deaconess	Mem C	Comunidad Cristiana Rockwall TX	(214)395-6222	SL-DEAC	2024
Barry Erin K Shidner	(562)676-7257 eshidner@gmail.com	3627 Lynbrook Dr Toledo OH 43614	OH	Teacher	Tchr	Trinity Toledo OH	(419)385-2651	IV	2000
Barry Katherine E Kitzerow	(763)290-9544 kbarry678@yahoo.com	321 Oak St North Chaska MN 55318	MNS	Teacher	C07/2016			MQ	2008
Bartell Marvin H Dr	(708)209-3133 marv.bartell@cuchicago.edu	1704 N 77th Ave Elmwood Park IL 60707	NI	Teacher	EM			RF	1961
Bartels Elizabeth	lbartels@stlorenz.org	23 Wilshire Dr Frankenmuth MI 48734	MI	Teacher	Tchr	St Lorenz Frankenmuth MI	(989)652-6141	SP	2015
Bartels Jack D	(240)604-6086 jackbartels@aol.com	209 Streamwood Dr Holly Springs NC 27540	SE	Teacher	EM			S	1966
Bartels Jennifer	(402)786-3474 jennkbartels@yahoo.com	10461 N 143rd St Waverly NE 68462	NEB	Teacher	Tchr	Faith Lincoln NE	(402)466-7402	S	2016
Bartels Judy K Gerken	(402)300-0153 bjbartels@yahoo.com	569 County Road U Tobias NE 68453	NEB	Teacher	EM			S	1971
Bartels Kathy L Bauman	(785)213-6154 kbartels818@gmail.com	1815 SW High Ave Topeka KS 66604	KS	Teacher	EM			S	1990
Bartels Kevin W	(573)579-7257	2116 County Road 350 Millersville MO 63766	MO	Teacher	Tchr	Immanuel Perryville MO	(573)547-6161	RF	1982
Bartels Renee L Groff	(952)467-3461	306 Oak Dr Young America MN 55397	MNS	Teacher	Tchr	St John Norwood Yng America MN	(952)467-3461	SP	1982
Bartelt Kristine S Redeker	(224)232-7090 kbartelt@immanuel-ed.org	132 N Wisconsin St Carpentersvle IL 60110	NI	Teacher	Tchr	Immanuel East Dundee IL	(847)428-1010	RF	1986
Bartelt Rebecca K	+886903337255 rebeccabartelt@hotmail.com	15005 Tibbles St Omaha NE 68116	NEB	Teacher	S Miss	Office of International Mission Saint Louis MO		CQ	2007
Barth Kyle T	(262)720-8676 kbarth@milwaukeelutheran.org	N86W15664 Shore Crest Dr Menomonee Falls WI 53051	SW	Teacher	Tchr	Milwaukee LHS Milwaukee WI	(414)461-6000	MQ	2010
Barthel Teresa L Heiden	(920)284-2286 teresabarthel@yahoo.com	1965 Lepak Dr Plover WI 54467	NW	Teacher	C02/2023			MQ	2000
Bartholomew Diana L Brunner	(414)588-4908 dianabartholomew13@gmail.com	10143 Haymarket Peak Ave. Las Vegas NV 89166	PSW	Teacher	C04/2024			MQ	1986
Bartholow Christian O	(321)704-6878 christianb@christ4u.net	c/o Christ The King Lutheran Church 3803 W Lake Houston Pkwy Kingwood TX 77339	TX	DCE	Mem C	Christ King Kingwood TX	(281)360-7936	AU	2017
Bartlett Krista A Reindel	(586)421-5313 kbartlett@immlutheran.org	4914 Brookside Ln Washington MI 48094	MI	Teacher	Tchr	Immanuel Macomb MI	(586)286-4231	CQ	2020
Bartok Kimberly J Reimann	(734)552-7858 kj2r@yahoo.com	2610 S Lilac St Ozark MO 65721	MO	DCE	C07/2016			RF	2004
Bartok Sarah M	smbartok@gmail.com		MO	Teacher	Tchr	Redeemer Springfield MO	(417)883-5717	AA	2014
Barton David F	(815)238-2427 dbarton5472@gmail.com	719 Alamo Dr Freeport IL 61032	NI	DCM	Mem C	Our Redeemer Freeport IL	(815)232-6934	CQ	2021
Barton Nicole Schuchman	(303)929-5976 nicolembarton@yahoo.com	10683 Braesheather Ct Hghlnds Ranch CO 80126	RM	Teacher	Tchr	Shepherd Hills Centennial CO	(303)798-0711	IV	2004
Bartz Bradley M	(325)260-1255 bradley.bartz777@gmail.com	3810 Radcliff Rd Abilene TX 79602	TX	DCE	C08/2021			SP	2013
Basham Megan M Coburn	(612)720-5376 mmbasham87@yahoo.com	14440 Quinn Dr NW Andover MN 55304	MNS	Teacher	Tchr	St John Corcoran MN	(763)420-2426	MQ	2009
Bass Gerod R	gerod@oslc.com	8004 65th Ave E Puyallup WA 98371	NOW	DCE	Mem C	Our Savior Tacoma WA	(253)531-2112	PO	1997
Bass Jamie L Kettler	(501)580-4006 jamie@jamieleecb.com	751 Soaring Dr Marietta GA 30062	FG	DCE	C07/2016			S	2008
Bass Katy R Grimes	(409)790-9835 katy.bass@gsmics.org	7506 Sika Deer Way Ft Myers FL 33966	FG	DCE	Mem C	St Michael Fort Myers FL	(239)939-1218	RF	2003
Bassett Nathan C	(402)570-2360 nbassett@lincolnlutheran.org	430 Hazelwood Dr Lincoln NE 68510	NEB	Teacher	Tchr	Lincoln Lincoln NE	(402)467-5404	S	1993
Bassuener Jennifer A Jording	(815)236-0928 jbassuen@gmail.com	580 Kennedy St Marengo IL 60152	NI	Teacher	EM			MQ	1990
Bates Andrew B	deaconbates@hotmail.com		MO	DCE	S Ex/S	The LCMS Corporate Saint Louis MO	(314)965-9000	RF	2000
Bates Janice A Grosskopf	(952)201-4074 janbates92@aol.com	17686 SE 92nd Grantham Ter The Villages FL 32162	MNS	Teacher	EM			SP	1987
Bates Lauren B Luedtke	(636)751-3422 laurenbethbates@yahoo.com	1217 Sonoma Way Pacific MO 63069	MO	DCE	Mem C	St Mark Eureka MO	(636)938-4432	S	2004
Bates Tracy M Jopp	(612)590-3468 t115332@gmail.com	14925 50th St Mayer MN 55360	MNS	Teacher	Tchr	Redeemer Wayzata MN	(952)473-1281	MQ	1999
Bathke Janice M Koehneke	(920)886-5116 jkoehneke@yahoo.com	2249 Vesterheim St Eau Claire WI 54703	NW	Teacher	EM			RF	1971
Battaile Laura J Beune	(330)591-5282 laurabattaile@gmail.com	19794 E Kerry Pl Strongsville OH 44149	OH	Teacher	Tchr	Royal Redeemer North Royalton OH	(440)237-7958	S	2003

*Multiple Assignments (See Church Worker Locator for Additional Details)
See Page 53 for the Table of Abbreviations for key to District, Classification, Position, and College abbreviations.
**C =Candidate; EM =Emeritus; the date following the C is the month and year the Candidate status began

NAME	TELEPHONE NUMBER EMAIL	STREET ADDRESS CITY/STATE/ZIP	DISTRICT	CLASS.	POSITION/ STATUS**	WHERE SERVING	OFFICE PHONE	COLLEGE/ UNIV/CQ	YR GRAD
Battle Joe L	(573)275-5213 joe.battle@outlook.com	4761 SW 1st Ter Ocala FL 34471	FG	Teacher	EM			RF	1963
Battu Rao Grace V Deac	raogv57@yahoo.com	1418 Whispering Creek Dr Ballwin MO 63027	SW	Deaconess	RSO	A Place Of Refuge Ministries Milwaukee WI	(414)438-2767	RF	2000
Batty Jennifer L Stock	(847)352-1837 jenstock78@aol.com	421 Chapel Dr Collinsville IL 62234	SI	Teacher	Tchr	Good Shepherd Collinsville IL	(618)344-3153	RF	2000
Bauck Diane K Sieling	(928)660-8496 diane.bauck@gmail.com	325 9th St SW Perham MN 56573	MNN	Teacher	EM			S	1975
Bauder Karen F Groteluschen	(224)587-6190 karenbauder1942@gmail.com	962 Oak Ridge Blvd Elgin IL 60120	NI	Teacher	EM			S	1964
Bauder Terri J Auger	(402)728-5261 terri_bauder@hotmail.com	202 Gordon St Waco NE 68460	NEB	Teacher	EM			SP	1981
Bauer Arlin J	(660)438-3250 arlinbauer@hotmail.com	800 S Fowler St Cole Camp MO 65325	MO	Teacher	EM			S	1966
Bauer Benjamin	(503)686-1258 thes5_11@hotmail.com	425 Northridge Dr Kalispell MT 59901	NOW	Teacher	Tchr	Forest Hills Cornelius OR	(503)359-4853	PO	2006
Bauer Elizabeth M Spencer	(402)641-2081 elizabeth.bauer@cune.org	P.O. Box 211 Kremmling CO 80459	RM	Teacher	C07/2016			S	2008
Bauer Heidi G Gruetzmacher	(414)322-3973 heidigbauer@hotmail.com	1394 Bluebird Dr Oconomowoc WI 53066	SW	Teacher	Tchr	Divine Redeemer Hartland WI	(262)367-3664	MQ	1995
Bauer Judith E Niemeyer	(219)432-7620	11323 Bittersweet Creek Run Fort Wayne IN 46814	IN	Teacher	EM			RF	1968
Bauer Kaitlin E Unruh	(561)405-1119 texasbauers@gmail.com	21 Founders Way Unit A Saint Louis MO 63105	TX	DCE	Tchr	Prince Of Peace Carrollton TX	(972)447-0532	CH	2010
Bauer Karen M Warkenthien	(312)209-8486 bauerkaren78@gmail.com	1001 Oeffling Ct McHenry IL 60051	NI	Teacher	EM			RF	1978
Bauer Kerry L Cullen	(503)686-1258 kerrylena@gmail.com	425 Northridge Dr Kalispell MT 59901	NOW	DCE	Mem C	Bethlehem Aloha OR	(503)649-3380	PO	2005
Bauer Kristi K Kuhl	kbauer@csp.edu	2020 Pine St Hastings MN 55033	MNS	DCE	S HS/C	Concordia University St Paul Saint Paul MN	(651)641-8278	SP	2013
Bauer Laura R Shoemaker Deac	(231)392-4267 laurabsdg@gmail.com	7511 Secor Rd Traverse City MI 49685	MI	Deaconess	RSO	Good Friend Ministries Traverse City MI	(231)590-8527	SL-DEAC	2025
Bauer Melissa M Miller	(443)618-5648 itroy@gmail.com	16193 County Road P Napoleon OH 43545	OH	Teacher	Tchr	St Paul Napoleon OH	(419)592-3535	S	2001
Bauer Noah L	(719)338-4364 noahsdg@gmail.com	7 Founders Way Unit A St. Louis MO 63105	EN	DCE	C07/2025			RF	2019
Bauer Todd D	(248)770-9836 toddandsteph2007@gmail.com	608 Ludlow Ave Rochester MI 48307	MI	Teacher	C09/2022			CQ	2006
Bauer Troy W	(443)618-5648 iptroy@gmail.com	1075 Glenwood Ave Napoleon OH 43545	OH	Teacher	Tchr	St Paul Napoleon OH	(419)592-3535	S	2000
Bauer Vivian V Harley	(707)765-0946	1736 E Madison St Petaluma CA 94954	CNH	Teacher	EM			S	1988
Bauern Kristen J De Gree	(714)721-0955 kristenbauern@gmail.com	10092 Sprit Cir Huntingtn Bch CA 92646	PSW	Teacher	Tchr	Christ Costa Mesa CA	(949)548-6866	IV	2003
Baugham Carol E Belitz	(757)867-6148 carolebteach@cox.net	101 Chanticlair Dr Yorktown VA 23693	SE	Teacher	EM			SP	1966
Baughman Kristina L Schulenburg	(317)407-7558 baughmanclan@att.net	3951 Fieldview Rd Lake Orion MI 48360	MI	Teacher	Prin	Northwest Rochester Hills MI	(248)856-0240	MQ	1996
Bauknecht Nathan J	(715)889-4213 njbauk@gmail.com	11520 Cty Rd M Crandon WI 54520	SW	Teacher	Tchr	First Immanuel Cedarburg WI	(262)377-6610	MQ	2023
Bauman Jacqueline N	(920)350-6900 jbauman@stjohnsportage.com	P.O. Box 55 Wyocena WI 53969	SW	Teacher	Tchr	St Johns Portage WI	(608)742-9000	CQ	2015
Bauman Michelle A Bridges	(812)350-2732 dmbauman@sbcglobal.net	3019 Revere Ct Columbus IN 47203	IN	Teacher	RSO	Lutherans for Life Nevada IA	(888)364-5433	S	1998
Baumann Gregory J	(320)543-2310 gbaumann429@yahoo.com	P.O. Box 492 Howard Lake MN 55349	MNS	Teacher	EM			S	1983
Baumann Joshua L	(314)302-6682 joshua.baumann@zionmayer.org	2203 Hope Ave Lester Pr MN 55354	MNS	Teacher	Prin	Zion Mayer MN	(952)657-2339	RF	2002
Baumann Katherine J Taege	(314)302-6663 katiebaumann@hotmail.com	2203 Hope Ave Lester Pr MN 55354	MNS	Teacher	C07/2016			RF	2003
Baumann Katie A	(864)784-8120 dce@gslcflock.org	9279 Lawford Way Apt. 203 Ooltewah TN 37363	MDS	DCE	Mem C	Good Shepherd Chattanooga TN	(423)629-4661	IV	2019
Baumann Leah M Olson	(507)830-0532 leaholson@yahoo.com	402 Smith Ave Heron Lake MN 56137	MNS	Teacher	C07/2016			CQ	2007
Baumann Russell G	(920)889-7395 baumann.russellg@gmail.com	4612 Lasley St Montague MI 49437	MI	DCM	Mem C	Saint James Montague MI	(231)894-8471	MQ	2010
Baumbach Nina L Klepacki	(218)464-8329 ninabaumbach@gmail.com	7204 S Heatherridge Ave Sioux Falls SD 57108	MNN	Teacher	C07/2016			S	2000
Baumgarn Carol Kolander	(320)276-8215 jrb0627@tds.net	15653 154th St NE Hawick MN 56273	MNN	Teacher	EM			S	1964
Baumgarn Jeanette S Friedrich	(507)227-5792 jenevergreen17@gmail.com	319 Meadow Lane Benson MN 56215	SW	Teacher	C02/2024			SP	1990
Baumgartel Ennis J	(760)219-2538 ennis444@gmail.com	P.O. Box 373 Idyllwild CA 92549	PSW	Teacher	EM			RF	1973
Baumgartel Jill M Saunders	(812)530-7095 baumsix@gmail.com	1214 W Park Ave Norfolk NE 68701	NEB	Teacher	Tchr	St John Battle Creek NE	(402)675-3605	S	2000
Baumgartel Jonathan J	(812)530-0044 jbaumgartel@stjohnbc.net	1214 W Park Ave Norfolk NE 68701	NEB	Teacher	Tchr	St John Battle Creek NE	(402)675-3605	S	1996
Baumgartner Brittany M Deac	(907)310-0341 brittybaum@gmail.com		NOW	Deaconess	Mem C	Our Redeemer Chugiak AK	(907)688-2157	FW-DEAC	2018
Bausch Rachel E Helland	(636)248-3559 rbausch@stjstl.net	567 Oaktree Crossing Ct Ballwin MO 63021	MO	Teacher	Tchr	Pathfinder Ellisville MO	(636)394-4100	S	1999
Baxter Juliann M Gust	(920)757-5722 julibaxter@shepherdhills.org	W6475 Greenville Dr Greenville WI 54942	NW	Teacher	Mem C	Shepherd Hills Greenville WI	(920)757-5722	SP	1974
Baxter Matthew J Dr	(541)620-1739 dr.baxter@alsalaska.org	320 High View Dr Anchorage AK 99518	NOW	Teacher	Tchr	Anchor Anchorage AK	(907)522-3636	CQ	2024

*Multiple Assignments (See Church Worker Locator for Additional Details)

See Page 53 for the Table of Abbreviations for key to District, Classification, Position, and College abbreviations.

**C =Candidate; EM =Emeritus; the date following the C is the month and year the Candidate status began

NAME	TELEPHONE NUMBER EMAIL	STREET ADDRESS CITY/STATE/ZIP	DISTRICT	CLASS.	POSITION/ STATUS**	WHERE SERVING	OFFICE PHONE	COLLEGE/ UNIV/CQ	YR GRAD
Baye Megan E Tindall	(248)759-8029 megan.baye@gmail.com	715 S Superior St De Pere WI 54115	NW	Teacher	C07/2016			MQ	2006
Baye Peter G	(920)246-3799 Peter@kingofkings.org	King Of Kings Lutheran Church 11615 I St Omaha NE 68137	NEB	Teacher	Tchr	King Of Kings Omaha NE	(402)333-6464	S	2009
Bayer Roxanne M Kudrna	(402)260-9393 rambayer@hotmail.com	1505 North St Marysville KS 66508	KS	Teacher	Tchr	Good Shepherd Marysville KS	(785)562-3181	S	1985
Bayles Johanna E Biggs	(217)201-9737	3611 N Woodridge Dr Decatur IL 62526	CI	Teacher	Tchr	Luth School Assoc Decatur IL	(217)233-2001	RF	1996
Bayless Ashley N Forseth Deac	(210)639-8746 anbayless@gmail.com	15326 E 22nd Ave Spokane Valley WA 99037	NOW	Deaconess	Aux	LLL/Lutheran Hour Ministries Saint Louis MO	(314)317-4100	SL-DEAC	2010
Beal Janelle C Arenz	(425)273-6315 janelle.christiana23@gmail.com	13002 44th Ave SE Everett WA 98208	NOW	Tch/DPM	Mem C	Lamb of God Seattle WA	(206)363-0110	CQ	2014
Beale Zeal Kirkpatrick	(504)427-3999 zealbeale@aol.com	2462 Burgundy St New Orleans LA 70117	SO	DCE	Mem C	St Paul New Orleans LA	(504)945-3741	CQ	2006
Beardsley Ronald L	(810)923-4023 beards.ronald0848@gmail.com	163 Shadowline Dr Apt 314 Boone NC 28607	SE	Teacher	EM			S	1958
Beaty Karen A Hamman	(636)795-5958 tkbeaty@hotmail.com	1670 Deergrass Dr Saint Charles MO 63303	MO	Teacher	EM			S	1972
Beaudean Talitha L Hoffstetter	(573)275-0481 tbeaudean@saxonylutheranhigh.org	208 Hinterland Dr Jackson MO 63755	MO	Teacher	Tchr	Saxony Jackson MO	(573)204-7555	CQ	2009
Beaudoin James M	(714)225-6300 jimbeaudoin37@yahoo.com	10531 S 181st Ave Goodyear AZ 85338	PSW	Teacher	EM			S	1982
Beaver Amanda K Johnson Dr	amanda.k.beaver@gmail.com		PSW	Teacher	Tchr	Trinity Litchfield Park AZ	(623)935-4665	CQ	2014
Beaver Elissa M Schulte	(314)952-1146 ebeaver@ilsc.org	1025 Pearview Dr Saint Peters MO 63376	MO	Teacher	Tchr	Immanuel Saint Charles MO	(636)946-0051	MQ	1998
Beaver-Perez Nichole L Beaver	(512)965-1864 nichole.perez@outlook.com	6713 Divers Loons St North Las Vegas NV 89084	PSW	Teacher	Tchr	Lamb Of God Las Vegas NV	(702)645-1626	MQ	2002
Beavers Jeffrey S Dr	(949)387-1199 dr.beavers@creanlutheran.org	4406 E Larkstone Cir Orange CA 92869	PSW	Teacher	Tchr	Crean Irvine CA	(949)387-1199	CQ	2002
Beccue Lester O	(760)807-9319 lester@beccue.com	1139 S Spruce St Escondido CA 92025	PSW	Teacher	EM			RF	1957
Beck Julia N Schaller	(260)414-4805 julia.beck68@gmail.com	6404 Oak Bridge Pl Fort Wayne IN 46835	IN	Teacher	RSO	Ascension Fort Wayne IN	(260)486-2226	CQ	2014
Beck Julie R Zipay	(314)605-4167 jbeck@ccls-stlouis.org	4200 Massabielle Dr Saint Louis MO 63129	MO	Teacher	Tchr	Christ Community Kirkwood MO	(314)822-7774	CQ	2023
Beck Leah R Matson	(763)360-6075 livingwithgraceandhope@live.com	17968 Tyler St NW Elk River MN 55330	MNS	Teacher	Tchr	St John Elk River MN	(763)441-6616	SP	2001
Beck Luke E	(608)415-1591 beckspot2000@yahoo.com	17216 N 33rd Ave Apt 2041 Phoenix AZ 85053	PSW	Teacher	Tchr	Atonement Glendale AZ	(623)374-3019	CQ	2006
Beckendorf Jana J	(952)457-3436 jana.beckendorf@stjohns-chaska.org	2190 Shamrock Pl Chaska MN 55318	MNS	Teacher	Tchr	Saint Johns Chaska MN	(952)448-2433	SP	2001
Becker Alvina C Chronis	(314)452-0287 wabecker73@gmail.com	2396 Daisy Tree Rd Saint Cloud FL 34771	S	Teacher	EM			S	1974
Becker Angela J Dobbertien	(402) 274-7259 Angbabe71@gmail.com	1815 23rd St Auburn NE 68305	NEB	Teacher	C07/2016			S	1994
Becker Beverly J Gerken	(440)864-5930 becker7375@gmail.com	4595 Ashbury Park Dr North Olmsted OH 44070	OH	Teacher	EM			S	1977
Becker Bryce E	(618)920-1500 brycebecker@stjls-mattoon.com	1300 S 12th St Apt 6 Mattoon IL 61938	CI	Teacher	Tchr	St Johns Mattoon IL	(217)234-4911	MQ	2022
Becker Carla J Oswald	(920)467-4967 cbecker80@me.com	14404 Soaring Hawk Trl Hoagland IN 46745	IN	Teacher	EM			RF	1984
Becker Carrie A	(956)532-4005 teachyteachy07@hotmail.com	471 W Hendricks St Shelbyville IN 46176	IN	Teacher	Tchr	St Peter Columbus IN	(812)372-1571	AA	2007
Becker Cena C Burdeen	(847)960-7226 cbecker@immanuel-ed.org	118 Indian Trl Lk In The Hls IL 60156	NI	Teacher	Tchr	Immanuel East Dundee IL	(847)428-4477	RF	1996
Becker Connie S Hadley	(501)920-8062 csbrltiks06@outlook.com	959 Wayside Rd Westphalia KS 66093	KS	Teacher	EM			S	1970
Becker Esther R Engelbrecht	(217)825-9854 erbecker86@gmail.com	9841 E 1600th Ave Effingham IL 62401	CI	Teacher	C04/2025			S	1972
Becker Gregory N	(920)207-4144	14404 Soaring Hawk Trl Hoagland IN 46745	IN	Teacher	EM			RF	1982
Becker Hannah M Schneiderman Deac	(814)421-8516 hannah.becker2714@gmail.com	8027 Butt Rd E Woodburn IN 46797	IN	Deaconess	Mem C	Promise Fort Wayne IN	(260)493-9953	CH	2015
Becker Jason P	(217)690-9102 beckerjpaul@gmail.com		MO	Teacher	Tchr	Lutheran North Saint Louis MO	(314)389-3100	Other	2017
Becker Jennifer N	(636)373-0485 jenniferbdce@gmail.com	1486 McKelvey Rd Maryland Heights MO 63043	MO	DCE	C12/2021			CH	2017
Becker Jeremy M	(954)873-3365 jbecker@stpaulweston.org	13349 NW 7th St Plantation FL 33325	FG	Tch/DCE	Mem C	St Paul Weston FL	(954)384-9096	RF	1999
Becker Joel C	(336)922-3316 jrunitas2@aol.com	3 E Ring Factory Rd Bel Air MD 21014	SE	Teacher	EM			RF	1965
Becker Julianne M Thompson	(414)377-5997 jillbecker@hotmail.com	N72W5321 Georgetown Dr Cedarburg WI 53012	SW	Teacher	EM			CQ	1985
Becker Kenneth J	(847)651-2482 k-becker@comcast.net	1951 Dorchester Ave Algonquin IL 60102	NI	Teacher	EM			RF	1968
Becker Kevin J	(847)508-1904 teacherbecker@hotmail.com	118 Indian Trl Lk In The Hls IL 60156	NI	Teacher	Prin	Immanuel East Dundee IL	(847)428-1010	RF	1996
Becker Kimberle L Wright	(517) 819-9630 kbecker@oursaviorlansing.org	2635 Little Hickory Dr Lansing MI 48911	MI	Teacher	Tchr	Our Savior Lansing MI	(517)882-8665	AA	1987
Becker Kristin A Stock	(314)520-4204 kbecker@oursaviorplantation.org	13349 NW 7th St Plantation FL 33325	FG	Teacher	Tchr	Our Savior Plantation FL	(954)473-6888	RF	1998

*Multiple Assignments (See Church Worker Locator for Additional Details)
See Page 53 for the Table of Abbreviations for key to District, Classification, Position, and College abbreviations.
**C =Candidate; EM =Emeritus; the date following the C is the month and year the Candidate status began

NAME	TELEPHONE NUMBER EMAIL	STREET ADDRESS CITY/STATE/ZIP	DISTRICT	CLASS.	POSITION/ STATUS**	WHERE SERVING	OFFICE PHONE	COLLEGE/ UNIV/CQ	YR GRAD
Becker Landon L	(512)665-3109 DCEBECKER@gmail.com	129 Pear Tree Ln Austin TX 78737	TX	DCE	C07/2018			RF	2002
Becker Mary J Koehn	(319)365-5290 mary3647@hotmail.com	3921 Red Cedar Dr NE Cedar Rapids IA 52402	IE	Teacher	EM			S	1974
Becker Michael D	(210)241-3955 beckertex@sbcglobal.net	7607 Stone Crop Ln San Antonio TX 78249	TX	Teacher	EM			RF	1983
Becker Michael R	(440)221-4321 Becke7573@gmail.com	4595 Ashbury Park Dr North Olmsted OH 44070	OH	Teacher	EM			S	1978
Becker Nicola R Rusnak	(314)972-4086 nbecker@sjlarnold.org	3077 Shelley Lynn Dr Arnold MO 63010	MO	Teacher	Tchr	St John Arnold MO	(636)464-7303	RF	2003
Becker Peter	(920)627-5126	8027 Butt Rd E Woodburn IN 46797	IN	Teacher	Tchr	Central New Haven IN	(260)493-2502	Other	2015
Becker Timothy J	(219)617-6663 tbecker@immanuelvalpo.org	156 John Glenn Dr Valparaiso IN 46383	IN	Teacher	Tchr	Immanuel Valparaiso IN	(219)462-8207	RF	1994
Becker William F	(618)282-2958 wdbecker@htc.net	1116 Teal Dr Red Bud IL 62278	SI	Teacher	Tchr	St John Red Bud IL	(618)282-3873	RF	1994
Beckman April H Clausen	(651)338-0354 beckmanal@hotmail.com	2111 Baihly Summit Dr SW Rochester MN 55902	MNS	DPM	Mem C	Redeemer Rochester MN	(507)289-5147	SP	2005
Beckman Austin T	(702)238-2658 austintbeckman@gmail.com	7622 Aspen Color St Las Vegas NV 89139	PSW	Teacher	Tchr	Faith Las Vegas NV	(702)804-4400	S	2011
Beckman Emily E Bernards	(714)281-8963	4 Vintage Way Trabuco Canyon CA 92679	PSW	Teacher	S HS/C	Concordia University Irvine Irvine CA	(949)854-8002	IV	1996
Beckman Gary L	(417)827-7273 gpjrbeckman@aol.com	3305 W Meadowlark St Springfield MO 65810	MO	Teacher	EM			S	1972
Beckman Jessica A Wendt	(414)517-0385 jezzy987@gmail.com	835 Apple Tree Ln Brookfield WI 53005	SW	Teacher	C06/2024			MQ	2004
Beckman Katherine S Krieger	(269)449-0151 justmemrsb@yahoo.com	19104 Three Oaks Rd Three Oaks MI 49128	MI	Teacher	EM			RF	1974
Beckman Loretta E Pooker	(636)677-3979 rclebeckman@prodigy.net	5168 Country Club Dr High Ridge MO 63049	MO	Teacher	EM			S	1968
Beckman Ronald C	(636)677-3979	5168 Country Club Dr High Ridge MO 63049	MO	Teacher	EM			CQ	1969
Beckmann Gail M Newby	(630)584-0593 gbeckmann@ilcsbatavia.org	912 Thornwood Dr. Saint Charles IL 60174	NI	Teacher	Tchr	Immanuel Batavia IL	(630)406-0157	CQ	2016
Beckwith Darla R Federwitz	(904)923-6931 bagofbagels@gmail.com	5421 Selton Ave Jacksonville FL 32277	FG	Teacher	Tchr	Lutheran Special Education Ministries Ann Arbor MI	(248)419-3390	RF	2001
Bedard Julie A Schwarz	(985)791-4448 bedard.julie@gmail.com	8235 SW 165th Ave Beaverton OR 97007	NOW	Teacher	Tchr	Pilgrim Beaverton OR	(503)644-8697	PO	1981
Beerman John W	(816)838-4261 splhjwb@yahoo.com	6181 Walkenhorst Rd Concordia MO 64020	MO	Teacher	EM			S	1971
Beermann Sandra R Braun	(414)801-7959 sbeermann04@gmail.com	2707 N 97th St Milwaukee WI 53222	SW	Teacher	EM			S	1970
Beery Brenda J Walter	(702)395-5238 beeryb@flhsemail.org	308 Huntly Rd Las Vegas NV 89145	PSW	Teacher	Tchr	Faith Las Vegas NV	(702)804-4400	S	1996
Beethe Ivan R	(616)881-1604 ivan.beethe@gmail.com	5910 Morning View Ln Weston WI 54476	NW	Teacher	EM			S	1976
Beethe Nathan A	(989)878-2103 nathan.beethe@proton.me	311 Short St Auburn MI 48611	MI	DPM	Mem C	Grace Auburn MI	(989)662-6161	S	2005
Beethe Rhonda J	(402)418-2866 rbeethe@goodshepherdks.org	307 S 5th St Marysville KS 66508	KS	Teacher	Tchr	Good Shepherd Luth School Marysville KS	(785)562-3181	S	1987
Beffrey Amy K Bennett	(989)751-7936 tabeffrey@gmail.com	733 Ivy Creek CV Fort Wayne IN 46804	IN	Teacher	Tchr	Holy Cross Fort Wayne IN	(260)483-3173	CQ	2017
Begley Janet L Schimke	(816)604-7853 jbegley4@gmail.com	4001 W 105th St Apt. 238 Overland Park KS 66207	KS	Teacher	Tchr	Hope Shawnee KS	(913)631-6940	S	1983
Behling Tamara J Hanson	(262)894-3789 tammie.jane@live.com	N77W7031 Oak St Cedarburg WI 53012	SW	Teacher	Tchr	First Immanuel Cedarburg WI	(262)377-6610	MQ	2005
Behlke Judith A Senn Wierman	(414)943-1200 judithbehlke1@gmail.com	8631 Halverson Rd Waterford WI 53185	EN	Teacher	EM			MQ	1985
Behm Constance R Rengstorf	(616)842-6518 ckbehm@yahoo.com	17864 Comstock St Grand Haven MI 49417	MI	Teacher	EM			SP	1969
Behmer Arlene M Kramer	(501)246-4037 arlenebehmer@att.net	2716 Old Forge Dr Little Rock AR 72227	MDS	Teacher	EM			RF	1972
Behmlander Todd G Dr	(812)522-3732 tgb@immanuelschool.org	1701 Northbrook Ct Seymour IN 47274	IN	Teacher	Prin	Immanuel Seymour IN	(812)522-3118	AA	1984
Behnke Caroline J Brogaard	(920)849-4286 behnkeacres@yahoo.com	534 Water St Apt 4 Chilton WI 53014	SW	Teacher	EM			RF	1967
Behnke Elaine A Heuer	(219)374-0171 ebehnke@sbcglobal.net	14024 Pickett Wat Cedar Lake IN 48303	IN	Teacher	EM			RF	1965
Behnke Fred H	(219)374-0171 fbehnke@sbcglobal.net	14024 Pickett Way Cedar Lake IN 46303	IN	Teacher	EM			RF	1965
Behnke John A Dr	behnkeja333@gmail.com	1255 Tarpon Center Dr #203 Venice FL 34285	FG	Teacher	EM			RF	1974
Behnke Kathryn E Otto	(319)279-3282 dktsaj@netins.net	2742 260th St Readlyn IA 50668	IE	Tch/DCE	EM			SP	1968
Behnken Donna D	(256)617-9846 ddbehnken47@gmail.com	305 Chateau Dr SW Huntsville AL 35801	SO	Teacher	EM			RF	1969
Behnken Phyllis I Breimeier	(907)345-3758 behnkenak@gmail.com	1401 Helen Dr Anchorage AK 99515	NOW	Teacher	EM			S	1967
Behny Mallory	(260)705-2622 mallory.behney@cuw.edu	8131 S 700 E Columbia City IN 46725	IN	Teacher	Tchr	St John-Emmanuel Monroeville IN	(260)639-0123	MQ	2025
Behrens Calvin M	(317)525-8946 behrens.calvin@yahoo.com	82268 Pine Acres Ln Bush LA 70431	SO	Teacher	EM			RF	1973
Beierwaltes Ruth E Muller	(708)531-0630 ruthbeierwaltes@hotmail.com	2328 Sherwood Ave Westchester IL 60154	NI	Teacher	EM			RF	1962

*Multiple Assignments (See Church Worker Locator for Additional Details)

See Page 53 for the Table of Abbreviations for key to District, Classification, Position, and College abbreviations.

**C =Candidate; EM =Emeritus; the date following the C is the month and year the Candidate status began

NAME	TELEPHONE NUMBER EMAIL	STREET ADDRESS CITY/STATE/ZIP	DISTRICT	CLASS.	POSITION/ STATUS**	WHERE SERVING	OFFICE PHONE	COLLEGE/ UNIV/CQ	YR GRAD
Beights Jennifer L Keck	(260)494-0596 jenny.keck@gmail.com	1612 Colony Dr Fort Wayne IN 46825	IN	Teacher	Tchr	Concordia Fort Wayne IN	(260)483-1102	CQ	2013
Beikmann David R	(402)200-9720 david.beikmann@cune.org	704 E Florence St Pierce NE 68767	NEB	Teacher		Nebraska District Seward NE	(402)643-2961	S	1999
Beikmann Diane M Wiese	(402)641-1221 diane.beikmann@gmail.com	704 E. Florence St Pierce NE 68767	KS	Teacher	C08/2017			S	2001
Beikmann Mildred L Marohn	(785)348-5464 mickbei@bluevalley.net	P.O. Box 303 Linn KS 66953	KS	Teacher	EM			S	1951
Beilstein Mary E Wamhof	(775)790-5190 mbeilnstein@charter.net	1011 Silveranch Dr Gardnerville NV 89460	CNH	Teacher	EM			CQ	2005
Beineke Thomas A Dr	(262)338-9356 thomas.beineke@yahoo.com	1329 Wolf Dr West Bend WI 53090	SW	Teacher	EM			CQ	2002
Beisel Matthew S	matt.beisel@cune.edu	1138 Sunrise Dr Seward NE 68434	NEB	Teacher	S HS/C	Concordia University Nebraska Seward NE	(402)643-3651	S	1992
Beisert Deborah K Boriack	(979)540-8144 dkbeisert@hotmail.com	4312 N US Highway 77 Giddings TX 78942	TX	Teacher	EM			S	1977
Beiswenger Roberta A Harthun	(952)440-4070	15852 Island View Rd NW Prior Lake MN 55372	MNS	Teacher	EM			S	1979
Beiter Ruth M Kahre	(714)630-8198 ruthkmb@yahoo.com	145 S Beth Cir Anaheim CA 92806	PSW	Teacher	EM			S	1969
Bejot Elizabeth M Hambrock	(260)615-6493 ebej86@gmail.com	10314 Copper Tree Pl Fort Wayne IN 46804	IN	Teacher	Mem C	Emmanuel Fort Wayne IN	(260)423-1369	S	2008
Belitz Larry F	(605)745-3902	12747 Oak Rd Hot Springs SD 57747	SD	Teacher	O-Sp Min	South Dakota District Sioux Falls SD	(605)361-1514	RF	1965
Bell Amanda L	(402)992-2502 abell@growingwithgrace.org	12737 Pearson Dr Waldorf MD 20602	SE	DCE	Mem C	Grace La Plata MD	(301)932-0963	AU	2007
Bell Andrea Queen	(303)807-9458 andreaqueenbell@gmail.com	1778 Presidio Dr Clermont FL 34711	FG	Teacher	Tchr	Woodlands Montverde FL	(407)469-2525	MQ	2016
Bell Daniel T	(217)440-4410 danbaell@trinluth.org	304 Clover Ct Bloomington IL 61704	CI	Teacher	Tchr	Trinity Bloomington IL	(309)829-7513	MQ	2009
Bell Julia D Weddell	(812)216-0851	5360 N County Road 200 E Seymour IN 47274	IN	Teacher	Tchr	Immanuel Seymour IN	(812)522-1301	CH	2009
Bell Kimberley K Garvin	(971) 506-8558 kimandrickbell@frontier.com	14896 SE North Ct Damascus OR 97089	NOW	Teacher	C07/2016			PO	2001
Bell Leslie A Guengerich	(309)545-2472 lesliebell08@gmail.com	304 Clover Ct Bloomington IL 61704	CI	Teacher	C03/2019			MQ	2007
Bell Peggy A Rood	(224)806-0218 pbell09@comcast.net	1705 Farmside Dr Carpentersville IL 60110	NI	DCM	EM			MQ	2009
Bellach Jeffrey P	(913)940-9697 bellachj@hotmail.com	c/o Bethel Lutheran Church 4102 Tiffany Trail Bryan TX 77845	TX	DCE	Mem C	Bethel Bryan TX	(979)822-2742	SP	2004
Belli Mark J	(734)353-5295 markbelli30@gmail.com	32430 Grandview Ave Westland MI 48186	MI	Teacher	Prin	Guardian Dearborn MI	(313)274-3665	MQ	1990
Bellin Sharon L Huff	(262)632-4102 wsnbellin@wi.rr.com	2601 Ole Davidson Rd Mt Pleasant WI 53405	SW	Teacher	EM			S	1973
Bellinger Melanie N Williams	(713)213-5522 mbellinger@trinitydt.org	1627 Scenic Ridge Dr Houston TX 77043	TX	Teacher	Tchr	St Mark Houston TX	(713)468-2623	S	2004
Belmas Lee A	lee.belmas@gmail.com	2214 Forest Grove Ave Kronenwetter WI 54455	NW	DCE	EM			SP	1985
Belofsky Ashley M Wang	(812)893-2887 ashleybelofshy@gmail.com	4400 Chadwick Rd Evansville IN 47710	IN	Teacher	Tchr	Evansville Evansville IN	(812)424-7252	CQ	2025
Belongia Nathan J	(734)716-9085 natebelongia@gmail.com	N6960 River Dr Shawno WI 54166	NW	Teacher	Prin	St James Shawano WI	(715)524-4213	CQ	2018
Belsha Diane L Bergmann	dianebelsha58@gmail.com	311 N Woodlawn Ave Kirkwood MO 63122	MO	Teacher	EM			CQ	2014
Beltran Alice A Hockemeyer	(916)967-1876 alicebeltran@aol.com	5026 Dewey Dr Fair Oaks CA 95628	CNH	Teacher	EM			CQ	1983
Beltz Tyler D	(863)875-8863 tylerbeltz14@msn.com	406 E Park Ave Norfolk NE 68701	FG	Teacher	C07/2016			S	2012
Bely Danielle N	(920)390-0371 dbely@goodshepherdwi.org	1200 Riverview Ln Watertown WI 53094	SW	Teacher	Tchr	Good Shepherd Watertown WI	(920)261-2579	MQ	2018
Benally Molly A Wilson	(623)512-0513 benallymolly@gmail.com	2505 S 117th Ave Avondale AZ 85323	PSW	Teacher	Tchr	Trinity Litchfield Park AZ	(623)935-4665	CQ	2003
Benda Amy L Luke		2505 Westminster Dr Valparaiso IN 46385	IN	Teacher	C07/2016			RF	1982
Benda Gretchen Lenning	(507)847-4784 gmbenda@earthlink.net	58958 850th St Alpha MN 56111	MNS	Teacher	Tchr	Immanuel Lakefield MN	(507)662-5860	SP	2004
Bender Angela J Stevens	(714) 271-4810 ajbender@mac.com	6327 E Bryce Ave Orange CA 92867	PSW	Teacher	Tchr	Saint Johns Orange CA	(714)288-4400	CQ	2013
Bender Cody W	(402)641-8159 dcebender@gmail.com	735 NE 1st Ave Grand Rapids MN 55744	MNN	DCE	Mem C	First Grand Rapids MN	(218)326-5453	S	2025
Bender Edgar L	(231)889-0839	9371 Coates Hwy Manistee MI 49660	MI	Teacher	EM			RF	1957
Bender Emilie R Howe	(989)780-0045 emilierhowe@gmail.com	40050 Romeo Plank Road Clinton Twp MI 48038	MI	Teacher	Tchr	Trinity Clinton Township MI	(586)463-2921	CH	2017
Bender Emily M Moravec	(773)891-6021 emilymariebender@gmail.com	9697 Huron Dr Olivette MO 63132	MO	Teacher	Tchr	Lutheran South Saint Louis MO	(314)631-1400	CH	2016
Bender Kendis D Prok	(440)967-1792 dbender6@gmail.com	4215 Telegraph Ln Vermilion OH 44089	OH	DCE	C08/2021			RF	1991
Bender Mark L Dr	(314)609-3584	104 Deer Meadows Ct Ballwin MO 63011	MO	Teacher	EM			RF	1974
Bender Michael H	(989)295-3364 mhbender65@gmail.com	11109 N Evergreen Dr Birch Run MI 48415	MI	Teacher	EM			RF	1987
Bender Rachel C	(440)787-7414 rcbender2@gmail.com	4215 Telegraph Ln Vermilion OH 44089	OH	Teacher	Tchr	Lutheran West Rocky River OH	(440)333-1660	MQ	2023

*Multiple Assignments (See Church Worker Locator for Additional Details)
See Page 53 for the Table of Abbreviations for key to District, Classification, Position, and College abbreviations.
**C =Candidate; EM =Emeritus; the date following the C is the month and year the Candidate status began

NAME	TELEPHONE NUMBER EMAIL	STREET ADDRESS CITY/STATE/ZIP	DISTRICT	CLASS.	POSITION/ STATUS**	WHERE SERVING	OFFICE PHONE	COLLEGE/ UNIV/CQ	YR GRAD
Benecke Vera L Frederking	(815)355-9396 hnvb4506@gmail.com	475 N Kewaunee Way Aurora CO 80018	RM	Teacher	EM			S	1965
Benedict Jeremy J	(920)680-8795 jbenedict@stjohnschicago.org	8963 Chestnut Ave. River Grove IL 60171	NI	Teacher	Tchr	St John Chicago IL	(773)736-1196	MQ	2009
Benedict Susan M Knoerr	(608)752-6127 suebe54@yahoo.com	1629 Edon Dr Janesville WI 53546	SW	Teacher	EM			CQ	2003
Benedum Charles E	(920)458-8268 rbenedum@charter.net	1224 Carmen Ave Sheboygan WI 53081	SW	Teacher	EM			RF	1969
Benes Sara R Mueller	(262)354-8105 sebenes@yahoo.com	756 Thackeray Trl Oconomowoc WI 53066	SW	Teacher	Tchr	St Paul Oconomowoc WI	(262)567-5001	CQ	2003
Benham Douglas E	(909)822-6799 doug.e.benham50@gmail.com	P.O. Box 571 Big Bear Lake CA 92315	PSW	DCE	EM			S	1973
Benne Bruce J	benne@creanlutheran.org	12471 Zig Zag Way Tustin CA 92780	PSW	Teacher	Tchr	Crean Irvine CA	(949)387-1199	S	1987
Benne Katherine L Schulenburg Davis	(714)721-6872 apotheosis.ck@gmail.com	12471 Zig Zag Way Tustin CA 92780	PSW	Teacher	C06/2020			IV	1986
Bennett Elisabeth A Kugel Behrend	txelisabeth@sbcglobal.net	11447 Glen Cross Dr Dallas TX 75228	TX	Teacher	EM			S	1963
Bennett Jonathan W	(949)413-4089 bennett@creanlutheran.org	218 E Palmdale Ave Orange CA 92865	PSW	Teacher	Tchr	Crean Irvine CA	(949)387-1199	IV	2014
Bennett Robert E	(660)463-7430 bobbennett100@hotmail.com	P.O. Box 16 Emma MO 65327	MO	Teacher	EM			S	1973
Benning Carl D	(618)349-6429 carlbenning@yahoo.com	813 N 1625 St Shobonier IL 62885	CI	Teacher	EM			S	1975
Benning Cathleen M Turis	(217)793-8765	325 Cartwright Dr Springfield IL 62704	CI	Teacher	EM			RF	1970
Benning Evelyn M Schulenburg	(317)292-3195 evecarl63@aol.com	4523 E County Road 200 S Avon IN 46123	IN	Teacher	EM			RF	1963
Benning Karen L Miessner	(618)349-6429 carlbenning@yahoo.com	813 N 1625 St Shobonier IL 62885	CI	Teacher	EM			S	1975
Benning Russell D	(217)306-3887 benning5@hotmail.com	325 Cartwright Dr Springfield IL 62704	CI	Teacher	EM			S	1968
Benscoter Andrew L Dr	(480)200-1037 andrew.benscoter@upbring.org	7235 N 13th Ln Phoenix AZ 85021	TX	Teacher	RSO	Luth Social Services South Inc Austin TX	(512)459-1000	S	2002
Benson Gene A	(713) 876-6414 pioneers92@myyahoo.com	6060 Fairmont Pkwy Apt 10301 Pasadena TX 77505	TX	Teacher	EM			S	1986
Benson Kristin N Matasovsky	(712)730-3927 kristin.matasovsky@gmail.com	3369 190th St. Newman Grove NE 68758	TX	Teacher	Tchr	Concordia San Antonio TX	(210)479-1477	S	2007
Benson Rachel L Vrudny	(715)869-2204 rachel.benson022@gmail.com	222 E Mitchell Hammock Rd Apt 1006 Oviedo FL 32765	S	Teacher	Tchr	St Lukes Oviedo FL	(407)365-3228	SP	2013
Benson Stephen E	mrb5six@gmail.com		NE	Teacher	EM			RF	1994
Benter Cassandra L Irwin	(248)495-2159 cassandra.irwin09@gmail.com	298 Maple Dr Oakland MI 48363	MI	Teacher	Tchr	St John Rochester MI	(248)402-8000	CH	2013
Bentley Tina J	(208)859-0629 tinateacher1@gmail.com	312 W Elm St Caldwell ID 83605	NOW	Teacher	C07/2016			S	2004
Benton Karen S Johnson	(314)691-6491 kbenton50@hotmail.com	1008 Yahkee Ct Warrenton MO 63383	MO	Teacher	EM			CQ	1993
Bents Jenna M Sorensen	(507)830-1467 ajbents20@gmail.com	29111 270th Street Worthington MN 56187	MNS	DCE	C08/2023			IV	2021
Bentz Terri L Taylor	(952)240-2056 terribentz@gmail.com	18165 County Road 50 Hamburg MN 55339	MNS	Teacher	C07/2016			S	1990
Benzler Catherine J Deac	(360)417-8003 sevenrivers7@aol.com	P.O. Box 2955 Port Angeles WA 98362	NOW	Deaconess	EM			SL-DEAC	2012
Beran Amber R Kucksdorf	(715)853-9600 aberan@stjamesshawano.org	270 Pearl Ave Shawno WI 54166	NW	Teacher	Tchr	St James Shawano WI	(715)524-4213	MQ	2004
Beran Madison R	(308)370-0903 madisonberan@lhsparker.org	19693 E Mann Creek Dr Apt C Parker CO 80134	RM	Teacher	Tchr	Colorado Lutheran High School Parker CO	(303)841-5551	S	2021
Berauer Karen R Rubel Deac	karen.rubel@gmail.com	847 S Addison Ave Villa Park IL 60181	NI	Deaconess	C07/2016			CH	2008
Berdis Juanita M Reynolds	(630) 605-8389 juanitaberdis54@gmail.com	1183 Parkview Ct Carol Stream IL 60188	NI	Teacher	EM			RF	1976
Berentsen Kurtis G	(503)358-5878 kberentsen@icloud.com	6637 SE 148th Ave Portland OR 97236	NOW	Teacher	EM			CQ	1996
Berg Alan M	(708)227-9727 sergeantpepper61@sbcglobal.net	8213 Bromley St Orland Park IL 60462	NI	Teacher	Tchr	Immanuel East Dundee IL	(847)428-1010	RF	1983
Berg Cara E Pirie	(360)773-8093 cberg@popfremont.org	356 Teddy Dr Union City CA 94587	CNH	Teacher	Tchr	Prince of Peace Fremont CA	(510)793-3366	PO	2007
Berg Carole J Schroeder	(920)395-2606 carolejberg@charter.net	4139 Cherrywood Ct Apt A103 Sheboygan WI 53081	SW	Teacher	EM			RF	1976
Berg Deborah G Linin	(630)323-5844 d4bergs@aol.com	17w170 Hillside Ln Willowbrook IL 60527	NI	Teacher	Tchr	Zion Hinsdale IL	(630)323-0384	RF	1986
Berg James N	(414)462-5871 jnrberg67@gmail.com	4645 N 103rd St Wauwatosa WI 53225	SW	Teacher	EM			S	1964
Berg Kathrine C Hodel	(303)797-0197 katie.berg@comcast.net	5151 Juniper St Littleton CO 80123	RM	Teacher	C07/2016			IV	1985
Berg Peter H	(360)773-7985 pberg@popfremont.org	356 Teddy Dr Union City CA 94587	CNH	DCE	Tchr	Prince of Peace Fremont CA	(510)793-3366	PO	2006
Berg Sarah A	(218)393-3279 sberg@crownchristianschool.com	26429 2nd St E Apt 305 Zimmerman MN 55398	MNN	Teacher	Tchr	Crown Saint Francis MN	(763)856-2099	SP	2013
Bergan Linda J Muckala	(952)270-0463 lbergan@live.com	2209 Grape Ct Great Falls MT 59404	MT	Teacher	EM			SP	1983
Bergdolt Karl J	(308)382-1598 kbergdolt3@gmail.com	4211 Vermont Ave. Grand Island NE 68803	NEB	Teacher	C05/2025			S	1988

*Multiple Assignments (See Church Worker Locator for Additional Details)
See Page 53 for the Table of Abbreviations for key to District, Classification, Position, and College abbreviations.
**C =Candidate; EM =Emeritus; the date following the C is the month and year the Candidate status began

NAME	TELEPHONE NUMBER EMAIL	STREET ADDRESS CITY/STATE/ZIP	DISTRICT	CLASS.	POSITION/ STATUS**	WHERE SERVING	OFFICE PHONE	COLLEGE/ UNIV/CQ	YR GRAD
Bergdolt Katherine M Justus	(402)314-2283 kate.bergdolt@cune.org	7201 Thomasbrook Cir Lincoln NE 68516	NEB	Teacher	C07/2025			S	1992
Bergdolt Kurt P	(402)314-1673 kurt.bergdolt@cune.org	7201 Thomasbrook Cir Lincoln NE 68516	NEB	Teacher	EM			S	1992
Bergelin Denise R	(920)889-4454 denise.bergelin@cuw.edu	10024 Acorn Ln Fort Wayne IN 46835	IN	Teacher	Tchr	Holy Cross Fort Wayne IN	(260)483-3173	MQ	2000
Bergelin Molly Marcis	(419)438-1879 mmarcis7@gmail.com	2928 Harvard Dr Janesville WI 53548	SW	DCE	Mem C	Mount Calvary Janesville WI	(608)754-4145	CH	2013
Berger David O	(314)997-6911 bergerd@csl.edu	800 Berry Hill Dr Olivette MO 63132	MO	Teacher	EM			RF	1962
Bergeron Janine M	(920) 254-0582 jbcouponqueen@aol.com	1534 Georgia Ave Sheboygan WI 53081	SW	DCE	EM			S	1993
Bergholt Matthew T			MO	Teacher	Pro Stf	Lutheran Church Extension Fund Saint Louis MO	(314)965-9000	CH	2007
Bergholt Melissa A Wittcop	(407)810-1648 mbergholt@wordoflifeschool.net	5281 Mild Dr Saint Louis MO 63129	MO	Teacher	Prin	Word of Life Saint Louis MO	(314)832-1244	Other	2008
Bergkoetter Molly A Schlechte	(248)394-1125 mabergkoetter@aol.com	8018 Sugarloaf Trl Clarkston MI 48348	MI	Teacher	EM			CQ	1993
Bergman Mary B	(951)297-1460 bergie10@hotmail.com	31130 S General Kearny Rd Spc 41 Temecula CA 92591	RM	Teacher	EM			S	1972
Bergman Peter M	(281)636-6794 dcepete@gmail.com	7126 Yardley Dr Katy TX 77494	TX	DCE	Mem C	NewChurch Katy TX	(832)786-8212	IV	1997
Bergmann Maureen J Huehn	(763)639-6846 momdad70@hotmail.com	23102 Kerry St NW Saint Francis MN 55070	MNS	Teacher	EM			SP	1968
Bergmann Peter A	(763)670-3059 momdad70@hotmail.com	23102 Kerry St NW Saint Francis MN 55070	MNS	Teacher	EM			SP	1968
Bergt Amanda L Cook	(507) 848-6863 amandabergt@martinlutherhs.com	814 Webster St Fairmont MN 56031	MNS	Teacher	Tchr	Martin Luther Northrop MN	(507)436-5249	S	1998
Bergt Carolyn S	(314)845-9138 bergtblueskies@aol.com	2512 Lindbergh Blvd Springfield IL 62704	MO	Teacher	EM			S	1967
Bergt David R	(507)238-2303 davidbergt@martinlutherhs.com	814 Webster St Fairmont MN 56031	MNS	Teacher	Tchr	Martin Luther Northrop MN	(507)436-5249	S	1995
Bergt Gerald A	(507)238-4035 gbergt@hotmail.com	622 Washington Ave Fairmont MN 56031	MNS	Teacher	EM			S	1969
Bergt Grace Deac	(618)580-3283 graceeb14@gmail.com	11 Parklands Dr Apt 925 Bluffton SC 29910	SE	Deaconess	Mem C	Island Hilton Head Island SC	(843)689-5200	SL-DEAC	2023
Bergt Pauline C Henschen	gbergt@hotmail.com	622 Washington Ave Fairmont MN 56031	MNS	Teacher	EM			S	1970
Bergt Richard D	(217)546-9323 rich.bergt@oslms.org	2512 Lindbergh Blvd Springfield IL 62704	CI	Teacher	EM			S	1973
Beringer Daniel W	(989)883-3824 pacrfan49@gmail.com	39 S Miller St Sebewaing MI 48759	MI	Teacher	EM			RF	1971
Beringer David C	(715)551-5740 dberinger@concordianc.org	929 43rd Avenue Ct NE Hickory NC 28601	SE	Teacher	Prin	Concordia Conover NC	(828)464-3324	RF	1984
Beringer Gloria L Gehner	(989)883-3824 pacrfan49@gmail.com	39 S Miller St Sebewaing MI 48759	MI	Teacher	EM			RF	1971
Berkesch Mary A Phillips	(260)437-3959 wmberkesch@gmail.com	481 Rabbit Run W Lafayette IN 47906	EN	Teacher	EM			RF	1977
Berlinski Donald W	(720) 427-4791 dberlinski@msn.com	6432 S Irvington Way Aurora CO 80016	RM	Teacher	EM			RF	1956
Bernardini Kate L O Hara	(216)441-5694	11090 Glamer Dr Parma OH 44130	OH	Teacher	C09/2020			RF	1990
Bernau Emily A	(507)339-1656 emilyabernau@gmail.com	414 W 6th St. Apt. E Spencer IA 51301	IW	Teacher	Tchr	Iowa Great Lakes Spencer IA	(712)262-8237	SP	2020
Bernau Jonathan P	(989)225-5974 jonbernau@gmail.com	1060 Englewood Dr Rantoul IL 61866	CI	Teacher	Tchr	St John Champaign IL	(217)359-1123	SP	2004
Bernau Marissa M	(507)339-2376 marissabernau@gmail.com	508 N Dugan St. Unit 6 Welcome MN 56181	MNS	Teacher	Tchr	St Martin Winona MN	(507)452-6928	SP	2022
Bernau Rebekah L	(262)527-5363 beckybernau@gmail.com	333 W. 1st St. Waconia MN 55387	MNS	Teacher	Tchr	St John Norwood Young America MN	(952)467-2740	MQ	2009
Bernau Stephen A	(507)995-6082 stephen.bernau@gmail.com	1318 Liggett Dr Saint Louis MO 63126	MO	Teacher	Tchr	Christ Community Kirkwood MO	(314)822-7774	MQ	2016
Berndt Clarence F Jr	(314)952-5056 crberndt2@gmail.com	8131 Watermark Ct West Chester OH 45069	OH	Teacher	EM			RF	1961
Berndt Holly R Rosselet	(414)476-7558 hberndt1981@hotmail.com	1416 N 67th St Wauwatosa WI 53213	SW	Teacher	EM			CQ	2002
Berner Jessica L Mangels	(636)405-3129 jl.berner@hotmail.com	424 Saint Thomas Isle Ln Wildwood MO 63040	MO	Teacher	Tchr	Christ Community Kirkwood MO	(314)822-7774	S	2000
Bernhardt Amy E Trinklein	(636)634-7226 abernhardt@zionharvester.org	3470 Beldeer Dr Saint Charles MO 63303	MO	Teacher	Tchr	Zion Saint Charles MO	(636)441-7425	RF	1994
Bernhardt David H	(636)922-5688 dbern37@sbcglobal.net	3401 Ridgeway Dr Saint Charles MO 63303	MO	Teacher	EM			RF	1960
Bernhardt Edythe E Voth	(636)922-5688 dbern37@aol.com	3401 Ridgeway Dr Saint Charles MO 63303	MO	Teacher	EM			RF	1960
Bernhardt Grace R	(636)328-5164 grace.bernhardt@cune.org	3470 Beldeer Dr Saint Charles MO 63303	MO	Teacher	Tchr	Christ Community Kirkwood MO	(314)822-7774	S	2021
Bernhardt Greta R Deac	(425)923-9353	P.O. Box 1825 Marysville WA 98270	NOW	Deaconess	Mem C	Immanuel Everett WA	(425)252-7038	SL-DEAC	2016
Bernhardt Jonathan D	(636)447-0453 jbernhardt@lhssc.org	3470 Beldeer Dr Saint Charles MO 63303	MO	Teacher	Tchr	St Charles Saint Peters MO	(636)928-5100	RF	1994
Berni Kathy A Ross	(760)536-3819 kberni@aol.com	1536 Peacock Blvd Oceanside CA 92056	PSW	Teacher	EM			RF	1974
Bernier Julie	(414)379-8380		PSW	Teacher	C07/2020			CH	2008

*Multiple Assignments (See Church Worker Locator for Additional Details)
See Page 53 for the Table of Abbreviations for key to District, Classification, Position, and College abbreviations.
**C =Candidate; EM =Emeritus; the date following the C is the month and year the Candidate status began

NAME	TELEPHONE NUMBER EMAIL	STREET ADDRESS CITY/STATE/ZIP	DISTRICT	CLASS.	POSITION/ STATUS**	WHERE SERVING	OFFICE PHONE	COLLEGE/ UNIV/CQ	YR GRAD
Berns Nancy E Jung	(313)241-7517 bnberns@sbcglobal.net	1788 Riverside Dr Monroe MI 48162	MI	Teacher	EM			RF	1971
Berns Sandra N	(561)891-0118 sberns@trinitydelray.org	413 Villa Circle Boynton Beach FL 33435	FG	Teacher	Tchr	Trinity Delray Beach FL	(561)276-8458	AA	2003
Berrey Bonnie L Sanders	(641)477-8222 teacherb@netins.net	1717 Jessup Ave Albion IA 50005	IE	Teacher	EM			CQ	1989
Berry Amanda M Hellwege Deac	deaconessberry@gmail.com		MO	Deaconess	Mem C	Concordia Sikeston MO	(573)471-5842	SL-DEAC	2021
Berry Jenna R Lipinski	(586)612-9668 jberry@immlutheran.org	46628 Featherstone Ridge Shelby Charter Township MI 48317	MI	DFLM	Mem C	Immanuel Macomb MI	(586)286-4231	AA	2018
Berry Kay S Schlehlein	(563)370-1614 jkberry79@gmail.com	2418 Wilkes Ave Davenport IA 52804	IE	Teacher	EM			RF	1974
Berry Peggy D Schneider	(979)366-2389 gberry@bluebon.net	1747 County Road 220 Giddings TX 78942	TX	Teacher	Tchr	Immanuel Giddings TX	(979)542-2918	S	1965
Berry Rachel B Polk Gilles	(630)251-0599 rachgilles@yahoo.com	435 Webster Street Berlin WI 54923	SW	Teacher	Tchr	St John Berlin WI	(920)361-0555	MQ	1994
Bersie Mark B	(773)817-3944 mbersie@comcast.net	3921 N Sayre Ave Chicago IL 60634	NI	Teacher	EM			RF	1978
Berson Susan D Prellwitz	(480)560-2825 sueberson@hotmail.com	6711 E Camelback Rd Unit 52 Scottsdale AZ 85251	PSW	Teacher	EM			SP	1977
Berta-Somogyi Sarah J Cusson	(916)784-9784 sarah.berta-somogyi@lcmsintl.org	Szirom Utca 6 Gyor 9025 HUNGARY	CNH	Teacher	S Miss	Office of International Mission Saint Louis MO		IV	2007
Berthold Ann L Williams	edannberthold@yahoo.com	9642 Peninsula Dr Traverse City MI 49686	MI	Teacher	EM			CQ	1986
Bertram Grace E	(507)399-3904 gbertram@fils.org	N163W19408 Cedar Run Dr Jackson WI 53037	SW	Teacher	Tchr	First Immanuel Cedarburg WI	(262)377-6610	MQ	2015
Bertrand Brenda L Kellogg	(301)540-1670 bbertrand@verizon.net	304 W 7th St Bethany Beach DE 19930	SE	Teacher	EM			AA	1990
Bertrand Elizabeth A	(281)433-1043 eabs5302@gmail.com	13102 Fallsview Ln Apt 5302 Houston TX 77077	TX	Teacher	Tchr	Pilgrim Houston TX	(713)432-7082	MQ	2000
Besel Ross E	rbesel76@gmail.com	1487 Olympus Pointe Pocatello ID 83201	NOW	Teacher	EM			PO	1985
Besel Travis W	(303)912-4099 tbaze03@gmail.com	1111 Louisville Ave Apt 1n Saint Louis MO 63139	MO	Teacher	Tchr	Lutheran South Saint Louis MO	(314)631-1400	S	2012
Bessert Bruce H	(414)526-8430 bruce.bessert@gmail.com	2044 N 113th St Wauwatosa WI 53226	SW	Teacher	EM			S	1977
Bessert Karla M Kirschenmann	(414)688-9555 karla.bessert@gmail.com	2044 N 113th St Wauwatosa WI 53226	SW	Teacher	EM			S	1978
Best Kevin A	(708)955-0088	9225 W Charleston Blvd Apt 1143 Las Vegas NV 89117	PSW	Teacher	Tchr	Faith Las Vegas NV	(702)804-4400	S	2001
Best Rebekah M Kretzmann	(219)241-9035 rebest@clspeoria.org	6633 N Randwick Rd Peoria IL 61615	CI	Teacher	Tchr	Christ Peoria IL	(309)637-5309	CH	2009
Bestian Isaak J	(970)412-9023 isaak.bestian@gmail.com	11330 N. Country Club Green Dr. Tomball TX 77375	TX	Teacher	Tchr	Concordia Tomball TX	(281)351-2547	AU	2019
Bethke Karen E Lorenz	(253)921-8199 mpb453@comcast.net	3119 Walker Rd Dupont WA 98327	NOW	Teacher	EM			S	1973
Bethke Paul H	(253)202-1505 mpb453@comcast.net	3119 Walker Rd Dupont WA 98327	NOW	Teacher	EM			S	1973
Bethke Susan Borkenhagen	(510)690-0238 bethke5@comcast.net	23401 Mona Marie Ct Hayward CA 94541	CNH	Teacher	EM			RF	1980
Bethke William R	(510)690-0238 bethke7@sbcglobal.net	23401 Mona Marie Ct Hayward CA 94541	CNH	Teacher	EM			RF	1967
Betterton Shelby A	(402)881-5194 sbetterton@stjohnlutheran. esu7.org	322 D St Schuyler NE 68661	NEB	Teacher	Tchr	St Johns Columbus NE	(402)285-0335	S	2020
Betts Brian J	(715)663-0804 bbetts@immanuelrapids.com	1021 Chester Ct Nekoosa WI 54457	NW	Teacher	Tchr	Immanuel Wisconsin Rapids WI	(715)423-3260	SP	1992
Betts Caleb J	(715)663-0806 cbetts@immanuelrapids.com	3320 Norton St Apt 202 Wisconsin Rapids WI 54494	NW	Teacher	Tchr	Immanuel Wisconsin Rapids WI	(715)423-0272	MQ	2021
Bever David P	(702)341-1597 lasvegasbevers@cox.net	9424 Summer Rain Dr Las Vegas NV 89134	PSW	Teacher	EM			S	1973
Beversdorf Andrea J Morlok	(402)724-2194	907 Rd 13 York NE 68467	NEB	Teacher	EM			S	1970
Beversdorf Bonnie J Borhart	(262)301-0521 bonniebeversdorf4@gmail.com	1100 Fountain Hills Dr Apt 233c Mount Pleasant WI 53406	SW	Teacher	EM			RF	1966
Beversdorf Janet L Kautz	(715)851-2226 jlbsdorf@gmail.com	W8499 County Road M Shawano WI 54166	NW	Teacher	EM			SP	1976
Beversdorf Melvin L	(262)342-5128 melvin.beversdorf@gmail.com	149 S Main St Burlington WI 53105	SW	Teacher	Mem C	St Peters Waterford WI	(262)534-6066	RF	2002
Beversdorf Richard A	(402)724-2194	907 Rd 13 York NE 68467	NEB	Teacher	EM			S	1968
Bevirt Cathy J Pruitt	(618)345-3904 clbevi@msn.com	473 S Mulberry Rd Collinsville IL 62234	SI	Teacher	Tchr	Holy Cross Collinsville IL	(618)344-3145	RF	1986
Beyer Anna M	(619)495-7068 anna.beyer@flhsemail.org	813 Elliott Park Ave North Las Vegas NV 89032	PSW	Teacher	Tchr	Faith Las Vegas NV	(702)804-4400	SP	1983
Beyer Beverly J Rollo	(805)443-1814 bevbeyer93036@gmail.com	2202 Desert Forest Ct Oxnard CA 93036	PSW	Teacher	EM			BR	1976
Beyer Gary A	(714)651-8510 gary.beyer@sbcglobal.net	5029 E Almond Ave Apt 1 Orange CA 92869	PSW	Teacher	EM			RF	1969
Beyer Kristen L Onsgard	(760)753-4776 paulasamson@stmarkchurch.net	552 S El Camino Real Encinitas CA 92024	PSW	DCO	Mem C	St Mark Encinitas CA	(760)753-4776	SP	2009
Beyer Rachel A	(920)538-4002 rchlbeyer81@yahoo.com	E7324 Little Creek Rd Manawa WI 54949	NW	Teacher	Tchr	St Paul Manawa WI	(920)596-2837	CQ	2018
Beyer Shirley A Wenholz	(763)442-0882 sabyr31@gmail.com	355 98th Ave NE Blaine MN 55434	MNS	Teacher	EM			SP	1964

*Multiple Assignments (See Church Worker Locator for Additional Details)
See Page 53 for the Table of Abbreviations for key to District, Classification, Position, and College abbreviations.
**C =Candidate; EM =Emeritus; the date following the C is the month and year the Candidate status began

NAME	TELEPHONE NUMBER EMAIL	STREET ADDRESS CITY/STATE/ZIP	DISTRICT	CLASS.	POSITION/ STATUS**	WHERE SERVING	OFFICE PHONE	COLLEGE/ UNIV/CQ	YR GRAD
Bickel Christine	(616)886-3000 cbickel26@yahoo.com	1230 Heather Ct Holland MI 49423	EN	Teacher	EM			MQ	2010
Bickel Connie S Laseter	(314)322-5585 csbickel15@gmail.com	35 Wilshire Ter Webster Groves MO 63119	MO	Teacher	EM			CQ	2009
Bickel Daniel A	(314)348-1950 danbickel@yahoo.com	1533 NE Amanda Ln Lee's Summit MO 64086	MO	Teacher	Tchr	Kansas City Kansas City MO	(816)241-5478	S	2007
Bickel Eric J	(660)674-2423 rcbckl@gmail.com	213 W 3rd St Alma MO 64001	MO	Teacher	Tchr	Trinity Alma MO	(660)674-2376	S	1992
Bickel Karen E Engel	(219)462-2030 pbickel2206@comcast.net	2518 Allison Cir Valparaiso IN 46383	IN	Teacher	EM			RF	1969
Bickel Kurt R	(407)423-1752 bickelkurt@aol.com	3811 Laguna St Orlando FL 32805	FG	DCE	C07/2016			S	1973
Bickel Lukas R	(937)594-3877 lukas.bickel@immanuelhamilton.com	555 N Dick Ave Hamilton OH 45013	OH	Teacher	P/Tchr	Immanuel Hamilton OH	(513)893-6792	AA	2006
Bickel Martha R Hussmann	(443) 787-5540 marthab309@gmail.com	2430 Johnson Mill Rd Forest Hill MD 21050	SE	Teacher	EM			S	1970
Bickel Nathan F	(262) 488-7657 nbickel@wi.rr.com	1423 Arthur Ave Racine WI 53405	SW	Teacher	EM			RF	1981
Bickel Philip G	(219)462-2030 pbickel2206@comcast.net	2518 Allison Cir Valparaiso IN 46383	IN	Teacher	EM			RF	1969
Bickel Randall J	(989)624-9204 midistythgath@yahoo.com	9449 Block Rd Birch Run MI 48415	MI	Teacher	Mem C	St Martin Birch Run MI	(989)624-9204	AA	1986
Bickel Reagan B Geno	(989)450-2100 rbbickel@outlook.com	4764 Richville Rd. Vassar MI 48768	MI	Teacher	Tchr	St Lorenz Frankenmuth MI	(989)652-6141	CQ	2023
Bickel Zachary D		1042 S Imperial Dr Hartland WI 53029	SW	Teacher	Tchr	Lake Country Hartland WI	(262)367-8600	CH	2009
Bickett Payton G	(262)720-6724 paytonbickett@gmail.com	W271 N2631 Orchard Ln Pewaukee WI 53072	SW	Teacher	Tchr	Immanuel Brookfield WI	(262)781-7140	MQ	2024
Bicondoa Candice A	(320)224-0862 candice.bicondoa@gmail.com	608 6th St NE Perham MN 56573	MNN	Teacher	Prin	St Pauls Perham MN	(218)346-2300	SP	2006
Biedinger Allyssa L Guynes	(254)457-8578 allyssag14@gmail.com	9821 Chapel Rd Waco TX 76712	TX	DCE	Mem C	Faith Georgetown TX	(512)863-7332	SP	2019
Biedinger Bruce R	(210)679-6737 bruce.biedinger@lhssa.org	18802 Real Rdg San Antonio TX 78256	TX	Teacher	Tchr	Lutheran San Antonio TX	(210)694-4962	RF	1985
Biel Kathy D Harms	(708)535-3716 kdbiel1@yahoo.com	665 Grace Ct New Lenox IL 60451	NI	Teacher	EM			RF	2002
Biel Larry R	(402)310-3098 flmlarry@gmail.com	239 N 4th St Seward NE 68434	NEB	Teacher	EM			S	1975
Bielby Sara Deac	(734)755-8975 smbielby@umich.edu	6413 Botsford Cir Howell MI 48855	EN	Deaconess	Mem C	Our Savior Hartland MI	(248)887-4300	FW-DEAC	2005
Bielec Heather N Uilk	(651)245-9778 hbielec@redeemerwayzata.org	169 4th St NW Delano MN 55328	MNS	Teacher	Tchr	Redeemer Wayzata MN	(952)473-5356	CQ	2006
Bien Heather E Deac	(850)902-2382 heatherbien@gmail.com	10 Holly Rd Crestview FL 32539	SO	Deaconess	Mem C	Our Savior Crestview FL	(850)682-3154	FW-DEAC	2019
Bienz Clinton E	(260)402-6619 clinton.bienz@gmail.com	423 Dale Ave Benton Harbor MI 49022	MI	Teacher	C02/2024			CH	2015
Bierbaum Daryl P	(719) 980-2054 dbierbaum@bresnan.net	918 Lowell Dr Rocky Ford CO 81067	RM	DCE	C07/2016			S	1994
Bierbaum Deanna J West	(719) 980-1045 dbierbaum@bresnan.net	918 Lowell Dr Rocky Ford CO 81067	RM	Teacher	C07/2016			S	1996
Bierbaum Edward W	(573)317-6250 debier66@yahoo.com	2050 W State Route 89a Lot 129 Cottonwood AZ 86326	PSW	Teacher	EM			S	1966
Bierbaum Pamela K Schneewind	(952)210-1764 pbierbaum@stjamesshawano.org	313 S Lincoln St Shawano WI 54166	NW	Teacher	RSO	Lutheran Special Education Ministries Ann Arbor MI	(248)419-3390	SP	1989
Bierbaum Timothy M	(952)406-0100 tbierbaum@wolfriverlhs.org	313 S Lincoln St Shawano WI 54166	NW	Teacher	Tchr	Wolf River Shawano WI	(715)745-2400	S	1992
Bierlein Beth N Kaufmann	(630)235-8268 mrsbierlein@gmail.com	E2641 Gatling Ct. La Valle WI 53941	SW	Teacher	Prin	St Peter Reedsburg WI	(608)524-4066	RF	1996
Bierlein Heather M Shirley	(989)737-4948 heatherbierlein@yahoo.com	242 E Kitchen Rd Pinconning MI 48650	MI	Teacher	Tchr	St Michael Richville MI	(989)868-4791	AA	2001
Bierlein Kimberly K	(352)408-2257 kbierlein@flcse.org	2702 Lakewood Ln Eustis FL 32726	FG	Teacher	Tchr	Faith Eustis FL	(352)589-5683	RF	1982
Bierlein Mary B Bauer	(989)284-3683 marybierlein14@gmail.com	10605 King Rd Frankenmuth MI 48734	MI	Teacher	EM			CQ	1993
Bierman Rachel V	(618)615-2816 rbierman@ilsperryville.org	302 N Kingshighway St Perryville MO 63775	MO	Teacher	Tchr	Immanuel Perryville MO	(573)547-8317	CQ	2021
Biermann-Miller Karen L Biermann	(815)405-3027 kmiller@hiscross.net	9166 Penman Rd Yorkville IL 60560	NI	Teacher	Tchr	Cross Yorkville IL	(630)553-7861	SP	1987
Bierwagen Sherry A Steinmetz	(314)942-8251 dsbierw@gmail.com	705 S Laclede Station Rd Apt 165 Saint Louis MO 63119	MO	Teacher	EM			S	1957
Biesendorfer Lynette K Roth	(314)422-7775 lynbeez02@gmail.com	1972 Sugar Hollow Court #1374 Marthasville MO 63357	MO	Teacher	EM			RF	1978
Bigon Katherine T Tucker	(210)416-3990 katherine.bigon@gmail.com	5814 Catina St New Orleans LA 70124	TX	Teacher	Tchr	Concordia San Antonio TX	(210)479-1477	AU	2018
Bilich Andrew J	(979)285-9313 ajbbwb@earthlink.net	215 Pansy Path St Lake Jackson TX 77566	TX	DCM	EM			MQ	1984
Billotte Pamela A	(217)529-8861	4101 W Iles Ave Apt 130 Springfield IL 62711	CI	Teacher	EM			S	1967
Bilodeau Mikala M Perino	(920)784-8105 perinomm@gmail.com	779 E Independence Dr Apt 6 Palatine IL 60074	NI	Teacher	Tchr	Immanuel Palatine IL	(847)359-1936	CH	2022
Bimler Kimberly A Jacobson	(847)840-8586 mrsbimler@gmail.com	6834 Hampshire Ct Maryville IL 62062	SI	Teacher	Tchr	Trinity Edwardsville IL	(618)656-7002	RF	1990
Bimler Rebecca E Schmidt	(402)641-9629 rebeccacdc2016@gmail.com	211 Deep Water Dr Lincoln NE 68527	NEB	Teacher	EM			S	1985

*Multiple Assignments (See Church Worker Locator for Additional Details)
See Page 53 for the Table of Abbreviations for key to District, Classification, Position, and College abbreviations.
**C =Candidate; EM =Emeritus; the date following the C is the month and year the Candidate status began

NAME	TELEPHONE NUMBER EMAIL	STREET ADDRESS CITY/STATE/ZIP	DISTRICT	CLASS.	POSITION/ STATUS**	WHERE SERVING	OFFICE PHONE	COLLEGE/ UNIV/CQ	YR GRAD
Bimler Richard W Dr	(630)924-1522 rbimler@gmail.com	336 W Hampshire Dr Bloomingdale IL 60108	NI	DCE	EM			CQ	1976
Binnie Meredith F Joyce	(702)326-5942 mrs.binnie@gmail.com	1376 Felspar St San Diego CA 92109	PSW	Teacher	Prin	St Pauls San Diego CA	(858)272-6282	IV	2002
Bira Carolyn I Spatz	(810)240-1614 carolynbira@gmail.com	6356 Queens Ct Flushing MI 48433	MI	DCE	EM			S	1978
Bird Debra F Marquardt	(507)330-3267 dbird06@gmail.com	514 Eagle Heights Rd Canon GA 30520	FG	DCE	C07/2016			SP	1984
Bird Terry L Smith	(913)244-8872 birdt88@yahoo.com	1549 N Cherry Dr Stevensville MI 49127	MI	Teacher	EM			S	1977
Birdsong John L	(713)937-8159 jbirdsong1@hotmail.com	9506 Lark Meadow Dr Houston TX 77040	TX	Teacher	Tchr	St Mark Houston TX	(713)468-2623	CQ	2002
Birge Laura A Dippel	(217)379-0619 brige@conxxus.com	536 S Vermillion St Paxton IL 60957	CI	Teacher	Tchr	St Johns Buckley IL	(217)394-2444	MQ	2006
Birk Amy C Werner	(573)225-5279 abirk@saxonylutheranhigh.org	75 Red Bird Ln Altenburg MO 63732	MO	Teacher	Tchr	Saxony Jackson MO	(573)204-7555	CQ	2005
Birkedal Ellen L Hente	(314)448-8129 ellen.birkedal@yahoo.com	6839 Casselberry Ct Saint Louis MO 63123	MO	Teacher	C07/2016			S	2011
Birkmire Amber N	(260)443-6464 anbirkmire@gmail.com	3508 Jackson Blvd Rapid City SD 57702	SD	Teacher	Tchr	Zion Rapid City SD	(605)342-5749	CH	2013
Birnbaum David C	(512)595-2262 teacherbirnbaum@hotmail.com	1104 N 4th St Ponca City OK 74601	KS	Teacher	Tchr	Trinity Atchison KS	(913)367-4763	AU	1990
Birnbaum Julie D Meier	(512)797-9376 jdbrinbaum@yahoo.com	504 N 12 St Atchison KS 66002	KS	Teacher	C06/2024			S	1994
Birner Jonathan G	(239)248-4321 musicdirector@graceofnaples.com	255 Burnt Pine Dr Naples FL 34119	FG	DPM	Mem C	Grace Naples FL	(239)261-7421	CQ	2014
Birner Sandra J Reif	(239)248-3229 birnerj@yahoo.com	255 Burnt Pine Dr Naples FL 34119	FG	Teacher	C07/2016			BR	1983
Birt Jena M Schwalenberg	(402)276-6374 jena.schwalenberg@cune.org	1414 Blue Spruce Dr Lincoln NE 68505	NEB	Teacher	Tchr	Faith Lincoln NE	(402)466-7402	S	2014
Bischoff Marianne	(419)575-6910 ecstatic22000@yahoo.com	9 Mason Rd Holyoke MA 01040	NE	Teacher	EM			RF	1972
Bishop Becky A Ward	(832)202-8073 bishopb@trinityklein.org	24141 Rustling Oaks St Magnolia TX 77355	TX	Teacher	Tchr	Trinity Spring TX	(281)376-5810	CQ	2014
Bishop Deanna L Mack	(309)382-1106 mamabishop13@yahoo.com	301 Beloit Rd Marquette Hts IL 61554	CI	Teacher	EM			CQ	2015
Bishop Heidi J Deac	(502)4679-6642 heidijoy0517@gmail.com	1720 Riverwood Dr Algonquin IL 60102	NI	Deaconess	S Miss	Office of International Mission Saint Louis MO		CH	2007
Bishop Mary J Lutz	(231)563-6642 micsbishop@yahoo.com	7190 Juniper Ct Norton Shores MI 49456	MI	Teacher	EM			RF	1967
Bishop Natalie D Eilers	(503)764-9597 nbishop@columbiachristian.com	16317 NE Multnomah St Portland OR 97230	NOW	Teacher	C07/2016			PO	1990
Bishop Rita L Burrow	(217)454-5016 rlb2b@att.net	660 Country Manor Dr Decatur IL 62521	CI	Teacher	EM			RF	1976
Bishop Sarah N Rathe	(209) 324-4157 sarah.rathe@yahoo.com	1185 Rosewood Ave San Carlos CA 94070	CNH	Teacher	Tchr	Redeemer Redwood City CA	(650)366-3466	IV	2004
Biskupski Alyssa M	(414)336-2784 alyssa.biskupski@cuw.edu	2548 S 98th St West Allis WI 53227	SW	Teacher	Tchr	First Immanuel Cedarburg WI	(262)377-6610	MQ	2019
Bisping Jerald L	(478)397-4669 bispingjerry@outlook.com	122 Holly Pointe Warner Robins GA 31088	FG	Teacher	Mem C	Mount Calvary Warner Robins GA	(478)922-1418	S	1964
Bissell Ann M Hetzner	(989)295-5856 abissell@firstlutheranschool.com	541 N Patton Ave Rockwood TN 37854	MDS	Teacher	Tchr	First Knoxville TN	(865)524-0308	AA	2007
Bitter Denise A Bondy	(785)224-9905 den@bittersweet2.com		NEB	Teacher	EM			S	1971
Bittner Carol S Witte	(260)724-9713	8550 NW Winchester Rd Decatur IN 46733	IN	Teacher	EM			RF	1964
Black April C	(715)524-4708	N5837 Lake Dr Shawano WI 54166	NW	Teacher	Tchr	Saint James Shawano WI	(715)524-4815	CQ	2006
Black David W	(720)425-0313 david.black@lhsparker.org	3767 Bucknell Cir Hghlnds Ranch CO 80129	RM	Teacher	Tchr	Lutheran Parker CO	(303)841-5551	MQ	1988
Black Gail D Gierke	(303)903-1008 gblack@sothfamily.org	3767 Bucknell Cir Hghlnds Ranch CO 80129	RM	DPM	Mem C	Shepherd Hills Centennial CO	(303)798-0711	MQ	1988
Black Kenneth W	(847)802-4937 mentorken1@comcast.net	13060 Crestview Dr Huntley IL 60142	NI	Teacher	EM			RF	1958
Black Sarah L Vandercook	(806)881-8935 sarahblacktexas@gmail.com	11950 E Fm 1151 Amarillo TX 79118	TX	Teacher	P/Tchr	Trinity Amarillo TX	(806)352-5620	AU	1994
Blackburn Craig A Dr	(925) 683-8364 cblackburn77@gmail.com	7493 Interlachen Ave San Ramon CA 94583	CNH	Teacher	C02/2025			IV	1987
Blackfeather Stephanie K Huelsman	ssblackfeather3@gmail.com	1519 S Wolf Rd Apt 207 Prospect Hts IL 60070	NI	Teacher	C11/2020			RF	1994
Blackford Bryan K	(636)346-2749 blackfordbryan@gmail.com	1468 Wilkesboro Dr O'fallon MO 63368	TX	Teacher	D Miss	Texas District Round Rock TX	(800)951-3478	S	2000
Blackley Jenny E Krans	(713)449-3537 jenny.krans@cune.org	1873 Round Rock St Friendswood TX 77546	TX	Teacher	Tchr	South Houston TX	(281)464-8299	S	2003
Blackwell Judith J Radtke	(734)304-9665 judyblackwe@gmail.com	24131 Ross St Dearborn MI 48124	MI	Teacher	Tchr	Emmanuel Dearborn MI	(313)565-4002	CQ	2005
Blackwell Kristine M Zobel Deac	(630)234-1491 kbwrk123@gmail.com	2917 Brentwood Ct Woodridge IL 60517	NI	Deaconess	EM			RF	1983
Blackwell Ruth M	(301)751-7114 rblackwell@growingwithgrace.org	8970 Mount Air Rd Newburg MD 20664	SE	Teacher	Tchr	Grace La Plata MD	(301)932-0963	BR	1992
Blain Amy K DuPont	(714)529-0892 mrsblain@clsbrea.com	1249 Desoto St Placentia CA 92870	PSW	Teacher	Tchr	Christ Brea CA	(714)529-0892	CQ	2006
Blair Rachel K	rachel.blair012@gmail.com	2925 227th St. SW Brier WA 98036	NOW	Teacher	C03/2019			IV	2017

*Multiple Assignments (See Church Worker Locator for Additional Details)
See Page 53 for the Table of Abbreviations for key to District, Classification, Position, and College abbreviations.
**C =Candidate; EM =Emeritus; the date following the C is the month and year the Candidate status began

NAME	TELEPHONE NUMBER EMAIL	STREET ADDRESS CITY/STATE/ZIP	DISTRICT	CLASS.	POSITION/ STATUS**	WHERE SERVING	OFFICE PHONE	COLLEGE/ UNIV/CQ	YR GRAD
Blake Jennifer L Breinig	(308)380-6570 jlb0997@gmail.com	18315 Harrow Hill Dr Houston TX 77084	TX	Teacher	Tchr	St Mark Houston TX	(713)468-2623	S	2001
Blake Mary A Bobb	(630)781-5011 mary.blake3@comcast.net	6728 Woodridge Dr Woodridge IL 60517	NI	Teacher	EM			RF	1968
Blake Patrick K	(325)518-0140 patrickblake@gmail.com	P.O. Box 11629 Spring TX 77391	TX	DCE	Mem C	St Timothy Houston TX	(281)469-2457	AU	2005
Blake Sarah E Williams	(325)280-5170 blakes@trinityklein.org	P.O. Box 11629 Spring TX 77391	TX	Teacher	Tchr	Trinity Spring TX	(281)376-5810	AU	2006
Blake Sharon E Rachow	(810)392-2694 fritz64@frontier.com	78101 Memphis Ridge Rd Richmond MI 48062	MI	Teacher	EM			RF	1964
Blanco Miriam K Roth	(914)779-3758 mkb@concordia-ny.edu	33 Cherokee Rd Yonkers NY 10710	AT	Teacher	Tchr	The Village Bronxville NY	(914)337-0207	BR	1977
Blanco Rebekah L Dorn	(402)643-3185 rldorn2@gmail.com	1175 Rainbow Ave Seward NE 68434	NEB	Teacher	EM			CQ	2002
Blank Emily C Schumacher	(702)233-9922 blanke@flhsemail.org	8309 Iron Anvil Ct Las Vegas NV 89129	PSW	Teacher	Tchr	Faith Las Vegas NV	(702)804-4400	RF	2005
Blank Heidi M	(407)242-6674 heidi.blank407@gmail.com	874 Washington Blvd Fremont CA 94539	CNH	Teacher	Tchr	Prince of Peace Fremont CA	(510)793-3366	IV	2012
Blank Jonathan H	(509)737-7348 jonboy24@gmail.com	1915 S Ione St Kennewick WA 99337	NOW	Teacher	Tchr	Bethlehem Kennewick WA	(509)582-5624	RF	1989
Blank Karen A Reiter Deac	(260)797-3348 karen.blank@southwestlutheran.org	1823 Griswold Dr Apt D21 Fort Wayne IN 46805	IN	Deaconess	Mem C	Southwest Fort Wayne IN	(260)436-4474	FW-DEAC	2008
Blank Karen M Roberts	(407)273-6558	14214 Cavelle Ct Orlando FL 32828	S	Teacher	Tchr	St Lukes Oviedo FL	(407)365-3228	RF	1983
Blank Kathleen D Fitzner	(507)225-9854	46687 478th St Nicollet MN 56074	MNS	Teacher	EM			SP	1967
Blank Laura A Elmshauser	(303)895-9478	207 Michael Dr Oviedo FL 32765	FG	Teacher	D Ex/S	Florida-Georgia District Orlando FL	(407)857-5556	S	2011
Blank Norma L Krueger	(510)278-4436 normablank@sbcglobal.net	1645 Via Ventana San Lorenzo CA 94580	CNH	Tch/DCE	EM			RF	1966
Blank Stephen M	(702)233-9922 sblankman@yahoo.com	8309 Iron Anvil Ct Las Vegas NV 89129	PSW	Teacher	Tchr	Faith Las Vegas NV	(702)804-4400	RF	1998
Blanke Mark S Dr	mark.blanke@cune.edu	189 Wildwood Rd Seward NE 68434	NEB	Tch/DCE	EM			S	1982
Blanken Ann M Stevenson	(402)833-8408 amarieblanken@gmail.com	P.O. Box 117 Winside NE 68790	NEB	Teacher	C06/2018			S	2010
Blase Marie L Brandes	(860)521-2682 hikebikegal@hotmail.com	94 Meadowbrook Rd West Hartford CT 06107	NE	Teacher	EM			S	1968
Blatt Janice M Lang	(630)420-6207 jrblatt@comcast.net	1272 Stonebriar Ct Naperville IL 60540	NI	Teacher	EM			S	1962
Blatt Richard H	(630)420-6207 jrblatt@comcast.net	1272 Stonebriar Ct Naperville IL 60540	NI	Teacher	EM			RF	1960
Blazek Robert A	(317)885-9426 r.blazer@comcast.net	4463 Silver Springs Dr Greenwood IN 46142	IN	Teacher	EM			RF	1964
Blazek Rosalyn J Doenges	(317)885-9426 r.blazer@comcast.net	4463 Silver Springs Dr Greenwood IN 46142	IN	Teacher	EM			RF	1964
Bleeke Fred A	(512)864-0517 bleeke2@peoplepc.com	P.O. Box 37 Walburg TX 78673	TX	Teacher	EM			RF	1967
Bleidistel Paige A Scanlon	(573)635-0882 bleidistel4@aol.com	251 Constitution Dr Jefferson Cty MO 65109	MO	Teacher	Tchr	Trinity Jefferson City MO	(573)636-6750	CQ	2012
Bleke Alyssa M	(260)402-7050 aibleke5@gmail.com	622 N Wheeler St Griffith IN 46319	IN	Teacher	Tchr	St Pauls Munster IN	(219)836-6270	MQ	2015
Bleke Renee S Salomon		7124 Thompson Rd Hoagland IN 46745	IN	Teacher	C07/2016			S	1984
Blessing Derek G	(702)505-7180 blessingdr7@gmail.com	10834 Monaco Beach Ave Las Vegas NV 89166	PSW	Teacher	Prin	Lamb Of God Las Vegas NV	(702)645-4998	S	2014
Blessing Rebecca A Snow	(636)399-9436	517 Proud Eagle Ln Las Vegas NV 89144	PSW	Teacher	Tchr	Lamb Of God Las Vegas NV	(702)645-4998	S	2014
Blickensdorf Jennifer L Bilbrey	(586)770-1113 jennifer@theblicks.com	55644 Placid Dr Macomb MI 48042	MI	Teacher	Tchr	Immanuel Macomb MI	(586)286-4231	AA	2001
Blindauer Megan I Tews	(507)312-4272 blindauer@lutheranhigh.com	1549 N 26th St Sheboygan WI 53081	SW	Teacher	Tchr	Sheboygan Sheboygan WI	(920)452-3323	MQ	2019
Blinn Kristen K	(847)846-0064 kblinn@stpeterlcms.org	308 E Schaumburg Rd Schaumburg IL 60194	NI	Teacher	Tchr	St Peter Schaumburg IL	(847)885-3350	RF	1997
Bliss David A	(402)306-0154 dbliss8@gmail.com	1002 Queen City Blvd Norfolk NE 68701	NEB	Tch/DCE	EM			S	1979
Bliss Marcia E Hubert	(402)306-0325 mebliss@msn.com	1002 Queen City Blvd Norfolk NE 68701	NEB	Teacher	EM			S	1978
Bliss Mary R Stechholz	(630)306-3637 mbliss@tlcs.org	3009 Blandford Court New Lenox IL 60451	NI	Teacher	Tchr	Trinity Tinley Park IL	(708)532-9395	RF	2003
Bloch Martha A Grein	(812)498-0962 mbloch@immanuelschool.org	1237 Hickory Hill Rd Seymour IN 47274	IN	Teacher	Tchr	Immanuel Seymour IN	(812)522-1301	S	1985
Block Jason R	(262)994-5808 jasonblock25@gmail.com	3520 Corona Dr Racine WI 53406	SW	Teacher	Prin	Lutheran High School Racine WI	(262)637-6538	MQ	1993
Block Marajean A Palmreuter	(734)568-0742 mblock4545@aol.com	6517 Black Diamond Ln Lambertville MI 48144	MI	Teacher	EM			RF	1967
Block Marlene V Menzel	(402)643-3324 marleneblock@hotmail.com	1261 N 1st St Seward NE 68434	NEB	Teacher	EM			CQ	1991
Block Melvin W	(708)366-3151 mmblock@sbcglobal.net	620 Beloit Ave Forest Park IL 60130	NI	Teacher	EM			RF	1961
Block Michelle R Nielsen	(989)652-6061 mblock@stlorenz.org	8145 S Block Rd Birch Run MI 48415	MI	Teacher	Tchr	St Lorenz Frankenmuth MI	(989)652-6141	S	1999
Blocker Holly B Wagner	(920)301-5283 blockerb@gmail.com	743 Lomond Dr NW Bagley MN 56621	MNN	Teacher	EM			S	1983

*Multiple Assignments (See Church Worker Locator for Additional Details)
See Page 53 for the Table of Abbreviations for key to District, Classification, Position, and College abbreviations.
**C =Candidate; EM =Emeritus; the date following the C is the month and year the Candidate status began

NAME	TELEPHONE NUMBER EMAIL	STREET ADDRESS CITY/STATE/ZIP	DISTRICT	CLASS.	POSITION/ STATUS**	WHERE SERVING	OFFICE PHONE	COLLEGE/ UNIV/CQ	YR GRAD
Blocker Jessica C Borchardt	(218)731-3425 dcejess@gmail.com		MNS	DCE	Mem C	St John Luverne MN	(507)283-2316	SP	2016
Bloebaum Mary T Schlecht	(309)828-8510 mtb1@trinluth.org	15 Stetson Dr Bloomington IL 61701	CI	DCE	Mem C	Trinity Bloomington IL	(309)828-6265	RF	1998
Blomenberg Nicholle R Harstad	(507)458-0338 lnblomenberg@gmail.com	4141 C St. Lincoln NE 68510	NEB	Teacher	C05/2025			S	2021
Blomenberg Paul M	(812)603-7944 6037944@gmail.com	1100 N 5th St Seward NE 68434	RM	Teacher	Tchr	Colorado Lutheran High School Parker CO	(303)841-5551	S	2007
Blomquist Barry E	(616)443-3676 bblomq@gmail.com	1820 Rowland Ave SE Grand Rapids MI 49546	MI	Teacher	EM			SP	1971
Bloom Julia M	jmbloom14@gmail.com		NEB	Teacher	Tchr	Concordia Omaha NE	(402)445-4000	S	2021
Bloomfield Anna C Meyer		5 Greenleaf Irvine CA 92604	PSW	Teacher	Tchr	Crean Irvine CA	(949)387-1199	S	2013
Blouch Kathleen E Barr	(816)858-5067 blouchkath@yahoo.com	12965 Ridgeview Dr Platte City MO 64079	MO	Teacher	Tchr	Martin Luther Kansas City MO	(816)734-1060	S	1986
Blue Emily K Lindsey	(920)400-9645 eklindsey3@gmail.com	314 Chestnut Street West Bend WI 53095	SW	Teacher	Tchr	St Johns West Bend WI	(262)334-3077	MQ	2021
Bluhm Don G	(715)848-5265 adbluhm@frontier.com	3011 Glendale Ave Wausau WI 54401	NW	Teacher	EM			S	1970
Bluhm Gerald A	(608)752-7595	606 S Franklin St Janesville WI 53548	SW	Teacher	EM			RF	1967
Blum Arthur P	(708)946-6477 arthurblum@att.net	36 Village Woods Dr Crete IL 60417	NI	Teacher	EM			RF	1962
Blume Kathryn L	(626)222-1047 kblume9204@aol.com	720 W Camino Real Ave Arcadia CA 91007	PSW	Teacher	Tchr	Zion Victorville CA	(760)245-9725	S	1980
Boatman Amy G Halbmaier Dr	(281)467-7812 aboatman@salem4u.com	15507 Stiller Park Dr Cypress TX 77429	TX	Teacher	Tchr	Salem Tomball TX	(281)351-8223	S	1994
Bobb Barry L Dr	(317)569-6784 barrylbobb@aol.com	14809 Fernwood Dr Carmel IN 46033	IN	Teacher	EM			RF	1973
Bobb Donna L Ferrebee	(317)569-6784 bobbdonna@yahoo.com	14809 Fernwood Dr Carmel IN 46033	IN	Teacher	EM			RF	1973
Boburka Carl M	(815)985-9869 bobnrok@hotmail.com	5537 El Palomino Dr Riverside CA 92509	PSW	Teacher	EM			RF	1975
Boburka Dustin P	(949)697-9348 dustin.p.boburka@gmail.com	3139 N River Mist Cir Orange CA 92865	PSW	Teacher	Tchr	Orange County Orange CA	(714)998-5151	IV	2004
Boburka Julie K Terrell	(805)890-9288 julie.boburka@gmail.com	3139 N River Mist Cir Orange CA 92865	PSW	Teacher	C07/2016			IV	2006
Bobzin John C	(660)463-7586 john_bobzin@yahoo.com	508 Travis St Concordia MO 64020	MO	Teacher	EM			S	1965
Boccalupo Christopher	(631)277-7986 youthwker@msn.com	280 Belmore Ave Apt 153 East Islip NY 11730	AT	DCE	Mem C	Trinity Islip NY	(631)277-1555	CQ	2009
Bocek Alissa D Johnson	(630)518-7798	8030 State Route 47 Yorkville IL 60560	NI	Teacher	Tchr	Cross Yorkville IL	(630)553-7861	RF	2005
Boche Benjamin A Dr	(630)835-2295 bennyboche@gmail.com	2606 Sears St. Valparaiso IN 46383	IN	Teacher	C12/2019			S	2005
Boche Darcia J Wenzel	(307)338-8842 gdboche@hotmail.com	2918 E J St Torrington WY 82240	WY	Teacher	C07/2016			S	2001
Bockelman James E	(402)643-7490 jbockelman@cune.edu	707 N 5th St Seward NE 68434	NEB	Teacher	S HS/C	Concordia University Nebraska Seward NE	(402)643-3651	S	1989
Bockelman Katie L	(402)890-0461 kbockel@yahoo.com	8971 Broken Spoke Dr Lincoln NE 68507	NEB	Teacher	Tchr	Lincoln Lincoln NE	(402)467-5404	S	1992
Bockelman Kelsey L Hizer	(720)335-7765 kelsey.bockelman@lhsparker.org	14424 Hop Clover Trl Parker CO 80134	RM	Teacher	Tchr	Colorado Lutheran High School Parker CO	(303)841-5551	S	2019
Bockelmann Louise A Radtke	(815)953-2425 lou717@hotmail.com	1416 W County Line Rd Beecher IL 60401	NI	Teacher	EM			RF	1970
Bode Joel R	(832)567-8733	2303 Timberknob Ct Magnolia TX 77355	TX	Teacher	Pro Stf	Concordia Pflugerville TX	(512)248-2547	MQ	1983
Bode Richard L	(262)994-1073 dickbode13@gmail.com	6611 Mariner Dr Ut #5 Mount Pleasant WI 53406	SW	Teacher	EM			S	1955
Bode Timothy A	(734)285-9695 tim@ctk.me	44100 Harris Rd Belleville MI 48111	MI	DCO	Tchr	Christ The King Southgate MI	(734)285-9695	SP	1984
Bodemann Daniel E	(914)484-1866 dbodemann@stpeters-columbus.org	1710 Maple St Columbus IN 47201	IN	DPM	Mem C	St Peter Columbus IN	(812)372-1571	AU	2016
Bodey Kevin M	(815)491-9554 kevinbodey1234@gmail.com	222 Roosevelt St Belvidere IL 61008	NI	DCM	Mem C	Christ The Rock Rockford IL	(815)332-7191	MQ	2023
Bodin Kathy D Metz	(281)460-4060 bodeight@gmail.com	122 Mimosa Silk Ct Montgomery TX 77316	TX	Teacher	EM			RF	1979
Boeck Susan A Dodge	(414)217-6055 saboeck@sbcglobal.net	3039 Dodger Dr # 302 Fort Dodge IA 50501	IW	Teacher	EM			RF	1979
Boeder Curtis I Jr	(208)859-2019 cibvikings@hotmail.com	211 Parkland Way Caldwell ID 83605	NOW	Teacher	EM			S	1977
Boeder Nicole M Decker	(618)615-8751 nicoleboeder@concordiaspfld.org	2819 Southfield Dr Quincy IL 62301	CI	Teacher	Tchr	Concordia Springfield IL	(217)529-3307	SP	2016
Boehle-Silva Pamela L Boehle Deac	(916)624-8185 deaconess@holycrossrocklin.org	4701 Grove St Rocklin CA 95677	CNH	Deaconess	Mem C	Holy Cross Rocklin CA	(916)624-8185	FW-DEAC	2011
Boehlke Christian J	(314)753-1333 christian.boehlke@lcms.org	4595 Green Valley Dr High Ridge MO 63049	MO	Teacher	S Ex/S	The LCMS Corporate Saint Louis MO	(314)965-9000	S	2000
Boehlke Christine M Seibert	(330)945-8074 tina.boehlke@gmail.com	322 Orrville Ave Cuyahoga Falls OH 44221	OH	Teacher	C06/2020			RF	1990
Boehlke Jeffrey K	(320)485-3317 principal@ccls.net	139 Westgate Dr Winsted MN 55395	MNS	Teacher	P/Tchr	Christ Community Watertown MN	(952)955-1419	RF	1992

*Multiple Assignments (See Church Worker Locator for Additional Details)

See Page 53 for the Table of Abbreviations for key to District, Classification, Position, and College abbreviations.

**C =Candidate; EM =Emeritus; the date following the C is the month and year the Candidate status began

NAME	TELEPHONE NUMBER EMAIL	STREET ADDRESS CITY/STATE/ZIP	DISTRICT	CLASS.	POSITION/ STATUS**	WHERE SERVING	OFFICE PHONE	COLLEGE/ UNIV/CQ	YR GRAD
Boehlke Keith W	(218)346-7109	908 Coney St W Apt 102 Perham MN 56573	MNN	Teacher	EM			S	1971
Boehlke Kristine M Schmid	(636)287-2147 kschmid13@hotmail.com	4594 Green Valley Drive High Ridge MO 63049	MO	Teacher	C07/2016			MQ	1999
Boehm Wendy R Deac	(260)415-8526 wmeyer.boehm@gmail.com	c/o Bethlehem Lutheran Church 6514 E 750 N Ossian IN 46777	IN	Deaconess	Mem C	Bethlehem Ossian IN	(260)597-7121	FW-DEAC	2019
Boehme Carolyn K Lefevre	(262)253-4808 ckboehme@aol.com	N91W17546 Saint Regis Dr Menomonee Fls WI 53051	SW	Teacher	EM			RF	1969
Boehme Joyce A Theilen	(217)787-5415 jboehme1010@gmail.com	8342 Bomke Rd Pleasant Plns IL 62677	CI	Teacher	EM			CQ	1995
Boehme Melissa M Wren	(217)503-8409 melissamboehme@gmail.com	2109 Kaskaskia Dr Springfield IL 62702	CI	Teacher	C05/2022			S	2010
Boehme Wendy S Brown	(217)891-5517 mrs.w.boehme@gmail.com	50 Harbauer Ln Springfield IL 62702	CI	Teacher	C12/2021			S	2012
Boehne Bruce K	(469)879-9874 bruceboehne@netscape.net	626 Wentworth Dr Richardson TX 75081	TX	Teacher	EM			CQ	1995
Boeka Cassie D	(308)530-5609 dce@trinityarapahoe.org	808 6th St. Arapahoe NE 68922	NEB	DCE	Mem C	Trinity Arapahoe NE	(308)962-7667	S	2018
Boenker Mary J Wolf	(630) 939-2210 mjboenker41@gmail.com	332 Lakemont Ct Bloomingdale IL 60108	NI	Teacher	EM			S	1963
Boerboom Anne Gifford	aboerboom@stmarksmilford.org	1133 Forest Run Dr Batavia OH 45103	OH	Teacher	Tchr	St Mark Milford OH	(513)575-0292	SP	2019
Boerger Karen L	(740)857-1535 karenboerger@aol.com	800 Rosedale Rd Irwin OH 43029	OH	Teacher	EM			AA	2003
Boerger Karen M Knapp	(317)919-7645 boergernp@icloud.com	6184 W Richman Ln New Palestine IN 46163	IN	Teacher	EM			S	1966
Boerger Kenneth M	(440)334-3893 ksboerger@sbcglobal.net	14722 Windsor Castle Ln Strongsville OH 44149	OH	Teacher	EM			S	1972
Boerger Megan L Genskow	(262)389-0913 megan.gen325@gmail.com	3870 N 88th St Milwaukee WI 53222	SW	Teacher	Pro Stf	Milwaukee LHS Milwaukee WI	(414)461-6000	MQ	2010
Boerger Susan J Stibrich	(440)876-7405 nonnyboerger@gmail.com	14722 Windsor Castle Ln Strongsville OH 44149	OH	Teacher	EM			S	1973
Boernke Debra Heitschmidt	(303)498-0321 dheitschmidt@hotmail.com	366 Matsuno St Brighton CO 80601	RM	Teacher	C07/2019			S	2001
Boerrigter Mary C Yung	(310)387-2935 cboerrigter54@gmail.com	3025 Lost Creek Rd N Montrose CO 81401	RM	Teacher	EM			S	1976
Boessling Jordan A	(512)542-1624 jordan.kristenb@gmail.com	311 Freshwater Drive Bastrop TX 78602	TX	Teacher	Mem C	Christ Austin TX	(512)442-5844	MQ	2003
Boester Andrea E	(618)322-3344 bboester@gmail.com	874 W Lebanon St Nashville IL 62263	SI	Teacher	Tchr	Trinity Hoffman IL	(618)495-2545	CQ	2006
Boetsch Christina N	(949)929-4765	22002 Tanbark Ln Lake Forest CA 92630	PSW	Teacher	Tchr	Light of Christ Irvine CA	(949)786-3326	IV	2010
Boettcher Christine S Pankow	(920)969-9386 paulandchrisboettcher@gmail.com	P.O. Box 2934 Frisco CO 80443	RM	Teacher	C07/2016			MQ	1987
Boettcher Joel W	(816)796-6916 g3bj@swbell.net	812 N Mohican Dr Independence MO 64056	MO	Teacher	EM			AA	1983
Boettcher Karen S Vogts	(316)719-1712 kboettcher@holycrosslutheran.net	1614 N Lakeside Ct Andover KS 67002	KS	Teacher	Prin	Holy Cross Wichita KS	(316)684-5201	S	1975
Boettcher Paul J	(970)445-2460 paulandchrisboettcher@gmail.com	P.O. Box 2934 Frisco CO 80443	RM	Teacher	C07/2016			S	1986
Boettcher Teddy M	(316)682-5193 tmbeduc@hotmail.com	1614 N Lakeside Ct Andover KS 67002	KS	Teacher	EM			S	1975
Boewe Amy E Marasus	(918)894-9180 amydce@gmail.com	8940 Jenny Lane Canadian Lakes MI 49346	MI	DCE	EM			SP	2012
Boggs Laura J Wykowski	lauraboggs@sbcglobal.net	929 S Chester Ave Park Ridge IL 60068	NI	Teacher	Tchr	St Andrews Park Ridge IL	(847)823-9308	RF	1983
Bogle Bethany N Duerr	(209)747-4432 bethanybogle20@gmail.com	2413 Hemlock Ct Merced CA 95340	CNH	Teacher	Tchr	St Paul Merced CA	(209)383-3301	IV	2015
Bohl Noreen F Brodersen	(712)859-3117 iacontryfolk@gmail.com	3734 280th St Graettinger IA 51342	IW	Teacher	EM			S	1972
Bohler Donald M	(618)667-9850 donmbohler@sbcglobal.net	316 Old Homestead Dr Troy IL 62294	MO	Teacher	EM			RF	1961
Bohler Lisa M Janssen	(218) 289-0025 lmbohler@icloud.com	800 Washington Ave Crookston MN 56716	MNN	Teacher	Tchr	Our Saviors Crookston MN	(218)281-5191	SP	1994
Bohlmann Allyson E Hoger	(708)288-1119 ahoger13@sbcglobal.net	54 Cloverdale Drive St Charles MO 63304	MO	Teacher	Tchr	Immanuel Saint Charles MO	(636)946-2656	Other	2017
Bohlmann Deborah A Schoof	(580)338-3820 debnote@hotmail.com	Rt 1 Box 80a Hooker OK 73945	OK	Teacher	EM			SP	1977
Bohlmann Derek G	(217)979-7568 gabesinvesting2@yahoo.com	408 S Railroad Ave Buckley IL 60918	CI	Teacher	Tchr	Christ Lutheran HS Buckley IL	(217)394-2547	S	1991
Bohmann Kari S Hottinger	(262)450-7516 kari.bohmann@mtolivemke.org	W243 S10285 Meadow Cir Big Bend WI 53103	SW	Teacher	Tchr	Mount Olive Milwaukee WI	(414)774-2200	MQ	1988
Bohn Stephanie N Kaiser	(314)640-3228 sbohn@mlslions.org	1802 English Oak Drive Lake St. Louis MO 63367	MO	Teacher	Tchr	Messiah Weldon Spring MO	(636)926-9773	MQ	2010
Bohnet Kathleen K Cotner	(618)910-1698 kathybohnet@gmail.com	6 Evergreen Ln Glen Carbon IL 62034	SI	Teacher	EM			S	1962
Bohnhoff Rachel K	(920)698-2732 rachel.bohnhoff@cune.org		SW	Teacher	C07/2022			S	2015
Bohning Roy W	(314)591-6528 rbohning6311@outlook.com	28240 Highway F Wright City MO 63390	MO	Teacher	EM			S	1976
Bohot Kim L Peterson	kbohot@mlchouston.org	9522 Walnut Glen Dr Houston TX 77064	TX	Teacher	Tchr	Memorial Houston TX	(713)782-6079	AU	1995
Bohren Elizabeth L Rogers	(651)328-1758 elizabeth.bohren@ concordiaacademy.com	2488 Arlington Ave E Maplewood MN 55119	MNS	Teacher	Tchr	Concordia Academy Roseville MN	(651)484-8429	S	2002

*Multiple Assignments (See Church Worker Locator for Additional Details)

See Page 53 for the Table of Abbreviations for key to District, Classification, Position, and College abbreviations.

**C =Candidate; EM =Emeritus; the date following the C is the month and year the Candidate status began

NAME	TELEPHONE NUMBER EMAIL	STREET ADDRESS CITY/STATE/ZIP	DISTRICT	CLASS.	POSITION/ STATUS**	WHERE SERVING	OFFICE PHONE	COLLEGE/ UNIV/CQ	YR GRAD
Bok Karen M Holmes	(443)285-1545 karen.bok87@gmail.com	341 Pinnacle Dr Lake Mills WI 53551	SW	Teacher	EM			RF	1983
Boldt Frederick F	(262)567-0034 fboldt@wi.rr.com	W117 Vista Dr Oconomowoc WI 53066	SW	Teacher	EM			RF	1968
Boldt Harold D	(281)255-2685 djboldt5@gmail.com	19107 Shale Creek Dr Tomball TX 77337	TX	Teacher	Tchr	Salem Tomball TX	(281)351-8223	MQ	1992
Boldt John P	(734)731-2456 jboldt@trinitylutheranmonroe.org	15385 Eastwood St Apt 3b Monroe MI 48161	MI	Teacher	Tchr	Trinity Monroe MI	(734)241-1160	S	1978
Bolger Lori L Ananias		7515 W Eden Ct Milwaukee WI 53220	SW	Teacher	EM			MQ	2010
Bolin Andrew B	(314)808-7576 andrew@thebolinfamily.com	2639 Sutton Blvd Saint Louis MO 63143	MO	DFLM	Mem C	Cong Chai v Shalom Saint Louis MO	(314)645-4456	AA	2002
Bolin Kaitlyn R Christensen	(262)237-9651 kaitlyn.bolin@cune.org	2948 Goldenrod Dr Grand Island NE 68801	NEB	Teacher	Tchr	Grand Island Grand Island NE	(308)385-3900	S	2019
Boline Kristin C Tarabochia	(206)612-7644 susakgirl@hotmail.com		NOW	Teacher	C07/2016			PO	2002
Boll Andrew V		7331 Sugar Beet Cir Billings MT 59106	MT	Teacher	C06/2024			S	2004
Boll Caroline A Timmerman	(507)259-2237 jcboll2103@charter.net	2103 Wyndham Park Dr Billings MT 59102	MT	Teacher	EM			S	1961
Boll David R	dave.boll@concordiaacademy.com	2965 165th Ln NE Ham Lake MN 55304	MNS	Teacher	Tchr	Concordia Academy Roseville MN	(651)484-8429	S	1987
Boll Jennifer Arend		325 Wyatt Circle Billings MT 59106	MT	Teacher	Tchr	Trinity Billings MT	(406)245-3984	S	2002
Boll John V	(651)485-3041 jcboll2103@charter.net	2103 Wyndham Park Dr Billings MT 59102	MT	Teacher	EM			S	1962
Boll Matthew D	(651)280-8677 matthew.boll@cune.org	2965 -165th Ln NE Ham Lake MN 55304	MNS	Teacher	Tchr	Trinity Lone Oak Eagan MN	(651)454-1139	S	2023
Boll Michael J	(701)955-8195 boll@lutherschools.org	114 Firebarn Rd Circle Pines MN 55014	MNS	Teacher	Tchr	King Of Kings Roseville MN	(651)484-5142	S	2016
Bolling Janine M Deac	dr.jay@bethlehemstlouis.org	c/o Bethlehem Lutheran Church 2153 Salisbury St Saint Louis MO 63107	MO	Deaconess	Mem C	Bethlehem Saint Louis MO	(314)231-4702	CH	2011
Bolling Lorenda Kirby	(217)737-1037 lbolling@wordoflifeschool.net	6974 Lindenwood Pl Saint Louis MO 63109	MO	Teacher	Tchr	Word of Life Saint Louis MO	(314)832-1244	CH	2014
Bollinger Sandra L Taylor		N59W38483 Kohl Ln Oconomowoc WI 53066	SW	Teacher	EM			CQ	2003
Bolognini Andrea C	(602)321-5979 abolognini@stmarkhouston.org	Saint Mark Lutheran Church 1515 Hillendahl Blvd Houston TX 77055	TX	DCE	Tchr	St Mark Houston TX	(713)468-2623	AU	2009
Bolosan Sherry L Hentze	(630)814-9103 sherrybolosan@ymail.com	614 W 16th St Sterling IL 61081	NI	DCE	C03/2023			RF	2003
Bolstad Solveig K	sbolstad@sjlsarnold.org		MO	Teacher	Tchr	St John Arnold MO	(636)464-7303	MQ	2007
Bolt Jeanine L Lutz	(719) 671-8004 trinity.rbolt@gmail.com	991 W Stallion Dr Pueblo West CO 81007	RM	Teacher	EM			S	1978
Bolt Jonathan M	(248)495-3655	3071 Navajo Xing New Haven IN 46774	IN	Teacher	Tchr	Central New Haven IN	(260)493-2502	AA	2005
Bolt R K	(630)935-0704 kirk.louise@sbcglobal.net	1803 Buckingham Green Ct Saint Charles MO 63303	MO	Teacher	EM			RF	1970
Bolton Sheila K Stuckwisch		4826 Auburn Frd Greenwood IN 46142	IN	Teacher	C07/2016			RF	1997
Bolwerk-Heien Anne C Heien	(309)409-6517 anneheien14@gmail.com	634 Finch Ct Walled Lake MI 48390	MI	Teacher	Mem C	St Matthew Walled Lake MI	(248)624-7676	MQ	2012
Bomareto Amy N Schaefer	(303)906-0370 amybom31@gmail.com	7123 Vivian Ct Arvada CO 80004	RM	Teacher	C07/2016			S	2002
Bond Gillian M Deac	(405) 310-0105 bondg@csl.edu	2808 Sandstone Dr Norman OK 73071	OK	Deaconess	EM			FW-DEAC	2010
Bonde Mary Deitemeyer	(612)217-4154 marybonde@gmail.com	5858 E County Road 1000 N Seymour IN 47274	IN	DPM	Mem C	Grace Columbus IN	(812)372-4859	MQ	2003
Bonderson Anne L	(619)871-5833 annebonderson@hotmail.com	8499 W Ross Ave Peoria AZ 85382	PSW	Teacher	Tchr	Atonement Glendale AZ	(623)374-3019	S	2004
Bonfield Dianna E Fenske Deac	(847)287-6624 dianna@lutheranchurchcharities.org	3020 Milwaukee Ave Northbrook IL 60062	NI	Deaconess	RSO	Lutheran Church Charities Northbrook IL	(866)455-6466	Other	1972
Bongard Stephanie	(219)921-9401 stephanie.bongard@sjdenver.org	7537 Dale Ave Saint Louis MO 63117	RM	Teacher	Tchr	St John's Denver CO	(303)733-3778	MW	2017
Bonine Natasha D	(620)615-1299	323 Buell Ave Ravenna NE 68869	WY	Teacher	C08/2024			S	2020
Bonk Eugene J	(760)855-3709 genejb@aol.com	130 W Strawberry Tree Ave Queen Creek AZ 85140	PSW	Teacher	C07/2016			S	1981
Bonner Susan K Gaiser	(623)877-3419 azbonner@aol.com	11528 W Rosewood Dr Avondale AZ 85392	PSW	Teacher	EM			S	1965
Boone Natalie E Weinhold	(636)698-2226 bnboone1113@gmail.com	275 Lakeview Farms Dr Saint Charles MO 63304	MO	Teacher	Tchr	Zion Saint Charles MO	(636)441-7424	Other	2017
Boor John M	jmboor.13@gmail.com	20662 S Graceland Ln Frankfort IL 60423	NI	Teacher	EM			RF	1975
Boos Manfred B Dr	(708) 334-0426 boos6014@gmail.com	1018 Home Ave Oak Park IL 60304	NI	Teacher	EM			RF	1970
Boos Sharon A Gerding	(708)848-3791 shrn.boos@gmail.com	1018 Home Ave Oak Park IL 60304	NI	Teacher	EM			RF	1970
Bopp Anne E Lehmann	(208)241-2611 abopp@gracepocatello.org	9383 W Autumn Ln Pocatello ID 83204	NOW	Teacher	Tchr	Grace Pocatello ID	(208)237-4142	PO	1986
Borchardt Diane M Heintz	(612)578-8288 mnirish@aol.com	13969 Edenwood Ct Apple Valley MN 55124	MNS	Teacher	EM			SP	1976

*Multiple Assignments (See Church Worker Locator for Additional Details)
See Page 53 for the Table of Abbreviations for key to District, Classification, Position, and College abbreviations.
**C =Candidate; EM =Emeritus; the date following the C is the month and year the Candidate status began

NAME	TELEPHONE NUMBER EMAIL	STREET ADDRESS CITY/STATE/ZIP	DISTRICT	CLASS.	POSITION/ STATUS**	WHERE SERVING	OFFICE PHONE	COLLEGE/ UNIV/CQ	YR GRAD
Borcherding David F	(402)570-8467 borcherding96@yahoo.com	6934 S 88th St Lincoln NE 68526	NEB	Teacher	EM			S	1989
Borcherding Gordon L	(847)577-9398	116 S Albert St Mt Prospect IL 60056	NI	Teacher	EM			RF	1958
Borcherding Kaylee M Vanness	(641)580-1173 kborcherding@stpaulslatimer.org	549 170th St. Latimer IA 50452	IE	Teacher	Tchr	St Pauls Latimer IA	(641)579-6046	CQ	2023
Borcherding Mark C	(317)966-4919 borchm53@gmail.com	10687 Jacks Way Indianapolis IN 46234	IN	Tch/DCE	EM			S	1977
Borcherding Wendy S Hopfensperger	(402)570-8939 wendy.borcherding@messiah.us	6934 S88th Lincoln NE 68526	NEB	Teacher	Tchr	Messiah Lincoln NE	(402)489-3024	RF	1993
Borchers Kevin L Dr	klborch@gmail.com	125 Lakeview Drive Unit 703 Bloomingdale IL 60108	NI	Tch/DCE	Pro Stf	Trinity Roselle IL	(630)894-3263	RF	1981
Borchin Jane C Crosbie	(570)848-1965 rogerborchin@hotmail.com	37 Windsor Rd Southhampton NJ 08088	NJ	Teacher	EM			RF	1971
Borchin Roger G	(570)848-1965 rogerborchin@hotmail.com	37 Windsor Rd Southhampton NJ 08088	NJ	Teacher	EM			RF	1965
Bordeaux Betty J	(314)695-4545 bjbordeaux@gmail.com	6844 Weber Rd Saint Louis MO 63123	MO	Teacher	EM			RF	1968
Bordeaux Joseph A Dr	(314)698-2196 bjbordeaux75@gmail.com	6844 Weber Rd Saint Louis MO 63123	MO	Teacher	EM			CQ	1972
Bordeleau Eileen L Natzke	(920)869-2540 perennialman@hotmail.com	472 Rose Hill Dr Hobart WI 54155	NW	Teacher	EM			S	1975
Bordeleau Jessica C Neary	(314)435-0506 jessica.bordeleau@gmail.com	2524 Saint Giles Rd Saint Louis MO 63122	MO	Teacher	C07/2016			MQ	1999
Borg Steven E	(561)734-1639 sborg@trinitydelray.org	172 SE 28th Ct Boynton Beach FL 33435	FG	Teacher	Tchr	Trinity Delray Beach FL	(561)276-8458	RF	1976
Borgers Karen J Bohlmann	(815)889-5223 ekborgers@hotmail.com	116 S Woodworth Rd Milford IL 60953	CI	Teacher	EM			RF	1969
Borgmann Audrey L Haynes	(541)647-7445 audrey.borgmann@gmail.com	20605 SE Meadowsweet Dr Bend OR 97702	NOW	Teacher	Tchr	Trinity Bend OR	(541)382-1850	S	2009
Boriack Anna C Witt Dr	(717)572-5030 annacwitt@gmail.com	2005 Old Rothsville Rd Lititz PA 17543	NEB	Teacher	S HS/C	Concordia University Nebraska Seward NE	(402)643-3651	S	2003
Boris Jennifer R Krueger	boris.jennifer@yahoo.com	950 Genesee St Waukesha WI 53186	SW	Teacher	Tchr	Divine Redeemer Hartland WI	(262)367-3664	MQ	1994
Boris Scott W	(262)574-9405 sboris@twc.com	950 Genesee St Waukesha WI 53186	SW	Teacher	Tchr	Zion Menomonee Falls WI	(262)781-7437	MQ	1995
Bork Kristin J	(314)550-3467 kbork@lhsn.org	14281 Cape Horn Pl Florissant MO 63034	MO	Teacher	Tchr	Luth High School Assn St Louis Saint Louis MO	(314)833-2904	S	2003
Bork Marilyn J Schmidt	(402)646-2174 nebraskabork@hotmail.com	1254 Rainbow Ave Seward NE 68434	NEB	Teacher	EM			S	1970
Bork Ronald D Dr	(402)613-1631 ronbork48@gmail.com	1254 Rainbow Ave Seward NE 68434	NEB	Teacher	EM			S	1970
Borlaug Katie M	(952)913-5328 principal@stpaulspriorlake.org	4506 Bulrush Blvd Shakopee MN 55379	MNS	Teacher	Prin	St Pauls Prior Lake MN	(952)447-2117	CQ	2022
Bormuth Sara B Doolen Deac	(360)510-6385 bormuth.sara5@gmail.com	1568 Barrell Springs Rd Bellingham WA 98229	NOW	Deaconess	EM			Other	1971
Bornheimer Alyssa A Healy	(734)883-7687 stephenalyssa@gmail.com	515 Stratton Rd Fort Wayne IN 46825	IN	Teacher	C07/2016			AA	2009
Bornheimer Stephen B		515 Stratton Rd Fort Wayne IN 46825	IN	Teacher	S HS/C	Concordia Theological Seminary Fort Wayne IN	(260)452-2100	AA	2010
Borth Elizabeth L Wilson Deac	(636)544-1926 bothborths@yahoo.com	11101 Oakshore Ln Clermont FL 34711	FG	Deaconess	C08/2022			CH	2007
Bortz Kimberly J Fries	(407)443-1880 tkbortz@bellsouth.net	432 Flyrod Cir Orlando FL 32825	FG	Teacher	C07/2016			RF	1992
Bortz Todd E	(407)443-6157 tkbortz@bellsouth.net	432 Flyrod Cir Orlando FL 32825	FG	Teacher	C07/2016			RF	1993
Bosma Cecelia F Koller	(480)369-2269 cfbosma@gmail.com	431 S Lila Cir Litchfield Pk AZ 85340	PSW	Teacher	C05/2018			CQ	2007
Bossaller Cindy K Dummer	thebossallers5@gmail.com	59 Durham Dr Washington MO 63090	MO	Teacher	EM			RF	1984
Bost Thomas H	(804)445-5345	11501 Courthouse Acres Rd Midlothian VA 23114	SE	Teacher	EM			CQ	2013
Bostic Sandra K Sprenger	(573)651-4064 sbostic@t-lutheranschool.org	1833 Marietta St Cpe Girardeau MO 63701	MO	Teacher	Tchr	Trinity Cape Girardeau MO	(573)334-1068	CQ	2009
Boston Vicki L Schwab	(618)344-6038 veboston@charter.net	2035 Greenbrier Dr Collinsville IL 62234	SI	Teacher	C07/2016			S	1975
Bott Renae Weaver	(785)747-7172 trbott@bluevalley.net	1740 3rd Rd Linn KS 66953	KS	Teacher	Tchr	Linn Linn KS	(785)348-5792	CQ	2023
Bottcher Ronald R		54 Briarwood Dr Belleville IL 62223	SI	Teacher	EM			S	1969
Bottrell Sandra M Blase	(217)498-7847 aeiouwy@hotmail.com	100 Deer Creek Rd Rochester IL 62563	CI	Teacher	EM			CQ	1983
Boudreau Noah J		3212 State St Apt 5 Quincy IL 62301	CI	DPM	Mem C	St John Quincy IL	(217)222-8579	SP	2020
Bouley Matthew L	(414)581-6756 trustmeicandoit@gmail.com	3040 Lilly Rd Brookfield WI 53005	SW	Teacher	Tchr	Wauwatosa Wauwatosa WI	(414)258-4558	MQ	2003
Bourgeois Janis K Pflantz	(618)493-6305 janbeau56@yahoo.com	186 N Main St Hoyleton IL 62803	SI	Teacher	EM			SP	1978
Bourgeois Julie A Schott	(410)271-7116 jbourgeois711@yahoo.com	526 W Main St Napoleon OH 43545	OH	Teacher	Tchr	St Paul Napoleon OH	(419)592-3535	RF	1989
Bourret Bonnie L Jensen	(308)879-4532 tbbourret@vistabeam.com	4470 Road 89 Potter NE 69156	WY	Teacher	EM			S	1981

*Multiple Assignments (See Church Worker Locator for Additional Details)
See Page 53 for the Table of Abbreviations for key to District, Classification, Position, and College abbreviations.
**C =Candidate; EM =Emeritus; the date following the C is the month and year the Candidate status began

NAME	TELEPHONE NUMBER EMAIL	STREET ADDRESS CITY/STATE/ZIP	DISTRICT	CLASS.	POSITION/ STATUS**	WHERE SERVING	OFFICE PHONE	COLLEGE/ UNIV/CQ	YR GRAD
Boutan Tonda M Jones	rtkcboutan@aol.com	199 Arapahoe Trl Carol Stream IL 60188	NI	Teacher	EM			CQ	1984
Bouy Sharon K Miller	(504)362-0132 spoohster@cox.net	913 Roberts St Gretna LA 70056	SO	Teacher	C07/2016			RF	1980
Boward Megan K	(979)324-8826 megan.boward@popcs.org	2426 April Sound Lane Frisco TX 75003	TX	Teacher	Tchr	Prince Of Peace Carrollton TX	(972)447-0532	CQ	2023
Bowdish Grant A	(810)569-5823 gbowdish@stmark.net	448 Sunset Blvd E Battle Creek MI 49017	MI	DPM	Mem C	St Mark Battle Creek MI	(269)964-0401	AA	2019
Bowen Carol L Mattfeld	carollbowen@icloud.com	18518 Branchdale Ln Spring TX 77379	TX	Teacher	Tchr	Trinity Klein Klein TX	(281)376-5773	AU	1998
Bower Edward R	(630)740-6118 ebower2453@sbcglobal.net	11835 Driftwood Dr Marion IL 62959	SI	Teacher	Prin	Immanuel Okawville IL	(618)243-6142	RF	1975
Bower Greta L Cutter	(734)516-4785 greta.bower@gmail.com	48024 Bemis Rd Van Buren Twp MI 48111	MI	Teacher	Tchr	Open Arms Belleville MI	(734)699-5000	AA	2006
Bower Kristine Nuoffer	kelbower@msn.com	1135 Ash St Broomfield CO 80020	RM	Teacher	Tchr	Mount Olive Aurora CO	(303)755-9123	IV	1994
Bowers Sandra J Miller Deac	(314)996-1741 sandra.bowers@lcms.org	c/o Lutheran Church-Missouri Synod 1333 S Kirkwood Rd Saint Louis MO 63122	MO	Deaconess	S Ex/S	Office of National Mission Saint Louis MO		SL-DEAC	2005
Bowland Brenna	(701)741-4748 brennanako@gmail.com	476 Morgan Dr Foley MN 56329	MNS	Teacher	C08/2023			CQ	2020
Bowlds Natasha A Westerman	(301)776-1775	6200 Goodman Rd Laurel MD 20707	SE	DCE	Mem C	Our Savior Laurel MD	(301)776-7670	CQ	2008
Bowles Debra D Yancey	(217)228-2197	3725 Tiffany Ln Quincy IL 62305	CI	Teacher	Tchr	St James Quincy IL	(217)222-8267	CQ	2007
Bowline Melanie S Pike		2724 Brienza Way Las Vegas NV 89117	PSW	Teacher	Tchr	Faith Las Vegas NV	(702)804-4400	S	1994
Bowman JoAnn Linn	(480)292-5899 jbowman@cglschool.org	1009 E Harvard Ave Gilbert AZ 85234	PSW	Teacher	Tchr	Christ Greenfield Gilbert AZ	(480)892-8521	CQ	2019
Bown Mary E Walker	(252)665-1372 maryebown2@gmail.com	723 E Union Ave Litchfield IL 62056	SI	Teacher	Tchr	Zion Litchfield IL	(217)324-2033	CQ	2015
Bowsher Monica L Carmean	(614)619-4693 mbowsher@sjsmarysville.org	20880 Collins Rd Milford Center OH 43045	OH	Teacher	Tchr	St Johns Marysville OH	(937)644-5540	CQ	2024
Boyce Deanne M Dahlke	deannemb@live.com	120 Colony Court Bastrop TX 78602	SW	Teacher	C06/2025			CQ	2012
Boyd Courtney N Mathieu	(918)859-8575 dcenikki@gmail.com	12206 E 79th St N Owasso OK 74055	OK	DCE	Mem C	Christ The Redeemer Tulsa OK	(918)492-6451	CQ	2007
Boyd Robert C	(863)603-8528 rboyd@stpaullakeland.org	8617 Backwater Dr Fort Wayne IN 46818	FG	Teacher	EM			CQ	1982
Boye Janet K	(402)438-9234 jboye15@neb.rr.com	4400 Waterbury Ln Lincoln NE 68516	FG	Teacher	C07/2016			S	1975
Boye Vicki L Dr	(402)643-3167 vboye@seward.cune.edu	1731 N 1st St Seward NE 68434	NEB	Teacher	S HS/C	Concordia University Nebraska Seward NE	(402)643-3651	S	1982
Boyer Deborah K Horenkamp	(636)922-3852 jboyer5272@aol.com	16 Trappers Way Saint Charles MO 63303	MO	Teacher	EM			CQ	1998
Boyer Linda R Krock	(217) 260-3127 linboyer51@gmail.com	1407 Woodridge Dr Danville IL 61832	CI	Teacher	EM			RF	1973
Boyer Lori L Bormet	(708)738-5593 lomobo1229@aol.com	1360 S Steware Ave Lombard IL 60148	NI	Teacher	Tchr	Walther Melrose Park IL	(708)344-0404	CQ	2023
Boyer Matthew P	(815)319-1581	PSC 305 Box 1878 Apo AP 96218	TX	Teacher	Tchr	Dallas Lutheran Sch Dallas TX	(214)349-8912	S	2012
Boyer Michele A Stewart	(415)586-4652 msbsf@yahoo.com	173 Majestic Ave San Francisco CA 94112	EN	Teacher	EM			RF	1971
Boyer Stephanie A Riggs	(989)860-8290 boyerst@ctkl.org	816 E Bay St Sebewaing MI 48759	MI	Teacher	Tchr	Christ The King Sebewaing MI	(989)883-3730	AA	2003
Boykin William O	(803)609-3424 billboykin@sc.rr.com	311 Newpark Pl Columbia SC 29212	SE	DCM	Mem C	Mount Olive Columbia SC	(803)781-5845	MQ	2010
Boylan Rachel E	rboylan1066@gmail.com	462 E Summer St Paxton IL 60957	CI	Teacher	C03/2019			S	2011
Boyle Kimberly K Hoppen	(660)687-9364 soundwind9@hotmail.com	507 S Travis St Concordia MO 64020	MO	Teacher	Tchr	Trinity Alma MO	(660)674-2376	S	1980
Braasch Allegra R Gunther	(720) 948-4012 allegrabraasch@gmail.com	16310 Saint Paul Dr Thornton CO 80602	RM	Teacher	Tchr	Bethlehem Lakewood CO	(303)238-7676	AA	2007
Braaten Lauren E Dorr Deac	(217)253-4539 laurenbraaten@gmail.com	706 E Northline Rd Tuscola IL 61953	CI	Deaconess	C07/2016			RF	2002
Braaten Rebecca L Schermer	(406)261-5221 becbraaten@gmail.com	1915 Okanogan Ave Wenatchee WA 98801	NOW	Teacher	Tchr	St Paul Wenatchee WA	(509)662-8790	PO	1982
Brackman Barbara J De Vries	(618)315-3589	1301 S Hackman St Staunton IL 62088	SI	Teacher	Tchr	Zion Staunton IL	(618)635-3060	CQ	1998
Brackman Diane M	(708)347-0050 dibrack@hotmail.com	3680 186th St Apt 404 Lansing IL 60438	NI	Teacher	EM			RF	1985
Brackman James E	(636)284-4973 jsbrackman@att.net	45 Little Creek Ln Saint Charles MO 63304	MO	Teacher	EM			S	1961
Brackman Jana M Holtmeier	(636)578-7599	867 McCauley Ct Saint Charles MO 63303	MO	Teacher	Tchr	Messiah Weldon Spring MO	(636)926-9773	S	1989
Brackman Timothy J Dr	(636)541-7977 tbrackman@lncrusaders.org	867 McCauley Ct Saint Charles MO 63303	MO	Teacher	Prin	Lutheran North Saint Louis MO	(314)389-3100	S	1989
Braddy Micah L	(636)734-8193 mlb823@gmail.com	12 Marcus Dr Saint Peters MO 63376	MO	Teacher	Pro Stf	St Charles Saint Peters MO	(636)928-5100	CH	2012
Bradley Carol J Buss	(713)943-2531	2914 Peach Ln Pasadena TX 77502	TX	Teacher	EM			S	1968
Bradley Donnell S Jernas	donnellsbradley@gmail.com	15848 Eastpark Ct Noblesville IN 46060	IN	Teacher	C07/2016			CQ	1999
Bradley Timothy	(303)475-9139 thetimothybradley@gmail.com	407 S Main St Concordia MO 64020	MO	Teacher	Tchr	St Paul Concordia MO	(660)463-2291	S	2012

*Multiple Assignments (See Church Worker Locator for Additional Details)

See Page 53 for the Table of Abbreviations for key to District, Classification, Position, and College abbreviations.

**C =Candidate; EM =Emeritus; the date following the C is the month and year the Candidate status began

NAME	TELEPHONE NUMBER EMAIL	STREET ADDRESS CITY/STATE/ZIP	DISTRICT	CLASS.	POSITION/ STATUS**	WHERE SERVING	OFFICE PHONE	COLLEGE/ UNIV/CQ	YR GRAD
Bradshaw Grace	(602)448-0102 gracebb33@gmail.com	7090 Simms St Unit 106 Arvada CO 80004	RM	Teacher	Tchr	Bethlehem Lakewood CO	(303)233-0401	AU	2020
Bradshaw James P	(785)273-5175 faithdce@hotmail.com	5839 SW 26th Terrace Topeka KS 66614	KS	Tch/DCE	EM			S	1982
Bradshaw Joanna D Gehrt	(785)273-5175 faithfam@swbell.net	5839 SW 26th Ter Topeka KS 66614	KS	Teacher	EM			S	1984
Bradshaw Maxine A Hoffman	maxinebradshaw@verizon.net	1611 County Road 216 Giddings TX 78942	TX	Teacher	Tchr	St Paul Serbin TX	(979)366-9650	AU	1992
Brakenhoff Benjamin P	(217)313-0320 bbrakenhoff@yahoo.com	1529 Edgewood Drive Milford IA 51351	SI	Teacher	C08/2020			S	2003
Bralley Kelsey Martinez	(623)377-2724 kbralley@stpaulmcallen.org	300 W Pecan Blvd McAllen TX 78501	TX	Teacher	Tchr	St Paul McAllen TX	(956)682-2345	S	2014
Brammeier Kathleen S Miller Stange	(515)276-3571 kathys5050@aol.com	6814 Jules Verne Ct Johnston IA 50131	IW	Teacher	EM			S	1970
Brammer Steven J	(815)735-7066 sbrammer@stpaulslutheran.net	1355 Eagle Bluff Dr Bourbonnais IL 60914	NI	Teacher	Tchr	St Paul Bourbonnais IL	(815)932-0312	CH	2014
Brand Alison M Keesaer	(417)840-6649 abrand@rlcmail.org	5841 S. Woodcliffe Dr. Springfield MO 65804	MO	Teacher	Tchr	Redeemer Springfield MO	(417)883-5717	S	1989
Brand Emma E	(417)841-7115 emma.brand@cune.org	109 Smithwood Ave #7 Catonsville MD 21228	SE	Teacher	Tchr	St Paul Catonsville MD	(410)747-1924	S	2020
Brand Gregory D	(507)564-1197 greg.brand@mchsi.com	602 Margaret St NE Chatfield MN 55923	MNS	Teacher	EM			SP	1986
Brand Lisa A Amb Deac	(507)469-5500 thisisthebrands@gmail.com	814 N McLellan St Bay City MI 48708	MI	Deaconess	Mem C	Immanuel Bay City MI	(989)893-4088	FW-DEAC	2014
Brand Michelle L Tschannen	(314)608-4291 michellebrand@gmail.com	5040 Castle Douglas Dr Saint Peters MO 63304	MO	Teacher	Tchr	Immanuel* Saint Charles MO	(636)946-0051	MQ	2007
Brand Susan L Gibson	sbrand04@gmail.com	P.O. Box 348 Mayfield MI 49666	MI	Teacher	EM			RF	1989
Brandenburg Keith B	(414)628-3413 kbrandenburg1@wi.rr.com	541 N 105th St Wauwatosa WI 53226	SW	Teacher	Tchr	Mount Olive Milwaukee WI	(414)774-2200	MQ	1991
Brandenburg Melissa M Potter	(512)541-5643 melca79@gmail.com	32338 Sea Raven Drive Rancho Palos Verdes CA 90275	PSW	Teacher	C07/2016			S	2002
Brandhorst Ronald L	(303)217-0286 rlbrandhorst@yahoo.com	12016 Prospect Ave Albuquerque NM 87112	RM	Teacher	EM			S	1966
Brandimore Layna M Schneider	(812)498-4233 laynabrandimore@gmail.com	4283 W Harrington St Bloomington IN 47404	IN	Teacher	C07/2016			RF	2011
Brandmahl Ashley C Jensema	(920)912-0462 brandmahls@gmail.com	566 S Main St Brillion WI 54110	SW	Teacher	C08/2019			CH	2011
Brandon Catherine A Grothe	(253)545-9864 mamakati@live.com	11122 N Country Club Green Dr Tomball TX 77375	TX	Teacher	Tchr	Salem Tomball TX	(281)351-8223	AU	2002
Brandon Katherine J Schneider Dr	(734)645-1477 kathy.j.brandon@gmail.com	11559 Pleasant Shore Dr Manchester MI 48158	MI	Teacher	EM			S	1972
Brandon Kevin J Dr	(734)660-6389 kbrandon50@gmail.com	11559 Pleasant Shore Dr Manchester MI 48158	MI	Teacher	EM			CQ	1983
Brandon Michael K	(253)737-7196 teachmike@gmail.com	20231 Galena Falls Dr Tomball TX 77375	TX	Teacher	Tchr	Salem Tomball TX	(281)351-8223	AU	2003
Brandon Ruth M Dubbe	(214)543-8203	859 Southern Shore Dr Peachtree Cty GA 30269	TX	Teacher	Tchr	Prince Of Peace Carrollton TX	(972)447-0532	IV	1986
Brandt Alla Shvetsova Deac	(248)504-9883 say691@yahoo.com	20413 NE 29th Ave Ridgefield WA 98642	RM	Deaconess	Mem C	Immanuel Roswell NM	(575)622-2853	FW-DEAC	2014
Brandt Barbara Rattelmuller	(618)789-1799 rattelmuller@gmail.com	7605 Stonebridge Golf Dr Maryville IL 62062	SI	Teacher	Tchr	St Paul Worden IL	(618)633-2202	S	1988
Brandt Dwaine C Dr	(971)409-2612	20100 SW Boones Ferry Rd Tualatin OR 97062	NOW	Teacher	EM			CQ	1966
Brandt Eunice F Mott	(402)640-3166 keeubr@hotmail.com	803 Skyview Cir Norfolk NE 68701	NEB	Teacher	EM			S	1970
Brandt Gilbert H	(317)787-5715 ghbgolf@hotmail.com	8663 Beechmill Ln Apt C Indianapolis IN 46227	IN	Teacher	EM			RF	1967
Brandt Jessica L Wilson	(317)628-4809 jbrandt616@gmail.com	6131 Thrushwood Circle Indianapolis IN 46250	IN	DPM	Mem C	Cornerstone Carmel IN	(317)814-4252	CH	2019
Brandt John E	(586)463-5183 jbrandt@lhsa.com	1419 Warrington St Mount Clemens MI 48043	MI	Teacher	Tchr	Lutheran North Macomb MI	(586)781-9151	AA	1985
Brandt John M Dr	(989)799-0201 brandt.john@sbcglobal.net	3665 W Winfield Dr Saginaw MI 48603	MI	Teacher	EM			RF	1977
Brandt Kathleen E Deeter	(317)460-9240 orangebrandt@gmail.com	9732 Chestnut Ln Indianapolis IN 46239	IN	Teacher	Tchr	Trinity Indianapolis IN	(317)897-0243	S	1991
Brandt Kimberly L Kappel	(660)335-4048 kbrandt@splhs.org	12730 Drift Ave Sweet Springs MO 65351	MO	Teacher	Tchr	Saint Paul Concordia MO	(660)463-2238	S	2002
Brandt Lillian C	(913)492-7564 alice.nurse17@gmail.com	c/o Alice Kasten 12130 W 100th St Lenexa KS 66215	KS	Teacher	EM			S	1961
Brandt Michael B	(317)460-9241 mbrandt@lhsi.org	9732 Chestnut Ln Indianapolis IN 46239	IN	Teacher	Prin	Indianapolis Indianapolis IN	(317)787-5474	S	1990
Brandt Pamela J Muehler	pjbrandt88@gmail.com	36399 Highway E Green Ridge MO 65332	MO	Teacher	Tchr	St Pauls Sedalia MO	(660)826-1925	S	1983
Brandt Paul M	(725)300-9583 pmbrandt@hotmail.com	1002 Country Club Dr Durham NC 27712	SE	Teacher	EM			RF	1979
Brandt Robert W	(417)235-0357 roshbrandt@gmail.com	4084 S Kelly Dr New Palestine IN 46163	IN	Teacher	EM			S	1960
Brandt Shirley M Biermann	(317)623-7016 roshbrandt@juno.com	4084 S Kelly Dr New Palestine IN 46163	IN	Teacher	EM			S	1958
Brandt Susan R Senske	(989)799-0201 brandt.john@sbcglobal.net	3665 W Winfield Dr Saginaw MI 48603	MI	Teacher	EM			RF	1977
Brannan Carol A Flom	(314)762-8015 brannan.carol@gmail.com	9911 Lakeford Ln Affton MO 63123	MO	Teacher	EM			SP	1971
Brantsch Robert J	(216)513-4252 dce@gloriadeihudson.org	3764 Elm Rd Stow OH 44224	OH	Tch/DCE	Mem C	Gloria Dei Hudson OH	(330)650-6550	RF	1995

*Multiple Assignments (See Church Worker Locator for Additional Details)

See Page 53 for the Table of Abbreviations for key to District, Classification, Position, and College abbreviations.

**C =Candidate; EM =Emeritus; the date following the C is the month and year the Candidate status began

NAME	TELEPHONE NUMBER EMAIL	STREET ADDRESS CITY/STATE/ZIP	DISTRICT	CLASS.	POSITION/ STATUS**	WHERE SERVING	OFFICE PHONE	COLLEGE/ UNIV/CQ	YR GRAD
Brase Alice A Sinclair	(507)317-1581 teachp34k@gmail.com	14861 557th Ave. Good Thunder MN 56037	MNS	Teacher	EM			SP	1978
Brase Jalynn M	(402)641-9551 jalynn.brase@cune.org	3578 Agnew Rd Staplehurst NE 68439	NEB	Teacher	Tchr	St John Seward NE	(402)643-4535	S	2018
Brase Janessa	(402)646-0530 janessa.brase@cune.org	3578 Agnew Rd Staplehurst NE 68439	NEB	Teacher	Tchr	St Paul Utica NE	(402)534-2121	S	2022
Brase Joel D	(402)643-5694 jbrase23@gmail.com	208 Shannon Rd Seward NE 68434	NEB	Teacher	C06/2023			S	2000
Brasher Tessa D Scheer	(870)239-9131 tessadbrasher@gmail.com	7101 Pine Dr Paragould AR 72450	MDS	DCE	Mem C	St John Lafe AR	(870)586-0319	CQ	2009
Brassie Alice M Wegner	(314)435-5460 aliloveskids@aol.com	2313 Winegarden Ct Wildwood MO 63011	MO	Teacher	EM			S	1969
Brauer Brian J	(414)828-1823 brianbrauer8085@gmail.com	2239 Brookside Dr Jackson WI 53037	SW	Teacher	C09/2020			MQ	1996
Brauer Frederick E	(925)312-2862 mrbrauer@sbcglobal.net	33585 Anderson Court Cross Lake MN 56442	CNH	Teacher	EM			SP	1978
Brauer Jennifer L		18680 Winston Detroit MI 48219	MI	Teacher	Tchr	Northwest Rochester Hills MI	(248)856-0240	AA	1999
Brauer Norman P	(775)265-5422 nvnk2b@yahoo.com	1940 Morgan Ct Gardnerville NV 89410	CNH	Teacher	EM			S	1967
Brauer Ranotta L Sylwester Schmidt	(208)640-4023 teach4joy@hotmail.com	4740 N Troy St Coeur D Alene ID 83815	NOW	Teacher	EM			RF	1978
Brauer Robert D	(402)534-2121	305 Colorado St Utica NE 68456	NEB	Teacher	EM			S	1979
Brauer Sheila K Littrell	(317)271-7638 easkb73071@yahoo.com	9822 Countryside Ct Avon IN 46123	IN	Teacher	EM			CQ	2002
Braun Andrew	(262)719-4164 andrewbraun@me.com	533 Hayley Marie Ln Knoxville TN 37920	SW	Teacher	Tchr	Milwaukee LHS Milwaukee WI	(414)461-6000	MQ	2012
Braun Bruce N Dr	(734)665-3791 bruce.braun1955@hotmail.com	2061 W Williams Cir Westland MI 48186	MI	Teacher	EM			RF	1978
Braun Carole J Germer	(262)781-1494 cadbraun@ieee.org	15780 Vernon Dr Brookfield WI 53005	SW	Teacher	EM			CQ	1990
Braun Douglas J	(702)232-5543 theologyguru@gmail.com	9641 Wexford Dr Ypsilanti MI 48198	MI	Teacher	Tchr	LHS Assn Of Greater Detroit Rochester Hls MI	(248)856-0240	RF	1995
Braun James R	(920)210-5951 arnie4900@gmail.com	W275 N4900 S Courtland Cir Pewaukee WI 53072	SW	Teacher	EM			SP	1971
Braun Jonathan A	(346)702-9067 jbraun1985@gmail.com	2017 Waters Edge Court Denton TX 76208	TX	DCM	Mem C	Lamb Of God Flower Mound TX	(972)539-5200	MQ	2008
Braun Linda S Klug	(682)716-1484 nanalindabraun7@gmail.com	2200 Acorn Bend Denton TX 76210	TX	Teacher	EM			MW	1980
Braun Rosemary A Hinck	(651)483-3157 alrosiebraun@gmail.com	2975 Highpointe Curv Roseville MN 55113	MNS	Teacher	EM			RF	1966
Braun Suzanne L Simpson	(512)799-5873 suzlbraun55@gmail.com	1014 Woodgate Dr Kirkwood MO 63122	MO	Teacher	EM			RF	1977
Braun Sylvia S	(573)821-5402 ssbraun94@gmail.com	c/o Dallas Lutheran School 8494 Stults Rd Dallas TX 75243	TX	Teacher	Tchr	Dallas Lutheran Sch Dallas TX	(214)349-8912	S	2017
Braun Theresa L Stout	(608)408-0550 theresabraun@saintpetersls.com	1133 14th St Reedsburg WI 53959	SW	Teacher	Tchr	St Peter Reedsburg WI	(608)524-4066	MQ	2004
Braunersreuther Rachel A Hartman	(314)541-0105 rbraunersreuether@gmail.com	23334 E Pine Ivy Ln Tomball TX 77375	TX	Teacher	EM			S	1984
Brautnick Janice M McGorman	(248)859-4852 jmbrautnick@gmail.com	41150 Fox Run Apt 525 Novi MI 48377	MI	Teacher	EM			SP	1965
Bray Merlin L Jr	(219)462-2715	713 Elmhurst St Valparaiso IN 46385	IN	Teacher	EM			RF	1954
Bray Nancy J DuBois	(217)725-9087 braynj62@gmail.com	4909 W Oakwood Dr Apt D McHenry IL 60050	NI	Teacher	C11/2023			CQ	2000
Brazeal Andrew J	(810)938-2208 abrazeal@trinityutica.com	15411 33 Mile Rd Armada MI 48005	MI	DFLM	Mem C	Trinity Utica MI	(586)731-4490	AA	2015
Brazeal Geraldine L Bock	geribrazeal@gmail.com	3701 S Lake Park Ave Chicago IL 60653	NI	Teacher	P/Tchr	Christ King Chicago IL	(773)536-1984	RF	1970
Brazelton William T Jr	(847)437-2782 wtbrazj@gmail.com	450 Sandy Ln Des Plaines IL 60016	NI	Teacher	EM			RF	1994
Brazgel Gregory S	(262)391-6321 gbrazgel@lakecountryhs.org	616 Cherry Ct Hartland WI 53029	SW	Teacher	Tchr	LHS Assn of Greater Milwaukee West Allis WI	(414)421-9100	MQ	1998
Brech Kathryn E Stahl	(520)991-2411 mrs.brech@gmail.com	821 N Barbara Worth Tucson AZ 85710	EN	Teacher	C07/2016			AA	1999
Bredehoeft Gloria J Haak	(317)299-3811 wgbredeh@sbcglobal.net	5351 Deer Creek Dr Indianapolis IN 46254	IN	Teacher	EM			S	1972
Bredehoeft Kathryn J Werth Vogts	(816)436-4734 lkwerth@yahoo.com	9019 N Mersington Ave Kansas City MO 64156	MO	Teacher	EM			S	1970
Bredehoeft Natasha N Torno	(870)805-0172 njbredehoeft@gmail.com	3276 Willington Dr Dublin OH 43017	OH	Teacher	Pro Stf	St John Dublin Dublin OH	(614)889-5893	S	2018
Bredehoft David P	(630)642-0570	3469 Robb Ave Cincinnati OH 45211	OH	Teacher	Mem C	Grace Cincinnati OH	(513)661-5166	S	1970
Bredehoft Dorothy R	(620)331-0810 dbredehoft12@cableone.net	1904 Patton Ct Independence KS 67301	KS	Teacher	EM			S	1973
Bredehoft George W	(503)293-6151 georgelaurie@msn.com	3733 SW Canby St Portland OR 97219	NOW	Teacher	EM			S	1976
Bredehoft John C	(520)981-5115 bredehoftjd@cox.net	9628 E Blue Ridge Mountain St Tucson AZ 85748	PSW	Teacher	EM			S	1970
Bredehoft Laura L	(858)272-6363 lbredehoft@stpaulspb.com	5252 Balboa Arms Dr Unit 104 San Diego CA 92117	PSW	DCE	Mem C	St Pauls San Diego CA	(858)272-6363	IV	2014
Bredehoft Susan L Pate	(909)988-3163 susan_bredehoft@msn.com	661 W Yale St Ontario CA 91762	PSW	Teacher	EM			RF	1987

*Multiple Assignments (See Church Worker Locator for Additional Details)

See Page 53 for the Table of Abbreviations for key to District, Classification, Position, and College abbreviations.

**C =Candidate; EM =Emeritus; the date following the C is the month and year the Candidate status began

NAME	TELEPHONE NUMBER EMAIL	STREET ADDRESS CITY/STATE/ZIP	DISTRICT	CLASS.	POSITION/ STATUS**	WHERE SERVING	OFFICE PHONE	COLLEGE/ UNIV/CQ	YR GRAD
Bredehoft Thomas A	(714)231-7334 blowitupdude@gmail.com	7200 S Victor Dr Tucson AZ 85757	PSW	Teacher	EM			RF	1982
Bredman Elizabeth	(218)304-1568 ejbredman@gmail.com	1509 Epsy Way Apt 103 Sheboygan WI 53081	SW	Teacher	Tchr	Sheboygan Sheboygan WI	(920)452-3323	MQ	2023
Bredow Gordon J	(636)357-0771 gordonbredow@gmail.com	213 Laurelwood Dr Saint Peters MO 63376	MO	Teacher	EM			S	1964
Bredow Rachel L Buescher	(720)981-3046 rachelbredow@gmail.com	3782 E Robin Ln Gilbert AZ 85296	PSW	Teacher	Tchr	Christ Greenfield Gilbert AZ	(480)892-8521	S	2003
Bredow Ryan J Dr	(303)895-9576 rjbredow@gmail.com	3782 E Robin Ln Gilbert AZ 85296	PSW	Teacher	C07/2018			S	2003
Brege Alissa A Smith	(310)940-2759 alissa.brege@gmail.com	1043 S Walker Ave San Pedro CA 90731	PSW	DCE	Tchr	Bethany Long Beach CA	(562)420-7783	IV	2006
Brege Paul C	(831)566-5413 pbrege@bethanylutheran.org	1043 S Walker Ave San Pedro CA 90731	PSW	Teacher	Tchr	Bethany Long Beach CA	(562)420-7783	IV	2021
Brehm Paul A		13664 Red Hill Ave Apt D Tustin CA 92780	PSW	Teacher	Tchr	Prince Of Peace Anaheim CA	(714)774-0993	IV	1988
Brehmer Tammy L Cullen	(920)849-3758 dtcejbrehmer@gmail.com	W945 Aebischer Rd Chilton WI 53014	SW	DCM	EM			MQ	1992
Brei Eric K	(563)949-9310 ericbreil@gmail.com	4574 34th Street Ct Bettendorf IA 52722	IE	DCE	Mem C	Our Savior Bettendorf IA	(563)332-5141	RF	1996
Breidert Dennis D	(303)940-9334 dbreidert@gmail.com	8458 Lewis Ct Arvada CO 80005	RM	Teacher	EM			S	1970
Breininger Terry	(260)444-3070	8442 Raceborg Pl Fort Wayne IN 46835	IN	Teacher	EM			RF	1971
Breitbarth Jonathan S	(651)641-8796 breitbarth@csp.edu	1282 Concordia Ave Saint Paul MN 55104	MNS	Teacher	S HS/C	Concordia University St Paul Saint Paul MN	(651)641-8278	SP	1997
Breite Christine L Meier	(573)651-3038 dcbreite@charter.net	2127 Derbyshire Ln Cape Girardeau MO 63701	MO	Teacher	EM			RF	1985
Breite Mary M Van Pelt	(501)786-1577 mary.breite@gmail.com	4 Lemoncrest Pl Little Rock AR 72210	MDS	Teacher	EM			S	1975
Breitenbach Molly A	(517)513-2876 mollyabreitenbach@gmail.com	c/o Living Word Lutheran Church 7539 Dustin Rd Galena OH 43021	OH	DFLM	Mem C	Living Word Galena OH	(740)965-3335	AA	2024
Breitwisch John A	(715)539-9831 breitwisch@worldnet.att.net	906 Adams St Merrill WI 54452	NW	Teacher	Tchr	St John Merrill WI	(715)536-7264	MQ	1993
Breitwisch Ruthann L Hackbarth	(715)539-9831	906 Adams St Merrill WI 54452	NW	Teacher	Tchr	St John Merrill WI	(715)536-7264	MQ	1993
Brekke Tais	(863)797-6386 taisbrekke@gmail.com	6207 Elm Sq W Lakeland FL 33813	FG	DCE	C07/2025			CH	2019
Bremer Alvin L	(219)929-7407 lptbr@aol.com	2621 White Pine Circle Valparaiso IN 46383	IN	Teacher	EM			S	1967
Bremer David A	(989) 640-1270 bremerda1950@yahoo.com	288 Bass Lake Rd Traverse City MI 49685	MI	Teacher	EM			RF	1972
Bremer David A	(308)379-3183 dbremer@tlsgi.org	1811 N Taylor Ave Grand Island NE 68803	NEB	Teacher	Tchr	Grand Island Grand Island NE	(308)385-3900	S	2011
Bremer Janet L Dore	(563)650-7217 janet.bremer54@gmail.com	2237 W Columbia Ave Davenport IA 52804	IE	Teacher	EM			RF	1977
Bremer Melinda K Hunsley	(219)928-1648 mindybremer@yahoo.com	2621 White Pine Circle Valparaiso IN 46383	IN	Teacher	EM			RF	1977
Bremer Sheila K	(503)419-7867	1021 N 2nd St Ponca City OK 74601	OK	Teacher	Tchr	First Ponca City OK	(580)762-9950	PO	1988
Bremer Valerie A	valerie.bremer@splgrafton.org	1108 Claern Ct Grafton WI 53024	SW	Teacher	Mem C	St Paul Grafton WI	(262)377-4659	S	1997
Brennan Jan L Heupel	(832)444-8652 sj_brennan@att.net	18523 Mellowgrove Ln Spring TX 77379	TX	Teacher	Tchr	Trinity Spring TX	(281)376-5810	S	1991
Brennan Kimberly D Goulart	(503)713-7951 brennank@fhlcs.org	3100 NE Glencoe Oaks Pl Hillsboro OR 97124	NOW	Teacher	Tchr	Forest Hills Cornelius OR	(503)359-4853	CQ	2017
Brenner Abigail Landskroener	(419)280-6137 a.landskroener12@gmail.com	15 Founders Way Unit D Saint Louis MO 63105	MO	Teacher	Tchr	Zion Saint Charles MO	(636)441-7424	AA	2025
Brenner Angela	(573)680-6461 angbrenn@hotmail.com	2723 Deardane Dr Jefferson City MO 65109	MO	DCE	Mem C	Trinity Jefferson City MO	(573)636-6750	CQ	2011
Brenner Emily G Butler	(404)433-7649 emily.brenner28@gmail.com	1797 Oakbrook Lane Kennesaw GA 30152	FG	Teacher	Tchr	Faith Marietta GA	(770)973-8877	CH	2017
Brenner Gerald R	(636)515-0242	1797 Oak Brook Ln NW Kennesaw GA 30152	FG	Teacher	Tchr	Faith Marietta GA	(770)973-8877	CH	2017
Brenner Mark D	(989)372-2123 brennermd11@yahoo.com	2828 55th Ave Unit 36 Kenosha WI 53144	SW	Teacher	Tchr	Lutheran High School Racine WI	(262)637-6538	AA	2003
Brenner Renee C Jenista	(989)372-2096 spanishtchr@yahoo.com	2828 55th Ave Unit 36 Kenosha WI 53144	SW	Teacher	Tchr	Lutheran High School Racine WI	(262)637-6538	AA	1996
Brenningmeyer Tammy S Lindsey	(636)332-5734 tbrenningmeyer@ilcsw.net	404 Wildflower Ridge Ct Wentzville MO 63385	MO	Teacher	Tchr	Immanuel Wentzville MO	(636)327-4416	CQ	2012
Brese Susan E Echtenkamp	(716)694-5681 susanbrese145@gmail.com	145 Lorelee Dr Tonawanda NY 14150	EA	Teacher	EM			RF	1964
Bresemann Brian R	(714)333-7899 brian.bresemann@christcm.org	505 N Hamlin St Orange CA 92869	PSW	Teacher	Tchr	Christ Costa Mesa CA	(949)631-1611	RF	2000
Bresemann Linda G Houren	(989) 213-4685 pab1@me.com	623 Franconian Dr E Frankenmuth MI 48734	MI	Teacher	EM			RF	1969
Bresemann Perry A Dr	(989)213-4685 pab1@me.com	623 Franconian Dr E Frankenmuth MI 48734	MI	Teacher	EM			RF	1970
Brettmann Linda M Loontjer	(402)643-4609 linda.brettmann@cune.org	705 Bader Ave Seward NE 68434	NEB	Teacher	EM			S	1970
Bretzmann Nancy L Rasmann Dr		124 Acushnet Ln Taylors SC 29687	SE	Teacher	EM			CQ	2002
Brevard Jennifer L Drush-Schmaltz	(314)409-7165 jldrush@yahoo.com	2075 Richardson Rd Arnold MO 63010	MO	Teacher	Tchr	St Marks Eureka MO	(636)938-4432	S	1996

*Multiple Assignments (See Church Worker Locator for Additional Details)
See Page 53 for the Table of Abbreviations for key to District, Classification, Position, and College abbreviations.
**C =Candidate; EM =Emeritus; the date following the C is the month and year the Candidate status began

NAME	TELEPHONE NUMBER EMAIL	STREET ADDRESS CITY/STATE/ZIP	DISTRICT	CLASS.	POSITION/ STATUS**	WHERE SERVING	OFFICE PHONE	COLLEGE/ UNIV/CQ	YR GRAD
Brewer Jennifer	(708)284-0400 thatjennybrewer@hotmail.com	1220 Silverwood Ct Saint Paul MN 55125	MNS	Teacher	Tchr	Trinity Lone Oak Eagan MN	(651)454-1139	RF	2006
Brewer Nathaniel C	(919)999-7978 nbrewer127@gmail.com	15508 W Bell Rd Ste 101-247 Surprise AZ 85374	EN	DCE	C03/2017			IV	2002
Brewer Pamela A Pobursky	(260)415-7510	7416 Golfway Ct Minocqua WI 54548	NW	Teacher	EM			S	1985
Brewer Patrick M	(651)247-1563 thatpatrickbrewer@hotmail.com	1220 Silverwood Ct Saint Paul MN 55125	MNS	DCE	Mem C	Woodbury Woodbury MN	(651)739-5144	CH	2006
Brewer Zachery C	(303)550-9648 zbrewer@zionbrighton.org	226 Chapel Hill Dr Brighton CO 80601	RM	DCE	Tchr	Zion Brighton CO	(303)659-2339	IV	1999
Brewner Linda S Gutman	(507)261-2497 librewner@gmail.com	25226 720th St Hayfield MN 55940	MNS	Teacher	EM			RF	1973
Brewster Charles M Jr	(636)485-1023 cbrewster@messiahnetwork.org	34 Breezy Knoll Ln Lake St Louis MO 63367	MO	Teacher	Tchr	Messiah Weldon Spring MO	(636)926-9773	CQ	2013
Brey Jeremy M	(605)520-4568 jeremy.brey@cune.org	900 E Central Ave Ponca City OK 74601	OK	Teacher		Oklahoma District Norman OK	(405)321-3443	S	2021
Brey Sarah M Benz	sarah.brey@stjohnsmayville.com	900 E Central Ave Ponca City OK 74601	SW	Teacher	Tchr	St Johns Mayville WI	(920)387-4310	S	2021
Breytung Barbara A Holle	(262)374-4398 bbreytung@gmail.com	318 W Wisconsin St Delavan WI 53115	SW	Teacher	EM			S	1975
Breytung James S	(262)745-3916 jsbreytung@gmail.com	318 W Wisconsin St Delavan WI 53115	SW	Teacher	EM			S	1975
Brice Alexander M	(636)627-8643 abrice2015@gmail.com	1150 Cedar Ave Elgin IL 60120	NI	DCE	Mem C	St Mark Saint Charles IL	(630)584-8638	CH	2020
Brice Madeline G Sunstrom	(443)900-4120 msunstrom2@gmail.com	1150 Cedar Ave Elgin IL 60120	NI	Teacher	Tchr	Trinity Roselle IL	(630)894-3263	CH	2019
Brickman Doris A	(206)568-1407 dbrickwa@hotmail.com	1429 Avenue D PMB 387 Snohomish WA 98290	NOW	Teacher	C07/2016			S	1963
Bridges Kristy K Jastram	(605)413-9073 kbridges@sflutheranschool.com	909 N Caleb Ave Sioux Falls SD 57103	SD	Teacher	Tchr	Sioux Falls Sioux Falls SD	(605)335-1923	S	2002
Bridges Michael R	(812)343-3352 mrb1954@aol.com	3020 Sherwood Ln Columbus IN 47203	IN	DCE	EM			S	1992
Brieschke Martin A	(502)290-5584 mabrieschke@yahoo.com	9108 Hensley Ct Prospect KY 40059	IN	Teacher	EM			S	1970
Briggs Cynthia M Teschendorf	(989)878-0189 mrsbriggs.trinity@gmail.com	1221 W Vassar Rd Reese MI 48757	MI	Teacher	P/Tchr	Trinity Reese MI	(989)868-9901	CQ	2013
Briggs Jessica A Hecht	(989)239-2771 jess_hecht@outlook.com	1600 Fox Knls Leonard MI 48367	MI	Teacher	Tchr	Trinity Utica MI	(586)731-4490	AA	2019
Brill Geraldine A Harnisch	(303)660-6584 pgbrill371@comcast.net	27005 County Road 5 Elizabeth CO 80107	RM	Teacher	EM			RF	2000
Bringold Levi R	(989)482-2296 lbringold@stjohnfraser.org	14723 Hannebauer Ct Sterling Heights MI 48313	MI	Teacher	Prin	St John Fraser MI	(586)293-0333	CQ	2011
Brink Mark A	(321)217-8112	608 S Main Ave Apt 8 Minneola FL 34715	FG	Teacher	EM			RF	1975
Brink Sally L Puls	(949)981-5109 sally.l.brink@gmail.com	2925 E Mayfair Ave Orange CA 92867	PSW	Teacher	Tchr	St Paul Orange CA	(714)637-2640	IV	2008
Brink Yvette	(989)977-2282 brinky@ctkl.org	4400 Volz Rd Sebewaing MI 48759	MI	Teacher	Tchr	Immanuel Sebewaing MI	(989)883-3050	CQ	2017
Brinker Sharon H LeDuc	(618)664-9547 ronbrinker@sbcglobal.net	422 Olde Cabin Rd Greenville IL 62246	MO	Teacher	EM			CQ	2004
Brinkley Carolyn S Schindler Deac	(260)622-9194 carolyn.brinkley@ctsfw.edu	8242 N 450 E Ossian IN 46777	IN	Deaconess	S HS/C	Concordia Theological Seminary Fort Wayne IN	(260)452-2100	FW-DEAC	2010
Brinkley Richard N	(260)622-9194 rbrink1950@yahoo.com	8242 N 450 E Ossian IN 46777	IN	Teacher	Mem C	Bethlehem Ossian IN	(260)597-7121	RF	1972
Brinkmann Jaime K Lange	(618)698-2789 jaime.brinkmann@gmail.com	2647 Overlook Dr Belleville IL 62221	SI	DCE	Mem C	Zion Belleville IL	(618)233-2299	RF	2004
Brinkmann Kevin Dr	(309)471-9020 kevin@kevinbrinkmann.com	1506 Brookcrest Ave Morton IL 61550	PSW	DCE	C07/2016			SP	2005
Brinneman Autumn L Lehman	aleman224@gmail.com	9429 Fireside Court Fort Wayne IN 46804	IN	Teacher	Tchr	St Peter-Immanuel Decatur IN	(260)623-6115	AA	2016
Brisbin Rae L Kunschke	(763)441-7549 rae.brisbin@charter.net	13419 Island View Dr NW Elk River MN 55330	MNS	Teacher	EM			S	1977
Brisbois Ruth M Jensen	(402)806-0119	1110 N 17th St Beatrice NE 68310	NEB	Teacher	EM			CQ	1983
Bristol Nancy E De Land	(909)732-9277 dkbristol01@aol.com	1668 Grasscreek Dr San Dimas CA 91773	PSW	Teacher	EM			S	1968
Bristow Kelly R Jacob Deac	(402)922-0708 kellyrbristow@gmail.com		ND	Deaconess	RSO	Dakota Boys and Girls Ranch Minot ND	(701)839-7888	SL-DEAC	2017
Britton John W	(217)609-1072 john.britton20@gmail.com	P.O. Box 444 Buckley IL 60918	CI	Teacher	EM			RF	1982
Britton Sarah M Wootton	(512)771-8448 sbrittondce@gmail.com	1902 Rivendell Circle Newbury Park CA 91320	PSW	DCE	C01/2025			S	2000
Broach Sara N Braatz	(414)899-5100 sara.broach@gls-hsv.org	9427 Ojay Dr SE Huntsville AL 35803	SO	Teacher	Tchr	Grace Huntsville AL	(256)881-0552	S	2011
Brocato Abigale	(636)485-5940 abigalebrocato@gmail.com	2204 Grit Court Washington MO 63090	MO	Teacher	Tchr	Immanuel Wentzville MO	(636)639-9887	MQ	2023
Brock Andrea R Hromowyk	(812)216-1078		IN	Teacher	C08/2019			MQ	2012
Brock Chloe E Cunningham	(830)353-9569 chloe.cunningham715@gmail.com	4584 Winkler Ave Apt 105 Fort Myers FL 33966	FG	Teacher	Tchr	Saint Michael Fort Myers FL	(239)939-1218	RF	2015
Brockberg Harold F Dr	(320)763-5679	Providence Place 815 Washington St #125 Grafton WI 53024	SW	Teacher	EM			S	1952
Brockberg Kevin H Dr	(248)895-2202 kevin.brockberg@gmail.com		IN	Teacher	C09/2024			RF	1978

*Multiple Assignments (See Church Worker Locator for Additional Details)
See Page 53 for the Table of Abbreviations for key to District, Classification, Position, and College abbreviations.
**C =Candidate; EM =Emeritus; the date following the C is the month and year the Candidate status began

NAME	TELEPHONE NUMBER EMAIL	STREET ADDRESS CITY/STATE/ZIP	DISTRICT	CLASS.	POSITION/ STATUS**	WHERE SERVING	OFFICE PHONE	COLLEGE/ UNIV/CQ	YR GRAD
Brockman Blake T	(715)350-9044 blak3br0ckman@gmail.com	7450 W 22nd Ave Lakewood CO 80214	NW	DCM	C08/2023			MQ	2016
Brockman Hannah F Arrigoni	(715)651-4522 hannahbrockman@gmail.com	7450 W 22nd Ave Lakewood CO 80214	MO	Teacher	C06/2025			MQ	2019
Brockmann Colleen D Woltz	cdbrockmann@stpaulwpne.org	921 11th Rd West Point NE 68788	NEB	Teacher	Tchr	St Paul West Point NE	(402)372-2355	CQ	2004
Brockmeier Ann S Spence	(314)724-1436 asbrockmeier@gmail.com	4533 Killdeer Dr Augusta MO 63332	MO	Teacher	EM			CQ	2015
Brockmeier Russel L	(801)750-0370 rbrockm@gmail.com	11025 S Grapevine CV Apt 204 Sandy UT 84070	RM	Teacher	C07/2016			S	1978
Brod Charles W	(708)366-7731 cwabrod@aol.com	628 Elgin Ave Forest Park IL 60130	NI	Teacher	EM			Other	1964
Brofford Eric M	(314)313-9932 ebrofford30@gmail.com	7264 Ravinia Saint Louis MO 63121	SI	Teacher		Southern Illinois District Belleville IL	(618)234-4767	RF	1988
Brogaard Jo Nette L Wilkening	(320)846-0984 brogaard@rea-alp.com	6158 County Road 11 NW Alexandria MN 56308	MNN	Teacher	EM			SP	1970
Brondos Marilyn	(708)341-4782 marilyn.brondos@gmail.com	234 Meadowbrook Court Geneseo IL 61254	CI	Teacher	EM			S	1981
Bronner Jill J Stamm	(989)652-3665 jbronner@stlorenz.org	430 E Tuscola St Frankenmuth MI 48734	MI	Teacher	Tchr	St Lorenz Frankenmuth MI	(989)652-6141	RF	1990
Brooks Erin	(812)569-2942 ebrooks@trinitycougars.org	9440 S 850 W Paris Crossing IN 47270	IN	Teacher	Pro Stf	Trinity Seymour IN	(812)524-8547	CH	2020
Brooks Jacquelin R Walsh	(734)934-3590 jbrooks@ctk.me	15600 Trenton Rd Southgate MI 48195	MI	Teacher	Tchr	Christ The King Southgate MI	(734)285-9695	AA	2011
Brooks Nora B Metzger	(262)323-6585 norabeth219@yahoo.com	354 S Maple Ln Saukville WI 53080	SW	Teacher	C07/2016			CH	2007
Brooner Katherine S Mueller	(314)971-4253 katie.brooner16@gmail.com	2118 Cromwell Court Arnold MO 63010	MO	Teacher	Tchr	Our Savior Fenton MO	(636)343-7511	CH	2011
Brosch Isabel	(316)765-5386 ibrosch@sbcglobal.net	261 NW Kessler Dr Apt 210 Lees Summit MO 64081	EN	DCE	Mem C	Beautiful Savior Lees Summit MO	(816)524-7288	S	2024
Brose Elizabeth E	(413)505-9615 eebrose@gmail.com	94-1063 Kaukahi Pl B-2 Waipahu HI 96797	CNH	Teacher	Tchr	Trinity Wahiawa HI	(808)621-6033	BR	2010
Brose Mary E Peddicord	(509)627-9006 maryeleanorebrose@gmail.com	3218 Florida St NE Albuquerque NM 87110	RM	Teacher	EM			RF	1965
Brosz Keith E	(573)651-8425 kbanchor@aol.com	3120 Independence St #425 Cape Girardeau MO 63703	PSW	Teacher	EM			S	1971
Brott Carolyn M Leckband	(402)228-7210 cmbrott@gmail.com	1707 Court St Beatrice NE 68310	NEB	Teacher	EM			S	1977
Brott Paul R	(425)908-7715 brottpaul@gmail.com	12215 NE 128th St #323 Kirkland WA 98034	NOW	Teacher	EM			S	1956
Brotzman Ruth E Maas	(713)851-7737 rbrotzman59@gmail.com	5915 Durango Ridge Ct Richmond TX 77469	TX	Teacher	EM			RF	1981
Brown Alexandra R	(734) 926-0720 lbrown@stpaulannarbor.org	495 Earhart Road Ann Arbor MI 48105	MI	DFLM	Mem C	St Paul Ann Arbor MI	(734)665-9117	AA	2020
Brown Alicia M Seltz	(989)600-9706 seltz.alicia@gmail.com	12813 Twyla Ln Hartland MI 48343	EN	Teacher	Tchr	Our Savior Hartland MI	(248)887-4300	CQ	2019
Brown Brian J	(651)245-7422 brian.bj651.brown@gmail.com	3010 Meadow Brook Dr Woodbury MN 55125	MNS	Teacher	C10/2022			SP	2002
Brown Brittni A Deac	(260)433-5631 bakoos90@gmail.com	8811 Nicole Dr Fort Wayne IN 46806	RM	Deaconess	Mem C	Our Savior* Lovington NM	(575)396-4549	FW-DEAC	2019
Brown Carol J Deac	(815)793-4968 carolbrown647@gmail.com	1433 Cambria Dr Dekalb IL 60115	NI	Deaconess	Mem C	St John Sycamore IL	(815)895-4477	FW-DEAC	2018
Brown Cheryl A Beilfuss	(330)794-4301	1568 18th St Cuyahoga Fls OH 44223	OH	Teacher	Tchr	Redeemer Cuyahoga Falls OH	(330)923-1445	AA	1986
Brown Christopher A	(218)342-3897 dcechristopher@arvig.net	1130 S Townline Rd Vergas MN 56587	MNN	DCE	Mem C	St Paul Perham MN	(218)346-7725	CQ	2013
Brown Cynthia A Seay-Hawley	(410)651-0217	27820 Mount Vernon Rd Princess Anne MD 21853	SE	Teacher	EM			S	1986
Brown Cynthia A Haller	(810)886-1585 principal@zionlcs.com	680 Lytle Ave Harbor Beach MI 48441	MI	Teacher	P/Tchr	Zion Harbor Beach MI	(989)479-3615	RF	1980
Brown David C	(313)388-9440 dbrown@lhsa.com	6860 Mayfair St Taylor MI 48180	MI	Tch/DCE	Tchr	Westland Westland MI	(734)422-2090	S	1981
Brown David E	dbrown@trinityct.org	37595 Ladue Street Clinton Twp MI 48036	MI	Tch/DCE	EM			RF	1975
Brown Erika P Heimsoth	(989)640-0811 principal@stpeterriley.org	6390 W Chadwick Rd Dewitt MI 48820	MI	Teacher	P/Tchr	St Peter Saint Johns MI	(989)224-3178	AA	2009
Brown Gail L Schauland	(712)276-6579 tgbrown1972@gmail.com	4619 Deer Shadow Trl Sioux City IA 51106	IW	Teacher	EM			S	1972
Brown Jared S	(309)231-0103 charredbrown14@gmail.com	532 S Olive St Apt 1 Waconia MN 55387	MNS	Teacher	Tchr	Mayer Mayer MN	(952)657-2251	Other	2018
Brown Jody R Johnson	(913)294-4926	1002 N Pearl St Paola KS 66071	KS	Teacher	EM			S	1974
Brown Justin T	(248)343-4958 jbrown@lhsa.com	21616 Flanders St Farmington Hills MI 48335	MI	Teacher	Prin	Westland Westland MI	(734)422-2090	CQ	2024
Brown Karen S Schaefer	(314)835-9098 kbrown@ccls-stlouis.org	502 Huntercreek Ridge Ct Des Peres MO 63131	MO	Teacher	Tchr	Christ Community Kirkwood MO	(314)822-7774	CQ	2016
Brown Kathleen A Reitz Deac	(405) 519-5049 Katbrown428@gmail.com	7408 NW 116th St Oklahoma City OK 73162	OK	Deaconess	Inst C	Oklahoma District Norman OK	(405)321-3443	Other	1977
Brown Kathryn L Moll	(314)544-5596 kathybrown@slcas.org	9131 Vasel Dr Saint Louis MO 63123	MO	Teacher	EM			S	1972
Brown Katie L Stiegemeier	(816)820-8358 katielynn6842@gmail.com	22812 E 28th St Ct Blue Springs MO 64015	MO	Teacher	Tchr	Kansas City Kansas City MO	(816)241-5478	S	2006
Brown Kenzie D Woltemath	(319)521-1085 kenzie.brown0217@gmail.com	517 Bluehaw Dr Georgetown TX 78628	TX	DCE	Mem C	King Of Kings Round Rock TX	(512)255-0829	S	2018
Brown Kirsten E	(317)370-7847 brown.kirsten12@gmail.com	4955 Waterhaven Dr Noblesville IN 46062	CI	Teacher	Tchr	Trinity Bloomington IL	(309)828-6265	CH	2012

*Multiple Assignments (See Church Worker Locator for Additional Details)

See Page 53 for the Table of Abbreviations for key to District, Classification, Position, and College abbreviations.

**C =Candidate; EM =Emeritus; the date following the C is the month and year the Candidate status began

NAME	TELEPHONE NUMBER EMAIL	STREET ADDRESS CITY/STATE/ZIP	DISTRICT	CLASS.	POSITION/ STATUS**	WHERE SERVING	OFFICE PHONE	COLLEGE/ UNIV/CQ	YR GRAD
Brown Larry G	(314)221-8644	182 Ameren Way Apt 364 Ballwin MO 63021	MO	Teacher	EM			S	1965
Brown Leta M	(941)209-0247 letabrown@hotmail.com	5840 Millington Rd Millington MI 48746	FG	Teacher	C07/2016			AA	2002
Brown Logan R	(281)793-7836 logan@christlittlerock.com	28 Point South Ct Little Rock AR 72211	MDS	DCE	Mem C	Christ Little Rock AR	(501)663-5232	AU	2012
Brown Mallory F Clausen	(504)919-3756 mallory.brown1987@gmail.com	2350 Morgans Point Road Belton TX 76513	SO	Teacher	C07/2016			AU	2010
Brown Mark A	(586)306-3637 mbrowntct@gmail.com	31255 Fairfield Dr Warren MI 48088	MI	Teacher	Prin	Trinity Clinton Township MI	(586)463-2921	AA	2001
Brown Martha L Weisenborn	(660)463-2174 mbrown1466@hotmail.com	511 NW 8th St Concordia MO 64020	MO	Teacher	Tchr	Immanuel Higginsville MO	(660)584-3541	RF	1988
Brown Shari K Schultz	(218) 457-0362 sharichris1998@gmail.com	1130 S Townline Rd Vergas MN 56587	MNN	Teacher	Tchr	St Paul Perham MN	(218)346-7725	CQ	2016
Brown Shirley A Mosshammer	(909)986-5424 bobandshirleybrown@gmail.com	1527 N Granite Ave Ontario CA 91762	PSW	Teacher	EM			RF	1960
Brown Susan C Leimer Deac	susan.brown@stmarkslife.org	826 Parkside Dr Wheaton IL 60187	NI	Deaconess	Mem C	St Mark Saint Charles IL	(630)584-8638	RF	2024
Brown Tamara L Gumm	(309)231-4876 talebrown@gmail.com	5393 County Rd 5 NW Alexandria MN 56308	MNN	Teacher	C06/2019			SP	1990
Brown Thomas D	(314)974-8373 tbrown@martinlutherhs.org	9400 W Wilbur Ave Milwaukee WI 53228	SW	Teacher	Tchr	Martin Luther Greendale WI	(414)421-4000	MQ	2019
Brown-Fickenscher Taylor Deac	taylor.brown@ctsfw.edu	c/o St Paul Lutheran Church 6045 E State St Columbus IN 47201	IN	Deaconess	Mem C	St Paul Columbus IN	(812)376-6504	FW-DEAC	2020
Browning Scott D	(817)689-9877 ilsprincipal@yahoo.com	4102 Laurel Grove Dr Seabrook TX 77586	TX	Teacher	Prin	South Houston TX	(281)464-8299	S	1996
Bruder Heidi M Albrecht	(763)259-8370 hmbruder@gmail.com	5809 Quin Ave NE Elk River MN 55330	MNS	DCO	C07/2016			SP	2001
Brudniak Paige M Kecseg	(630)841-3839 paigekecseg@gmail.com	18481 W Springwood Grayslake IL 60030	NI	Teacher	Tchr	Seeds of Grace Northbrook IL	(847)498-3060	RF	2015
Brueggemann Karen B Oswald	(262)375-1921 mkbrueggemann82@gmail.com	738 Lancaster Ct Grafton WI 53024	SW	Teacher	EM			RF	1982
Bruenger Marilyn J Weber	(785)217-6253	937 SW Woodbridge Pl Topeka KS 66606	KS	Teacher	EM			S	1965
Bruening Fayleen M Wessel	(573)335-3398	2000 SE Ranson Rd Lees Summit MO 64082	MO	Teacher	EM			S	1972
Bruening John S	(414)856-8186	6208 Middle Rd Caledonia WI 53402	SW	Teacher	EM			RF	1981
Bruggemann-Wong Charlene E	(650)588-2701	1016 Crestview Dr Millbrae CA 94030	EN	Teacher	EM			CQ	1987
Bruhn Paul R Dr	(216)382-1461 paul.bruhn@roadrunner.com	3433 Woodridge Rd Cleveland Hts OH 44121	OH	Teacher	EM			S	1978
Bruick George A II	(661)979-4749 georgebruick@gmail.com	11838 Silverado Dr Fishers IN 46037	OH	DCE	C09/2022			SP	1997
Brumfield Katie M	(460)880-4272 katiebrumfield@hotmail.com	1815 Paradise Street Escondido CA 92026	PSW	Teacher	C08/2022			IV	2003
Brumm Jeremy D			TX	Teacher	Prin	South Houston TX	(281)464-8299	S	2004
Brummer Rochelle M Gottberg	(402)476-7151 rochelle.brummer@messiah.us	5055 Constitution Ave Lincoln NE 68521	NEB	Teacher	Tchr	Messiah Lincoln NE	(402)489-3024	S	1982
Brummet Larry E	(574)849-9800 larrybrummet@trinityl.org	28637 Bender Dr Elkhart IN 46514	IN	Teacher	Tchr	Trinity Elkhart IN	(574)674-8800	RF	1990
Brune Brittany D Wolff	(260)413-4564 brittany.brune62@gmail.com	3421 Delray Dr Fort Wayne IN 46815	IN	Teacher	C07/2024			CH	2013
Brune Christopher R	(260)402-5809 cbrune62@gmail.com	3421 Delray Dr Fort Wayne IN 46815	IN	Teacher	Prin	St Peter's Fort Wayne IN	(260)749-5816	CH	2012
Brune Pamela J Schmook	(260)402-5834 pjbrune1@aol.com	6314 Treasure Cove Fort Wayne IN 46835	IN	Teacher	EM			RF	1976
Brune Richard F	(260)415-3111 brune1254@aol.com	6314 Treasure Cove Fort Wayne IN 46835	IN	Teacher	EM			S	1976
Brunette Janet Yungmann	(972)342-6013 jymbrunette@gmail.com	149 Northrup Ave Holts Summit MO 65043	MO	Teacher	EM			S	1967
Brunk Donna J	(586)871-6157 donnabrunk1@gmail.com	61282 Windwood Ct Washington MI 48094	MI	Teacher	EM			S	1975
Brunkhorst Kimberly A Plecker Myers	kimb@timothylutheran.com	22020 E R D Mize Rd Independence MO 64057	MO	Teacher	Tchr	Timothy Blue Springs MO	(816)228-5300	S	2002
Brunner Leslie A Kreissler	(573)896-5055 lbrunner@trinityjc.org	2845 Valley View Ter Jefferson Cty MO 65109	MO	Teacher	Tchr	Trinity Jefferson City MO	(573)636-6750	S	2001
Bruns Keziah A	(402)641-8210 keziah.bruns@cune.org	P.O. Box 214 1146 Alice St Goehner NE 68364	NEB	Teacher	C05/2023			S	2021
Bruns-Teske Loralee L Mundt	loralee_bruns@comcast.net	1319 Lily Ct Schererville IN 46375	IN	Teacher	EM			S	1972
Bruntjen Kathryn G Opperman	(217)737-5202 kathryn.bruntjen@gmail.com	402 E Chestnut St Mount Pulaski IL 62548	CI	Teacher	C08/2020			CQ	2017
Brunworth Gerald C Dr	gbrunworth16@gmail.com	8730 Westminister Terr Apt 3300 Dallas TX 75243	TX	Teacher	EM			RF	1960
Brusick William R Dr	(281)651-4845 brusickb@trinityklein.org	10707 Whisperwillow Pl The Woodlands TX 77380	TX	DPM	Mem C	Trinity Klein Klein TX	(281)376-5773	CQ	2012
Brutcher Kristen M Grotelueschen	(317)861-4775 thebrutcherboys@comcast.net	5634 High Acres North Ct New Palestine IN 46163	IN	Teacher	Tchr	Zion New Palestine IN	(317)861-4210	CQ	2009
Brutlag John D	(630)882-9927 dale.brutlag@gmail.com	305 Fairhaven Dr Yorkville IL 60560	NI	Teacher	EM			RF	1963
Brutlag Sarah	(314)482-6607 sarah.brutlag@redeemer.net		TX	Teacher	Tchr	Redeemer Austin TX	(512)459-1500	S	2019

*Multiple Assignments (See Church Worker Locator for Additional Details)

See Page 53 for the Table of Abbreviations for key to District, Classification, Position, and College abbreviations.

**C =Candidate; EM =Emeritus; the date following the C is the month and year the Candidate status began

NAME	TELEPHONE NUMBER EMAIL	STREET ADDRESS CITY/STATE/ZIP	DISTRICT	CLASS.	POSITION/ STATUS**	WHERE SERVING	OFFICE PHONE	COLLEGE/ UNIV/CQ	YR GRAD
Bryant Ann A Ammons	(503)754-3397 bryant5265@frontier.com	39663 Hilltop Cir Severance CO 80610	NOW	Teacher	EM			CQ	1987
Bryant Chad J	(636)949-8765 cosportsfan@yahoo.com	2512 Westside Ave Norfolk NE 68701	NEB	Teacher	Tchr	Christ Norfolk NE	(402)371-1210	MQ	2002
Bryant Elaine R Richter Dautenhahn Dr	(314)733-5157 elaineandvic13@gmail.com	711 S Laclede Station Rd Apt G104 Saint Louis MO 63119	MO	Teacher	EM			RF	1964
Bryant Janice L Bahlman	(217)423-5933 k9bryant@yahoo.com	222 N 16th St Decatur IL 62521	CI	Teacher	EM			RF	1966
Bryngelson Patricia A Muckala	(507)696-8780 pbryng@hotmail.com	66040 200th Ave Dodge Center MN 55927	MNS	Teacher	EM			CQ	2010
Bublitz Donald R	(715)526-5315 jodon3@charter.net	825 Cobblestone Ln Apt 307 Kimberly WI 54136	NW	Teacher	EM			RF	1958
Bublitz Rachel A Larson	(314)825-2139 rachel.larson312@gmail.com	5127 Romaine Spring Dr Fenton MO 63026	MO	Teacher	C08/2025			MQ	2020
Buboltz Lora J Wroge Woodford	lorajbuboltz@gmail.com	5331 County Road 7 SW Kensington MN 56343	MNN	Teacher	C07/2016			SP	2001
Bucciferro Lindsay P Beasley	(630)306-0906 lbeasley1993@gmail.com	3818 N Kenneth Ave Apt 2 Chicago IL 60641	NI	Teacher	C12/2023			CQ	2017
Buchheimer Paul D Dr	(512)817-7360 ppbuchh@yahoo.com	7818 Green Devon Dr Houston TX 77095	TX	Teacher	EM			RF	1968
Buchholz Aaron G	(260)452-0254 aaron.g.buchholz@gmail.com	536 South 10th Street Oostburg WI 53070	SW	Teacher	Tchr	Sheboygan Sheboygan WI	(920)452-3323	S	2015
Buchholz David A	(816)807-4295 dcnbuchholz@yahoo.com	6609 N Camden Ave Kansas City MO 64151	MO	Teacher	EM			S	1978
Buchholz Kurt S	kurt.buchholz@lhm.org		MO	DCE	Aux	LLL/Lutheran Hour Ministries Saint Louis MO	(314)317-4100	SP	2002
Buchholz Margaret L Feldt	(715)758-8715 buchholzpeggy@hotmail.com	511 E Green Bay St Bonduel WI 54107	NW	Teacher	Tchr	St Paul Bonduel WI	(715)758-8532	SP	1975
Buchholz Matthew D	(816)807-9252 matthew.buchholz@lhsparker.org	c/o Lutheran High School 11249 Newlin Gulch Blvd Parker CO 80134	RM	Teacher	Tchr	Lutheran Parker CO	(303)841-5551	S	2013
Buchholz Paige S Paige Bocherding	(402)570-3045 paigebuchholz716@gmail.com	6314 N. Wabash Avenue Kansas City MO 64118	MO	Teacher	Tchr	Martin Luther Kansas City MO	(816)734-1060	S	2020
Buchhorn Alice L Carlson	(254)527-3712	13520 Fm 487 Bartlett TX 76511	TX	Teacher	EM			AU	1988
Buchinger Dan	(260)353-1152 17buchs@gmail.com	7545 N 650 E Ossian IN 46777	IN	Teacher	EM			S	1975
Buchinger Lori A Haines	(989)395-2368 slsrsbuc@concentric.net	P.O. Box 130 Alger MI 48610	MI	Teacher	EM			S	1976
Buchinger Steven L	(989)395-2367 stevebuchinger@gmail.com	5872 Buffalo Trl P.O. Box 130 Alger MI 48610	MI	Teacher	EM			S	1976
Buchinger Susan J Damman	(260)353-1152 suebuchinger@gmail.com	312 E Dustman Rd Bluffton IN 46714	IN	Teacher	EM			S	1975
Buck Jane E Luekens	(262)827-0534 jelb2765@gmail.com	2765 Arbor Dr Brookfield WI 53005	SW	Teacher	EM			RF	1963
Buck Karen S	(402)643-3093 karen.buck@cune.org	1128 N 2nd St Seward NE 68434	NEB	Teacher	EM			RF	1965
Buck Mary L Mc Nally	(810)230-2825 mbuck@stpaulflint.com	1369 Hickory Hollow Dr Flint MI 48532	MI	Teacher	Prin	St Paul Flint MI	(810)239-6200	CQ	2009
Buck Roger L	(920)912-0788 buck@trinitysheboygan.org	1815 N 4th St Sheboygan WI 53081	SW	Teacher	EM			S	1973
Buck Thomas M Dr	(262)827-0534 tmbaux@gmail.com	2765 Arbor Dr Brookfield WI 53005	SW	Teacher	EM			RF	1964
Buckley Sara L Frankford	(618)600-4449 sbuckley@zionbethalto.org	523 Vermont St Bethalto IL 62010	SI	Teacher	Tchr	Zion Bethalto IL	(618)377-8314	CQ	2000
Budil Donna M Leitgeb	(847)271-0756 donnabudil@gmail.com	17369 W Dartmoor Dr Grayslake IL 60030	NI	Teacher	Tchr	Gloryland Grayslake IL	(847)548-0112	RF	1992
Budnik Adrienne R Wissmueller	(414)659-8910 adriennebudnik@gmail.com	4745 Camfield Dr Brookfield WI 53045	SW	Teacher	Tchr	Immanuel Brookfield WI	(262)781-7140	MQ	2003
Budnik Elizabeth A Reckelberg	(902)360-1338 bbudnik@stpaullux.org	824 Marys Court Luxemburg WI 54217	NW	Teacher	Tchr	St Paul Luxemburg WI	(920)845-2095	MQ	2023
Bueckman Blair K Bollmann	(636)717-1982 rbbueckman@gmail.com	9145 Valemount Dr Colorado Spgs CO 80924	RM	Teacher	EM			S	1975
Buelow Janis M Wagner	(586)789-6037 dcejanis@gmail.com	725 2nd St. Apt 153 Columbus IN 42701	IN	DCE	RSO	Camp Lakeview Seymour IN	(812)342-4815	S	2021
Bueltmann Kim C Deac	(262)825-2951 kim@bueltmann.org	602 S Main St Buffalo IL 62515	MO	Deaconess	S Miss	Office of International Mission Saint Louis MO		RF	2002
Bueltmann Tawn S Gudgel	(309)550-4440 blessedmom2abcd@gmail.com	P.O. Box 108 Hopedale IL 61747	PSW	Teacher	RSO	Shepherd's Canyon Retreat Inc Wickenburg AZ	(480)588-8837	S	1987
Buerck Bradley J	(303)695-3055 b_buerck@hotmail.com	5326 Oak Ct Arvada CO 80002	RM	Teacher	Tchr	Bethlehem Lakewood CO	(303)238-7676	S	2000
Buerger Jane R Dr	(708)681-1039 jr.buerger.3734@gmail.com	2916 S 12th Ave Broadview IL 60305	NI	Teacher	EM			CQ	1987
Buescher Barbara A Wiltenburg	(319)493-4959 barb.buescher@gmail.com	5573 Donald St Stevensville MI 49127	MI	Teacher	EM			S	1974
Buesing Richard G	(816)519-7048 buesing@att.net	17225 Endsley Rd Kearney MO 64060	MO	Teacher	EM			S	1962
Buetow Paul E	(636)386-5228 lancerprin@hotmail.com	587 E Katella Cir Nixa MO 65714	MO	Teacher	EM			CQ	1986
Buhler Pamela L Whiteway Deac	(972)342-7697 deaconess.buhler@gmail.com	8406 Talmage Court Fort Wayne IN 46835	IN	Deaconess	Mem C	Ascension Fort Wayne IN	(260)486-2226	FW-DEAC	2018
Buhman Jeana M Warneke	(402)564-1280 pbuhman@frontiernet.net	33359 126th Ave Columbus NE 68601	NEB	Teacher	EM			S	1989

*Multiple Assignments (See Church Worker Locator for Additional Details)

See Page 53 for the Table of Abbreviations for key to District, Classification, Position, and College abbreviations.

**C =Candidate; EM =Emeritus; the date following the C is the month and year the Candidate status began

NAME	TELEPHONE NUMBER EMAIL	STREET ADDRESS CITY/STATE/ZIP	DISTRICT	CLASS.	POSITION/ STATUS**	WHERE SERVING	OFFICE PHONE	COLLEGE/ UNIV/CQ	YR GRAD
Buhrke Gretchen	gretchenbuhrke@trinluth.org	19496 N 2600 East Rd Lexington IL 61753	CI	Teacher	Tchr	Trinity Bloomington IL	(309)828-6265	RF	2002
Buhrke Lynn D Rader	Lynnbuhrke@gmail.com	4215 SW Homestead Ct Lees Summit MO 64082	EN	Teacher	EM			RF	1968
Buikema Daniel J	(702)592-9137 buikemad@flhsemail.org	2071 Desert Prarie St Las Vegas NV 89135	PSW	Teacher	Tchr	Faith Las Vegas NV	(702)804-4400	CQ	2000
Bulava Adam J	(217)412-8185 ajbulava@gmail.com	910 South Macarthur Blvd. Springfield IL 62704	CI	Teacher	Tchr	Lutheran High Association Springfield IL	(217)546-6363	SP	2005
Bulgrien Rachel R Finck Deac	(810)837-2638 bulgrien@zionlcs.com	7385 Lakeshore Rd Palms MI 48465	MI	Deaconess	Mem C	Zion Harbor Beach MI	(989)479-3615	FW	2023
Bull Bernard D Dr	(262)751-4912 bernard.bull@gmail.com	507 Locust St Seward NE 68434	NEB	Teacher	S HS/C	Concordia University Nebraska Seward NE	(402)643-3651	MQ	1994
Buls Linda J Welshans	(830)438-4204 bulslinda43@gmail.com	26240 Silver Cloud Dr San Antonio TX 78260	PSW	Teacher	EM			S	1965
Bult Derek W	(402)641-4493 bult@lutheranhigh.com	1015 Hawthorne Dr Howards Grove WI 53083	SW	Teacher	Prin	Sheboygan Sheboygan WI	(920)452-3323	S	2005
Bultemeier Amy	(317)752-1659 amybult@hotmail.com	9833 Parkshore Dr Fishers IN 46038	IN	DCE	Mem C	Cornerstone Carmel IN	(317)814-4252	CQ	2025
Bultemeier Dianna L Bergelin	(260)639-7365 dlbergelin@yahoo.com	10424 Spotted Hawk CV Hoagland IN 46745	IN	Teacher	C07/2016			MQ	1998
Bultemeyer Daniel P	(260)450-2020 dan.bultemeyer@gmail.com	6628 Rockingham Dr Fort Wayne IN 46835	IN	Teacher	Tchr	Concordia Fort Wayne IN	(260)426-9922	RF	1988
Bumbleburg Sarah K Ulrich	(812)530-9801 sbumbleburg@immanuelschool.org	1994 Sophia Ln Seymour IN 47274	IN	Teacher	Tchr	Immanuel Seymour IN	(812)522-1301	RF	2001
Bumgardner Rebecca L Dancy Deac	(218)280-5236 rebecca.bumgardner@yahoo.com	1700 Fountain Ct #104 Columbus GA 31904	FG	Deaconess	C02/2020			FW-DEAC	2013
Bumgarner Maureen H Hernwall	(612)763-5355 smbumgar@embarqmail.com	2501 Sara Ave Alexandria MN 56308	MNN	Teacher	EM			SP	1970
Bunch Caren L Crary	(765)714-8897 caren.bunch@gmail.com	4209 S 900 E Lafayette IN 47905	IN	Teacher	P/Tchr	Saint James Lafayette IN	(765)423-1616	CQ	2023
Bundschuh Shirley L Vogel	(573)426-3767 shirleybund51@gmail.com	308 Traci Dawn Dr Rolla MO 65401	WY	Teacher	EM			S	1979
Bunge Merri L Deac	(216)905-2435 deaconessmerri@stpeterslc.org	6139 Saint Francis Dr Seven Hills OH 44131	OH	Deaconess	Mem C	St Peter Shaker Heights OH	(216)561-2511	FW-DEAC	2020
Bunke James E	(989)883-2539 cjbunke@yahoo.com	31 Auch St Sebewaing MI 48759	MI	Tch/DCE	EM			RF	1978
Bunkelman James O	(734)625-3344 jbunkelman@yahoo.com	852 Kings Park Rd Monroe MI 48161	MI	Teacher	EM			CQ	1984
Bunnett Jane E Wellman	(402) 202-9346 janeeb2640@gmail.com	4 Belmont Dr York NE 68467	NEB	Teacher	EM			S	1964
Buns Matthew T Dr	(651)468-4481 buns@csp.edu	700 Cretin Ave S Saint Paul MN 55116	MNS	Teacher	S HS/C	Concordia University St Paul Saint Paul MN	(651)641-8278	Other	2005
Bunte Maria L	(708)337-6393 rialb@sbcglobal.net	144 Gulfstream Ct Grayslake IL 60030	NI	Teacher	EM			RF	1977
Burandt Shelah J Stender	(952)456-1497 sjburandt@gmail.com	822 1/2 Fox Glove Terrace Waconia MN 55387	MNS	Teacher	EM			SP	1994
Burbrink Sandra L	(812)522-7666	508 E 14th St Seymour IN 47274	IN	Teacher	EM			S	1973
Burch Michelle M Urban-Waterfall	(260)409-1678 mwaterfallburch@gmail.com	6905 E Dela Balme Rd Columbia City IN 46725	IN	Teacher	C07/2016			RF	2000
Burchardt Zachery	(260)705-1247 zburchardt@stpetersfw.org	4518 Bruick Rd New Haven IN 46774	IN	Teacher	Tchr	St Peters Fort Wayne IN	(260)749-5811	CQ	2022
Burford Sandra L Schindler	(314)239-5129 sandyburford@gmail.com	1000 Arbor Pointe Dr Manchester MO 63088	MO	Teacher	EM			RF	1968
Burford Susan K	(314)544-1982	2622 Carousel Dr Saint Louis MO 63125	MO	Teacher	Tchr	St Paul Des Peres MO	(314)822-2771	CQ	2008
Burgdorf David P	dburgdorf@eartlink.net	1095 Loop Branch Claremont CA 91711	PSW	Teacher	C07/2016			S	1966
Burgdorf Susan L	(314)602-5915 slburgdorf@yahoo.com	2573 Grayland Walk Saint Louis MO 63129	MO	Teacher	Tchr	Our Savior Fenton MO	(636)343-2192	S	1982
Burgell Juliana V Hirsch Deac	(314)478-8064 julianavhirsch@gmail.com	421 Charlestowne Place Dr Saint Charles MO 63301	MO	Deaconess	C07/2024			SL-DEAC	2010
Burgener Abigail A Schult	(812)525-1416 aaschult00@gmail.com	1305 Gaiser Dr Seymour IN 47274	IN	DCE	C08/2024			CH	2023
Burgener Matthew G	(217)778-3152 mgburgener@gmail.com	1305 Gaiser Dr Seymour IN 47274	IN	DCE	C06/2025			CH	2022
Burger Stephen F	(352)404-6538 sburger77@gmail.com	10324 Vista Pines Loop Clermont FL 34711	SI	Teacher	EM			S	1975
Burgess Crystal D	(402)730-4836 teacher9775@gmail.com	2610 NW 52nd St Lincoln NE 68524	NEB	Teacher	Tchr	Trinity Lincoln NE	(402)466-1800	S	1997
Burgess David S	(414)534-1270	5720 W Allwood Dr Franklin WI 53132	SW	Teacher	EM			RF	1980
Burgess Kara M Mackenzie	(314)591-8866 kburgess@ccls-stlouis.org	559 Winding Bluffs Dr Fenton MO 63026	MO	Teacher	Tchr	Christ Community Kirkwood MO	(314)822-7774	CH	2024
Burgess Robert M	(713)825-1261 bburgess@stpaulannarbor.org	1863 Hunters Creek Dr Superior Twp MI 48198	MI	Teacher	Prin	St Paul Ann Arbor MI	(734)665-9117	CH	1984
Burghard Grace L Olfers	(210)363-7157 joglburg@gmail.com	3118 John Glenn Dr San Antonio TX 78217	TX	Teacher	EM			CQ	1995
Burhop Heather G Schmelz	(260)312-8436 heatherburhop@yahoo.com	7625 N Portsmouth Rd Saginaw MI 48601	MI	Teacher	Tchr	Immanuel Saginaw MI	(989)754-0929	AA	2003
Burk Daniel R	(734)425-0261 dan.burk@stmatthew.info	34372 Parkgrove Dr Westland MI 48185	MI	Teacher	Prin	St Matthew Westland MI	(734)425-0260	MQ	2002
Burkart Jeffrey E Dr	(651)484-7722 jburkart@csp.edu	433 Irene Ct Roseville MN 55113	MNS	Teacher	EM			RF	1971

*Multiple Assignments (See Church Worker Locator for Additional Details)

See Page 53 for the Table of Abbreviations for key to District, Classification, Position, and College abbreviations.

**C =Candidate; EM =Emeritus; the date following the C is the month and year the Candidate status began

NAME	TELEPHONE NUMBER EMAIL	STREET ADDRESS CITY/STATE/ZIP	DISTRICT	CLASS.	POSITION/ STATUS**	WHERE SERVING	OFFICE PHONE	COLLEGE/ UNIV/CQ	YR GRAD
Burkart Martha L Gaertner	(651)484-7722 marthalburkart@gmail.com	433 Irene Ct Roseville MN 55113	MNS	Teacher	EM			RF	1971
Burke Steven C	(480)823-5911 sburke.tahiti@gmail.com	1410 Creekview Dr Lewisville TX 75067	CNH	DCO	C07/2016			CQ	2006
Burke Susan N Bloom	(602)758-4560 prkybrky@gmail.com	11419 N 23rd St Phoenix AZ 85028	PSW	Teacher	EM			CQ	1995
Burkee Jeffrey R	(301)892-0459 lcmsprincipal@gmail.com	12354 Wensley Road Blackjack MO 63033	MO	Teacher	Prin	Salem Black Jack MO	(314)741-6781	RF	1981
Burkee John G	(414)517-4890 jack.burkee@gmail.com	8536 W Arthur Pl Milwaukee WI 53227	SW	Teacher	EM			MQ	1982
Burkhart Tammie L Meigs Dr	(949)680-7187 tammie.burkhart@cui.edu	68 Timberland Aliso Viego CA 92656	PSW	Teacher	S HS/C	Concordia University Irvine Irvine CA	(949)854-8002	IV	2019
Burmeister Janet M	(636)288-0244 janbur@aol.com	3520 Old Jacksonville Rd Apt 31 Springfield IL 62711	CI	Teacher	Tchr	Concordia Springfield IL	(217)529-3307	RF	1980
Burmeister Kelly E Szwandrok	(630)204-5370 kburmiel7@gmail.com	573 S Edgewood Ave Lombard IL 60148	NI	Teacher	Tchr	Immanuel Elmhurst IL	(630)832-1649	RF	2003
Burmeister Lishelle L Wagenknecht	(505)294-4636 llburmeister@msn.com	3100 Lykes Dr NE Albuquerque NM 87110	RM	Teacher	Tchr	Christ Albuquerque NM	(505)884-3876	S	1993
Burmeister Sylvia A Gunderson	(507)776-3827 dsburm@hotmail.com	620 Summit Dr Apt 306 Fairmont MN 56031	MNS	Teacher	EM			SP	1968
Burmester Ellen J Simmer	(707)252-8606 eburmester@stjohnsnapa.org	3187 Laurel St Napa CA 94558	CNH	Teacher	Tchr	St John Napa CA	(707)226-7970	SP	1975
Burmester Henry	(262)665-7077 h.burmester@stpaulbonduel.com	111 Meyer St Cecil WI 54111	NW	Teacher	Tchr	St Paul Bonduel WI	(715)758-8559	MQ	2021
Burnett Jennifer J Hueter Abrahamsen	(714)615-4943 j.burnett.ecdc@gmail.com	2605 E Rose Ave Orange CA 92867	PSW	Teacher	Tchr	Salem Orange CA	(714)633-2366	CQ	1996
Burnham Betsy L Jenks	(407)469-2525	15333 County Rd 455 Montverde Fl FL 34756	FG	DCE	Mem C	Woodlands Montverde FL	(407)469-2525	IV	2006
Burns Courtney L Auer	(702)296-1104 burnsc@flhsemail.org	916 Cambridge Cross Pl Las Vegas NV 89144	PSW	Teacher	Tchr	Faith Las Vegas NV	(702)804-4400	CQ	2006
Burns Jarred L	(317)449-1487 jarred.burns@cuw.edu	8322 Hartington Way Indianapolis IN 46259	IN	DCM	Mem C	St Pauls Indianapolis IN	(317)787-4464	MQ	2019
Burns Kim	(651)388-1379 k.burns@peaceantigo.org	1502 East 22nd Street Stuttgart AR 72160	NW	Teacher	Tchr	Peace Antigo WI	(715)623-2200	WN	1985
Burns Nichole L McKinney	(406)249-7155 nburns1640@gmail.com	752 4th Ave West N Kalispell MT 59901	MT	Teacher	Tchr	Trinity Kalispell MT	(406)257-6716	CQ	2023
Burns Pamela A Post	(410)303-2573	2013 Franklin St Kill Devil HI NC 27948	SE	Teacher	EM			CQ	2006
Burns Rebecca C Farrell	(319)277-1903 Rcfb29@gmail.com	1009 Grove St Cedar Falls IA 50613	IE	Teacher	EM			CQ	2005
Burow Peter J	(806)535-2977 peter.burow@oslmckinney.org	10308 Old Eagle River Ln McKinney TX 75072	TX	Teacher	C07/2016			AU	2000
Burroughs Daniel R	(734)646-7013 deanoinfo@gmail.com	2 Jackson Cir Festus MO 63028	MO	Teacher	EM			RF	1971
Burroughs Dorothy P Pralle	(832)398-9064 dpburroughs@sbcglobal.net	4141 S Braeswood Blvd Apt 616 Houston TX 77025	TX	Teacher	EM			RF	1975
Burrow Alexis N	burrowlexi@gmail.com		MO	Teacher	Tchr	Trinity Jefferson City MO	(573)636-7807	S	2019
Burtman Heather R Bartelt	(414)466-0065	3451 N 91st Street Milwaukee WI 53222	FG	Teacher	C09/2025			MQ	2000
Busacker William P	(970)231-3529 wbusacker@centurylink.net	920 Norway Maple Dr Loveland CO 80538	RM	Teacher	EM			S	1975
Busch Edna F Geuder	(727)328-9339 edna.busch@oursaviorfl.org	2560 York St N St Petersburg FL 33710	FG	Teacher	Mem C	Our Savior Saint Petersburg FL	(727)344-2684	BR	1982
Busch Erin M	(918)931-0454 erin.busch@cune.org	1207 E Normal St Tahlequah OK 74464	OK	Teacher	Tchr	Oklahoma District Norman OK	(405)321-3443	S	2012
Busch Joan L Hessel	(918)931-0975 buschfam@sbcglobal.net	1207 E Normal St Tahlequah OK 74464	OK	Teacher	EM			RF	1979
Busch Joanna N Rosenberg	(714)639-1946 jbusch@salemorange.com	3119 E Almond Ave Orange CA 92869	PSW	Teacher	Tchr	Salem Orange CA	(714)633-2366	IV	1997
Busch John E	(918)456-3974 jbusch2325@gmail.com	1207 E Normal St Tahlequah OK 74464	OK	Teacher	O-Sp Min	Oklahoma District Norman OK	(405)321-3443	CQ	1986
Busch Michael Dr	(949)214-3414 michael.busch@cui.edu	23 Greenbough Irvine CA 92614	PSW	DPM	S HS/C	Concordia University Irvine Irvine CA	(949)854-8002	IV	2003
Busch Michael J	(727)302-9339	2560 York St N St Petersburg FL 33710	FG	Teacher	Mem C	Our Savior Saint Petersburg FL	(727)344-2684	BR	1982
Buschena Wendy L Lorenzen	jwbuschena@yahoo.com	2140 41st St Fulda MN 56131	MNS	Teacher	EM			S	1981
Buser Shirley Miersch	(254)913-5717 sbuser5797@att.net	3114 Shady Hill Dr Temple TX 76502	TX	Teacher	EM			S	1965
Bush Rachel C Rottman	(661)361-3598 rachel.bush525@gmail.com	25911 Enchanted Dawn San Antonio TX 78255	TX	Teacher	Tchr	Shep Of The Hills San Antonio TX	(210)614-3741	AU	2009
Bushre Julie C Bacon	(309)945-8279 julie.bushre@gmail.com	2332 Judith Ln Waukesha WI 53188	SW	Teacher	Pro Stf	Christ The Life Waukesha WI	(262)547-1817	AA	2000
Buske Karlee J Hintsala	(231)944-5134 karlee.hintsala@gmail.com	3135 S Pinewood Creek Ct Apt 104 New Berlin WI 53151	SW	Teacher	Tchr	Immanuel Brookfield WI	(262)781-7140	MQ	2017
Buskirk Brandon W	(619)301-1473 buskirk623@gmail.com	4223 Canterbury Rd North Olmstead OH 44070	OH	Teacher	Tchr	Cleveland LHS Association Rocky River OH	(440)356-7155	CQ	2012
Buss Janice L Dummer	(812)350-7898 bussjan6@gmail.com	9854 S Randall Rd Columbus IN 47201	IN	Teacher	EM			RF	1975
Buss Mark A	mmjjj@live.com	9854 S Randall Rd Columbus IN 47201	IN	Teacher	EM			RF	1974
Buss Micah			IN	Teacher	Tchr	Office of International Mission Saint Louis MO		CH	2011

*Multiple Assignments (See Church Worker Locator for Additional Details)
See Page 53 for the Table of Abbreviations for key to District, Classification, Position, and College abbreviations.
**C =Candidate; EM =Emeritus; the date following the C is the month and year the Candidate status began

NAME	TELEPHONE NUMBER EMAIL	STREET ADDRESS CITY/STATE/ZIP	DISTRICT	CLASS.	POSITION/ STATUS**	WHERE SERVING	OFFICE PHONE	COLLEGE/ UNIV/CQ	YR GRAD
Buss Naomi M	(815)566-1332 nbuss@immanuelcl.org	1025 9th Ave Belvidere IL 61008	NI	Teacher	Tchr	Immanuel Crystal Lake IL	(815)459-1441	MQ	2020
Buss Timothy L	(970)712-1617 tim.buss207@gmail.com	20313 Youngstoun Ct Apt 2509 Hagerstown MD 21742	SE	DCE	Mem C	Concordia Hagerstown MD	(301)797-5955	IV	2024
Buss McDaniel Elizabeth R Buss			PSW	Teacher	Tchr	Office of International Mission Saint Louis MO		S	2012
Busse Dale A	(234)817-0011 bdale7052@gmail.com	402 E 14th St Lamar MO 64759	MDS	Teacher	EM			RF	1957
Busse Donald R	(734)558-3392 dbusse@splconline.com	3432 Anna Ave Trenton MI 48183	MI	DCE	Mem C	St Paul Trenton MI	(734)676-1565	SP	1985
Busse Kurt A	(309)532-3279 kurtbusse@trinluth.org	15365 Mountain Vw Heyworth IL 61745	CI	Teacher	Tchr	Trinity Bloomington IL	(309)829-7513	S	1983
Busse Mitchel J	(812)341-1091 mitchelbusse98@gmail.com	5350 E Deer Valley Dr Unit 3185 Phoenix AZ 85054	PSW	DCE	C11/2024			AU	2022
Buster Susan Hansen Dr	(951)204-0466 sue.buster@ilsroadrunner.org	6922 Ranch View Rd Riverside CA 92506	PSW	Teacher	Prin	Immanuel Riverside CA	(951)682-4211	IV	1982
Butcher Laura C Schwehn Deac	(225)773-6379 caitlynn.butcher@gmail.com	5302 Sloane Sq Williamsburg VA 23188	SE	Deaconess	Mem C	King of Glory Williamsburg VA	(757)258-9701	CH	2020
Butcher Nicholas A	(989)274-5953 nbutcher46440@gmail.com	5302 Sloane Sq Williamsburg VA 23188	SE	DCE	Mem C	King of Glory Williamsburg VA	(757)258-9701	S	2016
Butler Harmon R Jr	(989)280-4698 harmon.butler87@gmail.com	218 Kansas Ave Paxico KS 66526	KS	Teacher	P/Tchr	St John Alma KS	(785)765-3632	CQ	2014
Butler Kelli S Dettman	(828)322-2998	1291 Franklin St Newton NC 28658	SE	Teacher	Tchr	St Stephen Hickory NC	(828)256-9865	BR	1994
Butler Lori A Pickerill	(425)418-6271 lpickerill@aol.com	19010 92nd Ave NW Stanwood WA 98292	NOW	Teacher	EM			PO	1984
Butler Stacy A Phillips Dr	(713)553-9384 stacy.butler@lutheransouth.org	707 Shorewood Dr Seabrook TX 77586	TX	Teacher	Prin	South Houston TX	(281)464-8299	CQ	2024
Butterfield Jonathan M Dr	(314)740-2810 jlbutterfield@gmail.com	716 Spring Crest Ct Fenton MO 63026	MO	Teacher	Prin	Lutheran South Saint Louis MO	(314)631-1400	CQ	2005
Butterfield Michael W	(708)466-8391 michaelgwm@gmail.com	3104 Spyglass Cir Palos Heights IL 60463	NI	Teacher	EM			CQ	1995
Butz Thomas C	(949)433-4132 pswbutztc@aol.com	23442 El Toro Rd #w256 Lake Forest CA 92630	PSW	Teacher	EM			CQ	1993
Buuck Darlene L Simmer	(260)242-0054 disbuuck@gmail.com	917 Mannes Pine CV Fort Wayne IN 46814	IN	Teacher	EM			SP	1981
Buuck Lois C Reineck	(219) 794-4042 lobukmilwis800@att.net	3127 Maple Dr Highland IN 46322	IN	Teacher	EM			RF	1965
Buuck Paul A	(260)242-1962 paulbuuck@gmail.com	917 Mannes Pine CV Fort Wayne IN 46814	IN	Teacher	Tchr	Emmanuel-St Michael Fort Wayne IN	(260)422-6712	SP	1983
Buuck Steven J Dr	(702)804-4444 buucks@flhsemail.org	11537 Bohemian Forest Avenue Las Vegas NV 89138	PSW	Teacher	Tchr	Faith Las Vegas NV	(702)804-4400	MQ	1985
Bynum Autumn A Schmitt	(414)526-9593 abynum@immanuelbrookfield.org	W164N10422 Timberline Ct Germantown WI 53022	SW	Teacher	Tchr	Immanuel Brookfield WI	(262)781-7140	MQ	2009
Bynum Willie B III	(414)526-8389 bbynum@lwlhs.org	W164N10422 Timberline Court Germantown WI 53022	SW	Teacher	Tchr	Living Word Jackson WI	(262)677-9353	MQ	2006
Byrne Sherry L Dahlke	(920)606-2000 sbyrne@stpaullux.org	E2490 Church Rd Luxemburg WI 54217	NW	Teacher	Tchr	St Paul Luxemburg WI	(920)845-2095	MQ	1988
Cabrales Maria d Deac	(619)852-6346 espigadoradal@live.com	8961 W Marconi Ave Peoria AZ 85382	PSW	Deaconess	Mem C	Apostles Peoria AZ	(623)979-3497	SL-DEAC	2018
Cacciapuoti Melissa A Boring	(714)803-9719	1462 W Christopher Dr Meridian ID 83642	PSW	Teacher	Tchr	St Paul Orange CA	(714)921-3188	IV	2011
Cage Sara K Nessmann	(405)759-2210 bradandsara@cox.net	2309 SW 94th St Oklahoma City OK 73159	OK	Teacher	Prin	Messiah* Oklahoma City OK	(405)946-0681	MQ	1999
Cahill Kyle D	(714)307-8274 kylecahill@me.com		TX	DPM	Mem C	Concordia San Antonio TX	(210)479-1477	IV	2011
Cahill Matthew A	(330)635-2859	744 Verna Ave Newbury Park CA 91320	PSW	Teacher	C08/2017			CQ	2011
Cahill Robert A Sr	(210)473-7109 charlietcougar81@gmail.com	15150 W Mark Dr New Berlin WI 53151	SW	Teacher	Prin	Our Fathers Greenfield WI	(414)282-7500	RF	1981
Cahill Sara J Gonzales	(805)807-3447 sjcahill729@gmail.com	744 Verna Ave. Newbury Park CA 91320	PSW	Teacher	Tchr	Concordia Christian Granada Hills CA	(818)368-0892	IV	2006
Cain Caleb	(414)526-4537 ccain@lakecountryhs.org	1195 Rolling Hills Dr Rubicon WI 53078	SW	Teacher	Tchr	Lake Country Hartland WI	(262)367-8600	MQ	2016
Cain Corrianne G	(414)378-5963 ccain@hcl.org	W61 N953 Crescent Dr Cedarburg WI 53012	EN	Teacher	Tchr	Hales Corners Hales Corners WI	(414)529-6700	S	2020
Caithamer Betty M Pflug	(714)637-3646 bettymcaith@hotmail.com	1849 N Diamond St Orange CA 92867	PSW	Teacher	EM			RF	1965
Caldarella Kim S Duckett		4 Pritchard St Buffalo NY 14210	EA	Teacher	Tchr	Trinity West Seneca NY	(716)674-5353	CQ	2000
Caldwell Marsha R Ficken	(417)232-5180 marsharen@yahoo.com	533 W Dade 102 Lockwood MO 65682	MO	Teacher	P/Tchr	Immanuel Lockwood MO	(417)232-4642	S	2001
Calendo Tanya L Lawin Dr	(815)355-2143 tlcalendo@gmail.com	1219 Buckeye Cir Crystal Lake IL 60012	NI	Teacher	Prin	Immanuel Palatine IL	(847)359-1936	BR	1990
Calhoun Richard C Dr	(708)218-7789	11507 Burton Court Westchester IL 60154	NI	Teacher	EM			RF	1966
Callihan Juanita L Bromlow	(303)699-2155 juanitacallihan@msn.com	7548 S Shawnee St Aurora CO 80016	RM	Teacher	Tchr	Mount Zion Boulder CO	(303)443-4151	AU	1989
Camberg Christina L Knapp	(858)274-2976 chrisnap49@hotmail.com	3767 Balboa Ter Unit D San Diego CA 92117	PSW	Teacher	EM			RF	1972
Campbell Annette M Duske	(414)801-6697 annettecampbell@wi.rr.com	12590 W Lakeland Dr New Berlin WI 53151	EN	Teacher	EM			CQ	2019
Campbell April L	campbell_home@sbcglobal.net	31019 Raleigh Creek Dr Tomball TX 77375	TX	Teacher	Tchr	Trinity Klein Klein TX	(281)376-5773	CQ	2016

*Multiple Assignments (See Church Worker Locator for Additional Details)

See Page 53 for the Table of Abbreviations for key to District, Classification, Position, and College abbreviations.

**C =Candidate; EM =Emeritus; the date following the C is the month and year the Candidate status began

NAME	TELEPHONE NUMBER EMAIL	STREET ADDRESS CITY/STATE/ZIP	DISTRICT	CLASS.	POSITION/ STATUS**	WHERE SERVING	OFFICE PHONE	COLLEGE/ UNIV/CQ	YR GRAD
Campbell Dorothy A Schneider	(847)438-1356 doricampbell@yahoo.com	50 E Wilson St Palatine IL 60067	NI	Teacher	Tchr	Immanuel Palatine IL	(847)359-1936	RF	1993
Campbell Gary H	(989)482-8117 gcampbell@peacesaginaw.org	5199 Pebblestone Ln Saginaw MI 48603	MI	Teacher	EM			RF	1970
Campbell Irene C Crago Deac	(530)533-7504	2105 Park Ave Apt 27 Oroville CA 95966	CNH	Deaconess	EM			RF	1983
Campbell Jan E Jan Waugh	(239)322-9423	19 Climbing Aster Way Ashville NC 28806	FG	Teacher	C01/2020			CQ	2004
Campbell Joshua H	(440)870-1118 jcampbell@lutheranwest.com	21778 Eaton Rd Cleveland OH 44126	OH	Teacher	Tchr	Cleveland LHS Association Rocky River OH	(440)356-7155	MQ	2002
Campbell Nicole R Eme	(440)212-1611 omahacampbell@gmail.com	21778 Eaton Rd Fairview Park OH 44126	OH	Teacher	C07/2023			MQ	2002
Canez Joan M Gunder	(281)796-0690 joancanez@gmail.com	239a Birdsall St Houston TX 77007	TX	Teacher	EM			CQ	2001
Canjura Diana	(312)259-2279 dcanjura@stpeterlcms.org	857 Casa Solana Dr Wheaton IL 60189	NI	Teacher	Tchr	St Peter Schaumburg IL	(847)885-3350	CH	2023
Cannon Cristyn M Parolin	(314)401-7588 ccannon@stpaulsdesperes.org	812 Carman Woods Dr Manchester MO 63021	MO	Teacher	Tchr	St Paul Des Peres MO	(314)822-2771	CQ	2020
Capdeville Roy M	(512)943-9357 roycapdeville@yahoo.com	302 Allen Cir Georgetown TX 78633	TX	Tch/DCE	EM			RF	1968
Capouch Judith R Schroeder	(847)394-4690 eacapouch@aol.com	224 E Kerry Brook Ln Arlington Hts IL 60004	NI	Teacher	EM			RF	1964
Cappa Susan D Kovel	(708)655-1819 scappa64@gmail.com	6603 Chester Ave Hodgkins IL 60525	NI	Teacher	Tchr	St John's Lombard IL	(630)932-3196	RF	1989
Carbone Hannah J Lange	(715)846-3434 hannahj1521@gmail.com	1305 Olive Ln N Apt 127 Minneapolis MN 55447	MNS	Teacher	Tchr	St John Corcoran MN	(763)420-2426	CQ	2024
Carey Grant E Dr	(512)423-2033 grantdce@hotmail.com	1017 Lily Pad Ln Leander TX 78641	TX	DCE	Mem C	ACTS Leander TX	(512)337-6524	IV	2001
Carey Leah Quinlan	(724)470-5125 leahquinlan@gmail.com	P.O. Box 142 Ridgeville Corners OH 43555	IN	Teacher	Tchr	Central New Haven IN	(260)493-2502	AA	2023
Cargin Alexander C	(913)787-1547 alex.cargin@gmail.com	279 Stow St Fond Du Lac WI 54935	SW	DCE	Mem C	Grace Menomonee Falls WI	(262)251-0670	S	2017
Cargin Anna J Hirssig	(507)421-4777 carginanna@gmail.com		SW	Teacher	Tchr	St John Berlin WI	(920)361-0555	S	2016
Cariker Gretchen D Koehnke	(714)342-9257 g_cariker@att.net	1915 W Almond Ave Orange CA 92868	PSW	Teacher	EM			S	1979
Cario Meredith M Vincent	(928)580-5082	8904 119th Street Ct E Puyallup WA 98373	NOW	Teacher	C07/2016			S	2004
Cario William R Dr	(262) 527-5803 ccario@milwpc.com	4017 W Haven Ave Mequon WI 53092	SW	Teacher	EM			RF	1978
Carley Denise R O Brien Block	(319)446-7341	80 Cardinal Ave Atkins IA 52206	IE	Teacher	Tchr	Central Newhall IA	(319)223-5271	S	1996
Carlos Jack	(621)295-1793 carlostribe@gmail.com	6912 Russell Ave S Minneapolis MN 55423	MNS	DCO	EM			SP	1998
Carlove Patrick A	(214)995-9407 patrick.carlove@gmail.com	12017 Mira Vista Way Austin TX 78726	TX	Teacher	C04/2023			MQ	1991
Carls Lily R Lily Rebecca Franz		20749 Harford Way Lakeville MN 55044	MNS	DCO	Tchr	St Paul Prior Lake MN	(952)447-2117	SP	2023
Carlsen Christina Clark	(970)286-1031 cctmc@live.com	1914 Richards Lake Rd Fort Collins CO 80524	RM	Teacher	EM			CQ	1997
Carlson Elizabeth A Scheetz	(307)461-4575 elizabeth@carlsonplace.net	2519 Dry Ranch Rd Sheridan WY 82801	WY	Teacher	C07/2016			S	1997
Carlson James A	(314)723-2236	2020 Sibley St Saint Charles MO 63301	MO	Teacher	EM			S	1970
Carlson Jenny R DiGiorgio	(402)995-9691 jrosecarlson@gmail.com	4822 N 138th St. Omaha NE 68164	NEB	Teacher	Tchr	Concordia Omaha NE	(402)445-4000	S	2009
Carlson Phillip A	(402)860-0102 pcarlson@lhne.org	2412 W Madison Ave Norfolk NE 68701	NEB	Teacher	Tchr	Northeast Norfolk NE	(402)379-3040	S	2001
Carlson Robin E Unglaub	(952)292-7787 robinbird@frontiernet.net	7255 Stewart Ave Mayer MN 55360	MNS	Teacher	Tchr	Zion Mayer MN	(952)657-2339	SP	1989
Carlton Janet R Curtis	(404)558-8868 jancarlton@bellsouth.net	370 River Trail Dahlongega GA 30533	FG	Teacher	EM			RF	1975
Carlton Joann M Wiesehan	(321)359-1430 jo.carlton@juno.com	12203 Tullymore Dr Stanwood MI 49346	MI	Teacher	EM			RF	1972
Carlton Ruth M Kell	(248) 496-5994 jc4owat@sbcglobal.net	11138 Fieldcrest Meadows Ct White Lake MI 48386	MI	Teacher	Tchr	Christ Milford MI	(248)684-0895	AA	1984
Carmines Nicole F Young	(210)479-1477 nicolec@concordia-satx.com	1915 Oakline Dr San Antonio TX 78232	TX	Teacher	Mem C	Concordia San Antonio TX	(210)479-1477	CQ	2011
Carnahan Joshua R	joshua.carnahan@saints.org		NOW	Teacher	Tchr	Trinity Bend OR	(541)382-1850	CQ	2012
Carnahan Nathan A	nathan.a.carnahan@gmail.com	7013 Osprey Cir Bremerton WA 98312	NOW	Teacher	Tchr	Concordia Tacoma WA	(253)475-9513	IV	2011
Carnehl Janet E Kaiser	(847)359-7732 janetcarnehl@gmail.com	25 N Linden Ave Palatine IL 60074	NI	Teacher	EM			RF	1976
Carnehl Lisa G Greimann	(573)424-6853 lisacarnehl@gmail.com	319 Quaker Church Rd Randolph NJ 07869	NJ	Teacher	C09/2016			CH	2012
Carney Kelly J Meissner	(724)814-9960 kcarney@stlukecabot.org	2600 Plantation Dr Saxonburg PA 16056	EA	Teacher	Prin	St Luke Cabot PA	(724)352-2777	BR	1995
Carnoali Jean C Heerten	(402)631-7394 Jean.Carnoali2@gmail.com	705 4th St Adair IA 50002	IW	Teacher	C05/2022			S	1989
Carolus Holly S Roethler	(319)287-6814 ghcarolus@gmail.com	2810 Crestline Ave Waterloo IA 50702	IE	Teacher	C09/2025			CQ	2005
Carothers Cheryl L Kaiser	(812)371-0885 mccarothers@att.net	4800 E 300 S Columbus IN 47201	IN	Teacher	C07/2016			AA	1994
Carpenter Shirley A Schmohe	(908)233-5388 sc0601sc@aol.com	601 Graceland Pl Westfield NJ 07090	NJ	Teacher	EM			RF	1960

*Multiple Assignments (See Church Worker Locator for Additional Details)

See Page 53 for the Table of Abbreviations for key to District, Classification, Position, and College abbreviations.

**C =Candidate; EM =Emeritus; the date following the C is the month and year the Candidate status began

NAME	TELEPHONE NUMBER EMAIL	STREET ADDRESS CITY/STATE/ZIP	DISTRICT	CLASS.	POSITION/ STATUS**	WHERE SERVING	OFFICE PHONE	COLLEGE/ UNIV/CQ	YR GRAD
Carr Allison J Guse	(630)835-1282 allisoncarr26@gmail.com	3340 Parkway Dr Bay City MI 48706	MI	DFLM	C05/2022			AA	2016
Carr Brian M	(812)589-1030 bcarr0305@gmail.com	3159 Otter Lane Springfield IL 62712	CI	Teacher	Tchr	Concordia Springfield IL	(217)529-3307	CQ	2015
Carr Catherine G Brillinger	(734)977-2455 ccmickey45@yahoo.com	2449 Romar Dr Hermitage PA 16148	S	Teacher	EM			AU	1984
Carr Melissa L Scheer	(916)220-8661 thecarrshop@gmail.com	13086 Vanderwood Dr Black Jack MO 63033	CNH	DCE	C10/2019			S	2005
Carrabia Andrea M		3603 Fir Hollow Way Pearland TX 77581	TX	Teacher	Tchr	South Houston TX	(281)464-8299	CH	2014
Carrel Andrea K Winter	(618)553-4517 andreacarr@trinluth.org	311 Raleigh Ct Normal IL 61761	CI	Teacher	Tchr	Trinity Bloomington IL	(309)829-7513	RF	2005
Carretto Jessica E Otte	(561)504-8849 jecarretto@gmail.com	744 SW 7th St Boca Raton FL 33486	FG	Teacher	C07/2016			S	2006
Carrier Lori J Grimshaw	(810) 887-0206 loricarrier3@gmail.com	4115 Surrey Lane Fort Gratiot MI 48059	MI	Teacher	EM			S	1979
Carrillo Christina M Williams	(714)788-1722 christinamcarrillo@gmail.com	17781 Bishop Cir Villa Park CA 92861	PSW	Teacher	Tchr	Salem Orange CA	(714)633-2366	CQ	2018
Carroll Dorothy M Bartusch	(231)796-8522 dorothy-carroll@att.net	18170 Woodland Dr Big Rapids MI 49307	MI	Teacher	EM			RF	1972
Carson Lani L Seyfer Dr	(808)722-1020 lu2inhi@aol.com	94-121 Akaku Pl Mililani HI 96789	CNH	Teacher	Tchr	Trinity Wahiawa HI	(808)621-6033	CQ	2013
Carson Wende J Volkert	(402)518-0653 wcarsonorls@gmail.com	310 S Monroe St Pilger NE 68768	NEB	Teacher	EM			S	1978
Carter Beth D Lane	(314)803-4526 bcarter5881@gmail.com	12388 Harundale Ct Saint Louis MO 63146	MO	Teacher	EM			CQ	2004
Carter Deborah L Adam Dr	(540)656-3155	8 Revolutionary Rd Highland Fls NY 10928	AT	Teacher	C06/2021			BR	2016
Carter Debra J Dillon	(913)333-9851 debbiejt12@gmail.com	2520 SE Nottingham Drive Lees Summit KS 64063	KS	Teacher	Tchr	Bethany Overland Park KS	(913)648-2228	MQ	1994
Carter Gail R Dobberstein	(314)846-7473 cartergailr@aol.com	6240 Kings Ferry Pl Saint Louis MO 63129	MO	Teacher	EM			RF	1962
Carter Sarah M Steinborn	sarah.m.steinborn@gmail.com	20376 Twin Lakes Rd NW Elk River MN 55330	MNS	Teacher	Tchr	St John Corcoran MN	(763)420-2426	MQ	2018
Cartwright Marlys K Rempfer	(828)569-9291 mkc838@aol.com	1738 Meadow Ln Seward NE 68434	CNH	DCE	EM			S	1979
Carver Gail B Schrupp	(507)330-1519 tcarver0656@charter.net	122 Allen Ln Faribault MN 55021	MNS	Teacher	EM			SP	1979
Case Kimberly A Snyder	(314)304-2389 kcase@ccls-stlouis.org		MO	Teacher	Tchr	Christ Community Kirkwood MO	(314)822-7774	AA	2005
Case Susan G Baker Grau	(269)208-2467 sgcase531@gmail.com	621 Helena Street Dowagiac MI 49047	MI	Teacher	EM			S	1974
Cashmer Leah F	(734)934-6764 leahfcashmer@gmail.com	532 Des Plaines Ave. Apt. 1g Forest Park IL 60130	NI	Teacher	C08/2023			AA	2017
Cass Nicholas	(920)515-2623 ncass@immanuelrapids.com	1120 16th St S Wisconsin Rapids WI 54494	NW	DCO	Mem C	Immanuel Wisconsin Rapids WI	(715)423-3260	SP	2016
Casselman Lynn R Reifke-Seeman	(623)810-9821 lyncasselman@gmail.com	1014 12th St Eldora IA 50627	IE	Teacher	Tchr	Good Shepherd Eldora IA	(641)858-5928	RF	1984
Cassidy Matthew	(630)677-0692 mcassidy@ilcsbatavia.org	733 Burton Dr Batavia IL 60510	NI	DCM	Mem C	Immanuel Batavia IL	(630)879-7163	MQ	2024
Cassidy Shawn C	(262)387-0262	4447 River Vista Dr Cedarburg WI 53012	SW	Teacher	S HS/C	Concordia University Wisconsin Mequon WI	(262)243-5700	MQ	1993
Castens Maria A Schardt	(702)207-9509 mcastens@christlutheranchurch.org	5522 S 72nd St Lincoln NE 68516	NEB	Teacher	Mem C	Christ Lincoln NE	(402)483-7774	S	2003
Castillo Courtney M Lofink	(714)932-6238 clofink10@gmail.com	5003 E Lakeside Ave Orange CA 92867	PSW	Teacher	Tchr	St Paul Orange CA	(714)637-2640	CH	2019
Castleman Crystal L Boerger	ccastleman@clhscadets.com	22415 Hoagland Rd Monroeville IN 46773	IN	Teacher	Tchr	Concordia Fort Wayne IN	(260)483-1102	RF	1994
Catchpole Rebecca E Deac	(608)234-4747 beckellmew@gmail.com	4573 Emerald Valley Loop Fowlerville MI 48836	TX	Deaconess	D Miss	Texas District Round Rock TX	(800)951-3478	SL-DEAC	2015
Cattau Curt W Dr	(714)476-3995 curtcattau@gmail.com	4942 St Andrews Ct Loveland CO 80537	RM	Teacher	EM			S	1973
Cattau Daniel J	(702)280-3326 daniel.cattau@gmail.com	1125 Deer Valley Dr Friendswood TX 77546	TX	Teacher	Prin	South Houston TX	(281)464-8299	MQ	2009
Cattau Ruth A Klammer	(714)476-3997 ruthcattau@gmail.com	4942 Saint Andrews Ct Loveland CO 80537	RM	Teacher	EM			S	1972
Cavage Rebecca	(512)412-5676 rebecca.cavage@gmail.com	c/o Shepherd Of The Hills Lutheran School 6914 Wurzbach Rd San Antonio TX 78240	TX	Teacher	Tchr	Shep Of The Hills San Antonio TX	(210)614-3741	AU	2013
Cave Emily B Ringelberg Deac	(314)719-7696 emrunner@hotmail.com	4704 Glenn Ln Las Cruces NM 88007	PSW	Deaconess	C11/2021			SL-DEAC	2016
Ceder Katherine A	(765)342-7491 ceder@thecalvaryschool.org	5207 E Walnut Dr Mooresville IN 46158	IN	Teacher	Tchr	Calvary Indianapolis IN	(317)783-2000	CQ	2003
Cejas Amy A Yatsko	(412)849-8648 amy.yatsko@faithlasvegas.org	10217 Waseca Ave. Las Vegas NV 89144	PSW	Teacher	Tchr	Faith Community Las Vegas NV	(702)921-2700	CQ	2016
Ceplecha Paula I North	(989)479-3340 p.ceplecha@comcast.net	9677 Eastview Dr Harbor Beach MI 48441	MI	Teacher	EM			AA	1987
Cermak Leah M	(262)939-0473 leah.cermak@stjohnglendale.com	505 Lily Lane Grafton WI 53024	SW	Teacher	Tchr	St Johns Glendale WI	(414)352-4150	MQ	2014
Chabot Angela R Bock	(763) 237-4985 angichabot1970@yahoo.com	1230 Waters Way Watertown MN 55388	MNS	Teacher	EM			S	1997
Chaisson Kimberly A Schaller	(832)860-6212 kchaisson@salem4u.com	12938 Yorkmont Dr Cypress TX 77429	TX	Teacher	Tchr	Salem Tomball TX	(281)351-8223	CQ	2009

*Multiple Assignments (See Church Worker Locator for Additional Details)
See Page 53 for the Table of Abbreviations for key to District, Classification, Position, and College abbreviations.
**C =Candidate; EM =Emeritus; the date following the C is the month and year the Candidate status began

NAME	TELEPHONE NUMBER EMAIL	STREET ADDRESS CITY/STATE/ZIP	DISTRICT	CLASS.	POSITION/ STATUS**	WHERE SERVING	OFFICE PHONE	COLLEGE/ UNIV/CQ	YR GRAD
Chandler Allison L	(218)766-4830 ms.chandler@alsalaska.org	306 W Grant St Winthrop MN 55396	MNN	Teacher	C07/2020			MQ	2008
Chandler Kathryn A Whitney	(314)607-6187 kchandler825@gmail.com	845 Eckert Ln Columbia IL 62236	MO	Teacher	P/Tchr	Our Savior Fenton MO	(636)343-7511	CQ	2018
Chandler Tami L Bluschke	(308)380-6548 tamichandler@ymail.com	208 W. 13th Grand Island NE 68801	NEB	Teacher	Tchr	Trinity Grand Island NE	(308)382-5274	S	1990
Chaney Carin K Reinke	(320)293-5468	323 Creekside Dr Buffalo MN 55313	MNS	Teacher	EM			SP	1969
Chapa Matthew J			NW	Teacher	Tchr	Trinity Merrill WI	(715)536-7501	S	2016
Chapin Kathryne A Rau	(314)799-0768 kchapin@trinityof.org	2340 Banon Dr Saint Charles MO 63301	MO	Teacher	P/Tchr	Trinity Saint Charles MO	(636)250-3654	S	1996
Chapin Nancy K Elsen	(913)226-3219 chapinmj@swbell.net	12332 Russell St Overland Park KS 66209	KS	Teacher	EM			Other	1974
Chaplin Heidi U Klemm	(586)770-0175 1966chaplin@gmail.com	47779 Meadowbrook Dr Macomb MI 48044	MI	Teacher	Tchr	Peace Shelby Township MI	(586)731-4120	AA	1990
Chaplin Rebecca R	(586)764-8170 becky.chaplin@faithlasvegas.org	9470 Peace Way Unit 243 Las Vegas NV 89147	PSW	DFLM	Mem C	Faith Community Las Vegas NV	(702)921-2700	AA	2015
Chapman Darius M Dr	(702)840-8696 bochapman@gmail.com	1712 Havercamp Street Las Vegas NV 89117	PSW	DCE	Tchr	Faith Las Vegas NV	(702)804-4400	AU	2004
Chapman John J	(818)898-3346 j.pchapman@gmail.com	642 Harps St San Fernando CA 91340	PSW	DCE	Mem C	Our Savior First Granada Hills CA	(818)363-9505	IV	1992
Chapman Rosalie A Caldarera	(281)782-4495 chapmanrosalie1@gmail.com	10511 Dude Rd Houston TX 77064	TX	Teacher	Tchr	Our Savior Houston TX	(713)290-8277	AU	2017
Chappell Nicole Deac	(260)458-1292 nchappell118@gmail.com	117 Fox Chase Dr Arnold MO 63010	MO	Deaconess	Pro Stf	Christ Community Kirkwood MO	(314)822-7774	CH	2023
Charlton Kaitlyn M	(314)541-3188 ms.charlton4@gmail.com	1011a Sugar Creek Ct Saint Peters MO 63376	MO	Teacher	C07/2016			S	2008
Charogoff Carolyn E Milz	(734)652-1467 carolynmilz@gmail.com	17316 S Lucille Cir New Boston MI 48164	MI	Teacher	Tchr	Trinity Monroe MI	(734)242-2308	AA	2013
Charpentier Jaelle Rodenbeck	(708)663-4528 jcharpentier@racinelutheran.org	1717 Colony Dr Mt Pleasant WI 53406	SW	Teacher	Tchr	Lutheran High School Racine WI	(262)637-6538	S	2008
Charron Kelsey J	kcharron@trinityfreistadt.com		SW	Teacher	Pro Stf	Trinity Mequon WI	(262)242-2045	MQ	2018
Chase Jana J Koren	(260)246-2145 jana.chase@gmail.com	1031 13th St Carlyle IL 62231	MNS	Teacher	C07/2016			MQ	2007
Chatham Pamela D Inabinett	(808)372-8251 pchatham@hotmail.com	5 Winthrop Point Little Rock AR 72211	MDS	Teacher	C06/2023			CQ	2019
Chaveriat Charles A	(262)993-4832 chas.chaveriat@gmail.com	6470 37th Ave NW Apt 303 Rochester MN 55901	MNS	DPM	Prin	Rochester Central Rochester MN	(507)289-3267	S	2011
Cheadle Deanna L Deac	(740)804-1026 seohiodcs@yahoo.com	268 Ward Rd Chillicothe OH 45601	OH	Deaconess	Mem C	Our Savior Chillicothe OH	(740)775-2470	CQ	2005
Chellew Deborah S	(307)287-9597 deborah.chellew@gmail.com	2811 S Coral St Sioux City IA 51106	IW	Teacher	C08/2023			SP	1983
Cheney Mark R	(702)612-6724 cheneym@flhsemail.org	9325 Garden Springs Ave Las Vegas NV 89149	PSW	Teacher	Tchr	Faith Las Vegas NV	(702)804-4400	S	1999
Cheney Paul F	(281)380-7051 paulcheney@hotmail.com	19103 Logan Timbers Ln Tomball TX 77375	TX	Teacher	Mem C	Salem Tomball TX	(281)351-8223	Other	1999
Cherington Lynette K Roesel	(713)834-7408 lynettecherington@gmail.com	9418 Creek Vine Dr Houston TX 77040	TX	Teacher	Prin	Our Savior Houston TX	(713)290-8277	CQ	2022
Cherney Jenean J Williams			MNS	Teacher	C07/2023			S	2014
Cherry Robert P Jr	(949)212-0111 cherry@creanlutheran.org	289 W Pebble Creek Ln Orange CA 92865	PSW	Teacher	Tchr	Crean Irvine CA	(949)387-1199	CQ	2019
Childers Christina L Schaffer Deac	christina@visitgrace.org	7116 Arbor Trace Dr Apt 920 Knoxville TN 37909	MDS	Deaconess	Mem C	Grace Knoxville TN	(865)691-2823	SL-DEAC	2024
Childers Frances M Cashmer	francicashmer@gmail.com	13669 Phelps St Southgate MI 48195	MI	Teacher	Tchr	Christ The King Southgate MI	(734)285-9695	RF	1993
Childress Heather L Yardley	(618)226-3147 hchildress75@yahoo.com	10415 End Rd Shattuc IL 62231	SI	Teacher	Tchr	Trinity Hoffman IL	(618)495-2545	RF	1998
Chiles Jill	(702)882-5390 rcjc1519@gmail.com	2040 19th Avenue Dr NE Hickory NC 28601	MDS	Teacher	C07/2016			S	1999
Chiles Ross	(702)882-5369 rchiles@sslcms.org	2040 19th Avenue Dr NE Hickory NC 28601	SE	Teacher	Prin	St Stephen Hickory NC	(828)256-2166	S	1999
Chilman John III	(763)442-9898 chilmanj@flhsemail.org	10013 Long Cattle Ave Las Vegas NV 89117	PSW	Teacher	Tchr	Faith Las Vegas NV	(702)804-4400	SP	1992
Chilman Matthew J	(702)557-7106 matthew.chilman@flhsemail.org	10960 Kingston Fields Ave Las Vegas NV 89166	PSW	Teacher	Tchr	Faith Las Vegas NV	(702)804-4400	S	2018
Chin Barbara A Ramirez	(708)479-1262 bchin@tlcs.org		NI	Teacher	Tchr	Trinity Tinley Park IL	(708)532-3529	RF	2006
Chinberg Kathleen L Cordes	(636)579-1899 kldwchinberg@gmail.com	14938 Rutland Cir Chesterfield MO 63017	MO	Teacher	Mem C	King Of Kings Chesterfield MO	(314)469-2224	RF	1985
Chinchilla Erin D Radtke	(951)897-4934 erin.chinchilla@ilcs-riverside.org	5455 Alessandro Blvd. Riverside CA 92506	PSW	Teacher	Tchr	Immanuel Riverside CA	(951)682-7613	CQ	2017
Chittick Cari Dr	(949)400-4759 carichittick@hotmail.com	115 Chaumont Cir Foothill Rnch CA 92610	PSW	Teacher	S HS/C	Concordia University Irvine Irvine CA	(949)854-8002	S	1995
Choate Alyssa Deac	(713)818-6947 alyssa.lehenbauer@gmail.com	7508 E 83rd St Kansas City MO 64138	KS	Deaconess	Mem C	Bethany Overland Park KS	(913)648-2228	SL-DEAC	2025
Choate Carolyn R Horton	(501)425-0654 crchoate5@gmail.com	8008 Toltec Dr N Little Rock AR 72116	MDS	Teacher	EM			RF	2004
Choate Lauren N Wynn	(701)213-8630 lauren.n.choate@gmail.com	535 Country Ln Mount Vernon MO 65712	MO	Teacher	Tchr	Trinity Freistatt MO	(417)235-5931	CQ	2023
Choksi Pamela L Ruwald	(708)302-9419 pamela.choksi@comcast.net	18850 SE Crosswinds Ln Jupiter FL 33478	FG	Teacher	EM			S	1991
Cholak Stephanie A Blake	(314)952-3363 stephcholak@yahoo.com	5607 Deepcreek Ln Houston TX 77091	TX	Teacher	Tchr	Our Savior Houston TX	(713)290-8277	CQ	2018

*Multiple Assignments (See Church Worker Locator for Additional Details)
See Page 53 for the Table of Abbreviations for key to District, Classification, Position, and College abbreviations.
**C =Candidate; EM =Emeritus; the date following the C is the month and year the Candidate status began

NAME	TELEPHONE NUMBER EMAIL	STREET ADDRESS CITY/STATE/ZIP	DISTRICT	CLASS.	POSITION/ STATUS**	WHERE SERVING	OFFICE PHONE	COLLEGE/ UNIV/CQ	YR GRAD
Cholcher Norma J Hartner	(479)782-5788 n_cholcher@sbcglobal.net	4714 S X St Fort Smith AR 72903	MDS	Teacher	EM			S	1961
Choroba Katherine J Kuhl	(810)348-6410 cdc02@sbcglobal.net	2767 Buttercup Ct Howell MI 48843	MI	Teacher	EM			RF	1980
Chow Terry S Hyde	(818)601-8962 peppy1195@gmail.com	1317 Mandarin Ln Duarte CA 91010	PSW	Teacher	EM			RF	1977
Chrismer Emma P Gaither	emmapchrismer@gmail.com	4220 S Roberts Rd Fort Mohave AZ 86426	PSW	Teacher	C08/2017			S	2013
Christ Jaime L Hink	(716)860-7083	2501 Eggert Rd Tonawanda NY 14150	EA	Teacher	C07/2016			RF	1999
Christensen Diane V Avenson	(307)287-3346 dianechrist60@gmail.com	127 Cedar Ridge Dr Thermopolis WY 82443	WY	Teacher	C07/2016			SP	1983
Christensen Nancy J Rohlfs	(402)429-9043 jeffandnan75@gmail.com	3001 S 51st St Ct Unit 2204 Lincoln NE 68506	NEB	Teacher	EM			S	1974
Christian Bruce D	(832)465-5794 bruceandsuzanne@yahoo.com	733 Tonkawa Trl Fredericksbrg TX 78624	TX	Teacher	EM			CQ	2006
Christian Carl F Dr	(425)686-7390 cjchris52@gmail.com	17502 102nd Ave NE Apt 302 Bothell WA 98011	NOW	Teacher	EM			RF	1953
Christian David W	(314)348-6759 dandjonsidney@aol.com	809 68th St W Bradenton FL 34209	MO	Tch/DCE	EM			RF	1970
Christian Deborah R McClean	(281)827-4017 debchristi@yahoo.com	P.O. Box 1201 Blue Hill ME 04614	TX	Teacher	EM			RF	1980
Christian Donald A Dr	donald.christian@concordia.edu	P.O. Box 1201 Blue Hill ME 04614	TX	Teacher	EM			RF	1981
Christian Hannah L	(720)618-2807 christian@hopelutheran.org	12601 W 60th St Shawnee KS 66216	KS	Teacher	Tchr	Hope Shawnee KS	(913)631-6940	IV	2022
Christian Judith A Werman Dr	(314)378-7798 j.christian525@gmail.com	809 68th St W Bradenton FL 34209	MO	Teacher	EM			RF	1969
Christian Megan A Brunssen	(402)320-9550 christian.megana@gmail.com	6443 Windy Wheat Dr O Fallon MO 63368	MO	Teacher	Tchr	St Charles Saint Peters MO	(636)928-5100	S	2017
Christian Robert J	(586)615-0116 bobandlynn130@sbcglobal.net	130 S Highland St Mount Clemens MI 48043	MI	Teacher	EM			RF	1975
Christiansan-Ayers Deanna J Christiansan	(303)660-1487 dayers94@yahoo.com	926 Coral Ct Castle Rock CO 80104	RM	Teacher	P/Tchr	Trinity Franktown CO	(303)841-4660	IV	1998
Christiansen David L Dr	(847)271-7001 grampsy1685@startmail.com	405 N Washington Ave Park Ridge IL 60068	NI	Teacher	EM			CQ	2008
Christiansen Deirdre Batiansila Deac	(920)544-1616 lcmsugb@gmail.com	1400 Creekside Ln Green Bay WI 54311	NW	Deaconess	Mem C	Faith Green Bay WI	(920)435-5524	FW-DEAC	2023
Christman John T	(501)472-9056 christman.john@gmail.com	113 W Circle Dr Jefferson Cty MO 65109	MO	Teacher	Prin	Calvary Jefferson Cty MO	(573)638-0228	S	1999
Christopher Steven L Dr	(925)784-1272 cnhdce@aol.com	15491 Camino Del Parque N Sonora CA 95370	CNH	Tch/DCE	EM			S	1979
Chrysam Cynthia S Killenberger	(410)836-9623 cchrysam@baltimorelutheran.org	322 E Jarrettsville Rd Forest Hill MD 21050	SE	Teacher	Tchr	Concordia Towson MD	(410)825-2323	AA	1987
Chrzan Beth E Senechal	(818)653-2822 beth.chrzan@gmail.com	2971 E Stargazer Dr San Tan Valley AZ 85140	PSW	Teacher	EM			S	1977
Chudada Julie Propp	(414)517-1589 proppj@drlc.org	N14W27509 Silvernail Rd Pewaukee WI 53072	SW	Teacher	Tchr	Divine Redeemer Hartland WI	(262)367-3664	MQ	2006
Chuhran Kyle B Dr	(586)481-0252 kyle.chuhran@gmail.com	28090 Sunset Blvd W Lathrup Vlg MI 48076	MI	Teacher	S HS/C	Concordia University Ann Arbor Ann Arbor MI	(734)995-7300	AA	1987
Church Candace L Berry	(954)803-7794	111 Knoll CV Austin TX 78737	FG	Teacher	EM			S	1978
Churney Heather Lykins	(714)336-9490 churneyh@gmail.com	18825 E Indiana Ave Queen Creek AZ 85142	PSW	Teacher	S HS/C	Concordia University Irvine Irvine CA	(949)854-8002	CQ	2013
Cibulka Janine E Doering	(314)842-1082 jancibulka@hotmail.com	5081 Suson Hills Dr Saint Louis MO 63128	MO	Teacher	Tchr	Green Park Saint Louis MO	(314)544-4248	CQ	2002
Cid Jennifer D Zelt	(510)468-3540 mrsjcid@gmail.com	306 Turnstone Dr Livermore CA 94551	CNH	Teacher	P/Tchr	Our Savior Livermore CA	(925)447-1246	IV	2007
Cigelske Sara A Utecht	(920)286-3635 scigelske@gmail.com	1710 Van Buren St New Holstein WI 53061	SW	Teacher	C12/2023			MQ	2004
Cillick Diane R Bimler	(630)244-1187 diane.sillick@gmail.com	300 Forest Ave Roselle IL 60172	NI	Teacher	Tchr	Trinity Roselle IL	(630)894-3263	CQ	2021
Cimarusti Amy L Neumann	(847)334-5092 acimarusti@saint-pau.org	404 S Main St Mt Prospect IL 60056	NI	Teacher	Tchr	St Paul Mount Prospect IL	(847)255-6733	RF	1994
Cislo Jennifer L Schneewind	(954)560-2141 rjcislo@att.net	23331 Boca Trace Dr Boca Raton FL 33433	FG	DCE	C07/2016			S	1998
Clakley-Jonas Karen E Clakley	(818)472-0836 karenjonas@hotmail.com	27243 Sterling Grove Ln Canyon Cntry CA 91387	PSW	Teacher	C07/2016			Other	1987
Clapp Jill Pries	(650)218-4811 jillpriesclapp@gmail.com	16350 Hard Labor Saint John VI 00830	CNH	Teacher	EM			IV	1989
Clark Dennis W	(810)324-2877	7437 Imlay City Rd Clyde MI 48049	MI	Teacher	EM			RF	1982
Clark Gail A Dunajcik	(314)452-3870 jongail10@hotmail.com	162 Ameren Way Apt 423 Ballwin MO 63021	MO	Teacher	EM			CQ	1993
Clark Kristen R Zilz	(260)452-7678 krzilz@outlook.com	1595 E Poplar Rd Columbia City IN 46725	IN	Teacher	C07/2017			CH	2012
Clark Linda S Steinbrueck	(713)703-1054 lclark71914@gmail.com	1411 Mitchell Rd NW Cullman AL 35055	SO	Teacher	C06/2017			S	2009
Clark Lisa M Stock Dr	(314)659-7558 lisa.clark@cph.org	6724 Sutherland Ave Saint Louis MO 63109	MO	Teacher	Pro Stf	Concordia Publishing House Saint Louis MO	(314)268-1000	S	2004
Clark Lori D Pettiford	(248)930-7472 jwldclark@gmail.com	959 Hampstead Ln Rochester Hills MI 48309	MI	Teacher	Tchr	St John Rochester MI	(248)402-8000	AA	1992
Clark Lori J Riley	(918)287-8036 lclark@icaba.org	1101 S Hummingbird Ln Skiatook OK 74070	OK	Teacher	Tchr	Immanuel Broken Arrow OK	(918)251-5422	AA	1993

*Multiple Assignments (See Church Worker Locator for Additional Details)

See Page 53 for the Table of Abbreviations for key to District, Classification, Position, and College abbreviations.

**C =Candidate; EM =Emeritus; the date following the C is the month and year the Candidate status began

NAME	TELEPHONE NUMBER EMAIL	STREET ADDRESS CITY/STATE/ZIP	DISTRICT	CLASS.	POSITION/ STATUS**	WHERE SERVING	OFFICE PHONE	COLLEGE/ UNIV/CQ	YR GRAD
Clark Mary E Williams	(313)971-7120 kteachmary@aol.com	24802 Ashley Ct Redford MI 48239	MI	Teacher	EM			RF	1974
Clark Payton Woodruff	(317)698-0723 paytonw17@hotmail.com	8133 Yarmouth Way Indianapolis IN 46239	IN	Teacher	Tchr	Zion New Palestine IN	(317)861-4210	AA	2024
Clark Wendy D Duda	(407)365-3228 wclark@stlukes-oviedo.org	2451 Mikler Rd Oviedo FL 32765	S	Teacher	Tchr	St Luke Oviedo FL	(407)365-3408	CQ	2006
Clasen Alexandria M	(630)328-3813 aclasen@bethanylcs.com	3612 Becket Ln Naperville IL 60564	NI	Teacher	Tchr	Bethany Naperville IL	(630)355-6607	CH	2022
Claugherty Darlene J Ostrum	(651)674-6202	40605 Golden Ave North Branch MN 55056	MNN	Teacher	EM			SP	1967
Claus Donna M Oppermann	(989)791-3996 kfcdmoc@sbcglobal.net	1122 Lathrup Ave Saginaw MI 48638	MI	Teacher	EM			RF	1962
Claus Lori V	(217)836-4371 lori.claus@oursaviors-school.org	515 Illini Ct Springfield IL 62704	CI	Teacher	Tchr	Our Saviors Springfield IL	(217)546-4531	AA	1986
Clausen Karen A Von Fange	(402)534-5581 kclausen1964@gmail.com	600 Church St Seward NE 68434	NEB	Teacher	EM			S	1964
Clausen Vernon M Sr	(210)248-7925 hiflyer42@hotmail.com	455 County Road 385 San Antonio TX 78253	TX	Teacher	EM			S	1959
Clausing Catherine A	(703)899-7247 cclausing@trinitycp.org	238 Walnut Ln Crown Point IN 46307	IN	Teacher	Tchr	Trinity Crown Point IN	(219)663-1578	CQ	2023
Clausing Eleanor L	(636)875-8064 eleanor.clausing@gmail.com	34 Lincoln St Apt 321 Seward NE 68434	NEB	Teacher	C07/2025			S	2024
Clausing Karen A Rogner	(815)784-2105 wkclausing@hotmail.com	11318 Hill Rd Garden Pr IL 61038	NI	Teacher	EM			CQ	2005
Clawson Linda M Bilderback	(405)368-1883 lindyclaw@aol.com	13200 N 2780 Rd Dover OK 73734	OK	DCM	EM			MQ	2004
Clayton Anna S Thomack	(217)556-4755 aclayton@immanuelrapids.com	721 Witter St Wisconsin Rapids WI 54494	NW	Teacher	Tchr	Immanuel Wisconsin Rapids WI	(715)423-0272	MQ	2020
Clayton Lori J Aukamp	(618) 566-9093 kmcljcuac@yahoo.com	104 W State St Mascoutah IL 62258	SI	Teacher	C09/2025			RF	1995
Clegg Robert J	(501)368-0390	414 Crain Dr Searcy AR 72143	EN	Teacher	EM			RF	1960
Cleland Laura P Pugh	(214)682-3614 laurapcleland@gmail.com	14212 Orleans Dr Little Rock AR 72211	MDS	Teacher	EM			CQ	2007
Clemens Jennifer K Corey	(262)483-8838 jennifer.clemens@splgrafton.org	815 Overland Trl Grafton WI 53024	SW	Teacher	Tchr	St Paul Grafton WI	(262)377-4659	MQ	1995
Clement Laveta M Sunderman	(712)438-0195 lclement@cls.k12.ia.us	1858 T Ave Clarinda IA 51632	IW	Teacher	Tchr	Clarinda Clarinda IA	(712)542-3657	S	1984
Clements Taylor N Kaniuk	(586)295-2016 taylor.clements92@gmail.com	4934 Casey Rd Dryden MI 48428	MI	Teacher	C06/2021			AA	2014
Clements Tracey K Gove Kretzschmar	(443)325-3675 traceykclements@gmail.com	1810 Campbell Rd Forest Hill MD 21050	SE	Teacher	Tchr	St Pauls Kingsville MD	(410)592-8100	BR	1997
Clements Wayne E	(636)290-0028 wclements@yhti.net	612 Lohmann Forest Ln Saint Louis MO 63119	MO	Teacher	EM			S	1964
Clendenen Jennifer K Scott	(260)492-2996 jenclendenen@gmail.com	3505 Sun Valley Dr Fort Wayne IN 46804	IN	Teacher	Tchr	Emmanuel-St Michael Fort Wayne IN	(260)422-6712	CH	2015
Cleveland Kadie S	(251)404-4202 kadiecleveland@gmail.com	13051 Elm Tree Dr Apt 303 Herndon VA 20171	RM	DCE	C12/2024			AU	2012
Cleveland Tonja N Bolden	(314)769-2048 tonjacleveland@gmail.com	1845 Battlefield Dr Florissant MO 63031	MO	Teacher	C08/2024			MQ	2000
Clifford Morgan O Thorsen	(772)607-0677 morganoclifford@gmail.com	1818 Parkside Dr Anchorage AK 99501	NOW	Teacher		Northwest District Portland OR	(503)288-8383	AU	2015
Clift Tonja J Leerssen	(541)385-1282	2425 NE Jones Rd Bend OR 97701	NOW	Teacher	Tchr	Trinity Bend OR	(541)382-1850	CQ	2003
Clifton Margie E Pacey	(512)762-2308 mpacey1977@yahoo.com	599 Cactus St Giddings TX 78942	TX	Teacher	C05/2020			AU	2001
Clinard Randall R	(262) 259-2569 clinardrandall540@gmail.com	N50W17484 Mulberry Ln Menomonee Fls WI 53051	SW	Teacher	EM			RF	1969
Clinkenbeard Sandra K Zuckweiler	(979)530-3087 zclinksds@gmail.com	155 Duffy Dr Kerrville TX 78028	TX	Teacher	Tchr	Grace Brenham TX	(979)836-3475	S	1976
Clitty Cynthia S Syring	(320)493-2548	1623 Hurst Castle Rd Saint Cloud MN 56303	MNN	Teacher	Tchr	Prince Of Peace Saint Cloud MN	(320)251-1477	S	1979
Cloeter Christine A Ficken	(715)823-5323 dickchris80@gmail.com	W8287 Cloverleaf Lake Rd Clintonville WI 54929	NW	Teacher	EM			S	1980
Cloeter Janet R	(909)239-2757 jancloeter@aol.com	26316 Green Terr Dr Santa Clarita CA 91321	PSW	Teacher	EM			S	1976
Cloeter Robert C	(507)313-5653	915 40th Ave Winona MN 55987	MNS	Teacher	Mem C	St Martin Winona MN	(507)452-6928	SP	1977
Clonkey Elizabeth M	(262)722-0318 eclonkey@gslschool-et.org	S76W16906 Gregory Dr Apt E Muskego WI 53150	SW	Teacher	P/Tchr	Good Shepherd East Troy WI	(262)642-3310	SP	1995
Closner Kimberly J	(509)910-0234 kjclosner@yahoo.com	575 Columbia Point Dr Apt 108 Richland WA 99352	NOW	DCE	Tchr	Bethlehem Kennewick WA	(509)582-5858	PO	2008
Clow Kay J Bolte	(812)522-4520 gkclow@gmail.com	1822 E 950 S Columbus IN 47201	IN	Teacher	EM			RF	1971
Cluck Andrew J	(314)609-8289 a.j.cluck@gmail.com	8316 NW 138th Cir Oklahoma City OK 73142	OK	Teacher	Pro Stf	Holy Trinity Edmond OK	(405)348-3292	RF	2010
Cluck Kimberly A Poppitz	(314)620-4892 cluckfamily2012@gmail.com	8316 NW138th Circle Oklahoma City OK 73142	OK	Teacher	Tchr	Holy Trinity Edmond OK	(405)844-4000	RF	2009
Cluppert Elizabeth A Hass	(715)719-0167 bcluppert@gmail.com	1905 22 1/2 St Rice Lake WI 54868	NW	Teacher	C07/2016			SP	1998
Clymer Janice S Riepl	(719)260-8252	2290 Green Rush Pl Colorado Spgs CO 80919	RM	Teacher	Tchr	Rock Of Ages Colorado Springs CO	(719)632-9394	MQ	1986
Cmeyla William P	(989)450-2535 cmeylab@gmail.com	2747 Ziegler Rd Bay City MI 48706	MI	DCE	Pro Stf	Valley Saginaw MI	(989)790-1676	RF	2003
Cobb Kimberlee J Graef	(714)656-6716 kimberleejcobb@gmail.com	8812 S Carr Way Littleton CO 80128	RM	Teacher	Tchr	Bethlehem Lakewood CO	(303)238-7676	IV	2010

*Multiple Assignments (See Church Worker Locator for Additional Details)
See Page 53 for the Table of Abbreviations for key to District, Classification, Position, and College abbreviations.
**C =Candidate; EM =Emeritus; the date following the C is the month and year the Candidate status began

NAME	TELEPHONE NUMBER EMAIL	STREET ADDRESS CITY/STATE/ZIP	DISTRICT	CLASS.	POSITION/ STATUS**	WHERE SERVING	OFFICE PHONE	COLLEGE/ UNIV/CQ	YR GRAD
Coblentz Grace M Hartwig	(319)333-5725 gracecoblentz2@gmail.com	1606 Darby Ln New Haven IN 46774	IN	Teacher	Tchr	St John-Emmanuel Monroeville IN	(260)639-0123	CH	2021
Coburn Kristianna G	(907)854-8803 kcoburnak@gmail.com	18828 Moose Pl Chugiak AK 99567	NOW	DCE	C07/2018			PO	2016
Coburn Peggy L Pawelk	(763)757-3720 peggy-coburn@yahoo.com	14440 Quinn Dr NW Andover MN 55304	MNS	Teacher	EM			SP	1972
Cochran Krystal R Morrison	(801)268-3416 jameskrystal@hotmail.com	5962 S Ancestor Pl Taylorsville UT 84123	RM	Teacher	Tchr	Redeemer Salt Lake City UT	(801)467-4352	CQ	2003
Cochran Matthew D	(618)670-5391 matt@stjohnsconover.com	2369 Ellen St Granite Falls NC 28630	SE	DCE	Mem C	St John Conover NC	(828)464-4071	CH	2012
Cochran William D Jr Dr	(314)791-0433 bill.cochran@outlook.com	1430 Whispering Creek Dr Ballwin MO 63021	MO	Teacher	EM			S	1968
Cody Christopher B Dr	(414)238-1924 ccody@martinlutherhs.org		SW	Teacher	Prin	Martin Luther Greendale WI	(414)421-4000	MQ	2001
Cody Katelyn G Sievert	(989)780-3944 katelyncody3@gmail.com	603 N 8th St Seward NE 68434	NEB	Teacher	Tchr	St John Seward NE	(402)643-4535	S	2013
Cody Robert D	(719)580-4259 robert.cody@cune.org	603 N 8th St Seward NE 68434	NEB	Teacher	S HS/C	Concordia University Nebraska Seward NE	(402)643-3651	S	2014
Coe James F	(407)489-4668 jamesfcoe@gmail.com	P.O. Box 25687 Fort Wayne IN 46825	IN	Teacher	EM			S	1977
Coerber Teckla R Geyer	(970)219-8716 scotec@outlook.com	3890 McGuirk Ct Oviedo FL 32766	S	Teacher	C12/2024			S	2000
Coffey Jessica M Jacob	(317)883-3165 jcoffey@ourshepherd.org	79 Virgil Dr Greenwood IN 46142	IN	Teacher	C07/2016			AA	1992
Coffin Barbara L Worthington Deac	(804)332-8606 barbaralcoffin@yahoo.com	13437 Garden View Dr Apple Valley MN 55124	MNS	Deaconess	Mem C	Cross View Edina MN	(952)941-1094	CQ	2006
Coffin Stephanie	(702)540-6840 stephaniecoffin@hotmail.com	9550 W Cheyenne Ave Las Vegas NV 89129	PSW	Teacher	Tchr	Mountain View Las Vegas NV	(702)360-8290	IV	2005
Cohrs Christie L Volkman	(419)966-9728 christiecohrs88@gmail.com	K355 State Route 108 Napoleon OH 43545	OH	DFLM	Mem C	Immanuel Hamler OH	(419)274-4811	AA	2010
Cohrs Richard P	(636)288-4717 cohrs.rich@gmail.com	3750 Majestic Ct Saint Charles MO 63303	MO	Teacher	EM			RF	1971
Cole Amanda B	acole@rlcmail.org		MO	Teacher	Prin	Redeemer Springfield MO	(417)883-5717	CQ	2016
Cole Jane E Loza Deac	(913)269-9211 jcolejer2911@gmail.com	148 Netherwood Dr Jackson TN 38305	MDS	Deaconess	C01/2022			RF	1988
Cole Lisa M Schwecke	(507)834-6559 lisacole16@gmail.com	832 Clark Ave Gibbon MN 55335	MNS	Teacher	Mem C	Redeemer New Ulm MN	(507)233-3470	MQ	1991
Coleman Lisa M	(602)738-9798 lisa_marie_coleman@yahoo.com	8221 E Vernon Ave Scottsdale AZ 85257	PSW	Teacher	Tchr	Valley Phoenix AZ	(602)230-1600	CQ	2021
Coleman Sarah E Diekmann	(812)459-7902 sdiekmann@elsone.org	9629 Massey Dr Evansville IN 47725	IN	Teacher	Tchr	Evansville Evansville IN	(812)424-7252	CQ	2010
Collard Ann Marie	(239)994-1322 aajjsc@gmail.com	708 SW 9th St Cape Coral FL 33991	FG	Teacher	EM			CQ	2022
Collet Bruce G	(281)450-8548 goodgumbo@earthlink.net	133 Poland Ln Rockwood TN 37854	MDS	DCM	EM			MQ	1990
Colley Alison M Eichwedel	(630)863-6674 alicolley23@gmail.com	2915 Freedom Cir Crown Point IN 46307	NI	Teacher	C07/2025			CH	2011
Colley Ann M Fisher	(810)499-9616 cjcolley@hotmail.com	7091 Big Trail Rd Holly MI 48442	MI	Teacher	EM			AA	1984
Collier Cody M	(641)849-7884 cocollier09@gmail.com	503 S Akir St Latimer IA 50452	IE	Teacher	P/Tchr	St Paul Latimer IA	(641)579-6281	S	2013
Collins Hilary M	(920)627-0028 hpuksich@gmail.com	W63 N479 Hanover Ave Cedarburg WI 53012	SW	Teacher	Tchr	St Paul Grafton WI	(262)377-4659	CQ	2024
Collins Kristi G Koehler	(262)607-1333 kcollins4kids@yahoo.com	309 W 2nd St Waconia MN 55387	MNS	Teacher	Tchr	Trinity Waconia MN	(952)442-4165	RF	1984
Collins Laura G Heston	(317)294-2414 lauragcollins0727@gmail.com	157 S 7th Beech Grove IN 46107	IN	Teacher	Prin	Redeemer Kokomo IN	(765)864-6466	CQ	2024
Collins Marianne Oberton	(901) 219-8470 avballmom@aol.com	10116 Cliveden Cir N Collierville TN 38107	MDS	Teacher	EM			CQ	2002
Colross Ruth A Ermeling	(443) 286-2623 ruthcolross@gmail.com	14154 W Denny Blvd Unit 10 Litchfield Pk AZ 85340	PSW	Teacher	EM			S	1971
Colton Natasha A Preder, Campion	(860)948-0844 naptimetash@gmail.com	30 Tobey Ave Windsor CT 06095	NE	Teacher	C07/2016			AA	2006
Colwell Clinton C	(417)379-6436 ccolwell@splhs.org	405 S Faculty Ln Concordia MO 64020	MO	DCE	Pro Stf	Saint Paul Concordia MO	(660)463-2238	S	1992
Colyer Kenneth R	(209)952-6250	1138 Cypress Run Dr Stockton CA 95209	CNH	Teacher	EM			SP	1974
Combs Janice A Reinhardt	(317)410-5454	12668 Cerromar Ct Carmel IN 46033	IN	Teacher	C07/2016			S	1978
Combs Maggie E	(812)344-7215 maggiecombs93@gmail.com	1009 Redwing Dr Columbus IN 47203	IN	Teacher	C07/2022			CQ	2018
Comfort Jennifer Johnson	(262)391-0672 jen.johnson8099@gmail.com	10516 W Freistadt Rd Mequon WI 53097	SW	Teacher	Prin	Immanuel Brookfield WI	(262)781-7140	CQ	2013
Coneybeer Kristine O O Brien	(317)650-4417 coneybeer92@gmail.com	8256 S Franklin Rd Indianapolis IN 46259	IN	Teacher	EM			CQ	1985
Congemi Pamela H Harney	(504)837-1955	1463 N White St New Orleans LA 70119	SO	Teacher	C07/2016			CQ	2004
Conger Norene J Hass	(313)319-0318	633 S Higbie Pl Grosse Pt Wds MI 48236	MI	Teacher	EM			SP	1973
Coniglio Steven L	(307)857-2094	308 N Broadway Ave Riverton WY 82501	WY	Teacher	EM			AU	1997
Conner Brittany R Robinson	(618)553-9751 aliseighth2@alisrockets.com	1985 N 600th St Edgewood IL 62426	CI	Teacher	Tchr	Altamont Altamont IL	(618)483-6428	CQ	2020

*Multiple Assignments (See Church Worker Locator for Additional Details)

See Page 53 for the Table of Abbreviations for key to District, Classification, Position, and College abbreviations.

**C =Candidate; EM =Emeritus; the date following the C is the month and year the Candidate status began

NAME	TELEPHONE NUMBER EMAIL	STREET ADDRESS CITY/STATE/ZIP	DISTRICT	CLASS.	POSITION/ STATUS**	WHERE SERVING	OFFICE PHONE	COLLEGE/ UNIV/CQ	YR GRAD
Conner Lois J Grese	(309)966-9953 lconner853@gmail.com	7420 N. Brittany Park Place Peoria IL 61614	FG	Teacher	EM			RF	1975
Connick Sharon J Schamber	(916) 478-9399 connicksj@gmail.com	4812 Garden Homes Pl Elk Grove CA 95758	CNH	Teacher	C07/2016			S	1986
Connolly Patrick R	(925)784-6820 connollyp@flhsemail.org	9909 Garamond Ave Las Vegas NV 89117	PSW	Teacher	Tchr	Faith Las Vegas NV	(702)804-4400	IV	2013
Connors Diane	(563)332-1239 dconnors@trinity-lutheran-dav. pvt.k12.ia.us	4700 Village Dr Apt 107 Davenport IA 52807	IE	Teacher	EM			CQ	2003
Conover Barry F	(828)371-1374 bconover4@frontier.com	154 Bent Grass Cir Hayesville NC 28904	SE	DCM	EM			MQ	2003
Conover Charles W Jr	(341)392-9836	309 Kendall Ridge Ct Chesterfield MO 63017	MO	Teacher	EM			S	1967
Conover Liza G	(541)550-9057 liza.conover@saints.org	1968 Windy Tree Ct. Bend OR 97701	NOW	Teacher	Tchr	Trinity Bend OR	(541)382-1850	PO	2002
Conover Sharon M Milhous Deac	(207)660-5548 deaconess.smconover@gmail.com	89 Heritage Rd Oakland ME 04963	NE	Deaconess	Mem C	Resurrection Waterville ME	(207)872-5208	FW-DEAC	2016
Conrad Grace	(636)875-4828 dcegraceconrad@gmail.com	618 Breckenridge Ln Apt 4 Louisville KY 40207	IN	DCE	Mem C	Concordia Louisville KY	(502)585-4459	CH	2023
Conrad John A Sr	(847)414-4619 jconrad@immanuel-ed.org	638 Braeburn Rd East Dundee IL 60118	NI	Teacher	EM			S	1977
Conrad Lori L Hockemeyer	(260)341-8616 lconrad@spilutheran.org	827 Koehlinger Dr New Haven IN 46774	IN	Teacher	Tchr	St Peter-Immanuel Decatur IN	(260)623-6115	CQ	2022
Consoer Elizabeth J Eatherton Krieser	elizabethconsoer@slcas.org	9860 Zenith Dr Saint Louis MO 63123	MO	Teacher	Tchr	Salem Affton MO	(314)353-9242	S	2000
Consolino Jeanine E Weinrich	(314)583-8087 lv2teach4@sbcglobal.net	2827 Fireglow Dr Saint Louis MO 63129	MO	Teacher	EM			S	1973
Contreras Andrew J	(734)707-5985 acontreras@stpaulannarbor.org	5499 High Ridge Dr Ypsilanti MI 48197	MI	Teacher	Tchr	St Paul Ann Arbor MI	(734)665-9117	S	1991
Conway Samantha M Poet	(734)657-1379 sconway2314@gmail.com	305 Donna Dr Clinton MI 49236	MI	Teacher	Tchr	St Paul Ann Arbor MI	(734)665-9117	AA	2010
Cook Barbara L Gutz	(402)719-0029 bcook_45@yahoo.com	16304 Riggs St Omaha NE 68135	NEB	Teacher	EM			S	1971
Cook David A	(651)487-9015 rvmncook@usfamily.net	1975 Oxford St N Roseville MN 55113	MNS	Teacher	EM			S	1975
Cook Edward C	(618)980-2570 elc1974@yahoo.com	48 Foreman Dr Glen Carbon IL 62034	SI	Teacher	EM			CQ	1994
Cook Elizabeth A Hirssig		1235 Camelback Ct NE Rochester MN 55906	MNS	Teacher	C07/2020			S	2008
Cook Joanne M Cecere	(559)679-7489 cookvisalia@aol.com	2809 S Rova Ct Visalia CA 93277	CNH	Teacher	Tchr	Grace Visalia CA	(559)734-7694	BR	1989
Cook June M Sommerfeldt	(708)476-3846 jcook1915@yahoo.com	865 Campground Rd New Haven VT 05472	NI	Teacher	EM			SP	1985
Cook Kalli Wied	(940)636-4662 kwied95@icloud.com	2411 NE 2nd St Ocala FL 34470	FG	DCE	Mem C	St John Ocala FL	(352)629-1794	AU	2017
Cook Kevin T	(914)202-7548 kevincook@optonline.net	17 Sagamore Rd Bronxville NY 10708	AT	Teacher	EM			BR	1976
Cook Kristi L Slimick	(618)635-2460 kslim79@yahoo.com	518 Montana St Bethalto IL 62010	SI	Teacher	Tchr	Zion Staunton IL	(618)635-2880	CQ	2021
Cook Leslie A Christiansen	(224)361-5477 lachristiansen96@gmail.com	3819 Rugen Rd Glenview IL 60025	NI	Teacher	Tchr	St Andrews Park Ridge IL	(847)823-9308	MQ	2019
Cook Lisa M	(713)899-4954 lisacook921@yahoo.com	2816 N 69th St Omaha NE 68104	FG	Teacher	C07/2016			S	2002
Cook Lydia M	(573)768-0915 lcook@ilsperryville.org	1124 W North St Perryville MO 63775	MO	Teacher	Tchr	Immanuel Perryville MO	(573)547-6161	S	2021
Cook Mark A	dcecook@gmail.com	1235 Camelback Ct NE Rochester MN 55906	MNS	DCE	Mem C	Trinity Rochester MN	(507)289-1531	S	2009
Cook Pamela J Nielsen	(619)241-5449 pam.cook23@yahoo.com	7467 Mission Gorge Rd 141 Santee CA 92071	PSW	Teacher	EM			S	1972
Cook Shelley L Nielsen	(858)272-5327 stannshell91@aol.com	8920 Fair Ln Lakeside CA 92040	PSW	Teacher	Tchr	St Pauls San Diego CA	(858)272-6282	IV	1991
Cook Susan E Herrmann	(303)922-2721	1726 S Pierson St Denver CO 80232	RM	Teacher	C07/2016			S	1981
Cooksey Robert L	(402)990-1406 luhifremont@gmail.com	14714 Crown Point Ave Omaha NE 68116	NEB	Teacher	Mem C	Trinity Fremont NE	(402)721-5536	S	1984
Cooley Emily M Meyer	(507)351-0762 emilym474@yahoo.com	1147 Mayo Rd SW Pequot Lakes MN 56472	MNN	Teacher	C08/2018			CQ	2015
Coomer Hannah E	(734)516-7444 hcoomer@stjohnsgrandhaven.com	529 Tyler Ln Apt D5 Grand Haven MI 49417	MI	DPM	Mem C	St John Grand Haven MI	(616)842-4510	AA	2022
Coons Kevin W	(443)910-5029 coons2000@comcast.net	3156 Eden Dr Abingdon MD 21009	SE	Teacher	C07/2016			BR	2000
Cooper Amy M Morton	(989)395-2663 thecoopers2006@gmail.com	4440 Snowbell Dr Saginaw MI 48603	MI	Teacher	Pro Stf	Valley Saginaw MI	(989)790-1676	S	2004
Cooper Benjamin	(989)395-2787 bcooper@vlhs.com	4440 Snowbell Dr Saginaw MI 48603	MI	Teacher	Tchr	Valley Saginaw MI	(989)790-1676	S	2004
Cooper Carolyn M Smith	(219)558-2015 cmcooper29@yahoo.com	12463 W 87th Ave Saint John IN 46373	IN	Teacher	EM			S	1973
Cooper Craig L	(320)237-5507 craigcooper74@yahoo.com	360 Carlson Pkwy Apt. 301 Minnetonka MN 55305	MNN	DCO	EM			SP	1990
Cooper Dale E	(219)558-2015 dcoop319@yahoo.com	12463 W 87th Ave Saint John IN 46373	IN	Teacher	EM			S	1972
Cooper Jennifer L Johnson	(865)719-2621 jennyjohnsoncooper@gmail.com	461 Hidden Valley Rd Clinton TN 37716	MDS	Teacher	C06/2022			S	1995
Copeland Caitlin E			TX	Teacher	Tchr	Redeemer Austin TX	(512)459-1500	AU	2018

*Multiple Assignments (See Church Worker Locator for Additional Details)
See Page 53 for the Table of Abbreviations for key to District, Classification, Position, and College abbreviations.
**C =Candidate; EM =Emeritus; the date following the C is the month and year the Candidate status began

NAME	TELEPHONE NUMBER EMAIL	STREET ADDRESS CITY/STATE/ZIP	DISTRICT	CLASS.	POSITION/ STATUS**	WHERE SERVING	OFFICE PHONE	COLLEGE/ UNIV/CQ	YR GRAD
Copeland Laura J LaCombe	(956)874-8500 lcopeland@outlook.com	1204 Orange St McAllen TX 78501	TX	Teacher	Tchr	St Paul McAllen TX	(956)682-2345	AU	2015
Copp Michael A	(281)507-4913 copp.michael@icloud.com	28806 Ashbrook Ln Houston TX 77355	TX	Teacher	Tchr	Epiphany Houston TX	(713)896-1843	S	2009
Coppersmith Donna J Mathers	(760)567-7683 djc4him@aol.com	507 Dove Hollow Trl Georgetown TX 78633	TX	Teacher	EM			RF	1972
Corbett Melissa Beise	(612)532-2870 corbetts01@hotmail.com	818 Egret Ln Waconia MN 55387	MNS	Teacher	Tchr	Trinity Waconia MN	(952)442-4165	SP	1999
Cordani Sharon D Eilts	(217)324-4657 sharoncordani@hotmail.com	3230 N 15th Ave Litchfield IL 62056	SI	Teacher	EM			CQ	1997
Cordes Roy W	(815)304-5002	1108 S 6th Ave Kankakee IL 60901	NI	Teacher	EM			RF	1965
Cordova Connie L Ultz	(303)229-8991 ccordova53@gmail.com	82 S Newland Ct Lakewood CO 80226	RM	Teacher	EM			RF	1975
Cordt Victoria J Thierfelder	(214)986-9186 vcordt@me.com	18880 Coastal Shore Ter Land O Lakes FL 34638	FG	Teacher	EM			S	1979
Cordy Andrew A	(713)578-0507 andrew@pog.church	c/o Point Of Grace Lutheran Church 19507 Fm 685 Pflugerville TX 78660	TX	DCE	Mem C	Point Of Grace Pflugerville TX	(512)251-9095	AU	2016
Corker Lynn N	(586)615-2179 corkerlynn@gmail.com	5785 Meadowview St Ypsilanti MI 48197	MI	DFLM	C07/2016			AA	2003
Cornejo Kara A Clark	(314)974-4239 kcornejo@zionharvester.org	101 Berry Manor Cir Saint Peters MO 63376	MO	Teacher	Tchr	Zion Saint Charles MO	(636)441-7425	RF	2007
Cornett Ronald C	(913)515-3451	2029 S 47th Ter Kansas City KS 66106	KS	Teacher	EM			S	1962
Cornwell Kathryn M Strycker	(904)433-2046	504 Eventide Dr Pensacola Bch FL 32561	SO	Teacher	EM			RF	1962
Corrow Eleanor I Deac			MO	Deaconess	S Ex/S	The LCMS Corporate Saint Louis MO	(314)965-9000	FW-DEAC	2012
Cortright Kendall S	(314)413-9631 kendall.cortright@lcms.org		MO	DCE	S Ex/S	Office of National Mission Saint Louis MO		CQ	2020
Costenaro Lorilee Wendling	(219) 789-4007 lori@cosfam.com	8713 Lantern Dr Saint John IN 46373	NI	Teacher	EM			RF	1975
Cotter Emily A Hansen	(720)288-1218 emilyhcotter@gmail.com	419 E 9th Street Fremont NE 68025	NEB	Teacher	Tchr	St Paul Arlington NE	(402)478-4278	S	2010
Cotton Patricia A Dr	(260)498-0757 pcotton@holycrossfw.org	2906 Whitegate Dr Fort Wayne IN 46805	IN	DPM	Mem C	Holy Cross Fort Wayne IN	(260)483-3173	CQ	2016
Couchman Barbara G	(718)430-0913	1783 Tenbroeck Ave Bronx NY 10461	AT	Teacher	Tchr	Our Saviour Bronx NY	(718)792-5665	BR	1975
Coughlin Deborah S Potonik	(913)481-2965 tipper617@gmail.com	12802 W 123 Terr Overland Park KS 66213	KS	Teacher	Tchr	Christ Overland Park KS	(913)345-9700	CQ	2019
Cour Susan M Hoffmann	(715) 245-1084 scour@immanuelrapids.com	1490 Silver Canoe Trl Nekoosa WI 54457	NW	Teacher	Tchr	Immanuel Wisconsin Rapids WI	(715)423-3260	RF	1997
Courtney Angela N Neddenriep	(509)420-3217 chuckangela@charter.net	184 Edgewood Dr Richland WA 99352	NOW	Teacher	EM			S	1967
Courtney Elizabeth Scholz	(262)442-2476 betsycourtney1324@gmail.com	2808 Steamboat Loop #272 North Fort Myers FL 33917	FG	Teacher	Tchr	Saint Michael Fort Myers FL	(239)939-1218	CQ	2024
Courvoisier Elinor L Brisso	(949)422-2453 couvymom@gmail.com	3209 Minnesota Ave Costa Mesa CA 92626	PSW	Teacher	EM			RF	1971
Courvoisier Jeffrey M	(714)715-9637 jcouvy@gmail.com	242 S Crawford Canyon Rd. #31 Orange CA 92869	PSW	Teacher	Tchr	Saint Johns Orange CA	(714)288-4400	CQ	2015
Courvoisier Laura B Burkey	(714)325-3548 courvoisier.laura@gmail.com	3062 Club House Rd Costa Mesa CA 92626	PSW	DCE	S HS/C	Concordia University Irvine Irvine CA	(949)854-8002	IV	2008
Couser Thomas D	(972)484-7080 thomascouser@yahoo.com	2921 Meadow Green Dr Farmers Brnch TX 75234	TX	Tch/DCE	EM			RF	1969
Covarrubias Shanna L	(618)971-7420 shanna.covarrubias@melhs.org	1308 Gladys St Collinsville IL 62234	SI	Teacher	Tchr	Metro-East Edwardsville IL	(618)656-0043	CQ	2020
Covek Hannah J Creech	(712)209-1401 hannahcreech21@gmail.com	N53W14495 Aberdeen Dr Menomonee Falls WI 53051	SW	Teacher	Tchr	Immanuel Brookfield WI	(262)781-7140	MQ	2018
Covell Mary A Hein	mncovell@charter.net	826 Pine Grove Ave Traverse City MI 49686	MI	Teacher	EM			CQ	1994
Coverston Linda L Jacobi	(301)937-2014 rugdad@verizon.net	11406 Indigo Dr Beltsville MD 20705	SE	Teacher	EM			S	1968
Covert Christopher R	(580)823-0441 christopher.r.covert@gmail.com	10525 Essex Dr Unit 15 Johnston IA 50131	IW	Teacher	Tchr	Mount Olive Des Moines IA	(515)277-0247	S	2011
Cowan Beth A	brub@voyager.net	197 Hanrath St Frankfort MI 49635	MI	Teacher	EM			AA	1984
Cowan Mary T Palmreuter	(217)394-2632 mcowan@stjohnsbuckley.com	377 E 700 North Rd Buckley IL 60918	CI	Teacher	Tchr	St Johns Buckley IL	(217)394-2444	RF	1988
Cox Amy S Swartz	(920)840-6640 amy.cox@faithfv.org	2701 N McDonald St Appleton WI 54911	NW	DCM	Mem C	Faith Appleton WI	(920)739-9191	MW	2013
Cox Brenda K Kongslien	(909)720-5078 brenda.cox@mcldb.org	1140 Overden Pl Pomona CA 91766	PSW	Teacher	Tchr	Mt Calvary Diamond Bar CA	(909)861-2740	SP	1989
Cox Brenda R Brehm	(612)479-3312 bcox@ccls.net	5024 Perkinsville Rd Maple Plain MN 55359	MNS	Teacher	Tchr	Christ Community Watertown MN	(952)955-1419	SP	1990
Cox Camille Deac	(303)519-3971 deaconess.camille@gmail.com		FG	Deaconess	Mem C	Grace Saint Petersburg FL	(727)527-6213	FW-DEAC	2023
Cox Corey	(574) 329-1731	51290 Elm Rd Granger IN 46530	IN	Teacher	Tchr	Trinity Elkhart IN	(574)674-8800	CQ	2015
Cox Holly K Lustila Deac	(863)409-2269 deaconess@eternalshepherd.org	131 Whitman Way Easley SC 29642	SE	Deaconess	Mem C	Eternal Shepherd Seneca SC	(864)882-3209	SL-DEAC	2015
Cox Janell D Grage	(602)826-0591 janellcox87@gmail.com	1142 S Palomino Creek Dr Gilbert AZ 85296	PSW	Teacher	EM			MQ	1987
Cox John E		1140 Overden Pl Pomona CA 91766	PSW	Teacher	Tchr	Mt Calvary Diamond Bar CA	(909)861-2740	MQ	1988

*Multiple Assignments (See Church Worker Locator for Additional Details)

See Page 53 for the Table of Abbreviations for key to District, Classification, Position, and College abbreviations.

**C =Candidate; EM =Emeritus; the date following the C is the month and year the Candidate status began

NAME	TELEPHONE NUMBER EMAIL	STREET ADDRESS CITY/STATE/ZIP	DISTRICT	CLASS.	POSITION/ STATUS**	WHERE SERVING	OFFICE PHONE	COLLEGE/ UNIV/CQ	YR GRAD
Cox Lynn M Weerts	(262)853-1798 lweerts@juno.com	N86W17258 Joss Pl Menomonee Fls WI 53051	SW	Teacher	C08/2023			MQ	1998
Coxey Wendy C Moeller	(574)340-0126 twcoxey@gmail.com	2973 Dogwood Ct Bremen IN 46506	IN	Teacher	EM			MW	1980
Craig Joshua N	(734)799-7189 j-n-craig@live.com	9222 S 92nd East Ave Tulsa OK 74133	OK	DCE	Mem C	Grace Tulsa OK	(918)592-2999	AA	2017
Cramer Courtney P	(989)751-6937 ccramer@stlorenz.org	7955 Tuscola Rd Frankenmuth MI 48734	MI	Teacher	Tchr	St Lorenz Frankenmuth MI	(989)652-6141	CQ	2017
Crass Candace Kuenn	(414)828-7601 cacrass@att.net	2218 W Shore Dr Delafield WI 53018	SW	Teacher	Tchr	Beautiful Savior Waukesha WI	(262)542-2496	MQ	1992
Craven James A	(352)209-4862 craven906@gmail.com	906 Helen Dr Melrose Park IL 60160	NI	Teacher	EM			RF	1975
Craven Kathryn E Roberts	(352)209-4933 craven906@gmail.com	906 Helen Dr Melrose Park IL 60160	NI	Teacher	EM			RF	1974
Crawford Brenda Kreutz	(317)787-1451	7928 Grand Gulch Dr Indianapolis IN 46239	IN	Teacher	Tchr	Zion New Palestine IN	(317)861-5544	S	2002
Crawford Kathryn L Munson	(815)876-6426 katy.munson@gmail.com		IE	DCE	C10/2018			S	2012
Crenshaw Carrie M Buerges	(636)288-3936 ccrenshaw@zionharvester.org	2860 Danube Way Saint Charles MO 63301	MO	Teacher	Tchr	Zion Saint Charles MO	(636)441-7425	CQ	2014
Crespo Alicia K	(904) 928-9136 alicia_crespo@ graceltheraneagles.org	8812 Brighton Hill Cir E Jacksonville FL 32256	FG	Teacher	Tchr	Grace Jacksonville FL	(904)928-9136	CQ	2008
Creutz Kevin R	(260)443-3858 kcreutz@gmail.com	6626 Newburgh Pl Fort Wayne IN 46835	IN	Teacher	RSO	Lutheran Schools Services Inc Fort Wayne IN	(260)203-4500	RF	2003
Creutz Lauren R Brauer	(260)443-3958 whataday627@gmail.com	6626 Newburgh Pl Fort Wayne IN 46835	IN	Teacher	C07/2016			RF	2003
Crimmins Ruth E Moll	(847)989-7431 crimmins.ruth@gmail.com	3585 Winston Dr Hoffman Estates IL 60192	NI	Teacher	EM			RF	1987
Crisi David A	(503)310-7358 dcedave@aol.com	859 SE 58th Ave Hillsboro OR 97123	NOW	Tch/DCE	EM			PO	1988
Crist Andrew C	(417)569-3939 andrew@campomega.org	22750 Lind Ave Waterville MN 56096	MNS	DCE	RSO	Camp Omega Waterville MN	(507)685-4266	Other	2018
Crist Diane L Schoonover	(843)505-2711 dianebencrist@bellsouth.net	2209 Saint Joe Center Rd # 109 Fort Wayne IN 46825	IN	Teacher	EM			RF	1976
Critchley Danielle E	(440)453-3175 princessarya98@gmail.com	2736 Stardale Dr Apt 3 Fort Wayne IN 46816	MNS	DCE	C12/2021			SP	2021
Crites Tracy L Splete	(909)275-5822 critestracy@yahoo.com	10162 Brookhaven Ln. Brecksville OH 44141	OH	Teacher	C09/2020			CQ	2009
Cromley Joshua M	(720)614-2647 joshuacromley@mac.com	1566 Laverne Dr Arnold MO 63010	MO	DCE	C12/2023			S	2012
Cronauer Nicole A Hoene	(812)498-4629		IN	Teacher	Tchr	St Peter Columbus IN	(812)372-5266	CQ	2020
Cronauer Shirley J Herring	(317)272-4520 tcron@sbcglobal.net	1843 Thistle Ct Avon IN 46123	IN	Teacher	EM			S	1986
Cronkright Brandi L Mitti	(810)887-7723 bcronkright@stjohnrochester.org	109 Moross St Mount Clemens MI 48043	MI	Teacher	Tchr	St John Rochester MI	(248)402-8000	CQ	2022
Crosmer Jesse	(727)344-2500 jecrosmer@aol.com	5896 27th Ave N St Petersburg FL 33710	FG	Teacher	Prin	Our Savior Saint Petersburg FL	(727)344-1026	RF	1980
Cross Heidi A Scheck	(661)949-9320	44535 Loneoak Ave Lancaster CA 93534	PSW	DCE	Mem C	Grace Lancaster CA	(661)948-1018	S	1982
Cross Rachel L Gregg	(618)971-9611 rlc709@gmail.com	9 Oak Wood Ct Maryville IL 62062	SI	Teacher	C11/2023			S	2006
Crosson Stacey T Tasler	(571)326-5580 crossontasler@hotmail.com	547 Twin Lakes Ln Bumpass VA 23024	SE	DCE	C09/2019			SP	1995
Crouch Jamie L Mansholt	(217)851-5735 jamiecphotograph@gmail.com	84 Calstrada Dr Staunton IL 62088	SI	Teacher	P/Tchr	Zion Staunton IL	(618)635-2880	CQ	2021
Crouch Kellye M Koyn	(713)819-7583 kellye.crouch@gmail.com	2338 Keegan Hollow Ln Spring TX 77386	TX	DCE	Tchr	Immanuel Houston TX	(713)861-8787	AU	2012
Crouch Richard D	(281)635-0872 richard.crouch09@gmail.com	2338 Keegan Hollow Ln Spring TX 77386	TX	DCE	C07/2024			AU	2013
Crouse Karen S Dueker	(618)532-3545 rkcrouse@charter.net	15 Arline Dr Centralia IL 62801	SI	Teacher	EM			RF	1970
Crow Melinda L Stoelting	(505)856-6483 crow.mel@gmail.com	11209 Avenida Thomas La Mesa CA 91941	PSW	Teacher	Tchr	Christ La Mesa CA	(619)462-5211	S	1996
Crowder Jason D	(636)288-1920	9640 Spanish Steps Ln Las Vegas NV 89117	PSW	Teacher	Tchr	Faith Las Vegas NV	(702)804-4400	MQ	2000
Crowder Sarah M	(636)456-7406 crowders@flhsemail.org	9640 Spanish Steps Ln Las Vegas NV 89117	PSW	DCM	Tchr	Faith Las Vegas NV	(702)804-4400	MQ	2001
Crowe John	(630)728-7977 jcrowe737@gmail.com	306 E Union Ave Wheaton IL 60187	NI	DCM	Mem C	St John Wheaton IL	(630)668-0701	MQ	2011
Crowe Marrissa S Norland	(702)488-2339 marrissa8994@gmail.com	2211 3rd St S Nampa ID 83651	NOW	DCE	C05/2019			IV	2016
Crown Alyssa M Candioto	(480)737-1310 acrown@cclphoenix.org	13440 N 44th St Apt. 1057 Phoenix AZ 85032	PSW	Teacher	Tchr	Christ Phoenix AZ	(602)957-7010	IV	2021
Crown Luke I	(650)799-3523 lukelcrown@gmail.com	13440 N 44th St Apt 1057 Phoenix AZ 85032	PSW	Teacher	Tchr	Christ Phoenix AZ	(602)957-7010	IV	2022
Crutcher Susan Howard	(949)202-6800 scrutcher@sjlschool.org	15820 Carparzo Dr Bakersfield CA 93314	CNH	Teacher	Tchr	St John Bakersfield CA	(661)665-7815	IV	2007
Cruz Diane R Snyder	(219)369-8082 diane_r_cruz@yahoo.com	608 Center St Walkerton IN 46574	IN	DCE	Mem C	Our Redeemer Knox IN	(574)772-4186	RF	1998
Cruz Melissa K Waldie	(209)298-9918 misswaldie@gmail.com	4453 Darla Dr Bay City MI 48706	MI	Teacher	Tchr	Valley Saginaw MI	(989)790-1676	CH	2008
Cullen Christine H Bierly	(503)642-1198 ccullen820@hotmail.com	5795 SE Drake Rd Hillsboro OR 97123	NOW	Teacher	EM			RF	1973

*Multiple Assignments (See Church Worker Locator for Additional Details)
See Page 53 for the Table of Abbreviations for key to District, Classification, Position, and College abbreviations.
**C =Candidate; EM =Emeritus; the date following the C is the month and year the Candidate status began

NAME	TELEPHONE NUMBER EMAIL	STREET ADDRESS CITY/STATE/ZIP	DISTRICT	CLASS.	POSITION/ STATUS**	WHERE SERVING	OFFICE PHONE	COLLEGE/ UNIV/CQ	YR GRAD
Cullen Guelda E Buie	(281)298-1769 guelda.cullen@gmail.com	79 Woodhaven Wood Dr The Woodlands TX 77380	TX	Teacher	EM			CQ	1994
Cullen Kimberly E Lerche	(757)304-1551 kandjcullen@gmail.com	23 Chad Ave Sullivan IL 61951	CI	Teacher	C01/2025			CQ	2022
Cullen Michael P	(734)652-6757 mcullen@lsusfw.org	556 Courtney Dr New Haven IN 46774	IN	Teacher	Tchr	South Unity Fort Wayne IN	(260)744-0459	CH	2014
Cullen William G Dr	(815)399-3171 bcullen@mtolivelutheran.com	2001 N Alpine Rd Rockford IL 61107	NI	DCE	Mem C	Mount Olive Rockford IL	(815)399-3171	Other	1985
Cummins Le Ann J Wascher	(763)420-2317	9733 Alvardo Ln N Maple Grove MN 55311	MNS	Teacher	EM			SP	1966
Cunningham Judith E Trinklein	(561)501-5313	14030 Nesting Way Apt A Delray Beach FL 33484	FG	Teacher	EM			RF	1963
Cunningham Karen K Perr	(573)837-9220 kkc66@hotmail.com	116 S West Ln Jackson MO 63755	MO	Teacher	Tchr	St Paul Jackson MO	(573)243-2236	S	1990
Cunningham Lynn M Luehmann	(405)737-5208 jcunningham18@cox.net	2829 Woodcreek Rd Midwest City OK 73110	OK	Teacher	Tchr	Good Shepherd Midwest City OK	(405)732-0070	SP	1987
Cunningham Sara A Koehlinger	(219)916-4460 scunningham@immanuelvalpo.org	2711 White Pine Cir Valparaiso IN 46383	IN	Teacher	Tchr	Immanuel Valparaiso IN	(219)462-8207	S	1977
Curley Jennifer Edgington	(314)973-6004 Curleyfam21@gmail.com	904 N 10th St Atchison KS 66002	KS	Teacher	C06/2019			RF	2011
Curran Michaela J	(402)419-6331 michaela.curran@cune.org	1238 E Military Ave Fremont NE 68025	NEB	Teacher	C07/2018			S	2016
Currao Abigail	(812)216-8755 ossmyouth@osva.org	4203 Kings Mill Ln Annandale VA 22003	SE	DCE	Mem C	Our Savior Arlington VA	(703)892-4846	CH	2021
Curry Alexis	alliemustang16@aol.com	9515 Tesson Ferry Rd Saint Louis MO 63123	MO	Teacher	Tchr	Lutheran South Saint Louis MO	(314)631-1400	MQ	2020
Curtis Amber M Schauland	(262)424-1181 abccurtis@sbcglobal.net	1313 Riverdale Dr Oconomowoc WI 53066	SW	Teacher	Tchr	Divine Redeemer Hartland WI	(262)367-3664	MQ	1999
Curtis Tracy J Scheu	(507)399-3725 tcurtis@rlcmail.org	4395 E University St Springfield MO 65809	MO	Teacher	Tchr	Redeemer Springfield MO	(417)881-5470	CQ	2018
Cutler Joann L Schimmel	(406)212-7375 cutlerjoann@gmail.com	N7146 County Rd. TW Horicon WI 53032	SW	Teacher	C01/2020			S	1985
Cutler Sarah Groeling	(505)850-5040 sarah.groeling@cune.org	24 W Northview Loop Kalispell MT 59901	MT	Teacher	Tchr	Trinity Kalispell MT	(406)257-5683	S	2020
Cutler Stephanie T Storck	(414)639-5707 stephanie.cutler@drlc.org	1431 Blazing Star Dr Oconomowoc WI 53066	SW	DCM	Mem C	Divine Redeemer Hartland WI	(262)367-8400	MQ	2023
Cutrer Monica	(281)685-8831 mcutrer@salem4u.com	15524 Brown Rd Tomball TX 77377	TX	Teacher	Tchr	Salem Tomball TX	(281)351-8223	AU	2018
Cypher Alan J	(256)682-0024 alan.cypher@gmail.com	902 Highland Dr Madison AL 35758	SO	Teacher	EM			RF	1977
Czarapata Melody L	(715)432-5575 melody-czarapata@cuw.edu	621 32nd St N Apt 207 Wisc Rapids WI 54494	NW	Teacher	Tchr	Immanuel Wisconsin Rapids WI	(715)423-3260	MQ	2015
Czernicki Hillary R Troeger	(414)403-7074 hillaryczernicki@gmail.com	S110W20968 S Denoon Rd. Muskego WI 53150	EN	Teacher	C06/2023			MQ	2015
Daberkow Evelyn M	(719) 406-6524 emdaberkow@gmail.com	938 Cherrycrest Dr Pueblo CO 81005	RM	Teacher	EM			S	1972
Daenzer Charles G	(952)200-0802 cdaenzer1@comcast.net	4339 Wooddale Ave St Louis Park MN 55424	MNS	Teacher	EM			RF	1965
Dagel Julie K Eggiman	(402)451-0886	P.O. Box 12384 Omaha NE 68112	NEB	Teacher	EM			S	1978
Dahl Inese Pukste	(956)313-0133 idahl@stpaulmcallen.org	St Paul Lutheran Church 300 Pecan Blvd McAllen TX 78501	TX	DCE	Mem C	St Paul McAllen TX	(956)682-2345	S	2003
Dahl Joy L Perez	(707)287-7738 jdahl@stjohnsnapa.org	3027 Beecham St Napa CA 94558	CNH	Teacher	P/Tchr	St John Napa CA	(707)226-7970	CQ	2024
Dahl Luke A	(320)543-1086 ladahl71@gmail.com	P.O. Box 607 Howard Lake MN 55349	MNS	Teacher	Tchr	Saint James Howard Lake MN	(320)543-2766	SP	1995
Dahl Valerie A	(415)454-6238	45 Martens Blvd San Rafael CA 94901	CNH	Teacher	Tchr	Trinity San Rafael CA	(415)453-4526	S	1984
Dahlhauser Mary L Lauritsen	(402)478-4041 mpdahlhauser@gmail.com	750 White Feather Ct Arlington NE 68002	NEB	Teacher	EM			S	1975
Dahlia Mary E Borchard	musicmeri@gmail.com	2525 N Bourbon St Unit H4 Orange CA 92865	PSW	DCE	Tchr	Salem Orange CA	(714)639-1946	IV	1993
Dahlin Jeanette A Warnock	(714)366-2729	5785 Los Amigos St Buena Park CA 90620	PSW	Teacher	EM			S	1975
Dahlke Angelia P Denney	(256)708-1924 angedahlke@gmail.com	8161 Alabama Hwy 69 N Cullman AL 35058	SO	Teacher	EM			CQ	2014
Dahlke Betty L		1724 Wyn Cliff Dr NE Cullman AL 35058	SO	Teacher	EM			RF	1962
Dahlke Dorothy H	(320)864-3205	109 Andrew Dr Glencoe MN 55336	MNS	Teacher	EM			SP	1966
Dahlke Katelyn N Kardosh	(920)447-2188 kndahlke16@gmail.com	1845 Southeranwood Ln Indianapolis IN 46231	IN	Teacher	Tchr	Our Shepherd Avon IN	(317)271-9103	MQ	2016
Dahm Janet A Zastrow	(262)567-4415 janetdahm@charter.net	1194 Dorchester Dr Oconomowoc WI 53066	SW	Teacher	EM			RF	1964
Dahms Sara E Kuske		6915 Bentley Ave Darien IL 60561	NI	Teacher	C06/2025			RF	1986
Dahn Mary L Schleicher	(810)516-5958 douglasdahn@gmail.com	220 Cornwallis Way Fayetteville GA 30214	FG	Teacher	EM			AA	1982
Dahn Michael R	(217)429-1567 mdahn@lsadecatur.net	3163 Fair Oaks Dr Decatur IL 62526	CI	Teacher	Tchr	Luth School Assoc Decatur IL	(217)233-2001	RF	1999
Dahnke Michael J	(260)515-8126 mdahnke@sblschool.com	11826 N Star Pl Fort Wayne IN 46845	IN	Teacher	Tchr	Suburban Bethlehem Fort Wayne IN	(260)483-9371	MQ	2008
Dain Laura A	(618)401-2786 missdain@aol.com	5 Gerold Ln Belleville IL 62223	SI	Teacher	Tchr	Zion Bethalto IL	(618)377-8314	BR	1988

*Multiple Assignments (See Church Worker Locator for Additional Details)
See Page 53 for the Table of Abbreviations for key to District, Classification, Position, and College abbreviations.
**C =Candidate; EM =Emeritus; the date following the C is the month and year the Candidate status began

NAME	TELEPHONE NUMBER EMAIL	STREET ADDRESS CITY/STATE/ZIP	DISTRICT	CLASS.	POSITION/ STATUS**	WHERE SERVING	OFFICE PHONE	COLLEGE/ UNIV/CQ	YR GRAD
Dale Jennifer A	(585)451-6192 jwyant291@gmail.com	223 Dunbar Road Hilton NY 14468	EA	Teacher	Tchr	St Paul Hilton NY	(585)392-4000	CQ	2016
Dale Michelle L Miller	(402)440-2480 mldale79@gmail.com	2801 S 79th St Lincoln NE 68506	NEB	Teacher	Tchr	Christ Lincoln NE	(402)483-7774	S	2002
Daley Jeffrey D Dr	(847)844-3879 daley935@comcast.net	935 McConnoiche Ct West Dundee IL 60118	NI	Teacher	EM			RF	1966
Daley Sheila R Hendrikson	(630)991-0354 mojewski2@aol.com	150 Lake Blvd. Unit 116 Buffalo Grove IL 60089	NI	Teacher	EM			RF	1974
Dalpini Sharon L Novotny	(630)815-1189 sndalpini@aol.com	1585 Kaimy Ct Aurora IL 60504	NI	Teacher	Tchr	Immanuel Batavia IL	(630)406-0157	S	1978
Dame Christine M Meinert	(708)848-3196 christinedame@yahoo.com	1037 S East Ave Oak Park IL 60304	NI	Teacher	EM			RF	1973
Damery Dorothy A Lindstrom	(217)875-4956 ddamery@lsadecatur.net	200 Hickory Point Ct Forsyth IL 62535	CI	Teacher	EM			CQ	1993
Dammann Dean W Dr	(714)349-6590 deand12@ca.rr.com	25252 Parthenon Ave Mission Viejo CA 92691	PSW	Teacher	EM			S	1952
Damron Edith A Poppe	(301)864-1982 eadamron@comcast.net	6812 Wells Pkwy University Pa MD 20782	SE	Teacher	EM			S	1972
Damrow Kirsten M Smith	(414)333-5371 kiki.damrow@gmail.com	12521 Winnipeg Shores Minocqua WI 54548	NW	Teacher	EM			CQ	1987
Dancy Heidi L Scherfling	hldancy@gmail.com	10503 Lagoon Dr Grabill IN 46741	IN	Teacher	EM			RF	1976
Danek Jonathan D	mrdanek@tlsgi.org	344 E Delaware Ave Grand Island NE 68801	NEB	Teacher	Tchr	Grand Island Grand Island NE	(308)385-3900	S	2004
Daniell Sheri L Gross	(313)283-6185 gsd31195@yahoo.com	1161 Queens Dr Oxford MI 48371	MI	Teacher	Tchr	Trinity Utica MI	(586)731-4490	AA	1992
Daniels Allison D	(832)421-1924 allison.dayton91@gmail.com	127 Vanderbilt Ln Waxahachie TX 75165	TX	DCE	Mem C	Christ King Waxahachie TX	(972)938-1633	AU	2014
Daniels Amanda L Amanda Kellar	(618)207-5964 kellar.amanda@yahoo.com	109 W 5th St Hartford IL 62048	MO	Teacher	Tchr	Green Park Saint Louis MO	(314)544-4248	CQ	2024
Daniels Denise C	(618)696-7197 denisedaniels51@gmail.com	9 Whitechapel Ct Glen Carbon IL 62034	SI	Teacher	Tchr	Good Shepherd Collinsville IL	(618)344-3153	CQ	2002
Dankenbring David A	(414)534-5516 ddank5@hotmail.com	4530 E Farmdale Cir Mesa AZ 85206	PSW	Teacher	EM			S	1976
Dankenbring Nadine L Gumtow	(414)534-5515 ddank5@hotmail.com	4530 E Farmdale Cir Mesa AZ 85206	PSW	Teacher	EM			S	1974
Danley Korey D		1289 Travertine Ter Sanford FL 32771	S	DCE	C08/2024			S	2007
Danner Susanna R Kinsley	sdanner@hclk.org		NEB	DCE	Mem C	Holy Cross Kearney NE	(308)237-2944	SP	2019
Darby Megan E Leimer	(913)449-9271 mdarby@bethanyschool.net	c/o Bethany Lutheran School 9101 Lamar Ave Overland Park KS 66207	KS	Teacher	Tchr	Bethany Overland Park KS	(913)648-2228	S	2002
Darlage Clayton W	(812)528-3082 cdarlage@trinitycougars.org	261 N 500 E Seymour IN 47274	IN	Teacher	Prin	South Central Luth Assoc for Sec Ed Seymour IN	(812)524-8547	CQ	2020
Darlage Nell A Byers	(812)342-4868	5096 Dahlia Dr Plainfield IN 46168	IN	Teacher	EM			RF	1993
Darling Renae A Kragenbrink	(989)860-2952 darlingfam@yahoo.com	3641 Hensler Pl Saginaw MI 48603	MI	Teacher	Tchr	Peace Saginaw MI	(989)793-9025	CQ	2019
Darling Tara J McMiller Barrett			IE	DCE	Mem C	St Paul Mount Vernon IA	(319)895-8772	CQ	2010
Darlington Nathaniel D	(541)977-6262 nate.darlington1@gmail.com	4201 City Point Dr W #1224 North Richland Hills TX 76180	TX	DPM	Mem C	Crown of Life Colleyville TX	(817)421-5683	IV	2018
Dartmann Shelley K Gudgel	(402)699-6419 dartmanns@gmail.com	2701 Lakeview Circle Plattsmouth NE 68048	NEB	Teacher	Tchr	Concordia Luth Schools of Omaha Inc Omaha NE	(402)445-4000	S	1989
Dash Denise A Ziemer	(956)245-6195 trackmom55@hotmail.com	16263 Avocado Way Del Ray Beach FL 33484	FG	DCE	EM			BR	1977
Dashkevicz Shirley J Deac	(989)780-3036 shirley.dashkevicz@stpeter hemlock.org	2309 Milford Drive Saginaw MI 48603	MI	Deaconess	Mem C	St Peter Hemlock MI	(989)642-8188	FW-DEAC	2022
Davenport Chandler A	(734)679-3978 chandlerdavenport@yahoo.com	812 Michigan Ave #2 Monroe MI 48162	MI	Teacher	Tchr	Trinity Monroe MI	(734)242-2308	CH	2017
David Kelly R Linebrink	(512)994-6704 kelly.david@zionwalburg.org	308 Jake Dr Jarrell TX 76537	TX	Teacher	Tchr	Zion Georgetown TX	(512)863-3065	CQ	2007
Davidson Perris L Sherotski	(863) 899-6794 pdavidson@stpaullakeland.org	2208 Country Bend S Lakeland FL 33811	FG	Teacher	Tchr	St Paul Lakeland FL	(863)644-7710	CQ	2024
Davies Alissa A Anklam	(715)675-2124 alissa.davies15@gmail.com	514 Bugbee Ave Wausau WI 54401	NW	Teacher	C07/2023			MQ	2004
Davies Erica N Michaelson	(920)686-6559 erica.michaelson1@gmail.com	102 Amherst Dr Bartlett IL 60103	CI	DCE	Mem C	St Paul's Decatur IL	(217)423-6955	CH	2016
Davis Abigail A Haggard	(440)781-3827 abbyhaggard2@gmail.com	17000 Woodbury Ave Cleveland OH 44135	SI	Teacher	Tchr	Good Shepherd Collinsville IL	(618)344-3153	AA	2022
Davis Alanna K	(509)599-3835 davisalanna54@gmail.com		NOW	DCE	Mem C	Epiphany Kenmore WA	(425)488-9606	SP	2016
Davis Alyce L Hamilton	(712)899-3396 astrong459@gmail.com	203 Port Neal Rd Sergeant Bluff IA 51054	IW	Teacher	EM			S	1981
Davis Brandon J	(262)305-5035 bdavis@stjohnindy.org	7817 Rock Crk Avon IN 46123	IN	Teacher	Tchr	St John Indianapolis IN	(317)352-9196	MQ	2004
Davis Camela L Wichman	(828)244-3284 atticusharveybutler@yahoo.com	4102 Icard Ridge Rd Hickory NC 28601	SE	Teacher	C07/2016			AA	1986
Davis Christine S Holtz	(712) 840-0325 pastorswifecsd@gmail.com	2326 Story Ave Battle Creek IA 51006	IW	Teacher	EM			PO	1994
Davis Darlene B Goldammer	(402)371-9659 jtdne@telebeep.com	182 Ameren Way Apt 948 Ballwin MO 63021	NEB	Teacher	EM			S	1964

*Multiple Assignments (See Church Worker Locator for Additional Details)
See Page 53 for the Table of Abbreviations for key to District, Classification, Position, and College abbreviations.
**C =Candidate; EM =Emeritus; the date following the C is the month and year the Candidate status began

NAME	TELEPHONE NUMBER EMAIL	STREET ADDRESS CITY/STATE/ZIP	DISTRICT	CLASS.	POSITION/ STATUS**	WHERE SERVING	OFFICE PHONE	COLLEGE/ UNIV/CQ	YR GRAD
Davis Deborah K Oehlert	(314)809-8468 ddavis@lslanceres.org	5105 Towne Centre Dr Saint Louis MO 63128	MO	Teacher	Tchr	Lutheran South Saint Louis MO	(314)631-1400	CQ	2020
Davis Elizabeth M MacKenzie	(586)596-0115 elizabethdavis423@gmail.com	16575 Rosemary Fraser MI 48026	MI	Teacher	C07/2016			RF	1999
Davis Jeffrey M	(586)913-5993 jdavis@lhsa.com	16575 Rosemary Fraser MI 48026	MI	Teacher	Tchr	Northwest Rochester Hills MI	(248)856-0240	AA	1994
Davis Jennifer C Jennifer Wied	(832)643-1667 jennifercaroldavis@gmail.com	1206 Cambridge Dr Friendswood TX 77546	TX	Teacher	Tchr	South Houston TX	(281)464-8299	AU	2001
Davis Joan E Swanson -Darden Dr	(541) 570-5447 dr.yamma20@gmail.com	11863 Brighton Knoll Loop Riverview FL 33579	FG	Teacher	Prin	Immanuel Brandon FL	(813)685-1978	WN	1986
Davis John	(551)580-0410 john.davis@ctx.edu	8301 Artesian Springs Dr Fort Worth TX 76131	TX	DCE	Mem C	St Paul Fort Worth TX	(817)332-2281	AU	2017
Davis Kathryn R Koenig	(734)552-5460 dakrdavis877@gmail.com	95 Pinewood St Ortonville MI 48462	MI	Teacher	EM			RF	1977
Davis Leanne S Schlaefke	(989)652-6343	9445 Van Cleve Rd Vassar MI 48768	MI	Teacher	EM			RF	1989
Davis Mark A	(281)381-8781 mark.davis5151@gmail.com	10926 N Country Club Green Dr Tomball TX 77375	TX	Teacher	EM			S	1980
Davis Melissa C Gassman	(650)369-5198 tmjdavis@gmail.com	3340 Spring St Redwood City CA 94063	CNH	Teacher	Tchr	Bridge City Redwood City CA	(650)366-5892	CQ	2013
Davis Samantha M Wegner	(920)530-8638 dcesamanthadavis@gmail.com	18214 E Willow Oak Bend Dr Cypress TX 77433	MNS	DCE	Mem C	St John Woodbury MN	(651)436-6621	CH	2025
Davis Sarah A Krueger	(551)284-1745 sarahkrgr@gmail.com	8301 Artesian Springs Dr Fort Worth TX 76131	TX	DCE	Mem C	St Paul Fort Worth TX	(817)332-2281	AU	2018
Davis Sharon M Abend	(480)983-5887	2137 10th Ave Longmont CO 80501	PSW	Teacher	C07/2016			CQ	2002
Davis Shelly A Huber	(801)597-7188 shellyadavis@hotmail.com	5860 S 1900 E Salt Lake Cty UT 84121	RM	Teacher	EM			AA	1990
Davis Shirley A Merkle	(260)748-0635	8210 Grand Forest Ct Fort Wayne IN 46815	IN	Teacher	EM			RF	1971
Davis Shirley A Baumann	(210)822-3263 shirleyd@concordia-satx.com	118 Abiso Ave San Antonio TX 78209	TX	Teacher	Tchr	Concordia San Antonio TX	(210)479-1477	CQ	1995
Davis Stephanie L	sdavisyouthministry@gmail.com		MI	DFLM	Mem C	Trinity Utica MI	(586)731-4490	AA	2019
Davis Sue A Fehner	(817)313-4555 sueanndavis1979@gmail.com	7613 Skylake Dr Fort Worth TX 76179	TX	DCE	EM			SP	1982
Davis Terry M	(586)949-9261 terrymartindavis@gmail.com	23775 24 Mile Rd Macomb MI 48042	MI	Teacher	EM			RF	1968
Davis Tonya M Fellows	(281)704-3459 tfellows00@gmail.com	7823 Kleingreen Ln Spring TX 77379	TX	Teacher	Tchr	Salem Tomball TX	(281)351-8223	RF	2004
Davisson Haley A	(505)239-4490	5005 Georgi Ln Apt 39 Houston TX 77092	TX	DCE	Mem C	Trinity Houston TX	(713)224-0684	AU	2017
Davitt Jill M Kiessling	(503)828-7602 jillmdavitt6@gmail.com	18450 SW Kelly View Loop Aloha OR 97007	NOW	Teacher	Tchr	Pilgrim Beaverton OR	(503)644-8697	PO	1993
Dawn Russell P Dr	(708)209-3003 russell.dawn@cuchicago.edu		NI	Teacher	S HS/C	Concordia University Chicago River Forest IL	(708)771-8300	CQ	2015
Dawson Leah A Jaeger	(714)852-7225 leah.dawson@creanlutheran.org	26075 Las Flores Apt C Mission Viejo CA 92691	PSW	Teacher	Tchr	Crean Irvine CA	(949)387-1199	IV	2014
Dawson-Pappert Lavonne L Oberhelman			MO	Teacher	EM			CQ	2007
Day Tricia D Paull	(260)494-2986 daytricia23@yahoo.com	4821 Crystal Ridge Cove #305 Fort Wayne IN 46835	IN	Teacher	Tchr	Wyneken Memorial Decatur IN	(260)639-6177	CQ	2020
De Berard Mary I Betts	(970)241-0990	1356 29th St Lewiston ID 83501	RM	Teacher	Tchr	Messiah Grand Junction CO	(970)245-2838	S	1962
De Board Christina K Nolte	(618)532-6930 ckdeboard@yahoo.com	1470 State Route 161 Centralia IL 62801	SI	Teacher	Tchr	Trinity Centralia IL	(618)532-5434	RF	1990
De Cant Crystine Barthel	(847)716-0694 cdecant@comcast.net	705 N Dryden Ave Arlington Hts IL 60004	NI	Teacher	EM			RF	2005
De Cuir Gloria M Deac	(636)938-4735 gmdecuir@enonline.net	143 Shaw Dr Eureka MO 63025	MO	Deaconess	EM			SL-DEAC	2004
De Dominick Michael A	(206)794-0122 dedom421@gmail.com	513 Nightingale Ct Wake Forest NC 27587	NOW	DCE	C07/2016			PO	2008
de la Motte Heidi R Dietrich	(714)651-7797 heidi.delamotte@gmail.com	6 Riptide Ct Newport Beach CA 92663	PSW	Teacher	Tchr	St Paul Orange CA	(714)637-2640	IV	1993
de la Motte Jennifer M Swisegood	(209)324-9098 fishservant@hotmail.com	640 N Minaret Ave Turlock CA 95380	CNH	DCE	Mem C	Good Shepherd Turlock CA	(209)667-7712	PO	1999
De La Vega Maria E Mai			MDS	Teacher	C06/2019			PO	2016
De Lude Clarence A III	(808)265-8878 cdelude@me.com	5035 Big Red St Apt B Kapolei HI 96707	CNH	Teacher		California/Nevada/Hawaii District Livermore CA	(866)264-6079	PO	1985
De Pew Mary Wolf	(812)876-8472	6501 N Rhinestone Dr Ellettsville IN 47429	IN	Teacher	EM			RF	1965
De Simpelare Susan M Nobis	(440)320-1590 sdesimpelare@gmail.com	3965 Magnolia Pkwy Jackson MI 49201	MI	Teacher	C08/2021			AA	1991
De Voy Tanya M Walsh	devoy1021@gmail.com	41189 Clayton St Clinton Twp MI 48038	MI	Teacher	Tchr	Immanuel Macomb MI	(586)286-4231	AA	1999
Deadmond Jana S Traub	(618) 553-1047 jsdeadmond@yahoo.com	308 S 4th St Altamont IL 62411	CI	Teacher	Tchr	Altamont Altamont IL	(618)483-6428	CQ	1996
Dean Brenda K Nehrt	(312)520-5057 mbdean324@sbcglobal.net	1291 Riesling Lane Pevely MO 63070	MO	Teacher	Tchr	St John Arnold MO	(636)464-7303	RF	1986
Dean Karen A Werth	(248)841-3319	50316 Knoll Ct #286 Macomb MI 48044	MI	Teacher	EM			CQ	2000
Deardoff Daniel H Jr	(402)364-3568 dandeardoff@gmail.com	1362 S Pierson Ct Lakewood CO 80232	RM	Teacher	Tchr	Bethlehem Lakewood CO	(303)233-0401	S	2005

*Multiple Assignments (See Church Worker Locator for Additional Details)

See Page 53 for the Table of Abbreviations for key to District, Classification, Position, and College abbreviations.

**C =Candidate; EM =Emeritus; the date following the C is the month and year the Candidate status began

NAME	TELEPHONE NUMBER EMAIL	STREET ADDRESS CITY/STATE/ZIP	DISTRICT	CLASS.	POSITION/ STATUS**	WHERE SERVING	OFFICE PHONE	COLLEGE/ UNIV/CQ	YR GRAD
Deardoff Laura R Lehfeldt	(402)238-3261 lauradeardoff@gmail.com	9409 N 156th St Bennington NE 68007	NEB	Teacher	EM			WN	1985
DeBow Aaron M	(714)496-2452 amdebow@gmail.com	9822 Orchard Ln Villa Park CA 92861	PSW	Teacher	C08/2017			IV	2008
Debrick Marc W	(636)288-9450 mdebrick@sbcglobal.net	1131 Claycrest Cir Saint Charles MO 63304	MO	Teacher	EM			WN	1984
Decheim Sandra Niemi	(810)632-5224 sdee3223@gmail.com	P.O. Box 595 Hartland MI 48353	MI	Teacher	EM			RF	1963
Decker Elizabeth D Brammer	(618)973-5791 ed424261@gmail.com	4242 Saratoga Dr Janesville WI 53546	SW	Teacher	EM			RF	1983
DeDominick-Hill Catherine	(618)578-8532 cdedom5@gmail.com	2504 Baymont Pl Bremerton WA 98312	NOW	Teacher	Tchr	Peace Bremerton WA	(360)373-2116	PO	2010
Dedor Rhonda L	(641)423-6625	651 S Vermont Ave Mason City IA 50401	IE	Teacher	EM			S	1976
Deen Alyssa A Goehner		2105 S Baker St Santa Ana CA 92707	PSW	Teacher	C07/2016			IV	2001
Deen Daniel R	(949)394-5166	2105 S Baker St Santa Ana CA 92707	PSW	Teacher	S HS/C	Concordia University Irvine Irvine CA	(949)854-8002	CQ	2001
Deeter Christopher L Dr	(402)430-6227 cdeeter@lincolnlutheran.org	7636 Gulls Way Lincoln NE 68514	NEB	Teacher	EM			S	1986
Deeter Nicholas P	(402)430-4857 ndeeter@christlincoln.org	4330 N 11th St Lincoln NE 68521	NEB	Teacher	Tchr	Christ Lincoln NE	(402)483-7774	S	2014
DeForest Abigail H Jeppesen	(402)643-1166 abigail.jeppesen@cune.org	5 McKinley Ln Chico CA 95973	CNH	Teacher	C06/2023			S	2021
Degen Timothy M	(760)994-6672 musician328@yahoo.com	5914 Nova Ct Fort Wayne IN 46815	IN	Teacher	Mem C	St Peter's Fort Wayne IN	(260)749-5816	RF	2003
Degenhardt Michelle C Pierce	(512)595-4523 pierce19@yahoo.com	12119 Saybrook Point Ln Tomball TX 77375	TX	Teacher	Tchr	Salem Tomball TX	(281)351-8223	S	2003
Degg Pamela J Drzyzga	pdrzyzga@yahoo.com	317 S. Lincoln Bay City MI 48708	MI	Teacher	Tchr	Zion Bay City MI	(989)894-2611	CQ	2006
Degnan Dawn L Budnik	(262) 433-8299 djdeg2021@gmail.com	122 S Grandview Blvd Waukesha WI 53218	SW	Teacher	Tchr	LUMIN Milwaukee WI	(414)354-5126	MQ	2007
DeGroot Casey M Milller	(262)302-0334 degrootcasey@gmail.com	5887 County Highway Y West Bend WI 53095	SW	Teacher	Tchr	First Immanuel Cedarburg WI	(262)377-6610	MQ	2002
DeGroot Melissa A Nichols Deac	(401)301-1880 melissadegroot8@gmail.com	5804 San Miguel Dr NE Rio Rancho NM 87144	RM	Deaconess	C07/2016			FW-DEAC	2008
Dehn Linda M Bauer	(314)971-0629 ldehn0519@gmail.com	10950 Cedarberry Pl Saint Louis MO 63123	MO	Teacher	Prin	Our Savior Fenton MO	(636)343-2192	CQ	2002
Dehn Matthew T	(920)960-0290 mattdehn@saintpetersls.com	950 Krystle Ct Reedsburg WI 53959	SW	Teacher	Tchr	St Peter Reedsburg WI	(608)524-4066	MQ	2005
Dehne Jill M Boettcher	(573)270-7107 jdehne@stpauljackson.com	1561 Greenbrier St Cpe Girardeau MO 63701	MO	Teacher	Tchr	St Paul Jackson MO	(573)243-5360	RF	1994
Dehning Christopher J	(402)613-2456 chris.dehning@gmail.com	910 Mound St Winfield KS 67156	KS	Teacher	P/Tchr	Trinity Winfield KS	(620)221-9460	S	2010
Dehning Melanie L Wollslager	(402)613-2457 MelanieDehning@gmail.com	18 Muir St Eureka MO 63025	MO	DCE	EM			S	1981
Dehning Mervin W	(402)613-2436 mervdehning@gmail.com	18 Muir Street Eureka MO 63025	MO	Teacher	EM			S	1980
Dehnke Christine R Poynter	(314)803-0290 christinedehnke@yahoo.com	2558 Songbird Ln Grayson GA 30017	FG	Teacher	EM			RF	1971
DeHoyos Rebecca	(480)734-6869 db.dehoyos@gmail.com	1640 N Queensbury Mesa AZ 85201	PSW	Teacher	C06/2020			S	2013
Deinert Marilyn A Zeiger	(951)970-4983 marilyn.deinert@gmail.com	1790 E Campus Way Hemet CA 92544	PSW	Teacher	EM			CQ	1989
Deines Emma A	(636)542-2876 emma@stmfw.org	2219 Point West Dr Apt 2c Fort Wayne IN 46808	IN	DCE	Mem C	St Michael Fort Wayne IN	(260)432-2033	S	2023
Deines Jennifer Neary	(970)526-2068 j.deines@kci.net	14320 Greenway Dr Sterling CO 80751	RM	DCE	Mem C	Trinity Sterling CO	(970)522-5942	IV	2000
Delancy Lauran M Buddish	(913)488-5897 lauran.delancy@gmail.com	15417 W 149th Terr Olathe KS 66062	KS	DPM	Mem C	Beautiful Savior Olathe KS	(913)780-6023	MQ	2006
DeLeon Dehlia K Deac	dehliakd@gmail.com	5290 Lexi Ln S Dublin OH 43016	OH	Deaconess	Mem C	St John Dublin OH	(614)889-2284	CH	2013
Dellar Frances A Wilson	(847)903-4570 fad613@gmail.com	401 Ascot Dr Apt 1a Park Ridge IL 60068	NI	Teacher	EM			S	1971
Delleart Sarah M Scheer	(636)578-6335 sarahdelleart@yahoo.com	5713 Steutermann Rd Washington MO 63090	MO	Teacher	Tchr	Immanuel Washington MO	(636)239-1636	CQ	2018
Dellinger Carol C Schaefer	(614)582-5505 dellinger.caroll@gmail.com	16750 Middleburg Plain City Rd Marysville OH 43040	OH	Teacher	EM			S	1970
Delmotte Karen M Reichenbach	(586)212-4315 kadelmotte@yahoo.com	51528 Shadywood Dr Macomb MI 48042	MI	Teacher	Tchr	Trinity Utica MI	(586)731-4490	AA	1984
DeMaio Virginia C Fulghum	(301)464-1237 jennydemaio@hotmail.com	3126 Gracefield Rd Apt 202 Silver Spring MD 20904	SE	Teacher	EM			BR	1978
DeMario Helen I Isaksen Deac	(609)412-5049 hidemario@aol.com	188 Main St Port Republic NJ 08241	S	Deaconess	Mem C	Redeemer Manchester NJ	(732)657-2828	CH	2011
DeMarsh Amanda M	(847)975-2079 ademarsh@immanuel-ed.org	53 Edwards Ave West Dundee IL 60118	NI	Teacher	Tchr	Immanuel East Dundee IL	(847)428-4477	CQ	2019
Dembeck David E	chaparral2d@live.com	66 Moross St Mount Clemens MI 48043	MI	Teacher	EM			S	1974
Demel Debra J Ringers	(816)809-6312 djrdemel@gmail.com	1502 Shelby St Higginsville MO 64037	MO	Teacher	Tchr	Trinity Alma MO	(660)674-2376	S	1984
Demo Maida R Sevon	(810)513-3615 sevonmr@yahoo.com	5495 Stimson Rd Davison MI 48423	MI	Teacher	C07/2016			RF	1998
Denecke Suzanne B Degner	(414)588-6609 momof4@email.com	8487 N 66th St Brown Deer WI 53223	SW	Teacher	Pro Stf	Pilgrim Wauwatosa WI	(414)259-0190	RF	1985
Deneen Matthew W	(989)385-0188 mwdeneen@gmail.com	113 Auch St Sebewaing MI 48759	MI	Teacher	Tchr	Christ The King Sebewaing MI	(989)883-3730	AA	2014

*Multiple Assignments (See Church Worker Locator for Additional Details)

See Page 53 for the Table of Abbreviations for key to District, Classification, Position, and College abbreviations.

**C =Candidate; EM =Emeritus; the date following the C is the month and year the Candidate status began

NAME	TELEPHONE NUMBER EMAIL	STREET ADDRESS CITY/STATE/ZIP	DISTRICT	CLASS.	POSITION/ STATUS**	WHERE SERVING	OFFICE PHONE	COLLEGE/ UNIV/CQ	YR GRAD
Denholm George III	(812)343-4495 gdenholm@stpeters-columbus.org	4554 Hackberry Dr Columbus IN 47201	IN	DCE	Mem C	St Peter Columbus IN	(812)372-1571	RF	1983
Denkert Sally J Vyvyan	(414) 531-8398 sdenkert@att.net	11914 W Douglas Ave Milwaukee WI 53225	SW	Teacher	EM			CQ	2006
Dennert Katie M Wagenecht	(414)322-2144 kdennert@gmail.com	W133S6581 Fennimore Ln Muskego WI 53150	EN	Teacher	Tchr	Hales Corners Hales Corners WI	(414)529-6700	MQ	2000
Denney Rebecca R Fehl	(913)705-0019 rdenn7_8@yahoo.com	1707 Remington Ct Leavenworth KS 66048	MO	Teacher	Tchr	Martin Luther Kansas City MO	(816)734-1060	AU	1992
Denow Dennis K	66-86-046-0990 ddenow@yahoo.com	Baan Bunto 99/49 Chaengwattana Sisaman Rd Pak Kred Nontaburi THAILAND	PSW	Teacher	EM			RF	1970
Densmore Amanda J Wolff	ajwolff73@hotmail.com	724 Shawnee Rd Pocahontas IL 62275	SI	Teacher	Tchr	Zion Bethalto IL	(618)377-5507	RF	1995
Denson Amy M Benedict	(608)290-6743 adenson@stpaulsjanesville.com	6743 W. Wood Ridge Dr. Janesville WI 53548	SW	Teacher	Tchr	St Pauls Janesville WI	(608)754-4471	MQ	2003
Dent Andrea J Andrea Guse	(734)664-1678 andrea.dent@stpaulbaycity.org	1709 S Warner St Bay City MI 48706	MI	Teacher	Tchr	St Paul Bay City MI	(989)684-4450	CQ	2016
DePasquale Trisha L Engerer	(954)703-9318 trisha.depasquale@yahoo.com	2681 N Flamingo Rd Apt 2308 Sunrise FL 33323	FG	Teacher	Tchr	Our Savior Plantation FL	(954)370-2161	RF	2007
Deranleau Sarah L Ehlers	(641)344-0321 williamandsarah.deranleau@ gmail.com	2876 Red Oak Dr Perry OH 44081	IW	Teacher	C07/2016			S	2008
Derricks Linda S Lopnow	(414)863-6174 dlucky24@aol.com	3659 S Michiels Rd Denmark WI 54208	NW	Teacher	Tchr	Zion Wayside WI	(920)864-2463	MQ	1984
Derricks Serena M Little	(920)930-8273 serenaderricks@yahoo.com	P.O. Box 876 Forsyth MT 59327	MT	Teacher	RSO	Lutheran Bible Translators Inc Concordia MO	(660)225-0810	PO	2010
DeRuyter Rebecca L Helt	(920)889-4170 deruyter@stpaulsheboygan.org	2212 N 22nd St Sheboygan WI 53083	SW	Teacher	Tchr	St Paul Sheboygan WI	(920)452-6882	MQ	2022
DeSart-Strasser Denise R DeSart	(651)263-6878 denise.desart.strasser@gmail.com	1100 Cumberland St Saint Paul MN 55117	MNS	Teacher	C08/2018			CQ	2012
Deschaine Emily F	(989)798-3899 emily.sievert@cune.org	W201 N16520 Hemlock St Jackson WI 53037	SW	Teacher	Tchr	Living Word Jackson WI	(262)677-9353	S	2018
Deterding Faith	(218)205-5705 deterdif@csp.edu	1503 Glenmore Dr #205 Norfolk NE 68701	NEB	Teacher	Tchr	Christ Norfolk NE	(402)371-5536	SP	2024
Deterding Jo Ann K Hermann	(218)205-0835 jodeterding57@rocketmail.com	16700 Wellington Lakes Cir Fort Myers FL 33908	FG	Teacher	C07/2016			CQ	1982
Dettling Edward J Jr	(516)974-9387	65 Great Hill Dr Bethel CT 06801	AT	Teacher	EM			S	1977
Dettling Marie A Fluegge	(516)974-9386 Madettling@gmail.com	65 Great Hill Dr Bethel CT 06801	AT	Teacher	EM			BR	1975
Detviler Lauren T Fox-Montano	(949)244-7974 taylordetviler24@gmail.com	1423 E Lael Dr Orange CA 92866	PSW	Teacher	S HS/C	Concordia University Irvine Irvine CA	(949)854-8002	CQ	2024
DeVencenty Payton J			RM	DCE	Mem C	Holy Cross Colorado Springs CO	(719)596-0661	S	2019
Devenport Maria P Watson Brovick	(509)939-4866 maria@redeemerconnect.com	842 Littleleaf Dr Windsor CO 80550	RM	DCE	Mem C	Redeemer Fort Collins CO	(970)225-9020	IV	1997
Devine Connie J Spilker		1109 Quail Park Dr Austin TX 78758	TX	Teacher	EM			S	1977
Devine Rita J Bartels	(217)415-9336 devineritajo5@gmail.com	575 Old Walnut Br North August SC 29860	SE	Teacher	EM			S	1981
Devlin Anne C Schweppe	(714)287-9281 kindteacheranne@gmail.com	6735 Vista Loma Yorba Linda CA 92886	CNH	Teacher	EM			CQ	2008
DeVries Henry A	(516)935-0290 hdevries11801@yahoo.com	36 Raymond St Hicksville NY 11801	AT	Teacher	Tchr	Trinity Hicksville NY	(516)931-2211	CQ	1998
DeWerff Karol K Kroenke	(217)898-3506 kkdewerff@msn.com	17255 N 21st Ave Nokomis IL 62075	SI	Teacher	EM			RF	1980
DeWitt Andrew R	(847)309-0262 andydewitt83@gmail.com	168 Seabury Rd Bolingbrook IL 60440	NI	Teacher	P/Tchr	Trinity Burr Ridge IL	(708)839-1444	CH	2007
DeWitt Leann E Baker	(815)761-3854 leann.dewitt@gmail.com	168 Seabury Rd Bolingbrook IL 60440	NI	Teacher	Tchr	Trinity Burr Ridge IL	(708)839-1444	CH	2010
DeWitt Richard	(847)895-8975 rgdewitt@yahoo.com	1031 Lighthouse Dr Schaumburg IL 60193	NI	Teacher	EM			CQ	1999
Dexter Johanna L Hilfiker	(760)554-3888 johanna.dext@gmail.com		MI	DPM	Mem C	Holy Cross Jenison MI	(616)457-2420	IV	2013
DeYarmond Sara M Bennington	(517)202-7361 sdeyarmond@oursaviorlansing.org	6688 S Grove Rd Saint Johns MI 48879	MI	Teacher	Tchr	Our Savior Lansing MI	(517)882-8665	CQ	2016
Dhuse Anna Gain	(630)945-6824 acdcteaching@gmail.com	1300 Belt Line Rd Collinsville IL 62234	SI	Teacher		Southern Illinois District Belleville IL	(618)234-4767	MQ	2021
Dhyne James T	(914)261-9091 jimdhyne@gmail.com	101 W 81st St Apt 408 New York NY 10024	AT	Teacher	EM			S	1972
Diaz Jose J	(702)806-1073 mrdiazjj@yahoo.com	9113 Tantalizing Ave Las Vegas NV 89149	PSW	Teacher	Tchr	Faith Las Vegas NV	(702)804-4400	RF	1999
Diaz Linda K Kirkegaard	(210)264-5283 lindakdiaz71@gmail.com	6135 Feather Nest Ln San Antonio TX 78233	TX	Teacher	EM			AU	1994
Dibbern Sarah B	(651)271-3741	7303 Pioneers Blvd #621 Lincoln NE 68506	NEB	DCE	Mem C	Messiah Lincoln NE	(402)489-3024	SP	2015
Dibler Tiffany M Pedroley	(314)954-7237 tdibler@coglcs.com	8 Stable Rdg Saint Charles MO 63301	MO	Teacher	Tchr	Child Of God Saint Peters MO	(636)970-7080	Other	2018
Dicke Jeanne M Deac	(651)704-9464 jmdicke@live.com	8574 Quarry Ridge Ln Unit B Woodbury MN 55125	MNS	Deaconess	EM			Other	1979
Dicke Mark L	(507)469-3622 mdicke@immanuelcourtland.com	427 1/2 N Broadway St New Ulm MN 56073	MNS	Teacher	Tchr	Immanuel Courtland MN	(507)359-2534	SP	1990
Dickinson Matthew T	(231)645-9080 mtdickinson@tctrinityschool.org	429 Kratky Dr Traverse City MI 49696	MI	Teacher	Tchr	Trinity Traverse City MI	(231)946-2720	CQ	2010
Dickinson Melinda S Bathke	melinda_dickinson@yahoo.com	843 Woodcreek Blvd Traverse City MI 49686	MI	Teacher	EM			S	1976

*Multiple Assignments (See Church Worker Locator for Additional Details)
See Page 53 for the Table of Abbreviations for key to District, Classification, Position, and College abbreviations.
**C =Candidate; EM =Emeritus; the date following the C is the month and year the Candidate status began

NAME	TELEPHONE NUMBER EMAIL	STREET ADDRESS CITY/STATE/ZIP	DISTRICT	CLASS.	POSITION/ STATUS**	WHERE SERVING	OFFICE PHONE	COLLEGE/ UNIV/CQ	YR GRAD
Diebel Lois E Martin Deac	(321)536-0430 lois.diebel@gmail.com	P.O. Box 111616 Palm Bay FL 32911	S	Deaconess	Mem C	Hope Viera Melbourne FL	(321)622-6126	Other	1982
Dieckhoff Brent W	(316)618-9045 brent@tec21connect.com	302 E Hillcrest Dr Seward NE 68434	NEB	Teacher	C07/2016			S	1990
Dieckhoff Tashia L Helmer	(316)641-6764 tdieckhoff@gmail.com	302 E Hillcrest Dr Seward NE 68434	NEB	Teacher	Tchr	St John Seward NE	(402)643-4535	S	1989
Diefenbach Rebecca M Wittig	(725)208-9146	2135 Granada Dr Dayton OH 45431	OH	Teacher	C07/2024			S	2014
Dielmann Marilyn K	(714)529-2030 mkdielmann@gmail.com	2001 Westmoreland Dr Brea CA 92821	PSW	Teacher	EM			RF	1970
Diener Bethany J Heinecke	(440)554-6430 bethdiener@hotmail.com		MO	Teacher	Tchr	Immanuel Jefferson City MO	(573)496-3451	S	2009
Diepenbrock Ina J Kaul	(903)454-4336 inanray@hotmail.com	3253 Bent Oak St W Greenville TX 75401	TX	Teacher	EM			S	1964
Diepenbrock Ray L	(903)454-4336 inanray@hotmail.com	3253 Bent Oak St W Greenville TX 75401	TX	Teacher	EM			S	1964
Diercks Julie Krull	(636)392-8462 jdiercks@stpaulsdp.org	13 Founders Way Unit B Saint Louis MO 63105	MO	Teacher	Tchr	St Paul Des Peres MO	(314)822-2771	MQ	2025
Dierdorf Nancy C Young	(763)300-9996 dierdorfn@comcast.net	2110 Urbandale Ln N Plymouth MN 55447	MNS	Teacher	EM			S	1974
Dierker Stephen T	(707)290-7980 dcederk@yahoo.com	92 Calle Aragon Unit S Laguna Woods CA 92637	PSW	DCE	S HS/C	Concordia University Irvine Irvine CA	(949)854-8002	IV	1995
Dierks Connie J Gaff	(260)267-2324 cdierks088@gmail.com	7405 Derby Ln Fort Wayne IN 46815	IN	Teacher	EM			CQ	1996
Dierks Julie A Meyer	(952)467-4905 jules_ad@hotmail.com	121 Mackenthun Ln Norwood MN 55368	MNS	Teacher	EM			SP	1981
Dietel Joann H Riley	(765)464-2159 jtdietel@comcast.net	640 Hazelwood Dr West Lafayette IN 47906	IN	Teacher	EM			RF	1966
Dietrich Clifford A Dr	(260)415-3984 cliff.dietrich35@gmail.com	19262 Cooper St Clinton Twp MI 48038	MI	Teacher	EM			RF	1958
Dietrich Julie L Shoemaker	(812)371-4681 djdietrich@comcast.net	3664 Greenbriar Dr Columbus IN 47203	IN	Teacher	D Ex/S	Indiana District Fort Wayne IN	(800)837-1145	RF	1987
Dietrich-Fortkamp Mary R	(308)883-0376 mfortkamp@chasecountyschools.org	225 W. 17th Street Imperial NE 69033	NEB	Teacher	C07/2016			MQ	1998
Dietsch Gayle K Gerth	(309)868-1504 gayledietsch@trinluth.org	2212 E Olive St Bloomington IL 61701	CI	Teacher	Tchr	Trinity Bloomington IL	(309)829-7513	S	2003
Dietz Beverly G Grossmann	(414)331-8201 jbdietz@wi.rr.com	W277S4170 Green Country Rd Waukesha WI 53189	SW	Teacher	EM			S	1973
Dietz James C	(414)405-8201 jdietz@att.net	W277S4170 Green Country Rd Waukesha WI 53189	SW	Teacher	EM			S	1974
DiLiberto Jamie L Endorf	(626)224-1655 jendorf17@gmail.com	2731 Port Lewis Ave. Henderson NV 89052	PSW	Teacher	C07/2016			S	2005
Dill Susan E Marcis	(330)273-9707 susan_dill@adelphia.net	4625 Inverness Ave Brunswick OH 44212	OH	Teacher	C07/2016			CQ	2005
Dillabough Catherine A Wurster Deac	(705)406-5460 dillaboughcathi@gmail.com	31 2nd Ave S P.O. Box 413 Ashern MB R0C 0 CANADA	EN	Deaconess	EM			RF	1988
Dillahay Kathleen M Frentzel	(573)788-2519 kathy@ccilink.net	351 Quail Trl Uniontown MO 63783	MO	Teacher	EM			RF	1973
Dillman Susan J	(920)231-2801	1870 Woodstock St Oshkosh WI 54904	SW	Teacher	Tchr	Trinity Oshkosh WI	(920)235-1730	CQ	2004
Dillon Bethany J Stellwagen	(630)743-3450 bdillon@hcl.org	3923 W Jerelin Dr Franklin WI 53132	EN	Teacher	Tchr	Hales Corners Hales Corners WI	(414)529-6701	CQ	2022
Dillon Lori A Wanamaker Plummer	dillon11219@gmail.com	6600 Crooked Creek Dr Lincoln NE 68516	NEB	Teacher	Tchr	Lincoln Lincoln NE	(402)467-5404	CQ	2011
Dillon Wendy J Crady	(505)271-1685 rdillon@eudoramail.com	3304 Candlelight Dr NE Albuquerque NM 87111	RM	Teacher	C08/2017			S	1986
Dillow Denise D Schlesselman	(260)579-2942 bookanddoglover@yahoo.com	5714 Oak Park Rd Oakwood Hills IL 60013	NI	Teacher	Tchr	Zion Marengo IL	(815)568-5156	S	2001
Dills Megan Pergande	megandills101@gmail.com	N63 W12708 Grove St Menomonee Falls WI 53051	SW	Teacher	Tchr	Milwaukee LHS Milwaukee WI	(414)461-6000	MQ	2024
Dilzer Rhonda J	(602)628-8478 dilzerr@gmail.com	2725 E Houston Ave Gilbert AZ 85234	PSW	Teacher	C08/2016			CQ	2012
Dimmel Heather A Griffin		1792 380th Ave P.O. Box 281 Janesville MN 56048	MNS	Teacher	Mem C	Hosanna Mankato MN	(507)388-1766	SP	1999
Dimmel-Schultz Marcia K Schaetzke	(507)420-8964 jmschult@frontiernet.net	203 Prairie Ln Janesville MN 56048	MNS	Teacher	EM			SP	1972
Dinda Laura J Meyer	(512)851-3159 ljdinda@gmail.com	1103 E Applegate Dr Austin TX 78753	TX	Teacher	EM			SP	1964
Dinger Caitlin M May	(908)421-1946 cmdinger@gmail.com		MO	DCE	S HS/C	Concordia Seminary Saint Louis MO	(314)505-7000	PO	1996
Dinger Stephen P	spd2213@aol.com	1404 Linden Ave Nashville TN 37212	CNH	Teacher	EM			S	1971
Dippel Alexis E	(217)620-6649 aedippel1@yahoo.com	1660 Renaissance Commons Blvd Apt 2314 Boynton Beach FL 33426	FG	Teacher	Tchr	Trinity Delray Beach FL	(561)278-1737	CH	2016
Dippel David A	(281)350-4548 ddippel@houston.rr.com	3706 Ash Glen Dr Spring TX 77388	TX	Teacher	Tchr	Concordia Tomball TX	(281)351-2547	AU	2005
Dippel Lisa K Nielsen	(217)369-9842 lkdippel@yahoo.com	203 N Oak St Buckley IL 60918	CI	Tch/DCE	EM			RF	1982
Dirks Dennis J	(209)481-0281 dennis@dirks.email	19728 N Swan Ct Maricopa AZ 85138	PSW	Teacher	EM			SP	1971
Diroff Jayne K Kregel		3960 Geiman Rd Monroe MI 48162	MI	Teacher	Tchr	Holy Ghost Monroe MI	(734)242-0509	AA	1985
Dittman James B	(414)541-6251 jim@splcwa.org	2506 S 76th St West Allis WI 53219	SW	Teacher	Tchr	St Pauls West Allis WI	(414)541-6251	MQ	1984

*Multiple Assignments (See Church Worker Locator for Additional Details)
See Page 53 for the Table of Abbreviations for key to District, Classification, Position, and College abbreviations.
**C =Candidate; EM =Emeritus; the date following the C is the month and year the Candidate status began

NAME	TELEPHONE NUMBER EMAIL	STREET ADDRESS CITY/STATE/ZIP	DISTRICT	CLASS.	POSITION/ STATUS**	WHERE SERVING	OFFICE PHONE	COLLEGE/ UNIV/CQ	YR GRAD
Dittmer Cheryl L	(314)482-1960 cdittmer@ccls-stlouis.org	1509 Friar Ln Kirkwood MO 63122	MO	Teacher	EM			CQ	1998
Dittmer Omar H	(407)658-9815 odittmer892@gmail.com	70 W Lucerne Cir Apt 609 Orlando FL 32801	FG	Teacher	EM			S	1954
Divine Rebecca A Stuenkel	(970)531-3747 rstuenkel1@hotmail.com	2186 Empire St Ogilvie MN 56358	RM	Teacher	C07/2016			S	1999
Dixon Anthony J	(224)587-4813 tdixon@kingofkingscr.org	3195 7th St Marion IA 52302	IE	DCE	Mem C	King Of Kings Cedar Rapids IA	(319)393-2438	CH	2008
Dixon Jessica E Lynn	(414)614-6150 jedixon1@gmail.com		MO	DCE	C07/2016			AU	2007
Dixon Joshua A	(217)891-7161 joshdixon1980@gmail.com	32 Copper Mountain Ct Fenton MO 63026	MO	Teacher	Tchr	Green Park Saint Louis MO	(314)544-4248	S	2004
Dixon Scott P	(414)614-6130 sdixon@mlakc.com	7509 N. Wyandotte St Gladstone MO 64118	MO	Teacher	Prin	Martin Luther Kansas City MO	(816)734-1060	AU	2004
Dobbelaire Elizabeth N Deac	(505)884-3876 edobbelaire@clsabq.com	c/o Christ Lutheran Church 7701 Candelaria Rd NE Albuquerque NM 87110	RM	Deaconess	Mem C	Christ Albuquerque NM	(505)884-3876	FW	2024
Dobbelaire Laura L Anderson	ldobbelaire@goodshepherdpekin.com	1703 Summit Dr Pekin IL 61554	CI	Teacher	Tchr	Good Shepherd Pekin IL	(309)347-2020	CQ	2014
Dobberfuhl Marjorie L Kohlwey	(262)271-5270 tmdobbs@wi.rr.com	17510 Bedford Dr Brookfield WI 53045	SW	Teacher	EM			RF	1970
Dobberstein Mary E Vogt	(715)526-5732 marydobberstein47@gmail.com	N5990 Wolf River Rd Shawano WI 54166	NW	Teacher	EM			SP	1969
Dobbertien Glenda L Gierhan	(402)643-9394 glendad65@yahoo.com	1145 N 2nd St Seward NE 68434	NEB	Teacher	EM			S	1966
Dobbins Anne J Melvin	(321)355-9496 annejdobbins@gmail.com	317 Parker Dr Titusville FL 32780	FG	Teacher	Tchr	Prince Of Peace Orlando FL	(407)275-6703	CQ	2016
Dobbins Katherine B Schaefer	k.b.dobbins@sbcglobal.net	7717 Grassland Dr Fort Worth TX 76133	TX	Teacher	EM			WN	1985
Dobbs Jeraldine Scherer	(262)549-1648	810 Greenmeadow Dr Waukesha WI 53188	SW	Teacher	EM			MQ	2000
Dobbs Scot D	(605)430-0482 scot.dobbs@zionrc.org	818 E Iowa St Rapid City SD 57701	SD	Teacher	Tchr	Zion Rapid City SD	(605)342-5749	CQ	2018
Dobler Janet R Sanford	(316)648-4030 janetdobler@yahoo.com	2013 N Glen Wood Ct Wichita KS 67230	KS	Teacher	EM			CQ	2005
Dobler Lori A Holey	loridobler@gmail.com	1370 Linden CV Dewitt MI 48820	MI	Teacher	EM			RF	1983
Dodd Katie A Shinkwin	(209)605-9373 katie.a.dodd@gmail.com	1029 Johnston St Napa CA 94558	CNH	Teacher	C08/2019			SP	2010
Dodge Katherine A	(262)313-8232 katedodge92@gmail.com	2607 Meadowbrook Rd. Waukesha WI 53188	SW	Teacher	Tchr	Blessed Savior New Berlin WI	(262)786-6465	CQ	2024
Dodgers Betsy A Deac	(708)209-3502 betsy.dodgers@cuchicago.edu		NI	Deaconess	S HS/C	Concordia University Chicago River Forest IL	(708)771-8300	CH	2010
Doebele Mark E	(303)841-5551		RM	Teacher	Tchr	Lutheran Parker CO	(303)841-5551	S	2000
Doebler Lynda	(248)651-9226	828 Miller Ave Rochester MI 48307	MI	Teacher	EM			S	1973
Doede Gary E	(410)947-4645	415 N Rock Glen Rd Baltimore MD 21229	SE	Teacher	Tchr	Concordia Towson MD	(410)825-2323	BR	1989
Doederlein Karen A	(863)241-8547	145 Lowell Rd Winter Haven FL 33884	FG	Teacher	C07/2016			RF	1979
Doel Michele L Deac	(208)451-6237 doel.michele@gmail.com	3137 Hickory St Portage IN 46368	IN	Deaconess	Mem C	Saint Johns Laporte IN	(219)362-3726	SL-DEAC	2020
Doell Lorraine K Forslund	(715)758-8532 l.doell@stpaulbonduel.com	137 N Adams St Bonduel WI 54107	NW	Teacher	Tchr	St Paul Bonduel WI	(715)758-8532	MQ	1987
Doell Nathaniel D	(715)853-2458 claymaker34doell@gmail.com	176 Country Club Dr Clintonville WI 54929	NW	Teacher	Tchr	St Martin Clintonville WI	(715)823-6538	MQ	2016
Doelling Michelle L	(573)797-0158 mdoelling@trinityjc.org	1327 Westview Dr Jefferson Cty MO 65109	MO	Teacher	Tchr	Trinity Jefferson City MO	(573)636-6750	S	1999
Doellinger D D	(937)644-0576 weaverwood8@gmail.com	13498 Weaver Rd Marysville OH 43040	OH	Teacher	EM			RF	1978
Doellinger Janet S Schanbacher	(319)721-8014 jandoell@icloud.com	6843 Waterview Dr SW Cedar Rapids IA 52404	IE	Teacher	EM			S	1973
Doenges Joanne E Wing	(419)438-0444 doengesjoanne@gmail.com	5679 Monroe St Unit 1012 Sylvania OH 43560	OH	Teacher	EM			CQ	2004
Doepner Mark D	(260)615-5561 nate7791@aol.com	2020 Lakewood Dr Fort Wayne IN 46819	IN	Teacher	EM			RF	1976
Doering Brenda J Monsees	(314)330-1898 bdoering@doeringeng.com	4551 Kerth Forest Dr Saint Louis MO 63128	MO	Teacher	EM			CQ	2006
Doering Dwight R Dr	(949)376-7837 dwight.doering@cui.edu	3470 Westhampton Way Gainesville GA 30506	PSW	Teacher	S HS/C	Concordia University Irvine Irvine CA	(949)854-8002	RF	1980
Doering Matthew D	(832)260-4585 matt@narrative.church		TX	DCE	Mem C	Narrative Round Rock TX		AU	2013
Doering Michael D	(512)461-7409 mike.doering10@gmail.com	1009 Sue Ann Rose Dr Austin TX 78717	TX	Teacher	C07/2022			S	2004
Doering Sandra K Snyder Dr	(512)656-9057 sdoering@aol.com	2974 Wolfcreek New Braunfels TX 78130	TX	Teacher	EM			RF	1971
Doerr Faith R Schultze	(402)649-4358 faith.doerr@gmail.com	7212 N 140th Ave Omaha NE 68142	NEB	Teacher	Tchr	Concordia Omaha NE	(402)445-4000	CQ	2019
Doerr Kara L Krause	(414)581-2442 kdoerr@hcl.org	W223N2626 Springwood Lane Pewaukee WI 53186	EN	Teacher	Tchr	Hales Corners Hales Corners WI	(414)529-6701	MQ	2025
Doerr Paul A	(414)327-6894 pdoerr80@yahoo.com	2945 S 45th St Milwaukee WI 53219	SW	Teacher	EM			S	1980
Doerr Preston P	(402)394-7060 preston.doerr@gmail.com	7212 N 140th Ave Omaha NE 68142	NEB	Teacher	Tchr	Concordia Omaha NE	(402)445-4000	S	2013

*Multiple Assignments (See Church Worker Locator for Additional Details)
See Page 53 for the Table of Abbreviations for key to District, Classification, Position, and College abbreviations.
**C =Candidate; EM =Emeritus; the date following the C is the month and year the Candidate status began

NAME	TELEPHONE NUMBER EMAIL	STREET ADDRESS CITY/STATE/ZIP	DISTRICT	CLASS.	POSITION/ STATUS**	WHERE SERVING	OFFICE PHONE	COLLEGE/ UNIV/CQ	YR GRAD
Doesken Debra A Runke	(316)651-6462 debdoesken@flsderby.com	1046 N Kokomo Ave Derby KS 67037	KS	Teacher	Tchr	Faith Derby KS	(316)788-1715	S	1986
Doherty Patrick J III	(414)617-1985 pdo3424@yahoo.com	W125S9395 Prairie Meadows Dr Muskego WI 53150	EN	Teacher	Tchr	Hales Corners Hales Corners WI	(414)529-6701	MQ	2007
Dohring Margarete C Berndt	(360)427-3165 daycaremolc@comcast.net	2105 Laurel St. Shelton WA 98584	NOW	Teacher	Tchr	Mount Olive Shelton WA	(360)427-3165	PO	1984
Dohrmann Jane M Bergman	jane_dtrinity@yahoo.com	2213 S Van Buren Rd Reese MI 48757	MI	Teacher	EM			RF	1976
Dolak Allison K Fridley Dr	(402)617-2052 allisonkaydolak@gmail.com	713 Victorywynd Ct Lake St Louis MO 63367	MO	Teacher	Prin	Immanuel Wentzville MO	(636)639-9887	S	2002
Dolak Edward D Dr	(636)625-0456 edavid.dolak@gmail.com	2020 Paul Renaud Blvd Lake St Louis MO 63367	MO	Teacher	EM			S	1964
Dolan Gretchen E Hintze	gdolan17@gmail.com	16650 59th Ave N Plymouth MN 55446	MNS	Teacher	Tchr	St Johns Chaska MN	(952)448-2526	MQ	1998
Dolde Emma M Wendorff	(507)766-0073 emmadolde@gmail.com	P.O. Box 166 Grand Mound IA 52751	IE	Teacher	C06/2020			S	2018
Dolde Mark D	mdolde@clhscadets.com	7322 Winnebago Dr Fort Wayne IN 46815	IN	Teacher	Tchr	Concordia Fort Wayne IN	(260)483-1102	RF	1994
Dolen Lisa L Harris	(217)473-9401 dolen217@gmail.com	2416 Flaxen Mill Ct Springfield IL 62704	CI	Teacher	C04/2019			AA	1992
Dollevoet Nicole L Kunda	(920)540-1761 dcenicoled@gmail.com	526 Denison Cir Sheboygan Falls WI 53085	SW	DCM	Mem C	St Paul Sheboygan Falls WI	(920)467-6449	MQ	2000
Dolliver LaVonne M King	(972)977-5839 lmdolliver@yahoo.com	225 Woodside Ln Tallmadge OH 44278	OH	Teacher	EM			AU	2009
Domann Marsha D Wiese	(832)326-1952 mdwiese@hotmail.com	12116 E Parallel Rd Haven KS 67543	TX	Teacher	C08/2019			S	1998
Dombkowski Amy M Russell	(765)250-1804	2171 Kestral Blvd W Lafayette IN 47906	IN	Teacher	Tchr	St James Lafayette IN	(765)742-6464	CQ	1999
Dombrowski Renee K	(504)606-6208 rbrowski04@yahoo.com	3305 California Ave Kenner LA 70065	SO	Teacher	C07/2016			MQ	2004
Domeier Sue A Werling	(630)841-2541 dome27@sbcglobal.net	25w689 Macarthur Ave Carol Stream IL 60188	NI	Teacher	D Ex/S	Northern Illinois District River Forest IL	(708)449-3020	RF	1977
Domke Amelia V	amelia.domke@stjohnglendale.com		SW	Teacher	Tchr	St Johns Glendale WI	(414)352-4150	MQ	2023
Domsch Allison K Bork	(314)578-7145 allidomsch@gmail.com	16012 Fowler Ave Omaha NE 68116	NEB	Teacher	C07/2016			S	2005
Domsch Christopher L	(816) 916-1980 c.g.domsch@gmail.com	1955 S La Frenz Rd Liberty MO 64068	MO	Teacher	EM			S	1972
Domsch Nathan T	(402)445-4000 ndomsch@gmail.com	16012 Fowler Ave Omaha NE 68116	NEB	Teacher	Prin	Concordia Omaha NE	(402)445-4000	S	2004
Donal - Fisher Karyn M	(313)938-0560 kdonal4514@hotmail.com	1475 Walnut Ridge Cir Canton MI 48187	MI	Teacher	Tchr	St John Waltz MI	(734)654-6366	AA	1993
Donaldson Amy E Schneider	(224)321-2659 amylovesteaching@aol.com	1001 Georgian Place Bartlett IL 60103	NI	Teacher	Tchr	St Peter Schaumburg IL	(847)885-3350	RF	1994
Donnay Linda J Sommers	(320)510-4048 bltdonnay@gmail.com	1604 Birch Ave N Glencoe MN 55336	MNS	Teacher	Tchr	First Glencoe MN	(320)864-3317	SP	1986
Donnelly Laura J Keller	laura_d@earthlink.net	72 Bryan's Mill Way Catonsville MD 21228	SE	Teacher	EM			BR	1976
Donner Jennifer A Preusser	(314)445-8038 jdonner@zionharvester.org	1012 Pegasus Cir Saint Peters MO 63376	MO	Teacher	Tchr	Zion Saint Charles MO	(636)441-7425	CQ	2020
Dooley Karen M	(605)338-0849 karenmdooley@gmail.com	26715 Buffalo Butte Dr Hot Springs SD 57747	SD	Teacher	C06/2021			CQ	2006
Dopp Sherry E Eggert	(517)262-4839 dopp.sherry@gmail.com	9736 N 95th St Unit 223 Scottsdale AZ 85258	PSW	Teacher	EM			SP	1978
Doraska Mackenzie R Lindquist	(320)905-7135 doraska7916@gmail.com	2563 Cold Lake Trl W Mayer MN 55360	MNS	Teacher	Tchr	Trinity Waconia MN	(952)442-4165	SP	2016
Doring Lois R Prokopy	(973)347-3293 arthurard@yahoo.com	59 Church Ave Islip NY 11751	NJ	Teacher	EM			RF	1957
Dorlac Barbara Groppe	(561)716-1621 bdorlac@yahoo.com	9328 Sable Ridge Cir Apt C Boca Raton FL 33428	FG	Teacher	EM			RF	1970
Dorn Betty A Dierks	(936)273-4423 pbdorn6@gmail.com	6 Steep Trail Pl Conroe TX 77385	TX	Teacher	EM			SP	1980
Dorn Richard J	(979)450-3504 rjdorn@centurylink.net	6117 NW 49th St Johnston IA 50131	IW	Teacher	EM			RF	1962
Dorn Veloyce B Harnapp	(713)682-7168 rev.mpd@gmail.com	1016 Cheshire Ln Houston TX 77018	TX	Teacher	EM			S	1986
Dornak Holly M Barnes	hollydornak@mac.com	P.O. Box 607 El Campo TX 77437	TX	Teacher	Tchr	Memorial Houston TX	(713)782-4022	S	1999
Dorschner Bethany E	(507)329-7686 bethanydorschner.pvlc@gmail.com	711 N 1st St Apt G102 Eldridge IA 52748	IE	DCE/DCO	Mem C	Park View Eldridge IA	(563)285-9035	SP	2025
Dos Santos Fabiana A Deac	(469)803-0706 F.FabianaSantos@hotmail.com	108 Unbridled Trl Caddo Mills TX 75135	TX	Deaconess	Mem C	Comunidad Cristiana Rockwall TX	(214)395-6222	SL-DEAC	2024
Dosil Kelli Johnston	(602)478-6856 kcj33@hotmail.com	3041 E Grove Ave Mesa AZ 85204	PSW	Teacher	Tchr	Christ Greenfield Gilbert AZ	(480)892-8521	CQ	2017
Dost Nanette H Howard Deac	(314)766-6266 ndost60@hotmail.com	7564 Ahern Ave Saint Louis MO 63130	MO	Deaconess	EM			Other	1983
Dotson Michelle N Myslinski	(308)675-0586 mdotson513@gmail.com	4155 Iowa Ave Grand Island NE 68801	NEB	Teacher	C06/2024			S	2011
Dougherty Adam T	(360)801-3972 adougherty@salemorange.com		PSW	DCE	Mem C	Salem Orange CA	(714)633-2366	IV	2020
Dougherty Courtney A Rakow	(847)836-1182 courtneydougherty@sbcglobal.net	211 Howard Ave East Dundee IL 60118	NI	Teacher	Tchr	Immanuel East Dundee IL	(847)428-1010	CQ	2005
Dougherty Isabelle U Upchurch	(919)453-4466 isabelle.upchurch@gmail.com	18692 Villa Woods Cir Villa Park CA 92861	PSW	Teacher	Tchr	St Paul Orange CA	(714)637-2640	IV	2020
Dougherty Jo An M Stolzenburg Walling	(660)492-3957 jmwalling@live.com	P.O. Box 344 Okarche OK 73762	OK	Teacher	EM			S	1969

*Multiple Assignments (See Church Worker Locator for Additional Details)
See Page 53 for the Table of Abbreviations for key to District, Classification, Position, and College abbreviations.
**C =Candidate; EM =Emeritus; the date following the C is the month and year the Candidate status began

NAME	TELEPHONE NUMBER EMAIL	STREET ADDRESS CITY/STATE/ZIP	DISTRICT	CLASS.	POSITION/ STATUS**	WHERE SERVING	OFFICE PHONE	COLLEGE/ UNIV/CQ	YR GRAD
Douglas Chelsea E Sherman	(402)575-7476 chelseadouglas611@gmail.com	8 Amesbury Ct Saint Peters MO 63376	MO	Teacher	C08/2022			S	2016
Douglas Joshua D	(262)995-4511 joshua.douglas@cune.org	208 Cherry Lane P.O. Box 445 Cole Camp MO 65325	MO	Teacher	S Ex/S	The LCMS Corporate Saint Louis MO	(314)965-9000	S	2004
Douglas Melanie J Miller	(830)237-0531 mdouglas@satx.rr.com	287 Wendy Ln Grayling MI 49738	TX	Teacher	Tchr	Cross New Braunfels TX	(830)625-3969	RF	1978
Douglas Tracie N Tessendorf	(317)213-7238 traciedouglas678@gmail.com	2731 N Ridge Ave Arlington Heights IL 60004	NI	Teacher	C10/2023			CH	2008
Douglass Doni A Miller	(402)610-5536 ddouglass@christlincoln.org	200 S Vermont St Cortland NE 68331	NEB	Teacher	Tchr	Christ Lincoln NE	(402)483-7774	CQ	2009
Dowd Kourtney Pottschmidt	(502)551-1949 kourtney.pottschmidt@cune.org	1520 Corbin Dr Milford OH 45150	OH	Teacher	Tchr	St Mark Milford OH	(513)575-0292	S	2021
Dowdell Dorcel D Thrower Deac	(419)283-1434 ddowdell2002@yahoo.com	3331 Aldringham Rd Toledo OH 43606	OH	Deaconess	Mem C	St Philip Toledo OH	(419)475-2835	FW-DEAC	2010
Downey Michelle A Klinker Deac	michelledowney@concordia counseling.org	712 S Walnut St Seymour IN 47274	IN	Deaconess	RSO	Concordia Counseling A Lutheran Outreach Ministry Inc Seymour IN	(812)671-8704	FW-DEAC	2024
Downey Patrick J Jr	(920)222-1384 pdowney@trinitycougars.org	712 S Walnut St Seymour IN 47274	IN	Teacher	Pro Stf	Trinity Seymour IN	(812)524-8547	CQ	2023
Doyle Barbara E Stoll	(989)327-0270 bdoyle@vlhs.com	1101 Park Ave Bay City MI 48708	MI	Teacher	Tchr	Valley Saginaw MI	(989)790-1676	MQ	1995
Doyle Christa J Wehling	(953)373-7200 c.j.doyle2018@gmail.com	P.O. Box 112 West Point NE 68788	NEB	Teacher	Tchr	St Paul West Point NE	(402)372-2355	S	1997
Doyle Jonathan T	(602)540-7142 jdoyle@cclphoenix.org	5402 E Bloomfield Rd Scottsdale AZ 85254	PSW	Teacher	Tchr	Christ Phoenix AZ	(602)955-4830	IV	2000
Doyle Lori B Merritt Dr	(602)540-7149 lori.doyle@cui.edu	5402 E Bloomfield Rd Scottsdale AZ 85254	PSW	Teacher	S HS/C	Concordia University Irvine Irvine CA	(949)854-8002	IV	1998
Drachnik Amanda M Powers Dr	(314)308-0705 adrachnik@gmail.com		MO	Teacher	Tchr	Immanuel Saint Charles MO	(636)946-0051	CQ	2022
Draeger Linda M	(805)579-0624 lmdraeger@yahoo.com	1830 Rory Ln Unit 6 Simi Valley CA 93063	PSW	Teacher	EM			RF	1970
Dragel Denise Schroeder	(630)803-9676 sweet16.ds@gmail.com	1627 Gleneagle Dr Carpentersville IL 60110	NI	Teacher	EM			S	1989
Drager Christopher S	(262)672-7245 chrisdrager@gmail.com	1408 Hillcrest Cir Racine WI 53406	SW	DCE	Tchr	Concordia Sturtevant WI	(262)884-0991	SP	1990
Drake Chase J	(817)240-1766 drakec@csl.edu	1910 Meadow Creek Dr Pearland TX 77581	TX	DCE	C08/2023			AU	2015
Drake Jennifer L Schiemann	(440)357-5323 jennldrake@oh.rr.com	480 Cherrywood Ln Painesville OH 44077	OH	Teacher	Tchr	Our Shepherd Painesville OH	(440)357-7776	RF	1992
Drake Kristin R Meyer	(847)358-7648 huskerwife99@gmail.com	57 E Pepper Tree Dr Palatine IL 60067	NI	Teacher	Tchr	St Peter Arlington Heights IL	(847)259-4114	RF	1999
Dramstad Andrew A	(763)242-5699 aa.dramstad@gmail.com	P.O. Box 386 Trimont MN 56176	MNS	DCE	Mem C	St John Sherburn MN	(507)764-5312	CQ	2014
Draves Thomas J		24 E 2nd St Milan MI 48160	MI	Teacher	EM			RF	1980
Drees Emily A	(713)447-1054 emdrees0407@att.net	319 Little Dog Dr Montgomery TX 77356	TX	Teacher	Tchr	Our Savior Houston TX	(713)290-9087	AU	1997
Drees Leslie A	(402)440-6657 leslie.drees@gmail.com	P.O. Box 6 Daykin NE 68338	NEB	Teacher	C07/2025			S	2006
Dreessen Charles R	(636)349-4416 rdrunner007@juno.com	211 Laverne Dr Fenton MO 63026	MO	Teacher	EM			RF	1972
Dreessen Jean A Ellersieck	(636)349-4416 jdreessen46@gmail.com	211 Laverne Dr Fenton MO 63026	MO	Teacher	EM			RF	1973
Drefke Gary L	(402)371-4489 gldrefke@gmail.com	2612 Crestview Rd Norfolk NE 68701	NEB	Teacher	EM			S	1966
Drefs Katherine R Jeppesen	(605)933-2016 krdrefs@stpaulsconcordia.org	317 S College Drive Concordia MO 64020	MO	Teacher	Mem C	St Paul Concordia MO	(660)463-2291	S	2007
Drelleshak Jeremiah L	(503)984-7347 jeremiahdcm@gmail.com	3251 SE 179th Ave Portland OR 97236	NOW	DCE	Mem C	Ascension Portland OR	(503)665-8821	PO	2009
Drenkow Cassandra S	(608)387-5246 dcecassie@gmail.com		OH	DCE	Mem C	St Paul Napoleon OH	(419)592-3535	S	2010
Dresser Gary J Dr	(603)320-6437 gdresser1@gmail.com	11 Shirley Rd Swanzey NH 03446	NE	Teacher	EM			BR	1979
Dressler Ardyce M Petersen	(253)302-6065 djamdressler@comcast.net	8023 S A St Tacoma WA 98404	NOW	Teacher	Tchr	Concordia Tacoma WA	(253)475-9513	IV	1984
Dressler Justine Biermann	(828)206-4556 jkdressler0712@gmail.com	3775 Estates Dr Florissant MO 63033	SI	Teacher	C07/2016			MQ	2008
Dressler Kelly L	(636)297-5028 kelly.dressler@cune.org	2511 Oakview Rd Apt 13 Fort Smith AR 72908	MDS	Teacher	Tchr	First Fort Smith AR	(479)452-5330	S	2008
Dressler Ronald L	(989)327-4115 babybrenna1995@yahoo.com	8933 N Brookshire Dr Saginaw MI 48609	MI	Teacher	EM			RF	1971
Drevlow Henry J	(714)774-8146 hjdrev@aol.com	2222 E Lizbeth Ave Anaheim CA 92806	PSW	Teacher	EM			RF	1963
Drewiske Rebekah L Mc Collor	(715)213-3180 rebekah@drewiske.com	2531 Abby Ln Wisconsin Rapids WI 54494	NW	Teacher	Tchr	Immanuel Wisconsin Rapids WI	(715)423-0272	RF	1997
Drews Melanie A Reinke	(701)390-6074 farmersdaughter70@yahoo.com	316 N Sampson St Tremont IL 61568	CI	Teacher	Tchr	Bethel Morton IL	(309)263-2417	S	1992
Drews Ronald S	(646)522-7650 rdrews43@gmail.com	33 Ferris Estates Rd New Milford CT 06776	NE	Teacher	EM			S	1976
Dreyer Debra J Bierle	(515)955-5508 djdreyer@frontiernet.net	2242 140th St Fort Dodge IA 50501	IW	Teacher	EM			CQ	1993
Dreyer Nancy L Dressler	(314)882-4446 ndgrumpy@hotmail.com	1896 Pcr 414 Frohna MO 63748	MO	Teacher	Tchr	United in Christ Frohna MO	(573)824-5218	S	2001
Drier Marvin D	(260)701-4419 mddrier@gmail.com	19113 Stronach Dam Rd Wellston MI 49689	IN	Teacher	EM			AA	1984

*Multiple Assignments (See Church Worker Locator for Additional Details)

See Page 53 for the Table of Abbreviations for key to District, Classification, Position, and College abbreviations.

**C =Candidate; EM =Emeritus; the date following the C is the month and year the Candidate status began

NAME	TELEPHONE NUMBER EMAIL	STREET ADDRESS CITY/STATE/ZIP	DISTRICT	CLASS.	POSITION/ STATUS**	WHERE SERVING	OFFICE PHONE	COLLEGE/ UNIV/CQ	YR GRAD
Driessner Johnnie R Dr	(971)235-3608 jdriessner@comcast.net	674 SW 7th St Gresham OR 97080	NOW	Teacher	EM			S	1978
Driller Cathy A Altemann	(719)660-8552 ecdriller@gmail.com	2092 Burroughs Rd The Villages FL 32162	FG	Teacher	EM			S	1977
Drinan Lori J Weir	(989)245-6557 lwdrinan@gmail.com	5355 Nottingham Dr N Saginaw MI 48603	MI	Teacher	EM			RF	1983
Drinan MacKenzie W	(989)284-9473 mkdrinan@stlorenz.org	6 Wilshire Dr Frankenmuth MI 48734	MI	Teacher	Tchr	St Lorenz Frankenmuth MI	(989)652-6141	AA	2017
Driscoll John D	(724)816-6103 jdriscoll@redeemer-oakmont.org	565 Rainier Dr Pittsburgh PA 15239	EN	Teacher	Tchr	Redeemer Verona PA	(412)793-5884	CQ	2015
Driscoll Sarah J Holzer	(724)972-3548 sdriscoll@redeemer-oakmont.org	565 Rainier Dr Pittsburgh PA 15239	EN	Teacher	Tchr	Redeemer Verona PA	(412)793-5884	MQ	2007
Driskill William C Dr	(512)804-0842 williamdriskill69@gmail.com	2530 Muirlands Dr Austin TX 78744	TX	Teacher	EM			RF	1964
Droege Eleanor Baden	(301) 272-4582	9701 Veirs Dr 1-Md 1126 Rockville MD 20850	SE	Teacher	EM			RF	1954
Droegemueller Kim M Albrecht		3162 County Road 208 Giddings TX 78942	TX	Teacher	Tchr	St Paul Serbin TX	(979)366-2218	S	1998
Droegemueller Susan E Michael	(904) 923-9567 tsdroeg@gmail.com	7320 Lake Knoll Ct Cumming GA 30041	FG	Teacher	C07/2016			RF	1996
Droegemueller Wilma A Baden	(217)828-0057 wdrgmlr43@yahoo.com	1530 P B Ln Wichita Falls TX 76302	CI	Teacher	EM			S	1965
Droogsma Ruth E Gust	(763)315-4798		MNS	Teacher	EM			SP	1984
Drouillard Leatha E Jacobi	(336)768-2121 norman2nd@bellsouth.net	122 N Cliffdale Dr Winston Salem NC 27104	SE	Teacher	EM			S	1975
Druckhammer Jaclyn L Wiebold	(360)713-1129 jackie.druckhammer@gmail.com	3912 S 41st Pl Ridgefield WA 98642	NOW	DCE	Mem C	St John Vancouver WA	(360)573-1461	SP	2014
Drum Ruth K Deac	(507)621-8765 rkdrum3@gmail.com	P.O. Box 325 Trimont MN 56176	MNS	Deaconess	EM			RF	1997
Drumm Deborah K	(563)386-4495	3351 W Hayes St Davenport IA 52804	IE	Teacher	EM			RF	1974
Dubberke Robert D	(636)346-1924 coachd87@gmail.com	2705 Mayer Dr Saint Charles MO 63301	MO	Tch/DCE	Tchr	Immanuel Saint Charles MO	(636)946-2656	S	1988
Dubberke Ryan D	(636)489-9333 rdubberke@trinityjc.org	501 Belair Dr Jefferson City MO 65109	MO	Teacher	Tchr	Trinity Jefferson City MO	(573)636-6750	S	2015
Dubert Raymond S	(630)740-9070 raymond.dubert@gmail.com	42884 Ridgeway Dr Broadlands VA 20148	SE	DCE	Mem C	Our Savior's Way Ashburn VA	(703)858-9254	RF	2007
Dubke Benjamin D	(317)998-1315 bendubke@gmail.com	708 Hammond Ave Waterloo IA 50702	IE	Teacher	Tchr	Valley Cedar Falls IA	(319)266-4565	MQ	2023
Dubke Lisa M Brandt	(317)272-4855 dubke1@yahoo.com	8496 Charleston Ct Avon IN 46123	IN	Teacher	Tchr	Our Shepherd Avon IN	(317)271-9103	RF	1993
Duchac Rachel B Kuiper	(262)994-3250 rachelduchac@gmail.com	141 Old Pine Cir Racine WI 53402	SW	Teacher	Tchr	Lutheran High School Racine WI	(262)637-6538	RF	2005
Duclos Rebecca L Arnholt	(913)486-6767 becci.duclos@gmail.com	1725 Bastante Ct Nolensville TN 37135	MDS	Teacher	C07/2016			RF	2003
Duderstadt Lorna	(423)580-1562 tnduder@comcast.net	710 Astor Ln Chattanooga TN 37412	MDS	Teacher	EM			S	1970
Dueck Daniel R	(510)314-7597 ddueck75@gmail.com	9004 Hialeah Circle S North Richland Hills TX 76182	TX	Teacher	Prin	Crown Of Life Colleyville TX	(817)251-1881	S	1998
Dueck Erin L Kirchner	4duecks@att.net	9004 Hialeah Circle S North Richland Hills TX 76182	TX	Teacher	Tchr	Crown Of Life Colleyville TX	(817)251-1881	S	1996
Dueck-Stueber Denise A Dueck	(801)455-5795 stueberslc@msn.com	1905 E Brandon Park Ter Sandy UT 84092	RM	Teacher	C07/2016			S	1995
Dueker Julie K Schmidt	(515)710-6719 jdueker69@gmail.com	4500 Colt Dr West Des Moines IA 50265	IW	Teacher	Tchr	Mount Olive Des Moines IA	(515)277-0247	RF	1992
Dueker Karen L Bathke	(951)206-4838 kdueker@hephatha.net	760 N Shattuck Pl Apt D Orange CA 92867	PSW	Teacher	Tchr	Hephatha Anaheim CA	(714)637-0887	IV	1985
Duensing Beverly A Johnson	(402)228-3180 baduensing@yahoo.com	1818 Summit St Beatrice NE 68310	NEB	Teacher	EM			S	1970
Duensing Don W	(618)367-2101 dond68@hotmail.com	27218 Sandoval Rd Shattuc IL 62231	SI	Teacher	P/Tchr	Christ Our Rock Centralia IL	(618)226-3315	S	1992
Duensing Elden F	(402)643-6324	500 Heartland Park Dr # 212 Seward NE 68434	NEB	Teacher	EM			S	1953
Duensing Lonnie G	(402)228-3180 baduensing@yahoo.com	1818 Summit St Beatrice NE 68310	NEB	Teacher	EM			S	1970
Duensing-Werner Audrey M Duensing	(402)641-9810 dceaudrey@gmail.com	19220 Space Center Blvd Apt 513 Houston TX 77058	TX	DCE	Mem C	Gloria Dei Houston TX	(281)333-4535	SP	1992
Duerr Jasmine E Biermann	(314)546-8536 jasmineelise86@gmail.com	4937 Brookton Way Saint Louis MO 63128	SI	Teacher	C07/2016			MQ	2008
Duerr Margaret A Dunn	(714)310-0821 duerr@lhsoc.org	4604 E Blue Jay Ave Orange CA 92869	PSW	Teacher	Tchr	Orange County Orange CA	(714)998-5151	IV	1990
Duerr Paul L	(209)663-2715 pduerr@gmail.com	120 N California St Lodi CA 95240	CNH	Teacher	Tchr	St Peter Lodi CA	(209)333-2223	CQ	2016
Duerr Philip G		4604 E Blue Jay Ave Orange CA 92869	PSW	Teacher	Tchr	Salem Orange CA	(714)639-1946	IV	1987
Duesenberg Janyce S Schur	(314) 412-1848	9844 Eagle Hill Ln Saint Louis MO 63127	MO	Teacher	EM			CQ	2001
Duever Amy R Rengstorf	(785)614-3393 dueveramy@gmail.com	531 State Line Rd Marysville KS 66508	KS	Teacher	Tchr	Linn Linn KS	(785)348-5792	S	2001
Duff Sheryl K	(630)690-1201 sduff@stpeterlcms.org	1617 E Willow Ave Wheaton IL 60187	NI	Teacher	Tchr	St Peter Schaumburg IL	(847)885-3350	RF	1983
Duffy Colleen D Aakre	(651)434-3218 tcduffy5@outlook.com	9291 Avalon Path Inver Grove Heights MN 55077	MNS	Teacher	C07/2016			SP	1990
Duffy Daniel S	(402)984-7686 daniel.duffy@cune.org	1625 S Marion Ave Apt B102 Springfield MO 65807	MO	DCE	Mem C	Trinity Springfield MO	(417)866-5878	S	2023

*Multiple Assignments (See Church Worker Locator for Additional Details)

See Page 53 for the Table of Abbreviations for key to District, Classification, Position, and College abbreviations.

**C =Candidate; EM =Emeritus; the date following the C is the month and year the Candidate status began

NAME	TELEPHONE NUMBER EMAIL	STREET ADDRESS CITY/STATE/ZIP	DISTRICT	CLASS.	POSITION/ STATUS**	WHERE SERVING	OFFICE PHONE	COLLEGE/ UNIV/CQ	YR GRAD
Duffy Julie A Mueller	(303)993-2959	41120 Round Hill Cir Parker CO 80138	RM	Teacher	Tchr	St John's Denver CO	(303)733-3778	S	1988
Duffy Rosemarie	(832)603-0914	12170 Pebble View Dr Conroe TX 77304	TX	Teacher	Pro Stf	Concordia Tomball TX	(281)351-2547	CQ	2011
Duffy Sarah A Sarah Krause	(815)979-4697 sduffy@spbrookfield.org	501 S 8th St Maywood IL 60153	NI	Teacher	C01/2024			S	2019
Dufresne Elisa R Hebel	(760)207-7761 elisa.dufresne@lhssd.org	436 Vista Way Chula Vista CA 91910	PSW	Teacher	Tchr	Victory Chula Vista CA	(619)262-4444	IV	1992
Duggie Rachel Lamonica	(619)729-6640 rduggie@lutheranschool.org	1139 Pepper Dr El Cajon CA 92021	PSW	Teacher	Tchr	Christ La Mesa CA	(619)462-5211	CQ	2019
Duitsman Donald L	(402)560-2469 dduitsman@gmail.com	7024 Eagle Dr Lincoln NE 68507	NEB	Teacher	EM			S	1969
Duitsman Joyce E Reisenbichler	(913)367-7236 jim.duitsman@att.net	713 Mound St Atchison KS 66002	KS	Teacher	EM			S	1974
Duitsman Mark C	(303)249-7841 mark.duitsman4@gmail.com	3473 E Mesquite St Gilbert AZ 80134	RM	Teacher	C07/2022			S	2003
Duke Jacqueline A Villanis Deac	(401)338-5056	101 Greenwood Ln Kingsport TN 37663	MDS	Deaconess	EM			FW-DEAC	2011
Dukes Austin M	(816)456-6638 Austin.dukes@faithmarietta.org	2850 Delk Rd #11a Marietta GA 30067	FG	DCE	Mem C	Faith Marietta GA	(770)973-8877	S	2017
Dukes Erika R Borslien	(701)429-1245 erikardukes@gmail.com	3428 Tinker Pl Bellevue NE 68123	FG	Teacher	Tchr	Faith Marietta GA	(770)973-8877	S	2018
Dumar John E	(586)808-0462 jdumar@lhsa.com	115 Moross St Mount Clemens MI 48043	MI	Teacher	Tchr	Lutheran North Macomb MI	(586)781-9151	S	1982
Dumke Jane L Erickson	(513)277-1374 phil5du@fuse.net	2831 Hocking Dr Cincinnati OH 45233	OH	Teacher	EM			RF	1965
Dummann Matthew D	(262)993-3651 dummann11@hotmail.com	1400 Oakville Waltz Rd New Boston MI 48164	MI	Teacher	Mem C	Guardian Dearborn MI	(313)274-1414	MQ	2006
Dunahoo Lisa M Griffin	(920)562-8502 ms.lisagriffin@gmail.com	1256 Meadow View Ln De Pere WI 54115	NW	Teacher	Tchr	Northeastern WI Green Bay WI	(920)469-6810	MQ	2005
Dunbar Brooke M Garton	(951)232-2376 brooker313@aol.com	5025 Jade Ter Chino Hills CA 91709	PSW	Teacher	Tchr	Loving Savior Chino Hills CA	(909)597-2948	CQ	2005
Duncan Amy J Miles	(810)610-7292 amycldudncan@gmail.com	1426 Long Lake Dr Brighton MI 48114	MI	DPM	Mem C	University Chapel Ann Arbor MI	(734)663-5560	AA	2021
Duncan Sandra J Wiese	(317)502-9571 sanduncan@sbcglobal.net	2927 E Berwyn St Indianapolis IN 46203	IN	Teacher	EM			RF	1974
Dundek Hilary J York	(708)505-3818 dhdundek@hotmail.com	123 Acacia Cir Unit 612 Indianhead Pk IL 60525	NI	Teacher	EM			S	1976
Dunigan Elizabeth Tait	(414)748-8248 lizzydunigan@gmail.com	N132W17521 Rockfield Rd Germantown WI 53022	SW	Teacher	Tchr	Immanuel Brookfield WI	(262)781-7140	MW	2017
Dunkin Suzanne M Miller	(765)461-2760 dunkin6@comcast.net	1035 N Philips St Kokomo IN 46901	IN	Teacher	Prin	Zion New Palestine IN	(317)861-4210	CQ	2000
Dunklau Carol S Bottomley	(402) 372-7270 cpdunklau@gmail.com	1315 Elkhorn Dr Arlington NE 68002	NEB	Teacher	Tchr	St Paul Arlington NE	(402)478-4278	S	1988
Dunklau Edward H	(586)321-3050 dunklauel@comcast.net	16034 Haverhill Dr Macomb MI 48044	MI	Teacher	EM			S	1970
Dunklau Joyce E Greene	(402)277-0142 jdunklau@hotmail.com	21748 County Road P32 Arlington NE 68002	NEB	Teacher	EM			S	1983
Dunklau Linda J Bork	(586)247-5329 dunklauel@comcast.net	16034 Haverhill Dr Macomb MI 48044	MI	Teacher	EM			S	1970
Dunlop Barbara D Peterson	(314)966-5509 dunlopb@msn.com	2153 Pardoroyal Dr Des Peres MO 63131	MO	Teacher	Tchr	St Paul Des Peres MO	(314)822-0447	CQ	2016
Dunn Christine A	(775)443-8396 christine.gansberg@gmail.com	3721 Cattail Ct Northport AL 35473	SO	Teacher	C02/2021			MQ	2016
Dunn Steven E	(618)406-4152 edunn@trinitylutheranministries. org	240 Thomas Ter Edwardsville IL 62025	SI	DCE	Mem C	Trinity Edwardsville IL	(618)656-2918	S	2007
Dunnette Laurie A Sorbo	(618)696-2231 dunnettel@charter.net	2720 Stone Valley Dr Maryville IL 62062	MO	Teacher	Tchr	Salem Saint Louis MO	(314)352-4454	CQ	2015
Dunsmore Sharon K Bruns	(248)682-1792 skdunsmore@yahoo.com	28 Camley Dr Waterford MI 48328	MI	Teacher	Tchr	Our Shepherd Birmingham MI	(248)646-6100	AA	1982
Dunst Morgan N	(715)853-1871 dunstmo@gmail.com	4917 East Douglas Avenue Wichita KS 67218	KS	Teacher	Tchr	Holy Cross Wichita KS	(316)684-5201	MQ	2021
Dunt Abby L Blair	(309)824-8382 abbydunt@trinluth.org	2711 Six Points Rd Bloomington IL 61705	CI	Teacher	Tchr	Trinity Bloomington IL	(309)828-6265	MQ	2010
Dunwell Erin L Grotelueschen	edunwell@bethanylcs.org	24900 W Linda Ln Naperville IL 60564	NI	Teacher	Prin	Bethany Naperville IL	(630)355-6607	RF	1992
Duport Kyle J	(239)233-4994 coachduport@hotmail.com	18382 Manning Dr Tustin CA 92780	PSW	Teacher	Tchr	Saint Johns Orange CA	(714)288-4400	IV	1998
Duport Rebecca H Hirsch	(714)812-5352 dcemom@hotmail.com	18382 Manning Dr Tustin CA 92780	PSW	DCE	S HS/C	Concordia University Irvine Irvine CA	(949)854-8002	IV	1998
DuPree Ronald S Jr	(940)395-8434 DCERonbo@gmail.com	2321 Overlook Ln Denton TX 76207	TX	DCE	Mem C	St Paul Denton TX	(940)387-1575	IV	1996
Durham Richard E	(410)747-9291 rcdurham@verizon.net	6 Sweetgum Ct Catonsville MD 21228	SE	Teacher	Mem C	Emmanuel Catonsville MD	(410)744-0016	RF	1973
Durheim Cheryl M Biel	(540)841-3292 cheryldurheim@yahoo.com	16 Sanderling Ct Sacramento CA 95833	NEB	DFLM	S HS/C	Concordia University Nebraska Seward NE	(402)643-3651	SP	1997
Durheim Michelle R Sonntag	(985)641-7838 durheims@bellsouth.net	5608 Milmar Dr S Jacksonville FL 32207	FG	Teacher	C07/2016			S	1997
Durheim Steven W	(985)285-5486 steve.durheim@gmail.com	5608 Milmar Dr S Jacksonville FL 32207	FG	DCE	C02/2017			S	1997
Durkee Kay A Maasberg	(217)876-8041 kay.durkee@yahoo.com	591 Shadow Dr Decatur IL 62526	CI	Teacher	EM			CQ	1994
Durkovic Nancy J Nowak	abuelita7nancy@yahoo.com	2620 Forest Lk Santa Ana CA 92705	PSW	Teacher	EM			RF	1973

*Multiple Assignments (See Church Worker Locator for Additional Details)
See Page 53 for the Table of Abbreviations for key to District, Classification, Position, and College abbreviations.
**C =Candidate; EM =Emeritus; the date following the C is the month and year the Candidate status began

NAME	TELEPHONE NUMBER EMAIL	STREET ADDRESS CITY/STATE/ZIP	DISTRICT	CLASS.	POSITION/ STATUS**	WHERE SERVING	OFFICE PHONE	COLLEGE/ UNIV/CQ	YR GRAD
Durlacher Stacey L Hoffman	(260) 466-7934 stacey_durlacher@yahoo.com	3611 Three Oaks Dr Fort Wayne IN 46809	IN	Teacher	Tchr	Emmaus Fort Wayne IN	(260)459-7722	S	2004
Duseberg Amanda B Ziemblicki	amandaduseberg@yahoo.com		FG	Teacher	C07/2018			CQ	2013
Dutcher Alan J	(612)298-8958 al.dutcher@stjohns-chaska.org	504 1st Ave NW New Prague MN 56071	MNS	Teacher	Tchr	St Johns Chaska MN	(952)448-2526	S	1987
Dutton Karen Hempel	(216)341-4884 duttonk@oh.lcms.org	10112 Russell Ave Cleveland OH 44125	OH	Teacher	Tchr	St John Lutheran Garfield Heights OH	(216)587-4222	RF	1975
Duwenhoegger Jazmin L Roste	(320)766-5732 jduwenhoegger@ kingofkingsroseville.org	548 67th Ave NE Minneapolis MN 55432	MNS	Teacher	Tchr	King Of Kings Roseville MN	(651)484-5142	CQ	2019
Duxbury Kayla J	(507)458-2013 kaydux@gmail.com	221 Farmers St E Spring Valley MN 55975	MNS	Teacher	Tchr	St Johns Wykoff MN	(507)352-4671	SP	2025
Dvorak Jessica L Elsen	(785)249-8435 jessica.dvorak14@gmail.com	2010 Hawthorne Ct Plano IL 60545	NI	DCE	Mem C	Cross Yorkville IL	(630)553-7335	S	2016
Dwyer Garnet P Arlt	(616)902-0256 radngpd@gmail.com	57 Road 6 Ut Cody WY 82414	WY	Teacher	EM			RF	1963
Dwyer Michelle C Seris	(314)607-9900 michelle.dwyer@flhsemail.org	8148 Little Skye Ct Las Vegas NV 89166	PSW	Teacher	Tchr	Faith Las Vegas NV	(702)804-4400	CH	2011
Dwyer Timothy W	(636)294-0633 tdwyer@messiahnetwork.org	1474 Cochise Dr O Fallon MO 63366	MO	Teacher	Tchr	Messiah Weldon Spring MO	(636)926-9773	S	2002
Dybwad David B	(253)219-1785 dldybwad@nventure.com	7005 Homestead Ave Tacoma WA 98404	NOW	Teacher	EM			S	1972
Dybwad Linda E Braaten	(253)229-0821 dldybwad@gmail.com	7005 Homestead Ave Tacoma WA 98404	NOW	DFLM	EM			S	1972
Dyer Heather N Schepmann	(812)358-1714 ils8dyer@frontier.com	508 Kelly Dr Brownstown IN 47220	IN	Teacher	Tchr	Immanuel Seymour IN	(812)522-3118	AA	1999
Dykes Joyce L Theiss	(210)491-0128	14307 Walmer St San Antonio TX 78247	TX	Teacher	Tchr	Concordia San Antonio TX	(210)479-1477	CQ	1997
Dykstra Sharon L Studtmann	(715)572-4635 sldykstra5@gmail.com	11048 Meadowsweet Ln Roscoe IL 61073	NW	Teacher	EM			RF	1984
Dynneson Donald	(402)643-4486 ddynneson@seward.ccsn.edu	1483 252nd Rd Seward NE 68434	NEB	Teacher	EM			CQ	1978
Eads Lance R	(503)285-6448 sdae.ecnal@gmail.com	4915 N Houghton St Portland OR 97203	NOW	Tch/DCE	C07/2016			PO	1998
Earle Sarah E Fish Zahnow	(989)395-0154 searle@trinitymonitor.org	5807 Two Mile Rd Bay City MI 48706	MI	Teacher	Tchr	Trinity Monitor Bay City MI	(989)662-4891	MQ	2005
Earley Karen L Gross	(989)737-5194 kle291@aol.com	2820 N Raucholz Rd Hemlock MI 48626	MI	Teacher	EM			RF	1976
Easton Andrea L Nannenga	(219)798-4912 aeaston69@yahoo.com	4500 Liverpool Rd Lake Station IN 46405	IN	Teacher	C10/2022			CH	2021
Easton Janet E Fieselman	(303)995-7097 easton6147@q.com	21047 Hawthorne Ln Parker CO 80138	RM	Teacher	C07/2016			CQ	2001
Eatherton Lois C Wehling	(972)742-2845 eathertonlois@gmail.com	12 McCall Ter Saint Louis MO 63105	MO	Teacher	Tchr	St Paul Des Peres MO	(314)822-2771	S	1996
Eatherton Samuel J Dr	(469)435-1000 eathertons@csl.edu	#12 McCall Terrace Saint Louis MO 63105	MO	Teacher	S HS/C	Concordia Seminary Saint Louis MO	(314)505-7000	S	1996
Eaton Charles E	dceaton@sbcglobal.net	605 3100 Ave Abilene KS 67410	KS	Tch/DCE	EM			SP	1975
Eaton Cynthia A Nowicki	(417)438-7458 ceaton1193@gmail.com	507 Walton St Carl Junction MO 64834	MO	Teacher	EM			MQ	1992
Eaton Lynn D Danhauser Dr	(713)775-8235 leaton53@gmail.com	5319 Jason St Houston TX 77096	TX	Teacher	EM			CQ	2010
Ebel Anne M Frank	aebel@lhsa.com	1430 Burlington Dr Mount Clemens MI 48043	MI	Teacher	Tchr	LHS Assn Of Greater Detroit Rochester Hls MI	(248)856-0240	RF	1988
Ebel Hannah J	(586)828-3080 hannaheb145@gmail.com	1430 Burlington Dr Mount Clemens MI 48043	SW	Teacher		South Wisconsin District Milwaukee WI	(414)464-8100	MQ	2023
Ebel Kenneth K Dr	(714)614-2103 kenebel@gmail.com	35 Rocky Knl Irvine CA 92612	PSW	Teacher	EM			S	1968
Ebel William H Jr	(586)828-3078 webel@lhsa.com	1430 Burlington Dr Mount Clemens MI 48043	MI	Teacher	Tchr	Lutheran North Macomb MI	(586)781-9151	MQ	1987
Ebeling David G Dr	(812)339-6503 dave.ebeling@in.lcms.org	1724 E Windsor Dr Bloomington IN 47401	IN	Teacher	EM			RF	1963
Ebeling Melissa A	(707)227-6213 maebling16@gmail.com	3387 Antique Rose Dr Las Vegas CA 89135	CNH	Teacher	C09/2021			IV	2011
Ebeling Patricia A Bickel	(608)756-1459	1814 Saint George Ln Janesville WI 53545	SW	Teacher	EM			RF	1970
Ebeling Timothy J	(608)898-0829 ebelingtim@hotmail.com	1814 Saint George Ln Janesville WI 53545	SW	Teacher	EM			RF	1970
Eberhard Charlotte J Mueller	(989)293-5240 carlie1531@gmail.com	30328 Tigerwoods Dr Georgetown TX 78268	TX	Teacher	Tchr	Zion Georgetown TX	(512)863-5345	S	2018
Eberhard Marcia A Parr	(708)989-1867 marciaeb77@comcast.net	346 Foster Ave Wood Dale IL 60191	NI	Teacher	Tchr	Walther Melrose Park IL	(708)344-0404	MQ	2000
Eberhard Susan L Zoldak	(406)207-1128 eberhard.sue@gmail.com	224 Meadow Point Dr Grand Junction CO 81503	RM	Teacher	P/Tchr	Messiah Grand Junction CO	(970)245-2838	CQ	2014
Eberhardt Mary E Miller	(262)377-6174 marydave1104@gmail.com	2247 Seminole St Grafton WI 53024	SW	Teacher	EM			RF	1970
Eberhardt Melissa D Fehlauer	(414)331-5207 lissy-sweet@hotmail.com	4505 Gunderson Rd Waterford WI 53185	SW	Teacher	Tchr	Concordia Sturtevant WI	(262)884-0991	MQ	2001
Eberhart Robert W Jr	(812)626-0175 reberhart29@yahoo.com	9304 Darmstadt Rd Evansville IN 47710	IN	Teacher	EM			MQ	2004
Ebersole Carly M LeGere	(636)485-5859 ebersolecarly@gmail.com	54 Lauer Court Wentzville MO 63385	MO	Teacher	Tchr	Immanuel Wentzville MO	(636)639-9887	S	2013
Ebert Juanita M Deac	(402)643-4418 Jmebert20@gmail.com	531 N 5th St Seward NE 68434	NEB	Deaconess	EM			CQ	2003

*Multiple Assignments (See Church Worker Locator for Additional Details)
See Page 53 for the Table of Abbreviations for key to District, Classification, Position, and College abbreviations.
**C =Candidate; EM =Emeritus; the date following the C is the month and year the Candidate status began

NAME	TELEPHONE NUMBER EMAIL	STREET ADDRESS CITY/STATE/ZIP	DISTRICT	CLASS.	POSITION/ STATUS**	WHERE SERVING	OFFICE PHONE	COLLEGE/ UNIV/CQ	YR GRAD
Eberts Rosanne Gonzales		3663 Nasa Parkway #603 Seabrook TX 77586	TX	Teacher	Tchr	South Houston TX	(281)464-8299	S	1985
Ebke Harold D	(618)466-0608	5130 Riverwood Dr Godfrey IL 62035	SI	Teacher	EM			S	1962
Ebling Rose C Crockett	(502)442-1474 Eebling@gmail.com	5801 Hartford Ln Charlestown IN 47111	IN	Teacher	Mem C	Grace New Albany IN	(812)944-1267	CQ	2011
Eck Karen S Deac	(219)987-2358 ksue46@gmail.com	14451 N 950 W Demotte IN 46310	IN	Deaconess	EM			FW-DEAC	2012
Eckels Jonah M	(812)774-8883 jeckles@coglcs.com	12446 Lighthouse Way Dr Apt K Saint Louis MO 63141	MO	Teacher	Tchr	Child of God Saint Peters MO	(636)970-7080	MQ	2019
Eckels Patricia L Barton	(812)774-8882 peckels@elsone.org	2008 Joyce Ave Evansville IN 47714	IN	Teacher	Tchr	Evansville Evansville IN	(812)424-7252	S	1994
Eckert Connie M Krueger	(402)992-4056 connieeckert57@gmail.com	W5122 Joe Snow Rd Merrill WI 54452	NW	Teacher	EM			SP	1979
Eckert Dorothea C Fuchs	(956)428-4069	815 N 21st St Harlingen TX 78550	TX	Teacher	EM			RF	1966
Eckert Judith A Cummings	juditheckert1946@gmail.com	765 Summit Dr Waukesha WI 53186	SW	Teacher	EM			S	1968
Eckert Kenneth L	(314)298-3484	11210 Lakewood Crossing Dr Bridgeton MO 63044	MO	Teacher	EM			S	1965
Eckert Linn W	(864)757-8584 leck80msu@cox.net	2 Clear Lake Dr Simpsonville SC 29680	SE	Teacher	EM			S	1970
Eckert Lois C Bender	leenloispng@gmail.com	380 Willow Oak Dr Red Bud IL 62278	SI	Teacher	EM			RF	1962
Eckert Lorraine R Kissau	(616)927-6083 geckert01@sbcglobal.net	535 Lynwood Dr Benton Harbor MI 49022	MI	Teacher	EM			RF	1958
Eckert Michele K Verdon	(864)509-7841 leck80msu@cox.net	2 Clear Lake Dr Simpsonville SC 29680	SE	Teacher	EM			S	1978
Eckert Olga C Deac	(305)542-8714 deaconessolga@hotmail.com	9370 SW 53rd St Miami FL 33165	FG	Deaconess	Mem C	St Paul Miami FL	(305)271-3171	SL-DEAC	2012
Eckert Rodney A	(956)532-0257 raeckert@peoplepc.com	815 N 21st St Harlingen TX 78550	TX	Teacher	EM			RF	1966
Eckhoff Debra S Junkans	(573)377-4177 deckhoff@lsaschool.com	5877 Hwy 52 Versaille MO 65084	MO	Tch/DCE	P/Tchr	Luth School Assoc Cole Camp MO	(660)668-4614	S	1990
Eckhoff Eric A	(816)872-0156 eeckhoff@mlakc.com	6001 Harris Ave Raytown MO 64133	MO	Teacher	Tchr	Martin Luther Kansas City MO	(816)734-1060	CQ	2023
Eckhoff Sarah L Schroeder	(816)394-4329 barnums.mom@gmail.com	6001 Harris Ave Raytown MO 64133	MO	Teacher	Tchr	Martin Luther Kansas City MO	(816)734-1060	CQ	2024
Eckman Robbi L Menke	(636)239-3538 robbi.eckman@imlutheran.org	434 Michelle Dr Washington MO 63090	MO	Teacher	Tchr	Immanuel Washington MO	(636)239-1636	S	2005
Eckman Samuel W	(636)209-1379 sam.eckman22@gmail.com	434 Michelle Dr Washington MO 63090	MO	Teacher	Tchr	Immanuel Washington MO	(636)239-1636	S	2004
Eckstein Joshua T	(706)469-7931 dcejoshuae@gmail.com	1 Whispering Rock Ct O'fallon MO 63366	MO	DCE	Mem C	Chapel of the Cross Saint Peters MO	(636)928-5885	SP	2017
Eckstorm Kay E	(561)698-6027 ke620@yahoo.com	3262 Americo Dr West Palm Beach FL 33417	FG	Teacher	EM			AA	1983
Eden Amanda L Ramiz	(407)222-4354 amandalynneden@gmail.com	2303 Bastrop Circle Bryan TX 77808	FG	Teacher	C07/2016			AU	2010
Eden Joanna C Koopman	(630)743-9636 jjmmeden@gmail.com	1451 Suffolk Ave Westchester IL 60154	NI	Teacher	C12/2016			S	2002
Edenfield Marilyn J Kluck	(734)479-6337 edenfield2@comcast.net	19545 Wherle Dr Brownstown MI 48193	MI	Teacher	EM			RF	1968
Edgar Stephanie L Roegner	(314)640-8601 kumbawatta@gmail.com	11930 Canterwood Dr Jacksonville FL 32246	FG	Teacher	Tchr	Grace Jacksonville FL	(904)928-9136	SP	2007
Edge Aleen D	(913)522-9106 aedge123@aol.com	852 N Sycamore Ct Gardner KS 66030	KS	Teacher	C07/2016			SP	1979
Edge Michael A	(512)810-9173 mikeedge08@gmail.com	6759 W El Cortez Pl Peoria AZ 85383	PSW	DCE	Mem C	St Mark Phoenix AZ	(602)992-1980	AU	2009
Edgington Paige L Hershberger	(316) 617-4567 dcepaige@gmail.com		NEB	DCE	Mem C	Beautiful Savior Lavista NE	(402)331-7376	S	2013
Edmison Gordon D	(612)708-0173 weglaad@aol.com	2461 Deerwoods Ct Mayer MN 55360	MNS	Teacher	Tchr	First Glencoe MN	(320)864-3317	S	1985
Edmiston Mark J	(913)269-9576 principal@elcsmail.org	139 Creekview Rd Hendersonville NC 28792	SE	Teacher	Prin	Emmanuel Asheville NC	(828)252-1795	S	2010
Edmiston Melissa A Webb	(913)526-9989 melissa.edmiston2@gmail.com	139 Creekview Rd Hendersonville NC 28792	SE	Teacher	C09/2019			S	2009
Edwards Esther R Dunlop	(314)599-3882 davidandesther23@gmail.com	423 Shrike Dr Satellite Beach FL 32937	S	Teacher	C07/2025			CQ	2017
Edwards Jennifer L	(224)386-5557 jennifer.lynn9417@gmail.com	1145 N Sterling Ave Apt 115 Palatine IL 60067	NI	DCE	Mem C	Prince Peace Palatine IL	(847)359-3451	AU	2017
Efird Rebecca L Difatta	begird@ctk.me	7311 S Huron River Dr S Rockwood MI 48179	MI	Teacher	Tchr	Christ The King Southgate MI	(734)285-9695	AA	2000
Eggebrecht David W Dr	(262)377-3048 david.eggebrecht@cuw.edu	2362 Stoney Ln Grafton WI 53024	SW	Teacher	EM			RF	1960
Eggebrecht Paul A	peggebrecht@stpaulnapoleon.org	1011 W Washington St Napoleon OH 43545	OH	Teacher	Tchr	St Paul Napoleon OH	(419)592-5536	RF	1987
Eggebrecht Stephanie R Bernath	(419) 591-6087 seggebrecht@stpaulnapoleon.org	1011 W Washington St Napoleon OH 43545	OH	Teacher	Tchr	St Paul Napoleon OH	(419)592-3535	CQ	2006
Eggelmeyer Suzanne Klucas	(216)926-6638 seggelmeyer@bethanyparma.com	7480 Dover Ln Parma OH 44130	OH	Teacher	Tchr	Bethany Parma OH	(440)884-1230	CQ	2016
Egger Caitlin A Fuehne	(618)322-0976 caitlin.fuehne@cune.org	10175 Spring Mountain Rd. Unit 2059 Las Vegas NV 89117	PSW	Teacher	Tchr	Faith Las Vegas NV	(702)804-4400	S	2017
Egger Caleb T	(712)830-5229 caleb.egger@stjohnslanesville.com	1508 Saint Johns Church Rd NE Lanesville IN 47136	IN	Teacher	Tchr	Saint John Lanesville IN	(812)952-3711	S	2011
Egger Christian S	(712)210-5231 christian.egger@cune.org	10175 Spring Mountain Rd. Unit 2059 Las Vegas NV 89117	PSW	Teacher	Tchr	Faith Las Vegas NV	(702)804-4400	S	2018

*Multiple Assignments (See Church Worker Locator for Additional Details)

See Page 53 for the Table of Abbreviations for key to District, Classification, Position, and College abbreviations.

**C =Candidate; EM =Emeritus; the date following the C is the month and year the Candidate status began

NAME	TELEPHONE NUMBER EMAIL	STREET ADDRESS CITY/STATE/ZIP	DISTRICT	CLASS.	POSITION/ STATUS**	WHERE SERVING	OFFICE PHONE	COLLEGE/ UNIV/CQ	YR GRAD
Egger Kayla K Sombke	(712)371-2460 kayla.sombke@cune.org	1508 Saint Johns Church Rd NE Lanesville IN 47136	IN	Teacher	C07/2020			S	2016
Eggerman Laura E Kalbfleisch	(314)497-6686 lauraeggerman@gmail.com	28 Jo Ann Place Saint Louis MO 63126	MO	Teacher	Tchr	Mount Calvary Brentwood MO	(314)968-2360	CH	2012
Eggers David E	(314)355-3326 dossy2@juno.com	13237 Vanderwood Dr Black Jack MO 63033	MO	Teacher	EM			S	1971
Eggerstedt Kim L	(608)397-4901 kg8870@gmail.com	4630 Millatti Ln La Crosse WI 54601	SW	Teacher	EM			RF	1968
Eggert Christine L Stipe	(801)479-4177 eggertcl@aol.com	6314 Bybee Dr Ogden UT 84403	RM	Teacher	EM			CQ	2004
Eggert Jeanette Gibeson Dr	(503)331-1884 eggert.jeanette@gmail.com	12635 SE Lani Ln Boring OR 97009	NOW	Teacher	EM			RF	1975
Eggert Paul W	(708)712-1696 pkeggert@hotmail.com	330 E Butler Ave Grant Park IL 60940	NI	Teacher	EM			RF	1973
Eggold Cheryl B	(262)251-3046 cheryl@eggold.com	W167 N10976 Western Ave Germantown WI 53022	SW	Teacher	Tchr	Grace Menomonee Falls WI	(262)251-7140	MQ	1992
Eggold Hannah R Boehme	(636)357-3377	208 Limerick Ave Wentzville MO 63385	MO	Teacher	Tchr	Immanuel Wentzville MO	(636)327-4416	MQ	2017
Eggold Joshua M	(260)492-6367 eggolds@gmail.com	1810 Kensington Blvd Fort Wayne IN 46805	IN	Teacher	Tchr	Emmanuel-St Michael Fort Wayne IN	(260)422-6712	S	1994
Eggold Stephen F	(314)583-0376 stepheneggold@hotmail.com	520 Arctic Wolf Dr Imperial MO 63052	MO	Teacher	EM			S	1984
Ehle Holly S Gaston	(260)760-9909 hollyehle@frontier.com	2509 N River Run New Haven IN 46774	IN	Teacher	Tchr	St Peters Fort Wayne IN	(260)749-5811	CH	2010
Ehlers Cheryl K Blakeman	(602)803-3868 cheryl@garuna.org	11034 N 36th St Phoenix AZ 85028	PSW	Teacher	C08/2016			IV	2004
Ehlert Emily A	(920)809-9163 emily.ehlert@gmail.com	520 6th St Menasha WI 54952	SW	Teacher	Tchr	Trinity Menasha WI	(920)886-1083	MQ	2014
Ehlert Lorna M Rueth	(815)577-9452 grammamia@att.net	734 S Mecosta Ln Romeoville IL 60446	NW	Teacher	EM			RF	1972
Ehley Kim L Juergensen	(262)339-9873 kimehley@yahoo.com	447 Lilac Ct Grafton WI 53024	SW	Teacher	Tchr	Living Word Jackson WI	(262)677-9353	MQ	2002
Ehrhardt Monica L Heckmann	(713)303-6241 ehrhardtm@trinityklein.org	17902 Crampton Ln Spring TX 77379	TX	Teacher	EM			AU	1985
Ehrman Jennifer M Walker	(480)219-3544 jehrman@cclphoenix.org	17012 N 61st St Scottsdale AZ 85254	PSW	Teacher	Tchr	Christ Phoenix AZ	(602)955-4830	RF	1994
Eichert Carol Piske-Hanneman	(941)714-7863 ceichert@gmail.com	8807 Stone Harbour Loop Bradenton FL 34212	FG	Teacher	EM			RF	1977
Eichholz Diane M Scott	(913)268-8085 dmesaved@gmail.com	13410 W 72nd St Shawnee KS 66216	KS	Teacher	EM			S	2003
Eichinger Kenneth R	(574)248-2259 keneichinger@gmail.com	415 S Montgomery St Bremen IN 46506	IN	Teacher	EM			S	1973
Eickemeyer Lauren R	(713)204-7920 lauren.eickemeyer@gmail.com	11743 Northpointe Blvd. Apt 1233 Tomball TX 77377	TX	Teacher	Tchr	Salem Tomball TX	(281)351-8223	S	2012
Eickemeyer Lynnette L Bohning	(713) 204-7987 lynneickemeyer@hotmail.com	5031 Oak Shadows Dr Houston TX 77091	TX	Teacher	EM			RF	1977
Eickmann Marlene L Raap	marleneeickmann@hotmail.com	5605 Canyon View Dr Castle Rock CO 80104	RM	Teacher	EM			S	1954
Eickmann Nathan A	(720)242-9391 eickmann@msn.com	5605 Canyon View Dr Castle Rock CO 80104	RM	Tch/DCE	EM			S	1956
Eickstead Andrew A	(210)289-5723 andrew.eickstead@lhssa.org	9803 Kerrville St San Antonio TX 78251	TX	Teacher	Prin	Lutheran San Antonio TX	(210)694-4962	CQ	2022
Eickstead Frederick T	(210)415-6488 teickstead@shlutheran.org	10235 Whip O Will Way Helotes TX 78023	TX	Teacher	Mem C	Shepherd Hills San Antonio TX	(210)614-3742	RF	1980
Eid Christine R Krueger	(763)545-6190 christineeid@juno.com	2760 Medicine Ridge Rd Plymouth MN 55441	MNS	DCE	EM			CQ	1986
Eiden Matthew P	(712)229-1818 mpeiden7@gmail.com	4205 S 147 Plaza Apt. 102 Omaha NE 68137	NEB	DCE	C07/2016			S	2001
Eifert James M	(713) 715-9236 eifertjk@aol.com	5010 Bayou Vista Dr Houston TX 77091	TX	Teacher	Tchr	Our Savior Houston TX	(713)290-9087	AU	1992
Eifert Jonathan D Dr	(512)663-7157 prinzipale16@yahoo.com	14839 Craig Ct Warren MI 48088	MI	Tch/DPM	Mem C	Our Shepherd Birmingham MI	(248)646-6100	RF	1988
Eifert Kimberly D Schmidt	(832)266-7252	5010 Bayou Vista Dr Houston TX 77091	TX	Teacher	C03/2022			AU	1992
Eifert Mary M Webb	(512)663-5158 mmeifert1@gmail.com	14839 Craig Ct Warren MI 48088	MI	Teacher	Tchr	Our Shepherd Birmingham MI	(248)645-0551	RF	1988
Eifert Mikayla R	(281)546-3899 mikayla.eifert@cune.org	5010 Bayou Vista Dr Houston TX 77091	TX	Teacher	Tchr	Epiphany Houston TX	(713)896-1773	S	2018
Eigenfeld Janice R Blanchard	(224)595-0323 norskjan@aol.com	305 Chatham Ln Roselle IL 60172	NI	Teacher	EM			RF	1975
Eigenfeld Timothy P	(630)450-5287 tpeigenfeld@gmail.com		SW	Teacher	Tchr	Trinity Sheboygan WI	(920)458-8248	MQ	2015
Eilers Christine J	(808)636-0843	7329 129th Ave NE Kirkland WA 98033	TX	Teacher	EM			SP	1977
Einem Gary E	(281)844-4574 garyeinem@gmail.com	633 Apache Mountain Ln Georgetown TX 78633	TX	Teacher	EM			S	1972
Einem Randy H	(714)293-0126 randy.einem@gmail.com	2613 Willow Park Ln League City TX 77573	TX	Teacher	EM			S	1976
Einspahr Abby C	(510)861-3110 aeinspahr@yahoo.com	9271 ½ Park St Bellflower CA 90706	PSW	Teacher	Tchr	Bethany Long Beach CA	(562)421-4711	S	2006
Einspahr Beth A Lorentzen	(402)643-6305	1260 Eastridge Dr Seward NE 68434	NEB	Teacher	Tchr	St John Seward NE	(402)643-4535	S	1987
Einspahr Byron B	(727)202-8311 beinspahr@tampabay.rr.com	3618 16th Ave N St Petersburg FL 33713	FG	Teacher	EM			S	1972
Einspahr Donna M Pullmann	(775)901-6239 einsteacher@aol.com	9570 Dawning Heat St Las Vegas NV 89178	PSW	Teacher	Pro Stf	Mountain View Las Vegas NV	(702)360-8290	PO	1990

*Multiple Assignments (See Church Worker Locator for Additional Details)
See Page 53 for the Table of Abbreviations for key to District, Classification, Position, and College abbreviations.
**C =Candidate; EM =Emeritus; the date following the C is the month and year the Candidate status began

NAME	TELEPHONE NUMBER EMAIL	STREET ADDRESS CITY/STATE/ZIP	DISTRICT	CLASS.	POSITION/ STATUS**	WHERE SERVING	OFFICE PHONE	COLLEGE/ UNIV/CQ	YR GRAD
Einspahr Jack R	(303)922-5946	47 S Irving St Denver CO 80219	RM	Teacher		Rocky Mountain District Englewood CO	(303)695-8001	S	1989
Einspahr Karen L Klein	(480)370-0533 kleinspahr@yahoo.com	11303 S 213th Cir Gretna NE 68028	NEB	Teacher	EM			S	1979
Einspahr Karla M	(281)998-8834 karla.einspahr@lutheransouth.org	4514 Italy Ln Pasadena TX 77505	TX	Teacher	Tchr	South Houston TX	(281)464-8299	S	1985
Einspahr Kelvin W	(480)648-7632 keinspahr@yahoo.com	11303 S 213th Circle Gretna NE 68028	NEB	Teacher	EM			S	1978
Einspahr Kent Dr	(402)643-6305 kent.einspahr@cune.edu	1260 Eastridge Dr Seward NE 68434	NEB	Teacher	S HS/C	Concordia University Nebraska Seward NE	(402)643-3651	S	1979
Einspahr Kirk D	(509)699-9635 kdeins@yahoo.com	112 E Raymond St Chelan WA 98816	NOW	Teacher	C07/2016			PO	1984
Eisele Douglas J	(360)626-3091 deisele@plsbremerton.org	3030 Keel Ave Bremerton WA 98310	NOW	Teacher	P/Tchr	Peace Bremerton WA	(360)377-6253	S	1982
Eisele Shelley A Vitosh	(402) 239-0900 seisele@stpaulschoolbeatrice.org	40388 SW 75th Rd Odell NE 68415	NEB	Teacher	Tchr	St Paul Beatrice NE	(402)223-3414	S	2002
Eisenbraun Joel A	(832)326-3243 jeisenbraun4@yahoo.com	20907 Broad Hollow Ct Spring TX 77379	TX	Teacher	RSO	Lutheran Outdoors Min of TX La Grange TX	(979)968-1657	CQ	1998
Eisenbraun Kathryn A Wisroth	(812)372-7083 eisenbrp@juno.com	3106 16th St Columbus IN 47201	IN	Teacher	EM			S	1963
Eisenbraun Paul G	(812)372-7083 eisenbrp@juno.com	3106 16th St Columbus IN 47201	IN	Teacher	EM			S	1963
Eisenman Barbara M Kade	(313)806-3111 barb6eisenman@gmail.com	22209 Edison St Dearborn MI 48124	MI	Teacher	EM			RF	1977
Eisert Pamela S Oberdiek	(812)972-4711 pamela.eisert@gmail.com	3743 Lazy Creek Rd NE Lanesville IN 47136	IN	Teacher	EM			S	1975
Eising Christina E Guettler	(313)545-8349 ceising@mac.com	807 N Washington Ave Royal Oak MI 48067	MI	Teacher	Tchr	St Paul Royal Oak MI	(248)541-0613	AA	1986
Eisman Carl S	(414)870-2675 eisman.s0608@sbcglobal.net	134 Wildberry Ln Jackson MO 63755	MO	Teacher	EM			RF	1966
Eisman Kathleen S Ott	(989)708-7149 jkeisman@charter.net	2261 E Gordonville Rd Midland MI 48640	MI	Teacher	EM			RF	1970
Eitel Sandra F	(559)300-2499 dceforjesus@aol.com	2304 E Tulare Ave Visalia CA 93277	CNH	DCE	EM			SP	1995
Eitzmann Taylor M Johnson	(316)305-5314 candteitzmann@gmail.com	220 Greenwood Ave Seward NE 68434	NEB	Teacher	C07/2019			S	2015
Ekberg Christine Otte	(402)860-0725 christinee@oursav.org	2420 W Omaha Ave Norfolk NE 68701	NEB	DCE	Mem C	Our Savior Norfolk NE	(402)371-9005	S	2009
Eklund Rachel E Peterson			TX	Teacher	Tchr	Concordia Tomball TX	(281)351-2547	IV	2003
Eklund Todd E	eklund.todd@gmail.com		TX	Teacher	Prin	Concordia Tomball TX	(281)351-2547	IV	2002
Elfe Jenna M Newman	jmelfe@gmail.com	858 Bradley Dr Hudson WI 54016	NW	Teacher	C07/2022			MQ	2010
Elfman David H	(951)354-9896	10525 Stover Ave Riverside CA 92505	PSW	Teacher	EM			S	1968
Elkins Charlotte D Meyer	(812)371-2302 celkins@immanuelschool.org	3050 E 850 S Columbus IN 47201	IN	Teacher	Tchr	Immanuel Seymour IN	(812)522-1301	AA	1984
Elkjer Sarah R Lohmeyer	(402)440-8285 sarah.elkjer@gmail.com	14855 Thistledown Ln Perrysburg OH 43551	PSW	Teacher	Tchr	Lamb Of God Las Vegas NV	(702)645-4998	IV	2014
Ellefson James E	(630)291-0987 jamesellefson@comcast.net	644 Dordan Ct Gurnee IL 60031	NI	Teacher	EM			CQ	1978
Ellingsen Susan M	(262)896-0151 sellingsen@hcl.org	1707 Swartz Dr Waukesha WI 53188	EN	Teacher	Tchr	Hales Corners Hales Corners WI	(414)529-6700	CQ	2012
Elliott Benjamin C	(949)633-0506 bencelliott@gmail.com	2509 Felicita Rd Escondido CA 92029	PSW	Teacher	Prin	Grace Escondido CA	(760)745-0831	IV	2002
Elliott David W	dave.elliott1919@gmail.com	14801 Woodworth Redford MI 48239	MI	Teacher	Tchr	Westland Westland MI	(734)422-2090	IV	1993
Elliott Gayle L Ward	elliott92011@gmail.com		SD	Teacher	C07/2016			MQ	2006
Elliott Krista S Brandt	(949)520-0456 krista.s.elliott@gmail.com	387 N Clark St Orange CA 92868	PSW	Teacher	Tchr	Saint Johns Orange CA	(714)288-4400	CH	2004
Elliott Sammye L Jager	(573)364-8896 esammye@hotmail.com	11752 State Route Bb Rolla MO 65401	MO	Teacher	EM			SP	1988
Elliott Sarah E Hames Dr	(509)264-4437 docteacher@outlook.com	77 Konley Drive Kalispell MT 59901	MT	Tch/DCE	Tchr	Trinity Kalispell MT	(406)257-5683	PO	2003
Ellis Michael D	(402)965-3897 ellism@wolsa.org	10241 N 186th Ave Bennington NE 68007	NEB	Teacher	Tchr	Concordia Omaha NE	(402)445-4000	S	2002
Ellis Phyllis J Droege	(507)848-7547 del.and.phyllis@gmail.com	531 Copper Mountain Cir Brookings SD 57006	SD	Teacher	EM			RF	1980
Ellis Shannen G Boehler	(262)853-4458 sboehler2007@aol.com	S76 W 16415 Bellview Dr Muskego WI 53150	EN	Teacher	Tchr	Hales Corners Hales Corners WI	(414)529-6700	MQ	2016
Ellison Robert H	(586)610-8962 reelison@lhsa.com	176 Moross St Mount Clemens MI 48043	MI	Teacher	Tchr	LHS Assn Of Greater Detroit Rochester Hls MI	(248)856-0240	CQ	2020
Ellsworth Michael	(443)224-8771 michael.ellsworth@gmail.com	PSC 80 Box 20803 Apo AP 96367	NE	DFLM	C07/2016			AA	2005
Ellwein Kenneth L Dr	(714)606-1177 jkellwein@att.net	2311 Caper Tree Dr Tustin CA 92780	PSW	Teacher	EM			RF	1965
Ellwein Lisa J Rohmaller		398 N Fawnwood Ln Orange CA 92869	PSW	Teacher	Tchr	Salem Orange CA	(714)633-2366	S	1987
Elmhorst Brian D	(920)979-5410 brian.elmhorst@live.com	520 Grove St Manawa WI 54949	NW	Teacher	P/Tchr	St Paul Manawa WI	(920)596-2837	MQ	1998
Elmshauser John M IV	(303)690-8401 j_elmshauser@yahoo.com	1558 Sage Dr Eaton CO 80615	RM	Tch/DCE	C07/2016			S	1972

*Multiple Assignments (See Church Worker Locator for Additional Details)
See Page 53 for the Table of Abbreviations for key to District, Classification, Position, and College abbreviations.
**C =Candidate; EM =Emeritus; the date following the C is the month and year the Candidate status began

NAME	TELEPHONE NUMBER EMAIL	STREET ADDRESS CITY/STATE/ZIP	DISTRICT	CLASS.	POSITION/ STATUS**	WHERE SERVING	OFFICE PHONE	COLLEGE/ UNIV/CQ	YR GRAD
Elmshauser Rebecca A Kaaz	(618)334-4612 rebecca.kaaz@gmail.com	304 Bredall St Perryville MO 63775	RM	Teacher	Tchr	Lutheran Parker CO	(303)841-5551	S	2010
Elowsky Julianna L Pfeiffer	(586)321-2637	3 Jefferson Dr Spotswood NJ 08884	MO	Teacher	C10/2021			MQ	2018
Elsas Sandra L Carlstrom	(309)266-7517	217 Turtle Creek Trl Morton IL 61550	CI	Teacher	EM			CQ	1993
Elsey Hannah	(785)640-4299 hannah@fairmountministries.org	5340 N Cypress St Wichita KS 67226	KS	DCE	RSO	University Luth Mission Assoc Wichita KS	(316)684-5224	IV	2023
Eltiste Emily J	(714)290-0070 emilyjustine22@gmail.com		PSW	DCE	Pro Stf	Crean Irvine CA	(949)387-1199	IV	2012
Elwell Nancy K Langner Dr	(402)643-1289 nancy.elwell@cune.edu	402 135th Dr Amana IA 52203	NEB	Teacher	S HS/C	Concordia University Nebraska Seward NE	(402)643-3651	CQ	2015
Eman Kimberly A Titze	(303)439-2575 kimberlyeman@yahoo.com	10259 Garrison St Westminster CO 80021	RM	Teacher	EM			S	1976
Embree Karen S Reimer	(260)414-4853 kalenas49@yahoo.com	3893 W 900 S Warren IN 46792	IN	Teacher	EM			RF	1971
Emily Cory C	(515)865-8403 cory.emily@molcs.org	620 SE 15th St Grimes IA 50111	IW	Teacher	Prin	Mount Olive Des Moines IA	(515)277-8349	RF	2003
Emmack Susan J Gonder	sueemmack@trinityl.org	24526 Elmhurst Dr Elkhart IN 46517	IN	Teacher	Mem C	Trinity Elkhart IN	(574)674-8800	RF	1986
Enderle Amber L	(573)517-3800 aenderle@t-lutheranschool.org	914 May St Scott City MO 63780	MO	Teacher	Tchr	Trinity Cape Girardeau MO	(573)335-8224	CQ	2020
Endicott Joel	(480)550-1036 jsendicott@gmail.com	62459 Eagle Rd Bend OR 97701	NOW	DCE		Northwest District Portland OR	(503)288-8383	IV	1995
Endicott Ruth A Abbott Deac	(602) 623-9290 steveabendicott@gmail.com	6521 S Granite Dr Chandler AZ 85249	PSW	Deaconess	EM			CQ	2001
Endicott Steven K	(480)393-3801 steveabendicott@gmail.com	6521 S Granite Dr Chandler AZ 85249	PSW	Tch/DCE	EM			SP	1968
Endorf Ann F Erichsen	(218)652-3028 daendorf68@gmail.com	19296 Hilldale Ave Lakeville MN 55044	MNS	Teacher	EM			S	1987
Endorf Katherine M Raphelt	(817)821-7313 kendorf@ccls-st.louis.org	1008 Autumn Valley Ct Fenton MO 63026	MO	Teacher	Tchr	Christ Community Kirkwood MO	(314)822-7774	S	2010
Endrihs Cherie A Theis	(334)494-5807 cendrihs@gmail.com	103 Woodland Dr Enterprise AL 36330	SO	DCE	C07/2016			SP	1993
Enge Heidi A Seiter	(989)652-6329 Heidi_Enge@hotmail.com	11924 Ayre Ln Frankenmuth MI 48734	MI	Teacher	EM			IV	1990
Engebretson Rebekah M Deac	(715)527-0220 rengebretson24@gmail.com	2227 E151st St Apt 12 Carmel IN 46033	IN	Deaconess	Mem C	Epiphany Westfield IN	(317)815-3884	CH	2024
Engel Elizabeth Bandzak	(440)333-2759	2757 Carmen Dr Rocky River OH 44116	OH	Teacher	EM			RF	1974
Engel Nadine L Krupp	(815)468-8925 nadine55@icloud.com	503 Barry Turn Manteno IL 60950	NI	Teacher	EM			SP	1977
Engel Trisha R Wickland	(847)212-6681 trisha.wickland@gmail.com	1860 Great Lakes Dr Dyer IN 46311	IN	Teacher	Prin	St Pauls Munster IN	(219)836-6270	RF	2014
Engelbrecht Rachael A Paterick	(573)694-4479 sparty7178@hotmail.com	2740 Old Saginaw Hwy Grand Ledge MI 48837	MI	Teacher	Tchr	Our Savior Lansing MI	(517)882-8665	RF	2001
Engelby Paul J	(507)235-8173 pengelby@splfairmont.org	411 Martin Ct Fairmont MN 56031	MNS	Teacher	Tchr	St Paul Fairmont MN	(507)238-9492	MQ	1992
Engelhard Cynthia M Elston	engelhardc@gmail.com	5789 Clark Rd Unionville MI 48767	MI	Teacher	Tchr	St Paul Unionville MI	(989)674-8681	CQ	1997
Engelhard Marissa J	(989)977-0388 marissa.engelhard@gmail.com	124 Hamlet Rd Apt 302 Branson MO 65616	MO	Teacher	Tchr	Faith Branson MO	(417)334-2469	MQ	2008
Engelhardt Mark J	dcemarke@gmail.com	48 Connemara Rd Saint Peters MO 63376	MO	DCE	Mem C	Our Savior Saint Charles MO	(636)947-8010	S	1998
Engelking Cynthia L Schap Deac	(810)357-2170 davencindy01@gmail.com	3457 W Farm Road 168 Springfield MO 65807	MO	Deaconess	EM			FW-DEAC	2011
Engen Anthony M	(651)283-3478 tonyengen@gmail.com	14412 Portland Ave Burnsville MN 55337	MNS	DCE	C06/2022			SP	2016
Engerer-Halula Jamie E Engerer			NOW	Teacher	Tchr	Trinity Bend OR	(541)382-1850	MQ	2004
Engler Scott T	(317)617-0564 scengler1102@gmail.com	5807 River Run Trail Fort Wayne IN 46825	IN	Teacher	Tchr	St Pauls Fort Wayne IN	(260)424-0049	CH	2023
Engman Nathan	(281)795-9844 nathan@mlckaty.com	3102 Madison Elm St Katy TX 77493	TX	DCE	Mem C	Memorial Lutheran Katy TX	(281)391-0171	AU	2006
Engwall Hannah M	(727)423-5353 orgelspieler@outlook.com	2300 Hickory Street Casper WY 82604	WY	DPM	Mem C	Mount Hope Casper WY	(307)234-8428	MQ	2021
Ennis Cynthia A Butt	(262)355-6320 cennis@glwh.org	2381 Carriage Run Rd Kissimmee FL 34741	FG	Teacher	Tchr	Grace Winter Haven FL	(863)293-8447	MQ	2000
Enos Judy C Celestin	(504)756-0986 judycenos@gmail.com	300 Ridgelake Dr Apt 200 Metairie LA 70001	SO	Teacher	EM			CQ	2004
Ensrude Corey J	(618)972-2789 censrude@mlslions.org	68 Red Stone Ct O Fallon MO 63368	MO	Teacher	Tchr	Messiah Weldon Spring MO	(636)926-9773	CQ	2013
Enters Britney M Trettin	(262)751-0409 bmtrett@gmail.com	N68W26614 Wilderness Way Lisbon WI 53089	SW	Teacher	Tchr	Immanuel Brookfield WI	(262)781-7140	CQ	2014
Enters David	(414)795-9594	N68W26614 Wilderness Way Lisbon WI 53089	SW	Teacher	Tchr	Martin Luther Greendale WI	(414)421-4000	MQ	2013
Enters David T	(414)243-4211 david.enters@cuw.edu	12800 N Lake Shore Dr Mequon WI 53097	SW	DCM	S HS/C	Concordia University Wisconsin Mequon WI	(262)243-5700	MW	1980
Entzenberger Kathryn S Schmidt	(346)302-2744 kathy.entzenberger@leahdowntown.org	12922 Blackbrook Ln Houston TX 77041	TX	Teacher	Prin	Lutheran Education Association Friendswood TX	(281)617-5189	RF	1987
Enzinger Kimberly J Brock	(812)522-8976	104 W 1050 S Columbus IN 47201	IN	Teacher	Tchr	White Creek Columbus IN	(812)342-6832	CQ	2000

*Multiple Assignments (See Church Worker Locator for Additional Details)

See Page 53 for the Table of Abbreviations for key to District, Classification, Position, and College abbreviations.

**C =Candidate; EM =Emeritus; the date following the C is the month and year the Candidate status began

NAME	TELEPHONE NUMBER EMAIL	STREET ADDRESS CITY/STATE/ZIP	DISTRICT	CLASS.	POSITION/ STATUS**	WHERE SERVING	OFFICE PHONE	COLLEGE/ UNIV/CQ	YR GRAD
Epting Kim E Ostrander	(630)336-4153 EptingK@trinityroselle.com	316 Pinecroft Dr Roselle IL 60172	NI	Teacher	Prin	Trinity Roselle IL	(630)894-3263	CQ	2016
Erb Celeste M Drewes	cerb@trinitylutheranministries.org	481 Buena Vista St Edwardsville IL 62025	SI	Teacher	C04/2017			RF	1975
Erber Phyllis L Bluhm	(812)944-3122 pleas10275@aol.com	1217 Falls Creek Lndg New Albany IN 47150	IN	Teacher	EM			CQ	2004
Erdman Breanna M	(651)707-5494 berdman594@gmail.com	318 Owatonna St Apt 2 Mankato MN 56001	MNS	Teacher	Tchr	Concordia Classical North Mankato MN	(507)388-4336	MQ	2015
Erdman Cassandra E Shirk	(989)721-5107 cerdman@oursaviorhartland.org	P.O. Box 55 Vernon MI 48476	EN	Teacher	Tchr	Our Savior Hartland MI	(248)887-4300	CQ	2017
Erdman Daniel D	(507)351-3469 ils@newulmtel.net	50595 478th St Courtland MN 56021	MNS	Teacher	Tchr	Immanuel Courtland MN	(507)359-2505	SP	1983
Erdman Jacob S	(651)226-5714 jerdman@gslchurch.net	425 Taylor St Apt 1 Kimberly WI 54136	NW	DPM	Mem C	Good Shepherd Appleton WI	(920)734-9643	MQ	2016
Erdman Jerald S	(815)494-5289 coacherdman@yahoo.com	6179 Abington Dr Rockford IL 61109	NI	Teacher	C08/2024			MQ	1996
Erdman Rebecca	rebeccaerdman@saintpetersls.com	343 5th Street Apt. #3 Reedsburg WI 53959	SW	Teacher	Tchr	St Peter Reedsburg WI	(608)524-4066	MQ	2019
Erdman Susan L Darby	(507)359-4575 ils@newulmtel.net	50595 478th St Courtland MN 56021	MNS	Teacher	Tchr	Immanuel Courtland MN	(507)359-2534	SP	1984
Erdmann Brittany C	(952)594-9730 berdmann@lutheranwest.com	2885 Pease Dr Apt 301 Rocky River OH 44116	OH	Teacher	Tchr	Cleveland LHS Association Rocky River OH	(440)356-7155	S	2015
Erdmann Carly J Stramer	(612)916-8589 ccstramer@gmail.com	3811 Wehle Pl Saint Bonifacius MN 55375	MNS	Teacher	Tchr	Trinity Waconia MN	(952)442-4165	MQ	2021
Erdmann Clayton L	(636)447-1361 cerdmann@ilsolivette.org	3202 Eagles Hill Rdg Saint Charles MO 63303	MO	Teacher	Tchr	Immanuel Olivette MO	(314)993-2394	S	2007
Erfourth Lee E	leeerfourth@gmail.com	742 Woodlawn Ave Jackson MI 49203	MI	Teacher	P/Tchr	Trinity Jackson MI	(517)750-2105	RF	1979
Erger Lynne M Essman-Root	(406)256-1639 lynne43713@aol.com	3086 Saddleback Trl Billings MT 59106	MT	Teacher	EM			S	1976
Erickson Angela M Eberhard	(785)713-1108 angelaerickson9882@gmail.com	1106 Alston St Marysville KS 66508	KS	DCE	C11/2022			S	2005
Erickson Bradley K	(785)713-1047 kyleerickson0077@gmail.com	1106 Alston St Marysville KS 66508	KS	Teacher	Tchr	Good Shepherd Marysville KS	(785)562-3181	S	2005
Erickson Chelsea R King	(618)954-9933 cerickson62317@gmail.com	1718 Oakwood Dr O Fallon MO 63366	MO	Teacher	Tchr	King Of Kings Chesterfield MO	(314)469-2224	CH	2012
Erickson David L	(507)268-4329 david@davidericksonillustration. com	411 1st St Fountain MN 55935	MNS	Teacher	Tchr	St Johns Stewartville MN	(507)533-4420	SP	1987
Erickson Debra J	(712)541-7407 ericksondebra22@yahoo.com	2217 S 140th Plz Apt 23 Omaha NE 68144	NEB	Teacher	C06/2019			S	2011
Erickson Douglas	(712)541-7409 douglaserickson@concordia prepschool.org	19 Cedarburg Ct Apt. A Parkville MD 21234	SE	Teacher	Tchr	Concordia Towson MD	(410)825-2323	S	2014
Erickson Jennifer D	(712)541-7406 jennifer.erickson@cune.org	218 W Broadway St Apt 207 Winona MN 55987	MNS	Teacher	Tchr	St Martin Winona MN	(507)452-6928	S	2015
Erickson Katrina N	(920)461-2674 katrinaerickson@pilgrimluth.org	7522 Lone Pine Court Sobieski WI 54171	NW	Teacher	Tchr	Pilgrim Green Bay WI	(920)965-2244	MQ	2025
Erickson Lana L Oerman	(402)333-6953 ericksbl@aol.com	13826 Ames Ave Omaha NE 68164	NEB	Teacher	C07/2016			S	1994
Ericson Berit	(618)340-2846 berit.ericson@gmail.com	2763 Stonebridge Ct Maryvill IL 62062	CI	Teacher	C08/2024			CH	2016
Eriksen John F	(561)498-2339 johneriksen13@yahoo.com	1688 Fern Forest Pl Delray Beach FL 33445	FG	Teacher	C07/2016			S	1995
Eriksen Laurie B Schwarzrock	(561)498-2339 leriksen@trinitydelray.org	1688 Fern Forest Pl Delray Beach FL 33445	FG	Teacher	Tchr	Trinity Delray Beach FL	(561)278-1737	S	1996
Eriksen Tia L Pawlowski	(605)680-4895 teriksen@stjohnbc.net	107 N 6th St Battle Creek NE 68715	NEB	Teacher	Tchr	St John Battle Creek NE	(402)675-3605	CQ	2024
Erke Alan F	(708)805-2218 aerke@aol.com	18741 William St Lansing IL 60438	NI	Teacher	EM			RF	1971
Erke Lynn E Peters	(708)805-2216 aerke@aol.com	18741 William St Lansing IL 60438	NI	Teacher	EM			RF	1971
Erkkinen Linda N Jones	(314)313-5795 erkk51@aol.com	3230 Overlook Ct Columbus IN 47203	IN	Teacher	EM			RF	1973
Erlandson Kenneth W	(218)583-1035 kwerlandson@gmail.com	21099 Country Oak Loop Fergus Falls MN 56537	MNN	DCE	EM			SP	1985
Ermeling Lyndsay K	(480)383-9780 lermeling@gmail.com	1515 East Treasure Cove Dr Gilbert AZ 85234	PSW	Teacher	Tchr	Christs Greenfield Gilbert AZ	(480)892-8314	IV	1998
Ernest Erica C Hodge	(260)493-7235 eernest@cluth.org	1825 Greenstone Dr New Haven IN 46774	IN	Teacher	Tchr	Central New Haven IN	(260)493-2502	CQ	2002
Ernst Rebecca S	(815)621-4439 rebecky2@msn.com	7045 S Riverwood Blvd #103 Franklin WI 53132	SW	Teacher	Tchr	Martin Luther Greendale WI	(414)421-4000	IV	1996
Ernst Susan J Karpinsky	(262)242-3708 sjernst@yahoo.com	12243 N Farmdale Rd Mequon WI 53097	SW	Teacher	EM			S	1974
Ernst Thomas J	(314)383-9778 ternst@stpaulsdesperes.org	1536 Patterson Ln Manchester MO 63021	MO	Teacher	EM			S	1975
Ernst Timothy L	(269)429-7494 tim.ernst@discovertrinity.org	1655 Sun Prairie Dr Saint Joseph MI 49085	MI	Teacher	EM			S	1975
Ernstmeyer Craig A Dr	(573)576-6276 cernstmeyer@hotmail.com	10 Appaloosa Trail Ct Saint Peters MO 63376	MO	Teacher	Mem C	Messiah Weldon Spring MO	(636)926-9773	S	1996
Ernstmeyer Kayla J	(402)540-6176 kayla.ernstmeyer@cune.org	114 W 8th St Kearney MO 64060	KS	Teacher	C08/2025			S	2021
Ernstmeyer Scott J	(402)540-0888 sernstmeyer@gmail.com	903 N 86th St Lincoln NE 68505	NEB	Teacher	Mem C	Messiah Lincoln NE	(402)489-3024	S	1997
Ersland Benjamin E	(402)619-6410 beersland@hotmail.com	10240 N 186th Ave Bennington NE 68007	NEB	Teacher	Tchr	Concordia Omaha NE	(402)445-4000	S	2001

*Multiple Assignments (See Church Worker Locator for Additional Details)
See Page 53 for the Table of Abbreviations for key to District, Classification, Position, and College abbreviations.
**C =Candidate; EM =Emeritus; the date following the C is the month and year the Candidate status began

NAME	TELEPHONE NUMBER EMAIL	STREET ADDRESS CITY/STATE/ZIP	DISTRICT	CLASS.	POSITION/ STATUS**	WHERE SERVING	OFFICE PHONE	COLLEGE/ UNIV/CQ	YR GRAD
Ervin Katie J Dinkel	(260)431-9564 katie.j.ervin@gmail.com	8217 Astoria Hl Fort Wayne IN 46835	IN	Teacher	Tchr	St Peter's Fort Wayne IN	(260)749-5816	CQ	2013
Esala Keith M	(651)260-1563 keith.esala@gmail.com	7022 49th St N Oakdale MN 55128	MNS	Teacher	EM			SP	1976
Escandon Alec J	(440)752-8736 aescandon@lutheranwest.com	27008 1st St Westlake OH 44145	OH	Teacher	Tchr	Lutheran West Rocky River OH	(440)333-1660	AA	2023
Eschelbach Emily R Rodenbeck	(260)615-8125 emilyeschelbach@gmail.com	6896 Blue Star Hwy Coloma MI 49038	PSW	Teacher	EM			CQ	2013
Eschmann Paul D	(989)284-6047 pauleschmann@gmail.com	1029 River Forest Dr Saginaw MI 48638	MI	Teacher	Tchr	Valley Saginaw MI	(989)790-1676	S	1995
Esget Eileen J Sellen Deac	(612)817-9401 eileen.esget@gmail.com	6104 Fairview Farm Dr Unit 404 #404 Alexandria VA 22315	EN	Deaconess	EM			FW-DEAC	2021
Eskam Elaine B Feilmeier	(712)660-9816 elaine.feilmeier@gmail.com	6823 2nd St Frederick CO 80530	RM	Teacher	C07/2016			S	2011
Eskilson Edward W	(209)734-6353	1215 W Mary Ave Visalia CA 93277	CNH	Teacher	EM			RF	1962
Espinosa Faith D	(712)303-1422 faithespinosa17@gmail.com	104 South St Seward NE 68434	NEB	Teacher	Tchr	St Paul Utica NE	(402)534-2121	S	2025
Espinosa Lisa M Wagoner	(712)542-0074 lisaespi4@hotmail.com	2748 200th St Clarinda IA 51632	IW	Teacher	Tchr	Clarinda Clarinda IA	(712)542-3657	S	1991
Esqueda Michelle J Walker	(408)623-8747 mjesqueda14@yahoo.com	225 Carlene Dr Sparks NV 89436	CNH	Teacher	C09/2021			IV	2008
Esselman Adele T Bohnert	(573)986-1600 adele.esselman@gmail.com	5603 Sweet Springs Ct Jefferson City MO 65109	MO	Teacher	Tchr	Trinity Jefferson City MO	(573)636-7807	S	2010
Esselman Luke M	(217)899-1217 luke.esselman@yahoo.com	305 Cleveland St E Coopersville MI 49404	MI	DCE	Mem C	Grace* Coopersville MI	(616)837-7831	CH	2010
Essenburg Sheryl A Skuce	(716)390-2039 tsnburg@gmail.com	285 Robert Dr Apt 1 North Tonawanda NY 14120	FG	Teacher	C07/2016			CQ	2001
Esser Mark P	(612)720-6179 mark.patrick.esser@gmail.com	829 E Lake Ave Baltimore MD 21212	SE	Teacher	C08/2021			S	2018
Esser Paige N Stadler	(402)942-2164 esser.paige@gmail.com	829 E Lake Ave Baltimore MD 21212	SI	Teacher	Tchr	Zion Belleville IL	(618)233-2299	S	2019
Esser Tia M Lias	(605)321-3162 tesser@sflutheranschool.com	725 E 70th Pl Sioux Falls SD 57108	SD	Teacher	ExecDir	Sioux Falls Sioux Falls SD	(605)335-1923	CQ	2012
Essig James P	(407)446-7147 jim.essig@poporlando.com	304 Merin Ct Winter Garden FL 34787	FG	Teacher	EM			RF	1974
Essigman Melissa Parodi	(516)433-4075 melissa.essigman@luhi.org	165 Dartmouth Dr Hicksville NY 11801	AT	Teacher	Tchr	Long Island Brookville NY	(516)626-1735	CQ	2017
Esslinger Lynette E Grube	(260)622-6712 timlyness@aol.com	1803 Brook Ct Ossian IN 46777	IN	Teacher	EM			RF	1964
Esswein Ariana Sadeghipour	(714)998-5151 ariana.esswein@lhsoc.org	2222 N. Santiago Blvd. Orange CA 92867	PSW	Teacher	Tchr	Orange County Orange CA	(714)998-5151	IV	2017
Esterberg Parker A	(612)210-9647 parker.esterberg@mayerlutheran.org	110 Church Ave Green Isle MN 55338	MNS	Teacher	Tchr	Mayer Mayer MN	(952)657-2251	S	2022
Estes Heather L Hahn	(630)842-7151 heather.estes@ilselmhurst.org	0n050 Beverly St Wheaton IL 60187	NI	Teacher	Prin	Immanuel Elmhurst IL	(630)832-9302	RF	1998
Estrada Nancy L Deac	(630)401-6728 lissetnancy@gmail.com	905 E Lake St Aurora IL 60506	NI	Deaconess	C05/2023			SL-DEAC	2021
Ettner Susan K Beyer	(815)713-7058 teacher72@netzero.net	20015 Harmony Rd Marengo IL 60152	NI	Teacher	EM			RF	1972
Etzold Brenda D Dougherty	(573)576-0850 etzoldz@yahoo.com	50 Pcr 424 Uniontown MO 63783	MO	Teacher	EM			CQ	2015
Eubanks Laurie J Stoppenhagen	(618)792-8148 lauriejo72001@hotmail.com	985 W Adams St Nashville IL 62263	SI	Teacher	Tchr	Trinity Nashville IL	(618)327-3311	RF	1981
Euken Philip L	(719)495-0828 psblseuken@msn.com	12045 Greentree Rd Colorado Spgs CO 80908	RM	Teacher	C07/2016			IV	1985
Eustice-Brown Sara A	(360)254-5158 dce@vanflock.org	3115 NE 165th Place Vancouver WA 98682	NOW	DCE	Mem C	Good Shepherd Vancouver WA	(360)254-5158	PO	2007
Evangelista Judy E Kedzior Deac	(847)845-7471 judyevangelista@sbcglobal.net	436 O'hagan Dr Crown Point IN 46307	IN	Deaconess	EM			RF	1997
Evans Carrie L Merritt	(714)702-0701 cevans@bethanylutheran.org	3763 Lomina Ave Long Beach CA 90808	PSW	Teacher	Tchr	Bethany Long Beach CA	(562)421-4711	IV	2004
Evans Clifford H	(303)635-2082 hk2es64@hotmail.com	11559 Decatur St Apt B Denver CO 80234	RM	Teacher	EM			S	1969
Evans David W	evans4lvjc@comcast.net	4531 Excursion Dr Colorado Springs CO 80911	RM	DCM	C06/2022			MQ	2014
Evans Faith T Thorsen	(301)932-1230 bfrevans@gmail.com	7027 Oak Glen Dr Hughesville MD 20637	SE	Teacher	EM			S	1972
Evans Natalie M Brock	(913)752-7845 mrs.nmevans@gmail.com	3175 36 Ave Columbus NE 68601	NEB	Teacher	Prin	Immanuel Columbus NE	(402)564-8423	S	2010
Evans Susan K Workman	(303)635-2082 hk2es64@hotmail.com	11559 Decatur St Apt B Denver CO 80234	RM	Teacher	EM			S	1969
Evans Tracey L Timm	(314)503-1616 tracey@gmail.com	7012 Boyle Dr Austin TX 78724	TX	Teacher	Tchr	Redeemer Austin TX	(512)451-6478	MQ	2008
Evensen George H	(808)271-0490 georgeevensen.ret@gmail.com	3090 Emma Ln Mount Pleasant SC 29466	SE	Teacher	EM			S	1978
Everitt Lori R Nierman	(281)825-7247 everittl@trinityklein.org	1619 Leedscastle Mnr Spring TX 77379	TX	Teacher	Tchr	Trinity Spring TX	(281)376-5810	CQ	2014
Evert Catherine L Dugan	(713)302-2948 iloveteach@yahoo.com	12622 Orchard Summit Dr Sugar Land TX 77498	TX	Teacher	Tchr	Memorial Houston TX	(713)782-4022	AU	1984
Everts Eric N	(262)268-7592 eeverts24@hotmail.com	120 Friendship Ln Saukville WI 53080	SW	Teacher	Tchr	First Immanuel Cedarburg WI	(262)377-6610	MQ	1998
Ewald Gene K	(828)855-2793 cdgkewald@yahoo.com	565 39th Avenue Dr NW Hickory NC 28601	PSW	Teacher	EM			RF	1966

*Multiple Assignments (See Church Worker Locator for Additional Details)
See Page 53 for the Table of Abbreviations for key to District, Classification, Position, and College abbreviations.
**C =Candidate; EM =Emeritus; the date following the C is the month and year the Candidate status began

NAME	TELEPHONE NUMBER EMAIL	STREET ADDRESS CITY/STATE/ZIP	DISTRICT	CLASS.	POSITION/ STATUS**	WHERE SERVING	OFFICE PHONE	COLLEGE/ UNIV/CQ	YR GRAD
Ewald Mark M	(217)895-3103 markewald@aol.com	70 Shorts Dr Neoga IL 62447	CI	Teacher	EM			RF	1969
Ewald Wendy M Gutzke	(612)298-7991 wewaldkok@hotmail.com	9124 4th Ave S Bloomington MN 55420	MNS	Teacher	EM			SP	1979
Ewald William M	(708)848-3206 wm.ewald@cuchicago.edu	1000 N Harvey Ave Oak Park IL 60302	NI	Teacher	EM			RF	1965
Ewell Robert	(402)489-6373 bobandjudy2025@gmail.com	4341 S 45th St Lincoln NE 68516	NEB	Tch/DCE	EM			RF	1969
Ewert Christiana E Wolters Deac	(414)218-9478	714 Woodland Cir Waupaca WI 54981	NW	Deaconess	Mem C	St Paul Manawa WI	(920)596-2837	CH	2016
Exner Carol A Menger	(502)475-4460 jcexner27@gmail.com	1506 Cadet Ct Louisville KY 40222	IN	Teacher	EM			SP	1985
Exner Jeffrey L	(502)475-4452 jcexner@twc.com	1506 Cadet Ct Louisville KY 40222	IN	Teacher	EM			SP	1985
Eyer Susan W Werner Deac	(414)332-0649 sweyer@milwpc.com	4933 N Newhall St Milwaukee WI 53217	SW	Deaconess	EM			Other	1962
Eyerly Kathleen M Bremer	(507)238-1802 eyerly@hotmail.com	443 Lake Park Blvd Fairmont MN 56031	MNS	Teacher	EM			SP	1973
Eyerly Richard A Bremer	(507)238-1802 eyerly@hotmail.com	443 Lake Park Blvd Fairmont MN 56031	MNS	Teacher	EM			CQ	1972
Eyster Carol M Simmons	(989)397-7457 iteach333@hotmail.com	9149 Frankenmuth Rd Vassar MI 48768	MI	Teacher	EM			RF	1991
Eyster Katherine A Luepke	(314)660-0270 kaluepke@gmail.com	4301 Sunridge Dr Apt F Saint Louis MO 63125	MO	Teacher	Tchr	St Paul Des Peres MO	(314)822-0447	RF	2005
Eyster Timothy K	(989)397-4331 iteach4@hotmail.com	9149 Frankenmuth Rd Vassar MI 48768	MI	Teacher	EM			RF	1983
Eyth Sarah E Schurmann Strubbe	(217)491-7280 sarah.eyth@oursaviors-school.org	611 Garvey Ln Chatham IL 62629	CI	Teacher	Tchr	Our Savior's Springfield IL	(217)546-4531	MQ	2004
Ezell Charlotte A Helms	(757)766-2712 iconduct1@aol.com	228 Bayberry Ln Yorktown VA 23693	SE	Teacher	Mem C	Resurrection Newport News VA	(757)596-5808	BR	1975
Ezzo Susan K Phillips Hass	(440)230-5682 suekhass@yahoo.com	18237 Raccoon Trl Strongsville OH 44136	OH	Teacher	EM			SP	1975
Fackler Lisa M Streng	(314)724-4921 lisa.fackler113@gmail.com	85 Du Bourg Ln Florissant MO 63031	MO	Teacher	Tchr	Grace Chapel Bellefontaine Nghbrs MO	(314)868-3232	RF	1992
Faerber Janise M Lehl	(734)765-5172 janiseteach@gmail.com	10942 Buchanan St Belleville MI 48111	MI	Teacher	EM			S	1982
Faga Barry J	(847)890-9362 barryfaga@yahoo.com	636 S 7th St West Dundee IL 60118	NI	Teacher	EM			S	1970
Faga Carla J Cook	cfaga@immanuelloveland.org		RM	Teacher	Tchr	Immanuel Loveland CO	(970)667-7606	RF	1991
Fagalde Patricia	(630)674-6490 pfagalde65@gmail.com	4053 Abigail Way Indianapolis IN 46239	IN	Teacher	EM			RF	2011
Fahlsing Gloria D	(810)287-5311 gfahlsing@yahoo.com	3614 Aboite Lake Drive Fort Wayne IN 46804	IN	Teacher	EM			RF	1982
Fahr Julie K Grienke	(402)640-1645 jfahr5@gmail.com	2831 N Laverna St Fremont NE 68025	NEB	Teacher	EM			S	1989
Fahrmann Marilyn L Morische	(515)571-0367 lfahrmann@gmail.com	248 160th St Alexander IA 50452	IE	Teacher	EM			CQ	1984
Fair Diana K	(260)471-2043 dianafair1@frontier.com	2810 Farnsworth Dr Fort Wayne IN 46805	IN	Teacher	EM			RF	1967
Fairbank Jane Frisch	(805) 423-1974 Jfairbank943@gmail.com	943 Rolling Hills Rd Paso Robles CA 93446	CNH	Teacher	Prin	Trinity Paso Robles CA	(805)238-3702	CQ	2006
Fairchild Noel M Manske	(949)678-8915 dcenoel@gmail.com	14782 Elm Ave Irvine CA 92606	PSW	DCE	Mem C	Light of Christ Irvine CA	(949)786-3326	IV	1996
Faley Kimberly Auman	(260)446-1079 kfaley@esmeagles.com	6702 Shag Bark Court Fort Wayne IN 46835	IN	Teacher	Tchr	Emmanuel-St Michael Fort Wayne IN	(260)422-6712	CQ	2025
Falkner David A Dr	(520)722-9328 dafalkner@q.com	1595 N Saddleback Ave Tucson AZ 85715	PSW	Teacher	EM			CQ	1986
Fanara Annette R Boeck	tga2522@aol.com	15026 19th Ave Whitestone NY 11357	AT	Teacher	EM			RF	1980
Fangmann Dennis D	(314)704-7771 fangmadd@gmail.com	P.O. Box 580 New Harmony UT 84757	RM	Teacher	EM			S	1978
Fanning Kassidy L	(928)580-6569 kfanning@immanuelrapids.com	347 Wood Ave Nekoosa WI 54457	NW	Teacher	Tchr	Immanuel Wisconsin Rapids WI	(715)423-0272	S	2023
Fanta Amy L Carrier	(586)764-2285 amy@camprestore.org	10802 Old M3 5 Pelkie MI 49958	MI	Teacher	RSO	Camp RD Inc Detroit MI	(313)636-4422	S	2000
Fanuke Michael A	(586)255-4023 mike.fanuke@gmail.com	1410 Mill Rd Rockford IL 61108	NI	DCM	C05/2025			MQ	2021
Faris JeAnne M	(406)890-9878 mickeyj2828@yahoo.com	2266 Liberty Loop Rd Cantonment FL 32533	MT	Teacher	C01/2022			CQ	2010
Farless Erika Thompson	(949)697-5608 erikafarless@gmail.com	3209 S Center St Santa Ana CA 92704	PSW	Teacher	Pro Stf	Salem Orange CA	(714)633-2366	CQ	2021
Farley Jodie B Hurtgam	(585)281-3924 roses_14468@yahoo.com	158 East Ave Hilton NY 14468	EA	Teacher	Tchr	St Paul Hilton NY	(585)392-4000	BR	1998
Farrand Thomas J	(269)944-9008 tjcafarrand@comcast.net	23612 Hartwick Ln San Antonio TX 78259	TX	Teacher	EM			RF	1979
Farrar Deborah L Rieth Zaffke	(480)789-3506	8801 W Petersik St Milwaukee WI 53224	EN	Teacher	EM			CQ	1996
Farrell Myra A Schoenleber	(618)971-6645 myfarrell@ymail.com	5975 Eaton Ln Edwardsville IL 62025	SI	Teacher	EM			RF	1977
Farrington Jenna L Duff	(630)437-1039 jenna.farrington1@gmail.com	484 Rabbit Run W Lafayette IN 47906	IN	Teacher	C06/2023			CQ	2013
Farrow Aaron C	(903)814-3627 aaronfarrow@live.com	17 Founders Way Unit A Saint Louis MO 63105	TX	DCE	Mem C	Faith Sugar Land TX	(281)242-7729	AU	2015
Farwell Kristy R Heimsoth	(414)793-5788 kristyheimsoth@gmail.com	452 Town Center Blvd Gilberts IL 60136	NI	Teacher	Tchr	Immanuel Palatine IL	(847)359-1549	Other	2014

*Multiple Assignments (See Church Worker Locator for Additional Details)
See Page 53 for the Table of Abbreviations for key to District, Classification, Position, and College abbreviations.
**C =Candidate; EM =Emeritus; the date following the C is the month and year the Candidate status began

NAME	TELEPHONE NUMBER EMAIL	STREET ADDRESS CITY/STATE/ZIP	DISTRICT	CLASS.	POSITION/ STATUS**	WHERE SERVING	OFFICE PHONE	COLLEGE/ UNIV/CQ	YR GRAD
Fasnacht Hannah R Nissing	(636)448-0278 hfasnacht@stpaulsdp.org	406 Duckett Pl Saint Charles MO 63303	MO	Teacher	Tchr	St Paul Des Peres MO	(314)822-2771	S	2024
Fasshauer Kenneth E	(630) 607-2063 kfasshau@sbcglobal.net	1720 Trent Ct Wheaton IL 60189	NI	Teacher	EM			RF	1970
Fast Carla H Hufford	dook.dook@yahoo.com	567 East 12th Street St. Charles MN 55972	MNS	Teacher	EM			AU	1983
Faszholz Gary W	(586)207-1818 mfasz76@yahoo.com	665 N Fairgrounds Rd Imlay City MI 48444	MI	Teacher	EM			S	1976
Faszholz Mark A	(586)838-7924 mark.faszholz@cune.org	c/o Trinity Lutheran Church 45160 Van Dyke Ave Utica MI 48317	MI	Teacher	Tchr	Trinity Utica MI	(586)731-4490	S	2008
Fattig Ann K Hardin	(308)627-7195 bafattig@gmail.com	4114 I Ave Kearney NE 68847	NEB	Teacher	EM			CQ	2001
Faubion Stacey D Davison	(317)402-2832 faubion@thecalvaryschool.org	120 Sedona Drive Bargersville IN 46106	IN	Teacher	Tchr	Calvary Indianapolis IN	(317)783-2000	RF	2018
Faurot Hannah M Schult	(812)525-9967 hmschult95@gmail.com	140 Stevens Dr Seymour IN 47274	IN	Teacher	C01/2023			CH	2017
Fechik Carol A Voss	(269)624-1457 cafechik@aol.com	78169 Nesbit Dr Lawton MI 49065	MI	Teacher	EM			RF	1972
Fechner Rosemarie Filippi	(847)636-6509 rosiefechner@aol.com	1 S Highview Cir Hawthorn Wds IL 60047	NI	Teacher	EM			RF	1974
Fecht William G	(440)871-3806 wgfecht@aol.com	37882 Ashfield Way N Ridgeville OH 44039	OH	Teacher	EM			S	1969
Fedder Megan J Smith	40743789960 mjosies@hotmail.com	Strada Cezar Boliac 3a Brasov NO 50000 ROMANIA	EN	Teacher	C07/2016			PO	2005
Federwitz Allison A Urbach	(330)812-1296 ali.federwitz@lbt.org	1106 S Main St Concordia MO 64020	MO	Teacher	RSO	Lutheran Bible Translators Inc Concordia MO	(660)225-0810	RF	2000
Federwitz Nathan A	(651)202-6091 nathan.federwitz@lbt.org	8335 Loma Linda Ln Waxhaw NC 28173	MO	DCM	RSO	Lutheran Bible Translators Inc Concordia MO	(660)225-0810	MQ	2023
Federwitz Sarah R Deac	(973)906-2299 sarah.federwitz@lbt.org	8335 Loma Linda Ln Waxhaw NC 28173	MO	Deaconess	RSO	Lutheran Bible Translators Inc Concordia MO	(660)225-0810	FW-DEAC	2023
Federwitz Virginia C Topp	(715)823-3280 duwfed@frontiernet.net	N10048 Buelow Rd Clintonville WI 54929	NW	Teacher	EM			S	1971
Feek Amy S	a_feek@yahoo.com	1108 Village Rd Apt 16a Chaska MN 55318	MNS	Teacher	Tchr	St Johns Chaska MN	(952)448-2526	S	1994
Feenstra Bradley D	(616)844-0858 brad04_92@yahoo.com	14625 Fellsway Run Spring Lake MI 49456	MI	Teacher	P/Tchr	Trinity Muskegon MI	(231)755-1292	CQ	2009
Fehlhafer Stanley O	(402)560-3906 stan.fehlhafer@messiah.us	15700 Havelock Ave Lincoln NE 68527	NEB	Teacher	EM			S	1966
Fehn Kelley J Werderman	(989)295-5763 kelleyfehn@hotmail.com	14389 Grabowski Rd Saint Charles MI 48655	MI	Teacher	Tchr	St Peter Hemlock MI	(989)642-8188	AA	1993
Fehn Lynn A Knoll	(989)642-3047 fehnpk4@hotmail.com	3216 Pruess Rd Freeland MI 48623	MI	Teacher	Tchr	Good Shepherd Saginaw MI	(989)793-8201	AA	1993
Fehr Amber L Wisely	(309)507-2415 amfehr2@gmail.com	820 Grant St Chenoa IL 61726	CI	Teacher	C07/2016			S	2010
Fehrs Troy A	(314)837-7606 tfehrs@lhsn.org	2125 Pohlman Rd Florissant MO 63033	MO	Teacher	Tchr	Lutheran North Saint Louis MO	(314)389-3100	S	1989
Felbinger Darlene M	(716)691-8930 dmfelbinger50@yahoo.com	2a Sunmist Sq Amherst NY 14228	EA	Teacher	EM			SP	1972
Felderman Carol S Carlo	(402)332-6860 csf_oregon@yahoo.com	3207 Brown Rd Oregon OH 43616	OH	Teacher	EM			S	1979
Feldmann Jessica A Koenig Deac	(618)367-1511 feldmannw@gmail.com	4041 5 Mile Creek Rd Salem IL 62881	CI	Deaconess	Mem C	Salem Salem IL	(618)548-3190	SL-DEAC	2009
Fellers Jody Heinecke	(262)388-3014 jody.fellers123@gmail.com	516 Winnebago Dr Fond Du Lac WI 54935	SW	DCM	Mem C	St John West Bend WI	(262)334-4901	MQ	2021
Fellwock Geraldine R	(626)483-6260	825 W San Bernardino Rd #203 Covina CA 91722	PSW	Teacher	EM			SP	1979
Felske Randa R Schultz	(308)379-9302 randa.felske@gmail.com	1136 Sagewood Ave Grand Island NE 68803	NEB	Teacher	C07/2016			S	2004
Felten Daniel K	(661)992-9614	43647 Tranquility Ct Lancaster CA 93535	PSW	Teacher	EM			S	1975
Felten Daniel L	(989)652-4561 dfelten@stlorenz.org	535 Franconian Dr E Frankenmuth MI 48734	MI	Teacher	Tchr	St Lorenz Frankenmuth MI	(989)652-6141	RF	1999
Felten John C	(216)226-7516 jdfelten@att.net	38260 Revere Dr N Ridgeville OH 44039	OH	Teacher	EM			RF	1963
Felten Jolyn R Daenzer	(586)739-5510 jfelten@wowway.com	8991 Clinton River Rd Sterling Hts MI 48314	MI	Teacher	Tchr	Trinity Utica MI	(586)731-4490	AA	1997
Felten Mark G	(586)739-5510 mfelten@lhsa.com	8991 Clinton River Rd Sterling Hts MI 48314	MI	Teacher	Tchr	Lutheran North Macomb MI	(586)781-9151	AA	1996
Felten Michael J	(440)305-4775 feltenm@csl.edu	801 Seminary Pl. St. Louis MO 63105	MI	DFLM	C05/2024			AA	2021
Felten Scott A	(440)779-0219 sfelten@stpaulwestlake.org	3928 W 224th St Fairview Park OH 44126	OH	Teacher	Tchr	St Paul Westlake OH	(440)835-3050	AA	1993
Felton Charity	(260)494-6457 charity.felton4@gmail.com	1617 Gillieron Rd Fort Wayne IN 46825	IN	Teacher	Tchr	St Pauls Fort Wayne IN	(260)424-0049	AA	2021
Felton Faith A Aman	(260)490-6196 ffelton@clhscadets.com	1617 Gillieron Rd Fort Wayne IN 46825	IN	Teacher	Tchr	Concordia Fort Wayne IN	(260)483-1102	SP	1990
Felton Heidi N Gottschalk	(260)609-5294 hngottschalk@gmail.com	710 N Howard St Apt 402 Alexandria VA 22304	SE	Teacher	Tchr	Our Savior Arlington VA	(703)892-4846	Other	2017
Fenrick Jill L Ingraham	(608)754-1260	2140 Newman St Janesville WI 53545	SW	Teacher	Tchr	St Paul's Janesville WI	(608)754-4471	MQ	2002
Fenrick Mark O	(608)754-1260	2140 Newman St Janesville WI 53545	SW	Teacher	Tchr	St Paul's Janesville WI	(608)754-4471	MQ	1995
Fenske Emily K Fairbairn	(248)231-4805 e.fenske@peaceantigo.org	N2011 Old 26 Rd Antigo WI 54409	NW	Teacher	Tchr	Peace Antigo WI	(715)623-2200	MQ	2020

*Multiple Assignments (See Church Worker Locator for Additional Details)

See Page 53 for the Table of Abbreviations for key to District, Classification, Position, and College abbreviations.

**C =Candidate; EM =Emeritus; the date following the C is the month and year the Candidate status began

NAME	TELEPHONE NUMBER EMAIL	STREET ADDRESS CITY/STATE/ZIP	DISTRICT	CLASS.	POSITION/ STATUS**	WHERE SERVING	OFFICE PHONE	COLLEGE/ UNIV/CQ	YR GRAD
Fenske James L	(440)732-1410	28640 Bassett Rd Westlake OH 44145	OH	Teacher	EM			RF	1970
Fenton Nancy E Mohr	(813)814-9092	3641 15th St Riverside CA 92501	RM	Teacher	EM			RF	1959
Ferber Denise M Shelton	(314)709-0151 denise_ferber@yahoo.com	1934 Nightingale Ct Saint Paul MO 63366	MO	Teacher	EM			RF	1980
Ferg Emily J Hintz	(715)250-3449 eferg@stmlc.org	N11066 Meadow Lane Clintonville WI 54929	NW	Teacher	Tchr	St Martin Clintonville WI	(715)823-6538	IV	2010
Ferguson Carl J	(630)745-1229 teacherferguson@aol.com	144 S Martha St Lombard IL 60148	NI	Teacher	EM			RF	1981
Ferguson Lauren E Pankow	(414)364-1363 lpankow@stpeters-columbus.org	5020 Flintwood Cir Columbus IN 47203	IN	Teacher	Tchr	St Peter Columbus IN	(812)372-5266	S	2016
Ferguson Rose E Meinert	(586)808-7484 roseferguson615@gmail.com	5147 Sheridan Rd Saginaw MI 48601	MI	DFLM	C08/2023			AA	2012
Ferguson Scott A	(909)843-0601 saferguson77@gmail.com	1800 Ironwood Apt 21 Fairborn OH 45324	OH	Teacher	Prin	Bethlehem Fairborn OH	(937)878-7050	RF	1999
Ferrebee Duane R	(815)935-5503	1576 Carver Cir Bourbonnais IL 60914	NI	Teacher	Tchr	St Paul Bourbonnais IL	(815)932-0312	RF	1975
Ferrin Robert H			PSW	Teacher	S Miss	Office of International Mission Saint Louis MO		S	2002
Ferwerda Joseph R	(815)459-1670 ferwerdajoe@gmail.com	159 Ridge Ave Crystal Lake IL 60014	NI	DCE	Mem C	Immanuel Crystal Lake IL	(815)459-1441	CH	2007
Festa Dianne L Krause	(623)312-5999 tailskid@cox.net	3812 Saint Andrews Loop N Mobile AL 36693	SO	Teacher	EM			RF	1967
Festa Gerald R	(623)312-5999 tailskid@cox.net	3812 Saint Andrews Loop N Mobile AL 36693	SO	Teacher	EM			RF	1967
Fett Brenda D	(724)316-0504 bfett@zoominternet.net	116 W Water St Saxonburg PA 16056	EA	Tch/DCE	EM			S	1982
Fiala David A	(314)278-9750 david.fiala@lcms.org	734 Santschi Dr Herculaneum MO 63048	MO	Tch/DCE	S Ex/S	The LCMS Corporate Saint Louis MO	(314)965-9000	S	1999
Fiala Robert J	jfiala@ccls-stlouis.org	2129 Quarter Horse Crossing High Ridge MO 63049	MO	Teacher	Tchr	Christ Community Kirkwood MO	(314)822-7774	S	1989
Fiala Trevor R	(636)497-0828 trevorfiala@gmail.com	2228 January Ave Saint Louis MO 63110	MO	DCE	Mem C	Concordia Kirkwood MO	(314)822-7772	S	2022
Fichtner Anna M Bliese	(260)241-5582 ann.fichtner@yahoo.com	211 Caperiole Pl Fort Wayne IN 46825	IN	Teacher	EM			CQ	2009
Fick Jeffrey A	(515)230-6459 jeffrey.fick60@gmail.com	236 Sundew Dr Belleville IL 62221	SI	Teacher	D Ex/S	Southern Illinois District Belleville IL	(618)234-4767	RF	1982
Fick Kenneth W	(262)681-0414 fickkensport@aol.com	2425 Catherine Dr Racine WI 53402	SW	Teacher	EM			S	1974
Fick Matthew D	(262)344-2031 matthew.fick@gmail.com	215 E 3rd St Trenton IL 62293	SI	Teacher	Tchr	Trinity Hoffman IL	(618)495-2545	S	2007
Fick Patricia A Degner	(210)326-8632 patricia.fick@concordia.edu	1319 Piney Creek Ln Cedar Park TX 78613	TX	Teacher	Mem C	Redeeming Grace Austin TX	(512)695-2087	S	1984
Fick Rebecca S Troester	(262)664-3223 bfick@trinityracine.com	2425 Catherine Dr Racine WI 53402	SW	Teacher	Tchr	Trinity Racine WI	(262)632-1766	S	1974
Fiedler Leonard V	(573)833-6188 lenfiedler@gmail.com	1447 County Road 512 Altenburg MO 63732	MO	Teacher	EM			S	1967
Fields Jane Albers	(303)756-2932 fieldsthomas@comcast.net	5680 E Bates Ave Denver CO 80222	RM	Teacher	EM			RF	1967
Fields Sara E Schultz Deac	sistersara@christlutheranjack sonms.org	402 Pinewood Lane Ridgeland MS 39157	SO	Deaconess	Mem C	Christ Jackson MS	(601)366-2055	FW-DEAC	2016
Fiene Sheryl A Waddle	(402)689-7373 sherygrandma@gmail.com	9130 83rd St Apt 136 Pleasant Prairie WI 53158	NEB	Teacher	EM			SP	1968
Fiesman Carole Harris	(312)501-0223 cfiesman@yahoo.com	417 Williams Pl East Dundee IL 60118	NI	Teacher	Tchr	Immanuel Crystal Lake IL	(815)459-1444	CQ	2013
Filter Amanda J	(517)526-3445 amanda.filter@tlsmerrill.com	W3334 County Road P Apt 28 Merrill WI 54452	NW	Teacher	Tchr	Trinity Merrill WI	(715)536-5482	AA	2012
Finchum Luke		10511 Pintail Ln Indianapolis IN 46239	IN	Teacher	Tchr	Zion New Palestine IN	(317)861-5544	MQ	2005
Fincke Shannon M Dicke	(210)497-4556 shannonf@concordia-satx.com	1119 Button Bush San Antonio TX 78260	TX	Teacher	Tchr	Concordia San Antonio TX	(210)479-1477	AU	1994
Fingerle Suzanne K Deac	(815)713-9062 skfingerle@gmail.com	4910 Woodland Ln Sylvania OH 43560	TX	Deaconess	EM			RF	1985
Fink Deborah A Hoffmann	(253)852-2402 teacher_debbie@hotmail.com	10418 SE 196th St Renton WA 98055	NOW	Teacher	EM			PO	1983
Fink Jacob M	(562)305-0815 jacob.fink@concordiaomaha.org	15418 Hamilton St Omaha NE 68154	NEB	Teacher	Tchr	Concordia Omaha NE	(402)445-4000	S	2018
Fink Jessica G Jessica Schrank	(602)323-4726 jfink@stjohnsorange.org	308 S James St Orange CA 92869	PSW	Teacher	Tchr	Saint Johns Orange CA	(714)288-4400	IV	2017
Fink Karl J	(562)972-3454 kfink@bethanylutheran.org	5390 E Canton St Long Beach CA 90815	PSW	Tch/DCE	Mem C	Bethany Long Beach CA	(562)421-4711	S	1983
Fink Kristin K Mc Cann	(714)397-4025 kkfink29@gmail.com	2109 N Williams St Santa Ana CA 92705	PSW	Teacher	Pro Stf	St Johns Orange CA	(714)288-4406	IV	1992
Fink Mary E Dunn Dr	(562)420-5603 mfink@bethanylutheran.org	5390 E Canton St Long Beach CA 90815	PSW	Teacher	Prin	Bethany Long Beach CA	(562)421-4711	S	1983
Fink Mildred R Wheeler	(828) 783-8171 m.fink7161@gmail.com	202 Egrets Landing Carmel NY 10512	AT	Teacher	EM			RF	1960
Fink Nadine C Novotny	(830)708-7011 nfink@crosslcmsschool.org	2437 Angelina Dr New Braunfels TX 78130	TX	Teacher	Tchr	Cross New Braunfels TX	(830)625-3969	CQ	2007
Fink Nancy J Wilson	(573)330-1174 bj1bj2@gmail.com		MO	Teacher	EM			S	1979
Fink Robert J	(830)708-7848 duxwin@gmail.com	2437 Angelina Dr New Braunfels TX 78130	TX	Teacher	Tchr	Cross New Braunfels TX	(830)625-3969	S	1981

*Multiple Assignments (See Church Worker Locator for Additional Details)
See Page 53 for the Table of Abbreviations for key to District, Classification, Position, and College abbreviations.
**C =Candidate; EM =Emeritus; the date following the C is the month and year the Candidate status began

NAME	TELEPHONE NUMBER EMAIL	STREET ADDRESS CITY/STATE/ZIP	DISTRICT	CLASS.	POSITION/ STATUS**	WHERE SERVING	OFFICE PHONE	COLLEGE/ UNIV/CQ	YR GRAD
Fink Ryan W	(562)972-4766 ryan.fink@creanlutheran.org	308 South James Street Orange CA 92869	PSW	Teacher	Tchr	Crean Irvine CA	(949)387-1199	IV	2016
Fink Feys Kelly L Wiegand	(586)212-3357 kfink@lhsa.com	12840 Watkins Dr Shelby Twp MI 48315	MI	Teacher	Tchr	LHS Assn Of Greater Detroit Rochester Hls MI	(248)856-0240	CQ	2012
Finke Bonnie K Mielke	(507)279-1472 bonniefinke@yahoo.com	368 Knopp Valley Dr Winona MN 55987	MNS	Teacher	Tchr	St Martin Winona MN	(507)452-6928	S	1976
Finke Charles W	(414)379-6218 greenheadllc@gmail.com	763 Ravine Ridge Dr Colgate WI 53017	SW	Teacher	EM			RF	1958
Finke Elizabeth C Collins	(713)204-4479 elizabeth.finke@ctx.edu	4700 Shell Ridge Dr Fort Worth TX 76133	TX	DCE	Mem C	Christ Fort Worth TX	(817)370-6242	AU	2012
Finke Julie A	(832)641-4704 juliefinke42@yahoo.com	1831 John Arden #100 Waxahachie TX 76165	TX	Teacher	EM			RF	1990
Finke Larry L	(507)459-0173 finkelarry@gmail.com	368 Knopp Valley Dr Winona MN 55987	MNS	Tch/DCE	EM			S	1976
Finkel Aaron E	(608)415-9813 dceaaronfinkel@gmail.com	7261 Alvarado Ln North Maple Grove MN 55311	MNS	DCE	Mem C	St Michaels Bloomington MN	(952)831-5276	CH	2022
Finkel Linda L Callender	(989)428-3003	6517 N Lakeshore Rd Port Hope MI 48468	MI	Teacher	EM			S	1984
Finley Jennifer H Hogan	(303)520-2464 jennifer.finley@tlcas.org	5403 E Aspen Ave Castle Rock CO 80104	RM	Teacher	Tchr	Trinity Franktown CO	(303)841-4660	SP	2001
Finley Jessica L Buchholtz	(602)516-2180 jessica.finley@rocketmail.com	19 Carpenter St Fond Du Lac WI 54935	SW	DCE	Mem C	Hope Fond Du Lac WI	(920)922-5130	IV	2006
Finnegan Heather J Lewandowski	(708)323-8333 h.j.finnegan01@gmail.com	116 Linden Ln Delavan WI 53115	SW	Teacher	Tchr	Our Redeemer Delavan WI	(262)728-6589	RF	2000
Finnegan Peter C	(708)323-8334 peter.c.finnegan@gmail.com	116 Linden Ln Delavan WI 53115	SW	Teacher	C07/2016			RF	1995
Fischer Caleb D	(573)694-8610 caleb.fischer@lhsparker.org	12838 Arezzo Cir Parker CO 80134	RM	Teacher	Tchr	Colorado Lutheran High School Parker CO	(303)841-5551	S	2021
Fischer Catherine E Murdock	(801)272-1420 cathyfischer1947@gmail.com	5138 S Gurene Dr Salt Lake Cty UT 84117	RM	Teacher	EM			S	1969
Fischer Curtis E	(217)638-5347 fischerone@msn.com	1070 Randolph St Carlyle IL 62231	SI	Teacher	EM			S	1969
Fischer Daniel D	(760)567-5678 dan312fischer@gmail.com	12160 Piledriver Way Colorado Springs CO 80921	PSW	Teacher	EM			S	1973
Fischer Dennis H	(989)652-8394 denfisch09@gmail.com	5999 Elmwood Lake Dr Hudsonville MI 49426	MI	Teacher	EM			S	1970
Fischer Derek J	(414)915-2334 dfischer@lakecountryhs.org	2897 Winnebago Dr Summit WI 53066	SW	Teacher	Tchr	Milwaukee LHS Milwaukee WI	(414)461-6000	MQ	2002
Fischer Franklin J	(360)302-0133 frankfischer2323@comcast.net	2209 S Lloyd Ct Spokane WA 99223	NOW	Teacher	EM			S	1960
Fischer James A	(352)427-4773 jamietaylor814@gmail.com	1668 Walters Drive Grafton WI 53024	SW	Teacher	Tchr	St Paul Grafton WI	(262)377-4659	MQ	2010
Fischer Jonathan M	(972)247-4724	3449 Pebble Beach Dr Dallas TX 75234	TX	Tch/DCE	EM			S	1959
Fischer Karen E Murphy	(586)992-3799 kfischer25@yahoo.com	52175 Southview Rdg Macomb MI 48042	MI	Teacher	EM			CQ	1994
Fischer Karen K Nemmetz	(248)408-8714 kfisch21@yahoo.com	2314 Lake Aire Sheboygan WI 53081	SW	Teacher	EM			RF	1975
Fischer Kathleen D Heckmann	(832)688-9484 khfischer@hotmail.com	9419 Brenham Ct Houston TX 77064	TX	Teacher	EM			S	1969
Fischer Matthew P	(480)510-3757 matt.fischer@oslcnashville.org	6009 Romain Ct Spring Hill TN 37174	MDS	Teacher	Mem C	Our Savior Nashville TN	(615)833-1500	IV	2001
Fischer Melinda A Wiersig		4829 Cedar Spring Dr Highland IL 62249	SI	Teacher	Tchr	Zion Litchfield IL	(217)324-2033	S	1997
Fischer Melissa C Nathan	(720)244-4928 fischer720@gmail.com	4005 Yarrow St Wheat Ridge CO 80033	RM	Teacher	Tchr	Bethlehem Lakewood CO	(303)238-7676	S	2007
Fischer Michael N	(480)706-5119 mikefischer2014@gmail.com	3712 E Summerhaven Dr Phoenix AZ 85044	MO	Teacher	S Ex/S	The LCMS Corporate Saint Louis MO	(314)965-9000	S	1975
Fischer Michelle D Lamka	(720)203-1221 michelledfischer73@gmail.com	9535 Jack Bond Rd Lakeland TN 38002	MDS	Teacher	D Ex/S	Mid-South District* Cordova TN	(866)373-1343	PO	2010
Fischer Robert T	(352)687-1592 rofischer@stjohnocala.org	9 Silver Ter Ocala FL 34472	FG	Teacher	C07/2016			S	1973
Fischer Sheri L Wolken	(254)527-3560 zissfischer@yahoo.com	4050 Fischer Rd Bartlett TX 76511	TX	Teacher	EM			S	1993
Fischer Trina M Baker	(832)459-3241 tmbfischer@aol.com	8019 Oakwood Hollow St Houston TX 77040	TX	Teacher	Tchr	St Mark Houston TX	(713)468-2623	S	1965
Fischer William C	(334)365-0431	3525 N Neva Ave Chicago IL 60634	SO	Teacher	EM			RF	1951
Fischl Mary Jo Bergstrom	(650)544-7325 mjsfis.1967@yahoo.com	5757 Cypress Ave Apt 238 Carmichael CA 95608	EN	Teacher	EM			SP	1972
Fish Cynthia A Hackbarth	(660)621-2903 dcfish882@gmail.com	23887 Cedar Ave Coffey MO 64636	MO	Teacher	EM			RF	1983
Fish Dale W	(989)225-6450 dfish7278@att.net	7278 Blake Dr Bay City MI 48706	MI	Teacher	EM			CQ	1978
Fish Katie A Borcherding	(402)570-3346 katie.borcherding@gmail.com	13 Founders Way Unit D Saint Louis MO 63105	MO	Teacher	Tchr	Zion Saint Charles MO	(636)441-7424	MQ	2022
Fishburn Samuel P	(620)899-3109 educatorfishburn@gmail.com	1424 Highland Ridge Cir Brandon FL 33510	FG	Teacher	Tchr	Immanuel Brandon FL	(813)685-1978	S	2013
Fisher Benjamin P	(308)746-2850	136 Patria Ladera Ranch CA 92694	PSW	Teacher	Tchr	Crean Irvine CA	(949)387-1199	S	2013
Fisher Janet L	(708)705-8492 jlfisher353@att.net	5822 Balfour Cir Fort Wayne IN 46814	IN	Teacher	EM			Other	1976
Fisher Janie B Deac	(314)413-0543 jfisher@ilsw.org	2238 Paris Ave SE Grand Rapids MI 49507	MO	Deaconess	Mem C	Immanuel Wentzville MO	(636)327-4416	SL-DEAC	2022

*Multiple Assignments (See Church Worker Locator for Additional Details)
See Page 53 for the Table of Abbreviations for key to District, Classification, Position, and College abbreviations.
**C =Candidate; EM =Emeritus; the date following the C is the month and year the Candidate status began

NAME	TELEPHONE NUMBER EMAIL	STREET ADDRESS CITY/STATE/ZIP	DISTRICT	CLASS.	POSITION/ STATUS**	WHERE SERVING	OFFICE PHONE	COLLEGE/ UNIV/CQ	YR GRAD
Fisher Jessica E Fleck	(630)390-4276 jessifisher@aol.com	303 Heustis St Yorkville IL 60560	NI	Teacher	Tchr	Cross Yorkville IL	(630)553-7861	RF	2000
Fisher Kathryn A Matern	(518)883-6321 fisherkathryn06@gmail.com	155 Potter Hollow Rd Galway NY 12074	AT	Teacher	EM			BR	1979
Fisher Ruth A Heffelfinger Deac	(480)235-1473 rfisheraz@hotmail.com	14321 N 78th Ave Peoria AZ 85381	PSW	Deaconess	Mem C	Trinity Litchfield Park AZ	(623)935-4665	Other	1977
Fisk A C	(920)261-3119 acfandlafisk@charter.net	700 Welsh Rd Apt 13 Watertown WI 53098	SW	Teacher	EM			RF	1963
Fisk Harold T III	(217)789-2527 tfisk@lhssstl.org	8747 Maple Grove Rd Edwardsville IL 62025	MO	Teacher	Tchr	Lutheran South Saint Louis MO	(314)631-1400	RF	1994
Fisk Katrina A Blackwell	(213)398-9275	168 Taylor St Manistee MI 49660	MI	Teacher	Tchr	Trinity Manistee MI	(231)723-8700	RF	1984
Fisk Makenzie M	(253)495-0249 Makenzieflc@gmail.com	1740 E Fairview Ave Pmb1036 Meridian ID 83642	NOW	DCE	C12/2019			PO	2014
Fisk Rachel Pfotenhauer	(509)594-0203 rachelpfot@gmail.com	1116 Stone Bluff Dr Fenton MO 63026	MO	Teacher	Tchr	Christ Community Kirkwood MO	(314)822-7774	S	2004
Fitch Ricky J	(574)952-9797 rjfitch@hotmail.com	3971 S 550 W Columbus IN 47201	IN	Tch/DCE	EM			RF	1982
Fittje Ruth E Sharp	(402)285-0377 mfittje@telebeep.com	24427 385 St Humphrey NE 68642	NEB	Teacher	Tchr	St John Columbus NE	(402)285-0335	S	1998
Fitzgerald Cherilyn M	(314)749-2392 rogdesign@hotmail.com	11951 Majella Dr Bridgeton MO 63044	MO	Teacher	Tchr	Immanuel Olivette MO	(314)993-5004	CQ	2022
Fitzgerald Erin K Sharp	(714)454-8881 eksharp@yahoo.com	7477 E Calle Durango Anaheim CA 92808	PSW	Teacher	C07/2016			IV	1999
Fitzgerald Lisa J Hinz	(512)568-2462 lisa.fitzgerald@chsaustin.org	609 Wagon Wheel Trl Pflugerville TX 78660	TX	Teacher	Tchr	Concordia Pflugerville TX	(512)248-2547	S	2005
FitzHenry Wendy S Wedo	(541)504-4231 jadereyen@yahoo.com	2407 SW Indian Ave Redmond OR 97756	NOW	Teacher	Tchr	Trinity Bend OR	(541)382-1850	SP	1995
Fitzner Cynthia E	(507)848-5349 cefitzner@hotmail.com	234 N Central Ave Truman MN 56088	MNS	Teacher	Tchr	St Pauls Truman MN	(507)776-6541	SP	1978
FitzPatrick Theresa J Dr	(651)728-0448 fitzpatrick@csp.edu	832 Fairview Ave N Saint Paul MN 55104	MNS	DPM	S HS/C	Concordia University St Paul Saint Paul MN	(651)641-8278	SP	2001
Fitzsimons Annalisa	(407)927-9100 afitzsimons@sllcs.org	399 Brushwood Ln Winter Springs FL 32708	S	DCE	Mem C	St Luke Oviedo FL	(407)365-3408	S	2016
Fjeldsted Kristeen K Kirch	(801)599-5689 kris.fjeldsted@me.com	1074 W River Ridge Ln Spanish Fork UT 84660	RM	Teacher	EM			IV	2003
Fjelstad Jade C Peters	(605)598-7306 jfjelstad@sflutheranschool.com	207 Park St Worthing SD 57077	SD	Teacher	Tchr	Sioux Falls Sioux Falls SD	(605)335-1923	CQ	2024
Flach Robinette A Wendling	(815)791-0362 robiflach@alisrockets.com	14432 N 400th St Altamont IL 62411	CI	Teacher	Prin	Altamont Altamont IL	(618)483-6428	CH	2007
Fladland Paige M Fitzsimons	(219)808-8162 paigefitzsimons@gmail.com	2030 Wintergreen Ct Grand Forks ND 58201	MNS	DCE	C04/2023			CH	2015
Flammann Christine M Indorf	(585)802-9484 chris.flammann@gmail.com	62 Watkins Drive Sandy Hook CT 06482	NE	Teacher	EM			BR	1978
Flandermeyer Michael D	(636)925-0126 m71fland@sbcglobal.net	3010 Sherwood Ln Saint Charles MO 63301	MO	Teacher	EM			S	1975
Flandermeyer Roger H Dr	(660)463-2052 cte51761@centurytel.net	P.O. Box 78 Concordia MO 64020	MO	Teacher	EM			CQ	1982
Flanick Meghan L O Hara		201 N Bowery Ave Gladwin MI 48624	MI	DCE	C07/2020			Other	2016
Flatt Dawn C Zuberbier	dawnflatt@trinityl.org	322 Park Ave Mishawaka IN 46545	IN	Teacher	Tchr	Trinity Elkhart IN	(574)674-8800	CQ	2006
Flattley Blake A	(832)795-6423 blakeflattley@gmail.com	13962 Holt Ave Santa Ana CA 92705	PSW	DPM	Mem C	Bethany* Long Beach CA	(562)421-4711	IV	2017
Fleer Lavonne L Laaker	(402)329-6755 dlfleer@ptcnet.net	85482 558th Ave Pierce NE 68767	NEB	Teacher	EM			S	1977
Flegler Brenda K	(989)224-4274 fleglerbk@gmail.com	7422 Church Rd Saint Johns MI 48879	FG	Teacher	EM			S	1971
Flegler Samantha M Brown	(815)573-1888	3797 N Chapin Rd Merrill MI 48637	MI	DCE	C05/2022			Other	2017
Fleischfresser Sheri L Hartz	(262)337-1042 slfleisch1@gmail.com	518 Frederick Ct Oconomowoc WI 53066	SW	Teacher	Tchr	St Paul Oconomowoc WI	(262)567-5001	MQ	1985
Fleming Kate E Phillips	(515)201-7705 kate.fleming@lutheransouth.org	14927 Evergreen Ridge Way Houston TX 77062	TX	Teacher	Prin	South Houston TX	(281)464-8299	S	2010
Fleming Ruth A Grese	(309)589-1828 dflem3021@comcast.net	5632 W Grande Cir Peoria IL 61615	CI	Teacher	EM			RF	1967
Flenner Lorraine F Johnston	(239)248-1746 lfflenner@yahoo.com	4533 Caleb Xing Powder Springs GA 30127	FG	Teacher	EM			CQ	2004
Fletcher Carole A Sandford Prime	(727)433-0434 cfletcher44@gmail.com	230 Edgewater Dr Saint Marys GA 31558	FG	DCE	EM			CQ	1997
Fletcher Chloe Borg	(435)817-0816 chloe.borg435@gmail.com	44 Kihalani Pl Unit 3602 Kihei HI 96753	CNH	Teacher	Tchr	Emmanuel Kahului-Maui HI	(808)877-3037	CQ	2016
Flett Mary E	(310)644-6057 meflett78@gmail.com	1439 Gloucester Pt Kerrville TX 78028	PSW	Teacher	EM			RF	1978
Flicker Gaylord E	(208)241-7088 geflicker@cableone.net	451 Brassie Cir Pocatello ID 83204	NOW	Teacher	EM			S	1974
Flicker Kristin D Udy	kristin.flicker@gmail.com	2839 Margo Ln Pocatello ID 83201	NOW	Teacher	C07/2016			S	1999
Fliege Judith B Eilers	(217)787-9011 judy.fliege@gmail.com	4101 W Iles Ave Apt 101 Springfield IL 62711	CI	Teacher	EM			CQ	1986
Fliege Laura L Brietzke	(217)753-2308	21 Cabin Smoke Trl Springfield IL 62707	CI	Teacher	Tchr	Trinity Springfield IL	(217)787-2323	RF	1976
Floetke Jay W	(913)651-2764 floetke@hotmail.com	1010 Pawnee St Leavenworth KS 66048	KS	Teacher	EM			S	1970
Floetke Karl D	(863)944-3836 kdfloetke@yahoo.com	970 41st Ave NE St Petersburg FL 33703	FG	Teacher	EM			S	1972

*Multiple Assignments (See Church Worker Locator for Additional Details)
See Page 53 for the Table of Abbreviations for key to District, Classification, Position, and College abbreviations.
**C =Candidate; EM =Emeritus; the date following the C is the month and year the Candidate status began

NAME	TELEPHONE NUMBER EMAIL	STREET ADDRESS CITY/STATE/ZIP	DISTRICT	CLASS.	POSITION/ STATUS**	WHERE SERVING	OFFICE PHONE	COLLEGE/ UNIV/CQ	YR GRAD
Floetke Pamela B Russert	(913)651-2764 floetke@hotmail.com	1010 Pawnee St Leavenworth KS 66048	KS	Teacher	EM			S	1971
Flohra Christine C Petersen	(714)404-5310 mrs.flohra@gmail.com	1908 Hickory Glen Rd Knoxville TN 37932	MDS	Teacher	C06/2021			CQ	2010
Flomo Abigail	(651)424-9203 abigail.flomo21@gmail.com	2750 1st Ave S Apt 210 Altoona IA 50009	IW	DCE	Mem C	First English Spencer IA	(712)262-5598	SP	2025
Flores de Apodaca Lucille H Howard	(714)931-4902 luciflores@socal.rr.com	6140 E Canyon Ct # B Anaheim CA 92807	PSW	Teacher	EM			CQ	1999
Florine David A	(520)343-4156 dflorine@sjlarnold.org	1370 E State Road 250 Brownstown IN 47220	IN	Teacher	EM			RF	1978
Florine Sharon G Nehrt	(520)343-4557 sgflo78@gmail.com	1370 E State Road 250 Brownstown IN 47220	IN	Teacher	EM			RF	1978
Florip Eunice E Merz	(616)447-0509	735 Rehoboth Dr NE Grand Rapids MI 49505	MI	Teacher	EM			RF	1956
Flowers Rebecca J Sullivan	(828)455-7562 sullir_2000@yahoo.com	1751 Pipers Ridge Cir NW Conover NC 28613	SE	Teacher	Tchr	St Stephen Hickory NC	(828)256-2166	AA	2002
Fluegel Doyle W		917 Hudson Dr Garland TX 75043	TX	Teacher	Tchr	Dallas Lutheran Sch Dallas TX	(214)349-8912	CQ	1995
Fluegge Kathleen M Prinz	(260)485-9010 k.fluegge@worldnet.att.net	2504 Silver Wolf Trl Fort Wayne IN 46815	IN	Teacher	EM			RF	1976
Fluegge Samuel G	(949)244-8029 samuel.fluegge@eagles.cui.edu	N18 W6341 Carriage Trace #153 Cedarburg WI 53012	NOW	Teacher		Northwest District Portland OR	(503)288-8383	IV	2021
Fluga Benjamin	(708)921-5364 bfluga@gmail.com	8925 Willow Ter Dr Apt 2010 Orland Hills IL 60487	NI	Teacher	Tchr	Walther Melrose Park IL	(708)344-0404	RF	2022
Flynn Jacquelyn Kildale	(631)235-5763 jackie@stlukedixhiulls.org	16 Candlewood Path Dix Hills NY 11746	AT	Teacher	Tchr	St Luke Dix Hills NY	(631)499-8656	CQ	2015
Flynn Michael D	(314)302-7310 flynnm@csl.edu	158 Stonebridge Rd Saint Paul MN 55118	MNS	Teacher	S HS/C	Concordia Seminary Saint Louis MO	(314)505-7000	SP	1975
Flynn Priscilla J		1274 Miracle Ln Fort Myers FL 33901	FG	Teacher	Tchr	Saint Michael Fort Myers FL	(239)939-1218	CQ	2004
Foerster Robert C	(810)858-7771 foerster6@aol.com	6904 Griswold Rd Kimball MI 48074	MI	Teacher	EM			S	1971
Fogleman Susan M	(443)684-9386 smfogleman@gmail.com	6520 Huntingtown Rd Huntingtown MD 20639	SE	DCE	Mem C	First Huntingtown MD	(410)257-3030	RF	2008
Fogo Robert S	(702)569-5407 scott.fogo@leahschools.org	4307 Sweet Cicely Ct Houston TX 77054	TX	Teacher	ExecDir	Lutheran Education Association Friendswood TX	(281)617-5189	IV	1996
Foiles Lisa M Stange	(989)545-0773 lisafoiles1@gmail.com	2140 4th St Bay City MI 48708	MI	Teacher	Tchr	Faith Bay City MI	(989)684-3430	RF	2001
Foley Anna C	(515)230-7682 anna81@mac.com	7382 N 89th St Omaha NE 68122	CNH	Teacher	C07/2016			S	2005
Folken Laurie R Popp	(816)682-6884 lfolken7@gmail.com	4277 N Colorado Ave Kansas City MO 64117	MO	Teacher	Tchr	Martin Luther Kansas City MO	(816)734-1060	S	1983
Folkmann Stacy B Helming	(303)642-0993 sfolkmann@glutheran.com	54 Old Logging Rd Golden CO 80403	RM	Teacher		Rocky Mountain District Englewood CO	(303)695-8001	RF	2002
Follett Jennifer	jfollett@stlukes-ovideo.org	1621 Sapphire Star Dr Oviedo FL 32765	S	Teacher	Tchr	St Lukes Oviedo FL	(407)365-3228	CQ	2005
Fong Victoria A Coffer	(713)849-5518 vccrfong@aol.com	7914 Sonata Ct Houston TX 77040	TX	Teacher	Tchr	Salem Tomball TX	(281)351-8223	CQ	2009
Fontenot Angela A Kegley	(414)418-1798 afontenot@immanuelbrookfield.org	9408 W. Orchard Street West Allis WI 53214	SW	Teacher	Tchr	Immanuel Brookfield WI	(262)781-7140	CQ	2019
Foote Daniel R	(210)383-9393 daniel.foote777@gmail.com	2009 Meadowridge Dr Austin TX 78704	TX	Teacher	Tchr	Redeemer Austin TX	(512)451-6478	AU	2018
Foote Henry C	(716)930-7141 foote4@aol.com	1523 Shady Ln Schererville IN 46375	IN	Teacher	C08/2018			BR	1983
Foote Karen A Brese	(716)930-7122 foote4@aol.com	1523 Shady Ln Schererville IN 46375	IN	Teacher	Mem C	St Paul Munster IN	(219)836-6270	BR	1983
Footh Rita C Aho Deac	(701)453-3291 deacones@srt.com	P.O. Box 224 Berthold ND 58718	ND	Deaconess	EM			CQ	1998
Forbes Emmi J Schulze	(646)651-2746 emmi.forbes@gmail.com	200 7th St Saint James NY 11780	MO	Teacher	C08/2024			AA	2020
Ford Deana M	(763)755-3240	3875 119th Ave NW Apt 69 Minneapolis MN 55433	MNS	Teacher	Tchr	St John Elk River MN	(763)441-6616	CQ	2004
Ford Dorothea M Kutzbach	(727)442-3426 dortieford3@gmail.com	1457 Norwood Ave Clearwater FL 33756	FG	Teacher	EM			RF	1973
Ford Leslie C Green	(310)619-4042 lesliecford@gmail.com	126 Gladshire Ln Warrenton MO 63383	MO	Teacher	Tchr	Zion Saint Charles MO	(636)441-7424	RF	1988
Ford Lois J Elgert	(352)989-2188 loisjford@gmail.com	118 E Wilt Ave Eustis FL 32726	FG	Teacher	EM			BR	1975
Ford Rebecca M	(909)568-1572 yellowbecca@gmail.com	160 Crestwood Ct Alpharetta GA 30009	FG	Teacher	Tchr	Faith Marietta GA	(770)973-8877	MQ	2014
Ford Sophie E	(612)201-7347 sofaj1633@gmail.com	4104 Alabama Ave S Saint Louis Park MN 55416	MNN	Teacher	Tchr	Crown Saint Francis MN	(763)856-2099	SP	2025
Forguson Abby L Gersman	(636)288-3409 abbyforguson@att.net	429 Marble Fields Dr Wentzville MO 63385	MO	Teacher	Tchr	Immanuel Wentzville MO	(636)327-4416	CQ	2012
Forke Brian D	(262)212-7631	10198 N Granville Rd Mequon WI 53097	SW	Teacher	EM			S	1985
Forke Donna J	(801)879-4152 donna.forke@cune.org	4310 Driftwood Dr Colorado Spgs CO 80918	RM	Teacher	EM			S	1975
Formella Amy J	(920)288-2289 amy.formella@lbt.org	431 Orchard Ln Little Chute WI 54140	MO	DCM	RSO	Lutheran Bible Translators Inc Concordia MO	(660)225-0810	MQ	2015
Forrester Suanne K Coskey	(952)583-0031 suanne.forrester@gmail.com	1 Mockingbird Ct Merrimack NH 03054	TX	Teacher	C08/2019			CQ	2004
Forsberg Erin E Fritsch	(906)221-1160 erinf424@gmail.com	401 Iron St Norway MI 49870	NW	DCE	C07/2016			S	2008

*Multiple Assignments (See Church Worker Locator for Additional Details)
See Page 53 for the Table of Abbreviations for key to District, Classification, Position, and College abbreviations.
**C =Candidate; EM =Emeritus; the date following the C is the month and year the Candidate status began

NAME	TELEPHONE NUMBER EMAIL	STREET ADDRESS CITY/STATE/ZIP	DISTRICT	CLASS.	POSITION/ STATUS**	WHERE SERVING	OFFICE PHONE	COLLEGE/ UNIV/CQ	YR GRAD
Forshee Marlene J Goedde	(920)698-2971	W197N16578 Aspen Dr Jackson WI 53037	SW	Teacher	Tchr	Immanuel Brookfield WI	(262)781-7140	MQ	1988
Forst Sharon R Going	(507)474-9597	2019 Clinton Dr Winona MN 55987	MNS	Teacher	EM			S	1983
Fortenberry Nathalie F	(541)213-3008 nathaliefay.f@gmail.com	4931 N. 32nd St. Apt. 3b Lincoln NE 68504	NEB	Teacher	Tchr	Faith Lincoln NE	(402)466-7402	S	2025
Fortlage Kathleen R Nass	(920)474-3191 fortlagek@gmail.com	W2612 Elm St P.O. Box 79 Ashippun WI 53003	SW	Teacher	Tchr	St Peter Lebanon WI	(920)925-3547	CQ	2016
Fortmeyer Amelia A Munger	(816)385-0631 afortmeyer4@gmail.com	4225 Oakland Cir Saint Joseph MO 64506	MO	Teacher	EM			S	1980
Fortmeyer Bernard P	(816)294-7787 bafortmeyer@gmail.com	4225 Oakland Cir Saint Joseph MO 64506	MO	DCE	EM			S	1992
Foshee Dina S Stallings	(901)490-3189 Dinalee@bellsouth.net	1958 Wine Leaf Dr Germantown TN 38139	MDS	Teacher	Tchr	Faith Collierville TN	(901)853-4673	CQ	2014
Fosheim Cynthia M Murrell	(920)362-6859 cindyfosheim@gmail.com	803 W Cook St New London WI 54961	NW	Teacher	EM			MQ	2001
Fosheim Daniel T	(715)460-4560 fosheimd@newlhs.com	707 Bow Bells Rd. Oneida WI 54155	NW	Teacher	Tchr	Northeastern WI Green Bay WI	(920)469-6810	RF	2008
Fossum Robert B	(503)475-2827 bob_fossum@hotmail.com	63141 NE Hadleyplace Bend OR 97701	NOW	Tch/DCE	EM			S	1975
Fossum Robin G Heiden	(503)475-2830 rgfossum@hotmail.com	63141 NE Hadley Pl Bend OR 97701	NOW	DFLM	EM			CQ	2018
Foster Carmen M Dodge	(309)507-1847 cfoster19682003@yahoo.com	324 E Wells St Geneseo IL 61254	CI	Teacher	C07/2016			RF	1990
Foster Jeanette M Schueler	(920)918-6070 jeanettefoster30@yahoo.com	W1276 Fawn Dr Montello WI 53949	SW	Teacher	EM			CQ	1996
Foster Matthew J	(618)444-7276 matthewfoster@slcas.org	1759 Cherry Blossom Ct Pevely MO 63070	MO	Teacher	Prin	Salem Affton MO	(314)353-9242	S	2010
Fouch Janie L Pickens	(660)665-7986 janiefouch@yahoo.com	24732 Hedgepath Ln Kirksville MO 63501	MO	Teacher	EM			CQ	2005
Found James A	(970)663-5490 learner9696@yahoo.com	837 Libra Ct Loveland CO 80537	RM	Tch/DCE	EM			CQ	1980
Foushi Angela M Duey-Basel	(708)955-3351 afoushi14@gmail.com	2350 Hillcrest Ln Lowell IN 46356	IN	Teacher	EM			RF	1990
Fowler Eleanor L Harms	(817)781-5775 fowlerellie@gmail.com	800 N. Anthem Dr Sioux Falls SD 57110	SD	Teacher	EM			RF	1981
Fowlkes Brenda D Harms	(402)634-2941 awwsumm68@gmail.com	53640 833 Rd Meadow Grove NE 68752	NEB	Teacher	Tchr	Northeast Norfolk NE	(402)379-3040	S	1990
Fowls Robert W	(541)312-8784 bobf@nowlcms.org	2511 NE Ravenwood Dr Bend OR 97701	NOW	Teacher	EM			RF	1974
Fox George G	(623)266-4821 foxes456@sbcglobal.net	1783 W Morse Dr Anthem AZ 85086	PSW	Teacher	EM			RF	1971
Fox Kip A	(623)523-3445 kip.fox@cui.edu	8376 E Thoroughbred Trl Scottsdale AZ 85258	PSW	DPM	S HS/C	Concordia University Irvine Irvine CA	(949)854-8002	IV	2003
Fox Starlayne G Lange	(623)266-4821 foxes456@sbcglobal.net	1783 W Morse Dr Anthem AZ 85086	PSW	Teacher	EM			RF	1971
Foxe Gary W	(262)246-8233 gwfoxe@yahoo.com	W240N6532 Ash St Sussex WI 53089	SW	Teacher	EM			RF	1974
Fraker Jonathan D	(512)876-4875 jfraker@elcsh.org	1107 River Rock New Braunfels TX 78130	TX	Teacher	Prin	Epiphany Houston TX	(713)896-1773	AU	2013
Fraker Sharon H Hinz	(830)620-4723 frakerfamily@sbcglobal.net	1107 River Rock New Braunfels TX 78130	TX	Teacher	EM			RF	1980
Fralicker Caresse S Hendrix	(512)963-0182	P.O. Box 433 Thrall TX 76578	TX	Teacher	Tchr	Redeemer Austin TX	(512)451-6478	AU	2008
Francik Christopher D	(502)381-3643 chris.francik@gmail.com	508 S Williams St Royal Oak MI 48067	MI	Teacher	Prin	St Paul Royal Oak MI	(248)546-6555	S	1999
Francisco Adam S Dr	adamsfrancisco@aol.com	1315 Gamon Rd Wheaton IL 60189	NI	Teacher	C01/2023			CQ	2001
Franck Donna J Erber	(708)212-0541 djf1315@yahoo.com	1315 E Ironwood Dr Mt Prospect IL 60056	NI	Teacher	EM			RF	1972
Frank Ann M Voges	(618)282-6597 afrank@htc.net	1153 Jacob Dr Red Bud IL 62278	SI	Teacher	Mem C	Immanuel Waterloo IL	(618)939-6480	S	1971
Frank David J	(816)517-4882 davefrank@sbcglobal.net	808 SW Stonehenge St Blue Springs MO 64015	MO	Teacher	EM			S	1975
Frank George C	(517)792-4726	4470 Frank Rd Frankenmuth MI 48734	MI	Teacher	EM			RF	1964
Frank Heidi B Borg	(503)421-8184 heidibfrank@q.com	11102 NE Mason St Portland OR 97220	NOW	DCE	EM			PO	1981
Frank John R	(314)517-1957 47music@sbcglobal.net	1 Meramec Bluffs Dr Apt 638 Ballwin MO 63021	MO	Teacher	EM			S	1969
Frank Lindsey T	(262)674-4219 lindsey.frank@cuw.edu	W52N194 Pierce Ave Cedarburg WI 53012	SW	Teacher	Tchr	First Immanuel Cedarburg WI	(262)377-6610	MQ	2016
Frank Margaret A Hintze	edmarfrank@yahoo.com	2106 Haas Ln Austin TX 78728	TX	Teacher	EM			S	1975
Frank Rebecca J Hartmann	(785)765-3815 frankfamilyfour@embarqmail.com	28642 Wabaunsee Rd Alma KS 66401	KS	Teacher	EM			S	1987
Frank Susan F Schutt	(386)672-3612 tsfrank@cfl.rr.com	18 Southern Trace Blvd Ormond Beach FL 32174	FG	Teacher	EM			RF	1968
Frank Ted A	(386)672-3612 tsfrank@cfl.rr.com	18 Southern Trace Blvd Ormond Beach FL 32174	FG	Teacher	EM			RF	1968
Frank Warren G	(618)282-6597 pupperinsk@aol.com	1153 Jacob Dr Red Bud IL 62278	SI	Teacher	EM			S	1970
Franke Sandra R Meyer	(812)580-8210 srmfranke@gmail.com	9309 E County Road 100 N Seymour IN 47274	IN	Teacher	Tchr	Immanuel Seymour IN	(812)522-1301	RF	1984
Franke Tommy L Meneely	(260) 414-9516 tommyfranke@comcast.net	8630 Brookline Ct Fort Wayne IN 46835	IN	Teacher	EM			CQ	2001

*Multiple Assignments (See Church Worker Locator for Additional Details)
See Page 53 for the Table of Abbreviations for key to District, Classification, Position, and College abbreviations.
**C =Candidate; EM =Emeritus; the date following the C is the month and year the Candidate status began

NAME	TELEPHONE NUMBER EMAIL	STREET ADDRESS CITY/STATE/ZIP	DISTRICT	CLASS.	POSITION/ STATUS**	WHERE SERVING	OFFICE PHONE	COLLEGE/ UNIV/CQ	YR GRAD
Franklin John M	(773)653-5110 jfranklin123115@gmail.com	5949 W Belle Plaine Ave Chicago IL 60634	NI	Teacher	Tchr	Walther Melrose Park IL	(708)344-0404	RF	2003
Franklin Rachael Kretschmar	(920)912-8001 rfranklin@stjohnschicago.org	5949 W Belle Plaine Ave Chicago IL 60634	NI	Teacher	Tchr	St John Chicago IL	(773)736-1196	CH	2009
Frantz Kymberly Alexander	(480)577-1322 kfrantz@cglschool.org	8110 E Dartmouth St Mesa AZ 85207	PSW	Teacher	Tchr	Christ Greenfield Gilbert AZ	(480)892-8521	CQ	2019
Frantz Teresa D Dube	(512)964-8008 teridube2@gmail.com	1807 Valle Verde Dr Cedar Park TX 78641	TX	DCE	C07/2021			AU	2006
Franz Timothy S	(414)704-5806 tfranz22@icloud.com	605 Chardonnay Court Cambridge WI 53523	EN	Teacher	EM			S	1980
Franzen Karen J Nothwehr	(303)750-5496 kjfranzen@hotmail.com	2786 S Lisbon Way Aurora CO 80013	RM	Teacher	Tchr	Peace W Christ Aurora CO	(303)693-5618	S	1977
Franzen Kimberly D Brakenhoff	(402)276-1926 kimfranzen2025@gmail.com	2918 32nd St Columbus NE 68601	NEB	Teacher	EM			CQ	1998
Franzen Margaret A Fuchssteiner	(630)202-9486 marge.franzen@gmail.com	2764 Rolling Meadows Dr Naperville IL 60564	NI	DCM	EM			MQ	2003
Frasca Emily L	(915)442-2402 emily.frasca@eagles.cui.edu	4761 N. Goldenrod Rd Apt A Winter Park FL 32792	S	Teacher	Tchr	St Lukes Oviedo FL	(407)365-3228	IV	2023
Fratzke Lauren E Gieschen	(260)444-1043 lauren.gieschen@gmail.com	N50W14137 Fairmount Ave Menomonee Falls WI 53051	SW	Teacher	Tchr	Immanuel Brookfield WI	(262)781-7140	MQ	2019
Frazee Anna K Dickhut	(217)653-8247 adickhut@gmail.com	41 Main St Mayville WI 53050	SW	Teacher	C06/2022			CQ	2015
Frazier Catherine M Berry	(618)570-7688 catherine.frazier104@gmail.com	141 Forest Dr Eureka MO 63025	MO	Teacher	Pro Stf	St Mark Eureka MO	(636)938-4432	CQ	2015
Frazier Kyle J	(737)210-2061 kylefrazier1955@gmail.com	1633 Bovina Dr Leander TX 78641	TX	DCE	Mem C	Acts Austin TX	(512)263-8175	IV	2006
Fredenburg Martha A Mc Allister	(713)560-1283 mfredenbrg@aol.com	250 Schneider St Giddings TX 78942	TX	Teacher	Tchr	Immanuel Giddings TX	(979)542-2918	CQ	1990
Fredericks Amy K Stubbe	(920)457-0293 amykfredericks@yahoo.com	4028 S 12th St Sheboygan WI 53081	SW	Teacher	Tchr	St John Plymouth WI	(920)893-5114	MQ	1995
Fredericksen Gary J	freddymlhs@aol.com	21108 Ruxton Drive #7107 Georgetown DE 19947	AT	Teacher	Tchr	Martin Luther Maspeth NY	(718)894-4000	CQ	1993
Fredericksen Heather J Dunkerley	(703) 300-6337 kings.mill.lane@gmail.com	4203 Kings Mill Ln Annandale VA 22003	SE	Teacher	Tchr	Our Savior Arlington VA	(703)892-4846	BR	1987
Fredericksen Lynnette A Deac	(618)633-2739 lfreder@gmail.com	P.O. Box 301 Hamel IL 62046	SI	Deaconess	Mem C	St Paul Worden IL	(618)633-2209	FW-DEAC	2009
Frederickson Sharon K Augustin	(507)259-5478 oma.frederickson@gmail.com	407 8th St SW Plainview MN 55964	MNS	Teacher	EM			SP	1974
Frederiksen Diana L Karnstedt	(630)834-3892 j.frederiksen634@comcast.net	634 S Hawthorne Ave Elmhurst IL 60126	NI	Teacher	EM			RF	1961
Fredrich Peter D	(989)205-2502 pcfredrich@att.net	209 Ruth St Auburn MI 48611	MI	Teacher	EM			S	1975
Fredrick Anna M Schield	(218)830-0204 aschield@trinityfirst.org		MNS	Teacher	Tchr	Trinity First Minneapolis MN	(612)870-9487	SP	2014
Fredrick Mara Schleis	(920)588-0178 mara.fredrick.14@gmail.com	W2157 Wildflower Lane Brillion WI 54110	NW	Teacher	Tchr	Zion Of Wayside Greenleaf WI	(920)864-2468	MQ	2023
Fredrickson Jenna A	(785)614-0248 jfredrickson@ilsw.org	46201 Pomme De Terre Dr Lake Saint Louis MO 63367	MO	Teacher	Tchr	Immanuel Wentzville MO	(636)639-9887	S	2021
Freeberg Lindsay	(262)402-8590 lindsayfreebergl@gmail.com		MDS	Teacher	C06/2019			MQ	2016
Freed R M	(316) 737-6505 Rmichaelfreed@gmail.com	622 N Caddy Ln Wichita KS 67212	KS	Tch/DCE	EM			RF	1979
Freed Rebekah R	(402)643-7411		NEB	DCE	S HS/C	Concordia University Nebraska Seward NE	(402)643-3651	S	2011
Freel Debra S Timm	(785)286-2608 iraf@cox.net	3901 SW King Arthurs Rd Topeka KS 66610	KS	Teacher	EM			CQ	1979
Freeman Alan L	(314)996-1272 alan.freeman@lcms.org	1333 S Kirkwood Rd Saint Louis MO 63122	MO	Teacher	S Ex/S	The LCMS Corporate Saint Louis MO	(314)965-9000	CQ	1995
Freeman Lisa M Bassuener	(847)803-5493 jlmnrfreeman@astound.net	1710 N Beech Rd Mt Prospect IL 60056	NI	Teacher	EM			S	1985
Freeman Noah D	(541)419-5889 nfreeman@bethanylutheran.org	c/o Bethany Lutheran Church 4644 Clark Ave Long Beach CA 90808	PSW	Teacher	Tchr	Bethany Long Beach CA	(562)421-4711	S	2021
Freeman Paula J Tibbott	(503)703-8477 rich.paula.freeman@gmail.com	2815 B St Forest Grove OR 97116	NOW	Teacher	Tchr	Forest Hills Cornelius OR	(503)359-4853	RF	2004
Freese James W Dr	(414)378-4527 james.freese@cuw.edu	W165 N10277 Wagon Trl Germantown WI 53022	SW	Teacher	EM			Other	1978
Freese Samantha A Schmidt	(414)339-5538 freese.sam@gmail.com	1833 Old Richton Rd Petal MS 39465	SO	DCM	C07/2016			MQ	2009
Freidenberger Karen L Boies	(970)370-3001 kfreidenberger@gmail.com	732 Carol St Fort Morgan CO 80701	RM	Teacher	EM			S	1976
Freitag Gene R	(770)954-9648 gfreitag@lhsa.com	955 Airline Rd McDonough GA 30252	FG	Teacher	EM			S	1967
Fremder Barbara A Wahlert	(402)659-3802 skipbobabe@yahoo.com	1609 Halifax St Bellevue NE 68123	NEB	DPM	EM			S	1987
Fremder Linda K Fiedler	(260)493-8522 mlfremder@comcast.net	7603 Preakness CV Fort Wayne IN 46815	OH	Teacher	EM			S	1969
French Patricia S Stephens	(801)231-9844 trishastephens@hotmail.com	P.O. Box 900161 Sandy UT 84090	RM	Teacher	C07/2016			CQ	2004
Frenk Ellen L Schrader	(815)459-6499 billneli@aol.com	237 Edgewater Dr Crystal Lake IL 60014	NI	Teacher	EM			RF	1988
Frerich Harold A	(952)836-6731 andy@messiahonline.org	16254 Harvard Dr Lakeville MN 55044	MNS	DCE	Mem C	Messiah Lakeville MN	(952)431-5959	SP	1999
Frerichs Tammy J Culley	(435)467-3642 tfrerichs@ylscrusaders.org	10166 E 39th Way Yuma AZ 85365	PSW	Teacher	Tchr	Yuma Yuma AZ	(928)726-8410	PO	1991

*Multiple Assignments (See Church Worker Locator for Additional Details)
See Page 53 for the Table of Abbreviations for key to District, Classification, Position, and College abbreviations.
**C =Candidate; EM =Emeritus; the date following the C is the month and year the Candidate status began

NAME	TELEPHONE NUMBER EMAIL	STREET ADDRESS CITY/STATE/ZIP	DISTRICT	CLASS.	POSITION/ STATUS**	WHERE SERVING	OFFICE PHONE	COLLEGE/ UNIV/CQ	YR GRAD
Frerking Caitlin S Kruse	(660)624-3617 katie.kruse@hotmail.com	305 Laura Ln Concordia MO 64020	MO	Teacher	Tchr	St Pauls Concordia MO	(660)463-7654	S	2014
Frerking Christi A Davis	(281)851-2002 cadsummer@sbcglobal.net	26 Wenoah Loop Spring TX 77389	TX	Teacher	Tchr	Trinity Klein Klein TX	(281)376-5773	CQ	2018
Frerking Krystol R Longhenry	(605)877-3361	1529 Aurora Dr Rapid City SD 57703	SD	Teacher	Tchr	Zion Rapid City SD	(605)342-5749	S	2001
Frerking Lois A	(412)793-2299 lfrerking@hotmail.com	436 Cypress Hill Dr Pittsburgh PA 15235	EA	Teacher	EM			S	1974
Frerking Nathan D	(281)785-4810 frerkingn@trinityklein.org	8318 Autumn Willow Dr Tomball TX 77375	TX	Teacher	Tchr	Trinity Spring TX	(281)376-5810	S	1991
Frerking Patrick D	(260)403-4265 patrick.frerking@gmail.com	2612 Buckhurst Run Fort Wayne IN 46815	IN	Teacher	Prin	Concordia Fort Wayne IN	(260)483-1102	S	1987
Frerking Rachel	(262)443-4857 rachel.frerking@drlc.org	580 Foxtail Dr Apt 210 Pewaukee WI 53072	SW	Teacher	Tchr	Divine Redeemer Hartland WI	(262)367-3664	MQ	2024
Frese Ashley A Micek	(402)750-1848 afrese@christlutheran.esu7.org	20286 Frese Dr Columbus NE 68601	NEB	Teacher	Tchr	Christ Columbus NE	(402)564-3531	CQ	2024
Frese Leland G	(512)819-9599 ljfrese@aol.com	120 Daisy Path Georgetown TX 78633	TX	Teacher	EM			S	1959
Frese Paul M	(630)279-3095 paulfrese@sbcglobal.net	834 S Euclid Ave Villa Park IL 60181	NI	Teacher	EM			S	1963
Freshour Jodi L Price	(616)435-6789	65160 Youngs Prairie Rd Constantine MI 49042	IN	Teacher	Tchr	Trinity Elkhart IN	(574)674-8800	CQ	2001
Fretthold Kathleen	(716)867-4817 kathleenfretthold@gmail.com	425 Homestead Dr N Tonawanda NY 14120	EA	Teacher		Eastern District Williamsville NY	(716)634-5111	CQ	2020
Freudenberg Howard T	(815)978-4948 hberg375@yahoo.com	1904 Spring Brook Ave Rockford IL 61107	NI	Teacher	EM			S	1979
Freudenberg Karen J Jampsa	(815)965-6799 kjfberg@yahoo.com	1904 Spring Brook Ave Rockford IL 61107	NI	Teacher	EM			PO	1983
Freudenburg Benjamin F	(602)750-2762 ben.freudenburg@cuaa.edu	7446 Roxbury Dr Ypsilanti MI 48197	MI	Tch/DCE	EM			S	1972
Freudenburg Ernest F	(507)291-4717 ekfreud@gmail.com	2512 9th Ave NW Rochester MN 55901	MNS	DCO	EM			S	1969
Freudenburg Joan K Rodekohr	(309)691-5022 freudenburg08@comcast.net	5118 N Merrimac Ave Peoria IL 61614	CI	Teacher	EM			S	1957
Freudenburg Kathryn A Day	(507)282-4162 kafreud712@gmail.com	2512 9th Ave NW Rochester MN 55901	MNS	Teacher	EM			SP	1968
Freudenburg Lauren A Aufdembrink	(402)992-7439 lauren.aufdembrink@cune.org	304 S Willow St Norfolk NE 68701	NEB	Teacher	C07/2022			S	2014
Frey Carol D Sachs	(410)274-7803 cdsfrey@hotmail.com	7910 32nd St Baltimore MD 21237	SE	Teacher	EM			RF	1976
Frey Christin S Mickow	(507)259-0944 chfrey@rcls.net	2203 Telemark Ln NW Rochester MN 55901	MNS	Teacher	Tchr	Rochester Central Rochester MN	(507)289-3267	CQ	2018
Freymark Robert C	(319)538-4976 46rcfia@gmail.com	4414 Churchill Ct Marion IA 52302	IE	Teacher	EM			S	1968
Frick Dean D	(715)257-1351 principal@trinityathens.com	1009 Decker St Athens WI 54411	NW	Teacher	P/Tchr	Trinity Athens WI	(715)257-7526	SP	1991
Frick Deborah		1009 Decker St Athens WI 54411	NW	Teacher	Tchr	Trinity Athens WI	(715)257-7559	SP	1994
Frick Matthew T	mfrick@stjohnindy.org		IN	Teacher	Mem C	St John Indianapolis IN	(317)352-9196	CH	2007
Fricke John M Dr	(517)348-7175 jmfricke1@gmail.com	5985 Highgate Ave East Lansing MI 48823	MI	Teacher	EM			S	1966
Fridley Sandra K Oetting	(636) 439-8275	4111 Cherry Blossom Dr Dardenne Prairie MO 63368	MO	Teacher	EM			S	1969
Friedrich Eugene T	(260)749-5518 friedrich1@juno.com	7404 Trotters Chase Ln Fort Wayne IN 46815	IN	Teacher	EM			RF	1966
Friedrich Joan B Becker	(239)410-2585 jebf410@comcast.net	5323 Chippendale Cir E Fort Myers FL 33919	FG	Teacher	C07/2016			CQ	2003
Friedrich Laura M Mueller	(920)889-0805 lmueller630@gmail.com	W162N10492 Auburn Ln Germantown WI 53022	SW	Teacher	Tchr	Immanuel Brookfield WI	(262)781-7140	MQ	2010
Friedrich Laurie A Wogsland Dr	(402)641-5967 lfriedrich2017@gmail.com	1277 Dayton Ave Saint Paul MN 55104	MNS	Teacher	C07/2016			SP	1980
Friedrich Ronald P	(530)529-0127 rnfriedrich@sbcglobal.net	350 Gilmore Rd Spc 111 Red Bluff CA 96080	PSW	Teacher	EM			RF	1969
Friedrich Sandra S Wolf	(260)749-5578	7404 Trotters Chase Ln Fort Wayne IN 46815	IN	Teacher	EM			RF	1970
Friedrichs Frederick R	(858)531-2579 frederickleaches@gmail.com	3919 Kenosha Ave San Diego CA 92117	PSW	Teacher	EM			S	1982
Frieling Gary M	(972)832-9745 ganddfrieling@verizon.net	6200 Allegheny Trl Plano TX 75023	TX	Teacher	EM			S	1970
Frieling Kurt F	kurtfrieling@dallaslutheranschool.com	2983 Marlow Ln Richardson TX 75082	TX	Teacher	Tchr	Dallas Lutheran Sch Dallas TX	(214)349-8912	AU	1998
Fries Sharon M Cezus	(913)648-2228 sfries@bethanyschool.net	9101 Lamar Ave Overland Park KS 66207	KS	Teacher	Pro Stf	Bethany Overland Park KS	(913)648-2228	CQ	1993
Friesenhahn Judith L Trinklein	(210)723-4861 jfriesenhahn@shlutheran.org	6004 Trone Trl San Antonio TX 78238	TX	Teacher	Tchr	Shepherd Hills San Antonio TX	(210)614-3742	RF	1982
Frillmann Edna M Gugel	(904)226-8760	P.O. Box 732 Penney Farms FL 32079	AT	Teacher	EM			RF	1950
Fringer Eileen E Cordes	(612)306-4593 eileen.e.fringer@gmail.com	521 Lovell Ave Roseville MN 55113	MNS	Teacher	EM			SP	1967
Frisco Alexandra N Fisher	(313)300-0871 alex.frisco1@gmail.com	15306 Doyle Rd Hemlock MI 48626	MI	Teacher	Tchr	St Peter Hemlock MI	(989)642-5659	AA	2015
Friske Graham A	(952)412-9367 grahamfriske@gmail.com	5000 Snicker Lane Watertown MN 55388	MNS	Teacher	C07/2024			SP	2022
Fritsch Charlotte E Jentsch	(920)748-2242 ccharf@yahoo.com	526 Mayparty Dr Ripon WI 54971	SW	Teacher	Tchr	St John Berlin WI	(920)361-0555	MQ	1983

*Multiple Assignments (See Church Worker Locator for Additional Details)
See Page 53 for the Table of Abbreviations for key to District, Classification, Position, and College abbreviations.
**C =Candidate; EM =Emeritus; the date following the C is the month and year the Candidate status began

NAME	TELEPHONE NUMBER EMAIL	STREET ADDRESS CITY/STATE/ZIP	DISTRICT	CLASS.	POSITION/ STATUS**	WHERE SERVING	OFFICE PHONE	COLLEGE/ UNIV/CQ	YR GRAD
Fritsche Christopher R	(325)276-1283 cfritsche@immlutheran.org	52617 Wellington Valley Dr Macomb MI 48042	MI	Teacher	Pro Stf	Immanuel Macomb MI	(586)286-4231	Other	2007
Fritsche Clarion Deac	(224)410-2403 Clarion.Fritsche@lcms.org	11 McCall Ter Saint Louis MO 63105	MO	Deaconess	S Ex/S	Office of International Mission Saint Louis MO		FW-DEAC	2021
Fritsche Kirsten K Schueler	(608)448-1228 kirstenfritsche20@gmail.com	52617 Wellington Valley Dr Macomb MI 48042	MI	Teacher	Tchr	St Peter Macomb MI	(586)781-9296	MQ	2013
Fritsche Ronald W	(325)650-7422 ron@tlcsanangelo.com	2371 Sul Ross St San Angelo TX 76904	TX	Teacher	Prin	Trinity San Angelo TX	(325)947-1275	RF	1976
Fritz Andrew S	(847)359-4628 andyfritz71@gmail.com	1559 N Broadmoor Ct Palatine IL 60067	NI	Teacher	Tchr	Immanuel Crystal Lake IL	(815)459-1444	AA	1993
Fritz Ann R Mitchell	(260)409-0469 afritz@stpaulsfw.org	429 Englewood Ct Fort Wayne IN 46807	IN	Teacher	Tchr	St Pauls Fort Wayne IN	(260)424-0049	RF	1981
Fritz Anne M Krass	(352)552-6086 anmkr12@hotmail.com	1095 Vanderbilt Dr Eustis FL 32726	FG	Teacher	Tchr	Faith Eustis FL	(352)589-5683	RF	2003
Fritz Beverly A Knuth	(248)990-5167 dobefritz@att.net	24477 Lakeland St Farmingtn Hls MI 48336	MI	Teacher	EM			RF	1965
Fritz Gary A	(651)968-7970 gary.fritz@concordiaacademy.com	2729 Farrington St Roseville MN 55113	MNS	Teacher	Tchr	Concordia Academy Roseville MN	(651)484-8429	SP	1988
Fritz Jeremy J	(352)552-3354 eagleball24@hotmail.com	1095 Vanderbilt Dr Eustis FL 32726	FG	Teacher	Tchr	Faith Eustis FL	(352)589-5433	RF	2004
Fritz Karen D Wilson	(715)675-2132 firstfritzfamily@gmail.com	4800 N 32nd Ave Wausau WI 54401	NW	Teacher	EM			SP	1989
Fritz Sharlyn S Bumann	(713)778-9033	5763 Birdwood Rd Houston TX 77096	TX	Teacher	EM			S	1966
Fritz-Halsted Jimmy W	(520)237-0704 jim@azbeachboy.com	628 Nelson St Hildreth NE 68947	NEB	DCO	EM			SP	1989
Frobel David P	(248)909-8130 Dfrobel@stjohnrochester.org	2987 Muirwood Ct Waterford MI 48329	MI	Teacher	Tchr	St John Rochester MI	(248)402-8000	AA	1986
Froehlich Hannah L Gurnett	(847)691-3022 hlfroehlich@gmail.com	10800 Lakes Blvd Apt 1107 Baton Rouge LA 70810	SO	Teacher	C07/2022			MQ	2003
Froh Elizabeth J Deac	deaconessfroh@earthlink.net		IN	Deaconess		Indiana District Fort Wayne IN	(800)837-1145	FW-DEAC	2015
Fronk Eva M Oehrle	(414)651-5532 evafronk@yahoo.com	100 Oaklands Blvd Apt 206 Exton PA 19341	EN	Teacher	EM			CQ	2008
Fruend Elizabeth L Burch	(636)236-2701 efruend14@msn.com	3401 Riverchase Pkwy Saint Charles MO 63301	MO	Teacher	Tchr	St Charles Saint Peters MO	(636)928-5100	MQ	1992
Fruge Rachel E Mohr Deac	(214)532-6783 rachel.fruge@sharingnewlife.com	402 Brooks Ln Coppel TX 75019	TX	Deaconess	Mem C	St Paul Fort Worth TX	(817)332-2281	FW-DEAC	2020
Frusco Diane I Dombro	(352)631-5294 di2teach@aol.com	15483 Arvin Dr Brooksville FL 34604	FG	Teacher	Tchr	Holy Trinity Tampa FL	(813)839-6847	BR	1984
Frusti Kathleen H Robertson	khfrusti@gmail.com	3373 Eastlane St Jackson MI 49203	MI	Teacher	EM			S	1981
Frusti Philip J Dr	(979)702-0925 pfrusti@yahoo.com	N9332 Idle Hour Dr Randolph WI 53956	KS	Teacher	ExecDir	Lead a Child Society Olathe KS	(979)702-0925	AA	1983
Frusti Timothy M Dr	(734)255-4024 timfrusti@gmail.com	3373 Eastlane St Jackson MI 49203	MI	Tch/DCE	EM			SP	1977
Fry Jessica J Cattau		301 W Hilton St Marengo IA 52301	IE	Teacher	Tchr	Central Newhall IA	(319)223-5271	S	2006
Fryar Jane L Dr	(314)409-2258 janefryar@outlook.com	2019 Green Oak St Pacific MO 63069	MO	Teacher	EM			S	1972
Frydendall Sharon A Kahre	(714)906-1484 frycm@sbcglobal.net	2820 Corvo Pl Costa Mesa CA 92626	PSW	Teacher	EM			S	1982
Fuchs Lori J Breskvar	(440)223-4191 slbdfuchs2@rocketmail.com	32918 Titus Hill Ln Avon Lake OH 44012	OH	Teacher	EM			RF	1983
Fuchs Michael W	(817)368-4438 michaelfuchstexas@gmail.com	4205 Shadow Ridge Dr Colleyville TX 76034	TX	Teacher	EM			S	1970
Fuchs Steven M	(440)223-4191 slbdfuchs1@rocketmail.com	32918 Titus Hill Ln Avon Lake OH 44012	OH	Teacher	EM			S	1979
Fuchsberger Lindsey A	(414)902-0137 lindsey.fuchsberger@mtolivemke.org	1663 Redtail Dr Hartford WI 53027	SW	Teacher	Tchr	Mount Olive Milwaukee WI	(414)774-2200	MQ	2022
Fuemmeler Nancy K Linneman	nancyfuem@fuemmeler.net	21 Cloverhill Cir Bloomington IL 61705	CI	Teacher	EM			CQ	2001
Fugill Lindsey M Bengsch	(920)988-7962 lfugill@stpeters-columbus.org	4272 Princeton Park Dr Columbus IN 47201	IN	DPM	Mem C	St Peter Columbus IN	(812)372-1571	MQ	2019
Fugitt Gilbert A Jr Dr	(626)484-6875 gilbert.fugitt@cui.edu	2 Calle Tortuga San Clemente CA 92673	PSW	DCE	S HS/C	Concordia University Irvine Irvine CA	(949)854-8002	S	2001
Fuhrmann Amy B Thompson	(502)437-5114 afuhrmann@oslslouisville.com	830 Veechdale Rd Simpsonville KY 40067	IN	Teacher	Tchr	Our Savior Louisville KY	(502)426-1130	RF	1996
Fuhrmann Gerald W	(914)245-4172 Gerfuh7@yahoo.com	197 Granite Springs Rd Yorktown Hts NY 10598	AT	Teacher	EM			S	1965
Fuiten Pamela R Knauer	(217)871-2780 fuiten5@comcast.net	445 Mayfair Dr Lincoln IL 62656	CI	Teacher	EM			CQ	1979
Fujii Karen S Louie	(808)294-2016 mrs.fujii2003@gmail.com	801 S King St #4208 Honolulu HI 96813	CNH	Teacher	Tchr	Good Shepherd Honolulu HI	(808)523-2927	PO	1993
Fulcer Brittany L	brittany@fulcer.net	P.O. Box 94 1001 E Street Utica NE 68456	NEB	DCE	Mem C	St Paul Utica NE	(402)534-2200	S	2020
Fulkerson Rebecca L Nielsen	(815)878-1611 bfulkerson24@hotmail.com	4418 N Wyss Ln Peoria IL 61614	CI	Teacher	C04/2017			RF	2001
Fuller Jennifer L Grundmeier	(712)251-7197 jenn.fuller@outlook.com	505 1st Street NW Bondurant IA 50035	IW	DCE	Mem C	Gloria Dei Urbandale IA	(515)276-1700	S	2001
Fuller Katerina G	(214)667-6366 katerina.fuller@cune.org	10243 Lawler Rd Dallas TX 75243	RM	Teacher	Tchr	Christ Albuquerque NM	(505)884-3876	S	2020
Fuller Lynne E Eriksson	(248)644-4986	31552 Waltham Dr Beverly Hills MI 48025	MI	Teacher	EM			CQ	2000

*Multiple Assignments (See Church Worker Locator for Additional Details)
See Page 53 for the Table of Abbreviations for key to District, Classification, Position, and College abbreviations.
**C =Candidate; EM =Emeritus; the date following the C is the month and year the Candidate status began

NAME	TELEPHONE NUMBER EMAIL	STREET ADDRESS CITY/STATE/ZIP	DISTRICT	CLASS.	POSITION/ STATUS**	WHERE SERVING	OFFICE PHONE	COLLEGE/ UNIV/CQ	YR GRAD
Funck Lynne S Kreyling	(410)661-1763 signdovesf@mac.com	3201 Hiss Ave Baltimore MD 21234	SE	Teacher	EM			RF	1968
Funk Stanna K	(307)640-1226 stannaf@hotmail.com	1045 13th St Gering NE 69341	WY	Teacher	C07/2016			S	2000
Funke Caleb D	(812)525-0152 sprinter_22@hotmail.com	3620 Taft Ave Primghar IA 51245	IW	DPM	C07/2016			MQ	2007
Funke David M	(314)489-0650 dm.funke@gmail.com	444 Shady Ln Wisconsin Rapids WI 54494	NW	DCE	EM			SP	1981
Furr Jennifer L Anderson	(612)747-7655 furrjen@gmail.com	860 E Seward St Seward NE 68434	NEB	Teacher	S HS/C	Concordia University Nebraska Seward NE	(402)643-3651	S	1997
Furr Ruth C Smeeding	(303)424-4454 rfurr@peacelutheran.net	Peace Lutheran Church 5675 Field St Arvada CO 80002	RM	DCE	Mem C	Peace Arvada CO	(303)424-4454	S	2013
Fury Norma J Kopischke	(507)234-5788	105 Savanna Ln Janesville MN 56048	MNS	Teacher	EM			SP	1972
Gabbert Timothy A	(727)432-1885 timagabbert@gmail.com	78 N Highview Ave Hernando FL 34442	FG	Teacher	Prin	First Clearwater FL	(727)462-8000	S	1986
Gabel Sarah Sirgey Herdlein	(716)982-2586 sgabel@trinitywny.org	2099 Lenox Rd Collins NY 14034	EA	Teacher	Tchr	Trinity West Seneca NY	(716)674-5353	BR	2005
Gable Courtney J Clark	(715)630-8930 missclark4@gmail.com	5181 County Road Q Amherst WI 54406	NW	Teacher	C06/2023			MQ	2015
Gable Donna J Halstenberg	(901)387-0306	3350 Pembroke Ellis CV Bartlett TN 38133	MDS	Teacher	EM			RF	1959
Gable Gary G	(425)407-3128 gary.g.gable@gmail.com	4014 144th Street Ct NW Gig Harbor WA 98332	NOW	Teacher	EM			S	1962
Gable Kathleen A Maas	(425)760-4763 gary.g.gable@gmail.com	4014 144th Street Ct NW Gig Harbor WA 98332	NOW	Teacher	EM			RF	1963
Gace Sharon D	(281)935-5041	2820 Goodson Loop Pinehurst TX 77362	TX	Teacher	Tchr	Trinity Klein Klein TX	(281)376-5773	AU	2011
Gadbaw Elizabeth A Graham	egadbaw@gmail.com	39 5th Ave. NE Hutchinson MN 55350	MNS	Teacher	Tchr	Zion Mayer MN	(952)657-2339	AA	2000
Gade William E	(224)402-3164	415 Maiden Ln East Dundee IL 60118	NI	Teacher	Mem C	Immanuel East Dundee IL	(847)428-4477	CQ	1983
Gaede Valerie L Webb	(630)269-1986 val.webb.gaede@gmail.com	817 Grove Ave West Chicago IL 60185	NI	Teacher	EM			S	1979
Gaertner Mary B Matteson Dr	(281)900-8546	27002 Mesa Verde Dr Magnolia TX 77354	TX	Teacher	EM			CQ	2007
Gaffney Sarah E Utecht Deac	(708)785-8048 deaconesssarah1@gmail.com	19 Allen Ave P.O. Box 616 Hamel IL 62046	SI	Deaconess	Mem C	St Paul* Worden IL	(618)633-2209	RF	1993
Gagan Patrick S	(562)429-1538 psgag@verizon.net	4229 Iroquois Ave Lakewood CA 90713	PSW	Teacher	EM			S	1978
Gage Donna A Deac	(816)916-0458 donnag7001@gmail.com	1001 Burningtree Cir Indpendence MO 64055	MO	Deaconess	C07/2016			RF	1987
Gahgan Veronica A	(847)366-9564 veronica.gahgan@gmail.com	1651 Partridge St Waukegan IL 60087	NI	Teacher	Tchr	St John Chicago IL	(773)736-1196	CH	2013
Gaide Mary L	(720)375-2012 laura-li.gaide@zionwalburg.org	233 Falling Star Ln Georgetown TX 78628	TX	DCE	Mem C	Zion Georgetown TX	(512)863-3065	S	2019
Gakstatter Kari S Streeter	(989)980-8301 kgakstatter@yahoo.com	901 N Powell Rd Essexville MI 48732	MI	Teacher	Tchr	Immanuel Bay City MI	(989)893-4088	CQ	1997
Galchutt Kathryn M Dr	kathryn.galchutt@cui.edu	c/o Concordia University Irvine 1530 Concordia West Irvine CA 92612	PSW	Teacher	S HS/C	Concordia University Irvine Irvine CA	(949)854-8002	SP	1993
Galchutt Keri R Shepherd	(651)307-2759 keri.galchutt@stjohns-chaska.org	112511 Ramsey Ct Chaska MN 55318	MNS	Teacher	Tchr	St Johns Chaska MN	(952)448-2526	SP	2000
Galek Linda L	l_galek@yahoo.com	6530 W Irving Park Rd Apt 208 Chicago IL 60634	NI	Teacher	EM			RF	1974
Gallagher John J III	(231)725-9502 brownstea@aol.com	732 Mapleway Dr Norton Shores MI 49441	MI	Teacher	EM			CQ	2002
Gallagher Megan J	(586)907-1649 megsgalla@hotmail.com	4180 N Euclid Ave Bay City MI 48706	MI	Teacher	Tchr	St Paul Bay City MI	(989)684-4450	AA	2002
Gallegos Bethany J Rempfer	(720)217-7017 gallegoszion@gmail.com	881 Macaw St Brighton CO 80601	RM	Teacher	Tchr	Zion Brighton CO	(303)659-2339	S	2004
Gallert Frederick D	(616)780-1145 fdgallert@hotmail.com	11433 Hannibal St Commerce City CO 80022	RM	Teacher	EM			S	1975
Galligar Timothy J	(812)390-5474 timothy.galligar@gmail.com	7522 E 80th St Indianapolis IN 46256	IN	Teacher	C08/2021			MQ	2015
Gallmann Grace M Miller	(714)514-7655 gracegallmann@gmail.com	59697 E Ankole Dr Oracle AZ 85623	EN	Teacher	EM			IV	1985
Gallmeier Edward C	(713)204-0572 egallmeier@aol.com	100 Bluff View Dr Apt 306a Belleair Blf FL 33770	FG	Teacher	EM			S	1962
Gallmeier Elizabeth A Huber	(713)817-4696 egallmeier@aol.com	100 Bluff View Dr Apt 306a Belleair Blf FL 33770	FG	Teacher	EM			S	1962
Galloway Shannon M Bobo	(916) 261-7086 scienceshan@yahoo.com	8308 Grayledge Dr Austin TX 78753	TX	Teacher	C01/2020			AU	1999
Galucia LuAnn E Kaaz	(618)334-0613 lakaaz@gmail.com	988 Mount Hawley Ct Wentzville MO 63385	MO	DPM	EM			MQ	2008
Gamble Lori R Potratz	(712)320-3364 lorigamble02@gmail.com	2303 Jackson Ave Spirit Lake IA 51360	IW	DCE	EM			SP	1982
Gansberg Stephanie A	(775)461-6752 stephaniegansberg95@gmail.com	1211 Shady Oak Dr Carson City NV 89701	SO	Teacher	C07/2025			MQ	2018
Ganswindt Pamela K	(414)828-2658 pam.ganswindt@gmail.com	17654 W Lincoln Ave New Berlin WI 53146	SW	Teacher	C08/2022			CQ	1994
Garber Abigail C Keller	(219)916-1186 abigailgarber618@gmail.com	8810 Latitudes Dr Apt 819 Indianapolis IN 46237	IN	Teacher	Tchr	Holy Cross Indianapolis IN	(317)823-5801	CH	2015
Garber Darla R		3031 21st St Columbus NE 68601	NEB	Teacher	EM			S	1983

*Multiple Assignments (See Church Worker Locator for Additional Details)

See Page 53 for the Table of Abbreviations for key to District, Classification, Position, and College abbreviations.

**C =Candidate; EM =Emeritus; the date following the C is the month and year the Candidate status began

NAME	TELEPHONE NUMBER EMAIL	STREET ADDRESS CITY/STATE/ZIP	DISTRICT	CLASS.	POSITION/ STATUS**	WHERE SERVING	OFFICE PHONE	COLLEGE/ UNIV/CQ	YR GRAD
Garber Keri J Meyer	(309)360-2506	1436 Church Rd Eureka IL 61530	RM	Teacher	EM			MQ	2004
Garcia Bethany A Miller	(805)415-3009 bethanyconcordia@yahoo.com	1740 Huntington Dr Apt B S Pasadena CA 91030	PSW	Teacher	Tchr	Emmaus Alhambra CA	(626)289-3664	IV	2009
Garcia Brooke A Zarick	(812)525-8365 brooke.zarick@gmail.com	730 S Jackson Park Dr Seymour IN 47274	IN	Teacher	Tchr	St John Seymour IN	(812)523-3131	S	2015
Garcia Justin N	(989)686-2142	1311 S Mountain St Bay City MI 48706	MI	Teacher	Tchr	St Paul Bay City MI	(989)684-4450	CQ	2006
Garcia Susan	(405)432-7066 westwindscitylights@yahoo.com	16605 Valley View Earlsboro OK 74840	OK	Teacher	C09/2019			CQ	2010
Garcia Vanessa R Bakenhus	(832)584-7591 vrgarcia7@gmail.com	252 Gabriel Ct Thorndale TX 76577	TX	Teacher	Tchr	Immanuel Giddings TX	(979)542-2918	S	2008
Gardels Ann M	(402)534-2120 amgardels1955@gmail.com	355 Nebraska St Utica NE 68456	NEB	Teacher	EM			S	1991
Gardiner Linda L Dettmer	(714)966-9025 abcpro@juno.com	3291 Arizona Ln Costa Mesa CA 92626	PSW	Teacher	EM			RF	1961
Gardner-Scholz Jolynn R Miller	(308)687-6430 jolynngard@kdsi.net	3757 W Prairie Rd Grand Island NE 68803	NEB	Teacher	EM			S	2006
Garetson Mary H Wehmiller			CNH	Teacher	S Miss	Office of International Mission Saint Louis MO		S	1974
Garland Julie A Johnson	(770)517-3813 jagsmail@comcast.net	105 Waterford Falls Dr Canton GA 30114	FG	Teacher	C07/2016			S	1991
Garlock Rebecca Stoll	bgarlock@lakecountryhs.org	N82 W33607 Huckleberry Ln Oconomowoc WI 53066	SW	Teacher	Tchr	Lake Country Hartland WI	(262)367-8600	RF	1997
Garmatz Margaret P Born	(702)769-1818 mgarmatz@yahoo.com	1029 Weatherstone Ln Howell MI 48843	MO	Teacher	EM			S	1963
Garmon Martha L Isbell Machell Dr	(903)245-2980 martha_garmon@yahoo.com	3510 Darnell Dr. Paris TX 75462	TX	DPM	EM			CQ	2004
Garner Emily R Books	(512)573-3900 emilygarner1995@gmail.com	1104 Wandering Brook St Magnolia TX 77354	TX	DCE	Mem C	Salem Tomball TX	(281)351-8223	AU	2018
Garrabrant Rachel A Richert	(734)308-0366 rachel.garrabrant@gmail.com	15518 Pilgrim Hall Dr Friendswood TX 77546	TX	Teacher	Tchr	South Houston TX	(281)464-8299	AA	1998
Garrett Carol A Wuerflein	(316)712-1031 cmmgarrett@cox.net	6805 W Sheriac Cir Wichita KS 67209	KS	Parish Assist	EM			AA	1986
Garrett Ethel M Ellwein	(414)217-9645 ethelmg37@gmail.com	3308 Cathy Dr Joliet IL 60431	NI	Teacher	EM			RF	1975
Garrett Sheri L Mounts	(219)836-5231	231 Lawndale Dr Munster IN 46321	NI	Teacher	EM			RF	1970
Garrison Katrina L Dunker	(828)464-3011 kgarrison@concordianc.org	327 E Herman St Newton NC 28658	SE	Teacher	Tchr	Concordia Conover NC	(828)464-3324	AA	2013
Garrity Madeline R Schult	(636)577-7517 madelinegarrity@gmail.com	335 Valverde Dr South San Francisco CA 94080	CNH	Teacher	C06/2021			RF	2017
Garske John E	(402)641-4467 redeemgarske@clarks.net	432 S Columbia Ave Seward NE 68434	NEB	Teacher	EM			S	1972
Garvey Barbara A Zahrndt	davidandbarbg@sbcglobal.net	56 Piepers Glen Ct O Fallon MO 63366	MO	Teacher	EM			CQ	1992
Garvey Lydia W Wilcke	(712)369-1618 lydiadce@gmail.com	512 Williamsburg Ln Odenton MD 21113	TX	DCE	C07/2016			S	2008
Garvue Kimberly L Goetz	(217)698-2949 kgarvue@gmail.com	8 Pinto Dr Springfield IL 62702	CI	Teacher	Tchr	Trinity Springfield IL	(217)787-2323	MQ	1993
Gary Susan D Krackhardt	(210)452-8325 gary1092@sbcglobal.net	11225 S Foster Rd Lot 5 San Antonio TX 78223	TX	Teacher	EM			RF	1985
Gasau Ashley B Thomas	(262)488-1869 waterfallstars@yahoo.com	6639 Bobolink Rd Racine WI 53402	SW	Teacher	Tchr	St John Racine WI	(262)633-2758	CQ	2012
Gasau Nicholas W	(303)596-9129 nickmyson@yahoo.com	6639 Bobolink Rd Racine WI 53402	SW	Teacher	Tchr	Lutheran High School Racine WI	(262)637-6538	MQ	2002
Gass Stacie Kanning	(260)433-5507 stacie_gass@hotmail.com	12217 Sanctuary Trl Fort Wayne IN 46814	IN	Teacher	Tchr	Sub Bethlehem Fort Wayne IN	(260)484-7873	CQ	2019
Gasser Mary E	(618)531-1508 mary.gasser1025@gmail.com	1514 Apple Blossom Cir Osage Beach MO 65065	MO	Teacher	Tchr	The King's Academy Lake Ozark MO	(573)693-9245	CQ	2021
Gassner Nanette K Geschke	(920)387-3981	769 Green Bay Dr Unit 7 Mayville WI 53050	SW	Teacher	EM			CQ	2004
Gast Andrea C Andrea Hricko	(301)974-4090 agast524@gmail.com	6740 Marvin Ave. Sykesville MD 21784	SE	Teacher	Tchr	Emmanuel Catonsville MD	(410)744-0015	BR	2014
Gast Carolyn R Fischer	(586)745-7336 cmustang7@att.net	17173 Timber Dr Macomb MI 48042	MI	Teacher	EM			RF	1966
Gast Holly A Scheff	(320)492-0400 hgast12@gmail.com	12833 W Flower St Avondale AZ 85392	PSW	Teacher	Mem C	Crown Of Life Sun City West AZ	(623)546-6228	MQ	2006
Gast Randal C	(443)876-6707 rgast2979@gmail.com	2964 Dumbarton Dr Abingdon MD 21009	SE	Teacher	EM			S	1979
Gast Timothy R	(443)866-7676 thegasts4@gmail.com	12833 W Flower St Avondale AZ 85392	PSW	Teacher	Prin	Valley Phoenix AZ	(602)230-1600	S	2006
Gast Warren E Jr	(773)501-3838 wgast@stjames-lutheran.org	2026 W Bradley Pl Chicago IL 60618	NI	Teacher	EM			RF	1975
Gasteiner Nancy L Albrecht	(630)773-8220 nlg0924@aol.com	1917 E Lilac Ter Arlington Heights IL 60004	NI	Teacher	EM			RF	1973
Gastler Gregory L	(314)832-7696 glgastler@sbcglobal.net	6712 Alexander St Saint Louis MO 63116	MO	Teacher	EM			RF	1986
Gastler Susan E	(301)751-4865 sgastler@growingwithgrace.org	8970 Mount Air Rd Newburg MD 20664	SE	Teacher	Prin	Grace La Plata MD	(301)932-0963	S	1994
Gatchell Matthew W	(262)370-1186 Matthew.Gatchell1@gmail.com	735 Canterbury Cir Hartland WI 53029	SW	DCM	EM			MQ	1991
Gates Andra S Jacobsen Deac	(605)660-8146 andra.gates@gmail.com	706 E 2nd St Mountain Home AR 72653	MDS	Deaconess	Mem C	Redeemer Mountain Home AR	(870)425-6071	FW-DEAC	2018

*Multiple Assignments (See Church Worker Locator for Additional Details)
See Page 53 for the Table of Abbreviations for key to District, Classification, Position, and College abbreviations.
**C =Candidate; EM =Emeritus; the date following the C is the month and year the Candidate status began

NAME	TELEPHONE NUMBER EMAIL	STREET ADDRESS CITY/STATE/ZIP	DISTRICT	CLASS.	POSITION/ STATUS**	WHERE SERVING	OFFICE PHONE	COLLEGE/ UNIV/CQ	YR GRAD
Gath Edythe M Lemke	(716)694-6825 gath572@aol.com	572 Ward Rd N Tonawanda NY 14120	EA	Teacher	Tchr	St John North Tonawanda NY	(716)693-9677	CQ	1998
Gatlin Carlee M Hefta	(405)295-1731 cgatlin@holytrinityedmond.org	9100 NW 86th Ct Yukon OK 73099	OK	Teacher	Tchr	Holy Trinity Edmond OK	(405)844-4000	S	1999
Gatlin Connie E Eilers	(972)494-4875 conniegx3@gmail.com	1845 Westcreek Drive Garland TX 75042	TX	Teacher	EM			S	1979
Gaudi Robert D Jr Dr	(808)381-5426 dgaudi@smls-hawaii.org	739 Hahaione St Honolulu HI 96825	CNH	Teacher	Prin	St Mark Kaneohe HI	(808)227-3930	CQ	2002
Gaudineer Elizabeth O Oelfke	(952)934-4213	8941 Knollwood Dr Eden Prairie MN 55347	MNS	Teacher	EM			SP	1967
Gauss Alicia J Stueber	(630)739-7703 egauss@hiscross.org	2048 Deerpoint Ln Yorkville IL 60560	NI	Teacher	Tchr	Cross Yorkville IL	(630)553-7861	MQ	1999
Gavigan Brittney Ulik	(262)389-5970	2318 Park Ave West Bend WI 53090	SW	Teacher	Tchr	St John West Bend WI	(262)429-1061	MQ	2013
Gavrun Andrew G IV	(260)445-5020 andrew.gavrun@trinitydavenport.org	1001 W Hickory Ct Eldridge IA 52748	IE	Teacher	Tchr	Trinity Davenport IA	(563)322-5224	AA	2003
Gaylor Phillip C	(909)615-8370 cadce06@gmail.com	15 Christamon W Irvine CA 92620	PSW	DCE	Mem C	Redeemer Ontario CA	(909)986-2615	IV	1991
Gebers Bethany E Mrosko	(262)212-9223 bgebers@trinityoflincoln.org	1420 Washington St. Lincoln NE 68502	NEB	DCO	Mem C	Trinity Lincoln NE	(402)474-0606	SP	2021
Gebhardt Charles E	(801)867-7735 c.gebhardt.sllhs@gmail.com	640 S 2nd St Seward NE 68434	NEB	Teacher	EM			S	1991
Gebhardt Deborah E Wehling	debgeb36@msn.com	1341 Fairlane Ave Seward NE 68434	NEB	Teacher	Tchr	St John Seward NE	(402)643-4535	S	1993
Gebhardt Gretchen S Foth	(402)643-6989 gebhardt2@windstream.net	1434 Eastridge Ave Seward NE 68434	NEB	Teacher	EM			S	1975
Gebhardt Kathryn L Krohe	(630)405-9441 kathy.gebhardt@cuchicago.edu	990 Waterside Ct Aurora IL 60502	NI	Teacher	S HS/C	Concordia University Chicago River Forest IL	(708)771-8300	RF	1996
Gebhardt Macy R	(402)643-5009 macygebhardt01@gmail.com	4216 S Manhattan Ave Apt 201 Tampa FL 33611	FG	Teacher	Tchr	Holy Trinity Tampa FL	(813)839-0665	Other	2024
Gedvilas Leah K Meier	(708)321-0571 lgedvilas0571@gmail.com	1117 Beloit Ave Forest Park IL 60130	NI	Teacher	C07/2016			RF	2009
Gedvilase Emily C Meier	(734)740-1006 meiercemily@gmail.com	945 Circle Ave Forest Park IL 60130	NI	Teacher	Tchr	Immanuel Elmhurst IL	(630)832-9302	MQ	2020
Gehlen Joy K Nickel	(503)649-5644 gehlenj@fhlcs.org	23724 SW Aspen Lake Dr Sherwood OR 97140	NOW	Teacher	Tchr	Forest Hills Cornelius OR	(503)359-4853	CQ	2017
Gehm John W	(989)798-2839 jgehmmer@gmail.com	3755 N 100th St Milwaukee WI 53222	SW	Teacher	Tchr	Trinity Mequon WI	(262)242-2045	MQ	2013
Gehm Rebecca A	(989)798-5775 ragtime2022@gmail.com	11889 Rathburn Rd Birch Run MI 48415	MI	Teacher	Tchr	St Michaels Richville MI	(989)868-4809	MQ	2022
Gehm Stephanie A Zimmer	(952)200-0902 stephannzimmer@gmail.com	3755 N 100th St Milwaukee WI 53222	SW	Teacher	Tchr	Pilgrim Wauwatosa WI	(414)259-0190	CH	2009
Gehner Norma Jean H Geidel	(217)552-3225 njgehner@gmail.com	22805 Monke Rd Mount Olive IL 62069	SI	Teacher	EM			S	1968
Gehring David J	(206)937-9180 dgehr5803@aol.com	1737 Harbor Ave SW Unit S301 Seattle WA 98126	NOW	Teacher	EM			RF	1964
Gehring Irene H Volz	(206)937-9180 sebelady@aol.com	1737 Harbor Ave SW Unit S301 Seattle WA 98126	NOW	Teacher	EM			RF	1961
Gehring Mary A Ortmann	(602)380-3777	8313 E Citrus Way Scottsdale AZ 85250	PSW	Teacher	EM			CQ	1995
Gehring Susann M Erdman	(256)837-0610 sgehring4@gmail.com	115 Netherbury Ln Madison AL 35758	SO	DCE	C07/2016			S	1996
Gehrke Amy C	(971)344-1878 amy.c.gehrke@gmail.com	6125 NE Wasco St Portland OR 97213	NOW	Teacher	C08/2020			PO	1996
Gehrke Andrea	(503)720-2005 dceandrea@yahoo.com	5650 SW Hall Blvd Beaverton OR 97005	NOW	DCE	Mem C	Pilgrim Beaverton OR	(503)644-8697	IV	1999
Gehrke Daniel E	(303)625-3657 gehrke1818@yahoo.com	11142 Bayne Way Parker CO 80134	RM	Teacher	Tchr	Lutheran Parker CO	(303)841-5551	MQ	1995
Gehrke Dennis E	(262)354-8266 dgehrke2@sbcglobal.net	1090 Pine Ridge Ct Oconomowoc WI 53066	SW	Teacher	EM			SP	1970
Gehrke Dorothy J Kamphoefner	(262)354-8266 dgehrke2@sbcglobal.net	1090 Pine Ridge Ct Oconomowoc WI 53066	SW	Teacher	EM			SP	1970
Gehrke Kristin A Weddick	(720)979-6179 gehrke1818@yahoo.com	11142 Bayne Way Parker CO 80134	RM	Teacher	C07/2016			IV	1998
Gehrke Seth W	(209)602-7629 sethgehrke@gmail.com	13327 Shaft Dr Cypress TX 77429	TX	Teacher	Mem C	St John Cypress TX	(281)373-0503	SP	2004
Gehrke Stacy M Johnson	(414)630-0817 gehrkefamily04@gmail.com	11823 N Church Pl Mequon WI 53097	SW	Teacher	Tchr	Trinity Mequon WI	(262)242-2045	MQ	2002
Gehrs Kathleen A Sandfort	(989)890-5272 kagehrs@hotmail.com	400 Sunburst Dr Frankenmuth MI 48734	MI	Teacher	EM			RF	1973
Geidel David O	(402)304-7657 dave.geidel@sddlcms.org	40242 169th St Dimock SD 57331	SD	Teacher	EM			S	1972
Geidel Jeremy T	(402)646-2215 jtgeidel@gmail.com	184 E Seward St Seward NE 68434	NEB	Teacher	Prin	Lincoln Lincoln NE	(402)467-5404	S	1996
Geier Gary L	(920)892-2897 ggeier@wi.rr.com	P.O. Box 117 Two Rivers WI 54241	SW	Teacher	EM			RF	1966
Geiger Ruth Ann D Marl	(937)209-9647 rdgeiger48@gmail.com	12891 Brown Moder Rd Marysville OH 43040	OH	Teacher	EM			S	1970
Geihsler Verna B	(504)289-9113 vgeihsler@hotmail.com	409 Blossom St Terrytown LA 70056	SO	Teacher	EM			S	1971
Geikas Sarah M Kaufman	sarahg@immanuelbaycity.com	320 N Sherman St Bay City MI 48708	MI	DPM	Mem C	Immanuel Bay City MI	(989)893-4088	S	2004
Geil Jean R Sundell Hedrich	(248)652-7098 geilfamily@aol.com	1221 Miniature Ct Rochester Hls MI 48307	MI	Teacher	EM			RF	1964

*Multiple Assignments (See Church Worker Locator for Additional Details)
See Page 53 for the Table of Abbreviations for key to District, Classification, Position, and College abbreviations.
**C =Candidate; EM =Emeritus; the date following the C is the month and year the Candidate status began

NAME	TELEPHONE NUMBER EMAIL	STREET ADDRESS CITY/STATE/ZIP	DISTRICT	CLASS.	POSITION/ STATUS**	WHERE SERVING	OFFICE PHONE	COLLEGE/ UNIV/CQ	YR GRAD
Geisinger Donald W	(619)698-6045 geisinger@cox.net	9282 Golondrina Dr La Mesa CA 91941	PSW	Teacher	EM			S	1963
Geisler Carol A Dr	(657)221-0513 cgeisler7@aol.com	149 N Batavia St Unit 7 Orange CA 92868	PSW	Teacher	EM			S	1975
Geisler Deborah J Keller	(402)975-7993 drg531arm@yahoo.com	5346 NW Tudor Ln Lincoln NE 68521	NEB	DCE	EM			S	2005
Geisler Emily G Weimer	(970)518-0164 wwjd_chick2004@hotmail.com	3242 N. 52 St Lincoln NE 68504	RM	Teacher	Tchr	Immanuel Albuquerque NM	(505)242-0616	S	2008
Geisler George H	(949)215-2585 georgefineart@gmail.com	26595 Dolorosa Mission Viejo CA 92691	PSW	Teacher	EM			CQ	1986
Geisler Herbert G Jr Dr	(949)689-5391 hgeisler@icloud.com		PSW	Teacher	EM			CH	1970
Geisler Rebecca G	(925)961-4995 num62426@gmail.com	735 Watson Canyon Ct Apt 118 San Ramon CA 94582	CNH	DCE	Mem C	St Philip Dublin CA	(925)828-2117	S	2004
Geistfeld Christine K Meyer	(507)776-2452 christine.geistfeld@cune.org	43172 760th Ave Saint James MN 56081	MNS	Teacher	Tchr	St Paul Truman MN	(507)776-2801	S	1992
Geistfeld Sierra C	(507)432-6931 sierra.geisfeld@cune.org	4404 W Chippewa Circle Apt #11 Sioux Fall SD 57106	SD	Teacher	Tchr	Sioux Falls Sioux Falls SD	(605)335-1923	S	2023
Gellerman-Long Joanna I Gellerman	(425)591-5318 jogellermanlong@gmail.com	1609 Washington St Beatrice NE 68310	NEB	Teacher	Tchr	St Paul Beatrice NE	(402)223-3414	CQ	2010
Gemar Anna M Dauffenbach	dceanna@redeemermqt.org	1700 West Fair Avenue Marquette MI 49855	NW	DCE	Mem C	Redeemer Marquette MI	(906)228-9883	SP	2015
Generally Amber A Fountain	(636)744-4469 evenifg3@gmail.com	12767 Bluebird Street NW Coon Rapids MN 55448	MNS	Teacher	Tchr	Trinity First Minneapolis MN	(612)871-2353	S	2003
Gengler Constance C Koester	(989)450-1593 conjonge@yahoo.com	1625 Wilder Rd Auburn MI 48611	MI	Teacher	EM			RF	1970
Genig Dennis K Dr	(734)624-2110 genigd@hotmail.com	17723 Yorkshire Dr Riverview MI 48193	MI	Teacher	EM			RF	1974
Genrich Lee Ann E Stohs	(402)228-1357 rvlegenrich@alltel.net	322 N 21st St Beatrice NE 68310	NEB	Teacher	EM			S	1963
Genske Stephanie L Litfin	(952)442-4165 stephanie.genske@trinitywaconia.org	823 Quail Run Waconia MN 55387	MNS	Teacher	Tchr	Trinity Waconia MN	(952)442-4165	MQ	1988
Genszler Christopher M	(262)384-0031 cmgensz53095@gmail.com	3 Founders Way Unit C Saint Louis MO 63105	NW	Teacher	C07/2024			S	2018
Genter Helen L Zurstadt	(913)682-6434 lgenter63@gmail.com	724 W 7th St Leavenworth KS 66048	KS	Teacher	EM			RF	1965
Genthner Clinton F	(517)745-5386 clintgenthner@gmail.com	13380 Clinton Rd Onondaga MI 49264	MI	Teacher	Tchr	Trinity Jackson MI	(517)784-3135	AA	1995
Genthner Richard G Jr	(734)834-1129 rgenthner@trinitylutheran-rc.org	5155 E Marquette Trl Chase MI 49623	MI	Teacher	Tchr	Trinity Reed City MI	(231)832-5186	AA	1990
Genzlinger Hope M Hennies	(605)391-9046 hope.genzlinger@zionrc.org	1536 Tablerock Rd Rapid City SD 57701	SD	Teacher	Tchr	Zion Rapid City SD	(605)342-5749	S	1999
George Connie M Steffens	(219)242-4563 cmjbgeorge@msn.com	614 W Edwards St Springfield IL 62704	CI	Teacher	Tchr	Our Savior's Springfield IL	(217)546-4531	RF	1990
George Jill M Brehm	(262)347-6557 jgeorge2@wi.rr.com	N54W37034 Yale St Oconomowoc WI 53066	SW	Teacher	Tchr	St Paul Oconomowoc WI	(262)567-5001	CQ	2019
George Patricia S Starck	(503)763-1872	251 Hylo Rd SE Salem OR 97306	NOW	Teacher	EM			CQ	1987
Georgi Mary E Laney	(440)864-2739 marygeorgi68@gmail.com	36451 N Reserve Cir Avon OH 44011	OH	Teacher	EM			RF	1967
Georgius Angela J Krebs Baumann	(505)357-5321 angela.baumann@gmail.com	1723 Tamarack St. Plover WI 54467	NW	Teacher	Tchr	St Paul Stevens Point WI	(715)344-5660	MQ	2006
Geraci Rachel C Fickenscher Deac	(260)418-6196 rachel.geraci89@gmail.com	1295 Milan Oakville Rd Milan MI 48160	MI	Deaconess	C03/2020			FW-DEAC	2017
Gerard Dana S	(713)384-5873 danagerard64@gmail.com	5502 Oak Trail Ln Houston TX 77091	TX	Teacher	EM			S	1985
Gerard Lance D	(713)553-4365 lancegerard001@gmail.com	4807 Droddy St Houston TX 77091	TX	Teacher	EM			S	1986
Gerber Glenn D	(281)725-1130 glenn707480@gmail.com	40436 Via Estrada Murrieta CA 92562	PSW	Teacher	EM			RF	1974
Gerber Joan C Stresemann -Malotky	(619)565-7904 jcgerber49@gmail.com	694 Myra Ave Chula Vista CA 91910	PSW	Teacher	EM			S	1972
Gerberding Jill L Doerfler	jill.gerberding@gmail.com	11 W Fairview Ln Springfield IL 62711	CI	Teacher	EM			CQ	2005
Gerbers Craig T	(260)227-0801 craig.gerbers@gmail.com	3332 Vantage Point Dr Apt 2a Fort Wayne IN 46825	IN	Teacher	Tchr	Concordia Fort Wayne IN	(260)483-1102	RF	2011
Gerdes Drew D Dr	(417)848-3937 drew.gerdes@cune.edu	1048 Ironwood Drive Seward NE 68434	NEB	Teacher	S HS/C	Concordia University Nebraska Seward NE	(402)643-3651	SP	2000
Gerdes Katherine M Cluver	(580)301-4073 Hag88CTC@gmail.com	2651 Whyburn Dr Apt 1274 Flower Mound TX 75028	TX	Teacher	EM			RF	1962
Gerds Fredrick A	(248)549-3642 fmgerds@prodigy.net	4614 Hampton Blvd Royal Oak MI 48073	MI	Teacher	EM			RF	1964
Gerdts Terry L	(314)409-5453 terry.gerdts@outlook.com	P.O. Box 877 Concordia MO 64020	MO	Teacher	EM			S	1968
Geres Theone P Schultz	(805)428-3267 the1geres@yahoo.com	2063 Sheridan Ct Simi Valley CA 93065	PSW	Teacher	EM			S	1973
Gerhardt Matthew A	(314)822-0447 mgerhardt@stpaulsdp.org	1 Lookout Ave Valley Park MO 63088	MO	DPM	Mem C	St Paul Des Peres MO	(314)822-0447	MQ	2012
Gerig Susan E	(260)705-8620 sgmof3@comcast.net	15831 Platter Rd New Haven IN 46774	IN	Teacher	C08/2023			CQ	2018
Gerken Charles	(480)661-1585 mapapickel@msn.com	9340 E Wood Dr Scottsdale AZ 85260	PSW	Tch/DCE	EM			S	1974
Gerken Eric L	(402)620-5877 eric.gerken@poporlando.com	13305 Lake Turnberry Circle Orlando FL 32828	FG	DCE	Mem C	Prince Of Peace Orlando FL	(407)277-3945	S	1997

*Multiple Assignments (See Church Worker Locator for Additional Details)
See Page 53 for the Table of Abbreviations for key to District, Classification, Position, and College abbreviations.
**C =Candidate; EM =Emeritus; the date following the C is the month and year the Candidate status began

NAME	TELEPHONE NUMBER EMAIL	STREET ADDRESS CITY/STATE/ZIP	DISTRICT	CLASS.	POSITION/ STATUS**	WHERE SERVING	OFFICE PHONE	COLLEGE/ UNIV/CQ	YR GRAD
Gerken Joshua P	(419)966-9356 joshua.gerken@gmail.com	5418 Brighton Dr Fort Wayne IN 46825	OH	DCE	C07/2021			S	2005
Gerken Rachel E	(269)470-4475	5418 Brighton Dr. Fort Wayne IN 46825	IN	Teacher	Pro Stf	Central New Haven IN	(260)493-2502	MQ	2016
Gerken Terri N Neer	(269)277-8769 picklegirl6@gmail.com	942 Wedgewood Rd Saint Joseph MI 49085	MI	Teacher	EM			AA	2001
Gerlach Eileen K Altenburg	(734)476-1799 eijoger68@sbcglobal.net	17939 Woodside St Livonia MI 48152	MI	Teacher	EM			S	1968
Gerlach John W	(734)634-0818 eijoger68@gmail.com	17939 Woodside St Livonia MI 48152	MI	Teacher	EM			S	1968
Gerlach Linda M Luke	(716)472-5499 lgerlach49@yahoo.com	3959 Forest Pkwy Apt 227 N Tonawanda NY 14120	EA	Tch/DCE	EM			S	1971
Gerlach Lucas J	(920)245-1474 lgerrlach@yahoo.com	2507 Riviera Circle Fort Smith AR 72903	MDS	Teacher	Tchr	First Fort Smith AR	(479)785-2886	S	1996
Gerlach Michelle R	(920)245-1904 mgerlach412@gmail.com	2507 Rivirera Cir Fort Smith AR 72903	MDS	Teacher	Mem C	First Fort Smith AR	(479)785-2886	S	1999
Gerlach Robin K	rob.gerlach@redeemer.net	2261 Park Place Cir Round Rock TX 78681	TX	Teacher	Tchr	Redeemer Austin TX	(512)459-1500	S	1978
Gerlach Roxanne C Stenson	(262)995-5701	3700 Honey Tree Ln Milwaukee WI 53221	SW	Teacher	EM			CQ	1991
Germain Sarah E	(727)517-5961 sarah.germain@aol.com	4595 Grand Preserve Pl Palm Harbor FL 34684	FG	Teacher	Tchr	Grace Saint Petersburg FL	(727)527-6213	CQ	2016
Germain Timothy B	(651)295-9962 tcgerm93@gmail.com	1211 4th St E Saint Paul MN 55106	MNS	DCE	Mem C	Eastern Hghts Saint Paul MN	(651)735-4202	SP	2013
German Sue A Uffelman	(260)579-7126 suegerman11@gmail.com	7002 Blake Dr Fort Wayne IN 46804	IN	Teacher	EM			S	1978
Germann Kenneth R	(972)955-0897 krgermann@frontier.com	2209 Covered Wagon Dr Plano TX 75074	TX	Teacher	EM			RF	1965
Gernant Renea B Dr	(402)643-1113 renea.gernant@gmail.com	P.O. Box 105 Louisville NE 68037	NEB	Teacher	C07/2016			S	1988
Gerndt Donna M Manthei	(414) 731-1533 Donna.gerndt@outlook.com	W1237 N Blue Spring Lk Dr Palmyra WI 53156	SW	Teacher	EM			SP	1970
Gerner Steven W Dr	(414)355-2748 gernerx@gmail.com	8806 W Daventry Rd Mequon WI 53097	SW	Teacher	C10/2023			CQ	2011
Gerold Abby J Dawkins	(816)204-0342	19200 Mill Dr Fergus Falls MN 56537	MNN	DCO	C07/2016			SP	2007
Gerrard Claire A Deac	(540)553-5252 cgerrard5853@gmail.com	118 Grant Ave Apt A Garden City KS 67846	KS	Deaconess	Mem C	Trinity Garden City KS	(620)276-3110	FW-DEAC	2024
Gerth Caledonia M	(402)641-1861 caledonia.gerth@gmail.com	5812 Main St Apt 424 McCordsville IN 46055	IN	DPM	Mem C	Holy Cross Indianapolis IN	(317)823-5801	S	2011
Gerth Elsa Mauritz Deac	(618)251-1870 elsagerth@protonmail.com	N8076 County Road Ay # 2 Mayville WI 53050	SI	Deaconess	C06/2017			CH	2013
Gerth Joseph J	(618)660-4503 josephgerth@proton.me	N8076 Unit 2 Cty Ay Mayville WI 53050	SW	Teacher	Tchr	Immanuel Mayville WI	(920)387-5363	MQ	2010
Gerth Yvonne	(262)352-2268 ygerth@gmail.com	20880 George Hunt Cir Apt 436 Waukesha WI 53186	SW	Teacher	EM			S	1971
GeRue Valerie F Virchow	(920) 750-8711 vgerue@gmail.com	1018 N Hawthorne Dr Appleton WI 54915	SW	Teacher	Tchr	Trinity Menasha WI	(920)886-1083	MQ	1990
Gery Margit R Reetz	(330)722-8973 margitgery@aol.com	6340 Branch Rd Medina OH 44256	OH	Teacher	EM			RF	1970
Gesch David S	(612)968-6044 dgesch@redeemerwayzata.org	2459 Chateau Ln Mound MN 55364	MNS	Teacher	Tchr	Redeemer Wayzata MN	(952)473-5356	Other	1985
Gesch Joel T	(216) 215-6595 jtgesch@gmail.com	2560 Barkwood Dr Sheffield Vlg OH 44054	OH	Teacher	EM			S	1977
Gestrich Kristen M Bassett	(608)756-0527 kgestrich@stpaulsjanesville.com	444 Douglas St Janesville WI 53545	SW	Teacher	Tchr	St Pauls Janesville WI	(608)754-4471	CQ	2000
Getka-Sullivan Allison J	(262)749-4915 asullivan@centrallutheranschool.org	P.O. Box 261 Atkins IA 52206	IE	Teacher	Tchr	Central Newhall IA	(319)223-5271	MQ	2014
Gettelman Steven D	(262)853-7568 principal@graceoakcreek.org	W159N10785 Captains Dr Germantown WI 53022	SW	Teacher	Tchr	Grace Oak Creek WI	(414)762-3655	MQ	2005
Geu Daniel C		1634 N Garfield Ave Loveland CO 80538	RM	Teacher	Tchr	Immanuel Loveland CO	(970)667-4506	S	2011
Geurink Brenda R Bohannon	(515) 423-4422 brenda.geurink@yahoo.com	4681 Wakonda Dr Norwalk IA 50211	IW	Teacher	C07/2016			S	1996
Gewirz Betsy A Braun	(707)255-8498 iandb@cwnet.com	2452 Cabernet St Napa CA 94558	CNH	Teacher	Tchr	St John Napa CA	(707)226-7970	S	1974
Geye Cynthia A Schmidt	(224)456-4134 cindygeye@sbcglobal.net	1853 Water Birch Way Castle Rock CO 80108	NI	Teacher	EM			RF	1984
Geyer Marissa K Marler	(417)840-8895 marissakmarler@gmail.com	5626 S Farm Rd 59 Republic MO 65738	MO	Teacher	C07/2020			S	2009
Geyer Stephen H	(248)892-2651 geyerstephen@yahoo.com	2124 Hamilton Dr Granite City IL 62040	SI	Teacher	EM			S	1974
Geyer Thomas W	(623)337-6160 tom.geyer@yahoo.com	3330 De Torres Circle Round Rock TX 78665	TX	Teacher	EM			RF	1982
Giambalvo Nat Jr	(516)205-6842 sacrifice1980@yahoo.com	322 Harvest Mdw Temple TX 76502	AT	Teacher	C07/2016			BR	2008
Giammanco Leah J Meyers	(260)418-4459 ljoycm13@gmail.com	6563 Thoreau Dr Portage IN 46368	IN	Teacher	Tchr	Immanuel Valparaiso IN	(219)462-8207	RF	2015
Giammarino Beth A Bacon	(630)709-2384 bethgiammarino@gmail.com	739 S Princeton Ave Villa Park IL 60181	NI	Teacher	EM			RF	1984
Giannotta Carlo	(773)762-1234 cgiannotta@gcachicago.org	3133 Highland Ave Berwyn IL 60402	NI	Teacher	Prin	Grace Chicago IL	(773)762-1234	RF	1995
Giannotta Jill M Erdmann	mrsg123@gcachicago.org	3133 Highland Ave Berwyn IL 60402	NI	Teacher	Tchr	Grace Chicago IL	(773)762-1234	RF	1994

*Multiple Assignments (See Church Worker Locator for Additional Details)
See Page 53 for the Table of Abbreviations for key to District, Classification, Position, and College abbreviations.
**C =Candidate; EM =Emeritus; the date following the C is the month and year the Candidate status began

NAME	TELEPHONE NUMBER EMAIL	STREET ADDRESS CITY/STATE/ZIP	DISTRICT	CLASS.	POSITION/ STATUS**	WHERE SERVING	OFFICE PHONE	COLLEGE/ UNIV/CQ	YR GRAD
Gianonne Debra Waters		131 Brookville Rd Glen Head NY 11545	AT	Teacher	Tchr	Long Island Brookville NY	(516)626-1735	BR	2001
Gibbon Karen M Knorr	(215)428-9228 gibbonfamily@gmail.com	141 Winding Way Morrisville PA 19067	EA	Teacher	EM			RF	1981
Gibbons Allison N Jones	gibbonsa@newlhs.com		NW	Teacher	Tchr	Northeastern WI Green Bay WI	(920)469-6810	CH	2011
Gibbons Lana R Lorenz	(815)575-3094 lanagibbonsmusic@gmail.com	3014 Deerpass Rd Marengo IL 60152	NI	Teacher	Mem C	Trinity Huntley IL	(847)669-5780	RF	1976
Gibelyou Sherrie L Mael	(253)389-0349 sherriegibelyou@comcast.net	6202 59th Street Ct W University Pl WA 98467	NOW	Teacher	Tchr	Concordia Tacoma WA	(253)475-9513	CQ	2015
Gibson Daniel J	(913)326-4597 daniel.gibson@cune.org	1218 N Wheeler Ave Grand Island NE 68801	NEB	Teacher	Tchr	Grand Island Grand Island NE	(308)385-3900	S	2013
Gibson Denean A	(419)902-9370 dgibson@trinityvikings.org	613 Sackett St Maumee OH 43537	OH	Teacher	Tchr	Trinity Toledo OH	(419)385-2651	CQ	2017
Gibson Kathryn E Parks	(541) 771-1537 gibson.kathy.e@gmail.com	195 Temelec Cir Sonoma CA 95476	NOW	Teacher	EM			CQ	2001
Gibson Lisette L Lueker	(989)667-0852	4700 Fox Pointe Dr Unit 210 Bay City MI 48706	MI	Teacher	EM			RF	1967
Gibson Rebeca	(281)574-4149 rebeca.gibson@live.com	23702 Hawkins Creek Ct Katy TX 77494	TX	Teacher	Tchr	Westlake Lutheran Richmond TX	(281)341-9910	CQ	2012
Gierach Raymond C	(586)322-2015 rgierachlaw@gmail.com	21143 Lily Ln Clinton Township MI 48036	MI	Teacher	EM			RF	1976
Gierke Jennifer D Behling	(978)660-1288 jenngierke@verizon.net	36 Ranlett Lane Billerica MA 01821	NE	Teacher	Tchr	Of The Savior Bedford MA	(781)275-6013	S	1990
Gierse Emily C	(314)330-0764 emily.gierse@cune.org	7714 Sundance Dr Louisville KY 40222	IN	Teacher		Indiana District Fort Wayne IN	(800)837-1145	S	2011
Giertz Louise N	(618)391-7112 tlsteacher@yahoo.com	120 Northbay Ct Glen Carbon IL 62034	SI	Teacher	C09/2017			RF	1977
Gieschen Christopher J	(260)223-1557 playright2@yahoo.com	7620 Idlebrook Dr Fort Wayne IN 46835	IN	Teacher	EM			RF	1977
Gieschen Denise E Goeman	(313)330-6705 denise.gieschen@splgrafton.org	N108 W14569 Bel Aire Ln Germantown WI 53022	SW	Teacher	Tchr	St Paul Grafton WI	(262)377-4659	RF	1981
Gieseke Greta A	(402)570-6785 ggieseke@gmail.com	9734 Erskine Street Omaha NE 68134	NEB	Teacher	Tchr	Concordia Omaha NE	(402)445-4000	S	2007
Gieseke Richard W	(636)225-0210 rick.gieseke@gmail.com	835 Kentridge Ct Manchester MO 63021	MO	Teacher	EM			RF	1974
Gieseke Ruthann L	(314) 846-0765 ruthann.gieseke@gmail.com	2720 Cripple Creek Dr Saint Louis MO 63129	MO	Teacher	C07/2023			RF	1978
Giesselmann Duane L	(573)756-2249 dgiesselmann@stpaulgiants.com	P.O. Box 101 Doe Run MO 63637	MO	Teacher	EM			S	1969
Giff Lorayne P Knippenberg	(507)825-5539 lauriepg81@gmail.com	318 4th St SW Pipestone MN 56164	MNS	Teacher	EM			RF	1966
Gifford Charles J Sr	(907)378-9978 gbtrout@yahoo.com	P.O. Box 125 Alma MO 64001	MO	Teacher	EM			RF	1984
Gifford Teresa L Hyser	(816)565-1636 dynomom@yahoo.com	1693 Mel Dor Acres Dr Apt 58 Climax Cprings MO 65324	MO	Teacher	EM			RF	1983
Giguere Norman W	(410)747-1619 nwgiguere@gmail.com	6003 Keithmont Ct Baltimore MD 21228	SE	Teacher	EM			RF	1965
Gihring Barbara J		1428 NW Selbo Rd Bremerton WA 98311	NOW	Teacher	EM			S	1974
Gihring Diane A Arthurs	dianegihring@gmail.com	149 N Citrus St Orange CA 92868	PSW	Teacher	C04/2022			IV	1993
Gil de Rodriguez Perla Deac	(713)894-6148 pgdz22@gmail.com	2311 Churchill Cove Ln Pearland TX 77089	TX	Deaconess	Mem C	Gloria Dei Houston TX	(281)333-4535	SL-DEAC	2011
Gilbert Cheryl E Kuhl	(970)669-7914 cgilbert@immanuelloveland.org	2224 S Del Norte Dr Loveland CO 80537	RM	Teacher	Tchr	Immanuel Loveland CO	(970)667-7606	S	1990
Gilbert Joel M	(314)288-6429 jgilbert@lslancers.org	3643 Castleman Ave Saint Louis MO 63110	MO	Teacher	Tchr	Lutheran South Saint Louis MO	(314)631-1400	S	2005
Gilbert Kyle H	(541)678-1030 kyle.gilbert@saints.org	20648 SE Cougar Peak Dr Bend OR 97702	NOW	Teacher	Tchr	Trinity Bend OR	(541)382-1850	IV	2002
Gildersleeve Margaret R	(716)545-6367 margogilder@gmail.com	505 S 68th Ave Apt 3 Wausau WI 54401	NW	Teacher	EM			CQ	2003
Giles Donna L Krause	(623)512-0020 gilesj1221@gmail.com	16147 W Vista North Dr Sun City West AZ 85375	PSW	Teacher	EM			RF	1969
Giles Tiffany N Stutz	(619)322-3923 gtgiles@hotmail.com	7867 Orien Ave La Mesa CA 91941	PSW	Teacher	Tchr	Christ La Mesa CA	(619)462-5211	CQ	2016
Gill Dawn M	(260)557-4929 dawnmgill07@gmail.com	4034 Thorton Dr Fort Wayne IN 46815	IN	Teacher	C11/2021			CQ	2019
Gillam Jennifer L Barkman	(817)656-2675 gllmjn@sbcglobal.net	1811 Rolling Bend Dr Keller TX 76248	TX	Teacher	Tchr	Crown Of Life Colleyville TX	(817)251-1881	RF	1991
Gillam Linda A Mueller	(501)613-4267 lin.gillam33@gmail.com	7 Hidden Bluffs Dr Lake Saint Louis MO 63367	MO	Teacher	EM			S	1974
Gillard Michelle S Hausz			MNN	DCO	RSO	Lutheran Bible Translators Inc Concordia MO	(660)225-0810	SP	2000
Gillespie Angel L	(913)594-0565 angel.gillespie@gmail.com	3401 NW Cerrito Ln Riverside MO 64150	KS	DCE	C01/2022			S	2012
Gillet Christina A Deac	(859)229-5408 cturtles2@gmail.com	N8766 Lake View Dr Tomahawk WI 54487	NW	Deaconess	RSO	Lutherans for Life Nevada IA	(888)364-5433	FW-DEAC	2018
Gillingham Donald E	dongillingha53@gmail.com	4454 Doral Ct Loves Park IL 61111	NI	Teacher	EM			RF	1976
Gilliom Cassondra L	(260)413-5905 cwinsemann@gmail.com	4514 Greenridge Way New Haven IN 46774	IN	Teacher	C07/2023			CQ	2019
Gillis Christine M Whisler	(309)697-2391	1 Haylake Dr Pekin IL 61554	CI	Teacher	Tchr	Trinity Bloomington IL	(309)828-6265	MQ	2006
Gillis Jean A Barr	(954)472-2811 jean@stpaulweston.org	11361 Highway 87 N Milton FL 32570	FG	Teacher	Tchr	St Paul Weston FL	(954)384-9096	S	1981

*Multiple Assignments (See Church Worker Locator for Additional Details)
See Page 53 for the Table of Abbreviations for key to District, Classification, Position, and College abbreviations.
**C =Candidate; EM =Emeritus; the date following the C is the month and year the Candidate status began

NAME	TELEPHONE NUMBER EMAIL	STREET ADDRESS CITY/STATE/ZIP	DISTRICT	CLASS.	POSITION/ STATUS**	WHERE SERVING	OFFICE PHONE	COLLEGE/ UNIV/CQ	YR GRAD
Gillrup Hannah	(813)778-3427 hgillrup@gmail.com	8511 Lansdown Rd Henrico VA 23229	SE	DCM	D Ex/S	Southeastern District Henrico VA	(703)971-9371	MQ	2020
Gilmore Kendra A Honebrink	(763)248-3672 gilmorekendra@gmail.com	10725 County Road 152 Cologne MN 55322	MNS	Teacher	P/Tchr	Saint Johns Chaska MN	(952)448-2433	S	2008
Gilson Grace P	(810)728-8047 gracegilson@yahoo.com	810 Plate St Apt 105 Rochester MI 48307	MI	Teacher	Tchr	St John Rochester MI	(248)402-8000	AA	2018
Gingerich Kathleen L Weaver	(515)202-6309 gingericka@gmail.com	3842 52nd St Des Moines IA 50310	IW	Teacher	C07/2016			SP	1989
Ginkel Mary E Mussell	(952)412-7232 maryginkel@gmail.com	3350 Colfax Ave N Minneapolis MN 55412	MNN	DCE	EM			SP	1998
Gioe Christopher M	(989)652-3178 cgioe@att.net	564 Franconian Dr E Frankenmuth MI 48734	MI	Teacher	EM			RF	1970
Gioe Louise E Scheuerman	(989)652-3178 lgioe564@gmail.com	564 Franconian Dr E Frankenmuth MI 48734	MI	Teacher	EM			RF	1970
Giordano Jonathon	(618)656-0043 jon.giordano@melhs.org	20 Williamsburg Ln Glen Carbon IL 62034	SI	Teacher	Tchr	Metro-East Edwardsville IL	(618)656-0043	RF	1995
Giordano Lois L Bartell	lois.giordano627@gmail.com	2015 Washington Ave Cedarburg WI 53012	SW	Teacher	EM			RF	1970
Giordano Thomas A	(262)825-8033 tgio@frii.com	2015 Washington Ave Cedarburg WI 53012	SW	Teacher	EM			RF	1968
Gipple Leah K Meyer	(715)409-9458 lgipple@stjohnmerrill.org	W5286 Newport Ln Merrill WI 54452	NW	Teacher	Tchr	St John Merrill WI	(715)536-7264	MQ	2015
Girkant Abigail M Lessner	(219)713-3780 abtink76@yahoo.com	1004 Reyome Dr 2h Griffith IN 46319	IN	Teacher	C08/2023			RF	2000
Gjersvold Emma E	(714)225-3889 emma.gjersvold@eagles.cui.edu	6011 E Shenandoah Ave Orange CA 92867	PSW	Teacher	Tchr	St Johns Orange CA	(714)288-4406	IV	2022
Glackin Brittnie A	(303)912-1075 bbesel@ccls-stlouis.org	126 Carol Dr Eureka MO 63025	MO	Teacher	Tchr	Christ Community Kirkwood MO	(314)822-7774	S	2010
Glandorf Brenda K	(815)541-6997 gdorf@juno.com	119 Hampton Cir Williamsburg IA 52361	IE	Teacher	EM			CQ	1986
Glandorf Steven P	spglandorf@gmail.com	103 Hollyberry Ln Georgetown TX 78633	TX	Teacher	EM			S	1980
Glanzer John H	(407)451-7458 jaglanzer@yahoo.com	4174 Heirloom Rose Pl Oviedo FL 32766	S	Teacher	Tchr	St Lukes Oviedo FL	(407)365-3228	S	1990
Glaskey Lyla J Dover	(417)549-9012 lglaskey@martinlutherjoplin.com	3408 S Park Ave Joplin MO 64804	MO	Teacher	Tchr	Martin Luther Joplin MO	(417)624-1403	S	1997
Glaskey T J	(417)540-9011 dcejason@gmail.com	3408 S Park Ave Joplin MO 64804	MO	DCE	Mem C	Immanuel Joplin MO	(417)624-0333	S	1998
Glasnapp Susan M Maxwell		2905 Hampton Cir E Delray Beach FL 33445	FG	Teacher	EM			CQ	1997
Glassley Kaitlyn C Tibben	(270)853-1361 kaitlyn.glassley@gmail.com	1429 Woodridge Dr Danville IL 61832	SO	Teacher	C07/2016			S	2013
Glatczak Nancy E Koopman	(262)391-3082 glatczak@trinitysheboygan.org	737 N 26th St Sheboygan WI 53081	SW	Teacher	Tchr	Trinity Sheboygan WI	(920)458-8248	CQ	2003
Glause Emily R	(402)853-4637 emily.kohl@cune.org	4320 N 7th St. Apt 204 Lincoln NE 68521	NEB	Teacher	Tchr	Christ Lincoln NE	(402)483-7774	S	2019
Glaw Emilie F Wiegle	(563)608-6705 glawesome38@gmail.com	1624 Sky Blue Dr. Sun Prairie WI 53590	SW	DCE	Mem C	Living Christ Madison WI	(608)829-2136	SP	2008
Glawe Joel M	(920)858-5927	4866 S 81st St Milwaukee WI 53220	SW	Teacher	EM			RF	1973
Gleason Heather M Stippich	(507)456-5010 heathergleason@hotmail.com	1130 18th St SE Owatonna MN 55060	MNS	Teacher	Tchr	Good Shepherd Owatonna MN	(507)451-6821	CQ	2024
Glenn Dorothy E Naumann Deac	(314)495-7521 deacglenn@gmail.com	1468 Garden Glen Ct Gardnerville NV 89410	CNH	Deaconess	S HS/C	Sierra Carson City NV	(775)267-1921	CH	2013
Glessing Marlene K Bisping	(320)224-2152 teaching2long@gmail.com	11573 78th St SW Howard Lake MN 55349	MNS	Teacher	EM			SP	1978
Glessner Eric A	eglessner@lslancers.org	1719 Cedargate Way Imperial MO 63052	MO	Teacher	Tchr	Lutheran South Saint Louis MO	(314)631-1400	Other	1998
Glicker Jennifer Werner	(951)310-8125 jglicker@hephatha.net	830 Bayberry Dr Corona CA 92882	PSW	Teacher	Tchr	Hephatha Anaheim CA	(714)637-0887	CQ	2023
Glienke David H	(512)394-2391 dsglienke@sbcglobal.net	12213 Donington Dr Austin TX 78753	TX	Teacher	EM			S	1975
Glines Jackie L Fitzsimmons	(402)440-1516 jackie.glines@messiah.us	2318 N 74th St Lincoln NE 68507	NEB	Teacher	Tchr	Messiah Lincoln NE	(402)489-3024	S	1995
Glock Stephen L	(510)792-9956 katmandu4m@aol.com	37423 Stonewood Dr Fremont CA 94536	CNH	Teacher	EM			S	1966
Gloss Jacqueline A	(480)650-3599 jgloss@cglschool.org	4411 E Ridgewood Ln Gilbert AZ 85298	PSW	Teacher	Tchr	Christ Greenfield Gilbert AZ	(480)892-8521	CQ	2012
Glover Martha Lutz	(636)578-8856 glover2@mac.com	7 Scarsdale Manor Ct Saint Charles MO 63303	MO	Teacher	EM			RF	1972
Glover Sarah A Wright	(402)992-1382 theglovers2010@gmail.com	3123 N 168th Ave Omaha NE 68116	NEB	Teacher	Tchr	Concordia Luth Schools of Omaha Inc Omaha NE	(402)445-4000	S	2004
Glowinski Michael A	(303)408-4551 michael.glowinski@gmail.com	1063 Northeast 19th St Ocala FL 34470	FG	Teacher	P/Tchr	St John Ocala FL	(352)622-7275	RF	2000
Glumm Julie K Boes	julieglumm@gmail.com	4576 W Lewis Dr Bay City MI 48706	MI	Teacher	Tchr	Bethlehem Saginaw MI	(989)755-1144	CQ	2013
Gmirek Samuel W	(920)382-9757 sgmirek@trinityracine.com	2028 Marquette St Racine WI 53402	SW	Teacher	Tchr	Trinity Racine WI	(262)632-1766	MQ	2019
Gnagy Susan C Schumm	(303)237-9759 sgnagy@bethluth.net	2120 Vance St Lakewood CO 80214	RM	Teacher	Tchr	Bethlehem Lakewood CO	(303)233-0401	S	1978
Gnan Paul W	(414)745-1893 paul.gnan@cune.edu	1018 N 1st St Seward NE 68434	NEB	Teacher	S HS/C	Concordia University Nebraska Seward NE	(402)643-3651	MQ	1990
Gnan Peter D	(402)860-8936	1450 Ashwood Dr Elgin IL 60123	NI	Teacher	C03/2023			MQ	1992

*Multiple Assignments (See Church Worker Locator for Additional Details)
See Page 53 for the Table of Abbreviations for key to District, Classification, Position, and College abbreviations.
**C =Candidate; EM =Emeritus; the date following the C is the month and year the Candidate status began

NAME	TELEPHONE NUMBER EMAIL	STREET ADDRESS CITY/STATE/ZIP	DISTRICT	CLASS.	POSITION/ STATUS**	WHERE SERVING	OFFICE PHONE	COLLEGE/ UNIV/CQ	YR GRAD
Gnewuch Cynthia A Nerge	(248)840-8459 cindygnewuch@gmail.com	5481 Waters Bend Dr Belvidere IL 61008	NI	Teacher	Tchr	Immanuel Belvidere IL	(815)547-5346	RF	1986
Gobeli Jane E Emmerich	(414)861-0404 jane.gobeli@gmail.com	7103 Parke St Hobart IN 46342	SW	Teacher	Tchr	Wauwatosa Wauwatosa WI	(414)258-4558	CQ	2005
Godbold Ellen E Stamm	(616) 554-5792 godbold5@yahoo.com	7455 Carpet Rose Dr SE Caledonia MI 49316	MI	Teacher	Tchr	ISJ Grand Rapids MI	(616)363-0505	RF	1993
Godemann Dawn R	(801)718-1186 dawnrenae32@gmail.com	14491 Locust St Omaha NE 68116	NEB	Teacher	Tchr	St Mark Omaha NE	(402)391-6148	S	1998
Goecker Lowell R	(512)484-2387 lgoecker@icloud.com	2120 Flat Creek Dr Richardson TX 75080	TX	Teacher	EM			S	1967
Goecker Rebecca A Hayas	(812) 525-5994 bgoecker@immanuelschool.org	8 N State Road 11 Seymour IN 47274	IN	Teacher	Tchr	Immanuel Seymour IN	(812)522-1301	RF	1990
Goeckner Lori M Roberts		485 Iola Ln Farina IL 62838	CI	Teacher	Tchr	St Peter Saint Peter IL	(618)349-8888	CQ	2001
Goeden Amanda Kopetzky	(715)218-8747 goeden.amanda@gmail.com	801 Edgewater Dr Merrill WI 54452	NW	Teacher	Tchr	Trinity Merrill WI	(715)536-7501	MQ	2024
Goeglein Amber L Hopkins	(303)862-1188 amber.laree.hopkins@gmail.com	15125 Grant St Overland Park KS 66221	KS	Tch/DPM	Pro Stf	Christ Overland Park KS	(913)345-9700	S	2021
Goeglein DeLoy D	(303)233-5979 ddgbellman@gmail.com	11239 W 27th Ave Lakewood CO 80215	RM	Teacher	EM			RF	1962
Goeglein Donna F Vogel	(816)589-4799 dgoeglein3@gmail.com	11224 Grand Ave Kansas City MO 64114	MO	Teacher	EM			S	1972
Goeglein Sara A Winsemann	(260)580-0422 sgoeglein@clsfw.org	11063 State Road 37 E New Haven IN 46774	IN	Teacher	Tchr	Concordia Fort Wayne IN	(260)422-2429	CH	2007
Goehmann Heidi L Weirich Deac		7346 Golfwood Dr Ludington MI 49431	MI	Deaconess	C10/2020			CH	2002
Goehmann Rodney P	(906)484-8000	233 S Lake St Rogers City MI 49779	MI	Teacher	EM			S	1972
Goehmann Susan E	(734)756-9889 szgoehmann@gmail.com	26715 Whispering Willows Dr New Boston MI 48164	MI	Teacher	C04/2025			S	2024
Goehner Janice E Kraft	(410)652-5773 jangeohner@verizon.net	715 Mayton Ct Bel Air MD 21014	SE	Teacher	EM			BR	1979
Goeke David L	(210)690-3135 dgoeke984@sbcglobal.net	242 Early Trail Dr San Antonio TX 78228	TX	Teacher	EM			S	1970
Goekler Scheery L Renken	(405)471-2557 scheeryg@yahoo.com	1321 NW 185th St Edmond OK 73012	OK	Teacher	Tchr	Messiah Oklahoma City OK	(405)946-0681	CQ	2009
Goeman Marilyn H Osness	(414)377-1691 magoe@sbcglobal.net	815 Washington St Unit 111 Grafton WI 53024	SW	Teacher	EM			RF	1958
Goers Bethany L Ketcher	bgoers@tctrinityschool.org	4428 Silver Valley Ln Traverse City MI 49684	MI	Teacher	Tchr	Trinity Traverse City MI	(231)946-2720	RF	2005
Goetz Betty J Bokelheide	(785)273-0613 bjbok@sbcglobal.net	1918 SW Arrowhead Rd Topeka KS 66604	KS	Teacher	EM			SP	1966
Goetz Lois A Mortensen	(586)294-8137 loisgoetz@gmail.com	13748 Adams Ave Warren MI 48088	MI	Teacher	EM			RF	1974
Goetzke Janis M Heller	janisgoetzke@gmail.com	608 Carriage Hill Dr Watertown WI 53098	SW	Teacher	EM			RF	1970
Gohde Paul F	(262)784-8497 pfgohde@gmail.com	14332 Waters Edge Trl New Berlin WI 53151	EN	Teacher	EM			CQ	1985
Going Deborah L Bush	(812)376-6788 going-forth@hotmail.com	Urawa Lutheran School 1-22-18 Komaba Urawa-Ku Saitama-Shi-Ken 330-8 JAPAN	IN	Tch/DCE	S Miss	Office of International Mission Saint Louis MO		IV	2000
Going Pamela J Selke	(952)873-5591 goingnorth@aol.com	214 E Orchard St Belle Plaine MN 56011	MNS	Teacher	C07/2016			SP	1988
Going Thomas L Jr	(812)350-4483 tomdebigoing@gmail.com	4303 East Windsor Lane Columbus IN 47201	IN	Tch/DCE	S Miss	Office of International Mission Saint Louis MO		IV	2000
Golchert Kent R	(217)254-4102 kentgolchert@gmail.com	3010 Smiley Rd Bridgeton MO 63044	MO	Teacher	EM			S	1974
Goldammer Ashley A Theilen	(402)276-1059	8231 Tanner Bridge Rd Jefferson Cty MO 65101	MO	Teacher	Tchr	Immanuel Jefferson City MO	(573)496-3451	S	2010
Golden J R	(559)733-3855 bbwgolden1958@att.net	5912 W Whitley Ave Visalia CA 93291	CNH	Teacher	EM			RF	1958
Golden Tamara K Thornburg	(559)786-9180 tamijer2911@gmail.com	5912 W Whitley Ave Visalia CA 93291	CNH	Teacher	Tchr	Grace Visalia CA	(559)734-7694	S	1988
Goldgrabe Arthur D	(509)586-7193 artary@charter.net	524 N Ely St Apt F11 Kennewick WA 99336	NOW	DCE	EM			S	1957
Goldgrabe Eunice I Dr	(402)643-3814 egoldgrabe@neb.rr.com	1807 N Columbia Ave Seward NE 68434	NEB	Teacher	EM			S	1966
Goll Janet L Larsen	(580)716-2478 janetgoll@hotmail.com	1101 N Ash St Ponca City OK 74601	OK	Teacher	EM			S	1972
Goltermann Vicky L	(507)479-3145 vgoltermann@gmail.com	618 Long St Watertown WI 53098	SW	Teacher	Tchr	Good Shepherd Watertown WI	(920)261-2579	RF	1988
Goltl Amy M Brandon	(832)299-8087 amygoltl@gmail.com	5332 E Ashton St Wichita KS 67220	KS	Teacher	Tchr	Holy Cross Wichita KS	(316)684-4431	AU	2020
Golz Allison S Grube	(630)337-2144 nosilla328@aol.com	908 E Krage Dr Addison IL 60101	NI	Teacher	Tchr	Trinity Burr Ridge IL	(708)839-1444	RF	2002
Gomes Domingo G	(714)244-8403 domgomes11@gmail.com	1447 N Center St Orange CA 92867	PSW	Teacher	Tchr	St Paul Orange CA	(714)637-2640	IV	1999
Gomes Robin E Keylon	(714)244-8202 robin.gomes@cui.edu	1447 N Center St Orange CA 92867	PSW	Teacher	S HS/C	Concordia University Irvine Irvine CA	(949)854-8002	CQ	2007
Gomez Sarah M	(402)807-9277 sdinger@gracepocatello.org	1421 Bluebell Cir Pocatello ID 83201	NOW	Teacher	Tchr	Grace Pocatello ID	(208)237-4142	S	2013
Gomez William L Jr	(770)507-8314	175 N Main Dr Stockbridge GA 30281	FG	DCE	Mem C	Christ East Point GA	(678)900-6315	SP	1992
Gong Madeline Upchurch			PSW	DCE	D Ex/S	Pacific Southwest District Irvine CA	(949)854-3232	IV	2017

*Multiple Assignments (See Church Worker Locator for Additional Details)
See Page 53 for the Table of Abbreviations for key to District, Classification, Position, and College abbreviations.
**C =Candidate; EM =Emeritus; the date following the C is the month and year the Candidate status began

NAME	TELEPHONE NUMBER EMAIL	STREET ADDRESS CITY/STATE/ZIP	DISTRICT	CLASS.	POSITION/ STATUS**	WHERE SERVING	OFFICE PHONE	COLLEGE/ UNIV/CQ	YR GRAD
Gong Wesley			PSW	DCE	Tchr	Crean Irvine CA	(949)387-1199	IV	2017
Gonski Bethany J Jones	(504)376-7147 gonski.b@gmail.com	7028 Glenn St Metairie LA 70003	SO	Teacher	Prin	St John New Orleans LA	(504)488-6641	CQ	2007
Gontjes Abigail G	(586)879-8014 abigail.gontjes@gmail.com	38263 Greenwood St Westland MI 48185	MI	Teacher	Tchr	St Matthew Westland MI	(734)425-0260	MQ	2015
Gonzales Rachel E Jackson	(573)821-3114 mrs-gonzales@hotmail.com	c/o Bethany Lutheran Church 6041 Ridge Rd Parma OH 44129	OH	Teacher	Tchr	Bethany Parma OH	(440)884-1230	S	2007
Gonzales Stephan T	(573)690-1339 sgonzalesgsls@gmail.com	7207 Trevor Ln Cleveland OH 44129	OH	Teacher	Tchr	Bethany Parma OH	(440)884-1230	S	2007
Gonzales Stephen P	(573)645-4360 steven3155@hotmail.com	14 Dillow Ln Bella Vista AR 72714	MO	Teacher	EM			WN	1983
Gonzalez Anne M Podoll	(608)780-9852 dceanne@gmail.com	c/o Lutheran Church-Missouri Synod 1333 S Kirkwood Rd Saint Louis MO 63122	MO	DCE	S Ex/S	Office of International Mission Saint Louis MO		SP	2005
Gonzalez Suzanne	gonzalezs@concordiacrusaders.org	6365 Inez Ct Kernersville NC 27284	TX	Teacher	Tchr	Concordia Tomball TX	(281)351-2547	MQ	2001
Goodpasture Rachel L Micheel	(913)426-4007 rachel.micheel@cune.org	504 Laurel Dr Atchison KS 66002	KS	Teacher	C07/2017			S	2009
Goodspeed Amanda L Gillespie	(765)490-9558 amandag@stjameslaf.org	4437 Crossbow Ct W Lafayette IN 47906	IN	Teacher	Tchr	Saint James Lafayette IN	(765)423-1616	RF	2002
Goodwin Amanda Kindschy	(808)343-1855 amandagoodwin78@gmail.com	125 Hedgewick Way Tyrone GA 30290	FG	Teacher	Tchr	St Paul Peachtree City GA	(770)486-3545	IV	2002
Goodwin James	(714)349-0547 jamesegoodwin0@gmail.com	19844 Grace Haven Way Yorba Linda CA 92886	PSW	Teacher	C01/2021			IV	2018
Gorcyca Rebecca A Borchers		1329 Hazel Ct Des Plaines IL 60018	NI	Teacher	Tchr	Saint James Chicago IL	(773)549-1615	RF	1998
Gorka Katherine A	katie.gorka@gmail.com	197 E Baja Pl Casa Grande AZ 85122	PSW	DFLM	Mem C	Trinity Casa Grande AZ	(520)836-2451	AA	2010
Gorline Gretchen Daubendiek	(636)730-0845 gjgorline@gmail.com	244 Montecito Terrace Saint Peters MO 63304	MO	Teacher	C01/2019			S	1993
Gorney Stephanie D Weiss	(989)274-0893	323 S 3rd St Harbor Beach MI 48441	MI	Teacher	Tchr	Zion Harbor Beach MI	(989)479-3615	AA	2008
Gorr Karen E Maurer	(202)680-0935	6135 Bricker Ln Alexandria VA 22315	EN	Teacher	Tchr	Immanuel Alexandria VA	(703)549-0155	AA	2011
Gosa David G	(608)712-4275 principal@zionwayside.org	1540 McRea Cir Green Bay WI 54311	NW	Teacher	P/Tchr	Zion Of Wayside Greenleaf WI	(920)864-2468	MQ	2002
Gosch Denise A	(941)644-1379 camsokly@gmail.com	498 Cameo Dr Lakeland FL 33803	FG	Teacher	EM			S	1988
Gosch Gretchen S Maurer	(712)269-1370 gretchen.gosch@unityridge.org	201 Green St Deloit IA 51441	IW	Teacher	Tchr	Unity Ridge Denison IA	(712)393-2002	SP	2006
Gotshall Megan C Ehlers	(602)919-3448 greenbutterfliezzz@yahoo.com	13837 N 22nd St Phoenix AZ 85022	PSW	Teacher	C07/2023			IV	2010
Gottschalk Ann C Cisco	(708)354-5956 anngottschalk@hotmail.com	744 S Catherine Ave La Grange IL 60525	NI	Teacher	EM			CQ	1995
Gottschalk Ardelle D Wilken	(612)866-7099 ardellegottschalk@hotmail.com	1000 Station Trl Apt 228 Saint Paul MN 55123	MNS	Teacher	EM			RF	1964
Gottschalk Daniel L	(260) 804-3001 dehrab.gottschalk@gmail.com	8001 Westwood Dr Fort Wayne IN 46818	IN	Teacher	EM			RF	1990
Gottschalk David R	dgottschalk@martinlutherhs.org	10120 S. Chicago Rd. Oak Creek WI 53154	SW	Teacher	Tchr	Martin Luther Greendale WI	(414)421-4000	RF	2002
Gottschalk Ellen K Dittmer	(260) 479-7983 dehrab1407@gmail.com	8001 Westwood Dr Fort Wayne IN 46818	IN	Teacher	Tchr	Sub Bethlehem Fort Wayne IN	(260)484-7873	RF	1990
Gottschalk Janet C Zuelch	(516)775-4931 janetz18@aol.com	361 Garden City Rd Franklin Sq NY 11010	AT	Teacher	C08/2016			RF	1970
Gottschalk Roger A	(414)543-9714 randngott2@msn.com	2461 S 73rd St West Allis WI 53219	SW	Teacher	EM			RF	1966
Gough Kinsey V Hopf	(920)254-0813 kgough@sjlplymouth.com	514 Meadow Ln Sheboygan Falls WI 53085	SW	Teacher	Tchr	St John Plymouth WI	(920)893-5114	MQ	2018
Gove Andrew P Dr	(516)592-1059 gove.andrew@gmail.com	3250 Colby Ct Swansea IL 62226	AT	Teacher	C05/2017			S	2000
Gove Richard G	(618)233-7798 nick63gove@yahoo.com	3250 Colby Ct Belleville IL 62226	SI	Teacher	EM			RF	1964
Gowdy Karsin N	(619)677-4449 karsin14@gmail.com	2300 Grayson Dr #427 Grapevine TX 76051	TX	Teacher	Tchr	Crown Of Life Colleyville TX	(817)251-1881	IV	2019
Gowen Nancy E Sonheim	(808)688-1517 momika3391@gmail.com	94-1101 Kapukawai St Waipahu HI 96797	CNH	Teacher	Mem C	Our Savior Aiea HI	(808)488-3654	S	1983
Grab David A	(708)296-1326 d_grab@hotmail.com	12936 W 159th Apt 2c Homer Glen IL 60491	NI	Teacher	EM			S	1969
Grab Margaret A Keery	(708)212-7378 margegrab@hotmail.com	3115 Hillary Ct Joliet IL 60435	NI	Teacher	EM			S	1969
Grabenhofer Kaethe K Webern	+86 177 2748 7231 kgrabenhofer@gmail.com	W66N695 Madison Ave Cedarburg WI 53012	SW	Teacher	C07/2023			MQ	1993
Grabow Kathryn L Perepell Schulz	grabowkate@yahoo.com	N4159 State Road 67 Elkhorn WI 53121	SW	Teacher	EM			RF	2001
Grabowski Louise A Leeney	(847)696-2823 lagrabowski@att.net	125 Boardwalk Pl Unit 104 Park Ridge IL 60068	NI	Teacher	EM			RF	1963
Grace Christina L	(661)406-4938 christinalgrace@yahoo.com	12740 W. Indian School Rd. #I212 Litchfield Park AZ 85340	PSW	Teacher	Tchr	Trinity Litchfield Park AZ	(623)935-4665	IV	2008
Grack-Moritz Sarah A Strussenberg	(657)464-0735 sgrack@socal.rr.com	16175 Cache St Fountain Vly CA 92708	PSW	Teacher	Tchr	Saint Johns Orange CA	(714)288-4400	MQ	1998
Grady Robert L Jr	(708)990-5020 rgrady@tlbr.org	424 Circle Ave Willowbrook IL 60527	NI	Tch/DCE	Mem C	Trinity Burr Ridge IL	(708)839-1200	RF	1988
Graef Becky S	(219)386-1047 BSGoreo@proton.me	2400 Silhavy Rd Valparaiso IN 46383	IN	Teacher	EM			S	1975

*Multiple Assignments (See Church Worker Locator for Additional Details)

See Page 53 for the Table of Abbreviations for key to District, Classification, Position, and College abbreviations.

**C =Candidate; EM =Emeritus; the date following the C is the month and year the Candidate status began

NAME	TELEPHONE NUMBER EMAIL	STREET ADDRESS CITY/STATE/ZIP	DISTRICT	CLASS.	POSITION/ STATUS**	WHERE SERVING	OFFICE PHONE	COLLEGE/ UNIV/CQ	YR GRAD
Graefe Joseph A	(660)668-8380 jgraefe1961@gmail.com	1324 Victoria Dr Cape Girardeau MO 63701	MO	Teacher	EM			MQ	1985
Graf Ashley R Muehl	(260)450-5756 ashley.muehl@gmail.com	671 Vernier Rd Grosse Pointe Woods MI 48236	MI	Teacher	C08/2020			RF	2011
Graf Duane S	(414)543-8808 dsgraf@netzero.net	14627 W Hickory Hills Dr New Berlin WI 53151	SW	Teacher	EM			SP	1971
Graf Heidi K	(414)380-1886 hgraf@hclk.org	704 W 46th St Kearney NE 68845	NEB	DPM		Nebraska District Seward NE	(402)643-2961	MQ	2020
Graf Jennifer S Degner	(847)612-0255 jensue1225@gmail.com	555 W Madison St Apt 4104 Chicago IL 60661	NI	Teacher	EM			RF	1981
Graf Lynne M Pries	(402)910-2480 lgraf@neb.rr.com	1759 29th Ave Columbus NE 68601	NEB	Teacher	Tchr	Immanuel Columbus NE	(402)564-8423	S	1984
Graf Patricia S	(414)629-5926	3904 S Prairie Hill Ln #114 Greenfield WI 53228	SW	Teacher	EM			MQ	1991
Graf Susan R Homuth	(414)543-8808 dsgraf@netzero.net	14627 W Hickory Hills Dr New Berlin WI 53151	SW	Teacher	EM			RF	1971
Graff-Ermeling Genevieve J Graff Dr	(970)646-5106 genevieve.ermeling@gmail.com		RM	Teacher	C08/2021			IV	1993
Grage Glenn G	(989)906-0012 ggg777dce@yahoo.com	3465 Kiesel Rd Apt 65 Bay City MI 48706	MI	Tch/DCE	C08/2022			RF	1978
Grages Cynthia R Lang	(303)693-4048 dwgrages@hotmail.com	19368 E Quincy Pl Aurora CO 80015	RM	Teacher	EM			S	1973
Graham Betsy J Parbhoo	(214)402-2762 txbp27@yahoo.com	2326 Heatherwoods Way Carrollton TX 75007	TX	Teacher	Prin	Dallas Lutheran Sch Dallas TX	(214)349-8912	MQ	2001
Gramenz Carolyn S Roth	(618)965-3514	4942 Ballpark Rd Steeleville IL 62288	SI	Teacher	Tchr	Trinity Red Bud IL	(618)282-2883	S	1979
Gramenz Eric D	(618)317-1336 egramenz@splhs.org	310 S College Dr Concordia MO 64020	MO	Teacher	Tchr	Saint Paul Concordia MO	(660)463-2238	S	2011
Gramenz Karen M Rutz	(618)443-8355 vandkgramenz@gmail.com	5019 Ballpark Rd Steeleville IL 62288	SI	Teacher	Tchr	Immanuel Murphysboro IL	(618)684-3012	SP	1980
Grams Susan E Ripke	(920)883-9523 sgrams@mac.com	15737 S Central St Olathe KS 66062	KS	Teacher	C06/2024			AA	1997
Granholm Kathleen E Mueller	(630)892-9088 charlesgranholm@yahoo.com	32 Pasadena Dr Oswego IL 60543	NI	Teacher	EM			RF	1972
Granley Brenda S Becker	(414)630-8161 brenda.granley@gmail.com	10001 Netherton Dr Las Vegas NV 89134	PSW	Teacher	EM			S	1980
Granley Russell J	(414) 630-8160 russell.whitesoxfan@gmail.com	10001 Netherton Dr Las Vegas NV 89134	PSW	Teacher	EM			RF	1976
Grannis Glenna G Haemmerle	(260)432-7392 w.wanelanetrane@verizon.net	2811 Wane Ln Fort Wayne IN 46808	IN	Teacher	EM			S	1970
Grant Danna M Gade	dannagrant600@gmail.com	Senior Housing 119 W Galena Blvd Apt 216 Sugar Grove IL 60554	NI	Tch/DCE	EM			RF	1987
Grant Jon B	(262)721-7065 jonanigrant@att.net	3918 Matthew Dr Caledonia WI 53402	SW	Teacher	Tchr	St John Racine WI	(262)633-2758	CQ	2024
Grant Michelle R Poole	(214)563-9314 shell_poole@yahoo.com	1624 Crown Point Drive Frisco TX 75036	TX	Teacher	Tchr	Prince Of Peace Carrollton TX	(972)447-0532	S	1994
Grass Erin P	(660)553-0465 erinpgrass@gmail.com	1824 SW Brooklyn Ave Topeka KS 66611	KS	Teacher	Tchr	St John Topeka KS	(785)354-7132	S	2015
Grass John P	(715)573-8257 jgrass10@gmail.com	1664 E Heather Ave Gilbert AZ 85234	NW	Teacher	EM			RF	1969
Grass Joshua C	(660)233-0416 joshuagrass99@gmail.com	1824 SW Brooklyn Ave Topeka KS 66611	KS	Teacher	C05/2023			S	2014
Grass Larry E	(660)463-7686 lggg1974@gmail.com	209 N. Elm St. P.O. Box 139 Emma MO 65327	MO	Teacher	EM			S	1974
Grass Peter J	(630)221-9347 dpgrass@sbcglobal.net	1271 N 117th St Milwaukee WI 53226	NI	Teacher	EM			S	1974
Grass Rebekah E	(660)233-0058 rebekahgrass@splsconcordia.org	1003 S. Orange St. Concordia MO 64020	MO	Teacher	Tchr	St Paul Concordia MO	(660)463-2291	S	2016
Grasz Duane F	(719)570-9518 d_m_grasz@q.com	5016 S Raindrop Cir Colorado Spgs CO 80917	RM	Teacher	EM			S	1962
Grasz Michael J	michaeljgrasz@gmail.com	244 S Leandro St Anaheim CA 92807	PSW	Teacher	C07/2023			S	1989
Grasz Tanya M Kutansky	(714)321-8893 tanyagrasz@sbcglobal.net	244 S Leandro St Anaheim CA 92807	PSW	Teacher	C08/2023			IV	1992
Gratz Kathryn M Krugler	(507)238-2975 dkbbg@frontiernet.net	1115 240th Ave Fairmont MN 56031	MNS	Tch/DCE	Tchr	St Paul Fairmont MN	(507)238-9492	S	1985
Graudin Peter J	(952)200-8954 runningemt54@aol.com	704 Ravencroft Road Waconia MN 55387	MNS	Teacher	EM			S	1979
Graumann Natalie N Kumm	(605)393-7602 nataliegraumann@hotmail.com	24185 Assurance Lane Hermosa SD 57744	SD	Teacher	C10/2024			S	2009
Graves Christopher T	(513)231-1031 cgraves@zionlc.org	1262 Meadowbright Ln Cincinnati OH 45230	OH	Tch/DCE	Mem C	Zion Cincinnati OH	(513)231-2253	RF	1994
Graves Jean E Krieger	(630)247-0288 graves4him@yahoo.com	1138 S Luther Ave Lombard IL 60148	NI	Teacher	EM			RF	1968
Graves Madalyn E	(513)917-9249 maddiegraves81@gmail.com	1262 Meadowbright Lane Cincinnati OH 45230	OH	Teacher	Tchr	St Mark's Milford OH	(513)575-3354	CH	2022
Grawcock Alyssa K	(261)897-3194 grawcock.alyssa@gmail.com	2279 N 1100 E Avilla IN 46710	IN	Teacher	C07/2016			AA	2004
Gray Caroline C	(586)344-4402 mrsgray42107@yahoo.com	51 Stargazer Way Mission Viejo CA 92692	TX	DCE	Tchr	Trinity Spring TX	(281)376-5810	IV	2006
Gray Constance Sabo	(636)485-4157 connie.gray@att.net	141 Westleigh Manor Dr Wentzville MO 63385	MO	Teacher	Tchr	Immanuel Wentzville MO	(636)327-4416	RF	1989
Gray Janniece E Zinnel	(402)362-7560 jgray@efyork.org	1225 Kiplinger Ave York NE 68467	NEB	Teacher	EM			S	1976

*Multiple Assignments (See Church Worker Locator for Additional Details)

See Page 53 for the Table of Abbreviations for key to District, Classification, Position, and College abbreviations.

**C =Candidate; EM =Emeritus; the date following the C is the month and year the Candidate status began

NAME	TELEPHONE NUMBER EMAIL	STREET ADDRESS CITY/STATE/ZIP	DISTRICT	CLASS.	POSITION/ STATUS**	WHERE SERVING	OFFICE PHONE	COLLEGE/ UNIV/CQ	YR GRAD
Gray Robyn A Kitzerow	(563)508-2439 robyn.gray1982@gmail.com	3212 Dundee Ln Bettendorf IA 52722	IE	Teacher	C07/2025			RF	2004
Gray Shelly A Offill	(573)768-5776 sagray@live.com	1056 Pcr 338 Frohna MO 63748	MO	Teacher	Tchr	Immanuel Perryville MO	(573)547-6161	CQ	2013
Grays Jean M Overgaard	(313)571-5427 jograys@aol.com	5044 Oakman Blvd Detroit MI 48204	MI	Teacher	EM			SP	1978
Greaser Elyse N Cattau	(303)422-3741 ecattau@bethluth.net	12264 Hannibal St Commerce City CO 80603	RM	Teacher	Tchr	Bethlehem Lakewood CO	(303)233-0401	MQ	2011
Greatens Bethany A Erickson	(314)623-9663 bgreatens@gmail.com	11905 Barkman Dr Saint Louis MO 63146	MO	Teacher	Tchr	Immanuel Olivette MO	(314)993-2394	S	2006
Grebe Sarah M Rooker	(920)980-5854 grebe.sarah@gmail.com		SW	Teacher	Tchr	St John Plymouth WI	(920)893-5114	CQ	2020
Greder Gary L	(602)909-3858 glgreder@yahoo.com	4327 E Meadow Dr Phoenix AZ 85032	PSW	Teacher	EM			S	1980
Green Amanda M Waxdahl	(661)203-7462	9903 Iroquois Ln Bakersfield CA 93312	CNH	Teacher	Tchr	St John Bakersfield CA	(661)665-7815	IV	2010
Green Danny L	(630)450-0719 dangreen1720@yahoo.com	246 N Stewart Ave Lombard IL 60148	NI	Teacher	EM			RF	1988
Green Sheila M Patchett	(248)656-8984 greenda70@gmail.com	53774 Regency Hills Ct Shelby Twp MI 48316	MI	Teacher	EM			S	1972
Greene Jaime L Baese	(262)751-8953 jaimelynn581@hotmail.com	2893 S 96th St West Allis WI 53227	SW	DCE	Mem C	Blessed Savior New Berlin WI	(262)786-6465	S	2004
Greener Amy S Loppnow	(219)402-8179 greener.sbls@gmail.com	7006 Felger Rd Fort Wayne IN 46818	IN	Teacher	Prin	Sub Bethlehem Fort Wayne IN	(260)484-7873	AA	1990
Greener Melissa E	mgreener922@gmail.com	4108 Kimberwick Place Fort Wayne IN 46818	IN	Teacher	Pro Stf	Emmanuel-St Michael Fort Wayne IN	(260)422-6712	AA	2017
Greenfield Rebecca L Eichler	(515)832-7971 highschoolmusicalmaniac@ yahoo.com	2790 Little Wall Lake Rd Jewell IA 50130	IW	Teacher	C10/2017			S	2017
Greenfield Sophia K Drager	(262)417-4370 DCEGreenfield@gmail.com	503 College Ave Apt 319 Morris MN 56267	MNN	DCE	Mem C	Zion Morris MN	(320)589-2744	SP	2021
Greenwald Celia J	(760)468-5741 cj.greenwald@yahoo.com	2471 Sunrise Rd House 75 Round Rock TX 78664	TX	Teacher	EM			CQ	1996
Greer Theresa M Rosace	(734)397-0565 tgrr123@yahoo.com	908 Bendleton Dr Woodstock GA 30188	FG	Teacher	C07/2016			AA	1993
Gregoire LeAnn J Deac	(320)364-0376 jane56386@gmail.com	20931 370th Ave Hillman MN 56338	MNN	Deaconess	Mem C	Trinity Isle MN	(320)676-8774	FW-DEAC	2022
Gregory Kaitlyn R Kaitlyn Renee Zeilbeck	(763)222-9187 krzeilbeck@gmail.com	618 Sunrise Ln Green Bay WI 54301	NW	DCE	Mem C	Hope De Pere WI	(920)336-9843	SP	2023
Grein Linda L Popp Parrott	(303)659-2788 grein.linda@gmail.com	3693 Horiuchi Ct Brighton CO 80601	RM	Teacher	Tchr	Zion Brighton CO	(303)659-2339	S	1979
Grein Michael T	(562)706-5078 greinage@gmail.com	1535 W Linden Ave Fremont NE 68025	NEB	Teacher	C05/2024			S	2004
Grein Sara N DeFreece	(510)846-5643 sara.grein@cune.org	1535 W Linden Ave Fremont NE 68025	NEB	Teacher	Prin	Trinity Fremont NE	(402)721-5536	S	2004
Greinke Ann M	(678)365-6588 anngreinke@att.net	2360 Heritage Park Circle NW Kennesaw GA 30144	FG	Teacher	Tchr	Faith Marietta GA	(770)973-8877	RF	1979
Grelk Margaret C Rall	mgrelk55@gmail.com	2270 S Lombardy Ln New Berlin WI 53151	SW	Teacher	EM			RF	1977
Grelle Brandon D	(219)742-7408 brandongrelle@gmail.com	115 Cove Point Fortville IN 46040	IN	DCE	Mem C	Holy Cross Indianapolis IN	(317)823-5801	RF	2008
Gremel Bruce	(248)969-1113 bgremel@gmail.com	1615 W Leonard Rd Leonard MI 48367	MI	Teacher	EM			RF	1967
Gremel Darla J Metzger	(602)745-0049 darla.gremel@faith-lutheran.org	7034 E Kenyon Dr Tucson AZ 85710	EN	Teacher	Tchr	Faith Tucson AZ	(520)326-2262	S	1980
Gremillion Kelli B Bollinger	gremillt@cox.net	10 Woodlawn Ave Metairie LA 70001	SO	Teacher	Tchr	Atonement Metairie LA	(504)887-0225	CQ	2005
Gremmer Elizabeth R Damrow	(210)490-3238 egremmer@yahoo.com	P.O. Box 700871 San Antonio TX 78270	TX	Teacher	EM			S	1975
Gremminger Anna J Kasper	(586)914-0734 annagremminger11@yahoo.com	176 S Point Dr Avon Lake OH 44012	OH	Teacher	C06/2020			MQ	2015
Grenz Melinda S Scott	(734)309-6093 grenzmom@gmail.com	865 Riverbank St Wyandotte MI 48192	MI	DCE	Mem C	Trinity Wyandotte MI	(734)282-5877	RF	2000
Grenz Rachel A Detlaff		21250 N Lower Sacramento Rd Acampo CA 95220	CNH	Teacher	Tchr	St Peter Lodi CA	(209)333-2223	MQ	2015
Grepke Franklin L	(850)497-6993 jogrepke@gmail.com	8890 Ransley Station Blvd Apt 1113 Pensacola FL 32534	SO	DCM	EM			MW	1977
Grepke Joann E Underwood Deac	(850)497-6993 jogrepke@gmail.com	8890 Ransley Station Blvd Apt 1113 Pensacola FL 32534	SO	Deaconess	EM			Other	1970
Grepke Neil M	(702)354-7210 grepken@flhsemail.org	8605 Raindrop Canyon Ave Las Vegas NV 89129	PSW	Teacher	Tchr	Faith Las Vegas NV	(702)804-4400	AA	1993
Grese Susan J Turner	(734)358-2507 susangrese@sbcglobal.net	100 W Park Cir Dr Unit 2h Wheaton IL 60187	NI	Teacher	EM			RF	1972
Greve Donald G	(440)331-3521 dggreve@aol.com	4314 Grannis Rd Fairview Park OH 44126	OH	Teacher	EM			RF	1953
Greve Karen L Faszholz	(586)677-9822 grevegang@gmail.com	54257 Samara Dr Macomb MI 48042	MI	Teacher	EM			RF	1981
Greve Tim M	(586)703-3201 tgreve73@gmail.com	8141 Carriage Hill Dr Shelby Township MI 48317	MI	Teacher	Tchr	Lutheran North Macomb MI	(586)781-9151	MQ	2011
Greve Wendy F Fischer	(517)648-4879 wendyfgreve@gmail.com	530 W Jefferson St Dimondale MI 48821	MI	Teacher	EM			S	1971
Grewe Mark J	(319)325-4972 m.grewe59@gmail.com	2513 W 63rd St Davenport IA 52806	IE	Teacher	EM			RF	1981
Gridley Kathleen S Mills	(262)844-2406 kathleen.gridley@gmail.com	W53N803 Windsor Ct Cedarburg WI 53012	SW	DCE	Tchr	St Paul Grafton WI	(262)377-4659	S	2001

*Multiple Assignments (See Church Worker Locator for Additional Details)
See Page 53 for the Table of Abbreviations for key to District, Classification, Position, and College abbreviations.
**C =Candidate; EM =Emeritus; the date following the C is the month and year the Candidate status began

NAME	TELEPHONE NUMBER EMAIL	STREET ADDRESS CITY/STATE/ZIP	DISTRICT	CLASS.	POSITION/ STATUS**	WHERE SERVING	OFFICE PHONE	COLLEGE/ UNIV/CQ	YR GRAD
Griede Matthew D		5715 Baltimore Dr #1 La Mesa CA 91942	PSW	Teacher	Tchr	Victory Chula Vista CA	(619)262-4444	PO	2012
Griedl Mary S Griffith	(281)794-1220	9214 Bayou Bluff Dr Spring TX 77379	TX	Teacher	EM			CQ	1994
Griepentrog Joy M	(262)787-8501 joy.griepentrog@me.com	16540 Golf Pkwy Brookfield WI 53005	SW	Teacher	Tchr	Lake Country Hartland WI	(262)367-8600	SP	2009
Griesse Yvonne R Heiden	(509)307-8589 yvonne.griesse@gmail.com	381 Sinclair Ln Selah WA 98942	NOW	Teacher	EM			S	1979
Griffin Clare	(309)807-7749 cgriffin@sllcs.org	1537 Chipmunk Ln Oviedo FL 32765	S	Teacher	Tchr	St Luke Oviedo FL	(407)365-3408	MQ	2021
Griffin Kathryn K	(651)735-3736 kgriffin_01@icloud.com	917 W Northgate Dr Irving TX 75062	MNS	Teacher	C10/2024			MQ	2000
Griffin Peggy J	(863)307-5059 pgriffin@glwh.org	130 Avenue C SE Apt 41 Winter Haven FL 33880	FG	Teacher	Tchr	Grace Winter Haven FL	(863)293-9744	PO	2005
Griffin Peter W	(208)237-8119 p.griffin54@gmail.com	2386 Gooding St Pocatello ID 83201	NOW	Teacher	EM			SP	1980
Griffin Shirley A Grayson	(716)310-6213 mrsgriffin03@yahoo.com	1421 Tremont St Selma AL 36701	SO	Teacher	EM			BR	1975
Griffith Billie J Davis	(956)245-4328	2021 Theresa St Harlingen TX 78550	TX	Teacher	EM			CQ	1997
Griffith Daniel W	(618)670-8695 dan.griffith@ greenparklutheranschool.org	541 Braebridge Rd Manchester MO 63021	MO	Teacher	Tchr	Green Park Saint Louis MO	(314)544-4248	CQ	2022
Griffith Kimberly A Kassing	(618)407-3173 kgriff97@yahoo.com	7676 Cody Ln Bethalto IL 62010	SI	Teacher	Tchr	Zion Bethalto IL	(618)377-8314	CQ	2013
Grillot Morgan I	(314)852-1879 morgan.grillot@cune.org	2323 S State St Springfield IL 62704	CI	Teacher	Tchr	Trinity Springfield IL	(217)787-2323	S	2006
Grillot Sarah E Peters	(314)775-9795 sarah.grillot@cune.org	2323 S State St Springfield IL 62704	CI	Teacher	C07/2016			S	2006
Grim Rebecca R	(260)222-1888 bgrim67@gmail.com	511 Villa Park Court Fort Wayne IN 46808	IN	Teacher	C07/2022			RF	1990
Grim Stephen M	(260)497-9884 sgrim@clscubs.org	903 Easton Trl Fort Wayne IN 46825	IN	Teacher	Tchr	Concordia Fort Wayne IN	(260)426-9922	RF	1985
Grime Jennifer Schmidt	(419)551-2978 grimejen@gmail.com	23376 State Route 34 Lot 10 Stryker OH 43557	OH	DFLM	C07/2020			AA	2008
Grimes Harrison M	dceharrygrimes@gmail.com		NI	DCE	Mem C	Immanuel Downers Grove IL	(630)968-3112	CH	2020
Grimm Carol L Winternheimer	(812)550-2723 carol6870@att.net	3506 Sweetser Ave Evansville IN 47714	IN	Teacher	EM			RF	1968
Grimm Ellen K Dedert	(231)730-1726 harleyekglady@comcast.net	1835 Riegler Rd Muskegon MI 49445	MI	Teacher	EM			RF	1976
Grimm Jana K Fielder	jgrimm@bethanyschool.net	9101 Lamar Ave Overland Park KS 66207	KS	Teacher	Tchr	Bethany Overland Park KS	(913)648-2228	CQ	2005
Grimm Peggy L Nienhueser	(319)664-3038 grimm.peggy@gmail.com	2976 Kk Ave North English IA 52316	IE	Teacher	EM			S	1978
Grimmer Christine Schotte Deac	caschotte@gmail.com	1431 Sawgrass Ave Mitchell SD 57301	SD	Deaconess	C07/2016			FW-DEAC	2014
Grimpo Elizabeth J Schnake Dr	(402)525-3194 elizabeth.grimpo@cune.edu	5201 S 75th St Lincoln NE 68516	NEB	Teacher	S HS/C	Concordia University Nebraska Seward NE	(402)643-3651	CH	1999
Grimsley Joelle M Puckett		20717 Lake Hook Rd Hutchinson MN 55350	MNS	Teacher	Tchr	Mayer Mayer MN	(952)657-2251	SP	1989
Grissett Rose A Wiemken	(254)675-7761	6966 Mesa Springs Blvd Abilene TX 79606	TX	Teacher	EM			RF	1965
Grissom Amanda K Grandt	(847)253-2360	610 N Russel Mount Prospect IL 60056	NI	Teacher	Tchr	St Peter Arlington Heights IL	(847)259-4114	RF	2004
Griswold Rene A Zito	(952)938-6478 shesasox2@aol.com	21284 640th Ave Litchfield MN 55355	MNS	Teacher	EM			SP	1978
Grizzle Sarah E Bergen-Eckhardt	(636)300-7096 sgrizzle8618@gmail.com	479 Speyer Pl Saint Charles MO 63303	MO	Teacher	Tchr	Immanuel Saint Charles MO	(636)946-2656	S	2010
Grobelch Sheryl L Stewart	(949)852-1409	1436 Glacier Dr Allen TX 75002	PSW	Teacher	Tchr	Light of Christ Irvine CA	(949)786-3326	IV	2005
Grobelny Cheryl A Hoscheit	(586)781-9151 cgrobelny@gmail.com	16825 24 Mile Rd Macomb MI 48042	MI	Teacher	Tchr	Lutheran North Macomb MI	(586)781-9151	S	1981
Groeper Robin F Gahring	(832) 425-7813 rginchrist@hotmail.com	407 Colchester Ln League City TX 77573	TX	Teacher	Tchr	Hope Friendswood TX	(281)482-7943	RF	1996
Groggel Heather	(209)631-2334 heather.groggel@gls-hsv.org	404 Promenade Dr. SW Madison AL 35756	SO	Teacher	Tchr	Grace Huntsville AL	(256)881-0552	MQ	2005
Groleau Sandra J Lau	(320)385-0543 sjg190@gmail.com	1030 River Trail Circle Apt 10 Keil WI 53410	SW	DCM	EM			MQ	1997
Gromowski Amy R Vogel	(920)941-0539 agromowski@goodshepherdwi.org	1320 Dakota St Watertown WI 53094	SW	Teacher	Prin	Good Shepherd Watertown WI	(920)261-2579	CQ	2011
Gronewold Harold W	(708)890-4655 halmargron@aol.com	2957 192nd St Lansing IL 60438	NI	Teacher	EM			RF	1960
Groppe Eva E Schneider	(262)377-4321	1538 Green Valley Rd Grafton WI 53024	SW	Teacher	EM			MQ	1983
Grosnick Shannon M Stubbe	(715)573-5299 shannon.grosnick@gmail.com	531 West St Wausau WI 54401	NW	Teacher	Tchr	Trinity Wausau WI	(715)842-0769	MQ	2012
Gross Emilie Rospopo	(574)341-0547 emilie.gross@yahoo.com	2008 Javelin Dr La Porte IN 46350	IN	Teacher	Tchr	St John's La Porte IN	(219)362-6692	CQ	2024
Gross Jill S Kerr	(630)441-2674 jillgross840@yahoo.com	1353 Sager Rd Apt 52 Valparaiso IN 46383	NI	Teacher	EM			CQ	2020
Gross Larry E	(503)645-5012 larrygross626@comcast.net	4267 NW Silverleaf Dr Portland OR 97229	NOW	Teacher	EM			CQ	1990
Gross Nancy D Waldrop Bevins	(734)788-8601 katybeth63@aol.com	28524 Elwell Rd Belleville MI 48111	MI	Teacher	Tchr	Trinity Monroe MI	(734)242-2308	AA	1985

*Multiple Assignments (See Church Worker Locator for Additional Details)
See Page 53 for the Table of Abbreviations for key to District, Classification, Position, and College abbreviations.
**C =Candidate; EM =Emeritus; the date following the C is the month and year the Candidate status began

NAME	TELEPHONE NUMBER EMAIL	STREET ADDRESS CITY/STATE/ZIP	DISTRICT	CLASS.	POSITION/ STATUS**	WHERE SERVING	OFFICE PHONE	COLLEGE/ UNIV/CQ	YR GRAD
Gross Sherry M Bevirt	(618)514-9597 sherrymarie20@gmail.com	1022 Cobbler Lane Saint Peters MO 63303	MO	Teacher	C08/2022			CH	2014
Gross Stephanie L	(314)910-8211 stephanielgross14@gmail.com	16316 Truman Rd Unit 5217 Ellisville MO 63011	MO	Teacher	Tchr	St Paul Des Peres MO	(314)822-2771	CQ	2016
Grotelueschen Daniel R	(317)898-1281 lesleydgl@sbcglobal.net	900 N Fenton Ave Indianapolis IN 46219	IN	Teacher	EM			RF	1964
Grotelueschen David P	(317)861-8146 judycsa@comcast.net	2423 S Richman Ct New Palestine IN 46163	IN	Teacher	EM			RF	1966
Grotelueschen Judith L Severance	(317)861-8146 judycsa@comcast.net	2423 S Richman Ct New Palestine IN 46163	IN	Teacher	EM			RF	1966
Grotelueschen Lesley A Ryden	(317)402-8312 lesleydgl@sbcglobal.net	900 N Fenton Ave Indianapolis IN 46219	IN	Teacher	EM			RF	1964
Groth Dawn C Robbins	(720)557-3639 grothd@trinitycr.org	1365 1st Ave SW Cedar Rapids IA 52405	IE	Teacher	Tchr	Trinity Cedar Rapids IA	(319)362-6952	S	1997
Groth Jeanette L Schlegel Dr	(859)699-2131 ghanagroth@yahoo.com	6304 Brook Ln Savage MN 55378	MNS	Teacher	EM			RF	1970
Groth Justin T	(402)641-7044 justin.t.groth@gmail.com		NEB	Teacher	S HS/C	Concordia University Nebraska Seward NE	(402)643-3651	S	2011
Groth Lorraine E Beltz Deac	(402) 641-6998 legroth@yahoo.com	1289 Augusta Dr Seward NE 68434	NEB	Deaconess	EM			Other	1975
Groth Paul W	(317)877-2189 vgroth1749@gmail.com	9562 Sweet Clover Way Fishers IN 46038	IN	Teacher	EM			RF	1970
Groth Robert W	(317)787-6630 rwgroth@att.net	1015 Southwood Dr Indianapolis IN 46227	IN	Teacher	EM			S	1978
Grothaus Timothy A	(248)651-8986 tgrothaus@gmail.com	1187 Burgoyne Blvd Rochester Hls MI 48307	MI	Teacher	EM			S	1980
Grothman Darci A Durham	(419)966-7622 darci.durham@gmail.com	4914 Bristow Dr Annandale VA 22003	RM	Teacher	Prin	Mission Las Cruces NM	(575)522-0465	CH	2011
Grove Doug	(949)294-5355 doug.grove@concordiashanghai.org	458 Orion Way Newport Beach CA 92663	MO	Teacher	S Miss	Office of International Mission Saint Louis MO		CQ	2019
Grover Alison A Snyder	(618)656-5766 tobie5@aol.com	7625 Chardonnay Dr Edwardsville IL 62025	SI	Teacher	EM			CQ	1996
Groves Linda A Mowers	(308)530-1104 lgrovesorls@gmail.com	705 S McCabe Ave North Platte NE 69101	NEB	Teacher	Tchr	Our Redeemer North Platte NE	(308)532-6421	CQ	2004
Grubb Crislyn R Zimmerman	crgrubb@att.net	2467 NE 17th Ct Jensen Beach FL 34957	FG	Teacher	Tchr	Redeemer Stuart FL	(772)286-0911	S	1996
Grubbs Christine M Yock	(636)544-7144 cgrubbs@ilsw.org	315 Coley Ct Wentzville MO 63385	MO	Teacher	Tchr	Immanuel Wentzville MO	(636)327-4416	CQ	2019
Grube Aaron E	(269)271-2848 dcegrube21@gmail.com	1318 Merry Brook St Kalamazoo MI 49048	MI	DCE	Mem C	Zion Kalamazoo MI	(269)382-2360	RF	2008
Grube Edward C Dr	(630)220-5283 egrube@sbcglobal.net	19w020 Oak St Addison IL 60101	NI	Teacher	EM			RF	1975
Grube Renee L Vanick	(630)263-3494 rlgabc@aol.com	19w020 Oak St Addison IL 60101	NI	Teacher	EM			RF	1973
Gruben Hannah F Eatherton	(469)305-8525 hannah.f.eatherton@gmail.com	808 Indiana Ave Collinsville IL 62234	SI	Teacher	C06/2025			S	2023
Gruben Kathryn A Bremer	(920)627-3602 gruben@trinitysheboygan.org	1914 N 6th St Sheboygan WI 53081	SW	Teacher	Tchr	Trinity Sheboygan WI	(920)458-8248	RF	1990
Gruber Kathryn A Wirth	(608)362-5714 ckgruber@gmail.com	807 W Big Hill Rd Beloit WI 53511	SW	Teacher	EM			S	1965
Gruber Mary M Janssens	(734)770-9411 marygruber@hotmail.com	3700 East Dunbar Monroe MI 48161	MI	Teacher	EM			CQ	2006
Gruen Anna G	(651)395-9249 anna.gruen89@gmail.com	1202 Van Buren Ave Saint Paul MN 55104	MNS	Teacher	Pro Stf	Concordia University St Paul Saint Paul MN	(651)641-8278	MQ	2012
Gruen Axel	(503)805-6719 gruenaxel1@gmail.com	4232 Corvina St Richland WA 99352	NOW	Teacher	C09/2022			PO	2004
Gruendler Carl G	(708)345-1756 gruendler@sbcglobal.net	1602 N 9th Ave Melrose Park IL 60160	EN	Teacher	EM			RF	1953
Gruenhagen Judith K Calkin Deac	(218)414-0126 warrenjudy@brainerd.com	3604 Waldenbrook Rd Greensboro NC 27407	SE	Deaconess	EM			Other	1964
Gruenwald Beverly A Zschiegner	(314)440-6934 bevgruenwald@gmail.com	9072 Crest Oak Ln Saint Louis MO 63126	MO	Teacher	EM			RF	1984
Gruenwald Catherine J Hipple	(630)776-1112 c.gruenwald@comcast.net	311 W. Loy St Lombard IL 60148	NI	Teacher	C06/2025			RF	1988
Gruenwald Mark E Dr	(812)480-3127 mark.gruenwald@lcms.org	5021 Corisande Woods Dr Fenton MO 63026	MO	Teacher	S Ex/S	Office of National Mission Saint Louis MO		RF	1981
Gruenwald Matthew D	(812)470-6331 gruenwmd@gmail.com	9108 Damson Dr Saint Louis MO 63123	MO	Teacher	Tchr	Lutheran South Saint Louis MO	(314)631-1400	Other	2015
Gruett Laura B Hillman	(608)495-0448 hilaura04@gmail.com	W8881 Wisconsin 67 Plymouth WI 53073	SW	Teacher	Tchr	St John Plymouth WI	(920)893-5114	SP	2009
Gruetzmacher Paul M	(262) 606-5859 p.ggg@att.net	18295 Milwaukee Ave Brookfield WI 53045	SW	Teacher	EM			RF	1962
Grulke Travis G	(330)618-1220 travis.grulke@michigandistrict.org	1609 Zoey Ct. Superior Township MI 48198	MI	Teacher	D Ex/S	Michigan District Ann Arbor MI	(888)225-2111	AA	2001
Grundstrom Michael H	(605)391-1416 mhgrundstrom@gmail.com	4901 W 93rd Avenue Apt 2234 Westminster CO 80031	RM	Teacher	Tchr	Bethlehem Lakewood CO	(303)233-0401	S	2022
Grunow Karin B Brown	(503)780-4855 grunowk@aol.com	2746 County Road #113 Giddings TX 78942	NOW	Teacher	EM			RF	1975
Grunwald Karen W	(715)304-9236 packer713@hotmail.com	1127 S Weed St Shawano WI 54166	NW	Teacher	EM			SP	1967
Grupe Larry R	(586)566-1525 llgrupe@sbcglobal.net	44003 Partridge Creek Blvd Apt 109 Clinton Township MI 48038	MI	Teacher	EM			S	1962
Grupe Michael J	(314)721-4159 mdgrupe@sbcglobal.net	5466 Shale Rd Fitchburg WI 53711	MO	Teacher	EM			S	1976

*Multiple Assignments (See Church Worker Locator for Additional Details)
See Page 53 for the Table of Abbreviations for key to District, Classification, Position, and College abbreviations.
**C =Candidate; EM =Emeritus; the date following the C is the month and year the Candidate status began

NAME	TELEPHONE NUMBER EMAIL	STREET ADDRESS CITY/STATE/ZIP	DISTRICT	CLASS.	POSITION/ STATUS**	WHERE SERVING	OFFICE PHONE	COLLEGE/ UNIV/CQ	YR GRAD
Grupe Michele S Rebant	(586)412-5431 mgrupe@trinityutica.com	18040 Meadow Ct Ray MI 48096	MI	Teacher	Tchr	Trinity Utica MI	(586)731-4490	CQ	2005
Grupe Sandra J Shapaker	(817)235-8413 sandigrupe@gmail.com	1841 Windsong Cir Keller TX 76248	TX	DCE	Mem C	St Paul Fort Worth TX	(817)332-2281	CQ	2007
Guagliardo Joseph A	(321)432-6032 supermanjoeg@gmail.com	140 Florida Blvd Merritt Island FL 32953	FG	DCM	EM			CQ	1999
Gubanyi Joseph A Dr	(402)641-4642 joe.gubanyi@cune.edu	8700 SW 81st Street Ct Denton NE 68339	NEB	Teacher	EM			S	1972
Gude Mary A Bobb	(618)420-7902 maryannagude43@gmail.com	5180 Loop Rd Dorsey IL 62021	SI	Teacher	EM			RF	1965
Guebert Alexander M	(714)280-3113 aguebert@stjohnsorange.org	224 N Shattuck Pl Orange CA 92866	PSW	DPM	Mem C	Saint Johns Orange CA	(714)288-4400	IV	2021
Guebert Christian	(714)628-3112 cnguebert@gmail.com	26224 Hillsford Pl Lake Forest CA 92630	PSW	DPM	Mem C	Abiding Savior Lake Forest CA	(949)830-1460	IV	2016
Guebert Diana S Genske	(630)357-3759 goguebert4@aol.com	10435 Cantacielo Dr NW Albuquerque NM 87114	RM	Teacher	EM			RF	1988
Guebert Lois A	(847)993-3674 2guebert@usm2.edo	1722 E Hudson Bay Palatine IL 60074	IN	Teacher	EM			RF	1974
Guebert Megan Wright	(916)425-3930 meganguebert@gmail.com		PSW	Teacher	C09/2018			IV	2009
Guebert Susan J Schulenburg			PSW	Teacher	EM			CQ	2011
Guelzow Erin R Sorgatz	(501)282-5058 eringuelzow@gmail.com	5211 Carpenter St Downers Grove IL 60515	NI	Teacher	C07/2016			RF	1997
Guelzow Jonathan	(828)324-9575 jguelzow1@juno.com	602 7th Ave NE Hickory NC 28601	SE	Teacher	EM			RF	1968
Guelzow Stephanie J	(336)671-6300 dstsseiss@hotmail.com	1100 22nd St NE Unit 504 Hickory NC 28601	SE	Teacher	Tchr	Concordia Conover NC	(828)464-3011	RF	1994
Guelzow Timothy M	(561)704-0191 tmguelzow@gmail.com	1408 Lake Victoria Dr Lake Worth FL 33461	FG	Teacher	EM			AU	2007
Guenther Amy L	(402)326-0823 amy.guenther@cune.org	5921 Weiss Street Apt E4 Saginaw MI 48603	MI	Teacher	Tchr	Peace Saginaw MI	(989)793-9025	S	2021
Guenther Douglas D	(989)482-2202 dguenther@vlhs.com	5285 Seidel Rd Saginaw MI 48638	MI	Teacher	Tchr	Valley Saginaw MI	(989)790-1676	AA	1983
Guenther Mariah G	(763)242-9166 mariah.guenther11@gmail.com	17025 Eidelweiss St NW Andover MN 55304	MNS	Teacher	Tchr	King Of Kings Roseville MN	(651)484-9206	SP	2025
Guenther Marla L Lohrke	(763)753-0473	17025 Eidelweiss St NW Andover MN 55304	MNS	Teacher	Tchr	Family Christ Ham Lake MN	(763)434-7337	SP	1997
Guenther Scott A			NEB	Teacher	Mem C	Messiah Lincoln NE	(402)489-3024	AA	1985
Guenzler J T Dr	(314)221-0365 tom1400@netzero.net	2309 Fox Hound Ct Lake Saint Louis MO 63367	MO	Teacher	EM			CH	2013
Guerra Jennifer L Caithamer	yakimali@att.net	2226 E Madison Ave Orange CA 92867	PSW	Teacher	C07/2016			IV	1996
Guerra Noemi E Deac	(806) 777-0987 noemiguerra@me.com	4115 124th St Lubbock TX 79423	TX	Deaconess	D Ex/S	Texas District Round Rock TX	(800)951-3478	SL-DEAC	2013
Guest Elizabeth S Tinkey	(574)551-7019 etinkey.ils@gmail.com	6331 White Church Rd Okawville IL 62271	SI	Teacher	Tchr	Immanuel Okawville IL	(618)243-6216	CQ	2016
Gugel Robert A	(702)900-9248 grudge43@hotmail.com	2250 NW 114th Ave Unit 1p Pty 4179 Doral FL 33192	PSW	Teacher	EM			RF	1966
Guglielmi Valerie M Toth	(630)359-1651 chicagoguglielmis@yahoo.com	212 W Madison Ave Wheaton IL 60187	NI	Teacher	Tchr	St John Wheaton IL	(630)668-0701	RF	2001
Guidera George A Dr	(651)274-9670 guidera@csp.edu	1101 Sibley Memorial Hwy Apt 3 Saint Paul MN 55118	MNS	Tch/DCE	EM			RF	1969
Guilford Holly L Noack	(402)417-3822 hollyguilford42@gmail.com	2346 S 62nd St Lincoln NE 68506	NEB	Teacher	C09/2024			S	1995
Guilford Thomas K	(402)417-5828 guilford.tom70@gmail.com	2346 S 62nd St Lincoln NE 68506	EN	Teacher	EM			S	1992
Guldenstein Paul	(217)875-0271 DGuldens@insightbb.com	3777 N Ashley Ct Decatur IL 62526	CI	Teacher	EM			S	1968
Gullen Linda S Klitzing	(618)791-8688 gullenlinda@yahoo.com	641 W 1st St Aviston IL 62216	CI	Teacher	Tchr	Salem Jacksonville IL	(217)243-3419	S	1975
Gulley Katie M	(314)330-1336 kgulley10@yahoo.com	801 N Madison St Apt 6 Litchfield IL 62056	SI	Teacher	Tchr	Zion Litchfield IL	(217)324-2033	MQ	2004
Gullicksrud Timothy J	(507)250-2896 tjgullicksrud@gmail.com	6580 Kristin Lane NW Rochester MN 55901	MNS	Teacher	Tchr	Rochester Central Rochester MN	(507)289-3267	CH	2006
Gullidge Christa Knutson	cgullidge@immanueltf.org	202 Parkland Way Caldwell ID 83605	NOW	Teacher	Tchr	Immanuel Twin Falls ID	(208)733-7820	PO	2011
Gulliver Holly A	(989)714-5978 hgulliver500@gmail.com	1391 Dover Pl Saginaw MI 48638	MI	Teacher	EM			CQ	2009
Gummelt Michael W	(818)701-3070 thegummelts@yahoo.com	3466 Vicki Ct Simi Valley CA 93063	PSW	Teacher	EM			S	1979
Gundelach Mary Wiese	(415)366-0230	116 Stockbridge Ave Atherton CA 94027	CNH	Teacher	EM			S	1960
Gundell Arthur	(570)679-2980 art_GUNDELL@YAHOO.COM	340 Lewis Lake Rd Union Dale PA 18470	EA	Teacher	EM			S	1968
Gundell Katie L Meissner	(716) 940-2737 katie_gundell@stjohnnt.com	6777 Nash Rd N Tonawanda NY 14120	EA	Teacher	Prin	St John North Tonawanda NY	(716)693-9677	BR	1996
Gundell Kevin	(716)940-9867 mr.gundell@gmail.com	6777 Nash Rd N Tonawanda NY 14120	EA	Teacher	Tchr	Holy Ghost* Wheatfield NY	(716)731-3030	BR	1998
Gundermann Noah M	(612)638-7740 noahthegundermann@gmail.com	807 1/2 1st Ave NW Buffalo MN 55313	MNS	DPM	Mem C	St John Buffalo MN	(763)682-1883	SP	2024
Gundlach Kenneth L	(920)207-7929 kgundlach@charter.net	4020 S 15th St Sheboygan WI 53081	SW	Teacher	EM			RF	1966
Gunn Sarah E Lucht	(712)223-1238 sarah.gunn@cune.org	2204 S Patterson St Sioux City IA 51106	IW	Teacher	C07/2016			S	2002

*Multiple Assignments (See Church Worker Locator for Additional Details)

See Page 53 for the Table of Abbreviations for key to District, Classification, Position, and College abbreviations.

**C =Candidate; EM =Emeritus; the date following the C is the month and year the Candidate status began

NAME	TELEPHONE NUMBER EMAIL	STREET ADDRESS CITY/STATE/ZIP	DISTRICT	CLASS.	POSITION/ STATUS**	WHERE SERVING	OFFICE PHONE	COLLEGE/ UNIV/CQ	YR GRAD
Gunther Grace	(210)856-1152 gunthergrace0@gmail.com	5251 SW 89th St Ocala FL 34476	FG	Teacher	Tchr	St John Ocala FL	(352)629-1794	AU	2020
Gunther Krista L Hillman	(608)495-0130 misskhillman@gmail.com		SW	Teacher	Tchr	St Peter Reedsburg WI	(608)524-4066	MQ	2011
Gurganious Jadi G	(828)234-9236 jadigwen@gmail.com	1746 14th St NE Hickory NC 28601	SE	DCM	Mem C	St Stephen Hickory NC	(828)256-9865	MQ	2011
Gurgel Jonathan P	(414)355-9264 jgurgel.trinity@gmail.com	2306 E 100 North Rd Shumway IL 62461	CI	Teacher	Tchr	Trinity Stewardson IL	(217)682-5722	CQ	2009
Gurgel Tiffany	(630)310-0501 tiffg98@hotmail.com	5630 158th St Oak Forest IL 60452	NI	Teacher	Tchr	Trinity Tinley Park IL	(708)532-3529	MQ	1998
Gurney Adrienne A Thompson	(812)521-4120 adrienne.gurney@stjohnswaltz.org	26003 E Huron River Dr Flat Rock MI 48134	MI	Teacher	Prin	St John Waltz MI	(734)654-6366	CQ	2003
Gurnsey Jody L Fohr	(623)935-4611 jgurnsey@trinitylcs.org	16143 W Lane Ave Litchfield Pk AZ 85340	PSW	Teacher	Tchr	Trinity Litchfield Park AZ	(623)935-4665	CQ	2003
Guse Amy E Brill	(763)647-4454 amewng@izoom.net	25775 Sloth St NW Zimmerman MN 55398	MNN	Teacher	Mem C	Faith Community Zimmerman MN	(763)856-3600	SP	1997
Guse Earl W	(402)364-2576 erguse@msn.com	P.O. Box 239 Davenport NE 68335	NEB	Teacher	EM			S	1988
Guse Jonathan M	(765)438-9560 jonathan@bethelmorton.org	85 Forestview Rd Morton IL 61550	CI	DCE	Mem C	Bethel Morton IL	(309)263-2417	CQ	2012
Guse Paul B Sr	(734)812-9296 pjgoose2000@yahoo.com	3340 Parkway Dr Bay City MI 48706	MI	Teacher	Tchr	St Lorenz Frankenmuth MI	(989)652-6141	AA	1987
Gust Clara F Gaffke	(517)428-4845 c.gust@hotmail.com	7364 Dobson Rd Port Hope MI 48468	MI	Teacher	Tchr	Zion Harbor Beach MI	(989)479-3615	S	1986
Gustafson Georgia D Pagel	(715)722-0474 scottandgeorgia@hotmail.com	615 W Main St Merrill WI 54452	NW	Teacher	Tchr	Trinity Merrill WI	(715)536-5482	RF	1993
Gustafson Karen B Schuster	(312) 502-2490 akagusty@juno.com	9411 Willow Ln Mokena IL 60448	NI	Teacher	EM			RF	1981
Gustafson Rebecca J Schultz	(507)421-8567 regustafson@rcls.net	25183 Co Hwy 34 Kasson MN 55944	MNS	Teacher	Tchr	Rochester Central Rochester MN	(507)289-3267	CQ	2020
Gustin Kristopher L	(952)657-2251 kris.gustin@mayerlutheran.org	819 Elm St W Norwood MN 55368	MNS	Teacher	Tchr	Mayer Mayer MN	(952)657-2251	CQ	2007
Gutekunst Richard K	(985)785-5501 richfaith62@gmail.com	249 Arian Ln Covington LA 70433	SO	Tch/DCE	EM			SP	1986
Gutenkunst Gary A	(586)863-2586 ggutenkunst@lhsa.com	51347 Janee Dr Chesterfield MI 48051	MI	Teacher	Tchr	LHS Assn Of Greater Detroit Rochester Hls MI	(248)856-0240	S	1981
Guthman Delores J Mau	(715)223-5455 deeguthman@gmail.com	520 W North St Owen WI 54460	NW	Teacher	EM			SP	1970
Gutknecht Dianne C Marks	(218)367-2219 gutknecht@arvig.net	48326 Flicker Ln Ottertail MN 56571	MNN	Teacher	EM			SP	1967
Gutterman Jordan E Mahnken	(913)940-1942 j.mahnken8@gmail.com	29775 W 95th St Desoto KS 66018	MO	Teacher	Tchr	Calvary Kansas City MO	(816)595-4020	MQ	2021
Gutwein Manfred	(630)859-8245 bngutweins@sbcglobal.net	345 S Commonwealth Ave Aurora IL 60506	NI	Teacher	EM			S	1978
Gutwein Susan M Pfeifer	(630)546-6142 bngutweins@sbcglobal.net	345 S Commonwealth Ave Aurora IL 60506	NI	Teacher	EM			S	1978
Gutzler Donna J Osenberg	(815)721-4469 mdgteach1@comcast.net	7415 Mill Rd Rockford IL 61108	NI	Teacher	EM			RF	1970
Gutzler Mark D	(815)721-4469 mdgteach1@comcast.net	7415 Mill Rd Rockford IL 61108	NI	Teacher	EM			RF	1971
Gutzler Matthew M		1202 E Linden Ln Mt Prospect IL 60056	NI	Teacher	Tchr	St Paul Mount Prospect IL	(847)255-0332	SP	1996
Gwaltney Megan L Loomis	(828)514-7376 megan.loomis@gmail.com	916 Ramie Mitchell Rd Hiddenite NC 28636	SE	DCE	C07/2016			S	2007
Gynther J S	(805)444-6779 tjgynther@yahoo.com	40600 Estoril Ct Palmdale CA 93551	PSW	Teacher	EM			PO	1992
Gyurnek Sandra D Meyer	(419)784-9870 sdgyurnek@defnet.com	518 Jefferson Ave Defiance OH 43512	OH	Teacher	EM			S	1975
Haack Caleb J	(402)575-1183 calebjhaack@gmail.com	4325 Jeffers Rd Apt 29 Eau Claire WI 54703	NW	DCE	Mem C	Peace Eau Claire WI	(715)834-2486	S	2018
Haack Loren F	(209)367-8821 haackloren@yahoo.com	2069 Holt Dr Lodi CA 95242	PSW	Teacher	EM			RF	1969
Haak Armand L	(636)925-1274 ahaak02@aol.com	433 Nantucket Dr Saint Charles MO 63301	MO	Teacher	EM			S	1975
Haak Charles E	(773)927-7280 cehaak@sbcglobal.net	4446 S Trumbull Ave Chicago IL 60632	NI	Teacher	EM			RF	1971
Haak Lisa J	(630)291-9492 ljhaak@juno.com	447 Burlington Ave #4 Clarendon Hills IL 60514	NI	Teacher	Tchr	Trinity Burr Ridge IL	(708)839-1444	AA	1985
Haak Sally C Heath	mrs.haak@pax-domini.org	10860 E 750 S Elizabethtown IN 47232	IN	Teacher	EM			RF	1986
Haake Jean M Nothwehr	(515)408-0520	712 Kenyon Rd Apt 106 Fort Dodge IA 50501	IW	Teacher	EM			S	1986
Haan Eric D	(509)378-8493 ericdhaan@gmail.com	1520 W 41st Ave Kennewick WA 99337	NOW	Teacher	Prin	Bethlehem Kennewick WA	(509)582-5624	CQ	2005
Haar Barbara L Lutz	(410)944-0167 barbhaar47@gmail.com	1705 Chesterton Rd Baltimore MD 21244	SE	Teacher	Tchr	St Paul's Glen Burnie MD	(410)766-2283	S	1983
Haar Carolyn D Chrzan	(443)955-1298 carolyn.haar4@gmail.com	2971 E Stargazer Dr San Tan Valley AZ 85140	PSW	Teacher	Tchr	Christ Phoenix AZ	(602)955-4830	S	2010
Haas Deon	(505)830-2178	3301 Monroe St NE Unit A1 Albuquerque NM 87110	RM	Teacher	Tchr	Christ Albuquerque NM	(505)884-3876	CQ	2002
Haas Jane L Elling	(314)856-2367 janehaas7@gmail.com	1327 Libra Dr Arnold MO 63010	MO	Teacher	EM			S	1969
Haas Nichole J Kuerschner	(262)416-6884 nichole.haas52@gmail.com	151 W Lilac Ln Grafton WI 53024	SW	DCE	Tchr	St Paul Grafton WI	(262)377-4659	RF	1999
Haas Mc Cue De Ann L	(515)278-2554 deann@gloriadeionline.com	9112 Oakwood Dr Urbandale IA 50322	IW	Teacher	Mem C	Gloria Dei Urbandale IA	(515)276-1700	S	1985

*Multiple Assignments (See Church Worker Locator for Additional Details)
See Page 53 for the Table of Abbreviations for key to District, Classification, Position, and College abbreviations.
**C =Candidate; EM =Emeritus; the date following the C is the month and year the Candidate status began

NAME	TELEPHONE NUMBER EMAIL	STREET ADDRESS CITY/STATE/ZIP	DISTRICT	CLASS.	POSITION/ STATUS**	WHERE SERVING	OFFICE PHONE	COLLEGE/ UNIV/CQ	YR GRAD
Haase Lorily Mc Crillis	(913)522-1398 lhaase52@att.net	11000 Delaware Pkway Apt 2100 Kansas City KS 66109	MO	Teacher	Tchr	Martin Luther Kansas City MO	(816)734-1060	S	1997
Haase Madison	(509)475-8988 maddy.haase@gmail.com	9321 E Warner Rd Apt 2052 Mesa AZ 85212	PSW	DCE	Mem C	Christ Greenfield Gilbert AZ	(480)892-8521	IV	2019
Haase Pamela S Davis	(217)819-2287 phaase3@gmail.com	P.O. Box 574 Grinnell IA 50112	IE	Teacher	EM			S	1972
Haase Peggy L	(209)740-9531 peggyhaase91@gmail.com	3333 164th St SW Apt 814 Lynnwood WA 98087	NOW	Teacher	EM			RF	1974
Habeck Jennifer L Ude	jlhabeck@aol.com	P.O. Box 4223 Greenwood Village CO 80155	RM	Teacher	EM			S	1978
Habedank Carolyn M Schoessel	(585)902-6005 mrsch156@aol.com	24 S Shore Dr Alden NY 14004	EA	Teacher	EM			RF	1968
Habegger Susan	habegger.susan@gmail.com		IN	Teacher	S HS/C	Concordia Theological Seminary Fort Wayne IN	(260)452-2100	MQ	2023
Haberhern Dennis M	(931)210-0671	108 Knollwood Ln Crossville TN 38558	MDS	Teacher	EM			S	1970
Haberhern Jean A Stueck	(931) 210-0671 jah33148@gmail.com	108 Knollwood Ln Crossville TN 38558	MDS	Teacher	EM			S	1970
Haberkamp Sharon R	(320)587-6185 oslhaberkamp@hotmail.com	907 Dale St SW Apt 132 Hutchinson MN 55350	MNS	Teacher	EM			RF	1970
Hack Konrad W	(949)444-1204 konrad.hack@cui.edu	4101 Glenwood St Irvine CA 92604	PSW	Teacher	S HS/C	Concordia University Irvine Irvine CA	(949)854-8002	CQ	2011
Hackbarth Michael R	(414)254-4205 mhackbarth4@yahoo.com	2110 E Kaweah Ct Visalia CA 93292	CNH	Teacher	C07/2016			MQ	1999
Hackbarth Richard O	(269)757-1168 rich.hackbarth@gmail.com	102 E South St Williamsburg IA 52361	IE	Teacher	EM			S	1968
Hackbarth Samuel O	(734)430-6703 samuel.ohackbarth@gmail.com	47350 Romeo Plank Rd Macomb MI 48044	MI	Teacher	Tchr	LHS Assn Of Greater Detroit Rochester Hls MI	(248)856-0240	AA	2022
Hackbarth Tracey J Norenberg	(734)652-0303 thackbarth@trinitylutheranmonroe.org	3127 S Custer Rd Monroe MI 48161	MI	Teacher	Prin	Trinity Monroe MI	(734)241-1160	MQ	1994
Hackelberg Holly R Johnson	(630)531-5909 hrhack16@gmail.com	7 Oriole Ct Woodridge IL 60517	NI	Teacher	EM			RF	1982
Hackerd Ellen M	ellenhackerd54@gmail.com	31789 Lawrence St Lebanon OR 97355	NOW	Teacher	EM			CQ	2000
Hackmann Melissa Washington	(425)232-6944 m.hackmann@zionls.org	20529 Dubuque Rd Snohomish WA 98290	NOW	Teacher	Tchr	Zion Snohomish Cty Lake Stevens WA	(425)334-5064	CQ	2015
Hadle Joanna B Maurer	(913)783-4510 hadle.farm@juno.com	23289 W 239th St Paola KS 66071	KS	Tch/DCE	EM			S	1986
Hadley Linda K Scheel	(641)782-9546 lks1954@yahoo.com	1396 Osage St Creston IA 50801	IW	Teacher	EM			S	1976
Haegele Dennis F	(708)870-0992 dennis21.haegele@gmail.com	2128 Sunbird Ct Oviedo FL 32765	FG	Teacher	EM			RF	1969
Haertling Velda F Statler	(573)547-5054 frogs32@hotmail.com	4243 Pcr 210 Perryville MO 63775	MO	Teacher	EM			RF	1964
Haese Taylor C	(920)838-4757 taylor.haese@gmail.com	N6504 Penny Ln Greenbush WI 53026	SW	Teacher	Tchr	Trinity Mequon WI	(262)242-2045	MW	2016
Hafer Marsha J Kahre	(714)628-6547 mjhafer@gmail.com	9124 203rd Ave E Bonney Lake WA 98391	NOW	Teacher	EM			IV	1983
Hagemeier Jonetta E Debban	(402)228-1466 jhagemeier@stpaulschoolbeatrice.org	22878 SW 32nd Rd Beatrice NE 68310	NEB	Teacher	Tchr	St Paul Beatrice NE	(402)223-3414	CQ	1996
Hagen Jean M Haege	(608)577-5970	3304 Woodspring Ln Champaign IL 61822	CI	Teacher	EM			CQ	1986
Hagen M Allen	(253)232-5452 alhagen31@yahoo.com	2606 38th Ave SE Puyallup WA 98374	NOW	Teacher	EM			S	1975
Hagen Stephanie R Malkow	(206)848-5017 athagen45@yahoo.com	2606 38th Ave SE Puyallup WA 98374	NOW	Teacher	EM			S	1977
Hagenlocher Aenne E Keuch	almeidachickita@yahoo.com	30 Crehore Dr Newton Lower Falls MA 02462	CNH	Teacher	EM			CQ	1996
Hagenmueller Elaine Brutlag	(815)404-9599 hagenmueller1953@gmail.com	7400 Nighthawk Way Cary IL 60013	NI	Teacher	EM			RF	1978
Hagenow Eric M	(989)475-2808 eric.hagenow@stpeterhemlock.org	2323 N Raucholz Rd Hemlock MI 48626	MI	Teacher	P/Tchr	St Peter Hemlock MI	(989)642-8188	AA	2011
Hagenow Margaret A Schroeder		2323 N Raucholz Rd Hemlock MI 48626	MI	Teacher	Tchr	St Peter Hemlock MI	(989)642-5659	CQ	1996
Hagenow Ruth L Wagner	(920)864-2128	10911 N County Rd W Reedsville WI 54230	NW	Teacher	Tchr	Zion Wayside WI	(920)864-2463	SP	1980
Hagge John B	(615)479-1438 43johnhagge@gmail.com	3718 S Peach Hollow Cir Pearland TX 77584	TX	Tch/DCE	EM			S	1975
Hagge Nathaniel D	(702)267-7540 nate.hagge@lutheransouth.org	2880 Rocky Creek Ln Dickinson TX 77539	TX	Teacher	Tchr	South Houston TX	(281)464-8299	S	2004
Hahn Amanda L Deac	(563)349-6950 deac.hahn@gmail.com		CI	Deaconess	Mem C	Holy Cross Moline IL	(309)764-9720	FW-DEAC	2018
Hahn Ann Marie C Boehme	(414)617-6802 dranhahn@hotmail.com	N63 W33981 Lakeview Dr Oconomowoc WI 53066	SW	DCM	Mem C	Divine Redeemer Hartland WI	(262)367-8400	MQ	2025
Hahn Anna	(608)495-5179 anna.hahn@cuw.edu	1016 Carriage Ln Casper WY 82609	WY	Teacher	Tchr	Mount Hope Casper WY	(307)234-8428	MQ	2018
Hahn Carol A Kalthoff	(863)647-4654 carolannhahn67@gmail.com	6241 Thousand Oaks Dr Lakeland FL 33813	FG	Teacher	EM			S	1966
Hahn Cortney K Pascascio	(715)741-0304 chahn@immanuelrapids.com	1451 Woodbine St Wisc Rapids WI 54495	NW	Teacher	Tchr	Immanuel Wisconsin Rapids WI	(715)423-3260	CQ	2015
Hahn David M Dr	(518)871-1340 david.hahn@luhi.org	15 Sicada St Saratoga Spgs NY 12866	AT	Teacher	ExecDir	Long Island Brookville NY	(516)626-1735	RF	1975

*Multiple Assignments (See Church Worker Locator for Additional Details)
See Page 53 for the Table of Abbreviations for key to District, Classification, Position, and College abbreviations.
**C =Candidate; EM =Emeritus; the date following the C is the month and year the Candidate status began

NAME	TELEPHONE NUMBER EMAIL	STREET ADDRESS CITY/STATE/ZIP	DISTRICT	CLASS.	POSITION/ STATUS**	WHERE SERVING	OFFICE PHONE	COLLEGE/ UNIV/CQ	YR GRAD
Hahn Janet Cline	(518)871-1340 janet.hahn@luhi.org	15 Sicada St Saratoga Spgs NY 12866	AT	Teacher	EM			RF	1975
Hahn Jeffrey S	(630)553-6903 jphahn1@juno.com	510 W Washington St Yorkville IL 60560	NI	Teacher	Tchr	Cross Yorkville IL	(630)553-7861	AA	1989
Hahn Josiah J	(630)551-6309 josiah.hahn@splcwa.org	3288 Evergreen Ct Richfield WI 53076	SW	Teacher	Tchr	St Pauls West Allis WI	(414)541-6251	MQ	2017
Hahn Kathleen M Frerking	(715)212-1906 khahn0856@gmail.com	1700 E 12th St Merrill WI 54452	NW	Teacher	EM			S	1978
Hahn Kimberly		169 Briarwood Irvine CA 92604	PSW	Teacher	Tchr	Orange County Orange CA	(714)998-5151	CQ	2011
Hahn Nathanael	lutheranmathemagician@gmail.com	1016 Carriage Ln Casper WY 82609	WY	Teacher	Tchr	Mount Hope Casper WY	(307)234-8428	MQ	2020
Hahn Rachel D Menscher Dr	(636)485-9640 rachelmenscher@gmail.com	2205 Cournier St Saint Charles MO 63301	MO	Teacher	Mem C	Immanuel Saint Charles MO	(636)946-2656	CQ	2021
Hahn Rebekah L	(331)725-8615 bekahlhahn@gmail.com	510 W Washington Yorkville IL 60560	NI	Teacher	Tchr	Cross Yorkville IL	(630)553-7861	MQ	2019
Hainer Deborah L Meyer	(970)507-0034 deborahhainer@gmail.com	1106 Breckenridge St Mayville WI 53050	SW	Teacher	Tchr	St Johns Mayville WI	(920)387-4310	MQ	2007
Haines Theresa M Haas	(210)247-8045	5503 N 45th St Tacoma WA 98407	NOW	DCE	Mem C	Our Savior Tacoma WA	(253)531-2112	PO	2010
Hainey Jordan M White			RM	Teacher	C07/2023			CQ	2011
Halfmann Norma J Rhone	(813)792-8406 merwillow@aol.com	15212 Hammock Chase Ct Odessa FL 33556	FG	Teacher	EM			S	1976
Hall Amanda B Eberle	(208)241-5693 ahall@allabouthope.org	2852 Sandstone Dr Idaho Falls ID 83404	NOW	Teacher	Tchr	Hope Idaho Falls ID	(208)529-8080	S	1994
Hall Carl G	(734)869-5029 bacahall72@gmail.com	4904 Colf Rd Carleton MI 48117	MI	Teacher	EM			S	1972
Hall Claire M	(404)408-8052 imperfect.grace@yahoo.com	936 Mountain Creek Road Apt 89 Chattanooga TN 37405	MDS	Teacher	Tchr	Belvoir Chattanooga TN	(423)622-3755	CQ	2024
Hall George R Jr	(301)474-0555 kangarookrew@hotmail.com	6605 Ian St New Carrollton MD 20784	SE	Teacher	EM			RF	1970
Hall Jennifer R Jacobsen	(952)465-1092 jen.hall@sjlcas.com	11550 Arbor Lakes Pkwy N Unit 1129 Maple Grove MN 55369	MNS	DCE	Prin	St John Elk River MN	(763)441-6616	SP	1992
Hall Kevin J Dr	(507)210-3352 khall@csp.edu	14241 Davenport Path Rosemount MN 55068	MNS	DCE	S HS/C	Concordia University St Paul Saint Paul MN	(651)641-8278	SP	1983
Hall Steven L	(815)209-5982 shall@stpaulrochelleil.org	1118 Lincoln Highway Rochelle IL 61068	NI	Teacher	Prin	St Paul Rochelle IL	(815)562-6323	RF	1985
Hallemeier Paige E	(314)707-1241 phallemeier@immanuelstcharles.org	1049 Tompkins St Saint Charles MO 63301	MO	Teacher	Tchr	Immanuel Saint Charles MO	(636)946-2656	CQ	2018
Haller Jenifer E Reynolds	jhaller@ilsmemphis.com	220 Martha Cove Oakland TN 38060	MDS	Teacher	Tchr	Immanuel Memphis TN	(901)388-0205	CQ	2015
Hallett Kristin L Grudt	(949)929-3019 krick79@hotmail.com	1582 N Elmwood St Orange CA 92867	PSW	Teacher	C06/2022			IV	2001
Hallien Aaron M	ahallien@hotmail.com	417 Fremont St Washington MO 63090	MO	Teacher	Tchr	Immanuel Washington MO	(636)239-1636	RF	1999
Hallsted Natalee J Hanke Vollman	(727)461-1431 baileyboo98@hotmail.com	1101 Oakview Ave Clearwater FL 33756	FG	Teacher	Tchr	First Clearwater FL	(727)462-8000	AA	1985
Halter Carol L Deac			CNH	Deaconess	S Miss	Office of International Mission Saint Louis MO		Other	1965
Halvorson Peter J	(619)990-2229 peajay8ch@yahoo.com	1738 Elmhurst St Chula Vista CA 91913	PSW	Teacher	EM			RF	1969
Hamann Brad	(210)313-1787 BradH@concordia-satx.com	24519 Bliss Cyn San Antonio TX 78260	TX	Teacher	Tchr	Concordia San Antonio TX	(210)479-1477	S	2002
Hambaum Abigail E	(989) 274-9304 abigailhambaum@gmail.com		SW	DCM	RSO	A Place Of Refuge Ministries Milwaukee WI	(414)438-2767	MQ	2024
Hambaum Patricia S Stange	(989)293-1622 pathambaum@gmail.com		MI	Teacher	Tchr	Trinity Reese MI	(989)868-4501	RF	1992
Hambridge Deborah R Fink	(703) 795-7593 dhambridge@osva.org	1420 S Randolph St Arlington VA 22204	SE	Teacher	Tchr	Our Savior Arlington VA	(703)892-4846	BR	1989
Hambridge Les		1420 S Randolph St Arlington VA 22204	SE	Teacher	EM			IV	1982
Hamburg Diana K Maine	(580)572-8120 hamburg-diana@hotmail.com	10301 S Douglas Ave Oklahoma City OK 73139	OK	Tch/DCE	EM			WN	1971
Hamer Camille L Bolte	chamer@peacecolumbus.org		NEB	DCE	Mem C	Peace Columbus NE	(402)564-8311	S	2021
Hamer Jennifer L White	(718)791-3275 jenhamer262@yahoo.com	96 Wahoo Ln Oceanside CA 92058	AT	Teacher	C07/2016			AA	1995
Hamilton Cara J Post	(765)490-2168 carahamilton3@gmail.com	7571 Ridgeview Ln Lafayette IN 47905	IN	Teacher	C05/2025			RF	2002
Hammer Margaret M Szymaszek	(414)813-0787 mhammer@sbcglobal.net	S81W19364 Highland Park Dr Muskego WI 53150	EN	Teacher	EM			CQ	2007
Hammes Callie K Firminhac	(307)575-4078 cal.hammes@gmail.com	801 E 4th St Apt 110 Wayne NE 68787	NEB	Teacher	Mem C	Grace Wayne NE	(402)375-1905	S	2021
Hammes Debra L Ernst	(708)431-1385 debrahammes8@gmail.com	2101 Norfolk Ave Westchester IL 60154	NI	Teacher	EM			RF	1988
Hammes Neil R	(630)660-3550 neil.hammes@gmail.com	2101 Norfolk Ave Westchester IL 60154	NI	Teacher	EM			RF	1980
Hammon Cherry A Kaczor	(402)589-2020	P.O. Box 410 Spencer NE 68777	NEB	Teacher	EM			S	1962
Hammon John F	(419)599-2248 hamneggs@bright.net	915 Clairmont Ave Napoleon OH 43545	OH	Teacher	EM			RF	1972
Hammons Cynthia J Davis	(913) 680-9536 mohammons@gmail.com	710 Miami St Leavenworth KS 66408	KS	Teacher	Prin	St Paul Leavenworth KS	(913)682-5553	RF	1984

*Multiple Assignments (See Church Worker Locator for Additional Details)
See Page 53 for the Table of Abbreviations for key to District, Classification, Position, and College abbreviations.
**C =Candidate; EM =Emeritus; the date following the C is the month and year the Candidate status began

NAME	TELEPHONE NUMBER EMAIL	STREET ADDRESS CITY/STATE/ZIP	DISTRICT	CLASS.	POSITION/ STATUS**	WHERE SERVING	OFFICE PHONE	COLLEGE/ UNIV/CQ	YR GRAD
Hampton Daniel	(317)446-2523 dcedan@gmail.com	328 Winter Lake Ct Fenton MO 63026	RM	DCE	C05/2023			S	2009
Hampton Sandra E Thompson	(281)251-7817 hamptons0687@gmail.com	6615 Saffron Hills Dr Spring TX 77379	TX	Teacher	Tchr	Trinity Spring TX	(281)376-5810	IV	1986
Hamre Rachael E Klein	(580)362-0893 zlsrhamre@yahoo.com	8950 Boca Raton Ct North Richland Hills TX 76182	TX	Teacher	Tchr	Crown of Life Colleyville TX	(817)421-5683	S	1996
Hamrick Mary E Becker		206 Ashley Pl Apt 8 Edwardsville IL 62025	SI	Teacher	Tchr	Unity East Saint Louis IL	(618)874-6605	RF	1988
Hamrick Roy A	(779)238-2877 rhamrick@rockfordlutheran.com	2120 S Alpine Rd Rockford IL 61108	NI	Tch/DCE	Tchr	Rockford Rockford IL	(815)877-9551	RF	1984
Hand Gwen L Honebrink	(773)796-3717 ghonebrink19@yahoo.com	1468 E Walnut Ave Des Plaines IL 60016	NI	Teacher	C07/2016			RF	2002
Handlin Cinder Lerand	(715)570-3564 cinder.handlin@tlsmerrill.com	109 S State St Merrill WI 54452	NW	Teacher	Tchr	Trinity Merrill WI	(715)536-5482	CQ	2021
Handrich James A	(941)486-5416 jimhandrich@comcast.net	950 Tamiami Trail South Unit 504 Venice FL 34285	AT	Teacher	EM			RF	1966
Handrock Sarah J Bowen	(505)221-3111 sjhandrock@aol.com	2811 W Manitou Trl McHenry IL 60051	NI	Teacher	EM			CQ	2003
Handy Dena M Denton	(443)883-1625 dhandy@stpaulgb.org	809 Paradise Ln Glen Burnie MD 21061	SE	Teacher	C04/2025			BR	1995
Hanebutt Kathleen L Hentsch	(913)660-8897 rickhanebutt@aol.com	5207 Woodsonia Dr Shawnee KS 66226	KS	Teacher	EM			RF	1974
Hanebutt Richard C	(913)660-8897 rickhanebutt@aol.com	5207 Woodsonia Dr Shawnee KS 66226	KS	Teacher	EM			RF	1974
Haneline Sarah Streger	(813)777-6006 skh_aqui@yahoo.com	25243 Birchwood Springs Ave Porter TX 77365	FG	Teacher	C07/2016			AU	2006
Hanft Elizabeth M Veal	(970)371-1991 betsyhanft@gmail.com	1932 Markham Ct Loveland CO 80538	RM	Teacher	Tchr	Immanuel Loveland CO	(970)667-4506	S	2000
Hanke Elsie C Hesemann	(616)465-6520	9807 Jericho Rd Bridgman MI 49106	MI	Teacher	EM			WN	1957
Hanke John L	(251)213-3782 johnhanke7@gmail.com	1208 Sweet Laurel St Foley AL 36535	SO	Tch/DCE	EM			S	1976
Hanke Melinda J Truesdell	(314)520-8749 mindyhanke@sbcglobal.net	206 Almentor Ave Saint Louis MO 63119	MO	Teacher	Tchr	St Paul Des Peres MO	(314)822-0447	MQ	2005
Hankemeier Amanda S Rowland	(979)540-8143 amandahankemeier@gmail.com	15 Founders Way Unit A Saint Louis MO 63105	MO	Teacher	P/Tchr	Green Park Saint Louis MO	(314)544-4248	AU	2001
Hanlon-Hunt Kelly J Hanlon	(763)639-3123 hanlonhk@csp.edu	2532-223rd Ln NW Oak Grove MN 55011	MNS	Teacher	Tchr	Trinity Saint Francis MN	(763)753-1234	SP	2023
Hanna Kirstin A McClintock	(419)787-3554 khanna@trinityvikings.org	4125 Mockingbird Ln Toledo OH 43623	OH	Teacher	Tchr	Trinity Toledo OH	(419)385-2651	AA	2003
Hannemann Lauren J Sankey	(402)641-7007 hannemann85@yahoo.com	7938 Cistena Way Parker CO 80134	RM	Teacher	C06/2018			S	2008
Hannon Claire E Busby	(618)214-9491 cbusby148@gmail.com	942 N 11th St Decatur IN 46735	IN	Teacher	Tchr	St Peter-Immanuel Decatur IN	(260)623-6115	S	2021
Hansa Joseph G	(708)484-6928 joey101881@yahoo.com	3515 Scoville Berwyn IL 60402	NI	Teacher	Tchr	Grace Chicago IL	(773)762-1234	RF	2003
Hansard Christie L Deac	(810)750-8243 parishnurse@faithgb.org	103 N Howard St Fenton MI 48430	MI	Deaconess	Mem C	Faith* Grand Blanc MI	(810)694-9351	FW-DEAC	2021
Hansell Christopher G	(734)545-5319 chrishansell@tlsjackson.com	5043 Brookside Dr Jackson MI 49203	MI	Teacher	Tchr	Trinity Jackson MI	(517)784-3135	AA	2002
Hansen Abigail N Imlah	(517)231-7615 abigail.imlah@gmail.com	2207 N 52nd St Milwaukee WI 53208	SW	Teacher	Tchr	Mount Olive Milwaukee WI	(414)774-2200	MQ	2019
Hansen Ankara T Ankara Greenwood-Armstrong	(626)324-7926 ankara.hansen22@gmail.com	3848 N Center Rd Saginaw MI 48603	MI	DPM	Mem C	Good Shepherd Saginaw MI	(989)793-8201	IV	2021
Hansen Catherine M Dow	(636)928-6290 cathansen4@gmail.com	372 Mason Ridge Dr Saint Charles MO 63304	MO	Teacher	EM			CQ	2004
Hansen Cathi D	(219) 836-8013 linde749@hotmail.com	8636 Harrison Ave. Munster IN 46321	IN	Teacher	EM			RF	1977
Hansen Darren D	(661)964-7172 ldh1123@sbcglobal.net	1479 Ramsey Close Rockford IL 61007	NI	Teacher	Tchr	Rockford Rockford IL	(815)877-9551	S	1987
Hansen Dean R	(503)310-2164 hansendean90@gmail.com	1630 W Manor Dr Lincoln NE 68506	NEB	Teacher	EM			S	1973
Hansen Karen R Schmidt	(920)532-0928 raehansen@yahoo.com	405 Turner St Wrightstown WI 54180	NW	Teacher	Tchr	Zion Of Wayside Greenleaf WI	(920)864-2468	MQ	1995
Hansen Kathryn A Clausen	(310)597-0216 kathryn.clausen@eagles.cui.edu	337 N Sacramento St Orange CA 92867	PSW	Teacher	Tchr	Crean Irvine CA	(949)387-1199	IV	2021
Hansen Kelly A Kelso	(714)858-1458 kellyhanseninca@yahoo.com	2879 N Roxbury St Orange CA 92867	PSW	Teacher	Tchr	Salem Orange CA	(714)633-2366	IV	1991
Hansen Lori V Brown	(661)964-7170 ldh1123@sbcglobal.net	1479 Ramsey Close Rockford IL 61107	NI	Teacher	Tchr	Rockford Rockford IL	(815)877-9551	S	1988
Hansen Lynnette M Jass	(715)323-7986 lynnettehansen@pilgrimluth.org		NW	Teacher	Tchr	Pilgrim Green Bay WI	(920)965-2233	MQ	2006
Hansen Matthew W	(714)974-5579	3634 E Westridge Dr Orange CA 92867	PSW	Teacher	Tchr	Orange County Orange CA	(714)998-5151	IV	1984
Hansen Maxwell A	(602)384-3158 maxwellhansen93@gmail.com	120 Camelot Dr Apt F05 Saginaw MI 48638	MI	DPM	Mem C	Good Shepherd Saginaw MI	(989)793-8201	IV	2021
Hansen Nicholas	(815)821-9239 hansennicholas4@gmail.com	304 Walnut St Lindenwood IL 61049	NI	DPM	Mem C	St John Sycamore IL	(815)895-4477	CH	2024
Hansen Pamela J De Groot	(714)974-5579 pam.hansen@lhsoc.org	3634 E Westridge Dr Orange CA 92867	PSW	DPM	Pro Stf	Orange County Orange CA	(714)998-5151	CQ	2006
Hansen Rebecca Bertermann	(630)750-1312 bbertermann@sbcglobal.net	7188 Dexter Rd Downers Grove IL 60516	NI	Teacher	Tchr	Walther Melrose Park IL	(708)344-0404	RF	2004
Hansen Ryan W	(414)588-0522 foolish4christ@gmail.com	W201N17020 Chateau Dr Jackson WI 53037	SW	DCM	Tchr	Trinity Mequon WI	(262)242-2045	MQ	2010
Hansen Samantha	(262)939-1677 shansen@trinityracine.com	3206 Ruby Ave Racine WI 53402	SW	Teacher	Tchr	Trinity Racine WI	(262)632-1766	CQ	2022

*Multiple Assignments (See Church Worker Locator for Additional Details)
See Page 53 for the Table of Abbreviations for key to District, Classification, Position, and College abbreviations.
**C =Candidate; EM =Emeritus; the date following the C is the month and year the Candidate status began

NAME	TELEPHONE NUMBER EMAIL	STREET ADDRESS CITY/STATE/ZIP	DISTRICT	CLASS.	POSITION/ STATUS**	WHERE SERVING	OFFICE PHONE	COLLEGE/ UNIV/CQ	YR GRAD
Hansen Sarah J	(920)495-3016 hansens@newlhs.com	8130 County C Sturgeon Bay WI 54235	NW	Teacher	Tchr	Northeastern WI Green Bay WI	(920)469-6810	MQ	2013
Hansen Sheryl M	(314)435-3447 sheryl_hansen@yahoo.com	3039 S Ridgecrest Dr Apt E3 Springfield MO 65807	MO	Tch/DCE	EM			S	1983
Hansen Sierra L	(402)340-1374 shansen@zionlutheranpierce.com	54765 858th Rd Pierce NE 68767	NEB	Teacher	Tchr	Zion Pierce NE	(402)329-4658	CQ	2023
Hansen Teresa L Howard		710 Pointe Pacific Apt 2 Daly City CA 94014	EN	Teacher	C06/2019			S	1994
Hanson G D Riley	(317)435-9543 dhanson1966@gmail.com	876 Village Brook Ct Ballwin MO 63021	MO	Teacher	EM			CQ	2002
Hanson Kristine L Grewe Deac	(952)212-7237 kristine.hanson1@me.com	113 Cedar Lane Dr Jordan MN 55352	MNS	Deaconess	EM			FW-DEAC	2011
Hanson Laura G Wiederrich	(402)643-5808 laurahanson715@gmail.com	513 Hickory Manor Arnold MO 63010	MO	Teacher	Tchr	Lutheran South Saint Louis MO	(314)631-1400	S	2018
Hantula Erica M Demel	(714)998-5151 erica.hantula@lhsoc.org	3052 North Pinewood St Orange CA 92865	PSW	Teacher	Tchr	Orange County Orange CA	(714)998-5151	IV	2006
Hanusa Lois M	(712)325-4378	518 Elliott St Council Blfs IA 51503	IW	Teacher	EM			S	1975
Hapke Gerald D	(260)705-5613 aarons_hold@comcast.net	4227 Stillwood Dr Fort Wayne IN 46815	IN	Teacher	EM			RF	1964
Harbaugh Kara E Garvelink	(616)560-2940 harbaughkara@gmail.com	4300 Boulder Run NE Ada MI 49301	MI	Teacher	C06/2023			CQ	2016
Harbers Elizabeth J Salzberg	(636)675-9279 esalzberg@immanuelstcharles.org	107 Beacon Hill Dr Saint Charles MO 63301	MO	Teacher	Tchr	Immanuel Saint Charles MO	(636)946-2656	S	2013
Harbig Rachel A Pankow	(612)763-9423 rharbig@charter-internet.com	1407 N McKay Ave NE Alexandria MN 56308	MNN	Teacher	Tchr	Zion Alexandria MN	(320)763-4842	SP	1986
Harbke James M	(847)361-4902 youthleader@sbcglobal.net	4107 Owl Dr Rolling Mdws IL 60008	NI	Teacher	EM			RF	1970
Hardecopf Karen L Thanepohn	(630)222-2157 khardecopf@gmail.com	2137 Bluebird Ln Yorkville IL 60560	NI	DCM	EM			MQ	2004
Harder Jason D	(920)287-3197 jdharder77@gmail.com	608 N 40th St Sheboygan WI 53081	SW	Teacher	Tchr	Trinity Sheboygan WI	(920)458-8248	CQ	2012
Hardies Karla M Dorn	(586)610-4511 karlahardies@gmail.com	7709 Riverview Dr Apt 204 Jenison MI 49428	MI	Teacher	Prin	ISJ Grand Rapids MI	(616)363-0505	AA	2021
Hardies Michael A	(586) 610-4172 mhardies@hotmail.com	22010 Colony Dr Boca Raton FL 33433	MI	Teacher	C09/2025			RF	1994
Hardin Beth A Miller	(336)725-1651 beth.hardin@stjohnsws.org	4136 Greenmead Rd Winston Salem NC 27106	SE	Teacher	Tchr	St Johns Winston-Salem NC	(336)725-1651	RF	1982
Hardin Sandra M Messett	(951)318-2106 sandymh47@gmail.com	21107 Brookline Dr Walnut CA 91789	PSW	Teacher	EM			CQ	2002
Harding Corine A Vollmer	(630)336-9911 coriharding77@gmail.com	1428 Oldenburg Dr Mt Pleasant SC 29429	SE	Teacher	C07/2016			RF	1999
Harding Jacob H	(308)391-9360 jacobharding@concordiaprep school.org	9833 Lower Marine Rd Marine IL 62061	SE	Teacher	C06/2022			S	2020
Harding Nicolas J	(402)937-6301 nicolas.harding93@gmail.com	649 Carlton Rd Palmetto GA 30268	FG	Teacher		Florida-Georgia District Orlando FL	(407)857-5556	S	2016
Hardt James W	(402)992-5855 jhardt52@yahoo.com	800 W Klein Battle Creek NE 68715	NEB	Teacher	EM			S	1974
Hardt Kelly J Deac	(636)432-1332 kelly.hardt@imlutheran.org	1809 Jessica Hills Ct Washington MO 63090	MO	Deaconess	Mem C	Immanuel Washington MO	(636)239-4705	RF	2000
Hardy Kristin E Hirt	(586)822-7307 khardy@trinityct.org	44080 Boulder Dr Clinton Twp MI 48038	MI	DCE	C07/2016			RF	1998
Hardy Lucretia L Drews	(630)935-1030 llh764@sbcglobal.net	764 S Cambridge Ave Elmhurst IL 60126	NI	Teacher	EM			RF	2001
Hardy Timothy D	(586)822-7306 thardy@lhsa.com	44080 Boulder Dr Clinton Twp MI 48038	MI	Teacher	Tchr	Lutheran North Macomb MI	(586)781-9151	RF	1995
Harer April J Perr	(714)865-4230 mrsharer1@yahoo.com	22501 Chase Apt 11116 Aliso Viejo CA 92656	PSW	Teacher	Tchr	Abiding Savior Lake Forest CA	(949)830-1460	IV	2005
Harfst Herbert E II	(804)350-8952 herbert.e.harfst@richmond.edu	7416 Ewell Rd Mechanicsville VA 23111	SE	DCM	EM			CQ	2002
Harger Steven K	(510)512-5287 sharger@zionlutheran.net	19345 Brusk Ct Castro Valley CA 94546	CNH	Teacher	Tchr	Zion Piedmont CA	(510)530-4213	RF	1988
Harkins La Jean M Sparks	(217)341-4168 lajean.harkins@oursaviors-school.org	2616 Lemont Dr Springfield IL 62704	CI	Teacher	Tchr	Our Saviors Springfield IL	(217)546-4531	CQ	1998
Harkins Martha E Semanko	(701)793-7784 mesemanko@gmail.com	25992 10th St W Zimmerman MN 55398	MNS	DCE	Mem C	Mount Olive Anoka MN	(763)421-3223	CH	2020
Harkins Richard R II	(217)971-4844 rich.harkins@outlook.com	2616 Lemont Dr Springfield IL 62704	CI	Teacher	Tchr	Lutheran Springfield IL	(217)546-6363	RF	1986
Harks Theo E	(262)735-4740 harks_t@icloud.com	N78W17445 Wildwood Dr Apt 419 Menomonee Fls WI 53051	SW	Teacher	EM			SP	1967
Harling Carrie E Wyatt	(507)514-2713 carrieharling14@gmail.com	6155 Edgerly Ln Lincoln ND 58504	ND	Teacher	Tchr	Martin Luther Bismarck ND	(701)224-9070	MQ	2007
Harlow Archie R	(325)456-2100 harlow.archie@gmail.com	808 N Davidson St Brady TX 76825	TX	DCM	EM			MQ	1986
Harm Mary	(618)533-7790	2223 Hawks Landing Dr Lake Saint Louis MO 63367	SI	Teacher	Tchr	Trinity Centralia IL	(618)532-2614	RF	1973
Harman Anthony C	(928)317-0513 tharman@yumalutheranschool.org	2260 E 25th Pl Yuma AZ 85365	PSW	Teacher	Tchr	Christ Yuma AZ	(928)726-0773	S	1982
Harman Kristin M Allen	(309)840-4216 kmallen357@gmail.com	695 S Elwood St Forsyth IL 62535	CI	DCE	Mem C	St Paul's Decatur IL	(217)423-6955	RF	2016
Harman Tamara L Crumbaugh	(520)317-0560	2242 E San Marcos Dr Yuma AZ 85365	PSW	Teacher	Tchr	Yuma Yuma AZ	(928)726-8410	S	1985
Harmon Brittany	(708)595-2180	1311 New England Drive Fort Wayne IN 46815	IN	Teacher	Tchr	Concordia Fort Wayne IN	(260)426-9922	MQ	2018

*Multiple Assignments (See Church Worker Locator for Additional Details)

See Page 53 for the Table of Abbreviations for key to District, Classification, Position, and College abbreviations.

**C =Candidate; EM =Emeritus; the date following the C is the month and year the Candidate status began

NAME	TELEPHONE NUMBER EMAIL	STREET ADDRESS CITY/STATE/ZIP	DISTRICT	CLASS.	POSITION/ STATUS**	WHERE SERVING	OFFICE PHONE	COLLEGE/ UNIV/CQ	YR GRAD
Harms Amy R Streuter	amy.harms@cune.edu		NEB	Teacher	S HS/C	Concordia University Nebraska Seward NE	(402)643-3651	S	2005
Harms Hillard H	(262) 527-0103 hillardharms@yahoo.com	1427 Tullar Rd Apt 6 Neenah WI 54956	SW	Teacher	EM			SP	1969
Harms Paula L Robbins	(419)966-7006 pharms@stpaulnapoleon.org	1050 Westchester Ave Napoleon OH 43545	OH	Teacher	Tchr	St Paul Napoleon OH	(419)592-5536	AA	2003
Harms Sarah K	(636)577-0512 salli.kharms@gmail.com	3 Red Oaks Dr Saint Peters MO 63376	MO	DCM	C07/2021			MQ	2016
Harnden Melissa A Deac	(425)215-6969 harnden.ma@gmail.com	1220 Sunview Dr Unit 1280-17 Saint Johns MI 48879	MI	Deaconess	Mem C	St Peter Saint Johns MI	(989)224-3178	FW-DEAC	2025
Harney Rachel L Carpenter	(504)493-5358 rachelh5020@aol.com	7315 Beryl St New Orleans LA 70124	SO	Teacher	Tchr	Atonement Metairie LA	(504)887-0225	RF	1986
Harper Michaela E Wilaby	(952)232-7504 michaelawilaby@pilgrimluth.org	1628 W Main Ave Apt 8 De Pere WI 54115	NW	Teacher	Tchr	Pilgrim Green Bay WI	(920)965-2233	MQ	2021
Harper Sarah C Bedlan-Heislen	(702)569-5385 harpers@flhsemail.org	1715 Blue Sage Pkwy Elkhorn NE 68022	NEB	Teacher		Nebraska District Seward NE	(402)643-2961	S	1994
Harrell Katie A Gowen	(808)489-3722 katiepuanani@yahoo.com	5435 Del Norte Way Santa Maria CA 93455	CI	Teacher	C03/2025			BR	2019
Harries Cynthia L	(816)833-4872 charries53@yahoo.com	2131 S Norwood Ave Independence MO 64052	MO	Teacher	EM			S	1975
Harries Daniel L	(308)381-8142 theharriesparents@hotmail.com	404 Woodland Dr Apt 402 Grand Island NE 68801	NEB	Teacher	EM			S	1969
Harries Diane M Strohm	(913)888-4772 dineharries@yahoo.com	12691 W 82nd Ter Lenexa KS 66215	KS	Teacher	Tchr	Hope Shawnee KS	(913)631-6940	CQ	2009
Harries Terry L Hennis	(785)799-5849 terryharries2000@yahoo.com	353 5th Rd Marysville KS 66508	KS	Teacher	C07/2024			CQ	2002
Harrington Melissa M Martin Deac	(989)928-6748	1320 Road 12 1/2 Powell WY 82435	WY	Deaconess	C04/2024			FW-DEAC	2022
Harris Christine L	(585)822-0984 christine.harris28@yahoo.com	51 Briarwood Dr West Seneca NY 14224	EA	Teacher	Tchr	Trinity West Seneca NY	(716)674-5353	BR	1996
Harris Dawn M	(734)751-9947 dharris@trinityutica.com	3820 Hunt Club Ct Shelby Twp MI 48316	MI	Teacher	Tchr	Trinity Utica MI	(586)731-4490	CQ	2014
Harris Kallie N Adkins	(217)246-6222 Kharris@stjls-mattoon.com	408 Essex Ave Mattoon IL 61938	CI	Teacher	Tchr	St Johns Mattoon IL	(217)234-4911	Other	2016
Harris Katherine M Bandy	(260)388-7352 kate.harris712@gmail.com	4020 Pebble Way New Haven IN 46774	IN	Teacher	Tchr	St John-Emmanuel Monroeville IN	(260)639-0123	MQ	2008
Harris Kathleen D		3002 Palo Duro Dr San Angelo TX 76904	TX	Teacher	Tchr	Trinity San Angelo TX	(325)944-8660	AU	2009
Harris Linda C Zientara	(217)546-2924	8327 Spring Ridge Ln Indianapolis IN 46278	CI	Teacher	EM			CQ	1986
Harris Maggie D Deac	(558)338-2420 maggierny@gmail.com	942 Joseph Ave Rochester NY 14621	EA	Deaconess	EM			Other	1979
Harris Margaret L Vorwerk	(713)569-2375 margaret.vorwerk.harris@gmail.com	14215 Orion Dr Tomball TX 77375	TX	Teacher	EM			SP	1975
Harris Valerie J	(586)604-5853 valerieharris2008@comcast.net	14140 Merriweather St Apt 213 Sterling Hts MI 48312	MI	Teacher	EM			RF	1982
Harrison Amber J Navarrette Jackson			OK	Teacher	C07/2016			S	2006
Harrison Kenneth L Jr	(714)330-2270 kharrison@stjohnsorange.org	929 E Chestnut Ave Orange CA 92867	PSW	Teacher	Tchr	Saint Johns Orange CA	(714)288-4400	IV	2002
Harrison Molly E	(951)678-9449 mharrison@stjohnsorange.org	929 E Chestnut Ave Orange CA 92867	PSW	Teacher	Tchr	Saint Johns Orange CA	(714)288-4400	IV	2003
Harrison Rayann S		P.O. Box 111 Concan TX 78838	TX	Teacher	Tchr	Lutheran Education Association Friendswood TX	(281)617-5189	CQ	2003
Harstad Susan K Meyer	(507)259-5690 dansueharstad@gmail.com	1806 Koenigstein Ave Norfolk NE 68701	NEB	Teacher	Tchr	Zion Pierce NE	(402)329-4658	S	1985
Hart Charles M	(303)659-4954	287 S 13th Ave Brighton CO 80601	RM	Teacher	Tchr	Zion Brighton CO	(303)659-3443	S	1984
Hart Jamie C Sides	(314)368-3315 jamies410@sbcglobal.net	11256 Sherwood Oak Ct Saint Louis MO 63146	MO	Teacher	Tchr	Immanuel Olivette MO	(314)993-2394	CQ	2014
Hart Jennifer K Kuphal	(651)460-4247 hartgjlsh@gmail.com	20627 Cypress Dr Farmington MN 55024	MNS	Teacher	EM			S	1977
Hart Rachel C Deac	(620)352-1719 hartet@csl.edu	310 Woodland Dr Salem IL 62881	CI	Deaconess	Mem C	Salem Salem IL	(618)548-3190	SL-DEAC	2025
Hart Regina A Prail	(626)281-7517	1832 S 9th St Alhambra CA 91803	PSW	Teacher	Tchr	Emmaus Alhambra CA	(626)289-3664	SP	1964
Hart Susan A Ashby	(303) 304-9657 susan.hart728@gmail.com	287 S 13th Ave Brighton CO 80601	RM	Tch/DCE	C09/2020			S	1985
Hartfield Kathryn J Sattler	(269)429-5192	3404 Knox St Saint Joseph MI 49085	MI	Teacher	C08/2021			RF	1995
Hartje Deborah S Moore	(913)638-3894 deb.hartje@gmail.com	1920 Shawnee Dr Kansas City KS 66106	MO	Tch/DCE	C07/2016			RF	1987
Hartman Hanna F	hartman41@gmail.com		IN	Teacher	C09/2020			CQ	2019
Hartman Joanna E Nelson	(714)655-5092 jehartman4@hotmail.com	2313 Cheyenne Trail San Angelo TX 76903	TX	Teacher	Tchr	Trinity San Angelo TX	(325)947-1275	IV	2007
Hartman Kenneth W	(573)230-8243 kshartman73@gmail.com	26 Spring Time Ct Saint Charles MO 63303	MO	Teacher	EM			RF	1973
Hartman Patricia A	(716)627-9836 path95@verizon.net	95 Waterview Pkwy Hamburg NY 14075	EA	Teacher	EM			S	1968
Hartman Sally M Konsdorf	(573)230-9678 teacherTLS33@icloud.com	26 Spring Time Ct Saint Charles MO 63303	MO	Teacher	EM			RF	1973

*Multiple Assignments (See Church Worker Locator for Additional Details)

See Page 53 for the Table of Abbreviations for key to District, Classification, Position, and College abbreviations.

**C =Candidate; EM =Emeritus; the date following the C is the month and year the Candidate status began

NAME	TELEPHONE NUMBER EMAIL	STREET ADDRESS CITY/STATE/ZIP	DISTRICT	CLASS.	POSITION/ STATUS**	WHERE SERVING	OFFICE PHONE	COLLEGE/ UNIV/CQ	YR GRAD
Hartmann Dale W	(714)639-5863 dalehartmann@sbcglobal.net	2400 E Palm Ave Orange CA 92867	PSW	Teacher	EM			S	1954
Hartmann Dari R	dhartmann@saint-paul.org	810 E Shady Way Apt 310 Arlington Hts IL 60005	NI	DCE	Mem C	St Paul Mount Prospect IL	(847)255-0332	SP	1983
Hartmann Deidre J Walton	(573)987-9159 dhartmann91@yahoo.com	465 Jeffery Dr Jackson MO 63755	MO	Teacher	C08/2022			S	1995
Hartmann Dennis R	(573)243-3006 deedenhart@att.net	465 Jeffery Dr Jackson MO 63755	MO	Teacher	Tchr	Trinity Cape Girardeau MO	(573)334-1068	S	1995
Hartmann Esther Hepting	(573)334-4250	1339 Karen Dr Cpe Girardeau MO 63701	MO	Teacher	EM			S	1960
Hartmann Jennifer N Zoch	(832)331-5656	3331 Ewing Dr Manvel TX 77578	TX	Teacher	Tchr	South Houston TX	(281)464-8299	CQ	2013
Hartmann Robert T	(573)334-4250	1339 Karen Dr Cpe Girardeau MO 63701	MO	Teacher	EM			S	1954
Hartmann Royce R	(314)973-2864 rhartmann@ccls-stlouis.org	1001 Autumn Valley Ct Fenton MO 63026	MO	Teacher	Prin	Christ Community Kirkwood MO	(314)822-7774	AA	1991
Hartwig Britnee Fear	(308)539-9901 britnee.fear@gmail.com	813 N State St Merrill WI 54452	NW	Teacher	Tchr	Trinity Merrill WI	(715)536-5482	CQ	2021
Hartwig Sandra L Rummel	(630)543-2651	1283 W Lake St Apt 303 Addison IL 60101	NI	Teacher	EM			RF	1972
Harvey Lauren K Zahner	(207)313-9346 lauren.zahner@cuw.edu	112 W Althea Dr Grafton WI 53024	SW	Teacher	C07/2016			MQ	2009
Harvey Michael J Sr	(507)529-5463 dceorange@gmail.com	230 14th Ave SE Rochester MN 55904	MNS	DCE	Mem C	Redeemer Rochester MN	(507)289-5147	SP	2001
Harwell Lise A Strom	(970)294-6201 lise.harwell@gmail.com	1050 Mt Oxford Ave Severance CO 80550	RM	Teacher	C07/2016			S	2009
Harwell Matthew C	(970)294-6210 matt.harwell@gmail.com	1050 Mount Oxford Ave Severance CO 80550	RM	DCE	C07/2016			S	2010
Hasamear Melissa M Rosen	(618)581-9738 lissacombs@yahoo.com	2014 Greenbrier Dr Collinsville IL 62234	SI	Teacher	Tchr	Good Shepherd Collinsville IL	(618)344-3153	CQ	2007
Hashimoto Cynthia L Bergemann	cindihashimoto@yahoo.com	336 N Redwood Dr Mankato MN 56001	MNS	Teacher	C07/2016			SP	1992
Hasko Joyce L Vick	(262)554-1431 joycehasko@gmail.com	2815 Oregon St Mt Pleasant WI 53405	S	Teacher	EM			SP	1977
Hass Donna M Kellner	(785)246-0336 dvhass@juno.com	6300 SW 6th Ave Apt 204 Topeka KS 66615	KS	Teacher	EM			S	1960
Hass Kenneth E	(810)392-3640 kehass@hotmail.com	758 Memphis Ridge Rd Riley MI 48041	MI	Teacher	EM			S	1972
Hasseldahl Cynthia L Moderow	(573)529-6604 moderow@yahoo.com	2021 Chatham St Racine WI 53402	SW	Teacher	EM			S	1980
Hasseldahl David C	(815)506-3862 david.hasseldahl@cune.org	1124 Foxglove Ln Marengo IL 60152	NI	Teacher	Tchr	Zion Marengo IL	(815)568-5156	S	2009
Hasseldahl Gregory C	(573)529-6603 gchasseld@gmail.com	2021 Chatham St Racine WI 53402	SW	Teacher	EM			S	1981
Hasseldahl Jill N Ireton	(262)672-5257 jill.hasseldahl@cune.org	23 S Hillock Dr Mt Pleasant WI 53406	SW	Teacher	C08/2020			S	2006
Hasseldahl Kevin P	Kevin.Hasseldahl@cune.org	23 S Hillock Dr Mt Pleasant WI 53406	SW	Teacher	Tchr	Lutheran High School Racine WI	(262)637-6538	S	2005
Hasseldahl Lisa M Piel	(815)506-3862 lisa.hasseldahl@att.net	1124 Foxglove Ln Marengo IL 60152	NI	Teacher	C07/2018			RF	2008
Hassemer Jill E Borchardt	(920)360-1613 jhassemer@zionwayside.org	6757 Cascade Dr Greenleaf WI 54126	NW	Teacher	Tchr	Zion Of Wayside Greenleaf WI	(920)864-2468	MQ	2004
Hasstedt Frederick O	(618)920-7262 climberdude50@gmail.com	9 Gardenia Dr Belleville IL 62221	SI	Teacher	EM			S	1977
Hasstedt Jill A Muehlfelt	(618)920-6278 jhasstedt@gmail.com	9 Gardenia Dr Belleville IL 62221	SI	Tch/DCE	Mem C	Zion Belleville IL	(618)233-2299	S	1977
Hasz Barbara J Nierman	(731)423-5383 lunicho@aol.com	380 Henderson Rd Jackson TN 38305	MDS	Teacher	EM			RF	1962
Hatcher Beckie L Rathke	(913)269-0358 nebeckie@gmail.com	317 NE Woodbury Dr Lees Summit MO 64086	MO	Teacher	Tchr	Timothy Blue Springs MO	(816)228-5300	S	1989
Hathaway Mary M Hartman	(260)615-7388 ronandmaryhathaway@gmail.com	636 Hathaway Rd Fort Wayne IN 46845	IN	Teacher	EM			S	1971
Hathaway Tyler J	(602)531-4668	17049 N 42nd St Phoenix AZ 85032	PSW	Teacher	Tchr	Christ Phoenix AZ	(602)955-4830	IV	2004
Hauch James E	(815)985-0321 jimhauch84@gmail.com	254 Lily Ln Rockford IL 61107	NI	Teacher	EM			RF	1962
Hauch Melissa A Nennig	(920)980-0521 melihauch@gmail.com	2710 Main Ave Sheboygan WI 53083	SW	Teacher	Tchr	Trinity Sheboygan WI	(920)458-8248	RF	1999
Hauer Raymond P	(931)451-7009 rayhauer@gmail.com	409 Bruce Dr Spring Hill TN 37174	MDS	Teacher	EM			S	1965
Haug-Schulz Jacqueline J Haug Deac	(415)333-6743	421 Gennessee St San Francisco CA 94127	CNH	Deaconess	EM			Other	1961
Haupt Natalie A	(586)381-3959 nhaupt79@gmail.com	16890 25 Mile Rd Macomb MI 48042	MI	Teacher	Tchr	Lutheran North Macomb MI	(586)781-9151	AA	2002
Haupt Sarah E Johnson	(954)856-4219 sarahhaupt11@gmail.com	1596 Dublin Dr Hampshire IL 60140	FG	Teacher	C07/2016			MQ	2006
Hausch Michael F	(734)449-9493 mfhausch@gmail.com	10920 Tuthill Rd South Lyon MI 48178	EN	DCE	EM			S	1979
Hauser Janet L Johnson Stoll	(989)414-7727 janstoll5@yahoo.com	4737 Maplewood Dr Bay City MI 48706	MI	Teacher	EM			RF	1967
Hausler Eunice A Redeker	(618)478-2346 unicehausl@frontiernet.net	15611 State Route 127 Hoyleton IL 62803	SI	Teacher	EM			RF	1956
Hauter Donna R Felbinger	(806)676-2919 dhauter1953@gmail.com	8606 Baxter Dr Amarillo TX 79119	TX	Teacher	EM			SP	1975
Havekost Jeffrey C	(303)204-7585 jhavekost@bethluth.net	3297 S Emporia Ct Denver CO 80231	RM	Teacher	Tchr	Bethlehem Lakewood CO	(303)233-0401	S	1972

*Multiple Assignments (See Church Worker Locator for Additional Details)

See Page 53 for the Table of Abbreviations for key to District, Classification, Position, and College abbreviations.

**C =Candidate; EM =Emeritus; the date following the C is the month and year the Candidate status began

NAME	TELEPHONE NUMBER EMAIL	STREET ADDRESS CITY/STATE/ZIP	DISTRICT	CLASS.	POSITION/ STATUS**	WHERE SERVING	OFFICE PHONE	COLLEGE/ UNIV/CQ	YR GRAD
Havera Beverly A Swanson	(269)663-2309 chemistherbie@aol.com	26357 Acorn St Edwardsburg MI 49112	IN	Teacher	EM			SP	1965
Havers Brenda E Krzyske	(586)747-6336 bhavers7999@gmail.com	5661 Secord Lake Rd Dryden MI 48428	MI	Teacher	EM			AA	1985
Hawkins Wendy A Knox	whawkins@trinityutica.com	45781 Heather Ridge Dr Macomb MI 48044	MI	Teacher	Tchr	Trinity Utica MI	(586)731-4490	RF	1995
Hawthorne Nancy J	(805)444-9499 n.hawthorne@att.net	1532 Arabian St Simi Valley CA 93065	PSW	Teacher	EM			S	1977
Hayden Hannah D	(515)745-2436 hannahhayden0@gmail.com	2130 E Hamilton Ct Apt B203 Republic MO 65738	MO	DCE	Mem C	Redeemer Springfield MO	(417)881-5470	Other	2017
Hayes Aaron D	(208)241-3795 aarondhayes@proton.me	851 Park Ln Pocatello ID 83201	NOW	Teacher	Tchr	Grace Pocatello ID	(208)237-4142	CQ	2023
Hayes H R Dr	(708)227-0633 robert.hayes@cuchicago.edu	2350 Pepper Tree Ct Lisle IL 60532	NI	Teacher	EM			CQ	1974
Hayes Jaymes E	(217)722-1222 jaymeshayes20@gmail.com	1502 W 38th St Kearney NE 68845	NEB	DCE	Mem C	Holy Cross Kearney NE	(308)237-2944	CH	2010
Hayes Rachel C Saldate	(714)222-0164		PSW	Teacher	C07/2016			IV	2002
Haynes Coleen R Speidel	(503)304-9391 mickhaynes@comcast.net	3295 Jack St N Keizer OR 97303	NOW	Teacher	C07/2016			S	1992
Haynes David C	(541)419-9440 david.c.haynes@gmail.com	19889 Duck Call Ln Bend OR 97702	NOW	Teacher	Tchr	Trinity Bend OR	(541)382-1850	PO	2012
Haynes Shelli J Jolivette	(909)226-3179 shelli.haynes@mcstn.org	138 Eleanor Davis Dr. Maryville TN 37804	MDS	DCE	C08/2025			IV	1996
Haynes Travis M	(714)345-1590 travis.haynes.13@gmail.com	138 Eleanor Davis Dr Maryville TN 37804	MDS	Teacher	C07/2016			IV	1995
Hayter Jennifer	(253)797-6968 j.hayter@zionls.org	15823 3 Lakes Rd Snohomish WA 98290	NOW	Teacher	Tchr	Zion Snohomish Cty Lake Stevens WA	(425)334-5064	CQ	2017
Hayter Maryann M Oklejas Deac	(734)625-4432 deaconessmaryann@icloud.com	295 Lillian Ave Union MO 63084	MO	Deaconess	S Ex/S	Office of National Mission Saint Louis MO		SL-DEAC	2013
Hayward Janet K Augenstein	jhayward@cluth.org	8219 Roanoke Dr Fort Wayne IN 46835	IN	Teacher	Tchr	Central New Haven IN	(260)493-2502	CQ	1996
Hazelberg Faye M	(920)387-0315	520 Bridge St. Mayville WI 53050	SW	Teacher	Tchr	St Johns Mayville WI	(920)387-4310	MQ	1994
Headley Matthew C	(512)777-9322 com@gstx.org	3224 Venezia Vw Leander TX 78641	TX	DCE	Mem C	Good Shepherd Cedar Park TX	(512)258-6227	AU	1982
Heath Brandon W	(619)405-7476 brandon.w.heath@gmail.com	690 Live Oak Dr El Cajon CA 92020	NEB	DCE		Nebraska District Seward NE	(402)643-2961	S	2000
Hebel Harry G Jr	(949)348-2385 hhebel@hotmail.com	5200 Irvine Blvd Spc 267 Irvine CA 92620	PSW	Teacher	EM			S	1966
Hecht Annie R Buchanan	(269) 806-5034 ahecht2014@gmail.com	1410 Finleys Lane Vicksburg MI 49097	MI	Teacher	Tchr	St Michael Portage MI	(269)327-7832	AA	2009
Heck David P	(586)713-9559 nmouc414@comcast.net	52775 Kelly Dr Macomb MI 48042	MI	Teacher	EM			AA	2004
Heck Edwin G	(805)405-2560 edandbarb1@verizon.net	891 La Grange Ave Newbury Park CA 91320	PSW	Teacher	EM			S	1973
Heck Zonna L King	(231)679-4230 zlouheck@hotmail.com	438 N State St Big Rapids MI 49307	MI	Teacher	EM			RF	1981
Heckert Hannah G Seefeld	hgheckert@gmail.com		SW	Teacher	C10/2016			MQ	2010
Heckert Shawn B	(414)510-8449 sjheckert616@gmail.com	1505 S Indiana Ave West Bend WI 53095	SW	Teacher	Tchr	Milwaukee LHS Milwaukee WI	(414)461-6000	CQ	2022
Heckler Sandra L Lannan	(262)617-3156 momopapaw@yahoo.com	1941 Lakeside Dr Madison OH 44057	OH	Teacher	EM			CQ	1996
Heckman Shirley M Knobloch	(626)305-2408 shirleyheckman3@gmail.com	1763 Royal Oaks Dr Apt B24 Bradbury CA 91010	PSW	Teacher	EM			S	1958
Heckmann Michelle A		5523 Bryanhurst Ln. Spring TX 77379	TX	Teacher	Tchr	Trinity Klein Klein TX	(281)376-5773	AU	2009
Hecksel Shannon T	(651)226-5763 dcehex@gmail.com	109 Inverness Ct Mankato MN 56001	MNS	Teacher	Tchr	Hosanna Mankato MN	(507)388-1766	SP	2000
Hedemann Philip E		59 N Dade 91 Lockwood MO 65682	MO	Teacher	EM			S	1968
Hedges Amy L Lybarger	(317)852-0171	4423 East County Road 850 South Mooresville IN 46158	IN	Teacher	C06/2024			CQ	2011
Hedrick Jeremy L	(563)370-3299	188 Chestnut Ridge Dr Hartland WI 53029	SW	Teacher	Tchr	Lake Country Hartland WI	(262)367-8600	CH	2009
Hedrick Jessica L	hedrickjl2@gmail.com	806 S Concord St Davenport IA 52802	NOW	Teacher	C08/2022			CH	2013
Hedstrom Laura E	(507)407-0081 laura.hedstrom@gmail.com	87515 440th Ave Lakefield MN 56150	IN	DPM	C06/2021			S	2017
Heeren Lynelle M	(413)313-5651	32 Lower Westfield Road Apt 314 Holyoke MA 01040	NE	Teacher	EM			SP	1981
Heerssen Karla K Timmerman	(281)855-7763 lalakk@sbcglobal.net	6107 Aberton Forest Dr Houston TX 77084	TX	Teacher	EM			S	1977
Hefele Isabelle S	(314)919-6017 ihefe25@gmail.com	8150 N 61st Ave Apt 3086 Glendale AZ 85302	PSW	Teacher	Tchr	Valley Phoenix AZ	(602)230-1600	CH	2024
Heffelfinger Mark L		4204 Menomonee River Pkwy Wauwatosa WI 53222	SW	Teacher	EM			RF	1968
Heflin Roy W	(954)804-3438 dcemrh@mac.com	1808 Butterfly Pl Sun City Ctr FL 33573	FG	DCE	EM			SP	1995
Hegenauer Diane L Heyl	(734)595-1037 cdhege@comcast.net	439 S Bryar St Westland MI 48186	MI	Teacher	Tchr	St Michael Wayne MI	(734)728-1950	AA	1988
Heggemeier Lyle M	lheggemeier@gmail.com	7400 Goodman Dr Urbandale IA 50322	IW	Tch/DCE	EM			S	1978
Heibel Matthew S	(402)217-2313 matthew.heibel@gmail.com	1940 Pinedale Ave Lincoln NE 68506	NEB	Teacher	EM			S	1984

*Multiple Assignments (See Church Worker Locator for Additional Details)
See Page 53 for the Table of Abbreviations for key to District, Classification, Position, and College abbreviations.
**C =Candidate; EM =Emeritus; the date following the C is the month and year the Candidate status began

NAME	TELEPHONE NUMBER EMAIL	STREET ADDRESS CITY/STATE/ZIP	DISTRICT	CLASS.	POSITION/ STATUS**	WHERE SERVING	OFFICE PHONE	COLLEGE/ UNIV/CQ	YR GRAD
Heicher Ellyn S Buchholz	(262)513-8191	14540 W Maylore Ct New Berlin WI 53151	EN	Teacher	Tchr	Hales Corners Hales Corners WI	(414)529-6701	CQ	2011
Heide Rachel E	(602)517-7279 rachelheide1@gmail.com	2610 E Vista Dr Phoenix AZ 85032	PSW	Teacher	C07/2016			IV	2009
Heide William J Dr	(714)425-9568 wjmeadows@aol.com	526 E Meadowbrook Ave Orange CA 92865	PSW	Teacher	EM			RF	1973
Heideman Julie K Spencer	(317)841-9514 jheideman@hclc.info	14542 Shire Close Fishers IN 46037	IN	Teacher	Tchr	Holy Cross Indianapolis IN	(317)826-1234	RF	1989
Heider Wendy E Peirce	(308)383-7242 webheider23@gmail.com	4148 Springview Dr Grand Island NE 68803	NEB	Teacher	EM			S	1974
Heidlauf Joanne V Vimtrup	(847)245-4915 jvheidlauf@gmail.com	39031 N Cedar Crest Dr Lake Villa IL 60046	NI	Teacher	EM			RF	1965
Heidloff Linda S	(309)827-0713 lindasheidloff@gmail.com	824 McGregor St Apt 3 Bloomington IL 61701	CI	Teacher	EM			RF	1977
Heidorn Caroline Hannaman	(402)534-4191 pcheidn@windstream.net	600 Church St #107 Seward NE 68434	NEB	Teacher	EM			S	1973
Heidrich Melissa K	(405)255-9553 mkheidrich@yahoo.com	28 Butterfly Creek Blvd Edmond OK 73013	OK	Teacher	Tchr	Messiah Oklahoma City OK	(405)946-0462	CQ	2023
Heidtbrink Natalie A	(210)668-9030 Natalie.heidtbrink@messiah.us	1800 S 84th Street Lincoln NE 68506	NEB	Teacher	Mem C	Messiah Lincoln NE	(402)489-3024	CQ	2016
Heien David A	(309)678-5927 davidheien@aol.com	3545 W Saymore Ln Peoria IL 61615	CI	Teacher	EM			S	1970
Heien Janet M Bremer	(309)678-5727 janheien@aol.com	3545 W Saymore Ln Peoria IL 61615	CI	Teacher	EM			S	1974
Heil John O	(815)953-6450 joheil55@gmail.com	3093 Lowe Rd Kankakee IL 60901	NI	Teacher	EM			RF	1978
Heiliger Andrea L Chandler	(406)652-5092 andreaheiliger@trinitybillings.org	583 Sudan Pl Billings MT 59105	MT	Teacher	Tchr	Trinity Billings MT	(406)656-1021	SP	2008
Heiliger Cameron E	(406)647-8212 cameronheiliger@trinitybillings.org	583 Sudan Pl Billings MT 59105	MT	Teacher	Mem C	Trinity Billings MT	(406)245-3984	SP	2008
Heilman Deborah E	(352)408-0789 josh19deb@gmail.com	2702 Lakewood Ln Eustis FL 32726	FG	Teacher	Tchr	Faith Eustis FL	(352)589-5433	S	1979
Heilman Lisa M	(260)403-1109 lheilman@esmeagles.com	3232 Getz Rd Fort Wayne IN 46804	IN	Teacher	Tchr	Emmanuel-St Michael Fort Wayne IN	(260)422-6712	RF	2000
Heilman Ruth A Shoemaker	rheilman@mystandrew.org	1304 McPherson Ct Lutherville MD 21093	SE	Teacher	Mem C	St Andrew Silver Spring MD	(301)384-4394	RF	1985
Heimerl Heather	(920)590-1606 heimhm87@gmail.com	8884 Elm Rd Suring WI 54174	NW	Teacher	Tchr	St John Suring WI	(920)842-4443	MQ	2015
Heimlich Carrie M		5509 Leadville Ave Las Vegas NV 89130	PSW	Teacher	Tchr	Faith Las Vegas NV	(702)804-4400	RF	1997
Heimsoth Barbara R Kurth	(414)545-6618	2923 S 80th St West Allis WI 53219	SW	Teacher	EM			S	1980
Heimsoth Carla E Unrath	(847)259-2750 viccarla@juno.com	711 W Gettysburg Dr Arlington Hts IL 60004	NI	Teacher	EM			CQ	1987
Heimsoth Elroy L	(573)243-0092		MO	Teacher	EM			RF	1953
Hein Gail E Halstead	(970)443-3078 gheinsite@gmail.com	4860 Glen Isle Dr Loveland CO 80538	RM	Teacher	EM			PO	1982
Hein Martin A	(402)525-3774 Martyhein1@gmail.com	9016 Trader Dr Lincoln NE 68507	NEB	Teacher	EM			S	1984
Heine Mary L Nielsen	(402)380-4038 maryheine180@gmail.com	P.O. Box 308 Winside NE 68790	NEB	Teacher	EM			S	1978
Heine Melinda K Smith	(713)376-1765 heine.melinda@gmail.com	407 Janet Dr Lebanon IL 62254	SI	Teacher	EM			S	1979
Heinecke Joshua D	(970)901-1372 joshua.heinecke@redeemer lutheranschool.org	64430 Ranger Rd Montrose CO 81403	RM	Teacher	C07/2016			S	2003
Heinemann Brian W	(760)490-7518 bheinemann26@gmail.com	6460 E Hope Well St Prescott AZ 86314	PSW	Teacher	EM			S	1972
Heinemann Charles E	(828)302-9294 heinemannc@aol.com	14941 Wellwood Rd Silver Spring MD 20905	SE	Teacher	EM			RF	1970
Heinemann Jonathan B	(402)516-5383 heinemannjb@gmail.com	7803 N 164th St Bennington NE 68007	NEB	Teacher	Mem C	Beautiful Savior Lavista NE	(402)331-7376	CQ	2010
Heinemann Kimberly C Foss	(909)975-4967	1318 Leggio Ln Upland CA 91784	PSW	Teacher		Pacific Southwest District Irvine CA	(949)854-3232	S	1999
Heinen Rita Van Dyke	(414)722-7031 ritanoel10@gmail.com	4739 S 22nd Pl Milwaukee WI 53221	SW	Teacher	Tchr	Grace Oak Creek WI	(414)762-3655	CQ	2018
Heinert Karla S	(810)444-4826 kheinert67@gmail.com	4950 Fox Crk Apt 29 Clarkston MI 48346	MI	Teacher	Tchr	St John Rochester MI	(248)402-8000	AA	1990
Heinicke Miriam Paulus		705 E Heim Ave. Orange CA 92865	PSW	Teacher	Tchr	Orange County Orange CA	(714)998-5151	IV	1990
Heinicke Rebecca L Hanusa	(712)310-1472 becca.heinicke@splecc.org	1742 Ave F Council Bluffs IA 51501	IW	Teacher	C07/2016			S	2011
Heinicke William F Dr	(775)384-9202 ferdlou@charter.net	664 W Riverview Cir Reno NV 89509	CNH	Teacher	EM			S	1953
Heinitz Jan M Dr	jmheinitz@gmail.com	417 Madero Dr Thiensville WI 53092	SW	Teacher	EM			S	1976
Heinitz John R	johnheinitz@gmail.com	937 Coast Grade Street Wake Forest NC 27587	CNH	Teacher	EM			S	1980
Heinitz Ruth A Pabor	(510)569-9594 heinitz@packbell.net	3926 Delmont Ave Oakland CA 94605	CNH	Teacher	EM			S	1979
Heinlein Brian J	brian.heinlein@stpeter hemlock.org	311 Southridge Dr Hemlock MI 48626	MI	Teacher	Mem C	St Peter Hemlock MI	(989)642-8188	MQ	2001
Heinrich Stacy L Rutz	(832)215-9806 stacyheinrich@yahoo.com	S74W25400 High Ridge Dr Waukesha WI 53189	SW	Teacher	Tchr	Immanuel Brookfield WI	(262)781-7140	MQ	2002

*Multiple Assignments (See Church Worker Locator for Additional Details)
See Page 53 for the Table of Abbreviations for key to District, Classification, Position, and College abbreviations.
**C =Candidate; EM =Emeritus; the date following the C is the month and year the Candidate status began

NAME	TELEPHONE NUMBER EMAIL	STREET ADDRESS CITY/STATE/ZIP	DISTRICT	CLASS.	POSITION/ STATUS**	WHERE SERVING	OFFICE PHONE	COLLEGE/ UNIV/CQ	YR GRAD
Heins Dawn R Landmesser	(269)876-9637 drheins2@gmail.com	2841 Woodelm Dr Rochester Hills MI 48309	MI	Teacher	EM			S	1977
Heins Emily M Cicerale	(248)762-2694 heins@stjohnsracine.org	2925 Lake Vista Court Racine WI 53402	SW	Teacher	Prin	St John Racine WI	(262)633-2758	MQ	2007
Heins Joseph M	(248)720-9475 heins.joe@gmail.com	813 Western Star Dr Fort Worth TX 76179	TX	Teacher	Tchr	St Paul Fort Worth TX	(817)353-2929	MQ	2015
Heins Sheridan N Heyn	(989)598-7377 sheins@cglschool.org	5720 Cobb Creek Rd Rochester MI 48306	PSW	Teacher	Tchr	Christ Greenfield Gilbert AZ	(480)892-8521	MQ	2016
Heins Staci Larsen	(720)998-3946 brian_and_staci@hotmail.com	12775 Strawberry Cir Longmont CO 80503	RM	Teacher	C07/2016			S	2001
Heintz Marilyn J Arnos	(708)557-2032 marilyn.heintz@gmail.com	7626 Eagle Feather Pt Colorado Spgs CO 80923	RM	Teacher	EM			RF	1971
Heinz Francie A Rincker	(402)598-6464 mikenfran3@cox.net	4508 S 150th St Omaha NE 68137	NEB	Teacher	EM			S	1972
Heinz Julia S Brauer	(224)622-2814 jheinzddd@aol.com	503 Reese Ave East Dundee IL 60118	NI	Teacher	C08/2022			Other	1992
Heinz Suzanne Hubert	(618)637-2109 rheinz@madisontelco.com	8114 Heinz Rd New Douglas IL 62074	SI	Teacher	EM			CQ	2000
Heinze Frederick C	(256)462-3864 hbheinze@yahoo.com	1620 County Road 1069 Vinemont AL 35179	SO	Teacher	EM			S	1970
Heinze Hazel B Bachmann	(256)462-3864 hbheinze@yahoo.com	1620 County Road 1069 Vinemont AL 35179	SO	Teacher	EM			S	1966
Heinze Jennifer Buenconsejo	(847)414-7558 jenniferheinze111@gmail.com	111 S Elm St Mount Prospect IL 60056	NI	Teacher	EM			RF	1987
Heinze Michael E	(708)601-1643 mheinze@saint-paul.org	111 S Elm St Mount Prosprect IL 60056	NI	Teacher	Tchr	St Paul Mount Prospect IL	(847)255-0332	RF	1982
Heinzel Rozanne M Starke	(415)509-2659 rozheinzel@outlook.com	631 Orange St Daly City CA 94014	EN	Teacher	EM			RF	1964
Heirigs Joshua D	(507)923-6288 joshua.heirigs@gmail.com	602 3rd St SW Stewartville MN 55976	MNS	DCE	Mem C	Redeemer Rochester MN	(507)289-5147	S	2011
Heirigs Rachel L Miller	(605)310-2949 rachlynne11@gmail.com	602 3rd St SW Stewartville MN 55976	MNS	Teacher	C07/2016			S	2011
Heiser Paul M	(920)336-7735 pheiser@new.rr.com	340 Roselawn Blvd Green Bay WI 54301	NW	DPM	Mem C	Faith Green Bay WI	(920)435-5524	MQ	2008
Heislen Clara M	(702)292-8113 claraheislen@gmail.com	3300 Brookside Dr Apt 4 Anchorage AK 99517	NOW	Teacher		Northwest District Portland OR	(503)288-8383	SP	2024
Heiss Christina L Bodenstab	(812)528-1363 chrissyheiss@gmail.com	4400 Grandview Rd Kansas City MO 64137	KS	Teacher	Tchr	Hope Shawnee KS	(913)631-6940	CQ	2006
Heissenbuettel Brenda M	(734)934-4496 bheissenbuettel@gmail.com	26376 Ypsilanti St Apt 1 Flat Rock MI 48134	MI	Teacher	EM			RF	1987
Heissenbuettel Monica M Frank	(734)547-5192 musical_mommy@yahoo.com	3428 Oak Dr Ypsilanti MI 48197	EN	Teacher	Tchr	Our Savior Hartland MI	(248)887-4300	AA	1991
Heitmann Cheryl M Mundinger	(573)826-8356 mumu46@hotmail.com	704 Hollyhock Dr Fulton MO 65251	MO	Teacher	EM			RF	1968
Heitschmidt Katherine S Fink	(303)659-2698 kathyheitschmidt@prodigy.net	685 S 14th Ave Brighton CO 80601	RM	Teacher	EM			S	1971
Held David P Dr	(402)643-6330 david.held@cune.edu	372 Shannon Rd Seward NE 68434	NEB	Teacher	EM			S	1960
Held Elisabeth A Nahrwold	(260)615-8472 eheld1@yahoo.com	11535 Stonepine Meadow Ct Tomball TX 77375	TX	Teacher	Tchr	Concordia Tomball TX	(281)351-2547	MQ	2003
Held Jeffrey M Dr	(949)214-3420 jeff.held@cui.edu	14311 Morning Glory Rd Tustin CA 92780	PSW	Teacher	S HS/C	Concordia University Irvine Irvine CA	(949)854-8002	CQ	2001
Held Jonathan D	(281)451-1166 heldj@clhs-tx.org	11535 Stonepine Meadow Ct Tomball TX 77375	TX	Teacher	Tchr	Concordia Tomball TX	(281)351-2547	RF	2000
Heldman Sandra J Loose	(330)273-3218 sheldman@roadrunner.com	915 W Aurora Rd # 122 Northfield OH 44067	OH	Teacher	EM			RF	1965
Heldt Stephanie M Christensen	(503)841-2765 stephmarie989@gmail.com	7618 SW Mapleleaf St Portland OR 97223	NOW	Teacher	C06/2018			PO	2005
Helge Benjamin	(505)293-4439 benjamin.helge@lcmsintl.org	10505 Arvilla Ave NE Albuquerque NM 87111	RM	Teacher	S Miss	Office of International Mission Saint Louis MO		IV	2012
Hellbusch Maynard M	(251)978-5977 wiff63@yahoo.com	24036 Perdido Beach Blvd Apt 7 Orange Beach AL 36561	SO	Teacher	EM			S	1961
Heller Jennette E Morrison Deac	(515)447-5912 deaconessjheller@gmail.com		SI	Deaconess	C07/2016			FW-DEAC	2014
Hellmers Tina M Horenkamp	(504)638-2850 tinamariehellmers@gmail.com	233 Legrande Bayou Ln Kenner LA 70065	SO	Teacher	EM			S	1984
Hellyer Lisa M	(816)304-1657 lisa.hellyer@lhm.org	616 S Foxridge Dr Raymore MO 64083	MO	Tch/DCE	Aux	LLL/Lutheran Hour Ministries Saint Louis MO	(314)317-4100	RF	1987
Helm Kelly L	(712)221-1909 dcekellygirl01@yahoo.com	4501 47th Ave NW Mandan ND 58554	ND	DCE	C07/2016			S	1996
Helmer Joel W Dr	(402)641-4596 joel.helmer@cune.edu	1315 238th Seward NE 68434	NEB	Teacher	S HS/C	Concordia University Nebraska Seward NE	(402)643-3651	S	1992
Helmer Rebecca J	(832)334-9665 helmerrebecca@hotmail.com	3535 N 175th Ct Unit 126 Omaha NE 68116	NEB	Teacher	Tchr	Concordia Omaha NE	(402)445-4000	S	1998
Helmer Theodore N	(316) 734-1635 thelmer2@cox.net	401 S Clifton Ave Wichita KS 67218	KS	Teacher	EM			S	1967
Helmick Donna J Everett	(309)565-4506 donna@wibscockers.com	c/o Morning Breeze Retirement Center 950 N Lakeview Dr Greensburg IN 47240	CI	Teacher	EM			RF	1963
Helmkamp Amanda L Steele	(618)975-9134 amanda.helmkamp@gmail.com	1749 Michaelwood Ct Saint Charles MO 63303	MO	Teacher	Tchr	Zion Saint Charles MO	(636)441-7424	RF	2006
Helmkamp Barbara S Smetana Dr	(720)842-0126 barbara.helmkamp@gmail.com	9838 E Tom Tom Dr Parker CO 80138	RM	Teacher	C07/2016			CQ	2007
Helmkamp Robert K Dr	(720)272-4349	7651 Clayton Rd Apt 8411 Saint Louis MO 63117	RM	Teacher	EM			RF	1964

*Multiple Assignments (See Church Worker Locator for Additional Details)
See Page 53 for the Table of Abbreviations for key to District, Classification, Position, and College abbreviations.
**C =Candidate; EM =Emeritus; the date following the C is the month and year the Candidate status began

NAME	TELEPHONE NUMBER EMAIL	STREET ADDRESS CITY/STATE/ZIP	DISTRICT	CLASS.	POSITION/ STATUS**	WHERE SERVING	OFFICE PHONE	COLLEGE/ UNIV/CQ	YR GRAD
Helmke Richard A	(630)659-6838 helmkera@gmail.com	1486 Lake Holiday Dr Sandwich IL 60548	NI	Teacher	EM			RF	1970
Helmling Vicki J Tetro	(708)359-1104 vjhelmling@comcast.net	195 N Marion St #3 Oak Park IL 60301	EN	Teacher	EM			RF	1978
Helmreich Emily L Phillis	(248)685-9290 emily_helmreich@yahoo.com	P.O. Box 4912 Edwards CO 81632	EN	Teacher	EM			CQ	2000
Helmreich Harry J	(231)276-9594 bhelmreich@charter.net	1789 Fairfield Dr Grawn MI 49637	MI	Teacher	EM			RF	1980
Helms Carol M Koehl	(512)413-7486 chelms8294@gmail.com	11300 Songbird CV Austin TX 78750	TX	Teacher	EM			S	1968
Helpap Thomas E	(920)596-2641	N5905 Summit Ln Manawa WI 54949	NW	Teacher	EM			RF	1971
Helwig Bethany J Buchinger	(812)525-9516 bethjaneboo@yahoo.com	3729 S State Road 235 Vallonia IN 47281	IN	Teacher	C07/2016			S	2003
Hemler Heather A Giordano	hhemler@stpaulsdp.org	1328 Crossings Ct Unit C Ballwin MO 63021	MO	Teacher	Tchr	St Paul Des Peres MO	(314)822-0447	RF	1996
Hemmann Nicole D	(573)382-6134 n.hemmann@htlstampa.org	7616 W Courtney Campbell Cswy Unit 414 Tampa FL 33607	FG	Teacher	Tchr	Holy Trinity Tampa FL	(813)839-6847	S	2016
Hemme Barbara R Doerner Deac	(847)638-7444 brhemme@yahoo.com	1025 Grandview Ave Lockport IL 60441	EN	Deaconess	EM			CH	2010
Hemme Mathilda A Hinkelman	(206)767-3596 mathemme@juno.com	2805 S 125th St Apt 306 Burien WA 98168	NOW	Teacher	EM			S	1966
Hemmen Rosella K Nothwehr	(970)213-0313 r_hemmen@yahoo.com	1555 Platte Ct Loveland CO 80538	RM	Teacher	EM			S	1971
Hemmings Jenny R Crane	(714)488-2144 jennyrhemmings@gmail.com	5072 E Equestrian Ln Orange CA 92869	PSW	Teacher	Tchr	St Paul Orange CA	(714)637-2640	S	1994
Hempel Donn F	(708)442-1505 dfhlyons@gmail.com	8011 Salisbury Ave Lyons IL 60534	NI	Teacher	Tchr	Immanuel Hillside IL	(708)562-5580	RF	1976
Hempel Ruth R Dornfeld	(734)751-9301 ruthhempel@yahoo.com	28604 Sunnydale St Livonia MI 48154	EN	Teacher	EM			RF	1976
Hencye Lawrence K	(260)348-8483 lhencye@hotmail.com	3409 Merrimack Pl Fort Wayne IN 46815	IN	Teacher	EM			S	1972
Hendershot Diana A Zarro	(716)364-4851 dianahendershot@hotmail.com	5009 Hamden Ct Evans GA 30809	EA	Teacher	EM			CQ	1997
Henderson Jane M Post	(217)248-7724 janehenderson2011@gmail.com	3 Bellevue Dr Jacksonville IL 62650	CI	Teacher	EM			AA	1975
Henderson Julie A Bonnie	(505)288-0158 julie.henderson@hotmail.com	1815 War Admiral Dr SE Albuquerque NM 87123	RM	Teacher	Tchr	Christ Albuquerque NM	(505)884-3876	CQ	2024
Hendricks Stevan L Jr	shendricks@lhssc.org	471 Peregrine Ct Winfield MO 63389	MO	Teacher	Tchr	St Charles Saint Peters MO	(636)928-5100	S	1998
Hendrickson Abby K Schreader	(507)202-4984 abby.hendrickson@stjohns-chaska.org	6986 Tecumseh Ln Chanhassen MN 55317	MNS	Teacher	Tchr	St Johns Chaska MN	(952)448-2526	CQ	2022
Hendrickson Eunice M Fichte	(979)884-0200	1667 County Road 130 Ledbetter TX 78946	TX	Teacher	EM			S	1969
Hendrickson Grace E	(785)713-9378 grace.hendrickson@cune.org	1333 Sunrise Dr Seward NE 68434	NEB	Teacher	Tchr	St Paul Utica NE	(402)534-2121	S	2024
Hendrikson Paige E	(608)931-1717 pehsings11@gmail.com		SW	DCM	Mem C	St Peter Reedsburg WI	(608)524-4512	MQ	2023
Hengeveld Adam J	(469)964-8165 adam.campokoboji@gmail.com	2802 Delia Ln Milford IA 51351	IW	Teacher	RSO	Camp Okoboji Milford IA	(712)337-3325	S	2009
Hengeveld Elizabeth C Wallis	(210)347-1388 bethlyn84@gmail.com	2802 Delia Ln Milford IA 51351	IW	Teacher	C08/2024			RF	2006
Hengst Anthony	(414)232-5362 ahengst@graceoakcreek.org	7669 S Pennsylvania Ave Oak Creek WI 63154	SW	Teacher	Tchr	Grace Oak Creek WI	(414)762-3655	MQ	2021
Hengst Lisa Mirenda	(262)853-7568 principal@graceoakcreek.org	8537 S Pennsylvania Ave Oak Creek WI 53154	SW	Teacher	P/Tchr	Grace Oak Creek WI	(414)762-8990	MQ	2002
Henke Chad	(713)449-1322	2327 Heatherwoods Way Carrollton TX 75007	TX	Teacher	Tchr	Prince Of Peace Carrollton TX	(972)447-0532	AU	1999
Henke Heidi M Riske	(972)816-6211 heidiriske@hotmail.com	2327 Heatherwoods Way Carrollton TX 75007	TX	Teacher	Tchr	Prince Of Peace Carrollton TX	(972)447-0532	AU	1999
Henkell Joe D	(760)224-4470 jhenkell@aol.com	3424 E Russell St Mesa AZ 85213	PSW	Teacher	EM			RF	1967
Henkell Liane K Bade Brinkman	(480)313-0420 lkhenkell@gmail.com	190 E Bluejay Dr Chandler AZ 85286	PSW	Teacher	C06/2022			SP	1997
Henkes Michael	(801)568-9487 mjhenkes@netzero.net	331 E Chad Heights Ln Midvale UT 84047	RM	Teacher	EM			S	1975
Hennig Denise K Wehrman	(217)622-5128 dhenning22@gmail.com	22915 N Aut Ln Centralia IL 62801	SI	Teacher		Southern Illinois District Belleville IL	(618)234-4767	Other	1985
Hennig Suzanne Fischer	(425)277-1533 youth@kingofkings.org	12642 SE 169th Pl Renton WA 98058	NOW	DCE	Mem C	King Of Kings Renton WA	(425)226-1480	CQ	2016
Henning David W	(414)265-6596 dvhenning@wi.rr.com	3975 S 84th St Apt 7 Greenfield WI 53228	SW	Teacher	EM			RF	1973
Henning Donna J Kretzmann	(715)623-4702 djhenning@hughes.net	N7537 Black Oak Rd Deerbrook WI 54424	NW	Teacher	EM			S	1969
Henning James C	(715)623-4702 djhenning70@gmail.com	N7537 Black Oak Rd Deerbrook WI 54424	NW	Teacher	EM			S	1969
Henning Mary J Yost	(402)430-0804 mjroghenning@gmail.com	4401 Waterbury Ln Lincoln NE 68516	NEB	Teacher	EM			S	1969
Henning Michael A	(920)832-0942	230 W Park Ridge Ave Appleton WI 54911	NW	DCE	Mem C	Faith Appleton WI	(920)739-9191	CQ	2005
Henny Ann E	(660)492-0076 ann.henny@hotmail.com	2502 Westside Ave Norfolk NE 68701	NEB	DPM	Mem C	Christ Norfolk NE	(402)371-1210	S	2010
Henry Barbara A Batterman-Oppermann	(414)915-6259 rdbah68@gmail.com	W65N753 Washington Ave Cedarburg WI 53012	SW	Teacher	EM			RF	1973

*Multiple Assignments (See Church Worker Locator for Additional Details)

See Page 53 for the Table of Abbreviations for key to District, Classification, Position, and College abbreviations.

**C =Candidate; EM =Emeritus; the date following the C is the month and year the Candidate status began

NAME	TELEPHONE NUMBER EMAIL	STREET ADDRESS CITY/STATE/ZIP	DISTRICT	CLASS.	POSITION/ STATUS**	WHERE SERVING	OFFICE PHONE	COLLEGE/ UNIV/CQ	YR GRAD
Henry Deborah D Wolf	(314)359-7349 katiescarlettohara2001@gmail.com	310 Montesano Park Dr Imperial MO 63052	MO	Teacher	EM			S	1971
Henry Kelsey M	(805)233-1798 kelsey.michaela.henry@gmail.com	18192 Theodora Dr Tustin CA 92780	PSW	Teacher	Tchr	Crean Irvine CA	(949)387-1199	Other	2011
Henschen Daniel R	(217)529-7347 clschool@comcast.net	2376 County Road 11 Fremont NE 68025	CI	Teacher	EM			S	1973
Henschen Ellen Kottwitz	(618)656-4333 ehenschen@yahoo.com	1209 Richetta Dr Edwardsville IL 62025	SI	Teacher	EM			S	1974
Henschen Joel I	jhenschen@sjlno.org		SO	Teacher	Tchr	St John New Orleans LA	(504)482-2118	S	2010
Henschen Rebekah A	(605)228-3781 rebekahhenschen@gmail.com	1261 8th St. Apt. 203 West Des Moines IA 50265	IW	Teacher	Tchr	Mount Olive Des Moines IA	(515)277-0247	S	2022
Henschen Rhonda A Frohling	(605)290-5995 rhondahenschen@gmail.com	509 Park St P.O. Box 296 Bancroft NE 68004	NEB	Teacher	Tchr	Christ Norfolk NE	(402)371-5536	CQ	2012
Henschen Ronald J	(618)920-3992 ronh_50@yahoo.com	1209 Richetta Dr Edwardsville IL 62025	SI	Teacher	EM			S	1972
Hensel Tanya L Nygaard	(406)245-6050 tanyahensel@trinitybillings.org	1258 Nasturtium Dr Billings MT 59105	MT	Teacher	Tchr	Trinity Billings MT	(406)245-3984	CQ	2014
Hensel Tanya L Kolesar		5612 Castle Ct Apt 201 Racine WI 53406	S	Teacher	C07/2016			MQ	1998
Hensz Daniel J	(956)245-8408 danielhensz@gmail.com	c/o Saint Paul Lutheran Church 602 Morgan Blvd Harlingen TX 78550	TX	DCE	Mem C	St Paul Harlingen TX	(956)423-3924	AU	2012
Hente Brenda J	bhente@ILSOlivette.org	3226 Saint Joachim Ln Saint Ann MO 63074	MO	Teacher	Tchr	Immanuel Olivette MO	(314)993-2394	RF	1987
Hentges Aaron P	(816)352-9242 ahentges@splhs.org	312 S. College Drive Concordia MO 64020	MO	Teacher	Pro Stf	Saint Paul Concordia MO	(660)463-2238	S	2018
Henwood Jane D Coomer	(586)817-0774 ijhenwood@yahoo.com	3415 Bruceville Rd Vincennes IN 47591	IN	Teacher	EM			RF	1967
Henze Christopher L	(828)446-9639 chrishenze1970@gmail.com	1100 3rd Avenue SW Conover NC 28613	SE	DCE	Mem C	Concordia Conover NC	(828)464-3324	IV	1998
Hepburn Joyce A Long	jahepburn2@hotmail.com	214 Meadow Lakes Dr Shorewood IL 60404	NI	Teacher	EM			RF	1967
Heppe Phillip T	(217)899-5473 ptheppe@gmail.com	832 S Columbia Ave Springfield IL 62704	CI	Teacher	Tchr	Our Savior's Springfield IL	(217)546-4531	CH	2015
Heppe Rebecca L List	(217)494-2826 becky.heppe@oursaviors-school.org	4848 Cockrell Ln Springfield IL 62711	CI	Teacher	Tchr	Our Saviors Springfield IL	(217)546-4531	RF	1984
Herbrich Ben T	(718)740-2891 herbrich3@gmail.com	28 Atkins Ct Carmel NY 10512	AT	Teacher	EM			S	1964
Herbst Kathryn A Wellenkamp	(262)784-9575 normkathy@att.net	1155 Jewel St Brookfield WI 53005	SW	Teacher	EM			S	1966
Heren Andrew S	(715)831-9236 Rcktnut007@aol.com	3711 Brian St Eau Claire WI 54701	NW	Tch/DCE	C07/2016			RF	1987
Hereth Lynne A West	(425)327-7839 l.hereth@icloud.com	12747 Wedgewood Dr Burlington WA 98233	NOW	Teacher	EM			CQ	1986
Hering Ruth A Voigt	(920)458-9006 ruthhering2305@gmail.com	571 Mossy Creek Dr Venice FL 34292	SW	Teacher	EM			RF	1971
Herl Joseph Dr	(402)643-7454 joseph.herl@cune.edu	140 Hillcrest Dr Seward NE 68434	NEB	Teacher	S HS/C	Concordia University Nebraska Seward NE	(402)643-3651	CQ	2001
Herman Carol S Keller	(260)450-9410 herman_99@comcast.net	7131 Evansbrook Dr Fort Wayne IN 46835	IN	Teacher	EM			CQ	1996
Herman Kimberly A Vondran	(702)451-8769 mrsmommy24@gmail.com	303 Warm Front St Henderson NV 89014	PSW	Teacher	C07/2016			RF	1995
Herman Richard E	(630)302-8805 rick@weraise.org	15 Coleman St Weaverville NC 28787	SE	Teacher	EM			RF	1974
Herman Sandra K Troester	(260)492-9842 kskherman1@yahoo.com	10187 Chapmans CV Fort Wayne IN 46835	IN	Teacher	EM			S	1969
Herman Tiffany R Hart	tiffanyherman11281@yahoo.com	7628 Idlebrook Dr Fort Wayne IN 46835	IN	Teacher	Tchr	Central New Haven IN	(260)493-2502	AA	2004
Hermann Alfred L	(260)668-6729 ingeher64@gmail.com	4340 W 250 N Angola IN 46703	IN	Teacher	EM			RF	1964
Hermann Randi S Rush	(734)379-5431 randihermann@mac.com	32162 Covington Rd Rockwood MI 48173	MI	Teacher	EM			S	1977
Hernandez Jamie L Lumaye	(832)314-4431 jamie.hernandez1228@gmail.com	2660 Augusta #d308 Houston TX 77057	TX	Teacher	Tchr	Immanuel Houston TX	(713)864-2651	AU	2008
Herold Chris R	(503)724-7857 heroldck@gmail.com	17115 Merganser Dr Bend OR 97707	NOW	Teacher	C06/2018			PO	2002
Heroux Jerika T	(920)618-1105 jerika.heroux@gmail.com	107 W Stoney Ridge Way Saukville WI 53080	SW	Teacher	Tchr	St John West Bend WI	(262)429-1061	MQ	2023
Herre Norma E Schroeder	(317)531-1477 everlasting105@att.net	7110 Bel Moore Cir Indianapolis IN 46259	IN	Teacher	EM			S	1968
Herring Amy C Kottlowski	(630)886-6994 amyh851@gmail.com	22w120 Hillcrest Ter Medinah IL 60157	NI	Teacher	C01/2023			RF	1989
Herring Paul M	(574)383-2602 paulherring30@gmail.com	1310 6th Ave Des Moines IA 50314	IN	Teacher	C02/2024			S	1993
Herrmann Julie A Giesselmann	julie.herrmann@stjohns-chaska.org	106 Hazelwood Ave Cologne MN 55322	MNS	Teacher	Tchr	St Johns Chaska MN	(952)448-2526	MQ	1996
Hertel Delores L Carroll	(847)934-6266 stamping19@yahoo.com	629 W Hill Rd Palatine IL 60067	NI	Teacher	EM			RF	1961
Herther Ann P Kurtz	(605)357-8870 aherther@midco.net	2705 S Phillips Ave Sioux Falls SD 57105	SD	Teacher	EM			CQ	2001
Hertlein Laura K Wilson	(816)252-6138 lhertlein@msn.com	1608 SW 23rd St Blue Springs MO 64015	MO	Teacher	EM			CQ	2003

*Multiple Assignments (See Church Worker Locator for Additional Details)

See Page 53 for the Table of Abbreviations for key to District, Classification, Position, and College abbreviations.

**C =Candidate; EM =Emeritus; the date following the C is the month and year the Candidate status began

NAME	TELEPHONE NUMBER EMAIL	STREET ADDRESS CITY/STATE/ZIP	DISTRICT	CLASS.	POSITION/ STATUS**	WHERE SERVING	OFFICE PHONE	COLLEGE/ UNIV/CQ	YR GRAD
Hertling Barbara J Gehrke	(320)251-7195 hertlingbarb@gmail.com	2518 Serenity Dr Saint Cloud MN 56301	MNN	DCE	EM			SP	1979
Hertneky Margaret L Opperman	(262)490-9060 jmjkhert@hotmail.com	906 York Imperial Dr Oconomowoc WI 53066	SW	Teacher	Tchr	St Paul Oconomowoc WI	(262)567-5001	RF	1979
Herz Karen L Wallin	(262)424-4957 klherz31@gmail.com	W195S8610 Plum Creek Blvd Muskego WI 53150	EN	Teacher	EM			CQ	2004
Herzog Janet S Meyr	(708)705-1727 janetherzog@gmail.com	937 N Williams Dr Palatine IL 60074	NI	Teacher	EM			RF	1974
Herzog Phillip G	(414)687-1197 psherzog@msn.net	621 E Mary Ln Oak Creek WI 53154	SW	Teacher	EM			RF	1974
Hess Anne L Burger	(260)255-7687 panhess@icloud.com	12612 Brunson Rd Hoagland IN 46745	IN	Teacher	EM			S	1978
Hess Heidi L Scheck	(920)716-0251 hessh@trinitynet.org	609 Becker St Rothschild WI 54474	NW	Teacher	Tchr	Trinity Wausau WI	(715)848-0166	CH	2013
Hess Janna L Virus	(281)229-3994 jannahess@splsconcordia.org	407 S Sunset Hills Dr. Concordia MO 64020	MO	Teacher	Tchr	St Pauls Concordia MO	(660)463-7654	S	2008
Hess Jo Ann Nietfeldt	(815)922-9503 jahesshome@gmail.com	1620 Hunters Run Dr Bourbonnais IL 60914	NI	Teacher	EM			RF	1979
Hess Mark L		1620 Hunters Run Dr Bourbonnais IL 60914	NI	Tch/DCE	EM			S	1980
Hess Tara M Brune	(402)630-0360 tara.hess@gslcgretna.org	21767 Bobwhite Ave Gretna NE 68028	NEB	DCE	Mem C	Good Shepherd Gretna NE	(402)332-3345	S	2003
Hess Teresa M Rosso	(949)244-8224 teresa.hess@cui.edu	7028 Rockrose Terr Carlsbad CA 92011	PSW	Teacher	S HS/C	Concordia University Irvine Irvine CA	(949)854-8002	CQ	2024
Hesse Bonnie J Krause	(314)330-6612 bjkhesse@gmail.com	341 Oak Ridge Pkwy Arnold MO 63010	MO	Teacher	EM			RF	1973
Hesse Esther B Beineke	(262)334-3077	8548 Eagle Ridge Dr Kewaskum WI 53040	SW	Teacher	Tchr	St Johns West Bend WI	(262)334-3077	CQ	2001
Hesse Merlene J Blauert	(513)313-0138 hessemerlene@gmail.com	401 Maple St Aurora IN 47001	NW	Teacher	C09/2025			SP	1990
Hessenthaler Meaghan M Kane	(262)765-9553 meaghanhessen@gmail.com	15255 W Woodland Dr New Berlin WI 53151	EN	Teacher	EM			CQ	2005
Hessler Dorothy E Scheck	(650)722-8650 dehessler@comcast.net	0099 Hunters Ln Boyne City MI 49712	MI	Teacher	EM			RF	1960
Hessler Lindsey S Raney	(989)274-2087 lhessler1234@gmail.com	7412 W Greenleaf Ct Frankenmuth MI 48734	MI	Teacher	C07/2016			AA	2002
Hessong Amelia E	(812)498-3727 ahessongsauers@gmail.com	9830 Camino Villa Apt 623 San Antonio TX 78254	TX	Teacher	Tchr	Lutheran San Antonio TX	(210)694-4962	CH	2024
Hessong Susan M Lambring	(812)528-3674 smhessong@gmail.com	190 S County Road 475 E Seymour IN 47274	IN	Teacher	EM			AA	1986
Hett Nicolette M Johnson	(507)259-3476 dce@lordofglory.org		NI	DCE	Mem C	Lord Of Glory Grayslake IL	(847)548-5673	CH	2019
Hetzel Jeremy M	(719)243-3136 jhetzeldce@gmail.com	c/o Pathfinder Lutheran Church 15800 Manchester Rd Ellisville MO 63011	MO	DCE	Mem C	Pathfinder Ellisville MO	(636)394-4100	CQ	2007
Hetzner Jacquelyn R Liese	(847)287-6626 jackiehetzner@gmail.com	123 S Brockway St Palatine IL 60067	NI	Teacher	EM			RF	1978
Hetzner Timothy J	(866)455-6466 timhetzner@lutheranchurch charities.org	123 S Brockway St Palatine IL 60067	NI	DCE	Pro Stf	Lutheran Church Charities Northbrook IL	(866)455-6466	SP	1978
Heublein Metta F Bailey	(574)674-0131 mheublein@hotmail.com	53467 Valley Springs Ct Granger IN 46530	IN	Teacher	Tchr	Trinity Elkhart IN	(574)674-8800	RF	1974
Heublein Robert R	(574)674-0131 rrh@mr-h.com	53467 Valley Springs Ct Granger IN 46530	IN	Tch/DCE	EM			RF	1976
Heuer Amy J	dce.amy@fairlawnlutheran.org	153 Kenridge Rd Fairlawn OH 44333	EN	DCE	Mem C	Fairlawn Fairlawn OH	(330)836-7286	S	2000
Heuer Waldemar C	(414)574-0120 heuerinfranklin@gmail.com	6360 N Berkeley Blvd Milwaukee WI 53217	EN	DCM	EM			MW	1968
Heun Karissa A Weinrich	(402)719-7614	c/o Trinity Lutheran School 1200 N 56th St Lincoln NE 68504	NEB	Teacher	Tchr	Trinity Lincoln NE	(402)466-1800	S	2012
Heupel Tami W	(713)294-5003 brennant@clhs-tx.org	12723 Carriage Glen Dr. Tomball TX 77377	TX	Teacher	Tchr	Concordia Tomball TX	(281)351-2547	S	1994
Heupel Timothy J II	(618)975-5694 heupelt@flhsemail.org	10528 Waking Cloud Ave Las Vegas NV 89129	PSW	Teacher	Tchr	Faith Las Vegas NV	(702)804-4400	S	2002
Hewitt Frank E	(847)428-4211 fhewitt117@aol.com	325 Spring Point Dr Carpentersvle IL 60110	NI	DCM	EM			MQ	1992
Hewitt Susan K Bersie Dr	(612)280-2597 suehewitt4@gmail.com	106 Benchmark Dr Mountain Village CO 81435	RM	DCO	EM			CQ	2006
Hibbard Casault Mary A Deac	(586)764-3561 mhibbard@plcms.org	338 Old Hickory Dr Coldwater MI 49036	EN	Deaconess	EM			CQ	1996
Hickey Gary R Jr	(321)696-1468 ghickey@cyberfalcon.com	101 Coventry St Boca Raton FL 33487	FG	Teacher	Tchr	St Paul Boca Raton FL	(561)395-0433	MQ	2012
Hicks Bonnie A	(805)279-4115 Bhicksdce@gmail.com	1223 E Glendora Ave Orange CA 92865	PSW	DCE	D Ex/S	Pacific Southwest District Irvine CA	(949)854-3232	IV	1999
Hicks Jenna M Collins	(260)409-2360 jenna@thelutheranfoundation.org	6341 Sharon Dr Fort Wayne IN 46825	IN	Teacher	RSO	Lutheran Schools Services Inc Fort Wayne IN	(260)203-4500	MQ	2008
Hicks Judith A Vollmer	(309)840-2632	307 South St Pekin IL 61554	CI	Teacher	Prin	Good Shepherd Pekin IL	(309)347-2020	RF	1999
Hiddings Michael	(586)202-2290 mhiddings@lhsa.com	31829 York St Fraser MI 48026	MI	Teacher	Tchr	Northwest Rochester Hills MI	(248)856-0240	MQ	2016
Hiegel Connie J Kahle	(308)389-4551 cjhiegel4@gmail.com	404 E 19th St Grand Island NE 68801	NEB	Teacher	Tchr	Trinity Grand Island NE	(308)382-5274	S	1989
Hiegel Jack L	(502)345-1950 jackhiegel@yahoo.com	614 Heatherleigh Ln Louisville KY 40222	IN	Teacher	EM			S	1983

*Multiple Assignments (See Church Worker Locator for Additional Details)
See Page 53 for the Table of Abbreviations for key to District, Classification, Position, and College abbreviations.
**C =Candidate; EM =Emeritus; the date following the C is the month and year the Candidate status began

NAME	TELEPHONE NUMBER EMAIL	STREET ADDRESS CITY/STATE/ZIP	DISTRICT	CLASS.	POSITION/ STATUS**	WHERE SERVING	OFFICE PHONE	COLLEGE/ UNIV/CQ	YR GRAD
Hiegel Thomas A	(402)943-6913 thomas.hiegel55@gmail.com	8516 Spring Forest Dr Fort Wayne IN 46804	IN	Teacher	EM			S	1978
Highley Kristin E Schmidt	(951)775-6134 khighley@rslc.org	713 Gold Hill Dr Erie CO 80516	RM	DCE	Mem C	Risen Savior Broomfield CO	(303)469-3521	IV	2020
Highley Rachell M Gawlik Deac	(918)766-6745 rachell.highley@flcspc.com	2032 Lemon Tree Ln Ponca City OK 74604	OK	Deaconess	Mem C	First Ponca City OK	(580)762-1111	SL-DEAC	2024
Hight Steven R	(714)331-1350 srhight@sbcglobal.net	2064 N Cleveland St Orange CA 92865	PSW	Teacher	EM			S	1983
Hilchen Le Ann M Wessel	(971)222-4643 MusicMast3r1776@gmail.com	1722 NW Abilene Rd Ankeny IA 50023	IW	Teacher	EM			S	1990
Hildebrand Alice M	(314) 313-5888 mosunflwr@sbcglobal.net	1131 Claycrest Circle Saint Charles MO 63304	MO	Teacher	EM			RF	1974
Hildebrand Kevin J	(260)452-2193 kevin.hildebrand@ctsfw.edu	5014 Honey Oak Run Fort Wayne IN 46845	IN	Teacher	S HS/C	Concordia Theological Seminary Fort Wayne IN	(260)452-2100	RF	1995
Hildebrand Laura A Giger	(269)281-1182 samisydney@yahoo.com	10501 Garr Rd Berrien Sprgs MI 49103	MI	Teacher	C06/2023			AA	1996
Hilgendorf Duane H	(262)893-0942 duane.hilgendorf@cuw.edu	1125 Appian Dr Punta Gorda FL 33950	FG	Teacher	EM			S	1974
Hilgendorf Mary E Cash Dr	(262)893-0942 mary.hilgendorf@cuw.edu	1125 Appian Dr Punta Gorda FL 33950	FG	Teacher	EM			S	1973
Hilgendorf Thomas C Dr	(512)797-6179 thomas.hilgendorf@sbcglobal.net	1411 Amber Day Dr Pflugerville TX 78660	TX	Teacher	EM			S	1975
Hilger Ron O	(224)217-3236 mrhilger@hotmail.com	5542 W Celebrity Cir Hanover Park IL 60133	NI	Teacher	C02/2021			RF	2000
Hilk Miriam R Schedler	(612)442-5277 miriamhilk@gmail.com	7025 County Road 10 N Waconia MN 55387	MNS	Teacher	EM			SP	1974
Hilken John C	(734)243-2015 hilken.c3223@sbcglobal.net	1020 Donnalee Dr Monroe MI 48162	MI	Teacher	EM			RF	1978
Hill Kenneth S	(920)539-3977 kenhill0333@gmail.com	299 Breister Ave. Fond Du Lac WI 54935	SW	Teacher	EM			RF	1978
Hill Lori E Schlehuser-Smith	(812)350-1474 lorihill170@gmail.com	14625 S 300 W Columbus IN 47201	IN	Teacher	EM			RF	1985
Hill Lorna R V Reyelts Deac	(512)352-3363 specialtyknitsetc@yahoo.com	221 Hill Ave N Jasper MN 56144	MNS	Deaconess	EM			Other	1985
Hill Rachel L Mueller	(720)842-0458	7418 Huntington Dr Saint Louis MO 63121	RM	Teacher	Tchr	Lutheran Parker CO	(303)841-5551	S	2002
Hiller Kathryn R	(763)234-7236 krhiller918@gmail.com	15430 Argon St NW Ramsey MN 55303	MNS	Teacher	Tchr	Trinity First Minneapolis MN	(612)871-2353	SP	2024
Hiller Mary E Weinrich	(763)576-0839 mhiller@foclutheran.org	15430 Argon St NW Ramsey MN 55303	MNS	Teacher	Tchr	Family Christ Ham Lake MN	(763)434-7337	SP	1992
Hiller Peter E	(763)381-2001 philler@foclutheran.org	15430 Argon St NW Ramsey MN 55303	MNS	DCE	Mem C	Family Christ Ham Lake MN	(763)434-7337	SP	1991
Hiller Sally J Meyer Deac	sjhiller@aol.com	1536 Meyers Station Rd Odenton MD 21113	SE	Deaconess	EM			Other	1976
Hillhouse Roberta S Sauer Deac	(828)330-0053 srrobie@msn.com	1782 White Water Ct Hickory NC 28602	SE	Deaconess	EM			Other	1980
Hillman Charlotte M Schiefer	(608)393-7447 charhillman54@gmail.com	N4566 Iroquois Ct La Valle WI 53941	SW	Teacher	EM			RF	1976
Hillman Rebecca R Barz	(316)518-3266 rrhillman@hotmail.com	32615 W 55th St S Cheney KS 67025	KS	Teacher	EM			S	1980
Hills Jennifer A Brown	(703)971-2210 jennifer.hills@sjlc.com	4751 Shadow Oak Ct Montclair VA 22025	SE	DCE	Mem C	St Johns Alexandria VA	(703)971-2210	RF	1999
Hilsabeck Janet E Roberts	(586)431-1179 jhilsabeck1184@wowway.com	36348 Egan St Clinton Twp MI 48035	MI	Teacher	EM			AA	1982
Hilton Rosemary A			PSW	Teacher	C08/2021			IV	2014
Himelright Amy R Keilman	(812)952-1301 amy9500@yahoo.com	1205 Black Creek Rd SE Elizabeth IN 47117	IN	Teacher	Tchr	St Johns Lanesville IN	(812)952-2737	AU	2000
Himmler Gary W	(713)705-7895 gary.himmler@gmail.com	4730 Kipper Cir Pasadena TX 77505	TX	Teacher	EM			S	1981
Himmler Jonathan C	(281)386-6664 jonathanhimmler@gmail.com	216 Trailridge Rd Norfolk NE 68701	NEB	Teacher	Tchr	Christ Norfolk NE	(402)371-5536	S	2007
Hinchey Margaret R Rickers	(303)667-5671 mhinchey@aol.com	1961 Pikes Peak Dr Loveland CO 80538	RM	DCE	EM			SP	1975
Hinck Barbara A List	(734)775-3315 barbarahinck@stmatthew.info	41950 Trent Ct Canton MI 48188	MI	Teacher	EM			S	1981
Hinck Diane E	dhinck@zionschool.net	633 W Prairie St Marengo IL 60152	NI	Teacher	Tchr	Zion Marengo IL	(815)568-5156	RF	1986
Hinck John T	(734)716-1651 jthctnmi@att.net	41950 Trent Ct Canton MI 48188	MI	Teacher	EM			S	1974
Hinck Katarina M	hinck00@gmail.com		MO	Teacher	Tchr	St Pauls Des Peres MO	(314)822-9219	MQ	2023
Hinck Sandra S Schoenleber	(816)716-8833 sandrahinck@spslsconcordia.org	27231 Highway Aa Concordia MO 64020	MO	Teacher	EM			RF	1978
Hinckfoot Michael S	(812)344-3437 mhinckfoot@stpeters-columbus.org	1062 Coles Dr Columbus IN 47201	IN	DCE	Mem C	St Peter Columbus IN	(812)372-1571	CQ	1992
Hindenach Deanna J Brill	(269)657-4987 trinityschool@trinitylutheran.com	211 W North St Paw Paw MI 49079	MI	Teacher	Tchr	Trinity Paw Paw MI	(269)657-4840	CQ	1998
Hines Mary M Friedrich	(260)783-1487 mmsthines@frontier.com	903 Elnora Dr Fort Wayne IN 46825	IN	Teacher	EM			RF	1975
Hines Michelle C Brase	hahasmama2007@gmail.com	323 3rd Ave Atkins IA 52206	IE	Teacher	C07/2024			RF	2006
Hines Michelle L Krafft	(702)217-4784 jphmlk@aol.com	6258 Golden Rain St N Las Vegas NV 89031	PSW	Teacher	Tchr	Faith Las Vegas NV	(702)804-4400	CQ	2008

*Multiple Assignments (See Church Worker Locator for Additional Details)
See Page 53 for the Table of Abbreviations for key to District, Classification, Position, and College abbreviations.
**C =Candidate; EM =Emeritus; the date following the C is the month and year the Candidate status began

NAME	TELEPHONE NUMBER EMAIL	STREET ADDRESS CITY/STATE/ZIP	DISTRICT	CLASS.	POSITION/ STATUS**	WHERE SERVING	OFFICE PHONE	COLLEGE/ UNIV/CQ	YR GRAD
Hines Rachel L Culp	(714)227-7080 rachel.hines@outlook.com	1044 Concord St Costa Mesa CA 92626	PSW	Teacher	Tchr	Christ Costa Mesa CA	(949)631-1611	IV	2011
Hinkel Barbara K Thomson	(972)385-1904 bhinkel@ziondallas.org	13651 Spring Grove Ave Dallas TX 75240	TX	Teacher	Tchr	Zion Dallas TX	(214)363-1639	AU	1995
Hinrichs Stefanie A	(714)272-1717	6038 Village Rd Lakewood CA 90713	PSW	Teacher	Tchr	Bethany Long Beach CA	(562)421-4711	IV	2014
Hintz Debbie S	(715)851-2938 debhintz@yahoo.com	E8055 Wood Way New London WI 54961	NW	Teacher	Tchr	St Paul Manawa WI	(920)596-2837	CQ	2017
Hintz Dennis L	(785)235-9684 hintzdl@cox.net	816 SW Buchanan St Topeka KS 66606	KS	Tch/DCE	EM			S	1971
Hintz Gary H	(346)763-0053 bghhintz@sbcglobal.net	3622 Millspring Dr Houston TX 77080	TX	Teacher	EM			S	1960
Hintz Gretchen A Buchwald	travelgal1023@yahoo.com	N7468 4th Dr Westfield WI 53964	SW	Teacher	C06/2025			MQ	1993
Hintze Sarah V Radtke	(262)573-9812 sarahhintze321@gmail.com	324 Buffalo Cave Rd Georgetown TX 78628	TX	Teacher	C07/2020			MQ	2011
Hintzman Brandi L Smith	(970)587-8701	5825 Aspen View Ct Loveland CO 80538	RM	Teacher	Tchr	Immanuel Loveland CO	(970)667-7606	S	2002
Hinz Amy M Currao	(540)226-9150 amymhinz@aol.com	5 Osprey Ln Fredericksbrg VA 22405	SE	Teacher	C07/2016			BR	1990
Hinz Ann M Backhaus	(727)656-0226 ann.hinz487@gmail.com	2266 Grovewood Rd Clearwater FL 33764	FG	Teacher	Mem C	First Clearwater FL	(727)462-8000	RF	1982
Hinz Kenneth E	(217)429-3470 kennethhinz@aol.com	166 S Elder Ln Decatur IL 62522	CI	Teacher	EM			RF	1963
Hinz LeRae I Mossner	(989)671-7416 lerae.hinz@gmail.com	22400 Clairwood St St Clr Shores MI 48080	MI	Teacher	C06/2017			AA	2015
Hinz Rachel G Cousino	(734)693-3858 rachelghinz@gmail.com	1683 Timber Hollow Dr. Wildwood MO 63011	MO	Teacher	C07/2016			AA	2006
Hinz Tamara Schmidt	(715)509-2108 tamihinz@pilgrimluth.org	W3572 Old Dump Rd Bonduel WI 54107	NW	Teacher	Tchr	Pilgrim Green Bay WI	(920)965-2244	CQ	2014
Hinz William V Dr	(512)769-6791 wvhinz@gmail.com	606 Dartmouth CV Pflugerville TX 78660	TX	Teacher	D Ex/S	Texas District Round Rock TX	(800)951-3478	RF	1978
Hinze Adele L Hermanas	(815)549-8574 iteach_1st@hotmail.com	252 N Tomagene Dr Bourbonnais IL 60914	NI	Teacher	EM			RF	1977
Hipenbecker Timothy J	(262)951-5330 thipenbecker@gmail.com	1268 Huron Way Hartford WI 53027	NI	Teacher	C07/2024			MQ	1988
Hipple Eric C	(618)791-2855 ehipple@concordiapeoria.com	1859 W Teton Dr Peoria IL 61614	CI	Teacher	Tchr	Concordia Peoria IL	(309)691-8921	CH	1996
Hire Matthew J	(419)980-8221 hirematthew603@gmail.com	859 Bristol Ave NW Grand Rapids MI 49504	MI	DFLM	C08/2021			AA	2015
Hirsch Linda M Nolan Dr	(314)276-9250 lmrnhirsch@gmail.com	421 Parkshire Pl Dr O Fallon MO 63368	MO	Teacher	EM			S	1973
Hischke Kevin	(303)829-3279 krhischke@gmail.com	1941 E 129th Dr Thornton CO 80241	RM	Tch/DCE	EM			S	2007
Hischke Martha F Fischer	(303)829-1772 mkhischke@gmail.com	1941 E 129th Dr Thornton CO 80241	RM	Teacher	EM			S	1980
Hiske Beverly G	(989)354-8012	151 S North St Alpena MI 49707	MI	Teacher	EM			RF	1962
Hiskey William R	(270)843-1782 brhiskey@hotmail.com	290 Lamplighter Dr Bowling Green KY 42104	MDS	Teacher	Mem C	Holy Trinity Bowling Green KY	(270)843-9595	S	1987
Hittinger Catherine A Tripp	(626)824-5125 kithitt22@gmail.com	4309 Cedar Ave El Monte CA 91732	PSW	Teacher	Prin	Pacific Gardena CA	(310)538-6865	CQ	2002
Hittinger Mollie C	(626)824-7769 mollie.hittinger@flhsemail.org		PSW	Teacher	Tchr	Faith Las Vegas NV	(702)804-4400	MQ	2022
Hitzeman Jacqueline A Boklund	(260)485-6386 jhitzeman@frontier.com	3890 Bueschlng Dr Fort Wayne IN 46815	IN	Teacher	EM			RF	1970
Hoag Rachel H Brandmire	(253)579-7326 rachelhoag5@gmail.com	8507 Landsdowne Rd Henrico VA 23229	SE	DCE	Mem C	Trinity Richmond VA	(804)270-4626	IV	2020
Hoback Barbara A La Haine	bahoback@yahoo.com	2528 River Bend Trl Mayer MN 55360	MNS	Teacher	EM			S	1980
Hobbs Christiane D Zoch	(817)247-9023 chobbs@txlcms.org	4919 Havenside Way Mansfield TX 76063	TX	DCE	D Ex/S	Texas District Round Rock TX	(800)951-3478	SP	2001
Hobbs Nancy J Nielsen	(714)501-7376 nancyjhobbs@hotmail.com	2250 E South Redwood Dr Anaheim CA 92806	PSW	Teacher	Tchr	Mt Calvary Diamond Bar CA	(909)861-2740	IV	1993
Hobus David A	(406)300-2061 dbhobus@gmail.com	2185 Steel Bridge Rd Kalispell MT 59901	MT	Teacher	EM			S	1987
Hobus Steven R Dr	(414)531-8024 hobus57@gmail.com	8057 NE Sherman Rd Meriden KS 66512	KS	Teacher	EM			CQ	2001
Hoch Afton A	(586)876-8897 afton.hoch@lutheransouth.org	200 Water St. 21307 Webster TX 77598	TX	Teacher	Tchr	South Houston TX	(281)464-8299	MQ	2014
Hoch Arthur G	arthoch@charter.net	176 Parker Ave Alpena MI 49707	MI	Teacher	EM			SP	1971
Hoch Judith L Bohl		176 Parker Ave Alpena MI 49707	MI	Teacher	EM			SP	1991
Hoch Robert M	(586)899-6399 hoch.bob@outlook.com	55138 Estates Ln Macomb MI 48042	MI	Teacher	EM			SP	1976
Hock Kristine L Ulmer	(303)550-1815 krishock@comcast.net	1879 S Union Blvd Lakewood CO 80228	RM	Teacher	Tchr	Bethlehem Lakewood CO	(303)233-0401	S	1978
Hockemeyer Brooke N	(260)602-2018 b.hockemeyer123@gmail.com	68903 Farwell Ave Sturgis MI 49091	MI	Teacher	Tchr	Trinity Sturgis MI	(269)651-4245	CH	2022
Hockemeyer Phyllis A	(260)438-8788 phockemeyer@cluth.org	14431 Bremer Rd New Haven IN 46774	IN	Teacher	EM			RF	1981
Hodge Kristin J Casselman Deac	(260)318-4875 kristinhodge911@gmail.com	1516 E. Kammerer Road Kendalville IN 46756	IN	Deaconess	EM			FW-DEAC	2013
Hodge Susan M Koehler	(636)300-1542 sue@4hodge.com	8005 Knights Crossing Dr O Fallon MO 63368	MO	Teacher	EM			S	1969

*Multiple Assignments (See Church Worker Locator for Additional Details)
See Page 53 for the Table of Abbreviations for key to District, Classification, Position, and College abbreviations.
**C =Candidate; EM =Emeritus; the date following the C is the month and year the Candidate status began

NAME	TELEPHONE NUMBER EMAIL	STREET ADDRESS CITY/STATE/ZIP	DISTRICT	CLASS.	POSITION/ STATUS**	WHERE SERVING	OFFICE PHONE	COLLEGE/ UNIV/CQ	YR GRAD
Hodges Doreen M Seddon	(712)215-2533 dhodges@cls.k12.ia.us	702 Walnut St Shenandoah IA 51601	IW	Teacher	Tchr	Clarinda Clarinda IA	(712)542-3657	CQ	2007
Hodges Paige W Williams	(972)965-0763 faithpaige@verizon.net	1050 Paul Wilson Rd Wylie TX 75098	TX	Teacher	Tchr	Faith Plano TX	(972)423-7447	CQ	1999
Hodgson Carol I Scott	(913)262-2310 chodgsonkc@yahoo.com	4111 Elledge Dr Roeland Park KS 66205	MO	Teacher	EM			S	1979
Hodgson William E Jr	(602)402-8209 hodgson1@cox.net	3301 E Turney Ave Phoenix AZ 85018	PSW	Teacher	EM			S	1972
Hoech Kayla R	(949)527-8397 kayla.hoech@gmail.com	5828 N Lindenwood Dr. Apt. 2309 Peoria IL 61615	CI	Teacher	Tchr	Lutheran Central School Assoc Peoria IL	(309)691-8921	IV	2024
Hoeft James M	(313)574-1474 jhoeft1976@gmail.com	20491 Centralia Redford MI 48240	MI	Teacher	Tchr	Guardian Dearborn MI	(313)274-3665	AA	1999
Hoehne Bethany R	(734)620-4336 bethany.hoehne@lhsparker.org	19693 E Mann Creek Dr Apt C Parker CO 80134	RM	Teacher	Tchr	Colorado Lutheran High School Parker CO	(303)841-5551	Other	2021
Hoehne Matthew J	(734)679-4667 matthewhoehne92@gmail.com	16233 E Rosetta Dr Unit 43 Fountain Hills AZ 85268	MO	DPM	EM			RF	1992
Hoehner Erin R Trinklein	(636)541-0777 erinhoehner1@gmail.com	715 Napa Ln Saint Charles MO 63304	MO	Teacher	Tchr	Chapel of the Cross Saint Peters MO	(636)928-5885	RF	1997
Hoelzel Jennifer M Zirbel	(920)973-9915 jenhoelzel1019@gmail.com	1248 Wild Rose Ln Neenah WI 54956	NW	Teacher	Tchr	Zion Of Wayside Greenleaf WI	(920)864-2468	MQ	2004
Hoem Kristin E	(920)912-0852 thehoems@gmail.com	1910 Worthington Dr Fort Wayne IN 46845	IN	Teacher	Tchr	St Pauls Fort Wayne IN	(260)423-2496	MQ	2001
Hoener Janet L Schmidt	(303)904-0102 jan.hoener@comcast.net	5446 Knoll Pl Hghlnds Ranch CO 80130	RM	Teacher	EM			S	1975
Hoeppner Aaron C	(262)744-1006 aaron.hoeppner10@gmail.com	3804 S Bridlewood Mesa AZ 85212	PSW	Teacher		Pacific Southwest District Irvine CA	(949)854-3232	MQ	2007
Hoeppner Carrie E	(989)327-4061 choeppner@stmichaelsrichville.org	6700 E Holland Rd Saginaw MI 48601	MI	Teacher	Tchr	St Michael Richville MI	(989)868-4791	CQ	2016
Hoeppner Karen L	(260)705-8895 bkhoeppner@aol.com	5311 N State Road 101 Woodburn IN 46797	IN	Teacher	EM			CQ	2001
Hoeppner Michelle M Schmidt	(262)352-2946 mmhoeppner@gmail.com	3804 S Bridlewood Mesa AZ 85212	PSW	Teacher		Pacific Southwest District Irvine CA	(949)854-3232	MQ	2009
Hoeppner Shannon M Buck	(920)285-9878 panner84@hotmail.com	1109 Louisa St Watertown WI 53098	EN	DCM	Tchr	Faith Watertown WI	(920)261-8060	MQ	2006
Hoerauf Karen F Strickert	(586)247-5177 hoeraufdk@sbcglobal.net	15134 Congress Dr Sterling Hts MI 48313	MI	Teacher	EM			S	1973
Hoerner Miriam J Stock	(219)671-6455 miriam.hoerner@gmail.com	20080 White Oaks Dr. Clinton Township MI 48036	MI	Teacher	C06/2023			MQ	2015
Hoff Cary L	(469)733-3979 cary.hoff@gmail.com	11012 Canyon Rd E Ste 8 Puyallup WA 98373	NOW	DCE	Mem C	Our Savior Tacoma WA	(253)531-2112	AU	2012
Hoff Dereem M Miller	(805)844-4862 hoffd3@gmail.com	11012 Canyon Rd E Ste 8 Puyallup WA 98373	NOW	Teacher	Mem C	Our Savior Tacoma WA	(253)531-2112	CQ	2012
Hoff Laura R Schumm		103 German St West Newton PA 15089	EA	Teacher	Tchr	Calvary Murrysville PA	(724)327-2898	AA	1986
Hoffert Corinne P Will	(352)385-7231 cphoffert1@centurylink.net	2503 Natoma Blvd Mount Dora FL 32757	FG	Teacher	EM			RF	1975
Hoffert Erick K	(352) 978-4514 hoffert1@brighthouse.com	2503 Natoma Blvd Mount Dora FL 32757	FG	Teacher	EM			RF	1975
Hoffman Amy C	(602)570-4042 ahoffman@sjlschool.org	12513 Lautner Dr Bakersfield CA 93311	CNH	Teacher	Tchr	St John Bakersfield CA	(661)665-7815	MQ	2004
Hoffman Cherryll I Cook Deac	(712)276-7503 cherrycook@cableone.net	5620 Windsor Ave Sioux City IA 51106	IW	Deaconess	EM			Other	1960
Hoffman Craig C	(260)485-0602	5724 Bell Tower Ln Fort Wayne IN 46815	IN	Teacher	EM			S	1961
Hoffman Eric B	(602)570-4043 dahoffermn@gmail.com	12513 Lautner Dr Bakersfield CA 93311	CNH	Teacher	Tchr	St John Bakersfield CA	(661)665-7815	MQ	2003
Hoffman Justin E	(712)269-9780 hoffmanjustin@hotmail.com	1404 N 40th St Lincoln NE 68503	NEB	Teacher	C06/2023			S	2003
Hoffman Karisa G	(630)429-4756 karisahoffman01@gmail.com	1060 N Farnsworth Ave Apt 1206 Aurora IL 60505	NI	Teacher	C10/2023			MQ	2022
Hoffman LaDonna R Arnst	(708)341-9590 lhoffman10948@gmail.com	1206 Park Dr Melrose Park IL 60160	NI	Teacher	C02/2021			CH	1970
Hoffman Lance C	(260)515-8663 lhoffman@clhscadets.com	1322 County Road 20 Corunna IN 46730	IN	Teacher	S HS/C	Concordia Theological Seminary Fort Wayne IN	(260)452-2100	MQ	1990
Hoffman Nancy L Raap	(715)218-3037 nancyraaphoffman@gmail.com	522 S 1st Ave Wausau WI 54401	NW	Teacher	EM			SP	1977
Hoffman Patricia A Dr	(949)547-2333 hoffmanpa01@gmail.com	15710 W 62nd Street Shawnee KS 66217	KS	Teacher	EM			RF	1976
Hoffman Sarah R Koepke		353 SE 43rd Ave Hillsboro OR 97123	NOW	Teacher	Tchr	Forest Hills Cornelius OR	(503)359-4853	PO	1982
Hoffmann Kimberly	khoffman3@hotmail.com	2710 Santa Fe Trl Apt 202 Racine WI 53404	SW	Teacher	Tchr	St John Racine WI	(262)637-7011	RF	2003
Hoffmann Linda L Baker	(262)786-1203	20835 Brook Park Ct Brookfield WI 53045	SW	Teacher	EM			CQ	1994
Hoffmann Mackenzie R Thiesfeld	(952)913-7039 mthiesfeld11@gmail.com	1809 Judd Ave N Glencoe MN 55336	MNS	Teacher	Tchr	First Glencoe MN	(320)864-5522	SP	2019
Hoffmann Nicholas J	(303)921-1411 dcenickhoffmann@outlook.com	7862 E 131st Pl Thornton CO 80602	RM	DCE	C07/2016			S	2014
Hoffmann Shawn M	(309)530-0231 shawnhoffmann@trinluth.org	10 Ethell Pkwy Bloomington IL 61701	CI	Teacher	Prin	Trinity Bloomington IL	(309)829-7513	RF	1995
Hoffschneider Joel T	(260)748-4336 jhoffschneider@clsfw.org	6605 Centerton Dr Fort Wayne IN 46815	IN	Teacher	Tchr	Concordia Fort Wayne IN	(260)422-2429	RF	1988
Hoffschneider Larry E	(214)280-1116 lhoffschn@gmail.com	2360 Home Again Rd Apopka FL 32712	S	Teacher	EM			RF	1966

*Multiple Assignments (See Church Worker Locator for Additional Details)
See Page 53 for the Table of Abbreviations for key to District, Classification, Position, and College abbreviations.
**C =Candidate; EM =Emeritus; the date following the C is the month and year the Candidate status began

NAME	TELEPHONE NUMBER EMAIL	STREET ADDRESS CITY/STATE/ZIP	DISTRICT	CLASS.	POSITION/ STATUS**	WHERE SERVING	OFFICE PHONE	COLLEGE/ UNIV/CQ	YR GRAD
Hoffschneider Nancy M Achterberg	(214)280-1116 nancyberghof1@gmail.com	2360 Home Again Rd Apopka FL 32712	S	Teacher	EM			S	1968
Hofman Amy R Rullman	(828)446-1423 ahof@yahoo.com	3229 Land Hbr Newland NC 28657	SE	Teacher	EM			SP	1973
Hofman Laurene E Leistico Dr	(707)365-4665 lhofman.tls@gmail.com	1353 Plum Creek Dr Bourbonnais IL 60914	NI	Teacher	C07/2016			IV	1999
Hofman Lindsey R Knolhoff	(618)830-9873 lhofman@firstlutheranschool.com	3207 Mona Ln Knoxville TN 37914	MDS	Teacher	Tchr	First Knoxville TN	(865)524-0308	CH	2008
Hofman Mark D	(314)996-1315 mark.hofman@lcms.org	8530 Elgin Ave Saint Louis MO 63123	MO	Teacher	S Ex/S	The LCMS Corporate Saint Louis MO	(314)965-9000	S	1993
Hofman Sue E Endorf	(954)966-3739 charlesandsueh@att.net	1904 N 39th Ave Hollywood FL 33021	FG	Teacher	EM			S	1965
Hofmann Sandra E Wadenklee	(201)664-7667	645 Ridgewood Rd Twp Washinton NJ 07676	NJ	Teacher	Tchr	Zion Westwood NJ	(201)664-8060	RF	1969
Hofmeister Kurt R	(989)225-7385 khofmeister@vlhs.com	3389 Brentway Dr Bay City MI 48706	MI	Teacher	EM			CQ	1994
Hoft Bethany C Hoelz	hofthome4@gmail.com	205 Blackhawk Dr Eldridge IA 52748	IE	Teacher	C07/2016			MQ	1997
Hoft Lydia R Armbrecht	(319)720-5180 lydiahoft608@gmail.com	14 Founders Way Unit D St Louis MO 63105	MO	Teacher	Tchr	Child Of God Saint Peters MO	(636)970-7080	S	2025
Hogan-Gomez Elin L Gomez	(651)253-1484 ehogangomez@gmail.com	10 Newport Ave Saint Louis MO 63119	MO	DPM	C08/2019			SP	2009
Hoger Nadine L Mundt	(708)720-5524 nhoger@tlcs.org	5900 Lincoln Hwy Matteson IL 60443	NI	Teacher	Tchr	Trinity Tinley Park IL	(708)532-3529	RF	1985
Hohenstein Rebecca A Fritsche	(314)971-3247 hohenstein.becky@gmail.com	725 Settler Rd Fenton MO 63026	MO	Teacher	EM			RF	1978
Hohle Gwendolyn L Hinrichs	(512)924-9074 ghohle@gmail.com	327 Sycamore St Georgetown TX 78633	TX	Teacher	EM			AU	1983
Hohle Raymond L	(979)540-8474 schfr5@hotmail.com	4067 County Road 114 Lincoln TX 78948	TX	Teacher	EM			S	1954
Hohlfeld Elizabeth J	(309)686-0769 elizabeth0936@att.net	820 W Purtscher Dr Peoria IL 61614	CI	Teacher	EM			S	1965
Hohnbaum James M	(317)757-6417 loho828@comcast.net	8224 Rumford Rd Indianapolis IN 46219	IN	Teacher	EM			S	1968
Hohnstadt Elizabeth J Maxwell	(714)334-4122 lizhohnstadt30@gmail.com	533 SW 6th Ct Gresham OR 97080	NOW	Teacher	C07/2021			S	2016
Hohnstadt Kyra M	(248)296-6436 kyra.hohnstadt@gmail.com	5900 Meadows Dr Clarkston MI 49348	MI	Teacher	C06/2023			MQ	2022
Hohnstadt Rebecca S	(248)495-8338 rshohnstadt@gmail.com	W172 N11368 Division Rd Apt. D Germantown WI 53022	SW	Teacher	Mem C	Trinity Mequon WI	(262)242-2045	AA	1986
Hohnstadt Steven M	(816)500-1484 shohnstadt@ourshepherd.org	1929 N Avon Ave Avon IN 46123	IN	DPM	Mem C	Our Shepherd Avon IN	(317)271-9103	MQ	2007
Hokana Brittany L Virchow	(262)343-1425 bhokana@immanuelrapids.com		NI	Teacher	Tchr	Rockford Rockford IL	(815)877-9551	MQ	2019
Holdeman Kimberly S Frieling	(734)731-5461 kholdeman@oslcrockwall.org	1708 Cherrybrook Ln Wylie TX 75098	TX	DCE	Mem C	Our Savior Rockwall TX	(972)771-8118	S	2006
Holden Christine	(619)402-0268 ceholden@pobox.com	1887 Galway Pl El Cajon CA 92020	PSW	Teacher	Tchr	Christ La Mesa CA	(619)462-5211	CQ	2017
Holdorf Leanne R	lholdorf@sflutheranschool.com	5001 W Heritage Pl Apt 7 Sioux Falls SD 57106	SD	Teacher	Tchr	Sioux Falls Sioux Falls SD	(605)335-1923	CQ	2021
Holeso Cassidy L	(517)769-5084 dcecassidyholeso@gmail.com		OH	DCE	C07/2022			CH	2021
Holland Jill R Meyer	(314)497-1850 jill4mizzou@yahoo.com	1617 Shane Dr Imperial MO 63052	MO	Teacher	Tchr	St John Arnold MO	(636)464-7303	CQ	2011
Holland Kenneth L	(816)206-1627 kenholland04@outlook.com	1295 NW Lindenwood Dr Grain Valley MO 64029	MO	Teacher	Prin	Timothy Blue Springs MO	(816)228-5300	CQ	2023
Holland Taylor N Kelso	(714)928-9241 taynholland10@gmail.com	7748 E. Sandberg Lane Orange CA 92869	PSW	Teacher	C06/2024			IV	2018
Hollatz Jacob D Dr	(979)836-6578 jakehollatz@gmail.com	742 E Almond Ave Orange CA 92866	PSW	Teacher	Prin	Saint Johns Orange CA	(714)288-4400	SP	2000
Holle Kathryn A Ebel	(618)698-2453 kaebel8@gmail.com	4420 NE 16th St Ankeny IA 50021	IW	Teacher	Tchr	Mount Olive Des Moines IA	(515)277-0247	CQ	2015
Holle Lesley A Owens Deac	(505)710-7124 holle.lesley@gmail.com	10708 Nelle Ave NE Albuquerque NM 87111	RM	Deaconess	Mem C	Grace Albuquerque NM	(505)823-9100	FW-DEAC	2009
Hollenbeck Mark		17021 Bennett Dr Parker CO 80134	RM	Teacher	Tchr	Lutheran Parker CO	(303)841-5551	IV	1999
Hollendoner Emily A Adas Maki	ehollendoner@cglschool.org	2827 W Sable Ave Apache Junction AZ 85120	PSW	Teacher	Tchr	Christ Greenfield Gilbert AZ	(480)892-8521	CH	2009
Holler Nora F Ford	(630)464-6325 firstnora@comcast.net	4323 Coldsprings Dr Pensacola FL 32514	SO	Teacher	Prin	Redeemer Pensacola FL	(850)455-0330	RF	1980
Holliday Cynthia R Hoffmann	crholl23@gmail.com	1532 Harding Ave Berkeley IL 60163	NI	Teacher	Tchr	Walther Melrose Park IL	(708)344-0404	RF	1997
Hollman Linda M Kirchner	(734)812-3464 lindah@christoursavior.org	20691 Chestnut Cir Livonia MI 48152	MI	Tch/DCE/ DCO	Mem C	Christ Our Savior Livonia MI	(734)522-6830	S	1983
Hollmann Dorothea A Haynes	(260)432-1622 dollihollmann@gmail.com	611 W County Line Rd S # 317 Fort Wayne IN 46814	IN	Teacher	EM			RF	1974
Hollmann John E	(480)861-3453 hollmann4448@gmail.com	4215 E Aspen Ave Mesa AZ 85206	PSW	Tch/DCE	EM			S	1974
Holloway Lisa A	(480)310-1065 lholloway@cglschool.org	4316 E Millbrae Ln Gilbert AZ 85234	PSW	Teacher	Tchr	Christs Greenfield Gilbert AZ	(480)892-8314	S	1997
Hollrah Deanna S	(586)469-0168 d.hollrah@sbcglobal.net	294 Jones St Mount Clemens MI 48043	MI	Teacher	EM			S	1968
Hollrah Deborah L Schmidt	(203)770-1450 deb2guide@gmail.com	19 Beechwood Dr Danbury CT 06810	NE	Teacher	C07/2016			BR	1985
Hollrah Joyce E	(636)244-1943 joyeholl@charter.net	600 Breeze Park Dr Apt 294 Weldon Spring MO 63304	MO	Teacher	EM			RF	1960

*Multiple Assignments (See Church Worker Locator for Additional Details)

See Page 53 for the Table of Abbreviations for key to District, Classification, Position, and College abbreviations.

**C =Candidate; EM =Emeritus; the date following the C is the month and year the Candidate status began

NAME	TELEPHONE NUMBER EMAIL	STREET ADDRESS CITY/STATE/ZIP	DISTRICT	CLASS.	POSITION/ STATUS**	WHERE SERVING	OFFICE PHONE	COLLEGE/ UNIV/CQ	YR GRAD
Holman Freddie J Hall	(281)610-1401 holmanf@concordiacrusades.org	25111 Oak Hollow Blvd Hockley TX 77447	TX	Teacher	Tchr	Concordia Tomball TX	(281)351-2547	S	1998
Holman Matthew J	(608)217-2717 nordique72@yahoo.com	2202 Meadowland Dr Apt 103 Sheboygan WI 53081	SW	Teacher	Tchr	Sheboygan Sheboygan WI	(920)452-3323	S	2004
Holman Melissa M Shinn	melissa.holman2014@gmail.com	2803 Roscommon Dr Fort Wayne IN 46805	IN	Teacher	Tchr	Suburban Bethlehem Fort Wayne IN	(260)483-9371	CQ	2019
Holmes Jennifer Sleeter	(715)350-9415 jenny@theholmesnetwork.com	5871 Slate Rock Ct Las Vegas NV 89149	PSW	Teacher	Tchr	Faith Las Vegas NV	(702)804-4400	MQ	2000
Holmes Michelle E Meier	(972)235-9031 mholmes@flsplano.org	1701 E Park Blvd Plano TX 75074	TX	Teacher	Tchr	Faith Plano TX	(972)423-7448	CQ	2019
Holmlund James L	(612)834-4021 director@loveincheartland.org	9585 Ranchview Ln N Maple Grove MN 55369	MNS	Teacher	C08/2021			SP	1996
Holmlund Lauren M	(763)248-9780 lholmlund@rockfordlutheran.org	4041 Renn Hart Hills Rd Apt 52 Loves Park IL 61111	NI	Teacher	Tchr	Rockford Rockford IL	(815)877-9551	S	2022
Holschen Carl C Dr	(314)425-9420 holschcc@charter.net	716 Sterling Ridge Dr O Fallon MO 63366	MO	Teacher	EM			RF	1970
Holshouser Jennifer R Wilson	(636)233-3147 jenniferraewilson@hotmail.com	2131 Blendon Pl Saint Louis MO 63143	MO	Teacher	Tchr	Our Savior Fenton MO	(636)343-2192	AA	2005
Holst Larry R	(816)795-6015	18209 E 25th Ter S Independence MO 64057	MO	Teacher	EM			S	1968
Holste Cynthia K Meier	(440)321-6155 cinntoast95@gmail.com	1042 Richmond Rd Painesville OH 44077	OH	Teacher	Tchr	Our Shepherd Painesville OH	(440)357-7776	S	1995
Holste Kenneth E	(406)257-4374 ckholstel@gmail.com	375 3rd Avenue West N Kalispell MT 59901	MT	Teacher	EM			S	1969
Holste Richard W	(563)424-0660 Rick.holste@trinitydavenport.org	2311 W 29th St Davenport IA 52804	IE	Teacher	Tchr	Trinity Davenport IA	(563)322-5224	S	1982
Holt Daniel V	(415)299-9248 danielholt@sbcglobal.net	2860 Tipperary Ave S San Fran CA 94080	EN	Teacher	EM			RF	1985
Holt Deborah K Lax	(920)912-4463 debkholt@yahoo.com	3478 Samson Dr Milton WI 53563	SW	Teacher	Tchr	Our Redeemer Delavan WI	(262)728-6589	CQ	2014
Holt Jeffrey S			SW	Teacher	Tchr	Our Redeemer Delavan WI	(262)728-6589	MQ	1995
Holt Sherlyn J Anderson	(605)695-1743 sjholt28@gmail.com	21782 457th Ave Arlington SD 57212	SD	Teacher	C07/2016			SP	1994
Holt Stacey R Mahn	(712)292-9993 staceyholt4031@gmail.com	9637 Saint Gregory Cir Lincoln NE 68526	MO	DCE	C10/2022			S	2014
Holtan Alice M Sachtleben	(630)299-3740	2278 James Leigh Dr Aurora IL 60503	NI	Teacher	EM			RF	1961
Holtan Karen C Dux-Pfingsten	(507)259-6292 kaholtan@gmail.com	21412 State Highway 30 Hayfield MN 55940	MNS	Teacher	EM			SP	1979
Holtan Sarah E Gilbert Dr	(414)305-0270	910 Katherine Dr Elm Grove WI 53122	SW	Teacher	S HS/C	Concordia University Wisconsin Mequon WI	(262)243-5700	CQ	2011
Holten Ben H	(507)246-5183 benholten@yahoo.com	38616 State Highway 111 Nicollet MN 56074	MNS	Teacher	EM			SP	1986
Holten Jeanne L Tolzmann	(507)246-5183 jholten7@hotmail.com	38616 State Highway 111 Nicollet MN 56074	MNS	Teacher	C10/2022			SP	1986
Holten Rachel J	(507)766-7382 racheljholten@gmail.com	248 Harvest Ridge Blvd Elgin TX 78621	TX	Teacher	Tchr	Zion Georgetown TX	(512)863-5345	IV	2021
Holthus Emma K	(612)816-9854 emma.holthus@cune.org	13011 Arrowood Ln N Dayton MN 55327	MNS	Teacher	C03/2024			S	2022
Holthus Terry W	terry.holthus@gmail.com	1259 N Hickory St Wahoo NE 68066	NEB	Teacher	EM			S	1976
Holtmeier Aaron C	(636)699-3710 aaronholtmeier@ concordiaprepschool.org	33 Greenleaf Rd Parkville MD 21234	SE	Teacher	Tchr	Concordia Towson MD	(410)825-2323	MQ	2020
Holtmeier Michael G	(636)244-3481 mholtmeier@lhssc.org	639 River Moss Dr Saint Peters MO 63376	MO	Teacher	Tchr	St Charles Saint Peters MO	(636)928-5100	S	1980
Holtmeier Ronald G	(636)284-7436 holtmeier2@att.net	600 Breeze Park Dr Apt 386 Weldon Spring MO 63304	MO	Teacher	EM			CQ	1967
Holton Stacy L Kissling	(214)426-1174 stacyksu@sbcglobal.net	8928 Hackney Ln Dallas TX 75238	TX	DCO	C02/2017			SP	2004
Holtz Katie L Angle	(573)330-4880 kholtz@stpaulgiants.com	2211 Kyle Ct Farmington MO 63640	MO	Teacher	Tchr	St Paul Farmington MO	(573)756-7872	CQ	2019
Holtzen Lee R Dr	(402) 643-0449 janhojanho@msn.com	500 Heartland Park Dr #27 Seward NE 68434	NEB	Teacher	EM			S	1952
Holtzman Chad M	(319)215-9680 cmatthewh@yahoo.com	107 Berry Hill Rd Cedar Falls IA 50613	IE	Teacher	Tchr	Valley Cedar Falls IA	(319)266-4565	CQ	2003
Holz Kristin D Wittenberger	(303)589-1455 kristinholz225@yahoo.com	2370 Federalist Pl O Fallon MO 63368	MO	Teacher	Tchr	Zion Saint Charles MO	(636)441-7425	CH	2008
Holzer Gail J Auger	(412)793-5884 gholzer@redeemer-oakmont.org	364 McMahon Dr N Huntingdon PA 15642	EN	Teacher	Prin	Redeemer Verona PA	(412)793-5884	CQ	2009
Holzer Katie A Hermann	(734)673-0496 katesholzer@gmail.com	22538 Foxcroft St Woodhaven MI 48183	MI	Teacher	Tchr	Christ The King Southgate MI	(734)285-9695	AA	2008
Holzerland Barbara A Ulrich	(573)732-5776	2217 Country Hills Ct Rolla MO 65401	MO	Teacher	EM			S	1960
Holzheimer Allen J II	(920)889-9711 holzheimer@lutheranhigh.com	1622 N 27th Pl Sheboygan WI 53081	SW	Teacher	Prin	Sheboygan Sheboygan WI	(920)452-3323	MQ	1993
Homann Theodore R	(206) 818-7043 trhomann@hotmail.com	2260 Cascade Dr Atwater CA 95301	CNH	Teacher	EM			S	1969
Homrich Kaeleen R Sugden	(989)450-2889 kaeleen.homrich@gmail.com		MI	Teacher	Tchr	St Peter Hemlock MI	(989)642-5659	CQ	2023
Honebrink David		7634 Ockley Ln Indianapolis IN 46259	IN	Teacher	Tchr	Calvary Indianapolis IN	(317)783-2000	MQ	2007
Honeck Bill		11326 N Country Club Green Dr Tomball TX 77375	TX	Teacher	Tchr	Concordia Tomball TX	(281)351-2547	CQ	2010

*Multiple Assignments (See Church Worker Locator for Additional Details)

See Page 53 for the Table of Abbreviations for key to District, Classification, Position, and College abbreviations.

**C =Candidate; EM =Emeritus; the date following the C is the month and year the Candidate status began

NAME	TELEPHONE NUMBER EMAIL	STREET ADDRESS CITY/STATE/ZIP	DISTRICT	CLASS.	POSITION/ STATUS**	WHERE SERVING	OFFICE PHONE	COLLEGE/ UNIV/CQ	YR GRAD
Honeck Jennifer	(281)704-8179 honeckj@trinityklein.org	8017 Whisper Grove Dr Magnolia TX 77354	TX	Teacher	Tchr	Trinity Spring TX	(281)376-5810	AU	2018
Honeck Laura M Schlichting	(281)636-9681 lhoneck@salem4u.com	11322 N Country Club Green Dr Tomball TX 77375	TX	Teacher	Tchr	Salem Tomball TX	(281)351-8223	S	2008
Hong Janis T Thiemann	(904)635-0537 janisthiemann@gmail.com	7223 Bristol Ridge Dr Houston TX 77095	TX	Teacher	Tchr	St Mark Houston TX	(713)468-2623	S	2013
Honoree Cheryl C Coyner	(504)652-7379	559 Diplomat St Terrytown LA 70056	SO	Teacher	Tchr	Faith Harahan LA	(504)737-9554	RF	1980
Honoree Cheryl L	(573)225-9048 cherylhonoree@gmail.com	6339 Alameda Dr Shreveport LA 71119	SO	Teacher	EM			S	1981
Hood Kimberly L Koppe	(206)650-9057 koppehood@gmail.com	2383 N Waterberry St Orange CA 92865	PSW	Teacher	EM			IV	1988
Hood Matthew W	(206)554-1985	6322 38th Ave SW Seattle WA 98126	PSW	Teacher	Tchr	Crean Irvine CA	(949)387-1199	IV	2018
Hook Chelsea M Yamin	(586)627-4121 cmyamin727@gmail.com	511 N Main St Janesville MN 56048	MNS	Teacher	Tchr	Trinity Janesville MN	(507)231-6646	CH	2021
Hook Jennifer L Stocker	(520)777-4401 jennifer@hookcentral.com	13599 E Cienega Creek Dr Vail AZ 85641	PSW	Teacher	EM			S	1986
Hoolahan Connie E Schmidt	(904)262-0384 choolahan07@aol.com	9411 Genna Trace Trl Jacksonville FL 32257	FG	Teacher	C07/2016			RF	1989
Hooper Deborah L Runion		832 E Ada Ave Glendora CA 91741	PSW	Teacher	EM			CQ	1997
Hooper Mary E Hammell	(619)200-9763 maryehooper@yahoo.com	2613 Sir Percival Ln Lewisville TX 75056	TX	Teacher	EM			CQ	1993
Hooper Susan L Repp	(810)603-0744 rsjchoop@yahoo.com	6102 Kings Shire Rd Grand Blanc MI 48439	MI	Teacher	EM			S	1973
Hoover Alexa	(260)222-1441 alexahoov11@gmail.com	10276 Jamestown Dr Anchorage AK 99507	NOW	Teacher	Tchr	Anchor Anchorage AK	(907)522-3636	CH	2023
Hope-Hull Joseph B	(619)957-7145 joseph.hopehull@gmail.com	2906 Francis Ave Mansfield MA 02048	NE	DCE	C06/2023			S	2019
Hopfensperger Elizabeth G Paul	(262)665-4157 epaul@adventlutheran.org		EN	Teacher	Tchr	Advent Zionsville IN	(317)873-6318	MQ	2023
Hopfensperger Jacob C	(320)221-9440 jhop@adventlutheran.org	9546 Carlyle Dr Apt D Indianapolis IN 46240	EN	Teacher	Tchr	Advent Zionsville IN	(317)873-6318	MQ	2025
Hopfensperger Nick A	(636)239-1723 nick.hopfensperger@imlutheran.org	707 Ron Ave Washington MO 63090	MO	Teacher	Prin	Immanuel Washington MO	(636)239-1636	RF	2000
Hopkins Sofia K Kovalenko	(573)636-2604 sofiahopkins@hotmail.com	221 Madelines Park Cir Jefferson Cty MO 65109	MO	Teacher	EM			CQ	1996
Hopkirk Pamela J Wasley	(714)931-9764 hopkirkspd@gmail.com	2113 Catalina Ave. Santa Ana CA 92705	PSW	Teacher	EM			CQ	1993
Hopman Jordan C	(708)650-0899 jordanhopman@yahoo.com	270 Victoria Ct Decatur IL 62522	CI	Teacher	Tchr	Luth School Assoc Decatur IL	(217)233-2001	CH	2019
Hopman Susanna E Cluver	(217)521-3383 susannahopman@yahoo.com	270 Victoria Ct Decatur IL 62522	CI	Teacher	Tchr	Luth School Assoc Decatur IL	(217)233-2001	CH	2007
Hopp Jerry L	(248)506-7377 hoppjj@aol.com	602 S Manitou Ave Clawson MI 48017	MI	Teacher	EM			RF	1965
Hoppe Carl E	(708)396-2935 blueislandhoppe@yahoo.com	2136 121st Pl Blue Island IL 60406	EN	Teacher	EM			RF	1975
Hopper Linnea F Buchholz	linnea.buchholz@gmail.com		MO	Teacher	Tchr	Immanuel Wentzville MO	(636)327-4416	S	2021
Hopper Marilyn Duval	(765)473-1211	10428 E County Road 450 S Walton IN 46994	IN	Teacher	EM			SP	1967
Horak John B	(517)803-9043 jhorak@oursaviorlansing.org	11232 Brickand Dr Grand Ledge MI 48837	MI	Teacher	Tchr	Our Savior Lansing MI	(517)882-8665	S	1983
Horkey Marsha B Pankow	(712)898-4702 marsha.horkey@gmail.com	200 1/2 S Churchill Circle N Sioux City SD 57049	IW	Teacher	EM			SP	1978
Horn Jana S Long	(262)617-8325 jhorn@hcl.org	11220 Francis Ct W Franklin WI 53132	EN	Teacher	Tchr	Hales Corners Hales Corners WI	(414)529-6701	CQ	2010
Horn Jane E Kriel	(612)408-5133 janiehonk@gmail.com	8106 Highwood Dr Apr Y117 Bloomington MN 55438	MNS	Teacher	EM			SP	1973
Hornbuckle Rebekah G Rusert	(507)236-4272 rebekah.rusert@cune.org	P.O. Box 164 Sheldahl IA 50243	IW	Teacher	Tchr	Trinity Boone IA	(515)432-6912	S	2019
Hornburg Emily E	(573)529-4645 eehornburg@gmail.com	4654 W 94th St Oak Lawn IL 60453	NI	DCE	C07/2016			CH	2009
Horne Kayla K	(830)459-2901 kaylakhorne@gmail.com		TX	DCE	Tchr	Redeemer Austin TX	(512)451-6478	AU	2014
Horne Laurie A	(414)218-9160 lahwmin@aol.com	7102 W Jordan Ct Franklin WI 53132	EN	Teacher	EM			MQ	1988
Horning Brian C	(231)622-1430 bhorning@zionlutheranpetoskey.org	8930 Moore Rd Alanson MI 49706	MI	DFLM	Mem C	Zion Petoskey MI	(231)347-3438	AA	2009
Hornyak Kimberly A Malloy	(330)461-0605 kahornyak@gmail.com	338 E. Maple Street Granville OH 43023	EN	DCM	C06/2024			CQ	2015
Horrigan Karen J Amolsch	(913)814-8474 kmhorrigan@msn.com	13641 Manor Leawood KS 66224	KS	Teacher	Tchr	Christ Overland Park KS	(913)754-5813	WN	1985
Horrmann Ann L Burnside	ann.horrmann@gmail.com		MNS	DCE	C07/2016			SP	2005
Horst Jenna G	(720)243-7464 Jennavhyde@gmail.com	12 Founders Way Unit C Saint Louis MO 63105	MO	Teacher	C06/2023			CQ	2022
Horton Linda	(816)507-8408 lindahorton17@gmail.com	413 Tanglewood Dr. St. Joseph MO 64506	MO	DCE	Mem C	St Paul Saint Joseph MO	(816)279-1110	IV	2020
Horton Nancy L Albers	(254)760-5401 nlhorton2@gmail.com	401 Fm 575 N Goldthwaite TX 76844	TX	Teacher	EM			AU	1982
Horton Wallace W Dr	(703)425-2531 celloorgan@verizon.net	4320 Braeburn Dr Fairfax VA 22032	SE	Teacher	EM			CQ	1971

*Multiple Assignments (See Church Worker Locator for Additional Details)
See Page 53 for the Table of Abbreviations for key to District, Classification, Position, and College abbreviations.
**C =Candidate; EM =Emeritus; the date following the C is the month and year the Candidate status began

NAME	TELEPHONE NUMBER EMAIL	STREET ADDRESS CITY/STATE/ZIP	DISTRICT	CLASS.	POSITION/ STATUS**	WHERE SERVING	OFFICE PHONE	COLLEGE/ UNIV/CQ	YR GRAD
Horvath Brian	bhorvath@lhsa.com	34544 School Section Rd Richmond MI 48062	MI	Teacher	Tchr	LHS Assn Of Greater Detroit Rochester Hls MI	(248)856-0240	MQ	1999
Horvath Gail J Grundmeier	(636)495-9252 gail.j.horvath@gmail.com	5497 Regency Woods Mnr Imperial MO 63052	MO	Teacher	EM			S	1975
Horvath Kenneth E	(636)375-0493 kenneth.e.horvath@gmail.com	5497 Regency Woods Mnr Imperial MO 63052	MO	Teacher	EM			S	1976
Hoskey Brenda L Otto	(989)751-7117	5143 Dustine Drive North Saginaw MI 48603	MI	Teacher	EM			AA	1990
Hosmon Michele M Bohnke	(812)424-4725 mhosmon@elsone.org	4412 Stringtown Rd Evansville IN 47711	IN	Teacher	EM			S	1976
Hottinger Stacy L Hicks	(951)279-6682 shottinger@sbcglobal.net	c/o Loving Savior Of The Hills Lutheran Church 14816 Peyton Dr Chino Hills CA 91709	PSW	Teacher	Tchr	Loving Savior Chino Hills CA	(909)597-4668	CQ	2001
Houge Rhoda Luecht	(402)739-3489 claudehouge@msn.com	3656 Vermilion Ct N Eagan MN 55122	MNS	Teacher	EM			S	1971
Hougesen Cara D Wilson	(317)339-0891 rchougesen@att.net	3175 E Banta Rd Indianapolis IN 46227	IN	Teacher	Tchr	Holy Cross Indianapolis IN	(317)823-5801	RF	1989
House Andrew W	(301)218-3977 awhouse@verizon.net	1422 Perrell Ln Bowie MD 20716	SE	Teacher	EM			BR	2003
House Audrey M Johnson	(580)522-1085 ahouse4scouts@gmail.com	1607 N James St Guymon OK 73942	OK	Teacher	EM			S	1989
House James L	(972)948-3980 jimhouse57@gmail.com	951 Acorn St Giddings TX 78942	TX	Teacher	EM			S	1979
Houser Jillene A Stubenberg Deac	(402)679-5265	23247 New Maple Ridge Rd Blackduck MN 56630	MNN	Deaconess	C05/2021			FW-DEAC	2013
Houser Karen S Maassel	(260)515-3940 kghouser@aol.com	15836 Walnut St Huntertown IN 46748	IN	Teacher	EM			CQ	2008
Houston Rebecca J Wegener	(321)960-8916 baltmhou5@gmail.com	3111 Indian Trail Eustis FL 32726	FG	Teacher	Prin	Trinity Rockledge FL	(321)636-5431	CQ	2022
Hovatter Sarah A Reilly	(209)747-6241 shovatter@zionsf.org	443 9th Ave San Francisco CA 94118	CNH	Teacher	Tchr	Zion San Francisco CA	(415)221-7500	IV	2012
Hovland Stephenie M Mueller Deac	(920)264-8317	219 James St Portage WI 53901	SW	Deaconess	Mem C	St Johns Portage WI	(608)742-9000	MQ	1993
Howard Brent A	(913)322-6636 dcebrent@gmail.com	11428 W 117th Ter Overland Park KS 66210	KS	Tch/DCE	Mem C	Christ Overland Park KS	(913)345-9700	S	1996
Howard Jean M Augenstein	(260)615-4256		SE	Teacher	EM			CQ	1998
Howard Karen J Kroll	(920)287-8328 karenhoward@mac.com	1632 Ohio Ave Sheboygan WI 53081	SW	Teacher	EM			RF	1975
Howard Kathleen A Roberts	(208) 603-9439	1081 Lakeshore Dr Sagle ID 83860	NOW	Teacher	C07/2016			CQ	2002
Howard Kay H	(260)431-6659 kay.howard8@gmail.com	450 S Scott Rd Fort Wayne IN 46814	IN	Teacher	EM			RF	1979
Howard Kenneth D	(920)287-8385 ken.donald.howard@gmail.com	1632 Ohio Ave Sheboygan WI 53081	SW	Teacher	EM			RF	1975
Howard Marcus W	(727)459-7026 dcemarcushoward@gmail.com	1436 Rosetree Ct Clearwater FL 33764	S	DCE	C07/2024			IV	2021
Howard Michelle R Kilgore	(913)322-6636 michelle.howard@clcop.org	11428 W 117th Ter Overland Park KS 66210	KS	Teacher	Tchr	Christ Overland Park KS	(913)345-9700	S	2015
Howard Nancy J Gerling	(714)423-3642 howardnj72@yahoo.com	8899 Dahlia Drive Corona CA 92883	PSW	Teacher	EM			S	1973
Howard Roger A	(619)618-9576 rhowdpm@gmail.com	46 Lockspring San Antonio TX 78254	TX	DCE	Mem C	Shepherd Hills San Antonio TX	(210)614-3742	PO	1986
Howard Ryan L	(631)982-9082 rlhow8@gmail.com	24826 Broad Pine Dr Huffman TX 77336	TX	DCE	Mem C	Lamb Of God Humble TX	(281)446-8427	CH	2014
Howard Thomas A	(714)470-7685 howard@lhsoc.org	5927 E Creekside Ave Unit 4 Orange CA 92869	PSW	Teacher	Tchr	Orange County Orange CA	(714)998-5151	IV	2001
Howard Whitney J Holle	(785)268-0078 whollestjohnalma@gmail.com	319 W. 8th St Alma KS 66401	KS	Teacher	Tchr	St John Alma KS	(785)765-3632	S	2013
Howe Kenneth J	(949)351-1199	3298 S Patton Ct Denver CO 80236	RM	DPM	Mem C	Peace W Christ Aurora CO	(303)693-5618	IV	2007
Howell Vicki L Stuber	vickihowell67@gmail.com	855 Jefferson St Mondovi WI 54755	NW	Teacher	C07/2016			SP	1992
Hower Carol D Olson	(314)803-0674 chower@prudentialalliance.com	506 Westonridge Ct Wildwood MO 63021	MO	Teacher	EM			RF	1974
Howland Beth M Kalthoff	(602)561-7345 bmhowland@outlook.com	10029 E Alfalfa Dr Florence AZ 85132	PSW	Teacher	EM			IV	2002
Howland Jeri L Just	(818)235-7288 Jeri.l.howland@gmail.com	3740 Diamond Ct Simi Valley CA 93063	PSW	Teacher	C07/2021			IV	2009
Hoy Heather I Hoffman	(331)551-1406 heather.hoy74@gmail.com	2s411 Riverside Ave Warrenville IL 60555	NI	Teacher	Tchr	Walther Melrose Park IL	(708)344-0404	RF	1996
Hoy Lynn C Evans	(815)464-0736 lynn.hoy125@gmail.com	2s411 Riverside Ave Warrenville IL 60555	NI	Teacher	EM			RF	1968
Hoyer Connie A Lathers	(260)755-0739 choyer103@gmail.com	3010 Shelbourne Ct Fort Wayne IN 46825	IN	Teacher	EM			S	1969
Hoyer Dexter C	(260)755-0739 dexhoyer@gmail.com	3010 Shelbourne Ct Fort Wayne IN 46825	IN	Teacher	EM			S	1969
Hoyme Kristie L Jones	Kristie.hoyme@icloud.com	1406 Ripple Creek Rd Dell Rapids SD 57022	SD	Teacher	EM			CQ	2008
Hoyum Jerry L	(309)613-3050 jhoyum@comcast.net	3331 Kleinbrook Way Crandall TX 75114	CI	Teacher	EM			S	1985
Hoyum Lynette M Holtzen	(309)613-3778 jhoyum@comcast.net	3331 Kleinbrook Way Crandall TX 75114	CI	Teacher	EM			S	1981
Hrdlicka Leroy A	(331)551-4807	2s631 Gray Ave Lombard IL 60148	NI	Teacher	EM			RF	1969

*Multiple Assignments (See Church Worker Locator for Additional Details)

See Page 53 for the Table of Abbreviations for key to District, Classification, Position, and College abbreviations.

**C =Candidate; EM =Emeritus; the date following the C is the month and year the Candidate status began

NAME	TELEPHONE NUMBER EMAIL	STREET ADDRESS CITY/STATE/ZIP	DISTRICT	CLASS.	POSITION/ STATUS**	WHERE SERVING	OFFICE PHONE	COLLEGE/ UNIV/CQ	YR GRAD
Hruska Brittany A Feher	(440)346-7584	34676 Plantation Pl N Ridgeville OH 44039	OH	Teacher	Tchr	St Paul Westlake OH	(440)835-3050	RF	2009
Hsu Kan L Deac	(314)600-6572 kanlhsu@gmail.com	434 Shadybrook Dr St Louis MO 63141	MO	Deaconess	Mem C	Immanuel Olivette MO	(314)993-2394	SL-DEAC	2024
Hu Anna Y	(209)371-7162 annacello57@gmail.com	22024 N 59th Dr Glendale AZ 85310	PSW	Teacher	EM			RF	1980
Hua Margaret R Brodhagen	(262)525-8074 huam6010@gmail.com	7710 N Chadwick Rd Milwaukee WI 53217	SW	Teacher	Tchr	Living Word Jackson WI	(262)677-9353	MQ	2015
Huang Cynthia	(415)244-6239 mscynhuang@yahoo.com	61 Bolero Way Daly City CA 94014	CNH	Teacher	Tchr	Hope Daly City CA	(650)991-4673	IV	1998
Hubacek Carol L Jernberg			IN	Teacher	EM			RF	1970
Hubach Amy A Schuster	(208)407-8912	780 Bader Seward NE 68434	NEB	DCE	S HS/C	Concordia University Nebraska Seward NE	(402)643-3651	S	2001
Hubach Marlee A	(208)899-0896 marleehubach@gmail.com	1105 South 3rd Ave Pocatello ID 83201	NOW	Teacher	Tchr	Grace Pocatello ID	(208)237-4142	CQ	2023
Hubach Timothy P	(303)654-8219 myreddirt@aol.com	6554 Sage Ave Firestone CO 80504	RM	Teacher	EM			S	1970
Hubbard Christa E Merz	(804)288-0250 cmhub@hotmail.com	8005 River Rd Richmond VA 23229	SE	Teacher	EM			CQ	2001
Hubbard Terry L	(920)212-0052 tdhubbard49@twc.com	626 Trailview Xing Waterford WI 53185	SW	Teacher	EM			SP	1971
Hubeler Joshua O	jhubeler@lutheranwest.com	4159 W 204th St Cleveland OH 44126	OH	Teacher	Tchr	Cleveland LHS Association Rocky River OH	(440)356-7155	MQ	2002
Hubert Holly M Dr	(815)286-9075 hollyhubert@frontier.com	P.O. Box 300 Hinckley IL 60520	NI	Teacher	EM			CQ	2005
Hublick Angela E Lubbesmeyer Deac	(270)300-3229 ahublick@yahoo.com	451 Charles Crutcher Dr Vine Grove KY 40175	EN	Deaconess	C06/2023			FW-DEAC	2006
Hubmeier Bruce N	(734)552-9076 hubbameister3@hotmail.com	333 Colony Blvd #122 The Villages FL 32162	FG	Teacher	EM			RF	1968
Hubner Patricia J Hellwege	(765)376-1789	10577 W State Road 28 West Lebanon IN 47991	CI	Teacher	EM			S	1967
Hudak Lindsey M Pfanstiel	(618)340-6055 lindsey@stjohnsredbud.org	412 Country Club Dr Red Bud IL 62278	SI	DPM	Mem C	St John Red Bud IL	(618)282-3873	MQ	2008
Hudlin Trevor	(478)841-2468 trevorhudlin427@gmail.com	138 Greison Trl Apt 3209 Newnan GA 30263	FG	DCE	Mem C	St Paul Peachtree City GA	(770)487-0339	IV	2025
Hudnall Gail A Weiss	(480)619-8846 gailhud@gmail.com	7249 W Ring Perch Dr Boise ID 83709	NOW	Teacher	EM			CQ	1984
Hudock Carissa L Schlichtmann	(573)338-2262 CLHudock@gmail.com	11789 Harrow Pl N Royalton OH 44133	OH	Teacher	C06/2020			MQ	2008
Hudson Stephanie E Glanzer	(480)545-9985 ut98az04@yahoo.com	2829 Maryland Circle W Memphis TN 38133	MDS	Teacher	Tchr	Immanuel Memphis TN	(901)388-0205	S	1997
Hudson Tracie L King	(402)741-2305 tlhudson10@gmail.com	6120 Anderson Ave Manhattan KS 66503	KS	Teacher	C07/2016			S	2007
Huebner Kent L	(603)305-6982 huebnerkl@hotmail.com	16 Parkhurst Dr Hudson NH 03051	NE	DCM	Mem C	Grace Nashua NH	(603)888-7579	MQ	1997
Huebner Leland D	(320) 582-0143 lb2huebner@yahoo.com	19456 Cambria Ct. Farmington MN 55024	MNS	Teacher	EM			S	1970
Huebner Todd A	(516)801-3822 toddalan68@hotmail.com	128 Brookville Rd Glen Head NY 11545	AT	Teacher	Tchr	Long Island Brookville NY	(516)626-1735	MQ	1990
Huebschman Raymond R Dr	(402)643-4444 rdhuebschman@hotmail.com	500 Heartland Park Dr Seward NE 68434	NEB	Tch/DCE	EM			S	1963
Huebschman Timothy P	(920)892-6780 thuebschman@sjlplymouth.com	18 Grove St Plymouth WI 53073	SW	Teacher	Mem C	St John Plymouth WI	(920)893-3071	S	1989
Huehn Barbara J	(703)665-6610 bjhueinn@gmail.com	229 Woodmere Dr Unit A Williamsburg VA 23185	SE	Teacher	EM			RF	1974
Huelsman Jenny Z Deac	(402)564-4461 zoehuelsman@gmail.com	1699 June Dr Pittsburgh PA 15209	EN	Deaconess	Mem C	First Trinity Pittsburgh PA	(412)683-4121	SL-DEAC	2023
Huelsnitz Ingrid M Wilson		39510 Reeds Lake Rd Waseca MN 56093	MNS	Teacher	Tchr	Trinity Janesville MN	(507)231-6646	S	1987
Hueske Rebecca L	(303)358-6776 gr8fulheart12@gmail.com	2172 S Zeno St Aurora CO 80013	RM	Teacher	C06/2017			IV	2005
Huesmann Aaron C	(262)685-8777 ahuesmann@centrallutheranschool.org	5777 Ridgeview Dr SW Apt 738 Cedar Rapids IA 52404	IE	Teacher	Tchr	Central Newhall IA	(319)223-5271	S	2021
Huff Bethany M Melcher	(402)304-3352 bethany.huff@gmail.com	5239 Normal Blvd Lincoln NE 68506	NEB	DCE	C07/2016			S	2004
Huff Cathryn	(217)304-5297 cathy.huff@trinityadvancedlearning.org	1616 Skyline Danville IL 61832	CI	Teacher	Tchr	Trinity Danville IL	(217)442-4311	PO	2019
Huff Marcus S	(906)250-7219 marcus@copperluth.org	1010 4th St Hancock MI 49930	NW	DCO	Mem C	SS Peter and Paul Houghton MI	(906)482-4750	SP	2007
Huffman Elizabeth K Engelage	(618)343-1841 bhuffm@zionbethalto.org	6362 Oak Dr Moro IL 62067	SI	Teacher	Tchr	Zion Bethalto IL	(618)377-5507	RF	1994
Hufford Amy J Hepburn	cupohuff@gmail.com	1n138 Darling St Carol Stream IL 60188	NI	Teacher	Tchr	St John's Lombard IL	(630)932-3196	RF	1990
Hughes Donita G	(801)231-3411 donita.hughes@cune.org	1119 Ward Dr Greeley CO 80634	RM	Teacher	EM			S	1973
Hughes Jenny R Lucas	(714)351-3558 hughes.jennyr@gmail.com	684 N Lemon Hill Trl Orange CA 92869	PSW	Teacher	Tchr	Christ Brea CA	(714)529-2984	IV	1999
Hughes Kathryn M Asmus	(757)375-7728 k708hughes@gmail.com	506 Long Pt Chesapeake VA 23322	NE	Teacher	C07/2016			S	1990
Hughes Kimberly E Mitchell	(262)780-1044 hywelk@gmail.com	12850 W Balboa Dr New Berlin WI 53151	SW	Teacher	Tchr	Concordia Sturtevant WI	(262)884-0991	MQ	1986

*Multiple Assignments (See Church Worker Locator for Additional Details)

See Page 53 for the Table of Abbreviations for key to District, Classification, Position, and College abbreviations.

**C =Candidate; EM =Emeritus; the date following the C is the month and year the Candidate status began

NAME	TELEPHONE NUMBER EMAIL	STREET ADDRESS CITY/STATE/ZIP	DISTRICT	CLASS.	POSITION/ STATUS**	WHERE SERVING	OFFICE PHONE	COLLEGE/ UNIV/CQ	YR GRAD
Hughes Kristina A Hein	(573)544-7221 khughes@trinityjc.org	3209 Cassidy Rd Jefferson City MO 65101	MO	Teacher	Tchr	Trinity Jefferson City MO	(573)636-6750	CQ	2020
Hugo Donald G	(636)441-9954 dhugo46@yahoo.com	2 River Trl Saint Charles MO 63303	MO	Teacher	Mem C	Zion Saint Charles MO	(636)441-7425	RF	1967
Huie Katharine L Wahrle	(847)917-9013 huiek526@gmail.com	4019 Brunswick Ln Janesville WI 53546	SW	Teacher	Tchr	St Pauls Janesville WI	(608)754-4471	MQ	2008
Hulke Andrew J	(906)869-7550 andhulke@gmail.com	3107 Caleb Dr Weston WI 54476	NW	Teacher	Prin	Trinity Wausau WI	(715)848-0166	MQ	2009
Hull Mika A Patron Deac	(316)284-4251 deaconessmika@gmail.com		MI	Deaconess	C08/2024			FW-DEAC	2020
Hull Misti J Shafer	mistijhull@gmail.com		MO	Teacher	C06/2021			S	2006
Hull Renee N Rousselo	(708)261-5967 reneehull1@gmail.com	15456 Alameda Ave Oak Forest IL 60452	NI	Teacher	EM			RF	1982
Hulshof Valarie J Eilert-Johnson	(618)210-3768 valarie.hulshof@gmail.com	782 County Highway 311 Scott City MO 63780	MO	Teacher	C07/2016			S	2002
Hulvey Courtney K Eaton	(360)904-3584 courtney.hulvey@gmail.com	23808 112th Ave SE Kent WA 98031	NOW	Teacher	Tchr	Sunbeams Kent WA	(253)854-3240	PO	2009
Hulvey Jacqulyn J Trulove	(269)277-3907	8511 W 3rd Ave Kennewick WA 99336	NOW	Teacher	C08/2020			CH	2010
Humphrey Roxane M Gernant	(308)631-8241 roxanehumphrey@yahoo.com	2311 Stone St Falls City NE 68355	NEB	Teacher	EM			SP	1992
Hundertmark Jennifer L	(772)342-8117 jen100mark@gmail.com	894 Nettles Blvd Jensen Beach FL 34957	FG	Teacher	Tchr	Redeemer Stuart FL	(772)286-0932	BR	2017
Hunsley Diane S Weidler	(217) 737-5962 m.hunsley@comcast.net	1281 Richland Ave Lincoln IL 62656	CI	Teacher	Tchr	Zion Lincoln IL	(217)732-3946	RF	1984
Hunt Barbara N Nichols	(636)485-9004 bhunt@kokstl.org	2 Berkshire Ct Saint Charles MO 63301	MO	Teacher	Tchr	King Of Kings Chesterfield MO	(314)469-2224	CQ	2018
Hunt Edith J Janetzke	(580)765-9872 ehunt@poncacity.net	5250 N Union St Ponca City OK 74601	OK	Teacher	EM			S	1967
Hunt G Warren	(636)633-0507 whunt@sjlsarnold.org	2012 Elephant Walk Imperial MO 63052	MO	Teacher	Tchr	St John Arnold MO	(636)464-7303	RF	1993
Hunt Lindsay A Bartling	(402)719-4122 lindsayhunt2016@gmail.com	13400 Briarwick Dr Unit 303 Austin TX 78729	TX	Teacher	C06/2018			S	2011
Hunt Megan J	(260)760-9474 mhunt@clscubs.org	5132 Truemper Way Apt 6 Fort Wayne IN 46835	IN	Teacher	Tchr	Concordia Fort Wayne IN	(260)426-9922	CH	2008
Huntington Jeffrey D	(317)506-2880 jhuntington@stjohnindy.org	1312 Freemont Ln Greenwood IN 46143	IN	Teacher	Prin	St John Indianapolis IN	(317)352-9196	MQ	1997
Huntington Leslie A Moeller	(317)506-2245 lhuntin1@insightbb.com	1312 Freemont Ln Greenwood IN 46143	IN	Teacher	Tchr	Calvary Indianapolis IN	(317)783-2000	MQ	1997
Huonder Matthew T	(651)341-6842 mhuonder1@yahoo.com	545 Patton Drive Buffalo Grove IL 60089	NI	Teacher	C01/2022			CQ	2014
Hurd Loraine K Einspahr	(989)751-8823 lowraine48602@hotmail.com	203 S Andre St Saginaw MI 48602	MI	Teacher	EM			S	1970
Hurst James W	(440)842-8332 jndhurst@juno.com	34421 Bainbridge Rd North Ridgeville OH 44039	S	Teacher	Mem C	Calvary Parma OH	(440)845-0070	RF	1990
Hurst Nancy L Weber	(806)359-3731 nhurst@trinitylutheranschool.org	6101 Calumet Rd Amarillo TX 79106	TX	Teacher	Tchr	Trinity Amarillo TX	(806)352-5620	S	1987
Huscher Christian F		6580 Windmill Dr College Grove TN 37046	PSW	Teacher		Pacific Southwest District Irvine CA	(949)854-3232	IV	1985
Huse Daniel L	(815) 383-2940 dhuse@stpaulspk8.org	1061 E 1400 North Rd Onarga IL 60955	CI	Teacher	Tchr	St Paul Milford IL	(815)889-4209	CQ	2010
Huske Michele L	(847)345-7910 mhuske@sjlindy.org	5516 Ashview Dr #g Indianapolis IN 46237	IN	Teacher	Tchr	St John Indianapolis IN	(317)352-9196	RF	1993
Hussey Samantha N Stubblefield	(314)346-1966 shussey@ccls-stlouis.org	1081 Sandfort Farm Dr Saint Charles MO 63301	MO	Teacher	Tchr	Christ Community Kirkwood MO	(314)822-7774	CQ	2021
Hussong Andrea D Koenig	(563)441-0023 andrea.hussong@trinitydavenport.org	209 Northbrook Ct Davenport IA 52806	IE	Teacher	Tchr	Trinity Davenport IA	(563)322-5224	RF	1997
Huster Brenda K Palisch	(314)221-8047 brenda.huster@greenparklutheranschool.org		MO	Teacher	Tchr	Green Park Saint Louis MO	(314)544-4248	CQ	2015
Huster Scott A	(636)219-4633 thehusters@hotmail.com	2218 Zumbehl Rd. Saint Charles MO 63301	MO	Teacher	Prin	Immanuel Saint Charles MO	(636)946-2656	MQ	2002
Huston Allison N Westrem	(260)797-3795 ahuston@cluth.org	8711 Amberly Dr New Haven IN 46774	IN	Teacher	Tchr	Central New Haven IN	(260)493-2502	RF	2003
Huth Daniel R	(317)372-1160 daniel.r.huth@gmail.com	1107 Brighton Lake Rd Brighton MI 48116	MI	DCE	C12/2020			S	2011
Hutton William P	(507)202-6740 huttonb1959@gmail.com	1900 Lakeview Ct SW #202 Rochester MN 55902	MNS	Teacher	C07/2016			RF	1983
Huwyler Suzanne Carrotte	(281)799-0766 huwylers@yahoo.com	11215 N Country Club Green Dr Tomball TX 77375	TX	Teacher	EM			CQ	2003
Hwang Krista R Wille	(303)795-9368 techrkris@juno.com	1021 Willow Pl Louisville CO 80027	RM	Teacher	C07/2016			RF	2000
Hylton Holly L Eads	(206)714-1017 hollyleaf73@gmail.com	10612 19th Ave S Seattle WA 98168	NOW	Teacher	Tchr	Concordia Seattle WA	(206)525-7407	PO	1995
Hynous Terry A	(281)610-4672 thynous@hotmail.com	17 N Mossrock Rd The Woodlands TX 77380	TX	Teacher	EM			RF	1965
Hyslop Dora J Pingel	(989)860-0706 dorahyslop@gmail.com	9527 Highland View Dr Dallas TX 75238	TX	Teacher	Tchr	Zion Dallas TX	(214)363-1630	RF	1991
Hyslop Scott M Dr	(989)860-7846 Shyslop61@gmail.com	9527 Highland View Dr Dallas TX 75238	TX	DPM	Mem C	Zion Dallas TX	(214)363-1639	CQ	2006
Iannucelli Anna E Regan	(216)408-6653 aregan130@gmail.com	1010a Commodore Drive Saint Louis MO 63117	MO	Teacher	Tchr	Immanuel Olivette MO	(314)993-2394	MQ	2022
Ibe Scott W	(309)696-3555 scott.ibe@comcast.net	6714 N Talisman Ter Peoria IL 61615	CI	Teacher	Mem C	Redeemer Peoria IL	(309)691-2333	RF	1985

*Multiple Assignments (See Church Worker Locator for Additional Details)

See Page 53 for the Table of Abbreviations for key to District, Classification, Position, and College abbreviations.

**C =Candidate; EM =Emeritus; the date following the C is the month and year the Candidate status began

NAME	TELEPHONE NUMBER EMAIL	STREET ADDRESS CITY/STATE/ZIP	DISTRICT	CLASS.	POSITION/ STATUS**	WHERE SERVING	OFFICE PHONE	COLLEGE/ UNIV/CQ	YR GRAD
Ickstadt Kathleen L Moehrke	(219)395-6946 kickstadt@yahoo.com	1280 Golf View Dr Mondovi WI 54755	NW	Teacher	EM			RF	1982
Ickstadt William M	(219)395-6708 wickstadt@yahoo.com	1280 Golf View Dr Mondovi WI 54755	NW	Teacher	EM			RF	1981
Iehl Sandra S Goldsmith	(618)344-3216 iehlstamp@aol.com	138 Helen Pl Collinsville IL 62234	SI	Teacher	EM			CQ	1988
Ihssen Timothy C	tim.ihssen@gmail.com	1314 Berkeley Ave Fircrest WA 98466	NOW	DCE	C07/2016			PO	1992
Ihssen William F	(260)447-0227 bihssen@frontier.com	6723 S Anthony Blvd Apt E235 Fort Wayne IN 46816	IN	Teacher	EM			CQ	1969
Iliff Melissa L	(989)482-5267 melissa.iliff@hcls.org	1695 Seminole Ln Saginaw MI 48638	MI	Teacher	Tchr	Holy Cross Saginaw MI	(989)793-9795	CQ	2024
Illich Seth K	(815)236-9502 seth.illich@gmail.com	112 Prairie Song Ln Liberty Hill TX 78642	TX	DCE	C08/2025			Other	2012
Imes Kim R	(562)209-6782 skeeter321@gmail.com	1601 Pontontoc Trace #b Harker Heights TX 76548	PSW	Teacher	EM			RF	1978
Incitti Hannah M Shockey	(612)799-1237 hincitti@gmail.com	4910 Kirkwood Ln N Plymouth MN 55442	MNS	Teacher	Tchr	King Of Kings Roseville MN	(651)484-9206	MQ	2012
Inglehart Jana D Miller	(402)340-8544 jana.inglehart@lcmsintl.org	601 E Park Ave Norfolk NE 68701	NEB	Teacher	S Miss	Office of International Mission Saint Louis MO		CQ	2001
Ingram Nancy L House	ningram@flsplano.org		TX	Teacher	Tchr	Faith Plano TX	(972)423-7447	AU	1985
Ingwersen David J	(815)271-2560 dingwersen@juno.com	8542 Russell St Overland Park MO 66212	PSW	Tch/DCE	EM			SP	1975
Innes Kacie A Kacie Krause	(979)540-7445 kacie.krause12@gmail.com		TX	Teacher	Tchr	Prince Of Peace Carrollton TX	(972)447-0532	AU	2012
Inselmann Cynthia L Ellig Deac	(763)355-9559 cindyi@gvlc.net	12710 Oakhill Trl Dayton MN 55327	MNS	Deaconess	Mem C	Golden Valley Golden Valley MN	(763)544-2810	FW-DEAC	2011
Ipatenco Sara B Mallory	(720)308-9126 sipatenco@bethlehemdenver.com	11075 W 54th Ln Arvada CO 80002	RM	Teacher	Tchr	Bethlehem Lakewood CO	(303)238-7676	CQ	2016
Irish Christopher D	(262)783-9921	674 Petunia St Oconomowoc WI 53066	SW	Teacher	Tchr	Lake Country Hartland WI	(262)367-8600	MQ	2004
Irish Joy C Smith	(863)858-7191 jirish@stpaullakeland.org	8529 Indian Ridge Trl Lakeland FL 33810	FG	Teacher	Tchr	St Paul Lakeland FL	(863)644-7710	CQ	2007
Irish Mary E Rotermund	(262)894-1623 mary.irish721@gmail.com	1623 Switchgrass St Oconomowoc WI 53066	SW	Teacher	Tchr	Wauwatosa Wauwatosa WI	(414)258-4558	RF	1975
Irwin David W	(417)887-6252 ddirwin@sbcglobal.net	4834 S Ridgecrest Dr Springfield MO 65810	MO	Teacher	EM			S	1971
Irwin Deborah A Frese	(417)887-6252 ddirwin@sbcglobal.net	4834 S Ridgecrest Dr Springfield MO 65810	MO	Teacher	EM			S	1971
Irwin Jessica M	jirwin@firstlutheranschool.com	1616 Jefferson Ave Knoxville TN 37917	MDS	Teacher	Prin	First Knoxville TN	(865)524-0308	Other	2009
Irwin Kay M Nitschke	(865)274-1058 kmirwin@att.net	137 County Road 604 Athens TN 37303	MDS	Teacher	EM			RF	1980
Isbell Robert		4601 Spanish Oak Rd Temple TX 76502	TX	Teacher	Tchr	Prince Peace Carrollton TX	(972)447-9887	CQ	2000
Iteen Barbara S Ebe	(231)907-7177 babsiteen@sbcglobal.net	804 E Ludington Ave Ludington MI 49431	NI	Teacher	EM			RF	2002
Itzcovitch May Deac	(773)809-0477 itzcovitchm@gmail.com	4301 16th N St Petersburg FL 33703	FG	Deaconess	Mem C	Grace Saint Petersburg FL	(727)527-6213	FW-DEAC	2023
Iverson Jena L Boltmann	(320)282-1340 djiverson94@gmail.com	1045 Glen Echo Rd Winona MN 55987	MNS	Teacher	Tchr	St Martin Winona MN	(507)452-6928	MQ	1990
Ivie Angela M Weinhold	(816)633-2663 aivie@splhs.org	401 S. Bismark St. Concordia MO 64020	MO	Teacher	Tchr	Saint Paul Concordia MO	(660)463-2238	S	2009
Iwabuchi Amanda C Domel	(512)573-0931 amanda.iwabuchi@gmail.com		TX	Teacher	Tchr	Redeemer Austin TX	(512)459-1500	AU	2008
Jablinski Olivia D	(214)298-7148 olivia.jablinski@gmail.com	312 Apache Trl Apt. 121 Murphy TX 75094	TX	DCE	Mem C	Our Savior McKinney TX	(972)562-9944	AU	2013
Jabs David P	(216)339-9454 djabs@lutheraneast.org	1772 Donwell Dr South Euclid OH 44121	OH	Teacher	Tchr	Cleveland LHS Association Rocky River OH	(440)356-7155	S	2008
Jabs Joan I Goethke	(920)889-1032 jigjabs@gmail.com	2408 Poch Ave Plymouth WI 53073	SW	Teacher	EM			SP	1976
Jabs Rebecca J	(443)844-6321 rebeccajabs@gmail.com	4516 Birchwold Rd Cleveland OH 44121	OH	Teacher	Tchr	Lutheran West* Rocky River OH	(440)333-1660	S	2004
Jack Elizabeth J Dettmer	(812)390-2433 ejjack@att.net	14000 W Cedar Tree Dr Lot 83 Seymour IN 47274	IN	Teacher	EM			AA	1971
Jackemeyer Sarah	(269)431-0028 sarahmjack00@gmail.com	12197 Hills Rd Buchanan MI 49107	MI	Teacher	Tchr	Trinity Berrien Springs MI	(269)473-1811	AA	2022
Jacklin Robert M	(636)699-6566 rjacklin@lncrusaders.org	1010 Hollybend Dr Ballwin MO 63021	MO	Teacher	Tchr	Lutheran North Saint Louis MO	(314)389-3100	RF	1998
Jackson Aaron N	(903)724-2800 rlcmhmusic@gmail.com	1705 Honeysuckle Mountain Home AR 72653	MDS	DPM	Mem C	Redeemer Mountain Home AR	(870)425-6071	S	2021
Jackson Danielle R	(414)614-3264 ms.jackson044@gmail.com	3434 S 63rd St Milwaukee WI 53219	SW	Teacher	Prin	St Pauls West Allis WI	(414)541-6251	CQ	2013
Jackson Karin K Johnson	(414)416-0908 angelk65@msn.com	1921 Daisy Dr West Bend WI 53090	SW	Teacher	Tchr	St John Random Lake WI	(920)994-9190	MQ	1987
Jackson Kirsten R Howard	(920)254-6897 kirsten.howard@cuw.edu	29660 Tobaben Rd Cole Camp MO 65325	MO	Teacher	Tchr	Luth School Assoc Cole Camp MO	(660)668-4614	MQ	2011
Jackson Kristen M Nagy	(734)341-0320 kmj1206@gmail.com	4497 Colf Rd Carleton MI 48117	MI	Teacher	EM			AA	1991
Jackson Linda J Roenfeldt	(314)843-3224 ljjackson@mindspring.com	10761 Willinda Dr Saint Louis MO 63123	MO	Teacher	Tchr	St Pauls Des Peres MO	(314)822-9219	S	1985
Jackson Rhonda L Schultz	(985)276-4017 rhonjack@bellsouth.net	2644 W 15th Ave Covington LA 70433	SO	Teacher	EM			S	1974

*Multiple Assignments (See Church Worker Locator for Additional Details)
See Page 53 for the Table of Abbreviations for key to District, Classification, Position, and College abbreviations.
**C =Candidate; EM =Emeritus; the date following the C is the month and year the Candidate status began

NAME	TELEPHONE NUMBER EMAIL	STREET ADDRESS CITY/STATE/ZIP	DISTRICT	CLASS.	POSITION/ STATUS**	WHERE SERVING	OFFICE PHONE	COLLEGE/ UNIV/CQ	YR GRAD
Jackson Teri L Sievers	(414)375-4862 tjackson@fls.org	10480 Highlawn Ct Cedarburg WI 53012	SW	Teacher	Tchr	First Immanuel Cedarburg WI	(262)377-6610	MQ	1985
Jacob Dorothea B	(346)236-9250 blacksmith.shop@att.net	8742 Fairbend St Houston TX 77055	TX	Teacher	EM			RF	1957
Jacob Frederick R	(415)290-4072 sfjacob@att.net	1249 16th Ave Apt 6 San Francisco CA 94122	EN	Teacher	EM			IV	1987
Jacob John R	(309)219-6153 jjacob733@gmail.com	350 Dufelmeier Rd Groveland IL 61535	CI	Teacher	EM			RF	1987
Jacob Karen L Badertscher	(503) 815-1818 istuck@gmail.com	4050 Reaves Rd Kissimmee FL 34746	CNH	DCE	C07/2016			PO	1997
Jacob Sierra D	(402)922-1680 sjacob@flsweb.org		MNS	Teacher	Tchr	Faribault Faribault MN	(507)334-7982	S	2019
Jacobs Erika A Stein	(608)289-7507 eajacobs3@yahoo.com	12 Knightsbridge Way Stafford VA 22554	SE	Teacher	C07/2016			MQ	2004
Jacobs Louise C Rogers	(801)942-6081 2lcjacobs@gmail.com	8717 S Sugarloaf Dr Sandy UT 84093	RM	Teacher	EM			CQ	2005
Jacobs Robert J	(317)402-6883 coachjacobs1972@gmail.com	1480 Queensborough Drive Carmel IN 46033	IN	Teacher	C09/2023			CQ	2014
Jacobsen JoAn R Bethke	(660)463-0166 jcjacobsen@hotmail.com	301 S Sandia St Concordia MO 64020	MO	Teacher	EM			S	1964
Jacobsen John C	(660)463-0166 jcjacobsen@hotmail.com	301 S Sandia St Concordia MO 64020	MO	Teacher	EM			S	1965
Jacobsen Lynne M Weideman	(608)335-8712 polishnorske@gmail.com	1107 Morningside Dr Janesville WI 53546	SW	Teacher	EM			RF	1977
Jacobson Christopher R	(507)313-2716 chrisjacobson18@yahoo.com	150 Bluffview Dr Winona MN 55987	MNS	Teacher	C06/2025			CQ	2018
Jacobson Kay A Yagow	(352)638-2528 kayalene43@gmail.com	1728 Mountville Ct The Villages FL 32162	FG	Teacher	EM			RF	1966
Jacoby Douglas J	(920)889-7737 dougjacoby26@gmail.com	22 Hillside Cir Fond Du Lac WI 54937	NW	Teacher	C11/2023			MQ	1987
Jacoby Kristina L Jones	(262)492-0979 kristina.jacoby@cuw.edu	N239 County Road Cc Random Lake WI 53075	SW	Teacher	S HS/C	Concordia University Wisconsin Mequon WI	(262)243-5700	MQ	2004
Jacques Krista E Pfeiffer	(586)598-0498 timothy_jacques@comcast.net	49161 Morning Glory Dr Macomb MI 48044	MI	Teacher	EM			RF	1982
Jaech Renata A	(253)475-2654 renjaech@netzero.com	7368 S Alaska St Tacoma WA 98408	NOW	Teacher	C07/2016			PO	1989
Jaeger Christine R Young	(702)516-4806 jaegerc@lambofgodlv.com	9001 Tumblewood Ave Las Vegas NV 89143	PSW	Teacher	Tchr	Lamb Of God Las Vegas NV	(702)645-4998	MQ	1989
Jaeger Jessica	(714)403-8481 jessica.jaeger@creanlutheran.org	201 Follyhatch Irvine CA 92618	PSW	Teacher	Tchr	Crean Irvine CA	(949)387-1199	CQ	2024
Jaeger Lisa M Grabowski			FG	Teacher	C08/2025			CQ	2013
Jaeger Lori A Utke	(714)852-7996 tllm.jaeger@cox.net	43 Sorenson Irvine CA 92602	PSW	Teacher	S HS/C	Concordia University Irvine Irvine CA	(949)854-8002	RF	1986
Jaeger Timothy P	(714)838-5620 tim.jaeger@cui.edu	43 Sorenson Irvine CA 92602	PSW	Tch/DCE	S HS/C	Concordia University Irvine Irvine CA	(949)854-8002	RF	1986
Jagiello Kaitlin M Grott	(765)491-4031 kaitlin.jagiello@gmail.com	206 E Lakeside Dr Vernon Hills IL 60061	NI	Teacher	Tchr	St Peter Arlington Heights IL	(847)259-4114	MQ	2012
Jagler Kyle K	(920)207-9022 jaglerk@gmail.com	W173N8477 Robert Ave Menomonee Fls WI 53051	SW	Teacher	Tchr	Immanuel Brookfield WI	(262)781-7140	MQ	2006
Jagoda Pamela J Schramm Mendieta	(586)206-2464 pjagoda@lhsa.com	58396 Broughton Rd Ray MI 48096	MI	Teacher	Tchr	LHS Assn Of Greater Detroit Rochester Hls MI	(248)856-0240	RF	1988
Jahnke Amanda A Cone	ajahnkedce@gmail.com		SE	DCE	Tchr	Concordia Towson MD	(410)825-2323	SP	2012
Jahnke Danielle K Danielle Harstad	(507)273-7436 daniellejahnke2@gmail.com	1206 Ridgeview Ter NE Alexandria MN 56308	MO	Teacher	C07/2020			S	2017
Jahnke Jane A Pedersen	(414)241-9936 jajahnke34@gmail.com	15809 Brookshire Dr Urbandale IA 50323	IW	Teacher	EM			CQ	1991
Jahnke Lisa K Turner	(989)860-8118 lisa.jahnke1@gmail.com	7867 Teaberry Dr Freeland MI 48623	MI	Teacher	Tchr	Holy Cross Saginaw MI	(989)793-9723	CQ	2016
Jahnke Nancy M Netherton	(630)667-7563 jahnke_nancy@yahoo.com	601 Pleasant Dr Shorewood IL 60404	NI	Teacher	EM			CQ	2000
Jahnke Philip C	(763)568-4406 pjahnke34@gmail.com	12021 Belair Rd Kingsville MD 21087	SE	Teacher	Tchr	Concordia Towson MD	(410)825-2323	SP	2012
Jahnke Steven M	(512)825-1085 steven.jahnke@upbring.org	1431 Thibodeaux Dr Round Rock TX 78664	TX	Teacher	RSO	Luth Social Services South Inc Austin TX	(512)459-1000	AU	1995
Jahnke Susan R Uran	(701)281-9367 principal@glsfargo.org	325 Cherry Ct West Fargo ND 58078	ND	Teacher	Prin	Grace Fargo ND	(701)232-7747	SP	1986
Jahns Sandra E	(414)737-0054 sandra.jahns@cuw.edu	6704 Dellrose Ct Greendale WI 53129	EN	Teacher	S HS/C	Concordia University Wisconsin Mequon WI	(262)243-5700	CQ	2019
Jahr Rebecca J	rebecca.jahr@cune.org	1110 Lynde Dr NE Minneapolis MN 55432	MNS	Teacher	Tchr	King Of Kings Roseville MN	(651)484-9206	S	2014
Jakubs Alison J Schmidt	(517)214-6587 alisonjakubs@gmail.com	4022 Pearl St. Bridgman MI 49106	MI	Teacher	Tchr	Trinity Saint Joseph MI	(269)983-5000	AA	2015
James Levana L Gilmore	(501)553-1846 levanajames32@gmail.com	123 NW Canton St John Day OR 97845	SO	Teacher	C08/2018			MQ	2005
James Marjorie A Seeton	(330)492-4742 marjorie@neo.rr.com	3935 Logan Ave NW Canton OH 44709	OH	Teacher	EM			CQ	2011
James Patricia R	(219)493-7910	9051 Earlmont Dr Fort Wayne IN 46835	IN	Teacher	EM			S	1973
James Rachel L Paul	(414)232-8903 jamesr@calvarylhs.org	2 Coverdale Pl. Fort Wayne IN 46825	IN	Teacher	C05/2020			MQ	2019
Jamison Beverly S Friedrichs	(816)560-9140 bng_1989@hotmail.com	7702 Crescent Avenue Raytown MO 64138	MO	Teacher	EM			S	1980

*Multiple Assignments (See Church Worker Locator for Additional Details)

See Page 53 for the Table of Abbreviations for key to District, Classification, Position, and College abbreviations.

**C =Candidate; EM =Emeritus; the date following the C is the month and year the Candidate status began

NAME	TELEPHONE NUMBER EMAIL	STREET ADDRESS CITY/STATE/ZIP	DISTRICT	CLASS.	POSITION/ STATUS**	WHERE SERVING	OFFICE PHONE	COLLEGE/ UNIV/CQ	YR GRAD
Jammer Bonnie M	(989)600-0500 bjammer1957@hotmail.com	1760 11 Mile Rd Auburn MI 48611	MI	Teacher	EM			S	1979
Janda Sarah E Dagel	(320)493-4214 sjanda35@gmail.com	5301 Oregon Ave N New Hope MN 55428	MNS	Teacher	Tchr	Redeemer Wayzata MN	(952)473-5356	MQ	2009
Jander Louis C Dr	(512)629-7907 ljander@crownpnt.org	142 Ahrens Ave Brenham TX 77833	TX	Tch/DCE	EM			S	1966
Jander Martha S Streufert	(512)629-7269 mjander@crownpnt.org	142 Ahrens Ave Brenham TX 77833	TX	Teacher	EM			RF	1966
Janetzke Bruce D	(720)812-2142 brucenmary2@comcast.net	4714 Mulberry St Woodward OK 73801	OK	Teacher	EM			RF	1965
Janetzke Chad D	(281)620-5512 cjanetzke@martinlutherhs.org	6547 W Euclid Ave Milwaukee WI 53219	SW	Teacher	Tchr	LHS Assn of Greater Milwaukee West Allis WI	(414)421-9100	MQ	2003
Janetzke Emily L Bluege	(989)980-0005 emilyj529@yahoo.com	136 Seminole Dr Springfield IL 62704	CI	Teacher	C07/2016			RF	2004
Janetzke Erin E Heffelfinger	(281)620-5667 ejanetzke@yahoo.com	6547 W Euclid Ave Milwaukee WI 53219	SW	Teacher	Tchr	Martin Luther Greendale WI	(414)421-4000	RF	2002
Janetzke Gary A	(414)839-9458 gjanetzke@sbcglobal.net	W156 N11983 Pilgrim Rd Germantown WI 53022	PSW	Tch/DCE	EM			RF	1974
Janetzke Kari A Jensen	(309)696-0354 kajanetzke@gmail.com	968 Creekside Cir Naperville IL 60563	NI	Teacher	Tchr	Bethany Naperville IL	(630)355-6607	CH	2006
Janetzke Kristen S Billig	kjanetzke@stjohnrochester.org	1251 Washington Rd. Rochester Hills MI 48306	MI	Teacher	Tchr	St John Rochester MI	(248)402-8000	AA	1993
Janisko David A	hjanisko@gmail.com	68 Greene St Taylorsville NC 28681	SE	Teacher	EM			RF	1963
Jank Rachel M Mol	(402)570-5618 rachelmmol@gmail.com	1129 Plainview Ave Seward NE 68434	NEB	Teacher	Tchr	St John Seward NE	(402)643-4535	S	2009
Jank Timothy A	mwondering@gmail.com	307 Caperiole Pl Fort Wayne IN 46825	IN	DCE	Mem C	Sub Bethlehem Fort Wayne IN	(260)484-7873	S	1991
Janko Dennis L		2 Honeysuckel Ct Georgetown DE 19947	SE	Teacher	EM			RF	1960
Jankowski Nancy J Passarelli	(949)293-9681 jankowski@hopelutheran.org	7323 Park Street Shawnee KS 66216	KS	Teacher	Prin	Hope Shawnee KS	(913)631-6940	S	2000
Janousek Jennifer J Hellbusch Dr	(402)499-3512 jen.janousek@cune.edu	101 Goldenrod Ln Seward NE 68434	NEB	Teacher	S HS/C	Concordia University Nebraska Seward NE	(402)643-3651	CQ	2025
Jansen Aaron P	(301)865-5068 KantorAaron@stpaulsfallschurch.org	12403 Catoctin View Dr Mount Airy MD 21771	SE	DPM	Mem C	St Paul Falls Church VA	(703)573-0295	CQ	2011
Jansen Glory K Krause	(262)391-9283 gloryalleluia2002@yahoo.com	4091 W Menomonee Fls WI 53051	SW	Teacher	Tchr	Grace Menomonee Falls WI	(262)251-7140	MQ	2002
Jansen Mari-Beth Ingalls	(616)818-5885 Mbteachr@gmail.com	1621 Cambridge Dr SE Grand Rapids MI 49506	MI	Teacher	EM			RF	1982
Janson Jennifer M Smith	(989)980-1801 jennifermsmith14@gmail.com	9435 W Sanilac Rd Reese MI 48757	MI	Teacher	Tchr	St Michaels Richville MI	(989)868-4809	AA	2020
Janssen Frances A Torresdal	(530)722-0320 farjnsn@charter.net	2100 Deerfield Ave Redding CA 96002	CNH	Teacher	EM			CQ	1986
Janssen Gerald H	(530)605-0407 jerryjanssen64@yahoo.com	2491 Maywood Ln Redding CA 96003	CNH	Teacher	EM			RF	1959
Janssen Matthew C	(815)325-4940 matthewcjanssen@gmail.com	11106 Wedgestone Ct Saint Louis MO 63126	MO	Teacher	Mem C	Hope Saint Louis MO	(314)352-0014	S	2003
Janssen Richard W	(618)826-2683 richardjnssn@yahoo.com	518 W German St Chester IL 62233	SI	Teacher	EM			S	1967
Janssen Sharon R Krug	(217)287-1086 ejanssen@chipsnet.com	335 N 1250 East Rd Morrisonville IL 62546	CI	Teacher	Tchr	Trinity Taylorville IL	(217)824-8148	CQ	1993
Janus Lisa A Plopper	(920)296-4799 lisa.janus22@gmail.com	4435 Birdie Cir Slinger WI 53086	SW	Teacher	Tchr	St Stephen Horicon WI	(920)485-6687	MQ	1986
Janzen Gayle M Bartel	(920)889-8987 jesus_died4you2@yahoo.com	2305 Saddle Back Ct Fort Lupton CO 80621	RM	DCE	EM			RF	1974
Jardim Susan J Horn	(818)429-1459 susan.jardim38@gmail.com	17205 Donmetz St Granada Hills CA 91344	PSW	Teacher	Tchr	Our Redeemer Winnetka CA	(818)341-3460	CQ	1995
Jaremba Marcia S Sonnenberg	(810)655-8898	4347 Grand Blanc Rd Swartz Creek MI 48473	MI	Teacher	EM			AA	1976
Jareske Derek J	(402)369-1555 dejare01@icloud.com	804 Walnut Dr Wayne NE 68787	NEB	DCE	Mem C	Zion Pierce NE	(402)329-4313	IV	2022
Jarocki Jennifer A	(701)367-9466 jenniferjarocki625@gmail.com	22481 Canova Ct Farmington MN 55024	MNS	Teacher	C08/2025			CQ	2018
Jarocki Karen K Hansen	(928)342-9466 kkjarocki@hotmail.com	7887 E 37th St Yuma AZ 85365	PSW	Teacher	Tchr	Christ Yuma AZ	(928)726-0773	S	1980
Jaseph Rachel E Powell Deac	(443)454-1931 rachel.jaseph@gmail.com	1053 Cayer Dr Glen Burnie MD 21061	SE	Deaconess	C01/2024			CH	2014
Jasion Tina G	(410)557-7855 tjasion1@gmail.com	2501 Derby Dr Fallston MD 21047	SE	DCO	RSO	Lutheran Mission Society of MD Linthicum MD	(410)636-0123	CQ	2006
Jaster Emily C Kramer	(816)810-0228	1127 Whittier St Apt 7 Emporia KS 66801	KS	Teacher	C07/2016			S	2003
Jauss Lanett S Blunk Dr	(660)422-1298 marklanettjauss@gmail.com	59679 Walnut Pl New London MO 63459	CI	Teacher	EM			S	1980
Jean-Marcoux Mackenzie T	mjean@immanuelvalpo.org	1700 Monticello Park Dr Valparaiso IN 46383	IN	DCE	Mem C	Immanuel Valparaiso IN	(219)462-8207	CH	2024
Jedele Pauline A Schlichting	(620)440-1136 annchuck2000@yahoo.com	10819 W. Kent St Wichita KS 67209	KS	Teacher	EM			WN	1956
Jefferies Dorothy R Dyer	(720)876-1776 dottiejeff@msn.com	200 Glenwood Cir Apt 303 Monterey CA 93940	RM	Teacher	EM			CQ	1999
Jeffers Debra W Windle	(281)705-1746 debbie.jeffers@comcast.net	12871 Westleigh Dr Houston TX 77077	TX	Teacher	Tchr	Memorial Houston TX	(713)782-4022	CQ	2007

*Multiple Assignments (See Church Worker Locator for Additional Details)
See Page 53 for the Table of Abbreviations for key to District, Classification, Position, and College abbreviations.
**C =Candidate; EM =Emeritus; the date following the C is the month and year the Candidate status began

NAME	TELEPHONE NUMBER EMAIL	STREET ADDRESS CITY/STATE/ZIP	DISTRICT	CLASS.	POSITION/ STATUS**	WHERE SERVING	OFFICE PHONE	COLLEGE/ UNIV/CQ	YR GRAD
Jelneck Ruth A Seidel	(219)942-2522 raj32@comcast.net	909 E 8th St Hobart IN 46342	IN	Teacher	Mem C	Trinity Hobart IN	(219)942-2589	SP	1974
Jenkins Jessica R Werner	(602)653-5505 jessica.jenkins@lutheransouth.org	16731 Bending Creek Ln Friendswood TX 77546	TX	Teacher	Tchr	South Houston TX	(281)464-8299	S	2009
Jenkins Theron R Jr	(602)663-0958 rafejr@gmail.com	16731 Bending Creek Ln Friendswood TX 77546	TX	Teacher	Tchr	South Houston TX	(281)464-8299	S	2010
Jenks Brenda K	(920)594-1188 bjenks@wolfnet.net	P.O. Box 72 521 Mills St Manawa WI 54949	NW	Teacher	Tchr	St Paul Manawa WI	(920)596-2837	S	1986
Jenks Jon M	(507)432-5824 eyekinspel@yahoo.com	9330 Willowbrook Dr. Tillamook OR 97141	PSW	Teacher	C07/2022			CQ	2011
Jennings Jennifer L Myers	(760)953-5445 rsjasmom@yahoo.com	901 N 10th Humboldt KS 66748	KS	Teacher	C07/2016			IV	1993
Jennings Sarah Butts	(314)306-7108 sjennings@zionharvester.org	3274 Hyatt Court Saint Peters MO 63303	MO	Teacher	Tchr	Zion Saint Charles MO	(636)441-7424	CQ	2021
Jennings-Marousek Susan M Pabst	(562)884-2796 smjenningsca@gmail.com	3712 Allred St Lakewood CA 90712	PSW	Teacher	Tchr	Zion Anaheim CA	(714)535-1169	IV	1992
Jensen Daniel L	(262)885-5072 danlindajensen@hotmail.com	10223 278th Ave Trevor WI 53179	SW	Teacher	EM			S	1975
Jensen Deje K Greve	(563)659-6222 deje.jensen@trinitydavenport.org	1119 9th Ct De Witt IA 52742	IE	Teacher	Tchr	Trinity Davenport IA	(563)323-8001	MQ	1992
Jensen Frances S	frannyjensen2nd@gmail.com	5822 N Riverbay Rd Waterford WI 53185	SW	Teacher	Tchr	Immanuel Brookfield WI	(262)781-7140	MQ	2021
Jensen Heather			PSW	Teacher	Tchr	Grace Lancaster CA	(661)948-1018	MQ	2007
Jensen Karen E Sohn	(402)416-4757 karenejensen21@gmail.com	5965 Chandler Dr Rockford IL 61114	NI	Teacher	Tchr	Rockford Rockford IL	(815)877-9551	MQ	2002
Jensen Kelsey N Kleba	(262)443-5806 kelsey.kleba@gmail.com	4270 S 91st Pl Milwaukee WI 53228	SW	Teacher	Tchr	Martin Luther Greendale WI	(414)421-4000	MQ	2020
Jensen Marlene M Cleland	(208)336-8758 mmjensen41@yahoo.com	3395 W Monessen Ln Meridian ID 83646	NOW	Teacher	EM			RF	1964
Jensen Wayne E Dr	(407)256-1728 drjensen86@gmail.com	5822 N River Bay Rd Waterford WI 53185	SW	Teacher	Prin	Milwaukee LHS Milwaukee WI	(414)461-6000	CQ	1999
Jentsch Bradley S	(920)980-2124 bradjentsch@yahoo.com	2508 W Riverdale Ave Sheboygan WI 53081	SW	Teacher	C01/2020			CQ	2011
Jeppesen Rachel A Kruse	(320)220-7332 rachjepp@gmail.com	15671 140th St NW Sunburg MN 56289	MNN	Teacher	EM			SP	1990
Jerabek Pauline M Palmreuter	(715)823-2593 pjerabek@frontiernet.net	P.O. Box 197 Embarrass WI 54933	NW	Teacher	Tchr	St Martin Clintonville WI	(715)823-6538	RF	1985
Jerry Heidi L Guelzow	(501)952-6739	8331 Maple Acres Dr Houston TX 77095	TX	Teacher	Prin	St Mark Houston TX	(713)468-2623	RF	2002
Jeseritz Rebecca L Gudmundson	(402)981-1918 Rebecca.jeseritz@gmail.com	11918 Ashwood Dr Bennington NE 68007	NEB	Teacher	Tchr	Concordia Omaha NE	(402)445-4000	MQ	2004
Jeseritz Baker Laura A Miller	(920)342-0330 laura.jeseritz@yahoo.com	907 Shamrock Ln Watertown WI 53094	SW	Teacher	Tchr	Good Shepherd Watertown WI	(920)261-2579	MQ	2000
Jesgarz Frederick K	(231) 690-7930	2316 S Coyote Loop Washington UT 84780	RM	Teacher	EM			RF	1984
Jesgarz Sherri L Heise	(217)827-4579 trinitykclass@gmail.com	2114 E 875 North Rd Shelbyville IL 62565	CI	Teacher	Tchr	Trinity Stewardson IL	(217)682-3881	S	1992
Jessen Carol J Luepke	(630)567-4548 caroljjessen@gmail.com	16875 W 62nd Ln Arvada CO 80403	RM	Teacher	EM			S	1968
Jessop Michael K	(805)746-4343 mkjessop@gmail.com	7837 E Raleigh Ave Mesa AZ 85212	PSW	DCE		Pacific Southwest District Irvine CA	(949)854-3232	IV	2011
Jimerson Courteney A	(661)204-4694 courteney.mecomber@gmail.com	3316 Ashley Ct Bakersfield CA 93311	CNH	DPM	Mem C	St John Bakersfield CA	(661)665-7815	IV	2011
Jipp Andrew W	(402)681-0905 5jipps@gmail.com	17507 Tucker St Bennington NE 68007	NEB	Teacher	Tchr	Concordia Omaha NE	(402)445-4000	S	1999
Jiter Jerry L	(715)579-4144 jerryjiter5060@gmail.com	827 Deresch Street Antigo WI 54409	NW	Teacher	EM			CQ	1980
Jobe Delores R Boettcher	(262)255-5251 drjobe@att.net	N102W17488 Lone Oaks Dr Germantown WI 53022	SW	Teacher	EM			S	1966
Jobst Ann E Biberdorf	(414)791-3693 ajobst12@gmail.com	40097 S Lesio Ln Tucson AZ 85739	EN	Teacher	EM			SP	1977
Jobst Dwayne D	(414)791-3683 dwaynejobst29@gmail.com	40097 S Lesio Ln Tuscon AZ 85739	EN	Tch/DCE	EM			SP	1975
Joerz Lori L Luedeke	(917)363-6917 lljoerz@gmail.com	409 W Palm Dr Lakeland FL 33803	FG	Teacher	Tchr	St Paul Lakeland FL	(863)644-7710	BR	1989
Jofre Erica Deac	(970)466-2255 raquel_28_31@hotmail.com	800 Clark St Sterling CO 80751	RM	Deaconess	Mem C	Trinity Sterling CO	(970)522-5942	SL-DEAC	2018
Johns Katrina L	(920)892-0090 kjohns@sjlplymouth.com	763 Jennie Dr #1 Plymouth WI 53073	SW	DCE	Mem C	St John Plymouth WI	(920)893-3071	IV	2017
Johnsen Heidi	(661)203-4844 happilyheidi@att.net	30247 N 47th St Cave Creek AZ 85331	PSW	Teacher	Tchr	Christ Phoenix AZ	(602)955-4830	CQ	2019
Johnson Abby	abbymjohnson@hotmail.com	451 S. River Rd Apt 5 West Bend WI 53095	SW	Teacher	Tchr	St Johns West Bend WI	(262)334-3077	CQ	2018
Johnson Amy B Zenda	(651)686-5995 ajohnson@tsilink.net	774 Golden Meadow Rd Saint Paul MN 55123	MNS	Teacher	Tchr	Trinity Lone Oak Eagan MN	(651)454-1139	CQ	1997
Johnson Andrea E	(317)258-2554 ajohnson71287@gmail.com	227 Churchgrove Rd Frankenmuth MI 48734	MI	Teacher	Tchr	St Lorenz Frankenmuth MI	(989)652-6141	AA	2010
Johnson Andrea L Stoll	(810)227-9615 johnson.andrea.1117@gmail.com	3150 Old Orchard Dr Brighton MI 48114	EN	Teacher	EM			RF	1973
Johnson Anna E	(402)803-0123 ajohnson@bethanyschool.net	5306 Rosewood St Roeland Park KS 66205	KS	Teacher	Tchr	Bethany Overland Park KS	(913)648-2228	S	2024
Johnson Anna S Doeren Deac	(960)606-0075 anna.doeren@gmail.com	5740 Greenton Way Saint Louis MO 63128	MO	Deaconess	Pro Stf	Concordia Publishing House Saint Louis MO	(314)268-1000	CH	2010
Johnson Ardith J Cox	(406)250-6364 bajohnson65@hotmail.com	2233 N Records Way Apt 235 Meridian ID 83646	NOW	Teacher	EM			SP	1965

*Multiple Assignments (See Church Worker Locator for Additional Details)

See Page 53 for the Table of Abbreviations for key to District, Classification, Position, and College abbreviations.

**C =Candidate; EM =Emeritus; the date following the C is the month and year the Candidate status began

NAME	TELEPHONE NUMBER EMAIL	STREET ADDRESS CITY/STATE/ZIP	DISTRICT	CLASS.	POSITION/ STATUS**	WHERE SERVING	OFFICE PHONE	COLLEGE/ UNIV/CQ	YR GRAD
Johnson Barbara S Seddelmeyer	barbjohn815@yahoo.com	1506 Dunnagans Way New Haven IN 46774	IN	Teacher	EM			S	1970
Johnson Bethany M Woelmer	(469)400-4382 bjohnson@stjlcms.org	5116 SW Brentwood Rd Topeka KS 66606	KS	DPM	Mem C	Saint Johns Topeka KS	(785)354-7132	MQ	2015
Johnson Betty K Geist	(770)713-4382 bkj625@yahoo.com	231 Osmanthus Way Canton GA 30114	FG	Teacher	EM			RF	1970
Johnson Brent T	(410)960-0738 brentjohnson@ concordiaprepschool.org	521 Idlewild Rd Bel Air MD 21014	SE	Teacher	Pro Stf	Concordia Towson MD	(410)825-2323	S	2001
Johnson Brittany L	(630)632-8744 brittanyj@stmattsonline.com	1445 Downing Pl #O-3 Mundelein IL 60060	NI	DCM	Mem C	St Matthew Hawthorn Woods IL	(847)438-7709	MQ	2024
Johnson Carol R Umbach	(732)407-8616 cjorlnj@yahoo.com	66 Corey St Fords NJ 08863	NJ	Teacher	EM			RF	1978
Johnson Christine A Eberhard	(313)777-3834 tjohnson@stpeterslutheranchurch. net	27102 Maywood St Roseville MI 48066	MI	Teacher	Tchr	Saint Peters Eastpointe MI	(586)777-6300	S	1975
Johnson Clare L	(605)999-9738 clare.johnson@glsfargo.org	1822 14 1/2 St S Fargo ND 58103	ND	Teacher	Tchr	Grace Fargo ND	(701)232-7747	CQ	2024
Johnson Connie L Allen Deac	(715)834-6338 1deacclj@charter.net	550 Graham Ave Apt 509 Eau Claire WI 54701	NW	Deaconess	EM			Other	1962
Johnson Connie L Balzum	(720)339-7626 connie.johnson@pwclc.org		RM	Teacher	Tchr	Peace With Christ Aurora CO	(303)766-7116	MQ	1988
Johnson Cynthia A Reinking-Schwartz	(949) 302-0423 caljohnsons@hotmail.com	2309 Orange Ave Costa Mesa CA 92627	PSW	Teacher	Tchr	Light of Christ Irvine CA	(949)786-3326	RF	1971
Johnson David S	(714)336-8256 djondce@gmail.com	6003 Broadwater Dr Kernersville NC 27284	SE	DCE	Mem C	Fountain of Life Kernersville NC	(336)993-4447	SP	2012
Johnson Deborah L Gall	(847)912-5840 debl4@cs.com	8937 Robin Dr Des Plaines IL 60016	NI	Teacher	Tchr	Immanuel Glenview IL	(847)724-1034	RF	1985
Johnson Emily D Chapman	(616)405-4206 missemily726@yahoo.com	2044 Woodview Dr Wixom MI 48393	MI	Teacher	C07/2016			RF	2008
Johnson Emily L Stanley	(317)550-8065 ejohnson@holycrossfw.org	1305 N Anthony Blvd Fort Wayne IN 46805	IN	Teacher	Prin	Holy Cross Fort Wayne IN	(260)483-3173	AA	2008
Johnson Erica A Thiede	(262)389-6224 ethiede34@gmail.com	4530 County Road B Port Washington WI 53074	SW	Teacher	C07/2016			MQ	2008
Johnson Erin S	(406)885-8949 erinsjohnson7@gmail.com	121 Hawthorn Ave Apt 7 Kalispell MT 59901	MT	Teacher	Tchr	Trinity Kalispell MT	(406)257-5683	S	2021
Johnson Evan C	(417)217-6992 ecjohnson1998@gmail.com	345 S Monroe St Pilger NE 68768	NEB	DCE		Nebraska District Seward NE	(402)643-2961	S	2021
Johnson Evelyn E Walz	(317)437-8131 evelyn.johnson12@yahoo.com	3 Indian River Ave Apt 807 Titusville FL 32796	FG	Teacher	EM			RF	1968
Johnson Gregory K	gjohnson@mightymessengers.org	5351 East W Ave Vicksburg MI 49097	MI	Teacher	Prin	St Michael Portage MI	(269)327-7832	CQ	2006
Johnson Haley E	(928)304-8718 haleyj12@me.com	1931 E San Marcos Dr Yuma AZ 85365	PSW	Teacher	C05/2021			IV	2016
Johnson Heather E Engstrom	(847)637-3490 heatherjohnson129@yahoo.com	7101 Chenango Ln SW Cedar Rapids IA 52404	IE	Teacher	Tchr	Central Newhall IA	(319)223-5271	CQ	2021
Johnson Heather N Koepp	(405)219-9176 hjohnson612@gmail.com	728 Dana Dr Yukon OK 73099	OK	Teacher	C01/2025			S	2022
Johnson Hollie L	(260)760-1232 hleejohnson21@gmail.com	12321 W Washington Center Rd Fort Wayne IN 46818	IN	Teacher	Tchr	St Peters Fort Wayne IN	(260)749-5811	AA	2025
Johnson James J	johnsonj@concordiacrusaders.org	700 E Main St Tomball TX 77375	TX	Teacher	Tchr	Concordia Tomball TX	(281)351-2547	MQ	1997
Johnson Janet L Voehl Miller	(309)263-7752 jbhrhg@frontier.com	500 S Glen Ave Morton IL 61550	CI	Teacher	Tchr	Bethel Morton IL	(309)266-6592	S	1981
Johnson Janet S Adkins	(801)556-7424 tayaines@hotmail.com	3713 S Carolyn St Salt Lake Cty UT 84106	RM	Teacher	EM			S	1983
Johnson Janice L Bass-Enders	(402)875-1025 janicej7717@gmail.com	1603 Syracuse Ave Norfolk NE 68701	NEB	Teacher	EM			S	1973
Johnson Jeffery J	(920)660-9557 jjohns066@gmail.com	1420 Pat Tillman St De Pere WI 54115	NW	DCM	Mem C	St John Pulaski WI	(920)822-3511	MQ	2002
Johnson Jenna A Hempe	(414)975-9272	2401 Emslie Ct Waukesha WI 53188	SW	Teacher	Tchr	LUMIN Milwaukee WI	(414)354-5126	MQ	2010
Johnson Jenna L Karlin		10101 White Pine Rd Lincoln NE 68527	NEB	Teacher	Tchr	Faith Lincoln NE	(402)466-7402	S	2015
Johnson Joy C Gehring	(410)206-7501 joy.johnson773@gmail.com	521 Idlewild Rd Bel Air MD 21014	SE	Teacher	C07/2016			S	2002
Johnson Karen L Bunce	(562)945-5831 tootseeq@aol.com	13566 Starbuck St Whittier CA 90605	PSW	Teacher	Tchr	Hope Glendora CA	(626)335-5315	IV	1997
Johnson Karen M Braun	(805)630-6208 peppersk@roadrunner.com	3791 Fountain St Camarillo CA 93012	PSW	Teacher	EM			S	1962
Johnson Kari M Waterman	(402)657-5334 kari.johnson4220@gmail.com	1005 Dogwood Cir Bellvue NE 68005	NEB	Teacher	C10/2020			S	2001
Johnson Kayla E	(901)682-8405 kayla.johnson@ctkschool.com	1186 Ascend Dr Apt 201 Memphis TN 38119	MDS	Teacher	Tchr	Christ the King Memphis TN	(901)682-8405	S	2024
Johnson Keri A Witek	(312)767-1481 keri.witek.johnson@gmail.com	4622 Highview Dr Milton WI 53563	EN	DCE	C07/2016			SP	2007
Johnson Leah J Livo	ljohnson@ctk.me		MI	Teacher	Tchr	Christ The King Southgate MI	(734)285-9697	S	2006
Johnson Leann J		1509 W Franklin St Appleton WI 54914	NW	DCE	EM			SP	1992
Johnson Leslee L Lemke	(773)286-3188 johnsonglml1@yahoo.com	4141 N Parkside Ave Chicago IL 60634	NI	Teacher	EM			S	1976
Johnson Leslie J Tarr	(815)262-5419 ljohnson530@hotmail.com	5799 Capetown Ave Rockford IL 61108	NI	Teacher	Tchr	Rockford Rockford IL	(815)877-9551	CH	2011
Johnson Linda E Gotsch	(708)268-5869 lindaellenjohnson@att.net	5430 Bohlander Ave Berkeley IL 60163	NI	Teacher	EM			RF	1977

*Multiple Assignments (See Church Worker Locator for Additional Details)

See Page 53 for the Table of Abbreviations for key to District, Classification, Position, and College abbreviations.

**C =Candidate; EM =Emeritus; the date following the C is the month and year the Candidate status began

NAME	TELEPHONE NUMBER EMAIL	STREET ADDRESS CITY/STATE/ZIP	DISTRICT	CLASS.	POSITION/ STATUS**	WHERE SERVING	OFFICE PHONE	COLLEGE/ UNIV/CQ	YR GRAD
Johnson Lisa M Cisewski	(952)465-5242 lisajohnson@trinitymerrill.com	901 Johnson St Merrill WI 54452	NW	Teacher	Mem C	Trinity Merrill WI	(715)536-5482	SP	1997
Johnson Lynda P Dougherty	(314)781-9685	7610 Williams Ave Saint Louis MO 63143	MO	Teacher	Tchr	Abiding Savior Saint Louis MO	(314)892-4408	SP	1983
Johnson Marcia K Hansen	(903)240-1046 johnson.marcia72@yahoo.com	2845 S 63rd Dr Phoenix AZ 85043	PSW	Teacher	EM			CQ	2002
Johnson Melanie L Marshall	(313)289-2869 johnsonm@trinitycp.org	17029 Keppen Ave Allen Park MI 48101	IN	Teacher	Tchr	Trinity Crown Point IN	(219)663-1578	MQ	2004
Johnson Melody A Reed	(406)892-9822 brownbearcharters@charter.net	412 N Hilltop Rd Columbia Fls MT 59912	MT	Teacher	EM			S	1969
Johnson Michael R	(630)272-8391 wackydawg95@gmail.com	143 N Washington St Bonduel WI 54107	NW	Teacher	Tchr	St Paul Bonduel WI	(715)758-8559	MQ	2017
Johnson Mireya P Alvarez Deac	(251)752-4188 mireyajohnson@hotmail.com	30 Heritage Pointe Cir Fenton MO 63026	MO	Deaconess	Tchr	Lutheran South Saint Louis MO	(314)631-1400	CQ	2005
Johnson Myrene K Beune	(580) 651-2356 myrenejohnson@gmail.com	Rr 1 Box 83 Goodwell OK 73939	OK	Teacher	EM			S	1975
Johnson Nathan K	(269)366-9052 nathan.johnson@shepherdhills.org	4838 N Marlo Way Unit 29 Appleton WI 54913	NW	DPM	Mem C	Shepherd Hills Greenville WI	(920)757-5722	S	2022
Johnson Nathan L	(719)464-6335 the116life@gmail.com	630 Echoglen Ct Colorado Springs CO 80906	RM	DCE	C07/2016			AU	2007
Johnson Noel N	(863)633-8002 njohnsondce@gmail.com	7666 Vallhalla Dr Colorado Springs CO 80920	RM	DCE	C06/2017			CQ	2006
Johnson Olivia G	(913)299-7904 olivia.grace1698@gmail.com	5740 County Line Rd Kansas City KS 66106	KS	DCE	Mem C	Lord Of Life Leawood KS	(913)681-5167	S	2021
Johnson Pamela A Mueller	(630)830-4319 pamnrandy@comcast.net	621 Arnold Ave Streamwood IL 60107	NI	Teacher	EM			RF	1975
Johnson Pamela D Neubauer	(317)362-7056 ppphea@aol.com	6051 S Eaton Ave Indianapolis IN 46259	IN	Teacher	EM			RF	1976
Johnson Parley J III	(303)337-2052 jande81@gmail.com	3009 1/2 Royal Court Grand Junction CO 81504	RM	Teacher	EM			CQ	2000
Johnson Paul W	(317)937-2111 packrteach@aol.com	6051 S Eaton Ave Indianapolis IN 46259	IN	Teacher	EM			RF	1977
Johnson Phillip L Dr	(952)223-2161 phillip.johnson@mnsdistrict.org	1109 Woodridge Ct SE Lonsdale MN 55046	MNS	DCO	D Ex/S	Minnesota South District Burnsville MN	(952)435-2550	SP	1982
Johnson Rachael L Minick	(260)402-3320 rachaelljohnson53@yahoo.com	7827 Bartel Ct New Haven IN 46774	IN	Teacher	Tchr	Emmanuel Fort Wayne IN	(260)447-3005	CQ	2010
Johnson Rebecca E Rockrohr Deac	(414)813-1084 johnson.rebecca.elizabeth@gmail.com	3046 14th Ave S Moorhead MN 56560	NW	Deaconess	C09/2018			CH	2014
Johnson Rebekah A	(920)664-2999 rebekah.johnson@tlsmerrill.com	1208 Arctic Ln Wausau WI 54401	NW	Teacher	Tchr	Trinity Merrill WI	(715)536-5482	MW	2017
Johnson Robert D	(630)272-8904 r.johnson@stpaulbonduel.com	129 S Elm St Bonduel WI 54107	NW	Teacher	Tchr	St Paul Bonduel WI	(715)758-8559	SP	1988
Johnson Robert L Dr	(262)377-1460 robert.johnson@cuw.edu	W65N781 Washington Ave Cedarburg WI 53012	SW	Teacher	EM			CQ	2003
Johnson Ross E	(419)705-9736 ross49johnson@gmail.com	2800 County Road 5 Delta OH 43515	OH	Teacher	EM			RF	1971
Johnson Ruth A Laesch Swanagin	(205)807-9709 ruthinbham@gmail.com	1817 Mountain Woods Pl Vestavia AL 35216	SO	Teacher	Tchr	Vestavia Hills Vestavia Hills AL	(205)823-1883	RF	1986
Johnson Sarah K Schendel		289 Madelines Park Cir Jefferson Cty MO 65109	MO	Teacher	C08/2024			RF	1995
Johnson Scott R	(952)649-0206	901 Johnson St Merrill WI 54452	NW	Teacher	Prin	Trinity Merrill WI	(715)536-7501	SP	1995
Johnson Sharon A Gellerman	(402)690-1935 arjsaj1@cox.net	2949 Jack Cir Salina KS 67401	KS	Teacher	EM			S	1964
Johnson Stephen P	(262)354-4563 steveo236@gmail.com	2115 Cardinal Ct Waukesha WI 53186	SW	Teacher	C07/2016			RF	1996
Johnson Susan J Hoelz	(816)517-0155 sjhoelz@gmail.com	9706 Lily Pond Ln Hamel MN 55340	MNS	Teacher	C07/2016			RF	2001
Johnson Sylvia A Deac	(414)530-3150 stjohnslwml@gmail.com	12455 W Janesville Rd Unit 304 Muskego WI 53150	EN	Deaconess	EM			CQ	2001
Johnson Tanya J Laabs	(920)205-9510 totaljohnson@gmail.com	N9665 Darboy Dr Appleton WI 54915	NW	Teacher	Mem C	Good Shepherd Appleton WI	(920)734-9643	SP	1996
Johnson Thomas K	(402)616-0005 thomaskyjohnson@gmail.com	3840 W 5th St Goodview MN 55987	MNS	Teacher	Tchr	Hope Winona MN	(507)474-7799	S	2021
Johnson Wade S	(402) 469-5628 dcewade@yahoo.com	837 N Chestnut Ave Hastings NE 68901	NEB	DCE	Mem C	Faith Hastings NE	(402)462-5044	SP	1999
Johnson William R	(763)300-1521 billj1158@gmail.com	7095 Deerwood Ln N Maple Grove MN 55369	MNS	Tch/DCE	EM			SP	1980
Johnston Christopher J Dr	(703)256-7646 chris1223966@yahoo.com	7447 Little River Tpke Apt 104 Annandale VA 22003	SE	Teacher	C07/2016			RF	1998
Johnston Helen L Althoff	(573)364-3043 slvrhawk@embarqmail.com	1902 Saint Mathews Ct Unit C Rolla MO 65401	MO	Teacher	EM			RF	1968
Johnston Matthew S	(260)229-1387 msjiu84@gmail.com	3311 Jonquil Dr. Ft. Wayne IN 46815	IN	DPM	Mem C	Emmanuel Fort Wayne IN	(260)423-1369	CQ	2018
Johnston Hermann Julie Holz	(402)643-9656 julie.hermann@cune.edu	2025 Rainbow Ave Seward NE 68434	NEB	Tch/DCE	S HS/C	Concordia University Nebraska Seward NE	(402)643-3651	S	1982
Jolliff Katherine S Gramzow	(248)808-0766 ksgramzow@gmail.com	26097 Brettonwoods St. Madison Heights MI 48071	MI	Teacher	Tchr	LHS Assn Of Greater Detroit Rochester Hls MI	(248)856-0240	CQ	2024
Jonas Faith M	(424)212-3455 fjonas@shlutheran.org	3903 SE Military Drive Apartment 2308 San Antonio TX 78223	TX	Teacher	Tchr	Shep Of The Hills San Antonio TX	(210)614-3741	S	2023
Jonas Laurel M Frey	(608)981-2167 dramamama.jonas@gmail.com	W8095 Grouse Dr Portage WI 53901	SW	Teacher	EM			SP	1980

*Multiple Assignments (See Church Worker Locator for Additional Details)
See Page 53 for the Table of Abbreviations for key to District, Classification, Position, and College abbreviations.
**C =Candidate; EM =Emeritus; the date following the C is the month and year the Candidate status began

NAME	TELEPHONE NUMBER EMAIL	STREET ADDRESS CITY/STATE/ZIP	DISTRICT	CLASS.	POSITION/ STATUS**	WHERE SERVING	OFFICE PHONE	COLLEGE/ UNIV/CQ	YR GRAD
Jonason Jennifer Gross	(817)475-7551 jiffermg@gmail.com	20030 Goldeneye Way Rogers MN 55374	MNS	DCE	Mem C	Beautiful Savior Plymouth MN	(763)550-1000	AU	2013
Jones Amanda R Kaijala	(989)928-5675 amandaruthjones@yahoo.com	3310 Warringham Ave Waterford MI 48329	MI	Teacher	Tchr	St Paul Flint MI	(810)239-6733	AA	2002
Jones April M Anderson	(901)661-2173 ajones@mid-southlcms.com	9760 Monasco Rd Millington TN 38053	MDS	Teacher	C07/2025			S	2008
Jones Cathy J Spencer	(419)592-0015 cathyjjones@me.com	960 W Riverview Ave Napoleon OH 43545	OH	Teacher	EM			S	1973
Jones Crystal F	(863)838-3100 crystalfjones@gmail.com	1050 Shoreview Cir #206 Casselberry FL 32707	S	Teacher	Tchr	St Luke Oviedo FL	(407)365-3408	CH	2016
Jones David W	(920)498-0530	1144 Desnoyers St Green Bay WI 54303	NW	Teacher	EM			CQ	1986
Jones Edith J Nusser Dr	(325)944-1569 jones@csp.edu	6302 Stage Coach Trl San Angelo TX 76901	TX	Teacher	EM			CQ	2004
Jones Jennifer R Braeger	(828) 638-7936 jen71j@gmail.com	573 30th Avenue Cir NE Hickory NC 28601	SE	Teacher	C07/2016			RF	1994
Jones Juanita King	(251)401-8838	2722 Harper Ave Mobile AL 36617	SO	Teacher	EM			S	1979
Jones Katherine A Schafer	(517)449-5470 jones2326@att.net	310 Lama Cir Lansing MI 48911	MI	Teacher	EM			S	1976
Jones Kathryn L Peter	(651)246-7113 24kljones@gmail.com	2988 Pilot Knob Rd Eagan MN 55121	MNS	Teacher	EM			SP	1980
Jones Laurie A Fink	(314)229-0503 ljones@wordoflifeschool.net	4137 E Linda Ln Robertsville MO 63072	MO	Teacher	Tchr	Word of Life Saint Louis MO	(314)832-1244	CQ	2012
Jones Marilyn S	(515)279-7660 mjones2629@aol.com	1910 Merklin Way Des Moines IA 50310	IW	Teacher	EM			S	1971
Jones Mary A Aring	(815) 325-6091 mgojones5@yahoo.com	1012 Jacquelyn Ct Marengo IL 60152	NI	Teacher	EM			S	1975
Jones Nancy M Busch	n_jones1550@comcast.net	3639 Westport Dr New Haven IN 46774	IN	Teacher	EM			RF	1969
Jones Paula M Mertz	(240)672-8269 p2jones2@outlook.com	6301 Grant Chapman Dr La Plata MD 20646	SE	Teacher	Tchr	Grace La Plata MD	(301)932-0963	S	1991
Jones Ryan J	(602)819-6346 rjones@stjohnsorange.org	655 Baker St #z203 Costa Mesa CA 92626	PSW	Teacher	Tchr	St Johns Orange CA	(714)288-4406	IV	2022
Jones Sarah E Vogler	(920)740-1231 sqjones@gmail.com	225710 Buck Wood Ln Wausau WI 54401	NW	Teacher	C01/2022			MQ	2003
Jones Wesley D	(618)830-0324 wdjones_82@yahoo.com	6 Wagon Wheel Ct Collinsville IL 62234	SI	Teacher	Prin	Trinity Edwardsville IL	(618)656-2918	CH	2006
Jopp Jill M Kloempken	(612)910-3334 JillJopp@gmail.com	5121 Sundance Run Mayer MN 55360	MNS	Teacher	C07/2016			SP	1997
Jordan Amy M Johnston	(573)434-4636 amyjordan1975@yahoo.com	1083 S College Ave Newton NC 28658	MO	Teacher	C07/2024			CQ	2015
Jordan Jenny L Morner	(714)556-2396 jordanpl@juno.com	2210 W Moore Ave Santa Ana CA 92704	PSW	Teacher	Tchr	Christ Costa Mesa CA	(949)548-6866	S	1980
Jordan Rebecca E	(559)972-9378 rebecca.jordan@eagles.cui.edu	1452 W Settlers Way #21 Taylorsville UT 84109	RM	Teacher	Tchr	Redeemer Salt Lake City UT	(801)467-4352	IV	2017
Jordening Carol J Hessler	(714)420-8988 carol.jordening@faithlasvegas.org	788 Tillis Pl Las Vegas NV 89138	PSW	Teacher	Tchr	Faith Las Vegas NV	(702)921-2727	IV	1991
Jordening Jonathan D	(714)420-8987 jon.jordening@faithlasvegas.org	788 Tillis Pl Las Vegas NV 89138	PSW	Tch/DCE	Mem C	Faith Community Las Vegas NV	(702)921-2700	S	1987
Jorgensen Erin B Ponder	(765)860-7594 erin.b.jorgensen@gmail.com	2113 Saratoga Ave Kokomo IN 46902	IN	Tch/DCE	Tchr	Holy Cross Indianapolis IN	(317)823-5801	CH	2008
Josephson Donna K Lagerlef	(907)444-1171 mrs.josephson@alsalaska.org	4859 Pavalof St Anchorage AK 99507	NOW	Teacher	Tchr	Anchor Anchorage AK	(907)522-3636	WN	1986
Joslen Anna	(909)664-4994 ajoslen13@gmail.com	1117 Pinot Noir Dr Lodi CA 95240	CNH	Teacher	Tchr	St Peter Lodi CA	(209)333-2223	IV	2021
Jost Lauren A Troester	(402)730-7681 ljost@zionbethalto.org	201 S Donk Ave Maryville IL 62062	SI	Teacher	Tchr	Zion Bethalto IL	(618)377-8314	S	2016
Jost Sylvia M Aubuchon	(417)881-7257 sylviajost@hotmail.com	3830 S Jefferson Ave Apt L1 Springfield MO 65807	MO	Teacher	EM			S	1966
Jostes Jordan C Haroldson	(515)557-0143 jcharoldson@gmail.com	3631 Extreme Ct Las Vegas NV 89129	PSW	Teacher	Tchr	Lamb Of God Las Vegas NV	(702)645-1626	S	2013
Jostes Laura L Rowley Deac	(314)591-8664 laura.jostes@gmail.com	7138 Winona Ave Saint Louis MO 63109	MO	Deaconess	EM			SL-DEAC	2018
Jostes Steven P	(402)750-7169 steven.jostes@flhsemail.org	3631 Extreme Ct Las Vegas NV 89129	PSW	Teacher	Tchr	Faith Las Vegas NV	(702)804-4400	S	2012
Joyce Mark L Dr	(402)803-1020 markjoyce.designer@gmail.com	1710 Rainbow Ave Seward NE 68434	NEB	Teacher	EM			S	1970
Juergensen James D Dr	(262)243-4518 james.juergensen2@cuw.edu	W59N973 Essex Dr Cedarburg WI 53012	SW	Teacher	S HS/C	Concordia University Wisconsin Mequon WI	(262)243-5700	MQ	1993
Juergensen James J Dr	(262)751-7901 james.juergensen@cuw.edu	1014 Algoma Dr Prt Washingtn WI 53074	SW	Teacher	EM			S	1962
Juergensen Jessica L	(262)888-0632 jessica.juergensen@cune.org	1310 Rusk Dr Richardson TX 75081	TX	Teacher	Tchr	Zion Dallas TX	(214)363-1630	S	2022
Jung Ann M Hillmer	(682) 246-2925 annmjung80@gmail.com	6865 Dogwood Ct N Richlnd Hls TX 76182	TX	Teacher	EM			RF	1977
Jung Charlene E Fiedler	(260)755-6417 cjung@comcast.net	9625 Chapmans Blvd Fort Wayne IN 46835	IN	Teacher	EM			RF	1971
Jung Doris J	(414)870-1886	12455 W Janesville Rd Unit 103 Muskego WI 53150	EN	Teacher	EM			CQ	2003
Jung Sara M Anderson	(269)352-9154 sjung@stjohnrochester.org	1011 W University Dr Rochester MI 48307	MI	Teacher	Tchr	St John Rochester MI	(248)402-8000	CQ	2022
Jung Scott L	(317)460-5659 scjung1030@gmail.com	10488 Hunters Creek Dr Zeeland MI 49464	MI	DCE	Mem C	Zion Holland MI	(616)392-7151	S	1998

*Multiple Assignments (See Church Worker Locator for Additional Details)
See Page 53 for the Table of Abbreviations for key to District, Classification, Position, and College abbreviations.
**C =Candidate; EM =Emeritus; the date following the C is the month and year the Candidate status began

NAME	TELEPHONE NUMBER EMAIL	STREET ADDRESS CITY/STATE/ZIP	DISTRICT	CLASS.	POSITION/ STATUS**	WHERE SERVING	OFFICE PHONE	COLLEGE/ UNIV/CQ	YR GRAD
Jungklaus Rebecca A Deac	(713)852-7114 bjungklaus@lifebridgesealy.com	312 Morning Dove Trail Sealy TX 77474	TX	Deaconess	Mem C	LifeBridge Sealy TX	(979)885-7270	SL-DEAC	2023
Jungkuntz Sandra S Redemske	sjungkuntz@stpeterlcms.org	306 E Schaumburg Rd Schaumburg IL 60194	NI	Teacher	Tchr	St Peter Schaumburg IL	(847)885-3350	RF	1990
Jurchen Candace R	(402)641-3973 cjurchen@trinitylcms-lincoln.com	3127 N 41st St Lincoln NE 68504	NEB	Teacher	Tchr	Trinity Lincoln NE	(402)466-1800	S	2001
Jurchen Deborah E Perschbacher	(515)401-7275 djurchen@gmail.com	1078 N 7th St Seward NE 68434	NEB	Teacher	C08/2024			S	2006
Jurchen James A	(402)379-3127 james.jurchen@cune.edu	1051 Eastridge Dr Seward NE 68434	NEB	Teacher	S HS/C	Concordia University Nebraska Seward NE	(402)643-3651	S	1999
Jurchen John C Dr	(402)643-9491 john.jurchen@cune.edu	624 N 5th St Seward NE 68434	NEB	Teacher	S HS/C	Concordia University Nebraska Seward NE	(402)643-3651	S	1997
Jurchen Tamra L Wagner	(402)641-3133 tjurchen@gmail.com	3435 Old Cheney Rd Beaver Xing NE 68313	NEB	Teacher	EM			SP	1969
Jurica Katrina M Fricke	(217)691-6957 katrina.jurica@gmail.com	2847 N Long Ave Chicago IL 60641	NI	Teacher	Tchr	St John Chicago IL	(773)736-1196	Other	2014
Jurss Jacob B	(920)946-9730 jjurss@lutheranhigh.com	809 Panther Ave Sheboygan WI 53081	SW	Teacher	Tchr	Sheboygan Sheboygan WI	(920)452-3323	MQ	2019
Jurss Jared	(920)627-0090 jurss112@gmail.com	1123 6th Ave Grafton WI 53024	SW	Teacher	Tchr	Trinity Mequon WI	(262)242-2045	MQ	2022
Jurss Jason B	(262)375-0519 jjurss@milwaukeelutheranhs.org	W56N827 Meadow Ln Cedarburg WI 53012	SW	Teacher	Tchr	Milwaukee LHS Milwaukee WI	(414)461-6000	RF	1995
Jurss Jeffrey A	(414)458-6552 jurss@lutheranhigh.com	1726 Terry Andrae Ave Sheboygan WI 53081	SW	Teacher	Tchr	Sheboygan Sheboygan WI	(920)452-3323	RF	1989
Just Darrel D	(602)212-1658 darrel60@cox.net	2221 E Lincoln Dr Phoenix AZ 85016	PSW	Teacher	EM			RF	1969
Just Janet L Stuber	(818)314-6381 janj@pacbell.net	7946 Rudnick Ave Canoga Park CA 91304	PSW	DCE	EM			SP	1977
Justice Donald C	(248)867-9103 justicedon816@gmail.com	15206 Bratten Lane Webster TX 77598	TX	Teacher	Tchr	South Houston TX	(281)464-8299	S	1995
Kaber Jennifer D Haffer	(314)825-2191 jkaber@ccls-stlouis.org	179 Bertrand Dr Saint Louis MO 63129	MO	Teacher	Tchr	Christ Community Kirkwood MO	(314)822-7774	S	2005
Kabrick Bonnie J Meyer	(712)240-2555 bkabrick36@gmail.com	603 W 4th St Spencer IA 51301	IW	DCE	EM			CQ	2007
Kacmar Dawn S Gerike Deac	(269)756-9525 dskacmar@hotmail.com	610 Sherwood Ave Three Oaks MI 49128	MI	Deaconess	EM			Other	1976
Kading Douglas R	(712)260-3438 dougkading@gmail.com	1942 350th St Spencer IA 51301	IW	Tch/DCE	EM			S	1971
Kaelberer Edward B	(719)269-1783	10001 S Oswego St Apt 254 Parker CO 80134	RM	Teacher	EM			S	1955
Kaelberer Jennifer A Graumann	(307)250-5739 jenkaelberer@gmail.com	1007 Stampede Ave Cody WY 82414	WY	DCE	C07/2016			S	2006
Kaelberer Jerome T	(507)776-6487	82726 420th St Truman MN 56088	MNS	Teacher	EM			S	1961
Kaelberer Kent J	(262)627-0881 kkaelberer@immanuelbrookfield.org	4776 Monches Rd Colgate WI 53017	SW	Teacher	Tchr	Immanuel Brookfield WI	(262)781-7140	MQ	1992
Kaelberer Mary L Schulz	(303)750-7541 maryloukae@gmail.com	9831 E Cornell Ave Denver CO 80231	RM	Teacher	EM			SP	1969
Kaemmerer Angela K Flamion	(636)239-7790 angela.kaemmerer@lsportal.net	3019 Koch Ln Washington MO 63090	MO	Teacher	Tchr	Immanuel Washington MO	(636)239-1636	S	2002
Kaes Jane M Rummel	(208)733-6963	29656 Slade Rd Caldwell ID 83607	NOW	Teacher	EM			RF	1959
Kaestner Dorothy A Ahrens	(314)304-5752 dkaestner101@gmail.com	18650 N Thompson Peak Pkwy Unit 1083 Scottsdale AZ 85255	PSW	Teacher	EM			RF	1969
Kahl Lynn M Ehrenwerth	(312)890-0020 lynnkahl50@gmail.com	111 Acacia Dr Unit 414 Indianhead Pk IL 60525	NI	Teacher	EM			RF	1972
Kahler Micheal L	(636)561-8999 kahlerm@aol.com	60 Normandy Dr Lake St Louis MO 63367	MO	Teacher	EM			S	1975
Kahler Nancy S Blackburn	(714)875-6335 r.n.kahler@outlook.com	5402 E McKellips Rd Lot 152 Mesa AZ 85215	PSW	Teacher	EM			CQ	2001
Kahlfeldt Albert L	(262)227-6321 al.kahlfeldt@gmail.com	14080 W North Oak Blvd New Berlin WI 53151	EN	Teacher	EM			RF	1969
Kahre Lillian R Hardin	lrkahre@gmail.com	1912 Oak Shire Dr Pearland TX 77581	TX	Teacher	Tchr	South Houston TX	(281)464-8299	CQ	2003
Kaio Andrea M Katt	(808)281-7046 k.teacher@elcs-maui.org	2211 Keanu St Wailuku HI 96793	CNH	Teacher	Tchr	Emmanuel Kahului-Maui HI	(808)877-3037	CQ	2003
Kaiser David A	(715)304-1188 ejkdak@yahoo.com	308 E Center St Shawano WI 54166	NW	Teacher	Prin	Saint James Shawano WI	(715)524-4815	AA	1997
Kaiser Erika J Goebel	(715)304-1096 ejkdak2@yahoo.com	308 E Center St Shawano WI 54166	NW	Teacher	Tchr	Saint James Shawano WI	(715)524-4815	AA	1998
Kaiser Joanna L Rudlaff	(616)648-3288 joannarudlaff@hotmail.com	904 S Camino De Bravo Pueblo West CO 81007	RM	Teacher	C07/2016			RF	2000
Kalal Ruth L Panning	(630)932-9543 ruthkalal@sbcglobal.net	526 S Highland Ave Lombard IL 60148	NI	Teacher	Tchr	St Peter Schaumburg IL	(847)885-3350	RF	1984
Kalal Thomas C	(630)643-2827 thomaskalal@sbcglobal.net	526 S Highland Ave Lombard IL 60148	NI	Teacher	EM			RF	1985
Kalbas Pamela L Byerly	(512)429-5117 pamkalbas@gmail.com	1212 E Boynton St Hamilton TX 76531	TX	Teacher	Tchr	St Paul Thorndale TX	(512)898-5455	AU	2001
Kalbfleisch Melissa A Niemeyer	(314)650-7990 kalbfleisch.melissa@gmail.com	1218 Hyannis Dr Saint Louis MO 63146	MO	DPM	C08/2017			CH	2010
Kalkopf Joseph R	(414)333-2661 jkalkopf@milwaukeelutheran.org	W333N5467 Linden Cir W Nashotah WI 53058	SW	Teacher	Tchr	LHS Assn of Greater Milwaukee West Allis WI	(414)421-9100	MQ	2001

*Multiple Assignments (See Church Worker Locator for Additional Details)
See Page 53 for the Table of Abbreviations for key to District, Classification, Position, and College abbreviations.
**C =Candidate; EM =Emeritus; the date following the C is the month and year the Candidate status began

NAME	TELEPHONE NUMBER EMAIL	STREET ADDRESS CITY/STATE/ZIP	DISTRICT	CLASS.	POSITION/ STATUS**	WHERE SERVING	OFFICE PHONE	COLLEGE/ UNIV/CQ	YR GRAD
Kalmes Michael W	(734)572-0185 mwkalmes@yahoo.com		MI	Teacher	EM			S	1971
Kalous Keith L	(414)813-0070 kkalous@wi.rr.com	W144N4937 Stone Dr Menomonee Fls WI 53051	SW	Teacher	EM			RF	1978
Kamin Robin R Nicklaus	(630)887-1626 robinkamin@aol.com	529 W 58th Pl Hinsdale IL 60521	NI	Teacher	EM			RF	1974
Kamman Rebecca A Kassel	(502)254-1308 becky.kamman@insightbb.com	12002 Hillrose Cir Louisville KY 40243	IN	Teacher	Tchr	Our Savior Louisville KY	(502)426-1130	S	1990
Kamman Scott R	(502)254-1308 scott.kamman@gmail.com	12002 Hillrose Cir Louisville KY 40243	IN	Teacher	Tchr	Our Savior Louisville KY	(502)426-0864	AA	1987
Kamm-Dooley Suzette Christensen	(503)249-0506 kammsj@aol.com	4410 NE Ainsworth St Portland OR 97218	NOW	Teacher	EM			CQ	1984
Kammerlohr Joshua I	(720)226-3286 kam2lohr@yahoo.com	6505 Newland St Arvada CO 80003	RM	Teacher	C07/2016			S	2002
Kammerlohr Krista L Scheele	(720)226-3286	6505 Newland St Arvada CO 80003	RM	Teacher	C07/2016			S	2002
Kammerlohr William A	(217)525-0805 bkamclimb@gmail.com	3509 Angelo Springfield IL 62707	CI	Teacher	EM			S	1974
Kammeyer Laurel E Raatz	(660)463-7354	1204 S Maple St Concordia MO 64020	MO	Teacher	EM			MW	1969
Kammrath Julaine L Wendler	(630)844-0290 jkammrath@hotmail.com	319 Sunset Ave Aurora IL 60506	NI	Teacher	EM			RF	1971
Kammrath Mark R	(630)844-0290 kammrathmrk@msn.com	319 Sunset Ave Aurora IL 60506	NI	Teacher	EM			RF	1971
Kamprath Deanna D Bauer Jalas	(402)200-8767 dee.jalas@cune.org	416 State St Grand Island NE 68801	NEB	Teacher	Tchr	Trinity Grand Island NE	(308)382-5274	S	1996
Kamprath Elizabeth I Nolte	(920)540-1725 lkamprath72@gmail.com	1431 Linda Ave Menasha WI 54952	SW	Teacher	EM			SP	1968
Kamprath Lei L Michael	(571)850-7184 fredric@kamprath.net	2350 SW 17th Cir Delray Beach FL 33445	FG	Teacher	EM			S	1959
Kamprath Paulette G Luebke	(830)626-7577 jimkamprath@msn.com	3647 Archer Blvd New Braunfels TX 78132	TX	Teacher	EM			S	1969
Kamprath Ronald P	(920)208-1296 ronald@kamprath.net	2713 N 5th St Sheboygan WI 53083	SW	Teacher	EM			S	1965
Kamps Sallie J	(715) 499-1301 teddygrrl59@charter.net	1303 O Day St Apt 4 Merrill WI 54452	NW	Teacher	EM			RF	1981
Kampschnieder Yvette Rasmussen	(720)333-8043 ykampschnieder@gmail.com	6356 Otis St Arvada CO 80003	RM	Teacher	Prin	Bethlehem Lakewood CO	(303)238-7676	S	1994
Kamp-Schroeder Debra J Kamp	(715)250-0416 dkampschreoder4@gmail.com	N8627 Mill Creek Rd Clintonville WI 54929	NW	Teacher	EM			MQ	2007
Kamrath Angela S	(253)538-3886 angelakamrath@aol.com	5608 76th Street Ct E Puyallup WA 98371	NOW	Teacher	Tchr	Concordia Tacoma WA	(253)475-9513	MQ	1999
Kana Tamara S Daugherty	(352)292-4228 tamaraskana@gmail.com	21 Redwood Track Ter Ocala FL 34472	FG	Teacher	Tchr	St John Ocala FL	(352)629-1794	S	1990
Kane Debra L Henderson	(440)596-8011 karl.deb.kane@gmail.com	2214 S State St Unit 107 Saint Joseph MI 49085	NI	Teacher	EM			CQ	1993
Kangas Julie A Lindquist	(714)522-1962 julielind@yahoo.com	25107 Dovetail Cove Ct Tomball TX 77375	TX	Teacher	Prin	Concordia Tomball TX	(281)351-2547	IV	1992
Kangas Sean S	(714)615-5780 skangas12@aol.com	25107 Dovetail Cove Ct Tomball TX 77375	TX	Teacher	Tchr	Trinity Klein Klein TX	(281)376-5773	PO	1997
Kant Jaxson A	(402)992-3353 jaxsonkant@gmail.com	1906 N 26th St Norfolk NE 68701	NEB	Teacher	Tchr	Christ Norfolk NE	(402)371-5536	S	2025
Kapels Paula J Gutz	(402)276-0399 pjkapels@gmail.com	18989 445 St Creston NE 68631	NEB	Teacher	EM			S	1984
Karbash Emily E Grabow	(262)215-8284 eekarbash@gmail.com	1209 Bay De Noc Ct Green Bay WI 54311	NW	Teacher	Tchr	Green Bay Trinity Green Bay WI	(920)655-4673	MQ	2015
Karcher Wayne	(713)851-0144 gigikarcher@gmail.com	15 Grey Birch Pl The Woodlands TX 77381	TX	Teacher	EM			S	1968
Kard Jennifer A Ashby	(727) 510-9259 ashby_jennifer@hotmail.com	1221 43rd Avenue North Saint Petersburg FL 33703	FG	Teacher	Tchr	Grace Saint Petersburg FL	(727)527-6213	S	1994
Karges Caleb W Dr	(307) 346-7031 caleb.karges@lutherclassical.org	4021 Crystie Ln Casper WY 82609	WY	Teacher	Tchr	Mount Hope Casper WY	(307)234-6865	IV	2009
Karges Lonnie R	(775)720-5710 kargerosa@charter.net	171 Six Mile Canyon Rd Dayton NV 89403	CNH	Tch/DCE	Prin	Bethlehem Carson City NV	(775)882-5252	S	1982
Karges Zachary J	(775)230-6256 zachary.karges0202@gmail.com		IN	Teacher	Tchr	Emmaus Fort Wayne IN	(260)459-7722	CQ	2019
Karle Deloris	(708)259-5681	542 S Evergreen Ave Arlington Hts IL 60005	NI	Teacher	EM			RF	1961
Karner Bonnie E Grom	(314)258-4598 bonnie.karner@gmail.com	8613 Copper Knoll Ave Las Vegas NV 89129	PSW	Teacher	EM			S	1976
Karner Jennifer E	(702)686-3606 karnerj@flhsemail.org	11380 Belmont Lake Dr Unit 103 Las Vegas NV 89135	PSW	Teacher	Tchr	Faith Las Vegas NV	(702)804-4400	S	2006
Karner Steven D	skarner@martinlutherhs.org	6700 W Hayes Ave Milwaukee WI 53219	SW	Teacher	Tchr	Martin Luther Greendale WI	(414)421-4000	S	2005
Karolus Stephanie A	(715)350-9422 stephanie.karolus@gmail.com		CNH	DCE		California/Nevada/Hawaii District Livermore CA	(866)264-6079	RF	2013
Karpenko William O II Dr	(651)344-8579 bill.karpenko@gmail.com	15168 Claret Cir Rosemount MN 55068	MNS	Tch/DCE	EM			CQ	1977
Karpinsky Roy D	(262)634-6370 rkarpinsky@wi.rr.com	1703 Chatham St Racine WI 53402	SW	Teacher	EM			RF	1967
Karschnik Anna L Deac	(715)671-8432 annakarschnik@gmail.com	2501 Lancaster Ln N Apt 257 Plymouth MN 55441	MNS	Deaconess	C03/2022			FW-DEAC	2021
Karsten Kenneth P	(812)476-9991 ken@redeemerchurch.org	5611 Woodlawn Dr Newburgh IN 47630	IN	DCM	Mem C	Our Redeemer Evansville IN	(812)476-9991	MQ	2005

*Multiple Assignments (See Church Worker Locator for Additional Details)
See Page 53 for the Table of Abbreviations for key to District, Classification, Position, and College abbreviations.
**C =Candidate; EM =Emeritus; the date following the C is the month and year the Candidate status began

NAME	TELEPHONE NUMBER EMAIL	STREET ADDRESS CITY/STATE/ZIP	DISTRICT	CLASS.	POSITION/ STATUS**	WHERE SERVING	OFFICE PHONE	COLLEGE/ UNIV/CQ	YR GRAD
Karvelius Victor W	(815)229-8858 dv136@comcast.net	50 Arkansaw Traveller Rd Hardy AR 72542	MDS	Teacher	EM			RF	1970
Kaschinske Eric J	(260)492-2735 ekaschinske@clhscadets.com	6502 Landmark Dr Fort Wayne IN 46815	IN	Teacher	Tchr	Concordia Fort Wayne IN	(260)483-1102	RF	1996
Kaschinske Kenneth A	(989)793-3607 kaschinske@chartermi.net	4850 Hanover Dr Saginaw MI 48603	MI	Teacher	EM			RF	1967
Kaschube Elizabeth M Uekert	(616)821-6587 cbkaschube@netscape.net	1209 Oakes Ave Grand Haven MI 49417	MI	Teacher	Tchr	Trinity Muskegon MI	(231)755-1292	AA	2002
Kaspar Neal A	(970)201-3835	503 Riverview Dr Grand Junction CO 81507	RM	Teacher	EM			RF	1968
Kasper Deborah L Brandt	(734)340-4447 robertkasper45@yahoo.com	8145 Starling Ct Ypsilanti MI 48197	MI	Teacher	EM			SP	1985
Kasper Holly E Burggraf	(520)664-6203 hollyekasper@gmail.com	7606 Madrid Dr Lansing MI 48917	MI	Teacher	Tchr	Lutheran Special Education Ministries Ann Arbor MI	(248)419-3390	CQ	2012
Kasper Shelli R Kasper Stuewe	(512)293-7025 shelli51169@gmail.com	P.O. Box 7 Walburg TX 78673	TX	Teacher	EM			CQ	1994
Kassebaum Tina M Ziemnick	(314)732-7386 kassebaum.tina@gmail.com	1214 St. Jean Street Florissant MO 63031	SI	DCE	Prin	Immanuel Okawville IL	(618)243-6142	SP	1996
Kassel Robert G	bobkassel741@gmail.com	1542 Ontario Dr Waterloo IL 62298	SI	Teacher	EM			RF	1963
Kassl Linda M Brockett		801 S Madison St Bloomington IL 61701	CI	Teacher	Tchr	Trinity Bloomington IL	(309)828-6265	RF	1981
Kassulke Megan M	(816)810-3574 megan.homan@cune.org	12903 E 36th Terrace South Independence MO 64055	MO	Teacher	Tchr	Christ Platte Woods MO	(816)741-8031	S	2008
Kasten Benjamin J	(618)201-4919 bkasen@corlhs.org	214 N Park St Hoyleton IL 62803	SI	Teacher	Tchr	Christ Our Rock Centralia IL	(618)226-3315	S	2004
Kasten Frances H Bailey	(847)345-3439 fbailey@lincolnlutheran.org	214 N Park St Hoyleton IL 62803	SI	Teacher	Tchr	Trinity Hoyleton IL	(618)493-6226	MQ	2009
Kasten Robert R	(262)388-1856 rjkasten@hotmail.com	2486 Wallace Lake Rd West Bend WI 53090	SW	Teacher	EM			RF	1968
Kasten Ronald L	(636)432-1576 ronandl.kasten@gmail.com	639 Oak Crossing Dr Villa Ridge MO 63089	MO	Teacher	EM			RF	1958
Kasten Sandra L Rueger	(920)458-1058 ejohnson@excel.net	1904 Tivoli Ln Sheboygan WI 53081	SW	Teacher	Tchr	Bethlehem Sheboygan WI	(920)452-5071	RF	1975
Kastens Alice C Nobe	(314)892-0888 ackastens@gmail.com	5101 Kings Park Dr Saint Louis MO 63129	SI	Teacher	EM			CQ	1998
Kaster John H			TX	DCM	EM			MQ	1984
Katz Diane L Going	(630)336-7093 dianekatz77@yahoo.com	12809 Indigo Way Bradenton FL 34211	FG	Teacher	EM			RF	1980
Kaufman Kara L Gsell	(503)853-9750 kaufmanpls@gmail.com	3555 SE Lake Rd Portland OR 97222	NOW	Teacher	Tchr	Pilgrim Beaverton OR	(503)644-8697	PO	1999
Kaufmann Carlie L Rettke	(309)678-4682 carliekauf@gmail.com	1400 N Parkway Dr Pekin IL 61554	CI	Teacher	Tchr	Bethel Morton IL	(309)266-6592	CH	2019
Kaufmann Catherine M Consoer	(262)539-4250 mrs.kaufmann.4@gmail.com	8520 Fishman Rd Burlington WI 53105	SW	Teacher	EM			S	1969
Kaufmann Jonah T	(714)944-8784 jonahkaufmann@gmail.com	102 5th Ave Apt. 11-103 Milton WA 98354	NOW	DCE	Mem C	St Lukes Federal Way WA	(253)941-3000	IV	2021
Kaufmann Joy C Schutte	(714)944-7631 joyckaufmann@gmail.com	13027 W Telemark St Boise ID 83713	NOW	DCE	Mem C	Friendship Meridian ID	(208)288-2404	RF	1994
Kaufmann Katie M Deac	(217)503-7864 kkaufmann@lutheranlifevillages.org	4668 Craftsbury Cir Apt B Fort Wayne IN 46818	IN	Deaconess	RSO	Lutheran Homes Inc Fort Wayne IN	(260)447-1591	CH	2023
Kaufmann Timothy P	(714)944-6199 tkaufmann@friendshipcelebration.org	13027 W Telemark Boise ID 83713	NOW	DCE	Mem C	Friendship Meridian ID	(208)288-2404	RF	1992
Kaun Robert W Jr	rwkaun@gmail.com	5770 Eldon St Greendale WI 53129	EN	Teacher	EM			MW	1980
Kavugha Rehema B	(504)390-1801 rehema1983@gmail.com	5568 Pierre Ct. St. Louis MO 63128	MO	Teacher	Pro Stf	Lutheran Church Extension Fund Saint Louis MO	(314)965-9000	S	2007
Kayser Doris A Deac	jooyinjesus@gmail.com	2481 Abbington Dr SE Grand Rapids MI 49506	MI	Deaconess	EM			FW	2012
Keaton Gail F Fiske	gandmkeaton@gmail.com	391 Heritage Dr Rochester NY 14615	EA	Teacher	EM			RF	1974
Keck Robert A	(410) 925-5458 keck807@comcast.net	807 Hillen Rd Towson MD 21286	SE	Teacher	EM			BR	1976
Keefer Megan Stites	(260)715-7509 megk626@gmail.com	1735 Brandywind Trl Fort Wayne IN 46845	IN	Teacher	C07/2022			CH	2013
Keeley Julie M	(406)599-3280 juliekeeleybp@gmail.com	4251 Lariat Ln Grand Island NE 68803	NEB	DCM	C03/2024			MQ	2009
Keenan Carol A Beineke	(352)216-8106 fromhisflock@aol.com	8810 SE 141st Loop Summerfield FL 34491	FG	Teacher	EM			CQ	2002
Kegley Denise R Duvall	denisekegley@mac.com	2925 Crosswind Trl Jackson WI 53037	SW	Teacher	Tchr	St Johns West Bend WI	(262)334-3077	CQ	2002
Kegley Elizabeth Eberhart	(414)581-1156 bethlankegley@gmail.com	405 Garfield Ave Valparaiso IN 46383	IN	Teacher	C07/2016			MQ	2013
Kehe Michael J	(314)607-3735 michaelkehe@sbcglobal.net	10 S Elizabeth Ave Ferguson MO 63135	MO	Tch/DCE	EM			RF	1983
Kehr Mark A	(937)738-7073 fritzgone200@yahoo.com	453 Timberview Dr Marysville OH 43040	OH	Tch/DCE	EM			S	1972
Keilman Tamara S Schepmann	(812)524-2551 tsgk01@aol.com	617 Pineway Ct Seymour IN 47274	IN	Teacher	Tchr	Immanuel Seymour IN	(812)522-3118	AA	1993
Keily-Vann Katie E Keily	katie.vann@melhs.org	426 Tiffin Ave Ferguson MO 63135	SI	Teacher	Tchr	Metro-East Edwardsville IL	(618)656-0043	S	2013

*Multiple Assignments (See Church Worker Locator for Additional Details)
See Page 53 for the Table of Abbreviations for key to District, Classification, Position, and College abbreviations.
**C =Candidate; EM =Emeritus; the date following the C is the month and year the Candidate status began

NAME	TELEPHONE NUMBER EMAIL	STREET ADDRESS CITY/STATE/ZIP	DISTRICT	CLASS.	POSITION/ STATUS**	WHERE SERVING	OFFICE PHONE	COLLEGE/ UNIV/CQ	YR GRAD
Keinath Julie L Hooper	(989)882-5531 julie.keinath@stpaul-millington.org	4507 Main St Millington MI 48746	MI	Teacher	C07/2016			AA	2006
Keiper Christa F Kasten	(281)773-7931 keiperc@att.net	22906 Shieldhall Lane Tomball TX 77375	TX	Teacher	Tchr	Trinity Klein Klein TX	(281)376-5773	RF	1995
Keiper Gertrude M Lieder Dr	(979)450-6688 gert.keiper@concordia.edu	679 Partridge Cir Golden CO 80403	TX	Teacher	EM			CQ	1989
Keiper Paul E Dr	(281)773-7831 pek@tamu.edu	22906 Shieldhall Ln Tomball TX 77375	TX	Teacher	EM			MQ	1987
Keiper Val H Dr	(414)412-2531 val.keiper@cuw.edu	5413 N Navajo Ave Glendale WI 53217	SW	Teacher	S HS/C	Concordia University Wisconsin Mequon WI	(262)243-5700	PO	1980
Keithley Joshua J	(913)444-2397 dcejosh@lordoflifekc.com	1906 E 241st Street Cleveland MO 64734	KS	DCE	Mem C	Lord Of Life Leawood KS	(913)681-5167	S	2005
Keithley Kari Saving	(719)660-4474	1906 E 241st St Cleveland MO 64734	RM	Teacher	Tchr	Immanuel Colorado Springs CO	(719)636-5011	S	2005
Kelderman Laverne I Meyer	(319)266-3428 Laverne.kelderman@gmail.com	5415 Lemongrass Dr Cedar Falls IA 50613	IE	Teacher	EM			SP	1972
Kell Donald L Dr	(916)434-0759 kell.d@sbcglobal.net	2100 Redwood Rd Apt 203 Napa CA 94558	CNH	Teacher	EM			RF	1953
Kell Jeremy J		766 Greystone Dr Port Washington WI 53074	SW	Teacher	Tchr	St Paul Grafton WI	(262)377-4659	MQ	1998
Kellar Robert J	(618)616-5905 rkellar007@hotmail.com	1990 Mapleleaf Dr Collinsville IL 62234	SI	Teacher	EM			RF	1989
Kelle Grace E	(507)564-2196 gklainie@gmail.com	7585 W Drexel Ave Apt 223 Franklin WI 53132	EN	Teacher	Tchr	Hales Corners Hales Corners WI	(414)529-6701	MQ	2023
Keller Jennifer C	(561)632-5138 jenniferckeller@yahoo.com	3730 E Sandpiper Dr #3 Boynton Beach FL 33436	FG	Teacher	C07/2016			SP	2008
Keller Jennifer M	(425)647-5574 keller.jenniferm@outlook.com	23912 NE 113th Ln Redmond WA 98053	NOW	Teacher	EM			S	1996
Keller Megan R Friend	(812)521-0536 mkeller@immanuelschool.org		IN	Teacher	Tchr	Immanuel Seymour IN	(812)522-1301	CQ	2023
Keller Michael T	(989)860-4323 mkeller@stlorenz.org	2 Krafft Court Frankenmuth MI 48734	MI	Teacher	Tchr	St Lorenz Frankenmuth MI	(989)652-6141	Other	2013
Keller Stephanie L Gehrs	skeller1619@gmail.com	1155 S Ridge Ave Arlington Hts IL 60005	NI	Teacher	RSO	Lutheran Church Charities Northbrook IL	(866)455-6466	RF	1987
Kellerman Deanna M		3545 S Shore Dr Hubertus WI 53033	SW	Teacher	Tchr	Grace Menomonee Falls WI	(262)251-7140	MQ	2007
Kellerman Joel A	joelkellerman@gmail.com	2197 Cherokee St Grafton WI 53024	SW	Teacher	C07/2016			MQ	2003
Kelley Ashley N Myer	(573)275-3465 ashleykelley1219@gmail.com	610 W Cape Rock Dr Cape Girardeau MO 63701	MO	Teacher	Tchr	Trinity Cape Girardeau MO	(573)334-1068	CQ	2023
Kelling Lori A Rever	(414)315-7715 kelling.lori@gmail.com	10457 Shields Ct San Diego CA 92124	PSW	Teacher	Tchr	St Pauls San Diego CA	(858)272-6282	MQ	2010
Kelling Stephanie R Loseke	(414)339-3923 stephaniekelling4@gmail.com	9168 N Sacred Sky Pl Tucson AZ 85743	EN	Teacher	EM			S	1976
Kelly Jacob W	(316)218-2772 jkelly@holycrosslutheran.net	828 N Bedford Ct Wichita KS 67206	KS	Teacher	Tchr	Holy Cross Wichita KS	(316)684-5201	CQ	2018
Kelly Kimberly A		2021 S State St Saint Joseph MI 49085	MI	Teacher	Tchr	Trinity Saint Joseph MI	(269)983-5000	CQ	2008
Kelly Quinn M	(636)856-6656 quinnmk19@gmail.com	666 Dundee Ct Wentzville MO 63385	MO	Teacher	Tchr	Child Of God Saint Peters MO	(636)970-7080	CH	2024
Kelly Sarah J Hunt	(636)541-2622 skelly@messiahnetwork.org	666 Dundee Ct Wentzville MO 63385	MO	Teacher	Tchr	Messiah Weldon Spring MO	(636)926-9773	CQ	2014
Kelm George G	(262)877-8729 geona2@charter.net	404 Tindalls Nest Twin Lakes WI 53181	NI	Teacher	EM			SP	1971
Kelso Corey L	(714)624-1525 coreykelso7@gmail.com	2879 N Roxbury St Orange CA 92867	PSW	Teacher	Tchr	Salem Orange CA	(714)633-2366	IV	2015
Kelso Danielle C Klaub	(714)624-2618 danielle.kelso@lhsoc.org	5302 E Rural Ridge Cir Anheim Hills CA 92807	PSW	Teacher	Tchr	Orange County Orange CA	(714)998-5151	IV	1988
Kelso Darren L	(714)624-2617 darren.kelso@lhsoc.org	5302 E Rural Ridge Cir Anheim Hills CA 92807	PSW	Teacher	Tchr	Orange County Orange CA	(714)998-5151	IV	1986
Kelso Nicole J Zehnder	(916)622-7059 nicole.zehnder@eagles.cui.edu	2879 N Roxbury St Orange CA 92867	PSW	Teacher	Tchr	Salem Orange CA	(714)633-2366	IV	2015
Kelzer Debra S David	(612)619-8220	6785 Quartz Ave Mayer MN 55360	MNS	Teacher	EM			SP	1982
Kembel Sharon A Muehl	(970)768-2538 robertsharon69@msn.com	17557 County Road V Fort Morgan CO 80701	RM	Teacher	EM			RF	1969
Kemmis Sidney C	(309)236-5061 sckemmis@yahoo.com	28236 Ridge Rd Prophetstown IL 61277	NI	DCM	Mem C	St John Lena IL	(815)369-4035	MQ	2010
Kemnitz Alec M	(979)429-5685 aleckemnitz10@rocketmail.com	6102 Black Gum Dr Houston TX 77092	TX	Teacher	Tchr	Our Savior Houston TX	(713)290-8277	CQ	2013
Kemnitz Dirk A	(713)290-8277 dkemnitz@mac.com	946 Del Norte St Houston TX 77018	TX	Teacher	EM			S	1981
Kemp Stacy A Ulrich	(949)235-0171	2142 Border Ave Corona CA 92882	PSW	Teacher	Pro Stf	Crean Irvine CA	(949)387-1199	IV	2011
Kempe Jean M Beck	(951)682-7613 jean.kempe@ilcs-riverside.org	5455 Alessandro Blvd Riverside CA 92506	PSW	DCE	Mem C	Immanuel Riverside CA	(951)682-7613	SP	2002
Kemper Lorna B Koehnlein McAlpine	(480)559-0552 jlmcalpine@yahoo.com	3902 Westgate Dr Saint Joseph MO 64506	PSW	Teacher	EM			CQ	1996
Kempfert Elizabeth A Kaiser	(712)898-1361 liz.kempfert@unityridge.org	2235 200th St Denison IA 51442	IW	Teacher	Tchr	Unity Ridge Denison IA	(712)393-2002	CQ	2023
Kempff Elna M	(989)868-9921 ekboots@att.net	2252 Mallard Dr Reese MI 48757	MI	Teacher	EM			RF	1957
Kempff Mark N	(314)398-6153 kempffmr@gmail.com	4394 Olive St Saint Louis MO 63108	MO	Teacher	S HS/C	Concordia Seminary Saint Louis MO	(314)505-7000	S	1974

*Multiple Assignments (See Church Worker Locator for Additional Details)
See Page 53 for the Table of Abbreviations for key to District, Classification, Position, and College abbreviations.
**C =Candidate; EM =Emeritus; the date following the C is the month and year the Candidate status began

NAME	TELEPHONE NUMBER EMAIL	STREET ADDRESS CITY/STATE/ZIP	DISTRICT	CLASS.	POSITION/ STATUS**	WHERE SERVING	OFFICE PHONE	COLLEGE/ UNIV/CQ	YR GRAD
Kempin Karen L Chance	(989)708-6688 kkempin@sjlmidland.org	3801 Wintergreen Dr Midland MI 48640	MI	Tch/DCE	Mem C	St John's Midland MI	(989)835-5861	S	1994
Kendall Kendra R Fleck	(816)262-6749 kkendall@splcc.org	1313 S. 30th St. Saint Joseph MO 64507	MO	Teacher	P/Tchr	St Paul Saint Joseph MO	(816)279-1110	CQ	2020
Kennedy Harold W	(631)942-7238 harold.kennedy@luhi.org	14 Oakland Ave East Northport NY 11731	AT	Teacher	Tchr	Long Island Brookville NY	(516)626-1735	CQ	2018
Kennedy Susan Q Quisenberry	(301)502-4952 sqkennedy@aol.com	3150 Mallory Sq Port Republic MD 20676	SE	Teacher	Tchr	Grace La Plata MD	(301)932-0963	BR	1987
Kennell Charles	(414)354-6810 clkenn6470@att.net	6336 W Donges Ln Brown Deer WI 53223	SW	Teacher	EM			S	1965
Kennell Emily A Tlusty	emilykennell@gmail.com		MO	DCE	C07/2016			SP	2006
Kennell Linda J Rubke	(414)354-6810 lindak515@icloud.com	6336 W Donges Ln Brown Deer WI 53223	SW	Teacher	EM			RF	1970
Kenney Alyssa P Joerz	(631)603-9683 alyssa.joerz@outlook.com	4101 Player Cir 504 Orlando FL 32808	FG	Teacher	Tchr	Faith Eustis FL	(352)589-5433	BR	2014
Kenney John W III Dr	(714)289-7621	1219 E Vanowen Ave Orange CA 92867	PSW	Teacher	EM			CQ	2003
Kenniston Rita F Gantka	(541)420-7667 stanleykenniston@gmail.com	21035 Azalia Ave Bend OR 97702	NOW	Teacher	EM			CQ	1990
Kenow Peter D	(402)641-5700 pete.kenow@cune.edu	945 N 3rd St Seward NE 68434	NEB	Tch/DCE	S HS/C	Concordia University Nebraska Seward NE	(402)643-3651	S	1988
Kerkman Randall J	(512)554-5965 ranjokman@gmail.com	11716 Barchetta Dr Austin TX 78758	TX	Tch/DCE	EM			RF	1975
Kern Becky S Karr	(406)755-5144 beckykern@trinityed.org	6203 Shiloh Ave Unit A Whitefish MT 59937	MT	Teacher	EM			S	1978
Kern Bonnie L Leidel	(517)652-9445	3839 S Block Rd Frankenmuth MI 48734	MI	Teacher	EM			RF	1969
Kern Dennis L	(269)429-4979 kern_joan@hotmail.com	Q3 Cond Villas De Playa 1 Dorado PR 00646	MI	Teacher	EM			S	1972
Kern Edward A	(812)523-8554 ekern@cinergymetro.net	210 Vehslage Rd Seymour IN 47274	IN	Teacher	EM			RF	1964
Kern Hanna M Hoffbeck Deac	hanna.hoffbeck@gmail.com	9277 Slattery Rd Marlette MI 48453	MI	Deaconess	Mem C	Our Savior Marlette MI	(989)635-7994	FW-DEAC	2019
Kern Kimberly L	kernk@ourshepherd.net	1822 Elliott Ave Madison Hts MI 48071	MI	Teacher	Tchr	Our Shepherd Birmingham MI	(248)645-0551	AA	1987
Kern Loretta L Gehrke	(989)652-8579 franzkl@charter.net	236 Cherry St Frankenmuth MI 48734	MI	Teacher	EM			RF	1964
Kern Stuart C	(989)868-4026 kathystul@gmail.com	2229 Mallard Dr Reese MI 48757	MI	Teacher	EM			RF	1966
Kernkamp Lynn M	(954)242-4438 lkernkamp@aol.com	17510 Bedford Dr Brookfield WI 53045	FG	Teacher	EM			RF	1970
Kernstock Patricia J	(586)212-3337 pattyjk@yahoo.com		CI	Parish Assist	Pro Stf	Luth School Assoc Decatur IL	(217)233-2001	AA	1985
Kerr Homer U	(317)862-3690 rk1950@sbcglobal.net	4257 Wanamaker Dr Indianapolis IN 46239	IN	Teacher	EM			CQ	1986
Kerrins Melia R Hartmann	(508)946-9585 melialial@netzero.com	3301 S Goldfield Rd Lot 4086 Apache Junction AZ 85119	RM	Teacher	C07/2016			IV	1992
Kersten John V Jr	(314)583-1543 john.kersten@gmail.com	1935 Keelen Dr Saint Louis MO 63136	MO	Teacher	EM			S	1977
Kersten Lois M Heggemeier	(636)464-9760	1960 Parkton West Dr Barnhart MO 63012	MO	Teacher	EM			S	1964
Kersten Michael J			AT	Teacher	S Miss	Office of International Mission Saint Louis MO		S	2007
Kersten Robert A	(920)290-3193 rkersten49@yahoo.com	310 E Huron St Berlin WI 54923	SW	Teacher	EM			SP	1972
Kerwin Ellen R Baumann	(516) 849-0763 ekerwin@trinityhicksville.org	276 9th St Bethpage NY 11714	AT	Teacher	Tchr	Trinity Hicksville NY	(516)931-2225	BR	1984
Kesar Avery P	(531)210-2471 averykesar@concordiaprepschool. org	1145 Concordia Dr Towson MD 21286	SE	Teacher	Tchr	Concordia Towson MD	(410)825-2323	S	2021
Kesar Michael L	(402)452-8371 kesarmichael@gmail.com	2203 Silent Springs Court League City TX 77573	TX	Teacher	Mem C	Hope Friendswood TX	(281)482-7943	AA	1983
Kesar Vivian H Heldt	(402)203-6615 kesarvivian@gmail.com	2203 Silent Springs Court League City TX 77573	TX	Teacher	EM			AA	1985
Kesel Dawn B Bergelin	(573)616-9431 dbbergelin@yahoo.com	160 Lindenwood Pl Holts Summit MO 65043	MO	Teacher	Tchr	Trinity Jefferson City MO	(573)636-6750	MQ	1999
Keseman Andrew E	(618)207-0500 andrew.keseman@cune.org	1201 Greenlawn Drive Norfolk NE 68701	NEB	Teacher	Tchr	Northeast Norfolk NE	(402)379-3040	S	2014
Keseman Rachel E	(618)207-7286 rachelkeseman@gmail.com	815 Brookmead Drive O'fallon MO 63366	MO	Teacher	Tchr	Immanuel Wentzville MO	(636)639-9887	S	2017
Keseman Rena J Bertermann	(509)396-9436 renakes@gmail.com	3225 Kristin Ct West Richland WA 99353	NOW	Teacher	C07/2016			PO	1995
Keshishian Karen K Sylvester	(410)836-8111 kkeshish@comcast.net	409 Dellcrest Dr Forest Hill MD 21050	SE	Teacher	Tchr	St Pauls Kingsville MD	(410)592-8100	RF	1982
Keske Richard P	(815)874-7499 rpkeske@gmail.com	5575 Skywood Ter Rockford IL 61109	NI	Teacher	EM			RF	1968
Kessels Samantha N Coomer	(636)357-1755 samanthacoomer20@gmail.com	220 Allison Ln Winfield MO 63389	MO	Teacher	C07/2022			S	2018
Kester Brenda A Post	bkester2000@gmail.com	N205 Kester Rd Fremont WI 54940	NW	Teacher	EM			MQ	1986
Kester Laura A		621 32nd St N Apt 108 Wisconsin Rapids WI 54494	NW	Teacher	Tchr	Immanuel Wisconsin Rapids WI	(715)423-3260	SP	2016

*Multiple Assignments (See Church Worker Locator for Additional Details)
See Page 53 for the Table of Abbreviations for key to District, Classification, Position, and College abbreviations.
**C =Candidate; EM =Emeritus; the date following the C is the month and year the Candidate status began

NAME	TELEPHONE NUMBER EMAIL	STREET ADDRESS CITY/STATE/ZIP	DISTRICT	CLASS.	POSITION/ STATUS**	WHERE SERVING	OFFICE PHONE	COLLEGE/ UNIV/CQ	YR GRAD
Kester Olivia R	(920)250-0077 olivia.kester@oursaviors-school.org	1625 Westchester Blvd Apt #1 Springfield IL 62704	CI	Teacher	Tchr	Our Saviors Springfield IL	(217)546-4531	MQ	2019
Ketcher Karol R Mueller Deac	ketcher@trinitycp.org	391 Golden Oak Dr Crown Point IN 46307	IN	Deaconess	Mem C	Trinity Crown Point IN	(219)663-1578	FW-DEAC	2023
Ketcher Ronald L	(952)240-2107 excellentlawnkare@yahoo.com	54809 Pearl St Osage MN 56570	MNN	Teacher	EM			SP	1983
Ketterer John E	(586)945-3856 john.kettererdce@gmail.com	9814 North St Reese MI 48757	MI	DCE	Mem C	Trinity Reese MI	(989)868-9901	S	2018
Kettler Victoria A Piller		17 Walden Pond Dr Nashua NH 03064	NE	Teacher	EM			BR	2010
Kettner Warren W	(303)935-2969	3246 S Wolff St Denver CO 80236	RM	Teacher	EM			CQ	1963
Keuning Lynette L Arft	(515)789-4008 keuningll@iowatelecom.net	313 Marshall St Dexter IA 50070	IW	Teacher	C07/2016			RF	1986
Keup Aaron W	(734)678-0414 fortress_ak@yahoo.com	20777 Walnut Dr Reed City MI 49677	MI	Teacher	Tchr	Trinity Reed City MI	(231)832-5186	AA	2004
Keup Joel A	jkeup@peacesaginaw.org	1800 Wilson Ave Saginaw MI 48638	MI	Teacher	Tchr	Peace Saginaw MI	(989)792-2581	RF	1997
Keup Karen L Von Behren	(989)777-8321	5115 Sheridan Rd Saginaw MI 48601	MI	Teacher	EM			RF	1990
Keup Ronald W		5115 Sheridan Rd Saginaw MI 48601	MI	Teacher	EM			RF	1971
Keyne Lisa K Dr	(360)949-5118 lisakeyne@gmail.com	11608 NW 34th Ave Vancouver WA 98685	NOW	Tch/DCE	EM			SP	1981
Keyne-Michaels Lynn Keyne Dr	(360)600-2549 lkeyne-michaels@outlook.com	11118 NW 6th Ave Vancouver WA 98685	NOW	Teacher	EM			S	1978
Keys Carolyn R Kilian	(713)208-4076 crkeys@gmail.com	2002 Concord St Deer Park TX 77536	TX	Teacher	Tchr	Memorial Houston TX	(713)782-4022	S	1973
Kidd Alene R Deac			SO	Deaconess	Mem C	Prince Peace Pineville LA	(318)473-0812	SL-DEAC	2025
Kidd Michelle Y Walker	(260)438-1815 dmjckidd@gmail.com	1523 Faulkner Ct Fort Wayne IN 46815	IN	Teacher	C11/2019			CQ	2010
Kidd Tori A	(407)760-5507 tkidd@1stglencoe.org	13375 91st Pl N Maple Grove MN 55369	MNS	DCE	C07/2022			S	2016
Kidston Alicia A Stuckenschmidt Oates	(303)263-9245 astuke3@hotmail.com	17613 Hoyt Pl Parker CO 80134	RM	Teacher	Tchr	Lutheran Parker CO	(303)841-5551	S	2003
Kiehl Karen K Lassman	(480)246-1378 kathy.kiehl@gmail.com	10528 Waking Cloud Ave Las Vegas NV 89129	PSW	Teacher	EM			S	1967
Kiehl Peter J	(727)515-5543 peterkiehl@yahoo.com	8261 Summers St Utica MI 48317	MI	Teacher	Tchr	Trinity Utica MI	(586)731-4490	S	1997
Kiel Janice R	(812)525-0727 jankiel@msn.com	1001 Fontview Dr Columbus IN 47201	IN	Teacher	Mem C	St Peter Columbus IN	(812)372-1571	RF	1986
Kiel Stephanie J Brake	(336)692-5951 kiel.stephaniej@gmail.com	4001 Sundown Rd Gaithersburg MD 20882	SE	Teacher	Tchr	St Paul Catonsville MD	(410)747-1924	CQ	2009
Kieschnick Glen A	(512)657-5415 gkieschnick@gmail.com	116 Eisenhower Ct Georgetown TX 78633	TX	Teacher	EM			S	1973
Kiesel Richard C	(954)962-0332	140 NW 78th Ave Pembroke Pnes FL 33024	FG	Teacher	C07/2016			RF	1972
Kietzman Janna K	(218)507-0103 jkkietzman@gmail.com	31211 Hazel Rd Akeley MN 56433	MNN	Teacher	Tchr	Immanuel Walker MN	(218)547-4139	SP	1984
Kightlinger Timothy P	(515)278-2694 tim@gloriadeionline.com	180 80th St Unit 108 Wdm IA 50266	IW	DCE	Mem C	Gloria Dei Urbandale IA	(515)276-1700	S	1993
Kilgus Joel E	(309)251-6624	3075 Quail Ridge Rd Bettendorf IA 52722	IE	Teacher	Prin	Trinity Davenport IA	(563)322-5224	CQ	2015
Killian Lisa M Kath	(224)588-2077 lisakillian614@gmail.com	3032 Woods Creek Ln Algonquin IL 60102	NI	Teacher	Tchr	Zion Marengo IL	(815)568-6564	RF	1987
Kilpatrick Andrea D Kimble	(952)393-1259 AndreaDKilpatrick@gmail.com	13700 Foxfield Ln Little Rock AR 72211	MDS	Teacher	Tchr	Christ Little Rock AR	(501)663-5232	CH	2009
Kilps Lori L Gottschalk	(920)793-3368 lorikilps@gmail.com	3504 Pierce Ct Two Rivers WI 54241	SW	Teacher	EM			RF	1978
Kim Eugene P Dr	(949)333-9188 eugene.kim@cui.edu	35 Wild Trails Irvine CA 92618	PSW	Teacher	S HS/C	Concordia University Irvine Irvine CA	(949)854-8002	CQ	2018
Kim EunChu	(949)331-4308 eunchukim@yahoo.com	35 Wild Trails Irvine CA 92618	PSW	Teacher	D Ex/S	Pacific Southwest District Irvine CA	(949)854-3232	CQ	2015
Kimble Daniel F	(952)297-5505 danknya@gmail.com	303 4th Ave SW Young America MN 55397	MNS	Teacher	EM			RF	1972
Kimmel Sharon K	(716)637-5638 stskim@yahoo.com	2227 Sweden Walker Rd Hilton NY 14468	EA	Teacher	EM			CQ	1997
Kindred Allison K Seeliger	(405)760-6362 aseeliger@sllcs.org	2450 Cherry Laurel Dr Apt 218 Sanford FL 32771	S	Teacher	Tchr	St Lukes Oviedo FL	(407)365-3228	S	2018
King Amy L Martinez	(708)204-9078 amy.king@sharingnewlife.com	5532 Plata Ln Benbrook TX 76126	TX	Teacher	Tchr	St Paul Fort Worth TX	(817)332-2281	CQ	2021
King Carole R Deac	(219)775-5533 basenjimere94@yahoo.com	8210 W Sunbury Ct Milwaukee WI 53219	SW	Deaconess	Mem C	St Paul West Allis WI	(414)541-6250	CH	1986
King Dorothy L Riedel	(314)780-0270 takingjr@hotmail.com	600 Breeze Park Dr Apt 308 Weldon Spring MO 63304	MO	Teacher	EM			RF	1969
King Janis D Dorsch	(707)208-2996 janisellen1@gmail.com	12596 S Arezzo Way Nampa ID 83686	CNH	Teacher	EM			BR	1980
King Judith H Wiebold	(763)438-6123 jhkteacher2nd@yahoo.com	11969 Utah Ave N Champlin MN 55316	MNN	Teacher	Tchr	Prince Of Peace Saint Cloud MN	(320)251-1477	SP	1977
King Judith I Macholz	(310)701-7688 kinjudy@gmail.com	15318 Whitmore St Bennington NE 68007	NEB	Teacher	EM			S	1971
King Kristie L	(224)659-1633 k_King_@hotmail.com	11 Summit St East Dundee IL 60118	NI	Teacher	Tchr	Immanuel East Dundee IL	(847)428-1010	RF	2016
King Thomas A Jr	(314)780-0906 takingjr@hotmail.com	600 Breeze Park Dr Apt 308 Weldon Spring MO 63304	MO	Teacher	EM			RF	1968

*Multiple Assignments (See Church Worker Locator for Additional Details)
See Page 53 for the Table of Abbreviations for key to District, Classification, Position, and College abbreviations.
**C =Candidate; EM =Emeritus; the date following the C is the month and year the Candidate status began

NAME	TELEPHONE NUMBER EMAIL	STREET ADDRESS CITY/STATE/ZIP	DISTRICT	CLASS.	POSITION/ STATUS**	WHERE SERVING	OFFICE PHONE	COLLEGE/ UNIV/CQ	YR GRAD
King Tracy L LeMaster	(832)250-1435 tracylking30@GMAIL.COM	20803 Windy Briar Ln Spring TX 77379	TX	Teacher	Tchr	Trinity Spring TX	(281)376-5810	CQ	2012
Kingston Gayle M Utecht	(480)734-6568 asuprofmate@gmail.com	8440 West Tonto Ln Peoria AZ 85382	PSW	Teacher	EM			CQ	1989
Kinley Stephanie Deac	(804)840-4857 skinley@holycrossfw.org	5341 Brookfarm Pl Fort Wayne IN 46835	IN	Deaconess	Mem C	Holy Cross Fort Wayne IN	(260)483-3173	FW-DEAC	2025
Kinsel Jan L Sipos	(630)234-6190 jkinsel323@gmail.com	366 Poplar Dr Yorkville IL 60560	NI	DCM	Mem C	Cross Yorkville IL	(630)553-7335	MQ	2017
Kinsey Melissa A Hartmann	(314)452-2744 mkinsey@fils.org	W69N389 Evergreen Blvd Cedarburg WI 53012	SW	Teacher	Tchr	First Immanuel Cedarburg WI	(262)377-6610	S	1998
Kintz Rachel L Baumann	(402)640-2326 baumann.rachel1@gmail.com	114 Del Rio Ct Belleville IL 62221	SI	Teacher	Tchr	Zion Belleville IL	(618)234-0275	S	2012
Kinworthy John C Dr	(402)643-2592	714 N 1st St Seward NE 68434	NEB	Teacher	EM			RF	1963
Kipp Anita E	(314)540-3488 7777anita7777@gmail.com	1113 Victory Dr Saint Louis MO 63125	MO	Teacher	EM			S	1977
Kipp Marla R Kurth	(920)980-9829 mkipp@sjrl.org	N3332 Rock Rd Cascade WI 53011	SW	Teacher	Prin	St John Random Lake WI	(920)994-9190	MQ	2001
Kipp Michael R	(402)394-1557 kippmike@hotmail.com	2317 Fairview Dr Norfolk NE 68701	NEB	DCE	C10/2018			S	2008
Kirby Emilie S Schultz	(832)482-7348 emilie.schultz@cune.org	1139 Schulte Rd Saint Louis MO 63146	MO	Teacher	Tchr	St Pauls Des Peres MO	(314)822-9219	S	2012
Kirby Kathryn J Bergdolt	(217)682-5429 trinityteacher@hotmail.com	612 W North 1st St Stewardson IL 62463	CI	Teacher	Tchr	Trinity Stewardson IL	(217)682-3881	S	1984
Kirchenberg Jonathan W	(253)227-2359 jwkirche@gmail.com	8478 Sweet Cherry Ln Magnolia TX 77354	TX	Teacher	Tchr	Concordia Tomball TX	(281)351-2547	AA	2006
Kirchenberg Mark R	(231) 510-4202 mkirchenberg@trinitymanistee.com	664 Ravine Drive Manistee MI 49660	MI	Teacher	EM			RF	1976
Kirchenberg Ralph J	(708)345-9353 ralph.kirchenberg@cuchicago.edu	1000 N 2nd Ave Maywood IL 60153	NI	Teacher	EM			RF	1955
Kirchner Cheryl N Middlestadt	(952)210-0632 ritakirchner@comcast.net	150 Front St N Unit 225 Prescott WI 54021	MNS	Teacher	C09/2023			SP	1985
Kirin Wendy J Pelletier	(863)224-6949 wendy.kirin@gmail.com	139 Eloise Oaks Dr Winter Haven FL 33884	FG	Teacher	Tchr	Grace Winter Haven FL	(863)293-9744	RF	1983
Kirk Juliane M Mayo Deac	(251)680-3439 erbmem@bellsouth.net	740 Winesap Dr Fairhope AL 36532	SO	Deaconess	Mem C	Redeemer Fairhope AL	(251)928-8397	FW-DEAC	2017
Kirk Kristi Kasper	(512)659-7881	605 Pebblestone Walk Dr Cedar Park TX 78613	TX	Teacher	C04/2023			CQ	2019
Kirkpatrick Taylor	(541)913-9731 taylorskirkpatrick@gmail.com	2002 American Eagle Dr Unit 16 Slinger WI 53086	SW	Teacher	Tchr	First Immanuel Cedarburg WI	(262)377-6610	MQ	2019
Kirkwood Tiffany M Engler	(254)760-6795 kirkwoods61811@gmail.com	517 Arbors Circle Elgin TX 78621	TX	Teacher	P/Tchr	St Paul Thorndale TX	(512)898-5455	AU	2004
Kirsch Adam J	(262)994-8266 adamkirsch80@gmail.com	8043 W 122nd Terrace Overland Park KS 66213	MO	Teacher	Prin	Kansas City Kansas City MO	(816)241-5478	S	2003
Kirsch Lauren C Rodenburg	(262)944-8284 laurenkirsch2@gmail.com	8043 W 122nd Ter Overland Park KS 66213	KS	Teacher	C07/2016			S	2002
Kirsch Roger A	(847)343-6430 papakirsch5@gmail.com	275 Thrasher St Bloomingdale IL 60108	NI	Teacher	EM			RF	1971
Kirschner Christa M Lindeman	(303)913-7668	244 Bristol St Castle Rock CO 80104	RM	Teacher	C07/2016			S	2014
Kirst Donna J	(618)344-4095 annod62234@yahoo.com	370 Skyline View Dr Collinsville IL 62234	SI	Teacher	Tchr	Holy Cross Collinsville IL	(618)344-3145	RF	1983
Kirst Kathleen L Krenke	(920)467-4989 klk711@yahoo.com	N6184 Woodland Meadows Dr Sheboygan WI 53083	SW	Teacher	EM			SP	1970
Kirts Barbara J Morrison	(217)317-4558 seankirts@mchsi.com	221 N 35th St Mattoon IL 61938	CI	Teacher	C07/2016			CQ	1997
Kiser Karen D Quam	(503)713-3322 kkiser@princeofpeacelc.org	16584 SW Henderson Ct Beaverton OR 97007	NOW	Teacher	P/Tchr	Prince Of Peace Portland OR	(503)645-1211	PO	2000
Kisker Jonathan M	jonathanm.kisker@gmail.com		FG	Teacher	Tchr	St John Ocala FL	(352)629-1794	S	2020
Kissell Kelsey M Wood	(602)695-3617	8396 Sunset Trail Pl Unit A Rch Cucamonga CA 91730	PSW	Teacher	Tchr	Immanuel Riverside CA	(951)682-4211	IV	2011
Kisser David T	(908)782-2625 dave@stpaulnj.com	16 Reussner Rd Southington CT 06489	NE	Teacher	C07/2016			BR	1987
Kite Janalee R Meier	(952)380-6018	116 E Main St Waconia MN 55387	MNS	Teacher	C07/2016			S	2004
Kite Jessica M Joyce	(402)646-5346 jesskite@yahoo.com	19816 Acorn Dr Gretna NE 68028	NEB	Teacher	C06/2025			S	2002
Kittel Walter J	(239)939-5766	1263 Sunbury Dr Fort Myers FL 33901	FG	Teacher	EM			RF	1953
Kitten Aline R Schmerdtmann	jine4248@hotmail.com	4003 Sandalwood Dr Grand Island NE 68803	NEB	Teacher	EM			CQ	2003
Kittleman Joshua B	(586)453-9399 joshkittleman@gmail.com	8232 Rickie Ln Westland MI 48185	MI	DFLM	Mem C	Christ Our Savior Livonia MI	(734)522-6830	AA	2002
Kitzman Diana J Schmidt	(507)334-3632 dkitzman@flsweb.org	1407 19th Ave NW Faribault MN 55021	MNS	Teacher	Tchr	Faribault Faribault MN	(507)334-7982	CQ	2005
Kitzman Laura A Benson	laura.kitzman@gmail.com	1111 Minda Ct Walled Lake MI 48390	MI	Teacher	Tchr	St Michael Wayne MI	(734)728-1950	AA	1986
Kjos Kathleen M Schumann Cziok	(701)552-3866 ckfgoers@msn.com	86 25th Ave N Fargo ND 58102	ND	Teacher	EM			SP	1979
Klaas Joan E Hellmann	(920)205-4010 joancls@aol.com	1925 N Eugene St Appleton WI 54914	NW	Teacher	EM			RF	1969
Klammer Jane L Peuster	(858)231-7596 janeklammer493@gmail.com	2166 N Diamond St Orange CA 92867	PSW	Teacher	Tchr	Orange County Orange CA	(714)998-5151	S	1981

*Multiple Assignments (See Church Worker Locator for Additional Details)
See Page 53 for the Table of Abbreviations for key to District, Classification, Position, and College abbreviations.
**C =Candidate; EM =Emeritus; the date following the C is the month and year the Candidate status began

NAME	TELEPHONE NUMBER EMAIL	STREET ADDRESS CITY/STATE/ZIP	DISTRICT	CLASS.	POSITION/ STATUS**	WHERE SERVING	OFFICE PHONE	COLLEGE/ UNIV/CQ	YR GRAD
Klammer Joel R	(858)231-7596 joelklammer@gmail.com		PSW	Teacher	Tchr	Orange County Orange CA	(714)998-5151	AA	1985
Klappenback Anne E Schnake	(949)278-7907 aeklappenback@gmail.com	3141 N 158th Plaza Cir Omaha NE 68116	NEB	Teacher	Tchr	Concordia Omaha NE	(402)445-4000	IV	2004
Klappenback Lisa M Steinfeld	(702)370-6712 lisaklappenback@gmail.com	4436 E Sharon Dr Phoenix AZ 85032	PSW	Teacher	C05/2023			RF	2005
Klappenback Quinn A	(623)201-0130 qklappenback@nilfisk.com	4436 E Sharon Dr Phoenix AZ 85032	PSW	Teacher	C07/2016			IV	2005
Klatt Corrie L Stelmachowicz	(913)209-2111 corrieklatt@gmail.com	19411 W 201st Ter Spring Hill KS 66083	KS	Teacher	Mem C	Redeemer Olathe KS	(913)764-2359	IV	1990
Klatt Emmalynn C Rodriguez	(816)518-6527 emm.klatt@gmail.com	3030 W Greenfield Dr Freeport IL 61032	NI	Teacher	C07/2019			S	2015
Klauer Susan E Goebel	(586)295-2467 susan.klauer@hotmail.com	5803 Diamond View East Dr. Midland MI 48642	MI	Teacher	P/Tchr	Zion Auburn MI	(989)662-4264	CQ	1999
Klausmeier Caroline L Hartwig	(248)798-4052 cklausmeier@gmail.com	4487 Fairfield Dr Clarkston MI 48348	MI	Teacher	EM			RF	1955
Klausmeier Jacob A	(248)410-6232 jklausmeier@lhsa.com	227 Ogemaw Rd Pontiac MI 48341	MI	Teacher	Tchr	LHS Assn Of Greater Detroit Rochester Hls MI	(248)856-0240	MQ	2019
Klausmeier Veronica M MacKavich	(248)891-9651 veronicaklausmeier@gmail.com	4487 Fairfield Drive Clarkston MI 48348	MI	Teacher	Tchr	LHS Assn Of Greater Detroit Rochester Hls MI	(248)856-0240	CQ	2011
Kleb Michelle M Spohrer	(713)898-0344 edithmmsk@yahoo.com	19927 Indigo Lake Dr Magnolia TX 77355	TX	Teacher	C08/2024			AA	1999
Kleba Dale J	(262)271-5155 dale52kleba@aol.com	100 Main St Apt 101 Pewaukee WI 53072	SW	Teacher	EM			SP	1974
Kleber Susan K Edmison	(316)682-1894 skkleber@aol.com	8711 E 44th St N Wichita KS 67226	KS	Teacher	EM			S	1975
Kleckner Kimberly A Brockberg	(515)721-4738 kakleckner@att.net	3249 86th St Apt 622 Urbandale IA 50322	IW	Teacher	EM			RF	1979
Kleckner Pamela S Plegge	(618)635-2743 pkleck@hotmail.com	806 E Pennsylvania St Staunton IL 62088	SI	Teacher	Tchr	Zion Staunton IL	(618)635-3060	RF	1995
Kleiboeker Carole A Fortner	(417)285-4932 dckleiboeker@windstream.net	14579 Lawrence 1060 Stotts City MO 65756	MO	Teacher	EM			S	1999
Kleimola David A	(217)553-9632 dkleimola51@gmail.com	1006 Madison St Pawnee IL 62558	CI	Teacher	C07/2016			S	1973
Klein Amy T Eickmann	(636)399-7625 atklein09@yahoo.com	7 Bellerive Acres Saint Louis MO 63121	MO	Teacher	Pro Stf	Concordia Plans Services Saint Louis MO	(314)965-7580	MQ	1988
Klein Charles E	(415)752-9451	461 9th Ave San Francisco CA 94118	CNH	Teacher	EM			S	1963
Klein Cheryl M Kahle	(580)362-6821 opaandbunny@gmail.com	6501 North W St Newkirk OK 74647	OK	Teacher	EM			S	1970
Klein Dave R	(618)553-2130 daveklein05@gmail.com	11 Edgewood Ln N Centralia IL 62801	SI	Teacher	Tchr	Trinity Centralia IL	(618)532-2614	S	1984
Klein Donald E	(815)904-3708 coupleofkleins@gmail.com	725 Sheridan Dr Loves Park IL 61111	NI	Teacher	EM			RF	1965
Klein Doris J Braun	(707) 332-0818 dorisklein@comcast.com	2516 Grove Ave Napa CA 94558	CNH	Teacher	EM			S	1971
Klein Jeannine L Fuerstenau	(414)628-6231 jeannine.klein@concordialutheran school.net	4526 S Austin St Milwaukee WI 53207	SW	Teacher	Prin	Concordia Sturtevant WI	(262)884-0991	MQ	1986
Klein Linda G	(815)904-3708 coupleofkleins@gmail.com	725 Sheridan Dr Loves Park IL 61111	NI	Teacher	EM			RF	1966
Klein Miriam K Waech	(801)673-7952 brymir_26@msn.com	756 Ivory Rd SE Rio Rancho NM 87124	RM	Teacher	Tchr	Immanuel Albuquerque NM	(505)242-0616	S	1987
Kleine Racheal A		24655 Manila St Harrison Twp MI 48045	MI	Teacher	Tchr	Lutheran North Macomb MI	(586)781-9151	RF	1997
Kleinert Bruce	(209) 607-2893 busternjazzy@gmail.com	P.O. Box 208 Wallace CA 95254	CNH	Tch/DCE	EM			PO	1981
Kleinschmidt Wilbur H	(715)526-6292 wkleinschmidt6292@charter.net	31 E. North Water Street Apt 203 Neenah WI 54956	NW	Teacher	EM			RF	1952
Klekamp Patricia A	(214)729-9868 patkle57@gmail.com	13114 Sulphur Trl San Antonio TX 78253	TX	Teacher	Prin	Dallas Lutheran Sch Dallas TX	(214)349-8912	CQ	1985
Klement Alice M Albert	(210)563-2458 amklement@yahoo.com	3235 Castledale Dr San Antonio TX 78230	TX	Teacher	EM			SP	1969
Klemm Jennifer R Jennifer McDaniel			PSW	Teacher	Tchr	Faith Las Vegas NV	(702)804-4400	IV	2010
Klemm Karri L Primas	(561)703-4115 kklemm@trinitydelray.org	1690 Rnssnc Cmns Blvdapt 1514 Boynton Beach FL 33426	FG	Teacher	Tchr	Trinity Delray Beach FL	(561)276-8458	BR	1985
Klemm Olivia A	(224)232-9873 oliali@yahoo.com	10546 Elm Rd Waynesville IL 61778	CI	Teacher	C03/2019			MQ	2002
Klemm Rebecca	(317)446-7987 bklemmdce@gmail.com		IN	DCE	Mem C	Cornerstone Carmel IN	(317)814-4252	CH	2019
Klemp Garreth D	(414)242-6052 jlklemp@gmail.com	516 Alta Loma Dr Thiensville WI 53092	SW	Teacher	EM			RF	1967
Klemp Heather Batt	(618)334-6627 mrsklemp@gmail.com	95-1056 Puukoa St Mililani HI 96789	CNH	Teacher	Tchr	Trinity Wahiawa HI	(808)621-6033	MQ	2001
Klemp Jonathan W	(414)213-7783 jonathan.klemp@luhi.org	131 Brookville Rd Glen Head NY 11545	AT	Teacher	Tchr	Long Island Brookville NY	(516)626-1735	MQ	2006
Klemp Kyle D	(618)334-6628 hawaiipackfan@yahoo.com	95-1056 Puukoa St Mililani HI 96789	CNH	Teacher	Prin	Trinity Wahiawa HI	(808)621-6033	MQ	1999
Klemp Peter S	(402)651-6260 klempp@concordiaomaha.org	14905 Redman Ave Omaha NE 68116	NEB	Teacher	Tchr	Concordia Luth Schools of Omaha Inc Omaha NE	(402)445-4000	SP	1992
Klenke Luther M	(402)432-7440 luther.klenke@gmail.com	2489 N Columbia Ave Seward NE 68434	NEB	Teacher	EM			S	1968
Klenke Rebecca A	(260)728-4362	92 W Honeysuckle Ln Decatur IN 46733	IN	Teacher	Tchr	Wyneken Memorial Decatur IN	(260)639-6177	SP	1976

NAME	TELEPHONE NUMBER EMAIL	STREET ADDRESS CITY/STATE/ZIP	DISTRICT	CLASS.	POSITION/ STATUS**	WHERE SERVING	OFFICE PHONE	COLLEGE/ UNIV/CQ	YR GRAD
Klenz Alexander K	(414)238-8300 alex.klenz@flhsemail.org	1845 Derbyshire Dr Las Vegas NV 89117	PSW	Teacher	Tchr	Faith Las Vegas NV	(702)804-4400	S	2013
Klenz Tammy J Juergensen	(414)305-1911 tklenz@fils.org	679 S Fox Run Dr Saukville WI 53080	SW	Teacher	Tchr	First Immanuel Cedarburg WI	(262)377-6610	MQ	1990
Kletke Dale B	(913)244-2710 bkletke@yahoo.com	12411 Wornall Road Kansas City MO 64145	MO	Teacher	Tchr	Calvary Kansas City MO	(816)444-6908	WN	1985
Klick Emily A Driver	(815)861-8339 klickemilya@gmail.com	W151N8691 Marshall Dr Menomonee Falls WI 53051	EN	Teacher	C09/2021			CH	2016
Kline Andrew	(920)412-2464 klinea@trinitynet.org	1000 20th St #21 Mosinee WI 54455	NW	Teacher	Tchr	Trinity Wausau WI	(715)842-0769	MQ	2020
Kline Margaret Weber	margaret.weber@cune.org		IN	Teacher	Tchr	Holy Cross Indianapolis IN	(317)826-1234	S	2015
Klinge Rebecca Morton	(812)528-1147 rdmklinge@hotmail.com	8780 Pine Lake Ct Elizabethtown IN 47232	IN	Teacher	C07/2019			MQ	1999
Klingelhofer Carol Sturm	(847)803-9791 klingfamily2@sbcglobal.net	65 N 7th Ave Des Plaines IL 60016	NI	Teacher	EM			RF	1967
Klingsporn Kassidy J Rixstine	(402)643-2251 kassidyklingsporn@trinity fremont.org	126 Westgate Dr Ames NE 68621	NEB	Teacher	Tchr	Trinity Fremont NE	(402)721-5959	S	2015
Klinkenberg Kay M Schreiber	(714)504-0451 kklinkenberg@sbcglobal.net	5375 Via De La Zorra Yorba Linda CA 92887	PSW	Teacher	EM			RF	1962
Klinker Stephanie D Berning	(260)435-0760 stephanieklinker0@gmail.com	5219 N Sampson Rd Woodburn IN 46797	IN	Teacher	C09/2022			CH	2011
Klipfel Sanna L Struecker	(209)640-0778 sanna.klipfel@gmail.com	2772 Bitternut Cir Simi Valley CA 93065	PSW	Teacher	EM			S	1974
Klipp Allison M	(402)300-1998 allisonklipp98@gmail.com	1300 May St Marysville KS 66508	KS	Teacher	Tchr	Good Shepherd Marysville KS	(785)562-3181	S	2021
Klitzing Ashley M Smith			PSW	Teacher	Tchr	St Paul Orange CA	(714)637-2640	IV	2008
Klitzing Mark A	(949)922-1162 mark.klitzing@gmail.com	8 Cosenza Irvine CA 92614	PSW	Teacher	EM			S	1979
Klitzing Nathan J	nate.klitzing@lhsoc.org	803 E Van Bibber Ave Orange CA 92866	PSW	Teacher	Tchr	Orange County Orange CA	(714)998-5151	IV	2008
Klitzing Rachel Loesch	(949)852-0119 rachel.klitzing@psd-lcms.org	8 Cosenza Irvine CA 92614	PSW	Teacher		Pacific Southwest District Irvine CA	(949)854-3232	S	1979
Klitzke Angela E Shugart	(608)524-9091 angieklitzke@yahoo.com	2217 Winfield Dr Reedsburg WI 53959	SW	Teacher	C07/2016			CQ	2006
Klocke Elaine L Piehl	(952)906-1340	8312 Suffolk Dr Chanhassen MN 55317	MNS	Teacher	EM			S	1965
Klockziem Gloria Rupprecht	(863)838-9693 gklockziem@stpaullakeland.org	6329 Butternut Dr Lakeland FL 33813	FG	Teacher	EM			SP	1970
Kloess Gary M	(630)222-1578 gkloesscubfan@att.net	61 Evergreen St Elk Grove Vlg IL 60007	NI	Teacher	EM			RF	1975
Kloess Katrina E	(847)651-1578	8124 169th St Apt 1W Tinley Park IL 60477	NI	Teacher	Tchr	Trinity Tinley Park IL	(708)532-3529	RF	2005
Kloess Susan L Backsmeier	(847)269-1578 kloess5257@att.net	61 Evergreen St Elk Grove Vlg IL 60007	NI	Teacher	EM			RF	1979
Kloetzke Scott W	(612)859-2885 skloetzke@yahoo.com	1021 Glenhill Rd Shoreview MN 55126	MNS	Teacher	C07/2017			SP	1984
Klopke Julie S Streit	(847)529-8536 Julie.Klopke@gmail.com	4601 Magnolia Dr Rolling Meadows IL 60008	NI	Teacher	RSO	Lutheran Education Association River Forest IL	(708)209-3343	RF	1982
Klopke Philip J	(847)450-4593 philip.klopke@gmail.com	1623a Chase St Nashville TN 37216	TX	DCE	O-Sp Min	Texas District Round Rock TX	(800)951-3478	CH	2010
Klotz Debra A Timm	(479)246-1075 klotzdebbie2021@gmail.com	1606 S 24th St Rogers AR 72758	MDS	Teacher	EM			RF	1976
Klotz Lance W	(479)366-8140 lance.klotz@cox.net	1606 S 24th St Rogers AR 72758	MDS	DCO	C07/2016			SP	1991
Kluender Selma Hensiek	(812)849-9656	1112 W Oak St Mitchell IN 47446	IN	Teacher	EM			RF	1987
Kluesner Sheryl K Timm	(636)262-5071 stimm8@gmail.com	603 Steinhagen Rd Warrenton MO 63383	MO	Teacher	EM			SP	1985
Klug David H	(231)798-7932 klugdb@comcast.net	307 Farr Rd Norton Shores MI 49444	MI	Teacher	EM			CQ	1981
Klug Joshua A	(703)203-4464 jklug1717@yahoo.com	2530 N 25th St Sheboygan WI 53083	SE	Teacher	Prin	Bethlehem* Sheboygan WI	(920)452-5071	MQ	1998
Klug Kay E Wornardt	(715)536-9661 kklug1@frontier.com	409 E Taylor St Merrill WI 54452	NW	Teacher	EM			RF	1973
Klug Rachel R Finck	(314)780-7094 rrkteach@yahoo.com	731 Strafford Ridge Dr Ballwin MO 63021	MO	Teacher	Prin	Christ Community Kirkwood MO	(314)822-7774	CQ	2022
Klug Zachary A	(314)803-2731 zklug94@gmail.com	508 Brandywine Rd Springfield IL 62704	CI	Teacher	P/Tchr	Lutheran High Association Springfield IL	(217)546-6363	RF	1999
Kluge David A	(717)235-7879 dmkluge9@gmail.com	704 Bollinger Dr Shrewsbury PA 17361	SE	Teacher	EM			RF	1957
Klumb Deborah L Degner	(360)485-3022 deborah.klumb@gmail.com	935 Oakcrest Dr SE Lacey WA 98503	NOW	Teacher	EM			S	1976
Klumb Hannah L		935 Oakcrest Dr SE Lacey WA 98503	NOW	Teacher	C12/2022			PO	2009
Kluth Carol M Janes	(512)799-8197 cakluth@yahoo.com	2508 Plantation Dr Round Rock TX 78681	TX	Teacher	EM			SP	1973
Knaack Ruth E	(218)252-4702 rknaack@dishmail.net	11631 County 48 Park Rapids MN 56470	MNN	Teacher	EM			SP	1973
Knaak Anna B Smith	(815)529-4915 anna.smith1@cuw.edu	15 Teardrop Dr Saint Charles MO 63304	MO	Teacher	Tchr	Messiah Weldon Spring MO	(636)926-9773	MQ	2019
Knabach Justin	(314)489-3919 jdknabach@gmail.com	4765 Groveton Way Saint Louis MO 63128	MO	DPM	Mem C	Resurrection Sunset Hills MO	(314)843-6633	CH	2012

*Multiple Assignments (See Church Worker Locator for Additional Details)

See Page 53 for the Table of Abbreviations for key to District, Classification, Position, and College abbreviations.

**C =Candidate; EM =Emeritus; the date following the C is the month and year the Candidate status began

NAME	TELEPHONE NUMBER EMAIL	STREET ADDRESS CITY/STATE/ZIP	DISTRICT	CLASS.	POSITION/ STATUS**	WHERE SERVING	OFFICE PHONE	COLLEGE/ UNIV/CQ	YR GRAD
Knaggs William H	(440)327-6032	6845 Paradise Way N Ridgeville OH 44039	OH	Teacher	EM			S	1960
Knapp Andrew O	(406)381-0651	252 Black Ln Corvallis MT 59828	RM	Teacher	C07/2016			S	1995
Knapp Betty J Deac	(906)228-5180 dcsbjk@aol.com	230 W Ohio St Marquette MI 49855	NW	Deaconess	EM			Other	1979
Knapp Gayle L Dymond	(978)844-2280 galknapp@comcast.net	13 Porter Ln Marlborough NH 03455	NE	Teacher	EM			RF	1977
Knapp Lorraine C	(760)646-1038 yankeelori@gmail.com	14969 La Habra Rd Victorville CA 92392	PSW	Teacher	Tchr	Zion Victorville CA	(760)245-9725	CQ	2010
Knapp Ronald F	(479)283-8830 rknapp751@sbcglobal.net	3241 Chapel Downs Dr Dallas TX 75229	TX	Teacher	EM			S	1966
Knea Katherine E Boschee	(270)234-8839 billknea@yahoo.com	808 Foxfire Rd Elizabethtown KY 42701	IN	Teacher	EM			SP	1968
Knea Linda A Lyk	(612)709-5580	205 Washington St Young America MN 55397	MNS	Teacher	EM			SP	1969
Knea Mariana E Ebert	(847)394-8632 mknea@stpeter-ah.org	1710 S Arlington Heights Rd Unit 5a Arlington Heights IL 60005	NI	Teacher	Tchr	St Peter Arlington Heights IL	(847)259-4114	RF	1992
Knea Sara J Wells	(920)285-9719 sjwknea@yahoo.com	3433 S Van Buren Rd Reese MI 48757	MI	Teacher	Tchr	St Michaels Richville MI	(989)868-4809	RF	2000
Knea Stephanie C Bickmeier	(419)302-6916 sknea@gdlc.org	200 Whitehall Ln League City TX 77573	TX	Teacher	Mem C	Gloria Dei Houston TX	(281)333-4535	RF	1999
Knea William E	(270)234-8839 billknea@yahoo.com	808 Foxfire Rd Elizabethtown KY 42701	IN	Teacher	EM			SP	1968
Knego Keelie M Drenner	(714)267-0578 kknego@stjohnsorange.org	430 S Grand St Orange CA 92866	PSW	Teacher	Tchr	St Johns Orange CA	(714)288-4406	CQ	2024
Knehans Hannah L Biermann	hknehans@trinitylutheranspfd.org		MO	DFLM	Mem C	Trinity Springfield MO	(417)866-5878	AA	2020
Knehnetsky Raymond T	(310)968-9098	185 N Washington Ave Centereach NY 11720	AT	DPM	Mem C	Our Savior Centereach NY	(631)588-2757	IV	2016
Kneser Nicole Giovenco	(863)529-0370 nkneser@stpaullakeland.org	4310 Salt Springs Ln Lakeland FL 33811	FG	Teacher	Tchr	St Paul Lakeland FL	(863)644-7710	AU	2005
Knight Nancy J Morrow	(619)789-4804	643 W 13th Ave Escondido CA 92025	PSW	Teacher	Tchr	Ramona Ramona CA	(760)789-4804	S	1971
Knippenberg Kimberly M Meister		11724 Crab Apple Rd Indianapolis IN 46239	IN	Teacher	Tchr	Zion New Palestine IN	(317)861-4210	RF	1989
Knitter Susan K Kleinschmidt	(847)584-2777 knitfour@comcast.net	827 S Springinsguth Rd Schaumburg IL 60193	NI	Teacher	Tchr	Immanuel Elmhurst IL	(630)832-9302	RF	1981
Knobeck Kelly A Brewer	(260)223-4529 kaknobeck@gmail.com	7412 Golfway Ct Minocqua WI 54548	EA	Teacher	C06/2017			MQ	2014
Knoepfel Aimee J Dierks and Walsh	(815)793-0288 aimeeknoepfel@gmail.com	2024 SE 27th Rd. Ocala FL 34471	FG	Teacher	Tchr	Amazing Grace Oxford FL	(352)350-6449	RF	1996
Knoepfel James B	(402)317-1493 jim.knoepfel@gmail.com	2024 SE 27th Rd Ocala FL 34471	FG	Teacher	P/Tchr	St John Ocala FL	(352)622-7275	S	1987
Knoll Leah M Schiefer	(989)213-6589 lknoll@stlorenz.org	8182 E Curtis Rd Frankenmuth MI 48734	MI	Teacher	Prin	St Lorenz Frankenmuth MI	(989)652-6141	CQ	2000
Knoll Lois E Christian	(262)338-0809 leknoll@yahoo.com	901 Decker Dr West Bend WI 53090	SW	Teacher	EM			RF	1968
Knop Margaret E Gross	(618)826-3686 mknop5@hotmail.com	1415 Allendale Blvd Chester IL 62233	SI	Teacher	Tchr	St John Chester IL	(618)826-4345	S	1979
Knopf Linda A Rahdert	(260)485-9164 knopfd@aol.com	1717 Maplecrest Rd Apt 146 Fort Wayne IN 46815	IN	Teacher	EM			RF	1959
Knorp Brendan D	(314)698-3604 bknorp@mac.com	1419 Atlantic Crossing Dr Fenton MO 63026	MO	Teacher	Mem C	Concordia Kirkwood MO	(314)822-7772	AA	1996
Knorr Karl W	(262)227-2925 dr.karl.knorr@gmail.com	4341 Desert Dancer Way Las Vegas NV 89147	PSW	Teacher	EM			RF	1985
Knosher Bruce A	(630)222-1573 bknosher@yahoo.com	4 Fernwood Ct Bethalto IL 62010	MO	Teacher	EM			RF	1977
Knott Diane	(808)262-7139 lovefrogies@hotmail.com	711 Pahumele Way Kailua HI 96734	CNH	Teacher	EM			CQ	2001
Knotts Richard E Jr	(214)883-7845 rknotts2010@gmail.com	530 Bronco St Centerton AR 72719	MDS	Teacher	EM			AA	1984
Knowles Susan J Riemer Deac	(716)417-9013	8758 Jennings Rd Eden NY 14057	IN	Deaconess	Mem C	Concordia Theological Seminary Fort Wayne IN	(260)452-2100	FW-DEAC	2024
Knox Jennifer	(319)231-5919 jknox424@gmail.com	4778 S Forest Point Blvd New Berlin WI 53151	SW	Teacher	Tchr	Martin Luther Greendale WI	(414)421-4000	MQ	2008
Knox Jennifer N Kern	(630)370-5546 jnnk3@yahoo.com		NI	Teacher	C06/2017			RF	2001
Knudten George V	(847)281-7412 gknudten@knudten.com	901 Florsheim Dr Apt 113 Libertyville IL 60048	NI	Teacher	EM			S	1958
Knudten Jacqueline E Rosene	(919)800-7012 jackie@knudten.com	901 Florsheim Dr Apt 121 Libertyville IL 60048	NI	Teacher	EM			S	1977
Knueppel Carol L Georg	(260)625-4607 cknuep@aol.com	4422 Darnley Ct Fort Wayne IN 46814	IN	Teacher	EM			S	1966
Knuppenburg Kimberly R Laabs	(414)243-0704 kknuppenburg@ gracemenomoneefalls.org	N99W16743 Woodcock Rd Germantown WI 53022	SW	Teacher	Tchr	Grace Menomonee Falls WI	(262)251-7140	MQ	2004
Knuth Fred F	(269)429-5163 ffknuth@yahoo.com	2876 Kim St Saint Joseph MI 49085	MI	Teacher	EM			S	1964
Knuth Sara A Zastoupil	(608)314-1002 sknuth@spsflames.k12.wi.us	1202 Bruin Ln Janesville WI 53545	SW	Teacher	Tchr	St Paul's Janesville WI	(608)754-4471	MQ	2000
Knuth Sarah Noffke	(414)322-0139 sknuth@trinityfreistadt.com	8158 W. Holly Rd. Mequon WI 53097	SW	Teacher	Tchr	Trinity Mequon WI	(262)242-2045	MQ	2005
Knutson Francesca L Walker	(407)719-7743 fknutson12@gmail.com	318 Hang Loose Way Daytona Beach FL 32124	FG	Teacher	EM			RF	1984

*Multiple Assignments (See Church Worker Locator for Additional Details)
See Page 53 for the Table of Abbreviations for key to District, Classification, Position, and College abbreviations.
**C =Candidate; EM =Emeritus; the date following the C is the month and year the Candidate status began

NAME	TELEPHONE NUMBER EMAIL	STREET ADDRESS CITY/STATE/ZIP	DISTRICT	CLASS.	POSITION/ STATUS**	WHERE SERVING	OFFICE PHONE	COLLEGE/ UNIV/CQ	YR GRAD
Knutson Jeffrey R	(407)716-4216 knutson.jeffrey@gmail.com	318 Hang Loose Way Daytona Beach FL 32124	FG	Teacher	EM			RF	1986
Knutson Rachel Roell Flippo	(260)485-5096 olongolola@yahoo.com	423 Wisconsin Ave Wisconsin Dells WI 53965	SW	Teacher	Tchr	Trinity Wisconsin Dells WI	(608)253-3241	MQ	2002
Kober Caroline M Krenning	(314)221-9722 ckrenning@hotmail.com	7 Addison St Collinsville IL 62234	NEB	Teacher	S HS/C	Concordia University Nebraska Seward NE	(402)643-3651	S	1997
Kober Daniel B	(702)812-1632 koberd@flhsemail.org	9541 Sunken Reef Cir Las Vegas NV 89117	PSW	Teacher	Tchr	Faith Las Vegas NV	(702)804-4400	S	2010
Koboldt Mary E Dietzel	(989)799-1684 mkoboldt@peacesaginaw.org	2319 Gatesboro Dr W Saginaw MI 48603	MI	Teacher	Tchr	Peace Saginaw MI	(989)792-2581	AA	1986
Koch Beverly J	(248)852-1048 dvcbev@yahoo.com	120 Eastlawn Dr Rochester Hls MI 48307	MI	Teacher	EM			S	1978
Koch Gene E	(260)449-1678 genekoch1987@gmail.com	1311 W Branning Ave Fort Wayne IN 46807	IN	Teacher	EM			RF	1979
Koch Jessica L Hennig	(217)622-9355 jlh9217@gmail.com	927 N Benjamin St Port Washington WI 53074	SW	Teacher	Tchr	St Paul Grafton WI	(262)377-4659	MQ	2014
Koch Karen L Krenzke	kcklkoch@yahoo.com	1984 78th St Luck WI 54853	NW	Teacher	EM			S	1975
Koch Kenneth C	(715)716-0456 kckochsf@yahoo.com	1984 78th St Luck WI 54853	NW	Teacher	EM			S	1975
Koch Krista C Gerken	(260)745-0159 kkoch@clhscadets.com	1311 W Branning Ave Fort Wayne IN 46807	IN	Teacher	Tchr	Concordia Fort Wayne IN	(260)483-1102	S	1984
Koch Margene A	(253)472-3494 mkoch20@comcast.net	6829 Homestead Ave Tacoma WA 98404	NOW	Teacher	EM			S	1972
Koch Matthew P	(586)747-2092 kochmp87@gmail.com	36643 Suffolk Clinton Township MI 48035	MI	DFLM	C12/2018			AA	2010
Koch Neal S	(402) 641-7847 neal.s.koch@gmail.com	595 7th St Utica NE 68456	NEB	Teacher	EM			S	1972
Koch Sarah E Weisman	(217)520-5875 skoch@gmail.com	2306 Little Round Top Dr Edwardsville IL 62025	SI	Teacher	Prin	Zion Bethalto IL	(618)377-8314	S	2002
Koch Sherry L Anderson	(715)536-5723	1104 Saint Paul Dr Merrill WI 54452	NW	Teacher	Tchr	St John Merrill WI	(715)536-7264	RF	1987
Koch Shirlene L Bredehoft	lkoch.tle@gmail.com	413 Trotter Dr Hamel IL 62046	SI	Teacher	Tchr	Trinity Edwardsville IL	(618)656-7002	S	1972
Koch Stephen	(618)692-0703 19stevekoch54@gmail.com	413 Trotter Dr Hamel IL 62046	SI	Teacher	C07/2016			RF	2004
Koch William III	(434) 284-5798 carbilko@comcast.net	1384 Stone Creek Ln Apt 107 Charlottesvle VA 22902	SE	Teacher	EM			RF	1957
Kocsis Betsy A	(518)869-9897	11 Richards Dr Albany NY 12205	AT	Teacher	Tchr	Our Savior Colonie NY	(518)459-2248	CQ	2016
Koeberl Nelda E Newman	(573)824-5449 nkoeberl@att.net	P.O. Box 101 Frohna MO 63748	MO	Teacher	EM			CQ	2012
Koebert Jay W	(262)424-9866 jkoebert@wi.rr.com	W168N10338 Wildrose Ln Germantown WI 53022	SW	Teacher	Tchr	Milwaukee LHS Milwaukee WI	(414)461-6000	S	1987
Koehler Debra G	(630)967-4640 koehlerdeb@aol.com	1489c Woodcutter Ln Apt C Wheaton IL 60189	NI	Teacher	Tchr	Immanuel Elmhurst IL	(630)832-9302	RF	1982
Koehler Elizabeth C Crawford	(360)471-8728 elizabethc131@msn.com	14268 Raspberry Dr Rogers MN 55374	MNS	Teacher	C06/2022			PO	2007
Koehler Heidi E Werner	(816)519-0752 dceheidi@gmail.com	346 Rockport Dr Cape Girardeau MO 63701	MO	DCE	Mem C	St Andrew Cape Girardeau MO	(573)334-3200	IV	1998
Koehler Jacob D	(260)446-5776 jkoehler@holycrossfw.org	15211 East Tillman Road Fort Wayne IN 46816	IN	Teacher	Tchr	Holy Cross Fort Wayne IN	(260)483-3173	CH	2013
Koehler Kenneth W	(701)429-3092 dcekkoehler@ideal.net	307 10 1/2 Ave E West Fargo ND 58078	ND	DCE	EM			SP	1975
Koehler Mackenzie C Amerine	(701) 540-1010 kenzie@blcmail.org	155 Linwood Ave Ridgewood NJ 07450	NJ	DCO	Mem C	Bethlehem Ridgewood NJ	(201)444-3600	SP	2021
Koehler Nancy J Wietfeldt	(260)450-0741 nkoehler@clhscadets.com	15211 E Tillman Rd Fort Wayne IN 46816	IN	Teacher	Tchr	Concordia Fort Wayne IN	(260)483-1102	RF	2012
Koehlert Karen K	princ1@aol.com	715 Denzil Dr Apt 3 Columbia City IN 46725	IN	Teacher	Tchr	South Unity Fort Wayne IN	(260)744-0459	MQ	1987
Koehlert Marilyn E Saager	(847)426-7452 marilynkoehlert@hotmail.com	201 King Ave East Dundee IL 60118	NI	Teacher	EM			RF	1976
Koehlinger Mark R	(260)615-1834 markkoehlinger@gmail.com	6423 Langley Ct Fort Wayne IN 46815	IN	Teacher	EM			S	1983
Koehlinger Michelle E Reed	(260)615-4866 mekoehlinger@holycrossfw.org	6423 Langley Ct Fort Wayne IN 46815	IN	Teacher	C09/2024			S	1982
Koehne Robert E	(602)481-5649 koehne4@gmail.com	10908 W Wood St Tolleson AZ 85353	PSW	Teacher	Tchr	North Valley Phoenix AZ	(623)551-3454	CQ	2008
Koehneke Sarah E Bonnough	(239)961-2621 skoehneke@yahoo.com	5700 Cypress Hollow Way Naples FL 34109	FG	Teacher	C07/2016			AA	2002
Koehnke Paige A McFerran	(714)745-0377 paigekoehnke@gmail.com	1002 W Almond Ave Orange CA 92868	PSW	Teacher	C07/2016			IV	2007
Koelper Lawrence R	(260)478-7438 lkoelper@stpaulsfw.org	1619 Lakewood Dr Fort Wayne IN 46819	IN	Tch/DCE	EM			RF	1987
Koen Jessica M Zeller	(707)363-9322 jkoen@stjohnsnapa.org	1151 El Centro Avenue Napa CA 94558	CNH	Teacher	Tchr	St John's Napa CA	(707)255-0119	CQ	2021
Koen Laureen A Norris	(618)967-3773 laurikoen1959@gmail.com	911 Bayberry Ln Red Bud IL 62278	SI	Teacher	C07/2019			RF	1981
Koenemann Darin D	(260)486-3634 koened2000@gmail.com	7108 Evansbrook Dr Fort Wayne IN 46835	IN	Teacher	Tchr	Wyneken Memorial Decatur IN	(260)639-6177	AA	1999
Koenemann Julie A	(402)536-0114 juliekmusic@hotmail.com	20865 Flavin Circle Elkhorn NE 68022	NEB	Teacher	EM			CQ	1980
Koenen Genelle L Lucht	(515)298-2913 genellekoenen@hotmail.com	4534 Chickasaw Pass St. Charles MO 63304	MO	Teacher	EM			S	1980

*Multiple Assignments (See Church Worker Locator for Additional Details)

See Page 53 for the Table of Abbreviations for key to District, Classification, Position, and College abbreviations.

**C =Candidate; EM =Emeritus; the date following the C is the month and year the Candidate status began

NAME	TELEPHONE NUMBER EMAIL	STREET ADDRESS CITY/STATE/ZIP	DISTRICT	CLASS.	POSITION/ STATUS**	WHERE SERVING	OFFICE PHONE	COLLEGE/ UNIV/CQ	YR GRAD
Koenig Amy J Brandt	(563)343-5293 amy.koenig@trinitydavenport.org	1411 W 51st St Davenport IA 52806	IE	Teacher	Tchr	Trinity Davenport IA	(563)322-5224	RF	2005
Koenig Carol J Leimbach	(636)448-9716 vaa213@aol.com	3855 Indian Ridge Lane Defiance MO 63341	MO	Teacher	EM			RF	1974
Koenig Lynn R German	(260)485-4095 lrkoenig58@gmail.com	6426 Post Brook Ln Fort Wayne IN 46835	IN	Teacher	EM			BR	2021
Koenig Robyn J Brosz	(573)824-5157 rkoenig@hughes.net	265 Pcr 328 Farrar MO 63746	MO	Teacher	Tchr	United in Christ Frohna MO	(573)824-5218	S	1993
Koepke Alan R	(636)225-5975 aljosada@charter.net	907 Grove Hill Ct Fenton MO 63026	MO	Teacher	EM			S	1975
Koepke Joel L	(608)254-6864 jlk.scienceguy@gmail.com	1600 Ohio St # C Racine WI 53405	SW	Teacher	EM			RF	1970
Koepke Marlene E Roberts	(608)254-6864 musicbymarlene@gmail.com	1600 Ohio St # C Racine WI 53405	SW	Teacher	EM			S	1974
Koepke Roger A	(314)428-3416 stlkpky@aol.com	8616 Belhaven Dr Saint Louis MO 63114	MO	Teacher	EM			S	1960
Koepsell Tracy S Hilk	(952)210-5319 tracy.koepsell@stjohns-chaska.org	2655 Woods Dr. Victoria MN 55386	MNS	Teacher	Tchr	St Johns Chaska MN	(952)448-2526	CQ	2023
Koeritz Heidi S Halverson	(507) 848-6091 heidikoeritz@sjlnorthrop.com	P.O. Box 84 Northrop MN 56075	MNS	Teacher	Tchr	St James Northrop MN	(507)436-5289	S	1983
Koerner William S	(812)522-6224	934 Wendemere Dr Seymour IN 47274	IN	Teacher	EM			RF	1971
Koester Elizabeth A Deac	97ekoester@gmail.com	235 A Rue Sans Souci Bethalto IL 62010	SI	Deaconess	Mem C	St Paul Worden IL	(618)633-2209	CH	2020
Koester Jason P	(303)264-9115 jason.koester@sjdenver.org	2927 S Wolff St Denver CO 80236	RM	Teacher	Tchr	St John's Denver CO	(303)733-3778	CQ	2007
Koester Mari L Buss	(707)501-7518 mari.koester@sjdenver.org	2927 S Wolff St Denver CO 80236	RM	Teacher	Tchr	St John's Denver CO	(303)733-3778	S	2008
Koester Sandra L	(504)232-5175 slk2219@bellsouth.net	511 Hopscotch Road Covington LA 70433	SO	Teacher	EM			S	1979
Koester Sarah L Beineke	(618)282-4265 mkoester@htc.net	9400 S Prairie Rd Red Bud IL 62278	SI	Teacher	Tchr	Trinity Hoyleton IL	(618)493-6226	S	1991
Koffarnus Dallas L	(402)430-2551 ddmast@gmail.com	516 Terrace Road Lincoln NE 68505	NEB	Teacher	EM			SP	1973
Koffarnus Thomas L	(402)802-5329 tkoffarnus@gmail.com	1751 Deweese Drive Lincoln NE 68504	NEB	Teacher	Tchr	Christ Lincoln NE	(402)483-7774	CQ	2014
Kogelmann Gerald F	(479)872-6328 gfkogel@yahoo.com	P.O. Box 22 Ocheyedan IA 51354	MDS	Teacher	EM			RF	1964
Kogler Henry J	(224)587-4523 hkogler747@hotmail.com	733 E Glencoe St Palatine IL 60074	NI	Teacher	EM			RF	1973
Koglin Anna S Strei	(507)316-8177 aakoglin@gmail.com	1435 9th Ave SE Rochester MN 55904	MNS	Teacher	C07/2016			SP	2008
Kohler Ruth A Hafemann	(262)338-6392 pkrk21@hotmail.com	1222 N 14th Ave West Bend WI 53090	SW	Teacher	EM			MQ	2004
Kohlhof Sarah L Schluckebier	(402)540-8514 sarah.kohlhof@messiah.us	3919 S 31st Street Cir Lincoln NE 68502	NEB	Teacher	Tchr	Messiah Lincoln NE	(402)489-3024	CQ	2007
Kohlman Todd A	(920)912-5969 kohlman@cuslight.org	7107 W Dove Ct Milwaukee WI 53223	SW	Teacher	Tchr	LUMIN Milwaukee WI	(414)354-5126	CQ	2004
Kohlmeier James N	(414) 870-2445 jamie.kohlmeier@orlctosa.org	10926 W Derby Ave Wauwatosa WI 53225	SW	Teacher	Tchr	Wauwatosa Wauwatosa WI	(414)258-4558	AA	1992
Kohlmeier Sara J Bruening	(414)573-9683 skohlmeier@wi.rr.com	2239 S 106th St West Allis WI 53227	SW	Teacher	EM			RF	1984
Kohls Craig V	(320)290-1528 rkohls17@charter.net	1504 14th St SE Saint Cloud MN 56304	MNN	Teacher	EM			S	1971
Kohls Traci L	(952)457-8742 tracileighk@gmail.com	241 Wildhurst Rd Waconia MN 55387	MNS	DCE	Mem C	Trinity Waconia MN	(952)442-4165	SP	1997
Kohlwey Martin R	(402)643-0738 martin.kohlwey@lhsparker.org	7314 S Havana St Apt 3020 Centennial CO 80112	RM	Teacher	Tchr	Colorado Lutheran High School Parker CO	(303)841-5551	S	1983
Kohn Dawn M Rudnick	(231)578-3826 dwkohn@comcast.net	4858 Cedar Branch Ct Indianapolis IN 46234	IN	Teacher	EM			CQ	2009
Kohring Katherina		302 NW 112th St Seattle WA 98177	NOW	Teacher	Tchr	Lutheran Ministry Services Northwest Seattle WA	(206)450-7128	PO	2015
Kohrs Jonathan A	(847)209-8454 jkohrs811@gmail.com	1222 Chicago Ave Apt 606 Evanston IL 60202	NI	Teacher	C08/2023			RF	1985
Kohrs Stephen A	(262)844-5512 sakohrs@hotmail.com	15020 W Harcove Dr New Berlin WI 53151	SW	Teacher	EM			RF	1983
Kohtz Roger O	(313)581-5364 kohtzroger@gmail.com	7645 Ternes St Dearborn MI 48126	MI	Teacher	EM			S	1956
Kohtz Virginia R	(402)643-2727 virginia.kohtz@cune.org	1151 Fairlane Ave Seward NE 68434	NEB	Teacher	EM			S	1961
Kois Heather A Eden	(208)761-8858 kois.heather@gmail.com	3755 N Maywood Dr Boise ID 83704	CNH	Teacher	C06/2022			S	2012
Kokel Joyce L Timm	(281)216-4375 jlk6126@gmail.com	P.O. Box 84 Walburg TX 78763	TX	Teacher	EM			RF	1968
Kokel Sylvia J Haefker	(512)296-5718 sylviakokel5@gmail.com	15602 Giese Ln Manor TX 78653	TX	Teacher	EM			S	1971
Kolander Eugene E	ekolander@cox.net	15740 W Edgemont Ave Goodyear AZ 85395	PSW	Teacher	EM			S	1958
Kolander Kevin	(262)573-9301 kevin.kolander1@gmail.com	5745 Olin Rd Brandenburg KY 40108	IN	Teacher	C06/2020			S	1984
Kolb Arlene C	(586)219-7623 arlenekolb@outlook.com	2250 Tiverton Dr Sterling Hts MI 48310	MI	Teacher	EM			RF	1969
Kolb Linda A Heintz Smith Deac	(701)429-0838 linda.a.kolb@icloud.com	P.O. Box 172 Big Stone City SD 57216	SD	Deaconess	C07/2016			RF	1989

*Multiple Assignments (See Church Worker Locator for Additional Details)

See Page 53 for the Table of Abbreviations for key to District, Classification, Position, and College abbreviations.

**C =Candidate; EM =Emeritus; the date following the C is the month and year the Candidate status began

NAME	TELEPHONE NUMBER EMAIL	STREET ADDRESS CITY/STATE/ZIP	DISTRICT	CLASS.	POSITION/ STATUS**	WHERE SERVING	OFFICE PHONE	COLLEGE/ UNIV/CQ	YR GRAD
Kolb Thomas W	(919)986-1837 tkolb@se.lcms.org	7904 Netherlands Dr Raleigh NC 27606	SE	Teacher	D Ex/S	Southeastern District Henrico VA	(703)971-9371	CQ	1999
Kolberg Deborah L Ziebart	(616)842-7151 ddkolberg@yahoo.com	17445 Beech Hill Dr Grand Haven MI 49417	MI	Teacher	EM			RF	1977
Kolke Linaya	(505)220-9750 linaya@christlittlerock.com	415 Trumpler St Little Rock AR 72211	MDS	DCE	Mem C	Christ Little Rock AR	(501)663-5232	IV	2020
Kollbaum Angela M Johnson	(660)238-1751 angela.kollbaum@eagles.cui.edu	P.O. Box 371 Madison NE 68748	NEB	DCE	Mem C	Trinity Madison NE	(402)454-3532	IV	2021
Kollbaum Clarissa J Beving	(712)260-2419 clarissa.beving@cune.org	2719 S 40th St Lincoln NE 68506	NEB	Teacher	C07/2018			S	2016
Kollbaum Stephanie J Schroeder	skollbaum@stjohnbc.net	P.O. Box 262 Battle Creek NE 68715	NEB	Teacher	Tchr	St John Battle Creek NE	(402)675-3605	S	2015
Kollbaum Zachary E	(712)344-2228 zkollbaum@lincolnlutheran.org	2719 S 40th St Lincoln NE 68506	NEB	Teacher	Tchr	Lincoln Lincoln NE	(402)467-5404	S	2016
Kollipara Ian A	(402)904-0427 ian.kollipara@gmail.com	501 Lakeside Dr #302 Lincoln NE 68528	NEB	Teacher	S HS/C	Concordia University Nebraska Seward NE	(402)643-3651	S	2023
Kollmann Marcia E Littmann	(914)337-7554 marcia.kollmann@gmail.com	46 Rose Ave Eastchester NY 10709	AT	Teacher	Tchr	The Village Bronxville NY	(914)337-0207	BR	1977
Kollmeier Michelle M Voland	(516)746-4426 michelle.kollmeier@resgc.org	42 Marlborough Rd West Hempstead NY 11552	AT	DCE	Mem C	Resurrection Garden City NY	(516)746-4426	IV	2021
Kollmeyer Judith E Scheperle	(573)636-4377	2605 Dogwood Bluff Dr Jefferson Cty MO 65109	MO	Teacher	EM			RF	1972
Kollmeyer Tasha L Oetting	(573)230-6580 tkollmeyer@hotmail.com	6916 Spring Park Dr. Jefferson City MO 65109	MO	Teacher	Tchr	Trinity Jefferson City MO	(573)636-6750	CQ	2002
Kollmorgen Nicole M Braun-Leeland	(414)315-1708 n.kollmorgen@yahoo.com	W146S7785 Stags Leap Ct Muskego WI 53150	SW	Teacher	C07/2016			CQ	2003
Kollmorgen Paul G	(414)477-0215 pkollmorgen@martinlutherhs.org	W146S7785 Stags Leap Ct Muskego WI 53150	SW	Teacher	Tchr	Martin Luther Greendale WI	(414)421-4000	S	1994
Kollmorgen Rebecca J Lange	(419)861-7141 rebeccakollmorgen@gmail.com	1755 E Huntley Rd Goshen OH 45122	OH	Teacher	Tchr	St Mark's Milford OH	(513)575-3354	S	1987
Kollmorgen Rex T	(419)407-5445 rexkollmorgen@gmail.com	5840 W Benalex Dr Toledo OH 43612	EN	Tch/DCE	EM			S	1959
Kollmorgen Sandra J Morris	(419)407-5445	5840 W Benalex Dr Toledo OH 43612	EN	Teacher	EM			S	1960
Kollmorgen Timothy A	(513)575-3354 stmarksmilford@yahoo.com	1755 E Huntley Rd Goshen OH 45122	OH	Teacher	Prin	St Mark Milford OH	(513)575-0292	S	1988
Kolumban Robin L Eckert	(402)339-4115 meekmusch@hotmail.com	310 Laredo Rd Papillion NE 68046	NEB	Teacher	C07/2017			PO	1992
Kolusk Diane L Priskorn	(313)605-5039 dkolusk@stmichaellutheran.org	6676 Brookshire Dr Canton MI 48187	MI	Teacher	Tchr	St Michael Wayne MI	(734)728-1950	CQ	2019
Kolzow Janet L Boldt	(847)741-5478 jkolzow@gmail.com	332 W Exchange St Sycamore IL 60178	NI	Teacher	EM			S	1976
Komarnicki Carol B Kisenick	(631)692-8672 carolofcsh@gmail.com	17 Homeland Dr Huntington NY 11743	AT	Teacher	Tchr	Trinity Hicksville NY	(516)931-2211	BR	2003
Komorowski Kelsey Koepke	(414)458-0298 kelsey.koepke@cuw.edu	1058 Jackson Pl Racine WI 53406	SW	Teacher	Tchr	Lutheran High School Racine WI	(262)637-6538	MQ	2021
Konkel Hannah C Griffiths	(715)610-5633 hannah.griffiths8@gmail.com	P.O. Box 167 Finlayson MN 55735	MNN	Teacher	C08/2016			MQ	2015
Konkel Lynnette S Jensen	(734)413-3009 lskonkel@gmail.com	29156 Crawford Rd Romulus MI 48174	MI	Teacher	EM			S	1982
Konow Amy S Fair	(260)385-3703 akonow@eseagles.com	510 Greenlawn Ave Fort Wayne IN 46808	IN	Teacher	Tchr	Emmanuel-St Michael Fort Wayne IN	(260)422-6712	CQ	2021
Konz Julie A Firgens	(920)893-6320 juliekonz@gmail.com	N6264 Riverview Rd Plymouth WI 53073	SW	Teacher	Tchr	St John Plymouth WI	(920)893-5114	CQ	2004
Kooi Patti J Walter	(616)402-4377 pbkooi@charter.net	642 Pennoyer Ave Grand Haven MI 49417	MI	Teacher	EM			RF	1978
Koontz Charessa D Perdue	(804)317-2999 charessak@gmail.com	112 Ridge Line Austin TX 78737	TX	DCE	Mem C	Bethany Austin TX	(512)292-8778	S	2002
Koopman David L	(262)212-8456 dave.koopman48@gmail.com	2173 Yuma St Grafton WI 53024	SW	Teacher	EM			S	1970
Koopman Janice E Pooker	jan.koopman47@gmail.com	2173 Yuma St Grafton WI 53024	SW	Teacher	EM			S	1969
Koopman Karleen J	(308)850-7632 koopmankarleen@yahoo.com	101 Windsor Rd Loredo TX 78041	TX	Teacher	EM			SP	1987
Koopman Rachel L Cuttriss	(217)787-5765 r.koopman@spilunhi.org	609 Catskill Dr Springfield IL 62711	CI	Teacher	Tchr	Lutheran Springfield IL	(217)546-6363	S	1989
Koosman Jeremy W	jeremy.koosman@ stjlutheranschool.org	9141 County Road 101 Corcoran MN 55340	MNS	Teacher	Tchr	St John Corcoran MN	(763)420-2426	SP	2002
Koosmann Jason L	(612)816-2903 jason@redemptionmn.org	4253 W 140th Street Savage MN 55378	MNS	DCE	Mem C	Redemption Bloomington MN	(952)881-0035	CQ	2014
Kootz Jamie R Burmeister	(785)577-0827 jamie.kootz@cune.org	2841 Crystal Lake Dr Salina KS 67401	KS	Teacher	C07/2016			S	2006
Kopecky Jonathan	(209)712-5972 jonathankopecky@me.com	10129 34th Ave SW Seattle WA 98146	NOW	DCE	Mem C	Hope Seattle WA	(206)937-9330	S	2006
Koplin Joyce E Becker	(815)568-6386 jek4@charter.net	1209 Hale St Marengo IL 60152	NI	Teacher	EM			RF	1968
Kopp Amy L Ager	(260)445-6903 ameala@yahoo.com	2009 Timber Rd Jefferson City MO 65101	MO	Teacher	Tchr	Immanuel-Honey Creek Jefferson City MO	(573)496-3766	S	2003
Kopp Tyler J	(260)446-2820 tkopp654@yahoo.com		MO	Teacher	Prin	Immanuel-Honey Creek Jefferson City MO	(573)496-3766	S	2004
Kopper Jill M	(586)219-0636 kopperj4@gmail.com	54731 Marissa Way Shelby Twp MI 48316	MI	Teacher	Tchr	Trinity Clinton Township MI	(586)463-2921	AA	2001
Kopplin Elaine A Burrow	(618)483-5499 eakopplin@yahoo.com	3499 E 900th Ave Altamont IL 62411	CI	Teacher	Tchr	Altamont Altamont IL	(618)483-6428	RF	1989

*Multiple Assignments (See Church Worker Locator for Additional Details)
See Page 53 for the Table of Abbreviations for key to District, Classification, Position, and College abbreviations.
**C =Candidate; EM =Emeritus; the date following the C is the month and year the Candidate status began

NAME	TELEPHONE NUMBER EMAIL	STREET ADDRESS CITY/STATE/ZIP	DISTRICT	CLASS.	POSITION/ STATUS**	WHERE SERVING	OFFICE PHONE	COLLEGE/ UNIV/CQ	YR GRAD
Korff Lynn J	koof420@att.net	2945 Heatherwood Dr Schaumburg IL 60194	NI	Teacher	Tchr	Walther Melrose Park IL	(708)344-0404	RF	1985
Korntheuer Mark A	(708)217-1980 broncotennis@sbcglobal.net	706 N 2nd Ave Maywood IL 60153	NI	Teacher	EM			RF	1974
Koromhas Karen L		115 Van Breeman Dr Clifton NJ 07013	NJ	Teacher	EM			BR	1975
Korotka Joshua J	(920)407-0020 jkorotka@gmail.com	N2190 County Road X Weyauwega WI 54983	NW	Teacher	Tchr	St Paul Manawa WI	(920)596-2837	CQ	2017
Korte Don W Jr Dr	(262)707-1240 don.korte@gmail.com	2324 W Chestnut Rd Mequon WI 53092	SW	Teacher	EM			CQ	2000
Korte Faith C	(989)392-2307 korte.faith@gmail.com	7629 Trestlewood Dr Apt 3b Lansing MI 48917	MI	Teacher	Tchr	Our Savior Lansing MI	(517)882-8665	CH	2020
Korte Matthew L	(402)960-1055 kortem@cox.net	4840 N Shepherd Dr Apt 1302 Houston TX 77108	TX	Teacher	Pro Stf	Lutheran Education Association Friendswood TX	(281)617-5189	S	1991
Kortmeyer Leah R	(573)579-4134 dceleah@hotmail.com	920 Independence St Cape Girardeau MO 63703	MO	DCE	Mem C	Trinity Cape Girardeau MO	(573)335-8224	S	1993
Kortze Aaron D	(815)289-8652 akortze88@gmail.com	418 N Highland Ave Rockford IL 61107	NI	DPM	Mem C	Immanuel Belvidere IL	(815)544-8058	S	2012
Kortze Donald E	(815)742-9328 donkortze@yahoo.com	4712 Pepper Dr Rockford IL 61114	NI	Teacher	EM			S	1982
Kortze Matthew D	(815)871-0346 matt@stjohnlc.com	5304 NW Harney St Vancouver WA 98663	NOW	DCE	Mem C	St John Vancouver WA	(360)573-1461	S	2019
Kortze Sarah E	(815)289-7684 kortze@lhssc.org	1508 Garden Valley Drive Apt. B Saint Peters MO 63376	MO	Teacher	Tchr	St Charles Saint Peters MO	(636)928-5100	S	2014
Kortze Sarah E Wolff	(620)440-1405 mrssarahkortze@gmail.com	418 N Highland Ave Rockford IL 61107	NI	Teacher	C01/2022			S	2012
Kosberg Kasaundra M	(913)426-8081 kasaundra.kosberg@gmail.com		PSW	Teacher	Tchr	Faith Las Vegas NV	(702)804-4400	S	2019
Kosberg Makayla A	(913)938-2184 makayla.kosberg@flhsemail.org	650 S Town Center Dr Apt 2124 Las Vegas NV 89144	PSW	Teacher	Tchr	Faith Las Vegas NV	(702)804-4400	S	2020
Kosche Kenneth T Dr	(406)534-4380 kkosche@hotmail.com	3274 Banff Ave Billings MT 59102	MT	Teacher	EM			CQ	1986
Kosche Thomas P	(406)256-7956 tkosche@hotmail.com	588 Sudan Pl Billings MT 59105	MT	Teacher	Tchr	Trinity Billings MT	(406)656-1021	MQ	2002
Koschmann Mark E	(989)839-5181 mekosch@aol.com	710 Chatham Dr Midland MI 48642	MI	Teacher	EM			S	1976
Koscik Annette E Fleischer	(440)639-1881 akoscik72@gmail.com	9518 Graystone Ln Mentor OH 44060	OH	Teacher	EM			S	1972
Koscik Celeste A Montre	(714)366-9583 celeste.koscik@stlukemesa.com	807 N Stapley Dr Mesa AZ 85203	PSW	DCE	Mem C	St Luke Mesa AZ	(480)969-4414	PO	2005
Koscik James R	(440)639-1881	9518 Graystone Ln Mentor OH 44060	OH	Teacher	EM			S	1971
Kosciuk Sarah D Welemirov	(248)990-6784 deedee6597@yahoo.com	848 Norwich Dr Troy MI 48084	MI	Teacher	Tchr	Immanuel Macomb MI	(586)286-4231	Other	2005
Koslan Carolyn S Nobis	(979)716-8728 ckoslan@gmail.com	P.O. Box 448 Giddings TX 78942	TX	Teacher	EM			S	1977
Kosmala Diane L	(262)637-3684 kosmalajeff@aol.com	5110 Terrace High Racine WI 53406	EN	Teacher	EM			S	1976
Kosman Paul K	(269)651-2386 paul.kosman@gmail.com	605 Parkside Dr Sturgis MI 49091	MI	Teacher	EM			RF	1983
Kosmatka Amy B	(269)325-4776 sportsmom2303@hotmail.com	40419 La Grange Dr Sterling Hts MI 48313	MI	Teacher	Tchr	LHS Assn Of Greater Detroit Rochester Hls MI	(248)856-0240	RF	1989
Kosmatka Bruce J Dr	(586)246-4017 bruce4packers@gmail.com	7211 Yorktown Ln Shelby Twp MI 48317	MI	Teacher	EM			RF	1964
Kosmerchock Shellie L Bentzler	(402)270-7172 skosmerchock@gmail.com	1959 Scheuring Rd Apt 1 De Pere WI 54115	NW	Teacher	Tchr	St Paul Luxemburg WI	(920)845-2095	SP	1987
Kosmicki Andrea M Gibson	(785)307-3173 akosmicki85@gmail.com	2116 SE 36th St Topeka KS 66605	KS	Teacher	Tchr	St John Topeka KS	(785)354-7132	S	2007
Kothe Jacob E	(702)523-6579 kothej@flhsemail.org	10240 Turia Gardens Rd Las Vegas NV 89135	PSW	Teacher	Tchr	Faith Las Vegas NV	(702)804-4400	CQ	2000
Kotila Lisa L Hirsch	(320) 310-2877 lisakotila007@gmail.com	900 5th St N Dassel MN 55325	MNS	Teacher	Tchr	St James Howard Lake MN	(320)543-2630	SP	1993
Kottmeyer Lorna	(618)243-6280	15450 Robin Rd Nashville IL 62263	MO	Teacher	EM			RF	1973
Kottwitz Roger L	(808)572-3712 rlk1@hawaii.rr.com	PMB 8875 15-2662 Pahoa Village Rd #306 Pahoa HI 96778	CNH	Teacher	EM			S	1961
Kovtun George G	(586)677-4961 georgekovtun@comcast.net	52742 Paint Creek Dr Macomb MI 48042	MI	Teacher	EM			S	1980
Kowalke Julie A	(586)321-4473 kowajulielke@gmail.com	16743 Country Ridge Ln Macomb MI 48044	MI	Teacher	Tchr	St Peter Macomb MI	(586)781-3434	SP	1989
Kowalski Rebecca L Pahnke	rkowalskizionecec@gmail.com	255 N Ardmore Ave Villa Park IL 60181	NI	Teacher	Tchr	Zion Hinsdale IL	(630)323-0384	CH	2007
Kowalski Ruth A Bartels	(402)363-3960 ruthbartels@yahoo.com	P.O. Box 212 Bruning NE 68322	NEB	Teacher	C07/2016			S	2007
Kozisek Barbra J	(812)525-9464 bjkozisek@me.com	1585 290th St Garner IA 50438	IW	Teacher	EM			CQ	2022
Kraase Peggy A Wornardt	(262)293-9214 peggyak2002@yahoo.com	N115W16887 El Camino Dr Germantown WI 53022	SW	Teacher	EM			SP	1981
Kraatz Kathy J Wondero	(847)986-4669 rkraatz@sbcglobal.net	1003 Castleton Ct Grayslake IL 60030	NI	Teacher	EM			S	1973
Kraayenbrink Sally J Ebel	(515)571-4770 sjkraayenbrink@gmail.com	1561 National Ave Fort Dodge IA 50501	IW	Teacher	EM			S	1983
Krach Mary L Baumann	(626)622-2803 marykrach@icloud.com	968 S Orange Grove Blvd Unit C Pasadena CA 91105	PSW	Teacher	EM			S	1968

*Multiple Assignments (See Church Worker Locator for Additional Details)

See Page 53 for the Table of Abbreviations for key to District, Classification, Position, and College abbreviations.

**C =Candidate; EM =Emeritus; the date following the C is the month and year the Candidate status began

NAME	TELEPHONE NUMBER EMAIL	STREET ADDRESS CITY/STATE/ZIP	DISTRICT	CLASS.	POSITION/ STATUS**	WHERE SERVING	OFFICE PHONE	COLLEGE/ UNIV/CQ	YR GRAD
Kraemer Kristi L Rinkel	(618)553-8895 kkraemer.spls@gmail.com	P.O. Box 101 Saint Peter IL 62880	CI	Teacher	Tchr	St Peter Saint Peter IL	(618)349-8321	CQ	2020
Krafft Anna	(262)323-4020 anna.krafft@cuw.edu	1916 Brooks Ct West Bend WI 53090	SW	Teacher	Tchr	Living Word Jackson WI	(262)677-9353	MQ	2023
Krafft James E	(702)641-9599 jim.oramay@gmail.com	1213 Big Tree Ave N Las Vegas NV 89031	PSW	Teacher	EM			RF	1959
Krafft Joanne M	(702)656-5097	5509 Leadville Ave Las Vegas NV 89130	PSW	Teacher	Tchr	Faith Las Vegas NV	(702)804-4400	IV	1987
Krahn Hillary K Swanson	(920)864-2463 communications@zionwayside.org	10415 Belmar Ave Maribel WI 54227	NW	DCM	Mem C	Zion Wayside WI	(920)864-2463	MQ	2024
Krahn Suzanne C Adams Deac	(641)420-1787 katlazyk@yahoo.com	206 S Patricia St Waco TX 76705	TX	Deaconess	EM			FW-DEAC	2013
Krake Carrie A Fischer	(715)823-7996 ckrake@stmlc.org	E10708 County Road I Clintonville WI 54929	NW	Teacher	Tchr	St Martin Clintonville WI	(715)823-6538	MQ	2002
Krall Jayson S	(920)893-5533	4437 S 18th Sheboygan WI 53081	SW	Teacher	EM			S	1979
Krall Robert A	rak7292@gmail.com	3721a W Capital Ave Apt 209 Grand Island NE 68803	NEB	Teacher	Tchr	Grand Island Grand Island NE	(308)385-3900	S	2002
Kramer Carla J Aufdemberge	(405)615-3502 carjokra@gmail.com	1702 Hayworth Ct Columbia MO 65203	MO	Teacher	EM			S	1976
Kramer Connie L Baumgarten	(319)233-6461	741 E 1323rd Ln Liberty IL 62347	IE	Teacher	EM			CQ	1986
Kramer Frederick D Dr	(360)896-7247 fdkramer@msn.com	2911 SE Village Loop Apt 302 Vancouver WA 98683	NOW	Teacher	EM			RF	1949
Kramer Jane E Klitzing	(516)433-8315 sjk@trinityhicksville.org	45 Bobwhite Ln Hicksville NY 11801	AT	Teacher	Tchr	Trinity Hicksville NY	(516)931-2211	RF	1961
Kramer Kirsten J	kkramer@orlcs.org	217 Air Park Dr Apt 15 Watertown WI 53094	SW	Teacher	Tchr	Our Redeemer Delavan WI	(262)728-6589	RF	1991
Kramer Llewellyn J	(920)471-8630 llewellynkramerwr@gmail.com	428 Echo Hill Dr Green Bay WI 54166	NW	Teacher	EM			SP	1982
Kramer Marilyn M Schroeder	(208)655-4306 mdcars@filertel.com	2633 Paintbrush Dr Twin Falls ID 83301	NOW	Teacher	EM			S	1968
Kramer Michael W Dr	(405)637-6908 micwilkra@aol.com	1702 Hayworth Ct Columbia MO 65203	MO	Teacher	EM			S	1976
Kramer Patricia A Mueller	(567)277-1331 patcharl@bright.net	5336 County Rd 6 Delta OH 43515	OH	Teacher	EM			S	1972
Kramer Raquel L Daugherty	(405)328-8418 raquel.daugherty16@gmail.com	425 N 42nd St Apt 202 Grand Forks ND 58203	ND	Teacher	C08/2024			AU	2020
Kramer Sarah K	(415)246-9438 ms.sarah.kramer@gmail.com	23 Ravenwood Ln Napa CA 94558	CNH	Teacher	C07/2016			RF	2006
Kramer Sybil J	(913)217-7141 sybilkramer1@gmail.com	6121 West 53rd Plance Mission KS 66202	KS	Teacher	EM			S	1969
Kramer Wayne C Dr	(713)492-1990 waynekramer1950@outlook.com	119 West Silky Sephora Ct Montgomery TX 77316	TX	Teacher	EM			S	1972
Kranich Jeffrey D	(206)227-2730 jeff@princeofpeacelc.org	3944 NW 166th Dr Beaverton OR 97006	NOW	DCE	Mem C	Prince Of Peace Portland OR	(503)645-1211	PO	1980
Krans Dorothy L Boettcher Deac	(636)479-6855 dkrans@yahoo.com	122 Saint Benedict Pevely MO 63070	MO	Deaconess	S Ex/S	Office of National Mission Saint Louis MO		Other	1975
Kranz Bonnie J	(419)385-4894 bkranz@trinityvikings.org	2944 Lutaway Dr Toledo OH 43614	OH	Teacher	EM			RF	1972
Krass Kathleen G Mill	kkrass623@gmail.com	157 W Nicholai St Hicksville NY 11801	AT	Teacher	Tchr	Trinity Hicksville NY	(516)931-2211	RF	1968
Krato Kimberly A Bowers	(314)922-3486 kimkrato@sbcglobal.net	617 Charmont Dr Ferguson MO 63135	MO	Teacher	Tchr	Child of God Saint Peters MO	(636)970-7080	CQ	1996
Kratz Amanda L	(920)676-5215 amanda.kratz16@gmail.com	1750 Flower St Apt 3 Waterloo IA 50701	IE	Teacher	Tchr	Valley Cedar Falls IA	(319)266-4565	MQ	2013
Kratz Dean E	(586)329-9352 dkratz@lhsa.com	54777 Foss Rd Macomb MI 48042	MI	Teacher	EM			S	1973
Kratz Joshua R	(586)630-2246 jkratz@holycrossfw.org	3811 Stafford Dr Fort Wayne IN 46805	IN	Teacher	Tchr	Holy Cross Fort Wayne IN	(260)483-3173	MQ	2008
Kratz Kristina J Woods	(805)723-4991 twoods31@aol.com	15314 Fowler Ave Omaha NE 68116	NEB	Teacher	Tchr	Concordia Omaha NE	(402)445-4000	CQ	2015
Kratzer Michael J	(314) 392-8734 mjkratzer@gmail.com	136 Dornoch Dr Saint Charles MO 63301	MO	Teacher	EM			RF	1975
Kratzert Keith A	(703)250-4052 kratzert@aol.com	6305 Swan Landing Ct Burke VA 22015	SE	DCM	EM			MQ	2007
Krause Alan C	(517)627-8569 akrause@oursaviorchurch.org	11068 Broadbent Rd Lansing MI 48917	MI	Teacher	EM			RF	1964
Krause Alice Fortune	(509)452-0510	709 S Middle Creek Dr Nampa ID 83686	NOW	Teacher	EM			CQ	1987
Krause Barbara J Hoelmer	(469)644-1956 bjkrause51@gmail.com	9223 Flickering Shadow Dr Dallas TX 75243	TX	Teacher	EM			SP	1973
Krause Beth E Appold	(952) 994-7712 jbankrause@comcast.net	1022 Old Post Rd Grand Ledge MI 48837	MI	Teacher	EM			S	1976
Krause Bradley R	(214)729-2793 brkrause@sbcglobal.net	1063 Cydnie Ct Kennedale TX 76060	TX	Teacher	EM			S	1986
Krause Hanne E Norby	(619)886-8018 hkrause@gracepocatello.org	1375 Remington Rd Pocatello ID 83201	NOW	Teacher	Prin	Grace Pocatello ID	(208)237-4142	MQ	1993
Krause Hope M Lawlor Schaefer	(262)227-3062 hmjakrause@gmail.com	N65W14452 Redwood Dr Menomonee Falls WI 53051	SW	Teacher	EM			MQ	1984
Krause Jay A Dr	(602)369-3612 jay.krause@melhs.org	2077 Pinehurst Way Maryville IL 62062	SI	Teacher	Prin	Metro-East Edwardsville IL	(618)656-0043	S	1983
Krause Jennifer L Dietrich	(989)397-3190 jkrause@stmichaelsrichville.org	870 N Block Rd Reese MI 48757	MI	Teacher	Tchr	St Michael Richville MI	(989)868-4791	AA	1997
Krause Jerald A	(414)704-2787	N65W14452 Redwood Dr Menomonee Fls WI 53051	SW	Teacher	EM			S	1974

*Multiple Assignments (See Church Worker Locator for Additional Details)
See Page 53 for the Table of Abbreviations for key to District, Classification, Position, and College abbreviations.
**C =Candidate; EM =Emeritus; the date following the C is the month and year the Candidate status began

NAME	TELEPHONE NUMBER EMAIL	STREET ADDRESS CITY/STATE/ZIP	DISTRICT	CLASS.	POSITION/ STATUS**	WHERE SERVING	OFFICE PHONE	COLLEGE/ UNIV/CQ	YR GRAD
Krause Katherine A	(815)209-5845 katherine.krause128@gmail.com	709 N 4th St Seward NE 68434	NEB	Teacher	Tchr	St John Seward NE	(402)643-4535	S	2011
Krause Kristine A Plamann	(602)369-3989	2077 Pinehurst Way Maryville IL 62062	SI	Teacher	Tchr	Good Shepherd Collinsville IL	(618)344-3153	S	1984
Krause Pamela S Hembry	(979)366-2456 daniel.krause59@gmail.com	3106 County Road 208 Giddings TX 78942	TX	Teacher	Tchr	St Paul Serbin TX	(979)366-2218	S	1982
Krause Rebekah L	(402)641-9157 bekah.krause@gmail.com	319 Lafayette St Apt A Washington MO 63090	MO	Teacher	Tchr	Immanuel Washington MO	(636)239-1636	Other	2020
Krause Sandra L Grousnick	(517)792-2978 s.l.krause1@gmail.com	2825 Wieneke Rd Apt 106 Saginaw MI 48603	MI	Teacher	EM			AA	1987
Krause Steven J	(414)461-6000 skrause@milwaukeelutheran.org	9906 W Grantosa Dr Wauwatosa WI 53222	SW	Teacher	Tchr	Milwaukee LHS Milwaukee WI	(414)461-6000	MQ	1986
Krause Valerie G Hinck	(660)463-2238 vgkmom@gmail.com	31770 Highway Pp P.O. Box 688 Concordia MO 64020	MO	Teacher	EM			CQ	2001
Krauss Susan K Wilson	(314)591-8755 skrauss@lhssc.org	120 Dardenne Landing Ct O Fallon MO 63368	MO	Teacher	Tchr	St Charles Saint Peters MO	(636)928-5100	CQ	2018
Kravitz Heather M	(503)530-0219 hmkravitz@gmail.com	1407 Goldenrod Dr SE Olympia WA 98513	NOW	Teacher	Tchr	Faith Lacey WA	(360)491-3552	PO	2009
Krc Mary E	(301)693-3072 Mary.Krc@student.cune.edu	517 Sage Hen Way Frederick MD 21703	SE	Teacher	EM			S	2012
Krebbs Karen M Witte	(209)450-5839 karenkrebbs@gmail.com	1623 Albany Abe Modesto CA 95350	CNH	Teacher	C10/2016			MQ	2007
Krecklow Russell C	(520)825-4695 rkrecklow2@comcast.net	9005 N Oracle Rd Unit 211 Tucson AZ 85704	EN	Teacher	EM			S	1956
Kregar Deborah L Landheer	(815)718-1316 dkregar48@gmail.com	1504 Avenue J Sterling IL 61081	NI	Teacher	EM			S	1970
Kreger Nichol R Bagles	(262)237-4276		SW	Teacher	Tchr	St Stephen Horicon WI	(920)485-6687	MQ	2007
Kreienkamp Daniel A	(314)954-9085 daniel.kreienkamp@gmail.com	14 Weatherby Saint Peters MO 63376	MO	DCE	Tchr	St Charles* Saint Peters MO	(636)928-5100	S	2005
Kreis Rachel	(734)928-8898 rkreis01@gmail.com	4129 Cornwallis Dr Apt 102 Virginia Beach VA 23452	SE	DPM		Southeastern District Henrico VA	(703)971-9371	AA	2022
Kreiss Paul T Dr	(708)203-8436 shasenwinkel@comcast.net	1133 Bishops View Ln Knoxville TN 37932	NI	Teacher	EM			RF	1952
Kreizel Lexie L	(402)440-1664 lkreizel@christlincoln.org	2741 Dorothy Dr Lincoln NE 68507	NEB	Teacher	Tchr	Christ Lincoln NE	(402)483-7774	S	2024
Krekel Ronda L	(816)739-8718 rondakrek@gmail.com	1506 SW Twincreek Pl Blue Springs MO 64015	MO	Teacher	Tchr	Timothy Blue Springs MO	(816)228-5300	CQ	2017
Kremmel Mary Beth A Hessel	(314)707-2238 mbkremmel12@gmail.com	842 Country Stone Dr Manchester MO 63021	MO	Teacher	EM			CQ	2001
Krempler Jeffrey E Dr	(561)843-2053 jk13mets@gmail.com	1480 NW 12th Way Boca Raton FL 33486	FG	Teacher	EM			BR	1975
Krenning Marguerite M Snyder	(314)308-0831	13190 S Outer 40 Rd Apt 2108 Chesterfield MO 63017	MO	Teacher	EM			S	1958
Krentz Paul A	(737)444-1284 krentztx@gmail.com	103 Parque Vista Dr Georgetown TX 78626	TX	Tch/DCE	EM			S	1971
Krentz Rebecca J Fraser	(512)819-9575 dcebecky@verizon.net	103 Parque Vista Dr Georgetown TX 78626	TX	Teacher	EM			S	1971
Krenz Hannah M	(816)853-7988 hmk40@yahoo.com	4571 Short Putt Rd Carson City NV 89701	CNH	Teacher	Tchr	Sierra Carson City NV	(775)267-1921	S	2003
Krenzke Bette J Thompson Dr	(623)572-5490 bette.krenzke@cox.net	19420 N Westbrook Pkwy Unit 523 Peoria AZ 85382	NI	Teacher	EM			RF	1966
Krenzke Christine Buchinger Deac	(763)350-7215 christine.krenzke@gmail.com	49 Clubview Dr Hartford City IN 47348	IN	Deaconess	C07/2016			FW-DEAC	2008
Krenzke Thomas A	(262)391-0192 thomas.krenzke@cune.org	126 Oconomowoc Sq Oconomowoc WI 53066	SW	Teacher	EM			CQ	1975
Krenzke Timothy L Dr	(623)572-5490 tkrenzke@cox.net	19420 N Westbrook Pkwy Unit 523 Peoria AZ 85382	NI	Teacher	EM			RF	1966
Kress Miranda L Leksche	(312)497-3740 mkress@standrewlutheranschool.org	6232 N Broadway St Apt 3 Chicago IL 60660	NI	Teacher	Tchr	St Andrews Park Ridge IL	(847)823-9308	CQ	2019
Kressbach Frederick M	(586)549-8820 fkbach@yahoo.com	15721 Lorway Dr Clinton Twp MI 48038	MI	Teacher	EM			CQ	2003
Kretzmann David C	(916)482-6439 dckretzmann@gmail.com	4265 Carle Ln Sacramento CA 95841	CNH	Teacher	EM			PO	1980
Kretzmann Nathan O	(623)670-2269 nate.kretzmann@gmail.com	31222 Casa Grande San Juan Capistrano CA 92675	PSW	Teacher	Pro Stf	Crean Irvine CA	(949)387-1199	IV	1985
Kretzmann Norma J Rader Dr	(956)642-7351 njkretzmann@gmail.com	1905 S Lakeline Blvd Apt 128 Cedar Park TX 78613	TX	Teacher	EM			CQ	1998
Kretzmann Tabitha A Schmidt	(651)230-3742 kretzfam@hotmail.com	W8924 770th Ave River Falls WI 54022	MNS	DCO	C07/2016			SP	2001
Krey Tirzah A Deac	(809)501-6117 tirzah.krey@lcms.org	13517 NE 94th St Redmond WA 98052	MO	Deaconess	S Miss	Office of International Mission Saint Louis MO		FW-DEAC	2023
Krieger Randy J	(602)509-9123 rskrieger6@live.com	2329 N 39th Pl Phoenix AZ 85008	PSW	Teacher	EM			S	1982
Krieger Ruth A Dubke	(269) 313-4981 krieger.trinity@gmail.com	201 S Mechanic St Berrien Sprgs MI 49103	MI	Teacher	Tchr	Trinity Berrien Springs MI	(269)473-1811	RF	1982
Krieger Susan L Bauer	(602)513-1025 rskrieger6@live.com	2329 N 39th Pl Phoenix AZ 85008	PSW	Teacher	Tchr	Trinity Litchfield Park AZ	(623)935-4690	S	1982
Krienke Linda F Baule	(612)709-0510 krienkel@gmail.com	15302 Boulder Creek Dr Minnetonka MN 55345	MNS	Teacher	EM			SP	1967
Kringel Dorothy A Gugel	(302)233-2585 dorothykringel@yahoo.com	1516 NE 96th St Seattle WA 98115	NOW	Teacher	EM			S	1968
Krinke Arlen D	(763)441-4589 akrinke@yahoo.com	1948 W Wayzata Blvd Apt 102 Long Lake MN 55356	MNS	Teacher	EM			SP	1968

*Multiple Assignments (See Church Worker Locator for Additional Details)

See Page 53 for the Table of Abbreviations for key to District, Classification, Position, and College abbreviations.

**C =Candidate; EM =Emeritus; the date following the C is the month and year the Candidate status began

NAME	TELEPHONE NUMBER EMAIL	STREET ADDRESS CITY/STATE/ZIP	DISTRICT	CLASS.	POSITION/ STATUS**	WHERE SERVING	OFFICE PHONE	COLLEGE/ UNIV/CQ	YR GRAD
Kristofic Patricia L Akins Deac	bachp73@mac.com		RM	Deaconess	Mem C	Redeemer Salt Lake City UT	(801)467-4352	CQ	2001
Kroemer Karen J Miller	(319)363-3349 klkroemer@msn.com	3205 Willowridge Rd Unit B Marion IA 52302	IE	Teacher	EM			CQ	1987
Kroenke Marissa E Manor Deac	(309)310-5915 deaconess.marissa@gmail.com		MO	Deaconess	C10/2023			FW-DEAC	2022
Kroft David	(512)773-0383	716 Rocky Shadows Chattanooga TN 37421	TX	Teacher	EM			S	1970
Krohe Lois A	(734)735-4194 lkrohe@me.com	100 Bur Oak Ct Monroe MI 48162	MDS	Teacher	EM			RF	1973
Krohmer Brian M	(216)246-1292 bkrohmer123@gmail.com	611 Bridge Crossing Pl Apt B Indianapolis IN 46227	IN	DCE	Mem C	Calvary Indianapolis IN	(317)783-2000	RF	2024
Krohn Lindsey M Kobin	(262)984-7571 lindsey.m.krohn@gmail.com	344 Grant St. Elkhorn WI 53121	FG	Teacher	C07/2016			MQ	2009
Krohse Kenneth C	(630)495-4313 grace915@att.net	206 N Main St Lombard IL 60148	NI	Teacher	EM			CQ	1981
Krohse Ronald D	(217)488-6135	729 E Gibson St New Berlin IL 62670	CI	Teacher	EM			RF	1968
Kroll James W	(608)756-2286 jkroll@stpaulsjanesville.com	608 S Academy St Janesville WI 53548	SW	Teacher	Prin	St Pauls Janesville WI	(608)754-4471	RF	1978
Kroll Mary L De Haan	(630)986-8154 mlk259@comcast.net	259 S Prospect Ave Clarendon Hls IL 60514	NI	Teacher	EM			RF	1976
Kroll Sharon J Pasbrig	(763)355-5834 onebluelake@comcast.net	4572 58th Ave N Apt 275 Brooklyn Ctr MN 55429	MNS	Teacher	EM			RF	1969
Krome Allison P Wendling	allyplymouth@gmail.com		SE	Teacher	C01/2024			CH	2016
Kromminga Joyce M Dreyer	(507)330-4460	1667 Buckingham Path Faribault MN 55021	MNS	Teacher	EM			SP	1979
Krone James R	(248)907-5048 kronejim@gmail.com	19669 Gary Ln Livonia MI 48152	MI	Teacher	EM			RF	1981
Krone Shirley M Miller	(313) 701-7026 shirleykrone5@gmail.com	5 Scottsdale Pl Dearborn MI 48124	MI	Teacher	EM			S	1969
Krone Toni L Delventhal	(440)327-0111 tonikrone@yahoo.com	7557 Root Rd N Ridgeville OH 44039	OH	Teacher	EM			RF	1973
Krone Walter K	(313)730-8185	5 Scottsdale Pl Dearborn MI 48124	MI	Teacher	EM			RF	1966
Kroonblawd Hannah L Dr	(651)341-4151 hannah.kroonblawd@cune.org	722 N 3rd St Apt 1 Seward NE 68434	NEB	Teacher	S HS/C	Concordia University Nebraska Seward NE	(402)643-3651	S	2012
Krubsack David H	(414)321-8574	2960 S 96th St West Allis WI 53227	SW	Teacher	EM			RF	1958
Krueger Brendan J	(989)971-1617 brendankrueger0610@gmail.com	7159 Roedel Rd Frankenmuth MI 48734	MI	Teacher	Tchr	Bethlehem Saginaw MI	(989)755-1144	CH	2022
Krueger Cheryl R Knuth	(262)268-1502 teachercrr@hotmail.com	873 Ashley Ave Prt Washingtn WI 53074	SW	Teacher	Tchr	St John Fredonia WI	(262)692-2734	MQ	1999
Krueger Deborah B Blank	(860)585-9154 dj2hkrueger@gmail.com	437 Matthews St Bristol CT 06010	NE	Teacher	Tchr	Immanuel Bristol CT	(860)583-5631	CQ	2022
Krueger Janeen K Reinitz Lano	(612)360-3192 janeenkrueger@gmail.com	7613 Century Blvd Chanhassen MN 55317	MNS	Teacher	C07/2016			CQ	2001
Krueger Joleen G Baack	(812) 314-9849 sjkrueger5@comcast.net	12441 Willow Bnd Elizabethtown IN 47232	IN	Teacher	EM			S	1987
Krueger Jonathan L	(920)334-5533 jon.krueger@ourbethlehem.com	3627 S 10th St Sheboygan WI 53081	SW	Teacher	Tchr	Bethlehem Sheboygan WI	(920)452-5071	MQ	2004
Krueger Juanita L	trinitynm@yahoo.com	10620 215th St W Morristown MN 55052	MNS	Teacher	C07/2016			SP	1982
Krueger Julie M Jacobsen	(832)494-6759 juliek1314@gmail.com	2000 Eclipse CV Cedar Park TX 78613	TX	Teacher	Tchr	Redeemer Austin TX	(512)451-6478	AU	2010
Krueger Kenneth F	(570)617-8861 highvoltagekk@att.net	10 Sierra Dr. Glen Carbon IL 62034	SI	Teacher	Prin	Trinity Edwardsville IL	(618)656-2918	MQ	2005
Krueger Kurt J Dr	(949)525-5101 kurt.krueger@cui.edu	42395 Chisolm Trail Murrieta CA 92562	PSW	Teacher	EM			CQ	1971
Krueger Michael D	(618)288-3080 mkrueger@gslcs.org	116 Ridge Dr Maryville IL 62062	SI	Teacher	Tchr	Good Shepherd Collinsville IL	(618)344-3153	S	1991
Krueger Michelle L	(920)418-0031 14krumi95@gmail.com	4141 State Road 91 Apt 203 Oshkosh WI 54904	NW	Teacher	Tchr	St Paul Bonduel WI	(715)758-8559	MQ	2018
Krueger Nancy E Hagensick Bowman	(773)259-3298 nehbowmanmaed@gmail.com	5222 Wickfield Drive New Orleans LA 70122	SO	Teacher	Tchr	St John New Orleans LA	(504)488-6641	CQ	2009
Krueger Paul H	(920) 946-2118 paulkrueger2010@gmail.com	524 W Riverside Dr Kohler WI 53044	SW	Teacher	EM			S	1975
Krueger Richard C	(616)361-8626 rick.krueger@messiahgr.org	1659 Diamond Ct NE Grand Rapids MI 49505	MI	Parish Assist	Mem C	Messiah Grand Rapids MI	(616)363-2553	AA	1989
Krueger Robert J Dr	(651)641-8848 rkrueger@csp.edu	1064 Oakwood Road Newport MN 55055	MNS	Teacher	S HS/C	Concordia University St Paul Saint Paul MN	(651)641-8278	S	1993
Krueger Shannon L Nothelfer Wiegert	(920)994-9060 kruegsandwiegs@gmail.com	W8497 Brazelton Dr Random Lake WI 53075	SW	Teacher	Tchr	Trinity Mequon WI	(262)242-2045	RF	1996
Krueger Stephanie D Walther	(262)501-0150 nkrueger6@wi.rr.com	S25W26919 Winnebago Way Waukesha WI 53188	SW	Teacher	Tchr	Beautiful Savior Waukesha WI	(262)542-2496	MQ	2000
Krueger Steven R	(512)731-2697 steven.krueger@live.com	2000 Eclipse CV Cedar Park TX 78613	TX	DCE	Mem C	Redeemer Austin TX	(512)459-1500	AU	2009
Krueger Tracy M	(209)406-1788 tmkrueger@uwalumni.com	N87 W7019 Evergreen Ct #103 Cedarburg WI 53012	SW	DCE	Mem C	St Paul Grafton WI	(262)377-4659	RF	2005
Krueger Vera I Heckman	(303)452-3192	12457 Columbine Ct Thorton CO 80241	RM	Teacher	EM			S	1966
Krueger Walter E Dr	(503)522-2179 wkrueger@teleport.com	1963 SW Lake Pl Gresham OR 97080	NOW	Teacher	EM			RF	1968

*Multiple Assignments (See Church Worker Locator for Additional Details)

See Page 53 for the Table of Abbreviations for key to District, Classification, Position, and College abbreviations.

**C =Candidate; EM =Emeritus; the date following the C is the month and year the Candidate status began

NAME	TELEPHONE NUMBER EMAIL	STREET ADDRESS CITY/STATE/ZIP	DISTRICT	CLASS.	POSITION/ STATUS**	WHERE SERVING	OFFICE PHONE	COLLEGE/ UNIV/CQ	YR GRAD
Krueger William G	(309)353-7290	231 Maple Park Dr Pekin IL 61554	CI	Teacher	Mem C	St John Green Valley IL	(309)348-3180	S	1961
Kruger Anna C	(734)770-9700 annackruger@yahoo.com	3920 Gettysburg St Midland MI 48542	MI	DFLM	Mem C	St John's Midland MI	(989)835-5861	AA	2017
Kruger Nancy E	(586)251-6515 nancek1526@wowway.com	11342 Jacqueline Dr Sterling Hts MI 48313	MI	Teacher	EM			CQ	2001
Krumland Rick	(573)364-8599 rickkrumland@hotmail.com	3710 Oxford Rd Jefferson Cty MO 65109	MO	Teacher	EM			S	1971
Krumwiede Anastasia E Murray	(281)610-3646 stasiakrum@gmail.com	2971 Laurel Mill Way Houston TX 77080	TX	Teacher	C06/2024			CQ	2021
Krupski James F	(608)448-7387 jameskrupski@msn.com	10365 Wayborough Ln Lincoln NE 68527	NEB	Teacher	EM			RF	1982
Krupski Judith K	(858)613-1453 jykrupski@att.net	17430 Plaza Dolores San Diego CA 92128	PSW	Teacher	EM			RF	1964
Krupsky Harold K	(248)689-1554 hkrupsky@faithtroy.org	1238 Balmoral Dr Mount Clemens MI 48043	MI	Teacher	Mem C	Faith Troy MI	(248)689-4664	RF	1971
Kruse Ashley A	(816)344-6443 ashley.kruse@cune.org	505 E Meadow Ln Saint Joseph MO 64501	MO	Teacher	Tchr	St Paul Saint Joseph MO	(816)279-1118	S	2004
Kruse Daryl M	(404)791-7304 darylkruse@outlook.com	107 Farmstead Ct McHenry IL 60050	NI	Teacher	EM			RF	1979
Kruse Laura M Golnitz	(714)280-7524 laura.kruse@lhsoc.org	1445 E Trenton Ave Orange CA 92867	PSW	Teacher	Tchr	Orange County Orange CA	(714)998-5151	SP	1995
Kruse Lavern R	(248)756-0848 lavern.kruse@gmail.com	2270 Cedar Crest Blvd Commerce Twp MI 48390	MI	Tch/DCE	EM			S	1966
Kruse Robin F Geidel	(320)587-5440 rfkruse@gmail.com		MNS	Tch/DCE	C07/2016			S	1990
Kruse Sheryl M Endorf	(785)337-2308	3024 24th Rd Hanover KS 66945	KS	Teacher	EM			S	1971
Krutz Charles H	(402)643-3464	Rr 1 Seward NE 68434	NEB	Teacher	EM			S	1954
Krycho Steven P Jr	(469)525-9665 skrycho@flsplano.org	3809 Wintergreen Dr Plano TX 75074	TX	Teacher	Tchr	Faith Plano TX	(972)423-7447	MQ	2019
Krzesinksi Marjorie A Larsen	(913)422-2037 krzesinski@hopelutheran.org	730 S 9th St Edwardsville KS 66111	KS	Teacher	Tchr	Hope Shawnee KS	(913)631-6940	S	1985
Kuball Daniel C	(507)405-7059 dckuball@gmail.com	4742 Savannah Dr NW Rochester MN 55901	MNS	Teacher	Tchr	Rochester Central Rochester MN	(507)289-3267	SP	1992
Kuball Robin M	rrkuball@gmail.com	21636 Farwell Ave Faribault MN 55021	MNS	Teacher	C07/2016			CQ	2003
Kube Brian K	(779)423-8640 coachbkube@yahoo.com	22918 Ambassador Blve NW Saint Francis MN 55070	MNS	Teacher	Prin	Trinity Saint Francis MN	(763)753-1234	SP	1997
Kube Lisa J Heintz	(815)491-3400 mrsljkube@yahoo.com	22918 Ambassador Blve NW Saint Francis MN 55070	MNS	Teacher	Tchr	Trinity Saint Francis MN	(763)753-1234	SP	1990
Kuchenbecker Randall D	(209)365-0811 rdkteacher@gmail.com	1227 S Mills Ave Lodi CA 95242	CNH	Teacher	EM			S	1970
Kuck Glen T	(773)889-6518 gtkuck@gmail.com	2639 N Meade Ave Chicago IL 60639	NI	Teacher	EM			RF	1972
Kuck William E	(407)432-2018 bill_kuck@mac.com	779 Cypress Crossing Trail St. Augustine FL 32095	FG	Teacher	EM			RF	1969
Kuebler Eugene C	(989)245-3778 eugene.kuebler@yahoo.com	15531 W Oakridge Ct Surprise AZ 84374	PSW	Teacher	EM			S	1972
Kueck Jonathan R	(501)940-1594 jonkueck@yahoo.com	809 Acorn St Giddings TX 78942	TX	Teacher	Tchr	Faith Lutheran High School Warda TX	(979)242-2889	S	2003
Kueck Nicole D Vanderhoff	(501)940-6259 nicole.vanderhoff@cune.org	809 Acorn St. Giddings TX 78942	TX	Teacher	Prin	Faith Lutheran High School Warda TX	(979)242-2889	S	2008
Kuefner Benjamin R	(308)325-0490 bkuefner2@gmail.com	211 E 7th St Lexington NE 68850	MDS	Teacher	C06/2025			S	2022
Kuefner Marla R Otteman	(650)245-2871 54mrok@gmail.com	237 Aspen Grove Way Severance CO 80550	CNH	Teacher	EM			S	1977
Kuegele Laura J	(707)206-1818 dcelaura@me.com	11833 County Road 167 Tyler TX 75703	TX	DCE	Mem C	Trinity Tyler TX	(903)593-1526	IV	2002
Kuehl Mary L Jaeger	(262)349-3373 kuehl.sherherdsway@gmail.com	W310s749 Maple Ave Waukesha WI 53188	SW	Teacher	Tchr	Divine Redeemer Hartland WI	(262)367-8400	CQ	1988
Kuehm Carrie M Albrecht	(847)217-9879 ckuehm@standrewslutheran school.org	842 Cross Creek Dr N Apt A1 Roselle IL 60172	NI	Teacher	Tchr	St Andrews Park Ridge IL	(847)823-9308	RF	1995
Kuehne Tori C Anderson Deac	(763)244-7711 tori.kuehne@stjlutheran.org	10146 45th Pl NE Saint Michael MN 55376	MNS	Deaconess	C07/2016			FW-DEAC	2009
Kuehner Karl J	(630)632-0774 karljkuehner@gmail.com	1529 Harding Ave Berkeley IL 60163	NI	Teacher	C07/2016			RF	2007
Kuehner Rachel K Shaffer	(978)407-6657 rachelkuehner@gmail.com	1529 Harding Ave Berkeley IL 60163	NI	Teacher	Tchr	Walther Melrose Park IL	(708)344-0404	RF	2006
Kuehnert Michelle R McWilliams	(260)413-4057 mrkuehnert2@gmail.com	3225 Copper Hill Rn Fort Wayne IN 46804	IN	Teacher	C06/2022			CQ	2020
Kueker Linda C Pfister	(847)394-1798 ldkueker@gmail.com	4203 N Harvard Ave Arlington Hts IL 60004	NI	Teacher	EM			RF	1975
Kuerschner Edwin F	(816)876-3085 ekuersch@tahoo.com	1907 16th Ave Grafton WI 53024	SW	Teacher	EM			SP	1982
Kuerschner John P	(262)377-5706 JKuers2811@aol.com	N30W6078 Lincoln Blvd Cedarburg WI 53012	FG	Teacher	EM			RF	1966
Kuerschner Shirley A Schimelpfenig	(262)377-5706 JKuers2811@aol.com	N30W6078 Lincoln Blvd Cedarburg WI 53012	FG	Teacher	EM			SP	1971
Kuerschner Vernon C	(630)833-9695 vernkuersch@yahoo.com	261 N Illinois St Elmhurst IL 60126	NI	Teacher	EM			RF	1961
Kugler Anna M	(509)750-2838 annamkugler77@gmail.com	1244 Utah St. Wenatchee WA 98801	NOW	Teacher	Tchr	St Paul Wenatchee WA	(509)662-8790	S	1999

*Multiple Assignments (See Church Worker Locator for Additional Details)
See Page 53 for the Table of Abbreviations for key to District, Classification, Position, and College abbreviations.
**C =Candidate; EM =Emeritus; the date following the C is the month and year the Candidate status began

NAME	TELEPHONE NUMBER EMAIL	STREET ADDRESS CITY/STATE/ZIP	DISTRICT	CLASS.	POSITION/ STATUS**	WHERE SERVING	OFFICE PHONE	COLLEGE/ UNIV/CQ	YR GRAD
Kugler Colleen J Klahn	(616)426-4741	3856 Warren Woods Rd Three Oaks MI 49128	MI	Teacher	EM			S	1972
Kuhfahl Helen M Schubert	(847) 226-4711 hmkuhfahl@comcast.net	148 Bannock Ct East Dundee IL 60118	NI	DCM	EM			MQ	2012
Kuhl Amanda B Pullmann	(406)861-5933 amandakuhl44@gmail.com	8602 W Brittany Dr Littleton CO 80123	RM	Teacher	C07/2016			MQ	2011
Kuhlmann Bethany A Hargreaves	(402)440-3840 bethany.kohlmann1@gmail.com	105 E Division St Anthon IA 51004	IW	DCE	RSO	Lutheran Family Service Fort Dodge IA	(515)573-3138	S	2015
Kuhlmann Douglas J Dr	(314)497-3014 dkuhlmann@lhssc.org	17 Greenhurst Ct Saint Peters MO 63376	MO	Teacher	ExecDir	St Charles Saint Peters MO	(636)928-5100	S	1998
Kuhlmann Eloise S Stigge	(806)570-5965 eloiselwml@gmail.com	131 Wilmington Dr Fate TX 75189	TX	Teacher	EM			S	1967
Kuhlmann Linda J Howard	(503)351-0590 lkuhls@gmail.com	160 State Route 19 S Hermann MO 65041	MO	Teacher	EM			S	1972
Kuhn William F Dr	(402)641-4224 billkuhn78@gmail.com	17312 Edna Street Omaha NE 68136	NOW	Teacher	EM			RF	1977
Kuhnau Brenda S Christian	(715)897-6469 brendakuhnau@yahoo.com	N5738 County Road Y Chili WI 54420	NW	Teacher	Tchr	Immanuel Marshfield WI	(715)384-5121	SP	1998
Kuhnert Susan E	(630)730-4567 lizsue42@yahoo.com	7421 Blackburn Ave Apt 102 Downers Grove IL 60516	NI	Teacher	EM			CQ	1987
Kuiper Emily D Eastwood	(210)854-5447 eastwood@anthemcross.org	421 Woodland Ave Giddings TX 78942	TX	Teacher	Tchr	Immanuel Giddings TX	(979)542-2918	AU	2008
Kuiper Jason T	(262)498-2925 jkuiper@splch.com	421 Woodland Ave Giddings TX 78942	TX	Teacher	Tchr	Immanuel Giddings TX	(979)542-2918	S	2007
Kuker Gerald W	(574)323-8783 gwkuker@yahoo.com	901 Dublin Dr Mishawaka IN 46545	IN	Teacher	EM			RF	1967
Kulak Abigail C Malme	(920)791-1954 abbykulak@pilgrimluth.org	2271 Balsam Way Green Bay WI 54313	NW	Teacher	Tchr	Pilgrim Green Bay WI	(920)965-2244	CH	2020
Kulat Diane L Diehl	2mypie@gmail.com	455 W Front St 2-504 Wheaton IL 60187	NI	Teacher	EM			RF	1972
Kulat Terry L	terrykulat090@gmail.com	455 W Front St 2-504 Wheaton IL 60187	NI	Teacher	EM			RF	1972
Kulus Kenneth M	(402)740-3693 kulusk@concordiaomaha.org	15929 Rosewater Pkwy Bennington NE 68007	NEB	Teacher	Tchr	Concordia Omaha NE	(402)445-4000	CQ	2015
Kumke Allison C	(708)209-8207 akumke@mytlsonline.com	8932 W 140th St #3d Orland Park IL 60462	NI	Teacher	Tchr	Trinity Burr Ridge IL	(708)839-1200	RF	2018
Kumm David H	(402)610-4465 dhkumm@gmail.com	3100 N 68th St Lincoln NE 68507	NEB	Teacher	Prin	Trinity Lincoln NE	(402)466-1800	S	2001
Kun Christina R Ford	(909)568-1568 chriskun2011@gmail.com	1903 Ray Ave Caldwell ID 83605	NOW	Teacher	C01/2022			PO	2000
Kunde Casey L Lawyer	(619) 606-5145 caseykunde@gmail.com	5655 Tau St La Mesa CA 91942	PSW	Teacher	C07/2016			CQ	2003
Kundinger Debra J Bach	kundinde@ctkl.org	10298 Rescue Rd Sebewaing MI 48759	MI	Teacher	Tchr	Christ The King Sebewaing MI	(989)883-3730	AA	1986
Kunert Charles J Dr		21718 SW Oxford Ter Sherwood OR 97140	NOW	Teacher	EM			S	1969
Kunert Nancy A Vanderhorst	(808)959-9953 nanakunert@gmail.com	1092 W Kawailani St Hilo HI 96720	CNH	Teacher	EM			RF	1962
Kunkel Dustin			NOW	DCE	D Ex/S	Northwest District Portland OR	(503)288-8383	PO	1996
Kunkel Jesse H	(816)694-8053	505 S Leona St Concordia MO 64020	MO	Teacher	EM			S	1956
Kunkel Ruth M Schmid	(816)585-6768 rkunkel@calvarykc.com	12411 Wornall Road Kansas City MO 64145	MO	Teacher	Tchr	Calvary Kansas City MO	(816)444-6908	S	1984
Kunkel Sara A Vickery	(360)490-2911 kunkelfam99@gmail.com	3108 SW Thistle St Seattle WA 98126	NOW	Teacher	C07/2024			PO	1999
Kunz Marshall F	(507)289-2815 marlo4751@yahoo.com	6377 Freedom Ln NW Rochester MN 55901	MNS	Teacher	EM			SP	1971
Kunz Susan M Wille	(708)482-9040 suekunz@yahoo.com	416 S Ashland Ave La Grange IL 60525	NI	Teacher	EM			RF	1974
Kunze Caleb L	(320)345-0058 caleb@loveofchrist.org	31 Ben Nevis Ln Waite Park MN 56387	MNN	DCM	Mem C	Love Of Christ Saint Cloud MN	(320)253-7453	MQ	2017
Kunze Trevor S	(970)889-0718 kunzet19@gmail.com	468 N Wyndham Ave Greeley CO 80634	RM	DCM	C03/2019			MQ	2012
Kuphal Emmalee M	(507)301-4279 emkuph@gmail.com	P.O. Box 460 Lake Crystal MN 56055	MNN	DCE	C06/2024			SP	2013
Kuphal Myrna Knick	(320) 510-1760 kuphalm@yahoo.com	28740 505th Ave Winthrop MN 55396	MNS	Teacher	EM			CQ	2002
Kurek Stephen C	(815)625-5302 skurek1@aol.com	2612 Clover Ln Sterling IL 61081	NI	Teacher	EM			RF	1970
Kurien Rebekah L Bullock	(586)419-9920 rebekah.kurien@st-matthew.org	5480 Huron Hills Dr Commerce Twp MI 48382	MI	Teacher	Tchr	St Matthew Walled Lake MI	(248)624-7676	MQ	2004
Kurio Nancy A Northington	(512)255-4150	725 County Road 316 Georgetown TX 78626	TX	Teacher	EM			CQ	1993
Kurka Margie L Gerdts	(573)377-4646 margiekurka@aol.com	407 W 3rd St Stover MO 65078	MO	Teacher	EM			S	1981
Kurth Barbara T Schukat	(262)345-5083 btkurth26@wi.rr.com	N56W15891 Scott Ln Menomonee Fls WI 53051	SW	Teacher	EM			RF	1958
Kurth Elizabeth F Wachal	(773)736-9465 kurth.e@sbcglobal.net	3506 W 4th St Davenport IA 52804	NI	Teacher	EM			RF	1975
Kurth Lyle J Dr	(847)742-2454 ljrth@juno.com	600 Breeze Park Dr Apt 181 Weldon Spring MO 63304	MO	Tch/DCE	EM			S	1954
Kurth Ruth J Dr	(616)421-5010 kurthmi@comcast.net	3271 Gold Dust St NE Belmont MI 49306	MI	Teacher	EM			RF	1962
Kurtz Amy L Starks	(901)237-7759 akurtz@ilsmemphis.com	11910 Country Valley Cove Arlington TN 38002	MDS	Teacher	Prin	Immanuel Memphis TN	(901)373-4486	S	2001

*Multiple Assignments (See Church Worker Locator for Additional Details)

See Page 53 for the Table of Abbreviations for key to District, Classification, Position, and College abbreviations.

**C =Candidate; EM =Emeritus; the date following the C is the month and year the Candidate status began

NAME	TELEPHONE NUMBER EMAIL	STREET ADDRESS CITY/STATE/ZIP	DISTRICT	CLASS.	POSITION/ STATUS**	WHERE SERVING	OFFICE PHONE	COLLEGE/ UNIV/CQ	YR GRAD
Kurtz Nancy C Bromund	(734)671-9354 kurtznc@comcast.com	25489 Montebello Ct Woodhaven MI 48183	MI	Teacher	EM			AA	1984
Kurtz Neal I	(402)992-1791 nikurtz@outlook.com	330 W Fremont St Oneill NE 68763	NEB	Teacher	EM			S	1971
Kusch David S	(734)812-5843 dkusch23@gmail.com	750 Lawnview Ct Rochester Hls MI 48307	MI	Teacher	Tchr	Northwest Rochester Hills MI	(248)856-0240	AA	1984
Kuschmann Helmut P	(586)247-5299 hmkuschmann@sbcglobal.net	47635 Goldridge Ln Macomb MI 48044	MI	Teacher	EM			RF	1966
Kuschmann Margie A Linder	(586)247-5299 hmkuschmann@sbcglobal.net	47635 Goldridge Ln Macomb MI 48044	MI	Teacher	EM			RF	1966
Kuschnereit Gary J	(405)733-8921 luteaprin@aol.com	1402 Magnolia Ln Midwest City OK 73110	OK	Teacher	EM			S	1972
Kusel Jill C Jacobsen	(660)864-4992 jkusel@lutheranschool.org	210 Kens Road El Cajon CA 92021	PSW	Teacher	Tchr	Christ La Mesa CA	(619)462-5211	CQ	1995
Kusel Mark D	(660)624-4927 mkusel@lutheranschool.org	210 Kens Rd El Cajon CA 92021	PSW	Teacher	Tchr	Christ La Mesa CA	(619)462-5211	CQ	2001
Kuseske Cherice L Carrigan	(320) 209-1536 kuseskect@msn.com	11070 39th St N Apt 200 Lake Elmo MN 55042	MNS	Teacher	EM			SP	1968
Kuseske Thomas E	(320)209-1536 tkuseske@msn.com	The Fields At Arbor Glen 11070 39th St N Apt 200 Lake Elmo MN 55042	MNS	Teacher	EM			SP	1968
Kuske Kevin E	(920)737-7692 KKuske@bethanyschool.net	9101 Lamar Ave Overland Park KS 66207	KS	Teacher	Tchr	Bethany Overland Park KS	(913)648-2228	S	1983
Kuske Mary E Moll	(989)652-9806 mkuske@charter.net	649 Willow Ln Frankenmuth MI 48734	MI	Teacher	EM			RF	1954
Kusmierczak Elizabeth G Morley	(314)757-4246 lizk530@hotmail.com	629 Lubbock Ct Moscow Mills MO 63362	MO	Teacher	Tchr	Immanuel Wentzville MO	(636)327-4416	S	2010
Kusserow Mary Lou Mikulecky	(602)454-9298 tmlkusserow@yahoo.com	6932 S 825 E Midvale UT 84047	PSW	Teacher	EM			SP	1970
Kusserow Thomas E	(602)454-9298 tmlkusserow@yahoo.com	6932 S 825 E Midvale UT 84047	PSW	Teacher	EM			SP	1971
Kuster Lorien Pelletier	(808)220-3779 lkuster@rlcs-slc.org	1291 E Vine Gate Dr Apt 5 Salt Lake City UT 84121	RM	Teacher	Tchr	Redeemer Salt Lake City UT	(801)467-4352	PO	2014
Kutch Michael R	(269)953-2050 mrkutch44@gmail.com	504 Lincoln Lake Lowell MI 49331	MI	DPM	Mem C	Hope Dewitt MI	(517)669-3930	MQ	2015
Kutcher Steven R	(262)501-1260 skutcher@martinlutherhs.org	3289 S 147th St New Berlin WI 53151	SW	Teacher	Tchr	LHS Assn of Greater Milwaukee West Allis WI	(414)421-9100	CQ	2019
Kutschkau Sarah N	(636)233-3226 sarah.kutschkau@cune.org	c/o Bethany Lutheran 9101 Lamar Ave Overland Park KS 66207	KS	Teacher	Tchr	Bethany Overland Park KS	(913)648-2228	S	2012
Kutz Amy E Steffens	amykutz@gmail.com	3346 E Cheyenne St Gilbert AZ 85296	PSW	Teacher	C07/2023			S	2006
Kutz Amy J Olejniczak	(414)422-1907 akutz@hcl.org	S 76 W 17146 Deer Creek Ct Muskego WI 53150	EN	Teacher	Tchr	Hales Corners Hales Corners WI	(414)529-6701	MQ	2008
Kutz Cathy A Gerds	(586)792-3524	35737 Lucerne St Clinton Twp MI 48035	MI	Teacher	EM			S	1970
Kutz Doris M Peters	(612)763-5394	1812 Darling Ave E Apt 268 Alexandria MN 56308	MNN	Teacher	EM			S	1979
Kutz John C	(586)792-3524 jkutz48@gmail.com	35737 Lucerne St Clinton Twp MI 48035	MI	Teacher	EM			S	1970
Kwapis Nicholas A	(248)505-9049 nakwapis@gmail.com	3109 Wains Way Oakland MI 48363	MI	Teacher	Mem C	St John Rochester MI	(248)402-8000	MQ	2008
L Heureux Brian T	(712)269-0808 brian.lheureux@vlscrusaders.org	5005 Quesada Ave Cedar Falls IA 50613	IE	Teacher	Prin	Valley Cedar Falls IA	(319)266-4565	S	1996
L Heureux Mark J	(414)839-9379 marklheureux75@gmail.com	7211 Rutha Ln Lincoln NE 68516	NEB	Teacher	Prin	Christ Lincoln NE	(402)483-7774	S	1997
La Croix Timothy C	(260)415-2576 tlacroix@clhscadets.com	6205 Landover Pl Fort Wayne IN 46815	IN	Teacher	Tchr	Concordia Fort Wayne IN	(260)483-1102	RF	1985
La Fontaine Cindy R Havemeier	(810)610-5760 clafontaine60@gmail.com	4473 Brighton Dr Grand Blanc MI 48439	MI	Tch/DCE	Tchr	Faith Grand Blanc MI	(810)694-9351	SP	1985
La Rocque Janet E	(989)450-8936 jelarocque@yahoo.com	4640 Fox Pointe Dr Apt 231 Bay City MI 48706	MI	Teacher	EM			S	1978
Laabs Jonathan C Dr	(630)671-0306 laabsjc@lea.org	116 Cambrian Ct Roselle IL 60172	NI	Teacher	RSO	Lutheran Education Association River Forest IL	(708)209-3343	RF	1977
Laabs June M Meyer	(630)671-0306 laabsjc@att.net	116 Cambrian Ct Roselle IL 60172	NI	Teacher	EM			S	1975
Laabs Kathryn E Taylor	(405)532-3575 kathrynt2828@gmail.com	433 Larchbrook Dr Garland TX 75043	TX	Teacher	Tchr	Our Redeemer Dallas TX	(214)368-1465	S	2023
Laabs Sharon K Ruehl	(262)707-8584 rslaabs@yahoo.com	N114W17854 Blackstone Ct Germantown WI 53022	SW	Teacher	EM			CQ	2004
Laatsch Joel M Dr	(813)469-7328 jmlaatswch@gmail.com	3105 Thackery Ct Plant City FL 33566	FG	Teacher	C07/2016			S	1996
Labahn Kristen A Schilf	(219)616-9424 k76labahn@gmail.com	11109 Barclay CV Roanoke IN 46783	IN	Teacher	Tchr	Emmanuel-St Michael Fort Wayne IN	(260)422-6712	RF	1998
Labbus Paul	(715)212-2161 plabbus@gmail.com	N1685 Crestwood Rd Antigo WI 54409	NW	Teacher	EM			SP	1972
LaBelle Cheryl D Beaman-Knollman	(812)344-0092 Cheryldlabelle@gmail.com	5880 N State Highway 3 North Vernon IN 47265	IN	DCE	C12/2022			RF	2002
LaBrash Jewell B Gafken	(260)414-1227 labrashb@msn.com	4410 Arrow Dr Fort Wayne IN 46809	IN	Teacher	Tchr	Emmanuel-St Michael Fort Wayne IN	(260)422-6712	CQ	2005
Lacey Michael W	(504)889-7084 mclacey25@gmail.com	4732 Herrmann St Metairie LA 70006	SO	Teacher	C07/2016			AU	1986
Lachmann Susan E Schak	(847)439-1598 slach73@hotmail.com	805 S Busse Rd Mt Prospect IL 60056	NI	Teacher	EM			CQ	2004

*Multiple Assignments (See Church Worker Locator for Additional Details)

See Page 53 for the Table of Abbreviations for key to District, Classification, Position, and College abbreviations.

**C =Candidate; EM =Emeritus; the date following the C is the month and year the Candidate status began

NAME	TELEPHONE NUMBER EMAIL	STREET ADDRESS CITY/STATE/ZIP	DISTRICT	CLASS.	POSITION/ STATUS**	WHERE SERVING	OFFICE PHONE	COLLEGE/ UNIV/CQ	YR GRAD
LaCroix Bob A	(507)384-1597	22750 Lind Ave Waterville MN 56096	MNS	DCE	RSO	Camp Omega Waterville MN	(507)685-4266	SP	1995
LaCroix Jennifer A Thurk	(507)384-1079 jenlacx@gmail.com	22750 Lind Ave Waterville MN 56096	MNS	DCE	C07/2016			SP	1997
LaCroix Susan M Wegner	(262)414-7588	6205 Landover Pl Fort Wayne IN 46815	IN	Teacher	EM			RF	1985
Ladd Marcia A Spree	(314)842-8454 marcialadd@yahoo.com	9129 Desmond Dr Saint Louis MO 63126	MO	Teacher	EM			CQ	1998
Laesch William J	(414)313-4039 bill.laesch@gmail.com	920 Riverview Dr Apt 224 Rio Rancho NM 87124	SW	Teacher	EM			CQ	1976
Lafrentz Louise J Haefker	llafrentz@msn.com	3604 E 15th St Sioux Falls SD 57103	SD	Teacher	EM			S	1967
Lafrentz Randall W	bigtymers04@frontier.com	7227 Moeller Rd Lot 54 Fort Wayne IN 46806	IN	Teacher	EM			S	1973
Lagalo Ruth J Heinlein	(989)284-3475 rjheinle@svsu.edu	6500 Maple Rd Frankenmuth MI 48734	MI	Teacher	C07/2019			CQ	2015
Lahrman Sherri L	(734)255-9282 sherri.lahrman@gmail.com	7130 Country Hill Dr Fort Wayne IN 46835	IN	Teacher	Tchr	St Pauls Fort Wayne IN	(260)424-0049	AA	2007
Laib Brady M	(402)339-3668 dce.brady@1st-lutheran.org	420 N Washington St Papillion NE 68046	NEB	DCE	Mem C	First Papillion NE	(402)339-3668	S	2017
Lail Cheryl L Meissner	(636)219-5045 chris.lailfamily@gmail.com	158 Berry Manor Cir Saint Peters MO 63376	MO	Teacher	EM			RF	1976
Lail Rachel L Sattgast	(605)350-5227 rachel.lail@gmail.com	7019 N Fischer Ct Spokane WA 99208	NOW	Teacher	C05/2022			S	2005
Laingren Bailey R Bosman	(734)552-3835 bailey.bosman@gmail.com	15805 Lakeside Dr Apt 7 Southgate MI 48195	MI	Teacher	Tchr	Christ The King Southgate MI	(734)285-9697	MW	2017
Lakamp Faith L	(619)876-0534 flakamp@comcast.net	8383 W Pioneers Blvd Denton NE 68339	NEB	Teacher	C06/2022			CQ	2020
Lambert Debra R Wolka	(812)522-4320 jadelambert@comcast.net	212 Church Ave Seymour IN 47274	IN	Teacher	EM			RF	1976
Lamberti Jennifer R Mooney	(309)472-3384 clsjlamberti@yahoo.com	522 Fox Den CV Peoria IL 61607	CI	Teacher	Tchr	Christ Peoria IL	(309)637-1512	CH	2008
Lamberty Antonette M Kulesza	(773)763-5261 calambfam@att.net	6243 W Peterson Ave Chicago IL 60646	NI	Teacher	C07/2016			RF	1991
Lamberty Stephanie	(847)885-3350 slamberty@stpeterlcms.org	208 E Schaumburg Rd Schaumburg IL 60194	NI	Teacher	Tchr	St Peter Schaumburg IL	(847)885-3350	CH	2021
Lambrecht Jo A Coine	(402)489-1503 hislamb2@windstream.net	339 S 48th St Lincoln NE 68510	NEB	Teacher	EM			S	1968
LaMere Anastacia L Davis	(952)681-1555 hamnewt44@gmail.com	13273 Kipling Ave S Savage MN 55378	MNS	Teacher	Prin	Trinity Lone Oak Eagan MN	(651)454-1139	PO	2003
Lamkin Kelly A Van Hoorn	(651)357-6680 kalamkin@gmail.com	7495 269th Ave NW Saint Francis MN 55070	MNN	Teacher	P/Tchr	Crown Saint Francis MN	(763)856-2099	CQ	2004
Lamkin Melissa M	(763)360-1281 mlamkin@goodshepherd lutheranhs.org	16797 County Rd 83 Elk River MN 55330	MNN	DCM	RSO	Good Shepherd Lutheran High School Otsego MN	(651)357-6680	MQ	2006
LaMontagna Rachel M Solyom	(630)363-4336 rmlamontagna@gmail.com	848 S Linden Ave Elmhurst IL 60126	NI	Teacher	Tchr	Trinity Lombard IL	(630)629-8765	RF	2013
Lampe Diann V Gehring	(314)707-1243	4175 McRee Ave Apt 1w Saint Louis MO 63110	MO	Teacher	EM			SP	1965
Lams E T II	(708)485-3474 etlamsii@gmail.com	4211 Arthur Ave Brookfield IL 60513	NI	Teacher	EM			RF	1965
Lancaster Sophie R Kovachevich	(224)523-0877	737 Chesterfield Ln North Aurora IL 60542	NI	Teacher	Tchr	Immanuel Batavia IL	(630)406-0157	CH	2024
Landes Lydia L Gallup	(630)430-2708 llandes27@gmail.com	1239 Summer Springs Dr Middleburg FL 32068	FG	DPM	C12/2022			MQ	2012
Landfried Elizabeth A Rex	(512)924-5765 lizzy40rex@att.net	1714 Robinson Dr Brenham TX 77833	TX	Teacher	EM			S	1975
Landgraf Janet L Buesking	(314)791-4369 jlandgraf@stmarkseureka.org	107 S Edward Ct Eureka MO 63025	MO	Teacher	Tchr	St Marks Eureka MO	(636)938-4432	CQ	2000
Landgrave Aaron M	(708)261-4022 a.landgrave@stpaulbonduel.com	1812 N Winesap Ave Grand Chute WI 54914	NW	Teacher	Prin	St Paul Bonduel WI	(715)758-8532	RF	1985
Landon Beth D Daenzer	(314)341-6539 blandon85@gmail.com	540 E Hillcrest Dr Seward NE 68434	OH	Teacher	EM			S	1977
Landskroener Ellen A Schlueter	(419)930-8444 jimandellen@hotmail.com	7244 Hunters Chase Maumee OH 43537	OH	Teacher	EM			AA	1992
Landskroener James A	(517)231-9619 jlandskroener@trinityvikings.org	7244 Hunters Chase Maumee OH 43537	OH	Teacher	Prin	Trinity Toledo OH	(419)385-2651	S	1991
Landskroener Joel P	(952)913-0909 joel.landskroener@mayerlutheran.org	5188 Prairie Pt Mayer MN 55360	MNS	Teacher	Tchr	Mayer Mayer MN	(952)657-2251	S	1983
Landskroener Nathan L	(217)577-1868 nlands@hotmail.com	2414 Lindsey Ct Quincy IL 62305	CI	Teacher	EM			S	1980
Lane David M	(952)270-9075	9350 Morgan Ln Cologne MN 55322	MNS	Teacher	EM			CQ	1985
Lane Jenna R	(630)945-0430 jenna@lanehome.org	2434 Grey Fox Trl Bloomington IL 61705	CI	Teacher	C02/2022			Other	2018
Lane Kathleen R Remund	(920)740-1110 k.d.lane@outlook.com	884 129th Ln NE Blaine MN 55434	MNS	DCE	EM			SP	1978
Lane Katie M Worthington	(770)362-8903 klane@stpaulptc.org	336 Bur Oak Bend Newnan GA 30265	FG	Teacher	Tchr	St Paul Peachtree City GA	(770)487-0339	S	2013
Lane Rodrick R	(402)499-0807 lanerodrick@yahoo.com	9541 S 71st St Lincoln NE 68516	EN	DCE	Mem C	Redeemer Lincoln NE	(402)477-1710	SP	2010
Lang David W	(214)763-3929 david.lang@popcs.org	300 Woodcreek Dr Princeton TX 75407	TX	Teacher	Tchr	Prince Of Peace Carrollton TX	(972)447-0532	CQ	2012
Lang Emma J Gyle	(561)523-5186 elteaches@yahoo.com	10139 40th Ter S # 293 Boynton Beach FL 33436	FG	Teacher	Tchr	Trinity Delray Beach FL	(561)276-8458	RF	1968

*Multiple Assignments (See Church Worker Locator for Additional Details)
See Page 53 for the Table of Abbreviations for key to District, Classification, Position, and College abbreviations.
**C =Candidate; EM =Emeritus; the date following the C is the month and year the Candidate status began

NAME	TELEPHONE NUMBER EMAIL	STREET ADDRESS CITY/STATE/ZIP	DISTRICT	CLASS.	POSITION/ STATUS**	WHERE SERVING	OFFICE PHONE	COLLEGE/ UNIV/CQ	YR GRAD
Lang Hannah M Roth	(636)667-2152 hroth47@gmail.com	173 Coyote Crest Ln Augusta MO 63332	MO	DCE	Mem C	Messiah Weldon Spring MO	(636)926-9773	CH	2015
Lang Mary A Zuroweste	mcclang@aol.com	1805 Woodfill Way Louisville KY 40205	IN	Teacher	EM			S	1978
Lang Philip W	(714)971-0727 pwlang69@gmail.com	2153 S Anchor St Anaheim CA 92802	PSW	Teacher	EM			S	1969
Langbehn Marcia L Middendorf	(503)357-7613 langbehnm@fhls.org	3349 Cedar Edge Ct Forest Grove OR 97116	NOW	Teacher	EM			S	1975
Lange Janice A Mansholt	(618)327-3115 sjblange@charter.net	682 W Saint Louis St Nashville IL 62263	SI	Teacher	Tchr	Trinity Nashville IL	(618)327-3311	RF	1980
Lange Julia N Rivkin	(310)463-1239 jnlange20@gmail.com	20702 El Toro Rd #78 Lake Forest CA 92630	PSW	Teacher	Tchr	Crean Irvine CA	(949)387-1199	IV	2021
Lange Lori L Sorensen	(714) 488-7718 Llange@bethanylutheran.org	6430 Dominica Ave Cypress CA 90630	PSW	Teacher	Tchr	Bethany Long Beach CA	(562)421-4711	S	1990
Lange Maeson Lovie	(707)637-3711 mlange@cglschool.org	1633 E Lakeside Dr Unit 135 Gilbert AZ 85234	PSW	Teacher	Tchr	Christ Greenfield Gilbert AZ	(480)892-8521	IV	2018
Langefeld Richard A	(314)604-4980 richard.langefeld@gmail.com	2137 Dawson Lane NE Cullman AL 35058	SO	Teacher	EM			S	1974
Langendorf Megan N	(618)550-0898 mlangendorf@ trinitylutheranministries.org	407 Chapman Edwardsville IL 62025	SI	Teacher	Tchr	Trinity Edwardsville IL	(618)656-7002	CQ	2018
Langfield Tammy L Beyer	(414)708-6919 tlangfield64@gmail.com	N166W19521 Pheasant Lane Jackson WI 53037	SW	Teacher	EM			RF	1986
Langford Sherry S Payne	(636)529-9330 sherry_langford@att.net	3347 Chantarene Dr Pensacola FL 32507	MO	Teacher	EM			CQ	2004
Langlois Tonya M Fleming	(989)734-2155 tonyalanglois@gmail.com	2359 Schalk St Rogers City MI 49779	MI	Teacher	P/Tchr	St John Rogers City MI	(989)590-2643	AA	2001
Lanham Jenelle D	(865)919-4014 jlanham@elcsmail.org	306 Asheville Springs Cir Asheville NC 28806	SE	Teacher	Tchr	Emmanuel Asheville NC	(828)252-1795	RF	2005
Lanning Chantal M Kulczycki	(810)625-5326 c3lanning@gmail.com	47638 Andrea Ct Shelby Twp MI 48315	MI	Teacher	Tchr	Immanuel Macomb MI	(586)286-4231	RF	1993
Lanning Joyce A Owen	(248)310-2014 jannlanning@gmail.com	P.O. Box 538 Salome AZ 85348	PSW	Teacher	EM			CQ	1998
LaPerriere Sandra J Weig	(586)357-8787 slaperriere@splcs.net	46348 Swirling Leaves Ln Macomb MI 48044	MI	Teacher	Prin	St Peter Macomb MI	(586)781-9296	CQ	2024
LaPlant Emily L Parvey	(763)244-9917 emily.laplant@yahoo.com	707 Lower Johnson Cir Saint Peter MN 56088	MNS	Teacher	Tchr	Concordia Classical North Mankato MN	(507)388-4336	SP	2003
Lapp Fe B Heydenburg	(815)382-1517 lappfe@gmail.com	1494 Brentwood Pl Morganton NC 28655	NI	Teacher	EM			RF	1977
Lareva Nancy R Kilian	(714)997-7397 nlareva01@gmail.com	363 N Fern St Orange CA 92867	PSW	Teacher	EM			RF	1966
Lark Peter J	(714)538-5010	4401 E Kirkwood Ave Orange CA 92869	PSW	Teacher	Tchr	Orange County Orange CA	(714)998-5151	RF	1999
Larkin Dawn R Martin	(815)997-7333 dlarkin@lslancers.org	1404 S Theresa Ave Saint Louis MO 63104	MO	Teacher	Tchr	Luth High School Assn St Louis Saint Louis MO	(314)833-2904	S	2013
Larkin Robin L Weber	(920)334-0083 robinlarkin77@gmail.com	8602 E Cliffside Dr Apt 106 Anaheim CA 92808	PSW	Teacher	Tchr	Orange County Orange CA	(714)998-5151	MQ	2000
Larrabee Linda E	(720)232-5012	11916 Monroe St Thornton CO 80233	RM	Teacher	EM			S	1975
Larrabee Loren L	(303)726-3758 lllarrab2@gmail.com	118 1st Rd Clyde KS 66938	RM	Teacher	EM			S	1976
Larrabee Lu Ann E	(720)234-3106 luann@ecentral.com	6468 Trappers Trail Ave Parker CO 80134	RM	Teacher	C07/2016			S	1979
Larsen Kari L Tessendorf	(630)849-4127 dcekari@gmail.com	39w122 Shannon Square Geneva IL 60134	NI	DCE	Mem C	Immanuel Batavia IL	(630)879-7163	RF	2005
Larsen Kristi	(952)201-5389 klarsen1976@msn.com	1535 Sparrow Rd Waconia MN 55387	MNS	Teacher	Tchr	Trinity Waconia MN	(952)442-4165	CQ	2012
Larsen Michele L Gawinski	(586)431-1146 michelelynnlarsen@gmail.com	3015 Rennit Ct Raleigh NC 27603	SE	Teacher	C07/2016			MQ	2010
Larsen Phillips E	(623)229-3254 706phil@bellsouth.net	292 Mac Dougall Dr West End NC 27376	PSW	DCM	EM			Other	1987
Larsen Sara N Rotermund	(660)463-7464 numberonetexanfan@yahoo.com	1302 S Maple St Concordia MO 64020	MO	Teacher	Tchr	St Pauls Concordia MO	(660)463-7654	S	1998
Larsen Stacy A Lessman	(507)430-9644 stacyalarsen@gmail.com	702 Douglas Ave Henning MN 56293	MNN	Teacher	Tchr	Trinity Fergus Falls MN	(218)736-5847	SP	2005
Larsen-Roberts Tara N Larsen	(402) 982-9328 caseyandtararoberts@gmail.com	2431 N Nye Ave Fremont NE 68025	NEB	Teacher	C07/2024			S	2017
Larson Carol S Bennett	(847)910-6153 tthumpergirl@yahoo.com	11838 S Magic Stone Dr Phoenix AZ 85044	NI	Teacher	EM			CQ	1986
Larson Heather N Greseth	(952)232-8135 dhgemlarson@gmail.com	7237 Janero Avenue S Cottage Grove MN 55016	MNS	Teacher	C07/2016			S	2003
Larson Katherine M	(813)785-5377 irma1233@aol.com	6404 Santa Monica Dr Tampa FL 33615	FG	Teacher	Tchr	Holy Trinity Tampa FL	(813)839-6847	S	1997
Larson Lisa L Cellarius	(314)825-2138 lisallarson@msn.com	5127 Romaine Spring Dr Fenton MO 63026	MO	Teacher	Tchr	Christ Community Kirkwood MO	(314)822-7774	CQ	1999
Larson Mariah A Erdmann	(920)838-0611 mariah.erdmann@gmail.com	828 Ann Ct Apt 1 Plymouth WI 53073	SW	Teacher	Tchr	Trinity Sheboygan WI	(920)458-8248	MQ	2014
Larson Philip	(319)284-2494 plarson9715@gmail.com	1059 Parklane Rd Oelwein IA 50662	IE	DCM	EM			MQ	2006
Larson Stephanie C Ewald	(626)290-3382 slarson@stpaulspb.com	10014 Pebble Beach Drive Santee CA 92071	PSW	Teacher	Tchr	St Pauls San Diego CA	(858)272-6282	IV	2013
Lash Elizabeth M Kohl	(217)299-5569 betsy.kohl@gmail.com	8710 Gordon Dr Chatham IL 62629	CI	DCE	C09/2024			CH	2008
Lasseigne Diane E Stohs	(618)799-8757 diane0822@yahoo.com	1517 McCoy Dr Edwardsville IL 62025	SI	Teacher	Tchr	Trinity Edwardsville IL	(618)656-7002	WN	1984

*Multiple Assignments (See Church Worker Locator for Additional Details)

See Page 53 for the Table of Abbreviations for key to District, Classification, Position, and College abbreviations.

**C =Candidate; EM =Emeritus; the date following the C is the month and year the Candidate status began

NAME	TELEPHONE NUMBER EMAIL	STREET ADDRESS CITY/STATE/ZIP	DISTRICT	CLASS.	POSITION/ STATUS**	WHERE SERVING	OFFICE PHONE	COLLEGE/ UNIV/CQ	YR GRAD
Latin Keri M Urban	(231)250-1866 keri_latin@hotmail.com	212 Chisholm Place Fort Wayne IN 46825	IN	Teacher	Tchr	Emmanuel-St Michael Fort Wayne IN	(260)422-6712	RF	2002
Lato Jenae L Siebarth	(720)383-8771 jenaesiebarth@gmail.com	2019 S. Hannibal St. Unit A Aurora CO 80013	RM	Teacher	C07/2020			S	2006
Latzig Nona J Lehrke	(612)306-5319 nlatzig@gmail.com	17685 62nd St New Germany MN 55367	MNS	Teacher	Tchr	Christ Community Watertown MN	(952)955-1419	SP	2003
Latzke Laura L Rahe	(708) 203-6685 latzkelaura@gmail.com	1280 Village Dr Apt 221 Arlington Hts IL 60004	NI	Teacher	EM			RF	1966
Laubenstein Barbara A Strobel	(262)677-1041 barblaubenstein@gmail.com	W209N16590 Galloway Ct Jackson WI 53037	SW	Teacher	EM			SP	1972
Laubenstein Joan L Senechal		10016 E Elmwood Ct Sun Lakes AZ 85248	PSW	Teacher	EM			S	1973
Laubenstein Katherine N	(815)299-2438 katielaubenstein27@gmail.com	725 S Spring St Port Washington WI 53074	SW	Teacher	Tchr	Lutheran Classical Port Washington WI	(262)284-2131	MQ	2003
Laubenstein Larry P	(660)463-7831	314 S College Dr Concordia MO 64020	MO	Teacher	Tchr	Saint Paul Concordia MO	(660)463-2238	S	1970
Laubsch Jennifer M	(574)333-5976 jml1498@hotmail.com	995 Woodlane Dr Unit 6 Rochester Hls MI 48307	MI	Teacher	Tchr	St John Rochester MI	(248)402-8000	RF	1999
Laubsch Terry J	(989)652-6885 tlaubsch@stlorenz.org	9440 Junction Rd Frankenmuth MI 48734	MI	Teacher	EM			RF	1968
Lauersdorf Alex R	(262)269-9490 alauie052601@gmail.com	1510 Wolverine Trail #1 New Franken WI 54229	NW	Teacher	Tchr	Northeastern WI Green Bay WI	(920)469-6810	MQ	2023
Lauersdorf Robyn R	meyerr@greenbaytrinity.org		NW	Teacher	Tchr	Green Bay Trinity Green Bay WI	(920)655-4673	S	2014
Laufer Edith M Mager	(618)340-6712 edith.laufer@outlook.com	201 Eastlawn St New Athens IL 62264	SI	Teacher		Southern Illinois District Belleville IL	(618)234-4767	WN	1982
Laufer John E	(702)332-4367 johnlaufer@hotmail.com	1204 Fascination St Las Vegas NV 89128	PSW	Tch/DCE	EM			S	1981
Laufer Jonathan N	(402)641-9731	201 East Lawn New Athens IL 62264	SI	Teacher	Tchr	Trinity Centralia IL	(618)532-2614	S	2015
Laughlin Donna E Peterson	(415)297-6259 dlaughlin1968@gmail.com	1100 Averill Dr Batavia IL 60510	NI	Teacher	Prin	Immanuel Batavia IL	(630)879-7163	CQ	2003
Laughlin-Adler Barbara J Laughlin Dr	barb.adler@cuaa.edu	1404 Coventry Square Dr Ann Arbor MI 48103	MI	Teacher	EM			CQ	1984
Launer Pamela A Brown	(260)484-8623 pamlauner@gmail.com	8744 Raceborg Pl Fort Wayne IN 46835	IN	Teacher	EM			CQ	2008
Laurent Kristen K Zwick	(402)643-0102 kristenlaurent11@gmail.com	208 W. 13th Grand Island NE 68801	NEB	Teacher	Tchr	Trinity Grand Island NE	(308)382-5274	S	2007
Laurente Marvin L	(661)205-6711	1002 Duxbury Ct Bakersfield CA 93312	CNH	Teacher	EM			RF	1962
Laury Ann	(901)649-1474 alaury@bellsouth.net	7047 Santa Cruz Dr Memphis TN 38133	MDS	Teacher	Prin	Christ the King Memphis TN	(901)682-8404	CQ	2017
Lauterbach Emily Manack	(989)600-9276 elauterbach@stmikeschool.org	1409 Odell Farm Lane Vicksburg MI 49097	MI	Teacher	Tchr	St Michael Portage MI	(269)327-7832	CQ	2016
Laux Elizabeth A Krenz	(989)245-6860 llaux@stlorenz.org	4416 S Beyer Rd Frankenmuth MI 48734	MI	Teacher	Tchr	St Lorenz Frankenmuth MI	(989)652-6141	S	1999
Lavado Kimberly R Russell Dr	(843)251-2048 kim_lavado@yahoo.com	229 Ribbon Rd Summerville SC 29483	SE	Teacher	C07/2020			CQ	2007
Lavicka Jan M Cluver	(815)889-5540 janr@lavickaworks.com	1142 N 2050 East Rd Milford IL 60953	CI	Teacher	C07/2016			MQ	2002
LaVoie Kelli A Jensen	(218)820-9578 kelli.a.lavoie@gmail.com	9992 James Ave NE Otsego MN 55362	MNS	Teacher	Tchr	St John Elk River MN	(763)441-6616	SP	2008
Lavrenz Cynthia J Fredrickson	(620)271-8260 cindylavrenz@netins.net	310 S Illinois Box 113 Hubbard IA 50122	IE	DCE	EM			S	1999
Lavrenz Ruth H	(319)213-0120 ruthlavrenz@gmail.com	1905 Daleview Dr Marion IA 52302	IE	Teacher	EM			S	1979
Lawrence Gloria M Bendik	(262) 424-8277 gloria.lawrence27@gmail.com	1712 20th Ave N Fort Dodge IA 50501	EN	Teacher	EM			RF	1974
Lawrence Kyle R	(931)284-1105 kyle.lawrence1985@gmail.com	4613 Crossover Ln Memphis TN 38117	MDS	Teacher	C05/2019			MQ	2007
Lawrenz Denise L Dittmer	(501)215-0809 canddlawrenz@gmail.com	1332 Highland Dr McPherson KS 67460	KS	Teacher	C07/2016			S	1996
Lawrenz Jenna Lindeman	(303)913-3512 jenna.lindeman@cune.org	6621 S Yarrow St Littleton CO 80123	RM	Teacher	C07/2016			S	2010
Lawton Christine M Ross Dr	(360)880-7284 stinalawton@gmail.com	2908 NE 45th Street Vancouver WA 98663	NOW	DCE	C04/2020			CQ	2002
Lazarus Phyllene D Bachert	(847)276-8383 lazarus.phyllene@gmail.com	707 Edelweiss Dr Lake Zurich IL 60047	NI	Teacher	EM			CQ	1991
Le Blanc Christopher J	(504)400-3018 redfishpond@yahoo.com	559 Oak Glen Dr Gretna LA 70056	SO	Teacher	Tchr	Atonement Metairie LA	(504)887-0225	MQ	1996
Le Fevere Verlyn E	(319)377-0797 verlyn43@outlook.com	637 40th St NE Cedar Rapids IA 52402	IE	Tch/DCE	EM			RF	1966
Leahy Michelle L Novinger	(260)610-1778 mleahy@stpetersfw.org	5380 Hursh Rd Fort Wayne IN 46845	IN	DFLM	Mem C	St Peter's Fort Wayne IN	(260)749-5816	CQ	2013
Leapley Elizabeth G	(262)955-5688 eleapley26@gmail.com	6047 Bay Valley Rd Apt 3 Bay City MI 48706	MI	Teacher	Tchr	Valley Saginaw MI	(989)790-1676	S	2024
Leapley Kurt A	(262)366-4466 kurtleapley@gmail.com	330 Riverview Dr #3 Delafield WI 53018	SW	Teacher	Tchr	Beautiful Savior Waukesha WI	(262)542-2496	S	1986
Leapley Margaret S Bessert	(262)352-1233 faithleap@wi.rr.com	330 Riverview Dr #3 Delafield WI 53018	SW	Teacher	Tchr	Beautiful Savior Waukesha WI	(262)542-2496	S	1986
Leapley Michael S	(262)378-9958		SW	Tch/DCE	Mem C	Brookfield Brookfield WI	(262)783-4270	S	2021
Leatzow Edward A	(231)780-7665 ealeatzow@aol.com	736 Mapleway Norton Shores MI 49441	MI	Teacher	EM			SP	1968

*Multiple Assignments (See Church Worker Locator for Additional Details)

See Page 53 for the Table of Abbreviations for key to District, Classification, Position, and College abbreviations.

**C =Candidate; EM =Emeritus; the date following the C is the month and year the Candidate status began

NAME	TELEPHONE NUMBER EMAIL	STREET ADDRESS CITY/STATE/ZIP	DISTRICT	CLASS.	POSITION/ STATUS**	WHERE SERVING	OFFICE PHONE	COLLEGE/ UNIV/CQ	YR GRAD
LeBaube Laura J Rasmussen	(636)744-5453 lauralebaube@gmail.com	c/o Royal Redeemer Lutheran 11680 Royalton Rd N Royalton OH 44133	OH	DFLM	Mem C	Royal Redeemer North Royalton OH	(440)237-7958	AA	2011
LeBeau LuAnn M Kleinschmidt Platter	(260)446-1861 leadershipluann@gmail.com	7725 Payne Parkway Fort Wayne IN 46818	IN	Teacher	C07/2019			RF	1990
Lebeck Sandra I Hoemann	(815)471-2506 sandylebeck@gmail.com	W7196 Kettle Moraine Dr Whitewater WI 53190	SW	Teacher	EM			S	1981
LeBorious Nathan M	(478)396-4830 n.leborious@gmail.com	441 Enquirer Ct Apt 207 Cordova TN 38018	MDS	Teacher	Tchr	Christ the King Memphis TN	(901)682-8405	CH	2024
Lebrecht Phyllis T Tubesing	(714)529-5746 llebrecht@aol.com	700 Madison Ave Unit 210 Brea CA 92821	PSW	Teacher	EM			RF	1969
Lecakes Amy M	(518)928-0757 dermyfam@hotmail.com	895 Inman Road Niskayuna NY 12309	AT	Teacher	C12/2022			SP	1994
Leckband Lois E Hill	(402)992-0356 lois.leckband@gmail.com	1606 Skyline Dr Norfolk NE 68701	NEB	Teacher	EM			RF	1977
Leckband Paul R	(402)992-0578 pleckband@hotmail.com	1606 Skyline Dr Norfolk NE 68701	NEB	Teacher	EM			S	1975
Ledbetter Bobbie A Feldman	(281)485-7955 randy@ledbetter.net	P.O. Box 788 Pearland TX 77588	TX	Teacher	EM			S	1975
Ledebuhr James A	(618) 920-8821 jledebuhr@zionschoolbelleville.org	500 Millstone Dr Belleville IL 62221	SI	Teacher	Tchr	Zion Belleville IL	(618)234-0275	RF	1992
Lee Abigail R Gustafson	(262)365-7798 agustoafson21@yahoo.com	700 Prairie Ridge Dr Woodstock IL 60098	NI	Teacher	Tchr	Zion Marengo IL	(815)568-5156	MQ	2013
Lee Debra D Eckhardt	(406)452-0678 wee.disciples@gmail.com	3305 5th St NE Great Falls MT 59404	MT	Teacher	Tchr	Trinity Great Falls MT	(406)452-2121	CQ	2009
Lee Elizabeth K Reed	(989)600-1089 elee@osva.org	6582 Bermuda Green Ct Alexandria VA 22312	SE	Teacher	Tchr	Our Savior Arlington VA	(703)892-4846	AA	2006
Lee Jennifer L Louie			CNH	Teacher	Prin	Zion San Francisco CA	(415)221-7500	IV	2012
Lee Joanna R Johnson Deac	(828)514-2480 deaconessjoanna@gmail.com		EA	Deaconess	Mem C	Zion Bridgeville PA	(412)221-4776	FW	2024
Lee Jordan E Timian	(208)440-1321 jtimian@gracepocatello.org	193 Hawthorne Ave Pocatello ID 83204	NOW	Teacher	Tchr	Grace Pocatello ID	(208)237-4142	S	2024
Lee Kristin A	kristinlee684@gmail.com	5807 219th St SW Mountlake Ter WA 98043	NOW	Teacher	Tchr	Concordia Seattle WA	(206)525-7407	S	2005
Lee Nancy A Wolfe	(630)730-0093 nancy.lee051355@gmail.com	112 Sanchos Cir Dardenne Prairie MO 63368	NI	Teacher	EM			RF	1977
Leech Beth J Christensen	(308)385-8433 bleech@flcse.org	8973 Nautical Way New Haven IN 46774	FG	Teacher	Tchr	Faith Eustis FL	(352)589-5433	S	2003
Leech Debra J Scott	(573)230-9467	3832 Nottingham Dr Fort Wayne IN 46815	FG	Teacher	EM			SP	1978
Leech Timothy M	(260)248-0612 tleech@clscubs.org	8973 Nautical Way New Haven IN 46774	IN	Teacher	Prin	Concordia Fort Wayne IN	(260)426-9922	S	2007
Leech William A	(573)353-0369 blorls@hotmail.com	3832 Nottingham Dr Fort Wayne IN 46815	FG	Teacher	EM			S	1973
Leeds Emily R Duescher	(858)703-7799 emily.leeds12@gmail.com	2820 Summer Day Ave Castle Rock CO 80109	RM	DPM	Mem C	Our Father Centennial CO	(303)779-1332	IV	2013
Leeper Emily L Fehn	(989)573-1738 elfehn123@gmail.com	608 Bentwood Dr Marshall WI 53559	SW	Teacher	Tchr	Good Shepherd Watertown WI	(920)261-2579	S	2018
Leeper Karmen K Sahlhoff	(219)546-3310 ckleeper@embarqmail.com	120 Brant Dr Bremen IN 46506	IN	Teacher	C07/2016			AA	1989
Leese William C	(425)268-4268 bill.leese@gmail.com	1014 Hoyt Ave Everett WA 98201	NOW	DCE	C07/2016			CQ	1986
Leet Janet B Buerger	(314)973-1790 j.leet@att.net	302 Twinview Ter Manchester MO 63011	MO	Teacher	EM			CQ	1998
Leger Sandra K Hobratsch	(713)376-9783 rickyandsandy1228@att.net	7514 Mosewood Houston TX 77040	TX	Teacher	Tchr	Memorial Houston TX	(713)782-6079	AU	1984
Legler Ryan A	(316)573-2333 dcedrummer@gmail.com	13218 N 95th East Ave Collinsville OK 74021	OK	DCE	C11/2019			RF	2002
Lehenbauer Becky A Arp	(407)283-7107 becky@lehenbauer.us	884 Benchwood Dr Winter Springs FL 32708	S	Teacher	EM			S	1986
Lehenbauer Katie L Pederson	(262)618-2734 thelehenbauers@gmail.com	8900 W Bonniwell Rd Mequon WI 53907	SW	Teacher	C07/2016			RF	2003
Lehenbauer Louisa C Mehl	(314)799-9267 louisa.mehl@cune.org	404 South Saint Louis Street Concordia MO 64020	MO	Teacher	C07/2022			S	2014
Lehenbauer Steven L	(407)283-7107 slehenbauer@sllcs.org	884 Benchwood Dr Winter Spgs FL 32708	S	Teacher	Tchr	St Luke Oviedo FL	(407)365-3408	S	1985
Lehl Ella L	(209)369-7640 ellalehl@sbcglobal.net	10942 Buchanan St Belleville MI 48111	FG	Teacher	EM			S	1966
Lehman Arron L		911 W Crestview Ct Crown Point IN 46307	IN	Teacher	Tchr	Trinity Crown Point IN	(219)663-1578	S	1994
Lehman Janet R Roehrborn	(920)212-0923 janlehman@yahoo.com	1345 Dayton St Apt 7 Mayville WI 53050	SW	Teacher	EM			RF	1974
Lehmann Judith E Wandel	(402)206-6440 judy@reachfar.net	15972 Meredith Ave Omaha NE 68116	NEB	Teacher	EM			S	1960
Lehmann Kristin M Becker	(979)540-8223 lehmannk@flhstx.org	3610 Old Plum Hwy La Grange TX 78945	TX	Teacher	Tchr	Faith High Giddings TX	(979)242-2889	AU	2012
Lehner-Schwoch Jamie M Lehner	(920) 763-3984 jamieschwoch@yahoo.com	304 Cardinal Cir Mayville WI 53050	SW	Teacher	Tchr	St Johns Mayville WI	(920)387-4310	CQ	2005
Lehrke Dale A		515 Euclid Ave Unit 2204 Cleveland OH 44114	OH	Teacher	Tchr	Bethany Parma OH	(440)884-1010	RF	1984
Lei Ieng Rice Deac	(903)401-8615 glassthimble@gmail.com	22034 Audette St Dearborn MI 48124	MI	Deaconess	RSO	Ephphatha Lutheran Mission Society Hartland MI	(248)980-5741	CH	2018
Leibig Rebecca A Leder	(870)830-9092	1105 S Grand Ave Stuttgart AR 72160	MDS	Teacher	EM			RF	1968

*Multiple Assignments (See Church Worker Locator for Additional Details)

See Page 53 for the Table of Abbreviations for key to District, Classification, Position, and College abbreviations.

**C =Candidate; EM =Emeritus; the date following the C is the month and year the Candidate status began

NAME	TELEPHONE NUMBER EMAIL	STREET ADDRESS CITY/STATE/ZIP	DISTRICT	CLASS.	POSITION/ STATUS**	WHERE SERVING	OFFICE PHONE	COLLEGE/ UNIV/CQ	YR GRAD
Leible Deanna	(573)450-0745 deeleible@gmail.com	1101 Holgate Dr Manchester MO 63021	MO	Teacher	Tchr	Christ Community Kirkwood MO	(314)822-7774	S	2009
Leidecker Karla J Thanepohn	(586)634-0934 karlajean710@gmail.com	17871 22 Mile Rd Macomb MI 48044	MI	Teacher	Tchr	Saint Peters Eastpointe MI	(586)777-6300	AA	1998
Leidecker Shirley A Hantak	(586)727-9757 sleidecker@immlutheran.org	49576 Cosimo Ct Macomb MI 48042	MI	Teacher	EM			RF	1966
Leidich Roy E	(586)465-5475 irene@macdl.org	22800 Stair Dr Clinton Twp MI 48036	MI	Teacher	EM			RF	1968
Leiding Kristen L Kontak	(507)381-1282 kristen@leidings.com	708 Northwood Dr Janesville MN 56048	MNS	Teacher	C05/2024			SP	2006
Leighty Kelli N Borchelt	(260)452-9127 kleighty@holycrossfw.org	6507 Rockingham Dr Fort Wayne IN 46835	IN	Teacher	Tchr	Holy Cross Fort Wayne IN	(260)483-3173	RF	2002
Leimbach Stacy C Stuckenschmidt	(402)770-7168 sleimbach3@gmail.com	809 Manes Ct Lincoln NE 68505	NEB	Teacher	Tchr	Trinity Lincoln NE	(402)466-1800	S	1996
Leimbach William W	(713)858-0536 bcleimbach@aol.com	2215 Walnut Ln Pasadena TX 77502	TX	Teacher	EM			RF	1955
Leimer Ann E Bremer	(904)305-1730 djleimer@hotmail.com	8253 Catfield Ct Jacksonville FL 32277	FG	Teacher	Tchr	Grace Jacksonville FL	(904)928-9136	S	1996
Leimer David J	(904)305-1752 dave_leimer@gracelutheran eagles.org	8253 Catfield Ct Jacksonville FL 32277	FG	Teacher	Tchr	Grace Jacksonville FL	(904)928-9136	BR	1991
Leimer John F	(904)329-2395 jcleimer45@gmail.com	4274 Eagles View Ln Jacksonville FL 32277	FG	Teacher	EM			RF	1967
Leinberger David W	(586)781-5434 dmlein68@gmail.com	61892 Glenwood Trl Washington MI 48094	MI	Teacher	EM			RF	1961
Leinberger Timothy D	(586)428-9761 tleinberger@splcs.net	56548 Leeds Ln Macomb MI 48042	MI	Teacher	Prin	St Peter Macomb MI	(586)781-3434	RF	1997
Leininger Allison M Meinert	(440)213-9014 meinall05@hotmail.com	5228 Stonehurst Dr Brunswick OH 44212	OH	Teacher	Tchr	Royal Redeemer North Royalton OH	(440)237-7958	AA	2006
Leinss Jennifer L	(414)476-7109 j_bird_13@hotmail.com	9535 W Center St Milwaukee WI 53222	SW	Teacher	Tchr	Blessed Savior New Berlin WI	(262)786-6465	MQ	2005
Leising Emily J	(308)655-0648 leising.emily@gmail.com	727 East Reagan Parkway Apt 212 Medina OH 44256	EN	DCE	Mem C	Prince Peace Medina Township OH	(330)723-8293	S	2014
Leissinger Marilyn J Flakne	(504) 458-2203 hleissinger@cox.net	4616 Clearlake Dr Metairie LA 70006	SO	Teacher	EM			S	1969
Leitner Cheryl A	(224)484-8314 leitscj12@aol.com	1419 Karen Dr West Dundee IL 60118	NI	Teacher	Tchr	Immanuel East Dundee IL	(847)428-4477	CQ	2011
Leitner George W	(602) 703-6826 leitnergeorge@gmail.com	109 Marlin Ave Galveston TX 77550	TX	Teacher	EM			AU	1982
Leitner Linda D Ramming	(505) 814-8118 leitnerlindal@gmail.com	109 Marlin Ave Galveston TX 77550	TX	Teacher	EM			S	1973
Lelle John B	(440)867-2747 jblelle@yahoo.com	1120 Dartmouth Dr Painesville OH 44077	OH	Teacher	EM			S	1978
Lelle Wilberta J Rode	(440)867-2747 blelle@roadrunner.com	1120 Dartmouth Dr Painesville OH 44077	OH	Teacher	EM			S	1970
Lemerande Cynthia A Kasinski	(414)526-9907 clemerande@hcl.org	3360 S Highpointe Dr New Berlin WI 53151	EN	Teacher	Tchr	Hales Corners Hales Corners WI	(414)529-6701	CQ	2006
Lemke Cynthia M Rickman	(402)643-4210 cindy.lemke@cune.org	305 Grand Ave Seward NE 68434	NEB	Teacher	EM			S	1976
Lemke George F	(248)549-5208 gflemke@aol.com	4146 Normandy Rd Royal Oak MI 48073	MI	Teacher	EM			RF	1966
Lemke Jane E	(734)241-0639	415 Laurel Dr Monroe MI 48161	MI	Teacher	EM			S	1971
Lemke Linda M Daeke	lemkelinda@yahoo.com	2130 Sunray Cir Eau Claire WI 54703	NW	Teacher	EM			S	1973
Lemon Sara J Pollert Deac	(812)498-4409 saralemon@gmail.com	4310 Goose Rock Ct Indianapolis IN 46239	IN	Deaconess	C07/2016			RF	2007
Lenghart Susan M Mitchell	(248)363-4260 lenghart@ameritech.com	1916 Glen Iris Dr Commerce Twp MI 48382	MI	Teacher	EM			CQ	1988
Lenhart April R Mandel	(301)789-5835 lenhart.april@yahoo.com	3345 Beechwood Lane Marion IA 52302	IE	Teacher	Tchr	Trinity Cedar Rapids IA	(319)366-1569	MQ	1999
Lennington Monica J	(913)314-1081 monica.lennington@cune.org		KS	Teacher	Tchr	Trinity Atchison KS	(913)367-4763	S	2019
Lennox Debra L Peterson	deaconessdeb@gmail.com		SE	DCM	C04/2018			MQ	2007
Lentz Lori	(320)230-0673	1310 10th Ave N Saint Cloud MN 56303	MNN	Teacher	Tchr	Prince Of Peace Saint Cloud MN	(320)251-1477	CQ	2003
Lenz Emily E Krueger	(414)235-9922 emilylenz78@gmail.com	12265 W Barnard Ave Greenfield WI 53228	EN	Teacher	Tchr	Hales Corners Hales Corners WI	(414)529-6701	MQ	2001
Lenz Lisa A Bankson	(308)946-5068 ilspolk1886@gmail.com	54 Willowbend Marquette NE 68854	NEB	Teacher	Tchr	Immanuel Polk NE	(402)765-7253	S	1989
Lenz Rodney G	(605)261-3495 wingsrgl@yahoo.com	3206 W Keywest St Wichita KS 67204	KS	Teacher	EM			SP	1979
Lenz Tina M Hoyt	(605)261-0904 tmhoytlenz@yahoo.com	3206 West Keywest St Wichita KS 67204	KS	Teacher	EM			SP	1979
Leon Melissa J	(414)881-9848 melissa.leon@cuw.edu	6100 W Stonehedge Dr Apt 223 Greenfield WI 53220	SW	Teacher	Tchr	Journeys Hales Corners WI	(414)461-8500	MQ	2011
Leonard Chad S	(815)218-5791 chad.chapleonard@gmail.com	26w063 Armbrust Ave Wheaton IL 60187	NI	DCM	Mem C	Trinity Lisle IL	(630)964-1272	MQ	2011
Leonard Christine R Rueter	(610)442-6604 crrl56@gmail.com	846 E Independence St Jackson MO 63755	MO	Teacher	EM			RF	1981
Leonard Jonathan T Dr	jleonard2146@yahoo.com	409 Dalewood Dr Vincennes IN 47591	IN	Teacher	C07/2018			RF	1979
Lepley Wendi M Rittersdorf	(812)519-2047 lepleyw@gmail.com	3361 Rio Rogue Ln NE Belmont MI 49306	MI	Teacher	Tchr	Trinity Conklin MI	(616)899-2152	CQ	2013

*Multiple Assignments (See Church Worker Locator for Additional Details)

See Page 53 for the Table of Abbreviations for key to District, Classification, Position, and College abbreviations.

**C =Candidate; EM =Emeritus; the date following the C is the month and year the Candidate status began

NAME	TELEPHONE NUMBER EMAIL	STREET ADDRESS CITY/STATE/ZIP	DISTRICT	CLASS.	POSITION/ STATUS**	WHERE SERVING	OFFICE PHONE	COLLEGE/ UNIV/CQ	YR GRAD
Lerch Kathleen Phalon	(714)350-2664 ryka.lerch@gmail.com	2807 Garden River Ln Richmond TX 77406	TX	Teacher	EM			IV	1988
Lerret Brian W	(414)704-9322 blerret7@gmail.com	S97W13126 Champions Dr Muskego WI 53150	SW	Teacher	Tchr	Martin Luther Greendale WI	(414)421-4000	MQ	1998
Leseberg Jessica M	(402)230-0988 jessmarie33_@hotmail.com	23570 SW 75th Rd Beatrice NE 68310	NEB	Teacher	Tchr	St Paul Beatrice NE	(402)223-3414	S	2003
Lesher Holly A Boeding	(847)863-4209 hollylesher@yahoo.com	711 Lura Ln Marengo IL 60152	NI	Teacher	Tchr	Zion Marengo IL	(815)568-5156	CQ	2014
Leshney Thomas R	(623)680-4855 tleshney@yahoo.com	16445 W Monteverde Ln Surprise AZ 85374	PSW	Teacher	EM			CQ	2006
Leslie Kathryn Noack	(832)492-5576 lesliek@trinityklein.org	5518 Cobble Ln Spring TX 77379	TX	Teacher	Tchr	Trinity Spring TX	(281)376-5810	AU	1986
Leslie Richard A	(281)351-8517 leslietomball@aol.com	16430 Lutheran School Rd Tomball TX 77377	TX	Tch/DCE	EM			CQ	1988
Lettow Kari L Glaeseman	(801)910-3628 karileag@yahoo.com	354 Kowald Ln New Braunfels TX 78130	TX	Teacher	Tchr	Cross New Braunfels TX	(830)625-3969	SP	1998
Leupold Patrick H	(407)538-6026 huskerball1956@gmail.com	1213 Winter Springs Blvd Winter Spgs FL 32708	S	Teacher	C07/2016			S	1979
Leutner Jessica Rupprecht	(262)853-0998 rupprecht@cuspilgrim.org	2824 S 46th St Milwaukee WI 53219	SW	Teacher	Tchr	Pilgrim Wauwatosa WI	(414)259-0190	MQ	2011
Levenhagen Amy D Snider	(913)626-1811 amylevenhagen@yahoo.com	20503 Ashmont San Antonio TX 78258	TX	Teacher	Tchr	Concordia San Antonio TX	(210)479-1477	RF	1998
Levine Karina M Schlecht	(970)237-1088 karinalevine34@gmail.com	915 E North Bay St Tampa FL 33603	FG	Teacher		Florida-Georgia District Orlando FL	(407)857-5556	SP	2016
Levitt Alicia M Jipp	(260) 438-1831 jippam@hotmail.com	1220 Rangely Pass Fort Wayne IN 46845	IN	Teacher	Tchr	Lutheran Schools Services Inc Fort Wayne IN	(260)203-4500	RF	1997
Levy Albert D	(415)233-2695 davedce@gmail.com	33 Warner Ct San Rafael CA 94901	CNH	DCE	Mem C	Trinity San Rafael CA	(415)454-4135	IV	2000
Levy Natalie A Klotz		33 Warner Ct San Rafael CA 94901	CNH	Teacher	C07/2016			IV	1998
Levy Nicole Creutz	(330)904-7711 nlevy@lmslancers.org	4560 Sunset Oval Brooklyn OH 44144	OH	Teacher	Prin	Luther Memorial* Cleveland OH	(216)749-5300	AA	2009
Lewandowski Tera A Pfortmiller	(847)502-8017 tlewando13@gmail.com	508 Eagle Ct Valaparaiso IN 46383	IN	Teacher	Tchr	Immanuel Valparaiso IN	(219)462-8207	MQ	2009
Lewer Elizabeth A Brandt	(317) 610-1151 blewer@zionewpal.org	2828 Davis Rd Indianapolis IN 46239	IN	Teacher	Tchr	Zion New Palestine IN	(317)861-4210	S	1986
Lewer Steven F	(317) 476-5830 slewer@lhsi.org	2828 Davis Rd Indianapolis IN 46239	IN	Teacher	Tchr	Indianapolis Indianapolis IN	(317)787-5474	S	1985
Lewis Dana L Kaio	(808)281-6084 mrs.lihaulewis@gmail.com	670 Akakuu St Wailuku HI 96793	CNH	Teacher	Pro Stf	Emmanuel Kahului-Maui HI	(808)877-3037	S	2010
Lewis Ellen K Bobb	(352)303-8039 Husker5494@aol.com	5301 W Village Dr Glendale AZ 85308	PSW	Teacher	Tchr	Atonement Glendale AZ	(623)374-3019	S	1985
Lewis Heath L Dr	(651)603-6214 hlewis@csp.edu	1282 Concordia Ave Saint Paul MN 55104	MNS	DCE	S HS/C	Concordia University St Paul Saint Paul MN	(651)641-8278	S	2006
Lewis Heidi N Fingerlin	(901)493-6514 heidinlewis@gmail.com	5612 Finkman St Saint Louis MO 63109	MO	DCE	Mem C	St Trinity Saint Louis MO	(314)353-3276	S	1991
Lewis Ingrid E Tegeler	(216)409-1345 ticelewis@aol.com	14015 Erwin Ct Cleveland OH 44130	OH	Teacher	Mem C	Bethany Parma OH	(440)884-1230	RF	1986
Lewis Lori J Kell	(734)646-0141 jtl196728@gmail.com	5013 Ruby Dr Gladwin MI 48624	MO	Teacher	EM			AA	1989
Lewis Mildred C Schau	(480)421-8665 mclewis13@hotmail.com	2646 W Cholla Ridge Pl Tucson AZ 85742	PSW	Teacher	Tchr	Christ Greenfield Gilbert AZ	(480)892-8521	CQ	1995
Lewis Susan L Gray	sllewis366@hotmail.com	700 Bourn St Harvard IL 60033	NI	Teacher	EM			RF	1971
Lewiston Sunny Kan Deac	(715)501-4706 sunnyk94_99@yahoo.com	S36 Deer Run Road Mondovi WI 54755	NW	Deaconess	C07/2016			RF	1999
Leyva Colleen A Krueger	jleyva1@att.net	36 Meadows Cir Arden NC 28704	SE	Teacher	EM			RF	1984
Li Brandon	(415)374-9086 brandon.li@eagles.cui.edu	219 Topeka Ave San Francisco CA 84124	CNH	DPM	Mem C	Bridge City Redwood City CA	(650)366-5892	IV	2018
Liang Megan L Boyd	(979)492-5321 mliang@oslschool.org	3319 Allington Ct Houston TX 77014	TX	Teacher	Tchr	Our Savior Houston TX	(713)290-9087	AU	2021
Libka Robert J Dr	(847)980-2930 rjlibka@yahoo.com	97 Hilltop Dr Lk In The Hls IL 60156	NI	Teacher	EM			RF	1975
Librizzi Kathryn A Kleist	(414)545-3294	2117 S 96th St West Allis WI 53227	SW	Teacher	Tchr	St Pauls West Allis WI	(414)541-6251	MQ	1992
Lichtenegger Debbie M Jordan	(573) 390-5432 uclsdebbie@gmail.com	2267 Highway Y Frohna MO 63748	MO	Teacher	Tchr	United in Christ Frohna MO	(573)824-5218	CQ	2012
Lieb Abigail G	(573)353-5420 alieb@cglschool.org	1350 S Greenfield Rd Unit 1020 Mesa AZ 85206	PSW	Teacher	Tchr	Christs Greenfield Gilbert AZ	(480)892-8314	AU	2023
Lieb Trina K Montgomery	(573)634-0027 12345liebs@gmail.com	217 Hunters Run Jefferson Cty MO 65109	MO	Teacher	Tchr	Calvary Jefferson Cty MO	(573)638-0228	AU	1993
Liebenow Mark R	(512)669-0002 mark.liebenow@gmail.com	3015 Flower Hill Dr Round Rock TX 78664	TX	Teacher	EM			AU	2002
Liebnau Heather Heimsoth	(636)575-1927 hliebnau@gmail.com	16223 Marina Del Ray Ln Grover MO 63040	MO	Teacher	Tchr	Christ Community Kirkwood MO	(314)822-7774	S	1998
Lieder Charles H	(507)235-5328 chlieder@frontiernet.net	214 W Anna St Fairmont MN 56031	MNS	Teacher	EM			RF	1971
Lieder Elaine T Terhune	(507)235-5328 principal@splfairmont.org	214 W Anna St Fairmont MN 56031	MNS	Teacher	EM			RF	1972
Liefer Kelly J Gronewald	(262)339-8976 kellyliefer@gmail.com	14361 W Old Farm Rd New Berlin WI 53151	EN	Teacher	C07/2016			MQ	2007
Liefer Rebekah J	(618)282-7714 i_jhn_55@hotmail.com	4611 Horse Creek Rd Red Bud IL 62278	SI	Teacher	Tchr	St John Red Bud IL	(618)282-3873	RF	1993
Lienau Jane E Mund	(313)278-7351 jelienau@porchsidevineyard.com	P.O. Box 146 Old Mission MI 49673	MI	Teacher	EM			CQ	1995

*Multiple Assignments (See Church Worker Locator for Additional Details)

See Page 53 for the Table of Abbreviations for key to District, Classification, Position, and College abbreviations.

**C =Candidate; EM =Emeritus; the date following the C is the month and year the Candidate status began

NAME	TELEPHONE NUMBER EMAIL	STREET ADDRESS CITY/STATE/ZIP	DISTRICT	CLASS.	POSITION/ STATUS**	WHERE SERVING	OFFICE PHONE	COLLEGE/ UNIV/CQ	YR GRAD
Liermann Abigail E Bock	(262) 417-5731 abigail.liermann@gmail.com	9075 Rapps Road Woodruff WI 54568	NW	Teacher	C07/2021			RF	2011
Liescheidt Richard H	(917)699-4761 rliescheidt@aol.com	675 Portion Rd Apt 106 Ronkonkoma NY 11779	AT	Teacher	Prin	St John Staten Island NY	(718)761-1858	RF	1959
Liese Marc T	(440)799-0730 mliese3911@gmail.com	3911 Linden Rd Rocky River OH 44116	OH	Teacher	EM			RF	1982
Liese Stacey L Barbee	(309)423-9221 staceyliese@gmail.com	319 North Elm St Apt E Henderson KY 42420	IN	Tch/DCE	EM			RF	1987
Lieske Michele P Rioux Deac	michelelieske@gmail.com	609 N Lundys Ln Fergus Falls MN 56537	MNN	Deaconess	C09/2016			SL-DEAC	2010
Liess Chelsey A Bartels	(308)390-1849 kcliess2009@gmail.com	2419 Cochin St Grand Island NE 68801	NEB	Teacher	Tchr	Grand Island Grand Island NE	(308)385-3900	S	2007
Lietz Brenda L Schendel	dblietz73@gmail.com	2321 Iota Ave Cuyahoga Fls OH 44223	OH	Teacher	EM			S	1973
Lietzau Jeannette	(717)749-5055	c/o Parker House 6596 Orphanage Rd #101 Waynesboro PA 17268	SE	Teacher	EM			CH	1962
Lilienthal Payton M	(320)296-5837 paytonlilienthal@gmail.com	2956 120th St Plato MN 55370	MNS	Teacher	Tchr	First Glencoe MN	(320)864-3317	CQ	2023
Lilienthal Sue A Nichols	(715)341-0873 mamalilipad@yahoo.com	4845 Woodland Ct Plover WI 54467	NW	Teacher	Tchr	St Paul Stevens Point WI	(715)344-5660	MQ	1991
Lilley Joan E Gilbert	(619)742-8110 joan.lilley@hotmail.com	8991 Sovereign Rd San Diego CA 92123	PSW	DCE	EM			CQ	1992
Lillich Dennis M	(330)605-9932 dianalillich@yahoo.com	1349 Roslyn Ave SW Canton OH 44710	S	Teacher	EM			S	1973
Lillis Alexandra K	(703)451-5855 alex.lillis@poplc.org	8304 Old Keene Mill Rd Springfield VA 22152	SE	DCE	Mem C	Prince Of Peace Springfield VA	(703)451-5855	S	2020
Lillquist Judy	(414)852-3844	S78W16930 Bridgeport Cir Muskego WI 53150	EN	Teacher	EM			MQ	2002
Limback Jane	(913)220-9841 jane.limback@gmail.com	34065 W. 90th Circle De Soto KS 66018	KS	Teacher	Tchr	Bethany Overland Park KS	(913)648-2228	S	1984
Limback Sharon K Schmidt	(319)279-3443 sharonklimback@gmail.com	5032 E Gresham Rd Dunkerton IA 50626	IE	Teacher	EM			S	1973
Limmel Tamara J Stern	(952)442-2447 ftlimmel@embarqmail.com	205 Carver Sq Waconia MN 55387	MNS	Teacher	Tchr	Our Savior Excelsior MN	(952)474-5181	S	1984
Limmer Courtney K	(402)860-0581 courtneylimmer@gmail.com	9407 Crossland Way Highlands Ranch CO 80130	RM	DCE	Mem C	Our Father Centennial CO	(303)779-1332	S	2017
Lincoln Cynthia A Cone	(586)549-0942 cresourcer@yahoo.com	903 High Vista Dr Davenport FL 33837	FG	Teacher	EM			CQ	1977
Lind Amy K Kuhnau	(763)274-0363	19833 W Ford Brook Dr Anoka MN 55303	MNS	Teacher	Tchr	St John Elk River MN	(763)441-6616	SP	2001
Lindau Rebecca E		240 Marina Ct Unit 21 Waterford WI 53185	SW	Teacher	RSO	A Place Of Refuge Ministries Milwaukee WI	(414)438-2767	MQ	1994
Lindauer Steven J II	(407)797-7275 slindauer@sllcs.org	4545 Riverton Dr Orlando FL 32817	S	Teacher	Tchr	St Luke Oviedo FL	(407)365-3408	AU	2016
Lindberg Lisa Stueve	(951)719-6623 lisalindberg2020@gmail.com	1931 W 39th Ave Kennewick WA 99337	NOW	Teacher	C08/2021			IV	2012
Lindberg Ruth S	(414)491-8527 lindberg@cuspilgrim.org	1200 Rock Run Dr Apt 202 Crest Hill IL 60403	SW	Teacher	Tchr	LUMIN Milwaukee WI	(414)354-5126	SP	2019
Lindblad Cathy E		10715 Mission Lakes Ave Las Vegas NV 89134	PSW	Teacher	Tchr	Faith Community Las Vegas NV	(702)921-2700	CQ	2017
Lindblad Paul F	(847)420-9200 plindbladc@comcast.net	1861 Maple St Des Plaines IL 60018	NI	Teacher	Tchr	St John Forest Park IL	(708)366-3226	RF	1979
Lindeman Alise A Moravec	(303)425-0403	6424 W 82nd Dr Arvada CO 80003	RM	Teacher	C07/2016			S	1981
Lindeman Lois E Milbrath	(262)628-7395 lois.lindeman@outlook.com	6386 Liberty St Ave Maria FL 34142	FG	Teacher	EM			S	1971
Lindeman Timothy D	(303)912-9362 david.lindeman@cune.org	1752 Branching Canopy Dr Windsor CO 80550	RM	DCE	Mem C	Redeemer Fort Collins CO	(970)225-9020	S	2016
Lindemood Brett A	(208)982-1461 blindemood@gmail.com	1 Alturas Lake Rd Stanley ID 83278	NOW	DCE	RSO	Camp Perkins Ketchum ID	(208)788-0897	IV	2002
Lindemood Eileen H Nakatani	(208)598-5943 elindemood@gmail.com	Hc 64 Box 912 Ketchum ID 83340	NOW	Teacher	C07/2016			IV	2000
Lindenfelser Lynn M Duhl	(313)530-8899 lynn.lindenfelser@guardian lutheran.org	6741 Rockland St Dearborn Hts MI 48127	MI	Teacher	Tchr	Guardian Dearborn MI	(313)274-1414	AA	1999
Lindgren Amy M Wagner	(414)510-5966 amy.lindgren@cuw.edu	2469 N 67th St Wauwatosa WI 53213	SW	Teacher	S HS/C	Concordia University Wisconsin Mequon WI	(262)243-5700	MQ	2001
Lindhurst Katryne M Adas	(586)549-5275 klindhurst@trinityutica.com	15264 Yale Dr Clinton Twp MI 48038	MI	Teacher	Tchr	Trinity Utica MI	(586)731-4490	CQ	2015
Lindquist Bobby G	(281)795-3151 lindquistb@clhs-tx.org	4827 Diehlwood Pl Spring TX 77388	TX	Teacher	Tchr	Concordia Tomball TX	(281)351-2547	CQ	2007
Lindsey Dean J Jr	(920)400-9646 lcmsjay@gmail.com	1716 Autumnwood Ct Sheboygan WI 53081	SW	Teacher	EM			MQ	1991
Lindsey Jodi E Stefanovitz	(920)400-9644 lcmsjodi@gmail.com	1716 Autumnwood Court Sheboygan WI 53081	SW	Teacher	Tchr	St John Plymouth WI	(920)893-5114	MQ	1991
Linebrink Cheryl J Pieper	(512)868-5840 pixmike@hotmail.com	20 Freedom Dr Georgetown TX 78626	TX	Teacher	EM			RF	1971
Linebrink Michael G	(512)694-3639 pixmike@hotmail.com	20 Freedom Dr Georgetown TX 78626	TX	Teacher	EM			RF	1970
Lingafelter Janella	(618)581-7580 jbahr10@gmail.com	10 Spring Meadow Dr Edwardsville IL 62025	SI	Teacher	Tchr	Good Shepherd Collinsville IL	(618)344-3153	RF	2017
Lingenfelter Betty E Berndt	(417)622-7218 betberndt@hotmail.com	1520 Massachusetts Ave Joplin MO 64804	MO	Teacher	EM			S	1991

*Multiple Assignments (See Church Worker Locator for Additional Details)

See Page 53 for the Table of Abbreviations for key to District, Classification, Position, and College abbreviations.

**C =Candidate; EM =Emeritus; the date following the C is the month and year the Candidate status began

NAME	TELEPHONE NUMBER EMAIL	STREET ADDRESS CITY/STATE/ZIP	DISTRICT	CLASS.	POSITION/ STATUS**	WHERE SERVING	OFFICE PHONE	COLLEGE/ UNIV/CQ	YR GRAD
Lingenfelter Nancy L Brandt Deac	(814)342-1713 nllingenfelter@gmail.com	225 Dogwood Dr Apt 302 Philipsburg PA 16866	EA	Deaconess	EM			Other	1965
Link Kimberly C Paul	(952)303-4807 klink.01@hotmail.com	9935 Briar Rd Apt 223 Bloomington MN 55437	MNS	Teacher	Tchr	St Michaels Bloomington MN	(952)831-5276	MQ	2001
Linn Darla J Johnston	(541)388-5049 darla.linn@saints.org	19066 Choctaw Rd Bend OR 97702	NOW	Teacher	Tchr	Trinity Bend OR	(541)382-1850	CQ	2003
Linneman Michelle M	(636)634-6438 mlinneman@zionharvester.org	5 Quiet Trail Ct Saint Peters MO 63376	MO	Teacher	Tchr	Zion Saint Charles MO	(636)441-7425	CQ	2018
Linse Melissa	(920)946-8835 mlinse@stjohnberlin.org	173 Pierce St Berlin WI 54923	SW	Teacher	Prin	St John Berlin WI	(920)361-0555	SP	2014
Lintz Jene L Bertels			IN	Teacher	C07/2017			S	2009
Lipka Nancy J Copple	(812)525-0310 njolipka@yahoo.com	444 Manor Dr Seymour IN 47274	IN	Teacher	EM			S	1978
Lipke Kristen J Keat	(719)589-6155 cottonwoodtrees@yahoo.com	721 W 54th St Casper WY 82601	RM	Teacher	Tchr	Trinity Alamosa CO	(719)589-3271	S	2015
Lis Rogene A Peterson Deac	(630)940-6347 rogeneannlis@gmail.com	330 Williams St Roselle IL 60172	NI	Deaconess	EM			CQ	2004
Lisius Carl H	(708)687-6864 cctravelafar@gmail.com	15422 Ridgeland Ave Oak Forest IL 60452	NI	Teacher	EM			RF	1970
Lisius Charlotte M Knuth	(708)687-6864 cctravelafar@gmail.com	15422 Ridgeland Ave Oak Forest IL 60452	NI	Teacher	EM			RF	1970
List Janelle T Adams		5210 S 78th St Lincoln NE 68516	NEB	Teacher	Tchr	Faith Lincoln NE	(402)466-7402	S	2020
List Jessica R Findlay	(989)751-3523 jlist@stlorenz.org	304 Harlan Dr Frankenmuth MI 48764	MI	Teacher	Tchr	St Lorenz Frankenmuth MI	(989)652-6141	CQ	2012
List Katherine A Miller	(919)210-2477 klist@oursaviorlansing.org	3911 Marimba Rd Holt MI 48842	MI	Teacher	Tchr	Our Savior Lansing MI	(517)882-8665	CQ	2021
List Robert	(314)488-8997 robert.list@att.net	4822 Azalea Place Alton IL 62002	SI	DCM	EM			MW	1977
List Vicky L Schreiner	(989)652-3116 vlist22@gmail.com	728 Heine St Frankenmuth MI 48734	MI	Teacher	EM			RF	1982
Liston Carol A Sprehe	(650)291-6293 caleduc8r@hotmail.com	304 E Lincoln St Buckley IL 60918	CI	Teacher	EM			RF	1966
Little Rebecca A Sadler	(636)448-0412 beck06curf@aol.com	7358 Tannoia Dr Hazelwood MO 63042	MO	Teacher	Tchr	Grace Chapel Bellefontaine Nghbrs MO	(314)868-3232	RF	2006
Littmann Aaron M	(979)338-0326 aaron.littmann@gmail.com	4395 River Rd Columbus IN 47203	IN	DCE	Mem C	St Peter Columbus IN	(812)372-1571	CQ	2014
Litzau Katie M Kuball	(507)330-4020 katiekuball@gmail.com	121 Cedar Dr P.O. Box 303 Lester Pr MN 55354	MNS	DCM	Mem C	St John Norwood Young America MN	(952)467-2740	MQ	2010
Livingston Janet L Miller	(308)520-3022 jll54747@gmail.com	9131 W Front Rd North Platte NE 69101	NEB	Teacher	EM			S	1976
Livo Gilbert R	(970)522-1791 livo726@msn.com	18790 Koester St Riverview MI 48193	MI	Teacher	EM			S	1971
Livo-Biesanz Rebecca A Livo	(262)939-0962 becky.biesanz@ concordialutheranschool.net	1100 Indiana Street Racine WI 53405	SW	Teacher	Tchr	Concordia Sturtevant WI	(262)884-0991	S	1995
Lizarraga Kirsten M Smith	(714)612-2829 lizarragakirsten@gmail.com	492 S Grand St. Orange CA 92866	PSW	Teacher	Tchr	St Johns Orange CA	(714)288-4406	IV	2004
Lloyd Nicola R Ardrey Berg	(765)271-6731 mrslloyd211@gmail.com	677 Wren Avenue Palatine IL 60067	NI	Teacher	Tchr	St Paul Mount Prospect IL	(847)255-6733	RF	2004
Lobosky Pamela L Hewitt	(573)434-1165 plobosky@gmail.com	1536 Hawk Island Dr Osage Beach MO 65065	MO	Teacher	Tchr	The King's Academy Lake Ozark MO	(573)693-9245	CQ	2004
Lochhead Wendy L Hockemeyer	(618)826-5965 wlochhead2004@yahoo.com	416 Riverview Blvd Chester IL 62233	SI	Teacher	Tchr	Christ Jacob IL	(618)763-4663	RF	1984
Lochmann Nancy G Bunge	(618)540-9096 nlrecycle@yahoo.com	127 E Country Ln Collinsville IL 62234	SI	Teacher	EM			S	1975
Lochmann William J	(618)540-9096 nlrecycle@yahoo.com	127 E Country Ln Collinsville IL 62234	SI	Teacher	EM			S	1975
Lock Kathleen A Horky Deac	kathy.lock2016@gmail.com	2695 S Raleigh St Denver CO 80219	RM	Deaconess	EM			RF	1993
Locke Andrew G	(262)510-7983 alocke@lhsagm.org	2036 Erie St Grafton WI 53024	SW	Teacher	RSO	LHS Assn of Greater Milwaukee West Allis WI	(414)421-9100	MQ	1989
Locke George M Dr	(734)780-5458 george.locke@yahoo.com	101 Walnut Cir Apt 3527 Grafton WI 53204	SW	Teacher	EM			S	1962
Lockhart Carol E Jennejahn	(562)305-8604 jwlcel@aol.com	465 West River Park Drive West Branch MI 48661	MI	Teacher	EM			S	1967
Lockhart Susan J Smith	(586)321-4177 sjlock104@msn.com	1915 Hunt Club Dr Grosse Pt Wds MI 48236	MI	Teacher	EM			CQ	2012
Loeffler Esther M Weber	(314)941-2399	1765 Highway B Elsberry MO 63343	MO	Teacher	EM			RF	1985
Loeper Leslie A Booker	(909)373-6940 leslie.loeper@gmail.com	45120 Hwy 79 #110 Aguanga CA 92536	PSW	Teacher	EM			CQ	1999
Loesch Jonathan	(512)868-6814 Loeschfam@gmail.com	300 River Ridge Dr Georgetown TX 78628	TX	Tch/DCE	EM			S	1983
Loesel Allen H	(636) 448-2843 allenloesel@yahoo.com	4451 Hesters Way Saint Charles MO 63304	MO	Teacher	EM			S	1973
Loesel Christopher A	chris.loesel@lhsparker.org		RM	Teacher	Tchr	Colorado Lutheran High School Parker CO	(303)841-5551	S	2008
Loeslie Valerie A Buckland Deac	(605) 651-0953 valeriebuckland12@gmail.com	40201 270th St Dimock SD 57331	SD	Deaconess	C07/2016			CH	2009
Loewe Carol A Roberts	(612)219-8637 carolloewe@hotmail.com	5045 Johnson St NE Columbia Heights MN 55421	MNS	Teacher	EM			S	1967

*Multiple Assignments (See Church Worker Locator for Additional Details)
See Page 53 for the Table of Abbreviations for key to District, Classification, Position, and College abbreviations.
**C =Candidate; EM =Emeritus; the date following the C is the month and year the Candidate status began

NAME	TELEPHONE NUMBER EMAIL	STREET ADDRESS CITY/STATE/ZIP	DISTRICT	CLASS.	POSITION/ STATUS**	WHERE SERVING	OFFICE PHONE	COLLEGE/ UNIV/CQ	YR GRAD
Loewe Jennifer L Dash	(956)742-9583 jloewe@trinitydelray.org	16263 Avacado Way Delray Beach FL 33484	FG	Teacher	Tchr	Trinity Delray Beach FL	(561)276-8458	RF	2004
Loewe Jerald J	(612)219-8637 carol.loewe@lcms.org	5045 Johnson St NE Columbia Heights MN 55421	MNS	Teacher	EM			S	1967
Lofink Karen L Liibbe	(714)932-2858 karen.lofink@splsorange.org	144 S Waterwheel Way Orange CA 92869	PSW	Teacher	Tchr	St Paul Orange CA	(714)637-2640	S	1992
Lofink Mark C	(714)932-2889 mlofink@icloud.com	144 S Waterwheel Way Orange CA 92867	PSW	Teacher	C07/2021			IV	1995
Lofton Bobbette M Hill	(562)673-5423 bobbettelofton@yahoo.com	2311 Clark Ave Long Beach CA 90815	PSW	Teacher	EM			CQ	2009
Lohman James H	lohmanjh@gmail.com	1289 Oakshire Ln Saint Louis MO 63122	MO	Tch/DCE	EM			CQ	1983
Lohman Tessa C	(314)623-4092 tessa.c.lohman@gmail.com		PSW	Teacher	Tchr	Christ La Mesa CA	(619)462-5211	RF	2017
Lohmeyer Daryl J	(760)525-8721 dcedaryl@gmail.com	P.O. Box 3673 Running Springs CA 92382	PSW	DCE	C11/2017			IV	2001
Lohmeyer Jan W Dr		151 Sarahs Ln Waveland MS 39576	SO	Teacher	EM			S	1971
Lohmeyer Lisa G Shoemaker	(812)342-7975 llohmeyer@stpeters-columbus.org	9785 S State Road 58 Columbus IN 47201	IN	Teacher	Mem C	St Peter Columbus IN	(812)372-1571	RF	1979
Lombard Milo D	(636)922-0823 miloandalice@att.net	22 Pear Blossom Ct Saint Charles MO 63303	EN	Teacher	EM			RF	1961
Long Bradley J	(425)949-9753 bradlong00@gmail.com	1609 Washington St Beatrice NE 68310	NEB	Teacher	Tchr	St Paul Beatrice NE	(402)223-3414	S	2003
Long Christina Gonzales	(714)222-8756 christina.long@zionkearney.org	2521 Central Ave Kearney NE 68847	NEB	Teacher	Tchr	Zion Kearney NE	(308)234-3410	CQ	2022
Long Marcheta M Strelow	(402)675-1601	P.O. Box Mxy Glennallen AK 99588	NEB	Teacher	EM			S	1963
Long Stacey L Peters	(918)381-5160 goodshepherdehcres@gmail.com	12625 S 198th East Ave Broken Arrow OK 74014	OK	Teacher	C06/2024			S	2006
Longmire Aaron D	(920)585-6494 aaron.longmire3@gmail.com	135 Country Center Dr Suite F #105 Pagosa Springs CO 81147	RM	Teacher	Tchr	Our Savior Pagosa Springs CO	(970)731-3512	CQ	2016
Longmire Duane L	duanelongmire@gmail.com	1012 25 25 1/4 St Chetek WI 54728	NW	Teacher	Tchr	Pilgrim Green Bay WI	(920)965-2233	SP	1980
Longmire Kenny L	(920)639-2280 kenlongmire@pilgrimluth.org	N6931 River Dr Shawano WI 54166	NW	Teacher	EM			SP	1974
Longmire Sarah A Deac	(920)634-5464 sarah.longmire@gmail.com	1303 Hidden Ridge Cir Blue Springs MO 64015	MO	Deaconess	Mem C	St Matthew Lees Summit MO	(816)524-7068	CH	2008
Longmire Susan G Vogel	(715)304-9177	N6931 River Dr Shawano WI 54166	NW	Teacher	EM			RF	1976
Looker Mark S Dr	(313)665-9395 mark.looker@cuaa.edu	409 Mark Hannah Pl Ann Arbor Ann Arbor Ann Arbor MI 48103	MI	Teacher	EM			RF	1973
Looker Paul J	(248)867-9096 plooker@lhsa.com	20007 Hudson Bay Clinton Twp. MI 48038	MI	Teacher	ExecDir	Northwest Rochester Hills MI	(248)856-0240	AA	1983
Loomans Eunice P Tuschy	(608)524-2735	S 2504a Horkan Rd Reedsburg WI 53959	SW	Teacher	EM			RF	1963
Loomans Ted P	(406)259-6133 loomans95@msn.com	241 Burlington Ave Billings MT 59101	MT	Teacher	Tchr	Trinity Billings MT	(406)656-1021	MQ	1995
Loontjer Gary L	(952)836-6025 garyloontjer1@gmail.com	2613 N 191st Ave Elkhorn NE 68022	MNS	Teacher	EM			S	1975
Lopez Kayleigh M Belvery	(309)397-6583 kayleighlopez18@gmail.com	3320 Petaluma Long Beach CA 90808	PSW	DCE	Mem C	Bethany Long Beach CA	(562)421-4711	RF	2012
Lopez Stephanie L Klenz	(414)524-9110 stephanielopez614@gmail.com	679 S Fox Run Dr Saukville WI 53080	SW	Teacher	Tchr	LUMIN Milwaukee WI	(414)354-5126	MQ	2012
Lopez Susan W	(680)882-6292 queenslopez24@gmail.com	306 Garden Cir Yorkville IL 60560	NI	Teacher	EM			SP	1975
Loppnow Jessica J Gipp	(920)680-5689 jessica.loppnow@cuw.edu	2232 Edgewood Dr Grafton WI 63024	SW	Teacher	S HS/C	Concordia University Wisconsin Mequon WI	(262)243-5700	CQ	2021
Loppnow Matthew M	(812)786-2142 dceloppnow@gmail.com	176 Cruse Loop SE Corydon IN 47112	IN	DCE	Mem C	Saint John Lanesville IN	(812)952-3711	AU	2014
Loranger Laura L Cain	(949)709-4072 loranger@abidingsavior.com	25635 Horse Shoe Lake Forest CA 92630	PSW	Teacher	Tchr	Abiding Savior Lake Forest CA	(949)830-1460	IV	2004
Loren John M	(210)488-0260 john.m.loren@gmail.com	107 Dresden Wood Dr Boerne TX 78006	TX	DCE	C02/2023			AU	2020
Lorentz Deborah A Kjergaard	(618)971-8447 mrslorentz@msn.com	310 8th St Perry IA 50220	IW	Teacher	EM			SP	1980
Lorenz Elise A Swanke	(414)659-4043 swan2822@aol.com	W149N6311 Mineola Dr Menomonee Fls WI 53051	SW	Teacher	Tchr	Divine Redeemer Hartland WI	(262)367-3664	MQ	2002
Lorenz Michael W		9510 Tesson Ferry Rd Saint Louis MO 63123	MO	Teacher	Tchr	Luth High School Assn St Louis Saint Louis MO	(314)833-2904	S	2003
Lorenz Peter J	(414)403-3361 pjlorenz1982@gmail.com	4665 Imperial Dr Brookfield WI 53045	SW	Teacher	Prin	Zion Menomonee Falls WI	(262)781-7437	MQ	2005
Lorenz Sarah D Knosher	(262)497-2475 slorenz@zionbethalto.org	149 Woodcrest Dr Bethalto IL 62010	SI	Teacher	Tchr	Zion Bethalto IL	(618)377-8314	RF	2001
Lorenz Timothy M	(262)497-2436 tim.lorenz@melhs.org	149 Woodcrest Dr Bethalto IL 62010	SI	Teacher	Tchr	Metro-East Edwardsville IL	(618)656-0043	RF	1999
Lorenzen Micah	mlorenzen@lhsa.com		MI	Teacher	Pro Stf	LHS Assn Of Greater Detroit Rochester Hls MI	(248)856-0240	MQ	2009
Losee Anne E	(914)969-4406 aelosee@optonline.net	100 Diplomat Dr Apt 7I Mount Kisco NY 10549	AT	Teacher	C07/2016			CQ	1993
Loseke Mary A Huebner	(503) 730-5267	14155 SW Barlow Rd Beaverton OR 97008	NOW	Teacher	EM			S	1975

*Multiple Assignments (See Church Worker Locator for Additional Details)

See Page 53 for the Table of Abbreviations for key to District, Classification, Position, and College abbreviations.

**C =Candidate; EM =Emeritus; the date following the C is the month and year the Candidate status began

NAME	TELEPHONE NUMBER EMAIL	STREET ADDRESS CITY/STATE/ZIP	DISTRICT	CLASS.	POSITION/ STATUS**	WHERE SERVING	OFFICE PHONE	COLLEGE/ UNIV/CQ	YR GRAD
Losey Virgil L		22307 Mosswillow Ln Tomball TX 77375	TX	Teacher	EM			S	1966
Lott Lori A Appel	(913)651-7592	201 Sheldon St Leavenworth KS 66048	KS	Teacher	EM			S	1987
Lottes Jane M Demro	(516)650-2521 jane.lottes@luhi.org	5 Michael Ln Huntington Station NY 11746	AT	Teacher	Pro Stf	Long Island Brookville NY	(516)626-1735	S	1982
Lotz Jennifer L Loesel	(901)489-8939 jennifer.lotz@cune.org	204 Woodgate Blvd Baton Rouge LA 70808	SO	Teacher	C07/2018			S	1993
Loucks Autumn M	(810)347-9766 loucksmr@aol.com	2325 Tobias Rd Clio MI 48420	MI	Teacher	C09/2025			CQ	2016
Louden Sandra J Hyatt	(810)632-5768 sjlou2010@gmail.com	10497 Viewtop Ct Hartland MI 48353	MI	Teacher	EM			CQ	1986
Loughmiller Mitzi D	(504)455-8138	3864 17th St Metairie LA 70002	SO	Teacher	Tchr	Lutheran High School Metairie LA	(504)455-4062	S	2004
Love Anna M Wiesneski	(715)218-0703 amwiesneski@gmail.com	N5403 Bradley St Gleason WI 54435	NW	Teacher	Tchr	St John Merrill WI	(715)536-7264	MQ	2022
Love Antoine A	(518)300-0897 love.antoine@gmail.com	7823 N 152nd Ave Benningtin NE 68007	NEB	Teacher	Tchr	Concordia Luth Schools of Omaha Inc Omaha NE	(402)445-4000	CQ	2016
Love Diane K Ryherd	(616)863-1103 dianeklove@gmail.com	c/o Trinity Lutheran Church 4560 Glendale Ave Toledo OH 43614	OH	Teacher	Tchr	Trinity Toledo OH	(419)385-2651	RF	1992
Love Nicolai R	(574)979-4446 nicolai.love@cune.org	7912 N 154th St Bennington NE 68007	NEB	Teacher	Tchr	Concordia Omaha NE	(402)445-4000	S	2006
Love Sarah C Kohlmeier	(573)979-4655 sarahcklove@gmail.com	7912 N 154th St Bennington NE 68007	NEB	Teacher	Tchr	Concordia Omaha NE	(402)445-4000	S	2006
Loveless Aaron M	(414)313-6238 aaronloveless9999@gmail.com	5957 107th St Chicago Ridge IL 60415	NI	Teacher	C12/2024			CH	2015
Loveless Michael P	(414)418-6375 m.p.loveless@sbcglobal.net	10901 W Cobb Ave Hales Corners WI 53130	SW	Teacher	Tchr	Martin Luther Greendale WI	(414)421-4000	S	1989
Lovett Jillian K McNally	jillian.mcnally@gmail.com	8478 Michael David Dr Saginaw MI 48603	MI	Teacher	C07/2016			AA	2009
Lovhaug Brenda A Garbers	(612)272-3714 brendal@gvlc.net	6741 Brunswick Ave N Brooklyn Park MN 55429	MNS	Teacher	Tchr	Loving Shepherd Golden Valley MN	(763)544-0590	SP	1990
Lovie Jennie M Porter	(707)738-6924 jloviebug@gmail.com	1633 E Lakeside Dr Unit 135 Gilbert AZ 85234	PSW	Teacher	EM			CQ	2018
Lovig Dean S	(913)294-2083 dklovig@yahoo.com	306 E Wea St Paola KS 66071	KS	Teacher	EM			S	1968
Lovitsch Lisa	(630)212-0546 lisa.lovitsch@gmail.com	731 Duval Station Rd Ste 107-235 Jacksonville FL 32218	FG	Teacher	C07/2016			S	1990
Lowe Amanda D Rohlwing		7020 Autumnwood Trl Plano TX 75024	TX	DCE	Mem C	Prince Peace Carrollton TX	(972)447-9887	S	2000
Lowe Jayme K	(913)426-3353 jlowe@trinitycougars.org	581 N 600 E Seymour IN 47274	IN	Teacher	Tchr	Trinity Seymour IN	(812)524-8547	S	2019
Lowe Jeremy R Dr	(970)445-7799 jerlowe@gmail.com	7020 Autumnwood Trl Plano TX 75024	TX	Teacher	Prin	Prince Of Peace Carrollton TX	(972)447-0532	CQ	1999
Lowe Jill M McKinstry	(913)426-5810 jlowe@trinityatchison.org	1801 Cardinal Cir Atchison KS 66002	KS	Teacher	Tchr	Trinity Atchison KS	(913)367-2837	S	2006
Lowe Randy D	(763) 360-0302 rlowe31@hotmail.com	5484 Jason Ct Albertville MN 55301	MNS	Teacher	EM			RF	1971
Lower Joseph W	(517)490-5614 lowerjos@gmail.com	2588 Hartline Dr Rochester Hills MI 48309	MI	Teacher	Tchr	LHS Assn Of Greater Detroit Rochester Hls MI	(248)856-0240	CQ	2016
Lowing Heather M Graf	(224)321-9100 hlowing@trinitydelray.org	1140 Delray Lakes Dr Delray Beach FL 33444	FG	Teacher	Tchr	Trinity Delray Beach FL	(561)278-1737	RF	2003
Lozano Tauchen Suzanne M Toepke	(330)730-8802 mseamlozano@yahoo.com	2957 Kendall Rd Copley OH 44321	OH	DCO	C07/2016			SP	1996
Lu John		1530 Concordia Irvine CA 92612	PSW	Teacher	S HS/C	Concordia University Irvine Irvine CA	(949)854-8002	CQ	2009
Lua Andrea L Benich	(818)259-2459 luamom46@yahoo.com	6032 Larkellen Ct Oak Park CA 91377	PSW	Teacher	EM			S	1977
Lubner Adrianna	(920)948-5250 adriannalubner@ymail.com	W1963 Rustic Dr Campbellsport WI 53010	SW	Teacher	Tchr	St Paul Oconomowoc WI	(262)567-5001	MQ	2019
Lucas Cindy L Doede	(734)755-4328 lucas.clucas@yahoo.com	5539 Spitfire Ct Newport MI 48166	MI	Teacher	EM			S	1978
Lucas John K	(248)891-6364 johnlucas1987@gmail.com	5081 Orion Rd Rochester MI 48306	MI	Teacher	Tchr	Trinity Utica MI	(586)731-4490	AA	2010
Lucas Krista M Kuhl	(724)755-4295 4lucas.krista@gmail.com	3180 Paysage Pl Traverse City MI 49684	MI	Teacher	EM			RF	1977
Lucas Mark C	(360)793-4914 mark.lucas1951@gmail.com	115 10th St Sultan WA 98294	NOW	Tch/DCE	EM			RF	1974
Lucas Nathanael P	(619)464-3020 nplucas@cox.net	8041 Fairview Ave La Mesa CA 91941	PSW	Teacher	EM			S	1959
Lucas Priscilla E Schrank	(956)682-7630 lwilford@rgv.rr.com	1112 Martin Ave McAllen TX 78504	TX	Teacher	EM			CQ	1997
Luce Ronald E	ronluce58@gmail.com	195 1st St Utica NE 68456	NEB	Teacher	EM			S	1980
Luchterhand Karli	(262)939-7111 karli_luchterhand@hotmail.com	3545 County Rd H #2 Fransville WI 53126	SW	Teacher	Mem C	Prince Peace Racine WI	(262)639-1277	CQ	2022
Luckemeyer Amy N Ronning	amynoel85@gmail.com	212 Perennial Place Fallbrook CA 92028	PSW	DCE	C09/2016			IV	2008
Luckhardt Jennifer L Dankenbring	(262)408-9345 jluckhardt@cglschool.org	1464 S Stapley Dr Apt 1024 Mesa AZ 85204	PSW	Teacher	Tchr	Christ Greenfield Gilbert AZ	(480)892-8521	AA	2002
Luckow Emily A Sinks	(218)281-5907	18748 310th Ave SW Fisher MN 56723	MNN	Teacher	Tchr	Our Saviors Crookston MN	(218)281-5191	CQ	2004
Ludtke Alvin L	(562)923-4232 alvin.ludtke@gmail.com	7322 Quill Dr Unit 148 Downey CA 90242	PSW	Teacher	EM			CQ	1985

*Multiple Assignments (See Church Worker Locator for Additional Details)
See Page 53 for the Table of Abbreviations for key to District, Classification, Position, and College abbreviations.
**C =Candidate; EM =Emeritus; the date following the C is the month and year the Candidate status began

NAME	TELEPHONE NUMBER EMAIL	STREET ADDRESS CITY/STATE/ZIP	DISTRICT	CLASS.	POSITION/ STATUS**	WHERE SERVING	OFFICE PHONE	COLLEGE/ UNIV/CQ	YR GRAD
Ludvigsen Dee A Carlstrom	(402)317-7146 script1628@gmail.com	1114 N Bell St Fremont NE 68025	NEB	Teacher	EM			CQ	2000
Ludwig Brett L	(320)460-0072 bludwig@zionalex.org	1503 Irving St Alexandria MN 56308	MNN	Teacher	Tchr	Zion Alexandria MN	(320)763-4842	CQ	2022
Ludwig Katherine A Jacob	(828)320-4092 momludwig@aol.com	1974 12th Street Pl NE Hickory NC 28601	SE	Teacher	EM			RF	1961
Lueck John W	(208)265-5084 jwlueck@aol.com	316 Homestead Loop Sandpoint ID 83864	NOW	Teacher	EM			RF	1971
Luecke Audrey L Stewart	(319)759-6778 aud@luecke.net	3589 Jumprock Rd Indian Land SC 29707	SE	Teacher	EM			RF	1988
Luecke Matthew R	(440)387-3008 lueckemr@gmail.com	2029 Brown Rd Lakewood OH 44107	OH	Teacher	Tchr	Cleveland LHS Association Rocky River OH	(440)356-7155	AA	2012
Luecke Melinda A Taylor	(216)534-3856 mbell@royred.org	2029 Brown Rd Lakewood OH 44107	OH	Teacher	Prin	Royal Redeemer North Royalton OH	(440)237-7958	RF	2006
Luecke Rita V Timm	(952)381-4691 rita.luecke@hotmail.com	170 Morning Dr Mayer MN 55360	MNS	Teacher	EM			SP	1971
Luecke Robert K	robertluecke@live.com	170 Morning Dr Mayer MN 55360	MNS	Teacher	EM			SP	1971
Lueckemeyer Aliceson M Niemeyer	(281)826-1112 lueckemeyera@trinityklein.org	7802 Mayglen Ln Spring TX 77379	TX	Teacher	Tchr	Trinity Spring TX	(281)376-5810	CQ	2024
Luedders Larry A	(618)965-9283 llueddderssm@egyptian.net	11355 Oak Terrace Dr Steeleville IL 62288	SI	Teacher	EM			S	1972
Luedemann Sheri E Malzahn	(817)793-3022 sheri.luedemann@gmail.com	804 Tall Pine Ct Keller TX 76248	TX	Teacher	Tchr	St Paul Fort Worth TX	(817)332-2281	S	1996
Lueders Kayla J Blair	(218)298-1984	49459 330th Street Ottertail MN 56571	MNN	Teacher	C07/2016			SP	2015
Luedtke Janet A Wolff	(503)476-4076 janl32246@gmail.com	3317 E 500th Ave Mason IL 62443	CI	Teacher	EM			RF	1968
Luedtke William E Dr	(623)262-4614 bill0330.bl@gmail.com	3126 N Knoll Terrace Wauwatosa WI 53222	PSW	Teacher	EM			RF	1971
Luehmann Heath J	(314)210-4310 heath@luehmanngrowth.com	1907 Bentwood Ct Chesterfield MO 63005	MO	Teacher	C06/2023			Other	2012
Luehring Stacey L Doherty	(414)704-0887 sluehring@luminspi.org	5827 N 83rd St Milwaukee WI 53223	SW	Teacher	Prin	LUMIN Milwaukee WI	(414)354-5126	MQ	2009
Luehrs Marjorie L Struck	(510)278-9059 margieluehrs@yahoo.com	17348 Via Encinas San Lorenzo CA 94580	CNH	Teacher	EM			S	1974
Luepke Donald M	(260)495-1253 donluepke@juno.com	1057 S Clear Lake Dr Fremont IN 46737	IN	Teacher	EM			CQ	1967
Luepke James E	(260)797-2474 73jluepke@gmail.com	6014 Cardinal Creek Dr Saint Louis MO 63129	MO	Teacher	EM			S	1973
Luepke Melissa C Christian	(317)523-1419 melissaluepke@gmail.com	12062 Kingfisher Ct Indianapolis IN 46236	IN	DCE	Mem C	Cornerstone Carmel IN	(317)814-4252	RF	1999
Luerssen Holly A Hurtienne	(715)623-3110 theluerssens@g2a.net	702 Elm St Antigo WI 54409	NW	Teacher	Tchr	Trinity Merrill WI	(715)536-7501	MQ	1994
Luevano Matthew E	(832)506-8825 luevanom@trinityklein.org	25131 Haverford Rd Spring TX 77389	TX	Teacher	Tchr	Trinity Spring TX	(281)376-5810	S	2006
Luevano Michelle M Griedl	(832)506-9929 luevanomi@trinityklein.org	25131 Haverford Rd Spring TX 77389	TX	Teacher	Tchr	Trinity Spring TX	(281)376-5810	S	2009
Lukacs Katherine D Hoops Daenzer	(586)260-9553 katrina@daenzerglass.com	52749 Deerwood Dr Macomb MI 48042	MI	Teacher	EM			S	1976
Lukas Jessica	(352)283-2153 jessrelax@gmail.com	1021 Pearson Dr Oviedo FL 32765	FG	DCE	C07/2016			RF	2002
Lukas Rebekah L Karolus Deac	(715)216-9033 arleigh.kay@gmail.com	26 N Main St Clintonville WI 54929	NW	Deac/DCM	C07/2023			SL-DEAC	2021
Luker Joan E Stolle	(713)202-3472 jluker83112@yahoo.com	9225 Sequoia Dr Houston TX 77041	TX	Teacher	Tchr	Immanuel Houston TX	(713)864-2651	S	1976
Lukomski Lynn C Raymond Schaekel	lynnclu@icloud.com	905 South St New Athens IL 62264	SI	Teacher	EM			S	1973
Luksha Dale W Whitney	daleluksha@mail4me.com	5640 Capri Ln Morton Grove IL 60053	NI	Teacher	EM			RF	1974
Lull Alan S	(262)306-6702 alull@stjohnswestbend.org	1821 Jefferson St West Bend WI 53090	SW	DCM	Mem C	St John West Bend WI	(262)334-4901	CQ	2005
Luna Jose A	(998)970-5987 mr.luna@juno.com	P.O. Box 9613 Lowell MA 01853	NE	DCM	C07/2016			MQ	1999
Luna Marta Deac	(503)951-0778 martaluna1017@gmail.com	915 Paul St Mount Angel OR 97362	NOW	Deaconess	RSO	Lutheran Latino Ministries Mount Angel OR	(503)930-0386	SL-DEAC	2011
Lunak Brooke R Zeddies	(989)295-6207 blunak23@gmail.com	7645 W Cleveland Ave West Allis WI 53219	SW	Teacher	Tchr	St Pauls West Allis WI	(414)541-6251	CH	2012
Lunak Robert E	(815)403-9948 robert.lunak13@gmail.com	7645 W Cleveland Ave West Allis WI 53219	SW	Teacher	Pro Stf	South Wisconsin Dist Milwaukee WI	(414)464-8100	CH	2012
Lund Keith R	(903)357-3036 lundtx@gmail.com	P.O. Box 2302 Pottsboro TX 75076	TX	Teacher	EM			S	1976
Lunde Julie R Strasser	(708)275-9991 jstrasser626@gmail.com	114 Meadowlark Dr Countryside IL 60525	NI	Teacher	Tchr	St John's Lombard IL	(630)932-3196	CQ	2008
Lundin David W	(832)221-9456 dave.lundin@gmail.com	854 Rock Harbor Ln League City TX 77573	TX	Teacher	EM			CQ	1977
Lundquist Alexi K	(443)761-8866 alexklund2814@gmail.com	1 Rosecrest Court Asheville NC 28804	SE	DCE	Mem C	Emmanuel Asheville NC	(828)252-1795	Other	2018
Lundquist Emily A Longman	(443)761-2780 elundquist23@gmail.com	1 Rosecrest Court Asheville NC 28804	SE	Teacher	Tchr	Emmanuel Asheville NC	(828)281-8182	Other	2017
Lundquist Heidi K Garrett Deac	(610)844-7664 unashamed211@yahoo.com	87 Pheasant Dr Kutztown PA 19530	S	Deaconess	EM			CH	2016
Lunning Peyton L	(612)356-1291 plunning@kingofkingsroseville.org	6721 21st Ave S Lino Lakes MN 55038	MNS	Teacher	Tchr	King Of Kings Roseville MN	(651)484-5142	SP	2021
Lunsford Charlotte E Tamborello	(713)632-5895 lunsfordc@trinityklein.org	18410 Glenn Haven Estates Dr Spring TX 77379	TX	Teacher	Tchr	Trinity Spring TX	(281)376-5810	CQ	2024

*Multiple Assignments (See Church Worker Locator for Additional Details)

See Page 53 for the Table of Abbreviations for key to District, Classification, Position, and College abbreviations.

**C =Candidate; EM =Emeritus; the date following the C is the month and year the Candidate status began

NAME	TELEPHONE NUMBER EMAIL	STREET ADDRESS CITY/STATE/ZIP	DISTRICT	CLASS.	POSITION/ STATUS**	WHERE SERVING	OFFICE PHONE	COLLEGE/ UNIV/CQ	YR GRAD
Lunz Mindy L Steele	(989)598-5517 mindy.steele@lsport.net	7810 Maysville Rd Fort Wayne IN 46815	IN	Teacher	Tchr	St Peters Fort Wayne IN	(260)749-5811	CQ	2006
Luptak Andrew J Dr	(262)781-6655 andrew.luptak@gmail.com	N54W14381 Vera Ln Menomonee Fls WI 53051	SW	Teacher	EM			S	1966
Lusk Michael D	(469)471-4849 dallas_lusk@yahoo.com	2930 Kevin Lane Houston TX 77043	TX	Teacher	Mem C	St Mark Houston TX	(713)468-2623	CQ	2007
Luster-Bartz Melissa S Monn	(260)705-2888 mmonn2913@aol.com	53433 Stoneridge St Apt B South Bend IN 46637	IN	Teacher	Tchr	Resurrection South Bend IN	(574)272-2200	MQ	2002
Lustila Gerald J Jr	(863)409-3217 jacklustila@live.com	14500 Tamiami Tr E Lot 132 Naples FL 34114	FG	Teacher	EM			AA	1986
Lusty Eleanor M Strable	(262)316-9613 emstrable@gmail.com	232 Emerald Boulevard Apt 7 Saukville WI 53080	SW	Teacher	Tchr	St Johns West Bend WI	(262)334-3077	CH	2023
Lutringer Alvin E	(507) 649-2616 aelutringer51@outlook.com	415 6th Ave NE Plainview MN 55964	MNS	Teacher	EM			S	1973
Lutz Alan O	(714)310-7985 alutz51@hotmail.com	845 E Chestnut Ave Orange CA 92867	PSW	Teacher	EM			S	1973
Lutz David A	(203)241-8514 dalutz73@gmail.com	1546 Ewald Ave SE Salem OR 97302	NE	Teacher	EM			S	1968
Lutz Jennifer M	(918)513-2248 jlutz@martinlutherjoplin.com	2302 S Joplin Ave Joplin MO 64804	MO	Teacher	Tchr	Martin Luther Joplin MO	(417)624-1403	S	2014
Lutz Katherine S	(817)709-5006 katherine.lutz@sharingnewlife.com	2416 Via Bologna Apt 2326 Fort Worth TX 76109	TX	DCE	Mem C	St Paul Fort Worth TX	(817)332-2281	CH	2021
Lutz Katie E Lane	(952)270-8666 katieelizabethlutz@gmail.com	502 Bluffwood Ct Kernersville NC 27284	SE	DCM	C07/2016			MQ	2009
Lutz Nina L Anderson	(714)310-7983 ninalutz97@gmail.com	845 E Chestnut Ave Orange CA 92867	PSW	Teacher	EM			RF	1976
Lutze Sonya S Milburn	(815)786-6078	1230 County Rd R Colon NE 68018	NI	Teacher	Tchr	Cross Yorkville IL	(630)553-7861	S	1996
Lutzinger Norma J Milnikel	(623)536-6956 putterrtl@aol.com	9504 Eldwick Dr Brentwood TN 37027	CNH	Teacher	EM			RF	1956
Lyles Elizabeth L Welch	(562)644-5483	23551 Vista Way Menifee CA 92587	PSW	Teacher	Prin	Zion Anaheim CA	(714)535-1169	CQ	2021
Lynch James R	(425)334-3572 jimlyn70@hotmail.com	181 Ruby Rd Port Angeles WA 98362	NOW	Teacher	EM			S	1970
Lynch Stephanie A Taylor	(951)764-3824 slynch@stjohnshemet.org	41426 Crest Dr Hemet CA 92544	PSW	Teacher	Prin	St John Hemet CA	(951)925-7756	CQ	2015
Lynn Karen L Klemm	(757)404-8954 kareles1@hotmail.com	965 Norview Ave Norfolk VA 23513	SE	Teacher	EM			RF	1974
Lyon David R	david.lyon@concordiashanghai.org	620 Market St Oxford MI 48371	MI	Teacher	S Miss	Office of International Mission Saint Louis MO		AA	2001
Lyons Eileen S Rumsey	(512)554-1517	15220 Katies Corner Ln Pflugerville TX 78660	TX	Teacher	EM			RF	1975
Lyons Richard G	(716)208-1621 rick_lyons@stjohnnt.com	216 Werkley Rd Tonawanda NY 14150	EA	Teacher	Tchr	St John North Tonawanda NY	(716)693-9677	CQ	2013
Lyvers Alison R Barton	(815)235-2364 mrslyvers678@gmail.com	6236 N Unity Rd Lena IL 61048	NI	Teacher	C06/2020			CH	2009
Maack Susan R Kromphardt	mrsmaack50@gmail.com	16240 Cape Coral Dr Wimauma FL 33598	SE	DCE	EM			BR	1979
Maanum Jenna M Russell	(719)924-3214 ednjenna@gmail.com	2724 Minuteman Ln Knoxville TN 37920	RM	Teacher	C07/2016			RF	2002
Maas Allana M Blakeman	(402)540-4681 allana.maas@lhsparker.org	16990 Carlson Dr Unit 721 Parker CO 80134	RM	Teacher	Tchr	Colorado Lutheran High School Parker CO	(303)841-5551	S	2020
Maas John H	(816)289-9485 jnmaas@sbcglobal.net	5740 NE Wilson Blvd Kansas City MO 64118	MO	Teacher	EM			S	1981
Maas Nancy L Haak	(816)452-9097 jnmaas@sbcglobal.net	5740 NE Wilson Blvd Kansas City MO 64118	MO	Teacher	EM			S	1980
Maas Richard E Sr	(262)255-1862 richardmaas@att.net	N93W15358 Hillside Ln Menomonee Fls WI 53051	SW	Teacher	EM			RF	1950
Maas Terry P	(626)857-0321 maasterry@hotmail.com	3530 Damien Ave Spc 289 La Verne CA 91750	PSW	Teacher	C09/2016			S	1972
Maassel Shawn L Gsellman	(301)332-9801 smaassel@comcast.net	7440 Stone Ct Saint Leonard MD 20685	SE	DCE	EM			CQ	2006
Mac Lean Joyce L	(660)641-5389 joycemaclean55@gmail.com	910 S Whippoorwill Dr Marshall MO 65340	MO	Teacher	EM			CQ	2001
Mac Lean Judy L Watson Boehmer	(816)548-7275 jlynnmac@att.net	807 SE Moreland School Rd Blue Springs MO 64014	MO	Teacher	EM			S	1973
Macduff Grace Deac	(509)546-1630 gracem@blcbls.org	404 N Underwood St Kennewick WA 99336	NOW	Deaconess	Mem C	Bethlehem Kennewick WA	(509)582-5858	SL-DEAC	2025
MacGillis Elizabeth C Steinke	(414)916-6962 lmacgillis@sjlplymouth.com	W4343 Stoney Ln Plymouth WI 53073	SW	Teacher	Prin	St John Plymouth WI	(920)893-3071	MQ	2004
Machemer Andrea L Loesel	(260)408-4577 andrea.machemer83@gmail.com	3 Martin Luther Dr Fort Wayne IN 46825	IN	Teacher	C07/2016			CH	2006
Machemer Matthew A	(586)295-8944 matthew.machemer@ctsfw.edu	3 Martin Luther Dr Fort Wayne IN 46825	IN	DPM	S HS/C	Concordia Theological Seminary Fort Wayne IN	(260)452-2100	CH	2007
Machemer Melvin A	(586)295-8943 melvin.machemer@gmail.com	14246 Edshire Dr Sterling Hts MI 48312	MI	Teacher	EM			RF	1981
Machemer Susan M Teske	(586)295-8942 susan.machemer@gmail.com	14246 Edshire Dr Sterling Hts MI 48312	MI	Teacher	EM			RF	1981
MacIntosh-Beatson Joshua S	(832)495-8683 dcejosh@aol.com	211 Oldbridge Dr Hutto TX 78634	TX	DCE	Mem C	King Of Kings Round Rock TX	(512)255-0829	AU	2020
Mack Kelly J Rolf	(612)327-9692 kelly.mack@concordiaacademy.com	310 County Road B2 W Roseville MN 55113	MNS	Teacher	Tchr	Concordia Academy Roseville MN	(651)484-8429	SP	2005
Mack Martin M Jr	(507)288-7269 mmack21523@aol.com	1921 Alexander Rd NE Rochester MN 55906	MNS	Teacher	EM			S	1968

*Multiple Assignments (See Church Worker Locator for Additional Details)
See Page 53 for the Table of Abbreviations for key to District, Classification, Position, and College abbreviations.
**C =Candidate; EM =Emeritus; the date following the C is the month and year the Candidate status began

NAME	TELEPHONE NUMBER EMAIL	STREET ADDRESS CITY/STATE/ZIP	DISTRICT	CLASS.	POSITION/ STATUS**	WHERE SERVING	OFFICE PHONE	COLLEGE/ UNIV/CQ	YR GRAD
Macke Eric J	(727)641-9616 mackeeric@hotmail.com	2590 Tropical Shores Dr SE St Petersburg FL 33705	FG	Teacher	Tchr	Grace Saint Petersburg FL	(727)527-6213	BR	1999
Mackenthun Katherine M Collier	(952)210-3692 kathymackenthun@msn.com	1333 Dunsmore Dr Waconia MN 55387	MNS	Teacher	EM			RF	1980
MacKenzie Meg M	(260)494-8836 megmackenzie525@gmail.com	6 Tyndale Pl Fort Wayne IN 46825	IN	Teacher	EM			CQ	2004
Mackey Boyd Yvonne M Mackey	(314)307-1531 ymboyd26@gmail.com	8623 Church Rd Saint Louis MO 63147	MO	Teacher	Prin	River Roads Saint Louis MO	(314)388-0300	RF	2006
Mackie Allison N	(402)270-5996 allison.mackie@splco.org	914 State St Apt 3 Oconomowoc WI 53066	SW	DPM	Mem C	St Paul Oconomowoc WI	(262)567-5001	S	2019
Mackie Debra J McGowan	(630) 518-1289 dmackie178522@gmail.com	18180 Bluebonnet Ln Bowling Green MO 63334	NI	Teacher	EM			RF	1976
Mackie Ruth E Garchow	(507)304-3155 remackie816@gmail.com	2022 Marlee Ln Green Bay WI 54304	NW	Tch/DCE	Mem C	Pilgrim Green Bay WI	(920)965-2233	CQ	2007
MacKinnon Kasey R	(989)751-2268 kmackinnon@stlorenz.org	221 Ardussi St Frankenmuth MI 48734	MI	Teacher	Tchr	St Lorenz Frankenmuth MI	(989)652-6141	CQ	2017
Mackowski Elliot N	(602)448-4275 elliotnoel2@gmail.com	7303 Spring Cypress Rd 332 Spring TX 77379	TX	DCE	Mem C	Resurrection Spring TX	(281)353-4413	S	2023
MacLean Erin A Riggert	(660)668-7765	104 S Boonville St Cole Camp MO 65325	MO	Teacher	C07/2016			S	2000
Madden Noelle Geraghty	(650)366-1678 noellemadden@sbcglobal.net	551 Grand St Redwood City CA 94062	CNH	Teacher	Tchr	Bridge City Redwood City CA	(650)366-5892	CQ	2013
Maddick Amber A Morrison	(636)233-0215 amber.morrison@cune.org	54 Jamestown Dr Saint Peters MO 63376	MO	Teacher	Tchr	St Charles Saint Peters MO	(636)928-5100	S	2006
Maddick David L	(636)233-0110 david.maddick@cune.org	54 Jamestown Dr Saint Peters MO 63376	MO	Teacher	Tchr	Zion Saint Charles MO	(636)441-7424	S	2006
Maddick Melanie K Schuldt	(641)750-0211 teachermkm@hotmail.com	7 Reece Dr O Fallon MO 63366	MO	Teacher	EM			RF	1981
Maddux Paula D Price	(817)688-3596 paula.maddux@sharingnewlife.com	4540 Rush River Trl Fort Worth TX 76123	TX	Teacher	Tchr	St Paul Fort Worth TX	(817)353-2929	CQ	1998
Magalis Cara B Duensing	(260)494-6848 cduensing78@gmail.com	4503 Dunton Terrace Unit Q Perry Hall MD 21128	SE	Teacher	C07/2019			S	2009
Maggert Elizabeth J Guthrie	(660)463-7552 emaggert55@yahoo.com	908 S Main St Concordia MO 64020	MO	Teacher	EM			CQ	2001
Magness Phillip A	(630)759-0452 phillip.magness@protonmail.com	5001 Oak Bluff Drive High Ridge MO 63049	MO	DPM	Mem C	Village Ladue MO	(314)993-1834	RF	2014
Magnus Mary K Mueller	(417)988-2896 mmagnus3@gmail.com	1101 W Westview St Springfield MO 65807	MO	Teacher	EM			S	1974
Magnus-Duitsman Jennifer A Magnus	(402)432-3398 jduitsman@lincolnlutheran.org	3301 N 72nd St Lincoln NE 68507	NEB	Teacher	Tchr	Lincoln Lincoln NE	(402)467-5404	S	1999
Magnuson Jacquelyn	(651)261-4982 jqmagnuson@gmail.com	2200 Riverfront Dr Apt 1303 Little Rock AR 72202	MDS	DPM	Mem C	Grace Little Rock AR	(501)663-3631	CQ	2022
Mahler H J	(954)224-3825 jamesmahler@bellsouth.net	4365 15th Ave South Apt 310 Fargo ND 58103	FG	Teacher	C07/2016			SP	1995
Mahler Richard J Dr	(248)543-3528 rjmahler@wowway.com	6783 Alex Ln Cleveland OH 44130	OH	Teacher	EM			S	1969
Mahler William A Dr	(734)680-7809	6161 Schuss Xing Ypsilanti MI 48197	MI	DCM	EM			CQ	1983
Mahnken Carol A Johnson	(314)852-6192 cmahnken@immanuelstcharles.org	15 Godfrey Ln Ferguson MO 63135	MO	Teacher	EM			S	1972
Mahoney Judith Rose	(630)665-9285 judymahoney@gmail.com	1949 Richton Dr Wheaton IL 60189	NI	Teacher	EM			CQ	2004
Mahshi Tasha C	(714)788-2407 Tasha.Mahshi@gmail.com	7931 E Salinas Ct Orange CA 92869	PSW	DCE	Mem C	St Paul Orange CA	(714)637-2640	IV	2022
Maichel Emily L Metcalf	(314)591-3069 emilymetcalf33@gmail.com	7328 General Sherman Ln Saint Louis MO 63123	CI	Teacher	C07/2016			S	2013
Maier Denise E Schaus	(650)280-3520 dmaier5th@yahoo.com	120 Danbury Ln Redwood City CA 94061	CNH	Teacher	Tchr	Bridge City Redwood City CA	(650)366-5892	CQ	2013
Mailand Julia A Moody	(281)465-9886	10200 Six Pines Dr Apt 408 Shenandoah TX 77380	TX	Teacher	Tchr	Trinity Spring TX	(281)376-5810	CQ	2014
Maita Ruth C	(239)785-5239 ruthcmaita@gmail.com	Western Lakes # 2401 Mayaguez PR 00682	MO	Teacher	S Miss	Office of International Mission Saint Louis MO		CQ	2015
Major Cynthia C Schluckebier	(989)624-6008 cdisneyfan@yahoo.com	3856 Geranium Ave Haines City FL 33844	FG	Teacher	EM			RF	1986
Majorins Jeremiah D	(402)430-2580 jdmajorins@gmail.com	8033 Sanborn Drive Lincoln NE 68505	NEB	Teacher	Tchr	Christ Lincoln NE	(402)483-7774	S	2012
Makey Brian S	(716)923-3880 bmky3458@yahoo.com	2061 Billington Rd East Aurora NY 14052	EA	Teacher	EM			BR	1980
Makey Ellen S Fink	(716)961-8378 esmky23@yahoo.com	2061 Billington Rd East Aurora NY 14052	EA	Teacher	EM			BR	1980
Makowski Rebecca L Walker	(734)474-7664 beckielwalker@gmail.com	3162 Delevan Dr Saginaw MI 48603	MI	Teacher	Tchr	Peace Saginaw MI	(989)793-9025	AA	2011
Malady Kelley M Fischer	(636)357-3370 keli1010@sbcglobal.net	2824 Essex St Saint Charles MO 63301	MO	Teacher	Tchr	Assoc Spec Ed Saint Louis MO	(314)268-1234	S	2003
Malcman Kimberly E Smith	(847)647-3107 mrsmalcman@hotmail.com	7056 W Madison St Niles IL 60714	NI	Teacher	C02/2022			RF	2001
Malenke Julia R Bennett	(334)703-0325 juliamalenke@hotmail.com	1021 Palm Ave Wildwood FL 34785	FG	DCE	EM			S	1976
Malenke Norbert J	(281)687-6763 njmalenk1@comcast.net	14419 Leaning Aspen Ct Cypress TX 77429	TX	Teacher	EM			S	1972
Malinowski Christine Wager	(309)830-4424 dcewager@hotmail.com	11 McCormick Blvd Normal IL 61761	CI	DCE	Mem C	Trinity Bloomington IL	(309)828-6265	CQ	2000
Mallardi Janine R Blair	(620)795-2008 janine_j9@hotmail.com	28091 Heits Point Ave Lincoln MO 65338	MO	DCE	RSO	Heits Point Lutheran Camp Lincoln MO	(660)668-2363	S	2000

*Multiple Assignments (See Church Worker Locator for Additional Details)
See Page 53 for the Table of Abbreviations for key to District, Classification, Position, and College abbreviations.
**C =Candidate; EM =Emeritus; the date following the C is the month and year the Candidate status began

NAME	TELEPHONE NUMBER EMAIL	STREET ADDRESS CITY/STATE/ZIP	DISTRICT	CLASS.	POSITION/ STATUS**	WHERE SERVING	OFFICE PHONE	COLLEGE/ UNIV/CQ	YR GRAD
Mallegni Kimberly S Mallegni Van Bibber	(414)519-2104 kmmallegni@gmail.com	3540 S 15th St Milwaukee WI 53221	EN	Teacher	EM			IV	1985
Mallinson Jeffrey C Dr	(425)418-5222	1530 Concordia Irvine CA 92612	PSW	Teacher	S HS/C	Concordia University Irvine Irvine CA	(949)854-8002	IV	1996
Malm Erik K	(414)535-1445 emalm@lakecountryhs.org	13640 Acre View Dr Brookfield WI 53005	SW	Teacher	Tchr	LHS Assn of Greater Milwaukee West Allis WI	(414)421-9100	MQ	2000
Malone Christine C Oberdeck	(206)979-9693 bcmalone1030@gmail.com	14066 22nd Ave NE Seattle WA 98125	NOW	Teacher	Tchr	Concordia Seattle WA	(206)525-7407	MQ	2007
Malone Heidi A Brenenstuhl	(440)623-2464 hmalone@bethanyparma.com	4519 Broadale Rd Cleveland OH 44109	OH	Teacher	Tchr	Bethany Parma OH	(440)884-1010	Other	2006
Malone Rachel L Radtke	(260)639-2375 rmalone@esmeagles.com	11206 Lantern Lane Fort Wayne IN 46845	IN	Teacher	Tchr	Emmanuel-St Michael Fort Wayne IN	(260)422-6712	CQ	2025
Malone Walter D	(785)338-2158	3318 SW Lakeside Dr Topeka KS 66614	KS	Teacher	EM			S	1969
Malterer De Anne R Guse	(507)340-2097 demalterer@gmail.com	400 N West St Janesville MN 56048	MNS	Teacher	EM			CQ	2006
Malucky Maralyn B Ludwig	(626)318-0751 mmalucky@earthlink.net	1763 Royal Oaks Dr Apt C58 Bradbury CA 91010	PSW	Teacher	EM			S	1961
Maly Lonn D	(651)249-8605 maly@csp.edu	7989 Drake Bay Woodbury MN 55125	MNS	Teacher	S HS/C	Concordia University St Paul Saint Paul MN	(651)641-8278	SP	1981
Malzahn Robert W Dr	(817)562-2884 rwmalzahn@gmail.com	1508 Rush Creek Ct Keller TX 76248	TX	Teacher	EM			S	1971
Manahan Renee C Wolf	(636)795-4977 rmanahan8@gmail.com	1401 Norwood Hills Dr O Fallon MO 63366	MO	Teacher	Tchr	Christ Community Kirkwood MO	(314)822-7774	CQ	2008
Mancini Michael J	(650)400-7889 mmancini@redeemerrwc.org	446 Jeter St Redwood City CA 94062	CNH	Teacher	Tchr	Redeemer Redwood City CA	(650)366-3466	CQ	2003
Mandziara Nicole L	(586)530-1713 nmandziara@lhsa.com	16835 Huntington Woods Dr Macomb MI 48042	MI	Teacher	Tchr	Northwest Rochester Hills MI	(248)856-0240	CQ	2020
Mangels Anne D	(314)353-1043 adm929stl@aol.com	7332 Parkview Dr Apt 1 Saint Louis MO 63109	MO	Teacher	EM			RF	1965
Mangels Cheryl D Heine	(281)513-6061 cherylmangels@gmail.com	13027 N 41st St Phoenix AZ 85032	PSW	Teacher	Tchr	Christ Phoenix AZ	(602)955-4830	CQ	2005
Mangels Kenneth E Dr	(714)878-1973 ken.mangels@cui.edu	140 Dan Moody Trl Georgetown TX 78633	PSW	Teacher	S HS/C	Concordia University Irvine Irvine CA	(949)854-8002	S	1968
Mangels Verlin G	(573)576-1502 vgmangels@gmail.com	2411 State Highway B Oak Ridge MO 63769	MO	Teacher	EM			CQ	2007
Mangieri Gesine E Luecke	(864)361-6725 foxwood4@juno.com	4 Grist Mill Rd Medfield MA 02052	FG	Teacher	EM			RF	1963
Mangrum Lorre M O Neal	(541)295-4963	611 SW Balsam Rd Grants Pass OR 97526	NOW	Teacher	EM			S	1968
Manley Shannon M	(816)591-6213 smanley@bethanyschool.net	c/o St Paul Lutheran School 320 N 7th St Leavenworth KS 66048	KS	Teacher	Tchr	St Paul Leavenworth KS	(913)682-5553	MQ	2006
Mann Brian C	(620)202-3049 trinitylutheranbrian13@gmail.com	10680 Bookcliff CV New Haven IN 46774	IN	Teacher	EM			S	2007
Mann Christina A Keller	(520)481-2784 un4getable2@live.com	6340 N Pear Tree Rd Tucson AZ 85743	PSW	DCE	C07/2016			IV	1998
Mann Evelyn R Faske	(512)898-5278 eviemann@hotmail.com	215 Glacier Dr Cedar Park TX 78613	TX	Teacher	EM			RF	1970
Mann Julie A Rivers Reid	(612)578-7449 julie@iowadistrictwest.org	1057 N 31st Pl Fort Dodge IA 50501	IW	Teacher	D Ex/S	Iowa West District Fort Dodge IA	(515)576-7666	IV	1991
Mann Mark D	(520)450-9429 mdmann575@gmail.com	6340 N Pear Tree Rd Tucson AZ 85743	PSW	DCE	C07/2016			IV	2004
Mann Melissa R Fick	(515)230-6460 mrfmann@gmail.com	8209 Bancroft Ave Lincoln NE 68506	NEB	Teacher	C07/2016			S	2009
Mann Nancy L Priem	(503)465-2480 mdnlmann@yahoo.com	1161 SW 5th Way Troutdale OR 97060	NOW	Teacher	EM			SP	1972
Mannigel Timothy J	(260)750-2581 tmannigel@clhscadets.com	2909 Rivulet Run Fort Wayne IN 46818	IN	Teacher	Tchr	Concordia Fort Wayne IN	(260)483-1102	S	1996
Manning Amanda J Saurmann	(775)671-1307 amanning@blcs.org	888 W Bonanza Dr Carson City NV 89706	CNH	Teacher	Tchr	Bethlehem Carson City NV	(775)882-5252	RF	2006
Manning David M	(618)578-9061 david@davidmanning.net	225 S Hackman St Staunton IL 62088	SI	Teacher	C08/2020			AU	2005
Manning Heather H Wyneken	(714)685-9046 heathermanning@ searchlightministries.com	2710 N Gaff St Orange CA 92865	PSW	DCE	Mem C	Searchlight Fullerton CA	(714)871-1711	IV	1994
Manning Jarvis A	(775)461-3493 jarvis.manning@cune.org	888 W Bonanza Dr Carson City NV 89706	CNH	Teacher	Tchr	Bethlehem Carson City NV	(775)882-5252	S	2006
Manning Mary A Befi	(262)391-7545 tmanning237@gmail.com	W228 N3986 Crescent Dr Pewaukee WI 53072	SW	Teacher	EM			MW	1983
Manor Lisa M Himmelein	(414)708-1589 lmanor@fils.org	5426 W Hillcrest Dr Mequon WI 53092	SW	Teacher	Tchr	First Immanuel Cedarburg WI	(262)377-6610	MQ	2003
Manor Tiffany M Ornelis Dr	(314)996-1085 tiffany.manor@lcms.org	c/o Lutheran Church-Missouri Synod 1333 S Kirkwood Rd Saint Louis MO 63122	MO	Deaconess	S Ex/S	The LCMS Corporate Saint Louis MO	(314)965-9000	FW-DEAC	2012
Mansfield Cheryl L	(314)348-4233 cherimansfield63@gmail.com	12987 Vanderwood Dr Black Jack MO 63033	MO	Teacher	Tchr	Lutheran North Saint Louis MO	(314)389-3100	CQ	2015
Mansfield Erin E Vernoy	(714) 904-0273 emansfield@popfremont.org	845 Posada Way Fremont CA 94536	CNH	Teacher	Tchr	Prince of Peace Fremont CA	(510)793-3366	IV	2008
Mansk Daniel J	316dna@gmail.com	316 N 7th Ave Wausau WI 54401	NW	Teacher	EM			SP	1975
Manske Barbara M Amt Deac	(949)299-2904	c/o Noel Fairchild 14782 Elm Ave Irvine CA 92606	PSW	Deaconess	EM			Other	1961
Mantey Megan F Flannery	meganfmantey@gmail.com	3 Hillcrest St Hallowell ME 04347	NE	DCE	C02/2025			PO	2004

*Multiple Assignments (See Church Worker Locator for Additional Details)
See Page 53 for the Table of Abbreviations for key to District, Classification, Position, and College abbreviations.
**C =Candidate; EM =Emeritus; the date following the C is the month and year the Candidate status began

NAME	TELEPHONE NUMBER EMAIL	STREET ADDRESS CITY/STATE/ZIP	DISTRICT	CLASS.	POSITION/ STATUS**	WHERE SERVING	OFFICE PHONE	COLLEGE/ UNIV/CQ	YR GRAD
Manthei Gregory W	(734)740-3680 manthei54@hotmail.com	29964 Tamarack Dr Flat Rock MI 48134	MI	Teacher	Tchr	St John Waltz MI	(734)654-6366	AA	1991
Manwaring Veronica A Reitzel	(618)201-6168 vmanwaring@immanuelmurphy.com	815 N 6th St Murphysboro IL 62966	SI	Teacher	Tchr	Immanuel Murphysboro IL	(618)684-3012	CQ	2016
Manweiler Nancy D Asche	(801)230-4075 nasche33@msn.com	1259 M 2190 W St George UT 84770	RM	Teacher	C07/2016			S	1984
Mappes Doris M Awe Deac	(470)885-0101	4460 Celebration Blvd Apt 3207 Acworth GA 30101	IN	Deaconess	EM			Other	1958
Marbach Megan L Kearns	(260)385-6766 megan.l.kearns@gmail.com	8231 N 500 E Decatur IN 46733	IN	Teacher	Tchr	St Peter-Immanuel Decatur IN	(260)623-6115	CH	2014
Marburger Faith A Feltz Deac	(540)226-0673 faithalayne@gmail.com	35059 Germanna Heights Dr Apt 34 Locust Grove VA 22508	SE	Deaconess	EM			Other	1977
March John D	(518)817-7162 principal@wlsedu.org	1246 Bearpaw Dr Defiance OH 43512	IN	Teacher	P/Tchr	Woodburn Woodburn IN	(260)632-5493	AA	1997
March Tristiana	(608)322-7641 tristianamarch@gmail.com	1214 Hawthorne Ave Janesville WI 53545	SW	Teacher	Tchr	St Pauls Janesville WI	(608)754-4471	MQ	2019
Marchese Ruth A Moentmann	(240)731-3793 ruthmarchese@hotmail.com	352 Natsam Woods Way Wake Forest NC 27587	SE	Tch/DCE	C06/2020			RF	1992
Marchione Austin J	(248)496-2660 austin@marchionefamily.com	624 Colbarn Dr Fishers IN 46038	IN	DFLM	C02/2025			MQ	2021
Marcinkowski Susan C Streich	(708)602-4193 bsm77@att.net	10818 S Komensky Ave Oak Lawn IL 60453	NI	Teacher	EM			RF	1974
Marcis Erin M	(440)221-3756 erinmarcis@gmail.com	1752 Winston Blvd Toledo OH 43614	OH	Teacher	Tchr	Trinity Toledo OH	(419)385-2651	AA	2016
Marcsisak Thomas A	(952)649-1717 tommarcsisakzion@gmail.com	1325 Brenda Rd Waconia MN 55387	MNS	Teacher	EM			SP	1981
Maree-Bohm Patricia J Meltzer	(870)673-8634 momma.pat2@yahoo.com	410 S Broadway St Forest City IL 61532	CI	Teacher	C07/2016			CQ	1991
Margheim Rachel O			RM	Tch/DCE	Tchr	Trinity Greeley CO	(970)330-2485	S	2021
Margrett Deborah A Steffen	(262)641-0806 dmargrett@wi.rr.com	2620 El Rancho Dr Brookfield WI 53005	SW	Teacher	Tchr	St Pauls West Allis WI	(414)541-6251	RF	1990
Marinaccio Nicole M Hitchcock	(714)876-8523	5824 E Avenida Serra Anaheim CA 92807	PSW	Teacher	C05/2022			IV	2016
Marinko Paul B	(260)515-7620 pmarinko@frontier.com	6108 Ranger Trl Fort Wayne IN 46835	IN	Teacher	EM			RF	1986
Marino Kathleen Porter	(585)409-5887 kathleenrmarino@gmail.com	60 Gateway Rd Apt 142W Yonkers NY 10703	AT	Teacher	Mem C	The Village Bronxville NY	(914)337-0207	BR	2009
Marino Quentin	(734)663-3865 qcmarino@gmail.com	15941 E Sunflower Dr Fountain Hills AZ 85268	MI	Teacher	EM			CQ	1963
Markiewicz Hannah R	(989) 977-1551 hannahvolz193@gmail.com	10010 Huron Line Road Sebewaing MI 48759	MI	Teacher	Tchr	Christ The King Sebewaing MI	(989)883-3730	AA	2023
Markin Jerold D	(714)331-7088 jdmarkin@gmail.com	4042 Victoria Ln Lancaster CA 93536	PSW	Tch/DCE	EM			S	1970
Markin Karen J Fredericks	(661)480-3228 kjmarkin@gmail.com	4042 Victoria Ln Lancaster CA 93536	PSW	Teacher	EM			S	1984
Marko Sara R Doyle	(714)321-1778 smarko@stjohnsorange.org	777 N Lincoln St Orange CA 92867	PSW	Teacher	Tchr	Saint Johns Orange CA	(714)288-4400	IV	2011
Marks John B	(260)452-9152 jbmarksprin@aol.com	9508 Arundel Run Fort Wayne IN 46835	IN	Teacher	EM			CQ	1977
Markworth Douglas W	(773)505-3296 douglas.markworth77@gmail.com	770 Pearson St Unit 706 Des Plaines IL 60016	EN	Teacher	EM			S	1977
Markworth JoAn L Schimke	(773)919-1907 joanmarkworth@gmail.com	770 Pearson St Apt 706 Des Plaines IL 60016	EN	Teacher	EM			S	1977
Marlatt Kristine M Schmidt		7855 Wind Ridge Trl Mound MN 55364	MNS	Teacher	Pro Stf	Trinity Waconia MN	(952)442-4165	BR	1987
Marnholtz Laura M Roediger	(715)536-8492 larlamo@charter.net	1105 E 3rd St Merrill WI 54452	NW	Teacher	EM			RF	1985
Marohn Virginia A Metzger	(630)325-5166	1353 Avocet Dr Greenwood IN 46143	NI	Teacher	EM			RF	1958
Marolf Brandon D	(262)894-5541 bmarolf@zionharvester.org	16 Spring Leaf Ct Saint Peters MO 63376	MO	Teacher	Prin	Zion Saint Charles MO	(636)441-7424	MQ	2005
Marolf Shirley Haertel	(563)391-3019	2216 N Ohio Ave Davenport IA 52804	IE	Teacher	EM			RF	1967
Marose David P	(414)491-2970 dmarose@outlook.com	1700 S Craftsman Dr New Berlin WI 53146	SW	Teacher	EM			S	1982
Marose Natalie S Rehmer	(952)994-7063 nsmarose@gmail.com	9301 11th Ave S Bloomington MN 55420	MNS	Teacher	C07/2016			S	1987
Maroszek Gina M Natal	(715)675-7578 maroszekg@trinitynet.org	234428 N 96th Ave Wausau WI 54401	NW	Teacher	Tchr	Trinity Wausau WI	(715)848-0166	MQ	1985
Marotzke Judy L	(417)849-2246 rotzke84@yahoo.com	15698 Highway F Bruceton MO 65237	MO	Teacher	Tchr	Zion Bunceton MO	(660)838-6428	S	1984
Marousek Rebekah E Hart	(949)922-1277 RebekahMarousek@gmail.com	348 E Tudor St Covina CA 91722	PSW	Teacher	Tchr	Emmaus Alhambra CA	(626)289-3664	IV	2005
Marquardt Jamie J Nikodym	(402)746-0561 jamie.nikodym@zionkearney.org	3417 Ave W Kearney NE 68847	NEB	Teacher	Tchr	Zion Kearney NE	(308)234-3410	S	2019
Marquardt Joel A	joelamarquardt@gmail.com	4050 N 21st Lincoln NE 68521	NEB	DCE	Mem C	Christ Lincoln NE	(402)483-7774	S	2018
Marquardt Leonard M	(309)732-3160 llmarq@att.net	2105 Friendship Pl Rock Island IL 61201	CI	Teacher	EM			RF	1950
Marquardt Marcia A Bernthal Deac	(262)784-2062 marcia1@wi.rr.com	1980 N 166th St Brookfield WI 53005	SW	Deaconess	EM			Other	1982
Marquardt Meg	(714)904-9147 mmarquardt@salemorange.com	7745 E Briarwood Rd Orange CA 92869	PSW	Teacher	Tchr	Salem Orange CA	(714)633-2366	CQ	2017

*Multiple Assignments (See Church Worker Locator for Additional Details)

See Page 53 for the Table of Abbreviations for key to District, Classification, Position, and College abbreviations.

**C =Candidate; EM =Emeritus; the date following the C is the month and year the Candidate status began

NAME	TELEPHONE NUMBER EMAIL	STREET ADDRESS CITY/STATE/ZIP	DISTRICT	CLASS.	POSITION/ STATUS**	WHERE SERVING	OFFICE PHONE	COLLEGE/ UNIV/CQ	YR GRAD
Marquardt Paul J Dr	(714)904-8161 marquardt.paul@gmail.com	7745 E Briarwood Rd Orange CA 92869	PSW	Teacher	C08/2016			IV	1990
Marquardt-Smith Judy L	(815)455-4607 jlms91@yahoo.com	9109 Arthur St Crystal Lake IL 60014	NI	Teacher	C07/2016			CQ	1999
Marquart Lydia M Smith	(219)616-0299 l.marquart@alcsfw.org	10525 Oak Valley Rd Fort Wayne IN 46845	IN	Teacher	Tchr	Ascension Fort Wayne IN	(260)486-2226	CH	2024
Marriott Catherine C Gulbrandson	(414)870-4021 cnamarriott@hotmail.com	W225S3626 Foxcroft Ln Waukesha WI 53189	SW	Teacher	EM			MW	1980
Marschel Mary R Adam	(636) 283-8584 ruth.marschel@gmail.com	11 Valmont St Greenbrier AR 72058	MO	Teacher	EM			S	1965
Marsh Jerrode K Baker Dr	(816)605-5173 jmarsh@splhs.org	312 S Orange St Concordia MO 64020	MO	Teacher	Tchr	Saint Paul Concordia MO	(660)463-2238	CQ	2017
Marsh Keith A	(636)271-6648 the_marshes@hotmail.com	908 Silver Lake View Dr Pacific MO 63069	MO	Teacher	EM			S	1973
Marsh Meredith L Peters	(660)463-2238 mmarsh@splhs.org	907 S Gordon St Concordia MO 64020	MO	Teacher	Tchr	Saint Paul Concordia MO	(660)463-2238	S	2005
Marshall Christopher R	(414)690-5603 cmarshall0079@gmail.com	5328 Thornapple Ln Cedarburg WI 53012	SW	Teacher	Tchr	Milwaukee LHS Milwaukee WI	(414)461-6000	MQ	2012
Marshall Jennifer	(818)694-3538 jenniescraps1965@gmail.com	760 E Route 66 Apt 46 Glendora CA 91740	PSW	Teacher	Tchr	Hope Glendora CA	(626)335-5315	IV	1988
Marshall Patricia L	(419)782-1306	805 Kentner St Defiance OH 43512	OH	Teacher	Tchr	St John Defiance OH	(419)782-1751	S	1970
Martchenke Colleen A Dolan	(303)465-2315 cmartchenke@gmail.com	2745 Bethlehem Cir Broomfield CO 80020	RM	Teacher	C07/2016			S	2002
Martchenke William C	(952)447-2711 bmartchenke@hotmail.com	2745 Bethlehem Cir Broomfield CO 80020	RM	Teacher	C07/2016			SP	1993
Marten Dennis L	(913)991-2124 dennismarten@earthlink.net	5738 N 79th St Scottsdale AZ 85250	PSW	Teacher	EM			S	1998
Martens Gina R Oetting	(660)463-1337 cte56410@centurytel.net	26273 Duensing Rd Concordia MO 64020	MO	Teacher	Tchr	St Paul Concordia MO	(660)463-2291	S	1992
Martens Lisa M Jacobitz	(816)217-6199 lmartens@mlakc.com	7524 N Booth Ave Kansas City MO 64158	MO	Teacher	Pro Stf	Martin Luther Kansas City MO	(816)734-1060	S	1996
Martens Melanie M	(573)339-1936 melmar@clas.net	623 Sycamore Cir Apt 4 Cpe Girardeau MO 63701	MO	Teacher	EM			S	1981
Martens Rachel L Clayton	(660)238-6902 trumpetgirl1978@hotmail.com	27950 Old Hwy 40 Concordia MO 64020	MO	Teacher	Tchr	St Paul Concordia MO	(660)463-2291	RF	2002
Martens Sean P	(962)223-2152 sean.martens@mnsdistrict.org	13575 Harvest Ct Apple Valley MN 55124	MNS	Teacher	D Ex/S	Minnesota South District* Burnsville MN	(952)435-2550	S	1991
Marti Dianne S Pannier	(763)227-1111 dsonshine.marti@gmail.com	730 Cox Ct Leclaire IA 52753	IE	Teacher	EM			S	1974
Martin Anne L Brooks	(949)306-9565 gordanne@mac.com	25882 Vicar Way Lake Forest CA 92630	PSW	Teacher	C07/2016			CQ	1999
Martin Breanna Leonard	(208)602-1635 landen.bre.martin@gmail.com	669 S Blackoak Ave Kuna ID 83634	NOW	Teacher	C12/2020			IV	2003
Martin Caleb J	(260)445-4020 caleb.martin7701@gmail.com	17614 Rosa Drew Lane 4d Irvine CA 92612	PSW	Teacher	Tchr	St Johns Orange CA	(714)288-4406	CH	2023
Martin Douglas P	(815)397-0793	3306 Buckingham Dr Rockford IL 61107	NI	Teacher	Tchr	Rockford Rockford IL	(815)877-9551	S	1983
Martin Jayanne Placette	(281)907-2566 JAYANNEM@SBCGLOBAL.NET	12715 Sherborne Castle Court Tomball TX 77375	TX	Teacher	Mem C	Trinity Klein Klein TX	(281)376-5773	CQ	2014
Martin Joy Kiekhaefer	(920)664-7573 pjmartin@ameritech.net	180 N Bedford Rd Green Bay WI 54311	NW	Teacher	EM			RF	1970
Martin Kathy A	(989)892-4963 k77am54@aol.com	1507 S Chilson St Bay City MI 48706	MI	Teacher	EM			S	1976
Martin Keith D	(260)701-5943 kmartin@emmauslutheranfw.org	220 Lauren Ln Roanoke IN 46783	IN	Teacher	EM			CQ	1989
Martin Kerry J	(720)456-5465 kjmartin227@gmail.com	25826 S Hollygreen Dr Sun Lakes AZ 85248	PSW	Teacher	EM			RF	1978
Martin Lyn J	(623)703-8348 blitzen55555@gmail.com	15613 N 99th Dr Sun City AZ 85351	PSW	Teacher	EM			S	1971
Martin Margo M Luce	(317)247-1135 dancer0@sbcglobal.net	2009 Fullerton Dr Indianapolis IN 46214	IN	Teacher	EM			RF	1971
Martin Mary R Clikeman	(575)650-3302 marymartin01@yahoo.com	535 North Park Dr Las Cruces NM 88005	RM	Teacher	EM			CQ	2001
Martin Natalie K Conrad-Cheshier	(901)680-1922 natalie.martin917@gmail.com	2665 Greenmill Dr Memphis TN 38119	MDS	Teacher	C05/2022			CQ	2004
Martin Peter D	peter731@pdmz.com	18202 41st Ave SE Bothell WA 98012	NOW	Teacher	Tchr	Zion Snohomish Cty Lake Stevens WA	(425)334-5064	CQ	2004
Martin Wanda L Stockman	(573)291-1976 wmartin54jc@hotmail.com	5510 Bradford Ct Jefferson Cty MO 65101	MO	Teacher	EM			CQ	2001
Martinal Rebekah E Wrase	(517)416-3788 r.martinal@gmail.com	930 Vine St Adrian MI 49221	MI	DCE	Mem C	Hope Adrian MI	(517)263-4317	CQ	2013
Martinez Rosaura Deac	martinezr@trinityklein.org	6730 Lilacbrook Ct Spring TX 77379	TX	Deaconess	Mem C	Trinity Klein Klein TX	(281)376-5773	SL-DEAC	2013
Marting Eileen M	(760)271-5718 eileenmarting@gmail.com	17430 Plaza Dolores San Diego CA 92128	RM	Teacher	Tchr	Redeemer Salt Lake City UT	(801)467-4352	IV	1987
Martinson Lisa A Day	(715)768-5338 martinsondce@yahoo.com		NW	DCE	Mem C	Shep Of Valley Saint Croix Fls WI	(715)483-1186	SP	1988
Marton Kenneth R	(414)510-8663 biggdoggwisc@gmail.com	5813 Crosswinds Dr Unit 34 Norton Shores MI 49444	MI	Teacher	EM			RF	1978
Marts Jennifer L	(813)610-7253 jenmarts72@gmail.com	16940 Carlson Dr Apt 417 Parker CO 80134	RM	Teacher	C07/2016			S	1996
Marty Larry D	(314)947-4652 larrymarty21@gmail.com	1300 Country Club Rd Saint Charles MO 63303	MO	Teacher	EM			S	1972
Marty Matthew D	(314)541-8823 matthew.marty@gmail.com	1219 N 150th St Omaha NE 68154	NEB	Teacher	Tchr	Concordia Omaha NE	(402)445-4000	S	2004

*Multiple Assignments (See Church Worker Locator for Additional Details)

See Page 53 for the Table of Abbreviations for key to District, Classification, Position, and College abbreviations.

**C =Candidate; EM =Emeritus; the date following the C is the month and year the Candidate status began

NAME	TELEPHONE NUMBER EMAIL	STREET ADDRESS CITY/STATE/ZIP	DISTRICT	CLASS.	POSITION/ STATUS**	WHERE SERVING	OFFICE PHONE	COLLEGE/ UNIV/CQ	YR GRAD
Marut Janice B Beverley	(817)763-5212 jbmarut@gmail.com	6251 Stevenson Oaks Dr Fort Worth TX 76123	TX	Teacher	EM			CQ	1998
Marxhausen Kim D Weinhold Dr	(402)641-7203 kim@marxhausen.net	6211 Glendale Rd Lincoln NE 68505	NEB	Teacher	EM			S	1981
Masat Krista L Warneke	(402)929-0738 kmasat@conpoint.com	86482 527th Ave Brunswick NE 68720	NEB	Teacher	Tchr	Zion Plainview NE	(402)582-3312	S	1987
Masbruch Randal	(414)651-4048 rmasbruch@aol.com	4579 W Thorncrest Dr Franklin WI 53132	EN	DCM	EM			MQ	2009
Maschke Anna J Hasty	(925)628-9897 annamaschke@gmail.com	2288 Oak Ridge Dr Carson City NV 89703	CNH	Teacher	Tchr	Bethlehem Carson City NV	(775)882-5252	S	2001
Maschke Samuel R	(815)543-5876 maschke51@aol.com	242 Broadway # 406 Schenectady NY 12305	AT	Teacher	EM			RF	1974
Masengarb Virginia R Ungrodt	(219)688-7170 gmasengarb@gmail.com	842 Market St Unit 104 Saukville WI 53080	SW	Teacher	EM			RF	1969
Masenthin Timothy	tmasenthin@sbcglobal.net	6813 Kingswood Dr Cedarburg WI 53012	SW	DCE	C07/2016			RF	2002
Maser Kari E Stirtz	(402)312-6813 rkmaser@gmail.com	303 11th Ave Plattsmouth NE 68048	NEB	Teacher	C07/2021			S	2018
Maser M D	(651)399-0158 dcmaser@msn.com	4475 Watercolor Way Fort Myers FL 33966	MNS	Teacher	P/Tchr	Trinity Waconia MN	(952)442-4165	SP	1990
Mashuga Stephanie	(507)766-6152 stephanie.mashuga@gmail.com	126 N Lincoln St Apt 5 West Point NE 68788	NEB	Teacher	Tchr	St Paul West Point NE	(402)372-2355	S	2024
Masiello Debra R Patton	(914)410-4350 drm1207@gmail.com	65 Hillview Ave Yonkers NY 10704	AT	Teacher	EM			BR	1987
Maske Andrea J Rempert	(810)429-9141 gspdirector@gselgin.org	357 E Jackson Ave Hampshire IL 60140	NI	Teacher	Tchr	Good Shepherd Elgin IL	(847)741-7788	CQ	2011
Maske Kathy E Simmons	(618)980-1286 kathymaske@gmail.com	1307 W Old National Trl Greenville IL 62246	SI	Teacher	Tchr	Good Shepherd Collinsville IL	(618)344-3153	RF	2002
Mason Kristi M Georgi	(281)734-1077 kristilange79@gmail.com	12927 Dermott Dr Houston TX 77065	TX	Teacher	C01/2022			AU	2004
Mason Sharon L	(773)471-2424 smason3050@blackpearl.org	8230 S Whipple St Chicago IL 60652	NI	Teacher	EM			RF	1979
Massey Alaine L Holmes	(734)474-3609 amassey@sjlmidland.org	2610 W Whippoorwill Hollow Midland MI 48642	MI	Teacher	Tchr	St John's Midland MI	(989)835-5861	AA	1987
Massey Bradley R	(734)646-8553 masseyb@msn.com	2610 Whipporwill Hollow Midland MI 48642	MI	Teacher	Prin	St John's Midland MI	(989)835-5861	AA	1987
Massey Elizabeth K	(734)660-6603 lizzkmassey@gmail.com	1650 Chapel Hills Dr #n206 Colorado Springs CO 80920	RM	DCE	Mem C	Holy Cross Colorado Springs CO	(719)596-0661	AU	2022
Massey Katherine G Vogel	(813)459-2562 k.vogel@htlstampa.org	3717 Wenig Rd NE Cedar Rapids IA 52402	FG	Teacher	Tchr	Holy Trinity Tampa FL	(813)839-6847	S	2017
Massey Madison N	(989)751-7494 madisonnmassey@gmail.com	501 NE 5th Terrace Apt. 203 Ft. Lauderdale FL 33301	FG	Teacher	Tchr	St Paul Boca Raton FL	(561)395-8548	AA	2022
Massmann Adrienne M	(636)358-3870 adrienne.massmann@ imlutheran.org	604 Madison Ave Washington MO 63090	MO	Teacher	Tchr	Immanuel Washington MO	(636)239-1636	CQ	2022
Massmann Janice C Ambler Dr	(949)476-0770 jan.massmann@gmail.com	15 Las Cruces Irvine CA 92614	PSW	Teacher	EM			S	1969
Massmann Paul F Dr	pfmassmann@gmail.com	15 Las Cruces Irvine CA 92614	PSW	Teacher	EM			S	1968
Masters William L Jr	(402)841-2031 bill8156@telebeep.com	608 N 25th St Norfolk NE 68701	NEB	Teacher	EM			S	1979
Mastic Megan E Boeger	meganmastic@gmail.com		RM	Teacher	C07/2016			MQ	2005
Matasovsky Brenda L Bening	(507)662-6730 infinitecherrypi@gmail.com	75718 480th Ave Jackson MN 56143	MNS	Teacher	C07/2016			CQ	2007
Matasovsky Dina C Cristante	(734)673-5037 dmatasovsky@comcast.net	14356 Woodgrove Dr Belleville MI 48111	MI	Teacher	Tchr	St Michael Wayne MI	(734)728-1950	SP	1994
Mathews Brittany N Mikeska	(713)504-2143 bmathews@lhskc.com	17 E Hurt St Liberty MO 64068	MO	Teacher	Tchr	Kansas City Kansas City MO	(816)241-5478	S	2009
Mathews Eunice F Labbus	(941)527-5828 read2tim@gmail.com	3790 Pinebrook Cir Apt 508 Bradenton FL 34209	FG	Teacher	EM			SP	1977
Mathey Debra A Marks	(715) 330-5599 lcmsdcedeb@gmail.com	119417 Huckleberry Rd Edgar WI 54426	NW	DCE	C07/2016			SP	1999
Mathias Connie J Kopplin	(618)483-3400 cmathias22@gmail.com	9622 N 1st St Altamont IL 62411	CI	Teacher	Tchr	Altamont Altamont IL	(618)483-6428	CQ	1996
Mathiowetz Barbara E Townsend	(619)588-8642 dbmath1@cox.net	1834 Brabham St El Cajon CA 92019	PSW	Teacher	EM			CQ	1996
Mathison Kevin	(214)535-1716 mathisonkj@gmail.com	3573 Palomar Way Napa CA 94558	CNH	DCE	Mem C	St John's Napa CA	(707)255-0119	AU	2019
Mathison Megan A Perna	(707)637-6893 meganmathison2@gmail.com	3573 Palomar Way Napa CA 94558	CNH	Teacher	Tchr	St John's Napa CA	(707)255-0119	AU	2018
Mattes Craig R	(708)212-0388 craig.mattes.2819@gmail.com		NI	DCO	C01/2021			SP	2010
Mattes Scott W	(949)201-0335 bigwheeel71@gmail.com	3419 San Vicente Ln Katy TX 77450	PSW	Teacher	C08/2019			S	1996
Matthees Barbara J	(507)235-6021 bmatthees@midco.net	132 Linden Dr Fairmont MN 56031	MNS	Teacher	EM			SP	1970
Mattheus Ellen J Dory	(859)556-9899 ellenmattheus@yahoo.com	1477 Stillwater Blvd Saint Johns FL 32259	FG	Teacher	EM			CQ	2007
Matthews Kay L Brosowske	(708)567-7895 lambsteacher@hotmail.com	1841 Audra Cir Aurora IL 60504	NI	Teacher	EM			RF	2002
Matthews Larry A Dr	(402)643-2093	500 Heartland Park Dr # 134 Seward NE 68434	NEB	Teacher	EM			S	1958
Matthias Donley D	(224)361-6905 dmatth3055@aol.com	704 S Dryden Pl Arlington Hts IL 60005	NI	Teacher	EM			S	1958

*Multiple Assignments (See Church Worker Locator for Additional Details)
See Page 53 for the Table of Abbreviations for key to District, Classification, Position, and College abbreviations.
**C =Candidate; EM =Emeritus; the date following the C is the month and year the Candidate status began

NAME	TELEPHONE NUMBER EMAIL	STREET ADDRESS CITY/STATE/ZIP	DISTRICT	CLASS.	POSITION/ STATUS**	WHERE SERVING	OFFICE PHONE	COLLEGE/ UNIV/CQ	YR GRAD
Matthias John W	(313)570-5885 jmatt1718@msn.com	8944 Winston Redford MI 48239	MI	Teacher	Mem C	Peace Detroit MI	(313)882-0254	RF	1993
Matthis Lisa M Thaete	(303)815-9649 thaete@hotmail.com	3641 Amber Sun Cir Castle Rock CO 80108	RM	Tch/DCE	Mem C	Epiphany Castle Rock CO	(303)688-4435	S	2006
Matthys Naomi R Komarchuk	(254)547-1824 tmatthys@hot.rr.com	503 Yucca Dr Copperas Cove TX 76522	TX	Teacher	EM			S	1973
Mattila Haley K Babineau	(949)939-5061 hbabineau@abidingsavior.com	26571 Guadiana Mission Viejo CA 92691	PSW	Teacher	Tchr	Abiding Savior Lake Forest CA	(949)830-1460	IV	2020
Mattila Sarah J Dagel	sarah.mattila0385@gmail.com	409 Menage Ave Lakefield MN 56150	MNS	Teacher	Tchr	Immanuel Lakefield MN	(507)662-5718	S	2007
Mattle Elissa M Roberts	(210)845-4865 eroberts522@hotmail.com	17389 Nature Walk Trl Unit 301 Parker CO 80134	RM	Teacher	Tchr	Peace With Christ Aurora CO	(303)766-7116	AU	2008
Mattlin Tyler A	(816)308-5793 tyler.mattlin@cune.org	111 W Pocahontas Ln Kansas City MO 64114	MO	Teacher	Prin	Calvary Kansas City MO	(816)595-4020	S	2014
Mattoon Steven H	(714)496-7802 mattoons1515@gmail.com	327 E Jacaranda Ave Orange CA 92867	PSW	DCE	Pro Stf	Salem Orange CA	(714)639-1946	IV	1994
Matyas Valerie E	(248)227-3491 valerie.matyas@stpaulbaycity.org	2704 Ziegler Rd. Bay City MI 48706	MI	Teacher	Prin	St Paul Bay City MI	(989)684-4450	AA	2007
Matzke Sally L Ebert	(269)429-1545 sallymatzke@sbcglobal.net	3314 Lincoln Ave Saint Joseph MI 49085	MI	Teacher	EM			RF	1971
Mau Delmer J	(480)492-9308 brmj846@hotmail.com	36408 N Black Canyon Hwy # 577 Phoenix AZ 85086	PSW	Teacher	EM			SP	1968
Mau Jacqueline J Brandon	(480)492-9308 brmj846@hotmail.com	36408 N Black Canyon Hwy # 577 Phoenix AZ 85086	PSW	Teacher	EM			SP	1968
Mau Rita J Dargel	(847)391-9284 maushaus@juno.com	1780 E Algonquin Rd Des Plaines IL 60016	NI	Teacher	EM			S	1972
Maunula Sharon L Korpi	(320)676-3435 slkmmn@icloud.com	3941 State Highway 27 Wahkon MN 56386	MNN	Teacher	EM			SP	1983
Maurer Mary D Kliefoth	(503)389-2157 marydmaurer21@gmail.com	20344 Rae Rd Bend OR 97702	NOW	Teacher	EM			S	1977
Maurer Richard L	(765)427-8279 richmaurer@comcast.net	6705 Jeffry Ln Lafayette IN 47905	IN	Teacher	EM			S	1966
Mawhorter Julia M Hagthrop	(714)493-4572 juliemawhorter@hotmail.com	2689 Almanor Dr. Tracy CA 95304	PSW	Teacher	Tchr	Mt Calvary Diamond Bar CA	(909)861-2740	S	1985
Maxfield Melissa A Wehmeyer	(314)283-4461 melmaxfield@yahoo.com	5939 Loblolly Ct Saint Louis MO 63128	MO	Teacher	Tchr	Word of Life Saint Louis MO	(314)832-1244	CQ	2015
Maxon Sara S Stinnett	maxons@concordiaomaha.org	3036 S 159th Avenue Cir Omaha NE 68130	NEB	Teacher	Tchr	Concordia Omaha NE	(402)445-4000	CQ	2009
Maxson Karen Webber	(913)274-6888 mrsmaxson11@gmail.com	2106 S Stoneybrook St Wichita KS 67206	KS	Teacher	C07/2024			Other	2015
Maxson Stephanie C May	(260)672-9559 stephanie@stmfw.org	6833 Sweet Wood Ct Fort Wayne IN 46814	IN	Tch/DPM	Mem C	St Michael Fort Wayne IN	(260)432-2033	RF	1994
Maxwell Deryl R	(714)271-0081 deryl.maxwell@gmail.com	2336 N Bedford Dr Fullerton CA 92831	PSW	Teacher	Prin	St Paul Orange CA	(714)921-3188	S	1984
Maxwell John R III	(301)512-3660 jrmaxwell3@gmail.com	16406 Abbey Dr Bowie MD 20715	SE	Teacher	EM			S	1972
May Judy A Warneke	(260)403-3981 judy.6335m@comcast.net	6335 Dirwood Ct Fort Wayne IN 46804	IN	Teacher	EM			RF	1966
May Kimberly A Maas	(773)733-2328 kmay@stjames-lutheran.org	1002 N Mozart St Chicago IL 60622	NI	Teacher	Tchr	St James Chicago IL	(773)525-4990	RF	1995
May Kimberly A Grapatin	(317)437-6209 kmay@ourshepherd.org	1458 Labrot Ct Avon IN 46123	IN	Teacher	Tchr	Our Shepherd Avon IN	(317)271-9100	RF	1985
May Sharon L Doughty	(503)597-9066 boricagardens@comcast.net	742 SE Summerfield Pl Corvallis OR 97333	NOW	Teacher	EM			IV	1987
Mayer Diane K Graft	(813)362-6718 diane47@tampabay.rr.com	4231 Amber Ridge Ln Valrico FL 33594	FG	Teacher	EM			RF	1969
Mayer Heidi M	(718)324-3344 hmm1213@aol.com	7 Saint Marks Pl Yonkers NY 10704	AT	Teacher	Tchr	St Marks Yonkers NY	(914)237-4944	BR	1993
Mayeski Lark L Gunthert	(858)337-9985 lark.mayeski@gmail.com	10939 Salinas Way San Diego CA 92126	PSW	Teacher	EM			CQ	2009
Mayhew John R	(618)344-3153 gsls1@hotmail.com	2709 Sandstone Dr Maryville IL 62062	SI	Teacher	Prin	Good Shepherd Collinsville IL	(618)344-3153	RF	1979
Mayhew Patricia Hamilton	(817)680-9405 thamilton14@yahoo.com	8858 Comstock Ct Maple Grove MN 55311	MNS	DCE	C12/2022			CQ	2010
Maynard Patrick E	(512)851-7164	202 Oak Creek Dr League City TX 77573	TX	Teacher	Pro Stf	South Houston TX	(281)464-8299	PO	2002
Mayo Michael A	(513)358-8539 mike3462@hotmail.com	148 Magnolia Ave Northfield OH 44067	OH	Teacher	EM			S	1974
Mayrens Bonnie J Williams	(773)507-2264 bonniemayrens2@gmail.com	2631 Sarah St Franklin Park IL 60131	NI	Teacher	Tchr	St John Chicago IL	(773)736-1196	RF	1985
Mazariegos Karina L Deac	(331)575-6248 mazariegoskl@gmail.com	725 Morgan St Elgin IL 60123	NI	Deaconess	Mem C	Vida y Fe/Life Faith West Dundee IL	(224)802-2949	SL-DEAC	2023
Mazur Tammy E	(248)854-1191 tammytwo4@gmail.com	7124 Creekside Dr Lansing MI 48917	MI	Teacher	Tchr	Our Savior Lansing MI	(517)882-8665	RF	1997
Mc Auley Virginia M	(360)698-3359 mcauley@q.com	3696 NE Trout Brook Ln Bremerton WA 98311	NOW	Teacher	EM			CQ	2001
Mc Cain Jean A Geipel Deac	(636)529-1086 dcsjamc@yahoo.com	182 Ameren Way Apt 361 Ballwin MO 63021	MO	Deaconess	EM			RF	1955
Mc Camant Diane E Arndt	(817) 253-9209 diane.mccamat@me.com	2041 Glenco Ter Fort Worth TX 76110	TX	Teacher	Tchr	St Paul Fort Worth TX	(817)353-2929	CQ	1998
Mc Cann Timothy E	(714)876-4665 tkshmccann@gmail.com	13862 Mauve Dr Santa Ana CA 92705	PSW	Teacher	Tchr	St Paul Orange CA	(714)637-2640	CQ	1998
Mc Cartney Kristen R Klemz	wfmkrm80@att.net	2322 Silver Lane Dr Indianapolis IN 46203	IN	Teacher	EM			SP	1977
Mc Carty Eunice J Kimmel	(308)380-5813 Emccarty1955@gmail.com	4067 W Capital Ave Grand Island NE 68803	NEB	Teacher	EM			S	1978

*Multiple Assignments (See Church Worker Locator for Additional Details)

See Page 53 for the Table of Abbreviations for key to District, Classification, Position, and College abbreviations.

**C =Candidate; EM =Emeritus; the date following the C is the month and year the Candidate status began

NAME	TELEPHONE NUMBER EMAIL	STREET ADDRESS CITY/STATE/ZIP	DISTRICT	CLASS.	POSITION/ STATUS**	WHERE SERVING	OFFICE PHONE	COLLEGE/ UNIV/CQ	YR GRAD
Mc Carty Nancy Ann G Eberle	(763)688-1642 naneb507@outlook.com	500 1st Ave SE Apt 207 Stewartville MN 55976	MNS	Teacher	EM			SP	1980
Mc Carty Wendy L Going Dr	(308)390-2529 mcwendy@hotmail.com	2215 Del Mar Ave Grand Island NE 68803	NEB	Teacher	EM			S	1977
Mc Clain Leann E Carlson	(979)242-5097 leannmcclain@cvctx.com	107 Tomahawk Lane La Grange TX 78945	TX	Teacher	EM			S	1976
Mc Clain Mark A	(979)661-1181 markmcclain@cvctx.com	107 Tomahawk La Grange TX 78945	TX	Teacher	Mem C	St Michael's Winchester TX	(979)242-3444	S	1976
Mc Clatchey Rita I Simanis	(248)398-7171 ritamcc6@yahoo.com	28690 Diesing Dr Madison Hts MI 48071	MI	Teacher	EM			RF	1974
Mc Clellan James R	(920)819-7729 mcclellanj@newlhs.com	116 S Platten St Green Bay WI 54303	NW	Teacher	Tchr	Northeastern WI Green Bay WI	(920)469-6810	MQ	1993
Mc Clendon Greta A Kabat	(970)218-7143 greta_mcclendon@yahoo.com	P.O. Box 90 Franklin KY 42135	RM	Teacher	C07/2017			S	1991
Mc Collister David P	(636)949-2804 davemccollister@gmail.com	6 Archer Cir Saint Charles MO 63301	MO	Teacher	EM			S	1967
Mc Conkey Peggy M Haschemeyer	(309)692-5728	6806 N Wilshire Ct Peoria IL 61614	CI	Teacher	EM			CQ	1982
Mc Connell James H Dr	(512)567-2654 jim.mcconnell482@gmail.com	5832 Kenville Green Cir Kernersville NC 27284	TX	DCE	EM			S	1977
Mc Cormack Kristina R	(760)684-5350	18720 Munsee Rd Apple Valley CA 92307	PSW	Teacher	Tchr	Zion Victorville CA	(760)245-9725	PO	2004
Mc Cormick Sara A	(217)671-7904	404 W Jefferson St Mount Pulaski IL 62548	CI	Teacher	EM			RF	1993
Mc Coy Kathleen S Delventhal Deac	(561)601-0911 deackathy@aol.com	21 Marko Ln Independence OH 44131	FG	Deaconess	C07/2016			Other	1977
Mc Daniel Carol R Schroeder Dr	(949)439-1312 carolrsmcdaniel@icloud.com	9705 Standard Ave Las Vegas NV 89129	NEB	Teacher	C05/2022			S	1983
Mc Daniel Gary R Dr	(949)278-0404 garyrmcdaniel61@gmail.com	9705 Standard Ave Las Vegas NV 89129	NEB	Teacher	EM			S	1983
Mc Daniel Joyce A Koester	(618)420-9931 joycemcd64@gmail.com	5114 Plaza Pkwy Waterloo IL 62298	SI	Teacher	EM			RF	1986
Mc Donald Deborah M Crosby	(248)930-6148 debm820@gmail.com	10414 N 100 E Decatur IN 46733	IN	Teacher	EM			RF	1976
Mc Donald Ian K	ianm820@gmail.com	10414 N 100 E Decatur IN 46733	IN	Teacher	EM			RF	1973
Mc Farlin Jerry A	(708)767-0700	29872 New Castle Dr Elkhart IN 46514	IN	Teacher	EM			S	1971
Mc Farlin Vickie L Seeman	(708)331-5293	29872 New Castle Dr Elkhart IN 46514	IN	Teacher	EM			S	1971
Mc Ferran Caleb R	(714)559-2408 calebmcferran@gmail.com	20522 Montauk Circle Huntingtn Beach CA 92646	PSW	Teacher	C07/2019			IV	2007
Mc Ferran Peggy J Dickson	(636)296-4655 peggymcferran@gmail.com	3327 Amber Heights Ln Imperial MO 63052	MO	Teacher	EM			CQ	1992
Mc Ghee D M	(419)782-3533 hondomc@defnet.com	22711 Garman Rd Defiance OH 43512	OH	Teacher	EM			RF	1966
Mc Ghee Janice L Miessler	(419)782-3533 hondomc@defnet.com	22711 Garman Rd Defiance OH 43512	OH	Teacher	Tchr	St John Defiance OH	(419)782-1751	RF	1981
Mc Grath Janis M Movsesian	(586)925-2936 jmcgrath@splcs.net	50550 Bredenbury Dr Macomb MI 48044	MI	Teacher	Tchr	St Peter Macomb MI	(586)781-3434	CQ	2008
Mc Grew Katherine M Steinle	(918)251-5422 kmcgrew@icaba.org	1808 N 15th St Broken Arrow OK 74012	OK	DCM	Mem C	Immanuel Broken Arrow OK	(918)258-5506	MQ	2009
Mc Guan Sharon Loewlein	(716)803-3767 salmcg23@gmail.com	73 Dorchester Rd Buffalo NY 14222	EA	Teacher	EM			CQ	2001
Mc Guffey Christine G Wolfframm	(301)801-9751 tina@mcguffeyfamily.com	14003 Briarchip Ct Laurel MD 20708	SE	DCM	EM			MQ	2003
Mc Intosh Melody D Mayer	(210)279-0589 mellydawn@yahoo.com	123 Village Park Dr Georgetown TX 78633	TX	Teacher	Tchr	Zion Georgetown TX	(512)863-5345	AU	2001
Mc Keage Karla R Remmele Deac	pkmckeage@gmail.com	6692 Walkenhorst Rd Concordia MO 64020	MO	Deaconess	C02/2019			RF	1996
Mc Kim Gale F	(310)961-7197 gfmckim@gmail.com	28119 Pontevedra Dr Rch Palos Vrd CA 90275	PSW	Teacher	EM			RF	1972
Mc Kim Jon T	(541)771-3068 jtmckim74@gmail.com	63551 Brahma Ct S Bend OR 97701	NOW	Teacher	Tchr	Trinity Bend OR	(541)382-1832	PO	2004
Mc Kim Judy E Herndon	(310)739-8971 gjkmckim@gmail.com	28119 Pontevedra Dr Rancho Palos Verde CA 90275	PSW	Teacher	EM			RF	1971
Mc Kinney Elaine C Giro	(479)419-9788 mck004@aol.com	1801 Larkspur St Springdale AR 72764	MDS	Teacher	EM			S	1969
Mc Kinney Faith I Horn	(949)838-6959 rfmfim@aol.com	1102 Chestnut St Independence OR 97351	PSW	Teacher	EM			AU	1986
Mc Kinney Rebecca S Blanchard	bmckinney@centrallutheran school.org	501 5th St E Newhall IA 52315	IE	Teacher	Tchr	Central Newhall IA	(319)223-5271	CQ	2008
Mc Kinney Robert D	(805)390-8592 mckinr@gmail.com	1008 Hillview Cir Simi Valley CA 93065	PSW	Tch/DCE	EM			Other	1969
Mc Kinnon Margaret L Larson	(501)915-9464 mck742@sbcglobal.net	1158 Valley View Rd Lake City MN 55041	SI	Teacher	EM			CQ	1988
Mc Knight Jennifer A	(561)445-7083 jenamck@yahoo.com	976 Siesta Key Blvd Apt 315 Deerfield Bch FL 33441	FG	Teacher	C07/2016			S	2002
Mc Lain Margaret B Richter	(615)293-2211 margimclain@gmail.com	29 Calm Sea Dr Salem SC 29676	SE	Teacher	EM			SP	1975
Mc Laughlin Candace J Riddle	candymclaughlin@gmail.com	7022 White Oak Ave Hammond IN 46324	IN	Teacher	EM			RF	1982
Mc Laughlin Elizabeth H Katt Scherping	(209)629-4390 inhiminTX@gmail.com	6044 Holiday Ln North Richland Hills TX 76180	CNH	Teacher	Mem C	St Paul Tracy CA	(209)835-7438	S	1979
Mc Lay Renee E Rullman	(727)251-4271 rmclay58@gmail.com	1900 Tanglewood Dr NE St Petersburg FL 33702	FG	Teacher	Tchr	Grace Saint Petersburg FL	(727)527-6213	S	1992

*Multiple Assignments (See Church Worker Locator for Additional Details)
See Page 53 for the Table of Abbreviations for key to District, Classification, Position, and College abbreviations.
**C =Candidate; EM =Emeritus; the date following the C is the month and year the Candidate status began

NAME	TELEPHONE NUMBER EMAIL	STREET ADDRESS CITY/STATE/ZIP	DISTRICT	CLASS.	POSITION/ STATUS**	WHERE SERVING	OFFICE PHONE	COLLEGE/ UNIV/CQ	YR GRAD
Mc Loughlin Janet M Wooden	(248)321-2121 mclough3@ourshepherd.net	1357 Stonetree Dr Troy MI 48083	MI	Teacher	P/Tchr	Our Shepherd Birmingham MI	(248)645-0551	AA	1984
Mc Mahon Barbara H Heidemann	(910)284-3695	205 SE Service Rd Apt 127 Southern Pines NC 28387	CI	Teacher	EM			S	1969
Mc Martin Hugh H	(313)608-8160 goaliehugh@yahoo.com	4423 Willow View Ct Howell MI 48843	EN	DCM	EM			MQ	1992
Mc Michael Kristie L	(952)994-2620 kristie.mcmichael@gmail.com	3099 North Aquaview Terr Hernando FL 34442	FG	Teacher	EM			CQ	2006
Mc Nabb Sally A Van Pelt	(501) 690-8002 sallymcnabb85@gmail.com	4309 Oaks Bluff Dr Little Rock AR 72223	MDS	Teacher	EM			S	1974
Mc Nally Brian D	(586)295-5452 Royaloakk@yahoo.com	111 N Main St Unit 304 Royal Oak MI 48067	MI	Teacher	EM			S	1972
Mc Neil David A	davidmcneil@comcast.net	2944 Ridgeview St North Muskegon MI 49445	MI	Teacher	EM			S	1986
Mc Queen Carla J Wardin	(517)642-8829 mcqueencjm@aol.com	14540 Frost Rd Hemlock MI 48626	MI	Teacher	EM			S	1974
Mc Reynolds Ruth A Jones	(757)254-7742 ramcreynolds@yahoo.com	4800 N Courthouse Rd Providence Forge VA 23140	SE	Teacher	C07/2016			BR	1979
Mc Williams David L	(720)686-0751 dlmcwilliams@comcast.net	1543 Cherry St Brighton CO 80601	RM	Teacher	EM			S	2008
McArthur Rebecca A Winkler	(830)627-0062 rebeccamcarthur6@gmail.com	133 Ranch Estates Blvd New Braunfels TX 78130	TX	Teacher	Tchr	Cross New Braunfels TX	(830)625-3969	AU	1986
McBee Ethan J	(734)735-2502 emcbee@rockfordlutheran.org	209 Shaw St Rockford IL 61104	NI	Teacher	Tchr	Rockford Rockford IL	(815)877-9551	RF	2013
McCaig Kayla M Konow	(412)499-2212 kaylakonow@gmail.com	4315 Winding Way Fort Wayne IN 46835	IN	Teacher	C06/2023			CH	2015
McCall Erin M Balz	(651)587-3955 emccall@bcacademy.net	6803 Pine Dr Chattanooga TN 37421	MDS	Teacher	Tchr	Good Shepherd Chattanooga TN	(423)629-4661	MQ	2004
McCarthy Carrie L Rye	(443)415-2123 CARRIE.RYE@GMAIL.COM	P.O. Box 327 Wall SD 57790	SE	Teacher	Tchr	St Pauls Kingsville MD	(410)592-8100	CQ	2019
McCarthy Jennifer M Alexander	(414)217-0222 jenmc8914@gmail.com	W141N8314 Merrimac Dr Menomonee Fls WI 53051	SW	Teacher	Tchr	Zion Menomonee Falls WI	(262)781-7437	MQ	2007
McCarthy Steven J	(949)431-0020 steven.mccarthy@redeemer.net	6410 Shoal Creek Blvd Austin TX 78757	TX	DCE	Mem C	Redeemer Austin TX	(512)459-1500	IV	2017
McCartney Kassandra L	(402)322-0485 lowerkassi@gmail.com	P.O. Box 381 Kenesaw NE 68956	NEB	Teacher	Tchr	Christ Juniata NE	(402)744-4991	S	2014
McCauley Kristin R	(406)212-0485 kristinmccauley79@gmail.com	936 S Washington Shawano WI 54166	NW	Teacher	Tchr	Saint James Shawano WI	(715)524-4815	MQ	2002
McClanahan Andrea K	(573)516-0462 andreakmcc@gmail.com	3511 Cartee Rd Farmington MO 63640	MO	Teacher	Tchr	St Paul Farmington MO	(573)756-1715	S	2019
McClintock Matthew D	(952)686-4190		MNS	Teacher	Tchr	Mayer Mayer MN	(952)657-2251	CH	2008
McCloud Ian H	(712)363-1502 ian.mccloud@trinitydavenport.org	2943 E 18th St Davenport IA 52803	IE	Teacher	Tchr	Trinity Davenport IA	(563)322-5224	CQ	2024
McClure Kyle J	(828)302-1236 kmcclure@concordianc.org	4125 Hideaway Ct NE Hickory NC 28601	SE	Teacher	Tchr	Concordia Conover NC	(828)464-3324	CQ	2009
McClure Marilyn R Droege	(520)881-2252 gdmmac@aol.com	2012 E Monte Vista Dr Tucson AZ 85719	EN	Teacher	EM			RF	1967
McCollister Allison M Drake	(313)626-1038 antrimamd@yahoo.com	27010 Southwestern Hwy Redford MI 48239	MI	Teacher	Tchr	Guardian Dearborn MI	(313)274-3665	AA	1987
McComack Lara A Deac	(318)816-0642 lmccomack@calvarytopeka.org	2416 NE Grant St Topeka KS 66617	KS	Deaconess	Mem C	Calvary Topeka KS	(785)286-1431	SL-DEAC	2025
McCormick Heather N	(651)245-6938 dceheather@faithlutherantopeka.com	2613 SW 8th Ave Topeka KS 66606	KS	DCE	Mem C	Faith Topeka KS	(785)272-4214	SP	2014
McCormick Jamie L	(775)721-9628 jlmccormick314@gmail.com	11 Afton Place Boynton Beach FL 33426	FG	Teacher	Tchr	Trinity Delray Beach FL	(561)276-8458	S	2002
McCormick Micah D Owens	(812)343-8656 micahmccormick3@gmail.com	1151 N 475 E Columbus IN 47203	IN	Teacher	Tchr	St Peter Columbus IN	(812)372-1571	MQ	2011
McCown Rachel B Werner	(402)768-8826 rwerner2014@gmail.com	1744 Road 5200 Davenport NE 68335	NEB	Teacher	Tchr	Deshler Deshler NE	(402)365-7858	S	2014
McCoy Abigail M Wietfeldt	(260)385-6004 abbywietfeldt@gmail.com	15131 Peony Court Huntertown IN 46748	IN	Teacher	Tchr	Emmanuel-St Michael Fort Wayne IN	(260)422-6712	MQ	2018
McCoy Laura L Six	(406) 696-0042 teachermccoy6@gmail.com	2109 Trails End Rd Billings MT 59106	MT	Teacher	Tchr	Trinity Billings MT	(406)656-1021	S	1999
McCrory Christi L Neuf	(423)503-8168 clmccrory@gmail.com	3514 E Daley Ln Phoenix AZ 85050	PSW	Teacher	Tchr	Christ Phoenix AZ	(602)955-4830	CQ	2007
McCullough Gretchen M Krause	(907)235-7959 gretchen.mccullough@gmail.com	P.O. Box 393 Homer AK 99603	NOW	DCE	C07/2017			AU	2006
McDaniel Jonathan R			PSW	Teacher	Prin	Office of International Mission Saint Louis MO		S	2010
McDonald Mandy L Propst	(573)644-4405 mlmcdonald@embarqmail.com	8231 Tanner Bridge Rd Jefferson Cty MO 65101	MO	Teacher	Tchr	Immanuel Jefferson City MO	(573)496-3451	CQ	2006
McDonnell Debra L Moses	(440)476-9433 debra.mcdonnell10@gmail.com	9157 Katherine St N Ridgeville OH 44039	OH	Teacher	EM			RF	1983
McDonnell Ruth E Hooper Dr	(314)808-5556 ruth.mcdonnell@att.net	3615 Forest Dale Dr Saint Louis MO 63125	MO	Deaconess	Tchr	Salem Affton MO	(314)353-9242	SL-DEAC	2006
McDow Sarah M House	(985)774-9733 sarah.house007@gmail.com	665 Valentine Ct. Galt CA 95632	CNH	Teacher		California/Nevada/Hawaii District Livermore CA	(866)264-6079	AU	2012
McDowell Marsha A	(480)203-4208 martyann53@hotmail.com	3209 W Sentinel Rock Rd Phoenix AZ 85086	PSW	Teacher	EM			CQ	1993
McElroy Brenda M Oldenburg	(850)225-4185 furaha2005@outlook.com	1520 Kruse Dr Ft Walton Bch FL 32547	SO	DCO	C07/2016			SP	1997
McElroy-Breuer Paula J Mather	(414)614-0737 paula.breuer@att.net	9449 W Forest Home Ave Hales Corners WI 53130	SW	DCM	EM			MQ	1986

*Multiple Assignments (See Church Worker Locator for Additional Details)
See Page 53 for the Table of Abbreviations for key to District, Classification, Position, and College abbreviations.
**C =Candidate; EM =Emeritus; the date following the C is the month and year the Candidate status began

NAME	TELEPHONE NUMBER EMAIL	STREET ADDRESS CITY/STATE/ZIP	DISTRICT	CLASS.	POSITION/ STATUS**	WHERE SERVING	OFFICE PHONE	COLLEGE/ UNIV/CQ	YR GRAD
McEneely Angela Wiegert	(630)449-2090	1051 E Washington Blvd Lombard IL 60148	RM	Teacher	C07/2016			MQ	2003
McFall Kathleen A Lehman	(720)503-7275 tkmcfall@outlook.com	2598 E San Paulo Dr Casa Grande AZ 85194	PSW	Teacher	EM			SP	1975
McFarland Julie A	(630)222-2279 jmcfarland@ilcsbatavia.org	412 Ridgelawn Trl Batavia IL 60510	NI	Teacher	Tchr	Immanuel Batavia IL	(630)406-0157	CQ	2022
McGaffick Caitlin Smith	(414)759-3501 caitlin.mcgaffick@gmail.com		SW	Teacher	Tchr	Divine Redeemer Hartland WI	(262)367-3664	MQ	2018
McGehee Marinea Oliver	(225)907-4815 trinitylutheranschool@tlcbr.org	37451 S Park Ave Prairieville LA 70769	SO	Teacher	P/Tchr	Trinity Baton Rouge LA	(225)272-3110	CQ	2012
McGhee Stacy J Hoeft	(313)595-7762 stacyjm524@gmail.com	7966 River Run Dr Brighton MI 48116	MI	Teacher	RSO	Lutheran Special Education Ministries Ann Arbor MI	(248)419-3390	MQ	1996
McGirr Kristen B Hoffman	(574)575-9000 kristenmcgirr@trinityl.org	54845 Currant Rd Mishawaka IN 46545	IN	Teacher	Tchr	Trinity Elkhart IN	(574)674-8800	CQ	2020
McGowan Kayla E Lohman	kayla.e.lohman@gmail.com	98-325 Koauka Street Aiea HI 96701	CNH	DCE	Mem C	Our Savior Aiea HI	(808)488-3654	CH	2016
McIntosh Kathy M Nettling Franker	(913)406-1839 kathymc1113@yahoo.com	24706 W 75th Place Shawnee KS 66227	KS	Teacher	EM			RF	1978
McKinnon Brooke A Smith	(386)288-8830 bmckinnon@trinitydowntown.org	3309 E Esther St Orlando FL 32806	FG	Teacher	C06/2019			CH	2013
McKnight Allison M Heideman	(661)809-0732 allisonmmcknight@gmail.com	18420 Camborne Ave Edmond OK 73012	PSW	Teacher	C04/2025			IV	2011
McLaughlin Hannah E Birtell	(402)979-9170 dce@peacewaverly.org	520 E Vine St Yutan NE 68073	NEB	DCE	Mem C	Peace Waverly NE	(402)786-2345	S	2022
McLean Emily Deac	emclean@sllcs.org	2021 West State Rd 426 Oviedo FL 32765	S	Deaconess	Mem C	St Luke Oviedo FL	(407)365-3408	FW-DEAC	2021
McMahan Cassandra S Reinke	(402)770-1117 cmcmahan11@gmail.com	5124 Disbrow Ct Lincoln NE 68516	NEB	Teacher	EM			CQ	2010
McMahon Rachel M Leinhos	(303)641-8500 mcmahon.rachelm@gmail.com	5317 Weathervane Lane Flower Mound TX 75028	TX	Teacher	C07/2016			S	2012
McManus Austin J	(419)957-6200 austinmcmanus14@gmail.com	705 N Vernon St Dearborn MI 48128	MI	DPM	Mem C	Guardian Dearborn MI	(313)274-1414	AA	2019
McMillen Robin B Farris	(920)392-9839 robin.mcmillen18@gmail.com	3843 McCormick Village Dr Bremerton WA 98312	NOW	Teacher	Tchr	Faith Lacey WA	(360)491-3552	MQ	2006
McMullen Michelle L Davis	(712)265-0129 shellymcmullen04@gmail.com	14299 Manchester Pike Christiana TN 37037	MDS	DCE	C09/2020			S	2009
McNamara Erin M Fredenburg	(713)516-3746 themcnamaras2020@gmail.com		TX	Teacher	Tchr	Epiphany Houston TX	(713)896-1773	AU	2014
McNamara Joshua D	(832)577-8391 themcnamaras2020@gmail.com	c/o St. Paul Lutheran Church 1301 Hogan Lane Waco TX 76705	TX	DCE	Mem C	St Paul Bellmead TX	(254)799-3211	AU	2016
McNatt Kendra L	kendra.l.mcnatt@gmail.com		CNH	DCE	Mem C	Prince of Peace Fremont CA	(510)793-3366	S	2015
McPeak Aaron	(303)562-6544 thearg@aol.com	7645 Dunleer Dr Brownsburg IN 46112	IN	Teacher	C07/2022			CQ	2021
McPeak Julie A Heck Deac	(618)406-8084 jmcpeak@gracecolumbus.org	11694 N County Rd 1300 E Seymour IN 47274	IN	Deaconess	Mem C	Grace Columbus IN	(812)372-4859	RF	1998
McSwain Grant M	(314)660-6164 mcswain4077@gmail.com	2609 Brookridge Ln Saint Charles MO 63301	MO	Teacher	Tchr	Immanuel Saint Charles MO	(636)946-2656	AA	2001
McSwain Stephanie L Pottschmidt	(314)660-6163 slmcswain@yahoo.com	2609 Brookridge Lane Saint Charles MO 63301	MO	DPM	Prin	Our Savior Saint Charles MO	(636)947-8010	AA	2003
Mead Karen M	(970)214-9190 karenm@messiahlutherangj.org	620 Cris Mar St Grand Jct CO 81504	RM	Teacher	Tchr	Messiah Grand Junction CO	(970)245-2838	S	1993
Mead Katherine A	(586)651-7442 ktanne03@gmail.com	74261 Tietz St Armada MI 48005	MI	Teacher	C08/2023			CQ	2020
Meaden Lydia A	(713)857-9576	P.O. Box 8745 Houston TX 77249	TX	Teacher	Tchr	South Houston TX	(281)464-8299	MQ	2011
Meador Jill M Jaeger	(920)838-4703 jillmeador@hotmail.com	455 E Green Bay Ave Saukville WI 53080	SW	Teacher	S HS/C	Concordia University Wisconsin Mequon WI	(262)243-5700	MQ	1991
Meador Joseph K	(920)838-0809 joseph.meador96@gmail.com	113 Granville St Bethalto IL 62010	SI	Teacher	Tchr	Metro-East Edwardsville IL	(618)656-0043	MQ	2018
Mearling Stephen R	(812)401-7930 stemar@wowway.com	3015 Ivy Meadow Dr Evansville IN 47711	IN	Teacher	EM			RF	1971
Mech Katherine A Morgenson	(414)256-8171 mrsmech@hotmail.com	2630 N 86th St Milwaukee WI 53226	SW	Teacher	Tchr	Beautiful Savior Waukesha WI	(262)542-2496	MQ	2002
Mecker Karen L	(636)926-0936 kmecker@immanuelstcharles.org	581 Wyatt Dr Saint Peters MO 63376	MO	Teacher	Tchr	Immanuel Saint Charles MO	(636)946-0051	CQ	2009
Meckes Hannah K Maske	(734)773-7564 hkmeckes@gmail.com	1302 Saltbox Dr Chesterfield MO 63017	MO	Teacher	Tchr	Zion Saint Charles MO	(636)441-7424	CH	2013
Medack Madison R	(979)542-8191 medackm@trinityklein.org	6220 Fm 2920 Apt 714 Spring TX 77379	TX	Teacher	Tchr	Trinity Spring TX	(281)376-5810	CQ	2024
Medcalf Christine A Young	(630)487-1471 studentmin@grace-connect.org	N115W16877 El Camino Dr Germantown WI 53022	SW	Tch/DCE	Mem C	Grace Menomonee Falls WI	(262)251-0670	S	2017
Meder Karen A Toepke	(330)644-7493 kmeder@neo.rr.com	354 Cheshire Rd Akron OH 44319	OH	Teacher	EM			RF	1972
Meehl Mark W Dr	(402)643-5774 mark.meehl@cune.edu	628 N 2nd St Seward NE 68434	NEB	Teacher	S HS/C	Concordia University Nebraska Seward NE	(402)643-3651	S	1979
Meers Diana D Lee	(314)974-3794 dmeers07@gmail.com	4 Boenker Ct Saint Charles MO 63301	MO	Teacher	EM			CQ	1998
Meerstein Mark W	(920)461-7351 meersteinm@yahoo.com	1830 Juneberry Dr Green Bay WI 54311	NW	Teacher	Tchr	Northeastern WI Green Bay WI	(920)469-6810	MQ	1991
Mehl Hope C Colwell	(417)209-4420 hopecmehl@gmail.com		MO	Teacher	Tchr	Lutheran South Saint Louis MO	(314)631-1400	S	2017

*Multiple Assignments (See Church Worker Locator for Additional Details)
See Page 53 for the Table of Abbreviations for key to District, Classification, Position, and College abbreviations.
**C =Candidate; EM =Emeritus; the date following the C is the month and year the Candidate status began

NAME	TELEPHONE NUMBER EMAIL	STREET ADDRESS CITY/STATE/ZIP	DISTRICT	CLASS.	POSITION/ STATUS**	WHERE SERVING	OFFICE PHONE	COLLEGE/ UNIV/CQ	YR GRAD
Mehltretter Andrew W	(989)980-6795 andrew.mehltretter@gmail.com	1346 Glendale Ave Saginaw MI 48638	MI	Teacher	C07/2016			AA	2005
Mehring Rachel C	(618) 615-3453 mehring2008@live.com	8586 Ames Road Prairie Du Rocher IL 62277	SI	Teacher	C07/2016			S	2008
Mehrl Mary Jo Schmalz	(612)991-7729 marjomusic@aol.com	973 Winterberry Dr Woodbury MN 55125	MNS	DPM	Mem C	St John Woodbury MN	(651)436-6621	AA	1990
Meier Carisa D	(954)249-2259 carisa_meier@bellsouth.net	101 E McNab Rd Apt 310 Pompano Beach FL 33060	FG	Teacher	Tchr	Our Savior Plantation FL	(954)473-6888	RF	2004
Meier Cathleen J Penner	(714)330-8549 cathymeier84@gmail.com	11278 Lakehaven Dr White Lake MI 48386	PSW	Teacher	EM			S	1984
Meier David W	(847)274-5258 dmeier615@gmail.com	32w931 Hecker Dr Dundee IL 60118	NI	DCE	Mem C	Immanuel East Dundee IL	(847)428-4477	RF	2005
Meier Deborah A Vette	(618)344-0447 debmeier70@gmail.com	626 Lillian St Collinsville IL 62234	SI	Teacher	EM			S	1974
Meier Elisabeth E Maron	(630)892-0836 eem2meier@gmail.com	1958 Lakeside Dr Montgomery IL 60538	NI	Teacher	EM			RF	1977
Meier Jessica L Denninger	(571)217-4148 jlmeier717@gmail.com	8169 Barrington Dr Ypsilanti MI 48198	MI	Teacher	Tchr	St Paul Ann Arbor MI	(734)665-9117	RF	2006
Meier Kathy L Wessel	(952)994-7021 katky.meier.km@gmail.com	3430 Rodrick Cir Orlando FL 32824	FG	Teacher	EM			RF	1978
Meier Kristyna O Beine	(573)290-8940 kmeier@ilsperryville.org	623 Highway Y Altenburg MO 63732	MO	Teacher	Tchr	Immanuel Perryville MO	(573)547-6161	CQ	2023
Meier Lester T	(714)920-9278 meierfamilysocal@gmail.com	11455 N T Quarter Circle Prescott Valley AZ 86315	PSW	Teacher	Tchr	North Valley Phoenix AZ	(623)551-3454	S	1984
Meier Maureen E Pommer	(360)477-9869 maureenemeier@msn.com	1120 E 8th St Port Angeles WA 98362	NOW	Teacher	EM			RF	1969
Meier Michelle M Ronne	(816)898-2113 meiermm12@gmail.com	500 W Carrine Dr Lincoln NE 68521	NEB	Teacher	C07/2016			MQ	2001
Meier Paula K Vogts	paula5meier7@gmail.com	6757 N Woodland Ave Kansas City MO 64118	MO	Teacher	EM			CQ	1981
Meier Robert P	(650)796-0609 rpm.meier@gmail.com	1958 Lakeside Dr Montgomery IL 60538	NI	Teacher	EM			RF	1976
Meier Rosalie A Wille	roanwime@gmail.com	N76W14573 Fairfield Ct Menomonee Fls WI 53051	SW	Teacher	EM			S	1982
Meier Susan N Herbolsheimer	(847)525-6657 snmeier@gmail.com	32w931 Hecker Drive Dundee IL 60118	NI	Teacher	Tchr	Immanuel East Dundee IL	(847)428-1010	RF	2003
Meier William F	(734)740-1067 F00258141@gmail.com	4503 Washington St Midland MI 48642	MI	Teacher	Tchr	St Johns Midland MI	(989)835-7041	MQ	2013
Meineke David A	dtmeineke@aol.com	10831 Larry Dr Northglenn CO 80233	RM	Teacher	EM			RF	1977
Meineke Hannah R Ferry Dr	(414)708-7726 hmeinecke88@gmail.com	9413 Congress Park Ave Brookfield IL 60513	TX	Teacher	Pro Stf	Redeemer Austin TX	(512)459-1500	S	2010
Meinert Jill M	(507)313-1427 jmeinert@hbci.com	P.O. Box 541 Lewiston MN 55952	MNS	Teacher	Tchr	Immanuel Lewiston MN	(507)523-2228	S	1996
Meinz Gavin	(719)651-3493 gavinmeinz1@gmail.com	570 Green Meadows Dr Dallastown PA 17313	SE	DCE	Mem C	St John York PA	(717)840-0382	IV	2024
Meinzen Fern F Grotelueschen	(913)940-6462 fmeimusik@gmail.com	258 Sundance Rd Cape Fair MO 65624	MO	Teacher	EM			S	1975
Meinzen Katie L Leitermann	(414)217-2040 katiel1411@gmail.com	W132 S6838 Fennimore Ln Muskego WI 53150	SW	Teacher	Tchr	St Pauls West Allis WI	(414)541-6251	CH	2011
Meinzen Philip E	(262)707-4493 philip.meinzen@gmail.com	N96W14108 Knollcrest Cir Germantown WI 53022	SW	Teacher	EM			S	1977
Meisinger Ardel E	(336)765-2942 ardle@bellsouth.net	3110 Shannon Dr Winston Salem NC 27106	SE	Teacher	EM			S	1971
Meisinger Judith J Lange	(336)765-2942 jmeisinger@triad.rr.com	3110 Shannon Dr Winston Salem NC 27106	SE	Teacher	EM			S	1971
Meissner Daniel F	(941)776-7707 djmeissner1@hotmail.com	2525 Niagara Rd Niagara Falls NY 14304	EA	Teacher	P/Tchr	Holy Ghost Bergholtz NY	(716)731-3030	BR	2001
Meissner H D	(727)278-3269 Docmeiss76@gmail.com	3230 53rd St N St Petersburg FL 33710	FG	Teacher	Tchr	Our Savior Saint Petersburg FL	(727)344-2684	BR	1998
Meissner Herbert W	(716)731-1466 jemhwm@yahoo.com	2874 Albright Rd Ransomville NY 14131	EA	Teacher	EM			RF	1968
Meissner Karin M Strom	(303)888-8901 karin@meissnernet.com	16657 Tin Cup Ct Parker CO 80134	RM	DCE	Mem C	Our Father Centennial CO	(303)779-1332	S	2008
Meissner Laurence L Dr	(512)497-5625 laurencemeissner@gmail.com	450 Spring Valley St Hutto TX 78634	TX	Teacher	EM			S	1968
Meissner Rebekah L Hintzman	(708)414-0108 thanksgiving76@yahoo.com	7807 NE 54th Street Kansas City MO 64119	MO	Teacher	C07/2021			S	2000
Melcher Heather K Hume	(509) 988-0156 hkmelcher@yahoo.com	1658 N Kulm Rd Ritzville WA 99169	NOW	DCE	C07/2016			S	1999
Melcher Ryan S	(209)918-3511 rsmelcher@gmail.com	27319 Marigold Ct Hayward CA 94545	CNH	Teacher	Tchr	Prince of Peace Fremont CA	(510)793-3366	MQ	2004
Melendez Andrew A Jr	(612)702-1595 awmelendez@gmail.com	7141 York Ave S Apt 303 Minneapolis MN 55435	MNS	Tch/DCE	EM			CH	1959
Melin Elizabeth G Ashley Deac	(479)799-4398 lizmelin@protonmail.com	300 S H St Herington KS 67449	MO	Deaconess	RSO	Lutherans in Jewish Evangelism Saint Louis MO	(314)645-4456	SL-DEAC	2023
Mellecke Judith E Lemanski	(216)242-9525 jmellecke@mailfence.com	2108 Louis Circle Apt. B Jefferson City MO 65101	MO	Teacher	Tchr	Trinity Jefferson City MO	(573)636-7807	AA	1985
Mellen Brandie L McCallister	(660)723-4381 brandiemellen@outlook.com	29336 Highway Ae Cole Camp MO 65325	MO	Teacher	Tchr	Luth School Assoc Cole Camp MO	(660)668-4614	CQ	2020
Mellendorf Craig E	(414)840-2967 cmellendorf@gmail.com	627 Grand Ave Thiensville WI 53092	EN	Teacher	EM			S	1981
Mello Michael R	(321)888-7580 rmello@stpetersfw.org	17628 Gar Creek Rd New Haven IN 46774	IN	Teacher	Tchr	St Peters Fort Wayne IN	(260)749-5811	CH	2010

*Multiple Assignments (See Church Worker Locator for Additional Details)
See Page 53 for the Table of Abbreviations for key to District, Classification, Position, and College abbreviations.
**C =Candidate; EM =Emeritus; the date following the C is the month and year the Candidate status began

NAME	TELEPHONE NUMBER EMAIL	STREET ADDRESS CITY/STATE/ZIP	DISTRICT	CLASS.	POSITION/ STATUS**	WHERE SERVING	OFFICE PHONE	COLLEGE/ UNIV/CQ	YR GRAD
Mellor Paige D Keeling	(713)204-2907 sewawesome@live.com	15306 Streetcar Ct. Cypress TX 77429	TX	Teacher	Tchr	St Mark Houston TX	(713)468-2623	CQ	2016
Menashe Jack J Jr	(206)933-8893 menasheandsons@hotmail.com	944 13th St SE Puyallup WA 98372	NOW	Teacher	C03/2022			Other	2005
Mendez Edward W Dr	(949) 300-7738 buddy.mendez@cui.edu	32 Canopy Irvine CA 92603	PSW	Teacher	S HS/C	Concordia University Irvine Irvine CA	(949)854-8002	CQ	1996
Mendez Jennifer L Lebeck	(815)471-3006 jenniferlebeck@gmail.com	1715 N Sunnyslope Dr Mt Pleasant WI 53406	SW	Teacher	Tchr	Grace Oak Creek WI	(414)762-8755	CH	2016
Menke Hanah M Hanah Singer	(714)975-4885 hmenke@salem4u.com	2014 Woodgate Lane Tomball TX 77375	TX	Teacher	Tchr	Salem Tomball TX	(281)351-8223	AU	2020
Menke Joshua T	(563)340-9560 jmenke0711@gmail.com		TX	Teacher	Tchr	Immanuel Giddings TX	(979)542-2918	S	2011
Menke Thomas O	(512)228-9019 owennwa@aol.com	703 W Custers Creek Bnd Pflugerville TX 78660	TX	Teacher	EM			S	1982
Menke Wendy K Esterline	(812)604-5004 wendyesterline@sbcglobal.net	11540 Hwy 57 Evansville IN 47725	IN	Teacher	Tchr	Evansville Evansville IN	(812)424-7252	AA	1995
Mennicke Sally J Banning	(352)690-1623 sally.mennicke@stjohnocala.org	2101 SE 10th Ct Ocala FL 34471	FG	Teacher	EM			SP	1995
Menuge Angus J	(920)457-1605	1535 N 27th St Sheboygan WI 53081	SW	Teacher	S HS/C	Concordia University Wisconsin Mequon WI	(262)243-5700	CQ	2006
Menze Karla N Ilten	(847)394-3260 kmenze@gmail.com	211 N Eastwood Ave Mt Prospect IL 60056	NI	Teacher	Tchr	St Paul Mount Prospect IL	(847)255-0332	CQ	1995
Menzel Leah Schmidt	(321)765-4340	P.O. Box 102 1572 County Road 211 Giddings TX 78942	TX	Teacher	Tchr	St Paul Serbin TX	(979)366-9650	AU	2007
Menzel Lorna R Streufert	(256)759-8083 lormenz@aol.com	782 Honeycomb Valley Rd Grant AL 35747	SO	Teacher	EM			S	1971
Menzel Marianne Ellwein	(414)520-3542 garymenzel@att.net	10261 W Tower Ave Milwaukee WI 53224	SW	Teacher	EM			CQ	2001
Mercier Alissa	(217)899-6494 alissa.mercier@our saviors-school.org	124 Cypress Point Dr Springfield IL 62704	CI	Teacher	Tchr	Our Savior's Springfield IL	(217)546-4531	CQ	2017
Mercier Deborah Dunham Dr	(714)974-8718 drdebsmail@gmail.com	922 E Heim Ave Orange CA 92865	PSW	Teacher	EM			CQ	2003
Mercier Gary L	(262)506-8865 x749@hotmail.com	749 Homestead Trl Grafton WI 53024	SW	Teacher	EM			RF	1969
Mercier Nathan T			PSW	Teacher	Tchr	Crean Irvine CA	(949)387-1199	CQ	2010
Mercier Sandra K Fitzsimons	(714)227-1882 Mrs.Mercier77@outlook.com	22592 Revere Rd Lake Forest CA 92630	PSW	Teacher	S HS/C	Concordia University Irvine Irvine CA	(949)854-8002	IV	2006
Merker Elita Bohn	(920)224-5651 ebohn@clavarykc.com	12240 Holmes Rd Kansas City MO 64145	MO	Teacher	Tchr	Calvary Kansas City MO	(816)444-6908	MQ	2015
Merkord Deborah A Kretzmann	(210)497-7836	24819 Shining Arrow San Antonio TX 78258	TX	Teacher	Tchr	Concordia San Antonio TX	(210)479-1477	S	1977
Merkord Lanny D	(210)497-7836	24819 Shining Arrow San Antonio TX 78258	TX	Teacher	Tchr	Concordia San Antonio TX	(210)479-1477	S	1977
Merrell Linda S Gerler	(960)245-2876 lsmapn@aol.com	1133 SW Trail Ridge Dr Blue Springs MO 64015	MO	DCM	EM			MQ	2001
Merrill Kenlyn S Weller	(586)764-7546 ksm48066@yahoo.com	401 S. 17th Street Hot Springs SD 57747	SD	Teacher	EM			S	1968
Merriman Brittany E Closner	(509)307-7148 becmerriman@gmail.com	205 North 81st Ave Yakima WA 98908	NOW	DCE	Mem C	Pilgrim Spokane WA	(509)325-5738	PO	2008
Merriman Charles E	(479) 644-0374 chuck_elena@hotmail.com	35 Kirkcudbright Ln Bella Vista AR 72715	MDS	DCE	EM			S	2002
Merritt Bonnie A Judkins	(480)510-1808 bbmerritt@hotmail.com	7934 E Kenwood St Mesa AZ 85207	PSW	Teacher	EM			RF	1972
Merritt Gary E	(620)507-7040	2419 Hyatt Creek Ln Port Orange FL 32128	FG	Teacher	EM			S	1967
Merritt Karen M	karmerr12@gmail.com		TX	Teacher	Tchr	St Paul Fort Worth TX	(817)353-2929	CQ	2002
Merritt Robert A	(602)708-1972 bbmerritt@hotmail.com	7934 E Kenwood St Mesa AZ 85207	PSW	Teacher	EM			S	1970
Merritt Ronnie G	(417)869-9573	7040 W Lone Oak St Springfield MO 65803	MO	Teacher	EM			RF	1976
Merritt Timothy M		83 Circle Rd Pasadena MD 21122	SE	Teacher	Tchr	Emmanuel Catonsville MD	(410)744-0016	BR	1981
Merritt Timothy T	(972)881-4324	1701 E Park Blvd Plano TX 75074	TX	Teacher	Pro Stf	Faith Plano TX	(972)423-7448	IV	1994
Merten Polly I Olson	(503)860-3294 polly@merten.us	12900 SW Whitmore Rd Hillsboro OR 97123	NOW	Teacher	C06/2021			CQ	2016
Mertens Barbara J	(219)895-0158 barb.mertens@stjohnseward.org	2080 Star St Seward NE 68434	NEB	Teacher	Prin	St John Seward NE	(402)643-4535	S	1993
Mertens Bruce A	(507)317-3272 brucemertens64@gmail.com	402 N Main St Janesville MN 56048	MNS	Teacher	C07/2023			S	1995
Mertens Sarah J Strohschein	mertens.sj@gmail.com	15350 Ridgefield Lane Colorado Springs CO 80921	RM	Teacher	Tchr	Colorado Lutheran High School Parker CO	(303)841-5551	S	2007
Mertes John H	(559)585-8345 frog61535@aol.com	1935 N Chardonnay Pl Hanford CA 93230	CNH	DCE	EM			CQ	1992
Mertz Darryl H	(815)985-3177 darmar@ame.com	1035 Luanna Dr Rockford IL 61103	NI	Teacher	EM			RF	1984
Mertz Douglas S	(414)313-1038 dmertz1336@gmail.com	4576 W Alesci Dr Franklin WI 53132	EN	Teacher	EM			RF	1980
Mertz Joshua T	(414)303-6842 joshmertz12@gmail.com	4576 W Alesci Dr Franklin WI 53132	SW	Teacher	Tchr	Milwaukee LHS Milwaukee WI	(414)461-6000	MQ	2012
Mertz Victoria L Georgson	(414)313-0729	4576 W. Alesci Drive Franklin WI 53132	EN	Teacher	EM			RF	1981

*Multiple Assignments (See Church Worker Locator for Additional Details)
See Page 53 for the Table of Abbreviations for key to District, Classification, Position, and College abbreviations.
**C =Candidate; EM =Emeritus; the date following the C is the month and year the Candidate status began

NAME	TELEPHONE NUMBER EMAIL	STREET ADDRESS CITY/STATE/ZIP	DISTRICT	CLASS.	POSITION/ STATUS**	WHERE SERVING	OFFICE PHONE	COLLEGE/ UNIV/CQ	YR GRAD
Merz Jessica L Stoltenberg	crosseyed@juno.com	3987 Wakefield Rd Berkley MI 48072	MI	Teacher	C07/2016			CQ	2004
Merz Kathy M Miesner	(618)303-1049 kmmerz@hotmail.com	506 Cambridge Dr De Soto IL 62924	SI	Teacher	EM			S	1971
Meseck Julie A	(402)731-1923 meseck_j@msn.com	4829 Holmes St Apt 220 Omaha NE 68117	NEB	Teacher	EM			S	1968
Meseke Steven D	(586)468-0453 gymshoe52@gmail.com	37228 Ingleside St Clinton Twp MI 48036	MI	Teacher	EM			RF	1975
Messick Timothy A	(907)750-8992 tim.a.messick@gmail.com	2228 Gates Rd Hershey PA 17033	NOW	Teacher	EM			PO	1981
Messina Julie A	(708)296-3550 jmessina@stpeterlcms.org	Ono76 Woodland Ct Winfield IL 60190	NI	Teacher	Prin	St Peter Schaumburg IL	(847)885-3350	CQ	2025
Messing Elizabeth A Johnston Dankenbring	(402)768-3565 messingbetty@gmail.com	345 N 11th Street Hebron NE 68370	NEB	Teacher	C06/2022			S	1986
Mester Kim M Schultz	(563)322-5224 kim.mester@trinitydavenport.org	6140 N Linwood Ave Davenport IA 52806	IE	Teacher	Tchr	Trinity Davenport IA	(563)322-5224	S	1995
Metzger Kelsey E	(260)409-1400 k_metzger@icloud.com	1731 Highland Dr Grafton WI 53024	SW	Teacher	C08/2022			MQ	2015
Metzger Michelle R Dr	(402)525-2127 mmetzger613@gmail.com	524 E 13th St Storm Lake IA 50588	NEB	Teacher	C07/2016			S	1993
Meulendyke John A	(414)393-7690 john.meulendyke@cune.org	1407 Clearwater Dr Oconomowoc WI 53066	SW	Teacher	Tchr	Divine Redeemer Hartland WI	(262)367-3664	CQ	2013
Meunier Dennis M	(352)207-4258 meunierdennis1@gmail.com	2038 SE 16th Lane Ocala FL 34471	FG	Teacher	EM			RF	1971
Mews Amy L Batho	(260)460-7292 amymews5@gmail.com	11631 Culebra Rd Unit 158 San Antonio TX 78253	TX	Teacher	EM			SP	1977
Mews Gary R	(260)443-5390 grmews@gmail.com	11631 Culebra Rd Unit 158 San Antonio TX 78253	TX	Teacher	EM			SP	1996
Meyer Abigail R Friedrichs	(785)220-7626 ameyer@goodshepherdks.org	457 2nd Rd Bremen KS 66412	KS	Teacher	Tchr	Good Shepherd Marysville KS	(785)562-3181	CQ	2022
Meyer Aimee E	aimeehowe379@gmail.com	505 E 3rd St Neligh NE 68756	NOW	Teacher	C06/2024			S	2020
Meyer Arlene S	(847)550-6590 meyermemos@att.net	250 Mohawk Trl Apt 337 Lake Zurich IL 60047	NI	Teacher	EM			RF	1978
Meyer Arlyn	(309)262-9080 ameyer@ourshepherd.org	1385 Money Ln Danville IN 46122	IN	DCE	Mem C	Our Shepherd Avon IN	(317)271-9103	CQ	2009
Meyer Bethany C Brandvold	(320)333-5506 dcebethany@gmail.com	1379 Roselawn Ave W Roseville MN 55113	MNS	DCE	Mem C	Woodbury Woodbury MN	(651)739-5144	SP	2015
Meyer Betty J Beckman Fehlhafer		800 3rd P.O. Box 95 Utica NE 68456	NEB	Teacher	EM			S	1966
Meyer Brienna L Hirsch	(402)646-5872	3069 U St Lincoln NE 68503	NEB	Teacher	C07/2025			S	2014
Meyer Carol J Welck	cmeyer@netins.net	2647 G Ave Ladora IA 52251	IE	Teacher	EM			RF	1980
Meyer Charlotte H Hellbusch	(714)514-6326 pmeyer661@gmail.com	661 N Buttonbush Trl Orange CA 92869	PSW	Teacher	EM			S	1959
Meyer Christine A Freet	(815)889-6953 cbtlmeyer@gmail.com	11 Wildflower Dr Centerburg OH 43011	CI	Teacher	Tchr	St Paul Milford IL	(815)889-4209	AU	2000
Meyer Courtney A	(402)643-4774 courtney.meyer@cune.edu	1680 Edgewood Ln Seward NE 68434	NEB	Teacher	EM			S	1965
Meyer Cynthia F Gutz	(402)582-4741 meyercindy9101@gmail.com	86080 542nd Ave Osmond NE 68765	NEB	Teacher	Tchr	Zion Plainview NE	(402)582-3312	S	2004
Meyer Dana C Schmidt	(314)368-7187 dcsmeyer@yahoo.com	1256 Arbor Bluff Cir Ballwin MO 63021	MO	Teacher	Tchr	St Paul Des Peres MO	(314)822-2771	CQ	2018
Meyer Daniel C	(314)269-7114 dcedmeyer@gmail.com	823 Redwood Road Grand Island NE 68803	NEB	DCE	Mem C	Peace Grand Island NE	(308)384-5673	S	2005
Meyer David J	(989)354-5864 dhmeyer@charter.net	1115 Merchant St Alpena MI 49707	MI	Teacher	EM			RF	1956
Meyer David J	(616)227-0694 dmeyer@lhsa.com	47626 Clairmont Ln Chesterfield Township MI 48047	MI	Teacher	Tchr	Lutheran North Macomb MI	(586)781-9151	S	1995
Meyer David R	(206)799-0848 dmeyer.grace@gmail.com	6517 N 13th Dr Phoenix AZ 85013	PSW	Teacher	Tchr	Valley Phoenix AZ	(602)230-1600	PO	1989
Meyer Diane J Johnson	(612)799-0642 diane.j.meyer@gmail.com	26701 Muller Dr Bovey MN 55709	MNN	Tch/DCE	EM			SP	1982
Meyer Donna M Reinke	(402)364-3548 donnammcares@gmail.com	206 E 12th St Davenport NE 68335	NEB	Teacher	EM			S	1972
Meyer Emilie A Lewis	(918) 504-4005 emilieameyer@gmail.com	12193 S 104th East Ave Bixby OK 74008	RM	Teacher	C07/2016			S	2006
Meyer Eunice A Mueller	(972)394-1180	1945 Sussex Dr Carrollton TX 75007	TX	Teacher	Tchr	Prince Of Peace Carrollton TX	(972)447-0532	S	1979
Meyer Felicia R	(507)458-3223 feliciarmeyer@gmail.com	20569 County Rd 20 Lewiston MN 55952	MNS	Teacher	Tchr	Immanuel Lewiston MN	(507)523-2228	MQ	2016
Meyer Heather N Markle	(620)654-7146 hnmarkle@yahoo.com	515 Alexander St Winfield KS 67156	KS	Teacher	Tchr	Trinity Winfield KS	(620)221-9460	S	1997
Meyer Herman W	(314)892-6908 pkmeyer@postnet.com	5012 Cold Springs Ln Saint Louis MO 63128	MO	Teacher	EM			CQ	1966
Meyer James T	(760)443-5143	24030 Morella Cir Murrieta CA 92562	PSW	DCE	Mem C	Saint Johns Orange CA	(714)288-4400	IV	1995
Meyer James W			NW	DCM	Mem C	St Paul Bonduel WI	(715)758-8559	MQ	2023
Meyer Janet C	(512) 635-5097 janetmeyer9794@aol.com	1112 Chapote Ter Georgetown TX 78628	TX	Teacher	EM			S	1968
Meyer Jeaninne I Radke	(314)757-7747 meyerji@hotmail.com	1803 Rutger St Saint Louis MO 63104	MO	Teacher	EM			S	1971
Meyer Jeanne L Weber	(414)423-0010 meyorch@sbcglobal.net	5604 County Line Rd Franklin WI 53132	SW	Teacher	EM			CQ	1989

*Multiple Assignments (See Church Worker Locator for Additional Details)

See Page 53 for the Table of Abbreviations for key to District, Classification, Position, and College abbreviations.

**C =Candidate; EM =Emeritus; the date following the C is the month and year the Candidate status began

NAME	TELEPHONE NUMBER EMAIL	STREET ADDRESS CITY/STATE/ZIP	DISTRICT	CLASS.	POSITION/ STATUS**	WHERE SERVING	OFFICE PHONE	COLLEGE/ UNIV/CQ	YR GRAD
Meyer Jerome J Dr	(702)505-3776 meyerj@flhsemail.org	1525 Lucano Ln Las Vegas NV 89117	PSW	Teacher	Tchr	Faith Las Vegas NV	(702)804-4400	Other	2005
Meyer Jill D Borchardt-Hartman	(636)357-2214 jilldmeyer@yahoo.com	224 Hutchings Farm Blvd N O'fallon MO 63368	S	DCE	EM			SP	1986
Meyer JoAnne C Eberhardt	(203)268-2080 delsmeyer@sbcglobal.net	1950 S Wa Grimes Blvd Apt 214 Round Rock TX 78664	TX	Teacher	EM			RF	1959
Meyer Judith E Roehl	judithm624@gmail.com	18323 Sonterra Pl Apt 3205 San Antonio TX 78258	TX	DCM	EM			MQ	1999
Meyer Judith W Wangerin Dr	(314)725-5386 drjwm43@gmail.com	625 S Skinker Blvd Apt 1001 Saint Louis MO 63105	MO	Teacher	EM			RF	1965
Meyer Juliet L Scudder	mjcrmeyer@juno.com	1835 Abbey Ct Loveland CO 80538	RM	Teacher	EM			WN	1983
Meyer Kara J Steffens	(303) 218-0310 karasteffens@yahoo.com	3905 Carolewood Dr Cape Girardeau MO 63701	MO	Teacher	Tchr	Trinity Cape Girardeau MO	(573)335-8224	AA	2003
Meyer Karen K	(317)797-0061 kkmeyer66@gmail.com	295 Village Ln Apt 105 Greenwood IN 46143	IN	Teacher	EM			SP	1966
Meyer Karl F	(585)964-3434 kfmeyer1@gmail.com	1815 Lake Rd Hamlin NY 14464	EA	Teacher	EM			S	1969
Meyer Kay E	(316)833-2513 kaymeyer2232@rocketmail.com	4610 E Harry St Wichita KS 67218	KS	Teacher	EM			S	1988
Meyer Kellsey R Lee	(507)210-3207 kellseymeyer@gmail.com	3013 8th Ave NW Faribault MN 55021	MNS	Teacher	Tchr	Faribault Faribault MN	(507)334-7982	CQ	2018
Meyer Kevin E	(507)459-4803 kmeyer@immanuelsilo.org	20569 County Road 20 Lewiston MN 55952	MNS	Teacher	P/Tchr	Immanuel Lewiston MN	(507)523-2228	SP	1988
Meyer Kim M	(217)662-9092 kimmeterrn@hotmail.com	2509 Lindbergh Blvd Springfield IL 62704	CI	DCM	EM			MQ	2001
Meyer Kristin M Smolik	(319)329-2583 kmeyer@centrallutheranschool.org	107 Pheasant Ave Atkins IA 52206	IE	Teacher	Tchr	Central Newhall IA	(319)223-5271	CQ	2008
Meyer Lindsay J	(608)415-2299 lindsaymeyer@saintpetersls.com	395 East St Apt 13 Loganville WI 53943	SW	Teacher	Tchr	St Peter Reedsburg WI	(608)524-4066	MQ	2020
Meyer Lori A Hohenstein	(314)791-0157 lhohenstein85@gmail.com	1025 Stonecastle Drive O Fallon MO 63366	MO	Teacher	C05/2022			RF	2007
Meyer Mandy	(320)815-5460 kuhnaum@csp.edu	3350 Lake Victoria SE Alexandria MN 56308	MNN	Teacher	Tchr	Zion Alexandria MN	(320)763-4842	SP	2010
Meyer Mardelle M Juveland	(618)593-7932 drmeyer1987@gmail.com	4702 Storeyland Dr Alton IL 62002	SI	Teacher	Tchr	Trinity Edwardsville IL	(618)656-7002	SP	1986
Meyer Margaret E	(618)277-8728 dpmeyerblv@charter.net	1275 Baybrook Ct Belleville IL 62221	SI	Teacher	EM			CQ	1996
Meyer Mark J	(507)226-5495 mark.meyer@cune.org	504 6th Street South Waterville MN 56096	MNS	Teacher	Tchr	Faribault Faribault MN	(507)334-7982	S	2013
Meyer Mary L	(260)223-3019 traveling.teacher@sbcglobal.net	1259 Lily Ln Schererville IN 46375	IN	Teacher	EM			RF	1972
Meyer Neil H Jr	(619)922-3616 nhfmjr345@twc.com	5851 E 39th St Yuma AZ 85365	PSW	Teacher	EM			IV	1984
Meyer Peter J	pjmeyer72@comcast.net	716 Kinsmoor Ave Fort Wayne IN 46807	IN	Teacher	Tchr	Bethlehem Ossian IN	(260)597-7366	RF	1988
Meyer Rachel M			SW	Teacher	Tchr	Trinity Racine WI	(262)632-1766	Other	2008
Meyer Ruth P Thompson	(314)985-0805 ruth.thompson@melhs.org		SI	Teacher	Tchr	Metro-East Edwardsville IL	(618)656-0043	S	2004
Meyer Ryan D	(314)839-0306 rmeyer3422@gmail.com	3290 Kingsley Dr Florissant MO 63033	SI	DPM	Mem C	Zion Belleville IL	(618)233-2299	S	2004
Meyer Shannon E Mc Clure	(531)207-9556 shannonmeyer74@gmail.com	9215 Merryvale Dr Lincoln NE 68526	NEB	Teacher	Tchr	Messiah Lincoln NE	(402)489-3024	RF	2001
Meyer Stacey L Mueller	(402)720-9635 smeyer5@yahoo.com	6 Mayfair Ln Bella Vista AR 72715	MDS	Teacher	C05/2023			S	1993
Meyer Susan E Sharum	(931)277-5180 weems1@frontier.com	88 Cottage Cir Crossville TN 38558	MDS	Teacher	EM			RF	1972
Meyer Theresa M	(314)728-1107 tmeyer@ilsw.org	2047 Oaktimber Ct Kirkwood MO 63122	MO	Teacher	Tchr	Immanuel Wentzville MO	(636)639-9887	MQ	2022
Meyer William C	(563)514-4932 wmey5876@gmail.com	4605 Warren St Davenport IA 52806	IE	Teacher	C07/2025			S	1980
Meyerhofer Nancy L Urtel	(716)693-7253	259 Stenzil St # 1b North Tonawanda NY 14120	EA	Teacher	EM			BR	1975
Meyers Amy M Williams	(415)221-7500 awilliams@zionsf.org	445 9th Ave San Francisco CA 94118	CNH	Teacher	Tchr	Zion San Francisco CA	(415)221-7500	S	2010
Meyers Anita G Streufert	(616)897-0685 rsemeyers@gmail.com	144 Sudan Dr SE Lowell MI 49331	MI	Teacher	EM			RF	1960
Meyers Heidi Kriewaldt	(260)417-4074 nljcmom@gmail.com	3318 Walden Run Fort Wayne IN 46815	IN	Teacher	EM			RF	1977
Meyers Lisa H Dr	(989)790-1676 lmeyers@vlhs.com	3726 Dustine Dr E Saginaw MI 48603	MI	Teacher	Tchr	Valley Saginaw MI	(989)790-1676	S	1987
Meyers Rebekah N		W5062 Green Tree Rd Upper Plymouth WI 53073	SW	Teacher	Tchr	St John Plymouth WI	(920)893-5114	Other	2019
Meyr Christine A Roth	(314)477-3366 cmeyr@ilsolivette.org	10809 Waycroff Dr Saint Louis MO 63114	MO	Teacher	Tchr	Immanuel Olivette MO	(314)993-2394	S	1992
Meyr Dorothy R Lambky	(573)334-9239	1835 Niemann Dr Cpe Girardeau MO 63701	MO	Teacher	EM			S	1964
Meyr Teresa A Nash	(573)450-5997 tameyr@live.com	1731 Sherwood Dr Cape Girardeau MO 63701	MO	Teacher	EM			CQ	2002
Michael Patricia M Sadlon	(269)471-1761 PM8855@aol.com	2110 Courtside Ln Apt 205 Charlotte NC 28270	SE	Teacher	EM			RF	1968
Michaelsen Kim A Kemerling	(630)257-8853 ericmichaelsen@comcast.net	13455 Arctic Ln Lemont IL 60439	NI	Teacher	Tchr	Trinity Burr Ridge IL	(708)839-1200	RF	1985
Michel Susan J Schierbecker	(309) 373-2855 jonrebmom@yahoo.com	11 Windsor Terrace Palm Coast FL 32164	EN	Teacher	C07/2016			RF	1993

*Multiple Assignments (See Church Worker Locator for Additional Details)

See Page 53 for the Table of Abbreviations for key to District, Classification, Position, and College abbreviations.

**C =Candidate; EM =Emeritus; the date following the C is the month and year the Candidate status began

NAME	TELEPHONE NUMBER EMAIL	STREET ADDRESS CITY/STATE/ZIP	DISTRICT	CLASS.	POSITION/ STATUS**	WHERE SERVING	OFFICE PHONE	COLLEGE/ UNIV/CQ	YR GRAD
Michels Gerald L	(414)353-5370 jerrysfishroom@gmail.com	2143 Scenic Hill Trl Richfield WI 53076	SW	Teacher	EM			S	1968
Mick Beth A Kah Pyscher	(810)875-1764 bethannmick@gmail.com	4417 Wheatland Dr Swartz Creek MI 48473	MI	Teacher	Tchr	St John Rochester MI	(248)402-8000	CQ	2014
Mickelson Drew A	(608)438-7554 drew.mickelson68@gmail.com	726 Fairview Dr N West Bend WI 53090	SW	Teacher	Tchr	Living Word Jackson WI	(262)677-9353	MQ	2023
Mickley Ralph E	(573)719-3095 mickley1@comcast.net	123 Nighthawk Ln Hannibal MO 63401	CI	Teacher	EM			RF	1968
Middaugh Barbara A Kottlowski	(574)248-0664 bmiddaugh@stpaulsbremen.org	305 S Liberty Dr Bremen IN 46506	IN	Teacher	EM			RF	1973
Middleton Andrew C	(862)432-7775 acmidd23@gmail.com	405 Serrano Dr. Apt 12m San Francisco CA 94132	EN	Teacher	Tchr	West Portal San Francisco CA	(415)665-6330	MQ	2012
Middleton Mary P Hahn	(973)479-1270 mpmidd55@gmail.com	9000 Spring Mountain Way Fort Myers FL 33908	FG	Teacher	C07/2016			BR	1980
Mielke Abigail L	(574)350-3477 abbylynm@gmail.com	412 Spring Lake Blvd Granger IN 46530	IN	Teacher	Tchr	Trinity Elkhart IN	(574)674-8800	RF	2022
Mielke Hannah	(317)306-8231 hannahmielke01@gmail.com	7815 E Hanna Ave Indianapolis IN 46239	IN	DCM	RSO	Camp Lakeview Seymour IN	(812)342-4815	MQ	2023
Mielke Heidi P Algeier	(317)538-3958 hmielke@stjohnindy.org	7815 E Hanna Ave Indianapolis IN 46239	IN	DCE	C07/2016			RF	1997
Mielke Jon A Dr	(260)417-6957 jonmielke21@gmail.com	4024 Hemlock Ct Oshkosh WI 54904	SW	Teacher	EM			RF	1979
Mielke Judy M Pelz	(414)426-9446 jmielkedog@gmail.com	4024 Hemlock Ct Oshkosh WI 54904	SW	Teacher	EM			RF	1979
Mielke Karen J	(847)358-4429 kjmielke@me.com	833 E Kings Row Unit 4 Palatine IL 60074	NI	Teacher	EM			RF	1970
Mielke Mariah R	(317)358-9484 mariahrae622@gmail.com	7815 E Hanna Ave Indianapolis IN 46239	IN	Teacher	Tchr	St John Indianapolis IN	(317)352-9196	CH	2023
Mierow Douglas A	(952)447-8928 dmierow@integraonline.com	15221 Fairlawn Shores Trl SE Prior Lake MN 55372	MNS	Teacher	EM			SP	1971
Mierow John E	(414)861-8699 oflsprin@aol.com	768 Mailpouch Ln Nashville IN 47448	IN	Teacher	EM			S	1975
Mierow Nicolette K Barton	(260)418-6378 nmierow@ourshepherd.org	7115 Pluto Dr Indianapolis IN 46241	IN	Teacher	Tchr	Our Shepherd Avon IN	(317)271-9103	CH	2019
Miesner Diane L Thalacker	(573)327-0473 rainbowlanepk@yahoo.com	305 W Clinton St Napoleon OH 43545	OH	Teacher	EM			S	1979
Miesner Joshua P	(419)906-2002 joshua.miesner@gmail.com	703 W Washington St Napoleon OH 43545	OH	Teacher	Mem C	St Paul Napoleon OH	(419)592-3535	S	2008
Miesner Shannon R Mueller	(419)906-2006 shannon.miesner@gmail.com	703 W Washington St Napoleon OH 43545	OH	Teacher	Mem C	St Paul Napoleon OH	(419)592-3535	S	2008
Miesner Timothy G	(281)793-2949	6916 La Cantera Dr Fort Worth TX 76108	TX	Teacher	EM			S	1974
Miessler Megan Armstrong	(407)488-1919 mmiessler@gmail.com	2802 Strand Loop Ct Oviedo FL 32765	FG	DCE	RSO	Luth Counseling Services Inc Winter Park FL	(407)644-4692	CQ	2010
Mietzner Aaron	(702)460-1248 aaron.mietzner@eagles.cui.edu	7914 La Mesa Blvd #46 La Mesa CA 91942	PSW	Teacher	Tchr	Christ La Mesa CA	(619)462-5211	IV	2017
Mietzner Ellee T Ernst Deac	(336)944-2415 elleemietzner@gmail.com	80002a General Patton St Fort Drum NY 13603	NOW	Deaconess	C11/2022			SL-DEAC	2013
Mietzner Rebecca A Schell	(423)208-8417 bdmietzner@gmail.com	7970 Wilderness Way Ooltewah TN 37363	MDS	Teacher	EM			RF	1979
Mihm Susan V Lorenz	(217)493-6503 svmihm@aol.com	1105 Birkdale Dr Champaign IL 61822	CI	Teacher	EM			RF	1988
Mikelson Roxanne	(510)894-0397 roxiebell_2000@yahoo.com	37171 Sycamore St Apt 532 Newark CA 94560	CNH	Teacher	Tchr	Prince of Peace Fremont CA	(510)793-3366	IV	2006
Mikesell Donna L Imlah	(309)531-7987 dmikesell@mikesellonline.com	1315 E Washington St Bloomington IL 61701	CI	Teacher	EM			CQ	1992
Mikkelson Jacob R	(402)769-5730 jmikkelson98@gmail.com	13208 S 21st St Bellevue NE 68123	SI	Teacher		Southern Illinois District Belleville IL	(618)234-4767	S	2020
Miklos Jennifer L	(714)771-4027 miklos@lhsoc.org	466 W Linden Dr Orange CA 92865	PSW	Teacher	Tchr	Orange County Orange CA	(714)998-5151	IV	2004
Milam Marcia A Ebeling	(262)844-6151 mmilam@sjswb.org	313 Kames Ct Slinger WI 53086	SW	Teacher	Tchr	St Johns West Bend WI	(262)334-3077	MQ	1997
Milas Martha J Wienecke	(217)722-5469 mmilasster@gmail.com	2904 Garrison Avenue Port St Joe FL 32456	CI	Teacher	EM			RF	1979
Milbrath Elizabeth Easto	(281)701-4806 beth@epiphanypearland.org	3018 Elsbury Ln Pearland TX 77584	TX	DCE	Mem C	Epiphany Pearland TX	(281)485-7833	AU	2017
Milbrath Judith L Benedum	(414)466-1302 jmilbrath20@gmail.com	4152 Glenway St Wauwatosa WI 53222	SW	Teacher	EM			RF	1969
Mildred Erika E Schaibley	(309)230-4692 emildred1@hotmail.com	1532 Aylesbury Ln Plano TX 75075	TX	Teacher	Tchr	Faith Plano TX	(972)423-7447	RF	1999
Miles Barbara A Stromeyer	(716)694-5838 barbm1948@yahoo.com	1124 Niagara Falls Blvd N Tonawanda NY 14120	EA	Teacher	EM			CQ	1997
Miles Robert G Dr	(989)737-8106 rgmbaycity@charter.net	705 Park Ave Bay City MI 48708	MI	Teacher	EM			RF	1965
Miles Sharon R Droegemueller	miles.sharonr@gmail.com	2221 SW 1st Ave Apt 322 Portland OR 97201	NOW	Teacher	EM			RF	1968
Milinkovich Emilee R Gustin	(612)816-0433	900 E Orchard St Belle Plaine MN 56011	MNS	Teacher	C07/2025			CQ	2023
Millard Molly E	mmillard112@gmail.com		PSW	Teacher	Tchr	Christ Phoenix AZ	(602)955-4830	S	2011
Millen Jai D	(515)231-9498 jai.millen@gmail.com	1531 Edgewood Dr Milford IA 51351	IW	DCE	RSO	Camp Okoboji Milford IA	(712)337-3325	S	2016
Miller Alexandra A Schmidt	(989)295-1465 aamiller174@gmail.com	247 E Prairie Ave Lombard IL 60148	FG	Teacher	C07/2016			CH	2014
Miller Brinn E	(260)443-3766 brinn.miller.12@gmail.com		MO	Teacher	Tchr	Lutheran North Saint Louis MO	(314)389-3100	CH	2024

*Multiple Assignments (See Church Worker Locator for Additional Details)

See Page 53 for the Table of Abbreviations for key to District, Classification, Position, and College abbreviations.

**C =Candidate; EM =Emeritus; the date following the C is the month and year the Candidate status began

NAME	TELEPHONE NUMBER EMAIL	STREET ADDRESS CITY/STATE/ZIP	DISTRICT	CLASS.	POSITION/ STATUS**	WHERE SERVING	OFFICE PHONE	COLLEGE/ UNIV/CQ	YR GRAD
Miller Carrie	(414)737-5479 cmiller7307@gmail.com	316 N 111th St Wauwatosa WI 53226	SW	Teacher	Tchr	Immanuel Brookfield WI	(262)781-7140	MQ	1996
Miller Christal A Carpenter	(541)912-8790 christalamiller@yahoo.com	3695 Sanders St Eugene OR 97404	NOW	Teacher	C07/2016			CQ	2015
Miller Christine A Brown	(714)330-6851 camiller1127@gmail.com	1425 Madison St Tustin CA 92782	PSW	Teacher	Tchr	Crean Irvine CA	(949)387-1199	IV	1999
Miller Christine E Reed	(219)663-1578 millerc@trinitycp.org	250 S. Indiana Ave Crown Point IN 46307	IN	Teacher	Prin	Trinity Crown Point IN	(219)663-1578	RF	1996
Miller Cindy Roemer	(210) 724-7313 cindylmiller.2021@gmail.com	356 County Road 128 Floresville TX 78114	TX	Teacher	Tchr	Shepherd Hills San Antonio TX	(210)614-3742	AU	1982
Miller Corwin L	(303)241-5860	1515 N 18th St Grand Jct CO 81501	RM	Teacher	Tchr	Messiah Grand Junction CO	(970)245-2838	S	1975
Miller Curtis D	(605)929-0486 curtismiller@concordiaprepschool.org	c/o Concordia Prep School 1145 Concordia Dr Towson MD 21286	SE	Teacher	Tchr	Concordia Towson MD	(410)825-2323	S	2011
Miller Deanna L	(719)568-0607 miller.deanna85@gmail.com	1853 West Dr Arnold MO 63010	MO	Teacher	Tchr	St John Arnold MO	(636)464-7303	CQ	2018
Miller Deborah L Gerth	(260)557-8988 sunlover1952@aol.com	11827 Hoagland Rd Hoagland IN 46745	IN	Teacher	EM			S	1974
Miller Duane E	(414)334-9994 duaneandrose.miller@gmail.com	3905 Silver Bow Dr Green Bay WI 54313	NW	Teacher	EM			S	1970
Miller Ellen K Boda	(314)472-5122 emswmr78@gmail.com	2108 Crimson Oaks Ct Saint Louis MO 63129	MO	Teacher	EM			RF	1977
Miller Enid S Althaus	(970)216-4710 enidsue@gmail.com	1515 N 18th St Grand Jct CO 81501	RM	Teacher	EM			S	1975
Miller Eunice A Timm	(503) 886-9955 euniceam@msn.com	11275 Chelan Loop West Linn OR 97086	IN	Teacher	EM			RF	1964
Miller Hailey J Moore	students@memoriallutheran.net		SD	DCE	Mem C	Memorial Sioux Falls SD	(605)334-7133	S	2011
Miller Heather M	(605)359-7825 hmiller@sflutheranschool.com	1803 W 10th St Sioux Falls SD 57104	SD	Teacher	Tchr	Sioux Falls Sioux Falls SD	(605)335-1923	CQ	2012
Miller Heidi K Sanders	(760)221-3206 heidi.sanders@gmail.com	3814 Ferndale Ave Baltimore MD 21207	SE	Teacher	Tchr	Emmanuel Catonsville MD	(410)744-0015	S	2006
Miller James L	(262)696-4280 jimandkathymiller1982@gmail.com	16640 Cherry Hill Dr Brookfield WI 53005	SW	Teacher	EM			SP	1971
Miller James M	(224)254-3356 jskem@aol.com	764 Shivers Loop The Villages FL 34762	FG	Teacher	EM			S	1974
Miller Jane A	(630)947-9532 thirdgradestp@gmail.com	1301 E Indian Trl Apt 2 Aurora IL 60505	NI	Teacher	Tchr	Immanuel Palatine IL	(847)359-1936	CQ	1986
Miller Jane R Roloff	(262)345-5986 jane23513@gmail.com	N78 W17343 Wildwood Dr 518 Menomone Flls WI 53051	SW	Teacher	EM			RF	1959
Miller Jennifer A Oczepek	(931)626-2482	3205 Windy Cape Lane League City TX 77573	TX	Teacher	C07/2016			AA	1998
Miller Jennifer L Kaiser Deac	(847)401-0479 mrsjenimiller@gmail.com	35 Coopers Glen Dr SW Mableton GA 30126	EN	Deaconess	C07/2016			FW-DEAC	2009
Miller Joanne M Doan	(360)750-3886 jimjo9999@msn.com	9317 NE 86th St #208 Vancouver WA 98662	NOW	Teacher	EM			AA	1988
Miller John W	(314)472-5122 jmjazz2108@gmail.com	2108 Crimson Oaks Ct Saint Louis MO 63129	MO	Teacher	EM			RF	1976
Miller Jordan D	(281)734-7598 jordan.miller@cune.org	21718 Sarasota Spice St Tomball TX 77377	TX	DPM	Mem C	Salem Tomball TX	(281)351-8223	S	2015
Miller Julia A Ritter	kinderjam@hotmail.com	8026 S 2300 E Ogden UT 84405	RM	Teacher	Tchr	St Paul Ogden UT	(801)392-6368	SP	1981
Miller Kaitlyn Stradtmann	(779)300-0322 kaitlynmiller@concordiaprepschool.org	14 Glenamoy Rd Unit 202 Lutherville Timonium MD 21093	SE	Teacher	Tchr	Concordia Towson MD	(410)825-2323	S	2019
Miller Karen L Sheehan	(714)330-2278 teachermiller7@gmail.com	13242 Chestnut St Westminster CA 92683	PSW	Teacher	EM			IV	1997
Miller Karl G	(713)240-2286 dfm@fishersofmen.org	6602 Lussier Dr Sugar Land TX 77479	TX	DCM	Mem C	Fishers Of Men Sugar Land TX	(281)242-7711	MQ	2022
Miller Kimberly A Pellegrino	(214)448-9878 kimimiller24@gmail.com	15320 Roller Coaster Rd Colorado Spgs CO 80921	FG	DCM	C07/2016			MQ	2002
Miller Kristin A Bird	(440) 487-5617 kristinmiller1968@yahoo.com	1651 Mentor Ave Apt 3504 Painesville OH 44077	OH	Teacher	Tchr	Our Shepherd Painesville OH	(440)357-7776	RF	1990
Miller La Mar Jr	(507)776-2678 millersports5@frontier.com	414 N 3rd Ave E Truman MN 56088	MNS	Teacher	P/Tchr	St Paul Truman MN	(507)776-2801	S	1978
Miller Lawren L	(402)851-1951 miller.lawren@gmail.com	55043 840th Rd Norfolk NE 68701	NEB	Teacher	EM			S	1973
Miller LeAnn	(402)649-2846	234 W 5th St Gibbon MN 55335	MNS	DCE	Mem C	St Peter's Gibbon MN	(507)834-6676	S	2014
Miller Michael A	(210)647-7313 mamiller_98@yahoo.com	356 County Road 128 Floresville TX 78114	TX	Teacher	Prin	Lutheran San Antonio TX	(210)694-4962	CQ	1997
Miller Pamela S Loesch	(314)520-0603 milltown5223@att.net	1793 Woodwind Dr Imperial MO 63052	MO	Teacher	EM			S	1974
Miller Patti R Rezner Deac	(251)751-5209 reznermiller@yahoo.com	11530 Sandy View Drive Saint Louis MO 63146	MO	Deaconess	Mem C	Village Ladue MO	(314)993-1834	FW-DEAC	2022
Miller Paul M	(618)635-2964 pm7951@yahoo.com	8763 Klondike Rd Worden IL 62097	SI	Teacher	EM			CQ	1978
Miller Perry M	(402)750-4377 principal@1stglencoe.org	2906 Mach 1 Dr Norfolk NE 68701	MNS	Teacher	Prin	First Glencoe MN	(320)864-3317	IV	1989
Miller Rachel E Snyder	(618)473-2641 rmiller@stjohnsredbud.org	9441 Trappers Creek Dr Red Bud IL 62278	SI	Teacher	Tchr	Good Shepherd Collinsville IL	(618)344-3151	RF	1988
Miller Rachel J Mierow	(317)682-7464 rmierow@ourshepherd.org	1875 Windsor Ln Danville IN 46122	IN	Teacher	Prin	Our Shepherd Avon IN	(317)271-9100	RF	2005
Miller Rachel M	(303)909-2563	214 Missouri Ave Ellsworth KS 67439	RM	Teacher	C07/2016			SP	2008

*Multiple Assignments (See Church Worker Locator for Additional Details)
See Page 53 for the Table of Abbreviations for key to District, Classification, Position, and College abbreviations.
**C =Candidate; EM =Emeritus; the date following the C is the month and year the Candidate status began

NAME	TELEPHONE NUMBER EMAIL	STREET ADDRESS CITY/STATE/ZIP	DISTRICT	CLASS.	POSITION/ STATUS**	WHERE SERVING	OFFICE PHONE	COLLEGE/ UNIV/CQ	YR GRAD
Miller Richard J	(928)443-1784 rjmilla44@yahoo.com	3113 Briarwood Prescott AZ 86301	PSW	Teacher	EM			RF	1966
Miller Sarah E Lentz	(714)883-8148 sarah.miller0616@gmail.com	2425 E Powhatan Ave Anaheim CA 92806	PSW	Teacher	Tchr	Hephatha Anaheim CA	(714)637-0887	CQ	2019
Miller Shay J Watson	shayj.miller@gmail.com	1771 Highway 51 Bancroft NE 68004	IN	DCE	C07/2016			S	2011
Miller Stacy K Porter	(440)610-8131 smiller@bethanyparma.com	4025 Harding Dr Westlake OH 44145	OH	Teacher	Tchr	Bethany Parma OH	(440)884-1230	CQ	2021
Miller Stephanie M Schroeder	(815)289-5926 smiller@rockfordlutheran.org	4584 Cinnamon Ct Rockford IL 61114	NI	Teacher	C09/2025			RF	1998
Miller Susan	(410)298-8498 smiller@elsbaltimore.org	7819 Paddock Way Baltimore MD 21244	SE	Teacher	P/Tchr	Emmanuel Catonsville MD	(410)744-0015	CQ	2001
Miller Susan Z Zoeller	(937)707-5420 smiller@sjsmarysville.org	1380 Woodline Dr. Marysville OH 43040	OH	Teacher	Tchr	St John's Marysville OH	(937)644-5540	CQ	2019
Miller Tammy L Wendland	(248)396-2855 tammy@ststephenwaterford.org	3923 Reseda Rd Waterford MI 48329	MI	Teacher	Mem C	St Stephen Waterford MI	(248)673-6621	AA	1986
Miller Tessa L Pacilli	(970)683-8233 special5_me@yahoo.com	610 Cottage Meadows Ct Grand Jct CO 81504	RM	Teacher	Tchr	Messiah Grand Junction CO	(970)245-2838	MQ	2005
Milleville Judy A Kopplin	(618)483-5308	3512 E 900th Ave Altamont IL 62411	CI	Teacher	EM			CQ	1996
Mills Elaine E	(415)861-9333 millselaine149@gmail.com	1225 Appaloosa Way Sevierville TN 37876	EN	Teacher	EM			CQ	1994
Mills Kathleen V Loomis Deac	+61490397520 dcskathleen@gmail.com	2087 Morningside Dr Florence KY 41042	OH	Deaconess	C07/2016			FW-DEAC	2010
Millwood Teresa M Miesner	(812)568-9137 tmillwood722@gmail.com	12318 Wolf Run Rd Noblesville IN 46060	IN	Teacher	Pro Stf	Cornerstone Carmel IN	(317)814-4262	S	2003
Milnikel Jenifer J Engel	(269) 470-6532 jmilnikel@comcast.net	2845 Washington Ave Saint Joseph MI 49085	MI	Teacher	EM			SP	1973
Milosch Daniel P	(907)337-1541 dmilosch@alaska.net	7850 Linda Ln Anchorage AK 99518	NOW	Teacher	EM			RF	1974
Milroy Lori J Pless	(989)412-3666 lorimilroy4@gmail.com	427 Wiltshire Blvd Oakwood OH 45419	SE	Teacher	EM			CQ	2015
Milz Charlene K Bammann	(775)315-6720 cmilz717@gmail.com	1534 Oreana Dr Carson City NV 89701	CNH	Teacher	EM			CQ	1983
Minda Keith A	(989)326-1168 kminda@peacesaginaw.org	2825 Emerald Park Saginaw MI 48603	MI	Teacher	EM			S	1976
Mindach Rex A	(320)491-5864 rexmindach@gmail.com	48285 250th St Gaylord MN 55334	MNS	Teacher	Tchr	Immanuel Gaylord MN	(507)237-2804	SP	1985
Minshall Isabel E	(714)749-4922 isabel.minshall@gmail.com	6456 E Lookout Ln Anaheim CA 92807	PSW	Teacher	Tchr	Christ Brea CA	(714)529-0892	CQ	2024
Minster David	(480)286-1387 dce.davee@gmail.com	962 N Golden Key St Gilbert AZ 85233	PSW	DCE	Mem C	Gethsemane Tempe AZ	(480)839-0906	S	2012
Miranda Tracy M Oglesby	(815)370-3600 tracy.miranda@mymetronet.net	1994 Somerset Dr Romeoville IL 60446	NI	Teacher	Tchr	Immanuel Mokena IL	(708)479-5600	SP	1995
Mirly Ethan A	(907)982-2074 ethan.mirly@gmail.com	1621 S Bonanza St. Palmer AK 99645	NOW	DCE	Mem C	St John Palmer AK	(907)745-3338	S	2018
Mirly Timothy S	(573)576-2968 tmirlymail@gmail.com	374 N W Dewburry Ter Jensen Beach FL 34957	FG	Teacher	Prin	Redeemer Stuart FL	(772)286-0911	RF	1987
Mischnick Walter T	(574)303-9293 lead1221@yahoo.com	6215 Tezcuco Ct Granbury TX 76049	TX	Teacher	EM			RF	1972
Miske Shirley J Dr	(651)415-9715 smiske@pobox.com	2838 Lakeview Ave Saint Paul MN 55113	SI	Teacher	EM			RF	1976
Miskimen David M	(262)677-9353 dmiskimen@lwlhs.com	N4353 Oak Lawn Ests Iron Ridge WI 53035	SW	Teacher	Tchr	Living Word Jackson WI	(262)677-9353	MQ	1994
Miskimen Grace V Betts	(573)893-4981	1532 La Hacienda Ct Jefferson Cty MO 65101	MO	Teacher	EM			S	1962
Miskimen Harvey D	miskmo@aol.com	1532 La Hacienda Ct Jefferson Cty MO 65101	MO	Teacher	EM			S	1962
Mitchell Joel D	(281)240-8375	3111 Timber View Ct Sugar Land TX 77479	TX	Teacher	C07/2017			AU	1995
Mitsch Marlena J Ressie	(651)393-5114 jmmitsch08@gmail.com	1227 Skillman Ave W Roseville MN 55113	MNS	Teacher	Tchr	King Of Kings Roseville MN	(651)484-9206	SP	2002
Mitteis Mary A Hudnall	(618) 578-1014 maryannmitteis@gmail.com	17973 Staunton Bunker Hill Rd Staunton IL 62088	SI	Teacher	Tchr	Zion Staunton IL	(618)635-2880	IV	1985
Mittelstaedt Susan A	(260)267-2917 samjn146@aol.com	1227 W Branning Ave Fort Wayne IN 46807	IN	Teacher	EM			S	1977
Mitts Dawn A Michalk		775 County Road 140 Georgetown TX 78626	TX	Teacher	Tchr	Grace Killeen TX	(254)441-5519	AU	1996
Mitts Erika K	(402)730-7119 ektroester@gmail.com	1314 SW Georgetown Dr Lees Summit MO 64082	EN	DCE	C12/2024			S	2017
Mizel Danielle L	daniellemizel@gmail.com	3905 Goshawk Dr Rock Springs WY 82901	MO	DCE	Tchr	Office of International Mission Saint Louis MO		S	2008
Mlnarik Kathryn J Douglas	(701)680-9843 katie.mlnarik@gmail.com	804 E 64th St Sioux Falls SD 57108	SD	Teacher	Tchr	Sioux Falls Sioux Falls SD	(605)335-1923	S	2010
Mo Ku	(414)552-9259 kumo341@gmail.com	4921 S 26th St Milwaukee WI 53221	SW	Teacher	Tchr	Trinity Mequon WI	(262)242-2045	MQ	2022
Mockler Gaye L	(805) 238-0335 gmockler@trinitypaso.com	1811 Redwood Dr Paso Robles CA 93446	CNH	Teacher	Tchr	Trinity Paso Robles CA	(805)238-0335	S	1986
Mockler Heather A	(602)377-9127 hmockler@hotmail.com	3531 Taffrail Ln Oxnard CA 93035	PSW	Teacher	C07/2020			S	2001
Moe Jeana A Manning Deac	(260)416-8472 dcsjeana@yahoo.com	3055 Saint Louis Ave Fort Wayne IN 46809	IN	Deaconess	Mem C	Mount Calvary Fort Wayne IN	(260)747-4121	RF	1984
Moehle Sharilyn R Lueking	(618)633-2413 kmoehle@madisontelco.com	9143 Trio Ln Edwardsville IL 62025	SI	Teacher	EM			RF	1966

*Multiple Assignments (See Church Worker Locator for Additional Details)

See Page 53 for the Table of Abbreviations for key to District, Classification, Position, and College abbreviations.

**C =Candidate; EM =Emeritus; the date following the C is the month and year the Candidate status began

NAME	TELEPHONE NUMBER EMAIL	STREET ADDRESS CITY/STATE/ZIP	DISTRICT	CLASS.	POSITION/ STATUS**	WHERE SERVING	OFFICE PHONE	COLLEGE/ UNIV/CQ	YR GRAD
Moehlenkamp Marilyn E Dr	(708)702-5429 marilyn.moehlenkamp@cuchicago.edu	1800 N 74th Ct Elmwood Park IL 60707	NI	Teacher	EM			S	1969
Moehring Cheryl E	(361)946-5769 cmoehring@outlook.com	2246 Appellation New Braunfels TX 78132	TX	Teacher	EM			CQ	2018
Moehring David P	(231)398-9457 davmoeh@aim.com	822 Locust St Manistee MI 49660	MI	Teacher	EM			RF	1973
Moehring Judith A Siegert	(260)223-0487	2933 Old Orchard Rd Fort Wayne IN 46804	IN	Teacher	EM			RF	1978
Moehring Mary M Bahr	(231)398-9457 mmoehring@trinitymanistee.com	822 Locust St Manistee MI 49660	MI	Teacher	EM			S	1974
Moeller Amy L Varcoe	(630)667-7869 amoellerc3f3@gmail.com	2896 Stoney Creek Dr Elgin IL 60124	NI	Teacher	EM			RF	1978
Moeller Bonnie J Busacker	(503)430-5967 loubon@comcast.net	711 Kalex Ln Forest Grove OR 97116	NOW	Teacher	Tchr	Forest Hills Cornelius OR	(503)359-4853	S	1991
Moeller Janet K Biermann	(515)230-6676 janetmoeller75@gmail.com	9925 Marnewood Dr. Johnston IA 50131	IW	Teacher	EM			RF	1975
Moeller Jeffery R	(330)618-7837 dcemoeller@gmail.com	3239 Crecida Way Carlsbad CA 92010	PSW	Tch/DCE	C06/2018			S	1987
Moeller Marcy J Woerman	(619)913-8220 marcylamesa@yahoo.com	2211 Massachusetts Ave #6-G Lemon Grove CA 91945	PSW	Teacher	EM			S	1968
Moeller Steven W	(630)532-7739 smoeller618@gmail.com	2896 Stoney Creek Dr Elgin IL 60124	NI	Tch/DCE	EM			RF	1978
Moellering Dianne Rueger	(260) 413-1934 mrsdmoe@yahoo.com	10317 Greenwood Lakes Dr New Haven IN 46774	IN	Teacher	EM			S	1972
Moellering Thomas P	(219)483-3281 mrsdmoe@yahoo.com	10317 Greenwood Lakes Dr New Haven IN 46774	IN	Teacher	EM			S	1972
Moen Brittany D	(952)564-7440 brittanymoen@zion-cologne.org	1118 Skybrooke Ave Waconia MN 55387	MNS	Teacher	Tchr	Zion Cologne MN	(952)466-3379	CQ	2018
Moennig Amanda L	(417)388-0168 amoenning@slsfreistatt.org	16589 Lawrence 1030 Wentworth MO 64873	MO	Teacher	P/Tchr	Trinity Freistatt MO	(417)235-7300	CQ	2017
Moentmann Sherry L	(314)309-6632 ckarakan@gmail.com	2135 N. Western Ave Apt 7e Liberal KS 67901	KS	Teacher	C07/2016			S	2000
Moerbe Alicia L	(979)540-7447 amoerbe@stpaulserbinschool.org	P.O. Box 81 Warda TX 78960	TX	Teacher	Tchr	St Paul Serbin TX	(979)366-9650	CQ	2019
Moerbe Mary J Veith Deac	(580)262-0806 mary.jack@gmail.com	12218 Rocky Knoll Dr Houston TX 77077	TX	Deaconess	Tchr	Memorial Houston TX	(713)782-4022	FW-DEAC	2008
Moerbe Randall R	(979)822-2742 moerbe@suddenlin.net	9 Ranchero Rd College Sta TX 77845	TX	Tch/DCE	EM			S	1973
Moerbe Susan L Ritter	(361)522-6694 sulymo@msn.com	803 E Henderson St Bishop TX 78343	TX	Teacher	EM			S	1974
Moerer Lucille P	(248)652-9458 lmoerer@gmail.com	3250 Walton Blvd Apt 115 Rochester Hills MI 48309	MI	Teacher	EM			S	1970
Moesch Jason R	(414)464-5367	W183S6581 Jewel Crest Dr Muskego WI 53150	SW	Teacher	Tchr	Milwaukee LHS Milwaukee WI	(414)461-6000	MQ	1993
Moffitt Marissa R Logan	(330)926-7012 mmoffitt03@gmail.com	6318 W California Rd Fort Wayne IN 46818	IN	Teacher	Tchr	Sub Bethlehem Fort Wayne IN	(260)484-7873	MQ	2002
Mogelvang Kami J Kuesel	(239)272-6964 kueselk@gmail.com	7633 Welshire Blvd Fort Wayne IN 46815	FG	DCE	Mem C	Grace Naples FL	(239)261-7421	SP	2007
Mohlenhoff Richard W	(586)465-2645 rchrchm@aol.com	8350 Plumbrook Rd Apt 104 Sterling Heights MI 48313	MI	Teacher	EM			RF	1960
Mohr Renita A Bandelow	(217) 316-7044 drmamam4@comcast.net	2629 Rogers Ct Quincy IL 62301	CI	Teacher	EM			RF	1983
Mohr Rhonda J	(515)573-0010 rhonda@iowadistrictwest.org	409 Kenyon Rd Suite B Fort Dodge IA 50501	IW	Tch/DCE	D Ex/S	Iowa West District Fort Dodge IA	(515)576-7666	S	1986
Moilanen Karen K Hemming	(517)787-2274 kmoilanen@att.net	2012 Forest Park Dr Jackson MI 49201	MI	Teacher	EM			CQ	1999
Mol James M	(810)471-2736 jimmol@me.com	1117 Plainview Ave Seward NE 68434	NEB	Parish Assist	EM			AA	1982
Mol Rachel M Iltis	(989)860-1684 rachelmol220@gmail.com	244 Mistwood Ln North Aurora IL 60542	NI	Teacher	C07/2016			S	2013
Moldenhauer Allison R Gruhn	(936)446-7303 agruhn@hotmail.com	397 Shelton Rd Madison AL 35758	SO	Teacher	Tchr	Grace Huntsville AL	(256)881-0553	S	2002
Moldenhauer David J	(248)231-5802 david.moldenhauer@melhs.org	701 Copper Line Rd Maryville IL 62062	SI	Teacher	Tchr	Metro-East Edwardsville IL	(618)656-0043	CH	2014
Moldenhauer Donna L Sprehe	(217)438-3872 gmoldenhauer@yahoo.com	415 Pine View Dr Auburn IL 62615	CI	Teacher	Mem C	Trinity Auburn IL	(217)438-6820	RF	1995
Molin Douglas C	(504)390-0422 dougmolin@gmail.com	1120 W Lockeford St Apt 3 Lodi CA 95240	CNH	Teacher		California/Nevada/Hawaii District Livermore CA	(866)264-6079	SP	1982
Molinari Matthew	(916)580-5592 mattmolinari@me.com	2229 Eastwood Dr Roseville CA 95747	CNH	DCE	Pro Stf	Lutheran Church Extension Fund Saint Louis MO	(314)965-9000	IV	2005
Molitor Laura M Snyder	(314)443-4318 lsnyder0315@gmail.com	9107 Mauna Loa Ln Houston TX 77040	TX	Teacher	C07/2021			CH	2014
Molitor Lisa A Olson	(714)393-6871 lisaannmolitor@gmail.com	2509 N Meadow Grove Rd Orange CA 92867	PSW	Teacher	Tchr	Salem Orange CA	(714)633-2366	IV	2010
Moll Brett T	(217)341-0745 brett.t.moll@gmail.com	5412 Turnstone Rd Springfield IL 62711	CI	Teacher	Tchr	Trinity Springfield IL	(217)787-2323	CQ	2015
Moll Grace E Huesmann	(262)685-7997 grace.moll@orlcne.org	119 S 2nd Street Seward NE 68434	NEB	Teacher	Tchr	Our Redeemer Staplehurst NE	(402)535-2251	Other	2022
Moll Marion C	(505)286-2145 marionmoll7@msn.com	P.O. Box 1007 Cedar Crest NM 87008	RM	Teacher	EM			S	1967
Moll Patricia J Johnson	(505)286-2145 marionmoll7@msn.com	P.O. Box 1007 Cedar Crest NM 87008	RM	Teacher	EM			S	1967

*Multiple Assignments (See Church Worker Locator for Additional Details)
See Page 53 for the Table of Abbreviations for key to District, Classification, Position, and College abbreviations.
**C =Candidate; EM =Emeritus; the date following the C is the month and year the Candidate status began

NAME	TELEPHONE NUMBER EMAIL	STREET ADDRESS CITY/STATE/ZIP	DISTRICT	CLASS.	POSITION/ STATUS**	WHERE SERVING	OFFICE PHONE	COLLEGE/ UNIV/CQ	YR GRAD
Moll Thomas A	(260)487-1150 tmollicus@gmail.com	1510 Clearwater Ln Fort Wayne IN 46825	IN	DCE	RSO	Lutheran Ministries Media Inc Fort Wayne IN	(260)471-5683	S	2005
Mollak Krista N Stanford	(573)645-6968 mollakkn@gmail.com	1507 N 144th Ave Cir Omaha NE 68154	PSW	Teacher	C05/2024			S	2019
Mollwitz Katherine E	(262)305-7672 kmollwitz@trinityfreistadt.com	9827 N Melrose Ct Mequon WI 53097	SW	Teacher	Tchr	Trinity Mequon WI	(262)242-2045	MQ	2023
Molnau Kari A Dowell	(414)745-3232	20440 Hunters Run Brookfield WI 53045	SW	Teacher	Tchr	Divine Redeemer Hartland WI	(262)367-3664	MQ	2001
Molotla Elizabeth V Loch Deac	(773)870-1867 lisamolotla@gmail.com	412 N Cook Street Plano IL 60545	NI	Deaconess	C12/2018			CH	2014
Mondary Miranda S	(760)885-8510 mirandamondary@yahoo.com	9220 Acuff Ln Lenexa KS 66215	KS	Teacher	Tchr	Hope Shawnee KS	(913)631-6940	PO	2016
Mondragon Virginia I Carter	(310)548-4583 mondragon8@att.net	28605 Vista Madera Rch Palos Vrd CA 90275	PSW	Teacher	EM			S	1975
Monfre Susan E Sodemann	(414)861-1123 suemonfre@gmail.com	14225 W North Oak Blvd New Berlin WI 53151	EN	Teacher	EM			RF	1979
Monkemeyer Andrew W	(630)392-4303 dmonk2388@aim.com	7820 E Quintana Ave. Mesa AZ 85212	PSW	Teacher		Pacific Southwest District Irvine CA	(949)854-3232	CH	2011
Monroe Kelly M Muehlbrandt	(586)413-0126 monroerk@comcast.net	49478 Golden Park Dr Shelby Twp MI 48315	MI	Teacher	Tchr	St John Fraser MI	(586)293-0333	AA	1990
Monson Kathryn P Porisch	(507)834-6651 kmons@centurytel.net	63885 290th St Gibbon MN 55335	MNS	Teacher	EM			S	1972
Montag Mary J Borer	(724)352-9235 sarverbell@zoominternet.net	139 Keck Rd Sarver PA 16055	EA	Teacher	EM			RF	1972
Montanez Ramon E	(956)357-7107 f1sher0men@aol.com	5417 Plainview Dr El Paso TX 79924	RM	DCO	EM			SP	1998
Montgomery Andrew M	(812)552-1696 andy_montgomery30@hotmail.com	10928 Elata Dr Fort Worth TX 76108	TX	Teacher	Prin	St Paul Fort Worth TX	(817)353-2929	CH	2013
Montgomery Benjamin M	(308)660-1753 bmontgomery@stpaulnapoleon.org		OH	Teacher	Tchr	St Paul Napoleon OH	(419)592-3535	S	2016
Montgomery Deann L Hauch	(308)530-4603	1809 N Sherman Ave North Platte NE 69101	NEB	Teacher	Tchr	Our Redeemer North Platte NE	(308)532-6421	MQ	1987
Montgomery Laura B Roberts	(636)575-4252 lmontgomery@lesastl.org	3535 Possum Ridge Dr Imperial MO 63052	MO	Teacher	RSO	Lutheran Elem School Assn Saint Louis MO	(314)200-0790	CQ	2003
Montney Matthew R			MI	Teacher	Tchr	Westland Westland MI	(734)422-2090	CQ	2020
Moodie Keith E	(801)261-7406 kmmforever@yahoo.com	5406 S York St Murray UT 84117	RM	Teacher	EM			S	1977
Moody Jane A Markert	(978)887-9171 jamapple1@verizon.net	133 Fox Point Rd Newington NH 03801	NE	Teacher	EM			RF	1961
Moody Wanda E Nusser	(210)657-4201 wandam@concordia-satx.com	730 Sunrise Trl Spring Branch TX 78070	TX	Teacher	Tchr	Concordia San Antonio TX	(210)479-1477	CQ	1995
Mook Lynn M Krause	(561)736-2397 lmook@trinitydelray.org	9464 Longmeadow Cir Boynton Beach FL 33436	FG	Teacher	EM			SP	2008
Moon Emily N			NW	Teacher	C07/2024			MQ	2018
Moon Kathryn J Schlieger	(810)280-5109 kjmoon@stpaulflint.com	2388 S Elms Rd Swartz Creek MI 48473	MI	Teacher	Tchr	St Paul Flint MI	(810)239-6200	CQ	2006
Moon Tracy A Bresnahan	(262)397-7034 tracy.moon@cuw.edu	1704 Highland Dr Grafton WI 53024	SW	Teacher	C08/2017			MQ	2005
Mooney Erin E Taylor	(309)912-2991 mooney@lhssc.org	417 Nantucket Dr. Saint Charles MO 63301	MO	Teacher	Tchr	St Charles Saint Peters MO	(636)928-5100	CQ	2021
Mooney Jeanelle A Harfst	(573)634-2247	2300 Yorktown Dr Jefferson Cty MO 65109	MO	Teacher	EM			CQ	1996
Mooney Terry M Sr	(309)648-1549 tmoon1956@yahoo.com	11 Stahl Pl Bartonville IL 61607	CI	Teacher	P/Tchr	Christ Peoria IL	(309)637-1512	S	1978
Moore Bonnie K Burghard	(210)573-2292 bonniemoore8488@gmail.com	5010 Spring Forest Dr Houston TX 77091	TX	Teacher	Tchr	Our Savior Houston TX	(713)290-8277	AU	1988
Moore Cassandra A Hagerman			NOW	DCE	C11/2022			IV	2008
Moore Gary L	(417)380-1816 rom8.28@sbcglobal.net	1707 W Elfindale St Apt 9 Springfield MO 65807	MO	DCM	EM			MQ	2010
Moore George T	(650)348-7255 peguy5@comcast.net	2112 Hale Dr Burlingame CA 94010	EN	Teacher	EM			RF	1978
Moore Jesse Jesse Wisroth	jmoore@ielschool.org	865 W Works St Sheridan WY 82801	WY	Teacher	Tchr	Immanuel Alliance NE	(308)762-4663	S	2009
Moore Katherine L	(818)269-1123 katy.moore@concordiaschoolsla.org	14047 Saddle Ridge Rd Sylmar CA 91342	PSW	Teacher	Prin	Lutheran HS Assoc Southern CA Granada Hills CA	(818)368-0892	SP	1983
Moore Kelly L Schmidt	(817)919-6489 kmoore1374@gmail.com	4 Shiloh Pl Sherwood AR 72120	MDS	Teacher	Tchr	Grace Little Rock AR	(501)663-0755	CQ	2014
Moore Kimberly Sherwin Deac	(920)851-5873 deaconess@teamjesusliberty.org	518 N Grover St Liberty MO 64068	MO	Deaconess	Mem C	St Stephen Liberty MO	(816)781-3377	SL-DEAC	2017
Moore Kimberly A Webster	(317)859-0757	962 Vicksburg North Dr Greenwood IN 46143	IN	Teacher	Tchr	Calvary Indianapolis IN	(317)783-2305	S	1985
Moore Krista R Fricke	(360)771-3316 jkmoorejaz@msn.com	16507 NE 92nd Cir Vancouver WA 98682	NOW	Teacher	Tchr	Trinity Portland OR	(503)288-6403	PO	1996
Moore Linda M Ritterbusch-Redeker	(309)264-9459 moorelinda@rocketmail.com	36 Prairie Village Pl Morton IL 61550	CI	Teacher	EM			S	1974
Moore Lindsey A Chrismer	(636)627-1747 lmoore@ilsw.org	15321 Devils Boot Rd Marthasville MO 63357	MO	Teacher	Tchr	Immanuel Wentzville MO	(636)327-4416	CQ	2019
Moore Lisa M Reimer	(407)481-9601 lrmoore856@yahoo.com	2 Fountainebleau Cir Daytona Beach FL 32118	FG	Teacher	EM			RF	1978
Moore Pamela J	moore@hopeglendora.org	560 Teakwood Ave La Habra CA 90631	PSW	Teacher	Tchr	Hope Glendora CA	(626)335-5315	IV	1988
Moore Ronald W	(864)417-2963 rwmronald@gmail.com	101 Aberdeen Chase Dr Apt D Easley SC 29640	SE	DCO	EM			SP	2000

*Multiple Assignments (See Church Worker Locator for Additional Details)
See Page 53 for the Table of Abbreviations for key to District, Classification, Position, and College abbreviations.
**C =Candidate; EM =Emeritus; the date following the C is the month and year the Candidate status began

NAME	TELEPHONE NUMBER EMAIL	STREET ADDRESS CITY/STATE/ZIP	DISTRICT	CLASS.	POSITION/ STATUS**	WHERE SERVING	OFFICE PHONE	COLLEGE/ UNIV/CQ	YR GRAD
Moore Samuel D	(816)385-0589 sammoore@splsconcordia.org		MO	Teacher	Tchr	St Paul Concordia MO	(660)463-2291	S	2020
Moore Steven C	(920)843-2403 steve.moore@faithfv.org	W6025 Coral Ct Appleton WI 54915	NW	DPM	Mem C	Faith Appleton WI	(920)739-9191	CQ	2021
Moore Timothy P	(813)518-1634 tmoorep@reagan.com	508 S Park Ave Steeleville IL 62288	SI	Teacher	Prin	St Mark Steeleville IL	(618)965-3838	S	1997
Moorehouse Christine A Massey	chrisamo12@gmail.com	8101 Sendero Trail Apt 3734 Fort Worth TX 76177	TX	Teacher	Tchr	St Paul Fort Worth TX	(817)332-2281	CQ	2009
Moorman Colleen	(501)690-1359 colleen.moorman@sbcglobal.net	11404 Hickory Hill Rd Little Rock AR 72211	MDS	Teacher	EM			CQ	1999
Morales Ligia I Deac	liyetita@yahoo.com	c/o Prince Of Peace Lutheran Church 1515 S Semoran Blvd Orlando FL 32807	FG	Deaconess	Mem C	Prince Of Peace Orlando FL	(407)277-3945	SL-DEAC	2013
Moran Mark A	(920)427-4228 bugsymoran555@gmail.com	620 Wagon Wheel Ln Marysville OH 43040	OH	Teacher	Tchr	St John's Marysville OH	(937)644-5540	MQ	1987
Moran Valerie E Timler	(920)362-0793 valeriemoran@yahoo.com	620 Wagonwhell Ln Marysville OH 43040	OH	Teacher	Tchr	St John's Marysville OH	(937)644-5540	MQ	1987
Moravec Kathleen M Hinz		15233 Walnut Rd Oak Forest IL 60452	NI	Teacher	EM			RF	1979
Morden Karen T Walleman	(989)239-0087 karen.morden@hcls.org	3645 Frandor Pl Saginaw MI 48603	MI	Teacher	Tchr	Holy Cross Saginaw MI	(989)793-9723	CQ	2016
Moreno Lisa M Kuske	(402)371-3898 nebraskalisa@gmail.com	1401 Homewood Dr Norfolk NE 68701	NEB	Teacher	C07/2018			S	1989
Morey Sydney A	(812)344-5872 smorey@whitecreek.org	1433 W 950 S Columbus IN 47201	IN	Teacher	Tchr	White Creek Columbus IN	(812)342-6832	CQ	2025
Morgan Katie M	(785)230-4319 Katie.morgan@cune.org		RM	DCE	Mem C	Family Of Christ Colorado Springs CO	(719)481-2255	S	2011
Morgensen Shannon C Riley	(424)255-0036 s.c.morgensen@gmail.com	3765 San Anseline Ave Long Beach CA 90808	PSW	Teacher	Tchr	Bethany Long Beach CA	(562)420-7783	IV	2001
Morgenthaler Shirley K Kloha Dr	(708)302-2759 shirley.morgenthaler@gmail.com	1000 Sunset Ridge Rd Apt 323 Northbrook IL 60062	NI	Teacher	EM			RF	1959
Moriarity Linda R Herrmann		1568 Bent Creek Rd Concord VA 24538	PSW	Teacher	EM			RF	1970
Moritz Joel W	(815)321-3683 Jmoritz@ilcp.org	3630 N Alder Dr Hoffman Est IL 60192	NI	Teacher	Tchr	Immanuel Palatine IL	(847)359-1936	RF	1996
Moritz Lorelle R Baumgart	(269)858-8889 lorellemoritz@hotmail.com	P.O. Box 92 Marcellus MI 49067	MI	Teacher	EM			RF	1968
Moritz Todd J	toddjmoritz@gmail.com	16175 Cache St. Fountain Valley CA 82708	PSW	Teacher	D Ex/S	Pacific Southwest District Irvine CA	(949)854-3232	CQ	2010
Morlock Amie N Zillinger	amiemorlock@gmail.com	2800 SW Villa West Dr Apt 84 Topeka KS 66614	KS	Teacher	C08/2016			S	2012
Morlock Kristi J	(460)740-0079 kmorlock.calvary@yahoo.com	P.O. Box 363 Colstrip MT 59323	RM	Teacher	Tchr	Peace W Christ Aurora CO	(303)693-5618	PO	2005
Morner Andrew S	(714)686-7472 andrewmorner92@gmail.com	178 N Singingwood St. Unit 1 Orange CA 92869	PSW	Teacher	Tchr	St Johns Orange CA	(714)288-4406	IV	2015
Morner Leah M Busch	(714)697-7708 lmorner@yahoo.com	921 Grovemont St Santa Ana CA 92706	PSW	Teacher	Tchr	St Johns Orange CA	(714)288-4406	IV	1986
Morner Timothy S	(714)299-9678 mornerfamily@yahoo.com	921 Grovemont St Santa Ana CA 92706	PSW	Teacher	EM			IV	1987
Moro Martin L III	(734)756-1626 morom3@yahoo.com	29435 Evergreen St Flat Rock MI 48134	MI	Teacher	RSO	MOST Ministries Ann Arbor MI	(734)994-7909	S	1981
Morrill Stephen	(989)482-1900 sjm85@yahoo.com	595 Crying Bird Ave Las Vegas NV 89178	PSW	Teacher	Tchr	Faith Las Vegas NV	(702)804-4400	MQ	2008
Morris Cheryl J Gruenhagen	(989) 513-5366 wncmorris@charter.net	933 Poplar Dr Saginaw MI 48609	MI	Teacher	Tchr	St Peter Hemlock MI	(989)642-8188	SP	1983
Morris Edward W	(918)344-4588 ewmorris1027@gmail.com	311 Lakeview Drive Apt 208 Enid OK 73701	OK	DCE	EM			S	1996
Morris Leslie R		1932 E Waltann Ln Phoenix AZ 85022	EN	Teacher	EM			S	1964
Morris Sarah P	(214)384-4398 sarah.morris@ctx.edu	1990 Forest Hills Blvd Bella Vista AR 72715	MDS	DCE	Mem C	Bella Vista Bella Vista AR	(479)855-0272	AU	2011
Morris Wendy E Falkenberg	(615)480-4866 wendy.morris@oursaviorfl.org	4705 Alexandria Ct Palmetto FL 34221	FG	Teacher	Prin	Our Savior Saint Petersburg FL	(727)344-1026	RF	1989
Morrison Janet L Kozak	(440)884-7730 jan.morr@cox.net	2939 Whispering Shores Dr Vermilion OH 44089	OH	Teacher	EM			RF	1977
Morrison Jeri I Deac	blestmuch@yahoo.com	1749 Meadow Lane Drive Seward NE 68434	NEB	Deaconess	Mem C	St John Seward NE	(402)643-2983	RF	2002
Morrison Judy E Heiden	(317)753-8978 fishdrywall@gmail.com	8615 Aberdeenshire Ct Indianapolis IN 46259	IN	Teacher	EM			RF	1984
Morrison Laura R Wilson	(618)406-0121 laura.morrison@melhs.org	821 Andra Maryville IL 62062	SI	Teacher	Tchr	Metro-East Edwardsville IL	(618)656-0043	S	1996
Morrissey Erik S		9910 Green Valley Ln Houston TX 77064	TX	Teacher	Tchr	Our Savior Houston TX	(713)290-9087	S	1995
Morrissey Sarah R Ganze	(281)682-6863 smorrissey@oslschool.org	9910 Green Valley Lane Houston TX 77064	TX	Teacher	Tchr	Our Savior Houston TX	(713)290-8277	AU	2007
Morrow Vicki Reinisch	(310)569-6512 morrows6836@sbcglobal.net	8922 Fleetwing Ave Los Angeles CA 90045	PSW	Teacher	EM			RF	1976
Morschen Stephanie C Friske	(952)442-9205 lorenandsteph@aol.com	13310 County Road 32 Cologne MN 55322	MNS	Teacher	Tchr	Zion Cologne MN	(952)466-3379	S	1988
Mort Sarah B	(269)363-6938 s.mort@trinityberrien.org	5042 Woodward Coloma MI 49038	MI	Teacher	Tchr	Trinity Berrien Springs MI	(269)473-1811	AA	2019
Mortensen Gayle E Bergemann	(218)828-4007 mgkemort@gmail.com	8783 Dal Mar Dr Brainerd MN 56401	MNN	Tch/DCE	Mem C	Prince Of Peace Baxter MN	(218)829-7092	SP	1985
Mortenson Phyllis J Weise	(262)989-5027 pjmortenson@gmail.com	1813 Cloverview Street West Bend WI 53095	SW	Teacher	EM			RF	1977

*Multiple Assignments (See Church Worker Locator for Additional Details)

See Page 53 for the Table of Abbreviations for key to District, Classification, Position, and College abbreviations.

**C =Candidate; EM =Emeritus; the date following the C is the month and year the Candidate status began

NAME	TELEPHONE NUMBER EMAIL	STREET ADDRESS CITY/STATE/ZIP	DISTRICT	CLASS.	POSITION/ STATUS**	WHERE SERVING	OFFICE PHONE	COLLEGE/ UNIV/CQ	YR GRAD
Morthole Annika B	(410)747-2363 amorthole@stpauls-lutheran.org	1119 Baker Ave Baltimore MD 21207	SE	Teacher	EM			BR	1999
Morton Barbara E Dr	(949)433-1259 barbara.morton@cui.edu	1285 Luther Ln Apt 331 Arlington Heights IL 60004	NI	Teacher	EM			RF	1967
Morton Christina M Kuester	(949)292-4071 tinamorton6@gmail.com	8525 E Lindner Ave Mesa AZ 85209	PSW	Teacher	Tchr	Christ Greenfield Gilbert AZ	(480)892-8521	IV	1998
Morton Linda J Capps	(614)596-1363 lindamort300@sbcglobal.net	96 Pinebrooke Dr Westerville OH 43082	PSW	Teacher	EM			S	1973
Morton Rachel E	(903)353-2293 rmorton@stjohnswestbend.org	809 S 6th Avenue West Bend WI 53095	SW	DPM	Mem C	St John West Bend WI	(262)334-4901	MQ	2011
Mosemann Russell J Dr	(507)722-1364 russell.mosemann@cune.org	217 W Ferndale Dr Council Blfs IA 51503	IW	Teacher	EM			S	1984
Moses Elaine A Ristau	(216)835-0696 elaine.moses2011@gmail.com	1206 Brookview Blvd Parma OH 44134	OH	Teacher	EM			CQ	2001
Moses Lori J Rumsey	(812)343-7997 lmoses@trinigycougars.org	12792 W Old Nashville Rd Columbus IN 47201	IN	Teacher	Tchr	Trinity Seymour IN	(812)524-8547	IV	1992
Moses Timothy J	(216)469-8567 tmoses2015@gmail.com	6318 W California Rd Fort Wayne IN 46818	IN	Teacher	Tchr	Sub Bethlehem Fort Wayne IN	(260)484-7873	RF	2019
Moses William R	(216)835-0716 bill.moses2013@gmail.com	1206 Brookview Blvd Parma OH 44134	OH	Teacher	EM			CQ	2023
Mosley Anita R	anita_mosley@icloud.com	14896 N Escondido Cir Litchfild Prk AZ 85340	PSW	Teacher	Tchr	Trinity Litchfield Park AZ	(623)935-4665	IV	2005
Moss Abigail C	(813)789-7143 abbymoss@messiahtampa.com	3702 Carrollwood Place Cir Apt 305 Tampa FL 33624	FG	DFLM	Mem C	Messiah Carrollwood FL	(813)961-2182	AA	2006
Moss Corey J	(512)269-8908 corey.moss@popcs.org	3919 Walden Way Dallas TX 75287	TX	Teacher	Prin	Prince Of Peace Carrollton TX	(972)447-0532	AU	2002
Moss Emily L Hente	(314)315-0395 emilyhente@yahoo.com	5740 Hidden Stone Dr Saint Louis MO 63129	FG	DCE	C07/2016			S	2009
Moss Katie t Timm Dr	(763)496-5346 katie.moss@stjlutheran.org	9671 97th Pl N Maple Grove MN 55369	MNS	DPM	Mem C	St John's Corcoran MN	(763)420-2426	MQ	2010
Moss Nicklaus W	(863)608-0475 nmoss@stpaullakeland.org	5822 Oakmont Ln Lakeland FL 33812	FG	DCE	Mem C	St Paul Lakeland FL	(863)644-7710	S	2005
Mosser Rachel A Zimmerman	(618)635-7509	218 E 1st St Staunton IL 62088	SI	Teacher	Tchr	Zion Staunton IL	(618)635-2880	CQ	2015
Motter Brett A	(260)403-5453 brettmotter@frontier.com	1407 Sevan Lake Ct Fort Wayne IN 46825	IN	Teacher	Tchr	St Peter's Fort Wayne IN	(260)749-5816	CQ	2020
Motzkus Kyle M	(920)203-2298 gbay66@gmail.com	6011 162nd St Chippewa Falls WI 54729	SW	Teacher	Prin	Trinity Wisconsin Dells WI	(608)253-3241	MQ	1987
Moudy Lauren E Chumbley	(214)415-8939 laurenemoudy@gmail.com		TX	Teacher	C05/2022			S	2021
Mouis Jessica A Dawson	(630)802-3996 jessdawson@hotmail.com	6160 Red Gate Ln Yorkville IL 60560	NI	Teacher	Tchr	Cross Yorkville IL	(630)553-7861	S	2000
Moulds Russell G Dr	(402)803-6047 380sjave@gmail.com	1615 253rd Dr Seward NE 68434	NEB	Teacher	EM			S	1976
Mountford Mary J Falk	(713)825-7352 marymountford49@gmail.com	5500 Del Bello Ln Manvel TX 77578	TX	Teacher	EM			S	1971
Moyer Daniel E Dr	(714)595-2871 dan.moyer@creanlutheran.org	7710 Rockybrook Way Stanton CA 90680	PSW	Teacher	P/Tchr	Crean Irvine CA	(949)387-1199	IV	2000
Moyer Jean E	(562)429-8775	3085 Conquista Ave Long Beach CA 90808	PSW	Teacher	EM			IV	1991
Moyer Robin Deac	(870)476-2081 rmoyer@mid-southlcms.com	18828 Highway 141n Lafe AR 72436	MDS	Deaconess	D Ex/S	Mid-South District Cordova TN	(866)373-1343	SL-DEAC	2025
Moza Paulette J Hayes	(480)275-5934 paulettemoza@aol.com	2604 N Hogan Ave Mesa AZ 85215	NI	Teacher	EM			RF	1970
Mrosko Gary L	(507)332-9853 gbmrosko@charter.net	1311 10th St SW Faribault MN 55021	MNS	Teacher	EM			RF	1963
Muck Ruth E Ophardt	drlmuck@aol.com	1614 Calvary Cir Apt 201 Charlottesvle VA 22911	EA	Teacher	EM			S	1970
Muck Susan K Thumm	(517)265-7973	2349 Sword Hwy Adrian MI 49221	MI	Teacher	EM			RF	1968
Mudd Stephanie K	(314)210-0347 smudd@zionharvester.org	497 Coussot Parc Saint Charles MO 63303	MO	Teacher	Tchr	Zion Saint Charles MO	(636)441-7425	CQ	2017
Muehl Mark P	(260)241-4845 markmuehl62@gmail.com	1525 Rapids Way Fort Wayne IN 46825	IN	Teacher	Pro Stf	LCMS Foundation Saint Louis MO	(314)965-9000	RF	1984
Muehl Paul H		3220 Independence Dr Apt 312 Danville IL 61832	CI	Teacher	EM			S	1957
Muehler Faith E Deac	(314)278-3212 fmuehler@lutheranfamilyservice.org	3500 Edgewood Rd NE Apt 411 Cedar Rapids IA 52402	IE	Deaconess	RSO	Lutheran Family Service Fort Dodge IA	(515)573-3138	CH	2025
Muehler Hope V	(314)403-9684 muehlerh@trinitycr.org	3500 Edgewood Rd NE #411 Cedar Rapids IA 52402	IE	Teacher	Tchr	Trinity Cedar Rapids IA	(319)362-6952	CH	2024
Muehler Jesse C	(314)717-6201 jessemuehler@gmail.com	9921 Wayne Trace Fort Wayne IN 46816	IN	Teacher	Tchr	St John-Emmanuel Monroeville IN	(260)639-0123	CH	2022
Mueller Benjamin J	(262)370-6575 ben@splco.org	5561 Rd E Oconomowoc WI 53066	SW	Teacher	Tchr	St Paul Oconomowoc WI	(262)567-5001	CQ	2011
Mueller Bonnie J Neubauer	(518)369-1492 bonniemueller89@gmail.com	831 Hillary Ct Longwood FL 32750	AT	Teacher	Tchr	Our Savior Colonie NY	(518)459-2248	RF	1989
Mueller Bonnie L Stender Pevestorf	(573)824-5757 bonloumueller@aol.com	P.O. Box 485 Lester Pr MN 55354	SI	Teacher	EM			SP	1966
Mueller Brett A	(507)841-2132 brett4c99@gmail.com	485 May Valley Ln Apt 1 Fenton MO 63026	MO	Teacher	Tchr	Our Savior Fenton MO	(636)343-7511	S	2022
Mueller Carol A Chandler	(713)702-5364 muellerc@trinityklein.org	5414 Mineral Creek Ct Spring TX 77379	TX	Teacher	Tchr	Trinity Klein Klein TX	(281)376-5773	AU	1984
Mueller Carol R Krupski	(512)630-7908 crmueller@yahoo.com	8010 S. 97th St. Lincoln NE 68526	NEB	Teacher	EM			RF	1979

*Multiple Assignments (See Church Worker Locator for Additional Details)
See Page 53 for the Table of Abbreviations for key to District, Classification, Position, and College abbreviations.
**C =Candidate; EM =Emeritus; the date following the C is the month and year the Candidate status began

NAME	TELEPHONE NUMBER EMAIL	STREET ADDRESS CITY/STATE/ZIP	DISTRICT	CLASS.	POSITION/ STATUS**	WHERE SERVING	OFFICE PHONE	COLLEGE/ UNIV/CQ	YR GRAD
Mueller David W Dr	(512)630-7066 muellerdw@gmail.com	8010 S. 97th Street Lincoln NE 68526	NEB	Tch/DCE	EM			RF	1980
Mueller Dawn M Klein	(989)493-3148 dmueller3169@gmail.com	2850 Kennely Rd Saginaw MI 48609	MI	Teacher	Tchr	St Lorenz Frankenmuth MI	(989)652-6141	S	1992
Mueller Dawn M Olson	(630)346-7027 dmueller1231@gmail.com	6917 Celtic Ct Austin TX 78754	TX	Teacher	EM			S	1986
Mueller Dawn T Miehlke	(618)478-5544 dmuellerteacher@hotmail.com	15516 State Route 127 Nashville IL 62263	SI	Teacher	Tchr	Trinity-St John Nashville IL	(618)327-8561	AA	1983
Mueller Delores H I Mussler	(636)329-8955 erich.mueller@sbcglobal.net	600 Breeze Park Dr Apt 309 Weldon Springs MO 63304	MO	Teacher	EM			RF	1977
Mueller Donna K Schlichting	(832)236-3941 dmueller4@sbcglobal.net	3802 Evening Trail Dr Spring TX 77388	TX	Teacher	Tchr	Trinity Spring TX	(281)376-5810	S	1981
Mueller Glenn F	(402)727-1796 marymueller_99@yahoo.com	1924 Phelps Ave Fremont NE 68025	NEB	Teacher	EM			RF	1955
Mueller Gregory G	(309)795-9812 dcehog@derbyworks.net	14328 161st St W Taylor Ridge IL 61284	CI	Tch/DCE	Mem C	St Matthew Milan IL	(309)787-4295	RF	1979
Mueller Jackson S	(262)613-8287 jacksonmueller3232@gmail.com	1615 Parkwood Blvd Sheboygan WI 53081	SW	Teacher	Tchr	St John Plymouth WI	(920)893-5114	MQ	2021
Mueller Jill N Benitz	(308)762-9208 rmueller@bbc.net	1031 Dakota Ave Alliance NE 69301	WY	Teacher	Tchr	Immanuel Alliance NE	(308)762-4663	S	1987
Mueller Joann M Lowery	(262)293-3838 jmmueller6@gmail.com	W155N7021 Amberleigh Cir Menomonee Fls WI 53051	SW	Teacher	EM			RF	1969
Mueller John L	jnmueller@wi.rr.com	N80W13494 River Park Dr Menomonee Fls WI 53051	SW	Teacher	EM			RF	1956
Mueller John N	(909)936-3955 johnmueller12391@gmail.com	939 East Center Way Janesville WI 53545	SW	DCE	Mem C	St Paul's Janesville WI	(608)754-4471	CH	2014
Mueller Jonathan K	(314)368-4805 jon.mueller@lutheransouth.org	10202 Sagegate Dr Houston TX 77089	TX	Teacher	Tchr	Lutheran Education Association Friendswood TX	(281)617-5189	S	2007
Mueller Joy A Blasingame	(651)485-9694 joyannmueller@gmail.com	4650 Links Village Dr B102 Ponce Inlet FL 32127	FG	Teacher	EM			SP	1977
Mueller Kaja M Heinecke	(319)541-4827 kaja@ourredeemer.org	4530 580th St Lone Tree IA 52755	IE	DCE	Mem C	Our Redeemer Iowa City IA	(319)338-5626	SP	2004
Mueller Kathleen M	(330)808-5883 kmmuel@yahoo.com	3916 S Arlington Rd #1200 Uniontown OH 44685	OH	Teacher	EM			S	1972
Mueller Kirk H	(314)385-9277 kirk.mueller@lcms.org	4543 Nadine Ct Saint Louis MO 63121	MO	Teacher	Pro Stf	LCMS Foundation Saint Louis MO	(314)965-9000	S	1975
Mueller Kristen J Uffelman	(507)458-8261 joyful_202@hotmail.com	22551 County Rd 25 Lewiston MN 55952	MNS	Teacher	C06/2023			S	2002
Mueller Laura L	(262)527-1804 lauralmueller@yahoo.com	1048 Quinlan Dr Unit C Pewaukee WI 53072	SW	Teacher	EM			S	1984
Mueller Lindsay E Meyer	(989)450-8914 mueller7241@gmail.com		MI	Teacher	Tchr	Valley Saginaw MI	(989)790-1676	RF	2007
Mueller Lynn R	(573)824-5757	1315 Pcr 430 Frohna MO 63748	SI	Teacher	EM			S	1967
Mueller Mark S	(319)360-7401 Themarkmueller56@gmail.com	922 Iris Avenue NW Cedar Rapids IA 52405	IE	Teacher	C11/2023			S	1979
Mueller Mary M Zurstadt	(314)605-5054 gmmueller@charter.net	1739 Hawkins Rd Fenton MO 63026	MO	Teacher	EM			RF	1967
Mueller Matthew S	(402)972-6006 matt.mueller711@gmail.com	316 S College Dr Concordia MO 64020	MO	Teacher	Prin	St Pauls Concordia MO	(660)463-7654	S	2013
Mueller Mikayla J Lowe	(913)426-0855 mikayla.lowe52@gmail.com	604 Cross Creek Dr Apt D Saint Louis MO 63141	MO	Teacher	Tchr	Chapel of the Cross Saint Peters MO	(636)922-3728	S	2022
Mueller Nathaniel E	(989)930-8286 nmueller1204@gmail.com	18385 Babcock Rd Apt 1022 San Antonio TX 78255	TX	Teacher	Tchr	Lutheran San Antonio TX	(210)694-4962	S	2024
Mueller Pamela J	(630)334-2811 pjmueller87@gmail.com	1036 W Grove Way Coeur D'alene ID 83815	NOW	Teacher	EM			RF	1974
Mueller Patra S Pfotenhauer	(206)822-0825 patramueller@hopeseattle.org	8462 Tillicum Rd SW Seattle WA 98136	NOW	DCE	Mem C	Hope Seattle WA	(206)937-9330	SP	1990
Mueller Paul M	(618)314-3572 pmemueller@gmail.com	142 S Church Rd Kings IL 61068	NI	Teacher	C03/2025			SP	2012
Mueller Paula K Hemminghaus	(602)295-3622 pkmueller@cox.net	2944 N Manor Dr W Phoenix AZ 85014	EN	Tch/DCE	EM			S	1976
Mueller Randall H	(702)334-3529 rhmueller@cox.net	3825 Russet Falls St Las Vegas NV 89129	PSW	Teacher	EM			CQ	2000
Mueller Robert K	(989)714-0588 bobkmue.4@gmail.com	1011 S Thomas Rd Saginaw MI 48609	MI	Teacher	EM			AA	1984
Mueller Roland M Dr	(620)221-4306 rmueller22@cox.net	716 Tweed Apt 206 Winfield KS 67516	KS	Teacher	EM			RF	1951
Mueller Roxanna P Minster	rdmrdm@att.net	2027 N 5th St Sheboygan WI 53081	SW	Teacher	EM			RF	1967
Mueller Stephanie J Lohse	(260)348-5956 smueller@esmeagles.com	2902 Briardale Dr Fort Wayne IN 46825	IN	Teacher	Tchr	Emmanuel-St Michael Fort Wayne IN	(260)422-6712	S	1990
Mueller Taylor S	(319)538-1994 taylor.mueller@cune.org	P.O. Box 722 Lester Prairie MN 55354	MNS	Teacher	Tchr	Mayer Mayer MN	(952)657-2251	S	2017
Mueller Victoria L	(815)990-0945 psychfan7@aol.com	120 S Henry St Green Bay WI 54302	NW	Teacher	Tchr	Green Bay Trinity Green Bay WI	(920)655-4673	MQ	1997
Mueller Walter O	wm79855@gmail.com	79855 McFadden Rd Armada MI 48005	MI	Tch/DCE	EM			S	1981
Mueller-Roebke Jenny M Mueller Dr	(402)643-3013 jenny.roebke@cune.edu	200 Struthers Pl Seward NE 68434	NEB	Teacher	EM			S	1973
Muench Nicholas A	(708)220-6318 huskermuench@gmail.com	806 S Park Blvd Freeport IL 61032	NI	Teacher	Prin	Immanuel Freeport IL	(815)232-3511	S	2001
Muench Sandra J Stec	(708)712-1723 wrigleymuench@gmail.com	806 S Park Blvd Freeport IL 61032	NI	Teacher	Tchr	Immanuel Freeport IL	(815)232-3511	MQ	1999

*Multiple Assignments (See Church Worker Locator for Additional Details)

See Page 53 for the Table of Abbreviations for key to District, Classification, Position, and College abbreviations.

**C =Candidate; EM =Emeritus; the date following the C is the month and year the Candidate status began

NAME	TELEPHONE NUMBER EMAIL	STREET ADDRESS CITY/STATE/ZIP	DISTRICT	CLASS.	POSITION/ STATUS**	WHERE SERVING	OFFICE PHONE	COLLEGE/ UNIV/CQ	YR GRAD
Mues Candy-Lu B Brauer	cmues@immanuelvalpo.org	4630 Beringer Dr Lafayette IN 47909	IN	Teacher	Tchr	Immanuel Valparaiso IN	(219)462-8207	RF	1984
Muhl Carol M Anderson	(810)736-7973 fcmuhl2000@hotmail.com	4290 Bobwhite Dr Flint MI 48506	MI	Teacher	EM			RF	1968
Muhlenbruck Marvin R	(319)430-4133 mfm@iowatelecom.net	9354 10th St Mediapolis IA 52637	IE	Teacher	EM			RF	1966
Muich Andrew A	(703)656-6287 andy.muich@gmail.com	47549 Anchorage Cir Sterling VA 20165	SE	DCE	C11/2024			CH	2006
Mulder Nayva K Deac	(701)430-9049 nayva.mulder@ctsfw.edu	809 2nd Ave NW Jamestown ND 58401	ND	Deaconess	Mem C	Concordia Jamestown ND	(701)252-2819	FW-DEAC	2014
Muldowney Marybeth A Madsen	(847)530-9331 muldowneymb@gmail.com	2780 Calariva Dr Stockton CA 95204	CNH	Teacher	C07/2017			CH	2015
Mulholland Betty R Schmidt Deac	(970)461-7783 dcsbettyem98@yahoo.com	2265 Mt Meeker Ct Loveland CO 80537	RM	Deaconess	EM			Other	1955
Mull Lisa R	(217)766-4756 lbananabrain@gmail.com	1604 Oriole Lane Brentwood MO 63144	MO	Teacher	Tchr	Immanuel Olivette MO	(314)993-5004	RF	1987
Mullaney Joy A Schroeder Ross Dr	(630)379-7077 joymullaney@gmail.com	520 S Wheaton Ave Wheaton IL 60187	NI	Teacher	EM			CQ	2016
Mullen Susan J Lampe	(847)609-1575 susanjoymullen@gmail.com	1635 Arbor Ct Darien IL 60561	NI	DCM	EM			MQ	2008
Muller Donna E Steger	(615)566-8949 donnaemuller@gmail.com	3350 SW 109th Dr Gainesville FL 32608	FG	Teacher	C04/2018			CQ	2008
Mulligan Judy A Munstein	(310)487-8624 msjudy17@msn.com	204 E McMurray Blvd Casa Grande AZ 85122	PSW	Teacher	EM			CQ	2007
Mullikin Melissa M Johnson	(414)379-8187 m84johnson@gmail.com	9516 W Montana Ave West Allis WI 53227	SW	Teacher	Tchr	Zion Menomonee Falls WI	(262)781-7437	MQ	2007
Mullis Lindsay M Paluch	(231)750-1256 lmullis@whitecreek.org	5842 Madison Ct Columbus IN 47203	IN	Teacher	Tchr	White Creek Columbus IN	(812)342-6832	CH	2012
Mulso Zachary R	(651)895-6804 zach@colchurch.com	17374 N 89th Ave Apt #2002 Peoria AZ 85382	PSW	DCM	Mem C	Crown Of Life Sun City West AZ	(623)546-6228	MQ	2023
Mumm Amanda L Van de Kamp Deac	(208)733-7820 amandav@immanueltf.org	3515 E 3195 N Kimberly ID 83341	NOW	Deaconess	Mem C	Immanuel Twin Falls ID	(208)733-7820	CH	2016
Mumm Heidi S McCormick	(716)868-6320 islettеselite@aol.com	2155 Staley Rd Grand Island NY 14072	EA	Teacher	Tchr	St John North Tonawanda NY	(716)693-9677	CQ	2011
Mundt Allen F	(812)519-1592 mundt8576@gmail.com	8576 Rainier Rd Seymour IN 47274	IN	Teacher	EM			S	1966
Mundt Angela M McKeage	(816)665-1520 angiemundt@gmail.com	2816 SW 10th St. Lees Summit MO 64081	MO	Teacher	Pro Stf	Small Saints Liberty MO	(816)781-6994	S	1997
Mundt Hannah E	(816)200-4734 hannah.mundt@cune.org	112 W Washington Blvd Apt 430 Fort Wayne IN 46802	IN	Teacher	Tchr	Concordia Fort Wayne IN	(260)483-1102	S	2023
Mundt Janis M Pflueger	(812)519-1592 mundt8576@gmail.com	8576 Rainier Rd Seymour IN 47274	IN	Teacher	EM			RF	1969
Munoz Ariel W Wenz	(917)648-4429 babyjudah@hotmail.com	2112 123rd St Apt 1r College Point NY 11356	AT	Teacher	C07/2016			S	2000
Munoz Faustino T	(314)532-6772 Faustino.Munoz@Faithstl.org	1727 Leigh Loop Cantonment FL 32533	MO	DCE	Mem C	Faith Oakville MO	(314)846-8612	Other	2018
Munoz Valerie K Krueger	(520)248-4352 vjkmunoz@gmail.com	161 S Gold Mine Loop Tucson AZ 85748	PSW	Teacher	EM			CQ	2009
Munster Mervin D	(541)926-2010 mervin_munster@yahoo.com	628 Breezy Way NE Albany OR 97322	NOW	Teacher	EM			S	1970
Murdick Heather Gartzke	(262)490-1993 hcgartzke@gmail.com	W5480 S Round Lake Rd Wild Rose WI 54984	SW	Teacher	C07/2016			MQ	2010
Murphy Ashley L Scheele	(920)254-1963 amurphy@sjlplymouth.com	W4486 River Bend Drive Waldo WI 53093	SW	Teacher	Tchr	St John Plymouth WI	(920)893-5114	MQ	2017
Murphy Christopher L	(260) 348-2118 cmurphy@clhscadets.com	1309 Big Horn Pl Fort Wayne IN 46825	IN	Teacher	Tchr	Concordia Fort Wayne IN	(260)483-1102	RF	1985
Murphy Deanna M Bredehoft	(217)358-3201	94 N Country Club Rd Decatur IL 62521	CI	Teacher	EM			CQ	1993
Murphy Matthew J	(719)453-9415 matthew@anchoragelutheran.org	1111 Barrow St Apt A Anchorage AK 99501	NOW	DCE	Mem C	Anchorage Anchorage AK	(907)272-5323	S	2021
Murphy Vicki K Whipker	(812)350-2266 vmurphy@whitecreek.org	7275 S Midland Ave Columbus IN 47201	IN	Teacher	Tchr	White Creek Columbus IN	(812)342-6832	CQ	2023
Murray Elizabeth A Isenhour	(864)978-2156 bmurray@concordianc.org	2850 Snead Ct NE Conover NC 28613	SE	Teacher	Tchr	Concordia Conover NC	(828)464-3011	CQ	2004
Murray Jamie M	(702)471-8436	3207 Cherum St Las Vegas NV 89135	PSW	Teacher	Tchr	Faith Community Las Vegas NV	(702)921-2700	CQ	2008
Murray Kimberly D Griffith	(702)649-5956 bkmurraylv@gmail.com	6513 Summer Bluff Ct N Las Vegas NV 89084	PSW	Teacher	Tchr	Lamb Of God Las Vegas NV	(702)645-4998	CQ	2006
Musa Rahel Deac	(517)372-9629 rahel_m2003@yahoo.com	c/o St Luke Lutheran Church 5589 Van Atta Rd Haslett MI 48840	MI	Deaconess	Mem C	St Luke Haslett MI	(517)339-9119	CQ	2007
Musella Miriam L Wahlers	(909)896-0349 mimimusella@hotmail.com	1615 Juniper Ridge St Pomona CA 91766	PSW	Teacher	EM			S	1979
Musfeldt Jay N	(512)259-6649 moosejam@suddenlink.net	601 Las Colinas Dr Leander TX 78641	TX	Tch/DCE	EM			S	1963
Musgrove Kristen D Kruse-Salamone	(281)650-4538 kristen.musgrove@icloud.com	9839 Cobalt Cove Willis TX 77318	TX	Teacher	Tchr	Trinity Klein Klein TX	(281)376-5773	CQ	2008
Mussell Ann E Passow	(507)534-2115 bamussell@yahoo.com	625 West Broadway Plainview MN 55964	MNS	Teacher	EM			SP	1971
Mussell Leah M	(763)516-1934 leah.mussell@cune.org		SW	Teacher	Tchr	St Johns West Bend WI	(262)334-3077	S	2019
Mussmann Anna I Beck	(412)365-0256 annabookreader@gmail.com	21 Plum Crest Dr Pittsburgh PA 15239	EN	Teacher	C09/2016			MQ	2007
Muth Janet J	(618)391-7081 jmuth@stpaulhamel.org	1968 Raintree Trail Collinsville IL 62234	SI	Teacher	Tchr	St Paul Worden IL	(618)633-2202	PO	1985

*Multiple Assignments (See Church Worker Locator for Additional Details)

See Page 53 for the Table of Abbreviations for key to District, Classification, Position, and College abbreviations.

**C =Candidate; EM =Emeritus; the date following the C is the month and year the Candidate status began

NAME	TELEPHONE NUMBER EMAIL	STREET ADDRESS CITY/STATE/ZIP	DISTRICT	CLASS.	POSITION/ STATUS**	WHERE SERVING	OFFICE PHONE	COLLEGE/ UNIV/CQ	YR GRAD
Muth Timothy D	(920)208-3563 muth@lutheranhigh.com	4328 Lavalle Dr Sheboygan WI 53081	SW	Teacher	Tchr	Sheboygan Sheboygan WI	(920)452-3323	MQ	1990
Muther Cindy B Azinger	(920)609-8982 cindymuther@pilgrimluth.org	3561 Spring Green Rd Green Bay WI 54313	NW	Teacher	Tchr	Pilgrim Green Bay WI	(920)965-2233	S	1977
Muther Julia E Einspahr	(815)209-6518 jemuther@yahoo.com	1577 Honeysuckle Rd Apt 5 Hartford WI 53027	SW	Teacher	Tchr	Wauwatosa Wauwatosa WI	(414)258-4558	S	1983
Muther Pamela J Utech	(262)338-9435 pjmuther@yahoo.com	915 E Kilbourn Ave West Bend WI 53095	SW	Teacher	EM			S	1976
Muther Timothy A	(815)209-6517 lhswrestling@yahoo.com	1577 Honeysuckle Rd Apt 5 Hartford WI 53027	SW	Teacher	Tchr	Living Word Jackson WI	(262)677-9353	S	1984
Mycock Carol L Bischoff	(210)363-3314 christmascarol7@juno.com	129 Noble Woods Boerne TX 78006	TX	Teacher	EM			S	1973
Myers Elizabeth D	(314)596-1156 bettymyers300@gmail.com	9008 Villaridge Court Unit D Saint Louis MO 63123	MO	Teacher	EM			SP	1981
Myers Jenny A Ersland	(970)397-1088 jmyers@holycrosslutheran.net	1311 N Rutland Cir Wichita KS 67206	KS	Teacher	Mem C	Holy Cross Wichita KS	(316)684-5201	S	2007
Myers Matthew D	(813)699-0892 myersgeneral@gmail.com	729 Cory Dr Seward NE 68434	NEB	DCO	S HS/C	Concordia University Nebraska Seward NE	(402)643-3651	CQ	2011
Myers Paula M Heddle	(810)984-8872 pmyers@trinityutica.com	4157 Parker Rd Fort Gratiot MI 48059	MI	Teacher	Tchr	Trinity Utica MI	(586)731-4490	AA	1987
Naatz Thomas J	(256)527-0170 tommynaatz@gmail.com	15122 Balsam Dr SE Huntsville AL 35803	SO	Teacher	EM			S	1974
Naber Karyn L Martin Deac	(612)281-0385 knaber73@gmail.com	5105 Paul Mountain Dr Imperial MO 63052	MO	Deaconess	RSO	Lutheran Senior Services DBA EverTrue Brentwood MO	(314)968-9313	SL-DEAC	2024
Naber Katelyn M Catura	(262)957-0156 knaber@hcl.org	5868 Oriole Ln Greendale WI 53129	EN	Teacher	Tchr	Hales Corners Hales Corners WI	(414)529-6701	CQ	2022
Naber Mary Schneider	(414)940-2770 mnaber25@hotmail.com	W128S9572 Walter Hagen Dr Muskego WI 53150	EN	Teacher	EM			MQ	2008
Nack Jovita J Glandorf	(507)841-1132 jovnack@gmail.com	1803 N Main St Auburn IN 46706	IN	Teacher	Tchr	Woodburn Woodburn IN	(260)632-5493	S	1992
Nack Judith A Friesen	(219)661-3845 judyandruth@gmail.com	1071 Concordia Ln Crown Point IN 46307	IN	Teacher	EM			S	1965
Naegeli Sandra J Hetland	(262)884-4223 tsct34@sbcglobal.net	7540 Gittings Rd Mt Pleasant WI 53406	SW	Teacher	Tchr	St John Racine WI	(262)633-2758	CQ	2012
Nafzger Kathryn J McCoid	(651)303-5757 katie.nafzger@gmail.com	6 McCall Ter Saint Louis MO 63105	MO	Teacher	Tchr	Lutheran North Saint Louis MO	(314)389-3100	S	2000
Nagel Brittany A Arlow	(907)355-8931 bgnagel907@gmail.com		MNS	DCE	C07/2023			SP	2010
Nagel Judith E Thorgren	(773)883-7284 nagelj3@hotmail.com	311 Birchbrook Ct Glen Ellyn IL 60137	NI	Teacher	EM			CQ	2002
Nagel Marlise Halvorson	(914)844-5380 mollynagel80@gmail.com	5276 Plum Tree Irvine CA 92612	PSW	Teacher	Tchr	Abiding Savior Lake Forest CA	(949)830-1460	CQ	2020
Nagel Matthew C		3540 Oreana Ave Las Vegas NV 89120	PSW	Teacher	Tchr	Faith Las Vegas NV	(702)804-4400	S	1987
Nagy Krista F Fawcett	(260)797-8065 krista.nagy31@gmail.com	2253 E. Belmont Place Anaheim CA 92806	PSW	Teacher	C07/2020			RF	1989
Nail John R	(660)287-0673 johnnail50@gmail.com	1423 S Park Ave Sedalia MO 65301	MO	Teacher	EM			CQ	2002
Nale Charlotte W Williams	(924)443-1018 char@nale.org	370 Fontonett Ave Livermore CA 94550	CNH	Teacher	EM			RF	1980
Naleieha Michael M	(512)837-0685	11611 Parkfield Dr Austin TX 78758	TX	Teacher	EM			RF	1973
Namanny Cynthia A Raebel	(601)842-9865 cindynamanny@gmail.com	67 Springview Dr Brandon MS 39042	SO	Tch/DCE	EM			SP	1978
Nance Kelly A Albers	(720)626-3646 kellynance02@gmail.com	17589 E 111th Place Commerce City CO 80022	RM	Teacher	Tchr	Zion Brighton CO	(303)659-2339	S	2020
Napier Dawn L Mellenthine	(757)851-3278 dawnnapier55@gmail.com	302 Gaines Mill Ln Hampton VA 23669	SE	Teacher	EM			BR	1977
Nash Cora B Hernandez	(832)725-0137 cora@savinggracelc.org	23329 South 226th Way Queen Creek AZ 85142	PSW	Teacher	Tchr	Saving Grace Queen Creek AZ	(480)888-9673	CQ	2012
Nash Susan J Meyer	(507)272-1462 sjnash2001@yahoo.com	319 Gold St N Wykoff MN 55990	MNS	Teacher	EM			SP	2021
Natonick Marlys Jean Schiller	(302)448-9531 marlysnatonick@gmail.com	4615 The Station Blvd Sachse TX 75048	TX	Teacher	EM			CQ	2005
Natz Debra J Leopold	(608)754-0232 dnatz@stpaulsjanesville.com	2338 Garden Dr Janesville WI 53546	SW	Teacher	EM			CQ	2000
Natzke Robert A	(920)246-0936	8212 County Rd W Greenleaf WI 54126	NW	DCM	EM			MQ	1986
Naumann Cheryl D Freitag Deac	(412)983-6122 mrscherylnaumann@gmail.com	782 15th St Oakmont PA 15139	EN	Deaconess	S Miss	Office of International Mission Saint Louis MO		CQ	2004
Nauta Shelby J Schelk	(262)376-4225 sjnauta1971@yahoo.com	1650 S Pine St Grafton WI 53024	SW	Teacher	Tchr	St Paul Grafton WI	(262)377-4659	MQ	1994
Nauth Jackie L Pitchford	(612)283-3374 jackienauth@gmail.com	11301 Maple Knoll Way Apt 405 Maple Grove MN 55369	MNS	Teacher	Tchr	St John Corcoran MN	(763)420-2426	CQ	2021
Navarro Albert M	(847)254-6357 acnavarro309@gmail.com	309 S 2nd St West Dundee IL 60118	NI	Teacher	EM			RF	1993
Navas Candice S	(713)874-4858 cnavas@stmarkhouston.org	4613 Frontier Houston TX 77041	TX	Teacher	Tchr	St Mark Houston TX	(713)468-2623	CQ	2021
Navurskis Miriam E Mischnick	(605)354-7027 navurskism@trinitycr.org	216 31st St NW Cedar Rapids IA 52405	IE	Teacher	Tchr	Trinity Cedar Rapids IA	(319)362-6952	MQ	1998
Neafcy Jennifer N Matthys	(512)784-0630 jennifer.neafcy@gmail.com	10213 34th Ave SW Seattle WA 98146	NOW	Teacher	Tchr	Hope Seattle WA	(206)937-9330	AU	1992
Neagley Claire E Krans Deac	(717)343-6600 dcsclaire75@yahoo.com	560 Oak Dr, Apt 234 Harleysville PA 19438	EA	Deaconess	EM			Other	1975

*Multiple Assignments (See Church Worker Locator for Additional Details)
See Page 53 for the Table of Abbreviations for key to District, Classification, Position, and College abbreviations.
**C =Candidate; EM =Emeritus; the date following the C is the month and year the Candidate status began

NAME	TELEPHONE NUMBER EMAIL	STREET ADDRESS CITY/STATE/ZIP	DISTRICT	CLASS.	POSITION/ STATUS**	WHERE SERVING	OFFICE PHONE	COLLEGE/ UNIV/CQ	YR GRAD
Neal Danika Schmid	danika.neal624@gmail.com	2252 Waterford Pl Carson City NV 89703	CNH	Teacher	Tchr	Sierra Carson City NV	(775)267-1921	IV	2016
Nearman Kayla T Kayla Vrudny	(320)216-5309 kvrudny@gmail.com	5258 12th Ave NE # A Seattle WA 98105	NOW	Teacher	Tchr	Concordia Seattle WA	(206)525-7407	SP	2012
Nebel Cindy F Muehler	(618)237-8236 nebelfam@yahoo.com	107 S Biltz Dr Concordia MO 64020	MO	Teacher	Tchr	Trinity Alma MO	(660)674-2444	RF	1996
Nebel Clara A	(618)973-4987 clara.nebel@cune.org	2147 S County Road 750 E Seymour IN 47274	IN	Teacher	Tchr	St John Seymour IN	(812)523-3131	S	2021
Neben Amy E	(714)609-3950 amyneben7@gmail.com	406 N Swidler St Orange CA 92869	PSW	Teacher	Tchr	Saint Johns Orange CA	(714)288-4400	IV	2002
Neben Jason K Dr	(949)923-0600 jasonneben@gmail.com	21581 Vintage Way Lake Forest CA 92630	PSW	Teacher	S HS/C	Concordia University Irvine Irvine CA	(949)854-8002	CQ	2001
Neebe Allysha L	(951)642-9248 ally@neebe.com	24795 Rochelle Lane Lake Forest CA 92630	PSW	Teacher	Tchr	Abiding Savior Lake Forest CA	(949)830-1460	IV	2012
Nehrenz Sheila K Vorpagel	(260)615-7655 snehrenz@lsusfw.org	4620 Williamsburg Ct Fort Wayne IN 46804	IN	Teacher	Prin	South Unity Fort Wayne IN	(260)744-0459	RF	1979
Nehring Charles G	(920)494-0227 cgneh2@juno.com	1237 Reed St Green Bay WI 54303	NW	Teacher	EM			RF	1959
Nehrt Rebecca L Riemer	(618)780-5059 rlnehrt@yahoo.com	1665 Hookdale Ln Smithboro IL 62284	SI	Teacher	Tchr	Good Shepherd Collinsville IL	(618)344-3153	RF	1983
Neideffer Joy L	(262)455-0212 joyjoy2021@comcast.net	1525 Cheyenne Ave Unit G Grafton WI 53024	SW	Teacher	Tchr	St John Racine WI	(262)633-2758	MQ	2025
Neidhold Eunice P Rolf	(509)328-9521 neidhold60@q.com	6526 E 17th Ave Spokane Valley WA 99212	NOW	Teacher	EM			S	1958
Neidhold Gail M Elliott	neidhold@mindspring.com	P.O. Box 13519 Spokane Valley WA 99213	NOW	Teacher	C07/2016			PO	1984
Neidigk Matthew W	(832)257-9131 neidigkm@clhs-tx.org	9102 Marshall Ct Magnolia TX 77354	TX	Teacher	Tchr	Lutheran Education Association Friendswood TX	(281)617-5189	MQ	1997
Neilitz Anne M Guse	(920)629-9874 anne_m_neilitz@hotmail.com	465 Aberdeen Drive Waite Park MN 56387	MNN	Teacher	Prin	Prince Of Peace Saint Cloud MN	(320)251-1477	SP	2000
Neils Alicia R Benning Deac	(217)710-5865 aliciabenningneils@gmail.com	6956 Ashwood Road, Apt. 302 Woodbury MN 55125	MNS	Deaconess	Mem C	Rose Of Sharon Cottage Grove MN	(651)459-3551	SL-DEAC	2022
Neipp Hyun Nyo S Moon	(559)741-9917 sharineneipp@yahoo.com	4016 W Sweet Ct Visalia CA 93291	CNH	Teacher	Tchr	Grace Visalia CA	(559)734-7694	IV	1991
Neitsch Howard W	(863)224-1454 neitschs@yahoo.com	2800 W Lake Hamilton Dr Winter Haven FL 33881	FG	Teacher	EM			RF	1971
Nelsen Cynthia K Steinke	(715)381-1128 rcnelsen@netzero.net	1159 56th St Hudson WI 54016	MNS	Tch/DCE	Tchr	Trinity Hudson WI	(715)386-9313	SP	1987
Nelsen Rachel R Witt	(262)365-1540 rachelnelsen24@gmail.com	N173W20208 Crestview Dr Jackson WI 53037	SW	Teacher	Tchr	St Paul Grafton WI	(262)377-4659	MQ	2012
Nelson Amy A Bernhardt	(608)449-0379 nelson.chuck_amy@yahoo.com	38 W Elizabeth St Milton WI 53563	EN	DCM	C04/2025			MQ	2005
Nelson Angela L Rolf	(214)924-8873	7111 Wagon Top Ct Colorado Springs CO 80908	RM	Teacher	C07/2016			RF	1991
Nelson Ashley M Wangerin Deac	(405)762-3606 deaconess@splcs.org	735 Silver Leaf St Apt D Leavenworth KS 66048	KS	Deaconess	Mem C	St Paul Leavenworth KS	(913)682-0387	SL	2024
Nelson Becky J Fingerlin	(863)513-5908 beckhaven24@gmail.com	640 Cindy Dr. Twin Falls ID 83301	NOW	Teacher	C07/2016			SP	1983
Nelson Christie A Deac	(940)758-1451 christienelson21@yahoo.com		TX	Deaconess	EM			RF	1990
Nelson Christina Hodge	(229)291-1499 cnelson@royed.org	8050 Beaver Ridge Dr Apt 1201 North Royalton OH 44133	OH	DCE	Mem C	Royal Redeemer North Royalton OH	(440)237-7958	AU	2021
Nelson Christopher C	(920)471-5457 cnelson@racinelutheran.org	2721 Manor Ave Mt Pleasant WI 53406	SW	Teacher	ExecDir	Lutheran High School Racine WI	(262)637-6538	MQ	1994
Nelson Corey A	(507)358-5839 conelson@rcls.net	2121 50th St NW Rochester MN 55901	MNS	Teacher	Tchr	Rochester Central Rochester MN	(507)289-3267	S	1993
Nelson David A	(734)366-3206 dnelson1423@gmail.com		MI	DCE	Mem C	St Luke Ann Arbor MI	(734)971-0550	CH	2009
Nelson Eric M	(317)371-7649 eric@ctkcda.com	P.O. Box 1494 Coeur D'alene ID 83816	NOW	DCE	Mem C	Christ King Coeur D Alene ID	(208)664-9231	PO	2001
Nelson Erin C Cherpeski	(714)369-5636 erin.nelson@cui.edu	11 Timberbluff Aliso Viejo CA 92656	PSW	Teacher	S HS/C	Concordia University Irvine Irvine CA	(949)854-8002	CQ	2019
Nelson Gary R	(248)760-6197	1971 Cut Crystal Ln Shelby Twp MI 48316	MI	Teacher	EM			RF	1981
Nelson George W	(651)895-0201 gwnone@aol.com	217 Pralle Ln Saint Charles MO 63303	MO	Tch/DCE	Mem C	Chapel of the Cross Saint Peters MO	(636)928-5885	S	1971
Nelson Geraldine Menth	(989)255-4400 sjnelson04@charter.net	10770 E Grand Lake Rd Presque Isle MI 49777	MI	Teacher	EM			S	1970
Nelson Holly M Smith	(775)546-3347 mandhnelson@gmail.com	8639 Leslie Dr Sterling Heights MI 48314	MI	DCE	Mem C	Peace Shelby Township MI	(586)731-4120	S	2008
Nelson Kari L Loll	(714)420-4645 lollk@aol.com	8149 Shadyview Lane N Maple Grove MN 55311	MNS	Teacher	Tchr	Mount Olive Anoka MN	(763)421-9048	SP	1996
Nelson Katie A Maxson	(719)238-2459 k8emaxnelson@gmail.com	15524 E Tamarac Ct Wichita KS 67230	KS	Teacher	Tchr	Holy Cross Wichita KS	(316)684-4431	S	2006
Nelson Kristina L Sawicki	(615)895-1211 ttn9767@netzero.net	2206 Eastview Dr Murfreesboro TN 37128	SO	Teacher	C07/2016			AU	1995
Nelson Laura E Tatum	(714)397-3821 jlnelsonfamily@yahoo.com	2318 N Glennwood St Orange CA 92565	PSW	Teacher	Tchr	Saint Johns Orange CA	(714)288-4400	IV	2003
Nelson Laura L Cadwell	(515)864-6064 laura@stpaulankeny.org	1218 NW Cedarwood Dr Ankeny IA 50023	IW	DCM	Mem C	St Paul Ankeny IA	(515)964-1250	MQ	2025
Nelson Michael A	(248)977-7365 michael.a.nelson1983@gmail.com	8639 Leslie Dr Sterling Heights MI 48314	MI	Teacher	Prin	Peace Shelby Township MI	(586)731-4120	S	2006
Nelson Michael T	(281)687-1085 tnelson@mlchouston.org	15614 Country Fair Ln Cypress TX 77433	TX	Teacher	EM			RF	1970

*Multiple Assignments (See Church Worker Locator for Additional Details)

See Page 53 for the Table of Abbreviations for key to District, Classification, Position, and College abbreviations.

**C =Candidate; EM =Emeritus; the date following the C is the month and year the Candidate status began

NAME	TELEPHONE NUMBER EMAIL	STREET ADDRESS CITY/STATE/ZIP	DISTRICT	CLASS.	POSITION/ STATUS**	WHERE SERVING	OFFICE PHONE	COLLEGE/ UNIV/CQ	YR GRAD
Nelson Paul A	(402)910-6530 panelson94@gmail.com	1504 2nd St. NE Buffalo MN 55313	MNS	DCE	Mem C	St John Buffalo MN	(763)682-1883	S	2018
Nelson Rebecca J Schelp	rnelson@splhs.org	17707 Boulder Ave. Blackburn MO 65321	MO	Teacher	Tchr	Saint Paul Concordia MO	(660)463-2238	S	2013
Nelson Roberta L Bultmann Dr	(224)723-5791 drnelson10@sbcglobal.net	1066 Shermer Rd Apt 10 Northbrook IL 60062	NI	Teacher	EM			RF	1963
Nelson Sandra J Driska	(913)962-2461 sandrajnelson1@gmail.com	900 Edgewood Ave Columbia MO 65203	MO	Teacher	EM			CQ	1993
Nelson Scott D	(863)513-5908 brlymkgit@aol.com	640 Cindy Dr Twin Falls ID 83301	NOW	Teacher	EM			S	1983
Nelson Stephanie E	(916)768-8425 stephanie.nelson@cune.org	8826 Central Ave Orangevale CA 95662	CNH	Teacher	C07/2016			S	2011
Nelson Wayne R Jr	(262)664-3907 waynelson62@gmail.com	P.O. Box 372 Cedarburg WI 53012	SW	Teacher	Tchr	First Immanuel Cedarburg WI	(262)377-6610	MQ	1984
Nelson Wendy M Hurt	(630)761-9130 wnelson@immanuelbatavia.org	426 N Van Buren St Batavia IL 60510	NI	Teacher	Tchr	Immanuel Batavia IL	(630)879-7163	RF	1997
Nelson-McKenzie Kristen M Nelson Dr	(716)957-0469 knelsonmckenzie@gmail.com	5030 Bradford Rd Jacksonville FL 32217	FG	Teacher	C07/2016			CQ	1995
Nemec Carol A Stabler Deac	(765)376-2511 canemec@gmail.com	1991 Pioneer Rd Gaylord MI 49735	MI	Deaconess	EM			FW-DEAC	2011
Nemec Christianna N Eckstein Deac	(701)658-0329 christiannaeckstein@gmail.com	6218 26th St Lubbock TX 79407	TX	Deaconess	C07/2025			FW-DEAC	2023
Nemec Lisa B	(281)651-8606 longhornnemec@gmail.com	21002 La Arbre Ln Spring TX 77388	TX	Teacher	Pro Stf	Concordia Tomball TX	(281)351-2547	AU	2010
Nemeth Grace M Nickel	(562)697-2045	1234 Solejar Dr Whittier CA 90603	PSW	Teacher	EM			RF	1960
Nemeth Mary K Haecker	(219)766-0521 mhack9802@hotmail.com	136 E Junco Dr Kouts IN 46347	IN	Teacher	C07/2016			RF	2002
Nemoyer Nancy E Nicol Deac	(717)421-5741 nnemoyer@gmail.com	2406 Ken James Ct Napoleon OH 43545	OH	Deaconess	EM			RF	1985
Nesman Sharon A Rau-Paquette	(727)692-4416 snesman@grace-lutheran.com	2582 West Brook Ln Clearwater FL 33761	FG	Teacher	Tchr	Grace Saint Petersburg FL	(727)527-6213	CQ	2008
Netherton Dana J Truwe	(502)641-6082 dnetherton@bellsouth.net	2032 Goldsmith Ln Louisville KY 40218	IN	Teacher	Tchr	Our Savior Louisville KY	(502)426-1130	S	1994
Netherton Karen A Kochendorfer	(309)781-4693 nethertonka@gmail.com	2026 E Rusholme St Davenport IA 52803	IE	Teacher	EM			RF	1965
Nett Alyssa R Gipp	(920)680-5659 nett.alyssa@gmail.com	2828 E Ashby Rd Midland MI 48640	MI	Teacher	C08/2023			MQ	2011
Nettnin Kathleen L Brown	(585)964-8703 v_knettnin@frontiernet.net	1739 Apple Hollow Ln Hamlin NY 14464	EA	Teacher	EM			BR	1977
Neubauer Daniel J	(218)255-7397 dneubauer723@gmail.com	5040 S Greenbrook Terr 0209 Greenfield WI 53220	SW	Teacher	Tchr	Martin Luther Greendale WI	(414)421-4000	CH	2024
Neuendorf Christel A Deac	(734)277-6077 christel.neuendorf@lcms.org	1428 Calle Aloa Buena Vista Ponce PR 00717	MI	Deaconess	S Miss	Office of International Mission Saint Louis MO		FW-DEAC	2015
Neuenfeldt Jane D Mueller	(763)229-1541 jane9048@yahoo.com	1720 West Ln Anoka MN 55303	MNS	Teacher	EM			SP	1975
Neuenfeldt Melinda J Seifert	(763)232-5062 scoboscobs2@gmail.com	N99 W14422 Amber Dr Germantown WI 53022	SW	Teacher	Tchr	Trinity Mequon WI	(262)242-2045	SP	2010
Neuhart Norma D Burgess Deac	(810)239-7056 ndneuhart@gmail.com	262 Wig Ct Flint MI 48507	MI	Deaconess	EM			CQ	2002
Neuman Jeffrey B	(716)440-3217 jb.neuman@gmail.com	734 N 1st St Seward NE 68434	NEB	Teacher	C06/2024			AA	2007
Neuman Jessica L Selbe	(716)946-8864 jessicalin.neuman@gmail.com	734 N 1st St Seward NE 68434	NEB	Teacher	Tchr	St John Seward NE	(402)643-4535	AA	2007
Neumann Becky Plamann	(281) 300-3561 bneumann@stmarkhouston.org	16030 Kube Ct Jersey Village TX 77040	TX	Teacher	C09/2017			RF	1983
Neumann Gary J	(734)904-6592 gjneumann@hotmail.com	1640 E Cook Rd Fort Wayne IN 46825	MI	Teacher	EM			S	1974
Neumeyer Amanda J	(989)245-6207 ajneumeyer@gmail.com	145 N 74th St Unit 202 Mesa AZ 85207	PSW	Teacher	Tchr	Christ Greenfield Gilbert AZ	(480)892-8521	CQ	2015
Neumeyer Brianna M	(248)891-7767 briannamneumeyer@gmail.com	2295 Cole Rd Lake Orion MI 48362	MI	Teacher	Tchr	St John Fraser MI	(586)294-8740	MQ	2017
Neumeyer Dennis K	(989)274-4438 neumeyerdennis@gmail.com	2260 S Portsmouth Rd Saginaw MI 48601	MI	Teacher	EM			RF	1968
Neumeyer Joel K	jneumeyer@immlutheran.org	44521 Highgate Dr. Clinton Township MI 48038	MI	Teacher	Prin	Immanuel Macomb MI	(586)286-4231	Other	2008
Neumeyer Karen B Koenig	(248)207-7472 kneumeyer@stjohnrochester.org	2295 Cole Rd Lake Orion MI 48362	MI	Teacher	Tchr	St John Rochester MI	(248)402-8000	AA	1986
Neumeyer Marsha J Jastram	(989)274-1781 trost2260@gmail.com	2260 S Portsmouth Rd Saginaw MI 48601	MI	Teacher	EM			RF	1968
Neumeyer Paul L	(810)931-3840 paul.neumeyer524@gmail.com	1410 Inwood Rd Rochester MI 48306	MI	Teacher	Tchr	LHS Assn Of Greater Detroit Rochester Hls MI	(248)856-0240	AA	2016
Neumeyer Rosalie A Larson	(712)249-8015 mrneumeyer@yahoo.com	921 S 19th St Clarinda IA 51632	IW	Teacher	EM			S	1969
Neumeyer Scott R	(989)274-0963 scotthoops11@gmail.com	1371 McDivitt Ct Saginaw MI 48609	MI	Teacher	Tchr	St Peter Hemlock MI	(989)642-8188	AA	1994
Neumiller Craig C	(253)377-5405 c.neumiller@flschool.org	2309 Cantergrove Dr SE Lacey WA 98503	NOW	Tch/DCE	Prin	Faith Lacey WA	(360)491-3552	PO	1987
New Emilee R Nieman	(586)690-9658 emileerosenew@gmail.com	P.O. Box 295 Texico NM 88135	TX	Teacher	C07/2016			AA	2007
Neward Donna R Schmohe	(801)568-6877 dneward@earthlink.net	1932 E Stalbridge Cir Sandy UT 84093	RM	Teacher	EM			RF	1961
Newcom Heather C	(714)393-1105 marvinfrog@yahoo.com	760 N Shattuck Pl Apt C Orange CA 92867	PSW	Teacher	Tchr	Prince Peace Anaheim CA	(714)774-0993	IV	2011
Newell Johanna F Eschmann	(586)214-8910 jeschmann@hotmail.com	37208 Robert Dr Richmond MI 48062	MI	Teacher	Tchr	St Peter Richmond MI	(586)727-9080	S	1991

*Multiple Assignments (See Church Worker Locator for Additional Details)
See Page 53 for the Table of Abbreviations for key to District, Classification, Position, and College abbreviations.
**C =Candidate; EM =Emeritus; the date following the C is the month and year the Candidate status began

NAME	TELEPHONE NUMBER EMAIL	STREET ADDRESS CITY/STATE/ZIP	DISTRICT	CLASS.	POSITION/ STATUS**	WHERE SERVING	OFFICE PHONE	COLLEGE/ UNIV/CQ	YR GRAD
Newell Kristen A Peters Dr	(605)254-4079 newell.kristen@gmail.com	4924 S Kalen Pl Sioux Falls SD 57108	SD	Teacher	Prin	Sioux Falls Sioux Falls SD	(605)335-1923	S	2008
Newkirk Jennifer E Dahlinger	(405)216-5504 teacherjennifer2002@hotmail.com	2808 Palomino Dr Edmond OK 73034	OK	Teacher	C10/2019			SP	1999
Newman Daniel A	(920)358-9067 dan.newman@outlook.com	215 W Hurlbut St Charlevoix MI 49720	NW	DCM	C07/2024			MQ	2021
Newman Katherine G	(920)572-4771 kate.newman@stjohnswaltz.org	21819 Woodruff Rd Apt J-5 Rockwood MI 48173	MI	Teacher	Tchr	St John Waltz MI	(734)654-6366	MQ	2021
Newman Kimberly A La Bine	(586)383-3588 kanewman1962@gmail.com	33609 Terragona Dr Sorrento FL 32776	FG	Teacher	Tchr	Faith Eustis FL	(352)589-5433	RF	1985
Newman Mark P	(414)708-5539 mnewman@lakecountryhs.org	1142 Oriole Dr Oconomowoc WI 53066	SW	Teacher	Tchr	Lake Country Hartland WI	(262)367-8600	MQ	1996
Newman Sue L Gustafson	(541)382-1850 suemikenewman@msn.com	14555 SW Juniper Dr Powell Butte OR 97753	NOW	Teacher	EM			CQ	2005
Newsome Rhonda A Jentsch	(920)390-1205 rhonda@peaceantigo.org	634 Deleglise St Antigo WI 54409	NW	Teacher	Tchr	Peace Antigo WI	(715)623-2200	MQ	2001
Newton David M	(707)224-2473 Mnewton@stjohnsnapa.org	2572 Greenwood Ct Napa CA 94558	CNH	Teacher	Tchr	St John Napa CA	(707)226-7970	CQ	1986
Newton Janelle M Lutz	(707)224-2473	2572 Greenwood Ct Napa CA 94558	CNH	Teacher	C07/2016			S	1978
Newton LaRayne S Stanek	(989)799-1248 lnewton@stmichaelsrichville.org	2337 Gatesboro Dr W Saginaw MI 48603	MI	Teacher	Tchr	St Michael Richville MI	(989)868-4791	SP	1986
Newton Roselyn Hintz	(206)235-8953 rmnewton2@comcast.net	3712 NE 188th St Lk Forest Pk WA 98155	NOW	Teacher	EM			S	1969
Newton Sarah J Ludwig Deac	sarah.ludwig@cuw.edu	313 NW Waterview Ct Ankeny IA 50023	IW	Deaconess	C08/2022			SL-DEAC	2017
Neyer Mary C Tuskey	(630)333-2355 neyermary@gmail.com	134 Kawga Way Loudon TN 37774	NI	Teacher	C06/2023			RF	1989
Nguyen Brenda M Hill	(626) 493-5832 brendanguyen@verizon.net	236 W Mauna Loa Ave Glendora CA 91740	PSW	Teacher	Tchr	Hope Glendora CA	(626)335-5315	IV	1997
Niccolai Cynthia M	(630)542-7308 abcniccolai@aol.com	10329 Heritage Bay Blvd Apt 1634 Naples FL 34120	NI	Teacher	C08/2019			RF	2003
Nicholas Elizabeth L Kelly	elizabeth.kelly@cune.org	14816 Willow Creek Dr Omaha NE 68138	NEB	Teacher	C07/2016			S	2012
Nichols Lauri		6920 Crooked Creek Ct Lincoln NE 68516	NOW	Teacher	Tchr	Renton Prep Renton WA	(206)723-5526	S	2004
Nichols Mary L Bohnke	(260)459-7679 jerryandmary132@gmail.com	7789b W Jefferson Blvd Fort Wayne IN 46804	IN	Teacher	EM			RF	1960
Nichols Sara T Panagos	(314)780-0576 spanagos@sjlarnold.org	12883 Waggoner Road Festus MO 63028	MO	Teacher	Tchr	St John Arnold MO	(636)464-7303	CQ	2017
Nichols Shauna K	(503)693-8074 shauna.nichols@onemaildrop.com	300 NW 336th Ave Hillsboro OR 97124	NOW	Teacher	C07/2020			CQ	2016
Nicholson Gwendolyn R Tessmann	(262)567-5995 gwennicholson1@gmail.com	N8116 La Salle Cir Oconomowoc WI 53066	SW	Teacher	EM			RF	1961
Nickel Paul E	(502)458-7826 penickel@gmail.com	9215 Dayflower St Prospect KY 40059	IN	Teacher	EM			RF	1970
Nickel Scott G	(414)882-3780 skeenick@gmail.com	W151 S6799 Golden Country Dr Muskego WI 53150	EN	Teacher	EM			AA	1986
Nicks Amanda M Korthase Deac	(231)622-2506 akorthase@gmail.com		MDS	Deaconess	C06/2024			FW-DEAC	2021
Nicol Janet L Nist Deac	(614)561-7411 music.janet@gmail.com	1020 Lombard Chuckery Rd Plain City OH 43064	OH	Deaconess	RSO	Lutherans for Life Nevada IA	(888)364-5433	FW-DEAC	2017
Nicol Jodi L Ronschke	(937)243-0295 jnicol@sjsmarysville.org	13815 State Route 4 Marysville OH 43040	OH	Teacher	Tchr	St Johns Marysville OH	(937)644-5540	CQ	2024
Niebergall Carol E Martensen	(651)503-2839 wcniebergall@me.com	11070 39th St North Lake Elmo MN 55042	MNS	Teacher	EM			RF	1962
Niebergall Donald L	(419)598-8251 dkniebs@embarqmail.com	U014 County Road 16 Napoleon OH 43545	OH	Teacher	EM			S	1958
Niebergall William A Dr	(651)503-2839 wcniebergall@me.com	11070 39th St North Lake Elmo MN 55042	MNS	Teacher	EM			S	1957
Niebuhr Kurt W	(512)639-2941 kurtmagic777@gmail.com	301 Shale Dr Jarrell TX 76537	TX	DCE	EM			SP	1979
Niedfeldt Carol S Sbresny	(918)815-3727 carolsdickens@gmail.com	P.O. Box 3726 McAlester OK 74502	OK	Teacher	EM			CQ	2000
Nielsen Allan C	(626)201-9389	283 E Benwood St Covina CA 91722	PSW	Teacher	EM			RF	1965
Nielsen George R Dr	(605)394-0289 gnie857317@rap.midco.net	1132 Enchantment Rd Rapid City SD 57701	SD	Teacher	EM			S	1954
Nielsen Jeffrey D	(715)623-3324 nielsen@dwave.net	222 Gruber St Antigo WI 54409	NW	DCM	Mem C	Peace Antigo WI	(715)623-2200	MQ	2003
Nielsen Pamela J Reagin Deac	pamjniel@aol.com	645 Running Creek Dr Ballwin MO 63021	MO	Deaconess	C10/2021			RF	1985
Nieman Lenore Kelly	(810)796-2083 lenore.nieman@gmail.com	6090 Ada Van Dr Dryden MI 48428	MI	Teacher	EM			CQ	1998
Nieman Matthew W	(812)216-2424 mnieman@immanuelseymour.com	220 Emerson Dr Seymour IN 47274	IN	Teacher	Mem C	Immanuel Seymour IN	(812)522-3118	RF	1994
Niemann Carol S Schlie	(217)356-4146 ikuwai@hotmail.com	2605 Cherry Creek Rd Champaign IL 61822	CI	Teacher	EM			RF	1972
Niemann Claudia	(518)269-2752 claudianiemann@gmail.com	8808 Pardee Forest Dr Apt D Saint Louis MO 63123	MO	Teacher	EM			RF	1962
Niemann Randy L	(217)356-4146 ikuwai@hotmail.com	2605 Cherry Creek Rd Champaign IL 61822	CI	Teacher	EM			RF	1972
Niemann Sarah P Beard	(816)716-4835 sallyniemann618@yahoo.com	911 10th Ave Leavenworth KS 66048	KS	Teacher	Tchr	St Paul Leavenworth KS	(913)682-0387	CQ	2019
Niemeyer Bradley N	(515) 571-1640 niemeyerbrad@gmail.com	1662 N 25th St Fort Dodge IA 50501	IW	DCE	EM			SP	2006

*Multiple Assignments (See Church Worker Locator for Additional Details)

See Page 53 for the Table of Abbreviations for key to District, Classification, Position, and College abbreviations.

**C =Candidate; EM =Emeritus; the date following the C is the month and year the Candidate status began

NAME	TELEPHONE NUMBER EMAIL	STREET ADDRESS CITY/STATE/ZIP	DISTRICT	CLASS.	POSITION/ STATUS**	WHERE SERVING	OFFICE PHONE	COLLEGE/ UNIV/CQ	YR GRAD
Niemeyer Catherine A Nispel	(402)466-4291 cneimeyer@faithlincoln.org	7651 Maple Village Dr Lincoln NE 68510	NEB	Teacher	EM			CQ	1987
Nierman Joanne Henning	(970)286-8861 mjnierman@msn.com	3569 Harding Dr Loveland CO 80538	RM	Teacher	Tchr	Immanuel Loveland CO	(970)667-4506	S	1999
Niermann Elizabeth M Deac	(330)690-7011 campdeac@yahoo.com	4492 Fishcreek Rd Stow OH 44224	OH	Deaconess	C07/2016			RF	1990
Niesche Katie	kniesche@sothfamily.org	4821 S Center St Casper WY 82601	RM	Teacher	Tchr	Shepherd Hills Centennial CO	(303)798-0711	SP	2012
Nieting Kathryn A Bohl	(479)650-6530 kathynieting@icloud.com	2520 S 67th St Fort Smith AR 72903	MDS	Teacher	EM			S	1977
Nietubicz Lauren M Froehlich	(832)296-4336	21715 Flecherwood Ct Spring TX 77388	TX	DCE	C07/2016			AU	2005
Niewald Pamela J Smith	(314)878-0716 pamniewald@gmail.com	2179 Seven Pines Dr Saint Louis MO 63146	MO	Teacher	EM			CQ	1994
NIGH Rose E	(402)616-0621 rose.nigh@molcs.org	10505 Providence Dr Unit 103 Johnston IA 50131	IW	Teacher	Tchr	Mount Olive Des Moines IA	(515)277-0247	S	2022
Nihiser Jane A Wollenburg	(231)590-5285 jakeandjim2@juno.com	4945 Pinespar Trl Traverse City MI 49685	MI	Teacher	EM			S	1977
Niles Sara J Sara J Korte	(812)454-0900 sjkorte2@yahoo.com	5122 Hedera Dr Evansville IN 47711	IN	Teacher	Tchr	Evansville Evansville IN	(812)424-7252	AA	1986
Nilsson Lianna M Jordan	(530)966-2806 liannanilsson@gmail.com	11086 Telluride Court Commerce City CO 80022	RM	Teacher	C08/2021			IV	2016
Nimmer Joshua E			SW	Teacher	Tchr	Trinity Mequon WI	(262)242-2045	MQ	2011
Nimtz Faith D Hafercamp	(402)960-7854 faithnimtz14@gmail.com	302 N 27th St Ashland NE 68003	NEB	Teacher	Tchr	Peaceful Beginnings Waverly NE	(402)786-2345	AU	1982
Nimtz Mark A Dr	(248)224-1842 nimtzm@ourshepherd.net	1127 Shadow Dr Troy MI 48085	MI	Teacher	Mem C	Our Shepherd Birmingham MI	(248)646-6100	S	1981
Nimtz Wendy E Blus	(248)524-1619 nimtzw@ourshepherd.net	1127 Shadow Dr Troy MI 48085	MI	Teacher	Tchr	Our Shepherd Birmingham MI	(248)646-6100	SP	1988
Nisayas Eloise P Kieschnick	(281)252-3101 tiredteacher_2@hotmail.com	27407 Kathy Ln Magnolia TX 77355	TX	Teacher	EM			RF	1976
Nistler Kristin Zellers	kristin.nistler@gmail.com	1002 Constitution Dr Bismarck ND 58501	ND	Teacher	Mem C	Zion Bismarck ND	(701)223-8286	S	2002
Nitta Amber Amber Parrish		10700 SE 260th St F103 Kent WA 98030	NOW	Teacher	C06/2018			AU	2012
Nitz Angela M Haupt	(214)450-8169 dcenitz@usa.net	5665 Chippendale Ct Rockford IL 61107	NI	DCE	Mem C	Immanuel Belvidere IL	(815)544-8058	RF	1997
Nitz Kenlyn G	(469)900-6675 nitzkenlyn@gmail.com	5665 Chippendale Ct Rockford IL 61107	NI	Teacher	Tchr	Rockford Rockford IL	(815)877-9551	CH	2024
Nitz Todd E	(214)893-9352 toddnitz@usa.net	5665 Chippendale Ct Rockford IL 61107	NI	Teacher	Prin	Rockford Rockford IL	(815)877-9551	MQ	1991
Nixon Christine A Sears	(314)606-8517 cnixon1230@gmail.com	2944 Westborough Dr Saint Charles MO 63301	MO	Teacher	Prin	Immanuel Olivette MO	(314)993-2394	S	1994
Nixon Joann M Avey	(260)493-6344 nixonjmn@gmail.com	1222 Langley Pass Fort Wayne IN 46815	IN	Teacher	EM			RF	1971
Nixon Sarah K	(505)884-3876	11405 San Jacinto Ave NE Albuquerque NM 87112	RM	Teacher	Tchr	Christ Albuquerque NM	(505)884-3876	S	2008
Noack Dalton J	(512)569-0631 dndnoack@gmail.com	2306 Pleasant Rose Cir Bryan TX 77808	TX	Teacher	EM			S	1959
Noack Dorothy A Hutchins	(469)693-1951 dorothy.noack@gmail.com	123 Camp Dr Georgetown TX 78633	TX	Teacher	EM			CQ	2004
Noack Kristin Madsen	noack18@optonline.net	45 Greene Ave Sayville NY 11782	AT	Teacher	C07/2016			S	1998
Nobbe Rebecca L Ruebke	(618)443-8875 rebecca.nobbe@hotmail.com	307 Sycamore Drive Waterloo IL 62298	SI	Teacher	Tchr	Good Shepherd Collinsville IL	(618)344-3153	CQ	2016
Nobili Linda D Davidson Deac	(248)892-7405 dcslinda1492@gmail.com	5977 Anglers Dr Ortonville MI 48462	FG	Deaconess	EM			RF	2001
Nobis Judy A Hospodar	(616)558-8889 nobisjudy@yahoo.com	8541 Riverbend Dr Portland MI 48875	MI	Teacher	EM			CQ	2004
Nobis Lloyd B	(989)652-9039	1005 W Tuscola St Frankenmuth MI 48734	MI	Teacher	EM			RF	1970
Nobis Sharon K	(480)510-5825 snobis@cox.net	8659 E Via De Viva Scottsdale AZ 85258	EN	Teacher	EM			RF	1966
Noble Jennifer S Bonow	(605)213-0024 rjnoble97@yahoo.com	6608 E Steamboat Trl Sioux Falls SD 57110	SD	Teacher	C05/2020			CQ	2015
Noble Sandra J Shaw	(847)253-7381 snoble@sbcglobal.net	2305 Martin Ln Rolling Mdws IL 60008	NI	Teacher	EM			RF	1968
Noel Cynthia L Capps		31058 Ponderosa St Lake Elsinore CA 92530	PSW	Teacher	EM			S	1973
Noel Kimberly L Marino	(828)280-3429 knoel@elcsmail.org	1250 Little Ridge Dr Marshall NC 28753	SE	Teacher	Tchr	Emmanuel Asheville NC	(828)252-1795	CQ	2013
Noel Marie A Fetterer	(313)505-6052 mnoel914@hotmail.com	8414 Perrin Ave Westland MI 48185	MI	Teacher	EM			RF	1978
Noennig Mark T	(701)261-3003 dcemark20@gmail.com	120 2nd St S Sabin MN 56580	MNN	Teacher	EM			S	1978
Noffze Denise J	(720)922-3073	4574 S Estes St Littleton CO 80123	RM	Teacher	Tchr	Lutheran Parker CO	(303)841-5551	AA	1983
Noll Terry E Skok	(216)333-0872 terrinoll4@gmail.com	21382 Maplewood Ave Rocky River OH 44116	OH	Teacher	EM			CQ	1990
Nord Lois A Denninger	(319)573-0808 loisanord@gmail.com	825 27th St Marion IA 52302	IE	Teacher	EM			RF	1972
Nordbrock Janice A Vick	(602) 741-9260 vickinordbrock@msn.com	3827 W Phelps Rd Phoenix AZ 85053	PSW	Teacher	EM			RF	1982
Nordeen Mary A Natonick	(201)796-5540 marynordeen@optonline.net	10424 W Alabama Ave Sun City AZ 85351	NJ	Teacher	EM			RF	1966

*Multiple Assignments (See Church Worker Locator for Additional Details)

See Page 53 for the Table of Abbreviations for key to District, Classification, Position, and College abbreviations.

**C =Candidate; EM =Emeritus; the date following the C is the month and year the Candidate status began

NAME	TELEPHONE NUMBER EMAIL	STREET ADDRESS CITY/STATE/ZIP	DISTRICT	CLASS.	POSITION/ STATUS**	WHERE SERVING	OFFICE PHONE	COLLEGE/ UNIV/CQ	YR GRAD
Nordhausen Joanne R Zuch Dr	(585)747-2475	24 Wayne Dr Rochester NY 14626	EA	Teacher	EM			RF	1974
Nordling Sara A Bauman Deac	(260)348-8709 sanordling@hotmail.com	6015 Countess Dr Fort Wayne IN 46815	IN	Deaconess	C07/2016			RF	1985
Nordman Diane L Happel	dianenordman@ilcp.org	268 Galway Dr Cary IL 60013	NI	Teacher	Tchr	Immanuel Palatine IL	(847)359-1936	S	1983
Nordmeyer Richard C	(815)263-5757 rcnord@comcast.net	255 E Park St # 96 Chebanse IL 60922	NI	Teacher	EM			RF	1973
Norelius Sharon L	(516)922-0808 sharon.norelius@luhi.org	18 2nd Ave Bayville NY 11709	AT	Teacher	Tchr	Long Island Brookville NY	(516)626-1735	CQ	2017
Norris Pamela J Rhoda	(815)945-7736 pamela.j.norris@osfhealthcare.org	26317 N 2850 East Rd Chenoa IL 61726	CI	DCM	Mem C	St Paul Chenoa IL	(815)945-5331	CQ	2002
Norris Priscilla R Van Duzer	(661)992-9633 norrisp@trinityklein.org	35445 Woodtrace Circle Pinehurst TX 77362	TX	Teacher	Tchr	Trinity Spring TX	(281)376-5810	RF	2003
Norris Sharon E Huettner	(828)236-3957 clahen20@charter.net	40 Sydney Ln Asheville NC 28806	SE	Teacher	EM			S	1965
Norris Susan C Hess	(863)441-4169 s_norris123@yahoo.com	114 McKinley Ave Lake Placid FL 33852	FG	Teacher	Mem C	Trinity Lake Placid FL	(863)465-5253	BR	1980
Northcutt Bryan W	(208)541-8480 bwnorthcutt@outlook.com	61 Lakeside Dr Unit B-1 Pagosa Springs CO 81147	RM	Teacher	Tchr	Our Savior Pagosa Springs CO	(970)731-3512	CQ	2021
Norton Gary P	(619)741-4534 gary.norton@psd-lcms.org	8106 Vista Dr La Mesa CA 91941	PSW	Teacher	EM			S	1963
Norton John J II Dr	(979)370-3951 john.norton@cui.edu	19 Beacon Pt Ladera Ranch CA 92694	PSW	Teacher	S HS/C	Concordia University Irvine Irvine CA	(949)854-8002	CQ	2016
Norton Judith L Zafft	kumujudy2@yahoo.com	3293 Lost Mountain Rd Sequim WA 98382	NOW	Teacher	EM			S	1961
Norton Kenneth J	(206)258-4307 fishon8@comcast.net	5000 California Ave SW Apt 201 Seattle WA 98136	NOW	Teacher	EM			S	1959
Norton Kenneth S	(253)212-0522 dcenorton@comcast.net	9002 East F Street Tacoma WA 98445	NOW	DCE	EM			SP	2001
Norton Mary Thompson	(206)932-2768 jeff.norton1@attbi.com	1118 51st St NE Tacoma WA 98422	NOW	Teacher	Tchr	Hope Seattle WA	(206)935-8500	PO	1984
Norton Teri L Siewert	(414)614-1951 tlnorton66@gmail.com	W169 N 10650 Juniper Dr Germantown WI 53022	SW	Teacher	C07/2016			MQ	1988
Novak Brenna Krause	(414)690-1303 brennanovak19@gmail.com	17465 River Birch Dr Apt 112 Brookfield WI 53045	SW	Teacher	Tchr	Lake Country Hartland WI	(262)367-8600	MQ	2018
Novak Jan A	(360)691-3372 worship@lambofgod-lakestevens.org	13313 74th St NE Lake Stevens WA 98258	NOW	Teacher	Mem C	Lamb Of God Lake Stevens WA	(425)377-2173	IV	1988
Novak Julie M Spurgat	(734)218-2744 jnovak@stpaulannarbor.org	1921 Frances Way Ypsilanti MI 48198	MI	Teacher	Tchr	St Paul Ann Arbor MI	(734)665-0604	RF	1986
Novak Thelma A Lovelace	(410)638-6644 tnovak@stpaulskingsville.org	803 Kilber Ct Bel Air MD 21014	SE	Teacher	Tchr	St Pauls Kingsville MD	(410)592-8100	BR	1977
Novotny Vicki J Miller		5839 S Loomis Rd Waterford WI 53185	SW	Teacher	Tchr	St Pauls West Allis WI	(414)541-6251	MQ	1991
Nowicki Michael W	(321)439-2208 mwndrum@hotmail.com	985 Willow Run Ln Winter Spgs FL 32708	S	Teacher	C07/2016			MQ	1983
Nowicki Sarah E Bangert	(321)439-2298 sarah_nowicki@hotmail.com	2042 W State Road 426 Oviedo FL 32765	S	Teacher	EM			MQ	1982
Nowiszewski Nancy E Michels	(816)678-6557 novatn73@gmail.com	100 Porter Dr Smithville MO 64089	MO	DCM	EM			MQ	2012
Nuffer Patricia Squibb Deac	(260)402-4942 patnuffer@gmail.com	6527 Deepwater Point Rd Williamsburg MI 49690	MI	Deaconess	EM			FW-DEAC	2007
Nummela Pamela R Lehenbauer	(913)515-9276 pam.nummela@gmail.com	12462 Merrick Dr Saint Louis MO 63146	MO	Tch/DCE	EM			S	1974
Nummela Rachelle M Wilcox	(314)520-3852 rachelle.nummela@gmail.com	7206 General Sherman Ln Affton MO 63123	MO	Teacher	Tchr	Christ Community Kirkwood MO	(314)822-7774	S	2008
Nummela Thomas A	(913)940-8765 tom.nummela@gmail.com	12462 Merrick Dr Saint Louis MO 63146	MO	DCE	EM			S	1975
Nummela-Hanel Bethany		7517 Sloewood Dr Leesburg FL 34748	FG	Teacher	Tchr	Faith Eustis FL	(352)589-5683	S	2024
Nun Sandra J Oswald	(512) 925-8356 sjnun@sbcglobal.net	11803 Oak Trl Austin TX 78753	TX	Teacher	EM			RF	1971
Nunes Brenna L Deac	(312)952-6754 deaconunes@yahoo.com	4221 Bandice Ln Pflugerville TX 78660	SO	Deaconess	C04/2023			RF	2001
Nunez Stephanie J Rogers	(630)267-8961 stephanie.jean986@gmail.com	1725 Bayberry Lane Pingree Grove IL 60140	NI	Teacher	Tchr	St Peter Arlington Heights IL	(847)259-4114	CH	2009
Nunnally Wilma J Doster	(480)436-0764 wilmanunnally@icloud.com	1859 E Sesame St Tempe AZ 85283	PSW	Teacher	EM			CQ	1989
Nuoffer Marcelle D Dr	(818)403-0265 docnuoffer@gmail.com	6509 Brandywine Way Las Vegas NV 89107	PSW	Teacher	Tchr	Faith Las Vegas NV	(702)804-4400	IV	1994
Nyen Duane M	(435)632-0236 smudgeny@gmail.com	2921 Box Elder Cir Saint George UT 84790	RM	Teacher	EM			S	1988
O' Boyle Sharilyn M Specht	(248)709-6519 oboylesharilyn@gmail.com	20881 Knobs Hollow Dr Macomb MI 48044	MI	Teacher	EM			AA	1986
O Brien Kessler T	(480)404-8139 kessler.obrien@splsorange.org	354 N Brook Glen Ln Orange CA 92869	PSW	DCE	Mem C	St Paul Orange CA	(714)637-2640	IV	2023
O Conner Sarah M Kehr	(562)818-1511 smo17636@yahoo.com	6002 Gallup St Lakewood CA 90713	PSW	Teacher	Tchr	Bethany Long Beach CA	(562)421-4711	BR	1999
O Connor Dawn K Irvin	(262)395-4586 bd2010@sbcglobal.net	13800 W Park Central Blvd Apt 446 New Berlin WI 53151	SW	Teacher	EM			RF	1966
O Connor Sean E	(843)424-4812 sean.oconnor@risenchristacademy.com	1348 Reflection Pond Dr. Little River SC 29566	SE	Teacher	Prin	Risen Christ Myrtle Beach SC	(843)272-5845	CQ	2016
O Dell Katrina J Kois Thomas	(918)695-9674 katejoyodell@gmail.com	2713 S Chestnut Ave Broken Arrow OK 74012	OK	Teacher	C07/2016			S	2006

*Multiple Assignments (See Church Worker Locator for Additional Details)
See Page 53 for the Table of Abbreviations for key to District, Classification, Position, and College abbreviations.
**C =Candidate; EM =Emeritus; the date following the C is the month and year the Candidate status began

NAME	TELEPHONE NUMBER EMAIL	STREET ADDRESS CITY/STATE/ZIP	DISTRICT	CLASS.	POSITION/ STATUS**	WHERE SERVING	OFFICE PHONE	COLLEGE/ UNIV/CQ	YR GRAD
O Keefe Ruth E Riedel	(209)368-2090	1716 Reisling Dr Lodi CA 95240	CNH	Teacher	EM			S	1968
O Neill Christina M Chuma Larkin	(702)631-9062 christophersue@cox.net	3316 Big Sandy Cir Las Vegas NV 89129	PSW	Teacher	Tchr	Faith Community Las Vegas NV	(702)921-2777	CQ	2009
Oberdieck Brian N	(812)952-3098 inoberdieck@aol.com	1507 Saint Johns Church Rd NE Lanesville IN 47136	IN	Teacher	Tchr	St Johns Lanesville IN	(812)952-2737	RF	1992
Oberdieck Timothy L	(502)974-3382 tim.oberdieck@stjohnseward.org	541 N 5th St Seward NE 68434	NEB	DCE	Mem C	St John Seward NE	(402)643-2983	S	2022
Oberg Meghan K	(512)300-7672 meghan.oberg@redeemer.net	114 Bedrock Dr Liberty Hill TX 78642	TX	Teacher	Tchr	Redeemer Austin TX	(512)459-1500	AU	2017
Obermann Donna S Garber	(309)635-4275	21029 E Mewes Rd Queen Creek AZ 85142	PSW	Teacher	EM			S	1975
Obermeyer Barbara A Rusch	(314)221-4545 barbaraaobermeyer@gmail.com	8413 Meadow Dr Hillsboro MO 63050	MO	Teacher	Tchr	St John Ellisville MO	(636)779-2325	CQ	2015
Obermueller Elizabeth A Stork	(402)643-3977 elizabeth.obermueller@cune.org	1348 Rainbow Ave Seward NE 68434	NEB	Teacher	EM			S	1967
Obermueller Megan L	(651)324-7232 megan.obermueller@lhsparker.org	8395 Ponderosa Dr Parker CO 80138	RM	Teacher	Tchr	Lutheran Parker CO	(303)841-5551	S	2000
Obermueller Stanley R Dr	(402)643-3977 stan.obermueller@cune.edu	1348 Rainbow Ave Seward NE 68434	NEB	Teacher	EM			S	1968
Obersat Jane A Mason Deac	(979)716-7717 janeamason@hotmail.com	P.O. Box 245 Eden TX 76837	TX	Deaconess	C01/2025			CQ	2007
Obersat Magdalena R	(512)718-6893 magdalena.obersat@gmail.com		TX	Teacher	Tchr	Grace Brenham TX	(979)836-2030	MQ	2024
Oblinger Carolyn D Luedtke	(832)592-3790 ecmo@sbcglobal.net	8922 Forest Creek Dr Tomball TX 77375	TX	Teacher	Tchr	Trinity Spring TX	(281)376-5810	AA	1997
Oblinger Eric S Dr	(832)592-3745 oblingere@clhs-tx.org	8922 Forest Creek Dr Tomball TX 77375	TX	Teacher	Tchr	Concordia Tomball TX	(281)351-2547	CQ	2012
O'Brien Christian A	(812)746-6907 christianobrien527@gmail.com	1936 Eastland Dr Evansville IN 47715	IN	Teacher	Tchr	Evansville Evansville IN	(812)424-7252	CQ	2025
Ochnikowski Joshua J	(414)419-6213 ocho8soccer@gmail.com	13419 W Sunny View Dr New Berlin WI 53151	EN	Teacher	Tchr	Hales Corners Hales Corners WI	(414)529-6701	MQ	2013
Ochoa Abigail K Abigail Luerssen	(715)219-4939 akluerssen@gmail.com	2014 Greystem Cir Apt 203 Gurnee IL 60031	SW	Teacher	Tchr	Concordia Sturtevant WI	(262)884-0991	MQ	2021
Ochs David L	(316)744-9390	4119 N Edgemoor St Bel Aire KS 67220	KS	Teacher	EM			S	1980
Ochs Lauren G Brezina	(720)590-9544 lochs@redeemeralive.org	12211 E 25th Ave Spokane Valley WA 99206	NOW	DPM	Mem C	Redeemer Spokane WA	(509)926-6363	CQ	2024
Ochs Lisa B Schardt	(785)410-8513 lisaochs@gmail.com	11503 E Tipperary Wichita KS 67206	KS	Teacher	C07/2016			S	2006
Ockander Marli M	(605)376-6078 mockander@sflutheranschool.com	7121 W 56th St Apt 75 Sioux Falls SD 57106	SD	Teacher	Tchr	Sioux Falls Sioux Falls SD	(605)335-1923	S	2002
Ockander Remkea R	merrem77@hotmail.com	19420 Oakwood St Omaha NE 68135	NEB	Teacher	C05/2021			CQ	2006
O'Connor John D			SW	Teacher	Tchr	Divine Redeemer Hartland WI	(262)367-3664	MQ	2010
O'Connor Kristin A Kloess	(847)308-1578 kristinoconnor535@gmail.com	1205 E Hintz Rd Unit 209 Arlington Hts IL 60004	NI	Teacher	Tchr	Immanuel Crystal Lake IL	(815)459-1441	RF	2005
O'Connor Stephanie L Wisser			SW	Teacher	C07/2023			MQ	2010
O'Day Kathleen M Kearney Deac	kmkoday@gmail.com	10730 Keystone Ln Crown Point IN 46307	NI	Deaconess	RSO	Lutheran Church Charities Northbrook IL	(866)455-6466	CH	2017
Odemba Britt S Anderson	+254701862691 ecenut@gmail.com	Po Box 22 Karen 00502 KENYA	PSW	Teacher	S Miss	Office of International Mission Saint Louis MO		IV	1998
Odinga Ardith A Gerken	(989)714-6667 ardith.odinga@gmail.com	734 Lost Pine Dr Midlothian TX 76065	TX	Teacher	EM			S	1970
Odinga Kimberly E Michaelis	(832)326-1528 kimodinga@yahoo.com	24627 Raven Cliff Falls Dr Tomball TX 77375	TX	Teacher	Tchr	Concordia Tomball TX	(281)351-2547	MQ	2001
Odinga Michael D	(989)714-6667	734 Lost Pine Dr Midlothian TX 76065	TX	Teacher	EM			S	1969
Odle Susan H Heide	(714)401-9233 susanodle@aol.com	6007 E Mabury Ave Orange CA 92867	PSW	Teacher	EM			CQ	1985
Odle Timothy J	(714)363-1771 tim.odle@cui.edu	5626 E Valencia Dr Orange CA 92869	PSW	Teacher	S HS/C	Concordia University Irvine Irvine CA	(949)854-8002	CQ	2001
O'Donnell Aidan R	(262)720-2194 aidan.r.odonnell@gmail.com	N8052 Woody Ln Ixonia WI 53036	SW	Teacher	Tchr	Trinity Mequon WI	(262)242-2045	MQ	2022
Oechsner Bryan P	(253)888-0957 boeschner@lwlhs.com	N93W5103 Thornapple Ln Cedarburg WI 53012	SW	Teacher	Tchr	Living Word Jackson WI	(262)677-9353	CQ	2010
Oehlert George J	(850) 653-6261	1604 Duke St Beaufort SC 29902	FG	Teacher	EM			S	1967
Oerkfitz Kenneth J	(216)789-6436 kennjoerk@yahoo.com	18420 Bunker Hill Dr Strongsville OH 44136	EN	Teacher	EM			RF	1965
Oerman Rebecca L	(507)236-0955 rebeccaoerman@martinlutherhs.com	310 N 2nd Ave E Truman MN 56088	MNS	Teacher	Tchr	Martin Luther Northrop MN	(507)436-5249	S	1985
Oesch Joel C Dr	(512)619-4149 joel.oesch@cui.edu	P.O. Box 693 Silverado CA 92676	PSW	DCE	S HS/C	Concordia University Irvine Irvine CA	(949)854-8002	IV	1997
Oesterreich Allan C	(717)432-9147 atoest2@icloud.com	2107 Edgehill Circle Johnson City TN 37601	SE	Teacher	EM			RF	1959
Oesterreich Donna G Isaacson	(850)625-0573 donna.oesterreich@gmail.com	302 Eagle Drive P C Beach FL 32407	SO	Teacher	EM			SP	1980
Oestmann Marvin P	(303)408-0608 oestmanns@msn.com	14555 E Hampden Ave Apt 205 Aurora CO 80014	RM	Teacher	EM			CQ	1968
Oestriecher Diane J Karcher	(504)250-3011 doestriecher@yahoo.com	4217 Page Dr Metairie LA 70003	SO	Teacher	EM			CQ	1995

*Multiple Assignments (See Church Worker Locator for Additional Details)

See Page 53 for the Table of Abbreviations for key to District, Classification, Position, and College abbreviations.

**C =Candidate; EM =Emeritus; the date following the C is the month and year the Candidate status began

NAME	TELEPHONE NUMBER EMAIL	STREET ADDRESS CITY/STATE/ZIP	DISTRICT	CLASS.	POSITION/ STATUS**	WHERE SERVING	OFFICE PHONE	COLLEGE/ UNIV/CQ	YR GRAD
Oetting Aaron P	(815)209-7591 oettingat@gmail.com	3636 Spring Creek Rd Belvidere IL 61008	NI	Teacher	C08/2018			S	1998
Oetting Dennis D	(660)463-7516 doetting@mac.com	P.O. Box 24 Emma MO 65327	MO	Teacher	EM			S	1966
Oetting Tara M Hodge	(815)209-7593 oettingat@yahoo.com	3636 Spring Creek Rd Belvidere IL 61008	NI	Teacher	Tchr	Immanuel Belvidere IL	(815)544-8058	S	1997
O'Farrell Allison S	(262)720-2274 ofarrellally@gmail.com	23417 Beverly St St Clair MI 48082	MI	Teacher	Tchr	Lutheran Special Education Ministries Ann Arbor MI	(248)419-3390	MQ	2025
Offermann David K	(815)369-4035 office@stjohnslena.org	11889 N Christian Hollow Rd Winslow IL 61089	NI	Teacher	Mem C	St John Lena IL	(815)369-4035	RF	1991
Ogden Kathryn C Manahan	(636)448-5878 kcogden1@gmail.com	573 Oak Leaf Manor Ct Ballwin MO 63021	MO	Teacher	Tchr	Christ Community Kirkwood MO	(314)822-7774	CQ	2012
Ogilvie Kianna N	(719)963-9082 kianna.ogilvie@cune.org	211 5th Ave NE Hankinson ND 58041	MT	Teacher	C07/2025			S	2021
Oglialoro Kelly Triest Dr	(863)430-5418 koglialoro@stpaullakeland.org	5127 Meadowood Ln Mulberry FL 33860	FG	Teacher	Prin	St Paul Lakeland FL	(863)644-7710	CQ	2022
OHara Jacob T	(440)242-5690 jacobohara44@gmail.com	3522 Clague Rd. North Olmsted OH 44070	OH	Teacher	Tchr	Cleveland LHS Association Rocky River OH	(440)356-7155	CH	2012
O'Hara Rachel M Goodwin	(847)271-9938 rachelmgoodwin16@gmail.com	727 Green Tree Rd West Bend WI 53090	SW	Teacher	Tchr	St John West Bend WI	(262)429-1061	MQ	2021
O'Hara Rebecca L Matson	oharasohana@gmail.com		NOW	Teacher	EM			MQ	2002
Ohlemeyer Grace A	(314)296-7993 graceanna.ohlemeyer@gmail.com	835 White Rock Dr Des Peres MO 63131	MO	Teacher	Tchr	Lutheran South Saint Louis MO	(314)631-1400	MQ	2025
Ohling Lindsey E	(916)622-6491 lindsey.ohling@att.net	15720 E 4th Ave Apt D203 Spokane Valley WA 99037	NOW	DCE	Mem C	Redeemer Spokane WA	(509)926-6363	IV	2023
Ohlmann Glenn E	(402)643-2769 glenn.ohlmann@windstream.net	1318 N 2nd St Seward NE 68434	NEB	Teacher	EM			S	1963
Ohm Elisabeth R Allyn	eohm604@gmail.com	483 W Commonwealth Ln Elmhurst IL 60126	NI	Teacher	Tchr	Immanuel Elmhurst IL	(630)832-1649	RF	2003
Ohmann Jaclyn R Gronbach	(507)649-0888 ohmanndairy@gmail.com	2090 290th St E Randolph MN 55065	MNS	DCE	C01/2018			SP	2003
Ohmie Angela R Ruprecht	(636)498-9188 angela.ohmie@gmail.com	2 Scarsdale Manor Ct Saint Charles MO 63303	MO	Teacher	C07/2016			RF	2003
Okonski John S	(940)440-6311 johnokonski@att.net	2225 Rodgers Ln Aubrey TX 76227	PSW	Teacher	EM			S	1967
Oldehoeft Harold W	(402)675-7915 oldehoef@yahoo.com	1312 W Norfolk Ave Apt B Norfolk NE 68701	NEB	Teacher	EM			S	1964
Oldenburg Craig S Dr	(616)799-6360 coldenburg@gmail.com	8327 Foxtail Loop Pensacola FL 32526	SO	Tch/DCE	EM			RF	1981
Oldenburg Jonathan	(262)366-6802	214 Glen Oak Ct Delafield WI 53018	SW	Teacher	Tchr	Lake Country Hartland WI	(262)367-8600	MQ	2012
Oldenburg Mary K Brown	(616)799-6576 oldenburgs@hotmail.com	8327 Foxtail Loop Pensacola FL 32526	SO	Tch/DCE	EM			RF	1983
Oldenburg Michael P	(262)366-2871 mikeo@drlc.org	1009 Hilger Rd Hartland WI 53029	SW	Teacher	EM			RF	1976
Oldenettel Dawn D Kohls	(262)573-8315 dawnoldenettel@gmail.com	23 Newburgh Drive Bella Vista AR 72715	MDS	Teacher	EM			Other	2005
Oleson Cindy A	(224)659-2404 cindyoleson@yahoo.com	118 Emerson Dr Schaumburg IL 60194	NI	Teacher	EM			RF	1987
Oleson David G	(909)838-9825 olesda44@gmail.com	390 Cavaletti Lane Norco CA 92860	PSW	Teacher	EM			S	1967
Oliver Charles A	(308)227-0468 coliver@wvhs.org	888 S 6th Ave West Bend WI 53095	SW	Teacher	Tchr	Living Word Jackson WI	(262)677-9353	MQ	1990
Oliver Timothy D	(402)641-3094 toliver@immanuelknights.org	910 1/2 Warren Ave Belvidere IL 61008	NI	Teacher	Tchr	Immanuel Belvidere IL	(815)547-5346	S	1979
Olmstead Daisy L Steinke	(504)906-8586 dlolmstead623@gmail.com	70477 Chambly Ct Madisonville LA 70447	SO	Teacher	D Ex/S	Southern District Slidell LA	(504)282-2632	MQ	2005
Oloff Betty C Wiger	(208)522-1440 bcoloff@yahoo.com	3625 S Koester Rd Idaho Falls ID 83402	NOW	Teacher	EM			SP	1980
Oloff James L	(208)522-1440 jmslff@yahoo.com	3625 S Koester Rd Idaho Falls ID 83402	NOW	Teacher	EM			SP	1973
Olp Mariel S Nuckols	(402)875-0821 mariel.olp@gmail.com	N98W16822 Concord Rd Germantown WI 53022	SW	Teacher	Tchr	Immanuel Brookfield WI	(262)781-7140	S	2009
Olsen Brenda G Gold Deac	(206)852-5863 Bolsen60@gmail.com	7863 Wildwood Farms Ln Indianapolis IN 46239	IN	Deaconess	EM			Other	1977
Olsen Brenda J Mueller		2451 Lake Breeze Dr Unit 10 Manitowoc WI 54220	RM	Teacher	C07/2023			CH	2016
Olsen Chris M	(308)850-1692 colsen@flcse.org	1092 Remington Ave Eustis FL 32726	FG	Teacher	Tchr	Faith Eustis FL	(352)589-5683	S	2001
Olsen Heidi K Unglaub	(952)237-0807 holsen2215@gmail.com	2265 Coldwater Xing Mayer MN 55360	MNS	Teacher	Tchr	Saint James Howard Lake MN	(320)543-2766	SP	1995
Olsen Jessica L Westerhold	mrsolsenk12@gmail.com	10101 Crystal Lake Dr. Blair NE 68008	NEB	Teacher	C05/2020			S	2002
Olsen Lauren K Morgan Deac	(815)353-9414 deaclaurenolsen@gmail.com	3313 Stone Bend Dr Winterville NC 28590	SE	Deaconess	EM			RF	1987
Olsen Linda L Brandt	(720)338-6222 lindaolsen1948@gmail.com	4902 S Robb Way Littleton CO 80127	RM	Tch/DCE	EM			S	1982
Olsen Matthew W	(586)215-4222 matthewwolsen@yahoo.com	1873 Glen Iris Dr Commerce Twp MI 48382	MI	Teacher	EM			AA	1990
Olson Angela M Calvin	(702)885-4286 angieolson13@live.com	3838 Susan Circle W Hansen ID 83334	NOW	Teacher	Prin	Immanuel Twin Falls ID	(208)733-7820	CQ	2017
Olson Debra L Smith	(260)437-7423 smittyolson@gmail.com	1540 Golf Course Rd Columbus NC 28722	SE	Teacher	Tchr	Mt Pisgah Hendersonville NC	(828)698-5900	SP	1978

*Multiple Assignments (See Church Worker Locator for Additional Details)

See Page 53 for the Table of Abbreviations for key to District, Classification, Position, and College abbreviations.

**C =Candidate; EM =Emeritus; the date following the C is the month and year the Candidate status began

NAME	TELEPHONE NUMBER EMAIL	STREET ADDRESS CITY/STATE/ZIP	DISTRICT	CLASS.	POSITION/ STATUS**	WHERE SERVING	OFFICE PHONE	COLLEGE/ UNIV/CQ	YR GRAD
Olson Eric	(714)315-7879 olson@creanlutheran.org	23152 Tulip Lake Forest CA 92630	PSW	Teacher	Tchr	Crean Irvine CA	(949)387-1199	CQ	2019
Olson Gail R Maser	(651)983-3962 gmaser@yahoo.com	1836 Red Fox Rd Eagan MN 55122	MNS	Teacher	EM			SP	1978
Olson John R	(989)662-6635 johnolson38@gmail.com	3791 Carter Rd Auburn MI 48611	MI	Teacher	EM			RF	1971
Olson Judith C Constien	(816)935-5555 gjknkc@gmail.com	4116 NE 71st Ct Kansas City (gladstone) MO 64119	MO	Teacher	EM			RF	1980
Olson Katie A Hiesterman	(785)692-4276 kolson@bluevalley.net	623 Jade Rd Palmer KS 66962	KS	DCE	C07/2016			S	2001
Olson Kayla K	(309)202-2367 kolson319@gmail.com	325 Oak Creek Dr Apt 108 Apt 2 Wheeling IL 60090	NI	DCE	Mem C	St Peter Arlington Heights IL	(847)259-4114	RF	2016
Olson Morris L	(785)473-0099 mojosjoy@gmail.com	2228 Alta Dr Manhattan KS 66502	KS	DCO	EM			SP	2007
Olson Ruth E Kohtz	(208)829-4214	1002 S 1900 E Hazelton ID 83335	NOW	Teacher	EM			S	1962
Olson Sheryl B	(480)278-3823 solson2747@gmail.com	5830 E McKellips Rd Unit 15 Mesa AZ 85215	PSW	DCE	EM			CQ	1985
Olson Susan J	(708)217-0197 sjolson57@aol.com	17900 Poplar Ln Country Club Hills IL 60478	NI	Teacher	EM			CQ	2006
Olson Susan K Burmeister	(605)421-9826 dro1010@hotmail.com	13115 W 70th St Juniata NE 68955	NEB	Teacher	Tchr	Christ Juniata NE	(402)744-4991	S	1999
Olson Tanner J	(407)761-0820 tannerjolson14@gmail.com	2224 Monticello Dr Nashville TN 37207	MDS	DCM	C08/2019			MQ	2012
O'Meara Elizabeth E Plaehn	(586)263-3565 lomeara@immlutheran.org	46188 Peach Grove Ave Macomb MI 48044	MI	Teacher	Tchr	Immanuel Macomb MI	(586)286-7076	CQ	1998
Ommen Sharon T Thielker	(573)353-9016 dsommen.1982@gmail.com	P.O. Box 153 Gerald MO 63037	MO	Teacher	EM			CQ	2005
O'Neal Grace C	(712)339-3365 18graceoneal@gmail.com	1041 29th St Spirit Lake IA 51360	MO	Teacher	Tchr	Saint Paul Concordia MO	(660)463-2238	S	2022
O'Neil Haley Gruenhagen	hngruenhagen@gmail.com	S513 County Road 15 Napoleon OH 43545	OH	Teacher	Tchr	St John Napoleon OH	(419)598-8961	CQ	2013
Onnen Natasha B Otjen	(402)750-9052 natasha.otjen@cune.org	107 N Werner St Battle Creek NE 68715	NEB	Teacher	Tchr	St John Battle Creek NE	(402)675-3605	S	2006
Onnen Nicholas J	(402)364-3107 principal@stjohnbc.net	107 N Werner St P.O. Box 321 Battle Creek NE 68715	NEB	Teacher	Tchr	St John Battle Creek NE	(402)675-3605	S	2006
Opel Edgar L	(989)992-9303 opeledor@outlook.com	310 E 10600 S Unit 203 Sandy UT 84070	RM	Teacher	EM			S	1958
Opel R W	(586) 295-4074 warren.opel@gmail.com	7373 Sashabaw Rd Unit 303 Clarkston MI 48348	MI	Teacher	EM			S	1962
Opfer Shanna R Sander	(402)643-4676 shanna.opfer@cune.edu	2544 Timber Creek Dr Seward NE 68434	NEB	Teacher	S HS/C	Concordia University Nebraska Seward NE	(402)643-3651	S	1999
Ore Charles W Dr	(402)643-3569 charles.ore@cune.edu	2523 Bluff Rd Seward NE 68434	NEB	Teacher	EM			S	1958
Orlow-Brandt Vicki L	(503)460-3382 vickiobrandt@gmail.com	5844 NE 24th Ave Portland OR 97211	NOW	Teacher	C06/2019			MQ	1986
Orr Anna E Neumann	(715)533-1658 mommyoftsj@gmail.com	4322 Long Grove Dr. Seabrook TX 77586	TX	Teacher	Pro Stf	Lutheran Education Association Friendswood TX	(281)617-5189	MQ	2002
Orr Diana B Busby	(714)745-3678 dorr4sc@icloud.com	76580 Daffodil Dr Palm Desert CA 92211	PSW	Teacher	EM			CQ	2009
Orr Jonathan P	(715)577-2754 jorrflv@gmail.com	4322 Long Grove Dr Seabrook TX 77586	TX	Teacher	Pro Stf	Lutheran Education Association Friendswood TX	(281)617-5189	MQ	2004
Orr Rachel L Anderson	(651)210-7588	9611 Hamlet Ave S Cottage Grove MN 55016	MNS	Teacher	C07/2016			SP	2005
Orr Robert A	(612)281-6314 robert.orr@tloschool.org	9611 Hamlet Ave S Cottage Grove MN 55016	MNS	Teacher	Tchr	Trinity Lone Oak Eagan MN	(651)454-7235	CQ	2016
Ortado Renee M Daley Williams	(303)828-6735 rotado@tlgreeley.com	3605 29th St Unit 6 Greeley CO 80634	RM	Teacher	Tchr	Trinity Greeley CO	(970)330-2485	CQ	2015
Ortloff Grace C	(320)583-1710 grace.ortloff@gmail.com	575 Barley Street SW Hutchinson MN 55350	MNS	Teacher	Tchr	St Johns Chaska MN	(952)448-2526	SP	2025
Osbourn Jeffrey W	(443)417-5657 osbourn.jeff@gmail.com	41 Willow Path Ct Nottingham MD 21236	SE	Teacher	Tchr	St Pauls Kingsville MD	(410)592-8100	RF	2003
Osbourn Scott C	(314)517-7236 scosbourn@gmail.com	2803 Brockway Pl Kingsville MD 21087	SE	Teacher	Prin	St Pauls Kingsville MD	(410)592-8100	RF	1998
Osbourn William E III	(410)382-3183 sskiposb@hotmail.com	207 Bynum Ridge Rd Forest Hill MD 21050	SE	Teacher	EM			CQ	2002
Osbron Paige K Pomroy	(248)928-4913 paige.osbron@st-matthew.org	4725 Lindholm Dr White Lake MI 48383	MI	Teacher	Tchr	St Matthew Walled Lake MI	(248)624-7676	AA	2019
Osbun Nancy A Rogner	(260) 220-2458 sarahartburnd@yahoo.com	66354 State Road 331 Bremen IN 46506	IN	Teacher	EM			S	1966
Osell Rachel	(414)651-7225 rachel.osell@yahoo.com	2756 S 69th St Milwaukee WI 53219	SW	Teacher	Tchr	Living Word Jackson WI	(262)677-9353	MQ	2023
Osten Corby D	(402)980-2704	307 Hickory St Seward NE 68434	NEB	Teacher	S HS/C	Concordia University Nebraska Seward NE	(402)643-3651	S	2004
Oswald Eric M	(801)518-9411 ericmoswald@gmail.com	18865 SW Johnson St Aloha OR 97003	NOW	DCE	Mem C	Bethlehem Aloha OR	(503)649-3380	SP	2003
Othling-Carman Sharon L Seymour	sharoncarman@bellsouth.net	546 E Jefferson St Pulaski TN 38478	SO	Teacher	EM			S	1974
Ott Donna J Paris	(989)992-9046 djott27@yahoo.com	49 Tuscany Cir Saginaw MI 48603	MI	Teacher	EM			RF	1982
Otte Carolyn A Becker	(303)503-1504 otte623@gmail.com	2972 S Zenobia St Denver CO 80236	RM	Teacher	EM			S	1979
Otte Deanna A Bremer	(507)529-0989 whotte@frontier.net	909 18th Ave NE Rochester MN 55906	MNS	Teacher	EM			SP	1968

*Multiple Assignments (See Church Worker Locator for Additional Details)
See Page 53 for the Table of Abbreviations for key to District, Classification, Position, and College abbreviations.
**C =Candidate; EM =Emeritus; the date following the C is the month and year the Candidate status began

NAME	TELEPHONE NUMBER EMAIL	STREET ADDRESS CITY/STATE/ZIP	DISTRICT	CLASS.	POSITION/ STATUS**	WHERE SERVING	OFFICE PHONE	COLLEGE/ UNIV/CQ	YR GRAD
Otte Jill M Kovach	(816)905-4336 jjotte@hotmail.com	1105 SW Huntington Dr Blue Springs MO 64015	MO	Teacher	Tchr	Timothy Blue Springs MO	(816)228-5300	CQ	2000
Otte Paul R	(320)583-8873 paul.n.peeters@gmail.com	105 10th Ave NE Hutchinson MN 55350	MNS	Tch/DCE	EM			SP	1969
Otten Carl W	(573)943-2034 carlwotten@live.com	4259 Highway N Morrison MO 65061	MO	Teacher	EM			RF	1965
Otten Hans K	(920)803-9572	412 Bell Ave Sheboygan WI 53083	SW	Teacher	Tchr	Sheboygan Sheboygan WI	(920)452-3323	RF	1989
Otten Ruth A Reinking	(708)485-7074 theottens1@juno.com	9044 Sheridan Ave Brookfield IL 60513	NI	Teacher	EM			RF	1965
Otto Deanna L	dlo2870@aol.com	2142 Baltimore Circle Colorado Springs CO 80904	RM	Teacher	Mem C	Rock Of Ages Colorado Springs CO	(719)632-9394	S	1993
Otto Jane M	jotto930@gmail.com	636 Crest St Mount Clemens MI 48043	MI	Teacher	EM			S	1982
Otto Katelyn R	(309)838-0758	2254 CR 226 Giddings TX 78942	TX	DCE	Mem C	Immanuel Giddings TX	(979)542-2918	RF	2014
Otto Phyllis F Foreman	(616)240-3098 phyllisfotto43@gmail.com	2252 Hummingbird Ct SE Grand Rapids MI 49546	MI	Teacher	EM			SP	1965
Otto Reid A	(262)844-2690 reidotto81@gmail.com	1639 Redwood St West Bend WI 53095	SW	Teacher	Tchr	St Peter-Immanuel Milwaukee WI	(414)353-6800	CQ	2017
Overbeck Lindsey J	(573)803-7807 lindsey.overbeck@cune.org	2662 State Highway C Jackson MO 63755	MO	Teacher	C07/2024			S	2020
Overgaard Kim A	(812)519-3591 kimovergaard80@gmail.com	645 E 15th St Seymour IN 47274	IN	Teacher	EM			SP	1974
Overley Kathryn A Stanton	kaddm5@gmail.com	1006 W Madison Ave Milton WI 53563	SW	Teacher	EM			RF	1989
Owen Angela J Grim	(260)602-7979	10204 Chambord Knl Fort Wayne IN 46835	IN	Teacher	Tchr	Concordia Fort Wayne IN	(260)426-9922	RF	1986
Owen Christine A Heinemann	(402)841-9955 love2knit@cableone.net	804 W Walnut Ave Norfolk NE 68701	NEB	Teacher	Tchr	Christ Norfolk NE	(402)371-5536	S	1991
Owen Johanna C Ragland	johanna.owen@flhsemail.org	4438 Peaceful Harbor St Las Vegas NV 89129	PSW	Teacher	Tchr	Faith Las Vegas NV	(702)804-4400	S	2019
Owen Madison J	(712)830-5014 owen.maddie23@gmail.com	10505 Providence Dr Unit 103 Johnston IA 50131	IW	Teacher	Tchr	Mount Olive Des Moines IA	(515)277-0247	S	2023
Owen Spencer L	dcespencer@gmail.com	4438 Peaceful Harbor St Las Vegas NV 89129	PSW	DCE	Tchr	Faith Las Vegas NV	(702)804-4400	S	2018
Owens Anna M Reinhart	(910)340-1067 annie.m.owens@outlook.com		SO	DCE	C03/2022			IV	1989
Owens Ross M	(618)791-7312 owens.ross@gmail.com	1701 Camp Lone Star Rd La Grange TX 78945	TX	DCE	RSO	Lutheran Outdoors Min of TX La Grange TX	(979)968-1657	AU	2012
Owens Sharon M Bradley	(480)407-7009 smomacau@yahoo.com	625 N Hamilton St Unit 46 Chandler AZ 85225	PSW	DCE	Mem C	Hosanna Mesa AZ	(480)984-1414	S	2001
Oyedeji Oyeniran A	(678)478-1909 oyeniranoyedeji@ immanueldanbury.org	163 S St Unit 29 Danbury CT 06810	NE	DPM	Mem C	Immanuel Danbury Danbury CT	(203)748-3320	CQ	2023
Oyler Bertha J La Sell	(812)378-2075 oylerblo2003@yahoo.com	2657 Washington St Columbus IN 47201	IN	Teacher	EM			S	1965
Ozark La Donna S Dreyer	(573)547-9197	2664 Pcr 316 Perryville MO 63775	MO	Teacher	Tchr	Immanuel Perryville MO	(573)547-6161	CQ	1998
Paape Adam D Dr	(262)993-8301 adam.paape@cuw.edu	1420 Audubon Ave Grafton WI 53024	SW	Teacher	S HS/C	Concordia University Wisconsin Mequon WI	(262)243-5700	MQ	2000
Paape Barbara A Koschmann	(414)303-3313 tchrpaa@aol.com	N71W23588 Homestead Rd Sussex WI 53089	SW	Teacher	EM			MQ	1989
Paape Darcy Barnhart	(262)993-8401 dpaape@fils.org	1420 Audubon Ave Grafton WI 53024	SW	Tch/DCE	Mem C	First Immanuel Cedarburg WI	(262)377-6610	MQ	2000
Pabst Mary H Rennegarbe	(562)221-8524 mpabst1964@gmail.com	3712 Allred St Lakewood CA 90712	PSW	Teacher	EM			S	1964
Pace Serena A Anazagasty Dr			TX	DCE	Mem C	Grace Arlington TX	(817)274-1626	S	1997
Pacheco Amanda L Kosberg	(480)620-0372 alchase@mac.com	1683 N Westfall Trail Casa Grande AZ 85122	PSW	Teacher	C07/2016			S	1999
Pacilli Denise J Kolar	(253)347-4272 dpacilli@sunbeamslutheranschool. com	P.O. Box 9302 Covington WA 98042	NOW	Teacher	EM			S	1975
Packard Heather L	(630)483-0544 hpack75@gmail.com	5825 Charleston Ct Hanover Park IL 60133	NI	Teacher	C02/2021			RF	1997
Packard Mary M Casto	(630)483-0544 mmcp46@aol.com	5825 Charleston Ct Hanover Park IL 60133	NI	Teacher	C07/2016			CQ	1995
Packard Trudy G Stafne Finley	(510)828-5179 tpackard@hotmail.com	596 W Hickory Ct Sebewaing MI 48759	MI	Teacher	EM			S	1977
Packham Kathryn E	(714)916-8101 dkpackham@gmail.com	1424 Shamrock Ln Costa Mesa CA 92626	PSW	DPM	Tchr	Orange County Orange CA	(714)998-5151	IV	2014
Paetow Kenneth	(314)745-3352	814 N Deal Ave Newton NC 28658	SE	Teacher	C06/2023			S	2021
Pagano Mary Ann Sembach	maryannp8@yahoo.com	3228 Snow Rd Bridgman MI 49106	MI	Teacher	EM			RF	1974
Page Catherine M Schneider	(715)921-4396 catherinepage422@gmail.com	W5254 Pa-Tray Ln Merrill WI 54452	NW	Teacher	Tchr	St Mark Wausau WI	(715)848-5511	RF	1994
Pagels Doris E Meyermann	(517)552-8687 jimpagels08@comcast.net	1408 Catherines Way Howell MI 48843	MI	Teacher	EM			RF	1980
Pahl Debbie	(863)646-6130 kpahl@tampabay.rr.com	276 Fiddlers CV Blairsville GA 30512	FG	Teacher	Tchr	St Paul Lakeland FL	(863)644-7710	CQ	2005
Pahnke Heidi J Schneider	(920)536-0865 hschneider16@gmail.com	E2409 Kassner Rd Kewaunee WI 54216	NW	Teacher	Tchr	St Paul Luxemburg WI	(920)845-2095	SP	2007

*Multiple Assignments (See Church Worker Locator for Additional Details)
See Page 53 for the Table of Abbreviations for key to District, Classification, Position, and College abbreviations.
**C =Candidate; EM =Emeritus; the date following the C is the month and year the Candidate status began

NAME	TELEPHONE NUMBER EMAIL	STREET ADDRESS CITY/STATE/ZIP	DISTRICT	CLASS.	POSITION/ STATUS**	WHERE SERVING	OFFICE PHONE	COLLEGE/ UNIV/CQ	YR GRAD
Palazzari Alexandra M	(970)471-8168 alexi@palazzari.net	13630 Garfield St Unit E Thornton CO 80602	RM	DCE	Mem C	Summit Peace Thornton CO	(303)452-0448	IV	2019
Palisch Daniel E	(469)644-4440 ddpalisch@att.net	647 Oak Meadow Dr Jackson MO 63755	MO	Teacher	EM			S	1967
Palka Susan E Mc Creadie	(248)624-7677 susan.palka@st-matthew.org	1925 Ashstan Dr Commerce Twp MI 48390	MI	Teacher	P/Tchr	St Matthew Walled Lake MI	(248)624-7677	S	1984
Palkewick Nathaniel A	(203)546-8766 npalkewick@yahoo.com	8 Old Bridge Rd E New Fairfield CT 06812	NE	Teacher	C07/2016			BR	1998
Palm Justin M	(618)214-1103 jpalm@stjohnsredbud.org	1210 Flint St Red Bud IL 62278	SI	Teacher	Prin	St John Red Bud IL	(618)282-3873	CQ	2014
Palmer Mark T	(512)789-3482 marktpalmer@gmail.com	1566 Homewood Cir Round Rock TX 78665	TX	Teacher	C07/2016			AU	1991
Palmer Rachel M Dr	palmerrm@comcast.net	3271 Gold Dust St NE Belmont MI 49306	MI	Teacher	EM			RF	1968
Palmer Sara M Vogele	(651)214-4665 spalmer@gracels.com	5437 35th Ave S Fargo ND 58104	ND	Teacher	Tchr	Grace Fargo ND	(701)232-7747	SP	2003
Palmreuter David W	(989)890-2355 dpalmreuter@stlorenz.org	9025 Waterman Rd Vassar MI 48768	MI	Teacher	Tchr	St Lorenz Frankenmuth MI	(989)652-6141	RF	1991
Palmreuter Kathy R	(414)688-5282 kpalmreuter@esmeagles.com	6204 Cornwallis Dr Apt 3a Fort Wayne IN 46804	IN	Teacher	Tchr	Emmanuel-St Michael Fort Wayne IN	(260)422-6712	RF	1996
Palmreuter Kenneth R Dr	(303)908-5039 kpalmreuter@gmail.com	6201 Seminole Ln Rapid City SD 57702	SD	Teacher	EM			RF	1962
Palmreuter Martha M Zoellick	(303)840-9205 mardypalm@gmail.com	6201 Seminole Ln Rapid City SD 57702	SD	Teacher	EM			RF	1961
Palomaki Michael T	(402)641-9562 palomakim@clhs-tx.org	1000 Hicks St #208 Tomball TX 77375	TX	Teacher	Tchr	Concordia Tomball TX	(281)351-2547	S	2012
Paluch Allan E	(713)777-6571 polishal@sbcglobal.net	6123 Imogene St Houston TX 77074	TX	Teacher	EM			RF	1969
Paluch Beth A Hesterman	(231)750-9714 paluchfam@comcast.net	5404 E Spring Dr Columbus IN 47201	IN	Teacher	EM			RF	1981
Paluch Martin W	(832)465-2946 martypaluch22@gmail.com	15319 Hunters Bend Dr Tomball TX 77377	TX	Teacher	EM			RF	1977
Pangburn Cheryl	(518)355-0518	157 Cedarview Ln Watervliet NY 12189	AT	Teacher	Tchr	Our Savior Colonie NY	(518)459-2273	RF	1969
Pangburn Janet K Klusmann	(716)731-5991	5917 Shawnee Rd Sanborn NY 14132	EA	Teacher	EM			RF	1994
Pangrace Caroline Pintner	(440)773-4063 cpintner@lutheranwest.com	815 Alameda Ave Sheffield Lake OH 44054	OH	Teacher	Tchr	Lutheran West Rocky River OH	(440)333-1660	CQ	2008
Pankow Amy R Peplinski	(414)254-5909 amyrp4@gmail.com	16655 Willow Ridge Ln Brookfield WI 53005	SW	Teacher	Tchr	Grace Oak Creek WI	(414)762-3655	MQ	2014
Pankow Eric J	(414)364-4990 ejpankow@gmail.com	6088 E Pioneer Pl Columbus IN 47203	IN	Teacher	EM			RF	1983
Pankow Ethan J	(414)629-4297 ethanj.pankow@gmail.com		NEB	Teacher	Tchr	Lincoln Lincoln NE	(402)467-5404	S	2022
Pankow Matthew D	(414)217-9200 matthew.pankow77@gmail.com	300 Spruce Ct Delafield WI 53018	SW	Teacher	EM			MQ	2012
Panning Tamara L Lagemann	(260)740-9306 tpanning2015@gmail.com	375 Lane 140 Little Otter Lake Fremont IN 46737	IN	Teacher	C07/2021			CQ	2006
Panozzo Stephanie M Stork	(708)560-6340 spanozzo@tlcs.org	9826 Treetop Drive 2W Orland Park IL 60462	NI	Teacher	Tchr	Trinity Tinley Park IL	(708)532-3529	RF	2010
Papendorf Lisa A Habeck	(715)250-3865 tlpapendorf@gmail.com	N2931 County Road D Clintonville WI 54929	NW	Teacher	Tchr	St Martin Clintonville WI	(715)823-6538	MQ	1994
Paquet Beverly J Pfiffner	(314)894-8422 bevpaquet@hotmail.com	5728 Hidden Stone Dr Saint Louis MO 63129	MO	Teacher	EM			CQ	1992
Pariseau Stephanie R Baesler	(206)697-7965 6apariseau@gmail.com	18316 74th St E Bonney Lake WA 98391	NOW	Teacher	EM			PO	1989
Parker Alexander	(360)989-5335 alexanderrwparker@gmail.com	8938 Jamie Court Spring Valley CA 91977	PSW	DCE	Mem C	Concordia Chula Vista CA	(619)656-8100	PO	2018
Parker Daniel E	(940)357-9309 dan@stlhouston.org	14225 Hargrave Rd Houston TX 77070	TX	DCE	Mem C	St Timothy Houston TX	(281)469-2457	S	2005
Parker Kristina Long	(503)307-9226 kparker@gracepocatello.org	2919 Silverwood Pl Pocatello ID 83201	NOW	DCE	Mem C	Grace Pocatello ID	(208)237-0467	PO	2013
Parker Sally A McBrine	sallyp@concordia-satx.com		TX	Teacher	Tchr	Concordia San Antonio TX	(210)479-1477	AU	2003
Parker Tracy Schroeder			PSW	Teacher		Pacific Southwest District Irvine CA	(949)854-3232	CQ	2009
Parks Amanda	(414)617-2118 amanda.newman79@gmail.com	304 Garden Cmn Livermore CA 94551	CNH	Teacher	Tchr	Our Savior Livermore CA	(925)447-1246	CQ	2006
Parks Danette L Edwards	(310)433-0321 parksmail@aol.com	3612 Redwood Ave Los Angeles CA 90066	PSW	Teacher	C07/2019			IV	2005
Parks Jessica M Marquardt	(714)904-0527 jessicamqt@gmail.com	12927 Newport Ave Apt D Tustin CA 92780	PSW	Teacher	Tchr	St Paul Orange CA	(714)637-2640	IV	2016
Parks Trevor A			MI	Teacher	Tchr	Trinity Reese MI	(989)868-9901	CQ	2010
Parris Franklin O	fop5702@gmail.com	109 B Ave. P.O. Box 56 Newhall IA 52315	IE	Teacher	Tchr	Central Newhall IA	(319)223-5271	S	1989
Parrish Katherine A Mahlum	(612)308-8527 katherine.parrish2013@gmail.com	4540 W 131 1/2 St Savage MN 55378	MNS	Teacher	Tchr	St Paul Prior Lake MN	(952)447-2117	SP	2018
Parrish Madeline	(909)522-2205 madeline.parrish@splsorange.org	2150 S State College Blvd Apt 3076 Anaheim CA 92806	PSW	Teacher	Tchr	St Paul Orange CA	(714)637-2640	IV	2020
Parrott Craig H	(720)487-2825 craigparrott5@gmail.com	10115 S Peoria # 12-106 Parker CO 80134	RM	Teacher	Tchr	Colorado Lutheran High School Parker CO	(303)841-5551	S	1979
Parry Stephen E Dr	(309)533-5200 drparry07@icloud.com	20 Saint Ivans Cir Unit 100 Bloomington IL 61705	CI	Teacher	Prin	Zion Lincoln IL	(217)732-3977	RF	1990

*Multiple Assignments (See Church Worker Locator for Additional Details)
See Page 53 for the Table of Abbreviations for key to District, Classification, Position, and College abbreviations.
**C =Candidate; EM =Emeritus; the date following the C is the month and year the Candidate status began

NAME	TELEPHONE NUMBER EMAIL	STREET ADDRESS CITY/STATE/ZIP	DISTRICT	CLASS.	POSITION/ STATUS**	WHERE SERVING	OFFICE PHONE	COLLEGE/ UNIV/CQ	YR GRAD
Parscale Brenda L Benson	(501)227-8673 parscale@comcast.net	1323 Westcliffe Dr Little Rock AR 72210	MDS	Teacher	EM			CQ	1999
Parsons Daniel J	(602)622-0266 daniel.parsons@popcs.org	4051 Beltway Dr Apt 603 Addison TX 75001	TX	Teacher	Tchr	Prince Of Peace Carrollton TX	(972)447-0532	CQ	2017
Parsons Julia Hoerauf	(714)325-2989	728 S Ridgeview Rd Anaheim CA 92807	PSW	Teacher	Tchr	Orange County Orange CA	(714)998-5151	CQ	2013
Partipilo Audrey C Herrmann	(307)851-3423 audrey.partipilo@gmail.com	3011 Shalimar Circle Fort Wayne IN 46808	IN	Teacher	Mem C	Trinity Auburn IN	(260)925-2440	S	2009
Parton Laurie J Evans	(303)805-9163 teach4hope@yahoo.com	23911 Broadmoor Pl Parker CO 80138	RM	Teacher	C07/2016			S	1994
Parvey Linda L Kreger	(763)753-2441 lindaparvey@msn.com	19940 Xavis St NW Cedar MN 55011	MNS	Teacher	EM			S	1974
Paschal Ruth A Wittmus	(573)221-5977 rcpaschal@hotmail.com	11976 Old 79 New London MO 63459	EN	Teacher	EM			RF	1967
Pasche Dawn E Snaufer Deac	(260)255-9802 dawnpasche@hotmail.com	15530 Coldwater Rd Fort Wayne IN 46845	IN	Deaconess	RSO	Siberian Lutheran Mission Society Fort Wayne IN	(260)438-1385	FW-DEAC	2015
Paselk Renate E Erhardt	(586)383-1095 ppaselk@gmail.com	35462 Wellston Ave Sterling Hts MI 48312	MI	Teacher	EM			S	1973
Paszkiewicz Katie D	(507)313-3543 paszkiek@csp.edu	875 E 5th St Winona MN 55987	MNS	Teacher	C06/2025			SP	2014
Pata Ronda C Quamme	(310)259-9971 krchpata@aol.com	1019 Hidden Hills Dr Dripping Spgs TX 78620	TX	Teacher	EM			CQ	1995
Pate Ardelle L Voeltz Dr	(815)354-2863 ardelle.pate@CUChicago.edu	174 Pomeroy Ave Crystal Lake IL 60014	NI	Teacher	EM			CQ	2016
Pate Julie M Johnson	(817)914-0003 julie.pate@sharingnewlife.com	6032 Wessex Street North Richland Hills TX 76180	TX	Teacher	Tchr	St Paul Fort Worth TX	(817)353-2929	RF	2004
Paterson Mark R Dr	(319)389-3203 mark.paterson@cuw.edu	2021 Cold Springs Rd Saukville WI 53080	SW	Teacher	S HS/C	Concordia University Wisconsin Mequon WI	(262)243-5700	CQ	2023
Patrow Madison R	(218)244-2155 madisonpatrow@yahoo.com		MNS	DCE	Mem C	Beautiful Savior Plymouth MN	(763)550-1000	SP	2022
Patterson Joshua J	(214)687-1424 cubfan1984@gmail.com	4500 Wedgewood Dr McKinney TX 75070	TX	DCE	Mem C	Tangible Grace Allen TX	(972)246-8411	SP	2010
Patterson Judy E Frampton	(786)972-1161 lutheranmomthree@gmail.com	15802 Country Lake Dr Tampa FL 33624	FG	Teacher	Tchr	Messiah Carrollwood FL	(813)961-2182	SP	1994
Patterson Laura J Degner	(414)254-0571 ljdpatterson@yahoo.com	3267 N 88th St Milwaukee WI 53222	SW	Teacher	Tchr	Blessed Savior New Berlin WI	(262)786-6465	RF	1983
Patterson Myra R Ludwig	mrp1106@hotmail.com	1211 Kaweloka St Pearl City HI 96782	CNH	Teacher	EM			S	1966
Patton Cara M Deac	(406)533-9950 cmlpatton@gmail.com	432 Cloister Walk Kirkwood MO 63122	MO	Deaconess	S Ex/S	The LCMS Corporate Saint Louis MO	(314)965-9000	CH	2013
Patton Donna M Lampe	(720)244-6116 donnap727@me.com	2636 S. Jebel Way Aurora CO 80013	RM	DCE	Mem C	Peace W Christ Aurora CO	(303)693-5618	AU	2015
Paukner LaBree A Barclay	(815)742-4220 labree9@aol.com	1510 S 167th St New Berlin WI 53151	SW	Teacher	C10/2020			CH	2011
Paul Amy N Rivers	(575)910-6274 anpaul87@gmail.com	3719 Shadow Wick Ln Houston TX 77082	TX	Teacher	C07/2016			BR	2009
Paul Gregory L	(248)593-6587 glpaul3288@comcast.net	1045 E Long Lake Rd Bloomfield Hills MI 48304	MI	Teacher	Tchr	St Paul Royal Oak MI	(248)541-0613	S	1984
Paul Jen-Yi I Lee	(414)232-8903 irene64paul@gmail.com	No. 21 5F-1 Xinrong Road, Alley 35 Chiayi City NO 60002 TAIWAN	IN	Teacher	C07/2016			S	1990
Paul Kristina L Meggers Deac	(314)650-1753 kpaul@ckhome.org	651 Winding Bluffs Dr. Fenton MO 63026	MO	Deaconess	Mem C	Concordia Kirkwood MO	(314)822-7772	SL-DEAC	2010
Paul Marc J	(651)770-3630	2979 Chisholm Pkwy Maplewood MN 55109	MNS	Teacher	Tchr	Concordia Academy Roseville MN	(651)484-8429	CQ	2010
Paul Robin M Steinke	(920)246-1898 paulr@greenbaytrinity.org	2104 Jen Rae Rd Green Bay WI 54311	NW	Teacher	Tchr	Green Bay Lutheran School Association Inc Green Bay WI	(920)655-4673	RF	1996
Paul Warren F	(850)748-3469 warren_paul60@yahoo.com	535 E Lucy Ln Ellettsville IN 47429	SO	Teacher	EM			S	1969
Pauley Linda G Newman	(480)895-8555	4219 E. Lafayette Ave Gilber AZ 85298	PSW	Teacher	Tchr	Risen Savior Chandler AZ	(480)895-6782	CQ	2007
Pauli Elaine E	(248)651-4081 eepauli@icloud.com	875 Greenview Ct Unit 52 Rochester MI 48307	MI	Teacher	EM			RF	1970
Pauling Frederick J	(703)549-8062	411 Summers Dr Alexandria VA 22301	SE	Teacher	EM			S	1961
Pauling Melissa G Hulsey	(812)499-7140 mgpauling@gmail.com	807 Prince Andrew Ct Saint Charles MO 63304	MO	Teacher	Tchr	St Paul Des Peres MO	(314)822-2771	RF	2006
Paulison Elinor Bach			RM	DPM	Mem C	Peace W Christ Aurora CO	(303)693-5618	S	2004
Pauls Cambria J Deac	(925)997-3882 cambriajpauls@gmail.com	2101 174th St NE Apt Jj303 Marysville WA 98271	NOW	Deaconess	Mem C	Messiah Marysville WA	(360)659-4112	FW-DEAC	2024
Pauls Rebekah T Thoelke	(636)238-8520 rebekah.thoelke@gmail.com	52119-2 Shawnee Ct Fort Hood TX 76544	TX	Teacher	C08/2019			CH	2017
Paulsel Brenda K Dubs	(713)208-6429 paulselbrenda@gmail.com	25691 Chestnut Ln Splendora TX 77372	TX	Teacher	EM			S	1991
Paulsen Cynthia A Arnold	(928)344-1830 cynthiapaulsen@peoplepc.com	1715 E County 14 3/4 St Yuma AZ 85365	PSW	Teacher	EM			CQ	2001
Paulsen Michael A	(563)340-5495 mpaulsen@stpeterlcms.org	2318 N Clark St Davenport IA 52804	NI	Teacher	Mem C	St Peter Schaumburg IL	(847)885-3350	S	2016
Paulus John D	(303)750-5818 jdpaulus@gmail.com	15997 E Kepner Dr Aurora CO 80017	RM	Tch/DCE	EM			S	1978
Pautler Vera Laufer	(618)282-6636	310 Indiana St Red Bud IL 62278	SI	Teacher	Tchr	St John Red Bud IL	(618)282-3873	RF	1968
Pavasars Michelle C Sloan	(714)336-2956 michelle.psalm374@gmail.com	23520 Silver Spring Ln Diamond Bar CA 91765	PSW	DCE	Mem C	Christ Brea CA	(714)529-2984	IV	2004

*Multiple Assignments (See Church Worker Locator for Additional Details)

See Page 53 for the Table of Abbreviations for key to District, Classification, Position, and College abbreviations.

**C =Candidate; EM =Emeritus; the date following the C is the month and year the Candidate status began

NAME	TELEPHONE NUMBER EMAIL	STREET ADDRESS CITY/STATE/ZIP	DISTRICT	CLASS.	POSITION/ STATUS**	WHERE SERVING	OFFICE PHONE	COLLEGE/ UNIV/CQ	YR GRAD
Pavel Heidi L Brueggemann	(308)539-8441 hpavelorls@gmail.com	221 James Ave North Platte NE 69101	NEB	Teacher	Tchr	Our Redeemer North Platte NE	(308)532-6421	S	1985
Pavelski Suzanne R Schnell	(719)582-1353 spavelski1952@gmail.com	44 Douglas Ln Pueblo CO 81001	RM	Teacher	EM			CQ	1994
Pawelk Frederick G	(320)395-4244 F_pawelk@hotmail.com	18002 County Road 9 Lester Pr MN 55354	MNS	Teacher	EM			RF	1989
Pawlitz Carol J Mc Collum	(586)948-5169	50629 Cameron Dr Macomb MI 48044	MI	Teacher	EM			RF	1969
Pawlitz Gail E Youngblood	(314)223-4480 gpawlitz@gmail.com	4978 Arbors At Stonegate Drive Affton MO 63123	MO	Teacher	EM			S	1970
Pawlitz Gary L Dr	(586)212-2345 gcpawlitz5@att.net	50629 Cameron Dr Macomb MI 48044	MI	Teacher	EM			S	1968
Pawlitz Ronald H	(314)605-9154 rpawlitz@hotmail.com	4978 Arbors At Stonegate Affton MO 63123	MO	Teacher	EM			S	1970
Payne Joshua M	(619)828-0028 jpayne@lutheranschool.org	1976 Paradise St San Diego CA 92114	PSW	Teacher	Tchr	Christ La Mesa CA	(619)462-5211	CQ	2016
Payne Keah D Deac	(405)436-9664 keah.payne@gmail.com	7204 S Douglas Ave Oklahoma City OK 73139	MO	Deaconess	S Miss	Office of International Mission Saint Louis MO		FW-DEAC	2023
Payne Melissa L Mathis	(619)920-7979 mlpayne@clslm.org	1976 Paradise St San Diego CA 92114	PSW	Teacher	Tchr	Christ La Mesa CA	(619)462-5211	CQ	2018
Payne Nancy C Carter	(281)255-4080 paynen@concordiacrusaders.org	12818 Mossy Ledge Tomball TX 77377	TX	Teacher	Tchr	Concordia Tomball TX	(281)351-2547	CQ	2006
Payne Stephani A Bruening	(832)928-8999 spayne@oslschool.org	66 N Lochwood Way Tomball TX 77375	TX	Teacher	Tchr	Our Savior Houston TX	(713)290-8277	S	2024
Peacock Amber C	(217)530-8385 apeacock@stjohnsbuckley.com	123 N Union St Paxton IL 60957	CI	Teacher	Tchr	St John Buckley IL	(217)394-2422	S	2014
Peara Karen E Dreyer	(847)845-7763 peara8@juno.com	400 Lovell St Elgin IL 60120	NI	Teacher	C10/2021			RF	1984
Pearson Kathryn K	(989)225-1560 kathikraaipearson@gmail.com	4651 Richville Rd Vassar MI 48768	MI	Teacher	Tchr	Peace Saginaw MI	(989)793-9025	RF	1988
Pece Katie J Munguia	(630)247-8516 kpece@hotmail.com	2771 Woodmere Dr Darien IL 60561	NI	Teacher	S HS/C	Concordia University Chicago River Forest IL	(708)771-8300	CQ	2015
Peckman Janet A Mottershaw	(816)632-2493 peckman@centurytel.net	1106 Sam G Hiner Dr Cameron MO 64429	MO	Teacher	EM			S	1969
Pedde Joshua N	(317)517-2181 jpedde@cornerstonelutheran.church	4741 Minton Ct Carmel IN 46033	IN	DPM	Mem C	Cornerstone Carmel IN	(317)814-4252	CQ	2016
Pedersen Fred R	(586)746-9132 frblpedersen@ameritech.net	28719 Mercury Ln Chesterfield MI 48047	MI	Teacher	EM			RF	1983
Pedersen Melissa A Asmus	(636)233-7326 melpedersen@aol.com	1022 Knollcrest Dr Fort Dodge IA 50501	IW	Teacher	EM			S	1982
Pederson Jessica L Schneider			TX	Teacher	Tchr	St Mark Houston TX	(713)468-2623	RF	1999
Pedrosa Julia J	(262)497-6701 jpedrosa@racinelutheran.org	1332 Monroe Ave Racine WI 53405	SW	Teacher	Tchr	Lutheran High School Racine WI	(262)637-6538	MQ	2021
Peebles Carla J Brakhage	(918)706-1791 carlajo_brakhage@yahoo.com	14730 Doe Run Harvest AL 35749	SO	Tch/DCE	Mem C	Ascension Huntsville AL	(256)536-9987	S	1980
Pegues Agnes C Clark	(334)872-7102 pegues9@att.net	285 E Castlewood Dr Selma AL 36701	SO	Teacher	EM			S	1967
Pehl Hannah R Johnson	(262)323-6151 hannah.pehl@trinitywaconia.org	1945 Woods Pt Waconia MN 55387	MNS	Teacher	Tchr	Trinity Waconia MN	(952)442-4165	MQ	2012
Pehlke Todd M	(715)218-8838 tpehlke57@gmail.com	14129 Reston Dr South Beloit IL 61080	NI	Teacher	Prin	Immanuel Belvidere IL	(815)547-5346	SP	1997
Peiffer Claire Hoy	(970)305-6452 clairepeiffer@trinityed.org	324 Stillwater Loop Kalispell MT 59901	MT	Teacher	Tchr	Trinity Kalispell MT	(406)257-5683	S	2017
Peirce Laura K Seutter	(989)415-8091 lpeirce711@yahoo.com	9009 Busch Rd Birch Run MI 48415	FG	Teacher	C07/2016			S	2008
Peiser Anne L Jesgarz	(217)663-9272 jesgarzanne@gmail.com		CI	Teacher	Tchr	St Johns Mattoon IL	(217)234-4911	S	2019
Pelayo Emilie M Sanders	(501)339-8315 emsand0926@gmail.com		MDS	Teacher	C07/2021			AU	2016
Pelletier Lorine L Fink	(808)487-1194 llpell2001@yahoo.com	99-788 Aumakiki Pl Aiea HI 96701	CNH	Teacher	EM			S	1974
Pelletier Lynsey L	(808)225-0498 lynseyp@blcbls.org		NOW	Teacher	Tchr	Bethlehem Kennewick WA	(509)582-5858	IV	2017
Pelltier Carol A Rivera	(419)966-9661 carolpelltier@gmail.com	234 Hart Street Romeo MI 48065	MI	Teacher	Tchr	St Peter Macomb MI	(586)781-3434	AA	1987
Pelz Philip A	(260)402-4682 pelzpa@gmail.com	5322 Damask Rd Fort Wayne IN 46815	IN	DCE	C12/2023			IV	2021
Pena Janice Mitchell	(816)453-3527 jpjpena2@gmail.com	520 Dorsey Dr El Paso TX 79912	FG	Teacher	EM			S	1964
Penhallegon Gabriel C	(734)431-2877 gpenhallegon2017@gmail.com	10699 Strawberry Hill Ln Whitmore Lake MI 48189	MI	DPM	Mem C	Our Savior Chelsea MI	(734)475-1404	AA	2023
Penn Charlotte R Ross	(952)484-3377 charlottepenn00@gmail.com	3540 220th Street E. Prior Lake MN 55372	MNS	Teacher	Tchr	Redeemer Wayzata MN	(952)473-1281	SP	2006
Pennekamp Jacob E	(260)579-2720 jpennekamp@clhscadets.com	6212 Twisted Oak Ct Fort Wayne IN 46835	IN	Teacher	Pro Stf	Concordia Fort Wayne IN	(260)483-1102	RF	1996
Pennekamp Sarah A Smith	(260)486-6740 pennekamp6@yahoo.com	6212 Twisted Oak Ct Fort Wayne IN 46835	IN	Teacher	Mem C	Emmanuel Fort Wayne IN	(260)423-1369	RF	1996
Penney Kierra M	(715)680-1308 dce.bethanycr@gmail.com	4 Chapelridge Cir Apt F Marion IA 52302	IE	DCE	Mem C	Bethany Cedar Rapids IA	(319)364-6026	S	2023
Penniman Rebecca L Westergaard	(262)740-1701 babyesmom@pennfam.com	2012 Green Meadow Dr P.O. Box 213 Delavan WI 53115	SW	Teacher	Tchr	Our Redeemer Delavan WI	(262)728-4266	RF	1996
Pennington Nathan T	(210)556-5854 nathan.pennington@imlutheran.org	4047 Hwy T Marthasville MO 63357	MO	DPM	Mem C	Immanuel Washington MO	(636)239-4705	S	2023

*Multiple Assignments (See Church Worker Locator for Additional Details)

See Page 53 for the Table of Abbreviations for key to District, Classification, Position, and College abbreviations.

**C =Candidate; EM =Emeritus; the date following the C is the month and year the Candidate status began

NAME	TELEPHONE NUMBER EMAIL	STREET ADDRESS CITY/STATE/ZIP	DISTRICT	CLASS.	POSITION/ STATUS**	WHERE SERVING	OFFICE PHONE	COLLEGE/ UNIV/CQ	YR GRAD
Pennington Wilfred D	(618)339-3149 unclewilfred2001@yahoo.com	324 S Perrine Ave Centralia IL 62801	SI	Teacher	Tchr	Christ Our Rock Centralia IL	(618)226-3315	CQ	2010
Penny Amy R Woodman	(402)469-0538 amy.woodman@cune.org	4042 Regal Drive Grand Island NE 68803	NEB	Teacher	C05/2023			S	2011
Penny Michelle D Haegele	(708)275-0543 mrsmichellepenny@yahoo.com	206 W Maple St Lombard IL 60148	NI	Teacher	C07/2016			RF	2002
Penoske Sandra L Paprich	(812)524-7170 spenoske@comcast.net	131 Stevens Dr Seymour IN 47274	IN	Teacher	EM			CQ	1993
Penrose Kari J Reppert	(402)380-4567 karipenrose27@gmail.com	1784 H Road Lot #4 West Point NE 68788	NEB	Teacher	C06/2020			S	2000
Pensel Amanda L Mayfield	(573)382-2000 amayfield44@gmail.com	665 Lakeview Xing Cpe Girardeau MO 63701	MO	Teacher	Tchr	Immanuel Perryville MO	(573)547-6161	S	2012
Pepe Jessica E Fowls	(541)728-8079 j.e.fowls@gmail.com	5659 Silver Bell Lane Granite Falls NC 28630	SE	Teacher	Tchr	University Christian Hickory NC	(828)855-2995	PO	2005
Peperkorn Kathryn M Brandt	(262)705-5469 kpeperkorn@me.com	2624 Chichester Ln Fort Wayne IN 46815	IN	Teacher	C02/2024			S	1993
Peperkorn Renata	(916)316-8745 peperkorn@trinitysheboygan.org	732a Bell Ave Sheboygan WI 58083	SW	DPM	Tchr	Trinity Sheboygan WI	(920)458-8248	S	2024
Peppel Sofia Abel	(262)468-1029 sofia.peppel@splco.org	1121 Dickens Dr Oconomowoc WI 53066	SW	Teacher	Tchr	St Paul Oconomowoc WI	(262)567-5001	MQ	2024
Pera Jeremy J	j.pera@sbcglobal.net	616 Franklin St Clay Center KS 67432	KS	Tch/DCE	EM			S	1972
Peralta Anna R McDaniel			PSW	Teacher	Tchr	Faith Las Vegas NV	(702)804-4400	S	2015
Peregoy Spencer R	(661)617-7191 snrperegoy@gmail.com	3957 Thundercloud Dr Colorado Springs CO 80920	RM	Teacher	EM			S	1977
Perez Carolyn	(208)403-1509 joshua.carolynperez@gmail.com	1554 Avon Lane Idaho Falls ID 83401	RM	Teacher	C07/2016			S	2009
Perez Jessie Pedraja Deac	(786)426-5417 jessiep@baptisthelth.net	10301 SW 45th St Miami FL 33165	FG	Deaconess	Mem C	Concordia Miami FL	(305)235-6123	CQ	1994
Perez Sarah R Peterson	greenyesgirly@gmail.com	14163 Double Dutch Cir Parker CO 80134	RM	Teacher	C07/2016			IV	2004
Perkowski Karla R Kemerling	(470)723-4959 krkemerling@gmail.com	7511 NW Prairie View Rd. Platte Woods MO 64152	MO	Teacher	EM			S	1977
Perna Kari	(707)224-2886 kperna@stjohnsmapa.org	2432 Christie Court Napa CA 94558	CNH	Teacher	Tchr	St John's Napa CA	(707)255-0119	CQ	2011
Perr Lisa M Perich	(714)458-8656 lperich@aol.com	998 Oakcrest Ave Brea CA 92821	PSW	Teacher	Tchr	Christ Brea CA	(714)529-0892	IV	1986
Perr Orville R Jr		629 W Washington St Jackson MO 63755	MO	Teacher	Tchr	St Paul Jackson MO	(573)243-2236	S	1984
Perry Joseph W	(832)693-3800 perry_joey@ymail.com	3431 Nutwood Ln Spring TX 77389	TX	Teacher	Tchr	Salem Tomball TX	(281)351-8223	AU	2006
Perschbacher Gerald Dr	(314)849-5249 persch3@hotmail.com	8868 Rock Forest Dr Saint Louis MO 63123	MO	Teacher	EM			RF	1972
Persich Laurell L Ritter	(816)987-6114 lpersich@hotmail.com	903 Buckeye Ln Pleasant Hill MO 64080	MO	Teacher	Tchr	Calvary Kansas City MO	(816)444-6908	S	1980
Pesch Janet M	(262)456-0639 jntpesch7@gmail.com	158 Merrie Ln Racine WI 53405	SW	Teacher	Tchr	St John Racine WI	(262)633-2758	SP	1991
Pesick Deborah M Knepper	(574)265-5174	6109 Hunter Wood Dr Fort Wayne IN 46835	IN	Teacher	Tchr	Holy Cross Fort Wayne IN	(260)483-3173	MQ	2000
Pester Beth E Royuk Dr	(402)641-0584 beth.pester@cune.edu	722 N 5th St Seward NE 68434	NEB	Teacher	S HS/C	Concordia University Nebraska Seward NE	(402)643-3651	S	1996
Peter Tonya A Kirst	(314) 666-9237 tonya.peter@att.net	559 Brookhaven Ct Kirkwood MO 63122	MO	Teacher	Tchr	Mount Calvary Brentwood MO	(314)968-2360	RF	1991
Peter Victor K	(402)646-2033 vp11124@windstream.net	539 Bader Ave Seward NE 68434	NEB	Teacher	EM			S	1956
Petering Carol J Meyer	(314)821-2885 petering@sbcglobal.net	751 Club Ln Kirkwood MO 63122	MO	Teacher	EM			RF	1960
Peterman Charles E	(314)239-6878 cpeterman66@gmail.com	5519 Remington Villas Ct Saint Louis MO 63129	MO	Teacher	EM			RF	1965
Peterman Diane R Lohmeyer	(314)703-1777	5519 Remington Villas Ct Saint Louis MO 63129	MO	Teacher	EM			RF	1966
Peterman Karl F	(507)796-1072 kfpeterman@gmail.com	P.O. Box 143 Altura MN 55910	MNS	Teacher	EM			S	1972
Peterman Kyle P	(763)218-4110 petermak@granitemoon.com	9141 County Road 101 Corcoran MN 55340	MNS	Teacher	Tchr	St John Corcoran MN	(763)420-2426	SP	2000
Peters Cyan A Swank	(260)255-5833 cpeters@cluth.org	7 Tyndale Pl Fort Wayne IN 46825	IN	Teacher	Tchr	Central New Haven IN	(260)493-2502	MQ	2008
Peters Denis A	(260)489-3188	7980 Auburn Rd Fort Wayne IN 46825	IN	Teacher	EM			S	1965
Peters Donna S Verkler	(636)734-6091 dpetersmusic@yahoo.com	610 Callaway Ridge Dr Defiance MO 63341	MO	Teacher	EM			CQ	2008
Peters Elizabeth A Granzow	(605)759-4782 children@memoriallutheran.net	Memorial Lutheran 5000 S Western Ave Sioux Falls SD 57108	SD	DCE	Mem C	Memorial Sioux Falls SD	(605)334-7133	SP	1999
Peters Jana R Knight Deac	(262)214-0432 shepherdshandfwed@gmail.com	1596 S 150 W Albion IN 46701	IN	Deaconess	RSO	The Shepherds Hand Community Center Fort Wayne IN	(260)424-2224	RF	2006
Peters Jill R Rieches	(815)383-6037 jillpeters@trinluth.org	2197 2350th St Atlanta IL 61723	CI	Teacher	Tchr	Trinity Bloomington IL	(309)829-7513	CH	2007
Peters Joyce K Brueggemann	(712)454-0012 jkbriggs44@gmail.com	395 Partridge Cir North Sioux City SD 57049	SD	Teacher	EM			S	1966
Peters Karen S Priester	(630)671-1105 kpeters@saintlukeitaska.org	6n070 Keeney Rd Roselle IL 60172	NI	Teacher	Tchr	St Luke Itasca IL	(630)773-0509	RF	1996
Peters Linda J Hardt	(402)365-7795 lindapabc@yahoo.com	556 Road 5500 Deshler NE 68340	NEB	Teacher	EM			S	1976

*Multiple Assignments (See Church Worker Locator for Additional Details)
See Page 53 for the Table of Abbreviations for key to District, Classification, Position, and College abbreviations.
**C =Candidate; EM =Emeritus; the date following the C is the month and year the Candidate status began

NAME	TELEPHONE NUMBER EMAIL	STREET ADDRESS CITY/STATE/ZIP	DISTRICT	CLASS.	POSITION/ STATUS**	WHERE SERVING	OFFICE PHONE	COLLEGE/ UNIV/CQ	YR GRAD
Peters Mark G	(231)590-9733 cantorman26@gmail.com	1846 Sleepy Hollow Ln Interlochen MI 49643	MI	DPM	Mem C	Immanuel Leland MI	(231)256-9464	RF	2005
Peters Martha L Buckentin	(262)989-3161 martha.peters4boys@gmail.com	7616 Bull Rapids Rd Woodburn IN 46797	IN	Teacher	C07/2025			MQ	2002
Peters Pamela K Hoffmann	(414)461-7024 tweety1748@gmail.com	5881 N 39th St Milwaukee WI 53209	SW	Teacher	EM			S	1970
Peters Philfert L	(812)358-5155	3122 E County Road 400 S Brownstown IN 47220	IN	Teacher	EM			RF	1970
Peters Rebecca R Schuricht Dr	(714)287-2460 1becky.peters@gmail.com	1507 Hitch Wagon Dr Loveland CO 80537	PSW	Teacher	EM			RF	1973
Peters Timothy C Dr	(714)337-4397 peters1224@gmail.com	1507 Hitch Wagon Dr Loveland CO 80537	PSW	Teacher	EM			RF	1973
Peters Bonnett Le Anne M Peters		1129 S Rock Creek Rd Jefferson Cty MO 65101	MO	Teacher	Tchr	Immanuel Jefferson City MO	(573)496-3451	AU	1996
Petersen Connie M	cmpetersen@me.com	510 Wheelock Pkwy W Saint Paul MN 55117	MNS	Teacher	EM			SP	1967
Petersen Doris J Wacker	(765)392-4458 petersdj@hotmail.com	1194 S Hubert Cir W Martinsville IN 46151	IN	Teacher	EM			RF	1962
Petersen Enoch A	(217)720-5054 bigpbanddude@gmail.com	501 S Glenwood Ave Springfield IL 62704	CI	Teacher	C08/2020			RF	1992
Petersen Gary W Dr	(262)957-6401 gwpetersen11@outlook.com	10536 N Magnolia Dr Mequon WI 53092	SW	Teacher	EM			CQ	2012
Petersen Hannah L Zimmermann	(319)504-5410 hannahpetersen1@yahoo.com	1539 Highlandview Dr West Bend WI 53096	SW	DCE	C07/2016			Other	2005
Petersen Kathleen M Lindhorst	(402)910-8774 kpete@esu7.org	4001 87th St Columbus NE 68601	NEB	Teacher	EM			CQ	2005
Petersen Lorien B	(605)484-5521 lorien.petersen@zionrc.org	4550 Mount Rushmore Rd Rapid City SD 57701	SD	DCE	Mem C	Zion Rapid City SD	(605)342-5749	PO	2006
Petersen Marilyn A	(281)655-0564	6415 Jadecrest Dr Spring TX 77389	TX	Teacher	EM			S	1971
Petersen Michelle L Hagemeier	(270) 765-9038 gloriadei_michelle@yahoo.com	2180 Payneville Rd Brandenburg KY 40108	IN	Teacher	Tchr	Gloria Dei Elizabethtown KY	(270)769-5910	RF	1981
Petersen Sarah R Bierman	(402)640-2323 sarah.petersen@cune.org	845 Hickory Dr Arlington NE 68002	NEB	Teacher	Tchr	St Paul Arlington NE	(402)478-4278	S	2008
Petersen Scott M	(715)259-7168 scott.m.petersen@gmail.com	30237 S Bear Lake Dr Webb Lake WI 54830	NW	DCE	EM			RF	1983
Petersen Susan C Schlomann	(618)531-6546 suep310@gmail.com	99 Westmoreland St Collinsville IL 62234	SI	Teacher	Tchr	Good Shepherd Collinsville IL	(618)344-3151	CQ	2007
Peterson Amy C Becker	beckerac2@me.com	9124 Utica Ave S Bloomington MN 55437	MNS	Teacher	C06/2022			CH	2012
Peterson Callie L Reintsma	(406)794-7624 calliereintsma@yahoo.com	326 Westchester Sq N Apt C Billings MT 59105	MT	Teacher	Tchr	Trinity Billings MT	(406)656-1021	SP	2024
Peterson Christina D Hanley		W510 Bell School Rd East Troy WI 53120	EN	Teacher	Tchr	Hales Corners Hales Corners WI	(414)529-6701	MQ	1997
Peterson Dana B Dana Marie Louise Burkey	(949)214-3469 dana.peterson@cui.edu	1530 Concordia West Irvine CA 92612	PSW	DCE	S HS/C	Concordia University Irvine Irvine CA	(949)854-8002	IV	2011
Peterson Elia	(507)380-0308 3in1learningcenter@frontier.com	2982 Davis Rd Fairbanks AK 99709	NOW	DCE	Mem C	Zion Fairbanks AK	(907)456-7660	CQ	2009
Peterson Emily R	(218)892-0805 epeterson@trinitysf.org	23013 Kerry St NW #302 St. Francis MN 55070	MNS	Teacher	Tchr	Trinity Saint Francis MN	(763)753-1234	MQ	2013
Peterson Heidi S Stennfeld	(817)468-8573 kindergrace1@yahoo.com	3408 Forestway Ct Arlington TX 76001	TX	Teacher	Tchr	Grace Arlington TX	(817)275-5131	RF	1992
Peterson Janice L Richter	(863)318-0694	260 Alachua Dr Winter Haven FL 33884	FG	Teacher	C07/2016			RF	1985
Peterson Janis R Hartkopf	(805)522-6877 janisruth@gmail.com	3680 N Moorpark Rd # 114 Thousand Oaks CA 91360	PSW	Teacher	EM			RF	1967
Peterson Jon J	(863)318-0694 jpeterson@glwh.org	260 Alachua Dr Winter Haven FL 33884	FG	Teacher	Prin	Grace Winter Haven FL	(863)293-9744	RF	1985
Peterson Jonathan D	(253)293-9875 dce@mlgj.org	517 28 1/2 Rd 2a Grand Junction CO 81501	RM	DCE	Mem C	Messiah Grand Junction CO	(970)245-2838	IV	2023
Peterson Keith B	(708)846-1100 kpeterson22@gmail.com	25436 S Queen Palm Dr Sun Lakes AZ 85248	PSW	Teacher	EM			RF	1975
Peterson Kelly A Walz	(541)990-6472 kkpete93@gmail.com	17517 Rose Lane Rd Omaha NE 68136	NEB	Teacher	EM			S	1993
Peterson Kenzie M Peters	(414)510-8520 kenzers1590@gmail.com	3358 S 86th St Milwaukee WI 53227	SW	Teacher	Tchr	Mount Olive Milwaukee WI	(414)774-2200	CH	2014
Peterson Kimberley A Rebber	(612)600-3778 skspeterson@hotmail.com	11610 Aileron Court Inver Grove Heights MN 55077	MNS	Teacher	Tchr	King Of Kings Roseville MN	(651)484-9206	MQ	2001
Peterson LaDonna K Ressie	(319)230-0662 ladonnapeterson@immanuel lakefield.com	505 4th Ave S Lakefield MN 56150	MNS	Teacher	Tchr	Immanuel Lakefield MN	(507)662-5718	SP	1996
Peterson Ralph O	(708)216-5260 rolafpeterson@hotmail.com	65 Illinois Racine WI 53405	SW	Teacher	EM			MW	1980
Peterson Ruth A Mittelstaedt	(818)590-4737 rpeter27@aol.com	11018 Rhodesia Ave Sunland CA 91040	PSW	Teacher	EM			CQ	2013
Peterson Sheila K Kalm	(218)878-0442 mamasheila.peterson@mchsi.com	6149 Edgewood Ave Saint Paul MN 55125	MNN	DCO	EM			SP	1996
Peterson-Finster Sharon L Osenberg	(914)552-5150 simpkinp@aol.com	6503 Alderson St Weston WI 54476	AT	Teacher	EM			RF	1973
Petkewicz Karen K Singer	(630)724-0015 karenpetkewicz@gmail.com	4133 Washington Downers Grove IL 60515	NI	Teacher	C07/2016			RF	1984
Petree Andrea K Adams	(417)894-3399 apetree@trinityjc.org	69288 Red Fox Rd Tipton MO 65081	MO	Teacher	Tchr	Trinity Jefferson City MO	(573)636-7807	MQ	1998
Petrich Daniel J	(253)284-4433	2056 Sundance Pkwy Apt 9302 New Braunfels TX 78130	TX	DPM		Texas District Round Rock TX	(800)951-3478	SP	2016

*Multiple Assignments (See Church Worker Locator for Additional Details)

See Page 53 for the Table of Abbreviations for key to District, Classification, Position, and College abbreviations.

**C =Candidate; EM =Emeritus; the date following the C is the month and year the Candidate status began

NAME	TELEPHONE NUMBER EMAIL	STREET ADDRESS CITY/STATE/ZIP	DISTRICT	CLASS.	POSITION/ STATUS**	WHERE SERVING	OFFICE PHONE	COLLEGE/ UNIV/CQ	YR GRAD
Petrik Randi R Eggers	(319)491-4557 drpetrik4@gmail.com	9307 W 112th St Overland Park KS 66210	KS	DCE	C10/2020			S	2008
Petroff Gail C Batten	(763)786-2470 gailpetroff@q.com	8751 Tamarack St NW Coon Rapids MN 55433	MNS	Teacher	EM			SP	1975
Pett Ellen C Helmreich	(989)225-1864 ellenp@immanuelbaycity.com	347 Old Orchard Drive Essexville MI 48732	MI	Teacher	Tchr	Immanuel Bay City MI	(989)893-4088	CQ	2008
Pett Royden D	(989)482-7136 royden.pett@yahoo.com	347 Old Orchard Dr Essexville MI 48732	MI	Teacher	Tchr	Peace Saginaw MI	(989)793-9025	AA	2018
Pett Timothy W	(262)470-2152 timpett8@gmail.com	117 E Waushara St Apt 15 Berlin WI 54923	SW	Teacher	Tchr	St John Berlin WI	(920)361-0555	MQ	2002
Pettet Holly M	(865)776-1818	45 Knollwood Dr Rockledge FL 32955	FG	Teacher	Tchr	Trinity Rockledge FL	(321)636-5431	S	2009
Pettit Elizabeth L Inman	(660)229-1911	9941 SW 58th Ave Ocala FL 34476	SO	Teacher	C07/2016			S	2012
Petzold Julian H Dr	(248)931-5394 jpetzold90@gmail.com	24752 Victoria Ct Harrison Twp MI 48045	MI	Teacher	C06/2022			RF	1993
Petzoldt Lowell K	(419)966-0196 petzor01@hotmail.com	15942 County Road U Napoleon OH 43545	OH	Teacher	EM			S	1976
Peuster Barbara J Rehkop	(660)463-0001 jbpeuster@centurytel.net	305 S Sandia St Concordia MO 64020	MO	Teacher	EM			S	1982
Peyton Heather A Piescer	(714)614-5737 hpeyton@sjlschool.org	11926 Bouquet Dr Bakersfield CA 93311	CNH	Teacher	Tchr	St John Bakersfield CA	(661)664-8090	IV	2003
Pfabe Jerrald K Dr	(402)643-3278 jerry.pfabe@cune.edu	773 N Columbia Ave Seward NE 68434	NEB	Teacher	EM			RF	1960
Pfaff Kimberley J Lees	(281)413-6066 kipfaff@hotmail.com	711 Dresden Wood Dr Boerne TX 78006	TX	Teacher	EM			Other	2005
Pfannkuch Darrell L	(616)459-6190	1317 Emerald Ave NE Grand Rapids MI 49505	MI	Teacher	EM			RF	1964
Pfantz Lynne M Riese	(515)483-2663 llpfantz@gmail.com	2026 Hart Ave State Center IA 50247	IE	Teacher	EM			S	1980
Pfeiffer Ann M Kaiser	(734)721-3942 tomannpfeiffer@hotmail.com	161 Larchmont Dr Westland MI 48185	MI	Teacher	EM			S	1969
Pfeiffer Elena R Wolters	(218)234-1937 elena.pfeiffer1@gmail.com		OH	Teacher	Tchr	St Paul Milford Center OH	(937)349-5939	MQ	2010
Pfeiffer Linda M	(262)685-8915 lpfeiffer423@gmail.com	16380 Sudbury Ct Macomb MI 48044	MI	Teacher	Tchr	St Peters Eastpointe MI	(586)777-6300	RF	1993
Pfeiffer Megan M Gould	(618)616-8641 mpfeiffer@zionbethalto.org	104 Windsor Pl Bethalto IL 62010	SI	Teacher	Tchr	Zion Bethalto IL	(618)377-5507	S	2007
Pfeiffer Sara L Hauser	(563)639-4151 dsampfeiffer@msn.com	6675 Spring Creek Dr Bettendorf IA 52722	IE	Tch/DCE	EM			RF	1992
Pfeil Nathanael J	(319)929-1273 Nathanaeljpfeil@gmail.com	1215 Country Club Dr Marion IA 52302	IE	DPM	C05/2023			S	2014
Pfendler Ryan G	(919)608-7095 rpfendler@messiahnetwork.org	482 Oak Hill Dr Lake Saint Louis MO 63367	MO	DCE	Mem C	Messiah Weldon Spring MO	(636)926-9773	AU	2016
Pfenning Sara M	(414)531-8454 spfenning@sllcs.org	1537 Chipmunk Ln Oviedo FL 32765	S	Teacher	Tchr	St Luke Oviedo FL	(407)365-3408	MQ	2016
Pflieger R C Jr	(505)242-7657 rcpflieger@gmail.com	908 19th St NW Albuquerque NM 87104	RM	Teacher	EM			S	1984
Pflug Melissa D Deac	(812)599-1244 melissa.pflug@lcms.org	323 Hilcrest Dr Madison IN 47250	MO	Deaconess	S Miss	Office of International Mission Saint Louis MO		FW-DEAC	2024
Pflughoeft Casey L Van Deursen	(219)669-4853 pflughoeftc3@gmail.com	1905 Belshaw Rd Lowell IN 46356	IN	Teacher	C08/2022			CQ	2016
Pfund Roy E	(314)963-0602	701 Eckrich Pl Webster Grvs MO 63119	MO	Teacher	EM			RF	1959
Pfund Susan E Grush	(248)842-5176 pfundsusan@wowway.com	53333 Briar Dr Shelby Township MI 48316	MI	Teacher	Tchr	St John Rochester MI	(248)402-8000	AA	1984
Phelps Jason M	(713)299-0577 jasonmphelps@me.com		TX	DCE	Mem C	Gloria Dei Houston TX	(281)333-4535	S	2007
Phelps Kelly N Waterman	(920)785-1632 phelpsk@flhsemail.org	9320 Garden Springs Ave Las Vegas NV 89149	PSW	Teacher	Tchr	Faith Las Vegas NV	(702)804-4400	S	2006
Phelps Molly B Johnson	(217)871-1588 mollyphelps09@gmail.com	6405 Mardel Ave Saint Louis MO 63109	MO	Teacher	Tchr	Christ Community Kirkwood MO	(314)822-7774	MQ	2006
Phifer Jennifer J Millerwise		835 Cherokee Ave Port Neches TX 77651	TX	Teacher	C06/2024			CQ	2004
Philipp Diane P Anderson Deac	(847)336-8346 dianephilipp@att.net	825 Hickory St Waukegan IL 60085	NI	Deaconess	EM			CQ	1996
Philippi-Aden Melody Philippi	(402) 239-3489 melody.aden@gmail.com	1315 Paddock Ln Beatrice NE 68310	NEB	Teacher	Tchr	St Paul Beatrice NE	(402)223-3414	S	1990
Phillips Amelia A Schlichting	(402)307-0901 amelia.schlichting@cune.org	11545 N US Highway 27 Decatur IN 46733	IN	Teacher	Tchr	Bethlehem Ossian IN	(260)597-7121	S	2021
Phillips Anne M Hoft	(586)709-9513 annephillips28@yahoo.com	44240 Boulder Dr Clinton Twp MI 48038	MI	Teacher	Tchr	Lutheran North Macomb MI	(586)781-9151	AA	2003
Phillips Beth L Schmiesing	(410)626-8088	1131 Old Stone Ln Arnold MD 21012	SE	Teacher	EM			BR	1982
Phillips Karen M Horn	(847)363-9930 karen1228@comcast.net	1404 Knotty Pine Dr Elgin IL 60123	NI	Teacher	Tchr	Immanuel Belvidere IL	(815)547-5346	CQ	2019
Phillips Kathryn E Deac	(410)353-0673 deaconess.kphillips@proton.me	291 County Rd 489 Apt B Hanceville AL 35077	SO	Deaconess	Tchr	St Pauls Cullman AL	(256)734-6580	FW-DEAC	2021
Phillips Sarah A Stechholz	(801)500-7928 phillipss@lambofgodlv.com	7004 Dillseed Dr Las Vegas NV 89131	PSW	Teacher	Tchr	Lamb Of God Las Vegas NV	(702)645-4998	IV	2010
Philp Sharon D Meier	(314)226-5724 sharonphilp89@gmail.com	4792 Scharmen Rd Traverse City MI 49696	MI	Teacher	C09/2020			S	1997
Phoenix Emily M Norman			SE	DCE	C06/2020			S	2008

*Multiple Assignments (See Church Worker Locator for Additional Details)
See Page 53 for the Table of Abbreviations for key to District, Classification, Position, and College abbreviations.
**C =Candidate; EM =Emeritus; the date following the C is the month and year the Candidate status began

NAME	TELEPHONE NUMBER EMAIL	STREET ADDRESS CITY/STATE/ZIP	DISTRICT	CLASS.	POSITION/ STATUS**	WHERE SERVING	OFFICE PHONE	COLLEGE/ UNIV/CQ	YR GRAD
Piasecki Allison J Leach	(586)214-0839 teach314@comcast.net	45843 Keding St Utica MI 48317	MI	Teacher	Tchr	Crown Of Life Rochester Hills MI	(248)652-7720	CQ	2007
Piatti Norman F Dr	(651)641-8734 piatti@csp.edu		MNS	DCO	S HS/C	Concordia University St Paul Saint Paul MN	(651)641-8278	CQ	2022
Picciolo Jane C Arenson	(414)687-9629 jpicciolo@hcl.org	6501 Jessica Turn Calendonia WI 53402	EN	Teacher	Tchr	Hales Corners Hales Corners WI	(414)529-6701	CQ	2022
Pichan Daryl E	(585)615-8580 daryl2576@gmail.com	41 Westfield Cmns Rochester NY 14625	EA	Tch/DCE	EM			RF	1972
Pichan Thomas A	(734)751-7653	25227 Donald Redford MI 48239	MI	Teacher	Tchr	St Michael Wayne MI	(734)728-3315	AA	1989
Pickel Michele L Rodemeyer	(651)343-5016 pickel@csp.edu	1225 W Rondeau Lake Dr Forest Lake MN 55025	MNS	Tch/DCE	EM			SP	1977
Pickel Steven L	(651)493-0570 bigskymt2@hotmail.com	1225 W Rondeau Lake Dr Forest Lake MN 55025	MNS	DCE	EM			SP	1976
Pickelman Maureen R	(586)536-2631 maureenpickelman@gmail.com	138 Mark Dr Mount Clemens MI 48043	MI	Teacher	EM			RF	1967
Picker Rebekah M Adams	(509)572-7206 rebekahp@blcbls.org	6043 W 38th Ave Kennewick WA 99338	NOW	Teacher	Tchr	Bethlehem Kennewick WA	(509)582-5624	PO	2010
Pidsosny Mary L Fenske	(586)943-7585 pidsosnym@yahoo.com	4218 W Pebble Beach Ct Franklin WI 53132	SW	Teacher	EM			S	1980
Piehl Kerry K Knope	(715)524-2645	111 Forest Hill Ct Shawano WI 54166	NW	Teacher	EM			SP	1970
Piel Laura M	(847)302-0132 laura.m.piel@gmail.com	735 Alice Pl Elgin IL 60123	NI	Teacher	Tchr	Trinity Roselle IL	(630)894-3263	RF	2011
Piel Lianne M	(847)334-3491 lmp346@hotmail.com	735 Alice Pl Elgin IL 60123	NI	Teacher	Tchr	St Paul Mount Prospect IL	(847)255-6733	RF	2015
Piel Pamela J Daniel	(847)428-4013 pfpiel@sbcglobal.net	2331 Stewart Ln West Dundee IL 60118	NI	Teacher	EM			RF	1976
Piel Paul F	(847)428-4013 pfpiel@sbcglobal.net	2331 Stewart Ln West Dundee IL 60118	NI	Teacher	EM			RF	1983
Piepenbrink Allen C	(731)803-9397 Piepenbrinkallen@gmail.com	930 Buckingham Dr #2 Camdenton MO 65020	MO	Teacher	EM			S	1972
Piepenbrink Shirley A Meyer	(731)571-7368 spieps@gmail.com	930 Buckingham Dr Unit 2 Camdenton MO 65020	MO	Teacher	EM			S	1972
Pieper Anna Holle	(717)881-1478 anna@corrieshouse.org		TX	DCE	RSO	Lutheran Inter-City Network Houston TX	(713)426-2451	AU	2021
Pieper Dennis R	(708)759-4954 drpier@sbcglobal.net	322 Osage St Park Forest IL 60466	NI	Teacher	Tchr	Voice of Care Lombard IL	(630)231-3862	RF	1978
Pieper Kevin M	(281)635-2400 kpieper@salem4u.com	22407 Miramar Crest Dr Tomball TX 77375	TX	Teacher	Mem C	Salem Tomball TX	(281)351-8223	S	1980
Pieper Nancy A Kuehne	(763) 498-4509 nap_psteach@hotmail.com	5620 Royal Oaks Dr Shoreview MN 55126	MNS	Teacher	EM			SP	1974
Pieper Shelly S Faga	(224)678-9727 shelpiep6@gmail.com	1431 Lancaster Ln Algonquin IL 60102	NI	Teacher	Tchr	Immanuel East Dundee IL	(847)428-1010	RF	1993
Pierce Aaron V	(760)417-1700 dcepierce@yahoo.com		CNH	DCE	C07/2016			S	2000
Pierce Deborah A	(586)791-3447 debbie81992@yahoo.com	21448 Sunnyview St. Clinton Township MI 48035	MI	Teacher	Tchr	St Peters Eastpointe MI	(586)777-6300	AA	1991
Piering Donette M Mattfeld	(319)845-2093 dpiering@hotmail.com	215 Erusha Dr Walford IA 52351	IE	Teacher	EM			SP	1984
Piering Vernon C	(319)845-2093 vcpiering@hotmail.com	215 Erusha Dr Walford IA 52351	IE	Teacher	EM			RF	1969
Pierini Laurie A Schlecht	jlpierini3@gmail.com	159 S Middleton Ave Palatine IL 60067	NI	Teacher	EM			CQ	1986
Pierson Aubrie Bogle	(818)823-0053 aubrieb32@gmail.com	1701 E Park Blvd Plano TX 75074	TX	Teacher	Tchr	Faith Plano TX	(972)423-7447	IV	2017
Pierson Hannah J Weber		905 Beach St Webster City IA 50595	IW	Teacher	C05/2021			S	2016
Pierson Laura J	lpierson@salem4u.com	Salem Lutheran Church 22601 Lutheran Church Rd Tomball TX 77377	TX	DPM	Mem C	Salem Tomball TX	(281)351-8223	IV	2019
Pietsch Vicki L Hill	(972)345-6827 VickiPietsch@gmail.com	488 S Leon Giddings TX 78942	TX	Teacher	Tchr	Immanuel Giddings TX	(979)542-3319	AU	2015
Pifer Christine A Gentz	(586)596-1444 cpifer1016@gmail.com	17506 Eastland St Roseville MI 48066	MI	Teacher	Prin	St Paul Northville MI	(248)349-3140	RF	1983
Pikalek Gary E	(630)329-2881 gpikalek@netzero.com	13816 W Chase Ct Manhattan IL 60442	NI	Teacher	EM			RF	1972
Pike Brian N	(402)641-3256 bpike19@gmail.com	4114 Crofton St Lafayette IN 47909	IN	DCE	Mem C	Grace Lafayette IN	(765)474-1887	S	2011
Pike Kamie L Reinbold	(988)823-9925 kamiepike@yahoo.com	5175 Cottrell Rd Vassar MI 48768	MI	Teacher	Tchr	Trinity Reese MI	(989)868-4501	AA	1992
Pingel James A II Dr	(262)243-4214 james.pingel@cuw.edu	333 Blazing Star Cir Port Washington WI 53074	SW	Teacher	S HS/C	Concordia University Wisconsin Mequon WI	(262)243-5700	MQ	1992
Pingel Joshua J	(920)889-0068 jpingel@lutheranwest.com	21158 Norwood Ave Fairview Park OH 44126	OH	Teacher	Tchr	Cleveland LHS Association Rocky River OH	(440)356-7155	MQ	2019
Pingel Kathy M Tumm	pingelkathy@hotmail.com	3783 Canvasback Dr Janesville WI 53546	SW	Teacher	Tchr	St Paul's Janesville WI	(608)754-4471	SP	1990
Pinick Gregg A	(714)728-5054 gregg.pinick@gmail.com	19975 Voltera Pl Bend OR 97702	NOW	Teacher	EM			S	1980
Pinkerton Jan S Goodballet	(714)554-1779 janpinkerton@yahoo.com	15162 Reeve St Garden Grove CA 92843	PSW	Teacher	EM			IV	1989
Pinn Jon L	(605)941-3682 jpinn@sflutheranschool.com	2617 W Minnehaha Dr Sioux Falls SD 57105	SD	Teacher	Tchr	Sioux Falls Sioux Falls SD	(605)335-1923	S	2001
Pinn Madyson M Pralle	(507)271-0519 mmpinn.dce@gmail.com	2415 Dean Ave Bellingham WA 98225	NOW	DCE	Mem C	Trinity Bellingham WA	(360)734-2770	S	2023

*Multiple Assignments (See Church Worker Locator for Additional Details)
See Page 53 for the Table of Abbreviations for key to District, Classification, Position, and College abbreviations.
**C =Candidate; EM =Emeritus; the date following the C is the month and year the Candidate status began

NAME	TELEPHONE NUMBER EMAIL	STREET ADDRESS CITY/STATE/ZIP	DISTRICT	CLASS.	POSITION/ STATUS**	WHERE SERVING	OFFICE PHONE	COLLEGE/ UNIV/CQ	YR GRAD
Pinnow Barbara J	(312) 402-4826 bpinnow@hiscross.net	12009 Lisbon Rd Newark IL 60541	NI	Teacher	Tchr	Cross Yorkville IL	(630)553-7861	RF	1984
Pipho Donald M	(712)949-2268 dmpipho@tcaexpress.net	313 S Maple St P.O. Box 564 Paullina IA 51046	IW	Teacher	EM			S	1963
Pipkorn Alison L Brueggemann	(262)378-0458 apipkorn@fils.org	1505 13th Ave Grafton WI 53024	SW	Teacher	Tchr	First Immanuel Cedarburg WI	(262)377-6610	CQ	2012
Pipkorn Anne M Pederson	(262)305-2367 apipkorn@trinityfreistadt.com	11222 W Freistadt Rd Mequon WI 53097	SW	Teacher	Tchr	Trinity Mequon WI	(262)242-2045	CH	2006
Pirn Irene	(216)218-7296 irenepirn@gmail.com	1629 Eden Park Dr Apt 8 Hamilton OH 45013	OH	Teacher	Pro Stf	Immanuel Hamilton OH	(513)893-6792	BR	2021
Pister Ronnie J	(816)261-6634 rpister64@gmail.com	5021 Frederick Ave Saint Joseph MO 64506	MO	Teacher	Tchr	St Paul Saint Joseph MO	(816)279-1110	CQ	2007
Pister Teri J Olerud	(816)279-1115 tjpanic66@yahoo.com	5021 Frederick Ave Saint Joseph MO 64506	MO	Teacher	Tchr	St Paul Saint Joseph MO	(816)279-1118	CQ	2005
Pitsch Monte G	(660)463-2238 montepitsch@yahoo.com	313 S College Dr Concordia MO 64020	MO	Teacher	Tchr	Saint Paul Concordia MO	(660)463-2238	S	1994
Pittman Ellen M Struecker	emptlo@yahoo.com		MNS	Teacher	EM			SP	1969
Pittman Eric G	(248)840-7339 jandepittman@gmail.com	241 Harrington Dr. Troy MI 48098	MI	Teacher	EM			RF	1973
Pittman Heather M Rasch	(940)765-4632 heather.rasch@cune.org	131 N Virginia Ave Belleville IL 62220	SI	Teacher	Tchr	Zion Belleville IL	(618)233-2299	S	2019
Pittman Janel D Weisenbach	(989)497-0208	471 Canterbury Dr Saginaw MI 48638	MI	Teacher	Tchr	Peace Saginaw MI	(989)793-9025	CQ	2014
Pittock Stephanie M Gruhn	(936)435-5505	3905 105th Street Lubbock TX 79423	TX	DCE	C11/2022			CQ	2022
Pitts Michelle V	(912)247-9744 michelle13755@gmail.com	2090 Lyda Ln Loganville GA 30052	FG	DCE	Mem C	Our Savior Plantation FL	(954)473-6888	SP	2006
Pixley Joyce M Braun	(260)437-1735	1762 Cloister Dr Indianapolis IN 46260	IN	Teacher	EM			CQ	2003
Planker Rachel H Hosmon	(772)291-8553 rplanker@gmail.com	604 SE Krueger Pkwy Stuart FL 34996	FG	Teacher	C07/2016			RF	2004
Playter Kellie L Shaw	(951)818-0950 kellie.playter@cui.edu	11341 Reagan St. Los Alamitos CA 90720	PSW	Teacher	S HS/C	Concordia University Irvine Irvine CA	(949)854-8002	CQ	2016
Ploetz Melissa Kohlman	(920)912-8590 ploetzmelissa@gmail.com	650 S. Silverbrook Dr. West Bend WI 53095	SW	Teacher	Tchr	St John* West Bend WI	(262)429-1061	MQ	2016
Plopper Lisa A Kutz	(262)893-7536 lisaplopper@gmail.com	W279N7220 Millpond Way Hartland WI 53029	SW	Teacher	Tchr	Divine Redeemer Hartland WI	(262)367-3664	MQ	2003
Plopper Sydney A	(262)685-7962 sydney.plopper@gmail.com	16380 Sudbury Ct Macomb MI 48044	MI	Teacher	Tchr	Immanuel Macomb MI	(586)286-4231	CH	2021
Ploss Mark A	(317)294-7093 Frugalmap@aol.com	836 S Home Ave Franklin IN 46131	IN	Teacher	EM			RF	1979
Plourde Randall J	(906)235-6138 slingshot@campluther.com	1893 Koubenec Rd Three Lakes WI 54562	NW	DCM	D Ex/S	North Wisconsin District Wausau WI	(715)845-8241	MQ	2018
Plozizka Jeanette L	(217)585-0188	4101 West Iles Ave Rm 6312 Springfield IL 62711	CI	Teacher	EM			S	1969
Plucknett Terence M	(253)350-8783 terry.plucknett@ccatacoma.org	3860 SW 339th St Federal Way WA 98023	NOW	Teacher	Tchr	Concordia Tacoma WA	(253)475-9513	PO	2008
Plumb Donna S	(908)869-7550	19610 N 97th Ln Peoria AZ 85382	PSW	Teacher	Tchr	Christ Phoenix AZ	(602)955-4830	RF	1972
Plummer D Dean	(402)910-4191 djplummer76@gmail.com	3261 50th Ave Columbus NE 68601	NEB	Teacher	EM			S	1975
Plutat Angela L McAninch	(765)271-6557 aplutat@redeemerkokomo.org.in	2730 Tumbleweed Dr Kokomo IN 46901	IN	Teacher	Tchr	Redeemer Kokomo IN	(765)864-6466	CQ	2022
Plyler Anneliese Ploetz	(716)560-8699 anneliese.plyler@gmail.com	561 Tremont St. North Tonawanda NY 14120	EA	Teacher	C08/2024			S	2023
Podwils Carol M Bohning	(541)420-2698 cpodwils@gmail.com	2859 NE Pinnacle Pl Bend OR 97701	NOW	Teacher	EM			S	1975
Poehlmann Hilliary A Jaster	(979)251-2484 hpoehlmann@glsbrenham.com	2633 Triangle Z Ln Brenham TX 77833	TX	Teacher	Tchr	Grace Brenham TX	(979)836-3475	AU	2004
Pohl Jane A Roszell	(512)341-0201 jane_anne_pohl@yahoo.com	2904 Forest Meadow Dr Round Rock TX 78665	TX	Teacher	EM			S	1974
Pohlman Betty L	(847)437-4557 b.pohlman@yahoo.com	1145 S Arlington Heights Rd Arlington Hts IL 60005	NI	Teacher	EM			RF	1967
Poley Carol L Schefft	(440)333-4176 gpoles2@cox.net	1 S Hampton Ct Rocky River OH 44116	OH	Teacher	EM			CQ	1989
Politte Paula J	(503)806-1268 pjplmo13@gmail.com	8209 NE 7th St Vancouver WA 98664	NOW	Teacher	C07/2021			PO	1984
Polk Norma P Deac	(734)395-9357	535 Berkshire Dr Saline MI 48176	MI	Deaconess	Mem C	University Chapel Ann Arbor MI	(734)663-5560	SL-DEAC	2015
Pollan Rebecca S Raub	(901)756-0509	8277 Still Oaks CV Cordova TN 38018	MDS	Teacher	Tchr	Immanuel Memphis TN	(901)388-0205	CQ	2003
Pollatz Brian M	(248)376-4805 bpollatz@lhsa.com	31644 Campbell Rd Madison Hts MI 48071	MI	Teacher	Tchr	Northwest Rochester Hills MI	(248)856-0240	AA	1987
Pollert Karen L Bobb	(812)523-8025 kpollert@pollerts.com	106 E 2nd St Seymour IN 47274	IN	Teacher	EM			CQ	1993
Pollock Rachel L Messmann	(320)305-0924 mrsrachelpollock@gmail.com	4017 Hiawatha Blvd Fort Wayne IN 46809	IN	Teacher	C07/2016			MQ	1996
Pollom Cheri R Hartleben	(307)632-8917 cpollom@trinitycheyenne.org	1608 W Gopp Ct Cheyenne WY 82007	WY	Teacher	P/Tchr	Trinity Cheyenne WY	(307)635-2802	S	1993
Polson Jodi E Rolf	(303)949-5424 jodi.rolf@cune.org	9975 W 85th Pl Arvada CO 80005	RM	Teacher	Tchr	Trinity Franktown CO	(303)841-4660	S	2006
Polster Sheryl L Miller	(920)312-4831 spluvsjc@hotmail.com	N6251 County Road Oj Plymouth WI 53073	SW	Teacher	EM			MQ	2003
Polzin Bryan C	(612)787-5877 bryanpolzin@me.com	3326 US Highway 212 Plato MN 55370	MNS	Teacher	C07/2019			S	2006

*Multiple Assignments (See Church Worker Locator for Additional Details)

See Page 53 for the Table of Abbreviations for key to District, Classification, Position, and College abbreviations.

**C =Candidate; EM =Emeritus; the date following the C is the month and year the Candidate status began

NAME	TELEPHONE NUMBER EMAIL	STREET ADDRESS CITY/STATE/ZIP	DISTRICT	CLASS.	POSITION/ STATUS**	WHERE SERVING	OFFICE PHONE	COLLEGE/ UNIV/CQ	YR GRAD
Polzin David M	(612)801-5675 homebrew55122@yahoo.com	829 14th St E Glencoe MN 55336	MNS	Teacher	EM			SP	1975
Polzin Lauren A Wunder	(262)707-8559 lwunder@gracemenomoneefalls.org	1539 County Road A West Bend WI 53090	SW	Teacher	Tchr	Grace Menomonee Falls WI	(262)251-7140	MQ	2013
Polzin Megan L Hallowell Deac	(952)232-9844 mpolzin@1stglencoe.org	3326 US Highway 212 Plato MN 55370	MNS	Deac/Tch	Mem C	First Glencoe MN	(320)864-5522	FW-DEAC	2022
Pomerenke Lydia I		14410 Sandalfoot Street Houston TX 77095	TX	Teacher	Tchr	Our Savior Houston TX	(713)290-9087	S	2014
Pomerenke Micah J	(314)677-8574 micahpomerenke@gmail.com	83 Henry Avenue Ellisville MO 63011	MO	Teacher	Tchr	Lutheran North Saint Louis MO	(314)389-3100	S	2013
Pomroy Courtney L Wahl	(248)807-7084 azcourtney@gmail.com		MI	Teacher	Tchr	Christ The King Southgate MI	(734)285-9695	AA	2010
Ponder Ashley R Pedrosa	(573)837-2095 unitedinchristprincipal@att.net	9290 Main St Altenburg MO 63732	MO	Teacher	Prin	United in Christ Frohna MO	(573)824-5218	MQ	2011
Ponder Elaine J Frentzel	(756)438-9226 teader26@aol.com	3753 W 600 N Sharpsville IN 46068	IN	Teacher	EM			CQ	1998
Pontifes Matthew E	(832)552-2793 matthew.gracioussaviorchurch@gmail.com	c/o P.O. Box 250 Edwards CO 81632	RM	DCE	Mem C	Gracious Savior Edwards CO	(970)926-3550	AU	2018
Poore Betty A Dr	(314)849-0010 poores@sbcglobal.net	5372 Studer Ln Saint Louis MO 63128	MO	Teacher	EM			CQ	2003
Popenhagen Margie J Hildebrand	(319)396-8381	1726 Meiers Ct NW Cedar Rapids IA 52405	IE	Teacher	EM			S	1967
Popp Elaine D Carr	(727)524-4502 libbycarr@ij.net	2591 Keene Park Dr Largo FL 33771	FG	Teacher	Tchr	First Clearwater FL	(727)462-8000	RF	1980
Popp Jessa D Dorman	(904)535-0384 jessa_popp@gracelutheraneagles.org	1502 Arden Way Jax Bch FL 32250	FG	Teacher	Tchr	Grace Jacksonville FL	(904)928-9136	S	1999
Popp Sarah E Poertner	(210)632-1810 sarahp8791@gmail.com	1314 Grand Ave Spencer IA 51301	IW	Teacher	Prin	Iowa Great Lakes Spencer IA	(712)262-8237	RF	1991
Poppe Cheryl L Steinke	(440)465-0639 cherylpoppe@hotmail.com	4032 W 157th St Cleveland OH 44135	S	Teacher	Tchr	Grace Lakewood OH	(216)529-1081	AA	1997
Poppe Jonathan M	(262)383-1084 jmcpoppe@gmail.com	3506 Kendale Dr Fort Wayne IN 46835	NI	Teacher	C07/2022			CH	2013
Poppe Molly E Gowen	(707)346-7621 molly.gowen@gmail.com	801 Seminary Place St. Louis MO 63105	MO	Teacher	C07/2018			CH	2014
Poppe Nathanael W	(720)628-5461 nathanaelpoppe431@gmail.com	13 Founders Way Unit C Saint Louis MO 63105	MO	Teacher	C07/2025			CH	2013
Poppe Richard A	(317)576-0777 ripoppe@sbcglobal.net	6816 Cherry Laurel Ln Fishers IN 46038	IN	Teacher	EM			S	1961
Porath Jennifer L	(260)452-7335 jporath@clhscadets.com	8834 Seiler Rd New Haven IN 46774	IN	Teacher	Tchr	Concordia Fort Wayne IN	(260)483-1102	S	2017
Porath Kathleen A Jans	(402)615-3270 kporath@gmail.com	8331 SW 98th St Denton NE 68339	NEB	Teacher	EM			S	1974
Porisch Dorleen K Van Diest		3875 194th Ln NW Anoka MN 55303	MNS	Teacher	EM			CQ	2003
Porter Ellen L Walker	(863)514-6373 familyporter24@gmail.com	1179 Southcreek Dr Manteno IL 60950	PSW	Teacher	Tchr	Christ Phoenix AZ	(602)955-4830	RF	1997
Porterfield Sharon R Liebold	(847)636-6418 sporterfield77@gmail.com	2557 Spyglass Ct Edwardsville IL 62025	NI	Teacher	EM			CQ	2010
Portillo Panchita Deac	(308)391-0169 panchitaportillo@hotmail.com	915 E 6th St Grand Island NE 68801	NEB	Deaconess	Mem C	Cristo Cordero/Dios Grand Island NE	(308)391-0169	SL-DEAC	2014
Portwood Von E	(402) 750-7737	406 Market Pl Norfolk NE 68701	NEB	Teacher	Tchr	Christ Norfolk NE	(402)371-5536	S	1985
Post Kristen C Barthel	(425)353-0990 darren_post@msn.com	301 S Cabot Rd Everett WA 98203	NOW	Teacher	Tchr	Zion Snohomish Cty Lake Stevens WA	(425)334-5064	IV	2007
Postenrieder Gene R	(513)236-9274 weposts@yahoo.com	6605 Ponderosa Ave NE Albuquerque NM 87110	RM	Teacher	Tchr	Christ Albuquerque NM	(505)884-3876	CQ	2005
Postma Cecelia M Herrmann	(307)856-3620 cec_herrmann@hotmail.com	1007 N Broadway Ave Riverton WY 82501	WY	Teacher	EM			S	1985
Potratz Zachary J	(402)646-5930 zachary.potratz@cune.org	346 Roberts St Seward NE 68434	NEB	Teacher		Nebraska District Seward NE	(402)643-2961	S	2022
Potter Jeffrey E		7394 Panache Way Boca Raton FL 33433	FG	Teacher	Prin	St Paul Boca Raton FL	(561)395-0433	MQ	2008
Potter Margaret R Baumbach	(410)420-7526 hnybear1@verizon.net	1835 Beth Bridge Cir Forest Hill MD 21050	SE	Teacher	EM			CQ	1990
Potter Mary L Hockemeyer	(260)493-4872	15802 Slusher Rd New Haven IN 46774	IN	Teacher	Tchr	Central New Haven IN	(260)493-2502	RF	1985
Potthoff Matthew S	(714)765-9670 potthoff@lhsoc.org	2445 N Robinhood Pl Orange CA 92867	PSW	Teacher	Tchr	Orange County Orange CA	(714)998-5151	IV	2003
Potthoff Melissa A Mackey	(714)749-1833 lyssabow@sbcglobal.net	2445 N Robinhood Pl Orange CA 92867	PSW	Teacher	Tchr	Orange County Orange CA	(714)998-5151	IV	2004
Potts Randy L	(404)454-2942 youth@cts.org	4655 Webb Bridge Rd Alpharetta GA 30005	EN	Tch/DCE	Mem C	Christ Shepherd Alpharetta GA	(770)475-0640	S	1979
Pottschmidt Robert L	(812)358-2864 rj_pottschmidt@hotmail.com	2887 E State Road 250 Brownstown IN 47220	IN	Teacher	EM			RF	1973
Potvin Alicia A David		525 N Stewart Ave Lombard IL 60148	NI	Teacher	Tchr	St Peter Arlington Heights IL	(847)259-4114	CH	2004
Powell Connie S Reinert	(319)294-4458 powellc@trinitycr.org	2781 Tower Dr Cedar Rapids IA 52411	IE	Teacher	Tchr	Trinity Cedar Rapids IA	(319)362-6952	RF	1996
Powell Luella M Roth	(573)822-5490 powell.luella@yahoo.com	416 Janet Trl Palmyra MO 63461	MO	Teacher	EM			S	1972
Powers Gwyn L Schluckebier	(703)489-0087 gwyn.powers@gmail.com	3733 Birdwood Rd Richmond VA 23234	SE	Teacher	EM			S	1983

*Multiple Assignments (See Church Worker Locator for Additional Details)

See Page 53 for the Table of Abbreviations for key to District, Classification, Position, and College abbreviations.

**C =Candidate; EM =Emeritus; the date following the C is the month and year the Candidate status began

NAME	TELEPHONE NUMBER EMAIL	STREET ADDRESS CITY/STATE/ZIP	DISTRICT	CLASS.	POSITION/ STATUS**	WHERE SERVING	OFFICE PHONE	COLLEGE/ UNIV/CQ	YR GRAD
Powley Kaela	(618)615-3413 kpowley12@gmail.com	505 Solomon St Chester IL 62233	SI	Teacher	Tchr	St John Chester IL	(618)826-3545	CQ	2016
Poyner Stephanie A	(281)682-1347 stephanieannepoyner@gmail.com	1806 Rose Circle Lewisville TX 75077	TX	Teacher	Mem C	Lamb Of God Flower Mound TX	(972)539-5200	S	2001
Praeuner Danica R	(402)750-3282 praeunerdr@esu8.org	721 E Park Ave Norfolk NE 68701	NEB	Teacher	Tchr	Trinity Madison NE	(402)454-2651	CQ	2022
Prahl Holly A Swanson	(715)212-0241 prahlh@trinitynet.org	166251 Junction Rd Wausau WI 54403	NW	Teacher	Tchr	Trinity Wausau WI	(715)848-0166	MQ	1988
Prahlow Donald A Dr	(314)222-1990 janeprahlow@icloud.com	711 S Laclede Station Rd Apt 3104 Saint Louis MO 63119	MO	Teacher	EM			RF	1952
Prahlow James D	(314)681-0049 jprahlow@lncrusaders.org	6919 Jamestown Way Dr Florissant MO 63033	MO	Teacher	Tchr	Lutheran North Saint Louis MO	(314)389-3100	RF	1976
Pralle Eric A	(620)577-4581 eapralle87@gmail.com	2915 Crown Dr Independence KS 67301	KS	Teacher	Prin	Zion Independence KS	(620)332-3300	S	1992
Pralle Jacob C	(507)244-0821 jcpralle.dce@gmail.com	602 E 925 N Firth ID 83236	NOW	DCE	Mem C	St John Idaho Falls ID	(208)522-5650	S	2022
Pralle Marilyn A Mueller	(785)806-5734 mampralle@hotmail.com	3550 W Coleman Rd Ponca City OK 74601	OK	Teacher	EM			S	1963
Prange Deborah J Miller	(262)966-4953 djprange@gmail.com	W334N5897 Township Road M Nashotah WI 53058	SW	Teacher	EM			CQ	2006
Prange Debra J Stuenkel	(314)302-1183 debprange@msn.com	6915 Turnesa Ln Saint Louis MO 63129	MO	Teacher	EM			S	1975
Prange Michael	(314)620-5509 prangemj@gmail.com	175 Ameren Way Ballwin MO 63021	MO	Teacher	EM			S	1965
Prange Sherry L Hoffherr	(618)615-1630 ruma_sp@yahoo.com	9 Julie St Ruma IL 62278	SI	Teacher	EM			RF	1969
Prann William E	(602)930-7870 wprann@hotmail.com	4801 Anderson Ave Manhattan KS 66503	KS	DCE	Mem C	St Lukes Manhattan KS	(785)539-2604	S	2004
Pratt David J	(562)508-3373 davepratt@mac.com	10628 College Hill Ave Las Vegas NV 89166	PSW	Teacher	Tchr	Faith Las Vegas NV	(702)804-4400	S	2004
Pratt Diana M Palmer	(217)443-2981 dprtch2@comcast.net	161 Mauck Ln Danville IL 61832	CI	Teacher	EM			RF	1976
Pratt Ellen M Look	(562)633-7334 teacherel@gmail.com	10646 Cliff Ridge Ave Las Vegas NV 89129	PSW	Teacher	D Ex/S	Pacific Southwest District Irvine CA	(949)854-3232	CQ	1999
Pratt Jonathan D	(562)631-4303 jonathan.pratt@FLHSEMAIL.ORG	360 Purple Sandpiper St Las Vegas NV 89138	PSW	Teacher	Tchr	Faith Las Vegas NV	(702)804-4400	IV	2007
Prechel Dennis	(248)478-1381	20390 Purlingbrook St Livonia MI 48152	MI	Teacher	EM			S	1971
Precht Kenneth P	(810)765-0595 ruthandken_1957@yahoo.com	155 S Water St Apt 205 Marine City MI 48039	MI	Teacher	EM			RF	1956
Predoehl Susan M	(520)304-8813 smpredoehl@gmail.com	2303 S Cliff Dr Green Valley AZ 85614	EN	Teacher	C04/2017			SP	1996
Prelerson Karen K Cross	(402)592-6847 kppooh@cox.net	603 Laredo Rd Papillion NE 68046	NEB	Teacher	EM			S	1987
Preloger Joan Von Strohe	(812)523-8801	28 Carolyn Dr Seymour IN 47274	IN	Teacher	EM			RF	1970
Preloger Ronald R Dr	(812)523-8801	28 Carolyn Dr Seymour IN 47274	IN	Teacher	EM			RF	1970
Prentice Lindsey E	(812) 205-6673 linzeep@me.com	701 Keck Ave Evansville IN 47711	IN	Teacher	Tchr	Evansville Evansville IN	(812)424-7252	S	1999
Prentice Sarah N Lessman	(812)205-6865 sarah@redeemerchurch.org	701 Keck Ave Evansville IN 47711	IN	DCE	Mem C	Our Redeemer Evansville IN	(812)476-9991	S	2000
Preston Emily M Owen	(651)728-1107 epreston@cglschool.org	9535 E Rainbow Ave Mesa AZ 85212	PSW	DCO	Mem C	Christ Greenfield Gilbert AZ	(480)892-8521	SP	2009
Preston Matthew E	(210)284-1643 mattprestonmusic@gmail.com	9535 E Rainbow Ave Mesa AZ 85212	PSW	DPM	Mem C	Christ Greenfield Gilbert AZ	(480)892-8521	IV	2009
Prestwich Becka N	beckapres@gmail.com		FG	DCM	Mem C	Our Redeemer Augusta GA	(706)733-6076	MQ	2023
Prestwood Elizabeth A Petsch	(806)626-4591 eprestw927@sbcglobal.net	8230 Garrison Point Dr Houston TX 77040	TX	Teacher	Tchr	Our Savior Houston TX	(713)290-8277	CQ	2020
Preus Anna N Klitzing		1975 N Lassen Blvd Orange CA 92867	PSW	Teacher	D Ex/S	Pacific Southwest District Irvine CA	(949)854-3232	IV	2003
Preus Jacob A IV Dr	jack.preus@gmail.com		PSW	Teacher	Tchr	Orange County Orange CA	(714)998-5151	CQ	2003
Preus Janet E Bingaman	(763)438-2387 klemjan@comcast.net	299 Mile O Pne Grand Marais MN 55604	MNS	Teacher	EM			CQ	1995
Preus Julianne E Lams	(763)416-3789 julielamspreus@yahoo.com	7755 Polaris Ln N Maple Grove MN 55311	MNS	Teacher	EM			RF	1973
Preuss Judith C Walter Dr	(402)643-3115 jpreuss@neb.rr.com	1056 Plainview Ave Seward NE 68434	NEB	Teacher	EM			S	1960
Preuss Mary L Wellenkamp	(618) 210-6893 marypreuss@yahoo.com	6823 Kensington Dr Maryville IL 62062	SI	Teacher	EM			S	1960
Preuss Micah D	micahdpreuss@gmail.com	221 W 3rd St Sparta IL 62286	SI	Teacher	C07/2022			CH	2015
Preuss Timothy L Dr	(949)468-6176 tim.preuss@cune.edu	1737 Plainview Ave Seward NE 68434	NEB	Teacher	S HS/C	Concordia University Nebraska Seward NE	(402)643-3651	S	1983
Price Jodee M Frazier	(574)606-5665 jodeeprice@trinityl.org	50591 Elk Trl Granger IN 46530	IN	Teacher	Tchr	Trinity Elkhart IN	(574)674-8800	CQ	2020
Price Lora L Schwarz	(630)746-3841 llprice74@yahoo.com	1221 Willow Way Yorkville IL 60560	NI	Teacher	Tchr	Bethany Naperville IL	(630)355-6607	CQ	1997
Price Sandra M Seevers	(574)612-2000	22300 Heron CV Elkhart IN 46516	IN	Teacher	EM			RF	2001
Pride Sandra K Davis	(317)946-3946 jfskpride@sbcglobal.net	4920 Five Points Rd Indianapolis IN 46239	IN	Teacher	EM			S	1973
Priebe Bonnie S Spicer	(301)341-2788 bonnielass_us@yahoo.com	5600 Inwood St Cheverly MD 20785	SE	Teacher	EM			RF	1964

*Multiple Assignments (See Church Worker Locator for Additional Details)

See Page 53 for the Table of Abbreviations for key to District, Classification, Position, and College abbreviations.

**C =Candidate; EM =Emeritus; the date following the C is the month and year the Candidate status began

NAME	TELEPHONE NUMBER EMAIL	STREET ADDRESS CITY/STATE/ZIP	DISTRICT	CLASS.	POSITION/ STATUS**	WHERE SERVING	OFFICE PHONE	COLLEGE/ UNIV/CQ	YR GRAD
Priehs Karen L Kvorka	(586)707-2028 priehs6@yahoo.com	35656 Electra Sterling Heights MI 48312	MI	Teacher	EM			RF	1975
Priehs Warren W	(586) 202-9467 priehs6@yahoo.com	35656 Electra Dr Sterling Hts MI 48312	MI	Teacher	EM			RF	1974
Priem Sadie N McDaniel	(989)415-0104 spriem@zionbaycity.org	606 N Elevator Rd Linwood MI 48634	MI	Teacher	Tchr	Zion Bay City MI	(989)894-2611	CQ	2021
Priest Kimberly S Jonasch	(260)415-1871 k2priest@aol.com	7911 Hoagland Rd Hoagland IN 46745	IN	Teacher	EM			CQ	2012
Prigge Barbara J Johannes	(952)854-3158 rogbarprigge@msn.com	3601 W. Old Shakopee Rd Bloomington MN 55431	MNS	Teacher	EM			SP	1973
Prill Ann E Leininger	(760)987-5128 annprill@hotmail.com	2900 S Valley View Blvd Trlr 50 Las Vegas NV 89102	PSW	Teacher	EM			S	1973
Prill James C	(760)987-1237 jcprill51@me.com	2900 S Valley View Blvd Trlr 50 Las Vegas NV 89102	PSW	Teacher	EM			S	1973
Primeau Douglas A	(586)574-0369	11436 Newbern Dr Warren MI 48093	MI	Teacher	EM			S	1967
Primuth Kurt S Sawinski	kurtprimuth@gmail.com	1175 Sunset Dr Beresford SD 57004	SD	DCM	Pro Stf	South Dakota District Sioux Falls SD	(605)361-1514	MQ	2022
Prince Heather N Slayton	(714)328-7220 heather.prince2017@gmail.com	28275 Evening Star Dr Menifee CA 92585	PSW	Teacher	Tchr	Immanuel Riverside CA	(951)682-4211	IV	2013
Prince Michelle L Dobbertien	(414)552-4938 mlprince@hotmail.com	3242 Superior Ave East Troy WI 53120	SW	Teacher	Tchr	Good Shepherd East Troy WI	(262)642-3310	S	1992
Prindiville Hannah V Jeppson	(940)206-7831 hprindiville@log.org	3655 Fairview Dr Corinth TX 76210	TX	DCM	Mem C	Lamb Of God Flower Mound TX	(972)539-5200	MQ	2007
Prine Barbara M Morse	(708)207-1801 bprine876@gmail.com	826 S Hillside Elmhurst IL 60126	NI	Teacher	Tchr	Immanuel Elmhurst IL	(630)832-1649	CQ	2020
Pringle Johanna E Hubel	(810)407-3774 johanna.hubel@cuw.edu	1028 Kingston Ave Racine WI 53402	SW	Teacher	Tchr	Lutheran High School Racine WI	(262)637-6538	MQ	2008
Prinsen Samantha S Steger	(414)940-0070 sprinsen19@gmail.com	725 Chief Kewaskum Pl Kewaskum WI 53040	SW	Teacher	Tchr	St Johns West Bend WI	(262)334-3077	MQ	2018
Priskorn Gary J	(248)399-3313 garypam68@comcast.net	6577 Emerald Lake Dr Troy MI 48085	MI	Teacher	EM			RF	1968
Pritchard Emily M Hinck	(618) 409-4671 emmiep66@gmail.com	6072 S Circle Rd Stover MO 65078	SI	Teacher	Tchr	Good Shepherd Collinsville IL	(618)344-3153	RF	1989
Pritchard Wendy M Klug	(847)224-2896 wpritchard79@gmail.com	1321 Elm Street Alexandria MN 56308	MNN	Teacher	C07/2019			CQ	2004
Pritzl Korie M Sorenson	(262)497-7998 kbaganz@gmail.com	6123 State Highway 38 Caledonia WI 53126	SW	Teacher	Tchr	Concordia Sturtevant WI	(262)884-0991	RF	2004
Probst David A	(812)603-7970 dcedavidp@gmail.com	9163 Janelle Dr Seymour IN 47274	IN	DCE	C08/2022			S	1998
Probst Jennifer A Bierdeman	(765)491-7818 4probstfamily@gmail.com	9163 Janelle Dr Seymour IN 47274	IN	Tch/DCE	Pro Stf	St Paul Columbus IN	(812)376-6504	S	1998
Prochnow John R	(507)235-5926 jtprochnow@frontier.net	477 Meadow Ln Young America MN 55397	MNS	Teacher	EM			SP	1968
Proctor Jack M	(703)203-5510 proctor.jack@gmail.com	8506 Pioneer Gold San Antonio TX 78249	TX	DCE	Tchr	Concordia San Antonio TX	(210)479-1477	AU	2017
Profilet Janet L Heidloff	(314)412-6736 janet.profilet@gmail.com	2422 St Andrews Rd Urbana IL 61802	CI	Teacher	EM			RF	1985
Prohl-Keller Ellen E Prohl	(630)251-0795 eprohl71@gmail.com	1221 48th Ave N Saint Petersburg FL 33703	FG	DPM	Mem C	Grace Saint Petersburg FL	(727)527-6213	RF	2013
Prophete Jennifer J Mustard	(314)614-5210 jennifer.prophete@gmail.com	1109 Wildflower Ln Saint Charles MO 63304	MO	Teacher	Aux	LLL/Lutheran Hour Ministries Saint Louis MO	(314)317-4100	S	2002
Propst Elizabeth A Schanbacher	(314)303-5759 eschanbacher@gmail.com	901 Ihler Rd Jefferson City MO 65109	MO	Teacher	C07/2023			RF	2010
Prost Linda A Poellot	(262)376-3878 lppprost@gmail.com	N17 W5328 Garfield St Cedarburg WI 53012	SW	Teacher	Tchr	St Johns West Bend WI	(262)334-3077	MQ	1993
Prouty Kristi A Rettedal	(605)261-3435 kprouty@sflutheranschool.com	2500 W 66th St N Sioux Falls SD 57107	SD	Teacher	Tchr	Sioux Falls Sioux Falls SD	(605)335-1923	CQ	2024
Prozenko Emilie A Stoller Deac	(514)434-7436 stolleremilie@gmail.com	7992 Highway Unit 2 Musquodoboit Harbour NS B0J 2 CANADA	S	Deaconess	C09/2023			CH	2021
Pruhs Brenda D Kudick	(623)203-5068 loveisgolden@cox.net	14256 60th St Scottsdale AZ 85254	PSW	DCE	C10/2019			IV	1988
Pruhs Shea J Thorson Deac	(916)759-8827 sheap@christ4u.net	4210 Spring Palms Ct Kingwood TX 77345	TX	Deaconess	Mem C	Christ King Kingwood TX	(281)360-7936	SL-DEAC	2016
Prusak Kathleen A Hollmann	(313)333-1831 kh3772287@yahoo.com	4905 Middlesex St Dearborn MI 48126	MI	Teacher	EM			S	1977
Prybylski Dorothy Kruse Deac	(360)897-9313 gocken@centurytel.net	12620 232nd Ave E Buckley WA 98321	NOW	Deaconess	EM			Other	1971
Pryor Jami L	(217)324-9215 jpryor@zionlutheranlitchfield.com	315 North Chestnut St Litchfield IL 62056	SI	Teacher	Prin	Zion Litchfield IL	(217)324-3166	CQ	2003
Przybylski Sonja E Gullbrandsen	(630)926-2606 tchme3@gmail.com	5821 S. Menard Ave Chicago IL 60638	NI	Teacher	C03/2022			S	1993
Puccio Lawrence C	(516)557-3696 lawrencepuccio@gmail.com	876 Grand Blvd Westbury NY 11590	AT	Teacher	C07/2016			CQ	2006
Puckett Paul R	(952)210-2939 prpuckett63@embarqmail.com	426 5th NE Mayer MN 55360	MNS	Teacher	EM			S	1963
Pudell Lisa A Stange	(630)235-0307 lisap@mac.com	760 Duxbury Ln Bartlett IL 60103	NI	Teacher	EM			CQ	2001
Pudiwitr Kelly M Ballard	(661)477-2580 kpudiwitr@gmail.com	2718 Tami Ct Bakersfield CA 93314	CNH	Teacher	Tchr	St John Bakersfield CA	(661)665-7815	CQ	2020
Pudwell Kristin L Schumann	(901)603-0683	6515 Elmore Rd Memphis TN 38134	MDS	Teacher	EM			RF	1975
Puechner Amy L Nestle	(414)430-2542 amypuechner@yahoo.com	3120 N 82nd St Milwaukee WI 53222	SW	Teacher	EM			CQ	1999

*Multiple Assignments (See Church Worker Locator for Additional Details)

See Page 53 for the Table of Abbreviations for key to District, Classification, Position, and College abbreviations.

**C =Candidate; EM =Emeritus; the date following the C is the month and year the Candidate status began

NAME	TELEPHONE NUMBER EMAIL	STREET ADDRESS CITY/STATE/ZIP	DISTRICT	CLASS.	POSITION/ STATUS**	WHERE SERVING	OFFICE PHONE	COLLEGE/ UNIV/CQ	YR GRAD
Puelz Josie L	(402)601-1148 josiepuelz@gmail.com	2501 W Denton Rd Lincoln NE 68523	NEB	Teacher	Tchr	Lincoln Lincoln NE	(402)467-5404	S	2024
Pugh Tia M Williams	(515)710-1558 tia.pugh@gmail.com	621 51st St West Des Moines IA 50265	IW	DCE	Mem C	Shep Of The Valley West Des Moines IA	(515)225-1623	SP	2007
Pulfer Denise L Manning	(608)234-4744 mand_95687@yahoo.com	108 Honeysuckle Ln Pflugerville TX 78660	TX	DCE	EM			IV	1992
Pullen Susan D Bartram	pullenp@grc.nia.nih.gov	8800 Walther Blvd Apt 4506 Parkville MD 21234	SE	Teacher	EM			RF	1972
Pulliam Laura M Fusilier	(512)350-8130 laurampulliam@gmail.com	1918 Creston Dr. Spring TX 77386	TX	DCE	Mem C	Lazarus Spring TX	(210)643-4319	AU	2010
Pullmann Cameron A	(479)866-7994 cameron.pullmann@gmail.com	9635 Windborne Ave Las Vegas NV 89147	PSW	DCE	Tchr	Faith Las Vegas NV	(702)804-4400	IV	2012
Pullmann Paul M	paul.pullmann@gmail.com	3464 Gosling St Las Vegas NV 89117	PSW	Teacher	Tchr	Faith Las Vegas NV	(702)804-4400	RF	1985
Puls Aaron D	(760)401-5338		PSW	Teacher	Tchr	Crean Irvine CA	(949)387-1199	IV	2016
Puls Daniel W Dr	(562)556-9575 dpulspsyd@gmail.com	13454 Bailey St Whittier CA 90601	PSW	DFLM	C07/2016			IV	1984
Puls Douglas W	(215)595-6419 dpuls1026@gmail.com	26 Favored Ln Levittown PA 19055	EA	Teacher	EM			BR	1987
Puls Maryann Oester	(215)817-3950 mpuls528@gmail.com	26 Favored Ln Levittown PA 19055	EA	Teacher	Prin	Hope Levittown PA	(215)946-3467	AA	1989
Pummill Marriah S	(309)694-7247 pummill98@gmail.com	109 Kickapoo Dr. East Peoria IL 61611	CI	Teacher	Tchr	Lutheran Central School Assoc Peoria IL	(309)691-8921	CH	2024
Puryear Roberta A Mau Worley	(509)994-2055	P.O. Box 508 Liberty Lake WA 99019	NOW	Tch/DCE	C07/2016			PO	1986
Putnam Cynthia A Bratvogel	(262)894-0385 readandsew@live.com	W156N7727 Cherry Ct Menomonee Fls WI 53051	SW	Teacher	EM			MQ	1995
Putnam Danelle L Deac	+1 (809)902-9055 danelleputnam@gmail.com	Apartado 1356 Santiago 51000 DOMINICAN REPUBLIC	MO	Deaconess	S Miss	Office of International Mission Saint Louis MO		FW-DEAC	2014
Putnam Stephanee	(713)870-1903 stephaneejo@yahoo.com	37940 42nd St E Apt 100 Palmdale CA 93552	PSW	Teacher	EM			SP	1971
Pygman Patricia L Carroll	(708)354-6728 leepygman1@yahoo.com	111 E Cossitt Ave Apt 201 La Grange IL 60525	NI	Teacher	EM			RF	1975
Pyle Jennifer A Gallegos	jenniferpyle44@gmail.com	9430 W County Road 100 N Seymour IN 47274	IN	Teacher	Tchr	Immanuel Seymour IN	(812)522-3118	CH	2014
Quackenbush Randa S Haynes	(419)877-2848 randiquackenbush@gmail.com	6107 N Texas St Whitehouse OH 43571	OH	Teacher	EM			CQ	2008
Quade Gene W	(586)677-5954	11236 Concord Ln Washington MI 48094	MI	Teacher	EM			S	1961
Quade Karen J	(989)734-4520 missq48105@yahoo.com	2632 W Heythaler Hwy Rogers City MI 49779	MI	Teacher	EM			S	1972
Quandt Beth A	(618)288-7858	177 Somerset Dr Glen Carbon IL 62034	SI	Teacher	Tchr	Trinity Edwardsville IL	(618)656-2918	CQ	2015
Quick Donna A Mathey Longhauser	(319)360-3350 quick.donna@gmail.com	8320 SW 212th St Trimble MO 64492	MO	Teacher	EM			RF	1974
Quickel Dale E	(713)540-3110 dalequickel@yahoo.com	10251 N Laurel Branch Dr Houston TX 77064	TX	Teacher	EM			CQ	1999
Quickel Lisa L Hintz	(713)540-3111 lquickel@stmarkhouston.org	10251 N Laurel Branch Dr Houston TX 77064	TX	Teacher	Tchr	St Mark Houston TX	(713)468-2623	AU	1988
Quigg Juliann M Gauwitz	(217)670-4160	39202 E. Truman Rd. Oak Grove MO 64075	CI	Teacher	EM			S	1981
Quinlan Jennifer S			RM	DCE	Tchr	Lutheran Parker CO	(303)841-5551	IV	2002
Quiroz Blanca	(512)810-9172 blanca.quiroz@cui.edu	374 E Feather River Dr Fresno CA 93730	PSW	Teacher	S HS/C	Concordia University Irvine Irvine CA	(949)854-8002	CQ	2022
Raabe David L	(847)677-8976 daveraabe@aol.com	7915 Kostner Ave Skokie IL 60076	NI	Teacher	EM			RF	1978
Raabe Madison J Maria	madisonjraabe@gmail.com	4204 Stone Ridge Cir Berea OH 44017	OH	Teacher	C03/2023			MQ	2018
Raabe Natalie L Pieper	(763)568-3445 nataliepieper12@gmail.com	7535 Mark St Loretto MN 55357	MNS	Teacher	C10/2023			SP	2015
Raabe Paula J Ziehlsdorf	(847)677-8976 raabe618@aol.com	7915 Kostner Ave Skokie IL 60076	NI	Teacher	EM			RF	1979
Raabe Tyler D	(216)527-2244 raabet9@gmail.com	4204 Stone Ridge Cir Berea OH 44017	OH	Teacher	C04/2023			S	2018
Rabb Jacqueline M Britton	(763)202-3734 jacqueline.britton@cuw.edu	5202 Green Valley Trl San Angelo TX 76904	TX	Teacher	Tchr	Trinity San Angelo TX	(325)947-1275	MQ	2012
Rabb Tracy Welch		5214 Lawndale Dr San Angelo TX 76903	TX	Teacher	Tchr	Trinity San Angelo TX	(325)947-1275	CQ	2013
Rabel Donna L	(713)822-8108 drabel@salem4u.com	11743 Northpointe Blvd Apt 1022 Tomball TX 77377	TX	Teacher	Tchr	Salem Tomball TX	(281)351-8223	AU	1999
Raben-Rogers Sandra M Brodhagen	(715)551-1075 sandy.raben@splco.org	502 Greenmeadow Dr Waukesha WI 53188	SW	Teacher	Tchr	St Paul Oconomowoc WI	(262)567-5001	SP	1986
Rach Joanne M Ford	(630)728-2093 joken1@aol.com	2412 Joyce Ln Naperville IL 60564	NI	Teacher	C07/2016			RF	1984
Rachow Joel W	(810)335-0346 jrachow.osl@gmail.com	4260 Castle Rd North Branch MI 48461	MI	Teacher	Prin	St Michaels Richville MI	(989)868-4809	CQ	2017
Rachuy Terry L Miller	(520)891-3661 tlrach@aol.com	233 S London Station Rd Tucson AZ 85748	PSW	Teacher	EM			SP	1984
Radcliffe Elizabeth U	(313)720-9607 lradcliffe@hcl.org	2509 N 67th St Wauwatosa WI 53213	EN	Teacher	Tchr	Hales Corners Hales Corners WI	(414)529-6700	CQ	2020
Raddatz Lauren M Zimmer	(314)489-9155 laurenmraddatz@gmail.com	1s309 Windsor Ln Villa Park IL 60181	NI	Teacher	C08/2017			Other	2014

*Multiple Assignments (See Church Worker Locator for Additional Details)

See Page 53 for the Table of Abbreviations for key to District, Classification, Position, and College abbreviations.

**C =Candidate; EM =Emeritus; the date following the C is the month and year the Candidate status began

NAME	TELEPHONE NUMBER EMAIL	STREET ADDRESS CITY/STATE/ZIP	DISTRICT	CLASS.	POSITION/ STATUS**	WHERE SERVING	OFFICE PHONE	COLLEGE/ UNIV/CQ	YR GRAD
Radde Kathy M Klein	(952)334-7612 kmradde@gmail.com	1633 Liberty Ln Waconia MN 55387	MNS	Teacher	Tchr	Trinity Waconia MN	(952)442-4165	SP	1990
Raddemann Melissa S	(262)483-6034 melraddemann@gmail.com	810 Jurie St Cape Girardeau MO 63701	SW	Teacher	C07/2025			MQ	2004
Rademacher Jo Ann A Zimmerman	(734)558-0620 cjrad@comcast.net	18240 Raleigh Square Dr Southgate MI 48195	MI	Teacher	EM			S	1974
Rader Marianne L Nicholson Dr	(512)799-5679 ponygirlatcua@aol.com	350 Greenridge Rd Georgetown TX 78628	TX	Teacher	Prin	Concordia Pflugerville TX	(512)248-2547	CQ	2011
Radewahn Krista L Dobratz	(414)630-5834 klradewahn@gmail.com	N49 W17680 Christopher Ct Menomonee Falls WI 53051	SW	Teacher	C03/2025			CQ	2020
Radintz Jamie M Schutte	(651)261-0258 jschutte12@gmail.com	6890 Rolling Hills Road Hamel MN 55340	MNS	Teacher	C07/2016			SP	2001
Radloff Nancy L Krause	(414)630-3822 mrs.radloff@yahoo.com	P.O. Box 294 Lake Tomahawk WI 54539	NW	Teacher	EM			MW	1980
Radue Linda J Long	(262)370-8145	908 3rd Ave Grafton WI 53024	SW	Teacher	EM			RF	1977
Raebel Micah E	(219)613-6343 mraebel@stjohnsorange.org		PSW	DPM	Mem C	Saint Johns Orange CA	(714)288-4400	CQ	2018
Raedeke Henry W	(636) 219-2378 h.raedeke@sbcglobal.net	711 S Laclede Station Rd Apt 3115 Saint Louis MO 63119	MO	Teacher	EM			S	1968
Rael Jody L Brunkhardt	(702)956-0323 jody.rael@icloud.com	8585 W Craig Rd Las Vegas NV 89129	PSW	Teacher	Tchr	Faith Las Vegas NV	(702)804-4400	S	1999
Rafferty Brian C	(509)965-4958 pbrafferty@gmail.com	7103 Modesto Way Yakima WA 98908	NOW	Teacher	EM			S	1986
Ragaisis Dee Ann V Schmideler Dr	(832) 871-8036 deeannragaisis@gmail.com	1507 Pine Crest Drive Pearland TX 77581	TX	Teacher	EM			RF	1989
Ragland John H Jr	(815)713-9399 raggs75@yahoo.com	201 Main Street P.O. Box 2 Potter WI 54160	SW	Teacher		South Wisconsin District Milwaukee WI	(414)464-8100	S	1992
Rahberg David E	(972)768-2725 daverahberg@hotmail.com	811 Hancock Ct Fate TX 75189	TX	Tch/DCE	EM			S	1978
Rahn Gail K Grob	(714)832-9477 momrahn40@gmail.com	1 Witherspoon #232 Irvine CA 92604	PSW	Teacher	EM			RF	1962
Rahn Kreighton	(231)299-4424 krahn23@hotmail.com	8215 SW 62nd Ave Ocala FL 34476	FG	Teacher	C12/2022			AA	2018
Rainey Anthony G	(773)746-9460 arainey8059@yahoo.com	8059 S Talman Ave Chicago IL 60652	NI	Teacher	EM			RF	1986
Rains Heidi J Stafford	(515)314-2640 jhrains@gmail.com	3820 79th St Urbandale IA 50322	IW	Teacher	Tchr	Mount Olive Des Moines IA	(515)277-8349	CQ	2014
Rakow Christine M Davis	(630)706-1849 c.m.rakow@att.net	552 Claremont Ave West Chicago IL 60185	NI	Teacher	EM			RF	1966
Rambo Margaret E Glasgow	(636)394-3523	819 Auber Ln Ballwin MO 63011	MO	Teacher	EM			S	1966
Ramirez Caitlin Worden Deac	(269)830-2915 caitlin.worden@lcmsintl.org	2272 Ramblin Dr Battle Creek MI 49014	MO	Deaconess	S Miss	Office of International Mission Saint Louis MO		FW-DEAC	2015
Ramirez Kristen Kocsis	(334)791-0995 Kristenakocsis@gmail.com	1275 Fairview Ave Brentwood CA 94513	CNH	DCE	Mem C	Resurrection Brentwood CA	(925)634-5180	AU	2017
Ramirez Raquel E Eusebid Deac	(813)453-7662	c/o Messiah Lutheran Church 14920 Hutchison Rd Tampa FL 33625	FG	Deaconess	Mem C	Messiah Carrollwood FL	(813)961-2182	SL-DEAC	2013
Ramsey April L Bishop Deac	(281)703-9743 aprillynnkaty@yahoo.com	6402 Alicia Way Ln Katy TX 77493	TX	Deaconess	Mem C	Memorial Lutheran Katy TX	(281)391-0171	RF	2006
Ramsey Danielle N White	(618)322-1488 dramsey@lsusfw.org	1430 Irene Ave Fort Wayne IN 46808	IN	Teacher	Tchr	South Unity Fort Wayne IN	(260)744-0459	Other	2018
Ramsey Suzanne K Britton	(260)724-2816	1235 Oak Grove Pl Decatur IN 46733	IN	Teacher	EM			CQ	1995
Ramstad Mollie K Hanlin	(417)686-0391 mramstad@martinlutherjoplin.com	c/o Martin Luther School 2616 Connecticut Ave Joplin MO 64804	MO	Teacher	Prin	Martin Luther Joplin MO	(417)624-1403	S	2010
Ramthun Michael L	(715)297-5499 mikeramth@gmail.com	156463 E Wausau Ave Wausau WI 54403	NW	DCM	C05/2019			MQ	2017
Randall Claudia G Werfelmann	(626)422-8079 kcrand@aol.com	15713 N Little Spokane Dr Spokane WA 99208	PSW	Teacher	EM			SP	1968
Randall Kimberly A Sonnenberg	(949)459-2014 kimlovescats@hotmail.com	12 El Prisma Rcho Sta Marg CA 92688	PSW	Teacher	Tchr	Abiding Savior Lake Forest CA	(949)830-1461	IV	1990
Randall Lisa K Erke	(860)818-6546 lrandall133@gmail.com	7386 Blazing Star Ct Ooltewah TN 37363	MDS	Teacher	Tchr	First Chattanooga TN	(423)629-5990	CQ	2003
Randall Sally A Barry	(248)673-9512 salrandall@sbcglobal.net	3277 Alco Dr Waterford MI 48329	MI	Teacher	EM			RF	1969
Randt Miriam C Wroge	(320)867-6315 miriamrandt@gmail.com	1409 Elm St Glencoe MN 55336	MNS	Teacher	EM			S	1974
Rankin Peggy A Ness	mselliot12@gmail.com	1618 Elk Spring Dr Brandon FL 33511	FG	Teacher	Tchr	Immanuel Brandon FL	(813)685-1978	RF	1978
Rapp Kerri A Motley	kerri.rapp@lutheransouth.org	12555 Ryewater Dr Houston TX 77089	TX	Teacher	Tchr	Lutheran Education Association Friendswood TX	(281)617-5189	S	2003
Rapson Andrea K Beck	(989)712-0041 rapsonak@gmail.com	237 S Huron Ave Harbor Beach MI 48441	MI	Teacher	EM			SP	1982
Raschke Leonard R	(863)646-8451 lraschkebeach@gmail.com	315 Faye Cir N Lakeland FL 33813	FG	Teacher	EM			S	1970
Rashid Janet M Schott	(586)254-9485 jmrjanns@aol.com	4100 Montgomery Dr Shelby Twp MI 48316	MI	Teacher	EM			CQ	1986
Rasmussen Kimberly A Raymond	(505)610-6343 princessk321@hotmail.com	12016 Prospect Ave NE Albuquerque NM 87112	RM	Teacher	Tchr	Christ Albuquerque NM	(505)884-3876	IV	1988
Rasmussen Pamela C Nittsche	rasmussenp@sbcglobal.net	9623 Oak Thicket Dr Houston TX 77040	TX	Teacher	Tchr	Concordia Tomball TX	(281)351-2547	CQ	2010

*Multiple Assignments (See Church Worker Locator for Additional Details)
See Page 53 for the Table of Abbreviations for key to District, Classification, Position, and College abbreviations.
**C =Candidate; EM =Emeritus; the date following the C is the month and year the Candidate status began

NAME	TELEPHONE NUMBER EMAIL	STREET ADDRESS CITY/STATE/ZIP	DISTRICT	CLASS.	POSITION/ STATUS**	WHERE SERVING	OFFICE PHONE	COLLEGE/ UNIV/CQ	YR GRAD
Rasmussen Sarah E Wesemann	(314)939-6852 swesel1@aol.com	1382 Reading St Valparaiso IN 46385	IN	Teacher	C10/2018			Other	2010
Rasmussen Suzanne C Hoffert	(406)755-2493 no1teacher@hotmail.com	259 Commons Way Kalispell MT 59901	MT	Teacher	EM			S	1975
Rassbach Sharon J Gall	(314)843-3714	13457 Tesson Ferry Rd Apt 302 Saint Louis MO 63128	MO	Teacher	EM			SP	1965
Rast Amy C Engelbrecht Deac	(260)760-3707 rast.amyc@gmail.com	8120 Moss Grove Pl Fort Wayne IN 46825	IN	Deaconess	EM			FW-DEAC	2013
Rathe Andrew A	(402)335-7038 andrew.rathe@cune.org	4308 Stratford Pl Grand Island NE 68803	NEB	Teacher	Prin	Trinity Grand Island NE	(308)382-5274	S	2010
Rathe Katheryn M Leonhardt	(605)228-1589 katheryn.leonhardt@cune.org	4308 Stratford Pl Grand Island NE 68803	NEB	Teacher	C09/2016			S	2010
Rathje Lynda L Scarr	(810)650-2946 l_rathje@hotmail.com	2643 10th St Port Huron MI 48060	MI	Teacher	EM			S	1974
Rathje Michael L	(281)996-9631	16732 County Road 127 Pearland TX 77581	TX	Teacher	EM			S	1976
Rathke Aubrey E	(402)860-8808 aubrey.rathke@cune.org	2608 Addison Ln Johns Creek GA 30005	EN	DCE	Mem C	Christ Shepherd Alpharetta GA	(770)475-0640	S	2025
Rathman Devin D	(308)390-3728 devindrathman@gmail.com	5 Luddy Ct Apt A Parkville MD 21234	SE	Teacher	Tchr	Concordia Towson MD	(410)825-2323	S	2024
Rathman Loraine M Dr	(985)246-6108 drloraine@aol.com	350 Emerald Forest Blvd Unit 14204 Covington LA 70433	SO	Deaconess	EM			CQ	2003
Rathmann Dawn A Jensen	(314)603-1837 rodneyrathmann@gmail.com	15985 Clarkes Gap Rd Waterford VA 20197	SE	Teacher	EM			CQ	1992
Rathmann Rodney L Dr	(314)808-3838 rodneyrathmann@gmail.com	15985 Clarkes Gap Rd Waterford VA 20197	SE	Teacher	EM			SP	1974
Ratkovec Lori L Bakke	(262)758-9228 lori.bakke202@gmail.com	5408 Clearview Lane Waterford WI 53185	SW	Teacher	Tchr	Concordia Sturtevant WI	(262)884-0991	MQ	2019
Ratliff Emily A Laubenstein	(224)213-9202 eratliff@ilcp.org	185 W Brandon Ct Unit E Palatine IL 60067	NI	Teacher	Tchr	Immanuel Palatine IL	(847)359-1936	MQ	2006
Rattei Faith J Craig	(239)961-7278 coachfaithdco@gmail.com	118 Cott's Drive North Sioux City SD 57049	SD	DCO	C07/2020			SP	2004
Rau Christian W	(727)522-0839 cwrau@verizon.net	2638 Sumo Dr Clearwater FL 33764	FG	Teacher	EM			RF	1965
Rau Dalton J	(918)876-2104 Dalton.Rau@oursaviorbett.org	1405 19th St Bettendorf IA 52722	IE	DCE	Mem C	Our Savior Bettendorf IA	(563)332-5141	S	2024
Rau Donald R	don.r.rau@gmail.com	5 Kaffee Ct Palm Coast FL 32164	EN	DCM	EM			MQ	1994
Rauch Micah A	(309)256-2204 mrauch@clscubs.org	3001 Canterbury Blvd Fort Wayne IN 46835	IN	Teacher	Tchr	Concordia Fort Wayne IN	(260)422-2429	MQ	2017
Rauch Scott M	(309)251-2623 scottmrauch@gmail.com	116 Sara St East Peoria IL 61611	CI	Tch/DCE	Mem C	Trinity Peoria IL	(309)676-4609	S	1986
Rausch Henry G	(480)376-5940 hanksuerausch@gmail.com	847 308th Seward NE 68434	PSW	Teacher	EM			RF	1970
Rausch Joyce C Steeneck	(516)822-7456 joycerausch@optonline.net	14 Westmoreland Rd Hicksville NY 11801	AT	Teacher	EM			RF	1963
Rausch Richard M	(614)561-8685 rausch_r@yahoo.com	940 Walker Woods Ln Marysville OH 43040	OH	Teacher	Prin	St Johns Marysville OH	(937)644-5540	CQ	2023
Rausch Susan K Vedder	(480)492-2880 hanksuerausch@gmail.com	847 308th Seward NE 68434	PSW	Teacher	EM			RF	1970
Rauschert Cynthia K Appold	(989)684-5512 ckrauschert@gmail.com	1800 N Huron Rd Tawas City MI 48763	MI	Teacher	EM			CQ	2002
Rauworth Heidi L Hedrich Pawelk	(952)500-2744 heidi.pawelk@trinitywaconia.org	12920 50th Street Watertown MN 55388	MNS	Teacher	Tchr	Trinity Waconia MN	(952)442-4165	CH	1992
Ravanelli Renee	(660)463-2513 rav@centurytel.net	507 SW 7th Ter Concordia MO 64020	MO	Teacher	EM			S	1974
Rawlings James E	(715)218-7823 rawlingsj363@gmail.com	1523 Beechwood Dr Wausau WI 54401	NW	Teacher	EM			RF	1972
Rawlins Cheryl L Van Emon	(510)797-8186 scoop1995@hotmail.com	467 Flora Pl Fremont CA 94536	CNH	Teacher	Tchr	Prince Of Peace Fremont CA	(510)797-8186	RF	1968
Rawson Kathleen N Glade	(989)652-2745 drawson123@aol.com	1296 S Beyer Rd Saginaw MI 48601	MI	Teacher	EM			RF	1966
Raymond Gemma M Saenz	(702)921-2777 gemmamraymond@faithlasvegas.org	10513 Sunblower Ave Las Vegas NV 89135	PSW	Teacher	Tchr	Faith Community Las Vegas NV	(702)921-2777	CQ	2007
Reavis Lisa A Johnson	(301)805-4758 larteach@hotmail.com	8306 Satinleaf Ct Bowie MD 20715	SE	Teacher	C07/2016			BR	1989
Rebber Blaire M	(260)750-6805 blairerebber@yahoo.com	25620 Woodburn Rd Woodburn IN 46797	IN	Teacher	Tchr	St Pauls Fort Wayne IN	(260)424-0049	S	2024
Rebeck Douglas C	(708)460-1918 douglasrebeck@comcast.net	15722 Old Orchard Ct Unit 2w Orland Park IL 60462	NI	Teacher	EM			RF	1976
Rebentisch Barbara E Hibbing	(651)359-5107 barb.rebentisch@lcms.org	10181 Fox Run Rd Woodbury MN 55129	MNS	DCE	C04/2025			S	1984
Reber Carrie R Schriefer	(817)602-8541 creber2@gmail.com	7017 Bentley Ave Fort Worth TX 76137	TX	Tch/DCE	EM			SP	1984
Reck Jennifer D Glahn	(231) 720-5946 jennyglahnreck@aol.com	1901 Crestwood Ln Norton Shores MI 49441	MI	Teacher	Tchr	Trinity Muskegon MI	(231)755-1292	AA	1984
Reck Linda K Gray	lreck@stpeterlcms.org	N76W14382 Northpoint Dr Menomonee Falls WI 53051	NI	Teacher	EM			RF	1981
Reck Teri L Derango	(303)594-5383 treck@zionbrighton.org	521 S 16th Ave Brighton CO 80601	RM	Teacher	Tchr	Zion Brighton CO	(303)659-2339	CQ	2011
Reck-Meyer Carrie Reck	(314)651-2975 creckmeyer@gmail.com	10115 Glenfield Ter Saint Louis MO 63126	MO	Teacher	EM			CQ	1998
Recksiedler Ronald E	(619)729-7552 rrex2007@yahoo.com	1217 Peerless Dr El Cajon CA 92021	PSW	Teacher	EM			RF	1977

*Multiple Assignments (See Church Worker Locator for Additional Details)

See Page 53 for the Table of Abbreviations for key to District, Classification, Position, and College abbreviations.

**C =Candidate; EM =Emeritus; the date following the C is the month and year the Candidate status began

NAME	TELEPHONE NUMBER EMAIL	STREET ADDRESS CITY/STATE/ZIP	DISTRICT	CLASS.	POSITION/ STATUS**	WHERE SERVING	OFFICE PHONE	COLLEGE/ UNIV/CQ	YR GRAD
Reddeman Rachel	(734)674-4594 rer1118@gmail.com	43144 Applewood Rd Canton MI 48188	MI	Teacher	Tchr	Guardian Dearborn MI	(313)274-3665	AA	2022
Reddemann Richard W	(260)348-5708 reddemann@comcast.net	113 W Wayne St Apt 315 Fort Wayne IN 46802	IN	Teacher	EM			S	1965
Redmond Samantha L	(310) 850-6278 samantha.redmond@eagles.cui.edu	14037 Lemoli Ave Hawthorne CA 90250	PSW	Teacher	Tchr	Christ Rancho Palos Verdes CA	(310)831-0848	IV	2022
Reed Amanda K Graham	(260)312-3982 agraham@cluth.org	13235 Passerine Blvd Fort Wayne IN 46845	IN	Teacher	Tchr	Central New Haven IN	(260)493-2502	CQ	2015
Reed Amber R	amber@mlckaty.com	25063 Lake Park Ct Magnolia TX 77355	TX	DCE	Mem C	Memorial Lutheran Katy TX	(281)391-0171	AU	2019
Reed April A Fett	(952)240-6956 aprilreed2012@gmail.com	2114 Atlantic St Maplewood MN 55109	MNS	Teacher	C07/2016			S	1999
Reed Laurie D Robinson	(573)300-9467 laurie1777@gmail.com	713 Laramie St Atchison KS 66002	KS	Teacher	Tchr	Trinity Atchison KS	(913)367-2837	IV	1986
Reed Margaret A Adams	(210)735-4094	411 Green Meadow Blvd San Antonio TX 78213	TX	Teacher	Tchr	Concordia San Antonio TX	(210)479-1477	CQ	1997
Reed Pamela S Ahles	(949)713-2811 pavolleyball@hotmail.com	153 Via Vicini Rcho Sta Marg CA 92688	PSW	Teacher	C07/2016			RF	1990
Reed Rebecca D Limback	rlimback@hotmail.com	1451 Wood Haven Dr Saint Charles MO 63304	MO	Teacher	Tchr	Zion Saint Charles MO	(636)441-7425	S	2001
Reed Robert W	B.REED1945@YAHOO.COM	5225 Lowell Rd Tampa FL 33624	FG	Tch/DCE	EM			RF	1967
Reed Taylor K	(970)397-0509 tkreed46@yahoo.com	19290 22 Mile Rd Macomb MI 48044	MI	Teacher	Tchr	St John Fraser MI	(586)294-8740	MQ	2016
Reed William A		1281 SE 35th Avenue Hillsboro OR 97123	NOW	Teacher	C08/2021			PO	1996
Reemsnyder Sally J		35760 Timberlane Dr Solon OH 44139	OH	DCE	Mem C	Our Redeemer Solon OH	(440)248-4066	CQ	2007
Reeves Carol A	creevescuddles41@gmail.com	3270 Upton Ln Decatur IL 62521	CI	Teacher	EM			RF	1964
Reeves Cynthia L Meier	(216)469-8782 cwreeves3209@sbcglobal.net	6202 Nelwood Rd Cleveland OH 44130	OH	Teacher	Tchr	Luther Memorial Cleveland OH	(216)749-5300	CQ	2007
Reeves Sonja L Wall Deac	(406)542-8838 deaconesssonja@gmail.com	5751 Fox Trl Florence MT 59833	MT	Deaconess	Mem C	First Missoula MT	(406)549-3311	FW-DEAC	2015
Refenes James L Dr	(734)664-6394 jimrefenes@gmail.com	12240 Bethel Church Rd Manchester MI 48158	MI	Teacher	EM			RF	1982
Regan James	(516)992-5183 jregan@martinluthernyc.org	392 Hempstead Ave Rockville Ctr NY 11570	AT	Teacher	Tchr	Martin Luther Maspeth NY	(718)894-4000	CQ	2019
Reginelli Marcy J Muellner	(808)398-4651 mjreginelli@hotmail.com	99-788 Aumakiki Pl Aiea HI 96701	CNH	Teacher	EM			RF	1966
Rehbein Ann M Hintz Deac	decdocreh@aol.com	9844 Tender Blossom Way Stockton CA 95209	CNH	Deaconess	EM			Other	1981
Rehbein Erika N MacGregor	(406)471-9984 erika.rehbein@gmail.com	415 W Washington St Kalispell MT 59901	MT	Teacher	Tchr	Trinity Kalispell MT	(406)257-5683	S	2012
Rehbein Natalie L Kesar	(402)514-7389 natrehbein@gmail.com	15234 Bedford Ave Omaha NE 68116	NEB	Teacher	C05/2018			S	2015
Rehbein Timothy J	(402)238-4759 timothy.rehbein@gmail.com	415 W Washington St Kalispell MT 59901	MT	DPM	C08/2023			S	2013
Rehberg Gregory A	(260)414-4390 grehbert@clhscadets.com	10616 Unita Dr Fort Wayne IN 46804	IN	Teacher	Pro Stf	Concordia Fort Wayne IN	(260)483-1102	CQ	1987
Rehberger Louis A III	(760)521-7302 mrrseventh@gmail.com	2108 Golfcrest Ct Oceanside CA 92056	PSW	Teacher	EM			CQ	2011
Reher Danielle E Sedlmayr Deac	(317)643-0317 danielle.reher@gmail.com	1200 Peterson Rd Rapid City SD 57701	IN	Deaconess	C07/2016			FW-DEAC	2010
Rehkop Andrew T	(352)304-7448 drrehkop@gmail.com	67 Yarmouth Ln North East MD 21901	FG	Teacher	C07/2016			S	2006
Rehkop Annalisa M Mueller	(352)304-9456 darehk06@hotmail.com	67 Yarmouth Ln North East MD 21901	FG	Teacher	C07/2016			S	2006
Rehkop Thomas V	(314)306-4716 tomrehkop@yahoo.com	15822 Harris Ridge Ct Chesterfield MO 63017	MO	Teacher	EM			S	1977
Rehmer Edgar P	(715)383-8215 erehmer33@hotmail.com	10652 Wills Run Marshfield WI 54449	NW	Teacher	EM			RF	1967
Rehmer Loren W	(952)447-9954 lorehm@aol.com	17026 Pheasant Meadow Ln SW Prior Lake MN 55372	MNS	Teacher	EM			RF	1958
Rehmer Robert C	(763)424-4674 family72189@aol.com	11865 100th Pl N Maple Grove MN 55369	MNS	Teacher	EM			RF	1969
Rehwaldt Elizabeth E Sommer Hofman	(260)438-4381 elizabeth.rehwaldt@gmail.com	4326 Bridgetown Ct Fort Wayne IN 46804	IN	Teacher	Tchr	Central New Haven IN	(260)493-2502	S	2002
Reichert Caitlin E Cameron	(217)891-2074 creichert@trinity-lutheran.com	1711 S 4th St Springfield IL 62703	CI	Teacher	Tchr	Trinity Springfield IL	(217)787-2323	CQ	2016
Reick Myron H	(586)260-8753 mrsrmi@aol.com	447 Black Hawk Dr Marysville OH 43040	OH	Teacher	EM			S	1973
Reick Sandra L Krey	(586)260-0151 sandne06@gmail.com	447 Black Hawk Dr Marysville OH 43040	OH	Teacher	EM			S	1973
Reid Eileen M Pajkowski	(631)664-4674 eileenmried415@aol.com	10082 Paisley Dr Charlotte NC 28269	AT	Teacher	C07/2016			BR	1990
Reigles James D	(262)255-1833 1203klmv@att.net	1919 Hidden Hollow Ln Manitowoc WI 54220	SW	Teacher	EM			RF	1966
Reigles Karen L Baumgart	(414)255-1833 1203klmv@att.net	1919 Hidden Hollow Ln Manitowoc WI 54220	SW	Teacher	EM			RF	1966
Reihmann Anna K Anna Kreis	(239)898-9353 anna.reihmann@faithlasvegas.org	9642 Ponderosa Skye Ct. Las Vegas NV 89166	PSW	Teacher	Tchr	Faith Community Las Vegas NV	(702)921-2777	S	2011
Reikowski Ellen J Downard	(813)767-9407 ellenajo@msn.com	704 Hidden Lake Drive Brandon FL 33511	FG	Teacher	Tchr	Immanuel Brandon FL	(813)689-1787	AU	2015

*Multiple Assignments (See Church Worker Locator for Additional Details)
See Page 53 for the Table of Abbreviations for key to District, Classification, Position, and College abbreviations.
**C =Candidate; EM =Emeritus; the date following the C is the month and year the Candidate status began

NAME	TELEPHONE NUMBER EMAIL	STREET ADDRESS CITY/STATE/ZIP	DISTRICT	CLASS.	POSITION/ STATUS**	WHERE SERVING	OFFICE PHONE	COLLEGE/ UNIV/CQ	YR GRAD
Reiland Jana M Prill	(949)632-4791 jmreiland14@gmail.com	488 Towergrove Dr Corona CA 92879	PSW	Teacher	Tchr	Orange County Orange CA	(714)998-5151	S	1999
Reilly Kelly A Mc Colgan	(302)242-7459 kellyannreilly413@gmail.com	2419 Knight Island Dr Brandon FL 33511	FG	Teacher	Prin	Holy Trinity Tampa FL	(813)839-6847	S	2019
Reimann Mary J Luedtke	(614)208-1709 reimama3@gmail.com	1260 Purdue Ave. St. Louis MO 63130	MO	Teacher	EM			RF	1979
Reimer Andria J Ostovich	(414)380-9156 areimer@hcl.org	75296 W Grant St West Alles WI 53219	EN	Teacher	Tchr	Hales Corners Hales Corners WI	(414)529-6701	MQ	2023
Reimer Matthew T	(920)254-5339 mreimer@stmlc.org	79 Industrial Ave #7 Clintonville WI 54929	NW	Teacher	Tchr	St Martin Clintonville WI	(715)823-6538	MQ	1994
Reimers Nancy J Stegemann	(847)426-2431 njreimers@yahoo.com	18n640 Field Ct Dundee IL 60118	NI	Teacher	EM			RF	1973
Reimers Rhonda K	(574)896-3275 reimers@stpeternorthjudson.org	108 Hancock Ave North Judson IN 46366	IN	Teacher	P/Tchr	St Peter North Judson IN	(574)896-2025	S	1980
Reinbold Tricia K Mallory	(231)392-4619 trishreinbold888@gmail.com	210 Haral St Sturgis MI 49091	MI	Teacher	Prin	Trinity Sturgis MI	(269)651-4245	AA	1995
Reincke John M	(586)855-8410 john.reincke@gmail.com	362 Cambridge Dr Mount Clemens MI 48043	MI	Teacher	Prin	Lutheran North Macomb MI	(586)781-9151	RF	1990
Reinders Barbara L Benz	(920)954-0615 barbara.reinders@ celebrationlutheran.net	2821 S Carpenter St Appleton WI 54915	NW	Teacher	Tchr	Celebration Appleton WI	(920)734-8218	RF	1992
Reineck Marilyn E Fuss Dr	(612)271-7733 reineck@csp.edu	6022 131st St N Hugo MN 55038	MNS	Teacher	EM			S	1973
Reineke Anna C	(715)216-4162 annar@mypeacechurch.com	502 N Second St Alma WI 54610	NW	DCE	Mem C	Peace Eau Claire WI	(715)834-2486	SP	2021
Reineke David C	(715) 216-1964 davidreineke22@gmail.com	502 N 2nd St Alma WI 54610	NW	DCE	C07/2022			SP	1988
Reineke Jane A Accola	(715)216-7935 janeannette19@gmail.com	502 N Second St Alma WI 54610	NW	Tch/DCE	Mem C	Zion Mondovi WI	(715)926-3664	SP	1990
Reineke Zachary	reinekezach@gmail.com		CNH	Teacher	Tchr	Sierra Carson City NV	(775)267-1921	MQ	2022
Reinert Daniel M	(989)327-5518	12646 King Rd Frankenmuth MI 48734	MI	Teacher	Tchr	St Lorenz Frankenmuth MI	(989)652-6141	AA	1995
Reinertson Jerome A	(702)243-3103 princjar@aol.com	1640 Monrovia Ave Unit 343 Costa Mesa CA 92627	PSW	Teacher	EM			S	1968
Reinhardt Karen S Krohe	(734)625-2007 gkreinhardt@sbcglobal.net	122 Twin Lakes Dr Onsted MI 49265	MI	Teacher	EM			RF	1976
Reinhart Janet L Flechsig	(309)303-7176 jareinhart@clspeoria.org	2211 W Clarke Ave West Peoria IL 61604	CI	Teacher	EM			SP	1973
Reinisch Sheryl J Mueller Dr	(813)773-7814 sreinisch@cu-portland.edu	16130 Cape Coral Dr Wilmauma FL 33598	FG	Teacher	EM			RF	1980
Reinke Betty J Schneider	(208)420-0788 bettyreinke@gmail.com	1139 N College Rd W Twin Falls ID 83301	NOW	Teacher	EM			S	1964
Reinke Edward G	(402)643-4516	7239 S 41st St Lincoln NE 68516	NEB	Teacher	S HS/C	Concordia University Nebraska Seward NE	(402)643-3651	S	1985
Reinke Janette M Ruediger	(785)550-7771 janettereinke@gmail.com	6350 Hagan St Shawnee KS 66216	KS	DCE	C07/2016			S	1995
Reinke Juli A Gudgel	(402)364-2549 jajrejoice@gmail.com	1824 Road 5000 Davenport NE 68335	NEB	Teacher	Tchr	Deshler Deshler NE	(402)365-7858	S	1991
Reinke Kristine R Mueller	(715)758-8628 krreinke@gmail.com	130 N Church St Bonduel WI 54107	NW	Teacher	EM			CQ	1999
Reinke Tristin N	tristin.reinke@gmail.com	409 Clearwater Ct Great Falls MT 59405	MT	DPM	Mem C	Peace Great Falls MT	(406)761-7343	MQ	2013
Reinking Martha B Meineke	(720)308-6924 mreinking@trinityutica.com	13511 Cloverlawn Dr Sterling Heights MI 48312	MI	Teacher	Tchr	Trinity Utica MI	(586)731-4490	S	2012
Reinking Timothy J		2150 Owaissa Way Fort Wayne IN 46809	IN	Teacher	Tchr	Concordia Fort Wayne IN	(260)483-1102	RF	1983
Reinl Joseph M	(920)233-7539	3978 Highland Shore Ln Oshkosh WI 54904	SW	Teacher	P/Tchr	Trinity Oshkosh WI	(920)235-7440	CQ	2002
Reinowski Emilie C	(262)501-6103 eblanck@immanuelbrookfield.org	N70W28315 Huntington St Hartland WI 53029	SW	Teacher	Tchr	Immanuel Brookfield WI	(262)781-7140	MQ	2019
Reisdorf Marlys B Hockenberry	(209)832-5354 mpreisdorf@gmail.com	579 N Castellina Terrace Mountain House CA 95391	CNH	Teacher	C07/2016			IV	2003
Reisenbichler Audrey	(513)262-7314 rreisenb@hotmail.com	107 Amy Ct New Albany IN 47150	IN	Teacher	EM			S	1976
Reisenbichler Robert D	rreisenb@hotmail.com	107 Amy Ct. New Albany IN 47150	IN	Teacher	EM			S	1976
Reiser Sandra K	(734)735-4871 sreiser@emich.edu	4003 Stone Post Rd Newport MI 48166	MI	Teacher	C07/2016			AA	2006
Reisetter Richard C		306 S 1st St Apt D Savannah MO 64485	MO	DCO	EM			SP	1983
Reisler Bennett E	(715)851-7234 bennett.reisler@gmail.com	10000 Calumet St #14 Rothschild WI 54474	NW	Teacher	Tchr	Trinity Merrill WI	(715)536-7501	MQ	2022
Reisler Louise L Banaszynski	(715)758-7798 l.reisler@stpaulbonduel.com	120 S Elm St Bonduel WI 54107	NW	Teacher	Tchr	St Paul Bonduel WI	(715)758-8532	MQ	1994
Reiss Deborah L	(914)961-8821 dreiss@vlc-ny.org	80 E Hartsdale Ave Apt 522 Hartsdale NY 10530	AT	Teacher	Mem C	The Village Bronxville NY	(914)337-0207	BR	1984
Reiss Richard G	(314)631-7869 rreiss@hotmail.com	9872 Arv Ellen Dr Saint Louis MO 63123	MO	Teacher	EM			RF	1968
Reitmeier Angeline R Adensam Deac	(417)833-2194 reitmeier1861@att.net	1861 E Arlington Dr Springfield MO 65803	MO	Deaconess	EM			RF	1994
Reitsma Joy L	(954)319-1010 joyousoccasion@att.net	11a Eisenhower Dr Apt A Jacksonville IL 62650	CI	Teacher	P/Tchr	Salem Jacksonville IL	(217)243-3419	RF	1986
Relaz Kristen L Noble	krelaz@sbcglobal.net	6102 Dunroven Lakes Ct Carpentersvle IL 60110	NI	Teacher	Tchr	St Peter Schaumburg IL	(847)885-3350	RF	1995

*Multiple Assignments (See Church Worker Locator for Additional Details)

See Page 53 for the Table of Abbreviations for key to District, Classification, Position, and College abbreviations.

**C =Candidate; EM =Emeritus; the date following the C is the month and year the Candidate status began

NAME	TELEPHONE NUMBER EMAIL	STREET ADDRESS CITY/STATE/ZIP	DISTRICT	CLASS.	POSITION/ STATUS**	WHERE SERVING	OFFICE PHONE	COLLEGE/ UNIV/CQ	YR GRAD
Remmert Celeste P Green	(916)667-3689 pat.remmert@comcast.net	9637 Country Falls Ln Elk Grove CA 95757	CNH	Tch/DCE	EM			RF	1959
Rempfer Joel D	(618)980-5852 joel.rempfer@melhs.org	418 N Donk Ave Maryville IL 62062	SI	Teacher	Tchr	Metro-East Edwardsville IL	(618)656-0043	S	2005
Rempfer Joshua S	(801)391-6665 principal@elcs-maui.org	2740 Liholani Street #25 Pukalani HI 96768	CNH	Teacher	Prin	Emmanuel Kahului-Maui HI	(808)877-3037	S	2001
Rempfer Rachel S Royuk	(402)641-7674 rachel.royuk@cune.org	P.O. Box 121 Creston NE 68631	MO	Teacher	C06/2020			S	2016
Rendahl Karla K Konrad	(520) 576-7371 kkonrad61@gmail.com	2311 16th Street Vernon TX 76384	TX	DCE	EM			SP	1985
Renken Betty R		675 W Center St Nashville IL 62263	SI	Teacher	EM			CQ	1996
Renken Gayle R			CNH	Teacher	S Miss	Office of International Mission Saint Louis MO		CQ	2020
Renken Jo Ann M Langiewicz	(714)322-3633 jrenken56@gmail.com	174 Loch Lomond Rd. Rancho Mirage CA 92270	PSW	Teacher	EM			CQ	2001
Renken Randolph G	(260)492-8411 renken6@gmail.com	6335 Mapledowns Dr Fort Wayne IN 46835	IN	Teacher	EM			S	1985
Renn Peter C Dr	(708)543-0637 rennpc@gmail.com	11432 3rd Ave S Seattle WA 98168	NOW	Teacher	C08/2016			S	1992
Rennecker Stephanie L	(260)438-8671 slrennec@gmail.com	1198 Devonshire East Dr Apt B Greenwood IN 46143	IN	Teacher	Tchr	Indianapolis Indianapolis IN	(317)787-5474	CQ	2019
Rennegarbe Rebekkah L	rebekkah.rennegarbe@gmail.com	1121 Michigan Ave Napoleon OH 43545	OH	Teacher	C06/2023			IV	2013
Rennewanz Dustin	(815)592-0353 drennewanzteach@gmail.com	6095 Stone Pathway Bourbonnais IL 60914	NI	Teacher	C07/2016			CQ	2013
Reno Christopher L	(516)330-3314 chris.reno@luhi.org	244 W 17th St Deer Park NY 11729	AT	Teacher	Tchr	Long Island Brookville NY	(516)626-1735	S	1997
Renquest David W	(303) 475-8648 david.renquest@lhsparker.org	17353 E Cranesbill St Parker CO 80134	RM	Teacher	Tchr	Lutheran Parker CO	(303)841-5551	IV	1988
Rensner Josiah J	(217)690-8043 josiah.rensner@cune.org	21833 Zuni Dr Lake Forest CA 92630	PSW	Teacher	S HS/C	Concordia University Irvine Irvine CA	(949)854-8002	S	2019
Rensner Stephen E	(317)782-0650 rensner@thecalvaryschool.org	1191 Brookway Dr Avon IN 46123	IN	Teacher	Prin	Calvary Indianapolis IN	(317)783-2305	RF	1982
Repp Carl E	(512)926-8574 carlrepp@gmail.com	12910 Johnson Rd Manor TX 78653	TX	DCE	Mem C	Hope Austin TX	(512)926-8574	AU	2013
Reseburg Julie Anacker	(920)912-8135 juliereseburg@gmail.com	115 Forest Dr Apt 1004 Wisconsin Dells WI 53965	SW	Teacher	EM			CQ	1981
Resnick Kelsey Overbeck	(573)803-7826 koverbeck@live.com	39575 State Hwy A Truxton MO 63381	MO	DCE	C12/2016			S	2015
Ressler Amanda F	(440)596-7984 mandi.ressler@gmail.com	5839 Deepwood Ct Clarkston MI 48346	MI	DFLM	Mem C	St Trinity Clarkston MI	(248)625-4644	AA	2020
Ressler Christine M Stuart	(281)216-0464 mschristineressler@gmail.com	2439 Cedarcrest Place Valrico FL 33596	FG	Teacher	Tchr	Immanuel Brandon FL	(813)685-1978	MQ	1996
Rethwisch Jennifer M Schilmoeller	(319)550-6528 jrethwisch@lutheraninterparish.com	2653 Cc Ave Victor IA 52347	IE	Teacher	Tchr	Lutheran Interparish Williamsburg IA	(319)668-1711	CQ	2021
Rettig James F	(260)493-6783 jfrettig@frontier.com	9522 Shadecreek Pl Fort Wayne IN 46835	IN	Teacher	EM			RF	1956
Rettig Mandy K Raffety	(402)202-0135 mrettig9@gmail.com		NEB	Teacher	C06/2025			CQ	2021
Rettig Mary K	(419)966-6160 mrettig67@gmail.com	389 Independence Ct Napoleon OH 43545	OH	Teacher	EM			RF	1971
Retzlaff Marissa M Arndt Deac	(262)337-1414 retzlaffmarissa@gmail.com	3221 Shortridge Dr Caledonia WI 53402	S	Deaconess	C12/2020			SL-DEAC	2016
Reuille Wanda P Chin-Leaman	(260)456-4789 wreuille698@hotmail.com	7333 Hathaway Rd Churubusco IN 46723	IN	Teacher	EM			RF	1970
Revard Stephanie R Weldon	(989)624-9204 music@stmartinbirchrun.org	10995 Canada Rd Birch Run MI 48415	MI	DCE	Mem C	St Martin Birch Run MI	(989)624-9204	BR	1996
Reyes Amanda L Detviler	(714)306-5993	2166 N. Diamond Street Orange CA 92867	PSW	Teacher	Tchr	St Paul Orange CA	(714)921-3188	IV	2008
Reynolds Aaron	(260)452-0677 areynold216@gmail.com	7 Founders Way Unit D Saint Louis MO 63105	MO	Teacher	Tchr	Lutheran South Saint Louis MO	(314)631-1400	CH	2022
Reynolds Douglas R	(260)466-8551 dougrreynolds@gmail.com	9212 Ridgetree Dr Fort Wayne IN 46819	IN	Teacher	Pro Stf	Emanuel New Haven IN	(260)749-2163	S	1987
Reynolds Eileen E Rice	(661)347-9982 eileenreynolds1@yahoo.com	18701 Flying Tiger Dr Apt 242 Santa Clarita CA 91387	PSW	Teacher	Tchr	Concordia Christian Granada Hills CA	(818)368-0892	S	1975
Reynolds Jeannette M Breidert	(720)581-3439 jeannettembr@outlook.com	7100 Xavier St Westminster CO 80030	RM	Teacher	EM			S	1966
Reynolds Karen K Wells	(308)968-3452 kreynolds@gpcom.net	2224 Deadwood Trl Cotesfield NE 68835	NEB	Teacher	EM			S	1982
Reynolds Kelsey A Dunn	(808)269-1975 kelsey.hawaii@gmail.com	674 Riviera Bay Dr NE Saint Petersburg FL 33702	FG	Teacher	C09/2019			MQ	2010
Reynolds Natalie J Recks	(260)466-8552	9212 Ridgetree Dr Fort Wayne IN 46819	IN	Teacher	C07/2025			S	1987
Reynolds Sharon L Biermann	(618)407-3741 tripmomst@gmail.com	206 Villawood Dr Collinsville IL 62234	SI	Teacher	C09/2017			RF	1984
Rezek Robin R Rohder	(708)227-1588 robinrezek@comcast.net	14624 Coachmans Rd Homer Glen IL 60491	NI	Teacher	C04/2020			RF	1984
Rhein Sandra K Uffelman Deac	(574)360-6593 sandra.rhein@lcms.org	3164 Parnell Ave Fort Wayne IN 46805	IN	Deaconess	S Miss	Office of International Mission Saint Louis MO		FW-DEAC	2010
Rhinehart Charles M	(239)826-7181 mikecmr50@gmail.com	12944 Park Crescent Cir Pineville NC 28134	FG	Teacher	EM			S	1972
Rhoades Jean M Grant	(520)904-2640 jmrhoades22@cox.net	8357 E Louise Dr Tucson AZ 85730	PSW	Teacher	EM			CQ	1995

*Multiple Assignments (See Church Worker Locator for Additional Details)
See Page 53 for the Table of Abbreviations for key to District, Classification, Position, and College abbreviations.
**C =Candidate; EM =Emeritus; the date following the C is the month and year the Candidate status began

NAME	TELEPHONE NUMBER EMAIL	STREET ADDRESS CITY/STATE/ZIP	DISTRICT	CLASS.	POSITION/ STATUS**	WHERE SERVING	OFFICE PHONE	COLLEGE/ UNIV/CQ	YR GRAD
Rhoden Rebecca A Parks	(561)704-2926 beccarhoden@yahoo.com	9455 Woodbine Way Plain City OH 43064	OH	Teacher	Tchr	St John Dublin OH	(614)889-2284	RF	2003
Rhodes Jenna A Jenna Weingart	(813)404-8174 jenna.weingart@gmail.com	7517 Adams Ave Evansville IN 47715	IN	Teacher	Tchr	Evansville Evansville IN	(812)424-7252	MQ	2004
Ribar Vicki L Booker	(810)516-1832 vicki@tlcfenton.org	19420 Tipsico Lake Rd Fenton MI 48430	MI	DFLM	Mem C	Trinity Fenton Fenton MI	(810)629-7861	AA	2014
Rice Denise L Meyer	(314)608-8360 denise.rice@lea.org	835 La Bonne Pkwy Manchester MO 63021	MO	Teacher	RSO	Lutheran Education Association River Forest IL	(708)209-3343	AU	1984
Rice Tracey J Bossow	(407)883-6619 tbt_rice@yahoo.com	10215 Summer Elm Ave Clermont FL 34711	FG	Teacher	C07/2016			S	1997
Rich Mary B Aufdemberge	(586)665-0068 marytablet1@gmail.com	2497 Beacon Hill Dr Rochester Hls MI 48309	MI	Teacher	Tchr	St John Rochester MI	(248)402-8000	CQ	2015
Rich Monica K Sloan	(303)906-9521 richmonica14@gmail.com	15048 E Carolina Pl Aurora CO 80012	RM	Tch/DCE	C06/2023			IV	1987
Richards James K	(770)714-3404 jrichards@stpaulbocaschool.com	1124 SW 13th Dr Boca Raton FL 33486	FG	Teacher	Prin	St Paul Boca Raton FL	(561)395-0433	CQ	2000
Richards Katherine M Meyer	(630)719-9335 katherine@peacehome.org	1641 Apache Dr Naperville IL 60563	NI	Teacher	Tchr	Peace Lombard IL	(630)627-1101	RF	1991
Richardson Brenda C Koglin	(989)551-0814 bri6955@gmail.com	615 Cumberland Mount Clemens MI 48043	MI	Teacher	Tchr	St John Fraser MI	(586)293-0333	CQ	2009
Richardson Toria N Turner	(317)410-3859 tnjturner18@gmail.com	1051 N K St Fremont NE 68025	NEB	Teacher	Tchr	Trinity Fremont NE	(402)721-5959	S	2018
Richardt Myra K Schroeder	(979)702-0240	10428 Tiffany Village Ct # 25b Saint Louis MO 63123	MO	Teacher	EM			RF	1960
Richberg Connie L Wagner	oceaneastgardens@hotmail.com	3331 Burlington Pl SW Vero Beach FL 32968	FG	Teacher	C07/2016			MQ	1994
Richenburg Peter W		19 Indian Hill Rd Barnstable MA 02630	MO	Teacher	EM			S	1974
Richert James A	(317)882-4470 jarichert@hotmail.com	130 Canna Rd Indianapolis IN 46217	IN	Teacher	EM			RF	1977
Richert Susan M Gronewold	(463)224-7104 smrichert22@hotmail.com	130 Canna Rd Indianapolis IN 46217	IN	Teacher	EM			RF	1970
Richhart Julene C Hessler	(714)448-3957 jrichhart@salemorange.com	5594 E Vista Del Rio Anaheim CA 92807	PSW	Teacher	Tchr	Salem Orange CA	(714)639-1946	IV	1988
Richter Allison M Morton	(928)242-8405 allison.richter27@gmail.com	1156 Brentwood Rd Morton IL 61550	CI	Teacher	Tchr	Bethel Morton IL	(309)263-2417	S	2007
Richter Joseph B	(602)864-1047 joe.richter55@gmail.com	2941 W Northview Ave Phoenix AZ 85051	PSW	Teacher	EM			S	1978
Richter Nathan D	(217)620-8715 nrichter@bethluth.net	8767 W Cornell Ave Apt 2 Lakewood CO 80227	RM	Teacher	Prin	Bethlehem Lakewood CO	(303)233-0401	S	1999
Richter Richard G	richardgrichter@comcast.net	2325 Quaint Cottage Dr O Fallon MO 63368	NI	Teacher	S HS/C	Concordia University Chicago River Forest IL	(708)771-8300	RF	1972
Richter Ronald R Dr	(620)301-1535 rrichter59@gmail.com	807 Spey Winfield KS 67156	KS	Teacher	EM			S	1964
Richter Sharon L Luecke	(713)447-1322	20323 Bent Aspen Ct Cypress TX 77433	TX	Teacher	EM			S	1963
Richter Timothy D	(561)309-2268 trichter063@gmail.com	13383 Sylvan Ave Fort Myers FL 33919	FG	DCE	Mem C	Zion Fort Myers FL	(239)481-4040	S	2005
Ricke David W	dricke290@gmail.com	831 S Harrison St Papillion NE 68046	NEB	Tch/DCE	EM			S	1977
Rickman Eva N Morlok Deac	(714)235-7183 arthurandeva@gmail.com	c/o Doug Morlok 9030 Parrot Ave Downey CA 90240	IE	Deaconess	S Miss	Office of International Mission Saint Louis MO		SL-DEAC	2006
Rickman Susan J Schedler	(414)728-2247 susan_rickman@yahoo.com	209 Meadow Ct Delavan WI 53115	SW	Teacher	EM			SP	1977
Rickords Jeffery B	jrickords@lincolnlutheran.org	7931 Seth Ct Lincoln NE 68507	NEB	Teacher	Tchr	Lincoln Lincoln NE	(402)467-5404	S	1995
Rider Donna A Smith	(231)887-0009 donnasmith1140@gmail.com	824 S Washington St Delphi IN 46923	IN	Teacher	EM			AA	1988
Ridgeway Kayla Brigman	(618)541-1113 kridgeway@zionbethalto.org	1188 Tampico Dr Edwardsville IL 62025	SI	Teacher	Tchr	Zion Bethalto IL	(618)377-5507	CQ	2022
Ridley Stephanie C Conkling	(914)621-8291 stephanieridley87@gmail.com		TX	Teacher	C07/2020			BR	2010
Ridolf Helene Begovich	(516)822-9455	11 Emmet Pl Hicksville NY 11801	AT	Teacher	Tchr	Long Island Brookville NY	(516)626-1735	RF	1972
Rieck Marlene K Roebke	(715)891-0991 marlenerieck87@gmail.com	3700 Oneida Farms Rd Eagle River WI 54521	NW	Teacher	Tchr	Our Savior Eagle River WI	(715)479-6226	S	1988
Riedel Suzanne R Retzlaff	(402)371-1420 riedelsv@cableone.net	112 Hillside Dr Hadar NE 68701	NEB	Teacher	EM			S	1969
Riedl James M	(503) 314-3152 jimmer2446@yahoo.com	16337 NE Fargo Ct Portland OR 97230	NOW	Teacher	EM			S	1968
Riemenschneider Susan L Wischmeyer	sriemenschneider@zionharvester.org	7467 Pierside Dr Dardenne Prairie MO 63368	MO	Teacher	Tchr	Zion Saint Charles MO	(636)441-7424	RF	1994
Riemer Olivia G	(314)807-9326 oliviariemer13@gmail.com	1306 Autumn Wood Cir Ballwin MO 63011	MO	Teacher	Tchr	Zion Saint Charles MO	(636)441-7424	MQ	2023
Riese Rodney J	(715)845-3821 rriese24@frontier.com	152337 Lily Ln Wausau WI 54401	NW	Teacher	EM			S	1968
Riffel Kathleen M Meier	(219)464-1898	1307 Peachtree Dr Valparaiso IN 46383	IN	Teacher	EM			S	1969
Riffel Perry W Dr	(219)464-1898 riffel1307@comcast.net	1307 Peachtree Dr Valparaiso IN 46383	IN	Teacher	EM			S	1969
Riggert Mary L Swenson	(660) 537-3777 jariggert@sbcglobal.net	3702 Bedford Dr Columbia MO 65203	MO	Teacher	EM			S	1986
Riggs Timothy J	(561)752-2325	2740 Quaking Leaf Ln Boynton Beach FL 33436	FG	Teacher	EM			RF	1969

*Multiple Assignments (See Church Worker Locator for Additional Details)
See Page 53 for the Table of Abbreviations for key to District, Classification, Position, and College abbreviations.
**C =Candidate; EM =Emeritus; the date following the C is the month and year the Candidate status began

NAME	TELEPHONE NUMBER EMAIL	STREET ADDRESS CITY/STATE/ZIP	DISTRICT	CLASS.	POSITION/ STATUS**	WHERE SERVING	OFFICE PHONE	COLLEGE/ UNIV/CQ	YR GRAD
Riley Barbara A Alyea	(440)667-9654 riley467@yahoo.com	P.O. Box 156 Munger MI 48747	MI	Teacher	Tchr	Immanuel Saginaw MI	(989)754-4285	S	1997
Riley Elisabeth A Wright	(303)733-3777 rileymel1@gmail.com	5395 N Rosepoint Way Boise IA 83713	RM	Teacher	C07/2016			S	2007
Riley Jennifer L Hoffman	(608)617-5320 jvolley1@gmail.com	537 Lilac Ln West Bend WI 53095	SW	Teacher	Tchr	St Johns West Bend WI	(262)334-3077	MQ	2004
Riley Lukas K	(317)946-0664 lukasriley57@gmail.com	6897 Cardiff Dr McCordsville IN 46055	IN	Teacher	Tchr	Holy Cross Indianapolis IN	(317)826-1234	CQ	2021
Riley Melinda L Finkel	(586)419-7149 melinda.finkel@gmail.com	7080 Timbercrest Washingtn Twp MI 48094	MI	Teacher	Tchr	Immanuel Macomb MI	(586)286-4231	CQ	2017
Rincker Keith E	(618)345-5796 kprincker@att.net	414 Chapel Dr Collinsville IL 62234	SI	Teacher	Tchr	Good Shepherd Collinsville IL	(618)344-3153	S	1980
Rincker Loana M Timm	(217)682-3690 loanarincker6@gmail.com	314 E South 1st St Stewardson IL 62463	CI	Teacher	EM			S	1973
Rincker Peggy J Schulze	(618)345-5796 kprincker@att.net	414 Chapel Dr Collinsville IL 62234	SI	Teacher	Tchr	Good Shepherd Collinsville IL	(618)344-3153	S	1980
Rindt David R Dr	(510)579-9449 drindt2013@gmail.com	10231 S 77 St Lincoln NE 68516	NEB	Teacher	S HS/C	Concordia University Nebraska Seward NE	(402)643-3651	MQ	2008
Ringers Diana L Moore	(251)989-4878 dringers@gulftel.com	12521 Chicago St Elberta AL 36530	SO	Tch/DCE	EM			S	1980
Ringler Louise M Baack	(402)643-0037 louisembringler@yahoo.com	200 Windflower Cir Lincoln NE 68521	NEB	Teacher	EM			S	1964
Ringman Melanie D	(972)207-2177 Melanie@Ringman.org	4033 Sharondale Dr Flower Mound TX 75022	TX	Teacher	Tchr	Prince Of Peace Carrollton TX	(972)447-0532	CQ	2024
Rink Judith A Mindykowski	(630) 254-3865	114 N Pine St Elmhurst IL 60126	NI	DFLM	Mem C	Immanuel Elmhurst IL	(630)832-1649	CQ	2007
Rinkinen Jenna E	(248)249-3626 jennarinkinen5@gmail.com	4343 Deerwood Dr Traverse City MI 49686	MI	Teacher	Tchr	Trinity Traverse City MI	(231)946-2721	MQ	2014
Ripke Judith L Gardels	judyripke88@gmail.com	16004 E Exposition Dr Aurora CO 80017	RM	Teacher	EM			S	1977
Rippstein Timothy A Dr	(402)641-9254 tim.rippstein@gmail.com	2205 N Columbia Ave Seward NE 68434	NEB	DCE	EM			PO	1984
Risch Carl A	(260)724-8588	1024 Grenelefe Ct Decatur IN 46733	IN	Teacher	Tchr	Zion Decatur IN	(260)728-9995	S	1979
Risch David A	(708)209-3649 david.risch@cvchicago.edu	7400 Augusta St River Forest IL 60305	NI	Teacher	S HS/C	Concordia University Chicago River Forest IL	(708)771-8300	RF	1987
Riske Angela C	(989)450-7990 acriske@yahoo.com	1763 Carter Rd Midland MI 48642	MI	Teacher	Tchr	Zion Auburn MI	(989)662-4264	CQ	2019
Riske Curtis H	cdriske@verizon.net	2601 Marsh Lane Unit 243 Plano TX 75093	TX	Tch/DCE	Tchr	Prince Of Peace Carrollton TX	(972)447-0532	RF	1964
Riske Ralph H	(989)662-2538 ralph.riske@yahoo.com	2798 W North Union Rd Apt 39 Midland MI 48642	MI	Teacher	EM			S	1974
Ristau Edward J	(440)823-6052 edwardristau6712@gmail.com	22940 Mastick Rd Apt 101 Fairview Park OH 44126	OH	Teacher	EM			CH	2002
Ristow Beth A Aufdemberge	(231)881-2680 bethristow@gmail.com	103 Stanford Dr Monroe MI 48162	MI	Teacher	Tchr	Holy Ghost Monroe MI	(734)242-0509	AA	1986
Ristow Carolyn J Paulus		19925 E Lehigh Pl Aurora CO 80013	RM	DCE	Pro Stf	Colorado Lutheran High School Parker CO	(303)841-5551	IV	2009
Ristvedt Naomi E	(402)381-8104 Naomi.ristvedt@cune.org		NEB	Teacher	Tchr	Trinity Grand Island NE	(308)382-5274	S	2017
Rittenhouse Amy L Wickwire	(309)507-0959 amerpie84@gmail.com	140 Brookside Dr Glendale Heights IL 60139	NI	Teacher	C06/2020			CQ	2019
Rittenhouse Barbara L Klatt	(303)229-5511 barbrittenhouse@comcast.net	17483 E View Loop Foley AL 36535	RM	Teacher	EM			S	1986
Ritter Nadia C	(630)670-0936 nceleste.schmidt@gmail.com	803 Parkside Cir Streamwood IL 60107	NI	Teacher	Tchr	St Peter Schaumburg IL	(847)885-3350	CH	2009
Ritter Robyn L Gulden	(715)558-4075 ritter0806@gmail.com	5211 Hunters Ridge Dr Wisconsin Rapids WI 54494	NW	DCE	C06/2022			S	2005
Rittierodt Rachel E Hoffman	(561)454-9512 rrittierodt@trinitydelray.org	5243 Tennis Ln Delray Beach FL 33484	FG	Teacher	Tchr	Trinity Delray Beach FL	(561)278-1737	S	2001
Rittierodt Thomas C	(561)454-9310 dcetom@gmail.com	5243 Tennis Ln Delray Beach FL 33484	FG	DCE	C07/2016			AU	2009
Rittman Judith A Lorenz	(660)463-2461 mojudyr@yahoo.com	P.O. Box 911 Concordia MO 64020	MO	Teacher	EM			CQ	1986
Rittner Katherine E Blomquist Deac	(260)494-5382 katherine.rittner@ctsfw.edu	3415 Shoreline Dr Columbia City IN 46725	IN	Deaconess	S HS/C	Concordia Theological Seminary Fort Wayne IN	(260)452-2100	FW-DEAC	2019
Ritz Wanda L		11480 Michael Dr Washington MI 48094	MI	Teacher	EM			RF	1977
Ritzma Victoria L	(660)864-7342 victoria.ritzma@cune.org	278 E 5th St Winona MN 55987	MNS	Teacher	Tchr	Hope Winona MN	(507)474-7799	S	2023
Riveness Garret P	(713)681-6130	5115 Whittier Oaks Dr Friendswood TX 77546	TX	Teacher	Tchr	South Houston TX	(281)464-8299	PO	1992
Rivers Christine M Elliott	(217)649-3159 crivers@flsplano.org	139 Carolyn Ln Murphy TX 75094	TX	Teacher	Tchr	Faith Plano TX	(972)423-7448	RF	2001
Rivers Lisa M Pfund	(314)920-0719 jlrivers89@gmail.com	3216 Watson Rd Festus MO 63028	MO	Teacher	EM			S	1987
Rizzo Jennifer L Dr			PSW	Teacher	Tchr	Orange County Orange CA	(714)998-5151	CQ	2019
Roach Lorraine H Hingston Deac	(406)550-1900 lroach@thrgroup.com	P.O. Box 656 Stevensville MT 59870	MT	Deaconess	C08/2016			FW-DEAC	2012
Roan William T	(619)670-0479 roans4@cox.net	3818 Avenida Johanna La Mesa CA 91941	PSW	Teacher	EM			S	1971
Robbins Doris E Bremer	(507)358-3101 birdsoffour@hotmail.com	51839 Curly Dr Deer Creek MN 56527	MNN	Teacher	EM			SP	1968

*Multiple Assignments (See Church Worker Locator for Additional Details)

See Page 53 for the Table of Abbreviations for key to District, Classification, Position, and College abbreviations.

**C =Candidate; EM =Emeritus; the date following the C is the month and year the Candidate status began

NAME	TELEPHONE NUMBER EMAIL	STREET ADDRESS CITY/STATE/ZIP	DISTRICT	CLASS.	POSITION/ STATUS**	WHERE SERVING	OFFICE PHONE	COLLEGE/ UNIV/CQ	YR GRAD
Robbins Julie L Schaar	jrobbins@zionanaheim.org	4371 Dorthea St. Yorba Linda CA 92886	PSW	Teacher	Tchr	Zion Anaheim CA	(714)535-3600	IV	1992
Robbins Penny S Klingerman	(402)682-2312 pennyrobbins64@gmail.com	17472 County Road 134 Flint TX 75762	TX	Teacher	Tchr	Trinity Tyler TX	(903)593-1526	RF	1987
Robbins Stephen L	(623)693-6360 steohen.robbins@lhsparker.org	18213 Shadbury Ln Parker CO 80134	RM	Teacher	Tchr	Colorado Lutheran High School Parker CO	(303)841-5551	S	2006
Roberson Christine L Friedrich	christine.roberson@ celebrationlutheran.net		NW	Teacher	Tchr	Celebration Appleton WI	(920)734-8218	MQ	2007
Roberts Casey M	(785)844-3838 caseydce@gmail.com	2431 N Nye Ave Fremont NE 68025	NEB	DCE	Mem C	Trinity Fremont NE	(402)721-5536	S	2016
Roberts Gerald M	(616)957-9896 groberts@oursavior-gr.org	2525 Birchcrest Dr SE Grand Rapids MI 49506	MI	Teacher	Tchr	Our Savior Grand Rapids MI	(616)949-0710	CQ	1997
Roberts James E	(661)917-7808 james.e.roberts483.civ@army.mil	413 Vanguard White Sands Missile Range NM 88002	PSW	DCE	M Chap	Office of International Mission Saint Louis MO		SP	2002
Roberts Kimberly C Powers Hedding	(208)651-9373 k_c_roberts@outlook.com	6894 W. Bonnaire Loop Coeur D Alene ID 83815	NOW	DCE	C07/2016			S	2011
Roberts Lisa J Nelson	(262)282-8612	N34W23137 Circle Ridge Rd Apt 108 Pewaukee WI 53072	SW	Teacher	Tchr	Immanuel Brookfield WI	(262)781-7140	MQ	2007
Roberts Mary E Sandfort	(636)578-0577	1100 S 6th St Saint Charles MO 63301	MO	Teacher	EM			RF	1969
Roberts Sandra L Robinson	(847)302-5172 deaconbeac@aol.com	W4029 Glen Fern Ln Lake Geneva WI 53147	NI	Teacher	EM			CQ	1994
Roberts Susan E	(801)359-3386 susan.roberts.utah@gmail.com	252 E 11th Ave Salt Lake Cty UT 84103	RM	DCO	Mem C	Christ Murray UT	(801)266-8714	CQ	2007
Robertson Charlotte L Struecker	(417)434-6115 maestraluterana@gmail.com	25633 Ridge Rd Joplin MO 64801	MO	Teacher	EM			S	1971
Robertson Ruth E Bernau	(507)573-2743 ruth.e.robertson26@gmail.com	900 NE 9th St Madison SD 57042	SD	Teacher	C06/2021			MQ	2010
Robinett Candace K Mc Arthur	(573)636-5570 candyrobinett@hotmail.com	2100 Deer Trl Jefferson Cty MO 65101	MO	Teacher	Tchr	Trinity Jefferson City MO	(573)636-6750	CQ	2001
Robinette Laura E Renzelmann	(260)435-9701 lrobinette@cluth.org	1210 Daly Dr New Haven IN 46774	IN	Teacher	Tchr	Central New Haven IN	(260)493-2502	CH	2007
Robinson Alyssa K Teschendorf	(618)660-9897 aktesch08@gmail.com	114 Sugarmill Rd Troy IL 62294	SI	Teacher	Tchr	Holy Cross Collinsville IL	(618)344-3145	RF	2019
Robinson Ceres A Krohn	(510)387-4950 crobinson@ppfremont.org	378 Solano Ave Hayward CA 94541	CNH	Teacher	Tchr	Prince of Peace Fremont CA	(510)793-3366	CQ	2015
Robinson Claire W Fuhler	(314)422-2488 clairew.robinson@gmail.com	56242 Oak St Novelty MO 63460	MO	Teacher	C08/2022			S	2018
Robinson David P	(314)775-3036 david.robinson@pwclc.org	20431 E Princeton Ave Aurora CO 80013	RM	Teacher	P/Tchr	Peace With Christ Aurora CO	(303)766-7116	S	1995
Robinson Diane S Williamson	(317)894-3885	10656 N 850 W Fairland IN 46126	IN	Teacher	Tchr	Indianapolis Indianapolis IN	(317)787-5474	CQ	2008
Robinson Joel D	(713)248-4570 joeldrob2004@gmail.com	1214 Blackthorne Trail N Plainfield IN 46168	IN	Teacher	EM			S	1972
Robinson Nicole M Mente	(414)708-9084 nrobinson@lwlhs.com	N169 W20342 Georgetown Dr Unit 3 Jackson WI 53037	SW	Teacher	Tchr	Living Word Jackson WI	(262)677-9353	MQ	2002
Robinson Ruth A Bunge	(719)279-9739 swissrobinson415@yahoo.com	3081 Rock Creek Dr Broomfield CO 80020	RM	Teacher	EM			S	1976
Robinson Shannan T Landers	shannan.robinson@imlutheran.org	8 Brookshire Ln Washington MO 63090	MO	Teacher	Tchr	Immanuel Washington MO	(636)239-1636	CQ	2008
Robinson Suzie	(618)980-9108	213 Forest Ridge Ct Glen Carbon IL 62034	SI	Teacher	Tchr	Good Shepherd Collinsville IL	(618)344-3153	S	2016
Robison Elizabeth A Miller	(773)331-2678	21579 Kings Bend Dr Kingwood TX 77339	TX	Teacher	Tchr	Our Savior Houston TX	(713)290-9087	CH	2013
Robson Amy P	(480)329-1306 arjourney7@gmail.com	2414 W Comstock Dr Chandler AZ 85224	PSW	Teacher	Tchr	Christ Greenfield Gilbert AZ	(480)892-8521	MQ	2006
Robson Dawn M Trautmann	(602)622-1053 wlobsonl@yahoo.com	2414 W. Comstock Dr Chandler AZ 85224	PSW	Teacher	EM			SP	1976
Robson Wendell L	(602)622-1053 wlrobsonl@yahoo.com	2414 W Comstock Dr Chandler AZ 85224	PSW	Teacher	EM			SP	1976
Rocans Roberta L Raca	(847)778-1519 rrocans@yahoo.com	40 N 5th Ave Des Plaines IL 60016	NI	Teacher	EM			RF	1992
Rochlitz David W	(586)945-0297 daverochiltz@gmail.com	36190 Paddock Dr Clinton Twp MI 48035	MI	Teacher	EM			RF	1981
Rock Melissa K Taylor	(309)824-8507 melissarock@trinluth.org	300 W Wayne St Le Roy IL 61752	CI	Teacher	Tchr	Trinity Bloomington IL	(309)829-7513	S	1987
Rockensuess Larry H Sr	(734) 771-1721 larryrockensuess@yahoo.com	2972 Saint Paul St Trenton MI 48183	MI	Parish Assist	EM			AA	1984
Rockey Stephen J	(352)262-2848 sjrockey@gmail.com	9317 County Road 125d Wildwood FL 34785	FG	Teacher	C07/2016			AU	1983
Rockrohr Deborah L Roth Dr	(260)416-4150 deborah.rockrohr@gmail.com		IN	Deaconess	Tchr	Concordia Fort Wayne IN	(260)483-1102	RF	1984
Rockrohr Megan R Frisque	(608)449-6043 megan.frisque@gmail.com	224 Shields Rd Stafford VA 22554	SW	Teacher	C07/2016			MQ	2013
Rockwell Cindy L Eisenbraun	(970)640-3028 cindyroc@gmail.com	320 Old Hickory Blvd Apt 2109 Nashville TN 37221	RM	Teacher	Tchr	Messiah Grand Junction CO	(970)245-2838	SP	1985
Rockwell Lori L Laux	(989)401-2341 lllaux_goblue@hotmail.com	7947 Blackmar Rd. Birch Run MI 48415	MI	Teacher	Tchr	Immanuel Saginaw MI	(989)754-4285	AA	1991
Rodarte Stacy K Fischer	(714)856-5560 stafis27@gmail.com	21082 Larchmont Dr Lake Forest CA 92630	PSW	Teacher	Tchr	Abiding Savior Lake Forest CA	(949)830-1460	IV	2011
Rode Emily E Wagner	(317)258-1498 emilye82@aol.com	11335 N 600 W Fountaintown IN 46130	IN	Teacher	Tchr	St John Indianapolis IN	(317)352-9196	CQ	2023
Rode Mary	(714)821-6221 missrode.m@gmail.com	c/o St Paul Lutheran Church 700 Ardenlee Parkway Peachtree GA 30269	FG	Teacher	Tchr	St Paul Peachtree City GA	(770)486-3545	S	2001

*Multiple Assignments (See Church Worker Locator for Additional Details)
See Page 53 for the Table of Abbreviations for key to District, Classification, Position, and College abbreviations.
**C =Candidate; EM =Emeritus; the date following the C is the month and year the Candidate status began

NAME	TELEPHONE NUMBER EMAIL	STREET ADDRESS CITY/STATE/ZIP	DISTRICT	CLASS.	POSITION/ STATUS**	WHERE SERVING	OFFICE PHONE	COLLEGE/ UNIV/CQ	YR GRAD
Rodenbeck Allen G	(260)450-4549 rodeag01@yahoo.com	8203 Astoria Hl Fort Wayne IN 46835	IN	Teacher	EM			S	1976
Rodenbeck Edith F Knake	(219)485-0717	4728 Ottawa Dr Fort Wayne IN 46835	IN	Teacher	EM			RF	1961
Rodenbeck Jill D Broughton	(260)241-4831 jrodenbeck@gmail.com	8203 Astoria Hill Fort Wayne IN 46835	IN	Teacher	EM			S	1977
Rodgers Erin K		2323 Wilson Rd Apt K21 Knoxville TN 37912	MDS	Teacher	Tchr	First Knoxville TN	(865)524-0308	CH	2009
Rodgers Lauren A	(217)971-1986 program@cilca.org	4124 Camp Cilca Rd Cantrall IL 62625	CI	Teacher	C08/2024			CH	2014
Rodgers Lewis E III	(217)971-4487 trodgers@cidlcms.org	6 Knollcrest Ln Chatham IL 62629	CI	Teacher	D Ex/S	Central Illinois District Springfield IL	(217)793-1802	RF	1982
Rodgers Matthia Duryea	(970)846-0443 matthia.duryea@gmail.com	150 Veronica Dr Windsor CO 80550	RM	DPM	C03/2023			IV	2014
Rodis John		131 Brookville Rd Brokkville NY 11545	AT	Teacher	Tchr	Long Island Brookville NY	(516)626-1735	CQ	2007
Rodrigues Charles A Dr	(310)514-9338 charrodrig@gmail.com	17636 3/4 Virginia Ave Bellflower CA 90706	PSW	Teacher	S HS/C	Concordia University Irvine Irvine CA	(949)854-8002	CQ	2010
Rodriguez Elisebeth A Hovland			CNH	Teacher	C03/2022			SP	2016
Rodriguez Krista L Schmidt	(979)716-0143 2014kls@gmail.com	4703 N 15th St Ozark MO 65721	MO	Teacher	Tchr	Redeemer Springfield MO	(417)883-5717	S	2019
Rodriguez Kyla L Stigdon	(410)404-6482 dcekyla@gmail.com		MO	DCE	S Ex/S	Office of National Mission Saint Louis MO		Other	2013
Rodriguez Rachel L Cutler	(406)212-3219 rachel.rodriguez0619@gmail.com	114 Prospect Ave Iron Ridge WI 53035	SW	Teacher	C05/2020			S	2015
Roe Madison Hawkins	(402)515-3654 madison.hawkins@cune.org		PSW	Teacher	C06/2023			S	2016
Roeber John K	(402)944-7762	28211 Church Rd Murdock NE 68407	NEB	Teacher	EM			S	1966
Roedel Karen R Wessel	(248)697-1069 mkroedel@hotmail.com	W381 Golden Lake Park Cir Oconomowoc WI 53066	SW	Teacher	C02/2018			SP	1979
Roeder Joanne L Krause	(714)393-4033 cjroeder64@gmail.com	21370 Via Del Vaquero Yorba Linda CA 92887	PSW	Teacher	EM			RF	1964
Roeglin Zachary	(314)761-7283 zachary.roeglin@gmail.com	3685 Fiebrantz Dr Brookfield WI 53005	SW	Teacher	Tchr	Living Word Jackson WI	(262)677-9353	MQ	2023
Roekle Thomas H	(989)964-8044 troekle@juno.com	25807 Byron Dr. North Olmsted OH 44070	OH	Teacher	Tchr	Cleveland LHS Association Rocky River OH	(440)356-7155	S	1985
Roelfs Tabitha J Schauer	akcagirl2000@yahoo.com	10319 Stewart Dr Eagle River AK 99577	NOW	Teacher	C07/2016			IV	2005
Roemke Carol A Burandt	(518)438-3232	39 Washington Ave Albany NY 12205	AT	Teacher	EM			RF	1965
Roemke Thomas L	(518)438-3232 troemke@nycap.rr.com	39 Washington Ave Albany NY 12205	AT	Teacher	EM			RF	1965
Roepe Judith L Fritsche	(816)405-1679 judyroepe@splsconcordia.org	205 E. Maple St. P.O. Box 131 Emma MO 65327	MO	Teacher	Tchr	St Paul Concordia MO	(660)463-2291	AU	1990
Roepke Mary J Kirkholm	(818)823-0358 mjrrom828@yahoo.com	10125 Lasaine Ave Northridge CA 91325	PSW	Tch/DCE	EM			CQ	1990
Roesel Lori		7034 Pine Vista Ln Houston TX 77092	TX	Teacher	Tchr	St Mark Houston TX	(713)468-2623	CQ	2014
Roeske Jenna R Saleska Dr	(262)323-1367 jennaroeske@gmail.com	W712 Orchard Beach Drive Sheboygan WI 53083	SW	Teacher	C06/2025			MQ	2012
Roeske Kimberly S Koenemann	(907)259-5683 kimroeske82@mail.com	695 Park Ln Monroe WA 98272	NOW	Teacher	Tchr	Zion Snohomish Cty Lake Stevens WA	(425)334-5064	AA	1985
Roeske Robin L Rathke	(262)707-8070	1972 Granville Rd Cedarburg WI 53012	SW	Teacher	EM			MQ	1983
Roesler Joyce E Bultemeier	(410)647-0673 broeslerjr@verizon.net	204 Holland Rd Severna Park MD 21146	SE	Teacher	EM			S	1968
Roesler Kerrie R Kelling	(414)510-0370 kerrie.roesler@gmail.com	8206 Scoresby Manor Ct Spring TX 77379	TX	Teacher	Prin	Trinity Spring TX	(281)376-5810	MQ	2011
Roethel Kimberley L Ford	(920)946-0282 roethel.kim@gmail.com	300 N 8th St Oostburg WI 53070	SW	Teacher	Tchr	Trinity Sheboygan WI	(920)458-8248	CQ	2013
Roethler Heather N Hoffman	(308)250-2405 heather.hoffman@cune.org	1349 14th Ave N Fort Dodge IA 50501	IW	Teacher	Tchr	St Paul Fort Dodge IA	(515)955-7208	S	2016
Roettger Andrea L	andrearoettger@gmail.com		KS	DCE	Mem C	Bethany Overland Park KS	(913)648-2228	S	2002
Roettjer Jennifer M		3205 Spool Ln SW Huntsville AL 35805	SO	DCE	Mem C	Grace Huntsville AL	(256)881-0552	S	1999
Roettjer Stephanie R Stocker	dcesteph@hotmail.com		RM	DCE	C07/2016			IV	2000
Rogalski Susan	(901)756-6109 sue.rogalski@ctk.com	7274 Abercrombie Ln Memphis TN 38119	MDS	Teacher	EM			CQ	2008
Rogers Eric V	(630)308-1492 rogers9201@sbcglobal.net	106 Heathgate Rd Montgomery IL 60538	NI	Teacher	Tchr	Bethany Naperville IL	(630)355-6607	CQ	2005
Rogers Jamie L Abel	(608)617-5276 jrogers@stpaulsbremen.org	579 Jennifer Lane Bremen IN 46506	IN	Teacher	Tchr	St Pauls Bremen IN	(574)546-2790	CQ	2023
Rogers Phillip L	(608)415-7764 biscuitking34@gmail.com	502 Greenmeadow Dr Waukesha WI 53188	SW	Teacher	Tchr	Mount Olive Milwaukee WI	(414)774-2200	SP	1988
Rogers Randall J	(989)245-2053 runningrandyrogers@yahoo.com	5868 Chandler Dr Rockford IL 61114	NI	Teacher	Tchr	Immanuel Belvidere IL	(815)547-5346	RF	1983
Rogers Robert J	(918)688-7411 rjrogers494@gmail.com	10533 E 39th St Yuma AZ 85365	PSW	Teacher	Prin	Yuma Yuma AZ	(928)726-8410	CQ	2005
Roggow Annalisa Yarborough	(618)477-7090 aroggow@gmail.com	826 3rd St Alva OK 73717	OK	Teacher	EM			S	1989
Roggow Gloria A Deac	(580)395-0016 garoggow@yahoo.com	7665 E Eastman Ave Apt D302 Denver CO 80231	RM	Deaconess	C07/2016			RF	2000

*Multiple Assignments (See Church Worker Locator for Additional Details)

See Page 53 for the Table of Abbreviations for key to District, Classification, Position, and College abbreviations.

**C =Candidate; EM =Emeritus; the date following the C is the month and year the Candidate status began

NAME	TELEPHONE NUMBER EMAIL	STREET ADDRESS CITY/STATE/ZIP	DISTRICT	CLASS.	POSITION/ STATUS**	WHERE SERVING	OFFICE PHONE	COLLEGE/ UNIV/CQ	YR GRAD
Roggow Jacob T	(618)477-7091 jacob.roggow@cune.org	45075 Platt St Utica MI 48317	MI	DPM	C05/2025			S	2020
Rogner Andrea M Weiss	(989)529-8038 andrea.m.w01@gmail.com	173 Lakeshore Dr Clarkston MI 48348	MI	Teacher	C06/2024			S	2012
Rogner Calisse K Visser Petersen	(847)305-0340 calissek@gmail.com	4410 Buffalo Ridge Wickenburg AZ 85390	PSW	Teacher	EM			RF	1977
Rogner David Dr	(708)524-3364 david.rogner@cuchicago.edu	206 N Kenilworth Ave Apt 3 Oak Park IL 60302	NI	Teacher	S HS/C	Concordia University Chicago River Forest IL	(708)771-8300	RF	1982
Rohde Donald J	(414)365-1160	8109 N Celina St Milwaukee WI 53224	SW	Teacher	EM			RF	1970
Rohde Molly J Helmreich	(248)303-9680 mollyrohde@rocketmail.com	8355 Yager Rd Columbus MI 48063	MI	Teacher	Tchr	St Peter Richmond MI	(586)727-9693	S	2006
Rohde Rebecca A Helmreich	(260)437-2086 solfeger@frontier.com	2810 Briar Rose Ct Fort Wayne IN 46815	IN	Teacher	Tchr	Concordia Fort Wayne IN	(260)426-9922	AA	1997
Rohe Linda L Dyroff	(618)377-9910 linr1231@hotmail.com	27 Brooks Dr. Bethalto IL 62010	SI	Teacher	EM			RF	1968
Rohlfing Roxanne Krumland	(314) 623-7038 rrohlfing@hotmail.com	2 Lena Ct Saint Charles MO 63303	MO	Teacher	EM			CQ	1992
Rohlfing Terrence H	(788)521-3225 tershare@frontier.com	1928 Old Highway 50 Ottawa KS 66067	KS	Teacher	EM			RF	1968
Rohloff Astraea M Glover	(602)677-2810 astraearohloff77@gmail.com	3105 N Heritage St Buckeye AZ 85396	PSW	Teacher	Prin	Trinity Litchfield Park AZ	(623)935-4690	CQ	2022
Rohm Kristine R Emerson	(714)538-2374 krohm@immanuelorange.org	181 N Pine St Orange CA 92866	EN	Teacher	Tchr	Immanuel Orange CA	(714)538-2373	RF	1992
Rohmaller Betty J Kranich	(714)914-3860 betty.rohmaller@att.net	1008 Presidio Dr Costa Mesa CA 92626	PSW	Teacher	EM			S	1976
Rohr Sarah L Mundt	(812)523-1092 sarah.rohr@lsportal.net	562 N County Road 400 E Seymour IN 47274	IN	Teacher	Tchr	Lutheran Central Brownstown IN	(812)358-2512	S	1998
Rohrdantz Darcy L Brandenburg	(815)219-9856 darcyrohrdantz@yahoo.com	136 N Greenfield Ave Crystal Lake IL 60014	NI	Teacher	C07/2016			RF	1997
Rohren Sara M Wagnitz	(402)690-0954 sara.rohren@gmail.com	21126 Castlerock Ln Gretna NE 68028	NEB	Teacher	C06/2024			S	2005
Rohrich Jennifer L Howser	(402)649-6903 jrohrich@zionlutheranpierce.com	121 N 7th St Pierce NE 68767	NEB	Teacher	Tchr	Zion Pierce NE	(402)329-4658	CQ	2022
Rohwer Marletta M Stahn	(651)490-9035 mrohwer3@hotmail.com	1022 Tiller Ln Shoreview MN 55126	MNS	Teacher	EM			SP	1972
Rojas Irma S Marrero Deac	(409)399-7414 amigosrojas@aol.com	214 N Dean Rd Orlando FL 32825	FG	Deaconess	EM			CQ	1995
Rojas Raquel A Deac	(718)324-1288 dcsrojas@redeemerlutheranbronx.org	4360 Theodore Wittrock Crossing The Bronx NY 10466	AT	Deaconess	Mem C	Redeemer Bronx NY	(718)324-1288	FW-DEAC	2010
Rojas De Robles Alejandra Deac	(402)430-0177 alex.keinbaum@gmail.com	8834 Shell Island Dr. Jacksonville FL 32216	FG	Deaconess	C12/2020			FW-DEAC	2017
Roland Lydia M	(765)426-9985	121 S 30th St Lafayette IN 47904	IN	Teacher	EM			RF	1981
Roldan Lisa G Gordon	(972)824-8285 lroldan9@gmail.com	7910 Rabbit Drive Frisco TX 75034	TX	Teacher	Tchr	Dallas Lutheran Sch Dallas TX	(214)349-8912	CQ	2005
Rolf Cheryl J Hahn	(248)709-8148 crolf246@gmail.com	223 Pine St Rochester MI 48307	MI	Teacher	EM			S	1978
Rolf Cheryl L Gally	(509)630-5949 casagally@gmail.com	11433 Hannibal St Commerce City CO 80022	RM	Teacher	C07/2016			RF	1975
Rolf Joel A	(317)435-8300 joel.rolf@trinityindy.org	1415 Ash Way St. Anderson IN 46012	IN	Teacher	Tchr	Trinity Indianapolis IN	(317)897-0243	RF	1988
Rolf Kathryn A Wareham Dr	(651)336-1012 kathryn.rolf@gmail.com	412 Pleasant Ln Chaska MN 55318	MNS	DPM	Mem C	Saint Johns Chaska MN	(952)448-2433	SP	2003
Rolfsmeier Grant D	(402)641-0666 rolfsmeierg@flhsemail.org	4033 Laurel Flat Ct Las Vegas NV 89129	PSW	Teacher	Tchr	Faith Las Vegas NV	(702)804-4400	S	2012
Rolland Jack E	(402)570-9608 jack68526@gmail.com	10401 Natural Springs Ave Las Vegas NV 89129	PSW	Teacher	Tchr	Faith Community Las Vegas NV	(702)921-2777	S	2023
Roller Kaitlyn	(310)779-8704 kait.roller@gmail.com	5637 Hazeltine Ave Apt 202 Sherman Oaks CA 91401	PSW	DCE	C07/2016			CQ	2009
Rollin Justine		2141 Devonshire Dr Napa CA 94558	CNH	Teacher	Tchr	St John Napa CA	(707)226-7970	CQ	2024
Rollins Glenn K	(217)899-2640 glenn.rollins@lcms.org	109 Fairview St Watertown WI 53094	SW	Teacher	S Ex/S	The LCMS Corporate Saint Louis MO	(314)965-9000	S	1979
Rommel Gregory R	(314)277-2005 greg@rommel.net	5931 Carnaby Ln Rosenberg TX 77471	TX	Tch/DCE	S Ex/S	The LCMS Corporate Saint Louis MO	(314)965-9000	SP	1975
Romsa Jerad R	(818)881-5574 jerryromsa@hotmail.com	8132 Darby Pl Reseda CA 91335	PSW	Teacher	EM			S	1968
Rondema Patricia C Rhoads	(503)758-1997 jtrondema@hotmail.com	6526 SE 137th Ave Portland OR 97236	NOW	Teacher	EM			CQ	2001
Ronning Randall L	(804)516-3267 ranron22@aol.com	1615 Swinton Ln Richmond VA 23238	SE	Tch/DCE	EM			S	1983
Rooney John L Dr	(503)975-1666 jlroone@aol.com	2181 Kates Bridge Dr Reno NV 89521	PSW	Teacher	EM			IV	2002
Root Christopher S	(262)424-1703 root_christopher@yahoo.com	N89W27861 Twin Pines Cir Hartland WI 53029	SW	Teacher	RSO	LHS Assn of Greater Milwaukee West Allis WI	(414)421-9100	MQ	2005
Root Emily M Fetzer	(605)390-8572 roote@trinitycr.org	2175 26th St Marion IA 52302	IE	Teacher	Tchr	Trinity Cedar Rapids IA	(319)366-1569	S	2016
Root Katy L Lehfeldt	(262)894-6772 root_katy@yahoo.com	N89 W27861 Twin Pine Cir Hartland WI 53029	SW	Teacher	Tchr	Divine Redeemer Hartland WI	(262)367-3664	MQ	2006
Root Linda Boyd	(954)383-2454 lroot@oursaviorplantation.org	7521 Plantation Rd Plantation FL 33317	FG	Teacher	Prin	Our Savior Plantation FL	(954)473-6888	CQ	2020
Root Samantha M	(714)900-0308 sam.root93@yahoo.com	625 Stanley Ave Unit One Half Long Beach CA 90814	PSW	Teacher	Tchr	Bethany Long Beach CA	(562)420-7783	IV	2015

*Multiple Assignments (See Church Worker Locator for Additional Details)
See Page 53 for the Table of Abbreviations for key to District, Classification, Position, and College abbreviations.
**C =Candidate; EM =Emeritus; the date following the C is the month and year the Candidate status began

NAME	TELEPHONE NUMBER EMAIL	STREET ADDRESS CITY/STATE/ZIP	DISTRICT	CLASS.	POSITION/ STATUS**	WHERE SERVING	OFFICE PHONE	COLLEGE/ UNIV/CQ	YR GRAD
Rosamond Jerry D	(612)597-1504 jrosamond419@gmail.com	1117 77th St Victoria MN 55386	MNS	DCO	EM			SP	1987
Rosamond Kathy A Heiman	(952)412-8404 krosamond17@gmail.com	1117 77th St Victoria MN 55386	MNS	Teacher	EM			WN	1982
Rose Angeline M Mickelson	(305)296-6289	2906 Flagler Ave Key West FL 33040	FG	Teacher	EM			SP	1955
Rose Carol Moss	(612)961-7385	3530 Hazel Trl Unit F Woodbury MN 55129	MNS	Teacher	EM			SP	1979
Rose Dawn M Eichelberg	(303)349-6311 rdhbrose4@msn.com	9647 Osceola St Westminster CO 80031	RM	Teacher	C07/2016			S	2003
Rose Dwayne K	(262)255-3507 dewtamrose@wi.rr.com	W170N8736 Edgewood Pl Menomonee Fls WI 53051	SW	Teacher	EM			MQ	1984
Rose Patricia Krone Dr	(630)290-7155 patricia.rose@cuchicago.edu	342 W Greenfield Ave Lombard IL 60148	NI	Teacher	EM			S	1976
Roseboom Heather J Rothrock	(607)222-1702 smartteach32@hotmail.com	712 Prescott Ave Endicott NY 13760	EA	Teacher	C07/2018			BR	2000
Rosebrock Kimberly A Acton	(314)412-4313 kimarosebrock@gmail.com	1101 Forest Court Rochelle IL 61068	NI	DCO	C07/2016			SP	2006
Rosendahl Darla M	(402)934-1116	1229 N 147th Plz Omaha NE 68154	NEB	Teacher	EM			S	1973
Rosenthal Dennis L	(402)372-1978 drosenthal@q.com	1028 E Sherman St West Point NE 68788	NEB	Teacher	EM			S	1970
Rosenthal Sallie E Fowler	(402)372-1978 dlrosenthal14665@gmail.com	1028 E Sherman St West Point NE 68788	NEB	Teacher	EM			S	1970
Rosentreter Kathy E	(989)652-4494 katerose@airadv.net	5 Krafft Ct Frankenmuth MI 48734	MI	Teacher	EM			AA	1990
Rosenwinkel Sandra L De Long	(219)670-6448 sandyrosenwinkel@att.net	1970 Greenvalley Dr Crown Point IN 46307	IN	Teacher	EM			CQ	2002
Rosier Lindamarie Sobottke Epperson	(510)520-7171 lindamarierosier@aol.com	P.O. Box 7292 Carmel By The CA 93921	CNH	Teacher	EM			RF	1971
Rosin Aaron	(313)384-9723 aaronrosin1@gmail.com	2505 Corby Ave Fort Wayne IN 46815	IN	Teacher	Tchr	Concordia Fort Wayne IN	(260)426-9922	AA	2019
Rosin Michael P	(313)729-0730 rosindawg14@gmail.com	521 Thurston Ct Fort Wayne IN 46825	IN	Teacher	EM			RF	1985
Rosin Paul M	(313)729-1739 rosinp35@gmail.com	23392 Broadwood Dr Elkhart IN 46514	NI	Teacher	Prin	St John's Lombard IL	(630)932-3196	MQ	2010
Ross Diane M Hanggie List	(714)921-3188 diane.ross@splsorange.org	901 E Heim Ave Orange CA 92865	PSW	Teacher	Tchr	St Paul Orange CA	(714)637-2640	CQ	2012
Ross Laura E Sweere	(952)688-8301 lauraross8697@gmail.com	10151 Brinwood Dr Houston TX 77043	TX	DCE	Mem C	St Mark Houston TX	(713)468-2623	AU	2020
Ross Sarah A Brakke	(720)724-1016 sarahandrewkids@gmail.com	1691 Minorca Pl Costa Mesa CA 92626	PSW	Teacher	Tchr	Christ Costa Mesa CA	(949)548-6866	S	2002
Rossi Jennifer S Haglund	(989)295-5731 jennyhaglund18@gmail.com	7690 Lydia St Saginaw MI 48609	MI	Teacher	Tchr	Peace Saginaw MI	(989)793-9025	CH	2008
Roste Lucy M Golnitz	(320)762-2606	15628 SW Amelia Rd Glenwood MN 56334	MNN	Teacher	Tchr	Zion Alexandria MN	(320)763-4842	SP	1990
Rotermund Donald O Dr	(972)889-1117 dondor6@sbcglobal.net	605 Olympic Richardson TX 75081	TX	Teacher	EM			RF	1955
Roth Alfred R Dr	allormilor@gmail.com	17999 SE River Rd Apt 119 Portland OR 97267	NOW	Teacher	EM			CQ	1961
Roth Carlyn J Hodde	(313)802-1729 carlynjr@outlook.com	35552 Marina Dr Sterling Hts MI 48312	MI	Teacher	EM			S	1963
Roth Christopher D	(651)756-7420 chrisroth1@gmail.com	300 4th St E Apt 112 Saint Paul MN 55101	MNS	Teacher	Tchr	Concordia Academy Roseville MN	(651)484-8429	SP	1992
Roth Daniel C	(618)277-3649 danmicroth@charter.net	110 Foxbrush Dr Belleville IL 62221	SI	Teacher	EM			RF	1965
Roth Erin E Bray	(319)290-0065 ebray21@gmail.com	4925 S 186th Ave Omaha NE 68135	NEB	Teacher	C05/2023			S	2012
Roth James A	(586)978-9349 carlynjr@outlook.com	35552 Marina Dr Sterling Hts MI 48312	MI	Teacher	EM			S	1962
Roth Jeanine S Burke	(612) 200-8982 jrothretired@yahoo.com	3500 W 50th St Apt 417 Minneapolis MN 55410	MNS	Teacher	EM			RF	1963
Roth Leslie D	(989)652-2592 ROTHLC5125@ATT.NET	683 Eastgate Dr Frankenmuth MI 48734	MI	Teacher	EM			S	1965
Roth Marilyn J Schwartz	(618)277-3649 danmicroth@charter.net	110 Foxbrush Dr Belleville IL 62221	SI	Teacher	EM			CQ	1988
Roth Melanie J Dippold	(573)803-7429 mroth@saxonylutheranhigh.org	149 Kaskaskia Ln Jackson MO 63755	MO	Teacher	Tchr	Saxony Jackson MO	(573)204-7555	CQ	2020
Roth Rebecca E	(314)580-4828 rebeccaeroth154@gmail.com	658 Tempo Trail Drive Apt C Creve Coeur MO 63141	MO	Teacher	Tchr	Lutheran North Saint Louis MO	(314)389-3100	MQ	2023
Roth Ronald J	(419)599-0340 rjroth1948@gmail.com	244 Black Walnut Dr Westerville OH 43082	OH	Teacher	EM			RF	1969
Rothas Cynthia K Selby	(707)495-8912	504 S College St Hahira GA 31632	CNH	Teacher	C07/2016			SP	1984
Rothe Sarah B Chapman	(317)438-3537 sarah.b.rothe@gmail.com	4647 Big Run Ct Indianapolis IN 46239	IN	Teacher	C07/2016			AA	2002
Rottermond Linda I Zielke	(972)369-7068 linda.rottermond@gmail.com	5001 Berkley Dr McKinney TX 75070	TX	Teacher	EM			RF	1971
Rottmann Michael S	(815)519-7873 mrottmann@glwh.org	3126 Sugar Leaf Lane Lakeland FL 33810	FG	Teacher	Prin	Grace Winter Haven FL	(863)293-8447	MQ	1994
Rouland Megan E Bolt	(636)219-6404 merouland@zionharvester.org	1777 Michaelwood Ct Saint Charles MO 63303	MO	Teacher	Tchr	Zion Saint Charles MO	(636)441-7425	AA	2001
Roundey William G Jr	(636)795-3451 roundey@gmail.com	2 Melody Ln Mexico MO 65265	MO	Teacher	EM			S	1983
Rountree Scott R	(509)979-2885 reese.rountree10@gmail.com	63446 Mustang Rd Bend OR 97701	NOW	DCE	Mem C	Trinity Bend OR	(541)382-1832	IV	2023

*Multiple Assignments (See Church Worker Locator for Additional Details)

See Page 53 for the Table of Abbreviations for key to District, Classification, Position, and College abbreviations.

**C =Candidate; EM =Emeritus; the date following the C is the month and year the Candidate status began

NAME	TELEPHONE NUMBER EMAIL	STREET ADDRESS CITY/STATE/ZIP	DISTRICT	CLASS.	POSITION/ STATUS**	WHERE SERVING	OFFICE PHONE	COLLEGE/ UNIV/CQ	YR GRAD
Rouse Carolyn J	(972)826-2676 crouse@orlcs.com	10124 Wake Bridge Dr Frisco TX 75035	TX	Teacher	Tchr	Zion Dallas TX	(214)363-1630	RF	1987
Rousseau Donald L	(561)322-5211 don.lifehope@gmail.com	3924 Mesa Rd Destin FL 32541	FG	DCM	EM			MQ	1998
Rousu Amber L Sellin	(320)491-0047 arousu@zionalex.com	1808 Jasmine Dr Alexandria MN 56308	MNN	Teacher	Tchr	Zion Alexandria MN	(320)763-4842	CQ	2018
Rovak Meredith K Evans	(630)336-0545 meredithrovak@aol.com	502 Windett Ridge Yorkville IL 60560	NI	Teacher	C06/2019			CQ	2015
Rovey Karl M	(405)434-6518 kmrovey@yahoo.com	218 Regency Dr Clinton OK 73601	SI	DPM	Mem C	St John Chester IL	(618)826-3545	S	2019
Rowe Christine E Hand Dr	(914)617-9115 christi4rw@aol.com	902 Heritage Hls # C Somers NY 10589	AT	Teacher	EM			CQ	1997
Rowe Rebecca A Mooney	(309)825-5515 beckyrowe@bethellutheran school.org	520 E Adam St Morton IL 61550	CI	Teacher	Tchr	Bethel Morton IL	(309)266-6592	S	2007
Rowell Mary A Huebner Dr	(260)897-3387 mannrowell@gmail.com	1526 E Albion St Avilla IN 46710	IN	Teacher	EM			RF	1961
Rowland LeAnna H Christopher	(925)784-6043 lrowland@lutheranschool.org	6878 Navajo Rd. #97 San Diego CA 92119	PSW	Teacher	Tchr	Christ La Mesa CA	(619)462-5211	IV	2009
Rowley Mary G	(515)249-8604 mary.rowley13@gmail.com	1220 Manistique Ave South Milwaukee WI 53172	SW	DCM	C09/2019			MQ	2013
Rowsell David H	(319)396-1206 roz4450@yahoo.com	2530 Paulyn Ct NW Cedar Rapids IA 52405	IE	Teacher	EM			RF	1967
Royalty Leanna Burbrink	(812)569-2541 leannaroyalty@gmail.com	8576 E. County Road 200 N Seymour IN 47274	IN	Teacher	C05/2021			CH	2018
Roybal Linda A Spino	(303)934-7375	7170 W Calahan Ave Lakewood CO 80232	RM	Teacher	Tchr	Bethlehem Lakewood CO	(303)238-7676	CQ	2000
Royuk Amy E Martens	(402)643-9830 amy.royuk@cune.edu	1815 N Columbia Ave Seward NE 68434	NEB	DCM	S HS/C	Concordia University Nebraska Seward NE	(402)643-3651	S	2001
Royuk Barbarakay T Seckel	(402)478-4797 barbarakayr@yahoo.com	1285 W Dodge Ave Arlington NE 68002	NEB	Teacher	EM			S	1969
Royuk Brad R	(410)419-2688 broyuk@hotmail.com	929 Sorock Torrance CA 90502	PSW	Teacher	Tchr	Bethany Long Beach CA	(562)420-7783	S	1993
Royuk Brent R Dr	brent.royuk@cune.edu	142 Seward St Seward NE 68434	NEB	Teacher	S HS/C	Concordia University Nebraska Seward NE	(402)643-3651	S	1988
Royuk Elaine A Hummel	(402)641-3564 e_royuk@yahoo.com	334 N 1st St Seward NE 68434	NEB	Teacher	EM			S	1962
Royuk Sandra J Muehler	(402)646-0637 sandra.royuk@stjohnseward.org	142 Seward St Seward NE 68434	NEB	Teacher	Tchr	St John Seward NE	(402)643-4535	S	1988
Rozak David O	bestfroggy1@yahoo.com	171 Lariat Dr Gallipolis OH 45631	FG	Teacher	EM			S	1964
Rozelle Angela J Bickel	(716)550-6108 angroz14@gmail.com	400 Orchard Terrace Roselle IL 60172	NI	Teacher	Prin	Immanuel Palatine IL	(847)359-1936	AA	1998
Rua Angie N Hoffer	(702)343-0501 angierua94@gmail.com	6726 Lincoln Wood St Las Vegas NV 89149	PSW	Teacher	Tchr	Faith Las Vegas NV	(702)804-4400	PO	1998
Ruark Mark J	(573)335-9125 mruark@saxonylutheranhigh.org	475 Hilltop Rdg Cpe Girardeau MO 63701	MO	Teacher	Prin	Saxony Jackson MO	(573)204-7555	CQ	2016
Rubel Elaine M Petersen	(715)347-2417 onegoodstitch@gmail.com	2030 Adams St Plover WI 54467	NW	Teacher	EM			S	1970
Rubel John C	(715)347-8417 j.rubel@sbcglobal.net	2030 Adams St Plover WI 54467	NW	Teacher	EM			RF	1968
Rucker Karlee J Friend	(573)746-1562 kjane415@gmail.com	63 Beacon Hill Dr Lake Ozark MO 65049	MO	Teacher	C05/2024			CQ	2021
Rucks Lois E Klein	(715)424-4324 loisrucks@gmail.com	1229 90th St S Wisc Rapids WI 54494	NW	Teacher	EM			S	1973
Rudat Sheila K Richards	(217)201-1341 dce@stmarkedmond.org	1417 NW 181st St Edmond OK 73012	OK	DCE	Mem C	St Mark Edmond OK	(405)340-0192	RF	1996
Rudi Carol A Schneider		2303 Buroak Rdg San Antonio TX 78248	TX	Teacher	EM			RF	1975
Rudick Annette K	(989)662-7562 akrudick@gmail.com	313 W Elm St Auburn MI 48611	MI	Teacher	EM			SP	1989
Rudick Barbara A Klug	(616)850-0738 barb.rudick@gmail.com	1091 Aspen Dr Norton Shores MI 49441	MI	Teacher	EM			RF	1968
Rudick Pamela M	(217)352-7037 pmrudick@gmail.com	3304 Sylvan Dr Champaign IL 61821	CI	Teacher	Tchr	St John Champaign IL	(217)359-1123	RF	1993
Rudlaff Richard A	(712)735-4036	6676 Frederick Ave May City IA 51354	IW	Teacher	EM			S	1969
Rudnick Carlene E Helmkamp	(763)497-9177 miltcarl6@gmail.com	P.O. Box 192 Albertville MN 55301	MNS	Teacher	EM			RF	1960
Rudolph Alison L		25749 4th St W Apt 207 Zimmerman MN 55398	MNN	Teacher	Tchr	Crown Saint Francis MN	(763)856-2099	SP	2018
Rudolph Barbara R Summerer	barbrudolphkdg@gmail.com	9370 Viking Blvd NW Elk River MN 55330	MNS	Teacher	EM			S	1978
Rudolph Erin L	elrudolph08@gmail.com		MNN	Teacher	Tchr	Crown Saint Francis MN	(763)856-2099	SP	2013
Rudolph Lorna M Kreger	(763)441-4114	19915 Proctor Rd NW Elk River MN 55330	MNS	Teacher	EM			SP	1984
Rudsinski Amy C	(314)960-9701 two4amy@hotmail.com	1229 Trails Drive Fenton MO 63026	MO	Teacher	Tchr	St Paul Des Peres MO	(314)822-2771	RF	2000
Rudsinski Calvin H	(314)960-1908 eightozfilet@hotmail.com	2549 Buckley Ridge Ct Saint Louis MO 63125	MO	Teacher	EM			RF	1973
Rudsinski Carol A Hallemeier	(314)960-9702 carol_rudsinski@hotmail.com	2549 Buckley Ridge Ct Saint Louis MO 63125	MO	Teacher	EM			RF	1975
Rudy Sally L	(956)244-2623 peanutbrittlemaker@yahoo.com	6194 Whitcomb Dr Saginaw MI 48603	MI	Teacher	EM			S	1971

*Multiple Assignments (See Church Worker Locator for Additional Details)
See Page 53 for the Table of Abbreviations for key to District, Classification, Position, and College abbreviations.
**C =Candidate; EM =Emeritus; the date following the C is the month and year the Candidate status began

NAME	TELEPHONE NUMBER EMAIL	STREET ADDRESS CITY/STATE/ZIP	DISTRICT	CLASS.	POSITION/ STATUS**	WHERE SERVING	OFFICE PHONE	COLLEGE/ UNIV/CQ	YR GRAD
Rudzinski Aaron M			RM	Teacher	Tchr	Colorado Lutheran High School Parker CO	(303)841-5551	RF	2003
Rudzinski Emilie L Groth			RM	Teacher	C07/2016			RF	2005
Rudzinski Kevin R	(812)525-1878 kevin.r.rudzinski@gmail.com	5326 Wharfside Dr Imperial MO 63052	MO	Teacher	Tchr	St Paul Des Peres MO	(314)822-0447	RF	1996
Rudzinski Leroy F	(816)799-9106 marleenud@aol.com	9725 Winslow Pl Kansas City MO 64131	MO	Teacher	EM			RF	1971
Rudzinski Mark A	(920)619-7318 mark.rudzinski@lhsparker.org	11931 S Copper Creek Cir Parker CO 80134	RM	Teacher	Tchr	Colorado Lutheran High School Parker CO	(303)841-5551	RF	2004
Rueber Bruce E	(765)458-6198 gbjerseys@aol.com	2501 E County Road 200 S Liberty IN 47353	IN	Teacher	EM			RF	1968
Rueber Gloria J Becker	(765)458-6198 gbjerseys@aol.com	2501 E County Road 200 S Liberty IN 47353	IN	Teacher	EM			RF	1968
Ruehs Tara L Heintz	(623)434-8172 tara@ruehsclan.com	1018 E Renee Dr Phoenix AZ 85024	EN	DCE	C07/2016			SP	1996
Ruehs Taylor	(949)433-0400 ruehstaylor@gmail.com	1117 Pinot Noir Dr Lodi CA 95240	CNH	Teacher	Tchr	St Peter Lodi CA	(209)333-2225	IV	2023
Rueter David L Dr	(909)957-4565 dave.rueter@lhsparker.org	998 Wagoner Dr Livermore CA 94550	RM	DCE		Rocky Mountain District Englewood CO	(303)695-8001	IV	1996
Rueter Nancy J Oman	(562)461-2038 rueterroger@gmail.com	13732 Cornuta Ave Bellflower CA 90706	PSW	Teacher	EM			S	1968
Rueter Roger H	(562)461-2038 rueterroger@gmail.com	13732 Cornuta Ave Bellflower CA 90706	PSW	Teacher	EM			S	1966
Ruhmann Amanda R	(618)401-1840 ruhmannamanda@gmail.com	617 Country Club Dr Red Bud IL 62278	SI	Teacher	Tchr	St John Red Bud IL	(618)282-3873	RF	2006
Ruiz Miguel A	(719)849-0120 mruizmusic@gmail.com	1308 Whitley Rd Keller TX 76248	TX	DPM	Mem C	Messiah Keller TX	(817)431-2345	CQ	2014
Rull Kara L Ray	(618)910-2415 krull895@charter.net	104 Fairway Dr Maryville IL 62062	SI	Teacher	Tchr	Holy Cross Collinsville IL	(618)344-3145	RF	1984
Rullman Glenn L	(336)722-6278	2430 Maplewood Ave Winston Salem NC 27103	SE	Teacher	EM			RF	1965
Rumbold Sharon K Winkleman	(309)222-4085 sandkrumbold@gmail.com	709 N Bradley Ave Chillicothe IL 61523	CI	Teacher	EM			CQ	1990
Rumsch Rebecca D	(503)504-5600 rebalucky@yahoo.com	2511 S 248th St Apt B27 Kent WA 98032	NOW	Tch/DCE	C08/2023			PO	2009
Rumsey Angie C Schlueter	(714)336-5314 arumsey@salemorange.com	751 N Milford St Orange CA 92867	PSW	Teacher	Tchr	Salem Orange CA	(714)633-2366	IV	1994
Rumsey Annie M Thompson	(402)487-2648 thdrar@yahoo.com	56128 826 Rd Madison NE 68748	NEB	Teacher	EM			CQ	2001
Runge Alan P Dr	(314)445-7789 runge.alan@gmail.com	13122 Promontory Trail Roscoe IL 61073	NI	Teacher	ExecDir	Rockford Rockford IL	(815)877-9551	CQ	2009
Runge David K	(319)442-3459 drunge@centrallutheranschool.org	206 3rd Ave Keystone IA 52249	IE	Teacher	Tchr	Central Newhall IA	(319)223-5271	S	1996
Runge Michelle L Bahr	(708)275-0701 mrunge@stjohnschicago.org	4532 N Monitor Ave Chicago IL 60630	NI	Teacher	Prin	St John Chicago IL	(773)736-1196	RF	2004
Runyan Lillian E Hall	(714)469-5911 lillian.runyan24@gmail.com	1725 W Katella Ave Apt 428 Orange CA 92867	PSW	Teacher	Tchr	St Johns Orange CA	(714)288-4406	IV	2023
Rupe Dawn M Ruelle	(248)912-8680 drupe207@gmail.com	5909 Long Point Dr Davisburg MI 48350	MI	DCE	C04/2025			RF	1998
Rupnow Amy M Springer	arupnow@ststephen-lcms.org	N5208 County Road A Juneau WI 53039	SW	Teacher	Tchr	St Stephen Horicon WI	(920)485-6687	SP	1997
Rupp Donna C Menzel	(210)621-5482 dcrupp89@gmail.com	4839 Legend Well Dr San Antonio TX 78247	TX	Teacher	EM			AU	1987
Ruppert Ruth M Pickelman	(309)696-6888 ruthiemruppert@hotmail.com	434 Church St Seward NE 68434	NEB	Teacher	EM			RF	1966
Ruppert Thomas W	(309)696-7840 pickrupps@hotmail.com	434 Church St Seward NE 68434	NEB	Teacher	EM			RF	1967
Rupprecht Edward P	(630)888-4381 eprupprecht@gmail.com	8809 W Myrtle Ave Glendale AZ 85305	PSW	Teacher	EM			RF	1964
Rupprecht Holly Edwards	(618)670-3952 hrupprecht@gmail.com	5567 N State Route 159 Edwardsville IL 62025	SI	Teacher	Tchr	Zion Bethalto IL	(618)377-8314	CQ	2021
Ruscetta Janine L Case	(720)670-9428 jlruscetta@gmail.com	P.O. Box 910 Bennett CO 80102	RM	Teacher	C06/2017			S	2005
Rusch David L	(310)204-0366 ccdave48@gmail.com	4146 Center St Culver City CA 90232	PSW	Teacher	EM			RF	1970
Rusch Lydia J	(920)530-8127 lrusch@wolfriverlhs.org		NW	Teacher	Tchr	Wolf River Shawano WI	(715)745-2400	MQ	2018
Rusche Sarah T Johnson Deac	(501)733-8094 sarahtrusche@gmail.com	333 Jackson St Unit 1 Marengo IL 60152	NI	Deaconess	RSO	Redeeming Life Outreach Sanford FL	(407)790-9745	SL-DEAC	2023
Ruse Amy Bostelman	(419)966-6895 80snamenoshame@gmail.com	509 Meadows Parkway Avilla IN 46710	IN	Teacher	Tchr	Ascension Fort Wayne IN	(260)486-2226	CQ	2024
Rusert David G	(314)580-5252 david.rusert@ greenparklutheranschool.org	2012 Henley Woods Drive Arnold MO 63010	MO	Teacher	Tchr	Green Park Saint Louis MO	(314)544-4248	RF	1982
Rush Angela G Schneider	(317)341-2096 angie.rush1281@gmail.com	720 N Oklahoma Ave Morton IL 61550	CI	Teacher	Tchr	Bethel Morton IL	(309)266-6592	AA	2005
Rush James G II	821095135898 jamesrush.ltu@gmail.com	1432 Leisure Dr Flint MI 48507	MI	Teacher	C04/2019			MQ	2000
Rush Melissa M Vogt	(812)447-5921 melissarush721@gmail.com	8122 Buttermore Run Fort Wayne IN 46804	IN	Teacher	C07/2019			CH	2011
Rush Ranelle D	(817)431-3228 rushrickranelle@gmail.com	12133 Thicket Bend Dr Fort Worth TX 76244	TX	Teacher	EM			S	2002
Rush Raymond E	(507)469-8248 raybear@hickorytech.net	15568 550th Ave Good Thunder MN 56037	MNS	DCM	C07/2016			MW	1977

*Multiple Assignments (See Church Worker Locator for Additional Details)
See Page 53 for the Table of Abbreviations for key to District, Classification, Position, and College abbreviations.
**C =Candidate; EM =Emeritus; the date following the C is the month and year the Candidate status began

NAME	TELEPHONE NUMBER EMAIL	STREET ADDRESS CITY/STATE/ZIP	DISTRICT	CLASS.	POSITION/ STATUS**	WHERE SERVING	OFFICE PHONE	COLLEGE/ UNIV/CQ	YR GRAD
Rushton Leah K Martin	(510)332-0072 leah.kmartin@gmail.com	450 Bridgeport Drive Half Moon Bay CA 94019	CNH	Teacher	P/Tchr	Prince Of Peace Fremont CA	(510)797-8186	SP	2022
Rusnak Carolyn A Laesch Dr	(314)200-9797 crusnak@ckhome.org	4612 Misty Trail Ln Saint Louis MO 63128	MO	Teacher	Mem C	Concordia Kirkwood MO	(314)822-7772	RF	1982
Russ Kimberly M Bardales	(813)389-3229 tkruss8@msn.com	4623 San Paulo Ct Lakeland FL 33813	FG	Teacher	C07/2016			CQ	2005
Russell Charles P	(501)584-8508 cpr294@gmail.com	9290 Hamilton Circle Washington Township MI 48094	MI	DPM	Mem C	St Peter Macomb MI	(586)781-3434	MQ	2017
Russell Darci M Drilling	(319)230-3850 dce.darci@zionhiawatha.org	835 S 5th St Marion IA 52302	IE	DCE	Mem C	Zion Hiawatha IA	(319)393-2013	IV	2021
Russell Gordon A	(319)393-2438 grussell@kingofkingscr.org	2315 Linden Dr SE Cedar Rapids IA 52403	IE	DPM	Mem C	King Of Kings Cedar Rapids IA	(319)393-2438	CQ	2025
Russell Ieva C Deac	(636)541-2071 irussell@kingofkingscr.org	6610 Berry Rd SE Cedar Rapids IA 52403	IE	Deaconess	Mem C	King Of Kings Cedar Rapids IA	(319)393-2438	SL-DEAC	2025
Russell James R	(574)248-0075 russjimel@gmail.com	1636 W Grant St Bremen IN 46506	IN	Teacher	EM			RF	1972
Russell Katelyn E	(219)405-7150 kmartin12525@gmail.com	1704 Boca Lago Dr Valparaiso IN 46383	IN	Teacher	Tchr	Immanuel Valparaiso IN	(219)462-8207	CQ	2017
Russell Kathryn A Weber		15662 Mountain Track Rd Orange VA 22960	SE	Teacher	EM			S	1972
Rust Anna M Bean	(812)522-6937 arust@bcremc.net	7861 W Seymour Rd Seymour IN 47274	IN	Teacher	EM			CQ	1982
Rust Rebecca K Friedrich	(314)420-9423 rdoubledup@gmail.com	P.O. Box 1611 Ruidoso NM 88355	RM	DCE	C07/2016			IV	2003
Ruszkowski Alaina L	(407)233-9611 alaina@ccridgefield.com	P.O. Box 1446 Ridgefield WA 98642	NOW	DCE	Mem C	Christ Community Ridgefield WA	(360)727-3578	S	2018
Ruth David G	druth@lhsa.com	2221 N Melborn St Dearborn MI 48128	MI	Teacher	Tchr	LHS Assn Of Greater Detroit Rochester Hls MI	(248)856-0240	CQ	2000
Rutherford Jonathan C	(714)271-4250 rutherford@creanlutheran.org	25500 River Bend Dr Apt F Yorba Linda CA 92887	PSW	Teacher	Tchr	Crean Irvine CA	(949)387-1199	IV	2014
Rutowicz Katherine	(262)277-8971 krutowicz@stpaulhamel.org	1 B Country Ln P.O. Box 92 Hamel IL 62046	SI	Teacher	Tchr	St Paul Worden IL	(618)633-2202	MQ	2024
Ruwald Joan E Voges	(618)473-2650 mrhw@aol.com	P.O. Box 57 Hecker IL 62248	SI	Teacher	EM			RF	1965
Ruwisch Jennifer L Kettler Deac	(603)321-2106 jlruw87@gmail.com	7 Ronnie Dr Nashua NH 03062	NE	Deaconess	C07/2017			CH	2011
Ryan Brenda M Deac	(519)312-4162 ryan.brenda91@gmail.com	5475 Beach St Lambton Shores ON N0N-1 CANADA	EN	Deaconess	EM			IV	2000
Ryan Hannah	(518)439-4328 ryan@blcdelmar.com	111 Elm Ave Delmar NY 12054	AT	DCM	Mem C	Bethlehem Delmar NY	(518)439-4328	MQ	2024
Ryan Julie Hite	(503)331-6234 ryanj@fhlcs.org	1822 NW 9th Ave Hillsboro OR 97124	NOW	Teacher	Tchr	Forest Hills Cornelius OR	(503)359-4853	CQ	2021
Ryan Richard D	(806)570-7702 rickdryan6@gmail.com	3302 Fleetwood Dr Amarillo TX 79109	TX	Teacher	EM			AU	1982
Ryherd Ann C Collins	(217)972-1919 ann.ryherd@ greenparklutheranschool.org	3490 Brookstone View Dr St Louis MO 63129	NI	Teacher	C09/2025			PO	2012
Ryskowski Raymond J	(860)989-9972 rryskowski@yahoo.com	176 Seneca Rd Bristol CT 06010	NE	Teacher	EM			RF	1974
Ryskowski Rosemary J Mc Bride	(860)583-9842	176 Seneca Rd Bristol CT 06010	NE	Teacher	Tchr	Immanuel Bristol CT	(860)583-5631	RF	1982
Saalfeld Larry D	(281)813-8332 saalfeld@comcast.net	14159 Limerick Ln Tomball TX 77375	TX	Teacher	EM			S	1974
Sabal Barbara L Holls	(216)331-7315 jsabal@cox.net	19030 E Shoreland Ave Rocky River OH 44116	OH	Teacher	EM			RF	1968
Sabanosh Rachel A Wanagat	(908)358-2645 sabanosh@me.com	6 Redwood Ct Racine WI 53402	SW	Teacher	Tchr	Trinity Racine WI	(262)632-1766	MQ	1996
Sabbides Elizabeth Francis	(239)580-7581 betsy.sabbides@gmail.com	3281 Lindsey Lane #2 Naples FL 34109	FG	DCE	Mem C	Marco Marco Island FL	(239)394-0332	S	2008
Sabel Judith J Garwood		1126 Northlawn Dr Fort Wayne IN 46805	IN	Teacher	EM			S	1975
Sabol Natalie J Watt Deac	(507)525-6639 nj.sabol@gmail.com	14320 Dysprosium St NW Apt 319 Ramsey MN 55303	MNS	Deaconess	C07/2016			RF	1998
Sacco Sarah D Pierce Deac	(719)593-0138 sarahdsacco@live.com	3211 W Kiowa St Colorado Spgs CO 80904	RM	Deaconess	C07/2016			SL-DEAC	2008
Sachtleben Joyce L Helmkamp	(314)838-5491 rjsachtleben@msn.com	1345 Nashua Dr Florissant MO 63033	MO	Teacher	EM			RF	1967
Sachtleben Kristin N Liefer	(618)830-0469 kristin.sachtleben@gmail.com	8601 Segen Rd Red Bud IL 62278	SI	Teacher	C07/2016			RF	2006
Sachtleben Roger P	(314)838-5491 rjsachtleben@msn.com	1345 Nashua Dr Florissant MO 63033	MO	Teacher	EM			RF	1967
Sadlovsky Kelly R Smiley Dr	(651)592-9117 sadlovsky@csp.edu	1516 Southview Blvd South St Paul MN 55075	MNS	Teacher	S HS/C	Concordia University St Paul Saint Paul MN	(651)641-8278	CQ	2024
Sado Audrey V Mehl	a.v.mehl@gmail.com	411 Water Road Ocala FL 34472	FG	Teacher	Tchr	St John Ocala FL	(352)622-7275	S	2017
Saeger David R	djsaeger@gmail.com	3402 Amanda Dr Weston WI 54476	NW	Teacher	EM			RF	1965
Saeger Robert A	(402)366-6629 saeger001@windstream.net	P.O. Box 183 Waco NE 68460	NEB	Teacher	EM			S	1973
Saehler Chrysteena R Fay	(618)795-9017 chrysteenasaehler@gmail.com	122 E Rice St Owatonna MN 55060	MNS	Teacher	Pro Stf	Faribault Faribault MN	(507)334-7982	MQ	2016
Sagissor Chelsea B Durk	(920)316-0050 csagissor@yahoo.com	317 Burnham St Lowell IN 46356	IN	Teacher	C07/2016			S	2007
Sagissor Emily L Wolf	(701)866-4025 emilydce@gmail.com	424 Brook Ave S Moorhead MN 56560	MNN	DCE	Mem C	Our Redeemer Moorhead MN	(218)233-7569	S	2008

*Multiple Assignments (See Church Worker Locator for Additional Details)
See Page 53 for the Table of Abbreviations for key to District, Classification, Position, and College abbreviations.
**C =Candidate; EM =Emeritus; the date following the C is the month and year the Candidate status began

NAME	TELEPHONE NUMBER EMAIL	STREET ADDRESS CITY/STATE/ZIP	DISTRICT	CLASS.	POSITION/ STATUS**	WHERE SERVING	OFFICE PHONE	COLLEGE/ UNIV/CQ	YR GRAD
Sagissor Philip J	(920)316-0219 psagissor@trinitycp.org	317 Burnham St Lowell IN 46356	IN	Teacher	Tchr	Trinity Crown Point IN	(219)663-1578	S	2006
Sainz Tanya Guyer	(505)307-2836	2926 Arizona Pl NE Albuquerque NM 87110	RM	Teacher	Tchr	Christ Albuquerque NM	(505)884-3876	CQ	2013
Salathe Marie E	(504)288-5322	227 Alix St New Orleans LA 70114	SO	Teacher	EM			CQ	1995
Salchert Rachel M Winter	(201)275-5944 rachel.salchert@gmail.com	16441 Vescovo Ln Pflugerville TX 78660	TX	Teacher	Tchr	Redeemer Austin TX	(512)451-6478	SP	2010
Salefski Jeffrey F	(217)875-2901 jsalefski@yahoo.com	4666 Havenwood Ct Decatur IL 62526	CI	Teacher	Tchr	Luth School Assoc Decatur IL	(217)233-2001	RF	1985
Saleska Candice O Noelker	(812)530-7682 csaleska@gmail.com	245 Franconian Dr W Frankenmuth MI 48734	MI	Teacher	Tchr	St Lorenz Frankenmuth MI	(989)652-6141	MQ	2010
Saleska John T	(262)227-2808 johnt.saleska@cuw.edu	12203 W Shawnee Pass Mequon WI 53097	SW	Teacher	S HS/C	Concordia University Wisconsin Mequon WI	(262)243-5700	CQ	2023
Saleska Thomas J Dr	(262)844-7052 tom.saleska@cuw.edu	1777 Valley Rd West Bend WI 53090	SW	Teacher	EM			RF	1979
Saleska Vanessa M Ehlke	(262)323-1347 52020vanessa@yahoo.com	1777 Valley Rd West Bend WI 53090	SW	Teacher	EM			RF	1977
Salgado Felicia N	(318)505-0280 salgado.felicia.n@gmail.com	109 Eagle Wing Dr Decatur AL 35603	SO	DFLM	C01/2021			IV	2019
Salinas BethAnn E Bennett	(406)750-8868 bethannsalinas@rocketmail.com	317 Market St. Freeport PA 16229	EA	Teacher	C07/2016			AA	2006
Salmi Kristine M	(302)670-8123 krissalmi@gmail.com	162e E Clay St Scott Afb IL 62225	TX	Teacher	C08/2020			SP	1995
Salmon Courtney M Glynn	(308)750-2190 courtney.glynn@cune.org	P.O. Box 142 901 Plevna Street Palmer NE 68864	NEB	Teacher	Tchr	Trinity Grand Island NE	(308)382-5274	S	2007
Salo Andrea K Garfield	(248)840-9300 andreaksalo@gmail.com	6508 County Road 263 Hannibal MO 63401	CI	Teacher	Tchr	St James Quincy IL	(217)222-8267	CQ	2009
Salogga Brenda J Richter	(217)429-9183 dnbsal@comcast.net	4710 E Beacon Dr Decatur IL 62521	CI	Teacher	Tchr	Luth School Assoc Decatur IL	(217)233-2001	CQ	2016
Salzberg Sarah L Trinklein	sarah.salzberg@lhsoc.org		PSW	Teacher	Tchr	Orange County Orange CA	(714)998-5151	S	2007
Samsell Alva L Jr	(616)249-2069 samsusan.samsell@att.net	1811 Holliday Dr SW Wyoming MI 49519	MI	DCE	EM			S	1969
Samsell Christopher N	(989)321-0582 chriss@immanuelbaycity.com	2808 E Fisher Rd Bay City MI 48706	MI	Teacher	Tchr	Immanuel Bay City MI	(989)893-4088	MQ	1995
Samuels Kari A Retzlaff	(402)309-0143 Kari.Samuels@sewardschools.org	446 Rainbow Cir Seward NE 68434	NEB	Teacher	C07/2016			S	2003
Samuta Ashley C	(630)746-1564 ashleysamuta@gmail.com	590 Hillside Ave Glen Ellyn IL 60137	NI	Teacher	Tchr	St John's Lombard IL	(630)932-3196	MQ	2024
Sanabria Ashley L Meissner	(817)343-5942 ashleylsanabria@gmail.com	5201 Spring Cypress Rd Spring TX 77379	TX	Teacher	Tchr	Trinity Klein Klein TX	(281)376-5773	AU	2011
Sanabria Flor M Deac	(813)406-9003	c/o Messiah Lutheran Church 14920 Hutchison Rd Tampa FL 33625	FG	Deaconess	Mem C	Messiah Carrollwood FL	(813)961-2182	SL-DEAC	2013
Sanabria Yolima Deac	(813)770-6718	13723 Pimberton Drive Hudson FL 34669	FG	Deaconess	Mem C	Messiah Carrollwood FL	(813)961-2182	SL-DEAC	2013
Sanchez Leticia Deac	(817)709-5159 leticiasherrera369@gmail.com	5938 Wall Ave Haltom City TX 76117	TX	Deaconess	EM			SL-DEAC	2015
Sandau William H	(510)461-1714 besandau929@gmail.com	2682 Cub Lake Drive Loveland CO 80538	RM	Teacher	EM			RF	1962
Sandcork Robert R II	(507)523-2580 rsandcork@hopelhs.org	21498 Friendly Four Rd Lewiston MN 55952	MNS	Teacher	Prin	Hope Winona MN	(507)474-7799	SP	1997
Sandcork Sofia R	(507)429-2880 sofiasandcork@gmail.com	5600 137th St Apt 406 Overland Park KS 66223	KS	Teacher	Tchr	Bethany Overland Park KS	(913)648-2228	SP	2025
Sander Sharolyn M Schomburg	(630)222-8184 sharolynsander@aol.com	2544 Timber Creek Dr Seward NE 68434	NEB	Teacher	EM			S	1971
Sanders Kara C	(901)412-0516 karaharbin24@gmail.com	4630 N Maple Grove Rd Boise ID 83704	NOW	Teacher	C07/2022			AU	2018
Sanders Kenneth W	(717)887-2102 colonelmusic@comcast.net	14 Willomette Ct York PA 17402	SE	Teacher	EM			S	1971
Sanders Rebekah J Meyer	(217)840-0660 rebekah.meyer87@gmail.com	465 E 500 N Road Buckley IL 60918	CI	Teacher	C08/2020			S	2010
Sandersfeld Dineen S Oestreich	(262)391-1185 drmy2boys@gmail.com	2508 Plumadore Dr. Grand Island FL 32735	FG	Teacher	Tchr	Faith Eustis FL	(352)589-5433	MQ	1995
Sandersfeld Kip L	(815)988-6737 kipsandersfeld@gmail.com	2508 Plumadore Dr Grand Island FL 32735	FG	Teacher	Tchr	Faith Eustis FL	(352)589-5433	MQ	1995
Sandfort Mary E		5587 Sunrise Dr Fort Myers FL 33919	FG	Teacher	C07/2016			S	1990
Sandfort Melissa H Howard Dr	(314)640-0732 pgaphd@sbcglobal.net	3610 West Clay Saint Charles MO 63301	MO	Teacher	Prin	Child Of God Saint Peters MO	(636)970-7080	CQ	2022
Sandfort Melvin T	(812)350-9514 tisandfort@gmail.com	114 N Benton Ave Saint Charles MO 63301	MO	Teacher	EM			RF	1965
Sandfort Neil I Dr	(636)669-0079 neilsandfort@yahoo.com	2920 Homewood Ave Saint Charles MO 63301	MO	Teacher	EM			RF	1961
Sandifer Sarah J White	(503)729-6220 dcesarahj@gmail.com	5490 SW 191st Beaverton OR 97078	NOW	DCE	C07/2016			PO	2005
Sandlin Linda K Kane	lindakanesandlin@gmail.com	2117 Cedar Circle Carrollton TX 75006	TX	Teacher	Tchr	Prince Of Peace Carrollton TX	(972)447-0532	CQ	2010
Sandmann Danny C	(269)697-0200 snapsa@aol.com	1336 Honeysuckle Ln Niles MI 49120	IN	Teacher	EM			S	1970
Sandor Donald R	(989)293-1590 dksandor27@gmail.com	47 Maravista Ave. Greenville SC 29617	SE	Teacher	EM			RF	1962
Sanford Julianne L	(515)576-1248	1217 4th Ave S Fort Dodge IA 50501	IW	Teacher	Tchr	St Paul Fort Dodge IA	(515)955-7208	S	1985

*Multiple Assignments (See Church Worker Locator for Additional Details)

See Page 53 for the Table of Abbreviations for key to District, Classification, Position, and College abbreviations.

**C =Candidate; EM =Emeritus; the date following the C is the month and year the Candidate status began

NAME	TELEPHONE NUMBER EMAIL	STREET ADDRESS CITY/STATE/ZIP	DISTRICT	CLASS.	POSITION/ STATUS**	WHERE SERVING	OFFICE PHONE	COLLEGE/ UNIV/CQ	YR GRAD
Sanft Evan J	(314)604-7799 ejsanft@gmail.com	724 Caspian Ln St. Louis MO 63125	MO	Teacher	Tchr	Luth High School Assn St Louis Saint Louis MO	(314)833-2904	CH	2012
Sanft Nicole M Beran	(708)305-5386 nmsanft@gmail.com		MO	Teacher	Tchr	Christ Community Kirkwood MO	(314)822-7774	CH	2011
Sankey Kenneth T Dr	(224)500-0041 klsankey@hotmail.com	1060 N 7th St Seward NE 68434	NEB	Teacher	S HS/C	Concordia University Nebraska Seward NE	(402)643-3651	S	1980
Sankey Lorinda L Schomacker Dr	(224)500-0041 lorinda.sankey@cune.edu	1060 N 7th St Seward NE 68434	NEB	Teacher	S HS/C	Concordia University Nebraska Seward NE	(402)643-3651	S	1980
Sankey Mary A McCain	(321)368-6187 dcemary1@gmail.com	112 Five Fingers Ct Apt C Kodiak AK 99615	FG	DCE	C10/2018			IV	2017
Sansoucie Lori M Sanfilippo	(314)956-1709 lori@oshkoshgoodshepherd.org	5298 Cornhusk Lane Omro WI 54963	SW	DCE	Mem C	Good Shepherd Oshkosh WI	(920)231-0530	IV	2018
Santel Dorene J Otte	(618)334-3442	542 Berkshire Dr Troy IL 62294	SI	Teacher	EM			S	1967
Sapiro Deanna L Hopper	(414)350-5372 dsapiro@wauwatosalutheran.org	3232 N 88th St Milwaukee WI 53222	SW	Teacher	Tchr	Wauwatosa Wauwatosa WI	(414)258-4558	MQ	1993
Sarkkinen Amy A	(269)651-6171 nanydells@hotmail.com	1101 E Congress St Sturgis MI 49091	MI	Teacher	Tchr	Trinity Sturgis MI	(269)651-4245	AA	1995
Sarr Lisa L Purcell	(303)499-9012 lsarr1003@comcast.net	9673 Remington Ave Firestone CO 80504	RM	Teacher	Tchr	Immanuel Loveland CO	(970)667-7606	IV	1984
Sarrault Kelsey Kelsey Thomas	(810)834-9770 kelseythomas7@icloud.com	7529 Faith Haven Court Willow Spring NC 27592	SE	DFLM	C10/2018			AA	2016
Sasse Linda K Maitland	(904)382-5966 sassehome55@gmail.com	31278 Wellston Dr Warren MI 48093	MI	Teacher	EM			RF	1977
Sasso Christina R Sereda	(908)565-4744 christina.sereda@gmail.com	221 Brier Estate Dr Meridianville AL 35759	SO	Teacher	Tchr	Grace Huntsville AL	(256)881-0552	S	2015
Satek Pamela A Kreibaum	(630)258-1660 pams@satekwinery.com	160 Lane 620 Lake James Fremont IN 46737	IN	Teacher	EM			CQ	1997
Sato Stacy K	(702)553-5111 mraloha_99@yahoo.com	2482 Dragon Fire Lane Henderson NV 89052	CNH	Teacher	C07/2016			PO	1981
Satterlee Cassie E Bednar	(618)635-3269	18336 Windy Hill Rd Staunton IL 62088	SI	Teacher	EM			CQ	1998
Sattler Andrea S Langrehr	(618)713-1998 sattlera34@gmail.com	316 E Field Dr Red Bud IL 62278	SI	Teacher	Tchr	Trinity Red Bud IL	(618)282-2883	MQ	2008
Sattler Carol K Kettler	(262)642-5805 kcsattler77@gmail.com	2006 Division St East Troy WI 53120	SW	Teacher	EM			S	1977
Sattler Karl E	onwingslikeeaglesis4031@ gmail.com	2006 Division St East Troy WI 53120	SW	Teacher	EM			S	1978
Saucerman Emily E Benecke	(720)427-1408 emilysaucerman@centurylink.net	474 N Jamestown Way Aurora CO 80018	RM	Teacher	Tchr	Peace W Christ Aurora CO	(303)693-5618	RF	1999
Sauer Laura L Mountford	(818)489-9160 casauers@gmail.com	6906 Bluebell Ave N Hollywood CA 91605	PSW	Teacher	EM			RF	1976
Sauls Stephanie	(512)699-9050 sksauls@gmail.com	1908 Northwest Blvd Georgetown TX 78628	TX	Teacher	Tchr	Zion Georgetown TX	(512)863-3065	AU	2006
Saunders David R	(630)363-4356 vbdrs6@hotmail.com	2860 Northampton Dr Apt A2 Rolling Mdws IL 60008	NI	Teacher	Tchr	Immanuel Palatine IL	(847)359-1936	CQ	1980
Saurmann Melissa R Strong	(217)972-9883 msaurmann@unitydecatur.org	3185 Fair Oaks Dr Decatur IL 62526	CI	Teacher	Tchr	Luth School Assoc Decatur IL	(217)233-2001	RF	2003
Sausaman Pamela A Peper	(217) 652-9157 psausaman@trinity-lutheran.com	3790 Tozer Rd Springfield IL 62707	CI	Teacher	Tchr	Trinity Springfield IL	(217)787-2323	RF	1987
Saving David W	(913)558-9298 dsaving7@gmail.com	11325 Wornall Rd Kansas City MO 64114	KS	DCE	EM			SP	1978
Sawhill Julia N Burton	(713)553-1641 juliesawhill@hotmail.com	2224 Walnut Ln Pasadena TX 77502	TX	Teacher	EM			S	1977
Sawusch Pamela M	(847)373-3282		NI	Teacher	Tchr	St John Chicago IL	(773)736-1196	S	2004
Sawyer Kerrick P	(360)917-5992 principal@greenbaytrinity.org	1268 Weise St Green Bay WI 54302	NW	Teacher	Prin	Green Bay Trinity Green Bay WI	(920)655-4673	S	2014
Sawyer Rachel K Jones	(805)252-0207 racheljones1119@gmail.com	1268 Weise St Green Bay WI 54302	NW	Teacher	C06/2022			S	2015
Sayles Priscilla M Miller	(605)341-0505 bpsayles@gmail.com	11375 Sheridan Lake Rd Rapid City SD 57702	SD	Teacher	EM			RF	1971
Scaer Anyssa M Neustel	(720)951-7795 jascaer@gmail.com	8431 Bremen Way Fort Wayne IN 46825	IN	Teacher	Tchr	Concordia Fort Wayne IN	(260)483-1102	S	2017
Scagnoli Laurie B Bartelt	(260)241-3328 lbbartelt12@gmail.com	4720 Innsbruck Dr Fort Wayne IN 46835	IN	Teacher	Tchr	Concordia Fort Wayne IN	(260)422-2429	CQ	2018
Scannell Denis G	(516)567-3241 denis.scannell@luhi.org	131 Brookville Rd Glen Head NY 11545	AT	Teacher	Tchr	Long Island Brookville NY	(516)626-1735	CQ	2018
Scarlata Micaela Martinez	(518)275-8820	14 Elm St Newburgh NY 12550	AT	Teacher	C07/2016			BR	2001
Scepanski Kathleen E Okray	(414)750-3494 scepanskik@gmail.com	8100 W Tesch Ave Milwaukee WI 53220	SW	Teacher	Tchr	St Pauls West Allis WI	(414)541-6251	MQ	2003
Schaaf Martina N Nerger	(501)703-3317 mns77calendar@gmail.com	725 Flat Fork Rd Wartburg TN 37887	MDS	Teacher	C04/2023			RF	1999
Schaaf Robert R	(239)994-6180 bob.schaaf@smlcs.org	6756 Fairview St Fort Myers FL 33966	FG	Teacher	Tchr	Saint Michael Fort Myers FL	(239)939-1218	BR	1979
Schaar Dennis R	(909)592-7113 kasdrs1018@icloud.com	1802 Grasscreek Dr San Dimas CA 91773	PSW	Teacher	EM			RF	1967
Schaar Karen A Thorsen	(909)592-7113 kasdrs1018@icloud.com	1802 Grasscreek Dr San Dimas CA 91773	PSW	Teacher	EM			RF	1965
Schacht Margaret Meier	(414)510-3932 peg.schacht@gmail.com	13655 W Marquette Dr New Berlin WI 53151	EN	DCM	EM			MQ	2008
Schachtsiek Marcia E Schulz	(573)735-4159	6938 County Road 249 Palmyra MO 63461	MO	Teacher	EM			S	1966

*Multiple Assignments (See Church Worker Locator for Additional Details)

See Page 53 for the Table of Abbreviations for key to District, Classification, Position, and College abbreviations.

**C =Candidate; EM =Emeritus; the date following the C is the month and year the Candidate status began

NAME	TELEPHONE NUMBER EMAIL	STREET ADDRESS CITY/STATE/ZIP	DISTRICT	CLASS.	POSITION/ STATUS**	WHERE SERVING	OFFICE PHONE	COLLEGE/ UNIV/CQ	YR GRAD
Schadt Daren E de la Motte	(360)337-7786 getshandsdirty@yahoo.com	8645 Sungate Pl NE Bremerton WA 98311	NOW	Teacher	EM			S	1976
Schaefer Andrew P Bassett	(520)401-9652 andy.schaefer90@gmail.com	2060 Del Morro Dr Dacula GA 30019	NE	DCE	C03/2017			RF	2013
Schaefer Carol M Bussey	(717)324-9577 carolmayschaefer@gmail.com	1932 Outer Circle Dr Oviedo FL 32765	FG	Teacher	EM			S	1964
Schaefer Daniel V	(979)542-8301 schfr5@hotmail.com	4067 County Road 114 Lincoln TX 78948	TX	Teacher	Tchr	Faith High Giddings TX	(979)242-2889	S	1982
Schaefer Erin Q Batiansila	erinschaefer@pilgrimluth.com	3242 Brookside Dr Pulaski WI 54162	NW	Teacher	Tchr	Pilgrim Green Bay WI	(920)965-2244	MQ	1988
Schaefer Gary J	(314)348-8010 civbuffwar@gmail.com	310 Bayless Ave Saint Louis MO 63125	MO	Teacher	EM			S	1986
Schaefer Jeffrey M	(815)218-1279 jms.fishing61@gmail.com	604 Taylor Rdg Belvidere IL 61008	NI	Teacher	EM			S	1983
Schaefer Judy L Peterson	(815)218-1278 judy.schaefer@comcast.net	604 Taylor Rdg Belvidere IL 61008	NI	Teacher	EM			S	1981
Schaefer Linda E Bickel Deac	(217)648-2824 schaeferdeac@aol.com	P.O. Box 429 Atlanta IL 61723	CI	Deaconess	EM			Other	1970
Schaefer Margaret F	mars1045@sbcglobal.net	5212 Gadsden Ave Fort Worth TX 76244	TX	Teacher	EM			S	1968
Schaefer Michelle J	(541)231-8349 m1schaefer@hotmail.com	927 Silverbrook Rd Randle WA 98377	NOW	Teacher	C07/2016			PO	1998
Schaefer Rachel A	(812)929-2608 rschaefer@redeemer-oakmont.org	1917 W Evergreen Ave Apt 1f Chicago IL 60622	NI	Teacher	S HS/C	Concordia University Chicago River Forest IL	(708)771-8300	RF	2016
Schaefer Robyn R Maas	(319)330-0662 robschaefer4@gmail.com	471 11th Ave Box 8 Box 8 Conroy IA 52220	IE	Teacher	EM			S	1979
Schaefer Susan G Hohle	(979)716-7901 schfr5@hotmail.com	4067 County Road 114 Lincoln TX 78948	TX	Teacher	EM			S	1982
Schaeff Natalie M Yurgens	(989)233-5340 natalie.schaeff@gmail.com	8600 Janes Rd Saginaw MI 48601	MI	Teacher	Tchr	Peace Saginaw MI	(989)792-2581	CQ	2023
Schafer Charity C Espinosa	(248)653-4785 charity.schafer@orlcne.org	412 M St David City NE 68632	NEB	Teacher	Tchr	Our Redeemer Staplehurst NE	(402)535-2251	S	2018
Schafer Joyce L Unverfehrt	(517)673-2949 jlschafer50@gmail.com	4932 W Cedar Creek Dr New Palestine IN 46163	IN	Teacher	EM			S	1972
Schafer Katherine M Erickson	(317)599-6877 katieme_01@yahoo.com	14201 Princewood Dr Fishers IN 46037	IN	Teacher	C07/2016			MQ	2005
Schaff Andrew A	(402)750-2626 andrew.schaff@lcms.org	1712 E Sycamore Ave Norfolk NE 68701	MO	Teacher	S Miss	Office of International Mission Saint Louis MO		S	2004
Schaff John M	(309)868-3743 johnschaff10@gmail.com	17723 Elm Rd. Hoyleton IL 62803	SI	Teacher	Prin	Trinity Hoyleton IL	(618)493-6226	IV	1991
Schaff Noel B Sunderman	011-886-0901036661 noel.b.schaff@gmail.com	#31 Chien Kuo Rd Section 2 Minhsing Chia Yi 621 TAIWAN	MO	Teacher	Tchr	Office of International Mission Saint Louis MO		S	2004
Schaffer Joel P	(734)787-5559 jpstne@gmail.com	38108 Clydesdale Dr Romulus MI 48174	MI	Teacher	Tchr	St Johns Waltz MI	(734)654-6366	RF	1997
Schaffer Rebecca	(352)804-2333 becca_s_59@yahoo.com	c/o St Paul Lutheran School 701 W Palmetto Park Rd Boca Raton FL 33486	FG	Teacher	Tchr	St Paul Boca Raton FL	(561)395-0433	SP	2001
Schaidt Lauren A	(586)214-3116 schaidtl@gmail.com	42400 Park Ridge Way Clinton Twp MI 48038	MI	Teacher	Tchr	Lutheran North Macomb MI	(586)781-9151	MQ	2006
Schalk Linda S Hopp	(989)766-8073 wlschalk74@gmail.com	8138 S Rogers Rd Hawks MI 49743	MI	Teacher	EM			S	1973
Schaller Bruce H	(713)937-9144 bruceschaller@sbcglobal.net	16418 Jersey Dr Jersey Vlg TX 77040	TX	Teacher	EM			RF	1968
Schaller Karen L Diekhoff	(417)849-0424 kschaller.182@aol.com	1667 N East Ridge Dr Strafford MO 65757	MO	Teacher	EM			CQ	2005
Schaller Rita M Steeneck	(713) 305-7402 ritaschaller@sbcglobal.net	16418 Jersey Dr Jersey Vlg TX 77040	TX	Teacher	EM			RF	1968
Schallhorn Mark B	zippy2040@aim.com	107 W Chapel Chase Dr Decatur IN 46733	IN	Teacher	EM			RF	1978
Schallhorn Randy B	(952)913-7766 ranschall@yahoo.com	12455 W Janesville Rd Unit 405 Muskego WI 53150	EN	Teacher	EM			SP	1971
Schallhorn Valjean A Beck	(952)913-7767 vschallhorn@yahoo.com	12455 W Janesville Rd Unit 405 Muskego WI 53150	EN	Teacher	EM			S	1971
Schallhorn Vicki L Wiltenburg	(260)301-9096 vickilynn355@aol.com	107 W Chapel Chase Dr Decatur IN 46733	IN	Teacher	EM			RF	1977
Schallock Katherine J Prahl	(920)892-2280 schallocks22@yahoo.com	2306 N 5th St Sheboygan WI 53083	SW	Teacher	Tchr	Bethlehem Sheboygan WI	(920)452-5071	RF	2005
Schalow Kathleen S Rubin	(815)708-4424 kathyschalow@gmail.com	1416 Arden Ave Rockford IL 61107	NI	Teacher	Tchr	Immanuel Belvidere IL	(815)547-5346	RF	1985
Schamber Bonnie L Struck	(989)883-2518 schambeb@ctkl.org	5 Auch St Sebewaing MI 48759	MI	Teacher	EM			RF	1971
Schamber Gordon E	(225)266-1431 gschamber1@gmail.com	1505 Turret Dr Baton Rouge LA 70816	SO	Teacher	EM			S	1973
Schamber John G	(260)485-9104	6804 Briarcliff Dr Fort Wayne IN 46835	IN	Teacher	EM			S	1960
Schamber Kathleen A Bloch	(225)803-1635 kschamber44@gmail.com	1505 Turret Dr Baton Rouge LA 70816	SO	Teacher	EM			S	1973
Schamp Barbara A King	(303)669-5825 barb1st@q.com	7233 Deframe Ct Arvada CO 80005	RM	Teacher	EM			RF	1982
Schanbacher Tonya M Berns	(319)213-0432 tschanbacher@centrallutheran school.org	2929 72nd St Newhall IA 52315	IE	Teacher	Tchr	Central Newhall IA	(319)223-5271	CQ	2024
Scharlemann Sandra F Emmons Dr	(816)686-6446 jpczhar@aol.com	259 Candy Ln Redlands CA 92373	PSW	Teacher	EM			CQ	2007
Schatte Heidi J Arp	(281)517-0264	13302 Raven Flight Dr Cypress TX 77429	TX	Teacher	Tchr	Salem Tomball TX	(281)351-8223	CQ	2011

*Multiple Assignments (See Church Worker Locator for Additional Details)

See Page 53 for the Table of Abbreviations for key to District, Classification, Position, and College abbreviations.

**C =Candidate; EM =Emeritus; the date following the C is the month and year the Candidate status began

NAME	TELEPHONE NUMBER EMAIL	STREET ADDRESS CITY/STATE/ZIP	DISTRICT	CLASS.	POSITION/ STATUS**	WHERE SERVING	OFFICE PHONE	COLLEGE/ UNIV/CQ	YR GRAD
Schatte Rochelle K Davis		7525 Lake Rd Ponca City OK 74604	OK	Teacher	Tchr	First Ponca City OK	(580)762-9950	S	1979
Schatte William A II	(512)293-9167 william.schatte2@gmail.com	1110 Meadows Pl Jefferson Cty MO 65101	MO	Teacher	C07/2022			AU	1997
Schattschneider Allan R	(847)518-0927 s14al@comcast.net	516 N Home Ave Park Ridge IL 60068	NI	Teacher	EM			RF	1967
Schattschneider Susan J Rotermund	(847)518-0927 s14al@comcast.net	516 N Home Ave Park Ridge IL 60068	NI	Teacher	EM			RF	1967
Schatz Emily A Jung	(314)226-0917 emily.schatz1991@gmail.com	6732 Bear Creek Drive Saint Louis MO 63129	MO	DCE	Mem C	Webster Gardens Webster Groves MO	(314)961-5275	CH	2016
Schatz Gregory J	(812)327-8261 dcegreg@gmail.com	1908 N 30th St Norfolk NE 68701	NEB	DCE	Mem C	Our Savior Norfolk NE	(402)371-9005	CQ	2012
Schatz Holly G	(847)477-7252 schatzholly@gmail.com	175 N Main St South Elgin IL 60177	NI	Teacher	C07/2016			CH	2014
Schaubs Craig H	(414)333-8391 cschaubs@fils.org	W59N776 Highwood Dr Cedarburg WI 53012	SW	Teacher	EM			MQ	1983
Schaubs Kristine J Desotelle	(414)333-9047 kschaubs@yahoo.com	W59N776 Highwood Dr Cedarburg WI 53012	SW	Teacher	EM			MQ	1983
Schauer Angela K Lambrecht	(712)260-3039 spencerschauers@gmail.com	1618 Marks Ct Spencer IA 51301	IW	Teacher	Tchr	Iowa Great Lakes Spencer IA	(712)262-8237	SP	1990
Schauer Barbara J Stigge	(402)643-3145 arthurschauer@windstream.net	1441 Crestwood Dr Seward NE 68434	NEB	Teacher	EM			S	1967
Schauer Gideon M	(406)440-5593 gideon@trinitykalispell.org	121 Hawthorn Ave Apt 5 Kalispell MT 59901	MT	DCE	Mem C	Trinity Kalispell MT	(406)257-5683	S	2024
Schauer Hannah E Hannah Russell	(636)232-4573 dce.hr19@gmail.com		IE	DCE	C11/2023			CH	2019
Schauer Kimberly A	(507)358-1411 kischauer@rcls.net	18 Elton Ridge Ct NW Rochester MN 55901	MNS	Teacher	Tchr	Rochester Central Rochester MN	(507)289-3267	S	2000
Schaulat Ronald A Dr	(405)640-2564 batlshp@aol.com	8413 Sandpiper Rd Oklahoma City OK 73132	OK	Parish Assist	Mem C	Immanuel Oklahoma City OK	(405)525-5793	MQ	2011
Schaum Martha J Marquardt Deac	(256)349-8631 martharf95@gmail.com	223 Colorado Ave Muscle Shoals AL 35661	SO	Deaconess	C07/2016			RF	1995
Schaus Marvin W	(562)925-0132 mandsschaus@yahoo.com	13612 Woodruff Ave Bellflower CA 90706	PSW	Teacher	EM			S	1956
Schave Kimberly L Carr Deac	(513)309-3268 kimschave@hotmail.com	126 Peine Valley Ct Wentzville MO 63385	SW	Deaconess	S HS/C	Concordia University Wisconsin Mequon WI	(262)243-5700	FW-DEAC	2006
Scheck Dennis R Dr	(757)501-8019 drscheck@yahoo.com	12606 Pine Warbler San Antonio TX 78253	RM	Tch/DCE	M Chap	Office of International Mission Saint Louis MO		RF	1973
Schedler Jennifer K	(858)692-1752 jkschedler@gmail.com	2251 South Fort Apache Rd #2094 Las Vegas NV 89117	PSW	Teacher	Tchr	Faith Community Las Vegas NV	(702)921-2700	CQ	2013
Schedler Steven P	(858)229-1750 steve.schedler@psd.lcms.org	5940 Union Rd Pas Robles CA 93446	PSW	DCE	D Ex/S	Pacific Southwest District Irvine CA	(949)854-3232	IV	1984
Scheel Gretchen L Feuerborn	(630) 346-5528 gscheel@stjohnwheaton.org	1312 Anderson Dr Batavia IL 60510	NI	Teacher	Tchr	St John Wheaton IL	(630)668-0701	CQ	2016
Scheele Dean M	(952)250-1149 sdscheele@hotmail.com	809 16th St E Glencoe MN 55336	MNS	Teacher	EM			S	1985
Scheele Sheila J Friske	(320)296-0188 shescheele@hotmail.com	809 16th St E Glencoe MN 55336	MNS	Teacher	C07/2016			S	1983
Scheer Michelle A Smith	(281)990-9672 samscheer4@sbcglobal.net	15202 Ridgewell Dr Houston TX 77062	TX	Teacher	C07/2016			RF	1994
Scheeres Maribeth	(248)259-0302 bethscheeres@gmail.com	4115 Coolidge Hwy Royal Oak MI 48073	MI	Teacher	Tchr	St John Fraser MI	(586)293-0333	AA	1984
Schefft Sandra H Wulff	(419)343-2976 sschefft@bex.net	9564 Captiva Dr Sylvania OH 43560	OH	Teacher	EM			CQ	2001
Schefft Walter R	(618)420-4318 georgiawalt1@yahoo.com	904 Lillian St Collinsville IL 62234	SI	Teacher	EM			RF	1965
Scheiber Vernie W	(260)242-6210	117 S Morton St Kendallville IN 46755	IN	Teacher	EM			S	1974
Scheid Sherry A Boeck	(414)342-7750 sherryscheid1@gmail.com	2903 W State St Milwaukee WI 53208	SW	Teacher	EM			S	1976
Scheiderer Paul M	(812)521-3300 pscheiderer@immanuelseymour.com	1021 Gaiser Dr Seymour IN 47274	IN	Teacher	Mem C	Immanuel Seymour IN	(812)522-3118	AA	2002
Scheimann Robert E	(260)484-2821 rscheimann@aol.com	6723 S Anthony Blvd Apt E328 Fort Wayne IN 46816	IN	Teacher	EM			RF	1954
Scheiwe Jean R Rodammer	(989)684-4989 wascheiwe@charter.net	994 Amelith Rd Bay City MI 48706	MI	Teacher	EM			RF	1965
Scheiwe Robert N	(630)289-7279 scheiwer@trinityroselle.com	549 Harbor Ter Bartlett IL 60103	NI	Teacher	Tchr	Trinity Roselle IL	(630)894-3263	RF	1978
Scheiwe Warren A	(989)684-4989 wascheiwe@charter.net	994 Amelith Rd Bay City MI 48706	MI	Teacher	EM			RF	1964
Scheiwe Wendy A	(248)926-1323 wscheiwe@yahoo.com	1210 Amarillo St Wolverine Lk MI 48390	MI	Teacher	Tchr	St Matthew Walled Lake MI	(248)624-7677	RF	1990
Schelen Donna J Loesche	(817) 821-9337 donna97@sbcglobal.net	5617 Jamaica Cir N Richlnd Hls TX 76180	TX	Teacher	Tchr	Crown Of Life Colleyville TX	(817)251-1881	RF	1986
Schelen Rachel E	(682)715-9468 rachel99@att.net	3600 NW Expressway Oklahoma City OK 73112	OK	Teacher	Tchr	Messiah Oklahoma City OK	(405)946-0681	AU	2021
Schelen Rebecca A	(682)715-9415 beccaann99@sbcglobal.net	11500 Jollyville Rd Apt 312 Austin TX 78759	TX	Teacher	Tchr	Redeemer Austin TX	(512)459-1500	AU	2021
Scheller Brian M	(402)643-5147 bmscheller@me.com	2 Candlegate Ct Saint Peters MO 63376	MO	Teacher	Tchr	St Charles Saint Peters MO	(636)928-5100	S	2004
Scheller Sara A Safford	(314)616-1623 sscheller@immanuelstcharles.org	2 Candlegate Ct St. Peters MO 63376	MO	Teacher	Tchr	Immanuel Saint Charles MO	(636)946-2656	S	2004
Schelp Christopher P	(580)762-6579 splhcb67@yahoo.com	1413 De Soto St Ponca City OK 74604	OK	Tch/DPM	Mem C	First Ponca City OK	(580)762-1111	RF	2006

*Multiple Assignments (See Church Worker Locator for Additional Details)

See Page 53 for the Table of Abbreviations for key to District, Classification, Position, and College abbreviations.

**C =Candidate; EM =Emeritus; the date following the C is the month and year the Candidate status began

NAME	TELEPHONE NUMBER EMAIL	STREET ADDRESS CITY/STATE/ZIP	DISTRICT	CLASS.	POSITION/ STATUS**	WHERE SERVING	OFFICE PHONE	COLLEGE/ UNIV/CQ	YR GRAD
Schelp Keith A	(863)676-1157 kathleen.schelp@gmail.com	3544 Red Oak Ct Lake Wales FL 33898	FG	Teacher	EM			S	1974
Schempf Andrew M	(517)392-7208 andrew.schempf@gmail.com	4040 Hartford St Saint Louis MO 63116	MO	DPM	Mem C	Immanuel Saint Charles MO	(636)946-2656	CH	2007
Schempp Roberta A Hennig	(913)219-4331 schempp04@gmail.com	8417 Lewis Dr Lenexa KS 66227	KS	Teacher	EM			RF	1994
Schenaman Jennifer C	(402)802-1284 Jennifer.Schenaman@cune.org	3410 Russwood Ln Garland TX 75044	TX	Teacher	Tchr	Our Redeemer Dallas TX	(214)368-1371	S	2018
Schendel Elisa R Von Dielingen	(815)210-2917 ljschend@charter.net	71 Keywest Ct Four Seasons MO 65049	MO	Teacher	EM			S	1966
Schepker Karen L Steffens	(573)694-8793 ksteffens@gslscolumbia.org	8231 Tanner Bridge Rd Jefferson Cty MO 65101	MO	Teacher	Tchr	Immanuel Jefferson City MO	(573)496-3451	CQ	2001
Schepmann Gilbert F Sr	(513)519-7575 gschepmann@cinci.rr.com	7874 Golden Meadow Dr Mason OH 45040	OH	Teacher	EM			S	1969
Scherch Ronald C	(512)415-4737 ron.scherch@gmail.com	9504 Gunview Rd Nottingham MD 21236	SE	Tch/DCE	EM			RF	1973
Scherer Glenn D	(443) 463-7285 glenndscherer@gmail.com	16916 Flickerwood Rd Parkton MD 21120	SE	Teacher	EM			RF	1979
Schermbeck Cassandra J Pfeiffer	(512)818-1018 cschermbeck@ourfatherlutheran.net	6720 S Clermont St Centennial CO 80122	RM	DCE	Mem C	Our Father Centennial CO	(303)779-1332	S	1999
Scheske Melissa M Amling	(269)503-3696 mscheske@gmail.com	21425 Dogleg Dr Sturgis MI 49091	MI	Teacher	C06/2020			MQ	2006
Schettenhelm Karla J Witt	(734)462-8438 jknschett@aol.com	14326 Knolson St Livonia MI 48154	MI	Teacher	Tchr	Christ Our Savior Livonia MI	(734)513-8413	AA	1989
Scheuer James A	(414)595-1007 oconscheuer@gmail.com	4425 N 110th St Wauwatosa WI 53225	SW	Teacher	Tchr	Milwaukee LHS Milwaukee WI	(414)461-6000	MQ	1993
Scheuerman Doreen M Leptien Deac	(316)775-7301 dmlscheuerman@yahoo.com	100 Watson Angola St Coffeyville KS 67337	KS	Deaconess	EM			CQ	2005
Scheurman Linda L Piepenbrink	(847)352-2180 lscheurman48@gmail.com	620 Wileman Dr Edgerton WI 53534	EN	Teacher	EM			SP	1970
Schewe Sarah E Hinze	(319)480-3973 sschewe08@yahoo.com	18925 Hwy 38 Monticello IA 52310	IE	Teacher	C07/2016			MQ	2006
Schewe Sharon K Krueger	(651)485-0477 sharonks603@gmail.com	604 Shoreview Lane Norwood Young Americ MN 55397	MNS	Teacher	EM			S	1977
Schewe Sharyn J Meiers	(815)980-9715	877 Liddle Rd Rockton IL 61072	NI	Teacher	EM			RF	1972
Schiebel Josephine M Fabricius	(207)248-9051 schiebel.jo@gmail.com	802 Lakeview Dr China ME 04358	NE	Teacher	C07/2020			S	2001
Schieber Helmut E	(620)272-2001 chespirito0707@yahoo.com	1598 Tallulah Ter Wesley Chapel FL 33543	FG	DCE	C07/2016			S	1981
Schiefer Carl L	(561)393-7405 skatjoy@bellsouth.com	2036 S Conference Dr Boca Raton FL 33486	FG	Teacher	Tchr	St Paul Boca Raton FL	(561)395-8548	RF	1963
Schiefer Mark T	(989)971-9815 theschief@hotmail.com	P.O. Box 144 Richville MI 48758	MI	Teacher	EM			RF	1974
Schiefer Staci L Arnholt	(812)344-0564 staci.schiefer@stpeters-columbus.org	5645 E Fountain Way Columbus IN 47201	IN	DCE	Prin	St Peter Columbus IN	(812)372-5266	RF	2002
Schield Daniel N	(218)830-9840 danielschield@gmail.com		MNS	Teacher	Tchr	Trinity Lone Oak Eagan MN	(651)454-1139	SP	2010
Schiemann Kathleen R Wardin	(989)642-8923 krschiemann@juno.com	260 Doyle Rd Hemlock MI 48626	MI	Teacher	EM			RF	1972
Schiemann Michael T	(971)371-0143 mikets9729@gmail.com	61143 Splendor Ln. Bend OR 97002	NOW	Teacher		Northwest District Portland OR	(503)288-8383	CQ	2005
Schiestel Delaine S Hughes	(847)571-4042 delaineschiestel@gmail.com	7600 Teal Dr SW Huntsville AL 35802	SO	Teacher	C07/2025			RF	1988
Schildwachter Paul J	(443)686-0125 pschild15@gmail.com	2101 Albrook Ct Fallston MD 21047	SE	Teacher	Tchr	Concordia Towson MD	(410)825-2323	BR	1976
Schilf Kenneth M	(260)580-2599 schilfmeister@gmail.com	6723 S. Anthony Blvd. Apt. E128 Fort Wayne IN 46816	IN	Tch/DCE	EM			RF	1966
Schilf Paul R Dr	(605)376-0981 pauls@popplersmusic.com	2801 N Oak Rd Brandon SD 57005	SD	Teacher	EM			RF	1983
Schilke Nadine L Francis	(414)510-4932 nadine6109@icloud.com	9052 Westlake Dr Greendale WI 53129	EN	Teacher	EM			RF	1983
Schiller Angela L Berg	(314)276-6854 stlbluesfan07@gmail.com	5421 Anaheim Ave Pflugerville TX 78660	TX	Teacher	Prin	Redeemer Austin TX	(512)451-6478	CQ	2003
Schiller Charles A	(985)789-0766 sptiger4@hotmail.com	989 Beauregard Pkwy Covington LA 70433	SO	Teacher	EM			S	1973
Schilling Rebecca A Maassel	(586)863-7847 raschilling22@gmail.com	32071 Di Stefano Ct Fraser MI 48026	MI	Teacher	Tchr	Saint Peters Eastpointe MI	(586)777-6300	CQ	2005
Schilling Scott D	(708)269-4753	19451 Donelson Ln Westfield IN 46062	NI	Teacher	EM			RF	1980
Schilling Timothy R	(586)863-7863 curfhof@comcast.net	32071 Di Stefano Ct Fraser MI 48026	MI	Teacher	EM			RF	1984
Schilling Wendy L Lange	(952)846-9500 wschilling@ccls.net	1270 County Road 92 Maple Plain MN 55359	MNS	Teacher	Tchr	Christ Community Watertown MN	(952)955-1419	MQ	1985
Schimank Penny A Pfeiffer		1212 County Road 338 Lincoln TX 78948	TX	Teacher	Tchr	Immanuel Giddings TX	(979)542-3319	AU	1983
Schimke Pamela L Seeman	plschimke@gmail.com	19212 N 40th St Phoenix AZ 85050	PSW	Teacher	EM			S	1977
Schimm Alisha D Bohnert	(989)708-4851 alisha.bohnert@gmail.com	5212 Henry St Muskegon MI 49441	EN	DPM	C05/2021			S	2011
Schimm Naomi R Rush	(989)493-5835 nschimm@yahoo.com	P.O. Box 1095 Bay City MI 48706	MI	Teacher	EM			RF	1976
Schimm Peter A	(602)781-4519 pschm22@gmail.com	3394 Terry St Saginaw MI 48604	MI	Teacher	Mem C	St Paul Bay City MI	(989)684-4450	CH	2014

*Multiple Assignments (See Church Worker Locator for Additional Details)
See Page 53 for the Table of Abbreviations for key to District, Classification, Position, and College abbreviations.
**C =Candidate; EM =Emeritus; the date following the C is the month and year the Candidate status began

NAME	TELEPHONE NUMBER EMAIL	STREET ADDRESS CITY/STATE/ZIP	DISTRICT	CLASS.	POSITION/ STATUS**	WHERE SERVING	OFFICE PHONE	COLLEGE/ UNIV/CQ	YR GRAD
Schindler Belva J Walz	(520)243-0283 belvaschin@aol.com	2001 W Rudasill Rd Apt 1211 Tucson AZ 85704	EN	Teacher	EM			S	1962
Schingeck Briana M	(920)227-8308 brianaschingeck@gmail.com	E0958 County Road N Luxemburg WI 54217	NW	Teacher	Tchr	St Paul Luxemburg WI	(920)845-2095	CQ	2020
Schipper Stuart P	(585)377-0350	Fairport Baptist Home Room F316 4646 Nine Mile Point Road Fairport NY 14450	IN	Teacher	EM			SP	1977
Schipporeit Jeanette E	(402)379-2286 jschipporeit@gmail.com	825 S 9th St Norfolk NE 68701	NEB	Teacher	EM			S	1973
Schipull Douglas W Dr	(773)724-1257	5581 Shadow Grove Blvd Pensacola FL 32526	S	Teacher	EM			S	1969
Schirrmacher Mary L Boehlke	(949) 331-6488 mrs.schirrmacher@gmail.com	4942 Greencap Ave Irvine CA 92604	PSW	Teacher	Tchr	Saint Johns Orange CA	(714)288-4400	IV	1994
Schiwart Melvin E	(281)351-4234 schiwartm@hotmail.com	30619 Quinn Rd Tomball TX 77375	TX	Teacher	EM			S	1967
Schkade Juli A Wolfe	(214)727-3364 jschkade@ziondallas.org	10135 Plummer Dr Dallas TX 75228	TX	Teacher	Tchr	Zion Dallas TX	(214)363-1639	AU	1999
Schkade Kristi J Kriete	(618)409-4636 kristischkade@gmail.com	7104 Mastin St Merriam KS 66203	KS	Teacher	Tchr	Hope Shawnee KS	(913)631-6940	S	1998
Schlecht Jonathan E	(970)237-2463 jonathanschlecht@gmail.com	18213 French Creek Ave Parker CO 80134	RM	Teacher	Tchr	Colorado Lutheran High School Parker CO	(303)841-5551	MQ	2019
Schlecht Katherine R Johnson Dr	(970)203-4396 kschlecht@immanuelloveland.org	3306 Franklin Ave Loveland CO 80538	RM	DPM	Mem C	Immanuel Loveland CO	(970)667-4506	SP	1984
Schlehlein Joan K Treise	(262)895-7588 jtschlehlein@yahoo.com	26614 Waubeesee Lake Dr Wind Lake WI 53185	EN	Teacher	EM			SP	1972
Schleicher Amy L Walquist	(281)825-1948 amyschleicher81@gmail.com	22419 Willow Creek Bridge Ln Tomball TX 77375	TX	Teacher	C07/2016			S	2007
Schleicher Chelsea Vaudt	(832)702-5152	c/o Trinity Lutheran School 18926 Klein Church Rd Spring TX 77379	TX	Teacher	Tchr	Trinity Spring TX	(281)376-5810	S	2011
Schleicher Kimberly J Walquist	(281)475-9871 schleicherk@trinityklein.org	7810 Mayglen Ln Spring TX 77379	TX	Teacher	Tchr	Trinity Spring TX	(281)376-5810	S	2002
Schleicher Matthew J	(281)475-9870 mschleicher@elcsh.org	7810 Mayglen Ln Spring TX 77379	TX	Teacher	Prin	Epiphany Houston TX	(713)896-1843	MQ	2001
Schleifer Heidi A	(828)400-3956 haschleifer@gmail.com	51 Wilburn Pl Asheville NC 28806	SE	Teacher	Tchr	Emmanuel Asheville NC	(828)252-1795	MQ	2011
Schlesselman David A	(636)578-1766 daschlesselman@gmail.com	66 Dansbury Creek Ct Saint Peters MO 63376	MO	Teacher	EM			S	1970
Schlesselman Roberta W Winters	(608)687-8730	S 3104 N Shore Dr Fountain City WI 54629	MNS	Teacher	EM			RF	1975
Schley Calista Hoewisch	(920)810-5643 calschley@gmail.com	E8854 County Rd O Clintonville WI 54929	NW	Teacher	Tchr	St Martin Clintonville WI	(715)823-6538	MQ	2014
Schley Margaret J Trautmann	(586)612-7654 peggyjschley@gmail.com	32955 N River Rd Harrison Twp MI 48045	MI	Teacher	EM			CQ	1996
Schlicht Haley M	haleyschlicht@gmail.com		NW	Teacher	Tchr	Saint James Shawano WI	(715)524-4815	CH	2016
Schlichtemeier Kent A Dr	(714)944-2768 kent.schlichtemeier@cui.edu	32 Sorenson Irvine CA 92602	PSW	Teacher	S HS/C	Concordia University Irvine Irvine CA	(949)854-8002	S	1978
Schlichting Kevin R	(281)773-1171 schlichting3rd@gmail.com	11326 N Country Club Green Dr Tomball TX 77375	TX	Teacher	EM			S	1979
Schlichtmann Dian M	(715)315-4062 dschlichtmann@stpaulequips.com	3322 Wilson Ave Plover WI 54467	NW	Teacher	Tchr	St Paul Stevens Point WI	(715)344-5660	S	1990
Schlicker Christin C Simon	(702)219-2553 cschlicker@mvlcs.org	8505 Gold Flash Ave Las Vegas NV 89129	PSW	Teacher	Tchr	Mountain View Las Vegas NV	(702)360-8290	RF	2000
Schlicker David J	(218)826-6389 djschlick@gmail.com	29234 County Highway 45 Underwood MN 56586	MNN	Teacher	EM			S	1968
Schlicker Esther A Heintz	(218)826-6389 easchlick@gmail.com	29234 County Highway 45 Underwood MN 56586	MNN	Teacher	EM			S	1969
Schlicker Tavis J	(832)260-3729	2711 Crossbranch Ct Fort Wayne IN 46825	IN	Teacher	Mem C	Concordia Fort Wayne IN	(260)422-2429	S	2001
Schlie Abigail L Difatta	(414)748-1041 aschlie@hotmail.com	6709 Moss Ct Indianapolis IN 46237	IN	Teacher	Tchr	Indianapolis Indianapolis IN	(317)787-5474	AA	1995
Schlie Angela R Specht	(815)985-4537 angiehasemail@gmail.com	9658 S California Ave Evergreen Pk IL 60805	NI	Teacher	C01/2022			RF	1999
Schlie David J	(414)339-5658 aschlie@hotmail.com	6709 Moss Ct Indianapolis IN 46237	IN	Teacher	Tchr	Indianapolis Indianapolis IN	(317)787-5474	S	1993
Schlie Penny L Thomas	(816)806-4844 pshcls@yahoo.com	628 NE 96th Terr Kansas City MO 64155	MO	Teacher	EM			S	1974
Schlie Rachel C McCall	(830)992-1998 rachel.schlie@outlook.com	2898 Chapel Bend Dr Hixson TN 37343	MDS	Teacher	C07/2016			MQ	2009
Schlimpert Charles E Dr	(406)363-4488 orazmt@gmail.com	8597 E Arroyo Seco Rd Scottsdale AZ 85266	PSW	Teacher	EM			RF	1968
Schlotman Cindy L Puls O Hara	(440)829-7201 ctohara2@aol.com	5049 Fitch Dr Sheffield Vlg OH 44054	OH	Teacher	EM			RF	1985
Schlotterbeck Katherine L Mountford	(239)338-8462 katie.schlotterbeck@bvhs.org	17040 Carolyn Ln N Ft Myers FL 33917	FG	Teacher	EM			RF	1982
Schluckebier Lee E Dr	(402)643-6441 lees@tentcords.org	306 Bradford St Seward NE 68434	NEB	Teacher	EM			S	1968
Schluckebier Melinda D Sobek	mschluckebier@comcast.net	1606 Prairie Hawk Dr Longmont CO 80504	RM	DCE	C07/2016			RF	1994
Schlueter Mary K Lowke	(714)998-8864 mkschlueter14@gmail.com	234 E Woodvale Ave Orange CA 92865	PSW	Teacher	EM			S	1978
Schlueter Michelle J Wolfram	(515) 305-4542 michelles1914@outlook.com	195 Cari Cir Waukee IA 50263	IW	Teacher	C07/2016			SP	2002

*Multiple Assignments (See Church Worker Locator for Additional Details)
See Page 53 for the Table of Abbreviations for key to District, Classification, Position, and College abbreviations.
**C =Candidate; EM =Emeritus; the date following the C is the month and year the Candidate status began

NAME	TELEPHONE NUMBER EMAIL	STREET ADDRESS CITY/STATE/ZIP	DISTRICT	CLASS.	POSITION/ STATUS**	WHERE SERVING	OFFICE PHONE	COLLEGE/ UNIV/CQ	YR GRAD
Schmaltz Norman J Dr	(407)366-7280 schmaltzn@bellsouth.net	1525 Haven Dr Oviedo FL 32765	FG	Teacher	EM			RF	1954
Schmand Mary A Schrader	(901)481-3715 maryschmand@gmail.com	2462 E Hawthorne Rd Bartlett TN 38134	MDS	Teacher	EM			RF	1966
Schmeckpeper Cathy A Schoeling	(630)554-5652 ryanandcathy@sbcglobal.net	4830 Reservation Rd Oswego IL 60543	NI	Teacher	Tchr	Cross Yorkville IL	(630)553-7861	RF	1997
Schmeisser Chelsie K MacIntosh Deac	chelsieschmeisser@gmail.com	500 Berkey Ave Swanville MN 56382	MNN	Deaconess	C02/2024			FW-DEAC	2020
Schmelling Brenda Segovia	(408)512-8708 bschmelling@stlukes-church.com	17311 28th Ave E Tacoma WA 98445	NOW	DCE	Mem C	St Lukes Federal Way WA	(253)941-3000	IV	2015
Schmich Deborah K Pranschke	dkschmich@hotmail.com	1554 Roy Dr Arnold MO 63010	MO	Teacher	EM			CQ	1994
Schmid Erna I Baehr Deac	(520)578-2837 bobnerna@msn.com	6038 W Ten Star Rd Tucson AZ 85713	PSW	Deaconess	EM			RF	1992
Schmid John E	(815)319-5052 jschmid@mtolivelutheran.com	1736 Cumberland St Rockford IL 61103	NI	Teacher	Mem C	Mount Olive Rockford IL	(815)399-3171	S	1993
Schmid Jonathan P	(618)920-6373	1504 Westhampton Trce Belleville IL 62220	SI	Teacher	Tchr	Zion Belleville IL	(618)234-0275	S	1998
Schmid KerriAnn R Kothe	(618)222-1920 kkothe@zionbelleville.org	1504 Westhampton Trce Belleville IL 62220	SI	DCE	Mem C	Zion Belleville IL	(618)233-2299	S	2001
Schmid Steven P	(314)600-1217	1023 Scenic Oaks Ct Imperial MO 63052	MO	Teacher	Tchr	Lutheran South Saint Louis MO	(314)631-1400	MQ	1993
Schmidt Allan H Dr	(402) 643-5490 alla.schmi@gmail.com	1538 Eastridge Ave Seward NE 68434	NEB	Teacher	S Miss	Office of International Mission Saint Louis MO		RF	1960
Schmidt Amy M Cloeter	(734)904-6266 amycschmidt@gmail.com	1131 Stony Rapids Bay Lincoln NE 68505	NEB	Teacher	Tchr	Messiah Lincoln NE	(402)489-3024	S	2000
Schmidt Amy R Ruder	(515)556-9159 amy@amyrschmidt.com	8340 S 61st St Lincoln NE 68516	NEB	DCE	Mem C	Christ Lincoln NE	(402)483-7774	S	2006
Schmidt Andrea K Bodtke	aschmidt@splhs.org	1218 S Bismark St Concordia MO 64020	MO	Teacher	Tchr	Saint Paul Concordia MO	(660)463-2238	CQ	2003
Schmidt Brenda S Thoelke	(314)849-2156 mom1424@sbcglobal.net	13733 Hagemann Crossing Ct Saint Louis MO 63128	MO	Teacher	EM			CQ	2009
Schmidt Carla R Brandt Deac	(636)923-2364 carla.schmidt@lssliving.org	5601 Ravenwood Dr Jefferson Cty MO 65109	MO	Deaconess	Inst C	Lutheran Senior Services DBA EverTrue Brentwood MO	(314)968-9313	SL-DEAC	2010
Schmidt Casandra E Eberth	(913)333-9951 casandraeberth@gmail.com	4231 Tupelo Dr. St Louis MO 63125	MO	Teacher	Tchr	Word of Life Saint Louis MO	(314)832-1244	S	2019
Schmidt Deborah J Hays	(260)615-9385 dschmidt@cluth.org	15008 Prairie Park CV Hoagland IN 46745	IN	Teacher	Tchr	Central New Haven IN	(260)493-2502	CQ	2003
Schmidt Deborah L Doege	(219)923-8560 ctschm@hotmail.com	9143 Southmoor Ave Highland IN 46322	IN	Teacher	EM			S	1973
Schmidt Dennis M	(989)662-2477 dszion@gmail.com	4854 11 Mile Rd Auburn MI 48611	MI	Teacher	EM			S	1971
Schmidt Elizabeth A Dippel	(832)482-7209 mrs.elizabeth.schmidt@gmail.com	515 Pasadena Dr Lexington KY 40503	IN	Teacher	Tchr	St Johns Lexington KY	(859)275-1907	AU	2013
Schmidt Elizabeth R	(715)853-1969 schmidte@trinitynet.org	1111 S 50th Ave Apt 13 Wausau WI 54401	NW	Teacher	Tchr	Trinity Wausau WI	(715)848-0166	MQ	2023
Schmidt Erich L	(979)716-7568 schmidt@lutheranhigh.com	3917 Mendocino Ln Apt 110 Sheboygan WI 53083	SW	Teacher	Tchr	Sheboygan Sheboygan WI	(920)452-3323	S	2014
Schmidt Evelyn I Reuter	(785)380-1668	410 East 8th St Apt 8 Alma KS 66401	KS	Teacher	EM			S	1957
Schmidt Gail A Imhoff	(602)692-9153 azgaschmidt@gmail.com	3590 E Remington Dr Gilbert AZ 85297	PSW	Teacher	EM			RF	1975
Schmidt Gerald R	(715)509-0281 58g.schmidt@gmail.com	W3592 Old Dump Rd Bonduel WI 54107	NW	Teacher	EM			MQ	1982
Schmidt Grant L	(402)643-5534 gschmidt@ogt.org	637 Penrose Dr Lincoln NE 68521	NEB	Teacher	RSO	Orphan Grain Train Inc Norfolk NE	(402)371-7393	S	1983
Schmidt Harold J	(763)355-4024 halschmidt@outlook.com	26569 W Vista N Dr Buckeye AZ 85396	PSW	Teacher	EM			S	1978
Schmidt Heather M Haschka	(414)659-6809 heather@dsronline.com	7288 W Pineberry Rdg Franklin WI 53132	EN	Teacher	C06/2022			CQ	2007
Schmidt James A	(870)674-7572 james.schmidt@suddenlink.net	406 Louann Dr Mountain Home AR 72653	MDS	Teacher	EM			S	1965
Schmidt Joel H	(847)313-5048 joelschmidt@comcast.net	325 Foxfire Dr Lake Zurich IL 60047	NI	Teacher	EM			RF	1960
Schmidt John C	(347)281-9401 mschm82383@netscape.net	1835 Hone Ave Bronx NY 10461	AT	Teacher	EM			SP	1975
Schmidt Karen A Payer	(630)334-4206 kschmidt836@comcast.net	836 S School St Lombard IL 60148	NI	Teacher	EM			Other	1974
Schmidt Kenneth E Dr	(512)496-9717 kenandmargene@mac.com	3589 S Lisbon Ct Aurora CO 78665	RM	Teacher	EM			S	1967
Schmidt Kristen A Clausen	(949)854-4873	13 Evening Breeze Irvine CA 92603	PSW	Teacher	S HS/C	Concordia University Irvine Irvine CA	(949)854-8002	RF	1980
Schmidt Kristina M Christensen	(785)587-8213 kristinas@usd383.org	1800 Little Kitten Ave Manhattan KS 66503	KS	DCE	EM			IV	1993
Schmidt Kurt E	(586)764-5714 iiiontheprize@yahoo.com	33641 Utica Rd #6 Fraser MI 48026	MI	Teacher	Tchr	St Paul Royal Oak MI	(248)546-6555	S	1983
Schmidt Lester O Dr	(816)741-1520 lsch1571@gmail.com	9101 N Ambassador Dr Apt 1104 Kansas City MO 64154	KS	Tch/DCE	EM			RF	1962
Schmidt Lindsey M Burken	(651)592-1818 burkenschmidt@gmail.com	9409 Hale Ave S Cottage Grove MN 55016	MNS	DCE	Mem C	Woodbury Woodbury MN	(651)739-5144	SP	2005
Schmidt Lisa A Hembry	(979)716-7526 lschmidt1989@gmail.com	1572 County Road 211 Giddings TX 78942	TX	Teacher	C10/2020			S	1989
Schmidt Lu Ann L Schauer	(320)864-6523 schmidtlu13@gmail.com	16405 Garden Ave Glencoe MN 55336	MNS	Teacher	EM			CQ	2008

*Multiple Assignments (See Church Worker Locator for Additional Details)
See Page 53 for the Table of Abbreviations for key to District, Classification, Position, and College abbreviations.
**C =Candidate; EM =Emeritus; the date following the C is the month and year the Candidate status began

NAME	TELEPHONE NUMBER EMAIL	STREET ADDRESS CITY/STATE/ZIP	DISTRICT	CLASS.	POSITION/ STATUS**	WHERE SERVING	OFFICE PHONE	COLLEGE/ UNIV/CQ	YR GRAD
Schmidt Luther W Dr	(660)463-8090 lschmidt@splhs.org	1218 S Bismark St Concordia MO 64020	MO	Teacher	Tchr	Saint Paul Concordia MO	(660)463-2238	CQ	2006
Schmidt Mara R Rautenberg	maraschmidt@comcast.net	1342 Portsmouth Ave Westchester IL 60154	NI	Teacher	EM			RF	1979
Schmidt Martin E Dr			NEB	Teacher	S Miss	Office of International Mission Saint Louis MO		S	1990
Schmidt Mary E Bierlein	(847)757-7098 joelschmidt@comcast.net	325 Foxfire Dr Lake Zurich IL 60047	NI	Teacher	EM			RF	1960
Schmidt Mary J	(970)379-6135 smtnfam@aol.com	9511 Castle Ridge Cir Highlands Ranch CO 80129	RM	Teacher	C10/2017			S	1985
Schmidt Michael A	(715)509-0002 schmidtm@newlhs.com	2441 Wilder St Green Bay WI 54311	NW	Teacher	Tchr	Northeastern WI Green Bay WI	(920)469-6810	CQ	2006
Schmidt Miranda Spears	(618)301-0884 mspears91@gmail.com	3661 G Rd Fults IL 62244	MO	DCE	Mem C	Faith Oakville MO	(314)846-8612	RF	2015
Schmidt Paul M	(313)929-0338	19015 Henry St Melvindale MI 48122	MI	Teacher	EM			S	1964
Schmidt Phyllis L Parsons	(414)210-5564	3136 S 54th Milwaukee WI 53219	SW	Teacher	EM			RF	1962
Schmidt Ralph R	(847)394-0526 schmidtrrs@aol.com	1203 N Belmont Ave Arlington Hts IL 60004	NI	Teacher	EM			RF	1954
Schmidt Rebecca S Breyer Dr	(636)634-6559 becky.schmidt100@gmail.com	517 Muirfield Dr Saint Charles MO 63304	MO	Teacher	EM			CQ	1993
Schmidt Sandra J Toennies	(989)662-2477 sjschmidt4854@charter.net	4854 11 Mile Rd Auburn MI 48611	MI	Teacher	EM			RF	1976
Schmidt Sandra R Jessen Dawson	(479)601-6482 sanschmidt50@gmail.com	9465 Main St Altenburg MO 63732	MO	Teacher	EM			S	1973
Schmidt Shannon R Bloch	(417)889-9060 sschmidt@rlcmail.org	2941 W Highpoint St Springfield MO 65810	MO	Teacher	Tchr	Redeemer Springfield MO	(417)883-5717	CQ	2014
Schmidt Stephanie Baune	(949)870-0139 greatogo200@gmail.com	964 Lismore Dr Columbus GA 31904	FG	DCE	C07/2016			IV	2015
Schmidt Tanner C	tschmidt@lwlhs.com	725 Meadowbrook Dr West Bend WI 53090	SW	Teacher	Tchr	Living Word Jackson WI	(262)677-9353	MQ	2015
Schmidt Terry L	(314)846-5197 terrylschmidt06@yahoo.com	7251 Orchid Meadow Ct Saint Louis MO 63129	MO	Teacher	EM			RF	1972
Schmidt Victoria L Jerke	(408)679-2299 vschmidt@immanueltf.org	2171 Rusty Ct Twin Falls ID 83301	NOW	Teacher	Tchr	Immanuel Twin Falls ID	(208)733-7820	S	1998
Schmidt Warren R	(479)601-6458 wrschmidt25@gmail.com	9465 Main St Altenburg MO 63732	MO	Teacher	EM			S	1972
Schmidt Wayne A Dr	(623)252-9153 waschmidt50@gmail.com	3590 E Remington Dr Gilbert AZ 85297	PSW	Teacher	EM			RF	1972
Schmidt William G	(260)436-7021 williamgschmidt4@yahoo.com	6436 Covington Rd Fort Wayne IN 46804	IN	Teacher	EM			SP	1967
Schmidtgoessling Karen L Wysik	(513)451-2013 mamagoose52@gmail.com	2280 Townhill Dr Cincinnati OH 45238	OH	Teacher	EM			RF	1974
Schmidtke Beverly D Wolters	(507)384-1710 bev_schmidtke@hotmail.com	13909 Lake Ave Lakewood OH 44107	OH	Teacher	EM			S	1975
Schmidtke Nathaniel D	(314)809-8411 natschmidtke@clspeoria.org	3805 N Sheridan Rd Peoria IL 61614	CI	Teacher	Prin	Christ Peoria IL	(309)637-1512	SP	2016
Schmieding Suzanne K Rader	(618)277-3741 jschmieding@sbcglobal.net	1050 Fountain Lakes Dr Apt 320 O Fallon IL 62269	SI	Teacher	EM			S	1967
Schmiesing Valerie L Desena	(443)604-2139 teach407@comcast.net	18 Holden St Unit A Attleboro MA 02703	NE	Teacher	EM			RF	1974
Schmit Harvey M Dr	(734)896-0548 harvschmit@hotmail.com	2553 River Woods Dr N Canton MI 48188	MI	Teacher	EM			RF	1975
Schmit James D	(847)840-0007 jschmit14@yahoo.com	1280 Village Dr Apt 369 Arlington Heights IL 60004	NI	Teacher	EM			RF	1963
Schmit Steven P	(734)259-9126 schmitsteven@gmail.com	8273 Berkshire Dr Ypsilanti MI 48198	MI	Teacher	Tchr	St Paul Ann Arbor MI	(734)665-9117	AA	2011
Schmitt Ellen M Daniel	(847)401-9648 ellenmarieschmitt@gmail.com	1308 Mulberry St Yankton SD 57078	SD	Teacher	C08/2017			CH	2013
Schmitt Joshua M	(605)500-9247 joshuamichaelschmitt@gmail.com	1308 Mulberry St. Yankton SD 57078	SD	DCE	Mem C	St John Yankton SD	(605)665-7337	IV	2017
Schmitz Barbara M Schweizer	(828)712-7861 barbschmitz461@gmail.com	450 Blue Earth Ln Harrisburg IL 62946	SI	Teacher	EM			S	1989
Schmitz Betty E Isringhaus	(618)282-6836 bschmitz@stjohnsredbud.org	124 E Red Bud St Red Bud IL 62278	SI	Teacher	Tchr	St John Red Bud IL	(618)282-3873	CQ	1983
Schmitz Mark H	(920)980-9560 mark.schmitz@cuw.edu	2607 Mill Rd Sheboygan WI 53083	SW	Teacher	S HS/C	Concordia University Wisconsin Mequon WI	(262)243-5700	CQ	2019
Schmitzer Jill A Warnsholz	(563)340-5252 jill.schmitzer@trinitydavenport.org		IE	Teacher	Tchr	Trinity Davenport IA	(563)322-5224	CQ	2013
Schmucker Calvin F Dr	(231)492-2031 2cschmucker@gmail.com	12100 Cherry Ln South Lyon MI 48178	MI	Teacher	EM			CQ	2003
Schnabel Kirsten L Bowers	(630)707-6717 kschnabel23@gmail.com	250 Chatham Ln Roselle IL 60172	NI	Teacher	Tchr	St Luke Itasca IL	(630)773-0509	RF	1997
Schnack Deborah G Nelson	(734)358-3951 debbyschnack@gmail.com	3740 W Four Ridge Rd House Springs MO 63051	MO	Teacher	EM			RF	1975
Schnack John C	(734)358-3952 jcschnack@gmail.com	3740 W Four Ridge Dr House Springs MO 63051	MO	Teacher	EM			RF	1975
Schnackenberg Melvin P	(301)593-9460 schnackm@verizon.net	10011 Kinross Ave Silver Spring MD 20901	SE	Teacher	EM			RF	1956
Schnake Richard K I Dr	(262)241-9647 richard.schnake@cuw.edu	121 W Highview Dr Thiensville WI 53092	SW	Teacher	EM			S	1972
Schnakenberg Barbara L Schutte	(660)343-5359 bschnak@hotmail.com	32600 Schlobohm Smithton MO 65350	MO	Teacher	Tchr	Luth School Assoc Cole Camp MO	(660)668-4614	CQ	2003

*Multiple Assignments (See Church Worker Locator for Additional Details)

See Page 53 for the Table of Abbreviations for key to District, Classification, Position, and College abbreviations.

**C =Candidate; EM =Emeritus; the date following the C is the month and year the Candidate status began

NAME	TELEPHONE NUMBER EMAIL	STREET ADDRESS CITY/STATE/ZIP	DISTRICT	CLASS.	POSITION/ STATUS**	WHERE SERVING	OFFICE PHONE	COLLEGE/ UNIV/CQ	YR GRAD
Schnakenberg Laurie A Pautsch	(616)801-3121 laup547@yahoo.com	333 Valley Dr Zeeland MI 49464	RM	Teacher	Tchr	Trinity Greeley CO	(970)330-2485	S	2004
Schnare Dawn L Otten	(618)973-3169 zndschnare@gmail.com	414 Walnut St P.O. Box 303 Alhambra IL 62001	SI	Teacher	C08/2020			S	2007
Schnare Diane J Cook	(618)623-5887 tndschnare@gmail.com	P.O. Box 493 237 Hamel Avenue Hamel IL 62046	SI	Teacher	Tchr	St Paul Worden IL	(618)633-2209	S	1976
Schnare Zachariah D	(618)973-2426 zachariah.schnare@gmail.com	414 Walnut St P.O. Box 303 Alhambra IL 62001	SI	Teacher	S Ex/S	The LCMS Corporate Saint Louis MO	(314)965-9000	S	2009
Schnarre Amber R Kroening	(618)977-3104 alissecond@alisrockets.com	910 E 1425th Ave Beecher City IL 62414	CI	Teacher	Tchr	Altamont Altamont IL	(618)483-6428	CQ	2021
Schneck Joy C Stottlemyer	(360)624-8258 joybell13@aol.com	4 Founders Way Unit B Saint Louis MO 63105	OH	DCE	C07/2016			RF	2007
Schnegelberger Aaron M	(214)457-8644 aschnegelberger@gmail.com	444 Sheffield Richardson TX 75081	TX	Teacher	Tchr	Zion Dallas TX	(214)363-1639	S	2001
Schnegelberger Christine L Allyn	(303)776-0640	1526 Mallard Dr Johnstown CO 80534	RM	Teacher	Tchr	Immanuel Loveland CO	(970)667-7606	S	1971
Schnegelberger Emma F	(214)642-8186 eschnegelberger@zionharvester.org	3355 Ridgeway Drive St. Charles MO 63303	MO	Teacher	Tchr	Zion Saint Charles MO	(636)441-7424	CH	2024
Schnegelberger Rachel M		444 Sheffield Richardson TX 75081	TX	Teacher	Tchr	Zion Dallas TX	(214)363-1639	S	2001
Schneider Amanda R Zimmer	amandaschneider410@gmail.com	N45W24434 Lindsay Rd Stop 1 Pewaukee WI 53072	SW	Teacher	Tchr	Grace Menomonee Falls WI	(262)251-7140	MQ	2008
Schneider Carol S Swander	(913)206-3477 carolschneider75@gmail.com	17528 W 116th St Olathe KS 66061	KS	Teacher	EM			S	1979
Schneider Christopher A	(512)585-6784 aaron.schneider@lutheransouth.org	15003 Coral Sands Dr Houston TX 77062	TX	Teacher	Tchr	South Houston TX	(281)464-8299	AU	2007
Schneider Debra A Zuege	(262)781-6543 jrsdas77@gmail.com	4455 N 143rd St Brookfield WI 53005	SW	Teacher	EM			RF	1976
Schneider Deitt C Borrenpohl	(618)824-6335 deitt@stjohnsredbud.org	8549 Primrose Rd Venedy IL 62214	SI	Teacher	Tchr	St John Baldwin IL	(618)785-2344	RF	1976
Schneider Erin N	(903)423-8258 erinwoods31@gmail.com	PMB 329 4500 Williams Dr Ste 212 Georgetown TX 78633	TX	Teacher	Tchr	St Paul Thorndale TX	(512)898-5455	AU	2021
Schneider Janis E	(313)928-1094	9322 Niver Ave Allen Park MI 48101	MI	Teacher	EM			RF	1975
Schneider Kathryn Amendt	(515)210-6329 kathrynschneiderm@gmail.com		IW	DCE	Mem C	Zion Manning IA	(712)655-2352	AU	2013
Schneider Kristopher E	(707)761-0946 kschneider@mvlcs.org	3213 Paragon Pointe St Las Vegas NV 89129	PSW	Teacher	Prin	Mountain View Las Vegas NV	(702)360-8290	IV	1995
Schneider Leah A Ryan	(812)521-1059 schneiderleah@msn.com	5910 N US Highway 31 Seymour IN 47274	IN	Teacher	Tchr	Trinity Seymour IN	(812)524-8547	CQ	2012
Schneider Lori A Stockhaus	(847)498-3060 nutworks@verizon.net	3151 N Daniels Ct Arlington Hts IL 60004	NI	Teacher	Tchr	Seeds of Grace Northbrook IL	(847)498-3060	AA	2004
Schneider Mary A	(812)521-2984	16200 S 300 W Columbus IN 47201	IN	Teacher	Tchr	White Creek Columbus IN	(812)342-6832	CH	2008
Schneider Naomi M Kahle	(715)722-0152 nkahle2532@charter.net	W4755 Golf Dr Merrill WI 54452	NW	Teacher	Tchr	Trinity Merrill WI	(715)536-5482	MQ	2006
Schneider Patti G Boerger	(269)275-7610 patti.schneider55@gmail.com	10136 Corona Ln Plain City OH 43064	OH	Teacher	EM			Other	1977
Schneider Richard W	(608)566-5439 shebschnei67@gmail.com	310 Kristin Ct W Brookfield WI 53045	SW	Teacher	Tchr	Grace Menomonee Falls WI	(262)251-7140	RF	1989
Schneider Robert T	(715) 350-0961 rtsgm1945@gmail.com	W5129 Creek Ave Merrill WI 54452	NW	DCM	EM			MQ	2002
Schnepel Doreen R Bergelin	(920)889-0386 schnepel@stjohnsredbud.org	10471 Brickey Red Red Bud IL 62278	SI	Teacher	Tchr	St John Red Bud IL	(618)282-3873	MQ	2006
Schnorr Marcia A	(815)562-6823 marcyschnorr2009@gmail.com	1225 Springdale Dr Rochelle IL 61068	NI	DCM	Mem C	St Paul Rochelle IL	(815)562-2744	MQ	2001
Schnuell-Ruth Karen D Ragsdale	(313)938-2981 kschnuellruth@gmail.com	2975 Beaumont Dr Highland MI 48356	MI	Teacher	EM			RF	1975
Schnulle Valerie Hein	(608)743-0775 schnullevalerie@gmail.com	4417 Tanglewood Dr Janesville WI 53546	SW	Teacher	C07/2016			CQ	2011
Schnurstein David B	(760)524-7903 dschnurstein@hotmail.com	9236 Stony Creek Stockton CA 95219	CNH	Teacher	Prin	St Paul Tracy CA	(209)835-7438	RF	1981
Schober Nathanial	(775)624-4228 nateschober@gmail.com	5262 Cedarwood Dr Reno NV 89423	CNH	DCE	C07/2016			PO	2006
Schoedel Adam W		7430 Wellington Ave Saint Louis MO 63130	MO	Teacher	Tchr	Immanuel Olivette MO	(314)993-5004	CH	2013
Schoedel David W	(314)520-4838 dwalterschoedel@gmail.com	14 Rippling Water Ct Saint Charles MO 63303	MO	Teacher	EM			S	1980
Schoen Kristen M Wille	(507)236-3742 pkschoen@hotmail.com	404 N Osborne St Sherburn MN 56171	MNS	Teacher	Tchr	Saint James Northrop MN	(507)436-5289	CQ	2013
Schoenbeck Carl J Dr	(651)485-7070 carlschoenbeck@mac.com	316 Wedgewood Cir Hudson WI 54016	MNS	Teacher	EM			RF	1965
Schoenborn Marlys J Woinowski	(605)393-7474 mjschoenborn@gmail.com	5425 Meadowlark Dr Rapid City SD 57702	SD	Teacher	EM			SP	1969
Schoenefeld Karen M Sattler	(260)432-5282 kschoenefe@aol.com	2725 Covington Reserve Blvd Fort Wayne IN 46804	IN	Teacher	EM			RF	1968
Schoenherr Barbara I Jammer	(989)430-5491 bsch54_2000@yahoo.com	4092 11 Mile Rd Auburn MI 48611	MI	Teacher	EM			S	1976
Schoening Linda M Gnatzig		28202 Epperson Ave Silver City IA 51571	NEB	Teacher	EM			RF	1977
Schoenknecht Paul R	(517)871-2280 prschoenknecht@gmail.com	3825 Swaffer Rd Millington MI 48746	MI	Teacher	EM			RF	1976
Schoenleb Chris C Jr	(815)404-0039 flhsprincipal@gmail.com	2333 West Sienna Bouquet Place Phoenix AZ 85085	PSW	Teacher	Pro Stf	North Valley Phoenix AZ	(623)551-3454	Other	2007

*Multiple Assignments (See Church Worker Locator for Additional Details)
See Page 53 for the Table of Abbreviations for key to District, Classification, Position, and College abbreviations.
**C =Candidate; EM =Emeritus; the date following the C is the month and year the Candidate status began

NAME	TELEPHONE NUMBER EMAIL	STREET ADDRESS CITY/STATE/ZIP	DISTRICT	CLASS.	POSITION/ STATUS**	WHERE SERVING	OFFICE PHONE	COLLEGE/ UNIV/CQ	YR GRAD
Schoepp Mark L	(503)551-5055 fatherfitz@gmail.com	2555 Hamline Ave N Apt 506 Saint Paul MN 55113	NI	DCE	EM			S	1990
Schoerverth Gayle D	(216)401-1468 gschoerverth@yahoo.com	181 Dilworth St Elyria OH 44035	OH	DCM	Mem C	Shepherd Ridge North Ridgeville OH	(440)327-7321	MQ	1993
Schoettlin Jeffrey N	(402)419-6866 jschoettlin@lincolnlutheran.org	3303 N 92nd St Lincoln NE 68507	NEB	Teacher	Tchr	Lincoln Lincoln NE	(402)467-5404	S	2002
Schollmeyer Robert C	(989)652-8616 scholl8616@charter.net	151 Beyerlein St Frankenmuth MI 48734	MI	Teacher	EM			RF	1959
Scholz Christina L Drebes	(920)264-6147 clscholz97@gmail.com	7806 Whitetail Dr Mount Pleasant WI 53406	SW	Teacher	Tchr	Our Fathers Greenfield WI	(414)282-7500	S	1997
Scholz Ramona A Lapsley	(719)360-7721 bluefishmanitou@aol.com	1 Delaware Rd Manitou Spgs CO 80829	RM	Teacher	C07/2016			S	1986
Scholz Richard S	(623)363-0785 rick@vlhs.org	40601 N Acadia Ct Anthem AZ 85086	PSW	Teacher	Tchr	Valley Phoenix AZ	(602)230-1600	IV	1997
Scholz Robert W	(909)553-5973 bobscholz@aol.com	P.O. Box 3297 Lk Arrowhead CA 92352	PSW	DCE	Mem C	Mount Calvary Lake Arrowhead CA	(909)337-1412	IV	1995
Schoof Erin R	(260)409-0454 eschoof66@gmail.com	7810 Maysville Rd Fort Wayne IN 46815	IN	Teacher	Tchr	St Peters Fort Wayne IN	(260)749-5811	RF	2006
Schotte Mark L	(620)222-1451 markandbeckyschotte@msn.com	1425 E 4th Ave Winfield KS 67156	KS	Teacher	EM			WN	1982
Schotte Susan R Topolosky	(785)744-3235 susanschotte@yahoo.com	599 5th Road Bremen KS 66412	NEB	Teacher	Tchr	St Paul Beatrice NE	(402)223-3414	AA	2001
Schrader Aaron J	(801)707-6694 aschrade@hotmail.com	107a Glenn Ct. Elkton KY 42220	RM	Teacher	C07/2016			S	1999
Schrader Diana L	melighthouse@aol.com	678 Warburton Ave Apt 4f Yonkers NY 10701	AT	Teacher	EM			RF	1968
Schrader Erinn K Lampton Mousley	(801)487-6734 erinnklm811@gmail.com	107a Glenn Ct Elkton KY 42220	RM	Teacher	C07/2016			CQ	2004
Schrader Stephen P	(612)866-2323 spsc44@gmail.com	6633 Lynwood Blvd Richfield MN 55423	MNS	Teacher	EM			S	1972
Schramm Conni L Guntert	(949)702-1286 schramm828@gmail.com	20 Tierra Vis Laguna Hills CA 92653	PSW	Teacher	EM			CQ	1981
Schrampfer David A	(920)419-8429 david@stjohnlc.com	10715 NE 72nd Ave Vancouver WA 98686	NOW	DCE	Mem C	St John Vancouver WA	(360)573-1461	S	2020
Schrank Deborah A Hummel	(352)672-0631 deborahschrank@yahoo.com	1643 Apache Trl Colorado Spgs CO 80905	FG	Teacher	EM			CQ	2000
Schranz Emma L Wall	(314)412-9332 emma.schranz@gmail.com	1130 Wedgewood Dr Saint Charles MO 63303	MO	Teacher	Tchr	St Pauls Des Peres MO	(314)822-9219	S	2016
Schranz William A	(402)643-7209 Bill.Schranz@cune.edu	1932 448th Utica NE 68456	NEB	Teacher	S HS/C	Concordia University Nebraska Seward NE	(402)643-3651	S	1981
Schranz William B	(352)409-7050 william.schranz1@cune.org	23407 W Pine Ivy Ln Tomball TX 77375	TX	Teacher	Tchr	Concordia Tomball TX	(281)351-2547	S	2010
Schroeder Alicia M	(920)418-5119 alicia.schroeder@celebration lutheran.net	13 South 11th St Hilbert WI 54129	NW	Teacher	Tchr	Celebration Appleton WI	(920)734-8218	MQ	2025
Schroeder Amy I	(515)433-0409	1419 Harrison St Boone IA 50036	IW	Teacher	Tchr	Trinity Boone IA	(515)432-6912	S	1997
Schroeder Andrew J	(260)226-1626 24aschroeder@gmail.com	1596 S 150 W Albion IN 46701	IN	Teacher	RSO	Camp Lutherhaven Albion IN	(219)636-7101	S	2024
Schroeder Betsy M	(515)441-5701 betsy.marie526@gmail.com	233 N Redwood Rd #116 Salt Lake City UT 84116	RM	Teacher	Tchr	Redeemer Salt Lake City UT	(801)467-4352	S	2009
Schroeder Beverly D Wieseman	(618)223-1515 bschroeder56@hotmail.com	6307 Roman Hills Rd Edwardsville IL 62025	SI	Teacher	Tchr	Trinity Edwardsville IL	(618)656-7002	S	1978
Schroeder Bobby L	(314)560-6132 bobbyschroeder@kw.com	719 Wren Path Ct Ellisville MO 63021	MO	Teacher	Mem C	St Johns Arnold MO	(636)464-0096	AU	1990
Schroeder Bret A	(901)319-5289 bret.schroeder@lutheransouth.org	11902 Orchard Mountain Dr Houston TX 77059	TX	Teacher	Tchr	South Houston TX	(281)464-8299	S	1998
Schroeder Carol J Olday Deac	(561)252-4056 cjolday@yahoo.com	1270 Flat Rock Church Rd White Plains GA 30678	FG	Deaconess	Mem C	Trinity Athens GA	(706)546-0670	RF	1988
Schroeder Dawn L	(320)420-5754 dschroeder345@gmail.com	745 3rd St SW Plainview MN 55964	MNS	Teacher	Tchr	Immanuel Plainview MN	(507)534-3700	CQ	2004
Schroeder Deborah A Knoll	(314)409-5639 debschroeder1144@gmail.com	973 Fairway Dr Union MO 63084	MO	Teacher	EM			S	1975
Schroeder Donald A	(260)239-1072 dschroeder@stjohneagles.org	516 Freds Ct Kendallville IN 46755	IN	Teacher	Tchr	St John Kendallville IN	(260)347-2444	AA	1989
Schroeder Dorothy J Succop	(989)652-4183	Winter Village 255 Mayer Rd Apt 183 Frankenmuth MI 48734	MI	Teacher	EM			RF	1961
Schroeder Douglas R	(262)227-9935 dougschroeder2002@yahoo.com	3695 Mountain Dr Brookfield WI 53045	SW	Teacher	EM			SP	1971
Schroeder Ellen E Haas	(763)516-2666 ted-ellen@comcast.net	17954 75th Ave N Maple Grove MN 55311	MNS	Teacher	EM			SP	1975
Schroeder James E	(972)660-2669 jeschroeder27@gmail.com	2305 Wilmer Dr Grand Prairie TX 75052	TX	Teacher	EM			S	1968
Schroeder Julie A Helvey	(270)978-7383 julieschroeder12@gmail.com	444 Hillcrest Dr Seward NE 68434	NEB	Teacher	C07/2016			S	2001
Schroeder Karen L	(925)583-5560 kleighschroeder@earthlink.net	102 Windward Cmn Unit 4 Livermore CA 94551	CNH	Teacher	Mem C	Our Savior Livermore CA	(925)447-1246	IV	1989
Schroeder Katherine L	(586)747-6901 Kschroeder@immlutheran.org	47450 Lizabeth Chesterfield MI 48047	MI	Teacher	Tchr	Immanuel Macomb MI	(586)286-4231	CQ	2014
Schroeder Katrina P Schroeder Baese	(414)466-9749 trina61083@sbcglobal.net	4100 N 94th St Milwaukee WI 53222	SW	Teacher	Tchr	Mount Calvary Milwaukee WI	(414)873-3466	MQ	2003
Schroeder Kenneth W	(989) 255-3040 lenkenschroeder@hotmail.com	157 Hoeft Rd Rogers City MI 49779	MI	Teacher	EM			S	1982
Schroeder Kevin P	(260) 403-1590 kpschroeder131@gmail.com	3320 Jonquil Dr Fort Wayne IN 46815	IN	Teacher	Tchr	Holy Cross Fort Wayne IN	(260)483-3173	RF	1984

*Multiple Assignments (See Church Worker Locator for Additional Details)

See Page 53 for the Table of Abbreviations for key to District, Classification, Position, and College abbreviations.

**C =Candidate; EM =Emeritus; the date following the C is the month and year the Candidate status began

NAME	TELEPHONE NUMBER EMAIL	STREET ADDRESS CITY/STATE/ZIP	DISTRICT	CLASS.	POSITION/ STATUS**	WHERE SERVING	OFFICE PHONE	COLLEGE/ UNIV/CQ	YR GRAD
Schroeder Linda J	(423)499-9034 lindachatt@bellsouth.net	8790 Igou Gap Rd Chattanooga TN 37421	MDS	Teacher	EM			S	1965
Schroeder Linda L Wemhoener	(630)569-1900 schroederlinda06@gmail.com	2889 Stoney Creek Dr Elgin IL 60124	NI	Teacher	EM			S	1964
Schroeder Lori A Swanson	(952)442-3474 fishingfreaks64@hotmail.com	1422 Courtland W Waconia MN 55387	MNS	Teacher	Tchr	St John Norwood Young America MN	(952)467-2740	SP	1990
Schroeder Margaret A Baldwin	(260)582-9954 pschroeder@stjohneagles.org	516 Freds Ct Kendallville IN 46755	IN	Teacher	Tchr	St John Kendallville IN	(260)347-2444	CQ	2001
Schroeder Marilyn L Campbell	(920)468-7031 rmschroeder16@gmail.com	W5824 Cedar Ave Shawno WI 54166	NW	Teacher	EM			S	1972
Schroeder Mary P Pennekamp	(260)385-3449 mschroeder@trinitylcs.org	15400 W Monte Vista Rd Apt 2094 Goodyear AZ 85395	PSW	Teacher	Tchr	Trinity Litchfield Park AZ	(623)935-4690	S	2023
Schroeder Nancy E	(801)265-8036 neschroeder@msn.com	1259 N 2190 W Saint George UT 84770	RM	Teacher	EM			RF	1968
Schroeder Nancy L Ehlmann	(574)286-7584 nandan68.46@gmail.com	58270 Ash Rd Osceola IN 46561	IN	Teacher	EM			S	1968
Schroeder Nina R Johnson	schrades.11@gmail.com		SW	Teacher	EM			S	1978
Schroeder Nolan B	(402)364-3035 nolan.schroeder@cune.org	11301 Ralph Ave NE Albuquerque NM 87112	RM	Teacher	Tchr	Immanuel Albuquerque NM	(505)242-0616	S	2017
Schroeder Paula A Hetzel	(847)359-0548	157 S Fremont St Palatine IL 60067	NI	Teacher	Tchr	Immanuel Palatine IL	(847)359-1936	RF	1986
Schroeder Peggy S Schuelke	(715)853-2892 pianoe14@hotmail.com	911 S Main St Shawano WI 54166	NW	Teacher	Tchr	Saint James Shawano WI	(715)524-4815	RF	1975
Schroeder Phyllis A Kraft	(435) 215-8484 pschroed2@msn.com	125 W Commerce Dr Unit 115 Belle Plaine MN 56011	CNH	Teacher	EM			RF	1970
Schroeder Ronald M	(920)664-5733 enesters@new.rr.com	W5824 Cedar Ave Shawano WI 54166	NW	Teacher	EM			S	1972
Schroeder Ruth J Mueller	(260)223-9325 schroe6@gmail.com	16629 Minnich Rd Hoagland IN 46745	IN	Teacher	Tchr	Woodburn Woodburn IN	(260)632-5493	RF	1977
Schroeder Sarah K Wegener	(847)255-6733 swegener@saint-paul.org	927 E Slayton Dr Palatine IL 60074	NI	Teacher	Tchr	St Paul Mount Prospect IL	(847)255-6733	CH	2012
Schroeder Talitha J Elbert	(618)979-5928 talitha.elbert@cune.org	11301 Ralph Ave NE Albuquerque NM 87112	RM	Teacher	Tchr	Immanuel Albuquerque NM	(505)243-2589	S	2016
Schroeder Tammy S Brock	tsschroeder@stpaulwpne.org	2017 Highway 275 West Point NE 68788	NEB	Teacher	Tchr	St Paul West Point NE	(402)372-2355	S	1988
Schroeder Timothy A Dr	(270)978-6869 timothy.schroeder@cune.edu	444 Hillcrest Dr Seward NE 68434	NEB	Teacher	S HS/C	Concordia University Nebraska Seward NE	(402)643-3651	S	2001
Schroll George M	(812)216-5615 george.schroll@gmail.com	1203 2nd St NW Rochester MN 55901	MNS	Teacher	Tchr	Rochester Central Rochester MN	(507)289-3267	S	2003
Schroll Norma R Fischer	(314)843-8638	8300 S Laclede Station Rd Saint Louis MO 63123	MO	Teacher	EM			S	1970
Schroppel Kristy R Morner	kschroppel@gmail.com	420 Oneawa St Apt C Kailua HI 96734	CNH	Teacher	Tchr	St Mark Kaneohe HI	(808)227-3930	S	1985
Schrupp Stephanie A	(952)474-5541 lhs8588@aol.com	5950 Glencoe Rd Excelsior MN 55331	MNS	Teacher	Tchr	Redeemer Wayzata MN	(952)473-1281	SP	1993
Schubert Joy E Sievers	(573)352-0026 joy@livinghopega.com	2146 Merrimac Ct NW Acworth GA 30101	FG	Tch/DCE	Mem C	Living Hope Kennesaw GA	(770)425-6726	RF	1995
Schuck Kathleen A Alatalo	(906)249-1948 mkschuck@gmail.com	1456 Brigadoon Ct Apt 2 Traverse City MI 49686	MI	Parish Assist	EM			AA	1980
Schuemer Lisa S Adolfson	(630)336-8940 lschuemer@comcast.net	739 Hawthorne Cir Lombard IL 60148	NI	Teacher	Tchr	St John Chicago IL	(773)736-1196	RF	1990
Schuermann Chad	(715)410-7594 chad@lmcrf.org	2644 Hilltop Ln River Falls WI 54022	NW	DCE	Mem C	Luther Memorial River Falls WI	(715)425-2675	RF	2004
Schuessler Joel N	(651)248-1812 nozo@csp.edu	9210 Andrea Dr Saint Paul MN 55125	MNS	Teacher	S HS/C	Concordia University St Paul Saint Paul MN	(651)641-8278	SP	1983
Schuessler Norma H	(573)547-4014	623 Ann St Perryville MO 63775	MO	Teacher	EM			RF	1966
Schuette Jessica L	(262)389-0776 jschuette@goodshepherdpekin.com	3201 Court St Pekin IL 61554	CI	Teacher	Tchr	Good Shepherd Pekin IL	(309)347-2020	MQ	2013
Schuette Yvonne V Relien	(320)864-3237 schuettey@yahoo.com	1714 Cedar Ave N Glencoe MN 55336	MNS	Teacher	EM			SP	1983
Schuetz Glory J Pederson	(303)815-8743 gjschuetz@aol.com	676 Hedgerow Way Brighton CO 80601	RM	Teacher	EM			S	1974
Schuh Emily C	(920)838-1931 eschristine2000@gmail.com	8349 S. Newbury Dr. Apt. 1704 Oak Creek WI 53154	SW	Teacher	Tchr	Martin Luther Greendale WI	(414)421-4000	MQ	2023
Schuldheisz Daniel L	(509)586-1533 djschuldheisz@charter.net	2921 S Tacoma Pl Kennewick WA 99337	NOW	Teacher	EM			S	1967
Schuldheisz Jan R Miller	(509)586-1533 djschuldheisz@charter.net	2921 S Tacoma Pl Kennewick WA 99337	NOW	Teacher	EM			S	1967
Schuldheisz Mary Hertwig	(503) 703-6675 mschuldheisz@gmail.com	917 23rd St NW Puyallup WA 98371	NOW	Teacher	C07/2025			SP	1977
Schulenburg Carl L	(317)861-6389 cschulenburg@lhsi.org	5665 W High Acres West Ct New Palestine IN 46163	IN	Teacher	EM			RF	1970
Schulenburg Linda S Ott	(317)861-6389	5665 W High Acres West Ct New Palestine IN 46163	IN	Teacher	EM			RF	1971
Schuler Nancy A Folkerts	(303)775-2124 jnelraschuler@yahoo.com	1177 Princeton Dr Longmont CO 80503	RM	Teacher	C07/2016			S	1984
Schuler Rhoda G Grever Dr	schuler@rhodaschuler.com	1288 Marshall Ave Saint Paul MN 55104	MNS	Deaconess	EM			Other	1977
Schuler Yi Yi Fu	(949)331-6679 yi.schuler@gmail.com	20 Willow Tree Ln Irvine CA 92612	PSW	Teacher	S HS/C	Concordia University Irvine Irvine CA	(949)854-8002	CQ	2024
Schuller Beverly Richhart	(714)448-3930 beverly.richhart@gmail.com	5594 E Vista Del Rio Anaheim CA 92807	PSW	Teacher	Tchr	Orange County Orange CA	(714)998-5151	IV	2018

*Multiple Assignments (See Church Worker Locator for Additional Details)

See Page 53 for the Table of Abbreviations for key to District, Classification, Position, and College abbreviations.

**C =Candidate; EM =Emeritus; the date following the C is the month and year the Candidate status began

NAME	TELEPHONE NUMBER EMAIL	STREET ADDRESS CITY/STATE/ZIP	DISTRICT	CLASS.	POSITION/ STATUS**	WHERE SERVING	OFFICE PHONE	COLLEGE/ UNIV/CQ	YR GRAD
Schult Christopher J	(715)218-5659 schultc@csp.edu	5238 Sandhill Rd Racine WI 53402	SW	Teacher	Tchr	Trinity Racine WI	(262)632-1766	SP	2008
Schult Daniel L	(602)583-4260 danielschult@frontier.com	1503 S Walnut St Apt 531 Seymour IN 47274	IN	Teacher	EM			RF	1956
Schult Diane M Steinbronn	(715)722-3404 dmjcschu@charter.net	1004 N State St Merrill WI 54452	NW	Teacher	EM			S	1973
Schult Donald C Jr	(715)536-3580 dj@nwdlcms.org	3103 Seymour Ln Wausau WI 54401	NW	Teacher	D Ex/S	North Wisconsin District Wausau WI	(715)845-8241	CQ	2001
Schult Philip D	(407)462-6573 bandman5@yahoo.com	312 S Main St Granada MN 56039	MNS	Teacher	Tchr	Martin Luther Northrop MN	(507)436-5249	RF	1987
Schult Sherry A Stuckwisch	(812)525-1011 saschult@hotmail.com	1512 Robin Hood Dr Seymour IN 47274	IN	Teacher	C07/2016			RF	1991
Schulte Erin D Deac	(770)658-9603 erinschulte25@gmail.com	171 Leisure Lane Bremen GA 30110	MO	Deaconess	RSO	Lutheran Bible Translators Inc Concordia MO	(660)225-0810	SL	2023
Schulte Natalie M Davis	(608)921-5437 nschulte3520@gmail.com	3267 W Bridge St Greenfield WI 53221	SW	Teacher	Tchr	St Pauls West Allis WI	(414)541-6251	MQ	2011
Schulte Vicki A Van Vliet	(714)906-2792 vaschulte11@gmail.com	15022 N. 48th Way Scottsdale AZ 85254	PSW	Teacher	EM			IV	2001
Schulteis Benjamin C	(641)745-0505 schulteis.benjamin@gmail.com	17735 53rd St New Germany MN 55367	MNS	Teacher	Tchr	Mayer Mayer MN	(952)657-2251	S	2016
Schulteis Donald H	(909)702-8164 doschulteis@verizon.net	1655 W Lisbon St Upland CA 91784	PSW	Teacher	EM			RF	1965
Schulteis Ellen K Franzmeier	(712)299-4656 ellen.franzmeier@gmail.com	216 Central Ave Lester Prairie MN 55354	MNS	Teacher	Mem C	Saint Paul Lester Prairie MN	(320)395-2573	S	2016
Schulteis Julia	(303)845-2468 jschulteis@stpaulptc.org	250 Wagon Wheel Trl Senoia GA 30276	FG	Teacher	Tchr	St Paul Peachtree City GA	(770)486-3545	MQ	2025
Schulteis Melinda S Quandt Dr	melinda.schulteis@cui.edu	27051 Mariscal Ln Mission Viejo CA 92691	PSW	Teacher	S HS/C	Concordia University Irvine Irvine CA	(949)854-8002	IV	1995
Schulteis Michael W Dr	(949)951-3001 michael.schulteis@cui.edu	27051 Mariscal Ln Mission Viejo CA 92691	PSW	Teacher	S HS/C	Concordia University Irvine Irvine CA	(949)854-8002	IV	1995
Schulteis Michele L Hunter	(703) 835-5584 mschulteis@verizon.net	10500 Sierra Ridge Dr Parker CO 80134	RM	Teacher	EM			RF	1992
Schultz Amy E Carter	(913) 660-4330 amy.schultz@bslcks.org	12915 W 104th Ter Overland Park KS 66215	KS	Teacher	Tchr	Bethany Overland Park KS	(913)648-2228	RF	1990
Schultz Amy J Schinkel	schultza@immanuelalpena.org	1015 Golf Course Rd Alpena MI 49707	MI	DFLM	Tchr	Immanuel Alpena MI	(989)354-3443	AA	2010
Schultz Andrea J Harder	(989)598-6896 andreaschultz82@gmail.com	1419 Wiesner St Green Bay WI 54304	NW	Teacher	Tchr	Northeastern WI Green Bay WI	(920)469-6810	MQ	2004
Schultz Andrew M	(832)326-4607 aschultz87@gmail.com	2514 Hannover Way Spring TX 77388	TX	Teacher	Tchr	Concordia Tomball TX	(281)351-2547	S	2009
Schultz Beth M Brackmann	(720)341-8065 mrs.schultz720@gmail.com	114 Record St Mankato MN 56001	MNS	Teacher	Tchr	Concordia Classical North Mankato MN	(507)388-4336	S	2012
Schultz Colleen J Demas	(314)368-3051 schultzcolleen66@gmail.com	219 North State St Neshkoro WI 54960	SW	Teacher	EM			MQ	2004
Schultz David L	(512)249-0077 fschultz9@twc.com	9703 Quilberry Dr Austin TX 78729	TX	Teacher	EM			RF	1962
Schultz Dawn M Johnson	(317)346-0684 dschultz622@aol.com	4136 Hunt Club Pkwy Bargersville IN 46106	IN	Teacher	Tchr	Calvary Indianapolis IN	(317)783-2305	RF	1990
Schultz Dorothy R Nickel	(518)458-7231 ccnyrcs@aol.com	24 Whitestone Way Slingerlands NY 12159	AT	Teacher	EM			BR	1975
Schultz Elizabeth A Justus	(402)617-1180 lizschultz62@gmail.com	7130 Eagle Dr Lincoln NE 68507	NEB	Teacher	EM			S	1984
Schultz Eric M	(414)456-0268 eschultz7@wi.rr.com	11819 W Cherry St Wauwatosa WI 53226	EN	Teacher	EM			S	1974
Schultz Gwenith B Mitchell	(608)201-8777 gwenschultz@stjohnevc.org	832 E Centerway Janesville WI 53545	SW	DCM	Mem C	St John Edgerton WI	(608)884-3515	MQ	2009
Schultz Hannah M Thompson	(319)551-0880 hschultz523@gmail.com	203 4th Ave Keystone IA 52249	IE	Teacher	C05/2024			CH	2020
Schultz Jane E	(248)321-5370 jschultz737@gmail.com	45075 Platt St Utica MI 48317	MI	Teacher	Tchr	Trinity Utica MI	(586)731-4490	RF	2019
Schultz Jenna D Geyer	(248)892-2659 jschultz0330@gmail.com	1327 Vaughn Rd Wood River IL 62095	SI	Teacher	Tchr	St Paul Wood River IL	(618)259-0257	CH	2011
Schultz Jeremy J	(989)598-6847 judgeme82@gmail.com	1419 Wiesner St Green Bay WI 54304	NW	Teacher	Tchr	Pilgrim Green Bay WI	(920)965-2233	MQ	2005
Schultz Jesse J	(913)265-6274 jesseschultz10@gmail.com	7345 Field Ave Saint Louis MO 63116	MO	Teacher	Tchr	Christ Community Kirkwood MO	(314)822-7774	CH	2023
Schultz Jesse R	(920)980-9753 jesse.schultz@cuw.edu	W5787 County Rd N Waldo WI 53093	NW	Teacher	Tchr	St Paul Bonduel WI	(715)758-8532	MQ	2007
Schultz John E	(812) 455-6023 schultzj15q@gmail.com	2410 Larue Ln Green Bay WI 54313	NW	Teacher	EM			SP	1977
Schultz Jolene A	(314)660-5306 joschultz2@gmail.com	418 S Park Blvd Independence KS 67301	KS	Teacher	EM			S	1965
Schultz Jonathan P	(541)250-9572 Jonathan.Schultz@zioncorvallis.com	2498 Broadway St SW Albany OR 97321	NOW	Teacher	Tchr	Zion Corvallis OR	(541)753-7503	S	1982
Schultz Joshua E	(507)720-2403 josh.schultz231@gmail.com	18911 MN-22 Mankato MN 56001	MNS	Teacher	Tchr	Concordia Classical North Mankato MN	(507)388-4336	S	2014
Schultz Josiah D	(989)450-4385 josiahschultz@protonmail.com	207 E May St Apt 6 Gladwin MI 48624	MI	DCE	Mem C	Our Savior Gladwin MI	(989)426-9689	S	2020
Schultz Judy K Robbins	(414)456-0268 judyschmke@gmail.com	11819 W Cherry St Wauwatosa WI 53226	EN	Teacher	EM			S	1974
Schultz Laurie M Goers	(715)212-3522 schultzlaumar@gmail.com	646 Richardson Avenue Sheboygan Falls WI 53085	SW	Teacher	Tchr	Bethlehem Sheboygan WI	(920)452-5071	MQ	1996
Schultz Linda L Koch	(715)536-5796 lindy3342@frontier.com	1105 W 10th St Merrill WI 54452	NW	Teacher	EM			S	1963

*Multiple Assignments (See Church Worker Locator for Additional Details)
See Page 53 for the Table of Abbreviations for key to District, Classification, Position, and College abbreviations.
**C =Candidate; EM =Emeritus; the date following the C is the month and year the Candidate status began

NAME	TELEPHONE NUMBER EMAIL	STREET ADDRESS CITY/STATE/ZIP	DISTRICT	CLASS.	POSITION/ STATUS**	WHERE SERVING	OFFICE PHONE	COLLEGE/ UNIV/CQ	YR GRAD
Schultz Lowell E	(715)551-7744 lschultz1123@gmail.com	N736 Lake Rd Merrill WI 54452	NW	Teacher	EM			S	1966
Schultz Lydia	(636)212-5606 lydia.schultz@stjohncala.org	3611 SW 34th St Apt 230 Gainesville FL 32608	FG	Teacher	Tchr	St John Ocala FL	(352)629-1794	MQ	2021
Schultz Madison R Chiappetta	(913)302-1563 mchia01@gmail.com	W168N11529 El Camino Dr. Germantown WI 53022	SW	Teacher	Tchr	Milwaukee LHS Milwaukee WI	(414)461-6000	MQ	2023
Schultz Mark A	(715)432-0570 schultzmars@gmail.com	9298 Niver Ave Allen Park MI 48101	MI	Teacher	EM			SP	1980
Schultz Mark O	(502)558-9335 moschultz11@twc.com	10314 Whipps Mill Rd Louisville KY 40223	IN	Teacher	EM			SP	1978
Schultz Mary C Koch	(414)793-0369 mary.carolyn2@gmail.com	18 Newland Ln Jacksonville IL 62650	NW	Teacher	C08/2020			Other	2017
Schultz Mary L Mixon	(918)520-9331 iw2finish@yahoo.com	1318 W Pittsburg Place Broken Arrow OK 74012	OK	Teacher	EM			CQ	2007
Schultz Megan B	(248)763-1811 mbschultz42@gmail.com	825 Iroquois #c4 Detroit MI 48214	MI	DFLM	C03/2025			AA	2015
Schultz Melanie S Maxson	(719)231-0746 melanie.schultz@yahoo.com	2514 Hannover Way Spring TX 77388	TX	Teacher	Mem C	Trinity Klein Klein TX	(281)376-5773	S	2010
Schultz Michael J	(914)337-3202 macvlc@aol.com	25 North Rd Bronxville NY 10708	AT	Teacher	Prin	Chapel Bronxville NY	(914)337-3202	CQ	2002
Schultz Michelle N Hennig Deac	(217)572-6515 m4hennig@gmail.com	8518 Leesburg Rd Fort Wayne IN 46818	IN	Deaconess	Mem C	Sub Bethlehem Fort Wayne IN	(260)484-7873	CH	2020
Schultz Patricia A Nagel	(313)205-3792 n2kidz2@sbcglobal.net	34527 Summers St Livonia MI 48154	MI	Teacher	EM			S	1960
Schultz Rachel T	(254)290-9598 missrschultz@gmail.com	6061 Village Bend Dr Apt 2010 Dallas TX 75206	TX	Teacher	Tchr	Our Redeemer Dallas TX	(214)368-1465	RF	2006
Schultz Rebecca R Schlichting	(920)980-6687 rebeccaroseschultz@gmail.com	225 W Beech St Grafton WI 53024	SW	Teacher	C08/2022			CH	2013
Schultz Ronald P	(314)707-0001 rpshome1@gmail.com	312 Clayton Crossing Dr Apt 102 Ellisville MO 63011	MO	Teacher	EM			RF	1983
Schultz Ruth A Gartman	(618)259-4332 2mschultz@charter.net	1301 Vaughn Rd Wood River IL 62095	SI	Teacher	Tchr	Trinity Edwardsville IL	(618)656-7002	RF	1982
Schultz Ruth Ann	(608)755-0362 rschultz@stpaulsjanesville.com	1318 E Van Buren St Janesville WI 53545	SW	Teacher	Tchr	St Pauls Janesville WI	(608)754-4471	RF	1985
Schultz Ryan A	(832)560-9041 rschultz@stmarkhouston.org	11303 Valley Spring Dr Houston TX 77043	TX	Teacher	Tchr	St Mark Houston TX	(713)468-2623	MQ	2010
Schultz Sandra C Gilbreath	(414)507-4734 schultzrick@sbcglobal.net	9525 W Palmetto Ave Wauwatosa WI 53222	SW	Teacher	EM			S	1979
Schultz Sarah E Kleist	(612)710-9828 sarahschultz1986@gmail.com	223 Stafford St Plymouth WI 53073	SW	Teacher	Tchr	St John Plymouth WI	(920)893-5114	CH	2008
Schultz Sarah L	(812)454-9975 sschultz425@gmail.com	2410 Larue Ln Green Bay WI 54313	NW	Teacher	C08/2024			MQ	2010
Schultz Sarah M Deac	(231)633-2925 deacsarah@gmail.com		MI	Deaconess	C12/2022			FW-DEAC	2009
Schultz Shirley A Schneeberger	(407)408-3839 shirley.schultz27@gmail.com	10718 Sunrise Terrace Dr Orlando FL 32825	S	Teacher	EM			SP	1981
Schultz Stephanie A Karsten	(920)838-2020 stephanie_karsten@hotmail.com	N6556 Penny Ln Glenbeulah WI 53023	SW	Teacher	Tchr	St John Plymouth WI	(920)893-5114	MQ	2006
Schultz Susan E Wischmeier	(314)304-0556 jonathan.susan@att.net	9556 Parkfield Place Drive Saint Louis MO 63126	MO	Teacher	EM			RF	1990
Schultz Valerie D Kallio	valerieschultz023@gmail.com	8557 Ardennes Dr Fishers IN 46038	IN	Teacher	EM			RF	1979
Schultz Wyatt A	(832)257-9028 wyatt.schultz@lutheransouth.org	13923 Kensington Pl Houston TX 77034	TX	Teacher	Tchr	South Houston TX	(281)464-8299	SP	1978
Schultze Jennifer M	(650)520-6672 schultzejenny@yahoo.com	4279 Parkview Ct Vadnais Hts MN 55127	MNS	Teacher	Tchr	King Of Kings Roseville MN	(651)484-5142	S	2001
Schulz Cynthia L Sattel	(314)651-2110 schulzcynthia@yahoo.com	2498 Ashland Ave Saint Louis MO 63114	MO	Teacher	EM			CQ	1999
Schulz Janice M	(313)204-2854 jschulz@stpaulschoolfd.org	P.O. Box 113 Beecher IL 60401	NI	Teacher	EM			S	1964
Schulz Jennifer L	(815)459-4894 Jennyschulz@juno.com	410 Suffolk Dr Crystal Lake IL 60014	NI	Teacher	C06/2019			MQ	1998
Schulz Kathleen M Lindemeyer	(636)326-9854 kschulz_osl@hotmail.com	125 Parkside Acres Dr Fenton MO 63026	MO	Teacher	EM			S	1975
Schulz LeRoy E	(909)592-8409 lz-no-t@verizon.net	1807 Via Palomares San Dimas CA 91773	PSW	Teacher	EM			S	1954
Schulz Marlo A	(816)273-6864 marlo23schulz@gmail.com		NI	DCE	C02/2021			S	2005
Schulz Nancy J Hillmer	(913)231-4775 njschulz11@hotmail.com	8405 W 98th Cir Overland Park KS 66212	KS	Teacher	EM			SP	1982
Schulz Nathan E	(360)427-8876 n_schulz@msn.com	16625 1st Ave S Apt 226 Normandy Park WA 98148	NOW	Teacher	EM			S	1964
Schulz Paul A	(914)351-3990 pschulz56@gmail.com	18 Rose Ave. Patchogue NY 11772	AT	Teacher	EM			BR	1981
Schulz Shari L Buchholz	(414)425-1970 slschulz@rconnect.com	5614 Gatewood Ln Greendale WI 53129	SW	Teacher	C06/2023			MQ	1992
Schulze Betty J Dutschmann	(512)251-5129 pvilletx@reagan.com	504 Oak Ridge Dr Pflugerville TX 78660	TX	Teacher	EM			S	1968
Schulze Jacalyn A	(612)267-2925 jaschulze07@gmail.com	20949 Keokuk Ave Lakeville MN 55044	MNS	Teacher	EM			SP	1974
Schulze Kresha Payne	(503)939-4096 kresha.a.schulze@gmail.com	1602 E 1100 S Eden ID 83325	NOW	Teacher	C07/2016			AU	2003
Schulze Robert J Sr	(804)447-8883 bobschulze42@gmail.com	300 Twinridge Ln Apt 219 Richmond VA 23235	SE	Teacher	EM			S	1964
Schumacher Amy E Bert	(262)573-2016 amy.schumacher@splgrafton.org	2013 Carrier Ct Grafton WI 53024	SW	Teacher	Tchr	St Paul Grafton WI	(262)377-4659	MQ	2007

*Multiple Assignments (See Church Worker Locator for Additional Details)
See Page 53 for the Table of Abbreviations for key to District, Classification, Position, and College abbreviations.
**C =Candidate; EM =Emeritus; the date following the C is the month and year the Candidate status began

NAME	TELEPHONE NUMBER EMAIL	STREET ADDRESS CITY/STATE/ZIP	DISTRICT	CLASS.	POSITION/ STATUS**	WHERE SERVING	OFFICE PHONE	COLLEGE/ UNIV/CQ	YR GRAD
Schumacher Cynthia A Decker	(260)633-6081 caschumacher54@gmail.com	1109 Dakota Dr Fort Wayne IN 46845	IN	Teacher	EM			S	1976
Schumacher Gordon L	(574)249-0648 njschumachers@yahoo.com	852 N 600 East Rd Buckley IL 60918	CI	Teacher	EM			RF	1970
Schumacher Jacob W	schumacherj@flhsemail.org	9629 Towngate Ave. Las Vegas NV 89129	PSW	Teacher	Tchr	Faith Las Vegas NV	(702)804-4400	CH	2013
Schumacher James L	(989)671-2213 jlschu0132@att.net	417 Willow Bnd Auburn MI 48611	MI	Teacher	EM			RF	1966
Schumacher Jenafer Schafer	(317)359-1345	2323 Cole Wood Ct Indianapolis IN 46239	IN	Teacher	Tchr	Zion New Palestine IN	(317)861-5544	MQ	2007
Schumacher Jo Ann M Schanbacher	(319)721-2325 joschumbox@hotmail.com	3930 Georgia Ave NE Cedar Rapids IA 52411	IE	Teacher	EM			CQ	1996
Schumacher Joshua S	(734)417-5466 jschumachers@gmail.com		MI	Teacher	C01/2025			RF	2007
Schumacher Laura C Denninger	(702)524-8885	9 Benton Rd Saginaw MI 48602	PSW	Teacher	C07/2016			RF	2008
Schumacher Linda L Laux	(937)594-3010 laux_mgoblue@hotmail.com	29893 Dover St Garden City MI 48135	MI	Teacher	Tchr	Lutheran Special Education Ministries Ann Arbor MI	(248)419-3390	AA	1995
Schumacher Richard W Jr	(734)748-5253 rwschumacher@gmail.com	29893 Dover St Garden City MI 48135	MI	Teacher	RSO	Lutheran Special Education Ministries Ann Arbor MI	(248)419-3390	AA	1994
Schumacher Scott A	(812)344-4724 scott@lutheransgo.org	2930 Jordan Dr Columbus IN 47203	IN	Teacher	RSO	The Luth Scholarship Granting Org of IN Fort Wayne IN	(260)203-4509	RF	1993
Schumacher Steven R	(217)737-1858 stevenschumacher@gmail.com	2026 Trenton Ct Jefferson Cty MO 65101	MO	Teacher	EM			S	1976
Schumacher Timothy J	(714)313-1866 tjschu@gmail.com	1923 N 6th St Sheboygan WI 53081	SW	Teacher	Tchr	St Johns West Bend WI	(262)334-3077	RF	1987
Schumann Diane E Schmidt	(414)510-2541 dschumann314@gmail.com	917 Ridgeway Cir Fredonia WI 53021	SW	Teacher	Tchr	St Paul Grafton WI	(262)377-4659	MQ	1984
Schumann Lois J Gerke	(515)223-6517 dschum209@gmail.com	209 Jordan Dr W Des Moines IA 50265	IW	Teacher	EM			CQ	1989
Schumm Deborah A Castens	(484)889-7356 ces11deb@gmail.com	1798 Chateau Dr Green Bay WI 54304	EA	Teacher	EM			RF	1979
Schumm Karen R	(630)553-7821 krschumm@aol.com	304 Olsen St Apt B Yorkville IL 60560	NI	Teacher	EM			RF	1980
Schumm Kelly L Krueger	(920)634-8795 kellyschumm@pilgrimluth.org	1764 Susan Ln Green Bay WI 54303	NW	Teacher	Tchr	Pilgrim Green Bay WI	(920)965-2233	MQ	2010
Schumm Michael	(484)889-7244 mikeschumm@pilgrimluth.org	1764 Susan Ln Green Bay WI 54303	NW	Teacher	Tchr	Pilgrim Green Bay WI	(920)965-2233	MQ	2011
Schumpe James E	(812)523-3064	788 S County Road 1100 E Seymour IN 47274	IN	Teacher	EM			S	1969
Schuppan Marjorie C Nordbrock	(314)821-0371 mschuppan@42gmail.com	711 S Laclede Station Rd Apt G118 Saint Louis MO 63119	MO	Teacher	EM			RF	1964
Schurig Kathy A Fritz	(586)567-5697 jschurig2@comcast.net	14558 Maisano Dr Sterling Hts MI 48312	MI	Teacher	Tchr	Peace Shelby Township MI	(586)731-4120	RF	1977
Schuster Sally M Pritzl	(651)341-3830 sschuster@kingofkingsroseville.org	2236 German St Maplewood MN 55109	MNS	DCE	Mem C	King Of Kings Roseville MN	(651)484-5142	SP	2005
Schutt Elizabeth R Sprosty	(504)352-6309 churchoffice@alcs.org	9664 Mirada Blvd Fort Myers FL 33908	SO	DCE	Mem C	Atonement Metairie LA	(504)887-0225	CH	2010
Schutt Kathleen S Russo	(515)285-0699	3824 Wakonda Dr Des Moines IA 50321	IW	Teacher	EM			CQ	1975
Schutt Kim D	(734)675-6001 kim.schutt@stpaul-trenton.org	2672 Lenox St Trenton MI 48183	MI	DCE	Mem C	St Paul Trenton MI	(734)676-1565	SP	1980
Schutte Amy C Marsh	(651) 457-3929 amy@emanuellutheranchurch.org	2386 Whitefield Dr Woodbury MN 55125	MNS	DPM	Mem C	Emanuel Inver Grove Heights MN	(651)457-3929	SP	1999
Schutte Jay M	(702)372-0313 schuttej10@gmail.com	6432 49th St N Oakdale MN 55128	MNS	Teacher	Prin	King Of Kings Roseville MN	(651)484-5142	SP	2003
Schutte Rachel M Noennig	(763)350-0941 arschutte22@outlook.com	2816 107th Ave NE Blaine MN 55449	MNS	Teacher	Tchr	King Of Kings Roseville MN	(651)484-9206	SP	1999
Schwaegerle Judy L Matthews	(734)716-0823 schwaggs3@gmail.com	903 Flora Lane Frankenmuth MI 48734	MI	Teacher	Tchr	St Lorenz Frankenmuth MI	(989)652-6141	AA	1994
Schwalm Shelly S	(651)641-8213 schwalm@csp.edu	1282 Concordia Ave Saint Paul MN 55104	MNS	DCE	S HS/C	Concordia University St Paul Saint Paul MN	(651)641-8278	SP	2011
Schwan Lori A Lanning	(239)292-6544 lori.schwan@gsmlcs.org	1678 Moreno Ave Fort Myers FL 33901	FG	DCE	Mem C	St Michael Fort Myers FL	(239)939-1218	SP	1999
Schwan Paul A	(239)292-6029 paulschwan1@gmail.com	3062 Rain Dance Ln North Fort Myers FL 33917	FG	Tch/DCE	Tchr	Saint Michael Fort Myers FL	(239)939-1218	RF	1977
Schwanke Nancy K Braun	(320)469-1679 schwanke5@yahoo.com	1790 Sunrise Cir Mayer MN 55360	MNS	Teacher	Tchr	Zion Mayer MN	(952)657-2339	CQ	2003
Schwantz Richard G Jr	(260)493-1454 wishwewerekids@gmail.com	1931 S Tyland Blvd New Haven IN 46774	IN	Teacher	C07/2024			CQ	1993
Schwantz Yvonne M Brunow	(260)417-9081 wishwewerekids@gmail.com	1931 S Tyland Blvd New Haven IN 46774	IN	Teacher	Tchr	South Unity Fort Wayne IN	(260)744-0459	RF	1989
Schwanz Victoria K Ihssen	(715)212-1755 victoria.schwanz@gmail.com	2985 Wyndwood Way Sun Prairie WI 53550	NW	Teacher	Tchr	Trinity Athens WI	(715)257-7526	MQ	2010
Schwark Sadie A Nier	(920)676-8927 sadlienier@gmail.com	17440 Hans Dr Fraser MI 48026	MI	Teacher	Tchr	Peace Shelby Township MI	(586)731-4120	MQ	2017
Schwarting Amy B Korte	(402)895-3422 schwarting@concordiaomaha.org	7265 Timber Creek Rd. Fort Calhoun NE 68023	NEB	Teacher	Tchr	Concordia Omaha NE	(402)445-4000	CQ	2009
Schwartz Debra L Deardoff	(970)342-3104	1950 44th Ave Greeley CO 80634	RM	Teacher	C05/2020			S	2012
Schwartz Gretchen C Miesbach	(816)896-6797 nagrschwartz@gmail.com	1010 Double Eagle Ave SE Rochester MN 55904	MNS	Teacher	EM			S	1986

*Multiple Assignments (See Church Worker Locator for Additional Details)

See Page 53 for the Table of Abbreviations for key to District, Classification, Position, and College abbreviations.

**C =Candidate; EM =Emeritus; the date following the C is the month and year the Candidate status began

NAME	TELEPHONE NUMBER EMAIL	STREET ADDRESS CITY/STATE/ZIP	DISTRICT	CLASS.	POSITION/ STATUS**	WHERE SERVING	OFFICE PHONE	COLLEGE/ UNIV/CQ	YR GRAD
Schwartz Paula G Pyle	(303)489-2283 paulagary626@yahoo.com	5510 Barrington Park Dr Lincoln NE 68516	NEB	Teacher	EM			S	1976
Schwartz Roberta R Timm	(920)980-4417 rschwartz@sjlplymouth.com	253 Mead Ave Plymouth WI 53073	SW	Teacher	Tchr	St John Plymouth WI	(920)893-5114	CQ	2021
Schwartz Tammy J	(715) 384-3535 dcetammy@yahoo.com	1407 N Shawano Dr Marshfield WI 54449	NW	DCE	Mem C	Christ Marshfield WI	(715)384-3535	S	1993
Schwarz Lorinda L Anderson Deac	(541)276-9762 schwarz144@yahoo.com	73275 SE 54th St Pendleton OR 97801	NOW	Deaconess	EM			Other	1977
Schwarz Susan L Lenz	(618)571-0453 5sueschwarz@gmail.com	2154 State Route 154 Pinckneyville IL 62274	SI	Teacher	Tchr	St John Chester IL	(618)826-3545	S	1977
Schwarz Xavria A	(619)403-6819 xavria.schwarz@psd-lcms.org	6375 Lake Aral Dr San Diego CA 92119	PSW	Teacher	D Ex/S	Pacific Southwest District Irvine CA	(949)854-3232	IV	1996
Schwecke Shirley D Stuewe	schwecke2@yahoo.com	1960 Scenic Dr Canton MI 48188	MI	DCE	EM			S	1980
Schwecke Steven A	(313) 338-4390 schwecke.steven@gmail.com	1960 Scenic Dr Canton MI 48188	MI	Teacher	EM			S	1980
Schweda Ruth A Heller	(920)815-9114 noah.and.faiths.mom@gmail.com	1140 Merrill St Oshkosh WI 54901	NW	Teacher	Tchr	Northeastern WI Green Bay WI	(920)469-6810	IV	1996
Schweinler Lois M Quitmeyer	(828)551-2240 locious333@hotmail.com	1693 Holiday Dr Hendersonvile NC 28739	NE	Teacher	C07/2016			S	1975
Schwenneker Christopher W	(360)921-9031 c.schwenneker72@gmail.com	2101 N 5th Way Ridgefield WA 98642	NOW	DCE	C06/2017			SP	1995
Schwerin Daniel P	(810)730-7719 dschwerin6553@gmail.com	6553 Garden Dr Mount Morris MI 48458	MO	Teacher	EM			RF	1982
Schweyer Adam J	(260)755-8043 adamschweyer1@gmail.com	18 Clybourne Ct Towson MD 21204	SE	Teacher	Tchr	Concordia Towson MD	(410)825-2323	CH	2024
Scott Aaron M	(734)846-3519 aaron.m.scott3030@gmail.com	8234 Maple Valley Dr Fort Wayne IN 46835	IN	Teacher	Tchr	Holy Cross Fort Wayne IN	(260)483-3173	AA	2003
Scott Debora H Murray	(714)501-3662 d3bscott@gmail.com	2348 E Villa Vista Way Orange CA 92867	PSW	Teacher	Tchr	St Johns Orange CA	(714)288-4406	IV	1988
Scott Debra L Floyd	(630)261-9197 debfloyd65@yahoo.com	407 S Elizabeth St Lombard IL 60148	NI	Teacher	Tchr	St John's Lombard IL	(630)932-3196	S	1986
Scott Kimberly A Albrecht	(410)903-3229 kimsclanof5@gmail.com	68083 Hillside Ln Washington MI 48095	MI	Teacher	Tchr	Lutheran Special Education Ministries Ann Arbor MI	(248)419-3390	AA	1994
Scott Kristina A Dolbeare	(217)222-0841 kscott470@yahoo.com	1012 S 6th St Quincy IL 62301	CI	Teacher	Tchr	Saint James Quincy IL	(217)222-8447	CQ	2015
Scott Mary K Holl Dr	(714)998-5151 mary.scott@lhsoc.org	2222 N Santiago Blvd Orange CA 92867	PSW	Teacher	Pro Stf	Orange County Orange CA	(714)998-5151	RF	1980
Scott Megan P Pearce	(239)910-1293 meganpscott2020@gmail.com	601 Dogwood Trail Montgomery TX 77316	NOW	DCE	C05/2023			AU	2021
Scott Renee L Prill	(901)355-0471 rscott@ordallas.org	8109 Munich Drive Rowlett TX 75089	TX	Teacher	Tchr	Our Redeemer Dallas TX	(214)368-1371	S	2001
Scriven James A Jr	(907)350-9436 mrscriven@mac.com	1700 NE Knott Portland OR 97212	NOW	Teacher	D Ex/S	Northwest District Portland OR	(503)288-8383	SP	1990
Scriven Judy L Eickhoff	(907)350-9476 judescr@me.com	9221 NE 164th Ave Vancouver WA 98682	NOW	Teacher	Tchr	Grace Vancouver WA	(360)892-7850	SP	1990
Scungio Sara C Deac	(757)784-0657 saracscungio@gmail.com	105 Percussion Road Williamsburg VA 23185	SE	Deaconess	C04/2024			CH	2020
Seaman Nola D Felton	(562)225-6620 nola.seaman@yahoo.com	11221 Gardenaire Lane Garden Grove CA 92841	PSW	Teacher	EM			CQ	2002
Sebold Marcia L Mueller	(734)462-9621 mmsebold1979@yahoo.com	15561 Westbrook St Livonia MI 48154	MI	Teacher	EM			S	1977
Secker Karna A Kohtz Deac	(203)429-6739 karna@theseckers.net	35 Sherwood St Storrs Manfld CT 06268	NE	Deaconess	EM			Other	1962
Seddon Andrew K	(714)719-5478 drewseddon@hotmail.com	856 W Newgrove St Lancaster CA 93534	PSW	DCE	Tchr	Grace Lancaster CA	(661)948-1018	IV	2001
Seddon Tami E Westre Gansberg Dr	(775)722-8041 tseddon@slhs.com	1913 Foothill Rd Markleeville CA 96120	CNH	Teacher	Prin	Sierra Carson City NV	(775)267-1921	CQ	2010
Seefeld Marilyn R Blume	(414)698-7516 marilyn.r.seefeld@gmail.com	N110W14683 Preserve Heights Ct Germantown WI 53022	SW	Teacher	EM			S	1974
Seefeld Samuel J Dr	(414)213-2471	W182N8976 Princeway Drive Menomonee Falls WI 53051	SW	Teacher	Prin	Trinity Mequon WI	(262)242-2045	MQ	2009
Seehafer Mary D	(715)348-6858 mariachi11299@gmail.com	1880 10th Ave E Apt 109 Alexandria MN 56308	MNN	Teacher	Tchr	Zion Alexandria MN	(320)763-4842	MQ	2021
Seehafer Tyler N	(414)418-9562 tseehafer@stpaulannarbor.org	523 Riley St Dundee MI 48131	MI	DCM	Mem C	St Paul Ann Arbor MI	(734)665-9117	MQ	2010
Seelbach Rachel A	(618)635-6104	310 N Caldwell St Staunton IL 62088	SI	Teacher	Tchr	Zion Staunton IL	(618)635-2880	CQ	2017
Seeliger Michaela C	(405)550-8726 mcseeliger@gmail.com	2518 Deloak Dr #216 Saint Louis MO 63129	MO	DCE	Mem C	St Johns Arnold MO	(636)464-0096	AU	2017
Seelman Carol A	(404)295-4210 carolseelman@comcast.net	1373 Merrifield Ln Marietta GA 30062	FG	Teacher	EM			S	1970
Seeman Mylee S Spaude	(612)270-0792 pinky78.seeman@gmail.com	879 Wescott Sq Eagan MN 55123	MNS	Teacher	C08/2024			SP	2001
Seemann James W Dr	(651)226-8047 seemann@csp.edu	1075 Burgess St Saint Paul MN 55103	MNS	DCE	EM			CQ	1971
Seevers John J	(402)643-4703	2838 Adams Rd Seward NE 68434	NEB	Teacher	EM			S	1952
Seevers Scott M	scott.seevers@cune.edu	222 Wildwood Rd Seward NE 68434	NEB	Teacher	S HS/C	Concordia University Nebraska Seward NE	(402)643-3651	S	1989
Segert Richard R	(219)242-8137 richardsegert@gmail.com	2750 Aaran Quay Ter Valparaiso IN 46385	IN	Teacher	EM			RF	1975
Segrist Laisa A Lang	(909)210-2094 lsegrist@gmail.com	4890 Rigel Way Jurupa Valley CA 91752	PSW	Teacher	C07/2016			IV	1994

*Multiple Assignments (See Church Worker Locator for Additional Details)

See Page 53 for the Table of Abbreviations for key to District, Classification, Position, and College abbreviations.

**C =Candidate; EM =Emeritus; the date following the C is the month and year the Candidate status began

NAME	TELEPHONE NUMBER EMAIL	STREET ADDRESS CITY/STATE/ZIP	DISTRICT	CLASS.	POSITION/ STATUS**	WHERE SERVING	OFFICE PHONE	COLLEGE/ UNIV/CQ	YR GRAD
Seibel Martha K	(573) 900-7450 martha.seibel@concordia shanghai.org	1001 Pcr 701 Perryville MO 63775	MO	Teacher	S Miss	Office of International Mission Saint Louis MO		CH	2011
Seibert Ronald J		2411 Grove Ave Racine WI 53405	SW	Teacher	EM			S	1967
Seidel Haley D Waddington	(417)860-9086 haley.seidel14@gmail.com	71 Beacon Hill Dr Lake Ozark MO 65049	MO	Teacher	C07/2023			CQ	2021
Seider Candyce K Stelmachowicz Dr	(262) 424-2150 bseider@seider.com	N55W21121 Logan Dr Menomonee Fls WI 53051	SW	Teacher	EM			S	1972
Seider Courtney R Madden	(414)975-4303 courtneyrae11@gmail.com	1156 Mary Hill Circle Hartland WI 53029	SW	Teacher	C06/2023			CQ	2022
Seifert Vanessa M Dr	(402)580-1015 vanessa@vanessaseifert.com		NEB	DCE	D Ex/S	Nebraska District Seward NE	(402)643-2961	S	2003
Seils Ardis C Weyer	(773)960-0064 acseils@astound.net	11017 S Lawndale Ave Chicago IL 60655	NI	Teacher	EM			RF	1990
Seils Cynthia E Gall	(262)639-8603 cseils@wi.rr.com	2824 Rebecca Dr Racine WI 53402	SW	Teacher	C07/2016			RF	1988
Seim Daniel N	(480)673-5354 danielseim@mac.com	6601 E US Highway Space 759 Gold Canyon AZ 85118	PSW	Teacher	EM			S	1965
Seim John R	(402) 366-5137 johnseimsaints@gmail.com	934 Valley View Ct York NE 68467	NEB	Teacher	EM			S	1974
Seim Megan R	megan.seim@cune.org	2518 W Koenig St Grand Island NE 68803	NEB	Teacher	C05/2024			S	2018
Seim Robin	(308)380-4421 robin.seim@cune.org	2518 W Koenig St Grand Island NE 68803	NEB	Teacher	C07/2017			S	2008
Seiske Sarah A Laatsch	(920)730-6341	1609 E Pauline St Appleton WI 54911	NW	Teacher	Tchr	Celebration Appleton WI	(920)734-8218	MQ	2000
Selander Cheri L Strecker	(619) 980-0506 cselander@christlamesa.org	8110 Stadler St La Mesa CA 91942	PSW	Tch/DCE	Mem C	Christ La Mesa CA	(619)462-5211	S	1984
Selander Corinn E	(619)980-2536 corinn.selander@cune.org	3934 E Piccadilly Rd Unit 23 Phoenix AZ 85018	PSW	Teacher	Tchr	Christ Phoenix AZ	(602)955-4830	S	2019
Seleski Donald E Jr	(503)253-4055	2744 NE 60th Ave Portland OR 97213	NOW	Teacher	Tchr	Trinity Portland OR	(503)288-6403	PO	1981
Self Mary B Anderson	(913)963-8204 selfmb1966@gmail.com	3431 Old Stage Road Mayview MO 64071	MO	Teacher	Tchr	Timothy Blue Springs MO	(816)228-5300	S	2012
Self Rebekah	(816)529-8392 rebekah.self@cuw.edu	1247 S 96th St Apt 317 Mesa AZ 85209	SW	Teacher	Tchr	St John Plymouth WI	(920)893-5114	MQ	2023
Selle Haidee R kuehne	(651)295-8267 haidee.kuehne@gmail.com	318 8th St N Sartell MN 56377	MNS	DCO	C01/2022			SP	2010
Selle Jean E Senechal	(623)281-4660 jeanselle76@gmail.com	10016 E Elmwood Ct Sun Lakes AZ 85248	PSW	Teacher	EM			S	1972
Sellers Tammy L	sellerst@ourshepherd.net	36634 Park Place Dr Sterling Hts MI 48310	MI	Teacher	Tchr	Our Shepherd Birmingham MI	(248)646-6100	AA	1988
Sellke Carolyn R Rutz	(503)671-9926 crsellke339@frontier.com	550 NW 114th Ave Portland OR 97229	NOW	Teacher	EM			RF	1961
Sellke David E	(216)650-1332 sellkedavid@gmail.com	4410 Coral Gables Dr Parma OH 44134	OH	Teacher	EM			RF	1979
Sellke Donald H Dr	(651)490-0876 sellke@csp.edu	987 Tiller Ln Shoreview MN 55126	MNS	Teacher	EM			RF	1966
Sellmeyer David P	(608)254-2258 dsellwd@charter.net	732 Washington Ave Wisc Dells WI 53965	SW	Teacher	EM			RF	1971
Sellmeyer Vivian A Kellermeier	(608)254-2258 dsellwd@charter.net	732 Washington Ave Wisc Dells WI 53965	SW	Teacher	EM			RF	1971
Selph Sarah N Hirsch	(605)553-8320 sarahnselph@gmail.com	430 Keoniana St #202 Honolulu HI 98615	CNH	Teacher	Tchr	St Mark Kaneohe HI	(808)227-3930	SP	2017
Seltz Annamary	(507)454-3576 annamary.seltz@stmartinswinona.org	517 E 4th St Winona MN 55987	MNS	Teacher	EM			SP	1977
Selzer Anna Fuhrmann	(260)615-7710 aselzer@ziondecatur.com	2413 E US Highway 224 Decatur IN 46733	IN	Teacher	Tchr	Zion Decatur IN	(260)728-9995	CQ	2011
Semler Eric J Dr			TX	Teacher	S Miss	Office of International Mission Saint Louis MO		S	1994
Semler Karin L Nelson	(210)701-8320 eksemler@yahoo.com	24603 Fairway Spgs San Antonio TX 78260	TX	Teacher	Aux	LLL/Lutheran Hour Ministries Saint Louis MO	(314)317-4100	SP	1993
Senechal Carol A Forke	(801)231-1668 senfrank@aol.com	6326 Peak Vista Cir Colorado Spgs CO 80918	RM	Teacher	EM			S	1966
Senechal Christin J Maxson	(719)439-9200 senechalc@concordiaomaha.org	5433 N 160th Avenue Cir Omaha NE 68116	NEB	Teacher	Tchr	Concordia Luth Schools of Omaha Inc Omaha NE	(402)445-4000	S	2000
Senechal Mark D	(713)857-5753 mark.senechal@cmstl.org	3528 Kingsland Ct Saint Louis MO 63111	MO	Teacher	Mem C	Christ Memorial Saint Louis MO	(314)631-0304	BR	1984
Senechal Martin J	(402)504-1263 mareff11@yahoo.com	5433 N 160th Avenue Cir Omaha NE 68116	NEB	Teacher	Tchr	Concordia Omaha NE	(402)445-4000	S	2000
Sengele Lynn J Garrelts	(618)401-8100 lsengele@gslcs.org	722 Lake Ave Collinsville IL 62234	SI	Teacher	Tchr	Good Shepherd Collinsville IL	(618)344-3153	RF	1991
Sengele Mark S	(618)401-8200 mark.sengele@cph.org	722 Lake Ave Collinsville IL 62234	MO	Teacher	Pro Stf	Concordia Publishing House Saint Louis MO	(314)268-1000	AA	1983
Senkbeil Peter L Dr	(949)872-6508 peter.senkbeil@gmail.com	1402 E Oakmont Ave Orange CA 92867	PSW	Teacher	S HS/C	Concordia University Irvine Irvine CA	(949)854-8002	CQ	1997
Senne Dennis L	(952)890-5795 dmsenne@q.com	8104 Highwood Dr Apt G115 Minneapolis MN 55438	MNS	Teacher	EM			CQ	2004
Senne Roger P	(714)637-7579 Rpsenne@gmail.com	2329 N Glennwood St Orange CA 92865	PSW	Teacher	EM			S	1963
Senney Walter F III	(216)849-9303 treysenney@lea-hov.org	13909 Lake Ave Lakewood OH 44107	TX	Teacher	Tchr	South Houston TX	(281)464-8299	MQ	2006

*Multiple Assignments (See Church Worker Locator for Additional Details)
See Page 53 for the Table of Abbreviations for key to District, Classification, Position, and College abbreviations.
**C =Candidate; EM =Emeritus; the date following the C is the month and year the Candidate status began

NAME	TELEPHONE NUMBER EMAIL	STREET ADDRESS CITY/STATE/ZIP	DISTRICT	CLASS.	POSITION/ STATUS**	WHERE SERVING	OFFICE PHONE	COLLEGE/ UNIV/CQ	YR GRAD
Senske Al H Dr	(314)528-8057 alandruthsenske@gmail.com	711 S Lachlede Stn. Rd #2119 Saint Louis MO 63119	MO	Teacher	EM			S	1951
Senske Kurt M Dr	kurtsenske@gmail.com	200 Congress Ave Unit 16ac Austin TX 78701	TX	Teacher	EM			CQ	1994
Senter Jack E	jckss@gmail.com	633 Ramona Ave Spc 163 Los Osos CA 93402	CNH	DCM	EM			MW	1972
Sentesi Mary L Scheive	(281)376-1024 sentesi@aol.com	11206 Champion Wood Dr Tomball TX 77375	TX	Teacher	EM			RF	1969
Seppa-Gorwood Sonja L Seppa	(954)226-9636 ssgorwood7@yahoo.com	4490 NW 19th Ter Oakland Park FL 33309	FG	Teacher	EM			RF	1980
Septeowski Dale J Dr	(630)953-1175	342 Wabash Manor O Fallon MO 63366	MO	Teacher	EM			RF	1973
Septeowski Dawn I Pansegrau	(630)953-1175	342 Wabash Mnr O'fallon MO 63366	MO	Teacher	EM			RF	1973
Serbus Phaedra M Fisher Deac	(314)223-1873 pserbus@hotmail.com	850 Eddington Dr Sun Prairie WI 53590	SW	Deaconess	Tchr	Living Christ Madison WI	(608)829-3598	SL-DEAC	2007
Seris Philip C	(314)607-6145 philip.seris@gmail.com	3809 Creekside Ln Carrollton TX 75010	TX	Teacher		Texas District Round Rock TX	(800)951-3478	CH	2009
Sernett Gilbert L Dr	(940)365-1005 glsernett@gmail.com	4913 Glen Oaks Cir Aubrey TX 76227	TX	Teacher	EM			S	1967
Serola Gloria Gierach McQueen	(630)484-4583 gloriamcq@gmail.com	820 N Salem Ave Arlington Heights IL 60004	NI	Teacher	EM			RF	1972
Seta Savannah J Diroff	(734)735-5162 sdiroff@lhsa.com	3732 Academy St Dearborn MI 48124	MI	Teacher	Tchr	LHS Assn Of Greater Detroit Rochester Hls MI	(248)856-0240	AA	2017
Seter Guy L	(512)815-6892	222 N Woods St Sherman TX 76021	TX	DCE	Mem C	Grace Denison TX	(903)465-1016	AU	2008
Sever Rachel M Wisser	(708)374-2183 rsever86@gmail.com	5107 Deerpath Rd Oak Forest IL 60452	NI	Teacher	C10/2022			CH	2008
Severson Brenda J Wetzel	bjseverson@yahoo.com	2727 Little Texas Dr Humboldt IL 61931	CI	Teacher	EM			RF	1978
Severson Diane L	(832)651-6507 seversond@concordiacrusaders. org	19106 Avalon Springs Dr Tomball TX 77375	TX	Teacher	Tchr	Concordia Tomball TX	(281)351-2547	SP	1981
Seward Linda D Deac	(714)580-8075 linseward2@gmail.com	555 S Shaffer St Apt 111 Orange CA 92866	PSW	Deaconess	EM			CQ	2002
Seybold Sheryl A Wehmeier	(713)983-8321 sseybold@stmarkhouston.org	11107 Brandon Gate Houston TX 77095	TX	Teacher	Mem C	St Mark Houston TX	(713)468-2623	S	1988
Shadday Sarah C Rice	(314)330-3782 Sarah.Shadday@concordia-lcms. com	333 Springfield Circle Greenwood IN 46143	IN	DCE	Mem C	Concordia Greenwood IN	(317)881-4477	CH	2013
Shaffer Janel S Guebert-Blevins	(314)302-1447 jblevins@abidingsaviorlutheran.org	270 West Eldondale Drive P.O. Box 51 Hecker IL 62248	MO	Teacher	Tchr	Abiding Savior Saint Louis MO	(314)892-4408	S	1992
Shaffer Shelly S Von Ahsen	(319)721-1715 sshaffer@lutheraninterparish.com	2131 305th St North English IA 52316	IE	Teacher	Tchr	Lutheran Interparish Williamsburg IA	(319)668-1711	CQ	2007
Shane Brenda K Kuhnau	(320)808-9224 brenda.k.shane@gmail.com	2317 S Katie Ave Sioux Falls SD 57106	SD	Teacher	C03/2023			SP	2003
Shane Toni L Barnes	(314)308-9869 gmtshn@gmail.com	1914 Ontario Ct Mountain Home AR 72653	MDS	Teacher	EM			CQ	1998
Shanks Anette A Smith	(402)658-9563 anette.shanks@stjohnocala.org	644 SW 48th Ln Ocala FL 34471	FG	DFLM	Mem C	St John Ocala FL	(352)629-1794	AA	1982
Shapkauski Martha C Schmidt	(708)946-9094 mshapkauski@hotmail.com	220 Pelicans Nest Beecher IL 60401	NI	Teacher	C10/2022			RF	1995
Sharman Ian M	(989)482-9275 isharman98@gmail.com	765 N Block Rd Reese MI 48757	MI	Teacher	Tchr	St Lorenz Frankenmuth MI	(989)652-6141	CQ	2016
Sharman Lyle D	(402)563-2247	2620 21st St Columbus NE 68601	NEB	Teacher	EM			S	1970
Sharp Angela R Schurke	angela.sharp@lcms.org	203 Avenue A Denison IA 51442	SE	Teacher	S Miss	Office of International Mission Saint Louis MO		S	2002
Sharp Bridgette D Dreier Deac	(314)435-5231 deaconess.sharp@trinity-lutheran. com	2221 West Rd Dr Springfield IL 62711	CI	Deaconess	Mem C	Trinity Springfield IL	(217)787-2323	SL-DEAC	2024
Sharp Emily M	(816)745-3088 emilysharp7619@gmail.com		MO	Teacher	Tchr	Christ Platte Woods MO	(816)741-8031	S	2010
Sharp Lisa L Taylor	(618)635-2921	9441 Schaefer Rd Staunton IL 62088	SI	Teacher	Tchr	Zion Litchfield IL	(217)324-3166	CQ	2008
Sharp Mary K Kanning	(402)285-9009	24427 385 St Humphrey NE 68642	NEB	Teacher	EM			S	1962
Shaver Carolyn A Rehwaldt	(956)688-6134	4108 Carnation Ct McAllen TX 78501	TX	Teacher	EM			SP	1967
Shaver Kelly M Thiessen	(812)371-4164 kelly.shaver@cune.edu	430 Vale Ave Rockford IL 61107	NEB	Teacher	S HS/C	Concordia University Nebraska Seward NE	(402)643-3651	S	2012
Shaw Carol J St. Martin	(847)542-8907 shawcj114@yahoo.com	809 Trotter Ct Grayslake IL 60030	NI	Teacher	EM			SP	1965
Shaw Joy R Oetting	(573)987-8421 fullojoy@me.com	10099 E Chelsea Rd Stockton IL 61085	NI	Teacher	C02/2024			S	1993
Shaw Leah M Werling	(785)787-5543 leah@afamilyoffaith.com	P.O. Box 66 Holstein NE 68950	NEB	DCE	Mem C	Faith Hastings NE	(402)462-5044	Other	2020
Shea Jessica M Nehrt	(618)780-0266 jnehrt87@gmail.com	1942 Old Canton Rd Marietta GA 30062	FG	Teacher	Tchr	Faith Marietta GA	(770)973-8877	S	2010
Shea Jodene M Matthews	(407)230-1191 tjam89@bellsouth.net	14250 Deljean Cir Orlando FL 32828	FG	Teacher	C07/2016			CQ	2009
Sheafer Madeline C Osborne	(913)633-7505 olmosborne@gmail.com	14915 Bristlecone Ct Fort Wayne IN 46814	IN	Teacher	C09/2022			S	2017
Shearier Anne M Keiper	(303)947-8472 anne.shearier@gmail.com	8061 Capt Meriwether Lewis Dr Parker CO 80134	RM	Teacher	EM			CQ	2015

*Multiple Assignments (See Church Worker Locator for Additional Details)
See Page 53 for the Table of Abbreviations for key to District, Classification, Position, and College abbreviations.
**C =Candidate; EM =Emeritus; the date following the C is the month and year the Candidate status began

NAME	TELEPHONE NUMBER EMAIL	STREET ADDRESS CITY/STATE/ZIP	DISTRICT	CLASS.	POSITION/ STATUS**	WHERE SERVING	OFFICE PHONE	COLLEGE/ UNIV/CQ	YR GRAD
Shears Amanda R Shelton	(856)552-0768 shearsamanda@hotmail.com	15524 Honeybell Dr Winter Garden FL 34787	FG	Teacher	C07/2016			CQ	2009
Sheely Pamela A Osborn	(618)826-2720 rpsheely@hotmail.com	417 Riverview Blvd Chester IL 62233	SI	Teacher	EM			RF	1971
Sheets Corissa M Gerber			PSW	Teacher	Prin	Salem Orange CA	(714)633-2366	CQ	2009
Shelby Karla L Kuenzel	(760)945-4342 lilkidteacher2@gmail.com	1931 Lichens Rd Montague CA 96064	PSW	Teacher	Tchr	Grace Escondido CA	(760)747-3029	PO	1989
Sheldon David A	(586)260-6543 dsheldon@trinityutica.com	42994 Nebel Trl Clinton Twp MI 48038	MI	Teacher	EM			S	1972
Shelley Judy A Ehlers	jj5shells@yahoo.com	1241 Bellaire St Broomfield CO 80020	RM	Teacher	EM			S	1978
Shemanske Jo Anne Roders	(414)232-2778 jomoma3027@aol.com	8981 Woodbridge Dr Greendale WI 53129	SW	Teacher	EM			CQ	1996
Sheppard Amy D Tiefel	badshepps@gmail.com	1499 NE 19th St Gresham OR 97030	PSW	Teacher	C07/2016			S	1999
Sheppard Erin E Dr	(702)499-5499 astro.erin@gmail.com	574 Brinkburn Point Ave Las Vegas NV 89178	PSW	Teacher	C07/2016			PO	2007
Sheppard Jessica L Kaaz	(618)340-2455 jlkaaz@gmail.com	1515 S Wolcott Ct Denver CO 80219	RM	Teacher	Tchr	St John's Denver CO	(303)733-3778	S	2014
Sheppard Loren K Popke	(248)321-9774 lkpsheppard@gmail.com	1120 Erskine Way Waterford MI 48328	MI	Teacher	Tchr	Trinity Utica MI	(586)731-4490	AA	1983
Sheridan Darina L Lamont	(216)291-2793 dsheridan1384@gmail.com	1384 Plainfield Rd South Euclid OH 44121	OH	Teacher	EM			RF	1972
Sherman Katie B Bates	(540)588-9575 ksherman@stpaullakeland.org	6526 Evergreen Park Dr Lakeland FL 33818	FG	Teacher	Tchr	St Paul Lakeland FL	(863)644-7710	CQ	2022
Sherman Rodney D	(303)803-0302 rodsherman75@gmail.com	2167 N Diamond St Orange CA 92867	PSW	Teacher	Tchr	Orange County Orange CA	(714)998-5151	IV	1997
Sherrill Sharon L Oetting	ssherrill@stpaulgiants.com	20477 Straughn Rd Farmington MO 63640	MO	Teacher	Tchr	St Paul Farmington MO	(573)756-5147	S	1971
Sherry Patrice N Giltrop	(253)861-9437 patricesherry@gmail.com	3107 Oaklawn Park Saginaw MI 48603	MI	Teacher	Tchr	St Peter Hemlock MI	(989)642-5659	CQ	2022
Shevlin Erin G	(714) 299-8023 erin.shevlin@lhsoc.org	20206 Rockville Ct Yorba Linda CA 92886	PSW	DCE	Tchr	Orange County Orange CA	(714)998-5151	IV	2004
Shick Alexandria M Deac	(231)206-3177 ale391537@yahoo.com	117 Bent Oak Ct. Sanford FL 32773	FG	Deaconess	RSO	Redeeming Life Outreach Sanford FL	(407)790-9745	SL-DEAC	2022
Shideler Eileen K	(310)869-8170	P.O. Box 852 Paonia CO 81428	PSW	Teacher	C07/2016			S	1981
Shields Mark J	(412)461-0584 tandemcat@juno.com	1612 Greensprings Ave West Mifflin PA 15122	EA	Teacher	EM			RF	1986
Shiery Carolyn K Fischer	(714)538-5540 carolyn.shiery@cui.edu	1511 E Rose Ave Orange CA 92867	PSW	Teacher	S HS/C	Concordia University Irvine Irvine CA	(949)854-8002	CQ	2012
Shiffer Walter C Jr	(630)541-6086 wcshiffer@comcast.net	9 Wake Robin Ct Woodridge IL 60517	NI	Tch/DCE	C07/2016			CQ	1985
Shimek Jill M	(216)476-3362	18570 Merece Dr Brook Park OH 44142	OH	Teacher	Tchr	Lutheran West Rocky River OH	(440)333-1660	RF	1984
Shimkus Karen Muth	(618)345-0510 kjshimkus@charter.net	504 Sumner Blvd Collinsville IL 62234	SI	Tch/DCE	Pro Stf	Metro-East Edwardsville IL	(618)656-0043	PO	1985
Shimoi Ruth A Waetzig Deac	(206)851-7770 snowwoman91@hotmail.com	1022 Monroe Ave NE Renton WA 98056	NOW	Deaconess	EM			Other	1976
Shipler Katelyn J	(320)296-4396 katelynshipler@gmail.com	251 Luedtke Ave Racine WI 53405	SW	Teacher	Tchr	Lutheran High School Racine WI	(262)637-6538	SP	2023
Shipler Kirk A	(320)395-8462 kirk.shipler@gmail.com	71 Kennedy Ave S P.O. Box 509 Lester Pr MN 55354	MNS	Teacher	Tchr	Zion Mayer MN	(952)657-2339	SP	1996
Shipler Tracy M Prigge	(320)310-6040 tracy.shipler@zionmayer.org	P.O. Box 509 Lester Pr MN 55354	MNS	Teacher	Tchr	Zion Mayer MN	(952)657-2339	SP	1996
Shirley Angela K Paavola	(314)330-1116 ashirley@ccls-stlouis.org	5016 Oak Bluff Dr High Ridge MO 63049	MO	Teacher	Pro Stf	Christ Community Kirkwood MO	(314)822-7774	RF	1996
Shirley Karen S Keller	(419)367-6726 kshirley@trinityvikings.org	1559 Glenbrook Dr Toledo OH 43614	OH	Teacher	EM			RF	1975
Shirley Tessa J Bidinger	(920)912-5593 samtessashirley@gmail.com	W5772 Ember Dr Montello WI 53949	NW	DCM	C05/2022			MQ	2021
Shoaf Susan E Schmidt	(720)289-6324 susanshoaf7@gmail.com	5603 E Nichols Pl Centennial CO 80112	RM	Teacher	EM			S	1973
Shoemaker Kay E Scholz	(314)842-5775 keshoemaker@gmail.com	12006 Southwick Dr Saint Louis MO 63128	MO	Teacher	EM			RF	1978
Short Madalyn S Frank	(419)212-2760 madalyn_sue20@hotmail.com	114 S Madison St P.O. Box 603 West Unity OH 43570	OH	DFLM	C06/2023			AA	2017
Short Martha L Fritz	(651)968-7944 ml.short190@gmail.com	440 W 9th St North Bend NE 68649	NEB	Teacher	Tchr	St Peter Little Lamb North Bend NE	(402)652-8215	MQ	2017
Shoumaker Jeffry T	(309)657-1722 jeffs@redeemerlutheran.com	6714 N Hi Wood Ct Peoria IL 61614	CI	DCE	Mem C	Redeemer Peoria IL	(309)691-2333	S	1981
Shoumaker Lisa K Megown	(563)249-8760 lisa.shoumaker@gmail.com	1365 W 34th St Davenport IA 52806	IE	Teacher	EM			S	1981
Shreve Jennie L Arnold	(502)633-3472 jennie1213@bellsouth.net	426 Turnberry Ln Shelbyville KY 40065	IN	Teacher	EM			SP	1969
Shudy Amy L Luszowiak	(630)888-8761 alshudy@gmail.com	24 Basswood Ter Maumelle AR 72113	MDS	Teacher	Tchr	Christ Little Rock AR	(501)663-5232	CH	2009
Shull Allysa	(779)770-7173 allysaharding@gmail.com	1681 High Bluff Rd Grafton WI 53024	SW	Teacher	Tchr	St Paul Grafton WI	(262)377-4659	MQ	2022
Shull Hannah M	(812)483-1139 hannah.shull@lcmsintl.org	1101 Char Lee Dr Evansville IN 47712	IN	Teacher	S Miss	Office of International Mission Saint Louis MO		MW	2018
Shull Joshua P	(812)598-0451 joshua.shull@lhsparker.org	940 E Plum Creek Pkwy Apt 102 Castle Rock CO 80104	RM	Teacher	Tchr	Colorado Lutheran High School Parker CO	(303)841-5551	MQ	2023

*Multiple Assignments (See Church Worker Locator for Additional Details)

See Page 53 for the Table of Abbreviations for key to District, Classification, Position, and College abbreviations.

**C =Candidate; EM =Emeritus; the date following the C is the month and year the Candidate status began

NAME	TELEPHONE NUMBER EMAIL	STREET ADDRESS CITY/STATE/ZIP	DISTRICT	CLASS.	POSITION/ STATUS**	WHERE SERVING	OFFICE PHONE	COLLEGE/ UNIV/CQ	YR GRAD
Shull Tony E	(812)457-4708 tshull889@gmail.com	1101 Char Lee Dr Evansville IN 47712	IN	Teacher	EM			WN	1984
Shults Julianna C	(773)316-3404 julianna.shults@lcms.org	1333 S Kirkwood Saint Louis MO 63122	MO	DCE	S Ex/S	Office of National Mission Saint Louis MO		S	2005
Shults Marilyn J Voss	(785)220-4338 mjshults5@gmail.com	3600 Stonebridge Rd Wdm IA 50265	IW	Teacher	EM			S	1976
Shutts Abigail M Allen	(619)316-2774 abbyshutts@gmail.com	1767 Shady Crest Pl El Cajon CA 92020	PSW	Teacher	Tchr	Christ La Mesa CA	(619)462-5211	IV	2012
Sias Heidi D Mueller Deac	(406)720-0702 heidi@heidisias.com		MO	Deaconess	C07/2019			CH	2016
Sibley Megan M Jensen	(904)868-1018	943 N 4th St Ponca City OK 74601	OK	Teacher	Tchr	First Ponca City OK	(580)762-9950	S	2006
Sibley Sandra K Melvard	(904)382-9211 sksibly@aol.com	1609 Monument Rd Ponca City OK 74604	OK	Teacher	EM			CQ	2005
Sickles Diane L Severin	(309)647-4996 gsickles@peoplepc.com	2807 Ninovan Ln Minooka IL 60447	CI	Teacher	EM			S	1974
Siebarth Jolene R	(314)302-6673 dcejolene@gmail.com	6925 Sherwood Dr Jenison MI 49428	MI	DCE	Mem C	Holy Cross Jenison MI	(616)457-2420	RF	1998
Siebarth Monica L	(414)630-8242 msiebarth@milwaukeelutheran.org	10837 W Jeffrey Ln Milwaukee WI 53225	SW	Teacher	Tchr	Milwaukee LHS Milwaukee WI	(414)461-6000	RF	1996
Siebarth Pamela A Hahn	p4ams@aol.com	2019 S Hannibal St Unit A Aurora CO 80013	RM	Teacher	EM			S	1978
Siefker Roy D	(313)538-7749 rdsiefker@gmail.com	19443 Lancashire St Detroit MI 48223	MI	Teacher	EM			RF	1966
Siegel Geraldine F Krueger	(920)253-0062 grsiegel@yahoo.com	5869 Sekaly Ln Gillett WI 54124	NW	DCM	EM			MQ	1987
Sieger Barbara J Hempel	(440)833-0452 bsmw1991@aol.com	30128 Truman Ave Wickliffe OH 44092	OH	Teacher	Tchr	St John Cleveland OH	(216)531-1156	RF	1982
Siegert Laura A Lang	(714)654-5466 lrsgrt@gmail.com	160 N Mine Canyon Rd Unit G Orange CA 92869	PSW	Teacher	Tchr	Abiding Savior Lake Forest CA	(949)830-1460	IV	1992
Siegle Renee L Schneewind	(612)616-7063 renee.siegle@stjohns-chaska.org	201 SE 2nd St Nya MN 55397	MNS	Teacher	Tchr	Saint Johns Chaska MN	(952)448-2433	CQ	2020
Siegrist William C	(512)796-2766 billsiegrist@gmail.com	138 Palisades Dr Signal Mountain TN 37377	TX	DCE	EM			S	1981
Siekmann Joseph M	(714)313-2828 joseph.siekmann@mcldb.org	8812 Kings Canyon Street Chino CA 91708	PSW	Teacher	Tchr	Mt Calvary Diamond Bar CA	(909)861-2740	IV	2022
Siekmann Lori C Christiansen	(714)310-1739 lori.siekmann@cui.edu	11 Alcoba Irvine CA 92614	PSW	Teacher	S HS/C	Concordia University Irvine Irvine CA	(949)854-8002	RF	1989
Siekmann Stephen V	(920)465-0422 svsiekmann@live.com	547 Edelweiss Dr Green Bay WI 54302	NW	Teacher	C07/2016			RF	1974
Siekmann Timothy C	(586)254-4132 siekhimfirst@gmail.com	46504 Ben Franklin Dr Shelby Twp MI 48315	MI	Teacher	Tchr	Trinity Utica MI	(586)731-4490	RF	1985
Sielaff Andrew C	(623)337-1142 sielaffa@gmail.com	411 E Palm St Litchfield Pk AZ 85340	PSW	Teacher	C07/2016			CQ	2009
Sielaff Ann Meihak	(623)337-1385 sielaff6@hotmail.com	411 E Palm St Licthfield Park AZ 85340	PSW	Teacher	Tchr	Trinity Litchfield Park AZ	(623)935-4690	CQ	2019
Sielaff Jonah A	(623)666-2569 Jonah.sielaff@gmail.com	225 Fraser Pt Apt 307 Camarillo CA 93012	PSW	DCE	Mem C	Trinity Simi Valley CA	(805)526-2429	IV	2023
Sielaff Sara J Schiller	(217)737-6309 preschool62@gmail.com	1841 1235th Ave Lincoln IL 62656	CI	Teacher	Tchr	Good Shepherd Pekin IL	(309)347-2020	RF	1985
Siemen Rachel K Gehm	(989)293-0258 rgehm26@gmail.com	1018 Kensington Ave Flint MI 48503	MI	DFLM	C04/2023			AA	2015
Siemers Ilene V	(314)867-2818	624 Gleason Dr Saint Louis MO 63137	MO	Teacher	EM			SP	1968
Sienkiewicz Janet S Obermueller Gnam	(623)341-6482 jsienkiewicz@trinitylcs.org	13316 W Port Au Prince Ln Surprise AZ 85379	PSW	Teacher	C09/2025			S	1994
Sievers Ruth M Schmidt	(708)952-9902 ruthsievers@att.net	10853 Cook Ave Oak Lawn IL 60453	NI	Teacher	EM			RF	1961
Sievers Steven R	(414)379-6647 stevesievers@hotmail.com	1820 Alverno Dr Brookfield WI 53005	SW	Teacher	C07/2016			MQ	2000
Sievers Wendy H Pesch	(480)345-9383 rhapsody_930@msn.com	829 E McNair Dr Tempe AZ 85283	PSW	Teacher	EM			CQ	2008
Sievert Amy L Raabe	(812)530-7585 danandamys@hotmail.com	2115 College View Dr Norfolk NE 68701	NEB	Teacher	C05/2023			S	1995
Sievert Benjamin D	(989)293-4555 bdsievert@stlorenz.org	224 Franconian Dr W Frankenmuth MI 48734	MI	Teacher	Mem C	St Lorenz Frankenmuth MI	(989)652-6141	S	2015
Sievert Daniel M	(812)530-7587 dsievert@lhne.org	2115 College View Dr Norfolk NE 68701	NEB	Teacher	Prin	Northeast Norfolk NE	(402)379-3040	S	1994
Sievert Katherine E	(414)628-6110 katie.pahlkotter@vlscrusaders.org	2023 Crescent Dr Apt 5 Cedar Falls IA 50613	IE	Teacher	Tchr	Valley Cedar Falls IA	(319)266-4565	CH	2025
Sievert Kathryn A Reil	(408)655-0789 kat.sievert@gmail.com	20632 N 17th St Phoenix AZ 85024	PSW	DCE	Mem C	Desert Foothills Scottsdale AZ	(480)585-8007	IV	2006
Sievert Rachel J Mussell	(507)251-6587 rjsievert15@gmail.com	224 Franconian Drive W Frankenmuth MI 48734	MI	Teacher	Tchr	Valley Saginaw MI	(989)790-1676	S	2015
Sievert Raymond R	(253)878-5244 raykay@comcast.net	160 NE 13th Ave Canby OR 97013	NOW	Teacher	EM			S	1959
Siewert Dean K	(818)388-3665 dksiewert@gmail.com	54549 Sherwood Ln Shelby Township MI 48315	PSW	Teacher	EM			S	1985
Sifuentes Elly Deac	(224)500-0275 ellysifu@icloud.com	620 Newbury Ln Schaumburg IL 60173	NI	Deaconess	Mem C	St Matthew Chicago IL	(312)636-6496	SL-DEAC	2006
Silva Tiffany A Wiescamp	(860)739-7254 ctdce@sbcglobal.net	4 Miranda Way East Lyme CT 06333	NE	DCE	C07/2016			S	1998
Silvio Sara M Tiedgen	(505)888-2932 stiedgen@peoplepc.com	2209 Tyler St Hutchinson KS 67502	RM	Teacher	Tchr	Immanuel Loveland CO	(970)667-4506	IV	2003
Simela Phyllis N Ncube	(504)858-3248 psimela1974@gmail.com	7246 Tascosa Dr Flowery Br GA 30542	FG	Teacher	C07/2016			SEL	1998

*Multiple Assignments (See Church Worker Locator for Additional Details)
See Page 53 for the Table of Abbreviations for key to District, Classification, Position, and College abbreviations.
**C =Candidate; EM =Emeritus; the date following the C is the month and year the Candidate status began

NAME	TELEPHONE NUMBER EMAIL	STREET ADDRESS CITY/STATE/ZIP	DISTRICT	CLASS.	POSITION/ STATUS**	WHERE SERVING	OFFICE PHONE	COLLEGE/ UNIV/CQ	YR GRAD
Simkins Emily Doyle	(812)528-2656 em_gymgirl34@hotmail.com	7363 S State Road 39 Crothersville IN 47229	IN	Teacher	Tchr	St John Seymour IN	(812)523-3131	CQ	2020
Simmons Benjamin J	(443)789-6857 benjaminsimmons44@gmail.com	13781 Olive Blvd Chesterfield MO 63017	MO	DCE	Mem C	King Of Kings Chesterfield MO	(314)469-2224	CH	2023
Simmons Brandy M Ramm	(817)723-7343 bsimmons@log.org	3736 Bison Trail Krum TX 76249	TX	DCE	Prin	Lamb Of God Flower Mound TX	(972)539-5200	AU	2006
Simmons Jerry L	(520)554-6854 jerrysimmons10694@comcast.net	10694 N Hewitt Pl Oro Valley AZ 85737	PSW	Teacher	EM			S	1960
Simmons Lynnette D Wirt	(317)446-3761 ldsimmons06@gmail.com	6111 Hickorywood Dr Indianapolis IN 46224	IN	Teacher	EM			SP	1969
Simmons Michelle R Frerking	(260)557-2813 michellesimmons808@gmail.com	13781 Olive Blvd Chesterfield MO 63017	MO	Teacher	Tchr	Immanuel Saint Charles MO	(636)946-0051	CH	2022
Simmons Olivia E Laube	(515)729-2830 olivialaube19@gmail.com	3927 Oregon Ave N New Hope MN 55427	MNS	DCE	C03/2025			SP	2023
Simon Julie A Couch	(714)814-6894 jasimon03@gmail.com	25851 Chapel Hill Dr Lake Forest CA 92630	PSW	Teacher	Tchr	Abiding Savior Lake Forest CA	(949)830-1460	IV	1996
Simon Laura L		4714 W Caldwell Ave Apt B Visalia CA 93277	CNH	Teacher	EM			S	1958
Simon Lois E	(920)734-8413	3133 Tri Park Ct Apt 8 Appleton WI 54914	NW	Teacher	EM			S	1973
Simon Shirley A Bieberich-Lake	(301)249-7132 shirleysimon@verizon.net	15604 Peyton Ct Bowie MD 20716	SE	Teacher	EM			RF	1967
Simon Zane A	zanesimonmin@gmail.com	320 Fremont St #2 Caron MI 48723	MI	DFLM	Mem C	St Paul Caro MI	(989)673-4214	AA	2021
Simonis John A	(262)707-9081 jsimonis@lwlhs.com	3590 Saint Huberts Ct W Hubertus WI 53033	SW	Teacher	Tchr	Living Word Jackson WI	(262)677-9353	MQ	2008
Simonis Mallory L Edmonds	(231)288-8801 mallorysimonis1@gmail.com		SW	Teacher	Tchr	Immanuel Brookfield WI	(262)781-7140	MQ	2008
Simpson Amy Hamilton	(805)610-9598 ahamilton@crownofilfe.org	2128 Serene Ct Keller TX 76248	TX	Teacher	Tchr	Crown Of Life Colleyville TX	(817)251-1881	IV	2007
Simpson Carolyn D Moeschler	miscpooh@aol.com	29733 Maritime Way Menifee CA 92585	PSW	Teacher	EM			PO	1998
Simpson Colleen D Lipp	(419)276-1524 clsimpson@edtm.com	85847 577th Ave Wayne NE 68787	NEB	DCE	C07/2016			S	1987
Simpson Erin E Tomlinson	esimpson@splfairmont.org	101 W Innes St Fairmont MN 56031	MNS	Teacher	Tchr	St Paul Fairmont MN	(507)238-9491	SP	2006
Simpson Matthew E	(573)837-2457 msimpson@saxonylutheranhigh.org	270 Matt Ln Jackson MO 63755	MO	Teacher	Tchr	Saxony Jackson MO	(573)204-7555	S	2003
Simpson Pamela S Bray	(402)643-7983 pam.simpson@stjohnseward.org	215 2nd St P.O. Box 33 Bee NE 68314	NEB	Teacher	Tchr	St John Seward NE	(402)643-4535	S	1990
Simpson-Berman Laura	laursimps@aol.com	8 Birch St Flemington NJ 08822	AT	Teacher	C07/2016			BR	2006
Sims Sue E Ashe	(812)342-4840 sesims@hotmail.com	5620 W 700 S Columbus IN 47201	IN	Teacher	Tchr	Immanuel Seymour IN	(812)522-1301	RF	1984
Sinardi Catherine C Collins Dr	(562)235-9881 catherine.sinardi@cui.edu	8117 Meadowood Ln Knoxville TN 37919	PSW	Teacher	S HS/C	Concordia University Irvine Irvine CA	(949)854-8002	CQ	2017
Sinclair Brandon J	(812)521-0639 bsinclair@immanuelschool.org	1642 Finn Way Seymour IN 47274	IN	Teacher	Tchr	Immanuel Seymour IN	(812)522-1301	CQ	2015
Sines Ryan M	(920)973-5631 rsines21@gmail.com	1947 Waverly Court Sheboygan WI 53083	SW	Teacher	Tchr	Bethlehem Sheboygan WI	(920)452-5071	MQ	2007
Singer Connie L Ziegler	(989)871-2544	7574 Barkley Rd Vassar MI 48768	MI	Teacher	Tchr	St Paul Millington MI	(989)871-4581	RF	1989
Singler Susan Lilienkamp	(618)409-4091 ssingler@zionbethalto.org	123 Homestead Court Edwardsville IL 62025	SI	Teacher	Tchr	Zion Bethalto IL	(618)377-5507	S	2004
Singleton Lisa A	(616)304-9909 lsingleton_isj@yahoo.com	5900 S Rickfield Rd Jackson MI 49201	MI	Teacher	Prin	Trinity Jackson MI	(517)784-3135	CQ	2010
Sinn Michael G	(309)202-7522 msinn@stpaulwestlake.org		OH	DCE	Mem C	St Paul Westlake OH	(440)835-3050	CH	2015
Sipan Kelly			PSW	DCE	C07/2016			IV	2008
Sipes Marie A Schultz	(618)975-3568 2msipes@gmail.com	713 Sydney Court Washington MO 63090	MO	Teacher	C05/2023			CH	2019
Sipp Gabriela M Tino	(305)414-9671 gmtino12@gmail.com	12514 W Hadley St Avondale AZ 85323	PSW	Teacher	C07/2022			CQ	2018
Sirek Kathryn J Kamprath	kathysirek13@gmail.com	5625 La Salle St Lincoln NE 68516	NEB	Teacher	EM			S	1973
Sitas Rebecca L Hackbarth	(319)930-7376 rsitas@lutheraninterparish.com	104 E South St Williamsburg IA 52361	IE	Teacher	Tchr	Lutheran Interparish Williamsburg IA	(319)668-1711	RF	1997
Sitas William J Jr	(319)930-7377 wsitas@lutheraninterparish.com	104 E South St Williamsburg IA 52361	IE	Teacher	Prin	Lutheran Interparish Williamsburg IA	(319)668-1711	RF	1997
Sitze Casey C Jehn	(619)497-6945 jehn@hotmail.com	6222 Lake Albano Ave San Diego CA 92119	PSW	Teacher	Tchr	Christ La Mesa CA	(619)462-5211	IV	1997
Siudak Pamela S Oelkers	siudakp@greenbaytrinity.org	4566 Humboldt Rd Green Bay WI 54311	NW	Teacher	Tchr	Green Bay Trinity Green Bay WI	(920)655-4673	MQ	1992
Siukola Jennifer L Johnson Deac	(765)894-1791 jsiukola@adventlutheran.org	2745 W 146th St Carmel IN 46074	EN	Deaconess	Mem C	Advent Zionsville IN	(317)873-6318	FW-DEAC	2022
Sjostrand Maile Kaanoi	(808) 740-4260 maileroses@gmail.com		CNH	Teacher	Tchr	Emmanuel Kahului HI	(808)873-6334	CQ	2022
Sjurseth Janet A Schneider	(847)322-2123 janetrealmoms@gmail.com	1511 Ginny Ln Woodstock IL 60098	NI	Teacher	C09/2016			RF	1993
Skelton Benjamin S	(573)407-9983 bskelton08@gmail.com	7244 Abbey Ln Winter Park FL 32792	S	Teacher	C07/2023			S	2012
Skelton Megan Billos	(407)907-7937 mrsskelton12@gmail.com	7244 Abbey Ln Winter Park FL 32792	S	DCE	C08/2025			S	2013

*Multiple Assignments (See Church Worker Locator for Additional Details)
See Page 53 for the Table of Abbreviations for key to District, Classification, Position, and College abbreviations.
**C =Candidate; EM =Emeritus; the date following the C is the month and year the Candidate status began

NAME	TELEPHONE NUMBER EMAIL	STREET ADDRESS CITY/STATE/ZIP	DISTRICT	CLASS.	POSITION/ STATUS**	WHERE SERVING	OFFICE PHONE	COLLEGE/ UNIV/CQ	YR GRAD
Skibbe Annette K Engelhard	(574)896-2471 skibbe@stpeternorthjudson.org	3415 W 625 S North Judson IN 46366	IN	Teacher	Tchr	St Peter North Judson IN	(574)896-5933	AA	1991
Skinner Elizabeth A Fluegel	(304)258-7920 skinnerea@gmail.com	351 S Washington St Berkeley Spgs WV 25411	SE	Teacher	EM			RF	1977
Skinner Elizabeth M Manske	(630) 988-6118 lizskinner7@gmail.com	2027 Richton Dr Wheaton IL 60189	NI	Teacher	EM			CQ	1992
Skinner Sandra	(818)367-6611 sandyskinner@live.com	13972 Sayre St Sylmar CA 91342	PSW	Teacher	EM			S	1976
Skoch Erika J Williams	erikajbird@aol.com		AT	Teacher	Tchr	Trinity Hicksville NY	(516)931-2225	BR	2003
Skoog Karen L Asmus	(970)242-2986	2212 Victorian Ct Grand Jct CO 81507	RM	Teacher	Tchr	Messiah Grand Junction CO	(970)245-2838	CQ	1984
Skoog Letha Wallace			RM	Teacher	Tchr	Messiah Grand Junction CO	(970)245-2838	MQ	2019
Skov Fredrica A Nolte	(865)235-2716 fans842@gmail.com	7075 Woodgate Cir Fischers IN 46038	MDS	Teacher	EM			S	1964
Skov Neil M Dr	(734)971-7763 nskov@cuaa.edu	2728 Cranbrook Rd Ann Arbor MI 48104	MI	Teacher	EM			S	1969
Skrabanek Janel S Moore	(256)929-2916 janel.skrabanek@gmail.com	2708 Talsworth Dr College Station TX 77845	TX	Teacher	C07/2016			AU	1994
Skrastins Igor	(507)279-4389 iskrasti1@mac.com	10752 Torreys Peak Way Peyton CO 80831	RM	Teacher	EM			RF	1978
Skraznas Robbin R Reeve Kitashima	(720)220-8494 rskraznas@outlook.com	6752 W 65th Ave Arvada CO 80003	RM	Teacher	Tchr	Bethlehem Lakewood CO	(303)238-7676	CQ	1999
Skrocke Jacqueline Whittemore	jskrocke@wave.hicv.net	2434 Kamehameha V Hwy Kaunakakai HI 96748	RM	Teacher		Rocky Mountain District Englewood CO	(303)695-8001	CQ	1996
Skuda Deanna Behrman	(954)943-9114 dsskuda@gmail.com	430 SW 18th Ct Pompano Beach FL 33060	FG	Teacher	EM			RF	1968
Skura Kristen A Monson	(720)315-4104 kristen.skura@gmail.com	21400 Pointe Dr Rogers MN 55374	MNS	Teacher	P/Tchr	St John Corcoran MN	(763)420-2426	S	2001
Skvarenina Joseph L	(317)518-1467 jskvarenina@hotmail.com	523 N Swope St Greenfield IN 46140	IN	Teacher	EM			CQ	1997
Skyrm Donna L Nemec	(216)262-1432 dlskyrm@hotmail.com	26078 Crocker Rd Columbia Sta OH 44028	OH	Teacher	EM			CQ	1997
Slater Emily M Ball	(702)221-6319 ophelialives_99@yahoo.com	9101 W Sahara Ave Ste 105 Las Vegas NV 89117	PSW	Teacher	Tchr	Faith Las Vegas NV	(702)804-4400	RF	1999
Slavens Elizabeth A Schepers	(314)412-1085 lizslavens@yahoo.com	47015 Rose Cir Tea SD 57064	SD	Teacher	Tchr	Sioux Falls Sioux Falls SD	(605)335-1923	S	2002
Slaybaugh Ava M Schweninger	(210)501-7050 slaybaugh.ava@gmail.com	2501 Ashley Dr The Village OK 73120	OK	DCE	C04/2025			IV	2021
Slaybaugh Matthew P	(919)744-1433 slaybaugh.matt@gmail.com	2501 Ashley Dr Oklahoma City OK 73120	OK	DCE	C08/2024			CH	2017
Sleezer Meghan V Butterfield	(773)610-1014 meghan.sleezer@cuchicago.edu	457 N. Oak St. Elmhurst IL 60126	NI	Teacher	S HS/C	Concordia University Chicago River Forest IL	(708)771-8300	AU	2004
Sleighter David R	(206)914-2631 daversleighter@hotmail.com	1777 5th St Livermore CA 94550	CNH	Teacher		California/Nevada/Hawaii District Livermore CA	(866)264-6079	CQ	2019
Slettvedt Carol E Chancy-Cordero	(415)566-8870 carolslettvedt2659@comcast.net	2659 16th Ave San Francisco CA 94116	EN	Teacher	EM			CQ	1987
Slininger Kimberly R Deac	(207)356-4554 Kim@spiritwarrior.me	462 Main Rd S Hampden ME 04444	NE	Deaconess	Mem C	Hope Hampden ME		FW-DEAC	2016
Sloan Jo Anne E Otto	(714)993-4129 pavajerb@att.net	2866 Devonshire Ave Fullerton CA 92835	PSW	Teacher	EM			RF	1967
Slothower Elizabeth L Wolter	(402)740-5386 slothower.l@gmail.com	26314 Holly Ridge Dr Denham Spgs LA 70726	SO	Teacher	EM			SP	1970
Slupik Kathy E Jeschke	(773)792-2917 kathy.slupik@gmail.com	4848 N Merrimac Ave Chicago IL 60630	EN	Teacher	EM			RF	1977
Small Christine R Rodewald	(619)282-4561 csmallchris@aol.com	2204 Felton St San Diego CA 92104	PSW	Teacher	EM			S	1978
Small Laura R Laura Hayden	lauraraesmall@gmail.com	1 Eayrestown Rd Medford NJ 08055	NJ	Teacher	C08/2018			S	2004
Smallwood Carol J Scheller	(714)496-4805 csmallwood9126@gmail.com	9101 Avebury Ct Columbia IL 62236	PSW	Teacher	EM			S	1970
Smedal Nicholas E	(262)573-4385 nick.smedal@gmail.com	824 Schloemer Dr West Bend WI 53095	SW	Teacher	Tchr	Living Word Jackson WI	(262)677-9353	MQ	2023
Smelser Jonathan T	(701)261-0806 jon.smelser@outlook.com	4409 Sunset Blvd West Fargo ND 58078	ND	DCM	Mem C	Grace Fargo ND	(701)232-1516	MQ	2021
Smith Addison R	(402)646-0988 smith.addison1101@gmail.com	315 N 44th St #1005 Lincoln NE 68503	NEB	Teacher	Tchr	Lincoln Lincoln NE	(402)467-5404	S	2024
Smith Alice E Kratt	(989)295-8497 alicesaddress@yahoo.com	535 W Genesee St Unit E Frankenmuth MI 48734	MI	Teacher	EM			RF	1964
Smith Alison A Walunas	(972)824-1757 alison.smith@mlcatexas.org	10873 Hawks Landing Rd Haslet TX 76052	TX	Teacher	C11/2022			AA	1991
Smith Angela Trahin	(260)450-0011 ssmith@cluth.org	8682 Ashton Rd Woodburn IN 46797	IN	Teacher	Tchr	Central New Haven IN	(260)493-2502	CQ	2021
Smith Anna C Polson	(303)883-1431 annachristinepolson@gmail.com	83 County Rd 63 Keenesburg CO 80643	RM	Teacher	Tchr	Zion Brighton CO	(303)659-2339	S	2004
Smith Barbara J Maas	(317)897-2281 barbjsmith8305@yahoo.com	8305 Rumford Rd Indianapolis IN 46219	IN	Teacher	EM			CQ	1999
Smith Beverly J Secor	(512)868-9366 burgecarmon3@suddenlink.net	243 Bonham Loop Georgetown TX 78633	TX	Teacher	EM			RF	1960
Smith Breenna Abel	breennaabel@yahoo.com		IN	Teacher	Mem C	Trinity Darmstadt IN	(812)867-5279	CH	2013
Smith Charity R Olson	(804)874-1225 titus2.7and8@gmail.com	3 Schrader Farm Ct St. Peters MO 63376	MO	DCE	Mem C	Holy Cross O'fallon MO	(636)272-4505	CH	2011

*Multiple Assignments (See Church Worker Locator for Additional Details)
See Page 53 for the Table of Abbreviations for key to District, Classification, Position, and College abbreviations.
**C =Candidate; EM =Emeritus; the date following the C is the month and year the Candidate status began

NAME	TELEPHONE NUMBER EMAIL	STREET ADDRESS CITY/STATE/ZIP	DISTRICT	CLASS.	POSITION/ STATUS**	WHERE SERVING	OFFICE PHONE	COLLEGE/ UNIV/CQ	YR GRAD
Smith Charles E	(812)525-9756 csmith.ils@aol.com	823 Evergreen Dr Seymour IN 47274	IN	Teacher	Tchr	Immanuel Seymour IN	(812)522-1301	AA	1999
Smith Cory C	(770)846-9800 cory.smith@stjohnmansfield.org	1812 Fairfax Dr Mansfield TX 76063	TX	DCE	Mem C	St John Mansfield TX	(817)473-4889	S	1999
Smith Cristine M	(920)216-3630 cristinesmith1110@gmail.com	649 Richardson Ave Sheboygan Falls WI 53085	SW	Teacher	Tchr	St John Plymouth WI	(920)893-5114	AA	2017
Smith Devin L	(402)646-9037 devin.smith@cune.org	1038 Eastridge Dr Seward NE 68434	NEB	Teacher	S HS/C	Concordia University Nebraska Seward NE	(402)643-3651	S	1992
Smith Dustin R	(815)979-2113 smith@thecalvaryschool.org	74 Halldale Dr Whiteland IN 46184	IN	Teacher	Tchr	Calvary Indianapolis IN	(317)783-2305	MQ	2004
Smith Elizabeth A	(712)269-7078 elizabeth.smith@trinityfremont.org	2550 E Cuming St Fremont NE 68025	NEB	Teacher	Tchr	Trinity Fremont NE	(402)721-5959	CQ	2024
Smith Eric R	(989)928-8830 esmith@vlhs.com	826 Piper Dr Saginaw MI 48604	MI	DCE	Tchr	Valley Saginaw MI	(989)790-1676	RF	1996
Smith Gail H Graham	(734)558-8811	2448 Liberty St S Canton MI 48188	MI	Tch/DCE	EM			RF	1987
Smith Heather C Judd	(919)884-6282 hcsmith617@gmail.com	1145 Presto Ct Adams TN 37010	MDS	Teacher	C07/2017			AA	2003
Smith Heidi M Massa	(715)966-1298 hmm-497@hotmail.com	1407 26th St NW Rochester MN 55901	MNS	Teacher	Tchr	Rochester Central Rochester MN	(507)289-3267	MQ	2019
Smith James F	(231)679-4908 jsmith5621@aol.com	5619 Trishlyn CV Fort Wayne IN 46835	IN	Teacher	EM			RF	1968
Smith Janet E Kiefer	(260)413-3839 smithje0512@gmail.com	10350 Riverhouse Ln Grabill IN 46741	IN	Teacher	C04/2017			CQ	2015
Smith Jennifer L Meier	(773)984-0343 smithjen316@gmail.com	446 Woodfield Prairie Way Hobart WI 54155	NW	Teacher	C11/2023			CH	2006
Smith Jennifer M Schaedig	(989)595-6279 kjsmith012007@gmail.com	12732 S Coleman Rd Empire MI 49630	MI	Teacher	Tchr	Trinity Traverse City MI	(231)946-2720	AA	2006
Smith Jessica Matro	(231)668-2752 jessierue86@gmail.com	5155 Park Ave S Minneapolis MN 55417	MNS	Teacher	C07/2022			MQ	2009
Smith Jill E Schneider	(575)649-7659 circl@comcast.net	1243 Kingsbury Ct Las Cruces NM 88005	RM	Teacher	Tchr	Mission Las Cruces NM	(575)522-0465	S	1971
Smith Jill E Evans	(863)688-1181 jillsmith0349@gmail.com	1438 Country Oaks Ln Lakeland FL 33810	FG	Teacher	Tchr	St Paul Lakeland FL	(863)644-7710	CQ	2004
Smith Joanie L Schlie	(847)712-6760 jsmith@messiahnetwork.org	P.O. Box 1076 Lake Sherwood MO 63357	MO	Teacher	Prin	Messiah Weldon Spring MO	(636)926-9773	RF	1989
Smith Julie M Brege	(260)223-2623 julieb_40@outlook.com	726 N 3rd St Decatur IN 46733	IN	Teacher	Tchr	St Peter-Immanuel Decatur IN	(260)623-6115	CQ	2010
Smith Kari M Greseth	(563)210-5122 ksmith@lutheranfamilyservice.org	2036 E 48th St Davenport IA 52807	IW	Teacher	RSO	Lutheran Family Service Fort Dodge IA	(515)573-3138	S	1999
Smith Kevin G	(714)635-2726 paakamaa@gmail.com	837 S Lemon St Anaheim CA 92805	PSW	Teacher	EM			S	1979
Smith Kimberly D Page	(931)516-3391 kdsmith19@gmail.com	1810 Glenbridge Rd Bloomington IL 61704	MDS	Teacher	Tchr	Heavenly Host Cookeville TN	(931)526-3423	AU	1992
Smith Kurtis L	(763)607-3931 kurtisleonsmith@gmail.com	97 Blake Rd N Apt 111 Hopkins MN 55343	MNS	DCO	C04/2017			CQ	2000
Smith Kyle J	(989)464-7063 ksmith@tctrinityschool.org	12732 S Coleman Rd Empire MI 49630	MI	Teacher	Prin	Trinity Traverse City MI	(231)946-2720	AA	2006
Smith Lisa M Schneider	(630)880-8908 tsimplylisa@sbcglobal.net	2732 Quinn Pl Dyer IN 46311	IN	Teacher	Tchr	St Pauls Munster IN	(219)836-6270	RF	1992
Smith Lorna J Hartman	lornaandwalt@gmail.com	709 Cedar St Defiance OH 43512	OH	Teacher	EM			RF	1971
Smith Margaret E Blessen	(308) 450-6969 mencsmith@frontiernet.net	4306 Linden Dr Kearney NE 68847	NEB	Teacher	EM			S	1964
Smith Mary E Auernhamer	(260) 417-0006 mssmith@esmeagles.com	322 Red Eagle Pass Fort Wayne IN 46845	IN	Teacher	Tchr	Emmanuel-St Michael Fort Wayne IN	(260)422-6712	RF	1991
Smith Mavis J Scheetz	(605)254-3566 macmom85@hotmail.com	4251 33rd Ave S Apt 101 Fargo ND 58104	SD	DCE	C07/2016			S	1983
Smith Melissa A Horvath	(847)504-7598 melissa.ecedu@aol.com	760 S Ravinia Cir Palatine IL 60074	NI	Teacher	C09/2024			RF	2004
Smith Melissa D Dube	(713)906-1365 melissa.smith724@gmail.com	501 Lake Livingston Trail McKinney TX 75071	TX	Teacher	C07/2017			CQ	2016
Smith Mphatso M	(402)213-8036 mphasmith@gmail.com	950 French Dr Apt 4201 Valley Park MO 63088	MO	Teacher	Tchr	Christ Community Kirkwood MO	(314)822-7774	S	2024
Smith Nicolette L Lieske	(402)450-8022 dannick712@aol.com	2006 Independence Dr Lincoln NE 68521	NEB	Teacher	Tchr	Faith Lincoln NE	(402)466-7402	CQ	2011
Smith Patricia L Krause	(414)466-1349 trish.smith@orlctosa.org	4124 N 88th St Milwaukee WI 53222	SW	Teacher	Tchr	Wauwatosa Wauwatosa WI	(414)258-4558	MQ	1987
Smith Patricia W		209 Erskine Ct Cary NC 27511	SE	Teacher	EM			CQ	2004
Smith Randall	(727)577-4711	1566 86th Ave N St Petersburg FL 33702	FG	Tch/DCE	C07/2016			S	1969
Smith Rebecca E	(989)225-9596 rsmith@bethlehemsaginaw.org	791 Belair Dr. Saginaw MI 48638	MI	Teacher	Tchr	Bethlehem Saginaw MI	(989)755-1144	AA	2016
Smith Sandra L	(630)740-1994 sandy.smithandcats@yahoo.com	455 E George St Itasca IL 60143	NI	Teacher	EM			RF	1969
Smith Sara K Deac	(513)509-8108 dcs.sara3@gmail.com	7130 Flora St Arvada CO 80004	RM	Deaconess	C07/2020			FW-DEAC	2013
Smith Sarah Sample	(260)710-1295 ssmith@esmeagles.com	4122 Bulrush Ct Fort Wayne IN 46818	IN	Teacher	Tchr	Emmanuel-St Michael Fort Wayne IN	(260)422-6712	CQ	2025
Smith Sarah A Sunderman	(660)553-7213 sarah.sunderman@cune.org	202 N Huntsman Blvd Raymore MO 64083	IW	Teacher	C08/2016			S	2007
Smith Shandlyn Black	(636)299-2609 ssmith@messiahnetwork.org	1887 Lunenburg Dr Saint Peters MO 63376	MO	Teacher	Tchr	Messiah Weldon Spring MO	(636)329-1096	CQ	2016
Smith Sherrie M Kirst	s.smith.lwml@gmail.com	7418 Figura Dr Justice IL 60458	NI	Teacher	EM			RF	1982

*Multiple Assignments (See Church Worker Locator for Additional Details)
See Page 53 for the Table of Abbreviations for key to District, Classification, Position, and College abbreviations.
**C =Candidate; EM =Emeritus; the date following the C is the month and year the Candidate status began

NAME	TELEPHONE NUMBER EMAIL	STREET ADDRESS CITY/STATE/ZIP	DISTRICT	CLASS.	POSITION/ STATUS**	WHERE SERVING	OFFICE PHONE	COLLEGE/ UNIV/CQ	YR GRAD
Smith Shilo C	(575)650-1747 shilo.smith@mlschool.net	1957 Sheryl Way Las Cruces NM 88001	RM	Teacher	Tchr	Mission Las Cruces NM	(575)522-0465	S	2002
Smith Skylar F	(813)215-7008 skylarfsmith@gmail.com		SO	Tch/DCE	Mem C	St Paul's Decatur AL	(256)353-8759	AU	2017
Smith Susan M Orr	(989)245-4019 ssmith@faithbaycity.org	826 Piper Dr Saginaw MI 48604	MI	Teacher	C09/2025			RF	1995
Smith Tiffany A Swanson	(509)868-4815 tiffany.anne.smith@gmail.com	1397 Windsong Ct NW Salem OR 97304	NOW	Teacher	C06/2017			PO	2006
Smith William F Jr	(979)540-8738 smithwf63@gmail.com	3050 Fm 141 Giddings TX 78942	TX	Teacher	Tchr	Immanuel Giddings TX	(979)542-3319	CQ	2004
Smith-Davis Lydia E Prendeville	(949)307-4606 lsmithdavis@gmail.com	2215 Paseo De Las Americas Ste 25-M # 233 San Diego CA 92154	PSW	Teacher	EM			CQ	2012
Smithers Jennifer L Shaffer	(281)793-7699 j.smithers.texas@gmail.com	18347 Burkhardt Rd Tomball TX 77377	TX	Teacher	Tchr	Salem Tomball TX	(281)351-8223	MQ	1993
Smith-Hubbell Mary-Bethany A Smith	(989)450-8018 marybethanysmithhubbell@ gmail.com	2981 N. Fordney Rd Hemlock MI 48626	MI	Teacher	Tchr	Peace Saginaw MI	(989)793-9025	AA	1989
Smukowski Kelsey R Lindholm	(563)370-2968 klindholm11@gmail.com	1819 Marliz Dr Waukesha WI 53189	SW	Teacher	Tchr	St Paul Oconomowoc WI	(262)567-5001	MQ	2011
Smukowski Theresa		303 Cottage St Merrill WI 54452	NW	Teacher	Tchr	St John Merrill WI	(715)536-7264	MQ	1993
Snashall Doris M Deac	(619)920-6330 d_g_snashall@outlook.com	811 4th St Coronado CA 92118	PSW	Deaconess	Mem C	Grace San Diego CA	(619)299-2890	CQ	2006
Snider Charles A	(573)415-7688 chalsn52@hotmail.com	410 Virginia Rd P.O. Box 109 Alma MO 64001	MO	Teacher	EM			S	1974
Snodgrass Jennifer	jenzionpierce@gmail.com	221 W Florence St Pierce NE 68767	NEB	Teacher	Tchr	Christ Norfolk NE	(402)371-5536	CQ	2020
Snow Curtis D	(920)745-0244	152 E Marquette St Berlin WI 54923	SW	Teacher	EM			SP	1981
Snow Jennifer J Johnson	(813)503-1747 jsnow@familyofchristtampa.com	19102 Nature Palm Ln Tampa FL 33647	S	Teacher	Prin	Family Of Christ Tampa FL	(813)558-9343	CQ	2013
Snow Michele R Hoffman	(281)796-3388 cmrsnow@sbcglobal.net	22719 Bayleaf Dr Spring TX 77373	TX	Teacher	Tchr	Salem Tomball TX	(281)351-8223	CQ	1994
Snyder Arlene Encarnacion	(510)304-9218 aesnyder143@gmail.com	2428 Los Pinos Dr Spanish Springs NV 89441	CNH	Teacher	C06/2022			CQ	2014
Snyder Brigid A Bielski	snyder4life2@gmail.com		MI	Teacher	EM			CQ	2010
Snyder Frederick E III	(260)436-3283 fredthirdman@aol.com	318 Nordale Dr Fort Wayne IN 46804	IN	Teacher	EM			RF	1968
Snyder Joseph M	(314)504-0966 josephmsnyder59@gmail.com	13 Rippling Water Ct Saint Charles MO 63303	SI	Teacher	Prin	Zion Bethalto IL	(618)377-8314	RF	1981
Snyder Linda J Siesennop	(314)842-2436 jlsnyder2@msn.com	711 S Laclede Station Rd Apt G111 Saint Louis MO 63119	MO	Teacher	EM			RF	1964
Sochowski Mark D	(618)975-3850 mskaline@yahoo.com	104 Boulder Dr Red Bud IL 62278	SI	Tch/DCE	C07/2016			RF	1983
Soderbeck Faith	(414)760-8883 faith.soderbeck@orlctosa.org	1320 Goldenrod Way Oconomowoc WI 53066	SW	Teacher	Tchr	Wauwatosa Wauwatosa WI	(414)258-4558	S	1991
Soeken Kate M Luckemeyer	(830)708-8221 kate.soeken@gmail.com	1412 Genesis McPherson KS 67460	KS	DCE	C03/2017			S	2010
Soflin Montana L Hayes	(402)879-1488 montana.soflin@gmail.com	1620 Eastridge Seward NE 68434	NEB	Teacher	C07/2022			S	2015
Sohl James R	(608)393-0541 sohljames3@gmail.com	8561 SW 90th St Unit D Ocala FL 34481	FG	Teacher	EM			S	1970
Sohn David L	(714)319-6760 davidlsohn@gmail.com	4214 SW Vesta St Portland OR 97219	NOW	Teacher	C07/2016			S	1981
Sohn Kristine K De Boer	(678)313-3123	7550 Roxborough Lane Grand Ledge MI 48837	MI	Teacher	EM			S	1986
Sohn Lawrence E Dr	(414)727-3774 lsohn@wi.rr.com	8220 Harwood Av #343 Wauwatosa WI 53213	SW	Teacher	EM			RF	1959
Sohn Terry D Berg	(714)319-5434 terrydsohn@gmail.com	4214 SW Vesta St Portland OR 97219	NOW	Teacher	C07/2016			S	1982
Soignier Chloe E	(504)508-1276 chloesoignier@gmail.com	5241 Trenton St Metairie LA 70006	SO	Teacher	Tchr	Atonement Metairie LA	(504)887-0225	CH	2019
Sok Kelli E Kanaly	(815)245-0650 kellikanaly@yahoo.com	450 S Page St Marengo IL 60152	NI	Teacher	Tchr	Zion Marengo IL	(815)568-5156	CQ	2011
Sok Peter R		444 N American St Stockton CA 95202	CNH	DCM	Mem C	Trinity Stockton CA	(209)464-1936	CQ	1982
Soldner Amy Barker	(513)207-2630 amyrsoldner@gmail.com	181 Westfield Ave Hamilton OH 45013	OH	Teacher	Tchr	Immanuel Hamilton OH	(513)893-6792	CQ	2021
Soleta Stacie L Krenz	(507)853-4711 staciesoleta@immanuellake field.com	38629 790th St Lakefield MN 56150	MNS	Teacher	Tchr	Immanuel Lakefield MN	(507)662-5860	S	1994
Solheim Christine R Gregg	(707)292-3430 cdksolheim@gmail.com	7088 Hastings Pl Windsor CA 95492	CNH	Teacher	C07/2016			CQ	1984
Solinsky Ann C Oltmanns	(605)390-3092 ann.solinsky@zionrc.org	15116 Lower Spring Creek Rd Hermosa SD 57744	SD	Teacher	P/Tchr	Zion Rapid City SD	(605)342-5749	CQ	2003
Sollberger Lukas J	(402)658-6538 ljsollberger@gmail.com	2110 Duff Ave Cheyenne WY 82001	WY	Teacher	Tchr	Trinity Cheyenne WY	(307)635-2802	S	2022
Sollenberger James W	(812) 350-9336 jsollen71@gmail.com	3285 Forsythia Dr Columbus IN 47203	IN	Teacher	EM			S	1976
Sollenberger Karen A Jesse	(812)376-9034 jksollen@att.net	3285 Forsythia Dr Columbus IN 47203	IN	Teacher	EM			RF	1977
Sollenberger Reta M Livermore	(561)302-4034 retasbgr@aol.com	14808 NW 4th Ct Vancouver WA 98685	FG	Teacher	EM			CQ	1980

*Multiple Assignments (See Church Worker Locator for Additional Details)
See Page 53 for the Table of Abbreviations for key to District, Classification, Position, and College abbreviations.
**C =Candidate; EM =Emeritus; the date following the C is the month and year the Candidate status began

NAME	TELEPHONE NUMBER EMAIL	STREET ADDRESS CITY/STATE/ZIP	DISTRICT	CLASS.	POSITION/ STATUS**	WHERE SERVING	OFFICE PHONE	COLLEGE/ UNIV/CQ	YR GRAD
Sombke Deloris E	(317)375-1956	11050 Presbyterian Dr # 237 Indianapolis IN 46236	IN	Teacher	EM			S	1964
Sombke Kristie L Bruick	(419)203-7704 ksombke@hclc.info	13889 Vincent Dr McCordsville IN 46055	IN	Teacher	Pro Stf	Holy Cross Indianapolis IN	(317)826-1234	S	1989
Sommerer Lauren K Hofman	(402)643-4300 lauren.sommerer@gmail.com	663 N 7th St Seward NE 68434	NEB	Teacher	Tchr	St John Seward NE	(402)643-2983	S	1993
Sommerer Melanie J Liebmann	(618)594-8714 mjsommerer@gmail.com	1346 W Fremont St Galesburg IL 61401	CI	Teacher	C07/2016			S	1997
Sommerer Samuel E	(636)233-0586 remremmoss@gmail.com	548 N 6th St Seward NE 68434	NEB	Teacher	P/Tchr	St Paul Utica NE	(402)534-2121	S	1992
Sommerfeld Gene W	(515)570-2022 gene.sommerfeld@gmail.com	511 9th St NE Dilworth MN 56529	MNN	Teacher	EM			S	1970
Sommerfeld Jennifer L	(701)281-2768 jsommerfeld@gracels.com	4701 Preston Park Blvd Apt 1635 Plano TX 75093	ND	Teacher	Tchr	Grace Fargo ND	(701)232-7747	MQ	2003
Sommermeyer David A Dr	(281)352-7935 davesommermeyer@me.com	465 Wildflower Ct Ballwin MO 63021	MO	Teacher	EM			S	1966
Sommermeyer Joshua D	(260)446-7658 joshsommermeyer@pilgrimluth.org	1445 Waterford Dr Ashwanbenon WI 54313	NW	Teacher	Prin	Pilgrim Green Bay WI	(920)965-2244	MQ	1998
Sonlitner Glenn R	(630)978-7257 g.son-a.pav@sbcglobal.net	3472 Saint Barthelemy Ln Aurora IL 60504	NI	Teacher	EM			RF	1969
Sonnenberg E S	(949)922-1151 essonn@flash.net	4815 Camino Costado San Clemente CA 92673	PSW	Teacher	EM			S	1964
Sonntag Annette M Schult	(402)285-9100 amsonnttag74@gmail.com	39209 205th Ave Columbus NE 68601	NEB	Teacher	EM			S	1974
Sonntag Connie L Kundinger	(989)686-8854	3034 Linden Park Dr Bay City MI 48706	MI	Teacher	EM			CQ	2006
Sonntag Judith R Barton	(507)227-9136	1718 10th St SE Forest Lake MN 55025	MNS	Teacher	EM			S	1968
Sonstroem Emily K	(703)774-4327 emily@oswlc.org	324 Shenandoah St SE Leesburg VA 20175	SE	DCE	Mem C	Our Savior's Way Ashburn VA	(703)858-9254	CH	2014
Soo Rachel L Leising	rachel.soo@cui.edu	6 Sunridge Irvine CA 92604	PSW	Teacher	S HS/C	Concordia University Irvine Irvine CA	(949)854-8002	IV	2008
Soper Roderick B	(949)635-5773 rod.soper@cui.edu	201 Woodview Ln Sapulpa OK 74066	PSW	Teacher	S HS/C	Concordia University Irvine Irvine CA	(949)854-8002	CQ	2000
Sopko Darlene K Brockshus	(605)653-0242 sopkodarlene@gmail.com	4900 S Oxbow Ave Apt 204 Sioux Falls SD 57106	SD	Teacher	EM			S	1969
Sorenson Michelle A Mueller	mmueller1288@gmail.com	11630 W 930 S Seymour IN 47274	IN	DCE	C07/2016			S	2012
Sorg Amanda M Sullivan	(260)466-4811 asorg@cluth.org	10520 Franke Rd Monroeville IN 46773	IN	Teacher	Tchr	Central New Haven IN	(260)493-2502	CQ	2013
Sorgatz James F	(901)494-9113 jamessorgatz@gmail.com	146 Burwyck Park Dr Saline MI 48176	MI	Teacher	EM			RF	1967
Sorgatz Marian A Helmreich	(901)494-7669 marian.sorgatz@gmail.com	146 Burwyck Park Dr Saline MI 48176	MI	Teacher	EM			RF	1968
Soso-Goines Connie R Goines Deac	(951)275-1456 deaconessconnie@gmail.com	2705 Shadow Lake Dr Greenwood AR 72936	MDS	Deaconess	Mem C	Grace Greenwood AR	(479)996-7747	FW-DEAC	2015
Sottile Melissa L Cattau	(808)268-2811 mlcattau@gmail.com	8301 Boseck Dr Unit 117 Las Vegas NV 89145	PSW	Teacher	Tchr	Faith Las Vegas NV	(702)804-4400	MQ	2004
Souer Rebecca J Trautman	(701)261-8646	420 Globe St Oxford NE 68967	NEB	DCE	C06/2020			S	2018
Soulek Paul M	(402)643-5863 paul.soulek@stjohnseward.org	1240 N Columbia Ave Seward NE 68434	NEB	DPM	Mem C	St John Seward NE	(402)643-2983	S	2007
Souligny Cheryl A Dubbe	(208)309-3008 casouligny@gmail.com	125 W 220th St Jordan MN 55352	NOW	Teacher	EM			S	1978
Souligny Clint J	cjsoulignt@gmail.com	33 Mesquite Cir Belton TX 76513	NOW	Tch/DCE	EM			S	1980
Souza Connie R Hopp	(775)846-5931 souzanna59@hotmail.com	26440 Freeport Ave Wyoming MN 55092	MNN	Teacher	EM			SP	1973
Souza William F Jr	(775)313-3378 billsouza12@yahoo.com	26440 Freeport Ave Wyoming MN 55092	MNN	Teacher	EM			SP	1973
Sovitzky Peter J	(847)602-0105 psovitzky@stjohnwheaton.org	1408 N Walnut Ave Arlington Hts IL 60004	NI	DPM	Mem C	St John Wheaton IL	(630)668-0701	CQ	2022
Spaeth Carol R Kionka	(989)590-8211 carolrspaeth@hotmail.com	1604 Summit Dr Pekin IL 61554	CI	Teacher	EM			RF	1965
Spaeth Cori L Brock	(309)642-7657 cori.spaeth@gmail.com	19 Cardinal Crst Pekin IL 61554	CI	Teacher	C03/2019			S	2007
Spangler John L IV	(516)902-1545 jspangler@ccls-stlouis.org	6333 Monterey Dr Saint Louis MO 63123	MO	Teacher	Tchr	Christ Community Kirkwood MO	(314)822-7774	MQ	1996
Spanos Esther M Giese	estherspanos@gmail.com	10312 Lake Tahoe Drive Fort Wayne IN 46804	IN	Teacher	Prin	Emmaus Fort Wayne IN	(260)459-7722	AA	1995
Spatz Carol J	(920)544-5985 cspatz@new.rr.com	1787 Cecil Ave Wabeno WI 54566	NW	Teacher	Tchr	Green Bay Trinity Green Bay WI	(920)655-4673	RF	1982
Spaulding Rebekah J Schumacher	(586)460-5737 rjemelia@gmail.com	810 S Roosevelt Green Bay WI 54301	NW	DCM	Mem C	Pilgrim Green Bay WI	(920)965-2233	MQ	2012
Spear Alexandra R	(618)381-2989 aspear1997@gmail.com	4100 Bridgewood Ct #8 Louisville KY 40241	IN	Teacher	Tchr	Our Savior Louisville KY	(502)426-0864	AA	2020
Speck Justin J Dr	(414)524-9382 justin.speck@cuw.edu	125 Grand Ave Thiensville WI 53092	SW	Teacher	S HS/C	Concordia University Wisconsin Mequon WI	(262)243-5700	CQ	2023
Speckhard John W	(314)894-0757 jwspeckhard@cs.com	4655 Concord Oaks Dr Saint Louis MO 63128	EN	Teacher	EM			RF	1959
Speers Chelsea M Heap	(517)388-3769 chelsea.speers@gmail.com	2041 Thornburn St Holt MI 48842	MI	Teacher	Prin	St Matthew Holt MI	(517)694-0978	CH	2010
Speers Laura		158 East Ave Hilton NY 14468	EA	Teacher	Tchr	St Paul Hilton NY	(585)392-4000	CQ	2019

*Multiple Assignments (See Church Worker Locator for Additional Details)

See Page 53 for the Table of Abbreviations for key to District, Classification, Position, and College abbreviations.

**C =Candidate; EM =Emeritus; the date following the C is the month and year the Candidate status began

NAME	TELEPHONE NUMBER EMAIL	STREET ADDRESS CITY/STATE/ZIP	DISTRICT	CLASS.	POSITION/ STATUS**	WHERE SERVING	OFFICE PHONE	COLLEGE/ UNIV/CQ	YR GRAD
Spelde Emily B Burcman Deac	(317)695-9366 ebspelde@gmail.com	2495 Cardinal Dr Indianapolis IN 46227	IN	Deaconess	EM			FW-DEAC	2013
Speltz Tona T Schmidtke	(507)351-6231 tona.speltz@molcs.org	1806 NW Ashland Pkwy Ankeny IA 50023	IW	Teacher	Tchr	Mount Olive Des Moines IA	(515)277-8349	CQ	2014
Spenner Cynthia H Harvey	(618)534-8785 cindy.spenner1@gmail.com	12163 N Prairie Rd Nashville IL 62263	SI	Teacher	Tchr	Trinity Hoffman IL	(618)495-2246	CQ	1998
Spero Gail E Streit	(847)390-7071 ilsflames@aol.com	741 S Warrington Rd Des Plaines IL 60016	NI	Teacher	Tchr	St Peter Schaumburg IL	(847)885-3350	RF	1990
Sperry Mark J	(563)321-0674 msperry@gracedewitt.org	1315 Maple Wood Ct De Witt IA 52742	IE	DCE	Mem C	Grace Dewitt IA	(563)659-9153	S	1994
Spicer Tiffani	(913)706-0248 tspicer@cglschool.org	1043 E Phelps St Gilbert AZ 85295	PSW	Teacher	Tchr	Christ Greenfield Gilbert AZ	(480)892-8521	CQ	2017
Spiegel Christy L Wawrzyniak	(512)653-3515 cspiegel@lutheranwest.com	4568 Carsten Ln North Olmsted OH 44070	OH	Teacher	Tchr	Cleveland LHS Association Rocky River OH	(440)356-7155	AU	2009
Spiehs Clarissa A	(641)373-8706 spieh.clarissa@gmail.com	205 S Main St Concordia MO 64020	MO	Teacher	Tchr	Saint Paul Concordia MO	(660)463-2238	S	2023
Spiehs Shawna L Voelker	slfootprints@hotmail.com	17411 Doleen Dr Macomb MI 48044	MI	Teacher	Tchr	Trinity Utica MI	(586)731-4490	S	1997
Spieker Jordan E VonDielingen	(812)603-6356 jspieker@immanuelschool.org	1976 Austin James Ln Seymour IN 47274	IN	Teacher	Tchr	Immanuel Seymour IN	(812)522-1301	CH	2013
Spieler Andrew F	(573)788-2591 aspieler@ilsperryville.org	9638 State Highway B Friedheim MO 63747	MO	Teacher	Prin	Immanuel Perryville MO	(573)547-8317	S	2002
Spieler Brenda M Schilling	(678)350-4354 brendaspieler@gmail.com	5462 Hillsboro Hematite Rd Desoto MO 63020	MO	Teacher	Prin	St John Arnold MO	(636)464-7303	RF	2000
Spieler Cathy M Dawes	c_spieler@yahoo.com	930 Jackson Trl Jackson MO 63755	MO	Teacher	EM			S	1971
Spieler Jennifer D Seabaugh	(573)768-1171 jspieler@ilsperryville.org	9638 State Highway B Friedheim MO 63747	MO	Teacher	Tchr	Immanuel Perryville MO	(573)547-6161	S	2003
Spieth Kristen M Fromm	(312)305-0971 kfromm89@gmail.com	35 Lemans Dr. Napoleon OH 43545	OH	Teacher	Tchr	St Paul Napoleon OH	(419)592-3535	MQ	2011
Spieth Renee E Werling	(260)557-8663 srspieth@hotmail.com	19203 Edgerton Rd Woodburn IN 46797	IN	Teacher	Tchr	St John-Emmanuel Monroeville IN	(260)639-0123	RF	1994
Spilker Ruth A Siebert	(618)483-3414 alissecond@altamontlis.com	6339 N 475th St Altamont IL 62411	CI	Teacher	EM			CQ	1995
Spilker Vernon R	(618)483-3414 vspilker@frontiernet.net	6339 N 475th St Altamont IL 62411	CI	Teacher	EM			RF	1969
Spinner Donna L Heinkel	(217)972-1519 spinnerdonna@gmail.com	524 Park Place Dr Unit B Forsyth IL 62535	CI	Teacher	EM			RF	1964
Spitz Sandra J Harms	(217)781-1264 sandy_spitz@yahoo.com	244 E Center St Paxton IL 60957	CI	Teacher	Tchr	Christ Lutheran HS Buckley IL	(217)394-2547	CQ	2009
Spitz Shelby K	(303)841-5551 shelby.spitz@lhsparker.org		RM	Teacher	Tchr	Colorado Lutheran High School Parker CO	(303)841-5551	Other	2020
Spitzack James R	(612)866-1787 jimspit@hotmail.com	6245 3rd Ave S Richfield MN 55423	MNS	Teacher	EM			S	1965
Spiva Cynthia L Pfohl	(661)342-3546 cspiva@emmausalhambra.org	777 E Valley Blvd #153 Alhambra CA 91801	PSW	Teacher	Prin	Emmaus Alhambra CA	(626)289-3664	PO	1988
Spiva Daniel F	dspiva@emmausalhambra.org	777 E Valley Blvd Apt 153 Alhambra CA 91801	PSW	Teacher	Tchr	Emmaus Alhambra CA	(626)289-3664	S	1985
Splattstoesser Kelsey E Baarck	(989)293-0721 kelseybaarck@gmail.com	932 Eastgate Ct Frankenmuth MI 48734	MI	Teacher	Tchr	St Lorenz Frankenmuth MI	(989)652-6141	S	2019
Splittgerber Anthony B	(308)293-0168 anthony.splittgerber@zionkearney.org	3305 B Ave Kearney NE 68847	NEB	Teacher	Tchr	Zion Kearney NE	(308)234-3410	S	2000
Splittgerber Lisa R Schmidt	(308)627-4566 tolisplit@hotmail.com	3305 B Ave Kearney NE 68847	NEB	Teacher	Tchr	Zion Kearney NE	(308)234-3410	S	2000
Spohn Christine Javer	(419)385-4382 cjspohn50@gmail.com	4057 Autumn View Ct Toledo OH 43614	OH	Teacher	EM			RF	1972
Spomer Constance D Rawerts	(918)355-0218 cspomer@cox.net	3708 N Battle Creek Dr Broken Arrow OK 74012	OK	Teacher	EM			CQ	1963
Spors Alison S Riach	(714)290-9587 Alison.Spors@splsorange.org	N60W27208 Trappers Run Sussex WI 53089	SW	Teacher	Tchr	Divine Redeemer Hartland WI	(262)367-3664	S	2001
Spors Robert R	(714)393-2512 robertr.spors@gmail.com	N60W27208 Trappers Run Sussex WI 53089	SW	Teacher	Tchr	LHS Assn of Greater Milwaukee West Allis WI	(414)421-9100	RF	1984
Spottiswood Wesley J	(818)642-7570 wspottiswood@hopelutheranwf.org	108 Kent St Youngsville NC 27596	SE	DCE	Mem C	Hope Wake Forest NC	(919)554-8109	IV	2017
Sprecher Arlyn L	(913)515-6322 arlyn.sprecher@gmail.com	11522 W 143rd Ter Olathe KS 66062	KS	Tch/DCE	EM			S	1970
Spreitzer Katharine B	(516)592-2669	7242 73rd St Glendale NY 11385	AT	Teacher	Tchr	Redeemer Glendale NY	(718)456-5292	BR	2014
Sprengel Charise L Pritzel	(913)449-5067 charise.sprengel@gmail.com	2326 Bainbridge Rd Jackson MO 63755	MO	Teacher	Tchr	Immanuel Perryville MO	(573)547-6161	S	1995
Sprengel Jonathan R	(573)298-0300 jrsprengel@gmail.com	233 Eastland Dr Jefferson City MO 65101	MO	Teacher	Prin	Trinity Jefferson City MO	(573)636-6750	S	2002
Sprengel Roger A	(618)920-7519 rogdonsprengel@gmail.com	1925 Herby Ln Swansea IL 62226	SI	Teacher	EM			S	1973
Sprengeler Cathy S Jaeger	(515)230-2749 cathy_sprengeler@msn.com	615 Brookridge Dr Boone IA 50036	IW	Teacher	EM			RF	1982
Sprengeler Denise E	(913)704-9577 g2sprengeler@gmail.com	6190 Boulder Ridge Dr Rockford MN 55373	MNS	Tch/DCE	EM			SP	1981
Springer Hans G	(636)861-7229 hgs007@aol.com	1115 Oakleaf Cove Ct Fenton MO 63026	MO	Teacher	EM			BR	1977

NAME	TELEPHONE NUMBER EMAIL	STREET ADDRESS CITY/STATE/ZIP	DISTRICT	CLASS.	POSITION/ STATUS**	WHERE SERVING	OFFICE PHONE	COLLEGE/ UNIV/CQ	YR GRAD
Springer Mara L Fick	(314)966-0532 mara.springer@lutheran specialed.org	741 W Lockwood Ave Saint Louis MO 63122	MO	Teacher	Tchr	Assoc Spec Ed Saint Louis MO	(314)268-1234	CQ	2001
Springer Marie E Eisemann	(636)861-7229 mespring004@aol.com	1115 Oakleaf Cove Ct Fenton MO 63026	MO	Teacher	EM			RF	1965
Springer Matthew J	(314)966-0532 mgmspringer3@gmail.com	741 W Lockwood Ave Saint Louis MO 63122	MO	Teacher	Tchr	St John Arnold MO	(636)464-7303	RF	1987
Springfield Mary H Conway		905 Oakdale Cir Pflugerville TX 78660	TX	Teacher	Tchr	Redeemer Austin TX	(512)459-1500	AU	2005
Sprow Keith R	(586)839-9945	33602 Bayview Dr Chesterfield MI 48047	MI	Teacher	EM			S	1971
Spurgeon David M	(360)581-2714 davidspurgeon13@gmail.com	1172 Vallecito Loop NW Los Lunas NM 87031	RM	DCE	Mem C	Immanuel Albuquerque NM	(505)242-0616	PO	2014
St Clair Gary L	(317)250-6137 gstclair36@gmail.com	16760 Algonquin St Huntington Beach CA 92640	IN	Teacher	EM			RF	1976
St Clair Nancy J Siekmann	(317)862-3789 gstclair72@hotmail.com	16760 Algonquin St Huntington Beach CA 92640	IN	Teacher	EM			RF	1975
St Georges Alyssa D Deac	(260)229-9825 deacalyssa75@gmail.com	2471 W Keiser Rd Columbia City IN 46725	FG	Deaconess	C07/2016			FW-DEAC	2014
St Martin Ruby A	(618)537-8393 rstmartin10926@att.net	10926 Upland Terrace Dr Lebanon IL 62254	SI	Teacher	EM			SP	1965
St Peters Cynthia M Buhs	(618)410-7131 charj5@sbcglobal.net	34169 Teakwood Pl Brighton IL 62012	SI	Teacher	C07/2016			RF	1989
Staake Linda S Kolzow	(714)974-0994 hillsres@aol.com	5900 E Santa Ana Canyon Rd Anaheim CA 92807	PSW	Teacher	EM			RF	1970
Stackhouse Melynda E Bender	(727)225-7291 mindy.stackhouse@verizon.net	125 Fallen Spruce Dr Asheville NC 28806	SE	Teacher	Tchr	Emmanuel Asheville NC	(828)252-1795	RF	1995
Stackle Christina M Meyer	(314)520-0027 christinastackle@yahoo.com	2283 Wincanton Rd Saint Louis MO 63129	MO	DCE	Mem C	Peace Saint Louis County MO	(314)892-5610	SP	2000
Stacy Amanda M Wilson	(402)650-3132	215 S Marigold St Ishpeming MI 49849	NW	DCE	Mem C	Christ King Ishpeming MI	(906)485-4432	S	2006
Stacy Betsy	(419)944-4033 betsy@teamstacy.org	8245 Elkhorn Lane Toledo OH 43617	OH	Teacher	Tchr	Trinity Toledo OH	(419)385-2301	CQ	2022
Stade Lisa A Givens	(909)899-1453 lrst1990@gmail.com	5387 Wagon Way Fontana CA 92336	PSW	Teacher	Tchr	Mt Calvary Diamond Bar CA	(909)861-2740	IV	1987
Stadler Grant P	(402)942-3918 grantstadler15@gmail.com	10220 Baltimore Ave Saint Ann MO 63074	MO	Teacher	Tchr	St Charles Saint Peters MO	(636)928-5100	S	2022
Stadler Rebekah M Eatherton	(469)435-1468 rebekahstadler@gmail.com	10220 Baltimore Ave Saint Ann MO 63074	MO	Teacher	Tchr	Zion Saint Charles MO	(636)441-7424	S	2023
Stadler Richard L	(352)209-0440 rcstad@embarqmail.com	5380 Layton Dr Venice FL 34293	FG	Teacher	EM			RF	1968
Staedler Heather A Corn	(414)940-4055 heather_corn@yahoo.com	338 Birchwood Lane Theresa WI 53091	SW	Teacher	Tchr	Good Shepherd Watertown WI	(920)261-2579	MQ	2002
Staehlin Mary E Weinrich	(847)508-2670 mstaehlin@fulllifeinchrist.org	3511 Sigwalt St Rolling Meadows IL 60008	NI	Teacher	Tchr	St Peter Arlington Heights IL	(847)259-4114	RF	2001
Staehr Brian T	(308)258-1164 btja1991@gmail.com	625 2nd St Hampton NE 68843	NEB	Teacher	Tchr	Emmanuel-Faith York NE	(402)362-6575	S	1994
Staehr Caleb T	(417) 866-5878 caleb.staehr@cune.org		MO	Teacher	Mem C	Trinity Springfield MO	(417)866-5878	S	2019
Staehr Jerrita A Kahle	(308)258-1163 jastaehr@gmail.com	625 2nd St Hampton NE 68843	NEB	Teacher	S HS/C	Concordia University Nebraska Seward NE	(402)643-3651	CQ	2007
Stafford Julia A Wakeland	(260)403-5851 jastafford08@gmail.com	3140 Garden View Ter Apt E Danville IN 46132	IN	Teacher	Tchr	Our Shepherd Avon IN	(317)271-9103	MQ	2008
Stafford - Nunez Mary E Lightbody	(262)408-0669 dcemel@yahoo.com	17812 W Oak Dr New Berlin WI 53146	SW	Tch/DCE	Mem C	Brookfield Brookfield WI	(262)783-4270	RF	1991
Stahl Heather	(415)314-3673 h.stahl@zion.org	1811 92nd Dr SE Lake Stevens WA 98258	NOW	Teacher	Tchr	Zion Snohomish Cty Lake Stevens WA	(425)334-5064	CQ	2010
Stahlecker Brianne L	(816)752-1718 bstahlecker09@gmail.com	1027 E Independence St Apt 103 Giddings TX 78942	TX	Teacher	Tchr	Immanuel Giddings TX	(979)542-3319	S	2009
Stahlecker Karla M	(989)245-4461 knittedbug@gmail.com	2526 N Mason St Saginaw MI 48602	MI	Teacher	Tchr	Valley Saginaw MI	(989)790-1676	S	2013
Stallings Jennifer	(832)457-9179 jestallings18@gmail.com		TX	Teacher	Tchr	Redeemer Austin TX	(512)451-6478	AU	2011
Stallman Ronald H	(574)266-7116 stallman1638@comcast.net	1638e Cobblestone Blvd Elkhart IN 46514	IN	Teacher	EM			RF	1962
Stam Connie J Wegehaupt	(651)345-5789	909 S 6th St Lake City MN 55041	MNS	Teacher	EM			SP	1968
Stam Tracy A Hackman	(812)358-5619	2731 S County Road 400 E Brownstown IN 47220	IN	Teacher	C05/2023			CQ	2003
Stamm Joanne R Janssen	(217)394-2136	P.O. Box 342 Buckley IL 60918	CI	Teacher	EM			RF	1963
Stamp Ellen J Black	(972)394-6322 Mjej630@verizon.net	3715 Remington Dr Carrollton TX 75007	TX	Teacher	Tchr	Zion Dallas TX	(214)363-1639	S	1982
Stancliff Jane C Carr Deac	(618)304-0560 stancrafter@gmail.com	54 Chateau Dr Fairview Hts IL 62208	SI	Deaconess	EM			SL-DEAC	2009
Standerfer Malinda A	(317)674-6731 malinda.standerfer@gmail.com	548 Surby Ave Battle Creek MI 49015	RM	DCE	C02/2025			S	2017
Stange Jessica A	(586)321-2094 jstange@lhsa.com	690 Huntington Street Mount Clemens MI 48043	MI	Teacher	Tchr	Northwest Rochester Hills MI	(248)856-0240	CQ	2019
Stanhope Debra G Goodwin	(707)363-8089 dgstanhope@gmail.com	314 Carlson Way Napa CA 94558	CNH	Teacher	EM			S	1976
Stanley Lisa S	(989)751-5209 stanley_ls@yahoo.com	8729 Jonathan Dr North Royalton OH 44133	OH	Teacher	Tchr	Bethany Parma OH	(440)884-1010	AA	1986
Stanley Sharon J Rosenthal	(760)807-4294 shemastanley@cox.net	1411 Archwood Pl Escondido CA 92026	PSW	Teacher	C07/2016			S	1977

*Multiple Assignments (See Church Worker Locator for Additional Details)
See Page 53 for the Table of Abbreviations for key to District, Classification, Position, and College abbreviations.
**C =Candidate; EM =Emeritus; the date following the C is the month and year the Candidate status began

NAME	TELEPHONE NUMBER EMAIL	STREET ADDRESS CITY/STATE/ZIP	DISTRICT	CLASS.	POSITION/ STATUS**	WHERE SERVING	OFFICE PHONE	COLLEGE/ UNIV/CQ	YR GRAD
Stansbury Megan E McMullen	(815)822-8110	2419 W 57th St Davenport IA 52806	IE	Teacher	Tchr	Trinity Davenport IA	(563)323-8001	MQ	2024
Stanski Kristina J	(813)753-8932 kristy.stanski@lsportal.net	520 W Nelson St Apt 311 Marion IN 46952	FG	Teacher	C07/2016			CQ	2005
Stapleton Anna M	(920)243-3012 anna_2382@yahoo.com	514 Cedar Glen Dr Apt 4 Fort Wayne IN 46825	IN	Teacher	Tchr	Concordia Fort Wayne IN	(260)422-2429	S	2006
Stapleton Michael R	(920)378-3440 mrstapleton53@gmail.com	2110 N Peter Ln Little Shute WI 54140	NW	DCE	EM			S	1983
Stark Debora A Willing	(989)631-0163 dstark@sjlmidland.org	149 W Ashby Rd Midland MI 48640	MI	DCE	EM			CQ	2008
Stark Elizabeth A Christian	(913)345-9345 elizabeth.christian@cune.org	12019 Felt Pl Monroeville IN 46773	IN	Teacher	Tchr	St John-Emmanuel Monroeville IN	(260)639-0123	S	2009
Stark Linda J Muenchow	(678)215-3488 lstark@messiahokc.org	4328 NW 57th St Oklahoma City OK 73112	OK	Teacher	Tchr	Messiah Oklahoma City OK	(405)946-0462	RF	1989
Stark Muriel L Friedrich	(320)634-0136 mlfstark279@gmail.com	25132 250th Ave Glenwood MN 56334	MNN	Teacher	EM			SP	1972
Stark Paul A	paul.stark@popcs.org	c/o Salem Lutheran Church 22601 Lutheran Church Rd Tomball TX 77377	TX	Teacher	Tchr	Salem Tomball TX	(281)351-8223	S	1996
Starks Suzanne E Lehrke	(612)724-3684	5705 27th Ave S Minneapolis MN 55417	MNS	Teacher	S HS/C	Concordia University St Paul Saint Paul MN	(651)641-8278	SP	1989
Starr Dawn P Johnson	(708)302-8505	8335 High Point Circle #2 Port Richey FL 34668	FG	Teacher	EM			RF	2002
Stathakis Carol B Schnake	(586)747-2484 carol.stathakis@gmail.com	13883 Timberview Dr Shelby Township MI 48315	MI	Teacher	EM			S	1980
Statler Patricia	(317)771-4091 tstatler@cornerstonelutheran.church	12410 Huntington Dr Indianapolis IN 46229	IN	DCE	Mem C	Cornerstone Carmel IN	(317)814-4252	CQ	2024
Statza Diane L Berkhahn	(262)366-2989 dianestatza@gmail.com	W180 N9865 Riversbend Circle W Germantown WI 53022	EN	Teacher	C07/2016			RF	1981
Staub Arlys R Mandernach	(260)632-5567 arlysstaub@gmail.com	5318 N State Road 101 Woodburn IN 46797	IN	Teacher	EM			S	1973
Staub Jeremy J	(808)268-0415 jstaub@clhscadets.com	9512 Pinepark Pass New Haven IN 46774	IN	Teacher	Tchr	Concordia Fort Wayne IN	(260)483-1102	S	2009
Staub Michael S Dr	(713)204-7942 mstaub@mlchouston.org	10046 Burgoyne Rd Houston TX 77042	TX	Teacher	Tchr	Memorial Houston TX	(713)782-6079	S	2002
Staub Rebekah M Stein	(260)446-1613 rebekahmstein@gmail.com	9512 Pinepark Pass New Haven IN 46774	IN	Teacher	Tchr	Concordia Fort Wayne IN	(260)483-1102	RF	2007
Staub Scott M	(260)632-5567 sstaub7808@gmail.com	5318 N State Road 101 Woodburn IN 46797	IN	Teacher	EM			S	1972
Staube Julie L	(602)475-0185 juliestraube0823@gmail.com	8200 Sunbury Ln Apt 15S-1516 Houston TX 77095	TX	Teacher	Tchr	Our Savior Houston TX	(713)290-8277	IV	2024
Stayton Melissa M Smith-Brown	(812)216-1375 mstayton@immanuelschool.org	434 Alexander Dr Seymour IN 47274	IN	Teacher	Tchr	Immanuel Seymour IN	(812)522-3118	RF	1997
Stearns Grace E	(314)910-7202 gstearns@osva.org	935 S Taylor St Arlington VA 22204	SE	Teacher	Tchr	Our Savior Arlington VA	(703)892-4846	BR	2015
Stec Christa R Funke	(757)903-1040 christastec@yahoo.com	104 Telemark Drive Williamsburg VA 23188	SE	DCM	Mem C	King of Glory Williamsburg VA	(757)258-9701	MQ	2002
Stec Daniel J	(636)577-1355 stec@me.com	3804 Grey Fox Cir Apt K Williamsburg VA 23188	RM	Teacher	C07/2016			MQ	2002
Stec Steven J	(708)257-3529 luke104142@gmail.com	16311 Cherry Hill Ave Tinley Park IL 60487	NI	Teacher	EM			RF	1971
Stechholz Janet L Kaminske	(734)679-9146 davejan7@hotmail.com	14374 Pere St Livonia MI 48154	EN	Teacher	EM			RF	1975
Steege Susan M	(716)440-5025 ssteege@firsttrinity.com	80 Charter Oaks Dr Apt 1 Buffalo NY 14228	EA	Tch/DCE	Mem C	First Trinity Tonawanda NY	(716)835-2220	S	1984
Steele Alicia M Woock	(630)485-8874 alicia.steele2014@gmail.com	1600 Dogwood Ct Perryville MO 63775	MO	Teacher	Tchr	Immanuel Perryville MO	(573)547-8317	CQ	2020
Steele Ashley	(602)284-7614 asteele@cglschool.org	1426 E Mineral Rd Gilbert AZ 85234	PSW	Teacher	Tchr	Christ Greenfield Gilbert AZ	(480)892-8521	CQ	2018
Steele Nathan P	(920)918-9914 kantorsteele@gmail.com	1600 Dogwood Court Perryville MO 63775	MO	DPM	Mem C	Immanuel Perryville MO	(573)547-8317	MQ	2014
Steffen Lee H	(920)287-9875 leesteffen@charter.net	2216 S 11th St Sheboygan WI 53081	SW	Teacher	EM			RF	1961
Steffen Lindsay L Rose	(262)510-7275 lsteffen@immanuelbrookfield.org	11880 W Janesville Rd Apt 2g Hales Corner WI 53130	SW	Teacher	Tchr	Immanuel Brookfield WI	(262)781-7140	MQ	2012
Steffen Michaela S Grubb	(402)640-4505 msgrubb2013@gmail.com	2001 E Norfolk Ave Norfolk NE 68701	NEB	Teacher	Tchr	Trinity Madison NE	(402)454-2651	CQ	2020
Steffens Allyn G	(573)547-1225 stefags@earthlink.net	614 Bruce St Perryville MO 63775	MO	Teacher	EM			S	1969
Steffens Christie R	(573)547-1225 ancsteffens@att.net	614 Bruce St Perryville MO 63775	MO	Teacher	EM			S	1969
Steffens Heather A Dorn	(269)873-2576 heathersteffens@hotmail.com	1481 Timberlane Dr Saint Joseph MI 49085	MI	Teacher	Tchr	Christ Stevensville MI	(269)429-7111	RF	2001
Steffens Mark C	(269)429-5487	6033 Bonanza Dr Stevensville MI 49127	MI	Teacher	EM			S	1967
Steffens Pamela A Marrocco	(314)795-9021 pamelaas76@aol.com	1213 Jefferson St Washington MO 63090	MO	Teacher	EM			RF	1976
Steffens Wanda B Doberenz	(573)837-2454 wbsteffens@charter.net	806 Pheasant Cove Dr Cpe Girardeau MO 63701	MO	Teacher	EM			S	1969
Stegall Emma L Leistico	(573)880-8613 kantor.stegall@gmail.com	125 E 14 Mile Rd Apt 6 Birmingham MI 48009	EN	DPM	Mem C	Ascension/Christ Beverly Hills MI	(248)644-8890	IV	2025
Steger Lauren E Heck	(920)382-6086 lauren.steger@live.com	7440 Werner Rd West Bend WI 53090	SW	Teacher	C07/2016			MQ	2012

*Multiple Assignments (See Church Worker Locator for Additional Details)

See Page 53 for the Table of Abbreviations for key to District, Classification, Position, and College abbreviations.

**C =Candidate; EM =Emeritus; the date following the C is the month and year the Candidate status began

NAME	TELEPHONE NUMBER EMAIL	STREET ADDRESS CITY/STATE/ZIP	DISTRICT	CLASS.	POSITION/ STATUS**	WHERE SERVING	OFFICE PHONE	COLLEGE/ UNIV/CQ	YR GRAD
Stegman Megan G Clift	(541)410-2532 megangraceclift@gmail.com	2828 Landing Creek Dr Apt. 521 Fort Worth TX 76131	CNH	Teacher	Tchr	Emmanuel* Kahului-Maui HI	(808)877-3037	IV	2019
Stehle Michelle A Galfano	(630)355-9435	2281 Weatherford Ln Naperville IL 60565	NI	Teacher	Tchr	Bethany Naperville IL	(630)355-6607	CQ	2010
Stehle Rebecca S Baker		16163 NW Fescue Ct Portland OR 97229	NOW	Teacher	Tchr	Pilgrim Beaverton OR	(503)644-8697	S	1997
Steichen Jessica Svajhart	(580) 716-6331 jessica.steichen@cune.org	3111 N Pecan Rd Ponca City OK 74604	OK	Teacher	Tchr	First Ponca City OK	(580)762-9950	S	2008
Steider Jannese M	(402)499-5908 jannese4hockey@outlook.com	1015 N Nebraska Ave York NE 68467	NEB	Teacher	Tchr	Emmanuel-Faith York NE	(402)362-6575	S	1993
Steigerwalt Sherri L Tino	(810)923-5263 gs.steigerwalt@gmail.com	11837 Lexington Dr South Lyon MI 48178	EN	Teacher	EM			AA	1988
Stein Marla	(408)807-3544 missmarlastein@gmail.com	518 Palo Verde Cmns Fremont CA 94539	CNH	Teacher	Tchr	Prince of Peace Fremont CA	(510)793-3366	CQ	2015
Stein Mary K Holmes Dr	(501)920-2126 marykstein@yahoo.com	2406 N Fillmore St Little Rock AR 72207	MDS	Teacher	EM			AU	2002
Stein Tonya C Waite	(602)653-9747 tonyawaite88@gmail.com	4185 W Sandarac St Tucson AZ 85741	EN	DCE	C02/2024			AU	2022
Steinacher Deborah M Wohlers	(217)675-2517 steinacherds@yahoo.com	2629 Woodson Franklin Rd Franklin IL 62638	CI	Teacher	Tchr	Salem Jacksonville IL	(217)243-3419	RF	2001
Steinbach Carol L Klemp	(870)425-0309 arlons@centurytel.net	82 Critter Ln Mountain Home AR 72653	MDS	Teacher	EM			RF	1967
Steinbach Martha C Schiebel	(240)687-9192 martha.steinbach7@gmail.com	8713 Oxwell Ln Laurel MD 20708	SE	Teacher	Tchr	Our Savior Laurel MD	(301)776-7670	BR	1996
Steinbacher Angela R	(636)448-4113 arsteinbacher@gmail.com	2608 Sequoia Drive St. Peters MO 63376	MO	Teacher	Mem C	Zion Saint Charles MO	(636)441-7425	S	2017
Steinbacher David A	(636)477-4950 dsteinbacher@lhssc.org	1214 Kingstowne Pl Saint Charles MO 63304	MO	Teacher	Tchr	St Charles Saint Peters MO	(636)928-5100	S	1983
Steinbauer Sara Streufert	(504)905-5470 ssteinbauer@hotmail.com	1900 Woodberry Run Dr Snellville GA 30078	SO	Teacher	EM			RF	1974
Steinberg Tannis L	(507)523-2523 tsteinberg@ridge-runner.com	264 Benson Dr Lewiston MN 55952	MNS	Teacher	Tchr	Immanuel Lewiston MN	(507)523-2228	SP	2001
Steinborn Julie L Jones	(952)955-3346 jsteinborn@ccls.net	808 Hutchinson Rd Watertown MN 55388	MNS	Teacher	Tchr	Christ Community Watertown MN	(952)955-1419	AA	1988
Steinbrenner Connie K Hinz	(630)406-1579 gsteinbrenner@prodigy.net	1291 St John St Erie CO 80516	RM	Teacher	EM			RF	1973
Steinbrenner Glenn A	(630)334-1579 GLENN.STEINBRENNER@GMAIL. COM	1291 St John St Erie CO 80516	RM	Teacher	EM			RF	1973
Steinbrenner Lisa S	(406)270-1011 lisa.steinbrenner@gmail.com	7090 Simms St Unit 106 Arvada CO 80004	RM	Teacher	Tchr	Bethlehem Lakewood CO	(303)238-7676	RF	2004
Steinbrenner Mark A	(414)460-3090 mark.steinbrenner@gmail.com	5243 Morley Dr Greendale WI 53129	EN	DCM	EM			MQ	2008
Steinbrenner Rachael M Quinlan	(724)413-5010 rachaelmsteinbrenner@gmail.com	5526 Cara Ct Dublin OH 43016	OH	Teacher	C08/2017			AA	2011
Steinbrueck Jan M	(314)913-1240 jsteinbrueck21@gmail.com	2001 Wyoming Ave Apt 8 Sun Prairie WI 53590	SW	DCE	Mem C	Bethlehem Sun Prairie WI	(608)837-7446	S	2019
Steinbrueck Judith A Kuhasz	(813)684-7520 judysteinbrueck@gmail.com	3832 Spruce Pine Dr Valrico FL 33596	FG	Teacher	EM			RF	1966
Steinbrueck Kathryn F Lehman	(314)843-0618 kasteinbrueck@gmail.com	8237 Marvale Ln Affton MO 63123	MO	Teacher	Pro Stf	Lutheran South Saint Louis MO	(314)631-1400	SP	1981
Steinbrueck Kenneth P	(314)843-0618	8237 Marvale Ln Affton MO 63123	MO	Teacher	Tchr	Lutheran South Saint Louis MO	(314)631-1400	RF	1978
Steinbrueck Melissa Martin	(813)326-5252 mms1223@gmail.com	4414 Crystal Downs Ct Wesley Chapel FL 33543	S	Teacher	Tchr	Family Of Christ Tampa FL	(813)558-9343	CQ	2009
Steinbrueck Richard G	(813)684-7520 4oclockguy@gmail.com	3832 Spruce Pine Dr Valrico FL 33596	FG	Tch/DCE	EM			S	1966
Steinburg Susan J		3829 S 2940 E Salt Lake Cty UT 84109	RM	Teacher	Tchr	Redeemer Salt Lake City UT	(801)487-6283	S	1970
Steiner Amy L Acton	(630)780-8138 alacton98@gmail.com	N28W6284 Alyce St # 132 Cedarburg WI 63012	SW	Teacher	Tchr	St Paul Grafton WI	(262)377-4659	MQ	2021
Steiner Bethany L Maxson	(801)913-3960 bsteiner28@gmail.com	1303 Birch Dr Mayer MN 55360	MNS	Teacher	Tchr	Trinity Waconia MN	(952)442-4165	S	2004
Steiner Pamela S Currie	(209)263-2400 pams.steiner@gmail.com	3652 Tranquility Trl Castle Rock CO 80109	RM	Teacher	EM			S	1971
Steingraber Lori J Tatkenhorst	(715)383-2663 Lori.Steingraber@gmail.com	801 Seminary Pl Saint Louis MO 63105	MO	Teacher	Tchr	Immanuel Olivette MO	(314)993-5004	S	2004
Steinhaus Lydia			MO	Teacher	Tchr	Office of International Mission Saint Louis MO		CH	2025
Steinhaus Paul R	(507)236-9488 psteinhauslmb@gmail.com	608 W 4th St Shawano WI 54166	NW	Teacher	Prin	Wolf River Shawano WI	(715)745-2400	MQ	1996
Steinke Amanda M	(262)744-5455 amsteinke209@gmail.com	1350 S Greenfield Rd Unit 1020 Mesa AZ 85206	PSW	Teacher	Tchr	Christs Greenfield Gilbert AZ	(480)892-8314	S	2025
Steinke Eric D	(517)260-2760 ericdce1@gmail.com	4190 Kelsey Ave Adrian MI 49221	MI	DCE	C08/2022			CQ	2010
Steinke Katherine M Boerger	(281)255-9988 ksteinke95@gmail.com	14265 Mildale St Brookfield WI 53005	SW	Teacher	Tchr	Milwaukee LHS Milwaukee WI	(414)461-6000	S	1994
Steinke Laurie J Callies	ljsteinke1982@gmail.com		FG	Teacher	C07/2016			RF	1982
Steinke Terry A Lassman	(407)289-6020 stinkysteinke@yahoo.com	1357 Haven Dr Oviedo FL 32765	FG	Teacher	EM			RF	1968
Steinmann Christopher	(216)469-3057 csteinmann@clhsa.org	2306 Oak Park Ave Cleveland OH 44109	OH	Teacher	Tchr	Lutheran East Cleveland Heights OH	(216)382-6100	AA	2004
Steinmann Judith Schroeder	(618)656-7503 brynnsgram@yahoo.com	8325 Jerusalem Rd Edwardsville IL 62025	SI	Teacher	EM			S	1966

*Multiple Assignments (See Church Worker Locator for Additional Details)
See Page 53 for the Table of Abbreviations for key to District, Classification, Position, and College abbreviations.
**C =Candidate; EM =Emeritus; the date following the C is the month and year the Candidate status began

NAME	TELEPHONE NUMBER EMAIL	STREET ADDRESS CITY/STATE/ZIP	DISTRICT	CLASS.	POSITION/ STATUS**	WHERE SERVING	OFFICE PHONE	COLLEGE/ UNIV/CQ	YR GRAD
Steivang Tracey A Winn	(651)335-8973 traceysteivang@gmail.com	79 Tribute Ave Hudson WI 54016	MNS	Teacher	C07/2016			SP	1994
Stejskal Cheryl A	(562)715-9763 bellflowercat3@gmail.com	17724 Regency Cir Bellflower CA 90706	PSW	Teacher	EM			CQ	2007
Stelling Dwight D Dr	(515)255-7639 stellingd@aol.com	662 34th St Des Moines IA 50312	IW	Teacher	EM			CQ	1980
Stelling George E	(949)243-6328 kuwaa513@att.net	24921 Muirlands Blvd #165 Lake Forest CA 92630	PSW	Teacher	EM			RF	1958
Stelling Troy A	(904)629-5328 stelling@digital.net	2470 S Naples Way Aurora CO 80013	RM	Teacher	Tchr	Lutheran Parker CO	(303)841-5551	S	1990
Stellwagen Benjamin J Dr	(260)234-1320 bstellwagen@esmeagles.com	10712 Bayou Blvd Fort Wayne IN 46845	IN	Teacher	Prin	Emmanuel-St Michael Fort Wayne IN	(260)422-6712	CQ	2016
Stellwagen David R	(260)452-4974 dstellwagen@emmauslutheranfw. org	6526 Wakopa Ct Fort Wayne IN 46815	IN	Teacher	Tchr	Emmaus Fort Wayne IN	(260)459-7722	RF	1985
Stellwagen Laurie J Rosenwinkel	(812)219-8423 thestellwagens@gmail.com	10712 Bayou Blvd Fort Wayne IN 46845	IN	Teacher	C07/2016			MQ	2006
Stelmachowicz Cary L Dr	(913)499-8548 cstelmac@lhske.com	5448 W 130th Ter Leawood KS 66209	MO	Teacher	Pro Stf	Kansas City Kansas City MO	(816)241-5478	RF	1978
Stelmachowicz Casey R	(314)923-1032 caseystelmachowicz@gmail.com	3661 Metter St Las Vegas NV 89129	PSW	Teacher	Tchr	Faith Las Vegas NV	(702)804-4400	MQ	2007
Steltenpohl Gayle F Giardini	(815)568-2750 gsteltenpohl@icloud.com	110 Beacon Dr Belvidere IL 61008	NI	Teacher	EM			RF	1975
Steltenpohl William M	(815)568-2750 otispoodle@yahoo.com	110 Beacon Dr Belvidere IL 61008	NI	Teacher	EM			RF	1975
Stelter Ellen Vandre	(920)457-3813 mrsellenabc@yahoo.com	2618 Broadway Ave Sheboygan WI 53081	SW	Teacher	EM			RF	1971
Stelter Julie A	julie.stelter@stjohns-laporte.com	111 Kingsbury Ave La Porte IN 46350	IN	Teacher	Tchr	Saint Johns Laporte IN	(219)362-3726	AA	1986
Stelzer Kenneth R	krstelzer210@aol.com	120 River Bend Dr Apt 234 Georgetown TX 78628	TX	Teacher	EM			S	1980
Stelzer Wilbert P Dr	(631)946-1373 wil.stelzer@osnas.org	55 Arbor Lane Centereach NY 11720	AT	Teacher	Prin	Our Sav New American Centereach NY	(631)588-2757	CQ	2016
Stenbeck Susan K Barnes	(314)849-6497	7224 Marlton Ln Saint Louis MO 63123	MO	Teacher	EM			SP	1973
Stender Laura E Schrupp	(952)200-8113 laura.stender@stjohns-chaska.org	789 Tacoma Ave Young America MN 55397	MNS	Teacher	Tchr	St Johns Chaska MN	(952)448-2526	SP	2008
Stengel Lori L Leonard	(314)973-5891 stengell3lucy@gmail.com	225 East Park Avenue Kansas City MO 64119	MO	DCE	C07/2016			SP	2001
Stengl Richard G	(715)573-0175 dce10311517@gmail.com	2110 Victor Ln Kronenwetter WI 54455	NW	DCE	C06/2024			CQ	2011
Stenklyft Joshua T	(920)226-1353 joshua.stenklyft@gmail.com	N8971 Holmes Rd Apt 4 Brillion WI 54110	SW	Teacher	Tchr	Trinity Hilbert WI	(920)853-3134	MQ	2014
Stenklyft Terry N	(920)451-7794	889 Forest Ave Sheboygan WI 53081	SW	Teacher	EM			MQ	1984
Stennett Lyn M Ruppert	(801)879-5568	1245 Eastridge Dr Seward NE 68434	NEB	Teacher	Tchr	St John Seward NE	(402)643-4535	RF	1992
Stepanek Amanda J Tuell	(720)841-0822 castepanek@gmail.com	8237 Ruby Mountain Way Las Vegas NV 89128	PSW	Teacher	Tchr	Faith Las Vegas NV	(702)804-4400	S	2002
Stephens Elizabeth A	(316)213-8830 dcebeths@gmail.com		KS	DCE	Mem C	Trinity Mission KS	(913)432-5441	S	2016
Stephens Judy L Etling	(618)401-4648 jdytchz1@yahoo.com	16 S 19th St Belleville IL 62226	SI	Teacher	EM			CQ	1995
Stephens Kent W	(316)708-0693 kentst22@gmail.com	4321 Dellrose Circle Wichita KS 67220	KS	DCO	EM			IV	1981
Stephenson Bonnie C Zimmerman Deac	(319)318-5138 bonniestephenson@proton.me	1305 Donels Dr Vinton IA 52349	IE	Deaconess	EM			Other	1981
Stephenson Erica A Swenson Deac	(317)881-4477 dcs.erica@gmail.com	305 Howard Rd Greenwood IN 46142	IN	Deaconess	Mem C	Concordia Greenwood IN	(317)881-4477	FW-DEAC	2013
Sterling Daniel T	(314)869-6681	10046 Harwich Dr Saint Louis MO 63126	MO	Teacher	Tchr	St Paul Des Peres MO	(314)822-2771	RF	1986
Stetson Jessica R Nienhuser	(949)838-5769 jessicastetson2@gmail.com	647 Otono Dr. Boulder City NV 89005	PSW	DCE	Mem C	Christ Boulder City NV	(702)293-4332	IV	2008
Steuernagel Paula J	(219)218-7700 dpsteuernagel@comcast.net	3508 Leming Lane Jackson MO 63755	MO	DPM	Mem C	St Paul Jackson MO	(573)243-2236	CQ	2018
Stevens Beverly J Check			NOW	Teacher	Tchr	CAN HK Repulse Bay	011-852-2812- 5151	CQ	2022
Stevens Judith A Tucker	(713)944-2760	2200 S Lakeline Blvd Unit 112 Cedar Park TX 78613	TX	Teacher	EM			CQ	1996
Stevens Nathan A	(602)524-7279 nstevens@cglschool.org	4608 W Del Rio St Chandler AZ 85226	PSW	Teacher	Tchr	Christ Greenfield Gilbert AZ	(480)892-8521	IV	2015
Stevens Todd C	(918)770-3920 toddstevensdce@gmail.com	20231 E 141st St S Broken Arrow OK 74014	OK	DCE	Mem C	Immanuel Broken Arrow OK	(918)258-5506	S	1997
Stevenson Betty J Potts	(248)787-7590	2298 Woodlawn St Wolverine Lk MI 48390	MI	Teacher	EM			CQ	1984
Stevenson James N Dr	(512)695-8284 kodaiborn@yahoo.com	1002 Weeping Willow Dr Austin TX 78753	TX	Teacher	EM			S	1964
Stevens-Verdi Kathryn H Stevens		1704 Travis Ct Allen TX 75002	TX	Teacher	Tchr	Faith Plano TX	(972)423-7447	BR	1976
Steward Brian D	(309)243-7990 stew31@hotmail.com	1516 Macklin Dr De Witt IA 52742	CI	DCE	C07/2016			RF	2002
Stewart Amanda L	(714)313-5715 astewy21@sbcglobal.net	1406 W Ball Rd Anaheim CA 92802	PSW	Teacher	C06/2021			IV	1998
Stewart Christopher		99 Franklin Sq New Britain CT 06051	NE	Teacher	C07/2016			S	2001

*Multiple Assignments (See Church Worker Locator for Additional Details)

See Page 53 for the Table of Abbreviations for key to District, Classification, Position, and College abbreviations.

**C =Candidate; EM =Emeritus; the date following the C is the month and year the Candidate status began

NAME	TELEPHONE NUMBER EMAIL	STREET ADDRESS CITY/STATE/ZIP	DISTRICT	CLASS.	POSITION/ STATUS**	WHERE SERVING	OFFICE PHONE	COLLEGE/ UNIV/CQ	YR GRAD
Stewart Lamar Q	(828)455-3187 lqstewart@gmail.com	1537 Paradise Valley Dr High Ridge MO 63049	SE	DCE	C06/2024			S	2009
Stewart Lois A Bramstadt	(708)373-1086 lois.stewart@nidlcms.org	3737 168th St Country Club Hills IL 60478	NI	Teacher	D Ex/S	Northern Illinois District River Forest IL	(708)449-3020	RF	1983
Stewart Nicole D	(832)816-6188 newportnik@comcast.net	2325 N Springfield St Buckeye AZ 85396	PSW	DCE	Mem C	Summit Community Buckeye AZ	(623)535-0251	S	1994
Stewart Rebecca J Trost	(360)509-1231 becci.stewart@gmail.com	9411 Spring Water Path Jessup MD 20794	SE	Tch/DCE	Mem C	Our Savior Laurel MD	(301)776-7670	S	1997
Stibrich JoAnn Shimabukuro	(303)250-5990 jstibrich@comcast.net	2561 S Olathe Way Aurora CO 80013	RM	Teacher	EM			CQ	2001
Stichler Taylor H	(541)771-6584 taylorstich@gmail.com	6017 SW Reif Rd Powell Butte OR 97753	NOW	DCE	Mem C	Trinity Bend OR	(541)382-1832	PO	2016
Stidman Linda	(309)263-8757	201 E Lakewood St Morton IL 61550	CI	Teacher	Tchr	Bethel Morton IL	(309)266-6592	RF	2001
Stiek Jared E	(608)346-4984 jared.stiek@icloud.com	902 N Ventura Dr Palatine IL 60074	NI	DCE	S HS/C	Concordia University Chicago River Forest IL	(708)771-8300	S	2009
Stiek Katarina M Miller		902 N Ventura Dr Palatine IL 60074	NI	Teacher	Tchr	Immanuel Palatine IL	(847)359-1936	MQ	2014
Stigdon Stanley E	(301)830-0104 sstigdon@gmail.com	413 Lee Dr Catonsville MD 21228	SE	Teacher	Prin	St Paul Catonsville MD	(410)747-1924	RF	1985
Stigge Judith E Hollman	(620)218-2017 ajstigge@gmail.com	728 N Locust St Flagstaff AZ 86001	PSW	Teacher	EM			S	1969
Stiles Pamela J Wegener	(509)627-0734 pam.stiles@frontier.com	2513 Oak Hill Ct Richland WA 99352	NOW	Teacher	EM			S	1974
Still Kelly L Damro	(415)823-3040 still.kelly79@gmail.com		EN	Teacher	C06/2019			IV	2003
Stine Maria J Bacher	(217)691-4449 maria.bacher@cuw.edu	1838 Saratoga Blvd Jefferson City MO 65109	CNH	Teacher	C07/2022			MQ	2011
Stinson Edward L	(650)368-9504 edstinson48@gmail.com	230 Santa Clara Ave Redwood City CA 94061	CNH	Teacher	EM			SP	1971
Stinson Kathleen M Griep	(650)368-9504 kathystinson6@gmail.com	230 Santa Clara Ave Redwood City CA 94061	CNH	Teacher	EM			SP	1970
Stirn Todd E Dr	(630)651-2093 tstirn@gmail.com	741 Palace St Aurora IL 60506	NI	Teacher	C07/2016			AA	1986
Stirnaman Jamie R Jensen	(630)201-3123 jstirnaman@stpaulslutheran.net	915 Percy Dr. Bourbonnais IL 60914	NI	Teacher	Tchr	St Paul Bourbonnais IL	(815)932-0312	CQ	2019
Stirtz Bradley	(630)627-1101 brad@peacehome.org	1648 Kildeer Rd Naperville IL 60565	NI	DCE	Mem C	Peace Lombard IL	(630)627-1101	CQ	2000
Stirtz Lisa R Fullner	(402)657-0797 cstirtz@cox.net	21813 Bobwhite Ave Gretna NE 68028	NEB	Teacher	EM			S	1984
Stock Joseph A	(314)686-8132 arnie3119@gmail.com	391 Autumn Creek Dr Apt A Manchester MO 63088	MO	Teacher	Tchr	St John Ellisville MO	(636)779-2325	RF	2006
Stock Michael R	(920)494-5797 blazersad@yahoo.com	1133 Carraway Ct Collinsville IL 62234	NW	Teacher	EM			RF	1972
Stock Michele L Hinz	(618)910-4081 vbsbshelly@yahoo.com	710 Wilson Ave Collinsville IL 62234	SI	Teacher	Tchr	Holy Cross Collinsville IL	(618)344-3145	MQ	2004
Stock Robert M	(618)910-3906 rob.stock@melhs.org	710 Wilson Ave Collinsville IL 62234	SI	Teacher	Tchr	Metro-East Edwardsville IL	(618)656-0043	RF	2004
Stocker Cindy L Hartman Deac	(630)257-8770 stockerk@sbcglobal.net	13319 E Red Coat Dr Lemont IL 60439	NI	Deaconess	EM			RF	1976
Stocker Lee J	(281)957-9601 lkstocker@mac.com	2610 Baycrest Dr Houston TX 77058	TX	Teacher	EM			RF	1964
Stockhaus Elaine A	(216)226-4561 estockhaus@juno.com	1611 Belle Ave Lakewood OH 44107	OH	Teacher	EM			RF	1968
Stockinger Elizabeth A Kohl	(419)212-3034 bethstockinger@yahoo.com	9912 Agora Dr Fort Wayne IN 46804	IN	Teacher	Tchr	Emmaus Fort Wayne IN	(260)459-7722	CQ	2023
Stockman Jan N	jnaomis@hotmail.com	3007 Jace Dr Mankato MN 56001	MNS	Teacher	EM			SP	1978
Stockman Rozanna M Kehren	(860)583-8325 rstoc10593@cs.com	24 Smith St Terryville CT 06786	NE	Teacher	EM			SP	1972
Stockman Wade A	(507)231-4563 wstockman@trinityjanesville.com	511 Allyn Cir Janesville MN 56048	MNS	Teacher	P/Tchr	Trinity Janesville MN	(507)231-6646	SP	1985
Stockmeyer Heidi M Blickensdorf	(586)404-0863 sballheidi@hotmail.com	17815 Breezeway Fraser MI 48026	MI	Teacher	Tchr	Trinity Clinton Township MI	(586)463-2921	AA	2004
Stoeckman Bonita M Honebrink	(952)657-2541 bstoeckman@gmail.com	13880 County Road 30 Mayer MN 55360	MNS	Teacher	EM			SP	1971
Stoehr Nancy A Kriewaldt	(608)576-7621 nancy.stoehr@cuw.edu	11603 N Lake Shore Dr Mequon WI 53092	SW	Teacher	S HS/C	Concordia University Wisconsin Mequon WI	(262)243-5700	CQ	2023
Stoelting Daniel D	(231)631-8876 click1nship2@gmail.com	12372 S Lovell Ln Unit 104 Traverse City MI 49684	MI	Teacher	Tchr	Trinity Traverse City MI	(231)946-2721	AA	1987
Stoelting Lara D Birnstein	(231)252-3089 stoelti793@gmail.com	12372 S Lovell Ln Unit 104 Traverse City MI 49684	MI	Teacher	Tchr	Trinity Traverse City MI	(231)946-2720	BR	1990
Stoelting Lucille A Niermeier	(785)567-3205 lastoelting@gmail.com	202 35th Street Dr SE Apt 115 Cedar Rapids IA 52403	IE	Tch/DCE	EM			S	1970
Stoeppelwerth Barbara A Hartmeister	(405) 888-1000 bstoppy@bellsouth.net	3116 Grapevine St. Edmond OK 73034	OK	Teacher	EM			S	1971
Stoermer Rose M Weiser	(210)877-0819 roses@concordia-satx.com	12910 Ocean Glade San Antonio TX 78249	TX	Teacher	Tchr	Concordia San Antonio TX	(210)479-1477	AU	1989
Stoever Bethany H Lange Deac	(620)395-2692 bethany.stoever@protonmail.com	673 W 680th Ave Hepler KS 66746	KS	Deaconess	Mem C	Immanuel Hepler KS	(620)395-2692	FW-DEAC	2021
Stohlmann Rebekah E Pranschke	(347)307-5518 rstohlmann@martinluthernyc.org	5664 59th St Maspeth NY 11378	AT	Teacher	Tchr	Martin Luther Maspeth NY	(718)894-4000	AA	2001
Stohs Bonnie S Sieling	(218)346-3265 bstohs@arvig.net	812 7th Ave SW Perham MN 56573	MNN	Teacher	EM			SP	1970

*Multiple Assignments (See Church Worker Locator for Additional Details)
See Page 53 for the Table of Abbreviations for key to District, Classification, Position, and College abbreviations.
**C =Candidate; EM =Emeritus; the date following the C is the month and year the Candidate status began

NAME	TELEPHONE NUMBER EMAIL	STREET ADDRESS CITY/STATE/ZIP	DISTRICT	CLASS.	POSITION/ STATUS**	WHERE SERVING	OFFICE PHONE	COLLEGE/ UNIV/CQ	YR GRAD
Stokes Kathleen	(810)334-4097 kat.stokes@flhsemail.org	4478 Chessie Ct Unit A Las Vegas NV 89147	PSW	Teacher	Prin	Faith Las Vegas NV	(702)804-4400	CQ	2023
Stollenwerk Jennifer L Spangler	(262)370-4210 jenny.stollenwerk@ journeyslutheran.org	N8015 Woodland Ct Ixonia WI 53036	SW	Teacher	C09/2025			MQ	1997
Stollenwerk Michael P	(262)313-8611 junkerjorg1517@yahoo.com	N8015 Woodland Ct Ixonia WI 53036	SW	Teacher	Tchr	Journeys Hales Corners WI	(414)461-8500	MQ	1995
Stoltenberg Katie L Heupel	(262)888-0203 mrs.stoltenberg@gmail.com	W295N1806 Prairie Wood Ct. Pewaukee WI 53072	SW	Teacher	Tchr	Divine Redeemer Hartland WI	(262)367-3664	MQ	2006
Stoltenow Curtis J	(507)330-5627 curt@campomega.org	409 4th Ave SW Hankinson ND 58041	ND	Teacher	EM			SP	1966
Stoltzner Jennifer L Flory	(714)906-3370 stoltznerjennifer@gmail.com	2111 Cartlen Dr Placentia CA 92870	PSW	Teacher	Tchr	Salem Orange CA	(714)633-2366	CQ	2009
Stone Kamela S Floetke		2739 Goldenrod Dr Yorkville IL 60560	NI	Teacher	Tchr	Cross Yorkville IL	(630)553-7861	S	1998
Stoneburner Audrey	(281)253-1167 audrey.stoneburner83@gmail.com	1829 Camas Dr Austin TX 78728	TX	Teacher	EM			RF	1984
Stoneburner Gordon F	gstoneburn@gmail.com	1829 Camas Dr Austin TX 78728	TX	Tch/DCE	EM			RF	1984
Stonecipher Abbey A Zenk	(307)850-7036 abbeystonecipher@outlook.com	5119 McCue Dr Cheyenne WY 82009	SO	Teacher	Tchr	Redeemer Pensacola FL	(850)455-0330	MQ	2011
Storck Ellen R Koslofski	(217)433-4131 ellenstorck@comcast.net	100 Bay Shore Dr Decatur IL 62521	CI	Teacher	EM			RF	1972
Storck Kay T Melcher	(402)996-0722 kay_iluvkids@yahoo.com	3337 S 89th St Omaha NE 68124	NEB	Teacher	C05/2021			S	1999
Storck Rhoda T Thomas	(402)885-7506 tnrstorck75@gmail.com	809 South 173rd Plaza Omaha NE 68118	NEB	Teacher	EM			S	1970
Stordahl Jean A Weigt	jdstordahl@gmail.com	7426 Pinebluff Dr Spring Lake MI 49456	MI	Teacher	EM			RF	1973
Stork Annetta L	(260)484-8382 astork@holycrossfw.org	460 Dalgren Ave Fort Wayne IN 46805	IN	Teacher	EM			S	1969
Storm Christine M Durst	(636)233-3897 stormcm77@gmail.com	1068 Pearview Dr Saint Peters MO 63376	MO	Teacher	EM			RF	1981
Storm Cindy L	(712)274-1342 dcecindy@gmail.com	2205 S Patterson St Sioux City IA 51106	IW	DCE	EM			SP	1998
Storm Daniel	(815)751-2841 dstorm82@hotmail.com	1660 Foster Cir Algonquin IL 60102	NI	Teacher	C07/2016			RF	2000
Storm Robert W	(636)447-7647 2stormshelter@charter.net	890 Penny Ln Saint Peters MO 63376	MO	Teacher	EM			RF	1955
Stortz Charlene R Hiatt	(402)640-9630 charlenestortz@gmail.com	509 Central Ave E Hampton IA 50441	IE	Teacher	Tchr	St Paul Latimer IA	(641)579-6281	S	1996
Stottlemyer Kimberly A Schmidt	(419)576-0148 kimmystottlemyer@gmail.com	209 Catalina Dr Defiance OH 43512	IN	Teacher	Tchr	Woodburn Woodburn IN	(260)632-5493	MQ	2002
Stotts Nancy K Dammeier		913 S 3rd St Saint Charles MO 63301	MO	Teacher	Tchr	Immanuel Saint Charles MO	(636)946-0051	RF	1976
Stouder Jane M Hasenjager	(417)942-4274 jstouder@rlcmail.org	1848 Cedar Tree Ln Republic MO 65738	MO	Teacher	EM			CQ	1999
Stover Mark P	(216)251-5272	2929 Columbia Rd Westlake OH 44145	OH	Teacher	Tchr	Lutheran West Rocky River OH	(440)333-1660	RF	1986
Strackbein Aaron	(210)882-9268 aaron.strackbein@cune.org	7519 Beaver Tree San Antonio TX 78249	IN	DCE	C06/2022			S	2019
Stradtmann Amy A Dencklau	(815)298-8653 astradtmann@yahoo.com	1890 224th Seward NE 68434	NEB	Teacher	S HS/C	Concordia University Nebraska Seward NE	(402)643-3651	S	1991
Strahle William F	(847)259-9392 bestrahle@aol.com	1280 Village Dr Apt 201 Arlington Heights IL 60004	NI	Teacher	EM			RF	1963
Strakis Randall O	(765)497-1676 strakisk@frontier.com	10 Wake Robin Ct W Lafayette IN 47906	IN	Teacher	EM			S	1974
Strand Diana F Flory	(541)231-5062 dianastrand@gmail.com	1442 91st Ave SE Tumwater WA 98501	NOW	Teacher	Tchr	Faith Lacey WA	(360)491-3552	S	1995
Strang Donna J Reidenbach	(313)720-2718 donnastrang@yahoo.com	304 Springtime Dr Sebring FL 33870	FG	Teacher	EM			RF	1972
Strang William J	(313)720-6935 bstrangg@yahoo.com	304 Springtime Dr. Sebring FL 33870	FG	Teacher	EM			RF	1972
Stratton Rachell Dewell	(260)249-4246	3522 Countrydale Dr Fort Wayne IN 46815	IN	Teacher	Tchr	Concordia Fort Wayne IN	(260)426-9922	S	2013
Straub Matthew A	(713)298-4697 mstraub23@hotmail.com	11507 Indigo Creek Ln Tomball TX 77375	TX	Teacher	Tchr	Concordia Tomball TX	(281)351-2547	S	1999
Straub Vincent J	vjstraub52@comcast.net	5118 Sunlight Hill Ct Spring TX 77379	TX	Teacher	EM			S	1974
Stravers Kenneth W	(262)271-7644 kennethstravers@att.net	7801 Point Meadows Dr Unit 8408 Jacksonville FL 32256	FG	Teacher	EM			SP	1986
Strecker Ashley M Brunkhorst	(913)749-9619 akstrecker@gmail.com	307 S Sunset Hills Dr Concordia MO 64020	MO	Teacher	Tchr	St Paul Concordia MO	(660)463-2291	S	2010
Streeks Shaeli M Shaeli Neustel	(720)281-4687 shaeli.streeks@cune.org	4308 Walkers Ridge Fort Wayne IN 46818	IN	Teacher	C08/2025			S	2020
Streeter Kim E	(586)949-6204 streeterk@comcast.net	48602 Wheatfield St Chesterfield MI 48051	MI	Teacher	EM			RF	1978
Strehlke James L	(612)270-2628 jodelbua@gmail.com	17050 Utah Dr Mayer MN 55360	MNS	Teacher	Mem C	St John Winsted MN	(320)485-2522	S	1990
Strehlow Gloria J Speckman	gloriaryankari@sbcglobal.net	402 Monarch Trl Georgetown TX 78633	TX	Teacher	EM			RF	1981
Strehlow Ryan M	(262)496-6418 strehlowr@gmail.com	10548 Nantucket Ridge Ave Las Vegas NV 89166	PSW	DCE	Pro Stf	Faith Las Vegas NV	(702)804-4400	CH	2013

*Multiple Assignments (See Church Worker Locator for Additional Details)
See Page 53 for the Table of Abbreviations for key to District, Classification, Position, and College abbreviations.
**C =Candidate; EM =Emeritus; the date following the C is the month and year the Candidate status began

NAME	TELEPHONE NUMBER EMAIL	STREET ADDRESS CITY/STATE/ZIP	DISTRICT	CLASS.	POSITION/ STATUS**	WHERE SERVING	OFFICE PHONE	COLLEGE/ UNIV/CQ	YR GRAD
Strei Madeline R Reuss	(612)716-2231 madstrei@hotmail.com	2056 Bellaire Ln Mound MN 55364	MNS	Teacher	EM			SP	1976
Stresman Geoffery G	(281)732-2929 geoff.stresman@lutheransouth.org	23217 Zinfandel Drive Alvin TX 77511	TX	Teacher	Tchr	South Houston TX	(281)464-8299	AA	2002
Stresman Kenneth C	(989) 233-4644 kstresman@gmail.com	6700 Westside Saginaw Rd #602 Bay City MI 48706	MI	Teacher	EM			RF	1963
Stresman Kevin D	(989)233-4644 kstresman@gmail.com	3611 Tressla Rd Vassar MI 48768	MI	Teacher	EM			S	1981
Stresow Ruth E	(415)824-0628	1065 S Van Ness Ave Apt 308 San Francisco CA 94132	EN	Teacher	EM			RF	1961
Streufert Frank C	(423)504-3665 fstreufert@gmail.com	506 Las Lomas Dr Chattanooga TN 37421	MDS	Teacher	EM			RF	1976
Streuter Catherine L Roth	(618)980-1021 cstreuter@gmail.com	8 Trappers Way Saint Charles MO 63303	MO	Teacher	Tchr	Zion Saint Charles MO	(636)441-7425	S	2002
Streuter Martha S Krueger	(618)345-1168 weeteachr@gmail.com	429 Chapel Dr Collinsville IL 62234	SI	Teacher	EM			RF	1973
Strickland Andrew A	(612)298-7314 stricklandoo@gmail.com	1348 Brittneys Pl Alexandria MN 56308	MNN	Teacher	Prin	Zion Alexandria MN	(320)763-4842	SP	2000
Stricklin Pamela M Tosie	(314)315-7556 pamtosie@gmail.com	1762 Cherry Blossom Ct Pevely MO 63070	MO	Teacher	Tchr	Salem Affton MO	(314)353-9242	CH	2013
Strietelmeier I D	(812)372-7350	2554 California St Columbus IN 47201	IN	Teacher	EM			RF	1958
Strieter Hope B	(989)751-0723 hope.strieter@gmail.com		MI	Teacher	Tchr	St Lorenz Frankenmuth MI	(989)652-6141	CQ	2021
Strieter Rachel M Westendorf	(989)395-4473 rstrieter@stlorenz.org	7159 E Curtis Rd Frankenmuth MI 48734	MI	Teacher	Tchr	St Lorenz Frankenmuth MI	(989)652-6141	CQ	2017
Stripling Kevin	(612)418-7780 kevin.stripling@zionhopkins.org	4680 Orleans Lane N Plymouth MN 55442	MNS	DCE	Mem C	Zion Hopkins MN	(952)938-7661	MQ	2019
Stroh Deborah Schwab	(314)308-7446 strohdeb@aol.com	422 W Beechnut Pl Sun Lakes AZ 85248	PSW	Teacher	EM			S	1971
Stroh Lester E Jr	(314)308-7448 les@lesstroh.com	422 W Beechnut Pl Sun Lakes AZ 85248	PSW	Tch/DCE	EM			S	1971
Stroh Myrna L Kruckeberg		408 James St Cedar Hill TX 75104	PSW	Teacher	EM			RF	1962
Strohacker Charles J	(616)429-0964 cstrohacker@hotmail.com	2888 W Trail Ln Saint Joseph MI 49085	MI	Teacher	EM			RF	1974
Strohmeyer Heidi	(414)587-6864 hstrohmeter@hcl.org	5085 Saxony Ln Greendale WI 53129	EN	Teacher	Tchr	Hales Corners Hales Corners WI	(414)529-6700	CQ	2020
Strohschein Benjamin	(314)856-2864	408 N Beth St Unit B Anaheim CA 92806	PSW	Teacher	Tchr	Orange County Orange CA	(714)998-5151	CQ	2012
Strohschein Brittany E Sawyer	(248)230-0624 brittany.strohschein@cune.org	316 Leoni St New Smyrna Beach FL 32168	FG	Teacher	C04/2021			S	2012
Strohschein Karen K Mielke	(320) 290-7665 kkstroh@gmail.com	2492 65th St NE Sauk Rapids MN 56379	MNN	Teacher	EM			SP	1973
Strohschein Lonnie M Hendrickson	(507)252-5073	212 42nd Ave NW Rochester MN 55901	MNS	Teacher	Tchr	Rochester Central Rochester MN	(507)289-3267	SP	1995
Strohschein Robyn Gerber	(314)856-2865	408 N Beth St Unit B Anaheim CA 92806	PSW	Teacher	Tchr	Orange County Orange CA	(714)998-5151	CQ	2012
Strohschein Timothy J	(507)269-7527 coachstrohs@gmail.com	212 42nd Ave NW Rochester MN 55901	MNS	Teacher	C07/2016			SP	1994
Stroik Marilyn L	(414)762-4293 sbgm64@hotmail.com	1814 Manitoba Ave S Milwaukee WI 53172	EN	Teacher	EM			CQ	1987
Strom Julie M Petersen	(612)419-0264 jstrom922@gmail.com	9009 Jensen Ave S Cottage Grove MN 55016	MNS	Teacher	C07/2016			CQ	1998
Stroming Linda L Smitten	(763)350-0835 PURSEoot@gmail.com	27023 Ingrid Dr Park Rapids MN 56470	MNN	Teacher	EM			SP	1981
Stroming Theodore G	(320)587-4019 stroming@hutchtel.net	315 E Pishney Ln SW Hutchinson MN 55350	MNS	DCE	Mem C	Good Shepherd Glencoe MN	(320)864-6157	SP	1990
Stroming Timothy J	(612)220-4918 tjs@ourredeemercohasset.org	1505 Horseshoe Lake Rd Grand Rapids MN 55744	MNN	DCE	Mem C	Our Redeemer Cohasset MN	(218)328-5165	SP	1985
Strong Martha A Parris	(715)572-4324 masdce@gmail.com	17090 Lensman Drive St. Robert MO 65584	MO	DCE	O-Sp Min	Office of International Mission Saint Louis MO		S	1988
Stroup Donald R	(309)431-4440 drs612@hotmail.com	210 E Craig St Princeville IL 61559	CI	Teacher	EM			RF	1969
Strubbe Linda Deac	(217)886-2025 strubbe_lg@hotmail.com	2072 Benson Rd Jacksonville IL 62650	CI	Deaconess	Mem C	Salem Jacksonville IL	(217)243-3419	FW-DEAC	2022
Struck Barbara A Boerner-Palmer	(262)287-8170 bpclogginfrog@yahoo.com	5737 Randal Ln Racine WI 53402	SW	Teacher	Tchr	Trinity Racine WI	(262)632-1766	MQ	2002
Struck Christopher M	(262)664-1566 kcurts2@hotmail.com	5737 Randal Ln Racine WI 53402	SW	Teacher	Tchr	Trinity Racine WI	(262)632-1766	MQ	1996
Struckmeyer Andrew A	(352)339-5909 andrew.struckmeyer@westlakeprep.org	32930 Silver Meadow Way Brookshire TX 77423	TX	Teacher	Tchr	Westlake Lutheran Richmond TX	(281)341-9910	AU	2010
Strzemieczny Sylvia Kirkpatrick	(708)479-6069 strzsms@aol.com	11953 Brookshire Dr Orland Park IL 60467	NI	Teacher	EM			RF	1975
Stuart Paula L Urbach	(801)613-1554	2357 N 525 E Ogden UT 84414	RM	Teacher	EM			S	1975
Stubblefield Linda K Edwards	(217)520-4571	210 S Woodale Ave Decatur IL 62522	CI	Teacher	EM			CQ	1989
Stuckert Gordon S	(678)503-8417 mgstuckert@gmail.com	307 Parkside Meadow Drive SW Marietta GA 30064	EN	Teacher	EM			RF	1969
Stuckwisch David A	(479)650-3612 dcedave90@gmail.com	216 W 11th St Fairmont MN 56031	CNH	DCE	Prin	Martin Luther Northrop MN	(507)436-5249	AU	2013

*Multiple Assignments (See Church Worker Locator for Additional Details)
See Page 53 for the Table of Abbreviations for key to District, Classification, Position, and College abbreviations.
**C =Candidate; EM =Emeritus; the date following the C is the month and year the Candidate status began

NAME	TELEPHONE NUMBER EMAIL	STREET ADDRESS CITY/STATE/ZIP	DISTRICT	CLASS.	POSITION/ STATUS**	WHERE SERVING	OFFICE PHONE	COLLEGE/ UNIV/CQ	YR GRAD
Stuckwisch Jacqueline R Van Liew	(812)524-7457 dslmmom@hotmail.com	6415 S County Road 200 E Brownstown IN 47220	IN	Teacher	Tchr	Trinity Seymour IN	(812)524-8547	CQ	2005
Stuckwisch Sandra L Helmer	(815)457-2721 revdonsan@live.com	P.O. Box 14 Goodwine IL 60939	CI	Teacher	EM			RF	1967
Stuckwisch Shelby L	(812)528-5619 sstuckwisch@sjsauerslutheran.org	1336 N State Rd 11 Seymour IN 47274	IN	Teacher	Tchr	St John Seymour IN	(812)523-3131	CQ	2024
Studer Kiara M Kiara Denholm	(812)374-2163 kiaradenholm@gmail.com		SE	Teacher	Tchr	Emmanuel Asheville NC	(828)281-8182	CH	2011
Stuebe David F	(419)438-5475 dpstuebe@gmail.com	383 Bear Woods Dr Powell OH 43065	OH	Teacher	EM			S	1968
Stueber Matthew P	(402)217-2759 matt.stueber@messiah.us	710 Indian Hills Dr Lincoln NE 68520	NEB	Teacher	Prin	Messiah Lincoln NE	(402)489-3024	MQ	1995
Stueber Ross E Dr	(262)573-4622 ross.stueber@att.net	1966 Meadowlark Ln Yorkville IL 60560	NI	Teacher	EM			S	1968
Stuedeman Mary M Roepke	(612)518-2408 mstuedeman@gmail.com	1314 110th St Plato MN 55370	MNS	Teacher	Tchr	Emanuel Hamburg MN	(952)467-2788	CQ	2018
Stuemke April L	(618)483-5162	27 Fairlane Cir Altamont IL 62411	CI	Teacher	C09/2024			RF	1996
Stuenkel Katelyn E Butts	(406)260-3383 katelyn.butts@cune.org	510 South Magdalena Street Concordia MO 64020	MO	Teacher	Tchr	St Pauls Concordia MO	(660)463-7654	S	2012
Stuenkel Paul R	(832)788-4685 paul@paulstuenkel.com	9611 Kindletree Dr Houston TX 77040	TX	Teacher	EM			S	1974
Stuenkel Ruth A Stockman	(435)260-0080 rimvistas@gmail.com	3300 Hwy 23 P.O. Box 741 Concordia MO 64020	MO	Teacher	EM			RF	1974
Stueve Heather A Halm Dr	(541)930-7184	61725 Ten Barr Ranch Rd Bend OR 97701	NOW	Teacher	Mem C	Trinity Bend OR	(541)382-1832	CQ	1990
Stueven Marjorie A Viestenz Kephart	(612)418-5935 mmstu@hotmail.com	8520 30th St SW Howard Lake MN 55349	MNS	Teacher	EM			SP	1968
Stuewe David R	(714)227-9606 dstuewe@stjohnsorange.org	1501 Portola Ave Santa Ana CA 92705	PSW	Teacher	Tchr	Saint Johns Orange CA	(714)288-4400	IV	1990
Stuewe Isabel J Jones	(714)557-3110 gousc@micndan.com	1734 New Hampshire Dr Costa Mesa CA 92626	PSW	Teacher	EM			S	1962
Stuewe Kristin D	(512)689-5320 stuewekristin@gmail.com	4701 Fm 1105 Georgetown TX 78626	TX	Teacher	Tchr	Zion Georgetown TX	(512)863-5345	AU	2020
Stuewe Yvette K Antrim	(714)227-8909 yvette.stuewe@cui.edu	1501 Portola Ave Santa Ana CA 92705	PSW	Teacher	S HS/C	Concordia University Irvine Irvine CA	(949)854-8002	IV	2018
Stuhlman Anne E Dr	(860)806-1944 annestuhlman@gmail.com	1106 Adams St Jefferson City MO 65101	MO	Teacher	Prin	The King's Academy Lake Ozark MO	(573)693-9245	CQ	2021
Stuhr Lonnie J	(712)276-6628 lstuhr5148@aol.com	5519 Stone Ave Sioux City IA 51106	IW	Teacher	EM			S	1965
Stults Sheryl A Poppe	(303)325-1249 sheri.stults@gmail.com	8362 Sunnyside Pl Highlnds Ranch CO 80126	RM	Teacher	EM			S	1988
Stults Susan A Knust	(520)229-1880 sastults@msn.com	7813 N Calle De La Aldea Tucson AZ 85704	EN	Teacher	EM			RF	1964
Stumpf Andrew E	(402)840-1708 andy.stumpf77@gmail.com	7921 Thornview Rd Lincoln NE 68506	NEB	DCE	C05/2018			RF	2008
Stumpf Linda D Krueger	(630)772-0848 elstumpf@sbcglobal.net	10348 Marlou Dr Munster IN 46321	IN	Teacher	EM			RF	1970
Stupy Erin L	(714)308-9445 estupy@christbrea.com	7618 E Chapman Ave Orange CA 92869	PSW	Teacher	Tchr	Christ Brea CA	(714)529-2984	IV	2013
Sturgess Jacqueline M Montambeau	(586)255-6486 jackstur@yahoo.com	23805 Lorraine Ave Warren MI 48089	MI	Teacher	EM			CQ	1994
Sturm Joan M Nelson	(630)904-1803 jpsturm@sbcglobal.net	4811 Daggets Ct Naperville IL 60564	NI	Teacher	EM			RF	1963
Sturm Keaton D	(402)806-9191 keaton.sturm@concordiaomaha.org	16837 Browne Cir Omaha NE 68116	NEB	Teacher	Tchr	Concordia Omaha NE	(402)445-4000	S	2012
Sturm Loween R Aadland	(612)242-9547 billandloukids@yahoo.com	9205 85th Ave Milaca MN 56353	MNN	Teacher	EM			S	1970
Sturm Raymond T	(810)441-8799 rsturm773@gmail.com	207 Fox St Lapeer MI 48446	MI	Teacher	EM			CQ	2006
Sturm Theresa I Luening	(217) 979-3480	111 N Plum St Paxton IL 60957	CI	Teacher	Tchr	St Johns Buckley IL	(217)394-2444	CQ	1994
Sturtevant Cleone E Hladky-Flandermeyer	(812) 708-0332 flanderwc@gmail.com	3526 Allens Ln Evansville IN 47720	IN	Teacher	EM			S	1966
Sublette Emily R Meier	(816)309-2477 frauprofemeier@gmail.com	7916 E 58th St Kansas City MO 64129	MO	Teacher	Tchr	Kansas City Kansas City MO	(816)241-5478	MQ	2011
Sudol Donna S Heupel	(405)946-0605	22530 Cedar Ridge Rd Edmond OK 73025	OK	Teacher	EM			S	1982
Suelzle Amy West	(360)491-8738 wildwest8@yahoo.com	5111 81st Ave SE Olympia WA 98501	NOW	Teacher	Tchr	Faith Lacey WA	(360)491-1733	PO	1996
Sugden Rebecca J Eifert	rsugden@vlhs.com	4437 S 9 Mile Rd Auburn MI 48611	MI	Teacher	Tchr	Valley Saginaw MI	(989)790-1676	CH	2014
Suggs Michelle Y King	(443)619-0517 kandmsuggs@verizon.net	101 Fig Tree Rd Meridianville AL 35759	SE	Teacher	Tchr	Concordia Towson MD	(410)825-2323	CQ	2003
Sugita Hannah S	(308)258-0720 hannah2244@gmail.com	9201 E County Road 100 N Avon IN 46123	IN	Teacher	Tchr	Our Shepherd Avon IN	(317)271-9103	S	2018
Sugita Tetsuya	(979)822-2742 tsugita@bicbcs.org	1304 Portsmouth Ct College Station TX 77845	TX	DPM	Mem C	Bethel Bryan TX	(979)822-2742	IV	2004
Suhr John D Dr	(402)646-2167 suhrjohn030@gmail.com	129 Langworthy Ln Seward NE 68434	NEB	Teacher	EM			S	1960
Suhr Kirsten J Wachs	(402)800-8014 topekawaxy@gmail.com	801 S 212th St Elkhorn NE 68022	NEB	Teacher	C07/2021			S	1990
Sullivan Courtney E Hiegel	(308)380-7926 courtney.hiegel@cune.org	2020 Brent Valley Rd Holland OH 43528	OH	Teacher	Tchr	Trinity Toledo OH	(419)385-2651	S	2017

*Multiple Assignments (See Church Worker Locator for Additional Details)
See Page 53 for the Table of Abbreviations for key to District, Classification, Position, and College abbreviations.
**C =Candidate; EM =Emeritus; the date following the C is the month and year the Candidate status began

NAME	TELEPHONE NUMBER EMAIL	STREET ADDRESS CITY/STATE/ZIP	DISTRICT	CLASS.	POSITION/ STATUS**	WHERE SERVING	OFFICE PHONE	COLLEGE/ UNIV/CQ	YR GRAD
Sullivan Judith A Wendt	(608)754-4267 jsullps461@aol.com	815 Sussex Dr Janesville WI 53546	SW	Teacher	EM			CQ	1999
Sullivan Kimberly A Johnson	(812)521-1145 ksullivan@zionseymour.org	2248 W Co Rd 600 N Brownstown IN 47220	IN	Teacher	Prin	Zion Seymour IN	(812)522-5911	CQ	2020
Sullivan Kylee D	(619)251-8095 kylee.dce@faithlutheranmi.org	c/o Faith Lutheran Church 280 Merritt Ave Merritt Island FL 32953	FG	DCE	Mem C	Faith Merritt Island FL	(321)452-4080	S	2024
Sullivan Leslie M Leonard		12611 Jarvis Rd Cypress TX 77429	TX	DCE	Mem C	St John Cypress TX	(281)373-0503	SP	2004
Sullivan Lois J Riske	(985)893-4301 ljriske@aol.com	312 Westwood Dr Mandeville LA 70471	SO	Teacher	EM			S	1974
Sultvedt Abigail E Kuenzel	(952)297-7378 abby.sultvedt@gmail.com	6847 12th Ave Longville MN 56655	MNS	Teacher	Tchr	Cross View Edina MN	(952)941-1094	SP	2008
Summerset Catherine A Fiege	(520) 213-5478 cathy.summerset@faith-lutheran.org	7238 East Shoreline Drive Tucson AZ 85715	EN	Teacher	Tchr	Faith Tucson AZ	(520)326-2262	IV	1986
Sump Merrilee A	(712)854-0212 msump3@gmail.com	1951 390th St Westside IA 51467	IW	Teacher	EM			S	1978
Sunderman Brenda L Keely	(402)750-2037 rbsunder@gmail.com	1001 Eastridge St Norfolk NE 68701	NEB	Teacher	EM			S	1974
Sunderman Preston D	(402)750-1386 psunderman@lhne.org	1303 N 19th St Norfolk NE 68701	NEB	Teacher	Tchr	Northeast Norfolk NE	(402)379-3040	S	2013
Sundermann Dianne S	(586)566-0787 dsundermann@comcast.net	16156 Meadows Dr Macomb MI 48044	MI	Teacher	EM			RF	1968
Sundermann Tamara K Springer		10683 County Road O Napoleon OH 43545	OH	Teacher	EM			CQ	2005
Sunstrom Melissa Mears	(443)904-2098 melissaunstrom@yahoo.com	1208 S 7th Ave Saint Charles IL 60174	NI	Teacher	Tchr	Trinity Roselle IL	(630)894-3263	BR	1990
Surprenant Faith E Redlitz	(714)879-4959 faithron@twc.com	219 N Wanda Dr Fullerton CA 92833	PSW	Teacher	EM			RF	1971
Surridge Shelly Tallada	(714)288-9452 dmsurridge@yahoo.com	1286 N Jamestown Way Orange CA 92869	PSW	Teacher	Tchr	Salem Orange CA	(714)639-1946	PO	1982
Suter Karen A Deac	karensuter111@gmail.com	108 Ridge Rd Summerville SC 29485	SE	Deaconess	Mem C	Grace Summerville SC	(843)871-5444	CH	2016
Sutton Karie E Knea	(972)922-7276 ksutton@whitecreek.org	701 W 7th St Seymour IN 47274	IN	Teacher	Tchr	White Creek Columbus IN	(812)342-6832	RF	1997
Suydam Penelope L Thom	(312)343-4547 psuydam@ilcsbatavia.org	408 Iowa Ave Aurora IL 60506	NI	Teacher	Tchr	Immanuel Batavia IL	(630)406-0157	RF	1994
Svarc Renee C Busch	(949)233-4149 rcslvs2tch@hotmail.com	144 12th St Seal Beach CA 90740	PSW	Teacher	EM			CQ	1997
Svec Gay M Hannah	(708)287-9314 thesvecs@comcast.net	11100 Windsor Dr Westchester IL 60154	NI	Teacher	EM			RF	1982
Swafford Benjamin C	(512)630-4994 DCEBenSwaff@gmail.com	12803 West Ave #8107 San Antonio TX 78216	TX	DCE	Mem C	Concordia San Antonio TX	(210)479-1477	AU	2016
Swafford Hannah K Ryan	(806)570-7717 hannah.ryan_02@yahoo.com	12803 West Ave #8107 San Antonio TX 78216	TX	Teacher	Tchr	Lutheran San Antonio TX	(210)694-4962	AU	2016
Swales Rachel A Niemeier	(319)415-8032 raswales@gmail.com	1050 S State St Denver IA 50622	IE	Teacher	C07/2016			S	2002
Swan Sheila R	(763)786-3939 swan8006@comcast.net	8006 Terrace Rd NE Spring Lk Pk MN 55432	MNS	Teacher	Tchr	St John Elk River MN	(763)441-6616	SP	1987
Swanlund Nancy E	(909)856-3085 neswanlund@yahoo.com	P.O. Box 5833 Palm Springs CA 92263	PSW	Teacher	EM			S	1977
Swanson Craig W	(972)352-8169 craigswanson52@hotmail.com	43663 Buckeye Rd Temecula CA 92592	PSW	Teacher	EM			CQ	1987
Swanson Crystal I Niemann	(763)213-7740 cswanson3@hotmail.com	14635 50th Pl N Minneapolis MN 55446	MNS	Teacher	C05/2024			RF	1995
Swanson Rhonda J Hibbing	(507)662-5513 rhondaswanson56@gmail.com	86325 490th Ave Lakefield MN 56150	MNS	Teacher	EM			S	1978
Swanstrom Cathy L Saenger Mossbarger	(979)849-9256 cathyswanstrom@hotmail.com	128 Country Rd Angleton TX 77515	TX	Teacher	Tchr	Immanuel Houston TX	(713)864-2651	AU	1985
Swanstrom Verna M Baever	(206)246-0436 eldonswanstrom@msn.com	620 SW 139th St Burien WA 98166	NOW	Teacher	EM			S	1962
Swartz Dawn L Gilmore	(937)243-1092	2824 Birch Tree Dr Saint Charles MO 63301	MO	Teacher	Tchr	Child Of God Saint Peters MO	(636)970-7080	AA	2000
Swartz Diane L Hall	(520) 909-8742 jdlswartz@cox.net	1210 SE 65th Cir Ocala FL 34472	FG	Teacher	Tchr	St John Ocala FL	(352)629-1794	SP	1988
Swartz Joshua D	(937)243-0958 josh.swartz@mo.lcms.org	2824 Birch Tree Dr Saint Charles MO 63301	MO	Teacher	D Ex/S	Missouri District Saint Louis MO	(314)590-6200	AA	1999
Swazey Angela N Kelly	(734)812-9531 angelaswazey@gmail.com	32613 Windsor St Garden City MI 48135	MI	Teacher	Prin	St Michael Wayne MI	(734)728-1950	AA	2000
Swearingen Martha S Becker	(417)569-7844 swearmd@yahoo.com	4353 W Forest Ridge Rd Battlefield MO 65619	MO	Teacher	Tchr	Redeemer Springfield MO	(417)883-5717	S	1994
Swenson Debi A Akey	(661)204-4380 dswensonl@bak.rr.com	313 Bloomfield Dr Bakersfield CA 93312	CNH	Teacher	Tchr	St John Bakersfield CA	(661)664-8090	CQ	2004
Swenson Faith E Fretham Deac	(218)329-8515 deaconess.swenson@gmail.com	136 Sloat Blvd San Francisco CA 94132	EN	Deaconess	C06/2024			FW-DEAC	2014
Swett Jonathan A	(312)259-4562 jonswett@hotmail.com	2144 Cherrywood Circle Naperville IL 60565	NI	DPM	Mem C	Bethany Naperville IL	(630)355-2198	CQ	2011
Switch Kiah A Bakken	(612)516-9433 kabak17@gmail.com	1358 Foxtail Gln Mayer MN 55360	MNS	Teacher	C06/2025			MQ	2021
Sworts Sandra J	(716) 692-6862	875 Eggert Dr N Tonawanda NY 14120	EA	Teacher	Tchr	St Matthew North Tonawanda NY	(716)692-6862	BR	1986
Sykes Judy P Plawin	(757)622-4915 judy.sykes424@gmail.com	424 Mowbray Arch Norfolk VA 23507	SE	Teacher	EM			CQ	2008

*Multiple Assignments (See Church Worker Locator for Additional Details)
See Page 53 for the Table of Abbreviations for key to District, Classification, Position, and College abbreviations.
**C =Candidate; EM =Emeritus; the date following the C is the month and year the Candidate status began

NAME	TELEPHONE NUMBER EMAIL	STREET ADDRESS CITY/STATE/ZIP	DISTRICT	CLASS.	POSITION/ STATUS**	WHERE SERVING	OFFICE PHONE	COLLEGE/ UNIV/CQ	YR GRAD
Sylva Jael Buss	(812)521-4300 jaelsylva@gmail.com	5900 E 100 S Columbus IN 47201	IN	Teacher	Tchr	St Peter Columbus IN	(812)372-5266	CQ	2022
Sylwester Donald R Dr	(402)326-5657 syl@cune.edu	1060 Fairlane Ave Seward NE 68434	NEB	Teacher	EM			S	1971
Sylwester Suzanne C Whitehouse	sue.sylwester@cune.org	1060 Fairlane Ave Seward NE 68434	NEB	Teacher	EM			RF	1969
Symank Rebekah L Mehrley	(208)750-8062 rebekah.symank@eagles.cui.edu	21641 Canada Rd 10g Lake Forest CA 92630	PSW	Teacher	Tchr	Lutheran Special Education Ministries Ann Arbor MI	(248)419-3390	IV	2023
Symmank Gabrielle E Nelsen	(715)245-6426 nelsengabrielle@gmail.com	7229 Tulane Ave Apt. 1f Saint Louis MO 63130	MO	Teacher	Tchr	Assoc Spec Ed Saint Louis MO	(314)268-1234	MQ	2022
Symmank Rachel M Wehling	(651)472-1975 jaynrays@gmail.com	1921 59th Ct E Inver Grove Heights MN 55077	MNS	Teacher	Tchr	Trinity Lone Oak Eagan MN	(651)454-1139	S	1990
Synovec Michele L Wilsey	(402)720-0391 michele.synovec@trinityfremont.org	345 Jean Dr Fremont NE 68025	NEB	Teacher	Tchr	Trinity Fremont NE	(402)721-5959	CQ	2003
Sype Chara L	(402)318-9565 c_sype1998@yahoo.com	9011 S 72nd St Lincoln NE 68516	NEB	Teacher	Tchr	Faith Lincoln NE	(402)466-7402	S	2004
Szeto Edward K	(571)285-2067 ed.szeto@lcms.org	102 Lake Region Blvd N Winter Haven FL 33881	SE	DCM	S Ex/S	Office of National Mission Saint Louis MO		CQ	2007
Szeto Frances F Deac	(516)592-1136 frances.szeto@cuchicago.edu	4930 Douglas Road Downers Grove IL 60515	NI	Deaconess	S HS/C	Concordia University Chicago River Forest IL	(708)771-8300	CH	2006
Szoyka Tammy A Hopkins	(216)251-9299 hopwp@yahoo.com	3257 W 157th St Cleveland OH 44111	OH	Teacher	Tchr	Lakewood Lakewood OH	(216)221-6941	MQ	1993
Szwarc Elizabeth S Parrish	(612)499-1038 eszwarc14@gmail.com		MI	DCO	C03/2025			SP	2020
Taggart Linda J Lapinsky	(586)775-6915 ltaggart@ymail.com	34864 Windsong Ln Richmond MI 48062	MI	Teacher	EM			RF	1976
Taggatz Roxanne M Wurm	roxtag6@gmail.com	5419 Citation Ln Racine WI 53402	SW	Teacher	Tchr	Grace Oak Creek WI	(414)762-3655	MQ	2004
Tagge Nancy J	(520)825-5552 njtagge@hotmail.com	61123 E Arbor Basin Rd Oracle AZ 85623	EN	Teacher	EM			S	1977
Tally Rachel E White	(281)757-7950 rtally@salem4u.com	27202 Mesa Verde Dr Magnolia TX 77354	TX	Teacher	Tchr	Salem Tomball TX	(281)351-8223	AU	2005
Tamburello Pamela J Mickelson	(281)292-3180 ptamburello@elcsh.org	1610 Ashway Conroe TX 77385	TX	Teacher	Mem C	Epiphany Houston TX	(713)896-1773	RF	1984
Tammen Vance V Dr	(949)214-3271 vance.tammen@cui.edu	6 Vista Encanta San Clemente CA 92672	PSW	Teacher	S HS/C	Concordia University Irvine Irvine CA	(949)854-8002	CQ	2003
Tams Sandra K Porath	(605)334-5750 sktams@aol.com	253 N Meyer Ln Sioux Falls SD 57103	SD	Teacher	EM			CQ	2001
Tanczer Hailey M Robertson	(806)570-5275 hailey.robertson@ctx.edu	1761 Cove Cir W Lawrenceburg IN 47025	OH	DCE	C12/2020			AU	2013
Tangen Renae J Kaelberer	(218)346-2421 renaetangen@hotmail.com	45867 County Highway 8 Perham MN 56573	MNN	Teacher	Tchr	St Pauls Perham MN	(218)346-2300	SP	1988
Tanner Jennifer M Meyer	(904)710-0472 jtanner@flgadistrict.org	1850 Wedgewood Way Kissimmee FL 34746	FG	Teacher	D Ex/S	Florida-Georgia District Orlando FL	(407)857-5556	AU	1999
Tanney Catherine I	(314)413-9140 tanneymc@aol.com	405 W State Rd Island Lake IL 60042	MO	Teacher	Tchr	Christ Community Kirkwood MO	(314)822-7774	CQ	2019
Tanney Lucas R	(314)580-9204 lucas.tanney@vlscrusaders.org	1917 Downing Ave Waterloo IA 50701	IE	Teacher	Tchr	Valley Cedar Falls IA	(319)266-4565	S	2008
Tanney Nicole A Hill	nicoleatanney@gmail.com	26 Hickory Ln Cary IL 60013	NI	Teacher	C07/2024			S	2014
Tappendorf Julie B Gnuse	(217)621-5273 jtappendorf@hotmail.com	2104 Belmont Park Ln Champaign IL 61822	CI	Teacher	C07/2016			CQ	2002
Tarr Cassandra L Jahns Makela Dr	tarrcassie@gmail.com		SW	Teacher	Prin	Trinity Mequon WI	(262)242-2045	MQ	2006
Tarr Grace A Mowery	(636)209-3952 gracetarr@gmail.com	16463 Hollister Crossing Dr. Wildwood MO 63011	MO	DPM	Mem C	King Of Kings Chesterfield MO	(314)469-2224	RF	2006
Tarr Sue A	(435)313-0984 tarr830@gmail.com	121 S 2000 E Saint George UT 84790	RM	Teacher	Tchr	Trinity Saint George UT	(435)628-1850	S	1993
Tasler Charles R	(602)296-7511 ctasler@cclphoenix.org	2118 E Angela Dr Phoenix AZ 85022	PSW	Teacher	Tchr	Christ Phoenix AZ	(602)955-4830	S	1996
Tasler Deborah A Harman	(602)481-6038 dtasler@cclphoenix.org	2118 E Angela Dr Phoenix AZ 85022	PSW	Teacher	Tchr	Christ Phoenix AZ	(602)955-4830	S	1996
Tate Gary R	(815)321-9059 garytate695@hotmail.com	206 Fox Ln Belvidere IL 61008	NI	Teacher	EM			RF	1969
Tate Heidi L Bolter-Haack	(952)200-2496	628 128th St SW Apt 110 Everett WA 98204	NOW	Teacher	Tchr	Shepherd Hills Snohomish WA	(360)668-7881	SP	1996
Tate Karen L Sneller	(502)851-1010	13701 Broken Branch Way Louisville KY 40245	IN	Teacher	C09/2024			CQ	2009
Tate Tonia L Landini	(702)921-2727 tonia.tate@faithlasvegas.org	10405 Griffith Peak Dr Las Vegas NV 89135	PSW	Teacher	Tchr	Faith Community Las Vegas NV	(702)921-2700	CQ	2014
Tatomer Linda Byer	(801)930-9440 btatomer@aol.com	4590 S Farm Meadow Ln Salt Lake Cty UT 84117	RM	Teacher	C07/2016			CQ	2000
Tatum Linda C Overstreet	lindact@att.net	3217 SW 28th Ct Gresham OR 97080	NOW	Teacher	EM			CQ	1993
Taube Jo Ann Bamsey	(309)788-0085 rjt61201@earthlink.net	3143 34th St Rock Island IL 61201	CI	Teacher	EM			S	1963
Taube Timothy W	(260)484-1088 twtaube@gmail.com	11225 Pine Bank Ct Fort Wayne IN 46845	IN	Teacher	EM			S	1973
Tauscher Jane M Martin	(817)292-9618	4305 Cartagena Dr Fort Worth TX 76133	TX	Teacher	EM			CQ	2012
Tausz Lydia G	(630)644-2173 lgtausz@gmail.com	2678 Woodmeadow Dr SE Apt E Grand Rapids MI 49546	MI	Teacher	Tchr	Our Savior Grand Rapids MI	(616)949-0710	CQ	2023

*Multiple Assignments (See Church Worker Locator for Additional Details)

See Page 53 for the Table of Abbreviations for key to District, Classification, Position, and College abbreviations.

**C =Candidate; EM =Emeritus; the date following the C is the month and year the Candidate status began

NAME	TELEPHONE NUMBER EMAIL	STREET ADDRESS CITY/STATE/ZIP	DISTRICT	CLASS.	POSITION/ STATUS**	WHERE SERVING	OFFICE PHONE	COLLEGE/ UNIV/CQ	YR GRAD
Taylor Bret A Dr	(714)271-6278 cuimathprof64@gmail.com	21338 NE Eagle Crossing Ave Bend OR 97701	NOW	Teacher		Northwest District Portland OR	(503)288-8383	S	1987
Taylor Caleb T	(512)639-8403 calebtaylor6@gmail.com	14915 Penn Hills Ln Houston TX 77062	TX	Teacher	Tchr	South Houston TX	(281)464-8299	S	2011
Taylor Elizabeth A Mossbarger	(512)595-1941 etaylor@mlchouston.org	128 Country Rd Angleton TX 77515	TX	Teacher	Tchr	Memorial Houston TX	(713)782-6079	AU	2012
Taylor Emma Kindt	(314)941-4505 emma.nt.taylor@gmail.com	2145 S Compton Mesa AZ 85209	PSW	Teacher	Tchr	Christs Greenfield Gilbert AZ	(480)892-8314	CH	2015
Taylor Isaac A	(331)208-4266 iketaylor95@gmail.com	2145 S Compton Mesa AZ 85209	PSW	Teacher	Tchr	Christs Greenfield Gilbert AZ	(480)892-8314	Other	2017
Taylor Jennifer R Prahl	(317)590-6315 jtaylor2@zlnp.org	2439 S Briar Park View New Palestine IN 46163	IN	Teacher	C04/2025			RF	1994
Taylor Joseph K	(504)401-0253 tayloj@gmail.com	6135 Shelby Street Indianapolis IN 46227	IN	Teacher	Tchr	Indianapolis Indianapolis IN	(317)787-5474	AA	2005
Taylor Julie A Fromm	(201)791-1535 jtaylorloveschocolate@gmail.com	31-06 Morlot Ave Fair Lawn NJ 07410	AT	Teacher	EM			BR	1987
Taylor LaVona M Knehans	(952)445-6955 vonietaylor@aol.com	433 W 5th St Apt 321 Waconia MN 55387	MNS	Teacher	EM			S	1989
Taylor Lisa J Schilling	(720)980-9446 lisajeanschilling@msn.com	7074 S Grape Way Centennial CO 80122	RM	Teacher	EM			RF	1985
Taylor Makenna K	(612)396-3377 makenna.taylor@cune.org	1717 E Union Hills Dr Unit 1060 Phoenix AZ 85024	PSW	Teacher	Tchr	Christ Phoenix AZ	(602)957-7010	S	2021
Taylor Marcia D	(989)652-4244	255 Mayer Rd Apt M244 Frankenmuth MI 48734	MI	Teacher	EM			CQ	1989
Taylor Nicholas R	(281)898-8528	100 County Road 139a Burnet TX 78611	PSW	DPM	Mem C	Summit Community Buckeye AZ	(623)535-0251	AU	2014
Taylor Patricia A Schroeder	(920)437-9339 patricia.taylor@new.rr.com	704 Emilie St Green Bay WI 54301	NW	Teacher	EM			S	1964
Taylor Rebecca C Thurber	(507)238-4763 rebeccacaroltaylor@hotmail.com	2908 Lynn St Fairmont MN 56031	MNS	Teacher	Tchr	St Paul Fairmont MN	(507)238-9492	S	1996
Taylor Steven P Dr	(262)573-6434 steve.taylor@cuw.edu	1933 Tumbleweed Cir West Bend WI 53095	SW	Teacher	S HS/C	Concordia University Wisconsin Mequon WI	(262)243-5700	MQ	1998
Taylor Susan G Patton	(406)461-0272 suetaylor120@gmail.com	626 S Sanders St Helena MT 59601	MT	Teacher	C07/2025			Other	1991
Taylor Tom D	(507)848-1762 tomtaylor@martinlutherhs.com	2908 Lynn St Fairmont MN 56031	MNS	Teacher	Tchr	Martin Luther Northrop MN	(507)436-5249	S	1992
Tayon Dawn E Mueller	(618)222-7428 tayon@charter.net	1315 Pcr 430 Frohna MO 63748	SI	Teacher	Tchr	Zion Belleville IL	(618)233-2299	S	1983
Tayon Justin R	(618)334-0313 justin.tayon@cune.org	308 Pennsylvania Ave Apt B Belleville IL 62220	SI	Teacher	C06/2020			S	2015
Teague Judy L Merriman	(260)760-0876 jteague226@gmail.com	1300 Mercer Ave 947-1 Decatur IN 46733	IN	Teacher	EM			RF	1979
Teague Sharon L Deac	(513)290-3781 sharonlouteague@gmail.com	2334 Broken Wheel Ln New Braunfels TX 78130	TX	Deaconess	Mem C	Hope Austin TX	(512)926-8574	CQ	1998
Teal Karen A Hein	(901)757-0130 kat653@hotmail.com	2898 Belgrave Dr Germantown TN 38138	MDS	Teacher	EM			RF	1975
Teasdale Darcey Caciano	dteasdale@ccls-stlouis.org		MO	Teacher	Tchr	Christ Community Kirkwood MO	(314)822-7774	CH	2016
Teasdale Zechary J	(260)348-1566 zech@webstergardenschurch.org	8809 Anchorage Ln Saint Louis MO 63126	MO	DCE	Mem C	Webster Gardens Webster Groves MO	(314)961-5275	RF	2011
Tebbenkamp Marla P Nichols	(660)674-2353 mpn9994@hotmail.com	P.O. Box 235 Alma MO 64001	ND	Teacher	Tchr	Grace Fargo ND	(701)232-7747	S	2002
Tedesco Kimberly J Rickwalt	(810)444-5083 tedesco@stpaul-lapeer.org	1184 Lakeshore Dr Columbiaville MI 48421	MI	Parish Assist	Mem C	St Paul Lapeer MI	(810)664-6653	AA	1988
Teeple Gina K Locascio Deac	(260)687-8627 gkteeple@yahoo.com	2025 N 110 W Angola IN 46703	EN	Deaconess	C01/2021			FW-DEAC	2016
Tegeler Sharon D	(708)280-2978 stegeler5@comcast.net	9106 Del Prado Dr Apt 1W Palos Hills IL 60465	NI	Teacher	Tchr	Trinity Tinley Park IL	(708)532-3529	RF	1987
Teggatz Rachel Mueller	(616)710-2687 rteggatz@coglcs.com	650 Salt Lick Rd Saint Peters MO 63376	MO	Teacher	Tchr	Child Of God Saint Peters MO	(636)970-7080	CQ	2022
Tegtmeier Lynette J	(407)547-9505 ltegtmeier@sllcs.org	523 Evening Sky Dr Oviedo FL 32765	S	Teacher	Tchr	St Luke Oviedo FL	(407)365-3408	S	1989
Teinert Bonnie J Stenklyft	(920)853-3990 bjteinert@yahoo.com	54 N 3rd St Hilbert WI 54129	SW	Teacher	EM			RF	1975
Teitz Jerrica A	(402)380-8926 tietzjerrica@gmail.com	704 W Herman Battle Creek NE 68715	NEB	Teacher	Tchr	St John Battle Creek NE	(402)675-3605	S	2019
Tellman Cheryl M	(219)772-5326 cmt_78@hotmail.com	254 E New York St Knox IN 46534	IN	Teacher	EM			AA	1985
Tellock Rebecca D Rohan	(920)867-3084 beckytellock@gmail.com	N3222 State Road 110 Weyauwega WI 54983	NW	Teacher	Tchr	St Paul Manawa WI	(920)596-2837	CQ	2010
Telschow Jonathan P	(214)620-7958 jon.telschow@gmail.com	537 Beck Dr Lavon TX 75166	TX	Teacher	Tchr	Faith Plano TX	(972)423-7447	S	1998
Teltow Kelly N Laeder	(586)980-5993 kellyteltow@gmail.com	50557 Torrey Pines Macomb MI 48042	MI	Teacher	Tchr	St Peter Macomb MI	(586)781-9296	CQ	2024
Temme Ruth L			MO	Teacher	C06/2021			MQ	2017
Temple Elizabeth A Franz	(815)637-4486 eliza_temple@yahoo.com	3908 Toft St Rockford IL 61114	NI	Teacher	Tchr	Rockford Rockford IL	(815)877-9551	MQ	1999
Templin Lynette L Kutzke	(507)334-0364 lynette.templin846@gmail.com	717 Winter Dr Faribault MN 55021	MNS	Teacher	EM			SP	1966
Tenney Kim West	(407)365-3486 ktenney@stlukes-oviedo.org	140 Forest Trl Oviedo FL 32765	S	Teacher	Tchr	St Luke Oviedo FL	(407)365-3408	CQ	2007

*Multiple Assignments (See Church Worker Locator for Additional Details)
See Page 53 for the Table of Abbreviations for key to District, Classification, Position, and College abbreviations.
**C =Candidate; EM =Emeritus; the date following the C is the month and year the Candidate status began

NAME	TELEPHONE NUMBER EMAIL	STREET ADDRESS CITY/STATE/ZIP	DISTRICT	CLASS.	POSITION/ STATUS**	WHERE SERVING	OFFICE PHONE	COLLEGE/ UNIV/CQ	YR GRAD
Tennies Kierra D Kuehl	(262)689-4395 kierra.kuehl@cuw.edu	1364 State Road 175 Hubertus WI 53033	SW	Teacher	Tchr	LHS Assn of Greater Milwaukee West Allis WI	(414)421-9100	MQ	2017
Tennis Donna M Grimm	(708)489-2797 dtennis@stphiliplutheran.com	2542 New St Blue Island IL 60406	NI	Teacher	Tchr	St Philip North Chicago IL	(773)561-9830	RF	1988
TenPas Sonia M Steinhaus	sonia.tenpas@gmail.com	6133 Cart Path Rd Sheboygan WI 53081	SW	Teacher	Tchr	Bethlehem Sheboygan WI	(920)452-4331	MQ	1992
Tensmeyer Joseph P	(509)663-4945	2203 Ashley Brooke Wenatchee WA 98801	NOW	Teacher	EM			S	1965
Tepker Carol A Gessert	(661)205-9858	3413 E Utopia Rd Phoenix AZ 85050	PSW	Teacher	EM			S	1976
Tepker Paul E	(661)703-0961 ptepker@gmail.com	3413 E Utopia Rd Phoenix AZ 85050	PSW	Teacher	EM			S	1975
Tereszkiewicz Mary F Schauer	(904) 521-7932 mflbr8@gmail.com	101 W Cross St Apt 359 Baltimore MD 21230	FG	Teacher	C07/2016			RF	1984
Terhaar Mary B Batterman	(262)232-0636 mbterhaar3@gmail.com		EN	Teacher	EM			SP	1979
Terkula Carole A Brown Deac	(502)541-0534 cterkula@gmail.com	1440 St. John's Church Road NE Lanesville IN 47136	IN	Deaconess	C05/2025			FW-DEAC	2018
Ternus Karissa K	(605)929-2937 Karissa.ternus@cune.org	1131 Klaus St Green Bay WI 54302	SW	Teacher	Tchr	Sheboygan Sheboygan WI	(920)452-3323	S	2022
Terrell Virginia I Peters	(224)622-1540	535 Shagbark Dr Elgin IL 60123	NI	Teacher	EM			S	1968
Tesch Debra L Toelle	(414)313-0834	2012 Forest Dr Camden SC 29020	SE	Teacher	EM			S	1978
Tesch Ruth Hoffmann	(916)281-5301 ruthtesch625@gmail.com	1863 William Bird Ave Sacramento CA 95835	CNH	Teacher	EM			SP	1974
Teske Kara	(217)394-2630	P.O. Box 212 Buckley IL 60918	CI	Teacher	Tchr	St Johns Buckley IL	(217)394-2444	CQ	2011
Teske Ralph W	(309)369-6092 rwtmat@yahoo.com	7715 Mohawk Tr Peoria IL 61604	CI	Teacher	Tchr	Concordia Peoria IL	(309)691-8921	RF	1989
Tessaro Sarah J Tennant	(417)209-0546 sarahtennant@sbcglobal.net	3531 W. Beechwood Pl. Springfield MO 65807	MO	Teacher	Tchr	Redeemer Springfield MO	(417)883-5717	AA	1999
Tessendorf Karen K Lane	(608)448-1980 kktess78@gmail.com	2731 N Ridge Ave Arlington Heights IL 60004	SW	Teacher	EM			RF	1978
Tessendorf Roger W	(608)448-8210 srtess78@gmail.com	2731 N Ridge Ave Arlington Heights IL 60004	SW	Teacher	EM			RF	1978
Teut Dylan C Dr	(712)269-1362 dylan.teut@gmail.com	1833 Rainbow Ave Seward NE 68434	NEB	Teacher	Tchr	Christ Lincoln NE	(402)483-7774	S	2012
Tews Dana A Topp	(402)990-4924 danaarlene3@gmail.com	8250 Auburn Rd Fort Wayne IN 46825	EN	Teacher	Tchr	Redeemer Verona PA	(412)793-5884	Other	2014
Tews Larry N	(812)320-9652 tewslarry@gmail.com	5975 Conifer Ct Columbus IN 47201	IN	Teacher	EM			RF	1974
Thaemert Ferol S	(314)921-3277 mfthaemert@att.net	2860 Sussex Dr Florissant MO 63033	MO	Teacher	EM			S	1961
Thaete Lorraine R Pomerantz	(913)631-3573 lorthaete@everestkc.net	1835 Meadow Ln Seward NE 68434	KS	Teacher	EM			RF	1967
Thauland Darlene		4803 NW Vincola Ter Portland OR 97229	NOW	Teacher	C07/2020			RF	1993
Theimer Jessica L Strefling	(989)600-7747 jtheimer@sjlmidland.org	864 Crooked Tree Lane Midland MI 48640	MI	Teacher	Tchr	St John's Midland MI	(989)835-5861	RF	1999
Theis Melissa A	(713)864-6836 theismel@yahoo.com	P.O. Box 7202 Houston TX 77248	TX	Teacher	Tchr	Our Savior Houston TX	(713)290-8277	CQ	2008
Theiss Jacob D	(713)504-6908 theiss.j@gmail.com	13502 Pin Oak Glen Lane Cypress TX 77429	PSW	Teacher	C07/2018			AU	2014
Themer Susan R	(812)967-3810	11715 S Priddy Rd Pekin IN 47165	IN	Teacher	EM			RF	1979
Thews Melinda L	mindy.thews@gmail.com	5135 Coventry Ct Davenport IA 52807	CNH	Teacher	Tchr	Office of International Mission Saint Louis MO		MQ	1993
Thibodeau Rebecca L Waggoner	(317)985-8903 becky.thibodeau@trinityindy.org	6818 W 100 N Greenfield IN 46140	IN	Teacher	Tchr	Trinity Indianapolis IN	(317)897-0243	CQ	2004
Thibodeau Sandra J Reick	(765)412-6730 sthibodeau987@gmail.com		IN	Teacher	Tchr	St John Indianapolis IN	(317)352-9196	S	2003
Thiede Donna K Dammeyer	(262)377-1568 gdjethiede@gmail.com	756 6th Ave Grafton WI 53024	SW	Teacher	EM			S	1977
Thiel Gail S Brabender	(920)532-6432 gailthiel622@gmail.com	269 Patricia Ln Wrightstown WI 54180	NW	Teacher	Tchr	Angels of Hope De Pere WI	(920)336-9843	MQ	1987
Thies Anne C Dr	(815)524-5486 anne.thies@cuchicago.edu	218 E 6th St Lockport IL 60441	NI	Teacher	S HS/C	Concordia University Chicago River Forest IL	(708)771-8300	CQ	2021
Thies Carl N	(260)739-3458 cthies7130@gmail.com	8085 Gull Harbor Ct Apt 102 Fort Wayne IN 46804	IN	Teacher	EM			RF	1964
Thies Ronal L	(715)341-5091 jthies@coredcs.com	1840 Ashford Dr Plover WI 54467	NW	Teacher	EM			RF	1962
Thiesfeldt Jackson R	(714)323-6875 jthiesfeldt@gmail.com	2959 Longspur Dr Fullerton CA 92835	PSW	Teacher	C02/2025			CQ	2018
Thiessen Mariah L Schamp	(303)667-5491 Mariah.thiessen616@gmail.com	7233 Deframe Ct Arvada CO 80005	RM	DCE	Tchr	Bethlehem Lakewood CO	(303)233-0401	S	2016
Thoelke Kate E Hugo	kthoelke@oslschool.org	4019 Delta Rose St Houston TX 77018	TX	Teacher	Prin	Our Savior Houston TX	(713)290-9087	RF	1996
Thoelke Mark	(636)243-1085 mthoelke@zionharvester.org	14 Amanda Ct Saint Peters MO 63376	MO	Teacher	Mem C	Zion Saint Charles MO	(636)441-7425	RF	1989
Thole Kelly R Ohland	(651)894-4317 ohlandk@csp.edu	9347 Padgett Ave NE Otsego MN 55330	MNS	DCE	Mem C	St John Buffalo MN	(763)682-1883	SP	2007
Thom Mychal C	(260)797-8495 mychalthom@gmail.com	6799 Jensen Ave S Cottage Grove MN 55016	MNS	Teacher	S HS/C	Concordia University St Paul Saint Paul MN	(651)641-8278	CQ	2009

*Multiple Assignments (See Church Worker Locator for Additional Details)
See Page 53 for the Table of Abbreviations for key to District, Classification, Position, and College abbreviations.
**C =Candidate; EM =Emeritus; the date following the C is the month and year the Candidate status began

NAME	TELEPHONE NUMBER EMAIL	STREET ADDRESS CITY/STATE/ZIP	DISTRICT	CLASS.	POSITION/ STATUS**	WHERE SERVING	OFFICE PHONE	COLLEGE/ UNIV/CQ	YR GRAD
Thomack Erik P	(812)341-0656 et4mail@yahoo.com	7040 S 175 W Columbus IN 47201	IN	DCE	C07/2016			S	1995
Thomack Jo-Ann A Severin	(931)472-4558 david.thomack@att.net	3410 Poplar Hl Clarksville TN 37043	MDS	DCE	EM			S	1991
Thomack Nathan E	(715)938-6225 n.thomack24@gmail.com	303 Meyer Rd Apt 1003 West Seneca NY 14224	EA	DCM	Mem C	Trinity West Seneca NY	(716)674-9188	MQ	2022
Thomack Sheila M Dilling	(812)390-6116 dceimm@gmail.com	7040 S 175 W Columbus IN 47201	IN	DCE	EM			S	1992
Thomack Timothy E	(217)710-5997 tim.thomack@lhsparker.org	17059 Wellington Drive Parker CO 80134	RM	Teacher	Tchr	Lutheran Parker CO	(303)841-5551	MQ	2011
Thomas Barbara Akins	(410)868-7000 bjthomas56@gmail.com	6 Outrigger Dr Swansboro NC 28584	SE	Teacher	EM			S	1970
Thomas Danielle E Mahlum	(952)201-4938 danielle.mahlum@gmail.com	632 E 2nd St Waconia MN 55387	MNS	Teacher	C07/2025			SP	2021
Thomas Gwen D Fichtner	(316)200-6130 gthomas@hcwichita.net	3154 N Cranberry St Wichita KS 67226	KS	Teacher	Tchr	Holy Cross Wichita KS	(316)684-4431	S	1986
Thomas Janelle C Schoenleber	(618)558-8187 jthomas@mlslions.org	507 Gentle Breeze Dr Saint Peters MO 63376	MO	Teacher	Tchr	Messiah Weldon Spring MO	(636)926-9773	S	2002
Thomas Jean G	(989)327-5711 thomas.jeang@gmail.com	2015 Hennepin Ave N #214 Glencoe MN 55336	MNS	Teacher	EM			SP	1972
Thomas Jennifer N	(260)241-2356	800 Watermill Ct Waterloo IN 46793	IN	Teacher	C08/2021			MQ	2007
Thomas Julie R	(248)933-0328 julieruththomas@gmail.com	22214 Curie Ave Warren MI 48091	MI	Teacher	Tchr	St Paul Royal Oak MI	(248)541-0613	CQ	2018
Thomas Lisa K	(815)886-0514 listeac@sbcglobal.com	25203 Scott Dr Plainfield IL 60544	NI	Teacher	C07/2016			RF	2003
Thomas Margaret C Margaret Katherin Christmas Dr	(714)401-1161 christmasphd@gmail.com	2046 W Beltline Rd Cedar Hill TX 75104	PSW	Teacher	S HS/C	Concordia University Irvine Irvine CA	(949)854-8002	CQ	2024
Thomas Michael A Dr	(949)214-3194 michael.thomas@cui.edu	Concordia University Irvine 1530 West Concordia Irvine CA 92612	PSW	Teacher	S HS/C	Concordia University Irvine Irvine CA	(949)854-8002	CQ	2007
Thomas Rebecca W Wyatt	(586)747-7788 rlwyatt@gmail.com	43493 Heydenreich Rd Clinton Twp MI 48038	MI	DCM	Mem C	Trinity Clinton Township MI	(586)463-2921	MQ	2024
Thomas Richard M	(406)670-9668 rickandsuethomas@gmail.com	3328 Tahoe Dr Billings MT 59102	MT	Teacher	EM			S	1982
Thomas Terri M Smith	(586)212-7684 thomas5mi@hotmail.com	19796 McKishnie St Clinton Twp MI 48035	MI	Teacher	Tchr	Lutheran Special Education Ministries Ann Arbor MI	(248)419-3390	CQ	2010
Thomason Linnette D Schumacher	(909)247-6329 lindthom@aol.com	6522 Hollis St Eastvale CA 92880	PSW	Teacher	EM			SP	1973
Thomay Mia G Peuluhn	(314)363-6448 mpauluhn@lutrheranwest.com	21250 Robinhood Ave Cleveland OH 44126	OH	Teacher	Tchr	Lutheran West Rocky River OH	(440)333-1660	S	2012
Thomlinson Rebecca S Gruoner	(913)547-0145 rebecca.gruoner@gmail.com	304 Grant St P.O. Box 183 St. George KS 66535	KS	Teacher	C08/2017			S	2003
Thompson Amelia L	(260)431-4943 alwellman23@gmail.com	216 Division St Plymouth WI 53073	SW	Teacher	C08/2023			Other	2018
Thompson Braedon J	(605)400-5978 braedon@trinityhillsboro.com	2615 21st Ave Forest Grove OR 97116	NOW	DCE	Mem C	Trinity Hillsboro OR	(503)640-1693	MQ	2024
Thompson Carolyn M	(573)445-0203 princess123@centurylink.net	4601 Wren Wood Dr Columbia MO 65202	MO	DCE	EM			RF	1992
Thompson Dylan	(765)586-6872 dylan.thompson@cuw.edu	1376 Felspar St San Diego CA 92109	SW	Teacher	S HS/C	Concordia University Wisconsin Mequon WI	(262)243-5700	CQ	2018
Thompson Janette K	(715)851-4925 j.thompson@stpaulbonduel.com	W4451 Landstad Rd Bonduel WI 54107	NW	Teacher	Tchr	St Paul Bonduel WI	(715)758-8532	Other	2020
Thompson Jessica J Jaranowski Deac	(407)497-1620 JessJThomp24@gmail.com	8 Banbury Ct Saint Louis MO 63126	MO	Deaconess	RSO	Redeeming Life Outreach Sanford FL	(407)790-9745	CQ	2004
Thompson Juliet P Giebelman Deac	juliet3025@gmail.com	10575 Northgate Dr Palo Cedro CA 96073	CNH	Deaconess	C03/2022			FW-DEAC	2012
Thompson Mark P	(512)971-2241 dce@timothystl.org	6412 Printz Ct Saint Louis MO 63116	MO	DCE	Mem C	Timothy Saint Louis MO	(314)781-8673	CQ	2006
Thompson Michelle R	(713)471-5393 Michelle.Thompson@cui.edu		PSW	Teacher	S HS/C	Concordia University Irvine Irvine CA	(949)854-8002	RF	1993
Thompson Paul A	(618)978-6682 p.thompson@peaceantigo.org	W12281 State Highway 64 Antigo WI 54409	NW	Teacher	Prin	Peace Antigo WI	(715)623-2200	SP	1991
Thompson Steven L		3431 Brooklyn Ave SE Grand Rapids MI 49508	MI	Teacher	Tchr	WMLHS Wyoming MI	(616)455-2200	AA	1987
Thomson David L Dr	(972)743-8381 thomsondoc@gmail.com	2102 Kildare Dr Pearland TX 77581	TX	Teacher	Tchr	South Houston TX	(281)464-8299	CQ	2013
Thomson Jordan E Scifres	(317)217-0408 jthomson0821@gmail.com	12215 Southcreek Ct Indianapolis IN 46236	IN	Teacher	C07/2016			CH	2010
Thomson Paula K Bourque	(972)743-0114 paula-k@rocketmail.com	2102 Kildare Dr Pearland TX 77581	TX	Teacher	Tchr	South Houston TX	(281)464-8299	AU	1998
Thorman Jeff C Dr	(214)235-6364 jthorman@ziondallas.org	4106 Eider Dr McKinney TX 75070	TX	Teacher	Prin	Zion Dallas TX	(214)363-1639	CQ	2009
Thormodson Brittany M Wilaby	thorbrit2018@gmail.com		SE	Teacher	C07/2021			MQ	2018
Thorne Marlene	(417)627-9190 mthorne53@sbcglobal.net	1429 E 26th St Joplin MO 64804	MO	Teacher	EM			SP	1985
Thornsbrough Kurt A	(217)497-5610 mrmrst3@aol.com	403 Douglas St Catlin IL 61817	CI	Teacher	C07/2016			RF	1983
Thornton Kristen Fletcher	(702)285-4345 thorntonk@flhsemail.org	5881 Windy Sky Pass Las Vegas NV 89135	PSW	Teacher	Tchr	Faith Las Vegas NV	(702)804-4400	CQ	2008
Thorsen Mark F	(256)694-1360 mript@yahoo.com	2618 Bonnie Oaks Dr SW Huntsville AL 35803	SO	Teacher	EM			S	1974

*Multiple Assignments (See Church Worker Locator for Additional Details)
See Page 53 for the Table of Abbreviations for key to District, Classification, Position, and College abbreviations.
**C =Candidate; EM =Emeritus; the date following the C is the month and year the Candidate status began

NAME	TELEPHONE NUMBER EMAIL	STREET ADDRESS CITY/STATE/ZIP	DISTRICT	CLASS.	POSITION/ STATUS**	WHERE SERVING	OFFICE PHONE	COLLEGE/ UNIV/CQ	YR GRAD
Thorson Jennifer M Phillips Deac	(260)557-2064 jennifer@ethorson.com	7809 County Road 35 W Annandale MN 55302	MO	Deaconess	Mem C	Grace Lexington MO	(660)259-2932	CQ	2006
Thurau Rachel E Lambring	(727)742-3244 hoosiergram61@gmail.com	439 Christan Bend Road Church Hill TN 37642	FG	Teacher	C07/2016			AA	1983
Thurber Daniel C Dr	(402)643-6487 daniel.thurber@cune.edu	1340 Plainview Ave Seward NE 68434	NEB	Teacher	S HS/C	Concordia University Nebraska Seward NE	(402)643-3651	S	1968
Thuringer Colin E	(605)215-2572 cthuringer@lhsi.org	8444 Browning Dr Apt A Indianapolis IN 46227	IN	Teacher	Tchr	Indianapolis Indianapolis IN	(317)787-5474	S	2025
Thurman Richard S	(360)241-0760 scott@stjohnlc.com	9501 NE 19th St Vancouver WA 98664	NOW	Teacher	Mem C	St John Vancouver WA	(360)573-1461	PO	1987
Thurmond Patricia R Fischer	(303)794-3259 prthurmond@comcast.net	11925 W Brandt Pl Littleton CO 80127	RM	Teacher	EM			S	1964
Thurn Kathleen C Robertson	(219)365-7710 kcthurn28@comcast.net	6751 Cypress Rd Apt 108 Plantation FL 33317	IN	Teacher	EM			CQ	1988
Thurner Janice J Hochradel Deac	(608)752-6808	2105 S Chatham St Janesville WI 53546	SW	Deaconess	EM			Other	1967
Thyparambil Nancy J Lamborn	(402)484-7030 nancyjt353@gmail.com	P.O. Box 353 Blue Hill NE 68930	NEB	Teacher	EM			S	1976
Tibben Jessica M Long	(920)213-7429	1818 N Alvin St Appleton WI 54911	NW	DCM	Mem C	Shepherd Hills Greenville WI	(920)757-5722	MQ	2014
Tibben Pennela D	(217)446-2321	1429 Woodridge Dr Danville IL 61832	CI	Teacher	Tchr	Trinity Danville IL	(217)442-4311	S	2005
Tichich Rachel L Ehrhard	(314)277-4618 rachel.legoute@gmail.com	119 Magdalen Ln O Fallon MO 63366	MO	DCO	Aux	LLL/Lutheran Hour Ministries Saint Louis MO	(314)317-4100	SP	2003
Tidyman Gracie L Griffin	(478)319-1139 gracieleegrace99@gmail.com	8056 Country Squire Ln Cordova TN 38018	MDS	Teacher	Tchr	Christ the King Memphis TN	(901)682-8405	S	2022
Tieman Sharon A Marcis	(815)404-4685	409 Reserve Dr Crystal Lake IL 60012	NI	Teacher	EM			RF	1984
Tiemann Louise M Schneider	(636)349-5354 l_tiemann@hotmail.com	304 Arlington Glen Ct Fenton MO 63026	MO	Teacher	EM			S	1968
Tiemann Traci L Guinzy	(618)322-8469 traci.tiemann14@gmail.com	1501 Woods Ln Centralia IL 62801	SI	Teacher	Tchr	Trinity Hoyleton IL	(618)493-7754	MQ	2009
Tietmeyer Larry R	(209)832-5845 ltietmeyer@stpaulstracy.org	43 Turnbridge Ct Lakeview AR 72642	CNH	Teacher	EM			S	1970
Tietz Cheryl L Heiden	(402)440-8798 cheritietz@hotmail.com	4827 Bunker Hill Rd Lincoln NE 68521	NEB	Teacher	EM			S	1970
Tietz Joan M Petersen	(319)784-7478 joan.tietz@gmail.com	1434 Shootingstar Way W Lafayette IN 47906	IN	Teacher	EM			S	1975
Tietz Stuart D	(402)440-8798 stietz32@gmail.com	4827 Bunker Hill Rd Lincoln NE 68521	NEB	Teacher	EM			S	1970
Tiffee Kelly A Landstrom	(630)901-1579 ktiffee@ziondallas.org	1414 McKavett Rd Forney TX 75126	TX	Teacher	Tchr	Zion Dallas TX	(214)363-1639	CH	2012
Tillman Cynthia Y Mc Bride	(239)300-5401 ctillmanHawaii@gmail.com	2015 Granada Dr Florissant MO 63033	CNH	Teacher	Tchr	Our Savior Aiea HI	(808)488-3654	RF	1983
Timm Diane M	(262)353-3068 dtim1943@charter.net	101 Cedar Ridge Dr. Apt N347 West Bend WI 53095	SW	Teacher	EM			RF	1965
Timm Eunice M Wentzel	(423)624-2588	4010 Belvoir Dr Chattanooga TN 37412	MDS	Teacher	EM			S	1968
Timm Jody R	(402)606-4016 jrtimm57@gmail.com	3568 38th Ave Columbus NE 68601	NEB	Teacher	EM			CQ	1996
Timm Karen K Klama	(630)257-8311	1287 Saint Colette Ct Lemont IL 60439	NI	Teacher	EM			RF	1963
Timm Katherine J Leininger	(260)348-3020 jean.timm@hotmail.com	2707 Bond Dr Lafayette IN 47909	IN	Teacher	EM			SP	1974
Timm Lowell H	ltimm5@hotmail.com	2707 Bond Dr Lafayette IN 47909	IN	Teacher	EM			RF	1974
Timm Marcia L Bennett	(402)553-7845	5813 Charles St Omaha NE 68132	NEB	Teacher	EM			S	1965
Timm Natalie R	(507)282-4881 nrtimm50@gmail.com	4143 Trumpeter Dr SE Rochester MN 55904	MNS	Teacher	EM			S	1972
Timm Richard P	(952)432-7981 avtimms@gmail.com	5856 139th St W Apple Valley MN 55124	MNS	Teacher	EM			S	1966
Timm Suzanne M Starck	(630)886-6119 chipskimom@att.net	500 Oak St North Aurora IL 60542	NI	Teacher	EM			RF	1967
Timm Trevor E	(262)388-8541 trevor.timm@orlctosa.org	4145 N 96th St Wauwatosa WI 53222	SW	Teacher	Prin	Wauwatosa Wauwatosa WI	(414)258-4558	MQ	2012
Timm Tyler G	(262)993-5868 tylertimm@rlscary.org	262 Winston Pointe Dr Clayton NC 27520	SE	Teacher	C08/2025			CH	2010
Timmerman David M	(321)745-8687 timmerman.dave@gmail.com	12200 McCormick Rd Jacksonville FL 32225	FG	DCE	C08/2023			S	2005
Timmerman Floy A Heermann	(303)659-3698 floykent@hotmail.com	302 S 14th Ave Brighton CO 80601	RM	Teacher	EM			CQ	1988
Timmerman Sonya A Condon	timmermansonya@gmail.com	2684 Howden Court Jacksonville FL 32225	FG	Teacher	Prin	Grace Jacksonville FL	(904)928-9136	S	2005
Tinder Jane E Gwin	(608)440-3144 janeelainetinder@gmail.com	204 Market St Apt D Deforest WI 53532	FG	Teacher	C03/2018			CQ	2006
Tinker Diane F Dahlbom	(602)315-2287 diane.tinker@gmail.com	10020 N 75th St Scottsdale AZ 85258	PSW	Teacher	EM			CQ	2005
Tinkey Jamielynn R Deac	(809)754-0183 jamielynn.tinkey@lcms.org	1782 Hartzler St Warsaw IN 46580	MO	Deaconess	S Miss	Office of International Mission Saint Louis MO		FW-DEAC	2023
Tirmenstein Stephen W	(314)741-2633 T6241@aol.com	1923 Lakemont Ln Saint Louis MO 63138	MO	Teacher	EM			RF	1969
Titus Desiree J	(262)689-2907 dtitus@stjohnswestbend.org	641 S 3rd Ave. West Bend WI 53095	SW	Teacher	Tchr	St John West Bend WI	(262)429-1061	MQ	2014

*Multiple Assignments (See Church Worker Locator for Additional Details)
See Page 53 for the Table of Abbreviations for key to District, Classification, Position, and College abbreviations.
**C =Candidate; EM =Emeritus; the date following the C is the month and year the Candidate status began

NAME	TELEPHONE NUMBER EMAIL	STREET ADDRESS CITY/STATE/ZIP	DISTRICT	CLASS.	POSITION/ STATUS**	WHERE SERVING	OFFICE PHONE	COLLEGE/ UNIV/CQ	YR GRAD
Tjernagel Ellen M Radewahn	(574)268-2667 tjernagel@kconline.com	2080 Sunset Dr Warsaw IN 46580	IN	Teacher	EM			RF	1960
Tobaben Kara L Theis Dr	ktobaben@ordallas.org	17940 Benchmark Dr Dallas TX 75252	TX	Teacher	Prin	Our Redeemer Dallas TX	(214)368-1465	S	1996
Toberman Christina J Dobratz	(715)851-2881 christinaj8450@gmail.com	1308 S Washington St Janesville WI 53546	SW	Teacher	Tchr	St Pauls Janesville WI	(608)754-4471	MQ	2016
Todd Audrey J Ahrendt	(303)726-9990 atodd5111@gmail.com	5111 S Meade St Littleton CO 80123	RM	Teacher	EM			S	1978
Todd Caitlin R Rath	(847)977-7824 rathcr@gmail.com	503 Fox Run Ln Hampshire IL 60140	NI	Teacher	C07/2016			RF	2010
Todd Katie N Conradson	(714)240-5746 ktodd@stjohnsorange.org	3000 N Woods St Unit 6 Orange CA 92865	PSW	Teacher	Tchr	St Johns Orange CA	(714)288-4406	CQ	2006
Toenjes Deborah S Holle	(253)531-2112 deborah.holle@cune.org	4519 112th St E Tacoma WA 98446	NOW	DCE	Mem C	Our Savior Tacoma WA	(253)531-2112	S	2024
Toenjes Nathan J	(920)360-9695 nathan@calvarylincoln.org	2758 Franklin St Lincoln NE 68502	NEB	DCE	Mem C	Calvary Lincoln NE	(402)476-1567	S	2019
Toensing Jacob T	jtoensing@splhs.org	404 S Faculty Ln Concordia MO 64020	MO	Teacher	Tchr	Saint Paul Concordia MO	(660)463-2238	S	2015
Toepke Anita Papenberg	(309)682-3691	6901 N Galena Rd Apt 210 Peoria IL 61614	CI	Teacher	EM			RF	1960
Toepper Robert M Dr	(630)375-1032 randmtoepper@comcast.net	1612 Catalina Ln Aurora IL 60504	NI	Teacher	EM			RF	1962
Toerpe Allison C Gunlock	(989)714-6334 toerpe@trinitysheboygan.org	2015 N 5th St Sheboygan WI 53081	SW	Teacher	Tchr	Trinity Sheboygan WI	(920)458-8248	MQ	2007
Toerpe Craig S	(262)707-3005 ctoerpe7@gmail.com	915 Hawthorn Dr West Bend WI 53095	SW	Teacher	Pro Stf	LCMS Foundation Saint Louis MO	(314)965-9000	MQ	2000
Tollefson Tyler S	(913)961-4535 ttollefson@salem4u.com	1302 Orchard Ridge Ln Tomball TX 77375	TX	DCE	Mem C	Salem Tomball TX	(281)351-8223	S	2008
Toman Laura K	(248)880-4627 lauratoman85@gmail.com	1441 Dover Hl N Walled Lake MI 48390	MI	Teacher	Tchr	St Matthew Walled Lake MI	(248)624-7677	AA	1989
Tomashewsky Suzanne B Birkholz			MI	Teacher	Tchr	Trinity Bay City MI	(989)662-6093	MQ	1999
Tomich Nancy L Bennett	(352)694-1166 tomich@cox.net	4519 SE 6th Pl Ocala FL 34471	FG	Teacher	Tchr	St John Ocala FL	(352)622-7275	CQ	1996
Tomko Linda K Holland		42 Orleans Way Richmond Hill GA 31324	OH	Teacher	EM			S	1968
Tompkins Rachel Henke	(615) 887-9636 rachel.tompkins@oslanashville.org	718 Cowan Dr Nolensville TN 37135	MDS	Teacher	Tchr	Our Savior Nashville TN	(615)833-1500	MQ	2004
Tompkins Sarah M	(402)369-6286 sarahtompkins1@gmail.com	950 French Dr Apt 4201 Valley Park MO 63088	MO	Teacher	Tchr	St Pauls Des Peres MO	(314)822-9219	S	2024
Tompkins Sonya S Bauer	(402)699-8883 sonya@heritageind.com	414 W 4th St Wayne NE 68787	NEB	Teacher	Tchr	Christ Norfolk NE	(402)371-5536	S	2024
Toms Emily M Jordan	(916)749-0763 aetoms09@gmail.com	5048 Southland Dr Woodstock GA 30188	FG	Teacher	C07/2016			IV	2010
Tong Allan K	(415)350-8481 dceallantong@gmail.com	5080 Appalachia Creek Ave Las Vegas NV 89141	PSW	DCE	Tchr	Faith Las Vegas NV	(702)804-4400	IV	1997
Tonjes Bernard J Dr	(636)395-7018 tonjesbj@gmail.com	1608 Waterford Ln St.charles MO 63303	MO	Teacher	EM			S	1974
Tonn Stephanie M Ostrowski	(262)677-3366 stonn@milwaukeelutheran.org	N132W17380 Rockfield Rd Germantown WI 53022	SW	Teacher	Tchr	Milwaukee LHS Milwaukee WI	(414)461-6000	MQ	2004
Tonniges Marva R Borck	(720)475-1396 RTonniges@aol.com	6371 S Pierce Ct Littleton CO 80123	RM	Teacher	EM			S	1965
Tonniges Taylor C Friedel		10723 Drake Ridge Ave Las Vegas NV 89166	PSW	Teacher	Tchr	Faith Las Vegas NV	(702)804-4400	S	2012
Tonsager Janelle J Goettsch	(608)438-4978 sparkle1557@gmail.com	8401 Reid Dr Madison WI 53717	SW	Teacher	EM			SP	1979
Tooley Katherine A Taglauer	saviorsongmusicmaker@gmail.com	7215 Ocean Gateway Easton MD 21601	SE	Tch/DCE	C01/2019			RF	1990
Topel Matthew R	(586)214-6708 matthew.topel@st-matthew.org	3150 Terry St Commerce Twp MI 48390	MI	Teacher	Tchr	St Matthew Walled Lake MI	(248)624-7676	AA	2010
Topel Samantha J Schroeder	(815)762-6348 topel.samantha@gmail.com	3150 Terry St Commerce Twp MI 48390	MI	Teacher	Tchr	St Matthew Walled Lake MI	(248)624-7676	CH	2012
Topel Stanley R Dr	(586)939-8530 yel01nast@att.net	5710 Victory Cir Sterling Hts MI 48310	MI	Teacher	EM			S	1957
Topel Timothy L	(586)460-0141 twtopel@gmail.com	39031 Helena Ave Sterling Hts MI 48313	MI	Teacher	EM			S	1982
Topel Wendy S van Breda	(586)214-2715 stjohnwtopel@yahoo.com	39031 Helena Ave Sterling Hts MI 48313	MI	Teacher	EM			S	1982
Topp David W	(406)270-4917 daviddwt6@gmail.com	9014 N Hickory Valley Rd Chattanooga TN 37416	MDS	Teacher	Prin	Belvoir Chattanooga TN	(423)622-3755	CQ	1998
Toppe Sharon M Herz	(812)358-9701 tstoppel@frontier.com	100 Cardinal Dr W Seymour IN 47274	IN	Teacher	EM			RF	1969
Torbeck Larry P	(314)583-9901 lptorbeck@hotmail.com	6292 Whisper Bend Dr Saint Louis MO 63129	MO	Teacher	EM			RF	1971
Torbeck Stephanie L	(314)583-9926 sttorbeck@hotmail.com	118 Tori Pines Dr Saint Louis MO 63129	MO	Teacher	Tchr	Green Park Saint Louis MO	(314)544-4248	RF	1998
Torblaa Travis C	(636)744-5321 travis.torblaa@nblc.net	5601 Sunnywood Dr Cedar Hill MO 63016	MO	Teacher	Mem C	New Beginnings Pacific MO	(636)257-4455	SP	1998
Tornow Leah K Back	(949)903-5897 mrs.tornow@christcm.org	871 Capital St Costa Mesa CA 92627	PSW	Teacher	Tchr	Christ Costa Mesa CA	(949)548-6866	S	1998
Torreson Megan L Krohe	(708)212-2557 megan.torreson@unityridge.org	2697 Highway 59 Denison IA 51442	IW	Teacher	P/Tchr	Unity Ridge Denison IA	(712)393-2002	RF	2004
Torreson Taylor M Eaton	(734)644-1897 taylortorreson@gmail.com	10522 Belleau Dr Twinsburg OH 44087	OH	Teacher	Tchr	Royal Redeemer North Royalton OH	(440)237-7988	MQ	2015

*Multiple Assignments (See Church Worker Locator for Additional Details)
See Page 53 for the Table of Abbreviations for key to District, Classification, Position, and College abbreviations.
**C =Candidate; EM =Emeritus; the date following the C is the month and year the Candidate status began

NAME	TELEPHONE NUMBER EMAIL	STREET ADDRESS CITY/STATE/ZIP	DISTRICT	CLASS.	POSITION/ STATUS**	WHERE SERVING	OFFICE PHONE	COLLEGE/ UNIV/CQ	YR GRAD
Toth Cynthia L Crawford	(219)942-9640 cynthiatoth134@gmail.com	134 N Kelly St Hobart IN 46342	IN	Teacher	EM			CQ	2002
Totsky Adele M Jedlicka	adele.totsky@gmail.com	709 Prestige St Joilet IL 60435	NI	Teacher	Tchr	Cross Yorkville IL	(630)553-7335	MQ	1986
Tougas Julia K	(209)747-9347 juliaktougas@gmail.com	6601 Blue Oaks Blvd Apt 2903 Rocklin CA 95765	CNH	DCE	Mem C	St Matthew Rocklin CA	(916)435-0330	IV	2024
Tracey Julie A Klakamp	(812)522-7957 jtracey@cinergymetro.net	424 Hedge Ct W Seymour IN 47274	IN	Teacher	Tchr	Immanuel Seymour IN	(812)522-1301	CQ	1993
Tracy Marjorie K Kennell	(682)365-4926 margetracy@hotmail.com	501 Bourland Rd Apt 2126 Keller TX 76248	TX	Teacher	EM			S	1969
Tracy Samantha K Megna	(920)427-6633 samanthakaytracy@gmail.com	3208 McCulloch St Stevens Point WI 54481	NW	DCM	Mem C	St Paul Stevens Point WI	(715)344-5660	MQ	2010
Trah Nathanael W	ntrah@flcse.org	1718 Tudor Ln. Tavares FL 32778	FG	Teacher	Tchr	Faith Eustis FL	(352)589-5683	S	2007
Trah Richard H	(314) 288-6729 r5trahs@att.net	2705 Chalet Hill Dr Saint Louis MO 63129	MO	Teacher	EM			RF	1973
Trah Sheila E	(815)568-7481	975 Keppler Dr Marengo IL 60152	NI	Teacher	EM			RF	1975
Trampe Ronald C	(314) 956-0100 caroladele6@att.net	1114 Yorktown Dr Saint Charles MO 63303	MO	Teacher	EM			RF	1955
Tranum Carla J Winterstein	(360)471-7276 mrstranum@yahoo.com	249 NW Jasper St #2126 Dallas OR 97338	NOW	Teacher	EM			RF	1971
Trapp Dale M Dr	(651)373-1724 dtrapp@csp.edu	1286 Etna St Saint Paul MN 55106	MNS	Teacher	EM			CQ	1968
Trapp Lauri R Reid Schmeiser	(262)496-0092 classical_ed@yahoo.com	29412 Silver Lake Rd Salem WI 53168	SW	Teacher	C09/2018			RF	1981
Trapp Mark D	(630)347-7528 mtrapp@zionconcord.org	102 W Kenilworth Ave Villa Park IL 60181	NI	Teacher	P/Tchr	Concord Bensenville IL	(630)766-0228	S	1988
Traska Keith A	(314)341-9979 coachtraska@gmail.com	504 Acacia Dr Grafton WI 53024	SW	Teacher	C08/2025			MQ	2001
Traska Marie L Kinkel	(715)212-2644 traska5@charter.net	1899 Seville Rd Kronenwetter WI 54455	NW	Teacher	EM			SP	1973
Traub Gail A Froemming	(217)246-5609 gailtraub@yahoo.com	970 County Road 500 E Toledo IL 62468	CI	Teacher	EM			CQ	1993
Trautmann Melissa M Welther Roberts	(765)337-8149 mmtrautmann@outlook.com	1918 Castellan Dr Lafayette IN 47906	IN	Teacher	C08/2023			RF	2006
Trautner Donn W	(512)921-3989 dtrautner@gmail.com	1005 Pine Creek Dr Pflugerville TX 78660	TX	Teacher	EM			RF	1973
Travers Barbara N Noske	(443) 617-1839 btravers85@hotmail.com	1502 Honeysuckle Dr Bel Air MD 21014	SE	Teacher	EM			BR	1985
Tredray Christina M Strei	(952)212-6211 ctredray@trinityfirst.org	3943 Hubbard Ave N Minneapolis MN 55422	MNS	Teacher	Tchr	Trinity First Minneapolis MN	(612)871-2353	RF	2000
Trent Keith B	ktrent@stpaulwestlake.org	6480 Grayfair Dr Brookpark OH 44142	OH	Teacher	Prin	St Paul Westlake OH	(440)835-3050	CQ	2015
Tres Marlene J Rippy	(847)670-0665	1111 N Pine Ave Arlington Hts IL 60004	NI	Teacher	P/Tchr	Immanuel Palatine IL	(847)359-1936	RF	1983
Trettin Paul K	(847)302-0985 pkt161952@gmail.com	N1847 Highland Rd Lake Geneva WI 53147	SW	Teacher	EM			RF	1973
Trickel Donald R	(309)828-8046	906 S Madison St Bloomington IL 61701	CI	Teacher	EM			S	1960
Trimberger Elaine L	(920)759-0528 etrimberger@mymailstation.com	4 McFarland Pl Kaukauna WI 54130	SW	Teacher	EM			RF	1964
Trinche Lori Calkins Deac	(630)665-5238 ltrinche@yahoo.com	450 Warrenville Road Unit 317 Lisle IL 60532	NI	Deaconess	C02/2024			CH	2020
Trinklein Joyce M Fix	(516)921-8572 joytrink@gmail.com	168 Brookville Rd Glen Head NY 11545	AT	Teacher	C07/2016			BR	1979
Trinklein Kathryn B Herzog	(260)745-3172 ktrinklein@esmeagles.com	227 Deer Cliff Run Fort Wayne IN 46804	IN	Teacher	EM			S	1973
Trinklein Susan M Blattner		1619 Claystone Ct Zeeland MI 49464	MI	Teacher	EM			RF	1977
Triplett Amy L Ohmann	(651)214-9086 atriplett@immanuelsilo.org	320 Main St Lewiston MN 55952	MNS	Teacher	Tchr	Immanuel Silo Lewiston MN	(507)523-3143	SP	2007
Triplett Benjamin L	(716)531-3401 btriplett@lutheraneast.org	14523 Glencliffe Rd. Cleveland OH 44111	OH	Teacher	Tchr	Cleveland LHS Association Rocky River OH	(440)356-7155	S	2008
Tripp Allison D Chrismer Patton	(636)288-6487 tripp@lhssc.org	527 Prairie Creek Ct Wentzville MO 63385	MO	Teacher	Tchr	St Charles Saint Peters MO	(636)928-5100	S	2010
Tripp Mikhail B	(619)248-5099 catcher1234q@gmail.com	2730 Dale St N Apt 307 Saint Paul MN 55113	TX	Teacher	Tchr	Immanuel Giddings TX	(979)542-3319	SP	2023
Trittin Sandra J	(218)280-0935 grade3_4.oslds@midconetwork.com	707 N Main St Crookston MN 56716	MNN	Teacher	Tchr	Our Saviors Crookston MN	(218)281-5191	SP	1993
Trochinski Desiree C Walker	(414)405-8076 desiree.trochinski@mtolivemke.org	2505 Elmwood Rd Hartford WI 53027	SW	Teacher	Tchr	Mount Olive Milwaukee WI	(414)774-2200	MQ	2016
Troemel Molly C Peterson	(260)450-4635 mollytroemel@gmail.com	7146 Chandler Ct Indianapolis IN 46217	IN	Teacher	Tchr	Calvary Indianapolis IN	(317)783-2000	CH	2014
Trofka Michele E Luetkens	(920)680-5673 mtrofka@new.rr.com	3900 Lark Rd Suamico WI 54313	NW	Teacher	EM			RF	1979
Trombley Kimberly E Coe Deac	(317)498-7952 deaconesskimberly@gmail.com	7821 Decatur Rd Fort Wayne IN 46816	IN	Deaconess	C06/2024			FW-DEAC	2012
Trosper Pena Kendra A	(630)307-2397 kendra.trosper@trinityroselle.com	201 Freeport Drive Bloomingdale IL 60108	NI	Teacher	Tchr	Trinity Roselle IL	(630)894-3263	S	2004
Trout Vickie L Hubbard Farmer	vfarmer8@insightbb.com	1506 W Vernon Ave Springfield IL 62704	CI	Teacher	EM			S	1975

*Multiple Assignments (See Church Worker Locator for Additional Details)
See Page 53 for the Table of Abbreviations for key to District, Classification, Position, and College abbreviations.
**C =Candidate; EM =Emeritus; the date following the C is the month and year the Candidate status began

NAME	TELEPHONE NUMBER EMAIL	STREET ADDRESS CITY/STATE/ZIP	DISTRICT	CLASS.	POSITION/ STATUS**	WHERE SERVING	OFFICE PHONE	COLLEGE/ UNIV/CQ	YR GRAD
Trowbridge Marisa J	(952)288-3587 mtrowbridge@mtcalvaryrichfield. org	2100 Cliff Rd E Apt 222 Burnsville MN 55337	MNS	Teacher	Mem C	Mount Calvary Richfield MN	(612)866-5405	S	1998
Trower Linda R Eichstaedt	(314)283-9048 ltrower@abidingsaviorlutheran.org	423 Cerny Ct Eureka MO 63025	MO	Teacher	Tchr	Abiding Savior Saint Louis MO	(314)892-4408	RF	1987
Truesdell Gayle G Brauer Deac	(636)579-0769 gayletruesdell@gmail.com	436 Redwood Forest Dr Manchester MO 63021	MO	Deaconess	Mem C	Mount Calvary Brentwood MO	(314)968-2360	SL-DEAC	2006
Trunkhill Brenda E Offermann	(620)474-3228 brenda@trunkhill.org	2460 Kenwood Rd Dow City IA 51528	IW	Teacher	Tchr	Unity Ridge Denison IA	(712)393-2002	SP	1998
Truog David J	(231)349-0709 dtruog@charter.net	20615 Okemos Rd Big Rapids MI 49307	MI	Teacher	EM			S	1970
Truog Susan L Carroll	(231)349-0425 struog@charter.net	20615 Okemos Rd Big Rapids MI 49307	MI	Teacher	EM			S	1970
Truttschel Rebecca L Hemauer	(920)946-0640 btruttschel@gmail.com	N7016 Jennifer Dr Plymouth WI 53073	SW	Teacher	Tchr	Trinity Sheboygan WI	(920)458-8248	MQ	2004
Truwe Gary M	(317)590-2022 gftruwe@sbcglobal.net	1834 Zinnia Dr Indianapolis IN 46219	IN	Tch/DCE	EM			S	1969
Trzeciak Lorie G Flores	(863)510-1738 ltrzeciak@langleyit.com	15283 Appleton Blvd Port Charlotte FL 33981	FG	Teacher	Prin	Shep of the Coast Fort Lauderdale FL	(954)772-5468	CQ	2012
Tschudy Joy N Doerr	(618)420-3296 jtschudy34@gmail.com	1658 S 26th St Sheboygan WI 53081	SW	Teacher	C07/2016			MQ	2005
Tschudy Matthew D	(248)798-0131 matthew.tschudy@gmail.com	1658 S 26th St Sheboygan WI 53081	SW	Teacher	Tchr	Sheboygan Sheboygan WI	(920)452-3323	MQ	2006
Tubandt Nicole M Koenig	(402)321-5467 dcenicole@gmail.com	17850 Domingo Dr Parker CO 80134	RM	DCE	C07/2016			S	2007
Tubbs JoAnna I Pugh	(916)471-8138 pughjoanna@gmail.com	125 Wax Myrtle Ct Savannah GA 31419	FG	Teacher	C07/2016			IV	2013
Tucker Jodi M Werman	(863)670-6894 jtucker@stpaullakeland.org	6893 Hayter Dr Lakeland FL 33813	FG	Teacher	Tchr	St Paul Lakeland FL	(863)644-7710	SP	2001
Tucker Katherine L Taube	(317)455-2749 ktucker5406@yahoo.com	5406 Buckskin Dr Kokomo IN 46902	IN	Teacher	EM			RF	1969
Tucker Lori D Hegler	(989)297-8463 tuck2@sbcglobal.net	923 Wolcott Ave Saint Joseph MI 49085	MI	Teacher	Tchr	Lutheran Special Education Ministries Ann Arbor MI	(248)419-3390	CQ	1997
Tucker Susan K Hahn	(307)840-3460 susantucker59@hotmail.com	1048 Gasser Rd Riverton WY 82501	WY	Teacher	EM			CQ	2006
Tull Betty L Gehring		5151 Autumn Fern Dr Dublin OH 43016	NEB	Teacher	EM			S	1977
Tull Rhonda L Harms	(501)226-8103 rhonda.tull@gmail.com	19 Frontera Cir Hot Springs Village AR 71909	MDS	Teacher	EM			S	2018
Tumminello Janet F Myers	(561)716-8452 jjvct1@gmail.com	805 Plaza Atlantic Beach FL 32233	FG	Teacher	C03/2023			CQ	2008
Tuomi Bruce G	(630)660-2927 tuomdad@comcast.net	9942 272nd Ave Trevor WI 53179	NI	Teacher	EM			RF	1976
Turke Carolyn D Gnewuch		6801 Phil Lewis Way Middleton WI 53562	NW	Teacher	Tchr	Pilgrim Green Bay WI	(920)965-2244	RF	1966
Turner Angela R Hawley	(724)352-2221 aturner@stlukecabot.org	c/o Saint Luke Lutheran School 330 Hannahstown Rd Cabot PA 16023	EA	Teacher	Tchr	St Luke Cabot PA	(724)352-2221	CQ	2024
Tweeten Duane A	(262)844-3656 tweetend@gmail.com	21945 Mayrose Blvd Brookfield WI 53045	SW	Tch/DCE	EM			MQ	2002
Twillman Cynthia L	(816)805-1292 cindce@gmail.com	832 NE 66th St Gladstone MO 64118	MO	DCE	Mem C	King Of Kings Kansas City MO	(816)436-7680	SP	1996
Twork Clara J	(734)604-2364 cjtwork53@gmail.com	46056 Purple Sage Ct Belleville MI 48111	MI	Teacher	EM			S	1976
Tyson Madelyn M Rodenbeck	madelyntyson@gmail.com	150 Parker Rd Asheville NC 28805	FG	Teacher	C07/2016			S	1976
Uden Cynthia L Anderson	(402)469-5969 cindylou.uden@gmail.com	600 N Brooks Ave Kenesaw NE 68956	NEB	Teacher	EM			S	1979
Uden Lori D Hartmann	(402)460-0287 logosfromldu@hotmail.com	1203 E 5th St Hastings NE 68901	NEB	Teacher	EM			S	1985
Uden Michael D Dr	(262)252-0624 michael.uden@cuw.edu	3246 Elm Rd Cedarburg WI 53012	SW	Teacher	S HS/C	Concordia University Wisconsin Mequon WI	(262)243-5700	MQ	1989
Uecker Carol S Ohlendorf	(605)256-4372	12440 Willow Creek Rd Custer SD 57730	SD	Teacher	EM			SP	1975
Ueltzen Larry	(954)426-1607 lueltzen@prodigy.net	1319 SE 14th Ter Deerfield Bch FL 33441	FG	Teacher	EM			RF	1970
Ueltzen Vanessa L Wedgbury	(773)517-5802 ueltzen@prodigy.net	3340 N Neenah Ave Chicago IL 60634	NI	Teacher	Tchr	Walther Melrose Park IL	(708)344-0404	RF	1997
Uetrecht Donald G	duetrecht@gmail.com	8312 S. Laclede Station Rd. Saint Louis MO 63123	MO	Teacher	Tchr	Christ Community Kirkwood MO	(314)822-7774	S	1986
Uffelman Janell M Pirrie Dr	jmuffelman88@gmail.com	1214 Road V Waco NE 68460	NEB	Teacher	EM			S	1975
Uffman Jessie C Waterman	(785)747-2481	995 Thunder Rd Greenleaf KS 66943	KS	Teacher	C08/2021			S	2004
Uffmann Lynne A Fibiger	lynneauffmann@yahoo.com	18155 Aden Dr Robertsdale AL 36567	SO	Teacher	EM			RF	1969
Uffmann Matthew N	(251)404-6018 mruffmann@stjohnsnapa.org	4393 Plass Dr Napa CA 94558	CNH	Teacher	Tchr	St John Napa CA	(707)226-7970	PO	2011
Ugorek Emily A Allor	(630)747-3242 eallor@fulllifeinchrist.org	6n451 Cedar Ave Wood Dale IL 60191	NI	Teacher	Tchr	St Peter Arlington Heights IL	(847)259-4114	MQ	2011
Ullman James L	(563)676-8224 james.ullman@trinitydaven port.org	5456 Taylor St Davenport IA 52806	IE	Teacher	Tchr	Trinity Davenport IA	(563)322-5224	AA	2005

*Multiple Assignments (See Church Worker Locator for Additional Details)

See Page 53 for the Table of Abbreviations for key to District, Classification, Position, and College abbreviations.

**C =Candidate; EM =Emeritus; the date following the C is the month and year the Candidate status began

NAME	TELEPHONE NUMBER EMAIL	STREET ADDRESS CITY/STATE/ZIP	DISTRICT	CLASS.	POSITION/ STATUS**	WHERE SERVING	OFFICE PHONE	COLLEGE/ UNIV/CQ	YR GRAD
Ullman Laura J Vogler	(563)320-3780 laura.ullman@trinitydavenport.org	5456 Taylor St Davenport IA 52806	IE	Teacher	Tchr	Trinity Davenport IA	(563)322-5224	MQ	2003
Ulmer Laurie L Bonczkowski	(269)519-3137 mrslaurieulmer@gmail.com	1834 Sherwood Dr Stevensville MI 49127	MI	Teacher	EM			AA	1985
Ulrich Dean R	(815)670-2423 ulrich.stpaul@gmail.com	2612 Lorado Ln Rockford IL 61101	NI	Tch/DCE	EM			RF	1975
Ulrich Heather C Danner	(425)742-2729 heatherculrich@yahoo.com	3582 Chasewood Dr San Diego CA 92111	NOW	DCE	C07/2016			S	1992
Ulrich Miriam S Bickel	(630)292-2173 mulrich@hiscross.org	15661 S Stonewall Dr Newark IL 60541	NI	Teacher	Prin	Cross Yorkville IL	(630)553-7861	RF	2002
Umland Jean M	(715)853-5221 umlandjean@gmail.com	608 S Lincoln St Shawano WI 54166	NW	Teacher	Tchr	Saint James Shawano WI	(715)524-4815	S	1979
Umphenour Terry A	(314)679-0599 terryumphenour@slcas.org		MO	Teacher	Tchr	Salem Saint Louis MO	(314)352-4454	CQ	1993
Underwood Brian P	(714)552-1749	P.O. Box 1193 Genoa NV 89411	CNH	Teacher	ExecDir	Sierra Carson City NV	(775)267-1921	CQ	2013
Unger Allison M Meineke	(720)273-8616 aunger@lhsa.com	22526 Beech St Dearborn MI 48124	MI	Teacher	Pro Stf	Westland Westland MI	(734)422-2090	MQ	2007
Unger Andrea Walters	(313)410-6402 andreaunger@stmatthew.info	6401 Reuter St Dearborn MI 48126	MI	Teacher	EM			S	1974
Unger Daniel E		22526 Beech St Dearborn MI 48124	MI	Teacher	Tchr	Westland Westland MI	(734)422-2090	MQ	2007
Unger Michael E	(734)637-8559 munger@lhsa.com	6401 Reuter St Dearborn MI 48126	MI	Teacher	EM			S	1972
Unger Robert E	(919)239-9083	2400 Thurrock Dr Apex NC 27539	SE	Teacher	EM			RF	1979
Ungerecht Cynthia B Kietzman	(218)820-6309 cindyandcraig@yahoo.com	46047 255th Ave Laporte MN 56461	MNN	Teacher	Tchr	Immanuel Walker MN	(218)547-4139	SP	1995
Unruh Christine M Klug	(507)450-3182 cmarieklug@gmail.com	41 Wenonah Rd Minnesota City MN 55959	MNS	Teacher	C08/2020			MQ	2014
Unverfehrt Kathleen E Hanke	(828)464-6648 kunvertfehrt@concordianc.org	1165 Wind Bluff Ct Newton NC 28658	SE	Teacher	Tchr	Concordia Conover NC	(828)464-3011	S	1977
Unverfehrt William E	(828)238-4239 bunverfehrt@uchigh.com	1165 Wind Bluff Ct Newton NC 28658	SE	Teacher	EM			S	1978
Upchurch Alexis N Wood	(919)714-3065 awood@abidingsavior.com	1530 Concordia West Irvine CA 92612	PSW	DCE	Mem C	Abiding Savior Lake Forest CA	(949)830-1460	IV	2024
Urban Douglas R	dutrumpet@gmail.com	113 Hampton CV Boerne TX 78006	TX	Teacher	Tchr	Shep Of The Hills San Antonio TX	(210)614-3741	RF	1981
Urban Drew R	(281)229-3450 durban@clnorfolk.org	2410 Clearfield Norfolk NE 68701	NEB	Teacher	Prin	Christ Norfolk NE	(402)371-5536	S	2006
Urban Emily	(262)893-8592	W6112 Quarry Rd Appleton WI 54913	SW	Teacher	Tchr	New Hope Neenah WI	(920)725-8797	MQ	2004
Urban Lawrence W	(618)349-8735 urbansix@frontiernet.net	2356 E 800 Ave Saint Peter IL 62880	CI	Teacher	EM			SP	1967
Urban Mariann C Dustman	(708)366-6033 catie_urban@waltheracademy.org	512 Thomas Ave Forest Park IL 60130	NI	Teacher	Tchr	Walther Melrose Park IL	(708)344-0404	RF	1983
Urban Matthew T	(260)409-1680 murban14@yahoo.com	526 E Jefferson Street Columbia City IN 46725	IN	Teacher	Tchr	Concordia Fort Wayne IN	(260)483-1102	Other	2010
Urban Sara L Pittman	(309)452-7430	2504 Timber View Dr Bloomington IL 61701	CI	Teacher	Tchr	Trinity Bloomington IL	(309)829-7513	MQ	1994
Urbank Sharon N Pokol	(702)480-1648 suteach1st@aol.com	5108 Cutty Way Las Vegas NV 89130	PSW	Teacher	C06/2017			CQ	2002
Urbanski Amy M Holcomb	(331)645-7066 amy.holcomb@cuw.edu	17121 Rochelle Ln Tinley Park IL 60487	NI	Teacher	Tchr	Trinity Tinley Park IL	(708)532-3529	CH	2009
Urberg Allison M Parkhurst	(315)617-3258 allieurberg@gmail.com	122 Eagle Ridge Ct Eau Claire WI 54703	NW	DCE	C11/2024			S	2016
Urquhart Christopher M	(618)826-2098 curquhar@randolph.k12.il.us	2455 Trout Camp Rd Waterloo IL 62298	SI	Teacher	EM			RF	1970
Urschel Catelyn E Mefferd	(419)605-6610 mefferdc5@gmail.com	3130 Bellshire Way Fort Wayne IN 46815	IN	Teacher	C02/2025			CH	2018
Usadel Jessica M Kanz	(920)207-3260 jessica.usadel@ourbethlehem.com	W2165 Shamrock Dr Sheboygan WI 53083	SW	Teacher	Tchr	Bethlehem Sheboygan WI	(920)452-5071	MQ	2015
Utech Nickolas A	(954)263-5668 nickutech@gmail.com	15015 Michelangelo Blvd Apt 208 Delray Beach FL 33446	FG	Teacher	C08/2025			RF	2004
Utech Ralph A	(561)943-8803 ralph@utechfamily.net	1507 SW 21st St Boynton Beach FL 33426	FG	Teacher	EM			S	1972
Utech Richard W			RM	Teacher	EM			RF	1969
Utecht Beth J Degler	(952)240-4817 bdegler34@gmail.com	948 Lincoln Blvd Manitowoc WI 54220	NW	Teacher	C07/2016			MQ	2003
Utecht Justina M Strecker	(402)801-2334 ejutecht@gmail.com	3010 15th St Columbus NE 68601	NEB	Teacher	C08/2018			S	2014
Utecht Justus R	(402)389-2466 justus.utecht@cune.org	P.O. Box 1435 Madison NE 68748	NEB	Teacher	Tchr	Northeast Norfolk NE	(402)379-3040	S	2019
Utecht Katie A Wrege	(586)668-8902 katieautecht@gmail.com	727 Mustang Dr. Apt. 202 Belle Fourche SD 57717	SD	Teacher	C08/2022			S	2021
Uthoff Patricia R Holjevic	(314)910-0830 pruthoff@hotmail.com	4969 Quail Crest Ct Saint Louis MO 63128	MO	Teacher	EM			CQ	2001
Vaccaro Brenda L Schlacht	(541)312-3808 lyndie.vaccaro@bendnetworks.com	827 NE Robin Ct Bend OR 97701	NOW	Teacher	C07/2016			S	1987
Vahl Heather C Sell	(262)901-5333 heather.sell@cune.org	1215 Copenhill Dr Waukesha WI 53186	SW	DCE	Mem C	Immanuel Brookfield WI	(262)781-7140	S	2009
Valdez Nicole D Weeden	nvaldez@fils.org	1164 Knollwood Dr Grafton WI 53024	SW	Teacher	Tchr	First Immanuel Cedarburg WI	(262)377-6610	CQ	2001

*Multiple Assignments (See Church Worker Locator for Additional Details)

See Page 53 for the Table of Abbreviations for key to District, Classification, Position, and College abbreviations.

**C =Candidate; EM =Emeritus; the date following the C is the month and year the Candidate status began

NAME	TELEPHONE NUMBER EMAIL	STREET ADDRESS CITY/STATE/ZIP	DISTRICT	CLASS.	POSITION/ STATUS**	WHERE SERVING	OFFICE PHONE	COLLEGE/ UNIV/CQ	YR GRAD
Valencia Sarah A Pulliam	(210)668-2899 pulliamsarah27@gmail.com	13330 Birdcall Ln Cypress TX 77429	TX	DCE	Mem C	St John Cypress TX	(281)373-0503	AU	2017
Valente Elizabeth A Mooney		1115 Park Rd Jackson MI 49203	MI	Teacher	Tchr	Trinity Jackson MI	(517)750-2105	AA	1998
Valentine Debra L Schuldheisz	(541)233-6769 deblvalentine19@gmail.com	62365 Deer Trail Rd Bend OR 97701	NOW	Teacher	EM			PO	1994
Valleroy Stephanie R Phelps	(618)443-8107 stvalleroy@stjohnsredbud.org	264 Summit St Red Bud IL 62278	SI	Teacher	Tchr	St John Red Bud IL	(618)282-3873	Other	2019
Vallin Kurt R	(651)214-9523 krvallin6@gmail.com	2128 Carnelian Ln Eagan MN 55122	MNS	Teacher	C07/2016			S	1990
Vallin Stephanie K Vogel	(651)494-7847 kandsand4@gmail.com	2128 Carnelian Ln Eagan MN 55122	MNS	Teacher	Tchr	Trinity Lone Oak Eagan MN	(651)454-7235	S	1992
Van Andel Judith E Kramer	(612)263-4373 judyandrog@gmail.com	12532 Marquess Way N Lake Elmo MN 55042	MNS	Teacher	EM			S	1971
Van Andel Roger J	(406)570-0878 judyandrog@gmail.com	P.O. Box 5263 Bozeman MT 59717	MNS	Teacher	EM			S	1971
Van Bibber Brianna	(308)227-8566 vanbibberbrianna@gmail.com	515 Fairway Dr Apt 6 Milford NE 68405	NEB	Teacher	Tchr	Trinity Lincoln NE	(402)466-1800	S	2024
Van Blarcom Stephanie L Mc Cann	(714)458-6627 webevb@gmail.com	204 N California St Orange CA 92866	PSW	Teacher	EM			IV	1983
Van Dellen Carol A Harriman	(248)318-7534 c.vandellen@sbcglobal.net	930 Watersmeet Dr Oxford MI 48371	MI	Teacher	EM			CQ	1987
Van Dellen James R	(414)218-5575 vandellen@aol.com	940 Schloemer Drive West Bend WI 53095	SW	Teacher	Prin	St Johns West Bend WI	(262)334-3077	AA	1991
Van Etten Jodi L Buch	(319) 558-6499 jvanetten@lutheraninterparish.com	122 Country Club Rd Williamsburg IA 52361	IE	Teacher	Tchr	Lutheran Interparish Williamsburg IA	(319)668-1711	CQ	2021
Van Hulst Lynne A Winkelman	(262)534-7261 lynnevanhulst@gmail.com	4331 Valley View Ln Waterford WI 53185	SW	Teacher	EM			CQ	2001
Van Kanegan Lynette M Dittloff	(414)282-8205 lynettevankanegan@icloud.com	5637 S Lorene Ave Milwaukee WI 53221	SW	Teacher	EM			RF	1976
Van Luchene Darrell G Dr	(406)686-4350 dvan1946@gmail.com	15705 Horse Creek Rd Bozeman MT 59715	MT	Teacher	EM			S	1968
Van Luchene Sue Zann Denton	(406)686-4650 suevanl2002@yahoo.com	15705 Horse Creek Rd Bozeman MT 59715	MT	Teacher	EM			S	1969
Van Natta Kirk D	(253)538-7936 kirkvannatta@hotmail.com	2012 105th St E Tacoma WA 98445	NOW	Teacher	Inst C	Office of National Mission Saint Louis MO		CQ	2000
Van Rixel Abigail	(715)581-7582 abbyvanrixel@gmail.com	605 Alfred St Athens WI 54411	NW	Teacher	Tchr	Trinity Wausau WI	(715)848-0166	MQ	2024
Van Rixel Rebecca C Brice	(715) 297-2057 vanrixelb@gmail.com	605 Alfred St Athens WI 54411	NW	Teacher	Tchr	Trinity Athens WI	(715)257-7559	MQ	1995
Van Slett Kate M Viesselmann	(414)405-2168 kvanslett@zls-lincoln.org	1725 1400th Ave Lincoln IL 62656	CI	Teacher	Tchr	Zion Lincoln IL	(217)732-3977	MQ	2012
van Sliedrecht Tiffany Hoffmann	(414)839-9398 t_vansliedrecht@yahoo.com	3156 Dan Mor Ln Racine WI 53404	SW	Teacher	Tchr	St John Racine WI	(262)633-2758	RF	2001
Van Spankeren David W	(260)494-9884 dvanspankeren@cluth.org		IN	Teacher	Prin	Central New Haven IN	(260)493-2502	CQ	2019
Van Spankeren Rebecca L Messmann	(260)493-2502 rvanspankeren@cluth.org		IN	Teacher	Tchr	Central New Haven IN	(260)493-2502	RF	2004
Van Straten Kerri A Quade	(414)916-0893 kerri.quade@stjohnsmayville.com	454 S National Ave Fond Du Lac WI 54935	SW	Teacher	Tchr	St John Mayville WI	(920)387-3568	MQ	2013
Van Volkenburgh Candace A Brauer	cvan@calvarykc.com	12411 Wornall Road Kansas City MO 64145	MO	Teacher	Tchr	Calvary Kansas City MO	(816)444-6908	CQ	1985
Vance Cindy A Froehling	(217)394-2084	590 E 1100 North Rd Buckley IL 60918	CI	Teacher	EM			CQ	2004
Vance Marguerite R Walburg	(952)884-5252 peggyvance@hotmail.com	10508 Upton Cir S Bloomington MN 55431	MNS	Teacher	EM			SP	1972
Vande Voort-Schweim Amy L Vande Voort	alschweim@comcast.net	703 W Main Puyallup WA 98371	NOW	DCE	Mem C	Our Savior Tacoma WA	(253)531-2112	SP	1994
VanDeKeere Johannah L Miesner	(573)517-3937 miesnerjohannah@gmail.com	3822 Live Oak Blvd Fort Wayne IN 46804	IN	Teacher	Tchr	Emmanuel-St Michael Fort Wayne IN	(260)422-6712	S	2005
VanDenBerg Loren M	(402)881-6234 loren.vandenberg@gmail.com		NW	Teacher	Tchr	Northeastern WI Green Bay WI	(920)469-6810	MQ	2009
Vandercar Whitney E Powers	(812)371-3983 whitneyvandercar@gmail.com	8088 Lutheran Lake Rd Seymour IN 47274	IN	Teacher	Prin	White Creek Columbus IN	(812)342-6832	CQ	2009
Vandercook Ardith J Piehl	(806)236-7553 ajvandercook@yahoo.com	4504 Steffi Ct Amarillo TX 79110	TX	Teacher	EM			S	1971
Vandercook James L	(806)236-5363 james.vandercook@gmail.com	4504 Steffi Ct Amarillo TX 79110	TX	Teacher	EM			S	1971
Vandergriff Mackenzie P Wells	(812)374-6585 mackenziepaige@gmail.com	7015 Northfield Dr Evansville IN 47711	IN	Teacher	Tchr	Evansville Evansville IN	(812)424-7252	CH	2014
Vandergrifft Jordan L Redmond	(512)364-4282 jordan.redmond@ctx.edu	21401 Grand National Ave Pflugerville TX 78660	TX	Teacher	Tchr	Redeemer Austin TX	(512)459-1500	AU	2017
Vanderhyde Daniel C	(949)872-6372 daniel.vanderhyde@gmail.com	7365 Windwood Way Parker CO 80134	RM	Teacher	C07/2021			IV	2010
Vanderhyde Jessica A Siebert	(602)317-3254 jessica.vanderhyde@gmail.com	7365 Windwood Way Parker CO 80134	RM	Teacher	C07/2016			IV	2010
Vandrey Wanda J Whitworth	(661)802-1236 wanda@vandrey.com	2028 Holguin St Lancaster CA 93536	PSW	Teacher	EM			CQ	1995
VanDyke Ellen L Abel	(414)383-6218 ellenlavd@gmail.com	1612 S 30th St Milwaukee WI 53215	SW	Teacher	EM			S	1982
Vanic Patrick R	(920) 782-1130 prv1974hondas@gmail.com	1205 Stonebridge Dr Howards Grove WI 53083	SW	Teacher	Prin	Bethlehem Sheboygan WI	(920)452-5071	MQ	2005
Vanick Edward W	(586)778-3729 edwardvanick@comcast.net	18269 Glendale St Roseville MI 48066	MI	Teacher	EM			RF	1969

*Multiple Assignments (See Church Worker Locator for Additional Details)
See Page 53 for the Table of Abbreviations for key to District, Classification, Position, and College abbreviations.
**C =Candidate; EM =Emeritus; the date following the C is the month and year the Candidate status began

NAME	TELEPHONE NUMBER EMAIL	STREET ADDRESS CITY/STATE/ZIP	DISTRICT	CLASS.	POSITION/ STATUS**	WHERE SERVING	OFFICE PHONE	COLLEGE/ UNIV/CQ	YR GRAD
Vanness Melinda A Kleopfer	(515)580-0007 mvanness@stpaulslatimer.org	634 170th St Latimer IA 50452	IE	Teacher	Tchr	St Pauls Latimer IA	(641)579-6046	S	1985
Vannoy Lisa K Klemz	(402)875-0927 lvannoy1966@gmail.com	1504 Bonforte Blvd Pueblo CO 81001	RM	Teacher	Tchr	Trinity Pueblo CO	(719)542-1864	S	1995
VanSoest LeeAnna M Smith	(574)248-2263 leeanna.smith@cuw.edu	3751 Lakeshore Dr Bremen IN 46506	IN	Teacher	Tchr	St Paul Bremen IN	(574)546-2332	MQ	2011
VanTol Rebecca S Reed	(989)430-0036 rebecca.vantol@gmail.com	2814 Cass St Unionville MI 48767	MI	Teacher	C06/2024			AA	1998
VanVleet Anna E Anna Shaw	(314)757-2636 annavanvleet@gmail.com	1118 Maplewood Ct SW Isanti MN 55040	MNS	Teacher	Tchr	Trinity First Minneapolis MN	(612)871-2353	SP	2013
Vanwey Teresa L Thomas	(316)201-1392 terrivanwey@yahoo.com	2022 S Webb Rd Ste 227 Wichita KS 67207	KS	Teacher	EM			CQ	2007
Varner Jane M Luebbe	(402)643-9745 janevarner@neb.rr.com	500 Heartland Park Dr Seward NE 68434	NEB	Teacher	EM			S	1975
Varnes Linda L Going-Smith	(208)463-0798 varnesnxl@msn.com	2600 San Marco Way Nampa ID 83686	NOW	Teacher	EM			S	1970
Vasquez Angela C Stucky	(808)351-2083 acstucky@yahoo.com	3939 Briargrove Ln #2310 Dallas TX 75287	TX	Teacher	Tchr	Prince Of Peace Carrollton TX	(972)447-0532	S	2001
Vasquez Roman S	(208)819-2645 pfbikes60@gmail.com	4450 E Weatherby Ave Post Falls ID 83854	NOW	Teacher	C07/2016			S	1996
Vaudt Amanda B	(952)242-8819 amandavaudt23@yahoo.com		IN	Teacher	Pro Stf	Central New Haven IN	(260)493-2502	SP	2001
Vaughan Diana L Dyer	(580)761-8382 diana.vaughan@flcspc.com	9250 E Coleman Rd Ponca City OK 74604	OK	Teacher	Tchr	First Ponca City OK	(580)762-9950	MQ	1999
Vaughn Melanie L Trentsch	mvaughndce@gmail.com	105 Stow Rd Apt B4 Harvard MA 01451	NE	DCE	C07/2016			S	2007
Vaughn Sarah R Anderson	(303)829-0486 sarah.vaughn@trinityfremont.org	1187 Nickerson Rd Hooper NE 68031	NEB	Teacher	Tchr	Trinity Fremont NE	(402)721-5959	CQ	2012
Vaupel Christina Baisch	(505)363-6862 vaupelcjb@yahoo.com	302 Saw Mill Rd Royse City TX 75189	TX	Teacher	Mem C	Tangible Grace Allen TX	(972)246-8411	RF	1997
Vecsernyes Evelyn L Lustila	(734)223-0640 evecsern@umich.edu	2800 Blanche St Melvindale MI 48122	MI	Teacher	C07/2016			CQ	1991
Vedder David O	(815)546-9261 dved99@yahoo.com	1914 George Ct Glenview IL 60025	NI	Teacher	EM			RF	1973
Veen Rebecca R Peters	(574)296-9234	55939 Kathryn Dr Elkhart IN 46514	IN	Teacher	C09/2025			RF	2001
Vega Aaron J	(631)806-1730 ajvega93@gmail.com	2833 Central Park Blvd Denver CO 80238	RM	DCE	Mem C	St Johns Denver CO	(303)733-3777	AU	2016
Vega Kristen L Martin	(239)989-9531 kristen.martin@ctx.edu	2833 Central Park Blvd Denver CO 80238	FG	DCE	C07/2016			AU	2014
Vehmeier Kathleen A Meyer	(815)235-4239 kvehmeier3@gmail.com	707 W American St Freeport IL 61032	NI	Teacher	EM			RF	1987
Veith Gene E Jr Dr	(571)334-1695 geveith2@aol.com	6601 Clayton Rd. 1-W St. Louis MO 63117	IN	Teacher	EM			CQ	1987
Vendetti Dina C Dr	(302)730-1379 dina_vendetti@verizon.net	352 W Wind Dr Dover DE 19901	SE	Teacher	EM			BR	1985
Venteicher Benjamin D	(402)984-3937 benvdce@gmail.com	223 B Street Hampton NE 68843	NEB	DCE	Mem C	Zion Hampton NE	(402)725-3320	S	2007
Venzke Jeanette Mandel	(712)263-8271 jvenke@frontiernet.net	1715 26th St Central City NE 66826	IW	Teacher	EM			RF	1960
Vercruysse Britney C Birtell	(402)992-3153 bvercruysse@sflutheranschool.com	3900 S Faith Ave Sioux Falls SD 57110	SD	Teacher	Tchr	Sioux Falls Sioux Falls SD	(605)335-1923	S	2014
Verner Elizabeth L Crowder	(636)448-1511 elvrtv04@gmail.com	2014 Teresa Fields Ln Lake St Louis MO 63367	MO	Teacher	Tchr	Immanuel Wentzville MO	(636)327-4416	S	2001
Verseman Dennis H Dr	(760)660-3764 versemankd39@msn.com	19365 Cardene Way Northville MI 48167	MI	Teacher	EM			RF	1962
Versemann Calvin E	(636)978-9216 cmverse@aol.com	202 Fairgate Dr Saint Peters MO 63376	MO	Teacher	EM			RF	1962
Versemann Rachel S Stohs	(314)496-4348 rsverse@hotmail.com	532 Oxborough Ct Saint Peters MO 63376	MO	Teacher	C07/2016			RF	1991
Versteeg Krista K Freitag	(253)273-8700 freitagkrista@gmail.com	18914 77th Ave Ct E Puyallup WA 98375	TX	Teacher	C07/2018			MQ	2012
Vevia Jonathan K	(619)847-5006 jon.vevia@saints.org	63080 Dickey Rd Bend OR 97701	NOW	DPM	Mem C	Trinity Bend OR	(541)382-1832	CQ	2020
Vezner Anthony J	(815)985-8302	710 E Riverview Ave Orange CA 92865	PSW	Teacher	S HS/C	Concordia University Irvine Irvine CA	(949)854-8002	CQ	2011
Vezner Heather L Brackmann	(714)222-8209 heather.vezner@cui.edu	710 E Riverview Ave Orange CA 92865	PSW	Teacher	S HS/C	Concordia University Irvine Irvine CA	(949)854-8002	RF	1993
Vick Michael S	(949)716-7242 mvick@abidingsavior.com	26245 Morning Gln Lake Forest CA 92630	PSW	Teacher	Tchr	Abiding Savior Lake Forest CA	(949)830-1461	S	1983
Viehl Warren A	dcewarren@gmail.com	17524 Dayton St Omaha NE 68135	NEB	DCE	EM			S	2000
Vieregge Keith L	(586)871-5428 kvieregge@gmail.com	501 S West St Fenton MI 48430	EN	Teacher	EM			S	1981
Viergutz Erin R	(715)581-5859 eviergutz@stpaulmanawa.org	N12098 Cty Rd D Clintonville WI 54929	NW	Teacher	Tchr	St Paul Manawa WI	(920)596-2815	MQ	2024
Vierk Dennis L	(608)752-2495 vierkfamily@gmail.com	1017 Laramie Ln Janesville WI 53546	SW	Teacher	EM			RF	1966
Viets Aaron D Dr	(816)547-2544 aaron.viets@cuw.edu	110 Edmaro St Fredonia WI 53021	SW	Teacher	S HS/C	Concordia University Wisconsin Mequon WI	(262)243-5700	CQ	2023
Viets Deborah R Flath-Flynn			NOW	Teacher	EM			S	1971
Viets Lisa J		114 Claiborne Wright Way Bastrop TX 78602	TX	Teacher	Tchr	Pilgrim Houston TX	(713)432-7082	MQ	2000

*Multiple Assignments (See Church Worker Locator for Additional Details)
See Page 53 for the Table of Abbreviations for key to District, Classification, Position, and College abbreviations.
**C =Candidate; EM =Emeritus; the date following the C is the month and year the Candidate status began

NAME	TELEPHONE NUMBER EMAIL	STREET ADDRESS CITY/STATE/ZIP	DISTRICT	CLASS.	POSITION/ STATUS**	WHERE SERVING	OFFICE PHONE	COLLEGE/ UNIV/CQ	YR GRAD
Viets Martin W	(815)540-9172 oatbird@sbcglobal.net	2728 NE Cole Ave McMinnville OR 97128	NI	Teacher	EM			RF	1974
Viets Norma J Fischer	(815)382-7828 oatbird@sbcglobal.net	2728 NE Cole Ave McMinnville OR 97128	NI	Teacher	EM			RF	1974
Viliocco Thomas L	(314)221-1631 tviliocco@gmail.com	14482 Eddington Dr Chesterfield MO 63017	MO	DCM	EM			MQ	2005
Villarreal Britt A	(512)297-8063 coloradobav@aol.com	9980 Frederick Pl Eden Prairie MN 55347	RM	Teacher	C07/2016			AU	1998
Villegas Maria I Deac	(630)402-1324 marbelillo@yahoo.com	807 S Edgelawn Dr Aurora IL 60506	NI	Deaconess	C05/2023			SL-DEAC	2021
Vincent Eric T	evincent@lhsi.org	677 Downing Dr Greenwood IN 46143	IN	Teacher	Tchr	Indianapolis Indianapolis IN	(317)787-5474	S	1999
Vincent Heath D	(989)316-1405 hdvincent16@gmail.com	2817 Dunmore Dr Saginaw MI 48603	MI	Teacher	P/Tchr	Immanuel Bay City MI	(989)893-8521	CQ	2011
Vincent J M	(314)843-6576 mikev103@gmail.com	8819 Red Oak Dr Saint Louis MO 63126	MO	Teacher	EM			S	1970
Violette James R	(714)955-3943 jviolette@princeofpeaceana heim.org	890 N Fern St Orange CA 92867	PSW	Teacher	Prin	Prince Of Peace Anaheim CA	(714)774-0993	IV	1986
Viray Emmanuel	(737)610-0125 emanuelviray@yahoo.com		TX	DCM	C02/2020			MQ	2016
Virus Christopher A	(660)238-8733 big_red_virus@yahoo.com	30150 Emma Rd Concordia MO 64020	MO	Teacher	C06/2017			S	2000
Visser Diana J Tallan	(503)332-3858 pvanddv@gmail.com	22275 SW Dewey Dr Sherwood OR 97140	NOW	Teacher	EM			PO	1984
Vito Samantha N	sam.vito93@gmail.com	501 Belair Dr Jefferson City MO 65109	MO	Teacher	Tchr	Calvary Jefferson Cty MO	(573)638-0228	RF	2017
Voelker Carol S Keehn	(515)571-0676 carolvoelker62@gmail.com	948 170th St Latimer IA 50452	IE	Teacher	P/Tchr	St Pauls Latimer IA	(641)579-6046	S	1984
Voelker Carolyn R Lichtenwald	(618)345-2869 fc@thevoelkers.us	1009 Meadows Ct Maryville IL 62062	SI	Teacher	EM			RF	1961
Voelker Franklin A	(618)910-2624 fc@thevoelkers.us	1009 Meadows Ct Maryville IL 62062	SI	Teacher	EM			RF	1962
Voelker Howard E	(402)831-0869 hvoelksp@gmail.com	240 N Colfax St West Point NE 68788	NEB	Teacher	EM			S	1969
Voelker Kimberly J Foster	(714)469-4697 voelkerkj@gmail.com	10591 E Cerulean Way Tucson AZ 85747	PSW	Teacher	EM			CQ	2001
Voelker Mary E Lochmann Dr	(402)831-0822 marylochmannvoelker@gmail.com	240 N Colfax St West Point NE 68788	NEB	Teacher	EM			S	1970
Voelker Rodney W	(402)329-6359 jrvlkr@ptcnet.net	85639 552nd Ave Pierce NE 68767	NEB	Teacher	EM			S	1968
Voelker Ted C	(715)435-3816 tcvoelkr@wctc.net	6444 2nd Ave Rudolph WI 54475	NW	Teacher	EM			S	1973
Voeller Kristina L Brasher	(701)751-1963 kvoeller1@gmail.com	707 5th Ave NE Mandan ND 58554	ND	Teacher	Tchr	Martin Luther Bismarck ND	(701)224-9070	S	1994
Voelz Robert T	(313)689-8862 voelz6@wideopenwest.com	19342 Coachwood Rd Riverview MI 48193	MI	Teacher	EM			S	1973
Vogel Craig A	(262)633-2835 vogeltrain@sbcglobal.net	3753 Saint Andrews Blvd Racine WI 53405	SW	Teacher	EM			S	1969
Vogel Le Ann M Leins	(605)209-3540	14409 Dice Ct Rapid City SD 57701	SD	Teacher	Tchr	Zion Rapid City SD	(605)342-5749	SP	2007
Vogel Mary I de Bruler	(630)776-8607 mvogel1991@gmail.com	109 W Theodore Ln Itasca IL 60143	NI	Teacher	EM			CH	2006
Vogel Megan M Dierks	(419)340-7149 mrs.vogel.5@gmail.com	104 High St P.O. Box 204 Haskins OH 43525	OH	Teacher	C05/2025			CQ	2013
Vogel Philip A	(308)224-1441 Philip.vogel@cune.org	2527 N 165th Ave Omaha NE 68116	NEB	Teacher	Tchr	Concordia Omaha NE	(402)445-4000	S	2013
Vogeler Jason G	(843)478-0175 jvogeler@mlchouston.org	8515 Ashford Green Ln. Houston TX 77072	TX	Teacher	Tchr	Memorial Houston TX	(713)782-6079	CQ	2021
Vogt Caren M Meyer	(973)222-2152 carenvogt@gmail.com	412 Rowell Court Conway SC 29526	NJ	Teacher	EM			BR	1979
Vogt Katie E	(201)841-1092 vogtkatie@gmail.com	114 Smart Ave Yonkers NY 10704	AT	Teacher	Tchr	The Village Bronxville NY	(914)337-0207	CQ	2020
Vogt Lisa M Held	(214)450-8562 lisa.m.vogt3@gmail.com	2134 Meadfoot Rd Carrollton TX 75007	TX	Teacher	C07/2024			S	1995
Vogt Naomi M	(973)874-8562 nvogt@immanuelrapids.com	3561 Washington St Unit 3521107 Wisconsin Rapids WI 54494	NW	DCE	Tchr	Immanuel Wisconsin Rapids WI	(715)423-0272	CH	2008
Vogtmann Janet L Roth	(989)686-0356	3298 Parkway Dr Bay City MI 48706	MI	Teacher	EM			RF	1962
Voight Sharon J Pieper	(715) 536-7509 svoight1958@gmail.com	1814 River St Merrill WI 54452	NW	Teacher	EM			RF	1966
Voigt Peggy S Schaefer	(414)251-0840 jvoigt7@wi.rr.com	N78W15364 Haymeadow Rd Menomonee Fls WI 53051	SW	Teacher	EM			S	1979
Voisine Janet M Hintz	(860)589-2620	156 Harmony Rd Bristol CT 06010	NE	Teacher	EM			RF	1965
Volberding Gary L	(763)516-2247 volbsgary@aol.com	9334 Loon Ln Pequot Lakes MN 56472	MNS	Teacher	EM			S	1981
Volkert Bruce R	(815)519-3242 volkert4@sbcglobal.net	40816 Cascade Dr Sterling Hts MI 48313	MI	Teacher	Prin	Trinity Utica MI	(586)731-4490	RF	1988
Volkert Marianne E Kuschmann	(815)914-7862 mariannevolkert@yahoo.com	40816 Cascade Dr Sterling Heights MI 48313	MI	Teacher	Tchr	LHS Assn Of Greater Detroit Rochester Hls MI	(248)856-0240	RF	1989
Volkman Heather D	(419)906-0542 missvolkman@gmail.com	21945 Foxhaven Run Apt 1 Waukesha WI 53186	SW	Teacher	Tchr	Immanuel Brookfield WI	(262)781-7140	AA	1997
Vollbrecht Marilyn G Miller	(952)467-2722 mgv56@hotmail.com	18180 County Road 50 Hamburg MN 55339	MNS	Teacher	EM			SP	1978

*Multiple Assignments (See Church Worker Locator for Additional Details)
See Page 53 for the Table of Abbreviations for key to District, Classification, Position, and College abbreviations.
**C =Candidate; EM =Emeritus; the date following the C is the month and year the Candidate status began

NAME	TELEPHONE NUMBER EMAIL	STREET ADDRESS CITY/STATE/ZIP	DISTRICT	CLASS.	POSITION/ STATUS**	WHERE SERVING	OFFICE PHONE	COLLEGE/ UNIV/CQ	YR GRAD
Volmerding Heather M	(260)557-4532 heather.volmerding@gmail.com	1703 Greythorn Dr Fort Wayne IN 46815	IN	Teacher	Tchr	St Peter's Fort Wayne IN	(260)749-5816	MQ	2009
Volz Karen R Nitz	kvolz75@gmail.com	5110 Churchgrove Rd Frankenmuth MI 48734	MI	Teacher	EM			RF	1974
Volz-Iannarone Kristin R	(954)383-1007 kduckv@hotmail.com	7521 NW 8th Ct Plantation FL 33317	FG	Teacher	P/Tchr	Our Savior Plantation FL	(954)370-2161	CQ	2022
Volzke Betty C Ryden	(402)466-1990 bettyrv10@yahoo.com	3900 N 42nd St Lincoln NE 68504	NEB	Teacher	EM			CQ	1995
Von Ahsen Kenneth H	(636)724-1752 kvonahsen7@gmail.com	901 Penrose Ln Saint Charles MO 63301	MO	Teacher	EM			S	1976
Von Behren Linda R Salm	(309)389-2400 linvonbehren@glastel.net	15800 W Devils Washboard Rd Glasford IL 61533	CI	Teacher	Tchr	Christ Peoria IL	(309)637-1512	CQ	1999
Von Boeckman Jill C Grossweiler	(847)722-2933 jvb551@hotmail.com	511 N Elmhurst Rd Prospect Hts IL 60070	NI	Teacher	EM			CQ	2000
Von Der Ahe Jeanne M	(405)509-4233 jmvda@sbcglobal.net	2303 Maple Ridge Rd Little Rock AR 72211	MDS	Teacher	EM			SP	2000
von der Lage Mark F	(303)956-6613 mr.vonderlage@gmail.com	263 Rendezvous Dr Lafayette CO 80026	RM	Teacher	EM			S	1973
von der Lage Ruth A Meseke	(586)748-7016 ruthvonderlage@gmail.com	3311 Compton Rd Groesbeck OH 45251	IN	Teacher	Tchr	St Pauls Fort Wayne IN	(260)424-0049	AA	2005
Von Dielingen Heather D Schneider	(812)521-5892 heatherschneider15@gmail.com	139 S Cty Rd 700 E Seymour IN 47274	EN	Teacher	C07/2016			AA	2008
Von Dielingen Jean L Schanbacher	(812)530-0105 jvondielingen@yahoo.com	1839 20th Blvd Unit 8 Arkdale WI 54613	IN	Teacher	EM			S	1979
Von Dielingen Joyce L Simmering	(580)863-2846	17701 E Willow Rd Garber OK 73738	OK	Teacher	EM			CQ	1985
Von Fange Susan D	(586)320-4982 suvonf@gmail.com	37422 Stonegate Cir Clinton Twp MI 48036	MI	Tch/DCE	EM			S	1980
Von Hagel Patricia L Davis	(715)815-7123 pvonhagel@yahoo.com	635 Faxon St Superior WI 54880	MNN	Teacher	EM			SP	1978
von Holdt Kimberly N Spaulding	(303)862-0601 k_spaulding7@yahoo.com	8900 W 4th Ave Lakewood CO 80226	RM	Teacher	Tchr	Bethlehem Lakewood CO	(303)238-7676	S	2000
Von Kampen Kurt E Dr	(402)646-2243	782 Cory Dr Seward NE 68434	NEB	Teacher	S HS/C	Concordia University Nebraska Seward NE	(402)643-3651	S	1983
von Kampen Paul M	(949)424-9134 pvonkampen@gmail.com	1324 Marshall Ave Saint Paul MN 55104	MNS	Teacher	S HS/C	Concordia University St Paul Saint Paul MN	(651)641-8278	S	2011
Von Rentzell Paul D	(303)829-9225 pvonrentzell@concordianc.org	2283 Mount Olive Church Rd Newton NC 28658	SE	Teacher	Tchr	Concordia Conover NC	(828)464-3011	S	1984
Vonada Sharon A Gerken	sgvonada@aol.com	1804 Skyview Drive Auburndale FL 33823	FG	Teacher	EM			S	1973
vonStrohe Patricia J	(317)244-8928 pjvonstrohe@att.net	6570 Rainer Dr Apt B Indianapolis IN 46214	IN	Teacher	EM			AA	1986
Voorman Pamela J Burnside Deac	(402)540-5737 pam.voorman@gmail.com	218 Hampshire Dr Cranberry Twp PA 16066	EA	Deaconess	NMem C	Concordia Lutheran Ministries Cabot PA	(724)352-1571	FW-DEAC	2012
Vorck Jennifer A Canning	(714)329-6895 jennifervorck@gmail.com	1326 Whispering Trl Irvine CA 92602	PSW	Teacher	Tchr	Christ Costa Mesa CA	(949)631-1611	CQ	2021
Vorthmann Justin K	(608)205-7098 mr.vorthmann@gmail.com	1743 Bell Ford Dr W Seymour IN 47274	IN	Teacher	Tchr	Trinity Seymour IN	(812)524-8547	S	2003
Vorthmann Lindsey K Trah	lindsey.trah@cune.org	1743 Bell Ford Dr W Seymour IN 47274	IN	Teacher	Tchr	Trinity Seymour IN	(812)524-8547	S	2005
Vorwerk Dale H	(810)496-3313 vorwerk@charter.net	890 Johnson Dr Quincy MI 49082	MI	Teacher	EM			RF	1966
Vos Donald L	(914)643-7093 donvos@gmail.com	1100 N Kelsey Ave Evansville IN 47711	AT	Teacher	C07/2017			S	1983
Voshell Carolyn S Kirchner	(260)433-5363 cvoshell@wyneken.org	5971 N 400 W Decatur IN 46733	IN	Teacher	Tchr	Wyneken Memorial Decatur IN	(260)639-6177	CQ	2008
Voss Amanda J Ackermann	(507)215-5327	75726 400th Ave Lakefield MN 56150	MNS	Teacher	C07/2016			MQ	2010
Voss Amy R Schoof	(402)621-0153 amy.voss@hotmail.com	1315 2nd St Deshler NE 68340	NEB	Teacher	Tchr	Deshler Deshler NE	(402)365-7858	S	1992
Voss Cheryl D Specht	tandclivestrong@sbcglobal.net	1433 S Gasaway Dr Derby KS 67037	KS	Teacher	EM			CQ	2006
Voss Cynthia C Richter	(618)345-9103 macvoss@hotmail.com	95 Wendler Dr Collinsville IL 62234	SI	Teacher	EM			SP	1978
Voss Michael E	(618)345-9103 macvoss@hotmail.com	95 Wendler Dr Collinsville IL 62234	SI	Teacher	Tchr	Good Shepherd Collinsville IL	(618)344-3153	RF	1984
Voss Sharon L Dr	(989)792-2106 voss.sharon@yahoo.com	218 S Wheeler St Saginaw MI 48602	MI	Teacher	EM			RF	1973
Voss Todd M	(402)720-5590 todd.voss@deshlerluth.org	1315 2nd St Deshler NE 68340	NEB	Teacher	Prin	Deshler Deshler NE	(402)365-7858	S	1993
Vought Andrew L	(715)891-8494 andrewlvought@gmail.com	440 S 1st Ave Iowa City IA 52245	EN	Teacher	C06/2023			S	2019
Vought Gary L	(715)891-1447 garyvought@gmail.com	3660 Wyman Lk Ln Crandon WI 54520	NW	Teacher	Pro Stf	LCMS Foundation Saint Louis MO	(314)965-9000	RF	1988
Vought Keely J Rolbiecki	(262)443-8239 keelyjean2112@gmail.com	440 S 1st Ave Iowa City IA 52245	EN	Teacher	C06/2020			MQ	2017
Vradenburgh Shirley A	(206)932-7466 svradenburgh2022@gmail.com	3818 49th Ave SW Seattle WA 98116	NOW	Teacher	EM			RF	1966
Vroom Nola J Duvall	(949)233-4992 njvroom@yahoo.com	27531 Bocina Mission Viejo CA 92692	PSW	Teacher	EM			S	1973
Vyhanek Carol B Wegner	(312)693-5728 cvyhanek@ilcp.org	548 Lance Dr Des Plaines IL 60016	NI	Teacher	EM			RF	1978
Waak Vera Lovercamp	(586)939-6173	141 Beaver Shores Dr Lachine MI 49753	MI	Teacher	EM			S	1977

*Multiple Assignments (See Church Worker Locator for Additional Details)

See Page 53 for the Table of Abbreviations for key to District, Classification, Position, and College abbreviations.

**C =Candidate; EM =Emeritus; the date following the C is the month and year the Candidate status began

NAME	TELEPHONE NUMBER EMAIL	STREET ADDRESS CITY/STATE/ZIP	DISTRICT	CLASS.	POSITION/ STATUS**	WHERE SERVING	OFFICE PHONE	COLLEGE/ UNIV/CQ	YR GRAD
Wachholz Donald F	(773)498-2187 wachholzdon@gmail.com	5213 S Mobile Ave Chicago IL 60638	EN	Teacher	EM			RF	1964
Wachholz Eugene H	(815)953-9079 ewachholz@stpaulslutheran.net	343 S Winfield Ave Kankakee IL 60901	NI	Teacher	EM			RF	1965
Wachholz Judith E Maka	(402)641-3664 judy.wachholz@cune.org	3600 Zanzibar Ln N Minneapolis MN 55446	MNS	Teacher	EM			RF	1969
Wachholz Karen L Smith	(612)385-9552 klwachholz@comcast.net	6601 Neddersen Pkwy Brooklyn Park MN 55445	MNS	Teacher	Tchr	Mount Olive Anoka MN	(763)421-9048	SP	1995
Wachs Cynthia L Brieschke	(262)352-6671 cwachs262@gmail.com	W164N10977 Grey Fox Ct Germantown WI 53022	SW	Teacher	EM			S	1976
Wachter Jenny M Messersmith	(706)506-7083 jenny.wachter@att.net	419 Blue Smoke Trl Peachtree Cty GA 30269	FG	Teacher	Tchr	St Paul Peachtree City GA	(770)487-0339	AU	2000
Wacker Amanda J Stell		285 Curwick Dr Bourbonnais IL 60914	CI	Teacher	Tchr	Christ Lutheran HS Buckley IL	(217)394-2547	RF	2002
Wacker Daniel R	(641)750-0171 wackerdr@outlook.com	509 N Dubuque St Albion IA 50005	IE	Teacher	EM			RF	1973
Wacker David J	(970) 258-4427 djwdce@hotmail.com	1764 Freedom Way Montrose CO 81401	RM	DCE	EM			SP	1985
Wacker Sara J Potratz	(641)488-2797 swacker2@gmail.com		IE	Teacher	EM			SP	1984
Wackt Julia E Bollinger	(414)379-4611 juliawackt@gmail.com	1120 Pine Ridge Ct Oconomowoc WI 53066	SW	Teacher	Tchr	Good Shepherd Watertown WI	(920)261-2579	MQ	2006
Wade Christine L Koenig	(636)485-6858 christine.louise.wade@gmail.com	2606 Idlewood Drive Denison IA 51442	IW	Teacher	C07/2016			AA	2009
Wade Whitney K Leehey	(714)292-8616 tswkwade15@gmail.com	126 Caravel Ct Ballwin MO 63021	MO	Teacher	Tchr	St Paul Des Peres MO	(314)822-0447	IV	2015
Wadsworth Julie R	(320) 491-5867 julierenee55@gmail.com	1520a Clemson Dr Saint Paul MN 55122	MNN	DCE	EM			SP	1979
Wagener Cassandra R Jones	(952)442-2865 crwage@gmail.com	208 E 2nd St Waconia MN 55387	MNS	Teacher	EM			S	1972
Waggy Ashley M	(785)747-6658 alwaggy12@gmail.com	11222 Yerkes Dr Evansville IN 47725	IN	Teacher	Pro Stf	Evansville Evansville IN	(812)424-7252	S	2014
Waggy Logan M	(785)713-9324 lwaggy@elsone.org	11222 Yerkes Dr Evansville IN 47725	IN	Teacher	Tchr	Evansville Evansville IN	(812)424-7252	S	2013
Wagner Alicia L Timm	alicia.lynne.wagner@gmail.com	1254 N 1500 East Rd Unit 1 Onarga IL 60955	CI	Teacher	Tchr	St Pauls Milford IL	(815)889-4209	RF	2003
Wagner Allison L	(402)762-5850 mrs.allisonwagner@gmail.com	1475 45th Ave Columbus NE 68601	NEB	DCE	Tchr	Immanuel Columbus NE	(402)564-8423	CQ	2023
Wagner Crystal G	(618)540-8304 cwagner@stpaulhamel.org	5350 Quercus Grove Rd Edwardsville IL 62025	SI	Teacher	Tchr	St Paul Worden IL	(618)633-2209	CQ	2018
Wagner Douglas J	(636)448-7820 djlwagner@gmail.com	2941 Westerland Ct Saint Charles MO 63301	MO	Teacher	EM			S	1974
Wagner Erin R St Bernard	(734)693-9133 erinstb30@gmail.com	4128 Adams Dr. Shelby Twp MI 48316	MI	Teacher	Tchr	St John Fraser MI	(586)293-0333	AA	2009
Wagner James A	(703)728-2686 jwagner@familyofchrist.org	1335 Emerald Hill Way Valrico FL 33594	FG	Teacher	Tchr	Trinity* Delray Beach FL	(561)278-1737	MQ	1999
Wagner Jolene Liimatainen	(320)766-1009 wagsjol@runestone.net	P.O. Box 314 Deer Creek MN 56527	MNN	Teacher	P/Tchr	St Paul Perham MN	(218)346-7725	SP	1984
Wagner Lee A Kurth	(636)448-7820 lwagner@immanuelstcharles.org	2941 Westerland Ct St Charles MO 63301	MO	Teacher	EM			S	1978
Wagner Samantha L	(254)709-2232 samanthalynne210@gmail.com	2045 Queens Road Salina KS 67401	KS	DCE	Mem C	Christ King Salina KS	(785)827-7492	AU	2014
Wagoner Mary L Reddel	(712)542-5768 rmlwagoner@hotmail.com	2716 200th St Clarinda IA 51632	IW	Teacher	EM			S	1965
Wagoner Paulette M Rathkamp	(239) 292-2590 richwagoner@comcast.net	2481 P Ave Clarinda IA 51632	FG	Teacher	EM			SP	1971
Wahl Rhoda M Niesen	(402)560-4045 rnrwahl@gmail.com	10810 W. Manzanita Dr. Sun City AZ 85373	PSW	Teacher	EM			S	1976
Wahlers Joel D	(707)738-0019 joel@cnh-lcms.org	4445 Meadowlark Dr Napa CA 94558	CNH	Teacher	D Ex/S	California/Nevada/Hawaii District Livermore CA	(866)264-6079	S	1986
Wahlers Mark E Dr	(971)235-3609 mark@wahlersfamily.com	430 SW 13th Ave Apt 2307 Portland OR 97205	NOW	Teacher	C02/2018			S	1978
Wahrle Lois L Messerschmidt	(608)921-9095 lwahrle@att.net	3718 Goldenrod Pl Janesville WI 53546	SW	Teacher	EM			SP	1978
Waibel Kenneth J	(410)719-8689 kwaibel27@hotmail.com	733 Crosby Rd Baltimore MD 21228	SE	Teacher	EM			RF	1968
Wakeland Cathie J Stein	(260)348-3061 wakelandcj@gmail.com	3606 Oak Park Dr Fort Wayne IN 46815	IN	Teacher	EM			S	1978
Walcheski Jeffrey R	(561)400-4435 jwalcheski@stpaulbocaschool.com	289 SW 13th St Boca Raton FL 33432	FG	Teacher	Tchr	St Paul Boca Raton FL	(561)395-8548	SP	1984
Walcheski Michael J Dr	(612)603-6184 walcheski@luther.csp.edu	4888 Fable Hill Pkwy N Hugo MN 55038	MNS	Tch/DCE	S HS/C	Concordia University St Paul Saint Paul MN	(651)641-8278	SP	1983
Walcheski Monika Sponsel	(561)400-2786 mcwalcheski@gmail.com	289 SW 13th Street Boca Raton FL 33432	FG	Teacher	C02/2019			WN	1983
Waldburger Rachael E Plautz	rachaelwaldburger@gmail.com		NW	Teacher	C06/2025			MQ	2014
Waldmann Tove E Coburn	(636)405-1148 toveloni@hotmail.com	16960 Kingstowne Place Dr Wildwood MO 63011	MO	Teacher	EM			S	1972
Walkenhorst Jennifer A Mullane	(417)414-3932 walkenhorst@trinitysheboygan.org	2604 Elizabeth St Sheboygan WI 53083	SW	Teacher	Tchr	Trinity Sheboygan WI	(920)458-8248	CQ	2019
Walker Dawn M Cochran	(262)573-1130 the_walks@sbcglobal.net	924 Big Bend Station Dr Manchester MO 63088	MO	Teacher	Prin	St Paul Des Peres MO	(314)822-2771	MQ	1991
Walker Kelsi C Sousa	(714)600-2624 kcwcoaching@gmail.com	1601 Medina Lane Prosper TX 75078	TX	Teacher	Tchr	Prince Of Peace Carrollton TX	(972)447-0532	CQ	2021

*Multiple Assignments (See Church Worker Locator for Additional Details)

See Page 53 for the Table of Abbreviations for key to District, Classification, Position, and College abbreviations.

**C =Candidate; EM =Emeritus; the date following the C is the month and year the Candidate status began

NAME	TELEPHONE NUMBER EMAIL	STREET ADDRESS CITY/STATE/ZIP	DISTRICT	CLASS.	POSITION/ STATUS**	WHERE SERVING	OFFICE PHONE	COLLEGE/ UNIV/CQ	YR GRAD
Walker Louise A Fuchssteiner	(205)881-5515 grthree@yahoo.com	2306 Britain Ave SW Huntsville AL 35803	SO	Teacher	EM			RF	1976
Walker Roger L	(863)297-9118 rwalker@glwh.org	21 Lake Link Dr SE Winter Haven FL 33884	FG	Teacher	EM			RF	1976
Walker Sara R Day	(512)569-0574 saracua2003@yahoo.com	613 NE Windrose Ct Apt D Kansas City MO 64155	MO	Teacher	Tchr	Martin Luther Kansas City MO	(816)734-1060	AU	2008
Walker Sarah G Geyer	(512)988-0565 sarah.walker@redeemer.net	c/o Redeemer Lutheran School 1500 W Anderson Ln Austin TX 78757	TX	Teacher	Prin	Redeemer Austin TX	(512)451-6478	AU	2009
Walker Shelly A Baur		2955 Heatherwyn Way Cumming GA 30040	FG	Teacher	C07/2016			CQ	2008
Walkowicz Celia G	cgwalkowiczmin@gmail.com		MDS	DFLM	Mem C	Our Savior Nashville TN	(615)833-1500	MQ	2020
Wall Bruce M	(402)615-5798 bruce.wall@cune.org	2906 17th St Columbus NE 68601	NEB	Teacher	RSO	Camp Luther Schuyler NE	(402)352-5655	S	2004
Wall Elizabeth M Cross	beth.wall.44@gmail.com		IE	Teacher	C08/2021			MQ	2018
Wall Julie A Kielsmeier	(563)650-9207 folkinart@gmail.com	191 West Scott Street Eldridge IA 52748	IE	Teacher	C06/2025			CQ	2017
Walla Niccole M Sedlmayr	(701)805-5643 niccole.walla@cune.org	517 E Turnpike Ave Bismarck ND 58501	ND	Teacher	C07/2016			S	2007
Wallace Jeffery L	(269)932-5296 jwallace@christstevensville.com	1814 Trafalgar Dr Saint Joseph MI 49085	MI	Teacher	Tchr	Christ Stevensville MI	(269)429-7222	RF	1998
Wallace Katrina N Miller	(248)894-4425 katnmill01@gmail.com	6223 Southwood Ave Apt 1n Saint Louis MO 63105	MO	DPM	Mem C	Bethlehem Saint Louis MO	(314)231-4702	AA	2023
Wallace Linda M Johnson	(410)747-6321 lwallace_6321@msn.com	30935 Sandy Ridge Dr Lewes DE 19958	SE	Teacher	EM			RF	1975
Wallace Lydia F	(563)340-8145 lydia.wallace@cuw.edu	1017 W 11th St Spencer IA 51301	IW	Teacher	Tchr	Iowa Great Lakes Spencer IA	(712)262-8237	MQ	2018
Wallace Sharon L Altevogt	(414)687-7069 swallace@stpaulptc.org	100 Silverthorne Dr Tyrone GA 30290	FG	Teacher	Prin	St Paul Peachtree City GA	(770)487-0339	AA	1992
Wallen Mary M Johnson	mwallen@orlcs.org	1535 Smith Lane Delavan WI 53115	SW	Teacher	Tchr	Our Redeemer Delavan WI	(262)728-6589	MQ	2008
Wallinger Dennis E	(414)732-1231 dewallinger@gmail.com	15834 SW 13th Cir Ocala FL 34473	FG	Tch/DCE	EM			RF	1972
Wallingford Sheila L Psencik Muth	(281)889-0485 sheila.psencik@gmail.com	6833 Wildrye Rd Lincoln NE 68521	NEB	Teacher	Prin	Lincoln Lincoln NE	(402)467-5404	S	1996
Wallman JoAnn K Weber	(402) 890-7729	14207 S 46th St Roca NE 68430	NEB	Teacher	EM			S	1973
Wallman-Hidek Katherine A Wallman	(907)696-2466 kwallmanhidek@gmail.com	P.O. Box 771161 Eagle River AK 99577	NOW	Teacher	EM			S	1971
Wallner Heidi A Schmidt	(920)254-8267 wallnerclan21@gmail.com	2220 S 16th St Sheboygan WI 53081	SW	Teacher	Tchr	Bethlehem Sheboygan WI	(920)452-5071	MQ	1998
Wallschlaeger Martha L Rasmussen	(505)206-7854 mlwalls@live.com	8333 Comanche Rd NE Apt 5a Albuquerque NM 87110	RM	Teacher	EM			S	1983
Walo Karen A Rich	(702)569-1148 karenwalo@gmail.com	1214 Rowan Drive Georgetown TX 78628	TX	Teacher	EM			CQ	2014
Walquist Sarah N Peregoy	(402)238-4284 answalquist@gmail.com	18422 Weeping Spring Dr Cypress TX 77429	TX	Teacher	Tchr	Salem Tomball TX	(281)351-8223	S	2006
Walsh Hannah R	hwalsh@ourshepherd.net	580 Colony Dr. Apt 3 Troy MI 48083	MI	DFLM	Mem C	Our Shepherd Birmingham MI	(248)646-6100	AA	2017
Walsh Kimber L Richard	(440)309-8254 kimberrichard@gmail.com	920 Halstead Blvd Jackson MI 49203	MI	DFLM	Mem C	Redeemer Jackson MI	(517)750-3100	AA	2011
Walsh Margaret A Ruehle Deac	(407)790-1543 Ellagrace152@gmail.com	299 Kaymar Dr Amherst NY 14228	EN	Deaconess	C07/2021			FW-DEAC	2016
Walter Brenda Turner	(501)944-8673 walterbrenda54@gmail.com	2807 Charter Oak Dr Little Rock AR 72227	MDS	Teacher	EM			SP	1976
Walter Bret L	(702)499-4138 bretlwalter12@gmail.com	5122 Albany Shores Ln Fulshear TX 77441	TX	Teacher	RSO	Lutheran Education Association Friendswood TX	(281)617-5189	S	1997
Walter Johanna Hoover	(217)218-1990	c/o Trinity Lutheran School 1215 W 7th Ave Fort Morgan CO 80701	RM	Teacher	Tchr	Trinity Fort Morgan CO	(970)867-4931	CH	2012
Walter Jonathan S	(281)355-8580 walters@concordiacrusaders.org	12170 Pebble View Dr Conroe TX 77304	TX	Teacher	Tchr	Concordia Tomball TX	(281)351-2547	S	1994
Walter Melanie L Beck	(847)736-3082 mbeck@clsfw.org	927 Windsor Lake Dr Fort Wayne IN 46845	IN	Teacher	Tchr	Concordia Fort Wayne IN	(260)422-2429	MQ	2008
Walter Sandra K VonDielingen	(513)829-4346 rnwalter@3z.net	5808 Leslie Dr Fairfield OH 45014	OH	Teacher	EM			RF	1962
Walter Teresa I Holle	(989)871-9366	5427 Millington Rd Millington MI 48746	MI	Teacher	Tchr	St Paul Millington MI	(989)871-4581	S	1982
Walters Jamie L Jennemann	(907)355-1456 jwalters1982@gmail.com	20344 Chugach Park Dr Chugiak AK 99567	NOW	DCE	C02/2018			S	2005
Walters Mary B Miles	(863)632-2741 beth57walters55@gmail.com	3907 Muncie Rd Babson Park FL 33827	FG	Teacher	Tchr	Grace Winter Haven FL	(863)293-9744	RF	1977
Walters Paulette E	(269)221-1912 paulettewalters@trinitysturgis.com	66997 Stillwater Drive Sturgis MI 49091	MI	Teacher	Tchr	Trinity Sturgis MI	(269)651-4245	RF	1982
Walters Tarayca L	(307)259-3396 taraycal@msn.com	1327 S Cottonwood St Casper WY 82604	WY	Teacher	C09/2021			S	2000
Waltersdorf Judith C Golchert	(480)539-1341 jcwaltersdorf@yahoo.com	2227 E Sunnyside Dr Phoenix AZ 85028	PSW	Teacher	EM			RF	1968
Walther Benjamin M	(262)434-0247 benwalther.email@gmail.com	1235 Nasa Parkway Apt 1332 Houston TX 77058	TX	Teacher	Pro Stf	South Houston TX	(281)464-8299	MQ	2005
Walther Carol J Bauer	(618)558-2731 carolwaltherdce@gmail.com	5111 Kirkland Trl Sorento IL 62086	SI	Teacher	Mem C	Good Shepherd Collinsville IL	(618)344-3151	RF	1980

*Multiple Assignments (See Church Worker Locator for Additional Details)
See Page 53 for the Table of Abbreviations for key to District, Classification, Position, and College abbreviations.
**C =Candidate; EM =Emeritus; the date following the C is the month and year the Candidate status began

NAME	TELEPHONE NUMBER EMAIL	STREET ADDRESS CITY/STATE/ZIP	DISTRICT	CLASS.	POSITION/ STATUS**	WHERE SERVING	OFFICE PHONE	COLLEGE/ UNIV/CQ	YR GRAD
Walther Daniel H	(314)736-1314 dwalther08@yahoo.com	717 Eckrich Pl Webster Grvs MO 63119	MO	Teacher	EM			S	1961
Walther John F Dr	(262)505-5479	13750 W National Ave Apt 4409 New Berlin WI 53151	SW	Teacher	EM			S	1958
Walther Julie L Werkmeister	(956)493-9958 jwlynne@sbcglobal.net	1117 E Leggett Rd Harlingen TX 78550	TX	Teacher	EM			S	1985
Walther Mary L Aufdenberg	(573)579-3259 walthermary@hotmail.com	1487 County Road 325 Cpe Girardeau MO 63701	MO	Teacher	EM			S	1975
Walton Matthew L	(949)306-9118 youth@stjohnsdenver.org	1210 S Idalia St Unit C Aurora CO 80017	RM	Teacher	Mem C	St Johns Denver CO	(303)733-3777	IV	2001
Waltz Amy W Amy Louise Werth	(804)317-4999 amy.waltz@oslanashville.org	2008 Keene Cir Spring Hill TN 37174	MDS	Teacher	Tchr	Our Savior Nashville TN	(615)833-1500	CQ	2024
Waltz David E	(586)226-3962 dw48038@gmail.com	17327 Knollwood Dr Clinton Twp MI 48038	MI	Tch/DCE	EM			S	1978
Walworth Kelsey A Smith	(248)977-7004 kelsey.walworth@gmail.com	3 Adams Ln Dearborn MI 48120	IN	Teacher	C07/2016			S	2011
Walz Christine J	(774)271-1357 cjwalz4@hotmail.com	9702 Crawford Rd Columbus MI 48063	MI	Teacher	EM			S	1977
Walz Jeffrey S	(920)668-8430 jeff.walz@cuw.edu	48 Hickory Dr Cedar Grove WI 53013	SW	Teacher	S HS/C	Concordia University Wisconsin Mequon WI	(262)243-5700	CQ	2000
Walz Robert A	(541)757-1093 robert.walz@zioncorvallis.com	1935 SE Bethel St Corvallis OR 97333	NOW	Teacher	Tchr	Zion Corvallis OR	(541)753-7503	S	1992
Walz Timothy A	(817)706-1954 twalz@stjohneagles.org	119 Baker Ct Kendallville IN 46755	IN	Teacher	Prin	St John Kendallville IN	(260)347-2444	CQ	1992
Wanagat Carolyn L Liefer	(618)972-9791 cjwanagat@yahoo.com	2318 Nugent Cir Urbana IL 61802	SI	Teacher	EM			S	1966
Wanagat James M	(618)973-0049 cjwanagat@yahoo.com	401 Burwash Ave Apt 209 Savoy IL 61874	SI	Teacher	EM			S	1967
Wandel Melissa A Smith	(702)499-0401 mrwandel2@gmail.com	12272 Kings Eagle St Las Vegas NV 89141	PSW	Teacher	Tchr	Faith Las Vegas NV	(702)804-4400	CQ	2005
Wangelin Kristin J Dodge	(517)599-7052 kristinwangelin@gmail.com	7006 Captiva Dr Lansing MI 48917	MI	Teacher	C07/2016			AA	2002
Wanner Emily E	(417)350-2022 ewanner@faithlincoln.org	4923 N 32nd St 2b Lincoln NE 68504	NEB	Teacher	Tchr	Faith Lincoln NE	(402)466-7402	S	2023
Wanner Joshua M	(417)766-9520 jwanner@rlcmail.org	2985 W Darby St Springfield MO 65810	MO	Teacher	Tchr	Redeemer Springfield MO	(417)883-5717	RF	1999
Wanner Kari J Nielsen	(417)766-2610 kjwanner1299@hotmail.com	2985 W Darby St Springfield MO 65810	MO	Teacher	Tchr	Redeemer Springfield MO	(417)883-5717	RF	1998
Ward Abigail K Deac	(573)469-1656 abbykward99@gmail.com	12598 Hwy 28 W Vienna MO 65582	MO	Deac/Tch	Tchr	Calvary Jefferson Cty MO	(573)638-0228	CH	2023
Ward Donna J Feltner	(989)479-6439 warddonna24@gmail.com	P.O. Box 222 Harbor Beach MI 48441	MI	Teacher	EM			CQ	1984
Ward Jennifer A Buehring	(832)515-8741 jenward1029@gmail.com	3706 W Pine Orchard Dr Pearland TX 77581	TX	Teacher	Tchr	South Houston TX	(281)464-8299	S	1996
Ward Suzan E England	(573)335-3730 sward@t-lutheranschool.org	2536 Fairlane Dr Cpe Girardeau MO 63701	MO	Teacher	Tchr	Trinity Cape Girardeau MO	(573)335-8224	CQ	2010
Wareham Jon G	(321)480-1717 jgwareham@att.net	3914 Robin Ct Acworth GA 30101	FG	Teacher	Tchr	Faith Marietta GA	(770)973-8877	RF	1982
Wareham Joshua D	(678)773-2921 warehamj72@gmail.com	3914 Robin Ct Acworth GA 30101	FG	Teacher	C12/2021			CH	2015
Wargo Nicole N Hurttgam	(586)446-9239 wargo@me.com	54497 Egmont Key Ave Macomb MI 48042	MI	Teacher	Tchr	St Peter Macomb MI	(586)781-3434	RF	1998
Warmbier Gerald J	(313)300-7092 geraldwarmbier@gmail.com	34601 Elmwood St Apt 335 Westland MI 48185	EN	Teacher	EM			RF	1959
Warneke Arlan G	(402)329-6686 awarneke@ptcnet.net	415 N 6th St Apt 5 Pierce NE 68767	NEB	Teacher	EM			S	1958
Warneke Julie R	(402)270-4142 julie.warneke@yahoo.com	39346 205th Ave Columbus NE 68601	NEB	Teacher	Tchr	St Johns Columbus NE	(402)285-0335	S	1992
Warneke Kimberly K Vestweber	(241)543-0613 k_warneke@msn.com	6633 Oakmont Ct Plano TX 75093	TX	Teacher	Tchr	Prince Of Peace Carrollton TX	(972)447-0532	S	1993
Warneke Lindsey A	lindsey.warneke@cune.org	12055 Sabo Rd Apt 226 Houston TX 77089	TX	Teacher	Pro Stf	South Houston TX	(281)464-8299	S	2012
Warneke Sarah K Niemeier	sarah.niemeier@cune.org	312 W Central Ave Arkansas City KS 67005	KS	Teacher	Tchr	Trinity Winfield KS	(620)221-1820	S	2020
Warneke Timothy E	(310)987-0850 warno33@yahoo.com	1502 S Palm Ave Alhambra CA 91803	PSW	Teacher	EM			S	1977
Warner Kara A	(619)994-6071 kwarner@gracelcms.net	1260 Sundown Gln Escondido CA 92026	PSW	Teacher	Tchr	Grace Escondido CA	(760)745-0831	Other	1993
Warner Margaret E	(563)468-3042 warner.margaret.e@gmail.com	200 N 6th St Saint Charles MO 63301	MO	DCE	Mem C	Immanuel Saint Charles MO	(636)946-2656	CH	2021
Warner Stephanie M Hunt	(720)219-1167 stephwarner10@gmail.com	412 Miracle Rose Way Liberty Hill TX 78642	TX	DCE	C07/2016			S	2010
Warnick Harriet H Lange	(989)262-8287 warnick@charter.net	342 Clarmarc Dr Frankenmuth MI 48734	MI	Teacher	EM			RF	1960
Warnick Howard J	(989)327-0141 bachfan@charter.net	342 Clarmarc Dr Frankenmuth MI 48734	MI	Teacher	EM			RF	1960
Warnier Christina K	(618)401-3545 cwarnier09@gmail.com	531 Pinegrove Ln Apt B Fort Wayne IN 46807	IN	Teacher	Tchr	St John-Emmanuel Monroeville IN	(260)639-0123	S	2009
Warnke Katherine Deac	(706)974-8150 k.m.warnke15@gmail.com	7516 Watson Cir Locust Grove GA 30248	FG	Deaconess	Mem C	Christ Our Savior Griffin GA	(770)227-4082	SL-DEAC	2018
Warnken Melinda B Braden	(914)263-3673 k3mco@aol.com	346 Hutchinson Blvd Mount Vernon NY 10552	AT	Teacher	EM			BR	1985

*Multiple Assignments (See Church Worker Locator for Additional Details)
See Page 53 for the Table of Abbreviations for key to District, Classification, Position, and College abbreviations.
**C =Candidate; EM =Emeritus; the date following the C is the month and year the Candidate status began

NAME	TELEPHONE NUMBER EMAIL	STREET ADDRESS CITY/STATE/ZIP	DISTRICT	CLASS.	POSITION/ STATUS**	WHERE SERVING	OFFICE PHONE	COLLEGE/ UNIV/CQ	YR GRAD
Warren Thaddeus P	thad.warren@cune.edu	800 N Columbia Ave Seward NE 68434	NEB	Tch/DCE	S HS/C	Concordia University Nebraska Seward NE	(402)643-3651	S	1991
Warsinski Rebecca L	(972)695-5117 rlwarsinski@verizon.net	4270 Charles Rd Carrollton TX 75010	TX	Teacher	C07/2016			IV	2012
Wartick Ruth V Crosmer	(413)335-4144 rwartick@stmlc.org	79 McKinley Ave Clintonville WI 54929	NW	Teacher	Tchr	St Martin Clintonville WI	(715)823-6538	S	1982
Wascher Charridan A	cwascher@stlorenz.org	942 Eastgate Ct Frankenmuth MI 48734	MI	Teacher	Tchr	St Lorenz Frankenmuth MI	(989)652-6141	RF	1999
Wascher Erin M Block	(989)652-8071 blockerin@hotmail.com	942 Eastgate Ct Frankenmuth MI 48734	MI	Teacher	Tchr	St Lorenz Frankenmuth MI	(989)652-6141	RF	1999
Washburn Debra S Kohler	(586)557-3877 dwashburn3@yahoo.com	13098 Concord Dr Sterling Hts MI 48313	MI	Teacher	EM			AA	1984
Wasmund Gary W	(352)357-6814 gpwazz@comcast.net	1964 Outer Circle Dr Oviedo FL 32765	FG	Teacher	EM			RF	1968
Wassilak Kristin R Hannenberg Deac	(708)707-8813 kristin.wassilak@cuchicago.edu	1038 Hannah Ave Forest Park IL 60130	NI	Deaconess	S HS/C	Concordia University Chicago River Forest IL	(708)771-8300	RF	1986
Waterman Wayne L Jr	(657)205-6332 waynewtrmn@gmail.com	14802 Newport Ave Apt 16b Tustin CA 92780	PSW	Teacher	Tchr	St Paul Orange CA	(714)637-2640	IV	1996
Wathall Heather M Marhenke Deac	(708)323-6321 heather.marhenke@gmail.com	121 Layton Drive Butler PA 16001	EA	Deaconess	RSO	Concordia Lutheran Ministries Cabot PA	(724)352-1571	CH	2008
Watson Andrea J	(225)247-4805 andreawatson0318@gmail.com	1750 Charles Ave. Apt. 504 New Orleans LA 70130	SO	Teacher	Tchr	St John New Orleans LA	(504)482-2118	CQ	2019
Watson Janet D Woodburn	(443)684-0354 jwwatson5715@gmail.com	7847 Bagley Ave Baltimore MD 21234	SE	Teacher	EM			S	1979
Watson Marie C Buvelot	(616)429-6034 mcwatson51@sbcglobal.net	6180 Dreamcatcher Rd Stevensville MI 49127	MI	Teacher	EM			RF	1975
Watson Millard	(210)659-1298	11911 Stillstone Schertz TX 78154	TX	DCM	Mem C	Mount Calvary San Antonio TX	(210)824-8748	MQ	1996
Watson Thomas W	(410)665-8974 twwat@hotmail.com	7847 Bagley Ave Baltimore MD 21234	SE	Teacher	EM			S	1979
Watt Nathaniel H	(920)544-1366 natewatt@martinlutherhs.com	1833 210th Ave Fairmont MN 56031	MNS	Teacher	Tchr	Martin Luther Northrop MN	(507)436-5249	CQ	2009
Watt Suzanne S Stewart	(918)619-7490 suzanne.watt@ctrtulsa.org	2550 E 71st St Tulsa OK 74136	OK	DCE	Mem C	Christ The Redeemer Tulsa OK	(918)492-6451	RF	2007
Waugh Michael	(262)309-9100 mwaugh@lhsagm.org	N55W25308 Crescent Hill Dr Sussex WI 53089	SW	Teacher	Tchr	LHS Assn of Greater Milwaukee West Allis WI	(414)421-9100	CH	2024
Way Erika M Budd	(541)206-9530 bandeway@aol.com	1902 Innsbrook Ct Sutherlin OR 97479	NOW	Teacher	C09/2017			CQ	2015
Wayman Rachael M	(630)607-4407 waymanr@trinityroselle.com	410 Pierce Ave Roselle IL 60172	NI	Teacher	Tchr	Trinity Roselle IL	(630)894-3263	CQ	2021
Weander Isaac J	iweander@clhscadets.com	6745 Pointe Inverness Way Fort Wayne IN 46804	IN	Teacher	Tchr	Concordia Fort Wayne IN	(260)483-1102	S	2020
Weaver Debra S Nolin	(309)838-6741 deb@weaverclan.org	1505 Paddington Dr Bloomington IL 61704	CI	Teacher	EM			RF	1987
Weaver Hannah F Bjornstad	(570)604-1804 hfweaver4@gmail.com	702 S Orient St Fairmont MN 56031	MNS	DPM	Mem C	St Paul Fairmont MN	(507)238-9491	SP	2018
Weaver Jennifer L Tinkey	(574)551-7024 jweaver@thecalvaryschool.org	620 Valley Oaks Rd. Greenwood IN 46143	IN	Teacher	Tchr	Calvary Indianapolis IN	(317)783-2305	CH	2013
Webb Brittany P Thomas	(423)834-4976 bwebb@bcacademy.net	175 Blue Bird Ln Ringgold GA 30736	MDS	Teacher	Tchr	Belvoir Chattanooga TN	(423)622-3755	CH	2024
Webb Catherine E Dr	(714)519-8900 catherine.webb@cui.edu	5183 W 1275 S Cedar City UT 84720	PSW	Teacher	S HS/C	Concordia University Irvine Irvine CA	(949)854-8002	CQ	2017
Webb Hannah R Keuning	(515)729-6356 hkeuning@trinityutica.com	45668 Keding St. Utica MI 48317	MI	Teacher	Tchr	Trinity Utica MI	(586)731-4490	S	2015
Webb Janet M Brandt	(216)470-5625 teanatious@gmail.com	2423 Leisure World Mesa AZ 85206	PSW	Teacher	EM			S	1976
Webb Neil F	(586)646-0367 webbnf@gmail.com	4733 Woodland Dr Saint Joseph MI 49085	MI	Teacher	P/Tchr	Christ Stevensville MI	(269)429-7222	S	1998
Weber Ann M Hemke	(952)831-7670	7601 W 101st St Apt 109 Bloomington MN 55438	MNS	Teacher	EM			RF	1963
Weber Carol A Kamasis	(989)871-9975 c_weber_teacher@yahoo.com	6316 Barnes Road Millington MI 48746	MI	Teacher	Tchr	St Paul Millington MI	(989)871-4581	AA	1986
Weber Diane L Damrau	(865)382-6400 mowebers@yahoo.com	1155 Pcr 430 Frohna MO 63748	MO	DCE	EM			S	1996
Weber Diane L Fasching	diane.weber@trinitywaconia.org	8163 Petunia Victoria MN 55386	MNS	Teacher	Tchr	Trinity Waconia MN	(952)442-4165	SP	1988
Weber Donald C	(402)643-9842 donweber55@yahoo.com	1506 313th Seward NE 68434	NEB	Teacher	EM			S	1969
Weber Gary G	(402)649-7077 gwebmab43@yahoo.com	1211 Greenlawn Dr Norfolk NE 68701	NEB	Teacher	EM			S	1974
Weber Jennifer J	(480)280-1238 weberducky@hotmail.com	2009 16th St Columbus NE 68601	NEB	Teacher	Tchr	Immanuel Columbus NE	(402)564-8423	S	1997
Weber Justin T	(630)788-8727 Jweber500@gmail.com	1531 Edgewood Dr Milford IA 51351	MNS	DCE	Mem C	Saint Johns Chaska MN	(952)448-2433	CH	2025
Weber Karlton R I	(248)804-7031 kweber@lhsa.com	2822 Walsh Dr Rochester Hills MI 48309	MI	Teacher	EM			CQ	1997
Weber Katrina M Deardoff	(815)762-9372 katrinaweber4@gmail.com	505 NW 169th St Edmond OK 73012	OK	Teacher	Tchr	Messiah Oklahoma City OK	(405)946-0681	S	2003
Weber Kristine D	(248)804-7032 kweber1387@gmail.com	9407 E Sebring Ave Mesa AZ 85212	PSW	Teacher	Tchr	Christs Greenfield Gilbert AZ	(480)892-8314	MQ	2015
Weber Louise A Schini	(239)849-1427 luschweb@gmail.com	7820 Fanning Ct #231 Fort Myers FL 33907	FG	Teacher	EM			RF	1969

*Multiple Assignments (See Church Worker Locator for Additional Details)
See Page 53 for the Table of Abbreviations for key to District, Classification, Position, and College abbreviations.
**C =Candidate; EM =Emeritus; the date following the C is the month and year the Candidate status began

NAME	TELEPHONE NUMBER EMAIL	STREET ADDRESS CITY/STATE/ZIP	DISTRICT	CLASS.	POSITION/ STATUS**	WHERE SERVING	OFFICE PHONE	COLLEGE/ UNIV/CQ	YR GRAD
Weber Michael J	(239)565-9721 mchlwbr@gmail.com	7820 Fanning Ct 231 Fort Myers FL 33907	FG	Teacher	EM			RF	1969
Weber Nancy L Currie	(402)750-7726 iteach3cls@hotmail.com	1211 Greenlawn Dr Norfolk NE 68701	NEB	Teacher	EM			S	1974
Weber Sarah E Hinckfoot	(402)641-1656 sweber@stpeters-columbus.org	3533 Berkdale Dr Columbus IN 47203	IN	Teacher	Tchr	St Peter Columbus IN	(812)372-5266	S	2011
Weber Sarah L Masenthin	(260)246-9310 sarahweber@yahoo.com	7022 Bohnke Dr Fort Wayne IN 46815	IN	Teacher	Tchr	Holy Cross Fort Wayne IN	(260)483-3173	S	2000
Weber Timothy R	(956)212-8588 kettlebeller956@gmail.com	2809 Mynah Ave McAllen TX 78504	TX	Teacher	EM			RF	1979
Weber Victoria Behling	(952)838-5500 mvweber1@yahoo.com	10318 Rhode Island Cir Bloomington MN 55438	MNS	Teacher	C07/2016			SP	1991
Webinger Jennifer M Mau	(402)426-8852 website@gpcom.net	2738 Krejci Blvd Blair NE 68008	NEB	Teacher	EM			CQ	2004
Webster Lora J Blackwood	(517)392-5292 lorajwebster@gmail.com	2956 N Talman Ave # 2 Chicago IL 60618	NI	Teacher	Tchr	St James Chicago IL	(773)525-4990	CH	2008
Webster Marilyn G Long	marilyngwebster@gmail.com	1929 E Troon Dr Lake Havasu City AZ 86404	PSW	Teacher	EM			CQ	2004
Wedde Deborah D Keller	(269)473-6697 trucks3904@cs.com	205 S Mechanic St Berrien Sprgs MI 49103	MI	Teacher	EM			S	1978
Weddelman Michelle Rosebrock	(419)966-6115 mweddelman@sjl.org	16452 County Road 424 Napoleon OH 43545	OH	Teacher	Tchr	St John Napoleon OH	(419)598-8961	CQ	2021
Weerts Gretchen J Brockmann	(260)403-4545 Weertsgretchen@gmail.com	1727 Duart Ct New Haven IN 46774	IN	Tch/DCE	EM			S	1979
Weesner Gretchen A	(956)533-4453 gweezie@hotmail.com	300 N San Antonio St Rio Grande Cy TX 78582	TX	Teacher	S Miss	Office of International Mission Saint Louis MO		RF	1996
Wegener Barbara L Schmidt	(954)946-5389 daveandbarb@sum.net	2930 NE 8th Ter Pompano Beach FL 33064	FG	Teacher	Tchr	St Paul Boca Raton FL	(561)395-8548	S	1970
Wegener Luanne S	(989)948-4426 lwegener@charter.net	4526 Franklin St Auburn MI 48611	MI	Teacher	EM			RF	1977
Wegner Elizabeth M Boettcher	(651)353-4272 elizabethmwegner@gmail.com	1811 Van Buren Ave Saint Paul MN 55104	MNS	Teacher	Tchr	King Of Kings Roseville MN	(651)484-5142	SP	1987
Wegner Frank L	(715)526-2932 fwegner@charter.net	N5423 Poplar Rd Shawano WI 54166	NW	Teacher	EM			S	1968
Wegner James T	(715)570-2945 jwegner@splpoint.com	5473 Conifer Dr Stevens Point WI 54482	NW	Teacher	P/Tchr	St Paul Stevens Point WI	(715)344-5660	MQ	1995
Wegner Jeffrey P	wegsjp@gmail.com	314 Meadows Ave Cedar Grove WI 53013	SW	Teacher	Tchr	St Johns West Bend WI	(262)334-3077	MQ	1997
Wegner Jennifer L Hodges Maas	(262)353-1737 jwegner@immanuelrapids.com	5473 Conifer Dr Stevens Point WI 54482	NW	Teacher	Tchr	Immanuel Wisconsin Rapids WI	(715)423-3260	CQ	2001
Wegner Paulette E Palmquist	(303)358-5629 wegnerbp@gmail.com	18679 Oregon Cir Elkhorn NE 68022	NEB	DCE	EM			SP	1987
Wehling Alicia C Royuk	(402)646-0514 wehling.alicia@gmail.com	803 S. Boxelder St. Norfolk NE 68701	NEB	Teacher	C07/2022			S	2017
Wehling Miriam K Roggow	(620)655-2515 mimiam2k@gmail.com	2108 E 29th St Lawrence KS 66046	KS	Tch/DCE	D Ex/S	Kansas District Topeka KS	(785)357-4441	S	1988
Wehling Paula M Mueller	(402)795-5766 paulamarie42@yahoo.com	1041 154th Pleasant Dale NE 68423	NEB	Teacher	EM			S	1963
Wehmeier Sandra J Stalker	(262)679-5818 swehmeier@sbcglobal.net	W252N6642 Aspen Ln Sussex WI 53089	EN	Teacher	EM			CQ	1992
Wehmeyer Allison M	awehmeyer@stpaulsdp.org	3932 Walsh St Saint Louis MO 63116	MO	Teacher	Tchr	St Paul Des Peres MO	(314)822-2771	CQ	2003
Wehmeyer Barbara A Hinck	(636)947-4742 barb1263@juno.com	2256 Argonne Meadows Dr Lake St Louis MO 63367	MO	Teacher	EM			S	1972
Wehmeyer Kenneth G	(314)355-4449 kenlow2064@sbcglobal.net	11601 Doris Dr Saint Louis MO 63138	MO	Teacher	EM			S	1968
Wehmeyer Lois M Cheslock	(314) 749-7040 kenlow2064@sbcglobal.net	11601 Doris Dr Saint Louis MO 63138	MO	Teacher	EM			S	1968
Weidler Jean G Oelrich	(630)740-2765 Jweidler@gmail.com	1073 Ponca Dr Batavia IL 60510	NI	Teacher	EM			RF	1972
Weidler Peggy L	(479)221-0036 pweidler@hotmail.com	9200 Enid St Fort Smith AR 72903	MDS	Teacher	EM			S	1978
Weidner Christina M Hile		3483 Center St Reese MI 48757	MI	Teacher	Tchr	Trinity Reese MI	(989)868-9901	AA	2009
Weidner Lindsey A Howell	(907)317-3899 lindsey.weidner@gmail.com	1450 Rose Hill Ln Saint Peters MO 63376	MO	Teacher	Tchr	Child Of God Saint Peters MO	(636)970-7080	S	2009
Weier Kent G	(313)928-7350 kentweier@att.net	3237 Stuart Lane Dearborn MI 48120	MI	Teacher	EM			RF	1970
Weikum Lois J	(219)771-6541 weikteach@aol.com	6755 S 250 W North Judson IN 46366	IN	Teacher	EM			SP	1972
Weil Amanda G	(262)748-4016 mander_weil@yahoo.com	2880 11th Pl Unit 612 Kenosha WI 53140	SW	Teacher	Tchr	Trinity Racine WI	(262)632-1766	MQ	2003
Weil Michael R	(414)870-1739 michael.weil7@gmail.com	324 Precipice Way Georgetown TX 78626	TX	Teacher	Tchr	Concordia Pflugerville TX	(512)248-2547	CH	2013
Weilnau Jeanette N	(734)770-5025 jnweilnau@gmail.com	4088 Louise St Saginaw MI 48603	MI	Teacher	Tchr	Valley Saginaw MI	(989)790-1676	AA	2009
Weingarth Clara J	(919)564-9092 clara.weingarth@gmail.com	3677 W Bryce Ct Phoenix AZ 85086	PSW	Teacher	C07/2024			IV	2018
Weinhold Deborah A Hingst	(816)262-7035 weinhold.deb@gmail.com	540 Rolling Hills Dr Saint Charles MO 63304	MO	Teacher	EM			RF	1976
Weinhold John D Dr	(402)643-4924 jd.weinhold@cune.edu	7225 Orchard St Lincoln NE 68505	NEB	Teacher	EM			S	1957
Weinhold Rachel S	(816)262-6435 rachel.weinhold@gmail.com	52 Timberbrook Dr Saint Peters MO 63376	MO	DCE	C06/2021			S	2015

*Multiple Assignments (See Church Worker Locator for Additional Details)

See Page 53 for the Table of Abbreviations for key to District, Classification, Position, and College abbreviations.

**C =Candidate; EM =Emeritus; the date following the C is the month and year the Candidate status began

NAME	TELEPHONE NUMBER EMAIL	STREET ADDRESS CITY/STATE/ZIP	DISTRICT	CLASS.	POSITION/ STATUS**	WHERE SERVING	OFFICE PHONE	COLLEGE/ UNIV/CQ	YR GRAD
Weinlaeder Kenneth C	(319)775-1638 kcwnldr@gmail.com	6215 Poplar Bch Romulus NY 14541	PSW	Teacher	EM			S	1971
Weinrich Christopher A	(714)317-5986 cweinrich@salemorange.com	7808 E Teal Ln Orange CA 92869	PSW	Teacher	Tchr	Salem Orange CA	(714)639-1946	IV	1995
Weinrich Douglas D	dweinrich@redeemeralive.org	12739 E Apache Pass Rd Spokane WA 99206	NOW	DCE	Mem C	Redeemer Spokane WA	(509)926-6363	S	1995
Weinrich Kasey K Briglio	(714)744-4186	7808 E Teal Ln Orange CA 92869	PSW	Teacher	Tchr	Salem Orange CA	(714)633-2366	IV	2000
Weinrich Timothy P	(402)753-0617 timweinrich@yahoo.com	1506 Jones Dr Fremont NE 68025	NEB	Teacher	EM			S	1979
Weisenbach Janice L Dove Dr	weisjan@aol.com	1299 Allendale Dr Saginaw MI 48638	MI	Teacher	EM			CQ	1993
Weiser Joshua R	(970)390-1491 josh.gracioussaviorchurch@gmail.com	2207 Crazy Horse Cir Edwards CO 81632	RM	DCE	Mem C	Gracious Savior Edwards CO	(970)926-3550	AU	2017
Weishaar Sarah E Hettig			RM	DFLM	Mem C	Bethlehem Lakewood CO	(303)238-7676	AA	2018
Weisheit Carolyn Pomerenke	(913)825-1402 eweis10671@gmail.com	9000 Park St Apt 714 Lenexa KS 66215	PSW	Teacher	EM			RF	1978
Weismantel Paul O	(517)641-4128	2100 Wyndham Ln Alpena MI 49707	MI	Teacher	EM			RF	1963
Weiss Bethany A			MI	Teacher	C08/2023			CQ	2020
Weiss Charles L	(715)421-3477 cwbw@tznet.com	4220 16th Street South Wisc Rapids WI 54494	NW	Teacher	EM			RF	1962
Weiss Frederick J	(260)489-6712 retprincipal@frontier.com	1214 Ludwig Park Dr Fort Wayne IN 46825	IN	Teacher	EM			RF	1959
Weiss Jared L	(586)791-2217 jweiss7378@gmail.com	20866 Fleetwood Dr Clinton Twp MI 48035	MI	Teacher	EM			S	1977
Weiss Jeffery D			IN	Teacher	C02/2024			AA	2010
Weiss Kaila N	(714)883-8481 weiss.kaila@gmail.com	759 W 37th Pl Yuma AZ 85365	PSW	Teacher	C09/2023			IV	2010
Weiss Kathryn E Dueker	(951)206-7575 kweiss@sjlschool.org	5716 Giocondo Ave Bakersfield CA 93311	CNH	Teacher	Tchr	St John Bakersfield CA	(661)665-7815	IV	2010
Weiss Muriel J Pingel	(989)755-1818	6680 E Holland Rd Saginaw MI 48601	MI	Teacher	EM			SP	1975
Weiss Nicolas R	(972)922-5379 nick.weiss@popcs.org	5505 Green Hollow Ln The Colony TX 75056	TX	Teacher	Tchr	Prince Of Peace Carrollton TX	(972)447-0532	MQ	2006
Weiss Paula C Bauer	(704)541-1624 family@messiah-nc.org	8300 Providence Rd Charlotte NC 28277	SE	DCE	Mem C	Messiah Charlotte NC	(704)541-1624	SP	1982
Weiss Rebecca A Lehenbauer	(775)291-7046 mrsbeccaweiss@yahoo.com	94 Canfield Dr Mount Clemens MI 48043	MI	Teacher	Tchr	St John Fraser MI	(586)294-8740	S	2006
Weiss Rebecca J Haupt		5505 Green Hollow Ln The Colony TX 75056	TX	Teacher	Tchr	Prince Of Peace Carrollton TX	(972)447-0532	MQ	2005
Weiss Thomas H	(941)757-9032 weisstom@att.net	1700 3rd Ave. W. Apt 108 Bradenton FL 34205	FG	Teacher	EM			RF	1965
Weissmueller Amy M Eisman	(573)270-3017 aimes2763@yahoo.com	190 Wildberry Ln Jackson MO 63755	MO	Teacher	C07/2016			RF	2007
Welburn Staci M Guinn	(616)340-7240 staciwelburn@att.net	8221 Greencastle Dr Charlotte NC 28210	SE	DCE	C10/2019			SP	2001
Welch Briana M Jordan	(828) 302-6388 brianamjordan12@gmail.com	1083 S College Ave Newton NC 28658	SE	Teacher	Tchr	Concordia Conover NC	(828)464-3324	S	2019
Welch Donna M Felzien	(563)322-2510 dmwelch144@gmail.com	1003 W Central Park Ave Davenport IA 52804	IE	Teacher	EM			S	1970
Welch Jennifer J	(616)309-0369 jwelch@mychristianschool.com	4350 Alpenhorn Dr NW Apt 1d Comstock Park MI 49321	MI	Teacher	Tchr	ISJ Grand Rapids MI	(616)363-0505	RF	1994
Weldon Melissa J	(443)388-8453 melissaweldon@concordiaprepschool.org	5505 Catalpha Rd Baltimore MD 21214	SE	Teacher	Tchr	Concordia Towson MD	(410)825-2323	CQ	2007
Wellander Ronald E	(479)903-3584 lrwellander@yahoo.com	190 Wade Ln Apt 17 Pea Ridge AR 72751	MI	Teacher	EM			RF	1955
Wellen John B	(312) 758-5758 lauren.wellen@gmail.com	1044 N Lombard Ave Oak Park IL 60302	NI	Teacher	EM			RF	1967
Wellen Lauren A Clark Dr	(312)758-5758 lauren.wellen@gmail.com	1044 N Lombard Ave Oak Park IL 60302	NI	Teacher	EM			RF	1969
Wellmann Bradley A	(402)616-1416 bwellmann@efyork.org	668 East 8th St York NE 68467	NEB	Teacher	Prin	Emmanuel-Faith York NE	(402)362-6575	CQ	2022
Wellna Alan J	(920)980-9321	501 Hillcrest Rd Saukville WI 53080	SW	Teacher	Tchr	St Paul Grafton WI	(262)377-4659	MQ	2010
Wells Angela R	(660)641-7874 angiewells@trinitylutheranalma.com	210 NW 8th St Concordia MO 64020	MO	Teacher	Prin	Trinity Alma MO	(660)674-2444	CQ	2020
Wells David D Dr	(336)408-7475 dr.daviddwells@gmail.com	6947 Simmons Rd Rural Hall NC 27045	SE	Teacher	C07/2016			S	1990
Wells Mary Lou E Dey	mwells18@gmail.com	1919 Northfork Cir Clearwater FL 33760	FG	Teacher	EM			SP	1967
Wells Molly Ann A	(913)416-2241 molly-ann.wells@cune.org	629 N Edgemoor St Wichita KS 67208	KS	Teacher	Tchr	Holy Cross Wichita KS	(316)684-4431	S	2013
Wells Rodger D	(727)524-1145 rdwells38@gmail.com	1919 Northfork Cir Clearwater FL 33760	FG	Teacher	EM			SP	1972
Wells Susan G Fehlhafer	(913)290-0004 brususwells@yahoo.com	1233 High St Leavenworth KS 66048	KS	Teacher	Tchr	St Paul Leavenworth KS	(913)682-0387	S	1987
Welte John A	(248)787-0049 john.welte@st-matthew.org	2040 S Commerce Rd Walled Lake MI 48390	MI	Tch/DCE	Mem C	St Matthew Walled Lake MI	(248)624-7676	S	1990

*Multiple Assignments (See Church Worker Locator for Additional Details)
See Page 53 for the Table of Abbreviations for key to District, Classification, Position, and College abbreviations.
**C =Candidate; EM =Emeritus; the date following the C is the month and year the Candidate status began

NAME	TELEPHONE NUMBER EMAIL	STREET ADDRESS CITY/STATE/ZIP	DISTRICT	CLASS.	POSITION/ STATUS**	WHERE SERVING	OFFICE PHONE	COLLEGE/ UNIV/CQ	YR GRAD
Welter Crystal A Stelmachowicz	(262)573-0895 cwiswelt@gmail.com	1460 Cacao Ln Pensacola FL 32507	SO	Teacher	Tchr	Redeemer Fairhope AL	(251)928-8397	S	1983
Welter Leah M	(319)423-5358 welterdce@gmail.com	1111 Range St Unit 202 North Mankato MN 56003	MNS	DCE	Mem C	Hosanna Mankato MN	(507)388-1766	SP	2005
Welton Michael G	(815)369-5598 mwelton@ourgodwithus.com	119 E Main St Lena IL 61048	NI	Teacher	Tchr	Immanuel Freeport IL	(815)232-3511	CQ	1992
Wemlinger Thomas E	(515)209-9140 thomas.wemlinger@gmail.com	111 Poplar Ave Waterloo IA 50703	IE	DCO	EM			SP	2003
Wendelin Sandra M Hilbert	(303)880-2675 swendelin@bethlehemdenver.com	12429 W 17th Ave Lakewood CO 80215	RM	DCE	Mem C	Bethlehem Lakewood CO	(303)238-7676	SP	1990
Wendling Austin D	(618)354-1195 adwendling606@gmail.com	Saint James Evangelical Lutheran Church 8 West Overlea Ave Baltimore MD 21206	SE	Teacher	Tchr	Concordia Towson MD	(410)825-2323	CH	2023
Wendorf Kristine A Grunden	(956)244-8463 kristinewendorf@gmail.com	2814 Emerald Lake Dr Harlingen TX 78550	TX	Teacher	C07/2016			RF	2000
Wendt Elenita A Hofmann	(816)436-7170 ewendt@pcikc.com	6967 N Woodland Ave Gladstone MO 64118	MO	Teacher	EM			S	1968
Wendt Nikol S Ziegelbein	(605)939-0188 321cook@gmail.com	13732 47th Ave W Rapid City SD 57702	SD	Teacher	C07/2016			RF	2001
Wendt Paul R	(219)662-9317 faithteacher@ameritech.net	207 W Rush St Kendallville IN 46755	IN	DCE	Mem C	St John Kendallville IN	(260)347-2158	SP	1991
Wendt Richard L Jr	(414)543-9543 wendtr@mtcalvary-mke.org	2972 N 91st St Milwaukee WI 53222	SW	Teacher	Tchr	Mount Calvary Milwaukee WI	(414)873-3466	MQ	1997
Wendt Susan	(920)866-2396 wendts@newlhs.com	5165 Edgewater Beach Rd Green Bay WI 54311	NW	Teacher	Tchr	Northeastern WI Green Bay WI	(920)469-6810	CQ	2018
Wendte Susan K	(479) 461-1128	2511 S L St Fort Smith AR 72901	MDS	Teacher	EM			S	1972
Wenger Daniel P	(636)284-7385 dwenger@lhsnstl.org	500 Crown Passage Dr Saint Charles MO 63303	MO	Teacher	Pro Stf	Lutheran North Saint Louis MO	(314)389-3100	BR	1998
Wenger John W	johnwenger@comcast.net	192 Jade Trl N Unit 324 Lake Elmo MN 55042	MNS	Teacher	EM			CQ	1973
Wenger Kathleen T	(772)286-0911 kwenger@rlcsrams.com	3877 SW Sailfish Dr Palm City FL 34990	FG	DCO	Mem C	Redeemer Stuart FL	(772)286-0911	SP	2021
Wenger Margaret S Siering	(516)433-3712 pwenger@optonline.net	44 Primrose Ave Hicksville NY 11801	AT	Teacher	EM			S	1966
Wenger Patricia L Miller	(316)631-2558 pat.wenger@yahoo.com	1503 NE Craigievar Ct Blue Springs MO 64014	MO	Teacher	EM			S	1973
Wenger Paul F	(516)433-3712 pwenger@optonline.net	44 Primrose Ave Hicksville NY 11801	AT	Teacher	EM			S	1966
Wenke Carolyn A Vetter	(402)992-8742 cwenke70@yahoo.com	3614 Koenigstein Ave Ste 29 Norfolk NE 68701	NEB	Teacher	EM			S	1980
Wenndt Ashley A Deac	(715)340-6496 deaconess.ashley@yahoo.com	607 W Blodgett St Marshfield WI 54449	NW	Deaconess	C01/2024			FW-DEAC	2012
Wenninger Barbara A Straub	(507)276-7360 barbawenninger@yahoo.com	29770 State Highway 15 Winthrop MN 55396	MNS	Teacher	Tchr	Immanuel Gaylord MN	(507)237-2804	S	1984
Wente Steven F	(708)268-0730 stevenwente@gmail.com	709 N 5th Ave Maywood IL 60153	NI	Teacher	EM			RF	1975
Wenthe William D Jr	(210)325-8330 williamw4texans@gmail.com	5610 Spring Fire San Antonio TX 78247	TX	Teacher	Tchr	Shepherd Hills San Antonio TX	(210)614-3742	AU	1989
Wentland Kenneth H	(260)490-4298	3901 High St Logansport IN 46947	IN	Teacher	EM			RF	1969
Wentzel Aaron M	(616)591-7874 wentzel@stjohnsracine.org	3055 Caledonia St Racine WI 53402	SW	Teacher	Tchr	St John Racine WI	(262)633-2758	MQ	2020
Wentzel Anne C Natzke	(616)970-9645 wenmichigan@gmail.com	810 N Adams Litchfield IL 62056	SI	Teacher	C11/2023			MQ	1992
Wentzel Katrina A	(262)509-0122 kwentzel@christstevensville.com	6359 Jericho Road Stevensville MI 49127	MI	Teacher	Tchr	Christ Stevensville MI	(269)429-7222	MQ	2021
Wentzel Steven J	(419)966-5828 swentzel@bright.net	16840 Co Rd S Rt 4 Napoleon OH 43545	OH	Teacher	EM			RF	1973
Wentzel Vicki Blomenberg	(419)598-8818 vwentzel0310@gmail.com	16840 County Rd S Napoleon OH 43545	OH	Teacher	EM			RF	1973
Wenzel Arthur P	(260)602-7536	1086 Boulder Ridge Dr New Haven IN 46774	IN	Teacher	EM			RF	1974
Wenzel Gary E Dr	(708)383-7409 wenzelmr@hotmail.com	753 E Crescent Dr Arlington Heights IL 60005	NI	Teacher	EM			RF	1970
Wenzel Ruth Ellen Donovan	(718)461-7579 ptwenz@aol.com	12407 11th Ave College Point NY 11356	AT	Teacher	Tchr	Flushing And Bayside Bayside NY	(718)225-5502	BR	1976
Wenzelburger Garrett A	(414)303-2121 gwenzelburger@lhsa.com	27715 Riviera St Harrison Twp MI 48045	MI	Teacher	Tchr	LHS Assn Of Greater Detroit Rochester Hls MI	(248)856-0240	MQ	2016
Wenzelburger Jana L	(414)902-3699	52910 Romeo Plank Rd Macomb MI 48042	FG	Teacher	Tchr	Grace Winter Haven FL	(863)293-8447	MQ	2018
Wenzler Rebecca Gudas	(574)225-2774 wenzler@stpeternorthjudson.org	172 S 400 E Winamac IN 46996	IN	Teacher	Tchr	St Peter North Judson IN	(574)896-5933	CQ	2022
Wenzlick Angela J Sitz	(303)834-2652 gelajoy2518@hotmail.com	6566 Antelope Run Cir Apt 205 Colorado Springs CO 80924	MO	Teacher	C01/2024			CQ	2004
Werderman Amy L Rohde	(586)727-4123 nelswer@comcast.net	68756 S Forest Ave Richmond MI 48062	MI	Teacher	EM			S	1970
Werk Ann M I Meyer	(585)297-6608 annwerk@gmail.com	36 Trailside Dr Winona Lake IN 46590	IN	Teacher	EM			RF	1979
Werling Anna C	(260)415-5312 annaw2604@gmail.com	45 Hunting Creek Rd Saint Peters MO 63376	MO	Teacher	Tchr	Lutheran North Saint Louis MO	(314)389-3100	CH	2020
Werling Cathleen M Mueller	(260)415-0584 mcwerling@aol.com	14004 Harper Road New Haven IN 46774	IN	Teacher	EM			S	1990
Werner Bethany R Kuhnle	(712)310-7713 bethanyrwerner@gmail.com	1300 N 78th St Lincoln NE 68505	NEB	DCE	C12/2024			S	2011

*Multiple Assignments (See Church Worker Locator for Additional Details)
See Page 53 for the Table of Abbreviations for key to District, Classification, Position, and College abbreviations.
**C =Candidate; EM =Emeritus; the date following the C is the month and year the Candidate status began

NAME	TELEPHONE NUMBER EMAIL	STREET ADDRESS CITY/STATE/ZIP	DISTRICT	CLASS.	POSITION/ STATUS**	WHERE SERVING	OFFICE PHONE	COLLEGE/ UNIV/CQ	YR GRAD
Werner CherylAnne	(402)675-1265 cheriewerner6@yahoo.com	202 W Park St Battle Creek NE 68715	NEB	Teacher	Tchr	St John Battle Creek NE	(402)675-3605	S	1991
Werner Courtney M Dykema	(989)395-3194 courtneymdykema@gmail.com	569 Thornhill Ct. Belleville MI 48111	MI	Teacher	C07/2022			AA	2019
Werner Dauna L Goeman	(262)370-4539 sosaltybutsweet@gmail.com	3459 Knollwood Rd West Bend WI 53095	SW	Teacher	Tchr	St Paul Grafton WI	(262)377-4659	MQ	1987
Werner David J	(402)641-9014 djohnwerner@gmail.com	903 N 2nd St Seward NE 68434	NEB	Teacher	EM			S	1973
Werner Dorinda R Noack	(618)593-1419 dorinda830@gmail.com	2306 Pleasant Rose Cir Bryan TX 77808	TX	DCE	D Miss	Texas District Round Rock TX	(800)951-3478	SP	1985
Werner Elizabeth Kamprath	(402)641-9015 betsykwerner@gmail.com	903 N 2nd St Seward NE 68434	NEB	Teacher	EM			S	1973
Werner Karen L Kennedy	(562)400-9407 eduk8um813@aol.com	8050 E Tarma St Long Beach CA 90808	PSW	Teacher	EM			S	1973
Werner Michael C	(720)880-8424 mcw1956usa@gmail.com	1435 S Chambers Rd Unit 104 Aurora CO 80017	RM	Teacher	EM			S	1986
Werner Michael J	(402)641-9016 michaeljwerner4@gmail.com	1100 N 56th St Lincoln NE 68504	NEB	Teacher	Tchr	Lincoln Lincoln NE	(402)467-5404	CH	2012
Werner Pamela S Seevers	(403)984-0279	1723 Road 5300 Davenport NE 68335	NEB	Teacher	EM			S	1984
Wernsing Darrel G	(217)792-3961 darwer@frontiernet.net	508 N Lafayette St Mount Pulaski IL 62548	CI	Teacher	EM			RF	1962
Werschky Sharon L Schnitker	(989)977-0169 sharon.werschky@airadv.net	10675 Rescue Rd Sebewaing MI 48759	MI	Teacher	EM			CQ	2005
Wert Emilyann P Pool Deac	(513)283-9168 emilyann.wert@gmail.com	6919 Terra Cotta Dr SE Caldonia MI 49316	MI	Deaconess	C06/2024			FW-DEAC	2021
Wert Mary L Erbelding	(630)906-1899 mwert@immanuelbatavia.org	731 Lindsay Cir North Aurora IL 60542	NI	Teacher	Tchr	Immanuel Batavia IL	(630)879-7163	RF	1988
Werth Janice M Volkert	(716)731-7183 jan_werth@stjohnnt.com	2469 Stoelting St Niagara Falls NY 14304	EA	Teacher	Tchr	St John North Tonawanda NY	(716)693-9677	RF	1985
Wesenberg Deborah L Montroy Galford	(248)330-8536 debwesenberg@yahoo.com	6344 Marina Drive Algonac MI 48001	MI	Teacher	EM			CQ	2007
Wesley Ryan E	(586)781-9151 rwesley@lhsa.com	55130 Belle Rose Dr Shelby Twp MI 48316	MI	Teacher	Tchr	Lutheran North Macomb MI	(586)781-9151	AA	2001
Weslock Naomi Y Nao	(630)947-4309 wanderingweslocks@netzero.com	7000 Aston Gardens Dr Unit 206 Venice FL 34292	FG	Teacher	EM			RF	1964
Weslock Terry E	(630)222-8837 tweslock12@gmail.com	7000 Aston Gardens Dr Unit 206 Venice FL 34292	FG	Teacher	EM			RF	1965
Wessel Kathy Timler	(507)346-1073 twt68@juno.com	503 W Fremont St Spring Valley MN 55975	MNS	Teacher	EM			RF	1981
Wessler Jonathan M Dr	(617)360-1504 jonathan.wessler@flc-boston.org	12 Pine Hill Terrace Rockland MA 02370	NE	DPM	Mem C	First Boston MA	(617)536-8851	MQ	2018
Wessling Ruth L Glienke	(305)322-2254 catspawruth@gmail.com	7008 Flagstone Way Flowery Branch GA 30542	FG	Teacher	EM			S	1977
West Rebecca L Collins	(214)287-0853	406 Silver Springs Ln Lavon TX 75166	TX	Teacher	Tchr	Messiah Lambs Plano TX	(972)398-7560	AU	1992
West Rebecca S Seitchick			NEB	Teacher	C05/2025			CQ	2004
Westad Karen J Rosen	(320)593-1860 karbert@hutchtel.net	427 Tischler Ave SE Faribault MN 55021	MNS	Teacher	EM			SP	1980
Westby Jessica R Reed	(828)612-3322 jwestby@concordianc.org	5889 Crescent Drive Claremont NC 28610	SE	Teacher	Tchr	Concordia Conover NC	(828)464-3011	CQ	2020
Westendorf Karen S Renkert	(586)567-6586 jkwesty@hotmail.com	42141 Blairmoor Dr Sterling Hts MI 48313	MI	Teacher	EM			CQ	1997
Westol John L	(352)629-5769 jrstol@yahoo.com	2021 SE 38th St Ocala FL 34480	FG	Teacher	Tchr	St John Ocala FL	(352)622-7275	RF	1969
Weston Amy J Osborne	(248)787-1178 amy.weston@st-matthew.org	1715 Paramount St Novi MI 48377	MI	Teacher	Tchr	St Matthew Walled Lake MI	(248)624-7676	AA	1999
Weston Ashlea J	weston.ashlea@gmail.com	448 3rd St Manistee MI 49660	MI	Teacher	Prin	Trinity Manistee MI	(231)723-8700	AA	2009
Weston Laura A Glowiak	(630)809-4873 lauraweston@live.com	4316 Nutmeg Ln Apt 168 Lisle IL 60532	NI	Teacher	Tchr	St John's Lombard IL	(630)932-3196	CQ	2015
Westphal Renee M	(414)526-5651 westphaltwins@gmail.com	5706 S 104th St Hales Corners WI 53130	EN	Teacher	C06/2025			CQ	2020
Westphal Thomas A	(248)709-8617 twestphal98@gmail.com	705 Indiana Ave Collinsville IL 62234	SI	DCE	Mem C	Good Shepherd Collinsville IL	(618)344-3151	CH	2012
Westrem John M	(260) 615-5233 jjw6320@frontier.com	6320 Treasure CV Fort Wayne IN 46835	IN	Teacher	EM			S	1972
Westrup Susan J	(559)439-5318	330 W Sierra Ave Apt 112 Fresno CA 93704	CNH	Tch/DCE	EM			SP	1985
Wetherell Carri J Chambers	sparksmate@aol.com	25 Marjorie Trl Ormond Beach FL 32174	FG	Teacher	C07/2016			RF	1982
Wetherell Mark E	(386) 852-6061 hotwheelsparks@aol.com	25 Marjorie Trl Ormond Beach FL 32174	FG	Tch/DCE	C07/2016			RF	1984
Wetjen Dennis D	(619)254-9659 ddwetjen@yahoo.com	7735 Ropalt St La Mesa CA 91942	PSW	Teacher	EM			S	1973
Wetjen Tamara J Wachs	(319)330-0088 tjwetjen@yahoo.com	1677 Locust Dr Williamsburg IA 52361	IE	Teacher	EM			S	1980
Wetmore Melba L Heitgerd	(314)843-3112 chasmel2@sbcglobal.net	10353 Roscommon Dr Saint Louis MO 63123	MO	Teacher	EM			S	1973
Wetzel Linda K Happel	(507)281-3282	2521 23rd Ave SE Rochester MN 55904	MNS	Teacher	EM			S	1973
Wetzel Myron E	(507)281-3282	2521 23rd Ave SE Rochester MN 55904	MNS	Teacher	EM			S	1972
Wetzstein Joel C	(713)454-3963 wetzstein.joel@gmail.com	6645 Jeffery Bay S Cottage Grove MN 55016	MNS	DCM	Mem C	Woodbury Woodbury MN	(651)739-5144	MQ	2015

*Multiple Assignments (See Church Worker Locator for Additional Details)
See Page 53 for the Table of Abbreviations for key to District, Classification, Position, and College abbreviations.
**C =Candidate; EM =Emeritus; the date following the C is the month and year the Candidate status began

NAME	TELEPHONE NUMBER EMAIL	STREET ADDRESS CITY/STATE/ZIP	DISTRICT	CLASS.	POSITION/ STATUS**	WHERE SERVING	OFFICE PHONE	COLLEGE/ UNIV/CQ	YR GRAD
Wetzstein Sandra L Jensen	(720)493-8849 mswetzstein@gmail.com	7200 E Quincy Ave Apt 404 Denver CO 80237	RM	Teacher	EM			RF	1966
Weyer Edith C Chrysler	(847)280-9393 weweyer@aol.com	3165 E University Dr Lot 807 Mesa AZ 85213	PSW	Teacher	EM			RF	1987
Weyers Amanda Jacobsen	(715)307-2675 weyersba@gmail.com	1325 Ward Ave Hudson WI 54016	MNS	Teacher	Tchr	Trinity First Minneapolis MN	(612)871-2353	SP	2023
Weyhrich Randy J	(414)463-6481 rweyhrich@gmail.com	5239 N 108th Ct Milwaukee WI 53225	SW	Teacher	EM			CQ	1977
Weyhrich Richard L	(931)935-1548 teansymphony@blomand.net	231 Parks Thompson Rd Sparta TN 38583	MDS	Tch/DCE	Mem C	Shep Of The Hills Crossville TN	(931)484-3461	CQ	1984
Weymier Amy S Hoelke	(262)293-9045 amy.weymier@gmail.com	N63W15185 Pocahontas Dr Menomonee Fls WI 53051	SW	Teacher	Tchr	Zion Menomonee Falls WI	(262)781-7437	RF	1987
Wheeler Cynthia A Weander	(314)706-9102 magillone@sbcglobal.net	2172 Sante Fe Cir Arnold MO 63010	MO	Tch/DCE	EM			S	1979
Wheeler Julie A Bittner	(989)737-4472 joyjulie9999@gmail.com	9999 Overton St Reese MI 48757	MI	Teacher	EM			RF	1983
Wheeler Lynn A	(661)665-9451 lwheeler@sjlchurch.org	9700 Cimarron Trails Dr Bakersfield CA 93311	CNH	Teacher	P/Tchr	St John Bakersfield CA	(661)664-8090	PO	1982
Wheeler Taylor J	(719)569-4125 pic.youthmin@gmail.com	5007 Maple Grove Rd Duluth MN 55811	MNN	DCE	Mem C	Peace Christ Hermantown MN	(218)729-9473	SP	2017
Whelply Karen K Wrede	(949)857-6680	1 Windwood Irvine CA 92604	PSW	Teacher	EM			S	1965
Whipker Courtney A	(812)521-8967 cwhipker@trinitycougars.org		IN	Teacher	Tchr	Trinity Seymour IN	(812)524-8547	S	2012
Whipkey Robert E Jr		206 Westwood Dr Moro IL 62067	SI	Teacher	EM			RF	1969
Whirrett Andrew M	(260)417-2229 amwhirrett@gmail.com	8620 Sakaden Pkwy Fort Wayne IN 46825	IN	Teacher	Prin	St Pauls Fort Wayne IN	(260)424-0049	S	2001
Whitcomb Rhonda J Hintz	(320)582-2279 rwhitcomb@ylscrusaders.org	10145 S Dos Hermanas Yuma AZ 85367	PSW	Teacher	Tchr	Christ Yuma AZ	(928)726-0773	SP	1984
White Andrea J Christensen	(785)456-8737 andreajeanwhite@gmail.com	17228 Driftwood End Wamego KS 66547	KS	Teacher	C07/2016			S	2005
White Danielle C Moeller	dwhite@cluth.org	8208 Tewksbury Ct Fort Wayne IN 46835	IN	Teacher	Tchr	Central New Haven IN	(260)493-2502	CQ	2011
White Diane M Baker	(713)857-3743 awhite14@comcast.net	1023 W 30th St Houston TX 77018	TX	Teacher	Tchr	Our Savior Houston TX	(713)290-9087	RF	1996
White Elisabeth A Jobst	dcebethwhite@gmail.com		TX	DCE	Mem C	Trinity Weatherford TX	(817)613-1939	SP	2020
White Ellinor B Black Dr	(256)852-1102 ellinorbwhite@aol.com	2815 Carl T Jones Dr SE Apt 175 Huntsville AL 35802	SO	Teacher	EM			CQ	1998
White Emily L Rohlf	(402)270-3734	385 Tall Oaks Dr Branson MO 65616	MO	Teacher	Tchr	Faith Branson MO	(417)334-2469	S	1998
White Laura A Wagner	(503)807-4439 laurawhite@trinityed.org	33 Hillcrest Dr. Kalispell MT 59901	MT	Teacher	Prin	Trinity Kalispell MT	(406)257-5683	PO	1988
White Lauren E Sperry	(309)371-0413 lauren@shepherdlutheran.com		TX	DCE	Mem C	Shepherd Hills San Antonio TX	(210)614-3742	S	2019
White Lisa A Lipke	(573)225-2454 lalipke@hotmail.com	2562 Mansfield Pl Jackson MO 63755	MO	Teacher	Prin	St Paul Jackson MO	(573)243-5360	CQ	2022
White Mary P Andrzejczak	(630)908-0598	714 Nassau Dr Roselle IL 60172	NI	Teacher	C06/2023			CQ	2022
White Michael J	(512)699-5564 mikewhite1212@yahoo.com	18714 Jones St Elkhorn NE 68022	NEB	DCE	C12/2023			AU	2008
White Pamela K Ochs	(989)471-2248 tonywhite@chartermi.net	7553 US Highway 23 S Ossineke MI 49766	MI	Teacher	EM			S	1972
White Paul W	(321)704-4903 dcepaulwhite@gmail.com	17535 Say Rd Wamego KS 66547	KS	DCE	Mem C	Mount Calvary Wamego KS	(785)456-2444	S	2007
White Sarah G	(847)826-1765 sgwhite24@gmail.com	11700 Offaly Dr Austin TX 78754	TX	Teacher	Tchr	Redeemer Austin TX	(512)459-1500	MQ	2011
White Signe G	(208)720-4371 trekinjoy@gmail.com	225 Alturas Dr Hailey ID 83333	NOW	Teacher	RSO	Camp Perkins Ketchum ID	(208)788-0897	MQ	1994
Whitely Jennifer R Abernathy	(828)217-4941 jwhitely@charter.net		SE	DPM	C05/2025			CQ	2012
Whiteneck Elaine	(620)340-7535 ekwhitemlc@gmail.com	1717 W Wilman Ct Emporia KS 66801	KS	DCE	EM			S	1982
Whitener Abigail K	(402)942-5824 Abbywhitener25@gmail.com		MO	Teacher	Tchr	Abiding Savior Saint Louis MO	(314)894-9200	S	2018
Whitmore Jennifer M Wren	(812)799-6578 whitmore97@hotmail.com	49594 County Highway 53 Perham MN 56573	MNN	Teacher	C07/2016			RF	2001
Whitney Heather J Niedfeldt	(402)883-0083 whitney.heatherj@gmail.com	203 W. Ash St P.O. Box 548 Battle Creek NE 68715	NEB	Teacher	C07/2016			S	2013
Whitney Jaelyn N Adler	(970)520-5895 jaelyn.adler@gmail.com	10631 E Southern Ave Apt 2013 Mesa AZ 85208	PSW	Teacher	Tchr	Christs Greenfield Gilbert AZ	(480)892-8314	S	2023
Whitney Larry A	(970) 405-0785 lawman80634@yahoo.com	6912 18th St Greeley CO 80634	RM	Teacher	Tchr	Trinity Greeley CO	(970)330-2485	S	1970
Whitney Roger L	(407)719-6714	1344 Haven Drive Oviedo FL 32765	S	Teacher	EM			RF	1972
Whitney Steven B	(507)330-1559 steven.b.whitney@gmail.com	203 W Ash St Battle Creek NE 68715	NEB	DCE	Mem C	St John Battle Creek NE	(402)675-3155	S	2014
Whitsett Margaret E Claus Deac	(502)377-5007 margy.whitsett@twc.com	12113 Briargate Ln Goshen KY 40026	IN	Deaconess	Mem C	Our Savior Louisville KY	(502)426-1130	Other	1975
Whitson Janet S Ormerod Dr	(402)641-3138 janetwhitson8@gmail.com	91 Lakeview Shores Dr Coldspring TX 77331	TX	Teacher	EM			RF	1971
Whitson Kelley E Delph	(812)216-2996 kwhitson@immanuelschool.org	835 Redding Rd Seymour IN 47274	IN	Teacher	Tchr	Immanuel Seymour IN	(812)522-1301	MQ	2003

*Multiple Assignments (See Church Worker Locator for Additional Details)

See Page 53 for the Table of Abbreviations for key to District, Classification, Position, and College abbreviations.

**C =Candidate; EM =Emeritus; the date following the C is the month and year the Candidate status began

NAME	TELEPHONE NUMBER EMAIL	STREET ADDRESS CITY/STATE/ZIP	DISTRICT	CLASS.	POSITION/ STATUS**	WHERE SERVING	OFFICE PHONE	COLLEGE/ UNIV/CQ	YR GRAD
Whittington Joanna J Lutz	(575)291-5640 joannajoywhittington@gmail.com	13 E Darby Rd Dexter NM 88230	RM	Teacher	C05/2019			MQ	2006
Whittler Timothy B	(314)578-8455 twhittler@sjlarnold.org	1432 Coachlite Dr De Soto MO 63020	MO	Teacher	Tchr	St John Arnold MO	(636)464-7303	CQ	2022
Wichern Rebecca L Smith	(573)450-5958 wichern6618@gmail.com	11936 US Highway 61 Jackson MO 63755	MO	Teacher	Tchr	Saxony Jackson MO	(573)204-7555	CQ	2003
Wichman Donald L	(219)493-1364	2725 Kingsland Ct Fort Wayne IN 46815	IN	Teacher	EM			S	1975
Wickboldt Cynthia Buttke	(773)282-8211 cynthiawickboldt@gmail.com	6227 W Waveland Ave Chicago IL 60634	NI	Teacher	EM			RF	1974
Wickboldt Ingrid E Davies	(773)971-5060 ingrid.wickboldt@gmail.com	1211 Hazelcrest Dr Watertown WI 53094	SW	Teacher	Tchr	Good Shepherd Watertown WI	(920)261-2579	RF	2000
Wickboldt Mark W	(773)282-8211 mwwickboldt@gmail.com	6227 W Waveland Ave Chicago IL 60634	NI	Teacher	EM			RF	1974
Wickre Carol M Tointon	(507)884-9261	1905 50th Ave SE Rochester MN 55904	MNS	Teacher	EM			SP	1980
Wickre Paul N	(507)282-8006 pawickre@rcls.net	1905 50th Ave SE Rochester MN 55904	MNS	Teacher	EM			SP	1977
Wickre Koyiol Rachel S	(507)990-9939 wickre@csp.edu	744 Tiffany Ln Waconia MN 55387	MNS	Teacher	Tchr	Trinity Waconia MN	(952)442-4165	SP	2012
Wicks Janice L	(414)421-0416 janice_wicks@att.net	7780 W Grange Ave Apt 313 Greendale WI 53129	SW	Teacher	EM			SP	1968
Widjojo Victoria A Swanson	(760)846-6381 vwidjojo@gracelcms.net	2954 West Canyon Ave San Diego CA 92123	PSW	Teacher	Tchr	Grace Escondido CA	(760)745-0831	S	2006
Wiebold Judith A Mahler	(858) 342-1220 showpark@aol.com	8196 Laborie Ln Wellington FL 33414	FG	Teacher	EM			RF	1965
Wiebold Linda J Hanson	(612)247-7900	6817 Lorena Ln Eden Prairie MN 55346	MNS	Teacher	EM			SP	1976
Wiechers Faith D Decker	(618)973-7066 fwiechers@stpaulnapoleon.org	T105 County Road 17 Napoleon OH 43545	OH	Teacher	Tchr	St Paul Napoleon OH	(419)592-3535	CH	2011
Wiedenkeller Hilbert W	(414)525-5546 hib@steepleview.org	12455 W Janesville Rd Unit 315 Muskego WI 53150	EN	Teacher	EM			RF	1960
Wiedenmann Ruth E	(407)754-4522 rjwiedfl@aol.com	P.O. Box 521776 Longwood FL 32752	S	Teacher	Tchr	St Lukes Oviedo FL	(407)365-3228	RF	1976
Wiederhold Chelsea S Volk	(708)822-2165 chelsea.volk@cune.org	2613 County Road 205 Giddings TX 78942	TX	Teacher	Tchr	St Paul Serbin TX	(979)366-9650	S	2014
Wiederkehr Stephen E		1701 Mimosa St Enid OK 73701	OK	Tch/DCE	EM			SP	1977
Wiegmann Mira L Roeder Dr	(971)255-0461 mira.wiegmann@cune.org	2750 SW 89th Ave Portland OR 97225	NOW	Teacher	EM			S	1969
Wiegmann Richard W	(971)255-0461 richard.wiegmann@cune.org	2750 SW 89th Ave Portland OR 97225	NOW	Teacher	EM			S	1962
Wiemann Thomas E	(847) 564-6320 tomwie@yahoo.com	12 W Lonnquist Blvd Mt Prospect IL 60056	NI	Teacher	EM			S	1974
Wiemer Abigail J Burkee	(303)416-0756 burskill@gmail.com	210 Cypress Point Washington IL 61571	CI	DCE	C10/2022			CH	2014
Wiemer Rebecca M Drewitz	(660)620-1832 dcewiemer@gmail.com	1513 N 16th St Sheboygan WI 53081	SW	DCE	C07/2023			Other	2018
Wiemer Thomas R	(309)620-3530 mrwiemer1@gmail.com	1513 N 16th St Sheboygan WI 53081	SW	Teacher	Tchr	St Paul Sheboygan WI	(920)452-6882	CH	2018
Wienberg Marie A Fischer	(816)405-8640 mwienberg@splhs.org	11886 Amazon Ave Concordia MO 64020	MO	Teacher	EM			CQ	2001
Wiencke Dorothy C Costley	(314)604-6462 dcwink@yahoo.com	2 Founders Way Unit B Clayton MO 63105	MO	Teacher	Tchr	Assoc Spec Ed Saint Louis MO	(314)268-1234	S	2000
Wieneke Lori S Mac Kay		7487 Emerald Woods Dr SE Byron Center MI 49315	MI	Teacher	Mem C	St Matthew Grand Rapids MI	(616)942-9091	AA	1998
Wientge Jennifer L Messmer Deac	(314)369-3667 sixkidsplusdog@yahoo.com	4248 Union Terr Dr Saint Louis MO 63125	MO	Deaconess	Inst C	Lutheran Senior Services DBA EverTrue Brentwood MO	(314)968-9313	SL-DEAC	2020
Wier Barry L	(608)752-9330 barlee22@hotmail.com	2277 N Hawthorne Park Dr Janesville WI 53545	SW	Teacher	EM			RF	1976
Wier Ruth A Staubitz	(608)752-9330 brwier1@gmail.com	2277 N Hawthorne Park Dr Janesville WI 53545	SW	Teacher	EM			RF	1975
Wier Timothy A	(708)829-4544 tim.wier@gmail.com	16 E Pine Ave Bensenville IL 60106	NI	Teacher	S HS/C	Concordia University Chicago River Forest IL	(708)771-8300	RF	2005
Wierman Judith A Deac	(815)922-2482 jawierman@yahoo.com	5316 Brindlewood Dr Plainfield IL 60586	NI	Deaconess	C06/2017			FW-DEAC	2016
Wierschke Leah J Kangas	(308)327-3103 leahwierschke@yahoo.com	P.O. Box 546 Rushville NE 69360	WY	Teacher	C07/2016			MQ	1995
Wiersig Christine C AuBuchon	(734)525-2859 wdwiersig@aol.com	28944 Savoie Ct Livonia MI 48154	MI	Teacher	EM			S	1969
Wiersig W D	(734)525-2859 wdwiersig@aol.com	28944 Savoie Ct Livonia MI 48154	MI	Teacher	EM			S	1968
Wiese Curtis J	(850)651-1022 familylifeminister@gslcshalimar.org	1 Meigs Dr Shalimar FL 32579	SO	DCE	Mem C	Good Shepherd Shalimar FL	(850)651-1022	S	2003
Wiest Kathryn S Schardt	(308)532-4801 rkwiest@msn.com	1212 Crown Road Norfolk NE 68701	NEB	Teacher	EM			S	1978
Wietfeldt Cathy L	(314)591-0103 cwietfeldt@hotmail.com	18560 S Fox Creek Ln Pacific MO 63069	MO	Teacher	EM			RF	1975
Wieting Bruce L	(970)356-2590 wwieting@yahoo.com	140 23rd Ave Lot 30 Greeley CO 80631	RM	Teacher	EM			S	1989
Wiggenhorn Andrew D	dwiggenhorn5564@gmail.com		SI	Teacher	C05/2019			Other	2018

*Multiple Assignments (See Church Worker Locator for Additional Details)
See Page 53 for the Table of Abbreviations for key to District, Classification, Position, and College abbreviations.
**C =Candidate; EM =Emeritus; the date following the C is the month and year the Candidate status began

NAME	TELEPHONE NUMBER EMAIL	STREET ADDRESS CITY/STATE/ZIP	DISTRICT	CLASS.	POSITION/ STATUS**	WHERE SERVING	OFFICE PHONE	COLLEGE/ UNIV/CQ	YR GRAD
Wiggins Karen Y	(404)931-1607 kwiggins007@gmail.com	P.O. Box 1973 Cedar Hill TX 75106	AT	Teacher	C06/2019			AU	1987
Wilaby Kevin L	(952)426-8496 kevin.wilaby@mayerlutheran.org	2519 River Bend Trl Mayer MN 55360	MNS	Teacher	Tchr	Mayer Mayer MN	(952)657-2251	S	1987
Wilber Brittany J Newton	(815)985-7958 brittanyjnewton@gmail.com	1700 Albatross Rd Princeton TX 75407	TX	Teacher	Tchr	Faith Plano TX	(972)423-7447	CH	2009
Wilbert Lori A Deac	(815)254-2352 loriwilbert@sbcglobal.net	2302 Buttercup Ln Crest Hill IL 60403	NI	Deaconess	EM			RF	1984
Wilcox Susan L Koenen	(402)641-4875 susan.wilcox1989@gmail.com	1889 N Columbia Ave Seward NE 68434	NEB	Teacher	EM			S	1981
Wilcoxen Lydia Temme			SI	Teacher	C07/2017			MQ	2013
Wildauer Beverly J Bremer	(308)850-5111 bevwildauer85@gmail.com	4310 Claussen Rd Grand Island NE 68803	NEB	Teacher	EM			S	1996
Wildauer Charles	(214)662-5747 donadei@sbcglobal.net	301 Droinwich Cir Allen TX 75002	TX	Teacher	EM			S	1970
Wildauer Cheryl A Helmlinger	paxdomini311@sbcglobal.net	301 Droinwich Cir Allen TX 75002	TX	Teacher	EM			S	1969
Wildauer Sarah B Dreessen	(573)270-1670 sarah.wildauer@gmail.com	1919 Sherwood Dr Cape Girardeau MO 63701	MO	Teacher	C07/2016			RF	2005
Wilde Elyse A Gunderman	(319)400-1676 ewilde@lutheraninterparish.com	2983 225th St Williamsburg IA 52361	IE	Teacher	Tchr	Lutheran Interparish Williamsburg IA	(319)668-1711	S	1994
Wilde Stephanie L Deac	(218)371-5644 deaconess.stephanie.wilde@ gmail.com	419 E Oak St Parkers Prairie MN 56361	ND	Deaconess	RSO	Dakota Boys and Girls Ranch Fargo ND	(701)237-3123	FW-DEAC	2021
Wiley-Pearce Jarryn D Wiley	(660)441-1212 jarrynw@yahoo.com	203 S Logan St Dow City IA 51528	IW	DCE	Mem C	Our Savior Denison IA	(712)263-3282	S	2006
Wilgers Karen A Poland	(316)214-3130 karenwilgers@hotmail.com	715 N Crest Ridge Ct Wichita KS 67230	KS	Teacher	EM			CQ	2003
Wilharm Keith A	(847)529-8614 KeithWilharm@yahoo.com	207 N Walnut St Elmhurst IL 60126	NI	Teacher	EM			RF	1976
Wilharm Rebecca I Wykert	(708)408-2718 rwykert@yahoo.com	925 N 68th St Philadelphia PA 19151	EA	Teacher	C06/2023			MQ	2016
Wilhelm Marlene E Ebel	(352)801-8169 mee1012@netzero.com	21534 Prince Albert Ct Leesburg FL 34748	FG	Teacher	EM			RF	1958
Wilke Carolyn M Mueller	(832)237-2915	10818 White Oak Creek Ct Cypress TX 77429	TX	Teacher	EM			RF	1962
Wilke Christian T	(832)813-2051 cwilke387@gmail.com	11110 Opal Glen Ct Houston TX 77075	TX	Teacher	Tchr	South Houston TX	(281)464-8299	CH	2015
Wilke Jane P Mussell	(651)337-1943 janewilke@comcast.net	1275 Waters Path Woodbury MN 55129	MNS	Teacher	EM			SP	1975
Wilke Julie A	(612)720-8626 jwilke316@gmail.com	203 Yellowstone Ave Billings MT 59101	CNH	Teacher	Tchr	St Peter Lodi CA	(209)333-2223	SP	2000
Wilke Kenneth R	(206)937-2146	9603 California Ave SW Seattle WA 98136	NOW	Teacher	EM			RF	1969
Wilke LeRoy R Dr	(651)337-1943 lrwilke@comcast.net	1275 Waters Path Woodbury MN 55129	MNS	DCE	EM			SP	1972
Wilke Nancy E	(989)823-2143 newilke@charter.net	125 Timber Ridge Dr Vassar MI 48768	MI	Teacher	EM			RF	1974
Wilke Paul M	(832)237-2915	10818 White Oak Creek Ct Cypress TX 77429	TX	Teacher	Mem C	Epiphany Houston TX	(713)896-1773	MQ	1990
Wilke Phillip M	(281)351-2547 wilkep@clhs-tx.org	12b Leah Dr Montgomery TX 77316	TX	Teacher	Tchr	Concordia Tomball TX	(281)351-2547	MQ	1988
Wilke Sarah R Ragland	(224)358-9561 srose1324@yahoo.com	251 Luedtke Ave Apt 4b Racine WI 53405	SW	Teacher	Tchr	Lutheran High School Racine WI	(262)637-6538	S	2022
Wilkerson Jessica A Henke	(615)364-4860 jeci3376@yahoo.com	6532 Westfall Dr Nashville TN 37221	MDS	Teacher	C07/2016			MQ	2006
Wilkie Alicia E	(561)901-5910 aewilkie78@gmail.com	1665 Eden Park Dr Apt 10 Hamilton OH 45013	OH	Teacher	Tchr	Immanuel Hamilton OH	(513)895-9212	RF	2000
Wilkie Melba J Hallow	(812)584-7076	9963 Oak Circle Dr Aurora IN 47001	IN	Teacher	EM			RF	1962
Wilks Myril A	(586)838-6405 myrilwilks@gmail.com	11463 Birch Ct Washington MI 48094	MI	Teacher	EM			S	1971
Will Debra A Bertulis	(708)532-4116 willtrigger@comcast.net	7459 Cashew Dr Orland Park IL 60462	NI	Teacher	EM			RF	1978
Will Marlene G Staehr	(219)851-1798 mgwill3654@gmail.com	1710 Indiana Ave La Porte IN 46350	IN	Teacher	EM			S	1984
Wille Linda J Torney	(319)430-7051 lwille@lutheraninterparish.com	2836 260th St Williamsburg IA 52361	IE	Teacher	Tchr	Lutheran Interparish Williamsburg IA	(319)668-1711	CQ	2004
Wille Margaret L Stueber	(920) 941-0107 dmusic102047@gmail.com	1216 Hus Dr Watertown WI 53098	SW	Teacher	EM			S	1969
Wille Melvin	(630)554-3194 melwille@aol.com	327 Prairieview Dr Oswego IL 60543	NI	Teacher	EM			RF	1965
Wille Ronald G	(920)206-8842 ronwille5647@gmail.com	1216 Hus Dr Watertown WI 53098	SW	Teacher	EM			S	1970
Willer Kirsten M Damrow	(262)720-9274 willerkirsten@gmail.com	15905 Brentwood Dr Brookfield WI 53005	SW	Teacher	Tchr	Grace Menomonee Falls WI	(262)251-7140	CQ	1999
Willers Darcy J Cattau	(308)293-4540 darcywillers@gmail.com	2860 99th Street Pl Kearney NE 68845	NEB	Teacher	Tchr	Zion Kearney NE	(308)234-3410	S	2005
Willert Kathryn A Habedank	kwillert@trinitywny.org	156 Reserve Rd Buffalo NY 14224	EA	Teacher	Tchr	Trinity West Seneca NY	(716)674-5353	BR	1995
Willert Mark E	(716)608-8907 mkwillert@aol.com	156 Reserve Rd Buffalo NY 14224	EA	Teacher	Tchr	Trinity West Seneca NY	(716)674-5353	BR	1995
Willett Carolyn R Stahl	(714)273-4523 lyn2178@hotmail.com	536 N Pine St Orange CA 92867	PSW	Teacher	Tchr	Saint Johns Orange CA	(714)288-4400	RF	2000

*Multiple Assignments (See Church Worker Locator for Additional Details)

See Page 53 for the Table of Abbreviations for key to District, Classification, Position, and College abbreviations.

**C =Candidate; EM =Emeritus; the date following the C is the month and year the Candidate status began

NAME	TELEPHONE NUMBER EMAIL	STREET ADDRESS CITY/STATE/ZIP	DISTRICT	CLASS.	POSITION/ STATUS**	WHERE SERVING	OFFICE PHONE	COLLEGE/ UNIV/CQ	YR GRAD
Williams Abigail Schuldheisz	(503)784-4358 abbywilliams503@gmail.com		NOW	Teacher	Tchr	Concordia Seattle WA	(206)525-7407	PO	2012
Williams Allan A	(586)254-3304 awlutheran@yahoo.com	8335 Canal Rd Utica MI 48317	MI	Tch/DCE	EM			S	1977
Williams Amy M Bethel	(636)357-0773 watj@sbcglobal.net	110 Wimbledon Ct O Fallon MO 63368	MO	Teacher	C06/2023			CQ	2010
Williams Brent	(661)304-2518 bhstrumpet182@gmail.com	3810 Ames Ln Bakersfield CA 93311	CNH	Teacher	Tchr	St John Bakersfield CA	(661)665-7815	CQ	2021
Williams Droxsan J		4600 14th St SW Loveland CO 80537	RM	Teacher	Tchr	Immanuel Loveland CO	(970)667-7606	S	1999
Williams Elizabeth V	elizwms25@aol.com	35133 Meadow Ln Farmington Hls MI 48335	MI	Teacher	EM			RF	1972
Williams Hillary A Wichmann	(714)876-8772 hillarywichmann@yahoo.com	6234 East Coral Circle Anaheim CA 92807	PSW	Teacher	Tchr	Hephatha Anaheim CA	(714)637-0887	CQ	2015
Williams Janice A Auer	janwms@aol.com	7518 E Pinewood Pl Tucson AZ 85750	AT	Teacher	C07/2016			RF	1965
Williams Janice B Schaff	(408)559-7508 rcwilliams55@sbcglobal.net	2299 Sunrise Dr San Jose CA 95124	CNH	Teacher	EM			S	1962
Williams Janice L Spates	(586)430-0900 jankteacher@yahoo.com	8335 Canal Rd Utica MI 48317	MI	Teacher	EM			S	1977
Williams Jennifer L Crawley	(417)655-1782 williamsj0525@gmail.com	924 E Sunshine St Springfield MO 65807	MO	Teacher	Tchr	Redeemer Springfield MO	(417)883-5717	CQ	2024
Williams Judy E Harmoning	(586)946-7754 williamsjudy40@gmail.com	214 Thornwhistle Pl Garner NC 27529	SE	Teacher	EM			CQ	1999
Williams Kari L Krueger	(920)615-6892 kariw1546@gmail.com	1546 Spencers Xing Green Bay WI 54313	NW	Teacher	Tchr	Pilgrim Green Bay WI	(920)965-2233	RF	2004
Williams Kari L Strehlow	(414)248-9777 strehlow.kari@gmail.com	3404 Rooba St Austin TX 78728	TX	Teacher	Tchr	Redeemer Austin TX	(512)451-6478	CH	2014
Williams Kelly E Engelking	(847)641-1018 kengelking@sjlchurch.org	3810 Ames Ln Bakersfield CA 93311	CNH	Teacher	Tchr	St John Bakersfield CA	(661)665-7815	CH	2012
Williams Lewis E	(520)722-7966 wmslew@aol.com	7518 E Pinewood Pl Tucson AZ 85750	AT	Teacher	C07/2016			RF	1967
Williams Lissa K Oster	(314)591-2304 lwilliams@coglcs.com	3673 Sweetwater Crossing Pl Saint Charles MO 63301	MO	Teacher	Tchr	Child Of God Saint Peters MO	(636)970-7080	CQ	2023
Williams Mary E	(775)229-1101 willi126@me.com	4591 Spring Dr Reno NV 89502	CNH	DCE	C01/2021			S	2010
Williams Robert E	(989)245-9811 bob.williams@sharingnewlife.com	1113 Sam Bass Rd Willow Park TX 76087	TX	Teacher	Mem C	St Paul Fort Worth TX	(817)332-2281	RF	1987
Williams Sherry L Scheiwe	(414) 870-1969 slscheiwe@yahoo.com	2918 N 91st St Milwaukee WI 53222	SW	Teacher	Tchr	Mount Calvary Milwaukee WI	(414)873-3466	RF	1991
Williams Sina	swilliams@sothfamily.org	9481 E Mansfield Ave #108 Aurora CO 80014	RM	DCE	Mem C	Shepherd Hills Centennial CO	(303)798-0711	IV	2005
Williamson David M	(414)213-4627 david.williamson@orlctosa.org	W224N2286 Elmwood Dr Waukesha WI 53186	SW	Teacher	Tchr	Wauwatosa Wauwatosa WI	(414)258-4558	MQ	2003
Williamson June C Eschbach	(630)988-1428 junewilliamson1st@yahoo.com	2360 West Dusty Wren Dr Phoenix AZ 85085	PSW	Teacher	Tchr	Atonement Glendale AZ	(623)374-3019	CQ	1997
Williamson Katie L Widstrand	(586)944-8690 kwidstrand@yahoo.com	12355 Watkins Dr Shelby Township MI 48315	MI	Teacher	Tchr	St John Fraser MI	(586)293-0333	RF	2002
Williamson Pamela A Ling	(847)922-5022 pwplace@gmail.com	5640 Lucore Rd Marion IA 52302	IE	Teacher	EM			RF	1979
Willig Cheryl L Doty	(317)403-3254 clwillig@hotmail.com	5398 Guadeloupe Way Naples FL 34119	IN	Teacher	EM			RF	1974
Willig Fredrick J	(317)979-4697 fwilligpiman@hotmail.com	5398 Guadeloupe Way Naples FL 34119	IN	Teacher	EM			RF	1975
Willis Lisa M Rueter	(812)882-1322 willislm@hotmail.com	1266 S Oliphant Ave Vincennes IN 47591	IN	Teacher	EM			RF	1985
Willis Sarah A Van Duser	(402)641-2684 sarah.willis@trinitywaconia.org	2553 Coldwater Xing Mayer MN 55360	MNS	DCE	Mem C	Trinity Waconia MN	(952)442-4165	S	2021
Willman Jennifer Porath	(414)254-7855 willman.jennifer@gmail.com	1752 Manchester Dr Grafton WI 53024	SW	Teacher	Tchr	St Paul Grafton WI	(262)377-4659	CQ	2015
Willman Meghan E Groppe	(262)498-4378 willmanfam18@gmail.com	314 Hummingbird Ln Grafton WI 53024	SW	Teacher	C06/2022			MQ	2018
Willmann Joseph T	(219)669-9683 jtwillmann@gmail.com		NI	Teacher	Pro Stf	Lutheran Church Extension Fund Saint Louis MO	(314)965-9000	CQ	2017
Wills Herman C	(573)768-1024 hn.wills2@gmail.com	1505 S Walnut St Apt 303 Seymour IN 47274	IN	Teacher	EM			RF	1959
Wills Paul R	(734)645-4302 pawprw@gmail.com	9133 Cottage Trl Richland MI 49083	MI	Teacher	EM			S	1971
Willweber David E	(808)358-2945 dwillweber@gmail.com	1135 Mokapu Blvd Kailua HI 96734	CNH	Teacher	C07/2016			S	1992
Willweber Marie A Obermueller	(808)358-2946 marie.willweber@gmail.com	1135 Mokapu Blvd Kailua HI 96734	CNH	Teacher	C07/2016			S	1993
Willweber Sharon A Brandt	(559)310-9093 sharon@willweber.net	1135 Mokapu Blvd Kailua HI 96734	CNH	Teacher	EM			RF	1959
Wilschetz Susan M Huelskoetter	(619)694-6180 the4wlshtz@aol.com	5110 Franklin Pike Nashville TN 37220	MDS	DCE	C07/2016			RF	1994
Wilshek Gail A Sieveking	dgwilshek@gmail.com	5160 Country Club Dr High Ridge MO 63049	MO	Teacher	EM			RF	1984
Wilshire Grace A	(412)452-7333 gwilshire20@gmail.com	120 Cobblestone Dr Plum PA 15239	EN	Teacher	Tchr	Redeemer Verona PA	(412)793-5884	MQ	2023
Wilshusen Chad E	(402)719-0772 chad.wilshusen@flhsemail.org	9599 W Charleston Blvd Apt 2021 Las Vegas NV 89117	PSW	Teacher	Tchr	Faith Las Vegas NV	(702)804-4400	S	2010
Wilshusen Loren W	(402)719-0869 loren.wilshusen@gmail.com	1331 Stanford Ave Fremont NE 68025	NEB	Teacher	EM			S	1972

*Multiple Assignments (See Church Worker Locator for Additional Details)
See Page 53 for the Table of Abbreviations for key to District, Classification, Position, and College abbreviations.
**C =Candidate; EM =Emeritus; the date following the C is the month and year the Candidate status began

NAME	TELEPHONE NUMBER EMAIL	STREET ADDRESS CITY/STATE/ZIP	DISTRICT	CLASS.	POSITION/ STATUS**	WHERE SERVING	OFFICE PHONE	COLLEGE/ UNIV/CQ	YR GRAD
Wilson Amanda	(314)646-9884 awilson@ilsolivette.org	112 Spring Tree Ct Saint Charles MO 63303	MO	Teacher	Tchr	Immanuel Olivette MO	(314)993-5004	CH	2020
Wilson Brenda S Frank	(989)493-2351 bwilson@bethlehemsaginaw.org	2777 Hermansau Rd Saginaw MI 48604	MI	Teacher	Prin	Bethlehem Saginaw MI	(989)755-1144	CQ	2014
Wilson Brianna L Sonnenberg	(269)449-1834 mrsblwilson@gmail.com	41311 W Elm Dr Maricopa AZ 85138	PSW	Teacher	C01/2018			AA	2011
Wilson Christopher	(510)586-8893 Christophus.wilson@gmail.com	1730 Douglas St Rockford IL 61103	NI	Teacher	Tchr	Rockford Rockford IL	(815)877-9551	S	2016
Wilson Diane V Fagenbaum	(808)572-8224 dianeruss@msn.com	175 Awakea Loop Makawao HI 96768	CNH	Teacher	Tchr	Emmanuel Kahului-Maui HI	(808)877-3037	SP	1985
Wilson Elizabeth E Nimtz	(248)915-8999 nimtz.elizabeth@gmail.com	1069 E 14 Mile Rd Clawson MI 48017	MI	Teacher	Tchr	Our Shepherd Birmingham MI	(248)646-6100	CH	2020
Wilson Gina M Lyon	(510)406-2041 gina6474@yahoo.com	19056 Santa Maria Ave Castro Valley CA 94546	CNH	Teacher	Tchr	Bridge City Redwood City CA	(650)366-5892	PO	1997
Wilson Jodi S Renner	(952) 467-2780 jwilson@emanuelschool.org	P.O. Box 44 Green Isle MN 55338	MNS	Teacher	Tchr	Emanuel Hamburg MN	(952)467-2780	SP	1987
Wilson Katelyn M	(714)883-9628 katelynmwilson1414@gmail.com	19682 Ridgewood Pl Yorba Linda CA 92886	PSW	Teacher	Tchr	St Johns Orange CA	(714)288-4406	IV	2023
Wilson Kathrine N Onnen	(417)527-2006 k4mwilson@gmail.com	2006 Cedarcrest Dr Louisville KY 40242	IN	Teacher	C05/2023			CQ	2013
Wilson Lindsey R Kinstler	(650)207-1170 lwilson1221@gmail.com	5920 Silkwood Way Granite Bay CA 95746	CNH	Teacher	C09/2022			CQ	2013
Wilson Mackensi J	(231)287-3106 mackensiwilson@gmail.com	3682 Karen Parkway Apt 201 Waterford MI 48328	EN	Teacher	Tchr	Our Savior Hartland MI	(248)887-3836	AA	2024
Wilson Rebecca A Steffens	(314)550-0147 bawilson96@me.com	10911 Rustic Creek Dr Bakersfield CA 93312	CNH	Teacher	C08/2017			CQ	2012
Wilson Sara Denninger	(571)217-4678 sarawilson613@gmail.com	7978 Revenna Ln Springfield VA 22153	SE	Teacher	C07/2016			CH	2010
Wilson Steven R	(231)287-4432 wilsos@live.com	5134 Saint Richard Dr Shelby Twp MI 48316	EN	DCE		English District Farmington MI	(248)476-0039	CQ	2007
Wilson Thomas J	(515)890-9058 dcezionhumboldt@gmail.com	609 13th Ave South Humboldt IA 50548	IW	DCE	Mem C	Zion Humboldt IA	(515)332-3279	S	2018
Wilson Fluegge Marie E	(314)740-7868 marieme@gmail.com	7817 Benmore St Saint Louis MO 63123	MO	Teacher	Tchr	St John Arnold MO	(636)464-7303	CQ	2023
Wilt John T	(832)440-0660 J602TW@yahoo.com	4828 Lj Pkwy Apt 330 Sugar Land TX 77479	TX	Teacher	EM			CQ	1994
Wilt Mark B	(724)352-2747 mwilt@stlukecabot.org	31 Boston Ln Palm Coast FL 32137	EA	Teacher	EM			BR	1975
Wiltse Matthew W	(702)503-0421	1000 Twin Ridge Rd Lincoln NE 68510	NEB	Teacher	Tchr	Messiah Lincoln NE	(402)489-3024	CQ	2003
Wimberley Linda H Hegwer	(713)851-1221 lwimbels@gmail.com	16129 Crawford St Jersey Vlg TX 77040	TX	Teacher	EM			AU	1996
Wimmer Kimberly D Lyskawa	(262)227-6709 kim.lyskawa@gmail.com	8418 Linden Ridge Rd Allenton WI 53002	SW	Teacher	Tchr	LHS Assn of Greater Milwaukee West Allis WI	(414)421-9100	MQ	2012
Winegarden Alan D Dr	(651)295-0575 alan.winegarden@gmail.com	352 Chatham Ct Nekoosa WI 54457	MNS	DCE	EM			S	1979
Wingert Angela S Harstad	(507)273-5453 angelawingert@icloud.com	3027 N. Woods St. Orange CA 92865	PSW	Teacher	Tchr	Orange County Orange CA	(714)998-5151	S	2013
Wingert Matthew J	(714)222-7250 mjwingert@icloud.com	3027 N Woods St Orange CA 92865	PSW	DCE	S HS/C	Concordia University Irvine Irvine CA	(949)854-8002	AU	2017
Wingfield Nathan M	(414)795-0314 nathanm.wingfield@gmail.com	1229 Maxine Drive Fort Wayne IN 46807	IN	Teacher	D Ex/S	Indiana District Fort Wayne IN	(800)837-1145	CQ	2018
Winiger Kristin L Johann	(812)455-3036 jojohann@hotmail.com	10650 Old State Rd Evansville IN 47711	IN	Teacher	Tchr	Evansville Evansville IN	(812)424-7252	S	1997
Winkelman Amanda R	(217)720-7963 amandawink@msn.com	1396 Pinecone Cir Mayer MN 55360	MNS	DCE	Tchr	Trinity Waconia MN	(952)442-4165	RF	2003
Winkelman Steven R			TX	Teacher	S Miss	Office of International Mission Saint Louis MO		AU	1993
Winkelman Summer L Schmidt	(618)580-0636 summerschmidt27@gmail.com	205 Wagon Wheel Trl Georgetown TX 78628	TX	Teacher	Tchr	Zion Georgetown TX	(512)863-5345	AU	2022
Winkelman Suzan H Paskett	(512)771-2328 suzan.winkelman@gmail.com	802 W 10th St Georgetown TX 78626	TX	Teacher	Prin	Zion Georgetown TX	(512)863-5345	AU	1988
Winkelman Tristan M	(512)887-0211 tristan.winkelman@ctz.edu	205 Wagon Wheel Trl Georgetown TX 78628	TX	Teacher	Tchr	Concordia Pflugerville TX	(512)248-2547	AU	2021
Winkelmann Jennifer L Harder	(262) 853-3255 jwinkelmann@ gracemenomoneefalls.org	3973 Windemere Dr Colgate WI 53017	SW	Teacher	Tchr	Grace Menomonee Falls WI	(262)251-7140	MQ	2005
Winkelmann Kristine M Tuscany	(608) 697-1191 kwinkelmann@stjohnsportage.com	579 E Slifer St Portage WI 53901	SW	Teacher	Tchr	St Johns Portage WI	(608)742-9000	RF	1988
Winkler Karl	(254)721-6166 kwinkler@tlctyler.org	15719 Brittain Ct Lindale TX 75771	TX	DCE	Mem C	Trinity Tyler TX	(903)593-1526	AU	2007
Winkler Kayla C Cowan	(254)228-7252 kaymc84@gmail.com	6901 Fm 972 Bartlett TX 76511	TX	DCE	Tchr	Concordia Pflugerville TX	(512)248-2547	AU	2006
Winningham Carolyn R Guengerich	(217)313-0220 winninghamfam@gmail.com	3836 Highway E Perryville MO 63775	SI	Teacher	C08/2019			MQ	2005
Winningham Patrick A	(317)376-2216 pwinningham@gmail.com	2175 4th St Bay City MI 48708	MI	Teacher	Tchr	Valley Saginaw MI	(989)790-1676	AA	2002
Winscher Susan A Jaggi	(909)240-4814 suewinscher2000@yahoo.com	100 Pont Julienn Ct Edmond OK 73034	PSW	Teacher	EM			CQ	2009
Winsemann Kristen M Manck	(260)402-0897 kriswin29@gmail.com	11527 Tall Oak Run Fort Wayne IN 46845	IN	Teacher	C07/2023			CH	2008
Winston Valerie J	(313)610-7941 valeriejwinston@mac.com	4594 15 Mile Rd Apt 201 Sterling Heights MI 48310	MI	Teacher	Tchr	St Peters Eastpointe MI	(586)777-6300	RF	1984

*Multiple Assignments (See Church Worker Locator for Additional Details)

See Page 53 for the Table of Abbreviations for key to District, Classification, Position, and College abbreviations.

**C =Candidate; EM =Emeritus; the date following the C is the month and year the Candidate status began

NAME	TELEPHONE NUMBER EMAIL	STREET ADDRESS CITY/STATE/ZIP	DISTRICT	CLASS.	POSITION/ STATUS**	WHERE SERVING	OFFICE PHONE	COLLEGE/ UNIV/CQ	YR GRAD
Winter Catherine Grandt	(901)848-5959 cathwinter@hotmail.com	6398 Trafalgar Rd Memphis TN 38134	MDS	Teacher	EM			RF	1971
Winter Elizabeth A Turanski	(989)295-0055 winterbess@gmail.com	4055 Barnard Rd Saginaw MI 48603	MI	Teacher	Tchr	Valley Saginaw MI	(989)790-1676	AA	1995
Winter Ellis A	(901)386-0389 ellis_winter@yahoo.com	6398 Trafalgar Rd Memphis TN 38134	MDS	Teacher	EM			RF	1971
Winter Erin R	(636)399-5529 ewinter24@hotmail.com	12021 Bel Air Rd Apt B Kingsville MD 21087	SE	Teacher	Tchr	St Pauls Kingsville MD	(410)592-8100	CQ	2006
Winter Frank E IV	(402)992-7493 frank4winter@gmail.com	2246 N 128 Cir Omaha NE 68164	NEB	Teacher	Tchr	Concordia Omaha NE	(402)445-4000	CQ	2019
Winter Heather J Strong	(920)254-0440 hdwinter02@gmail.com	3615 S 17th Street Sheboygan WI 53081	SW	Teacher	Tchr	St Paul Sheboygan WI	(920)452-6882	MQ	2001
Winter Peggy J	(952)200-2711 winterflakes16@gmail.com	13505 485th Ave Parkers Pr MN 56361	MNN	Teacher	EM			SP	1974
Winter Stacy A Sundell	(612)714-3835 mswin2@comcast.net	1464 Parkwood Dr Woodbury MN 55125	MNS	DCE	C07/2016			SP	1987
Winterroth Pamela J Westra	pjwinterroth@sbcglobal.net	778 Lenox Ave Bolingbrook IL 60490	NI	Teacher	Tchr	Trinity Burr Ridge IL	(708)839-1444	RF	1996
Winterstein George R	(253)840-1790 dickwinterstein@gmail.com	6719 96th St E Puyallup WA 98371	NOW	Teacher	EM			RF	1962
Winterstein Jill N Topham	(810)569-0015 jilltopham@gmail.com	315 N Haas St Frankenmuth MI 48734	MI	Teacher	Tchr	St Lorenz Frankenmuth MI	(989)652-6141	AA	2013
Winterstein Katherine A Hudnall	(480)862-0734 googkatie@gmail.com	6629 S Solar Ave Boise ID 83709	NOW	Teacher	C07/2016			MQ	2012
Winterstein Thomas J	(517)304-4484 twinterstein@stlorenz.org	315 N Haas St. Frankenmuth MI 48734	MI	DPM	Mem C	St Lorenz Frankenmuth MI	(989)652-6141	CQ	2021
Wippich David D	(219)608-0508 whipit58@hotmail.com	221 Farmwood Ln La Porte IN 46350	IN	Teacher	EM			SP	1980
Wippich Sarah J Schildwachter	(651)402-2269 dswippich@yahoo.com	3860 Scheuneman Rd Saint Paul MN 55110	MNS	Teacher	Prin	Trinity First Minneapolis MN	(612)871-2353	MQ	1987
Wirsing Angela F Fulbright	(309)533-9220 afwirsing@gmail.com	2014 Lake Bluff Rd Bloomington IL 61704	CI	DPM	Mem C	Trinity Bloomington IL	(309)828-6265	CQ	2019
Wischmeier Henry A	(812)376-6899 henrywischmeier@att.net	5550 E 275 S Columbus IN 47201	IN	Teacher	EM			RF	1966
Wischmeyer Donald H	(636)385-6214 donwisch63@gmail.com	110 Grenache Ct O Fallon MO 63368	MO	Tch/DCE	EM			RF	1963
Wiseman Levi C	(402)300-1189	69834 Hidden Valley Ln Cove OR 97824	NOW	Teacher	C12/2017			S	2012
Wisneski Amy L Miesner	(816)390-2059 amywisneski@splcc.org	3409 Duncan St Saint Joseph MO 64507	MO	Teacher	Tchr	St Paul Saint Joseph MO	(816)279-1118	S	2002
Wisneski Jean M Beehler	(515)971-1063 gnjwisneski456@gmail.com	N6141 Alpine Road Sheboygan Falls WI 53085	SW	Teacher	EM			SP	1965
Wisnieski Rebecca R Rosso	(734)347-6783 horsegirl44@hotmail.com	2118 Scio Rd Dexter MI 48130	MI	Teacher	EM			CQ	2007
Wisniewski Brady R	(715)470-2735 bwisniewski@stpaulequips.com	1926 Center St Stevens Point WI 54481	NW	Teacher	Tchr	St Paul Stevens Point WI	(715)344-5660	MQ	2021
Wissmueller Adam L	(414)659-7770 adam.wissmueller@gmail.com	4440 Coral Dr Brookfield WI 53045	SW	Teacher	Tchr	Milwaukee LHS Milwaukee WI	(414)461-6000	MQ	2006
Wissner Larry O	(214)551-8102 larrywissner6@gmail.com	3351 Virginia Pkwy #4202 McKinney TX 75202	TX	Teacher	EM			S	1969
Witchger Ann G Gerstacker	(989)274-7760 sajcmw@sbcglobal.net	1190 N Frost Dr Saginaw MI 48638	MI	Teacher	EM			CQ	2002
Witek Cheryl A Cicona	(414)554-6626	4634 Edgewater Dr Mt Pleasant WI 53403	SW	Teacher	Tchr	St John Racine WI	(262)633-2758	CQ	2010
Withee Jane M Krohn	(970)309-7957 janewitheel@gmail.com	3260 N 12th St Apt 221 Grand Junction CO 81506	SD	Teacher	EM			S	1978
Withee Roxanne J Hinrichs	(605)786-4237 roxi.withee@gmail.com	3230 Dover St Rapid City SD 57702	SD	Teacher	EM			S	1977
Witt Joel J	(507)412-0821 jwitt6719@gmail.com	13235 W 70th St Juniata NE 68955	NEB	Teacher	Prin	Christ Juniata NE	(402)744-4991	S	1993
Witt Steven C Dr	(262)573-2740 steven.witt@cuw.edu	4714 County Road Kw Prt Washingtn WI 53074	SW	Teacher	S HS/C	Concordia University Wisconsin Mequon WI	(262)243-5700	IV	2006
Witt Sylvia E White Deac	(313)333-1053 sew0146@gmail.com	1001 E Cold Spring Ln Baltimore MD 21212	SE	Deaconess	C11/2019			SL-DEAC	2013
Wittcop Ernest J	(863)324-4762 jeffwittcop@msn.com	2553 Partridge Dr Winter Haven FL 33884	FG	Teacher	Mem C	Grace Winter Haven FL	(863)293-8447	RF	1976
Wittcop Jessica	(615)691-3867 jlwittcop@gmail.com	2715 Rutledge Ct Winter Haven FL 33884	FG	Teacher	Tchr	Grace Winter Haven FL	(863)293-9744	MQ	2006
Wittcop Patricia A Svorec	(863)325-6477 pwittcop@glwh.org	2553 Partridge Dr Winter Haven FL 33884	FG	Teacher	Tchr	Grace Winter Haven FL	(863)293-8447	RF	1977
Witte Dennis E Dr	(708)846-8300 witte@cuchicago.edu	223 Callaway Dr Monroe MI 48162	MI	Teacher	EM			RF	1973
Witte Kenneth L	(414)719-7011 kenwittel@hotmail.com	1369 E Hawthorne Dr Fredonia WI 53021	SW	Teacher	EM			RF	1977
Witte Lucie E Stelter	witte.lucie@yahoo.com	80 Waterford Blvd Fairborn OH 45324	MI	Teacher	EM			RF	1972
Witte Megan R Abbott	(501)366-5319 megan.witte@gmail.com	63 Belle Meadow Ln Little Rock AR 72210	MDS	Teacher	Tchr	Christ Little Rock AR	(501)663-5232	RF	2006
Wittig David L	(808) 728-9488 ddub808@gmail.com	8504 Berkley Hall St Las Vegas NV 89131	PSW	Teacher	EM			S	1980
Wittig Evelyn D Sell	(989)781-9067 wittigevelyn@gmail.com	2825 Wieneke Rd Apt 75 Saginaw MI 48603	MI	Teacher	EM			RF	1967
Wittig Marsha J Rau	(808)235-9488 mdub808@gmail.com	8504 Berkley Hall St Las Vegas NV 89131	PSW	Teacher	EM			S	1979

*Multiple Assignments (See Church Worker Locator for Additional Details)
See Page 53 for the Table of Abbreviations for key to District, Classification, Position, and College abbreviations.
**C =Candidate; EM =Emeritus; the date following the C is the month and year the Candidate status began

NAME	TELEPHONE NUMBER EMAIL	STREET ADDRESS CITY/STATE/ZIP	DISTRICT	CLASS.	POSITION/ STATUS**	WHERE SERVING	OFFICE PHONE	COLLEGE/ UNIV/CQ	YR GRAD
Wittler Ronald T	(713)562-3460 rwittler@lncrusaders.org	26 Tamma Ln Hazelwood MO 63042	MO	Teacher	Tchr	Lutheran North Saint Louis MO	(314)389-3100	S	1993
Wittman Anthony A	(847)894-6501 awitty12345@gmail.com	147 Kings Creek Dr Bluffton SC 29909	IN	Teacher	EM			RF	1985
Wittmann Roger A	(618)344-9454 rogerwittmann@hotmail.com	5878 Sugar Loaf Rd Collinsville IL 62234	SI	Teacher	EM			RF	1968
Witto Gregory P	(217)259-2936 gregwitto1@gmail.com	c/o Christ Our King Lutheran Church 3255 Saline Waterworks Rd Saline MI 48176	MI	Parish Assist/ DFLM	Mem C	Christ Our King Saline MI	(734)429-9200	AA	1994
Witto Katherine I	(636)233-4176 kwitto@lutheranfamily.org	1331 N Grant Ave Indianapolis IN 46201	IN	Teacher	Mem C	Cornerstone Carmel IN	(317)814-4252	RF	1990
Wittrock John H	(248)647-7142 jhwittrock@ameritech.net	1599 Bowers St Birmingham MI 48009	MI	Teacher	EM			S	1965
Wittrock Yvonne K Lemke	(208)380-9770 ywittrock@gmail.com	4200 Angelica Trl Johnstown CO 80534	RM	Teacher	EM			SP	1976
Wo Michelle A Seibert	(773)842-4054 kdgnfun@comcast.net	2850 W Farragut Ave #2 Chicago IL 60625	NI	Teacher	Tchr	St John Chicago IL	(773)736-1196	RF	1993
Woebke Kimberly S Helm	(612)384-2245 woebkekim@gmail.com	10009 Goodrich Rd Bloomington MN 55437	MNS	Teacher	Tchr	Trinity Waconia MN	(952)442-4165	SP	1989
Woelfel Emily M	(920)268-7773 em_woelfel@hotmail.com	140 Linden Lane #4 Thienville WI 53092	SW	Teacher	Tchr	Trinity Mequon WI	(262)242-2045	MQ	2006
Woelfel Laura E Doell	(715)853-6220 doelllaura7@gmail.com	89 Torrey St Clintonville WI 54929	NW	Teacher	Tchr	St Martin Clintonville WI	(715)823-6538	MQ	2018
Wolbert Janet A	(407)595-3676 janet.wolbert@cuchicago.edu	2826 Regal Ln Oviedo FL 32765	NI	Teacher	S HS/C	Concordia University Chicago River Forest IL	(708)771-8300	RF	1996
Wolf Alexa	(585)629-8296 alexawolf@stpaulhilton.org	17192 Roosevelt Hwy Kendall NY 14476	EA	Teacher	Tchr	St Paul Hilton NY	(585)392-4000	CQ	2023
Wolf Charles H	(586)876-4100	135 S Christine Cir Mount Clemens MI 48043	MI	Teacher	EM			RF	1975
Wolf Jennifer R Jaeger	(414) 916-8942 jennyrwolf@yahoo.com	1156 Auburn Rd West Bend WI 53090	SW	Teacher	EM			CQ	1988
Wolf Lisa J Seider	(414)588-8140 lwolf@immanuelbrookfield.org	W144N7074 Terrace Dr Menomonee Fls WI 53051	SW	Teacher	Tchr	Immanuel Brookfield WI	(262)781-7140	MQ	1985
Wolf Melissa L Altevogt	(660)679-1015 5487mwof@gmail.com	208 E Illinois St Highland KS 66035	KS	Teacher	Tchr	Trinity Atchison KS	(913)367-4763	RF	1986
Wolf Michelle P Pozdol	(630)269-2214 mwolf72@yahoo.com	250 W Maple Ave Roselle IL 60172	NI	Teacher	Tchr	Trinity Roselle IL	(630)894-3263	RF	1994
Wolf Miriam A	(314)704-7729 miriamwolf290@gmail.com	2103 Dalton Dr Apt A Jefferson City MO 65109	MO	Teacher	Tchr	Trinity Jefferson City MO	(573)636-7807	S	2022
Wolf Robert J	(623)824-1051 fbcoach61@hotmail.com	573 Lakewood Dr S Saint Paul MN 55119	MNS	Teacher	Tchr	Concordia Academy Roseville MN	(651)484-8429	SP	1994
Wolf Tara L Rooney	(970)999-8657 tara@redeemerconnect.com	5851 Dripping Rock Ln Unit B-104 Fort Collins CO 80528	RM	DCE	Mem C	Redeemer Fort Collins CO	(970)225-9020	IV	2003
Wolfanger Mildred Sunderman	(630)893-5383 heartwmr@aol.com	6n534 Glendale Rd Medinah IL 60157	NI	Teacher	EM			S	1954
Wolfe Emily C Gau	(586)242-4740 emily.gau@gmail.com	35747 Parklawn Ct Round Hill VA 20141	SE	DFLM	C07/2016			AA	2009
Wolfe Michelle D Chunn	(503)545-7704 mchunn1@hotmail.com	414 West St Frohna MO 63748	MO	Teacher	Tchr	United in Christ Frohna MO	(573)824-5218	S	2002
Wolfe Morgan T Brandt	(920)254-6042 wolfe.morgant@gmail.com	2111 Creekside Ct Sheboygan WI 53081	SW	Teacher	Tchr	Divine Redeemer Hartland WI	(262)367-3664	MQ	2016
Wolfe Shaunna L Reynolds	(303)505-0289 swolfe@zionbrighton.org	10180 Truckee Way Commerce City CO 80022	RM	Teacher	Tchr	Zion Brighton CO	(303)659-3443	S	1995
Wolfe Thomas	(402)564-6330	3914 25th St Apt 18 Columbus NE 68601	NEB	Teacher	EM			S	1969
Wolff Garry F	(618)483-5877	5108 N 600th St Mason IL 62443	CI	Teacher	EM			RF	1963
Wolff Jennifer Foster	(414)365-1206 jennywolff81@yahoo.com	N58W23426 Aster Dr Sussex WI 53089	SW	Teacher	Prin	Beautiful Savior Waukesha WI	(262)542-2496	MQ	2003
Wolff Sara M Pietrangelo	(414)719-0969 wolff.sara@yahoo.com	8520 N 66th St Brown Deer WI 53223	SW	Teacher	Tchr	St Johns Glendale WI	(414)352-4150	MQ	1999
Wolff Stephanie F Frederick	(812)376-3227 swolff@stpeters-columbus.org	13420 E 200 S Columbus IN 47203	IN	Teacher	Tchr	St Peter Columbus IN	(812)372-5266	RF	2002
Wolfgram Barbara R Hentz	(440)638-9302 bwavon121@hotmail.com	1440 Pamela Ln La Habra CA 90631	PSW	Teacher	EM			SP	1983
Wolfgram Dale A	(440)360-0637 dwlalhs@gmail.com	1440 Pamela Ln La Habra CA 90631	PSW	Teacher	EM			S	1975
Wolfgram Dane E	(701)400-5044 dane.wolfgram@cune.org	2228 January Ave Saint Louis MO 63110	MO	DCE	Mem C	Abiding Savior Saint Louis MO	(314)894-9200	S	2022
Wolfgram Grace E	(701)400-5071 grace.wolfgram@cune.org	949 East Central Avenue Apt 5 Bismarck ND 58501	ND	DCE	C05/2024			S	2023
Wolfinbarger Mary K Doyle	(949)264-6889 mwolfy@att.net	21156 Prairie View Ln Trabuco Cyn CA 92679	PSW	Teacher	D Ex/S	Pacific Southwest District Irvine CA	(949)854-3232	CQ	2011
Wolfram Mark	(314)556-7589 markjwolfram@gmail.com	719 Westglen Village Dr Ballwin MO 63021	MO	Teacher	S Ex/S	The LCMS Corporate Saint Louis MO	(314)965-9000	IV	2013
Wolfram Tim	(865)522-0951 timwolfram@bellsouth.net	1104 Glenmora Grove Way Knoxville TN 37923	SO	Teacher	EM			SP	1971
Wolfram William R I	(402)643-2535 wwolfram@windstream.net	1036 Sunrise Dr Seward NE 68434	NEB	Teacher	EM			CQ	1959
Wolgast Gregg A	(316) 285-4400 gwolgast@hcwichita.net	2752 N Beacon Hill Ct Wichita KS 67220	KS	Teacher	Tchr	Holy Cross Wichita KS	(316)684-4431	S	2014
Wolkenhauer Kimberly Deac	(509)475-1659 kimcoramdeo@gmail.com	12909e San Juan Ln Spokane WA 99206	NOW	Deaconess	Mem C	Hope Spokane Valley WA	(509)924-1630	FW-DEAC	2020
Wollberg Barbara L Vogts	(816)468-5295 bwollberg@gmail.com	301 NW 80th St Kansas City MO 64118	MO	Teacher	EM			S	1974

*Multiple Assignments (See Church Worker Locator for Additional Details)
See Page 53 for the Table of Abbreviations for key to District, Classification, Position, and College abbreviations.
**C =Candidate; EM =Emeritus; the date following the C is the month and year the Candidate status began

NAME	TELEPHONE NUMBER EMAIL	STREET ADDRESS CITY/STATE/ZIP	DISTRICT	CLASS.	POSITION/ STATUS**	WHERE SERVING	OFFICE PHONE	COLLEGE/ UNIV/CQ	YR GRAD
Wollenberg Katherine E Cox	(314)910-7793 katie.wollenberg@gmail.com	191 N Main St Hoyleton IL 62803	SI	Teacher	Tchr	Christ Our Rock Centralia IL	(618)226-3315	MQ	2009
Wollenburg Jerry L Witt	(618)222-6899 jerwoll@charter.net	2340 Fourlakes Dr Belleville IL 62220	SI	Teacher	EM			RF	1979
Woller Robert W	(414)796-1227 kwollerbslc@gmail.com	3145 S Thornapple Ln New Berlin WI 53146	SW	Teacher	EM			CQ	1987
Wollin Kenneth E		260 Prairie Ln Forsyth IL 62535	SI	Teacher	EM			Other	1965
Wollman Cynthia K Schroeder	(410)569-9237 cindywol@verizon.net	1004 Old Joppa Rd # A Joppa MD 21085	SE	Teacher	EM			S	1976
Wollman Gayle J Thaete	(208)989-4869 gwollmanzls@gmail.com	1104 11th St S Nampa ID 83651	NOW	Teacher	EM			PO	1984
Wolske Clee K	(402)368-5966 wolskeclee@gmail.com	83830 Highway 45 Tilden NE 68781	NEB	Teacher	EM			S	1973
Wolske Monique A Schlecht	(402)368-5966 mawolske0@gmail.com	83830 Highway 45 Tilden NE 68781	NEB	Teacher	EM			S	1973
Wolter Anthony V	(989)395-5812 anthonywolter12@gmail.com	3344 Binscarth Ave Saginaw MI 48602	MI	Teacher	Tchr	St Peter Hemlock MI	(989)642-8188	S	2020
Wolter Cynthia K Schultz	(507)893-4523	1911 270th Ave Granada MN 56039	MNS	Teacher	Tchr	St James Northrop MN	(507)436-5289	S	1992
Wolter Roger W	(989)751-2381 roger.wolter@hcls.org	3344 Binscarth Ave Saginaw MI 48602	MI	Teacher	P/Tchr	Holy Cross Saginaw MI	(989)793-9723	S	2000
Wolters Ann E	(660)463-7382 woltersann5siblings@gmail.com	205 S Sunset Hills Dr Apt 222 Concordia MO 64020	MO	Teacher	EM			S	1964
Woltmann Corinne R Timmerman	(507)456-5380 yacminister@gmail.com	1004 Nord St Norfolk NE 68701	NEB	DCE	Mem C	Christ Norfolk NE	(402)371-1210	S	2009
Woltmann Ruth M Hausch	(218)343-6528 picyouthministry@gmail.com	7315 168th Circle NW Ramsey MN 55303	MNS	DCE	Mem C	Family Christ Ham Lake MN	(763)434-7337	S	2007
Wombold Dawn L Bauermeister-Fendrick	dawnwombold@gmail.com	1601 Mount Rushmore Rd # 3-114 Rapid City SD 57701	SD	Teacher	C07/2016			S	1997
Wondrasch Brittany A Sell	brittany.wondrasch@gmail.com	4110 Wenzel Ln St. Louis MO 63129	MO	Teacher	C07/2024			MQ	2016
Wong Ashley Y	(415)866-3861 ashleywong1917@yahoo.com	2400 Noriega St San Francisco CA 94122	CNH	DCE	Mem C	Holy Spirit San Francisco CA	(415)661-1120	IV	2011
Wong Christine A Irwin	(417)576-8979 christine.wong12@yahoo.com	4943 S Tanager Ave Battlefield MO 65619	MO	Teacher	Tchr	Redeemer Springfield MO	(417)883-5717	SP	2001
Wong Paula H Stadelman	(412)230-6380 pstadelman@yahoo.com	411 Monroeville Ave Turtle Creek PA 15145	EA	Teacher	C03/2021			RF	2000
Woock Dale D	(847)650-9488 dale.woock@gmail.com	1133 Clover Hill Ln Elgin IL 60120	NI	Teacher	Mem C	Saint John's Elgin IL	(847)741-0814	SP	1980
Woock Emily	(847)650-9181 emily.woock@gmail.com	1133 Clover Hill Ln Elgin IL 60120	NI	DPM	S HS/C	Concordia University Chicago River Forest IL	(708)771-8300	CH	2008
Wood Amanda L White	(512)214-7339 amandaw@fastmail.com	1824 Holling Dr Omaha NE 68144	NEB	DCE	C09/2025			AU	2012
Wood Bethany H Mattil	(623)225-5526 scottandbethanywood@gmail.com	1409 Nutmeg Ct Fort Worth TX 76131	PSW	DCE	C07/2016			AU	2006
Wood Christopher M	(636)395-3394 cwood@zionharvester.org		MO	DCE	Mem C	Zion Saint Charles MO	(636)441-7425	IV	2024
Wood Christy L Silveria	(415)265-4411 wooste@comcast.net	3956 Dunhill St Napa CA 94558	CNH	Teacher	Prin	St John's Napa CA	(707)255-0119	IV	1997
Wood Dale F	(414)353-5086	11917 W Appleton Ave Unit 6 Milwaukee WI 53224	SW	DCM	EM			MQ	1985
Wood Ellen L Bellinger	ewood@abidingsavior.com	54 Via Madera Rcho Sta Marg CA 92688	PSW	Teacher	Tchr	Abiding Savior Lake Forest CA	(949)830-1461	CQ	1995
Wood Janice M	(734)752-1809 jwjanicewood@gmail.com	27961 Southpointe Rd Grosse Ile MI 48138	MI	Teacher	EM			AA	1985
Wood Rachael A Hartmann	(260)705-1195	8937 Nautical Way New Haven IN 46774	IN	Teacher	C07/2020			RF	2011
Woodall Emily M Kollbaum	(660)238-4755 emily.kollbaum@cune.org		NEB	Teacher	Tchr	Northeast Norfolk NE	(402)379-3040	S	2017
Woodley Jacqueline F Demmin	(716)205-8703 woodley8286@yahoo.com	2526 Stoelting St Niagara Falls NY 14304	EA	Teacher	Tchr	Holy Ghost Bergholtz NY	(716)731-3030	BR	1977
Woods Amy B Bobzin	(660)641-1069 amywoods@splsconcordia.org	506 S Faculty Ln Concordia MO 64020	MO	Teacher	Tchr	St Paul Concordia MO	(660)463-2291	S	1995
Woods Carol D Frisch	(310)532-9847 carol4asc@earthlink.net	15612 Ruthelen St Gardena CA 90249	PSW	Teacher	EM			CQ	2001
Woods Donna M Callahan	(775) 309-8449 dwoods719@gmail.com	944 Springfield Dr Gardnerville NV 89460	CNH	Teacher	EM			CQ	2007
Woods Lydia N	(402)917-7112 lydianoelwoods@gmail.com	17506 Cinnamon St Omaha NE 68135	NEB	DCE	Mem C	Lord Of Life Elkhorn NE	(402)289-3437	IV	2022
Woodward Melissa	(763)516-7490 mwoodward@trinitylcs.org	2712 N 153rd Dr Goodyear AZ 85395	PSW	Teacher	Tchr	Trinity Litchfield Park AZ	(623)935-4690	SP	2008
Wooldridge Ashley L Moerbe	(979)249-7567 ashleymoerbe@gmail.com	11726 Winthrop River Trl Richmond TX 77406	TX	Teacher	Tchr	Westlake Lutheran Richmond TX	(281)341-9910	AU	2011
Woolery Pamela J Heitmann	(319)486-2311 pamela.woolery@gmail.com	619 Stephan Ave Waterloo IA 50701	IE	Teacher	C07/2016			S	2003
Woolery Stephen J	(319)486-2380 stephenwoolery81@gmail.com	619 Stephan Ave Waterloo IA 50701	IE	Teacher	Tchr	Valley Cedar Falls IA	(319)266-4565	S	2003
Woolley Annette M	(425)293-4132 gaetha@hotmail.com	17909 Trombley Rd Snohomish WA 98290	NOW	Teacher	C07/2021			CQ	2018
Wooster Larry D Dr	(661)992-0487 ldwooster@gmail.com	508 East Third St Saint Peter IL 62880	CI	Teacher	Prin	St Peter Saint Peter IL	(618)349-8321	S	1982
Worden Shelly A Stresman	(916)835-1808 shelly.worden@icloud.com	4209 Oslo Ct Antelope CA 95843	CNH	Teacher	C07/2019			S	1981

*Multiple Assignments (See Church Worker Locator for Additional Details)

See Page 53 for the Table of Abbreviations for key to District, Classification, Position, and College abbreviations.

**C =Candidate; EM =Emeritus; the date following the C is the month and year the Candidate status began

NAME	TELEPHONE NUMBER EMAIL	STREET ADDRESS CITY/STATE/ZIP	DISTRICT	CLASS.	POSITION/ STATUS**	WHERE SERVING	OFFICE PHONE	COLLEGE/ UNIV/CQ	YR GRAD
Worm Maralyse K Bedroske	(920)379-4380 maralyse.bedroske@gmail.com	48911 County Road 380 Grand Junction MI 49056	MI	Teacher	Tchr	St Michael Portage MI	(269)327-7832	CH	2015
Wormington Dana M Berg	(417)737-1012 dana_berg87@hotmail.com	7952 Lawrence 2150 Mount Vernon MO 65712	MO	Teacher	Tchr	Trinity Freistatt MO	(417)235-5931	CQ	2011
Worral Carolyn R Trittin	carolynworral@gmail.com	2814 Hickory St N Fargo ND 58102	ND	Teacher	Tchr	Grace Fargo ND	(701)232-1516	SP	1986
Worral Hannah E Davis	(763)498-9534 hannah.davis@cune.org	978 York Ct Brainerd MN 56401	MNN	Teacher	C06/2020			S	2019
Worthing Brianna	(512)402-4514 brianna.worthing@ctx.edu	382 N Grimes St Giddings TX 78942	TX	Teacher	Tchr	St Mark Houston TX	(713)468-2623	AU	2015
Worthington Tamara S Avery	(770)362-8848 tamieworthington@gmail.com	140 Annabelle Ln Tyrone GA 30290	FG	Teacher	C07/2016			CQ	2002
Wottrich Sharon L Vogel	(294)694-8620 swottrich@aol.com	294 Thousand Oaks Dr P.O. Box 365 Whitney TX 76692	TX	Tch/DCE	EM			CQ	1986
Wrase William R	(313)244-1917	189 Lake Huron Dr Mulberry FL 33860	MI	Teacher	EM			S	1969
Wrege Thomas W Dr	(586)381-2738 twrege@sbcglobal.net	1327 Ascot St Georgetown TX 78626	TX	Teacher	C08/2024			S	1985
Wright Alexander T	(224)343-1467 wrightal@csp.edu	1236 Emilie St Green Bay WI 54301	NW	DCE	Mem C	Faith Green Bay WI	(920)435-5524	SP	2015
Wright Bethann C Hall	(260)749-4206 jbwright1@verizon.net	10605 Wadsworth Ct Fort Wayne IN 46845	IN	Teacher	Tchr	Emmanuel-St Michael Fort Wayne IN	(260)422-6712	RF	1995
Wright Blake A	blakewright11@icloud.com	543 Providence Blvd Deltona FL 32725	S	DFLM	Mem C	Holy Cross Lake Mary FL	(407)333-0797	AA	2018
Wright David M	(517)282-4996 dwright@oursaviorlansing.org	326 S Waverly Rd Eaton Rapids MI 48827	MI	DFLM	Mem C	Our Savior Lansing MI	(517)882-8665	CQ	2015
Wright Denise M	(717)757-6707 dwright@blazenet.net	650 S Hampton At Waterford York PA 17402	SE	Teacher	Tchr	St John York PA	(717)840-0382	BR	1979
Wright Janice M Kamtz	(303)791-8614	476 McArthur Dr Lone Tree CO 80124	RM	Teacher	Tchr	Shepherd Hills Centennial CO	(303)798-0711	S	1968
Wright Kate E	(505)264-0337	799 Snyder Mountain Rd Evergreen CO 80439	RM	Teacher	Tchr	Zion Brighton CO	(303)659-2339	S	2004
Wright Kenneth	(619)421-5140 kwwright1@juno.com	991 Rutgers Ave Chula Vista CA 91913	PSW	Teacher	EM			S	1970
Wright Lisa A Dye	(303)506-5471	501 W Medina St Cario NE 68824	NEB	Teacher	C12/2023			CQ	2001
Wright Lucinda M Hahn	(651)335-3517 cindywi785@gmail.com	P.O. Box 243 Almena WI 54805	MNS	Tch/DCE	EM			SP	1976
Wright Ridell M Schneider	(714)582-2627 ridellwright@hotmail.com	932 Newhall Ter Brea CA 92821	PSW	Teacher	EM			CQ	1995
Wright Sarah J Scherer	(402)380-5495 mrssarahjwright@hotmail.com	5620 Dove Circle Lincoln NE 68516	NEB	Teacher	Tchr	Christ Lincoln NE	(402)483-7774	S	2004
Wright Stacy R Stuckwisch	(812)521-7200 stacywright8220@gmail.com	1501 Gaiser Dr Seymour IN 47274	IN	Teacher	Tchr	Zion Seymour IN	(812)522-5911	RF	1994
Wright Steven A	(262)565-7027 swright.tko@gmail.com	19 Woodcrest Way Oxford OH 45056	OH	Teacher	EM			S	1979
Wright Tammie J Calloway	(949)322-9416 tammie_wright1@msn.com	1022 Drava Ln Houston TX 77090	TX	Teacher	Tchr	Our Savior Houston TX	(713)290-9087	IV	2007
Wrobleski Richard E	(989)975-6186 richandvera@gmail.com	628 E Main St Apt 10 Sebewaing MI 48759	MI	Teacher	EM			RF	1961
Wrucke Wesley J	(260)413-3359 weswrucke@gmail.com	2525 Vista View Dr Evansville IN 47711	IN	Teacher	EM			RF	1980
Wrye Karen A Sasser	(503)284-4991 rkwrye@gmail.com	6306 NE 26th Ave Portland OR 97211	NOW	Teacher	EM			RF	1966
Wrye Richard F	(503)284-4991 dickwrye@gmail.com	6306 NE 26th Ave Portland OR 97211	NOW	Teacher	EM			RF	1967
Wu Cheryl L Crabbs	(720)935-6888 cheryl@mtzionboulder.org	3715 Broadway St Boulder CO 80304	RM	Teacher	Prin	Mount Zion Boulder CO	(303)443-8477	S	1985
Wudtke Deborah A Marriott	(618)830-5071 deb@wudtke.net	248 Lakeview Acres Dr Collinsville IL 62234	SI	Teacher	Tchr	Metro-East Edwardsville IL	(618)656-0043	MQ	1991
Wudtke Marie E Haufler	(618)345-0338 marie@wudtke.net	9 Chapel Ct Collinsville IL 62234	SI	Teacher	EM			CQ	1992
Wudtke Sarah E Rethwisch	(515)227-1805 sarahwudtke620@gmail.com	346 Cheval Dr Gallatin TN 37066	MDS	DCE	C05/2020			S	2018
Wudy James R	(260)479-9721 manistee35@yahoo.com	1407 Edenton Dr Fort Wayne IN 46804	IN	Teacher	EM			SP	1971
Wuebbels Richard E Jr	(636)497-2455 warrior.wuebbels@gmail.com	305 Schmidt Dr Wentzville MO 63385	MO	Teacher	Tchr	Immanuel Wentzville MO	(636)639-9887	CQ	2021
Wuestenberg Danna N Soto	(563)221-1678 gdwuestenberg@gmail.com	4022 Cresthill Dr Davenport IA 52806	IE	Teacher	C07/2016			MQ	1997
Wuggazer Heidi L Bierlein	(904)866-1552 heidibierlein@hotmail.com	4516 Mainmast Ln Jacksonville FL 32277	FG	DCE	C07/2016			SP	1999
Wulfkuhle Elizabeth M Prichard	(920)917-0105 elizabeth.prichard14@gmail.com	1031 4th Avenue Grafton WI 53024	SW	Teacher	Tchr	St Paul Grafton WI	(262)377-4659	MQ	2020
Wunderlich Alan W	(636)221-1105 alan.wunderlich@imlutheran.org	2203 NE Greenwich Ct Blue Springs MO 64014	MO	Teacher	EM			RF	1980
Wunderlich Diane L Umland	dwunder1@aol.com	4207 Pinewood Ln Matteson IL 60443	NI	Teacher	EM			CQ	2003
Wunderlich Tyson A	(617)943-7093 tysonwunder@hotmail.com	2863 Alta Cuesta Dr Cpe Girardeau MO 63701	MO	Teacher	C08/2021			CQ	2010
Wurdeman Shaina M Mitchell Deac	(949)285-6388 dcs.smm@gmail.com	6585 Bismark Rd Colorado Spgs CO 80922	RM	Deaconess	C03/2020			FW-DEAC	2008
Wutke Mari Mc Allister	(619)229-8984 mariwutke@gmail.com	7553 Milky Way Pt San Diego CA 92120	PSW	Teacher	EM			CQ	2000

*Multiple Assignments (See Church Worker Locator for Additional Details)
See Page 53 for the Table of Abbreviations for key to District, Classification, Position, and College abbreviations.
**C =Candidate; EM =Emeritus; the date following the C is the month and year the Candidate status began

NAME	TELEPHONE NUMBER EMAIL	STREET ADDRESS CITY/STATE/ZIP	DISTRICT	CLASS.	POSITION/ STATUS**	WHERE SERVING	OFFICE PHONE	COLLEGE/ UNIV/CQ	YR GRAD
Wyatt Quincy E	(217)690-1630 wyatt@lutheranschools.org	336 Telstar Dr Bicmarck ND 58503	ND	Teacher	Tchr	Martin Luther Bismarck ND	(701)224-9070	S	2016
Wycherley Scott P	(715)276-3920 scottdew@centurytel.net	P.O. Box 38 Townsend WI 54175	NW	Tch/DCE	Mem C	St John Townsend WI	(715)276-7214	BR	1978
Wyeth Susan L Unger	(630)643-6540 suewyeth1@att.net	2476 W Downer Pl Aurora IL 60506	NI	Teacher	EM			RF	1983
Wykert Thomas A	(708)408-2789 twykert@yahoo.com	4630 Hawthorne Ave Lyons IL 60534	NI	Teacher	Tchr	St John's Lombard IL	(630)932-3196	RF	1991
Wykert Victoria J Schoenbeck	(708)408-2759 vwykert@sbcglobal.net	4630 Hawthorne Ave Lyons IL 60534	NI	Teacher	C07/2025			RF	1990
Wyman Kelly A Blomstrom	(989)233-3559 kellyanneblomstrom@yahoo.com	1024 Malzahn St Saginaw MI 48602	MI	Teacher	Tchr	St Paul Bay City MI	(989)684-4450	AA	2003
Wyse Lydia Schroeder	(419)591-6506 lschroeder@stpaulnapoleon.org	1075 Glenwood Ave Napoleon OH 43545	OH	Teacher	Tchr	St Paul Napoleon OH	(419)592-5536	AA	2022
Wysocki James E	(815)451-1583 jwysocki79@gmail.com	2200 Spring Brook Ave Rockford IL 61107	NI	Teacher	C07/2020			RF	2001
Wysocki Korey L Meyer	(815)980-8216 korey.wysocki@gmail.com	2200 Spring Brook Ave Rockford IL 61107	NI	DCE	Mem C	Mount Olive Rockford IL	(815)399-3171	RF	2001
Wyss Kristen H Lehman	(260)409-1489 kristen323@hotmail.com	9630 Pinto Ln Fort Wayne IN 46804	IN	Teacher	Tchr	Concordia Fort Wayne IN	(260)422-2429	RF	2002
Wyzard Debra J Davidson	(309)264-0089 dwyzard33@gmail.com	5214 Deerwood Lake Dr Springfield IL 62703	CI	Teacher	EM			RF	1980
Wyzard Kristen M	kwyzard@zionbethalto.org		SI	DCE	Mem C	Zion Bethalto IL	(618)377-8314	RF	2009
Yaeger Margaret A Grauer	(630)852-0971 margybob@comcast.net	1575 Belvidere St Apt 251 El Paso TX 79912	NI	Teacher	EM			RF	1959
Yagow Carmen E		2202 Cormorant Dr Springfield IL 62711	CI	Teacher	Prin	Our Saviors Springfield IL	(217)546-4531	CH	2012
Yagow Daniel P	dyagow.dls@gmail.com	22219 Carltons Dell Rd Danville IL 61834	CI	Teacher	EM			S	1981
Yagow James S	(920)809-4445 jimyagow@aol.com	N3494 Hooyman Ct Freedom WI 54913	NW	Teacher	EM			S	1975
Yagow Lisa M	(630)539-6559 yagowlisa@gmail.com	1171 W Bryn Mawr Ave Roselle IL 60172	NI	Teacher	C07/2016			RF	1999
Yahr Kathyrn H	dwinkkyahr@aol.com		NW	Teacher	EM			CQ	2006
Yakimow Miriam R Sailer Deac	(503)908-2589 miriam@stpaulhamburg.com	6095 Sundance Trail Brighton MI 48116	MI	Deaconess	Mem C	St Paul Hamburg Whitmore Lake MI	(810)231-1033	Other	1994
Yamaguchi Joan P Crow	(720)365-9284 mjpaez2@gmail.com	4082 W Greenwood Pl Denver CO 80235	RM	Teacher	C07/2016			RF	1973
Yamate Amanda Z Iliadis	(773)972-6141 amanda.yamate@gmail.com	6661 N Octavia Ave Chicago IL 60631	NI	Teacher	Tchr	St John Chicago IL	(773)736-1196	RF	2010
Yarrington Edgar J	(757)930-3007 ed.yarrington@gmail.com	616 Burcher Rd Newport News VA 23606	SE	DCM	EM			MQ	2003
Yatckoske Jacob L	(612)708-7323 jyatckoske@gmail.com	3505 Fishers Dr Anoka MN 55303	MNN	Teacher	Tchr	Good Shepherd Lutheran High School Otsego MN	(651)357-6680	CQ	2022
Yee Phyllis Deac	(845)642-6165 phyllis.mc1107@gmail.com	1110 150th St Whitestone NY 11357	AT	Deaconess	Tchr	Martin Luther Maspeth NY	(718)894-4000	FW-DEAC	2017
Yoakum Marilyn J Walde	(641)344-6609 myoak10@gmail.com	41089 291st Ave Russell IA 50238	IW	Teacher	EM			S	1961
Yochum Lawrence H III	(636)212-5322 lyochum3@gmail.com	2036 San Angelo Dr Arnold MO 63010	MO	DCE	Mem C	St Johns Arnold MO	(636)464-0096	RF	2003
Yocius Sarah M Watts	(630)207-4050 sarah.yocius@gmail.com	2313 Massachusetts Ave Naperville IL 60565	NI	Teacher	C01/2018			CQ	2013
Yoder Jennifer A Gremel	(989)529-8608 yoderj@ctkl.org	6415 Center St Unionville MI 48767	MI	Teacher	P/Tchr	Christ The King Sebewaing MI	(989)883-3730	CQ	2013
Yoder Marian R Schrupp	(419)782-1281 nap_npub_my@nwoca.org	2170 Hawthorne Dr Defiance OH 43512	OH	Teacher	EM			SP	1969
Yohannes Saron Woldehaimanot Deac	(240)205-6629 Saronyo12@gmail.com	6000 Denton Ct Springfield VA 22152	SE	Deaconess	Mem C	Our Savior Arlington VA	(703)892-4846	SL-DEAC	2011
Yost Janice Kirner Stone	(949)701-7625 janicejyost@yahoo.com	23955 Raleigh St Lake Forest CA 92630	PSW	DCE	EM			S	1977
Youmans Christy A Lemon	(512)293-0201 christyyoumans@yahoo.com	4049 Canyon Glen Cir Austin TX 78732	PSW	Teacher	C07/2016			IV	1998
Youmans Jacob L Dr	(512)284-2129 jacob.youmans@concordia.edu	4049 Canyon Glen Cir Austin TX 78732	TX	DCE	C04/2023			IV	1997
Youmans Kim D	(702)219-0720 sky6grand@gmail.com	7624 Oyster Cove Dr Las Vegas NV 89128	PSW	Tch/DCE	EM			S	1973
Youmans Sandra B Geiger	(702)370-2889 sbgymusic@gmail.com	7624 Oyster Cove Dr Las Vegas NV 89128	PSW	Teacher	EM			S	1973
Young Ann C Marcsisak	(952)467-3792 acyoung56@gmail.com	606 Robert Ave Hamburg MN 55339	MNS	Teacher	EM			SP	1978
Young Brian A	(989)893-2486 bbyoung32@gmail.com	1460 Calmac Ct Bay City MI 48708	MI	Teacher	EM			RF	1967
Young Courtney A Campbell	(989)225-5698 ccyoung1024@gmail.com	539 Summit Dr West Bend WI 53095	SW	Teacher	Tchr	St Johns West Bend WI	(262)334-3077	RF	2009
Young Daniel B	(612)616-2964	606 Robert Ave Hamburg MN 55339	MNS	Teacher	EM			SP	1981
Young Eric A	(224)244-3834 eyoung@saint-paul.org	319 N Elm St Mt Prospect IL 60056	NI	Teacher	Tchr	St Paul Mount Prospect IL	(847)255-6733	RF	1997
Young Heide E Kollmorgen	heide.young@splgrafton.org	423 W Seacroft Ct Mequon WI 53092	SW	DPM	Tchr	St Paul* Grafton WI	(262)377-4659	IV	2012
Young Krista L Adler	(314)745-2381 krista.young@lcms.org	790 Safari Dr Sylvia NC 28977	SE	DCE	S Ex/S	The LCMS Corporate Saint Louis MO	(314)965-9000	SP	1993

*Multiple Assignments (See Church Worker Locator for Additional Details)
See Page 53 for the Table of Abbreviations for key to District, Classification, Position, and College abbreviations.
**C =Candidate; EM =Emeritus; the date following the C is the month and year the Candidate status began

NAME	TELEPHONE NUMBER EMAIL	STREET ADDRESS CITY/STATE/ZIP	DISTRICT	CLASS.	POSITION/ STATUS**	WHERE SERVING	OFFICE PHONE	COLLEGE/ UNIV/CQ	YR GRAD
Young Michael E Dr	(949)231-2032 michael.young@cuw.edu	423 W Seacroft Ct Mequon WI 53092	SW	Teacher	S HS/C	Concordia University Wisconsin Mequon WI	(262)243-5700	CQ	2008
Young Norman E Dr	(414)235-9311 ncyoung49@att.net	S 77 W 12929 McShane Dr Apt #d211 Muskego WI 53150	SW	Teacher	EM			RF	1956
Young Patricia J Hall	pattyjeanyoung@gmail.com	3145 N Hearthside St Orange CA 92865	PSW	Teacher	EM			S	1976
Young Renee P Skerkowski Deac	(580)304-2069 donrenee1984@gmail.com	2412 Donner Ave Ponca City OK 74604	OK	Deaconess	EM			CQ	2005
Young Teresa L	(308)520-6772 lntyoung@msn.com	3353 Bartlett Blvd Bartlett TN 38134	MDS	Teacher	Tchr	Immanuel Memphis TN	(901)388-0205	CQ	2024
Younghouse Kurt R	(217)620-1809 kyounghouse@unitydecatur.org	10 Edgewood Ct Decatur IL 62522	CI	Teacher	Tchr	St John Decatur IL	(217)875-3656	MQ	2004
Yount Sandra J Zwingelberg	(316)260-9639 syount.105@cox.net	940 N Woodlawn St Wichita KS 67208	KS	Teacher	EM			WN	1982
Yox Alison C Ebel	(406)698-0630 ayox@bethlehemdenver.com	11746 W Chenango Dr Apt 2 Morrison CO 80465	RM	Teacher	Tchr	Bethlehem Lakewood CO	(303)233-0401	S	2019
Yuen Grace	(415)664-4500	3830 Noriega Street San Francisco CA 94122	CNH	Teacher	C09/2020			IV	2011
Yung Janice J	(713)927-7706 janyung44@gmail.com	20659 Stone Oak Pkwy Apt 1607 San Antonio TX 78258	TX	Teacher	EM			CQ	1990
Yurk Amanda Dietrich	(920)360-5863 ayurk@flcse.org	12584 Wedgefield Dr Grand Island FL 32735	FG	Teacher	Tchr	Faith Eustis FL	(352)589-5683	CQ	2023
Yurk Michael J	(262)618-4827 mikejoyyurk@gmail.com	188 W Acorn Dr Grafton WI 53024	SW	Teacher	Prin	St Paul Grafton WI	(262)377-4659	MQ	1992
Yurk Michael T	(678)773-1844 myurk@flcse.org	12584 Wedgefield Drive Grand Island FL 32735	FG	DCE	Mem C	Faith Eustis FL	(352)589-5433	CH	2014
Zabel Martin W	(561)641-4274 martyzabel@trinitydelray.org	13636 Eridanus Dr Orlando FL 32828	FG	Teacher	EM			SP	1972
Zabel Mary P Boucher	(561)641-4274 maryzabel@att.net	13636 Eridanus Dr Orlando FL 32828	FG	Teacher	EM			SP	1972
Zabinsky Lee A Lemmon	(760)638-1575 lzabinsky@gracelcms.net	31017 Rosebush Ln Valley Center CA 92082	PSW	Teacher	EM			RF	1979
Zacho John E	(325)944-4336	P.O. Box 1182 Hext TX 76848	TX	Teacher	EM			S	1968
Zachrich Ann E Koschmann	(330)958-3160 aezdrz@att.net	1573 Timbertop Dr Tallmadge OH 44278	OH	Teacher	EM			RF	1971
Zagel James R	(303)252-1485	16168 Dallas St Brighton CO 80602	RM	Teacher	Tchr	Zion Brighton CO	(303)659-3443	S	1979
Zahn Crystal K Lepp	(262)355-6254 cbobowski16@gmail.com	726 Belmont Dr. Watertown WI 53094	SW	Teacher	Tchr	Divine Redeemer Hartland WI	(262)367-3664	MQ	2013
Zahrte Hannah R		7610 York Ave S #3202 Edina MN 55435	MNS	DCM	Mem C	Cross View Edina MN	(952)941-1094	MQ	2018
Zamora Alma Deac	(817)713-6699 zamora.alma@yahoo.com	1600 Village Dr Apt 1217 Euless TX 76039	TX	Deaconess	Mem C	Our Redeemer Irving TX	(972)255-0595	SL-DEAC	2011
Zamorano Rachel K Bahn	(309)533-1737 rzamorano@clcfamily.org	830 W. Lincoln Ave Unit 290 Escondido CA 92026	PSW	DCE	Mem C	Community Escondido CA	(760)739-1650	IV	2021
Zander Joel R	(231)343-2960 jzander@faithgb.org	6401 Kings Pointe Grand Blanc MI 48439	MI	DCE	Mem C	Faith Grand Blanc MI	(810)694-9351	SP	2000
Zander Tyler J	(320)237-3005 tz9113@gmail.com		SW	Teacher	Tchr	Martin Luther Greendale WI	(414)421-4000	S	2013
Zanta Patricia A Tyler	(520)444-4556 ptzanta@gmail.com	7921 E Scarlett St Tucson AZ 85710	EN	Teacher	EM			S	1984
Zappitell Kathleen M Gerber	jkzapp@wowway.com	4154 Shorebrook Sterling Heights MI 48314	MI	Teacher	EM			CQ	1992
Zaring Alexandra K Carmichael	(812)216-0778 azaring@immanuelschool.org	405 Lasher Dr. Seymour IN 47274	IN	Teacher	Tchr	Immanuel Seymour IN	(812)522-1301	CQ	2024
Zastrow Margaret B Bode	(573)459-6432 mzastrow@fidmail.com	804 Meadowlark Dr Washington MO 63090	MO	Teacher	EM			S	1972
Zavalis Elizabeth A Spilman	(610)647-0858	7 Pickwick Ln Malvern PA 19355	EA	Teacher	EM			RF	1966
Zbytniewski Timothy A	(262)305-7506 tzbytniewski@lwlhs.com	N169W20342 Georgetown Drive Apt 3 Jackson WI 53037	SW	Teacher	Tchr	Living Word Jackson WI	(262)677-9353	CH	2012
Zeckzer Bethany D	(260)438-5569 bzeckzer@lincolnlutheran.org	1943 Battista Ave Lincoln NE 68521	NEB	Teacher	Tchr	Lincoln Lincoln NE	(402)467-5404	S	2022
Zeckzer Callie	(260)452-9851 cjhoover02@gmail.com	2634 44th St F Highland IN 46322	IN	Teacher	Tchr	St Pauls Munster IN	(219)836-6270	CH	2025
Zeckzer Deborah L Eifert	(260)493-2143 dzeckzer@cluth.org	4016 Bridgewood Ct New Haven IN 46774	IN	Teacher	Tchr	Central New Haven IN	(260)493-2502	S	1989
Zeddies Michael F	(989)293-7292 mzeddies@icloud.com	378 Frank Rd Frankenmuth MI 48734	MI	Teacher	EM			RF	1981
Zehendner Jacqulyn J Erickson	cjtjczehendner@gmail.com	23765 Grand Island Rd Pleasanton NE 68866	NEB	Teacher	Tchr	Grand Island Grand Island NE	(308)385-3900	S	1995
Zehendner Jessica A	(308)627-6075 jazehendner10@gmail.com	515 N York Avenue Apt. 2 York NE 68467	NEB	Teacher	Tchr	Emmanuel-Faith York NE	(402)362-6575	S	2025
Zehnder James W	(517)290-9133 walripz@gmail.com	8884 Rossman Hwy Dimondale MI 48821	MI	Teacher	EM			RF	1965
Zehnder Jason A	(407)963-8152 jason.zehnder@gsmlcs.org	1452 Oakley Ave Fort Myers FL 33901	FG	Teacher	Tchr	Saint Michael Fort Myers FL	(239)939-1218	CQ	2023
Zehnder Kathleen S Miller	(440)729-3217 ktzehn@yahoo.com	12104 Parker Dr Chesterland OH 44026	OH	Teacher	EM			CQ	1977
Zehnder Stephen P	(402)980-0082 szdawg1@gmail.com	2010 Orchid St Sugar Land TX 77498	TX	Teacher	Prin	Westlake Lutheran Richmond TX	(281)341-9910	CQ	2006

*Multiple Assignments (See Church Worker Locator for Additional Details)

See Page 53 for the Table of Abbreviations for key to District, Classification, Position, and College abbreviations.

**C =Candidate; EM =Emeritus; the date following the C is the month and year the Candidate status began

NAME	TELEPHONE NUMBER EMAIL	STREET ADDRESS CITY/STATE/ZIP	DISTRICT	CLASS.	POSITION/ STATUS**	WHERE SERVING	OFFICE PHONE	COLLEGE/ UNIV/CQ	YR GRAD
Zehnder Wilma S Moeckel	(517)290-1399	8884 Rossman Hwy Dimondale MI 48821	MI	Teacher	EM			RF	1965
Zeitler Kristen S Frick	(920)606-0586 kristenzeitler32@gmail.com	422 Brookview Dr Luxemburg WI 54217	NW	Teacher	Tchr	St Paul Luxemburg WI	(920)845-2095	MQ	1991
Zell Kathi K Bartel	(715)592-3701	E1048 Bartel Rd Waupaca WI 54981	NW	Teacher	Tchr	St Paul Stevens Point WI	(715)344-5660	MQ	1995
Zellar David M	(507)257-2175 dave.zellar58@gmail.com	440 Thomas Dr Eagle Lake MN 56024	MNS	DCE	EM			CQ	1988
Zellar Jonathan D	(507)317-9256 jon.zellar@gmail.com	637 Grayhawk Dr Mankato MN 56001	MNS	DCE	Mem C	Hosanna Mankato MN	(507)388-1766	S	2012
Zellmer Judith Kettner	(414)427-1965 judizellmer@gmail.com	14195 W North Oak Blvd New Berlin WI 53151	EN	Teacher	EM			CQ	2004
Zellmer Sarah K Jagler	(920)207-7886 zellmers712@hotmail.com	201 N Porter Ave Waukesha WI 53186	SW	Teacher	Tchr	St Pauls West Allis WI	(414)541-6251	MQ	2004
Zellmer Susan C Turner	(507)435-2431 zcsue@yahoo.com	47360 132nd St Lewisville MN 56060	MNS	Teacher	EM			SP	1972
Zemke Frieda J Mindach	(708)334-2652 friedazemke@gmail.com	812 N 6th Ave Maywood IL 60153	NI	Teacher	EM			RF	1975
Zemke Stasia M Ahmann	(509)844-3757 stasiazemke@gmail.com	308 SW 3rd Ave Battle Ground WA 98604	NOW	Teacher	C07/2016			PO	2005
Zernicke Hannah E	(715)701-0789 zernickeh@trinitynet.org	3502 Mount View Ave Apt 11 Schofield WI 54476	NW	Teacher	Tchr	Trinity Wausau WI	(715)848-0166	Other	2020
Zersen Rolf M	(414)254-7309 rolfzersen@gmail.com	N59W24673 Quail Run Ln Sussex WI 53089	EN	Teacher	C07/2016			MQ	1997
Zeuner Christina L Sowatsky	(920)467-6733 preschool@paulfalls.com	2402 N 34th St Sheboygan WI 53083	SW	Teacher	Tchr	St Paul Sheboygan Falls WI	(920)467-6449	RF	1985
Zeuner Richard P	zeuner@lutheranhigh.com	2402 N 34th St Sheboygan WI 53083	SW	Teacher	Tchr	Sheboygan Sheboygan WI	(920)452-3323	RF	1985
Zeuner-Wunderlich Brenda M Consoer	(815)737-8100 zeuner.brenda@yahoo.com	21332 Burr Oak Rd Harvard IL 60033	SW	Teacher	EM			SP	1980
Zhang Helen Deac	(636)893-6976 qiu.yonghe@gmail.com	1353 Kiefer Bluffs Dr Ballwin MO 63021	MO	Deaconess	Mem C	Immanuel Olivette MO	(314)993-2394	SL-DEAC	2024
Zickfield James G	(573)382-1819 zickfield@gmail.com		MO	DCO	Mem C	St Paul Jackson MO	(573)243-2236	CQ	2007
Zickler Anela K Kristalik	(314)849-0209 zickler@sbcglobal.net	10538 Mimosa Ln Saint Louis MO 63126	MO	Teacher	EM			RF	1973
Zickuhr Jarianne L	(301)864-5869 jzickuhr@verizon.net	5026 37th Ave Hyattsville MD 20782	SE	Teacher	EM			RF	1963
Zieba Lori A Boren		1687 County Road 435 Jackson MO 63755	MO	Teacher	EM			S	1989
Ziebart Thomas A	(352)324-2541 tomziebart@aol.com	1006 Hamlin Ave Howey In Hls FL 34737	FG	Teacher	C07/2016			RF	1979
Ziebarth Kathie O Oakes Deac	(763)350-4557 dbkathiez@gmail.com	16280 227th Ave NW Elk River MN 55330	MNN	Deaconess	EM			RF	1987
Ziech William A	(630)768-6371 bziech26@gmail.com	1545 Phillips Rd Lebanon TN 37087	NI	DCE	EM			CQ	2008
Ziegelbein Annie C Hinck	(573)298-0817 annie.hinck@cune.org	8416 E Lohman Rd. Lohman MO 65053	MO	Teacher	Tchr	Trinity Jefferson City MO	(573)636-6750	S	2008
Ziegelbein Samuel L	(573)680-6887 ziegelbein@calvarylhs.org	1328 Westview Dr Jefferson City MO 65109	MO	Teacher	Tchr	Calvary Jefferson Cty MO	(573)638-0228	CQ	2018
Ziegler Constance J Hardt	(239)980-4680 conziegler22@gmail.com	2139 N 2nd St Seward NE 68434	NEB	Teacher	EM			S	1980
Ziegler Heidi M Blair	(425)361-8207 hblair4@hotmail.com	2025 Primrose St Eugene OR 97402	NOW	Teacher	C06/2017			PO	2013
Ziegler Kathryn K Deac	+542291434186 kathryn.ziegler@ctsfw.edu	Calle 44 No 411 Miramar Buenas Aires 7607 ARGENTINA	MO	Deaconess	S Miss	Office of International Mission Saint Louis MO		FW-DEAC	2014
Ziegler Robert J	(239)910-5072 rjziegler2@gmail.com	2139 N 2nd St Seward NE 68434	NEB	Teacher	D Ex/S	Nebraska District Seward NE	(402)643-2961	S	1981
Zielinski Carolyn K Staubitz	(715)573-6010 ckz54476@gmail.com	2848 Little Rapids Rd De Pere WI 54115	NW	Teacher	EM			RF	1971
Zielinski Jason R	(920)639-2019 jzielinski@wdpsd.com	640 County Line Rd De Pere WI 54115	NW	Teacher	C07/2016			MQ	1996
Zielinski Sandra N Glace	(760)390-6367 snzielinski@yahoo.com	21 Wingfield Way Benicia CA 94510	PSW	Teacher	EM			CQ	1990
Zielinski Sara L Dahlheimer	sarazielinski@hotmail.com	232 W 130th St Brunswick OH 44212	OH	Teacher	Tchr	Cleveland LHS Association Rocky River OH	(440)356-7155	RF	2000
Zielke Adolph E	(734)709-2582 zielkeade@gmail.com	610 Country Ridge Sq Woodstock IL 60098	NI	Tch/DCE	EM			RF	1971
Zielke Brian H	(630)209-4263 bzielke@lolchurch.net	221 E Shannon St Elburn IL 60119	NI	DCE	Mem C	Lord of Life Elburn IL	(630)513-5325	CQ	2012
Zielke Philip J	(630)577-7694 philz@philsfriends.org	501 Longmeadow Cir Saint Charles IL 60174	NI	Teacher	RSO	Phil's Friends NFP Inc Crown Point IN	(244)653-8315	RF	2004
Zielke Stephen P	(224)239-6164 steve.zielke@att.net	255 E Elmhurst Ave Elmhurst IL 60126	NI	Teacher	EM			RF	1978
Zielske Scott D	(561)702-7416 zoriolesfan1957@att.net	4760 NW 10th Ct Apt 104 Plantation FL 33313	FG	Teacher	C07/2016			BR	1986
Ziemba Stephanie E Lindblom	(262)994-6270 stephanieziemba77@gmail.com	6420 111th Ave Kenosha WI 53142	SW	Teacher	C07/2017			CH	2005
Ziemer Matthew M	(920)360-8723 matthew.ziemer@cuw.edu	1200 S 50th Ave Apt 8 Wausau WI 54401	NW	Teacher	Tchr	Trinity Wausau WI	(715)848-0166	MQ	2022
Ziems Lyle L	(402)417-8241 lziems@lincolnlutheran.org	820 N 58th St Lincoln NE 68505	NEB	Teacher	Tchr	Lincoln Lincoln NE	(402)467-5404	S	1989
Zieroth Geremy D	(608)742-2956 htoreizdg@gmail.com	W8032 Whitetail Dr Pardeeville WI 53954	SW	DPM	Mem C	St Peter Arlington WI	(608)635-4825	CQ	2014

*Multiple Assignments (See Church Worker Locator for Additional Details)

See Page 53 for the Table of Abbreviations for key to District, Classification, Position, and College abbreviations.

**C =Candidate; EM =Emeritus; the date following the C is the month and year the Candidate status began

NAME	TELEPHONE NUMBER EMAIL	STREET ADDRESS CITY/STATE/ZIP	DISTRICT	CLASS.	POSITION/ STATUS**	WHERE SERVING	OFFICE PHONE	COLLEGE/ UNIV/CQ	YR GRAD
Zieroth Taylor R Schmidt	(816)590-8315 taylorzieroth@gmail.com	3467 Glencove Lane Dubuque IA 52002	IE	Teacher	C05/2021			MQ	2019
Zieschang Zachary M	(512)626-2436 zzieschang@gmail.com	24171 New York St Dearborn MI 48124	MI	DPM	Mem C	Emmanuel Dearborn MI	(313)565-4002	CH	2014
Zillinger Sara J Senechal Dr	sarazillinger@gmail.com	2680 Emerald Ridge Dr Colorado Springs CO 80920	RM	Teacher	C07/2016			S	1997
Zillman Lynne Velguth	(708)343-5817 lynne.zillman@gmail.com	1670 Candlewick Dr SW Poplar Grove IL 61065	NI	Teacher	EM			RF	1976
Zillman O J Dr	(708)227-9197 john.zillman@gmail.com	1670 Candlewick Dr Poplar Grove IL 61065	NI	Teacher	EM			RF	1976
Zills Candis C	(920)360-2467 c.zills@stpaulbonduel.com	N9695 Willard Rd Berlin WI 54923	NW	Teacher	Tchr	St Paul Bonduel WI	(715)758-8559	MQ	2018
Zilm John H	(618)920-1924 jzilm88@gmail.com	916 Meadow Ln Godfrey IL 62035	SI	Teacher	Tchr	Zion Bethalto IL	(618)377-8314	S	2011
Zilm Sharon Henning	(618)466-4729 sharon.zilm@gmail.com	1111 White Oak Trl Godfrey IL 62035	SI	Teacher	EM			CQ	2007
Zilz Peggy E Leiter	pezilz@hotmail.com	1595 E Poplar Rd Columbia City IN 46725	IN	Teacher	C12/2023			CQ	2000
Zimbrick Charles R	(510)651-5836 czimbrick@hotmail.com	4764 Stratford Ave Fremont CA 94538	CNH	Teacher	EM			RF	1975
Zimbrick Emilie A Bain	(510)673-3858 ezimbrick@sbcglobal.net	4764 Stratford Ave Fremont CA 94538	CNH	Teacher	EM			RF	1977
Zimdahl Bernard W	(630)659-5926 zimdahb@yahoo.com	1100 Thatcher Trl West Dundee IL 60118	NI	Teacher	EM			RF	1969
Zimdahl Janet R Truemper	(224)402-4453 jzimdahl@sbcglobal.net	1100 Thatcher Trl West Dundee IL 60118	NI	Teacher	EM			RF	1968
Zimmer Carol A Eckert	(708)343-4866 zimmerra2@aol.com	909 Helen Dr Melrose Park IL 60160	NI	Teacher	EM			RF	1966
Zimmer Dennis W	(708)227-3112 dzimmer7@gmail.com	5521 Bohlander Ave Berkeley IL 60163	NI	Teacher	Mem C	St Paul Lockport IL	(815)838-1832	RF	1985
Zimmer Jenifer R Nahnsen	(952)994-4262 zimmom1@aol.com	N57W24927 Clover Dr Sussex WI 53089	SW	Teacher	EM			RF	1990
Zimmer Mark A	(317)408-8476 pasqua720@att.net	4602 Fairhope Dr Indianapolis IN 46237	IN	Teacher	EM			RF	1977
Zimmer Martin K	(219)322-8584 mzimmer@stplmunster.com	513 Sycamore Dr Dyer IN 46311	IN	Teacher	EM			RF	1979
Zimmer Michael J	(952)200-0898 mikezimmer731@gmail.com	N57W24927 Clover Dr Sussex WI 53089	SW	Teacher	EM			RF	1982
Zimmerman Anna L Reincke	(586)746-7611 zimmermanna29@gmail.com		MI	DCO	C12/2019			SP	2015
Zimmerman Dennis K	(651)793-0311	793 Nebraska Ave E Saint Paul MN 55106	MNS	Teacher	EM			CQ	2002
Zimmerman Gary E	(608)314-7818 nbfzman@hotmail.com	6344 Weathervane Ln Machesney Park IL 61115	NI	Teacher	C03/2022			MQ	2006
Zimmerman Gloria N Merz	(425)226-4089 g.zimmerman@comcast.net	7003 S 132nd St Seattle WA 98178	NOW	Teacher	EM			RF	1971
Zimmerman Jennifer D Klinge	(952)797-2307 ajzimmerman2012@gmail.com	3670 350th St Farnhamville IA 50538	IW	Teacher	C07/2016			S	2005
Zimmerman Lea J	(832)715-0987 leazimmerman@hotmail.com	8611 Gander Bayshore Ln Houston TX 77040	TX	Teacher	Tchr	Memorial Houston TX	(713)782-6079	S	1987
Zimmerman Margaret E Paulson	(707)294-2033 zimelaine@comcast.net	2520 Trower Ave Napa CA 94558	CNH	Teacher	EM			RF	1964
Zimmerman Michael P	(972)686-0525 zmptexas@att.net	1931 Robert Jones Dr Mesquite TX 75150	TX	Teacher	Tchr	Dallas Lutheran Sch Dallas TX	(214)349-8912	CQ	1995
Zimmermann Donna D Petermann	(920)733-0635	1043 E Moorpark Ave Appleton WI 54911	NW	Teacher	Tchr	Celebration Appleton WI	(920)734-8218	RF	1981
Zimmermann Joseph T	(715)551-2397 dcojoseph@gmail.com		NW	DCO	C07/2016			SP	2000
Zink Charlene J Little	(248)918-8978 cjzink@aol.com	1895 Woodland Ave Sylvan Lake MI 48320	MI	Teacher	EM			S	1980
Zink Janet S Nelson	(309)314-0377 tlzinksr@att.net	5 Blackhawk Hills Dr Rock Island IL 61201	CI	Teacher	EM			CQ	1981
Zinnel Nora L Schinnerer	(925)408-0592 oldmustangmoma@aol.com	P.O. Box 38 Stromsburg NE 68666	NEB	Teacher	EM			S	1974
Zirbel Jennifer J Thompson	(414)688-3171 jzirbel0925@gmail.com	830 Taft Ter Hartford WI 53027	SW	Teacher	Tchr	Grace Menomonee Falls WI	(262)251-7140	MQ	2005
Ziska Katherine D Reinke	(262)442-0358 tomandkathyz41@gmail.com	4112 Grady Ter The Villages FL 32163	SW	Teacher	EM			RF	1974
Zittergruen David L	(952)353-0136 zittergruendavid@gmail.com	6317 Lakeside Dr Chaska MN 55318	MNS	Teacher	EM			CQ	2003
Zobel Carol L Eickhoff	(618)708-7598 cubs@egyptian.net	602 Hillandale Dr Steeleville IL 62288	SI	Teacher	EM			RF	1975
Zobel James R	(618)708-7471 cubs@egyptian.net	602 Hillandale Dr Steeleville IL 62288	SI	Teacher	Tchr	Immanuel Murphysboro IL	(618)684-3012	S	1981
Zobel Rebecca N	(608)212-9806 zobelnrebecca@gmail.com	325 Hartridge Dr Hartland WI 53029	SW	Teacher	Tchr	Divine Redeemer Hartland WI	(262)367-3664	MQ	2023
Zobel Suzanne E	(586)405-3872 suzanne.zobel@gmail.com	114 Poplar Dr Yorkville IL 60560	NI	DCE	EM			S	1983
Zoch Anita M Seemann	(979)716-4078 anitazoch@gmail.com	P.O. Box 462 Giddings TX 78942	TX	Teacher	EM			RF	1985
Zoch Dylan C	(979)716-8550 dylanczoch15@gmail.com	6810 Blenheim Rd Apt B Baltimore MD 21212	SE	DCE	C06/2023			AU	2019
Zoch Elizabeth A Londenberg	(512)926-5377 tefzoch@aol.com	7205 Fred Morse Dr Austin TX 78723	TX	Teacher	EM			AU	1984

*Multiple Assignments (See Church Worker Locator for Additional Details)
See Page 53 for the Table of Abbreviations for key to District, Classification, Position, and College abbreviations.
**C =Candidate; EM =Emeritus; the date following the C is the month and year the Candidate status began

NAME	TELEPHONE NUMBER EMAIL	STREET ADDRESS CITY/STATE/ZIP	DISTRICT	CLASS.	POSITION/ STATUS**	WHERE SERVING	OFFICE PHONE	COLLEGE/ UNIV/CQ	YR GRAD
Zoch Eva J Schmidt	(713)466-7868	11122 Melba Ln Houston TX 77041	TX	Teacher	EM			RF	1964
Zoch Riley W	(979)540-8404	100 Park Pl Apt 617 Marshall TX 75672	TX	Teacher	Tchr	Redeemer Austin TX	(512)459-1500	AU	2016
Zoellick Jeffrey L	(630)913-9233 jzoellick@oursavior.com	606 Topeka Ct Carol Stream IL 60188	NI	DCM	Mem C	Our Savior Carol Stream IL	(630)830-4833	MQ	1995
Zook Randall J	(407)282-2366 zookrj@aol.com	919 Grassy Island Ln Orlando FL 32825	FG	Teacher	C07/2016			PO	1982
Zorena Kevin C	zorenak@calvarylhs.org		MO	Teacher	Tchr	Calvary Jefferson Cty MO	(573)638-0228	RF	2017
Zorumski Susan K	(636)441-0127 szorumski@charter.net	63 Park Charles Blvd S Apt B Saint Peters MO 63376	MO	Teacher	Tchr	Immanuel Wentzville MO	(636)327-4416	RF	1993
Zubke Holly Goetze	(218)209-0002	11004 Harmony Rd NW Laporte MN 56461	MNN	Teacher	Tchr	Immanuel Walker MN	(218)547-4139	MQ	2006
Zuch Thomas A	(503)788-1412	10317 SE Rex St Portland OR 97266	NOW	Teacher	EM			RF	1961
Zucker Denys M Erickson	(262)227-4611 denys.zucker@gmail.com	3191 Woodvalley Dr Flushing MI 48433	MI	DCE	EM			SP	1993
Zuehlsdorf James F	(414)303-0812 zuehlsdorfwoodworks@wi.rr.com	8279 N 46th St Brown Deer WI 53223	SW	Teacher	EM			SP	1972
Zuehlsdorf Mary A Manthey	(414)333-7408 zuehlsdorfwoodworks@wi.rr.com	8279 N 46th St Brown Deer WI 53223	SW	Teacher	EM			SP	1972
Zuehsow Angela Bockelman	angi.zuehsow@gmail.com	3909 Acklin Dr Plano TX 75025	TX	Teacher	EM			S	1976
Zuelsdorf Anthony E	(518)459-5020	22 Laing St Albany NY 12205	AT	Teacher	EM			RF	1962
Zuelsdorf Betty J Klatt	(518)459-5020	22 Laing St Albany NY 12205	AT	Teacher	EM			RF	1962
Zuelsdorff Billy J	(715)630-4659 bzuelsdorff@immanuelplain view.org	100 4th Ave SW Plainview MN 55964	MNS	Teacher	Prin	Immanuel Plainview MN	(507)534-2108	SP	1991
Zum Hofe Allen W	(763)784-5454 azumhofe@aol.com	96 South Dr Apt. 304 Circle Pines MN 55014	MNS	Tch/DCE	EM			SP	1969
Zum Hofe Laurie L Dr	(402)314-7492 zumlow@gmail.com	825 S 34th St Lincoln NE 68510	NEB	Teacher	C06/2024			S	1996
Zumhofe Joan M Kuphal	(651)470-9575 jmzumhofe@gmail.com	54157 246th St Winthrop MN 55396	MNS	Teacher	EM			S	1976
Zumwalt Mary E Budde	(618)483-5519 mezumwalt@yahoo.com	1500 E 900th Ave Altamont IL 62411	CI	Teacher	Tchr	Altamont Altamont IL	(618)483-6428	RF	1977
Zunker Morgan Marnholtz			SW	Teacher	C08/2022			MQ	2019
Zutz Ellen S Lau	(920)418-5557 eszutz@gmail.com	3311 Whitetail Run Brillion WI 54110	SW	Teacher	EM			RF	1984
Zwernemann Madelynn D Mc Ginnis	(860)575-1539 bonniez57@yahoo.com	4460 Celebration Boulevard Apt # 5304 Acworth GA 30101	AT	Teacher	EM			RF	1961

*Multiple Assignments (See Church Worker Locator for Additional Details)
See Page 53 for the Table of Abbreviations for key to District, Classification, Position, and College abbreviations.
**C =Candidate; EM =Emeritus; the date following the C is the month and year the Candidate status began

DIRECTORY OF HIGH SCHOOLS AND JUNIOR HIGH SCHOOLS

Corrected to September 18, 2025

Schools are listed according to the state and physical town, village, or city in which the school building is located. School enrollments are shown for schools that reported in the most recent collection cycle.

CITY	SCHOOL	ADDRESS	PHONE	EMAIL WEBSITE	PRINCIPAL/ ADMINISTRATOR	YEAR ORG.	RSO	NLSA	GRADES OFFERED	ENROLL
ALASKA										
ANCHORAGE	*ANCHOR*	8100 ARCTIC BLVD 99518	(907)522-3636	office@alsalaska.org www.alsalaska.org	Mya Woodard	1978	R	N	EC-12	363
ARIZONA										
GILBERT	*CHRISTS GREENFIELD*	425 N Greenfield Rd 85234	(480)892-8314	info@cglschool.org school.cglchurch.org	Albert J Amling IV	1986		N	K-12	463
PHOENIX	*NORTH VALLEY*	33655 North 27th Dr 85085	(623)551-3454	Chriss@northvalleyca.org northvalleyca.org	Chris C Schoenleb Jr	2010	R	N	EC-12	781
	VALLEY	5199 N 7th Ave 85013	(602)230-1600	info@vlhs.org www.vlhs.org	Timothy R Gast	1981	R	N	9-12	122
ARKANSAS										
JONESBORO	*ALL SAINTS*	1812 S Rains 72401	(870)935-2001	headmaster@allsaintsjonesboro.org allsaintsjonesboro.org/school					1-12	13
CALIFORNIA										
CHULA VISTA	*VICTORY*	810 Buena Vista Way 91910	(619)262-4444	scott.dufresne@victorysouthbay.org www.victorysouthbay.org	Scott R Dufresne	1975	R	N	K-12	319
GARDENA	*PACIFIC*	1473 W 182nd St 90248	(310)538-6865	office@paclutheran.com pacificlutheranhigh.com	Catherine A Hittinger		R		6-12	131
IRVINE	*CREAN*	12500 Sand Canyon Ave 92618	(949)387-1199	moyer@creanlutheran.org www.creanlutheran.org	Dr Daniel E Moyer	2007	R	N	9-12	1126
NORWALK	*LUTEC*	11943 Rosecrans Ave 90650	(562)204-6538	todd.moritz@lutec.org www.lutec.org	Todd J Moritz	2022			9-12	6
ORANGE	*ORANGE COUNTY*	2222 N Santiago Blvd 92867	(714)998-5151	info@lhsoc.org www.lhsoc.org	Dr Jacob A Preus IV	1961	R	N	9-12	1515
RIDGECREST	*OUR SAVIOR'S*	725 N Fairview St 93555	(760)375-7921	dayschool@oslc-rc.org www.oslc-rc.org	Clinton S Hoff				K-9	
COLORADO										
LOVELAND	*IMMANUEL*	4650 Sunview Dr 80538	(970)667-7606	schooloffice@immanuelloveland.org school.immanuelloveland.org	Cheryl E Gilbert	1977		N	EC-9	143
PARKER	*LUTHERAN*	11249 Newlin Gulch Blvd 80134	(303)841-5551	jodi.hoehne@lhsparker.org www.lhsparker.org	Daniel E Gehrke	1955	R	N	9-12	
FLORIDA										
NORTH FORT MYERS	*GOOD SHEPHERD*	4770 Orange Grove Blvd 33903	(239)995-7711	pastordavis@goodshepofnfm.com www.goodshepofnfm.org		1967		N	EC-12	281
OCALA	*ST JOHN*	1915 SE Lake Weir Ave 34471	(352)622-7275	jim.knoepfel@stjohnocala.org www.stjohnocala.org	James B Knoepfel	1963		N	EC-12	499
SANFORD	*HOLY CROSS ACADEMY*	100 Aero Lane 32771	(407)936-3636	cmoon@thehcla.org www.thehcla.org		1999		N	EC-12	532
IDAHO										
NAMPA	*ZLS-NAMPA-ID*	1012 12th Ave Rd 83686	(208)466-9141	zlsoffice1@gmail.com zlsnampa.org	Joshua Swigart	1960		N	EC-9	32
POCATELLO	*GRACE*	1350 Baldy Ave 83201	(208)237-4142	glsoffice@gracepocatello.org www.gracepocatello.org	Robert Raschke	1959		N	EC-12	545
ILLINOIS										
BUCKLEY	*CHRIST LUTHERAN HS*	201 W Lincoln St 60918	(217)394-2547	christlutheranhs@yahoo.com www.christlutheranbuckley.com	Sandra J Spitz	1997	R		9-12	
CENTRALIA	*CHRIST OUR ROCK*	9545 Shattuc Rd 62801	(618)226-3315	corlhs@corlhs.org www.corstallions.org	Don W Duensing	2002	R		9-12	107
DECATUR	*LUTH SCHOOL ASSOC*	2001 E Mound Rd 62526	(217)233-2001	frontoffice@unitydecatur.org www.unitydecatur.org		1959	R		EC-12	393
EDWARDSVILLE	*METRO-EAST*	6305 Center Grove Rd 62025	(618)656-0043	jay.krause@melhs.org www.melhs.org	Dr Jay A Krause	1977	R	N	9-12	
MATTOON	*ST JOHNS*	100 Broadway 61938	(217)234-4911	mhagen@stjls-mattoon.com www.stjls-mattoon.com	Meghan Hagen	1956		N	EC-11	
MELROSE PARK	*WALTHER*	900 Chicago Ave 60160	(708)344-0404	tim_bouman@waltheracademy.org www.walther.com	Tim Bouman	1954	R	N	6-12	306
MORTON	*BETHEL*	325 E Queenwood Rd 61550	(309)266-6592	school@bethellutheranschool.org www.bethellutheranschool.org	John R Jacob	1982			EC-12	
ROCKFORD	*ROCKFORD*	3411 N ALPINE RD 61114	(815)877-9551	info@rockfordlutheran.org www.rockfordlutheran.org	Dr Alan P Runge	1963	R	N	EC-12	691
SPRINGFIELD	*LUTHERAN*	3500 W Washington St 62711	(217)546-6363	z.klug@spiluhi.org www.spiluhi.org		1978	R	N	9-12	104

*Indicates Boarding High School
R = Recognized Service Organization (RSO)
N = National Lutheran Schools Accreditation (NLSA)

CITY	SCHOOL	ADDRESS	PHONE	EMAIL WEBSITE	PRINCIPAL/ ADMINISTRATOR	YEAR ORG.	RSO	NLSA	GRADES OFFERED	ENROLL
WORDEN	ST PAUL	6961 W Frontage Rd 62097	(618)633-2202	principal@stpaulhamel.org school.stpaulhamel.org	Deac Lynnette A Fredericksen	2014			EC-12	
INDIANA										
FORT WAYNE	CONCORDIA	1601 Saint Joe River Dr 46805	(260)483-1102	jpennekamp@clhscadets.com www.clhscadets.com	Jacob E Pennekamp	1935	R	N	9-12	687
	REDEEMER CLASSICAL	202 W Rudisill Blvd 46807	(260)255-6375	redeemerclassicalschool@gmail.com www.fortwayneclassical.com	Nathaniel Pullmann		R	N	1-10	51
INDIANAPOLIS	INDIANAPOLIS	5555 S Arlington Ave 46237	(317)787-5474	admissions@lhsi.org www.lhsi.org	Michael B Brandt	1975	R	N	9-12	276
SEYMOUR	TRINITY	1 Trinity Way 47274	(812)524-8547	info@trinitycougars.org trinitycougars.org	Clayton W Darlage	2000	R	N	9-12	189
IOWA										
CEDAR FALLS	VALLEY	4520 Rownd St 50613	(319)266-4565	info@vlscrusaders.org www.vlscrusaders.org	Brian T L Heureux	2002	R	N	K-12	177
DENISON	UNITY RIDGE	1004 1st Avenue South Suite B 51442	(712)393-2002	megan.torreson@unityridge.org www.unityridge.org	Megan L Torreson	2022	R		EC-12	121
LATIMER	ST PAULS	404 W Main 50452	(641)579-6046	leadteacher@stpaulslatimer.org www.stpaulslatimer.org	Cody M Collier	1925		N	K-12	41
KANSAS										
BASEHOR	RISEN SAVIOR	14750 Leavenworth Rd 66007	(913)724-2900	weinkauf@rslcms.church risensaviorlcms.org					K-12	55
WICHITA	CONCORDIA ACADEMY	909 S Market 67211	(316)202-8989	CAW_info@cawichita.org CAWichita.org	Dan Snyder			N	9-12	10
LOUISIANA										
METAIRIE	LUTHERAN HIGH SCHOOL	3864 17TH ST 70002	(504)455-4062	cchristen@lutheranhighschool.net www.lutheranhighschool.net		1970	R	N	8-12	
MARYLAND										
TOWSON	CONCORDIA	1145 Concordia Dr 21286	(410)825-2323	brentjohnson@concordiaprepschool.org www.concordiaprepschool.org	Brent T Johnson	1965	R		6-12	492
MICHIGAN										
BIG RAPIDS	ST PETER	408 W Bellevue St 49307	(231)796-6684	office@stpetersbr.org stpetersbr.org		1871			EC-12	99
MACOMB	LUTHERAN NORTH	16825 24 Mile Rd 48042	(586)781-9151	jreincke@lhsa.com www.lutherannorth.com	John M Reincke	1972	R	N	9-12	624
ROCHESTER HILLS	NORTHWEST	1000 Bagley Ave 48309	(248)856-0240	plooker@lhsa.com www.lutherannorthwest.com	Kristina L Baughman	1978	R	N	9-12	285
SAGINAW	VALLEY	3560 Mc Carty Rd 48603	(989)790-1676	akaul@vlhs.com www.vlhs.com		1977	R	N	9-12	297
WESTLAND	WESTLAND	33300 Cowan Rd 48185	(734)422-2090	jbrown@lhsa.com www.lutheranwestland.com	Micah Lorenzen		R	N	9-12	181
WYOMING	WMLHS	150 50th St SW Suite 2 49548	(616)455-2200	kangers@wmlhs.org www.wmlhs.org	Kristine A Angers	2004	R	N	7-12	14
MINNESOTA										
MAYER	MAYER	306 7th St NE 55360	(952)657-2251	info@mayerlutheran.org www.mayerlutheran.org	Kevin L Wilaby	1960	R	N	5-12	198
NORTHROP	MARTIN LUTHER	315 Martin Luther Dr 56075	(507)436-5249	principal@martinlutherhs.com www.martinlutherhs.com	David A Stuckwisch	1983	R	N	7-12	64
OTSEGO	GOOD SHEPHERD LHS	15670 90th St NW Ste B 55330	(320)319-0626	office@goodshepherdlutheranhs.org gslhighschool.org	Melissa M Lamkin		R	N	9-12	
ROSEVILLE	CONCORDIA ACADEMY	2400 Dale St N 55113	(651)484-8429	tim.berner@concordiaacademy.com www.concordiaacademy.com	Dr Timothy A Berner	1959	R	N	9-12	341
THIEF RIVER FALLS	ST JOHN	15671 158th St NE 56701	(218)681-7753	Schooloffice@stjohntrf.com	Tammy Ballard	2003			EC-12	12
WINONA	HOPE	312 E. Broadway St 55987	(507)474-7799	office@hopelhs.org www.hopelhs.org	Robert R Sandcork II	2003	R	N	9-12	74
MISSOURI										
COLE CAMP	LUTH SCHOOL ASSOC	204 E Butterfield 65325	(660)668-4614	office@lsaschool.com www.lsaschool.com	Debra Eckhoff	1961	R	N	K-12	75
CONCORDIA	SAINT PAUL	205 S Main St 64020	(660)463-2238	pmehl@splhs.org www.splhs.org	Paul M Mehl	1883	R	N	9-12	157
FARMINGTON	ST PAUL	4337 Showplace Dr 63640	(573)756-1715	asherrill@stpaulgiants.com stpaullutheranhs.com	Andrew R Sherrill		R	N	9-12	
JACKSON	SAXONY	2004 Saxony Dr 63755	(573)204-7555	mruark@saxonylutheranhigh.org saxonylutheranhigh.org	Mark J Ruark	1998	R	N	9-12	
JEFFERSON CTY	CALVARY	2525 ROUTE B 65101	(573)638-0228	administrator@calvarylhs.org www.calvarylhs.org	John T Christman	2005	R	N	9-12	117
KANSAS CITY	KANSAS CITY	12411 Wornall Rd 64145	(816)241-5478	akirsch@lhskc.com lhskc.com	Adam J Kirsch	1978	R		9-12	113

*Indicates Boarding High School
R = Recognized Service Organization (RSO)
N = National Lutheran Schools Accreditation (NLSA)

CITY	SCHOOL	ADDRESS	PHONE	EMAIL WEBSITE	PRINCIPAL/ ADMINISTRATOR	YEAR ORG.	RSO	NLSA	GRADES OFFERED	ENROLL
PLATTE CITY	*OUR SAVIOR*	14155 N Highway 64079	(816)866-1597	oursavioracademy@yahoo.com oursavioracademy.org	Lori Albright	2004		N	EC-12	46
SAINT LOUIS	*ASSOC SPEC ED*	3558 S Jefferson Ave 63118	(314)268-1234	bj.wiemer@lutheranspecialed.org lutheranspecialed.org	B J Wiemer	1956	R	N	EC-12	
	LUTHERAN NORTH	5401 Lucas and Hunt Rd 63121	(314)389-3100	tbrackman@LNCrusaders.org www.LNCrusaders.org	Dr Timothy J Brackman	1946	R	N	6-12	358
	LUTHERAN SOUTH	9515 Tesson Ferry Rd 63123	(314)631-1400	jbutterfield@lslancers.org www.lslancers.org	Dr Jonathan M Butterfield	1957	R		9-12	565
SAINT PETERS	*ST CHARLES*	5100 Mexico Rd 63376	(636)928-5100	jbernhardt@lhssc.org lutheranhighstcharles.com	Dr Douglas J Kuhlmann	1981	R	N	9-12	
SPRINGFIELD	*SPRINGFIELD LUTH HS*	1415 South Holland Ave 65807	(417)370-7975	info@springfieldlutheranhs.org springfieldlutheranhs.org	Stephanie Grandestaff		R		9	
				NEBRASKA						
ALLIANCE	*IMMANUEL*	1312 E 10th St 69301	(308)629-1601	office@ielschool.org immanuelevlutheran.org	Shaun M Daugherty	2014			EC-9	108
FREMONT	*FREMONT*	1546 N Luther Rd 68025	(402)990-1406	luhifremont@gmail.com luhifremont.org/	Robert L Cooksey				9-12	0
GRAND ISLAND	*GRAND ISLAND*	3900 W Husker Hwy 68803	(308)385-3900	principal@heartlandlutheran.org cnlutheran.org/	Chelsey A Liess	2000		N	7-12	58
LINCOLN	*LINCOLN*	1100 N 56th St 68504	(402)467-5404	swallingford@lincolnlutheran.org www.lincolnlutheran.org	Jeremy T Geidel	1962	R	N	6-12	385
NORFOLK	*NORTHEAST*	2010 N 37th St 68701w	(402)379-3040	dsievert@lhne.org www.lhne.org	Daniel M Sievert	1996	R	N	9-12	124
OMAHA	*CONCORDIA*	15656 Fort St 68116	(402)445-4000	nathan.domsch@concordiaomaha.org concordiaomaha.org	Nathan T Domsch	2001	R	N	K-12	670
PAPILLION	*FAITH LUTHERAN ACADE*	420 N Washington St 68046	(402)339-3668	pkz@1st-lutheran.org faithlutheranacademy.substack.com/	Karl P Ziegler				EC-12	
SEWARD	*TRINITY*	800 N Columbia Ave 68434	(402)643-7255	trinityacademy@cune.edu trinityacademycune.org/	Gabriel Haley				9-12	
				NEVADA						
CARSON CITY	*SIERRA*	3601 Romans Rd 89705	(775)267-1921	admin@slhs.com www.slhs.com	Micah Glenn	2001	R	N	9-12	166
LAS VEGAS	*FAITH*	2015 Hualapai Way 89117	(702)804-4400	buucks@flhsemail.org www.faithlutheranlv.org	Kathleen Stokes	1978	R	N	6-12	2182
				NEW MEXICO						
ROSWELL	*IMMANUEL*	1405 N Sycamore 88201	(575)622-2853	lcms_row_r@plateautel.net www.immanuelroswell.org/school		2006		N	EC-9	
				NEW YORK						
BRONX	*OUR SAVIOUR*	1734 Williamsbridge Rd 10461	(718)792-5665	kfamulare@oursaviourbronx.org www.oursaviourbronx.org	Matthew R Gonzalez	1942			1-12	
BROOKVILLE	*LONG ISLAND*	131 Brookville Rd 11545	(516)626-1735	info@luhi.org www.luhi.org	John Buck III	1960	R		6-12	
CENTEREACH	*OUR SAV NEW AMERICAN*	140 Mark Tree Rd 11720	(631)588-2757	dolores.reade@osnas.org osnas.org	Dr Wilbert P Stelzer	1967			K-12	
MASPETH	*MARTIN LUTHER*	60-02 Maspeth Ave 11378	(718)894-4000	schapman@martinluthernyc.org www.martinluthernyc.org	Sean C Chapman	1960	R		6-12	
				NORTH CAROLINA						
HICKORY	*UNIVERSITY CHRISTIAN*	602 7th Avenue NE 28601	(828)855-2995	uchs@uchigh.com uchigh.com	Colin Barrett	2009	R	N	9-12	132
				OHIO						
CLEVELAND HEIGHTS	*LUTHERAN EAST*	3565 Mayfield Rd 44118	(216)382-6100	csteinmann@clhsa.org www.lutheraneast.org		1948	R	N	9-12	386
HAMILTON	*IMMANUEL*	1285 Main St 45013	(513)895-9212	jaan.pirn@immanuelhamilton.com immanuelhamilton.com	Lukas R Bickel	1953		N	EC-9	234
ROCKY RIVER	*LUTHERAN WEST*	3850 Linden Rd 44116	(440)333-1660	joel.bahr@lutheranwest.com www.lutheranwest.com	Joel S Bahr	1948	R	N	6-12	718
SPRINGFIELD	*RISEN CHRIST*	41 E Possum Rd 45502	(937)323-3688	breid@risenchristschool.com www.risenchristschool.com	Rebecca S Reid	1993		N	EC-9	112
				OKLAHOMA						
BROKEN ARROW	*IMMANUEL*	400 North Aspen 74012	(918)251-5422	tberwaldt@icaba.org www.ilcanews.org		2002	R	N	K-12	160
MIAMI	*MOUNT OLIVE*	2337 N Main St 74354	(918)540-3456	mt.oliveschool@yahoo.com mtoschool.org		1956		N	EC-12	23
				OREGON						
BEND	*TRINITY*	2550 NE Butler Market Rd 97701	(541)382-1850	mike.schiemann@saints.org www.saints.org	Gregg A Pinick	1959		N	EC-12	649
				PENNSYLVANIA						
VERONA	*REDEEMER*	700 Idaho Ave 15147	(412)793-5884	gholzer@redeemer-oakmont.org www.rlspittsburgh.org	Gail J Holzer	1983	R	N	EC-12	
				SOUTH CAROLINA						
MYRTLE BEACH	*RISEN CHRIST*	10595 N Kings Hwy 29572	(843)272-8163	info@risenchristacademy.com risenchristacademy.com	Sean E O Connor	1976			EC-12	141
				SOUTH DAKOTA						
SIOUX FALLS	*SIOUX FALLS*	6715 S. Boe Lane 57108	(605)335-1923	tesser@sflutheranschool.com www.siouxfallslutheran.com	Tia M Esser	1977	R	N	EC-12	515

*Indicates Boarding High School
R = Recognized Service Organization (RSO)
N = National Lutheran Schools Accreditation (NLSA)

CITY	SCHOOL	ADDRESS	PHONE	EMAIL WEBSITE	PRINCIPAL/ ADMINISTRATOR	YEAR ORG.	RSO	NLSA	GRADES OFFERED	ENROLL
TEXAS										
BRENHAM	*GRACE*	1212 W Jefferson St 77833	(979)836-2030	schooloffice@glsbrenham.com www.glsbrenham.com/	Isaac S Schuller	1947			EC-12	104
CARROLLTON	*PRINCE OF PEACE*	4004 Midway Rd 75007	(972)447-0532	school.receptionist@popcs.org www.popcs.org	Dr Jeremy R Lowe	1980	R	N	EC-12	749
DALLAS	*DALLAS LUTHERAN SCH*	8494 Stults Rd 75243	(214)349-8912	office@dallaslutheranschool.com dallaslutheranschool.com	David J Bangert	1976	R	N	7-12	
GIDDINGS	*FAITH HIGH*	600 FM 1482 78942	(979)242-2889	kueckn@flhstx.org www.flhstx.org	Nicole D Kueck	2016	R	N	9-12	23
HOUSTON	*MEMORIAL*	5800 Westheimer Rd 77057	(713)782-4022	rpaul@mlchouston.org www.memoriallutheranschool.org		1980		N	EC-12	
	OUR REDEEMER	215 Rittenhouse St 77076	(713)694-0332	paintbrush4@att.net www.alivewithchrist.org		1954			5-12	
	SOUTH	12555 Ryewater Dr 77089	(281)464-8299	info@lutheransouth.org www.lutheransouth.org	Scott D Browning	1949	R	N	EC-12	853
NEWARK	*VICTORY IN CHRIST*	508 Main St 76071	(817)489-5400	schooloffice@viccla.org www.viccla.org		2010			K-2; 4-5; 9	
PFLUGERVILLE	*CONCORDIA*	1201 S Heatherwilde Blvd 78660	(512)248-2547	shelly.guentzel@chsaustin.org www.chsaustin.org	Dr Marianne L Rader	2002	R	N	9-12	115
PLANO	*FAITH*	1701 E Park Blvd 75074	(972)423-7448	school@flsplano.org www.flsplano.org	Stephen W Kieser	1972		N	EC-12	
RICHMOND	*WESTLAKE LUTHERAN*	23300 Bellaire Blvd 77406	(281)341-9910	stacey.walter@westlakelutheran.org westlakelutheran.org	Stacey M Walter	2008	R	N	EC-9	206
SAN ANGELO	*TRINITY*	3516 YMCA Dr 76904	(325)947-1275	trinityschool@tlcsanangelo.com trinityschoolsa.com	Ronald W Fritsche	1951		N	EC-12	185
SAN ANTONIO	*LUTHERAN*	18104 Babcock Rd 78255	(210)694-4962	info@lhssa.org www.lhssa.org	Andrew A Eickstead	1994	R	N	9-12	
TOMBALL	*CONCORDIA*	700 E Main St 77375	(281)351-2547	info@clhs-tx.org www.clhs-tx.org	Todd E Eklund	1982	R	N	9-12	564
WYLIE	*VERITAS ACADEMY*	1345 E. FM 544 75098	(469)661-8002	jhotopp@veritasacademics.org www.veritasacademics.org	Jennifer Hotopp	2017			EC-11	
WASHINGTON										
RENTON	*RENTON PREP*	200 Mill Ave S Ste 110 98057	(206)723-5526	drzimmerman@rentonprep.org www.rentonprep.org	Dr Michelle R Zim- merman	1968			EC-10	
TACOMA	*CONCORDIA*	202 E 56th St 98404	(253)475-9513	cindy.bowers@ccatacoma.org www.concordiachristianacademy.org	Sherrie L Gibelyou	1939	R	N	K-12	218
WENATCHEE	*ST PAULS*	312 Palouse 98801	(509)662-4757	office@stpaulslutheranschool.com www.stpaulslutheranschool.com	Tara Breidert	1978			EC-9	136
WISCONSIN										
GREEN BAY	*NORTHEASTERN WI*	1311 S Robinson Ave 54311	(920)469-6810	info@newlhs.com www.newlhs.com	Christopher C Nelson	1976	R	N	9-12	
GREENDALE	*MARTIN LUTHER*	5201 S 76th St 53129	(414)421-4000	ccody@martinlutherhs.org www.martinlutherhs.org	Dr Wayne E Jensen	1968	R	N	9-12	663
HALES CORNERS	*JOURNEYS*	5425 S 111th St 53130	(414)461-8500	info@journeyslutheran.org www.journeyslutheran.org	Jenny Stollenwerk	1986	R	N	3-12	111
HARTLAND	*LAKE COUNTRY*	401 Campus Dr 53029	(262)367-8600	kbaganz@lakecountryhs.org www.lakecountryhs.org	Kathryn Baganz	1999	R	N	9-12	362
JACKSON	*LIVING WORD*	2230 Living Word Ln 53037	(262)677-9353	dmiskimen@lwlhs.com www.lwlhs.com	David M Miskimen	2001	R	N	9-12	270
MILWAUKEE	*BEAUTIFUL SAVIOR*	3205 N 85th St 53222	(414)292-0740	Lunak@swd.lcms.org swd.lcms.org/LNS/	Robert E Lunak				K-9	11
	MILWAUKEE LHS	9700 W Grantosa Dr 53222	(414)461-6000	wjensen@milwaukeelutheran.org www.milwaukeelutheran.org	Dr Wayne E Jensen	1955	R	N	9-12	855
RACINE	*LUTHERAN HIGH SCHOOL*	251 Luedtke Ave 53405	(262)637-6538	cnelson@racinelutheran.org racinelutheran.org	Jason R Block	1944	R	N	9-12	346
SHAWANO	*WOLF RIVER*	W7467 River Bend Rd 54166	(715)745-2400	office@wolfriverlhs.org www.wrlhs.org	Paul R Steinhaus	2004	R	N	9-12	31
SHEBOYGAN	*SHEBOYGAN*	3323 University Dr 53081	(920)452-3323	bult@lutheranhigh.com www.lutheranhigh.com	Derek W Bult	1977	R	N	9-12	
WEST ALLIS	*TRINITY CLASSICAL*	2500 S 68th St 53219	(414)321-3640	bkoble@trinitylutheranclassical.org trinitylutheranclassical.org	Brandon W Koble	2023	R		9-12	14
WYOMING										
CASPER	*MOUNT HOPE*	2300 Hickory St 82604	(307)234-6865	mounthopecasper@aol.com www.mounthopecasper.com	Andrew P Richard	1984			K-12	85
CHEYENNE	*TRINITY*	1111 E 22nd St 82001	(307)635-2802	finance@trinitycheyenne.org www.trinitycheyenne.org	John C Preus				EC-12	

*Indicates Boarding High School
R = Recognized Service Organization (RSO)
N = National Lutheran Schools Accreditation (NLSA)

HIGH SCHOOL ASSOCIATIONS

The following is a list of Lutheran High School Associations not already listed in the high school section. The names, cities, and states of high schools within each association are included here and may be used to find more detailed information in the high school section.

North Valley Christian Academy
33655 N 27th Dr.
Phoenix, AZ 85085
North Valley Christian Academy — Phoenix, AZ

Valley Lutheran High School Association
5199 N. 7th Ave.
Phoenix, AZ 85013
Valley Lutheran High School — Phoenix, AZ

The Center for Lutheran Education DBA Victory Christian Academy
810 Buena Vista Way
Chula Vista, CA 91910-6853
Victory Christian Academy — Chula Vista, CA

Pacific Lutheran High School Association of the Greater Torrance Area, Incorporated
1473 W. 182nd St
Gardena, CA 90248
Pacific Lutheran Jr./Sr. High School — Gardena, CA

Lutheran High School Association of Southern California
16603 San Fernando Mission Blvd.
Granada Hills, CA 91344
Concordia Preschool, Elem. & Junior High — Granada Hills, CA

Lutheran High South—Orange County, Incorporated
12500 Sand Canyon Ave.
Irvine, CA 92618
Crean Lutheran High School — Irvine, CA

Lutheran High School Association of Orange County
2222 N. Santiago Blvd.
Orange, CA 92867-2552
Orange Lutheran High School — Orange, CA

The Colorado Lutheran High School Association
11249 Newlin Gulch Blvd.
Parker, CO 80134
Lutheran High School — Parker, CO

East Central Illinois Lutheran High School Association DBA Christ Lutheran High School
201 W. Lincoln St.
Buckley, IL 60918
Christ Lutheran High School — Buckley, IL

Christ Our Rock Lutheran High School Association
9545 Shattuc Rd.
Centralia, IL 62801
Christ Our Rock Lutheran High School — Centralia, IL

The Lutheran School Association of Decatur, Illinois, Incorporated
2001 E. Mound Rd.
Decatur, IL 62526-9305
Lutheran School Association of Decatur — Decatur, IL
Unity Christian School — Decatur, IL

Metro East Lutheran High School Association, Incorporated
6305 Center Grove Rd.
Edwardsville, IL 62025-3317
Metro East Lutheran High School — Edwardsville, IL

Walther Lutheran High School Association, Incorporated
900 Chicago Ave.
Melrose Park, IL 60160-4120
Walther Christian Academy — Melrose Park, IL

Lutheran High School Association of the Greater Rockford Area
3411 N. Alpine Rd.
Rockford, IL 61114-4801
Rockford Lutheran School-Jr./Sr. HS — Rockford, IL

Lutheran High School Association of the Greater Springfield Area
5200 6th St. Frontage Rd. E
Springfield, IL 6270
Lutheran High School — Springfield, IL

Concordia Educational Association, Incorporated
1601 St. Joe River Dr.
Fort Wayne, IN 46805
Concordia Lutheran High School — Fort Wayne, IN

Greater Indianapolis Association for Lutheran Secondary Education, Incorporated
5555 S. Arlington Ave.
Indianapolis, IN 46237-2366
Lutheran High School of Indianapolis — Indianapolis, IN

South Central Lutheran Association for Secondary Education, Incorporated
1 Trinity Way
Seymour, IN 47274-1929
Trinity Lutheran High School — Seymour, IN

Eastern Iowa Lutheran High School Association
4520 Rownd St.
Cedar Falls, IA 50613-7924
Valley Lutheran School — Cedar Falls, IA

Lutheran High School Association of Greater New Orleans
3864 17th St.
Metairie, LA 70002-4440
Lutheran High School — Metairie, LA

Baltimore Lutheran High School Association, Incorporated
1145 Concordia Dr.
Baltimore, MD 21286-1714
Concordia Preparatory School — Baltimore, MD

Lutheran High School Association of Greater Detroit
1100 Bagley
Rochester Hills, MI 48309
Lutheran High School North — Macomb, MI
Lutheran High School Northwest — Rochester Hills, MI
Lutheran High School Westland — Westland, MI

Saginaw Valley Lutheran High School Association
3560 McCarty Rd.
Saginaw, MI 48603-2239
Valley Lutheran High School — Saginaw, MI

West Michigan Lutheran High School Association
601 36th St. SW
Wyoming, MI 49509
West Michigan Lutheran High School — Wyoming, MI

Lutheran High School Association in Mayer, Minnesota
306 7th St. NE
Mayer, MN 55360
Mayer Lutheran High School — Mayer, MN

The Martin Luther High School Association
315 Martin Luther Dr.
Northrop, MN 56075
Martin Luther High School — Northrop, MN

Good Shepherd Lutheran High School
15670 90th St. NW, Suite B
Otsego, MN 55330
Good Shepherd Lutheran High School — Ostego, MN

Concordia Academy Association of Lutheran Schools
2400 N. Dale St.
Roseville, MN 55113-4598
Concordia Academy — Roseville, MN

Hope Lutheran High School
312 E. Broadway St,
Winona, MN 55987
Hope Lutheran High School — Winona, MN

Saint Paul Lutheran High School, Incorporated
205 S. Main St.
Concordia, MO 64020-0719
Saint Paul Lutheran High School — Concordia, MO

St. Paul Lutheran High School Association, Incorporated
4337 Showplace Dr.
Farmington, MO 63640
St. Paul Lutheran High School — Farmington, MO

Saxony Lutheran High School
2004 Saxony Dr.
Jackson, MO 63755-8535
Saxony Lutheran High School — Jackson, MO

Lutheran High School Association of Mid-Missouri
2525 Rte. B
Jefferson City, MO 65101-8902
Calvary Lutheran High School — Jefferson City, MO

Lutheran High School Association of the Greater Kansas City Area, Incorporated
12411 Wornall Rd.
Kansas City, MO 64145-1119
Lutheran High School of Kansas City — Kansas City, MO

Lutheran High School Association of St Louis
5401 Lucas & Hunt Rd., Ste. 103
St. Louis, MO 63121
Lutheran High School North — St. Louis, MO
Lutheran High School South — St. Louis, MO

Lutheran High School Association of St. Charles County, Incorporated
5100 Mexico Rd.
St. Peters, MO 63376-1617
Lutheran High School of St. Charles County — St. Peters, MO

Lincoln Lutheran School Association, Incorporated of Lincoln, Nebraska
1100 North 56th St.
Lincoln, NE 68504-3251
Lincoln Lutheran Middle/High School — Lincoln, NE

Lutheran High School Association of Northeast Nebraska, Incorporated
2010 N. 37th St.
Norfolk, NE 68701-3108
Lutheran High Northeast — Norfolk, NE

Concordia Lutheran Schools of Omaha, Incorporated
15656 Fort St.
Omaha, NE 68116
Concordia Junior High School — Omaha, NE
Concordia Senior High School — Omaha, NE

Sierra Lutheran High School Association
3601 Romans Rd.
Carson City, NV 89705-8009
Sierra Lutheran High School — Carson City, NV

Lutheran Secondary School Association of Clark County, Nevada, Incorporated
2015 S. Hualapai Way
Las Vegas, NV 89117-6949
Faith Lutheran Middle School and High School — Las Vegas, NV

Lutheran High School Association of Nassau and Suffolk Counties
131 Brookville Rd.
Brookville, NY 11545-3329
Long Island Lutheran Middle and High School — Brookville, NY

The Martin Luther School
60-02 Maspeth Ave.
Maspeth, NY 11378
Martin Luther School — Maspeth, NY

University Christian High School, Incorporated
602 7th Ave. NE
Hickory, NC 28601
University Christian High School — Hickory, NC

The Cleveland Lutheran High School Association, Incorporated
3870 Linden Rd.
Rocky River, OH 44116-4099
Lutheran High School East — Cleveland Hgts, OH
Lutheran High School West — Rocky River, OH

Immanuel Ministry and Education Corporation
400 N. Aspen Ave.
Broken Arrow, OK 74102
Immanuel Ministry and Education Corp. — Broken Arrow, OK

Redeemer Lutheran School
700 Idaho Ave.
Verona, PA 15147
Redeemer Lutheran School — Verona, PA

Prince of Peace Christian School
4004 Midway Rd.
Carrollton, TX 75007
Prince of Peace Christian School — Carrollton, TX

Lutheran Secondary Association of Dallas, Incorporated
8494 Stults Rd.
Dallas, TX 75243-4006
Dallas Lutheran School — Dallas, TX

Faith Lutheran High School of Central Texas, Incorporated
600 FM 1482
Giddings, TX 78942
Faith Lutheran High School — Giddings, TX

Lutheran Education Association of Houston
225 E. Edgewood Dr.
Friendswood, TX 77546
Lutheran South Academy — Houston, TX
LEAH Downtown Academy — Houston, TX
Westlake Preparatory Lutheran Academy — Richmond, TX

Lutheran School Association of the Greater Austin Area DBA Concordia High School
1201 S. Heatherwilde Blvd.
Pflugerville, TX 78660
Concordia High School — Pflugerville, TX

Lutheran High School Association of San Antonio
18104 Babcock Rd.
San Antonio, TX 78255
Lutheran High School of San Antonio — San Antonio, TX

Concordia Lutheran High School of North Harris County
700 E. Main St.
Tomball, TX 77375-6721
Concordia Lutheran High School — Tomball, TX

Concordia Christian Academy
202 E. 56th St.
Tacoma, WA 98404
Concordia Christian Academy — Tacoma, WA

Northeastern Wisconsin Lutheran School Association of the Greater Green Bay Area, Incorporated
1311 S. Robinson Ave.
Green Bay, WI 54311-5545
Northeastern Wisconsin Lutheran School — Green Bay, WI

Living Word Lutheran High School, Incorporated
2230 Living Word Ln.
Jackson, WI 53037
Living Word Lutheran High School — Jackson, WI

The Lutheran High School Association of Racine Corporation
251 Luedtke Ave.
Racine, WI 53405-1899
Racine Lutheran High School — Racine, WI

East Central Wisconsin Lutheran High School Association of the Greater Shawano Area, Incorporated
W. 7467 River Bend Rd.
Shawano, WI 54166
Wolf River Lutheran High School — Shawano, WI

Lutheran High School Association of the Greater Sheboygan Area, Incorporated
3323 University Dr.
Sheboygan, WI 53081-4761
Sheboygan Lutheran High School — Sheboygan, WI

The Lutheran High School Association of Greater Milwaukee
10427 W. Lincoln Ave., Ste. 1300
West Allis, WI 53227
Martin Luther High School — Greendale, WI
Milwaukee Lutheran High School — Milwaukee, WI
Mt. Calvary Lutheran School — Milwaukee, WI
Lake Country Lutheran High School — Hartland, WI

Western Heritage Lutheran Academy
611 E. Main St.
Riverton, WY 82501
Western Heritage Lutheran Academy — Riverton, WY

DIRECTORY OF EARLY CHILDHOOD SCHOOLS AND ELEMENTARY SCHOOLS

Corrected to September 18, 2025

Schools are listed according to the state and physical town, village, or city in which the school building is located. School enrollments are shown for schools that reported in the most recent collection cycle.

CITY	SCHOOL	ADDRESS	PHONE	EMAIL WEBSITE	PRINCIPAL/ ADMINISTRATOR	YEAR ORG.	RSO	NLSA	GRADES OFFERED	ENROLL
ALABAMA										
BIRMINGHAM	*VESTAVIA HILLS*	201 Montgomery Hwy S 35216	(205)823-1883	bheisler@vestavialutheran.org vestavialutheran.org		1987			EC	
CULLMAN	*ST PAULS*	510 3rd Ave SE 35055	(256)734-6580	rgaub@stpaulscullman.com stpaulscullman.com		1954		N	EC-6	
DAPHNE	*ASCENSION CHRISTIAN*	8888 County Road 64 36526	(251)348-7510	ascension.schooldaphne@gmail.com					EC	
DECATUR	*ST PAULS*	1700 Carridale St SW 35601	(256)353-1353	preschool@stpaulsdec.com www.stpaulsdec.com	Bethany Eze	1995		N	EC	
ELBERTA	*GOOD SHEPHERD*	13220 N Main Street 36530	(251)987-1966	gsls2017@yahoo.com		2004			EC	26
FAIRHOPE	*VERITAS*	200 S. Section St 36532	(251)979-3389	admin@veritaslutheran.org veritaslutheran.org	Taylor Winston				K-6	
HUNTSVILLE	*ASCENSION*	3803 Oakwood Ave NW 35810	(256)536-5245	dcm@ascensionhsv.org cdc.ascensionhsv.org	Carla J Peebles	1978			EC	
	GRACE	3321 Memorial Park SW 35801	(256)881-0553	allison.merrill@gls-hsv.org www.gls-hsv.org/Child_Development_ Center	Jessica McGuire			N	EC	
	GRACE	3321 S Memorial Pkwy 35801	(256)881-0553	gls@gls-hsv.org www.gls-hsv.org	Delaine S Schiestel	1963		N	EC-8	
MOBILE	*TRINITY*	2668 Berkley Ave 36617	(251)456-7960	mlambert@trinitylutheranmobile.org www.trinitylutheranmobile.org	Theron Florence Jr	1955			EC-5	
ALASKA										
ANCHORAGE	*ANCHOR*	8100 ARCTIC BLVD 99518	(907)522-3636	office@alsalaska.org www.alsalaska.org	Mya Woodard	1978	R	N	EC-12	363
FAIRBANKS	*OPEN ARMS*	2980 Davis Rd 99709	(907)455-9466	epeterson@openarmsfairbanks.org www.openarmsfairbanks.org	Elia Peterson	2000			EC	
HOMER	*FAITH*	1000 Soundview Ave 99603	(907)235-7600	preschool@faithhomer.org faithhomer.org	Diane Bartz	1996			EC	26
ARIZONA										
CASA GRANDE	*TLC*	1428 N Pueblo Dr 85122	(520)836-2451	katherine.gorka@tlcscg.org www.tlcscg.org	Katherine A Gorka	2000			EC	42
CHANDLER	*RISEN SAVIOR*	23914 S Alma School Rd 85248	(480)802-1505	linda.pauley@risensavioraz.org www.risensaviorpreschool.org	Linda G Pauley	2002			EC-K	138
COTTONWOOD	*HILLTOP*	2021 E Fir St 86326	(928)634-7759	cottonwoodhilltoppreschool@yahoo.com cottonwoodfaithlutheran.org	Windy Mickle	1975			EC	43
GILBERT	*CHRIST GREENFIELD*	425 N Greenfield Rd 85234	(480)892-8314	tspicer@cglschool.org christgreenfield.school		1986		N	EC	142
	CHRISTS GREENFIELD	425 N Greenfield Rd 85234	(480)892-8314	info@cglschool.org school.cglchurch.org	Albert J Amling IV	1986		N	K-12	463
GLENDALE	*ATONEMENT*	4001 W Beardsley Rd 85308	(623)374-3019	school@atonementlc.org atonementlutheranschool.org	Megan M Larson	1987		N	EC-8	112
LITCHFIELD PARK	*TRINITY*	830 Plaza Cir E 85340	(623)935-4690	accounts@trinitylcs.org trinitynewthinking.org	Astraea M Rohloff	1999		N	EC-8	406
MESA	*LITTLE PALMS*	9601 E Brown Rd 85207	(480)986-9436	admin@littlepalmsschool.com www.hosanna-lcms.com	Anne E Anderson	2002			EC	30
PAGE	*SHEPHERD OF DESERT*	331 S Lk Powell Blvd 86040	(602)645-9398	shepherdpreschool@scinternet.net	Donna Johnson	1984			EC	
PHOENIX	*CHRIST*	3901 E Indian School Rd 85018	(602)957-7010	jdoyle@cclphoenix.org www.clsphx.org	Jonathan T Doyle	1955		N	EC-8	626
	FAMILY OF CHRIST	3501 E Chandler Blvd 85048	(480)759-4047	pastor@familyofchristlutheranaz.org www.familyofchristschool.org		1992			EC-K	
	NORTH VALLEY	33655 North 27th Dr 85085	(623)551-3454	Chriss@northvalleyca.org northvalleyca.org	Chris C Schoenleb Jr	2010	R	N	EC-12	781
	ST MARK	3030 E Thunderbird Rd 85032	(602)992-1980	kgrandprey@Hopephx.com www.stmarkphx.org/preschool	Kathy Grandprey	1963			EC	29
PRESCOTT VALLEY	*GODS WORLD*	3950 N Valorie Dr 86314	(928)772-0460	gods.worldtlc@ymail.com		1984			EC	129
QUEEN CREEK	*SAVING GRACE*	24414 S Ellsworth Rd 85142	(480)793-7380	cora@savinggracelc.org www.savinggracepreschool.org		2023			EC	88
SCOTTSDALE	*DESERT FOOTHILLS*	29305 N Scottsdale Rd 85266	(480)585-8007	martha@dflc.org www.dflc.org	Martha A Betcher	1998			EC-K	53
	SHEP OF THE DESERT	9400 E Mountain View Rd 85258	(480)860-0488	jmarmaduke@sotdaz.org shepherdaz.school	Jennifer Marmaduke	1983		N	EC	171
SEDONA	*PRECIOUS STONES*	390 Dry Creek Rd 86336	(928)282-4091	info@sedonalcms.com www.preciousstonespreschool.org		2002			EC	46
SURPRISE	*WORD OF LIFE*	17525 W Bell Rd 85374	(623)544-4608	director@wolschool.org www.wolschool.org	Ericca S Stoetzel	2004			EC	78
TEMPE	*GETHSEMANE*	1035 E Guadalupe Rd 85283	(480)839-0906	srosenbaum@gatempe.org gatempe.org	Sandy Rosenbaum	1978			EC-K	94
TUCSON	*ASCENSION*	1220 W Magee Rd 85704	(520)742-6229	e.russell@alcs-az.org www.ascensiontucson.org		1984			EC-K	
	FAITH	3925 E 5th St 85711	(520)881-0670	schooloffice@faith-lutheran.org www.faith-lutheran.org	Esther Lang	1952			EC-8	

R = Recognized Service Organization (RSO)
N = National Lutheran Schools Accreditation (NLSA)

CITY	SCHOOL	ADDRESS	PHONE	EMAIL WEBSITE	PRINCIPAL/ ADMINISTRATOR	YEAR ORG.	RSO	NLSA	GRADES OFFERED	ENROLL
VAIL	*CREATION*	14600 E Colossal Cave Rd 85641	(520)468-7075	creationschool@christlutheranvail.org www.creationschool.org	Jennifer L Hook				EC-5	95
YUMA	*YUMA*	2555 S Engler Ave 85365	(928)726-8410	jrogers@ylscrusaders.org www.yumalutheranschool.org	Robert J Rogers	1957		N	EC-8	473

ARKANSAS

CITY	SCHOOL	ADDRESS	PHONE	EMAIL WEBSITE	PRINCIPAL/ ADMINISTRATOR	YEAR ORG.	RSO	NLSA	GRADES OFFERED	ENROLL
BENTON	*FIRST*	18181 I-30 Frontage Rd 72015	(501)317-1325	Admin@Flsbenton.com flsbenton.com/	James D Burns				K-3	22
FAYETTEVILLE	*ST JOHN*	2730 E Township Rd 72703	(479)443-3620	stjohnschildren@aol.com stjohnschildren.com		1988			EC	41
FORT SMITH	*FIRST*	2407 Massard Rd 72903	(479)452-5330	sfishburn@1stlutheran.com 1stlutheran.com	Samuel P Fishburn	1853		N	EC-8	109
JONESBORO	*ALL SAINTS*	1812 S Rains 72401	(870)935-2001	headmaster@allsaintsjonesboro.org allsaintsjonesboro.org/school					1-12	13
LITTLE ROCK	*CHRIST*	315 S Hughes St 72205	(501)663-5212	csteely@christlittlerock.com christlittlerockschool.com		1870		N	EC-8	208
	GRACE	5124 Hillcrest Ave 72205	(501)663-0755	ecdc@gracelutheranlr.org www.gracelutheranlr.org	Colleen Moorman	1990			EC	65
ROGERS	*HOLY TRINITY PARENTS*	1101 W Hudson Rd 72756	(479)636-1135	pdo@holytrin.org holytrin.org/pdo	Leah Grimaldi O'Ryan				EC	33
SPRINGDALE	*SALEM*	1800 W Emma Ave 72762	(479)751-9500	staceymeyer272@gmail.com salemspringdale.com/	Kris Busch	1964			EC	46
STUTTGART	*ST JOHN*	2019 S BUERKLE ST 72160	(870)673-7096	sjlsstuttgart@gmail.com		1885			EC-6	192

CALIFORNIA

CITY	SCHOOL	ADDRESS	PHONE	EMAIL WEBSITE	PRINCIPAL/ ADMINISTRATOR	YEAR ORG.	RSO	NLSA	GRADES OFFERED	ENROLL
ALHAMBRA	*EMMAUS*	840 S Almansor St 91801	(626)289-3664	cspiva@emmausalhambra.org www.emmausalhambra.org	Cynthia L Spiva	1941		N	EC-8	131
ANAHEIM	*HEPHATHA*	5900 E Santa Ana Canyon Rd 92807	(714)637-0887	jglicker@hephatha.net www.hephatha.net	Jennifer Glicker	1983		N	EC-8	316
	PRINCE OF PEACE	1421 W Ball Rd 92802	(714)774-0993	mmilla@princeofpeaceanaheim.org	Maria E Milla	1993		N	EC	25
	PRINCE OF PEACE	1421 W Ball Rd 92802	(714)774-0993	jviolette@princeofpeaceanaheim.org princeofpeaceanaheim.org	James R Violette	1962		N	K-8	70
	TRINITY	4101 E Nohl Ranch Rd 92807	(714)637-8370	staceydavis@tlcanaheim.com www.trinityanaheim.com	Stacey L Davis				EC	96
	ZION	222 N East St 92805	(714)535-1172	smarousek@zionanaheim.org www.zionanaheim.org	Susan M Jennings-Marousek	1972		N	EC	32
	ZION	1244 E Cypress St 92805	(714)535-3600	school@zionanaheim.org www.zionanaheim.com	Amy Jacobson	1909		N	K-8	103
ARROYO GRANDE	*PEACE*	244 Oak Park 93420	(805)489-9644	director@peacearroyogrande.com www.peacearroyogrande.com	Doris Angel	1981			EC	
BAKERSFIELD	*ST JOHN*	4500 Buena Vista Rd 93311	(661)664-8090	eanwyl@sjlschool.org www.sjlschool.org	Evan S Anwyl	1977		N	EC-8	
	WONDER WINDOW	8001 Panorama Dr 93306	(661)871-7051	wonderwindow@lcop.org www.lcop.org	Vanessa Stewart	1972			EC	24
BARSTOW	*CONCORDIA*	420 Avenue E 92311	(760)256-8979	concordiaschoolbarstow@gmail.com www.concordialutheranbarstow.org	Debbie Barajas	1985			EC	58
BENICIA	*NOAHS ARK*	201 Raymond Dr 94510	(707)746-1868	BLCNoahsArk@sbcglobal.net www.benicialutheranchurch.com	Hebu Abu Ghazaleh	1993			EC	
BREA	*CHRIST*	820 W Imperial Hwy 92821	(714)529-0892	mrsblain@clsbrea.com www.clsbrea.com	Amy K Blain	1969		N	EC-8	251
BRENTWOOD	*WEE CARE*	1275 Fairview Ave 94513	(925)634-5180	farber.sabrina@yahoo.com	Adrienne L Lough	2004			EC	
BURLINGAME	*TRINITY*	1505 Sherman Ave 94010	(650)580-2349	preschooloffice@trinityburlingame.org trinity-lutheran-preschool.org	Jam Eyvazov	2012			EC	54
CAMARILLO	*PEACE*	71 Loma Dr 93010	(805)987-1613	preschool@peacecamarillo.com peacecamarillo.com	Rachael Ylizaliturri	1979			EC	23
CANYON COUNTRY	*BETHLEHEM*	27265 Luther Dr 91351	(661)251-6027	preschool@bethlehemscv.com bethlehemscvpreschool.com	Marsha MacIntyre	1985			EC	52
CARLSBAD	*REDEEMER BY THE SEA*	6604 Black Rail Rd 92011	(760)431-8293	director@redeemerbythesea.org www.redeemerkp.com	Lindsey Malloy	2005			EC-K	147
CERRITOS	*CONCORDIA*	13633 183rd St 90703	(562)926-2491	school@concordia.org concordia.org	Elizabeth Medina	1980			EC	9
CHINO HILLS	*LOVING SAVIOR*	14816 Peyton Dr 91709	(909)597-2948	vwend@lovingsavior.org www.lovingsavior.org/school.html	Valorie Wend	1993		N	EC-8	449
CHULA VISTA	*CONCORDIA*	1695 Discovery Falls Dr 91915	(619)656-8100	director@concordiachurch.com www.concordiaschool.org	Rexanna M Blas				EC	103
	VICTORY	810 Buena Vista Way 91910	(619)262-4444	scott.dufresne@victorysouthbay.org www.victorysouthbay.org	Scott R Dufresne	1975	R	N	K-12	319
CONCORD	*FIRST*	4006 Concord Blvd 94519	(925)798-5330	director@flpsconcord.org www.flpsconcord.org	Jeni Smith	1993			EC	43
CORONA	*GRACE*	1114 W Ontario Ave 92882	(951)737-2187	gracelutherancorona@gmail.com	Lisa Hatton	2014			EC-K	70
COSTA MESA	*CHRIST*	760 Victoria St 92627	(949)548-6866	robbie.bouslaugh@christcm.org www.school.christcm.org	Robbie Bouslaugh	1953		N	EC-8	314
CUPERTINO	*AGNUS DEI*	5825 Bollinger Rd 95014		agnusdeilca@lcos.org agnusdeilutheranclassicalacademy.org/	Yvonne Belloncle				K-8	
DALY CITY	*HOPE*	55 San Fernando Way 94015	(650)991-4673	preschool@hopedalycity.org www.hopedayschool.org	Cynthia Huang	1987			EC	145
DIAMOND BAR	*MT CALVARY*	23300 E Golden Springs Dr 91765	(909)861-2740	brenda.cox@mcldb.org www.mcldb.org	Deryl R Maxwell	1983		N	EC-8	267
DUBLIN	*ST PHILIP*	8850 Davona Dr 94568	(925)829-3857	cthung@stphilipchurch.com www.stphiliplutheranschool.com	Raymond E Zinnel	1984			EC-K	

R = Recognized Service Organization (RSO)
N = National Lutheran Schools Accreditation (NLSA)

CITY	SCHOOL	ADDRESS	PHONE	EMAIL WEBSITE	PRINCIPAL/ ADMINISTRATOR	YEAR ORG.	RSO	NLSA	GRADES OFFERED	ENROLL
EL CAJON	*FIRST*	867 S Lincoln Ave 92020	(619)444-0559	preschool@youhaveaplace.com www.youhaveaplace.com/our-preschool/	Ramona Van Deweghe	1986			EC	
EL SEGUNDO	*ST JOHN'S*	1611 E Sycamore Ave 90245	(310)615-0211	josie@stjohnspreschooles.org www.stjohnspreschooles.com	Josie Meade	1967			EC	38
ENCINITAS	*ST MARK*	556 S El Camino Real 92024	(760)231-1917	aconrad@stmarkpreschool.org stmarkpreschool.org	Annette Conrad	2006			EC	50
ESCONDIDO	*COMMUNITY*	3575 E Valley Parkway 92027	(760)739-8649	lhaskell@clclfamily.org clcfamily.org/preschool	Lori Haskell	1993			EC	
	GRACE	643 W 13th Ave 92025	(760)747-3029	vlippman@gracelcms.net www.graceschoolescondido.org	Benjamin C Elliott	1957		N	EC-8	242
EXETER	*LITTLE LAMBS*	420 Sequoia Dr 93221	(559)592-1935	Littlelambsexeter@gmail.com	Christina Clark	1991			EC-K	
FAIR OAKS	*FAITH*	4000 San Juan Ave 95628	(916)961-6069	lmanges@faithfairoaks.com www.faithfairoaks.com	Lisa Manges	1955			EC	38
FALLBROOK	*ZION*	1405 E Fallbrook St 92028	(760)723-3500	zionschool@zlcs.org zionfallbrookpreschool.org	Lana L Janey	1985			EC-K	106
FREMONT	*PRINCE OF PEACE*	38451 FREMONT BLVD 94536	(510)797-8186	school@popfremont.org www.popfremont.org	Leah K Rushton	1957		N	EC-8	399
FULLERTON	*IREMNANT*	1521 W Orangethorp Ave 92833	(714)992-5008	iremnantpreschool@gmail.com iremnantpreschool.com					EC	68
	SEARCHLIGHT	2311 E Chapman Ave 92631	(714)871-6641	preschool@searchlightministries.com	Barbara C Williams	1971			EC	24
GARDENA	*PACIFIC*	1473 W 182nd St 90248	(310)538-6865	office@paclutheran.com pacificlutheranhigh.com	Catherine A Hittinger		R		6-12	131
GLENDORA	*HOPE*	1041 E Foothill Blvd 91741	(626)335-5315	principal@hopeglendora.org www.hopeglendora.org	Brenda M Nguyen	1960		N	EC-8	199
GOLETA	*GOOD SHEPHERD*	380 N Fairview Ave 93117	(805)967-6101	kreckertgsps@gmail.com	Susan L Huthsing	1985			EC	43
GRANADA HILLS	*CONCORDIA CHRISTIAN*	16603 San Fernando Mission Blvd 91344	(818)368-0892	katy.moore@concordiaschoolsla.org www.concordiagranadahills.com	Katherine L Moore	1954	R		EC-8	170
HEALDSBURG	*LITTLE LAMBS*	1402 University Ave 95448	(707)433-5779	director@mylittlelambspreschool.com	Ana Alvarenga	2003			EC	
HEMET	*PRINCE OF PEACE*	701 N Sanderson 92545	(951)925-9798	popschool2014@hotmail.com www.princeofpeace.org	Lucy Coronado	2009			EC-K	46
	ST JOHN	26410 Columbia St 92544	(951)925-7756	nbellamy@stjohnshemet.org www.stjohnshemet.org	Nancy J Bellamy	1983		N	EC-8	298
HUNTINGTON BEACH	*CHILD OF FAITH*	8200 Ellis Ave 92646	(714)962-1864	desiree.robles@christhb.org www.childoffaith.org	Desiree Robles	1985			EC	
	REDEEMER	16351 Springdale St 92649	(714)840-7117	preschool.director@redeemer-lutheran.net www.redeemer-lutheran.net	Melinda Weiss	1986			EC	14
IRVINE	*LIGHT OF CHRIST*	18182 Culver Dr 92612	(949)786-3997	bruehs.loc@gmail.com lightofchristpreschool.com	Sheryl L Grobelch	1980		N	EC	53
LA MESA	*CHRIST*	7929 La Mesa Blvd 91942	(619)462-5211	mbrouker@lutheranschool.org www.lutheranschool.org		1957		N	EC-8	222
LAKE FOREST	*ABIDING SAVIOR*	23262 El Toro Rd 92630	(949)830-1461	dlucas@abidingsavior.com abidingsavior.com	Donna Lucas	1974		N	EC-8	354
LANCASTER	*GRACE*	856 W Newgrove St 93534	(661)948-1018	principal@gracelancaster.org www.gracelancaster.org	Karen J Markin	1958		N	EC-8	70
LIVERMORE	*OUR SAVIOR*	1385 S Livermore Ave 94550	(925)447-1246	oslm@oslm.net www.oslm.net	Julie Knight	1975		N	EC-8	510
LODI	*ST PETER*	2400 Oxford Way 95242	(209)333-2225	dmunsch@stpeterlodi.org www.stpeterlodi.com	Dale Munsch	1904		N	EC-8	355
	ZION CHILDCARE	105 S Ham Lane 95242	(209)369-1910	jennifer@ziclodi.org zlclodi.org	Jennifer Sawyer	2009			EC	
LONG BEACH	*BETHANY*	4644 Clark Ave 90808	(562)429-7335	tsimpson@bethanylutheran.org www.bethanylutheran.org	Tamara A Simpson	1974		N	EC	91
	BETHANY	5100 E Arbor Rd 90808	(562)420-7783	principal@bethanylutheran.org www.bethanylutheran.org		1947		N	K-8	191
	ST PAULS	2285 Palo Verde 90815	(562)598-4729	preschool@stpaulslb.org www.stpaulslb.org		2000			EC	
LOS GATOS	*HOLY CROSS*	15885 Los Gatos Almaden Rd 95032	(408)356-6828	childrenscenter@holycrosslosgatos.com holycrosslosgatos.com	Cynthia J Fehrenbach	1990			K-5	116
MANHATTAN BEACH	*FIRST CIRCLE OF LOVE*	1100 N Poinsettia Ave 90266	(310)545-5653	director@first-lutheran.com www.FLCOL.org		1986		N	EC	111
MENLO PARK	*LITTLEST ANGELS BETH*	1095 Cloud Ave 94025	(650)854-4973	katieo@bethany-mp.org www.bethany-mp.org	Kathie O' Malley	1996			EC	45
MERCED	*ST PAUL*	2916 MCKEE RD 95340	(209)383-3302	school@stpaulmerced.com www.stpaulmerced.com	Ruth Sebastian	1988		N	EC-6	107
MODESTO	*GRACE*	617 W Orangeburg Ave 95350	(209)522-6393	preschool@gracemodesto.org www.gracelutheranschool.com	Cindy Steele	1983			EC	29
MONROVIA	*FIRST*	1227 S Magnolia Ave 91016	(626)303-3950	flprem@gmail.com preschool.lutheranmonrovia.org/	Joana Afuang	1949			EC	23
MONTEBELLO	*ST JOHN*	425 N 18th St 90640	(323)722-9885	stjohns323@gmail.com stjohnsmontebello.info	Bernadette Galindo	1913			EC	60
MORENO VALLEY	*SHEP OF THE VALLEY*	11650 Perris Blvd 92557	(951)924-3422	psdirector@svlcmoval.net www.svllearningcenter.com	Linda M Williamson	1985			EC-K	
MOUNTAIN VIEW	*ST PAUL*	1075 El Monte Ave 94040	(650)969-2696	cdc@st-paul.org st-paul.org/cdc		1988			EC-K	
NAPA	*ST JOHN*	3521 Linda Vista Ave 94558	(707)226-7970	jdahl@stjohnsnapa.org www.stjohnsnapa.org	Christy L Wood	1938		N	EC-8	293
NEWBURY PARK	*CHRIST THE KING*	3947 W Kimber Dr 91320	(805)499-7022	ctkkids@ctknp.com christthekingpreschoolnp.com		1982			EC	29
NORWALK	*TRINITY*	11609 Studebaker 90650	(562)864-2319	torres.debbie@yahoo.com www.tlc-norwalk.org	Debbie Torres				EC	25

R = Recognized Service Organization (RSO)
N = National Lutheran Schools Accreditation (NLSA)

CITY	SCHOOL	ADDRESS	PHONE	EMAIL WEBSITE	PRINCIPAL/ ADMINISTRATOR	YEAR ORG.	RSO	NLSA	GRADES OFFERED	ENROLL
NORWALK	TRINITY	11507 Studebaker 90650	(562)864-3712	dlove@tcstigers.net www.tcstigers.net					EC-8	92
ONTARIO	REDEEMER	920 W 6th St 91762	(909)986-6510	pthompson@redeemer4me.com www.redeemer4me.com	Monica Osorio	1952			EC	20
ORANGE	IMMANUEL	147 S Pine St 92866	(714)538-2374	preschool@immanuelorange.org www.immanuelorange.com/preschool		1922			EC	64
	SALEM	6411 E Frank Ln 92869	(714)639-1946	csheets@salemorange.com www.salemorange.com	Corissa M Sheets	1983		N	EC-8	574
	ST JOHNS	154 S Shaffer St 92866	(714)288-4406	jhollatz@stjohnsorange.org www.sjls.org	Dr Jacob D Hollatz	1882		N	EC-8	824
	ST PAUL	901 E Heim Ave 92865	(714)921-3188	www.splsorange.org	Jackson R Thiesfeldt	1908		N	EC-8	383
	ST PAUL'S	1250 E Heim Ave 92865	(714)637-2416	heidi.delamotte@splsorange.org www.splsorange.org		1985		N	EC	173
PASO ROBLES	TRINITY	940 Creston Rd 93446	(805)238-0335	principal@trinitypaso.com www.trinitypaso.com		1962		N	EC-8	156
PLEASANT HILL	FAITH FOOTPRINTS	50 Woodsworth Dr 94523	(925)685-7353	mary@welcome2faith.com	Mary Margaret Robbers				EC	
POWAY	MT OLIVE	14280 Poway Rd 92064	(858)679-8169	mtolive.hfangon@gmail.com www.mtolivepreschool.net	Heather Fangon	1983			EC	68
RAMONA	RAMONA	520 16th St 92065	(760)789-4804	office@ramonalutheran.org www.ramonalutheran.org	Melissa Hunsberger	1976			EC-7	63
RANCHO PALOS VERDES	CHRIST	28850 S Western Ave 90275	(310)831-0848	office@clschool.org www.christrpv.com	Charlene Soon	1955		N	EC-8	209
	MOUNT OLIVE	5975 Armaga Spring Rd 90275	(310)377-8821	mtolivepreschool@aol.com www.mtoliverpv.com	David Welch	1991			EC	65
REDDING	TRINITY	2440 Hilltop Dr 96002	(530)221-6686	crystal@reddingtlc.org	Crystal Connor	1990			EC	41
REDLANDS	CHRIST THE KING	1505 Ford St 92373	(909)793-8722	scoectk@yahoo.com www.ctkredlands.org	Sheri Coe	1981			EC-K	290
REDWOOD CITY	REDEEMER	468 Grand St 94062	(650)366-3466	info@redeemerrwc.org www.redeemer-school.org	Michael J Mancini	1956		N	EC-8	150
RIDGECREST	OUR SAVIOR'S	725 N Fairview St 93555	(760)375-7921	dayschool@oslc-rc.org www.oslc-rc.org	Clinton S Hoff				K-9	
RIVERSIDE	IMMANUEL	5455 Alessandro Blvd 92506	(951)682-4211	www.immanuelriverside.com	Dr Susan Buster	1957		N	EC-6	245
ROCKLIN	HOLY CROSS	4701 Grove St 95677	(916)624-2123	director@hclarocklin.org www.hclarocklin.org	Kim Lunsford	2007			EC-K	100
RUNNING SPRINGS	MOUNT CALVARY	32054 Hunsaker Way 92382	(909)337-7750	mckids3335@gmail.com www.mclutheranschools.com	Kimberly R Kopecky	1989			EC-2	61
SACRAMENTO	ANGELS NEST	475 Florin Rd 95831	(916)428-4651	angelsnestschool@sbcglobal.net www.angelsnestcdc.com	Kim McDonald	2001			EC	
SALINAS	OUR SAVIOR	1230 Luther Way 93901	(831)422-4614	info@salinaspreschool.com www.SalinasPreschool.com	Susan M Klemsz	1999			EC	23
SAN DIEGO	CHRIST CORNERSTONE	9028 Westmore Rd 92126	(858)566-1741	accounting@ctc-academy.org www.ctc-academy.org	Tammy Peters	1978			EC-5	113
	ST PAULS	1376 Felspar St 92109	(858)272-6282	mbinnie@stpaulspb.com www.stpaulspb.com	Meredith F Binnie	1946		N	EC-8	187
SAN FRANCISCO	HUG	3830 Noriega Street 94122	(415)664-4500	hug3830@gmail.com www.hugpreschool.com	Krissel Potter	2018			EC	
	WEST PORTAL	200 Sloat Blvd 94132	(415)665-6330	school@wplsf.com wplsf.com		1951		N	K-8	348
	ZION	495 9th Ave 94118	(415)221-7500	principal@zionsf.org www.zionsf.org	Jennifer L Lee	1947		N	K-8	155
SAN JOSE	SHEP OF THE VALLEY	1281 Redmond Ave 95120	(408)997-4848	www.shepherdofthevalleypreschool.org	Kennedy N Tania	1981			EC	
SAN LUIS OBISPO	ZION PRESCH	1010 E Foothfill Blvd 93405	(805)549-4441	preschool.director@zionslo.com zionpreschoolslo.com	Ella Batson				EC	
SAN RAFAEL	TRINITY	333 Woodland Ave 94901	(415)453-4526	natalie@trinitypreschool.com trinitypreschool.com	Natalie Levy	1987			EC	76
SANTA CRUZ	MESSIAH	801 High St 95060	(831)458-1498	messiahlc@sbcglobal.net	Gretchen Thigpen	1982			EC	
SANTA MARIA	GRACE	420 E Fesler St 93454	(805)922-5419	glpreschool93454@gmail.com	Crystal Corken	1966			EC	
	OUR SAV UPWARD BOUND	1040 Patterson Rd 93455	(805)938 5121	upwardbound.lcos@gmail.com www.lcos.net	Hether Frias	2000			EC	29
SANTA ROSA	ST LUKE	905 Mendocino Ave 95401	(707)545-6772	pre-k@stluke-lcms.org www.stluke-lcms.org	Jeanne Gerhardt	1975			EC	
SHERMAN OAKS	SHERMAN OAKS	14847 Dickens St 91403	(818)784-9480	sochildrenscenter@sbcglobal.net lutheranchildrenscenter.org	Diane J Nixon	1974			EC	
SIMI VALLEY	GOOD SHEPHERD	2949 Alamo St 93063	(805)526-2482	admin@gsls-simi.com gsls-simi.com	Karen E Clakley-Jonas	1979		N	K-5	52
	TRINITY	2949 Alamo St 93063	(805)526-5975	klauner@tlcsimi.com	Kerri Launer	1978			EC	102
STOCKTON	NEWDAY	4910 Claremont Ave 95207	(209)957-4089	Newday@stalc.org standrewsstockton.org	Marla Rivas	1975			EC	29
TEHACHAPI	GOOD SHEPHERD	329 S Mill St 93561	(661)823-7740	gspstehachapi@yahoo.com gslctehachapi.com	Kristen Arnecke	1994			EC	56
TEMECULA	TRINITY	30470 Pauba Rd 92592	(951)676-1492	kkennedy@trinitytemecula.info www.trinityisone.com	Kerry Kennedy	1997			EC-K	147
TERRA BELLA	ZION	10368 Road 256 93270	(559)535-4346	zionlutheran@ocsnet.net www.zionterrabella.org	Jacob W Dandy	1909			K-6	
TORRANCE	ASCENSION	17910 S Prairie Ave 90504	(310)371-3531	schooloffice@ascensiontorrance.org ascensiontorrance.org	Briana Minton-Jensen	1960			EC	29
TRACY	BELLA VISTA	1635 Chester Dr 95376	(209)835-7438	ljackson@stpaulstracy.org www.bellavistaca.com	Lisa Jackson	2000		N	EC-8	354

R = Recognized Service Organization (RSO)
N = National Lutheran Schools Accreditation (NLSA)

CITY	SCHOOL	ADDRESS	PHONE	EMAIL WEBSITE	PRINCIPAL/ ADMINISTRATOR	YEAR ORG.	RSO	NLSA	GRADES OFFERED	ENROLL
VACAVILLE	BETHANY	1011 Ulatis Dr 95687	(707)451-6683	myschool@gobethany.com www.gobethany.com	Alex Poole	1974		N	EC-8	139
VICTORVILLE	ZION	15342 Jeraldo Dr 92394	(760)243-3074	pastor@zionvv.org zionvv.org	Lewis M Busch	1982			EC-6	42
VISALIA	GRACE	1111 S Conyer St 93277	(559)734-7694	principal@gracechristianvisalia.org gracechristianvisalia.org	Joanne M Cook	1977			EC-8	111
WESTCHESTER	OUR SAVIOR	6705 W 77th St 90045	(310)215-3166	childrenofoursavior@gmail.com oursaviorwestchester.org/church/calendar/preschool/	Chisela Tembo	2002			EC	25
WINNETKA	OUR REDEEMER	8520 Winnetka Ave 91306	(818)700-0390	school@our-redeemer.org www.our-redeemerschool.org	Gennievie Ada-Atilon	1984			EC	36
WOODLAND	ST PAUL	625 W Gibson Rd 95695	(530)662-1935	preschool@stpaulswoodland.org stpaulswoodland.org/preschool	Jill Hardin	1983			EC	30
COLORADO										
ALAMOSA	TRINITY	52 El Rio Dr 81101	(719)589-3271	trinangels@yahoo.com lutheranchurchschoolalamosa.org	Mary L Conner	1982			EC-2	
ARVADA	PEACE	5675 Field Street 80002	(303)431-4494	earlylearning@peacelutheran.net www.peacelutheran.net		2004		N	EC-K	
AURORA	MOUNT OLIVE	11500 E Iliff Ave 80014	(303)750-9856	ececmtolive@gmail.com www.mtolc.org/preschool		1972			EC	41
	PEACE WITH CHRIST	3290 S Tower Rd 80013	(303)766-7116	pwccs@pwclc.org www.pwccs.org	David P Robinson	1994		N	EC-8	218
	PEACE WITH CHRIST	3290 S Tower Rd 80013	(303)699-8687	elc@pwclc.org		1987		N	EC	
BOULDER	MOUNT ZION	1680 Balsam Ave 80304	(303)443-8477	office@mtzionboulder.org www.mtzionboulder.org	Cheryl L Wu	1986			EC	26
BRIGHTON	ZION	1400 Skeel St 80601	(303)659-3443	school@zionbrighton.org www.brightonzls.org		1899		N	EC-8	261
BROOMFIELD	BEAUTIFUL SAVIOR	6995 W 120th Ave 80020	(303)469-2049	bslsstars@gmail.com www.beautifulsaviorbroomfield.org	Sonya Acker	1980			EC-5	
CARBONDALE	FAITH	1340 Hwy 133 81623	(970)510-5694	childcare@faithcarbondale.com	Cindi Maynard	2014			EC	
CENTENNIAL	OUR FATHER	6335 S Holly St 80121	(303)779-4910	hhenz@ourfatherlutheran.net www.oflc.net		1999			EC	161
	SHEPHERD HILLS	7691 S University Blvd 80122	(303)798-0711	info@sothfamily.org www.shepherdhillselc.org		1985			EC	
COLORADO SPRINGS	FAMILY OF CHRIST	675 Baptist Rd 80921	(719)481-0796	cdcinfo@foccs.net www.foccs.net	Amy J Campbell	1998			EC-K	
	HOLY CROSS	4125 Constitution Ave 80909	(719)596-0661	hcls@holycrosscs.org holycrosscs.org	Deborah A Schrank	1999			EC	30
	ROCK OF AGES	120 N 31st St 80904	(719)632-9394	rockofagespreschool@gmail.com roalcms.org		1983			EC-K	25
CORTEZ	TRINITY	208 N Dolores Rd 81321	(970)565-3166	trinitylpdirector@gmail.com www.tlpcortez.org	Misty Judson	1983			EC	32
DELTA	TINY TREASURES	1000 Pioneer Rd 81416	(970)874-3052	tinytreasures.lcms@gmail.com www.redeemerlutheranschool.org		2001			EC-6	95
DENVER	CHRIST	2695 S Franklin St 80210	(303)722-1424	sheri@littlelambs.academy www.christlutherandenver.org		1984			EC	22
	ST JOHN'S	700 S Franklin St 80209	(303)733-3778	k-8info@sjdenver.org www.sjdenverschool.org		1888		N	EC-8	
FORT COLLINS	OPEN ARMS	305 E Elizabeth St 80524	(970)482-1357	openarms@stjohnsfc.org www.openarmsfc.org	Kandy Wise	1994			EC	30
	REDEEMER	7755 Greenstone Tr 80525	(970)206-0381	teckla@redeemerconnect.com www.redeemerconnect.com	Teckla R Coerber	1994			EC	
FORT MORGAN	TRINITY	1215 W 7th Ave 80701	(970)867-4931	school.secretary@trinitylutheranfort morgan.com trinitylutheranfortmorgan.com	Carri Brown	1979			EC-5	
FRANKTOWN	TRINITY	4740 N Highway 83 80116	(303)841-4660	trinityschool@tlcas.org tlcas.org	Deanna J Christiansan-Ayers	1993		N	EC-8	121
GRAND JUNCTION	MESSIAH	840 N 11th St 81501	(970)245-2838	admin@mlgj.org www.messiahlutherangj.org	Susan L Eberhard	1979		N	EC-8	76
GREELEY	TRINITY	3000 35th Ave 80634	(970)330-2485	office@tlgreeley.com tlsgreeley.org		1945			EC-5	64
LAKEWOOD	BETHLEHEM	2100 Wadsworth Blvd 80214	(303)233-0401	bethlehemdenver.com	Yvette Kampschnieder	1940		N	EC-8	276
	CONCORDIA	13371 W Alameda Pkwy 80228	(303)989-5260	preschool@concordialcms.org www.concordialcms.org	Linda Capaldo-Smith	1987			EC-K	
LITTLETON	ASCENSION	1701 W Caley Ave 80120	(303)730-2514	director@alcpreschool.com alcpreschool.com	Kelly Lafferty				EC	13
LOVELAND	IMMANUEL	4650 Sunview Dr 80538	(970)667-7606	schooloffice@immanuelloveland.org school.immanuelloveland.org	Cheryl E Gilbert	1977		N	EC-9	143
PAGOSA SPRINGS	OUR SAVIOR	56 Meadows Dr 81147	(970)731-3512	annettemcinnis@yahoo.com www.oslcpagosa.org/our_savior_lutheran_school.htm	Anette Mc Innis	1992			EC-1	
PUEBLO	TRINITY	701 W Evans Ave 81004	(719)542-1864	trinity.dibarra@gmail.com www.trinitylutheranpueblo.org	Derion Ibara	1893			K-5	75
	TRINITY	701 W Evans Ave 81004	(719)562-9235	trinitychildcarectr@gmail.com		1999			EC	
RIFLE	EMMANUEL	652 E 5th St 81650	(970)625-4978	elprifle@gmail.com	Trixy Falke	1999			EC-3	48
STERLING	TRINITY	732 CLARK ST 80751	(970)522-5942	tleec2015@gmail.com	Tamara Dugan	1998			EC	166
WOODLAND PARK	FAITH	1310 Evergreen Hgts Dr 80863	(719)687-8060	preschool@faithteller.org www.faithteller.org	Megan Osborn	1999			EC	

R = Recognized Service Organization (RSO)
N = National Lutheran Schools Accreditation (NLSA)

CITY	SCHOOL	ADDRESS	PHONE	EMAIL WEBSITE	PRINCIPAL/ ADMINISTRATOR	YEAR ORG.	RSO	NLSA	GRADES OFFERED	ENROLL
CONNECTICUT										
AMSTON	*CHRIST*	330 Church St 06231	(860)228-5134	director@clecchebron.org www.CLECCHebron.org	Polly J Simon	2004			EC	
BRISTOL	*IMMANUEL*	154 Meadow St 06010	(860)583-5631	dkrueger@ilcs.org www.ilcs.org/school	Dr Anne E Stuhlman	1898		N	EC-8	159
CHESHIRE	*LITTLE CHERUBS*	660 West Main Street 06410	(203)272-1150	littlecherubs@cheshirelutheran.org www.cheshirelutheran.org/preschool.asp		1997			EC	
DANBURY	*IMMANUEL*	18 Clapboard Ridge Rd 06811	(203)748-7823	schooloffice@immanueldanbury.org www.immanueldanbury.org		1881		N	EC-8	65
MERIDEN	*ST JOHN*	520 Paddock Ave 06450	(203)630-3997	office@saintjohnmeriden.org		1971			EC	26
MIDDLETOWN	*GRACE*	1055 Randolph Rd 06457	(860)346-0766	glpdirector1055@gmail.com gelcps.org	Diana Cathcart	1988			EC	49
SOUTH WINDSOR	*OUR SAVIOR*	239 Graham Rd 06074	(860)644-6458	OSPCC_admin@oursaviorct.org www.oursaviorchildcare.com/		1985			EC	79
TRUMBULL	*HOLY CROSS*	5995 Main St 06611	(203)268-6471	preschool@holycrosstrumbull.com www.holycrosstrumbull.org	Michele Glennon	1987			EC	
WALLINGFORD	*LITTLE ZION*	235 Pond Hill Rd 06492	(203)269-0401	littlezionpreschool@hotmail.com www.littlezionpreschool.com		1986			EC	
WEST HARTFORD	*BETHANY*	1655 Boulevard 06107	(860)521-8782	nurseryschool@blcwh.org www.blcwh.org	Mari L Mikulastik	1959			EC	
WESTPORT	*ST PAUL*	41 Easton Rd 06880	(203)227-7920	school@stpaulwestport.org stpaulchristianschool.org		1976			EC-K	60
DELAWARE										
BEAR	*FAITH*	2265 Red Lion Rd 19701	(302)834-3417	preschool@faith-lutheran.church www.faith-lutheran.chuch/preschool/	Diana Roman	1996			EC	
WILMINGTON	*CONCORDIA*	3003 Silverside Rd 19810	(302)478-3004	director@concordiapreschool.org concordiapreschool.org		1980			EC	
FLORIDA										
BOCA RATON	*ST PAUL*	701 W Palmetto Park Rd 33486	(561)395-8548	jrichards@stpaulbocaschool.com www.stpaulbocaschool.com	James K Richards	1962		N	EC-8	422
BRANDON	*IMMANUEL*	2913 John Moore Rd 33511	(813)685-1978	office@ilsbrandon.com www.ilsbrandon.com	Dr Joan E Davis	1980		N	EC-8	222
CLEARWATER	*FIRST*	1644 Nursery Rd 33756	(727)462-8000	schooloffice@flcclearwater.org flcclearwater.org	Jack Lustilla	1975		N	EC-8	
DAVIE	*GLORIA DEI*	7601 SW 39th St 33328	(954)475-8584	wendy.turpin@gloria-dei.org www.gloriadeiacademy.org	Wendy Turpin	1979		N	EC	45
DELRAY BEACH	*TRINITY*	400 N Swinton Ave 33444	(561)276-8458	hlowing@trinitydelray.org trinitydelray.org	Heather M Lowing	1948		N	EC-8	460
ENGLEWOOD	*REDEEMER*	6970 Mineola Rd 34224	(941)475-2631	rlcc@ewol.com www.redeemerfl.com/childcare.htm	Wendy Horvath	1998			EC-6	99
EUSTIS	*FAITH*	2727 S Grove St 32726	(352)589-5683	tleech@flcse.org www.faitheustis.com	Timothy M Leech	1965		N	EC-8	285
FORT LAUDERDALE	*SHEP OF THE COAST*	1901 E Commercial Blvd 33308	(954)772-5468	dharvin@shepherdofthecoast.org sotcfl.org	Faith Granbow	1974		N	EC-8	
FORT MYERS	*SAINT MICHAEL*	3595 Broadway 33901	(239)939-1218	kati.miser@gsmlcs.org www.smlcs.org	Kati Miser	1956		N	EC-8	507
	ZION	7401 Winkler Rd 33919	(239)481-4040	bethw@zionfm.org zlsfm.org		2007		N	EC-7	82
FORT PIERCE	*OPEN ARMS*	2015 S 13th St 34950	(772)489-4800	loretta.gibbonsoa@gmail.com openarms4kids.com	Angela Thrasher	2011			EC-2	
GAINESVILLE	*ABIDING SAVIOR*	9700 W Newberry Rd 32606	(352)331-7770	barden@abidingsavior.info www.abidingsavior.info	Brenda K Arden	1994			EC	186
	OPEN ARMS	1823 NW 5th Ave 32603	(352)373-5856	amburrx2@yahoo.com flcgainesville.org	Angie Burr	2008			EC	82
GULF BREEZE	*GOOD SHEPHERD*	4257 Gulf Breeze Pkwy 32563	(850)932-9127	goodshepherdlutheranschool.1@gmail.com www.goodshepherdgb.com		1998			EC-6	81
HIALEAH	*FAITH*	293 Hialeah Dr 33010	(305)885-2845	schooloffice@faithlutheranhialeah.org www.faithlutheranhialeah.org	Zaida Valdes	1975		N	EC-8	79
HOBE SOUND	*BETHEL*	7905 SE Federal Hwy 33455	(772)546-7506	bethel_preschool@bellsouth.net www.bethel-lutheranhobesound.org/	Elizabeth Brown	1986		N	EC	109
JACKSONVILLE	*GRACE*	12200 Mc Cormick Rd 32225	(904)928-9136	principal@gracelutheraneagles.org www.gracelcms.com	Sonya Timmerman	1998		N	EC-8	223
JACKSONVILLE BEACH	*BETHLEHEM*	1423 8th Ave N 32250	(904)249-1204	bethlehemcenter@bellsouth.net	Patricia May	1986			EC	114
KEY WEST	*GRACE*	2713 Flagler Ave 33040	(305)296-8262	amydonaldson.glskw@gmail.com www.glskw.org	Amy Donaldson	1951			EC-8	127
LAKE PLACID	*TRINITY TOTS*	25 Lakeview St 33852	(863)465-6313	trinitytotslp@yahoo.com		1989		N	EC	43
LAKE WORTH	*EPIPHANY*	4460 Lyons Rd 33467	(561)968-3627	director@epiphanylakeworth.com www.epiphanylakeworth.com	Erica Agosta	1988		N	EC	73
LAKELAND	*ST PAUL*	4450 Harden Blvd 33813	(863)644-7710	gsawyer@stpaullakeland.org www.splslakeland.org	Gregory L Sawyer	1964		N	EC-8	508
LARGO	*CHRIST THE KING*	11220 Oakhurst Rd 33774	(727)595-2112	SchoolOffice@CTKLM.org CTK.School	Nichole DuBois	2007		N	EC-1	37
LUTZ	*LITTLE LAMBS*	20741 Leonard Rd 33558	(813)949-3611	dawnmariebernicky@verizon.net www.holytrinitylutz.com	Dawn M Bernicky	1997			EC-5	106
MERRITT ISLAND	*FAITH*	290 E Merritt Ave 32953	(321)452-4143	meredith.leon@faithlutheranmi.org faithlutheranmi.org		1966			EC	34

R = Recognized Service Organization (RSO)
N = National Lutheran Schools Accreditation (NLSA)

CITY	SCHOOL	ADDRESS	PHONE	EMAIL WEBSITE	PRINCIPAL/ ADMINISTRATOR	YEAR ORG.	RSO	NLSA	GRADES OFFERED	ENROLL
MIAMI	*CONCORDIA*	8701 SW 124th St 33176	(305)235-0160	fernanda@concordiaschool.net concordiaschool.net	Jennifer Lature	1961			EC	125
MONTVERDE	*WOODLANDS*	15333 County Road 455 34756	(407)469-2525	elcdirector@woodlandschurch.com www.woodlandschurch.com	Andie Bell	1993		N	EC	112
NAPLES	*GRACE*	860 Banyan Blvd 34102	(941)261-7700	julie.gracelutheranpreschool@gmail.com graceofnaples.org	Julie Crews	1994			EC	24
	LAMBS OF FAITH	4150 Goodlette Rd N 34103	(239)434-9277	lambsoffaith@flcnaples.com www.flc-naples.org	Karen Graham	1990			EC	
	PEACE	9850 Immokalee Rd 34120	(239)354-9140	info@peacekidsnaples.org www.peacekidsnaples.org	Betty Hernandez				EC	128
NORTH FORT MYERS	*GOOD SHEPHERD*	4770 Orange Grove Blvd 33903	(239)995-7711	pastordavis@goodshepofnfm.com www.goodshepofnfm.org		1967		N	EC-12	281
NORTH MIAMI	*HOLY CROSS*	650 NE 135th St 33161	(305)893-0851	cselby@holycross-nm.org www.holycrosslions.org	Christine Selby	1951		N	EC-8	316
NORTH PALM BEACH	*FAITH*	301 Ebbtide Dr 33408	(561)842-2487	ptucker@faithnpb.com www.faithnpb.com	Pilar Tucker	1962		N	EC	60
OCALA	*ST JOHN*	1915 SE Lake Weir Ave 34471	(352)622-7275	jim.knoepfel@stjohnocala.org www.stjohnocala.org	James B Knoepfel	1963		N	EC-12	499
OKEECHOBEE	*PEACE*	750 NW 23rd Ln 34972	(863)763-7566	okee.peace25@gmail.com peacelutheranschool-okeechobee.org		1982		N	EC-K	86
ORLANDO	*CHRIST THE KING*	4962 S Apopka-Vineland Rd 32819	(407)876-8155	whavens@ctkpreschool.net ctkpreschool.net	Wendy Havens	1996			EC	32
	HOPE	2600 N Dean Rd 32817	(407)657-4556	office@hopeoforlando.org www.hopeoforlando.org	Tina M Eaton	2002			EC	24
	PRINCE OF PEACE	1515 S Semoran Blvd 32807	(407)275-6703	preschool@poporlando.com www.poporlando.com/preschool	Anne J Dobbins	1959		N	EC	50
	TRINITY	420 Ruth Ln 32801	(407)849-3680	colby.howard@trinitydowntown.org www.trinitydowntown.org	Patty Moser	1953		N	EC	
OVIEDO	*ST LUKES*	2025 W State Rd 426 32765	(407)365-3228	rjackson@sllcs.org stlukeslutheranschool.org		1947		N	EC-8	878
OXFORD	*AMAZING GRACE*	4886 County Road 472 34484	(352)350-6449	elc.director@amazinggracelc.org www.amazinggracelc.org/	Aimee J Knoepfel	2018			EC	119
PENSACOLA	*AMAZING GRACE*	6601 N 9th Ave 32504	(850)505-7735	preschool@gracepensacola.org gracepensacola.org	Amy Onkka	2000			EC	23
	REDEEMER	333 Commerce St 32507	(850)455-0330	rls@redeemerschoolpensacola.org redeemerschoolpensacola.org	Nora F Holler	1955		N	EC-8	
PLANTATION	*OUR SAVIOR*	8001 NW 5th St 33324	(954)370-2161	lroot@oursaviorplantation.org oslplantation.school	Linda Root	1963		N	EC-8	198
ROCKLEDGE	*FAITH VIERA*	5550 Faith Dr 32955	(321)636-9333	preschool@faithviera.org www.faith-viera.org	Sheila M Fournier	2001		N	EC	56
	TRINITY	1330 S Fiske Blvd 32955	(321)636-5431	school@trinity-rockledge.org trinity-rockledge.org	Theresa Barnewall	1959		N	EC-6	110
SAINT CLOUD	*GRACE*	1123 Louisiana Ave 34769	(407)892-9814	director@graceofstcloud.org gscfla.org/school.html	Rijean Smith	1998			EC	
SAINT PETERSBURG	*GRACE*	4301 16th St N 33703	(727)527-6213	nclifton@grace-lutheran.com www.glsfl.org	Nicole Clifton	1956		N	EC-8	
	OUR SAVIOR	5843 4th Ave S 33707	(727)344-1026	school.office@oursaviorfl.org www.osls.net	Wendy E Morris	1982		N	EC-8	256
SANFORD	*HOLY CROSS ACADEMY*	100 Aero Lane 32771	(407)936-3636	cmoon@thehcla.org www.thehcla.org		1999		N	EC-12	532
SARASOTA	*GOOD SHEPHERD*	5651 Honore Ave 34233	(941)922-8164	gsls@comcast.net www.goodshepherdsarasota.org	Jennifer Oberlin	2003		N	EC	156
SEBRING	*FAITH*	2740 Lakeview Dr 33870	(863)385-3232	faithchilddevcenter@gmail.com www.faithlutheransebring.org	Ribed Calderon	2009			EC	23
STUART	*REDEEMER*	2450 SE Ocean Blvd 34996	(772)286-0932	kmcchrystal@rlcsrams.com www.redeemerstuart.com	Karyn McChrystal	1978		N	EC-8	235
TALLAHASSEE	*EPIPHANY*	8300 Deerlake Rd West 32312	(850)385-9822	lingram@epiphanystar.org epiphanytally.org/	Lisa L Ingram	1981		N	EC	78
TAMPA	*FAMILY OF CHRIST*	16190 Bruce B Downs Blvd 33647	(813)558-9343	school@familyofchrist.org FOC-knights.com	Jennifer J Snow	1999		N	EC-8	500
	HOLY TRINITY	3712 W El Prado Blvd 33629	(813)839-0665	principal@htlstampa.org www.htlstampa.org	Kelly A Reilly	1958		N	EC-7	249
	MESSIAH	14920 Hutchison Rd 33625	(813)968-9534	preschooldirector@messiahtampa.com www.messiahpreschool.org	Judy E Patterson	1987		N	EC	44
TITUSVILLE	*GOOD SHEPHERD*	2073 Garden St 32796	(321)264-1069	heather@titusvillelutherans.org www.titusvillelutherans.org	Telena Cooper	1987		N	EC	37
WESTON	*ST PAUL*	580 Indian Trce 33326	(954)384-9096	kathy@stpaulweston.org www.stpaulweston.org	Kathy Henze	1993			EC	101
WINTER HAVEN	*GRACE*	320 Bates Ave SE 33880	(863)293-9744	mrottmann@glwh.org school.glwh.org	Michael S Rottmann	1966		N	EC-8	457
				GEORGIA						
ALPHARETTA	*OPEN ARMS*	4655 WEBB BRIDGE RD 30005	(770)475-6570	openarms@cts.org www.cts.org	Barbara B Bowler	1990			EC-5	
ATHENS	*TRINITY*	2535 Jefferson Rd 30607	(706)546-0670	academy@trinity-athens.org www.trinitylutheranacademy.com	Kim Mall	1987		N	EC	74
ATLANTA	*OPEN ARMS*	4000 Roswell Rd NE 30342	(404)256-1330	business.manager@openarmsbuckhead. org www.openarmsbuckhead.org		1989			EC	
DOUGLASVILLE	*PRINCE OF PEACE*	3988 Hwy 5 30135	(770)627-5562	poplcprek@gmail.com	Renee Turner	2005			EC	

R = Recognized Service Organization (RSO)
N = National Lutheran Schools Accreditation (NLSA)

CITY	SCHOOL	ADDRESS	PHONE	EMAIL WEBSITE	PRINCIPAL/ ADMINISTRATOR	YEAR ORG.	RSO	NLSA	GRADES OFFERED	ENROLL
MARIETTA	*FAITH*	2111 Lower Roswell Rd 30068	(770)973-8921	faithls@faithmarietta.org		1958		N	EC-8	99
PEACHTREE CITY	*ST PAUL*	700 Ardenlee Pkwy 30269	(770)486-3545	swallace@stpaulptc.org www.stpaulptc.org	Sharon L Wallace	1997		N	EC-8	230
PERRY	*CHRIST*	208 Langston Rd 31069	(478)987-6016	christlutheranperry@gmail.com christlutheranperry.org		2022			K-4	9
WOODSTOCK	*TIMOTHY*	556 Arnold Mill Rd 30188	(770)924-7995	tlc.ecedirector@comcast.net www.tlcwoodstock.org	Kristin Freeman	1986		N	EC	90
HAWAII										
AIEA	*OUR SAVIOR*	98-1098 Moanalua Rd 96701	(808)488-0000	office@osls-hawaii.org www.osls-hawaii.org		1970			EC-8	104
HONOLULU	*GOOD SHEPHERD*	638 N Kuakini St 96817	(808)533-3088	gspdirector@gmail.com goodshepherdpreschoolhonolulu.com		1970			EC	
KAHULUI	*EMMANUEL*	520 W One St 96732	(808)873-6334	principal@elcs-maui.org www.elcs-maui.org		1978			EC-8	246
KANEOHE	*SAINT MARK*	45-725 Kamehameha Hwy 96744	(808)247-5589	dgaudi@smls-hawaii.org www.smls-hawaii.org	Dr Robert D Gaudi Jr	1956		N	EC-8	
WAHIAWA	*TRINITY*	1611 California Ave 96786	(808)621-6033	office@tls-hawaii.org www.tls-hawaii.org	Kyle D Klemp	1953		N	EC-8	142
IDAHO										
BOISE	*BEAUTIFUL SAVIOR*	2981 E Boise Ave 83706	(208)331-3040	bslcpreschool@yahoo.com	Christine M Eden	1990			EC	22
	BEGINNING YEARS	2981 E Boise Ave 83706	(208)338-0000	beginningyearscc@gmail.com beginningyearsscc.com	Lindsay Shaffer	1985			EC-K	
BUHL	*CLOVER TRINITY*	3552 N 1825 E 83316	(208)326-5198	office@cloverchristiansch.org cloverchristiansch.org	Wendy Barckholtz	1915			EC-5	33
CALDWELL	*GRACE*	2700 S Kimball Ave 83605	(208)459-4191	graceonkimball@gmail.com gracelutherancaldwell.org		1976			EC	21
COEUR D ALENE	*CHRIST THE KING*	1700 Pennsylvania Ave 83814	(208)765-6736	elc@ctkcda.com www.ctkcda.com		2002			EC	
EDEN	*TRINITY*	1602 E 1100 S 83325	(208)825-5277	preschool@trinitylutheraneden.org	Karla Saldivar	2014			EC	
IDAHO FALLS	*HOPE*	2071 12th St 83404	(208)529-8080	hlcs@allabouthope.org www.allabouthope.org		1958			EC-8	41
KIMBERLY	*XROSSWAY*	400 Irene St 83341	(208)423-5319	dannelle@xrossway.org xrossway.org/kidzworld					EC	
MERIDIAN	*CHRIST*	1406 W Cherry Ln 83642	(208)888-1622	preschool@clcmeridian.org www.clcmeridian.org					EC	19
	FRIENDSHIP	765 E Chinden Blvd 83646	(208)288-2404	preschool@friendshipcelebration.org www.friendshipcelebration.org	Jenny Coleman	1998			EC	
NAMPA	*ZION*	404 Nectarine 83686	(228)466-9446	bbhanway@yahoo.com nampalutheran.org				N	EC	
	ZLS-NAMPA-ID	1012 12th Ave Rd 83686	(208)466-9141	zlsoffice1@gmail.com zlsnampa.org	Joshua Swigart	1960		N	EC-9	32
POCATELLO	*GRACE*	1350 Baldy Ave 83201	(208)237-4142	glsoffice@gracepocatello.org www.gracepocatello.org	Robert Raschke	1959		N	EC-12	545
RATHDRUM	*SHEPHERD OF THE HILL*	13541 W Hwy 53 83858	(208)687-1809	apiettesothpreschool@gmail.com www.shepherdofthehills-rathdrum.org/ soth-pre-school	Anna Piette	1990			EC	
RUPERT	*TLC*	923 8th St 83350	(208)436-3412	tlcpreschoolrupert@gmail.com	Dr James A Von Busch				EC-K	
SANDPOINT	*LITTLE LAMBS*	1900 W Pine St 83864	(208)255-1514	faith@corsandpoint.org www.corsandpoint.org		1990			EC-K	
TWIN FALLS	*IMMANUEL*	2055 Filer Ave E 83301	(208)733-7820	immanuel@immanueltf.org immanueltfschool.org	Michelle Jund	1946			EC-5	176
	IMMANUEL	2055 Filer Ave E 83301	(208)734-3420	cdc@immanueltf.org immanueltf.org		1990			EC	
ILLINOIS										
ALTAMONT	*ALTAMONT*	7 S Edwards St 62411	(618)483-6428	robiflach@alisrockets.com www.alisrockets.com	Robinette A Flach	1973	R	N	K-8	172
ARENZVILLE	*TRINITY*	200 W Frederick St 62611	(217)997-5535	breannawinkelman@gmail.com trinityarenzville.org	Breanna L Winkelman	1872			EC-6	
ARLINGTON HEIGHTS	*LAMBS OF FAITH*	431 S Arlington Heights Rd 60005	(847)253-4839	faithlutheranpreschool@ymail.com www.faithlutheran-ah.org	Jori Reuter	2013			EC	
	ST PETER	111 W Olive St 60004	(847)259-4114	schooloffice@fulllifeinchrist.org www.stpetermyschool.com	Paul Goffron	1864		N	EC-8	483
AUBURN	*TRINITY*	1201 W Jackson 62615	(217)438-6823	tlp@mwii.net www.trinityauburn.org	Teresa A Todt	2006			EC	21
BATAVIA	*IMMANUEL*	950 Hart Rd 60510	(630)406-0157	school@immanuelbatavia.org www.ilsbatavia.org/	Donna E Laughlin	1989		N	EC-8	275
BELLEVILLE	*ZION*	1810 Mc Clintock Ave 62221	(618)234-0275	zionoffice@zionschoolbelleville.org www.zionschoolbelleville.org	Ananda C Baron	1861		N	EC-8	
BELVIDERE	*IMMANUEL*	1225 E 2nd St 61008	(815)547-5346	tpehlke@immanuelknights.org www.immanuelknights.org	Cheryl Gieseke	1953		N	EC-8	275
BENSENVILLE	*CONCORD*	865 S Church Rd 60106	(630)766-0228	acastellanos@zionconcord.org www.zionconcord.org	Paul Feddersen	1989		N	EC-8	43
BERWYN	*CONCORDIA/LAMBS*	3144 Home Ave 60402	(708)795-7563	director@concordiaberwyn.org	Monica R Latkowski	1992			EC	
BETHALTO	*ZION*	625 Church Dr 62010	(618)377-5507	schooloffice@zionbethalto.org zlsbethalto.org	Joseph M Snyder	1962		N	EC-8	312
BLOOMINGTON	*TRINITY*	1102 W Hamilton 61704	(309)829-7513	tlsbloomington@trinluth.org www.trinitylutheranlcms.org	Shawn M Hoffmann	1858			EC-8	384

R = Recognized Service Organization (RSO)
N = National Lutheran Schools Accreditation (NLSA)

SCHOOLS

CITY	SCHOOL	ADDRESS	PHONE	EMAIL WEBSITE	PRINCIPAL/ ADMINISTRATOR	YEAR ORG.	RSO	NLSA	GRADES OFFERED	ENROLL
BOURBONNAIS	*ST PAUL*	1780 Career Center Rd 60914	(815)932-0312	bporter@stpaulslutheran.net www.stpaulslutheran.net	Brian Porter	1864		N	EC-8	204
BROOKFIELD	*ST PAUL*	9035 Grant Ave 60513	(708)485-6987	stpaulbrookfield@comcast.net www.spbrookfield.org		1902			K-8	32
BUCKLEY	*ST JOHN*	206 E Main St 60918	(217)394-2422	principal@stjohnsbuckley.com www.stjohnsbuckley.com	Gordon L Schumacher	1870			EC-8	113
BURR RIDGE	*TRINITY*	11503 German Church Rd 60527	(708)839-1444	trinitylutheranschool@comcast.net www.mytls.org	Andrew R DeWitt	1883		N	EC-8	68
CARLYLE	*MESSIAH*	1091 13th St 62231	(618)594-8991	messiahpslcc@gmail.com	Janet Kahre				EC	
CARY	*HOLY CROSS*	2107 Three Oaks Rd 60013	(847)639-6533	principal@holycrosscary.org www.holycrosscary.org	Christina Heiss	1989			EC-5	31
CENTRALIA	*TRINITY*	203 S Pleasant Ave 62801	(618)532-5434	tlssecretary@trinitycentralia.org www.trinitycentralia.org	Christina K De Board	1897			EC-8	55
CHAMPAIGN	*ST JOHN*	509 S Mattis Ave 61821	(217)359-1714	cblack@stjohnls.com stjohnls.com	Cheryl Black	1983			EC-8	103
CHARLESTON	*IMMANUEL*	902 S Cleveland 61920	(217)345-3042	preschool@consolidated.net immanuelcharleston.com		1973			EC	
CHATHAM	*ST JOHN*	1225 N Main St 62629	(217)483-2612	stjohnsprek@comcast.net stjohnschathamil.org	Catherine Davis	1967			EC	24
CHESTER	*ST JOHN*	302 W Holmes St 62233	(618)826-4345	kpowley@sjshornets.com sjshornets.com	Kaela Powley	1849			EC-8	80
CHICAGO	*BETHESDA*	6803 N Campbell Ave 60645	(773)743-0800	mschaetzlein@biachicago.com biachicago.com	Mark Schaetzlein	1952			EC-8	76
	CHRIST THE KING	3701 S Lake Park Ave 60653	(773)536-1984	geribrazeal@gmail.com www.ctkluthchicago.comcastbiz.net	Geraldine L Brazeal	1973			EC-8	
	GOOD SHEPHERD	3740 W Belden Ave 60647	(773)342-5854	rsalgado@gscachicago.org www.goodshepherdchristianacademy chicago.com	Jo Ellen T Hoffmann	2017			EC-8	59
	GRACE	4106 W 28th St 60623	(773)762-1234	admin@gcachicago.org GCAChicago.org	Carlo Giannotta	1896	R		EC-8	
	ST JAMES	2101 N Fremont St 60614	(773)525-4990	smeyer@stjames-lutheran.org www.stjames-lutheran.org	Lynda Runge	1857		N	EC-8	214
	ST JOHN	4939 W Montrose Ave 60641	(773)736-1196	principal@stjohnschicago.org stjohnschicago.org	Michelle L Runge	1876		N	EC-8	168
	ST PAUL	7621 S Dorchester Ave 60619	(773)721-1438	della.weaver@stpauldorchester.com stpauldorchester.com	Dr Robyn Jacks-DuBose	1889			EC-8	61
	ST PHILIP	2500 W Bryn Mawr Ave 60659	(773)561-9830	dtennis@stphiliplutheran.com www.stphiliplutheran.com	Donna M Tennis	1937			EC-8	
CLINTON	*CHRIST*	701 South Mulberry 61727	(217)935-4675	lutheranpreschool.1997@gmail.com		1997			EC	
COLLINSVILLE	*GOOD SHEPHERD*	1300 Belt Line Rd 62234	(618)344-3153	gsls1@hotmail.com www.gslcs.org	John R Mayhew	1983		N	EC-8	362
	HOLY CROSS	304 South St 62234	(618)344-3145	information@holycross.collinsville.org www.holycross-collinsville.org		1848		N	EC-8	160
COLUMBIA	*ST PAUL*	227 N Goodhaven St 62236	(618)281-4190	preschool@stpauls-lcms.org		1992			EC	
CRYSTAL LAKE	*IMMANUEL*	300 S Pathway Ct 60014	(815)459-1444	thipenbecker@immanuelcl.org www.immanuelcl.org	Carole Fiesman	1875		N	EC-8	256
	MY FATHERS WORLD	932 Mchenry Ave 60014	(815)455-3200	myfathersworld@prince-of-peace.org prince-of-peace.org/about-our-preschool/		1993			EC	44
DANVILLE	*IMMANUEL*	1930 N Bowmann Ave 61832	(217)442-5036	ils.preschooloffice@gmail.com	Michael Heidle				EC	
	TRINITY	824 E Main 61832	(217)442-4311	tls@trinityadvancedlearning.org trinitylutheranschool.com	Evelyn Rodgers				1-5;7-8	
DE KALB	*LITTLE LAMBS*	511 Russell Rd 60115	(815)756-6669	katiem@immanueldekalb.com www.littlelambsdekalb.org/		1996			EC	43
DECATUR	*LUTH SCHOOL ASSOC*	2001 E Mound Rd 62526	(217)233-2001	frontoffice@unitydecatur.org www.unitydecatur.org		1959	R		EC-12	393
	MOUNT CALVARY	2055 S Franklin Street Rd 62521	(217)428-0641	preschool@mtcalvarydecatur.org www.mtcalvarydecatur.org/preschool		1971			EC	32
	ST PAUL	1 Bachrach Ct 62526	(217)424-9183	daycare@spldecatur.org www.spldecatur.org	Kim Newingham	1998			EC-5	
DOWNERS GROVE	*IMMANUEL*	5211 Carpenter St 60515	(630)324-6797	jrogoz2529@gmail.com www.ilcdg.org	Jamie Rogoz	1996			EC	56
EAST DUNDEE	*IMMANUEL*	5 South Van Buren 60118	(847)428-1010	kevinbecker@immanuel-ed.org www.immanuel-ed.org	Kevin J Becker	1863		N	EC-8	221
EAST SAINT LOUIS	*UNITY*	1600 N 40th St 62204	(618)874-6605	aaron-dickerson@att.net www.unityesl.org	Aaron L Dickerson		R	N	EC-8	
EDWARDSVILLE	*TRINITY*	600 Water St 62025	(618)656-7002	kkrueger@trinitylutheranministries.org www.trinitylutheranministries.org		1901		N	EC-8	546
EFFINGHAM	*ST JOHN*	901 West Jefferson Ave 62401	(217)342-4334	carrie.collier@stjohnslcms.net www.stjohnslcms.net	Carrie Collier	1997			EC	44
EL PASO	*TRINITY*	533 W 3rd St 61738	(309)527-4333	Trinitylutheranelpaso@gmail.com www.trinitylutheranpreschoolelpaso.com	Valerie Boehne	2011			EC	26
ELBURN	*LORD OF LIFE*	40W605 Rt 38 60119	(630)513-7346	preschool@lolchurch.net	Marliss Laughridge	1994			EC	109
ELGIN	*GOOD SHEPHERD*	195 Nesler Rd 60124	(847)697-4745	gspdirector@gselgin.org gselgin.org	Andrea J Maske	1961			EC	96
	ST JOHN	109 N Spring St 60120	(847)741-7633	mrpatrick@stjohns-school-elgin.org www.stjohns-school-elgin.org	Robert Patrick	1866		N	EC-1	21
ELMHURST	*IMMANUEL*	148 E 3rd St 60126	(630)832-9302	heather.estes@ilselmhurst.org www.ilselmhurst.org	Heather L Estes	1879		N	EC-8	

R = Recognized Service Organization (RSO)
N = National Lutheran Schools Accreditation (NLSA)

CITY	SCHOOL	ADDRESS	PHONE	EMAIL WEBSITE	PRINCIPAL/ ADMINISTRATOR	YEAR ORG.	RSO	NLSA	GRADES OFFERED	ENROLL
FERRIN	BETHLEHEM	12903 Clara St 62231	(618)545-9542	bethlehemferrinchurch@gmail.com www.bethlehemlutheranferrin.org		1995			EC	
FREEPORT	IMMANUEL	1964 W Pearl City Rd 61032	(815)232-3511	nmuench@ourgodwithus.com www.ourgodwithus.com/school	Nicholas A Muench	1877		N	EC-8	115
GALESBURG	MOUNT CALVARY	1372 W Fremont St 61401	(309)342-7083	office@mclcgalesburg.org mclcgalesburg.org	Jean J Whittle	1977			EC	30
GENESEO	CONCORDIA	316 S Oakwood Ave 61254	(309)944-3993	concordia@geneseolutheranchurch.com geneseolutheranchurch.com		2000			EC	
GENOA	TRINITY	33930 N State Rd 60135	(815)784-2522	tlcpreschool@tlcgenoa.org www.tlcgenoa.org		1995			EC	14
GLENVIEW	IMMANUEL	1850 Chestnut Ave 60625	(847)724-6092	oadirector@openarmsglenview.org www.openarmsglenview.org	Jessica Dinkelman			N	EC	52
GRAYSLAKE	GLORYLAND	607 W Belvidere Rd 60030	(847)548-0112	preschool@lordofglory.org www.glorylandpreschool.com	Donna Budil	2000			EC	49
GURNEE	BETHEL	5110 Grand Ave 60031	(847)244-9672	preschool@bethelgurnee.org www.bethelgurnee.org	Donna Stutzman	1985			EC	35
HAMEL	ST PAUL	125 Wolf Ave 62046	(618)633-3252	speclc@madisontelco.com school.stpaulhamel.org	Ronda Johnson	2005			EC	
HAWTHORN WOODS	ST MATTHEW	24480 N Old Mc Henry Rd 60047	(847)438-6103	connolly@stmattsonline.com www.stmatts.net		1863		N	EC	34
HERSCHER	LITTLE LAMBS	255 E 3rd St 60941	(815)426-2262	director@littlelambsherscher.org www.littlelambsherscher.org		2004			EC	27
HILLSIDE	IMMANUEL	2329 S Wolf Rd 60162	(708)562-5580	principal@immanuel-hillside.org www.immanuel-hillside.org	Patricia Jackson	1852			EC-8	61
HINSDALE	ZION	204 S Grant 60521	(630)323-0065	zionlutheranecec@gmail.com www.zionhinsdale.org	Elizabeth Reilley	2005		N	EC-K	102
HOFFMAN	TRINITY	8701 Huey Rd 62250	(618)495-2246	tlshoffice@trinityhoffman.org trinityhoffman.org		1874		N	EC-8	65
HOMEWOOD	SALEM	18328 Ashland Ave 60430	(708)206-0350	salemlutheranhomewood@gmail.com		1993			EC	10
HOYLETON	TRINITY	155 N Main St 62803	(618)493-7754	schaff@trinityhoyleton.org trinityhoyleton.org		1867		N	EC-8	
ITASCA	ST LUKE	410 S Rush St 60143	(630)773-0509	wschoenfuhs@saintlukeitasca.org www.saintlukeitasca.org	Walter Schoenfuhs	1885		N	EC-8	177
JACKSONVILLE	SALEM	222 E Beecher 62650	(217)243-3419	J.Reitsma@Salemjaxschool.net www.salemjax.net	Joy L Reitsma	1859			EC-8	57
JOLIET	OUR SAVIOR	1910 Black Rd 60435	(815)725-1688	oursaviorlutheranpk@gmail.com www.oursaviorlutheranpk.com		1991			EC-K	
LA GRANGE	ST JOHNS	505 S Park Rd 06525	(708)354-1690	school@stjohnslagrange.org www.stjohnslagrange.org		1886		N	EC-8	101
LEXINGTON	ST PAUL	107 E Chatham 61753	(309)365-5200	splpreschool11@yahoo.com www.stpaul-lex.org	Polly A Walcott	1997			EC	
LINCOLN	ZION	1600 Woodlawn Rd 62656	(217)732-3977	principal@zls-lincoln.org www.zls-linc.org	Dr Stephen E Parry	1975			EC-8	76
LISLE	TRINITY	1101 Kimberly Way 60532	(630)964-1276	trinitypreschool@tlc4u.org www.trinitypreschoollisle.org	Cassie Sund	1974			EC	41
LITCHFIELD	ZION	1301 N State St 62056	(217)324-3166	jpryor@zionlutheranlitchfield.com www.zionlutheranlitchfield.com	Timothy P Moore	1888		N	EC-8	
LOMBARD	PEACE COMMUNITY	21W500 Butterfield Rd 60148	(630)627-1135	pclc@peacehome.org pclckids.org	Anmaree Mora	1980			EC	30
	ST JOHN'S	220 S Lincoln St 60148	(630)932-3196	sjschooloffice@sjleagles.com www.stjohnslombard.com	Paul M Rosin	1888		N	EC-8	235
	TRINITY	1165 Westmore Meyers Rd 60148	(630)627-5601	principal@tlslombard.org trinitylombard.org	Julie A Messina	1860		N	EC-8	68
MACHESNEY PARK	CONCORDIA	7424 N 2nd St 61115	(815)633-6450	runge@concordiamp.com www.ConcordiaMP.com	Sherri Runge	1961			EC-5	
MARENGO	ZION	408 Jackson St 60152	(815)568-5156	office@zionschool.net www.zionschool.net	Dan J Bertrand	1888		N	EC-8	314
MASCOUTAH	ZION	101 S Railway 62258	(618)566-7345	zionpreschooldirector2020@gmail.com www.zionmascoutah.org/	Vikki Harms	1982			EC	
MASON CITY	LITTLE LAMB/CHRIST	114 E Walnut St 62664	(217)737-3987	christlumc@casscomm..com		1991			EC	
MATTOON	ST JOHNS	100 Broadway 61938	(217)234-4911	mhagen@stjls-mattoon.com www.stjls-mattoon.com	Meghan Hagen	1956		N	EC-11	
MC HENRY	ZION	4206 W Elm St 60050	(815)385-4488	office@zionmchenry.org zionmchenry.org	Mark T Buetow	1983			EC-3	62
MELROSE PARK	WALTHER	900 Chicago Ave 60160	(708)344-0404	tim_bouman@waltheracademy.org www.walther.com	Tim Bouman	1954	R	N	6-12	306
MILFORD	ST PAULS	108 W Woodworth 60953	(815)889-4209	office@stpaulspk8.org stpauls.weebly.com		1872		N	EC-8	
MOKENA	IMMANUEL	10731 W LA Porte Rd 60448	(708)479-5600	preschool@immanuelmokena.org immanuelmokena.org/preschool	Tracy M Miranda	1975			EC	76
MORTON	BETHEL	325 E Queenwood Rd 61550	(309)266-6592	school@bethellutheranschool.org www.bethellutheranschool.org	John R Jacob	1982			EC-12	
MOUNT PROSPECT	ST PAUL	18 S School St 60056	(847)255-6733	school@saint-paul.org saint-paul.org	Dawn Koenig	1913		N	EC-8	278
MOUNT PULASKI	ZION	203 S Vine St 62548	(217)792-5715	office@zionmp.org www.zionmp.org	Lori Allen	1851			EC-8	
MURPHYSBORO	IMMANUEL	1915 Pine St 62966	(618)684-3012	twalker@immanuelmurphy.com www.immanuelmurphy.com	James R Zobel	1897			EC-8	

R = Recognized Service Organization (RSO)
N = National Lutheran Schools Accreditation (NLSA)

CITY	SCHOOL	ADDRESS	PHONE	EMAIL WEBSITE	PRINCIPAL/ ADMINISTRATOR	YEAR ORG.	RSO	NLSA	GRADES OFFERED	ENROLL
NAPERVILLE	*BETHANY*	1550 Modaff Rd 60565	(630)355-6607	edunwell@bethanylcs.org www.bethanylcs.org	Erin L Dunwell	1930		N	EC-8	247
	TRINITY	2244 W 95th St Ste 101 60565	(630)946-6313	marcia.mckee@tlc4u.org www.tecc4u.org		2015			EC	62
	WORD OF LIFE	879 Tudor Dr 60563	(630)355-7648	director@wordoflife.net wordoflife.net		1989			EC	53
NASHVILLE	*TRINITY-ST JOHN*	680 W Walnut St 62263	(618)327-8561	principal@tsjlutheran.org tsjlutheran.org	Amy L Kurtz	1974		N	EC-8	
NEW LENOX	*TRINITY*	508 N Cedar Rd 60451	(815)485-6973	tlcsecretary508@gmail.com www.trinitynewlenox.org	Taylor Miller	1982			EC	
NORTH PLATO	*LITTLE SAINTS*	43W301 Plank Rd 60140	(847)464-5134	preschool@stpetersnorthplato.org www.littlesaintspreschool.com		1996			EC	23
NORTHBROOK	*SEEDS OF GRACE*	2245 Walters Ave 60062	(847)498-3060	lschneider@gracenorthbrook.org www.gracenorthbrook.org	Lori A Schneider				EC	74
OKAWVILLE	*IMMANUEL*	606 S Hanover St 62271	(618)243-6142	principal@immanuelokawville.org immanuelokawville.org	Dennis R Fancher	1908		N	EC-8	75
ORLAND PARK	*CHRIST*	14700 S 94th Ave 60462	(708)349-0171	whitneylcorbin@yahoo.com clewspreschool.com	Patricia A Bareither	1983			EC	47
	LIVING WORD	16301 S Wolf Rd 60467	(708)403-9673	intouchlwlc@yahoo.com www.livingwordorland.org	Diana Motel	1994			EC	4
PALATINE	*IMMANUEL*	200 N Plum Grove Rd 60067	(847)359-1936	kbauder@ilcp.org immanuelpalatine.org/	Tanya Calendo	1870		N	EC-8	200
PARIS	*GRACE*	712 S Central Ave 61944	(217)466-1234	slboyars@aol.com www.graceparis.org/cdc.aspx	Steve Boyars	1998			EC	65
PARK RIDGE	*ST ANDREWS*	260 N Northwest Hwy 60068	(847)823-9308	lboggs@standrewslutheranschool.org www.standrewsparkridge.org	Laura J Boggs	1911		N	EC-8	165
PEKIN	*GOOD SHEPHERD*	3201 Court St 61554	(309)347-2020	office@goodshepherdpekin.com www.goodshepherdpekin.com	Joel E Kilgus	1980	R		EC-8	
PEORIA	*CHRIST*	1311 S Faraday Ave 61605	(309)637-1512	school@clspeoria.org www.clspeoria.org	Terry M Mooney Sr	1892			EC-8	170
	CONCORDIA	2000 W Glen Ave 61614	(309)691-8921	ecraine@concordiapeoria.com www.concordiapeoria.com	Emily Craine	1959	R	N	K-8	
	REDEEMER	6801 N Allen Rd 61614	(309)691-2333	sue.skahill@redeemerlutheran.com www.redeemerlutheran.com	Sue Skahill	1953			EC	110
PRAIRIETOWN	*ST PETER*	7182 Renken Rd 62021	(618)888-2252	mburns@madisontelco.com saintpeterslutheran.org	Melissa A Burns	1855			EC-8	27
PROSPECT HEIGHTS	*SONSHINE*	304 W Palatine Rd 60070	(847)520-1116	sonshinepreschool@sbcglobal.net www.ourredeemerprospectheights.org	Danielle Snyder	1982			EC	
QUINCY	*ST JAMES*	900 S 17th St 62301	(217)222-8267	schooloffice@stjamesquincy.org www.stjamesquincyschool.org		1851			EC-8	104
RED BUD	*ST JOHN*	808 S Main St 62278	(618)282-3873	office@stjohnsredbud.org www.stjohnsredbud.org/school	Deitt C Schneider	1859		N	EC-8	288
	TRINITY	10247 S Prairie Rd 62278	(618)282-2881	office@trinityredbud.com www.trinityredbud.com		1842		N	EC-8	40
RIVER FOREST	*CONCORDIA*	7400 Augusta St 60305	(708)209-3099	Jamie.Hayley@CUChicago.edu www.cuchicago.edu/earlychildhood	Catherine J Gruenwald	1976		N	EC-K	202
ROANOKE	*RB AT TRINITY*	202 W Lincoln St 61561	(309)923-5251	trinity_roanoke@frontier.com		2000			EC	21
ROCHELLE	*ST PAUL*	1415 10th Ave 61068	(815)562-6323	shall@stpaulrochelleil.org www.stpaulrochelle.org	Steven L Hall	1961		N	EC-8	168
ROCKFORD	*CHRIST THE ROCK*	8330 Newburg Rd 61108	(815)332-7191	doreen.peterson@hotmail.com www.CTRockford.org		1996			EC	30
	ROCKFORD	3411 N ALPINE RD 61114	(815)877-9551	info@rockfordlutheran.org www.rockfordlutheran.org	Dr Alan P Runge	1963	R	N	EC-12	691
ROSELLE	*TRINITY*	405 Rush St 60172	(630)894-3263	tls@trinityroselle.com www.tlsroselle.com/	Kim E Epting	1899		N	EC-8	196
SADORUS	*NOAHS ARK*	101 E Church St 61872	(217)598-2259	stpaulsadorus@aol.com www.stpaulsadorus.com	Cindy Priest	1992			EC-K	
SAINT CHARLES	*ST MARK*	101 S 6th Ave 60174	(630)584-4850	PRESCHOOL@STMARKSLIFE.ORG www.stmarkssstc.org		1980			EC	90
SAINT PETER	*ST PETER*	701 E 3rd St 62880	(618)349-8888	Office@stpeterstpeter.org www.stpeterstpeter.org		1872			EC-8	88
SALEM	*LITTLE LAMB*	1401 Hawthorn Rd 62881	(618)548-3190	salemllps@salemlc.org salemlc.org	Jessica Feldmann	1988			EC	42
SCHAUMBURG	*ST JOHN*	1800 S Rodenburg Rd 60193	(847)524-9746	lauralicht@stjohnschaumburg.org	Mark J Brockhoff	1998			EC	
	ST PETER	208 E Schaumburg Rd 60194	(847)885-3350	jmessinna@stpeterlcms.org www.stpeterlcms.org	Julie A Messina	1847		N	EC-8	221
SHERMAN	*GOOD SHEPHERD*	500 S Sherman Blvd 62684	(217)496-3149	churchoffice@gsslcms.org gsslcms.org/preschool	Mindy Poehls	1983			EC	
SPARTA	*ST JOHN*	1110 N Market St 62286	(618)443-2010		Ann L Luedders	1980			EC	27
SPRINGFIELD	*CONCORDIA PRESCHOOL*	2300 E Wilshire Rd 62703	(217)529-3307	school@concordiaspfld.org www.concordiacares.org	Janet M Burmeister	1931			EC	11
	OUR SAVIORS	2645 Old Jacksonville Rd 62704	(217)546-4531	info@oursaviors-school.org www.oursaviors-school.org	Jill L Gerberding	1962		N	EC-8	189
	TRINITY	515 S MacArthur Blvd 62704	(217)787-2323	school@trinity-lutheran.com www.trinity-lutheran.com	Zachary A Klug	1860		N	EC-8	210
STAUNTON	*ZION*	220 W Henry St 62088	(618)635-3060	office@zion-school.org www.zion-luth.org	David M Manning	1858			EC-8	
STEELEVILLE	*ST MARK*	504 N James St 62288	(618)965-3838	stmarkssteeleville@gmail.com www.stmarksteeleville.com	Timothy P Moore	1874			EC-8	

R = Recognized Service Organization (RSO)
N = National Lutheran Schools Accreditation (NLSA)

CITY	SCHOOL	ADDRESS	PHONE	EMAIL WEBSITE	PRINCIPAL/ ADMINISTRATOR	YEAR ORG.	RSO	NLSA	GRADES OFFERED	ENROLL
STERLING	*CHRIST*	2000 18th Ave 61081	(815)625-3800	administration@clseagles.net www.christlutheranschool.com		1983			EC-8	45
STEWARDSON	*TRINITY*	318 E S 1st 62463	(217)682-3881	trinitylutheranchurchandschool@hotmail.com www.trinitystewardsonil.org		1868			EC-8	89
STREATOR	*HOLY TRINITY*	101 Trinity Dr 61364	(815)672-2393	preschool@holytrinitystreator.org www.holytrinitystreator.org		1982			EC	20
TAYLORVILLE	*TRINITY*	1010 N Webster St 62568	(217)824-8148	trinitychurch@tlctaylorville.com	Jessica Mills	1974			EC	13
	TRINITY	1010 N Webster St 62568	(217)287-2229	childcareplus@ctitech.com	Rachelle Stickle	2002			EC	
TINLEY PARK	*TRINITY*	6850 159th St 60477	(708)532-3529	school@tlcs.org www.tlcs.org	Tiffany Gurgel	1859		N	EC-8	235
TROY	*ST PAUL*	112 N Border St 62294	(618)667-6314	lcraig@saintpaulstroy.org www.saintpaulstroy.org		1864		N	EC	
URBANA	*WEE DISCIPLES*	701 East Florida Ave 61801	(217)607-2096	weedisciplespreschool@yahoo.com www.trinity-urbana.org		1997			EC	13
WASHINGTON	*OUR SAVIOR*	1209 Kingsbury Rd 61571	(309)444-4030	secretary@oslwashington.org www.oslwashington.org		1988			EC	
WATERLOO	*IMMANUEL*	110 Hoener Ave 62298	(618)939-6480	ilcwprek@gmail.com immanuelwaterloo.org	Linda Polansky	1979			EC	
WATSEKA	*CALVARY*	120 E Hickory St 60970	(815)432-4137	calvarypreschoolwatseka@gmail.com		1984			EC	
WESTMONT	*BETHEL*	36 N Grant St 60559	(630)968-3232	bethelearlylearningcenter@yahoo.com bethelwestmont.org	Lisa Graziano	2004			EC	42
WHEATON	*ST JOHN*	410 N Cross 60187	(630)668-0701	preschool@stjohnwheaton.org www.stjohnwheaton.org	Gretchen L Scheel	1956			EC	26
WOOD RIVER	*ST PAUL*	1327 Vaughn Rd 62095	(618)259-0055	preschool@stpaulwoodriver.com stpaulwoodriver.com	Tammy L Plummer	1974			EC	
WORDEN	*ST PAUL*	6961 W Frontage Rd 62097	(618)633-2202	principal@stpaulhamel.org school.stpaulhamel.org	Deac Lynnette A Fredericksen	2014			EC-12	
YORKVILLE	*CROSS*	8535 State Route 47 60560	(630)553-7861	www.hiscross.org	Miriam S Ulrich	1881		N	EC-8	404
				INDIANA						
AUBURN	*TLC*	1801 N Main 46706	(260)925-6544	preschool@trinitylutheran-auburn.org www.tlcearlylearning-auburn.com					EC	35
AURORA	*ST JOHN*	222 Mechanic St 47001	(812)926-2656	office@sjlsaurora.com stjohnlcms.com		1864		N	EC-8	75
AVON	*OUR SHEPHERD*	9201 E CR 100 N 46123	(317)271-9100	principal@ourshepherd.org www.ourshepherd.org	Rachel J Miller	1982		N	EC-8	256
BEDFORD	*CALVARY*	3705 Austin Dr 47421	(812)275-5488	calvarylutheranprek.bedford.in@gmail.com		1979		N	EC	25
BLOOMINGTON	*FAITH*	2200 S High St 47401	(812)334-2209	faithlutheranps@gmail.com www.faithbtown.org	Rachel Stults	1995			EC	109
BREMEN	*ST PAULS*	605 S Center St 46506	(574)546-2790	schools@stpaulsbremen.org stpaulsbremen.church	Nathan Miller	1846		N	EC-8	66
BROWNSBURG	*CHRIST*	701 E Tilden Dr 46112	(317)852-3343	celc701@gmail.com www.christlutheran-indy.org	Roberta Hoffer	1989			EC	18
BROWNSTOWN	*LUTHERAN CENTRAL*	415 N Elm St 47220	(812)358-2512	jami.stuckwisch@lcsaints.net lcsaints.net	Jami Stuckwisch	1966	R	N	EC-8	212
CARMEL	*CORNERSTONE*	4850 E Main St 46033	(317)814-4262	tmillwood@cornerstonelutheran.church www.cornerstonelutheran.church	Teresa M Millwood	1985		N	EC	125
COLUMBUS	*FAITH*	6000 W State Road 46 47201	(812)342-3587	preschool@faithontheweb.org www.faithontheweb.org	Indu Samuel	1981			EC	54
	ST PAUL	6045 E State St 47201	(812)376-6504	director@stpaulcolumbus.org www.stpaulcolumbus.org		1981		N	EC-K	71
	ST PETER	719 5th St 47201	(812)372-5266	pmeredith@stpeters-columbus.org www.stpeterscolumbus.org	Scott A Schumacher	1863		N	K-8	440
	WHITE CREEK	16270 S 300 W 47201	(812)342-6832	wvandercar@whitecreek.org www.whitecreek.org	Whitney E Vandercar	1840		N	K-8	110
CROWN POINT	*TRINITY*	250 S Indiana Ave 46307	(219)663-1578	millerc@trinitycp.org www.trinitycp.org	Christine E Miller	1868		N	EC-8	215
DECATUR	*ST PETER-IMMANUEL*	3845 E 1100 N 46733	(260)623-6115	principal@spilutheran.org spilutheran.org	Robert Reynolds Jr	1969	R	N	EC-8	78
	WYNEKEN MEMORIAL	11565 N US Highway 27 46733	(260)639-6177	office@wyneken.org www.wyneken.org	Casey Nidlinger	1969	R	N	EC-8	228
	ZION	1022 W Monroe St 46733	(260)728-9995	jheckler@ziondecatur.com www.ziondecatur.com		1955		N	EC-8	91
DEMOTTE	*FAITH*	1700 S Halleck St 46310	(219)987-3430	faithprek987@gmail.com www.faithlutheranindemotte.com	Patricia K Sojka	1994		N	EC	59
ELKHART	*TRINITY*	30888 CR 6 46514	(574)674-8800	office@trinityl.org trinityl.org/school-home/		1874		N	EC-8	495
EVANSTON	*SON SHINE*	12308 E CR 1160 N 47531	(812)547-9620	sonshine4kids@gmail.com stjohnsevanston.com	Kimberly Pearson	2005			EC	
EVANSVILLE	*EVANSVILLE*	111 E VIRGINIA ST 47711	(812)424-7252	web@evansvillelutheranschool.com evansvillelutheranschool.com		1971	R	N	K-8	158
	REDEEMER	1811 Lincoln Ave 47714	(812)476-9991	office@redeemerchurch.org redeemerchurch.org		1978			EC	18
	TRINITY	1403 W Boonville-New Harmony Rd 47725	(812)867-5279	preschool@tldarm.org www.trinitylutheranpreschooldarmstadt.com	Breenna Smith	2019			EC	34
FORT WAYNE	*ASCENSION*	8811 Saint Joe Rd 46835	(260)486-2226	office@alcsfw.org www.alcsfw.org		1997		N	EC-8	74

R = Recognized Service Organization (RSO)
N = National Lutheran Schools Accreditation (NLSA)

CITY	SCHOOL	ADDRESS	PHONE	EMAIL WEBSITE	PRINCIPAL/ ADMINISTRATOR	YEAR ORG.	RSO	NLSA	GRADES OFFERED	ENROLL
FORT WAYNE	*CONCORDIA*	4245 Lake Ave 46815	(260)426-9922	mrosin@clscubs.org www.clscubs.org	Michael P Rosin	1900		N	EC-8	
	EMMANUEL	9909 Wayne Trace 46816	(219)447-3036	soestdaycare@gmail.com emmanuelchildcarministries.weebly.com	Amanda Van Osdale	1998			EC	47
	EMMANUEL-ST MICHAEL	1123 Union St 46802	(260)422-6712	bstellwagen@esmeagles.com esmeagles.com	Benjamin Stellwagen	1867		N	EC-8	442
	EMMAUS	8626 Covington Rd 46804	(260)459-7722	principal@emmauslutheranfw.org www.emmauslutheranfw.org	Keith D Martin	1901		N	EC-8	215
	FAITH OF JACOBS WELL	10707 Coldwater Rd 46845	(260)637-9957	faith.preschool@jacobswell.us gotothewell.org/preschool/home	Judy Berggren	2014			EC	
	HOLY CROSS	3425 Crescent Ave 46805	(260)483-3173	ejohnson@holycrossfw.org www.holycrossfw.org		1946		N	EC-8	473
	LITTLE PRAISERS	1115 W Dupont Rd 46825	(260)490-9529	littlepraisers@praiselutheran.org		1998			EC	134
	PEACE	4900 Fairfield Ave 46807	(260)456-6605	preschool@peacelutheranfw.org www.peacelutheranfw.org	Barbara J Bradtmueller	1973			EC	16
	REDEEMER CLASSICAL	202 W Rudisill Blvd 46807	(260)255-6375	redeemerclassicalschool@gmail.com www.fortwayneclassical.com	Nathaniel Pullmann		R	N	1-10	51
	SOUTH UNITY	5401 S Calhoun St 46807	(260)744-0459	abahr@lsusfw.org www.lsusfw.org	Amber D Bahr	2009	R	N	K-8	178
	ST PAULS	1125 Barr St 46802	(260)424-0049	school@stpaulsfw.org school.stpaulsfw.org	Andrew M Whirrett	1836		N	EC-8	153
	ST PETERS	7810 Maysville Rd 46815	(260)749-5811	wildcats@stpetersfw.org www.splswildcats.org		1855		N	EC-8	290
	SUBURBAN BETHLEHEM	6318 W California Rd 46818	(260)483-9371	agreener@sblschool.com www.suburbanbethlehem.org	Amy S Greener	1882		N	EC-8	268
FREMONT	*WEE CREATIONS*	355 E State Road 120 46737	(260)495-6162	director@weecreations.org www.plcms.org/	Sara C Miller	1992			EC	
GARRETT	*ZION*	1349 S Randolph St 46738	(219)357-4658	mrs.julie@hotmail.com	Julie K Faulkner	1979			EC	
GARY	*ASCENSION*	1150 W 49th Ave 46408	(219)887-5031	reeves@ascensionlutheranschool.org www.ascensionlutheranschool.org	Stephanie Reeves	2017	R	N	K-5	
GEORGETOWN	*SHEPHERD HILLS*	5231 SR 62 47122	(812)945-3046	preschool@sothluth.org sothluth.org	Linda Darnstaedt	1999			EC	16
GREENFIELD	*FAITH*	200 W Mckenzie Rd 46140	(317)468-0610	rshanton.faithpreschool@gmail.com www.faithgreenfield.org	Rebecca Shanton	1992			EC	24
GREENWOOD	*CONCORDIA*	305 N Howard Rd 46142	(317)881-4477	concordia@concordia-lcms.com www.concordia-lcms.com	Jill Scifres	1979			EC	
HOBART	*TRINITY*	891 S Linda St 46342	(219)942-3147	marroyo.tls@trinityhobart.org www.trinityhobart.org	Molly M Arroyo	1880		N	EC-8	90
HUNTERTOWN	*OUR HOPE*	1826 Trinity Dr 46748	(260)338-1121	ourhopeprek@aol.com www.ourhopelutheran.com	Gina Pippenger	1998			EC	
INDIANAPOLIS	*CALVARY*	6111 Shelby St 46227	(317)783-2305	www.choosecalvary.com	Stephen E Rensner	1950		N	EC-8	290
	CORNERSTONE	6100 N Raceway Rd 46234	(317)858-3733	tmillwood@cornerstonelutheran.church www.cornerstonelutheran.church		2023		N	EC	
	HOLY CROSS	8115 Oaklandon Rd 46236	(317)826-1234	msearcy@hclc.info www.hclcindy.org		1991		N	EC-8	599
	LITTLE WINGS	6612 SOUTHEASTERN AVE 46203	(317)352-9196	lforgey@stjohnindy.org	Lori Forgey	2005			EC	36
	ST JOHN	6630 Southeastern Ave 46203	(317)352-9196	info@stjohnindy.org www.stjohnindy.org	Jeffrey D Huntington	1852		N	EC-8	223
	TRINITY	8540 E 16th St 46219	(317)897-0243	rebecca.hoff@trinityindy.org www.trinityindy.org	Rebecca A Hoff	1872		N	EC-8	179
KENDALLVILLE	*ST JOHN*	301 S Oak St 46755	(260)347-2444	school@sjlc.net www.stjohneagles.org	Timothy A Walz	1981		N	EC-8	133
KNOX	*LITTLE LAMBS*	1600 S Heaton St 46534	(574)806-4568	littlelambsorlc@gmail.com www.knoxlutheran.org	Karen Zimmerman	1985			EC	
KOKOMO	*REDEEMER*	705 E Southway Blvd 46902	(765)864-6466	www.redeemerlutheranschoolkokomo.org	Ruth H Lavrenz	1983		N	EC-8	171
LA PORTE	*ST JOHN'S*	111 Kingsbury Ave 46350	(219)362-6692	schooloffice@stjohns-laporte.com www.stjohnslaporte.org	Julie Berndt	1857		N	EC-8	133
LAFAYETTE	*ST JAMES*	615 N 8th St 47901	(765)742-6464	principal@stjameslaf.org www.mysjls.org	Heather Brooks	1850		N	EC-8	208
LANESVILLE	*ST JOHNS*	1507 Saint Johns Church Rd NE 47136	(812)952-2737	school@stjohnslanesville.com school.stjohnslanesville.com	Jeff Smitley	1861		N	EC-8	116
MARTINSVILLE	*PRECIOUS PLAYMATES*	3496 E Morgan St 46151	(765)342-2220	Preciousplaymatesdaycare@gmail.com www.popmartinsville.org	Brenda Frederick				EC	
	PRINCE OF PEACE	3496 E Morgan St 46151	(765)349-8873	popschoollcms@hotmail.com www.poppreschoolmartinsville.org		1998			EC	19
MONROEVILLE	*ST JOHN-EMMANUEL*	12912 Franke Rd 46773	(260)639-0123	principal@stjohn-emmanuel.com www.stjohn-emmanuel.com	Suzanne M Dunkin		R	N	EC-8	117
MUNSTER	*ST PAULS*	8601 Harrison Ave 46321	(219)836-6270	stplschool@stplmunster.com www.stplmunster.com	Barbara J Mertens	1886		N	EC-8	209
NEW ALBANY	*GRACE*	1787 Klerner Ln 47150	(812)941-1912	info@gracelutheran.school www.gracelutheran.school		1982			EC	
NEW HAVEN	*CENTRAL*	900 Green St 46774	(260)493-2502	office@cluth.org www.cluth.org	David W Van Spankeren		R	N	EC-8	401
	MARTINI KIDS CLUB	333 Moeller Rd 46774	(260)749-0014	martinikidsclubministry@gmail.com	Lisa Andrews				EC	74
NEW PALESTINE	*ZION*	6513 W 300 S 46163	(317)861-4210	principal@zionnewpal.org www.zionnewpal.org	Kristie L Sombke	1863		N	EC-8	274
NORTH JUDSON	*ST PETER*	810 W Talmer Ave 46366	(574)896-5933	reimers@stpeternorthjudson.org stpeternorthjudson.org	Rhonda K Reimers	1880		N	EC-8	156

R = Recognized Service Organization (RSO)
N = National Lutheran Schools Accreditation (NLSA)

CITY	SCHOOL	ADDRESS	PHONE	EMAIL WEBSITE	PRINCIPAL/ ADMINISTRATOR	YEAR ORG.	RSO	NLSA	GRADES OFFERED	ENROLL
OSSIAN	BETHLEHEM	7545 N 650 E 46777	(260)597-7366	principal@bethlsossian.org www.bethlehemossian.org	Mark B Schallhorn	1897		N	K-8	
	NEW HOPE	8824 N State Rd 1 46777	(260)622-7954	new_hopelutheran@yahoo.com		1977			EC	24
PERU	ST JOHN	181 W Main St 46970	(765)473-3373	2013beginningnew@gmail.com www.stjohnsperu.org	Charlene Beattie	1860			EC-K	
PLAINFIELD	LVNG CHRIST FOR KIDS	726 Moon Rd 46168	(317)837-9998	LCKchildcare@yahoo.com	Kimberly Willis	2004			EC	89
PLYMOUTH	CALVARY	1314 N Michigan St 46563	(574)936-2903	preschool@calvarylutheranplymouth.org calvarylutheranplymouth.org		1988			EC	48
RENSSELAER	ST LUKE	704 E Grace St 47978	(219)866-7681	stlukelcms@centurylink.net		1978			EC	
REYNOLDS	ST JAMES	Hwy 24 And 421 47980	(219)984-5994	stjameschildcarereynolds@yahoo.com		1996			EC	
ROANOKE	FAITH	3416 E 900 N 46783	(260)414-6928	pohlerua3@yahoo.com	Teresa Pohler				EC	34
SEYMOUR	IMMANUEL	605 S Walnut St 47274	(812)522-3118	hwolka@immanuelseymour.com	Heather Wolka				EC	
	IMMANUEL	520 S Chestnut St 47274	(812)522-1301	llister@immanuelschool.org www.immanuelschool.org	Dr Todd G Behmlander	1874		N	K-8	316
	ST JOHN	1058 S County Road 460 E 47274	(812)523-3131	klambring@sjsauerslutheran.org sjsraiders.com	Trisha R Engel	1840		N	EC-8	139
	ZION	1501 Gaiser Dr 47274	(812)522-5911	ksullivan@zionseymour.org www.zionschoolseymour.org	Kimberly A Sullivan	1974		N	EC-3	208
SOUTH BEND	RESURRECTION	6840 Nimtz Pkwy 46628	(574)272-2200	lisa@rlasouthbend.com www.rlasouthbend.com	Michelle Megyese	1998	R	N	EC-8	118
VALPARAISO	IMMANUEL	1700 Monticello Park Dr 46383	(219)462-8207	jbachman@immanuelvalpo.org www.immanuelvalpo-school.org	Joshua K Bachman	1950		N	EC-8	297
VINCENNES	ST JOHN	707 N 8th St 47591	(812)882-1861	stjohn_sec@sbcglobal.net	Sylvia J Saucerman	1866			EC	60
WARSAW	LITTLE STEPS	1720 E Center ST 46580	(514)267-5656	little_steps@redeemerwarsaw.org					EC	
WOODBURN	WOODBURN	4502 N State Rd 101 46797	(260)632-5493	woodburnlutheran@wlsedu.org www.woodburnlutheranschool.org	John D March	1954	R	N	EC-8	146
ZIONSVILLE	ADVENT	11250 N Michigan Rd 46077	(317)873-6318	dtrewartha@adventlutheran.org www.adventlutheran.org		2000			EC-6	121

IOWA

CITY	SCHOOL	ADDRESS	PHONE	EMAIL WEBSITE	PRINCIPAL/ ADMINISTRATOR	YEAR ORG.	RSO	NLSA	GRADES OFFERED	ENROLL
ADEL	FAITH'S FLOCK	602 S 14th St 50003	(515)993-3848	preschool@faithadel.com adelpreschool.com/		1981			EC	40
ALTOONA	CHILDREN OF CHRIST	600 1St Ave N 50009	(515)967-3349	childrenofchristpreschool@gmail.com christthekingaltoona.com	Rochelle Clifton	1978			EC	
AMES	ST PAUL	610 15th St 50010	(515)233-1914	education@saintpaulames.org saintpaulaimes.org/preschool/	Lori J Jenks	2004			EC	69
AUDUBON	ST JOHN	815 E Division 50025	(712)563-2114	St.johnscp@gmail.com		1978			EC	31
BELLE PLAINE	FIRST	1523 Sunset Dr 52208	(319)444-2849	flckidskingdom@gmail.com		2003			EC	
BETTENDORF	OUR SAVIOR	3775 Middle Rd 52722	(563)332-4648	oslpdir@oursaviorbett.org www.oursaviorbett.org	Lisa Piotter	1998			EC	295
BOONE	TRINITY	712 12th St 50036	(515)432-6912	aschroeder@tlsboone.us www.tlsboone.us/		1872		N	EC-8	150
CARROLL	LITTLE LAMB	1844 Highland Dr 51401	(712)792-4354	durene@mchsi.com www.stpaul-ia.com	Durene K Eisenbacher	1991			EC	
CEDAR FALLS	IMMANUEL	4820 Oster Pkwy 50613	(319)260-2000	preschool@immanuelcf.com www.immanuelpreschool.org		1879			EC	70
	VALLEY	4520 Rownd St 50613	(319)266-4565	info@vlscrusaders.org www.vlscrusaders.org	Brian T L Heureux	2002	R	N	K-12	177
CEDAR RAPIDS	SHARE AND CARE	4210 Johnson Ave NW 52405	(319)396-9148	shareandcarepreschool@gmail.com www.shareandcarepreschool.com		1980			EC	
	TRINITY	1361 7th Ave SW 52404	(319)362-6952	trinitycr.org	Jan Doellinger	1884		N	EC-8	252
CHEROKEE	TRINITY	1825 530th St 51012	(712)225-4332	preschool@trinitycherokee.org www.trinitycherokee.org	Virginia Horvath				EC	34
CLARINDA	CLARINDA	707 W Scidmore St 51632	(712)542-3657	lclement@cls.k12.ia.us www.clarindalutheranschool.com	Laveta M Clement	1988	R	N	K-8	77
	ST JOHNS NOAHS ARK	301 N 13th St 51632	(712)542-5501	stjohn.noahsark@gmail.com stjohnclarinda.org/noahsark.html		1982			EC	
CLINTON	ST JOHN	416 Main Ave 52732	(563)242-5588	csperry@stjohn-clinton-ia.org www.stjohn-clinton-ia.org		1971			EC	15
CLIVE	LITTLE FRIENDS	2180 NW 142nd St 50317	(515)556-5576	sandy.littlefriends@gmail.com www.livingfaithclive.com/little-friends		2003			EC	112
CORALVILLE	PRINCE OF PEACE	1701 8th St 52241	(319)887-3333	poppreschool@msn.com popcoralville.com	Jennifer Bounds	2005			EC	7
COUNCIL BLUFFS	ST PAUL	1500 N 16th St 51501	(712)322-3294	becca.heinicke@splecc.org www.splecc.org		2008			EC	39
CRESTON	TRINITY	800 N Sumner Ave 50801	(515)782-5095	jbrown@trinitycreston.org www.trinitycreston.org	Dayna Joy J Brown	1986			EC	25
DAVENPORT	RISEN CHRIST	6021 Northwest Blvd 52806	(319)386-1738	LBDC@rclcqc.org www.risenchristdavenport.org		1997			EC	40
	TRINITY	1122 W Central Park Ave 52804	(563)322-5224	molly.ruhnke@trinitydavenport.org www.trinitydavenport.org	William C Meyer	1870		N	EC-8	88
DENISON	UNITY RIDGE	1004 1st Avenue South Suite B 51442	(712)393-2002	megan.torreson@unityridge.org www.unityridge.org	Megan L Torreson	2022	R		EC-12	121
DES MOINES	HOPE	3857 E 42nd St 50317	(515)265-2057	preschool@hopelutheran-dsm.org www.hopelutheran-dsm.org		1977			EC	22
	MOUNT OLIVE	5625 Franklin Ave 50310	(515)277-0247	school.office@molcs.org www.molcs.org	Orval E Spence	1960		N	EC-8	264

R = Recognized Service Organization (RSO)
N = National Lutheran Schools Accreditation (NLSA)

CITY	SCHOOL	ADDRESS	PHONE	EMAIL WEBSITE	PRINCIPAL/ ADMINISTRATOR	YEAR ORG.	RSO	NLSA	GRADES OFFERED	ENROLL
DEWITT	*GRACE*	415 10th St 52742	(563)659-9153	preschool@gracedewitt.org	Christine Greve	2009			EC	36
DUBUQUE	*OUR REDEEMER*	2145 John F Kennedy Rd 52002	(563)588-1247	orlpreschool@gmail.com www.orlpreschool.org	Amy Kruse	1971			EC	44
ELDORA	*GOOD SHEPHERD*	1109 Washington St 50627	(641)858-5928	gspeldora@gmail.com		1974			EC	23
ELDRIDGE	*SHARE AND CARE*	14 Grove Rd 52748	(563)285-7111	shareandcarechristianpreschool1977@ gmail.com www.pvlcms.org		1977			EC	32
FAIRFIELD	*IMMANUEL*	1601 S Main St 52556	(641)469-6634	mdo6634@gmail.com www.ilcms.com	Jennifer McLain	1983			EC	31
FORT DODGE	*LITTLE LAMBS*	1436 21st Ave N 50501	(515)576-6308	littlelambs@goodshepfortdodge.org goodshepfortdodge.org	Joan Arndt	2003			EC	34
	ST PAUL	1217 4th Ave S 50501	(515)955-7208	stpaulsc@stpaulschoolfd.org www.stpaulschoolfd.org		1863		N	EC-8	135
FREDERICKSBURG	*FUN IN THE SON*	109 E Railroad 50630	(563)237-6117	funinthesonkids@gmail.com	Janiece A Kramer	1993			EC	82
GARNER	*LITTLE LAMBS*	870 State St 50438	(641)923-2300	littlelambstpaul@gmail.com	Alesha Lentz	1976			EC	
GREENFIELD	*IMMANUEL LITTLE LAMB*	505 NE Dodge St 50849	(641)745-5155	kristenkwalker@hotmail.com	Kristen K Walker	1981			EC	
HIAWATHA	*LITTLE LAMBS*	201 First Ave 52233	(319)393-8507	littlelambs@zionhiawatha.org	Kari Boyle	1981			EC	57
IOWA CITY	*OUR REDEEMER*	2301 E Court St 52245	(319)338-3949	preschool@ourredeemer.org ourredeemer.org/preschool/		1981			EC	22
JOHNSTON	*LOVING ARMS CHILDREN*	6270 Merle Hay Rd 50131	(515)270-0150	director@lovingarmschildrenscenter.com www.lovingarmschildrenscenter.com	Holly Randell	2001			EC	
LATIMER	*ST PAULS*	404 W Main 50452	(641)579-6046	leadteacher@stpaulslatimer.org www.stpaulslatimer.org	Cody M Collier	1925		N	K-12	41
MANNING	*ZION*	1204 Center St 51455	(712)655-2352	zionmanningpreschool@gmail.com		1985			EC	
MASON CITY	*SUNBEAM*	419 N Delaware Ave 50401	(641)424-7073	scccbl@gmail.com www.bethlcms.org	Rhonda L Dedor	1978			EC	44
MOUNT PLEASANT	*SON SHINE ACADEMY*	910 Mapleleaf Dr 52641	(319)385-7336	sonshineacademy52641@gmail.com www.faithsonshine.com		1999			EC	38
NEWHALL	*CENTRAL*	310 3rd St W 52315	(319)223-5271	principal@centrallutheranschool.org www.centrallutheranschool.org		1965	R	N	EC-8	178
OGDEN	*LITTLE MIRACLES*	319 W Elm St 50212	(515)275-3249	zionelmstreetpreschool@gmail.com		1999			EC	34
OSCEOLA	*OVER THE RAINBOW*	101 E View Pl 50213	(641)342-3121	lindakw1964@outlook.com		1983			EC	
PAULLINA	*ZION-ST JOHN*	103 W Bertha St 51046	(712)949-3915	zsj@tcaexpress.net www.zsjpaullina.org		1976	R	N	EC-8	30
POLK CITY	*BEAUTIFUL BEGINNINGS*	1701 W Jester Park Dr 50226	(515)984-6146	beautiful_beginnings1@yahoo.com www.beautifulbeginnings.info	Jessica A Paulin	1999			EC	
READLYN	*COMMUNITY*	2681 Quail Ave 50668	(319)279-3541	office@communitylutheranschool.com www.communitylutheranschool.com	Shari Ambrose	1977	R	N	EC-8	75
SCHLESWIG	*IMMANUEL*	501 Glad St 51461	(712)676-2235	immanuelschleswig@gmail.com	Leslie Gustafson	1984			EC	28
SIOUX CITY	*KINDER COTTAGE*	3204 S Lakeport St 51106	(712)276-1125	kcpreschool1976@gmail.com www.redeemersiouxcity.com	Tara Vander Weil	1976			EC	
	ST PAULS	614 Jennings St 51101	(712)258-6325	office@stpaulssiouxcity.org www.siouxcitystpauls.org		1880		N	EC-5	38
SPENCER	*FIRST ENGLISH*	1311 E 18th St 51301	(712)262-3699	felcpreschool1979@gmail.com		1979			EC	58
	IOWA GREAT LAKES	1311 E 18th St 51301	(712)262-8237	principal@igllstech.com www.iglls.org	Sarah E Popp	1999	R	N	K-8	134
SPIRIT LAKE	*JOYFUL JOURNEYS*	2300 27th St 51360	(712)336-2228	joyfuljourneyspreschool.ilc@gmail.com	Kari Jacobsen				EC	78
STORM LAKE	*GRACE*	1407 W 5th St 50588	(712)732-5005	lutherangrace1951@gmail.com		1982			EC	25
SWEA CITY	*OURSAVIOR LITTLELAMB*	301 3rd St N 50590	(515)272-4696	littlelambs@ringtelco.com		1994			EC	
URBANDALE	*TINY TREASURES*	8301 Aurora Ave 50322	(515)276-1700	heather.schmitz@gdlc.church www.gdlc.church		2005			EC	74
VENTURA	*REDEEMER*	301 S Main St 50482	(641)829-3615	redeemerdaycare@cltel.net	Kari R Johnson-Markla	1984			EC-6	
VINTON	*TLC*	1002 E 13th St 52349	(319)472-5571	tlcpreschoolvinton@yahoo.com trinitylcmsvinton.org	Gail Gerber	1984			EC	
WEBSTER CITY	*ST PAUL*	1005 Beach St 50595	(515)832-3043	stpaulwebstercity@gmail.com		1969			EC	37
WEST DES MOINES	*SHEPHERDS FLOCK*	3900 Ashworth Rd 50265	(515)225-1952	diane@sotv-wdm.org		1992			EC-K	114
WILLIAMSBURG	*LUTHERAN INTERPARISH*	804 Court 52361	(319)668-1711	mmiller@lutheraninterparish.com www.lutheraninterparish.com	William J Sitas Jr	1967	R	N	EC-8	131
WILTON	*ZION*	117 E Prairie St 52778	(563)732-2912	zionscl@netwtc.net www.zionwilton.org	Sheila Freie	1983			EC	21

KANSAS

CITY	SCHOOL	ADDRESS	PHONE	EMAIL WEBSITE	PRINCIPAL/ ADMINISTRATOR	YEAR ORG.	RSO	NLSA	GRADES OFFERED	ENROLL
ALMA	*ST JOHN*	206 W 2nd 66401	(785)765-3914	schoolofficestjohnalma@gmail.com stjohnalma.org	Harmon R Butler Jr	1873		N	K-8	46
ATCHISON	*TRINITY*	611 N 8th St 66002	(913)367-4763	bothborths@yahoo.com www.tlsks.org		1869			EC-8	144
ATWOOD	*GODS LITTLE SAINTS*	808 S 1st St 67730	(785)626-3178	redluth03@gmail.com	Riley A Merz	1999			EC	34
BASEHOR	*RISEN SAVIOR*	14750 Leavenworth Rd 66007	(913)724-2900	weinkauf@rslcms.church risensaviorlcms.org					K-12	55
	TRINITY FAMILY	16928 Evans Rd 66007	(913)724-4441	tflcdirector@gatheringinchrist.org www.gatheringinchrist.org	Jennifer Pierce	2006			EC	52
BURLINGTON	*TRINITY*	902 Kennedy St 66839	(620)364-2857	secretarytlcburlington@gmail.com	Lisa Booth	1988			EC	16
CHANUTE	*SONSHINE*	24 N Larson 66720	(620)431-0007	sonshinepreschoolZION@gmail.com	Samantha James	1988			EC	
CHENEY	*ST PAUL*	621 Lincoln St 67025	(316)542-3584	beckyh@stpaulscheney.com stpaulscheney.com	Rebecca R Hillman	1894			EC-8	39

R = Recognized Service Organization (RSO)
N = National Lutheran Schools Accreditation (NLSA)

CITY	SCHOOL	ADDRESS	PHONE	EMAIL WEBSITE	PRINCIPAL/ ADMINISTRATOR	YEAR ORG.	RSO	NLSA	GRADES OFFERED	ENROLL
CLAY CENTER	ST PAUL	816 9th St 67432	(785)632-5301	splpreschool@ymail.com www.claycenterlutheran.com					EC	
ELLINWOOD	ST JOHN	615 N Main 67526	(620)564-2885	sjohnschildcaredirector@gmail.com stjohnellinwood.org	Lisa Rector	1994			EC	
EMPORIA	THE LORDS LAMB	1348 Trailridge Rd 66801	(316)342-4669	lordslambs@gmail.com www.faithemporia.org	Lea Ann Guion	1982			EC	
FAIRVIEW	ST PAUL	110 East Maple 66425	(785)467-8816	rygaardgina@yahoo.com	Regina Rygaard	1985			EC	
FORT SCOTT	PRECIOUS LAMBS	2824 Horton St 66701	(620)223-3596	preciouslambsfs@gmail.com	Emelia Whiteaker	1989			EC	
GARDEN CITY	TRINITY	1010 Fleming St 67846	(620)276-3110	tlpreschool@cox.net	Tammy J Lampe	1984			EC	12
GARDNER	OPEN ARMS	306 E Madison 66030	(913)856-4250	openarmsdirector@kingofkings.org www.kingofkingsks.org	Shonda Williams	2003		N	EC-2	
HERINGTON	OUR REDEEMER	802 East Trapp Street 67449	(785)258-3122	orelcpreschool@gmail.com ourredeemerherington.org	Jamie Schrader	1995			EC	9
INDEPENDENCE	ZION	301 S 11th St 67301	(620)332-3331	lutheranschool@zionindy.com www.zionindy.com	Eric A Pralle	1884		N	EC-8	47
JUNCTION CITY	IMMANUEL	630 S Eisenhower Dr 66441	(785)238-5921	ileccjc@gmail.com	Jennifer Kohlmann	1954			EC	51
KANSAS CITY	OUR SAVIOUR	4153 Rainbow Blvd 66103	(913)236-6228	preschool@oskc.org oursaviourkcpreschool.org	Donna M Bottemuller	1931			EC	11
KENSINGTON	FIRST ST JOHN	332 N Adams 66951	(785)476-2247	connie.synoground@gmail.com www.1stjohnlutheran.com		1984			EC	
LEAVENWORTH	ST PAUL	320 N 7th St 66048	(913)682-5553	school@splcs.org splschool.org/	Cynthia J Hammons	1863			EC-8	81
LEAWOOD	LORD OF LIFE	3105 W 135th St 66224	(913)681-5167	meghan.lordlife@gmail.com www.lordoflifekc.com		1994		N	EC	
LINN	LINN	112 Church St 66953	(785)348-5792	secretary@linnlutheran.eduk12.net linnlutheranschool.org	Kelsey Hatesohl	1967	R		EC; 1-8	97
MANHATTAN	ST LUKE	355 Delaware 66502	(785)539-2604	centerdirector@stlukesmanhattan.org www.stlukesmanhattan.org	Betsy Molinary Martinez	1981			EC	50
MARYSVILLE	GOOD SHEPHERD	206 S 17th St 66508	(785)562-3181	kerickson@goodshepherdks.org goodshepherdks.eduk12.net/		1995	R		EC-8	70
NEWTON	ZION	225 S Poplar St 67114	(316)283-1441	zionpreschool@zionnewton.com www.zionnewton.com	Missy Ratzlaff	1988			EC	
OLATHE	BEAUTIFUL SAVIOR	13145 Blackbob Rd 66062	(913)780-6889	preschool@bslcks.org www.bslcks.org	Amy E Schultz	2001		N	EC	134
	REDEEMER	920 S Alta Ln 66061	(913)780-9912	rlecc@redeemerolathe.org www.redeemerolathe.org	Lori Belden	1985			EC	47
OTTAWA	FAITH	1320 W 15th St 66067	(785)242-7366	preschool@faithottawa.org	Stephanie E Circle	1980			EC	43
OVERLAND PARK	BETHANY	9101 Lamar Ave. 66207	(913)648-2228	frontdesk@bethanyschool.net www.bethanyschool.net	Sharon M Fries	2000			K-8	197
OVERLAND PARK	BETHANY	9101 Lamar Ave 66207	(913)648-2228	janderson@bethany-joco.org www.bethany-joco.org	Laurie Wyssmann	1966			EC	141
	CHRIST	11720 Nieman Rd 66210	(913)754-5813	michelle.howard@clcop.org www.clcop.org	Michelle R Howard	1988			EC	74
	CHRIST	11720 Nieman Rd 66210	(913)754-5888	ben.lausman@clclop.org www.clsop.org/	Dr David R Rindt	2001		N	K-8	133
PAOLA	SON SHINE	401 E Piankishaw St 66071	(913)294-5925	sonshine@firstlutheran-paola.org www.firstlutheran-paola.org	Kris Fuchs	2007			EC	
SABETHA	FIRST	225B S Second St 66534	(789)284-3570			1989			EC	30
SHAWNEE	HOPE	6308 Quivira Rd 66216	(913)631-6940	school.office@hopelutheran.org hopelutheran.org/school	Nancy J Jankowski	1983		N	EC-8	167
	TRINITY	21320 Midland Dr 66218	(913)563-5280	joann@tlcms.org www.tlcms.org	Jo Ann Emerson	1955		N	EC	73
TOPEKA	CALVARY	4211 NW Topeka Blvd 66617	(785)783-2121	Cllctopekadirector@gmail.com www.calvarytopeka.org		2006			EC	19
	PRINCE OF PEACE	3625 SW Wanamaker Rd 66614	(785)271-0913	ahoytalpopp@gmail.com	Amy Hoytal	1990			EC	98
	ST JOHN	901 SW Fillmore 66606	(785)354-7132	secretary@stjlcms.org stjohnlcmstopeka.org/learning/st-johns-classical-lutheran-school/		2023			K-6	11
WICHITA	ASCENSION	842 N Tyler Rd 67212	(316)722-4694	preschool@ascension-lcms.org www.ascension-lcms.org	Kendra D Herbig	1965			EC	40
	BETHANY	1000 W 26th St S 67217	(316)265-3033	blsoffice3033@gmail.com www.bethanylutheranwichita.org/school	Danita Seamars	1958			EC	
	HOLY CROSS	600 N Greenwich 67206	(316)684-4431	office@hcwichita.net www.lovemyschool.net	Karen S Boettcher	1959		N	EC-8	276
	OPEN ARMS	12885 W Maple 67235	(316)721-5675	ericam@openarmswichita.com www.ascension-lcms.org	Erica M Mason	2002			EC	
WINFIELD	TRINITY	910 Mound St 67156	(620)221-1820	principaldehning@trinitylutheranwinfield.org trinitylutheranwinfield.com	Christopher J Dehning	1888			EC-8	71
KENTUCKY										
ASHLAND	CHRISTS KIDS	1320 Bath Ave 41101	(606)324-7729	christskidspreschool@gmail.com	Mary Robinson	2010			EC	21
BOWLING GREEN	HOLY TRINITY	553 Ashmoor Ave 42101	(270)843-1001	school.admin@htlc-bg.org www.htlsbg.com	William R Hiskey	1967			EC-6	201
ELIZABETHTOWN	GLORIA DEI	1711 Ring Rd 42701	(270)769-5910	office.gloriadei@gmail.com gloriadeietown.org	Michelle L Petersen	2000			EC	
LEXINGTON	LEXINGTON	425 Patchen Dr 40517	(859)268-7787	lutheranschooloflex@gmail.com www.lutheranpreschoollex.com		2005	R		EC	

R = Recognized Service Organization (RSO)
N = National Lutheran Schools Accreditation (NLSA)

CITY	SCHOOL	ADDRESS	PHONE	EMAIL WEBSITE	PRINCIPAL/ ADMINISTRATOR	YEAR ORG.	RSO	NLSA	GRADES OFFERED	ENROLL
LEXINGTON	*OUR REDEEMER*	2255 Eastland Parkway 40505	(859)299-9615	kristinttarry@gmail.com www.preschool.orlutheran.com	Lisa Saylor	2005			EC	
	ST JOHNS	516 Pasadena Dr 40503	(859)275-1907	preschool@stjohnslexington.org stjohnslexington.org/education/preschool/		1986			EC	24
LOUISVILLE	*OUR SAVIOR*	8307 Nottingham Pkwy 40222	(502)426-0864	oursaviorschool@oslslouisville.com www.oslslouisville.com	Wesley J Wrucke	1990		N	EC-8	
				LOUISIANA						
BATON ROUGE	*TRINITY*	10925 Florida Blvd 70815	(225)412-4102	jcozzi@tlcbr.org www.tlcbr.org	Jordan Cozzi	2007			EC	
COVINGTON	*HOLY TRINITY*	1 N Marigold Dr 70433	(985)892-6146	schooladmin@htlministries.org htlministries.org		1991			EC	130
HARAHAN	*FAITH*	300 Colonial Club Dr 70123	(504)737-9554	fls-office@att.net faithlutheran-school.com	Lois Rost	1958		N	K-8	
LAKE CHARLES	*ST JOHN LITTLE LAMB*	600 University Dr 70605	(337)478-2659	stjohnslittlelambs@hotmail.com	Rebecca Yelverton	1980			EC	
METAIRIE	*ATONEMENT*	6500 Riverside Dr 70003	(504)887-0225	schooloffice@alcs.org www.alcs.org		1960			EC-8	
	LUTHERAN HIGH SCHOOL	3864 17TH ST 70002	(504)455-4062	cchristen@lutheranhighschool.net www.lutheranhighschool.net		1970	R	N	8-12	
NEW ORLEANS	*ST JOHN*	3937 Canal St 70119	(504)488-6641	mbinkley@sjlno.org www.StJohnLutheranNola.com	Bethany J Gonski	1854		N	K-8	105
SLIDELL	*OPEN ARMS*	1300 8th St 70458	(985)646-0974	janet@openarmsslidell.org www.openarmsslidell.com	Janet Lewis	2010			EC	86
				MARYLAND						
BALTIMORE	*PILGRIM CHRISTIAN*	7200 Liberty Rd 21207	(410)484-9240	pcds@bcpl.net www.bcpl.net/~pcds/index.html	Samuel Pettijohn	1948			EC-5	
BEL AIR	*ST MATTHEW*	1200 E Churchville Rd 21014	(410)838-3178	preschool@smlc.org www.smlcprek.org	Maryanne Shulman	1972			EC	
CATONSVILLE	*EMMANUEL*	929 Ingleside Ave 21228	(410)744-0015	smiller@elsbaltimore.org www.emmanuelbaltimore.org	Susan Miller	1956			K-8	
	ST PAUL	2001 Old Frederick Rd 21228	(410)747-1924	principal@stpaulcatonsville.org school.stpaulcatonsville.org	Suzanne Alms	1957		N	EC-5	132
GERMANTOWN	*MESSIAH*	13901 Clopper Rd 20874	(301)972-5428	mlpsoffice@gmail.com www.messiahlutherangermantown.org/preschool	Jeannine Shannon	2003		N	EC	28
GLEN ARM	*ST JOHN*	13300 MANOR RD 21057	(410)592-8019	director@stjohnslcms.org	Janet D Watson	1955			EC-K	63
GLEN BURNIE	*ST PAUL*	308 Oak Manor Dr 21061	(410)766-5790	rgast@stpaulsgb.org www.stpaulsgb.org/school/home	John R Maxwell III	1950		N	EC-8	340
HAGERSTOWN	*OPEN ARMS*	17906 Garden Ln 21740	(301)797-5955	openarms.hagerstown1@gmail.com www.concordia-hagerstown.org	Karla A Baker	2009			EC	
HUNTINGTOWN	*LITTLE LAMBS*	6300 Southern Md Blvd 20639	(410)257-3530	directorllps@firstlutheranchurch.org www.firstlutheranchurch.org	Angie Hohl	2000		N	EC	72
KINGSVILLE	*ST PAULS*	12022 Jerusalem Rd 21087	(410)592-8100	sosbourn@stpaulskingsville.org www.stpaulseagles.org	Scott C Osbourn			N	EC-8	177
LA PLATA	*GRACE*	1200 Charles St 20646	(301)932-0963	sgastler@growingwithgrace.org www.growingwithgrace.org	Jeffrey R Burkee			N	EC-8	266
LAUREL	*OPEN ARMS*	13611 Laurel Bowie Rd 20708	(240)568-9352	openarms@oslclaurel.org www.openarmslaurel.org	Rebecca J Stewart	2005			EC	120
LEXINGTON PARK	*LITTLE SONBEAMS*	46707 Shangri La Dr 20653	(301)862-4571	office@littlesonbeams.com littlesonbeams.com		1989			EC	41
OLNEY	*SHEPHERD'S CARE*	4200 Olney-Laytonsville Rd 20832	(301)570-7566	sccc@olneygoodshepherd.org www.olneygoodshepherd.org	Sandra Pernie	1997			EC	
PASADENA	*GALILEE*	4652 Mountain Rd 21122	(410)255-3504	t.merritt@glcpasadena.org www.glcpasadena.org	Jennifer Farrelly	1973			EC	56
PRESTON	*IMMANUEL*	242 Main St 21655	(410)673-7107	immanuellutheranpreston@verizon.net	Sarah Durham	1979			EC	30
SILVER SPRING	*ST ANDREW*	15300 New Hampshire Ave 20905	(301)384-2660	lcsapreschool@yahoo.com www.mystandrew.org	Lia Mai Puskar	1964			EC	
TOWSON	*CONCORDIA*	1145 Concordia Dr 21286	(410)825-2323	brentjohnson@concordiaprepschool.org www.concordiaprepschool.org	Brent T Johnson	1965	R		6-12	492
	HOLY CROSS	8516 Loch Raven Blvd 21286	(410)825-7905	holycross_director@comcast.net	Chris Diehl	1976			EC	
				MASSACHUSETTS						
ACTON	*MOUNT CALVARY*	472 Massachusetts 01720	(978)263-0337	krlarson19@gmail.com www.mtcalvaryacton.org	Wendy G Smutok	1987			EC	
BEDFORD	*OPEN ARMS*	426 Davis Rd 01730	(781)271-1148	openarmsbedford@aol.com www.lcsavior.org/#/open-arms-preschool	Donna Wilson	1996			EC	
DEDHAM	*ST LUKES*	950 East St 02026	(781)326-1346	stlukespreschooldedham@gmail.com	Elaine MacNeil	1964			EC	
FITCHBURG	*MESSIAH*	780 Rindge Rd 01420	(978)345-5954	mlc_learningcenter@verizon.net www.messiahfitchburg.com/ministries		1988			EC	
HANOVER	*OF THE CROSS*	77 Rockland St 02339	(781)826-6107	lutherannurseryschool@verizon.net www.lutheranpreschoolhanover.org	Vicki Gorder	1968			EC	
				MICHIGAN						
ADRIAN	*ST JOHN*	3448 N Adrian Hwy 49221	(517)266-2425	daycare@stjohnsadrian.org		1847			EC	25
ALBION	*LITTLE LAMBS JESUS*	615 S Dalrymple St 49224	(517)629-7699	littlelambsofjesus@outlook.com	Chelsea Siedzik	1984			EC	38
ALLEN PARK	*MOUNT HOPE*	5323 Southfield Rd 48101	(313)565-9140	mthopeluthschool@hotmail.com www.mthopepreschool.com		2006			EC	15
ALPENA	*IMMANUEL*	355 Wilson St 49707	(989)354-4805	school@immanuelalpena.org school.immanuelalpena.org	Joshua M Schultz	1874		N	EC-8	144

R = Recognized Service Organization (RSO)
N = National Lutheran Schools Accreditation (NLSA)

CITY	SCHOOL	ADDRESS	PHONE	EMAIL WEBSITE	PRINCIPAL/ ADMINISTRATOR	YEAR ORG.	RSO	NLSA	GRADES OFFERED	ENROLL
ANN ARBOR	ST PAUL	495 Earhart Rd 48105	(734)665-0604	priehs6@yahoo.com school.stpaulannarbor.org		1963		N	EC-8	278
AUBURN	ZION	1557 W Seidler Rd 48611	(989)662-4264	office@zionauburn.com www.zionbeaver.com	Susan E Klauer	1887		N	EC-8	107
BAD AXE	OUR SAVIOR	123 W Irwin St 48413	(989)269-7642	oslcbadaxe@gmail.com www.oursaviorlutheranchurch-badaxemi.org		1983			EC	4
BATTLE CREEK	WORLD FOR CHILDREN	114 E Minges Rd 49015	(269)965-4051	mhuisinga@stmarkbattlecreek.org owc.stmarkbattlecreek.org		2002			EC	188
BAY CITY	FAITH	3033 Wilder Rd 48706	(989)684-3448	ssmith@faithbaycity.org www.faithlutheranbc.org/		1961		N	EC-8	163
	IMMANUEL	247 N Lincoln St 48708	(989)893-8521	ils@immanuelbaycity.com www.immanuelbaycity.com	Heath D Vincent	1863		N	EC-8	139
	ST JOHN AMELITH	1664 Amelith Rd 48706	(989)686-0176	office@amelith.org www.amelith.org	Jonathan Korpi	1852			EC-8	22
	ST PAUL	6094 Westside Saginaw Rd 48706	(989)684-4450	office@stpaulbaycity.org stpaulbaycity.org	Valerie E Matyas	1848		N	EC-8	140
	TRINITY MONITOR	20 E Salzburg Rd 48706	(989)662-4891	school@trinitymonitor.org trinitymonitor.org/School.html		1880		N	EC-8	106
	ZION	1707 S Kiesel St 48706	(989)893-5793	pbaerwolf@zionbaycity.org zionbaycity.org		1903		N	EC-8	94
BELLEVILLE	OPEN ARMS	7865 Belleville Rd 48111	(734)669-5000	gbower@openarmscenter.com www.openarmscenter.com		2003			EC	111
BERRIEN SPRINGS	TRINITY	9123 George Ave 49103	(269)473-1811	school@trinityberrien.org www.trinityberrien.org	Mike Shembarger	1925			EC-8	143
BEVERLY HILLS	ASCENSION OF CHRIST	16935 W 14 Mile Rd 48025	(248)644-8890	cookc@ascensionofchrist.org www.ascensionofchrist.org/#/welcome-to-aoc					EC	
BIG RAPIDS	ST PETER	408 W Bellevue St 49307	(231)796-6684	office@stpetersbr.org stpetersbr.org		1871			EC-12	99
BIRCH RUN	PEACE OF MIND	10995 Canada Rd 48415	(989)624-0298	peaceofmind@stmartinbirchrun.org	Megan Schrubbe	2003			EC	19
BIRMINGHAM	OUR SHEPHERD	1658 E Lincoln St 48009	(248)645-0551	schooloffice@ourshepherd.net ourshepherd.net	Janet M Mc Loughlin	1956		N	EC-8	319
	WESTMAPLE	1800 W Maple Rd 48009	(248)646-5155	westmaple@redeemerbirmingham.org		1954			EC	94
BRIDGEPORT	FAITH	4241 Williamson Rd 48722	(989)777-2600	faithluthchurch@yahoo.com faithlutheranbridgeport.org		1970			EC	37
BRIDGMAN	IMMANUEL	9650 Church St 49106	(269)465-3351	barb.ackerman@immanuelbridgman.org		1896			EC	104
BRIGHTON	SHEPHERD OF THE LAKE	2101 S Hacker Rd 48114	(810)227-6473	school@sotlschool.com www.sotlschool.com	Juli Van Deven	1982		N	EC-8	280
CADILLAC	JOYFUL HEARTS	11198 E M-55 49601	(231)775-3898	joyfulhearts@emmanuelcadillac.org	Jayne R Foster	2004			EC	60
CALEDONIA	ST PAUL	8436 Kraft Avenue SE 49316	(616)891-8688	julie@stpaulcaledonia.org www.stpaulcaledonia.org	Julie Rop				EC	20
CASSOPOLIS	OPEN ARMS	305 W State St 49031	(269)228-8037	dpd6026@yahoo.com www.stpaulcass.org	Amy Wiggins	1997			EC	55
CHARLOTTE	FIRST	712 Paine Dr 48813	(517)543-3828	flpddirector@gmail.com	Rebekah Simmons	1986			EC	40
CLARKSTON	ST TRINITY	7925 Sashabaw Rd 48348	(248)620-6154	sttrinitypreschool@gmail.com www.sainttrinitylutheran.com		1983			EC	43
CLINTON TOWNSHIP	TRINITY	38900 Harper Ave 48036	(586)468-8511	csteenkamp@trinityct.org www.trinityct.org		1885		N	K-8	223
	TRINITY	38900 Harper Ave 48036	(586)463-8803	jplatte@trinityct.org www.trinityct.org		1997		N	EC	130
COLDWATER	SONSHINE KIDS	95 W State St 49036	(517)278-8061	churchoffice@stpaulcoldwater.com www.stpaulcoldwater.com	Lisa L Dove				EC	38
COLOMA	SALEM	275 Marvin St 49038	(269)468-6567	salem_lcms@comcast.net salemcoloma.org/our-preschool/		1974			EC	34
CONKLIN	TRINITY	1401 Harding St 49403	(616)899-2152	school@tlc-conklin.org www.tlc-conklin.org	Britney Ritz	1869			EC-5	40
DEARBORN	EMMANUEL	22425 Morley Ave 48124	(313)561-6265	baerwolfp@gmail.com emmanuelschool.net		1944		N	EC-8	33
	GUARDIAN	24544 Cherry Hill St 48124	(313)274-3665	principal@guardianlutheran.org www.guardianlutheran.org	Matthew D Dummann	1959			EC-8	244
DETROIT	EVERGREEN	8680 Evergreen Ave 48228	(313)584-0450	william20418@yahoo.com	Vera Brown	1956			K-8	9
DRYDEN	HOLY REDEEMER	4538 Dryden Rd 48428	(810)796-3951	jkdtrip@charter.net		1996			EC	
EASTPOINTE	ST PETERS	23000 Gratiot Ave 48021	(586)777-6300	school@stpeterslutheranchurch.net www.stpeterslutheranchurch.net		1850			EC-8	222
FLAT ROCK	CREATIVE LEARNING	23984 Gibraltar Rd 48134	(734)782-0563	office@clcflatrock.com www.clcflatrock.com		2001			EC	8
FLINT	ST PAUL	402 S Ballenger Hwy 48532	(810)239-6733	mbuck@stpaulflint.com stpaulflint.com	Mary L Buck	1924		N	EC-8	161
FRANKENMUTH	ST LORENZ	140 Churchgrove Rd 48734	(989)652-6141	jfrank@stlorenz.org stlorenz.org		1846		N	EC-8	643
FRASER	ST JOHN	16339 E 14 Mile Rd 48026	(586)294-8740	lbringold@stjohnfraser.org www.stjohnfraser.org	Levi R Bringold	1864		N	EC-8	268
GRAND BLANC	FAITH	12534 Holly Rd 48439	(810)694-9351	clafontaine@faithgb.org www.faithgb.org		1996			EC	70
GRAND HAVEN	ST JOHN	525 Taylor Ave 49417	(616)842-0260	lharvey@stjohnsgrandhaven.com www.stjohnsgrandhaven.com		1946			EC-8	73
GRAND RAPIDS	ISJ	2066 Oakwood NE 49505	(616)363-0505	isjoffice@mychristianschool.com www.isjacademy.org	Karla M Hardies	1859	R		EC-6	70

R = Recognized Service Organization (RSO)
N = National Lutheran Schools Accreditation (NLSA)

CITY	SCHOOL	ADDRESS	PHONE	EMAIL WEBSITE	PRINCIPAL/ ADMINISTRATOR	YEAR ORG.	RSO	NLSA	GRADES OFFERED	ENROLL
GRAND RAPIDS	*MESSIAH*	2727 5 Mile Rd NE 49525	(616)363-2553	smestadv@messiahgr.org www.messiahgrpreschool.org	Diane J Oppenneer	1987			EC	20
	OUR SAVIOR	1916 Ridgewood Ave SE 49506	(616)949-0710	jhabrecht@oursavior-gr.org www.oslsgr.org		1955		N	EC-8	61
GREENVILLE	*MT CALVARY*	908 W Oak St 48838	(616)754-8046	mccpc908.org@gmail.com www.mccpc908.org	Jennifer Neumann	1980			EC	36
GROSSE POINTE WOODS	*CHRIST THE KING*	20338 Mack Ave 48236	(313)402-2844	mrfc143@gmail.com www.christthekinggp.org	Melissa Pieper	1986			EC	
HARBOR BEACH	*ZION*	299 Garden 48441	(989)479-3615	principal@zionlcs.com www.zionlcs.com	Cynthia A Brown	1882		N	EC-8	158
HARTLAND	*OUR SAVIOR*	13667 W Highland Rd 48353	(248)887-3836	schooloffice@oursaviorhartland.org www.oursaviorhartland.org		1979			EC-8	151
HASLETT	*LITTLE LAMBS*	5589 Van Atta Rd 48840	(517)339-2333	jpurkiss@knowingjesus.org knowingjesus.org		1992			EC	37
HEMLOCK	*ST PETER*	2440 N Raucholz Rd 48626	(989)642-5659	eric.hagenow@stpeterhemlock.org www.stpeterhemlock.org	Eric M Hagenow	1881		N	EC-8	194
HILLMAN	*ST JOHN*	22000 County Rd 452 49746	(989)742-4400	stjohnhillman@speedconnect.com	Debra A Miller	2004			EC	19
HOLT	*HOLT*	2418 Aurelius Rd 48842	(517)694-3182	principal@hlsmi.org www.hlsmi.org	Chelsea M Speers	1972			K-8	86
	MESSIAH	5740 W Holt Rd 48842	(517)694-7344	mcdckids@messiahlutheranholt.org www.messiahlutheranholt.org	Kelly Marble	2002			EC	39
	SONSHINE	2418 Aurelius Rd 48842	(517)694-3182	sonshine.ecc@gmail.com www.sonshineecc.org		2006			EC-6	53
HOUGHTON	*SS PETER AND PAUL*	1010 Madeleine St 49931	(928)231-1268	preschool@copperluth.org www.copperluth.org.elc					EC	
HOWELL	*HEART OF SHEPHERD*	228 N Burkhart Rd 48843	(517)552-7218	courtni@hotshepherd.org www.hotshepherd.org	Courtni Holst	2006			EC	54
HUBBARD LAKE	*SMALL WONDERS*	6891 Nucholson Hill Rd 49747	(989)727-2496	childcaredirector@stpaulhubbardlake.org	Debbie Choe				EC	15
HUNTINGTON WOODS	*HUNTINGTON WOODS*	12935 W 11 Mile Rd 48070	(248)542-3031	hwlcpreschool@gmail.com		1975			EC	56
IRONWOOD	*TRINITY*	E5104 E Margaret St 49938	(906)932-3080	childcare@trinityironwood.org www.trinityironwood.org		1981			EC	
ISHPEMING	*CHRIST THE KING*	440 Stoneville Rd 49849	(906)485-4432	dce@christking-ish.org www.ctkishpeming.org		1996			EC	
JACKSON	*TRINITY*	4900 Mc Cain Rd 49201	(517)750-2105	office@tlsjackson.com www.tlsjackson.com	Lisa A Singleton				EC-8	66
KALAMAZOO	*FRIENDS OF JESUS*	2122 Bronson Blvd 49008	(269)382-2360	www.friendsofjesuspreschool.com	Jennifer LaPorte	1976			EC	17
KENTWOOD	*ST MARK*	1934 52nd St SE 49508	(616)455-5320	agust@saintmarkgr.org saintmarkpreschool.org		1967			EC	55
LAKE ORION	*GOOD SHEPHERD*	1950 S Baldwin Rd 48360	(248)391-1170	preschool@gsls.org www.goodshepherdlakeorion.com		1996			EC	105
LANSING	*OUR SAVIOR*	7910 E St Joe Hwy 48917	(517)882-8665	mcouser@oursaviorlansing.org www.oursaviorlansingschool.org		1957		N	EC-8	259
	TRINITY	501 W Saginaw St 48933	(517)372-3003	childcaretrinity@gmail.com childcaretrinity.org/		1994			EC	17
LAPEER	*ST PAUL*	90 Millville Rd 48446	(810)664-0046	james@stpaul-lapeer.org www.stpaulspirits.org		1987		N	EC-8	215
LIVONIA	*CHRIST OUR SAVIOR*	14175 Farmington Rd 48154	(734)513-8413	preschool@christoursavior.org www.christoursavior.org		1982			EC	81
MACOMB	*IMMANUEL*	47120 Romeo Plank Rd 48044	(586)286-7076	jneumeyer@immlutheran.org www.immlutheran.org	Joel K Neumeyer	1853		N	EC-8	547
	ST PETER	17051 24 Mile Rd 48042	(586)781-9296	slaperriere@splcs.net www.stpetermacomb.com	Sandra J LaPerriere	1877		N	EC-8	710
MANISTEE	*TRINITY*	420 Oak St 49660	(231)723-8700	trinityk8@trinitymanistee.com trinitymanistee.com	Ashlea J Weston	1870			EC-5	41
MARQUETTE	*REDEEMER*	1700 W Fair Ave 49855	(906)228-9883	rlecc@redeemermqt.org www.redeemermqt.org	Carmen Albert	1984			EC	83
MARSHALL	*CHRIST*	440 West Dr N 49068	(269)781-5842	clcsecretary1@att.net www.christlutheranmarshall.com/		1980			EC	22
MIDLAND	*ST JOHNS*	505 E Carpenter St 48640	(989)835-7041	bmassey@sjlmidland.org sjlmidland.org	Bradley R Massey	1946		N	EC-8	94
MILFORD	*CHRIST*	620 General Motors Rd 48381	(248)684-6773	preschool@christlutheranmilford.org www.christlutheranmilford.org		1999			EC-K	38
MILLINGTON	*ST PAUL*	4941 Center St 48746	(989)871-4581	school.office@spmill.org www.stpaul-millington.org	Barbara A Riley	1905		N	EC-8	141
MONROE	*HOLY GHOST*	3563 Heiss Rd 48162	(734)242-0509	holyghostmonroe@gmail.com holyghostmonroe.org		1844			EC-8	88
	TRINITY	315 Scott St 48161	(734)241-1160	thackbarth@trinitylutheranmonroe.org tlsmonroe.org	Tracey J Hackbarth	1844		N	EC-8	256
MONTAGUE	*GOOD SHEPHERD*	8945 Stebbins St 49437	(231)894-8471	stjamestz@frontier.com stjamesmontague.org		1983			EC	29
MOUNT PLEASANT	*ZION*	3401 E River Rd 48858	(989)772-1516	croe@zionmpmi.org www.zionlutheranpreschoolecc.com	Christina Roe	1972			EC	87
MUNISING	*GOOD SHEPHERD*	E9035 E STATE HIGHWAY M28 49862	(906)387-3579	goodshepherd@jamadots.com		2001			EC	
MUSKEGON	*WEST SHORE*	3225 Roosevelt Rd 49441	(231)755-1048	westshorelutheran@gmail.com westshorelutheran.com	Bradley D Feenstra	1995			EC-8	144
NORTHVILLE	*ST PAUL*	201 Elm St 48167	(248)349-3146	school@stpaulnorthville.org stpaulnorthville.org		1959			EC-8	32

R = Recognized Service Organization (RSO)
N = National Lutheran Schools Accreditation (NLSA)

CITY	SCHOOL	ADDRESS	PHONE	EMAIL WEBSITE	PRINCIPAL/ ADMINISTRATOR	YEAR ORG.	RSO	NLSA	GRADES OFFERED	ENROLL
ONAWAY	*HOLY CROSS*	3786 Glasier Rd 49765	(989)733-8412	holycrossonaway@gmail.com		2002			EC	6
OXFORD	*JOURNEY*	136 S Washington St 48371	(248)628-2011	roxann@journeylutheran.church www.journeylutheran.church		1964			EC	48
PAW PAW	*TRINITY*	725 Pine St 49079	(269)657-5921	jltuls@trinitylutheran.com trinitylutheran.com	Jody Tuls	1985			EC-5	97
PETOSKEY	*ZION*	500 W Mitchell 49770	(231)347-2757	preschool@zionlutheranpetoskey.org	Kimberlea Timm				EC	17
PORTAGE	*ST MICHAEL*	7211 Oakland Dr 49024	(269)327-0512	gjohnson@mightymessengers.org www.stmikeschool.org		2001		N	EC-8	227
PORTLAND	*WEE GROW*	8867 Kent St 48875	(517)647-4473	skpeabody@gmail.com	Sandy K Peabody	1993			EC	30
REED CITY	*TRINITY*	19778 US Hwy 10 49677	(231)832-5186	office@trinitylutheran-rc.org www.trinitylutheran-rc.org	Richard Saldin	1880			EC-8	75
REESE	*TRINITY*	9858 North St 48757	(989)868-4501	mrsbriggs.trinity@gmail.com www.trinityreese.com		1921		N	K-8	75
	TRINITY	9858 North St 48757	(989)868-4501	mrsbriggs.trinity@gmail.com www.trinityreese.com		2003		N	EC	46
RICHMOND	*SEASONS OF LEARNING*	67055 Gratiot Ave 48062	(586)248-4949	office@seasonsoflearning.org www.seasonsoflearning.org	Denise Hall		R		EC	31
	ST PETER	37601 31 Mile Rd 48062	(586)727-9080	hhaller@splschoolrichmond.org stpetersrichmond.org	Heather B Haller	1872		N	K-8	108
RICHVILLE	*ST MICHAELS*	9444 W Saginaw Rd 48758	(989)868-4809	smr@stmichaelsrichville.org www.stmichaelsrichville.org	Joel W Rachow	1851		N	EC-8	254
ROCHESTER	*ST JOHN*	1011 W University Dr 48307	(248)402-8000	school@stjohnrochester.org www.stjohnrochester.org	Todd M Pehlke	1943		N	EC-8	445
ROCHESTER HILLS	*CROWN OF LIFE*	2975 Dutton Rd 48306	(248)652-7720	preschool@crownoflifechurch.org www.crownoflifechurch.org	Allison J Piasecki				EC	38
ROCKFORD	*ST PETER'S*	310 E Division St 49341	(616)866-3700	preschoolstpeters@yahoo.com		1986			EC	87
ROGERS CITY	*ST JOHN*	145 N 5th St 49779	(989)734-3580	sjlsrogerscity@gmail.com StJohnSoars.com		1916		N	EC-8	68
ROMEO	*GRACE*	7525 32 Mile Rd 48065	(586)752-9800	preschool@graceromeo.com www.graceromeo.com		2010			EC	21
ROSEVILLE	*BETHLEHEM*	29675 Gratiot Ave 48066	(586)777-9130	blelc09@yahoo.com		1957			EC	26
ROYAL OAK	*ST PAUL*	508 Williams St 48067	(248)546-6555	principal@stpaulroyaloak.org www.stpaulroyaloak.org	Christopher D Francik	1916		N	EC-8	55
SAGINAW	*BETHLEHEM*	2777 Hermansau Rd 48604	(989)755-1144	bwilson@bethlehemsaginaw.org bethlehemsaginaw.org	Nicole Frederick	1914		N	EC-8	154
	GOOD SHEPHERD	5335 Brockway Rd 48623	(989)793-8252	ecc@goodshepherdsaginaw.com goodshepherdsaginaw.com		1957			EC-K	75
	HOLY CROSS	610 Court St 48602	(989)793-9795	school@hcls.org www.hcls.org	Roger W Wolter	1853		N	EC-8	75
	IMMANUEL	8220 E Holland Rd 48601	(989)754-4285	school@frankentrost.org frankentrost.org	Rachel M Abraham	1847		N	EC-8	128
	PEACE	3161 Lawndale Rd 48603	(989)792-2581	mhauser@peacesaginaw.org www.peacesaginaw.org/school	Matthew J Hauser	1940		N	EC-8	330
	ST MARK	2565 N Miller Rd 48609	(517)781-3205	stmark@stmarksaginaw.org www.stmarksaginaw.com	Megan Reinig	1999			EC	14
SAINT CLAIR	*IMMANUEL*	415 N 9th St 48079	(810)329-7174	preschool@immanuelsc.org immanuelsc.org		1997			EC	89
SAINT CLAIR SHORES	*REDEEMER*	30003 Jefferson Ave 48082	(586)944-2014	redeemerpreschoolscs@gmail.com	Michelle Rabideau				EC	
SAINT JOHNS	*ST PETER*	8990 Church Rd 48879	(989)224-3178	School@stpeterriley.org www.stpeterriley.org		1941			EC-8	61
SAINT JOSEPH	*TRINITY*	613 Court St 49085	(269)983-3056	Amy.Roth@discovertrinity.org trinitystjoe.org		1867		N	EC-8	187
SANDUSKY	*PEACE*	58 Flynn St 48471	(810)648-2485	peaceluthteacher@gmail.com www.peacelutheransandusky.com		1984			EC	24
SAWYER	*TRINITY*	5791 Sawyer Rd 49125	(269)426-3151	trinity_lutheran@yahoo.com trinitylutheransawyer.com	Jennifer L Lockman	1913			EC	36
SEBEWAING	*CHRIST THE KING*	612 E Bay St 48759	(989)883-3730	principal@ctkl.org www.ctklschool.org	Jennifer A Yoder	1998		N	EC-8	123
SHELBY TOWNSHIP	*PEACE*	6580 24 Mile Rd 48316	(586)731-4120	kdomerese@peaceshelby.org www.peaceshelby.org	Michael A Nelson	1969		N	EC-8	301
SOUTH LYON	*CROSS OF CHRIST*	24155 Griswold Rd 48178	(248)437-0871	cross-christ@att.net crossofchristlutheran.org	Janelle Rapson-Lach	1990			EC	45
SOUTHGATE	*CHRIST THE KING*	15600 Trenton Rd 48195	(734)285-9697	kkapp@ctk.me ctkpanthers.com	Kelli Kapp-Heifner	1957		N	EC-8	272
SPRING LAKE	*ST MATTHEW*	15395 Rannes St 49456	(616)846-4019	director.footsteps@gmail.com www.smslm.org	Sam Wilson	2005			EC	21
STEVENSVILLE	*CHRIST*	4333 Cleveland Ave 49127	(269)429-7111	nwebb@christstevensville.com christ-luth.org		1956		N	EC-8	95
STURGIS	*TRINITY*	406 S Lakeview Ave 49091	(269)651-4245	school@trinitysturgis.com www.trinitylutheransturgis.com	Tricia K Reinbold	1978			EC-8	129
TRAVERSE CITY	*TRINITY*	1003 S Maple St 49684	(231)946-2721	ksmith@tctrinityschool.org www.tctrinityschool.org		1950		N	EC-8	140
TRENTON	*ST PAUL*	2550 Edsel Dr 48183	(734)676-2918	pbayer@splconline.com splconline.com	Penny Bayer	1992			EC	197
TROY	*FAITH*	37635 Dequindre Rd 48083	(248)689-4664	kelliott@faithtroy.org www.faithtroy.org	Keri L Elliott	1975			EC	38
	ST AUGUSTINE	5475 Livernois 48098	(248)879-2893	staugps@yahoo.com Saltchurch.net		1998			EC	16

R = Recognized Service Organization (RSO)
N = National Lutheran Schools Accreditation (NLSA)

CITY	SCHOOL	ADDRESS	PHONE	EMAIL WEBSITE	PRINCIPAL/ ADMINISTRATOR	YEAR ORG.	RSO	NLSA	GRADES OFFERED	ENROLL
UTICA	*TRINITY*	45160 Van Dyke Ave 48317	(586)731-4490	schooloffice@trinityutica.com www.trinityutica.com	Bruce R Volkert	1882		N	EC-8	510
WALLED LAKE	*ST MATTHEW*	2040 S Commerce Rd 48390	(248)624-7677	Susan.Palka@st-matthew.org www.stmatthewlutheranschool.com	Susan E Palka	1957		N	EC-8	178
WALTZ	*ST JOHN*	28320 Waltz Rd 48164	(734)654-6366	schooloffice@stjohnswaltz.org www.stjohnswaltz.org	Adrienne A Gurney	1870			EC-8	111
WASHINGTON	*LITTLE LAMBS*	8600 27 Mile Rd 48094	(586)781-5567	littlelambs@ourredeemer-lcms.org ourredeemer-lcms.org		1983			EC	112
WAYNE	*ST MICHAEL*	3003 Hannan Rd 48184	(734)728-3315	schooloffice@stmichaellutheran.org www.stmichaelmustangs.org		1982		N	EC-8	199
WEST BLOOMFIELD	*SHEPHERD KING*	5300 W Maple Rd 48322	(248)626-2121	shepherdkingpreschool@gmail.com www.shepherdkinglcms.org	Pam Hughes	1992			EC	
WESTLAND	*ST MATTHEW*	5885 N Venoy Rd 48185	(734)425-0261	dan.burk@stmatthew.info www.stmatthew.info	Daniel R Burk	1949		N	EC-8	172
WIXOM	*HEARTS AND HANDS*	48380 Pontiac Trail 48393	(248)624-9525	karen.kosky@st-matthew.org www.st-matthew.org		2000			EC	53
WYOMING	*WMLHS*	150 50th St SW Suite 2 49548	(616)455-2200	kangers@wmlhs.org www.wmlhs.org	Kristine A Angers	2004	R	N	7-12	14

MINNESOTA

CITY	SCHOOL	ADDRESS	PHONE	EMAIL WEBSITE	PRINCIPAL/ ADMINISTRATOR	YEAR ORG.	RSO	NLSA	GRADES OFFERED	ENROLL
ALBERTVILLE	*LIFE IN CHRIST*	5015 Main Ave NE 55301	(763)497-5174	angie@lifeinchristpreschool.com lifeinchristpreschool.com	Angie M Underthun	2006			EC	23
ALEXANDRIA	*ZION*	300 Lake St 56308	(320)763-4842	astrickland@zionalex.org zionalexschool.org	Andrew A Strickland	1890		N	EC-8	224
ANOKA	*MOUNT OLIVE*	700 Western St 55303	(763)421-9048	cari@mtolive-anoka.org www.mtolive-anoka.org/school/index.htm	Cari Schommer	1981			EC	90
BEMIDJI	*TLC/GROWING TREE*	123 29th St NE 56601	(218)444-4442	tlcpre@paulbunyan.net www.trinitybemidji.com	Virginia Kurtzweg				EC	
BLOOMINGTON	*OPEN ARMS*	201 E 104th St 55420	(952)888-5116	info@openarmsecc.org www.openarmsecc.org	Dawn M Regan	1994		N	EC	55
	ST MICHAEL'S	9201 Normandale Blvd 55437	(952)230-2035	psdirector@smlcb.org www.smlcb.org	Kristi Lueth	1966			EC	31
BROWNTON	*NOAHS ARK*	700 Division St 55312	(320)328-5325	vickiattheark@yahoo.com www.immanuelbrownton.org	Vicki L Herrmann	1990			EC	25
BUFFALO	*NOAHS ARK*	302 NE 2nd St 55313	(763)682-1883	chelsey@stjohnsbuffalo.org stjohnsbuffalo.org/preschool	Chelsey Erickson	1988			EC	39
CHASKA	*ST JOHNS*	300 E Fourth St 55318	(952)448-2526	kendra.gilmore@stjohns-chaska.org www.sjschaska.org	Kendra A Gilmore	1886		N	EC-8	274
CLOQUET	*OUR REDEEMER*	515 Skyline Blvd 55720	(218)879-3380	preschool@orlcp.com www.orlcp.com		1990			EC	
COHASSET	*OUR RDMR LITTLE LAMB*	35568 Foxtail Ln 55721	(218)999-7193	littlelambs@ourredeemercohasset.org www.ourredeemercohasset.org		2004			EC	
COLOGNE	*ZION*	14735 County Road 153 55322	(952)466-3379	office@zion-cologne.org school.zion-cologne.org	Tom Marcsisak	1873		N	EC-8	79
COLUMBIA HEIGHTS	*DAVIDS*	4101 Washington St NE 55421	(763)789-4030	julie.sventek@stmatthew-ch.org www.dclearningcenter.org	Julie Sventek				EC	46
CORCORAN	*ST JOHN*	9141 County Road 101 N 55340	(763)420-2426	secretary@stjlutheran.org www.stjlutheranschool.org	Gretchen E Dolan	1864		N	EC-8	180
COTTAGE GROVE	*ROSEBUDS*	6875 Jamaica Ave S 55016	(651)459-4526	director@rosebudselc.com rosebudsearlylearningcenter.com	Jenessa A Miller				EC	35
COURTLAND	*IMMANUEL*	50605 478th St 56021	(507)359-2534	ils@newulmtel.net www.immanuelcourtland.com	Daniel D Erdman	1864			EC-8	61
CROOKSTON	*OUR SAVIORS*	217 S Broadway 56716	(218)281-5191	school_sec.oslds@midconetwork.com www.oursaviorslutheranschool.org	Sandra J Trittin	1983			EC-6	
DODGE CENTER	*GRACE*	404 Central Ave N 55927	(507)633-2253	gracedc@icloud.com	Patricia K Marquardt	1973			EC-3	23
EAGAN	*TRINITY LONE OAK*	2950 Highway 55 55121	(651)454-1139	school@trinityloneoak.org www.tloschool.org	Kathryn L Jones	1883		N	EC-8	120
EDINA	*CROSS VIEW*	6645 Mc Cauley Trl W 55439	(952)941-0009	stacey@crossview.net crossview.net	Anastacia L LaMere	1987		N	EC	82
	ST PETERS	5421 France Ave S 55410	(952)927-8400	jpitkanen@stpetersedina.org www.stpetersedina.org	Dr Tosca Grimm				EC	48
ELK RIVER	*GUIDING HANDS*	1506 Main St 55330	(763)441-2555	emmanluther@nsatel.net emmanuel-elkriver.org		1998			EC	
	ST JOHN	9243 Viking Blvd NW 55330	(763)441-6616	michelle.gueldner@sjlcas.com www.linkingliveselkriver.com	Jennifer R Hall	1888		N	EC-8	159
ESKO	*LITTLE ESKOMOS*	4 Elizabeth Ave 55733	(218)879-3510	stmattsesko@aol.com stmatthewsesko.org	Sybil Halvorson				EC	
EXCELSIOR	*OUR SAVIOR*	23290 Highway 7 55331	(952)474-5181	director@oslcs.org www.oursaviorschool.org		1984			EC-K	95
FAIRMONT	*ST PAUL*	201 Oxford St 56031	(507)238-9492	principal@splfairmont.org splfairmont.org	Elaine T Lieder	1895		N	EC-8	173
FARIBAULT	*FARIBAULT*	526 4th St NW 55021	(507)334-7982	flsoffice@flsweb.org flsweb.org	Chrysteena R Saehler	1996		N	K-8	140
	PEACE	213 SW 6th Ave 55021	(507)334-5999	peace.preschool@hotmail.com	Shermayne L Cross	1974			EC	83
FERGUS FALLS	*TRINITY*	1150 W Cavour 56537	(218)736-5847	info@preschoolattrinity.org www.preschoolattrinity.org	Diane V Christensen	1983			EC	
GAYLORD	*IMMANUEL*	417 High Ave 55334	(507)237-2804	immanuel@ilsgaylord.org www.ilsgaylord.org	Michelle L King	1882			EC-8	56
GLENCOE	*FIRST*	1015 14th St E 55336	(320)864-3317	malsleben@1stglencoe.org www.firstglencoe.org	Perry M Miller	1884			EC-8	165

R = Recognized Service Organization (RSO)
N = National Lutheran Schools Accreditation (NLSA)

CITY	SCHOOL	ADDRESS	PHONE	EMAIL WEBSITE	PRINCIPAL/ ADMINISTRATOR	YEAR ORG.	RSO	NLSA	GRADES OFFERED	ENROLL
GOLDEN VALLEY	LOVING SHEPHERD	5501 Glenwood Ave 55422	(763)544-0590	earlylearningcenter@gvlc.net www.gvlc.net	Brenda A Lovhaug	1989		N	EC	69
GOOD THUNDER	ST JOHN	311 Sherman St 56037	(507)278-3635	sjldaycare@gmail.com www.SJGT.org	Angela Groehler	1875			EC	40
HAM LAKE	FAMILY OF CHRIST	16345 Polk St NE 55304	(763)413-5037	mhiller@foclutheran.org www.foclutheran.org	Mary E Hiller	2004			EC	210
HAMBURG	EMANUEL	18155 County Road 50 55339	(952)467-2780	principalels@emanuelschool.org www.emanuelschool.org	Todd Bentz	1860		N	EC-8	55
	SONSHINE HOUSE	18169 County Road 50 55339	(952)467-9000		Stephanie Worm	2003			EC-4	
HASTINGS	HOPE	16898 Michael Ave 55033	(651)480-2417	preschool@hopeofhastings.com www.hopeofhastings.com/#/preschool	Katherine Bonnie	2001			EC	43
HERMANTOWN	PEACE IN CHRIST	5007 Maple Grove Rd 55811	(218)729-9473	peaceinchristpreschool@gmail.com	Kari Collins				EC	
HIBBING	CHILDREN OF GRACE	4010 9th Ave W 55746	(218)263-3955	childrenofgracecec@gmail.com	Bonnie L Nelson	2003			EC	
HINCKLEY	ST PAUL LITTLE LAMBS	405 2nd St NW 55037	(320)384-6267	littlelambsprek@gmail.com		1999			EC	
HOPKINS	ZION	241 5th Ave N 55343	(952)938-7661	zecc@zionhopking.org zionhopkins.org		2001			EC	
HOWARD LAKE	ST JAMES	1000 6th Ave 55349	(320)543-2630	school@stjameshl.org www.stjameshl.org	Mark S Loder	1918		N	EC-8	120
HUTCHINSON	LITTLE LAMBS	400 Franklin St SW 55350	(320)587-2629	Office@plchutch.org www.littlelambsmn.com	Rhonda Hulzebos	1983			EC	
	OUR SAVIOR	800 Bluff St NE 55350	(320)587-3318	osl@hutchtel.net www.oslhutch.com	Reyne Oster	1961			EC	80
JANESVILLE	TRINITY	501 N Main St 56048	(507)231-6646	info@trinityjanesville.com www.tlsjanesville.com	Wade A Stockman	1890		N	EC-8	116
LAKEFIELD	IMMANUEL	620 Bush St 56150	(507)662-5860	immanuel@immanuellakefield.com www.immanuellakefield.com		1899		N	EC-8	111
LEWISTON	IMMANUEL SILO	22591 County Rd 25 55952	(507)523-3143	siloschool@immanuelsilo.org immanuelsilo.org		1862		N	EC-8	122
LONG PRAIRIE	TRINITY	610 2nd Ave SE 56347	(320)732-2238	preschool@trinitylp.com trinitylp.com	Michelle Hentges	2008			EC	
LUVERNE	LITTLE LAMBS	803 N Cedar St 56156	(507)283-2316	littlelambs@stjohnluverne.org www.stjohnlutheranluverne.org	Rebecca L DeBoer	1982			EC	39
MAPLE GROVE	SHEPHERDS CARE	11875 W Eagle Lake Dr 55369	(763)493-3623	aislinn@shepherdscarechildcare.com www.shepherdscarechildcare.com	Aislinn R Anderson	1989			EC	70
MAYER	MAYER	306 7th St NE 55360	(952)657-2251	info@mayerlutheran.org www.mayerlutheran.org	Kevin L Wilaby	1960	R	N	5-12	198
	ZION	209 Bluejay Ave 55360	(952)657-2339	joshua.baumann@zionmayer.org www.zionmayer.org	Joshua L Baumann	1912		N	EC-8	155
MINNEAPOLIS	TRINITY FIRST	1115 E 19th St 55404	(612)871-2353	info@trinityfirst.org trinityfirstschool.org	Sarah J Wippich	1859		N	EC-8	136
MOORHEAD	OUR REDEEMER	1000 14th St S 56560	(218)233-8270	orcccdirector@outlook.com www.ourredeemermoorhead.org		1985			EC-3	
MORA	ZION	401 Highway 65 S 55051	(320)679-1094	zionlc.preschool@gmail.com		1993			EC	11
MORRIS	KIDS IN CHRIST	315 S Columbia Ave 56267	(320)585-5067	jjmiller@runestone.net		2004			EC	17
MORRISTOWN	TRINITY	10500 215th St W 55052	(507)685-2200	info@northmorristown.org northmorristown.org	Juanita L Krueger	1892			K-6	14
MOUNDS VIEW	MESSIAH	2848 County Road H2 55112	(763)784-1786	messiah@messiah-lutheran.org www.messiah-lutheran.org	Annie Bilski	1973			EC	61
NEW ULM	KINDER HAUS	718 S Broadway 56073	(507)766-1285	kinderhaus.rlc@gmail.com www.redeemernewulm.net	Jeanne L Holten	2000			EC	13
NEW YORK MILLS	TRINITY	424 E Gilman St 56567	(218)385-2450	bev.witt@nymtrinity.org www.nymtrinity.org		1988			EC	35
NORTH MANKATO	CONCORDIA CLASSICAL	2101 Lor Ray Dr 56003	(507)388-4336	ccamankato@gmail.com www.ccamankato.org	Barbra J Kozisek	2001			K-8	90
NORTHROP	MARTIN LUTHER	315 Martin Luther Dr 56075	(507)436-5249	principal@martinlutherhs.com www.martinlutherhs.com	David A Stuckwisch	1983	R	N	7-12	64
	ST JAMES	108 S James St 56075	(507)436-5289	sjlnorthrop@gmail.com sjlnorthrop.com		1892		N	EC-6	51
NORWOOD YNG AMERICA	ST JOHN	27 1st St NW 55397	(952)467-3461	schooloffice@stjohnsnya.org stjohnsnya.org	Keith A Traska	1875		N	EC-8	91
OWATONNA	GOOD SHEPHERD	2500 7th Ave NE 55060	(507)451-6821	gspreschool@msn.com goodshepherdowatonna.com	Heather M Gleason	1996			EC	42
PARK RAPIDS	ST JOHN ABC	803 W 1st St 56470	(218)732-9783	revneu@unitelc.com		1987			EC	
PERHAM	ST PAULS	500 6th Ave SW 56573	(218)346-2300	candice.bicondoa@stpaulsperham.org stpaulsschoolperham.org	Candice A Bicondoa	1910		N	EC-8	88
PINE CITY	GROWING IN GRACE	410 Main St S 55063	(320)629-3683	zionpinecity@gmail.com	Jenine M Preston	2004			EC	
PIPESTONE	ST PAUL	621 W Main St 56164	(507)825-5271	stpaul@iw.net stpaulpipestone.com/preschool	Shelly Tuinstra	1989			EC	40
PLAINVIEW	IMMANUEL	30 S Wabasha 55964	(507)534-2108	bzuelsdorff@immanuelplainview.org immanuelplainview.org	Rick Arguto	1921			EC-8	72
PLYMOUTH	BEAUTIFUL SAVIOR	5005 Northwest Blvd 55442	(763)235-7626	cdc@beautifulsaviorlc.org beautifulsaviorlc.org	Jan N Stockman				EC	
PRIOR LAKE	ST PAULS	5634 Luther Rd SE 55372	(952)447-2117	principal@stpaulspriorlake.org www.splspriorlake.org	Katie M Borlaug	1982		N	K-8	70
RED WING	LITTLE FOOTPRINTS	1811 Bush Street 55066	(651)388-5447	hiskidschildcare@yahoo.com hiskidschildcare.weebly.com	Kathey Warren	1999			EC	12
RICHFIELD	MT CALVARY	6541 16th Ave S 55423	(612)869-9441	mtrowbridge@mtcalvaryrichfield.org www.mtcalvaryedu.org	Marisa J Trowbridge				EC	15

R = Recognized Service Organization (RSO)
N = National Lutheran Schools Accreditation (NLSA)

CITY	SCHOOL	ADDRESS	PHONE	EMAIL WEBSITE	PRINCIPAL/ ADMINISTRATOR	YEAR ORG.	RSO	NLSA	GRADES OFFERED	ENROLL
ROCHESTER	*ROCHESTER CENTRAL*	2619 9th Ave NW 55901	(507)289-3267	nicatevenis@rcls.net www.rcls.net	Charles A Chaveriat	1959	R	N	EC-8	438
ROSEMOUNT	*OUR SAVIOR*	14980 Diamond Path W 55068	(651)423-5590	kidskool@osfamily.org www.oursaviorelc.com	Tamara Ristow	1987			EC	76
ROSEVILLE	*KING OF KINGS*	2330 Dale St N 55113	(651)484-9206	kingofkingsschool@kingofkingsroseville.org www.kingofkingslutheranschool.org		1964		N	EC-8	172
SAINT CHARLES	*ST MATTHEW*	555 E 12th St 55972	(507)932-4246	smcpreschool@yahoo.com smcpreschool.org	Kelli Loveless	1983			EC	34
SAINT CLOUD	*PRINCE OF PEACE*	4770 County Rd 120 56303	(320)251-1477	office@princeofpeacels.org www.princeofpeacels.org	Anne M Neilitz	2000	R	N	EC-8	
SAINT FRANCIS	*CROWN*	7515 269th Ave NW 55070	(763)856-2099	info@crownchristianschool.com www.crownchristianschool.com	Kelly A Lamkin	1883			EC-8	
	TRINITY	3812 229th Ave NW 55070	(763)753-1234	office@trinitysf.org www.trinityschoolsf.org	Brian K Kube	1980			EC-8	73
SAINT PAUL	*HAND IN HAND*	1250 Concordia Ave 55104	(651)641-8491	wellens@csp.edu handinhand.csp.edu		1982			EC	33
	OPEN ARMS	616 Ruth St 55119	(651)735-4202	openarmsst.paul@gmail.com www.openarmssaintpaul.com	Michelle L Emmons	2000			EC	65
SLAYTON	*TRINITY*	2105 King Ave 56172	(507)836-8129	bacarlson77@hotmail.com trinityslayton.net/pre-k	Beth Carlson	1984			EC	35
THIEF RIVER FALLS	*ST JOHN*	15671 158th St NE 56701	(218)681-7753	Schooloffice@stjohntrf.com	Tammy Ballard	2003			EC-12	12
TRUMAN	*ST PAULS*	114 E 4th St N 56088	(507)776-6541	stpaulsschooltruman@frontiernet.net stpaulslutherantruman.com/school/	Marty Miller	1900		N	EC-8	63
VERGAS	*JESUS LITTLE LAMBS*	301 E Altona Ave 56587	(218)342-3402	jllpreschool@gmail.com www.lcms-vergas.org		2000			EC	
WACONIA	*TRINITY*	601 E 2nd St 55387	(952)442-4165	dan.maser@trinitywaconia.org www.trinitywaconia.org	M D Maser	1865		N	EC-8	411
WALKER	*IMMANUEL*	4656 State 200 NW 56484	(218)547-4139	info@immanuellutheranwalker.com www.immanuellutheranwalker.com	Janna K Kietzman	1998		N	EC-8	
WATERTOWN	*CHRIST COMMUNITY*	512 County Rd 10 SE 55388	(952)955-1419	Office@ccls.net www.ccls.net	Jeffrey K Boehlke	1949	R		EC-8	177
WAYZATA	*REDEEMER*	115 Wayzata Blvd W 55391	(952)473-5356	acacka@redeemerwayzata.org www.redeemerchristianacademy.org		1978			EC-8	127
WHITE BEAR LAKE	*SOUTH SHORE TRINITY*	2480 S Shore Blvd 55110	(651)429-4293	sstrinity@visi.com www.sstwbl.org	Jolene Erickson	1948			EC	40
WILLMAR	*REDEEMER*	1401 6th St SW 56201	(320)235-4685	mcorti@redeemerwillmar.org www.redeemerlutheranpreschool.org		2003		N	EC	19
WINONA	*ST MARTIN*	253 Liberty St 55987	(507)452-6928	office@stmartinswinona.org www.stmartinswinona.org	Sharon R Forst	1866			K-8	125
WOODBURY	*WOODBURY*	7380 Afton Rd 55125	(651)739-5146	mulsos@wlc.church www.woodburylutheran.org		1968			EC	134
WYKOFF	*ST JOHNS*	245 S Line St 55990	(507)352-4671	school@stjohns-wykoff.com stjohns-wykoff.org		1875			K-8	32
				MISSISSIPPI						
FLOWOOD	*GOOD SHEPHERD*	6035 Hwy 25 39232	(601)992-4752	www.gslc-gsls.com	Carolyn K Sawyer	1995			EC-4	
				MISSOURI						
AFFTON	*SALEM*	5025 Lakewood Ave 63123	(314)353-9242	matthewfoster@slcas.org www.slcas.org	Matthew J Foster	1909		N	EC-8	142
ALMA	*TRINITY*	304 N Waverly 64001	(660)674-2444	angiewells@trinitylutheranalma.com www.trinitylutheranalma.com	Angela R Wells	1878		N	EC-8	160
	TRINITY DAYCARE INC	209 W 3rd St 64001	(660)674-2233	ashleyhemme@trinitylutheranalma.com trinitylutheranalma.com	Ashley Hemme		R		EC	
ARNOLD	*ST JOHN*	3511 Jeffco Blvd 63010	(636)464-7303	bspieler@sjlarnold.org www.stjohnsarnold.org	Brenda M Spieler	1848		N	EC-8	280
BELLEFONTAINE NGHBRS	*GRACE CHAPEL*	10015 Lance Dr 63137	(314)867-6564	kwilliams@gracechapelstl.org graceschoolstl.org		1955		N	EC-8	205
BLACK JACK	*SALEM*	5190 Parker Rd 63033	(314)741-8220	jburkee@salembjmo.org www.salembjmo.org/school	Jeffrey R Burkee	1861		N	EC-8	43
BLUE SPRINGS	*TIMOTHY*	301 E Wyatt Rd 64014	(816)228-5300	kenh@timothylutheran.com www.timothylutheranschool.com	Kenneth L Holland	1975		N	EC-8	142
BOONVILLE	*IMMANUEL*	1001 Immanuel Dr 65233	(660)882-2208	glendag1960@icloud.com immanuelboonvillemo.church	Glenda Gerhardt	1977			EC-K	
BRANSON	*FAITH*	221 Malone Dr 65616	(417)334-2469	ewhite@faithbranson.org www.faithls.org		2023			K-3	6
BRENTWOOD	*MOUNT CALVARY*	9321 Litzsinger Rd 63144	(314)968-2360	preschool@mtcalvarylcms.org	Jennifer Cross	1974			EC	60
CALIFORNIA	*ST PAUL*	207A N Owen 65018	(573)796-1997	spccc@stpaulslutheran1860.com	Marie Wickham	2007			EC-K	
CAMERON	*NOAHS ARK*	209 Little Brick St 64429	(816)632-7904	princeofpeacelutherancameron@gmail.com		2004			EC	3
CAPE GIRARDEAU	*TRINITY*	55 N Pacific St 63701	(573)334-1068	nglass@t-lutheranschool.org www.t-lutheranschool.org	Neil Glass	1854		N	EC-8	150
CHESTERFIELD	*KING OF KINGS*	13765 Olive Blvd 63017	(314)469-2224	bhunt@kokstl.org www.kokstl.org	Barbara N Hunt	1980		N	EC	93
	LORD OF LIFE	15750 Baxter Rd 63017	(636)532-0400	preschool@lordoflifelcms.org www.lolstl.org		1993			EC	
COLE CAMP	*LUTH SCHOOL ASSOC*	204 E Butterfield 65325	(660)668-4614	office@lsaschool.com www.lsaschool.com	Debra Eckhoff	1961	R	N	K-12	75
	TRINITY	104 E Butterfield Trl 65325	(660)668-2364	grandmacpetersen@gmail.com www.trinitycolecamp.org	Cheryl Petersen	2004			EC	20

R = Recognized Service Organization (RSO)
N = National Lutheran Schools Accreditation (NLSA)

CITY	SCHOOL	ADDRESS	PHONE	EMAIL WEBSITE	PRINCIPAL/ ADMINISTRATOR	YEAR ORG.	RSO	NLSA	GRADES OFFERED	ENROLL
COLUMBIA	*TRINITY*	2201 W Rollins Rd 65203	(573)445-1014	TLCLC@trinity-LCMS.org www.TLCLCkids.com		1979			EC	96
CONCORDIA	*ST PAULS*	407 Main St 64020	(660)463-7654	nathanaelpoppe@splsconcordia.org www.stpaulsconcordia.org	Nathanael W Poppe	1840		N	EC-8	194
DES PERES	*ST PAUL*	1300 N Ballas Rd 63131	(314)822-2771	school@stpaulsdp.org www.stplutheranschool.org	Dawn M Walker	1849		N	K-8	244
	ST PAULS	823 N Ballas Rd 63131	(314)822-9219	jbangert@g.stpaulsdp.org www.stpaulsdesperes.org	Jessica E Bangert	1992		N	EC	150
ELLISVILLE	*ST JOHN*	15800 Manchester Rd 63011	(636)779-2325	jbergtholdt@stjstl.net stjls.org/		1853		N	EC-8	303
EUREKA	*ST MARKS*	500 Meramec Blvd 63025	(636)938-4432	www.stmarkseureka.org	Megan Deines	1982		N	EC-8	105
FARMINGTON	*ST PAUL*	608 E Columbia St 63640	(573)756-5147	sbieser@stpaulgiants.com stpaulgiants.com	Dustin R Murray	1874		N	EC-8	243
FENTON	*OUR SAVIOR*	1500 San Simeon Way 63026	(636)343-7511	ldehn@oursaviorlcs.org www.oursaviorlcs.org	Linda M Dehn	1964		N	EC-8	175
FESTUS	*IMMANUEL*	19 N 3rd St 63028	(636)937-0043	ilchildcare@hotmail.com immanuellutheranchildcare.com		1993			EC	88
FREISTATT	*TRINITY*	218 N Main 65654	(417)235-5931	amoennig@tlsfreistatt.org www.trinity1874.com		1875		N	EC-8	142
FROHNA	*UNITED IN CHRIST*	10158 Hwy C 63748	(573)824-5218	unitedinchristprincipal@gmail.com	Ashley R Ponder	2011	R	N	EC-8	74
GRANDVIEW	*HOLY TRINITY*	5901 E 135th St 64030	(816)763-3211	churchofficeholytrinity@gmail.com		1995			EC	12
HANNIBAL	*ST JOHN'S*	1317 Lyon St 63401	(573)221-0615	school@stjohnshannibal.org www.stjohnshannibal.org	Joanne Conoyer	1860		N	EC-8	
HIGGINSVILLE	*IMMANUEL*	1500 Lipper St 64037	(660)584-2854	lflorence@ilswildcats.com www.ilswildcats.com	Linda Florence	1951	R	N	EC-8	108
HIGH RIDGE	*HOPE*	2308 Gravois Rd 63049	(636)677-8688	hopelecc@gmail.com www.hopehighridge.org/ECC	Stephanie Dexter	1999			EC	70
HOLTS SUMMIT	*GRACE*	618 Hallfax Rd 65043	(573)896-8824	Joydawn1993@gmail.com www.gracelutheranchurchholtssummit.org					EC	
JACKSON	*ST PAUL*	216 S Russell Street 63755	(573)243-5360	lisawhite@stpauljackson.com www.stpauljackson.com	Lisa A White	1893		N	EC-8	265
JEFFERSON CITY	*IMMANUEL-HONEY CREEK*	8231 Tanner Bridge Rd 65101	(573)496-3766	principal@midmoimmanuel.com www.midmoimmanuel.com	Tyler J Kopp	1868		N	EC-8	112
	TRINITY	812 Stadium Blvd 65109	(573)636-7807	school@trinityjc.org www.trinityjc.org	Jonathan R Sprengel	1870		N	EC-8	270
JOPLIN	*MARTIN LUTHER*	2616 Connecticut Ave 64804	(417)624-1403	mramstad@martinlutherjoplin.com www.martinlutherjoplin.com	Mollie K Ramstad			N	EC-8	78
KANSAS CITY	*CALVARY*	12411 Wornall Road 64145	(816)595-4020	principal@calvarykc.com calvaryschoolkc.com	Tyler A Mattlin	1948			EC-8	292
	GROW IN PEACE	8240 Blue Ridge Blvd 64138	(816)353-3910	director@gipchildcare.org www.gipchildcare.org		1996			EC	62
	HOLY CROSS	2003 NE Englewood Rd 64118	(816)452-9113	ecc@holycrosskc.org www.holycrosskc.org		1964			EC	62
	KING OF KINGS	1701 NE 96th St 64155	(816)436-7680	elcdirector@kokkc.org www.kingofkings-lcms.net	Joan Skare	1996			EC-K	
	MARTIN LUTHER	7112 N Overland Dr 64151	(816)734-1060	sdixon@mlakc.com www.martinlutheracademy.org	Scott P Dixon	2000	R	N	K-8	183
KIRKSVILLE	*FAITH*	1820 S Baltimore St 63501	(660)665-8166	faithlutherankids@gmail.com faithlutheranschoolkv.org		1976			EC-8	125
KIRKWOOD	*CHRIST COMMUNITY*	110 W Woodbine Ave 63122	(314)822-7774	mhoehner@ccls-stlouis.org ccls-stlouis.org	Dr Matthew J Hoehner	1973	R	N	EC-8	654
LA GRANGE	*ST PETER*	300 S 7th St 63448	(573)655-4416	stpeterslg@gmail.com www.facebook.com/stpeterslg/	Carolyn Feldkamp	1978			EC	6
LADUE	*VILLAGE*	9237 Clayton Rd 63124	(314)993-6743	preschool@villagelutheranchurch.org www.vlcpre.org		1979			EC	31
LAKE OZARK	*THE KING'S ACADEMY*	1700 Bagnell Dam Blvd 65049	(573)693-9245	principal@kingsacademylo.com www.kingsacademylo.com	Dr Anne E Stuhlman	2003		N	EC-8	165
LEES SUMMIT	*ABOUNDING LOVE*	615 SE Todd George Pkwy 64063	(816)524-7288	alpreschool@beautifulsavior-lcmo.org www.abounding-love.com	Katherine Palmer	2011			EC	
	ST MATTHEW	700 NE Chipman Rd 64063	(816)524-4354	stmatthewps@gracefaithlove.org www.gracefaithlove.org	Mary Lammers	1999			EC	67
LEMAY	*PEACE*	737 Barracksview Rd 63125	(314)892-8844	earlychildhood@peacelutheranstl.org www.peacelutheranstl.org		1977			EC	
LEXINGTON	*GRACE*	806 S Business Hwy 13 64067	(660)259-2932	preschool@gracelutheranlexington.org www.gracelutheranlexington.org/preschool	Lori Thornburg	1986			EC	
LIBERTY	*SMALL SAINTS*	205 N Forest Ave 64068	(816)781-6994	smallsaints@teamjesusliberty.org www.teamjesusliberty.org	Angela M Mundt	1988			EC	132
LOCKWOOD	*IMMANUEL*	212 W 4th St 65682	(417)232-4530	principal@immanuellcms.net www.immanuellcms.net	Terri A Tafoya	1882		N	EC-8	80
LONE ELM	*ZION*	17321 Lone Elm Rd 65237	(660)838-6307	mbtg8082@gmail.com	Marcia B Toellner	1896			1-8	
MARSHALL	*BRIGHT BEGINNINGS*	361 W Summit 65340	(660)831-0526	brightbeginnings@orlutheran.org orlutheran.org		2008			EC	22
MARYLAND HEIGHTS	*ZION*	12075 Dorsett Rd 63043	(314)739-6121	preschool@zionmh.org www.zionmh.org	Joni Wallace	2003			EC	16
NIXA	*REDEEMER*	911 W Mount Vernon 65714	(417)725-4288	npdirector@rlcmail.org www.redeemernixa.org/preschool	Shannon Dodson	2013			EC	24
O FALLON	*HOLY CROSS*	8945 Veterans Memorial Pkwy 63366	(636)272-4505	preschool@hcross.com www.hcross.com	Darlene E Birk	2003			EC	
OAKVILLE	*FAITH*	6101 Telegraph Rd 63129	(314)846-5942	fecc@faithstl.org feccstl.org	Amanda Hallsten	1977			EC	

R = Recognized Service Organization (RSO)
N = National Lutheran Schools Accreditation (NLSA)

SCHOOLS

CITY	SCHOOL	ADDRESS	PHONE	EMAIL WEBSITE	PRINCIPAL/ ADMINISTRATOR	YEAR ORG.	RSO	NLSA	GRADES OFFERED	ENROLL
OLIVETTE	*IMMANUEL*	9733 Olive Blvd 63132	(314)993-5004	school.office@ilsolivette.org www.ilsolivette.org	Christine A Nixon	1894		N	EC-8	157
OZARK	*OPEN ARMS*	1200 E McCracken Rd 65721	(417)582-0067	koverstreet@mchsi.com www.openarmsozark.org	Kim Overstreet				EC	45
PALMYRA	*ZION*	120 S Spring St 63461	(573)769-3739	zionpreschoolpalmyra@gmail.com www.zionpalmyra.com	Brandy J Schneider	1866			EC	36
PERRYVILLE	*IMMANUEL*	225 W South St 63775	(573)547-6161	aspieler@ilsperryville.org	Andrew F Spieler	1866		N	EC-8	
PLATTE CITY	*OUR SAVIOR*	14155 N Highway 64079	(816)866-1597	oursavioracademy@yahoo.com oursavioracademy.org	Lori Albright	2004		N	EC-12	46
PLATTE WOODS	*CHRIST*	6700 NW 72nd St 64151	(816)741-8031	christpkadmin@christlc.com www.christlc.net	Kristina Fredde	1972		N	EC	90
RAYMORE	*GUIDING STAR*	301 Johnston Parkway 64083	(816)322-3606	fdesneux@bethlehem-raymore.org www.bethlehem-raymore.org/preschool.html	Felecia Desneux	1993			EC	84
REPUBLIC	*HOPE*	218 E Hwy 174 65738	(417)732-9162	preschool@hopelc.com	Autumn Stevens				EC	27
ROCKVILLE	*ZION*	10135 SE COUNTY ROAD 9526 64780	(660)598-6213	zlsrockville@gmail.com		1868			EC-8	23
ROSEBUD	*IMMANUEL*	300 N 1st St 63091	(573)764-3495	contact@immanuelk8.org immanuelk8.org	Julie Wilson	1904			EC-8	84
SAINT CHARLES	*IMMANUEL*	115 S 6th St 63301	(636)946-0051	shuster@ilsc.org www.immanuelstcharles.org	Scott A Huster	1848		N	EC-8	575
	OUR SAVIOR	2800 W Elm St 63301	(636)947-8010	director.ecc79@gmail.com www.oslcecc.org	Stephanie L McSwain	1976		N	EC	112
	TRINITY	4689 N Highway 94 63301	(636)250-3654	kchapin@trinityof.org www.trinityorchardfarm.com/school	Kathryne A Chapin	1862		N	EC-8	
	ZION	3866 S Old Hwy 94 63304	(636)441-7424	www.zionharvester.org/school	Marc W Debrick	1851		N	EC-8	567
SAINT CLAIR	*HOLY TRINITY*	1502 S Outer Rd 63077	(636)629-6337	htcclcdirector@yahoo.com		1988			EC	32
SAINT JOSEPH	*ST PAUL*	4715 Frederick Ave 64506	(816)279-1118	stpaullutheran@splcc.org www.splcc.org	Kendra R Kendall	1987		N	EC-8	249
SAINT LOUIS	*ABIDING SAVIOR*	4353 Butler Hill Road 63128	(314)892-4408	bryherd@abidingsaviorlutheran.org www.aslsonline.org		1984		N	EC-8	212
	ASSOC SPEC ED	3558 S Jefferson Ave 63118	(314)268-1234	bj.wiemer@lutheranspecialed.org lutheranspecialed.org	B J Wiemer	1956	R	N	EC-12	
	BETHLEHEM	2153 Salisbury St 63107	(314)231-4702	dr.jay@bethlehemstlouis.org bethlehemstlouis.org	Deac Janine M Bolling				EC-5	
	CHRIST MEMORIAL	5250 S Lindbergh 63126	(314)631-0992	ana.irby@cmstl.org www.cmchildcare.org	Ana Irby	1979		N	EC	89
	GREEN PARK	4248 Green Park Rd 63125	(314)544-4248	lisa.waltenberger@greenparklutheranschool.org www.greenparklutheranschool.org	Lisa M Waltenberger	1961	R	N	EC-8	277
	LUTHERAN NORTH	5401 Lucas and Hunt Rd 63121	(314)389-3100	tbrackman@LNCrusaders.org www.LNCrusaders.org	Dr Timothy J Brackman	1946	R	N	6-12	358
	RIVER ROADS	8623 Church Rd 63147	(314)388-0300	ymboyd26@gmail.com www.riverroadslutheranschool.org	Yvonne M Mackey Boyd	1869	R	N	EC-8	76
	ST LUCAS	7100 Morganford Rd 63116	(314)832-2307	laurie.riley@stlucaslcms.org stlucaslcms.org/ecc		2019		N	EC	35
	WORD OF LIFE	6535 Eichelberger St 63109	(314)832-1244	mbergholt@wordoflifeschool.net www.wordoflifeschool.net	Melissa A Bergholt	1973	R	N	EC-8	215
SAINT PETERS	*CHAPEL OF THE CROSS*	907 Jungermann Rd 63376	(636)922-3728	erin.hoehner@chapelofthecrosslutheran.org www.chapelofthecrosslutheran.org	Erin R Hoehner	2017			EC	27
	CHILD OF GOD	650 Salt Lick Rd 63376	(636)970-7080	msandfort@coglcs.com www.coglcs.com	Dr Melissa H Sandfort	1999		N	EC-8	280
SALISBURY	*IMMANUEL*	124 W 3rd St 65281	(660)388-5192	monakothe@yahoo.com	Ramona Kothe	1983			EC	6
SAPPINGTON	*RESURRECTION*	9907 Sappington Rd 63128	(314)843-4980	lcrstl.org	Stephanie G Cain	1977			EC	136
SEDALIA	*ST PAULS*	701 S Massachusetts Ave 65301	(660)826-1925	principal@sedaliastpauls.net sedaliastpauls.org	Mary Walters	1958		N	EC-8	74
SPRINGFIELD	*REDEEMER*	2852 S Dayton Ave 65807	(417)883-5717	sls@rlcmail.org slssaints.org	Amanda B Cole	1984		N	EC-8	206
STOVER	*ST PAUL*	305 N Forrest 65078	(573)377-2690	ehrichs@stpaulpanthers.com www.stpaulpanthers.com	Michelle Ehrichs	1865			EC-8	36
UNION	*ST PAUL*	208 W Springfield Ave 63084	(636)583-2209	st.paulpreschool@outlook.com www.inunionwithchrist.org		1987			EC	49
WARRENTON	*LITTLE LAMBS*	950 S Highway 47 63383	(636)456-2888	littlelambsstj@gmail.com www.stjohnwarrenton.org	Lisa Rausch	1987			EC	56
WASHINGTON	*IMMANUEL*	214 W 5th St 63090	(636)239-1636	nick.hopfensperger@imlutheran.org www.imlutheran.org	Nick A Hopfensperger	1862		N	EC-8	243
WELDON SPRING	*MESSIAH*	5911 S Hwy 94 63304	(636)329-1096	jsmith@mlslions.org mlslions.org	Joanie L Smith	1997		N	EC-8	406
WENTZVILLE	*IMMANUEL*	632 E Hwy N 63385	(636)639-9887	adolak@ilcsw.net www.ilcsw.net	Dr Allison K Dolak	1880		N	EC-8	

MONTANA

CITY	SCHOOL	ADDRESS	PHONE	EMAIL WEBSITE	PRINCIPAL/ ADMINISTRATOR	YEAR ORG.	RSO	NLSA	GRADES OFFERED	ENROLL
BILLINGS	*MOUNT OLIVE*	2336 Saint Johns Ave 59102	(406)656-2635	businessmanager@mountolive.com www.mountolive.com		1993			EC	
	MOUNT OLIVE	2336 St Johns Ave 59102	(406)656-6687	businessmanager@mountolive.com mountoliveschool.org/		2007			K-8	30
	TRINITY	2802 Belvedere Dr 59102	(406)656-1021	school@trinitybillings.org trinitybillings.org	Stacy L Hall	1954			EC-8	317

R = Recognized Service Organization (RSO)
N = National Lutheran Schools Accreditation (NLSA)

CITY	SCHOOL	ADDRESS	PHONE	EMAIL WEBSITE	PRINCIPAL/ ADMINISTRATOR	YEAR ORG.	RSO	NLSA	GRADES OFFERED	ENROLL
COLUMBIA FALLS	KINGS KIDS	640 7th St W 59912	(406)892-0070	preschool@ourredeemerlc.org ourredeemerlc.org/kingskids/		1999			EC	14
GLENDIVE	OSLCCM	322 North River Ave 59330	(406)377-1190	oslccm@midrivers.com	Lesa L Schock	2000			EC	49
GREAT FALLS	WEE DISCIPLES	1226 1St Ave N 59401	(406)452-2121	wee.disciples@gmail.com www.trinity-mt.org	Debbie Lee	1991			EC	48
HAMILTON	GRACE	275 Hattie Ln 59840	(406)363-1924	gracellc@live.com www.gracelutheranhamilton.com	Teresa Bauder	1994			EC	
HELENA	FIRST	2231 E Broadway St 59601	(406)442-6913	school@firstlutheranhelena.org www.firstlutheranhelena.org		1979			EC	20
KALISPELL	TRINITY	495 5th Ave WN 59901	(406)257-6716	office@trinityed.org www.trinityed.org	Laura A White	1958		N	EC-8	241
MILES CITY	TRINITY	221 S Center Ave 59301	(406)234-4983	trinity@midrivers.com trinitylutheranchurch.360unite.com/trinity-lutheran-classical-school		1988			EC-8	81
MISSOULA	FIRST	2808 South Ave W 59804	(406)549-3311	flcmissoula@aol.com		1955			EC	16
	FIRST	2808 S Ave W 59804	(406)549-3311	info@flcschool.org www.flcschool.org		2009			EC-8	16
PARK CITY	LITTLE FISHES	301 1st St SW 59063	(406)633-2356	StPaulParkCity@gmail.com	Donna Mohr	1994			EC	
POLSON	MOUNT CALVARY	1609 2nd St W 59860	(406)883-4041	mtcalvarypreschool@hotmail.com		1992			EC	
RONAN	LITTLE LAMBS	35681 Terrace Lake Rd E 59864	(406)676-8283			1982			EC	6
STEVENSVILLE	OUR SAVIOR	184 Pine Hollow Rd 59870	(406)777-5625	oursaviorstevi@gmail.com	Mary A Beilke	1994			EC	
THREE FORKS	GRACE	305 S 5th Ave 59752	(406)285-6865	holytrinitygrace@gmail.com www.gracethreeforks.org	Amber Veltkamp	1987			EC	
NEBRASKA										
ALLIANCE	IMMANUEL	1312 E 10th St 69301	(308)629-1601	office@ielschool.org immanuelevlutheran.org	Shaun M Daugherty	2014			EC-9	108
ARLINGTON	ST PAUL	8951 Co Rd 9 68002	(402)478-4278	pdunklau@stpaulsarlington.org www.stpaulsarlington.org	Dr Larry D Wooster	1876			EC-8	83
BATTLE CREEK	ST JOHN	102 W Martin 68715	(402)675-3605	principal@stjohnbc.net www.stjohnbc.net		1882		N	EC-8	131
BEATRICE	ST PAUL	930 Prairie Ln 68310	(402)223-3414	aduever@stpaulbeatrice.org stpaulbeatrice.org/school					EC-5	158
BELLEVUE	PILGRIM	2311 Fairview Rd 68123	(402)291-2848	directorpilgrimlutheran@gmail.com	Shanna Smith	1993			EC	56
BURWELL	NOAHS ARK	350 N 8th St 68823	(308)346-5060	tswitzer@nctc.net	Teresa A Switzer	1996			EC	
CHAMBERS	HANDS OF HOPE	102 W Wry 68725	(402)482-5835	notnats4@hotmail.com	Terry J Makelin				EC	
COLUMBUS	CHRIST	32312 - 122nd Ave 68601	(402)564-3531	clsadmin@christlutheran.esu7.org www.christcolumbus.org		1871			EC-8	90
	FIRST STEPS	2720 28th St 68601	(402)562-8437	firststeps@peacecolumbus.org www.peacecolumbus.org	Lisa C Thomas	1998			EC	18
	IMMANUEL	2865 26th Ave 68601	(402)564-8423	nevans@immanuel.esu7.org www.immanuelweb.org	Natalie M Evans	1893		N	EC-8	183
	ST JOHNS	39346 205th Ave 68601	(402)285-0335	jwarneke@stjohnlutheran.esu7.org sites.google.com/stjohnlutheran.esu7.org/stjohns-columbus-ne/home		1888		N	EC-8	82
CRETE	LAMBS OF CHRIST	837 Hawthorne 68333	(402)826-4375	lambsofchristcrete@gmail.com lambsofchristcrete.com	Cheri K Chalupa	1991			EC	26
DAVID CITY	REDEEMER	695 N 9th St 68632	(402)367-3089	redeemerlutheran1234@gmail.com www.redeemerlcms-dc.com/		2003			EC	6
DESHLER	DESHLER	509 E Hebron 68340	(402)365-7858	todd.voss@deshlerluth.org www.DeshlerLuth.org	Todd M Voss	1889			K-8	52
ELKHORN	LORD'S LAMBS	20844 Bonanza Blvd 68022	(402)289-9291	lizcroson@gmail.com www.lordslambselkhorn.org	Denise Kempnich				EC	
ELWOOD	JESUS LAMBS	704 Smith Ave 68937	(308)785-2875	jesuslambspreschool@gmail.com	Jennifer Wolff	1999			EC	14
FREMONT	TRINITY	1546 N Luther Rd 68025	(402)721-5959	sara.grein@trinityfremont.org www.tlsfremont.org/		1884		N	EC-8	128
GERING	FAITH	2055 U St 69341	(308)436-4307	preschool@keepfaithlutheran.org		1998			EC	17
GORDON	LITTLE LAMBS	801 N Elm St 69343	(308)282-0584	pastorsherman@outlook.com		1987			EC	
GRAND ISLAND	GRAND ISLAND	3900 W Husker Hwy 68803	(308)385-3900	principal@heartlandlutheran.org cnlutheran.org/	Chelsey A Liess	2000		N	7-12	58
GRAND ISLAND	PEACE	1710 N North Rd 68803	(308)850-2146	ddupler@peacepreschoolgi.org www.peacepreschoolgi.org	Dee Ann Dupler	1982		N	EC	
	TRINITY	208 W 13th St 68801	(308)382-5274	principal@tlsgi.org cnlutheran.org/	Judy K Bartels	1881		N	EC-6	228
GRETNA	WEE LAMBS	11204 S 204th Street 68028	(402)332-3267	carol.theall@gslcgretna.org		2002			EC	105
HASTINGS	ZION CLASSICAL	465 S Marian Rd 68901	(402)462-5012	principal@zionclassical.org www.zionclassical.org		1900	R	N	EC-6	59
HOOPER	IMMANUEL	27053 Co Rd 12 68031	(402)654-3663	happyheartsofimmanuel@gmail.com www.immanuelhooper.com	Christy J Tenkley	1881			EC	20
HYANNIS	NOAHS ARK	609 N Hwy 61 69350	(308)458-2565	lvivion@yahoo.com		2004			EC	16
JUNIATA	CHRIST	13175 W 70th St 68955	(402)744-4991	jwitt@christjuniata.org	Joel J Witt	1890		N	EC-8	76
KEARNEY	HOLY CROSS	3315 11th Ave 68845	(308)237-2944	dkitzelman@hclk.org	Deanna D Kitzelman	1981			EC	43
	ZION	2421 Avenue C 68847	(308)234-3410	anthony.splittgerber@zionkearney.org zionkearney.org		1930		N	EC-8	178
LA VISTA	MEADOWLARK	7706 S 96th St 68128	(402)331-2681	jheinemann@bslcomaha.org www.kidnect.org	Rebeccah A Bradley	1974			EC	159

R = Recognized Service Organization (RSO)
N = National Lutheran Schools Accreditation (NLSA)

SCHOOLS

CITY	SCHOOL	ADDRESS	PHONE	EMAIL WEBSITE	PRINCIPAL/ ADMINISTRATOR	YEAR ORG.	RSO	NLSA	GRADES OFFERED	ENROLL
LEIGH	*ZION COMMUNITY*	405 N Main St 68643	(402)487-2502	zion.preschool405@gmail.com zionleigh.org	Nichole Lerch	1987			EC	16
LINCOLN	*CHRIST*	4325 Sumner St 68506	(402)483-7774	jmajorins@christlincoln.org www.christlincolnschools.org	Mark J L Heureux	1979		N	EC-5	188
	FAITH	8701 Adams 68507	(402)466-7402	kbarnhouse@faithlincoln.org www.faithlincoln.org	Krista K Barnhouse	1983		N	EC-5	179
	LINCOLN	1100 N 56th St 68504	(402)467-5404	swallingford@lincolnlutheran.org www.lincolnlutheran.org	Jeremy T Geidel	1962	R	N	6-12	385
	MESSIAH	1800 S 84th St 68506	(402)489-3024	matt.stueber@messiah.us school.messiah.us	Matthew P Stueber	1930		N	EC-5	415
	TRINITY	1200 N 56th St 68504	(402)466-1800	dkumm@trinityoflincoln.org www.trinityoflincoln.org	David H Kumm	1882		N	EC-5	133
MADISON	*TRINITY*	705 W 6th St 68748	(402)454-2651	praeunerdr@esu8.org trinitylutheranmadison.com	Emily L White	1906		N	EC-8	19
MC COOK	*CREATIVE*	411 E 6th St 69001	(308)345-2595	mycreativepreschool@gmail.com plcmccook.org		1979			EC	31
NORFOLK	*CHRIST*	511 S 5th St 68701	(402)371-5536	durban@clnorfolk.org tiger.clnorfolk.org	Drew R Urban	1871		N	EC-8	364
NORTH BEND	*ST PETER LITTLE LAMB*	920 Linden Dr 68649	(402)652-8215	ml.short190@gmail.com	Kiley Frana				EC	20
NORTH PLATTE	*BEAUTIFUL SAVIOR*	402 S Baytree Ave 69101	(308)534-7004	wilcoxannie@hotmail.com	Anne Wilcox	1984			EC	10
	OUR REDEEMER	1400 East E St 69101	(308)532-6421	mmohrorls@gmail.com ourredeemerschoolnp.com	Mindee Mohr	1927			EC-8	100
O NEILL	*LEAP AT CHRIST*	129 N 7th St 68763	(402)379-1648	jomomanelson@gmail.com christlutheranoneill.org/		2008			EC	
OGALLALA	*ST PAUL*	312 W 3rd St 69153	(308)284-2944	s.peck@stpaulsogallala.org www.stpaulsogallala.org	Drucilla L Lutkehus	1943			EC-5	37
OMAHA	*CONCORDIA*	15656 Fort St 68116	(402)445-4000	nathan.domsch@concordiaomaha.org concordiaomaha.org	Nathan T Domsch	2001	R	N	K-12	670
	KING OF KINGS	11615 I St 68137	(402)333-6464	ronda@kingofkingsomaha.org		1981			EC	
	LITTLE LAMB	15005 Q St 68137	(402)714-3950	rhonda@dsomaha.org littlelambomaha.org/	Rhonda DeVries	1984			EC	136
	ST MARK	1821 N 90th St 68114	(402)391-6148	school@stmarkomaha.org www.stmarkomaha.org	Eric L Jay	1985			EC-5	79
OSMOND	*IMMANUEL*	808 Fulton Street 68765	(402)748-3303	preschool.slagle@gmail.com www.immanuelosmond.com	Julie A Slagle	1906			EC	14
PAPILLION	*FAITH LUTHERAN ACADE*	420 N Washington St 68046	(402)339-3668	pkz@1st-lutheran.org faithlutheranacademy.substack.com/	Karl P Ziegler				EC-12	
	FIRST	420 N Washington St 68046	(402)339-1178	cindy.reilly@centurylink.net firstlutheran.360unite.com	Cindy Reilly	1990			EC	26
PIERCE	*ZION*	520 E Main St 68767	(402)329-4658	principal@zionlutheranpierce.com www.zionlutheranpierce.com	Lavonne L Fleer	1903		N	EC-8	124
PLAINVIEW	*ZION*	102 N 6th St 68769	(402)582-3312	zionplvw@plvwtelco.net www.zionlutheranplainview.org					EC-6	25
POLK	*IMMANUEL*	2406 E 26th Rd 68654	(402)765-7253	ilspolk1886@gmail.com ilspolk.weebly.com		1886			EC-8	36
SAINT PAUL	*LITTLE LAMBS*	1022 Elm St 68873	(308)754-5135	littlelambs@clcstpaulne.org		2011			EC	
SEWARD	*ST JOHN*	877 N Columbia Ave 68434	(402)643-4535	barb.mertens@stjohnseward.org www.stjohnseward.org	Barbara J Mertens	1884		N	EC-8	267
STAPLEHURST	*OUR REDEEMER*	425 South St 68439	(402)535-2251	harlan.anson@orlcne.org www.orlcne.org	Harlan D Anson	1966			EC-8	74
TILDEN	*LITTLE LAMBS*	103 W 5th St 68781	(402)368-2234	stephanie.reikofski@gmail.com ilctilden.com	Heather Hansen	1984			EC	49
UTICA	*ST PAUL*	1100 D St 68456	(402)534-2121	ssommerer@stpaulutica.com stpaulutica.com	Robert D Brauer	1900			EC-8	67
WAVERLY	*PEACEFUL BEGINNINGS*	9831 N 145th St 68462	(402)786-2345	director.pbecc@peacewaverly.org www.peacewaverly.org	Kayla Baker				EC	102
WAYNE	*FISHER OF KIDS*	909 Main St 68787	(402)375-5130	keilafolson@gmail.com www.gracewayne.com	Keila Olson	2003			EC	10
WEST POINT	*ST PAUL*	325 N Colfax 68788	(402)372-2355	squick@stpaulwpne.org www.stpaulwp.org	Susan Quick	1883			EC-8	49
WINNEBAGO	*JESUS OUR SAVIOR*	208 W Mercer 68071	(402)878-2110	jesusoursaviorschool@gmail.com jesusoursaviorwinnebago.org	Wende J Carson	1998	R		EC	12
YORK	*EMMANUEL-FAITH*	806 N Beaver Ave 68467	(402)362-6575	bwellmann@efyork.org www.emmfaith.org	Bradley A Wellmann	1957		N	EC-8	159

NEVADA

CITY	SCHOOL	ADDRESS	PHONE	EMAIL WEBSITE	PRINCIPAL/ ADMINISTRATOR	YEAR ORG.	RSO	NLSA	GRADES OFFERED	ENROLL
BATTLE MOUNTAIN	*CHRIST*	55 Bastian Rd 89820	(775)635-2290	clc_lcms48@yahoo.com	Rebecca Love	2002			EC	13
BOULDER CITY	*LITTLE LAMBS CHRIST*	1401 5th St 89005	(702)293-4332	littlelambsbcnv@gmail.com	Jessica R Stetson	1999			EC	72
CARSON CITY	*BETHLEHEM*	1837 N Mountain St 89703	(775)882-5252	dwinkelman@blcs.org www.blcs.org	Debbie Winkleman	1988			EC-8	178
ELKO	*ST MARK*	277 Willow St 89801	(775)738-4750	smlps.elko@gmail.com stmarkelko.com	Shawn Cavaness	1988			EC	65
FALLON	*ST JOHN*	1170 S Taylor St 89406	(775)423-6325	rmtogrow@cccomm.net	Tami Bennett	1993			EC	
GARDNERVILLE	*TRINITY*	1174 Mill St 89410	(775)782-5437	director@trinitygv.com tlchildcare.com	Joanne Tabor	1983			EC-K	
HENDERSON	*GRACE*	2657 W Horizon Ridge Parkway 89052	(702)492-4701	gracelutheranhenderson.org/glca/	Jamie L DiLiberto				K-8	22
LAS VEGAS	*ABC*	1730 N Pecos Rd 89115	(702)642-5176	abcpsrles@gmail.com www.redeemerlasvegas.com	Kimberly Warren	1973			EC	15

R = Recognized Service Organization (RSO)
N = National Lutheran Schools Accreditation (NLSA)

SCHOOLS

CITY	SCHOOL	ADDRESS	PHONE	EMAIL WEBSITE	PRINCIPAL/ ADMINISTRATOR	YEAR ORG.	RSO	NLSA	GRADES OFFERED	ENROLL
LAS VEGAS	*FAITH*	10405 Griffith Peak Dr 89135	(702)921-2727	carol.jordening@faithlasvegas.org www.faithpreschoollv.org/	Carol J Jordening	2002		N	EC	237
	FAITH	2015 Hualapai Way 89117	(702)804-4400	buucks@flhsemail.org www.faithlutheranlv.org	Kathleen Stokes	1978	R	N	6-12	2182
	FAITH COMMUNITY	2700 S Town Center Dr 89135	(702)921-2777	Daniel.smith@faithlasvegas.org www.faithlutheranacademy.org		2002		N	K-5	432
	LAMB OF GOD	6232 N Jones Blvd 89130	(702)645-1626	info@lambofgodlv.com www.lambofgodlv.org		1995			EC-5	302
	MOUNTAIN VIEW	9550 W Cheyenne Ave 89129	(702)233-9323	kschneider@mvlcs.org mvlcs.org	Kristopher E Schneider	1990		N	EC-5	231
MESQUITE	*MESQUITE*	450 Turtleback 89027	(702)346-3954	director@mesquitelutheran.org www.mesquitelutheran.org	Brandy Templeton	2007			EC	34
WINNEMUCCA	*ZION*	3205 N Highland Dr 89445	(775)623-3796	zionpscc.wmca.nv@sbcglobal.net www.zionwinnv.360unite.com	Jana Sperry	1972			EC	
				NEW HAMPSHIRE						
KEENE	*TRINITY*	100 Maple Ave 03431	(603)352-9403	tcs@tcskeene.com tcskeene.com		1955		N	EC-8	
NEW IPSWICH	*OUR REDEEMER*	200 Ashby Rd 03071	(603)878-1837	orlcnh@comcast.net www.ourredeemernh.com		1987			EC	
				NEW JERSEY						
BASKING RIDGE	*GENTLE SHEPHERD*	350 Lake Rd 07920	(908)766-1430	gscp@shlc.net www.gentleshepherd.net	Krissy Hosler	1993			EC	
BLAIRSTOWN	*GOOD SHEPHERD*	168 Rt 94 07825	(908)362-5819	goodshepherd94@gmail.com	Kathleen Belton	1988			EC	
BORDENTOWN	*HOLY CROSS*	280 Crosswicks Rd 08505	(609)298-2880	preschool@hclconline.org www.hclconline.org	Michelle Koehl	1977			EC	24
CLARK	*ZION*	559 Raritan Rd 07066	(732)382-1630	marini1120@gmail.com www.zionlutheranclark.com		1996			EC	54
EAST BRUNSWICK	*CROSSROADS*	114 Old Stage Rd 08816	(732)251-3221	crossroadselc@verizon.net www.crossroadsearlylearningcenter.com	Crystal Sanchez	1981			EC	90
FAIR LAWN	*OUR SAVIOR*	1-22 Hartley Pl 07410	(201)797-1585	nurseryschool@oursaviornj.org www.oursaviornj.org	Katie Giacomarro	1954			EC	14
FLEMINGTON	*ST PAUL*	201 State Route 31 08822	(908)782-3979	robyn@stpaulnj.com www.stpaulnj.com	Dorothy Davidson	1962			EC	
GALLOWAY TOWNSHIP	*PEACE*	328 E Great Creek Rd 08205	(609)748-0094	peacepre@gmail.com www.new.peacegallowaynj.org/		2002			EC	40
HACKETTSTOWN	*GETHSEMANE*	409 E Baldwin St 07840	(908)852-2156	gethsemanehtown.com	Elizabeth Yaremczak	1973			EC	12
LAMBERTVILLE	*ST PETER*	1608 Harbourton Rocktown Rd 08530	(609)466-6511	director.stpeter@gmail.com www.stpeterns.org		1996			EC	25
LANOKA HARBOR	*LITTLEST ANGELS*	701 Western Blvd 08734	(609)693-6010	vlclittlestangels@gmail.com	Angela Lafferty	2001			EC	
MANCHESTER	*REDEEMER*	2309 Route 70 08759	(732)657-0333	rlnsmanchester@gmail.com www.redeemermanchester.org/nursery-school	Danielle Wagner	1995			EC	15
MOUNTAIN LAKES	*KING OF KINGS*	145 Rt 46 W 07046	(973)334-4085	kofkpres@optonline.net		1970			EC	54
NEWTON	*REDEEMER*	37 Newton Sparta Rd 07860	(973)383-0217	redeemerpreschool@gmail.com www.redeemerpreschoolnewton.com	Krista Geisendorfer	1974			EC	57
OLD BRIDGE	*GOOD SHEPHERD*	3139 County Road 516 08857	(732)679-8887	Marianne@gs4nj.org www.obgscc.com		1968			EC-K	136
POINT PLEASANT	*GOOD SHEPHERD*	708 Ocean Rd 08742	(732)746-3164	GSNSpointpleasant@gmail.com www.gsppnj.org	Kathryn Roach				EC	
RIDGEWOOD	*BETHLEHEM*	155 Linwood Ave 07450	(201)444-6678	office@BELC.org	Elizabeth Hasbrouck	2003			EC-K	
RINGWOOD	*CHRIST THE KING*	50 Erskine Rd 07456	(973)962-6767	sheerin24@ive.com www.forministry.com/USNJLUCMSCTKLC	Dr Georgette L Gretina	1972			EC	
TINTON FALLS	*LUTHER MEMORIAL*	818 Tinton Ave 07724	(732)542-7447	lmcpreschool818@gmail.com lmcnj.org		1993			EC	27
WESTWOOD	*ZION*	64 1st Ave 07675	(201)664-8060	staff@zionlutheranschool.org www.zionlutheranschool.org	Michele D Meisten	1969			EC	
				NEW MEXICO						
ALBUQUERQUE	*CHRIST*	7701 Candelaria Rd NE 87110	(505)884-3876	principal@clsabq.com www.clsabq.com	Kimberly A Rasmussen	1989		N	EC-8	151
	IMMANUEL	300 Gold Ave SE 87102	(505)243-2589	principal@immanuelabq.org immanuelabq.org	Michael K Brandon	1924		N	EC-8	
ALBUQUERQUE	*LAMBS OF GRACE*	7550 Eubank Blvd NE 87122	(505)823-9100	logpreschool@gmail.com lambsofgracepreschool.org	Holle Lesley	2007			EC	
CLOVIS	*IMMANUEL*	1008 N Lea St 88101	(575)763-1952	immanuelprekteacher@gmail.com sites.google.com/site/clovisimmanuel preschool/		1992			EC	2
LAS CRUCES	*MISSION*	2752 Roadrunner Parkway 88011	(575)532-5489	office@mlschool.net www.mlschool.net	Darci Grothman	1997		N	EC-6	49
ROSWELL	*IMMANUEL*	1405 N Sycamore 88201	(575)622-2853	lcms_row_r@plateautel.net www.immanuelroswell.org/school		2006		N	EC-9	
SANTA FE	*GENTLE SHEPHERD*	207 E Barcelona Rd 87505	(505)983-9383	dkescue@aol.com	Laura Escue	1989			EC	
				NEW YORK						
BATAVIA	*ST PAUL*	31 Washington Ave 14020	(585)343-0488	stpaulbataviaprincipal@gmail.com www.stpaulbatavia.org	Jason Clark	1966			EC-6	
BAYSIDE	*FLUSHING AND BAYSIDE*	36-01 Bell Blvd 11361	(718)225-5502	www.lsfb.org	Marian Pia Haselbach	1991	R		EC-8	
BETHPAGE	*LITTLE GOSPEL LIGHTS*	449 Stewart Ave 11714	(516)933-4446	9334him@stpaulbethpage.com 9334him.wixsite.com/lglpreschool	Cheryl Hydo	1999			EC	63

R = Recognized Service Organization (RSO)
N = National Lutheran Schools Accreditation (NLSA)

CITY	SCHOOL	ADDRESS	PHONE	EMAIL WEBSITE	PRINCIPAL/ ADMINISTRATOR	YEAR ORG.	RSO	NLSA	GRADES OFFERED	ENROLL
BRONX	*OUR SAVIOUR*	1734 Williamsbridge Rd 10461	(718)792-5665	kfamulare@oursaviourbronx.org www.oursaviourbronx.org	Matthew R Gonzalez	1942			1-12	
BRONXVILLE	*CHAPEL*	172 White Plains Rd 10708	(914)337-3202	mschultz@thechapelschool.org www.thechapelschool.org	Michael J Schultz	1947		N	EC-8	217
BROOKLYN	*GREAT COMMISSION*	1187 E 92nd St 11236	(347)659-7562	soniapram@yahoo.com	Sonia Singh				1-4; 6	
	ST PETER	105 Highland Pl 11208	(718)647-1014	dhbad@aol.com www.spbklyn.org		1975			EC	
BROOKVILLE	*LONG ISLAND*	131 Brookville Rd 11545	(516)626-1735	info@luhi.org www.luhi.org	John Buck III	1960	R		6-12	
CAIRO	*JOYFUL*	Route 23B & 32 186 Main St 12413	(518)622-3286	rlc.office.lj@gmail.com www.rlc.life/preschool	Victor H Nelson Jr	1983			EC	25
CANANDAIGUA	*LITTLE LAMBS*	320 S Pearl St 14424	(585)394-2760	ewe@frontiernet.net goodshepherdcdga.org		1993			EC	16
CENTEREACH	*OUR SAV NEW AMERICAN*	140 Mark Tree Rd 11720	(631)588-2757	dolores.reade@osnas.org osnas.org	Dr Wilbert P Stelzer	1967			K-12	
CENTRAL ISLIP	*LITTLE LAMBS*	75 Calebs Path 11722	(516)232-3272	lambs75@aol.com www.angelfire.com/ny/littlelambs		1994			EC	
COLONIE	*OUR SAVIOR*	63 Mountain View Ave 12205	(518)459-2273	jrichardson@oursaviors.com oursaviors.com		1956			EC-8	
CORTLAND	*ST PAUL*	49 Hamlin St 13045	(607)753-7101	stpaulluthns@gmail.com		1989			EC	
DIX HILLS	*ST LUKE*	20 Candlewood Path 11746	(631)462-5216	director@stlukedixhills.org www.stlukedixhills.org	Beth Krass	1966			EC	
EAST MEADOW	*CALVARY*	36 Taylor Ave 11554	(516)520-4067	nurseryschool@calvarylc.org calvarylc.org/nurseryschool	Joanna Reilly	1981			EC	19
FAIRPORT	*RISEN CHRIST*	1000 Moseley Rd 14450	(585)223-5757	rclc.office@gmail.com risenchrist-preschool.com/		1982			EC	
FARMINGTON	*ST JOHN*	153 Church Ave 14425	(315)986-3045	preschool@pumpkinhook.com www.pumpkinhook.org		1968			EC	
FISHKILL	*LITTLE LAMBS*	1400 Rte 52 12524	(845)897-4423	preschool@oursaviorlutheran.org littlelambsofoslc.org		1995			EC	
GARDEN CITY	*RESURRECTION*	420 Stewart Ave 11530	(516)741-6447	jean@resgc.org resgc.org/preschool		1962			EC-K	
HAWTHORNE	*TRINITY*	292 Elwood Ave 10532	(914)773-1108	trinitypreschool292@gmail.com www.trinity-preschool.com		1995			EC	
HICKSVILLE	*TRINITY*	40 W Nicholai St 11801	(516)931-2211	jforte@trinityli.org www.trinityli.org	Jennifer Forte	1954		N	EC-8	97
HILTON	*ST PAUL*	158 East Ave 14468	(585)392-4000	principal@stpaulhilton.org www.stpaulhilton.org	Mark D Ball	1956			EC-8	226
HOLBROOK	*ST JOHN*	1675 Coates Ave 11741	(631)588-4347	sjnurseryschool@outlook.com sjnurseryschool.com	Christine McCarthy	1976			EC	
ISLIP	*TRINITY*	111 Nassau Ave 11751	(631)277-5855	trinitypreschoolislip@gmail.com trinitypreschoolislip.org	Kathryn Cantanno	1985			EC	
MASPETH	*MARTIN LUTHER*	60-02 Maspeth Ave 11378	(718)894-4000	schapman@martinlutherny c.org www.martinlutherny c.org	Sean C Chapman	1960	R		6-12	
MONROE	*ST PAUL*	21 Still Rd 10950	(845)783-1068	school@stpaulmonroe.net www.stpaulmonroe.net	Ramona Adams	1975			EC-2	
NORTH TONAWANDA	*ST JOHN*	6950 Ward Rd 14120	(716)693-9677	office@stjohnnt.com www.stjohnnt.com	Katie L Gundell	1853		N	EC-8	171
	ST MARK	1135 Oliver St 14120	(716)693-3715	officeadmin@stmarknt.org www.stmarknt.org		1891			EC	14
	ST PAUL	453 Old Falls Blvd 14120	(716)692-3255	beckyorlowski73@gmail.com www.stpaulnt.com	Rebecca Orlowski	1973			EC	27
OLD WESTBURY	*THE LIFE*	1 Old Westbury Rd 11568	(516)333-3355	dayschool@thelifeny.org thelifeny.org/dayschool		1991			EC	
PATCHOGUE	*EMANUEL*	179 E Main St 11772	(631)758-2250	mainoffice@emanluthpatchsc.org emanluthpatchsc.org		1956			EC	30
PENFIELD	*FAITH*	2576 Browncroft Blvd 14526	(585)385-2360	info@fccnschildcare.com www.fccnschildcare.com		1986			EC-5	
PUTNAM VALLEY	*ST LUKE*	65 Oscawana Lk Rd 10579	(845)526-3560	mail@stlukesputnamvalley.org www.stlukesputnamvalley.org		1982			EC	
REGO PARK	*OUR SAVIOUR*	64-33 Woodhaven Blvd 11374	(718)897-4343	school@our-saviour.org osnyec.org	Warren Castellani	1945			EC	
ROCHESTER	*HOPE*	1301 Vintage Ln 14626	(585)723-4673	kelliehudson@sharethehope.org www.sharethehope.org	Kellie L Hudson	1962			EC	168
SAINT JAMES	*ST JAMES*	229 Second Ave 11780	(631)862-8934	meredithpreschool@stjlc.com www.stjames-preschool.com	Meredith Johansson	1969			EC	
SARATOGA SPRINGS	*ST PAUL*	149 Lake Ave 12866	(518)584-0904	CCC@SpaLutheran.org spalutheran.org/preschool	Christy Albertin	1996			EC	
SPENCERPORT	*TRINITY*	191 Nichols St 14559	(585)352-3143	marilyn.mcmullen79.mm@gmail.com www.tlcspencerport.com		1986			EC	
SPRINGVILLE	*SALEM*	91 W Main St 14141	(716)592-9067	amyslpccc@gmail.com	Amy Tillinghast	2000			EC	52
STATEN ISLAND	*ST JOHN*	663 Manor Rd 10314	(718)761-1858	kay977@aol.com stjohnslutheransi.org/school/	John W Van Camp	1952			EC-8	
TONAWANDA	*FIRST TRINITY*	1570 Niagara Falls Blvd 14150	(716)835-2220	lhorn@firsttrinity.com www.firsttrinitypreschool.com		1961			EC	63
UTICA	*TRINITY*	2620 Genesee St 13502	(315)732-7869	trin1@juno.com www.trinitylutheranutica.com		1974			EC	
VESTAL	*GRACE*	709 Main St 13850	(607)748-0840	gracelc@gracevestal.org www.gracevestal.org		1969			EC	

R = Recognized Service Organization (RSO)
N = National Lutheran Schools Accreditation (NLSA)

CITY	SCHOOL	ADDRESS	PHONE	EMAIL WEBSITE	PRINCIPAL/ ADMINISTRATOR	YEAR ORG.	RSO	NLSA	GRADES OFFERED	ENROLL
WELLSVILLE	*TRINITY*	470 N Main St 14895	(585)593-3820	tcdwellsville@gmail.com		1985			EC	
WEST SENECA	*TRINITY*	146 Reserve Rd 14224	(716)674-5353	jbabcock@trinitywny.org www.trinitywny.org		1851		N	EC-8	99
WHEATFIELD	*HOLY GHOST*	6630 Luther St 14304	(716)731-3030		Kevin Gundell	1843		N	EC-8	130
WOLCOTTSVILLE	*ST MICHAEL*	6379 Wolcottsville Rd 14001	(716)542-2886	smpreschoolakron@gmail.com www.stmichaelsakron.org		1995			EC	
YONKERS	*ST MARKS*	7 St Marks Place 10704	(914)237-4944	smly2011@live.com www.smlsyonkers.com	Jennifer Cave	1962			EC-8	64
				NORTH CAROLINA						
ASHEVILLE	*EMMANUEL*	51 Wilburn Pl 28806	(828)281-8182	principal@elcsmail.org www.emmanuellutheranschool.org	Mark J Edmiston	1958		N	EC-8	233
CARY	*RESURRECTION*	100 W Lochmere Dr 27518	(919)851-7270	director@rlpcary.org rlpcary.org		1984			EC	
	RESURRECTION	100 W Lochmere Dr 27518	(919)851-7271	rlsadmin@rlscary.org www.rlscary.org		2002		N	EC-8	172
CHARLOTTE	*MESSIAH*	8300 Providence Rd 28277	(704)541-1624	preschool@messiah-nc.org	Alyssa Breuer	1987			EC	58
CLAYTON	*OPEN ARMS*	2920 NC Hwy 42 W 27520	(919)553-7227	openarms@earthlink.net www.holycrossclayton.com		2006			EC	
CONOVER	*CONCORDIA*	215 5th Ave SE 28613	(828)464-3011	admin@concordianc.org school.concordianc.org/	David C Beringer	1878		N	EC-8	258
	ST JOHN	2126 St Johns Church Rd 28613	(828)459-6468	misssuzannestuchspreschool@gmail.com www.stjohnsconover.com/preschool	Suzanne M Zastrow	1996			EC	
FRANKLIN	*GREAT BEGINNINGS*	38 Wayah St 28734	(828)369-2411	mygreatbeginningsrlc@gmail.com www.mygreatbeginnings.org		1990			EC	
HENDERSONVILLE	*MT PISGAH*	2606 Chimney Rock Rd 28792	(828)698-5900	mtppreschool@gmail.com		2004			EC	
HICKORY	*ST STEPHEN*	2304 Springs Rd NE 28601	(828)256-2166	school@sslcms.org sslswarriors.org	Ross Chiles	1943		N	EC-8	221
JACKSONVILLE	*CALVARY*	206 Pine Valley Rd 28546	(910)353-4016	calvaryprek@outlook.com	Jennifer Kamaris	1988			EC	
KERNERSVILLE	*FOUNTAIN OF LIFE*	323 Hopkins Rd 27284	(336)993-4447	preschool@folcp.com www.cometothefountain.com	Shannon Valentine	1991			EC	124
WAKE FOREST	*HOPE*	3525 Rogers Rd 27587	(919)453-0388	preschool@hopelutheranwf.org hopelutheranwf.org		1997			EC	172
WINSTON-SALEM	*ST JOHNS*	2415 Silas Creek Pkwy 27103	(336)725-1651	sdavidson@stjohnsws.org stjohnsfalcons.org	Tiffany Banks	1951		N	EC-5	102
				NORTH DAKOTA						
BISMARCK	*MARTIN LUTHER*	413 E Ave D 58501	(701)224-9070	office@lutherschools.org www.lutherschools.org	Denise Wolfgram	1995	R		EC-8	492
FARGO	*GRACE*	1025 14th Ave S 58103	(701)232-7747	principal@glsfargo.org www.glsfargo.org	Susan R Jahnke	2003	R	N	EC-8	
GRAND FORKS	*IMMANUEL*	1710 Cherry St 58201	(701)746-8112	iccc@immanuelgf.org www.immanuelgf.org	Marie M Remz	1999			EC-5	108
				OHIO						
AKRON	*FAIRLAWN*	3415 W Market St 44333	(330)864-7724	Katie.Bungard@fairlawnlutheran.org www.fairlawnlutheran.org		1997		N	EC-K	91
	HOPE	999 Portage Lakes Dr 44319	(330)644-3522	jackielangenek@hopelcmsakron.org www.hopeakron.org	Jackie Langenek	1997			EC	18
AMHERST	*ST PAUL*	115 Central Dr 44001	(440)988-5427	mmuresan0123@gmail.com www.stpaulamherst.com	Elizabeth Naro	1978			EC	43
ARCHBOLD	*ST JAMES*	22881 Monroe St 43502	(419)445-4750	alongthepathoflearning@gmail.com saintjamespreschool.yolasite.com	Sue Macdonald				EC	19
AURORA	*HOPE*	456 S Chillicothe Rd 44202	(330)562-8260	jennifer@lynagh.com	Jennifer Lynagh	1974			EC	
AVON	*FAITH*	2265 Garden Dr 44011	(440)934-2465	preschool@faithavon.com www.faithavon.com	Michele Herner	1976			EC	40
CHAGRIN FALLS	*VALLEY*	87 E Orange St 44022	(216)247-0390	j.congdon@valleychristianpreschool.org www.valleychristianpreschool.org		1995			EC	87
CHARDON	*PEACE*	12686 Bass Lake Rd 44024	(440)286-3310	pcps@windstream.net	Andrea Johnson	1979			EC	0
CHESTERLAND	*ST MARK*	11900 Chillicothe Rd 44026	(440)729-1668	preschool@stmarkchester.org www.stmarkchester.com		1976			EC	
CINCINNATI	*LITTLE BUD*	3301 Compton Rd 45251	(513)385-8404	tsedam@christ-lcms.org www.christ-lcms.org		1998			EC	41
CLEVELAND	*HOLY CROSS*	4260 Rocky River Dr 44135	(216)941-2770	secretary@hcwpls.org.in www.hclcas.org	Dr Michael D Scheer	1981			K-8	
	LUTHER MEMORIAL	4464 Pearl Rd 44109	(216)749-5300	dgaglione@lmslancers.org www.lmslancers.org	David Gaglione	1948	R	N	EC-8	199
CLEVELAND	*ST JOHNS*	1027 E 176th St 44119	(216)531-8204	ksauline@sjnschool.net www.stjohnnottingham.org	Kathryn Speigner	1892		N	K-8	42
COLUMBIA STATION	*HOSANNA*	13485 W River Rd 44028	(440)236-8900	tanyarindfleisch@yahoo.com hosannakids.com	Dana Petry	2005			EC	13
COLUMBUS	*ATONEMENT*	1621 Francisco Rd 43220	(614)451-5212	alpsdirector@atonementchurch.com www.atonementchurch.com	Carmen Fryman	1989			EC	
CUYAHOGA FALLS	*REDEEMER*	2141 5th St 44221	(330)923-1280	alenczewski@redeemerlutheran.us www.redeemerlutheran.us		1958		N	EC-8	187
DEFIANCE	*ST JOHN*	655 Wayne Ave 43512	(419)782-1751	principal.sjl@stjohntigers.com www.stjohntigers.com	Kristina Phipps	1873		N	EC-1	46
DUBLIN	*ST JOHN DUBLIN*	6135 Rings Rd 43016	(614)889-5893	amber.furr@stjohndublin.org stjohndublin.org		1985		N	EC-5	91

R = Recognized Service Organization (RSO)
N = National Lutheran Schools Accreditation (NLSA)

CITY	SCHOOL	ADDRESS	PHONE	EMAIL WEBSITE	PRINCIPAL/ ADMINISTRATOR	YEAR ORG.	RSO	NLSA	GRADES OFFERED	ENROLL
ELMORE	TRINITY	412 Fremont St 43416	(419)862-7010	tlcpreschool5@gmail.com	Migdalia Sanchez	1989			EC	19
ELYRIA	GRACE	9685 E River Rd 44035	(440)322-5497	graceelyria@gmail.com www.gracelcelyria.org	Stacy Zifcak	1970			EC	37
FAIRBORN	BETHLEHEM	1240 S Maple Ave 45324	(937)878-7050	sferguson@mybethlehemschool.com www.mybethlehemschool.com	Scott A Ferguson	1999			EC-8	130
FLORIDA	ST PETER	K-980 County Rd 17D 43545	(419)762-5075	stpeterpreschool123@gmail.com	Brittany Morgan	1988			EC	17
GENEVA	ST JOHN	811 S Broadway 44041	(440)466-2473	stjohnsgeneva20@gmail.com stjohnsgeneva.org	Diane S Gruber	1994			EC	26
HAMILTON	IMMANUEL	1285 Main St 45013	(513)895-9212	jaan.pirn@immanuelhamilton.com immanuelhamilton.com	Lukas R Bickel	1953		N	EC-9	234
HOLGATE	ST JOHN	501 N Wilhelm St 43527	(419)264-4641	christine.k.stober@gmail.com	Christine K Stober	1979			EC	28
HUDSON	GLORIA DEI	2113 Ravenna St 44236	(330)650-6550	mpolak@gloriadeihudson.org www.gloriadeihudson.org	Megan Polak	1987			EC	49
LAKEWOOD	GRACE	13030 Madison Ave 44107	(216)529-1081	gracepreschool@truevine.net www.grace-preschool.net	Bonita Sears	2008			EC	
	LAKEWOOD	14560 Madison Ave 44107	(216)221-6941	tszoyka@lakewoodlutheranschool.com www.lakewoodlutheranschool.com	Carolyn Potantus	1905		N	K-8	26
LANCASTER	REDEEMER	1400 Concordia Dr 43130	(740)653-9727	redeemerlutheranschool@yahoo.com www.redeemerlancaster.com	Cathryn Jurecki	1959			EC-K	62
LIBERTY CENTER	ST PAUL	8074 County Road T 43532	(419)533-3041	stpaulpreschool@embarqmail.com	Laura Bergstedt	1969			EC	26
LIBERTY TOWNSHIP	ROYAL REDEEMER	7127 Dutchland Pkwy 45044	(513)779-4740	diannabowers@royalredeemer.org www.royalredeemer.org/school/	Dianna Bowers				EC	37
MARYSVILLE	ST JOHNS	12809 State Route 736 43040	(937)644-5540	rrausch@sjsmarysville.org www.sjsmarysville.org	Richard M Rausch	1843		N	EC-8	571
MASON	KING OF KINGS	3621 Socialville Foster Rd 45040	(513)398-6089	ecemadmin@koklcms.org www.koklcms.org	Vicky Lesiak	1995		N	EC-K	140
MILFORD	ST MARK'S	5849 Buckwheat Rd 45150	(513)575-3354	principal@stmarksmilford.org www.stmarksmilford.org		1997		N	EC-8	250
MILFORD CENTER	ST PAUL	7960 State Route 38 43045	(937)349-5939	stpaulearlychildhoodcenter@gmail.com www.stpaulcheuckery.curch	Belinda Allen	1892			EC	
NAPOLEON	ST JOHN	16035 County Road U 43545	(419)598-8702	tgermann@sjl.org www.sjl.org	Tracy Germann	1869		N	EC-7	135
	ST PAUL	1075 Glenwood Ave 43545	(419)592-5536	jbourgeois@stpaulnapoleon.org www.stpaulnapoleon.org	Julie A Bourgeois	1933		N	EC-8	207
NORTH CANTON	HOLY CROSS	7707 Market Ave N 44721	(330)494-6478	michelle@holycrossnorthcanton.org www.holycrossnorthcanton.com	Michelle Voina	1994			EC	75
NORTH OLMSTED	ASCENSION	28081 Lorain Rd 44070	(440)777-6365	ascnecc@gmail.com www.alcecc.com	Laurie Schneider	1977			EC	
NORTH ROYALTON	ROYAL REDEEMER	11680 Royalton Rd 44133	(440)237-7988	mluecke@royred.org www.royred.org		1984		N	EC-8	323
OREGON	PRINCE OF PEACE	4155 Pickle Rd 43616	(419)693-8661	preschool@princeofpeaceoregon.com www.princeofpeaceoregon.com	Wendy Kelly	1989			EC	39
PAINESVILLE	OUR SHEPHERD	508 Mentor Ave 44077	(440)357-7776	mcarlson@oslpainesville.org www.oslpainesville.org	Paul Goodwin	1980	R	N	K-8	116
	ST PAUL	250 Bowhall Rd 44077	(440)354-3000	preschool@splcpainesville.org www.stpaulspainesville.com	Amy Marizek	1969		N	EC	35
PARMA	BETHANY	6041 Ridge Rd 44129	(440)884-1010	mschiemann@bethanyparma.com bethanyparmaschool.org	Michael T Schiemann	1935		N	EC-8	357
POWELL	BEAUTIFUL SAVIOR	3924 Home Rd 43065	(740)938-4246	preschool@bslcoh.org www.bslcoh.org	Elizabeth Shelton				EC	25
ROCKY RIVER	LUTHERAN WEST	3850 Linden Rd 44116	(440)333-1660	joel.bahr@lutheranwest.com www.lutheranwest.com	Joel S Bahr	1948	R	N	6-12	718
	ST THOMAS	21211 Detroit Rd 44116	(440)331-4426	principal@stls.net www.stls.net	A C Cipollo	1959		N	EC-K	40
SHAKER HEIGHTS	CLASSICAL ACADEMY	18000 Van Aken Blvd 44122	(216)561-2511	heather.vallier@cca-shaker.org www.cca-shaker.org/	Heather Vallier				K-5	0
SHEFFIELD VILLAGE	HOPE	4792 Oster Rd 44054	(440)949-2537	hopepreschoolsheffield@gmail.com www.hopeofsheffield.com/preschool	Jacqueline Dennison	1986			EC	8
SOLON	OUR REDEEMER	7196 SOM Center Rd 44139	(440)248-4066	orlcpreschool@sbcglobal.net www.orlcsolon.org		1975			EC-K	34
SPRINGFIELD	RISEN CHRIST	41 E Possum Rd 45502	(937)323-3688	breid@risenchristschool.com www.risenchristschool.com	Rebecca S Reid	1993		N	EC-9	112
TALLMADGE	TALLMADGE	759 East Ave 44278	(330)633-4908	Lmiller@tlcoh.org tcp.tlcoh.org	Laura Miller	1995			EC	60
TOLEDO	CONCORDIA	3636 S Detroit Ave 43614	(419)382-0410	office@concordiatoledo.org	Tammy Vogt	1968			EC	60
	TRINITY	4560 Glendale Ave 43614	(419)385-2301	jlandskroener@trinityvikings.org trinityvikings.org	James A Landskroener	1874		N	EC-8	198
WAUSEON	EMMAUS	841 N Shoop Ave 43567	(419)337-8471	emmauschristianpreschool@yahoo.com www.emmauslutheranchurch.com	Jennifer Rodriguez	1971			EC	9
WESTLAKE	ST PAUL	27981 Detroit Rd 44145	(440)835-3051	ktrent@stpaulwestlake.org www.stpaulwestlake.school		1858		N	EC-8	211
YOUNGSTOWN	ST MARKS	280 Mill Creek Dr 44512	(330)788-9599	bowdie3819@gmail.com		1997			EC	0
ZANESVILLE	TRINITY	128 S 7th St 43701	(740)453-0744	oliviaearich@gmail.com		2003			EC	8
OKLAHOMA										
BROKEN ARROW	IMMANUEL	400 North Aspen 74012	(918)251-5422	tberwaldt@icaba.org www.ilcanews.org		2002	R	N	K-12	160
EDMOND	HOLY TRINITY	308 NW 164th St 73013	(405)844-4000	school@holytrinityedmond.org www.holytrinityedmond.org	Jeff Nemcock	1987		N	EC-8	249

R = Recognized Service Organization (RSO)
N = National Lutheran Schools Accreditation (NLSA)

CITY	SCHOOL	ADDRESS	PHONE	EMAIL WEBSITE	PRINCIPAL/ ADMINISTRATOR	YEAR ORG.	RSO	NLSA	GRADES OFFERED	ENROLL
EDMOND	*ST MARK*	1501 N Bryant 73034	(405)340-0192	dce@stmarkedmond.org www.stmarkedmond.org	Sheila K Rudat	2000			EC	60
EL RENO	*TRINITY*	500 S Country Club Rd 73036	(405)953-5989	elrenotlc@gmail.com	Ashley Baker				EC	
ENID	*SAINT PAUL'S*	1626 E Broadway Ave 73701	(580)234-6646	office@stpaulsenid.com www.stpaulsenid.com		1926			EC-5	75
FAIRMONT	*ZION*	507 Fairmont Rd 73736	(580)358-2291	zlcfairmont@gmail.com		1985			EC	
GUYMON	*TRINITY*	1212 N Crumley St 73942	(580)338-6000	office@trinitylutheranchurch.com		1962			EC	
LAWTON	*HOLY CROSS*	2105 NW 38th St 73505	(580)357-9005	holycrosslearning2105@gmail.com	Candace Howard	1984			EC	
	ST JOHN	102 SW 7th St 73501	(580)280-2580	stjohnpreschool609@gmail.com www.stjohnlutheranpreschoollawton.com		1997			EC	
MIAMI	*MOUNT OLIVE*	2337 N Main St 74354	(918)540-3456	mt.oliveschool@yahoo.com mtoschool.org		1956		N	EC-12	23
MIDWEST CITY	*GOOD SHEPHERD*	700 N Air Depot Blvd 73110	(405)732-0070	van.guillotte@gslsmwc.com www.mylutheran.school	Van Guillotte	1982		N	EC-8	
MOORE	*ST JOHN*	1032 NW 12th St 73160	(405)794-8686	LRichards@sj-ls.org www.sj-ls.org	LaRhonda Richards	1997		N	EC-8	24
NORMAN	*TRINITY*	603 Classen Blvd 73071	(405)329-1503	tlsnormansec@gmail.com www.tlsnorman.com	Cheryl Anderson	1989			EC	
OKARCHE	*ST JOHN*	201 S 5th 73762	(405)263-4488	stjohnslutherancdc@gmail.com stjohnsokarche.com		1893			EC	
OKLAHOMA CITY	*MESSIAH*	3600 NW Expressway 73112	(405)946-0462	scage@messiahokc.org www.messiahlutheranschool.com	Sara K Cage	1989		N	EC-8	118
PONCA CITY	*FIRST*	1104 N 4th St 74601	(580)762-9950	lutheransecretary2022@gmail.com www.flcspc.com		1953		N	EC-8	174
TULSA	*ABLAZE*	4901 S 177 E Ave 74134	(918)248-1292	info@aca-ba.org aca-ba.org	Kara Castorena				EC	
	IMMANUEL	400 N Aspen 74012	(918)258-7622	khuggins@icaba.org www.ilcanews.org	Keisha R Huggins	1977			EC	146
				OREGON						
ALOHA	*BETHLEHEM*	18865 SW Johnson St 97003	(503)649-3380	mrs.laiva.hoffman@gmail.com blpaloha.org		1962			EC	32
BEAVERTON	*PILGRIM*	5650 SW Hall Blvd 97005	(503)644-8697	school.office@pilgrimbeaverton.com www.pilgrimbeaverton.com/school		1981		N	EC-8	131
BEND	*TRINITY*	2550 NE Butler Market Rd 97701	(541)382-1850	mike.schiemann@saints.org www.saints.org	Gregg A Pinick	1959		N	EC-12	649
CORNELIUS	*FOREST HILLS*	4221 SW Golf Course Rd 97113	(503)359-4853	office@fhlcs.org www.fhlcs.org	Kim Luna	1994		N	K-8	165
CORVALLIS	*ZION*	2800 NW Tyler Ave 97330	(541)753-7503	schooloffice@zioncorvallis.com zioncorvallis.com	Charlotte Bohlmann	1907		N	EC-8	147
DAMASCUS	*CHRIST THE VINE*	18677 SE Highway 212 97089	(503)658-5650	sbloemer.ctv@gmail.com ctvlutheranschool.org	Seanna Bloemer	1985			EC-2	36
FOREST GROVE	*MOUNT OLIVE*	2327 17th Ave 97116	(503)357-2511	preschool@mtolivefg.org www.mtolivefg.org	Linda Holscher	2005		N	EC	24
HERMISTON	*BETHLEHEM*	515 SW 7th St 97838	(541)567-7829	blps.hermiston@gmail.com bethlehemhermiston.org	Teresa Adams	1978			EC	70
HILLSBORO	*TRINITY*	2194 SE Minter Bridge Rd 97123	(503)846-1319	preschool@trinityhillsboro.com www.trinitypreschoolhillsboro.com		2001			EC	48
	ZION	178 NE Evergreen Rd 97124	(971)724-6539	zionpreschoolhillsboro@gmail.com www.zionhillsboro.org/preschool	Cyndi Biamont	1993			EC	
LA GRANDE	*SHINE PRESCHOOL*	104 S 12th St 97850	(541)963-2831	lgshinepreschool@gmail.com lgfaithlcms.org/shinepreschool		2017			EC	
LAKE OSWEGO	*KINGS CHILDREN*	4700 SW Lamont Way 97035	(503)636-8683	cherylbpackard@comcast.net tklc-lcms.org	Cheryl Packard	1994			EC	34
MEDFORD	*ST PETER*	1020 E Main St 97504	(541)858-1699	kc.osberg@gmail.com		1990			EC	
PORTLAND	*PRINCE OF PEACE*	14175 NW Cornell Rd 97229	(503)645-1211	school@princeofpeacelc.org www.princeofpeacelc.org	Karen D Kiser	1983			EC-K	80
	TRINITY	5520 NE Killingsworth St 97218	(503)288-6403	office@trinityportland.org www.trinityportland.org	Marsha Wolfe	1890		N	K-8	52
ROSEBURG	*ST PAUL*	750 W Keady Ct 97471	(541)673-7212	churchoffice@stpaulroseburg.org www.stpaulroseburg.org		1969			EC	23
SALEM	*REDEEMER*	4663 Lancaster Dr NE 97305	(503)393-7121	office@redeemer-lcms.org redeemer-lcms.org/preschool	Patricia Haneberg	1962			EC	
	ST JOHN	1350 Court St NE 97301	(503)588-0171	sjlc@teleport.com www.stjohnlcms.org	Kelly Crabtree	1961			EC-K	
SCAPPOOSE	*GRACE*	51737 S Columbia River Hwy 97056	(503)543-2734	gccc@gracescappoose.org www.gracescappoose.org	Karen Kenehan	1993		N	EC	152
SHERWOOD	*ST PAUL*	17500 SW Cedarview Way 97140	(503)625-6648	office@stpaulsherwood.org www.stpaullcms.net		1990			EC	
TIGARD	*OUR REDEEMER*	13401 SW Benish St 97223	(503)524-6646	ourredeemertigard@gmail.com orlc.net		2008			EC	38
TUALATIN	*LIVING SAVIOR*	8740 SW Sagert St 97062	(503)692-3303	lspdirector@living-savior.org living-savior.org	Christina Hermann	1980			EC-K	
				PENNSYLVANIA						
ALBION	*HOLY TRIN PRESCHOOL*	80 3rd Ave 16401	(814)756-3426	holytrinityps@gmail.com www.holytrinitylutheranalbion.org/holy-trinity-preschool	Michael S Taylor	1981			EC	
BRIDGEVILLE	*ZION*	3197 Washington Pike 15017	(412)221-4776	megan@zlcb.org www.zlcb.org		1980			EC	

R = Recognized Service Organization (RSO)
N = National Lutheran Schools Accreditation (NLSA)

CITY	SCHOOL	ADDRESS	PHONE	EMAIL WEBSITE	PRINCIPAL/ ADMINISTRATOR	YEAR ORG.	RSO	NLSA	GRADES OFFERED	ENROLL
CABOT	*ST LUKE*	330 Hannahstown Rd 16023	(724)352-2221	stlukeschool@stlukecabot.org www.school.stlukecabot.org	Angela R Turner	1866			EC-8	197
EASTON	*FAITH*	2012 Sullivan Trl 18040	(610)253-1572	faithlcms@outlook.com		1995			EC	
FREEDOM	*PRINCE OF PEACE*	60 Rochester Rd 15042	(724)728-3881	preschool@princeofpeacefreedom.com www.princeofpeacefreedom.com		1976			EC	
HOP BOTTOM	*GRACE*	351 Greenwood St 18824	(717)289-4921	hbgracepastor@echoes.net	Paulette Adams	1985			EC	22
LEVITTOWN	*HOPE*	2600 Haines Rd 19055	(215)946-3467	info@hopelcs.org www.hopelcs.org	Maryann Puls	1953			EC-8	166
MACUNGIE	*CONCORDIA*	2623 Brookside Rd 18062	(610)965-3265	preschoolconcordia@gmail.com www.concordia-preschool.com		1991			EC	77
MALVERN	*CHRIST MEMORIAL*	89 Line Rd 19355	(610)296-0650	office@christmemorial.us www.christmemorial.us	Jodie Merow	1974			EC-K	172
MORRISDALE	*ST JOHN*	3471 Winburne-Munson Rd 16858	(814)345-5741		Kelly L Williamson	1980			EC	26
MURRYSVILLE	*CALVARY*	4725 Old William Penn Hwy 15668	(724)327-2898	www.calvarylcms.org	Laura R Hoff	1996			EC-K	
PITTSBURGH	*GOOD SHEPHERD*	418 Maxwell Dr 15236	(412)884-5960	preschool@goodshepherdpittsburgh.org www.gslcpittsburgh.org	Jennifer L Meyer	1993			EC	
SCRANTON	*IMMANUEL*	238 Reese St 18508	(570)342-3374	immanuelscranton@verizon.net		2004			EC	
	THE LUTHERAN ACADEMY	1546 Monsey Ave 18509	(570)507-9108	info@thelutheranacademyscranton.org www.thelutheranacademyscranton.org	Janet Wells	2007			K-8	
STATE COLLEGE	*GOOD SHEPHERD*	851 N Science Park Rd 16803	(814)234-1388	goodshepherdscps@comcast.net www.goodshepherdsc.org	Dianne E Sefter	1993			EC	
VERONA	*REDEEMER*	700 Idaho Ave 15147	(412)793-5884	gholzer@redeemer-oakmont.org www.rlspittsburgh.org	Gail J Holzer	1983	R	N	EC-12	
WELLSBORO	*TRINITY*	53 West Ave 16901	(570)724-7723	trinitylutheran16901@yahoo.com www.trinitylutheranwellsboro.org		1981			EC-6	130

RHODE ISLAND

CITY	SCHOOL	ADDRESS	PHONE	EMAIL WEBSITE	PRINCIPAL/ ADMINISTRATOR	YEAR ORG.	RSO	NLSA	GRADES OFFERED	ENROLL
ASHAWAY	*TRINITY*	110 High St 02804	(401)377-4216	kmills613@yahoo.com trinityashaway.org	Kelly Mills	1984			EC	

SOUTH CAROLINA

CITY	SCHOOL	ADDRESS	PHONE	EMAIL WEBSITE	PRINCIPAL/ ADMINISTRATOR	YEAR ORG.	RSO	NLSA	GRADES OFFERED	ENROLL
COLUMBIA	*MOUNT OLIVE*	1541 Lake Murray Blvd 29212	(803)781-7180	preschool@mtolivesc.org mtolivesc.org/preschool	Anna Brent	2007			EC	
MYRTLE BEACH	*RISEN CHRIST*	10595 N Kings Hwy 29572	(843)272-8163	info@risenchristacademy.com risenchristacademy.com	Sean E O Connor	1976			EC-12	141
SENECA	*LITTLE LAMBS*	220 Carson Rd 29678	(864)882-3202	preschool@eternalshepherd.org www.eternalshepherd.org	Gina Cote	2001			EC	
SIMPSONVILLE	*IMMANUEL*	2820 Woodruff Rd 29681	(864)501-6822	admin@ils-sc.com www.immanuellutheranschool.net		1994			EC	116

SOUTH DAKOTA

CITY	SCHOOL	ADDRESS	PHONE	EMAIL WEBSITE	PRINCIPAL/ ADMINISTRATOR	YEAR ORG.	RSO	NLSA	GRADES OFFERED	ENROLL
ABERDEEN	*THE LIGHTHOUSE*	215 7th Ave SW 57401	(605)725-1855	directorlhph@stpaulsaberdeen.org www.stpaulsaberdeen.org	Rhonda A Henschen	2009			EC	15
BLACK HAWK	*DIVINE SHEPHERD*	7308 Wedgewood Dr 57718	(605)791-1131	dslceccdirector@divineshep.org www.divineshep.org	Suzanne Mayer				EC	58
BRANDON	*BLESSED REDEEMER*	705 S Sioux Blvd 57005	(605)582-2396	michelle.ternus@blessedredeemer.com www.blessedredeemer.com	Michelle Ternus	1995			EC	62
BROOKINGS	*PEACE*	1104 22nd St 57006	(605)692-5272	peacelut@brookings.net		1997			EC-3	
CANISTOTA	*ZION*	350 W Elm 57012	(605)296-3166	saint_johns_lutheran_church@hotmail.com		1997			EC	5
DAKOTA DUNES	*HOLY CROSS*	149 Bison Trl 57049	(605)235-1688	holycrosseducation@longlines.com www.holycrossdakotadunes.org		1995			EC	33
FLANDREAU	*REDEEMER*	508 West 1st Ave 57028	(605)997-3848	peacelut@brookings.net		2003			EC	
GROTON	*ST JOHN*	308 N Second St 57445	(605)397-2386	keithtricia69@icloud.com	Tricia J Keith	2005			EC	
HARTFORD	*TRINITY*	46448 263rd St 57033	(605)526-4021	director@hartfordtlc.org www.hartfordtlc.org		2007			EC	
HOT SPRINGS	*BETHESDA*	1537 Baltimore Ave 57747	(605)745-6676	Heather.Hunsaker@k12.sd.us www.bethesdalutheranchurchandschool.com		1980		N	EC-5	35
HURON	*MOUNT CALVARY*	688 Dakota Ave S 57350	(605)461-9222	daycare.mclc@midconetwork.com www.mtcalvaryhuron.org		1994			EC	45
MILBANK	*EMANUEL*	701 S First St 57252	(605)432-9555	elcpreschool@itcmilbank.com www.elcmilbank.org		1979			EC	
PIERRE	*FAITH*	714 N Grand Ave 57501	(605)224-2216	faith@faithluth.com faithluth.com	Shelby Bergeson	1979			EC	
RAPID CITY	*ZION*	4550 Mount Rushmore Rd 57701	(605)342-5749	zionschool@zionrc.org zionrc.org	Ann C Solinsky	1957			EC-5	176
SIOUX FALLS	*HIS ARK*	5500 W 26th St 57106	(605)361-7200	director@hisarksf.com	Jodene A Baker	2010			EC	
	SIOUX FALLS	6715 S. Boe Lane 57108	(605)335-1923	tesser@sflutheranschool.com www.siouxfallslutheran.com	Tia M Esser	1977	R	N	EC-12	515
TEA	*RISEN SAVIOR*	1401 N Main Ave 57064	(605)498-5050	rspreschool605@gmail.com www.risensaviortea.org/preschool		2004			EC	22
YANKTON	*ST JOHN*	1009 Jackson St 57078	(605)665-7337	stjohns@iw.net stjpreschool.org		1992		N	EC	23

TENNESSEE

CITY	SCHOOL	ADDRESS	PHONE	EMAIL WEBSITE	PRINCIPAL/ ADMINISTRATOR	YEAR ORG.	RSO	NLSA	GRADES OFFERED	ENROLL
CHATTANOOGA	*BELVOIR*	800 Belvoir Ave 37412	(423)622-3755	dtopp@bcacademy.net www.bcalions.org	David W Topp	1887		N	EC-8	196
CLARKSVILLE	*GRACE*	2041 Madison St 37043	(931)647-6750	preschool@glctn.org	Linda Cribbs	2000			EC	72

R = Recognized Service Organization (RSO)
N = National Lutheran Schools Accreditation (NLSA)

SCHOOLS

CITY	SCHOOL	ADDRESS	PHONE	EMAIL WEBSITE	PRINCIPAL/ ADMINISTRATOR	YEAR ORG.	RSO	NLSA	GRADES OFFERED	ENROLL
COLLIERVILLE	*FAITH*	507 N Byhalia Rd 38017	(901)853-0050	flpfaithcollierville@gmail.com www.faithcollierville.com	Dina S Foshee	1994		N	EC	242
COLUMBIA	*TLC*	5001 Trotwood Ave 38401	(931)381-7843	tlcchildcare@trinitycolumbia.org www.trinitycolumbia.org	LaDonna Lyons	1986			EC	47
COOKEVILLE	*HEAVENLY HOST*	777A S Willow Ave 38501	(931)520-3766	eccmbrock@heavenlyhostlcms.org heavenlyhostlcms.org		1993			EC	121
CROSSVILLE	*SHEP LITTLE FLOCK*	1461 Sparta Hwy 38572	(931)707-0508	slf@sothmail.org www.shepherdcrossville.com	Sabrina Gunderson				EC	48
KNOXVILLE	*FIRST*	1207 Broadway St NE 37917	(865)524-0308	office@firstlutheranschool.com www.firstlutheranschooltn.com	Jessica M Irwin	1869		N	EC-8	144
MEMPHIS	*CHRIST THE KING*	5296 Park Ave 38119	(901)682-8405	ann.laury@ctkschool.com www.ctkschool.com	Ann Laury	1960		N	EC-8	182
	IMMANUEL	6319 Raleigh Lagrange Rd 38134	(901)388-0205	schooloffice@immanuelmemphis.org www.ilsmemphis.org	Michelle D Fischer	1947		N	EC-8	164
NASHVILLE	*OUR SAVIOR*	5110 Franklin Rd 37220	(615)833-1500	amy.waltz@oslanashville.org oslanashville.org	Amy W Waltz	1996			EC	101
TULLAHOMA	*FAITH*	900 Greenwood Ave. 37388	(931)393-2869	faithdaycare@lighttube.net www.faithtullahoma.org	Ruby D Brewer				EC	20
WARTBURG	*ST PAUL*	222 S Church St 37887	(423)346-3554	stpaulluthrn@highland.net		1981			EC	18
				TEXAS						
ABILENE	*ALL GOD'S CHILDREN*	2801 Antilley Rd 79606	(325)437-5437	sara@allgodschildrencdc.com www.zion-abilene.org	Sara R Shaw				EC	
AMARILLO	*CHRIST*	2400 N Coulter 79124	(806)351-0458	bilderback.rose@yahoo.com	Rose M Bilderback	2001			EC	
	TRINITY	5005 I-40 W 79106	(806)352-5620	principal@trinitylutheranschool.org www.trinitylutheranschool.org	Richard D Ryan	1948		N	EC-5	134
ARLINGTON	*GRACE*	308 W Park Row Dr 76010	(817)275-5131	lscott@grace.lc gracesaints.net		1982			EC	
AUSTIN	*BETHANY*	3701 W Slaughter Ln 78749	(512)615-4147	linda.shirley@bethanyaustin.com Bethanyaustin.com		2005			EC	
	MOUNT OLIVE	10408 Highway 290 W 78736	(512)288-2330	preschool@connectwithJesus.org mtolivepreschool.org		1991		N	EC	63
	REDEEMER	1500 W Anderson Ln 78757	(512)451-6478	cmueller@redeemer.net www.redeemerschool.net	Thomas W Geyer	1954		N	EC-8	555
	UPBRING	3407 Red River St 78705	(512)472-3313	audrey.walker@upbring.org www.upbring.org	Audrey Walker		R		EC-K	
BAYTOWN	*REDEEMER*	702 N 11th St 77520	(281)422-2252	redeemerccbaytown@gmail.com www.rlcbaytown.org	Rhonda Scott	2000			EC-5	
BEAUMONT	*REDEEMER*	4330 Crow Rd 77706	(409)892-2518	rlccdirector@yahoo.com	Carolyn Taylor	1990			EC	
BOERNE	*MESSIAH'S KIDS*	9401 Dietz Elkhorn 78015	(830)755-2460	ghuskey@messiahboerne.org messiahkidstx.org		2009		N	EC	157
BRENHAM	*GRACE*	1212 W Jefferson St 77833	(979)836-2030	schooloffice@glsbrenham.com www.glsbrenham.com/	Isaac S Schuller	1947			EC-12	104
BRYAN	*BETHEL*	4221 Boonville Rd 77802	(979)485-9835	preschool@blcbcs.org www.blcbcs.org	Shelly Schultz	2012			EC	
CARROLLTON	*PRINCE OF PEACE*	4004 Midway Rd 75007	(972)447-0532	school.receptionist@popcs.org www.popcs.org	Dr Jeremy R Lowe	1980	R	N	EC-12	749
CEDAR PARK	*KIDS KOUNT*	700 W Whitestone Blvd 78613	(512)258-7602	kheadley@gstx.org www.PathwaysChristianPreschool.com	Kelly Headley	1979			EC	
CISCO	*REDEEMER*	1711 Conrad Hilton Ave 76437	(254)442-1955	rclccisco@gmail.com		1997			EC	45
CLEBURNE	*NEXT GENERATION*	205 S Ridgeway Dr 76033	(817)645-9452	carrie@ascensioncleburne.org www.ascensioncleburne.org	Carrie Villalobos				EC-2	33
COLLEGE STATION	*HOLY CROSS*	1200 Foxfire Dr 77845	(979)777-5262	school@holycrossbcs.org www.holycrossbcs.org	Michelle Hafer				EC	
COLLEYVILLE	*CROWN OF LIFE*	6605 Pleasant Run Rd 76034	(817)251-1881	ssama@crownoflife.org www.colschool.org	Laura P Cleland	1995		N	EC-8	131
CORPUS CHRISTI	*LORD OF LIFE*	1317 Flour Bluff Dr 78418	(361)937-6414	director@lordoflifecorpuschristi.org lordoflifecorpuschristi.org		1991			EC	20
CYPRESS	*ST JOHN*	15237 Huffmeiser 77429	(281)304-5546	tbunker@stjohn.tv www.stjohn-lutheran.net	Tiffany Bunker	1982		N	EC	181
DALLAS	*BETHEL*	11211 E Northwest Hwy 75238	(214)348-8375	elcdirector@betheldallas.org www.bethelelc.com	Takanya Spencer	1959			EC	
	DALLAS LUTHERAN SCH	8494 Stults Rd 75243	(214)349-8912	office@dallaslutheranschool.com dallaslutheranschool.com	David J Bangert	1976	R	N	7-12	
	OUR REDEEMER	7611 Park Ln 75225	(214)368-1465	cmoss@ordallas.org ordallas.org	Dr Kara L Tobaben	1960		N	EC-6	242
	ZION	6121 E Lovers Ln 75214	(214)363-1630	jthorman@ziondallas.org www.ZLSdallas.org		1948		N	EC-8	296
DENTON	*ST PAUL*	703 N Elm St 76201	(940)387-6651	clc@splcdenton.org www.splcdenton.org		1977			EC	
EDNA	*ST PAUL*	108 E Gayle St 77957	(361)782-3364	stpaulpreschooltx@att.net	Debbie Littlefield				EC	75
EL PASO	*ASCENSION*	6520 Loma De Cristo Dr 79912	(915)691-4472	ascensionlutheranpreschoolelp@gmail.com www.alconnect.faith	Pamela Olivas	1964			EC	62
	ZION	2800 Pershing Dr 79903	(915)565-7999	ziondayschool@gmail.com	Nancy Cagann	1995			EC-K	
FARWELL	*LIFE IN CHRIST ACAD*	725 CR DD 79325	(806)825-2409	lifeinchristacademylariat@gmail.com	Tina Symm	1999			EC	14
FLOWER MOUND	*LAMB OF GOD*	1401 Cross Timbers Rd 75028	(972)539-0055	preschool@log.org www.log.org		1989		N	EC	104
FORT WORTH	*ST PAUL*	1800 West Fwy 76102	(817)353-2929	stpaul@sharingnewlife.com stpauleagles.org	Andrew M Montgomery	1969		N	EC-8	

R = Recognized Service Organization (RSO)
N = National Lutheran Schools Accreditation (NLSA)

CITY	SCHOOL	ADDRESS	PHONE	EMAIL WEBSITE	PRINCIPAL/ ADMINISTRATOR	YEAR ORG.	RSO	NLSA	GRADES OFFERED	ENROLL
FRIENDSWOOD	*TINY TREASURES*	1804 S Friendwood Dr 77546	(281)482-7943	tinytreasures@hope-lutheran.org www.hope-lutheran.org		1990			EC	
GEORGETOWN	*FAITH*	4010 Williams Dr 78628	(512)863-2634	director@flpreschool.com www.flpreschool.com	Angela Cummings	1996			EC	
	ZION	6101 FM 1105 78626	(512)863-5345	suzan.winkelman@zionwalburg.org www.zionwalburg.org	Suzan Winkelman	1882		N	EC-8	248
GIDDINGS	*IMMANUEL*	382 N Grimes St 78942	(979)542-3319	school@ilgtx.com www.ilgtx.com		1882		N	EC-8	134
GRANBURY	*CROSS TOWN*	1400 North Meadows Dr 76048	(817)776-2074	ctp1400@gmail.com www.OurSavior.us	Mary Strickland	2001			EC	
GUN BARREL CITY	*ST PETER*	130 Luther Ln 75156	(903)887-5077	stpeterpreschool@yahoo.com stpeterlcms.net		2005			EC	
HAMILTON	*ST JOHN*	122 Cheyenne Mesa 76531	(254)386-3332	stjohnlutheranpreschool@gmail.com stjohnhamilton.org		1999			EC-K	
HARLINGEN	*GREAT BEGINNINGS*	602 Morgan Blvd 78550	(956)425-6330	gb@splch.com stpaultexas.com	Carla Wisdom	1973			EC	
HASLET	*NEW CREATIONS*	1500 FM 156 South 76052	(817)439-2100	newcreationsprek@sbcglobal.net newcreationspreschool.com/	Mary Visaggio	2005			EC	
HOUSTON	*BRIGHT BEGINNERS*	14225 Hargrave Rd 77070	(281)469-2913	kim@stlhouston.org www.thirstyforjesus.org		1978			EC	
	CHRIST MEMORIAL	14200 Memorial Dr 77079	(281)497-2055	barb@christmemorialhouston.church www.christmemorialeclc.org/		1969		N	EC-K	185
	DAY ONE	18220 Upper Bay Rd 77058	(281)333-3323	svindas@dayonechristianacademy.org www.dayonechristianacademy.org	Shani Vindas	1980		N	EC	138
	EPIPHANY	14423 West Rd 77041	(713)896-1843	jfraker@elcsh.org www.epiphanylutheranschool.org	Jonathan D Fraker	1986		N	EC-8	183
	GETHSEMANE	4040 Watonga Blvd 77092	(713)688-8346	kim.a.perry@sbcglobal.com www.gethsemanelutheran.org		1992		N	EC	96
	IMMANUEL	1440 Cortlandt St 77008	(713)861-8787	ecesecretary@immanuelhouston.org immanuelhouston.org		1927		N	EC-K	56
	LEAH DOWNTOWN	1316 Washington Ave 77002	(832)301-3100	LEAHDowntown.org	Kathryn S Entzenberger	2021	R		EC	
	MEMORIAL	5800 Westheimer Rd 77057	(713)782-4022	rpaul@mlchouston.org www.memoriallutheranschool.org		1980		N	EC-12	
	MESSIAH	5103 Rose St 77007	(713)864-5394	messiahdirector@yahoo.com mlhouston.org		1982			EC	
	MOUNT OLIVE	10310 Scarsdale Blvd 77089	(281)922-4453	ece@mountolivehouston.org www.mountolivehouston.org	Bobbie A Ledbetter	1994			EC	
	OUR REDEEMER	215 Rittenhouse St 77076	(713)694-0332	paintbrush4@att.net www.alivewithchrist.org		1954			5-12	
	OUR SAVIOR	5000 W Tidwell Rd 77091	(713)290-8277	school@oslschool.org www.oslschool.org	Kate E Thoelke	1945		N	EC-8	343
	SOUTH	12555 Ryewater Dr 77089	(281)464-8299	info@lutheransouth.org www.lutheransouth.org	Scott D Browning	1949	R	N	EC-12	853
	ST ANDREW	1353-A Witte Rd 77055	(713)468-0026	ecc@standrew-lcms.org www.standrew-lcms.org		1992			EC	
	ST MARK	1515 Hillendahl Blvd 77055	(713)468-2623	hjerry@stmarkhouston.org www.stmarkhouston.org		1949		N	EC-8	508
	THE FAMILY OF FAITH	16710 FM 529 77095	(281)855-2950	cora@tfof.org www.thefamilyoffaith.org	Cora B Nash	2004			EC	
HUMBLE	*LAMB OF GOD*	1400 FM 1960 Bypass East 77338	(281)446-5262	office@lambofgod.net www.lambofgod.net	Greg Toth	1981			EC	
HUNTSVILLE	*FAITH*	111 Sumac Rd 77340	(936)291-1706	school@flshuntsville.org www.faithhuntsville.org	Cheryl G Bailes	1987		N	EC-4	158
HURST	*RED APPLE*	941 W Bedford Euless Rd 76053	(817)284-7833	lisaholley@redappleschool.org www.redappleschool.org	Lisa Holley	1966			EC-K	
KATY	*CROSSROAD*	700 Westgreen Blvd 77450	(281)945-5133	asanders@crosspt.org www.crosspt.org	Amy Sanders	2000		N	EC-K	233
	MEMORIAL	5815 4th St 77493	(281)391-0172	psdirector@mlckaty.com mlckaty.com	Linda Stahmer	1993		N	EC	140
KELLER	*LIGHT OF THE WORLD*	8750 N Riverside Dr 76244	(817)750-0442	liz@lotwchurch.org www.lotwchruch.org	Liz Homans	2001			EC-K	
	MESSIAH	1308 Whitley Rd 76248	(817)431-5486	schooloffice@mlcatexas.org www.mlcatexas.org		1993		N	EC-8	87
KILLEEN	*GRACE*	1007 Bacon Ranch Rd 76542	(254)441-5519	school@gracelcs.com www.glckilleen.com	Denise Pennington	1978			EC-K	55
KINGWOOD	*KIDS OF THE KINGDOM*	3803 W Lake Houston Pkwy 77339	(281)360-0288	tonib@christ4u.net www.christ4u.net	Toni Byrge	1992			EC-K	88
LA GRANGE	*MOUNT CALVARY*	800 N Franklin St 78945	(979)968-5913	preschool@mtcalvary-lcms.org www.mtcalvary-lcms.org	Janice Teinert	1981			EC	49
LUBBOCK	*HOPE*	5700 98th St 79424	(806)798-2747	hope@hopelubbock.com www.hopelubbock.com		1988			EC	212
MANSFIELD	*ST JOHN*	1218 E Debbie Ln 76063	(814)473-0303	preschool@stjohnmansfield.org www.stjohnmansfield.org	Sharon Johnson	1990			EC-K	147
MC ALLEN	*ST PAUL*	300 W Pecan Blvd 78501	(956)682-2345	schoolsecretary@stpaulmcallen.org www.stpaulmcallen.org/school		1943		N	EC-7	228
MCKINNEY	*OUR SAVIOR*	2708 W Virginia Pkwy 75071	(972)562-9944	florene.west@oslmckinney.org www.oursaviorpreschoolmackinney.com	Carolyn Schneider	1992			EC	
MERCEDES	*IMMANUEL*	703 W 3rd St 78570	(956)565-1518	immanuelmercedes@sbcglobal.net lutheranmercedes.com		1996			EC-5	

R = Recognized Service Organization (RSO)
N = National Lutheran Schools Accreditation (NLSA)

CITY	SCHOOL	ADDRESS	PHONE	EMAIL WEBSITE	PRINCIPAL/ ADMINISTRATOR	YEAR ORG.	RSO	NLSA	GRADES OFFERED	ENROLL
MIDLAND	*GRACE*	3000 W Golf Course Rd 79701	(432)694-3063	ecp@gracelutheranmidlandtx.org grace4yall.org		1982		N	EC-K	93
NAVASOTA	*TRINITY*	1530 East Washington 77868	(936)825-9244	preschool@tlcnavasota.com www.trinitynavasota.com	Betty J Discher	1997			EC	34
NEDERLAND	*HOLY CROSS*	2711 Helena Ave 77627	(409)722-2177	lutheran_ece@sbcglobal.net www.holycrosstexas.org	Kay Brown	1982			EC	
NEW BRAUNFELS	*CROSS*	2171 E Common St 78130	(830)625-3969	principal@crossnbtx.org crossnbtx.org		1973		N	EC-8	
NEWARK	*VICTORY IN CHRIST*	508 Main St 76071	(817)489-5400	schooloffice@viccla.org www.viccla.org		2010			K-2; 4-5; 9	
PEARLAND	*MOTHERS DAY OUT*	5515 W Broadway St 77581	(281)485-7896	mdo@epiphanypearland.org www.shiningthelight.org	Becky Broussard	1994			EC	
PFLUGERVILLE	*LITTLE HANDS GRACE*	19507 FM 685 78660	(512)720-8026	b.watson@littlehandsofgrace.com www.littlehandsofgrace.com	Brenda Watson	2016			EC	59
PLANO	*FAITH*	1701 E Park Blvd 75074	(972)423-7448	school@flsplano.org www.flsplano.org	Stephen W Kieser	1972		N	EC-12	
	MESSIAH LAMBS	1801 W Plano Pkwy 75075	(972)398-7560	amyers@messiahlutheran.com www.messiahlutheran.com	Amy C Myers	1961			EC-K	150
	ST PAUL	6565 Independence Pkwy 75023	(972)491-5443	barbshakal@yahoo.com		1995			EC	
RICHMOND	*WESTLAKE LUTHERAN*	23300 Bellaire Blvd 77406	(281)341-9910	stacey.walter@westlakelutheran.org westlakelutheran.org	Stacey M Walter	2008	R	N	EC-9	206
RIESEL	*TRINITY*	264 CR 143 76682	(254)896-7105	eclc@tlcriesel.org		1996			EC	
ROANOKE	*ST PETER*	15701 Cleveland Gibbs Rd 76262	(817)491-2015	info@stpeterfw.org www.stpeterfw.org	Jennifer Murff	2010			EC	61
ROUND ROCK	*KING OF KINGS*	17000 Smyers Ln 78681	(512)255-0446	clc@kingofkingstx.org www.kingofkingstx.org		1985			EC	
SAN ANGELO	*TRINITY*	3516 YMCA Dr 76904	(325)947-1275	trinityschool@tlcsanangelo.com trinityschoolsa.com	Ronald W Fritsche	1951		N	EC-12	185
SAN ANTONIO	*CHRIST OUR SAVIOR*	5323 Blanco Rd 78216	(210)733-9444	ececdir@grandecom.net christoursavior-sa.org	Rosalinda Sonnen-Kopecky	1998			EC	
	CONCORDIA	16801 Huebner Rd 78258	(210)479-1477	susank@concordia.cc concordia.school	Susan Kirby	1952		N	EC-8	463
	CROWN OF LIFE	19291 Stone Oak Pkwy 78258	(210)490-9860	preschool@crownoflifesa.org www.crownoflifesa.org		1984			EC	135
	KING OF KINGS	13888 Dreamwood Dr 78233	(210)656-6509	lisa.avila@sakingofkings.com www.sakingofkings.com	Lisa Avila	1975			EC-5	
	SHEP OF THE HILLS	6914 Wurzbach Rd 78240	(210)614-3741	school@shlutheran.org www.shlutheran.org	Katy Rohr	1979		N	EC-8	280
	ST PAUL	2302 S Presa St 78210	(210)534-8577	deborahs@stpaulsa.org		1913			EC	
SEALY	*TRINITY*	402 Atchison St 77474	(979)627-7846	preschool123@tlcsealy.org www.tlcsealy.org	Magdalena Kent	1992			EC	
SEGUIN	*GRACE*	935 E Mountain St 78155	(830)372-0641	secretary@graceseguin.org		1979			EC	
SERBIN	*ST PAUL*	1578 CR 211 78942	(979)366-2218	jhouse@stpaulserbinschool.org www.stpaulserbinschool.org	James L House	1856		N	EC-8	125
SMITHVILLE	*GRACE*	401 Wilkes 78957	(512)360-2800	gracelutheranlearn@att.net www.glcs.org		1992			EC	
SPRING	*RESURRECTION*	1612 Meadow Edge Ln 77388	(281)353-4415	christine@churchthatcares.org www.churchthatcares.org	Chrsitine Armstrong	1975			EC	
	TRINITY	18926 Klein Church Rd 77379	(281)376-5810	eagles@trinityklein.org www.trinityklein.org	Kerrie R Roesler	1874		N	EC-8	731
STEPHENVILLE	*FAITH SCHOOL*	3000 Northwest Lp 76401	(254)968-2344	Lauren.johnson@faithschoolstephenville. com www.faithlutheranstephenville.com					EC	
SUGAR LAND	*LITTLE FISHERS*	2011 Austin Pkwy 77479	(281)265-5656	linda@fishersofmen.org www.littlefisherspreschool.org		1996			EC	
TAYLOR	*TRINITY*	3505 N Main St 76574	(512)365-2381	trinitycdctaylor@gmail.com	Ginger Schneider	1996			EC	
THE WOODLANDS	*LIVING WORD*	9500 N Panther Creek Dr 77381	(281)363-2628	bev@lwlc.org www.lwlc.org	Beverly Childs	1998			EC	58
THORNDALE	*ST PAUL*	101 N 3rd St 76577	(512)898-2711	tiffanykirkwood@stpaulthorndale.com www.stpaulthorndale.com		1890		N	EC-8	173
TOMBALL	*SALEM*	22601 Lutheran Church Rd 77377	(281)351-8223	salemschool@salem4u.com www.salemlutheran.com	Dr Amy G Boatman	1853		N	EC-8	573
	ZION	911 Hicks St 77375	(281)255-6203	zionlutheranschool@yahoo.com ecc.ziontomballtx.org/		1935			EC	
TYLER	*TRINITY*	2001 Hunter St 75701	(903)593-7465	ecm@tlctyler.org www.tlctyler.org		1951		N	EC	90
VERNON	*ST PAUL*	4405 Hospital Dr 76384	(940)552-6651	spls.vernon@gmail.com	Amy Koch	1912			EC-K	
VICTORIA	*GRACE*	9806 NE Zac Lentz Pkwy 77904	(361)573-0867	office@gracelutheran-tx.org www.gracelutheran-tx.org	Stacey Aschenbeck				EC	
WYLIE	*VERITAS ACADEMY*	1345 E. FM 544 75098	(469)661-8002	jhotopp@veritasacademics.org www.veritasacademics.org	Jennifer Hotopp	2017			EC-11	

UTAH

CITY	SCHOOL	ADDRESS	PHONE	EMAIL WEBSITE	PRINCIPAL/ ADMINISTRATOR	YEAR ORG.	RSO	NLSA	GRADES OFFERED	ENROLL
RIVERTON	*CONCORDIA*	13249 S Redwood Rd 84065	(385)249-6739	admin@holytrinityut.org concordialearningcenter.holytrinityut.org/	Sarah A Earhart	2012		N	EC-6	82
SAINT GEORGE	*TRINITY*	2260 E Red Cliffs Dr 84790	(435)628-6115	office@trinitystgeorge.org trinitystgeorge.org	Duane M Nyen	1993		N	EC-7	36
SALT LAKE CITY	*REDEEMER*	1955 E Stratford Ave 84106	(801)487-6283	jjohnson@rlcs-slc.org www.rlcs-slc.org		1961		N	EC-8	51

R = Recognized Service Organization (RSO)
N = National Lutheran Schools Accreditation (NLSA)

CITY	SCHOOL	ADDRESS	PHONE	EMAIL WEBSITE	PRINCIPAL/ ADMINISTRATOR	YEAR ORG.	RSO	NLSA	GRADES OFFERED	ENROLL
SALT LAKE CITY	*ST JOHN*	475 Herbert Ave 84111	(801)364-4874	amanda@stjohnsccdc.org www.stjohnslutheranslc.org	Chaney Zinn	1997		N	EC	
SANDY	*GRACE*	1815 E 9800 S 84092	(801)572-3793	school@gracesandy.org www.gracesandy.org	Shelly A Davis	1984		N	EC-8	37

VIRGINIA

CITY	SCHOOL	ADDRESS	PHONE	EMAIL WEBSITE	PRINCIPAL/ ADMINISTRATOR	YEAR ORG.	RSO	NLSA	GRADES OFFERED	ENROLL
ALDIE	*VINE AND BRANCHES*	25615 Lennox Hale Dr 20105	(571)267-5900	frontdesk@vablc.org vineandbranches.school/	Natasha Jackson				EC	
ALEXANDRIA	*BETHANY*	2501 Beacon Hill Rd 22306	(703)765-8687	preschool@bethany-lcms.org www.blps-tots.com		1959			EC-1	
	IMMANUEL	109 Belleaire Rd 22301	(703)549-0155	school@immanuelalexandria.org ilsalexandria.org		1945		N	EC-8	148
	ST JOHN	5952 Franconia Rd 22310	(703)971-3581	ecec@sjlc.com sjlc.com/ecec	Stephanie Schillero	1983			EC	
ARLINGTON	*OUR SAVIOR*	825 S Taylor St 22204	(703)892-4846	office@osva.org www.osva.org	Joshua A Klug	1952		N	EC-8	149
ASHBURN	*OPEN ARMS*	43115 Waxpool Rd 20148	(703)729-9144	director@openarms-ccdc.org www.openarms-ccdc.org	Carrie A Jiridly	1999		N	EC	
CHESTERFIELD	*OPEN ARMS*	14851 Hull Street Rd 23832	(804)639-6248	director@thenewhope.com openarmschesterfield.com					EC	
FAIRFAX STATION	*LIVING SAVIOR*	5500 Ox Rd 22039	(703)352-4208	preschool@livingsaviorlutheran.org www.livingsaviorlutheran.org	Elizabeth Smith	1991			EC	
FALLS CHURCH	*ST PAUL*	7426 Idylwood Rd 22043	(703)573-0494	splpreschool@aol.com www.splpreschool.com	Melinda Cagle	1994			EC	
FREDERICKSBURG	*REDEEMER*	5120 Harrison Rd 22408	(540)376-7513	preschool@redeemerfxbg.org www.redeemerfxbg.org	Ellen Church	1994			EC	12
HERNDON	*GOOD SHEPHERD*	1133 Reston Ave 20170	(703)437-4511	preschool@gslcva.org www.gslcva.org	Susie Hardwick	1981			EC	
KING GEORGE	*PEACE*	5590 Kings Hwy 22485	(540)775-7529	pastor@peacekg.com www.peacekg.com	Johnna Seale	1975			EC	
LEESBURG	*CHRIST COMMUNITY*	818 S King St 20175	(571)223-6736	info@christcommunityleesburg.org christcommunityleesburg.org	Morgan Smallwood	2008			EC	137
MIDLOTHIAN	*GOOD SHEPHERD*	1401 Old Hundred Rd 23114	(804)897-0260	cashton@goodshepherdmidlo.com goodshepherdchild.com	Cathy Ashton	2009			EC-5	
NEWPORT NEWS	*RESURRECTION*	765 J Clyde Morris Blvd 23601	(757)596-5808	school@rlcnn.org www.rlcnn.org/school	Melanie Mesick	2001			EC	
NORTH CHESTERFIELD	*REDEEMER*	9400 Redbridge Rd 23236	(804)272-7824	chunter@redeemerric.org www.redeemercdc.org	Caycee Hunter	1971		N	EC	
RICHMOND	*TRINITY*	2315 N Parham Rd 23229	(804)270-5042	tlcrvapreschool@gmail.com www.tlcpreschool.org	Joanne Garner	1995			EC	
ROANOKE	*GOOD SHEPHERD*	1887 Electric Rd 24018	(540)774-8746	office@gslcp.org gslcp.org	Kathy Thomas	1990			EC	
SPRINGFIELD	*PRINCE OF PEACE*	8306 Old Keene Mill Rd 22152	(703)451-6177	school@poplc.org www.poplc.org/school	Lisa Wentzel	1969		N	EC-K	146
STAFFORD	*LIVING HOPE*	325 Courthouse Rd 22554	(540)657-4105	office@livinghopestafford.org www.livinghopestafford.org	Robin Stafford	2010			EC	
VIRGINIA BEACH	*HOPE*	5350 Providence Rd 23464	(757)424-4894	school@hopevabeach.org	Bev Yoakum	1987			EC-K	
	PRINCE OF PEACE	424 Kings Grant Rd 23452	(757)340-3033	school@princeofpeacevb.org princeofpeacevb.net	Alicia Mangels	1964			EC	59
WAYNESBORO	*BETHANY*	100 Maple Ave 22980	(540)941-8853	bethanyecec@bethanylcw.org bethanylcw.org	Jayme Wikinson	1878			EC	
WILLIAMSBURG	*KING OF GLORY*	4897 Longhill Rd 23188	(757)258-1070	school@kogva.org kogpk.org	Michelle Swain-Clauberg	1999		N	EC	144

WASHINGTON

CITY	SCHOOL	ADDRESS	PHONE	EMAIL WEBSITE	PRINCIPAL/ ADMINISTRATOR	YEAR ORG.	RSO	NLSA	GRADES OFFERED	ENROLL
ABERDEEN	*CALVARY*	2515 Sumner Ave 98520	(360)532-3980	calvary@techline.com www.calvarylutheranaberdeen.org		1983			EC	
BATTLE GROUND	*PRINCE OF PEACE*	14208 NE 249th St 98604	(360)687-2448	preschool@princeofpeacebg.com www.battlegroundpreschool.com		1990			EC-K	70
BELLEVUE	*ALL SAINTS*	5501 148th Ave NE 98007	(425)869-6487	preschool@allsaints-lcms.com allsaints-lcms.com	Paix Irigon	1993			EC	14
	JOY	10420 SE 11th St 98004	(425)454-4790	joy@joylutheranpreschool.org joylutheranpreschool.org/		1992			EC	
BELLINGHAM	*REDEEMER*	858 W Smith Rd 98226	(360)384-5923	office@redeemerbellingham.com		1978			EC	
	TRINITY	119 Texas St 98225	(206)734-2770	church@trinitybellingham.org www.trinitybellingham.org	Lisa Burgess	1970			EC	
BLAINE	*GRACE*	702 G St 98230	(360)332-6589	preschool@bglutheran.com blaine-grace-lutheran.org		1972			EC	
BREMERTON	*PEACE*	1234 NE Riddell Rd 98310	(360)373-2116	deisele@plsbremerton.org www.peacebremerton.org	Sheri Juszczak			N	EC-8	174
CHEHALIS	*PEACE*	2071 Bishop Rd 98532	(360)748-4108	Peacelc@yahoo.com	Katie Foss	1995			EC	
DEER PARK	*PRECIOUS LITTLE LAMB*	214 S Weber Rd 99006	(509)276-5268	pllambs@yahoo.com www.deerparkfaithlutheran.com	Kim A Ferrell	1986			EC	33
EAST WENATCHEE	*FAITH*	171 Eastmont Ave 98802	(509)888-3316	flp.laurar@gmail.com faithlutheranpreschoolewen.com	Laura L Rosentrater	2009			EC	
FEDERAL WAY	*LIGHT OF CHRIST*	2400 SW 344th St 98023	(253)874-3506	preschool@thelight.org www.thelight.org	Judi Potter	1992			EC	24
	ST LUKES	515 S 312th St 98003	(253)941-3000	church@stlukes-church.com www.stlukes-church.com	Mary Schuldheisz	1968			EC-K	85

R = Recognized Service Organization (RSO)
N = National Lutheran Schools Accreditation (NLSA)

CITY	SCHOOL	ADDRESS	PHONE	EMAIL WEBSITE	PRINCIPAL/ ADMINISTRATOR	YEAR ORG.	RSO	NLSA	GRADES OFFERED	ENROLL
KENMORE	ARROWHEAD INGLEMOOR	16450 Juanita Dr NE 98028	(425)488-9800	janis@epiphanyonline.org	Janis Armfield	1986			EC	
KENNEWICK	BETHLEHEM	2505 W 27th Ave 99337	(509)582-5624	principal@blcbls.org www.blcbls.org	Eric D Haan	1911		N	EC-8	245
KENT	PEACE	18615 SE 272nd St 98042	(253)631-5876	preschool.peace@comcast.net peacecovington.org	Kathleen Qualey	1992			EC	29
	SUNBEAMS	23810 112th Ave SE 98031	(253)854-3240	office@sunbeamslutheranschool.com www.sunbeamslutheranschool.com	Denise J Pacilli	1978		N	EC-5	74
LACEY	FAITH	7075 Pacific Ave SE 98503	(360)491-1733	administrator@flschool.org www.flschool.org	Ann Ashe	1971		N	EC-8	150
LAKE STEVENS	ZION SNOHOMISH CTY	3923 103rd Ave SE 98258	(425)334-5064	office@zionls.org www.zionls.org	Peter D Martin	2002	R	N	EC-8	
MALTBY	SHEPHERD OF THE HILL	9225 212th St SE 98296	(360)668-7881	preschool.soth@gmail.com		1986			EC	
MILTON	BEAUTIFUL SAVIOR	2306 Milton Way 98354	(253)922-6977	preschool@mybslc.com www.mybslc.com		1980			EC	
MONROE	LITTLE DOVES	202 Dickinson St 98272	(360)794-7230	littledovespreschool@gmail.com www.littledovespreschool.com	Linda Herman	1986			EC-K	36
MOUNT VERNON	TLC	301 S 18th St 98273	(360)421-0800	teacherjulie@tlcmv.com tlcmv.com		2003			EC	167
PORT ANGELES	ST MATTHEW	132 E 13th St 98362	(360)457-4122	stmatthewlutheranpreschool@gmail.com	Sara Reed	1983			EC	8
PROSSER	MESSIAH	823 Luther Ln 99350	(509)786-2011	messiahprosseer@gmail.com messiahprosser.com		1993			EC	
PULLMAN	CONCORDIA	1765 NE Lower Dr 99163	(509)332-2830	preschool@concordiapullman.org concordiapullman.org/preschool					EC	34
PUYALLUP	IMMANUEL LEARNING	720 W Main 98371	(253)848-4548	Michelle@oslc.com oslc.com	Michelle Barger	1995			EC	59
RENTON	RENTON PREP	200 Mill Ave S Ste 110 98057	(206)723-5526	drzimmerman@rentonprep.org www.rentonprep.org	Dr Michelle R Zimmerman	1968			EC-10	
SEABECK	EVERGREEN	3200 Seabeck Holly Rd 98380	(360)830-4180	evergreenlutheranpreschool@yahoo.com www.seabecklutheran.com		1995			EC	37
SEATTLE	BEAUTIFUL SAVIOR	16919 33rd Ave S 98188	(206)246-9533	beautifulsaviorls@gmail.com		1993			EC	
	CONCORDIA	7040 36th Ave NE 98115	(206)525-7407	admin@concordiaseattle.com www.concordiaseattle.com	Christine C Malone	1905	R	N	EC-8	
	HOPE	4456 42nd Ave SW 98116	(206)935-8500	kokabayashi@hopeseattle.org www.hopeseattle.org		1959		N	EC-8	
SEQUIM	FAITH	354 W Cedar St 98382	(360)681-7126	faithlutheranpreschool@hotmail.com www.flcsequim.org		1994			EC	
SHELTON	MOUNT OLIVE	206 E Wyandotte Ave 98584	(360)427-3165	daycaremolc@comcast.net www.mtoliveshelton.org	Margarete C Dohring	1996			EC	31
SPOKANE	BEAUTIFUL SAVIOR	4320 S Conklin St 99203		school@beautifulsaviorspokane.org www.beautifulsaviorschool.org	Jennifer Stewart	1970			EC-K	61
	MEADOWLANE	5810 S Meadowlane Rd 99224	(509)327-4441	bookkeeper@sjlspokane.org www.meadowlanechristian.com	Jolee Wilke	1902	R		EC	
	REDEEMER	3606 S Schafer Rd 99206	(509)926-6363	ebarton@redeemeralive.org redeemeralive.org		1965			EC-K	51
	SON SHINE	7307 N Nevada St 99208	(509)483-4218	secretary@holycrosslcms.net www.sonshineearlychildhoodcenter.com		1991			EC	10
SUNNYSIDE	CALVARY	804 S 11th St 98944	(509)837-6771	Calvary_lc@hotmail.com www.calvarylutheranchurchsunnyside.org		1979			EC	25
TACOMA	CONCORDIA	202 E 56th St 98404	(253)475-9513	cindy.bowers@ccatacoma.org www.concordiachristianacademy.org	Sherrie L Gibelyou	1939	R	N	K-12	218
	GOOD SHEP LITTLE LAM	140 E 56th St 98404	(253)474-4214	preschool@goodshepherdluth.com www.littlelambstacoma.com	Bonnie J Huset	2005		N	EC	
	OUR SAVIOR	4519 112th St E 98446	(206)531-2112	lissa@oslc.com www.oslc.com		1972			EC	14
VANCOUVER	GRACE	9900 E Mill Plain Blvd 98664	(360)254-0663	childcare@gracevancouver.org www.gracelutheranchildcare.org	Judy L Scriven	1984		N	EC	25
	ST JOHN	11005 NE Highway 99 98686	(360)574-4900	director@stjohnschildcare.com www.stjohnlc.com		1979			K-3	
WENATCHEE	ST PAULS	312 Palouse 98801	(509)662-4757	office@stpaulslutheranschool.com www.stpaulslutheranschool.com	Tara Breidert	1978			EC-9	136
YAKIMA	MOUNT OLIVE	7809 Tieton Dr 98908	(509)966-2190	info4me@mountoliveyakima.org mountoliveyakima.org		1992			EC	

WISCONSIN

CITY	SCHOOL	ADDRESS	PHONE	EMAIL WEBSITE	PRINCIPAL/ ADMINISTRATOR	YEAR ORG.	RSO	NLSA	GRADES OFFERED	ENROLL
ALTOONA	LITTLE STAR	2245 Hayden Ave 54720	(715)832-1513	krystina.littlestar@gmail.com www.altoonalittlestar.com	Krystina E Schumacher	1993			EC	
ANTIGO	PEACE	300 Lincoln St 54409	(715)623-2200	p.thompson@peaceantigo.org peaceantigo.org	Paul A Thompson	1888		N	EC-8	
APPLETON	CELEBRATION	3100 E Evergreen Dr 54913	(920)734-8218	school@celebrationlutheran.net www.celebrationlutheran.net	Sarina Randazzo	1998	R	N	EC-8	91
	FAITH	601 E Glendale Ave 54911	(920)739-7772	fccoffice@faithchildcare.com www.faithchildcare.com		1989			EC	
ARLINGTON	ST PETER	303 Park St 53911	(608)635-4825	stpeterluth@gmail.com stpetersarlington.org	Tiffany Amoriello	1994			EC-5	29
ASHLAND	LITTLE FRIENDS JESUS	1114 12th Ave West 54806	(715)682-6075	lfoj@zionashland.com lfoj.org		1991			EC	
ATHENS	ST JOHN	486 County Rd F 54411	(715)536-1810	childcare@trinityathens.net		1994			EC	
	TRINITY	301 Elm St 54411	(715)257-7559	principal@trinityathens.com www.trinityathens.net	Dean D Frick	1901		N	EC-8	110

R = Recognized Service Organization (RSO)
N = National Lutheran Schools Accreditation (NLSA)

CITY	SCHOOL	ADDRESS	PHONE	EMAIL WEBSITE	PRINCIPAL/ ADMINISTRATOR	YEAR ORG.	RSO	NLSA	GRADES OFFERED	ENROLL
BARABOO	*OUR SAVIOR*	1120 Draper St 53913	(608)355-0852	oskidsadm@gmail.com www.oskidswi.com	David Zins	2000			EC	
BARRON	*SALEM*	1360 E Lasalle Ave 54812	(715)537-3011	salembarron@gmail.com		1982			EC	46
BERLIN	*ST JOHN*	146 Mound St 54923	(920)361-0555	school@stjohnberlin.org www.stjohnberlin.org	Melissa Linse	1867		N	EC-8	84
BONDUEL	*ST PAUL*	240 E Green Bay St 54107	(715)758-8532	a.landgrave@stpaulbonduel.com www.stpaulbonduel.com	Aaron M Landgrave	1863		N	EC-8	192
BROOKFIELD	*IMMANUEL*	13445 Hampton Rd 53005	(262)781-7140	aamling@immanuelbrookfield.org www.immanuelbrookfield.org	Jennifer Comfort	1950		N	EC-8	431
BURLINGTON	*IN HIS ARMS*	417 S Kane St 53105	(262)763-3883	IHA.LEARNING@GMAIL.COM www.oursaviorburlington.com	Linda Wingreen	1995			EC	61
CEDARBURG	*FIRST IMMANUEL*	W67N622 Evergreen Blvd 53012	(262)377-6610	filsprincipal@fils.org www.filschool.org	Joel Bahr	1853		N	EC-8	456
CHIPPEWA FALLS	*FAITH*	733 Woodward Ave 54729	(715)723-7754	faithcp733@gmail.com www.faithlutherancf.org/	Tresa J Juedes	1978			EC	
CLINTONVILLE	*ST MARTIN*	100 S Clinton Ave 54929	(715)823-6538	stmlc.org	Emily J Ferg	1886		N	EC-8	207
COLBY	*ZION*	301 N 2nd St 54421	(715)223-2166	daycare@zionlutheranchurchcolbywi.com www.zionlutheranchurchcolbywi.com		1981			EC	21
CUDAHY	*ST JOHN*	4850 S Lake Dr 53110	(414)482-0554	stjdaycare@yahoo.com www.stjohncudahy.org		1970			EC	46
DE PERE	*ANGELS OF HOPE*	700 S Superior St 54115	(920)336-9843	preschool@hopedepere.org www.hopedepere.org					EC	
DELAVAN	*OUR REDEEMER*	416 W Geneva St 53115	(262)728-6589	kanclam@orlcs.org www.orlcs.org	Kenneth A Anclam	1983		N	EC-8	89
EAST TROY	*GOOD SHEPHERD*	1936 Emery St 53120	(262)642-3310	gslschool@wi.rr.com www.gslet.org	Elizabeth M Clonkey	1980			EC-8	35
EAU CLAIRE	*REDEEMER*	601 Fall St 54703	(715)835-5528	twensel@ecasd.k12.wi.us www.redeemereauclaire.com	Terri Wensel	1976			EC	
	SHEPHERDS FOLD	601 Fall St 54703	(715)835-9314	daycare@epiphanyec.org					EC	
FALL CREEK	*ST PAUL*	721 S State St 54742	(715)877-3501	littlelambs.fallcreek@yahoo.com littlelambschildcare.org	Kathleen J Heinkel	1991			EC	
FOND DU LAC	*HOPE*	260 Vincent St 54935	(920)922-5130	Lschell@lifeathope.org www.lifeathope.org/preschool.html		1982			EC	
FREDONIA	*ST JOHN*	824 Fredonia Ave 53021	(262)692-2734	stjohnpreschool824@gmail.com www.stjohnfredonia.org		1991			EC	65
FREMONT	*ST PAUL*	107 Tustin Rd 54940	(920)446-3633	kdelwiche@stpaulfremontwi.org stpaulfremontwi.org	Nancy Bleck	1998			EC	30
GLENDALE	*ST JOHNS*	7877 N Port Washington Rd 53217	(414)352-4150	principal@stjohnglendale.com stjohnglendale.com	Jennifer Comfort	1888		N	EC-8	110
GRAFTON	*ST PAUL*	701 Washington St 53024	(262)377-4659	info@splgrafton.org www.splgrafton.org	Michael J Yurk	1851		N	EC-8	379
GREEN BAY	*FAITH*	2335 S Webster Ave 54301	(920)965-0795	faithpreschoolgb@gmail.com faithpreschoolgb.com		1993	R	N	EC	
	GREEN BAY TRINITY	120 S Henry St 54302	(920)655-4673	principal@greenbaytrinity.org www.greenbaytrinity.org	Kerrick P Sawyer	2003	R	N	EC-8	145
	OUR SAVIOUR	120 S Henry St 54302	(920)468-4065	joanne@oslc-gb.org www.oslc-gb.org		1977			EC	16
	PILGRIM	1731 Saint Agnes Dr 54304	(920)965-2244	joshsommermeyer@pilgrimluth.org www.pilgrimluth.org	Duane E Miller	1981		N	EC-8	321
GREENFIELD	*OUR FATHERS*	6023 S 27th St 53221	(414)282-7500	nwang@ourfatherslutheran.org www.ofls.org	Robert A Cahill Sr	1964		N	EC-8	177
GREENLEAF	*ALLELUIA BLESS CHILD*	6725 Elmro Rd 54126	(920)532-3892	alleluia.office@gmail.com alleluiawrightstown.org	Asby Cafleur				EC	39
	ZION OF WAYSIDE	8374 County Rd W 54126	(920)864-2468	school@zionwayside.org www.zionwayside.org	David G Gosa			N	EC-8	159
GREENVILLE	*HILLSIDE*	N1615 Meadowview Drive 54942	(920)757-5722	hillsidecooperativepreschool@gmail.com www.shepherdhills.org		1977			EC-K	
HALES CORNERS	*HALES CORNERS*	12300 W Janesville Rd 53130	(414)529-6701	ckogutkiewicz@hcl.org hclschools.org		1960		N	EC-8	
	JOURNEYS	5425 S 111th St 53130	(414)461-8500	info@journeyslutheran.org www.journeyslutheran.org	Jenny Stollenwerk	1986	R	N	3-12	111
HARTLAND	*DIVINE REDEEMER*	31385 W Hill Rd 53029	(262)367-3664	janet.bahr@drlc.org www.drlc.org	Janet L Bahr	1980		N	EC-8	538
HILBERT	*TRINITY*	N6081 W River Rd 54129	(920)853-3134	office@trinityrantoul.org www.trinityrantoul.org	Tanya J Johnson	1867		N	EC-8	62
	TRINITY	N6079 W River Rd 54129	(920)853-7142	daycare@trinityrantoul.org	Debbie L Kline			N	EC-4	21
HORICON	*ST STEPHEN*	505 N Palmatory St 53032	(920)485-6687	ststeph@ststephen-lcms.org www.ststephen-lcms.org	Amy M Rupnow	1864		N	EC-8	52
HOWARDS GROVE	*TRINITY*	W2776 Hwy 32 53083	(920)565-3669	preschool@trinityhowardsgrove.org www.trinityhowardsgrove.org		1990			EC	
HUDSON	*TRINITY*	1205 6th St 54016	(715)386-9349	ajohnson@trinityhudson.org www.trinityacademyofhudson.org	Alison Johnson	1977			EC-8	352
JACKSON	*LIVING WORD*	2240 Living Word Ln 53037	(262)677-9774	tamara.breckenfelder@mylivingword.com www.mylivingword.com	Kelly Patterson	2002			EC	139
JANESVILLE	*ST PAULS*	210 S Ringold St 53545	(608)754-4471	schooloffice@stpaulsjanesville.com www.stpaulsjanesville.com	James W Kroll	1865		N	EC-8	241
LADYSMITH	*ST JOHN*	515 College Ave W 54848	(715)532-5780	stjohnladysmith@centurylink.net		1987			EC	10
LEBANON TOWNSHIP	*LEBANON*	N 534 County Rd R 53098	(920)925-3791	lebanon.llsoffice@gmail.com llsedu.org	Hannah Walters	1985		N	EC-6	49

R = Recognized Service Organization (RSO)
N = National Lutheran Schools Accreditation (NLSA)

CITY	SCHOOL	ADDRESS	PHONE	EMAIL WEBSITE	PRINCIPAL/ ADMINISTRATOR	YEAR ORG.	RSO	NLSA	GRADES OFFERED	ENROLL
LUXEMBURG	ST PAUL	N4118 County Rd AB 54217	(920)845-2095	secretary@stpaullux.org www.stpaullux.org		1884		N	EC-8	94
MADISON	LIVING CHRIST	110 N Gammon Rd 53717	(608)829-3598	pserbus@living-christ.org www.living-christ.org		1990			EC	37
MADISON	MT OLIVE	110 N Whitney Way 53705	(608)238-5656	Atroia@molconline.org www.molc.us	Andrea Troia	1987			EC	6
MANAWA	ST PAUL	750 Depot St 54949	(920)596-2815	stplschl@wolfnet.net www.stpaulmanawa.org		1891		N	EC-8	108
MANITOWOC	REDEEMER	1712 Menasha Ave 54220	(920)684-3989	preschool@redeemermanty.com www.redeemermanty.com		1988			EC	40
MARINETTE	FAITH	4009 Irving St 54143	(715)732-9903	flpmarinette@gmail.com faithmarinette.org	Cindy Nickerson	1984			EC	11
MARSHFIELD	IMMANUEL	604 S Chestnut Ave 54449	(715)384-5121	info@immanuelmarshfield.org www.immanuelmarshfield.org	Dr Karen E Bahn	1886		N	EC-8	
MAYVILLE	IMMANUEL	N8076 Cty Hwy AY 53050	(920)387-5363	admissions@immanuelmayville.com www.immanuelmayville.com		1854			EC-7	57
	ST JOHNS	520 Bridge St 53050	(920)387-4310	principal@stjohnsmayville.com www.stjohnsmayville.com	Heather A Staedler	1892		N	EC-8	197
MENASHA	TRINITY	300 Broad St 54952	(920)886-1083	kgerue@trinitymenasha.com trinitymenasha.com	Keith E Ge Rue	1945			EC-8	60
MENOMONEE FALLS	GRACE	N87W16173 Kenwood Blvd 53051	(262)251-7140	schooloffice@gracemenomoneefalls.org www.grace-connect.org	Nicole Schmidt	1963		N	EC-8	237
	ZION	N48 W18700 Lisbon Rd 53051	(262)781-7437	plorenz@zioninthefalls.org www.zioninthefalls.org	Peter J Lorenz	1883		N	EC-8	79
MEQUON	TRINITY	10729 W Freistadt Rd 53097	(262)242-2045	trinity@trinityfreistadt.com trinitymequon.org/school/	Dr Cassandra L Tarr	1839		N	EC-8	445
MERRILL	ST JOHN	1104 E 3rd St 54452	(715)536-7264	schooloffice@stjohnmerrill.org www.stjohnmerrill.org	Kathleen M Hahn	1883		N	EC-8	188
	TRINITY	611 W Main St 54452	(715)536-7501	scott.johnson@tlsmerrill.com www.trinitymerrill.org	Scott R Johnson	1886		N	EC-8	154
MILWAUKEE	BEAUTIFUL SAVIOR	3205 N 85th St 53222	(414)292-0740	Lunak@swd.lcms.org swd.lcms.org/LNS/	Robert E Lunak				K-9	11
	COVENANT	8121 W Hope Ave 53222	(414)438-9712	covenantkids1@sbcglobal.net covenantlutheranmke.com		1995			EC	
	GRANVILLE	8242 N Granville Rd 53224	(414)354-6601	meinzer@luminschools.org www.granvillelutheran.org	Nicole Zick-Washington	2005	R	N	EC-8	241
	MOUNT CALVARY	2862 N. 53rd St 53210	(414)873-3466	thoward@mtcalvaryschool.org mtcalvary-mke.org		1925	R	N	EC-8	212
	MOUNT OLIVE	5301 W Washington Blvd 53208	(414)774-2200	erin.ballard@mtolivemke.org mtolivemke.org/cds	Stephen M Rosebrock	1950		N	EC-8	139
	NORTHWEST	4119 N 81st St 53222	(414)463-4040	sirmons@northwestlutheran.org www.northwestlutheran.org	Takeyla Sirmons	1957	R	N	EC-8	275
	ST PETER-IMMANUEL	7801 W Acacia St 53223	(414)353-6800	www.schoolspi.org	Stacey L Luehring	1973	R	N	EC-8	173
NEENAH	NEW HOPE	1850 American Dr 54956	(920)725-8797	nhcs@newhopeconnect.org www.nhcsneenah.org	Laurie M Prewitt	1991			EC-8	261
NEW BERLIN	BLESSED SAVIOR	15250 W Cleveland Ave 53151	(262)786-6465	jleinss82@gmail.com www.blessedsaviorwi.org		1990			EC	59
	LITTLE LAMBS-PEACE	17651 W Small Rd 53146	(262)679-1441	preschool@peacelutheran.org www.peacelutheran.org	Laurie A Kieliszewski	1989			EC	
NORTH PRAIRIE	ST JOHN	312 N Main St 53153	(262)392-9334	ps-dcdirector@stjohnsnp.org www.stjohnsnp.org	Catherine McNeil-Reinke	1987			EC	34
OAK CREEK	GRACE	8537 S Pennsylvania Ave 53154	(414)762-3655	school@graceoakcreek.org www.graceoakcreek.org	Steven D Gettelman	1980		N	EC-8	111
	GRACE	3381 E Puetz Rd 53154	(414)762-8755	eccdirector@graceoakcreek.org graceoakcreek.org	Rachel Miliacca	1999			EC	84
OCONOMOWOC	ST PAUL	210 E Pleasant St 53066	(262)567-5001	school@splco.org splco.org	Jill M George	1877		N	EC-8	127
OMRO	GRACE	720 Jackson Ave 54963	(920)685-2621	graceomro@att.net graceomro.com		1988			EC	
ONALASKA	SHEPHERDS FLOCK	1215 Redwood St 54650	(608)781-9445	shepherdsflockonalaska@gmail.com www.sothonalaska.org	Page Nickell	1982			EC	20
OSHKOSH	TRINITY	819 School Ave 54901	(920)235-1730	school@trinityoshkosh.org trinityoshkosh.org	Joseph M Reinl	1856		N	EC-8	36
PLYMOUTH	ST JOHN	222 N Stafford St 53073	(920)893-5114	office@sjlplymouth.com www.sjlseagles.com	Dean J Lindsey Jr	1864		N	EC-8	197
PORT WASHINGTON	LUTHERAN CLASSICAL	217 N Freeman Dr 53074	(262)284-2131	lutheranclassicalacademy.com	Richard M Gaub				K-8	
PORTAGE	ST JOHNS	430 W Emmett St 53901	(608)742-9000	kwinkelmann@stjohns.portage.com www.stjohnsportage.com	Kristine M Winkelmann	1865		N	EC-8	142
RACINE	PRINCE OF PEACE	4340 6 Mile Rd 53402	(262)639-1277	poppscc.racine@gmail.com www.princeofpeaceracine.com	Carla Abel	1978			EC	50
	RENAISSANCE	6150 Taylor Ave 53403	(262)554-6768	gordon@rlschools.org www.luminschools.org	Tiffany Vanegas		R	N	EC-8	426
	ST JOHN	510 Kewaunee St 53402	(262)633-2758	jntpesch7@gmail.com www.stjohnsracine.org	Janet M Pesch	1863		N	EC-8	244
	TRINITY	2065 Geneva St 53402	(262)632-1766	pamling@trinityracine.com www.trinityracine.com		1905		N	EC-8	239
RANDOM LAKE	ST JOHN	W5407 Hwy Ss 53075	(920)994-9190	principal@sjrl.org www.stjohnrandomlake.org	Marla R Kipp	1855		N	EC-8	31
REEDSBURG	ST PETER	345 N Pine St 53959	(608)524-4066	stpetersreedsburg@gmail.com stpetersreedsburg.com/	Beth N Bierlein	1867		N	EC-8	302

R = Recognized Service Organization (RSO)
N = National Lutheran Schools Accreditation (NLSA)

SCHOOLS

CITY	SCHOOL	ADDRESS	PHONE	EMAIL WEBSITE	PRINCIPAL/ ADMINISTRATOR	YEAR ORG.	RSO	NLSA	GRADES OFFERED	ENROLL
RICE LAKE	*FIRST*	15 E Sawyer St 54868	(715)234-7505	kidsatfirst@firstlutheranricelake.com www.firstlutheranricelake.com		1995			EC	
SHAWANO	*ST JAMES*	324 S Andrews St 54166	(715)524-4213	principal@stjamesshawno.org stjames-shawano.org	David A Kaiser	1889		N	EC-8	289
SHEBOYGAN	*BETHLEHEM*	1121 Georgia Ave 53081	(920)452-5071	infoschool@ourbethlehem.com www.ourbethlehem.com	Patrick R Vanic	1890		N	EC-8	158
SHEBOYGAN	*ST PAUL*	1819 N 13th St 53081	(920)452-6882	ann.blasczyk@stpaulsheboygan.org www.stpaulsheboygan.org		1889		N	EC-8	65
	TRINITY	824 Wisconsin Ave 53081	(920)458-8248	principal@trinitysheboygan.org www.trinitysheboygan.org	Dr Jenna R Roeske	1853		N	EC-8	191
SHEBOYGAN FALLS	*ST PAUL*	730 County Rd PPP 53085	(920)467-6733	preschool@stpaulfalls.com stpaulfalls.com/ecc/		1986			EC	57
SPOONER	*FAITH*	W7148 Luther Rd 54801	(715)635-2261	spoonerflps@gmail.com	Erin Burch	1984			EC	
STEVENS POINT	*ST PAUL*	1919 Wyatt Ave 54481	(715)344-5660	office@splpoint.com splpoint.com		1955		N	EC-8	204
STURTEVANT	*CONCORDIA*	8500 Durand Ave 53177	(262)884-0991	office@concordialutheranschool.net www.concordialutheranschool.net	Jeannine L Klein	1970	R	N	EC-8	237
SURING	*ST JOHN*	8945 Saint Johns Rd 54174	(920)842-4443	stjohns@stjohnlutheranhayes.org www.stjohnlutheranhayes.org/		1886			EC-8	58
SUSSEX	*PEACE*	W240 N6145 Maple Ave 53089	(262)246-3200	office@peacesussex.org www.peacesussex.org	Brennick T Christiansen	1995			EC-8	23
WALES	*BETHLEHEM*	470 N Oak Crest Dr 53183	(262)201-4092	preschool@bethlehemfamily.org www.LearningAtBethlehem.com		1989			EC	35
WATERFORD	*ST PETERS*	145 S 6th St 53185	(262)534-6066	www.stpeterswaterford.com	Kimberly M Trieglaff	1991			EC	12
WATERTOWN	*FAITH*	626 Milford St 53094	(920)261-8060	schooloffice4faithlutheran@gmail.com	Judi G Hoeppner	1988			EC-5	
	GOOD SHEPHERD	1611 E Main St 53094	(920)261-2579	www.goodshepherdwi.org	Amy R Gromowski	1983		N	EC-8	194
WAUKESHA	*BEAUTIFUL SAVIOR*	1205 S East Ave 53186	(262)542-2496	jwolff@bsl-school.org www.beautifulsaviorwaukesha.org	Jennifer Wolff	1986		N	EC-8	94
	CHRIST THE LIFE	3031 Summit Ave 53188	(262)547-7315	ECoffice@christthelife.com www.christthelife.com	Julie C Bushre	1997			EC	33
WAUPUN	*IN HIS HANDS*	315 S Madison St 53963	(920)324-3321	ihhpreschool@pellalutheran.org www.pellalutheran.org		1997			EC	
WAUSAU	*ST JOHN*	164923 Co Hwy Z 54403	(715)842-5212	school.secretary@stjohnofwausau.org www.stjohnofwausau.org	Mary J Prahl	1920		N	EC-8	
	ST MARK	600 Stevens Dr 54401	(715)848-5511	cpage@stmarkslcms.org stmarkslcms.org	Carolyn K Zielinski	1973			EC	71
	TRINITY	501 Stewart Ave 54401	(715)848-0166	info@trinitynet.org www.trinitywausau.org		1908		N	EC-8	165
WAUWATOSA	*PILGRIM*	6717 W Center St 53210	(414)259-0190	springer@cuspilgrim.org www.luminschools.org	Kimberly Springer		R	N	EC-8	258
	WAUWATOSA	10025 W North Ave 53226	(414)258-4558	school@orlctosa.org www.orlctosa.org	Trevor E Timm	1931		N	EC-8	104
WEST ALLIS	*ST PAULS*	7821 W Lincoln Ave 53219	(414)541-6251	principal@splcwa.org www.splswa.com	Danielle R Jackson	1926		N	EC-8	155
WEST BEND	*ST ANDREW*	7750 State Rd 144 N 53090	(262)335-4200	st.andrewecc@gmail.com standrewecc.square.site		1997			EC	20
	ST JOHN	899 S 6th Ave 53095	(262)429-1061	njanisse@stjohnswestbend.org www.stjohnswestbend.org		2003		N	EC	127
	ST JOHNS	899 S 6th Ave 53095	(262)334-3077	office@sjswb.org www.stjohnswestbend.org	James R Van Dellen	1872		N	EC-8	403
WESTFIELD	*LITTLE LAMBS*	302 S Charles St 53964	(608)296-2088	LittleLambs@ielcw.net		2004			EC	5
WESTON	*MOUNT OLIVE*	6205 Alderson St 54476	(715)359-5546	melissa@mtoliveweston.org www.mtoliveweston.org		1976			EC	
WEYAUWEGA	*CHRIST*	N6412 State Rd 49 54983	(920)867-3263	secretary@christlutheranwestbloomfield.com www.christlutheranwestbloomfield.com		1873			EC-8	20
WISCONSIN DELLS	*TRINITY*	728 Church St 53965	(608)253-3241	office@trinitydells.org www.trinitydells.org	Kyle M Motzkus	1958			EC-6	26
WISCONSIN RAPIDS	*IMMANUEL*	111 11th St N 54494	(715)423-0272	bbetts@immanuelrapids.com www.immanuelrapids.com	Brian J Betts	1884		N	EC-8	198
	ST LUKE	2011 10th St S 54494	(715)423-5990	preschool@stlukeslutheran.com www.stlukeslutheran.com		1972		N	EC	39

WYOMING

CITY	SCHOOL	ADDRESS	PHONE	EMAIL WEBSITE	PRINCIPAL/ ADMINISTRATOR	YEAR ORG.	RSO	NLSA	GRADES OFFERED	ENROLL
CASPER	*MOUNT HOPE*	2300 Hickory St 82604	(307)234-6865	mounthopecasper@aol.com www.mounthopecasper.com	Andrew P Richard	1984			K-12	85
CHEYENNE	*OUR SAVIOR*	5101 Dell Range Blvd 82009	(307)632-2580	preschool@oursaviorcheyenne.org www.oursaviorcheyenne.org	Laurie S Anderson	1963			EC	
	TRINITY	1111 E 22nd St 82001	(307)635-2802	finance@trinitycheyenne.org www.trinitycheyenne.org	John C Preus				EC-12	
CODY	*CHRIST THE KING*	1207 W Stampede 82414	(307)587-5774	prekdirector@ctkcody.org ctkcody.org	Stacey Grenz	1987			EC	34
POWELL	*IMMANUEL*	675 Avenue D 82435	(307)899-2310	ilcoffice3168@gmail.com www.immanuellutheranpowellwy.org		1992			EC	18
RIVERTON	*TRINITY CLASSICAL*	419 E Park Ave 82501	(307)857-5710	lutheran@wyoming.com tlsriverton.org	Stephen W Kieser	1991		N	EC-8	45
SHERIDAN	*MARTIN LUTHER*	1325 Burton St 82801	(307)674-6434	immanuellutheran82801@gmail.com sheridanmlgs.blogspot.com		2003			K-8	27

R = Recognized Service Organization (RSO)
N = National Lutheran Schools Accreditation (NLSA)

AUXILIARIES

Auxiliaries are organizations described in and subject to the conditions set forth in section 6.1 of the Bylaws of The Lutheran Church—Missouri Synod. Listing of an auxiliary organization in *The Lutheran Annual* is not a guarantee on the part of the Synod for the fiscal solvency of the auxiliary or any financial responsibility for such organization or for services expressly or impliedly offered.

International Lutheran Laymen's League

Lutheran Hour Ministries International Headquarters
Phone: (314) 317-4100
660 Mason Ridge Center Drive
St. Louis, MO 63141
Website: lhm.org

Chairman: Kurt Senske
Vice-Chairman: Donald Scifres
Secretary: Linda Arnold
Treasurer: Kirk Farney
Pastoral Advisor: Rev Tom Pfotenhauer

Board of Directors:
Karl Abraham
Linda Arnold
Melanie Braun
Ryan Bredow
Jim Dankenbring
Mark Duesenberg
Kirk Farney
Heidi Hove
Vincent James
Virginia Miller
Donald Scifres
Kurt Senske
Gordon Tresch

Staff Members:
CEO:
Kurt Buchholz
Chief Research & Innovation Officer:
Anthony Cook
Global Chief Administrative Officer:
Lara Heisohn-Sidorski
Global Chief Ministry Officer:
Karin Semler
Managing Director, Lutheran Laymen's League—Canada:
Lisa Jackson
The Speaker of The Lutheran Hour:
Michael Zeigler

District Presidents:
California-Nevada-Hawaii: Glen Butler
Capital: Yvette Moy
Central Illinois: James Blessman, Jr.
Eastern: Steven Klafehn
Grand Canyon: Gale Cynova
Indiana: Richard Hoffmann
Iowa East: Richard Hoelz
Iowa West: John Tews
Kansas: Joseph Chretien
Lone Star: T.C. Lipe
Michigan: Dennis Engelhard
Mid-Atlantic: Mark Dunlop
Minnesota North: David Gilster
Minnesota South: Doyle Benson
Missouri: Richard Schmidt
New England: Paul Martin
North Dakota: Kirk Rosin
North Wisconsin: Neal Schalow
Ohio: Eldon Gerken
Oregon: Darrel Nagel
South Wisconsin: Mark Roeder
Southern California: Richard Gast
Tennessee: Ray Musgrave
Utah-Idaho: Dale Bentley
Washington-Alaska: David Dybwad

Lutheran Women's Missionary League

Phone: (800) 252-LWML (5965)
General Office
801 Seminary Place. Ste L 010
St. Louis, MO 63105
Email: lwml@lwml.org
Website: lwml.org

President: Eden Keefe
Vice President of Christian Life:
Shari Miller
Vice President of Communication:
Linda Guteres
Vice President of Gospel Outreach:
Anne Hartman
Vice President of Organizational Resources:
Arlene Naasz
Vice President of Special Focus Ministries:
Karol Selle
Recording Secretary: Dianna Just
Treasurer: Nila Rodriguez
Sr. Pastoral Counselor: Mark Maas
Jr. Pastoral Counselor: Michael Schmidt
Meeting Manager: Leslie Colligan
PR Director: Debbie Yocky
Strategic Plan Facilitator: Cheryl Mattil

District Presidents:
Atlantic: Raquel Rojas
California-Nevada-Hawaii: Roxan Schwab
Carolinas: Paula Daniels
Central Illinois: Cheryl Long
Chesapeake: Christine Maconachy
Eastern: Dee Grzyb
English: Carol Klein
Florida-Georgia: Elizabeth Borth
Gulf States: Cherie Endrihs
Indiana: Sarah Rippy
Iowa East: Martha Hartwig
Iowa West: Penny Schuessler
Kansas: Elaine Engelman
Louisiana-Mississippi: Leslie Koenck
Michigan: Ruth Steele
Mid-South: Sandie Harjala
Minnesota North: Kathy Brandt
Minnesota South: Lisa Kamrath
Missouri: Marian Hoehner
Montana: Cheryl Stensrud
Nebraska North: LaDonna Stanosheck
Nebraska South: Vicky Van Velson
New England: Dr. June Merwin
New Jersey: Arlene Price
North Dakota: Alissa Arndt
North Wisconsin: Joan Berquist
Northern Illinois: Gayle Thanepohn
Ohio: Karen Shanahan
Oklahoma: Lori Steele
Oregon: Debbie Weaver
Pacific Southwest: Nancy Heredia
Rocky Mountain: Shelly Stewart
SELC: Carol Miksad
South Dakota: MaryJo Stier
South Wisconsin: Cinda Poppe
Southern Illinois: Carol Walther
Texas: Sally Krueger
Utah-Idaho: Terri Bentley
Washington-Alaska: Carolyn Holbrook
Wyoming: Terri Denniston

RECOGNIZED SERVICE ORGANIZATIONS

Recognized Service Organizations (RSOs) are organizations described in and subject to the conditions set forth in Bylaw 6.2 of the Synod Bylaws. The Lutheran Church—Missouri Synod makes no representations or guarantees about the fiscal solvency or financial responsibility of any recognized organization or for any services expressly or implicitly offered by it. The RSOs are listed by the type of services they provide. RSOs not listed here are included in other sections, including Schools and Retreat Centers and Summer Camps.

Organization Contact Name	Address City State Zip	Phone	Email Website

Communication Organizations

Organization Contact Name	Address City State Zip	Phone	Email Website
Crucial Productions Peter Slayton, Executive Director	1208 Holgate Dr Manchester, MO 63021	(815) 603-0209	peter@crucialproductions.org crucialproductions.org
IRIS Lending Library for the Blind Inc (dba: Lutheran Library for the Blind) Julia Neimes, President	5543 Fort Caroline Rd Jacksonville, FL 32277	(904) 404-8504	info@irisllb.org irisllb.org
Lutheran Ministries Media Inc DBA Worship Anew Matthew Leighty, Executive Director	5 Martin Luther Dr Fort Wayne, IN 46825	(260) 471-5683	info@worshipanew.org worshipanew.org

Educational Organizations

Organization Contact Name	Address City State Zip	Phone	Email Website
Concordia Catechetical Academy Inc Peter Bender, President	W240N6145 Maple Ave PO Box 77 Sussex, WI 53089	(262) 246-3200	info@lutherancatechesis.org lutherancatechesis.org
Concordia Deaconess Conference Jillene Houser, President	PO Box 247 Hamel, IL 62046	(402) 679-5265	cdcpresidentofficial@gmail.com concordiadeaconess.org
David's Harp: A Center for Musical Development Trey Stickler, Director of Operations	239 Frank St Council Bluffs, IA 51503	(712) 322-4729	admin@davidsharpmusic.org davidsharpmusic.org
Friends of Pioneer Inc DBA Pioneer of the Lake Rachel Petrick, Executive Director	9324 Lake Shore Rd Angola, NY 14006	(716) 383-6157	president@pioneeronthelake.com pioneeronthelake.com
High Impact Movement, Inc Amos Gray, Director of Family Engagement	200 Oakwood Ave Hot Springs, AR 71913	(501) 693-8232	him.inc2018@gmail.com highimpactinc.org
Immanuel Lutheran Church Child Care Center Darla Strege, Director	PO Box 509 Hankinson, ND 58041	(701)242-7668	ilcchildcarecenter@gmail.com
Little Hands Loving Hearts CDC Ann Mutzenberger-Willoughby, Board President	c/o Our Savior Lutheran Church 3705 11th St SW Minot, ND 58701	(701) 852-5454	lhlh@srt.com
Lutheran Education Association Jonathan Laabs, Executive Director	7400 Augusta St River Forest, IL 60305	(708) 209-3343	lea@lea.org lea.org
Lutheran Education Association of Houston R Scott Fogo, Executive Director	225 E Edgewood Dr Friendswood, TX 77546	(281) 617-5189	scott.fogo@leahschools.org leahschools.org
Lutheran Elementary School Association Elizabeth Gutberlet, CEO	11123 South Towne Square Ste F Saint Louis, MO 63123	(314) 200-0790	info@lesastl.org lesastl.org
Lutheran School Services Organization Inc DBA The Lutheran Schools Partnership Kevin Creutz, Executive Director	1601 St Joe River Fort Wayne, IN 46805	(260) 203-4500	admin@tlspartnership.org thelutheranschools.org
Lutheran Special Education Ministries (LSEM) Stacy McGhee, CEO	3773 Geddes Rd Ann Arbor, MI 48105	(248) 419-3390	lsem@luthsped.org luthsped.org
Lutheran Urban Mission Initiative Inc Shaun Luehring, President/CEO	8242 N Granville Rd Milwaukee, WI 53224	(414) 354-5126	luehring@luminschools.org luminschools.org
National Association of Directors of Christian Education Maria Davenport, Board Chairperson	505 S Kirkwood Rd Saint Louis, MO 63122	(509) 939-4866	nadce2013@gmail.com nadcewildapricot.org

Organization Contact Name	Address City State Zip	Phone	Email Website
National Lutheran Outdoors Ministry Association Inc John Busch, President	22750 Lind Ave Waterville, MN 56096	(918) 822-7405	president@nloma.org nloma.org
S.O.S. Center Inc Lydia Beasley, Executive Director	4620 W North Ave Milwaukee, WI 53208	(414) 449-9964	lydia@bba-accountant.com soscenterinc.org
St Johns College Alumni Association Larry Junker, Executive Director	PO Box 376 Winfield, KS 67156	(620) 221-1572	sjcaa1@cox.net stjohnsalumni.org
The Body of Christ and the Public Square Christopher Thoma, Executive Director	PO Box 119 Hartland, MI 48353	(810) 423-8591	revthoma@bocps.org bodyofchristandpublicsquare.org
The Chicagoland Lutheran Educational Foundation Janet Klotz, Executive Director	861 S Church Rd Bensenville, IL 60106	(630) 595-9310	clef@clefchicago.org clefchicago.org
The Consortium for Classical and Lutheran Education, Inc Stephen Kieser, President/Board Chairman	610 East Park Avel Riverton, WY 82501	(307) 851-0670	pastorkieser@gmail.com ccle.org
Western Heritage Lutheran Academy (WHLA) Paul Skrbac, Treasurer	PO Box 2080 Riverton, WY 82501	(307)240-4154	western_heritage@yahoo.com whla.us
Wittenberg Academy Inc J. Justin Benson, President	1103 Winona St SE Chatfield, MN 55923	(855) 362-3634	mrbenson@wittenbergacademy.org wittenbergacademy.org

Mission Organizations

Organization Contact Name	Address City State Zip	Phone	Email Website
ACTS 1:8 Ministry Incorporated Jeff Van Beaver, President	2145 S Oneida St Green Bay, WI 54304	(920) 494-2289	jeffvanbeaver@acts18.org acts18.org
All Nations Society of Atlanta	1155 N Highland Ave NE Atlanta, GA 30306	(615) 477-8461	ansamission.org
Ambassadors of Reconciliation Dwight Schettler, President	PO Box 81662 Billings, MT 59108	(844) 447-2671	dwight@aorhope.org aorhope.org
Amigos Ministries of SWFL Inc DBA Pelican Ministries of SW FL Mark Eisold, Sr Pastor	5800 Golden Gate Pkwy Naples, FL 34116	(239) 455-2520	pastormarknaples@gmail.com pelicancommunitycenter.org
Applerus US Inc DBA WORDrus Andrew Bartelt, President	8619 Grantwood Trails Ct Saint Louis, MO 63123	(314) 255-6114	bartelta@csl.edu wordrus.org
Arabic Lutheran Ministries (ALM) Abjar Bahkou, Executive Director	1565 Summer Chase Lane Fenton, MO 63026	(817) 680-1794	frabjarbahkou@gmail.com arabiclutheranministries.org
Belize Mission Society Cathy Dulgar, Executive Director	2822 Karr Rd Belvidere, IL 61008	(815) 979-7288	director@belizemissionsociety.net belizemissionsociety.net
Capstone Ministries Inc Daniel Schmelzer, Director	PO Box 2080 Oakdale, CA 95361	(860) 306-6111	capstoneministries@gmail.com capstoneministries.org
Central Ohio Lutheran Immigrant Mission (COLIM) Berhanu Arsse, Executive Director	PO Box 182 Galena, OH 43021	(614) 377-8350	arsseber@gmail.clom colim.us
Chinese Lutherans in Mission Building (CLIMB) Steve Law, Vice Chairman	550 Hancock St Quincy, MA 02170	(617) 773-5482	steve@wlchurch.org climb-lutheran.org
Christian Friends of New Americans Stanish Stanley, Executive Director	5515 S Grand Blvd Saint Louis, MO 63111	(314) 351-1740	mail@cfna-stl.org cfna-stl.org
Christian Senior Ministries Inc Carol-Joy Motisi, President	511 Russell Rd DeKalb, IL 60115	(630) 664-8005	cj.cmsc@gmail.com
Confessional Lutherans for Christ's Commission Inc Rob Jarvis, Executive Director	1202 Folsom St Boulder, CO 80302	(763) 280-4904	pastor@universitylutheranchapel.com theclcc.org
Eritrean Evangelical Lutheran Mission Society in North America Eskender Abraham, Chairperson	5900 Balcones Dr, Ste 100 Austin, TX 78731	(909) 609-7717	4eelms@gmail.com eelms.org
Evangelical Lutheran Mission Society for the Chinese Inc Michael Paul, Chairman	100 E Michigan St Evansville, IN 47711	(812) 455-0241	elmsc9@gmail.com lutheranchinese.org

Organization Contact Name	Address City State Zip	Phone	Email Website
Family Shield Ministries Inc Mark Frith, Board Chairman	PO Box 8571 Saint Louis, MO 63126	(314) 772-6070	witnesstofamily@gmail.com familyshieldministries.com
Higher Things Inc Crysten Sanchez, Executive Director of Operations	PO Box 175 Lisbon, IA 52253	(888) 482-6630	info@higherthings.org higherthings.org
Hmong Mission Society Lang Yang, President	PO Box 143 Richville, MI 48758	(989) 239-4758	hmongmissionsociety@gmail.com hmongmissionsociety.org
International Student Ministry Inc Sue Hasselbring, Ministry Catalyst	c/o Ascension Lutheran Church 5347 Donovan Ave Saint Louis, MO 63109	(715) 869-6460	isminc@isminc.org isminc.org
John 1334 Ministries DBA La Mesa Ministries Rick McClellan, Executive Director	425 Greenfield Rd Gilbert, AZ 85264	(480) 590-4622	rick@lamesaministries.org lamesaministries.org
LAMP Ministry Inc Steve Schave, Executive Director	PO Box 480167 New Haven, MI 48048	(800) 307-4036	office@lampministry.org lampministry.org
Lead a Child Society Philip Frusti, Executive Director	13145 S Black Bob Rd Olathe, KS 66062	(979) 702-0925	executivedirector@leadachild.org leadachild.org
LINC Ministries Intl Inc Ben Griffin, CEO	800 Houston Ave Houston, TX 77007	(713) 426-2451	info@linc.org linc.org
Lutheran Bible Translators Inc Richard Rudowske, Executive Director	PO Box 789 Concordia, MO 64020	(660) 225-0810	info@lbt.org lbt.org
Lutheran Braille Workers Inc Dr. Robert Hartwell, CEO	PO Box 5000 Yucaipa, CA 92399	(909) 795-8977	rob@lbwloveworks.org lbwloveworks.org
Lutheran Campus Mission Association Curt Dwyer, Chair	444 Abbot Rd East Lansing, MI 48823	(517) 332-0778	contact@golcma.org golcma.org
Lutheran Deaf Mission Society Edwin Bergstresser, Executive Director	PO Box 434038 Saint Louis, MO 63143	(614) 429-1351	LDMS@deafjesus.org deafjesus.org
Lutheran Heritage Foundation Matthew Heise, Executive Director	51474 Romeo Plank Rd Macomb, MI 48042	(800) 554-0723	info@lhfmissions.org lhfmissions.org
Lutheran Hispanic Missionary Institute Rodrigo Fernandez, Executive Director	420 Thunderbird Dr Ste E El Paso, TX 79912	(915) 275-4155	rfernandez@missionaryinstitute.org www.missionaryinstitute.org
Lutheran Latino Ministries Pam Bridgehouse, President	PO Box 293 Mount Angel, OR 96362	(503) 930-0386	lutheranlatinoministries@gmail.com lutheranlatinoministries.org
Lutherans in Jewish Evangelism Inc DBA Burning Bush Kevin Parviz, Executive Director	6327 Clayton Ave Saint Louis, MO 63139	(314) 645-4456	revkevye@aol.com lije.org
Ministry in Mission Jaclyn Rychel, President	13442 Shady Ln Chesterland, OH 44026	(440) 463-0594	jackie@ministryinmission.org ministryinmission.org
Mission Opportunities Short Term—MOST Ministries Martin Moro, Executive Director	655 Phoenix Dr Ann Arbor, MI 48108	(734) 994-7909	most@mostministries.org mostministries.org
Muslims for the Messiah DBA The Messiah for Muslims Hesham Shehab, President	405 Rush St #1 Roselle, IL 60172	(331) 645-0650	pastorheshamshehab@gmail.com messiahformuslims.org
Ongoing Ambassadors for Christ Inc Martin Herzberg, Executive Director	PO Box 712 Greenville, IL 62246	(618) 664-4056	oafcdirector@gmail.com oafc.org
Philadelphia Lutheran Ministries Inc Robert Kieselowsky, Executive Director	PO Box 15155 Philadelphia, PA 19130	(215) 992-9102	info@phillyministries.org phillyministries.org
Pittsburgh Area Lutheran Ministries Adam Thompson, President	535 N Neville St Pittsburgh, PA 15213	(412) 407-3306	directors@palmpa.org palmpa.org
Rural Gospel Initiative Ray Larson, President	214 SW 7th Ave Aberdeen, SD 57401	(605) 225-1847	rclarson@nrctv.com ruralgospel.org
Saint Philip Lutheran Mission Society Jesse Burns, President	301 South Main St Ventura, IA 50482	(641) 829-3650	pastorburns10@protonmail.com splms.org

Organization Contact Name	Address City State Zip	Phone	Email Website
Siberian Lutheran Mission Society Inc Robert Kiefer, Secretary/Treasurer	c/o Ascension Lutheran Church 8811 St Joe Rd Fort Wayne, IN 46835	(260) 438-1385	bobkiefer51@gmail.com siberianlutheranmissions.com
Springfield Lutheran Student Center Inc	848 S National Springfield, MO 65804	(417) 866-5543	director@thelsc.org thelsc.org
The Apple of His Eye Mission Society Steve Cohen, Founder	2349 Candle Ridge Trl Georgetown, TX 78626	(636) 326-4040	steve.cohen@appleofhiseye.org appleofhiseye.org
The Garuna Foundation Jeff Ehlers, Chairman	11034 N 36th St Phoenix, AZ 85028	(602) 765-7613	jeff@garuna.org garuna.org
The Saint Timothy Society Gordon Bynum, Chaplain	2355 Fairview Ave #326 Roseville, MN 55113	(307) 242-5400	info@sainttimothysociety.org sainttimothysociety.org
The Summit Mission Alliance Lawrence McGurer Jr, Executive Director	PO Box 3314 Breckenridge, CO 80424	(303) 902-6370	larry@summitmissionalliance.org summitmissionalliance.org
The Wyneken Project Inc Elliott Robertson, President	100 W Henrietta St Baltimore, MD 21230	(443) 745-9200	wynekenproject@gmail.com wynekenproject.org
University Lutheran Chapel of Hope Inc Michelle May, Ministry Director	PO Box 1465 Cape Girardeau, MO 63702	(636) 795-5747	lutheranchapelofhope@gmail.com
University Lutheran Ministry Association Hanna Elsey, Director	3815 E 17th St N Wichita, KS 67208	(316) 684-5224	info@fairmountministries.org fairmountministries.org
Warrensburg Lutheran Campus Ministry Inc Jon-Michael Schweigert, Pastor/Director	215 S Holden St Warrensburg, MO 64093	(660) 747-7603	ucmlutherans@gmail.com ucm-lsc.org

Camps

Information is listed in the Retreat Centers and Summer Camp section of *The Lutheran Annual*. See pages 876–77

Schools

Information is listed in the Directory of High School and Junior High Schools and Directory of Early Childhood Schools and Elementary Schools sections of *The Lutheran Annual*. See pages 803–06 and 810–50

Social Ministry Organizations-Headquarters

Name Contact	Address City State Zip	Phone	Email Website
A Place of Refuge Ministries of South Wisconsin Inc Grace Rao, Executive Director	PO Box 240695 Milwaukee, WI 53224	(414) 438-2767	apor.ministries.swd@gmail.com aplaceofrefuge.org
AAA Academy for Children Inc Larry Chenault, Board President	49 Flanders Bartely Rd #114 Flanders, NJ 07836	(973) 970-5696	Larrydc99@cs.com aaaacademyforchildren.org
Amboss Inc Jerry Winegarden, Chairman	429 E DuPont Road #57 Fort Wayne, IN 46825	(260) 295-1714	hello@ambossinc.org ambossinc.org
Amigos En Cristo Inc DBA Amigos Center Lindsay Ray, Executive Director	1560 Matthew Dr Ste A Fort Myers, FL 33907	(239) 274-0401	ray@amigoscenter.org amigoscenter.org
Bethany Lutheran Home Chandra Gustafson, Administrator	7 Elliott St Council Bluffs, IA 51503	(712) 328-9500	gustafson@blhs.care blhs.care
Bethesda Lutheran Disability Ministries Karen Carter, President	W18054 Stuve Rd Whitehall, WI 54773	(608) 864-3310	kseecarter@gmail.com
Camp RD Inc DBA Camp Restore Detroit Amy Fanta, Executive Director	PO Box 5577 Detroit, MI 48205	(313) 636-4422	detroit@camprestore.org camprestore.org
Cedar Lake Inc Rick Davis, CEO	9901 Linn Station Rd Ste 901 Louisville, KY 40223	(502) 495-4944	rdavis@cedarlake.org cedarlake.org
College Hill Foundation Fred Kimbrough, President	2141 East John Saint Louis, MO 63107	(314) 330-6414	fredkimbrough@gmail.com collegehillfoundation.org
Compass Facilities Inc Andrew Neumann, President/CEO	20935 W Swenson Dr Ste 101 Waukesha, WI 53186	(262) 542-9546	andrew.neumann@openskyeducation.org openskyeducation.org
Concordia Center for the Family Todd Biermann, Executive Director	3773 Geddes Rd Ann Arbor, MI 48105	(888) 553-5133	office@concordiafamily.org concordiacenterforthefamily.org
Concordia Counseling: A Lutheran Outreach Ministry Inc Michelle Downey, Executive Director	504 N Walnut St Seymour, IN 47274	(812) 671-8704	michelledowney@concordiacounseling.org concordiacounseling.org
Concordia Lutheran Ministries Keith Frndak, President/CEO	134 Marwood Rd Cabot, PA 16023	(724) 352-1571	kfrndak@concordialm.org concordialm.org
Crest View Corporation DBA Crest View Senior Communities Gabrielle Anderson, Interim CEO	4444 Reservoir Blvd NE Columbia Heights, MN 55421	(763) 782-1645	administration@crestviewcares.org crestviewcares.org
Cross Connections Inc Kirk Reber, Executive Director	4618 E State Blvd Ste 300 Fort Wayne, IN 46815	(260) 373-0213	kirkreber@crossconnectionscounseling.com crossconnectionscounseling.com
Dakota Boys and Girls Ranch Joy Ryan, President/CEO	PO Box 5007 Minot, ND 58702	(701) 839-7888	info@dakotaranch.org dakotaranch.org
DOXOLOGY: The Lutheran Center for Spiritual Care and Counsel Beverly Yahnke, Executive Co-Director	3415 Tall Oaks Dr Brookfield, WI 53045	(262) 955-0822	byahnke@doxology.us doxology.us
eliseo Brian MacDuff, Executive Director	1301 N Highlands Pkwy Tacoma, WA 98406	(253) 752-7112	bmacduff@eliseo.org eliseo.org
Ephphatha Lutheran Mission Society Brant Engel, President	1860 Korte St Hartland, MI 48353	(248) 980-5741	baecoach@comcast.net elms-deaf.org
Fellowship Square Foundation Inc Christy Zeitz, CEO	11260 Roger Bacon Dr Ste 20 Reston, VA 20190	(703) 860-2536	czeitz@fellowshipsquare.org fellowshipsquare.org
Florida-Georgia Lutheran Early Response Inc Joel Mathews, Board Chair	2021 W State Road 426 Oviedo, FL 32765	(321) 300-6794	jmathews@fgler.org fgler.org

Name Contact	Address City State Zip	Phone	Email Website
Forged by Fire Services Inc Paul Ernewein, Director/President	766 Fair Hill Loop Covington, LA 70433	(985) 607-4332	forgedbyfireservices@gmail.com FBF501C3.com
Franklin Avenue Mission Shannon Liddell, Business Manager	2210 N Franklin Ave Flint, MI 48506	(810) 285-9598	hansenclaudia49@hotmail.com franklinavemission.org
Good Friend Ministries Mark Hannemann, Executive Director	1994 Carroll Rd Traverse City, MI 49686	(231) 590-8527	mark@goodfriendministries.org goodfriendministries.org
Good Shepherd Lutheran Home of Sauk Rapids MN DBA Good Shepherd Community Michael Stordahl, President/CEO	1115 4th Ave N Sauk Rapids, MN 56379	(320) 252-6525	michaelstordahl@gsc-mn.org goodshepherdcampus.org
GracePoint Institute for Relational Health Mark Hannemann, President	1510 Q. St Lincoln, NE 68508	(402) 614-6287	mark@relationalhealth.org relationalhealth.org
Graceworks Lutheran Services Judy Budi, President/CEO	6430 Inner Mission Way Dayton, OH 45459	(937) 433-2140	information@graceworks.org graceworks.org
Humanitri Lorri Holtgrieve, Executive Director	PO Box 6512 Saint Louis, MO 63125	(314) 772-7720	l.holtgrieve@humanitri.org humanitri.org
Immigrant Mission Field Network Inc Matthew Buse, Executive Director	8811 St Joe Rd Fort Wayne, IN 46835	(260) 305-7444	immigrantmissionfieldnetwork@gmail.com immigrantmissionfieldnetwork.wildapricot.org
Inspiritus Inc John Moeller, CEO	731 Peachtree St NE Ste B Atlanta, GA 30308	(404) 875-0201	john.moeller@weinspirit.org weinspirit.org
KingsPath Senior Ministries Inc Greg Fictum, President	504 W Juneau Ave Milwaukee, WI 52303	(612) 963-6845	gfictum@speroseniorliving.org speroseniorministries.org
Liberty Lutheran Services Luanne Fisher, President/CEO	7002 Butler Pike Ambler, PA 19002	(267) 464-7700	lfisher@libertylutheran.org libertylutheran.org
Luther Care Services Mary Woolson, Executive Administrator	1555 Hull Ave Des Moines, IA 50316	(515) 262-5639	mwoolson@lutherparkcommunity.org lutherparkcommunity.org
Lutheran Association for Developmentally Disabled Inc Susan Lichtenthal, President	646 N French Rd Ste 3 Amherst, NY 14228	(716) 631-9212	s.lichtenthal@lssofny.org
Lutheran Care Center Corporation Emily Miller, Administrator	702 W Cumberland Rd Altamont, IL 62411	(618) 483-6136	emily@altamontlcc.org altamontlcc.org
Lutheran Child and Family Services of IN/KY Inc Sven Schumacher, CEO	1525 N Ritter Ave Indianapolis, IN 46219	(317) 359-5467	sschumacher@lutheranfamily.org lutheranfamily.org
Lutheran Child and Family Service of Michigan DBA Wellspring Lutheran Services David Gehm, President/CEO	2825 Wieneke Rd Saginaw, MI 48603	(989) 652-3470	info@wellspringlutheran.com wellspringlutheran.com
Lutheran Church Charities Christopher Singer, President/CEO	3020 Milwaukee Ave Northbrook, IL 60062	(866) 455-6466	lcc@lutheranchurchcharities.org lutheranchurchcharities.org
Lutheran Community Home, Inc Karyn Fleetwood, Executive Director	111 W Church Ave Seymour, IN 47274	(812) 522-5927	kfleetwood@lutherancommhome.org lutherancommhome.org
Lutheran Counseling and Family Services of WI Carol Flanary, CEO	3800 N Mayfair Rd Wauwatosa, WI 53222	(414) 536-8333	reception2@lcfswi.org lcfswi.org
Lutheran Counseling Services Inc Megan Meissler, Executive Director	1505 Orchid Ave Winter Park, FL 32789	(407) 644-4692	admin@lcsfl.com lcsfl.com
Lutheran Development Group Inc Christopher Shearman, Executive Director	3100 Chippewa St Saint Louis, MO 63118	(314) 396-6800	ldg@ldgstl.org ldgstl.org
Lutheran Disaster Care Inc David Ricks, President	5901 New York Ave Arlington, TX 76018	(214) 563-5298	dricks@lutherandisaster.care lutherandisaster.care
Lutheran Family & Children's Services of Missouri Charles Duggar, President/CEO	9666 Olive Blvd Ste 400 Saint Louis, MO 63132	(314) 787-5100	MikeD@lfcs.org lfcsmo.org
Lutheran Family Service Max Phillips, Executive Director	409 Kenyon Rd Ste C Fort Dodge, IA 50501	(515) 573-3138	info@lutheranfamilyservice.org lutheranfamilyservice.org

Name Contact	Address City State Zip	Phone	Email Website
Lutheran Family Services of Colorado DBA Lutheran Family Services Rocky Mountains James Horan, President/CEO	1035 Osage St Ste 700 Denver, CO 80204	(303) 922-3433	james.horan@lfsrm.org lfsrm.org
Lutheran Family Services of Nebraska Inc Christopher Tonniges, President/CEO	7929 W Center Rd Omaha, NE 69144	(402) 342-7038	chris.tonniges@onelfs.org oneLFS.org
Lutheran Foundation of Saint Louis Matthew Miller, President/CEO	8860 Ladue Rd 200 Ste 200 Saint Louis, MO 63124	(314) 231-2244	info@lutheranfoundation.org lutheranfoundation.org
Lutheran Haven Inc Jerry Griffing, President/CEO	2041 W State Rd 426 Oviedo, FL 32765	(407) 365-5676	jgriffing@lutheranhaven.org lutheranhaven.org
Lutheran Homes Inc DBA Lutheran Life Villages Alex Kiefer, President/CEO	6701 S Anthony Blvd Fort Wayne, IN 46816	(260) 447-1591	akiefer@lutheranlifevillages.org lutheranlifevillages.org
Lutheran Homes of Michigan Inc—DBA Wellspring Lutheran Services David Gehm, President/CEO	2825 Wieneke Rd Saginaw, MI 48603	(989) 652-3470	info@wellspringlutheran.com wellspringlutheran.com
Lutheran Homes Society Inc. DBA Genacross Lutheran Services Richard Marshall, President/CEO	2021 N McCord Rd Toledo, OH 43615	(419) 861-4990	rmarshall@@genacross.org genacrosslutheranservices.org
Lutheran Legal League William Huseman, President	9310 Old Kings Rd S Jacksonville, FL 32257	(904) 591-4822	whuseman@jaxattys.com lutheranlegalleague.org
Lutheran Metropolitan Ministry Mark Charvat, CFO	Richard Sering Center 4515 Superior Ave Cleveland, OH 44103	(216) 696-2715	mcharvat@lutheranmetro.org lutheranmetro.org
Lutheran Ministries of Mercy Inc Terri Rodriguez, President/CEO	PO Box 187 Williston, OH 43468	(419) 836-7741	trodrig@lutherhome.org lutheranministriesofmercy.org
Lutheran Ministry Services Northwest Donald Sundene, Executive Director	7040 36th Ave NE Seattle, WA 98115	(206) 450-7128	lms@lmsnw.org lmsnw.org
Lutheran Mission Society of Maryland Lucas Witt, CEO	PO Box 438 Linthicum, MD 21090	(410) 636-0123	lms@compassionplace.org compassionplace.org
Lutheran Pastoral Counseling Ministry Inc DBA Lutheran Counseling Center Elizabeth Geiling, Co-Executive Director	132 Jefferson Ave Mineola, NY 11501	(516) 741-0994	e.geiling@lccny.org lccny.org
Lutheran Scholarship Granting Organization of Ohio Andrew Zubin, Executive Director	3870 Linden Rd Rocky River, OH 44116	(440) 356-7155	azubin@clhsa.org lsgoohio.org
Lutheran Senior Citizens Inc DBA Concordia Life Care Community Danny Eischen, CEO	7707 W Britton Rd Oklahoma City, OK 73132	(405) 720-7200	deischen@concordiaseniorliving.com concordiaseniorliving.com
Lutheran Senior Services DBA EverTrue Adam Marles, President/CEO	1150 Hanley Industrial Ct Brentwood, MO 63144	(314) 968-9313	adam.marles@evertrueliving.org evertrueliving.org
Lutheran Servants for Christ Wayne Puls, President/Executive Director	108 Chesterton Dr Goose Creek, SC 29445	(843) 730-4420	wayne.puls@gmail.com
Lutheran Services Florida Inc Samuel Sipes, CEO	3627 W Waters Ave Tampa, FL 33614	(813) 875-1408	ssipes@lsfnet.org lsfnet.org
Lutheran Social Services Inc DBA Lutheran Social Services of Indiana Angie Moellering, President/CEO	333 E Lewis St Fort Wayne, IN 46802	(260) 426-3347	amoellering@lssin.org lssin.org
Lutheran Social Services of Alaska Alan Budahl, Executive Director	1303 W 33rd Ave Anchorage, AK 99503	(907) 272-0643	lssa@lssalaska.org lssalaska.org
Lutheran Social Services of Central Ohio Rachel Lustig, President/CEO	1105 Schrock Rd Ste 100 Columbus, OH 43229	(614) 228-5200	info@lssnetworkofhope.org lssnetworkofhope.org
Lutheran Social Services of New York Inc Damyn Kelly Jr, President/CEO	475 Riverside Dr Ste 1244 New York, NY 10115	(212) 870-1100	dkelly@lssny.org lssny.org
Lutheran Social Services of Northern California Carol Roberts, CEO	1465 Civic Ct Building D Ste 810 Concord, CA 94520	(925) 825-1060	croberts@lssnorcal.org lssnorcal.org

Name Contact	Address City State Zip	Phone	Email Website
Lutheran Social Services of Southern California LaSharnda Beckwith, President/CEO	999 Town and Country Rd Ste 100 Orange, CA 92868	(714) 685-1800	lasharnda.beckwith@lsssc.org lsssc.org
Lutheran Social Services of the National Capital Area Kristyn Peck, CEO	1730 Rhode Island Ave NW Ste 712 Washington, DC 20036	(202) 723-3000	peckk@lssnca.org lssnca.org
Lutheran Social Services of the South Inc DBA Upbring Michael Loo, President/CEO	PO Box 140767 Austin, TX 78714	(512) 459-1000	michael.loo@upbring.org upbring.org
Lutheran Social Services of the Southwest Kevin Meyer, Director of Philanthropic Engagement	2502 E. University Dr Ste 125 Phoenix, AZ 85035	(480) 396-3795	kmeyer@lss-sw.org lss-sw.org
Lutherans For Life Aric Fenske, Executive Director	1101 5th St Nevada, IA 50201	(888) 364-5433	info@lutheransforlife.org lutheransforlife.org
Lutherans in Medical Missions Sharon Thomas, Executive Director	PO Box 766 Concordia, MO 64020	(816) 699-1875	limm@limm.org limm.org
Martha and Mary Lutheran Services Lynette Ladenburg, CEO	PO Box 127 Poulsbo, WA 98370	(360) 779-7500	info@mmhc.org marthaandmary.org
Niagara Lutheran Health System Christopher Koenig, President/CEO	5959 Broadway Lancaster, NY 14086	(716) 684-0202	info@niagaralutheran.org niagaralutheran.org
Open Sky Education Inc Andrew Neumann, Executive Chair/CEO	20935 W Swenson Dr Ste 101 Waukesha, WI 53186	(262) 542-9546	info@openskyeducation.org openskyeducation.org
Orphan Grain Train Inc Grant Schmidt, Vice President	PO Box 1466 Norfolk, NE 68702	(402) 371-7393	info@ogt.org ogt.org
Our Place After School Care Inc Adeline Johnson, Executive Director	837 N Chestnut Hastings, NE 68901	(402) 519-5197	director@ourplacecare.org ourplacecare.org
Phil's Friends, NFP Inc Philip Zielke, Founder/President	1249 Arrowhead Ct Crown Point, IN 46307	(224) 653-8315	info@philsfriends.org philsfriends.org
RAI Ministries Inc DBA Camp Restore Renee Rolland, Executive Director	9301 Chef Menteur Hwy New Orleans, LA 70127	(504) 242-2636	info@camprestore.org camprestore.org
Rebecca's Garden of Hope Inc Sanya Parson, Executive Director	2212 S Chickasaw Trail Ste 114 Orlando, FL 32825	(407) 273-0101	sanya@rebeccasgardenofhope.org rebeccasgardenofhope.org
Rebuilding the Breach Ministries Inc Judson Salmon, President/Executive Director	PO Box 1092 Crown Point, IN 46308		judsonsalmon@gmail.com lydia-house.com
Redeeming Life Outreach Ministries Inc Sheryl DeWitt, Executive Director	PO Box 1496 Sanford, FL 32772	(407) 790-9745	office@rlom.org rlom.org
Riverview Lutheran Home of Spokane Washington DBA Riverview Terrace Danie Monaghan, President/CEO	1801 E Upriver Dr Spokane, WA 99207	(509) 483-6483	dmonoghan@riverviewretirement.org riverviewretirement.org
Shepherd of the Valley Lutheran Retirement Services Inc Richard Limongi, CEO	5525 Silica Rd Austintown, OH 44515	(330) 530-4038	rlimongi@shepherdofthevalley.com shepherdofthevalley.com
Shepherd's Canyon Retreat Inc Kevin Bueltmann, Executive Director	PO Box 222 Wickenburg, AZ 85358	(480) 588-8837	kevin@shepherdscanyonretreat.org shepherdscanyonretreat.org
Shepherds Heart Ministry Inc Eric Hollar, Interim Director	2884 Shell Hollar Rd Claremont, NC 28610	(828) 244-7201	hollar76@yahoo.com shmserves.org
Silent Word Media Resources Warren Schif, Director	200 N Plum Grove Rd Palatine, IL 60067	(847) 359-1549	pastorwarren@ilcp.org silentwordvideo.org
St Luke Homes and Services Inc David West, Administrator/CEO	1301 St Luke Dr Spencer, IA 51301	(712) 262-5931	dwest@stlukelh.com stlukelh.com
St Luke Lutheran Community Kathleen Langer-Champlin, Executive Director	220 Applegrove St NE North Canton, OH 44720	(330) 499-8341	kathleenchaplin@stllc.org stllc.org

Name Contact	Address City State Zip	Phone	Email Website
Stepping Stone Mission Inc Joseph Song, President	PO Box 3101 Duluth, GA 30096	(404) 429-9072	helper@steppingstonemission.net
The Foundation for Called Workers DBA Ministry FOCUS Ken Krueger, President	1716 Linkside Dr Columbia, MO 65201	(480) 528-5296	ken@ministryfocus.org ministryfocus.org
The Hispanic Lutheran Mission Society of Metropolitan Washington DC Inc Aurelio Magarino, Executive Director	3041 Dubarry Ln Brookville, MD 20833	(240) 603-3371	amagarino62@gmail.com
The Lutheran Care Network Inc Laraine Fellegara, CEO	700 White Plains Rd Ste 300 Scarsdale, NY 10583	(914) 365-6365	lfellegara@tlcn.org tlcn.org
The Lutheran Foundation Inc Mark Dixon, CEO	3024 Fairfield Ave Fort Wayne, IN 46807	(260) 458-2112	mark@thelutheranfoundation.org thelutheranfoundation.org
The Lutheran Home for the Aged Association East Diane Gloede, COO	PO Box 559 Vinton, IA 52349	(319) 472-4211	d.gloede@lhaa-e-org lhaa-e.org
The Lutheran Home for the Aged Association West DBA Perry Lutheran Homes Max Phillips, CEO	2323 E Willis Ave Perry, IA 50220	(515) 465-5342	rev.max.phillips@gmail.com perrylutheranhomes.org
The Lutheran Home Inc Kathy Cavers, President/CEO	7500 W North Ave Wauwatosa, WI 53213	(414) 258-6170	kathy.cavers@thelutheranhome.org thelutheranhome.org
The Lutheran Mission of the Good Shepherd DBA Lutheran Urban Mission Agency Phil Cook, Executive Director	PO Box 412594 Kansas City, MO 64141	(816) 844-5900	admin@lumakc.org lumakc.org
The Lutheran Retirement Home of Greater Seattle DBA The Hearthstone Reggie Mullis, CEO	6720 E Green Lake Way N Seattle, WA 98103	(206) 525-9666	rmullis@hearthstone.org hearthstone.org
The Lutheran Scholarship Granting Organization of Indiana Inc Scott Schumacher, Executive Director	PO Box 5174 Fort Wayne, IN 46895	(260) 203-4509	scott@lutheransgo.org lutheransgo.org
The Lutheran Service Society of New York Susan Lichtenthal, Executive Director	PO Box 1963 Williamsville, NY 14231	(716) 631-9212	luthsvc@aol.com lssofny.org
The Providence Place Inc Jenny Gall, Administrator	815 Washington St Grafton, WI 53024	(262) 377-9900	jgall@theprovidenceplace.org theprovidenceplace.org
The Shepherds Hand Community Outreach Center Jana Peters, Executive Director	1231 S Anthony Blvd Fort Wayne, IN 46803	(260) 424-2224	shepherdshandfwed@gmail.com shepherdshandfw.org
The SON Experience Mark Wrightsman, President	1254 140th Ave New Richmond, WI 54017	(651) 341-0907	mwrightsman@p2gcapital.com soneexperience.org
Voice of Care Melvin Faulkner, Executive Director	c/o Immanuel Lutheran Church 310 E Main St Dundee, IL 60118	(630) 231-3862	office@voiceofcare.org voiceofcare.org
Wartburg—Mt Vernon Inc David Gentner, President/CEO	1 Wartburg Place Mount Vernon, NY 10552	(914) 699-0800	dgentner@wartburg.org wartburg.org
We Raise Foundation Paul Miles, President	1 Pierce Pl Ste 250-E Itasca, IL 60143	(630) 766-9066	wrmail@weraise.org weraise.org
WLC Management Company Inc Timothy Wismar, President/CEO	47 Weston Ave Quincy, MA 02170	(617) 733-8659	tim@townbrookhouse.org wlchurch.org
Ysleta Lutheran Mission Human Care Karla Gonzalez, Interim Executive Director	301 S Schutz Dr El Paso, TX 79907	(915) 858-2588	karla.gonzalez@ylm.org ylm.org

Social Ministry Organizations

Dorothy Krans, Director, Recognized Service Organizations
1333 S Kirkwood Rd, St. Louis, MO 63122
lcms.org/how-we-serve/mercy/recognized-service-organizations

Social Ministry Organizations are granted "Recognized Service Organization" status by the LCMS Office of National Mission when they are in a responsible relationship with The Lutheran Church—Missouri Synod and the appropriate District(s) and comply with established criteria. Social Ministry Organizations minister, in the name of Jesus Christ, to the needs of people with a variety of services. The types of services offered by each Social Ministry Organization are identified according to the following key:

1. Information and Referral
2. Counseling and Mental Health
3. Children and Youth Services
4. Foster Care
5. Adoption
6. Pregnancy Counseling
7. Emergency Services and/or Relief
8. Abuse and/or Neglect Prevention/Treatment
9. Substance Abuse and Other Addiction Prevention/Treatment
10. Immigrant, Asylee, or Refugee Resettlement and Support
11. Aging/Elderly Services
12. Services for the Developmentally Disabled
13. Services for the Hearing or Visually Impaired
14. Chaplaincy Services
15. Life Enrichment Programs and Services
16. Volunteer Service Programs
17. Advocacy and Planning
18. Organizational Consultation and Development
19. Housing and Community Development
20. Broadcast Ministry
21. Hospice
22. Disaster Preparedness and Response
23. Granting
24. Trauma Intervention
26. HIV-AIDS Ministry
130. Veterans Services
132. Camps
133. Early Childhood (EC)
134. Elementary (EL)
135. High School (HS)
136. College/University
138. Other Education
140. Other
141. Bible Translation
142. Special Education
145. Evangelism
146. Resources for Campus Outreach
147. Maternity Home

[NOTE: For contact information, use the SMO names listed below to search alphabetically in the SMO HEADQUARTERS that immediately precedes this section.]

State	City	SMO Name	Type of Service
ALABAMA	BIRMINGHAM	Inspiritus Inc	10 - 12 - 15 - 16
	KIMBERLY	Shepherds Heart Ministry Inc	16 - 22
ALASKA	ANCHORAGE	Lutheran Social Services of Alaska	1 - 7 - 16 - 19 - 22
ARIZONA	DOUGLAS	Lutheran Social Services of the Southwest	11 - 12
	GLENDALE	Lutheran Social Services of the Southwest	7
	MESA	Lutheran Social Services of the Southwest	1 - 3 - 15 - 16 - 133
	NOGALES	Lutheran Social Services of the Southwest	11 - 12
	PHOENIX	Lutheran Social Services of the Southwest	1 - 3 - 4 - 5 - 10 - 15 - 16 - 22 - 133
	TUCSON	Lutheran Social Services of the Southwest	3 - 10 - 11 - 12 - 15
	WICKENBURG	Shepherd's Canyon Retreat Inc	2 - 15
ARKANSAS	HOT SPRINGS	High Impact Movement Inc	3 - 15 - 18 - 134 - 135 - 138
CALIFORNIA	BIG BEAR	Lutheran Social Services of Southern California	1 - 2 - 3 - 4 - 8 - 9 - 15 - 16 - 22
	CHULA VISTA	Lutheran Social Services of Southern California	1 - 7 - 11 - 15 - 16 - 135
	CONCORD	Lutheran Social Services of Northern California	1 - 22 - 140
	LONG BEACH	Lutheran Social Services of Southern California	1 - 2 - 3 - 7 - 11 - 15 - 16 - 19
	ORANGE	Lutheran Social Services of Southern California	1 - 15 - 17 - 22
	PASADENA	Lutheran Social Services of Southern California	1 - 12 - 15
	REDDING	Lutheran Social Services of Northern California	1 - 140
	RIVERSIDE	Lutheran Social Services of Southern California	1 - 2 - 19
	SACRAMENTO	Lutheran Social Services of Northern California	1 - 140
	SAN BERNARDINO	Lutheran Social Services of Southern California	1 - 3 - 7 - 9 - 14 - 15 - 16 - 19 - 26
	SAN FRANCISCO	Lutheran Social Services of Northern California	1 - 140
	SANTA ANA	Lutheran Social Services of Southern California	1 - 2 - 19
	STOCKTON	Lutheran Social Services of Northern California	1 - 22 - 140
	THOUSAND OAKS	Lutheran Social Services of Southern California	1 - 15
COLORADO	COLORADO SPRINGS	Lutheran Family Services of Colorado DBA Lutheran Family Services Rocky Mountains	1 - 3 - 4 - 5 - 6 - 8 -10 - 22
	DENVER	Lutheran Family Services of Colorado DBA Lutheran Family Services Rocky Mountains	1 - 3 - 4 - 5 - 6 - 7 - 10 - 11 - 22
	EVANS	Lutheran Family Services of Colorado DBA Lutheran Family Services Rocky Mountains	10
	FLORISSANT	Lutheran Valley Retreat Inc	3 - 15 - 16 - 18 - 19 - 133 - 134 - 138
	FORT COLLINS	Lutheran Family Services of Colorado DBA Lutheran Family Services Rocky Mountains	1 - 3 - 4 - 5 - 6 - 8 - 24
	GREELEY	Lutheran Family Services of Colorado DBA Lutheran Family Services Rocky Mountains	3 - 4 - 8 - 15

State	City	SMO Name	Type of Service

[NOTE: For contact information, use the SMO names listed below to search alphabetically in the SMO HEADQUARTERS that immediately precedes this section.]

State	City	SMO Name	Type of Service
DISTRICT OF COLUMBIA	WASHINGTON	Lutheran Social Services of the National Capital Area	1 - 3 - 4 - 5 - 10 - 15 - 16 - 17 - 18 - 132
FLORIDA	BELLE GLADE	Lutheran Services Florida Inc	1 - 3 - 133
	BELLEVIEW	Lutheran Services Florida Inc	6 - 147
	BRADENTON	Lutheran Services Florida Inc	11
	CLEARWATER	Lutheran Counseling Services Inc	2 - 11
	CRESTVIEW	Lutheran Services Florida Inc	1 - 3 - 17
	FORT LAUDERDALE	Lutheran Services Florida Inc	2 - 3 - 7 - 8 - 9
	FORT MYERS	Amigos En Cristo Inc DBA Amigos Center	10
		Lutheran Services Florida Inc	1 - 2 - 3 - 8 - 9 - 10 - 11
	JACKSONVILLE	Lutheran Legal League	1 - 7 - 10 - 17
		Lutheran Services Florida Inc	1 - 2 - 9
	LAKELAND	Lutheran Counseling Services Inc	2 - 11
	LARGO	Lutheran Services Florida Inc	1 - 3 - 8 - 133
	MIAMI	Lutheran Services Florida Inc	1 - 3 - 10
	MILTON	Lutheran Services Florida Inc	1 - 2 - 3 - 17
	MONTVERDE	Lutheran Counseling Services Inc	2 - 11
	NAPLES	Lutheran Services Florida Inc	1 - 10
	OAKLAND PARK	Lutheran Services Florida Inc	2 - 3
	ORLANDO	Florida-Georgia Lutheran Early Response Inc	22
		Lutheran Counseling Services Inc	2 - 11
		Rebecca's Garden of Hope Inc	3 - 16 - 18
	OVIEDO	Lutheran Counseling Services Inc	2 - 11
		Lutheran Haven Inc	11 - 14 - 16 - 17 - 21 - 130 - 140
	PENSACOLA	Lutheran Services Florida Inc	1 - 2 - 3 - 7 - 8 - 11 - 12 - 17
	SAINT PETERSBURG	Lutheran Services Florida Inc	10
		Lutheran Counseling Services Inc	2 - 11
	SANFORD	Redeeming Life Outreach Ministries Inc	6 - 7 - 15 - 16 - 19 - 140 - 147
	SARASOTA	Lutheran Services Florida Inc	1 - 3 - 8 - 10 - 11 - 12 - 17
	TAMPA	Concordia Lutheran Ministries	11
		Lutheran Services Florida Inc	1 - 2 - 3 - 7 - 10 - 17 - 140
	WEST PALM BEACH	Lutheran Services Florida Inc	1 - 2 - 3 - 7 - 133
	WINTER HAVEN	Lutheran Services Florida Inc	2 - 3 - 9
	WINTER PARK	Lutheran Counseling Services Inc	2 - 11
GEORGIA	ATLANTA	Inspiritus Inc	1 - 3 - 4 - 8 - 10 - 12 - 15 - 16 - 17 - 19 - 22
	DECATUR	Inspiritus Inc	1 - 3 - 7 - 8 - 10 - 15 - 16 - 24
	CLARKSTON	Inspiritus Inc	1 - 3 - 7 - 8 - 10 - 15 - 16 - 24
	CONYERS	Stepping Stone Mission Inc	1 - 7 - 15 - 16 - 19 - 132
	ROME	Inspiritus Inc	3 - 4 - 12 - 15 - 19
	SAVANNAH	Inspiritus Inc	1 - 3 - 10 - 12 - 16 - 19
ILLINOIS	ALTAMONT	Lutheran Care Center Corporation	3 - 11 - 14 - 15 - 16 - 19
	BELLEVILLE	Lutheran Senior Services DBA EverTrue	11 - 14 - 16 - 19
	EAST DUNDEE	Redeeming Life Outreach Ministries Inc	6 - 7 - 15 - 16 - 19 - 140 - 141
	EAST MOLINE	Lutheran Family Service	1 - 2 - 5 - 6 - 8 - 9 - 24
	GLEN CARBON	Lutheran Senior Services DBA EverTrue	11 - 14 - 16
	HAMEL	Concordia Deaconess Conference	1 - 15
	ITASCA	We Raise Foundation	18 - 23
	LOMBARD	Voice of Care	1 - 3 - 11 - 12 - 13 - 14 - 16 - 17 - 132 - 138
	NORTHBROOK	Lutheran Church Charities	1 - 3 - 7 - 10 - 11 - 14 - 15 - 16 - 17 - 18 - 19 - 20 - 22 - 24 - 130 - 138 - 140
	PALATINE	Silent Word Media Resources	13 - 15
	PEORIA	Lutheran Senior Services DBA EverTrue	11 - 14 - 16
	SPRINGFIELD	Lutheran Senior Services DBA EverTrue	11 - 14 - 16
	VILLA PARK	Voice of Care	1 - 3 - 11 - 12 - 13 - 14 - 16 - 17 - 132 - 138
	WHEATON	Phil's Friends, NFP Inc	15 - 16
INDIANA	COLUMBUS	Graceworks Lutheran Services	16 - 19
	CROWN POINT	Phil's Friends, NFP Inc	15 - 16
		Rebuilding the Breach Ministries Inc	7
	FORT WAYNE	Amboss Inc	1 - 7 - 16 - 17
		Cross Connections Inc	2 - 3 - 6 - 8 - 9 - 15 - 16 - 24 - 130
		Lutheran Homes Inc DBA Lutheran Life Villages	3 - 11 - 14 - 15 - 16 - 19
		Lutheran Social Services Inc DBA Lutheran Social Services of Indiana	1 - 2 - 3 - 6 - 7 - 8 - 9 - 15 - 17 - 24 - 133 - 140
		The Lutheran Foundation Inc	140
		The Lutheran Scholarship Granting Organization of Indiana Inc	18 - 23 - 133 - 134 - 135 - 140
		The Shepherds Hand Community Outreach Center	1 - 3 - 15 - 16 - 140
	GREENFIELD	Graceworks Lutheran Services	16 - 19
	GREENSBURG	Graceworks Lutheran Services	16 - 19
	INDIANAPOLIS	Lutheran Child and Family Services of IN/KY Inc	3 - 7 - 14 - 16 - 19 - 24

State	City	SMO Name	Type of Service

[NOTE: For contact information, use the SMO names listed below to search alphabetically in the SMO HEADQUARTERS that immediately precedes this section.]

State	City	SMO Name	Type of Service
INDIANA	KENDALLVILLE	Lutheran Homes Inc DBA Lutheran Life Villages	3 - 11 - 14 - 16
	LAWRENCEBURG	Graceworks Lutheran Services	16 - 19
	MADISON	Graceworks Lutheran Services	16 - 19
	NEW CASTLE	Graceworks Lutheran Services	16 - 19
	RICHMOND	Graceworks Lutheran Services	16 - 19
	RUSHVILLE	Graceworks Lutheran Services	16 - 19
	SCOTTSBURG	Graceworks Lutheran Services	16 - 19
	SEYMOUR	Concordia Counseling: A Lutheran Outreach Ministry Inc	2
		Lutheran Community Home, Inc	11 - 16
	UNION CITY	Graceworks Lutheran Services	16 - 19
IOWA	BETTENDORF	Lutheran Family Service	1 - 2 - 3 - 5 - 6 - 8 - 9 - 24
	CARROLL	Lutheran Family Service	1 - 2 - 5 - 6 - 8 - 24
	COUNCIL BLUFFS	Bethany Lutheran Home	1 - 11 - 14 - 19 - 21
		David's Harp: A Center for Musical Development	18 - 138
		Lutheran Family Service	1 - 2 - 5 - 6 - 8 - 24
		Lutheran Family Services of Nebraska Inc	1 - 2 - 5 - 6 - 10 - 133 - 138
	DAVENPORT	Lutheran Family Service	1 - 3
		The Lutheran Home for the Aged Association East	1 - 11 - 14 - 16 - 19 - 21
	DES MOINES	Luther Care Services	11
	DUBUQUE	Lutheran Family Service	1 - 2 - 5 - 6 - 8 - 9 - 24
	FORT DODGE	Lutheran Family Service	1 - 2 - 5 - 6 - 8 - 9 - 11 - 15 - 24 - 132
	JEFFERSON	Lutheran Family Service	1 - 2 - 5 - 6 - 8 - 24
	MANNING	Lutheran Family Service	1 - 2 - 5 - 6 - 8 - 9 - 24
	NEVADA	Lutherans for Life	1 - 2 - 3 - 15 - 17
	OSKALOOSA	Lutheran Family Service	1 - 2 - 5 - 6 - 8 - 9 - 24
	PERRY	Lutheran Family Service	1 - 2 - 5 - 6 - 8 - 9 - 24
		Lutheran Home for the Aged Association West DBA Perry Lutheran Homes	2 - 3 - 7 - 11 - 14 - 16 - 21 - 130 - 133 - 134 - 140
	SPENCER	St Luke Homes and Services Inc	11 - 14 - 21 - 130
	URBANDALE	Lutheran Family Service	1 - 2 - 5 - 6 - 8 - 9 - 15 - 24
	VINTON	The Lutheran Home for the Aged Association East	1 - 11 - 14 - 16 - 18 - 19 - 21 - 140
KANSAS	WICHITA	Lutheran Family Services of Nebraska Inc	5
KENTUCKY	LAGRANGE	Cedar Lake Inc	1 - 12 - 14 - 16 - 19
		Graceworks Lutheran Services	16 - 19
	LOUISVILLE	Cedar Lake Inc	1 - 12 - 14 - 16 - 19
	MAYSVILLE	Graceworks Lutheran Services	16 - 19
	NEW CASTLE	Cedar Lake Inc	1 - 12 - 14 - 16 - 19
LOUISIANA	NEW ORLEANS	Lutheran Social Services of the South Inc DBA Upbring	3 - 19
		RAI Ministries Inc DBA Camp Restore	1 - 11 - 16 - 18 - 19 - 132
	SLIDELL	Forged by Fire Services Inc	22
MARYLAND	ANNAPOLIS	Lutheran Mission Society of Maryland	1 - 7 - 14 - 16 - 19
	BALTIMORE	Lutheran Mission Society of Maryland	1 - 7 - 14 - 16
	BROOKEVILLE	The Hispanic Lutheran Mission Society of Metropolitan Washington DC Inc	1 - 7 - 10 - 14 - 17 - 20 - 24 - 140
	BROOKLYN PARK	Lutheran Mission Society of Maryland	1 - 2 - 16
	ESSEX	Lutheran Mission Society of Maryland	1 - 7 - 14 - 16
	FREDERICK	Lutheran Social Services of the National Capital Area	1 - 7 - 10
	GREENBELT	Lutheran Social Services of the National Capital Area	1 - 2 - 3 - 4 - 7 - 10 - 15 - 16
	HAVRE DE GRACE	Lutheran Mission Society of Maryland	1 - 7 - 14 - 16
	HICKORY	Lutheran Mission Society of Maryland	1 - 7 - 14 - 16
	HYATTSVILLE	Lutheran Mission Society of Maryland	1 - 7 - 14 - 16
	LA PLATA	Lutheran Mission Society of Maryland	1 - 7 - 16
	UPPER MARLBORO	Fellowship Square Foundation Inc	7 - 8 - 11 - 12 - 14 - 15 - 16 - 19
MASSACHUSETTS	QUINCY	WLC Management Company Inc	1 - 2 - 11 - 12 - 19
MICHIGAN	ANN ARBOR	Concordia Center for the Family	15 - 18 - 20 - 23 - 132 - 138 - 140
		Lutheran Special Education Ministries (LSEM)	3 - 12 - 13 - 15 - 23 - 138
	BAY CITY	Lutheran Child and Family Service of Michigan DBA Wellspring Lutheran Services	1 - 4 - 5 - 8
	BINGHAM FARMS	Lutheran Child and Family Service of Michigan DBA Wellspring Lutheran Services	1 - 3 - 4 - 5 - 8
	CLARE	Lutheran Child and Family Service of Michigan DBA Wellspring Lutheran Services	1 - 5 - 8
	DETROIT	Camp RD Inc DBA Camp Restore Detroit	3 - 15 - 16 - 19 - 132 - 138
	FAIRVIEW	Lutheran Homes of Michigan Inc DBA Wellspring Lutheran Services	11 - 19
	FLINT	Franklin Avenue Mission	1 - 3 - 7 - 15 - 16 - 17 - 19 - 24 - 132 - 140
	FRANKENMUTH	Lutheran Homes of Michigan Inc DBA Wellspring Lutheran Services	11 - 12 - 14 - 16 - 21

State	City	SMO Name	Type of Service

[NOTE: For contact information, use the SMO names listed below to search alphabetically in the SMO HEADQUARTERS that immediately precedes this section.]

State	City	SMO Name	Type of Service
MICHIGAN	GAYLORD	Lutheran Child and Family Service of Michigan DBA Wellspring Lutheran Services	1 - 4 - 5 - 8
	GIBRALTAR	Lutheran Homes of Michigan Inc DBA Wellspring Lutheran Services	11 - 19
	HARTLAND	Ephphatha Lutheran Mission Society	13 - 138
	KENTWOOD	Lutheran Child and Family Service of Michigan DBA Wellspring Lutheran Services	1 - 3 - 4 - 8
	LANSING	Lutheran Child and Family Service of Michigan DBA Wellspring Lutheran Services	1 - 4 - 5 - 8
	LIVONI	Lutheran Child and Family Service of Michigan DBA Wellspring Lutheran Services	1 - 3
	MIO	Lutheran Child and Family Service of Michigan DBA Wellspring Lutheran Services	1 - 8
	MONROE	Lutheran Homes of Michigan Inc DBA Wellspring Lutheran Services	11 - 14 - 16
	SAGINAW	Lutheran Child and Family Service of Michigan – DBA Wellspring Lutheran Services	1 - 3 - 4 - 5 - 6 - 8
		Lutheran Homes of Michigan Inc DBA Wellspring Lutheran Services	1 - 3 - 4 - 5 - 6 - 8 - 11 - 14 - 15 - 16 19 - 21
	SAULT SAINTE MARIE	Lutheran Child and Family Service of Michigan DBA Wellspring Lutheran Services	1 - 8
	TEMPERANCE	Lutheran Homes Society Inc DBA Genacross Lutheran Services	11 - 19
	TRAVERSE CITY	Good Friend Ministries	2
		Lutheran Child and Family Service of Michigan DBA Wellspring Lutheran Services	1 - 4 - 8
	WESTLAND	Lutheran Homes of Michigan Inc DBA Wellspring Lutheran Services	11 - 19
MINNESOTA	BECKER	Good Shepherd Lutheran Home of Sauk Rapids MN DBA Good Shepherd Community	11 - 14 - 15 - 16 - 19
	BLAINE	Crest View Corporation DBA Crest View Senior Communities	11
	COLUMBIA HEIGHTS	Crest View Corporation DBA Crest View Senior Communities	8 - 11 - 14 - 15 - 18 - 19 - 21
	LAKEVILLE	KingsPath Senior Ministries Inc	11 - 12 - 18 - 19 - 130
	SAINT PAUL	The SON Experience	133 - 134 - 140
	SAUK RAPIDS	Good Shepherd Lutheran Home of Sauk Rapids MN DBA Good Shepherd Community	11 - 14 - 15 - 16 - 19
MISSOURI	BALLWIN	Lutheran Senior Services DBA EverTrue	11 - 14 - 16 - 21
	BRENTWOOD	Lutheran Senior Services DBA EverTrue	7 - 11 - 14 - 15 - 16 - 17 - 19 - 21 - 22
	CAPE GIRARDEAU	Lutheran Family & Children's Services of Missouri	1 - 2 - 3 - 5 - 6 - 15 - 17 - 18
	CHESTERFIELD	Lutheran Senior Services DBA EverTrue	11 - 14 - 16 - 21
	COLUMBIA	Lutheran Family & Children's Services of Missouri	1 - 2 - 3 - 5 - 6 - 15 - 17 - 18
		Lutheran Senior Services DBA EverTrue	11 - 14 - 16
		The Foundation for Called Workers DBA Ministry FOCUS	23
	CONCORDIA	Lutherans in Medical Missions	15 - 16 - 23
	EUREKA	Lutheran Senior Services DBA EverTrue	11 - 14 - 16 - 19
	FENTON	The Foundation for Called Workers DBA Ministry FOCUS	23
	FLORISSANT	Lutheran Family & Children's Services of Missouri	2
		Lutheran Senior Services DBA EverTrue	11 - 14 - 16 - 19
	HILLSBORO	Lutheran Family & Children's Services of Missouri	2
	JOPLIN	Lutheran Family & Children's Services of Missouri	1 - 2 - 3 - 5 - 6 - 15 - 17
	KANSAS CITY	Lutheran Family & Children's Services of Missouri	1 - 2 - 3 - 5 - 6 - 15 - 17
		The Lutheran Mission of the Good Shepherd DBA Lutheran Urban Mission Agency	1 - 7 - 10 - 15 - 16 - 17 - 23 - 138 - 140
	KIRKWOOD	Lutheran Senior Services DBA EverTrue	11 - 14 - 16 - 19
	LAKE OZARK	Shepherd's Canyon Retreat Inc.	2 - 15
	LINCOLN	Heits Point Lutheran Ministries Inc	3 - 16 - 132 - 140
	SAINT LOUIS	College Hill Foundation	16 - 19 - 132
		Humanitri	15 - 16 - 19
		Lutheran Development Group Inc	19
		Lutheran Family & Children's Services of Missouri	1 - 2 - 3 - 4 - 5 - 6 - 8 - 15 - 16 - 17 - 18 - 133
		Lutheran Foundation of Saint Louis	23
		Lutheran Senior Services DBA EverTrue	7 - 11 - 14 - 16 - 19
	SAINT PETERS	Lutheran Family & Children's Services of Missouri	2 - 4 - 5
	SPRINGFIELD	Lutheran Family & Children's Services of Missouri	1 - 2 - 3 - 5 - 6 - 15 - 17 - 18 - 24
	UNION	Lutheran Family & Children's Services of Missouri	1 - 2 - 3 - 4 - 5 - 6 - 8 - 15 - 24
	WEBSTER GROVES	Lutheran Senior Services DBA EverTrue	11 - 14 - 15 - 16 - 21
	WELDON SPRING	Lutheran Senior Services DBA EverTrue	11 - 14 - 16 - 21
MONTANA	BILLINGS	Lutheran Family Services of Colorado DBA Lutheran Family Services Rocky Mountains	10
NEBRASKA	BLAIR	Lutheran Family Services of Nebraska Inc	1 - 2 - 3 - 5 - 6 - 9 - 16 - 19 - 24
	FREMONT	Lutheran Family Services of Nebraska Inc	1 - 2 - 4 - 5 - 6 - 7 - 8 - 9 - 10 - 15 - 16 - 17 - 18 - 24 - 133
	GRAND ISLAND	Lutheran Family Services of Nebraska Inc	1 - 2 - 6 - 10 - 15 - 24 - 130
	HASTINGS	Our Place After School Care Inc	3 - 12 - 15 - 16 - 140

State	City	SMO Name	Type of Service

[NOTE: For contact information, use the SMO names listed below to search alphabetically in the SMO HEADQUARTERS that immediately precedes this section.]

State	City	SMO Name	Type of Service
NEBRASKA	LEXINGTON	Lutheran Family Services of Nebraska Inc	1 - 2 - 5 - 6 - 9 - 10 - 24
	LINCOLN	GracePoint Institute for Relational Health	2
		Lutheran Family Services of Nebraska Inc	1 - 2 - 3 - 5 - 6 - 7 - 8 - 9 - 10 - 11 - 12 - 13 - 15 - 16 - 17 - 18 - 19 - 24 - 26 - 130 - 133 - 134
	NORFOLK	Orphan Grain Train Inc	16 - 22 - 140
	NORTH PLATTE	Lutheran Family Services of Nebraska Inc	1 - 2 - 5 - 6 - 9 - 24 - 130
	OMAHA	Lutheran Family Services of Nebraska Inc	1 - 2 - 3 - 4 - 5 - 6 - 7 - 8 - 9 - 15 - 16 - 17 - 18 - 22 - 24 - 130 - 133 - 138 - 140
NEW MEXICO	ALBUQUERQUE	Lutheran Family Services of Colorado DBA Lutheran Family Services Rocky Mountains	10
	LAS CRUCES	Lutheran Family Services of Colorado DBA Lutheran Family Services Rocky Mountains	10
NEW YORK	AMHERST	Lutheran Association for Developmentally Disabled Inc	12
		The Lutheran Service Society of New York	1 - 5 - 11 - 12 - 15 - 17 - 24
	BRONX	Lutheran Social Services of New York Inc	1 - 2 - 3 - 8 - 9 - 12 - 15 - 16 - 17 - 19 - 133 - 134 - 135 - 138
	BRONXVILLE	Lutheran Pastoral Counseling Ministry Inc DBA Lutheran Counseling Center	2 - 6 - 8 - 16 - 22- 24 - 26 -130
	BROOKLYN	Lutheran Pastoral Counseling Ministry Inc DBA Lutheran Counseling Center	2 - 6 - 8 - 16 - 22 - 24 - 26 - 130
		Lutheran Social Services of New York Inc	1 - 2 - 3 - 6 - 7 - 8 - 9 - 12 - 15 - 16 - 17 - 19 - 133
		The Lutheran Care Network Inc	11 - 15 - 19
	DELMAR	The Lutheran Care Network Inc	11 - 14 - 15 - 17- 19
	DIX HILLS	Lutheran Pastoral Counseling Ministry Inc DBA Lutheran Counseling Center	2 - 6 - 8 - 16 - 22 - 24 - 26 - 130
	FARMINGDALE	Lutheran Pastoral Counseling Ministry Inc DBA Lutheran Counseling Center	2 - 6 - 8 - 24 - 26
	KINGS PARK	The Lutheran Care Network Inc	11 - 15 - 19
	LANCASTER	Niagara Lutheran Health System	11 - 18
	MINEOLA	Lutheran Pastoral Counseling Ministry Inc DBA Lutheran Counseling Center	2 - 6 - 8 - 16 - 22 - 24 - 26 - 130
	MOUNT VERNON	Wartburg—Mt Vernon Inc	11 - 14 - 15 - 16 - 19 - 21 - 130 - 140
	NEW YORK	Lutheran Pastoral Counseling Ministry Inc DBA Lutheran Counseling Center	2 - 6 - 8 - 16 - 22 - 24 - 26 - 130
		Lutheran Social Services of New York Inc	1 - 2 - 3 - 4 - 8 - 9 - 10 - 15 - 16 - 18 - 19 - 133 - 134 - 147
	PATCHOGUE	Lutheran Pastoral Counseling Ministry Inc DBA Lutheran Counseling Center	2 - 6 - 8 - 16 - 22 - 24 - 26 - 130
	PAWLING	The Lutheran Care Network Inc	11 - 15 - 19
	POUGHKEEPSIE	The Lutheran Care Network Inc	11 - 14 - 15 - 16 - 17 - 19 - 21
	REXFORD	The Lutheran Care Network Inc	11 - 14 - 15 - 19
	SCARSDALE	The Lutheran Care Network Inc	1 - 11 - 18 - 19
	UNIONDALE	Lutheran Social Services of New York Inc	7 - 15
	WOODSIDE	Lutheran Pastoral Counseling Ministry Inc DBA Lutheran Counseling Center	2 - 6 - 8 - 16 - 22 - 24 - 26 - 130
NORTH DAKOTA	BISMARCK	Dakota Boys and Girls Ranch	2 - 3 - 8 - 14 - 17 - 24 - 134 - 135
	FARGO	Dakota Boys and Girls Ranch	2 - 3 - 8 - 14 - 17 - 24 - 134 - 135
	MINOT	Dakota Boys and Girls Ranch	2 - 3 - 8 - 14 - 15 - 24 - 134 - 135
	SAINT JOHN	Shepherds Hill Retreat Inc	132
OHIO	AKRON	St Luke Lutheran Community	11 - 16
	ASHLAND	Lutheran Social Services of Central Ohio	11 - 14 - 15 - 16 - 17 - 19
	AUSTINTOWN	Shepherd of the Valley Lutheran Retirement Services Inc	11
	BELLEFONTAINE	Graceworks Lutheran Services	16 - 19
	BOARDMAN	Shepherd of the Valley Lutheran Retirement Services Inc	11 - 14
	BRIDGEPORT	Lutheran Social Services of Central Ohio	11 - 19
	BUCYRUS	Lutheran Homes Society Inc DBA Genacross Lutheran Services	11 - 19
	CENTERBURG	Lutheran Social Services of Central Ohio	11 - 19
	CINCINNATI	Graceworks Lutheran Services	1 - 11 - 12
	CLEVELAND	Lutheran Metropolitan Ministry	1 - 2 - 3 - 4 - 7 - 8 - 9 - 11 - 15 - 16 - 17 - 19 - 24 - 130 - 138
	COLUMBUS	Lutheran Social Services of Central Ohio	1 - 7 - 8 - 11 - 12 - 13 - 14 - 15 - 16 - 17 - 19 - 130
	COPLEY	Concordia Lutheran Ministries	11 - 14 - 16
	DAYTON	Graceworks Lutheran Services	1 - 2 - 11 - 12 - 14 - 15 - 16 - 17 - 18 - 19
	DELAWARE	Lutheran Social Services of Central Ohio	11 - 19
	GIBSONBURG	Lutheran Homes Society Inc DBA Genacross Lutheran Services	11 - 19
	GIRARD	Shepherd of the Valley Lutheran Retirement Services Inc	11 - 14 - 19
	GROVE CITY	Lutheran Social Services of Central Ohio	11 - 19
	GROVEPORT	Lutheran Social Services of Central Ohio	11 - 19

State	City	SMO Name	Type of Service

[NOTE: For contact information, use the SMO names listed below to search alphabetically in the SMO HEADQUARTERS that immediately precedes this section.]

State	City	SMO Name	Type of Service
OHIO	HOLLAND	Lutheran Homes Society Inc DBA Genacross Lutheran Services	1 - 2 - 3 - 11 - 14
	LAKEWOOD	Lutheran Metropolitan Ministry	1 - 3 - 4 - 7 - 8 - 15
	LANCASTER	Lutheran Social Services of Central Ohio	1 - 7 - 11 - 15 - 16 - 17 - 19 - 130
	LIMA	Lutheran Homes Society Inc DBA Genacross Lutheran Services	11 - 19
	MANSFIELD	Lutheran Social Services of Central Ohio	11 - 19
	MARION	Lutheran Social Services of Central Ohio	11 - 19
	MILFORD	Graceworks Lutheran Services	16 - 19
	MINERVA	St Luke Lutheran Community	11 - 16
	NAPOLEON	Lutheran Homes Society Inc DBA Genacross Lutheran Services	11 - 14
		Lutheran Ministries of Mercy Inc	1 - 8 - 11 - 12 - 13 - 14 - 15 - 16 - 17 - 19
	NORTH CANTON	St Luke Lutheran Community	11 - 16
	NORWALK	Lutheran Homes Society Inc DBA Genacross Lutheran Services	11 - 19
	OAK HARBOR	Lutheran Homes Society Inc DBA Genacross Lutheran Services	11 - 19
	OREGON	Lutheran Homes Society Inc DBA Genacross Lutheran Services	11 - 19
	POLAND	Shepherd of the Valley Lutheran Retirement Services Inc	11 - 14 - 19
	SPRINGFIELD	Lutheran Social Services of Central Ohio	11 - 19
	TOLEDO	Lutheran Homes Society Inc DBA Genacross Lutheran Services	1 - 2 - 3 - 11 - 14 - 19
		Lutheran Ministries of Mercy Inc	1 - 2 - 3 - 6 - 7 - 8 - 9 - 11 - 15 - 16 - 18 - 24 - 130 - 135
	URBANA	Graceworks Lutheran Services	16 - 19
	WARREN	Lutheran Social Services of Central Ohio	11 - 19
		Shepherd of the Valley Lutheran Retirement Services Inc	11 - 14 - 19
	WILLISTON	Lutheran Ministries of Mercy Inc	1 - 2 - 3 - 7 - 8 - 9 - 11 - 12 - 13 - 14 - 15 - 16 - 17 - 19 - 24 - 130 - 135
OKLAHOMA	OKLAHOMA CITY	Lutheran Senior Citizens Inc DBA Concordia Life Care Community	11 - 15 - 19
PENNSYLVANIA	ALLENTOWN	Lutheran Senior Services DBA EverTrue	11 - 14 - 16
	ALLISON PARK	Concordia Lutheran Ministries	11
	AMBLER	Liberty Lutheran Services	1 - 7 - 11 - 14 - 15 - 16 - 17 - 18 - 19 - 21 - 22 - 130 - 132 - 138
	BADEN	Concordia Lutheran Ministries	11 - 14 - 16
	BALA CYNWYD	Liberty Lutheran Services	1 - 11 - 14 - 15 - 16 - 21 - 130
	BRIDGEVILLE	Concordia Lutheran Ministries	11 - 14 - 16
	BUTLER	Concordia Lutheran Ministries	11 - 14 - 16
	CABOT	Concordia Lutheran Ministries	3 - 11 - 14 - 16 - 23 - 140
	CARLISLE	Lutheran Senior Services DBA EverTrue	11 - 14 - 16
	CHESWICK	Concordia Lutheran Ministries	11 - 14 - 16
	GREENSBURG	Concordia Lutheran Ministries	11 - 14 - 16
	INDIANA	Concordia Lutheran Ministries	11 - 14 - 16
	JAMISON	Liberty Lutheran Services	11 - 15 - 16
	LEWISBURG	Lutheran Senior Services DBA EverTrue	11 - 14 - 16
	LIGONIER	Concordia Lutheran Ministries	11 - 14 - 16
	MARS	Concordia Lutheran Ministries	11 - 14 - 16
	MEADVILLE	Concordia Lutheran Ministries	11 - 14 - 16
	MONROEVILLE	Concordia Lutheran Ministries	11 - 14 - 16
	PHILADELPHIA	Liberty Lutheran Services	1 - 11 - 14 - 15 - 16 - 21 - 130
	PITTSBURGH	Concordia Lutheran Ministries	11 - 14 - 16
	SEWICKLEY	Concordia Lutheran Ministries	11 - 14 - 16
	STATE COLLEGE	Liberty Lutheran Services	11 - 15 - 16 - 21 - 130
	TOPTON	Lutheran Senior Services DBA EverTrue	11 - 14 - 16
	VALENCIA	Concordia Lutheran Ministries	3 - 14 - 16 - 21
	WASHINGTON	Concordia Lutheran Ministries	11 - 14 - 16
	WEXFORD	Concordia Lutheran Ministries	11 - 14 - 16 - 21
SOUTH DAKOTA	BLACKHAWK	Lutheran Family Service	2
	DEADWOOD	Lutheran Family Service	1 - 2 - 5 - 6 - 8 - 9 - 24
	RAPID CITY	Lutheran Family Service	1 - 2 - 5 - 6 - 8 - 9 - 24
	SIOUX FALLS	Lutheran Family Service	1 - 2 - 5 - 6 - 8 - 9 - 24
TENNESSEE	NASHVILLE	Inspiritus Inc	1 - 7 - 10 - 15 - 16 - 19 - 22
TEXAS	AMARILLO	Lutheran Social Services of the South Inc DBA Upbring	4 - 5
	ARLINGTON	Lutheran Disaster Care Inc	16 - 22
	AUSTIN	Lutheran Social Services of the South Inc DBA Upbring	3 - 4 - 5 - 7 - 8 - 14 - 15 - 16 - 19 - 133 - 134
	CANYON LAKE	Lutheran Social Services of the South Inc DBA Upbring	2 - 3 - 8 - 14 - 16
	CORPUS CHRISTI	Lutheran Social Services of the South Inc DBA Upbring	2 - 3 - 4 - 10 - 14 - 16
	EL PASO	Lutheran Social Services of the South Inc DBA Upbring	2 - 3 - 4 - 5 - 10 - 14 - 16
		Ysleta Lutheran Mission Human Care	1 - 7 - 10 - 14 - 15 - 16 - 17 - 20 - 140
	FORT WORTH	Lutheran Social Services of the South Inc DBA Upbring	4 - 5
	HARLINGEN	Lutheran Social Services of the South Inc DBA Upbring	4 - 5
	HOUSTON	Lutheran Social Services of the South Inc DBA Upbring	4 - 5
	KATY	Lutheran Social Services of the South Inc DBA Upbring	2 - 3 - 4 - 10 - 14 - 16

State	City	SMO Name	Type of Service

[NOTE: For contact information, use the SMO names listed below to search alphabetically in the SMO HEADQUARTERS that immediately precedes this section.]

State	City	SMO Name	Type of Service
TEXAS	LAREDO	Lutheran Social Services of the South Inc DBA Upbring	4 - 5
	LUBBOCK	Lutheran Social Services of the South Inc DBA Upbring	1 - 2 - 4 - 5 - 7 - 11
	MCALLEN	Lutheran Social Services of the South Inc DBA Upbring	2 - 3 - 4 - 5 - 10 - 14 - 16
	RICHARDSON	Lutheran Social Services of the South Inc DBA Upbring	4 - 5
	SAN ANTONIO	Lutheran Social Services of the South Inc DBA Upbring	4 - 5
	TYLER	Lutheran Social Services of the South Inc DBA Upbring	4 - 5
	VICTORIA	Lutheran Social Services of the South Inc DBA Upbring	4 - 5
UTAH	SALT LAKE CITY	Lutheran Family Services of Colorado DBA Lutheran Family Services Rocky Mountains	10
VIRGINIA	ALEXANDRIA	Lutheran Social Services of the National Capital Area	1 - 7 - 10 - 15 - 16
	FAIRFAX	Lutheran Social Services of the National Capital Area	1 - 2 - 3 - 4 - 7 - 10 - 15 - 16
	RESTON	Fellowship Square Foundation Inc	7 - 8 - 11 - 12 - 14 - 15 - 16 - 17 - 19
	WOODBRIDGE	Fellowship Square Foundation Inc	7 - 8 - 11 - 12 - 14 - 15 - 16 - 19
WASHINGTON	POULSBO	Martha and Mary Lutheran Services	11 - 14 - 16 - 19 - 21 - 133
	SEATTLE	Lutheran Ministry Services Northwest	1 - 11 - 14 - 15
		The Lutheran Retirement Home of Greater Seattle DBA The Hearthstone	11
	SPOKANE	Riverview Lutheran Home of Spokane Washington DBA Riverview Terrace	11 - 19
	TACOMA	eliseo	11 - 13 - 14 - 15 - 16 - 21 - 130
WISCONSIN	BROOKFIELD	DOXOLOGY: The Lutheran Center for Spiritual Care and Counsel	2 - 15 - 18 - 132 - 138
	CUDAHY	Lutheran Counseling and Family Services of WI	2 - 3 - 5 - 6 - 8
	FITCHBURG	Lutheran Counseling and Family Services of WI	2 - 3 - 5 - 6 - 8
	GRAFTON	Lutheran Counseling and Family Services of WI	2 - 3 - 5 - 6 - 8
	MILWAUKEE	A Place of Refuge Ministries of South Wisconsin Inc	1 - 6 - 7 - 15 - 16 - 17 - 18 - 138 - 140 - 147
		Lutheran Urban Mission Initiative Inc	134
		S.O.S. Center Inc	1 - 3 - 16 - 138 - 140
	PORTAGE	Lutheran Counseling and Family Services of WI	2 - 3 - 5 - 6 - 8
	RACINE	Lutheran Urban Mission Initiative Inc	134
	REEDSBURG	Lutheran Counseling and Family Services of WI	2 - 3 - 5 - 6 - 8
	SHAWANO	Lutheran Counseling and Family Services of WI	2 - 3 - 6 - 8
	SUN PRAIRIE	Lutheran Counseling and Family Services of WI	2 - 3 - 5 - 6 - 8
	WAUKESHA	Compass Facilities Inc	138
		Open Sky Education Inc	3 - 134 - 135
	WAUWATOSA	Lutheran Counseling and Family Services of WI	2 - 3 - 5 - 6 - 8 - 9
		Lutheran Urban Mission Initiative Inc	134
		The Lutheran Home Inc	1 - 3 - 11 - 14 - 16

INTER-LUTHERAN ENTITIES

Name Contact	Address City State Zip	Phone Fax	Email Website
Lutheran Services in America (LSA) Alesia Frerichs, President	100 Maryland Ave NE Ste 500 Washington, DC 20002	(202) 499-5836 (703) 898-4981	lsa@lutheranservices.org lutheranservices.org

OTHER LUTHERAN RESOURCES

Name	Phone	Website
Lutheran Federal Credit Union	(314) 394-2790	lutheranfcu.org

CAMPUS MINISTRY

LCMS U
1333 S Kirkwood Rd
St Louis, MO 63122-7295
Website: lcms.org/lcmsu
Email: lcmsu@lcms.org

The following list identifies Campus Ministries by state, city, ministry name, physical address, schools serving, contact, phone, email, and website. Students and others can locate a campus ministry contact by using the "Find a Campus Ministry" link found on www.lcms.org/lcmsu.

State City	Ministry Name	Address, Zip Code	Schools Serving	Contact	Phone	Email Website
ALABAMA						
Auburn						
	Luth Stdnt Fllwshp	446 S. Gay St, 36832	Auburn U	Katie Olszowy	(334) 887-3901	lsfellowship@tlcauburn.org tlcauburn.org/college
Mobile						
	Holy Cross LSF	3900 Airport Blvd, 36608	U of S AL Springhill College	Suzy Cleveland	(251) 342-8755	church@holycrosslcms.org holycrosslcms.org
Tuscaloosa						
	U LC	911 5th Ave, 35401	U of AL Shelton State	Kay Holden	(205) 752-8784	uniluchap@bellsouth.net tuscaloosaulc.org
ARIZONA						
Flagstaff						
	PLC Connect	3430 N Fourth St, 86004	NAU, Flagstaff	William Weiss, Jr.	(928) 526-9578	plcflagstaff@gmail.com peacelutheranflagstaff.org
Mesa						
	Campus Mission Coalition Phoenix	9601 E Brown Rd, 85207	AZ State	Sharon Owens	(480) 407-7009	sharon.cmcphx@gmail.com
Tempe						
	Campus Mission Coalition Phoenix	1035 E Guadalupe Rd, 85283	AZ State	Abby Schwichtenberg	(480) 839-0906	abbys@gctempe.org gctempe.org/index.php/the-garden
	The Garden	1035 E Guadalupe Rd, 85283	AZ State, Grand Canyon	Ethan Jones	(480) 349-5357	ejones@gctempe.org gctempe.org
Tucson						
	LCMSU AZ	3925 E 5th St, 85711	U of AZ, Pima CC	M. Todd Zill	(520) 400-3470	toddzillarising@gmail.com lcmsuarizona.org
ARKANSAS						
Conway						
	Luth Stdnt Fllwshp	800 S Donaghey Ave, 72034	U of Central AR Conway	Jason Hancock	(501) 329-3854	JHancock@conwaycorp.net peaceconway.org
Fayetteville						
	Lutherans and Friends	2730 E Township St, 72704	U of AR	J. D. Zischke	(210) 601-0682	jd.zischke@gmail.com
CALIFORNIA						
Chico						
	Redeemer LC	750 Moss Ave, 95926	CA State U Chico, Butte College	Brennan DeForest	(801) 910-6937	Pastorbd4est@gmail.com redeemerchico.org/
Monterey						
	BLC	800 Cass St, 93940	Defense Lang Inst; CA State Monterey Bay	Josh Schmidt	(314) 261-3180	pastor@blcmonterey.org
San Jose						
	Assoc of Confessing Christians	374 South 3rd St, 95112	San Jose State	Isaac Schuller	(408) 292-5404	pastorschullerfilc@gmail.com firstimmanuel.org
COLORADO						
Boulder						
	U Luth Chapel and Stdnt Ctr	1202 Folsom St, 80302	U of CO—Boulder	Rob Jarvis	(763) 280-4904	pastor@universitylutheranchapel.com universitylutheranchapel.com
Fort Collins						
	Christlife	305 E Elizabeth St, 80524	CO State U	Shawn Nettleton	(970) 482-5316	nettleton@stjohnsfc.org stjohnsfc.org
FLORIDA						
Gainesville						
	First LC	1801 NW 5th Ave, 32603	U of FL	John Glover	(352) 376-2062	office@flcgainsville.org
Oviedo						
	St. Luke's Lighthouse Min	2021 W State Rd 426, 32765	U of Central FL	Samuel Shick	(407) 365-3408	sshick@sllcs.org sllcs.org
Tallahassee						
	U LC	925 W Jefferson St, 32303	FL State U, FL A & M U Tallahassee State College	Jay Winters	(850) 778-5854	pastor@universitylutheranchurch.org universitylutheranchurch.org

State City	Ministry Name	Address, Zip Code	Schools Serving	Contact	Phone	Email Website
GEORGIA						
Athens						
	Christus Victor LC & Stdnt Ctr	1010 S Lumpkin St, 30605	U of GA	Greg Michael	(706) 543-3801	pastor.christusvictor@gmail.com christusvictor.net
Dahlonega						
	Luth Stdnt Fllwshp	109 Tipton Dr, 30533	U of N GA	David Kruger	(706) 864-6001	pastor.stpeterlutheran@gmail.com
ILLINOIS						
Carbondale						
	Luth Stdnt Fllwshp	700 S University Ave, 62901	S IL U—Carbondale	Jay Holden	(618) 549-1694	lutheran@siu.edu oslcdale.org
Champaign						
	U LC & Stdnt Ctr	604 E Chalmers St, 61820	U of IL—Urbana- Champaign, Parkland C	Michael Schuermann	(217) 344-1558	churchoffice@uniluchampaign.org uniluchampaign.org
Charleston						
	Immanuel Lutheran Campus Ministry	902 Cleveland Ave, 61920	E IL U, Lakeland CC	Ken Hoover	(217) 345-3008	pastorken@immanuelcharleston.com ilcm.info
Chicago						
	St James LC	2010 Fremont, 60614	DePaul U, Loyola, Columbia, Roosevelt	Joel Hess	(773) 525-4990	pastorhess@stjames-lutheran.org stjames-lutheran.org
DeKalb						
	Immanuel LC (Refuge)	511 Russell Rd, 60115	N IL U, Kishwaukee C	Marty Marks	(815) 756-6669	rev@godwithusilc.org immanueldekalb.com/
Edwardsville						
	LCMS U at SIUE	600 Water St, 62025	S IL U—Edwardsville	Jess Biermann	(314) 255-8066	lcmsuatsiue@gmail.com siuelutherans.com
Macomb						
	Immanuel Luth Stdnt Ctr	303 N Clay St, 61455	W IL U	Glenn Busse	(309) 337-2707	glennbusse@comcast.net immanuelmacomb.com
Normal						
	Wittenberg Luth Ctr	201 S Main St, 61761	IL State U, IL Wesleyan U, Heartland CC	Wm. Jensen	(309) 452-5971	wittenbergLCMS@gmail.com wittenberg-LCMS.org wittenberglutherancenter.com
Peoria						
	LCMS U (Trinity)	135 NE Randolph Ave, 61606	Bradley U	Mark Nelson	(309) 676-4609	pastornelson@trinitypeoria.com trinitypeoria.com
INDIANA						
Bloomington						
	U LC/LCMS U IN	607 E 7th St, 47408	IN U—Bloomington, Ivy Tech S	Timothy Winterstein	(812) 336-5387	indianalutheran@gmail.com indianalutheran.com
Evansville						
	Faith in Action	1811 Lincoln Ave, 47725	U of Evansville	Jeremy Seger	(812) 476-9991	jeremy@redeemerchurch.org
Ft Wayne						
	LCMS U	1145 S Barr St, 46801	Purdue U-FW	Thomas Sabel	(260) 438-6057	geoff.robinson@in.lcms.org
Indianapolis						
	LCMS U Indy	2525 E 11th St, 46201	Butler U, IUPUI, U of Indianapolis, Marian	Seth Mierow	(317) 638-7245	prmierow@gmail.com stpetersindy.org
Muncie						
	Ball State LCMS U	610 N Reserve St, 47303	Ball State U, IN Acdmy, Taylor U	(Vicar)	(765) 282-2537	gracelutheran2@sbcglobal.net gracemuncielcms.com
Terre Haute						
	LCMS U Terre Haute	645 Poplar St, 47807	IN State U, Rose-Hulman Inst of Tech Ivy Tech CC; Saint Mary-of-the- Woods C	Kurt Cockran	(812) 232-4972	pastorcockran@ielcth.org ielcth.org
Valparaiso						
	Valpo LCMS U	1600 Chapel Dr, 46383	Valparaiso U	James Wetzstein	(219) 464-6794	james.wetzstein@valpo.edu valpo.edu/chapel
West Lafayette						
	U LC	460 Northwestern Ave, 47906	Purdue U	Justin Herman	(765) 743-2472	ulutheranchurch@gmail.com ulupurdue.org
IOWA						
Ames						
	Memorial LC & Stdnt Ctr	2228 Lincoln Way, 50014	IA State U	David Beagley	(515) 292-5005	drbeagley@gmail.com memoriallutheranchurch.org/
Cedar Falls						
	LCMS U at UNI	2322 Olive St, 50613	U of N IA	John Wegener	(319) 266-1274	prwegener@cfu.net college-hill.org
Iowa City						
	St Paul's Luth Chapel & U Center	404 E Jefferson St, 52245	U of IA	W Max Mons	(319) 337-3652	stpaulschapel.iowacity@gmail.com stpaulic.com
Waverly						
	Wartburg Walther League	415 4th St SW, 50677	Wartburg C	Jon Ellingworth	(319) 352-2314	pastorellingworth@gmail.com

State / City	Ministry Name	Address, Zip Code	Schools Serving	Contact	Phone	Email / Website
KANSAS						
Emporia						
	Luth Stdnt Org	1 Kellogg Cir, 66801	Emporia State U	Gwen Larson	(620) 341-5528	glarson1@emporia.edu
Garden City						
	Trinity LC	1010 Fleming St, 67846	Garden City CC	Michael Hageman	(620) 276-3110	trinitygcks@gmail.com tlcgck.org
Lawrence						
	Luth Stdnt Fllwshp	2104 Bob Billings Pkwy, 66049	Kansas U, Baker, Haskell	Andrew Wehling	(785) 843-0620	immanuellutheran@ilcandusc.org immanuellawrence.org
	Redeemer LC	2700 Lawrence Ave, 66047	Kansas U, Baker, Haskell	Sean Kilgo	(785) 843-8181	redeemer.lutheran@att.net redeemer-lawrence.org
Manhattan						
	LCMS U KSU	354 N Delaware Ave, 66502	KS State U	Jessica Jones	(785) 539-2604	office@stlukesmanhattan.org stlukesmanhattan.org
Salina						
	Trinity LC	702 S Ninth, 67401	Kansas Wesleyan, Bethany, Kansas State—Salina	Mark Boxman	(620) 441-8342	markdboxman@gmail.com trinitysalina.org
Topeka						
	Christ LC	3509 SW Burlingame Rd, 66611	Washburn	Ben Micheel	(785) 266-6263	pastormicheel@christlcms.org christlcms.org
	Faith LC	1716 SW Gage Blvd, 66604	Washburn, Washburn Inst of Tech	Heather McCormick	(785) 272-4214	DCEHeather@faithlutherantopeka.com faithlutherantopeka.com
Wichita						
	Fairmount Ministries	3815 E 17th St N, 67208	Wichita State U, Butler CC, WSU Tech	Hannah Elsey	(316) 684-5224	info@fairmountministries.org fairmountministries.org
Winfield						
	Trinity LC & S	910 Mound St, 67156	Southwestern	Seth A Meyer	(620) 221-1820	revsahmeyer@gmail.com trinitylutheranwinfield.com
KENTUCKY						
Lexington						
	St John's Campus Ministry	516 Pasadena Dr, 40503	U of KY	Michael Hartley	(859) 277-6391	DCE@stjohnslexington.org
Richmond						
	Eastern LCMS U	511 Spinnaker Dr, 40475	Eastern KY	Vernon Wendt, Jr	(616) 717-0882	outreachkentucky@gmail.com www.tlcrk.360unite.com
LOUISIANA						
Baton Rouge						
	LCMS U at LSU (Chapel of the Cross)	3235 Dalrymple Dr, 70802	LA State U	Gary Peterson	(225) 978-2965	chapelcrossluthbr@yahoo.com
MARYLAND						
Baltimore						
	LC of Our Savior	3301 The Alameda, 21218	John Hopkins U, U of Baltimore, Morgan State	Roy A Coats	(410) 235-9553	oslbaltimore@yahoo.com oursaviourbaltimore.org
Pasadena						
	Luth Campus Min	236 Beachwood Rd, 21122	Gallaudet	Andrew Petajan	(202) 459-6680	andrew-petajan@gallaudet.edu gallaudet.edu/student-center-program-services/office-of-campus-ministries/lutheran-campus-ministry
MASSACHUSETTS						
Boston						
	FLC Stdnt & Early Career Min	299 Berkeley St, 02116	Colleges/Univ of Greater Boston	Miguel Barcelos	(617) 536-8851	youngadults@flc-boston.org
MICHIGAN						
Ann Arbor						
	CUAA Campus	4090 Geddes Rd, 48105	Concordia U—Ann Arbor	Randall Duncan	(734) 968-9339	randall.duncan@cuaa.edu
	U Luth Chapel	1511 Washtenaw Ave, 48105	U of MI	Marcus Lane	(743) 663-5560	info@ulcannarbor.org ulcannarbor.org
Big Rapids						
	LCMS—U Ferris State	408 W Bellevue, 49307	Ferris State U	Tyson Bentz	(231) 796-6684	LCMSU.fsu@gmail.com
East Lansing						
	Martin Luther Chapel	444 Abbot Rd, 48823	MI State U, Lansing CC	James Robinson	(517) 332-0778	robinsonj@martinlutherchapel.org martinlutherchapel.org
Houghton						
	Concordia Stdnt Min	217 Blanche St, 49931	MI Tech U	Marcus Huff	(906) 482-4750	marcus@copperluth.org copperluth.org/college-ministry
Jenison						
	Campus Lutherans	9628 48th Ave, 49428	Grand Valley State U	Marin Cerchez	(616) 201-7305	stjohn.pastormc@gmail.com stjohnlutherans.org
Kalamazoo						
	Solid Grounds Stdnt Ministries	1720 W. Michigan Ave, 49006	Western MI U	Mark Couch	(319) 505-0930	savannah@zionkazoo.org

State / City	Ministry Name	Address, Zip Code	Schools Serving	Contact	Phone	Email / Website
Marquette						
	Redeemer Campus Ministry	1522 Lincoln Ave, 49855-1605	Northern MI U	Anna Gemar	(906) 228-9883	dceanna@redeemermqt.org redeemermqt.org/nmu
Mount Pleasant						
	Christ the King Luth Chapel	1401 S Washington St, 48858	Central MI U		(989) 773-5050	christthekingatcmu.org
West Olive						
	Campus Lutherans	15424 Lake Michigan Dr, 49460	Grand Valley State U, Hope	Scott Benjamin	(616) 534-0805	office@christevangelicallutheran.org christevangelicallutheran.org
Ypsilanti						
	Cross and Resurrection the Chapel at EMU	812 Ann St, 48197	Eastern MI U, Washtenaw CC, Concordia U AA	Bryan Schindel	(734) 474- 1626	pastor@crossandres.org emuchapel.com
MINNESOTA						
Duluth						
	Luth Stdnt Fllwshp	2012 E Superior St, 55812	U of MN—Duluth, C of St Scholastica, Lake Superior C	Rachel Franck	(218) 724-2500	revfranck@msn.com mtoliveduluth.org
Marshall						
	Good Shep Campus Min	1600 E College Dr, 56258	SW MN State U	James Stefanic	(507) 532-4857	pastor@gslcmarshall.org gslcmarshall.org
Minneapolis						
	U Luth Chapel	316 10th Ave SE, 55414	U of MN, Concordia St Paul, Augsburg, U of St Thomas, Hamline	David Kind	(612) 331-2747	lutheran@umn.edu ulcmn.com
Morris						
	Zion Campus Ministry	315 S Columbia Ave, 56267	U MN Morris	Sophia Greenfield	(262) 417-4370	DCEGreenfield@gmail.com zion-morris.360unite.com/campus-ministry
Northfield						
	Trinity LC	803 Winona St, 55057	Carleton, St Olaf	Lisa Martinson	(507) 645-4438	dce.lisa@trinitynorthfield.org
St Cloud						
	Luth Stdnt Fllwshp	3000 County Rd 8 SE, 56303	St Cloud State U	Joshua Reber	(320) 227-4026	joshua.reber@ctsfw.edu faithstcloud.org/lsf
Winona						
	Luth Stdnt Fllwshp	328 E Broadway St, 55987	Winona State U	Ruth Badciong	(507) 452-6928	church@stmartinswinona.org
MISSISSIPPI						
Oxford						
	Luth Stdnt Fllwshp	407 W Jackson Ave, 38655	U of MS, NW MS CC	Jake Bennett	(662) 234-6568	peacelcmsu@gmail.com peaceoxford.ctshost.org/lsf
MISSOURI						
Cape Girardeau						
	U Luth Chapel of Hope	903 College Hill Pl, 63701	SE MO State U	Sheryl Spiecker	(573) 225-3986	lutheranchapelofhope@gmail.com
Columbia						
	Campus LC	304 S College Ave, 65201	U of MO, Stephens C, Columbia C Moberly Area CC	Kent Pierce	(573) 442-5942	lsf@campuslutheran.org campuslutheran.org
Kirksville						
	Luth Stdnt Fllwshp	1307 S Florence St, 63501	Truman State U	David Lukefahr	(660) 665-6122	lsftruman@gmail.com lsf.truman.edu/
Point Lookout						
	Luth Stdnt Fllwshp	100 Opportunity Ave, 65726	College of the Ozarks	Joe Western	(417) 690-2469	jwestern@cofo.edu
Rolla						
	Luth Stdnt Fllwshp	801 W 11th St, 65401	MO U of Sci and Tech	Eric Swyres	(573) 364-4525	ilc@ilcrolla.org
Saint Louis						
	Luth Stdnt Fllwshp	9237 Clayton Rd, 63124	Wash U—Danforth Campus Saint Louis U	Patti Miller	(314) 993-1834	deaconess@villagelutheranchurch.org
	Reliant	3500 Caroline St, 63104	WU, STL	Nathan Schultz	(734) 770-4181	nathan.schultz@cmstl.org reliantchurch.org
Springfield						
	Luth Stdnt Ctr	848 S National Ave, 65804	MO State U, Ozarks Tech CC, Drury U, Evangel U	Becky Edwards	(417) 866-5543	director@thelsc.org lsc-springfield.wixsite.com/lsc-springfield
Warrensburg						
	Luth Stdnt Ctr	215 S Holden St, 64093	U of Central MO	Jon-Michael Schweigert	(660) 747-7603	UCMLutherans@gmail.com
MONTANA						
Bozeman						
	Luth Stdnt Fllwshp	225 S Black Ave, 59715	Montana S U	Matt Schiermann	(406) 586-5374	lsfbozeman@gmail.com

State City	Ministry Name	Address, Zip Code	Schools Serving	Contact	Phone	Email Website
NEBRASKA						
Curtis						
	Harvest Fields	504 Wallace Ave, 69025	NE College of Tech Ag	James Peterson	(785) 302-0685	pastorpeterson8@gmail.com sjlc-ec.faithlifesites.com
Kearney						
	Holy Cross C Min	3315 11th Ave, 69025	U of NE—Kearney, Central CC Kearney	Megan Barone	(308) 237-2944	mbarone@hclk.org holycrosskearney.org
Lincoln						
	U Luth Chapel	1510 Q St, 68508	U of NE	Mike Giddings	(701) 306-9584	pastormike@lutheranchapel.org www.chapellunl.org
Wayne						
	Cup of Grace (Luth Stdnt Fllwshp)	117 E 10th St, 68787	Wayne State C	Erik Christensen	(402) 375-1905	pastorerik@gracewayne.com gracewayne.com
NEW JERSEY						
Princeton						
	Luth Campus Min	407 S Nassau St, 08540	Princeton U Princeton Theological Seminary	Martin Erhardt	(609) 924-3642	lcmprinceton@gmail.com princetonlutheranchurch.org
NEW MEXICO						
Portales						
	Faith in Christ LC	1024 W 14th Ln, 88130	E NM U	Gary Piepkorn	(575) 356-2510	ficlc@yucca.net
NEW YORK						
Fredonia						
	St Paul LC	334 Temple St, 14063	SUNY-Fredonia	Matthew Schettler	(716) 672-6731	mcschettler@gmail.com stpaulfredonia.org
Ithaca						
	Trinity Luth Stdnt Fllwshp	149 Honness Ln, 14850	Cornell U, Ithaca C, TC-3, Wells	Pastor Rob Foote	(607) 273-9017	TLC@Trinityithaca.org trinityithaca.org
NORTH DAKOTA						
Fargo						
	Luth Stdnt Fllwshp	1258 N Broadway, 58102	ND State U	Scott Johnson	(701) 293-7979	immanuel.fargo@gmail.com immanuelfargo.360unite.com
Grand Forks						
	Wittenberg Luth Chapel	3120 5th Ave N, 58203	U of ND	Daniel Suelzle	(701) 772-3992	wittenbergchapel@gmail.com wittenbergchapel.com
OHIO						
Columbus						
	LCMS U at OSU	766 S High St, 43206	OH State U	Alex Hinojosa	(614) 444-3456	office@zionlcms.org
Hamilton						
	Immanuel Luth Bible Study Fllwshp	1285 Main St, 45013	Miami U—Ohio	Kaleb Yaeger	(513) 309-1550	pastorjud@hotmail.com immanuelhamiltonchurch.com
Toledo						
	Good Shepherd LC	3934 W Laskey Rd, 43623	U of Toledo	Brad Scott	(419) 474-0529	gslcms@bex.net goodshepherdtoledo.org
OKLAHOMA						
Norman						
	LCMS U	603 S Classen Blvd, 73071	U of OK	Jonathan Anderson	(405) 429-9327	tlcnormanvicar@gmail.com tlcnorman.org/LCMSU
PENNSYLVANIA						
Philadelphia						
	Logos LC	628 N Broad St, 19130	U of PA, Temple U, Villanova U, Drexel U	Robert Kieselowsky	(215) 992-9102	revrobert@phillyministries.org phillyministries.org/campusministry
Pittsburgh						
	Luth Stdnt Fllwshp	533 N Neville St, 15213	The U of Pittsburgh, Carnegie Mellon U, Chatham U	Eric Andrae	(412) 683-4121	ericandrae@gmail.com lsfpgh.com
Slippery Rock						
	All Saints LC & Stdnt Ctr	351 S Main St, 16057	Slippery Rock U, Grove City C, Westminster	Augusta Mennell	(724) 794-4334	rocklutheran@gmail.com rocklutheran.org
State College						
	Revive PSU	851 N Science Park Rd, 16803	Penn State U	Byran Spang	(814) 234-8177	pastorbspang@gmail.com slaybaugh.matt@gmail.com goodshepherdsc.org
SOUTH CAROLINA						
Columbia						
	Holy Trinity Stdnt Fllwshp	2200 Lee St, 29205	U of SC, Midlands Tech, Benedict Allen U: Columbia C	Christopher Burger	(803) 799-7224	holytrinitylcms.contactus@gmail.com
SOUTH DAKOTA						
Brookings						
	Mount Calvary Student Fellowship	629 9th Ave, 57006	SD State U	Micah Bauer	(605) 692-2678	pastormicahbauer@gmail.com mountcalvary1.org
Sioux Falls						
	Our Redeemer Campus Ministry	2200 S Western Ave, 57105	U of Sioux Falls, Augustana U	Pastor	(605) 338-6957	office@ourredeemersf.org ourredeemersf.org
Spearfish						
	St Paul LC	846 N 7th St, 57783	Black Hills State U	Thomas Brown	(605) 642-2929	stpspear@rushmore.com stpaul-spearfish.org
Vermillion						
	Concordia LC and Student Center	7 S University, 57069	U of SD	Matthew Bless	(605) 624-3459	pastor@lcmsvermillion.org lcmsvermillion.org

State City	Ministry Name	Address, Zip Code	Schools Serving	Contact	Phone	Email Website
TENNESSEE						
Nashville						
	Our Savior LC	5110 Franklin Pike, 37220	Belmont, Lipscomb, Vanderbilt	Matt Fischer	(615) 833-1500	matt.fischer@oslcnashville.org oslcnashville.org
TEXAS						
Alpine						
	Luth Stdnt Ministry	1003 W Holland Ave, 79830	Sul Ross U	Philip Frank	(432) 279-0744	atxredeemer@yahoo.com redeemeralpinetx.com/
Austin						
	U LC	2100 San Antonio St, Ste 110, 78705	U of TX, Austin CC	Richard Mittwede	(512) 461-3425	richard@ulcaustin.com ulcaustin.com
Canyon						
	WT Luth Campus Min	2600 4th Ave, 79015	W TX A & M U	Brian Shane	(806) 655-4086	blauterbach1872@gmail.com lutheranchurchstpaul@hotmail.com
College Station						
	U Luth Chapel	802 Eisenhower St, 77841	TX A & M, Blinn C—Bryan	John Karle	(979) 846-6687	universitylutherancs@gmail.com ulctamu.org
Denton						
	Luth Stdnt Fllwshp	703 N Elm St, 76201	U of N TX, TX Women's U,	Ron DuPree	(940) 387-1575	dce@splcdenton.org splcdenton.org
Huntsville						
	Ratio Christi	111 Sumac Rd, 77340	Sam Houston State U	Darren Williams	(936) 577-0407	shsu@ratiochristi.org faithhuntsville.org
Lubbock						
	The Lutheran Student Center of Lubbock	2615 19th St, 79410	Texas Tech U	Jeff Jenkins	(806) 763-3644	lsclubbock@gmail.com lsftech.org
Nacogdoches						
	Redeemer LC & Stdnt Ctr	2306 Appleby Sand Rd, 75965	Stephen F Austin State U	John Cain	(936) 564-6759	rlcnac@yahoo.com redeemerlutherannacogdoches.com
Waco						
	Luth Doing Life Together	1301 Hogan Ln, 76705	Baylor, McLennan County Comm, Texas State Tech	Brian Hesse	(254) 799-3211	pastorhesse@splcwaco.com splcwaco.com/college
VIRGINIA						
Buena Vista						
	Concordia Luth Mission	34 Ben Salem Ln., 24416	VA Military Inst, WA & Lee U	Mark Schroeder	(540) 784-5622	markgnat@gmail.com concordiaandkoinonia.wordpress.com
Charlottesville						
	Immanuel LC	2416 Jefferson Park Ave, 22903	U of VA, Piedmont Valley Comm	Ben Maton	(434) 295-4038	churchoffice@immanuelcharlottesville.com immanuelcharlottesville.com
Fairfax						
	Christ on Campus at St Athanasius LC	3057 Nutley St, Ste 822, 22031	George Mason U, Patrick Henry	James Douthwaite	(703) 455-4003	salchurch7@gmail.com saint-athanasius.org/campusministry
Fairfax Station						
	The Breath	5500 Ox Rd, 22039	George Mason U	Ethan Frost	(703) 352-1421	thebreathgmu@gmail.com
Lynchburg						
	Our Savior LC	2940 Link Rd, 24501	Liberty U	Aaron Yaeger	(434) 384-6651	lsf@oursaviorlynchburg.org oursaviorlynchburg.org
Roanoke						
	Luth Outreach at VA Tech	(Mailing) 1887 Electric Rd, 24018 (Meeting) 601 Drillfield Dr, Blacksburg, 24060	VA Tech	Nathaniel Hall	(540) 774-8746	cma.lovt@gmail.com lovt.wordpress.com
WASHINGTON						
Cheney						
	Eagles LCMS U	216 W 5th St, 99004	Eastern Washington U	Marc DiConti	(951) 490-8680	marc.diconti@gmail.com
Pullman						
	Concordia Campus Min	1015 NE Orchard Dr, 99163	WA State U & U of Idaho	Matt Gulseth	(509) 332-2830	info@concordiapullman.org concordiapullman.org
WISCONSIN						
Eau Claire						
	St. Matthew Luth Stdnt Fllwshp	1915 Hogeboom Ave., 54703	U of WI Eau Claire UW-Green Bay, St. Norbert, Bellin	Jeff Kazmierski	(715) 834-4028	rev.kazmierski@gmail.com stmatthewec.org/index.html
Green Bay						
	LCMSU- Green Bay	2335 S. Webster Ave., 54301	Northeast WI Tech	Deirdre Batiansila	(920) 544-1616	lcmsugb@gmail.com
La Crosse						
	Faith LC & Stdnt Ctr	1407 Main St, 54601	U of WI—La Crosse, Viterbo U, W Tech C	Jacob Eichers	(608) 782-3696	lcmsu@faithonmain.com faithonmain.com
Madison						
	Calvary Luth Chapel	701 State St, 53703	U of WI—Madison	Rev. Allen Strum	(608) 255-7214	calvary@calvarymadison.org calvarymadison.org
Mequon						
	Campus Min Ldrshp Team	12800 N Lake Shore Dr, 53097	Concordia U WI	Jonathan Bakker	(262) 243-4532	jonathan.bakker@cuw.edu
Oshkosh						
	Connected Through Christ	2450 W 9th Ave, 54904	U of WI—Oshkosh	Greg Koepsell	(920) 231-0530	pastor@oshkoshgoodshepherd.org

State Cit	Ministry Name	Address, Zip Code	Schools Serving	Contact	Phone	Email Website
Platteville						
	Luth Stdnt Fllwshp	1096 N. Mainstreet, 53581	U of WI—Platteville	Mark Kufahl	(920) 209-3382	krauselo@uwplatt.edu alcplatteville.wordpress.com/lsf
Shorewood						
	Luther Memorial Chapel & U Stdnt Ctr	3833 N Maryland Ave, 53211	U of WI—Milwaukee, Concordia U W	Michael Larson	(414) 530-5732	mlarson@lmcusc.org lmcusc.org
Stevens Point						
	Peace Luth Campus Ctr	1517 Maria Dr, 54481	U of WI—Stevens Point	Andy Weden	(715) 345-6510	peacelutherancampuscenter@gmail.com
WYOMING						
Laramie						
	St Andrew's LC & Campus Ctr	1309 E Grand Ave, 82070	U of WY, WY Technical Institute	Tim Hu	(307) 745-5892	rso_student@standrewslaramie.org standrewslaramie.org

RETREAT CENTERS AND SUMMER CAMPS

For information regarding seasons, workshops, seminars, and evaluations of camps and programs—
contact National Lutheran Outdoors Ministry Association (NLOMA) (RSO)

Website: nloma.org
Email: nloma@nloma.org

The names and addresses of the following camps are provided as a convenience for congregations that are members of The Lutheran Church—Missouri Synod and for the individual members of those congregations. While some may be operated by or affiliated with Districts of the Synod or may be Recognized Service Organizations subject to the conditions set forth in Bylaw 6.2 of the Synod Bylaws, the inclusion of the names and addresses in the *Annual* does not constitute an endorsement of the camps by the Synod, and the Synod makes no representations or guarantees about the fiscal solvency or financial responsibility of any such camp or with respect to any services implied or expressly offered by any camp. It is the sole responsibility of any organization or individual that might want to use the service of such a camp, to otherwise contract with such a camp, or to make contributions to such a camp to make appropriate inquiries about the camp and its relationship, if any, to any District of the Synod.

(RSO) after the name indicates the retreat center or summer camp is a Recognized Service Organization

ALABAMA
Camp Dixie
29711 Josephine Dr
Elberta, AL 36530
(251) 987-1201
Email: director@campdixieministries.org
Website: campdixieministries.org

ARIZONA
Camp ALOMA
PO Box 3
Prescott, AZ 86302
(928) 778-1690
Email: office@campaloma.com
Website: campaloma.com

ARKANSAS
Lutheran Camp on Petit Jean Mountain (Camp Trinity) (RSO)
110 Montgomery Trace
Morrilton, AR 72110
(501) 652-6304
Email: director@lutherancamp.org
Website: lutherancamp.org

COLORADO
Lutheran Valley Retreat Inc (RSO)
PO Box 9042
Woodland Park, CO 80866-9042
(719) 687-3560
Email: LVR@LVR.org
Website: LVR.org

Family Adventure and Recreational Ministry (RSO)
9620 Chipita Park Rd
Chipita Park, CO 80809
(719) 238-9800
Email: rudysdg@gmail.com
Website: farmministry.org

Trinity Woods Summer Day Camp
1899 Tucker Rd
Macon, GA 31220-5399
(478) 474-8393
Email: campdirector@trinitywoods.org
Website: trinitywoods.org

IDAHO
Lutherhaven Ministries
3258 W Lutherhaven Rd
Coeur D'Alene, ID 83814-1327
(208) 667-3459
Email: info@lutherhaven.com
Website: lutherhaven.com

Shoshone Mountain Retreat
& Ranch
29216 Coeur D'Alene River Rd
Wallace, ID 83873
(208) 682-2267
Email: uptheriver@lutherhaven.com
Website: lutherhaven.com

Camp Perkins Lutheran Outdoor Ministries Inc (RSO)
HC 64 PO Box 9384
Ketchum, ID 83340
(208) 788-0897
Email: info@campperkins.org
Website: campperkins.org

ILLINOIS
Central Illinois Lutheran Camp Association (RSO)
4124 Camp CILCA Rd
Cantrall, IL 62625
(217) 487-7497
Email: office@cilca.org
Website: cilca.org

Camp Wartburg
5705 LRC Rd
Waterloo, IL 62298
(618) 939-7715
(618) 207-3929 Fax
Email: robert_polansky@lcfs.org
Website: campwartburg.com

Walcamp Outdoor Ministries Inc (RSO)
32653 Five Points Rd
Kingston, IL 60145-8443
(815) 784-5141
Email: office@walcamp.org
Website: walcamp.org

INDIANA
South Central Lutheran Camp Association of IN, Inc (RSO)
DBA Lakeview Ministries
13500 W Lake Rd
Seymour, IN 47274
(812) 342-4815
Email: office@lakeview.camp
Website: lakeview.camp

Lutheran Camp Association Inc (RSO)
1596 S 150 W
Albion, IN 46701-9695
(260) 636-7101
(260) 636-3032 Fax
Email: camp@lutherhaven.org
Website: lutherhaven.org

IOWA
Camp Io-Dis-E-Ca
3271 Sandy Beach Rd NE
Solon, IA 52333-9333
(319) 848-4187
(319) 848-4165 Fax
Email: office@campiodiseca.org
Website: campiodiseca.org

Camp Okoboji Lutheran Association (RSO)
1531 Edgewood Dr
Milford, IA 51351-7306
(712) 337-3325
(866) 449-3326 Fax
Email: adam.campokoboji@gmail.com
Website: campokoboji.org

MICHIGAN
Camp Arcadia
PO Box 229
Arcadia, MI 49613-0229
(231) 889-4361
(888) 753-1922 Fax
Email: info@camp-arcadia.com
Website: camp-arcadia.com

Camp Concordia Inc (RSO)
13400 Pinewood St NE
Gowen, MI 49326
(616) 754-3785
Email: office@campconcordia.org
Website: campconcordia.org

Camp Lu Lay Lea Inc. (RSO)
92 Ohio St
Lupton, MI 48635
(989) 971-4810
Email: director@camplulaylee.com
Website: camplulaylea.org

MINNESOTA
Camp Omega, Inc (RSO)
22750 Lind Ave
Waterville, MN 56096-9320
(507) 685-4266
(507) 685-4401 Fax
Email: info@campomega.org
Website: campomega.org

Lutheran Island Camp
45011 230th St
Henning, MN 56551-9449
(218) 583-2905
Email: info@islandcamp.org
Website: islandcamp.org

MISSOURI
Camp SEMO Wappapello
2060 Wayne 522
Wappapello, MO 63966
(573) 222-8279
Website: campsemowappapello.org

Camp Trinity
439 Camp Trinity Dr
New Haven, MO 63068-2213
(573) 237-2072
Email: camptrinity73@yahoo.com
Website: camptrinity.org

Heit's Point Lutheran Ministries Inc (RSO)
28345 Heit's Point Ave
Lincoln, MO 65338
(660) 668-2363
Email: info@heitspoint.org
Website: heitspointlutheran.org

MINISTRIES

MONTANA
Trinity Lutheran Camp
450 Pierce Lane
Bigfork, MT 59911
(406) 257-5683
Email: trinitycampdirector@gmail.com
Website: trinitylutherancamp.org

NEBRASKA
Camp Luther of Nebraska Inc (RSO)
1050 Road 4
Schuyler, NE 68661-7145
(402) 352-5655
(888) 442-5655 Fax
Email: campluther@campluther.org
Website: campluther.org

NEW YORK
Friends of Pioneer Inc Center (RSO)
9324 Lake Shore Rd
Angola, NY 14006
(716) 383-6157
Email: office@pioneeronthelake.com
Website: pioneeronthelake.com

NORTH CAROLINA
Camp Linn Haven Inc. (RSO)
PO Box 1096
Linville, NC 28646
(828) 320-2840
Email: camplinnhaven@gmail.com
Website: camplinnhaven.org

NORTH DAKOTA
Shepherd's Hill Retreats Inc (RSO)
502 Shepherds Hill Dr
St John, ND 58369
(701) 244-5225
(701) 244-2152 Fax
Email: director@shretreat.org
Website: shretreat.org

OKLAHOMA
Camp Lutherhoma
23197 East 742 Rd
Tahlequah, OK 74465
(918) 458-0704
Email: lutherhoma@lutherhoma.com
Website: lutherhoma.com

Lutherhaven Retreat Center
C/O Trinity Lutheran Church
1212 N. Crumley St
Guymon, OK 73942
(580) 423-7224
Email: wescoattmd@gmail.com
Website: facebook.com/profile.php?id=
100064772584008

OREGON
Camp Lutherwood
22960 Highway 36
Cheshire, OR 97419-9741
(541) 998-6444
Email: office@lutherwoodoregon.org
Website: lutherwoodoregon.org

Camp Serene
91707 Poodle Creek Rd
Noti, OR 97461
(541) 998-2593
Website: facebook.com/SereneDiscGolf/

TENNESSEE
First Lutheran Church Camp
1621 Lee Pike
Soddy-Daisy, TN 37379
(423) 629-5990
Email: flccamp@aol.com
Website: first4U.org

TEXAS
Lutheran Outdoors Ministry of Texas, Inc (RSO)
DBA Camp Lone Star
2016 Camp Lone Star Rd
LaGrange, TX 78945
(979) 968-1657
Email: info@camplonestar.org
Website: camplonestar.org

UTAH
Camp Lutherwood of Utah
US 89 & Utah Rt. 14
Long Valley Junction, UT 84710
(800) 205-4887
Email: lutherwoodutah@aol.com
Website: camplutherwoodutah.org

WASHINGTON
Lutherwood Camp and Retreat Center
1185 Roy Rd
Bellingham, WA 98229
(360) 734-7652
Email: office@camplutherwood.org
Website: camplutherwood.org

Valley Camp Ministries
49515 SE Middle Fork Rd
North Bend, WA 98045
(425) 888-1852
Email: info@valleycamp.org
Website: vallleycamp.org

WISCONSIN
Camp Luther
1889 Koubenic Rd
Three Lakes, WI 54562
(715) 546-3647
Email: info@campluther.com
Website: campluther.com

Camp LuWiSoMo, Inc (RSO)
W5421 Aspen Rd
Wild Rose, WI 54984
(920) 622-3350
Email: camp@luwisomo.org
Website: luwisomo.org

ECCLESIASTICAL RELATIONS OF THE LCMS

The following church bodies are listed by category and in alphabetical order by country. If you would like further background or contact information about a specific church body, please email the LCMS Office of the President, Attention: Church Relations, at michael.fr
ese@lcms.org or georgia.endicott@lcms.org.

SISTER CHURCHES IN ALTAR AND PULPIT FELLOWSHIP (44)

ARGENTINA
Ev. Lutheran Church of Argentina (IELA)

BELGIUM
Ev. Lutheran Church in Belgium (ELKB)

BOLIVIA
Evangelical Christian Lutheran Church of Bolivia (ICEL)

BRAZIL
Ev. Lutheran Church of Brazil (IELB)

CANADA
Lutheran Church–Canada (LCC)

CHILE
Confessional Lutheran Church of Chile (ILCC)

DENMARK
Ev. Lutheran Free Church in Denmark (ELFCD)

ENGLAND
Ev. Lutheran Church of England (ELCE)

FINLAND
Evangelical Lutheran Mission Diocese of Finland (ELMDF)

FRANCE
Ev. Lutheran Church–Synod of France (EELSF)

GERMANY
Independent Ev. Lutheran Church (SELK)

GHANA
Ev. Lutheran Church of Ghana (ELCG)

GUATEMALA
Lutheran Church of Guatemala (ILG)

HAITI
Evangelical Lutheran Church of Haiti (ELCH)

HONG KONG
The Lutheran Church–Hong Kong Synod (LCHKS)

INDIA
India Evangelical Lutheran Church (IELC)

KAZAKHSTAN
Evangelical Lutheran Church in Almaty (ELCA)

KENYA
Ev. Lutheran Church in Kenya (ELCK)

KOREA
Lutheran Church in Korea (LCK)

LATVIA
Ev. Lutheran Church of Latvia (LELB)

LIBERIA
Evangelical Lutheran Church in Liberia (ELCL)

LITHUANIA
Ev. Lutheran Church of Lithuania (LELB)

MEXICO
Lutheran Synod of Mexico (SLM)

NIGERIA
Lutheran Church of Nigeria (LCN)

NORWAY
Lutheran Church in Norway and Iceland (LKNI)

PAPUA NEW GUINEA
Gutnius Lutheran Church (GLC)

PARAGUAY
Ev. Lutheran Church of Paraguay (IELP)

PHILIPPINES
Lutheran Church in the Philippines (LCP)

PORTUGAL
Portuguese Evangelical Lutheran Church (IELP)

RUSSIA
Evangelical Lutheran Church of Ingria in Russia (ELCIR)

RUSSIA (Cont.)
Siberian Evangelical Lutheran Church (SELC)

SOUTH AFRICA
Confessional Lutheran Church of South Africa (CLCSA)

Free Evangelical Lutheran Synod in South Africa (FELSISA)

Lutheran Church in Southern Africa (LCSA)

SOUTH SUDAN
Evangelical Lutheran Church of South Sudan/ Sudan (ELCSS/S)

SPAIN
Evangelical Lutheran Church of Spain (IELE)

SRI LANKA
Ceylon Evangelical Lutheran Church (CELC)

TAIWAN
China Evangelical Lutheran Church (CELC)

TOGO
Lutheran Church of Togo (ELT)

UGANDA
Lutheran Church of Uganda (LCU)

UKRAINE
Evangelical Lutheran Church of Ukraine (ELCU)

UNITED STATES
American Association of Lutheran Churches (AALC)

URUGUAY
Lutheran Church of Uruguay (ILU)

VENEZUELA
Lutheran Church of Venezuela (ILV)

ASSOCIATE CHURCH BODIES (36)

(Non-Fellowship, Cooperating) Working toward Altar and Pulpit Fellowship through Theological Dialogue/Education/Mercy Work

AUSTRALIA
Lutheran Mission – Australia (LM-A)

BENIN
Lutheran Church in Africa—Synod of Benin (ELA-SBE)

BURKINA FASO
Evangelical Lutheran Church of Burkina Faso (EELBF)

BURUNDI
Lutheran Church in Africa — Synod of Burundi (ELA-SBU)

CAMBODIA
Cambodia Lutheran Church (CLC)

CONGO, DEM. REP. OF
Evangelical Lutheran Church in East Congo (CELCE)

CONGO, DEM. REP. OF (Cont.)
Evangelical Lutheran Confessional Church in the Congo (EELCC)

CONGO, REP. OF
Evangelical Lutheran Church in Congo (EELC)

COTE D'IVOIRE
Lutheran Church in Africa – Synod of Cote D'Ivoire (ELA-SCI) (Ivory Coast)

CZECH REPUBLIC
Evangelical Church of the Augsburg Confession in the Czech Republic (ECAVvCR)

Silesian Evangelical Church of the Augsburg Confession (SCEAV) (Czech Republic)

ERITREA
Evangelical Lutheran Church Eritrea (ELCE)

ETHIOPIA
Ethiopian Evangelical Lutheran Church (EELC)

GAMBIA
The Lutheran Church of The Gambia (LCG)

GUINEA
Evangelical Lutheran Church of Guinea (EELG)

INDIA
Bible Faith Lutheran Church (BFLC)

INDIA (Cont.)
Manipur Evangelical Lutheran Church (MELC)

INDONESIA
The Indonesian Christian Lutheran Church (GKLI)

JAPAN
West Japan Ev. Lutheran Church (WJELC)

KYRGYZSTAN
Lutheran Church Concordia (LCC)

MADAGASCAR
Malagasy Lutheran Church (FLM)

MALAWI
Confessional Lutheran Church—Malawi Synod (CLC-MS)

MALAYSIA
Evangelical Lutheran Church in Malaysia (ELCM)

NICARAGUA
Lutheran Church Synod of Nicaragua (ILSN)

NORWAY
The Evangelical Lutheran Diocese in Norway (DELSIN)

PANAMA
Evangelical Lutheran Church of Panama (IELPA)

PERU
Evangelical Lutheran Church—Peru (IEL-P)

RWANDA
Lutheran Mission in Africa— Synod of Thousand Hills (LMA—STH) (Rwanda)

SIERRA LEONE
Christ Evangelical Lutheran Church—Sierra Leone (CELC-SL)

SOUTH SUDAN
South Sudan Evangelical Lutheran Church (SSELC)

SWEDEN
Mission Province in Sweden (MPS)

SWITZERLAND
Confessional Lutheran Church in Switzerland (CLCS)

TANZANIA
Lutheran Church in East Africa (LCEA)

South East of Lake Victoria Diocese (SELVD-ELCT)

TURKEY
Istanbul Lutheran Church (ILK)

UNITED STATES
The Lutheran Ministerium and Synod (LMSUSA) (U.S.)

OTHER CHURCHES WORKING TOWARD FAITHFUL ECUMENISM AND JOINT STATEMENTS (24)

AUSTRALIA
Lutheran Church of Australia (LCA)

BANGLADESH
Bangladesh Northern Evangelical Lutheran Church (BNELC)

BELARUS
Independent Evangelical Lutheran Church in Belarus (IELCB)

BURUNDI
Hope Evangelical Lutheran Church in Burundi (HELCB)

COLOMBIA
Iglesia Confessionnal de Colombia (ICC)

CONGO, DEM. REP. OF
Church of Faithful Confessing Lutherans in Congo (CFCLCO)

ETHIOPIA
Ethiopian Evangelical Church Mekane Yesus (EECMY)

Gambella Evangelical Lutheran Church in Ethiopia (GELCE)

JAPAN
Japan Lutheran Church (JLC)

KAZAKSTAN
Evangelical Lutheran Church in the Republic of Kazakhstan (ELCRK)

KENYA
Evangelical Lutheran Conference and Ministerium of Kenya (ELCMK)

NEPAL
Himalayan Evangelical Lutheran Fellowship (HELF) (Nepal)

NORWAY
Evangelical Lutheran Church Society (DELK) (Norway)

Norwegian Lutheran Mission (NLM)

RWANDA
Lutheran Church of Rwanda (LCR)

SINGAPORE
Lutheran Church in Singapore (LCS)

TAIWAN
Lutheran Church of the Republic of China (LCROC)

UNITED STATES
Anglican Church of America (ACA)

Anglican Catholic Church (ACC)

Anglican Church in North America (ACNA)

Anglican Province of America (APA)

Evangelical Lutheran Synod (ELS)

North American Lutheran Church (NALC)

Wisconsin Evangelical Lutheran Synod (WELS)

SYNODICAL INFORMATION

Synodical Officers, Past and Present

A. Presidents

C. F. W. Walther, 1847–50; 1864–78
  Residence: St. Louis
F. C. D. Wyneken, 1850–64
  Residence: St. Louis, 1850–59; Friedheim, IN, 1859–64
H. C. Schwan, 1878–99
  Residence: Cleveland, OH
Franz Pieper, 1899–1911
  Residence: St. Louis
F. Pfotenhauer, 1911–35
  Residence: Chicago
J. W. Behnken, 1935–62
  Residence: Oak Park, 1935–51; St. Louis, 1951–62
Oliver R. Harms, 1962–69
  Residence: St. Louis
J. A. O. Preus, 1969–81
  Residence: St. Louis
Ralph A. Bohlmann, 1981–92
  Residence: St. Louis
Alvin Barry, 1992–2001
  Residence: St. Louis
Robert T. Kuhn, 2001
  Residence: St. Louis
Gerald B. Kieschnick, 2001–10
  Residence: St. Louis
Matthew C. Harrison, 2010–

B. Vice-Presidents

Wm. Sihler, 1847–54; 1864–69; 1874–78
Th. Brohm, 1851–57; 1860–64; 1869–74
H. C. Schwan, 1857–60
C. J. H. Fick, 1874–78
C. H. R. Lange, 1878–81
Carl Gross, 1878–79
Otto Hanser, 1881–84
C. H. Loeber, 1884–87
Henry Succop, 1887–90; 1905–8
H. C. Sauer, 1890–93
J. P. Beyer, 1893–99
C. C. Schmidt, 1899–1908
P. Brand, 1899–1917
F. Pfotenhauer, 1908–11
J. W. Miller, 1908–29
J. C. Strasen, 1908–14
John Hilgendorf, 1911–20
H. Speckhard, 1914–17
Fred Brand, 1917–29
H. P. Eckhardt, 1917–26
G. A. Bernthal, 1920–26
Wm. Dallmann, 1926–32
F. J. Lankenau, 1926–39
J. W. Behnken, 1929–35
Fred Randt, 1929–37
Henry Grueber, 1932–47
Karl Kretzschmar, 1935–38
Hermann Harms, 1938–59
A. J. Brunn, 1941–49
G. Chr. Barth, 1941–47
F. A. Hertwig, 1947–56
W. F. Lichtsinn, 1947–59
E. J. Friedrich, 1949–50
A. H. Grumm, 1950–59
Oliver R. Harms, 1956–62
R. P. Wiederaenders, 1959–73
George W. Wittmer, 1959–69
Arthur C. Nitz, 1959–65
Theo F. Nickel, 1962–77
W. Harry Krieger, 1965–69; 1972–74
Paul W. Streufert, 1965–72
Victor L. Behnken, 1969–71
Edwin C. Weber, 1969–81
Guido A. Merkens, 1971–83; 1986–89
Walter A. Maier Jr., 1973–95
August Bernthal, 1974–77
Robert C. Sauer, 1977–86; 1989–95
George Wollenburg, 1977–81; 1983–89
Gerhardt W. Hyatt, 1981–85
Joseph G. Lavalais, 1981–83
Robert H. King, 1986–2007
August Mennicke, 1986–95
Eugene W. Bunkowske, 1989–98
Robert T. Kuhn, 1995–2001; 2013–15
Dale A. Meyer, 1995–98
Wallace Schulz, 1995–2004
Roger Pittelko, 1998–2001
William Weinrich, 1998–2004
Daniel Preus, 2001–4; 2010–19
Paul Maier, 2001–13
William R. Diekelman, 2004–10
Dean W. Nadasdy, 2004–10
David D. Buegler, 2004–10
John C. Wohlrabe Jr., 2007–
Herbert C. Mueller Jr., 2010–19
Scott R. Murray, 2010–
Nabil S. Nour, 2013–
Christopher S. Esget, 2015–
Benjamin T. Ball, 2019–
Peter K. Lange, 2019–

C. Secretaries

F. W. Husmann, 1847–50; 1854–60
L. W. Habel, 1850–54
J. A. F. W. Mueller, 1860–66
Geo. Kuechle, 1866–74
Aug. Rohrlack, 1874–1905
R. D. Biedermann, 1905–20
M. F. Kretzmann, 1920–56
Walter C. Birkner, 1956–65
Herbert A. Mueller, 1965–83
Walter L. Rosin, 1983–98
Raymond L. Hartwig, 1998–2016
John W. Sias, 2016–

D. Treasurers/Chief Financial Officer

F. W. Barthel, 1847–57
Ferd. Boehlau, 1857–63
J. F. Schuricht, Sr., 1863–81
E. F. W. Meier, 1881–1902
J. F. Schuricht Jr., 1902–14
Edmund Seuel, 1914–42
W. H. Schlueter, 1942–58
Martin E. Strieter, 1958–62
Milton Carpenter, 1962–77
Norman Sell, 1977–99
Paul W. Middeke, 1999–2001
Thomas W. Kuchta, 2001–10
Jerald C. Wulf, 2011–20
Frank Simek (interim), 2022
Nathan Haak, 2022–

E. Chief Administrative Officers

Bradford L. Hewitt, 1998–2003
Ronald P. Schultz, 2005–17
Frank Simek, 2017–23
Felix Loc, 2023–

F. Chief Mission Officers

Gregory K. Williamson, 2011–14
J. Bart Day (interim), 2014–15
Kevin P. Robson, 2015–25
Dan Galchutt (interim), 2025—

General and Delegate Conventions of the Synod

General Convs.	Delegate Convs.	Year	Place
1	—	1847	Chicago
2	—	1848	St. Louis
3	—	1849	Fort Wayne
4	—	1850	St. Louis
5	—	1851	Milwaukee
6	—	1852	Fort Wayne
7	—	1853	Cleveland
8	—	1854	St. Louis
9	—	1857	Fort Wayne
10	—	1860	St. Louis
11	—	1863	Fort Wayne
12	—	1864	Fort Wayne
13	—	1866	St. Louis
14	—	1869	Fort Wayne
15	—	1872	St. Louis
16	1	1874	Fort Wayne
17	2	1878	St. Louis
18	3	1881	Fort Wayne
19	4	1884	St. Louis
20	5	1887	Fort Wayne
21	6	1890	Milwaukee
22	7	1893	St. Louis
23	8	1896	Fort Wayne
24	9	1899	St. Louis
25	10	1902	Milwaukee
26	11	1905	Detroit
27	12	1908	Fort Wayne
28	13	1911	St. Louis
29	14	1914	Chicago
30	15	1917	Milwaukee
31	16	1920	Detroit
32	17	1923	Fort Wayne
33	18	1926	St. Louis
34	19	1929	River Forest
35	20	1932	Milwaukee
36	21	1935	Cleveland
37	22	1938	St. Louis
38	23	1941	Fort Wayne
39	24	1944	Saginaw
40	25	1947	Chicago
41	26	1950	Milwaukee
42	27	1953	Houston
43	28	1956	St. Paul
44	29	1959	S. Francisco
45	30	1962	Cleveland
46	31	1965	Detroit
47	32	1967	New York
48	33	1969	Denver
49	34	1971	Milwaukee
50	35	1973	New Orleans
51	36	1975	Anaheim
52	37	1977	Dallas
53	38	1979	St. Louis
54	39	1981	St. Louis
55	40	1983	St. Louis
56	41	1986	Indianapolis
57	42	1989	Wichita
58	43	1992	Pittsburgh
59	44	1995	St. Louis
60	45	1998	St. Louis
61	46	2001	St. Louis
62	47	2004	St. Louis
63	48	2007	Houston
64	49	2010	Houston
65	50	2013	St. Louis
66	51	2016	Milwaukee
67	52	2019	Tampa
68	53	2023	Milwaukee

Place	Number
St. Louis	21
Fort Wayne	13
Milwaukee	8
Chicago	4
Cleveland	3
Denver	1
Detroit	3
Houston	3
New Orleans	1
New York	1
Saginaw	1
St. Paul	1
San Francisco	1
Anaheim	1
Dallas	1
Indianapolis	1
Wichita	1
Pittsburgh	1
Tampa	1
	68

Origin of Synodical Districts

Name	*First Meeting*	*Branched Off (from Division of)*	*Districts That Have Branched Off*
Alberta-British Columbia°°°	1921	Minnesota	—
Argentine°°	1928	Brazil	—
Atlantic	1907	Eastern	New England, 1971 New Jersey, 1971
Brazil°	1904	—	Argentine, 1927
California-Oregon†	1887	Western	Oregon-Wash, 1899 Calif-Nevada, 1899
Calif-Nev-Hawaii*	1899	Calif-Oregon	Southern Calif, 1930
Central†	1855	—	Indiana, 1963 Ohio, 1963
Central Illinois	1909	Illinois	—
Eastern	1855	—	Atlantic, 1907
English	1911	—	Southeastern, 1939
Florida-Georgia	1948	Southern	—
Illinois†	1875	Western	Tripartition, 1909
Indiana	1963	Central	—
Iowa†	1879	Western	Division, 1936
Iowa East	1936	Iowa	—
Iowa West	1936	Iowa	—
Kansas	1888	Western	Colorado, 1921 Oklahoma, 1924
Manitoba-Saskatchewan°°°†±	1922	Minnesota	
Michigan ("Northern" prior to 1881)	1882	Northern	
Mid-South	1966	Western	—
Minnesota-Dakota ("Minnesota" since 1910)†	1882 1910	Northwestern N. Dakota-Montana	South Dakota, 1906
Minnesota North	1963	Minnesota	—
Minnesota South	1963	Minnesota	—
Missouri	1966	Western	—
Montana	1945	N. Dak.-Montana	—
Nebraska†	1882	Western	Division, 1922
Nebraska	1970	N. and S. Nebr. Merged	Wyoming, 1970
New England	1971	Atlantic	—
New Jersey	1971	Atlantic	—
North Dakota	1945	N. Dak.-Montana	—
North Dakota-Montana†	1910	Minnesota-Dakota	Division, 1945
North Wisconsin	1918	Wisconsin	—
Northern†	1855	—	Northwestern, 1875 Canada, 1879 Michigan, 1882
Northern Illinois	1909	Illinois	—
Northern Nebraska†	1922	Nebraska	—
Northwest ("Oregon-Washington" before 1948)	1899	Calif-Oregon	—
Northwestern†	1874	Northern	Minnesota-Dakota, 1882 Wisconsin, 1882
Ohio	1963	Central	—
Oklahoma	1924	Kansas	—
Ontario°°°†±± ("Canada" before 1923)	1879	Northern	
Pacific Southwest***	1930	Calif-Nevada	—
South Dakota	1906	Minnesota-Dakota	—
South Wisconsin	1918	Wisconsin	—
Southeastern	1939	Eastern & English	—
Southern	1882	Western	Texas, 1906 Florida-Georgia, 1948
Southern Illinois	1909	Illinois	—
Southern Nebraska†	1922	Nebraska	—
SELC	1971	—	—
Texas	1906	Southern	—
The Rocky Mountain**	1921	Kansas	—
Western†	1855	—	Illinois, 1875 Iowa, 1879 Nebraska, 1882 Southern, 1882 California-Oregon, 1887 Kansas, 1888 Mid-South, 1966 Missouri, 1966
Wisconsin†	1882	Northwestern	Division in 1918
Wyoming	1970	Nebraska	—

†=no longer in existence
±=currently called "Central"
±±=currently called "East"
*=name changed from California-Nevada in 1977
**=name changed from Colorado in 1983
***=name changed from Southern California in 1989
°=partner church status, Jan. 1, 1980
°°=partner church status, July 1986
°°°=district of LCC partner church, 1989

Congregations Received into Synodical Membership

2023

TX Epiphany, Bastrop, TX

2024

CNH Redeeming Grace, Santa Clara, CA
EA St. John's, Ambridge, PA
EN Christ, West Olive, MI
St. Paul, Paris, TX
St. Thomas, Magnolia, TX
FG Conexion, Naples, FL
IW Christ, Denison, IA
South Lake, League City, TX
MI The Vine, Grand Rapids, MI
MNS Royal Family, Minneapolis, MN
PSW Trinity, Anaheim, CA
S New City, Orlando, FL
TX Comunidad Cristiana, Rockwall, TX
Gathering, Robinson, TX

2024 SUMMARIZED TOTALS OF CONGREGATION REPORTS

District	Parish Pastors	% of Total in U.S.	Congregations		% of Total in U.S.	New Church Starts	Average Weekly Attendance	Baptized Members	% of Total in U.S.	Compared with 2023	% of Change	Confirmed	% of Total in U.S.	Compared with 2023	% of Change	Rank in % Change
			Members of Synod	Total												
3 Atlantic	73	1.47	91	91	1.57	0	6,033	22,795	1.39	-713	-3.03%	17,740	1.37	-590	-3.22%	18
5 California/Nevada/Hawaii	139	2.80	176	178	3.07	2	12,075	25,229	1.54	-1,305	-4.92%	20,396	1.57	-1,143	-5.31%	27
7 Pacific Southwest	234	4.71	260	263	4.54	3	27,893	58,942	3.60	-1,560	-2.58%	48,590	3.75	-1,075	-2.16%	26
12 Eastern	87	1.75	122	122	2.11	0	7,973	27,445	1.68	-805	-2.85%	21,740	1.68	-585	-2.62%	16
14 English	152	3.06	159	160	2.76	1	12,263	34,312	2.10	-844	-2.40%	28,061	2.17	-445	-1.56%	12
16 Florida-Georgia	175	3.52	184	193	3.33	9	19,076	40,878	2.50	-1,688	-3.97%	33,008	2.55	-1,420	-4.12%	29
20 Central Illinois	115	2.31	148	149	2.57	1	13,904	50,375	3.08	-3,483	-6.47%	39,280	3.03	-2,708	-6.45%	32
22 Northern Illinois	199	4.00	202	202	3.49	0	22,194	77,143	4.72	-562	-0.72%	60,266	4.65	-352	-0.58%	10
24 Southern Illinois	73	1.47	92	93	1.61	1	8,646	33,401	2.04	-1	0.00%	26,447	2.04	-193	-0.72%	6
26 Indiana	229	4.61	216	217	3.75	1	27,988	83,542	5.11	-355	-0.42%	64,956	5.01	-590	-0.90%	19
28 Iowa East	93	1.87	117	117	2.02	0	9,144	33,064	2.02	-379	-1.13%	25,956	2.00	-327	-1.24%	8
30 Iowa West	124	2.49	166	166	2.87	0	13,612	49,419	3.02	-811	-1.61%	39,259	3.03	-510	-1.28%	13
32 Kansas	129	2.59	155	155	2.68	0	13,925	42,493	2.60	-600	-1.39%	33,631	2.60	-786	-2.28%	22
37 Michigan	364	7.32	345	348	6.01	3	45,760	146,863	8.98	-2,791	-1.86%	114,503	8.84	-2,699	-2.30%	31
38 Mid-South	120	2.41	118	119	2.05	1	10,798	23,445	1.43	67	0.29%	19,991	1.54	27	0.14%	3
39 Minnesota North	124	2.49	195	195	3.37	0	12,119	43,586	2.67	-467	-1.06%	34,510	2.66	-695	-1.97%	21
41 Minnesota South	214	4.30	229	230	3.97	1	27,608	96,183	5.88	-3,999	-3.99%	75,189	5.80	-3,141	-4.01%	35
43 Missouri	267	5.37	288	288	4.97	0	35,730	106,922	6.54	-2,740	-2.50%	84,549	6.53	-1,253	-1.46%	28
44 Montana	45	0.91	69	69	1.19	0	3,576	10,265	0.63	-601	-5.53%	8,261	0.64	-513	-5.85%	14
47 Nebraska	200	4.02	231	232	4.00	1	29,503	88,974	5.44	-2,556	-2.79%	68,495	5.29	-2,460	-3.47%	30
49 New England	56	1.13	66	66	1.14	0	4,022	11,430	0.70	-1,259	-9.92%	9,395	0.73	-947	-9.16%	24
51 New Jersey	32	0.64	47	47	0.81	0	2,326	7,499	0.46	-169	-2.20%	6,235	0.48	-113	-1.78%	4
53 North Dakota	42	0.84	77	77	1.33	0	4,415	16,133	0.99	-695	-4.13%	12,841	0.99	-339	-2.57%	9
55 Northwest	183	3.68	242	242	4.18	0	16,881	36,340	2.22	-734	-1.98%	29,785	2.30	-618	-2.03%	20
56 Ohio	123	2.47	153	154	2.66	1	14,167	40,351	2.47	-1,030	-2.49%	32,522	2.51	-809	-2.43%	23
58 Oklahoma	57	1.15	78	78	1.35	0	5,329	14,136	0.86	-575	-3.91%	11,131	0.86	-277	-2.43%	7
60 Rocky Mountain	151	3.04	166	166	2.87	0	14,350	34,667	2.12	-552	-1.57%	27,903	2.15	-587	-2.06%	17
61 South Dakota	69	1.39	105	105	1.81	0	7,724	25,989	1.59	-288	-1.10%	20,513	1.58	195	0.96%	1
63 Southeastern	198	3.98	213	219	3.78	6	20,126	49,881	3.05	-1,100	-2.16%	39,037	3.01	-1,013	-2.53%	25
65 Southern	112	2.25	147	147	2.54	0	8,593	18,785	1.15	-663	-3.41%	15,328	1.18	-527	-3.32%	15
67 Texas	341	6.86	344	381	6.58	37	42,615	102,168	6.25	-403	-0.39%	81,942	6.32	96	0.12%	2
76 North Wisconsin	159	3.20	213	213	3.68	0	22,547	80,938	4.95	-1,848	-2.23%	63,287	4.88	-2,992	-4.51%	34
78 South Wisconsin	204	4.10	199	200	3.45	1	24,485	79,717	4.88	-3,014	-3.64%	63,493	4.90	-2,824	-4.26%	33
79 Wyoming	46	0.93	60	60	1.04	0	3,153	8,324	0.51	-624	-6.97%	6,641	0.51	-420	-5.95%	11
97 SELC	43	0.86	52	52	0.90	0	5,164	13,442	0.82	-92	-0.68%	10,751	0.83	-127	-1.17%	5
Grand Totals	4,972		5,725	5,794		69	555,717	1,635,076		-39,239	-2.34%	1,295,632		-32,760	-2.47%	

4,516 congregations returned statistical reports for 2024. For congregations that did not report 2024 figures, their most recently reported statistics were used to calculate the totals listed in this table.

2024 SUMMARIZED TOTALS OF CONGREGATION REPORTS (Continued)

District	Children Baptized*	Compared with 2023	Juniors Confirmed*	Compared with 2023	Adults Confirmed*	Compared with 2023	Total Gained from Outside*	Sunday Schools			Vacation Bible Schools			Weekday Religion Classes		
								Number	Pupils**	Compared with 2023	Number	Pupils**	Children of Non-Members	Number	Enrollment**	Children of Non-Members
3 Atlantic	295	-5	157	26	258	152	497	54	2,109	-94	31	2,393	1,492	56	1,932	284
5 California/Nevada/Hawaii	229	-30	116	12	217	116	399	111	3,678	-406	36	3,700	2,512	103	2,894	605
7 Pacific Southwest	942	10	339	1	629	-18	1,228	166	7,996	175	70	6,267	3,841	161	5,968	1,309
12 Eastern	259	25	161	11	132	25	259	84	4,138	977	33	2,330	1,676	71	1,806	589
14 English	321	40	191	13	241	135	508	105	4,232	-600	39	2,008	947	93	3,510	896
16 Florida-Georgia	619	45	284	32	469	112	1,066	154	6,602	64	70	4,129	2,665	147	7,053	2,197
20 Central Illinois	410	11	305	10	192	-14	277	106	6,180	-851	45	3,054	1,479	101	3,105	263
22 Northern Illinois	672	-148	436	-41	343	38	756	154	7,458	101	81	6,074	3,220	147	6,028	1,231
24 Southern Illinois	164	13	181	23	86	16	154	60	2,687	-454	33	2,040	1,095	57	1,451	256
26 Indiana	803	-73	620	-18	439	60	664	156	11,156	-31	78	4,847	2,433	154	5,842	893
28 Iowa East	202	-277	194	-16	142	40	231	70	4,235	54	44	2,252	1,059	64	1,900	173
30 Iowa West	503	-106	409	22	165	-2	370	120	6,579	-2	82	4,271	2,276	111	3,320	333
32 Kansas	428	69	342	77	229	57	449	113	7,069	-171	69	4,148	2,215	100	3,831	517
37 Michigan	1,673	-92	1,039	-8	1,012	95	1,968	267	14,276	442	163	11,783	6,682	262	12,749	2,375
38 Mid-South	229	11	165	68	310	56	562	88	4,220	-777	36	1,397	712	78	2,478	407
39 Minnesota North	308	38	241	7	42	-4	249	124	4,955	-362	74	2,651	1,152	125	3,096	531
41 Minnesota South	768	-82	695	66	314	143	980	182	10,393	47	106	6,550	3,325	167	7,865	849
43 Missouri	994	-58	695	30	679	137	1,119	124	9,426	-2,375	80	6,340	3,451	121	5,990	1,367
44 Montana	88	-9	53	-12	77	-14	140	48	1,476	-287	19	946	423	46	1,035	123
47 Nebraska	1,166	-109	827	-85	495	123	913	175	12,366	101	122	9,207	3,831	168	8,584	706
49 New England	120	-8	53	-14	251	215	335	45	1,650	91	15	637	367	39	660	117
51 New Jersey	87	-3	64	28	183	171	269	34	851	20	13	455	301	37	597	74
53 North Dakota	114	-10	112	-7	48	18	136	43	1,922	-164	29	920	406	42	1,003	64
55 Northwest	282	11	139	18	205	43	488	153	5,560	393	63	3,380	2,351	149	3,947	783
56 Ohio	434	20	229	-2	230	82	581	116	5,803	-90	62	3,609	2,105	111	3,066	480
58 Oklahoma	127	12	56	-38	91	-7	152	57	2,604	298	29	1,543	989	48	1,141	181
60 Rocky Mountain	420	56	239	-30	295	23	529	118	7,415	-249	56	3,920	2,564	109	4,684	826
61 South Dakota	196	-6	135	-22	51	2	150	76	3,779	178	39	1,603	550	79	1,808	56
63 Southeastern	506	15	295	18	449	102	955	164	9,206	1,275	81	5,049	2,962	144	5,891	929
65 Southern	204	94	132	62	284	194	460	109	4,038	-224	47	2,021	1,028	88	1,601	171
67 Texas	1,203	201	702	7	1,030	360	1,787	261	20,306	-1,180	128	11,296	6,396	224	8,586	1,172
76 North Wisconsin	791	131	626	80	241	81	982	159	7,863	620	87	4,139	1,589	147	6,315	993
78 South Wisconsin	735	125	654	204	275	41	836	163	7,596	-156	85	4,641	2,080	155	6,379	1,276
79 Wyoming	92	-2	62	3	35	-6	88	41	1,584	179	17	505	252	41	797	40
97 SELC	175	9	89	7	224	24	378	34	1,075	-93	16	1,504	776	32	1,004	259
Grand Totals	16,559	-82	11,037	532	10,363	2,596	20,915	4,034	212,483	-3,551	2,078	131,609	71,202	3,777	137,916	23,325

Those columns marked with an asterisks (*) include totals only for the 4,516 congregations that reported for 2024. All other columns include totals for congregations that reported 2024 figures and the most recent figures for congregations that did not report for 2024.

**Enrollment includes adults and children.

2024 GAINS OR LOSSES IN CONFIRMED MEMBERSHIP

District	MEMBERSHIP INCREASE: Juniors Confirmed: Member Children	Juniors Confirmed: Non-Member Children	Adults Confirmed or Baptized	Reinstated/Prof. of Faith	Received from: Sister Congregations	Received from: Other Lutheran Bodies	TOTAL INCREASE	MEMBERSHIP DECREASE: By Death of Confirmed Members	Defections, Removal from Roster	Released to: Sister Congregations	Released to: Other Lutheran Bodies	TOTAL DECREASE	NET GAIN/LOSS
3 Atlantic	135	22	303	165	52	52	729	214	176	65	11	466	263
5 California/Nevada/Hawaii	100	16	301	127	121	39	704	218	406	155	18	797	-93
7 Pacific Southwest	304	35	997	375	476	189	2,376	663	907	366	94	2,030	346
12 Eastern	143	18	171	97	66	12	507	230	522	56	19	827	-320
14 English	184	7	300	208	272	52	1,023	301	588	231	22	1,142	-119
16 Florida-Georgia	264	20	602	481	628	96	2,091	648	947	354	83	2,032	59
20 Central Illinois	297	8	253	64	377	13	1,012	491	1,489	400	25	2,405	-1,393
22 Northern Illinois	419	17	425	339	392	57	1,649	667	1,105	377	76	2,225	-576
24 Southern Illinois	165	16	114	33	197	19	544	245	127	135	2	509	35
26 Indiana	597	23	571	184	852	18	2,245	696	878	681	15	2,270	-25
28 Iowa East	190	4	164	73	257	12	700	340	267	254	53	914	-214
30 Iowa West	388	21	219	131	471	53	1,283	570	496	334	90	1,490	-207
32 Kansas	326	16	273	168	538	36	1,357	499	382	396	38	1,315	42
37 Michigan	966	73	1,295	759	1,414	124	4,631	1,990	2,364	1,244	91	5,689	-1,058
38 Mid-South	156	9	371	222	448	21	1,227	294	635	209	21	1,159	68
39 Minnesota North	227	14	70	159	292	34	796	335	675	226	51	1,287	-491
41 Minnesota South	619	76	412	357	673	233	2,370	929	1,218	597	209	2,953	-583
43 Missouri	650	45	822	341	983	54	2,895	879	2,131	895	57	3,962	-1,067
44 Montana	52	1	103	51	117	11	335	115	517	92	3	727	-392
47 Nebraska	760	67	605	259	887	92	2,670	910	1,563	793	107	3,373	-703
49 New England	51	2	283	68	94	14	512	117	224	56	2	399	113
51 New Jersey	63	1	194	52	27	33	370	93	66	34	4	197	173
53 North Dakota	110	2	74	53	182	33	454	159	315	123	63	660	-206
55 Northwest	131	8	345	244	283	31	1,042	384	371	205	28	988	54
56 Ohio	210	19	306	246	299	86	1,166	487	522	223	56	1,288	-122
58 Oklahoma	53	3	112	45	159	13	385	166	253	137	4	560	-175
60 Rocky Mountain	220	19	428	202	363	13	1,245	321	325	354	51	1,051	194
61 South Dakota	133	2	75	77	224	20	531	209	708	192	38	1,147	-616
63 Southeastern	271	24	538	337	458	145	1,773	438	1,001	299	100	1,838	-65
65 Southern	126	6	314	129	266	41	882	219	444	162	11	836	46
67 Texas	626	76	1,306	586	1,089	95	3,778	924	1,757	853	97	3,631	147
76 North Wisconsin	590	36	305	474	556	231	2,192	753	2,745	466	149	4,113	-1,921
78 South Wisconsin	604	50	348	400	742	111	2,255	848	1,477	742	265	3,332	-1,077
79 Wyoming	61	1	55	38	172	14	341	117	104	90	13	324	17
97 SELC	77	12	322	128	110	14	663	145	155	195	4	499	164
Grand Totals	10,268	769	13,376	7,672	14,537	2,111	48,733	16,614	27,860	11,991	1,970	58,435	-9,702

All columns in this table include totals only for the 4,516 congregations that reported for 2024.

2024 School Enrollment Summary

Students Enrolled	2024-2025*	2023-2024	2022–2023	2021–2022	2020–2021	2015-2016
Child Care (Full Day) & Pre–K	71,719	77,508	71,689	76,800	63,483	84,558
Grades K–8	72,518	76,181	68,333	67,977	62,989	89,267
Grades 9–12	16,790	18,877	17,099	17,388	16,124	17,515
Total Students	161,027	172,566	157,121	162,165	142,596	191,340

2024 LCMS School Summary

Number of Lutheran Schools	2024-2025	2023-2024	2022–2023	2021–2022	2020–2021	2015-2016
Early Childhood Centers	971	1,001	1,045	1,075	1,099	1,173
Elementary Schools	660	674	677	681	689	804
High Schools	114	109	105	99	98	91
Total Lutheran Schools	1,745	1,784	1,827	1,855	1,886	2,068

*This data is reported from schools for the 2024–2025 school statistical year
and represents a 71% response rate.
It does not include unreported student data (29%).

Definitions: For the purpose of these statistics, the following definitions apply:
Early Childhood = Have any combination of Child Care, Pre–K, or Kindergarten, but no grades 1 or above
Elementary Schools = Have at least grades 1, 2, 3, 4, 5, 6, 7, or 8 with other early childhood, but not grades 9–12
High Schools = Have at least grades 9, 10, 11, or 12

SIZE OF STATIONS ANALYZED BY DISTRICTS 2024

District	Av. Size Membership		Classified According to Confirmed Membership																			
	Baptized	Confirmed	Total Cong	0	1–49	50–99	100–199	200–299	300–399	400–499	500–599	600–699	700–799	800–899	900–999	1000–1099	1100–1199	1200–1299	1300–1399	1400–1499	1500–1999	2000+
3 Atlantic	250	195	91	0	30	25	9	6	6	6	3	1	0	2	2	0	0	0	0	0	1	0
5 California/Nevada/Hawaii	142	115	178	7	51	55	35	17	5	4	0	3	0	0	1	0	0	0	0	0	0	0
7 Pacific Southwest	224	185	263	1	81	69	53	21	14	5	4	3	3	2	0	0	1	0	1	1	3	1
12 Eastern	225	178	122	0	26	32	33	11	9	3	0	2	1	1	0	3	1	0	0	0	0	0
14 English	214	175	160	5	45	38	31	17	7	7	5	1	2	1	0	0	0	0	0	0	0	1
16 Florida-Georgia	212	171	193	4	45	37	54	25	10	10	1	2	1	0	1	1	1	0	0	0	1	0
20 Central Illinois	338	264	149	1	21	20	47	19	13	9	6	2	3	1	2	0	1	1	0	1	1	1
22 Northern Illinois	382	298	202	2	27	39	45	30	19	6	7	7	5	2	1	0	0	3	1	1	6	1
24 Southern Illinois	359	284	93	0	16	9	24	17	5	6	2	4	4	1	0	1	2	1	1	0	0	0
26 Indiana	385	299	217	1	27	38	53	33	18	12	9	4	7	3	2	2	1	1	1	1	0	4
28 Iowa East	283	222	117	0	20	20	27	23	10	7	4	2	1	0	1	1	0	0	1	0	0	0
30 Iowa West	298	237	166	0	23	32	43	28	16	4	7	4	3	1	2	1	1	0	0	0	0	1
32 Kansas	274	217	155	1	22	30	47	21	15	6	3	2	2	2	0	0	1	2	1	0	0	0
37 Michigan	422	329	348	1	46	66	72	51	32	19	11	7	10	3	3	9	4	2	2	2	3	5
38 Mid-South	197	168	119	0	27	28	31	14	11	3	1	0	0	1	2	0	0	1	0	0	0	0
39 Minnesota North	224	177	195	0	34	47	55	24	15	7	3	7	3	0	0	0	0	0	0	0	0	0
41 Minnesota South	418	327	230	0	15	37	59	38	24	19	7	6	9	3	4	1	0	1	3	1	1	2
43 Missouri	371	294	288	1	51	57	70	31	17	18	11	7	2	2	1	1	1	5	1	2	7	3
44 Montana	149	120	69	0	31	15	11	5	3	2	0	1	0	0	0	0	1	0	0	0	0	0
47 Nebraska	384	295	232	1	24	44	65	34	21	10	6	6	3	3	2	5	1	0	1	0	2	4
49 New England	173	142	66	1	15	13	19	11	4	2	0	1	0	0	0	0	0	0	0	0	0	0
51 New Jersey	160	133	47	0	14	14	7	6	5	0	0	1	0	0	0	0	0	0	0	0	0	0
53 North Dakota	210	167	77	0	15	22	22	5	5	4	2	0	0	1	1	0	0	0	0	0	0	0
55 Northwest	150	123	242	5	59	69	70	19	7	9	2	1	0	0	1	0	0	0	0	0	0	0
56 Ohio	262	211	154	0	17	37	47	25	12	6	2	1	2	1	1	0	1	0	0	0	1	1
58 Oklahoma	181	143	78	0	22	21	14	10	6	4	0	0	1	0	0	0	0	0	0	0	0	0
60 Rocky Mountain	209	168	166	2	46	43	37	15	9	5	0	2	2	2	1	0	0	1	0	0	0	1
61 South Dakota	248	195	105	0	21	26	25	16	3	6	3	0	3	0	0	0	0	0	0	2	0	0
63 Southeastern	228	178	219	7	47	44	64	23	13	7	2	2	4	2	1	0	0	0	0	0	3	0
65 Southern	128	104	147	2	48	37	40	14	1	4	1	0	0	0	0	0	0	0	0	0	0	0
67 Texas	268	215	381	27	82	80	88	39	14	9	12	5	8	5	2	2	0	0	3	0	2	3
76 North Wisconsin	380	297	213	1	22	36	63	31	22	9	3	4	2	8	2	0	1	2	0	3	1	3
78 South Wisconsin	399	317	200	0	21	32	57	29	16	14	4	3	5	2	2	2	3	2	2	1	4	1
79 Wyoming	139	111	60	0	20	13	17	6	4	0	0	0	0	0	0	0	0	0	0	0	0	0
97 SELC	259	207	52	0	14	15	11	6	1	1	1	0	1	1	0	0	0	0	0	0	0	1
Totals and Averages	282	224	5,794	70	1,125	1,240	1,445	720	392	243	122	91	87	50	35	29	21	22	18	15	36	33
% of Totals						67%			23%			6%						4%				

4,516 congregations returned statistical reports for 2024. For congregations that did not report 2024 figures, their most recently reported statistics were used to calculate the totals listed in this table.

2024 WEEKDAY RELIGION AND CONFIRMATION CLASSES

District	Number of Classes	Enrollment by Grades						Total Enrollment**	Non-Member Children
		Preschool	Grades 1–2	Grades 3–4*	Grades 5–6*	Grades 7–8*	High School*		
3 Atlantic	9	291	53	53	110	274	101	882	155
5 California/Nevada/Hawaii	21	84	68	117	193	334	140	936	355
7 Pacific Southwest	31	115	96	122	272	620	341	1,566	407
12 Eastern	14	400	35	36	98	233	41	843	471
14 English	18	606	178	170	326	461	110	1,851	736
16 Florida-Georgia	40	577	141	145	335	719	316	2,233	1,188
20 Central Illinois	28	121	60	79	198	567	182	1,207	141
22 Northern Illinois	32	429	154	198	407	882	236	2,306	542
24 Southern Illinois	12	131	43	112	179	374	14	853	192
26 Indiana	20	298	242	243	476	1,019	119	2,397	664
28 Iowa East	20	30	36	95	252	362	120	895	75
30 Iowa West	35	76	47	201	571	815	180	1,890	134
32 Kansas	37	192	149	201	331	561	252	1,686	274
37 Michigan	63	1,088	587	724	1,015	1,889	415	5,718	1,392
38 Mid-South	13	76	69	70	198	263	167	843	238
39 Minnesota North	33	129	96	165	334	681	262	1,667	376
41 Minnesota South	46	454	173	220	784	1,592	787	4,010	465
43 Missouri	28	841	201	220	508	1,013	172	2,955	1,054
44 Montana	12	33	8	21	91	115	85	353	55
47 Nebraska	76	456	367	573	1,015	2,083	738	5,232	461
49 New England	5	60	5	6	22	99	24	216	68
51 New Jersey	5	0	1	2	60	119	14	196	10
53 North Dakota	9	26	24	36	122	200	36	444	27
55 Northwest	24	207	51	241	211	302	242	1,254	494
56 Ohio	25	109	83	88	290	475	122	1,167	264
58 Oklahoma	19	19	32	62	134	163	125	535	81
60 Rocky Mountain	29	329	147	167	328	485	201	1,657	593
61 South Dakota	23	14	30	78	266	439	172	999	32
63 Southeastern	27	405	99	137	320	677	396	2,034	401
65 Southern	10	15	13	8	76	196	60	368	46
67 Texas	58	396	168	224	536	1,318	593	3,235	521
76 North Wisconsin	46	318	253	241	657	1,679	458	3,606	656
78 South Wisconsin	27	442	250	282	503	1,186	163	2,826	903
79 Wyoming	12	18	4	43	145	97	25	332	30
97 SELC	8	116	7	12	48	139	45	367	178
Grand Total	915	8,901	3,970	5,392	11,411	22,431	7,454	59,559	13,679

4,516 congregations returned statistical reports for 2024. For congregations that did not report 2024 figures, their most recently reported statistics were used to calculate the totals listed in this table.

*Grades 3rd through 12th include confirmation classes.

**Total enrollment only includes preschool to high school children.

2024 SUNDAY CLASSES AND BIBLE STUDY GROUPS

Districts	Number of Sunday Classes	Pre-Confirmation Classes							Post-Confirmation Classes		Total Pupils Enrolled	Nursery Roll	
		Ages 2–3	Ages 4–5	Grades 1–2	Grades 3–4	Grades 5–6	Junior High Grades 7–8	Physical or Developmental Disabilities	High School Grades 9–12	Adult		Number	Enrollment
3 Atlantic	54	107	198	211	225	217	195	70	166	660	2,049	11	60
5 California/Nevada/Hawaii	111	166	197	258	302	238	176	57	260	1,979	3,633	17	45
7 Pacific Southwest	166	388	505	653	650	494	391	138	428	4,139	7,786	40	210
12 Eastern	84	197	336	334	487	244	250	41	368	1,830	4,087	15	51
14 English	105	137	285	269	292	300	215	220	326	2,074	4,118	27	114
16 Florida-Georgia	154	236	357	366	411	348	347	131	459	3,785	6,440	43	162
20 Central Illinois	106	278	378	473	410	392	390	49	551	3,062	5,983	35	197
22 Northern Illinois	154	324	557	644	619	530	516	91	628	3,360	7,269	39	189
24 Southern Illinois	60	176	199	248	244	216	207	1	264	1,075	2,630	14	57
26 Indiana	156	503	573	602	627	593	551	100	823	6,509	10,881	46	275
28 Iowa East	70	202	281	320	327	323	296	133	420	1,828	4,130	26	105
30 Iowa West	120	387	550	615	730	643	544	44	793	1,976	6,282	45	297
32 Kansas	113	307	390	447	474	460	463	46	657	3,667	6,911	32	158
37 Michigan	267	706	980	1,101	1,106	990	840	410	1,054	6,791	13,978	64	298
38 Mid-South	88	152	201	232	205	239	180	81	299	2,565	4,154	21	66
39 Minnesota North	124	270	398	451	528	444	366	15	555	1,713	4,740	39	215
41 Minnesota South	182	534	949	1,148	1,130	994	771	88	1,083	3,436	10,133	56	260
43 Missouri	124	614	715	820	808	685	624	67	1,043	3,756	9,132	46	294
44 Montana	48	53	84	113	118	76	60	0	84	865	1,453	9	23
47 Nebraska	175	1,028	1,150	1,280	1,168	1,079	903	177	1,161	3,956	11,902	55	464
49 New England	45	85	134	138	122	113	94	35	153	713	1,587	18	63
51 New Jersey	34	57	53	66	71	105	71	25	73	287	808	6	43
53 North Dakota	43	97	180	168	197	194	164	40	187	640	1,867	12	55
55 Northwest	153	248	268	258	293	285	283	154	421	3,222	5,432	43	128
56 Ohio	116	359	530	497	457	413	379	59	597	2,338	5,629	34	174
58 Oklahoma	57	83	94	122	145	146	136	16	219	1,591	2,552	17	52
60 Rocky Mountain	118	307	350	386	396	437	320	78	545	4,427	7,246	41	169
61 South Dakota	76	206	301	336	359	324	283	28	381	1,434	3,652	25	127
63 Southeastern	164	496	567	568	576	557	594	307	775	4,506	8,946	65	260
65 Southern	109	145	187	173	192	196	195	85	287	2,512	3,972	29	66
67 Texas	261	855	1,090	1,245	1,371	1,228	984	189	1,623	11,276	19,861	96	445
76 North Wisconsin	159	385	644	845	846	804	757	307	898	2,169	7,655	35	208
78 South Wisconsin	163	324	586	676	682	573	614	53	675	3,183	7,366	38	230
79 Wyoming	41	62	89	89	119	82	66	32	103	918	1,560	9	24
97 SELC	34	114	63	64	96	95	48	4	119	427	1,030	10	45
Grand Total	4,034	10,588	14,419	16,216	16,783	15,057	13,273	3,371	18,478	98,669	206,854	1,158	5,629

4,516 congregations returned statistical reports for 2024. For congregations that did not report 2024 figures, their most recently reported statistics were used to calculate the totals listed in this table.

TWO DECADES OF CHANGE

Fields of Activity	2004	2014	2024
Number of Districts	35	35	35
Number of Circuits	650	640	598
Number of countries served	75	35	71
Pastors			
Total number on clergy roster	8,936	9,471	9,006
Pastors, missionaries, and teachers	5,261	5,400	5,021
Serving Synod, Districts, and others	754	519	519
Entered the ministry (graduates)	191	156	155
Congregations			
Number of stations	6,151	6,105	5,794
Average size in baptized members	401	346	282
Average size in confirmed members	306	271	224
Membership			
Baptized members	2,463,747	2,097,258	1,635,076
Change over previous decade	-5.39%	-14.88%	-22.04%
Confirmed members	1,880,213	1,641,679	1,295,632
Change over previous decade	-3.59%	-12.69%	-21.08%
Christian Education			
Elementary Schools: Number*	1,028	842	660
Pupils enrolled	143,322	80,145	**72,518
Teachers—Men	N/A	N/A	N/A
Teachers—Women	N/A	N/A	N/A
Community High Schools: Number	101	85	114
Pupils enrolled	19,638	14,872	**16,790
Teaching staff	N/A	N/A	N/A

	2004	2014	2024
Colleges and Seminaries: Number	12	11	7
Students enrolled	18,721	37,022	24,254
Teaching staff	1,536	3,555	2,063
Sunday Schools: Number	5,330	4,581	4,034
Pupils and adults enrolled	451,414	307,026	212,483
Weekday Religion Schools: Number	4,152	4,314	3,777
Pupils and adults enrolled	198,054	202,524	137,916
Children of non-members	26,660	31,789	23,325
Vacation Bible Schools: Number	3,985	3,124	2,078
Sacred Acts* **			
Children baptized	32,851	25,551	16,559
Juniors confirmed	25,325	18,585	13,376
Adults confirmed or baptized	19,153	14,856	10,363
Total gains from outside	38,513	29,986	20,915
Contributions			
For work at home	$1,186,000,747	$1,229,158,978	$1,341,859,404
Average per confirmed member	$630.78	$748.72	$1,035.68
For work at large	$121,763,263	$118,292,783	$114,180,364
Average per confirmed member	$64.76	$72.06	$88.13
Total for all purposes****	$1,307,764,010	$61,489,324	$1,456,039,768
Average per confirmed member	$695.54	$37.46	$1,123.81
Remitted for Synod's budget	$20,881,843	$15,157,377	$13,012,818
Average per confirmed member	$11.11	$9.23	$10.04

*The number of elementary schools and enrollment exclude early childhood education.

**This data is reported from schools for the 2024-2025 statistical year and represents a 71% response rate. It does not include unreported student data (29%).

***Includes only figures from those congregations that reported current numbers for the given report year.

****Total for all purposes were incorrect on this table for statistical years 2014-2017 and 2019. The Non-Budget total was used in error. For 2014, it read $61,489,324 and should have been $1,347,451,761; for 2015, it read $65,465,202 and should have been $1,413,399,155; for 2016, it read $65,580,170 and should have been $1,431,379,355; for 2017, it read $66,893,447 and should have been $1,464,444,400; for 2019, it read $58,958,446 and should have read $1,381,593,136.

MISSOURI SYNOD BY STATES AND COUNTRIES — 2024

State and Countries	*Number of Pastors	Number of Stations	Baptized Members	Confirmed Members	Sunday School Pupils	Total Contributions	Av. per Confirmed
1 ALABAMA	47	54	7,101	5,632	2,036	$8,842,921	$1,570.12
2 ALASKA	10	13	2,203	1,682	163	$3,162,754	$1,880.35
3 ARIZONA	76	75	21,444	17,691	3,337	$30,283,393	$1,711.80
4 ARKANSAS	53	58	9,731	8,513	1,509	$10,640,593	$1,249.92
5 CALIFORNIA	310	364	59,553	48,298	7,478	$70,609,011	$1,461.94
6 COLORADO	121	113	28,644	22,992	6,433	$35,340,093	$1,537.06
7 CONNECTICUT	29	35	6,296	5,219	620	$5,654,820	$1,083.51
8 DELAWARE	4	7	1,111	887	110	$1,354,957	$1,527.57
9 DISTRICT OF COLUMBIA	3	4	471	340	57	$298,038	$876.58
10 FLORIDA	178	179	45,987	36,977	5,815	$57,036,943	$1,542.50
11 GEORGIA	42	46	6,971	5,751	1,951	$12,984,948	$2,257.86
12 HAWAII	10	10	966	804	210	$1,129,845	$1,405.28
13 IDAHO	34	43	6,859	5,606	1,434	$8,312,008	$1,482.70
14 ILLINOIS	432	467	164,133	128,735	16,636	$123,411,967	$958.65
15 INDIANA	229	206	82,493	64,212	10,859	$70,171,158	$1,092.80
16 IOWA	266	283	82,483	65,215	10,814	$48,955,416	$750.68
17 KANSAS	152	156	42,546	33,690	7,043	$40,311,930	$1,196.55
18 KENTUCKY	24	29	4,754	3,808	944	$6,337,263	$1,664.20
19 LOUISIANA	41	53	7,087	5,827	1,025	$6,454,163	$1,107.63
20 MAINE	3	3	297	250	46	$271,564	$1,086.26
21 MARYLAND	63	72	14,531	10,876	2,185	$19,378,627	$1,781.78
22 MASSACHUSETTS	19	19	3,092	2,444	655	$3,538,206	$1,447.71
23 MICHIGAN	426	389	155,193	121,180	15,520	$136,872,633	$1,129.50
24 MINNESOTA	389	422	138,254	108,605	15,135	$91,195,685	$839.70
25 MISSISSIPPI	20	23	2,136	1,800	392	$1,701,922	$945.51
26 MISSOURI	296	293	109,927	86,938	9,754	$70,112,402	$806.46
27 MONTANA	59	66	10,081	8,101	1,367	$8,641,673	$1,066.74
28 NEBRASKA	257	253	92,565	71,430	12,886	$74,158,448	$1,038.20
29 NEVADA	23	25	6,253	5,507	1,241	$4,637,548	$842.12
30 NEW HAMPSHIRE	6	6	959	825	222	$1,351,920	$1,638.69
31 NEW JERSEY	40	58	8,559	7,095	1,007	$7,232,189	$1,019.34
32 NEW MEXICO	22	32	3,001	2,444	574	$4,327,305	$1,770.58
33 NEW YORK	145	175	43,174	33,740	5,249	$26,136,326	$774.64
34 NORTH CAROLINA	56	64	17,507	14,219	3,589	$16,666,453	$1,172.13
35 NORTH DAKOTA	67	78	16,226	12,919	1,991	$9,902,317	$766.49
36 OHIO	141	169	43,228	34,942	6,070	$37,966,986	$1,086.57
37 OKLAHOMA	62	79	14,168	11,153	2,630	$14,166,012	$1,270.15
38 OREGON	65	82	10,349	8,652	1,470	$13,689,526	$1,582.24
39 PENNSYLVANIA	58	70	10,769	8,742	1,697	$9,723,792	$1,112.31
40 RHODE ISLAND	2	3	589	514	68	$591,594	$1,150.96
41 SOUTH CAROLINA	19	17	3,029	2,615	907	$4,951,420	$1,893.47
42 SOUTH DAKOTA	113	106	26,039	20,559	3,779	$16,209,802	$788.45
43 TENNESSEE	68	56	12,551	10,537	2,527	$18,906,264	$1,794.27
44 TEXAS	360	388	103,231	82,713	20,516	$140,466,074	$1,698.23
45 UTAH	10	14	1,939	1,670	195	$1,948,255	$1,166.62
46 VERMONT	2	2	347	293	63	$352,931	$1,204.54
47 VIRGINIA	55	54	13,508	10,284	2,360	$19,940,560	$1,938.99
48 WASHINGTON	84	107	16,888	13,840	2,521	$23,857,577	$1,723.81
49 WEST VIRGINIA	3	5	375	316	75	$616,173	$1,949.91
50 WISCONSIN	424	411	165,401	130,702	15,881	$126,953,179	$971.32
51 WYOMING	42	40	5,567	4,425	1,203	$6,164,537	$1,393.12
52 BAHAMAS	1	1	195	125	24	$35,846	$286.77
53 CANADA	16	16	4,095	3,148	156	$1,820,334	$578.25
54 HONG KONG	2	1	220	150	54	$261,467	$1,743.11
Grand Totals	5,479	5,794	1,635,076	1,295,632	212,483	$1,456,039,768	$1,123.81

4,516 congregations returned statistical reports for 2024. For congregations that did not report 2024 figures, their most recently reported statistics were used to calculate the totals listed in this table.

*If a pastor is working in a multi-congregation parish in two different states, he is reflected once in each state.

SUMMARY OF CONTRIBUTIONS DURING 2024

District	Total Contributions (Work at Home & Work at Large)						TOTAL FOR WORK AT HOME					
	Totals 2024	Compared with 2023	Per Confirmed Member Avgs.				Totals 2024	Compared with 2023	Per Confirmed Member Avgs.			
			2019	2023	2024	District Rank			2019	2023	2024	District Rank
3 Atlantic	$13,175,559	$1,222,565	$649.14	$652.10	$742.70	32	$12,378,107	$1,282,706	$530.86	$605.31	$697.75	29
5 California/Nevada/Hawaii	$34,687,342	-$1,167,077	$1,375.03	$1,664.63	$1,700.69	2	$31,395,337	-$1,342,934	$1,261.10	$1,519.95	$1,539.29	2
7 Pacific Southwest	$67,195,577	$4,360,521	$1,209.12	$1,265.18	$1,382.91	9	$63,371,761	$4,267,176	$1,132.37	$1,190.07	$1,304.21	9
12 Eastern	$19,259,403	-$996,912	$786.96	$907.34	$885.90	26	$17,140,628	-$376,923	$703.31	$784.66	$788.44	26
14 English	$34,609,986	$1,450,346	$981.24	$1,163.25	$1,233.38	12	$32,851,264	$1,605,882	$914.94	$1,096.10	$1,170.71	12
16 Florida-Georgia	$54,270,205	-$26,522	$1,313.68	$1,577.11	$1,644.15	4	$49,596,301	-$864,925	$1,191.42	$1,465.70	$1,502.55	4
20 Central Illinois	$37,675,558	-$1,100,861	$794.24	$923.51	$959.15	24	$34,541,487	-$379,334	$703.09	$831.69	$879.37	24
22 Northern Illinois	$66,602,173	$326,876	$882.05	$1,093.33	$1,105.14	18	$61,771,802	-$500,834	$821.84	$1,027.30	$1,024.99	19
24 Southern Illinois	$16,207,358	-$1,332,832	$599.24	$658.42	$612.82	35	$15,099,602	-$1,240,124	$560.51	$613.35	$570.94	35
26 Indiana	$71,177,903	$4,614,923	$935.17	$1,015.52	$1,095.79	19	$66,696,775	$5,370,826	$860.77	$935.62	$1,026.80	18
28 Iowa East	$18,615,341	$2,734,725	$640.10	$604.22	$717.19	33	$17,106,635	$2,657,584	$570.45	$549.75	$659.06	32
30 Iowa West	$30,340,075	-$10,629,737	$598.10	$1,030.19	$772.82	29	$27,367,365	-$10,681,749	$547.73	$956.75	$697.10	30
32 Kansas	$40,368,423	$894,441	$1,001.17	$1,146.93	$1,200.33	14	$37,268,921	$1,007,730	$932.38	$1,053.58	$1,108.17	13
37 Michigan	$130,611,487	$5,380,726	$895.27	$1,068.50	$1,140.68	17	$121,237,114	$5,227,033	$819.26	$989.83	$1,058.81	17
38 Mid-South	$31,271,169	$174,357	$1,217.21	$1,557.64	$1,564.26	6	$28,442,580	$1,834,410	$1,109.09	$1,332.81	$1,422.77	6
39 Minnesota North	$23,618,455	-$407,692	$581.33	$682.46	$684.39	34	$21,712,060	-$583,367	$534.01	$633.30	$629.15	33
41 Minnesota South	$68,590,403	$1,339,649	$809.11	$858.56	$912.24	25	$63,187,850	$1,526,918	$748.44	$787.19	$840.39	25
43 Missouri	$67,910,264	-$8,877,542	$894.82	$894.94	$803.21	27	$62,006,138	-$7,686,401	$830.89	$812.25	$733.38	27
44 Montana	$8,824,997	$775,451	$1,136.88	$917.43	$1,068.27	20	$8,148,461	$903,144	$1,069.95	$825.77	$986.38	20
47 Nebraska	$71,160,571	$4,540,841	$786.71	$938.90	$1,038.92	22	$64,276,139	$4,048,151	$704.03	$848.82	$938.41	22
49 New England	$10,959,965	-$260,481	$1,073.11	$1,084.94	$1,166.57	15	$10,268,410	-$213,598	$1,004.06	$1,013.54	$1,092.97	15
51 New Jersey	$6,245,667	$460,048	$648.69	$911.41	$1,001.71	23	$5,771,888	$489,495	$609.57	$832.14	$925.72	23
53 North Dakota	$9,718,993	-$256,763	$651.68	$756.89	$756.87	30	$7,743,699	-$906,173	$564.54	$656.29	$603.04	34
55 Northwest	$49,065,188	$4,380,795	$1,209.93	$1,469.74	$1,647.31	3	$45,685,697	$4,952,521	$1,094.95	$1,339.77	$1,533.85	3
56 Ohio	$34,476,975	-$1,435,068	$916.54	$1,077.44	$1,060.11	21	$31,505,111	-$141,692	$825.31	$949.47	$968.73	21
58 Oklahoma	$14,021,332	$1,957,364	$1,153.77	$1,057.50	$1,259.67	11	$13,125,868	$1,874,640	$1,068.32	$986.26	$1,179.22	11
60 Rocky Mountain	$42,614,362	$2,808,224	$1,276.42	$1,397.20	$1,527.23	7	$39,564,915	$2,318,115	$1,202.47	$1,307.36	$1,417.94	7
61 South Dakota	$16,209,802	-$172,235	$639.64	$806.28	$790.22	28	$14,244,633	$320,705	$519.37	$685.30	$694.42	31
63 Southeastern	$61,395,093	$5,846,328	$1,329.87	$1,386.99	$1,572.74	5	$56,774,233	$5,644,017	$1,234.43	$1,276.66	$1,454.37	5
65 Southern	$21,001,518	-$6,979,149	$1,340.40	$1,764.79	$1,370.14	10	$19,151,580	-$7,418,837	$1,231.93	$1,675.84	$1,249.45	10
67 Texas	$139,521,504	$5,267,285	$1,411.34	$1,640.33	$1,702.69	1	$128,466,937	$5,087,311	$1,298.04	$1,507.46	$1,567.78	1
76 North Wisconsin	$47,415,772	$4,309,591	$584.21	$650.37	$749.22	31	$44,242,856	$4,540,552	$536.71	$599.02	$699.08	28
78 South Wisconsin	$73,675,927	$9,831,595	$858.49	$962.71	$1,160.38	16	$68,271,003	$9,304,534	$790.76	$889.16	$1,075.25	16
79 Wyoming	$8,176,660	$622,277	$737.01	$1,069.87	$1,231.24	13	$7,323,596	$472,978	$654.34	$970.21	$1,102.79	14
97 SELC	$15,368,761	$1,538,548	$1,184.73	$1,271.39	$1,429.52	8	$14,122,651	$1,196,529	$1,096.72	$1,188.28	$1,313.61	8
Grand Totals	$1,456,039,768	$31,194,605	$939.73	$1,072.61	$1,123.81		$1,341,859,404	$33,596,066	$861.53	$984.85	$1,035.68	

4,516 congregations returned statistical reports for 2024. For congregations that did not report 2024 figures, their most recently reported statistics were used to calculate the totals listed in this table.

SUMMARY OF CONTRIBUTIONS DURING 2024 (Continued)

District	TOTALS FOR WORK AT LARGE (Including District, Synod and Other At-Large Purposes)									
	Totals 2024	Compared with 2023	Av. Per Confirmed Member	District Rank	Synod's Budget	Av. Per Confirmed Member	District Rank	Non-Budget Purposes	Av. Per Confirmed Member	District Rank
3 Atlantic	$797,452	-$60,141	$44.95	34	$54,528	$3.07	34	$344,372	$19.41	34
5 California/Nevada/Hawaii	$3,292,005	$175,857	$161.40	1	$134,472	$6.59	23	$1,795,085	$88.01	1
7 Pacific Southwest	$3,823,816	$93,345	$78.70	23	$149,715	$3.08	33	$2,296,124	$47.26	17
12 Eastern	$2,118,775	-$619,989	$97.46	13	$52,481	$2.41	35	$1,558,231	$71.68	4
14 English	$1,758,722	-$155,536	$62.67	30	$245,125	$8.74	19	$777,237	$27.70	29
16 Florida-Georgia	$4,673,904	$838,403	$141.60	3	$390,169	$11.82	14	$2,387,896	$72.34	3
20 Central Illinois	$3,134,071	-$721,527	$79.79	22	$501,112	$12.76	11	$1,715,002	$43.66	20
22 Northern Illinois	$4,830,371	$827,710	$80.15	21	$287,802	$4.78	29	$3,195,069	$53.02	15
24 Southern Illinois	$1,107,756	-$92,708	$41.89	35	$208,359	$7.88	20	$380,553	$14.39	35
26 Indiana	$4,481,128	-$755,903	$68.99	29	$463,832	$7.14	22	$2,481,556	$38.20	23
28 Iowa East	$1,508,706	$77,141	$58.13	31	$160,000	$6.16	26	$689,470	$26.56	30
30 Iowa West	$2,972,710	$52,012	$75.72	25	$631,800	$16.09	7	$1,561,522	$39.77	22
32 Kansas	$3,099,502	-$113,289	$92.16	15	$449,450	$13.36	10	$1,620,822	$48.19	16
37 Michigan	$9,374,373	$153,693	$81.87	19	$1,428,000	$12.47	12	$4,555,638	$39.79	21
38 Mid-South	$2,828,589	-$1,660,053	$141.49	4	$479,640	$23.99	1	$1,219,191	$60.99	10
39 Minnesota North	$1,906,395	$175,675	$55.24	32	$600,544	$17.40	5	$730,140	$21.16	32
41 Minnesota South	$5,402,553	-$187,269	$71.85	27	$871,186	$11.59	15	$3,407,019	$45.31	18
43 Missouri	$5,904,126	-$1,191,141	$69.83	28	$530,148	$6.27	25	$3,796,633	$44.90	19
44 Montana	$676,536	-$127,693	$81.90	18	$143,411	$17.36	6	$180,208	$21.81	31
47 Nebraska	$6,884,432	$492,690	$100.51	12	$767,000	$11.20	16	$4,617,342	$67.41	8
49 New England	$691,555	-$46,883	$73.61	26	$37,055	$3.94	30	$333,241	$35.47	24
51 New Jersey	$473,779	-$29,447	$75.99	24	$39,145	$6.28	24	$211,589	$33.94	25
53 North Dakota	$1,975,294	$649,410	$153.83	2	$291,148	$22.67	2	$888,628	$69.20	5
55 Northwest	$3,379,491	-$571,726	$113.46	10	$153,773	$5.16	28	$2,051,481	$68.88	6
56 Ohio	$2,971,864	-$1,293,376	$91.38	16	$115,834	$3.56	31	$1,768,633	$54.38	14
58 Oklahoma	$895,464	$82,724	$80.45	20	$150,000	$13.48	9	$330,915	$29.73	28
60 Rocky Mountain	$3,049,447	$490,109	$109.29	11	$92,924	$3.33	32	$2,066,146	$74.05	2
61 South Dakota	$1,965,169	-$492,940	$95.80	14	$383,705	$18.71	4	$690,711	$33.67	26
63 Southeastern	$4,620,860	$202,311	$118.37	8	$481,718	$12.34	13	$2,322,680	$59.50	11
65 Southern	$1,849,938	$439,688	$120.69	7	$80,108	$5.23	27	$853,937	$55.71	12
67 Texas	$11,054,567	$179,974	$134.91	5	$1,297,001	$15.83	8	$5,331,440	$65.06	9
76 North Wisconsin	$3,172,916	-$230,961	$50.14	33	$611,140	$9.66	18	$1,321,681	$20.88	33
78 South Wisconsin	$5,404,924	$527,061	$85.13	17	$460,493	$7.25	21	$3,504,116	$55.19	13
79 Wyoming	$853,064	$149,299	$128.45	6	$150,000	$22.59	3	$219,724	$33.09	27
97 SELC	$1,246,110	$342,019	$115.91	9	$120,000	$11.16	17	$732,624	$68.14	7
Grand Totals	$114,180,364	-$2,401,461	$88.13		$13,012,818	$10.04		$61,936,656	$47.80	

4,516 congregations returned statistical reports for 2024. For congregations that did not report 2024 figures, their most recently reported statistics were used to calculate the totals listed in this table.

2024 SUMMARIZED TOTALS OF CONGREGATION MINISTRY

District	New Church Starts*						Satellite Worship Sites					Specialized Worship Services**			Specialized Ministries**			
	2024 Year-End Total	% of Total in U.S.	2023 Year-End Total	New During 2024	Became LCMS Member	Closed During 2024	2024 Year-End Total	% of Total in U.S.	2023 Year-End Total	New During 2024	Closed During 2024	Hearing Impaired	Vision Impaired	Ethnic/ Language	Education Ministries***	Human Care Ministries	Media Ministries	Special Needs Support
3 Atlantic	0	0.00	0	0	0	0	5	1.63	5	0	0	4	2	6	356	281	148	48
5 California/Nevada/Hawaii	2	2.90	2	0	0	0	10	3.26	8	2	0	22	5	38	503	389	243	167
7 Pacific Southwest	3	4.35	3	0	0	0	18	5.86	15	4	1	28	3	32	940	689	443	227
12 Eastern	0	0.00	0	0	0	0	3	0.98	2	1	0	13	1	0	332	308	178	108
14 English	1	1.45	2	0	0	1	17	5.54	19	1	3	7	2	9	420	331	193	109
16 Florida-Georgia	9	13.04	9	1	0	1	6	1.95	7	0	1	39	8	17	695	537	325	171
20 Central Illinois	1	1.45	1	0	0	0	10	3.26	8	2	0	16	1	1	433	313	235	109
22 Northern Illinois	0	0.00	0	0	0	0	13	4.23	13	0	0	21	4	11	718	508	327	174
24 Southern Illinois	1	1.45	1	0	0	0	2	0.65	2	0	0	9	1	1	306	209	128	75
26 Indiana	1	1.45	1	0	0	0	10	3.26	9	1	1	31	15	6	677	424	320	164
28 Iowa East	0	0.00	0	0	0	0	5	1.63	5	0	0	3	2	0	317	170	126	52
30 Iowa West	0	0.00	1	0	0	0	5	1.63	5	0	0	6	1	4	474	362	276	125
32 Kansas	0	0.00	0	0	0	0	13	4.23	12	2	1	20	7	3	490	340	228	136
37 Michigan	3	4.35	4	0	1	0	28	9.12	27	2	1	39	5	4	1,347	987	602	303
38 Mid-South	1	1.45	1	0	0	0	7	2.28	6	1	0	15	4	1	349	290	184	95
39 Minnesota North	0	0.00	0	0	0	0	13	4.23	13	0	0	8	1	1	505	357	257	153
41 Minnesota South	1	1.45	1	0	0	0	18	5.86	17	1	0	26	3	6	807	562	421	206
43 Missouri	0	0.00	0	0	0	0	10	3.26	11	1	2	22	6	7	939	656	443	199
44 Montana	0	0.00	0	0	0	0	4	1.30	5	0	1	8	3	1	165	112	72	45
47 Nebraska	1	1.45	1	0	0	0	8	2.61	6	3	1	5	0	1	777	519	328	180
49 New England	0	0.00	0	0	0	0	3	0.98	3	0	0	4	1	0	186	130	92	45
51 New Jersey	0	0.00	0	0	0	0	0	0.00	0	0	0	0	0	0	126	119	69	35
53 North Dakota	0	0.00	0	0	0	0	1	0.33	1	0	0	2	0	1	202	135	92	58
55 Northwest	0	0.00	0	0	0	0	19	6.19	19	2	2	17	6	10	778	574	351	195
56 Ohio	1	1.45	1	0	0	0	8	2.61	11	0	3	19	5	1	502	365	239	117
58 Oklahoma	0	0.00	0	0	0	0	1	0.33	2	0	1	7	3	4	256	174	105	59
60 Rocky Mountain	0	0.00	0	0	0	0	4	1.30	4	0	0	5	2	5	546	370	276	112
61 South Dakota	0	0.00	0	0	0	0	6	1.95	4	2	0	7	0	3	278	140	116	53
63 Southeastern	6	8.70	6	0	0	0	12	3.91	8	4	0	14	6	12	694	674	334	176
65 Southern	0	0.00	0	0	0	0	3	0.98	4	0	1	13	1	2	390	324	191	77
67 Texas	37	53.62	40	4	4	3	12	3.91	15	0	3	36	12	75	1,064	765	487	233
76 North Wisconsin	0	0.00	0	0	0	0	17	5.54	14	3	0	26	2	2	661	467	293	161
78 South Wisconsin	1	1.45	0	1	0	0	7	2.28	7	0	0	45	7	8	761	517	331	201
79 Wyoming	0	0.00	0	0	0	0	2	0.65	2	0	0	2	0	0	182	112	82	45
97 SELC	0	0.00	0	0	0	0	7	2.28	6	1	0	0	1	4	132	108	70	32
Grand Totals	69		74	6	5	5	307		295	33	22	539	120	276	18,308	13,318	8,605	4,445

New Church Starts are reported by LCMS District Offices. All other figures in this table are based on reporting by individual congregations.
*Includes adjustments received from Districts in 2025.

** Specialized Worship Services and Specialized Ministries are based off the collection of June 2025; all other figures are based on 2024 year-end reports.
***Education Ministries includes parochial schools and all other specialized educational ministries to any age- and/or people-group.

SUMMARIZED STATISTICS — 1994 to 2024

(North American Districts Only)

Year	Parish Pastors	Congregations		Members		Communed Average Times	Membership Gains				Early Childhood & Elementary Schools			
		Members of Synod	Total Stations	Baptized	Confirmed		Children Baptized	Juniors Confirmed	Adults Confirmed or Baptized	Total Gain from Outside	Number	Pupils	Men Teachers	Women Teachers
1994	5,304	5,991	6,168	2,604,037	1,950,305	9	47,763	32,280	26,265	52,138	1,990	203,413	2,086	9,567
1995	5,263	5,995	6,175	2,601,753	1,948,700	_	49,728	33,051	29,018	54,927	2,031	210,270	2,188	10,140
1996	5,290	6,004	6,191	2,601,144	1,951,730	_	47,971	32,648	28,934	55,554	2,076	201,980	2,120	9,285
1997	5,230	6,022	6,215	2,603,036	1,951,391	_	46,984	32,399	29,508	55,504	2,149	214,079	2,178	11,099
1998	5,187	6,022	6,218	2,594,404	1,952,020	_	46,808	32,481	29,549	53,218	2,200	222,308	2,227	11,810
1999	5,170	6,121	6,220	2,582,440	1,945,846	_	45,901	32,195	29,479	51,931	2,226	229,951	2,163	12,310
2000	5,303	6,043	6,150	2,553,971	1,934,116	_	33,865	25,322	21,746	41,496	2,332	246,904	2,313	13,046
2001	5,235	6,039	6,150	2,540,045	1,920,949	_	32,606	24,534	19,964	40,947	2,738	250,841	2,190	14,074
2002	5,222	6,033	6,142	2,512,714	1,907,923	_	35,606	27,399	21,506	44,031	2,389	270,582	2,173	11,741
2003	5,281	6,043	6,160	2,488,936	1,894,822	_	33,959	25,542	19,197	38,379	2,427	268,921	2,708	13,037
2004	5,323	6,040	6,151	2,463,747	1,880,213	_	32,851	25,325	19,153	38,513	2,425	268,876	N/A	N/A
2005	5,343	6,044	6,144	2,440,864	1,870,659	_	31,701	24,572	18,684	38,525	2,423	271,525	N/A	N/A
2006	5,318	6,073	6,155	2,417,997	1,856,783	_	28,507	21,493	16,092	32,287	2,488	280,426	N/A	N/A
2007	5,356	6,075	6,167	2,383,084	1,835,064	_	27,913	20,673	13,869	29,389	2,382	254,649	N/A	N/A
2008	5,359	6,021	6,123	2,337,349	1,803,900	_	29,039	21,079	14,112	31,061	2,342	252,045	N/A	N/A
2009	5,407	6,075	6,178	2,312,111	1,784,139	_	24,745	19,104	13,067	33,347	2,345	236,721	N/A	N/A
2010	5,462	6,058	6,158	2,278,586	1,764,024	_	23,464	17,770	12,221	27,828	2,292	226,564	N/A	N/A
2011	5,669	6,040	6,145	2,231,858	1,731,522	_	28,627	20,883	15,770	33,306	2,257	213,519	N/A	N/A
2012	5,752	6,048	6,155	2,196,788	1,707,509	_	24,917	18,470	14,735	29,522	2,247	212,884	N/A	N/A
2013	5,678	6,026	6,136	2,163,698	1,685,597	_	21,318	15,877	10,789	23,189	2,165	201,647	N/A	N/A
2014	5,575	5,992	6,105	2,097,258	1,641,679	_	25,551	18,585	14,856	29,986	2,032	141,850	N/A	N/A
2015	5,524	5,990	6,101	2,060,514	1,609,100	_	23,500	16,830	14,147	27,621	1,977	173,825	N/A	N/A
2016	5,492	5,968	6,084	2,017,834	1,584,251	_	21,155	15,629	11,994	23,366	1,943	168,409	N/A	N/A
2017	5,432	5,936	6,046	1,968,641	1,545,124	_	21,087	15,512	14,105	26,236	1,905	167,343	N/A	N/A
2018	5,378	5,895	5,991	1,913,015	1,504,610	_	19,605	14,974	14,971	27,735	1,854	182,990	N/A	N/A
2019	5,234	5,875	5,975	1,864,800	1,470,208	_	16,871	13,282	10,991	18,866	1,817	164,949	N/A	N/A
2020	5,251	5,834	5,921	1,807,408	1,433,378	_	12,649	12,010	7,483	11,072	1,788	126,472	N/A	N/A
2021	5,159	5,798	5,883	1,770,655	1,399,363	_	15,059	11,895	6,640	15,456	1,756	144,777	N/A	N/A
2022	5,087	5,809	5,888	1,712,696	1,358,354	_	16,152	11,245	7,606	18,112	1,722	140,022	N/A	N/A
2023	5,021	5,767	5,841	1,674,315	1,328,392	_	16,641	10,505	7,767	18,125	1,675	153,689	N/A	N/A
2024	4,899	5,725	5,794	1,635,076	1,295,632	_	16,559	11,037	10,363	20,915	1,631	**144,237	N/A	N/A

**This data is reported from the 2024–2025 school statistical reports and represents a 71% response rate.
It does not include unreported student data (29%).

SUMMARIZED STATISTICS — 1994 to 2024 (Continued)

(North American Districts Only)

Year	Weekday Rel. Classes		Sunday Religion Classes			Enrollment in All Bible Study Groups	Vacation Classes		Contributions					
	Number	Pupils	Number	Pupils	Teachers and Officers		Number	Pupils	Work at Home	Average per Conf. Mem.	Work at Large	Average per Conf. Mem.	Synod's Budget	Average per Conf. Mem.
1994	4,872	135,919	5,754	565,213	76,708	377,230	4,322	311,113	$817,412,113	$419.12	$96,048,560	$49.25	$26,369,155	$13.52
1995	4,921	143,941	5,735	547,550	74,858	332,179	4,281	304,622	$832,701,255	$427.31	$98,139,835	$50.36	$26,295,995	$13.49
1996	4,954	141,580	5,742	540,902	74,525	345,881	4,245	305,226	$855,461,015	$438.31	$104,076,876	$53.33	$25,748,616	$13.19
1997	4,813	141,926	5,729	533,573	72,835	350,998	4,134	296,460	$887,928,255	$455.02	$110,520,917	$56.64	$24,919,551	$12.77
1998	4,702	130,422	5,688	502,807	70,061	339,691	4,157	295,931	$933,949,566	$478.54	$121,536,226	$66.26	$24,925,239	$12.76
1999	4,601	127,508	5,645	492,005	69,040	341,239	5,645	294,807	$986,295,136	$506.87	$123,632,549	$27.17	$25,233,082	$12.93
2000	4,878	200,702	5,658	505,690	74,440	_	4,197	299,216	$1,101,690,594	$569.61	$127,554,235	$65.95	$25,312,219	$13.09
2001	4,546	192,744	5,623	492,751	68,949	_	4,119	306,685	$1,092,453,907	$568.71	$124,703,387	$64.92	$24,293,120	$12.65
2002	4,230	195,198	5,269	469,003	65,205	_	3,968	282,509	$1,086,223,370	$569.32	$117,110,167	$61.38	$23,055,031	$12.08
2003	4,243	199,698	5,330	471,492	63,375	_	3,991	289,947	$1,131,212,373	$597.00	$125,169,844	$66.07	$21,830,193	$11.52
2004	4,152	198,054	5,330	451,414	62,612	_	3,985	286,648	$1,186,000,747	$630.78	$121,763,263	$64.76	$20,881,843	$11.11
2005	3,922	184,934	5,106	423,958	72,884	_	3,804	276,965	$1,176,649,592	$629.00	$120,169,146	$64.24	$20,457,455	$10.94
2006	3,905	185,060	5,189	425,638	58,231	_	3,849	276,775	$1,229,709,733	$662.00	$126,213,053	$67.97	$20,339,175	$10.95
2007	3,872	178,694	5,196	415,066	56,840	_	3,811	267,527	$1,278,836,855	$696.89	$120,937,847	$65.90	$19,428,812	$10.59
2008	3,571	169,644	4,839	371,204	51,521	_	3,544	248,710	$1,223,607,882	$678.31	$119,478,393	$66.23	$19,375,287	$10.74
2009	3,601	171,379	4,913	375,213	50,909	_	3,611	252,921	$1,234,616,467	$692.00	$126,921,340	$71.14	$18,486,508	$10.36
2010	3,602	172,805	4,944	363,389	49,997	_	3,562	249,313	$1,254,192,118	$710.98	$121,592,097	$68.93	$17,281,299	$9.80
2011	3,676	172,127	4,893	355,945	48,391	_	3,520	247,499	$1,255,443,938	$725.05	$120,711,376	$69.71	$15,805,477	$9.13
2012	4,519	210,089	5,080	360,897	_	_	3,576	250,736	$1,295,271,716	$758.57	$128,071,113	$75.00	$15,715,266	$9.20
2013	4,636	220,742	5,106	347,003	_	_	3,518	244,721	$1,290,994,013	$765.90	$128,693,151	$76.35	$15,456,539	$9.17
2014	4,314	202,524	4,581	307,026	_	_	3,124	220,466	$1,229,158,978	$748.72	$118,292,783	$72.06	$15,157,377	$9.23
2015	4,548	201,913	4,778	309,099	_	_	3,173	223,380	$1,289,412,334	$763.88	$123,986,821	$73.51	$14,921,446	$9.27
2016	4,588	202,499	4,863	295,844	_	_	3,191	219,836	$1,304,816,023	$823.62	$126,563,332	$79.89	$14,703,651	$9.28
2017	4,603	200,513	4,865	288,560	_	_	3,089	210,530	$1,336,341,138	$864.88	$128,103,262	$82.91	$14,201,323	$9.19
2018	4,693	181,925	4,713	285,351	_	_	2,844	199,731	$1,289,640,060	$857.13	$120,454,921	$80.06	$13,768,167	$9.16
2019	4,472	171,820	4,545	278,433	_	_	2,682	185,613	$1,266,628,750	$861.53	$114,964,386	$78.20	$13,148,618	$8.94
2020	4,261	133,446	4,067	251,007	_	_	1,072	59,270	$1,247,029,346	$869.99	$104,470,813	$72.88	$13,830,567	$9.65
2021	3,876	136,019	4,149	213,222	_	_	1,793	100,282	$1,307,012,568	$934.01	$139,963,894	$100.02	$13,120,038	$9.38
2022	3,901	135,685	4,198	217,287	_	_	2,013	122,371	$1,297,926,239	$955.51	$111,904,920	$82.38	$13,436,360	$9.89
2023	3,772	134,264	4,097	216,034	_	_	2,038	128,443	$1,308,263,338	$984.85	$116,581,825	$87.76	$13,153,367	$9.91
2024	3,777	137,916	4,034	212,483	_	_	2,078	131,609	$1,341,859,404	$1,035.68	$114,180,364	$88.13	$13,012,818	$10.04

FEDERAL INCOME TAX EXEMPTION
THE LUTHERAN CHURCH—MISSOURI SYNOD

The Internal Revenue Service has issued rulings under Internal Revenue Code Section 501 (c) (3), that recognize the exempt status of the Synod and its component parts and grant a blanket federal income tax exemption to member corporations, their unincorporated elementary schools, and those incorporated elementary schools and high schools that consent in writing to their inclusion in the group ruling. These rulings are dated June 3, 1992, and any reference to the Synod's exempt status or to the group ruling should refer to that date. Also, the Synod's group ruling is identified by the number 1709. The existing rulings are applicable to all of the following:

1. All of the Synod's boards, commissions, and councils, including:

Office of National Mission
Programs:
All Nations Ministry
Campus Ministry LCMSU
Church Planting Ministry
Deaconess Ministry
Disaster Response/Training
Discipleship Ministry
Family Ministry
Life & Health Ministry
Revitalization
School Ministry
Specialized Spiritual Care Ministry
Stewardship Ministry
Veterans and Soldiers of the Cross
Witness & Outreach Ministry
Worker Wellness
Worship
Youth Ministry

Office of International Mission
Programs:
Deaconess Ministry (International)
Disaster Response (International)
Global Safety & Security
Grants
Ministry to the Armed Forces
Missionary Services
Missionary Recruitment
Regional Operation
Short-Term Mission Services

2. Concordia Historical Institute
3. Concordia International Foundation
4. Concordia Plan Services
   Concordia Plan Services Ancillary Program Agency
5. Concordia University System
6. Lutheran Church Extension Fund—Missouri Synod
7. The Lutheran Church—Missouri Synod Foundation
8. Radio Station KFUO
9. Synodical Districts operating in the United States, to wit:

Atlantic
California-Nevada-Hawaii
Central Illinois
Eastern
English
Florida-Georgia
Indiana
Iowa East
Iowa West
Kansas
Michigan
Mid-South
Minnesota North
Minnesota South
Missouri
Montana
Nebraska
New England
New Jersey
North Dakota
North Wisconsin
Northern Illinois
Northwest
Ohio
Oklahoma
Pacific Southwest
Rocky Mountain
SELC
South Dakota
South Wisconsin
Southeastern
Southern
Southern Illinois
Texas
Wyoming

10. Incorporated church extension funds of districts, to wit:
    Central Illinois District Lutheran Church Extension Fund, Inc.
    Church Extension Fund of the Michigan District of The Lutheran Church—Missouri Synod
    Southern District Church Extension Fund, Inc.

11. The education institutions of the Synod, to wit:
    Concordia Seminary (the legal name of which is Concordia College), St. Louis, MO
    Concordia Theological Seminary, Fort Wayne, IN
    Concordia University, Irvine, CA
    Concordia University Wisconsin/Ann Arbor, Mequon, WI
    Concordia University Chicago, River Forest, IL
    Concordia University, St. Paul, MN
    Concordia University Nebraska, Seward, NE

12. The congregations of The Lutheran Church—Missouri Synod located in the United States and including those listed, by states, in the Directory of Congregations set forth on prior pages of this *Annual*, as well as those in the formative stages of membership, as established by records that exist in the offices of the Synod's districts listed above.

13. The elementary schools, middle schools and junior high schools, and high schools (a) that are operated by member congregations of the Synod and are not separately incorporated, as well as those (b) that are either separately incorporated or are otherwise identified as entities separate from congregations and that have consented in writing to be included in Synod's group ruling.

The separately incorporated preschools and day care centers that are controlled by member congregations of the Synod and that have consented to the inclusion in the group exemption ruling of the Synod, while not expressly included within the scope of the rulings listed above, like separately incorporated elementary schools, middle schools, junior high schools, and high schools that are operated by member congregations of the Synod, are listed among the organizations covered by the federal income tax exemption of the Synod because they are controlled by congregations of the Synod and are teaching ministries of those congregations.

The programs listed under the Office of National Mission and the Office of International Mission and the Radio Station KFUO are not expressly included within the scope of the rulings listed above. However, they are active programs of The Lutheran Church—Missouri Synod, and thus are listed among the entities covered by the federal income tax exemption of the Synod.

PUBLICATIONS

The following directory includes publications that are affiliated with The Lutheran Church—Missouri Synod. For more information about subscriptions, content, and frequency, contact the publisher at the address immediately above the section where the publication is listed, or at the phone number or email address found in the listing.

The Lutheran Church—Missouri Synod
International Center
1333 S. Kirkwood Rd.
St. Louis, MO 63122-7295

Publication	Publisher	Editor	Phone	Email
Annual Ministry Report	The LCMS Foundation	David O'Brien	(314) 996-1681	david.obrien@lfnd.org
Interest Time Magazine	LCEF	Laura Vivian	(314) 885-6486	laura.vivian@lcef.org
Journal of Lutheran Mission	Communications	Roy S. Askins	(314) 996-1227	roy.askins@lcms.org
LCEF Annual Report	LCEF	Joe Russo	(314) 885-6568	joe.russo@lcef.org
Lutherans Engage the World	Communications	Megan K. Mertz	(314) 996-1234	lutheransengage@lcms.org
Reporter	Communications	Cheryl Magness	(314) 996-1231	cheryl.magness@lcms.org
So Help Me God	Ministry to the Armed Forces	Steven C. Hokana	(314) 996-1337	lcmschaps@lcms.org
The Lutheran Witness	Communications	Stacey Eising	(314) 996-1230	stacey.eising@lcms.org
youthESource	Office of National Mission	Julianna Shults	(314) 996-1158	julianna.shults@gmail.com
Warning Order	Ministry to the Armed Forces	Steven C. Hokana	(314) 996-1337	lcmschaps@lcms.org

Concordia Publishing House (CPH)
3558 S. Jefferson Ave.
St. Louis, MO 63118

Publication	Publisher	Editor	Phone	Email
Concordia Pulpit Resources	Concordia Publishing House	Scot Kinnaman	(314) 268-1000	scot.kinnaman@cph.org
Happy Times	Concordia Publishing House	Lisa Clark	(314) 268-1000	lisa.clark@cph.org
My Devotions	Concordia Publishing House	Mark Sengele	(314) 268-1000	mark.sengele@cph.org
Portals of Prayer	Concordia Publishing House	Scot Kinnaman	(314) 268-1000	portals@cph.org
Strength for the Day	Concordia Publishing House	Scot Kinnaman	(314) 268-1000	scot.kinnaman@cph.org
Today's Light	Concordia Publishing House	Peggy Kuethe	(314) 268-1000	peggy.kuethe@cph.org

Lutheran Braille Workers
P.O. Box 5000
Yucaipa, CA 92399

Publication	Publisher	Phone	Email
Hope-Full Living (Large Print)	Worship Anew	(909) 795-8977	LBW@LBWloveworks.org
Lutheran Witness (Braille & Large Print)	Concordia Publishing House	(909) 795-8977	LBW@LBWloveworks.org
LWML Quarterly (Braille & Large Print)	Lutheran Women's Missionary League	(909) 795-8977	LBW@LBWloveworks.org
Mustard Seed Series Braille & Large Print)	Lutheran Women's Missionary League	(909) 795-8977	LBW@LBWloveworks.org
My Devotions (Large Print)	Concordia Publishing House	(909) 795-8977	LBW@LBWloveworks.org
Portals of Prayer (Braille & Large Print)	Concordia Publishing House	(909) 795-8977	LBW@LBWloveworks.org
Today's Light (Braille & Large Print)	Concordia Publishing House	(909) 795-8977	LBW@LBWloveworks.org

Other Publications

Publication	Publisher Address City, State ZIP	Editor	Phone	Email
Concordia Historical Institute Quarterly	Concordia Historical Institute 804 Seminary Place St. Louis, MO 63105-3014	John C. Wohlrabe Jr.	(207) 400-2017	editorchiq@gmail.com
Concordia Journal	Concordia Seminary 801 Seminary Place St. Louis, MO 63105-3199	Kevin Golden	(314) 505-7131	cj@csl.edu
Concordia Theological Quarterly	Concordia Theological Seminary 6600 N. Clinton St. Ft. Wayne, IN 46825-4996	Charles Gieschen	(260) 452-2104	CTQ@ctsfw.edu
For the Life of the World	Concordia Theological Seminary 6600 N. Clinton St. Ft. Wayne, IN 46825-4996	Kristine Bruss	(260) 452-2150	FLOW@ctsfw.edu
Historical Footnotes	Concordia Historical Institute 804 Seminary Place St. Louis, MO 63105-3014	Daniel N. Harmelink	(314) 505-7911	dharmelink@concordia historicalinstitute.org
The Deaf Lutheran	Lutheran Deaf Mission Society 305 Liberty St. Fridley, MN 55432	Janet Gehlbach	(612) 386-4824	janetgehlbach@gmail.com

TOPICAL INDEX